BEREISHIS
VOL. I(b)

ויצא	VAYEITZEI
וישלח	VAYISHLACH
וישב	VAYEISHEV
מקץ	MIKEITZ
ויגש	VAYIGASH
ויחי	VAYECHI

BEREISHIS

GENESIS / A NEW TRANSLATION WITH A COMMENTARY ANTHOLOGIZED FROM TALMUDIC, MIDRASHIC AND RABBINIC SOURCES.

Published by

Mesorah Publications, ltd

ArtScroll Tanach Series®

A traditional commentary on the Books of the Bible

Rabbi Nosson Scherman/Rabbi Meir Zlotowitz
General Editors

Translation and commentary by
Rabbi Meir Zlotowitz

Overviews by
Rabbi Nosson Scherman

FIRST EDITION — SIX VOLUMES
Two Impressions . . . June, 1977 - November, 1982

SECOND EDITION — COMPLETE IN TWO VOLUMES
First Impression . . . June, 1986
Second Impression . . . April, 1988
Third Impression . . . May, 1989
Fourth Impression . . . July, 1991
Fifth Impression . . . September, 1995

Published and Distributed by
MESORAH PUBLICATIONS, Ltd.
4401 Second Avenue
Brooklyn, New York 11232

Distributed in Europe by
J. LEHMANN HEBREW BOOKSELLERS
20 Cambridge Terrace
Gateshead, Tyne and Wear
England NE8 1RP

Distributed in Israel by
SIFRIATI / A. GITLER—BOOKS
4 Bilu Street
P.O.B. 14075
Tel Aviv 61140

Distributed in Australia & New Zealand by
GOLDS BOOK & GIFT CO.
36 William Street
Balaclava 3183, Vic., Australia

Distributed in South Africa by
KOLLEL BOOKSHOP
22 Muller Street
Yeoville 2198, Johannesburg, South Africa

THE ARTSCROLL TANACH SERIES®
BEREISHIS / GENESIS SECTION II

ISBN
Two Volume Set 0-89906-362-4 (hard cover)

Typography by CompuScribe at ArtScroll Studios, Ltd.
1969 Coney Island Avenue / Brooklyn, N.Y. 11223 / (718) 339-1700

Printed in the United States of America by Moriah Offset
Bound by Sefercraft, Inc., Brooklyn, NY

This work on Sefer Bereishis
is lovingly dedicated by the author
to the momory of his mother

הרבנית פרומא בת ר׳ חיים צבי ע״ה

Rebetzin Fannie Zlotowitz ע״ה

נפ׳ יב טבת תשמ״ה

*Like multitudes of Jews, she and her husband came to America
in the days of steerage and tenements, over half a century ago.
But unlike most, they held fast to their roots.
Her pride was her husband, the gaon, שליט״א,
who plumbed undisturbed the depths of Talmudic wisdom.
She inspired him in his learning and his commitment
to maintain the highest standards of rabbinical service.
Together they helped prepare the American soil
for today's lush crop of Torah scholars and communities.
Her ambition was that her children grow up
to bring pride to her forebears.
Her duty was to help the institutions and individuals who depended
on her warm heart and respected leadership.
She succeeded as did few others.
Wise, devoted, noble and kind;
she was the quintessential Jewish matriarch.
And the vineyard she planted will honor her memory
for generations to come.*

תנצב״ה

מכתב ברכה

משה פיינשטיין

ר"מ תפארת ירושלים

Rabbi Moshe Feinstein

455 F. D. R. Drive

New York, N. Y. 10002

בע"ה

הנה ידידי הרב הנכבד מאוד מהור"ר מאיר יעקב בן ידידי הרב הגאון ר' אהרן זלאטאוויץ שליט"א כבר נתפרסם בספריו על חמש מגילות, ספר יונה, ופרשיות בראשית בשפה האנגלית המדוברת פה במדינה, אשר קבץ פנינים יקרים ורעיונות נשגבים מספרי חז"ל ורבותינו הראשונים והאחרונים ז"ל המעוררים לאוהבת התורה וקיום המצוות ומחזיקים האמונה בהשי"ת, ויש בזה תועלת גדול לקרב לב הרחוקים לאבינו שבשמים, וגם ראה חיבוריו בני הרה"ג ר' דוד שליט"א וגם חיבורו הנוכחי ושבחוהו מאד שנלקט ונסדר בטוב טעם, וזה ביאור חשוב על המקרא. ועכשיו מברך על המוגמר שסיים ספר בראשית אשר על כן דבר טוב הוא שמדפיסו ומוציאו לאור עולם להגדיל אהבת השי"ת ותורתו הקדושה והאמונה הטהורה ולעורר על קיום המצוות. ואני מברכו שבזכות הרבצת התורה יתן השי"ת רפו"ש ואריכת ימים לאביו הרה"ג שליט"א ולאמו תחי' עמו"ש, ויתן לו השי"ת נחת מבניו יחי' וכל ב"ב, ושיהיה לו כח ומנוחת הנפש להמשיך הלאה בעבודת הק' לפרש ולסיים גם ספר שמות וכל ספרי התנ"ך ועוד ספרים חשובים אשר מוציאים לאור חברת ארטסקרול שהוא תחת הנהלתו, שזה לתועלת גדול להרבה אינשי, שהוא ממזכי הרבים, וזכותו גדול.

וגם אני מברך את ידידי הרב הנכבד מהור"ר נתן שערמאן שליט"א אשר הוסיף פתיחה חשובה לכל סדרה בענינים חשובים מהושכין את הלב לתורה ויראת השי"ת שיצליח מאד בכל מעשיו ובפרט בעבודת הקודש אשר עוסק בזה בכל כחו לקדש שם שמים.

וע"ז, בעה"ח [illegible]

[illegible] משה פיינשטיין

מכתב ברכה

יעקב קמנצקי
RABBI J. KAMENECKI
38 SADDLE RIVER ROAD
MONSEY, NEW YORK 10952

בע"ה,

יום ה' לסדר במדבר תשמ"א

כבוד ידידי הרבנים הנכבדים, הרה"ג הנעלה מוה"ר נתן שליט"א
והרה"ג הנעלה מוה"ר מאיר יעקב זלאטאוויץ שליט"א

שלום וברכת כל טוב

שמחתי באומרים לי שהנכם מתכוננים לגמור הפירוש והליקוט שלכם על ספר בראשית מיוסד על דברי חכמינו ז"ל ראשונים ואחרונים, עם הקדמות לכמה ענינים יסודיים בהשקפה.

הנני יודע נאמנה שעבודתכם עבודה תמה וכנה היא, וכמה מספקותיכם הוצעו לפני גדולי ישראל לפענחן על טהרת הקודש, ומאד הצלחתם להרביץ תורה בין יראי ה' וחושבי שמו ובין אלו שהיו רחוקים ונתקרבו.

ואומר לכם יישר חילכם לאוריתא, וכשם שמצאתם ברכה במעשי ידיכם כן תזכו להמשיך הלאה בעבודה זו על חמשה חומשי תורה וכן בעבודתכם בכמה מקצועות התורה בהשתתפות תלמידי חכמים מובהקים.

כעתירת ידידכם המברכם מתוך הנפש בהוקרה,

יעקב קמנצקי

מכתב ברכה

RABBI JACOB I. RUDERMAN
400 MT. WILSON LANE
BALTIMORE, MD. 21208

יעקב יצחק הלוי רודרמן
באלטימאר, מד.

יום שהוכפל בו כי טוב
כ"ג למטמונים, תשמ"א

כבוד הרבנים החשובים
מרביצי תורה למופת
הרב מאיר יעקב זלאטאוויץ שליט"א
והרב נתן שרמאן שליט"א,

בקשתם ממני לכתוב מכתב ברכה לכבוד החבור שהנכם מסיימים בו הפירוש לחומש בראשית, והנני קורא על הזדמנות זו "דבר בעתו מה טוב". הלא בימים אלו שכל ישראל מכין את עצמו לקבלת התורה באה ברכה על גמרה של תורה ממעמקים. ובפרט כשגמר זה אינו אלא התחלה להמשיך עבודתכם בקודש לקרב לבות אחינו בני ישראל לתורה ולתעודה. והנני אוחז בזה מנהגו של אביי באמרו (שבת קיח:) דכי חזינא צורבא מרבנן דשלים מסכתא עבידנא יומא טבא לרבנן, והנני משתתף בשמחתכם ומברך אתכם שתלכו מחיל אל חיל ויפוצו מעינותיכם חוצה להגדיל תורה ולהאדירה.

החותם לכבוד התורה ולומדיה,

יעקב יצחק הלוי רודרמן

יעקב יצחק הלוי רודרמאן
נר ישראל
ראש הישיבה

מכתב ברכה

בעזהשי"ת

הרב אהרן זלאטאוויץ

Rabbi Aron Zlotowitz

CONGREGATION ETZ CHAIM ANSHEI LUBIN
EXECUTIVE DIRECTOR: BOARD OF ORTHODOX RABBIS OF BROOKLYN

RESIDENCE
1134 EAST 9 STREET
BROOKLYN, N.Y. 11230
(212) 252-9188

ט' סיון התשמ"ג

אחזיקינן טיבותא לבני היקר והחביב הרב ר' מאיר יעקב שליט"א
שבס"ד חיבר מגודת ספרים על חמש מגילות ונתפרסם באולם בחיבורין
הקדושים הנ"ל ומובן נתקבלו בחיבה · ועכשיו מברך על המוגמר
שסיים חיבורו על ספר בראשית ומתחיל מיד ספר שמות בס"ד
בלי עיכוב. כבראותו בטור או"ח סימן תרס"ט הסברי מפני מה
קורין בשמחת תורה בסוף שני בראשית שלא יהא פתחון פה
לשטן המקטרג לומר כבר סיימו אותה ואינם רוצים לקרותה עוד ·
ומשום זכות זה בודאי יעזור לו הקב"ה בספר שמות. ג"כ כמו
בחיבוריו הקודמים כדי לקרב לב הרחוקים לאבינו שבשמים ·
במה שאסף ולקט מן הרבה ספרים הנה שופרו דשופריה ופולת
ישבאו ויתמזגו מטובו. כל אחד ואחד ימצא מה שלבו חפץ
והכל בלשון צח ונקי חכו ממתקים וכולו מחמדים · ומבאר כל
המאמרים בדברי רש"י הקדוש ורמב"ן ז"ל על התורה אשר מדברי ראשונים
וגדולי האחרונים וספרי דרוש שונים ועדיו המדוייקות ומאסף כל
דברים הנעימים אשר ערבים לשומעיהם עם הרבה הערות
אשר חנן ה' אותו. וברכה לבני הנ"ל שליט"א שיזכה להמשיך
להפיץ מעיינותיו חוצה בטובים ובנעימים לזכות את ישראל בספרין
הנפלאים אשר הדור כה צריך להם. ויזכה להמשיך בעבודתו
עבודת הקודש שנטל על עצמו ויצליח בכל מעשה ידיו אמן ·
ואני נותן שבח והודי' להקב"ה שזכיתי שיקוים בו מאמר
החכם מכל האדם אם חכם בני ישמח לבי גם אני ·

גם אני מברך את כבוד ידידי הרב מהו"ר נתן שערמאן שליט"א
איש הוגה בהקדמה לכל ספריו בעיונים חשובים להמשיך את הלב לתורה
נפלאות שמים. ובזכות זה יתן לו הקב"ה הצלחה בכל מעשה ידיו ונחת אכי"ר.

ברגשי כבוד והערכה אהרן זלאטאוויץ החותם
מנהל ומזכיר ועד הרבנים דברוקלין יצ"ו
וסגן נשיא דאגודת הרבנים דארצות הברית וקנדה.

RABBI A. ZLOTOWITZ

מכתב ברכה

מרדכי גיפטער
ישיבת טלז
RABBI MORDECAI GIFTER
28570 NUTWOOD LANE
WICKLIFFE, OHIO 44092

בע"ה — ד' חיי-שרה, תשמ"ב.

מע"כ ידידי, אהובי, **הרב הנעלה ר' מאיר, נר"ו, והרב הנעלה ר' נתן, נר"ו** יחד עם כל הצוות אשר עמכם, יחיו, שלום וברכה נצח!

תגדל שמחתי בשמועה טובה שתדשן עצם שהנכם עומדים בעבודתכם בתרגום וביאור החומש, לסיים ספר בראשית. הגם שס' בראשית אין בו אלא שלש מצוות מתרי"ג והן — פרי' ורבי', מילה, וגיד הנשה — הנה הוא ספר הראשית אשר בו מגלה ה' לעמו שרשי בריאה ותכלית בריאה, אשר הוא הרקע להתגלות עמו הנבחר שעבורו הוריד תורתו לעולם הזה.

ידעתי היטב, גם ידעתי שבעבודה קדושה זו משקיע ידידי הרב ר' מאיר, נר"ו, מיטב כחותיו ועמלו הרב בשימת לילות כימים ממש בתורת ה', וכל מעיין יראה שיש כאן פרי עמל רב מקיבעא ולא מקופיא. וחשיבות מיוחדת נודעת לעבודה זו שיש בה לא רק תרגום וביאור באנגלית, אלא שהמקור שבלה"ק כפי שניתן בסיני הוא יסוד העבודה אשר עליו סובב הולך התרגום והביאור. וכל הלומד בו לומד את החומש — תורת ה' — כפי שניתן בסיני. ועוד ענין נכבד ומעלה יתירה יש בו, שהתרגום והביאור בנוי ביסודו על דברי רש"י, ועליו נוספים ביאורי ופרושי רבותינו הראשונים והאחרונים ז"ל. שידוע שלימוד החומש היינו „חומש-רש"י" כפי הנודע משמי' דהגרי"ז איש בריסק ז"ל, ועיין דברי רבינו הרא"ש ז"ל בפ"ק דברכות ובס' ארחות חיים אות ל"ז. ואי לזאת יתברך ידידי בתוספת אומץ ועוז להמשיך בעבודתו לרוות צמאונם של מבקשי ה'.

למותר להעיר שיש בעבודתכם משום הפצת תורת ה' לצמאים לדברו, והנכם מקרבים אותם למקורות ע"י הגשת הדברים בשפתם המדוברת ובצורה המעוררת לב ונפש לאמונה טהורה בדור שמפלצת הכפירה והמינות גוברת בו למאד, בהיותו עומד סמוך וקרוב לגילוי אורו ית' בביאת משיח צדקנו בב"א.

יהא ה' בעזרכם להמשיך בעבודתכם בקדש כפי התכנית שהתויתם לכם ותוסיפו להביא דרכה לבית ישראל.

מנאי, אוהבכם מלונ"ח, הכו"ח לכבוד התורה ולומדי' ומפיצי',

מרדכי גיפטער

מכתב ברכה

RABBI SHNEUR KOTLER
BETH MEDRASH GOVOHA
LAKEWOOD, N. J.

בע״ה

שניאור קוטלר
בית מדרש גבוה
לייקוואוד, נ. דז.

ברכה לראש משביר, סגל חבורת ,,ארטסקרול״ לרגל סיום חלק מיצירתם הגדולה, השלמת התרגום והביאור לס׳ בראשית — ספר היצירה ,,יצירת כל נוצר ובמקרי האבות שהם כענין יצירה לזרעם״ [רמב״ן בסיום לס׳ בראשית והקדמה לס׳ שמות]. וזכו לבנות בנין משוכלל כלול בהדרו, מפורש ושום שכל. ובעבודתם פתחו שערים בעיר לאמרי׳ של תורה וקריאתה בראש הומיות, לחבב ד״ת ולהשמיע רנתם. ואם אחז״ל בזמן שהתורה חביבה על לומדי׳ פזר — הרי בתקופה זו גדולה המשימה להעיר ולעורר את האהבה הישנה עד שתחפץ — ללבות גחלים עוממות, ולדלות את הצפון וגנוז בלב כל אחד מישראל, לחשוף את העקידה הפוחמית ולהעלותה למרומי ההכרה.

יישר חילו של מע״כ ידידי הנעלה, איש אשר רוח בו, הרה״ג, איש האשכלות, **מוה״ר נתן שרמן שליט״א**, אשר להורות נתן בלבו [עי׳ אב״ע ואוה״ח שם], לשאוב מים ממעינות, ולחתות אש התורה ונשמות ישראל מיקוד — ללבות גחלים עוממות ולהדליק נר מצוה באור תורה. — ואפריון נמטי למע״כ ידידי הרה״ג יקר רוח **מוה״ר מאיר יעקב זלטוביץ שליט״א** המנצח על המלאכה, שתרגם ופירש ספר זה, מפורש ושום שכל.

תחזקנה ידיהם לתורה ולתעודה, ויזכו להמשיך בעבוה״ק ללמוד וללמד להגדיל תורה ולהאדירה בקרב ישראל עד יבא שילה ומלאה הארץ דעה בב״א.

הכו״ח לכבוד התורה, ג׳ לס׳ מטות, י״ט תמוז התשמ״א

יוסף חיים שניאור קוטלר

מכתב ברכה

דוד קאהן
ביהמ"ד גבול יעבץ
ברוקלין, נוא יארק

"ויותר שהיה קהלת חכם עוד למד דעת את העם ואזן וחקר תקן משלים הרבה" (קהלת יב-ט) ואזן דברי תורה וחקר דברי תורה עשה אזנים לתורה... עד שלא עמד שלמה לא היה אדם יכול להשכיל דברי תורה וכיון שעמד שלמה התחילו הכל סוברין תורה.

אמר רבי שילא לקיתון גדול שהוא מלא רותחין ולא היה לו אזן לטלטלו ובא אחד ועשה לו אזן והתחיל לטלטלו על ידי אזנו. אמר רבי חנינא לבאר עמוקה מלאה מים והיו מימיה צוננין ומתוקין וטובים ולא היתה בריה יכולה לשתות ממנה בא אדם אחד וספק לה חבל בחבל משיחא במשיחא ודלה ממנה ושתה התחילו הכל דולין ושותין... א"ר יודן ללמדך שכל מי שהוא אומר דברי תורה ברבים זוכה שתשרה רוח הקודש עליו וממי אתה למד משלמה שעל ידי שאמר דברי תורה ברבים זכה ששרתה עליו רוח הקודש ואמר שלשה ספרים משלי קהלת ושיר השירים (שיר השירים רבה א')

בס"ד

כבוד ידידי הנאמנים
הרב מאיר יעקב זלטוביץ נ"י והרב נתן שרמן נ"י
ה' עליהם יחיו

המאמרים המוזכרים למעלה מתארים רגשות לבי לקראת הופעתו של האבן העזר הלזה (עיין שמואל א ז-יב) בשדה היהדות, הלא היא הדפסת הכרך הששי שעל ידו נגמר הפירוש שלכם על חומש בראשית. חומש זה מיוחד הוא בין חמשה חומשי תורה שלמרות שהוזכרו בו מצוות מועטות הוא שרש האמונה, וזכיתם להפיץ השקפה שגושפנקא של ישראל סבא חתומה עליה.

תקופת שלמה המלך משמשת דוגמא של אחרית הימים. המלך המשיח יושב על כסאו, ישראל שרוי על אדמתו, ובונים מקדש להקב"ה. (אין ספק שזהו הטעם שמפטירים בשלמה בשמיני עצרת המסמל אחרית הימים אחרי אבדון של שבעים אומות העולם.) ובימיו מתגלים מבועי תורה, כמבואר במדרש, והוא דולה ומשקה מהם לרוות צמאון בני ישראל לדברי תורה.

כן בעקבתא דמשיחא יתגלו רזי תורה על ידי מלכים - מאן מלכי רבנן - שיקשרו חבל בחבל ומשיחא במשיחא וישאבו מים לאלו שבלעדיהם לא יוכלו לשתות מימי הבאר שחפרוה שרים.

אשריכם שזכיתם לכך לדלות מי תורה מהבארות אשר לעולם לא יכזבו מימיהם.
ואני תפלה שכשם שסיימתם ספר בראשית כן תזכו להתחיל ספרים אחרים ולסיימם ללמוד וללמד לשמור ולעשות.

אוהבכם ומוקירכם
הדורש שלומכם ושלום תורתכם
דוד קאהן
ל"ג בעומר תשמ"א

Table of Contents

◄§וישלח/Sidrah Vayishlach

◆§ סדר וישב / Sidrah Vayeishev

◆§ סדר מקץ / Sidrah Mikeitz

◈ סדר ויגש / Sidrah Vayigash

◈ סדר ויחי / Sidrah Vayechi

PREFACE TO THE FINAL VOLUME OF THE ORIGINAL SIX-VOLUME EDITION

ברוך שהחיינו וקימנו והגיענו לזמן הזה

It is with special feelings of humility and joyous gratitude to the Ribono Shel Olam that we present this, the sixth and last volume of the ArtScroll BEREISHIS, *to the Torah-learning public.*

The volume culminates the first plateau in the ongoing commentary to the Chumash, which I have the z'chus to write in association with Reb Nosson — the selection and preparation of the commentary being done by me, and the editing as well as the beautiful and stimulating Overviews prepared by him. It also marks the twelfth sefer which we have done together, and the forty-fifth in the ArtScroll Series בלע״ה כ״י.

What began nearly six years ago with a volume on Megillas Esther written as a memorial to a dear friend, Reb Mair Fogel ע״ה, *has* ב״ה *emerged into a major vehicle for disseminating Torah to the English-speaking world; a project deemed worthy of endorsement by the major Roshei Yeshivah and Gedolei Yisroel* שליט״א, *among them:* MARAN HAGAON R' MOSHE FEINSTEIN, MARAN HAGAON R' YAAKOV KAMENETZKY, MARAN HAGAON R' YAAKOV YITZCHAK HALEVI RUDERMAN, MARAN HAGAON R' MORDECHAI GIFTER, MARAN HAGAON R' SHNEUR KOTLER, *and* להבחל״ח MARAN HAGAON R' GEDALIAH SCHORR זצ״ל. *They who bear much of the burden of Jewish servival, and whose wisdom defines the means by which the nation of Torah sustains itself, have seen fit to give their approval, encouragement, time, and guidance to our work. They have graciously described the ArtScroll Series as one of the great contributions to the world of Torah, and we accept the heavy responsibility of being worthy of their confidence.*

Baruch Hashem, the series as a whole has attracted authors from the front ranks of English-speaking Torah-scholars and thinkers. Thanks to their participation, it has branched out from the Five Megillos and Chumash to many other areas. The series now includes works on Tanach, Mishnah — with one of the broadest anthologized commentaries ever produced, YAD AVRAHAM *— in memory of Avraham Yosef Glick* ע״ה *— under the patronage of* MR. AND MRS. LOUIS GLICK שיחיו; *the liturgy; Judaica classics; biographies, and even a new Youth Series. The impact of the Series has been profound, and we thank the Ribono Shel Olam for allowing us to be a conduit for spreading His Word to those who thirst for it.*

Work has already begun on Sefer Shemos, and is steadily progressing on the Siddur. In addition, the next year should אי״ה *see the publication of Yehoshua; the balance of Tehillim; Mishnayos Shabbos, Eruvin and Beitzah — thereby completing Seder Moed; Mishnah Yevamos in Seder Nashim; the final volumes of R' Zevin's* Festivals in Halachah *and* Treasury of Chassidic Tales on the Festivals; *Ezra; Nechemiah; a treasury of Biographies of Rishonim and Acharonim; and the first volume of Divrei HaYamim and of I Shmuel. An ambitious program, indeed; one that will require* סייעתא דשמיא *and great team effort to accomplish. But if our work can continue to make Torah study the province of English-speaking Jews — authentic, unalloyed Torah, as our Sages understood Hashem's Word, without watering down by non-traditional sources — then the thousands of hours invested will have been fully justified.*

ACKNOWLEDGMENTS

At this joyous time of fulfillment — the Siyum of Sefer Bereishis — I wish again to emphasize that if this work is in any way worthy of the reader's attention, it is because I have the honor of benefitting from the friendship and personal counsel of some of the most scholarly and intellectually gifted personalities on the contemporary Torah scene. I am deeply indebted to:

My father HARAV HAGAON ARON ZLOTOWITZ שליט״א, *of whose erudition and scholarship I have always stood in awe. He has discussed significant portions of the work with me and allowed me to benefit from his wisdom and hashkafah. May my dear mother* הרבנית פרומא בת אסתר גיטל תחי׳ *be granted a* רפואה שלמה, *so that they can resume their active lives together and enjoy much nachas from their children, grandchildren, and great grandchildren* עד מאה ועשרים שנה.

I wish especially to record my warmest gratitude to רבי ומורי, HARAV HAGAON R' DAVID FEINSTEIN שליט״א, *a self-effacing gaon of encyclopedic knowledge, who has given of himself and his sage counsel tirelessly and enthusiastically. He has generously torn days from his busy schedule to read the manuscript, note discrepancies, clarify difficult concepts, and point out new material and insights. More than once has saved me an embarrassing error, and has guided me to insights I might never have known without him. He has made himself totally available on every and any occasion to discuss a fine point in p'shat, and has sharply honed my sensitivity in areas of exegesis and presentation. His warm concern and encouragement have pervaded this entire undertaking. Words do not suffice to convey my feelings of gratitude and admiration.*

Similarly, my profound mentor, HARAV HAGAON R' DAVID COHEN *שליט״א, a rare blend of phenomenal breadth of knowledge and clarity of thought, has always made himself totally available — far beyond the bounds of friendship — to discuss and investigate concepts and approaches of the material prior to publication. It was Reb David who, many years ago, inspired in me a profound love for sefarim and meticulous research.*

Both HARAV FEINSTEIN *and* HARAV COHEN *encouraged this work at times of great frustration, and much of the z'chus of the ArtScroll publications must be credited to them. Though their comments are frequently quoted throughout the commentary and Overviews, their influence pervades the work far out of proportion to the times they are mentioned by name. The positive aspects of the work bears their imprint; the shortcomings are my own.*

Additionally, I must express gratitude to a group of distinguished leaders whose personal support and encouragement have been immeasurably important: R' MOSHE SHERER, R' MICHAEL L. MUNK, R' JOSEPH ELIAS, R' PINCHAS STOLPER, R' BORUCH B. BORCHARDT, MR. DAVID H. SCHWARTZ, MR. AARON L. HEIMOWITZ.

My colleagues, co-workers — and friends — at Mesorah Publications, RABBI AVIE GOLD *and* MR. STEPHEN BLITZ, *each in his respective role, exemplifies the very high standards we have set for ourselves — Avie in the literary area, and Steve in the organizational and developmental areas. Their loyal professional efforts, cheerfully expended, are gratefully appreciated and are very important in the success of the Series. Moreover, the office and production staff —* YOSEF TIMINSKY, *my sister* MRS. SHIRLEY KIFFEL, MRS. FAIGIE WEINBAUM, LEA FREIER, CHANEE FREIER, EDEL STREICHER, *and* ESTHER GLATZER, *have cheerfully performed their respective functions in a competent, cooperative, and professional manner, demanding production schedules notwithstanding. The finished products bear eloquent testimony to their efforts.*

I am also grateful to our Distributors in Europe and Israel, R' JOSEPH LEHMANN *(of Gateshead), and my long-time very dear friends* MR. AND MRS. JOSHUA GROSSMAN *(of Bayit Vegan). Their competence in bringing the ArtScroll Series to the attention of readers throughout the world is most sincerely appreciated.*

Mention must also be made of the sincere efforts and encouragement of dear friends [listed alphabetically]: R' JOSEPH BERLINER, R' ZUNDEL BERMAN, R' YISRAEL H. EIDELMAN, R' CHARLES GRANDOVSKY, R' RONALD GREENWALD, R' NAFTALI HIRSCH, R' MEIR HOLDER, R' BURTON JAFFA, *my brother-in law* R' YAAKOV KIFFEL, R' YAAKOV KORNREICH, R' YERUCHEM LAX, R' MICHAEL LEVI, R' JAY MARCUS, R' ELI MUNK, R' TZVI NEUBERGER, DR. ALLAN D. NOVETSKY, *my brother-in-law* R' SOL SCHOLAR, R' JUDAH SEPTIMUS, R' AVI SHULMAN, R' DAVID SINGER, R' YOSEF WEINBAUM, R' NISSON WOLPIN. *Their friendship and concern is warmly appreciated.*

During the course of publication of the ArtScroll Series, I have been privileged to make the acquaintance and to work closely with several great Talmidei Chachomim — veritable treasurehouses of Torah knowledge and hashkafah — whose association as contributors to the Series and as friends, has meant a great deal to me: R' HERSH GOLDWURM, R' MOSHE EISEMANN, R' YOSEF RABINOWITZ, R' J. DAVID BLEICH, R' AVROHOM CHAIM FEUER, R' AVROHOM YOSEF ROSENBERG, R' YISROEL GORNISH, R' YAAKOV SALOMON, R' REUVEN DRUCKER.

Most of all I am grateful for the very close association that has flowered between myself and REB NOSSON: ידיד נכבד, *mentor, critic, and chaver par excellence. Words simply cannot reflect the relationship. Suffice it to note that were it not for his eloquence, breadth, clarity of presentation of the most sublime thoughts of our Sages, and scope of his knowledge, this Series would never have gained the level of prominence it has had the z'chus to achieve. Every word of the ArtScroll Series bears testimony to his artistry and scholarly general editorship. Moreover, he has been the moving force behind my work, and has been a source of inspiration to me in many areas. I regret that I am unable to adequately express my gratitude to him. — O to be blessed with his felicity for just this one moment!*

My good friend, REB SHEAH BRANDER, *has constantly striven to make the Series one of beauty and esthetic excellence; and he has succeeded immensely — every volume bears testimony to his graphic artistry. Sheah's input is not limited to graphics; as a talmid chochom who delivers shiurim in his community, he has a zeal for the subject matter and frequently contributes comments and insights. During our decade-long association he has been a chaver and colleague in every sense of the words, and his friendship is appreciated beyond words.*

אחרון אחרון חביב. *I thank the Ribono Shel Olam for His chessed in granting me an* עקרת הבית *who has created a home for our children and me which is conducive to Torah study and Yiras Shamayim, and which, to her delight, has become a* בית ועד לחכמים, *a gathering place for scholars. To paraphrase R' Akiva who credited his accomplishments in Torah learning to his wife: "*שלי ... שלה*, Whatever I have accomplished is hers."* ROCHEL *has patiently borne the burden of domestic responsibilities, allowing — no, encouraging — me to devote myself to this project. The children, too, — Gedaliah, Esther, Faigie, Dvorah, Tziviah, Yisroel and Baruch — have cheerfully cooperated in every way they could. May Hashem reward us that our children dwell in the 'tent of Torah' and righteousness.*

The past year has unfortunately witnessed the taking of my dear father-in-law, R' Chaim Chaikel Shulman זצ״ל, *to whose memory this volume is lovingly dedicated. The spreading of Torah was his life's ideal, and he did it with a generosity of spirit that left an indelible memory with all who were warmed by his friendship. May the Torah learning this volume will engender be a z'chus for his neshamah, and may he be a* מליץ יושר *for the entire family, especially for his aishes chayil, my dear mother-in-law, Chaya* תחי׳*. May she be returned to full health so that she can continue to enjoy unlimited nachas from the family to whom she means so much.*

I close with a tefillah like that traditionally recited at the Siyum of a volume of the Talmud:

> *May it be Your will, HASHEM my God, that just as you have helped us complete Sefer Bereishis, so may You help us begin other Books and complete them. May we be enabled to study, teach, observe, perform and uphold all the words of Your Torah lovingly. May the merit of the Prophets, Sages, and commentators stand by us that the Torah may not depart from our mouths and from the mouths of our children and grandchildren forever. May there be fulfilled in us the verses: "When you journey it [the Torah] shall guide you, when you recline it shall protect you, and when you awaken it shall be your discourse. For through Me your days shall multiply and your days of life shall increase. Lengthy days are in its right, and in its left are wealth and honor. May HASHEM give strength to His people; may HASHEM bless His people with peace."*

Meir Zlotowitz

Tammuz, 5741 / July, 1981

◆§ סדר ויצא

◆§ Sidrah Vayeitzei

— *The Overviews*

Several topics in this Sidrah have been treated in Overviews to earlier volumes. Among them are:

Jacob's role — *Lech-Lecha and Toldos*
Tests — *Lech Lecha*
Reuben's sin — *Ruth*
Exile — *Eichah and Daniel*

The role of the twelve tribes will א״ה *be discussed in future volumes.*

An Overview —
Jacob: Vision and Exile*

וַיֵּצֵא יַעֲקֹב מִבְּאֵר שָׁבַע וַיֵּלֶךְ חָרָנָה, וּכְתִיב וַיִּפְגַּע בַּמָּקוֹם — כִּי מָטָא לְחָרָן אָמַר: אֶפְשָׁר עָבַרְתִּי עַל מָקוֹם שֶׁהִתְפַּלְּלוּ אֲבוֹתַי וַאֲנִי לֹא הִתְפַּלַּלְתִּי ... כַּד צָלֵי בָּעֵי לְמֵיהֲדַר, אָמַר הקב״ה צַדִּיק זֶה בָּא לְבֵית מְלוֹנִי וְיִפָּטֵר בְּלֹא לִינָה? מִיָּד בָּא הַשֶּׁמֶשׁ.

'Jacob left Beer Sheba and went to Charan' [*i.e., he arrived there*] *(28:10). And it is written, 'He encountered the place'* [*i.e., he came not to Charan but to Bethel/Moriah*] *(ibid. v. 11). — When he arrived in Charan he said, 'Can it be that I passed by the place where my fathers prayed, without my praying?' ... After he prayed, he wanted to return* [*to Charan*]. *The Holy One, Blessed be He, said, 'This tzaddik has come to My dwelling; shall he be allowed to leave without spending the night?' Immediately, the sun set* [*ibid.*] *(Chullin 91b).*

I. The Well

Dimensions of Exile

In *Vayeitzei* we read a narrative of dual significance. Jacob begins a personal exile with his flight from Esau to begin a twenty-year sojourn with Laban. There, in Charan, he would marry and give birth to all of his children except for Benjamin. He would arrive penniless and emerge with a great fortune. But despite his success in Charan he would always remain conscious that he was in exile from *Eretz Yisrael* and his parents' home, and that he was sub-

* This Overview is based on a *Schmuess* of Harav Gedaliah Schorr זצ״ל. All of its components, unless specifically credited, may be found in *Sfas Emes*.

ject to the constant machinations and swindles of Laban. That is one thread in this tale of exile, the *personal* travail of hounded, homeless Jacob. The second thread is the *national* aspect of this exile, for Jacob's flight must be seen in the context of the four hundred years of Jewish exile decreed upon Abraham's offspring [15:13], and as preparation for the future millenia of Jewish wandering and subjugation. Jacob, as the only Patriarch who experienced the brunt of exile's harsher manifestations, prepared the way for his posterity, for as we shall see in this and succeeding *sidros* Jacob set the precedents for Jewish behavior in exile.

Jacob, as the only Patriarch who experienced the brunt of exile's harsher manifestations, prepared the way for his posterity.

Jacob remained fully conscious all the while that he was in *galus. Vayeitzei* is unusual in that it contains not a single space between paragraphs. In the masoretic order of the Torah Scroll, the entire *sidrah* is written as a single 145-verse paragraph. This is meant to imply that Jacob never ceased his concentration on the predicament of being parted from the Holy Land. To forget that one is in exile is to make peace with the situation. Of course, *galus* is in great measure a geographical fact. Mordechai and Esther were in exile despite their greatness, while the humblest farmhand who returned to *Eretz Yisrael* with Ezra was not — but there are also intellectual and emotional dimensions to *galus*. In a very real sense, the well established, secure, happy person of affairs in the Diaspora feels less *galus* than the *tzaddik* and sage in the heart of the Holy City who weeps every midnight as he pours out his prayers for the coming of the Messiah and the building of the Temple. Jacob never ceased agonizing over the fact that he lived in Charan instead of Beer Sheba; to maintain such awareness is a major factor in enduring — and *surviving* — exile with one's spirit intact.

Mordechai and Esther were in exile despite their greatness, while the humblest farmhand who returned to Eretz Yisrael with Ezra was not.

Jacob's Oath

Jacob entered his personal exile with further resolve, as well. The *Midrash* expounds,

וַיֵּצֵא יַעֲקֹב מִבְּאֵר שָׁבַע ... יָצָא מִבְּאֵרָה שֶׁל שְׁבוּעָה

Jacob *departed from Beer Sheba* [28:10] ...

he departed from the well [בְּאֵר] *of* [*his*] *oath* [שְׁבוּעָה=שֶׁבַע] (*Bereishis Rabbah* 68:8).

Many commentators teach that the word שְׁבוּעָה, *oath,* is related to, and derived from שֶׁבַע, *seven.* When a person undertakes an oath, all his שֶׁבַע מִדּוֹת, the *seven attributes* of his personality, thought, and action processes become mortgaged to the execution of his pledge or to the truth of his statement. The oath is, so to speak, a lien on his entire being and resources. In Hebrew grammar, therefore, the taking of an oath is not an *active* word, it is a passive word; the grammatical implication is that when one swears he becomes possessed by his oath. We find the word נִשְׁבַּע or יִשָּׁבַע, literally *he was sworn* or *he will be sworn,* for all his seven attributes become subservient to the oath. [For a discussion of the seven attributes, see ArtScroll *Zemiroth* pp. 226-235.]

When one swears he becomes possessed by his oath.

The *Midrashic* exegesis is that Jacob left home with an oath that the concepts symbolized by Beer Sheba would never leave his awareness despite its distance from Charan in miles and its even greater distance in holiness and morality. But Jacob is not content merely to swear. He goes to Charan with a strong cognizance of בְּאֵרָה שֶׁל שְׁבוּעָה, *the* **source of the oath.** A sincere oath exerts a powerful control on a person's actions.But even more significant in the long run is that one remain powerfully attached to the set of beliefs, values, and goals which motivated his oath in the first place. Such a continuing awareness assures that the oath will retain its force even after the passage of years and the onslaughts of antagonistic people and circumstances. Merely to remember a resolve while forgetting the reason for making the resolution is a fragile crutch. Jacob entered a foreign land with the indelible memory of his upbringing and his knowledge of God's word — that memory was the source of his oath.

Merely to remember a resolve while forgetting the reason for making the resolution is a fragile crutch.

Jacob was a product of Isaac and Rebecca. He had chosen to dedicate his life to the Patriarchal ideal and he solidified his choice with fourteen years of study in the Academy of Eber before he dared venture from

Beer Sheba's holiness to Charan's impurity. These were the *'well'*, the source of Jacob's personal attributes, and Jacob remained cognizant wherever he was that he came from there — and that he *must* remain there emotionally and intellectually, if not physically.

Jacob, before descending to the spiritual depth of Charan, anchored himself to the holiness of Eretz Yisrael by means of an oath...

The *Zohar* compares Jacob to someone climbing down into a deep and treacherous well. Before attempting his descent, he must secure himself to the surface with a strong rope, otherwise he may fall and be lost forever. Jacob, before descending to the spiritual depth of Charan, anchored himself to the holiness of *Eretz Yisrael* by means of an oath, a resolve that he would never cut his ties with the source of his strength.

II. Jacob's Vision

כִּי מָטָא לְחָרָן אָמַר: אֶפְשָׁר עָבַרְתִּי עַל מָקוֹם שֶׁהִתְפַּלְּלוּ אֲבוֹתַי וַאֲנִי לֹא הִתְפַּלַּלְתִּי? כַּד יָהֵיב דַּעְתֵּיהּ לְמֵיהֲדַר, קָפְצָה לֵיהּ אַרְעָא — מִיָּד וַיִּפְגַּע בַּמָּקוֹם.

When he [Jacob] arrived at Charan he said, 'Can it be that I passed by the place where my fathers prayed, without my praying?' As soon as he decided to return, the earth jumped toward him — immediately, [28:11] he encountered the place (Chullin 91b).

The Place

The immediate prelude to Jacob's exile was his night at Bethel/Moriah, the place that he would recognize as the *House of God* and the *Gate of Heaven*, the place where God revealed Himself, and where Jacob made the vow that would sustain him for his twenty-two years away from home. The very fact that he came to Bethel/Moriah was in itself a testimony to the 'strong rope' by which he had secured himself to his 'well'. Jacob was already in Charan when he decided to pray at the place where Abraham and Isaac had prayed. As *Rashi* explains,

God brought Bethel/Moriah to meet Jacob. Geographic realities disappeared and the laws of physics were set aside as Jacob found himself where he wanted to be. It was Divine recognition that, in the spiritual sense, Jacob *was* in the place his fathers had sanctified; so powerful was his desire to emulate them.

In our confused state of understanding, we are so tightly bound to physical reality, that we cannot conceive of such an event taking place: If Jacob was in Charan, how could Bethel/Moriah come to meet him? *People* can move, but places cannot move, can they? That such assumptions are so axiomatic to us is a symptom of the unfortunate fact that we are conditioned to accept only the physical world as the 'real' world. Instead of seeking spiritual causes to explain physical occurrences, we seek physical reasons to explain miracles. But if spiritual existence has its own reality — as indeed it has — why should that not be the *prime* mode of existence, and why shouldn't laws of physics bend to accommodate spiritual needs?

Instead of seeking spiritual causes to explain physical occurrences, we seek physical reasons to explain miracles.

Unchanging Truth

Whatever the case, Jacob was at the place, prayed there, and slept there before his long sojourn in Charan. It was there that he had his great vision. To understand the vision, we must never forget that it was revealed to *Jacob*, and it must therefore be comprehended in the light of the uniqueness of the person for whom it was intended. Jacob's primary characteristic was מִדַּת הָאֱמֶת, *the attribute of truth,* as the prophet says תִּתֵּן אֱמֶת לְיַעֲקֹב, *give truth to Jacob (Micah* 7:20). [For a discussion of this quality within the context of the Patriarchal mission, see *Overview* to *Lech Lecha* and *Toldos.*]

An essential characteristic of truth is that it never changes.

An essential characteristic of truth is that it never changes, for if it were to change then it could never have been true. It may have been 'suitable,' 'apt,' or the best possible response to a set of circumstances, but it could not have been 'true' unless it were eternally true. Jacob, as the exponent of truth had to be consistent; he could not change his attitudes and aspirations according to moods and settings. Indeed, only because Jacob was the symbol of truth, could, his image be engraved on God's כִּסֵא הַכָּבוֹד, *Throne of Glory (Bereishis Rabbah* 82:2). God's Own seal is truth [חוֹתָמוֹ שֶׁל הקב״ה אֱמֶת] (*Shabbos* 55a), so only a human personification of His seal can be indelibly inscribed on His throne. Because that was Jacob's characteristic, he could accept only a prophetic vision that was entirely consistent with his comprehension of the Divine truth.

Three Visions

In the Torah's description of Jacob's vision, the word הִנֵּה, *behold!*, appears three time: וְהִנֵּה סֻלָּם, *behold! there was a ladder;* ... וְהִנֵּה מַלְאֲכֵי אֱלֹהִים, *behold! angels of God* ...; and וְהִנֵּה ה׳ נִצָּב עָלָיו, *behold! HASHEM stood over him* [28:12-13]. That word always signifies something strikingly new, therefore its three-fold appearance indicates that Jacob was shown three different levels of prophetic vision.

Chovos Halevavos explains that Jacob was shown a ladder to indicate a means by which he could attain an understanding of God.

First, there was a ladder standing on earth and extending up to heaven. *Chovos Halevavos* explains that Jacob was shown a ladder to indicate a means by which he could attain an understanding of God. With rigorous intellectual effort one can study the natural world and arrive at the inescapable conclusion that there must be a Creator. Such analysis can lead him rung by rung up the intellectual and spiritual ladder until he arrives at the most sublime understanding open to man. Abraham did it as a child when he said, in the famous *Midrashic* figure of speech ?תֹּאמַר לְבִירָה זוֹ בְּלֹא מַנְהִיג, *Can you say that this palace has no master? (Bereishis Rabbah* 39:1). Many of the classic commentators attempted to prove the existence of God and explain the commandments by means of philosophical inquiry.

But Jacob would not accept this revelation. His passion for truth could not be satisfied by a form of revelation which is based on human inquiry.

But Jacob would not accept this revelation. His passion for truth could not be satisfied by a form of revelation which is based on human inquiry for, in the final analysis, such knowledge of God is circumscribed by human limitations. The person who has attained such knowledge has accomplished much, but he still lacks an experience of the Divine.

Physical process can be reduced to mathematical formulae, but the most brilliant thesis cannot take the place of a sunrise. The score of a symphony is not equivalent to a concert.

Test of Sleep

Why was Jacob shown this vision for which he had no desire? God was testing his dedication to seek the ultimate level of truth — how consistent was it? The vision of this ladder of philosophical knowledge was a great challenge to Jacob. He was asleep. Of necessity, his perceptions were dulled. The self-control one exercises in wakefulness is not possible during sleep. A drowsy person can be seduced by arguments he would never accept and be induced to do foolish things he could never do while awake. But *some* things are so basic to people that they will never do them — in their dreams, in a daze, under hypnosis. A person who affects a dignified tone of voice and a sophisticated accent will slip into his natural speech pattern when his guard is down. But he will not commit murder.

Awake, Jacob would have no interest in philosophical speculation.

Awake, Jacob would have had no interest in philosophical speculation, for it did not measure up to his ideal of truth. But if he were to accept such a revelation while asleep, that would prove that his dedication to truth, while certainly sincere, was then still external. Were it truly part of his being, he could not have accepted anything that fell short; Jacob did *not* accept it.

A Higher Level

God tested him again with a second level of revelation, a heightened one — Godly angels ascended and descended the ladder. Now Jacob saw true spirituality, for angels are but a step removed from God. Now he saw a level of holiness that far transcended the philosophical ladder. But Jacob was not moved by the sight of angels. His craving for spiritual truth required more than angels could provide.

Centuries later, Moses, too, could not bring himself to accept the guidance of an angel in place of God. After Israel had sinned by building and worshiping the Golden Calf, God withdrew His Own Presence and dispatched an angel to lead the people. But Moses pleaded that he could not be guided by an angel. This was not a case of a refusal to obey God's word ח״ו; the prophet who had spoken to God 'face to face' *could* not — not *would* not — find commensurate spiritual sustenance in a 'mere' angel. Moses prayed:

אִם אֵין פָּנֶיךָ הֹלְכִים אַל תַּעֲלֵנוּ מִזֶּה

If Your Face [*i.e., Your Own Presence*] *will not come, do not cause us to travel from here (Exodus* 33:15*).*

Why was Jacob dissatisfied with the revelation of angels?

Why was Jacob dissatisfied with the revelation of angels? He recognized that they were not a true vision of God. We can best understand the deficiency of the angelic revelation by comparing it to something more familiar — a human being.

We know that a person consists of body and soul, and that the body blocks our perception of the soul's essence; we know the soul is there, but we cannot see it. In Kabbalistic terminology, this concept is known as לְבוּשׁ, *garment*. When a fully dressed, heavily bundled person engages in a vigorous activity, we do not see his arms and legs, hands and feet. We see only sleeves and pants, gloves and shoes. We *know* that a *body* is under the clothing, but a creature which had never seen a human body could have only a faint, and very erroneous, idea of what the organs look like. Going a step further, we know that the vital organs — brain, heart, glands and so on — are inside the body, but only a tiny fraction of the population has ever *seen* them in any form. A soul is there, too, but no human being has ever seen the soul; it is buried beneath the 'garb' of the body.

Similarly, Jacob recognized that even an angel is merely a 'garment' within which there existed the basic glory of God. Jacob was not content to see garments and imagine what lay within. He wanted to know God Himself. It is interesting and illuminating that the *Midrash* (69:1) interprets that word כָּבוֹד, literally *glory*, as Jacob's term for a direct vision of God. In *Psalms* 16:9, the human soul is referred to as

Jacob was not content to see garments and imagine what lay within. He wanted to know God Himself.

כָּבוֹד. Clearly, the highest form of glory is often obscured: God's holiness by angels, and man's soul by his body.

God urged Jacob to ascend the ladder — meaning that he should accept the levels of prophecy that had been offered him. God promised that if Jacob were to 'ascend,' he would never fall from that particular level of holiness, and his children would never be exiled. For Jacob to insist on a more intense level of revelation invited a grave risk, because the greater the aspiration, the greater the possibility that he or his offspring might fail to achieve it or maintain it. Why not content himself with what intellectual speculation and vision of angels could give him, and be secure that Israel would never fall from that great, though limited height? Why insist on the greatness of an elevation that might be too rarefied?

For Jacob to insist on a more intense level of revelation invited a grave risk.

But Jacob could not be content with such a guarantee. His passion for truth required him to know God Himself. However, an angel is not God. Just as the material nature and animal needs of the human body prevent our perception of the soul that resides within it, so the mere fact that an angel exists as a separate creature obscures the God Who created it.*

Jacob wanted direct knowledge of God. He wanted to be shown the ultimate truth for which he had striven all his life. He was shown it: וְהִנֵּה ה׳ נִצָּב עָלָיו, *and behold! HASHEM was standing over him.* Let the nations and the forces of nature be led by guardian angels — Jacob and the Jewish nation are guided directly by God.

כִּי חֵלֶק ה׳ עַמּוֹ יַעֲקֹב חֶבֶל נַחֲלָתוֹ
For HASHEM's portion is His nation; Jacob is His firm heritage (Deut. 32:9).

---

* There are other interpretations of God's urging that Jacob ascend. Furthermore, the *Midrash* quotes an opinion that Jacob sinned in not obeying. See *Sfas Emes, Netzach Yisrael,* and *Michtav MeEliyahu* vol. III. Furthermore, there are many other interpretations of the vision, most of which are cited in the commentary. The oft-stated principle remains: the words of the Torah are rich in meaning, all of them equally valid.

III. Prayer and Fulfillment

Jacob's Contribution

There is a tradition that the Patriarchs originated the three daily prayers: Abraham introduced שַׁחֲרִית [*Shacharis*], the *Morning Prayer;* Isaac introduced מִנְחָה [*Minchah*], the *Afternoon Prayer;* and Jacob — there at Bethel/Moriah [see *comm.*] — introduced מַעֲרִיב [*Maariv*], the *Evening Prayer (Berachos* 26b). *Shem MiShmuel* explains the uniqueness of Jacob's contribution to the world of prayer, a uniqueness that flowed from his perception that God must be seen behind all the garments that seem to reveal, but truly obscure, Him.

Shacharis and *Minchah* were instituted in the morning and afternoon corresponding to the morning and evening תְּמִידִים, *continual daily sacrifices* in the Temple. *Maariv* parallels the burning on the altar of the parts of the sacrifices that were left from the day's service. There is a basic difference between the daytime service and the nighttime burning of the parts. The actual sacrificial service is clearly holy. Its symbolism is widely perceived by the classic commentators as representing the dedication of souls and human states, it provides atonement and cleansing from the effect of sin. The blood of the offerings symbolizes the soul of the people seeking atonement.

Such sacrificial service is forbidden in the evening; it is valid only by day. It would seem as though the burning of the parts on the altar is lower in holiness, as though it were little more than a necessary way to dispose of the leftover parts.

He infused holiness into the mundane, or better said, he recognized that holiness was present in the mundane.

Jacob demonstrated otherwise. He infused holiness into the mundane, or better said, he recognized that holiness was *present* in the mundane. By fighting spiritual struggles to reach the *ultimate* glory of God's Own Presence, he meant to show that behind every occurrence and phenomenon in the universe God's presence can and must be seen. This teaching carried special significance for Jacob on his way to exile. What he did then was intended to be a lesson to the Jewish People in all future exiles. There are times when the nation considers itself forlorn and bereft of God's Providence; times that seem like the nighttime of our existence, when light is absent, and holiness seems far away. When that happens, we take heart from Jacob's example. Even in darkest night, he prayed, saw God, absorbed holiness. So must we.

Even in darkest night, he prayed, saw God, absorbed holiness. So must we.

The Sages teach that when God promised Jacob the entire land upon which he lay, He folded all of *Eretz Yisrael* beneath the sleeping Jacob to symbolize that it would be his (*Chullin* 91b; see *comm.* to 28:13). Why was this necessary in view of the Talmudic principle that a new owner need make a קִנְיָן, *act of acquisition,* in only part of a tract of land in order to acquire possession of the entire property? If so, the fact that Jacob lay on one small part of Bethel/Moriah should have been sufficient to enforce Israel's eventual ownership of the entire land.

Holy of Holies

By so folding the land, God signified that more than legal possession was intended. As the commentary sets forth, Jacob lay upon the eventual site of the קֹדֶשׁ הַקֳּדָשִׁים, *Holy of Holies. Eretz Yisrael* could have easily become his without the symbolism of placing all of it beneath him, but Jacob's vision — and the mission he had adopted by seeking the truth behind all 'garments' — required that the utmost holiness be found in every aspect of life. God wanted Jacob to know that every corner of *Eretz Yisrael* was to be invested with the utmost degree of holiness. Jews must never be content to find sanctity only on occasional excursions to Jerusalem and the Temple; they must infuse every nook and cranny with holiness.

Jews must never be content to find sanctity only on occasional excursions to Jerusalem and the Temple; they must infuse every nook and cranny with holiness.

Perhaps we may extend this concept to embrace Jacob himself. He was prepared to become the father of the tribes, the progenitor of the Jewish nation. Only then was he ready to begin the task, for only then had he merited to be shown God's Presence above him. All of *Eretz Yisrael* had to be subsumed under the overriding concept of Holy of Holies, and all of *Bnai Yisrael* had to be subsumed in the person of a Patriarch who saw and infused holiness into every aspect of his life. From such a father could be born such children. Of such a person could it be said that מִטָּתוֹ שְׁלֵמָה — all products of his home were righteous.

His Family— Two Camps

What sort of family would he produce? The answer is found in the last comments of *Ramban* and *Sforno* to *Vayeitzei*. The Torah tells us how Jacob saw a company of angels as he finally left Laban and set out for *Eretz Yisrael*. In their honor, he named the place *Machanaim*, literally *two camps:* his own camp and the angelic one (32:3).

Grammatically, however, the proper form should have been מַחֲנוֹת [*Machanos*], in the feminine plural form. But Jacob's intention was not to indicate the *numerical* fact that there was more than one camp. Rather he meant to stress the *quality* of the two camps.

In Hebrew there is a special suffix which *appears* to be masculine, but actually connotes 'pair of'. Thus, פַּעֲמַיִם means *two times* or a *pair* of times; יָדַיִם means a pair of hands, and מַחֲנַיִם means a *pair of camps.* When two things are called a pair, the implication is that both items are identical, or at least similar.

The exterior of the angels was a garment that clothed God's Presence— and so was the exterior of his family!

Jacob saw before him two camps: that of his wives, children, and possessions; and that of the angels. Knowing observer that he was, he could assess the *quality* of the camps as well as their size. And he saw that they were a pair! The exterior of the angels was a garment that clothed God's Presence — and so was the exterior of his family! Jacob had produced a family that was the parallel of the angels. In *Vayishlach* we will read of Jacob's encounter with, and conquest of, an angel. That was Jacob — but his children? Yes, his children. Perhaps they could not triumph over angels as could their father, but the conqueror of angels had produced a family — a camp

— that was the fitting equivalent on earth of an angelic camp above.

The promise of his vision had been fulfilled. He had lain on earth and perceived that the place where God is served on earth is the gateway to the heavens [28:17]. Now he had gone a major step further and perceived that the nation that serves God consistently and truthfully is equivalent to a company of angels.

Jacob's attribute was truth without compromise. He developed it in the home of Isaac and the Academy of Eber.

Jacob's attribute was truth without compromise. He developed it in the home of Isaac and the Academy of Eber, but only in situations that were anathema to truth — Laban, Esau, and Egypt — could his dedication to truth be tested in the most difficult circumstances imaginable. Now, his first test was over. Laban was behind him. Before him was Machanaim, proof that his vision was being fulfilled, for he stood facing a *pair* of equally holy camps.

An Overview /

Jacob, Rachel, and Leah

I. Jacob's Preparations for Marriage

His Particular Mission

Hardly a chapter in the Torah confronts our image of the Patriarch with as much difficulty as does that of Jacob's relationship with his two primary wives, Rachel and Leah. We read the Torah's narrative and wonder how to reconcile it with our faith in the greatness of the Patriarchs and Matriarchs. We know that Jacob was the בְּחִיר שֶׁבָּאָבוֹת, *chosen one of the Patriarchs,* the ideal human being whose wishes were motivated only by truth — yet the Torah implies that Jacob loved Rachel for her beauty and disdained Leah for her lack of it [29:17-18]; that he disliked Leah [29:31], and even after Rachel's early death he would not give Leah — mother of half his sons — the courtesy of raising her status above that of Rachel's handmaid, Bilhah [35:22, see *comm.*].

We tend to interpolate our own less-than-perfect reactions to real-life situations into the lives of our forebears.

As so often occurs, however, the translation of these episodes is not indicative of what was really happening. True, the episodes *seem* so simple and straightforward; in our own experience we are not surprised to hear of marriages based on physical attraction, of enduring resentments, and of jealousy among wives and relatives. Therefore we tend to interpolate our own less-than-perfect reactions to real-life situations into the lives of our forebears. We are quite prepared to acknowledge that Jacob's vision of the ladder cannot be understood superficially, because we recognize our own insufficiency to deal with prophetic visions, angels, the word of God, and the other unnatural events surrounding the vision. But his domestic life? — that is part of our own experience and it is inviting to see our ancestors in that familiar light. Let us attempt to demonstrate from the narrative itself that the 'simple understanding' is obviously inadequate. Then we shall seek the guidance of our Sages and commentators in arriving at a true comprehension of this complex chapter of our history.

To the believer, to the seeker of truth, what meets the eye in skimming the narrative is but a tantalizing invitation to plumb beneath the surface to seek the truth.

Harav Aharon Kotler זצ״ל saw this chapter as a prime example of the dangers inherent in superficial readings of Torah narratives, because of the above tendency to *humanize* our ancestors. To the believer, to the seeker of truth, what meets the eye in skimming the narrative is but a tantalizing invitation to plumb beneath the surface to seek the truth. *Harav Kotler* goes on to say that there are various interpretations given by the Sages and elucidated by the commentators in the light of their words. He offers this approach:

As we know, the Jewish *nation,* did not yet exist before Jacob's time. True, Abraham and Sarah had produced an Isaac, but Abraham also had an Ishmael and the children of Keturah. Isaac and Rebecca had produced a Jacob, but they had also had an Esau. *Israel* in its eternal sense was begun with Jacob. Of *that* Israel, God was to say that וְעַמֵּךְ כֻּלָּם צַדִּיקִים, *Your nation is entirely righteous (Isaiah* 60:21). There may be individual sinners among Israel, indeed sometimes the great majority of the nation is composed of such straying individuals, but the nation as a unit is considered righteous because its bond with holiness remains intact no matter what grievous temporary results are caused by temptation, persecution, and exile.

It was not enough for Jacob to think of marriage and family; he had to prepare himself for perfection.

Jacob knew that he was to be the father of the Twelve Tribes of Israel, and that every single one of his children would have to be great enough to be the forebear of one of the nation's components. It was not enough for Jacob to think of marriage and family; he had to prepare himself for *perfection.* Of him it would be said מִטָּתוֹ שֶׁל יַעֲקֹב אָבִינוּ שְׁלֵמָה, *the offspring of our father Jacob's marriage were perfect.* That could be possible only if he were to be the quintessence of the Patriarchal ideal, if he strove and labored to bring himself to a zenith of personal greatness. The Jacob whose portrait was etched on God's throne was the architect of the nation; as such he had to mold, craft, and refine his earthly self to match that heavenly visage.

All for the Purpose

That is why Jacob did not marry at forty in imitation of Isaac, as did Esau [26:34]. Even forty is a fairly advanced age for marriage, but Jacob could not think in terms of chronology alone; before he could marry he had to attain a spiritual level commensurate with his mission. When he was given Isaac's blessings and sent to Laban's home to find a mate, he was already sixty-three, but even then, he tarried. Jacob spent fourteen years of uninterrupted study in the Academy of Eber before venturing to Charan. Already when he was an adolescent, the Torah had described him as אִישׁ תָּם יֹשֵׁב אֹהָלִים, *a wholesome man, abiding in tents* [25:27]; he strove to unite himself with God's wisdom and he became the Patriarch who remains the very symbol of Torah, but he did not feel ready to go to Laban until he had spent fourteen years of uninterrupted study without even the luxury of bed and sleep [see *comm.* to 28:11].

How much preparation is necessary to become the father of Israel? None of us can even imagine, but Jacob knew. When he arrived at Laban's home, he was seventy-seven years old. Had he felt that he was ready for the cosmic task awaiting him, he would have insisted on an immediate marriage. After all, the plan that Jacob should work for seven years *before* marrying his bride was *Jacob's* suggestion, not Laban's. Why did Jacob offer to postpone his marriage even further, without even hearing Laban's terms? Certainly, Laban would have demanded an exorbitant payment, but if the Divine plan had called for the seventy-seven year old Patriarch to marry immediately, then the haggling over terms would not have been an impediment. Bethuel and Laban had been less than anxious to let Rebecca leave their home, but God did not permit them to prevent the

If the Divine plan had called for the seventy-seven year old Patriarch to marry immediately, then the haggling over terms would not have been an impediment.

inevitable. True, Jacob was penniless, but the man who single-handedly pushed boulders from well-mouths and routinely used angels as his emissaries could surely have found a way to send back to Isaac for whatever payment was required to satisfy the avaricious Laban.

Instead, Jacob *chose* to work for seven years before marrying. He *knew* — as we cannot even hope to understand — that his preparations were not yet complete. He needed seven years of unremitting labor and dedication. He needed seven years of punishing work during which he would voluntarily undertake unprecedented degrees of financial responsibility [31:38-40]. He knew that these preparations, too, were necessary prerequisites to the birth of Israel. The Torah he had studied with Isaac had to be augmented with a Torah of exile; the years with Eber would somehow make it possible for his future generations to endure and prevail during centuries of exile among the Labans and Esaus of history. His insistence on uncompromising standards of honesty as Laban's employee would instill in his progeny the fortitude to maintain its own uncompromising integrity despite the provocations of future taskmasters and tax assessors. [See next *Overview.*]

The Torah he had studied with Isaac had to be augmented with a Torah of exile.

Therefore, he did not long for Rachel while tending the sheep. What should have seemed like seven endless years passed כְּיָמִים אֲחָדִים, *like a few days* [29:20] because he *was* engaged in his mission. Whether in the fields and pasture lands of Paddan Aram preparing the way for his future children, or living with his wives to beget those children, he was involved with the same task. Had he busied himself with some senseless pursuit, he would indeed have felt each day to be another wasted eternity in his longing for Rachel — but not because he was in the field! The years spent tending the sheep were as much a part of his mission as would be the years he spent with his wives and children. The days passed quickly because they were filled with purpose.

The years spent tending the sheep were as much a part of his mission as would be the years he spent with his wives and children.

Without Delay

Finally, when he was ready, Jacob was not in the least reticent or ashamed to demand the wife for whom he had worked — הָבָה אֶת אִשְׁתִּי כִּי מָלְאוּ יָמָי וְאָבוֹאָה אֵלֶיהָ, *deliver my wife for my term is fulfilled, and I will consort with her* [29:21]: How *unseemly!* As *Rashi* remarks, quoting the *Midrash,* even a boorish lout would not speak so indelicately! Esau, the lustful murderer and adulterer, would have spoken like the perfect gentleman, yet Jacob, the truly perfect human, speaks like one overcome by lust and passion ח"ו! Are we to picture Jacob as a common laborer completing his term of service and roughly demanding his pay — his *human* pay? No, of course not!

As *Rashi* explains, Jacob said, 'I am already eighty-four years old; when will I beget twelve tribes?'

Let us understand this well. In Beer Sheba, Jacob had been sixty-three years old, but it was not *he* who spoke of the need to marry; Isaac and Rebecca *sent* him to seek a wife. He had patiently spent fourteen years in Eber's academy and another seven years with Laban's sheep — twenty-one years of *voluntary* delay — but we find no sign that he was impatient to unite with his chosen or to get about the task of begetting the twelve tribes. Was he even *then* a youngster who could afford such patience? And why the sudden almost embarrassing haste; having been patient for so many years, could he not have delayed the few hours or even days demanded by simple propriety and dignity?

Having been patient for so many years, could he not have delayed the few hours or even days demanded by simple propriety and dignity?

Indeed, if we understand his demand in superficial, literal terms, it is puzzling in the extreme. But the very question suggests its own answer. Jacob never thought in terms of his need for the physical companionship of a beloved partner. Had that been his motivation, he would not have waited until he was eighty-four, nor could his emotions have endured seven years of tending sheep while his Rachel awaited him.

Jacob existed for his mission: Twelve tribes. The nation of Israel. The fulfillment of God's purpose.

The people which would accept the Torah. Perfectly righteous offspring. The inner strength to endure and survive every manner of exile. Those were the visions and goals that preoccupied Jacob from the day he was old enough to know that the birthright had to be his with all its privileges and responsibilities. To become equal to them required more than half a lifetime of preparation. But when he *was* ready, what right had he to delay? Abraham had arisen early in the morning to prepare for the *Akeidah* [22:3], hadn't he? When a *mitzvah* is to be done, it must be accomplished promptly. If that were true even of the commandment for a father to slaughter his only son, surely it was true of the aging Patriarch about to lay the foundation of the Jewish People. Jacob had not wasted a moment in the Academy of Eber; he had not allowed night, cold, heat, or fatigue to deter him from tending Laban's sheep — now he would not allow a moment to be frittered away when he was ready for the next step in the process that began sixty-nine years earlier when he purchased the birthright from Esau. *'Give me my wife ... !'*

But unknown to Jacob, his mission required him to marry Leah too.

But unknown to Jacob, his mission required him to marry Leah too. Laban's greed and lack of scruple motivated him to substitute Leah for Rachel, and Rachel's almost incomprehensible kindness and sensitivity moved her to give her sister all the proofs of identity that she and Jacob had designed to thwart such a deception; and Leah's pure desire to be part of the building of Israel and her obedience to a father who did not deserve her respect forced her to accede to the scheme — but ultimately God's Providence made the plan succeed, because His Master Plan required it. That, and Jacob's preoccupation with the spiritual, cosmic implications of the wedding night. Had his purpose been physical, no amount of conspiracy could have deceived him. But his purpose was to fulfill the Divine mission of producing the nation of Israel. His spiritual antennae were not alerted because *he was in fact carrying out God's plan,* though he knew not — because it mattered not —

with whom. [The above is based on a lecture by *Harav Kotler* to a Torah Umesorah teachers seminar. It has been translated in its entirety, and published under the title *'How to Teach Torah.'*]

II. Rachel and Leah

Two Concepts

It still remains for us to learn why Jacob chose Rachel over Leah to be his partner. Were Leah not part of God's plan for him, we could understand: the righteous Jacob knew that Rachel was to be the mother of Israel and Leah was not. But this was not the case. Half the tribes, including Levi and Judah, the bearers of priesthood and monarchy, were Leah's children. Leah, not Rachel, would be his partner in the Cave of Machpelah. And it is axiomatic in our perception of the Patriarchs that Rachel's physical beauty could not have played a role in his choice.

He chose Rachel because she was his proper partner at that particular stage of his life. Jacob represents two concepts, as indicated by his names, Jacob and Israel. He was born as Jacob, but after nearly a hundred years of intensive and unremitting self-perfection, he accomplished and then transcended the mission represented by that name.

He was born as Jacob, but after nearly a hundred years of intensive and unremitting self-perfection, he accomplished and then transcended the mission represented by that name.

His initial task was to recognize this world as a separate entity, but to utilize it solely for God's sake. The world is full of potential and pleasure, and it is not easy to sublimate one's every urge and activity purely to a spiritual purpose. To do so was his task as a *'Jacob'* and, as we shall see in the next *Overview,* Jacob strove continuously to perfect this aspect of his being. His task was not fully done until he had endured his twenty years with Laban and was on his way back to *Eretz Yisrael.* Then he was able to conquer not only human impediments but even angels.

Having outgrown the status implied in the name Jacob, he was given the additional name Israel, signifying that this world had no independent existence for him; by then he had come to recognize it only in terms of its spiritual content and utility. It is one thing to make an inventory of one's possessions, recognize them as his *own,* but know that he is to use them to serve God alone; it is quite another to see everything as *God's* own, just as the angels and luminaries are His, and to see oneself as nothing more than His caretaker. The former sacrifices to God, the latter does not sacrifice at all, for whatever he touches is God's. Of course, it is *he* who signs the check for a charity, and *he* who dedicates his resources to a sacred purpose, but how is he different from the clouds that release rain because of his prayers or the sun that shines because of his service of God? The clouds and sun are not his, but they, like everything in the universe, respond to man's performance — or lack of performance — of God's will. Man, too, can so sublimate his perception of property that he recognizes everything as God's and himself as the mover, not the master. Jacob was born to utilize his *own* possessions for God's sake. Having achieved that mission, he went beyond it and recognized everything as God's — then he became Israel in recognition of his changed and elevated status *(Michtav MeEliyahu).*

The former sacrifices to God, the latter does not sacrifice at all, for whatever he touches is God's.

Two Roles

Just as the names Jacob and Israel represented two facets of Jacob's service, so were Rachel and Leah their complements. Husband and wife are partners in a mission. Their differences and similarities, even their conflicts, should ideally point toward the achievement of their joint goal. Rachel and Leah were different, just as Jacob and Israel were different.

There are two aspects of the Jewish nation.

1 — There is an unchanging degree of holiness shared by all Jews. It represents the zenith of our mission and it is the undying, inextinguishable spark of holiness that exists in all Jews, even the most sinful. When the *shofar* of the Messiah blows — the great *shofar* of the End of Days — and even the most forlorn and forsaken sons and daughters of Israel return from their Egypts and Assyrias to bow at God's mountain in Jerusalem, it will be this eternal

spark of Israel that the *shofar* will call forth. This aspect of Israel emanates from the most exalted sources of holiness; it is the ultimate holiness from which God began creation and which remains the ultimate goal of creation to reveal. Israel is the product on earth of this degree of holiness. Within it, there is no room for progress or regress; it is absolute and unchanging. Man's performance does not affect it; he can attain it or fall short, but he cannot alter it.

Israel is the product on earth of this degree of holiness.

2 — Israel's second facet is its responsibility to live in accordance with the Torah. This facet is never static; just as human performance changes, so this level of holiness is always changing, depending on Israel's degree of success in bringing its eternal spark of holiness into every area of its life and activity. It can be elevated to Israel's exalted state at Sinai or in Solomon's golden era, and it can plummet to the level before the two destructions or the times during the various exiles when it could fairly be asked, as the Angel of the Sea asked in Egypt, 'Both these and those are iniquitous, why should one be spared and the other destroyed?'

These two characteristics of Israel are represented by Leah and Rachel. Leah is the quiet, unseen holiness of Israel. The Kabbalists refer to the world of Leah as the עָלְמָא דְאִתְכַּסְיָא, *Hidden World.* Her world goes unnoticed in the hurly-burly of human activity, because it is holy and sublime beyond ordinary human comprehension. Her world is the soul of the universe as well as its ultimate goal, but it does not lower its standard to deal with the perceived 'reality' of human activity. It is unseen. Scripture alludes to this when it speaks of Leah's eyes as being weak [29:17] — figuratively, the 'vision' needed to perceive the nature of Leah is too weak, too clouded by the tangible world that constantly occupies its attention.

Rachel represents Israel's role of dealing with this world, elevating it and ultimately conquering it.

Rachel represents Israel's role of dealing with this world, elevating it and ultimately conquering it. The actor playing this role changes according to his performance, and all of creation changes with him. This task is visible; moment by moment it challenges us to decide what to think; what to do, what to dream, what to pursue. Rachel was the sister who caught people's attention, she was the 'beautiful' one who attracted the notice of people occupied with the activity of this world — and of a spiritual Jacob who occupied himself with turning the resources of his material world toward God.

A Wife for Jacob

The *Midrash* declares כָּל עַצְמוֹ שֶׁל יַעֲקֹב לֹא עָבַד אֶלָּא בִּשְׁבִיל רָחֵל, *Jacob's entire being dedicated itself to work* [*for Laban*] *only because of Rachel.* The *Midrash* stresses that *Jacob's* being, not Israel's, was dedicated to gaining Rachel as a wife. Because it was Jacob's task to sanctify the material universe, to use it exclusively for God's will and transform it into a sacrifice dedicated to Him, he *had* to unite himself with Rachel. *His* entire being was suited to the fulfillment of this goal. Of course, he was attracted by her beauty, for there is no greater beauty than a person ideally suited for a task he must perform or an object ideally suited to the need of the person to whom it is directed. In terms of the union between man and woman, Rachel's beauty is unsurpassed, because she symbolizes the successful dedication to the task of directing this world's resources and activity toward its goal. She is עַלְמָא דְאִתְגַּלְיָא, the *Revealed World.* She was Jacob's עֲקֶרֶת הַבַּיִת, *his primary wife.*

But Leah was Jacob's helpmeet in the loftier status of Israel. Once he had conquered man and angel, and recognized that all earthly possessions are but God's spirit in a material guise, Leah was the mate who best complemented him *(R' Moshe Chaim Luzzatto, Sefer HaK'lallim* 32; *Michtav MeEliyahu).*

A Wife for Israel

It is striking that Rachel died soon after Jacob was given the name Israel. Without a doubt, one factor in this phenomenon was that henceforth Leah, not Rachel, symbolized Jacob's ascendant mission. True, Jacob maintained Rachel's symbolic status as his primary wife by moving his personal belongings to the tent of Bilhah, Rachel's handmaid; despite his new status, the task of living with the exigencies of this world never end as long as one is alive. He was given the *additional* name Israel, but his name Jacob remained with him because life on earth remains a challenge that one can never ignore as long as he lives. Just as God does not associate His Name with a living *tzaddik,* because life includes the unending possibility of sin, so the attainment of Israel-status did not negate Jacob-status. Leah is the wife of Israel, but she becomes his primary companion only in the hidden holiness of the Cave of Machpelah after all of earth's temptations have been conquered.

Leah is the wife of Israel, but she becomes his primary companion only in the hidden holiness of the Cave of Machpelah after all of earth's temptations have been conquered.

There is a constant refrain going through most of chapters 29-30: the task of bringing the twelve tribes into the world. The commentary makes clear that this all-consuming goal concerned Jacob constantly and led to the intense rivalry among his wives to be instrumental in attaining this objective.

That this was his mission — indeed, that it was the primary purpose of his being in Charan — was implied to him as he lay at Bethel/Moriah on the way from Beer Sheba to Charan. The *Midrash* relates that Jacob put twelve stones around his head as he prepared to go to sleep, and the many stones coalesced into one. This incident showed Jacob that he would give birth to twelve sons who would become the separate tribes that form a unified nation.

III. Building Blocks

Words and Sons

Chiddushei HaRim on *Berachos* 2a comments that the word אֶבֶן, *stone,* has deep esoteric meanings. *Sefer Yetzirah* describes letters as אֲבָנִים, *stones.* In other places, children are referred to that way; indeed, the word בֵּן, *child,* is closely related to אֶבֶן, *stone.* The similarity is not coincidental. Stones are the material of constructing buildings; children are the human blocks of which nations and history are built; letters are the stuff of which words are made. The *Talmud, (Menachos* 29b) teaches that God created the spiritual universe with the letter י, *yud,* and the material universe with the letter ה, *hey*. Letters can create words and worlds, and can communicate the meaning of life from God to man and from man to man.

Jacob's twelve stones represented his twelve tribes, but they also represented twelve words that were essential to the oneness symbolized and proclaimed by his sons. As Jacob lay on his deathbed, he summoned all his sons with the intention of revealing to them what would occur to Israel at the End of Days. But his vision of the final redemption left him — and he was distraught: Was there, after all, an unworthy member of his family? Had he failed to produce a totally righteous family? Had he, despite all his agonizing years of preparation and striving to prepare for a Godly marriage, given birth to an Ishmael or an Esau, as had Abraham and Isaac?

His children reassured him, proclaiming: 'שְׁמַע יִשְׂרָאֵל ה׳ אֱלֹהֵינוּ ה׳ אֶחָד, *Hear, O Israel* [our father], *HASHEM our God, HASHEM is One.* Just as your heart is filled with nothing but the realization of God's Oneness — so do we recognize without doubt that HASHEM is One.'

Jacob responded: 'בָּרוּךְ שֵׁם כְּבוֹד מַלְכוּתוֹ לְעוֹלָם וָעֶד, *Blessed is the name of His glorious kingdom forever and ever.*'

The two verses of that climactic dialogue between the last Patriarch and the first Jewish generation contain twelve words. Those words express the idea that God is One and that we, the Children of Israel, dedicate all our faculties and resources to His service. And they express the hope and conviction that His kingdom will reign forever; that the time will come when every living creature will recognize that He is its Creator.

The universe belongs to God whether or not people prefer to acknowledge it.

The universe belongs to God whether or not people prefer to acknowledge it. But in the world as we know it, the perception of His Presence is fragmented. He gives life and existence to everything, but only here and there is some of His Presence recognized or proclaimed. God is One — of course! — but if we perceive Him in creation, we can, at best, recognize only varying forms of His manifestations. The heavens proclaim one aspect of His glory, the lion another, and the frog yet another. Taken all together, the entirety of the universe proclaims His Oneness. Similarly, each tribe of Israel is a separate and unique entity. Jacob and Moses each blessed them tribe by tribe, assigning each its own role in the national destiny, but the *totality* of Israel proclaims, 'ה׳ אֶחָד, *HASHEM is One.*'

Becoming a Community

Avnei Nezer notes that Jacob's doubt and his children's affirmation made the point that the tribes are separate but one, like the limbs and organs that are part of a single being. This concept was tellingly symbolized at the dedication of the Tabernacle in the Wilderness. Each prince brought a special sacrifice on behalf of his own tribe. Each had an intention and symbolism uniquely suited to his own tribe, even though the make-up of all the offerings was identical. What is more, the one whose turn fell on the Sabbath was permitted to bring his offering on that holiest of days although normally only קָרְבְּנוֹת צִבּוּר, *offerings required of the entire nation,* supersede the prohibitions of the Sabbath. Had each offering been solely that of a single tribe, it could not have been brought on the Sabbath. But because all the tribes are *ultimately* one, the offering of each transcended the particularity of an individual tribe and became a national sacrifice.

Jacob and the family he was destined to establish represented a complete unity of purpose.

Jacob and the family he was destined to establish represented a complete unity of purpose. So did the two wives he was to take. Leah, the representation of heavenly sanctity, and Rachel, the representation of earthly striving, had to be combined into a single Jewish nation. Indeed, as set forth in the previous *Overview,* Jacob's greatness was that he could embody in himself the concept of מַחֲנָיִם, *dual camp,* that unites heaven and earth. The coalescence of the stones declared to Jacob that he would succeed in forming twelve tribes that would act separately yet be one in their essence, and that the twelve words of God's Oneness and eternity would be embodied in his family (*Harav Gedaliah Schorr* זצ״ל).

Understanding the ideal represented by the twelve tribes, we can see why Jacob and the Matriarchs were so anxious to bring them into being, and why each of his four wives wanted so much to be a part of doing so. To bring a new generation into the world is an ambition worthy of any mother; Jacob's wives were giving birth to a nation.

The Same but Different

R' Yosaif Yehudah Leib Bloch (Shiurei Da'as Vol. 3) notes that basic human emotions remain with the human race throughout millennia. Jealousy has always existed, as has generosity. Selfishness is not new, nor is idealism. But these traits are put to different uses by different people. Jealousy is a base emotion, yet קִנְאַת סוֹפְרִים תַּרְבֶּה חָכְמָה, *jealousy of scholars increases the store of wisdom,* as they compete with one another and grow as a result. A giving, self-effacing nature is praiseworthy, but if a scholar does not care to compete and prove his mettle, not only he will lose — the universe which lives by the merit of Torah study will be the greatest loser. The unknowing observer may fail to see a difference between the hustler aggressively seeking to outdo his fellow merchant and the scholar who spares no effort to know Torah more thoroughly. Both display the same characteristics, don't they? They do, yet they are worlds apart. Or, better said, one builds the world while the other destroys it if he allows his desire to overcome his scruples.

The same casual observer may read the story of Rachel and Leah and smile as he recalls sibling rivalries and wifely jealousies that are the familiar fare of life and gossip.

The same casual observer may read the story of Rachel and Leah and smile as he recalls sibling rivalries and wifely jealousies that are the familiar fare of life and gossip. How superficial an observation! Of course they were jealous of one another. Of course, each tried to outdo the other. Of course, each wanted a greater share of Jacob's attention. All that, the Torah says very clearly. But to what purpose did they compete? To be jealous of another's clothing and furniture is base. To be jealous and try to outdo another's attainment in charity, dedication, and holiness is commendable — even though the same emotion is at the root of both feelings. Rachel and Leah were two worlds in complementary competition to build the future of Israel. They had human feelings because they were human, but they utilized their emotions for historic accomplishments — because they were great.

An Overview /

A Tzaddik and His Possessions

צָמְאָה לְךָ נַפְשִׁי כָּמַהּ לְךָ בְשָׂרִי ... רַבָּנָן אָמְרֵי, כְּשֵׁם שֶׁנַּפְשִׁי צְמֵאָה לְךָ, כֵּן רְמַ״ח אֵבָרִים שֶׁיֵּשׁ בִּי צְמֵאִים לְךָ

[Jacob said,] My soul thirsts for You, my flesh longs for You [Psalms 63:2] ... The Rabbis said: Just as my soul thirst for You, so do my 248 organs thirst for You (Bereishis Rabbah 69:2).

I. Jacob Sanctifies Labor

As Laban's Shepherd

We are not surprised that Jacob's soul thirsted for God: the soul is spiritual; of course, it thirsts to be reunited with the Source of all holiness. But the organs of Jacob's body? — the body interposes itself between the soul and its Creator; the body stands in contradiction to the soul. Why should Jacob's body yearn for God? [See above *Overview*: Jacob: Vision and exile.]

Jacob taught that every facet of earthly existence must be sanctified.

As we have seen above, Jacob taught that every facet of earthly existence must be sanctified. Not only can the soul survive its sojourn in the body with its holiness intact, it can elevate the body and, by making it the servant of holiness, transform it into something that is itself holy. To such an extent can this be done, that the body can be conditioned to become virtually an appendage of the soul and long for God's closeness as much as the soul does.

It would appear that Jacob had a unique mission to demonstrate how a man of truth, Torah, and holiness must react to the most earthly of earth's activities. Abraham and Isaac were men of wealth and property, but only Jacob was a common laborer. For twenty years from the ages of seventy-seven to ninety-seven, he was a shepherd for Laban. And what a shepherd he was! *Rambam* concludes his laws of the obligations of workmen with these words:

... וְכֵן חַיָּב לַעֲבוֹד בְּכָל כֹּחוֹ שֶׁהֲרֵי יַעֲקֹב הַצַּדִּיק אָמַר: ,,כִּי בְּכָל כֹּחִי עָבַדְתִּי אֶת אֲבִיכֶן״

... *So, too, is* [*a worker*] *required to work with all his might, for the righteous Jacob said* [31:6]: *'... For you know that it was with all my might that I served your father'* (*Hilchos Sechirus* 13:7).

Laban, for all his chicanery and fraudulent dealings, never disputed these claims of Jacob.

Jacob's own description of his dedication to Laban's work [31:6, 38-40] paints the portrait of a laborer who was conscientious in the extreme. Laban, for all his chicanery and fraudulent dealings, never disputed these claims of Jacob. Furthermore, the Patriarch accepted upon himself a degree of liability which goes beyond that of an ordinary shepherd. One can perhaps expect such excessive zeal for the sake of a benevolent, beloved employer, but Laban subjected Jacob to an incessant series of fraud and deception while he glibly masked his double-dealing with silkily pious speeches about how immoral it was to give a younger daughter before an older one, or how a doting father and grandfather had been duped out of the chance to kiss his daughters and grandchildren good-bye. Laban paraded himself as the very soul of upright integrity while all the while he attempted at every turn to cheat Jacob and leave him destitute. Surely a lesser person than Jacob would have considered himself justified in counteracting Laban's double-dealing by acting in kind. Or at the very least, Jacob could have followed the letter of the law by refusing to accept excessive liability, or invest excessive effort for the sake of the thieving Laban.

A Taste of Dishonesty

But no! Jacob, in an extraordinary manifestation of his מִדַּת הָאֱמֶת, *attribute of truth,* refuses to lower himself to Laban's standard of conduct. [As the commentators point out in Chapter 30, Jacob's tactics with the sticks were above board, his success in gaining large herds and flocks was miraculous, and he took pains to be sure that Laban would not be wiped out.] The lesson Jacob taught in the pastures of Charan is no less vital to the future of the nation of Israel than the lesson he taught while absorbing the heavenly vision at Bethel/Moriah. A Jew dares not sanctify his personal heaven while profaning his personal earth. Integrity is indivisible even when dealing with a Laban; one relaxes his standards of honesty only at the greatest peril to his inner self. When the soul thirsts for God as it should, then all 248 limbs and organs must thirst along with it.

The lesson Jacob taught in the pastures of Charan is no less vital to the future of the nation of Israel than the lesson he taught while absorbing the heavenly vision at Bethel/Moriah ... Integrity is indivisible even when dealing with a Laban.

Harav Dovid Cohen suggests that it was this lesson of Jacob's that the Sages had in mind when they criticized one of their colleagues *(Berachos* 5b). The great *amora* R' Huna suffered a substantial loss when four hundred barrels of wine turned into vinegar. His comrades urged him to examine his deeds to find a sin that had caused the punishment. R' Huna was taken aback that they suspected him; as *Tosafos* [*ibid.* s.v. דינא] explains, many righteous people suffer losses or illness without apparent cause. The rabbis persisted. Did *they* know of a possible cause, R' Huna asked?

'We have heard that you do not give your foreman his rightful share of the prunings from your vines,' they said.

R' Huna protested that it was known that his foreman stole from him; by retaining the prunings, he was only regaining part of his losses.

True, the rabbis replied, but this sort of case is illustrated by the proverb: בָּתָר גַּנְבָא גָּנִיב וְטָעִים טַעְמָא, *On who steals from a thief feels the taste of thievery.* [Therefore, such retaliation, while legal, was sinful for a man of R' Huna's caliber.]

Jacob's lesson: an honest man dares not taint himself by dishonest dealings, no matter how just his cause.

II. Seeds of Victory

A Jug's Value

An examination of Jacob's story through the portions of *Vayeitzei* and *Vayishlach* leads to the conclusion that the attainment of his highest degree of spiritual perfection paralleled — perhaps was an outgrowth — of his concept of property. Let us trace the pattern from the time that Jacob left Laban after twenty years of integrity under the most trying and tempting circumstances.

At the ford of Jabbok, Jacob is preparing to face Esau who heads a murderous army of four hundred men. Jacob has divided his people into two camps and has carried his children and valuables across the ford. Now he is alone:

> וַיִּוָּתֵר יַעֲקֹב לְבַדּוֹ. אָמַר רַבִּי אֶלְעָזָר שֶׁנִּשְׁתַּיֵּר עַל פַּכִּין קְטַנִּים. מִכָּאן לְצַדִּיקִים שֶׁחָבִיב עֲלֵיהֶם מָמוֹנָם יוֹתֵר מִגּוּפָם. וְכָל כָּךְ לָמָּה? לְפִי שֶׁאֵין פּוֹשְׁטִין יְדֵיהֶן בְּגָזֵל.
>
> *And Jacob remained alone* [32:25]. *R' Elazar said, He remained [behind] because of small jugs [i.e., insignificant items (Mizrachi; Gur Aryeh)]; from here we see that righteous people are more concerned with their possessions than with their personal safety. Why to such an extent? Because they do not extend their hands to stolen property (Chullin* 91a).

The Torah does not distinguish between petty and grand larceny.

A Jacob assesses his goods not according to their monetary value, but according to the moral values they represent. The Torah does not distinguish between petty and grand larceny. All thievery is a violation of the same negative commandment — the Torah says simply: *You may not steal,* neither a diamond nor a *perutah.* The judge is commanded to be as scrupulous with cases involving pittances as with those involving fortunes: יְהֵא חָבִיב עָלֶיךָ דִּין פְּרוּטָה כְּדִין שֶׁל מֵאָה מָנֶה, *Be as devoted to a case involving a perutah as to the case involving 100 maneh (10,000 sela'im) (Sanhedrin* 8a). The small earthenware jugs of the righteous have a significance out of proportion to their monetary value. They were acquired with strict adherence to all the laws governing civil relationships between man and his neighbor. The jug of a Jacob represents the entire *Choshen Mishpat* [The Code of Civil and Criminal Law]. Can one put a price on the *Choshen Mishpat?* Can one say that one rescues a Torah Scroll only if it is valuable, but not if there is no market for it?

Special Affection

The value Jacob attached to materially insignificant items can be better appreciated in the light of *R' Tzaddok HaCohen's* explanation of a Talmudic dictum:

> שְׁלֹשָׁה חִנּוֹת הֵן: חֵן מָקוֹם עַל יוֹשְׁבָיו, חֵן אִשָּׁה עַל בַּעְלָהּ, חֵן מֶקַּח עַל לוֹקְחוֹ
>
> *There are three varieties of affection: the affection of a dweller for his native place, the affection of a man for his wife, and the affection of a purchaser for his purchase (Sotah* 47a).

While nearly everyone has experienced one or all of these affections, the juxtaposition of the three seems strange. *R' Tzaddok* explains that every person has a distinct and unique mission on earth. God provides each of us with the tools we need to perform our personal roles. These 'tools' take the form of resources — homeland, family, neighbors, intellectual capacity, physical strength, mate — in short, whatever a person takes for granted as part of his milieu may well be essential to the performance of his Divinely ordained mission. Someone may drift from country to country or village to village until he finds a place to 'fall in love with' and call his own. When that happens, it may well indicate that his spiritual self recognizes that patch of earth as having been designated as 'his.' The same is true of objects and even of husbands and wives. Whatever other attractions people and objects possess, there can also be a spiritual significance in the sense that this man and that woman, this farm and that person, this object and that owner were destined for one another.

When this is true, it can be indicated by a warm affection for the person or possession.

Negative Esau There Jacob was, alone beyond the river, when a 'man' — the angel of Esau, Satan, the embodiment of evil — grappled with him, intent on destroying him and, failing that, to maim his posterity. [For a discussion of the struggle, see *Overview, Vayishlach.*] Jacob prevailed — and thereby proved that he was worthy of the name Israel, the name that expressed his superiority to the heavenly beings.

Surely it is not coincidental that Jacob's triumph came immediately after he signified that every bit of personal property must be made sacred. Esau represented greed, gluttony, selfishness. To him, a pot of beans was more valuable than his birthright — provided he desired the beans. Later, when he wanted the return of the birthright and the Patriarchal blessings — the attainment of that desire was more valuable than the blood of his brother and all his family. To Esau, there was no regulatory force, there was only desire. Jacob was the opposite. His measuring rod was the word of Torah. His desires flowed from the Torah; if his wish conflicted with God's law, then the law remained intact and his desire was set aside.

Jacob's small jugs epitomized what he stood for, and symbolized the crux of the conflict between the two brothers.

Perhaps Providence delayed Esau's onslaught until Jacob could spiritually conquer Esau by subduing — and thereby sanctifying — the desire for possessions; while Esau deified — and thereby contaminated — the perfectly normal human need for the means of livelihood and comfort.

III. Shelter of Succoth

Compassion for Sheep Having met Esau and escaped him unscathed, Jacob proceeded to Succoth where he built houses for his people and shelters for his livestock.

To commemorate the סֻכּוֹת, *shelters*, he named the place Succoth [see *comm.* to 33:17].

Why were the shelters of his livestock so significant that he named the place in their honor?

Gur Aryeh and others ask the obvious question: Why were the shelters of his livestock so significant that he named the place in their honor? *Or HaChaim* comments that Jacob may have been the first person to show compassion for his animals, that he went to the trouble and expense to build shelters to protect them from the blazing sun. Jacob named the place as a reminder of this new dimension of concern for animals.

Many of the Kabbalistic masters associate the Succoth where Jacob sojourned with the Succoth festival which the Torah would later ordain to commemorate God's protective עֲנָנֵי הַכָּבוֹד, *Clouds of Glory*, with which He shielded Israel when it left Egypt. Jacob protected his sheep; God protected His. Indeed, in one esoteric Kabbalistic comment, it is said that Jacob possessed 600,000 sheep, symbolizing the 600,000 adult males who left Egypt. God protected the people; Jacob, whose image graced the Heavenly Throne, protected the sheep.

The Succah's Power

There is a particular significance in the commandment to live in a *succah* seven days a year; the *succah* contributes something to its inhabitants. The *Zohar* refers to the *succah* as צִלָּא דִמְּהֵמְנוּתָא, *the protective shelter*, which means, as the commentators explain, that the fragile shade of the *succah* has the spiritual power to reinforce faith in God's Providence. The *succah* reminds us that God's Will protected an entire helpless nation against elements and enemies, thus, it 'preserves' the effect of a Divine act. Israel left Egypt fortified only by faith in God's Word; He protected the nation in return, and the *succah* helps us preserve that faith and continue to earn its Heavenly recompense. Jacob, too, was the beneficiary of God's help based on his prior faith. He was unconcerned with the laws of jungles or economics — only with *God's* law. To him, the pitiful jug was precious because it symbolized his adherence to God's Will; in return, God gave him victory over Esau's guardian angel.

Dangers of Success

Finally, Jacob was free of the menace of Esau. He was enormously wealthy as he slowly guided his flocks back toward Beer Sheba and the home of Isaac and Rebecca. Now that he was rich and secure for the first time in over twenty years, would he forget the recent past and become a wealthy gentleman farmer? Wealth and tranquility have all too often been the lethal enemies of spiritual stature. The Torah warns that וַיִּשְׁמַן יְשֻׁרוּן וַיִּבְעָט ... וַיִּטֹּשׁ אֱלוֹהַּ עָשָׂהוּ, *Yeshurun* [i.e., Israel] *will grow fat and kick aside ... and forsake God Who made it* [*Deut.* 32:15].

Jacob understood the dangers of success just as he had understood the temptations of victimization and the challenge of fear. He built protective covers over his sheep. Those shelters represented compassion as opposed to avarice; even more, they represented his wish to preserve his concept of property with the *shelter of faith* which would protect and deepen the perception that helped him defeat the angel and hold Esau at bay. *That* was the concept that he made eternal by his choice of a name. Property was a sacred trust because it was acquired with fidelity to God's Will — that recognition was demonstrated in the place where he celebrated his new freedom with devotion to the ideal that made him free from the shackles of material life!

Property was a sacred trust because it was acquired with fidelity to God's Will.

Then, Perfection

When he left Succoth for Shechem, the Torah tells us he was שָׁלֵם, *intact* [33:18]. As *Rashi* explains, his health was intact for he had recovered from the injury inflicted by the angel; his fortune was intact despite the generous gifts he had given Esau; and his Torah was intact, for he had forgotten nothing during his twenty work-filled years with Laban.

As many commentators have said, there is a deeper connotation in the expression שָׁלֵם, *intact.* The word also refers to Jacob's שְׁלֵמוּת, *spiritual wholeness*, his *perfection.* Jacob was never static. Always he was striving and advancing. And now he had finally attained the level of *perfection*. After his years with Isaac, he had not been called שָׁלֵם, *perfect* — nor after his years of study with Eber, nor after his vision at Bethel/Moriah. Until then, his life had been purely spiritual, but God did not call him perfect. Only after mastering the temptation to be less than totally dedicated to a dishonest employer, after besting the alluring chimera of wealth, and after taking measures to preserve the spiritual fruit of his victories — only then could he be called perfect.

Then [see *Rashi; Rambam;* and *R' Bachya* to 33:20], God Himself could call Jacob *El*, [literally, *God*, but also meaning *Master*] saying, 'I am the Master of everything on High and you are the master of everything below!'

◆§ סדר ויצא

◆§ Sidrah Vayeitzei

י וַיֵּצֵא יַעֲקֹב מִבְּאֵר שָׁבַע וַיֵּלֶךְ חָרָנָה:
יא וַיִּפְגַּע בַּמָּקוֹם וַיָּלֶן שָׁם כִּי־בָא הַשֶּׁמֶשׁ

SIDRAH VAYEITZEI

⌘ Jacob's flight to Charan. His dream at Bethel.

The Torah now resumes its narrative of Jacob's departure which was begun in *v.*5. The narrative had been interrupted by the parenthetical digression of verses 6-9 telling of Esau's marrying in reaction to Isaac's displeasure with the Canaanite women *(Rashi).*

10. וַיֵּצֵא יַעֲקֹב מִבְּאֵר שָׁבַע — [*And*] *Jacob departed from Beer Sheba.*[1]

[As has often been emphasized, the Torah is not a history book; it tells us only what is necessary to convey the sense of the narrative. Hence every seemingly superfluous detail must be measured to elicit the message suggested by its inclusion]:

It would have sufficed for the Torah to have stated simply: וַיֵּלֶךְ יַעֲקֹב חָרָנָה, *Jacob went to Charan.* What is the significance of adding וַיֵּצֵא, [*and he*] *departed?* — The Torah thereby teaches us that the departure of a righteous person from a place leaves a void: As long as a righteous person lives in a city, he constitutes its glory, its splendor, and its beauty; when he departs, its glory, splendor, and beauty depart with him. This, too, is the purpose of mentioning Naomi's departure in *Ruth* 1:7 [see *comm.* there] *(Rashi).*

In the *Midrash* the question is asked how the effects of Jacob's departure could be compared to that of Naomi. Naomi's departure left a noteworthy void in Moab because she had been the only righteous person there; in Jacob's case, however, the righteous Isaac still remained in Beer Sheba after Jacob's departure! — The answer is that the merit of a single righteous person cannot be compared to that of two [i.e., although Isaac remained, Jacob's departure still left a noticeable mark.]

The commentators explain that the mere *presence* of a righteous man in a place affects the moral behavior of the other residents; he acts as a deterrent against blatant sinfulness. When he departs, this restraining factor is gone.

The *Midrashim* also explain why Jacob's departure is mentioned here again although *v.* 7 specifically stated that Jacob had gone to Paddan Aram. One of the answers follows the view that Isaac had been living in Hebron at this time [see *Ramban* to *v.* 17]. Accordingly, after Isaac and Rebecca sent him to Charan, Jacob went from Hebron to Beer Sheba [site of Abraham's *eishel* and altar, and the site where assurances had been given to Isaac (26:4)] to seek permission from God to leave the land — as Isaac had

1. Five miracles were wrought for our father Jacob on the occasion of his departure from Beer Sheba:

1) The hours of the day were shortened and the sun set prematurely since [God's] Word wished to communicate with him;

2) The four stones which Jacob used for his pillow had, by morning become one stone [according to other versions there were twelve stones];

3) He was able to roll away the heavy stone covering the mouth of the well single-handedly [upon his arrival in Charan];

4) The well continued to overflow abundantly during the entire period that he was in Charan;

5) The earth contracted before him so that he traversed the distance to Charan in one day *(Targum Yonasan).*

28
10-11

[10] Jacob departed from Beer Sheba and went toward
Charan. [11] He encountered the place and spent
the night there because the sun had set. He took from

done before descending to Gerar. Jacob wanted to ascertain whether it was indeed in consonance with God's Will that he forsake the holy environs of *Eretz Yisrael* to go abroad and have children. Therefore, our verse specifies that he departed from *Beer Sheba* [after having apparently received the needed assurance]. Additionally, implicit in this repetition of Jacob's departure is that Jacob resumed his journey after his fourteen year interruption to study Torah in the academy of Eber [see *Ha'amek Davar* below].

Beer Sheba was a place that had long been associated with oaths. Its very name was given it by Abraham in commemoration of his oath with Abimelech [21:31], and Isaac was there when he reaffirmed the oath [26:33]. The *Midrash* finds in this background a further reason for Jacob's departure from Beer Sheba; he feared the possibility that he would be pressed to undertake undesirable oaths were he to remain there. First, he was afraid that Abimelech would insist that he affirm the oaths of his ancestors. This, Jacob was unwilling to do because Abraham's unwarranted pact with Abimelech had resulted in a Divinely decreed delay of seven generations before Abraham's descendants could occupy *Eretz Yisrael*. Jacob wished to avoid a similar punishment [see *footnote* to 11:28, p. 775]. Furthermore, he feared that Esau might seek to exact an oath nullifying Jacob's right to the birthright which he, Esau, had sworn to cede to Jacob [25:33]; and he feared that Esau would try to coerce him to renounce by oath the Patriarchal blessings which Isaac had sworn would be his.

Da'as Zekeinim notes that the Masoretic division of this *parshah* is סְתוּמָה, *closed* [i.e., the *parshah* contains no paragraph divisions within it, and does not even begin on a new line. Thus, the beginning appears to be obscure and hidden]. This alludes to the stealthy and concealed manner in which Jacob fled his home.

Furthermore, this *parshah* is 'closed' to allude to Jacob's having been 'closed up' in the academy of Eber *(Chizkuni)*.

Chatzi Menasheh [quoted by *Torah Sheleimah*] cites an interpretation that the proximity of verses 9 and 10: לוֹ לְאִשָּׁה, *as a wife for himself* ... and וַיֵּצֵא יַעֲקֹב, *and Jacob departed*, suggests that one may leave *Eretz Yisrael* only to study Torah or to seek a wife.

וַיֵּלֶךְ חָרָנָה — *And went toward Charan.*

[Jacob went to his uncle Laban in Paddan Aram, in obedience to his mother's wish (27:43) that he escape the wrath of Esau; and in fulfillment of his father's charge that he take a wife from there (*v.* 2).]

As noted in the *comm.* to *v.* 9, according to the traditional rabbinic chronology [see *Seder Olam* chap. 2; *Midrash*], Jacob did not go *directly* to Charan when he departed from his parents. Rather, he detoured and spent fourteen years in seclusion studying under Eber. He was sixty-three years old when he received his father's blessing and fled; when he finally set off toward Charan he was seventy-seven. This was in the year 2185 from Creation. [Eber died two years later in 2187, while Shem had died in 2158 when Jacob was fifty years old. See *Chronology / Timeline* on page xii of Vol. I.]

As *Midrash HaGadol* comments:

'Jacob first spent fourteen years secluded in the Land, clarifying his studies under his ancestor Eber. It was only after he clarified his studies that he departed from the land.'

The commentators perceive that Jacob's long and intensive years of study in the Academy of Eber were meant to prepare him spiritually for the personal exile he would endure in Charan.

Ha'amek Davar observes that Jacob's detour is implicit in the very fact that the Torah mentions his journey again after having already mentioned his departure in *v.* 7. The Torah seems to be implying that after having left his parents' home, Jacob made a *second* departure, thus alluding to the fact that before completing his trip to Charan, he went to the academy of Eber for a period of fourteen years.

This follows the assumption [see e.g., *Maskil l'David*] that the academy of Eber was located in Beer Sheba.

The translation *'toward' Charan* rather than *'to' Charan* follows *Rashbam* and *Rashi* who render: *he set out 'to go to' Charan,* but not that he arrived there. This interpretation is inspired by the sequence of the narrative itself. Since the next verse speaks of events that occurred during the course of his journey, it would seem clear that he had not yet arrived in Charan *(Mizrachi).*

As the *Midrash* observes, we say colloquially 'So-and-so has gone to Caesaria' when in fact he is still preparing for the journey.

Ibn Ezra interprets similarly, explaining that first the Torah mentions the intended destination, and then details the events that occurred en-route. Apparently he would render more literally: *He went to Charan,* the implication being that he was on his way when the following events took place.

[However, the Talmud cites an interpretation that *after* arriving in Charan, Jacob *returned to the site* mentioned in the following verses. This interpretation is discussed by *Rashi* in the *comm.* to *v.* 17, below.]

Furthermore, the *Midrash* derives from the proximity in our verse of the descriptions of Jacob's leaving Beer Sheba and arriving in Charan, that the earth contracted for him (קָפְצָה לוֹ הַדֶּרֶךְ) and in several hours he miraculously completed what would ordinarily be a seventeen day journey. [See *Rashi's* interpretation of this *Midrash* cited in his commentary to *v.* 17 below.]

⌘ Jacob's material possessions.

As evidenced by Jacob's later statement [32:11] כִּי בְמַקְלִי עָבַרְתִּי אֶת הַיַּרְדֵּן, *but with my staff I crossed the Jordan,* he fled from his father's house with the barest of necessities.

Ibn Ezra to 25:34 conjectures that Isaac and Rebecca sent off Jacob with neither fine clothing nor silver and gold, because Isaac was impoverished in his old age. Jacob, therefore, had to sustain himself by tending Laban's flocks. *Ramban* there disagrees sharply, and in a long dissertation illustrates that, to the contrary, the Patriarchs are depicted as wealthy and were regarded as princes by other kings who made treaties with them. Rather, he explains, the wealthy Isaac did not give valuables to Jacob because he wanted him to flee without attracting Esau's attention, and without tempting brigands to ambush and rob him. The latter fear is borne out by a *Midrashic* interpretation that Jacob *did* carry valuables with him, but was robbed at the outset of his journey. [See *Rashi* to 29:11.][1]

There is, however, a *Midrash* [*Tanchuma Yashan*] which relates that

1. *R' Hirsch* perceives in the literal flow of the narrative the introduction to Jacob's independent life and to his role as the forerunner of the Jewish nation. For, although Abraham represents the nation's roots and Isaac its growth, Jacob represents the nation's trunk; indeed, we are called the Children of *Israel,* not the Children of Abraham.

Like Abraham, Jacob was commanded to leave his home. But unlike Abraham who left with his wife, retinue, and wealth, Jacob left without anything at all. He preferred to leave everything behind to demonstrate that the advantage conferred by the blessings of the birthright was not material, but spiritual. He took with him only his personality, for the

God admonished Isaac for not bequeathing Jacob everything he had as his father had done to him [see 25:5]. Isaac should not have let Jacob leave empty-handed. The *Midrash* records that, as a consequence of this, the *Shechinah* departed from Isaac and did not communicate with him again until he was about to die.

11. וַיִּפְגַּע בַּמָּקוֹם — [And] *he encountered* [in] *the place.*

The Torah does not tell us *which* place. — Instead it uses the definite article בַּמָּקוֹם, [which is equivalent to בְּהַמָּקוֹם] **in the** *place,* implying that the identity of the place was so well known that it need not be specified. This indicates that it refers to the site referred to elsewhere by the designation *the place:* Mt. Moriah, of which it is said [22:4]: *he saw the place* [הַמָּקוֹם] *from afar (Rashi).*

Rashi's comment, as explained by his commentators, is based on several factors:

(a) There is a rule that 'the Torah does not come to conceal but to explain' [i.e., a Scriptural passage is intended not to be obscure but to instruct (see *Rashi* to 10-25 and 21:34)]. Accordingly, a reference to a place emphasized by the definite article 'the' must refer to some previously specified place *(Tzeidah laDerech).*

(b) It cannot refer to any place other than Mt. Moriah since the Torah itself refers to that holy site as מָקוֹם, *place,* in several places [22:4; and as *Ralbag* notes, the future Temple site on Mt. Moriah is also obliquely referred to in the Torah as *the 'place' HASHEM shall select (Deut.* 16:16 and frequently).] Accordingly, by its reference to *place* here, the allusion to Moriah is clear *(Mizrachi).*

(c) It is an application of the hermeneutic rule of *gezerah shavah* [i.e., the use of a common expression with regard to two different subjects can be taken to imply that a rule which is mentioned with regard to one of the subjects should be applied to the other one as well].

(d) Moriah was — by virtue of the *Akeidah* — the only site sacred enough for such a divine revelation; it was the supreme 'place' *par-excellence (Be'er Mayim Chaim).*

(e) Place names generally refer either to something about the owner or to a characteristic of the place. Because the prime significance of Mt. Moriah would not become known until the future when it would be the site of the Temple, it was called simply 'the place,' as if to imply that it was as yet unknown *(Kli Yakar).*

The traditional rabbinic interpretation that *the place* was *Mount Moriah* would seem to conflict with the simple sense of the narrative which would seem to imply that the place was *Luz-Bethel.* A reconciliation is offered by *Rashi* in *v.* 17 *(Or HaChaim).*

The translation of וַיִּפְגַּע *as encountered* follows *Rashi* who — as explained by his supercommentators — interprets the word as implying the *meeting of two objects moving toward one another,* synonymous with the verb וַיִּפְגַּשׁ. *Rashi* explains that the verb פגע is also used for *inanimate objects,* as, for example in *Joshua* 16:7 where it is used of boundaries: וּפָגַע בִּירִיחוֹ, and it *reached* Jericho; and similarly in *Joshua* 19:11: *it reached* (וּפָגַע) *to Dabesheth* [or in our case where it refers to the encounter of a person with a place.]

Rashi continues that our Sages [*Berachos* 26b] interpreted the term וַיִּפְגַּע [which, as in 23:8, also means *interceded*] to denote *prayer,* as it does in *Jeremiah* 7:16: וְאַל־תִּפְגַּע־בִּי, *and do not intercede with Me.* Accordingly, Jacob is credited with instituting עַרְבִית, the Evening Prayer [see *comm.* to 19:27 that Abraham instituted שַׁחֲרִית, the Morning Prayer; and 24:63 that Isaac instituted מִנְחָה, the Afternoon Prayer]. The Torah used the general term וַיִּפְגַּע to denote this prayer rather than וַיִּתְפַּלֵּל, the more

Jewish home is founded upon personal qualities. He demonstrated that God is to be found above all in the Jewish home. That is why he described the place of God's presence as בֵּית אֵל and בֵּית אֱלֹהִים, the *House* of God; God must be found in the place where people spend their lives and bring their possessions.

specific term for prayer, since the Torah also wanted to intimate by use of this term [which implies an unexpected meeting] that the way 'jumped' [or: contracted] before him as explained in *Chullin* 91b. [See *Rashi* to *v.* 17.]

According to the interpretation that וַיִּפְגַּע means *he prayed,* the word מָקוֹם would be a reference to God by His designation of מָקוֹם, *Omnipresent* [literally: *The Place*]. [As the *Midrash* explains, God is referred to as *Makom* — 'The Place' — because 'He is the place of the universe and the universe is not His place,' i.e., God is not limited by space nor encompassed by it; rather He encompasses everything and therefore is present everywhere.] Accordingly, the expression וַיִּפְגַּע בַּמָּקוֹם means: *he prayed to* [lit. *interceded with*] *the Omnipresent* (*Mizrachi*; see *Rashi* to *v.*17).

Pirkei d'Rabbi Eliezer explains in this context that God's designation as *Makom, Place,* intimates that God is to be found in every *place* where there are righteous men [see *Exod.* 20:21].

In his introduction to *Esther, Ibn Ezra* explains that He is called *Makom* since 'the whole world is full of His glory.'

However, *Ibn Ezra* denies that in the *literal sense* וַיִּפְגַּע means *he prayed* or that our verse refers to God as *Makom.* He maintains that God is not referred to anywhere in Scripture *in the literal sense* as מָקוֹם, *Place,* but only as מָעוֹן, *Dwelling Place* [see *Psalms* 90:1]. The only exception is a *Rabbinic* allusion to the word *Place* in *Esther* 4:14. He suggests that the definite term *'the* place' was used in the time of Moses to refer to Beth El, a place that had come to be well known because of this incident.

Sforno explains the definite article as denoting *the place* well known to travellers — i.e., the inn which each hamlet used to maintain in the square for travellers.

Onkelos, Rashbam, and *Sforno* interpret the phrase to mean that he happened upon an unnamed place where it had not been his intention to go.

וַיָּלֶן שָׁם כִּי־בָא הַשֶּׁמֶשׁ — *And* [he] *spent the night there, because the sun had set,* [and he did not have enough time to go on to the next city *(Rashbam)*].

Rashi observes that a more sequentially accurate word order would have been: וַיָּבֹא הַשֶּׁמֶשׁ וַיָּלֶן שָׁם, [first] *the sun set,* [and therefore] *he spent the night there.* As it reads, the phrase כִּי בָא הַשֶּׁמֶשׁ, *because the sun had set,* implies that the sun was caused to set unexpectedly — not in its proper time — in order to force Jacob to spend the night there.

[Actually, it would have sufficed for the Torah to state simply וַיָּלֶן שָׁם, *and he spent the night there,* it being self-evident that a traveler encamps for the night when darkness comes.] That the Torah finds it necessary to inform us that he slept there *because the sun had set,* indicates that he had not thought of stopping there since the sun was still high in the sky. Miraculously, the sun set prematurely forcing him to spend the night there *(Rashi* to *Chullin* 91b and *Sanhedrin* 95b; *Mizrachi).*

By not narrating the events in their sequential order, and by inserting the seemingly superfluous fact that the sun had set, the Torah indicates that there was an *untimely* setting *(Maskil l'David).*

the stones of the place which he arranged around his

Baal HaTurim notes that the initial letters of the word כִּי בָא הַשֶּׁמֶשׁ form the word כִּבָּה, *He extinguished*, alluding to the untimely snuffing out of the sun's light before its time.

In fact, some *Midrashic* commentators draw attention to the similar sound of the words כִּי בָא and כִּבָּה.

Cf. the *Midrash:*

... This teaches that the Holy One, Blessed be He, caused the sun to set prematurely in order to 'speak' in privacy, as it were, with our father Jacob.

— After Jacob prayed [see *comm.* to וַיִּפְגַּע בַּמָּקוֹם above] he wished to proceed, but the Holy One, Blessed be He, said: 'This righteous man has come to My habitation [the place, as noted, was Mt. Moriah, the future site of the Temple]; shall I allow him to depart without a night's rest?' — At once *the sun set* — prematurely *(Sanhedrin* 95b).

וַיִּקַּח מֵאַבְנֵי הַמָּקוֹם — [*And*] *he took from the stones of the place.*

Most commentators render that *he took* **one** *of the stones of the place (Rashbam, Ibn Ezra, Radak, Ralbag* and *Tosafos Chullin* 91b s.v. כְּתִיב).

Midrashically, however, the Sages render that *he took* **several** *of the stones of the place (Chullin* 91b, *Pirkei d'Rabbi Eliezer* §35, *Midrash,* and *Rashi).* This would appear to contradict verse 18, below, which speaks of only *one* stone. Therefore, *Rashi,* citing the *Talmudic* and *Midrashic* interpretation that there were originally *several* stones, comments:

The stones began quarreling with one another, each one saying, 'Upon *me* shall this righteous man rest his head.' Thereupon God combined them all into one stone. That is why verse 18 reads: *and he took 'the stone'* [singular].[1]

Gur Aryeh defends the *Talmudic* interpretation that Jacob took *many* stones by commenting that if only *one* stone were meant the Torah should merely have said וַיִּקַּח אֶבֶן, *he took a stone.* The phraseology *he took of the stones of the place,* by its very ambiguity implies that more than a single stone was taken. Since verse 18 mentions only *one* stone, the *Talmudic* interpretation quite accurately reflects even the *literal* intent of the narrative. [See *HaKsav V'haKaballah* who also defends the literal sense as implying plural, since the following phrase מְרַאֲשֹׁתָיו, *around his head,* denotes an arrangement of more than a single stone.]

The *Midrash* comments further that Jacob took *twelve* stones, saying: 'God has declared that twelve tribes should spring forth. Now, neither Abraham nor Isaac has produced them. If these twelve stones cleave to one another, then I know that I will produce the twelve tribes.'

Pirkei d'Rabbi Eliezer adds that Jacob took these twelve stones from the altar upon which his father had been bound. When these stones — which indicated to him that twelve tribes would descend from him — coalesced into one stone, he perceived that all the tribes were destined to become one people [i.e., indivisible and unique] on the earth, as it is said [*I Chron.* 17:21] 'And who is like Your people Israel — *a nation that is one on the earth.*'

1. [Although it is difficult to comprehend how inanimate stones can quarrel, this interpretation must be perceived, as are the 'defiance' of the waters, moon, and trees during the Six Days of Creation (see *comm.* 1:9; 11, 16), as a moral lesson to man. Thus we are taught that every person should strive to be of service to the righteous.]

More specifically, however, [as noted in the Overview to *Sidrah Bereishis*] all of God's creations — including the inanimate ones — are overseen by angels on high; and it is these 'guardian angels' that argue on behalf of their inanimate charges *(Tzeidah laDerech;* see *Gur Aryeh* who discusses the spiritual implications).

יב וַיִּשְׁכַּב בַּמָּקוֹם הַהוּא: וַיַּחֲלֹם וְהִנֵּה סֻלָּם
מֻצָּב אַרְצָה וְרֹאשׁוֹ מַגִּיעַ הַשָּׁמָיְמָה וְהִנֵּה
יג מַלְאֲכֵי אֱלֹהִים עֹלִים וְיֹרְדִים בּוֹ: וְהִנֵּה

According to another opinion he took *three* stones saying, 'God united His name with Abraham [i.e., He is referred to as *God of Abraham*], and similarly with Isaac. If these three stones will coalesce, then I am assured that God's Name will be united with me, too.' And so it was. [Other versions in the *Midrash* mention *two* stones; *Targum Yonasan* mentions *four* stones which *Yalkut Shimoni Job* 899 explains as alluding to the unity and perfection among the sons of his four wives.]

R' Eliyahu Kitov ז״ל suggests that these *Midrashim* are not mutually exclusive. Jacob was groping in the dark for matching stones with which to construct a shelter. Unbeknownst to him, he picked up the same stones which his grandfather had used in the altar. When Jacob picked up the second stone a certain symbolic thought occurred to him. Similarly, when he picked up the third, fourth, and twelfth, other symbolisms struck, as are recorded in the various versions.

The *Midrash* concludes that the stones that Jacob placed under his head became soft as pillows.[1]

Sforno also interprets that there were *several* stones. Following his comment that *the place* refers to the town inn, he explains that the stones were among those kept in the guest house for use by guests to eat or sleep on.

וַיָּשֶׂם מְרַאֲשֹׁתָיו — *Which he arranged* [lit., *and he placed*] *around his head.*

He arranged the stones in the form of a rain gutter around his head because he was afraid of wild beasts *(Midrash; Rashi).*

— But if only his *head* was protected, the *rest* of his body still remained exposed to wild beasts! Actually, we must assume that for this purpose Jacob constructed a barrier protecting his *whole* body. The Torah mentions only his head to intimate that it was only with regard to his *head* — the most important part of his body — that the stones began quarreling with one another; regarding the rest of his body, however, the Torah — which economizes on its every word — had no need to mention that he protected himself with stones *(Divrei David).*

The word מְרַאֲשֹׁתָיו is explained by some to mean either *beneath* his head, or *around it.* Our rendering follows *Rashi*, who, citing our Sages, explains that Jacob arranged the stones *around* his head to form a shield.

HaKsav V'haKaballah, citing *Heidenheim*, defends this definition by citing *I Samuel* 26:7: *Saul lay sleeping ... and his spear stuck in the ground* מְרַאֲשֹׁתָיו [*around (or near) his head*]; and *I Kings* 19:6 *And* [*Elijah*] *looked and behold there was cake ... and a cruse of water* מְרַאֲשֹׁתָיו [around his head]. In both of these cases the context proves that מְרַאֲשֹׁתָיו does not mean *beneath* his head.

וַיִּשְׁכַּב בַּמָּקוֹם הַהוּא — *And* [*he*] *lay down in that place.*

— I.e., in that spot whose sanctity made it entirely suitable for the prophetic dream he was about to experience *(Or HaChaim).*

The Sages in the *Midrash* explain that the Torah mentioned this detail to intimate a *limitation.* As *Rashi* explains: The word הַהוּא, *that*

1. *Kli Yakar* interprets the premature setting of the sun as foreshadowing to Jacob that the First Temple would be destroyed two years before its appointed end. Betokening his mourning over this sadness, Jacob placed a rock under his head. This is the origin of the *Tishah B'Av* custom of sleeping with a stone under one's head.

28
12
head, and lay down in that place. 12 *And he dreamt,*
and behold! A ladder was set earthward and its top
reached heavenward. And behold! Angels of God
were ascending and descending on it.

[*place*], suggests *only there* but not *else*where: Only in *that* place did Jacob lay down to sleep, but during the previous fourteen years, when he studied in the Academy of Eber, he did not *lie down* [to sleep in a bed; instead he would snatch a casual nap whenever necessary] — so engrossed was he in Torah study.

According to another view in the *Midrash*, the implication was that only in *that* place did Jacob *lie down* to sleep, but not during the twenty years that he was in Laban's house.

Why, then, did Jacob lie down *now? Divrei David* suggests that Jacob lay down to sleep now, perhaps because he perceived that the premature setting of the sun was a Divine portent that he should lie down and spend the night there.[1]

12. וַיַּחֲלֹם — *[And] he dreamt.*

Dreams mentioned by Scripture are understood to be vehicles of prophecy; otherwise the Torah would not cite them. Cf. *Job* 33:15, 16: *In a dream, in a vision of the night ... [God] opens the ears of man.*

Rambam, in *Hilchos Yesodei HaTorah* writes: All the prophets [except Moses] experienced prophetic manifestations only in dreams — at night, or by day after a deep sleep had fallen upon them, as it is said, *I make Myself known unto him in a vision; I speak with him in a dream* [*Numbers* 12:6 see *comm.* there.] When they had a prophetic experience their limbs trembled, their physical strength failed them, their thoughts became confused. As a result the mind was left free to comprehend the vision it saw, as occurred to Abraham [*Gen.* 15:12] and Daniel [*Dan.* 10:8]. [See also *Moreh Nevuchim* 2:36-38; *Derech Hashem* 3:5.]

וְהִנֵּה סֻלָּם מֻצָּב אַרְצָה וְרֹאשׁוֹ מַגִּיעַ הַשָּׁמָיְמָה — *And behold! A ladder was set earthward, and its top reached heavenward.*

[The commentators draw attention to the phrase מֻצָּב אַרְצָה, *set earthward*, i.e., *'toward' the ground,* (rather than עַל הָאָרֶץ, *'on' the ground)* implying that the ladder originated in *heaven* and extended down *toward the earth.*]

The connecting ladder clearly intimated that there was a means of communication upwards from the earth. But the ladder did not come there by chance. It was מֻצָּב, *set;* a Higher Power had placed it אַרְצָה, facing *earthward* to imply that the will and power that emplaced it were not earthly but heavenly. Nevertheless, the ladder was meant

1. *Kli Yakar* infers that Jacob's refusal to lie down until he reached this place was in the nature of an oath that he would permit himself no rest until he found the place where God's Presence would eventually find its resting place on earth.

Similarly, in vowing that he would not rest in his *bed* until he had found the place where the Temple would be built, David referred to the God of Jacob, an allusion to the similar vow made earlier by Jacob. Thus David vowed: *If I allow sleep to my eyes, slumber to my eyelids, until I find a place for* HASHEM, *a resting place for the Strong One of Jacob* (*Psalms* 132:4, 5).

to provide a means for people to raise themselves spiritually: וְרֹאשׁוֹ מַגִּיעַ הַשָּׁמָיְמָה, *and its top reached heavenward (Hirsch).* [See Symbolism of the Dream, below.]

וְהִנֵּה מַלְאֲכֵי אֱלֹהִים עֹלִים וְיֹרְדִים בּוֹ — *And behold! Angels of God were ascending and descending on it.*

First *ascending* and then *descending?* [We would expect to find angels of God *descending* first since they originate from heaven.] — The angels who escorted Jacob in *Eretz Yisrael* were not permitted to leave the precincts of the Land; they therefore *ascended* to heaven and others *descended* to escort him in the course of his travels outside the Holy Land *(Rashi* citing *Midrash).*

[This is based on the tradition that two angels are assigned to escort man at all times. See *Psalms* 91:11; *Orach Chaim* §3; and *Maharsha* to *Chullin* 91b. It was these angels whom Jacob saw in his dream.]

According to another opinion in the *Midrash,* the angels whom Jacob now saw ascending were the ministering angels who, 138 years earlier at the overthrow of Sodom, had revealed God's plan to Lot and boasted that *they* were going to overthrow the place [19:13]. They had been banished from the Divine Presence for all these 138 years. Now they were finally permitted to ascend to be given a new mission. Having received their new assignment, they descended again. [See *comm.* to 19:13, page 689, for the calculation of these 138 years.]

[There are opinions among the *Midrashic* commentators that the 'wings' of these angels were 'clipped' — in the deeply esoteric sense — and therefore they could not ascend on their own. Now they perceived the descent of this heavenly ladder as a Divine invitation, as it were, for them to finally reascend and descend with a new mission. According to others (see *Yafeh Toar* and *Etz Yosef*) these banished angels were the same ones who accompanied Jacob in *Eretz Yisrael.* Having completed their mission of escorting Jacob, they ascended.]

In the *literal* sense, however, no deduction need be drawn from the prior mention of *ascending* for it is respectful to speak first of an ascent *(Ralbag).*

The phrase עֹלִים וְיֹרְדִים בּוֹ is usually interpreted in its simple sense: *were ascending and descending on it* — i.e., on the ladder. There is a view in the *Midrash* that בּוֹ is to be interpreted *on* **him** — i.e., the ascent and descent of the angels was dependent *upon Jacob* because in heaven, he who speaks in Israel's favor is exalted; in his disfavor is debased. Thus, some angels were *ascending* because they exalted Jacob, but others *descended* because they maligned him. On earth, however, the reverse is true: He who speaks in Israel's favor is debased, while he who speaks in Israel's disfavor is exalted. [See *comm.* to ArtScroll *Lamentations* 1:5 citing *Gittin* 56a: 'Whoever causes Israel distress attains leadership'.]

☙ The Symbolism of the Dream.

Pesikta Zutresa observes that Jacob's dream is unusual in that its interpretation — unlike the other prophetic dreams recorded in Scripture — is not given in the Torah.

The Sages in the *Midrash* have variously interpreted the imagery of Jacob's dream, as have the later classical commentators. Although a thorough representation would take a volume by itself, a selection of the various interpretations follow. [The subject is also discussed in the *Overview.*]

In general, the expositors agree that the vision was a disclosure of the future of the Jewish nation. Accordingly, the interpretations that follow are not mutually exclusive: all of these allusions — and perhaps others that remain unrevealed to us — were concurrently implied in Jacob's prophetic dreams.

[It would seem that it was particularly important that this prophetic dream be shown Jacob only now when he was fleeing Esau's wrath. At this perilous time, Jacob was given this assurance that his father's blessings would be fulfilled through his progeny who would be born in exile. God wanted to reveal to him that He would be with Jacob even far from Isaac's home.]

☐ **Sinaitic Vision.** The סֻלָּם, *ladder,* represents a prophetic allusion to סִינַי, *Sinai* — both words having the same numeric value [130]; the angels represent Moses and Aaron, and God's stance upon the ladder refers to the revelation of the *Shechinah* atop Sinai *(Midrash).* [Accordingly, we may see the Torah, given at Sinai, as the bridge connecting heaven and earth through the agency of Torah sages as represented by Moses and Aaron.]

☐ **The Altar.** Another interpretation (ibid.): The ladder represents the altar; its top in heaven refers to the fragrance of the sacrifices which ascends on high; ascending and descending angels allude to the High Priests performing the service; God's stance above it is reminiscent of *Amos* 9:1: *I saw my Lord standing above* [נִצָּב עַל] *the altar.*

☐ **The Four Kingdoms.** *Pirkei d'Rabbi Eliezer,* in the best known of all the interpretations, equates the import of this vision with Abraham's vision at the Covenant Between the Parts [see 15:9-18]. Jacob was symbolically shown [as was Abraham (see *Ramban* to 15:12 and *footnote* to 14:1, page 474)] the Four Kingdoms which would, after the Egyptian bondage, successively *ascend* to subjugate Israel, and then *descend,* and fall from power. The angels accordingly represent the guardian angels of the nations [which are chosen by God to be the 'rod of His anger' by becoming His earthly agents to punish Israel. Thus, as *Abarbanel* explains, the vision of these angels traversing the heavenly ladder intimated that their dominion was influenced from Heaven.] ...

Accordingly, Jacob was shown the angel of the Babylonian Empire ascending 70 rungs [one for each year that Israel would be subjugated during the Babylonian Exile], and then descending. Then the angel of Media ascended 52 rungs and descended; the angel of Greece climbed 180 rungs and descended, representing the years of their respective domination of Israel. Jacob was then shown the angel of Edom [=Rome. Traditionally this refers to the current, lingering exile amid Western Civilization]. Edom ascended an undetermined number of steps, boasting that he would climb to the utmost heights and be like God Himself [see *Isaiah* 14:14], but Jacob did not see him descend. [This uninterrupted ascendancy alluded to the unspecified duration of the Edomite Exile.] Jacob became frightened that Edom's dominion would last forever ... God assured him that Edom's angel would ultimately cease [for as God assured Jacob in *v.* 15, He would be with Jacob — throughout his descendants' exiles — to guard him wherever he would go, and return him to the Land *(Abarbanel).*] [Cf. slightly different versions in *Sh'mos Rabbah* 32; *VaYikra Rabbah* 29; and *Ramban* to *v.* 13. (Cf. *Avodah Zarah* 9a according to which the Medes ruled 34 years.) This *Midrash* does not appear in *Radal's* edition of *Pirkei d'Rabbi Eliezer.* Apparently it was excised by Christian censors.][1]

[The interpretation that Jacob's dream represented the Four Monarchies assumes that there were four angels, each the guardian angel of one of the monarchies. That there were four is the view of the Sages in *Chullin* 91b and *Midrash.* It is based on this reasoning: Unless Scripture specifies otherwise, we must assume that the use of a plural form indicates that there were two. This assumption derives from the principle that the Torah comes not to conceal, but to

1. In *Vayikra Rabbah* 29:2 the *Midrash* continues:

The Holy One, Blessed be He, then ordered Jacob: 'You ascend as well.'

Jacob grew frightened and said: 'Perhaps, Heaven forfend, just as these are destined to descend, so, too, will I?'

God reassured him that once he would ascend there would be no descent for him.

Jacob would not believe, so he did not ascend [i.e., he had no confidence in his ability to remain sinless; he was apprehensive that his eventual sins might cause the forfeiture of the

יהוה נִצָּב עָלָיו וַיֹּאמַר אֲנִי יהוה אֱלֹהֵי

clarify; had more than two been meant, the number would have been specified. Thus, since we are told that *angels* ascended and other *angels* descended, we must assume that there were a total of four angels.]

Tosafos HaRosh Hadar Zekeinim cites a version that God also showed Jacob the angelic prince of the Egyptian monarchy ascending 210 rungs, and then descending. [This represented the 210 years of bondage in Egypt. See *comm.* and footnote to 15:14 on page 527, and *Rashi* to 42:2.]

☐ **The Land's Greatness.** *Rashi,* reflecting the exposition of the Sages, comments that the dream was designed to emphasize to Jacob the spiritual superiority of *Eretz Yisrael* over all other lands. Because Jacob was destined to spend more of his mature life outside of the Land then did the other Patriarchs, God wanted to instill within him an intense desire to return to the Land. Therefore, Jacob was shown that the angels of *Eretz Yisrael* are of such an exalted spiritual level that they cannot leave the Land. Instead, they return to heaven and are replaced by lesser angels (as explained by *Abarbanel*).

☐ **God's Emissaries.** *Ibn Ezra* cites two interpretations:

(a) The ladder symbolizes the soul which descends from above; the angels represent wise thoughts *(R' Shlomo Ibn Gabirol);*

(b) The ladder represents the vehicle by which one's prayer ascends to heaven and by which salvation descends from heaven *(R' Yehoshua ben Yehudah).*

Ibn Ezra concludes, however, that the most acceptable interpretation is that the ladder is emblematic of the link between the earthly and heavenly spheres. Nothing is hidden from God, and temporal matters are dependent on the celestial. The ladder, then, is the vehicle on which the angels return to the heavens to report on the missions entrusted to them on earth ... The symbolism is that of a king's courtiers reporting to their monarch although, of course, God requires no one to inform Him of what has transpired.

☐ **Wisdom for Earthly Use.** *Rambam* in *Moreh Nevuchim* 1:15 explains that the ladder symbolizes the vehicle which may be climbed by all who wish to attain a knowledge of Him Who is permanently above the summit of the ladder [see *Rambam's* explanation of נִצָּב עָלָיו in *v.* 13.] The *angels* in this context represent the prophets [i.e. emissaries of God]. The *ascendancy* — the *attainment* of a certain height of the ladder [i.e. of wisdom] — precedes the *descent* — the *application* of the knowledge thus acquired, for the training and instruction of mankind. [See *Rambam's* interpretation of the term ירד, *descent,* in *Moreh Nevuchim* 1:10.]

[In *Hilchos Yesodei HaTorah* 7:3, however, *Rambam* mentions only the interpretation that the angels on the ladder symbolized the Four Kingdoms and their successive oppressions of Israel (see *Pirkei d'Rabbi Eliezer* above). He explains that 'although matters communicated in a prophetic vision are communicated to a prophet in allegorical form, its interpretation is impressed upon his mind simultaneously with the vision, as was the case with Jacob, who dreamt symbolizing the Monarchies and their oppression of Israel.']

promise, and deprive him of God's blessing *(Radal). Ramban* explains (footnote to 15:2, page 506), the righteous never take their righteousness for granted and are never confident of their deservedness in this world. (See also *comm.* to קָטֹנְתִּי in 32:11.]

'Had you believed and ascended,' God said, 'you would never have come down. Now, however, your descendants are destined to be enslaved to the Four Monarchies in this world!'

Jacob was frightened. 'Will this endure forever?' he asked.

God assured him that it would not; that He would ultimately redeem Israel.

[13] *And behold! HASHEM was standing over him, and He said, 'I am HASHEM, God of Abraham your*

☐ **Jacob's Uniqueness.** *Ramban* generally concurs with *Ibn Ezra.* He explains that this prophetic dream was meant to convey to Jacob that whatever happens on earth is effected by angels *whom HASHEM has sent to walk the earth to and fro* [see *Zechariah* 1:10-11], and who act on Divine instructions. They do nothing, however, without first *ascending* to 'report' to God and receive His charge whereupon they *descend* to follow His command. As for Jacob, however, God assured him that he would be חֵבֶל נַחֲלָתוֹ, *God's portion.* Accordingly he would not be under the power of the angels, but under God's *direct* protection. [See *comm.* to *v.* 15; see also *footnote* on page 340.] *Abarbanel,* citing this view, adds that in his freedom from the control of angels, Jacob would be greater than other righteous men of whom it is written [*Psalms* 91:11] that God will give His *angels* charge over them.] *Ramban* also cites the view of *Pirkei d'Rabbi Eliezer* that this vision paralleled that of the vision shown Abraham in the Covenant between the Parts.

☐ **God's Superior Insight.** *R' Hirsch* writes that the angels were ascending and descending בּוֹ, *against* Jacob, for the angels came from heaven with the celestial image of man as he *should* be. The vision of man as he *is* — falling short of the goal assigned him— turns the angels against him. In the case of Jacob, the Sages teach that the angels were angered by the fact that he had the temerity to sleep in so holy a place. Instead, the sanctity of the place should have awakened in him a desire for greatness. Therefore, the angels prepared to 'endanger his life' (*Chullin* 91b). Then God appeared standing at the top of the ladder. The word נִצָּב, *standing,* suggests undivided attention. The implication is that God gives His attention to the person in a manner of which the angels are not capable. He sees man's potential and protects him even though man's current performance falls short of the goals toward which he must strive.

13. וְהִנֵּה ה׳ נִצָּב עָלָיו — *And behold! HASHEM was standing over him.*

— To protect him *(Rashi).*[1]

According to *Chullin* 91b, the angels were jealous of Jacob because they perceived his image on the Throne of Glory [which implied that he was on a higher plane than they] and they wished to harm him. Therefore, as the verse says, *Behold HASHEM was standing above him* [to protect him *(Rashi).*] The *Talmud* continues that were this fact not expressly stated in Scripture, we would not dare picture God standing like a human father fanning his son [to protect him from the sun's burning rays *(Rashi;* see *Maharsha).*].

Thus, *Maharsha* concludes, it would appear that in this exegesis *Rashi* goes according to the view that the angels ascended and descended בּוֹ on *Jacob,* as the *Midrash* interprets above. However, in his comment to verse 12, *Rashi* apparently follows the interpretation that Jacob's escorting angels ascended and descended the *ladder,* not to harm Jacob, but because the angels of the Holy Land were replaced by those from outside the Land.

According to *Mizrachi,* however, *Rashi's* two comments are consistent. When the escorting angels ascended, Jacob was left unprotected until the other escorting angels

1. The *Midrash* derives from this that idolators must stand over and protect their deities, whereas the True God protects His adherents:

Rav Yochanan said, The wicked stand over their gods, as it says [41:1]: *And Pharaoh dreamed, and behold, he stood over the river* [i.e. the Nile, which the Egyptians worshipped]; but the God of the righteous stands over them, as it says, *And behold, HASHEM was standing over him.*

אַבְרָהָם אָבִיךָ וֵאלֹהֵי יִצְחָק הָאָרֶץ אֲשֶׁר אַתָּה שֹׁכֵב עָלֶיהָ לְךָ אֶתְּנֶנָּה וּלְזַרְעֶךָ׃

descended. To fill this void, HASHEM Himself stood guard over Jacob.

Why, then, did the second group of angels not descend first, so Jacob would not be left unprotected? — One 'kingdom' may not encroach even for a moment upon another; i.e., Jacob could not be served simultaneously both by angels of *Eretz Yisrael* and by those of outside lands. Therefore, the first escorting angels had to depart before the others could replace them *(Gur Aryeh).*

The translation *was standing over him* is literal. Actually, as *Rashi* explains in 18:2, the phrase means standing *near* him, but when the Deity is the subject, the respectful term *upon* is used to avoid the implication that the divine and human are on equal footing.

The *Midrash* in commenting upon the depiction of God being *upon* him, notes that the Patriarchs are the 'chariot' of God; thus He may indeed be described as being 'upon' them. [See also *Rashi* to 17:2.]

Rambam in *Moreh Nevuchim,* 1:15 explains that the verb נצב is a homonym which depending on the context, means either *to stand, place oneself,* or to be *continuous* or *permanent* as in *Psalms* 119:89: דְּבָרְךָ נִצָּב בַּשָּׁמָיִם, Your word is *established* in Heaven. When the word refers to God it must be understood in the latter sense, as in our verse: *And behold,* HASHEM *was standing upon it* [the ladder], appearing as *eternal* and *everlasting* [see *Rambam's* interpretation of the symbolism of the dream, above.]

The word וְהִנֵּה, *behold,* occurs five times in this vision. This frequent use is explained by the commentators to emphasize that Jacob's vision was more than a mere fantastic dream: The word הִנֵּה, *behold,* is used only to introduce something of perceptive *substance (Akeidas Yitzchak).*

Ha'amek Davar notes that Jacob was shown angels before seeing the *Shechinah* to emphasize that God conducts His government much like that of earthly monarchs [in the sense that one sees the king's entourage before seeing the king himself.]

אֲנִי ה׳ — *I am HASHEM.*

[See *comm.* to 15:7 where it is explained that God's identification of Himself as *HASHEM* does not conflict with *Exodus* 6:3 where God tells Moses: *By My Name HASHEM I did not make Myself known to them* (i.e., the Patriarchs).]

אֱלֹהֵי אַבְרָהָם אָבִיךָ וֵאלֹהֵי יִצְחָק — *God of Abraham your father and God of Isaac.*

[Abraham was not Jacob's *father* — Isaac was. Even if father is interpreted to mean *ancestor,* the verse should have more properly read: *God of Abraham and Isaac your fathers*]·

The appellation *father* for Abraham is meant to suggest that Abraham is considered to be Jacob's father *only,* since Abraham's heritage would pass on *in its entirety* through Isaac to Jacob. Abraham's other biological offspring—Ishmael and Esau—are not considered to be his 'children' in the full sense of the word *(Radak).* [See *comm.* to 21:12: כִּי בְיִצְחָק יִקָּרֵא לְךָ זָרַע and to *v.* 15 below s.v. אֵת אֲשֶׁר.]

And as *Abarbanel* notes, Abraham is referred to as Jacob's *father* because the promise that Isaac gave to Jacob [28:4] was originally given to Abraham. Thus, in effect, Isaac but served as a conduit to Jacob and so Abraham, even more than Isaac, was therefore considered Jacob's spiritual father.

28
13 father and God of Isaac. The ground upon which you are lying, to you will I give it and to your descen-

Hirsch notes, in a similar vein, that nowhere else is a grandfather called a father, while the *true* father is not so described. Obviously, the relationship so depicted is not the physical one. In effect, therefore, Jacob was told that he should consider himself the spiritual heir of Abraham to whom God said, הִתְהַלֵּךְ לְפָנַי וֶהְיֵה תָמִים, *walk before Me and be perfect* (17:1). Abraham's mission attained its initial realization with Jacob, the one who established the first Jewish household.

Tosafos HaRosh suggests that *your father* refers to both Abraham and Isaac, the implication of the passage being: *I am the God of your father: God of Abraham and God of Isaac.*

Ha'amek Davar refers to *Exodus* 3:6 and 15 where he shows that the expression 'God of Abraham' refers especially to God as the Protector of Israel, while 'God of Isaac' refers to Him as the Provider of Sustenance. In Jacob's present predicament, he needed primarily an assurance of safety from the dangers of the journey and from his mortal enemy Esau. Therefore, although God implied assurance of both his safety and sustenance by describing Himself as the God of Abraham *and* of Isaac, He stressed Jacob's need for protection by the additional appellation אָבִיךָ, *your father,* with regard to Abraham.

Rashi notes that it is exceptional for God to associate Himself with a living person. Indeed, such a relationship is found nowhere else, in keeping with the principle *He puts not trust even in His Holy Ones* [*Job* 15:15 — i.e., since even the righteous can succumb to temptation while they are still alive, God does not allow His Name to be associated in a permanent manner with potential sinners]. In this case, however, God *did* associate His name with Isaac. However, since Isaac was blind and confined to his home, he was regarded as dead in the sense that the Evil Inclination left him and it was unlikely that he would be further subject to temptation [*Tanchumah*].

[Cf. references to this verse in 32:10 where Jacob later invokes this promise.]

הָאָרֶץ אֲשֶׁר אַתָּה שֹׁכֵב עָלֶיהָ — *The ground* [or: *land*] *upon which you are lying.*

I.e., the land of Canaan *(Sforno).*

[Are we to intimate from this verse that Jacob was promised no more than the piece of ground upon which he lay? *(Rashi, Chullin* 91b)]:

— God 'folded' the whole of *Eretz Yisrael* beneath him as a token that it would be as easily conquered by his descendants (*Chullin* 91b) as the four-cubit piece of ground upon which he lay *(Rashi).*[1]

1. *Tur* cites his father, the *Rosh,* that the site upon which Jacob lay was later to be the Temple [*Pesachim* 88a] and beneath him was the אֶבֶן שְׁתִיָּה, *Foundation Stone* [the first part of earth to be created and from which the rest of the earth sprang forth, and upon which the Ark of the covenant rested in the Holy of Holies in the Temple (see *Yoma* 54b and *Ramban* to 1:2 and further *v.* 17).] This was the center of the earth, and from there the ground unfolded [see *Pirkei d'Rabbi Eliezer* 35] to the four 'ends of the earth.'

Accordingly, since God bequeathed to Jacob this nucleus of earth, then *ipso facto* the rest of the land would be his, too. Therefore, God did not draw a comparison with the *stars of the*

יד וְהָיָה זַרְעֲךָ כַּעֲפַר הָאָרֶץ וּפָרַצְתָּ יָמָּה
וָקֵדְמָה וְצָפֹנָה וָנֶגְבָּה וְנִבְרְכוּ בְךָ כָּל־

The *Midrash* derives from the phraseology [the term שכב also refers to *burial*] that the Land would belong to Jacob's descendants only on the condition that he would be buried there [see *Etz Yosef*.]

Because, following this *Midrash*, the inheritance of the Land would be dependent on his burial there, Jacob insisted, prior to his death, that he not be buried in Egypt [47:29]. He could not be content, as was Joseph, with a pledge that his remains would be taken to *Eretz Yisrael* after the Exodus [50:25], because unless he, Jacob, was buried there. Israel would not have received the Land *(R' David Cohen)*.

לְךָ אֶתְּנֶנָּה וּלְזַרְעֶךָ — *To you will I give it and to your descendants.*

To you — potentially, *and to your descendants* — in actuality; *descendants* here meaning future descendants *(Ibn Caspi)*.

[This is yet another example of God's reiteration to each of the Patriarchs of His promise of the Land.]

The promise *to you* carries within it the implicit assurance that though Jacob was now fleeing the Land, *he* would yet return to *dwell* in it. However, it would be only *his descendants* who would actually *possess it (Da'as Soferim)*.

You will be considered a prince of God by its inhabitants as were Abraham [see 23:6] and Isaac [apparently a reference to 26:28] *(Sforno)*.

[Apparently *Sforno* intends to explain the significance of the blessing *here* during Jacob's flight. Although Jacob was now without worldly possessions and had but a few stones beneath him, he was assured that he would some day possess the Land and be considered a prince of God in it among its inhabitants as were his forefathers.][1]

14. וְהָיָה זַרְעֲךָ כַּעֲפַר הָאָרֶץ — *[And] your offspring shall be as the dust of the earth.*

— I.e. as *numerous* as the dust of the earth *(Onkelos)* [This, of course, is meant only in the figurative sense; since mankind — with its *lebensraum* needs could never be literally as numerous as the dust *(HaKsav V'haKabalah)*.]

... And Israel will be as basic to earthly existence as the dust. From the earth all is built and to it, all ultimately return. Not an atom of it is ever lost *(Hirsch)*.

heaven as He did with Abraham [see 15:5], but with the *dust of the earth* in all directions — as if to intimate: Just as the elements scattered in all directions from the spot where you lay, so will your descendants scatter to the west, east, north, and south.

1. Compare *Sanhedrin* 111a:

The Holy One, Blessed be He, said to Moses, 'Alas for those' [i.e., the Patriarchs] who are gone and no more to be found! For how many times did I reveal Myself to the Patriarchs ... and they did not question My Attributes [i.e., My 'dealings' with man] ... I said to Jacob: *The ground upon which you are lying, to you will I give it and to your descendants,* yet [upon his return from Paddan Aram] Jacob sought a place to pitch his tent and did not find one until he purchased it for *a hundred kesitah* [33:191].

[A similar observation is made of Abraham, who, notwithstanding God's many promises to *give* him the Land, was landless and had to *purchase* a burial plot to bury his wife. Nevertheless he never doubted God's ways (see *footnote* page 868). Similarly, though God promised to bless Isaac in Gerar (26:3), his servants still had to engage in controversy when seeking water to drink (26:20). Nevertheless, Isaac never doubted God's ways.]

28
14 *dants.* [14] *Your offspring shall be as the dust of the
earth, and you shall spread out powerfully westward,
eastward, northward and southward; and all the*

[See *comm.* to parallel blessing to Abraham in 13:16, page 470.]

Sforno connects this phrase with the following one, rendering: *Only after your offspring shall have become as degraded as the dust of the earth* [*see Isaiah* 51:23] *shall they spread out powerfully to the west, east, north, and south.* For, as the Sages have taught, God's future salvation will come only after Israel has experienced much degradation. [See *Overview* to *ArtScroll Daniel.*]

[This follows an interpretation in *Sh'mos Rabbah* 25 which cites *I Samuel* 2:8: *He raises up the poor out of the dust.*]

R' Bachya interprets similarly. God compared them to the dust of the earth rather than to the stars in heaven [as He did when He blessed Isaac in 26:4] to intimate that Israel will be like dust in ways other than abundance. Dust has the connotation of lowliness inasmuch as Israel would be downtrodden like the dust while in exile. Also, like dust, however, they would endure everything and prevail, just as the earth survives all those who tread on it [see footnote.] As Isaiah foretold [*Isaiah* 26:5]: *He brings it to the dust,* yet it is from the dust that Israel will be redeemed, as it is written [ibid. 52:2]: *Shake yourself from the dust, arise ... O Jerusalem.*[1]

וּפָרַצְתָּ — *And you shall spread out powerfully.*

Following the above interpretation that the subject of the verse is Jacob's offspring — for it is they who will multiply, be degraded, and expand — the phrase should have read וְיִפְרוֹצוּ, *and* **they** *shall.* Since it reads in the singular, the verse apparently refers to Jacob. It alludes to the *Midrashic* comment [see *comm.* to ArtScroll *Eichah* 2:3 s.v. וַיִּבְעַר בְּיַעֲקֹב] that 'when punishment comes into the world, no one feels it as much as Jacob and when there is good in the world no one rejoices as much as Jacob' [see *Psalms* 14:7] *(Kli Yakar).*

The commentators vary in their definition of the verb פרץ, which in its most literal sense, connotes *breaking forth* through narrow confines *(Radak).* According to *Ibn Ezra,* the connotation of וּפָרַצְתָּ is *increase numerically* [i.e., outgrow your premises].

Our translation, as always, follows *Rashi,* who, like *Onkelos* explains the connotation of the word to be: *you shall spread out powerfully,* as in *Exodus* 1:12: וְכֵן יִפְרֹץ, *and so he became powerful.* [Thus *Rashi* distinguishes the positive connotation here from the negative connotation of the same word in *Exodus* 19:22 and 19:24 פֶּן יִפְרָץ בָּם, (where *Rashi* explains *break forth against them* as connoting *bring death to them) (Mizrachi).*]

The implication of *Rashi,* then, is that the intent of the blessing is: May you [through your descendants] have the unrestricted strength to overflow and populate any area of their choice: West, east, north and south *(R' David Feinstein).*

יָמָּה וָקֵדְמָה וְצָפֹנָה וָנֶגְבָּה — *Westward, eastward, northward, and southward.*

I.e. to the four corners of the world *(Rashbam).*

1. The comparison of Jacob's descendants to the dust of the earth is appropriate, notes *Tzror HaMor:* Everyone tramples the ground; but in the end the earth swallows them all.

Furthermore, all trample the earth but all are sustained through it *(Sefer HaBris).*

טו מִשְׁפְּחֹת הָאֲדָמָה וּבְזַרְעֶךָ: וְהִנֵּה אָנֹכִי
עִמָּךְ וּשְׁמַרְתִּיךָ בְּכֹל אֲשֶׁר־תֵּלֵךְ

— An unbounded heritage [נַחֲלָה בְּלִי מְצָרִים] — unlike the delineated territory promised to Abraham [13:17], or to Isaac [26:3] *(Shabbos* 118b).[1]

The sequence of directions reflects the order of conquest led by Joshua. First, they advanced *westward* capturing the entire territory from the *eastern* border to the west. Then they turned *southward*, capturing the entire land from the south *(Malbim).*

Abarbanel comments that the blessing of the four directions is an allusion to the four encampments into which Jacob's descendants would be divided in the wilderness [see *Numbers* 2].

In 13:14 the directions are listed in a different sequence: *HASHEM said to Abram ... 'Raise now your eyes and look out from where you are: northward, southward, eastward and westward.'*

Tosafos HaRosh Hadar Zekeinim conjectures that to Abraham, who was moving [from Bethel to Hebron] in a southerly direction, God first mentioned the direction he was leaving — north — and then the direction towards which he was heading — south. Similarly, to Jacob who was headed toward Charan, God first mentioned west, the direction from which he was coming, and then east, the direction in which he was heading. [This does not account, however, for the use of east-west to Abraham, and west-east here. See also the entirely different sequence in God's communication with Moses in *Deut.* 3:27: West, north, south, east — רצ״ע.]

וְנִבְרְכוּ בְךָ ... וּבְזַרְעֶךָ — *And all the families of the earth shall bless themselves by you and by your offspring.*

And by your offspring was not said to Abraham [12:3] ... but it was added here because Jacob had no unworthy children *(Midrash HaBiur, Torah Sheleimah* §105).

This translation of וְנִבְרְכוּ as *shall bless themselves* follows *Rashi's* interpretation of this expression throughout Scripture: A man will bless his son by saying, 'Be like Jacob and his descendants.' And, as *Rashi* concludes, 'this is the meaning wherever the expression appears.'

[See extensive commentary to the virtually parallel blessing to Abraham in 12:3 and 18:18.]

Among other interpretations are: And all the families of the earth *shall be blessed* through your righteousness [i.e., by your merit] and the righteousness of your offspring (*Targum Yonasan;* see *Ramban* to 12:3).[2] All the families of the earth will wish to *intermingle* [from the Mishnaic verb ברך, *graft*] with you *(Rashbam).*

Radak interprets: *Because of you* and your offspring will all the families of the earth be blessed. Thus, the offspring of Jacob, by virtue of fulfilling God's commandments and recognizing Him Alone as Master of the universe, are responsible for the survival of the whole world.

15. וְהִנֵּה אָנֹכִי עִמָּךְ — [And] *behold, I am with you.*

Rambam, Moreh Nevuchim 3:18

1. He who delights in the Sabbath, is given an unbounded heritage, as it is written [*Isaiah* 54:13-14]: *If ... you call the Sabbath a delight ... then I will ... feed you with the heritage of Jacob your father.* The *heritage of Jacob* is mentioned because unlike the promises to Abraham and Isaac, the heritage promised to Jacob in our verse was boundless and unrestrained — [to the very ends of the earth, as it were] *(Shabbos* 118b).

In a homiletical vein, *Kli Yakar* notes that the boundless heritage of Jacob is mentioned both in connection with the Sabbath and, in our verse with the dust of the earth. Just as the Torah ordains that the land must rest every seventh year, so must Israel rest every seventh day.

28
15
families of the earth shall bless themselves by you
and by your offspring. [15] *Behold, I am with you; I*
will guard you wherever you go, and I will return

explains that this expression — which recurs often in Scripture (see for example 26:3) — is an explicit affirmation of Providence watching over the details of man's various activities according to the measure of man's perfection.

[From Jacob's later paraphrase of this promise in 32:13 as אֵיטִיב עִמָּךְ it would appear that this was a general affirmation that God would 'do good' with him.]

Jacob required God's reassurance since he was afraid of Esau and Laban *(Rashi).*

According to *Ramban* [*v.* 12] God's assurance indicated that Jacob would be under God's *direct* protection, and not under the power of the angels who perform God's will on earth [see *Abarbanel's* comment in this regard, cited at the end of *v.* 12.]

[Apparently this follows the usual interpretation that the pronoun אָנֹכִי (in comparison with the more subdued pronoun אֲנִי) has an emphatic connotation: 'I Myself — *and no other* — am with you.']

וּשְׁמַרְתִּיךָ בְּכֹל אֲשֶׁר־תֵּלֵךְ — *And I will guard you wherever* [lit. *in all that*] *you go.*

In your flight from Esau, and during your refuge with Laban and your return from him *(Radak).*

[In the prophetic historical sense]: I will guard you (=your descendants) in your wanderings,

2. *Or HaChaim* interprets: The nations of the world *will prosper* from the very day of your arrival. He notes far-reaching implications of this blessing. As the Sages tell us, Charan was hard-pressed for water, but when Jacob arrived, water became abundant. Similarly, when Jacob arrived in Egypt the famine ended.

This condition held true with Jacob's *offspring* as well: As the Sages note [*Sukkah* 55b], the nations of the world owed their prosperity to the descendants of Jacob who offered seventy bullocks every Succos [Tabernacles] in the Temple to atone for the seventy nations of the world. As Rav Yochanan said: 'Woe to the nations for they suffered a loss [by having destroyed the Temple] and do not realize the extent of the loss. While the Temple existed, the altar atoned for them, but now [that it is destroyed] who will atone for them?'

Ralbag synthesizes several views by rendering: *Through you and your offspring shall all the families of the earth be blessed* [i.e., blessings will proliferate among the families of the earth because of you and your offspring], because, in fact, when people will wish to bless one another they will say, 'May you be like Jacob and his children.'

[See also commentary to the *hispa'el* form, וְהִתְבָּרְכוּ, in 22:18 and 26:4.]

According to *Ha'amek Davar:* Even when Israel will be in exile, the families of the earth will bless themselves by you and your offspring inasmuch as the nations will recognize that the miracle of Jewish survival is possible only because its great Shepherd stands watch over it.

This would not have been as obvious were the world in peace and tranquility, for then the nations would attribute Israel's success to good fortune or natural prowess. Jacob's lot under Laban and Israel's lot in exile, however, were such that God's Providence was obvious to all.

R' Hirsch interprets that the blessing will emanate from a combination of Jacob *and* his offspring. The blessed spiritual influence of Jacob will be perceived by the nations only when successive generations of his offspring have demonstrated that their homes and their material labors have been founded upon the teachings and commandments of God.

Me'am Loez cites *Mishkenos Yaakov* who perceives a different implication in this verse: וְהָיָה זַרְעֲךָ כַּעֲפַר הָאָרֶץ, *Even when your descendants are downtrodden like the dust of the earth,* וּפָרַצְתָּ יָמָּה וָקֵדְמָה וְצָפֹנָה וָנֶגְבָּה, *and you are scattered to the four corners of the earth* — nevertheless, וְנִבְרְכוּ בְךָ כָּל מִשְׁפְּחֹת הָאֲדָמָה וּבְזַרְעֶךָ, *all the families of the earth will be blessed* [or: *bless themselves (Rashi)*] *through you and your offspring.*

וַהֲשִׁבֹתִיךָ אֶל־הָאֲדָמָה הַזֹּאת כִּי לֹא
אֶעֱזָבְךָ עַד אֲשֶׁר אִם עָשִׂיתִי אֵת אֲשֶׁר־
טז דִּבַּרְתִּי לָךְ: וַיִּיקַץ יַעֲקֹב מִשְּׁנָתוֹ וַיֹּאמֶר

and rescue you from your exiles among the nations *(Ramban* to *v.* 12 in citing *Pirkei d'Rabbi Eliezer's* interpretation that Jacob saw the future ascendancies of the Four Empires who would subjugate his descendants).

וַהֲשִׁבֹתִיךָ אֶל־הָאֲדָמָה הַזֹּאת — *And I will return you to this soil.*[1]

[Both in the personal sense: when Esau's wrath will cool; and in the national sense: when God will redeem your descendants from their future exiles.]

This does not suggest that once God had returned Jacob to the land, he could not be exiled again, as was indeed the case when Jacob, in the face of famine, had to go to Egypt *(Haamek Davar).*

God said, 'to this *soil'* rather than 'to this *land'* to hint that eventually Jacob would return from Egypt to be *buried* in the *soil* of *Eretz Yisrael (Meshech Chochmah).*

כִּי לֹא אֶעֱזָבְךָ — *For I will not forsake you.*

In the contextual sense: *I will not forsake you* while you are traveling, for a man needs more than usual protection while he is en route *(Rashbam).*

According to the *Midrash,* the concept of *forsaking* applies to sustenance as intimated in *Psalms* 37:25: *I have not seen the righteous* נֶעֱזָב, *forsaken* [lacking sustenance] *nor his seed begging bread.* Thus, by promising not to forsake him, God anticipated even Jacob's prayer for *bread to eat and clothing to wear* [*v.* 20].

עַד אֲשֶׁר אִם־עָשִׂיתִי — *Until [that/when] I have done.*

I.e., fulfilled *(Radak).*

The Hebrew, which literally means *until that/when* (or: *if) I have done* is idiomatic since, as *Radak* observes, the words אֲשֶׁר אִם would have sufficed; the redundancy implies emphasis. The translation in this context of אִם as *when* [rather than *if*] follows *Rashi.*

Sforno renders the phrase: *while I have not yet done,* the word עַד having the meaning of עוֹד, *while,* as in *Song of Songs* 1:12: עַד שֶׁהַמֶּלֶךְ בִּמְסִבּוֹ, *while the king was still at his table.* [He apparently interprets אִם *(if)* as meaning *not.* This follows *Sforno's* view in 14:23 that the word אִם *(if),* where it is not followed by a condition, has the implication of an oath, the meaning being *will not.* Thus in 14:23 the phrase וְאִם אֶקַּח means *nor shall I take.*]

Accordingly the assurance was that God would *never* forsake him nor his descendants since the promises He made concerning Jacob were eternal — embracing his descendants after him *forever (Radak).*

אֵת אֲשֶׁר־דִּבַּרְתִּי לָךְ — *What I have spoken about you.*

I.e. to Abraham. Whatever promises I made to Abraham concerning his descendants applied to *you,* not to Esau. I did not say to him יִצְחָק יִקָּרֵא לְךָ זָרַע, *'Isaac' will be*

1. The Holy One, Blessed be He, answers the righteous before they call upon Him, as it is written [*Isaiah* 65:24]: טֶרֶם יִקְרָאוּ וַאֲנִי אֶעֱנֶה, *Before they call I will answer.*

Thus, God told Jacob וּשְׁמַרְתִּיךָ, *and I will guard you,* before Jacob said [*v.* 20] וּשְׁמָרַנִי, *and He will guard me;* and He said וַהֲשִׁבֹתִיךָ, *and I will bring you back,* before Jacob said וְשַׁבְתִּי בְשָׁלוֹם, *and I return in peace (Midrash Ner Hasechalim — Torah Sheleimah* 110 [see *Bereishis Rabbah* 69:61]).

28 *you to this soil; for I will not forsake you until I have*
16 *done what I have spoken about you.'*
[16] *Jacob awoke from his sleep and said, 'Surely*

considered your offspring [which would have intimated that *all* of Isaac's descendants — including Esau — would be so regarded] but I said [21:12]: בְיִצְחָק, *'in'* Isaac, implying that only *part* of Isaac's offspring, not all of them, are included in the blessing. [This is explained in the footnote on p. 758] *(Rashi).*

According to *Rashi,* the flow of the assurance is: Do not fear Esau or Laban because I am with you and will not forsake you *until I have completed what I promised regarding you.* I promised Abraham to give this land to his offspring [12:7] and it is only through you — not through Esau — that this promise will be fulfilled. It is accordingly an *integral part of the promise* that I watch over you and assure your safe return *(Ibn Caspi).*

[Also inherent in this promise is that God would find a suitable wife for Jacob to assure the continuity of the Abrahamitic blessing.]

R' David Cohen similarly explains that this was Abraham's intent when he told his servant Eliezer when dispatching him to find a wife for Isaac: *HASHEM, God of heaven... who swore to me saying 'To your offspring will I give this land,' He will send His angel before you and you will take a wife for my son from there.* That is, in order for God to fulfill His many promises concerning my progeny, He will surely bring success to your mission of finding a *suitable* wife to build the House of Israel.

The translation of דִּבַּרְתִּי לָךְ [lit. *I have spoken* **to** you] as *I have spoken* **about** you, follows *Rashi* who explains that whenever the verb דִּבֵּר is followed by the pronoun לִי, לְךָ, לוֹ, or לָהֶם, it means to speak *concerning* rather than *to.* [This is enunciated more fully in *Rashi's* comm. to 24:7, page 900 s.v. וַאֲשֶׁר דִּבֶּר לִי]. Our verse proves this grammatical rule, *Rashi* continues, since the phrase cannot mean 'I have spoken *to* you,' because God had never spoken to Jacob before this occasion.

Others suggest that the phrase literally *does* mean: that I have *just spoken to you.* [*Rashi* does not subscribe to this view on grammatical grounds and because, had the reference been to the promises just given, it should have been put in present tense: אֵת אֲשֶׁר אֲנִי מְדַבֵּר אֵלֶיךָ, *what I am telling you (Mizrachi)*].

— The reference is to God's promise that He will bring him back to the soil *(Rashbam).*

— *I will not forsake you until I will have fulfilled My promise that you* [i.e., *your descendants*] *shall spread out powerfully to* the ends of the earth. Even after that, however, God's Mercy will prevail and He will remain in their midst as He promised [*Leviticus* 26:12]: וְהִתְהַלַּכְתִּי בְּתוֹכְכֶם, *And I will manifest Myself among you (Sforno).*[1]

16. וַיִּיקַץ יַעֲקֹב מִשְּׁנָתוֹ — *[And] Jacob awoke from his sleep.*

Jacob did not awake and say 'It was a dream,' as if to say that it had

1. According to *R' Hirsch,* too, the reference is to the fulfillment of the just given blessings reflecting the destiny of Jacob's descendants for all time:

— הִנֵּה אָנֹכִי עִמָּךְ, *I am with you,* and although you possess nothing but your staff, you may rely on My protection. Jacob was not given the promise of a great name as had Abraham (12:2), because, unlike Abraham, he was embarking on a long exile. Rather, he was promised protection from all the potential dangers of his new condition. He was further promised that God would not *forsake* either him or his descendants until the time comes for all the families of the earth to be blessed through Israel.

אָכֵן֙ יֵ֣שׁ יהוה בַּמָּק֣וֹם הַזֶּ֑ה וְאָנֹכִ֖י לֹ֥א
יָדָֽעְתִּי׃ יז וַיִּירָא֙ וַיֹּאמַ֔ר מַה־נּוֹרָ֖א הַמָּק֣וֹם
הַזֶּ֑ה אֵ֣ין זֶ֗ה כִּ֚י אִם־בֵּ֣ית אֱלֹהִ֔ים וְזֶ֖ה שַׁ֥עַר

little significance. Instead he treated it as a prophecy, for when prophets are shown a vision in a dream, they recognize it to be a communication from God, as did Jacob when he awoke exclaiming: *'Surely HASHEM is present in this place' (Moreh Nevuchim* 2:45).

The *Midrash* interprets homiletically: *And Jacob awoke* מִמִּשְׁנָתוֹ, *from his studies* [i.e. he had fallen asleep while studying *(Radal).*]

R' Hirsch explains יקץ as designating the moment when man has regenerated his exhausted body with sleep. It is as if he had returned himself to nature to replenish his depleted energies, then tears himself away from nature and returns again to an independent existence.

אָכֵן יֵשׁ ה' בַּמָּקוֹם הַזֶּה — *Surely HASHEM is present in this place.*

Targum Yonasan renders: Surely the Glory of God's *Shechinah* dwells in this place.

I.e., God is more imminent here than anywhere else *(Or HaChaim).*

Sforno interprets: Undoubtedly, *this place* is conducive to prophecy for I have seen a prophetic vision here even though I had not prepared myself for prophecy. The prophetic intellect is affected by changes of place and climate; some places can promote prophetic vision more than others. As the Sages have taught: אֲוִירָא דְאַרְעָא יִשְׂרָאֵל מַחְכִּים, *the atmosphere of Eretz Yisrael makes wise.*

Thus, Jacob perceived that the prophetic spirit descended upon him solely because of the intrinsic nature of the *place,* even though he had not made the necessary preparations *(Malbim).*

Jacob's first realization was that God's Presence is in this *place.* He modestly assumes that *the place,* rather than *he* was responsible for God's proximity. His next realization was that God seeks bearers of His Presence among human beings *(R' Hirsch).*

The translation of אָכֵן as *surely* follows the implication of *Onkelos, Targum Yonasan* and *Radak* who, in rendering בְּקוּשְׁטָא, *in truth,* interpret the word as an affirmative exclamation. The root word כֵּן, *yes,* is itself affirmative, meaning in certain contexts *correct* or *just,* as for example *Numbers* 27:7: כֵּן בְּנוֹת צְלָפְחָד דֹּבְרֹת; *Joshua* 2:4: כֵּן בָּאוּ אֵלַי הָאֲנָשִׁים *(Karnei Or).*

See *Rashbam* who explains אָכֵן as composed of two words: אַךְ כֵּן, *but, it is so.* Idiomatically the connotation is a conversive one: אַךְ *not* as I thought previously [that the place is not sacred], but כֵּן *it is so,* that HASHEM is present in this place. This meaning of אָכֵן as expressing a new, changed perception is the sense of the word throughout Scripture. See *Exodus* 2:14: אָכֵן נוֹדַע הַדָּבָר, *surely* [not as I thought that my deed had gone unnoticed] — *rather the thing is known* [i.e. Moses realized that he had been mistaken in his earlier belief that no one knew he had killed the Egyptian taskmaster].

וְאָנֹכִי לֹא יָדָעְתִּי — *And I did not know!*

— Had I known I would not have slept here! *(Midrash; Rashi).*

Or HaChaim suggests that *Rashi's* interpretation is insufficient. Why should Jacob have regretted sleeping there? — Had he not slept he would not have had the prophetic dream! Furthermore, what did Jacob mean to imply by this exclamation that he had been unaware of the place's holiness; was it surprising that he was not aware of this hidden Presence of God? Did he then presume to be privy to God's ways?

28
17

HASHEM is present in this place and I did not know!'
17 *And he became frightened and said, 'How awesome is this place! This is none other than the abode of God and this is the gate of the heavens!'*

Rather, the exclamation reflects Jacob's understanding in *retrospect* that the sudden sunset upon his arrival had been Divinely prepared in order to have him there for the prophecy. Thus, what he had not comprehended earlier now became clear to him. The implication is that *had he known,* he would have prepared himself to reach the degree of prophecy to which such a place is conducive. Moreover, he bemoaned his lack of awareness because, with adequate preparation, he might have prophesied while *awake* and would have avoided sleeping in that holy place.

[Although certain *Midrashim* cited above would seem to imply that Jacob *did* know that he was at the site of his father's *Akeidah* — which his grandfather named HASHEM Yireh [22:14] implying that God reveals Himself prophetically there — Jacob's remark implies he had been unaware of the *full* holiness of the place.]

Akeidas Yitzchak interprets: I was unaware that God's presence is more manifest in some places than in others.

Ibn Ezra interprets similarly and concludes that he cannot expound upon the sublime mystery that God manifests Himself in some places more than in others, although *the whole world is full of His Glory* [*Isaiah* 6:3].

17. וַיִּירָא — *[And] he became frightened.*

He feared for himself because he might not have comported himself with the dignity proper to so sacred a site *(Radak).*

HaKsav V'HaKabbalah suggests that it was not *fear of punishment* like that which Jacob experienced further in 33:8. Rather, the connotation of this fear is that Jacob experienced a feeling of *reverential awe* in the sense of וּמִקְדָּשִׁי תִּירָאוּ, *revere* [lit. *fear*] *My Sanctuary (Lev.* 19:30).

That he had received the prophetic inspiration though he was unprepared, instilled within him an awe of the immense holiness of the *place (Malbim).*

מַה נּוֹרָא הַמָּקוֹם הַזֶּה — *How awesome is this place!*

The place in which I have been shown such a great vision certainly commands the awe befitting so holy a place *(Radak).*

Onkelos renders: מַה דְּחִילוּ אַתְרָא הָדֵין, *O the fearfulness of this place!* דְּחִילוּ, *fearfulness,* is a noun (שֵׁם דָּבָר) [although it ends with a ו which, as a verbal suffix, usually indicates the past-tense third person plural: *How they feared this place*]. This noun-usage is similar to the nouns סוּכְלְתָנוּ, *understanding* [*Exodus* 31:3], and כְּסוּ, *garment (Rashi).*

[The above interpretation of *Rashi's* understanding of *Onkelos* follows *Mizrachi.* Our translation *How awesome is this place* follows *Gur Aryeh* and *Heidenheim* who take שֵׁם דָּבָר here to signify an *adjective* (=שֵׁם תּוֹאַר) since the Hebrew word נוֹרָא is really a *Niphal* participle.]

אֵין זֶה כִּי אִם־בֵּית אֱלֹהִים — *This is none other than the abode* [lit. *house*] *of God.*

— This is not an ordinary place, but the Sanctuary of God's Name, a suitable place for prayer *(Targum Yonasan).*

That is, this is a place where man

should pray in time of need, since it had been selected for that purpose (*Ibn Ezra*).[1]

In the context of the awesomeness of the place, Jacob intentionally used the Name אֱלֹהִים, *God*, which signifies the Source of awe, as it says [*Ecclesiastes* 3:14]: *God* [אֱלֹהִים] *has acted so that man should stand in awe* [שֶׁיִּרְאוּ] *of Him (Or HaChaim)* — [and as the *Talmud* explains (*Shabbos* 31b): God's whole purpose in creating the world was that man should stand in awe of Him!]

וְזֶה שַׁעַר הַשָּׁמָיִם — *And this is the gate of the heavens.*

— A propitious place for prayer (*Pirkei d'Rabbi Eliezer*).

It is the gate through which prayers and sacrifices ascend to heaven (*Rashi; Ramban*).

Of course this description is figurative; the heavens have no gates in the literal sense (*Mizrachi*).

Rashi adds that Midrashically the gate' at Bethel-Jerusalem implies that the Heavenly Temple is situated immediately opposite the Earthly Temple. [Hence the figurative designation for that site as 'the gate of the heavens' is quite appropriate (*Nachlas Yitzchak*).]

In summation, the *Midrashic* connotation would be: *this*, i.e. the Temple on earth, *is the Abode of God, and this*, i.e. the Heavenly Temple, *is the gate of the heavens* Gur Aryeh).

The *Midrash* [as explained by *Maharzu*] perceives this verse as a dialogue: Jacob said, '*This is ... the Abode of God*,' and God replied, '*This is the gate of the heavens* — and will be opened for many other righteous men like you.'

◆§ The site of Jacob's dream.

As noted earlier, the Sages, in their various *Talmudic* and Midrashic interpretations of this narrative maintain that the site at which Jacob slept was Mount Moriah, where Isaac was bound to the altar by Abraham, and where the future Temple in Jerusalem would be built. The text of the Torah would seem to imply, however, that the place was Luz-Bethel, *not* Jerusalem. In the following Midrashic dissertation, accordingly, *Rashi* attempts to reconcile the various Rabbinic views with the simple sense of the narrative (*Sefer HaZikaron*).

[The complexity of the treatment given the subject by *Rashi* and *Ramban* has caused many students of *Chumash* to forgo serious study of the question. It is felt, therefore, that a complete discussion of the topic, although lengthy, would be a valuable contribution.]

☐ *Rashi* quotes the *Midrash:* Rav Yose ben Zimra said, the ladder stood in Beer Sheba and [the middle of] its slope was over the site of the Temple.

[The above bracketed words 'the middle of' are inserted by *Rashi* based on his interpretation of the *Midrash*.]

Rashi goes on to explain his contention that the *middle* of the ladder was over Jerusalem. Bethel, over which Jacob saw the ladder's *top*, is north of Jerusalem while Beersheba where Jacob saw its *base*, is to the south. It follows, therefore, that the *mid-point* of the ladder's slope was over Jerusalem, the site of the future Temple

Although the text (next verse) seems to imply that Jacob spent the night in *Luz*, *Rashi* proceeds to cite two Talmudic interpretations indicating that he was in *Jerusalem*. The first of these is the interpretation [*Sanhedrin* 95b; *Chullin* 91b, (cited above in *v.* 11 s.v. וַיָּלֶן שָׁם)] that Jacob wished to proceed

1. The word בַּיִת does not necessarily mean house or abode in the *structural* sense. Rather it denotes a physical or spiritual entity which contains something. Thus, the inside of a container is called בַּיִת [as is a family which comprises many members all of whom are formed by and share the values of the family unit]. In this sense, the as-yet-unbuilt place was called an *abode* because there was a unique suitability for prayer and holiness within its boundaries (*Or Yohel*).

from *the place* mentioned in *v.* 11 and that God said: 'This righteous man has come to My habitation [an obvious reference to Mt. Moriah in Jerusalem], shall I allow him to depart without spending the night?' [Thereupon, the *Talmud* records God caused the sun to set prematurely in order to detain Jacob.] The second Talmudic interpretation is the implication from *Pesachim* 88a [cited below] that Jacob gave the name Bethel to *Jerusalem* rather than to Luz as the text would seem to indicate.

To reconcile this Rabbinic view [Bethel/Luz=Jerusalem] with the simple meaning of the text, [Bethel/Luz is distinct from Jerusalem], *Rashi* cites the following Talmudic interpretation [*Chullin* 91b]: וַיֵּלֶךְ חָרָנָה, *he went to Charan, (v. 10),* means that when Jacob departed from Beersheba he actually *arrived* in Charan. Then, he remorsefully said, 'Is it possible that I passed the place where my father prayed [i.e. Mount Moriah] without myself praying there?' He resolved to return there, and immediately קָפְצָה לוֹ הָאָרֶץ, *the earth 'contracted' for him,* with the result that וַיִּפְגַּע בַּמָּקוֹם, *he encountered the place* (*v.* 11).[1]

Rashi explains the latter to mean that when Jacob reached Charan he decided to return to Mt. Moriah, and traveled as far as Luz-Bethel, whereupon קָפְצָה לוֹ הָאָרֶץ, literally the earth *'jumped* toward him' — i.e., *Mount Moriah was removed from its place and transported toward Jacob.* The two met in Luz-Bethel. This is the implication of the expression וַיִּפְגַּע בַּמָּקוֹם, *he encountered the place,* since, as *Rashi* explains in *v.* 11, the term וַיִּפְגַּע is used to denote the *encounter of two objects* [in this case, Jacob and the Temple Mount] *moving toward one another.*

[Thus, in effect, *Rashi* in our verse differs from the common interpretation of קְפִיצַת הָאָרֶץ, which is generally understood to mean *not* that a site was *uprooted* and *jumped* toward someone, but that a person covered a great distance in a surprisingly short time because the earth *contracted*, so to speak, to speed his arrival *(Sefer HaZikaron).*]

Accordingly, *Rashi* proves Midrashically that because the earth 'jumped' toward him, Jacob was in Luz-Bethel and Moriah-Jerusalem *at the same time.* [Accordingly, both places in effect, were brought to one site so that Jacob could pray at both simultaneously *(Mizrachi)*]. Because Mt. Moriah had been transported to Luz, the *Talmud* refers to the site as *God's habitation* and implies that the place which Jacob named Bethel was indeed Jerusalem.

[Some editions of *Rashi* conclude that this is not the *Bethel near Ai* mentioned in 12:8, but that Bethel is a descriptive term meaning 'House of God.' Jacob gave that description to Luz because the future site of the Temple 'met' him there (See *Maharsha, Chullin* 91b and *Ramban* (b) below).]

Rashi offers a *further* proof that the site named Bethel by Jacob was indeed Mt. Moriah: In interpreting the verse, *Come let us go to the mountain of HASHEM, and the House of God of Jacob (Micah* 4:2), the *Talmud (Pesachim* 88b) explains that in that context HASHEM is referred to specifically as the God of Jacob, because Jacob, in our verse, gave the name *house* to the site of the future Temple. Clearly, therefore, the Sages understand the Bethel of our verse as a reference to Jerusalem.

[**Conclusions:** (a) Luz was to the north of Jerusalem; (b) The meaning of קְפִיצַת הָאָרֶץ in this case is that Mount Moriah 'jumped' toward Jacob and settled in Luz where Jacob prayed. It was that *dual holy site,* Moriah—Luz, where Jacob spent the night, dreamt, and erected the stone, which he named Bethel. (c) This is why the Sages referred to Luz-Bethel as God's 'habita-

1. *Rashi* explains: Should you ask, why did God not detain Jacob at the site of the Temple earlier, when he passed it on his outward journey from Beer Sheba to Charan? — The answer is: If it never entered Jacob's mind to pray at the place where his fathers prayed, why should Heaven make him stop there?

הַשָּׁמָיִם: יח וַיַּשְׁכֵּם יַעֲקֹב בַּבֹּקֶר וַיִּקַּח אֶת־

tion', and why, although he was in Luz, Jacob is described as having given the name Bethel to *Jerusalem.*]

□ *Ramban* cites *Rashi's* interpretation and differs with him on several counts:

(a) *Ramban* maintains that קְפִיצַת הָאָרֶץ can mean only that the earth *contracted* for him as the phrase is interpreted in the case of Eliezer [see on 24:42]; hence, the Temple Mount was not transported to meet him at Luz. *Chullin* 91b is to be interpreted that as soon as Jacob resolved to return to the site where his fathers prayed, *he was speeded there.* For, if *Rashi* is correct, why should the Temple Mount immediately 'spring' to Bethel [and wait while Jacob journeyed for several days to arrive there (*Abohab*)]; why did it not spring all the way to Charan to spare Jacob the trip to Luz? [*Mizrachi* answers this objection by explaining that according to *Rashi* the Temple Mount 'jumped' to the easternmost border of *Eretz Yisrael*; to have 'jumped' all the way to Charan would have taken the Temple Mount outside the Holy Land!]

(b) *Ramban* further counters that Bethel, as noted in 12:8, was at the *western* part of *Eretz Yisrael;* how can *Rashi* imply that Bethel was in the *easterly* direction toward Charan? [*Mizrachi* answers that the Luz which Jacob named was not the *Bethel near Ai* mentioned in 12:8. This site was on the northeastern side of Jerusalem and Jacob named it Bethel — House of God — to commemorate that the Temple Mount had 'jumped' there to meet him. *Maharsha* in *Chullin* 91b interprets similarly.]

(c) What is the significance of the *center* of a ladder's slope? [*Gur Aryeh* answers that the *center* was over Jerusalem to signify that the Temple was the central point of this 'ladder' which spanned heaven and earth. (Nevertheless, *Gur Aryeh* agrees with *Ramban* that *Rashi's* interpretation of R' Yose ben Zimra's Midrashic exposition of the sloping ladder does not blend with the contextual flow of the *Midrash*).]

Based on the *Midrashim, Ramban* suggests that Isaac lived in Hebron at the time [see 35:27]. Before departing for Charan, Jacob went to Beer Sheba to seek Divine permission to leave the Land. It was *there*, according to R' Yose ben Zimra, that he dreamt and received tacit permission to depart, as implied by the assurance in *v.* 15. Thus, the foot of the ladder was in Beer Sheba where he lay, and the end of the slope (which is the *top* of the ladder) reached a point opposite the Temple, supported in heaven at the gate through which the angels enter and exit. Jacob perceived God standing over him and he knew that *Beer Sheba* was the gate of heaven — because it was there that his prayer had been offered and accepted — and the Temple was the House of God. He erected the monument not in Beer Sheba but in Bethel, formerly Luz, which was Jerusalem, opposite the head of the ladder's slope. [He carried the monument there from Beer Sheba *(Radal).*] Thus, R' Yose ben Zimra would distinguish between the Bethel—Jerusalem named now by Jacob, and the Bethel near Ai which, as 12:8 implies, already carried that name prior to Abraham's time.

[It is not clear, according to this interpretation why this Bethel is identified in *v.* 19 and 35:6 with the unknown site *Luz* rather than *Jerusalem.* Possibly Luz, in this view, was not a place name, but an adjective. This view is supported by *Midrash HaGadol* which comments: From the time of Jacob onward it was *Bethel,* the House of God, but previously it was *Luz,* 'perverse' and 'estranged' from God. Thus, the verse tells us not that the city had been *called* Luz earlier, but that it was described as *'estranged'* from the possibility of holiness.]

Further, *Ramban* proceeds to cite the *differing* view of R' Yehudah ben R' Simon in the *Midrash* who maintains

[18] *Jacob arose early in the morning and took the*

that 'The ladder stood at the *Temple site* and its slope reached *Bethel.' Ramban* explains that according to this view: (a) The 'place' where Jacob was detained by the premature setting of the sun was *Mount Moriah;* (b) as the *Talmud* relates (*Chullin* 91b and *Sanhedrin* 95b) Jacob had gone all the way to Charan when he decided to return to the place where his fathers had prayed. Thereupon the earth 'contracted' for him and miraculously transported him there in a twinkling. When Jacob awoke, he exclaimed that the place where he had slept was the House of God, an excellent site for prayer. The site opposite the slope of the ladder — Bethel in Luz where he erected the pillar — was the gate of heaven and a suitable place for the service of God since 'it is the opinion of all the Rabbis that he erected it [the pillar] opposite the slope of the ladder.'

[Thus, according to this view, Bethel-Luz is *distinct* from Moriah; but this interpretation assumes (as *Radal* explains), that Jacob took the coalesced stones which had lain around his head and transported them to Bethel-Luz. That he perceived it to be a sacred place is evidenced by the reverence Jacob showed for the place many years later when he returned to *Eretz Yisrael* (see chapt. 35).]

Finally, *Ramban* cites *Pirkei d'Rabbi Eliezer* as further proof for this latter view of R' Simon that Mount Moriah was the 'place' where the sun set prematurely, and where Jacob spent the night, gathered the stones from the altar on which his father had been bound, and saw the vision. When Jacob awoke, he declared that the House of God was there, and exclaimed, *How awesome is this place!* From this we learn that whoever prays in Jerusalem is as if he prays before כִּסֵּא הַכָּבוֹד, *the Throne of Glory,* for the gate of heaven is open there to receive the prayers of Israel. Jacob found that the stones on which he rested were coalesced into one and so he set it up as a pillar. Then God caused the stone to be sunk deep into the earth. This stone is called אֶבֶן שְׁתִיָּה, *The Foundation Stone,* since it is the center of the earth, and it forms the foundation of the Temple. [This differs from the view (*cf. Yoma* 54b and *Ramban* to 1:2) that the Foundation Stone was the first part of earth to be created and from which the rest of earth sprang forth. See also footnote to *v.* 13.] From Moriah, the earth 'contracted' for Jacob and he found himself in Charan in a twinkling of an eye.

[According to the latter, again, Bethel is identified with Mount Moriah in Jerusalem, which leaves unexplained why the Torah in *v.* 19 uses the reference name *Luz* instead of Jerusalem unless, as suggested above, Luz is an adjective describing Moriah, rather than a proper noun. See *Chizkuni; Mizrachi;* and *Gur Aryeh.*]

18. וַיַּשְׁכֵּם יַעֲקֹב בַּבֹּקֶר — *[And] Jacob arose early in the morning.*

[It is noteworthy that after waking from his dream and exclaiming how awesome the place was, Jacob apparently waited until daybreak, when he *rose up early in the morning.* Until then, he made no effort to set up the pillar and pray in commemoration of the auspicious vision of the evening.]

Meshech Chochmah interprets Jacob's delay until morning in consonance with the rabbinic interpretation that the deeds of the Patriarchs were symbolic of the deeds of their descendants. Jacob's erection of the altar foreshadowed the construction of the Temple on this very site by his descendants. Jacob did not set up the altar at night [after he initially awoke from his dream (*v.* 17), but waited until

הָאֶבֶן אֲשֶׁר־שָׂם מְרַאֲשֹׁתָיו וַיָּשֶׂם אֹתָהּ
יט מַצֵּבָה וַיִּצֹק שֶׁמֶן עַל־רֹאשָׁהּ: וַיִּקְרָא

he arose early in the morning] since the Sanctuary may not be constructed at night as the Sages [*Shevuos* 15:2] derived from *Numbers* 9:15: *On the 'day' that the Tabernacle was erected.*

The early morning is a propitious time for prayer and sacrifice. It was during his prayers that Jacob verbalized his vow of the following verses *(Haamek Davar).*

וַיִּקַּח אֶת הָאֶבֶן אֲשֶׁר שָׂם מְרַאֲשֹׁתָיו — *And [he] took the stone that he had placed around his head.*

The *stone* is singular. The many stones he had collected earlier (*v.* 11) had coalesced into one stone *(Pirkei d'Rabbi Eliezer;* see *comm.* to *v.* 11).

This stone, as noted by the *Midrashim* above [*Pirkei d'Rabbi Eliezer* cited in *v.* 11], symbolized the unity of the future tribes of Israel *(Malbim).*

According to Abaye in *Zevachim* 116b, one may not construct an altar from materials used for such secular purposes as that to which these stones had been put by Jacob. However, such materials were permitted for a *bamah* [lit. *high place,* a private altar the use of which was permissible before the establishment of a central Sanctuary] *(Tur).*

וַיָּשֶׂם אֹתָהּ מַצֵּבָה — *And [he] set it up* [lit. *placed it*] *as a pillar* [more literally: *standing stone.*]

[Cf. dissertation in *v.* 17 "The site of Jacob's dreams" for the various views of *where* Jacob set up this pillar. According to several of the Midrashic opinions cited there, Jacob carried the stone from the place he slept — Beer Sheba or Mount Moriah (see *Ramban* there) — to the site he now named Bethel.]

According to *Sforno* the implication of *set* is that Jacob *consecrated the stone* [in the sense of *set it aside* for future use] so that on his return [when presumably he would not be pursued] he would erect it. Indeed, Scripture attests that he later did [see 34:14].

⸙ Permissibility of the pillar

[The Sages often emphasize that the Patriarchs scrupulously observed the Torah even before it was given. How, then, could Jacob have set up a pillar, inasmuch as the Torah later forbade such pillars and ordered them destroyed *(Exod.* 23:24; *Lev.* 26:1; *Deut.* 16:22)]?

The answer lies in the dissertation on the subject of the Patriarchs' observance of the Torah, see above, page 1083, where *Ramban* to 26:5 explains that in the time of the Patriarchs the erection of pillars was *permitted;* it became prohibited only later when such forms of sacrificial service became particularly associated with heathen idolatry (see *Sifre* to *Deut.* 16:22).] Note in this connection that Moses also set up pillars (*Exodus* 24:4).

Ramban cites *Yerushalmi Avodah Zarah* 4:5 [see also *Rashi* to *Deut.* 12:3] that the difference between מַצֵּבָה, *a pillar* and מִזְבֵּחַ, *an altar,* is that the former consists of *one* stone while the latter is composed of *many* stones. It would seem that *pillars* were used for libations but not for sacrifices, whereas *altars* were used for sacrifices. Since the Canaanites had established pillars for their idolatrous cult worship to a greater extent than altars, God later prohibited the erection of pillars. Though they

stone that he placed around his head and set it up as a
pillar; then he poured oil on its top. [19] *And he named*

were commanded to destroy the Canaanites' *altars* as well, God did not prohibit the Israelites from making their own altars. Perhaps God did not want to prohibit [opportunity for private sacrifices] entirely, and allowed them altars, which are fit for both libations and sacrifices.

R' Hirsch perceives a philosophical concept in the changing status of pillars. A *pillar*, since it is a single, natural stone unaltered by man, represents nature. An *altar*, because it is built of many stones, represents man's alteration of the raw material of nature. Before the Torah was given, God's rule was evident in man's subservience to nature. The use of a pillar, therefore, symbolized man's unaltered submission to God's will. With the giving of the Torah, however, God wished to be known by man's utilization of nature's bounty to do His will. This is symbolized by the use of altars, but *not* pillars, which imply helpless obedience to nature.

וַיִּצֹק שֶׁמֶן עַל רֹאשָׁהּ — *Then* [lit. *and*] *he poured oil on its top.*

To distinguish this stone from all others, so that on his return he might recognize the site and build an altar there. [He could not tarry there *now* to build an altar since he feared Esau's pursuit.] He used oil since its penetrating stain would not wash away in rainy weather, and it would remain recognizable. Perhaps he poured the oil as an act of service just as he did upon his return [35:14] similar to נֶסֶךְ הַיַּיִן, *libations of wine.* All these acts displayed proprietorship in the land since no one disturbed his monument, and the residents concurred in his changing the name of the area from Luz to Bethel *(Radak;* similarly *Ibn Ezra; Ralbag; R' Bachya* cites the first interpretation in the name of *R' Saadiah Gaon).*

[Possibly, Jacob wished to show ownership of the stone to deter the idolatrous Canaanites from coming upon and utilizing this stone for their worship. They would not have performed acts of idolatry with an object used in the service of another deity.]

Rashbam suggests that the oil served to *consecrate* the stone so that it could be used for sacrifices on his return. Such was the requirement in the case of the Tabernacle and its utensils of which it is written [*Numbers* 7:1]: *he anointed them and consecrated them.*[1]

According to *Malbim,* who notes that the coalesced stone represents the unity of Jacob's progeny, the oil represents God's spiritual bounty. Thus, Jacob symbolized that God's blessing would descend upon Israel if it were to be unified.

Jacob had virtually nothing with him but his staff; where did he get oil?

1. *R' Hirsch,* too, offers both possible interpretations of Jacob's pouring of oil — as consecration or as libation — but he explains the philosophical intent of the two deeds. When oil is mixed with another liquid, it remains apart. This represents the separate status of the anointed object; it is set apart and raised above all others. In the sense of libation, if wine is used, it represents the concept that all joy [wine Talmudically represents joy] derives from God. If water is used, it represents that acknowledgment that even such an insignificant gift as a drop of water is God's gift. An oil libation demonstrates one's recognition that health and well-being come from God.

אֶת־שֵׁם־הַמָּקוֹם הַהוּא בֵּית־אֵל וְאוּלָם
כ לוּז שֵׁם־הָעִיר לָרִאשֹׁנָה: וַיִּדַּר יַעֲקֹב נֶדֶר

— *Pirkei d'Rabbi Eliezer* suggests that some anointing-oil miraculously flowed to him from heaven. [Thus he anointed only *its top (Radal)*]. Cf. *Midrash Rabbah* that the oil was supplied to him from heaven in abundance.

Pesikta Zutresa and *Sechel Tov* conjecture that Jacob secured the oil from the city closest to that site.

[In 31:13 Jacob's anointing the stone is referred to with the verb משח, which Rashi explains in the sense of elevating in eminence as in the anointment of a king. There, Jacob consecrated the stone for use as an altar.]

19. וַיִּקְרָא אֶת שֵׁם הַמָּקוֹם הַהוּא בֵּית־אֵל — *And he named that place Bethel* [lit. *House of God*].

According to the various opinions enumerated in the commentary to verse 17, the site designated as Bethel can refer either to:

(a) the city of Bethel near Ai mentioned in 13:8;

(b) a city bearing the same name but further north in the later territory of Joseph [*Rashi* in *Josh.* 18:13 makes this distinction];

(c) not a city, but the designation — *House of God* — given to the dual site Jerusalem-Luz;

(d) Mount Moriah which was miraculously uprooted and 'jumped' to meet Jacob in Luz when he returned from Charan to pray at the site where his fathers prayed;

(e) a site identified with Jerusalem since it contained the House of God.

The *Vilna Gaon* to *Joshua* 16:2 lists three different locations that Jacob named Bethel: the site of his dream (here); *El Bethel* (35:7); and *Elohim Bethel* (35:15). *Mount Bethel* (*Joshua* 16:1) refers to the site [near Ai] which was already called Bethel in Abraham's time (13:8).

Rashbam suggests that it was the *outskirts* of the city, the site where Jacob slept, that he named Bethel. The city itself, too, subsequently came to be called by that name.

וְאוּלָם לוּז שֵׁם הָעִיר לָרִאשֹׁנָה — [*And*] *Luz was the city's name originally.*

The *Talmud* and *Midrashim* give many interpretations to the significance of the name Luz, a selection of which follows:

[However, many commentators suggest that the reference is to the Luz mentioned in *Judges* 1:24, which they claim is different from the Luz-Bethel mentioned here. *Torah Sheleimah* (§138 and §140) points out, however, that in current editions of *Midrash Rabbah* these comments are attached to the mention of Luz *in our* verse. Others suggest that the Luz mentioned in *Judges* 1:24 is our Luz, and it was to it that the *Midrashic* interpretations applied. Later, when the original Luz was destroyed (ibid. *v.* 25) the special properties attributed to the old city became manifest in the new city named Luz (ibid. *v.* 26).]

The word Luz literally means *almond tree.* According to the *Midrash,* an almond tree concealed the city's entrance, keeping outsiders away [see *Judges* 1:25.] The tree was hollow, and through it one entered a cave which led to the entrance of the city.

Luz is also the Aramaic name for the *os coccyx*, the 'nut' of the spinal column. The Rabbis explained that this is the only part of the body that is indestructible. This one bone does not decompose after death, and it will form the nucleus for the resurrection of the body [תְּחִיַּת הַמֵּתִים] (see *VaYikra Rabbah* 17, and *Koheles Rabbah* 12).

28 *that place Bethel. However, Luz was the city's name*
20 *originally.*
[20] *Then Jacob took a vow, saying, 'If God will be*

Just as God made this one *luz* bone impervious to the ravages of death, God set aside one spot on earth — *Luz* — where the Angel of Death has no power, and where people do not die. When a person was very old, and wanted to die, he would leave the city and there he would die [see *Sotah* 46b]. [As pointed out above, the city's entrance remained hidden — known only to its inhabitants — until the incident recorded in *Judges* 1:25.] It was, furthermore, in Luz where the *techeles* was dyed. It was not overthrown in Sennacherib's invasion, nor razed to the ground in Nebuchadnezzar's. The location of the city is now unknown.

According to *Midrash HaGadol* cited in the *footnote* to *v.* 17, Luz in this case was not the *name* of a place but an *adjective* describing the *perverse estrangement from God* [נִילוֹז וּמֵלִיז] that prevailed there before Jacob's time when the site was designated *Bethel* — the House of God.

20. Jacob's vow.

וַיִּדַּר יַעֲקֹב נֶדֶר לֵאמֹר — *Then* [lit. *and*] *Jacob took* [lit. *vowed*] *a vow, saying.*

As noted often in the commentary [see, for example 15:1] the word לֵאמֹר, *saying* (lit. *to say*) indicates that the statement was intended to be transmitted to others. In this case, Jacob was alone and there was no one to whom the message could be conveyed. The *Midrash,* therefore, interprets that Jacob undertook a vow at this time לֵאמֹר, *to say,* by example, to later generations that they should follow suit and vow to perform a righteous act in times of distress, and moreover that it is meritorious to do so.[1]

Or HaChaim suggests that לֵאמֹר, *saying,* implies that Jacob actually *verbalized* his vow. A contemplated vow is ineffective.

⁂ Why are vows efficacious in times of trouble?

Yafeh Toar explains that although one does not actually do anything when he makes a vow, the merit of the *intended* good deed protects him and rescues him from trouble. As the Sages also proclaimed [*Kiddushin* 40a]: מַחֲשָׁבָה טוֹבָה הקב״ה מְצָרְפָהּ לְמַעֲשֶׂה, *God considers a good intention as tantamount to a deed.*

1. [It is generally the practice to *refrain* from taking vows (see *Ecclesiastes* 5:4) for as the Sages noted (*Nedarim* 77b), it is better for a good deed to be done without having taken a vow to do it; and as *Ran* to *Nedarim* 22a comments, the Sages compare one who makes a vow to one who sinfully erects a בָּמָה, *private altar,* when such altars are forbidden (*Deut.* 12:13; see *Ramban* above, *v.* 18) because both sins are of a similar nature: both perpetrators think they can please God by doing something beyond what He has commanded. Nevertheless, we derive from here that it is meritorious to undertake a vow to perform a meritorious or charitable act *in times of distress.*]

Torah Temimah notes that in citing this *Midrash, Tosafos Chullin* 2b implies that not only is it *permissible* to make a vow in times of distress but *meritorious.* He finds it noteworthy, however, that as codified in *Yoreh Deah* § 203, the language used for this *halachah* is that oaths are 'permissible,' rather than 'meritorious,' at such times.

לֵאמֹר אִם־יִהְיֶה אֱלֹהִים עִמָּדִי וּשְׁמָרַנִי
בַּדֶּרֶךְ הַזֶּה אֲשֶׁר אָנֹכִי הוֹלֵךְ וְנָתַן־לִי
כא לֶחֶם לֶאֱכֹל וּבֶגֶד לִלְבֹּשׁ: וְשַׁבְתִּי בְשָׁלוֹם
אֶל־בֵּית אָבִי וְהָיָה יהוה לִי לֵאלֹהִים:

The commentators emphasize, however, that in general — not in times of distress — one should refrain from taking a vow because one can incur severe punishment if he does not fulfill the pledge. Therefore, many people say בְּלִי נֶדֶר, *'without a vow,'* when expressing their intention to perform a deed.

The *Midrash* notes additionally that Jacob was the first to offer a vow. Therefore he is credited with formulating the solemn, binding nature of vows. Thus in *Psalms* [132:2]: *How he swore unto* HASHEM *, and vowed unto the Mighty One of Jacob,* it is not Abraham or Isaac who is mentioned, but Jacob.

אִם יִהְיֶה אֱלֹהִים עִמָּדִי — *If God will be with me.*

— I.e., if He will fulfill His promises to be with me [*v.* 15] *(Rashi).*

Ramban explains that Jacob's mode of expression, *'if' God will...,* does not imply that Jacob *doubted* God's promise. Rather, Jacob was apprehensive that his own sins might cause the *forfeiture* of the promises [שֶׁמָּא יִגְרֹם הַחֵטְא]. (See *comm.* and footnote to 32:8.)

This follows the *Midrash* which notes that after God specifically promised Jacob to be with him [*v.* 15], Jacob nevertheless said: *If* God will be with me, implying that there is no assurance for the righteous in this world [as *Ramban* explains in the *footnote* to 15:2, page 506, the righteous never take their righteousness for granted and are never confident in this world. See also *Rashi* and *comm.* to 32:10,11 where Jacob's later apprehensions are similarly dealt with and explained.]

In the literal sense, however, *Ramban* goes on to suggest [like *Rashi* in *v.* 15 above] that the word אִם in this context does not express doubt — *'if'* it occurs — but has the meaning of *when* it shall occur, as in *Numbers* 36:4: *When* [וְאִם] *there shall be the jubilee of the children of Israel.* Thus, Jacob implied: *When* God's promises will be fulfilled, etc.

Sforno interprets the intent to be: *If God will be with me* and keep me from those obstacles which lead man astray from Him, as the Sages [*Eruvin* 41b] proclaimed: 'Three things deprive a man of his senses and of a knowledge of his Creator: Idolators, an evil spirit, and oppressive poverty.' [*Sforno* ties these in with the following conditions of the vow; see further.]

וּשְׁמָרַנִי בַּדֶּרֶךְ הַזֶּה אֲשֶׁר אָנֹכִי הוֹלֵךְ — *[And if He] will guard me on this way that I am going.*

— As He said [*v.* 5]: *And I will guard you wherever you go (Rashi).*

— *If He guards me* from the evil persons [=the idolators referred to above] who force one to reject Him *(Sforno).*

The Sages in the *Midrash* explain — by citing parallel allusions throughout Scripture — that Jacob's various expressions intimated protection from *idolatry, adultery, bloodshed,* and *slander.*

וְנָתַן־לִי לֶחֶם לֶאֱכֹל וּבֶגֶד לִלְבֹּשׁ — *[And if He] will give me bread to eat and clothes to wear.*

As He said [ibid.]: *For I will not forsake you.* [This promise intimated protection from hunger]

28 *with me, will guard me on this way that I am going;*
21 *will give me bread to eat and clothes to wear;* [21] *and I*
return in peace to my father's house, and HASHEM

since one who is forced to beg for bread is called *forsaken,* as in *Psalms* 37:25, *I have never seen a righteous man forsaken* (נֶעֱזָב) *nor his children begging for bread (Rashi:* see *Midrash* cited to *v.* 15 s.v. כִּי לֹא אֶעֱזָבְךָ).

The commentators explain that *Rashi's* intent is that God would provide *all* Jacob's *daily necessities.* Keeping him from *hunger for bread* in the literal sense, was but one intimation of God's earlier promise not to 'forsake' him. Actually, keeping him *clothed* and *generally maintained* was implicit in that blessing as well; hence Jacob's inclusion of *clothes to wear* although it had not been explicitly promised him.

— And if He will give me bread to eat and clothing to wear so that poverty will not lead me to rebel *(Sforno).*

Radak notes that Jacob asked only for life's barest necessities — bread and clothing; he asked for no luxuries. He had no need to ask for water since that is usually freely available to travelers.

21. וְשַׁבְתִּי בְשָׁלוֹם אֶל־בֵּית אָבִי — *And* [*if*] *I return in peace* [i.e., *safely (Radak)*] *to my father's house.*

— As He said [*v.* 15]: *I will bring you back to this soil (Rashi).*

Rashi explains בְּשָׁלוֹם [*in peace*] to imply: 'perfect' [שָׁלֵם] from sin; that I do not learn from Laban's ways.

— This is intimated by God's earlier promise to *bring him back to this soil;* implicit in this was that God return him in a state of sinlessness, as he had left *(Gur Aryeh).* If Jacob were not to return sinless, none of the promises God *spoke concerning him* [*v.* 15] to Abraham could have found fulfillment in him or his progeny *(Nachalas Yitzchak).*

Since Jacob attributed the return to his *own* power: And *I* will return, it was necessary for him to add בְּשָׁלוֹם [*in peace;* sinless] *(Gur Aryeh).* The physical *return* would be in *God's* hands; the *sinlessness* would be in Jacob's since 'Everything is in the hands of Heaven but the fear of Heaven' *(Divrei David;* see *Berachos* 33b).

Furthermore, though God had promised to bring Jacob back to the soil, this did not *necessarily* mean בְּשָׁלוֹם, *in peace,* i.e., whole in body rather than wounded. Furthermore, God promised only to return him to the *soil* [i.e., to the country itself]. Jacob added *to my father's house (Haamek Davar).*

This follows *Sforno,* who explains that בְּשָׁלוֹם, *in peace,* refers to coming back spiritually *whole,* not suffering from diseases [=the evil spirit referred to above] which keep men away from Him.

[Cf. 33:18.]

⇨ Why did Jacob attribute this act to himself — *and 'I' will return* — rather than to God — *and He will bring me back* — which would have been more in consonance with the other conditions?

Gur Aryeh comments that it would have been disrespectful for Jacob to have ascribed to God the physical chore of bringing him back, as if He were Jacob's porter; therefore, he said *'I' will return.* This alteration also accounts for Jacob's addition of the word בְּשָׁלוֹם, *in peace.* By definition, whatever God does is perfect; when God promised to return Jacob, it was implicit that His return would be in a state of peace and perfec-

כב וְהָאֶבֶן הַזֹּאת אֲשֶׁר־שַׂמְתִּי מַצֵּבָה יִהְיֶה
בֵּית אֱלֹהִים וְכֹל אֲשֶׁר תִּתֶּן־לִי עַשֵּׂר

tion. This cannot be said, however, of a human agency. When Jacob ascribed the return to himself, therefore, he had to add the hope that it would be *in peace.*

וְהָיָה ה׳ לִי לֵאלֹהִים — *And HASHEM will be a God to me.*

As reflected in the translation, *Rashi* interprets this as one of the *conditions* set by Jacob: *And* [if] *HASHEM will be a God to me.* Jacob asked that God cause His Name to rest upon his offspring forever in the sense that no blemish will be found in his posterity. This alludes to God's promise above [*v.* 15]: *that which I have spoken regarding you,* which refers to the promise made to Abraham [17:7]: *to be a God to you and to your offspring after you.*

Rashi offers this interpretation rather than the other possible interpretation that this was part of the *vow,* a *promise* by Jacob to remain loyal to God — because that would imply: If God will do all the above, *HASHEM will be a God to me,* i.e., only *then* will I recognize Him as my God, but not otherwise ח״ו. Such a blasphemous statement can clearly not be attributed to Jacob. Thus *Rashi* emphasizes that Jacob intended this as part of the *condition*: If God, Who is my God in any event, will allow His name to rest on me... *(Gur Aryeh).*

Rashbam, like *Rashi,* construes this as part of the condition: *If HASHEM will be a God to me* — by helping me in all my undertakings [the Name אֱלֹהִים, *God,* referring to Him in His aspect of Dispenser of providential assistance to all His creatures.]

Kli Yakar in one opinion suggests that the intimation is: If it be in His manifestation of *HASHEM* [His aspect of Mercy] that He will be my *God* [Dispenser of Justice]. That is, if He will deal with me in a manner of constantly tempering His justice with mercy.

Ramban, however, perceives this not as one of the *conditions* but as part of the *vow,* the implication being: If I return in peace to my father's house, *then I will serve the One God* in the Chosen Land at the site of this stone which will be as a House of God for me, and *there will I set aside tithes.*

Ramban continues that hidden in this is the esoteric rabbinic dictum [*Kesubos* 110b]: 'He who dwells outside *Eretz Yisrael* is like one who has no God' [the implication in our context being that only when Jacob returned to his father's house in *Eretz Yisrael,* would Hashem be his God in the fullest sense. See *Overview* to *Lech Lecha, Gen.* 12].

While noting that according to *Ramban,* Jacob's pledge should have begun a new verse, *Haamek Davar* explains why the promise is contingent upon his return to his father's home. In Charan — an alien and potentially hostile land — Jacob would surely place his trust in God, for what alternative could he have? But upon returning to *Eretz Yisrael* and the security of his father's home, it would be human nature to forget about his dependence on God. Therefore Jacob pledged, that his allegiance to God would continue even *after* his return home.

According to *Sforno* who also construes this as the vow, the implication is — if God shall do all the above *then HASHEM shall be to me* אֱלֹהִים, *my Judge,* i.e., He shall judge me if I do not serve Him with all my might. That is, I accept upon myself that in such a case HASHEM, the Merciful One, should thenceforth deal with me in strict justice as *Elohim.*

28 *will be a God to me —* 22 *then this stone which I have*
22 *set up as a pillar shall become a house of God, and*
whatever You will give me, I shall repeatedly tithe to
You.

22. וְהָאֶבֶן הַזֹּאת — *Then* [lit. *and*] *this stone ...*

The translation of the conjunctive ו as *then* follows *Rashi*, according to whom this is the beginning of the vow; i.e., if He will do all the above for me *then* I, too, will do the following.

יִהְיֶה בֵּית אֱלֹהִים — *Shall become a house of God.*

Rashi explains [that this is not to be taken literally as a vow to build a *House of God (Mizrachi)*; but] as *Onkelos* renders: *And at this stone ... will I worship before God* [i.e., this place will become a center for serving God *(Gur Aryeh)*.] This is what Jacob later did when he returned from Paddan Aram: He returned to Bethel [35:1] *and set up a pillar ... and poured a libation thereon.*

Did this imply that if the conditions were not met Jacob would not serve God? — No; it implied that *this stone,* which symbolized the site of the promises, could have a special significance only upon fulfillment of the promises associated with it. If, however, Jacob were not to merit such blessings, then the stone would remain an unvenerated object *(Divrei David).*

Radak explains this as a promise to build an *altar* which would become an inspirational center for those who wish to worship God.

According to *Abarbanel,* this statement was a prophetic prognostication that on that site a House of God would be built by his descendants. Or, as *Radak* writes, that he would charge his children with the duty of building a Sanctuary when they would inherit the Land.

[Concerning the *Midrash* that God sunk that stone into the earth to become the אֶבֶן שְׁתִיָּה, *Foundation Stone* on which the Ark rested, see end of *Ramban* to *v.* 17.]

וְכֹל אֲשֶׁר תִּתֶּן־לִי עַשֵּׂר אֲעַשְּׂרֶנּוּ — *And whatever You will give me, I shall repeatedly tithe* [lit. *tithe I shall tithe*] *to You.*

This pledge includes a tenth of my children, whom I shall dedicate to Your service. Specifically, this was Levi, who, more than his brothers, was involved in serving God, and to whom Jacob imparted the esoteric teachings and wisdom of the Torah *(Radak* citing *Midrash;* see *Pirkei d'Rabbi Eliezer* 37; *Tanchuma Re'eh* 14; *Targum Yonasan* 32:25).[1]

1. A Cuthean asked R' Meir. 'Do you not maintain that Jacob was truthful?'
'Certainly,' R' Meir replied.
'But did he not vow to give a tenth of *everything* God gave him?', the Cuthean asked.
'Yes, and he therefore even separated to God the tribe of Levi, which represented a tenth of the tribes,' R' Meir replied.
'Why did he not separate a tenth of the remaining two tribes?,' the Cuthean insisted.
Were there only *twelve* tribes?' R' Meir countered, 'there were *fourteen,* since Jacob considered Ephraim and Menasseh to be his own, 'like Reuben and Simeon' [48:5] ... Now there were four Matriarchs, and the first-born of each must be deducted from the fourteen, since the first-born are holy and no tenth is needed to exempt what is already holy.'
'Happy are the people in whose midst you dwell!,' the Cuthean exclaimed.

°שני א אֲעַשְּׂרֶנּוּ לָךְ: °וַיִּשָּׂא יַעֲקֹב רַגְלָיו וַיֵּלֶךְ
ב אַרְצָה בְנֵי־קֶדֶם: וַיַּרְא וְהִנֵּה בְאֵר בַּשָּׂדֶה

[*Ibn Ezra* notes that this is the homiletical and not the *literal* sense of the passage. In the literal sense, the Torah does not require one to tithe his children. The intent was that he would tithe his material possessions.]

The translation of עַשֵּׂר אֲעַשְּׂרֶנּוּ reflects the *literal* implication of the compound infinitive verbal form [lit. *tithe I will tithe*] which Scripturally denotes an emphatic significance: *I will surely tithe,* or as *Hirsch* renders, *I will repeatedly tithe,* the compound emphasizing the action. Cf. 2:16 אָכֹל תֹּאכֵל; 2:18 מוֹת תָּמוּת; 15:13 יָדֹעַ תֵּדַע.

R' Nachman in *Kesubos* 50a interprets in this case the compound *'tithe I will tithe'* as meaning that Jacob vowed to give a *double* tithe — that is, a fifth. This forms the basis for the ruling that even one who wishes to give liberally should not distribute more than a fifth of his wealth to charity. The purpose of this ruling was to prevent the donor from impoverishing himself and requiring assistance from others. The *Talmudic* sages are recorded as having, on various occasions, stopped others from giving away more than a fifth of their wealth.

Imrei Shefer refers this to the double tithe the Torah would later require — a tenth for the Levites and another tenth for the poor.

This was not a conditional vow but a separate statement: I will surely tithe regardless of what happens *(Devek Tov).*

Maharshal suggests that though Jacob would tithe from his gains whether or not the promises were fulfilled, the implication was that if he were not to forfeit the blessings by sinning, he would give a *double* tithe [עַשֵּׂר אֲעַשְּׂרֶנּוּ]. Otherwise, he would still give the tithe required by law.

[That Jacob actually set aside the tithe he vowed is mentioned by *Rashi* in 32:33 and *Ibn Ezra* in 35:14.]

לָךְ — *To You.*

— I.e., I will give my tithes to a person worthy of receiving them for the glory of God *(Ibn Ezra).*

According to *Rashbam*: By offering sacrifices to You.

⧫Jacob did not yet have riches; how could he pledge the transfer of דָּבָר שֶׁלֹּא בָּא לָעוֹלָם, *something that had not yet come into existence?* **Even in a commercial transaction, such an obligation would be invalid unless, according to some opinions, it was upheld by an oath.** [See *comm.* to 25:33.]

Rambam in *Hilchos Arachin* 6:32 maintains that were one to say: 'I pledge myself to donate [to charity] all that I earn this year,' or something similar, he is bound, because of his vow, to consecrate it after that which he pledged has come into existence. He draws evidence for this ruling from our case of Jacob which in 31:13 God acknowledges as having been a valid vow. *Rambam* goes on to explain that these and similar utterances belong to the class of נְדָרִים, *vows,* and not to the class of הַקְדָּשׁוֹת, *consecrations.* The difference between the two categories is this: A *vow* is a pledge to do something; a person can so obligate himself. However, *consecration* means that someone wishes to place a condition of sanctity on an object and to transfer it to sacred ownership. This, like all transfers of property, can be done only when something is in existence.

29
1-2

So Jacob lifted his feet, and went toward the land of
the Easterners. 2 *He looked, and behold — a well in*

XXIX

1. Jacob meets Rachel

וַיִּשָּׂא יַעֲקֹב רַגְלָיו — *So* [lit. *and*] *Jacob lifted* [or lit. *carried*] *his feet.*

I.e., he lifted his feet with agility and proceeded on his journey *(Targum Yonasan).*

At the good tidings which he had received assuring him of God's protection, his heart 'lifted his feet' and he felt very light as he continued his journey *(Rashi* citing *Midrash).*

This is an idiomatic expression for traveling joyfully and briskly *(Rashbam).*

[*Sforno* perceives the connotation to be that having perceived such Divine closeness and received God's assurances of protection, Jacob proceeded on his journey confident and without reluctance. He writes:]

When we mean to imply that a person goes willingly, we may rightly say that he 'carries his feet.' But if a person goes reluctantly, we say rather that 'his feet carry him.' Cf. *Isaiah* 47:9: Pass over to Tarshish; howl you inhabitants of the coastland. Is this your joyous city whose *feet* in antiquity, in ancient days, *carried her* afar to sojourn?

וַיֵּלֶךְ אַרְצָה בְנֵי קֶדֶם — *And went toward the land of the Easterners* [lit. *children of the east*].

The reference is to Abraham's ancestral home — the regions east of *Eretz Yisrael*: Aram, Ur Kasdim, etc. See *comm.* to 25:6.

2. וַיַּרְא — [*And*] *he looked* [lit. *saw*].

וְהִנֵּה בְאֵר בַּשָּׂדֶה — *And behold, a well in the field!*

The Torah narrates this incident at length to illustrate how those who wait [confidently] for God shall renew their strength [*Isaiah* 40:31]. For though Jacob was weary from his long journey, he was able to roll away the stone unassisted, a task which usually required the combined effort of all the shepherds *(Ramban).*[1]

1. **The symbolism of this incident.**

Ramban again expounds on the principle that whatever happened to the Patriarchs foreshadowed events in the future of their descendants. This is the reason why the Torah relates at length seemingly unimportant incidents in their lives. [See *footnote* on page 436, and *Overview* to *Lech-Lecha* (Vol. II page 383).]

Citing the *Midrash,* he explains that *the well* symbolized the Temple, the *three flocks of sheep* are symbolic of the pilgrims ascending to the Temple during the three pilgrimage festivals [=*Pesach, Shavuos,* and *Succos*; see *Deut.* 16:16]; *from that well they would water the flocks* represented the spiritual influence emanating from the Temple. Or, it may be that the *water* symbolized the Torah, which has been likened to water [*Isaiah* 55:1, *Bava Kamma* 17a], emanating from Zion along with God's Word [*Isaiah* 2:3]. Having enjoyed the water, they *replaced the stone,* until the next festival.

Other allegorical interpretations recorded in the *Midrash* are:

The well in the field represented the Sanhedrin [source of spiritual sustenance to Israel]; *the three flocks of sheep* symbolize the three rows of scholars who sat in front of the Sanhedrin during their deliberations; *from that well they watered the flocks:* it was there the *halachah*

וְהִנֵּה־שָׁם שְׁלֹשָׁה עֶדְרֵי־צֹאן רֹבְצִים
עָלֶיהָ כִּי מִן־הַבְּאֵר הַהִוא יַשְׁקוּ הָעֲדָרִים
ג וְהָאֶבֶן גְּדֹלָה עַל־פִּי הַבְּאֵר: וְנֶאֶסְפוּ־
שָׁמָּה כָל־הָעֲדָרִים וְגָלֲלוּ אֶת־הָאֶבֶן מֵעַל
פִּי הַבְּאֵר וְהִשְׁקוּ אֶת־הַצֹּאן וְהֵשִׁיבוּ אֶת־
ד הָאֶבֶן עַל־פִּי הַבְּאֵר לִמְקֹמָהּ: וַיֹּאמֶר

וְהִנֵּה שָׁם שְׁלֹשָׁה עֶדְרֵי־צֹאן רֹבְצִים עָלֶיהָ — *And behold! Three flocks of sheep lay there beside* [lit. *upon*] *it.*

The translation of עָלָיו, [*upon* it] as *'beside* it' follows *Radak* who cites such similar idiomatic usage in *Numbers* 2:20: וְעָלָיו מַטֵּה מְנַשֶּׁה. *and beside him shall be the tribe of Menasseh.*

The connotation of עָלָיו, *upon it* in contexts such as our verse is: *dependent upon it,* i.e., the sheep lay there *dependent* upon the water of that well *(R' David Feinstein).*

יַשְׁקוּ הָעֲדָרִים — *They would water the flocks.*

[The future tense יַשְׁקוּ, lit. *will water,* is in the imperfect tense and expresses a continual action]: *They,* i.e., the shepherds, *used to water the flocks;* this verse uses an elliptical phrase *they would water* [omitting the implied subject: the shepherds] *(Rashi;* see next verse).

וְהָאֶבֶן גְּדֹלָה עַל־פִּי הַבְּאֵר — *Now* [lit. *and*] *the stone over the mouth of the well was large.*

Had the Torah merely wanted to tell us that the stone was large rather than small, the expression would have been וְאֶבֶן גְּדֹלָה עַל פִּי הַבְּאֵר, *and* [there was] *a large stone over the mouth of the well.* Reading as it does וְהָאֶבֶן גְּדֹלָה, *and the stone ... was a large one,* the syntax emphasizes the *very* large size of the stone. The intent is to accent Jacob's God-given strength in effortlessly rolling off the stone as described in *v.* 10 *(Or HaChaim).*

[Apparently, many wells in that region were regularly kept covered with boulders — as is still the case today. The syntax indicates that the

was expounded by the Sanhedrin; *the stone over the well was large:* the Court's leading scholar, who defined the Law; *all the flocks would be assembled there:* the other scholars of *Eretz Yisrael; they would roll the stone:* they, too, would hear the Law expounded in the Sanhedrin; *then they would return the stone upon the mouth of the well in its place:* they would discuss each rule until it was thoroughly clarified.

[Other interpretations too lengthy to include here interpret the *well* as symbolizing the well which accompanied the Israelites in the desert; the three flocks allude to Moses, Aaron and Miriam, etc. Another *Midrash* allegorizes the *well* as alluding to Mount Sinai; and the *three flocks* as alluding to the priests, Levites, and ordinary Israelites who heard the Commandments given there.]

Kli Yakar cautions that none of these *Midrashic* interpretations mean to negate the literal sense of the verse (אֵין הַמִּקְרָא יוֹצֵא מִידֵי פְּשׁוּטוֹ). Rather, the Sages perceive that Jacob's encounter with the shepherds could not have been mere coincidence. Recognizing that God was showing Jacob what the future would hold for his children, the Sages seek to interpret the symbolism of the incident.

the field! And behold! Three flocks of sheep lay there beside it, for from that well they would water the flocks. Now the stone over the mouth of the well was large. 3 *When all the flocks would be assembled there they would roll the stone from the mouth of the well and water the sheep. Then they would put back the stone over the mouth of the well, in its place.*

Torah stresses *not* that a stone was used to protect the well — that was quite common, but that the stone was גְּדֹלָה, *so large,* that it could be moved only by the collective effort of all the shepherds.]

The commentators offer the reasons for use of such a large boulder:

— Because this was the town's only source of water, they wanted to ensure that no water was drawn until *all* the flocks were assembled; this would prevent wastage of water in the troughs which would occur if each flock were watered individually *(Radak).*

— As a safety measure to prevent creatures and objects from falling into the well, and to prevent unauthorized persons from drawing its water *(Chizkuni).*

R' Hirsch observes, however, that generally the cover of a public well is made to be removed easily to facilitate its use. That this well was made so inaccessible gives us an insight into the base character of the Arameans — no one trusted the other, nor would allow another to gain even the slightest advantage. Fearing that someone might take more than his share of water, they made the cover so heavy that only by their combined effort could the well be used.

From this description of the extreme precautions employed to guard the well, the Sages infer that the region was short of water and the residents were compelled to water all their sheep from that one well. Yet, after Jacob arrived, the fountains were blessed and water was in abundance as is evident from the mention of watering-troughs [plural] in 30:38 *(Midrash HaGadol;* see *Targum Yonasan* cited to 27:10).

3. וְנֶאֶסְפוּ שָׁמָּה כָל הָעֲדָרִים — *When* [lit. *and*] *all the flocks would be assembled there.*

As *Rashi* explains, they *regularly* assembled there because the boulder was so heavy.

וְגָלְלוּ אֶת הָאֶבֶן — *They* [i.e., the shepherds *(Radak)*] *would roll the stone.*

Though the verb is in past-conversive, it has a frequentive sense: *they used to roll,* and it is so rendered by *Onkelos:* וּמְגַנְדְּרִין. Frequent action is conveyed by the [imperfect] future or [perfect] past tenses, because every continuous action has already happened and will happen again *(Rashi).*

וְהֵשִׁיבוּ אֶת הָאֶבֶן — *Then* [lit. *and*] *they would put back the stone.*

Again, the verb is rendered in the 'frequentive' tense: they *used* to return the stone, as indicated by *Onkelos'* use of the participle: וּמְתִיבִין *(Rashi).*

לָהֶם֙ יַעֲקֹ֔ב אַחַ֖י מֵאַ֣יִן אַתֶּ֑ם וַיֹּ֣אמְר֔וּ
ה מֵחָרָ֖ן אֲנָֽחְנוּ׃ וַיֹּ֣אמֶר לָהֶ֔ם הַיְדַעְתֶּ֖ם אֶת־
ו לָבָ֣ן בֶּן־נָח֑וֹר וַיֹּאמְר֖וּ יָדָֽעְנוּ׃ וַיֹּ֥אמֶר לָהֶ֖ם
הֲשָׁל֣וֹם ל֑וֹ וַיֹּאמְר֣וּ שָׁל֔וֹם וְהִנֵּה֙ רָחֵ֣ל
ז בִּתּ֔וֹ בָּאָ֖ה עִם־הַצֹּֽאן׃ וַיֹּ֗אמֶר הֵ֥ן ע֙וֹד
הַיּ֣וֹם גָּד֔וֹל לֹא־עֵ֖ת הֵאָסֵ֣ף הַמִּקְנֶ֑ה הַשְׁק֥וּ

4. וַיֹּאמֶר לָהֶם יַעֲקֹב — *[And] Jacob said to them.*

I.e., to the shepherds already assembled there *(Ralbag).*

אַחַי — *My brothers.*

A congenial form of address given even to non-relatives and strangers to initiate a feeling of friendliness and peaceful intentions; compare Lot's remark in 19:8 *(Radak).*[1]

5. לָבָן בֶּן־נָחוֹר — *Laban the son of Nachor.*

Actually Laban's father was *Bethuel*; he was Nachor's *grandson* [see 22:20 ff. and 24:29]...

R' Bachya suggests that the use of *son* instead of *grandson* is common since, as the Sages note [*Yevamos* 62b]: 'Grandchildren are considered as children.' See 20:12 where this interpretation is cited in the case of Abraham who referred to Sarah as *my father's daughter* when, in reality, she was his father's *granddaughter.*

Ramban, taking *son* in the sense of 'descendant,' offers three reasons for identifying Laban with his grandfather: (a) Laban was better known through his grandfather, Nachor, than through his father, Bethuel, since Nachor was an important personage and the head of the family as evidenced by 31:53: *God of Abraham and god of Nachor*; (b) possibly Laban preferred to be identified with Nachor because Bethuel was a dishonorable person. This would explain why Laban answered before his father [24:50]; or (c) perhaps it was to demonstrate their connection with

1. The *Midrash* perceives in this passage an allusion to the later dispersion of Israel when Jacob would address his descendants, so to speak:

My brothers — i.e., conduct yourselves as *brothers*; from *where are you from?* — Why are you dispersed and scattered?

... *We are from Charan* — we are fleeing from God's wrath [*Charon*].

Do you know Laban? — Do you recognize your sins and do you know that only He can make your sins whiter [*lavan*] than snow [cf. *Isaiah* 1:18]?

We know — and confess our sins.

The Peace is His! — He is the personification of Peace ... may He grant you peace and settle you in the habitation of peace.

Peace — through whose merit shall it come about?

See! ... Rachel is coming with the flock — — peace shall come by her merit as it says [*Jeremiah* 31:15-17]: *Rachel is weeping for her children ... Restrain your voice from weeping and your eyes from shedding tears; for there is reward for your labor and they shall return from the enemy's land. And there is hope for your future, says* HASHEM, *and your children shall return to their own border (Midrash HaGadol).*

[4] *Jacob said to them, 'My brothers, where are you
from?' And they said, 'We are from Charan'.* [5] *He
said to them, 'Do you know Laban the son of
Nachor?' And they said, 'We know.'* [6] *Then he said,
'Is it well with him?' They answered, 'It is well. And
see — his daughter Rachel is coming with the flock!'*
[7] *He said, 'Look it is still broad daylight; it is not
yet time to bring the livestock in. Water the sheep*

their illustrious relative Abraham that his family preferred to trace its lineage to *Nachor brother of Abraham* [see 22:23].

6. הֲשָׁלוֹם לוֹ — *Is it well with him?* [lit. *is there peace to him?*].

I.e., in what circumstances does he find himself? Jacob's sensitivity prompted him to ask this question. He was about to visit Laban and he wanted to know how to approach him according to his circumstances *(Sforno).*

וְהִנֵּה רָחֵל בִּתּוֹ בָּאָה עִם הַצֹּאן — *And see — his daughter Rachel is coming with the flock!*

The shepherds' answers, as the *Midrash* observes, were curt and to the point.

They realized that Jacob's curiosity about Laban would involve more details about his personal life than they could supply. They therefore pointed out his daughter, as if to say: *Look, his daughter is coming* — perhaps you should ask *her* your questions directly! *(Haamek Davar).*

Compare the *Midrash:* Jacob said to them הֲשָׁלוֹם לוֹ, *is there peace* between you and *him? And they said: There is peace.* And if you are anxious for gossip: *See, there is his daughter Rachel coming with the sheep*— for women are fond of gossiping.

[On Rachel's role as shepherdess, see *v.* 9.]

The word בָּאָה in our verse is accented on the second syllable אָ, indicating that it is *present* tense: [*she*] *is coming,* as *Onkelos* renders אָתְיָא; while in verse 9 the accent is on the first syllable בָּ, indicating that it is *past* tense: *she arrived,* as *Onkelos* renders: אֲתַת *(Rashi).*

[Cf. *Rashi* to בָּאָה in 16:17 and שָׁבָה in *Ruth* 1:15.]

7. הֵן עוֹד הַיּוֹם גָּדוֹל — *Look, it is still broad daylight* [lit. *the day is yet great.*]

Seeing the assembled flocks lying around, Jacob assumed that the shepherds had gathered the sheep to bring them home without intending to let them graze any longer. He therefore reminded them that עוֹד הַיּוֹם גָּדוֹל, *it was still early,* and if they were being paid by the day they had not yet completed a day's work. On the other hand even if you *own* the sheep: לֹא עֵת הֵאָסֵף הַמִּקְנֶה, *it is not yet time to bring in the livestock.* Therefore, [take advantage of the additional hours of grazing]: הַשְׁקוּ הַצֹּאן וּלְכוּ רְעוּ, *water the sheep and go on grazing* them *(Rashi* based on *Midrash).*

— He called the livestock מִקְנֶה, *property,* [from קנה, *own*], thereby reminding them of their duty towards the owner of the sheep. They should not be allowed to lie about idle, but should be taken to the pastures *(R' Hirsch).*

ח הַצֹּאן וּלְכוּ רְעוּ: וַיֹּאמְרוּ לֹא נוּכַל עַד
אֲשֶׁר יֵאָסְפוּ כָּל־הָעֲדָרִים וְגָלֲלוּ אֶת־
הָאֶבֶן מֵעַל פִּי הַבְּאֵר וְהִשְׁקִינוּ הַצֹּאן:
ט עוֹדֶנּוּ מְדַבֵּר עִמָּם וְרָחֵל | בָּאָה עִם־הַצֹּאן
י אֲשֶׁר לְאָבִיהָ כִּי רֹעָה הִוא: וַיְהִי כַּאֲשֶׁר
רָאָה יַעֲקֹב אֶת־רָחֵל בַּת־לָבָן אֲחִי אִמּוֹ

Jacob's attitude illustrates how a righteous man objects to a wrong being done even to strangers, as it is said [*Proverbs* 29:27]: *An unjust man is an abomination to the righteous (Sforno).*

הַשְׁקוּ הַצֹּאן וּלְכוּ רְעוּ — *Water the sheep and go on grazing* [i.e. until night falls.]

According to *Haamek Davar,* Jacob wished to converse with Rachel privately, so he suggested that the shepherds leave.

8. לֹא נוּכַל — *We will be unable to.*

I.e., *we cannot* water the flocks because the boulder is heavy [and we are not strong enough to move it ourselves] *(Rashi).*

That is, do not assume that we are shirking our responsibilities; we did not conspire to congregate idly by the well rather than graze our flocks. We have no choice: it is physically *impossible* for us to water our flocks, since the weight of the boulder forces us to wait for the others to come and help us roll the stone from atop the well *(Mizrachi; Tzeidah laDerech).*

וְגָלֲלוּ אֶת הָאֶבֶן מֵעַל פִּי הַבְּאֵר — *And they* [i.e. the shepherds] *will roll the stone off* [lit. *from upon*] *the mouth of the well.*

[See *comm.* end of *v.* 2.]

In another grammatical note *Rashi* observes that [in contrast to *v.* 3 where וְגָלֲלוּ is rendered in the frequentive sense] here it is rendered by *Onkelos* in the future tense וִיגַנְדְּרוּן, *they will roll.*

9. עוֹדֶנּוּ מְדַבֵּר עִמָּם — [*While*] *he was still speaking with them.*

This phrase implies that Rachel arrived while *he* [Jacob] *was still speaking,* but the context of the verses indicates that she came during the *shepherds' reply* of verse 8. If so, our verse should read עוֹדָם מְדַבְּרִים עִמּוֹ, *While 'they' were still speaking with 'him'.* It may be that Jacob is kept as the subject of the verse because he is the main character of the entire series of chapters. Or it may be that Rachel arrived as Jacob was addressing his remonstrance to the shepherds [*v.* 7], but, out of respect to Jacob, Scripture gives their answer to him before reverting to the arrival of Rachel *(Or HaChaim).*

וְרָחֵל בָּאָה עִם הַצֹּאן אֲשֶׁר לְאָבִיהָ — [*And*] *Rachel had arrived with her father's sheep.*

The implication is that she came leading *all* his sheep; obviously Laban's flock was small since Rachel alone was able to lead them all. This would corroborate Jacob's later remark to Laban [30:30]: *For the little which you had before* [*my arrival*] *has now increased into a great multitude.* That such a young maiden could lead a flock of even such a size also displays Rachel's

and go on grazing.' [8] *But they said, 'We will be un-*
able to, until all the flocks will have been gathered
and they will roll the stone off the mouth of the well.
We will then water the sheep.'
[9] *While he was still speaking with them Rachel had*
arrived with her father's sheep, for she was a
shepherdess. [10] *And it was, when Jacob saw Rachel,*
daughter of Laban his mother's brother, and the

skill as a shepherdess [see *Targum Yonasan* below] *(Alshich; Or HaChaim).*

The *Midrash* draws a comparison between the region of Midian where Jethro's *seven* daughters who came to water their flocks were driven away by the other shepherds [*Exodus* 2:17], and the district of Charan where Rachel coming *alone* was unmolested even though she was beautiful [*v.* 17]. This is indicative of the influence which the righteous Abraham's residence in that region (almost a century earlier) had still exerted in their spiritual life (following *Matnos Kehunah*). (Cf. *Ramban* below.)

The accent here is on the first syllable בָּאָה, indicating past tense. See *Rashi* to *v.* 6.

כִּי רֹעָה הִוא — *For she was a shepherdess.*

She *alone* tended the flocks as there was no other shepherd. Leah did not share this chore, either because the sun might have been harmful to her weak eyes [see *v.* 17], or because she was older — of marriageable age — and Laban was afraid to let her mix with the shepherds. It could be that Laban — being of Abraham's family — was more modest than Jethro and would not allow his more mature daughter to venture among the shepherds. In the case of Rachel, however, there was no apprehension since she was still too young for the shepherd boys to take an interest in her *(Ramban).*

The Torah adds the description of Rachel as a shepherdess to intimate that Rachel tended her father's sheep only *because she was a skilled shepherdess* and was eminently qualified for this task. Otherwise, Rachel would not have undertaken such a chore since she was not a יַצְאָנִית, a type who liked to appear in public. Therefore the Torah uses the verb בָּאָה, *came,* [rather than the uncomplimentary וַתֵּצֵא, *she went out,* from which it might be inferred that she enjoyed going out and was lacking in modesty. For such connotations of the word וַתֵּצֵא, see *Rashi;* 34:1] *(Or HaChaim).*

According to *Kli Chemdah,* since Laban was a notorious swindler no one would work for him. Therefore, he thrust the responsibility on his younger daughter.

Targum Yonasan records that there had been a divine plague which wiped out Laban's flocks except for these few sheep. He therefore dismissed his shepherds and entrusted the remaining sheep to Rachel *who was a shepherdess* at that time.

10. כַּאֲשֶׁר רָאָה יַעֲקֹב אֶת רָחֵל — *When Jacob saw Rachel ...*

... But he did not roll it off *sooner.* He was apprehensive that if he did, the shepherds would water

וְאֶת־צֹאן לָבָן אֲחִי אִמּוֹ וַיִּגַּשׁ יַעֲקֹב וַיָּגֶל
אֶת־הָאֶבֶן מֵעַל פִּי הַבְּאֵר וַיַּשְׁקְ אֶת־צֹאן
יא לָבָן אֲחִי אִמּוֹ: וַיִּשַּׁק יַעֲקֹב לְרָחֵל וַיִּשָּׂא
יב אֶת־קֹלוֹ וַיֵּבְךְּ: וַיַּגֵּד יַעֲקֹב לְרָחֵל כִּי אֲחִי

only their own three flocks and would not wait to assist the others *(Sforno).*

[One can only imagine Jacob's exhilaration over 'happening' to meet — at that very moment — the daughter of the uncle to whom he was traveling in search of a wife and in flight from Esau. Jacob surely perceived this as an act of Providence guiding him to his destined wife. He must have compared his experience to that of Eliezer who 'happened' upon Rebecca when *he* was searching for a wife for Isaac nearly one hundred years earlier.]

בַּת־לָבָן אֲחִי אִמּוֹ וְאֶת צֹאן לָבָן אֲחִי אִמּוֹ — *Daughter of Laban his mother's brother, and the sheep of Laban his mother's brother.*

That Laban was *his mother's brother* is repeated three times in this verse to emphasize clearly that Jacob's every action was prompted not by the mere sight of Rachel but by his love for his mother *(R' Bachya; Abarbanel).*

As *R' Hirsch* explains: Jacob's every act was motivated by devotion to his mother whom he saw before him in the person of her relative. The frequent stress on this relationship provides an understanding of Jacob's reason for kissing Rachel. Otherwise, it would have been taken as an act of gallantry toward a pretty shepherdess. [See next verse.]

וַיִּגַּשׁ יַעֲקֹב וַיָּגֶל ... — [*And*] *Jacob came forward* [lit. *approached; drew near*] *and rolled the stone off* [lit. *from upon*] *the mouth of the well.*

— Unaided *(Rashbam).*

— As effortlessly as one draws a stopper from the mouth of a bottle. This illustrates Jacob's great physical strength *(Rashi.* [See *Ramban* to *v.* 2.]).

According to *Tzror HaMor,* it was the sight of Rachel, his mother's niece, under these circumstances that stirred him to perform this feat of great physical prowess. [*Malbim* comments similarly.]

Mizrachi offers that *Rashi's Midrashic* interpretation comparing Jacob's feat to the drawing of a stopper from the mouth of a bottle is based on the use of וַיָּגֶל literally, *he revealed,* instead of וַיְגַלְגֵּל, *he rolled.* He suggests that וַיָּגֶל comes from the root גלה *uncover* rather than גלל *roll,* and the verb is suggestive of the ease with which Jacob plucked off the stone and uncovered the well.

However, the word וַיָּגֶל is generally interpreted by the commentators [*Onkelos, Ibn Janach, Radak*] as *rolled.*

Accordingly, *Sifsei Chachamim* suggests that *Rashi* derives his interpretation from the proximity of the two verbs: וַיִּגַּשׁ וַיָּגֶל, *he drew near and rolled,* implying that no sooner had he drawn near than he rolled the stone away, as if no effort were required.

HaKsav V'HaKabalah cites an interpretation that this exegesis is based on the nonemphatic from וַיָּגֶל instead of ויגלל which, by virtue of the intensive form would have suggested a strenuous rolling rather than the effortless one implied here.

R' Hirsch notes that the word וַיָּגֶל is in *hiph'il* [=causative]: *he* [effortlessly] *let it roll away.* This root occurs nowhere else in the *hiph'il.* It designates

*sheep of Laban his mother's brother, Jacob came
forward and rolled the stone off the mouth of the
well and watered the sheep of Laban his mother's
brother.* 11 *Then Jacob kissed Rachel; and he raised
his voice and wept.* 12 *Jacob told Rachel that he was*

the ease with which he pushed the great stone aside.

וַיַּשְׁקְ אֶת צֹאן לָבָן אֲחִי אִמּוֹ — *And watered the sheep of Laban his mother's brother.*

The *Midrash* notes that unlike the case of Moses where it specifically says that he *drew* the water [*Exodus* 2:19], here in the case of Jacob, when he rolled the stone off the mouth of the well, the water in the well rose up and flowed over the sides to water Laban's sheep. This is the intent of the omission of any mention of his having drawn water from the well. The shepherds who witnessed this were astonished at his strength when they had difficulty in removing the stone *collectively*. Jacob viewed the overflowing water as a heavenly sign that he was now meeting his pre-destined wife (*Pirkei d'Rabbi Eliezer; Pirkei d'Rabbeinu HaKadosh; Zohar* 2:151).

According to *Targum Yonasan*, in Jacob's merit the water continued overflowing for twenty years [i.e., the total duration of Jacob's stay in Charan].

11. וַיִּשַּׁק יַעֲקֹב לְרָחֵל — *Then* [lit. *and*] *Jacob kissed Rachel.*

Rachel was still too young to arouse one's passion, and Jacob's kiss should be perceived in that context. Or, as *Ibn Ezra* [to 27:27] interprets, when the verb נשק, *kiss*, is followed by the prefix ל [as in our verse: וַיִּשַּׁק יַעֲקֹב לְרָחֵל] it means that he kissed her *not* on the mouth, but on the head or on the shoulder [or on the cheek as was the customary greeting of the region (see *Ibn Ezra* to *Song of Songs* 1:2)] (*Ramban* to *v.* 9).

As may be inferred from *Rashi* below in *v.* 13 however, this opinion is not universal, and according to most commentators, the verb *kiss* in Scripture regardless of what follows it, denotes a kiss on the *mouth*.

[Notwithstanding the above, the *halachah*, (*Even HaEzer* ch. 21) forbids such intimacy even with members of one's family unless they are very young children, except between parent and child.]

וַיֵּבְךְּ — *And* [*he*] *wept.*

— Because he foresaw through the prophetic spirit that she would not be buried with him [in the Cave of Machpelah.] [He also perceived that she would be buried along the highway and would lament as her descendants passed her grave on their way into exile. At the thought of their long exile, he wept *(Yafeh Toar).*] Another reason he wept was because he came empty-handed. He thought: Eliezer, who was only my grandfather's *servant* came for my mother laden with riches, while I come here destitute. Esau's son

אָבִיהָ הוּא וְכִי בֶן־רִבְקָה הוּא וַתָּרָץ
יג וַתַּגֵּד לְאָבִיהָ׃ וַיְהִי כִשְׁמֹעַ לָבָן אֶת־שֵׁמַע

Eliphaz took everything I had (*Rashi* citing *Midrash*).[1]

According to *Sforno* Jacob wept at the thought of his not having merited to have married her in his youth and to already have had children born to him as a young man.

Following *R' Hirsch:* Jacob's tears show the motive for his kiss. He did not see her beauty; he saw a relative after a long and lonely journey. [See above (28:10) that Jacob had studied at the Academy of Eber for fourteen years after leaving his parents' house.] The sight of his mother's niece moved him to tears and to a show of affection. Because Rachel must have been mystified, he withdrew and, in the next verse, explained the cause of his emotion.[2]

Haamek Davar similarly explains the tears after the kiss. He adds, however, that regarding Jacob's destitution, it would seem, according to the literal sense, that Jacob's riches would have dwindled away during his fourteen years at the Academy of Eber.

12. וַיַּגֵּד יַעֲקֹב לְרָחֵל... — [*And*] *Jacob told Rachel that he was her father's relative.*

[Our translation interprets the order of events as having occurred as indicated by the verses: first, he kissed her (*v.* 11), then he identified himself (*v.* 12).]

Ibn Ezra renders in past-perfect: *had* told. Only *after* telling her of their relationship (*v.* 12) did he kiss her (*v.* 11). [*Ralbag* and *Abarbanel* render similarly.]

According to *Sforno*, however, the sequence of events is as related in the narrative. He told her that he was her relative to assure her that he had not acted improperly by kissing her. [*Chizkuni* renders similarly; see also *R' Hirsch* above.]

[In 24:23 the verb הגד, *tell*, denotes the transmission of a comprehensive fully detailed conversation, in contrast with אמר, *say*, which has a more superficial connotation.]

כִּי אֲחִי אָבִיהָ הוּא וְכִי בֶן־רִבְקָה הוּא — *That he was her father's relative, and that he was Rebecca's son.*

The translation of אֲחִי [lit.

1. The *Midrash* records that when Jacob fled, Esau ordered his son Eliphaz to pursue Jacob and kill him. Eliphaz obeyed and overtook Jacob.

Since Eliphaz had been brought up on Isaac's lap, however, he refrained from slaying Jacob, but at the same time he realized that he would have to answer to his father for not obeying his command.

'I do not want to kill you, but what shall I do regarding my father's order?' Eliphaz asked.

'Take everything that I have', Jacob suggested, 'and leave me destitute. Then you will have obeyed your father's orders since a poor man is considered as dead' (*Rashi*).

2. There is a view in the *Midrash* that Jacob wept in response to the reaction of the onlookers who started whispering to one another, accusing him of introducing immorality there by kissing a girl in public. His weeping was to emphasize that his kiss was not a frivolous one, but that of a kinsman. The *Midrash* derives from this episode that one must reckon with what people may think as well as with what is right before Heaven (*Mishnas Rabbi Eliezer* 7; cf. *Midrash Rabbah*).

We find, accordingly, that one who is the victim of unwarranted accusation should weep. The *Talmud* [*Yoma* 19b] relates that the High Priest who was admonished against performing the rites like a Saduccee would separate himself and weep at the fact that he was under suspicion. Similarly Joseph wept [45:2] because, as the *Pesikta* explains, his brothers suspected him of planning to seek vengeance for their having sold him into slavery (*Yalkut Yehudah*).

29 *her father's relative, and that he was Rebecca's son.*
12 *Then she ran and told her father.*

brother] as *relative* follows *Rashi* who cites a similar usage in 13:8: *for we are kinsmen* [אַחִים, lit. *brothers.*] *Rashi* then goes on to explain the apparently redundant description of himself as both her father's brother *and* Rebecca's son, when one would have sufficed, by citing the *Midrashic* interpretation:

— Should your father wish to deceive me then *I am his brother* in deceit, [i.e. I am a match for him.] If, however, he is an honorable man, then I, too, am a son of his honorable sister Rebecca [and I will reciprocate accordingly.][1]

In answer to how a righteous man like Jacob could threaten to reciprocate Laban's deceit, *Or HaChaim* suggests that the intimation of the above *Midrash* is: 'If Laban acts treacherously with me, I will outwit him in an honest, legal manner. By behaving with integrity and according to the law, I will prevent him from cheating me.' Jacob alluded to this intention by describing himself as Rebecca's son; he had no intention of disgracing her righteous reputation. This is the inner meaning of the verse, *wisdom will give life to its possessor (Koheles* 7:12).

The *Talmud* [*Bava Basra* 123a; see footnote] records in this connection that when Rachel asked him if a righteous man may resort to deceit, he cited the verse *'with the righteous act righteously, and with the crooked act crookedly,* [II *Samuel* 22:2].

According to *Sforno*, as noted, he mentioned that he was her father's relative to allay any apprehension over his having kissed her. He added mention of Rebecca although Rachel did not know her, so that she might thus inform her father.

He mentioned his relationship to her father to intimate their physical kinship; the mention of his well-known righteous mother served to establish the spiritual kinship since the righteous rejoice in a kindred soul *(Or HaChaim).*

וַתָּרָץ וַתַּגֵּד לְאָבִיהָ — *Then she ran and told her father.*

— Because her mother was dead and she had no one else to tell but him *(Rashi* following *Midrash).*

[See *comm.* to 24:28 that Rebecca, in contrast, ran to her *mother's* tent because, as *Rashi* notes there, a girl tends to confide only in her mother. The *Midrash* there notes that Rachel's mother had died and she had no one else to confide in but her father.]

Ramban suggests however, that according to the plain meaning of the verses, Rachel went to her father so that he should go and welcome his relative. Her mother was not Jacob's relative; what would *she* do for him? On the other hand, *Rebecca* ran to her *mother* first, specifically to show her the jewels Eliezer had given her [24:28] as girls customarily do.

1. According to *Bava Basra* 123a it was on this occasion that Jacob asked Rachel's hand in marriage. She consented, but warned him that she had an older sister and that her cunning father would not allow her to be married before her sister. Jacob reassured her that he was her father's 'brother' in cunning, and he entrusted her with certain identifying passwords [by which he would identify her in the dark.] These were the signs Rachel later compassionately entrusted to Leah on her marriage night in order to prevent her humiliation if Laban's ruse were to be discovered. [See *Megillah* 13b, and *comm.* to *v.* 25.]

יַעֲקֹב בֶּן־אֲחֹתוֹ וַיָּרָץ לִקְרָאתוֹ וַיְחַבֶּק־לוֹ
וַיְנַשֶּׁק־לוֹ וַיְבִיאֵהוּ אֶל־בֵּיתוֹ וַיְסַפֵּר לְלָבָן
יד אֵת כָּל־הַדְּבָרִים הָאֵלֶּה: וַיֹּאמֶר לוֹ לָבָן
אַךְ עַצְמִי וּבְשָׂרִי אָתָּה וַיֵּשֶׁב עִמּוֹ חֹדֶשׁ

13. אֵת שֵׁמַע יַעֲקֹב בֶּן־אֲחֹתוֹ — *The news of Jacob his nephew* [lit. *sister's son*].

— I.e., the news that Jacob had rolled away the stone *(Sforno).*

— The account of Jacob's strength and piety; how he had procured the birthright and blessings from his brother; how HASHEM had revealed Himself to him at Bethel; how he had removed the boulder and how the well had overflowed ... *(Targum Yonasan).*

וַיָּרָץ לִקְרָאתוֹ — [*And*] *he ran toward him.*

Laban thought that Jacob must be loaded with money seeing that a mere household servant [Eliezer] had [years earlier] come with ten richly laden camels [24:10] *(Rashi).*

[This comment, like the comment on Laban's hurry to greet Eliezer in 24:29 is based on the sinister manner which Laban emerges in traditional Rabbinic perspective. It was known that Laban was not righteous, and that he was not simply being *hospitable*; his effusive welcome is accordingly interpreted as motivated by the sort of avarice he displayed in his later treatment of Jacob.]

As *R' Hoffmann* comments: We already know Laban [see 24:29] as a self-centered, greedy person. It was only the glitter of jewels on his sister's arm that had prompted him [97 years earlier!] to run and invite the stranger — Eliezer — into his home. Now, too, his attention was focused on the possible wealth he hoped Jacob had brought with him. But as he was soon to learn to his great disappointment, his nephew had come to him empty-handed!

וַיְחַבֶּק־לוֹ — [*And*] *he embraced him.*

Seeing that Jacob was empty-handed, Laban thought that he might have the money hidden on his person. He therefore *embraced* him [to frisk him and discover any hidden treasures] *(Rashi* based on *Midrash).*

This inference is drawn from a knowledge of Laban's personality and from the fact that the Torah should normally have expressed these actions more economically as וַיְחַבְּקֵהוּ וַיְנַשְּׁקֵהוּ. The use of the word לוֹ, which can be translated *for himself* prompted the Rabbis to interpret our phrase to imply that Laban embraced Jacob לוֹ, *for his* [Laban's] *own benefit;* in search of riches *(Maskil l'David).*[1]

וַיְנַשֶּׁק־לוֹ — [*And he*] *kissed him.*

When Laban felt nothing on Jacob's person, *he kissed him* thinking that his wealth might consist of

1. [*Maskil l'David's* inquiry into *Rashi's* justification for this interpretation points up a fundamental principle of *Rashi's* commentary throughout Scripture. Since *Rashi* to our verse quotes *Midrash Rabbah*, one might wonder why, instead of seeking a textual basis for *Rashi's* interpretation, *Maskil l'David* did not say simply that *Rashi* relied on the *Midrash*. Such an approach, however, would not be consonant with *Rashi's* own intention.

Above [on 3:8], *Rashi* explained his guiding principle in the choice of *Midrashic* interpretation: יֵשׁ מִדְרְשֵׁי אֲגָדָה רַבִּים וּכְבַר סִידְּרוּם רַבּוֹתֵינוּ עַל מְכוֹנָם בִּבְרֵאשִׁית רַבָּה וּבִשְׁאָר מִדְרָשׁוֹת, וַאֲנִי לֹא בָאתִי אֶלָּא לִפְשׁוּטוֹ שֶׁל מִקְרָא, וּלְאַגָּדָה הַמְיַישֶּׁבֶת דִּבְרֵי הַמִּקְרָא דָּבָר דִּבּוּר עַל אוֹפַנָּיו., *There are many homiletic expositions and our Rabbis have arranged them in an orderly manner in* Bereishis

29
13-14

*[13] And it was, when Laban heard the news of Jacob
his nephew, he ran toward him, embraced him,
kissed him, and took him to his house. He recounted
to Laban all these events. [14] Then Laban said to him,
'Nevertheless, you are my flesh and blood!' And he
stayed with him a month's time.*

precious stones carried in his mouth *(Rashi).*

This long, searching kiss is intimated by the intensive *pi'el,* וַיְנַשֶּׁק, instead of the more simple, *kal* form וַיִּשַּׁק used above in *v.* 11 *(Heidenheim; Hoffmann).*

[See *Ibn Ezra* cited to *v.*11 who maintains that the prefix indicates that the kiss was not on the mouth. *Rashi* here, however, certainly echoes the Rabbinic interpretation that Laban kissed Jacob on the *mouth.*]

וַיְסַפֵּר לְלָבָן אֵת כָּל־הַדְּבָרִים הָאֵלֶּה — [*And*] *he* [i.e., Jacob] *recounted to Laban all these events.*

What did Jacob recount?

He explained that he had come only because he was being persecuted by his brother, and that he had come penniless because all his money had been taken from him by Eliphaz *(Rashi).*

He explained that his parents had sent him to his family *(Rashbam).*

He related how it came about that he had received his father's blessings *(Ibn Ezra).*

14. Laban invites Jacob to reside with him

אַךְ עַצְמִי וּבְשָׂרִי אָתָּה — *Nevertheless you are my flesh and blood!* [The translation conveys the English idiom. The Hebrew is literally: *my bone and flesh*].[1]

[The connotation of אַךְ which implies a conversive to that which precedes it is:] Because you come penniless I am under no obligation to show you hospitality. *Nevertheless,* [i.e., although you are poor] *you are my relative,* and I will therefore put up with you for one month's time. And thus he did. But even that month was not free: Jacob earned his keep by tending Laban's flocks [as implied by the next verse] *(Rashi).*

Sforno interprets: *Although* you can earn your living as a shepherd elsewhere, since *you are my flesh and blood* you should stay and work for me.

Hoffmann suggests that אַךְ has the connotation of אָכֵן: *'Indeed* you are my

Rabbah *and the other* Midrashic *works. However, I have come only to explain the* plain *meaning of Scripture and to cite such* Midrashim *as explain each word of Scripture within its proper context.*

Accordingly, *Rashi* selected only such *Midrashic* expositions as are necessary to clarify the simple meaning of the verse. For this reason, the commentators to *Rashi* will often seek to find the *textual* consideration which compelled him to cite a particular *Midrash.*]

1. The *Vilna Gaon* cites the *Talmudic* dictum [*Niddah* 31a] that there are three partners in man: God, his father and his mother ... The father supplies the substance out of which are formed the child's bones ... while his mother supplies the substance out of which is formed his flesh ...

Accordingly, the Gaon explains the connotation of Laban's remark to be: You are related to me both from your father's side [=the *bone,* through Nachor/Abraham] and from your mother's side [=the *flesh,* through Rebecca].

טו יָמִים: וַיֹּאמֶר לָבָן לְיַעֲקֹב הֲכִי־אָחִי אַתָּה
וַעֲבַדְתַּנִי חִנָּם הַגִּידָה לִּי מַה־מַּשְׂכֻּרְתֶּךָ:
טז וּלְלָבָן שְׁתֵּי בָנוֹת שֵׁם הַגְּדֹלָה לֵאָה וְשֵׁם
יז הַקְּטַנָּה רָחֵל: וְעֵינֵי לֵאָה רַכּוֹת וְרָחֵל

flesh and blood' and [though you are penniless] I recognize my duty to you as a kinsman. [See *comm.* to אָכֵן in 28:16.] *Targum Yonasan* also renders in the affirmative: *Indeed.*

You were quite right to come to me *(Rashbam).*

According to *Kli Yakar,* when Laban heard Jacob's account of how he outwitted Esau to obtain the blessings, he proudly said, *'Indeed, you are my flesh and blood* [i.e., a man after my own heart] — you are a deceiver like me. I must therefore take you under my wing.'

Malbim, following *Alshich,* explains that Laban meant: 'Have no fear that Esau is pursuing you, Jacob, it is only *you* whom I consider my flesh and blood, not Esau. I love whomever my sister Rebecca loves, and if Esau comes to harm you, I will come to your defense.'

The expression *my bone and my flesh* implies: You are as dear to me as my own body *(HaRechasim leBik'ah).*

וַיֵּשֶׁב עִמּוֹ חֹדֶשׁ יָמִים — *And he* [=Jacob] *stayed with him a month's time* [lit. *a month of days*].

— Working for him (*Sforno;* see *Rashi* above and *Ramban* next verse).

The idiom *month of days* means a full cycle of days, when that same day falls out on the following month (*Ibn Ezra* above 4:3).

15. וַיֹּאמֶר לָבָן לְיַעֲקֹב — *Then* [lit. and] *Laban said to Jacob.*

[Presumably after the abovementioned thirty days.]

הֲכִי־אָחִי אַתָּה וַעֲבַדְתַּנִי חִנָּם — *Just because you are my relative* [lit. brother], *should you serve me for nothing?*

The Torah had not said that Jacob had been working for him; it is implied from this remark. Apparently, from the time Jacob first watered Rachel's flocks at the well [*v.*10] he took over her work and tended her flocks out of compassion to spare her the chore, so great was his love for her. Alternatively, Jacob may indeed have been a nonworking guest for a month. Knowing that Jacob would not continue to support himself at another's expense, Laban now connived to elicit from him an offer to work for his keep *(Ramban).*

Jacob had worked free of charge all month long for Laban rather than accept charity. Indeed, his work must have been very profitable if Laban, who surely computed the cost of Jacob's room and board still described Jacob's labor as having been *for nothing (R' Hirsch).*

The translation of this passage as an incredulous question follows *Rashi,* who also expounds the grammatical rule that a past-tense verb to which the conversive-prefix ו is added may change the verb, depending upon the context, to future. Hence עֲבַדְתַּנִי [past-tense, lit. *you served me*] *with the* ו conversive becomes *that you will* [or: *should serve me*].

According to *R' Bachya,* הֲכִי does not imply a question but an affirmation, as in 27:36 [following *Ibn Ezra* and *Radak* cited at top of page 1152], and וַעֲבַדְתַּנִי denotes the past tense. Thus, Laban's statement was: *Indeed you are my relative, and you have served me this past month for nothing.* Now, should you wish to remain here, then tell me what wage you desire.

[15] *Then Laban said to Jacob, 'Just because you are*
my relative should you serve me for nothing? Tell
me: What are your wages?'
[16] *(Laban had two daughters. The name of the*
older one was Leah and the name of the younger one
was Rachel. [17] *Leah's eyes were tender, while Rachel*

הַגִּידָה לִּי מַה מַּשְׂכֻּרְתֶּךָ — *Tell me: What are your wages?*

Although Jacob had been working without pay, Laban preferred to pay him — and get him to commit himself to continue on the job rather than risk losing such a capable worker *(R' Hirsch).*

But, at the same time, Laban was apprehensive that if he did not set a price *now,* Jacob would later demand more than he was prepared to pay *(Malbim).*

Others interpret that Laban wished to increase Jacob's liability for losses. A paid watchman [שׁוֹמֵר שָׂכָר] is liable for theft and loss while an unpaid watchman [שׁוֹמֵר חִנָּם] is liable only for negligence. Thus, by paying Jacob, Laban would get better protection for his assets *(Tur).*

16. וּלְלָבָן שְׁתֵּי בָנוֹת — [*And*] *Laban had two daughters.*

Before recording Jacob's response to Laban's inquiry, the Torah interjects these parenthetical verses to inform us that Laban had two daughters, the younger of whom Jacob loved. This digression prepares us for Jacob's response in verse 18 where he requested the younger daughter in marriage *(Rashbam).*

The *Midrash* by a slight revowelization homiletically reads בָּנוֹת, *daughters* as בּוֹנוֹת, *builders* — for it was they who built the Jewish nation, since the great personages of the nation descended from them: Moses, Joshua, Samson, David, Solomon and the royal house of Israel.

שֵׁם הַגְּדֹלָה לֵאָה — *The name of the older one was Leah.*

The name is related to the cognate root לאה meaning *wearied. Midrash Sechel Tov* perceives the name as an allusion to Leah's *weariness* over her constant weeping and praying to avert her marriage to Esau [as explained below]. *Midrash HaBiur* [cited in *Torah Sheleimah*] interprets the name as an abbreviation of *m'leah, full,* signifying that she was full of wisdom and knowledge.

וְשֵׁם הַקְּטַנָּה רָחֵל — *And the name of the younger one was Rachel.*[1]

The word means *sheep,* and she was so named for her skill in tending her father's sheep *(Sechel Tov);* according to *Yalkut Reuveni,* the name is a contraction which

1. Following the traditional Rabbinic chronology in *Seder Olam,* Leah and Rachel were twins, Leah being the elder of the two. They were born, according to the most prevalent Rabbinic view, when Jacob received the blessings. Accordingly, their age at marriage was twenty-two [the *Vilna Gaon* reads: twenty-one.].

According to *Pirkei d'Rabbi Eliezer,* Bilhah and Zilpah [whom Jacob later married] were also Laban's daughters, but by his concubines, and were therefore treated as servants [see verse 24]. Rachel and Leah were his daughters by his wife, and were older than Bilhah and Zilpah *(Yafeh Toar).*

implies that she was filled with רוּחַ אֵל, a *Divine* [prophetic] *spirit.*

Midrash HaBiur explains the connotation of the name to be that she was worthy that the Shechinah might rest [שֶׁתָּחוּל=רָחֵל] upon her.

The *Midrash* interprets הַגְּדֹלָה in the literal sense as the *greater sister,* suggesting that Leah was *great* in the gifts granted to her offspring. She received [through Levi and Judah respectively] the priesthood and royalty for all time [since even the future Messianic King will be descended from the House of David]. Rachel, in contrast, was the *small* sister -- *small* in her gifts. Joseph held sway for but a time, and Saul [who was a descendant of Benjamin] reigned for but a short time [neither founding a dynasty]. Compare *Psalms* 78:67: *He rejected the tabernacle of Joseph and chose not the tribe of Ephraim.* [See *footnote* next verse.]

17. וְעֵינֵי לֵאָה רַכּוֹת — [*And*] *Leah's eyes were tender* [lit. *watered; soft; weak*].

— Through constant weeping at the prospect of marrying Esau. People used to say that since Rebecca has two sons and Laban two daughters, the elder daughter would be married to the elder son, while the younger daughter would be married to the younger son *(Rashi).*

[This view is followed by *Targum Yonasan, Ibn Ezra, Ralbag,* and *Abarbanel.* The implication of *Ramban* in *v.* 9, too, is that Leah's eyes were *weak* and that was one reason that Rachel, and not she, tended the sheep.]

Rashi's interpretation is based on Rav's view in *Bava Basra* 123a. The *Talmud* reasons that it would be inconceivable for the Torah to record a disparaging blemish on the righteous Leah for no reason at all. Even when listing forbidden animals (*Gen.* 7:8), the Torah uses the longer, more euphemistic expression אֲשֶׁר אֵינֶנָּה טְהוֹרָה, *not clean,* rather than the shorter, but disparaging, expression טְמֵאָה, *contaminated.*

Accordingly, the *Talmud* seeks an alternative translation of רַכּוֹת, and an explanation of the blemish that would do *credit* to Leah. Rav in *Bava Basra ibid.* maintains that Leah's eyes were indeed *weak.* As *Rashbam* there explains, they were *watered; full of tears,* a condition that reflected her excessive weeping 'until her eyelashes fell out' over the prospect that she might be married to the wicked Esau. Thus, the weakness of her eyes was not a defect, but a symptom of her spiritual greatness.[1]

According to the Midrashic version, Leah used to weep as she prayed: 'May it be Your will that I do not fall to the lot of that wicked man [Esau]'. R' Huna said: Great is prayer that it annulled the decree [i.e., her original destiny to be Esau's wife] and she even took precedence over her sister [i.e., she was the first to marry Jacob and she bore most of his children].

Others perceive the sense of the descriptions not as a contrast between ugliness and beauty, but between relative types of attractiveness:

Instead of saying Leah was not so beautiful, it very delicately praises her good points. Her *eyes* were soft and

1. The other view cited by the *Talmud* is R' Elazar's. The word עֵינֵי refers not to *eyes,* but figuratively to *leaders* as we find the word interpreted in *Leviticus* 4:13, *Numbers* 15:24, and frequently in *Song of Songs.* The word רַכּוֹת is a shortened version of אֲרֻכּוֹת, *long.* The implication, as more clearly explained in *Tanchuma Yashan* and the *Midrash* above is that the blessing of *leadership* — priesthood and royalty — that would descend from her would be of *long duration.*

29 *was beautiful of form and beautiful of appearance.)*
18 [18] *Jacob loved Rachel, so he said, 'I will work for*

tender whereas Rachel was *altogether* beautiful. This follows *Onkelos* who translates: *the eyes of Leah were beautiful* [יָאַיִן] *(Tur).*

Tur continues, however, that some explain that weak eyes were Leah's *only* blemish, while Rachel, on the other hand, was *entirely* beautiful.

Rashbam also takes it in the sense as *beautiful, gleaming* and cites the *Talmud* [*Taanis* 24a] that if a bride's eyes are beautiful no further description is necessary.

Haamek Davar also interprets it this way, but suggests that Leah's eyes were also tender and sensitive to the sun with the result as *Ramban* explains, that she could not tend the sheep.

יְפַת תֹּאַר וִיפַת מַרְאֶה — *Beautiful of form and beautiful of appearance.*

I.e., possessing beautiful features and a radiant appearance [complexion] (*Rashi* and almost all commentators).

[See *comm.* to יְפַת מַרְאֶה in 12:11 and טֹבַת מַרְאֶה in 24:16.]

— *Altogether* beautiful, in comparison with Leah whose tender eyes were her *only* mark of beauty (*Abarbanel, R' Hirsch.* See *Tur* above).

18. וַיֶּאֱהַב יַעֲקֹב אֶת רָחֵל — *[And] Jacob loved Rachel.*[1]

— Since he foresaw that she was his preordained wife *(Zohar).*

The *Zohar* notes that Jacob's foreordained wife, Rachel, was encountered at a well as were Moses' and Isaac's. Leah, however, came to be Jacob's wife only in a devious manner. This was because Leah was the mate who was suited to Jacob's higher spiritual nature; had he met her first, he would not have shown any subsequent interest in Rachel. Providence ordained that he meet and come to love Rachel before Leah since his marriage to Leah would have taken place in any event. [See *Overview.*]

אֶעֱבָדְךָ שֶׁבַע שָׁנִים — *I will work for you seven years.*

'Do you think it is money that I seek?' Jacob replied to Laban's request that he specify his wage. 'It is your daughter for whom I came here!' *(Chasam Sofer).*

◈§ Jacob's voluntary separation from his parents.

[As was noted in the *comm.* to 28:5 and will be elaborated upon further in *Sidrah Vayeshev* אי״ה, Jacob was away from his parents for a total of thirty-six years, of which fourteen were spent studying in the Academy of Eber. For those years of study, he was not considered negligent for failing to honor his parents. For the other twenty-two years, however, during which he failed to return home [twenty years of service and two years of journeying] the Sages hold that Jacob was derelict. His punishment was that Joseph remained separated from him for a like number of years. As *Rashi* writes in 37:36: 'These twenty years that I have been with you,' Jacob alluded to Laban [31:41], 'were לִי, *for me,* i.e., the responsibility of them *lies upon me* and I shall yet be punished for an equal period of time.'

As explained, it was apparently Isaac's intention that Jacob stay away only long enough to take a wife, and that he be prepared to return as soon as Isaac felt it was safe enough to send for

1. [In the order of synagogue Torah reading, verse 17 is the conclusion of the second part of the *Sidrah.* Thus, there is a clear separation between the verse describing Rachel's beauty and the verse describing Jacob's love for her. The intention may be to point out that Jacob's love was not motivated by Rachel's physical beauty, but by her spiritual qualities.]

יט שָׁנִים בְּרָחֵל בִּתְּךָ הַקְּטַנָּה: וַיֹּאמֶר לָבָן
טוֹב תִּתִּי אֹתָהּ לָךְ מִתִּתִּי אֹתָהּ לְאִישׁ
כ אַחֵר שְׁבָה עִמָּדִי: וַיַּעֲבֹד יַעֲקֹב בְּרָחֵל

him. There is an interpretation that his mother had sent her nurse to fetch him one year after he arrived at Laban's home, but he did not leave because he was still obligated to serve Laban [see also *Rashi* to 35:8]. By *volunteering seven years of work* for Rachel — when a lesser amount might have sufficed — Jacob revealed a lack of sensitivity for his parents, and was therefore punished for *all* the years he was away from his father's service (except for the fourteen years of studying.)

The question arises, therefore, why Jacob obligated himself for so long a period? It is doubly difficult because the Sages infer from *Isaiah* 16:14 that one should not hire himself out for more than *three* years. [See *Overview.*]

[See *Tosafos Kiddushin* 17a; *Mordechai* ibid., *RaMA, Choshen Mishpat* 333:3, and *Ibn Ezra* to *Deut.* 15:18. See *Shach* in *Choshen Mishpat* ibid: that for sustenance which would apparently include the case of marriage it is permitted even longer. Cf. *Minchas Chinuch* 42, and *Pardes Yosef.*]

☐ *Rashi,* following the *Midrash,* suggests that Jacob's offer to work for seven years was based on his understanding of Rebecca's charge when she instructed him to flee to Laban. She spoke of *a few days* [27:44] and, as noted in the commentary there, the Torah often uses *days* to mean *years.* That Jacob had this understanding is alluded to in verse 20 when the Torah says that these seven years *seemed to him like a few days* [i.e., they were like the *few days* of which his mother had spoken *(Mizrachi).*]

☐ The *Zohar* suggests that Jacob volunteered such a long period of servitude to prove that his desire for the beautiful Rachel was not based on physical lust. Had he felt lust he could not have suppressed his passions for so long.

☐ Perhaps Rachel was still a young child [*R' Bachya* cites a version that she was but five years old at the time!] and Jacob wanted to delay the marriage until she was capable of child-bearing so his relation with her would be fruitful and entirely 'for the sake of Heaven.' Indeed, Reuben was the product of the first intimacy of Jacob's subsequent marriage *(R' Chananel).*

[As noted in the footnote to *v.* 16, however, the most common Rabbinic chronology, based on *Seder Olam,* has Rachel and Leah as 21 or 22 at the time of their marriage.]

☐ Jacob might have volunteered fewer years of service, but he never thought that he could gain such an extraordinary woman for less than such a long period *(Chizkuni).*

☐ Jacob suggested this long waiting period because it was common knowledge that *Leah* had been destined for Esau. Jacob wanted Esau to have sufficient time to come and claim *his* wife, so Jacob would be free to then marry Rachel. What indeed, prevented Esau from coming and marrying Leah? — Leah's tears and prayers [see comm. to *v.* 16, and *Tanchuma* below] *(Tanchuma Yashan).*

☐ *Or HaChaim,* in a mystical interpretation, comments that the righteous Jacob constantly sought to humble himself absolutely [i.e., since the number seven symbolizes completion, seven acts of contusion represents total self-abnegation]. Similarly, Jacob bowed seven times before Esau [33:3]. After such total nullification of self, the righteous man is helped by God as Scripture states, *For seven times the righteous one falls, but he arises* [*Prov.* 24:16].

בְּרָחֵל בִּתְּךָ הַקְּטַנָּה — *For Rachel your younger daughter.*

29
19 you seven years, for Rachel your younger daughter.'
[19] Laban said, 'It is better that I give her to you
than that I give her to another man. Remain with me.'

Because he knew Laban's cunning, Jacob took care to be very explicit, saying [literally]: *Rachel your daughter, the younger.* He said that he would work for *Rachel,* but lest Laban wish to deceive him by substituting another woman named Rachel, Jacob specified *your daughter.* To prevent Laban from deceiving him by changing Leah's name to Rachel, Jacob specified your *younger* daughter. But all these precautions were to no avail; Laban deceived him after all *(Rashi).*

Jacob might have further suspected Laban of changing Zilpah's name to Rachel and substituting her for the bride — for, as the Sages note Zilpah was Laban's youngest daughter by his concubine. However, Jacob did not suspect Laban of stooping *so* low *(Sifsei Chachomim;* see *Maskil l'David).*

Jacob intended that during the seven years Rachel would reach marriageable age and in the interim Laban will be able to find a husband for Leah. This he implied by describing Rachel as *younger:* in seven years time the legitimate needs of the older Leah could be filled and the young Rachel would have matured *(Sforno).*

Furthermore, by הַקְּטַנָּה Jacob implied: *your insignificant* [lit. *small*] *daughter,* the one who is not as precious in your eyes as Leah, seeing that you made her a shepherdess *(Chizkuni).*

Jacob did not ask for Leah because he was afraid that if he married the older daughter [who had originally been destined for Esau], it would provoke Esau to confront Jacob with the claim: Was it not enough that you took my birthright and blessings? Must you take my destined wife as well? *(Tanchuma).*

[The expression רָחֵל בִּתְּךָ הַקְּטַנָּה, *Rachel your younger daughter* has accordingly become idiomatic for 'clearly spelled out terms' of a deal.]

19. טוֹב תִּתִּי אֹתָהּ לָךְ מִתִּתִּי אֹתָהּ לְאִישׁ אַחֵר — *[It is] better that I give her to you than that I [should] give her to another man.*

— Since it was considered preferable to marry one's daughter to a relative *(Radak).*

Possibly the deceitful Laban wished to suggest by this that someone else had sought Rachel's hand in marriage. However, Laban's use of 'give' in this case where Jacob would spend seven years of hard *labor* for her, needs amplification. In retrospect, this implication was part of Laban's cunning, for the trickster implies that he is 'giving' something away when he is in fact selling it as part of a hard bargain. [Compare Ephron's use of *give* in Chapter 23.] Somehow it seems easier to renege on a *gift* than on an *obligation.* Laban intended to 'allow' Jacob to marry Rachel in return for his work; therefore, he avoided implying in any way that a *deal* had been struck in which he was *obligated* to grant Jacob her hand. He would *give* her to *him* instead of to a stranger, but merely out of courtesy; Jacob would not have a legal hold on her. The only assurance Laban intended was that in return for Jacob's service he would give him prime consideration over anyone else when the time came for Rachel's marriage *(Or HaChaim; Malbim* explains similarly).

שְׁבָה עִמָּדִי — *Remain* [or: *abide*] *with me.*

Laban's deceitful, insincere *in-*

שֶׁבַע שָׁנִים וַיִּהְיוּ בְעֵינָיו כְּיָמִים אֲחָדִים
כא בְּאַהֲבָתוֹ אֹתָהּ: וַיֹּאמֶר יַעֲקֹב אֶל־לָבָן
הָבָה אֶת־אִשְׁתִּי כִּי מָלְאוּ יָמָי וְאָבוֹאָה

timation was, 'I agree to your terms: Work for me seven years and I will give you my younger daughter Rachel in marriage'. However, as noted above, Laban never specifically verbalized his *agreement* to the terms; he kept his response vague and open to later reinterpretation. So, when Laban later defended his substitution of Leah by telling Jacob that giving the younger daughter before the elder was contrary to local practice, Jacob could not point to an earlier *agreement* on Laban's part to the contrary; there was, in fact, none *(Alshich; Malbim)*.

Laban's advice was only a stalling tactic, implying: 'Stay with me and work until it is time for her marriage' *(Haamek Davar)*.

20. וַיַּעֲבֹד יַעֲקֹב בְּרָחֵל שֶׁבַע שָׁנִים — *So Jacob worked seven years for* [lit. *in*] *Rachel.*

The Torah repeats *for Rachel* because Jacob constantly let it be known throughout his service that he was working *for Rachel.* He wanted the bargain to be known to all so Laban could not deny their deal later *(Or HaChaim)*.

וַיִּהְיוּ בְעֵינָיו כְּיָמִים אֲחָדִים — *And they seemed to him* [lit. *and they were in his eyes*] *like a few days.*

Like the *few days* his mother had intended *(Mizrachi;* see *Rashi* to *v.* 18).

בְּאַהֲבָתוֹ אֹתָהּ — *Because of his love for her.*

It was only his profound affection for Rachel that permitted Jacob to consider these seven long years as if they were only the *few days* his mother had described; had he not had this great love for Rachel, they would have truly seemed to be the many years that they were *(Mizrachi)*. [See *Overview.*]

... For 'love upsets the rule of normal conduct' [*Sanhedrin* 105b] *(Sforno;* [cf. *Rashi* to 22:3 s.v. וַיַּחֲבֹשׁ]).

In his love for her — Jacob's love for her accordingly exceeded his love for *himself (Machazeh Avraham)*.

Midrash Lekach Tov contrasts this with the afflictive period of Egyptian servitude which the Torah notes were of *'many' days* [*Exodus* 2:23].

The seven years seemed but a few days — because Jacob thought that he should have given an even bigger dowry [i.e. work an even *longer* period of time] for her *(Sforno)*.

Tzeidah laDerech interprets to the contrary, that in Jacob's great love for her, the time went so *slowly* that they seemed like single *days* rather than *years.* Thus, Jacob said later: for my *days* are fulfilled.

21. וַיֹּאמֶר יַעֲקֹב אֶל־לָבָן — [*And*] *Jacob said to Laban.*

After seven years, Laban said nothing; Jacob was forced to approach Laban to remind him of their arrangement *(Ralbag)*.

הָבָה אֶת אִשְׁתִּי כִּי מָלְאוּ יָמָי — *Deliver* [lit. *give*] *my wife* [i.e. the woman we designated to be my wife *(Haamek Davar)*] *for my term is* [lit. *my days are*] *fulfilled.*

29
20-21

[20] *So Jacob worked seven years for Rachel and they seemed to him a few days because of his love for her.*
[21] *Jacob said to Laban, 'Deliver my wife for my term is fulfilled, and I will consort with her.'*

The term of my work is fulfilled *(Onkelos).*

I.e., the term [=the *days*] to which my mother referred [when she sent me to you is now complete. I can procrastinate no longer: I must return home *(Mizrachi; Tzeidah laDerech)*]. Another interpretation: **'my** *days* [i.e., the years of my life] *are full.* I am already 84 years old [Jacob was 63 when he left home+14 years in the Academy of Eber+7 years of service with Laban=84], and unless I marry now I may be too old to have twelve tribes. [Jacob knew prophetically that he would have twelve sons. See *comm.* to 28:16 that it was indicated by the coalescing of the twelve stones.] This is what Jacob meant by adding the seemingly indelicate term וְאָבוֹאָה אֵלֶיהָ, *and I will consort with her* [see below] *(Rashi).*

Ramban (v. 27) objects to both of *Rashi's* interpretations. If Jacob would have asked Laban to let the marriage take place before the seven years were over, he would have to advance reasons such as his mother's wishes or his advancing age. But since, according to *Rashi,* the seven years were over, Jacob required no special indulgence from Laban; he should have said simply, as *Onkelos* renders our verse, *'my term of service is complete,* and I am entitled to my bride.' For, indeed, his fulfillment of the agreement was surely a stronger argument than either Rebecca's wish or his age!

Mizrachi defends *Rashi,* saying that the crafty Laban could invent reasons to delay the marriage even though the seven years were up. Jacob therefore considered it necessary to present his claim to Rachel together with a factor that ruled out any consideration of further delay.

The dispute between *Rashi* and *Ramban* hinges partly on the interpretation of מַלֵּא שְׁבֻעַ זֹאת, *complete this period of seven* [*v.* 27]. *Rashi,* following *Onkelos,* interprets it as *the week of this one,* i.e., the seven days of this bride's marriage feast. However, the word שְׁבֻעַ could also be rendered as *this period of seven* **years,** since it is a collective noun that refers to an indefinite group of seven; what 'seven' means always depends on the context. If so, Jacob's special request in our verse could be understood differently: Jacob had *not* completed his stipulated years of service, but because of his mother's wish or because of his own age, he asked Laban to permit the marriage. Though Laban acquiesced, he nevertheless demanded that before Jacob would be permitted to Rachel in addition to Leah, that Jacob complete *this seven-year period* **of work** [*v.* 27].

In another interpretation, *Ramban* notes that the Torah does not specifically say וַיְהִי בִּמְלֹאות הַיָּמִים, *and it came to pass after the days were fulfilled.* Accordingly, he suggests that Jacob approached Laban in the seventh, and final [calendar] year of the agreement, and asked for his wife. Jacob reasoned that a term which was nearly complete may be considered fulfilled for all practical purposes, and that he could be trusted to continue his service for the remaining days of his obligation. [*Haamek Davar* takes this in the sense that Jacob waited seven 354-day lunar years, while Laban insisted on full 365-day solar years. See also *comm.* to *v.* 27].

Ralbag interprets similarly, that Jacob was married before the conclusion of the seven years. As proof he cites his version of the chronology of years during which Jacob's children were born. (This will be dealt with in the following chapter.) *Abarbanel* insists however that interpretations such as the above take too many liberties with the simple context of the verse, which would seem to indicate that he *did* fulfill the term, and as

כב אֵלֶיהָ: וַיֶּאֱסֹף לָבָן אֶת־כָּל־אַנְשֵׁי הַמָּקוֹם
כג וַיַּעַשׂ מִשְׁתֶּה: וַיְהִי בָעֶרֶב וַיִּקַּח אֶת־לֵאָה
כד בִתּוֹ וַיָּבֵא אֹתָהּ אֵלָיו וַיָּבֹא אֵלֶיהָ: וַיִּתֵּן
לָבָן לָהּ אֶת־זִלְפָּה שִׁפְחָתוֹ לְלֵאָה בִתּוֹ

Rashi interprets, Jacob referred to his advancing years.

וְאָבוֹאָה אֵלֶיהָ — *And I will consort with her.*

[As *Rashi* notes above, Jacob's primary concern was that he was advancing in years]. That is why he added *'I will consort with her'*, for surely even the commonest of people would not use such an expression! Jacob wanted to emphasize that he was intent on begetting offspring [to fulfill his Providential destiny, and not that he was concerned with physical gratification] *(Rashi* following *Midrash).*[1]

— 'Let us proceed directly with the marriage instead of making the customary waiting period after the betrothal,' such was Jacob's urgent desire to acquire the Godly heritage of chilren *(Sforno).*

Or HaChaim writes that Jacob added this seemingly immodest remark to avoid a misapprehension. It would have seemed logical that the valuable labor of seven years would serve as the money which would affect the betrothal. This form of betrothal Jacob could not consider since wages due for services rendered are halachically considered a loan, and loans are not valid for betrothal (see *Rambam, Ishus* 5:20). Therefore, Jacob used the expression, *and I will consort with her* to imply that the betrothal would be consummated by בִּיאָה, *cohabitation,* which is one of the three means of betrothal. [See *Mishnah Kiddushin* 1:1; *Even HaEzer* 28:16; and *Malbim.*]

According to *Ramban* [*v.* 27 (see above)] who holds that Laban gave Leah to Jacob *before* the completion of the seven years. Jacob's statement should be rendered literally וְאָבוֹאָה אֵלֶיהָ, *and I will come to her.* His intent was, 'Do not fear that I will take my bride and leave your service. Rather, *I will come to her,* because I must remain here to complete my term of service. [Accordingly, as *Ramban* explains there, Laban later told Jacob that before he could marry Rachel he must first מַלֵּא שְׁבֻעַ זֹאת, *complete the balance of the seven year term for this* [*wife* i.e., *Leah*] *(v.* 27) and then marry Rachel.]

Abarbanel, too, renders the literal sense: *And I will come to her,* i.e. I will make a home with her *and come home to her* after working in the field, and no longer feel like a boarder in your home.

22. Leah is married to Jacob

וַיַּעַשׂ מִשְׁתֶּה — *And made a feast.*

The *Midrash* notes that *Laban as-*

1. *R' Bachya* explains that Jacob's remark can be considered improper only to the standards of ordinary people, of whom such talk would betray loose morals and a loose tongue. The Patriarchs, however, were above physical lust. They determined their actions by the dictates of their intellect.

To Jacob, cohabitation was not an animalistic act, but the means of fulfilling God's will that he have twelve sons. Similarly, Adam and Eve needed no clothing before their sin, because *all* organs of their bodies were above lust and were dedicated to the service of God.

29
22-24

22 *So Laban gathered all the people of the place and
made a feast.* 23 *And it was in the evening, that he
took Leah his daughter and brought her to him. And
he consorted with her.*
24 *— And Laban gave her Zilpah his maidservant —
a maidservant to Leah his daughter.*

sembled all the people of that place to tell them of his plan to substitute Leah. Laban knew that the Charanite economy had improved drastically since Jacob's arrival. Charan had been plagued with drought, and now all the wells were brimming over. Realizing that this had resulted from Jacob's merit, Laban devised this scheme to force Jacob to spend another seven years there in order to gain permission to marry Rachel whom he loved.

[The term מִשְׁתֶּה, from the verb שתה, *drink*, refers to a feast where wine is served as *Sforno* explains in 19:3 and 21:8].

This wine-feast was but another of Laban's deceitful ploys: He desired to muddle Jacob so that Leah could be substituted unnoticed. Note that he did not make such a feast at the marriage of Rachel since this was not necessary *(Daas Zekeinim).*

Furthermore, the presence of so many people would reassure Jacob that no trickery was being perpetrated and he would not consider it necessary to scrutinize his bride. Additionally, since so many guests would concur in effect, with Laban's later claims that older sisters must be married first, Jacob would be ashamed to divorce her when he realized the deception *(Malbim).*

23. וַיְהִי בָעֶרֶב — *And it was in the evening.*

The word וַיְהִי is often Midrashically interpreted to suggest trouble [וַי הָיָה=וַיְהִי, *there was woe;* see *comm.* to *Esther* 1:1; *Ruth* 1:1]. Here, too, there was an element of tragedy in that evening of deception *(Or HaChaim).*

וַיִּקַּח אֶת־לֵאָה בִתּוֹ וַיָּבֵא אֹתָהּ אֵלָיו — *Then* [lit. *and*] *he,* [=Laban] *took Leah his daughter.*

The phraseology suggests that Leah had no desire to deceive Jacob but Laban *took* her against her will. Or it suggests that he *persuaded* her [this being the Biblical connotation of *take* as explained in the *comm.* to 2:15 and 12:5] *(Or HaChaim).*

וַיָּבֹא אֵלֶיהָ — *And he* [=Jacob] *consorted with her* [i.e., consummated his marriage with her.]

— In sanctity, silence, and in the darkness of night as the laws of modest conduct demand. Thus, he did not recognize her *(Chizkuni; Or HaChaim).*

24. Laban presented Zilpah to Leah on the wedding night *(Radak).*

וַיִּתֵּן לָבָן לָהּ ... לְלֵאָה בִתּוֹ שִׁפְחָה — *And Laban gave* [*to*] *her ... a maidservant to Leah his daughter.*

The Torah interjects this fact because giving Zilpah to Leah on the wedding night played an important part in Laban's scheme to deceive Jacob: Zilpah was younger than Bilhah and should have gone to Rachel the younger daughter.

כה שִׁפְחָה: וַיְהִי בַבֹּקֶר וְהִנֵּה־הִוא לֵאָה
וַיֹּאמֶר אֶל־לָבָן מַה־זֹּאת עָשִׂיתָ לִּי הֲלֹא
בְרָחֵל עָבַדְתִּי עִמָּךְ וְלָמָּה רִמִּיתָנִי:
כו וַיֹּאמֶר לָבָן לֹא־יֵעָשֶׂה כֵן בִּמְקוֹמֵנוּ לָתֵת

That she was presented to the bride was another factor in Laban's deception of Jacob *(Midrash Aggadah).*

The syntax of the Hebrew is difficult, and apparently redundant.

Or HaChaim infers that Bilhah and Zilpah had been the personal maidservant of Laban's late wife and she had bequeathed them, one to Leah and the other to Rachel. Laban, however, in his normally overbearing, deceitful manner, acted as though *he* were their owner and to 'give' Zilpah to Leah as indicated in the first half of the verse. But in reality, the verse goes on to inform us, Zilpah was already Leah's property because her mother had given her *to Leah his daughter as a maidservant.*

R' Hirsch observes that the Torah emphasizes that Laban was careful to give Zilpah לָהּ, *to her, not to Jacob,* but expressly לְלֵאָה, *to Leah* as her own personal property. This has later significance, for when Jacob married Zilpah a few years later, he could have done so only on the initiative of Leah, to whom she belonged.

אֶת זִלְפָּה שִׁפְחָתוֹ — *Zilpah his maidservant.*

As noted in the *comm.* to *v.* 16 Zilpah was Laban's *daughter* by a concubine. Such offspring were commonly referred to as 'maidservants' *(Chizkuni* based upon *Pirkei d'Rabbi Eliezer).*

Her mother had been a maidservant; hence she, too, is called *maidservant (Midrash HaBiur; Torah Sheleimah* note 73).

Zilpah's name was appropriate, for her eyes, too, flowed with tears [מְזַלְּפוֹת דְּמָעוֹת] in sympathy for her mistress, Leah, who had been assumed to be Esau's future bride *(Sechel Tov; Torah Sheleimah* ibid.).

25. וַיְהִי בַבֹּקֶר וְהִנֵּה־הִוא לֵאָה — *And it was, in the morning, that* [lit. *and*] *behold it was Leah!*

— But at *night* she was not [distinguishable as having been] Leah because Jacob had given Rachel a prearranged sign [by which he could always recognize her; see *footnote to v.* 12]. When Rachel saw that they were about to substitute Leah for her, she confided the sign to her so that she would not be put to shame *(Rashi* from *Megillah* 13b).

According to the version in *Eichah Rabbah,* [Proem 14], already before the wedding Rachel had discovered the planned deception and got word of it to Jacob. In order to frustrate Laban's plan, she gave a sign by which he would be able to distinguish between her and her sister Leah. Later, however, Rachel had pity on Leah. She therefore, disclosed the secret signal to her sister so Jacob should think Leah was she. Furthermore, she even hid in the bridal chamber and answered whenever Jacob spoke so that he could not recognize Leah by her voice ... [1]

1. The *Midrash* [*Eichah Rabbah ibid.*] records in this context that when the Temple was destroyed and Israel was exiled, each of the Patriarchs and Moses came to implore God to be compassionate on their sinful descendants for their sake. Each of them related the suffering he had endured without questioning God's justice. But they all failed to stir God's Mercy.

Then the Matriarch Rachel related to God that on her long-awaited wedding night, she sup-

25 *And it was, in the morning, that behold it was
Leah! So he said to Laban, 'What is this you have
done to me? Was it not for Rachel that I worked for
you? Why have you deceived me?'
26 *Laban said, 'Such is not done in our place, to*

מַה־זֹּאת עָשִׂיתָ לִּי — *What is this you have done to me?*

[An incredulous rhetorical outburst, as if to say, 'How could you have perpetrated such a great injustice against me?' Comp. God's similar rebuke to Cain in 4:10; Pharaoh's and Abimelech's to Abraham in 12:18 and 20:9; and to Isaac in 26:10.]

הֲלֹא בְרָחֵל עָבַדְתִּי עִמָּךְ — *Was it not for Rachel that I worked for* [lit. *with*] *you?*

— As I kept making clear throughout my period of service! (*Or HaChaim* to *v.* 20).

Why did you not give me the woman for whom I worked? (*Malbim*).

וְלָמָּה רִמִּיתָנִי — [*And*] *why have you deceived me?*

— Why did you give me the daughter I did not want? (*Malbim*).

Why did you have to accomplish your desire by resorting to deceitful methods; you could have approached me regarding Leah in a rational manner. It is unseemly for a man to marry the woman with whom he will spend the rest of his life, in such an underhanded way (*Or HaChaim*).

26. Laban justifies his wicked act by shifting responsibility. He portrays himself as having been pressured into it because the community or some vague body to which he belongs compelled him to act in this way (*Hoffmann*):

לֹא־יֵעָשֶׂה כֵן בִּמְקוֹמֵנוּ — *Such is not done in our place.*

Our citizenry will not permit it (*Ramban*, end of *v.* 27); the people would not allow me to keep my word [they would prevent me from giving you Rachel, even if I wanted to] (*Sforno*).

According to the *Midrash*, this excuse was false, since, as noted in *v.* 22, the townspeople had agreed to back any course designed to force the continued blessed presence of Jacob. Convinced that their prosperity was dependent on his

pressed her desire and disclosed her secret signal to her sister to spare her from becoming humiliated. She concluded: 'And if I, a creature of flesh and blood, formed of dust and ashes, was not envious of my rival and did not expose her to shame and contempt, why should You, a King Who lives eternally and is Merciful, be jealous of vain idolatry, and exile my children? You have let them be slain by the sword, and their enemies have done with them as they wished!'

Immediately, the mercy of the Holy One, Blessed be He, was stirred, and He said, 'For your sake, Rachel, I will restore Israel to their place.' And so it is written [*Jeremiah* 31:14ff]: ... *A voice is heard in the upper spheres, lamentation and bitter weeping, Rachel weeping for her children, refusing to be consoled for her children for they are gone.*

This is followed by: *Thus said HASHEM, 'Withhold your voice from weeping, and your eyes from tears; your deeds shall be rewarded ... and there is hope for your future', said HASHEM 'and your children shall return to their own border.'* [*Rashi* to *Jeremiah* 31:14 records a slightly different version of the *Midrash.*]

כו הַצְּעִירָה לִפְנֵי הַבְּכִירָה: מַלֵּא שְׁבֻעַ זֹאת
כז וְנִתְּנָה לְךָ גַּם־אֶת־זֹאת בַּעֲבֹדָה אֲשֶׁר

residence among them, they were ready to concur in any tactic chosen by Laban.

The fact that Jacob accepted Laban's excuse teaches that local custom prevails over other conditional arrangements (see *Shach, Choshen Mishpat* 61:4, cf. SMA. See also version in *Yerushalmi Yevamos* 12:1; *Bavli Menachos* 32a). [For additional references regarding marriage to a younger sister before the elder see note to *Torah Sheleimah* 77.][1]

לָתֵת הַצְּעִירָה לִפְנֵי הַבְּכִירָה – *To give the younger* [i.e. in marriage] *before the elder* [or: *firstborn*].[2]

This would be considered a shameful act by them *(Ramban,* ibid.).

Laban said: 'It is the custom in this area, that if someone asks to marry a younger sister, he automatically includes the unmarried elder one, as we do not consider it correct to marry a younger sister before the older one. Therefore, in order to get the younger daughter, one first marries the elder. It's all perfectly in order: After Leah's marriage comes Rachel's' *(R' Hirsch).*

'Do not imagine that I have reneged on my promise to give you Rachel, or that I wished to force you to marry Leah. On the contrary, I have done this in order to *keep my promise* to you regarding Rachel. You see, in our place I cannot give you Rachel until Leah is married. Of course, I could allow someone else to marry her in return for seven years of service, but then you have to delay your marriage to Rachel for seven years because I will not trust another person to keep his promise *after* having married Leah. Thus, by giving you Leah now, I am making it possible

1. Certain halachic ramifications are elicited by the *Poskim* from Laban's remark.

R'vid HaZahav cites a halachic dispute on this matter recorded by the *Tosafists* in *Kiddushin* 52a. A question came before Rabbeinu Tam regarding the son of R' Oshaya HaLevi who betrothed a certain woman by saying to her father, 'Your daughter is betrothed to me,' without specifying *which* daughter. Rabbeinu Tam decided that in any event the *oldest* daughter was thereby betrothed since, as Laban's statement demonstrates, it is improper to marry off a younger child before an older one. Others, however, disagree.

That a *halachah* is derived from the behavior of the devious *Laban* rather than from the example of the righteous Jacob who, in fact, *did* want to marry the younger daughter first, is explained by *Maharsham:* Laban's insistence on not embarrassing his older daughter was purely a matter of נִימוּס וְדֶרֶךְ אֶרֶץ בִּלְבַד, *propriety and etiquette.* It is for this reason that we follow suit.

Similarly, the Sages derived several other laws from Laban: That אֵין מְעָרְבִין שִׂמְחָה בְשִׂמְחָה, *one festive occasion cannot be mingled with another,* is derived in *Yerushalmi Moed Katan* from מַלֵּא שְׁבֻעַ זֹאת, *complete the week of this one (v.* 27), i.e., the marriage of Rachel was to be delayed until Leah's festivities were over. That a maiden is entitled to twelve months to prepare for marriage is derived from תֵּשֵׁב הַנַּעֲרָה יָמִים, *let the maiden remain with us a year*

Similarly, from the fact that Laban had blessed his sister Rebecca prior to her marriage to Isaac [ibid. *v.* 60], the Sages in *Tractate Kallah* derive that bride and groom should be blessed [בִּרְכַּת חֲתָנִים].

It is not surprising, therefore, that the custom of Laban's people to marry off the older daughter first should have been adopted as a Jewish custom in the absence of extenuating circumstances.

2. Some perceive in Laban's emphasis on the qualifying phrase *our place* and on *firstborn* rather than *elder* a snide reference to Jacob's dealing with Esau:

Perhaps in *your* place such things are done, that the younger takes precedence over the firstborn; that his portion is taken away and given to another, and that the younger is given the status of firstborn. But such things are not done *in our place, to give the younger* before the firstborn! *(Maasei HaShem).*

29 27 *give the younger before the elder.* [27] *Complete the week of this one and we will give you the other one*

for you to marry Rachel now *(Malbim).*

[Of course, Laban's pieties were transparently dishonest. He had entered into an arrangement with Jacob without informing him of the local 'custom'. Furthermore, he had had seven years in which to arrange Leah's marriage.]

27. A new agreement is made for Rachel

מַלֵּא שְׁבֻעַ זֹאת — *Complete the week of this one.*

— *The week,* i.e. the seven days of the marriage feast, *of this woman* [Leah] as noted in *Yerushalmi Moed Katan (Rashi).*

Rashi goes on to explain that this translation is demanded by the punctuation, since שְׁבֻעַ is in the construct state: *week of.* Accordingly זֹאת implies: *of this woman.* It could not mean *this* [calendar] *week,* for two reasons: it would then have to be punctuated שָׁבֻעַ, and furthermore since שָׁבֻעַ is masculine the phrase would have had to read שָׁבֻעַ זֶה. Accordingly, the word שְׁבֻעַ which connotes a unit of *seven* [see *Rashi* on *Exodus* 10:22] here refers to *the seven days of the wedding feast* for זֹאת, *this wife.*

[Thus, as is derived in the *Yerushalmi* cited in the footnote to *v.* 26, since two celebrations should not be mixed, Laban directed Jacob to wait until the seven days of feasting for Leah would be completed, and then he could marry Rachel. *Yafeh Toar* observes that though these were the deceitful Laban's words, the *halachah* that אֵין מְעָרְבִין שִׂמְחָה בְשִׂמְחָה, *one period of rejoicing may not be mixed with another,* may still be derived from them, for if they did not conform to the Law, they would not have been included in the Torah.]

Ramban, in a long dissertation, cites *Yerushalmi Kesubos* 1:1 that the seven-day rejoicing period after a marriage feast was an ordinance established by *Moses* [and not introduced by Laban]. He suggests, however, that already in the time of the Patriarchs the custom may have been practiced, as also was the seven-day period of mourning [see 50:10]. And while in the *Yerushalmi* [*Moed Katan* 1:7] and *Midrash* the Sages deduce from *this* incident of Laban and Jacob that two celebrations should not be mixed [see *footnote* to *v.* 26], their deduction is merely a סָמַךְ בְּעָלְמָא, *a Scriptural allusion;* the *halachic requirement,* however, is not deduced from our verse. In our *Gemara, (Bavli, Moed Katan* 9) the Sages derived the halachic requirement not from Laban's statement, but from Solomon's feasts at the dedication of the Temple. He celebrated a total of fourteen days — seven in honor of the new Temple, and seven in honor of Succos [*I Kings* 8:65]. That Solomon did not combine both occasions into a single seven-day celebration is taken to indicate that every period of rejoicing is entitled to the exclusive attention of its celebrants. See *Tosafos ibid.* 8b.

[As noted in the *comm.* to *v.* 21, *Ramban* holds the שְׁבֻעַ in our verse refers to the *seven years of service,* not the seven days of feasting. Thus, according to the interpretations that Laban *claimed* to have — or actually *had* — given him Leah before the expiration of the seven years, his offer in our verse was as follows: Since Jacob had not yet completed the stipulated seven years of service, he should finish that initial period in payment for Leah, then begin a new period in payment for Rachel. Perhaps Laban was intimating a suspicion that Jacob might retaliate for the deception by refusing to work the balance of the seven years.][1]

1. *Malbim* interprets differently: *Complete this week,* i.e., the seven days of feasting, and then be free to marry Rachel by virtue of the years you have *already* worked. As far as Leah is

תַּעֲבֹד עִמָּדִי עוֹד שֶׁבַע־שָׁנִים אֲחֵרוֹת׃
כח וַיַּעַשׂ יַעֲקֹב כֵּן וַיְמַלֵּא שְׁבֻעַ זֹאת וַיִּתֶּן־לוֹ
כט אֶת־רָחֵל בִּתּוֹ לוֹ לְאִשָּׁה׃ וַיִּתֵּן לָבָן לְרָחֵל
בִּתּוֹ אֶת־בִּלְהָה שִׁפְחָתוֹ לָהּ לְשִׁפְחָה׃
ל וַיָּבֹא גַּם אֶל־רָחֵל וַיֶּאֱהַב גַּם־אֶת־רָחֵל

וְנִתְּנָה לְךָ גַּם אֶת זֹאת — *And we will give* [to] *you the other one* [lit. *this one*] *too.*

— Immediately after the seven days of marriage festivities for Leah (see *Rashi below).*

The use of the plural *we* possibly reflects the manner of speakers as if they speak in the name of many [i.e., the so-called plural of majesty; see 1:26 *(Radak)*].

Specifically by using the plural *we* will give, Laban might have been intimating that although marriage to the younger daughter before the elder had the disapproval of the residents of that place since it violated their conventions, this new arrangement regarding marriage to Rachel would have the approval of the entire community: *we will all* take part in the event. We shall all honor you, and give you a banquet as we did at the first wedding *(Ramban).*

As *R' Hirsch* explains, by saying 'we,' Laban tries to make it sound as if his duplicitous proposal was the accepted legal procedure.

The translation of וְנִתְּנָה in first-person plural, synonymous with וְנִתֵּן, *and we will give* follows *Rashi* who cites the similar forms נֵרְדָה, *let us go down,* וְנִשְׂרְפָה, *and let us burn* [11:3,7], the ו being merely conjunctive. *Ibn Ezra* and *Rashbam* interpret the word in the *niph'al* [passive] tense with the ו being conversive — changing it from past to future: And this one too *shall be given* to you.

[*Be'er Yitzchak* suggests that *Rashi* chose this rendering because if it were in the *niph'al,* the accusative article אֶת which always stands before the direct object would be grammatically superfluous (accordingly, most commentators adopt *Rashi's* first interpretation, while *Radak* cites both).]

בַּעֲבֹדָה אֲשֶׁר תַּעֲבֹד עִמָּדִי — *For the work which you will perform for me.*

I.e., *we will give you the other one* [=Rachel] *too* — immediately after the seven days of marriage festivity; — in exchange for the work you will do for me *after* your marriage *(Rashi, Rashbam).*

That Jacob was first given Rachel and *then* worked the additional seven years is clearly corroborated by *v.* 30 *(Mizrachi).*

עוֹד שֶׁבַע שָׁנִים אֲחֵרוֹת — *Yet another seven years.*

[This time it was *Laban* not Jacob who set the term. Because Jacob and Rachel were to be married *before* the work would begin, it was now to Laban's advantage that there be no ambiguities, so he made sure the terms were clearly agreed upon.]

28. Jacob acquiesces.

וַיַּעַשׂ יַעֲקֹב כֵּן — *So Jacob complied* [lit. *and Jacob did so*].

Jacob apparently perceived the hand of Providence. He therefore,

concerned, וְנִתְּנָה לְךָ גַּם אֶת זֹאת, *this one has already been given* (past tense) *to you.* In payment for the marriage which has already taken place, you must give me seven years of work. I would not make such an arrangement with anyone else — but I know you are honest and will keep your word. I am doing this so that you can marry Rachel immediately.

too, for the work which you will perform for me yet
another seven years.'
[28] *So Jacob complied and he completed the week*
for her. And he gave him Rachel his daughter as his
wife for him. [29] *And Laban gave Rachel his daughter*
Bilhah his maidservant — to her as a maidservant.
[30] *He consorted also with Rachel and loved Rachel*

acquiesced to Laban's suggestion, although in normal circumstances he would not have consented to marry two sisters *(Tanchuma;* see footnote, further).

וַיְמַלֵּא שְׁבֻעַ זֹאת — *And he completed the* [bridal] *week for her* [i.e., for Leah].

Following *Rashi;* according to *Ramban:* He completed the *initial* seven years of service.

וַיִּתֶּן לוֹ אֶת־רָחֵל בִּתּוֹ לוֹ לְאִשָּׁה — *And he* [=Laban] *gave him Rachel his daughter as a wife for* [lit. *to*] *him.*[1]

I.e. a woman suitable to be לוֹ לְאִשָּׁה, a wife *to him (Lekach Tov);* a wife who would be his helpmeet in building a home as we find in 25:20 in the case of Isaac and Rebecca. In the case of Leah, however, the expression לוֹ, *to him,* does not appear for she could not be called a wife in the sense of becoming his partner so long as he was not aware of her identity and agreeable to accept her *(Haamek Davar).*

29. **וַיִּתֵּן לָבָן לְרָחֵל בִּתּוֹ ... לָהּ לְשִׁפְחָה** — *And Laban gave* [*to*] *Rachel his daughter ... to her as a maidservant.*

[See comm. to *v.* 24].

אֶת־בִּלְהָה שִׁפְחָתוֹ — *Bilhah his maidservant.*

She was the older of Laban's daughters from his concubine *(Pirkei d'Rabbi Eliezer; see comm.* to *v.* 24).

Her name which incorporates the root בהל, *alarm;* implies that she was *alarmingly beautiful,* or that she was alarmed and distressed [בַּלָּהָה; cf. *Isaiah* 17:14] at her mistress' inability to conceive *(Sechel Tov; Torah Sheleimah* 82).

30. **וַיָּבֹא גַּם אֶל רָחֵל** — *He* [=Jacob] *consorted* [i.e. consummated his marriage] *also with Rachel.*

— As he had with Leah *(Radak).*

וַיֶּאֱהַב גַּם־אֶת רָחֵל מִלֵּאָה — *And* [*he*] *loved Rachel even* [lit. *also*] *more than* [lit. *from*] *Leah.*

The Torah mentions this because

1. The question of how Jacob, who kept the entire Torah before it was given, married two sisters, which is forbidden in *Leviticus* 18:18 is discussed in the commentary to 26:5 on page 1083. [Cf. footnote to 35:19.]

There is a further opinion that Rachel and Leah were considered as גֵּרִים, *proselytes,* and hence all former familial ties were severed. Accordingly, they were not considered sisters in the legal sense, and were permitted to him (*Chizkuni;* cf. *comm.* to 32:5).

There is a reference in *Pesachim* 119b that at the great feast God will make in the World to Come, Jacob will be offered the cup with which to lead the Grace after Meals. He will demur saying, 'I cannot lead because I married two sisters, which is forbidden by the Torah.

Jacob's refusal on those grounds is explained by *Gur Aryeh* to 46:10 to mean that though Jacob might not have been subject to the prohibition, he felt it would be improper for him to lead the Grace at the greatest banquet in the world. [See *Maharsha Pesachim,* ibid.]

מְלֵאָה וַיַּעֲבֹד עִמּוֹ עוֹד שֶׁבַע־שָׁנִים
לא אֲחֵרוֹת: וַיַּרְא יהוה כִּי־שְׂנוּאָה לֵאָה
לב וַיִּפְתַּח אֶת־רַחְמָהּ וְרָחֵל עֲקָרָה: וַתַּהַר

it is common for a man to feel more love for that woman with whom he lived first, just as the Sages observed [*Sanhedrin* 22b] that a woman's primary emotional commitment is to him who marries her first. That Jacob's love for Rachel was an exception to the rule is inferred by the superfluous word גַּם, *even* [which always implies an extension; as if to imply: Though he consorted first with Leah he *still* (גַּם) loved Rachel more] *(Ramban).*

R' Hirsch derives from the phraseology that Jacob loved Leah too, realizing, perhaps that she, like him, may have been deceived by Laban, that she was not a party to any *willful* deception. [See ויקח in *v.* 23.] The verse is telling us that although he loved Leah, *Jacob also loved Rachel* — and indeed — more than Leah. [This is in agreement with *Bereishis Zuta* and *Radak* who explain that the reference in *v.* 31 to Leah's being 'hated' was only in the *relative* sense: it seemed that way compared to Jacob's intense love for Rachel; cf. *Haamek Davar.*]

וַיַּעֲבֹד עִמּוֹ עוֹד שֶׁבַע שָׁנִים אֲחֵרוֹת — *And he worked for him yet another seven years.*

The apparently superfluous word **אֲחֵרוֹת**, ***another,*** is included in order to draw a comparison with the first seven year period: In this second period of seven years he served with the same loyalty as in the first seven, although they were the consequence of deceit *(Rashi).*

31. The Birth of the Tribes

Hoffmann perceives great significance in the alternating use of the Names HASHEM and ELOHIM, representing, respectively, God in His manifestation of Mercy, and in His manifestation as the Judge and as the Ruler of Nature.

When Leah gives birth to her first four sons, the Heavenly gift of children is described as having come from HASHEM, the Attribute of Mercy, in response to Leah's wounded feelings as the less loved wife. On the other hand, when Rachel protested to Jacob concerning her barrenness, he responded that ELOHIM, not he, had deprived her of children. This response must be understood in the light of the Sages' tradition that all the Matriarchs were naturally barren (*Yevamos* 64a; *Bereishes Rabbah* 45:5; *Tanchuma Vayeitzei* 7). Jacob told Rachel that she was no different from Sarah and Rebecca who had likewise been created by the God of nature without the ability to conceive. The implication was that Leah would have been no different had her personal plight not inspired God's mercy.

This theme will be followed through in the commentary as the narrative proceeds:

וַיַּרְא ה׳ — [*And*] *HASHEM saw* [i.e., perceived].

It was only HASHEM Who saw; Leah herself noticed nothing *(Or*

29
31

even more than Leah. And he worked for him yet
another seven years.
31 *HASHEM saw that Leah was unloved, so He*
opened her womb. But Rachel remained barren.

HaChaim), since Jacob was fulfilling his obligation to her in an entirely commendable manner *(Haamek Davar).*

It was in His Aspect of HASHEM — Dispenser of Mercy — that God perceived that insufficient love was accorded Leah *(Hoffmann).*

Rambam in *Moreh Nevuchim* 1:48 explains that the phrase *HASHEM saw* should be anthropomorphically explained as: *It became manifest to HASHEM.*

Ramban, however, interprets it in this context to imply: *God had compassion on her* because she was unloved [see below].

כִּי שְׂנוּאָה לֵאָה — *That Leah was unloved* [lit. *hated*].

Jacob resented the fact that she cooperated with her father's scheme and pretended to be Rachel; she should have let Jacob known whom she was. Indeed, the *Midrash* teaches that he decided to divorce her. God, however, knew that her motivation was pure. She wished to be married to the righteous Jacob *(Ramban).*

Ramban goes on to cite the opinion of *Radak* that *hated* is used in the *relative* sense. Leah noted Jacob's intense love for Rachel (*v.* 30), and in comparison she *felt* hated. Therefore God saw her 'affliction'.

וַיִּפְתַּח אֶת רַחְמָהּ — *So* [lit. *and*] *He opened her womb.*

According to the *Midrash* expounded by *Ramban:* Since God perceived that Leah cooperated in her father's scheme because of her intense desire to marry the righteous Jacob [rather than her destined husband, the wicked Esau (see *v.* 16)], He had compassion on her and gave her children so Jacob would not divorce her. As the *Midrash* states: When the Holy One, Blessed be He, remembered Leah by giving her children, Jacob said, 'Shall I divorce the mother of these children?'.

According to *Radak's* interpretation, God saw Leah's suffering as the less loved wife, and He compassionately gave her children. The expression *He opened her womb* implies that before that act of God, she, too, was barren.

וְרָחֵל עֲקָרָה — *But* [lit. *and*] *Rachel* [remained] *barren.*

The word *'remained'* is not in the Hebrew but its implied presence follows *Radak* who explains that both Leah and Rachel were barren, but God had pity on Leah as explained above. Rachel, however, *remained* barren until God opened *her* womb much later (see 30:22). [*Sforno* interprets similarly.][1]

The Torah mentions this fact

1. Not only Rachel, but all the Matriarchs were naturally barren but finally conceived. Only Leah, for the reason stated, and in *HASHEM's Mercy,* was allowed to conceive soon after her marriage. See *footnote* to page 542; *comm.* to 25:21 and *footnote* to page 1050 for reasons that the Matriarchs were so long barren.

Among the reasons for the Matriarch's barrenness cited in 25:21 from *Yevamos* 64a, is

לֵאָה֙ וַתֵּ֣לֶד בֵּ֔ן וַתִּקְרָ֥א שְׁמ֖וֹ רְאוּבֵ֑ן כִּ֣י

now to prepare us for Rachel's outburst in 30:1 *(Rashbam).*

According to the *Midrash,* the term עֲקָרָה is related to עִיקָּרָה, *the principal* of the household. Even though Leah bore children, רָחֵל עֲקָרָה, Rachel remained the mainstay of the household.

32. Reuben.

וַתַּהַר לֵאָה וַתֵּלֶד בֵּן — [*And*] *Leah conceived and* [*she*] *bore a son.*

Leah conceived — from their first union — *and she bore a son* seven months later *(Midrash).*

The proximity of the two terms וַתַּהַר, *and she conceived,* and וַתֵּלֶד, *and she bore,* indicates the swiftness with which the births took place, after a pregnancy of only seven months. This phrase appears in the case of all the children who were born in Charan [with the exception of Zilpah's pregnancies — see *Rashi* to 30:10]. All those children were born after seven month pregnancies. The exception was Benjamin who was born on the way back to Canaan *(R' Bachya).*

[See 30:17 where the *Tanchuma* notes that whenever the terms וַתַּהַר וַתֵּלֶד appear together, they imply painless childbirth. Just as the conception was painless, so was the birth.]

[The chronology follows chapter 2 of *Seder Olam; Pirkei d'Rabbi Eliezer* chapter 36. Cf. *Yalkut, Exodus* 1.]

Furthermore, *Pirkei d'Rabbi Eliezer ibid.* notes that with each child, a partner [i.e., future wife] was born [they were twins — male and female; see ibid. chapt. 39]. No partner was born with Joseph, for Asenath, Dinah's daughter, was destined to be his wife, nor was a partner born with Dinah.

This follows one opinion in the Talmud [*Sanhedrin* 58b] that marriage to a *maternal* sister is permitted a Noachide [a designation which included even our ancestors before the giving of the Torah]. However, the *halachah* as codified by *Rambam* in *Hilchos Melachim* 9:5 follows the other view; though marriage to a *paternal* sister was permitted a Noachide, marriage by a Noachide to his *maternal* sister was prohibited. See *Rashi* to 20:12. On this *Midrash* regarding marriage of the tribal ancestors to twin sisters, see *comm.* to 37:35 and 38:2 where *Ramban* advances the opinion that the intent was that the sons of Leah married the twin sister of the other children.

וַתִּקְרָא שְׁמוֹ רְאוּבֵן — *And she named him* [lit. *called his name*] *Reuben* [literally meaning *'see a son.'*]

— *See* the finely built, clever *son* that the Holy One, Blessed be He, has given me! *(Pirkei d'Rabbi Eliezer).*

[The first reason for the name is as given by the Torah; *For* HASHEM

'Because the Holy One, Blessed be He, longs to hear the prayer of the righteous,' i.e., because such prayers publicize the efficacy of prayer. God therefore gives them cause to pray so He can miraculously and publicly fulfill their requests.

Malbim here takes the view that *Leah* was destined to be the barren sister, but since she was the unloved one, Jacob presumably would not have prayed for her. Accordingly, God's purpose in causing the Matriarchs to be barren — to evoke the prayers of their righteous husbands — would have been negated. He therefore, opened *Leah's* womb and let Rachel remain the barren one.

29 *[32] Leah conceived and bore a son, and she named*
32 *him Reuben, as she had declared, 'Because HASHEM*

has seen my humiliation. Similarly, the Torah gives reasons for all the names Leah gave her other children. The Sages, however, perceived deeper significance in this name which Providence placed in her mouth and which was appropriate to Reuben's destiny]:

The Sages interpreted Reuben's name to mean: רְאוּ בֵין, *see between.* Leah [prophetically] declared: *See* the difference *between* my son and the son of my father-in-law [i.e., Isaac's son Esau] who sold his birthright to Jacob [voluntarily, and yet later hated him (27:41)] whereas my son did not [voluntarily] sell his birthright to Joseph [see below], but he did not complain concerning his loss. Moreover, he even tried to save Joseph from the pit [see 37:21]. [As the firstborn, Reuben should have had the distinction of being considered *two* tribes. However, *because Reuben defiled his father's couch* (see *comm.* to 35:22) his birthright was given to the sons of Joseph (*I Chron.* 5:1) with the result that Ephraim and Menashe became separate tribes (*Rashi* from *Berachos* 7b).][1]

The *Vilna Gaon* explains why the Sages *(ibid.)* offered a new interpretation of Reuben's name, but did not feel compelled to do so for the other names. He explains that it is the custom of Scripture to state a reason or cause, and *then* to state the result. For example, in the case of Simeon, Leah first said that HASHEM had heard her despair, then she gave the name which alluded to God's response. In Reuben's case, the name is given before the reason. This prompted the Sages to infer that the name was based upon some cause in addition to that given later in the verse *(Kol Eliyahu).*

Torah Temimah notes that of all the names of Jacob's children, the Sages in the *Talmud* interpret only Reuben's name. He explains that Reuben's name appears to have particular significance because, according to the reason Leah gave: *Because HASHEM saw my humiliation,* the name should have been *Reu-anyi.* Therefore, the Sages sought an additional prophetic interpretation of the name Reu-ben [see *Maharsha*].

כִּי אָמְרָה — *As she had declared.*

Usually, the future conversive is used: וַתֹּאמֶר. The past-perfect כִּי אָמְרָה, as she *had* said [which is how *R' Hirsch* renders the phrase] might imply that *already during pregnancy* Leah had said that her imminent childbirth proved that HASHEM saw her affliction and vindicated her *(Daas Soferim).*

1. *The Halachah* is clear that בְּנֵי תְמוּרָה, children born of a union during which the husband thought of another woman — even another one of his wives — are considered blemished.

Since Jacob thought he was with *Rachel* the first night, why was Reuben not included in this blemished category?

Magen Avraham to *Orach Chaim* 240:2 explains that this applies only to a case where one's mind is on one person and he consummates the act with another. In the case of Jacob, however, he saw Leah at the wedding ceremony and his intention was focused on the woman he married, but he thought that her name was Rachel. Thus, his case was distinct from one who thought of anyone other than the woman whom he knew to be with him.

אָמְרָה כִּי־רָאָה יהוה בְּעָנְיִי כִּי עַתָּה
לג יֶאֱהָבַנִי אִישִׁי: וַתַּהַר עוֹד וַתֵּלֶד בֵּן
וַתֹּאמֶר כִּי־שָׁמַע יהוה כִּי־שְׂנוּאָה אָנֹכִי
וַיִּתֶּן־לִי גַּם־אֶת־זֶה וַתִּקְרָא שְׁמוֹ שִׁמְעוֹן:
לד וַתַּהַר עוֹד וַתֵּלֶד בֵּן וַתֹּאמֶר עַתָּה הַפַּעַם
יִלָּוֶה אִישִׁי אֵלַי כִּי־יָלַדְתִּי לוֹ שְׁלשָׁה

כִּי רָאָה ה׳ בְּעָנְיִי — *Because* [i.e., I am giving him this name because] *HASHEM has discerned my humiliation* [following *Onkelos;* others render *affliction, suffering*].

— God saw *my humiliation* in that my husband suspected me of *willfully* deceiving him that night. Thus, by granting me children [of that very same union] God vindicated me, as it were *(Sforno).*

Leah specifically acknowledges that this child — as well as the next — was granted her by God in His Attribute of HASHEM — the Dispenser of Mercy *(Hoffmann).*

In the case of her second child, Leah later declares that HASHEM *heard* that she was unloved, while here, speaking of her humiliation, she uses the term *saw* which describes the perception of something more substantial. Leah's feelings of rejection before the birth of Reuben were so plain that they could be *seen.* That she remained relatively *unloved* until the birth of her second child was more *subtle* — the condition could only be *heard* [in the tone of Jacob's voice] (*Tanchuma;* see *Kli Yakar v. 33).*

As *R' Hirsch* explains, the successive names show how Jacob's attitude toward Leah became increasingly loving with each child she presented him. At first רָאָה ה׳ בְּעָנְיִי, *HASHEM has 'seen' my humiliation,* because Jacob's preference for Rachel was so obvious that it was visible. With the birth of Reuben, that degree of preference dissipated, but Leah detected in the tone of Jacob's voice to Rachel, that she, Leah, still did not possess Jacob's full love, so sne called her second son: Simeon, from the verb שמע, *hear.*

Emphasizing how the names of the tribes prognosticated the destiny of her descendants, *Targum Yonasan* adds: For my affliction has been manifested before God as will be the affliction of my children before God when they shall be enslaved in the land of Egypt.[1]

1. The name of each tribe incorporates a reference to Israel's redemption. [The *Midrash* cites only nine names, however]:

Reuben recalls the verse [*Exodus* 3:7]: *I have surely seen* [=רָאֹה רָאִיתִי] *the affliction of My people;*

Simeon [=Shimon] — *God heard* [=שָׁמַע] their groaning [*Exodus* 2:24];

Levi — *And many nations shall join themselves* [=נִלְווּ] *to HASHEM* [*Zech.* 2:15];

Judah [=Yehudah] — *And in that day you shall say, 'HASHEM, I will praise* [=אוֹדְךָ] *You'* [*Isaiah* 12:1];

Dan — *But also upon the nation which they shall serve will I execute judgment* [=דָן] [*Gen.* 15:14];

Naftali — *sweetness drips* [=תִּטֹּפְנָה] *from your lips* [*Song of Songs* 4:11];

Gad, recalls the Manna, described as being like coriander [=גַד] seed [*Numbers* 11:7];

Asher, recalls the redemption — And all *the nations shall call you fortunate* [=ואשרו] [*Malachi* 3:12];

Joseph — *And it shall come to pass in that Day that HASHEM shall set His hand again* [=יוֹסִיף] *the second time to recover the remnants of His people* [*Isaiah* 11:11.]

has discerned my humiliation, for now my husband will love me.'

33 *And she conceived again and bore a son and declared, 'Because HASHEM has heard that I am unloved, He has given me this one also.' And she named him Simeon.*

34 *Again she conceived, and bore a son and declared, 'This time my husband will become attached to me for I have borne him three sons.'*

כִּי עַתָּה יֶאֱהָבַנִי אִישִׁי — *For now my husband will love me.*

— As much as he loves my sister *(Radak).*

It is axiomatic that when one has two wives, God will cause the less beloved wife to bear the first son. This will draw her husband's love to her because the firstborn son is the one who performs God's service [as was done before the *Kohanim* were appointed], and this will cause his father to exult, as *Abarbanel* explains in *Deuteronomy* 21:15: *and the firstborn is hers that is hated (Kli Yakar).*

— *God has seen my humiliation* and vindicated me; does it not follow that עַתָּה יֶאֱהָבַנִי אִישִׁי, *my husband will now love me? (Ralbag).*

The *pasach* vowel under the ב [instead of the more usual form: יֶאֱהָבֵנִי] is similar to the vowelization of תִּדְבָּקַנִי [above, 19:19] *(Ibn Ezra);* and יַבְדִּילַנִי [*Isaiah* 56:3] *(Radak).* [Cf. *HaKsav V'HaKabbalah.*]

33. Simeon

וַתַּהַר עוֹד וַתֵּלֶד בֵּן — *[And] she conceived again and bore a son.*

He was born within the following seven months *(Seder Olam).*

וַתֹּאמֶר כִּי שָׁמַע ה׳ כִּי שְׂנוּאָה אָנֹכִי — *And declared, 'Because HASHEM has heard that I am unloved.'*

Although Leah had hoped that her husband would *love* her because of Reuben's birth [*v.* 32], now that she again referred to herself as *unloved* she apparently realized that she had been wrong. The very fact that God gave her a *second* child before Rachel gave birth to her *first* indicated to her that she was still hated. She was unaware of it, but שָׁמַע ה׳, *HASHEM* — Who searches the innermost recesses of the heart — *'heard' it* and responded with this child *(Kli Yakar,* cf. *Or HaChaim).*

וַיִּתֶּן לִי גַּם אֶת זֶה — *[And] He has given me this one also.*

To make me more beloved to my husband and eradicate any last traces of ill feeling he might have had toward me *(Kli Yakar).*

וַתִּקְרָא שְׁמוֹ שִׁמְעוֹן — *And she named him Simeon.* [Hebrew *Shim'on,* from the root שמע, *to hear.*]

Just as You heard that I was hated and You gave me this child, so may You hear the prayers of my descendants when they are enslaved in Egypt *(Targum Yonasan).*

34. Levi.

עַתָּה הַפַּעַם יִלָּוֶה אִישִׁי אֵלַי — *This time my husband will become attached* [Hebrew *yilaveh,* literally: *will join; escort;* or: *will become associated*] *to me.*

— In a bond of affection stronger

לה בָּנִ֑ים עַל־כֵּ֥ן קָרָֽא־שְׁמ֖וֹ לֵוִֽי׃ וַתַּ֨הַר ע֜וֹד

than the one with my sister (Radak).

The intent is that his *principal dwelling* will now be with me (*Heidenheim*).

— The Matriarchs were prophetesses and knew that Jacob was to beget twelve tribes by four wives.[1] Now that Leah had three children she said, 'Now my husband will have no cause for complaint against me, for I have given him my full share of children' (*Rashi*).

— Now she emphasized the *positive* aspect of her relationship with her husband and expressed her hopes for *full* recognition (*Ralbag*).

With the birth of her third son, she was confident that her relationship with Jacob would henceforth be one of pure, undiluted love. This concept is expressed by the name Levi which is related to לְוָיָה, *association*, and לוֶה, *debtor*. When two people are ideally attached to one another, each feels indebted to the other for his happiness and very life. The significance of this attitude is pointed up by the fact that Jacob himself conferred the name as the verse clearly states: קָרָא, *he*, called (*R' Hirsch*) [see *comm.* below].

— This time my husband will be united to me because I have borne him three sons; so may my children be united to serve God (*Targum Yonasan*).

According to the *Zohar*, it was a known tradition that only *one* of Jacob's wives would be buried along with him in the Cave of Machpelah. Her outburst here reflected her joy at the prognostication that since she bore three sons [before any of the others], now her husband will be joined to *her*, and it would be *she* of Jacob's wives who would share eternal repose alongside him in the Cave of Machpelah.

[The verb לוה in its meaning of *join, be joined*, occurs often in Scripture. Compare its various connotations, for example, in *Ecclesiastes* 8:15 יִלְוֶנּוּ; *Esther* 9:27 נִלְוִים; *Isaiah* 56:3 הַנִּלְוָה אֶל ה׳, *joined to HASHEM*. As *R' Hirsch* explains above, the cognate verb meaning *borrow* accordingly refers to the fact that the borrower considers himself *beholden* to the lender.]

כִּי יָלַדְתִּי לוֹ שְׁלֹשָׁה בָנִים — *For I have borne him three sons.*

— And the righteous take wives in order to have children (*Radak*).

Now that I have borne three children, I established that I am capable of bearing many, for, as the Sages said [*Bava Metzia* 106b]: A presumption [*chazakah*] is established when it occurs three times and this will ensure that my husband will cleave to me (*Sforno*).

עַל־כֵּן קָרָא שְׁמוֹ לֵוִי — *Therefore He named him Levi.*

In the case of the others it is stated *she called*, while here the tense is masculine: *He called*. The subject here is God. The *Midrash*

1. Actually, of all the Matriarchs, only Sarah is listed in the *Talmud* [*Megillah* 14a] among the seven prophetesses. That *Rashi* describes *all* the Matriarchs as prophetesses is no contradiction. The Talmudic list includes only those who were prophetesses to society; however, there were many others — the Matriarchs among them — who prophesied in matters that concerned themselves and their families (*Maharshal*).

Maharsha ibid. cites Rebecca as an example of this rule. Although not a prophetess, she was credited with a momentary surge of Divine Inspiration as explained in the *comm.* to 27:45 s.v. לָמָה אֶשְׁכַּל.

Torah Temimah, however, cites *Midrashic* opinions — for example *Yerushalmi Berachos* 9:5; *Midrash Shocher Tov* 105; *Seder Olam* 21 — which maintain that the Matriarchs *were* prophetesses.

29 34 *Therefore He named him Levi.*

Devarim Rabbah states that God dispatched Gabriel to bring the infant before Him, whereupon God named him Levi because his offspring would be *'escorted'* throughout history by the twenty-four priestly gifts. [These gifts include various sacrificial gifts and tithes which are given by Israel to the *Kohanim*, the offspring of Levi] *(Rashi).*

— And *this* child, not the firstborn Reuben, would accordingly be endowed with the role of performing God's service *(Or HaChaim).*

Kli Yakar raises the point that the Midrashic reason is at variance with the one stated by the verse. He explains that, in the days when the Divine service was performed by the firstborn, parents felt a special pride in their firstborn sons, a pride that would express itself in an attachment to the mothers who had borne them. As noted above, Reuben was to lose this privilege as a result of his future behavior. The performance of this service would be conferred upon Levi with the result that Jacob would feel indebted to Leah, mother of the tribe.

According to those who pursue the *simple* meaning of Scripture [e.g. *Radak, Rashbam, Abarbanel, R'Hirsch* (see above) *Malbim*] *'he'* refers to *Jacob* who acquiesced to Leah's declaration and in acknowledgment, named the child Levi.

As *Radak* explains: Jacob named him in accordance with Leah's wish because he rejoiced in the birth of Levi. It may also be that Jacob saw prophetically that Levi's offspring would be servants of God and teachers of the Torah, and as such, would be attached to God.

Thus, as the *Midrash* notes, the name *Levi* signifies that he was destined to 'lend' [*l'lavos* — the *hiphil* conjugation of the root of Levi] his sons to the service of their Heavenly Father. [Alternate translation: He was destined to *escort* his children to their Heavenly Father.]

Rashi, citing the *Midrash*, notes that all those sons in connection with [whose naming] Scripture uses the expression עַל כֵּן, *therefore,* became very populous tribes. Levi was an exception because the Ark consumed so many [of the Levites who were careless in safeguarding its holiness when they carried it in the wilderness *(Gur Aryeh)*] *(Rashi).*

[Cf. also incident with Uzza in *II Samuel* 6:6-7.]

The expression עַל כֵּן was used in connection with three tribes: Judah, Dan, and Levi. Judah and Dan were, indeed, the most populous of the tribes at the time of the Exodus, but Levi was small even then (see *Numbers* Ch. 2 and 3). *Gur Aryeh* explains that there were two factors in the great population growth of the Jews in Egypt: the normal blessing of God, because of which Levi, too, grew out of proportion to normal expectations; and a special blessing in response to Pharaoh's attempts to deplete the Jewish population through enslavement. Levi was not included in this second blessing because the tribe never volunteered for servitude. Therefore, had Pharaoh not attempted to kill Jews, Levi, Judah, and Dan would have been the largest of the tribes. As it was, Levi still grew at a far greater than normal rate.

Sefer HaParshiyos adds that *Rashi's* comment concerning the death of Levites can apply only to the family of Kehas which carried the holiest parts of the Tabernacle.

Harav David Feinstein notes that the population figures in *Numbers* would seem to contradict *Rashi's* assertion that the labors around the Tabernacle depleted the Levites. In *Numbers* 3:39, the population of the tribe is given as 22,000 while forty years later, it stood at 23,000 (ibid. 26:62). *Harav Feinstein*

וַתֵּלֶד בֵּן וַתֹּאמֶר הַפַּעַם אוֹדֶה אֶת־יהוה
עַל־כֵּן קָרְאָה שְׁמוֹ יְהוּדָה וַתַּעֲמֹד
א מִלֶּדֶת: וַתֵּרֶא רָחֵל כִּי לֹא יָלְדָה לְיַעֲקֹב

submits that since only the Kehasites died from carelessness around the Tabernacle, we may assume that *that* family decreased during the forty years while the Levite families of Gershon and Merari grew in accordance with the blessing accruing to the tribe of Levi.

Torah Sheleimah cites a version in *Bereishis Rabbah* that this exegesis refers only to those places where it says עַל כֵּן קָרְאָה, therefore *'she called'*, a formula which occurs only in the case of Judah and Dan, both of whom were, indeed, populous.

35. Judah.

הַפַּעַם אוֹדֶה אֶת ה׳ — *This time let me gratefully praise* [Hebrew *odeh*, related to *Yehudah*] HASHEM.

Because [with the birth of this, Jacob's *fourth child*] *I have had more* than my share [inasmuch as I have borne him more than a quarter of the twelve tribes he is destined to beget (see *Rashi v.* 34)]. I should henceforth thank HASHEM *(Rashi);* [bracketed additions are from the *Midrash*].[1]

— Because His bounty suffices me, and I will desire no more *(Ibn Ezra).*

The *Talmud* [*Berachos* 7b] mentions that 'from the day the Holy One, Blessed be He, created His world, no man praised Him until Leah came and praised Him.' [See *Maharsha* and *Torah Temimah*].

With the birth of the three previous sons, she considered how each would benefit her personal situation. By now she was secure in her position in the household — she could now enjoy her new baby for

1. As cited in the *Overview* to ArtScroll Ruth [page xxxvii], *Rashi* explains that when Leah gave birth to her fourth son, she gave *special* thanks because God had given her more than her share. That is why Jews are called *Yehudim* (implying that they are descended from Judah) no matter what tribe they belong to. Even Mordechai, a Benjaminite, is referred to in *Megillas Esther* as *Morechai haYehudi.* We are Yehudim because we always thank God for giving us *more* than our share, *more* than we deserve. The Jew is ever conscious of the graciousness and mercy of God. To him, health, prosperity — life itself — are never his by right; he thanks God for everything, for it is all an undeserved gift *(Chiddushei HaRim* in *Sefer haZechus).*

The strength of Judah lay in his readiness to be a willing receptacle of God's talent, blessing, and responsibility while ascribing nothing to himself. His very name indicates this quality. The Hebrew spelling of Judah's name, יְהוּדָה, contains the sacred four-letter name of God — plus one more letter, a ד, *dalet.* The word דַּל, *dal,* in Hebrew means a pauper. Judah has within himself the majesty of his Creator; his kingship is no less than the kingship, in a mortal guise, of God Himself, — but in his own eyes, Judah remains דַּל, a pauper. No matter how exalted his position, whatever he has is an undeserved gift of God.

David, first of the Judean kings and model for all his successors, embodies the same concept in his name. It begins with *dalet* and ends with a *dalet.* For all his grandeur and achievement, for all the love his Maker bore for him and the holiness that made even the blood of his war victims seem like holy offerings before the altar of God, David, from beginning to end, considered himself a pauper, an impoverished mortal who carried only the gifts of God, but nothing of his own. The future Mashiach is described by Zechariah as עָנִי וְרוֹכֵב עַל חֲמוֹר, *a poor man riding a donkey.* He will finally fulfill the purpose of creation by bringing the Kingdom of Heaven to earth and by crowning God as King of all mankind — but he is a pauper riding the humblest of domestic beasts of burden.

Such kings represent the final stage of revelation. They are themselves but an embodiment of God's will on earth *(Sfas Emes, Vayigash).*

29
35

[35] *She conceived again, and bore a son and*
declared, 'This time let me gratefully praise
HASHEM.' Therefore she named him Judah. Then she
stopped giving birth.

30
1

Rachel saw that she had not borne children to
Jacob, so Rachel became envious of her sister. She

its own sake. She exclaimed, 'Now I can thank God for the gift of a child' — and she named him accordingly *(R' Hirsch)*.

This time will I give praise before God; from this son, kings shall descend and from him shall spring King David who will offer praise to God *(Targum Yonasan)*.

עַל־כֵּן קָרְאָה שְׁמוֹ יְהוּדָה — *Therefore she named him Judah* [Hebrew: *Yehudah*.]

— Which contains letters referring to HASHEM's Name as well as to 'thankfulness' and 'praise' *(Sforno*; see footnote).

וַתַּעֲמֹד מִלֶּדֶת — *Then she stopped [from] giving birth.*

For the following interim period. This was part of the Divine scheme, in order to allow even the maidservants to bear Jacob's children *(Radak)*.

[The commentators note that our verse seems to link her expression of thanksgiving with the cessation of her childbearing, as if the thanks was the *cause* of the cessation.]

Ibn Ezra comments that her thanks contained the implication that she was satisfied to have given birth to four sons and desired none more. Her lack of desire to participate further in the building of Israel caused her to be punished by being temporarily denied further children.

Abarbanel goes further, commenting that she had already achieved her purpose of being loved by Jacob, and felt no need for more children.

Others give more universal reasons for this occurrence:

— *Maor VaShemesh* comments that whenever one thanks God for past benefits, he should also pray for continued Heavenly goodness, lest he imply that he no longer needs God. Leah failed to do so with the result that she ceased to conceive.

— The *Chozeh of Lublin* comments that the time to give thanks does not come while God's blessings continue to flow. While the blessing is in progress, one should accept it. The time for thanks is when God *completes* the blessings. By thanking God prematurely, Leah indicated that she wanted no further blessing.

XXX

1. Jacob marries Bilhah.

וַתֵּרֶא רָחֵל כִּי לֹא יָלְדָה לְיַעֲקֹב — [And] *Rachel saw that she had not borne [children] to Jacob.*

וַתְּקַנֵּא רָחֵל בַּאֲחֹתָהּ — *So* [lit. *and*] *Rachel became envious of her sister.*

[Although envy is a prohibited trait, the *Midrash* explains that

ויצא
ל/ב

וַתְּקַנֵּא רָחֵל בַּאֲחֹתָהּ וַתֹּאמֶר אֶל־יַעֲקֹב
הָבָה־לִּי בָנִים וְאִם־אַיִן מֵתָה אָנֹכִי:
ב וַיִּחַר־אַף יַעֲקֹב בְּרָחֵל וַיֹּאמֶר הֲתַחַת
אֱלֹהִים אָנֹכִי אֲשֶׁר־מָנַע מִמֵּךְ פְּרִי־בָטֶן:

Rachel's envy was wholesome and laudable:] She envied Leah's *good* traits thinking, 'Had Leah not been more righteous than I, she would not have deserved to bear children' *(Rashi).*

הָבָה־לִּי בָנִים – *Give me children.*

I.e., Pray on my behalf! *(Ibn Ezra).*

[She attributed her barren state to Jacob's failure to pray for her as Isaac did for Rebecca:] Did your father act this way toward your mother? Did he not pray on her behalf? *(Rashi).*

Rachel intended this remark to urge Jacob to implore God even more vigorously than he might have already been doing; that he should fast, don sackcloth and ashes, and persist in prayer until she would be granted a child ... Furthermore, her implication was that the matter was up to *him,* for Jacob was of no lesser stature than his father who had successfully implored God to end his wife's barrenness *(Ramban,* verses 1 and 2).

וְאִם־אַיִן מֵתָה אָנֹכִי – *Otherwise* [lit. *and if not*], *I am dead.*

'If you do not pray and gain children for me, I will remain childless and be regarded as dead.' Knowing of his love for her, she sought to goad him by frightening him with her death from grief *(Ramban).*

From this description it is learned that he who is childless may be regarded as dead *(Rashi).*[1]

The *Midrash* [see *Yafeh Toar; Akeidas Yitzchak*] continues: Jacob tried to console her by explaining that only the *wicked* are regarded as dead if they are childless since they leave nothing positive behind them after their death. When someone like Rachel is childless, however, her good deeds are considered her offspring. But Rachel was not comforted, and continued her pleas.

Her remark is to be understood in the same spirit as that of the eunuch who says [*Isaiah* 56:3]: *Behold I am a dry tree (Sforno).*

The word מֵתָה, *dead,* is accented on the second syllable and is in the present tense with a future connotation: *I will be considered* [*as*] *dead.* In 48:7, however, where the accent is on the first syllable, the connotation is past tense: מֵתָה עָלַי רָחֵל, *Rachel died on me (Rashbam).*

[In many *Chumashim,* however, the cantillation of מֵתָה in 48:7 is erroneously over the ה: in correct editions following the Mesorah, however, there is a double cantillation over both the מ and ה, with a Masoretic marginal note that the *first* syllable is to be accented indicating the past tense. See *Minchas Shay.*]

2. וַיִּחַר־אַף יַעֲקֹב בְּרָחֵל – *Jacob's anger flared up at Rachel.*

Jacob was angered by her

1. The Sages [*Nedarim* 64b; *Midrash*] taught that four may be regarded as dead: The leper, the blind, he who is childless, and he who is impoverished.

Rashi cites the latter three in our Sidrah: the blind in 28:13 s.v. וֵאלֹהֵי יִצְחָק; the childless here; the impoverished in 29:11 s.v. וַיֵּבְךְּ. That a leper may be regarded as dead is derived from *Numbers* 12:12.

30

2

said to Jacob, 'Give me children — otherwise I am dead.'

2 *Jacob's anger flared up at Rachel, and he said, 'Am I instead of God Who has withheld from you fruit of the womb?'*

implication that it was in his absolute power as a righteous man to assure her children, and by her improper tactics in attempting, like a spoiled wife, to frighten him with her death *(Ramban).*

Radak and *Sforno* similarly suggest that he was angered by her insinuation that *he* had God-like power to grant her children. In his zeal for the honor of God, he disregarded his love for his wife. Had she said, 'Pray for me,' *Radak* continues, her request would have been quite valid and Jacob would not have been provoked to anger.

According to *Or HaChaim* Jacob's anger was aroused because Rachel uttered a curse against herself by saying she would die unless she could give birth. Even in such subtle ways, a righteous person's remarks are effective. (See 31:32 regarding Jacob's curse and how it later affected Rachel.) This is why the verse adds בְּרָחֵל, *at Rachel,* i.e., Jacob's anger at her remark was intended for her own sake, to spare her from the result of her careless remark.

[That a righteous person's *unintentional* prognostications can be fulfilled as if by prophesy is discussed in the *footnote* on pages 1164-5 citing the dictum from *Moed Katan:* בְּרִית כְּרוּתָה לִשְׂפָתַיִם, *a covenant has been made with the lips.*]

The phrase וַיִּחַר אַפּוֹ is idiomatic and metaphorically means *and his nostrils flared. Rashi* in *Exodus* 15:8 explains that this expression is used to describe *fierce anger* since, when one is angry, the nostrils flare up and become 'hot.' Conversely, when one's anger subsides, he is described as נִתְקָרְרָה דַעְתּוֹ, *his mind became cooled.*

The word וַיִּחַר, from the root חרה [adj. חָרוֹן] has several connotations. *Rashi* in *Numbers* 16:15 explains it as meaning *grief, annoyance* (נִצְטַעֵר מְאֹד). *Onkelos* to *Exodus* 15:7 renders the term וּתְקֵיף לֵיהּ, *and he became angered. Rashi* to *Exodus* 15:8 explains the root חרה to denote *burning,* hence *heated anger* [see below]. *R' Hirsch* to *Gen.* 4:5 similarly renders *burnt,* denoting 'irritation by something we consider unfair.'

Generally speaking, the anger described as חֲרוֹן אַף, *flared up anger* [or burning wrath] or אַף, *anger,* refers to outwardly displayed vexation, while terms such as חֵמָה, *burning wrath,* describe the harsher, deepseated but repressed *inner* anger. [See *Radak Shorashim; Ibn Janach; Malbim* to 27:45.]

הֲתַחַת אֱלֹהִים אָנֹכִי אֲשֶׁר־מָנַע מִמֵּךְ פְּרִי־בָטֶן — *Am I instead* [following *Rashi;* lit. *beneath*] *of God Who has withheld from you fruit of the womb?*

There are several connotations here:

Why do you complain to *me.* Am *I* to blame for your condition? Am I in God's place? It is *He* not I, *Who has withheld children from you!* Moreover, *I* am not the barren one — it is from *you* that God withheld children, not from me; I already have children *(Radak; Abarbanel; Malbim).*

[Continuing the dialogue

ג וַתֹּאמֶר הִנֵּה אֲמָתִי בִלְהָה בֹּא אֵלֶיהָ
וְתֵלֵד עַל־בִּרְכַּי וְאִבָּנֶה גַם־אָנֹכִי מִמֶּנָּה׃

recorded in the *Midrash*]:

You say that I should do as my father did [and pray on your behalf]. But I am unlike my father: He had no children at all [therefore his prayer for himself was efficacious (see *Ramban* below)]; but *I* have children. God has withheld children from *you* — not from me *(Rashi)*.

Within the context of this Midrashic dialogue cited by *Rashi*, *Ramban* wonders at Jacob's response and remarks: Do not the righteous pray on behalf of others? Elijah and Elisha prayed even on behalf of strange women! [*I Kings* 18:2; *II Kings* 4:33].

Ramban concludes, therefore, that on account of this insensitive response the Sages took Jacob to task, stating in the *Midrash:* The Holy One, Blessed be He, said to Jacob, 'Is this the way to answer an aggrieved person? By your life! Your children [by your other wives] are destined to stand humbly before her son Joseph!'[1]

Ramban goes on to suggest that Jacob undoubtedly prayed for her, but his prayer had gone unanswered. Accordingly, Jacob's 'anger' was meant to admonish her for her improper outburst, and to emphasize that the righteous have no *absolute* power that their prayers would be answered, regardless of any other considerations. Accordingly, it was not in *his* power to grant her children but in God's, since *He* had withheld children from her. Moreover, Jacob wanted to stress that her reference to Isaac's prayers was inappropriate; Isaac's prayer had to be heard because he was destined to have children, whereas Jacob already had children so it was unlikely that his prayer would be answered. Furthermore, it was from *Rachel* that God withheld children.

... The result, *Ramban* concludes, was that the righteous Rachel went to pray on her own behalf. This is implied by *v.* 22: *And God listened to* **her**.

Similarly, we do not find that Elkanah prayed on behalf of Hannah. Presumably the reason was the same: he already had children by Peninah, so Hannah had to pray on her own behalf [*I Samuel* chapt. 1.]

Rashi discards the literal translation *Am I 'beneath' God?* because *all* people are indeed beneath God. Therefore, he renders *am I instead of God (Devek Tov)*.

1. Several answers are offered to *Ramban's* question:

— *Mizrachi* contends that prayer is appropriate only to fill a void: one may pray for something he lacks or that someone else lacks. However, one cannot pray for something which he *has*. In the case of Jacob and Rachel, any offspring granted to her by God would be Jacob's child as much as hers. Therefore, Jacob, who already *had* children of his own, could not properly pray as if he were a childless person begging God to fill a void in his life. *Nimukei Shmuel*, however, objects to *Mizrachi's* limitation on the efficacy of prayer commenting: 'Is God's power limited?' Rachel assumed that she was capable of bearing children, but that God had decreed that she not do so.

— *Maaravi* comments that Jacob knew prophetically that he would have a total of twelve sons no matter who their mothers would be. For him to pray that *Rachel* have children would be, in effect, a request that the privilege of giving birth to them should be taken away from other potential mothers. It is improper to pray for one person at the expense of another.

— *Divrei David* suggests that she pleaded with Jacob to pray that God rescind His *decree*. Jacob replied that it was not a case of a *decree* at all, rather she lacked the *physical capability* of conceiving and carrying a child. In that case, Jacob's prayer would be tantamount to asking God to create a new being. That is not ordinarily within a *tzaddik's* power.

30
3

[3] *She said, 'Here is my maid Bilhah, consort with her that she may bear upon my knees and I too may be built up through her.'*

The *Shaloh,* however, explains the connotation of *am I beneath God?* to be: Am I then in *Eretz Yisrael* which is considered directly 'beneath' God in merit, that my prayers should be answered, as were those of Abraham and Isaac whose prayers *were* offered in the Holy Land? It is not *my* fault that my many prayers on your behalf have gone unanswered!

3. הִנֵּה אֲמָתִי בִלְהָה — *Here is my maid Bilhah.*

— According to the *Midrash,* Rachel's offer was preceded by the following dialogue continued from above. Rachel said:

'[You say your circumstances are unlike your father's because your father had no children.] But your grandfather Abraham already *had* children from Hagar and yet he *girded his loins* [i.e., actively interceded to pray] on Sarah's behalf!'

Jacob answered, '[Then do as my grandmother did.] My grandmother took a rival wife into the house.'

'If that is the only impediment,' Rachel said, *'Here is my maid, Bilhah, consort with her ... and I, too, may be built through her,* just as Sarah was built through her maidservant.' *(Rashi;* [bracketed additions are from the *Midrash*]*).*[1]

The Hebrew term אָמָה, *maid,* which Rachel used for Bilhah is more delicate than the term שִׁפְחָה [*maidservant; slavewoman*] which Sarah used of Hagar. This was because, as noted in 29:29, Bilhah was Rachel's half-sister, Laban's daughter by a concubine *(Baal HaTurim).*

בֹּא אֵלֶיהָ — *Consort with her* [i.e. *marry her* (see on 16:2).]

וְתֵלֵד עַל־בִּרְכַּי — *That* [lit. *and*] *she may bear upon my knees.*

[This is a figurative expression meaning] *and I* will *rear* [the children she will bear] *(Onkelos; Rashi).*

וְאִבָּנֶה גַם־אָנֹכִי מִמֶּנָּה — *And I, too, may be built up through her.*

The word *too* implies: *just as Sarah was built through her maid-*

1. Actually, we find it nowhere explicitly stated that Abraham prayed for a child through Sarah after Ishmael was born. In fact the reverse seems to have been the case: When given the news that the covenant would be maintained by the son whom *Sarah* would bear, Abraham exclaimed, 'O that Ishmael might live before you!' [17:16-31].

Gur Aryeh suggests that it is axiomatic that the righteous Abraham prayed for such a son, since God would not have granted such an unsolicited favor. If God granted him a son through Sarah, Abraham *must* have strongly desired it and prayed for it though it is not recorded in the narrative [Compare *Gur Aryeh* to 2:5 where he explains that no rain fell on earth before Adam existed since there was no one to appreciate it, 'and it is prohibited to bestow a favor on one who will not apprecieate it.' God therefore waited for man to recognize the need and pray for rain. Only then did He grant it.]

Sefer HaZikaron suggests that Abraham's prayer might be *alluded* to in the expression [17:3] *Abram fell upon his face,* which immediately precedes God's promise of Isaac. [*Rashi* there, however, explains that Abraham literally *fell* to the ground since he was uncircumcised and unable to stand in God's Presence.]

R' David Cohen suggests that since the reason our Matriarchs were barren was, 'because the Holy One Blessed be He longs to hear the prayers of the righteous,' [*Yevamos* 64a], it is axiomatic that Abraham prayed for his barren wife.

ד וַתִּתֶּן־לוֹ אֶת־בִּלְהָה שִׁפְחָתָהּ לְאִשָּׁה
ה וַיָּבֹא אֵלֶיהָ יַעֲקֹב: וַתַּהַר בִּלְהָה וַתֵּלֶד
ו לְיַעֲקֹב בֵּן: וַתֹּאמֶר רָחֵל דָּנַנִּי אֱלֹהִים וְגַם
שָׁמַע בְּקֹלִי וַיִּתֶּן־לִי בֵּן עַל־כֵּן קָרְאָה
ז שְׁמוֹ דָּן: וַתַּהַר עוֹד וַתֵּלֶד בִּלְהָה שִׁפְחַת
ח רָחֵל בֵּן שֵׁנִי לְיַעֲקֹב: וַתֹּאמֶר רָחֵל

servant Hagar (Rashi; see above).

According to *Radak* and *Sforno*, the implication is: *'I, as well as my sister ...'*

The experience may stimulate me to normal bearing *(Sforno).*

The expression אִבָּנֶה, *I may be built,* is the same expression used by Sarah under similar circumstances in 16:2. The translation *built up* follows *Rashi* there, that since a childless person may be regarded as demolished, the reward of earning God's compassion by bringing a rival into the house will be that one will be 'built up' by having children.

Most others, however, [see *Rambam* to *Mishnayos Nazir* 2; *Ibn Ezra*] interpret אִבָּנֶה as a play on the word בֵּן, *son,* and render: And I too *may have children* through her. For, as *Midrash Sechel Tov* explains, in ancient times the servant bore and the mistress raised the child and was regarded as its mother.

4. וַתִּתֶּן־לוֹ אֶת־בִּלְהָה שִׁפְחָתָהּ לְאִשָּׁה – *So* [lit. *and*] *she gave him Bilhah her maidservant as a wife.*

Rachel *freed* her, so she would become his *full* wife in order that there should be no trace of servitude in Jacob's progeny as would have been the case had any of the children been born of a maidservant *(Zohar; Targum Yonasan)* [See on *v.* 5: וַתֵּלֶד לְיַעֲקֹב, *and she bore to Jacob.*]

5. וַתַּהַר בִּלְהָה – [And] *Bilhah conceived.*

[See comm. of *Heidenheim* cited to 16:4, page 542.]

וַתֵּלֶד לְיַעֲקֹב בֵּן – *And bore* [*to*] *Jacob a son.*

In the case of all the maidservants, it is emphasized that they bore a son *to Jacob* to indicate that he desired those children and acknowledged their status as equal to his sons. [This is evidenced by the blessings he gave them before his death, treating everyone with full equality. Also, these children, like those of Leah and Rachel, produced leaders and judges *(Radak)*]. The same phrase is used also of Leah's fifth and sixth sons [verses 17 and 19] to emphasize that though she had borne many children, Jacob nevertheless desired and befriended all of them; for this reason this phrase is not used in connection with the earlier children [of *Leah* since it is *obvious* that Jacob desired and showed affection to them] *(Ramban).*

Sforno compares the attitude of Rachel and Leah with that of Sarah. Because God would declare that only Isaac could be considered Abraham's spiritual heir, Hagar was

4 *So she gave him Bilhah her maidservant as a wife*
and Jacob consorted with her. 5 *Bilhah conceived and*
bore Jacob a son. 6 *Then Rachel said, 'God has judged*
me, He has also heard my voice and has given me a
son.' She therefore named him Dan.
7 *Bilhah, Rachel's maidservant conceived again*
and bore Jacob a second son. 8 *And Rachel said,*

not set free even after marrying Abraham [see 16:3]. In the case of Jacob's family, however, the sons of Bilhah and Zilpah would be of equal status with the others. Therefore, Rachel and Leah did not want them to bear the stigma of subservience.

6. Dan.

וַתֹּאמֶר רָחֵל — *Then* [lit. *and*] *Rachel said.*

— [Bilhah had borne the child, but it is accounted to Rachel, so it is she who gives the name as she did in the case of Bilhah's second child in verse 8. Similarly, in the case of Zilpah's children in verses 11 and 13, it is Leah who names them.]

דָּנַנִּי אֱלֹהִים — *God has judged me.*

[The verb דון, *judge*, has the connotations of *find guilty* or *vindicate. Rashi,* following the *Midrash,* takes the word here in both senses:]

He originally judged me and found me guilty [causing me to be barren; He judged me again] and vindicated me [and listened to my voice] *(Rashi.* Brackets are from the *Midrash).*

Thus, according to *Gur Aryeh's* interpretation of *Rashi's* exegesis, the connotation of דָּנַנִּי is entirely positive: Although God had *previously* found me guilty as evidenced by my barren state, *now He vindicated me* and gave me children.

Be'er Yitzchak questions the above interpretations in the light of the superfluous וְגַם, *and also,* He suggests that *Rashi's* Midrashic exegesis takes דָּנַנִּי here only in its usual sense of *guilt:* דָּנַנִּי אֱלֹהִים, *God had judged me as guilty* and made me barren; then subsequently — וְגַם, *and also* שָׁמַע בְּקוֹלִי, *He listened to my voice* and vindicated me. As a result, He *has given me a son* [through my maidservant] *(Hirsch* renders similarly).

וְגַם שָׁמַע בְּקֹלִי — [*And*] *He has also heard* [*in*] *my voice.*

I.e., he accepted my prayer (see *Sforno* above).

[Literally: 'heard *in* my voice' — i.e., God heard the *inner* intent and the justice of my pleas (based on *Haamek Davar's* comment to בְּקוֹלָהּ in 21:12).]

Sforno interprets: God was righteous in his judgment by not granting me a child, וְגַם, *but nevertheless,* שָׁמַע בְּקֹלִי, *He accepted my prayer.*

וַיִּתֶּן־לִי בֵּן — *And* [He] *has given me a son.*

— One to whom I can be at least a *spiritual* mother. Although I am not his natural mother, I can care for him and raise him as my contribution to Jacob's family *(R' Hirsch).*

עַל־כֵּן קָרְאָה שְׁמוֹ דָּן — *She therefore named him Dan.*

[See footnote end of 29:32].

On the phrase עַל־כֵּן signifying abundant progeny see *Rashi* to end of 29:34.

7. Naftali.

וַתֵּלֶד בִּלְהָה שִׁפְחַת רָחֵל — *And Bilhah, Rachel's maidservant, bore.*

Although Rachel freed her [*v.* 4], the Torah still refers to her *as*

נַפְתּוּלֵ֨י אֱלֹהִ֧ים ׀ נִפְתַּ֛לְתִּי עִם־אֲחֹתִ֖י גַּם־
ט יָכֹ֑לְתִּי וַתִּקְרָ֥א שְׁמ֖וֹ נַפְתָּלִֽי׃ וַתֵּ֣רֶא לֵאָ֔ה
כִּ֥י עָֽמְדָ֖ה מִלֶּ֑דֶת וַתִּקַּח֙ אֶת־זִלְפָּ֣ה
שִׁפְחָתָ֔הּ וַתִּתֵּ֥ן אֹתָ֛הּ לְיַעֲקֹ֖ב לְאִשָּֽׁה׃

Rachel's maidservant to suggest that Bilhah continued to treat her still childless mistress with respect. She was unlike Hagar who, after having a child, began to hold her still childless mistress in low esteem *(Haamek Davar).*

8. נַפְתּוּלֵי אֱלֹהִים נִפְתַּלְתִּי עִם־אֲחֹתִי — *Sacred schemes have I maneuvered to equal my sister.*

The phrase is difficult and open to several interpretations. The translation attempts to reflect the sense of *Rashi's own* interpretation below.

Rashi first cites the view of the grammarian *Menachem ben Seruk* who explains נַפְתּוּלֵי as derived from the root פתל [meaning *bound together*] as in the phrase [*Numbers* 19:15]: צָמִיד פָּתִיל, a cover *tightly bound.* Our verse would accordingly be rendered: נַפְתּוּלֵי אֱלֹהִים, [*with*] *Godly bonds* נִפְתַּלְתִּי עִם אֲחֹתִי, *have I been bound with my* sister [Leah, i.e., put on an equal plane with her] to merit children [through Bilhah].

Rashi disagrees, and as reflected in our translation prefers to render it in the sense of עִקֵּשׁ וּפְתַלְתּוֹל, *crooked and twisted* [*Deut.* 32:5], Rachel's intent being:

'I have attempted every possible scheme to influence God to grant me children as He did my sister' [Rachel prayed, blamed Jacob, sought to intimidate him with the threat of her literal or figurative 'death,' and finally gave him Bilhah.] She refers to these varying attempts to influence God as 'schemes and maneuvers.'

Rashi goes on to cite the view of *Onkelos* who explains the term to mean תְּפִלָּה, *prayer,* as if it read: נַתְפּוּלֵי אֱלֹהִים נִתְפַּלְתִּי. *Onkelos* renders the sense of Rachel's declaration: God accepted my supplication when I prayed with desirable prayers that I have a child like my sister.

Rashi rejects both *Menachem's* and *Onkelos'* interpretations because according to *Menachem,* the phrase *and I prevailed* is superfluous, while according to *Onkelos,* one must rearrange the letters in נַפְתּוּלֵי to נַתְפּוּלֵי for the purpose of interpretation, a practice *Rashi* prefers to avoid in elucidating the *simple meaning* of Scripture *(Tzeidah laDerech; Maskil l'David).*

Ibn Ezra also takes the word in the sense of *twisted* but with the connotation of *struggled, wrestled, contested.* He renders our verse: *With struggles to God have I struggled with my sister.* The reference to *God* suggests either that it was in *honor of God* that she gave her maidservant, or that God assisted her in her struggle.

Radak renders similarly but explains that *God* in this context is merely the Hebrew idiom for the superlative, the connotation being: *Enormous struggles.* When Scripture wishes to emphasize something's size or importance it idiomatically attaches God's Name to the noun, as in [*Jonah* 3:3]: עִיר־גְּדוֹלָה לֵאלֹהִים, *an enormously large* [lit. *large to God*] *city;* [*Psalms* 36:7: הַרְרֵי־אֵל, *enormously high mountains* [lit. *mountains to God*].

Abarbanel renders: *Struggles, O God have I struggled,* etc.

A sacred 'wrestling competition' did I

30 *'Sacred schemes have I maneuvered to equal my*
9 *sister, and I have also prevailed!' And she named him*
Naftali.
[9] *When Leah saw that she had stopped giving birth*
she took Zilpah her maidservant and gave her to

wage with my sister: for the sacred privilege of having a share in building Jacob's family, I struggled to be on an equal footing with my sister *(R' Hirsch).*

Malbim, like *Menachem* cited above relates נַפְתּוּלֵי to *Numbers* 19:15 פָּתִיל, *tightly bound,* but explains it to refer to matters that are shut off from human understanding: Divine mysteries. Thus, נַפְתּוּלֵי אֱלֹהִים, *Divine secrets* נִפְתַּלְתִּי, *have been hidden from me* עִם אֲחֹתִי, *regarding my sister.* — Why does she have children and not I?

Sforno renders: With Godly, sacred cleaving did I cleave to my husband עִם אֲחֹתִי, *together with my sister,* since we *both* gave Jacob our handmaids to facilitate the birth of the twelve sons whom Providence destined for him.

[According to *Sforno,* therefore, Leah had given Zilpah to Jacob before Naftali was born to Bilhah. His chronology is based on the tradition *(Seder Olam; Pirkei d'Rabbi Eliezer)* that eleven sons and Dinah were born during Jacob's second seven-year period of service. Accordingly, *Sforno* assumes that Leah gave her maidservant to Jacob *before* Naftali was born. Otherwise, if the sequence of the chapter is followed literally, there would be insufficient time — following *Sforno's* interpretation — for normal pregnancies. Such an interpretation presents no difficulty, since it is axiomatic that the Torah does not necessarily record events in sequential order. Cf. *'Jacob's Children'* in *comm.* to *v.* 24.]

גַּם־יָכֹלְתִּי — *And I have also prevailed.*

— I.e. He has yielded to my importunities *(Rashi)* [by granting me a child through my maidservant.]

I have attained my intentions by giving my maidservant to my husband *(Sforno).*

R' Hirsch: I have been able to do it. By giving Bilhah to Jacob I have come as close as possible to being the mother of part of Jacob's family.

According to *Malbim,* render: *And I endured them* [my predicament and lack of understanding] joyfully, for God is righteous.

וַתִּקְרָא שְׁמוֹ נַפְתָּלִי — *And she named him Naftali.*

[See *footnote* end of 29:32.]

9. Jacob marries Zilpah.

וַתֵּרֶא לֵאָה כִּי עָמְדָה מִלֶּדֶת — *When* [lit. *and*] *Leah saw that she had stopped giving birth* [as noted in 29:35].

— And that in the interim Rachel had had two children by her maidservant *(Alshich)*...

וַתִּקַּח אֶת זִלְפָּה שִׁפְחָתָהּ — [*And*] *she took Zilpah her maidservant.*

Leah who had children of her own did not have Rachel's motive for giving her maid to Jacob, nor is it plausible for a woman to want her husband to take another wife. Therefore, we must conclude with the *Midrash* [see *comm.* to 29:34] that the Matriarchs were prophetesses who knew that Jacob was destined to have twelve sons. Leah gave Jacob her maidservant so the majority of the children would be from her and her maidservant who was subject to her. This was her implication further in verse 18 — that God had given her her reward because she gave her maidservant to Jacob [i.e., her willingness to endure the anguish of maintaining a rival wife in her

י וַתֵּלֶד זִלְפָּה שִׁפְחַת לֵאָה לְיַעֲקֹב בֵּן:
יא וַתֹּאמֶר לֵאָה °בָּגָד וַתִּקְרָא אֶת־שְׁמוֹ גָּד:
יב וַתֵּלֶד זִלְפָּה שִׁפְחַת לֵאָה בֵּן שֵׁנִי לְיַעֲקֹב:
יג וַתֹּאמֶר לֵאָה בְּאָשְׁרִי כִּי אִשְּׁרוּנִי בָּנוֹת

° בָּא גָד

house earned her the merit of bearing another child.] Jacob also knew that he was destined to have twelve sons, and therefore he agreed to marry Zilpah.

... Furthermore, Jacob took many wives to increase his progeny because he was aware that the 'fourth generation' [see 15:16] had to return and take possession of the Promised Land. Therefore, Leah gave him her maidservant so that he would not wed a stranger *(Ramban).*

10. Gad.

וַתֵּלֶד זִלְפָּה שִׁפְחַת לֵאָה – *Zilpah, Leah's maidservant bore.*

Of Zilpah, it does not say וַתַּהַר *and she conceived* [i.e. *became pregnant*] as it does of the others, because she was the youngest of them all – a mere child whose pregnancy was not noticeable. Laban had given her to Leah in order to further deceive Jacob into thinking that Leah was Rachel, the younger sister, as noted in the *comm.* to 29:24 *(Midrash; Rashi).*

I.e., because of her youth, the early months of her pregnancy were not recognizable through missed menstrual cycles, and it was not until her last months that she became *obviously* pregnant *(Yafeh Toar).* [Or because of her youth one would attribute her changed physiognomy not to *pregnancy,* but to weight gain, or other natural symptoms of developing maturity. Furthermore, pregnancy does not affect a vigorous young girl as it does an older woman.]

On her designation here as *maidservant* though she had been freed, see on *v.* 7.

לְיַעֲקֹב בֵּן – [*To*] *Jacob a son.*

[See *Ramban* cited to this phrase in *v.* 5.]

11. בָּגָד – *Good luck has come!* [Hebrew: *bagad,* in assonance with the name Gad.]

I.e. an unexpected piece of luck has come. This son was one which Leah could not have expected under usual circumstances. Only Rachel's example had given Leah the idea of giving her maidservant to Jacob which led to the birth of Gad *(R' Hirsch).*

The translation follows *Rashi* who, following the *Mesorah,* treats בָּגָד as composed of two words: בָּא גָד. He cites the Talmudic meaning of גָּד as *luck* [*Shabbos* 67b], and its use in *Isaiah* 65:11: לַגַּד, *for fortune.* [*Targum Yonasan, Rashbam,* and *Radak* render similarly.]

Rashi continues that the word has the Midrashic connotation of *cut down* (as in *Daniel* 4:11 גֹּדוּ), and implies that he *came* (i.e., was born) *already cut-down,* i.e., he was born circumcised.

According to the version in *Tanchuma* [*Noach* 5], seven major Scriptural figures were born already circumcised: Adam, Seth, Noah, Jacob, Joseph, Moses, Job. *Avos d'Rabbi Nosson* [ch. 2] lists: Job, Adam, Seth, Noah, Shem, Jacob, Moses, Balaam, Samuel, David, Jeremiah, Zerubabel. *Rashi's* exegesis which includes Gad in this category appears in *Midrash Aggadah.*

Jacob as a wife. [10] *Zilphah, Leah's maidservant bore*
Jacob a son. [11] *And Leah declared, 'Good luck has*
come!' So she named him Gad.
[12] *Zilpah, Leah's maidservant bore a second son to*
Jacob. [13] *Leah declared, 'In my good fortune! For*
women have deemed me fortunate!' So she named

Ibn Ezra also interprets בָּגָד as composed of two words בָּא גָד, just as בָּבֶל, *Babel,* is composed of בָּא בֵל, *confusion has come* [see 11:9 where בל is defined as a form of בלל. Cf. the word בָּנו = בָּאנו, *we came,* in *I Sam.* 25:8].

However, *Ibn Ezra* interprets גָּד as derived from גְּדוּד, *troops,* our phrase accordingly meaning: *a troop has come,* i.e. now I have many children — a *troop,* as it were.

The traditional *reading* [*k'ri*] of the word is בָּא גָד, *ba gad.* Thus it is interpreted as two words: גָּד, *gad (luck* or the other interpretations cited above) בָּא, *has come,* since in Scripture the primary interpretation of a word follows its reading. The traditional *spelling* [*k'siv*], however, is one word בָּגָד, *bagad=treachery, faithlessness.*

Rashi concedes that he does not understand why the two words are traditionally spelled as one. However, he proceeds to cite an interpretation which accounts for the one-word written form: בָּגָד, which means *faithless:* [Leah told Jacob], 'You have been faithless to me, the wife of your youth, by accepting my maidservant. [You should have refused her since I was already the mother of several children.]'

וַתִּקְרָא אֶת־שְׁמוֹ גָּד — *So* [lit. *and*] *she named him Gad.*

[See *footnote* end of 29:32.]

12. Asher.

שִׁפְחַת לֵאָה — *Leah's maidservant.*

In contrast with Hagar, Zilpah continued to treat her mistress in a respectful manner. Thus, although Leah had freed her and she had already borne a child, the Torah continues to refer to her as Leah's *maidservant.* As indicated above [30:4,7], Bilhah behaved similarly *(Haamek Davar).*

13. בְּאָשְׁרִי כִּי אִשְּׁרוּנִי בָּנוֹת — *In my good fortune! For women* [lit. *daughters*] *have deemed me fortunate.*

I.e., this son represents another instance of the good fortune about which the women have been praising me (*Rashbam; Ibn Ezra; Sforno*).

Thus, the expression בְּאָשְׁרִי should be interpreted in the same spirit as בָּגָד — in this case, בָּא אָשְׁרִי, *my good fortune has come (Yohel Or).*

Unlike Sarah or my sister, I did not *have* to bring a rival wife into my home. That I did so even though I had children of my own, is בְּאָשְׁרִי, *to my great fortune,* since *the women will praise me for it (Akeidas Yitzchak).*

R' Hirsch explains אשר in the sense of *progress* [see his *comm.* to אַשְׁרֵי in *Psalms* 1:1]: Just as the births of my own children demonstrated my progress to personal happiness, so do the births of my ex-maidservant prove that I am still progressing toward that goal. The women have praised me for this progress as represented by the birth of these children.

Targum Yonasan perceives that this child will be praised in the

°רביעי יד וַתִּקְרָא אֶת־שְׁמוֹ אָשֵׁר: °וַיֵּלֶךְ רְאוּבֵן
בִּימֵי קְצִיר־חִטִּים וַיִּמְצָא דוּדָאִים בַּשָּׂדֶה

future for the good fruit which will grow in his portion of *Eretz Yisrael* [see 49:20].

וַתִּקְרָא אֶת שְׁמוֹ אָשֵׁר — *So* [lit. *and*] *she named him Asher.*

[See *footnote* end of 29:32.]

14. The dudaim.

The incident of the *dudaim* is one of the most puzzling in the Torah. It is filled with questions we cannot answer: What were the *dudaim?* Why were they so important to Rachel, Leah, and Reuben? Why did the Torah devote so many verses to an affair whose meaning eludes us?

It is clear beyond doubt that this chapter is filled with mysteries and secrets of the Torah. Of other verses, it is *axiomatic* that human intelligence is capable of only a superficial understanding of God's word; of the verses of the *dudaim,* it is *obvious* beyond doubt, for the Sages and commentators found many teachings in these cryptic verses.

Nevertheless, although we cannot comprehend them fully, we accept the privilege and responsibility of attempting to expound what we can, and acknowledge that the rest is a Divine mystery *(Sefer HaParshiyos).*

וַיֵּלֶךְ רְאוּבֵן בִּימֵי קְצִיר־חִטִּים — [*And*] *Reuben went out in the days of the wheat harvest.* — In Sivan [late spring].

According to *Sforno,* Reuben *deliberately* went out in quest of the *dudaim* which were believed to have fertility-inducing powers (see below. He wanted them for his mother, Leah, because he perceived that she was grieving over the cessation of her childbearing activity [*v. 9*].

Perhaps Reuben had overheard the popular, but false notion, that the herb induced fertility, and so he went out in search for them *(Radak).*[1]

The story of the *dudaim* is told in praise of Jacob's children. Although it was harvest time when mature wheat and barley were abundant, Reuben did not touch private property. Instead, he brought home only wild *dudaim* about which no one is concerned *(Midrash; Rashi).*

This lesson is further indicated by the fact that he found these *dudaim* בַּשָּׂדֶה, *in the field,* implying that they grew wild and were not taken from *private* property *(Malbim).*

וַיִּמְצָא דוּדָאִים בַּשָּׂדֶה — [*And*] *he found dudaim in the field.*

[The Hebrew word *dudaim* refers to a fragrant plant (see *Song of Songs* 7:14) the *exact* identity of which is lost to us. Since a *definitive* translation of the term is impossible, we have merely *transliterated,* not translated the term.]

1. There are various chronologies regarding the birth of the tribes. According to *Midrash Lekach Tov,* followed by *Tzemach David* and *Shalsheles HaKabbalah,* Reuben found the flowers in Sivan 2197 when he was *four* years old.

[The above is certainly the prevailing Rabbinic view inasmuch as the Rabbinic chronologies agree that all of Jacob's children except Benjamin were born in the seven year period of servitude to Laban. Since Leah had two more children after this incident of the *dudaim,* Reuben could not have been more than five and a half years old at the time.]

30 *him Asher.*
14 [14] *Reuben went out in the days of the wheat harvest. He found dudaim in the field and brought*

Rashi defines *dudaim* as a plant: סִיגְלֵי [=violets (ויאול״ש) see *Rashi* to *Sanhedrin* 99b, and *Shulchan Aruch Orach Chaim* 216:8], which is called *jasmine* in Arabic.

[This follows the view of Levi in *Sanhedrin* 99b].

Ramban differs from *Rashi's* identification of the Rabbinic term סִיגְלֵי *(violets)* with the Arabic *jasmine*. He maintains that *jasmine* is also the *Rabbinic* name for sesame seeds as mentioned in *Shabbos* 50b. It is quite distinct from סִיגְלֵי *(violets)* mentioned in *Berachos* 43b, which is a fragrant herb for the smell of which one recites the blessing בּוֹרֵא עִשְׂבֵי בְשָׂמִים, ... *who created fragrant herbs.* Furthermore, the season of jasmine is not during the *wheat harvest.* With regard to the last objection, however, [*Rashi* would possibly maintain that] Reuben found them growing by chance, out of season.

Mizrachi attempts to defend *Rashi's* interpretation, claiming that some *distinguish* between the Arabic and Talmudic plants named jasmine. The Arabic jasmine is the Aramaic סַמְלָק, *jasmine,* while the Talmudic jasmine, mentioned in *Shabbos ibid.* is a sesame ointment, as *Rashi* explains there. Further, *Mizrachi* suggests a possible scribal error in the text of *Rashi.* Accordingly, *Rashi's* comment should read not סִיגְלֵי, but סַמְלָק, which *Rashi* interprets as the Arabic *jasmine.*

[See *Berachos* 43b where these two terms are mentioned as *different* plants requiring different blessings. *Rashi* there interprets סַמְלָק as *jasmine,* and סִיגְלֵי as *violets,* an interpretation which is clearly at odds with our texts of *Rashi* in *Chumash* (the text upon which *Ramban* bases his comment) where *Rashi* interprets סִיגְלֵי as *jasmine.*

The *Gilyon HaShass* in *Berachos* ibid. takes note of this discrepancy. See *Sifsei Chachomim* to *Berachos* ibid, who cites the *Aruch* where it is suggested that the Arabic designation *jasmine* on s.v. סַמְלָק was originally a marginal note, not in *Rashi's* text. See also *Kaf HaChaim, O. Ch.* §216:8.

Furthermore, *Rashi's* primary comment in our verse that *dudaim* are סִיגְלֵי, *violets,* follows, as noted, one view in *Sanhedrin* 99b. Thus, *Mizrachi's* textual emendation would negate this citation, and as *Maharsha* ibid. comments, such textual emendation would necessarily require other emendations throughout the *Talmud* itself, certainly an impractical solution. The difficulty remains unreconciled.]

Ramban proceeds to suggest that it is best to follow *Onkelos* who, as does *R' Chiya* in the *Midrash* translates *dudaim* as יַבְרוּחִין, [commonly, but only conjecturally defined as *mandrakes,* a plant that was reputed in Oriental lands to have magical powers. See below]. These are known as *yavruach* in Arabic. [The above also follows the primary view in *Sanhedrin* 99b.]

According to *Ibn Ezra,* who agrees with *Onkelos'* interpretation of יַבְרוּחִין [*mandrakes (?)*], the species were very fragrant, as mentioned in *Song of Songs* 7:14. They resemble the human form, and some maintain that they are an aid to pregnancy, although *Ibn Ezra* questions their efficacy on medicinal grounds.[1]

Ramban makes the same observation as *Ibn Ezra* and adds that if *dudaim* do indeed promote conception as some claim, it may be in the manner of a charm, not by its *natural* quality.

In any event, *Ramban* insists that

1. [However, the legends attributing magical properties to the plant identified by some as mandrakes, are widespread. Josephus in *Wars* 7:183 refers to a plant having medicinal properties which was uprooted by tying a dog to its roots. The animal pulling them out, im-

וַיָּבֵא אֹתָם אֶל־לֵאָה אִמּוֹ וַתֹּאמֶר רָחֵל
אֶל־לֵאָה תְּנִי־נָא לִי מִדּוּדָאֵי בְּנֵךְ׃
טו וַתֹּאמֶר לָהּ הַמְעַט קַחְתֵּךְ אֶת־אִישִׁי
וְלָקַחַת גַּם אֶת־דּוּדָאֵי בְּנִי וַתֹּאמֶר רָחֵל

Reuben brought only the fragrant *fruit* of the *dudaim,* not the stem which supposedly has these magical powers. No potion was involved. Rather, Rachel desired them only for the delight of their fragrance, for Rachel was blessed with children through prayer, not by medicinal methods.

It would accordingly seem that it is the Biblical intention to emphasize that *dudaim* do *not* possess these reputed powers, and that conception and childbirth are a Divine gift as is clearly set forth in verses 17 and 22 which mention *God heeding* **their prayers**. See *comm.* there *(Radak).*

[See below for two additional alternate interpretations offered by *Ramban.*]

Rashbam interprets *dudaim* in the sense of 'baskets of figs', citing *Song of Songs* 7:15.

[See *Rashi* there and *Eruvin* 21a quoting *Jeremiah* 24:1: And behold two דּוּדָאֵי תְאֵנִים, *baskets of figs,* where דוּדָאִים has this meaning of *baskets.*]

Sforno, as noted, follows the interpretation that *dudaim* were fragrant herbs which promoted conception.

וַיָּבֵא אֹתָם אֶל־לֵאָה אִמּוֹ – *And [he] brought them to Leah his mother.*

Although it is normal for young boys to bring found objects to their *fathers* as noted in *Bava Metzia* 12a, in this case the young Reuben displayed his discretion in realizing that this object would be more applicable to his *mother.* This incident is the derivation of the Talmudic description in *Gittin* 89b of a mature minor as one who attained לִפְלַגּוֹת רְאוּבֵן, *the divisions of Reuben* [see *Judges* 5:15], i.e., the age of discretion, personified by Reuben in this matter *(Haamek Davar).*

[It is *Radak* and *Sforno's* view that Reuben did not merely 'happen' upon the *dudaim.* Accordingly, Reuben's judgment in this matter would be emphasized by his *initial* display of maturity in seeking the *dudaim* in response to his mother's desire to have more children. Selflessly suppressing the normal sibling unwillingness to share the parents' affection with new children, Reuben sought a way

mediately met a vicarious death for its master. *R' Yitzchak Caro,* grandfather of the author of the *Shulchan Aruch,* mentions this legend in *Toldos Yitzchak: Vayechi. Yerushalmi Shabbos* 6:2 forbids the recital of Biblical verses while uprooting the mandrake. *Rambam* in *Moreh Nevuchim* 3:29 mentions the 'superstitions of the deluded' about mandrakes.

Furthermore, *Karnei Or* cites *Rav Pe'alim* that *dudaim* provide a wonderful cure for weak eyesight, and its roots were a charm to facilitate pregnancy. Accordingly, he surmises that Leah and Rachel both were interested in these *dudaim* each for her own reason: Leah for her weak eyes, and Rachel for her barrenness.

Many in this context draw attention to the fact that the word *dudaim* is related to the word *dod,* love, recalling its purported aphrodisiac properties.

30 *them to Leah his mother. Rachel said to Leah, 'Please*
15 *give me some of your son's dudaim.'* [15] *But she said*
to her, 'Was your taking my husband insignificant?
— And now to take even my son's dudaim!' Rachel

to help his mother conceive again. *Or HaChaim* notes that this same selflessness motivated him to relocate his father's bed in the incident related below in 35:22.]

The *Midrash* [which does not ascribe fertility powers to the *dudaim*] makes the observation that the young Reuben's respect for his mother was noteworthy. Although the fruit of *dudaim* are delectable, the youngster did not even taste any himself, but, as the verse attests, brought his mother whatever he found.

תְּנִי־נָא לִי מִדּוּדָאֵי בְּנֵךְ — *Please give me* [*some*] *of your son's dudaim.*

Not *all* of the *dudaim,* as it is rude to request *all* that another has; Rachel asked for only *some* of them *(Haamek Davar).*

Possibly she wanted to perfume Jacob's couch in the customary manner [see *Proverbs* 7:17] ... or as some say *dudaim,* which is derived from the word *dodim* [love], are herbs which act as a stimulant to the husband *(Ramban v.* 15).

[Why didn't Rachel avoid this whole conflict and pick her own *dudaim?*

— Perhaps these flowers were not common or easily accessible, and it was immodest for a women to go out in the fields alone.]

15. הַמְעַט קַחְתֵּךְ אֶת־אִישִׁי — *Was your taking of my husband insignificant?*

— I.e. that you act in a manner that would make it appear that you are the wife and I the handmaid? *(Ramban).*

— 'Are you not satisfied with attracting my husband's affection toward yourself?' Leah alluded to the fact noted by the Sages that Jacob's primary residence was with Rachel notwithstanding Leah's many children *(Shocher Tov).*[1]

[He was my husband before he was yours. Once I was already married to him] you should never have consented to become my rival-wife *(Sforno).*

וְלָקַחַת גַּם אֶת־דּוּדָאֵי בְּנִי — *And now to take even my son's dudaim!* [lit. *and to take also my son's dudaim*].

— As though you were in fact my mistress? *(Ramban).*

[And by your use of its aphrodisiac qualities] you would also *increase* his love for you and hatred for me *(Sforno).*

The rendering of this elliptic phrase as an incredulous question follows *Rashi* who accounts also for the infinitive form וְלָקַחַת, *to take,* rather than the second person feminine וְלָקַחַתְּ, *you would take:* Is it a small thing that you took my husband ... would you *also*

1. *Midrash Aggadah* renders the implication similarly and provides Rachel's response to Leah's accusation: 'He is not your destined husband but mine, for it was only for *my* sake that he came here from Beer Sheba. Only because I told you pre-arranged signs [see on 29:25] did he become your husband at all. Nevertheless ... *he shall lie with you tonight in return for your son's dudaim.'*

לָכֵן יִשְׁכַּב עִמָּךְ הַלַּיְלָה תַּחַת דּוּדָאֵי בְנֵךְ׃
טז וַיָּבֹא יַעֲקֹב מִן־הַשָּׂדֶה בָּעֶרֶב וַתֵּצֵא לֵאָה
לִקְרָאתוֹ וַתֹּאמֶר אֵלַי תָּבוֹא כִּי שָׂכֹר
שְׂכַרְתִּיךָ בְּדוּדָאֵי בְּנִי וַיִּשְׁכַּב עִמָּהּ

seek לָקַחַת, *to take* my son's *dudaim*? [Cf. *Targum Yonasan*.]

וַתֹּאמֶר רָחֵל לָכֵן יִשְׁכַּב עִמָּךְ הַלַּיְלָה תַּחַת דּוּדָאֵי בְנֵךְ — [*And*] *Rachel said, 'Therefore,* [i.e., to allay your suspicions] *he shall lie with you tonight in return for your son's dudaim.'*[1]

Jacob was to have stayed that night with Rachel but she ceded the privilege to Leah in exchange for the *dudaim*. Because Rachel made light of being with that righteous man she was not privileged to be buried [i.e. to lie in eternal repose] with him *(Rashi)*.

[It would appear that *Rashi* cites this *Midrashic* interpretation to emphasize one of the several underlying reasons why this seemingly unimportant incident was recorded in the Torah.]

In 49:8, *Rashi* seems to contradict himself. There he explains that Rachel was buried by the roadside where her descendants were destined to trudge away to Babylonian exile after the Destruction. When they passed her tomb, her soul would beseech God for mercy upon them, and He would respond with the reassurance that they would one day return to their land. If so, her failure to be buried in the Cave of Machpelah with Jacob was not a punishment but a Divine manifestation of mercy for the future exiles.

The commentators explain that *Rashi's* two comments are not contradictory but complementary. It is true that the choice of her resting place in Bethlehem was for the sake of prayers for Israel, but had she not belittled the company of the *tzaddik*, she would have had the even greater privilege of being buried with him. [In that case, God would have provided another source of mercy for the exiles.] Furthermore, since it would have been demeaning for Jacob to have been buried with two sisters since the Torah would later forbid such marriages, the choice of *which one* would be buried with him was decided by individual merit. Thus, it was Rachel's making light of Jacob's companionship that determined that it would be *she* who would be destined to forfeit the privilege of being buried near Jacob in the Cave of Machpelah, and not Leah [see *Overview*] *(Mizrachi; Gur Aryeh)*.

Radak is of the opinion that Jacob had made his primary residence with Rachel in the hope that she would be blessed with conception by his constant presence. Each time they were together Rachel prayed that it would lead to pregnancy, as did Leah. Therefore, when they both finally conceived the Torah says of each that her *prayers* were responsible; of Leah [*v.* 17]: *God heeded Leah's* [prayer]; and of Rachel [*v.* 22]: *God heeded her.*

1. That night was the sixth of Sivan *(Shavuos)* the day on which the Torah would later be given at Sinai. The Patriarchs were very aware that the child who would be conceived on that propitious night would merit to spend his life immersed in Torah study. Leah was eager to merit such a child and Rachel — as usual — capitulated to her older sister's request.

Issachar was the product of this union [see footnote to *v.* 18] *(Alshich)*.

said, 'Therefore, he shall lie with you tonight in return for your son's dudaim.'

16 When Jacob came from the field in the evening, Leah went out to meet him and said, 'It is to me that you must come for I have clearly hired you with my

16. וַיָּבֹא יַעֲקֹב מִן הַשָּׂדֶה בָּעֶרֶב — *When* [lit. *and*] *Jacob came from the field in the evening.*

The *Midrash* notes how dedicated a worker Jacob was even during this second seven-year period when he had already married both Rachel and Leah. He did not return from the field until *evening,* in observance of the law obliging a day laborer to work until darkness sets in.

It was his custom to eat his evening meal in the tent of the wife with whom he was to spend that particular night. As noted, however, his primary residence was with Rachel *(Abarbanel; Akeidas Yitzchak).*

וַתֵּצֵא לֵאָה לִקְרָאתוֹ — *And Leah went out to meet* [lit. *toward*] *him.*

The Sages viewed Leah's *going out* unfavorably, as an immodest act. The *Midrash* gives Leah the uncomplimentary designation of יַצְאָנִית, 'one who is fond of going out.' See *Rashi* to 34:1.

Nevertheless, the *Zohar, Radak* and most commentators in the simple sense, defend Leah's action in going out to meet Jacob. Since Jacob had no idea of what had transpired he intended to go to his primary residence in Rachel's tent [see *Radak* above and *Rashi* to 35:22], where he was to have spent that night. It was certainly more delicate for her to go out and *intercept* him, *before* he entered Rachel's tent rather than force Rachel to endure the embarrassment of informing Jacob that she had given up his company for the sake of a few *dudaim.*

Furthermore, Leah was apprehensive that Rachel might seek to postpone fulfillment of her promise to another night since she had not said [*v.* 15] הַלַּיְלָה הַזֶּה, *this very* night, but the less specific *the* night *(Or HaChaim).*

אֵלַי תָּבוֹא — *It is to me that you must come.*

I.e. it is to *my* tent that you must come, since each of the wives had her own tent *(Radak; Abarbanel;* see *HaKsav V'HaKabbalah; Sforno; Eruvin* 100b).

כִּי שָׂכֹר שְׂכַרְתִּיךָ בְּדוּדָאֵי בְּנִי — *For I have clearly hired you* [lit. *hire have I hired you* (the compound infinitive verb idiomatically denotes a forceful emphasis)] *with my son's dudaim.*

I.e., [In order to have you spend the night in my tent], I have paid Rachel the hire she demanded for you *(Rashi).*

Rashi makes this comment so that one is not led to incorrectly interpret שְׂכַרְתִּיךָ, *I have hired you,* in the sense that I have *received* a fee for hiring you out *(Mizrachi).*

'For I have hired you with my son's *dudaim* — and your visit will not deprive Rachel of her rights, because the arrangement was made with her consent.' To those who brazenly misinterpret the Torah, this incident may appear immodest. Its purpose is to emphasize that the Patriarchs viewed marital intimacy with an innocence

יז בַּלַּיְלָה הוּא: וַיִּשְׁמַע אֱלֹהִים אֶל־לֵאָה
יח וַתַּהַר וַתֵּלֶד לְיַעֲקֹב בֵּן חֲמִישִׁי: וַתֹּאמֶר
לֵאָה נָתַן אֱלֹהִים שְׂכָרִי אֲשֶׁר־נָתַתִּי
שִׁפְחָתִי לְאִישִׁי וַתִּקְרָא שְׁמוֹ יִשָּׂשכָר:

similar to that of Adam and Eve prior to their sin: There was no thought of physical gratification; they were solely motivated by the desire to bear children and produce offspring to serve God. Furthermore, the incident demonstrates the favor with which God looked upon the deeds and pure intentions of the Matriarchs. Their sole motive was to share in the building of Israel; to do so they sought every *natural* avenue, such as asking Jacob to take other wives, and seeking the properties of the *dudaim*. Therefore, God accepted their prayers for it is proper for the *tzaddik* to combine effort and prayer *(Sforno)*.

[The assonance of *sachor secharticha* is alluded to in the name given to the offspring of this union: Issachar.]

וַיִּשְׁכַּב עִמָּהּ בַּלַּיְלָה הוּא — *So* [lit. *and*] *he lay with her that night* [*he*].

The word הוּא, *he*, at the end of the phrase intimates: with his full consent and desire, fully cognizant of her pure and lofty motives *(Sforno; Or HaChaim)*.

Radak notes that although it is uncommon for the definite article הַ [בַּלַּיְלָה הַהוּא] to be omitted, it is nevertheless an acceptable form. Compare, for example *II Samuel* 6:3: אֶת הָעֲגָלָה חֲדָשָׁה [=הַחֲדָשָׁה]; *Numbers* 28 הַכֶּבֶשׂ אֶחָד [=הָאֶחָד].

[However, the Sages perceived a deeper connotation here. According to the *Talmud (Niddah* 31a) the use of the anomalous form הוּא, *he*, instead of the regular הַהוּא refers to God, the *He* par excellence]:

It teaches that the Holy One, Blessed be He, sent His assistance: with *His* help Issachar was born *(Rashi)* [Comp. similar interpretation of הוּא, *He*, in 19:33.]

The *Talmud* goes on to explain that God 'assisted' in the matter by initially inspiring the donkey Jacob had been riding upon, to head toward Leah's tent, where she intercepted him. The Sages cite Jacob's later blessing to Issachar: יִשָּׂשכָר חֲמוֹר גָּרֶם [familiar interpretation: *Issachar is a strong-boned donkey*] which the Sages perceive in this context to imply: *As for Issachar, a donkey was instrumental* [גָּרֶם lit. *was the cause*.]

Nachalas Yitzchak adds that the 'assistance' was that God caused the donkey to *bray loudly* as it neared Leah's tent so she would be aware that Jacob was approaching and go out to meet him. Nevertheless, he feels that *Rashi's primary* implication of God's assistance was that He ensured that Leah would conceive from that night's intimacy and beget Issachar.

17. Issachar.

וַיִּשְׁמַע אֱלֹהִים אֶל־לֵאָה — [And] *God hearkened to Leah.*

I.e., He received her constant prayers for another child *(Targumim; Radak)*.

She had eagerly desired, and sought means, to increase the number of the tribes *(Midrash; Rashi)*.

— This specifically dispels any notion regarding the efficacy of *dudaim* in promoting fertility. The verse specifically teaches us that it was because *God hearkened to Leah* that she conceived and bore this child. Children are a gift *of God (Radak; R' Chananel)*.

son's dudaim.' So he lay with her that night.
[17] *God hearkened to Leah. She conceived and bore Jacob a fifth son.* [18] *And Leah declared, 'God has granted me my reward because I gave my maidservant to my husband.' So she named him Issachar.*

Or HaChaim adds that the further implication is that God recognized the pure motivation of Leah's ostensibly improper behavior. In her overpowering love of God and His commandments, she overstepped the bounds of propriety and lowered herself by inviting Jacob to her tent. Measure for measure, God rewarded her love by giving her two sons more than she normally would have had.

וַתַּהַר וַתֵּלֶד לְיַעֲקֹב בֵּן חֲמִישִׁי — *And she conceived and bore* [to] *Jacob a fifth son.*

[I.e. his fifth son *from her;* in total this was his *ninth* son.]

Whenever the terms וַתַּהַר וַתֵּלֶד, *conceived and bore* appear together, they imply painless childbirth: just as the conception was painless, so was the birth (*Tanchuma;* cf. *Sotah* 12a).

[On the expression לְיַעֲקֹב, *to Jacob,* see *Ramban* cited in *v.* 5.]

18. נָתַן אֱלֹהִים שְׂכָרִי אֲשֶׁר נָתַתִּי שִׁפְחָתִי לְאִישִׁי — *God has granted me my reward* [Hebrew: *sachar*] *because* [lit. *that*] *I gave my maidservant to my husband.*

Her willingness to endure a rival in her home proved her selflessness in wanting to foster the birth of the tribes. Now she interpreted God's gift of another child to *her* as a reward for her virtuous deed (*R'Avraham ben HaRambam; Ralbag;* see *Ramban* to *v.* 9).[1]

יִשָּׂשכָר — *Issachar* [=Yissachar].

I.e., יֵשׁ שָׂכָר *(yesh sachar) there is reward* for my good deed *(Radak).*

[The two letters שׂ intimate] a double *sachar.* [The word *sachar* means *reward* as well as *hire*]: one, referring to the *hiring out* of the *dudaim,* and one referring to her *reward* for giving up her handmaid to her husband *(Rashbam).*

☙ The pronunciation of Yissachar.

As noted, One of the 'rewards' *(sachar)* alluded to by the double שׂ in Issachar refers to her statement *I have clearly 'hired'* [*sachor secharticha*] *you.* Since this has an uncomplimentary connotation, one שׂ is silent and not pronounced. [Thus the name is pronounced *Yissachar* and not, as written *Yissas'char*] *(Daas Zekeinim; Chizkuni; Baal HaTurim).*

1. The *Midrash* observes that as a result of this incident of the *dudaim* there arose two great tribes in Israel: Issachar and Zevulun.

Issachar engaged in Torah study while Zevulun went to sea and shared his profits with him; thus did Torah knowledge increase in Israel. [On this Issachar-Zevulun partnership of Torah-study and commerce, see *comm.* to 49:13-14 and *Deut.* 33:18.]

The *Zohar* similarly notes that the *dudaim* did not make Rachel bear children, but God used them as an instrument to cause Rachel — who had always clung to Jacob — to release him to Leah that night. The result of this *dudaim* exchange was the birth of Issachar who clung to the Torah more than all the other tribes, and through whom the fragrance of the Torah ascended to the Almighty, in harmony with the allusion in *Song of Songs* 7:14: *The dudaim give forth fragrance.*

יט וַתַּ֤הַר עוֹד֙ לֵאָ֔ה וַתֵּ֥לֶד בֵּן־שִׁשִּׁ֖י לְיַעֲקֹֽב׃
כ וַתֹּ֣אמֶר לֵאָ֗ה זְבָדַ֨נִי אֱלֹהִ֥ים | אֹתִי֮ זֵ֣בֶד
טוֹב֒ הַפַּ֙עַם֙ יִזְבְּלֵ֣נִי אִישִׁ֔י כִּֽי־יָלַ֥דְתִּי ל֖וֹ
שִׁשָּׁ֣ה בָנִ֑ים וַתִּקְרָ֥א אֶת־שְׁמ֖וֹ זְבֻלֽוּן׃
כא וְאַחַ֖ר יָ֣לְדָה בַּ֑ת וַתִּקְרָ֥א אֶת־שְׁמָ֖הּ דִּינָֽה׃

Why then did Leah give her child a name with a double ש to commemorate *both* of these incidents, including the uncomplimentary one of 'hiring' him? — *She* knew how lofty her motives were, and she had no cause for shame; therefore, she had no hesitation in *giving* the name. *Others,* however, might misinterpret her motivations and read an indecent connotation into her remark. Therefore, the other ש is not pronounced *(Yalkut Yehudah).*

Another reason advanced for the silent ש is that Issachar had a son named יוב, *Yov* [46:13] which Issachar later realized to be a disgraceful name [inasmuch as it was the name of a heathen god *(Devek Tov* to *Numbers* 26:24).] Issachar thereupon gave him a letter (ש) of his name, and renamed him יָשׁוּב, *Yashuv* [see genealogy in *Numbers* ibid]. Hence Issachar's name is pronounced as if it were spelled with one ש: יִשָּׂכָר *(Daas Zekeinim).*

Ibn Ezra to *Exodus* 1:3 defends this pronunciation *grammatically* by stating that since the two consonants follow one another, the second is silent, as in the word מַחְצְצְרִים in *I Chron.* 15:24 which is pronounced מַחֲצְרִים. This is the only other such case in Scripture.

[There are various customs regarding this matter. Some pronounce the name *fully the first time it appears in the Torah,* and in subsequent passages pronounce it Yissachar. Others — and this is the prevailing custom — *always* pronounce it Yissachar. *Torah Sheleimah* §63 discusses this at length and cites a custom whereby some pronounce it fully until *Numbers* 26:24 where the name *Yashuv* appears the first time, and then only Yissachar.]

19-20. Zevulun.

זְבָדַנִי אֱלֹהִים אֹתִי זֵבֶד טוֹב — *God has endowed me* [*with*] *a good endowment.*

God was generous to me because my intentions in the matter of the *dudaim* were lofty; I acted only for His honor *(Sforno).*

— And his descendants, too, will receive a good portion in *Eretz Yisrael (Targum Yonasan).*

The translation *a good endowment* [lit. *a good portion*] follows *Onkelos* cited by *Rashi;* and *Rashbam* who deduces this meaning from the context.

Ramban notes that there is no Hebrew source known for the word זֵבֶד. He treats the word as a composite of the two words זֶה בַּד, *this is a tree-branch* for me. She figuratively describes the child as the *branch* of her family-tree. *Rambam* cites similar usages in *Job* 18:13; *Isaiah* 16:6, where בַּד similarly refers to *children.* She calls the child *good* because 'he will be the cause of my husband dwelling with me permanently.'

Regarding *Targum's* translation of זֵבֶד as a *portion, Ramban* observes that *Targum* treats the word as if it were spelled with a ו, זֵוֶד, which is Aramaic for צֵידָה, *provisions* [see 42:25]. *Targum's* intent is that God made this son like a generous store of provisions, assuring her of happiness and security, because now that she had given

[19] *Then Leah conceived again and bore Jacob a*
sixth son. [20] *Leah said, 'God has endowed me with a*
good endowment. Now my husband will make his
permanent home with me for I have borne him six
sons.' So she named him Zebulun. [21] *Afterwards, she*
bore a daughter and she named her Dinah.

birth to half of his ordained number of sons, Jacob would live mainly with her.

Hoffmann perceives the word זבד to be related to זבל, both verb forms having the essential meaning of *exalted* [usually in connection with abode]. The substance of Leah's declaration was: 'God exalted me with this good endowment. Therefore my husband, too, will exalt me and consider me his primary wife.'

הַפַּעַם יִזְבְּלֵנִי אִישִׁי כִּי יָלַדְתִּי לוֹ שִׁשָּׁה בָנִים — *Now* [i.e., henceforth (see *Rashi* to same word in 29:34)] *my husband will make his permanent home with me* [Hebrew: *Yizbeleni*, in assonance with *Zebulun*] *for I have borne him six sons.*

Now that I have presented him with as many children as the rest of his wives *together*, his primary residence will be with me. The word יִזְבְּלֵנִי [denoting dwelling-place] is related to the phrase בֵּית זְבוּל *a house for dwelling* in *I Kings* 8:13 *(Rashi).*

Hence, I will provide him with his בֵּית זְבוּל, *lofty abode*, and his love for me will ever increase *(Radak).*

[See *Hoffmann* above who renders: *now my husband will exalt me...*]

According to *Malbim:* now my husband will take me into his tent because I have borne him six sons and I have outgrown my premises.

21. Dinah.

וְאַחַר יָלְדָה בַּת — [*And*] *afterwards, she bore a daughter.*

The Torah, as noted often in this commentary, is not merely a history book, and does not generally mention the birth of a daughter. Dinah's birth is mentioned because she plays an important role later on in the narrative [see chapt. 34] and the Torah now introduces her to us *(Hoffmann).*

It would appear that Dinah was Zebulun's twin because the Torah simply states: *Afterwards she bore a daughter,* without mentioning that she *conceived* again *(Ibn Ezra; Radak; Chizkuni).*

[According to the Rabbinic interpretation cited by *Rashi* below, it might be possible that the Torah did not tell us that **she conceived** *and bore a daughter* because in fact she did not *conceive* a *daughter:* she conceived a *son* and later *bore* a daughter. (I later saw this interpretation in *Haamek Davar* and *Torah Temimah).* Furthermore, the *Talmud's* interpretation is attached to the word אַחַר, *afterward,* i.e. *after* she passed judgment on herself *she bore a daughter,* not *after* the birth of Zebulun. The matter of *conception* is irrelevant to the point made by the verse. See further.]

וַתִּקְרָא אֶת שְׁמָהּ דִּינָה — *And* [*she*] *named her Dinah.*

No reason for this name is given in the Torah. *Targum Yonasan* supplies it: For she said: 'Judgment [דִּין] proceeds from God that there shall be from me [only] half the tribes.'

כב וַיִּזְכֹּר אֱלֹהִים אֶת־רָחֵל וַיִּשְׁמַע אֵלֶיהָ
כג אֱלֹהִים וַיִּפְתַּח אֶת־רַחְמָהּ: וַתַּהַר וַתֵּלֶד
בֵּן וַתֹּאמֶר אָסַף אֱלֹהִים אֶת־חֶרְפָּתִי:

Rashi [citing *Berachos* 60a] comments that Leah 'passed judgment' *(danah)*: '[Jacob is destined to beget twelve tribes. I have already borne six and each of the handmaids have already borne two, making a total of ten.] If the child I am carrying turns out to be a male, then Rachel will not even be equivalent to one of the handmaids.' She therefore prayed concerning him, and he was changed to a female. [The bracketed addition is from the *Talmud, ibid.*][1]

[The Midrashic version of Dinah's birth is different. According to the *Midrash*, the cause of Dinah's birth as a female was *Rachel's* prayer after the birth of Joseph that she be granted another son [*v.* 24]. (*Maharzu* notes accordingly, that although the Torah groups all of Leah's later children together, Dinah was born *after* Joseph [see chart end of *v.* 24]).][2]

22. Rachel conceives; the birth of Joseph.

וַיִּזְכֹּר אֱלֹהִים אֶת רָחֵל — [*And*] *God remembered Rachel.*

[As fully explained in the commentary to the parallel expression regarding Noah above, 8:1 (pages 260-261) since there is no forgetfulness before God the term 'remembering' when applied to Him is a human term describing the manifestation of His benevolence on earth. According to *Rashi* following the *Midrash* the term *remember* implies that He took cognizance of some virtuous act. Hence *Rashi's* comment here]:

He took cognizance of Rachel's self sacrifice in having transmitted the secret sign to Leah [see 29:25]; He also remembered Rachel's recurring fear that Jacob might divorce her on account of her barrenness and that she would then have to marry Esau. Indeed Esau had entertained this hope when he heard Rachel was childless.

According to *Sforno*, God 'remembered' her efforts in bringing her handmaid into her house, and the incident of the *dudaim*.

Cf. *Ramban* to 21:1 [p. 744] who notes that 'remembering' is used in reference to all barren women who later gave birth, as in the case of Hannah [*I Sam.* 1:19]. See also footnote there on the terms זְכִירָה and פְּקִידָה.

1. The *Talmud* adds that God's response to Leah's prayer was a miracle. Therefore, it does not contradict the *Mishnah's (ibid.* 54a) rule that it is vain for a man to pray that his already pregnant wife should give birth to a male. Alternatively, Leah's prayer might have occurred within the first forty days after conception when the embryo's sex is considered as yet undetermined; then it is indeed proper to pray for a male child [see *Mizrachi*].

Cf. *Divrei David* who suggests that the Mishnah's rule applies only to a case where one prays that his wife bear a male, for how can the female she is carrying be born a male? However, when one specifically prays *for God's intervention* to change the sex of the embryo then it is not a vain prayer, for nothing is beyond God.

2. Our version in the *Midrash* records that Dinah's name commemorates how *all* the Matriarchs assembled and prayed: 'We have sufficient [*dayeinu*] males, let Rachel be remembered!'

22 *God remembered Rachel. God hearkened to her and He opened her womb.* 23 *She conceived and bore a son, and said, 'God has taken away my disgrace.'*

According to *Rosh Hashanah* 11a, the use of the term *remembrance* suggests that this event occurred on Rosh HaShanah, the day of 'remembrance of the *teruah.*'

Rosh HaShanah is the day God 'remembers' His people, and it was on this day that Sarah, Rachel, and Hannah were remembered *(Tanchuma; Midrash).*

[On the use here of the Name *Elohim* which describes God as Dispenser of Justice instead of the more appropriate Name *HASHEM* which designates Him as a *Merciful* God, see *Rashi* and *footnote* to 8:1: 'Happy are the righteous who transform the Attribute of Justice into the Attribute of Mercy' for even as *God (Elohim)* — Dispenser of Strict Justice — He compassionately remembered Rachel.]

וַיִּשְׁמַע אֵלֶיהָ אֱלֹהִים — [*And*] *God hearkened to her.*

— I.e. received her prayers *(Targum).*

As *Ramban* in *v.* 2 observes, when Rachel saw that she could not rely on Jacob's prayer, she proceeded to pray on her own behalf.

— These prayers were now answered, after Rachel had done everything in her power to bear children *(Alshich).*

וַיִּפְתַּח אֶת רַחְמָהּ — *And He opened her womb.*[1]

[It was not the reputed fertility powers of the *dudaim* that resulted in Rachel's womb being opened. As emphasized in the commentary to *v.* 14, this verse makes clear that *God remembered* Rachel; *God hearkened to her prayers;* and it was *He — Alone —* Who opened her womb. Children are clearly a gift of God.]

23. אָסַף אֱלֹהִים אֶת חֶרְפָּתִי — *God has taken away* [*Hebrew: asaph,* in assonance with *Yosef,* Joseph] *my disgrace.*

I.e. my disgrace as a barren woman. I had become an object of reproach for people were saying that I would eventually become Esau's wife [and now there was no further danger of that happening] *(Tanchuma; Rashi).*[2]

— *My disgrace* in that people used to reproach me, saying: Were Rachel really pious, she would have borne children *(Midrash HaGadol).*

According to *Sforno,* the *disgrace*

1. The *Talmud (Taanis* 2b) notes that the Holy One, Blessed be He, retains control of three 'keys' and does not entrust them to agents: The keys of rain, childbearing, and sustenance. Our verse [which unlike the earlier reference in 29:31 contains the words וַיִּפְתַּח אֱלֹהִים, *God opened,* in uninterrupted sequence *(Maharsha)*] is cited in the case of childbearing. [Cf. version in *Pirkei d'Rabbi Eliezer* cited on p. 744.]

2. *Rashi* also cites the Midrashic interpretation that God *has taken away my disgrace* by providing Rachel with a child to blame for her faults:

Before a woman has a child she has no one on whom to blame her faults. When, however, she has a child, she puts it on him:

'Who broke this article?' — 'Your son!'

'Who ate these figs?' — 'Your son!'

[*Harav Gedalia Schorr* זצ"ל has explained this apparently banal expression of gratitude at having a child. Rachel meant to say that God's blessing was utterly complete. So complete was it that it extended from the loftiest spheres down to the most trivial — such as providing an excuse for mishaps at home.]

כד וַתִּקְרָא אֶת־שְׁמוֹ יוֹסֵף לֵאמֹר יֹסֵף יהוה
כה לִי בֵּן אַחֵר: וַיְהִי כַּאֲשֶׁר יָלְדָה רָחֵל אֶת־
יוֹסֵף וַיֹּאמֶר יַעֲקֹב אֶל־לָבָן שַׁלְּחֵנִי

was that God had accepted Leah's prayers and not hers.

The mockers of that generation would taunt Rachel by saying that Jacob gave the beautiful Rachel a potion to keep her from childbearing for he desired her only as a mistress. It was the custom in those times for some men to marry two women: one for children and the other, who would be sterilized, for beauty [see *comm.* to 4:19]. To be considered a living ornament is a disgrace to a woman; with the birth of her child, Rachel was finally vindicated *(HaKsav V'HaKaballah* citing *R' Y. Caro).*

She prophetically added: As my son has removed my disgrace, so Joshua, his descendant, will remove the 'disgrace' from the children of Israel when he circumcises them beyond the Jordan River before they enter the Holy Land [see *Joshua* 5:9] *(Targum Yonasan).*

The translation of אָסַף as *taken away* — in the sense of *laid it up somewhere out of sight* follows *Rashi* who cites this meaning of the verb in *Isaiah* 4:1; *Exod.* 9:9; *Joel* 4:13; and *Isaiah* 60:20.

Ibn Ezra interprets it in the sense of *vanish* as in *Isaiah* 16:10: *Joy and gladness will vanish* (וְנֶאֱסַף).

Ramban agrees with *Onkelos* that the verb אָסַף should be understood in its plain sense: *gathered.* In our context the phrase would mean that God has *gathered up* her disgrace, i.e., she would no longer be discussed publicly.

Of course, the verb cannot be understood *simply* in its literal sense as *gathered up,* with the connotation of piling up in one place for all to see. That is why *Rashi* qualified his interpretation by adding: laid it up somewhere *out of sight (Mizrachi).*

24. יוֹסֵף — *Joseph.*

— Hebrew: *Yosef.* The name thus contains allusions both to the past: *God has taken away ['asaf'] my disgrace,* coupled with Rachel's prayer for the future: *May HASHEM add on ['yosef'] another son (Rashbam; Radak).*

לֵאמֹר יֹסֵף ה׳ לִי בֵּן אַחֵר — *Saying* [i.e. as if to imply], *'May HASHEM add on* [Hebrew: *yosef*] *for me another son.*

— [Here she invokes God in His Aspect as *HASHEM* — Dispenser of *Mercy.*]

She asked for only *one* more son because she knew prophetically that Jacob would have twelve sons, and eleven of them were already born.] The intent, then, of her prayer was: May that son which Jacob is yet destined to bear issue from *me (Rashi).*[1]

Following the *Midrash* cited above [end of *v.* 21], Joseph was born while Leah was pregnant with a male embryo. As a result of Rachel's prayer, the embryo was transformed into Dinah.

1. The word *Yosef* means 'increase'. Prophetess that she was, Rachel forsaw that she would have a second son. But an increase added on by God is usually larger than the original itself. Thus, Benjamin, the second son, whom Rachel regarded merely as a supplement, had ten sons while Joseph begot only two. These twelve together may be regarded the twelve tribes borne by Rachel *(Tanchuma Yashan).*

According to *Yelamdeinu* § 20, Rachel prophesied that Joseph would be the ancestor of the *Messiah ben Joseph* who would arise at the 'end of days'. Thus, בֵּן אַחֵר, *another son,* is to be understood as an eschatological reference to the בֵּן אַחֲרוֹנוֹ שֶׁל עוֹלָם, one who would function at the end of world history.

[24] *So she named him Joseph saying, 'May HASHEM*
add on for me another son.'
[25] *And it was, when Rachel had given birth to*
Joseph, Jacob said to Laban, 'Grant me leave that I

☙ Jacob's Children.

Ibn Ezra appends a note that except for Benjamin all of the tribes — and Dinah as well—were born in the seven year period. The assumption then is that they were born barely seven months apart [total 7 years = 84 months÷12 children=7 months each.] If so, the Text is probably not in strict chronological sequence: Leah may have given her handmaid Zilpah to Jacob before Naftali was born, and Rachel conceived before Zebulun was born. In any event we are not told when Dinah was born.

[Summing up, quite probably only *Leah's* first four children were born seven months apart; Jacob may have married the handmaids while Leah was pregnant with other children and each of them carried a full nine month period. See *Seder Olam* chapter 2; *Pirkei d'Rabbi Eliezer* chapter 36; *Ibn Ezra* to *Exod.* 2:2.]

The following table lists Jacob's children born in that period:

[The overlapping sequence is conjectural]

Yr.	LEAH	BILHAH	ZILPAH	RACHEL
1	*Reuben*			
2	*Simeon*			
3	*Levi*			
4	*Judah*	*Dan*		
5		*Naftali*	*Gad*	
6	*Issachar*		*Asher*	
7	*Zebulun* *Dinah*			*Joseph*

[There is, furthermore, an opinion recorded in *Pirkei d'Rabbi Eliezer* that each of the children except Joseph was born with a twin sister. See *Bereishis Rabbah* 82:8, 84:21. *Tosafos Bava Basra* 123a records that the sons intermarried with daughters of the other wives (i.e. with their half-sisters from their fathers, which was permitted Noachides, and which was not prohibited until the giving of the Torah — see *Ramban* cited in *comm.* to 37:35 and 38:2 for a full discussion of this opinion). Dinah, however, who according to this view, was not born with a twin, did not marry any of her half-brothers, and as we shall see Joseph later married Asenath who our Sages teach was Dinah's daughter by Shechem (see 41:45). Cf. also the Midrashic view in 34:26 and 46:10 that Simeon married Dinah.]

25. Jacob wishes to depart. A new agreement is concluded with Laban.

וַיְהִי כַּאֲשֶׁר יָלְדָה רָחֵל אֶת יוֹסֵף — *And it was, when Rachel had given birth to Joseph.*

By this time the additional seven years of service for Rachel had ended *(Rashbam).*

It will be recalled that when Jacob fled from Esau his mother promised to send for him when she perceived that the threat from Esau had subsided. Actually, we find no *specific* reference *in the text* of Jacob having received such a call [aside from the Midrashic tradition cited by *Rashi* in 35:8 that Rebecca had sent her nurse Deborah for the purpose of summoning Jacob.][1] Possibly Jacob felt that now that his *beloved*

1. At this time, Jacob was 91 years old. Isaac was 151, and Rebecca was 114.
Sefer HaYashar holds that it was at *this* time that Rebecca sent her nurse Deborah and two

כו וְאֵלְכָה אֶל־מְקוֹמִי וּלְאַרְצִי׃ תְּנָה אֶת־
נָשַׁי וְאֶת־יְלָדַי אֲשֶׁר עָבַדְתִּי אֹתְךָ בָּהֵן
וְאֵלֵכָה כִּי אַתָּה יָדַעְתָּ אֶת־עֲבֹדָתִי אֲשֶׁר
כז עֲבַדְתִּיךָ׃ וַיֹּאמֶר אֵלָיו לָבָן אִם־נָא
מָצָאתִי חֵן בְּעֵינֶיךָ נִחַשְׁתִּי וַיְבָרְכֵנִי יהוה

wife had borne a child, it was a propitious sign that he return home though his mother's call had not yet come *(Hoffmann).*

According to the *Midrash,* [although Jacob's period of service had ended and he was theoretically free to leave at any time] Jacob waited specifically until Joseph was born because it was only after the birth of Joseph, whom Jacob prophetically foresaw to be Esau's conqueror, that Jacob felt he could safely return home and brave Esau's wrath.

As *Rashi* expresses it: *When Rachel had given birth to Joseph* — who was the [destined] adversary of Esau [i.e., the power that would defeat him], as it is written [*Obadiah v.* 18]: *And the House of Jacob shall be fire, and the House of Joseph flame, and the House of Esau shall be straw. Fire* [=Jacob] without a *flame* [=Joseph] is ineffective from afar [i.e. only with the birth of Joseph who was like a flame could Jacob hope to defeat Esau.] Accordingly, only when Joseph was born did Jacob place his trust in God and decide to return home. [Cf. *Bava Basra* 123b.]

Radak suggests that Jacob waited until Rachel gave birth so that Laban could not ask him to leave her behind because she was childless [in which case Laban would then marry her to someone else *(Haamek Davar).*]

Jacob knew that he would have twelve tribes [as evidenced by the coalesced stones in 28:11]. Accordingly, once Rachel had borne Joseph and had been assured another son [*v.* 24], he was unafraid of Esau because Providence would surely keep him alive at least until he begot the twelfth tribe *(Kli Yakar).*

The *Zohar* suggests that Jacob did not wait for the birth of Benjamin since he knew that Benjamin would be born in *Eretz Yisrael.*

שַׁלְּחֵנִי וְאֵלְכָה אֶל מְקוֹמִי וּלְאַרְצִי — *Grant me leave* [following *Radak;* lit. *send me*] *that I may go* [lit. *and I will go*] *to my place and to my land.*

I.e., *to my place which is in my land, Eretz Yisrael.* Jacob thus made it abundantly clear to Laban that he did not consider *his place* to be Charan even though it was his grandfather's ancestral home, and the birthplace of his mother, wives, and children *(Hoffmann).*

[Compare *R'Bachya's* interpretation of *my place* in 18:33.]

26. תְּנָה אֶת־נָשַׁי וְאֶת יְלָדַי ... וְאֵלְכָה — *Give* [*me*] *my wives and my children ... and I will go.*

[We find nowhere that Laban was *physically detaining* Jacob's wives. Therefore, the expression *'give'*

of Isaac's servants to fetch Jacob. Jacob heeded them and requested leave from Laban, but Laban convinced him to stay on.

When Isaac's servants saw that Jacob would not return with them, they departed. Deborah, however, remained with Jacob and resided with his wives until six years later when Jacob left.

Deborah died during the journey home. [See *Rashi* to 35:8.]

may go to my place and to my land. [26] *Give me my*
wives and my children for whom I have served you,
and I will go. For you are aware of my service that I
labored for you.'
[27] *But Laban said to him, 'If I have found favor*
with you! — I have learned by divination that
HASHEM has blessed me on account of you.' [28] *And*

must be understood as 'give me permission to leave with my wives and children' *(Mizrachi; Tzeidah laDerech)*]:

— I have no wish to leave except with your permission *(Rashi).*

Though I labored for them, I still request your permission *(Sechel Tov).*

כִּי אַתָּה יָדַעְתָּ אֶת עֲבֹדָתִי אֲשֶׁר עֲבַדְתִּיךָ — *For you are aware of my service that I labored for you.*

You cannot capriciously detain them. I served you for them, and I must take them back with me to my land *(Radak).*

Hoffmann interprets: You are fully cognizant of the benefits you reaped as a result of my devoted service to you for them.

27. [Laban is reluctant to part with Jacob who, as he admits, served him well, and in whose merit God had blessed him]:

אִם־נָא מָצָאתִי חֵן בְּעֵינֶיךָ — *If I have found favor with you* [lit. *in your eyes*].

I.e., 'If you love me to the degree that our kinship would warrant' [the implication being]: You would not leave me *(Sforno).*

נִחַשְׁתִּי — *I have learned by divination.*

Laban was a diviner, and the verb means: 'I have discovered by my art of divination' *(Rashi).*

The term נחש refers to a form of occult art, of the categories mentioned in *Deut.* 18:10-11. *Rashi* there explains it as one who foretells or interprets omens: 'that the bread fell from his mouth, or that a deer crossed his path, or that his stick fell from his hand.' In *Lev.* 19:26, *Rashi* adds to this category those who elicit omens from the cry of a weasel, and from the [formation or twittering of] birds. [See *Sanhedrin* 65b and *Rambam Hilchos Avodah Zarah* 11:4,5.]

Ramban, following *Targum Yonasan* and *Radak* holds that the word basically connotes *testing. Ibn Ezra* suggests that it implies testing specifically by use of divinations with *teraphim* [see *comm.* to 31:19]: i.e. *I have tested the matter with my occult powers* through the medium of my *teraphim and conclude that HASHEM has blessed me on account of you.*

Laban hypocritically speaks in self-righteous tones, not admitting that he would like to keep Jacob *because of his great ability.* In those terms, he would have been compelled to make some concrete business proposal. Instead, Laban informs Jacob that he is moved by a ניחוש, a sort of superstitious belief. Laban believes that the God of Jacob has blessed him on account of such a pious servant *(R' Munk).*

וַיְבָרְכֵנִי ה' בִּגְלָלֶךָ — *That HASHEM has blessed me on account of you.*

I.e. on account of you and your

°חמישי

כח בִּגְלָלֶֽךָ׃ °וַיֹּאמַ֑ר נָקְבָ֧ה שְׂכָרְךָ֛ עָלַ֖י וְאֶתֵּֽנָה׃
כט וַיֹּ֣אמֶר אֵלָ֔יו אַתָּ֣ה יָדַ֔עְתָּ אֵ֖ת אֲשֶׁ֣ר
ל עֲבַדְתִּ֑יךָ וְאֵ֛ת אֲשֶׁר־הָיָ֥ה מִקְנְךָ֖ אִתִּֽי׃ כִּ֡י
מְעַט֩ אֲשֶׁר־הָיָ֨ה לְךָ֤ לְפָנַי֙ וַיִּפְרֹ֣ץ לָרֹ֔ב
וַיְבָ֧רֶךְ יהוה֛ אֹתְךָ֖ לְרַגְלִ֑י וְעַתָּ֗ה מָתַ֛י
לא אֶֽעֱשֶׂ֥ה גַם־אָנֹכִ֖י לְבֵיתִֽי׃ וַיֹּ֕אמֶר מָ֖ה אֶתֶּן־

merit for you are a righteous man *(Ramban).*

'It is through you that I have been blessed. When you first came here I had no sons, now I have sons.' That Laban had no sons prior to Jacob's arrival is obvious since he certainly would not have allowed a little girl, *Rachel,* to tend the flocks if he had had sons [29:6]. Now he had sons as stated in 31:1 *(Rashi).*

— I have this superstitious notion that HASHEM, the God Whom you serve, has brought me luck because you are so righteous. That is why I do not like to let such a pious man depart from me *(R' Hoffman).*

28. Laban had hoped the pious man would be flattered by this acknowledgment of Heavenly intervention, and declare himself willing to remain without asking for pay. But when Jacob remained silent, Laban realized that he would have to offer an inducement. Accordingly, he asked Jacob to stipulate his terms *(R' Hirsch).*

נָקְבָה שְׂכָרְךָ עָלַי וְאֶתֵּנָה — *Specify your wage to me* [עָלַי here having the sense of אֵלַי *(Heidenheim)*] *and I will give it.*

The term נָקְבָה שְׂכָרְךָ is to be interpreted as *Onkelos* renders it: פָּרֵשׁ אַגְרָךְ, *state clearly your wage (Rashi).*

Harav David Feinstein notes the use of the word עָלַי, literally *upon me,* related to עוֹל, *yoke,* an unpleasant burden that is placed upon an unwilling bearer. To Laban, the very idea that someone had the right to demand fair payment for services rendered, constituted a heavy, onerous yoke.

29. Jacob reiterates his position:

אַתָּה יָדַעְתָּ אֵת אֲשֶׁר עֲבַדְתִּיךָ — *You know* [lit. *have known*] *how I served you.*

I.e., the loyalty and full strength with which I served you *(Ramban).*

[See *R'Hirsch* in *footnote* next verse.]

וְאֵת אֲשֶׁר הָיָה מִקְנְךָ אִתִּי — *And what your cattle were with me.*

I.e. and you are fully aware of the small number of your cattle that were originally entrusted to me *(Rashi).*

Or: And you are aware of ... *how long your sheep were under my care* — for it was indeed many years *(Abarbanel).*

Others render: *And how your cattle fared with me (Ralbag).*

30. כִּי מְעַט אֲשֶׁר־הָיָה לְךָ לְפָנַי וַיִּפְרֹץ לָרֹב — *For the little that you had before I came* [lit. *before me*] *has expanded substantially* [lit. *and it has spread forth to abundance*].

The translation follows *R Hirsch.* Jacob declared that before he arrived, Laban had small

30
29-31 *he said, 'Specify your wage to me and I will give it.'*
29 *But he said to him 'You know who I served you*
and what your cattle were with me. 30 *For the little*
that you had before I came has expounded substan-
tially as HASHEM has blessed you with my coming.
And now, when will I also do something for my own
house?'
31 *He said, 'What shall I give you?' And Jacob said,*

numbers of animals, but that his livestock had increased dramatically as a result of his, Jacob's labors.

— Laban's flock had increased in a supernatural way *(Ramban).*

וַיְבָרֶךְ ה׳ אֹתְךָ לְרַגְלִי — *As* [lit. *and*] *HASHEM has blessed you with my coming* [lit. *to my foot*].

I.e., the blessing has come to you on account of my having *set foot* here. Compare the similar use of רֶגֶל in *Exodus* 11:8: *The people who have come with you* [בְּרַגְלֶיךָ lit. *at your feet*]; *Judges* 8:5: *the people that come with me* [בְּרַגְלַי, lit. *at my foot*] *(Midrash; Rashi).*

— Only HASHEM's blessing makes one rich [*Proverbs* 10:22], and that blessing was manifest from the time I set foot in your house *(Ibn Ezra; Ramban).*

[The word לְרֶגֶל, *at the foot of,* is figuratively understood in the sense of *on account of.* Cf. *Rashi Yoma* 38b s.v. רַגְלֵי חֲסִידָיו. *Rambam (Moreh Nevuchim* 1:8) similarly explains the connotation: *because of me* or *as a kindness to me.*]

R'Hirsch explains the connotation to mean *after my ways.*[1]

מָתַי אֶעֱשֶׂה גַם־אָנֹכִי לְבֵיתִי — *When will I also do something for my own house?*

— My sons *alone* have been providing for me up to now. The time has come when I must join with them and assist them. גַם־אָנֹכִי, *I also* must bear the responsibility of earning a living for my own family *(Rashi).*

Ramban and *Radak* understand גַּם as modifying *my house*: Jacob argued, 'When shall I provide for my house *also*, as I have provided for your house up to now?' Since even Jacob's oldest child was only six at this time, *Ramban* considers it unlikely that Jacob's children were shepherds. [The word גַּם does not always precede the word it is accentuating. Hence *Ramban* renders our passage as if it were written מָתַי אֶעֱשֶׂה אָנֹכִי גַם לְבֵיתִי.] Cf. *Numbers* 22:33 where גַּם אוֹתְכָה הָרַגְתִּי [lit. *also you I would have slain*] is interpreted as if it were written גַּם הָרַגְתִּי אוֹתְכָה, *also I would have slain you* [see *Rashi* there].

31. [Laban presses further]:

מָה אֶתֶּן־לָךְ — *What shall I give you?*

[You are concerned now about providing for your own household.] *What shall I give you* to compensate for what you could expect to earn

1. Jacob says: You have no need to attribute your blessed prosperity to an abstract idea that God provided for you, as you put it, בִּגְלָלִי, *for my sake.* You can just as well attribute your blessing to a more tangible factor: לְרַגְלִי, [*according to the pattern*] *taken by my feet.* Day and night I served you, following your flocks and caring for them. God took account not of my piety, but of my diligence. Now the time has come when I must utilize my industriousness to provide for my family *(R' Hirsch).*

לָךְ וַיֹּאמֶר יַעֲקֹב לֹא־תִתֶּן־לִי מְאוּמָה
אִם־תַּעֲשֶׂה־לִּי הַדָּבָר הַזֶּה אָשׁוּבָה
לב אֶרְעֶה צֹאנְךָ אֶשְׁמֹר: אֶעֱבֹר בְּכָל־צֹאנְךָ
הַיּוֹם הָסֵר מִשָּׁם כָּל־שֶׂה | נָקֹד וְטָלוּא
וְכָל־שֶׂה־חוּם בַּכְּשָׂבִים וְטָלוּא וְנָקֹד

[if you were to work for yourself]? *(Sforno).*

Jacob consents to remain.

[He proceeds to propose an arrangement by which, in the natural order of events, he would gain little]:

לֹא תִתֶּן לִי מְאוּמָה — *Do not give me anything* [or: *You will not give me anything.*]

Do not give me anything of the flocks you *now* possess; whatever you profited from my past work is yours because I worked for the right to marry your daughters. My wage for *continuing* to tend your flocks will come from those unnaturally colored animals which will be born *in the future (Rashbam).*

Whatever I gain as a result of our agreement will not come from *you*; God's grace to me will not diminish your possessions in any way. As the Sages proclaimed [*Yoma* 38b]: אֵין אָדָם נוֹגֵעַ בְּמוּכָן לַחֲבֵרוֹ, *No man can touch what is prepared for his fellow (Sforno).*

R' Hirsch interprets differently. Jacob did not wish to be dependent on Laban to *give* him his wages when they became due. Jacob had experienced too much of Laban's deception, and finding ways to avoid payment of debts. Therefore, Jacob insisted on an arrangement whereby he would rely on his own exceptional skill as a shepherd, and his wages would automatically be his property without the need to collect it from Laban.

אִם תַּעֲשֶׂה לִּי הַדָּבָר הַזֶּה — *If you will do this thing for me.*

[I.e. that which I am about to propose to you].

[*Rashi*, in *Bavra Metzia* 94a s.v. כָּל תְּנַאי שֶׁיֵּשׁ בּוֹ מַעֲשֶׂה בִּתְחִילָּתוֹ, cites Jacob's stipulation as a classic example of a condition which is preceded by an action. See *Mishnah* and commentaries there.]

אָשׁוּבָה אֶרְעֶה צֹאנְךָ אֶשְׁמֹר — [Then] *I will resume pasturing and guarding your flocks* [lit. *I will return, I will pasture your flock, I will guard.*]

According to *Midrash Lekach Tov* the terms *pasture* and *guard* are not redundant, there are shepherds who *pasture* but do not keep *guard.* I will both feed *and* keep guard.

According to *R'Bachya* the addition of אֶשְׁמֹר, *I will guard,* implies: I will become a שׁוֹמֵר שָׂכָר, *a hired guardian* [with the accompanying obligations. As the *Mishnah* states in *Shavuos* 49a, a hired guardian is responsible for loss and theft, while a שׁוֹמֵר חִנָּם, *unpaid guardian,* is not, provided, of course, he has not been deliberately negligent.]

HaKsav V'HaKabballah notes that the cantillation of אָשׁוּבָה [תְּבִיר] is disjunctive, indicating that the word is not attached to those that follow. Therefore, he interprets each part of this phrase as a separate thought: אָשׁוּבָה, *I shall withdraw* my decision to return to Canaan; אֶרְעֶה צֹאנְךָ, *I will pasture your flock;* אֶשְׁמֹר, *I will await* your execution of the agreement between us. The term שמר is used in the sense of *await* or *anticipate* in 37:11.

32. Jacob's wages.

[Although the commentators dif-

30
32

'Do not give me anything. If you will do this thing
for me, I will resume pasturing and guarding your
flocks: 32 Let me pass through your whole flock today. Remove from there every speckled or spotted
sheep, every brownish lamb among the sheep and the

fer as to the precise interpretation of *every* detail of the narrative, the arrangement by which Jacob agrees to work is *basically* as follows: Laban will remove from the flocks in Jacob's care certain animals of *abnormal color,* leaving the normally colored ones with Jacob. Of the animals to be born in the future from the flocks he was tending, Jacob would be permitted to keep the *abnormally* colored ones. All others would belong to Laban. See alternate interpretation in footnote, end of *v.* 35.]

הָסֵר מִשָּׁם — *Remove from there.*

The commentators differ on whether the word הָסֵר, *remove,* is to be interpreted in the imperative: *you remove,* or as an infinitive participle: I will pass through your whole flock today *removing* [i.e., and *I* (Jacob) *will remove*] *from there.* Our translation, in the imperative, follows *Rashi* here and in *v.* 35, *Radak, Ramban* and most classical commentators.

Malbim [following the alternate view cited in footnote end of *v.* 35] maintains that *Jacob* would himself *pass through and remove* all these unnaturally colored sheep.

כָּל שֶׂה נָקֹד וְטָלוּא — *Every speckled or* [lit. *and*] *spotted sheep.*

[The Hebrew word שֶׂה is a collective term that refers both to a young כֶּבֶשׂ, *lamb,* and a young עֵז, *kid,* regardless of sex, as is clear from *Exodus* 12:5. Hence the need for further clarification of שֶׂה עִזִּים, *young goat,* and שֶׂה כְּבָשִׂים, *young sheep.* See *Rashi* there and *Mishnah Bechoros* 1:5. The term כֶּבֶשׂ occurring alone refers to a sheep within its first year.]

According to *Ramban's* interpretation of *Rashi* [see end of verse] the designation שֶׂה here refers specifically to the *he-goats* (תְּיָשִׁים) mentioned below in *v.* 35, while עִזִּים, *goats,* mentioned further in our verse refers to the *she*-goats. Following this interpretation, Jacob's pay came only from goats, not from sheep.

In his own interpretation, *Ramban* [end of verse] suggests that שֶׂה refers to the *sheep.*

Many commentators — cf. *Radak, Sforno, Haamek Davar, Hoffmann* — interpret שֶׂה as a collective term for both the lambs and kids [see above]. First Jacob makes this *general* statement regarding the unnaturally colored *young* animals, then he goes on to *specify* exactly which distinguishing discolorations will apply respectively to the lambs and goats.

The term נָקֹד, *speckled,* refers to animals marked with *small* dot-like specks, while טָלוּא, *spotted* is related to טְלָאִים, *patches,* and has the meaning of *wide* patches (*Rashi*).

The translation 'speckled **or** spotted' follows *Ramban.*

וְכָל־שֶׂה־חוּם בַּכְּבָשִׂים — [*And*] *every brownish lamb among the sheep.*

Rashi explains that חוּם is related to the term שָׁחוּם, *reddish brown; rouge* in Old French.

Ibn Ezra and *Radak* render חוּם as

ויצא
ל/לג

לג בָּעִזִּים וְהָיָה שְׂכָרִי׃ וְעָנְתָה־בִּי צִדְקָתִי
בְּיוֹם מָחָר כִּי־תָבוֹא עַל־שְׂכָרִי לְפָנֶיךָ כֹּל
אֲשֶׁר־אֵינֶנּוּ נָקֹד וְטָלוּא בָּעִזִּים וְחוּם

black, but *Ramban* disagrees since, according to him, *most* sheep in that warm region are black and there would be nothing attractive in Jacob's offering. He agrees with *Onkelos* and *Rashi* that the word denotes *reddish brownish*, and that חום is related to חַמָּה, *sun*, which has a reddish cast.

חום [lit. *warm*] does not occur elsewhere as a color. In any case it means *dark;* either because dark colors keep warmer, or because white turns dark through heat. According to Jacob's terms, small spots or large patches apply to both sheep and goats; חום, *dark*, probably *black*, only for sheep. The normal color of wool is white (cf. *Isaiah* 1:18). In *Song of Songs* 4:1, 2, flowing black tresses are compared to a herd of goats hurrying down the mountain, and the teeth to a flock of sheep coming up from bathing. From that we can deduce, in opposition to *Rambam* that the normal color of sheep is *white* and that of goats is *black (R' Hoffmann)* [see also *Rashi* to *Shabbos* 77b].

Radak further limits the designated animals: חום [blackish] markings would apply only to their head and neck in any case.

וְטָלוּא וְנָקֹד בָּעִזִּים – *And the spotted or* [following *Ramban;* lit. *and*] *speckled among the goats.*

Most goats as noted, are black. Here, too, he would be segregating those with unnatural colors. *Spotted* and *speckled* in this case would refer to black goats which had *white* markings *(Hoffmann).*

וְהָיָה שְׂכָרִי – *That will be my wage.*

I.e., that kind of abnormally colored animal – the *speckled* and *spotted* among the *goats* and the *brownish* ones among the sheep shall be my wage. Remove the presently existing animals of such coloration to the care of your sons so you will not be able to claim that any such animals born later were in the flock previously. Another reason to segregate the flocks is that you should not complain that your abnormally colored males caused similar ones to be born *(Rashi).*

[According to the view of *Or Zarua* this group of *existing* unnaturally colored sheep *as well* as their future offspring would immediately become Jacob's hire. See *footnote* to the end of verse 35.]

Ramban notes that *Rashi* above includes only the *brownish sheep* and *speckled or spotted goats* among the offspring that would belong to Jacob. *Rashi* does not mention the opening category כָּל־שֶׂה נָקֹד וְטָלוּא, *every speckled or spotted* שֶׂה [*seh*].

[Since *seh* is a collective term which can designate either sheep or goats (see *Deut.* 14:4)], *Ramban* cites the specific mention in *v.* 35 of תְּיָשִׁים, *he-goats*, which is absent here, and suggests that following *Rashi's* interpretation – shared by *Ibn Ezra* – the expression *speckled or spotted 'seh'* refers to *he*-goats, while the later designation וְטָלוּא וְנָקֹד בָּעִזִּים, *spotted or speckled among the goats*, refers to the *she-goats*.

Thus, *Ramban* maintains, according to *Rashi's* exegesis above, the coloration of sheep and goats would not be the same: from the *goats* he would receive spotted or speckled kids, while from the *sheep* he would receive brownish lambs.

Ramban therefore finds this difficult since if Jacob were to receive only brownish sheep, why didn't he take steps to produce *brownish* lambs? Furthermore, *brownish* sheep were not shown him in his dream mentioned in 31:10. [Additionally, *Tur* wonders why the Torah interrupted the sequence by in-

30 *spotted or speckled among the goats — that will be*
33 *my wage.* [33] *Let my integrity testify for me in the*
future when it comes before you regarding my wage.
Any among the goats that is not speckled or spotted,

serting the reference to sheep between the descriptions of male and female goats.]

Accordingly, *Ramban* suggests that *'seh'* in the beginning of the verse refers to the *speckled* or *spotted sheep.* An additional request was the inclusion of the *brownish* ones among the sheep, while among the *goats* the criteria was limited to *speckled or spotted.* Thus *three* mutations of *sheep* would be considered Jacob's: *speckled, spotted,* and *brownish,* while among the goats only the *spotted* and *speckled ones.*

The reason he added the brownish to the category of *sheep* is that it is not in the nature of *sheep* to be born with the same discolorations as *goats.* [Therefore, had Jacob left himself with only *spotted and speckled sheep,* his gains would have been minimal. On the other hand, such discolorations are not uncommon among goats.] But he omitted *brownish goats* because such colored goats are quite unusual. However, *Ramban's* solution fails to solve the problem he, himself, raised. Since only brownishness is a fairly common mutation among *sheep,* why didn't Jacob set brownish sticks to assure himself of some gains among the sheep? *(Tur).* [See *R' Bachya* in *footnote* to *v.* 37.]

33. וְעָנְתָה־בִּי צִדְקָתִי בְּיוֹם מָחָר — *Let my integrity testify for me in the future* [lit. *on the day of the morrow*].

Should you in the future suspect me of taking any animals that are yours, my integrity will answer for me [i.e., any investigation will prove that I always deal honestly] *(Rashi).*

Hirsch interprets: The dedication that is expected of me will testify בִּי, *against me,* should I betray my standards of integrity.

Jacob added this assurance because knowing Laban's personality, he was sure that as early as בְּיוֹם מָחָר, *on the morrow,* there would arise some dispute regarding this seemingly clear-cut agreement *(Daas Soferim).*[1]

כִּי תָבוֹא עַל שְׂכָרִי לְפָנֶיךָ — *When it comes* [lit. *will come*] *before you.*

— When *it* — my integrity — will be questioned by you, it will come with the following demonstration of my honesty: You will find in my herd only abnormally colored animals ... *(Rashi).*

According to many commentators [*Rashbam; Radak; Sforno; R' Hirsch*] the word תָבוֹא is not in third person feminine referring to Jacob's righteousness — when *it* comes, but second person singular — when *you* (referring to Laban) *will come.* Thus: *when in the future you come to review my* wages which lies *before you,* i.e., by inspecting my flocks.

1. The *Mesorah* notes that the phrase בְּיוֹם מָחָר, lit. *on the day of the morrow,* occurs twice in Scripture: here, and in *Proverbs* 27:1: אַל תִּתְהַלֵּל בְּיוֹם מָחָר, *Boast not of yourself regarding the morrow.* The Holy One, Blessed be He, said to Jacob: You boast to Laban regarding the morrow; do you then know what the morrow will bring? *Boast not of yourself regarding the morrow,* for on the morrow [i.e. in the near future] your daughter Dinah will go out and be humbled [34:1ff] *(Midrash; Baal HaTurim).*

לד בַּכְּשָׂבִים גָּנוּב הוּא אִתִּי: וַיֹּאמֶר לָבָן הֵן
לה לוּ יְהִי כִדְבָרֶךָ: וַיָּסַר בַּיּוֹם הַהוּא אֶת־
הַתְּיָשִׁים הָעֲקֻדִּים וְהַטְּלֻאִים וְאֵת כָּל־
הָעִזִּים הַנְּקֻדּוֹת וְהַטְּלֻאֹת כֹּל אֲשֶׁר־לָבָן
בּוֹ וְכָל־חוּם בַּכְּשָׂבִים וַיִּתֵּן בְּיַד־בָּנָיו:

כֹּל אֲשֶׁר אֵינֶנּוּ נָקֹד...גָּנוּב הוּא אִתִּי — *Any among the goats that is not speckled or spotted, or among the sheep that is not brownish may be regarded as stolen if in possession* [lit. *it is stolen* with me].

— I.e. if any normal monochrome animal is found among *my* flocks it may be presumed that I have stolen it [from your flocks] *(Rashi).*

— Should you ask, if all such spotted animals are eliminated, from where shall *my* animals come in the future, let that be my worry. I will rely on my righteousness. God has blessed me until now for *your* benefit, and He will do the same for *my* benefit. This will be demonstrated later and no normal monochrome animal will remain in my possession. Otherwise you may count it as stolen *(Alshich).*

34. [Laban apparently assumed that the pure white and pure black animals left with Jacob would bear only a trifling percentage of miscolored young. Such would have indeed been the case were it not that Jacob — betrayed by Laban's changing of the terms — adopted special measures as will be explained later. Laban is gratified at the apparently advantageous terms and agrees to them at once]:

הֵן — *Agreed!* [lit. *yes*].

Following *Rashi:* an expression denoting agreement with a suggested proposition.

לוּ יְהִי כִדְבָרֶךָ — *If only it would remain as you say* [lit. *like your words*].

If only you would remain satisfied with this! *(Rashi).*

Woe to the wicked whose own words are perverse — state the Sages — and who imagine others to be like themselves. Here Laban expressed the hope that *Jacob* would abide by his word, but afterwards it was said of *Laban* [31:7]: *But your father cheated me, and changed my wages ten times! (Midrash HaGadol).*[1]

35. [In practice, Laban does not allow Jacob to remove the colored animals (see *v.* 32). Furthermore, the deceitful Laban removes more of the flock than he was entitled to under the original terms]:

וַיָּסַר בַּיּוֹם הַהוּא — *So* [lit. *and*] *he removed on that very day.*

[The subject is Laban.] No time is wasted: The devious Laban, taking no chances, proceeds to divide his flock *that very day (Ralbag).*

[See alternate view of *Or Zarua* cited in footnote, end of this verse.]

Malbim interprets the original deal in

1. *Sefer HaParshiyos* preserves a *Midrashic* interpretation that there was something sinister even in this 'innocent' remark of the deceitful Laban. Following as it does Jacob's statement: גָּנוּב הוּא אִתִּי, *It may be regarded as stolen if in my possession,* Laban's response implied: *'Yes, may it be as you say* — may I discover a monochrome animal unjustly in your possession, giving me grounds to nullify our whole agreement!'

30
34-35 *or among the sheep that is not brownish may be regarded as stolen if in my possession.'*

[34] *And Laban said, 'Agreed! If only it would remain as you say.'*

[35] *So he removed on that very day the ringed and spotted he-goats and all the speckled and spotted goats — every one that contained white, as well as all the brownish ones among the sheep, and he left them*

verse 32 to imply that it was *Jacob* himself who was to remove certain unnaturally colored animals, but in this verse, he interprets that *Laban* is the subject. Laban immediately proceeded to make unilateral changes in the terms agreed upon in verse 32. Although Jacob had specified that all existing spotted and speckled animals were to be given him, Laban took possession of them for himself. Furthermore, Jacob wanted multi-colored animals to remain intermixed with the flocks, but Laban removed them as well, leaving only the monochrome animals from whom the birth of the agreed-upon mutations would be highly improbable. Lastly, by taking the initiative in reneging on his agreements, Laban set the precedent *on that very day* which allowed him to change the terms whenever it suited him to do so. He did this by constantly reading new interpretations and shadings into the terms to which he had agreed.

הַתְּיָשִׁים הָעֲקֻדִּים וְהַטְּלֻאִים — *The ringed and spotted he-goats.*

The term עֲקֻדִּים [*ringed*] literally means *bound,* and refers to those animals which are differently colored at the point where animals are usually bound by their owners: the ankles of their forelegs and hindlegs *(Rashi v.* 39).

In 22:9, the verb וַיַּעֲקֹד, *he bound,* occurs in reference to Abraham's binding of Isaac's hands and feet behind him. *Rashi* there refers to the word עֲקֻדִּים in our verse which he similarly explains as meaning: whose ankles were [ringed] white, so that the place where they are bound can be plainly recognized.

The terminology here differs markedly from the arrangement formulated in *v.* 32. As *Ramban* explains there [differing from *Ibn Ezra*], in the original deal no reference was made specifically to *he*-goats, yet, *Ramban* points out, Laban now took the he-goats as well so as to avoid the genetic influence of the spotted and speckled males. He went further and [besides the *spotted* goats], he even removed those with ringed markings on their legs.

In effect he was making it almost impossible for Jacob to earn any animals within the terms of the agreement. Indeed, only by a miracle would any new animals be born with any markings whatsoever! *(R' Hirsch).*

In the interpretation of *Rashi* according to which he-goats *were* originally referred to by the designation שֶׂה, Laban similarly deviated from the original terms by taking even those with *ringed markings,* as well as any that had even the slightest marking of white [see further].

Following *Sforno,* Laban deviated by taking not only the *young,* but even the *mature* animals with those mutations.

וְאֵת כָּל־הָעִזִּים הַנְּקֻדּוֹת וְהַטְּלֻאֹת — *And all the spotted and speckled goats.*

These refer, as in *v.* 32, to the *she*-goats *(Ramban).*

כֹּל אֲשֶׁר־לָבָן בּוֹ וְכָל חוּם בַּכְּבָשִׂים — *Every one that contained white* [i.e a white spot *(Rashi)*], *as well as* [lit. *and*] *all the brownish ones among the sheep.*

The translation follows *Ramban* who renders this phrase as referring entirely to the sheep [which according to *Ramban* were usually

לו וַיָּשֶׂם דֶּרֶךְ שְׁלֹשֶׁת יָמִים בֵּינוֹ וּבֵין יַעֲקֹב
וְיַעֲקֹב רֹעֶה אֶת־צֹאן לָבָן הַנּוֹתָרֹת׃
לז וַיִּקַּח־לוֹ יַעֲקֹב מַקַּל לִבְנֶה לַח וְלוּז

dark in those regions]: Laban went beyond the original terms and removed whatever sheep had even the slightest white spot *in addition to* the brownish sheep which he was entitled to.

Ramban continues that it is also possible that the phrase *every one that had white in it* is connected with the *earlier* part of the verse and refers to the *goats,* in which case the *brownish sheep* were *in addition* to the speckled and spotted ones [which, according to *Ramban,* in *v.* 32 applied to the sheep as well]. The brownish *sheep,* as noted, were originally stipulated by Jacob because such color in sheep was highly improbable [and it made Laban even more eager to accept the deal. But now, taking no chances, Laban removed even those few brownish sheep in addition to the speckled and spotted ones, to diminish Jacob's chances as much as possible. It further exposes the cunning of Laban].

וַיִּתֵּן בְּיַד־בָּנָיו — *And he* [=Laban] *left* [*them*] *in the charge of his sons* [lit. *and he gave in the hand of his sons*].[1]

36. [As an additional precaution, Laban places a considerable distance between the flocks he separated and the flocks he left with Jacob]:

וַיָּשֶׂם דֶּרֶךְ שְׁלֹשֶׁת יָמִים בֵּינוֹ וּבֵין יַעֲקֹב — *And he* [Laban] *put a distance of three days* [lit. a three days' journey] *between himself and* [*between*] *Jacob.*

[For fear that there might be contact between these flocks and those tended by Jacob.]

וְיַעֲקֹב רֹעֶה אֶת צֹאן לָבָן הַנּוֹתָרֹת — *And Jacob tended* [the Hebrew רֹעֶה denotes a constant action: *was*

1. There is an alternate interpretation of this incident mentioned by the early halachic codifier *R' Yitzchak* of Vienna [ca. 1200 – 1270] in his work *Or Zarua,* Responsa 769. It is basically also the view of *Sefer HaYashar,* and cited with differences by *Abarbanel* followed by *Malbim.*

According to it, Jacob's wage included the *existing* unnaturally colored sheep separated from Laban's flock *as well as* the offspring which would later be born of them. The verb הָסֵר in *v.* 32 is not imperative but an infinitive participle, and refers to Jacob himself: *I will pass through your flocks today, removing them.* Accordingly, the expression *that will be my wage,* refers to these sheep that *Jacob* would thus separate from Laban's flocks. Consequently, the subject of the phrase *and he left them in the charge of his sons* is Jacob, who separated these animals and placed them in the care of his *own* children, Reuben and Simeon.

Following this view, Jacob could be accused of no trickery whatsoever since he used the peeled rods to influence only *his own flocks.* According to this interpretation even the *monochrome* offspring of Jacob's own flocks would remain his, but Jacob went beyond the strict letter of the arrangement and used the rods to assure that *all* his own flocks would be born spotted and speckled, thereby making it impossible for Laban to accuse him of stealing monochrome animals.

Jacob segregated the unnaturally colored sheep born of Laban's flocks which Jacob separated [*v.* 40] to assure that too many of Laban's newborn animals would not be colored unnaturally. Jacob's dream was intended to show him that Divine influence caused Laban's monochrome

in the charge of his sons. [36] *And he put a distance of*
three days between himself and Jacob; and Jacob
tended Laban's remaining flock.
[37] *Jacob then took himself a fresh rod of poplar*

tending or *would tend*] *Laban's remaining flock.*

— [The word נוֹתָרֹת, *remaining*, is interpreted in the *Midrash* as connoting the *leftover, inferior* sheep]:

Laban's remaining sheep — the defective, sickly and barren animals among them, which were nothing but the leftovers — these Laban handed over to Jacob *(Rashi).*

[Laban was confident that even under these circumstances — given Jacob's devoted service and the blessing of his presence — Jacob would be able to increase the flocks even from these sickly animals. This indeed took place, but Laban did not expect that Jacob would respond to his trickery in kind by enlarging his *own* flocks as well, although scrupulously adhering to the letter of the deal between them.]

37. The peeled rods.

[Jacob resorts to several devices to outwit his uncle and regain what was rightfully his under the original terms of the arrangement. He places colored rods in front of the flocks at the time they conceived, so that they would bear lambs having the same markings as the rod they were facing. Cf. *Megillah* 13b which justifies Jacob's actions by citing *Psalms* 18:27: *with the trustworthy, act trustingly; and with the crooked, act perversely.* See footnote to *v.* 42, and *Overview.*]

R' Bachya — and many early commentators — emphasize that Jacob did not resort to the device of the peeled rods on his own initiative but *after* the angel informed him in a dream [31:12]: *Raise your eyes ... and see that all the he-goats mounting the flocks are ringed,* Although the dream is described later, it preceded Jacob's peeling of the rods described now. As we have often seen, the Torah is not always written in chronological sequence.

מַקַּל לִבְנֶה לַח — *A fresh* [lit. *moist*] *rod of poplar.*

The word לִבְנֶה, *poplar*, refers to a tree by that name mentioned also in *Hoshea* 4:13. It is referred to in Old French as *tremble* [=trembling poplar; aspen, a species of poplar] which is white [hence the name *livneh* from *lavan*, white]. He took it while it was still fresh *(Rashi).*

R'Bachya explains it as a rod of

sheep to bear so many spotted and speckled offspring. This interpretation of verses 41-42 takes the term מְקֻשָּׁרוֹת to imply the unnaturally colored sheep, before whom Jacob placed the peeled sticks, while with עֲטוּפִים, *monochrome flocks*, Jacob did nothing.

Ramban in *v.* 30 and *Ibn Ezra* in *v.* 35 disagree with the above view [known to them apparently from earlier sources since *R' Yitzchak* of Vienna lived after them]. They maintain that *v.* 35 could not refer to Reuben and Simeon because they were mere children while Laban's sons were older. Accordingly, הָסֵר, *remove*, in *v.* 32 must be imperative, as explained in the mainstream of the commentary. [See *Malbim.*]

There are, in general, many difficulties with the above interpretation, which led *Riva* to maintain that it is more of a justification of Jacob's actions than a reflection of the simple sense of the verses.

וְעַרְמוֹן וַיְפַצֵּל בָּהֵן פְּצָלוֹת לְבָנוֹת
לח מַחְשֹׂף הַלָּבָן אֲשֶׁר עַל־הַמַּקְלוֹת: וַיַּצֵּג
אֶת־הַמַּקְלוֹת אֲשֶׁר פִּצֵּל בָּרְהָטִים
בְּשִׁקֲתוֹת הַמָּיִם אֲשֶׁר תָּבֹאןָ הַצֹּאן
לִשְׁתּוֹת לְנֹכַח הַצֹּאן וַיֵּחַמְנָה בְּבֹאָן

the cedar trees of the type which grow in Lebanon.[1]

וְלוּז וְעַרְמוֹן — *And* [rods of (following *Rashi*)]: *hazel and chestnut.*

The term לוז is familiarly translated as *almond* (so *Ibn Ezra*). As always, however, our translation follows *Rashi* who renders the term here as "a tree upon which small nuts grow; in Old French *coudre*" [= *coudrier*, the hazel tree.]

Rashi translates עַרְמוֹן as *castenoir* [= black chestnut.] [Some others identify it with the sycamore tree.]

וַיְפַצֵּל בָּהֵן פְּצָלוֹת לְבָנוֹת — [*And*] *he peeled white streaks* [lit. peelings] *in them.*

The word פְּצָלוֹת means *peelings.* He made many peelings which resulted in giving them a streaked appearance *(Rashi).*

[Some of the species, as noted, have white barks in which case the exposed peeled portion was dark. This passage speaks of the dark species in which he peeled *white* streaks.]

מַחְשֹׂף הַלָּבָן אֲשֶׁר עַל־הַמַּקְלוֹת — *Laying bare the white of* [lit. *which was upon*] *the rods.*

I.e. by peeling off portions of the [dark] bark, he uncovered the peeled portions which were white *(Rashi).*

38. וַיַּצֵּג אֶת־הַמַּקְלוֹת אֲשֶׁר פִּצֵּל — *And he set up the rods which he had peeled.*

The verb וַיַּצֵּג [set up] is translated by *Onkelos* וְדָעִיץ, which means *inserting, setting up (Rashi).*

בָּרְהָטִים בְּשִׁקֲתוֹת הַמָּיִם אֲשֶׁר תָּבֹאןָ הַצֹּאן לִשְׁתּוֹת — *In the runnels, in the watering receptacles to which the flocks came* [lit. *would* (regularly) *come*] *to drink.*

[The verb רהט is the Aramaic of רוץ, *run*]: בָּרְהָטִים, *in the runnels,* i.e. in the currents [מְרוּצוֹת, *running streams*] of water running in gutters made in the earth, where the sheep regularly came to drink *(Rashi)* ...

Rashi thus defines רְהָטִים, the Aramaic for *run,* as *running streams,* and he defines שִׁקֲתוֹת הַמָּיִם as *gutters* dug in the earth *(Mizrachi).* [The above is apparently offered to distinguish between the closely related terms רְהָטִים and שִׁקֲתוֹת הַמָּיִם. However, when the word רְהָטִים occurs *alone* as further in verse 41, it is familiarly rendered *runnels,* or, as *Ibn Ezra* suggests, *watering troughs.*]

[Comp. the allegorical interpretation of *Song of Songs* 7:7: מֶלֶךְ אָסוּר בָּרְהָטִים (lit. a king bound in *tresses*) where the Hebrew word *rehatim,* tresses, is esoterically related to the *rehatim,* watering troughs, of our episode: *God* (the 'King') is bound in love to Israel (i.e., Jacob) who peeled the rods in the *rehatim,* watering troughs.]

לְנֹכַח הַצֹּאן — *Facing the sheep.*

[This modifies the *placing of the*

1. We do not find that Jacob used חום, *reddish-brown,* colored rods to influence the birth of such sheep. Apparently he did not find any such naturally colored trees, and he would not risk the chance of painting such a color on other trees lest he arouse the curiosity of Laban's people *(R' Bachya).*

and hazel and chestnut. He peeled white streaks in
them, laying bare the white of the rods. [38] *And he set*
up the rods which he had peeled, in the runnels — in
the watering receptacles to which the flocks came to
drink — facing the sheep, so they would become
stimulated when they came to drink. [39] *Then the*

rods in the beginning of the verse]: I.e., there, in the watering troughs Jacob set up the rods *facing the sheep (Rashi).*

[*Rashi* means to negate the following misreading of the verse: ... *to the watering receptacles to which the flocks came to drink facing the sheep*. Such a literal reading of the verse would mean that one group of sheep came to drink facing another group of sheep *(Mizrachi).*]

Malbim differs. In his interpretation, the sheep *were* positioned so that they faced one another as they drank. As he emphasizes, the birth of the discolored animals was purely miraculous as revealed to Jacob in 31:12. Jacob's purpose was merely to perform a physical act which would 'assist', so to speak, the performance of the miracle. Such symbolic acts are often found in connection with prophecies and miracles. Jacob's intention, therefore, was to arouse the sheep through the sight of other spotted and speckled sheep and thereby influence their pigmentation. The groups faced one another, and *the peeled rods which Jacob set up between them* created the optical illusion that the sheep which they were facing were spotted and speckled as well. [See footnote below.]

וַיֵּחַמְנָה בְּבֹאָן לִשְׁתּוֹת — *So* [lit. *and*] *they would become stimulated* [lit. *heated;* i.e. excited; startled] *when they came to drink.*

When the female animals would see the rods [in their watering troughs] they would become startled and would recoil backwards. At that moment, the males would mount them, and they would later give birth to lambs having the same markings as the rod they were facing *(Rashi).*[1]

Others render the word וַיֵּחַמְנָה to mean *mated* or *bred,* the verse informing us that the flocks were accustomed to breed when they congregated to drink water.

This, too, was one of the miracles

1. [The physiological principle harnessed by Jacob in this episode illustrates a practical familiarity with parapsychological phenomena influencing the pigmentation of flocks through visual stimulus.

Indeed, the *Talmud* and *Midrash* provide many examples where even among *humans* meditation during marital intimacy can have major effects on the conceived child (see *R' Bachya* cited in commentary, next page).

From 31:12 it emerges that these laws of heredity were revealed to Jacob when an angel, appearing to him, opened his eyes to a comprehension of the subject.

There are opinions, noted later in the commentary, that the discolored pigmentations were the result of a miracle designed to preserve him from Laban's trickery. (In fact in *Midrash Tehillim* 8:6 the implication is that Jacob was able to make the sheep come out as he pleased through pure meditation). Jacob, however, used the rods so that the miracle could be achieved in a natural way (comp. *Ramban's* explanation regarding Noah's ark in 6:19).

Jacob's action, then, did not *bring forth* the miracle but only *accompanied* it. Similarly, Moses and Aaron stretched out their rods for the plagues in Egypt. Nothing is more exclusively in God's power than life, breeding, and giving birth. In the final analysis, only *He* can cause spotted cattle to be born (cf. Midrash HaGadol).]

לט לִשְׁתּוֹת׃ וַיֶּחֱמוּ הַצֹּאן אֶל־הַמַּקְלוֹת
וַתֵּלַדְןָ הַצֹּאן עֲקֻדִּים נְקֻדִּים וּטְלֻאִים׃
מ וְהַכְּשָׂבִים הִפְרִיד יַעֲקֹב וַיִּתֵּן פְּנֵי הַצֹּאן
אֶל־עָקֹד וְכָל־חוּם בְּצֹאן לָבָן וַיָּשֶׁת לוֹ
עֲדָרִים לְבַדּוֹ וְלֹא שָׁתָם עַל־צֹאן לָבָן׃

of the episode, that the flocks should be aroused to mate just on that occasion *(Malbim).*

R' Bachya observes that this concept contains an important lesson. If the imagination is a determining factor for the nature of the unborn lambs, as this verse describes, then how much more important will it be when sensitive, thinking human beings procreate! Therefore, when husband and wife unite, they must keep their minds purged of all impure thoughts and every element which is foreign or which concerns third parties. The degree of their moral and spiritual purity will have repercussions on the souls of their children *(R' Munk).*

Rashi proceeds to cite the view of R' Hoshaia that the water the animals drank changed miraculously into semen, and they did not require a male [to impregnate them.]

Gur Aryeh explains that R' Hoshaia's interpretation has two bases: 1) The verse attaches the stimulation of the sheep to their *coming to drink* rather than to the rods; b) The word וַיֵּחַמְנָה is a combination of the male form, וַיֶּחֱמוּ, and the feminine form וַתֵּחַמְנָה. This implies that the male and female functions were combined in the same animals.

Possibly R' Hoshaia holds that the verb וַיֵּחַמְנָה means *they became pregnant* when they came to drink *(Mizrachi).*

39. [Having provided a general description of Jacob's device, the Torah now proceeds to further detail the actual procedure]:

וַיֶּחֱמוּ הַצֹּאן אֶל הַמַּקְלוֹת — *Then* [lit. *and*] *the flocks became stimulated by* [lit. *toward*] *the rods.*

I.e. at the appearance of the [stripped] rods *(Rashi).* [As *Rashi* explains above in his primary interpretation, the startled sheep would recoil backwards at which time the males would mount them and they would conceive.]

Malbim observes that the fact that they were influenced by the speckled rods rather than by the more numerous monochrome animals was a further manifestation of God's Hand in this matter.

וַתֵּלַדְןָ הַצֹּאן עֲקֻדִּים נְקֻדִּים וּטְלֻאִים — *And the flocks gave birth to ringed ones, speckled ones, and spotted ones.*

[I.e. to offspring having the same markings as the rod they were facing *(Rashi v.* 38).]

[The terms *ringed, spotted and speckled* are defined in verses 32 and 35.]

40. [Jacob separates the flocks, making the newborn spotted ones lead the monochrome ones, so the latter would be influenced by the leaders and bear similar offspring]:

וְהַכְּשָׂבִים הִפְרִיד יַעֲקֹב — *Jacob segregated the lambs* — that were thus born ringed and spotted.

— And he formed them into a separate flock *(Rashi).*

וַיִּתֵּן פְּנֵי הַצֹּאן אֶל־עָקֹד וְכָל־חוּם בְּצֹאן לָבָן — *And he made the sheep face the ringed ones and all the brownish*

30 *flocks became stimulated by the rods and the flocks*
40 *gave birth to ringed ones, speckled ones and spotted*
ones. [40] *Jacob segregated the lambs and he made the*
sheep face the ringed ones and all the brownish ones
among Laban's flocks. He formed separate flocks of
his own and did not mingle them with Laban's sheep.

ones among Laban's flocks.

That is, he separated these ringed and spotted sheep [i.e. *lambs,* which, according to most interpretations of *Rashi* in *v.* 32, did not belong to Jacob, as only the newborn *brownish* lambs were to be his *(Gur Aryeh)*] and made them head the flock of monochrome sheep' [a collective term for ungulates including both sheep *and* goats] so that the latter would look at these ringed and spotted lambs as well as at the brownish ones [i.e., goats, see below] which Laban had left him *(Rashi).*

Following *Ramban's* interpretation of *Rashi's* exegesis, Jacob's intention was that the sight of these particular animals [i.e., the ringed and spotted *lambs* and brownish *goats,* both of which did not belong to Jacob, according to this interpretation of *Rashi*] would, like the rods, stimulate the remaining monochrome flocks to bear particolored offspring of the species which *would* belong to him, viz. ringed and spotted *goats* and brownish *lambs.*

The *'brownish ones'* mentioned by *Rashi* refer to those brownish *goats* left him by Laban. It could not refer to the brownish *sheep* since verse 35 explicitly mentions that Laban removed them. Laban had not removed the brownish *goats* since they would not belong to Jacob in any event [*v.* 32], just as in verse 35, according to this interpretation, Laban had not removed the ringed and spotted *sheep (Tzeidah LaDerech;* see *Sifsei Chachomim; Mizrachi).*

[Jacob's intention in taking these goats was that when the white *sheep* would gaze at the brownish *goats,* they would bear brownish offspring. These newborn brownish sheep would be Jacob's since, following this interpretation, he was to keep *only* the brownish ones among the sheep.]

According to *Ramban's* own interpretation of the episode [i.e. that the ringed sheep as well as the brownish sheep were included in Jacob's wage], Jacob took extra pains to influence the birth of such sheep. He did not content himself with having the sheep gaze at rods because lambs are sturdier than goats and they require more signs to stimulate them, and because there were no brownish sticks for him to set up [see footnote to *v.* 37.] Therefore he caused the lambs to gaze upon brownish goats. The intent of the verse is that Jacob separated the monochrome, unspotted lambs and caused these *lambs* — referred to collectively as *flocks* rather than again as *lambs* — to gaze upon the ringed flocks as well as upon the brownish ones. Following this interpretation, the term בְּצֹאן לָבָן, *among Laban's flocks* does not imply that these spotted flocks *belonged to Laban,* for in fact they did not. Rather it intimates: *so did he do with all of Laban's flocks.*

וַיָּשֶׁת לוֹ עֲדָרִים לְבַדּוֹ — [And] *he formed* [lit. *placed*] *separate flocks of his own* [lit. *by himself.*]

[Of these separated sheep] as explained above *(Rashi)*

[Cf. *Gur Aryeh*].

וְלֹא שָׁתָם עַל צֹאן לָבָן — *And did not mingle* [lit. *place*] *them with* [lit. *on*] *Laban's sheep.*

So that he would not be subject to suspicion. Jacob's flocks were clear-

מא וְהָיָה בְּכָל־יַחֵם הַצֹּאן הַמְקֻשָּׁרוֹת וְשָׂם
יַעֲקֹב אֶת־הַמַּקְלוֹת לְעֵינֵי הַצֹּאן
מב בָּרְהָטִים לְיַחְמֵנָּה בַּמַּקְלוֹת: וּבְהַעֲטִיף
הַצֹּאן לֹא יָשִׂים וְהָיָה הָעֲטֻפִים לְלָבָן

ly segregated and Laban would have no cause for complaint that Jacob was using his own animals to promote the birth of animals with a similar tendency among Laban's flocks *(Chizkuni).*

41-42. [Jacob did not apply these measures indiscriminately. He set up the peeled rods only when the early-bearing sturdier flocks were about to mate, thus securing the hardiest animals for himself.]

41. בְּכָל־יַחֵם הַצֹּאן הַמְקֻשָּׁרוֹת — *Whenever the early-bearing* [i.e. sturdier *(Ramban; Lekach Tov)*] *animals became stimulated.*

I.e., were about to mate in their prime season *(Radak).*

Understanding Jacob's procedure outlined in these two verses requires familiarity with the premise that sheep drop two litters annually: They mate in *Nissan* [=March-April] and have a litter in *Av* [=July-August]; they mate again in *Tishrei* [=September-October] and have a litter in *Adar* [=February-March].

Ramban [*v.* 37] explains that those *early-bearing sheep,* i.e. those who mated in *Nissan,* were the *sturdier sheep* referred to here. It was only with *these* sheep that Jacob resorted to the rods [to assure himself a sturdy flock]; with the *weaker, later-bearing sheep* who mated in *Tishrei* he did nothing since setting up the rods *twice* a year would have aroused the animosity of Laban's shepherds. Furthermore, had Jacob *always* resorted to this practice, Laban would have been left with absolutely no flocks whatsoever.

Ramban then cites *Radak's* father that in the *first year* of the agreement Jacob did not resort to this device, as many spotted animals were born to him that year by God's blessing [see 31:12]. It was only when these newborn sheep that were *already rightfully his* under the terms of the arrangement were ready to mate that he used the rods to influence them to produce similarly spotted offspring which would *remain* his. At the same time, Laban would be prevented from claiming that Jacob had stolen his flock which Laban certainly would have done had Jacob's animals produced monochromed lambs and kids.[1]

The ambiguous term מְקֻשָּׁרוֹת occurs in this form only here in all of Scripture. *Rashi* follows *Onkelos* who renders it בְּכִירוּת, *the firstlings,* i.e. *the early-bearing sheep* [or: sheep who bore for the first time *(Lekach Tov)*]. He cites *Menachem* who relates the

1. [The above is the only mention made by the early commentators regarding the status of the *offspring* of those spotted animals born to Jacob. Apparently, even *their* offspring would not automatically belong to Jacob unless they, too, were spotted. The monochrome offspring of even the spotted animals born under the terms of the deal would revert to Laban even if only for the purpose of maintaining visible proof of Jacob's compliance.]

Accordingly, *Ramban* continues, the animals referred to in our verse are those *firstlings* born to Jacob's by God's blessing: It was only with *these* that Jacob used the rods; with the *weaker ones,* i.e., those of Laban's flocks not granted him by God's blessing, he did not use this device, thereby leaving their offspring to Laban.

41 *Whenever the early-bearing animals became stimulated, Jacob would place the rods in the runnels, in full view of the flock to stimulate them among the rods.* 42 *But when the sheep were late-bearing he would not emplace. Thus, the late-bearing ones went to Laban and the early-bearing ones to Jacob.*

word to קֹשְׁרִים, *conspirators*, in *II Sam.* 15:13, the connotation being those sheep who *banded together* [=conspired] in order to accelerate their pregnancy [i.e., become early-bearing sheep.]

Ibn Ezra defines these sheep as those which mate in *Nissan*. *Ramban*, although agreeing with *Onkelos* and *Rashi* that it refers to the stronger, early-bearing sheep, suggests that the phrase refers to the virile and potent sheep who *constantly* desire to mate and are, consequently, always קְשׁוּרָה, *bound up*, following the females.

לְיַחֲמֶנָּה בַּמַּקְלוֹת — *To stimulate them* [i.e., cause them to mate *(Ibn Ezra)*] *among the rods.*

[See *Rashi* to *v.* 38 s.v. וַיֵּחַמְנָה.]

42. וּבְהַעֲטִיף הַצֹּאן לֹא יָשִׂים — *But when the sheep were late-bearing he would not emplace.*

[I.e., he would not set up the rods before the late-bearing, feebler, flocks. Accordingly, they did not produce spotted or speckled offspring.]

These were the sheep who bore late, as *Onkelos* renders וּבְלַקִּישׁוּת [from לקש, *late, slow, retarded* (compare the term מַלְקוֹשׁ, late rain).] *Menachem*, relating it to the root עטף, *wrapping*, figuratively explains this as referring to those animals who are 'well-wrapped in their furs' and do not desire — until later — to be 'warmed' by the males *(Rashi)*.

Ibn Ezra, too, defines these as those sheep who mated in *Tishrei*. They and their offspring are less sturdy, and the term עטף has the meaning of *feeble, languish*, weak [cf. *Psalms* 107:5; *Lam.* 2:19].

According to *Radak's* interpretation, cited by *Ramban* above, this was the season that Laban usually visited the newborn flocks. Jacob did not want him to see the rods even though they were set up in front of Jacob's flocks only, since Laban would accuse him of using such measures among *all* the flocks.

וְהָיָה הָעֲטֻפִים לְלָבָן וְהַקְּשֻׁרִים לְיַעֲקֹב — *Thus, the late-bearing ones went to Laban and the early-bearing ones to Jacob.*

For, in effect, the late-bearing feeble ones who were not exposed to the peeled rods did not give birth to spotted offspring. The early bearing ones as well as their spotted offspring born under the influence of Jacob's rods, remained with Jacob *(Ramban)*.[1]

Summary: The Validity of Jacob's Actions

1. Upon concluding the narrative of Jacob's dealings with Laban, one is struck by this question: How could the patriarch who epitomizes אֱמֶת, *truth* have stooped to such scheming? It is axiomatic, however, that since Jacob *does* represent the attribute of truth, his behavior must be understood in that light. Furthermore, the above arrangement lasted for six years, yet we find nowhere that Laban ever accused Jacob of cheating him, even in 31:26-30 when his ire was aroused. As outlined in the *Overview*, precisely *because* Jacob had to maintain his in-

ל/מג
לא/א

מג וְהַקְּשֻׁרִים לְיַעֲקֹב: וַיִּפְרֹץ הָאִישׁ מְאֹד
מְאֹד וַיְהִי־לוֹ צֹאן רַבּוֹת וּשְׁפָחוֹת
א וַעֲבָדִים וּגְמַלִּים וַחֲמֹרִים: וַיִּשְׁמַע אֶת־
דִּבְרֵי בְנֵי־לָבָן לֵאמֹר לָקַח יַעֲקֹב אֵת כָּל־
אֲשֶׁר לְאָבִינוּ וּמֵאֲשֶׁר לְאָבִינוּ עָשָׂה אֵת

43. The result of all the above is that Jacob prospered immensely:

וַיִּפְרֹץ הָאִישׁ מְאֹד מְאֹד – *The man became exceedingly prosperous* [lit. *spread out exceedingly;* or: *became exceedingly strong* (as *Rashi* explains the verb פרץ in 28:14).]

As noted in the commentary to 28:14 the verb פרץ in its most literal sense connotes *breaking forth* through narrow confines, or *increasing numerically* [*Radak* and *Ibn Ezra*].

– The connotation here is that

tegrity, he was tested by being thrown in with the arch-swindler of the era. Nevertheless, we must seek to understand the basis for his actions.

□ As viewed by the Sages, Jacob's action was necessary to defend himself against the trickery of Laban whose constant changes of the terms of the arrangement would have made it impossible for Jacob to earn any offspring for himself. Jacob's resort to trickery was permissible in consonance with the teaching of the Sages [*Megillah* 13b citing *Psalms* 18:27]: עִם־נָבָר תִּתָּבָר וְעִם־עִקֵּשׁ תִּתְפַּתָּל, *with the trustworthy act trustingly and with the crooked act perversely.* Compare *Rashi's* comment on 29:12 citing the *Midrash*: Jacob said to Rachel, 'Should your father wish to deceive me, I am his brother [i.e., his match] in deceit; but should he treat me fairly, I am the righteous Rebecca's son and I know how to reciprocate his righteousness' *(Mizrachi v.* 39).

□ *Ramban* [to *v.* 37] maintains that once they had agreed that certain mutations would belong to Jacob, Jacob had a right to seek to ensure such births and promote his interests. It is even possible that the procedure was distinctly stipulated for use only during the *Nissan* mating season [see *comm.* to *v.* 42].

□ *Radak,* citing his father, maintains that in the first year God blessed Jacob with an abundant flock of speckled and spotted animals without resort to peeled rods. It was *after* the vision of the angel [31:32; see *comm.* above, *v.* 37] that Jacob set up the peeled rods in front of his *own* spotted animals so that they in turn should produce similar ones. [According to this opinion Jacob did not have to do this because even the monochrome sheep born to Jacob's own speckled flock would remain Jacob's, nevertheless] Jacob used this device to prevent Laban from accusing him of stealing his monochrome animals, as Laban would undoubtedly have done had he discovered such offspring among Jacob's separated flocks. [See *Or Zarua* cited in *footnote* end of *v.* 35.]

□ Many commentators cited in the commentary point to the Providential aspect of this episode, and maintain that the mutants were merely the result of a miracle designed to protect Jacob from Laban's trickery. The rods were merely a symbolic manifestation of the miracle which Jacob understood after the vision described in 31:32, designed to disguise the miraculous aspect and clothe it in an aura of natural phenomena. Compare Elisha's instructions to Gehazi [*II Kings* 4:29] to lay his staff on the face of the child [as if the staff would be effective in reviving the child]. Similarly, as noted in the footnote to verse 38, the rods did not *bring forth* the miracle, but merely *accentuated* it, for the use of the rods made it plain that the birth of the mutants was not merely a freakish, but natural event. Only *God* can cause spotted cattle to be born (see *Mizrachi v.* 39).

Jacob, himself, later attributed his success to Providence. When he said [31:5] *the God of my father was with me,* he implied that, were it not for the miracle and Divine assistance, the matter could not have been accomplished merely with the peeled rods. He further suggested this when he said [ibid. *v.* 9]: *God has taken away your father's cattle and given them to me (R' Bachya).*

30
43 [43] *The man became exceedingly prosperous and he attained fecund flocks, maidservants and servants, camels and donkeys.*

31
1 [1] *Then he heard the words of Laban's sons saying, 'Jacob has taken all that belonged to our father, and from that which belonged to our father he amas-*

his wealth metaphorically caused him to *burst forth through barriers* to the extent that the region could no longer contain him: he outgrew his premises *(Radak).*

— He exceeded the limitations to prosperity usually associated with shepherding *(Sforno).*

צֹאן רַבּוֹת — *Fecund flocks.*

I.e. flocks which were prolific and which multiplied more than any other *(Tanchuma; Rashi).*

Rashi's interpretation takes רַבּוֹת as a participle: flock *which multiplied.* He does not render it as an adjective: *many* flocks, because the *numerical abundance* is already suggested by the prosperity mentioned earlier in the verse *(Mizrachi);* furthermore, had it been an adjective the phrase should have read צֹאן רַב *(Be'er Mayim Chaim).*

The feminine form רַבּוֹת is used because it describes the fecundity of the animals, and it is the females who bear *(Radak).*

וּשְׁפָחוֹת וַעֲבָדִים — [*And*] *maidservants and servants,* etc.

All of which he bought by selling his sheep at a high price *(Rashi).*

XXXI

1. Jacob's flight from Charan.

וַיִּשְׁמַע אֶת־דִּבְרֵי בְנֵי־לָבָן — *Then* [lit. *and*] *he* [Jacob] *heard the words of Laban's sons.*

Jacob heard their slanderous remarks against him, caused by their jealousy of him *(Sforno).*[1]

[The implication is either that Jacob *overheard* their taunts which were spoken between themselves, or that they complained directly to him.]

This, too, was part of God's Providential plan. The time had come for Jacob to depart, so God precipitated Jacob's discomfort *(Malbim).*

That Laban had *sons* is already noted above in 30:35. *(Ibn Ezra;* [see also *Rashi* ibid. *v.* 27]).

לָקַח יַעֲקֹב אֵת כָּל־אֲשֶׁר לְאָבִינוּ — *Jacob has taken all that belonged to our father.*

— I.e., he even took over the devious ways of our father, and used our father's own methods to outwit him *(Kli Yakar).*

וּמֵאֲשֶׁר לְאָבִינוּ עָשָׂה אֵת כָּל־הַכָּבֹד הַזֶּה — *And from that which belonged to our father he amassed all this wealth* [lit. *honor*].

'He would never have attained such wealth had he not resorted to his trickery, or if he had con-

1. Why does the Torah first mention the attitude of the sons and then of the father?

Possibly Laban's arrogance toward *his* father [see 24:50, 55] was avenged by his sons' behavior toward him; just as Laban gave the orders in Bethuel's household, so his sons now decided how to treat Jacob *(R' Hirsch).*

ב כָּל־הַכָּבֹד הַזֶּה: וַיַּרְא יַעֲקֹב אֶת־פְּנֵי לָבָן
ג וְהִנֵּה אֵינֶנּוּ עִמּוֹ כִּתְמוֹל שִׁלְשׁוֹם: וַיֹּאמֶר
יהוה אֶל־יַעֲקֹב שׁוּב אֶל־אֶרֶץ אֲבוֹתֶיךָ
ד וּלְמוֹלַדְתֶּךָ וְאֶהְיֶה עִמָּךְ: וַיִּשְׁלַח יַעֲקֹב

centrated on tending our father's flocks properly.' But their taunts were unjustified, as we soon learn *(Haamek Davar).*

The verb עָשָׂה, lit. *made,* means in this context *gathered, amassed,* as in *I Samuel* 14:48: וַיַּעַשׂ חַיִל, *he gathered troops (Rashi);* cf. *Rashi* to 12:5.

Onkelos renders the word in the sense of *acquired.*

The translation of כָּבֹד, lit. *honor,* as *wealth* [*Onkelos:* נִכְסַיָּא] follows the *Midrash* which explains the word in our context as referring to gold and silver. The word has the same meaning in *Nachum* 2:10 [where it is also spelled 'defectively' as כָּבֹד without the *vav* (כָּבוֹד) *(Tanchuma)*][1]

Wealth is figuratively referred to by the term *honor, Yafeh Toar* observes, because people tend to honor wealthy men.

Rashbam cites the use of the adjective כָּבֵד, *laden,* denoting abundance of wealth, in 13:2. [See *comm.* there.]

This monetary wealth came to Jacob from selling his unusually fecund flocks, as noted in 30:43 *(Tanchuma).*

2. [The dissatisfaction at Jacob's prosperity is visible in Laban's disposition]:

וַיַּרְא יַעֲקֹב אֶת־פְּנֵי לָבָן — *Jacob also noticed* [i.e. perceived, scrutinized] *Laban's disposition* [lit. *face*].

The crafty Laban's displeasure is more internalized than that of his brash sons, but he cannot completely *disguise* his frustration. A man's face is the barometer of his feelings *(Akeidas Yitzchak).*

According to *Sforno:* It was apparent from Laban's face that he had accepted his sons' vilifications.

וְהִנֵּה אֵינֶנּוּ עִמּוֹ כִּתְמוֹל שִׁלְשׁוֹם — *That, behold, it was not toward* [lit. *with*] *him as in earlier days* [lit. *as yesterday* (and) *the day before.*]

A mere look at Laban's face made it apparent that he was not as well disposed toward Jacob as he had been formerly *(Radak).*

According to *Onkelos,* then, the subject is Laban's face: *Its expression was not with him,* etc.

3. HASHEM commands Jacob to depart.

וַיֹּאמֶר ה׳ אֶל־יַעֲקֹב — *And HASHEM said to Jacob.*

This prophetic revelation came to Jacob while he was still reflecting on

1. The *Vilna Gaon* points out that the interpretation of citing *'honor'* as wealth, (*Nachum* 2:10) is contradicted by *Pirkei Avos* [6:3] where the Sages proclaimed: אֵין כָּבוֹד אֶלָּא תוֹרָה, *'honor' refers to nothing but Torah.*

He explains that the Torah generally uses the 'full' spelling for כָּבוֹד — with a ו — implying that it refers to a full measure of honor. Such honor can mean only Torah; the epitome of greatness. In our verse and in *Nachum,* it is spelled defectively, indicating that the 'honor' is deficient in nature. Such defective honor is the one given because of wealth.

[*Reb Avie Gold* notes that both our passage and the one in *Nachum* reflect a particular philosophy. In our verse, Laban's sons are speaking. In *Nachum,* the subject of the prophecy is Nebuchadnezzar. To such people, the only true 'honor' is the amassing of more and more wealth.]

sed all this wealth.' 2 Jacob also noticed Laban's dis-
position that behold, it was not toward him as in
earlier days. 3 And HASHEM said to Jacob, 'Return to
the land of your fathers and to your native land and I
will be with you.'

their changed attitude *(Radak).*

Jacob ignored the taunts of Laban's sons because they were children. But when he perceived a difference in *Laban's* attitude, he grew worried and God appeared to him to reassure him *(Tz'ror HaMor).*

Radak suggests that this revelation came to Jacob through the medium of an angel who, as God's emissary, delivers His message in first person.

[Comp. the angel's address to Hagar in 16:10 and *Rashi* to 18:10. This concept is explained in the footnote to 22:13, page 804. Perhaps *Radak's* comment is based on the premise that the presence of the Shechinah is limited to the Holy Land, or, more probably, this is the same vision given by Jacob in more detail further in *v.* 11 where it is specifically attributed to an angel (cf. *Chizkuni). See also Sforno* to 35:9.]

שׁוּב אֶל־אֶרֶץ אֲבוֹתֶיךָ וּלְמוֹלַדְתֶּךָ — *Return to the land of your fathers and to your native land.*

[The term מוֹלֶדֶת is familiarly translated *birthplace,* or, as we translate it here, *native land.* In 12:1 (see pp. 426-7) we translate it *relatives:* According to *Abarbanel,* there, it signifies: 'your loved ones among whom you were born and raised.' Since Jacob would be returning only to Isaac and Rebecca (who was still living at this time), *native land* is preferable in our context.]

Return to the land of your fathers — your father waits for you; *your 'moledes'* [homiletically: 'she who bore you'] — your mother — waits for you; *and I will be with you* — I, too, am waiting *(Midrash).*

וְאֶהְיֶה עִמָּךְ — *And I will be with you.*

This expression is an explicit affirmation of Providence watching over the details of man's various activities *(Moreh Nevuchim* 3:18; [see *comm.* to 28:15]).

— I will protect you from all harm during the journey *(Sforno).*

[The continuity of the verse is]: *There* — when you return to the land of your fathers — *I will be with you,* but [here], while you are still associated with the unclean [Laban], My Shechinah will not rest upon you *(Midrash; Rashi).*

— Therefore, My Providential protection appears to have been removed from you in *this* place, as evidenced by the disfavor of Laban and his sons. This I did to provoke your departure to the land of your fathers where I will once again protect you *(Malbim).*

That God promised to be *with him* was meant to imply that, contrary to Rebecca's fears for Jacob's safety, God would protect him from Esau *(Haamek Davar).*

4. Jacob summons his wives and explains his position to them. Jacob knew how difficult it is for people to uproot themselves from their home. Women find this especially difficult. He therefore consulted with his wives to convince them of the dishonesty of their wicked father, and to impress upon them

וַיִּקְרָא לְרָחֵל וּלְלֵאָה הַשָּׂדֶה אֶל־צֹאנוֹ׃
ה וַיֹּאמֶר לָהֶן רֹאֶה אָנֹכִי אֶת־פְּנֵי אֲבִיכֶן
כִּי־אֵינֶנּוּ אֵלַי כִּתְמֹל שִׁלְשֹׁם וֵאלֹהֵי אָבִי
ו הָיָה עִמָּדִי׃ וְאַתֵּנָה יְדַעְתֶּן כִּי בְּכָל־כֹּחִי
ז עָבַדְתִּי אֶת־אֲבִיכֶן׃ וַאֲבִיכֶן הֵתֶל בִּי

the necessity of an expedient departure since only God's protection had prevented Laban from harming him until now *(Tz'ror HaMor)*.[1]

וַיִּשְׁלַח יַעֲקֹב — *Jacob sent.*

According to *Targum Yonasan*, Jacob sent the fleet-footed Naftali to summon them. He intended to carry out the divine command without a moment's delay *(R' Munk)*.

וַיִּקְרָא לְרָחֵל וּלְלֵאָה — *And summoned* [lit. *called to*] *Rachel and* [*to*] *Leah.*

Rachel is mentioned first for she was the עֲקֶרֶת הַבַּיִת, *mainstay of the household* [i.e. his principal wife; see on 29:31 s.v. וְרָחֵל עֲקָרָה], since it was for her sake that Jacob became associated with Laban. Even Leah's descendants, as represented by Boaz and his court who though they were descendants of Leah's son Judah, gave precedence to Rachel when they said [*Ruth* 4:11]: *May* HASHEM *make the woman who is coming into your house like Rachel and like Leah, both of whom built up the House of Israel (Rashi).*

According to *Chizkuni*, Jacob did not have to *summon* Bilhah and Zilpah for they assisted him with his flocks and were already in the field.

הַשָּׂדֶה אֶל־צֹאנוֹ — *To the field, to his flock.*

I.e., that they should come to him in the field where he was tending his flocks *(Radak)*.

To the field where he could converse without being overheard since, as people say, 'the walls have ears' *(Midrash Aggadah)*.[2]

Ibn Caspi comments that Jacob summoned them to *his own* flock

1. Jacob first presented his wives with a frightening picture of their status with Laban, and only *then* did he tell them that God had commanded him to return to Canaan. They responded similarly: only *after* emphasizing their inferior status with Laban did they say *'whatever God has said to you, do.'* This was כְּדֵי לְהַקְטִין אֶת הַנִּסָּיוֹן, *to diminish the severity of the test.*

Generally it is considered more meritorious to overcome severe tests to one's faith, rather than to diminish them, however, as the masters of *mussar* teach, there are times when one should seek ways to strengthen his resolve by introducing inducements to do the right thing or by advancing arguments to diminish the apparent severity of the test.

Furthermore, it is basic to an understanding of any God-given test that it is calibrated to correspond to the person being tested. Therefore, a fair challenge to one person will be too difficult or too simple for most others. God's command here was given to *Jacob* — he needed no further inducement. But for Rachel and Leah, further arguments may have been needed. (For a fuller discussion of the nature of tests see *Overview — The Akeidah*, p. 599).

2. R' Akiva says, For three things I like the Medes: When they cut meat they cut it only on the table [and not simply while holding it; see *Maharsha*]; when they kiss [as a sign of respect] they kiss only on the back of the hand [and not on the mouth *(Rashi*; cf. *Maharsha)*]; and

[4] *Jacob sent and summoned Rachel and Leah to the field, to his flock,* [5] *and said to them, 'I have noticed that your father's disposition is not toward me as in earlier days; but the God of my father was with me.*
[6] *Now you have known that it was with all my might that I served your father,* [7] *yet your father mocked*

for it was the subject of his conflict with Laban. As *Haamek Davar* explains: Jacob summoned them specifically while he was tending *his own* flocks rather than Laban's, so Laban's shepherds should not become suspicious.

5. It is quite evident from your father's appearance that he is not as well-disposed toward me as before ...

וֵאלֹהֵי אָבִי הָיָה עִמָּדִי — *But* [lit. *and*] *the God of my father was with me.*

Although your father resents my success, his animosity toward me is unwarranted. My prosperity was not the result of my having stolen anything from him; *God* has been with me. *He* has given me everything I possess *(Rashbam; Sforno).*

Here Jacob emphasizes the role of Providence in his success, making no mention of the peeled rods. Only God's role in the miraculous result was the determining factor. This is further manifested in the dream Jacob reveals in *v.* 10 *(R' Bachya;* see footnote to 30:42).

6. Jacob reiterates Laban's repeated ingratitude for his faithful service:

וְאַתֵּנָה יְדַעְתֶּן — *Now you have known.*

[The sense of this form is: *If anyone knows, it is you, my dear wives* ...]

כִּי בְּכָל־כֹּחִי עָבַדְתִּי אֶת אֲבִיכֶן — *That it was with all my might that I served your father.*

— As Jacob says below [*v.* 40]: *By day scorching heat consumed me, and frost by night; my sleep drifted from my eyes (Radak).*[1]

7. וַאֲבִיכֶן הֵתֶל בִּי — *Yet* [lit. *and*] *your father mocked me.*

— By taking advantage of me *(Ibn Caspi).*

The translation *mocked* follows *Ibn Ezra* and *Radak* who relate the word to its use in *I Kings* 18:27: וַיְהַתֵּל בָּהֶם אֵלִיָּהוּ, *Elijah mocked*

when they take counsel, they do so only in the field [(secluded from all passers-by) for, as people say, 'the walls have ears' *(Rashi)*] *(Midrash; Berachos* 8b).

[Cf. *Aggadas Esther* 4:6 that Hasach went out to Mordechai *unto the city square* where no one could spy on them and overhear their conversation.]

1. Just as an employer is prohibited from depriving the poor worker of his wage or withholding it from him when it is due, so is a worker prohibited from depriving the employer of the benefit of his work by idling away his time, a little here and a little there, thus wasting the whole day deceitfully.

Indeed, a worker must be very punctual in the matter of time, seeing that the Sages were so solicitous in this matter that they exempted a worker from saying the fourth benediction of *Bircas HaMazon.* A worker must work with all his strength, as the righteous Jacob said, *It was with all my might that I served your father,* and he received his reward for his loyalty in this world too as it is written [30:43]: *And the man prospered exceedingly (Rambam, Hil. S'chirus* 13:7).

וְהֶחֱלִף אֶת־מַשְׂכֻּרְתִּי עֲשֶׂרֶת מֹנִים וְלֹא־
ח נְתָנוֹ אֱלֹהִים לְהָרַע עִמָּדִי: אִם־כֹּה יֹאמַר
נְקֻדִּים יִהְיֶה שְׂכָרֶךָ וְיָלְדוּ כָל־הַצֹּאן
נְקֻדִּים וְאִם־כֹּה יֹאמַר עֲקֻדִּים יִהְיֶה
ט שְׂכָרֶךָ וְיָלְדוּ כָל־הַצֹּאן עֲקֻדִּים: וַיַּצֵּל
י אֱלֹהִים אֶת־מִקְנֵה אֲבִיכֶם וַיִּתֶּן־לִי: וַיְהִי

at them. They derive it from the root החל.

HaRechasim Lebik'ah gives it the sense of: tried to *outwit* me; deceive or cheat. Citing this connotation in *Job* 13:8, *Heidenheim* goes to great lengths to assert that the root is תול and the prefix ה denotes the *hiphil* (as הֵחֵל=חלל) in the sense of *Psalms* 137:3 וְתוֹלָלֵינוּ, *our tormentors.* Accordingly, the verb here means [*your father*] *tormented me. R' Hirsch* derives the verb similarly, but interprets it to mean *let down* in ruin (comp. תֵּל, *a heap* of ruins), hence: *deceive,* renege on promises.

וְהֶחֱלִף אֶת מַשְׂכֻּרְתִּי עֲשֶׂרֶת מֹנִים — *And* [he] *changed my wage a hundred (times)* [lit. *ten tens*].

[I.e., Laban made attempt after attempt to alter the conditions to serve his own ends.]

Actually, *R' Munk* notes, the Torah alludes to only *one* such example of Laban's deceit [see 30:35]. However, as *Ramban* emphasizes, there must have been many such instances even though the Torah does not enumerate them. This is evidenced by Jacob's direct reproach to Laban regarding his constantly changing the wage in verse 41, a reproach which Laban did not deny. It is often the case that the Torah does not supply all details. For example in the episode of the *dudaim* [30:14ff] we are not told explicitly that Leah actually gave the *dudaim* to Rachel [although it is later implicit in *v.* 16 that she did so].

The translation of עֲשֶׂרֶת מֹנִים as *a hundred times* follows the Midrashic view cited by *Rashi* that the term *monim,* related to *minyan,* literally means a unit of ten. Hence the phrase עֲשֶׂרֶת מֹנִים, *ten monim,* means that Laban changed his conditions one hundred times [=ten times ten.]

Sifsei Chachomim [in the unabridged editions printed with *Mizrachi* and *Gur Aryeh*] gives a detailed calculation of the one hundred possibilities of changes in the terms.

Ibn Ezra relates the word מֹנִים to the verb מנה *count,* interpreting: *ten times,* [lit. *ten counts*]; thus, Laban deceived Jacob ten times, not a hundred. [*Rashbam* renders similarly as does *Onkelos,* זִימְנִין.] He also offers that 'ten' might be used as a round number rather than an exact total.

Radak asserts similarly, that *ten* is idiomatic and only signifies 'many,' as it does in *Lev.* 26:26. The number *ten* is used in this sense since it represents the transition point from single digits to multiple units.

He then cites his father, *R' Yosef Kimchi,* that it means *exactly ten.* Jacob worked for Laban a total of six years under this bargain. In the first year, when Laban saw that Jacob produced prodigious flocks for himself, he changed the terms; during each of the subsequent four years he changed the terms twice (once after each of Jacob's successful mating seasons), making a total of nine times in the first five years; and once more in the final year before this confrontation took place and Jacob finally fled.

According to *Midrash Maayan Ganim* cited in *Torah Sheleimah* 31:17 the number ten represents the fact that there were a total of five categories:

me and changed my wage a hundred times. But God
did not permit him to harm me. [8] *If he would*
stipulate: "Spotted ones shall be your wages," then
the entire flock bore spotted ones; and if he would
stipulate: "Ringed ones shall be your wages," then
the entire flock bore ringed ones. [9] *Thus, God took*
away your father's livestock, and gave them to me.

עֲקֻדִּים, *ringed;* נְקֻדִּים, *spotted;* בְּרֻדִּים, *checkered* [see further *v.* 10]; טְלוּאִים, *speckled;* and חוּם, *brownish.* In effect Laban changed the conditions regarding each of these five categories twice: first when originally offering, and then when withdrawing that particular category. Thus, there were a total of *ten* changes.

וְלֹא נְתָנוֹ אֱלֹהִים לְהָרַע עִמָּדִי — *But God did not permit* [lit. *give*] *him to harm me* [lit. *to do evil with me.*]

That is, none of Laban's attempts to cheat Jacob succeeded, because God was always generous to Jacob and frustrated Laban's plans, as Jacob proceeds to show *(Ramban).*

[See *Rashi* to 20:6 concerning this use of *give* with the figurative meaning *grant the power to do something,* hence: *permit.*]

8. אִם כֹּה יֹאמַר נְקֻדִּים יִהְיֶה שְׂכָרֶךָ ... וְיָלְדוּ כָל הַצֹּאן נְקֻדִּים... — *If he would stipulate* [lit. *if he would say thus*]: *'Spotted ones shall be your wages,' then the entire flock bore spotted ones; and if he would stipulate* [lit. *if he would say thus*]: *'Ringed ones shall be your wages,' then the entire flock bore ringed ones.*

Although the original agreement provided that *three* categories of mutations would go to Jacob, Laban constantly refused to give more than *one* mutation. Even that single *one,* he would change each year. But the flocks would always bear the kind finally allotted to Jacob *(Ramban).*[1]

9. וַיַּצֵּל אֱלֹהִים אֶת־מִקְנֵה אֲבִיכֶם וַיִּתֶּן־לִי — *Thus, God took away your father's livestock, and gave them to me.*

It was clearly by *God's approval* that Jacob's wealth increased in the face of Laban's every deceitful effort to frustrate the deal, and not by virtue of Jacob's resort to the peeled rods *(Ramban).*

The term מִקְנֶה from the root קנה, literally means *possessions, property* (so *R' Hirsch);* it therefore has the connotation of *cattle, livestock,* which in Biblical times was man's most important possession *(Ibn Janach).*

[On וַיַּצֵּל, *took away, salvaged,* literally connoting *set aside,* see *Rashi* on הִצִּיל in *v.* 16.]

R' Hirsch, interpreting the word as *rescued, salvaged,* comments: God gave part of your father's fortune to me in

1. The *Midrash* expounds in this context that when Laban saw the sheep pregnant he would constantly change the conditions, and God would cause a miracle, making the unborn lambs conform to whatever Laban would stipulate.

Therefore the expression used here is not in the past tense: אִם כֹּה אָמַר, *if he stipulated,* but in the future imperfect: *If he would stipulate.* God anticipated Laban's *future* demands and caused the unborn sheep to conform to his ultimate condition.

[The implication, as *Ramban* concludes, is that it was God's intervention in the face of Laban's every deceitful effort to cheat Jacob, and not the natural effect of the peeled rods that caused Jacob's success and prosperity.]

בְּעֵת יַחֵם הַצֹּאן וָאֶשָּׂא עֵינַי וָאֵרֶא
בַּחֲלוֹם וְהִנֵּה הָעַתֻּדִים הָעֹלִים עַל־הַצֹּאן
יא עֲקֻדִּים נְקֻדִּים וּבְרֻדִּים: וַיֹּאמֶר אֵלַי
מַלְאַךְ הָאֱלֹהִים בַּחֲלוֹם יַעֲקֹב וָאֹמַר
יב הִנֵּנִי: וַיֹּאמֶר שָׂא־נָא עֵינֶיךָ וּרְאֵה כָּל־
הָעַתֻּדִים הָעֹלִים עַל־הַצֹּאן עֲקֻדִּים
נְקֻדִּים וּבְרֻדִּים כִּי רָאִיתִי אֵת כָּל־אֲשֶׁר
יג לָבָן עֹשֶׂה לָּךְ: אָנֹכִי הָאֵל בֵּית־אֵל אֲשֶׁר

order to *save* it from falling into other hands. Or, whatever I have of your father's possessions was *saved* from falling into *his* hands, because it is rightfully mine in return for my labor. Moreover, I *earned* it with my work; it was not a dowry which is an unearned windfall.

10. [Jacob reveals for the first time that he had been shown in a prophetic dream that the birth of parti-colored young was God's compensation for Laban's ill-treatment of him].

וַיְהִי בְּעֵת יַחֵם הַצֹּאן — [*And*] *it* [*once*] *happened at the mating time of the flock* [lit. *at the time the flock would become heated*].

This dream had occurred at the beginning of the six-year period, after Laban began changing Jacob's wages. This is indicated by the angel's reference [*v.* 12] to *all that Laban is doing* [present tense] to you *(Ramban;* see *v.* 13).

וָאֶשָּׂא עֵינַי וָאֵרֶא בַּחֲלוֹם — *That* [lit. *and*] *I raised my eyes and saw in a dream:*

[A form of prophetic experience. On the significance of dreams as a vehicle of prophecy, see *comm.* to 28:12.]

וְהִנֵּה הָעַתֻּדִים הָעֹלִים עַל הַצֹּאן — [*And*] *Behold! The he-goats that mounted the flock.*

Laban had removed all of these he-goats so that flocks under Jacob should not bear similar offspring [see 30:35], but angels took them from his sons' flocks and returned them to Jacob's flocks *(Rashi).*

The word וְהִנֵּה, *Behold!* [as noted also in the *comm.* to 28:13] emphasizes that Jacob's dream was not a mere fantasy; the term: הִנֵּה, *Behold,* is used only to introduce something of *substance.* The vision was an assurance that Laban's capricious changes would not harm Jacob, and that his flocks would bear offspring of whatever coloration Jacob would need *(Ramban).*

The Hebrew terms for he-goats: תְּיָשִׁים (30:35) and עַתֻּדִים are synonymous *(Radak).* Both are rendered by *Onkelos:* תְּיָשַׁיָּא, *he-goats.*

Ramban adds that rams (male *sheep*) as well as he-*goats* are included in this term. It refers to all the adults in the flock; and figuratively, as well, to leaders among men, as in *Isaiah* 14:9: *the chieftains* (עַתּוּדֵי) *of the earth.*

עֲקֻדִּים נְקֻדִּים וּבְרֻדִּים — *Were ringed, spotted, and checkered.*

The dream did not portray the he-goats as being composed of a conglomeration of all the above.

[10] It once happened at the mating time of the flock that I raised my eyes and saw in a dream — Behold! The he-goats that mounted the flock were ringed, spotted, and checkered. [11] And an angel of God said to me in the dream, "Jacob!" And I said, "Here I am." [12] And he said, "Raise your eyes, if you please, and see that all the he-goats mounting the flocks are ringed, spotted, and checkered, for I have seen all that Laban is doing to you. [13] I am the God of Bethel

Rather, the flock was first shown him to be *ringed;* later it was portrayed as *spotted,* and finally *checkered (Ramban).*

[On the first two terms, see 30:32-35.]

The term בְּרֻדִּים occurs only here throughout Scripture. The translation *checkered* seems to be most faithful to *Rashi* who cites *Onkelos'* rendering פְּצִיחַ [lit. *open*] which he explains as *faissie* in Old French [=*faisceau* (?), things linked, checkered]: It refers to a white streak going around their body composed of open, interlinked spots.

Targum Yonasan renders the word: וְגַבֵּיהוֹן חִיוּוֹרִין, *their backs were white.*

The בְּרֻדִּים here are in place of the טְלוּאִים, *speckled,* of 30:32. The term בְּרֻדִּים signifies that their blotches were *white* related to בָּרָד, *hail.*

Minchah Belulah explains that the בְּרֻדִּים were in contrast to the נְקֻדִּים, *spotted ones.* The latter were white with black spots; the former were black with white spots.

11. וַיֹּאמֶר אֵלַי מַלְאַךְ הָאֱלֹהִים בַּחֲלוֹם יַעֲקֹב — *And an angel of God said to me in the dream, 'Jacob!'*

In enumerating the eleven degrees of prophecy, *Rambam* in *Moreh Nevuchim* 2:45 states that the sixth level of prophecy is communication from an angel in a dream, as in our verse, and that it is a form of prophecy 'which applies to most of the prophets.

הִנֵּנִי — *Here I am.*

Such is the response of the pious. The expression denotes both humility and readiness *(Rashi* 22:2).

12. שָׂא־נָא עֵינֶיךָ וּרְאֵה כָּל הָעַתֻּדִים ... — *Raise your eyes, if you please, and see that all the he-goats mounting the flocks are ringed, spotted and checkered.*

As noted above [see *v.* 10], this was God's implicit assurance that they would bear similar offspring, and that Jacob need no longer resort to the use of peeled rods *(Ramban).*

According to *R' Bachya* [to 30:38] however, the intent is to the contrary: Jacob understood that the angel would never have instructed him to gaze upon animals while they are mating — an immodest act prohibited by Torah law as formulated in *Avodah Zarah* 2:2 — unless he were meant to draw a practical lesson from the sight. He perceived that he was being shown an impending miracle so that he would be inspired to peel the rods in order to conceal God's miraculous intervention. See footnote to 30:42.

כִּי רָאִיתִי אֵת כָּל־אֲשֶׁר לָבָן עֹשֶׂה לָּךְ — *For I have seen all that Laban is doing* [present tense; see *v.* 10] *to you.*

— And accordingly I [as God's emissary] wish to assure you that all of Laban's designs against you will be rendered futile *(Ramban).*

מָשַׁחְתָּ שָּׁם מַצֵּבָה אֲשֶׁר נָדַרְתָּ לִּי שָׁם
נֶדֶר עַתָּה קוּם צֵא מִן־הָאָרֶץ הַזֹּאת וְשׁוּב
יד אֶל־אֶרֶץ מוֹלַדְתֶּךָ: וַתַּעַן רָחֵל וְלֵאָה
וַתֹּאמַרְנָה לוֹ הַעוֹד לָנוּ חֵלֶק וְנַחֲלָה

The angel speaks in the first-person, as he is God's emissary (*Radak;* see *comm.* to *v.* 3 and cross-references cited there).

13. According to *Ramban,* there were two separate dreams: the first (*vs.* 10-12) occurred during the early part of his six-year service, and the second (*v.* 13) occurred the night before Jacob related it to Rachel and Leah. Now, he told them both dreams to strengthen their resolve to leave with him, by informing them that God had caused his prosperity and that He had now commanded him to return to Canaan see footnote to *v.* 4]. The speaker in the second dream is still the angel who, as God's emissary, speaks in the first-person.

אָנֹכִי הָאֵל בֵּית־אֵל – *I am the God of Bethel.*

I.e., the God *Who appeared to you* in Bethel [see 28:13] (*Radak; R' Bachya*).

— And Who there promised you My protection, assuring you that I would bring you back to that land (*Malbim*).

Since the phrase הָאֵל בֵּית אֵל is in the construct state: the God *of* Bethel, the definite article הָאֵל, *the* God, is unnecessary in Hebrew.

Rashi accordingly notes that the ה is grammatically superfluous and the passage should be interpreted as if it read אָנֹכִי אֵל בֵּית אֵל, *I am God of Bethel.* Similar forms are [*Numbers* 34:2]: הָאָרֶץ כְּנָעַן [=אֶרֶץ כְּנָעַן, *land of Canaan*]. [Also (*Joshua* 3:14) הָאָרוֹן הַבְּרִית, *Ark of the Covenant* (*Radak*).][1]

Ibn Ezra interprets the phrase as being elliptic, rendering it as if it were written: אָנֹכִי הָאֵל, אֵל בֵּית אֵל, *I am the God* [*Who is the*] *God of Bethel.* This is similar to 2:9: עֵץ הַדַּעַת טוֹב וָרָע, which is interpreted as if it had an implied adjectivial phrase: *The tree of knowledge, i.e., knowledge of good and bad.*

Rambam in *Moreh Nevuchim* 1:27 interprets the phrase to imply: 'I am the *emissary* of the God of Bethel', i.e., an angel of the God Who appeared to you at Bethel. (Similarly, *Midrash HaGadol*).

אֲשֶׁר מָשַׁחְתָּ שָּׁם מַצֵּבָה – *Where you anointed a pillar* [lit. *a standing stone*].

— By anointing it, you sanctified it to be an altar [cf. 28:18], just as anointing a person for kingship exalts him above the common people (*Rashi*).

אֲשֶׁר נָדַרְתָּ לִּי שָׁם נֶדֶר – [And] *where you made* [lit. *vowed*] *Me a vow.*

I.e., you made a vow to God in Whose Name I (the angel) speak (*Radak*).

1. *Divrei Shaul,* however, comments that the ה serves a definite purpose. Jacob doubted that his dream was truly prophetic, because there is a general rule that prophetic revelation does not take place outside of *Eretz Yisrael.* Nevertheless, the Sages teach that once prophecy has begun in *Eretz Yisrael,* it may be continued even in other lands, as was the case with Ezekiel and Jonah [see *Moed Katan* 25a]. This, then, was the intent of God's opening statement to Jacob: I am הָאֵל, *the God* [i.e, in continuation of some vision] Who appeared to you in Bethel — the present vision is a continuation of that prophetic promise of your future.

31
14 *where you anointed a pillar and where you made Me*
a vow. Now — arise, leave this land and return to
your native land."'
[14] *Then Rachel and Leah replied and said to him,*
'Have we then still a share and an inheritance in our

It is now time for you to fulfill your vow, for in saying that the place would be *God's House* [28:22] you implied thereby that you would offer sacrifices there *(Rashi)*.

— And if you further delay the fulfillment of your vows, you might yet incur God's wrath [see *Eccles.* 5:5] *(Ramban)*.

It is interesting to note that when God commanded Jacob to leave Charan (*v.* 3), He omitted mention of this vow. In any event, now that Jacob was reminded of it in his dream he felt compelled to reveal the matter of his vow to his wives, since the neglect of it could affect them. *Meshech Chochmah* cites the dictum in *Rosh Hashanah* 6a: 'Whoever leaves a vow unfulfilled, his wife dies.' Indeed, it is the *Meshech Chochmah's* opinion that delay of the vow's fulfillment was a cause in Rachel's death. [Cf. *v.* 32.]

עַתָּה קוּם צֵא מִן הָאָרֶץ הַזֹּאת — *Now — arise, leave this land.*

I.e., accordingly, it is time for you to depart *(R' Meyuchas)*.

... I have carried out what I promised you, now it is up to you to do your part, to keep your promise — צֵא מִן הָאָרֶץ הַזֹּאת, *leave this land.* Here in Aram, the family life which God wants of you cannot develop *(R' Hirsch)*.

14. Rachel and Leah consent.

וַתַּעַן רָחֵל וְלֵאָה — *Then* [lit. *and*] *Rachel and Leah replied.*

The Hebrew literally means: *Then Rachel replied* (singular) *and Leah.* Rachel answered and Leah concurred *(Ralbag)*.

Cf. *Targum Yonasan:* And Rachel replied with the consent of Leah.

Rachel consented at once because she loved Jacob as dearly as he loved her [and was therefore immediately ready to follow him] *(Radak)*.

[Possibly the singular form of the verb implies that they both answered in one voice, implying *mutual* consent. Cf. *Exodus* 10:3, *Moses and Aaron came* (וַיָּבֹא, singular).]

The *Midrash* discusses the question of how Rachel answered before her older sister [see 35:19]. R' Yudan maintains that because Rachel answered before her [older] sister, she died first. R' Yosi countered that she answered first because she was summoned first. According to the latter, Rachel died first because of the curse implied in Jacob's statement to Laban [see below *v.* 32]: *With whomever you find your gods, he shall not live,* which was like the inadvertant command of a ruler [i.e., an unintentional prognostication.]

הַעוֹד לָנוּ חֵלֶק וְנַחֲלָה בְּבֵית אָבִינוּ — *Have we then still a share and an inheritance in our father's house?*

— What possible reason can we have for attempting to delay your departure? Have we any hope of inheriting anything of our father's estate together with his sons? *(Rashi)*.

— Since he has sons, we shall not receive any share or inheritance, for

טו בְּבֵית אָבִינוּ: הֲלוֹא נָכְרִיּוֹת נֶחְשַׁבְנוּ לוֹ
כִּי מְכָרָנוּ וַיֹּאכַל גַּם־אָכוֹל אֶת־כַּסְפֵּנוּ:
טז כִּי כָל־הָעֹשֶׁר אֲשֶׁר הִצִּיל אֱלֹהִים
מֵאָבִינוּ לָנוּ הוּא וּלְבָנֵינוּ וְעַתָּה כֹּל אֲשֶׁר
° ששי יז אָמַר אֱלֹהִים אֵלֶיךָ עֲשֵׂה: °וַיָּקָם יַעֲקֹב
וַיִּשָּׂא אֶת־בָּנָיו וְאֶת־נָשָׁיו עַל־הַגְּמַלִּים:
יח וַיִּנְהַג אֶת־כָּל־מִקְנֵהוּ וְאֶת־כָּל־רְכֻשׁוֹ

daughters do not inherit when there are sons *(Midrash Aggadah).*

[Regarding why they first offered these rationales and did not *immediately* say, 'Whatever God has said to you, do,' see footnote to *v.* 4.]

Some commentators treat the expression חֵלֶק וְנַחֲלָה, lit. *a share and an inheritance,* as a hendiadys, meaning: *an heir's portion.*

However, *R' Hirsch* perceives חֵלֶק, *share,* to imply: will our father give us anything now, during his lifetime, or נַחֲלָה, *an inheritance,* in the future? *Or HaChaim* interprets *share* — from our mother's estate, and *inheritance* — from our father's.

15. הֲלוֹא נָכְרִיּוֹת נֶחְשַׁבְנוּ לוֹ כִּי מְכָרָנוּ — *Are we not considered by him as strangers? For he has sold us.*

Instead of treating us like daughters and giving us a dowry upon marriage, he treated us like strangers and sold us to you in return for your work *(Rashi).*

וַיֹּאכַל גַּם־אָכוֹל אֶת כַּסְפֵּנוּ — *And* [*he*] *even totally consumed our money!*

The money we should have received upon our marriage *(Radak).*

— He withheld the wages due you for your labor *(Rashi).*

— After having used us to drive a hard bargain and extract fourteen years free service from you, it would have been no financial loss to utilize the value of your work as our dowry. Even that did not enter his mind; whatever we earned for him, he retained! *(R' Hirsch).*

[The translation *even totally consumed* reflects the emphatic form of the Hebrew which employs the infinitive: *and he consumed also consumed.*]

16. כִּי כָל־הָעֹשֶׁר אֲשֶׁר הִצִּיל אֱלֹהִים מֵאָבִינוּ לָנוּ הוּא וּלְבָנֵינוּ — *But, all the wealth that God has taken away from our father, belongs to us and to our children.*

The translation of the conjunctive כִּי as *but,* follows the implication of *Rashi.* [It is similar to 18:15: כִּי צָחָקְתְּ, *But you laughed,* i.e. you laughed indeed, see *Rashi* there.] The meaning of our passage is: We will receive nothing of our fathers estate. However, that which God has already taken from our father [and given to you] is ours and our children's.

— Consequently there is no reason we should not accompany you right now *(Alshich).*

The word הִצִּיל, *taken away* literally means *set aside, separate.* [The word usually connotes *rescue*] since one [who rescues a person] thereby *separates* him from misfortune and from the enemy *(Rashi).*

Onkelos renders similarly אַפְרֵשׁ, *separated,* while *Yonasan* renders רוֹקֵן, *removed,* as does *Radak:* עִנְיַן הֲסָרָה.

כֹּל אֲשֶׁר אָמַר אֱלֹהִים אֵלֶיךָ עֲשֵׂה — *Whatever God has said to you, do.*

I.e., proceed! You do not need

father's house? 15 *Are we not considered by him as*
strangers? For he has sold us and even totally con-
sumed our money! 16 *But, all the wealth that God has*
taken away from our father belongs to us and to our
children. So now, whatever God has said to you, do.'
17 *Jacob arose and lifted his children and wives*
onto the camels. 18 *He led away all his livestock and*
all the wealth which he had amassed — his purchased

permission; rely only on God's words *(Sforno).*

[*Sforno* might mean either: Seeing that God has so commanded you, you do not need *our* permission, or you do not need *Laban's* permission.]

17. Jacob's flight.

וַיִּשָּׂא אֶת־בָּנָיו וְאֶת־נָשָׁיו עַל־הַגְּמַלִּים — *And lifted his children and* [*his*] *wives onto the camels.*

Jacob gave precedence to the males over the females whereas Esau gave precedence to the women, as it is written [36:6]: *and Esau took his wives and his sons (Rashi).*

Gur Aryeh explains the different order of priority. Esau took wives only to satisfy his personal lust. The birth of children was a secondary outcome of his marriages; to him the women remained paramount. Jacob married because he was the forerunner of the Jewish nation and it was his responsibility to give birth to children; to him the children came first because they were the reason for his marriages. That Moses gave precedence to his wife over his children (*Exodus* 4:20) was because his sons were still infants who depended on their mother for all their needs. Jacob evacuated his wives across the river to escape Esau before he took his children across (32:23), specifically because the adults could be more easily taken across the river than the weaker, less agile children. *Gur Aryeh* concludes, however, that the order of preference is material only when one plans to settle down and build a future; then one's priorities reflect his values. In the cases of Moses and of Jacob in 32:23, loading for travel is a matter of convenience, and precedence is immaterial. [Cf. *Levush; Maskil l'David; Divrei David.*]

18. וַיִּנְהַג אֶת־כָּל־מִקְנֵהוּ וְאֶת־כָּל־רְכֻשׁוֹ אֲשֶׁר רָכָשׁ — *He led away all his livestock and all the* [lit. *his*] *wealth which he had amassed.*[1]

Jacob purposely left in a grand manner — leading his flocks and systematically gathering all his wealth — so as not to arouse the suspicions of Laban's people. Anyone who saw him leaving so openly would assume that he was departing with Laban's full knowledge and consent. Had he gone stealthily, he would have been stamped as a fugitive *(Abarbanel).*

The translation of *livestock* for מִקְנֶה [lit. *acquisition*] follows *R' Hirsch* who explains that when that word occurs together with רְכוּשׁ [*lifeless, movable property* (see *R' Hirsch* to 12:5)] it refers to living property, herds and flocks.

1. In these verse the Torah elaborates on Jacob's manner of leaving Paddan Aram, because it strikingly portends the departure of his descendants from Egyptian bondage.

Just as Jacob left with great wealth, so his descendants left Egypt בִּרְכֻשׁ גָּדוֹל, *with great wealth,* as God promised Abraham [15:14]. Just as Laban learned of Jacob's departure only after three days, so Pharaoh discovered only later כִּי בָרַח הָעָם, *that the people had fled* [with no intention of returning] (*Exodus* 14:5). Laban pursued Jacob, who was saved because of God's intervention; Pharaoh pursued Israel which was saved by the miracle at the Sea of Reeds. Thus, this is another illustration of the principle that the events in the lives of the Patriarchs were forerunners of their children's future history (*Hoffman;* cf. *Tanchuma Lech-Lecha* 9).

אֲשֶׁר רָכָשׁ מִקְנֵה קִנְיָנוֹ אֲשֶׁר רָכַשׁ בְּפַדַּן
אֲרָם לָבוֹא אֶל־יִצְחָק אָבִיו אַרְצָה כְּנָעַן:
יט וְלָבָן הָלַךְ לִגְזֹז אֶת־צֹאנוֹ וַתִּגְנֹב רָחֵל
כ אֶת־הַתְּרָפִים אֲשֶׁר לְאָבִיהָ: וַיִּגְנֹב יַעֲקֹב

מִקְנֵה קִנְיָנוֹ אֲשֶׁר רָכַשׁ בְּפַדַּן אֲרָם — *His purchased property* [lit. *the purchase of his acquired property*] *which he had amassed in Paddan Aram.*

I.e., the slaves and maidservants, camels and donkeys which he had purchased [מִקְנֵה] with the proceeds of the sale of קִנְיָנוֹ, *his flocks* [lit. *his acquired property.* (Cf. *comm.* to 30:43)] *(Rashi).*

[*Here, Rashi* explains that מִקְנֵה means *acquisition,* not *livestock (Be'er Mayim Chaim).*]

The Torah thus bears testimony that all of Jacob's wealth which he took along with him was legitimately his, i.e., possessions which he legally acquired in exchange for his own property *(Hoffmann).*

Haamek Davar perceives מִקְנֵה קִנְיָנוֹ [lit. *the purchase of his acquired possessions*] to mean *the possessions acquired by his slaves* [the term קִנְיָן being applied to *slaves* who are themselves acquired, as in *Lev.* 22:11.] He explains that Jacob himself did not engage in bartering his flocks for wealth; this was done by his talented slaves.

לָבוֹא אֶל יִצְחָק אָבִיו אַרְצָה כְּנָעַן — *To go* [lit. *come*] *to his father Isaac, to the land of Canaan.*

— For it was to both that he yearned to return: his father's house, and to the Holy Land *(Haamek Davar).*

19. וְלָבָן הָלַךְ לִגְזֹז אֶת־צֹאנוֹ — [*And*] *Laban had gone to shear his sheep.*

— Which were pasturing under the charge of his sons, a three-day distance away from Jacob's flocks [see 30:36] *(Rashi).*

Sheep-shearing was an occasion of festivity for the entire family as evident from *II Samuel* 13:23ff and other places in Scripture. Accordingly, since Laban was away with his entire household, the time was most opportune for Rachel to enter his house and steal his *teraphim,* and for Jacob to flee *(Haamek Davar).*

וַתִּגְנֹב רָחֵל אֶת הַתְּרָפִים אֲשֶׁר לְאָבִיהָ — *And Rachel stole the teraphim that belonged to her father.*

— To keep him from idol-worship *(Rashi).*

Rachel's intention was noble for she said to herself: Can I depart and leave my father to worship such idols? Accordingly, the Torah records this episode *(Midrash).*

Rachel thought that her intention of weaning her father from idolatry could be accomplished by her theft. If the supposed 'gods' lacked even the power to protect themselves against thieves, how could they protect the household of their owners? *(R' Hirsch).*

— She stole them to keep them from telling Laban that Jacob wished to flee, since as implied by *Hoshea* 3:4 and *Zechariah* 10:2, they were used for divination *(Rashbam).*

Although both of the above interpretations reflect varying — and not necessarily mutually exclusive views — *Ibn Ezra* inclines to the latter reason. If her intention was to stop Laban's idol-worship, she

property which he had amassed in Paddan Aram — to go to his father Isaac, to the land of Canaan.
19 *Laban had gone to shear his sheep, and Rachel stole the teraphim that belonged to her father.*

should have *hidden* and not taken them with her.

Among the answers offered to justify *Rashi's* interpretation is that Rachel would have attracted too much attention had she stopped to bury the *teraphim;* she therefore took them along — contemptuously placing them beneath her — and awaited a more propitious time to dispose of them *(R' Yosef Caro: Toldos Yitzchak).* According to *Gur Aryeh* she was afraid that Laban might refuse to believe Jacob's protestations that no member of his company had stolen the *teraphim.* Laban might become so vehement that she would be forced to return them in order to appease him. To prepare herself for such an eventuality, she did not destroy them.

Onkelos delicately renders the term *stole* in this verse, and next as וְכַסִּי, *concealed.* [See *Nesinah laGer* who suggests that this might be the primary meaning of the verb גנב, and that the connotation of *steal* is therefore applied to one who conceals other people's possessions for his own selfish use, while in this case Rachel clearly took them for loftier purposes.]

✎§ Teraphim

The etymology of this word, which occurs only in the plural, is obscure.

Ibn Janach, as does *Onkelos,* merely defines them as *images, idols,* but offers no clue to the etymology of the word. *Ramban* derives it from the root רפה meaning *weak* [see *Exod.* 5:17] alluding to the 'weakness' of their prognostications, as the prophet declared [*Zechariah* 10:2]: *For the teraphim have spoken vanity.* The Zohar interprets the word as being related to תרף and תורפה, denoting *obscenity* the term being a contemptuous one suggesting that the *teraphim* were the objects of obscenity, and filth. [Similarly, *Tanchuma*].

The *Zohar* [cited below] suggests that the idols were made in the form of a male and female [hence the plural form of the word *teraphim*]. *Radak,* who is of the opinion that they were a kind of clock which foretold fortunes, conjectures that the plural form is used since they were composed of several tablets. *Hoffmann* explains that the form may be regarded as a majestic plural; since the *teraphim* were regarded as gods, they were referred to in the plural.

That the *teraphim* were considered *gods* is evident from verse 30 where Laban called them *my gods.* As the *Zohar* notes, Laban was a great sorcerer who practiced the occult arts, and it was by such means that he learned whatever he wished to know.

Many consider them to have been a kind of household god supposed to be the protector of the home similar to the later Roman *Penates;* they were consulted for oracular purposes *(R' Hirsch). Ramban* [below] suggests that not all *teraphim* mentioned in Scripture were venerated as idols.

One of the earliest descriptions of *teraphim* is found in *Pirkei d'Rabbi Eliezer* 36. [It does not appear in the *Radal* edition, however; probably the result of censorship]:

'What are *teraphim?* — They would slay a firstborn man, remove his head and soak it in salt. They would write the name of an unclean spirit on a golden plate, place it under his tongue, and set him up on a wall. They would light candles, burn incense before it and bow down to it; it would then speak to them by magic. Unto such an object, did Laban bow down. How do we know that *teraphim* speak? For it is written

אֶת־לֵב לָבָן הָאֲרַמִּי עַל־בְּלִי הִגִּיד לוֹ כִּי
בֹרֵחַ הוּא: כא וַיִּבְרַח הוּא וְכָל־אֲשֶׁר־לוֹ

[*Zechariah* 10:2]: *the teraphim have spoken vanity.* For that reason Rachel stole them so they should not tell Laban that Jacob had fled, and furthermore, to remove idolatrous worship from her father's house. [A similar description appears in *Targum Yonasan, Midrash Tanchuma.* See also *Aruch,* s.v. תרף].

[*Ralbag* suggests that the *teraphim* did not actually speak. Rather, they served as the medium by which some sort of magical, occult voice was heard. See also *Ibn Ezra* below.]

The *Zohar* maintains, however, that the *teraphim* did possess certain powers which were the result of magical arts. According to Rav Yehudah, these powers were implanted in the objects by making them with scrupulous adherence to the magical properties of certain times and moments for striking and for holding off. At one moment the craftsman would use his hand to beat it into shape, and at another he would relax. Hence the term *teraphim,* akin to *hereph* [relax] (*II Sam.* 24:16). For when the craftsman was making it, the man who knew the proper seconds and hours stood over him, saying at one moment "strike", and at the other moment: "stay". There is no other work which requires to be timed in this way. This magic idol continually uttered evil counsel, and prompted mischief, and Rachel therefore feared that it might counsel her father to do mischief to Jacob. The *Teraphim* were a male and a female image, and a number of ceremonies had to be performed before them before they would speak. Among these ceremonies were that the area in front of it had to be swept and cleaned. Therefore, when Rachel contemptuously sat on them [*v.* 34 below] they could not speak. Hence Laban delayed three days before pursuing, because he had not been told of Jacob's flight.

Ibn Ezra cites an opinion that the *teraphim* were bronze instruments used for determining the time of day [so *Radak*]. He also cites the view of others that they were images made by astrologers, which at certain times had the power of speech. The latter is inferred from a literal interpretation of *Zechariah* 10:2: the teraphim *spoke* vanity. *Radak* differs from this interpretation of *Zechariah;* he interprets it *figuratively* as meaning: the teraphim *instructed* vanity [by magical means other than speech] [cf. *Ralbag*]. He offers only that they were a kind of dummy in the form of a human being which was capable of absorbing higher powers. His proof that the images were in the shape of a human is that Michal deceived David's pursuers by putting *teraphim* in the bed, which they mistook for David [*I Samuel* 19:13 ff.]

Ramban deduces from the story of Michal that not *all teraphim* were worshipped as idols, for if so, David would certainly not have possessed them. He follows the opinion, therefore, that they were a type of time-measuring instrument which were used to magically foretell fortunes. Men of little faith therefore venerated them as idols, and consulted them rather than God, as evidenced by such references in Scripture as *Judges* 17:5 and ibid. 18:5.

That Laban was a diviner, *Ramban* continues, is evident from his remark [above 30:27]: *I have learned by divination.* He came from a land of diviners [see reference in *Isaiah* 2:6 to land of the east which was inhabited by soothsayers and which was a center of the occult sciences. Charan, too, was in *the east* (29:1)]. Balaam the diviner [Laban's grandson *(Midrash)*] hailed from Aram [see *Numbers* 23:7]. Hence Laban venerated this time-measuring object of occult powers as a god.

[Note that in 30:27 *Ibn Ezra* maintains that Laban used his *teraphim* for the divination mentioned there.]

20 *Jacob deceived Laban the Aramean by not telling him that he was fleeing.* 21 *Thus, he fled with all he*

20. וַיִּגְנֹב יַעֲקֹב אֶת־לֵב לָבָן הָאֲרַמִּי — *Jacob deceived* [lit. *stole the heart of*] *Laban the Aramean.*

I.e. he stole Laban's mind [i.e., deceived him]. 'Heart' is figuratively used in this sense, since the seat of the intellect [in Biblical idiom] is the heart *(Ibn Ezra).*

Cf. *Targum Yonasan: He stole the knowledge of Laban;* while *Onkelos,* as noted above s.v. וַתִּגְנֹב רָחֵל renders: *Jacob concealed from Laban.*

Jacob deceived Laban by not revealing that he realized that Laban was no longer well disposed toward him [*v.* 2]. Jacob acted in this concealed manner because he knew that Laban was a cheat and would have taken measures to prevent Jacob's flight had his suspicions been aroused. [Therefore the Torah mentions again in this context that Laban was *Aramean,* which, as noted in the *comm.* and *footnote* to 25:2 is Midrashically interpreted as if it read *ramai,* rogue or cheat] *(Sforno).*

According to *Ramban* [*v.* 24], Laban is again referred to as the רַמַּאי, *cheat,* to intimate in a contemptuous manner that although Laban was the 'Aramean' — who prided himself as a diviner and master of *teraphim* — he was still deceived by Jacob.

עַל־בְּלִי הִגִּיד לוֹ כִּי בֹרֵחַ הוּא — *By not telling him* [lit. *in that he did not tell him*] *that he was fleeing.*

Obviously, if he would *tell* him, it could not be called *fleeing!* The intent is that Jacob never gave Laban any cause to *suspect* that he would ever flee *(Or HaChaim).*

— He did not *tell* him he was *planning* to depart; he fled instead *(Radak).*

[Jacob justifies his action in *v.* 31 *(Sforno).*]

According to *Me'am Loez* [cf. *Chomas Anach*], Jacob had duped Laban by not telling him *when he first arrived* כִּי בֹרֵחַ הוּא, *that he was a fugitive* from his brother Esau, and that his stay would be only of a limited duration until it was safe for him to leave. Therefore, Laban trusted him and never suspected that he would flee from him.

Haamek Davar perceives *Laban's heart* as the subject of this phrase, the interpretation of the passage being: Jacob deceived [lit. *stole the heart of*] Laban the Aramean, *in that Laban's heart did not reveal to Laban that Jacob would flee* — and he therefore was not on guard against it.

21. וַיִּבְרַח הוּא וְכָל אֲשֶׁר לוֹ — *Thus* [lit. *and*] *he fled with all he had.*

Jacob assumed that God would keep the knowledge of his departure from Laban. As has often happened in Jewish history, however, God did not act as people wanted Him to. Instead, Laban learned of Jacob's flight, pursued and caught him — but God saved Jacob through another means. This eventual protection, too, is a common thread in Jewish history *(Haamek Davar).* [See *footnote* to *v.* 23.]

The Hebrew term for fleeing, ברח, suggests flight from a place in anticipation of *future* danger and in cases where there is no *pursuer;* the term נוס indicates flight from a *pursuer* and a *clear and present* danger *(Sforno).*

וַיָּקָם וַיַּעֲבֹר אֶת־הַנָּהָר וַיָּשֶׂם אֶת־פָּנָיו
כב הַר הַגִּלְעָד׃ וַיֻּגַּד לְלָבָן בַּיּוֹם הַשְּׁלִישִׁי כִּי
כג בָרַח יַעֲקֹב׃ וַיִּקַּח אֶת־אֶחָיו עִמּוֹ וַיִּרְדֹּף
אַחֲרָיו דֶּרֶךְ שִׁבְעַת יָמִים וַיַּדְבֵּק אֹתוֹ

וַיָּקָם וַיַּעֲבֹר אֶת הַנָּהָר — *And proceeded to cross the river* [lit. *and he arose and he crossed the river.*]

I.e., the Euphrates *(Onkelos; Targum Yonasan).*

According to *Midrash Sechel Tov,* the word וַיָּקָם [lit. *and he arose*] connotes that after his departure from Aram, *he arose* spiritually [cf. וַיָּקָם in 23:17.]

וַיָּשֶׂם אֶת־פָּנָיו הַר הַגִּלְעָד — [*And*] *he set his direction* [lit. *face*] *toward Mount Gilead.*

His retinue was growing tired and he set his sight on the fertile pastures of Gilead to afford his people and livestock the opportunity of resting *(Haamek Davar).*

— He chose Mount Gilead because he prophetically foresaw that his descendants would win a great victory there in the time of יִפְתָּח, Jephtah [see *Judges* 11:29] *(Targum Yonasan).*

The territory soon to be named Gilead plays an important role in later Biblical history. It is a most fertile region, and lies east of the Jordan River. It was not named Gilead until later [*v.* 47]. The Torah uses the name by which it was already called in the days of Moses *(Abarbanel).*

Jacob wished to avoid the arduous and dangerous task of crossing the Jordan with his large camp. He intended to travel southward along the east bank of the Jordan to the southeast corner of *Eretz Yisrael* and enter by the land route to the Negev region via Mount Seir, to Hebron where his father was. Cf. his reference to Seir in 33:14. Ultimately, however, he changed his route and took a shortcut by crossing the Jordan opposite Shechem *(HaRechasim leBikah).*

22. [Laban is informed of Jacob's departure. He pursues him and overtakes him in Gilead.]

וַיֻּגַּד לְלָבָן בַּיּוֹם הַשְּׁלִישִׁי — [*And*] *it was told to Laban on the third day.*

On the *third day* — because that was the distance between Jacob and Laban's flocks *(Rashi);* see on *v.* 19.

Ba'al HaTurim cites a *Midrash* that the informant was Amalek, a grandson of Esau, who also later informed Pharaoh that the Jews had fled [see *Exod.* 14:5. In both verses the expression וַיֻּגַּד...כִּי בָרַח occurs.] The numerical value of כִּי בָרַח [=240] equals עֲמָלֵק, *Amalek.*

According to *Targum Yonasan,* Laban's shepherds told Laban after perceiving that the abundant blessing that had come to their region had ceased. They reasoned that Jacob must have left, and brought the news to Laban:

'After Jacob had gone, the shepherds went to the well but found no water; they waited three days in case it would again overflow but it did not. So they came to Laban on the third day and he knew that Jacob had fled because through his righteousness it had overflowed for twenty years' [see footnote to

31 ל had and proceeded to cross the river, and he set his
22-23 direction toward Mount Gilead.
[22] *It was told to Laban on the third day that Jacob*
had fled. [23] *So he took his kinsmen with him and*
pursued him a distance of seven days, catching up

28:10; and *comm.* to 29:2 s.v. וְהָאֶבֶן גְּדֹלָה].

23. וַיִּקַּח אֶת אֶחָיו עִמּוֹ — *So* [lit. *and*] *he took his kinsman* [lit. *brothers*] *with him.*

[The translation of 'brothers' as *kinsman* follows *Rashi. Ramban* in *v.* 46 observes that Laban's kinsmen were Jacob's kinsmen through marriage as well, and in that they were descended from Nachor, Abraham's brother.]

Laban's act of *taking his kinsman with him* in pursuit proves his aggressive intentions. As *Midrash Tanchuma* observes:

When Laban set out in pursuit of Jacob he intended to kill him, and the Torah accordingly speaks of Laban as if he had actually done so, as it says: אֲרַמִּי אֹבֵד אָבִי *An Aramean, was the destroyer of my father* [*Deut.* 26:5]. For the gentile nations, God equates evil intentions with actions [because their general performance justifies the assumption that they would indeed do so if they had the opportunity] *(Rashi, Deut.* ibid.).[1]

Pharaoh also pursued the Jews. The events in Jacob's life were a prognostication for his descendants *(Rimzei HaTorah, Torah Sheleimah* 31:50).

וַיִּרְדֹּף אַחֲרָיו דֶּרֶךְ שִׁבְעַת יָמִים — *And* [he] *pursued him a distance of seven days.*

During the three days that the messenger traveled toward Laban, Jacob had been proceeding on his journey. Consequently, by the time the messenger reached Laban, there was a six-day distance between them. On the seventh day [i.e., the next day, the day when Jacob covered the stretch of ground which made him seven travel-days apart from Laban's starting point *(Sifsei Chachomim)*], Laban overtook him. Thus, the distance Jacob would have traveled in seven days, Laban covered in one. [Hence, it says and he pursued him a *distance* of seven days; not that he actually pursued him *for seven days.* (This bracketed addition is not in all editions)] *(Rashi).*[2]

Rashbam points out that this was natural since Jacob would be traveling slowly on account of his flocks. He implies, however, that the interpretation is that Laban overtook Jacob after Jacob

1. Laban's cruelty is the reason why Jacob could not *remain* in Paddan Aram in fulfillment of God's prophecy to Abraham that his children would endure a long exile [15:13]. An allusion to this may be found in the verse אֲרַמִּי אֹבֵד אָבִי וַיֵּרֶד מִצְרַיְמָה, *An Aramean was the destroyer of my father, and he went down to Egypt (Deut.* 26:5); because of Laban the Aramean, Jacob was forced to undergo his exile *in Egypt* rather than in Aram *(R' Munk).*

2. Why did Jacob not enjoy קְפִיצַת הַדֶּרֶךְ, *contraction of the way,* as he had on his way to Charan and as even Eliezer experienced when he was dispatched to seek a wife for Isaac? Had such a miracle recurred, Jacob would have been spared the ordeal of being overtaken by Laban.

By not giving him supernatural speed God demonstrated to Jacob that he need not fear any

כד בְּהַר הַגִּלְעָד׃ וַיָּבֹא אֱלֹהִים אֶל־לָבָן
הָאֲרַמִּי בַּחֲלֹם הַלָּיְלָה וַיֹּאמֶר לוֹ הִשָּׁמֶר
לְךָ פֶּן־תְּדַבֵּר עִם־יַעֲקֹב מִטּוֹב עַד־רָע׃

had actually traveled seven days [i.e. Laban covered in *four* days the distance Jacob covered in seven].

Ramban suggests that Laban overtook Jacob after *Laban* had travelled seven days. First, he had to return to his city to get his kinsmen [thus, in effect, covering in seven days what Jacob traveled in ten days]. He cites *Pirkei d'Rabbi Eliezer* in support of his view. *Ramban* agrees, however, that according to the *Midrash* cited by *Rashi,* Laban began his pursuit without first returning to the city.

Tosafos HaRosh maintains that the episode occurred as follows:

Jacob first returned to the city where he and Laban lived. (It was there that Rachel stole Laban's *teraphim).* Jacob fled from there, and the messenger set out on the three day journey to inform Laban. Laban first returned home, a journey of three days, and also discovered that his *teraphim* were missing. By this time, Jacob was six travel days away. Laban set out in hot pursuit, overtook Jacob on the next day, covering in one day what had taken Jacob a week.

[Most estimate the distance Jacob traveled — from Charan to Gilead — at about thirty miles.]

וַיַּדְבֵּק אֹתוֹ בְּהַר הַגִּלְעָד — *Catching up with him* [lit. *and he became attached to him*] *on Mount Gilead.*

— Where Jacob had stopped to pasture his flocks *(Haamek Davar).*

— Where Jacob had been offering praise and praying to God *(Targum Yonasan).*

On the eve of the seventh day Laban reached the foot of the mountain and he saw Jacob encamped at a distance. That night as he slept below Jacob's camp, he dreamt the following dream *(Ramban).*

The translation of וַיַּדְבֵּק as *catching up with him* follows *Ramban* and others who hold that Laban did not actually *overtake* Jacob until *after* God's warning in the following dream. [Cf. *Ibn Ezra* next verse.]

The Hebrew refers to the point at which one can sight the other from afar *(HaRechasim leBik'ah).*

The *entire plain* was known as Mount Gilead. Therefore, as soon as Laban reached that plain where, although from afar, Jacob was encamped, he is said to have *caught* him; he did not actually *overtake* or *confront* him until the following morning [*v.* 25] *(Haamek Davar).*

24. God's warning to Laban.

וַיָּבֹא אֱלֹהִים אֶל לָבָן הָאֲרַמִּי בַּחֲלֹם הַלָּיְלָה — *But* [lit. *and*] *God had come to Laban the Aramean in a dream by* [lit. *of the*] *night.*

Through His angel Michael, brandishing a sword *(Pirkei d'Rabbi Eliezer).*

Before Laban even *caught up with* Jacob, God *had already* come to Laban. There are many such verses [which are not in strict chronological sequence, but which

harm from Laban even if there were to be a successful pursuit. To the contrary, if God had contracted the way for Jacob, it would have appeared as if ח״ו it was not in His power to protect Jacob from a direct confrontation with Laban. Other benefits of this natural course were that Laban was forced to pledge that he would not harm Jacob, and that Rachel would be buried on the road where she would pray for Israel when it trudged into Babylonian Exile [see *comm.* 35:19] *(Or HaChaim).*

31 *with him on Mount Gilead.* [24] *But God had come to*
24 *Laban the Aramean in a dream by night and said to*
him, 'Beware lest you speak with Jacob either good or
bad.'

parenthetically revert to an earlier incident to supply us with more detailed information. They are omitted from the original narrative in order not to break the *initial continuity* of the story] *(Ibn Ezra).*

[This differs from *Ramban* cited above, that the verses here *do* reflect the correct sequence, and that Laban did not *overtake* Jacob until *v.* 25. Apparently, *Ibn Ezra* — like *Onkelos* — holds that וַיַּדְבֵּק and וַיַּשֵּׂג are synonymous and both connote *overtook;* hence he explains the redundancy of verses 23 and 25 by explaining the interim verse as paranthetical. *Ramban* apparently maintains that וַיַּדְבֵּק connotes approaching closely; not until *v.* 25 did he *overtake* (וַיַּשֵּׂג) Jacob.]

Laban is again referred to as הָאֲרַמִּי [the *Aramean,* Midrashically interpreted as if it read הָרַמַּאי, *the cheat*]*:* Though Laban was a *cheat* and his townspeople were idolators and diviners [see on *v.* 19 and 20], yet the prophetic dream came to him in honor of the righteous Jacob *(Ramban).*

— For just as God had come to Abimelech [20:3] in honor of Abraham, so did He come to Laban in honor of Jacob *(Radak).*

[Cf. *Radak* to 20:3 that to protect the honor of the righteous, God comes to gentiles in prophetic dreams. The *Midrash* similarly observes that God appears to heathens only at *night.* This was the case also with Balaam (see *Numbers* 22:20), since the deeds of the wicked are as dark as night.][1]

הִשָּׁמֶר לְךָ פֶּן תְּדַבֵּר עִם־יַעֲקֹב — *Beware lest you speak with Jacob.*

— Even *speech* is forbidden you *(Sforno).*

According to the *Zohar,* speech was forbidden him because it had been Laban's intent not to wage *physical* war on him since Jacob was more powerful than he — but to kill Jacob through his *words* by casting a spell upon him. Thus God cautioned him not to communicate with Jacob *at all (Zohar).*

According to *Divrei David,* the intent in the literal sense was not that Laban avoid any communication, but that he avoid conversing on the matter of Jacob returning to Charan.

מִטּוֹב עַד רָע — *Either good or bad* [lit. *from good until bad.*]

[He should not even speak *good*] because [even] the goodness of the wicked is evil to the righteous. Since the righteous despise any benefits they may derive from wicked people, the benefit itself is not truly good *(Rashi* based on *Yevamos* 103b).

— Since the righteous man knows the enmity the wicked holds for him. What may appear to be an act of goodness is in reality, sinister in intent *(Kli Yakar).*

— In this case: What *you* might

1. Cf. also *Moreh Nevuchim* 2:51 that the phrase *God came to ... in a dream by night* does not indicate a prophecy, and the person mentioned in the phrase is not a prophet. The expression merely informs us that the attention of that person was called by God — through an angel — to a certain thing, and that this occurred at night.

... For just as God may cause a person to move in order to save or kill another person, so may He cause, according to His will, certain things to rise in man's mind in a dream by night.

כה וַיַּשֵּׂג לָבָן אֶת־יַעֲקֹב וְיַעֲקֹב תָּקַע אֶת־
אָהֳלוֹ בָּהָר וְלָבָן תָּקַע אֶת־אֶחָיו בְּהַר
כו הַגִּלְעָד: וַיֹּאמֶר לָבָן לְיַעֲקֹב מֶה עָשִׂיתָ
וַתִּגְנֹב אֶת־לְבָבִי וַתְּנַהֵג אֶת־בְּנֹתַי
כז כִּשְׁבֻיוֹת חָרֶב: לָמָּה נַחְבֵּאתָ לִבְרֹחַ
וַתִּגְנֹב אֹתִי וְלֹא־הִגַּדְתָּ לִּי וָאֲשַׁלֵּחֲךָ
כח בְּשִׂמְחָה וּבְשִׁרִים בְּתֹף וּבְכִנּוֹר: וְלֹא
נְטַשְׁתַּנִי לְנַשֵּׁק לְבָנַי וְלִבְנֹתָי עַתָּה

consider an act of goodness, such as enticing him to return with you to Charan, is really evil as far as he is concerned since the Divine Presence will not rest on him so long as he is associated with the wicked *(Sifsei Chachomim).*

Maskil l'David observes that the intent of the *Gemara Yevamos* 103b upon which *Rashi* based his exposition explains that God ordered Laban not to speak to Jacob even of good because he might seek to involve Jacob in a discussion about idols. Indeed, in verse 30, Laban *did* refer to the *teraphim* as gods.

According to *Ramban,* the literal sense is: *Either good* — i.e., neither entice him by promising to treat him well if he returns with you; *or bad* — nor threaten him with harm if he does not, for it is I Who commanded him to return to his land.

This explains how Laban *conversed* with Jacob at all after God's warning. But he avoided any mention of Jacob returning with him to Charan *(Divrei David).*

HaRechasim leBik'ah explains the expression *either good or bad* as idiomatically meaning *anything,* as in 24:50. [However, Laban ignored this implication of God's command and conversed with Jacob anyway, avoiding only the question of returning with him to Charan.]

The result of God's warning, as noted by *Midrash Aggadas Bereishis* [*Torah Sheleimah* §551] is that Laban did not carry out his villainous plan of killing Jacob.

25. וַיַּשֵּׂג לָבָן אֶת יַעֲקֹב — [And] *Laban overtook Jacob.*

In *v.* 23 Laban merely reached *close* to him; but now, in the morning, he actually *overtook* him and they met in a face-to-face confrontation *(Lekach Tov).* [Cf. *Ibn Ezra* and *Ramban* above.]

וְיַעֲקֹב תָּקַע אֶת אָהֳלוֹ בָּהָר — [*And*] *Jacob had pitched his tent on the mountain.*

On the slope of the mountain itself *(Haamek Davar).*

[I.e. Mount Gilead, as further identified at the end of the verse *(Ramban* to 30:40).]

וְלָבָן תָּקַע אֶת אֶחָיו בְּהַר הַגִּלְעָד — *While Laban had stationed his kinsmen on Mount Gilead* [following *Onkelos.*]

— Jacob had taken tents with him for his family and servants, but Laban and his kinsmen had not. Laban stationed his entourage at the foot of the mountain. He was still at a distance from Jacob even though the entire plain is referred to as the hill country of Gilead *(Haamek Davar).*

Ibn Ezra interprets the word אָהֳלוֹ, *his tent,* to refer to both Jacob

25 Laban overtook Jacob. Jacob had pitched his tent
on the mountain, while Laban had stationed his
kinsmen on Mount Gilead. 26 Laban said to Jacob,
'What have you done that you have deceived me and
led my daughters away like captives of the sword?
27 Why have you fled so stealthily, and cheated me?
Nor did you tell me — for I would have sent you off
with gladness, with songs, with timbrel, and with
lyre! 28 And you did not even allow me to kiss my
sons and daughters. Now you have acted foolishly.

and Laban: *Jacob pitched his tent and Laban pitched his with his kinsmen on Mount Gilead.*

26. [Laban reproaches Jacob for having stolen away with his daughters as if they were captives taken in war]:

מַה עָשִׂיתָ וַתִּגְנֹב אֶת לְבָבִי — *What have you done that* [lit. *and*] *you have deceived me* [lit. *stolen my heart*]?

What crime have you committed that compelled you to deceive me and flee? *(Abarbanel).*

וַתְּנַהֵג אֶת בְּנֹתַי כִּשְׁבֻיוֹת חָרֶב — *And* [*you*] *led my daughters away like captives of the sword?*

[I.e., like prisoners of war], 'sword' is a synonym for war *(Rashi).*

— Thus, preventing them from bidding farewell to their father and brothers *(Alshich).*

Laban feigns injured innocence in portraying himself as the aggrieved father by bringing up the matter of his daughters before the matter of Jacob's fleeing or the theft of his *teraphim (Haamek Davar).*

27. לָמָּה נַחְבֵּאתָ לִבְרֹחַ וַתִּגְנֹב אֹתִי — *Why have you fled so stealthily* [lit. *why have you been stealthy to flee*] *and cheated me?* [lit. *and stole from me*]:

— And stole my *heart* [i.e. deceived me] as in *v.* 26 *(Rashi; Radak).*

— And stole my *teraphim (Haamek Davar).*

וָאֲשַׁלֵּחֲךָ בְּשִׂמְחָה וּבְשִׁרִים בְּתֹף וּבְכִנּוֹר — *For I would have sent you off with gladness,* [*and*] *with songs, with timbrel and with lyre.*

The question was rhetorical, the implication being: It was foolish of you to flee without telling me, for had you asked me I would have given you permission and made a gala farewell celebration for you *(Malbim).*

28. וְלֹא נְטַשְׁתַּנִי לְנַשֵּׁק לְבָנַי וְלִבְנֹתָי — *And You did not* [even] *allow me to kiss my sons and daughters.*

— *To kiss* — i.e., a farewell kiss *(Ralbag);* or in the sense of יִשַּׁק in 41:40: *sustain,* render: *and you did not allow me to make provision for my sons and daughters (Chizkuni).*

My sons here obviously means *my grandchildren,* for grandchildren are like children *(Radak).*

עַתָּה הִסְכַּלְתָּ עֲשׂוֹ — *Now, you have acted foolishly.*

[The phrase is idiomatic. The

כט הִסְכַּלְתָּ עֲשׂוֹ׃ יֶשׁ־לְאֵל יָדִי לַעֲשׂוֹת
עִמָּכֶם רָע וֵאלֹהֵי אֲבִיכֶם אֶמֶשׁ | אָמַר
אֵלַי לֵאמֹר הִשָּׁמֶר לְךָ מִדַּבֵּר עִם־יַעֲקֹב
ל מִטּוֹב עַד־רָע׃ וְעַתָּה הָלֹךְ הָלַכְתָּ כִּי־
נִכְסֹף נִכְסַפְתָּה לְבֵית אָבִיךָ לָמָּה גָנַבְתָּ
לא אֶת־אֱלֹהָי׃ וַיַּעַן יַעֲקֹב וַיֹּאמֶר לְלָבָן כִּי

Hebrew which treats *foolish* as a verb, and *acted* in the infinitive, would literally be translated: *Now, you have been foolish to do,* עֲשׂוֹ = עֲשׂה.]

— You have always been the sensible one; *now,* in this instance, you have acted foolishly *(Radak).*

How did you not expect that I would pursue you? *(Haamek Davar).*

29. יֶשׁ־לְאֵל יָדִי לַעֲשׂוֹת עִמָּכֶם רָע — *It is within my power* [lit. *there is the power in my hand*] *to do you all* [עִמָּכֶם, second person plural] *harm.*[1]

[The phrase is equivalent to יֵשׁ אֵל לְיָדִי]: *I have the strength and power in my hand* to harm you. The word אֵל [which in this case is a non-sacred noun] signifies *strength and abundance of power,* and it is in this sense that אֵל, *El,* is used as a Name of God [since He is the sum of all Power] *(Rashi).*

[That Laban made such a bold, confident statement implies that he was accompanied by a band of kinsmen large enough to have carried out the implied threat.]

However, the *Midrashim* cite Jacob's extraordinary strength [see on 29:10 and *v.* 45 below], and claim that Laban was merely boasting and glorifying himself; it was to Jacob's credit that Jacob allowed himself to be subjected to Laban's wickedness and that he responded humbly instead of seeking a physical test of strength.

There are other opinions that notwithstanding the phenomenal power of Jacob and his household, he feared a confrontation with Laban because he knew Laban's notorious capacity to do evil. Although Jacob had faith that God would be with him, he was hesitant, since one should not rely on a miracle, and he was apprehensive that perhaps he had committed some sin which would cause him to lose God's grace (see on 32:11). [Cf. *Sefer HaParshiyos*].

וֵאלֹהֵי אֲבִיכֶם — *But* [lit. *and*] *the God of your* [plural] *father.*

— To Whom I [too] give honor *(Rashbam).*

The intent is: It is only because of *Him* that I show you forbearance; you do not deserve it seeing how you departed without my permission, and deceived me in doing so *(Sforno).*

אֶמֶשׁ אָמַר אֵלַי לֵאמֹר — *Addressed me* [lit. *said to me*] *last night saying.*

As noted often in the commentary, the word לֵאמֹר, *saying* [lit. *to*

1. *Me'am Loez,* following *Tz'ror HaMor* suggests that when making this statement Laban turned to *Jacob's sons* and addressed them all. Hence the plural: I have it in my power to harm all of you [עִמָּכֶם]; also the use of *the God of* אֲבִיכֶם, *your* (plural) *father.* The implication is: "The God of your father [Jacob] addressed me last night and said, 'Beware not to speak *to Jacob'*; but to *you,* his sons, I can do as I please."

[29] *It is within my power to do you all harm. But the God of your father addressed me last night saying, "Beware of speaking with Jacob either good or bad."*
[30] *Now — you have left because you longed greatly for your father's house. But why did you steal my gods?'*

[31] *Jacob answered and said to Laban, 'Because I*

say] has several connotations: *clearly, unambiguously; the communication is meant to be conveyed to others* [i.e., לֵאמֹר, *to retell*].

In this case, *Midrash Lekach Tov* interprets that God addressed this communication to Laban, as Laban himself admits, לֵאמֹר לְדוֹרוֹת, *to convey to future generations* [i.e. God's warning not to mistreat Jacob applies eternally to all gentiles who come in contact with Jacob's descendants] as it is written [*Psalms* 105:15]: *Touch not My anointed ones, and do My prophets no harm.*

30. וְעַתָּה הָלֹךְ הָלַכְתָּ כִּי־נִכְסֹף נִכְסַפְתָּה לְבֵית אָבִיךָ — [*And*] *Now — you have left because you longed* [lit. *were longed for*] *greatly for your father's house.*

[Both verbs are in the infinitive compound: lit. *leave you have left ... longing you have longed* to emphasize that Jacob's going was a *fait accompli.*]

The word נכסף meaning *desire* [*long; yearn*] occurs often in Scripture, for example: *Psalms* 84:3: *My soul yearns* (*נִכְסְפָה...נַפְשִׁי*); *Job* 14:15: *You desire* (תִּכְסֹף) *your handiwork* (*Rashi; Ibn Ezra* cites additional references).

The reason the verb is in the *niphal*-passive form [lit. *you were longed for greatly*] is to suggest the familiar principle that feelings between people are reciprocated; since Jacob was longed for by his parents, he felt a parallel longing for them (*Karnei Or*).

לָמָּה גָנַבְתָּ אֶת אֱלֹהָי — [*But*] *why did you steal my gods?*

[The preposition *but* is not in the Hebrew, but implied. The sense of the passage is]: Granted that you were motivated to leave because of the great longing you had for your father's house, *but how does that justify your stealing my gods?! (Sforno).*

— The gods could be of no possible value in your father's house. Accordingly, your theft of the *teraphim* must have been a wanton, provocative act *(Haamek Davar).*

When the tribal ancestors [i.e. Jacob's sons] heard their grandfather [Laban] say this, they exclaimed, 'We are ashamed of you, grandfather, that in your old age you can refer to them as your gods!' *(Midrash).*[1]

1. 'Laban had planned to uproot everything' *(Haggadah).* Laban, by his own admission [see also further, *v.* 29] was frustrated in his intention to murder Jacob and his family only by God's warning *(Vilna Gaon,* see ArtScroll *Haggadah* p. 101).

In his accusation, Laban was the prophetic forerunner of the old European potentates who so frequently hurled at Jacob's descendants the accusation 'Why did you steal my gods?' and used the allegation of stealing images or communion wafers as an opportunity to take the lives of the Jews and seize their property ... (Harav Miller: *Behold A People*).

יָרֵאתִי כִּי אָמַרְתִּי פֶּן־תִּגְזֹל אֶת־בְּנוֹתֶיךָ
לב מֵעִמִּי: עִם אֲשֶׁר תִּמְצָא אֶת־אֱלֹהֶיךָ לֹא
יִחְיֶה נֶגֶד אַחֵינוּ הַכֶּר־לְךָ מָה עִמָּדִי וְקַח־
לג לָךְ וְלֹא־יָדַע יַעֲקֹב כִּי רָחֵל גְּנָבָתַם: וַיָּבֹא

31. כִּי יָרֵאתִי — *Because I was afraid.*

Jacob answered the questions in order. This was his answer to Laban's first question [*v.* 26]: *What have you done that you led my daughters away? (Rashi).*

כִּי אָמַרְתִּי פֶּן־תִּגְזֹל אֶת־בְּנוֹתֶיךָ מֵעִמִּי — *For I thought* [lit. *said*], *perhaps you might* [lit. *lest you would*] *steal your daughters from me.*

Because you claim that you did not allow me to marry your daughters only to have me take them away from you, you prove that you would have thought yourself justified in detaining them, as well as my children and possessions. (This in fact appears to have been Laban's intention as is evident in *v.* 43). Furthermore, had I remained with you in Charan where you are influential, you could more easily get others to help you than you could if I am out of your country *(Sforno).*

Note that Jacob does not add insult to injury or provoke anger against his wives — Laban's daughters — by mentioning that they had *encouraged* him to flee [*v.* 14] *(Haamek Davar).*

32. עִם אֲשֶׁר תִּמְצָא אֶת אֱלֹהֶיךָ — *With whomever you find your gods.* [*Onkelos* renders this differently; see below.]

The following is Jacob's response to Laban's latter accusation that he stole the gods *(Rashbam).*

לֹא יִחְיֶה — [*He*] *shall not live.*

This is construed by the *Midrashim* as a prayer, in the sense of an imprecation: *May he not live:* — He will die prematurely *(Targum Yonasan; Pirkei d'Rabbi Eliezer).*

The Sages in the *Midrash* perceive this curse which left the lips of the righteous Jacob, to have been — although unintentional — a prognostication of the future. In consequence of this curse, Rachel died on the journey *(Rashi* citing *Midrash).*[1]

[In *v.* 14 above, an additional reason is offered: Rachel presumptuously answered before her older sister, and so died before her. Cf. also *Meshech Chochmah* to *v.* 13 that 'whoever leaves a vow unfulfilled, his wife dies.' Regarding Rachel's having died *on the way* rather than merit being buried in the Cave of Machpelah, see *Rashi* to 31:15 and 49:8.]

Rashbam, however, takes the literal sense of Jacob's remark to be: *He will not live* — I will physically exact

1. This must be understood in light of the dictum in *Moed Katan* 18:9: בְּרִית כְּרוּתָה לִשְׂפָתַיִם, *a covenant has been made with the lips,* i.e., the spoken word, even if uttered unintentionally, may unwittingly be fulfilled as if by prophecy.

And, just as one word uttered by a king can cause irreparable damage [see *comm.* to ArtScroll *Ecclesiastes* 10:5], the way in which something is expressed — even by a commoner — may contain a portent for the future. Accordingly, it behooves man to choose his words carefully.

The dictum in *Makkos* 11a may be cited in this connection: A curse of a wise man, even though uttered without cause, takes effect. [Although in this case the idols were not *found* in Rachel's possession and thus *technically* the condition of the imprecation was not met,

31 was afraid, for I thought, perhaps you might steal
32 your daughters from me. [32] With whomever you find
your gods, he shall not live; in the presence of our
kinsmen ascertain for yourself what is with me and
take it back.' (Now Jacob did not know that Rachel
had stolen them.)

vengeance upon him; *Ibn Ezra* interprets: *I will kill him*, while *Radak* is of the opinion that the implication is that the culprit will be placed in *Laban's* hands for retribution.

Jacob uttered this curse because he was convinced that the one who stole it had relapsed into idolatry *(Akeidas Yitzchak;* similarly, *Sforno* below).

Onkelos explains the imprecation to be not against the *person* with whom the gods are found, but against the *place.* He renders our passage: *The place where you find your deities will not endure* [i.e. *that place* will be destroyed. The word יִחְיֶה, *live,* referring to inanimate objects is similar to *Nechemiah* 3:34: *Will they revive* (הַיְחַיּוּ) *the stones?* The concept of inanimate objects being subject to 'death' is reminiscent of the pronouncement in *Bava Kamma* 54a: Regarding inanimate objects — their breaking is their death *(Nesinah laGer).*]

נֶגֶד אַחֵינוּ — — *In the presence of our kinsmen* [following *Rashi;* lit. *brothers.*]

Although the reference is to the people who accompanied Laban, they are called *our* kinsmen because they were related to Jacob as well, both through marriage and because they were descended from Nachor, the brother of Abraham (*Ramban* to *v.* 46).

הַכֶּר־לְךָ מָה עִמָּדִי — *Ascertain for yourself* [lit. *recognize to yourself*] *what is with me.*

I.e., what *of yours* is in my possession *(Rashi).*

— If something other than the *teraphim* was stolen, *take it back (Ralbag).*

וְקַח לָךְ — *And take it back* [lit. *and take to yourself*].

— And we will indeed have been proven to be the culprits *(Akeidas Yitzchak).*

Jacob was not as firm regarding other property as he was regarding Laban's idols. Regarding the idols he said absolutely: 'Whoever took it is certainly an idolator and must die.' But he could not be so certain that one of the servants had not stolen something else; in that case, should Laban discover *any* of his property he should take it back *(Haamek Davar).*

וְלֹא יָדַע יַעֲקֹב כִּי רָחֵל גְּנָבָתַם — *Now Jacob did not know that Rachel had stolen them.*

The Torah thus parenthetically testifies that Jacob uttered the im-

nevertheless the curse took effect. See *Tosafos* s.v. אֲפִילוּ.]

In this context, the *Midrash* notes that Rachel's death ensued because of Jacob's words ... and that Samuel's sons did not succeed their father because of what Eli said to him [see *I Samuel* 3:17; 4:11; 8:1 ff. Cf. also *comm.* to 22:5 s.v. וְנִשְׁתַּחֲוֶה, and *Rashi* to 27:45 s.v. לָמָה אֶשְׁכַּל].

— This is what Jacob meant when he lamented [48:7]: מֵתָה עָלַי רָחֵל, *Rachel died through me* — i.e. through the imprecation of my curse *(Lekach Tov).*

Cf. also *Sefer Chassidim* §924 that though her motives in taking the *teraphim* were noble, since Jacob was present she should have inquired of Jacob, for whenever a wise man is available, his advice should be sought before any action is taken.

לָבָ֜ן בְּאֹ֧הֶל־יַעֲקֹ֣ב ׀ וּבְאֹ֣הֶל לֵאָ֗ה וּבְאֹ֛הֶל
שְׁתֵּ֥י הָאֲמָהֹ֖ת וְלֹ֣א מָצָ֑א וַיֵּצֵא֙ מֵאֹ֣הֶל
לד לֵאָ֔ה וַיָּבֹ֖א בְּאֹ֥הֶל רָחֵֽל׃ וְרָחֵ֞ל לָקְחָ֣ה
אֶת־הַתְּרָפִ֗ים וַתְּשִׂמֵ֛ם בְּכַ֥ר הַגָּמָ֖ל וַתֵּ֣שֶׁב
עֲלֵיהֶ֑ם וַיְמַשֵּׁ֥שׁ לָבָ֛ן אֶת־כָּל־הָאֹ֖הֶל וְלֹ֥א
לה מָצָֽא׃ וַתֹּ֣אמֶר אֶל־אָבִ֗יהָ אַל־יִ֙חַר֙ בְּעֵינֵ֣י

precation because he had suspected that the culprit was a servant who had relapsed into idolatry and had stolen the *teraphim* to worship in secret. If Jacob would have had even the slightest notion that *Rachel* had stolen them, he would: *(a)* never have had the audacity to deny it so boldly; and *(b)* never have uttered a curse since he never would never have suspected her of idolatrous motives. He would have been certain that her motive was lofty — to wean her father from idol worship *(Akeidas Yitzchak; Sforno; Alshich).*

33. וַיָּבֹא לָבָן בְּאֹהֶל־יַעֲקֹב — [And] *Laban came into Jacob's tent.*

This was Rachel's tent, the tent where Jacob was generally found. [Rachel's tent was Jacob's usual home because she was his *primary* wife (see on 29:31 וְרָחֵל עֲקָרָה; and *Rashi* to *v.* 4 s.v. וַיִּקְרָא לְרָחֵל וּלְלֵאָה)]. Accordingly, in the genealogies of chapt. 46, only Rachel is referred to as *Jacob's wife,* a designation not given the other wives. When the verse concludes by saying that Laban went to Rachel's tent, it means that he returned for a second search of this tent *(Rashi).*

According to *Midrash Lekach Tov,* this was Jacob's *own* tent which he used for prayer.

Ramban similarly maintains that the tents of Jacob and Rachel cannot be one and the same, since it would be incorrect for a tent to be variously called by two different names in the same verse, first *Jacob's* and then further *Rachel's* tent. He maintains, accordingly, that this refers to Jacob's *own* tent where he would dine with his children and members of the household.

וּבְאֹהֶל לֵאָה וּבְאֹהֶל שְׁתֵּי הָאֲמָהֹת וְלֹא מָצָא — *And into Leah's tent and into the tent of the two maidservants* [=Bilhah and Zilpah] *but he found nothing* [lit. *and he did not find*].

Most commentators [*Rashi; Ibn Ezra; Ramban; Ralbag*] contend that, sequentially, Laban searched Rachel's tent *before* those of the maidservants. However, the Torah first mentions *all* the uneventful searches before going into the search of Rachel's tent because it was there that there was much to report. The search of *Rachel's* tent [according to *Rashi*, the second such search] is described last since the continuing narrative of the following verses focuses on her [see below].

Ibn Ezra cites an opinion that the singular form *'tent' of the two maidservants* indicates that one tent served them both. *Ramban,* however, leans to the opinion that we must conclude that to preserve modesty — see *Niddah* 17a — each of Jacob's four wives had a separate tent.

*33 Laban came into Jacob's tent, and into Leah's
tent and into the tent of the two maidservants, but he
found nothing. When he had left Leah's tent, he
came into Rachel's tent. 34 Now Rachel had taken the
teraphim, put them into the camel's packsaddle and
sat on them. Laban rummaged through the whole
tent, and found nothing. 35 She said to her father, 'Let*

Akeidas Yitzchak suggests that the maidservants indeed had separate compartments within the same larger tent, a fact which is inferred from the singular designation *'tent'*. Also, besides their respective separate entrances into their mistresses' tents, they had direct access to *each other's tents* so that they could assist one another in their duties.

וַיֵּצֵא מֵאֹהֶל לֵאָה וַיָּבֹא בְּאֹהֶל רָחֵל — *When* [lit. and] *he had left Leah's tent,* [*and*] *he came into Rachel's tent.*

He returned to Rachel's tent for a second search directly after leaving Leah's tent, because he recognized that she was a מַשְׁמְשָׁנִית, *one who touches everything (Rashi).*

[Thus, *Rashi* perceives the order of Laban's search to be: The tents of Jacob (=Rachel), Leah, Rachel a second time, and finally the maidservants. As noted above, the Torah reserves the mention of Rachel for the last because the narrative of the following verses focuses on her.]

Ramban, in following *Ibn Ezra* and most other commentators that Jacob had his own tent, maintains that the sequence was: the tent of Jacob; Leah; Rachel; the maidservants.

In the primary opinion cited by *Ibn Ezra,* but rejected by *Ramban,* the order of Laban's visits was as listed in the Torah: Jacob; Leah; the maidservants; Leah again, and Rachel.

R' Bachya takes the order literally: Jacob; Leah; the maidservants; Rachel. He conjectures why the Torah again mentions that Jacob left Leah's tent after that of the maidservants, when it would appear more proper to mention that he left the tent of the *maidservants* and entered Rachel's tent. He suggests that the tent of Leah was the largest of them all, and together with the tent of the maidservants, it formed sort of a compound. Accordingly, when he left the maidservants he was still technically within Leah's tent.

34. וְרָחֵל לָקְחָה אֶת הַתְּרָפִים — *Now* [lit. *and*] *Rachel had taken the teraphim.*

In the interim; before Laban entered her tent, Rachel had taken the *teraphim* in order to hide them *(Chizkuni).*

וַתְּשִׂמֵם בְּכַר הַגָּמָל — [And she] *put them inside the camel's packsaddle.*

The word כַּר literally means *pillow;* the rendering *packsaddle* follows *Onkelos (Rashi).*

וַתֵּשֶׁב עֲלֵיהֶם — *And* [*she*] *sat on them.*

In display of her utter contempt for Laban's 'gods', Rachel placed the idols beneath her *(Zohar).*

[And, as we see later, since 'the way of women' was upon her she knew Laban would not trouble her to rise.]

וַיְמַשֵּׁשׁ לָבָן אֶת־כָּל־הָאֹהֶל וְלֹא מָצָא — [And] *Laban rummaged* [lit. *felt*] *through the whole tent and found nothing* [lit. *and he did not find*].

Laban perceived from the withdrawn way Rachel was sitting on the camel's packsaddles, that 'the way of women was upon her'. He

אֲדֹנִי כִּי לוֹא אוּכַל לָקוּם מִפָּנֶיךָ כִּי־דֶרֶךְ
נָשִׁים לִי וַיְחַפֵּשׂ וְלֹא מָצָא אֶת־הַתְּרָפִים:
לו וַיִּחַר לְיַעֲקֹב וַיָּרֶב בְּלָבָן וַיַּעַן יַעֲקֹב
וַיֹּאמֶר לְלָבָן מַה־פִּשְׁעִי מַה חַטָּאתִי כִּי
לז דָלַקְתָּ אַחֲרָי: כִּי־מִשַּׁשְׁתָּ אֶת־כָּל־כֵּלַי

therefore did not ask her to rise *(Akeidas Yitzchak).*

35. אַל־יִחַר בְּעֵינֵי אֲדֹנִי — *Let not my lord find it annoying* [lit. *let it not annoy* (or: *anger) in the eyes of my lord*].

[The translation *annoy* for יִחַר follows *Rashi* to *Numb.* 16:15; see *comm.* above to 4:5 וַיִּחַר לְקַיִן, *this annoyed Cain. Onkelos* renders it in the sense of *let it not anger my lord.* Cf. *comm.* to וַיִּחַר אַף in 30:2.][1]

כִּי לוֹא אוּכַל לָקוּם מִפָּנֶיךָ — *That I cannot rise up before you.*

— To kiss your hand *(Ramban).*

Some see in the 'full' spelling לוא an allusion that Rachel was not utterly telling an untruth; her intention was a double-entendre as if she were combining the two words לֹא, *not,* and לוֹ, *for him.* She was suggesting: כִּי לוֹא אוּכַל לָקוּם, for *to him* [to my father] I can not rise up — but to others, indeed I could (see *Meshech Chochmah).*

כִּי דֶרֶךְ נָשִׁים לִי — *For the way of women is upon me.*

According to most, this is a euphemism for menstruation, similar to the expression אֹרַח כַּנָּשִׁים, *the manner of women,* in 18:11 *(Michlol Yofi).*

— What kind of excuse was it? Do menstruant women not stand up? — Perhaps she meant that her condition had made her feel ill, as is not uncommon for some women *(Ramban).*

Ramban continues that this must be understood in the context of ancient times when menstruant women were kept in isolation. This fact is indicated by the very designation given them — *niddah* [lit. *shunned*] for even talking to them was avoided [see *Ramban* to *Lev.* 18:19; and cf. *Resp. Chasam Sofer O. Ch.* 23 regarding these measures in our times].

... Accordingly, Rachel intimated that though it would ordinarily have been proper for her to rise and kiss his hands, her status as a menstruant prevented her from doing so. And since one did not then converse with a *niddah,* Laban kept silent and did not answer her.

Tur cites an interpretation that by *the way of women,* Rachel meant that she was *pregnant,* for she was carrying Benjamin at the time. [This differs with the traditional rabbinic chronology according to which Benjamin was born two years later.]

וַיְחַפֵּשׂ וְלֹא מָצָא אֶת הַתְּרָפִים — *Thus* [lit. *and*] *he searched but* [lit. *and he*] *did not find the teraphim.*

[Due to her condition, he did not search *beneath* her, but he continued to search elsewhere in the tent.]

1. [This is one of the few places in Scripture where the verb חרה occurs in conjunction with עֵינַיִם, *eyes;* the usual idiom attaches it to אַף, *nostrils.*]

Haamek Davar accordingly comments that idiomatically, when the verb חרה occurs in conjunction with *eyes,* as here, and in *Jonah* 4:2, the connotation is *smarting* and *fierce displeasure,* rather than *anger.* The idiom here, *annoy in the eyes,* refers to the *smarting* one feels when one focuses his gaze on something for a prolonged period. Here, Rachel asked her father not to be displeased at the sight of her sitting passively while he was actively engaged in his search. Therefore, she implied: Please do not stare at me so; *I cannot rise up before you,* etc.

not my lord find it annoying that I cannot rise up before you, for the way of women is upon me.' Thus he searched but did not find the teraphim.

[36] *Then Jacob became angered and he took up his grievance with Laban. Jacob spoke up and said to Laban, 'What is my transgression? What is my sin that you have hotly pursued me?* [37] *When you rum-*

It was certainly a display of Divine Providence that Laban did not discover his *teraphim* in Rachel's possession. Besides the embarrassment she would have experienced, who knows what he would have done? *(Haamek Davar).*

36. [The Torah does not record whether or not Laban searched through the belongings of his grandchildren and every servant as well. Perhaps we are to assume that he did; or possibly Laban felt that none but Jacob or his wives — who were Laban's daughters — would have had the audacity to enter his tent and steal his 'gods.' Nevertheless when Laban had finished ransacking Jacob's belongings and failed to find what he was searching for, the outraged Patriarch — who had painfully maintained his silence all these years — could contain himself no further, and became indignant]:

וַיִּחַר לְיַעֲקֹב וַיָּרֶב בְּלָבָן — *Then* [lit. *and*] *Jacob became annoyed* [or and this *angered Jacob;* see above *v.* 35 and *comm.* to 30:2], *and he took up his grievance* [lit. *argued, upbraided*] *with Laban.*

—Since Laban did not believe him, but searched through all his possessions. Although Jacob had *invited* Laban to make the search, he felt that Laban should have had the good manners not to do so *(Radak).*

Ramban observes, however, that although Laban might have been justified in making the search after he had been invited to do so, Jacob had originally made the offer because he had thought that one of the members of his household might have stolen the *teraphim.* Now that they were not found, he suspected that the whole charge was a pretext by Laban to enable him to make a general search, and Jacob's indignation was accordingly aroused [similarly *Sforno*].

מַה־פִּשְׁעִי מַה חַטָּאתִי — *What is my transgression? What is my sin...?*

[I.e., in what way have I wronged you? ...]

— [*Transgression* is a worse offense that *sin* in that the former is committed in a spirit of *rebellion,* while the latter denotes an *inadvertent* trespass (see *comm.* to *Exodus* 34:7 where the various terms for *sin* are defined).]

כִּי דָלַקְתָּ אַחֲרָי — *That you have hotly pursued* [after] *me?*

— As one pursues a thief? *(Ramban).*

[The verb דלק in its literal sense means *to kindle.*] Cf. the use of this verb in the figurative sense of *pursuit* in *Lam.* 4:19; and *I Sam.* 17:53 *(Rashi).*

From parallel uses of the verb דלק throughout Scripture, *HaRechasim leBikah* maintains that the connotation is *hot pursuit* with intent to kill.

37. כִּי מִשַּׁשְׁתָּ אֶת־כָּל־כֵּלַי — *When you rummaged through all my things* [lit. *utensils*].

Jacob urged: 'When a son-in-law

מַה־מָּצָאתָ מִכֹּל כְּלֵי־בֵיתֶךָ שִׂים כֹּה נֶגֶד
לח אַחַי וְאַחֶיךָ וְיוֹכִיחוּ בֵּין שְׁנֵינוּ: זֶה
עֶשְׂרִים שָׁנָה אָנֹכִי עִמָּךְ רְחֵלֶיךָ וְעִזֶּיךָ
לֹא שִׁכֵּלוּ וְאֵילֵי צֹאנְךָ לֹא אָכָלְתִּי:
לט טְרֵפָה לֹא־הֵבֵאתִי אֵלֶיךָ אָנֹכִי אֲחַטֶּנָּה

lives with his father-in-law, can he possibly avoid benefitting himself by at least a single item? Here, however, *when you rummaged through all my things what did you find of all your household objects?* — Nothing! Not even a needle or a hook!' *(Midrash).*

שִׂים כֹּה — *Set it here.*

— [Either: any object of contention between us, or more generally]: publicly state any grievances you might have now *(Radak).*

נֶגֶד אַחַי — *Before my kinsmen* [lit. *brothers*].

— I.e. the shepherds and other men who accompanied Jacob [see *v.* 23] *(Radak).*

וְיוֹכִיחוּ בֵּין שְׁנֵינוּ — *And let them decide between the two of us!*

— I.e., let them decide which of us is right; in Old French: *eprouver* [prove] *(Rashi).*

[*Rashi* thus distinguishes the meaning of the verb יכח in our verse (where it means *prove; decide*) from its other meaning of *reprove; chastise* (הוֹכָחָה) as below in *v.* 42.]

[*Haamek Davar* refers this, not to asking the kinsmen to decide who was right in their *general* relationship, but, to a request for a judgment on the particular points of conflict]:

'Perhaps we will disagree over the ownership of a certain article: they will be the arbiters and decide which of us is right' *(Haamek Davar).*

38. Jacob proceeds to justify himself indignantly, by recounting the hardship he endured while in Laban's service. Laban's suspicion that Jacob would steal his gods — or *anything* of his, for that matter — was wholly unjustified as Jacob proceeds to emphasize *(Haamek Davar):*

זֶה עֶשְׂרִים שָׁנָה אָנֹכִי עִמָּךְ — *These twenty years I have been with you.*

— And had I been dishonest, it would have been discovered sooner; no one can conceal dishonesty for so long. Furthermore, these twenty years were spent עִמָּךְ, with *you,* the ultimate rogue. No one is better able to sniff out chicanery than you. Had I ever attempted to cheat you, you would have known immediately *(Or HaChaim).*

רְחֵלֶיךָ וְעִזֶּיךָ לֹא שִׁכֵּלוּ — *Your ewes and she-goats never* [lit. *have not*] *miscarried.*

— Because of deficient pasture or negligence *(Rashbam).*

The care I gave them was exemplary; I always allowed them to travel at their own pace, without rushing them *(Chizkuni).*

According to *Midrash Lekach Tov:* They never miscarried, since your flocks were blessed because of me. [Cf. Laban's remark (30:27): *HASHEM has blessed me on your account.*]

וְאֵילֵי צֹאנְךָ לֹא אָכָלְתִּי — *Nor did I eat rams of your flock.*

— As other shepherds allow themselves to do *(Sforno).*

[The term אַיִל, *ram,* (lit. *the*

maged through all my things, what did you find of all
your household objects? Set it here before my
kinsmen and your kinsmen, and let them decide
between the two of us.
38 *'These twenty years I have been with you, your*
ewes and she-goats never miscarried, nor did I eat
rams of your flock. 39 *That which was mangled I*
never brought you — I myself would bear the loss,

strong) refers to male sheep. When the word is used to describe animals eligible for sacrificial use, it refers to a sheep older than thirteen months and one day old. A *yearling* is referred to as כֶּבֶשׂ or שֶׂה (see *Rashi* to *Numbers* (15:11; *Tosafos Bava Kamma* 65b s.v. איל, and *Toras Kohanim* cited by *Mizrachi).* In the *Talmud* a yearling is called טָלֶה *(lamb;* see *Bava Kamma* ibid. 'if one stole a טָלֶה, *lamb,* and it grew into an אַיִל, *ram...').* From Jacob's statement that he did not eat from the *rams of the flock,* it is deduced (see *Rashi* below) that אַיִל, *ram,* when used in a general, non-sacrificial sense (as *Tosafos* ibid. explains), refers to the male of the sheep *irrespective of age.*]

As *Rashi* explains: From this remark [which Jacob intended to be to his credit] the Sages [*Bava Kamma* 65b] deduced that a male sheep even when one day old is called an אַיִל, *ram.* Otherwise, it would be incongruous for Jacob to substantiate his honesty by saying that he did not steal animals older than thirteen months — while omitting from his disclaimer younger animals. Are we otherwise to infer that he proudly protested that he did not eat [grown] *rams, but did eat smaller* ones? Certainly not! If so he would have been a thief! [Rather, as the Sages point out אַיִל, *ram,* in this context signifies *even very young ones.* 'Even these,' said Jacob, 'I did not eat.']

Convention permitted shepherds who were a long distance from home, and where other foods could not be bought, to eat rams which were too young to give birth and were therefore more expendable than the more mature animals. 'But I never availed myself of this right,' said Jacob *(Chizkuni).*

Lekach Tov offers that Jacob said this to differentiate himself from other shepherds who habitually ate rams and claimed that wolves had devoured them. [Furthermore, as Jacob says in the next verse, he voluntarily paid for such genuine losses even though shepherds are not responsible for them.] Why did shepherds use this alibi specifically with the *rams?* — Because, as noted in *Shabbos* 53b, rams travel at the head of the flock and are thus more prone to attack; they are also fatter and more tempting than ewes. Also, the haughty walk of rams rouses the ire of wolves. [Thus a claim that a ram had been attacked by a wolf would be a plausible one.]

39. טְרֵפָה לֹא הֵבֵאתִי אֵלֶיךָ — *That which was mangled* [lit. *torn*] *I never brought* [*to*] *you.*

Mangled — by a lion or a wolf *(Rashi).*

For a shepherd is not required to combat such vicious animals even if he observes them in the act *(Haamek Davar).*

מִיָּדִי תְּבַקְשֶׁנָּה גְּנֻבְתִי יוֹם וּגְנֻבְתִי לָיְלָה:
מ הָיִיתִי בַיּוֹם אֲכָלַנִי חֹרֶב וְקֶרַח בַּלָּיְלָה
מא וַתִּדַּד שְׁנָתִי מֵעֵינָי: זֶה־לִּי עֶשְׂרִים שָׁנָה

If an animal is mangled by wild beasts while in a shepherd's care, it is termed אוֹנֵס, *beyond his control.* Jacob would have been exempt from payment in such a case if he could corroborate his claim through witnesses or by a display of limbs of the mangled animal [see *Exodus* 22:12]. However, because Jacob accepted this added responsibility while guarding the flocks, he never even bothered bringing Laban mangled animals. Likewise, Laban held him accountable *(Nachalas Yitzchak).* [*Cf. Sforno* below.]

R' Bachya infers from this statement that Laban's flocks were never attacked by wild beasts, so exemplary was Jacob's care.

אָנֹכִי אֲחַטֶּנָּה — *I myself would bear.*

I.e., the financial loss from such accidents would have been mine, since מִיָּדִי תְּבַקְשֶׁנָּה, *you exacted it from me* [lit. *from my hand* (i.e., you demanded restitution)] *(Rashi).*

— And I paid you though not legally required to *(Ramban v.* 36).

Cf. this use of the verb in *Judges* 20:16: וְלֹא יַחֲטִא, *shall not miss;* and *I Kings* 1:21: *I and my son Solomon are* חַטָּאִים [=חַסֵרִים], *lacking* [in authority]. *Onkelos,* too paraphrases: 'that which was missing (שְׁגָיָא) from the count' [i.e., when something was miscalculated inadvertently, and I thought there were less sheep than there really were, you always insisted on exacting payment according to the lower, erroneous, count *(Karnei Or);* see *Nesinah LaGer*]. *Onkelos* evidently takes the verb in the sense of *something missing,* synonymous with the verb נִפְקַד, *missing,* in *Numbers* 31:49 *(Rashi).*

Ibn Ezra relates the word to חֵטְא, *sin,* and renders the phrase as if it were spelled אָנֹכִי אֲחַטְאֶנָּה: if there was a mangled animal *I was considered to have sinned* through negligence — and you exacted compensation from me.

Cf. *Targum Yonasan:* Something mangled by wild beasts I did not bring to you; *for had I sinned, from my hand you would have sought it.*

Sforno also interprets the verb as connoting *sinful negligence,* but explains the syntax differently: I did not bring to you any animal which was mangled אָנֹכִי אֲחַטֶּנָּה, because of any *sinful negligence on my part* [such losses I made good as a matter of course]. I brought you only those whose mangling I could not prevent and for which I could not be held liable, but even for those you [injustly] demanded restitution.

גְּנֻבְתִי יוֹם וּגְנֻבְתִי לָיְלָה — *Whether it was stolen by day or stolen by night.*

— I repaid *everything (Rashi).*

What was stolen in the day by men — that I made good, and what was stolen in the night by wild beasts I also made good *(Targum Yonasan).*

[The rule is that a paid watchman is legally responsible for theft. If so, why did Jacob mention obligations that would have fallen upon any comparable worker?]

— *Tur* interpets this phrase as referring back to *mangled* animals, for which a paid watchman is not liable on the grounds that it is beyond his power to fight off wild, carnivorous animals. Thus, the flow of the verse is: 'I would bear the expense of mangled livestock whether they were stolen [by wild animals]

from me you would exact it, whether it was stolen by day or stolen by night. 40 *This is how I was: By day scorching heat consumed me, and frost by night; my sleep drifted from my eyes.* 41 *This is my twenty*

during the day or night.'

— Among the many instances listed by Jacob, he was legally responsible for some, such as theft, and not responsible for others. His intent in expressing this pent-up reproach was to illustrate the dimensions of the plight into which he had entered in order to win his two wives. [See *comm.* of *R' Shmuel ben Chafni Gaon; Bava Metzia* 93b; *Choshen Mishpat* §303.]

— *Rashi* explains that the suffix י in the word גְּנֻבְתִי is superfluous [=גְּנֻבַת] similar to the י in *Lam.* 1:1 רַבָּתִי [=רַבַּת] and שָׂרָתִי; *Isaiah* 1:21 מְלֵאֲתִי; and *Hoshea* 10:11 אֹהַבְתִּי. *Ibn Ezra* interprets similarly as do *Rashbam* and *Radak* who add that if the י were the first person pronominal suffix [=*my* גְּנוּבַת], the word would have been vowelized with a *kametz:* גְּנֻבָתִי.

Heidenheim submits, however, that grammatically it is possible for the י to be a first person pronoun, the passage meaning: you exacted from me *that which was stolen from me by day and that which was stolen from me by night.*

The *Midrash* translates: 'I was called a thief [גַּנָּב] by day and by night.' [People who saw the phenomenal increase of your flocks constantly taunted me and accused me of stealing animals for your benefit from other people.]

Onkelos enigmatically interprets the passage: נְטָרִית בִּימָמָא נְטָרִית בְּלֵילְיָא, *I watched by day and I watched by night* [see *Nesinah l'Ger* who cites *Machberes Menachem* where it is suggested that this is a euphemism for 'that which was hidden from me by day ... and night.']

40. הָיִיתִי — [*This is how*] *I was* .

בַיּוֹם אֲכָלַנִי חֹרֶב — *By day scorching heat consumed me.*

— The metaphor of heat *consuming* [*lit. eating*] is similar to [*Deut.* 4:24]: אֵשׁ אֹכְלָה, *consuming fire* *(Rashi).*

וְקֶרַח בַּלָּיְלָה — *And frost by night.*[1]

The word קֶרַח lit. *ice* in the figurative sense of *frost* occurs in *Psalms* 147:17: מַשְׁלִיךְ קַרְחוֹ כְפִתִּים, *He casts forth His ice like morsels* [where it refers to the effects of cold weather, as in our verse] *(Rashi).*

וַתִּדַּד שְׁנָתִי מֵעֵינָי — [*And*] *my sleep drifted from my eyes.*

— Because of my super-vigilance *(Ralbag);*

— In constant alert lest you deceive me *(Lekach Tov).*

[The word וַתִּדַּד derives from the verb נדד, lit. *wandering*, and figuratively refers to insomnia. Comp. *Esther* 6:1: נָדְדָה שְׁנַת הַמֶּלֶךְ, *sleep eluded the king* (lit. *the king's sleep wandered).*

According to one view in the *Midrash*, during those sleepless nights

1. The *Talmud* [*Bava Metzia* 83b] discusses Jacob's statement in the context of the obligations incumbent upon a paid watchman. Was Jacob required to see to the flock's protection day and night, or was he going beyond the *halachic* requirement? According to one view, this kind of vigilance is required only of the night watchman of a city [since the responsibility for all the citizens' security is his (*Rashi* ad.loc.)]. Accordingly, Jacob was referring to the *super-vigilance* with which he guarded Laban's flocks, as though he were a city watchman.

The prevailing view in the *Talmud*, however, is that any paid watchman must exercise such care. This requirement is derived from Jacob's own description of his duties. See *Choshen Mishpat* §303.

בְּבֵיתֶךָ עֲבַדְתִּיךָ אַרְבַּע־עֶשְׂרֵה שָׁנָה
בִּשְׁתֵּי בְנֹתֶיךָ וְשֵׁשׁ שָׁנִים בְּצֹאנֶךָ וַתַּחֲלֵף
מב אֶת־מַשְׂכֻּרְתִּי עֲשֶׂרֶת מֹנִים: לוּלֵי אֱלֹהֵי
אָבִי אֱלֹהֵי אַבְרָהָם וּפַחַד יִצְחָק הָיָה לִי

Jacob said the fifteen *Shir HaMaalos* [*Songs of Ascents*] *(Psalms* 120-134); the constantly recurring word *Israel* in those psalms refers to the *Patriarch* Israel. [*Maharzu* observes that contemplation of those psalms would yield many subtle parallels relating to Jacob's experience.]

41. זֶה לִּי עֶשְׂרִים שָׁנָה בְּבֵיתֶךָ — *This is my twenty years in your household* [lit. *this is to me twenty years in your home.*]

[I.e., Jacob's twenty years in Laban's home comprised the two time periods given later in the verse.]

These twenty years that I spent in your house are לִי, *to me* — the responsibility for them is *upon me;* I will yet be punished for these years by suffering for an equal period. [I.e., Jacob was away from his parents for these twenty years plus the two years that elapsed during his trip home. His punishment was that Joseph was separated from him for twenty-two years] (*Rashi* to 37:34; see *Chronological Deductions* appended to 28:9).

Above [*v.* 38] when Jacob initially described his twenty years of work, he did not use the word לִי, *to me*. There, in speaking to Laban he said עִמָּךְ, *with you.* The effects of those years can be seen from two viewpoints: Jacob's and Laban's. In verse 38, Jacob describes Laban's point of view [עִמָּךְ]: for Laban, Jacob's twenty years were blessed, productive, and profitable. But from Jacob's standpoint [our verse], they were years of unrelieved travail, swindle, and danger *(Heidenheim).*

עֲבַדְתִּיךָ אַרְבַּע עֶשְׂרֵה שָׁנָה בִּשְׁתֵּי בְנֹתֶיךָ — *I served you fourteen years for your two daughters.*

One detects here a note of bitterness as Jacob alludes to Laban's trickery which caused him to work *fourteen* instead of *seven* years for his wife. Jacob is not more explicit, however, in consideration of Leah's feelings *(Hoffmann).*

וְשֵׁשׁ שָׁנִים בְּצֹאנֶךָ — *And six years for your flocks.*

[Thus, whatever flocks you see here are rightfully mine; I worked six hard years for them.]

וַתַּחֲלֵף אֶת מַשְׂכֻּרְתִּי עֲשֶׂרֶת מֹנִים — *And you changed my wage a hundred times.*

You constantly altered our agreement by changing the terms from spotted to speckled, and from ringed to checkered *(Rashi).*

[For the translation of *a hundred times,* and the explanation of this charge, see *comm.* to parallel passage above *v.* 7.]

— The contextual implication of the passage is: Although I served you faithfully, and as your son-in-law should have been treated with consideration, the opposite was the case: *For you changed my wage a hundred times (R' Bachya).*

There is no doubt that Laban was indeed guilty of this. Otherwise Jacob would never have accused him of it to his face. Moreover, were the charge not true, Laban would have vigorously denied it *(Abarbanel).*

31
42

years in your household: I served you fourteen years
for your two daughters, and six years for your
flocks; and you changed my wage a hundred times.
42 *Had not the God of my father — the God of*
Abraham and the Dread of Isaac — been with me,

42. לוּלֵי אֱלֹהֵי אָבִי ... הָיָה לִי — *Had not the God of my father ... been with* [lit. *to*] *me.*

[The expression *God ... being with me* denotes God's Providential protection, as in His promise: אָנֹכִי עִמָּךְ, *I am with you;* see *comm.* to 28:15. Specifically, here it refers to God's Providence assuring — notwithstanding Laban's constant changes of terms — that the flocks bore whatever mutations which would belong to Jacob (see verses 8 and 9 above). For were it not for this Divine intervention, Laban's trickery would have indeed resulted in Jacob's being sent away empty-handed.]

By citing various verses in which the term לוּלֵי [lit. *if not*] occurs, the *Midrash* concludes that the term introduces a prayed-for source of protection or merit. In our verse, it refers to the merit of the Patriarchs; elsewhere it refers to the merit of the Divine Name or of faith [*Psalms* 22:13]; and the merit of the Torah [*ibid.* 119:92.]

וּפַחַד יִצְחָק — *And the Dread of Isaac.*

I.e., the *Awe of Isaac;* He Whom Isaac feared. This use of פַּחַד, *Dread,* as an appellation for God, occurs again in *v.* 53 (*R' Bachya*). [This, also, is the implication of *Onkelos* who renders וּדְדָחִיל־לֵהּ יִצְחָק *He Whom Isaac dreads.*]

Jacob avoided saying *God of Isaac* because [as noted in the *comm.* to 28:13] God does not associate His name with a *living* righteous person. Although God referred to *Himself* in 28:13 as *God of Isaac,* it was, as noted, because Isaac was blind and could be regarded as dead. Jacob, however, was afraid to use this designation, and substituted *the Dread (Rashi).*

Ibn Ezra interprets: The merit of Isaac's fear of God [יִרְאַת ה׳] has helped me, for the merit of the father helps the son [in This World; it is only in the World to Come that the Sages in *Sanhedrin* 104a proclaimed that a son's merit helps a father (because it is assumed that the father's teaching or example was instrumental in the son's deed), but not *vice versa (Rif* ad. loc.; see *Maharsha* and *Ein Yaakov).*]

Below in *v.* 53, however, *Ibn Ezra* interprets the expression like *Onkelos* cited above: *He Whom Isaac dreads.*

Radak suggests that by using the expression *Dread of Isaac,* Jacob was referring to the purest form of Awe of God that inspired Isaac to submit himself to the *Akeidah* [Chapt. 22] (similarly *Ibn Ezra* [*v.* 53]; *Pesikta Zutresa).*[1]

— It was also the merit of the *physical* fear experienced by Isaac at the *Akeidah* that was his support *(Lekach Tov).*

R' Hirsch interprets the express-

1. Alternately, *Radak* suggests that by this appellation Jacob was referring to his own *fear* that he might not see Isaac alive unless he returned home immediately. Jacob thereby insinuated that it was for two reasons that he was not thrown out of Laban's household empty-handed: *(a)* because the God of Abraham had been with him during his service; *(b)* because of his premature departure out of fear that he might not find his father alive; otherwise Jacob

כִּי עַתָּה רֵיקָם שִׁלַּחְתָּנִי אֶת־עָנְיִי וְאֶת־
מג יְגִיעַ כַּפַּי רָאָה אֱלֹהִים וַיּוֹכַח אָמֶשׁ: °וַיַּעַן
°שביעי לָבָן וַיֹּאמֶר אֶל־יַעֲקֹב הַבָּנוֹת בְּנֹתַי
וְהַבָּנִים בָּנַי וְהַצֹּאן צֹאנִי וְכֹל אֲשֶׁר־אַתָּה

ion similarly: the sacred Awe felt by Isaac at the *Akeidah*. In this interpretation, the *dread* of our verse refers to Isaac's *feeling* when he felt the knife at his throat. He conquered his instinctive fear, and dedicated himself to God's will. Thus Jacob found merit in the God of Abraham and the merit of Isaac.

כִּי עַתָּה רֵיקָם שִׁלַּחְתָּנִי — *You would surely have now sent me away empty handed.*

— [Your constant changing of my wages and other deceits you perpetrated against me would otherwise surely have resulted in my now being sent away empty-handed.]

אֶת עָנְיִי וְאֶת־יְגִיעַ כַּפַּי רָאָה אֱלֹהִים — *God saw my wretchedness* [lit. *affliction*] *and the toil of my hands.*

I.e., He perceived that whatever I achieved was by great toil and He pitied me, and vindicated me accordingly.

From this passage the *Midrash* derives that labor is more precious than ancestral merit, for 'ancestral merit saved wealth whereas labor saved life' [i.e., that Jacob was not sent away empty-handed he attributed to the God of his father (*'had not the God of my father,'* etc.); but God's warning that Laban dare not harm Jacob, he attributed to the *toil of his hands*, which God had 'seen' and rewarded.].

Accordingly, *Tanchuma* notes that one must not have the attitude that he need do nothing and that Heaven will provide for his needs. Rather man must first toil with his hands, and then God will send His blessing. Cf. *Psalms* 128:2 *When you eat the labor of your hands* [*then*] *you shall be happy and it shall go well with you.*

[The term 'seeing' when applied to God connotes intellectual perception. See *footnote* to 1:10. Cf. also 16:11 and 29:32.]

The key factor in God's defense of Jacob was *his wretchedness*. Had not Jacob endured so much suffering, God would have exercised His Attribute of אֶרֶךְ אַפַּיִם, *patient withholding of anger*; Laban would have succeeded and Jacob would have earned even greater reward for the World to Come. But due to Jacob's *wretchedness*, God paid him his wages on the day they were due [*Deut.* 24:15], so to speak, and reprimanded Laban *(Or HaChaim)*.

וַיּוֹכַח אָמֶשׁ — *So* [*Targum Yonasan;*

might have remained longer and Laban would surely have found some way to swindle him out of his entire fortune.

Accordingly it was this obsession with his father's well-being that, as noted above in *v.* 30 [*You have left because you longed greatly for your father's house*], caused him to depart immediately without prior notice.

Chizkuni [followed by *Kli Yakar*] submits that Jacob was attributing his relative well-being to *Laban's* fear of Isaac who had a reputation as a powerful potentate, as well as the protection of the God of Abraham.

31
43 *you would surely have now sent me away empty-*
handed. God saw my wretchedness and the toil of my
hands, so He admonished you last night.'
43 *Then Laban spoke up and said to Jacob, 'The*
daughters are my daughters, the children are my
children and the flock is my flock, and all that you

lit. *and*] *He admonished* [*you* (not in the Hebrew, but implied)] *last night.*

[This refers to God's warning to Laban (*v.* 24) not to harm Jacob, to which Laban himself made reference in verse 29.]

The translation of וַיּוֹכַח as *admonished* follows *Rashi* who insists that in this context the word implies תּוֹכָחָה, *rebuke, reproof,* and not הוֹכָחָה, *clarification, proof* as the verb means above in *v.* 37. [This is because in our context *Rashi* holds that there was no question that had to be clarified.]

Ramban, however, interprets: *and He rendered* **it**, i.e., *judgment, last night.* He maintains that there *was* indecision clarified by God's appearance to Laban, for Jacob had said [*v.* 38] that those present should *decide* between them. Now he observed that God, Who knows the hidden secrets, *did* [by revealing himself to Laban] decide between them. If the word meant *admonish, Ramban* concludes, the passage should more properly have read וַיּוֹכַח אוֹתְךָ אָמֶשׁ, *He reprimanded* you *last night.*

R' Hirsch interprets the phrase as does *Ramban* and renders: *And He proved it last night.*

According to *Kli Yakar: And last night He proved it.* Do not say that whatever you are doing is out of the goodness of your heart. Your statement regarding last night proves that you have no kind feelings towards me. By your own admission; only God's warning of last night prevents you from harming me [*v.* 29].

43. הַבָּנוֹת בְּנֹתַי וְהַבָּנִים בָּנַי – *The daughters are my daughters,* [and] *the children* [lit. *sons*] *are my children* [lit. *sons*].

— The girls whom you married are my daughters, and the children whom they bore will be considered as mine, and the sheep are my sheep (*Targum Yonasan*).

Some perceive in Laban's words a claim based on the primitive custom of their region whereby the head of the family was the nominal owner of all that belonged to its members. Unable to answer Jacob's reproaches, Laban invokes this weak quasi-legal claim which — by implication — also entitled him to examine all of Jacob's possessions. He then pretends to be solicitous for the welfare of his daughters and grandchildren, and suggests a pact [see *Hoffmann* and *Eisenstein*].

וְהַצֹּאן צֹאנִי – *And the flock is my flock.*

All the animals came into your possession by fraud, so even if I had *changed your wage a hundred times* or would have *sent you away empty-handed,* I would have been well within my rights (*Sforno*).

רֹאֶה לִי הוּא וְלִבְנֹתַי מָה־אֶעֱשֶׂה לָאֵלֶּה
מד הַיּוֹם אוֹ לִבְנֵיהֶן אֲשֶׁר יָלָדוּ׃ וְעַתָּה לְכָה
נִכְרְתָה בְרִית אֲנִי וָאָתָּה וְהָיָה לְעֵד בֵּינִי
מה וּבֵינֶךָ׃ וַיִּקַּח יַעֲקֹב אָבֶן וַיְרִימֶהָ מַצֵּבָה׃

לִי הוּא — *Is mine.*

This is an instance where לִי, lit. *to me;* means שֶׁלִּי, mine (*Rashi* to 32:18 s.v. לְמִי אַתָּה).

וְלִבְנֹתַי מָה אֶעֱשֶׂה לָאֵלֶּה הַיּוֹם — *Yet to my daughters — what could I do to them* [lit. *to these*] *this day?*

— [I.e., they are, nevertheless, my daughters; my own flesh and blood] —How could I possibly conceive of harming them. [By separating them from their husband, or their children from their father]? *(Rashi; Mizrachi; Tzeidah laDerech).*

According to *Ramban,* it was a question: *What can I do for them?* Laban was defending himself against Jacob's charges, and claimed that he had pursued him merely to see his daughters and determine if there was anything he could do to *benefit* them, since his mercies were greatly stirred by them. He went on to suggest a covenant for this purpose.

The expression לָאֵלֶּה, *to these,* is somewhat superfluous, following as it does the word וְלִבְנֹתַי, *to my daughters.* The translation follows *Ibn Ezra* and *Radak* who view the word לָאֵלֶּה, *to these* as constituting additional clarification, similar to *I Samuel* 20:42 נִשְׁבַּעְנוּ שְׁנֵינוּ אֲנַחְנוּ, lit. *we have sworn, the two of us, we.*

Ramban as noted above explains the significance of the passage by interpreting: ... *And for my daughters, what can I do* לָאֵלֶּה, *for these* who are in my presence — since I am deeply stirred by them and their children?

According to *Sforno,* the flow is: *All that you see is mine;* וְלִבְנֹתַי, *and it should go to my daughters* as their dowry. But if I took it from you as I rightfully could, מָה אֶעֱשֶׂה לָאֵלֶּה, *what could I do for them* to provide for their future well-being? Therefore, since I do not wish to harm you, *Come, let us make a covenant* to assure that you do not harm me either.[1]

אוֹ לִבְנֵיהֶן אֲשֶׁר יָלָדוּ — *Or to their children whom they have borne?*

— For they were born while in my house and they are like my own children *(Ramban).*

[*HaKsav V'HaKaballah* interprets Laban's oblique reference to his grandchildren as having a contemptuous connotation; see footnote.]

44. Laban proposes a treaty.

לְכָה וְנִכְרְתָה בְרִית אֲנִי וָאָתָּה — *Come, let us make a covenant, I and you.*

[Literally, the phrase reads *let us 'cut' a covenant.* As explained above in *Rashi* and the footnote on 15:9, p. 519, this was the idiomatic expression for entering into a covenant. The usage was based on the ancient custom of cutting an animal to seal the agreement. Although no such 'cutting' was involved in our

1. *HaKsav V'HaKaballah* differs and wonders why we should seek to impute to the wicked Laban such commendable instincts as compassion for his daughters? This is the same Laban whom tradition describes as more of a rogue than Pharaoh in that he wished to totally uproot everything! [Cf. ArtScroll *Haggadah* p. 100ff.]

He suggests that everything about Laban's remarks bespoke bitterness: Only God's warning to him prevented him from annihilating even his own flesh and blood who dared follow their husband and leave him. He added לָאֵלֶּה, *to these,* in the contemptuous manner of one who speaks of an enemy and cannot even bring himself to look at him directly; similarly he made an oblique reference to *the children she bore* as if they were total strangers.

*see is mine. Yet to my daughters — what could I do to
them this day? Or to their children whom they have
borne!* 44 *So now, come, let us make a covenant, I and
you, and He shall be a witness between me and you.'*
45 *Then Jacob took a stone and raised it up as a*

verse, the idiom is retained.]

This is the good I can do for my daughters by assuring that you will not afflict them and will take no other wives in addition to them *(Ramban).*

— Since I intend you no harm, I want to make this covenant to assure that you will likewise not harm me *(Sforno).*

Hoffmann notes that *two* distinct agreements were concluded by Laban and Jacob: (1) that Jacob would in no way ill-treat Laban's daughters (*vs.* 48-50); (2) that neither Laban nor Jacob would pass the mound of stones raised up as a landmark, with hostile purpose toward the other (*vs.* 51-53).

Haamek Davar cites *Sh'mos Rabbah* 3:3 that use of the word לְכָה (rather than לֵךְ) with the suffix ה, implies that the task at hand could be performed only by the person being addressed. Thus, Laban was implying to Jacob, 'You are the only one whom I would trust to make a pledge concerning the well-being of my precious children, and to make a commitment never to engage in hostile acts against me.'

וְהָיָה לְעֵד בֵּינִי וּבֵינֶךָ — *And He shall be a witness between me and you.*

The translation which treats God as the subject follows *Rashi.*

Ramban offers two interpretations: (a) that the subject is the בְּרִית, *covenant — The 'covenant' shall be a witness;* whoever violates it shall be accursed; (b) or possibly the intent is that Laban was suggesting that they set up a דָּבָר קַיָּם, *a tangible monument,* which would be a permanent symbol attesting to the covenant For that purpose, Jacob took the stone that was described as *the witness (v.* 52). Compare the stone which Joshua set up as a witness in *Joshua* 24:27. [See *Tosafos* cited on footnote to *v.* 52.]

[Note that also in *v.* 48 below it is the *mound* (not God) that is called the witness. However, in *v.* 50 it is *God* Who is invoked as witness.]

R' Hirsch maintains [with *Rashi*] that this passage can refer only to God to Whom Jacob had referred and Who had already intervened. It could not mean that the 'covenant' should be the witness since the word בְּרִית is feminine; thus the verb should have been וְהָיְתָה, *not* וְהָיָה. Perhaps this is why *Ramban* above offers his second interpretation that the subject is not the בְּרִית, *covenant,* but the implied דָּבָר קַיָּם, *something tangible.*

45. וַיִּקַּח יַעֲקֹב אָבֶן וַיְרִימֶהָ מַצֵּבָה — *Then* [lit. *and*] *Jacob took a stone and raised it up* [as a] *monument*

... Note further in this context how Laban wryly said: 'what could I do to them הַיּוֹם, *this day?' — Today,* I cannot harm them because God warned me only yesterday. But, as *Sefer HaYashar* notes, Laban nursed his hatred. It was he who later summoned Esau to intercept them on their way to Canaan [see footnote to 32:2].

For the moment, however, the frustrated and sinister Laban feigned compassion and, in the manner of a true rogue, piously spoke of a peace treaty.

[Perhaps *Rashi, Ramban* and others who view Laban as compassionate would similarly agree that he was basically insincere. Following God's warning, this demeanor was the only way he could depart and save face.]

מו וַיֹּאמֶר יַעֲקֹב לְאֶחָיו לִקְטוּ אֲבָנִים וַיִּקְחוּ
אֲבָנִים וַיַּעֲשׂוּ־גָל וַיֹּאכְלוּ שָׁם עַל־הַגָּל׃
מז וַיִּקְרָא־לוֹ לָבָן יְגַר שָׂהֲדוּתָא וְיַעֲקֹב קָרָא
מח לוֹ גַּלְעֵד׃ וַיֹּאמֶר לָבָן הַגַּל הַזֶּה עֵד בֵּינִי

[more literally: *a standing stone* (see on 28:18)].

I.e., he put it on a high part of the mountain where it could be seen from afar. Therefore the word וַיְרִימֶהָ, *raised* is used, not וַיָּשֶׂם, *set up;* [as in 28:18] *(Radak).*

The word מַצֵּבָה, *monument* or *pillar* is related to the root יצב, *to stand.* He raised it up [as a *standing stone*] to symbolize that the matter would stand permanently *(Sforno).*

Ibn Ezra renders: He raised it by standing it up [שֶׁהִצִּיב אוֹתָהּ].

As soon as Laban spoke of a covenant and invoked God as a witness, Jacob raised a stone as a monument. Laban needed no such tangible evidence of the covenant — to him, Jacob's word was sufficient. But Jacob, knowing with whom he dealt, put more faith in the physical evidence than in Laban's word *(R' Hirsch).*

According to *Midrash Tanchuma,* it was Jacob *alone* who, in a display of extraordinary strength, took the boulder and raised it up as a pillar. This proved to Laban that it was really *not* in Laban's power to do him harm as he had boasted in verse 29. [See *comm.* there regarding Jacob's having *voluntarily* assumed a role of humility in his dealings with Laban.]

46. לְאֶחָיו — *To his brethren.*

— The reference is to *Jacob's sons* who were 'brethren' to him, standing by him in trouble and battle *(Rashi)*

Rashi pursues this interpretation rather than the possible interpretation that Jacob ordered *Laban's* kinsmen to gather stones (see below). *Rashi* holds it would have been improper for Jacob to issue orders to strangers; or for him to refer to these people as 'brethren' while they were still ready to harm him at Laban's command. After the covenant was concluded, however (*v.* 54), he *could* call them his 'brethren' *(Gur Aryeh).*[1]

Cf. the *Midrash:* Jacob had only one brother, who would have been better off buried! Rather the term *brethren* refers to Jacob's *sons* who, in the Holy Tongue are here called brothers. *R' Huna* said, [They are called his *brethren*] in the sense that they were as valiant and righteous as he. *R' Yudan* said, 'when a man puts on his father's garment, [follows in his footsteps] he becomes his equal.'

According to *Ramban,* the reference is to *Laban's kinsmen* who, as noted in verse 23 above, had accompanied him. They were either his *companions* whom the Torah refers to as *brethren,* or they were his *kinsmen,* descendants of

1. *Haamek Davar* agrees with *Rashi's* interpretation that it refers to Jacob's *sons,* since as *Gur Aryeh* notes, had it referred, as it does in *v.* 23 to Laban's *kinsmen,* it would have been improper for Jacob to order *strangers* to gather stones.

What message then is to be derived from the fact that the Torah calls them *brothers* instead of *sons?* Furthermore, why did Jacob have his sons rather than his servants do this menial task? — Jacob acted true to form in refusing to be outraged by Laban's impudence. Instead, he sought to create a friendly atmosphere by inviting his adversaries to a meal. This was a trait he wanted to inculcate into his children. Therefore, he wanted *them* to make the necessary preparations and — rather than allow them to act only out of obedience to a 'father's' command — he addressed them as comrades as if to say 'do this because it is good,' not because it is commanded.

31 *monument.* [46] *And Jacob said to his brethren, 'Gather*
46-48 *stones!' So they took stones and made a mound, and*
they ate there on the mound. [47] *Laban called it Yegar-*
sehadusa, but Jacob called it Gal-ed.
[48] *And Laban declared, 'This mound is a witness*

Nachor, brother of Abraham. [See *comm.* to *v.* 23]. According to the latter view, these men were related to Jacob as well as to Laban. But out of respect to his father-in-law, Jacob addressed his instructions to gather stones to *them* rather than to Laban. [See also *v.* 54.] A similar usage [of a pronoun not referring to the first subject in a verse] occurs in 47:3 *And Pharaoh said to 'his' brothers,* i.e. to *Joseph's* brothers.

לִקְטוּ אֲבָנִים — *Gather stones.*

— And make a mound upon which we will eat to commemorate our friendship, and which will also serve as a witness when we make the covenant *(Ramban;* see below).

וַיַּעֲשׂוּ גָל — *And [they] made a mound.*

[— A heap of stones set up as a landmark, pillar, etc.]

וַיֹּאכְלוּ שָׁם עַל הַגָּל — *And they ate there on* [or: *by* (cf. 24:13)] *the mound.*

A meal was part of the ceremony of the covenant signalling the mutual acceptance of the pact (*Radak* to 26:30; *Rashbam* to 25:31).

Ramban explains that they partook of a small meal to commemorate the event, or perhaps it was customary for parties who entered a covenant to share a loaf of bread to signal their camaraderie. *After* they finalized the covenant they would offer sacrifices and make a great feast. Possibly, the meal included the offering mentioned below in verse 54.

47. וַיִּקְרָא לוֹ לָבָן יְגַר שָׂהֲדוּתָא — *Laban called it Yegar-sahadusa.*

— [I.e., he *referred* to the mound-memorial in *Aramaic* as *Yegar-sahadusa* which means 'the mound is a witness' and which, as *Rashi* notes, is the Aramaic equivalent of the Hebrew name Gal-ed. The actual *naming* (קָרָא שְׁמוֹ) came later (next verse).]

The *Midrash* notes that the value of the Aramaic [סוּרְסִי, *Syrian=Aramaic.* Cf. *Aruch; Tosaf. Bava Kamma* 83a; *Rashi Sotah* 49b] language must not be underestimated because God paid it the honor of including it in the Torah [here], the Prophets [*Jeremiah* 10:11], and in the Writings [much of *Daniel* and *Ezra* is written in Aramaic].

[See *Ibn Ezra* to 30:37 and *Karnei Or* that Arabic, Hebrew, and Aramaic are closely related.]

וְיַעֲקֹב קָרָא לוֹ גַּלְעֵד — *But Jacob called it Gal-ed* [the *Hebrew* for 'the mound is a witness'].

— Jacob retained the Hebrew language and did not abandon it *(Sforno).*

[See *comm.* to 14:13 that *Ivri* refers to Jacob's branch of Abraham's family, who remained loyal to the language of Eber, Hebrew; while Eber's *other* descendants, through Nachor, spoke Aramaic. The latter are therefore referred to as Arameans.]

The use of the conversive ו, and subject-verb arrangement of our verse [וְיַעֲקֹב קָרָא instead of the more common וַיִּקְרָא יַעֲקֹב] serves to emphasize the contrast with the previous statement — *Laban called* ... *but Jacob called.* See *comm.* to 14:18 s.v. וּמַלְכִּי־צֶדֶק, *but* Malchizedek.

וּבֵינְךָ הַיּוֹם עַל־כֵּן קָרָא־שְׁמוֹ גַּלְעֵד:
מט וְהַמִּצְפָּה אֲשֶׁר אָמַר יִצֶף יהוה בֵּינִי
נ וּבֵינֶךָ כִּי נִסָּתֵר אִישׁ מֵרֵעֵהוּ: אִם־תְּעַנֶּה
אֶת־בְּנֹתַי וְאִם־תִּקַּח נָשִׁים עַל־בְּנֹתַי אֵין

48-50. [The first part of the treaty: That Jacob will in no way ill-treat Laban's daughters]

48. הַגַּל הַזֶּה עֵד בֵּינִי וּבֵינְךָ הַיּוֹם – *This mound is a witness between me and you today.*

– Of what I am about to say *(Sforno).*

Laban apparently uttered these words in Hebrew, hence the significance of the mutually agreed-upon name *(Ramban;* see below).

עַל־כֵּן קָרָא שְׁמוֹ גַּלְעֵד – *Therefore he named it Gal-ed.*

A combination of the two words גַּל עֵד, *the mound is a witness (Rashi).*

Laban subordinated himself to Jacob by agreeing to the Hebrew name. It is possible, however, that Laban may have also said this in Aramaic, but the Torah gives the Hebrew version *(Ramban).*

This name later evolved into גִּלְעָד, *Gilead,* as the mountain is referred to today *(Hoffmann).*

49. וְהַמִּצְפָּה – *And* [*as for*] *the Mitzpah* [=watchtower].

According to *Rashi* as explained by *Ramban,* the *watchtower* was a high, conspicuous structure on the mountain; it was *not* the mound or pillar. Thus, our passage is elliptic: it additionally explains that the structure was called *Mitzpah, Watchtower,* because... (See *Judges* 11:29.)

[Thus, according to *Rashi* the sense is: *And as for the Mitzpah, it was so called because he said* (i.e., one said to the other), *'May HASHEM keep watch.'*]

Ramban's own opinion is that *Mitzpah* was another name given to Jacob's monument, and our passage is to be connected to the previous verse: *Therefore he named it Gal-ed and* [*also*] *Mitzpah* – i.e., he gave the monument both names (following *Tur).*

R' Eisenstadt explains *Ramban* as follows: The *mound* which the 'brethren' gathered was called *Gal-ed,* while the monument that Jacob set up was called *Mitzpah* ... Comp. *Yalkut Mayan Ganim (Torah Sheleimah* §118): 'The mound was for Laban, and the pillar for Jacob.' Cf. also *Radal* in *Pirkei d'Rabbi Eliezer* 36:112 citing *Vilna Gaon.*[1]

There is an opinion that the ancient Hebrews erected pillars or monuments which consisted of one boulder while the Arameans made mounds consisting of many stones. Therefore Jacob himself erected the *pillar* but instructed Laban's kinsmen to make a *mound.* Consequently, although Laban made several references to the pillar as well as to the mound, the essential aspect of the

1. Jacob made a covenant with the people of the land because Laban said to him, 'I know that God will give your descendants all these lands in the future. Make a covenant with me that they will not take possession of the land of Aram ... nor will they enter the land of Aram with evil intent, nor shall the Arameans enter *Eretz Yisrael* with evil intent.'

When David reigned he wished to enter Aram but was prevented from doing so on account of Jacob's oath until he broke the monument. [Although David's justification for doing so is

31
49-50

between me and you today'; therefore he named it
Gal-ed. 49 *And as for the Mitzpah — because he said,*
'May HASHEM keep watch between me and you
when we are out of each other's sight. 50 *If you will*
ill-treat my daughters or if you will marry wives in
addition to my daughters — though no man may be

pact as far as he was concerned, consisted of not passing over the *mound* [*v.* 52] (see *Karnei Or* par. 36).

אֲשֶׁר אָמַר יִצֶף ה׳ בֵּינִי וּבֵינֶךָ — *Because he said, 'May HASHEM keep watch* [Hebrew *Yitzef,* associated with *Mitzpah*] *between me and* [*between*] *you.'*

According to *Ibn Ezra,* this reverts to Laban: Jacob named it Mitzpah because *Laban* said, 'May HASHEM keep watch, etc.'

כִּי נִסָּתֵר אִישׁ מֵרֵעֵהוּ — *When we are out of each other's sight* [lit. *when we are hidden, man from his comrade.*]

— And will not see [i.e. not be able to watch] one another *(Rashi).*

Indeed, they never again saw one another after they parted on the morrow *(Pesikta).*

50. אִם תְּעַנֶּה אֶת בְּנֹתַי — *If you will ill-treat* [lit. *afflict*] *my daughters.*

— By denying them their conjugal rights *(Rashi, Yoma* 77b).

[That *affliction* refers to this form of abstinence is evidenced by the *halachah* that abstinence from marital union is one of the *afflictions* mandated on Yom Kippur. (See *Torah Temimah* and *comm.* to *Lev.* 16:29).]

— By marrying other women while my daughters are alive *(Midrash;* this view is disputed by the *Talmud* above which maintains that only the *second* clause refers to rival wives).

Ibn Ezra and *Radak* take it in the literal sense: By ill-treating them, subjecting them to indignity, deprivations, or compelling them to do things they dislike.

[On אִם see below.]

וְאִם תִּקַּח נָשִׁים עַל בְּנֹתַי — *Or if you will marry* [lit. *take*] *wives in addition* [lit. *upon;* cf. 28:9] *to my daughters.*

— Even after my daughters die *(Midrash).*

The verse mentions *my daughters* twice [when grammatically, since *daughters* is the obvious subject, in our phrase the pronoun *them* would have sufficed]. This emphasizes that the oath was to refer to a second set of daughters, Bilhah and Zilpah, for, as noted in the commentary to 29:24,29, they were his daughters from a concubine *(Rashi* [*Midrash*]*).*

אֵין אִישׁ עִמָּנוּ — *Though no man* [*may*] *be among us.*

— Since we will live in separate countries there will be no man who will be able to ensure that you keep the covenant and bring you to account should you break it *(Radak).*

not recorded in Scripture, the treaty was already null and void because it had been abrogated by the Arameans. Similarly, in a recorded incident, it was the Philistines who first violated the oath. See *I Chron.* 18:3 and *Radal* here *(Pirkei d'Rabbi Eliezer).*]

[Compare the effects of Abraham's oath with Abimelech in *footnote* on page 771, and of Isaac's oath in *footnote* on page 1108.]

אִישׁ עִמָּנוּ רְאֵה אֱלֹהִים עֵד בֵּינִי וּבֵינֶךָ׃
נא וַיֹּאמֶר לָבָן לְיַעֲקֹב הִנֵּה ׀ הַגַּל הַזֶּה וְהִנֵּה
נב הַמַּצֵּבָה אֲשֶׁר יָרִיתִי בֵּינִי וּבֵינֶךָ׃ עֵד הַגַּל
הַזֶּה וְעֵדָה הַמַּצֵּבָה אִם־אָנִי לֹא־אֶעֱבֹר
אֵלֶיךָ אֶת־הַגַּל הַזֶּה וְאִם־אַתָּה לֹא־
תַעֲבֹר אֵלַי אֶת־הַגַּל הַזֶּה וְאֶת־הַמַּצֵּבָה
נג הַזֹּאת לְרָעָה׃ אֱלֹהֵי אַבְרָהָם וֵאלֹהֵי

Or: *Since there is no one among us who is fit to act as witness to our pact* [— either morally, or since kinsmen are invalid witnesses] *(Chizkuni)* ...

[Or possibly since guardians cannot be appointed over matters of marital intimacy and no one could therefore possibly be appointed to assure that you do not deprive my daughters of their conjugal rights] ...

Sforno formulates a rule in his *comm.* to 14:23 s.v. אִם מִחוּט [comp. also *comm.* to 21:23 s.v. אִם תִּשְׁקֹר and 26:29 s.v. אִם תַּעֲשֵׂה], that the word אִם, *if,* where it is not explicitly followed by a condition has the implication of an oath. Accordingly, the meaning of Laban's statement would be not *if,* but *that,* i.e., you are forbidden to do so. In our verse then, the implication would be that you are hereby adjured by a sacred oath that *you will not* ill-treat my daughters and that *you will not* marry wives in addition to my daughters.

[According to *Ramban's* interpretation in 21:33, the word אִם, *if,* when used in connection with oaths, signifies an implied consequential imprecation. Tailored to our verse, this would mean: *If you will ill-treat my daughters* — then *God Who is a witness between me and you* will punish you appropriately. For, as *Ramban* notes in 21:33: 'In all such cases the Torah shortens the expression, leaving the threatened consequences to the imagination rather than explicitly stating them.' (Cf. *comm.* to 26:29 s.v. אִם תַּעֲשֵׂה).]

רְאֵה אֱלֹהִים עֵד בֵּינִי וּבֵינֶךָ — [*But* (not in the Hebrew, but exegetically implied)] *see, God is a witness between me and* [*between*] *you.*

— Therefore, *God* shall serve as witness to the terms of our pact *(Radak).*

— And He will exact retribution from you, for, [since He is a witness,] being false to me is equivalent to being false to *Him (Sforno).*

51-53. [The second part of the treaty: That neither Laban or Jacob will pass the mound of stones thrown up as a landmark, with hostile intention toward the other]

51. הִנֵּה הַגַּל הַזֶּה וְהִנֵּה הַמַּצֵּבָה אֲשֶׁר יָרִיתִי... — *Here is this mound, and here is the monument which I have cast* [following *Rashi* (see below); *Rashbam* renders: *set up*] *between me and* [*between*] *you.*

Although *Jacob* set up the monument and mound, Laban speaks of *himself* as having done so since Jacob acted on Laban's advice by suggesting the covenant. Furthermore, as noted above [see *Ramban's* interpretation of 'brethren' in *v.* 46 above], *Laban's* kinsmen gathered the stones to make the mound; therefore Laban takes credit for the

*among us — but see! God is a witness between me
and you.'* 51 *And Laban said to Jacob, 'Here is this
mound, and here is the monument which I have cast
between me and you.* 52 *This mound shall be witness
and the monument shall be witness that I may not
cross over to you past this mound, nor may you cross
over to me past this mound, with hostile purpose.*

action of his subordinates *(Radak).*

Rashi interprets ירה in the sense of *cast,* 'like one who casts an arrow' [i.e., *heaped up* effortlessly Laban thus boasts of his prowess as if setting up the monument and mound were an effortless act which he himself had done. However, see *Midrash Rabbah* ad loc] *(Yafeh Toar).*

52. עֵד הַגַּל הַזֶּה וְעֵדָה הַמַּצֵּבָה — *This mound shall be witness and the monument shall be witness.*

In the literal sense: These landmarks will serve as reminders. Should any of us wish to violate our covenant, when we see them we will be reminded of our pact *(Ibn Caspi).*[1]

אִם־אָנִי לֹא אֶעֱבֹר אֵלֶיךָ אֶת הַגַּל הַזֶּה ... לְרָעָה — *That I may not cross over to you past this mound ... with hostile purpose* [lit. *for evil*].

For evil — i.e., for doing evil. But for purposes of trade, you *may* cross over *(Rashi; Midrash).*

The translation follows *Rashi* and *Ibn Ezra* who render אִם [usually *if*] as meaning in this case אֲשֶׁר, *that,* as in 24:33: עַד אֲשֶׁר=עַד אִם, *until that.*

Tur cites an interpretation of אִם in the sense of *if,* and לְרָעָה as meaning: *in the event of trouble.* The implication is that they made a mutual defense treaty and this passage implies a euphemistic imprecation: 'This mound shall be a witness [and may some unmentioned disaster befall me] if I will

1. Such oaths have spiritual as well as legal force. The Sages attached particular significance to oaths taken upon objects, for these 'witnesses' can avenge the violation of the oath for which they take responsibility, so to speak. In this regard, *Daas Zekeinim* cites a touching story from *Rashi* and *Tosafos, Taanis* 8a, s.v. בחולדה:

A girl on the way to her father's house fell into a well. A young man passing by her asked, 'If I get you out, will you marry me?' She agreed, and they swore to one another that neither would marry anyone else. 'But,' they said, 'who will be the witness to our oath?' There was a weasel passing by, so they agreed that the well and the weasel would be their witnesses.

The girl kept her promise, but the young man married someone else. His wife gave birth to a boy — but a weasel bit him and he died. She had another child — but he fell into a well and died. The distraught mother exclaimed, 'What is it that causes us to suffer so much more than others!'

Her husband remembered his long-forgotten oath and told her about it. She said, 'If so, divorce me and marry her.'

In this context, *Hadar Zekeinim* records that Jacob and Laban thrust a sword into the heap to be an additional 'witness'. Balaam son of Beor [the latter is Midrashically identified as Laban while according to *Sefer HaYashar,* Beor is identified as Laban's son] who, years later, crossed the mound to curse Israel, was indeed struck by these very 'witnesses'. The wall against which Balaam's foot was crushed [see *Numbers* 22:25] was this same heap, and with this sword that they now thrust into the heap, he was ultimately killed, for it is written [*ibid.* 31:8]: 'They slew Balaam son of Beor with *the* sword' — implying a sword well-known from days of yore ... Support for this concept is found in the verse [*Deut.* 17:7]: *The hands of the 'witnesses' shall be first to put him to death* [*cf. Bereishis Zuta; Tur; Torah Sheleimah* §117].

נָחוֹר יִשְׁפְּטוּ בֵינֵינוּ אֱלֹהֵי אֲבִיהֶם וַיִּשָּׁבַע
נד יַעֲקֹב בְּפַחַד אָבִיו יִצְחָק׃ וַיִּזְבַּח יַעֲקֹב
זֶבַח בָּהָר וַיִּקְרָא לְאֶחָיו לֶאֱכָל־לָחֶם
°מפטיר א וַיֹּאכְלוּ לֶחֶם וַיָּלִינוּ בָּהָר׃ °וַיַּשְׁכֵּם לָבָן
בַּבֹּקֶר וַיְנַשֵּׁק לְבָנָיו וְלִבְנוֹתָיו וַיְבָרֶךְ
ב אֶתְהֶם וַיֵּלֶךְ וַיָּשָׁב לָבָן לִמְקֹמוֹ׃ וְיַעֲקֹב

not cross this mound [to help you] in the event of trouble, or if you fail to cross it [to help me] in the case of trouble.' [Cf. interpretation of אִם in *v.* 50.]

53. אֱלֹהֵי אַבְרָהָם וֵאלֹהֵי נָחוֹר יִשְׁפְּטוּ בֵינֵינוּ אֱלֹהֵי אֲבִיהֶם – *The God of Abraham and the god of Nachor judge between us — the god of their father* [=Terach].

The passage should be understood as if it read: *The God of Abraham and the god of Nachor, the god of their father, judge between us (R' Bachya).*

Laban thus proposed to invoke both the *God of Abraham* [Jacob's grandfather] as well as the *god of Nachor* [Laban's grandfather] with the explanation that he included the latter because he was also the *god of their* [=Abraham and Nachor's] mutual *father,* Terach *(Sforno).*

Although the phrase *god of their father* [Terach] is separated by the phrase *may judge between us,* it reverts to and modifies *god of Nachor.* It thus refers to Terach's *idolatrous* gods [rather than to Abraham's God]. This is evident from *Joshua* 24:2 where Terach and Nachor are described as serving other gods *(Ibn Ezra; Karnei Or).*

Laban mentioned Abraham and Nachor because they were more renowned than Isaac and Bethuel *(Radak).*

According to *Ibn Ezra,* the phrase *the god of their father* is a parenthetic interpolation which explains that each invoked his *own God:* Jacob, the God of his grandfather Abraham; and Laban, the god of his grandfather Nachor [see *Yohel Or*].

The capitalization of the word *God* in its first appearance, referring it to HASHEM, and the subsequent use of the lower-case *god,* referring it to an idol, follows *Rashi* citing the *Midrash: Rashi* comments that the word אֱלֹהֵי in *God of Abraham* is sacred [i.e. refers to HASHEM and may not be erased *(Mizrachi)*]; the designation *god of Nachor* is non-holy [i.e. אֱלֹהֵי in his case is a designation for an idol and may be erased]; *god of their father* is similarly non-sacred [since this designation includes Terach's idols (see *Soferim* 4)].

וַיִּשָּׁבַע יַעֲקֹב בְּפַחַד אָבִיו יִצְחָק – *And Jacob swore by the Dread of his father Isaac.*

I.e., the God whom his father feared *(Targum Yonasan).*

[On the term *Dread of Isaac* see *comm.* to parallel designation in *v.* 42.]

Since Laban proposed to invoke idolatrous deities in his oath, Jacob refused to swear with the formula devised by Laban. Instead, *he* took the oath by the True God — the God of *Isaac* who was not Terach's son [and therefore his God would not be coupled with the idols invoked by Laban] *(Sforno).*

54. וַיִּזְבַּח יַעֲקֹב זֶבַח בָּהָר – *Then* [lit. *and*] *Jacob slaughtered an animal on the mountain.*

The term זֶבַח [*slaughter*] usually

31
53-54
32
1-2

[53] *May the God of Abraham and the god of Nachor*
judge between us — the god of their father.' And
Jacob swore by the Dread of his father Isaac. [54] *Then*
Jacob slaughtered an animal on the mountain and
summoned his kinsmen to break bread. And they
broke bread and spent the night on the mountain.
[1] *And Laban awoke early in the morning; he kissed*
his sons and his daughters and blessed them. Then
Laban went and returned to his place. [2] *Jacob went on*

has a ritualistic sacrificial connotation, in which case the passage would be rendered: *Then Jacob offered a sacrifice.* The translation follows *Rashi* who explains it in the sense of: *slaughtered cattle for a feast (Radak* interprets similarly: He prepared a farewell feast).

Rashi pursues this line of interpretation since Jacob would certainly not have shared a sacrificial feast with the idolatrous Laban and his companions *(Gur Aryeh).*

וַיִּקְרָא לְאֶחָיו — *And summoned his kinsmen* [lit. *brothers*].

— *Laban's* kinsmen, i.e., the companions who had accompanied Laban [see *v.* 23] *(Targum Yonasan; Rashi).*

After the covenant they are *all* properly referred to as 'brothers' *(Radak).*

Jacob addressed the invitation to the entire group, rather than to Laban individually, out of respect to them, so as not to intimate to Laban that all of them were subject to his authority *(Ramban* to *v.* 46).

Rashi here does not suggest, as he does in *v.* 46, that 'kinsmen' refers to Jacob's *sons* since our verse says that Jacob *summoned* them. This would not apply to Jacob's *sons* whom we must presume were at Jacob's side throughout these events, whereas Laban's companions were not and had to be *summoned* to partake of the meal *(Divrei David).*

לֶאֱכָל לָחֶם — *To break* [lit. *eat*] *bread.*

[I.e., to partake of a meal]. *Bread* connotes *food* in general, as for example in *Daniel* 5:1: לְחֶם רַב, *a great feast; Jeremiah* 11:19; עֵץ בְּלַחְמוֹ, *a tree with its produce (Rashi;* comp. *Rashi* to *Lev.* 21:21; cf. *Radak, Shorashim* s.v. לחם).

His intention was that they should part on good terms after having entered into a treaty, and that they should spend the night there *(Ramban, v.* 46).

וַיֹּאכְלוּ לֶחֶם — *And they broke* [lit. *ate*] *bread.*

[I.e., ate a meal, *bread* being considered the primary staple.]

XXXII

1. וַיַּשְׁכֵּם לָבָן בַּבֹּקֶר — [And] *Laban awoke early in the morning.*

לְבָנָיו — *His sons.*

That is, his *grandsons (Ibn Ezra)* — *Jacob's* son's *(Targum Yonasan).*

וַיְבָרֶךְ אֶתְהֶם — *And* [*he*] *blessed them.*

Although the Sages have taught that even the blessing of a common person — like Laban — should not be denigrated, Scripture has a deeper purpose in mentioning Laban's blessing. It is meant to teach how effective a blessing can be when it is conferred with total sincerity, for Laban was surely sincere in blessing

הָלַךְ לְדַרְכּוֹ וַיִּפְגְּעוּ־בוֹ מַלְאֲכֵי אֱלֹהִים:
ג וַיֹּאמֶר יַעֲקֹב כַּאֲשֶׁר רָאָם מַחֲנֵה אֱלֹהִים
זֶה וַיִּקְרָא שֵׁם־הַמָּקוֹם הַהוּא מַחֲנָיִם:

his own daughters. Such selfless commitment is efficacious because it is an expression of the Godly nature of man's soul *(Sforno).*

וַיֵּלֶךְ וַיָּשָׁב לָבָן לִמְקֹמוֹ — *Then* [lit. *and*] *Laban went and returned to his place.*

— I.e., to his former state of poverty, as he was before Jacob came to him [cf. 30:27 where Laban himself attributes his prosperity to Jacob's presence]. Robbers entered his house and impoverished him *(Midrash).*

According to others, the implication is that he returned to his *wickedness (Bereishis Zuta).*[1]

2. וְיַעֲקֹב הָלַךְ לְדַרְכּוֹ — [And] *Jacob went on his way.*

— On his way of righteousness unaffected by his exposure for the past twenty years to the rogue, Laban *(Tzror HaMor).*

[As noted in the *comm.* to 28:10, the commentators attribute Jacob's unaffected spiritual survival in alien Charan to his fourteen years of preparatory Torah study in the Academy of Eber.]

וַיִּפְגְּעוּ־בוֹ מַלְאֲכֵי אֱלֹהִים — *And angels of God encountered him.*[2]

— To assist him on his journey *(Ibn Ezra).*

— They were angels who minister in *Eretz Yisrael.* Tey came to meet him to accompany him into the Holy Land *(Midrash; Rashi).*

[The angels who accompanied Jacob outside *Eretz Yisrael* escorted him back

1. What did the devious Laban do after this ostensibly 'peaceful' departure from Jacob and his children?

— When he returned home he dispatched his son and a representative delegation of his family to Esau. He ordered them to incite Esau by relating a tale of how Jacob came penniless to Laban's house seeking refuge after outwitting Esau; how Laban befriended him and gave him his two daughters in marriage; and how Jacob prospered immensely and fled secretly while Laban went to shear his sheep — and even stole Laban's *teraphim!*

'I left him with everything he owns,' the message to Esau concluded, 'at the mountain of the brook of Jabbok. If you wish, you can intercept him there and do to him as you please.'

Laban's messengers related the message to Esau who became incensed. His old hatred toward Jacob was ignited again as he heard their words, and he set out with a mightily armed camp.

Laban's messengers then went to Canaan and told Rebecca that Esau was advancing on Jacob with an armed camp of four hundred men to slay him and take all his possessions.

Rebecca then dispatched seventy-two men who met Jacob, and Jacob said when he met them: *this camp is destined me from God* [see 32:2]. They related to him about his parents' welfare and then gave him Rebecca's message regarding Esau with the advice that Jacob take steps to placate Esau: '... when he approaches you, supplicate him. Do not speak rashly to him, and give him a present from what God has blessed you with ... Conceal nothing of your personal affairs from him, perhaps he will be appeased and you will be spared. It is your duty to consider his dignity for he is your elder brother.'

When Jacob heard his mother's message, he wept bitterly and proceeded to follow her instructions [see *Sidra Vayishlach*] *(Sefer HaYashar).* [*HaKsav V'Hakabbalah* makes reference to the incident of Laban's inciting Esau when he negated Laban's sincerity in his *comm.* cited at the end of 31:43.]

[The above does not follow the general Rabbinic opinion cited by *Midrash Tanchuma* that Jacob *himself* was taken to task for 'taking the dog by the ears' by sending emissaries and attracting Esau's attention who presumably would otherwise not have been attracted to him.]

32
3

his way, and angels of God encountered him.
3 *Jacob said when he saw them, 'This is a Godly camp!' So he named that place Machanaim.*

as far as the border. There he was greeted by a fresh band of angels who were to escort him in *Eretz Yisrael*. The reverse occurred when he departed from the Holy Land, since as noted in the *comm.* to 28:12, angels who minister in the Holy Land cannot go beyond the frontier. Apparently then, *Rashi* is of the opinion that when Jacob left Mount Gilead for the region he named Machanayim, he was in the environs of *Eretz Yisrael* and presumably the mound heaped up by Jacob marked this boundary line. *R' Bachya* to 31:52 also maintains that Gilead was the border between Aram and *Eretz Yisrael*. In support, he cites *Deut.* 34:1: *And HASHEM showed him all the land of Gilead until Dan.* As noted *ibid.* 3:12, this was later in the Transjordan.]

Ramban differs in certain respects with several of the geographic conclusions stated above [see *Mizrachi* and *comm.* to 32:23 and 35:18]. He offers, therefore, that Jacob was still a long way from the Holy Land, and after crossing the Ford of the Jabbok [below 32:33] he still had to pass the boundary of Ammon and Moab before reaching Shechem [33:18]. Accordingly, this vision of the angels came to him when he entered enemy territory to assure him that the angels would be with him against his enemies [and that he need not fear Esau, since now, with the troops of angels, Jacob outnumbered him *(Abarbanel)*.]

[According to the selection from *Sefer HaYashar* cited in the footnote to *v.* 1, these מַלְאָכִים were *human messengers* sent to him by Rebecca to warn him of Esau's impending arrival.]

3. כַּאֲשֶׁר רָאָם — *When he saw them.*

[The use of the singular verb רָאָם, *he* saw them, denotes that] Jacob was the only one who saw them *(Ibn Ezra)*. [*Targum Yonasan* implies otherwise; see below.]

They were the angels he had previously seen ascending and descending the ladder of his dream [28:12]. The sense here of כַּאֲשֶׁר רָאָם, *when he recognized them,* since he had already 'seen' them *(R'Bachya)*.

מַחֲנֵה אֱלֹהִים זֶה — *This is a Godly camp.*

This remark was meant to assure those with him: 'These are not the troops of Esau or Laban coming to attack us; they are camps of holy angels which God sent from on high to protect us from the likes of our enemies' *(Targum Yonasan; Targum Yerushalmi)*.

The word אֱלֹהִים in this passage is sacred *(Soferim* 4). [I.e., it refers to God, thus the word אֱלֹהִים cannot be interpreted as the ad-

2. Twenty years earlier, when Jacob was on the way from Isaac's home to Laban's, וַיִּפְגַּע, *he* [Jacob] *encountered* the Divine [see *comm.* to 28:11]. Now, the angels encountered *him*. Then, it was an auspicious event that a man was told by God that it was his mission to make the earth a suitable habitat for the *Shechinah*. Now, when Jacob was finally free from the fetters of Laban, the angels were privileged to come and greet *him* — he represented the first human family that was fitting home for the *Shechinah*.

This follows *R' Bachya* who adds that the angels' mission was to guard Jacob, as in the verse [*Psalms* 91:11]: *For He shall give His angels charge over you to guard you in all your ways. They shall carry you in their hands lest you dash your foot against a stone.*

As the *Midrash* observes: Who is greater, the guardian, or the one who is guarded? Certainly the one who is being guarded. Who is greater, those who carry, or he who is being carried? Certainly the latter. Likewise, Jacob who was being met was greater than those [=the angels] who were meeting him.

jective *mighty* with the passage meaning: this is a mighty camp. See *Sefer HaYashar* in footnote to *v.* 1: *This is a camp destined to me by God.*]

מַחֲנָיִם — *Machanaim.*

Lit. *a pair of camps* referring to the two camps of angels: those who ministered outside the Holy Land who accompanied him thus far, and those of the Holy Land who now came to meet him *(Tanchuma; Rashi).*

This is the Machanaim across the Jordan mentioned in *II Samuel* 17:24, which is part of the Holy Land *(Haamek Davar,* differing from *Ramban;* see *Herchev Davar).*

According to *Ramban* [who differs with the view that the angels were of two categories], the *-im* suffix of the name Machanaim does not necessarily imply a plural since it is common for proper nouns to end with *-im* [as for example *Mitzraim*]. However, if there *is* a plural connotation to be derived from Machanaim, then it refers to two camps: Jacob's own camp and the camp of the higher beings [angels]. This suggests that both the human and the angelic are camps of God in that both bless Him and assert His unity. [The righteous ones on earth are equated to angels in heaven in their fulfillment of His will *(R' Bachya* 53:2).]

R' Hirsch explains similarly: Jacob and his family and entourage were on their way to a homeland where God would be with them as He had promised. They were a מַחֲנֶה, *temporary camp,* in search of God's Presence. The angels, too, were a *camp* in search of something: they sought a human community where God could dwell on earth. When these two camps met, Jacob named the place Machanaim, the *two camps* — מַחֲנֵה יִשְׂרָאֵל, *the camp of Israel,* and מַחֲנֵה אֱלֹהִים, *the camp of God* [see *Overview*].

Machanaim was to become one of the most important cities in Gilead. It was a city of Levites [*Josh.* 21:36], the royal city of Ishbosheth son of Saul [*II Sam.* 2:8], and the city where King David settled when he fled from his son Absalom [ibid. 17:24, 27]. It was located within Gad's territory, close to that of the half tribe of Menashe in the Transjordan [*Jos.* 13:26-30]. Notwithstanding the above references, it is difficult to pinpoint its exact location although it is generally assumed to lay between the streams of Jabbok and Yarmuk in line with Beth She'an *(Hoffmann).*

The *Midrash* cites an opinion that there were sixty myriads [=600,000] of angels who preceded Jacob when he entered the Land since God's Presence does not rest in Its fullness on less than that number [equal to the number of the Israelite camp at Mount Sinai at the Giving of the Torah]. According to the Sages, however, the plural form *Machanaim* implies that there was a *double* camp: 120 myriads. [See *comm.* to ArtScroll *Shir HaShirim* 7:1 s.v. כִּמְחֹלַת הַמַּחֲנָיִם, *like a dance of the camps.*]

According to the Masoretic note appearing at the end of the *Sidrah* there are 148 verses in the *Sidrah* numerically corresponding to the mnemonics חלק״י and מחני״ם, each of which totals 148. The Jewish People are referred to as God's חֵלֶק, *portion,* as in כִּי חֵלֶק ה׳ עַמּוֹ, *HASHEM's portion is His People* [*Deut.* 32:9]. Thus the birth of eleven of the twelve tribes, as described in this *Sidrah* constitutes the nation that God describes as חֶלְקִי, *My portion.* Additionally, the final word of the *Sidrah* is מַחֲנָיִם, *Machanaim,* the name Jacob gave to the place where he saw the two companies of angels. It also alludes to Jacob's abundant, flourishing growth, a condition which he was to describe in 32:11 as having grown into שְׁנֵי מַחֲנוֹת, *two camps.*] The *Haftorah* begins with *Hoshea* 12:13 וַיִּבְרַח יַעֲקֹב.

נשלם סדרה ויצא בעזרת האל

◆§ סדר וישלח

◆§ Sidrah Vayishlach

— *The Overviews*

Several topics in this Sidrah have been treated in Overviews to earlier volumes. Among them are:

Visions of Exile — *Daniel*
Reuben's sin — *Ruth*
Esau's Monarchy — *Yechezkel*

An Overview —
Jacob — Alone and Secure*

מַה הקב״ה כָּתוּב בּוֹ וְנִשְׂגַּב ה׳ לְבַדּוֹ, אַף יַעֲקֹב וַיִּוָּתֵר יַעֲקֹב לְבַדּוֹ

What is written of the Holy One, Blessed be He: HASHEM **alone** *shall be exalted [Isaiah 2:17]. Of Jacob, too, it is written: and Jacob remained* **alone** *(Bereishis Rabbah 77:1).*

I. Jacob's Consistency

A Contradiction

As *Ramban* notes in his introductory words to *Vayishlach,* this is the chapter of Israel's subjugation to Edom. Jacob's behavior in the face of a mortal threat from the stronger Esau is to guide our conduct in similar circumstances, and his salvation is our assurance that God will save Israel from destruction by Esau's powerful offspring until the eventual complete redemption by Messiah.

Jacob undertook three simultaneous courses: דּוֹרוֹן, *tribute,* תְּפִלָּה, *prayer,* and מִלְחָמָה, *battle.* He sent a *tribute* to appease Esau, he *prayed* to God, and prepared to engage in *battle* [*Rashi* to 32:8; see *comm.*]. At first glance such activities seem to involve contradictory emotions. One who dispatches a lavish tribute to a murderous enemy evidences abject submission; in effect, he humbles himself and throws himself at the mercy of his invincible foe. In preparing for war, he is ready to fight, to kill, and to win, refusing to acknowledge his opponent's supremacy. When someone prays sincerely, he throws his lot with God, manifesting a recognition that neither submission nor armed might can carry the fray — only God determines the outcome of human events.

When someone prays sincerely, he throws his lot with God.

* This Overview is based on a *schmuess* by *Harav Gedaliah Schorr* זצ״ל.

The average human being *can* adopt three contradictory policies, but because they involve irreconcilable emotional and intellectual responses to a situation, he will not be able to bring total commitment to each of the three. The hopeless pleading for mercy suggested by the tribute will interfere with the total trust that God is the *Master of war* [*Exodus* 15:3] before Whom an army is but an array of matchsticks; and one who sends groveling tribute can hardly muster the zeal needed for effective combat.

Jacob and Truth

It is true, of course, that contradictory actions are commonly undertaken by people, but we all know that many of them are insincere. Jacob was different. In understanding him at any juncture of his life, we must always recall an axiom that often eludes us: As the epitome of truth, Jacob does not pay mere lip service to ideals; what he says he means. Even where he was forced to make statements that were intended to mislead the listener, he remained as close to the truth as circumstances would allow, so much so that his words in and of themselves were absolutely true if understood properly. Thus, when he presented himself to Isaac saying אָנֹכִי עֵשָׂו בְּכֹרֶךָ, *It is I, Esau your firstborn* (27:19), his words could be understood as *literally* true, or as meaning that because of his righteousness and Esau's wickedness, God had decreed that the position originally meant for Esau had been assumed by Jacob [see *comm.* to 27:19]. And when he said that he would eventually come to Esau in Seir [see *comm.* to 33:14], Jacob had in mind the longed for time when Messiah would lead a triumphant Jewish nation to occupy the mountain of Esau.

Even where he was forced to make statements that were intended to mislead the listener, he remained as close to the truth as circumstances would allow.

Indeed because his frequent reference to Esau אֲדֹנִי עֵשָׂו, *my lord, Esau,* was so sincere, Jacob suffered for it. *Yalkut Shimoni* declares that because Jacob conferred that title of honor upon Esau eight times during his attempts at appeasement, Esau's descendants produced eight kings before Jacob's produced even one (see 36:31ff). By inculcating himself with the honest conviction that Esau was indeed his superior, Jacob lowered his own status to the point where Esau could indeed demonstrate a degree of superiority (*Shiurei Daas* part I). Offhand, insincere flattery could not have carried such major implications. Clearly any statement of a Jacob must be taken to reflect the innermost man.

That Jacob could dedicate himself with conviction to three contradictory courses of action is testimony to the greatness of his self-discipline.

That Jacob could dedicate himself with conviction to three contradictory courses of action is testimony to the greatness of his self-discipline. He was able to compartmentalize his emotions to such an extent that he could cast his lot with God, yet not fail to make the necessary human responses to a crisis; to recognize an element of justice in Esau's hurt at losing the blessings, yet prepare for an attack as if there were no defense but his own strong arms. This chapter teaches that Israel in exile must always be willing to recognize the varying and sometimes conflicting elements in any situation. Only in this way can we understand the plight of R' Yannai who always interceded with Rome on behalf of Israel. He never went without studying this chapter — except once, when he suffered disastrous results (see *comm.*). Surely, R' Yannai remembered the events of the chapter at least as well as we do; but there are lessons in Jacob's conduct that are apparent only to people of the highest caliber and even then, only if they rigorously study the chapter in the light of each particular event.

II. Incitement to Evil

Above and Alone

The highlight of the chapter is Jacob's combat with the angel of Esau posing as a 'man' [32:25-31]. The narrative tells us that Jacob remained 'alone' whereupon the angel attacked him. Understood superficially, the story is quite straightforward: the angel waited until Jacob was defenseless and vulnerable, whereupon he ambushed him. There are much deeper implications here, however.

וַיִּוָּתֵר יַעֲקֹב לְבַדּוֹ וַיֵּאָבֵק אִישׁ עִמּוֹ ... ר׳ בְּרַכְיָה

בְּשֵׁם ר׳ סִימוֹן אוֹמֵר: אֵין כָּאֵל יְשֻׁרוּן. אֵין כָּאֵל.
וּמִי כָאֵל? יְשֻׁרוּן, יִשְׂרָאֵל סָבָא. מַה הקב״ה כָּתוּב
בּוֹ וְנִשְׂגַּב ה׳ לְבַדּוֹ, אַף יַעֲקֹב וַיִּוָּתֵר יַעֲקֹב לְבַדּוֹ.
Jacob was left alone and a man wrestled with him ... [32:25]. R' Berachiah said in behalf of R' Simon: There is none like the God of Israel [*Deut.* 33:26]. [*This means:*] *there is none like God! But who is like God? — Israel! This refers to the Patriarch Israel* [*Jacob*]. *What is written of the Holy One Blessed be He: HASHEM* **alone** *shall be exalted* [*Isaiah* 2:17]. *Of Jacob, too, it is written: Jacob remained* **alone** *(Bereishes Rabbah* 77:1*).*

The *Midrash* sees a new element in Jacob's isolation. He was, so to speak, as far removed from the mundane affairs of his contemporaries, as glorious in his exaltation on earth, as is God Himself. Man, by nature, is a gregarious animal. He craves company. He may be shy and withdrawn, but his mind is always involved with human beings whether relating to family, business, politics or whatever. He may be alone on a desert island, but his thoughts always drift to human affairs. Jacob was different. He was above all that. As *Chovos Halevavos* says of the חָסִיד, *truly devout person:* Even when he is part of the crowd, his heart and mind are above every concern but what truly matters.

The angel attacked this Jacob — not the man, but this characteristic of rising above every situation by remaining alone even in the midst of turmoil.

The angel attacked *this* Jacob — not the man, but this characteristic of rising above every situation by remaining alone even in the midst of turmoil. Had Jacob been part of the crowd, the angel of evil could easily have ignored him even when he was defenseless; one more man named Jacob is no cause for concern to the forces of evil. It was Jacob's God-like *aloneness* that the angel could not tolerate. That Jacob's image was engraved on the Heavenly Throne [*Chullin* 91a] was proof that no impediment stood between him and the highest level of holiness available to man. When the angel saw a man capable of rising so far above earthly affairs, he had to attack, because the angel of evil exists to prevent such spiritual accomplishment.

This relationship between Jacob and God's throne operates in both directions.

This relationship between Jacob and God's Throne operates in both directions. Jacob's image on the Throne is proof enough of his stature, but it also demonstrates that his goal in life was to bring holiness into earthly affairs; he existed to bring that Heavenly image down to earth where it would influence the affairs of man. He was dedicated to removing the barriers that prevent Godliness from finding a home on earth [see Overview to *Vayeitzei:* 'A Tzaddik and His Possessions.']

To the Highest Level

The struggle between Jacob and the angel had truly cosmic implications. The *Talmud* derives this from the expression וַיֵּאָבֵק, *and he wrestled,* which is related to the word אָבָק, *dust* [32:26]:

> אָמַר ר׳ יְהוֹשֻׁעַ בֶּן לֵוִי: מְלַמֵּד שֶׁהֶעֱלָה אֲבַק מַרְגְלוֹתָם עַד כִּסֵּא הַכָּבוֹד.
>
> *R' Joshua ben Levi said: This teaches that the dust of their feet rose up to the Throne of Glory (Chullin 91a).*

Rashba explains that 'feet' alludes to first causes, 'dust', to the results churned up by an event, and the 'Throne of Glory' refers to the highest possible spiritual levels. The bout between Jacob and the angel had repercussions that went infinitely beyond the sands of Jabbok. The angel succeeded in setting in motion a chain of events that would affect Jacob's offspring thousands of years into the future [see next Overview], and its implications would affect world history until God would take his place on the thrones of judgment revealed to Daniel:

The angel succeeded in setting in motion a chain of events that would affect Jacob's offspring thousands of years in the future.

> חָזֵה הֲוֵית עַד דִּי כָרְסָוָן רְמִיו וְעַתִּיק יוֹמִין יְתִב ... דִּינָא יְתִב וְסִפְרִין פְּתִיחוּ
>
> *I [Daniel] watched until thrones were set up, and the Ancient of Days sat ... The judgment was set and the books were opened (Daniel 7:9-10).*

Throughout time the cause-and-effect processes set in motion by their struggle would reverberate, coloring, molding, determining history until God's final day of judgment. In terms of the struggle's intensity, it extended throughout every spiritual level, from the lowest all the way up to God Himself.

Power to Obscure

'Dust' also represents a dulling, covering substance. A brightly polished object loses its sheen with the first light covering of dust. Eventually, as the dust accumulates on them, gold and clay both look the same. Esau's angel tried to obscure the luster of God's holiness with all the dust of delusion. Why acknowledge God's power if Nature can be put in its place? Why guide one's actions by God's decree if man can assume absolute power? Why accept a Heavenly code of morality if man can adapt a philosophy tailored to his own lusts and preconceptions? Esau's duststorm has spread and risen until it has nearly obscured even the Throne, for those whose eyes see creation through dust-coated lenses. All the while, Jacob labors to cleanse and polish, but the angel battles him.

Evil's very existence is based on this ability to obscure the truth and deceive man into accepting falsehood.

Evil's very existence is based on this ability to obscure the truth and deceive man into accepting falsehood. If man could only realize that Satan's wares are all package and no content! But he doesn't. He sees their surface attractiveness and believes there is depth and legitimacy to Satan's message. And Satan Himself? —

יוֹרֵד וּמַתְעֶה וְעוֹלֶה וּמַרְגִיז נוֹטֵל רְשׁוּת וְנוֹטֵל נְשָׁמָה ... הוּא שָׂטָן הוּא יֵצֶר הָרַע הוּא מַלְאַךְ הַמָּוֶת

[*Satan*] *descends and seduces man* [*to sin*], *then he rises to anger* [*God by prosecuting man for his sinfulness*], *then he receives permission, and takes man's life ... Satan, the Evil Inclination, and the Angel of Death are one and the same (Bava Basra* 16a*).*

Satan's deceptions succeed in seducing virtually everyone, at least to some extent, for no man lives without falling short of his maximum goals [see *Koheles* 7:20], such are his powers. But Jacob would not be taken in by the surface allures of Satan. The angel persevered; he demonstrated all his might to

Jacob. As the *Midrash* relates the spiritual struggle between the two of them, the angel caused fire to bubble from the ground, whereupon Jacob responded, 'You seek to frighten me with fire? I am *all* fire,' as Scripture says [*Obadiah* 1:18]: *The house of Jacob shall be a flame ... (Bereishis Rabbah* 77:2). The angel could make a fire come out of nothing. But Jacob was superior to him, for he recognized that the fire had come from nothing, that it had no inner value. But Jacob, himself, who epitomized God's purpose in creating man — Jacob was *all* spiritual flame.

But Jacob was superior to him, for he recognized that the fire had come from nothing, that it had no inner value.

This *Midrashic* allegory represents the essence of their struggle. The power of evil and the exponent of good peeled away all the outer layers that concealed their respective essences. The angel sought to kick up dust storms that would obscure the ultimate value of things, but Jacob would not be deceived. The angel stormed and flashed, but for every attack Jacob had a response — and his ultimate response was 'You are a sham and I am the truth; you cover your falsehood with a veneer of philosophical, spiritual fire, but I *am* God's fire.'

III. Perceiving the Essence

Unprecedented Intensity

Never before had the fight between good and evil been fought with such intensity, with such a descent into the essence of both sides. This explains Jacob's remark in naming the place in commemoration of his fight with the angel. He said:

כִּי רָאִיתִי אֱלֹהִים פָּנִים אֶל פָּנִים וַתִּנָּצֵל נַפְשִׁי
For I have seen the Divine face, yet my life was saved (32:31).

On the surface it seems like a strange remark. Jacob was no stranger to angels; he had seen them in *Eretz Yisrael* and in Charan, he had even sent them as his messengers to Esau. Why was he now so impressed at having survived the sight of an angel? In the light of the above, we understand. The key word is פָּנִים, *face* — a word which also alludes to פְּנִימִיּוּת,

the innermost being. Jacob had seen angels, but he had never before glimpsed the *spiritual essence* of any angel, much less that of the personification of evil. To have survived such a sight is no small accomplishment, it is worthy of being a landmark, even in the life of Jacob.

Truth Eternal

But Jacob is not done. His attribute, as we know, is אֱמֶת, *truth.* The emanation following truth is נֶצַח, *eternity,* a word which also has the connotation of נִצָּחוֹן, *victory.* The concepts of truth, eternity, and triumph are closely related. Truth can never accept defeat, because no false victor can ever endure. By definition, truth *must* be eternal, because if it were ever to change, it could never have been true. Because truth is eternal it must triumph in the long run, even if the crowd accepts the alluring goddess of falsehood. God's purpose in creating evil was that it should be defeated. Satan has the mission of attempting to deceive man so that man should reach deep into his spiritual resources and refuse to believe the lie. In the long distance race of life, the purpose of such obstacles is that the racer should succeed in hurdling them. If man falls over each successive obstacle, the run is a failure. Satan places every manner of hindrance in man's path, but Satan, too, recognizes God's will; he, too, longs for the man who will face him down, for the man who will respond to surface fire with inner fire.

God's purpose in creating evil was that it should be defeated.

When the angel was defeated he said to Jacob:

שַׁלְּחֵנִי ... מַלְאָךְ אֲנִי וּמִיּוֹם שֶׁנִּבְרֵאתִי לֹא הִגִּיעַ זְמַנִּי לוֹמַר שִׁירָה עַד עַכְשָׁיו

Let me go ... I am an angel, and from the day I was created until now, my time had not come to recite songs of praise [*before God*] *(Chullin* 91b*).*

An angel's existence is its mission. It was created for mission, it exists for a mission, and its 'song of praise' to God is the successful completion of its mission. The angel of evil had been created by God from the beginning with the mission of surrounding itself with a false fire intended to test man — but God *wants* man to resort to his inner store of true fire, and defeat the angel. Finally, the angel had totally fulfilled its mission. It had faced Jacob with every wile, argument, and force at its command, and it had been vanquished by the power of truth. The man whose image graced God's Throne had vindicated creation, so now Satan could ascend to God not to prosecute man, anger God, and obtain permission to slay the straying soul, but to sing the praise of the man — *God's* man — who had overcome humans and defeated angels.

The man whose image graced God's Throne had vindicated creation.

That done, Esau had no power to harm Jacob who could now proceed on his way into *Eretz Yisrael.* As *Ramban* explains, this alludes to Israel's ultimate emergence from all manner of persecution. In his portentious life, Jacob symbolized all the future exiles of Israel, but he also symbolized that Israel might suffer but would never be defeated; in the end, its exile would end and it would enjoy the fruits of its victory over evil.

The Essential Trait

It was Jacob's greatness that provoked the angel to engage him in the climactic battle. The trait that exemplified his greatness was his **aloneness!** — וַיִּוָּתֵר יַעֲקֹב לְבַדּוֹ, *Jacob was left alone.* Jacob could elevate himself above exigencies and remain above every condition that threatened to pull him from the Throne of Glory to the gutter of material values. That quality had to survive in order for Israel to survive. Even Balaam saw that:

> ... הֶן עָם לְבָדָד יִשְׁכֹּן וּבַגּוֹיִם לֹא יִתְחַשָּׁב
> *... behold it is a nation that dwells apart; among the nations it does not reckon itself (Numbers 23:9).*

Throughout our history, Israel in its greatest moments has been proud of and treasured its uniqueness. The nation that was chosen to be priestly and holy has no need to prove that it could imitate the nations. To the contrary, Israel could serve them best by holding itself separate, the better to fulfill the mission for which Abraham's seed had been chosen. The bulk of the decrees and prohibitions found in the

Talmud have the purpose of maintaining Israel's separation to avoid intermarriage and adoption of non-Jewish ways of life. The same is true of the body of sacred Jewish custom that has been built over the centuries. This quality was stressed by Moses in his final words:

וַיִּשְׁכֹּן יִשְׂרָאֵל בֶּטַח בָּדָד

And Israel shall dwell secure, apart (Deut. 33:28*).*

To the extent that it is apart, it will be secure; to the extent that it seeks to become united with the nations, it will be insecure.

So vital is this isolation to the survival of Israel, that God imposes it if Israel fails to see its wisdom.

So vital is this isolation to the survival of Israel, that God imposes it if Israel fails to see its wisdom. *Meshech Chochmah* [*Lev.* 26:44] describes the entire panorama of Jewish history in exile in these terms: We are a bedraggled, wandering rabble forced from our home in a helpless and pitiful fate. We establish homes and communities in a new land, build our Torah and religious institutions to an undreamed of extent. Then, as time goes on, we look outward at our host society and seek to become accepted by it and eventually to become part of it. Eventually we make *it* our source of culture, we say 'Berlin is the true Jerusalem.' With these fearfully prophetic words, *Meshech Chochmah* says that God is left with only one way to preserve us — he must turn our hosts against us, have *them* remind us who we are, even expel us. Painful, tragic — but, in that way we are forced to preserve our identity, and begin the process anew. There is no better explanation for mindless anti-Semitism. It is God's preservative for His people. As David says of Egypt's hatred of the Jews who contributed so much to their land: הָפַךְ לִבָּם לִשְׂנֹא עַמּוֹ, *He* [*God*] *transformed their heart to hate His people (Psalms* 105:25).

As the days of Messiah draw closer, may we heed Jacob's lesson. A Jew is different. He is above the fray and, because he is, he triumphs.

An Overview —
Torah—Satan's Objective

הַלְוַאי אֹתִי עָזָבוּ וְתוֹרָתִי שָׁמָרוּ — שֶׁאִילוּ תוֹרָתִי שָׁמָרוּ ... הָיְתָה מַחֲזִירָן אֶצְלִי

[*God says,*] *if only they had forsaken Me but observed* [*the study of*] *My Torah ... it would have brought them back to Me (Yalkut Shimoni Jeremiah 282).*

... כְּעוֹבֵד כּוֹכָבִים נִדְמֶה לוֹ ... כְּתַלְמִיד חָכָם נִדְמֶה לוֹ

[*The angel*] *seemed like an idolator* [*to Jacob*] *... He seemed like a Torah scholar to him (Chullin 91a).*

I. The Angel's Victory

The First Target

The 'man' who struggled with Jacob was not a human being, nor was he an ordinary angel. As *Rashi* comments, the 'man' was Samael, the guardian angel of Esau. The Sages teach that Samael represents evil as does no other angel [see preceding *Overview*]. If that is Samael, then we can understand why he tried to destroy Jacob. He was fighting not merely Esau's twin brother, not merely the brother who had gained the blessings sought by Esau, not merely the heir to the inheritance Esau coveted — he was fighting the man who climaxed the Patriarchal tradition. Jacob was הַחוּט הַמְשֻׁלָּשׁ לֹא בִמְהֵרָה יִנָּתֵק, *the tripled-thread* [which] *will not be broken easily* (*Koheles* 4:12). Because Jacob combined within himself the qualities of all three Patriarchs, he was the unyielding, unbreakable pillar upon which the Jewish future could be built.

Because Jacob combined within himself the qualities of all three Patriarchs, he was the unyielding, unbreakable pillar upon which the Jewish future could be built.

That Esau's angel had to fight Jacob, we understand. What is difficult, however, is why the power

---

* This section of the *Overview* is based on an essay by *Harav Elchanan Wasserman* הי"ד.

Why did it wait until triply-strong Jacob came on the scene instead of mounting an offensive against Abraham or Isaac?

of evil waited so long? Why did it wait until triply-strong Jacob came on the scene instead of mounting an offensive against Abraham or Isaac? Of course, it is an overstatement to say that Abraham and Isaac went unmolested by the power of evil. They had tests and obstacles — indeed, the most difficult of Abraham's ten tests, the *Akeidah*, was prompted by Satan's insistence that Abraham's devotion to God was not without limit [see *Overview* to ArtScroll *Tashlich*]. But the fiercest, most direct onslaught was against Jacob. Why?

The analogy of armies at war will help us understand. Two worthy countries will win and lose their share of battles. Even a major defeat will not force the surrender of the loser provided its war-making capacity is not mortally struck. Military history is filled with stories of countries that lost battle after battle, but were still able to come back to counterattack and win. But once a combatant's capacity to fight is destroyed, the war is over. In medieval combat, victory belonged to the warrior who could unsword or unhorse his opponent. In modern conventional warfare, a major objective is to cripple the military-industrial complex of the enemy; if it could not build and transport the implements of war, it could not fight. Remove the antagonist's means of warfare, and his defeat is assured.

Man — particularly Israel — is locked in constant war with his Evil Inclination. God says, בָּרָאתִי יֵצֶר הָרַע בָּרָאתִי לוֹ תּוֹרָה תַּבְלִין, *I have created the Evil Inclination, I have created Torah as its antidote* (*Kiddushin* 30b). The Sages teach that Israel's most far-reaching sin is neglect of Torah study. This is derived from a verse in *Jeremiah:*

... עַל מָה אָבְדָה הָאָרֶץ נִצְּתָה כַמִּדְבָּר מִבְּלִי עֹבֵר? וַיֹּאמֶר ה׳ עַל עָזְבָם אֶת תּוֹרָתִי ... מָצִינוּ שֶׁוִּתֵּר הקב״ה עַל ע״ז עַל ג״ע וְעַל ש״ד וְלֹא וִתֵּר עַל מָאֲסָה שֶׁל תּוֹרָה ... הַלְוַאי אֹתִי עָזָבוּ וְתוֹרָתִי שָׁמָרוּ — שֶׁאִלוּ תוֹרָתִי שָׁמָרוּ מִתּוֹךְ שֶׁהָיוּ מִתְעַסְקִין בָּהּ הָיְתָה מַחֲזִירָן אֶצְלִי

... Why was the land destroyed, left desolate as a desert without passerby?

HASHEM said, 'Because they forsook My Torah ... (Jeremiah 9:11-12). We find that the Holy One, Blessed be He, overlooked idolatry, adultery, and bloodshed, but He would not overlook the debasement of Torah ... [God says] if only they had forsaken Me but observed [the study of] My Torah — for if they had observed My Torah, as a result of having involved themselves with it, it would have brought them back to Me (Yalkut Shimoni Jeremiah 282).

Torah represents the Jews' capacity to fight the war against evil.

Such is the spiritual strength inherent in the study of Torah that it can affect even sinners: שֶׁהַמָּאוֹר שֶׁבָּהּ מַחֲזִירָן לְמוּטָב, *for the spiritual illumination within it will bring them back to righteousness (Yerushalmi Chagigah* 1:7). Torah represents the Jews' capacity to fight the war against evil. Compared to the absolutely vital nature of Israel's adherence to the *study* of Torah, the important struggles to strengthen observance of individual commandments take on the nature of skirmishes in a constant battle. Skirmishes are significant, but they are not equivalent to the life-and-death struggle to defend the indispensable capacity to continue fighting.

But Not Torah

Satan is like a chief-of-staff planning his overall strategy. He prefers not to lose a division, a platoon, not even a sentry. But he knows that some losses are inevitable. And he knows further that no victory matters more than one that destroys the heart of the enemy's fighting ability. That being so, he will be prepared to allow the enemy spectacular advances and victories, as long as they do not interfere with the overall strategy.

This attitude is not limited to the military field. All large and most small enterprises operate in the same manner. A country undertakes measures to improve its standard of living or overcome economic reverses. No policy can be successful in every area; the intelligent, strong leader is ready to accept hardship, as long as he is convinced that the long-term goals will be met. Parents decide how they wish to raise their children. Whatever course they choose will require at least some agony along the way, but if they re-order their goals every time their child faces a painful obstacle, they will merely trade one difficulty for another and sacrifice the goal in the long run. Satan has a goal, as well. The goal is to destroy Israel's capacity to achieve God's purpose. Can Satan succeed without a single defeat? No intelligent general expects that, nor does Satan. So he adopts the wise course of assigning priorities to his objectives. What are his priorities?

The *Chofetz Chaim* used to say, 'The Evil Inclination doesn't mind if a Jew fasts, weeps, and prays all day long — provided he does not study Torah!'

Abraham represented kindness and Isaac represented service. Those are mighty pillars of the world (*Avos* 1:2), but they are not the crucial ones. Jacob represented Torah — and without Torah, the battle is lost.

Too many tragic eras in our history bear this out. In many countries, Jews contributed heroically to every manner of charity — food, clothing, health care, recreation, social services. They erected magnificent synagogues and maintained ancient traditions of lengthy and fervid services. But they failed to invest equivalent dedication in Torah institutions. The result was a steady erosion in the quality of their Jewish life — all too often ending in near total assimilation. Such Jewish communities fell by the wayside. Only communities that put primary emphasis on Torah study for adults and Torah education for children were able to survive and thrive despite exile and the blandishments of surrounding society.

Only communities that put primary emphasis on Torah study for adults and Torah education for children were able to survive and thrive.

Jacob, as the personification of Torah striving and achievement, *had* to be the prime target of Satan.

Students and Patrons

Although the angel could not defeat Jacob, he succeeded in injuring his thigh. Like so much else in the lives of the Patriarchs, this was portentious of the nation's future. The thigh symbolizes two categories:

(a) because it is in the area of the reproductive organs, it alludes to future generations, and (b) because the body is supported by its legs, Jacob's thigh represents the factors that provide support to Torah institutions. Jacob — and in turn the future nation — was shown that Satan would not rest. He had failed to defeat Jacob, but he would have a measure of future success in these two areas.

Times would come — and have *come — when Jacob's ideal, Torah education, would be under siege. Jacob's offspring would be torn from their dedication to Torah.*

Times would come — and *have* come — when Jacob's ideal, Torah education, would be under siege. Jacob's offspring would be torn from their dedication to Torah. A variety of challenges and temptations would arise to 'prove' to them that other activities and other forms of intellectual stimulation were more desirable. Jewish philanthropy, the strong, muscular legs that had supported Torah in all its wanderings, would look around and see 'better' places for its largesse. Funds which should have flowed to Torah institutions would be directed toward causes that would seem to be 'more worthwhile.'

These new courses of action would seem to be not only eminently logical, but utterly compelling. Such are the wiles of Satan that he is most powerful when he does not mount frontal assaults. The *Vilna Gaon* teaches that the people are most vulnerable to sin under two conditions, both of which do not appear to be open rebellions against God's will. Sometimes, Satan's course will be presented as a *mitzvah*, as the greatest benefit for the individual and the community. Or, one may know that his course is wrong, but he may be swept along by a powerful tide of general practice and opinion. Can — dare — someone antagonize his neighbors and community for the sake of conscience? Shouldn't conscience move over for the sake of peace and general acceptance? Such have been the arguments that attack Jacob's thigh — his Torah students and their supporters — at various times throughout history, and especially when the potential for Exile's end draws closer and closer *(Even Shlomo).*

Shouldn't conscience move over for the sake of peace and general acceptance?

II. Duplicitous Kidnapper

In Two Guises

ר׳ שְׁמוּאֵל בַּר נַחְמָנִי אָמַר: כְּעוֹבֵד כּוֹכָבִים נִדְמָה לוֹ ... רָבָא בַּר עוּלָּא אָמַר: כְּתַלְמִיד חָכָם נִדְמָה לוֹ

R' Shmuel bar Nachmani said: [The angel] seemed like an idolator [to Jacob] ... Rava bar Ula said: He seemed like a Torah scholar to him (Chullin 91a*).*

The seductive power of Esau's angel was an element of the very first confrontation with Jacob. An enemy as powerful as an Esau, and certainly an angel with the powerful force of evil behind him, would be a formidable enough adversary for Jacob. Certainly the millenia-long struggle between Jacob and Esau that was portended by that struggle at Jabbok would have been terrifying enough for Jacob's descendants even if we were to know the evil nature of the enemy. But we don't.

His role is to convince Israel to neglect its mission by whatever means may be effective.

Jacob saw someone in front of him. It was an angel in human form, but in what guise did he appear? The *Talmud* gives two versions: He may have appeared in the form of an idolator seeking to attack everything Jacob stood for, or he may have appeared as a Torah scholar sharing Jacob's very own goals. The two viewpoints of the *Talmud* are not in conflict. Esau's angel *does* appear in both forms. His role is to convince Israel to neglect its mission by whatever means may be effective. He may bare his fangs as a bitter enemy seeking to uproot all of Israel's values, like Rome in R' Akiva's time, Spain with its Inquisition, Russia with its czars and commissars, Germany with its Crusades and Holocaust. Or he may come with a smile and a kiss as Esau did when he finally met Jacob, and as other nations have done with the expressed or implied message: 'Come join us and become part of us. Tear down your walls of separation and we shall demolish our ghettoes. Our schools, businesses, agencies, and homes are open to you. The world we share is too small for us to be divided.'

The name of Esau's angel alludes to this dual identity, this mixture of good and evil. His name is סַמָאֵל, *Samael,* a combination of the two words סַם, *poison,* and אֵל, *a Godly angel.* The angel of evil is indeed both, and because he is, he varies his methods to suit the needs of the situation. When he confronted Jacob he came as both, but when Jacob defeated him, he dropped his guise of the fearsome idolator and adopted the pose of the angel insisting that Jacob release him to sing God's praises. Moreover, he insisted, as *Rashi* notes [see *comm.*] that from that moment of his creation, he had been awaiting this very dawn, the very first time he was to be given the privilege of praising God. This, too, was part of his ruse; having lost, let him lull the *tzaddik* with protestations of innocence and friendship, until the time was ripe to strike again.

The angel of evil is indeed both, and because he is, he varies his methods to suit the needs of the situation.

When the angel begged for permission to leave, Jacob restrained him saying derisively, קוּבְיוּסְטוּס אַתָּה?, *are you a kidnapper* [*that you fear the light of day*]? *(ibid., Rashi).* Jacob's choice of invective was most apt. The angel was indeed a kidnapper who, having failed in his primary goal of subjugating Jacob himself sought to inflict mortal damage on the Jewish future by contaminating Jewish children. This he symbolized by the wound he inflicted on Jacob — he wrenched loose the area of the body from which new generations are born. Truly have our Sages seen throughout the ages that the main battleground between Jacob and Esau, between good and evil, is the Jewish child. Jacob spent a lifetime of preparation, hard labor, and exile to produce a generation that was totally righteous; Esau's angel sought, seeks, and *will* seek until the End of Days to uproot it by anger or by guile, by cruelty or by generosity, by the lash or by the kiss *(Sh'lah HaKadosh, Vayishlach).*

The angel was indeed a kidnapper who, having failed in his primary goal of subjugating Jacob himself, sought to inflict mortal damage on the Jewish future by contaminating Jewish children.

The Sinew and the Day

The masters of Kabbalah have taught that the 248 positive commandments and the 248 organs and limbs [רְמַ״ח אֵבָרִים] are physical manifestations of higher spiritual entities. Each *mitzvah* provides the spiritual sustenance of a specific part of the body and, in turn, the good deed and the limb performing its function have beneficial effects on high. The 365 negative commandments, like the number of major sinews and blood vessels [שְׁסָ"ה גִידִין] and the 365 days of the solar year, are earthly manifestations of 365 spiritual forces of strict judgment. The observance of a particular negative commandment has the effect of restraining the destructive effect of Heavenly judgment on its particular day of the year.

The 365 negative commandments, like the number of major sinews and blood vessels and the 365 days of the solar year, are earthly manifestations of 365 spiritual forces of strict judgment.

Which day is intertwined with the commandment not to eat גִיד הַנָּשֶׁה, *the Sinew of the thigh?* According to the Kabbalah, that day is *Tishah B'Av*, the day of Jewish suffering. Samael, the angel of evil, tried every possibility to harm Jacob. Nowhere could he succeed except in that one place — his success meant that the Ninth of Av had been touched and contaminated by the forces of evil. Having fallen, at least to a degree, under the sway of evil, *Tishah B'Av* became prey to the forces of judgment throughout the ages [see *Overview* to ArtScroll *Eichah*] *(Sh'lah HaKadosh, Vayishlach).*

It may well be that the sources of these destructions lay in the angel's ability to affect Jacob's progeny. Only if Torah students and their patrons are swayed by Satan can *Tishah B'Av* be his day of joyful triumph. Let those who study and those who support them be weakened in their loyalty to the Torah represented by Jacob and tears will continue to flow. But let them be loyal to Torah and Satan will have no sway. May the sacrifices endured by Jacob to produce his own perfect generations be translated into the new generations that will forever remove the blemish of the sinew and the tragedy-laden day it inaugurated.

But let them be loyal to Torah and Satan will have no sway.

— *Rabbi Nosson Scherman*

סדר וישלח
Sidrah Vayishlach

ד וַיִּשְׁלַח יַעֲקֹב מַלְאָכִים לְפָנָיו אֶל־עֵשָׂו
ה אָחִיו אַרְצָה שֵׂעִיר שְׂדֵה אֱדוֹם: וַיְצַו

SIDRAH VAYISHLACH

4. Jacob dispatches angels to Esau.

This episode is recorded to illustrate how God sent an angel to save His servant from the hand of a stronger enemy. Furthermore, it shows that Jacob did not rely on his own righteousness, but strove mightily, by taking *practical* measures to ensure his safety ...

Additionally, the story applies to future generations, since everything that happened to Jacob with his brother Esau foreshadows the future experiences of Israel with Esau's descendants. [This is consistent with *Ramban's* view that the events in the lives of the Patriarchs presaged events that would occur to their descendants (cf. *footnote* to 12:6, p. 436).] Accordingly, we should follow his example by making a threefold preparation in our struggles with Esau's descendants [=Edom; an allusion to the nations in whose lands we are currently exiled]: through the means of **prayer** (see *v.* 10); **gifts** [=appeasement] (see *v.* 13); and **battle** (see *v.* 9) as shall be noted in the commentary *(Ramban).*

וַיִּשְׁלַח יַעֲקֹב מַלְאָכִים לְפָנָיו – *Then* [lit. *and*] *Jacob sent angels ahead of him.*

In order to simultaneously impress and terrify Esau *(Midrash).*

The word מַלְאָכִים may equally refer to *angels* or *human emissaries.* The translation *angels* follows *Rashi.*

Rashi's view that Jacob sent actual *angels* follows an opinion in the *Midrash.* This is supported by the continuity of the narrative, since in the previous verses מַלְאָכִים refers to the *angels* who had come to escort Jacob. He apparently dispatched some of *these* angels. This is suggested by the apparently superfluous לְפָנָיו, *ahead of him* [lit. *before him*] a word which does not occur in parallel passages which speak of *human* emissaries, as for example: *Numbers* 20:14, 21:21; *Josh.* 7:22; *Judges* 9:31. Accordingly, לְפָנָיו implies that he selected from those מַלְאָכִים who were *before him* — i.e., the *aforementioned accompanying angels* (Cf. *Mizrachi; Gur Aryeh; Levush; Tzeidah laDerech; Kli Yakar).*

R' Bachya suggests that we may infer that they were *angels* from *v.* 7 which states that *the 'malachim' returned,* without even having mentioned that they left — suggesting that they accomplished their mission in a fleeting moment as only angels can; they had hardly left when they returned.

Ibn Ezra, Radak, and *Ralbag* following the other view in the *Midrash* — and apparently also *Onkelos* who does not render מַלְאָכַיָּא, *angels,* but אִזְגַּדִּין, *runners, messengers* — explain that these were *human* emissaries selected from among Jacob's servants.

According to one opinion in *Tanchuma,* Jacob wanted to dispatch *human* emissaries to meet Esau. All of Jacob's men, however, were afraid to accept the mission. Jacob therefore sent angels [possibly ministering angels, to escort the human emissaries *(Etz Yosef).*]

This teaches that the righteous are greater than even the ministering angels, for when Jacob had a mission to accomplish he summoned ministering angels and they performed his bidding *(Tanchuma).*

Jacob allowed himself to dispatch angels because he viewed God's having sent him these angels for no apparent reason at that moment as a Providential sign that they were intended for this very purpose *(Midrash; Akeidas Yitzchak).*

4 Then Jacob sent angels ahead of him to Esau his brother to the land of Seir, the field of Edom.

אֶל עֵשָׂו אָחִיו — *To Esau his brother.*

Though he was *Esau,* he was still *his brother* [and Jacob hoped he would treat him as such] *(Midrash).*

⇐§Why did Jacob risk rekindling old hatred by initiating this contact?

According to *Ramban,* since Isaac lived in the southern part of Canaan [see 24:62] near Edom, Jacob had to pass through or near Edom on his return journey [see comm. to *v.* 1]. He feared that Esau would learn of his presence, and he therefore took the *initiative* of sending messengers to conciliate him. The Sages in the *Midrash* criticized Jacob for 'taking the dog by the ears' [since apparently Jacob could have taken a different route and avoided Esau entirely]: '... Esau was going about his business and you send him messengers to say, "Thus said your servant Jacob." [By so doing, of your own accord you make yourself his servant]!' *Ramban* observes additionally that the Hasmonean kings similarly brought about the downfall of the Jewish state during the Second Temple by sending ambassadors to seek a political alliance with Rome [=Edom]. The result was that Rome took control of the country.

According to the *Zohar,* Jacob took the initiative in attempting a reconciliation *now* because he felt that it would be advantageous to confront the situation while Isaac was still alive. Esau had great respect for their father — Jacob reasoned — and would never do anything to grieve him [see 27:41].

Following the selection from *Sefer HaYashar* cited in the *footnote* to *v.* 1, Jacob's action was not at his *own* initiative but in compliance with the advice of his mother's delegation which had warned him of Esau's rekindled intentions to kill him. [This also explains how Jacob knew of Esau's whereabouts.]

Abarbanel suggests that Jacob met a caravan traveling north from Seir. They apprised him that Esau had fortified himself with four hundred men and was preparing a military action against him. [These members of the caravan, according to *Abarbanel,* were the מַלְאֲכֵי אֱלֹהִים, *(human) emissaries of God,* referred to above. Jacob considered them to have been dispatched by God because they forewarned him. Accordingly, he sent emissaries to intercept Esau and assuage him.]

אַרְצָה שֵׂעִיר — *To the land of Seir.*

[The region encompassing the mountainous regions from the Dead Sea southward toward the Gulf of Aqaba. It was the home of Esau and his Edomite descendants (see 14:6). This was the fertile land alluded to in Isaac's blessing (see *Radak* cited in 27:39).]

The word אַרְצָה is synonymous with לָאָרֶץ, *to the land.* The ל prefix [to indicate *to*], is often replaced in Scripture with the suffix ה. [Thus: לַחוּץ=חוּצָה; לְמִצְרַיִם=מִצְרַיְמָה] *(Rashi* citing *Yevamos* 13b).

שְׂדֵה אֱדוֹם — *The field of Edom.*

I.e., to the particular region of the land of Seir that was inhabited by Esau [=Edom (see 25:30; 36:8)]. It was referred to as the *field* [=region or plain] *of Edom,* to distinguish it from the other regions of Seir which were still inhabited by the Seirites.

Originally, Seir the Horite inhabited the entire land named after him [see 14:6; 36:20]. At about this time Esau went to Seir, which was noted for its excellent hunting grounds, and dwelt in the *plain* — here referred to as the *field* of Edom — apparently because the inhabitants of the fortified mountain of Seir would not let him settle higher

אֹתָם לֵאמֹר כֹּה תֹאמְרוּן לַאדֹנִי לְעֵשָׂו
כֹּה אָמַר עַבְדְּךָ יַעֲקֹב עִם־לָבָן גַּרְתִּי

up. Esau's children and wives, however, remained in Canaan, and Esau would commute between these residences in order to honor his father and to supply his needs. After Jacob returned to Canaan, Esau moved his whole family to Seir. Eventually he conquered the entire region — including Mount Seir — driving away the Horites and making it his principal residence [36:8]. It remained Esau's possession by Divine sanction [see *Deut.* 2:5; 2:21] *(Midrash Aggadas Bereishis; Ramban* to 36:6; *Sforno* here; *Haamek Davar).*

Chizkuni suggests that Esau obtained this region as a dowry when he married Oholibamah, a great-granddaughter of Seir [see 36:20-25]. It was referred to as *field* to allude to Esau's vocation as a *man of the field* [25:27] and hunter.

Although the *field of Edom* was not yet, as noted, Esau's *permanent* residence, Jacob was apparently aware that Esau visited there regularly, and would now be there *(HaRechasim leBik'ah).*

5. וַיְצַו אֹתָם לֵאמֹר — [*And*] *he charged them as follows* [lit. *to say*]:

Jacob told his messengers לֵאמֹר, to give the following message *verbatim,* in his name, so Esau would realize that the message was exactly as Jacob had uttered it, and that the emissaries were adding nothing of their own *(Or HaChaim).*[1]

[The general intent of Jacob's message, as we shall see, is to appease Esau. Jacob attempts in subtle ways to impress Esau that he had not benefited from his purchase of the birthright or from Isaac's blessing. Jacob still renders him the honor due an older brother, and Esau's continued hatred is therefore unjustified. Jacob tries to represent himself, his experiences, and his condition as insignificant.]

כֹּה תֹאמְרוּן לַאדֹנִי לְעֵשָׂו — *Thus shall you say, 'To my lord, to Esau.'*

The punctuation of the translation follows *Radak* and *Or HaChaim* who comment that it was Jacob's intention that his emissaries make clear to Esau that he, Jacob, always referred to him as 'my lord, Esau.'

Ramban suggests that Jacob commanded them to begin their message by saying these words: *'To my lord Esau.'* Jacob meant for them to imply: 'We are our lord Esau's' — i.e., 'we belong to our lord Esau', or: 'we were dispatched to our lord Esau'. Support for this interpretation is in *v.* 18 where Jacob ordered his people to answer Esau's questions regarding the the lavish gift by saying: '... *it is a present sent to my lord Esau'.* Thus, Jacob wanted Esau to understand that he was held in the highest esteem and respect by Jacob and his entire retinue.

... By recording this, the Torah

1. *Midrash Lekach Tov* understands לֵאמֹר, *to say,* as implying that the passage contains a message for future generations as well: *To say* — i.e., to future generations that [in their dealings with Esau's descendants] they should, in a figurative sense, not stand stiffly in front of the approaching wave, for whoever does so will be engulfed; rather they should bend, for if one bends the wave will pass over him. [Comp. exegesis to לֵאמֹר in 28:20 and parallels cited there.]

[5] *He charged them as follows: 'Thus shall you say,*
"To my lord Esau. So said your servant Jacob: I have
lodged with Laban and have lingered until now. [6] *I*

teaches that one must accord honor to royalty *(R' Bachya).*

Alternately, the phrase *'to my lord, to Esau'* was not part of what the emissaries directly quoted, but Jacob's third person reference to his brother. Jacob referred to Esau gratuitously as *my lord* in the presence of his emissaries to impress upon them Esau's commanding position so that they, in turn, would address him accordingly *(Ibn Ezra).* Furthermore, by referring to Esau as *'my lord,'* Jacob cautioned them indirectly not to speak of Esau in any but a respectful manner *even when not in his presence (Ramban).*

עַבְדְּךָ יַעֲקֹב — *Your servant Jacob.*

Jacob paid Esau this honor by referring to him as *my lord* and to himself as *your servant.* Jacob emphasized thereby that notwithstanding the transfer of the birthright and Isaac's blessings — the reasons for Esau's hatred — the younger brother still honored the older brother [see *Kesubos* 103a and *comm.* to *Exodus* 20:12]. Accordingly, the implication was that Esau had no cause to hate him since Jacob did not consider the sale to be binding *(Ramban).*[1]

Jacob was basically sincere in this matter; already earlier he had decided to leave the benefit of the blessing to his descendants, and to reserve it as a legacy for the future *(Zohar).*

The Sages in the *Midrash* nevertheless took Jacob to task for demeaning himself before his wicked brother Esau:

When Jacob called Esau 'my lord' the Holy One, Blessed be He said to him: 'You have abased yourself and referred to Esau as *my lord* eight times. I will accordingly raise up eight kings of *his* descendants before *your* descendants [will have their first king]!' (See genealogy in 36:31).

[See also *Midrash* cited by *Ramban* in *v.* 4, and *footnote* to 25:23 (page 1057): Because Jacob so utterly demeaned himself notwithstanding God's promise that *the elder shall serve the younger* (25:23), God caused his words to materialize — Esau's descendants dominate Jacob's in this world, while Jacob's will dominate Esau's in the World to Come.]

עִם־לָבָן גַּרְתִּי — *I have lodged with Laban.*

The verb גַּרְתִּי, *lodged,* implies staying as a *stranger* [גֵּר=*alien*].

— I was but an *alien* and had no

1. R' Yehudah the Prince, the president of the *Sanhedrin,* once instructed R'Afes to write a letter in his name to the Roman Emperor Antoninus.

R' Afes began the letter with the words: 'From Judah the Prince to our lord the Emperor Antoninus.'

When R' Yehudah read the letter, he tore it up and wrote instead: 'From *your servant Yehudah* to our lord the Emperor Antoninus.'

'Why do you treat your honor so lightly?' R'Afes asked.

'Am I better than the Patriarch Jacob?,' R' Yehudah countered. 'Did he not instruct his men to say, thus said *your servant* Jacob?' *(Midrash).*

R' Bachya adds that when Antoninus received the letter he responded, 'Are you then my servant? If only I could be *your* servant in the World to Come!'

— 'No,' R' Yehudah replied. 'Neither am I greater than my ancestor [Jacob], nor are you less worthy than your ancestor [Esau], for Jacob similarly sent to Esau saying, *Thus said your servant Jacob.'*

ו וְאֵחַר עַד־עָתָּה: וַיְהִי־לִי שׁוֹר וַחֲמוֹר
צֹאן וְעֶבֶד וְשִׁפְחָה וָאֶשְׁלְחָה לְהַגִּיד
ז לַאדֹנִי לִמְצֹא־חֵן בְּעֵינֶיךָ: וַיָּשֻׁבוּ

rest. Indeed, *by day I was consumed by the scorching heat, and at night by the frost* [31:40] *(Lekach Tov).*

I have become neither a great prince nor have I achieved status ... I remained merely an alien. Therefore, you need not hate me for Father's blessing [27:29]: *Be a lord to your kinsmen,* since it has not been fulfilled in me. Another interpretation: the numerical value of the word גַּרְתִּי equals תרי״ג, 613, as if to intimate: *Though I have lodged* (גַּרְתִּי) *with Laban,* I have observed תַּרְיַ״ג מִצְוֹת, *the 613 Divine Commandments,* and have not learned from his evil ways *(Rashi).*

Both interpretations offered by *Rashi* are not mutually exclusive, but complement one another: The blessings have been ineffective for me; I achieved no prominence in spite of them but remained merely a גֵּר, *alien,* throughout my long period with Laban. However, do not think that the blessings were ineffective because I was not worthy; on the contrary: תַּרְיַ״ג מִצְוֹת שָׁמַרְתִּי, *I observed all 613 precepts,* while with Laban, and I *still* remained but a גֵּר, *alien.* Obviously, then, father's blessing can rest only upon you for whom they were originally intended. Therefore, you have no further cause to hate me *(Kli Yakar).*

Minchah Belulah interprets Jacob's allusion to the 613 commandments as an indirect way of conveying another message to Esau: 'Isaac promised you that if I fail to observe the Torah, you will throw off my yoke (see 27:40). Do not trifle with me, Esau, for I remain loyal to the commandments.'

That Jacob married two sisters does not conflict with his describing himself here as fulfilling all 613 precepts — which included the prohibition of such marriages [*Lev.* 18:18]. Since Jacob undertook these marriages with Divine sanction, in effect, even this was in compliance with the Torah *(Gur Aryeh).*

Levush holds that having been weaned from their father's idolatrous ways, Rachel and Leah were considered as converts, who have the halachic status of newborn children without former familial ties. Thus they were not *legally* sisters when Jacob married them. [See *comm.* on page 1083: *'To what extent the Patriarchs observed the Torah'*, and Gur Aryeh's *comm.* on page 1084. Cf. also footnotes to 29:28, and to 35:19.]

[Regarding Jacob's anxiety over having been absent from *Eretz Yisrael* and deprived of the *mitzvah* of honoring his parents (noted in the *Midrash* and *Da'as Zekeinim* to *v.* 8), we might conjecture that since his initial departure was at his parents' command, even in his absence he may be regarded as having honored them, and hence rightfully claim that he observed all 613 *mitzvos.* However, it is difficult to reconcile this with the fact that because of his staying away from his father's service, Jacob was punished with the similar extended absence of his beloved son Joseph. רצ״ע.]

Chemdos HaYamim explains the application of Jacob's remark to be: I accept upon my posterity the obligation to observe all 613 commandments.

According to *Rashbam: 'I have been staying with Laban* — as you know, at the command of Father and Mother.' Jacob said this so that Esau should not think that he had fled because of him.

Alshich interprets the connotation to be: 'Do not think I am merely a naive tent-dweller! I survived these twenty years with the rogue Laban!'

וָאֵחַר עַד־עָתָּה — *And [I] have lingered until now.*

— Therefore I have not come to pay my respects to you sooner *(Sforno).*

have acquired oxen and donkeys, sheep, servants, and maidservants and I am sending to tell my lord to gain favor in your eyes."'

Until now — that is, until Joseph, Esau's adversary, was born *(Tanchuma)*. [For as noted in the *comm.* to 30:25, it was only after the birth of Joseph whom Jacob prophetically saw was destined to be Esau's adversary, that Jacob felt he could safely return home and brave Esau's wrath.]

R' Hirsch comments that Jacob was informing Esau that his living and working conditions with Laban were so unreasonably difficult that he had to struggle for twenty years before he could accumulate whatever possessions he now had. Esau should recognize, therefore, that this twenty-year history should be sufficient atonement for any past grievances he had been nursing.

6. וַיְהִי־לִי שׁוֹר וַחֲמוֹר צֹאן וְעֶבֶד וְשִׁפְחָה — *[And] I have acquired* [lit. *there was to me*] *oxen and donkeys, sheep, servants and maidservants.*

My father blessed me with *the dew of the heavens and the fatness of the earth* [27:28] — but my human and animal possessions come from neither heaven or earth [so, in effect, the presence of these flocks does not negate my earlier contention that Father's blessings have not been fulfilled; these possessions did not come to me as a result of his *blessings* so there is no longer any reason for you to hate me on account of them] *(Rashi).*

All the Hebrew nouns in this passage are in the singular: *an ox and a donkey ... a servant and a maidservant.* The translation of the terms in *plural* follows *Rashi* who understands these in the *collective* sense as referring to many. For as the *Midrash* notes, in colloquial Hebrew, people refer to many *oxen* by the singular collective term: *ox.* Similarly, one does not say, 'The cocks crowed during the night,' but 'the cock crowed'.[1]

וָאֶשְׁלְחָה לְהַגִּיד לַאדֹנִי — *And I am sending to tell* [*to*] *my lord.*

[I.e., and I am sending this group of emissaries] to inform you that I am coming to you *(Rashi).*

[See alternate interpretations below.]

לִמְצֹא חֵן בְּעֵינֶיךָ — *To gain favor in your eyes.*

For I am at peace with you and seek your friendship *(Rashi).*

Rashi's intent is that the elliptic phrase *I am sending to tell my lord* is unrelated to the above report of Jacob's wealth. Rather it connects with the later phrase: To *gain favor in your eyes* — the sense being: I am sending to inform my lord that I am coming to gain your favor, and to

1. Verse 15 below specifically indicates that Jacob had *many* oxen and donkeys. That Jacob used the *singular* in describing his wealth is additionally viewed as a matter of etiquette: The righteous always minimize their assets while the wicked always boast about their possessions. Compare Esau's remark [32:9]: *I have plenty.* This tendency is expressed in *Proverbs* 33:9: *Some pretend to be rich but have nothing; while some pretend to be poor yet possess great wealth (Tanchuma).*

At the same time, the extent of the possessions is subtly left undefined through the use of these singular nouns with the force of collectives *(Tzeidah laDerech).*

הַמַּלְאָכִים אֶל־יַעֲקֹב לֵאמֹר בָּאנוּ אֶל־
אָחִיךָ אֶל־עֵשָׂו וְגַם הֹלֵךְ לִקְרָאתְךָ
ח וְאַרְבַּע־מֵאוֹת אִישׁ עִמּוֹ: וַיִּירָא יַעֲקֹב

do whatever you command (*Ramban*).

In his advancing his own opinion however, *Ramban* disagrees, suggesting that the passage reverts to the preceding phrase which describes Jacob's wealth. The sense is: *'I am sending to tell my lord* that I own all of these possessions *to gain your favor* — for you may do with them as you desire.' He thereby intimated that he would send Esau gifts from these possessions. Thus, when Esau later asked [33:8]: *'What do you mean by that whole camp that I met?,'* Jacob answered: *'To find favor in the eyes of my lord.'*

Sforno, too, interprets that the news of Jacob's *aforementioned wealth* is the subject of the passage: *'I have acquired oxen and donkeys* ... and *I am sending to tell my lord* [about my wealth] *to find favor in your eyes* — for I am confident that you will be pleased to hear of my good fortune, and that I would find favor by telling you this.'

For as *Be'er Yitzchak* notes, the only thing by which Jacob could have hoped to impress the materialistic Esau, was by his wealth.

— Since Jacob proclaimed himself Esau's *servant,* and it is known that 'whatever property a servant acquires belongs to his master,' Esau would surely be thrilled to learn that his 'servant' has many possessions (*Kli Yakar*).

Another reason Jacob mentioned his wealth was that he did not want his brother Esau to suspect that these emissaries were dispatched to him because Jacob was impoverished and really wanted alms. Jacob therefore instructed them to mention his wealth *at the outset* so Esau would understand that Jacob was independently wealthy and the mission was a sincere one (*Kol Yehudah*).

7. וַיָּשֻׁבוּ הַמַּלְאָכִים אֶל־יַעֲקֹב לֵאמֹר — [*And*] *the angels* [see *v.* 4] *returned to Jacob, saying.*

We may take it for granted that they carried out their mission, but it was unnecessary for the Torah to relate more details than necessary (*Ramban; cf. however, Ramban's* own opinion cited below).

The Torah mentions *they returned* without first informing us that *they went. R' Bachya* writes that this omission proves that they were *angels* and in effect accomplished their mission instantaneously. Since in a sense, they returned as soon as they left, there was no need to mention their departure. These myriads of angels were disguised as royal troops, the *Midrash* records. Some were clad in armor, others were horsemen, others were charioteers. All with one goal: To frighten Esau.

בָּאנוּ אֶל אָחִיךָ אֶל עֵשָׂו — *We came to your brother, to Esau.*

We came to this person whom you regard as a *brother,* but who behaves toward you as a wicked *Esau* — he still harbors hatred (*Midrash; Rashi*).

In addressing Jacob, the emis-

[7] *The angels returned to Jacob saying, 'We came to*
your brother, to Esau. Moreover, he is heading
toward you, and four hundred men are with him.'
[8] *Jacob became very frightened, and it distressed*

saries did not refer to Esau as *your lord Esau* for it is disrespectful for a servant to use the expression 'your lord' when addressing his master. Compare the etiquette of the rabbi-student relationship noted in *Rosh Hashanah* 31b: It is not polite for students to say to their teacher, 'your teacher' *(Haamek Davar).*

וְגַם הֹלֵךְ לִקְרָאתְךָ — *Moreover* [lit. *and also*] *he is heading* [lit. *going*] *toward you.*

The actual exchange between the angelic emissaries and Esau is not recorded. *Ramban* [*v.* 8] conjectures that Esau did not even receive the emissaries *personally,* but ignored them; for had an exchange taken place the Torah would surely have recorded Esau's response concerning his intentions, etc.* Evidently, Esau still bore Jacob a grudge and was waiting for an opportunity to take his revenge, and for this purpose took along his army. It was from their inquiries in the camp that the emissaries learned this. This is the force of וְגַם, *and moreover,* — i.e., *We came to your brother,* and he did not acknowledge us, *and moreover he is heading toward you* with might and an army.' This of course only intensified Jacob's misgivings. The text therefore notes [next verse] that *Jacob became very frightened and it distressed him.* [That Esau's intentions in coming to Jacob were to wage war also follows the opinion of the Sages and is implicit in *Rashi* and most commentators.]

Radak similarly observes that since Esau was coming with a force of *four hundred men* his intentions were certainly not peaceful. *Sforno* concurs, and draws a parallel from *Numbers* 20:20 **וַיֵּצֵא אֱדוֹם לִקְרָאתוֹ** בְּעַם כָּבֵד, *Edom went out* **toward** [=against] **him** *with a massive force.*

וְאַרְבַּע־מֵאוֹת אִישׁ עִמּוֹ — *And four hundred men are with him.*

Esau brought four hundred men as a smokescreen. Should Jacob be killed or injured, Esau would be able to disassociate himself from his men's action, and disclaim responsibility for the massacre. Compare the czars of today [18th century Russia] who 'innocently' feign ignorance of the spontaneous 'unplanned' pogroms by their populace *(Tiferes Yonasan).*

8. וַיִּירָא יַעֲקֹב מְאֹד וַיֵּצֶר לוֹ — [*And*] *Jacob became very frightened, and it distressed him.*

He heard that Esau had sent no message of goodwill, and what is more (וְגַם), was coming to meet him with a force of four hundred men. He knew that Esau's purpose in taking the four hundred men was to wage war against him so he feared greatly for his life *(Ramban).*

In the literal sense, the repetition

*[Thus, *Ramban's own* opinion of what occurred — that Esau did not give the emissaries a proper welcome and possibly did not even allow them to come into his presence — differs from his earlier *general* observation that the emissaries surely fulfilled their mission but the Torah found it pointless to relate the details.]

frightened ... distressed emphasizes the intensity of Jacob's fear (*Radak*).

Jacob's fear was such that his limbs became soft as wax (*Tanchuma Yashan*).

However, according to *Rashi,* following the *Midrashim,* the double phraseology describes different emotions:

He became very frightened — lest he be slain; *and it distressed him* — that he might be compelled to slay others (*Rashi*). For it was obvious to Jacob that if a battle would ensue, each of them would have to slay or be slain (*Midrash*).

Distress is a stronger emotion than *fear.* The thought that he might be compelled to kill pained Jacob even more than the thought that he himself might be killed (*Ralbag*).

Why — following *Rashi's* interpretation — was Jacob distressed at the thought that he might slay the wicked Esau if forced into battle? — Because he might thereby incur the wrath of Isaac who was still fond of Esau (*Tanchuma;* cf. *Mizrachi*).

Furthermore, though it may be argued that Jacob's action in killing Esau — or even his men — would be in self-defense, he was distressed at the circumstances which would cause him to kill. As the Sages note: מְגַלְגְלִין חוֹבָה עַל יְדֵי חַיָּיב, *Guilt is brought about through an evil* [lit. *guilty*] *person.* [If he were thrust into a situation where he had to kill someone, it would tend to prove that he, too, was an evil person; otherwise he would not be put into such a position] (*Divrei David*). [Cf. similar apprehension in ArtScroll *Jonah* 4:1.]

According to the *Midrash* and *Daas Zekeinim: He became very frightened* — since he was apprehensive that Esau would be fortified with the merit of having honored his father and mother these past twenty years, while Jacob had not. [Though Jacob had gone with the consent of his parents, he might have overstayed the intended time.] Furthermore, Jacob became very frightened at the thought that Esau would come fortified with the merit of having dwelt in *Eretz Yisrael* while he had lived outside the Land.

... *It distressed him.* That is, the very fact that *he became very frightened* of the approaching Esau distressed him since he had received assurances from God [31:3], and such fear would imply a lack of trust. For the pious Jacob felt that in the wake of God's promise, he should have feared no mortal, as Isaiah prophesied (*Isaiah* 54:12): *I* (God), *I am He that comforts you — who are you that you should be afraid of mortal man ... and have forgotten HASHEM?* That he *did* experience fear distressed him for he felt that he would be held accountable for his lack of trust, and no miracle would be performed for him. He therefore took to prayer and natural precaution.

Alternatively, news of Esau's impending attack *distressed him* since Esau had initially said that he would wait till the days of his father's mourning would be at hand before he would avenge himself on Jacob [see 27:41]. Now that Jacob was informed of Esau's approach he was distressed for he interpreted it to mean that the aged Isaac had died. This explains why Jacob mentioned the God *of Isaac* in his ensuing prayer [*v.* 10], an appellation he would not have used had he thought his father to be still alive, since [as noted in the *comm.* to 31:42] God does not usually associate His Name with the living (*Daas Zekeinim*).

Mizrachi asks: Since Isaac *was* still alive, why did Esau seek to harm Jacob when he had disavowed the exercise of such vengeance during his father's lifetime? — He suggests that possibly, Esau's original intention was that he would refrain from violence while in Isaac's *proximity;* in this case, however they were far away from Isaac.

According to *Haamek Davar: it distressed him* — because he interpreted the wave of fear that swept him, to portend that trouble lay ahead. Possibly, Jacob became distressed at this news because he now realized from the turn of events that he had erred in dispatching conciliatory emissaries to Esau.

According to *Rashbam's* interpretation that the emissaries reported that Esau was coming in Jacob's honor and that his intentions were ostensibly peaceful, Jacob was mistrustful that no matter how peaceful Esau *appeared* to be, his intentions were really hostile.

The *Zohar* offers that God instilled this fearful response in Jacob, so that he would be drawn to prayer, since 'God yearns for the prayer of the righteous.' [See comm. to ArtScroll *Song of Songs* p. 111.]

☙ Forfeiture by sin.

Furthermore, as *Rashi* himself explains in *v.* 11 s.v. קָטֹנְתִּי [based on *Berachos* 4a and *Shabbos* 32a], Jacob's fear in this verse resulted from his apprehension that his sins of the last twenty years might have caused him to forfeit God's promises of protection. Thus, Jacob's fears were not indicative of a lack of trust in God, but rather a lack of confidence *in himself*, in his own worthiness for a miracle to be wrought on his behalf, and in his own righteous conduct. For, as the *Midrash* observes, there is no assurance for the righteous in this world.[1]

Alternatively, God's promise in 28:15 assured Jacob of God's protection until

1. **Prophetic promises and forfeiture by sin. / A synopsis.**

Several fundamental concepts emerge from *Rashi's* Midrashic interpretations here and in *v.* 11, and the commentators dwell extensively on them.

One may ask why Jacob felt such fear that he might be slain in view of God's earlier promise when he left his father [28:15]: *I am with you; I will guard you wherever you go — And I will return you to this soil; for I will not forsake you until I have done what I have spoken about you.*

— This question is discussed in the *Talmud* [*Berachos* 4a] and as noted in the commentary, the answer offered is that the righteous never take their virtue for granted. Jacob was therefore apprehensive that some sin he committed *after* having received God's promise might have caused him to forfeit that promise. As noted in the *comm.* above [*Midrash* and *Daas Zekeinim*] Jacob was anxious that for the past twenty years he had not honored his father and mother and had not lived in *Eretz Yisrael*, while Esau *had* both of these merits to fortify him. Compare also the suggestions offered by *Ramban* and *Kli Yakar* respectively that Jacob feared that he might have sinned by entering into a covenant with Laban and by flattering Esau. Abraham felt similar fears, and needed constant assurance that he had not become unworthy of God's blessings. See *footnote*, p. 507, and cf. *Rashi* and *Ramban* to verse 11 s.v. קָטֹנְתִּי and *Shabbos* 32a cited there.

Similarly, the *Midrash* remarks in its exposition on 28:20 [see *comm.* there]: Notwithstanding God's promise [28:15]: *I am with you*, Jacob said [ibid. *v.* 20], If *God will be with me.* — From here we learn that there is no guarantee for the righteous man in This World.

Consequently, Jacob knew that a Divine promise was not an inviolable decree that Hashem *must* honor irrespective of circumstances; it was liable to be cancelled should his deeds and conduct demand it.

What then of the seemingly contradictory dictum [*Berachos* 7a]: 'No word of blessing that issued from the mouth of the Holy One, Blessed be He, even if conditional, was ever withdrawn by Him'?

Rambam (Yesodei HaTorah 10:4, and preface to *Peirush HaMishnayos)* deals with this question at length. He explains that sin *may* cause God to withhold even a promise for good, but only when the promise was to remain a private communication between God and the prophet. If, however, it was communicated to the prophet for transmission to others as a good tiding, God would not withdraw it 'because otherwise there would be no way to establish the validity of prophecy [for if promises were always subject to change, a prophet's inaccuracy could never be held against him and he could never be established as a true prophet]. But the Holy One, Blessed be He, gave us as a principle of His Torah [see *Deut.* 18:21-22] that the prophet can be tested by the realization of his assurances.' This is evident from Jeremiah's dialogue with Hananiah, son of Azur, when the former prophesied evil while the latter prophesied good. Jeremiah said to Hananiah: If my words [prophesying *evil*] are not conhe reached the borders of *Eretz Yisrael* — which he had already done; the promise did not guarantee his safety until he reached his father's house *(Sifsei Chachomim).*

Additionally, there was no promise that this protection would extend to his children. Perhaps Esau would kill Jacob's young children, and God's promises regarding Jacob's descendants [28:15] would apply to other children who would be born after Jacob returned to *Eretz Yisrael (Ibn Ezra; Binnah leIttim).* [*Ramban* rejects this, maintaining that the promise would necessarily extend to his children; rather Jacob's apprehension was that he might have forfeited God's promise by sinfulness.]

⁂ What 'sin' could have made Jacob apprehensive?

Daas Zekeinim, cited above, mentions that for twenty years Jacob had not honored his parents, nor lived in the Holy Land.

However, all of these references to Jacob's apprehension over the possible loss of God's protection recall His promise of *twenty years earlier* when Jacob left Beersheba (28:15). But they do not explain the fact that only*a few days ago* God had *reiterated* [in 31:3] the essence of His promise to 'be' with Jacob! What grave sin could Jacob have committed *in these few days* to forfeit the renewed promise of God's protection?

firmed by events, that will not prove that I am a false prophet. But should your predictions [prophesying *good*] not be fulfilled, you will be proved a false prophet; as it is said: *Nevertheless listen to this word that I speak, ... the prophet that prophesied of peace* [i.e. good fortune] *when the word of the prophet shall come true, then shall the prophet be known that HASHEM really sent him.* [See *Jeremiah* 28:7-9.]

Therefore, the failure of such a prophecy to be realized proves that the prophet is a false one. But when he predicts *calamity,* the non-fulfillment of his forecast does not discredit him, since God in His mercy is relentful; or it may be that the sinners repented and were forgiven, as happened to the people of Nineveh. Or possibly the sentence was merely *deferred,* as in the case of Hezekiah.

This is akin to Jacob's case. God's word to Jacob had come as a personal promise — and no prophet's veracity was at stake. Hence Jacob's apprehension that as a result of some sin he might have forfeited that assurance.

There is, however, an exception to this rule that a private communication is contingent upon the possibility that sin may cause it to be nullified: When God promises a good thing, and guarantees it with a שְׁבוּעָה, *vow,* or בְּרִית, *covenant,* then there is no longer a doubt as to the outcome. [See *Ramban* to 15:7; also *Ohel David* II to *Psalms* 89:35).

Akeidas Yitzchak (gate 96) takes issue with *Ramban's* thesis that prophetic predictions for the good must unequivocally be fulfilled because of a passage in *Jeremiah* 18:9 (also see *Ramban* to 15:7; *Ralbag and Ibn Chasdai,* cited by *Akeidas Yitzchak). ... And at another time I speak concerning a nation ... to build and to plant ... but if it does evil in My sight, and does not obey My voice, then I repent of the good with which I said I would benefit them.* [Hence the implication that God could withdraw a promise for the good. *Rambam,* however, would interpret this verse that such withdrawal of a promise for good would not conflict with the general rule, because it had been a private communication to the prophet (see *Mizrachi;* and *Maharsha, Berachos* 4a).]

There is a seemingly blatant exception to *Rambam's* rule that prophecy for the good is never withdrawn. The *Talmud (Shabbos* 55a) tells us: Never has a favorable word gone forth from the mouth of the Holy One, Blessed be He, which He revoked, except during the destruction of the First Temple, when He promised the righteous that they would not perish with the wicked [see *Ezekiel* 9:4ff], *but He changed His plan.* For, as the *Talmud* there explains, the righteous during the First Temple period suffered for their failure to rebuke the wicked. [Thus, the implication is that sin *could* cause forfeiture of God's promise.]

According to most editions to *Rambam, Yesodei HaTorah* 10:4, he himself takes note of this passage, and cites it as the *sole* exception to the rule. Others claim, however, [see *Avodas HaMelech,* Krakovsky, ibid.] that this is actually a contradiction that a copyist noted on the margin which was mistakenly incorporated in the text. (For a full treatment of this problem — see *Mizrachi; Lechem Mishnah, ibid.; Gevuros Hashem,* ch. 7. See also *Ohel David II* to *I Chronicles* 22:9, 23:17; *Ezekiel* 9:4; and *Jonah* 3:4).

[Noteworthy in this context is the opinion of *R' Nissim* on 15:2 that God does not withdraw

Ramban [end of *v.* 13] is aware of this difficulty and offers that Jacob was apprehensive that he might have sinned by entering into a covenant with the wicked Laban, or in some other matter for *who can discern errors?* [*Psalms* 19:13].

Kli Yakar also discusses the above difficulty and cites the Talmudic dictum that one who flatters the wicked will eventually fall into his hands. This flattering of Esau is what Jacob feared would cause him to lose God's protection, since he should have piously trusted in God.

[However cf. *Sotah* 41b and *Midrash HaGadol,* where Jacob's flattery of Esau is justified. Similarly, *Pirkei d'Rabbi Eliezer* ch. 38 cites Jacob as justifying his flattery of Esau by saying, 'Lord of all the Universe! My intention in flattering a rogue to prevent him from killing me.' Our verse is the source of the Rabbinic dictum that: One may flatter the wicked in This World for the sake of peace.]

Abarbanel expresses difficulty with *Rashi's* basic premise that Jacob's fear was motivated by apprehension that some sin might have caused him to forfeit God's promise.

Among the several difficulties he poses is that if Jacob's underlying concern was that sinfulness might have caused him to forfeit God's promise, why did he not *specifically* mention remorse in his prayer in *v.* 11, or why did God not reassure him that he need not be apprehensive?

a favorable blessing if it is *unequivocally* favorable. But in cases where a benefit to A will be detrimental to B, God would withdraw it should A not be worthy or should B repent. For example, if A is to defeat B in battle, the benefit promised A can come about only by B's disaster. In such cases, either A's sins or B's repentance is sufficient cause for God to reappraise His pledge. (Thus, though Abraham had not asked for a sign when God promised him children —a promise that affected no one adversely — he *did* ask for a sign when God promised him the Land — for his acquisition of the land depended upon it being first taken away from the Canaanites, and should they repent they might retain it).]

A remaining difficulty is the exegesis in *Berachos* 4a that Israel would have *two* equally triumphal entries into *Eretz Yisrael,* one at the time of Joshua and one when Ezra would lead them back from the Babylonian Exile. This is derived there from Moses' prophetic statement: עַד יַעֲבֹר עַמְּךָ ה׳ עַד יַעֲבֹר עַם זוּ קָנִיתָ, *Until Your nation passes over, HASHEM, until this nation which You have acquired passes over (Exodus* 15:16). The repetitive יַעֲבֹר, *pass over,* is interpreted as a prophecy that both entries into the Land would be of equal magnitude. The Sages comment: The Israelites were worthy to have a miracle performed for them in the time of Ezra in the same manner as was performed for them in the time of Joshua, but *sin was the cause,* [that Ezra's miracle was forfeited, and they entered *Eretz Yisrael* as vassals of Cyrus.]

Thus, we have a case where even a *prophet's* [Moses'] public statement was repudiated because of sinfulness, even though it would cast aspersions on the efficacy of prophecy.

Maharal (Gevuros Hashem, ch. 7) makes a distinction between this Biblical prophecy which refers to *general* good tidings, and a *specific guarantee.* Only a specific promise carries with it the unequivocal guarantee.

Cf. also *Lechem Mishnah* to *Yesodei HaTorah* 9:4, who maintains that the forfeiture of Moses's prediction expounded in *Berachos* 4a does not contradict *Rambam's* thesis, since that prediction is not attributed directly to God but to Moses. Thus the Sages in *Berachos* 7a (cited above) were careful to say: 'No word of blessing that issued *from the mouth of the Holy One, Blessed be He,* even if based on a condition was ever withdrawn by him.' For only to those prophecies that the Torah *specifically* attributes to Hashem does this dictum apply. [See also *Mizrachi* and *Levush.*]

Others [see *Maaseh Rokeach*] maintain that the guarantee that a prophecy for the good will unequivocally be fulfilled as a means of testing the veracity of a prophet was not applicable to Moses, since his infallibility was unquestionable [see *Yesodei hatTorah.* Therefore, it would be clear to all that the repudiation of Moses's statement was due to their sinfulness and was not a reflection of his veracity.

Maharal, however, takes exception to *Rambam* because of the *Midrash,* cited above, that there is not guarantee for the righteous man in This World. [*Ramban,* however, would qualify that the *Midrash* applies only when the communication was a personal prophecy — see above]. He differentiates between הַבְטָחָה, *promise,* and נְבוּאָה, *prophecy,* when a righteous man is given a promise because of a righteous quality or act, this promise is subject to the

מְאֹד וַיֵּצֶר לוֹ וַיַּחַץ אֶת־הָעָם אֲשֶׁר־אִתּוֹ
וְאֶת־הַצֹּאן וְאֶת־הַבָּקָר וְהַגְּמַלִּים לִשְׁנֵי
ט מַחֲנוֹת: וַיֹּאמֶר אִם־יָבוֹא עֵשָׂו אֶל־
הַמַּחֲנֶה הָאַחַת וְהִכָּהוּ וְהָיָה הַמַּחֲנֶה
י הַנִּשְׁאָר לִפְלֵיטָה: וַיֹּאמֶר יַעֲקֹב אֱלֹהֵי

Abarbanel therefore interprets that the above questions are academic since Jacob's fear did not result from lack of faith; his trust in God was genuine and strong. Rather, Jacob was like a hero who recognizes his emotions and is prepared for a brave death. A soldier who considers himself immortal is not a hero, but a fool; just as one who dispenses charity to demonstrate a scorn for money is not a philanthropist, but a spendthrift. One should dread death, but be ready to face it for a sufficient cause. It was thus with Jacob. Were he to think Esau would treat him as a loving brother, his readiness to confront Esau would not have indicated trust in God. To the contrary, because he was fully aware of Esau's murderous hatred, and because he feared death, his greatness becomes apparent. Despite the danger, his trust in God overcame his fear and he made ready to meet Esau. Such a person can be called a believer in God's prophecy.

Jacob did not despair nor did he rely on a miracle. Rather, he took all possible steps to protect himself and those with him. The Torah elaborates on his behavior to teach us how one should act in the face of danger.

◈ Military preparations.

וַיַּחַץ אֶת הָעָם ... לִשְׁנֵי מַחֲנוֹת — *So* [lit. *and*] *he divided the people ... into two camps.*

Jacob divided the camp in such a manner that each camp had some of his men, maidservants, and cattle. He did not separate his wives and children however; they remained together in the same camp. Jacob's strategy was that he would station the camp which did not contain his wives and children at the forefront — in the direction from which Esau and his men were most likely to approach: They would serve, in effect, as a buffer between Jacob's family and Esau *(Abarbanel).*

Or HaChaim emphasizes that Jacob's every action was inspired by a desire to minimize reliance on a miracle. [See *Shabbos* 32a cited in *v.* 11 s.v. קָטֹנְתִּי.]

R' Chiya the Elder said: We learn from Jacob's action in dividing his property that one should not keep all one's wealth in a single place *(Midrash).*

Cf. the prudent advice given in *Bava*

tzaddik being free from sin. However, if the information is transmitted as a prediction, it is unqualified.

According to *Ramban (Genesis* 12:6; see *R' Chavel)* it would seem that there is a distinction between a prophecy where an act was done by the prophet to 'fortify', or 'act out' part of the prophecy.

Some qualify the words of *Ramban (Ran, Derashos* 2) that this applies only where the prophecy contains bad tidings, while others disagree (see *Ohel David* to *II Chronicles* 22:9 for an explanation of *Ramban).*

[Admittedly, the above treatment is an oversimplification of a fundamental philosophic doctrine. Readers are urged to consult the original Hebrew sources whenever possible. See also the *Overview* to this Sidrah where the *hashkafah* implications are discussed.]

32
9

him. So he divided the people with him, and the
flocks, herds, and camels, into two camps. [9] *For he*
said, 'If Esau comes to the one camp and strikes it
down, then the remaining camp shall survive.'

Metzia 42a: One should always divide one's wealth into three parts: investing a third in land, a third in merchandise, and keeping a third available for use.

[*Tanchuma* offers that the term יחץ, *divided,* connotes that each *person* was, in a sense, divided in two]:

What did Jacob do? — He armored them underneath, and clothed them in white without. [Thus, they were *outwardly* dressed for a friendly meeting, but were prepared for battle should it prove necessary.]

R' Hirsch notes the striking contrast between Jacob's confidence throughout his twenty-year ordeal with Laban, and his fear of confrontation with Esau. He comments that Jacob's despondency was caused by the knowledge that, no matter how innocent and righteous his behavior, Esau had felt personally injured by him.

◆§ Preparation for Battle.

9. אִם־יָבוֹא עֵשָׂו אֶל הַמַּחֲנֶה הָאַחַת וְהִכָּהוּ — *If Esau comes to the one camp and strikes it down.*

The phrase הַמַּחֲנֶה **הָאַחַת**, *the one camp,* is in the feminine gender, while **וְהִכָּהוּ**, *smite it* [lit. smite *him*] is in the masculine. *Rashi* explains that the word מַחֲנֶה, *camp,* can be either masculine or feminine, as evidenced from *Psalms* 28:3 where the feminine gender is used, and below, 33:8, where the masculine gender occurs. Other nouns which occur in Scripture in both the male and female gender are שֶׁמֶשׁ, *sun;* רוּחַ, *wind, spirit;* אֵשׁ, *fire.*

Whenever dual-gendered words appear, the masculine form is used to indicate its essential nature while the feminine is used with regard to non-essential characteristics. In the case of an aggressive attack on a camp, the result can be damage and casualties — indicated by the feminine form — or total annihilation — indicated by the masculine form. Therefore, both forms are used in our verse *(Gur Aryeh).*

וְהָיָה הַמַּחֲנֶה הַנִּשְׁאָר לִפְלֵיטָה — *Then the remaining camp shall survive* [lit. *shall be for survivors*].

— It will survive despite his attack, *because I will fight him.* Accordingly, Jacob prepared himself for three things לְדוֹרוֹן, *for a gift* [i.e., appeasement] — see verses 13-22; לִתְפִלָּה, *for prayer* — see *v.* 10; לַמִּלְחָמָה, *for battle* — as in our passage [for I will fight him' *(Tanchuma)*] *(Rashi).*

Unlike the appeasement and prayer which are literally derived from the verses cited, the third preparation: *battle,* is not stated *explicitly* in our verse which merely mentions *surviving.* Rather, there was a tradition among the Sages that there were the three preparations listed by *Rashi* above, and that of *battle* is attached to our verse. Based on this tradition, *Rashi* adds the comment that the other camp would survive despite his attack *because I will fight him (Mizrachi).*

Sforno suggests that as a natural result of Esau's preoccupation with the first camp, the second will have time to flee.

Ramban offers that in the *literal* sense of the verse, Jacob is not threatening battle, but is expressing the *hope* that one camp would be

אֲבִי אַבְרָהָם וֵאלֹהֵי אָבִי יִצְחָק יהוה
הָאֹמֵר אֵלַי שׁוּב לְאַרְצְךָ וּלְמוֹלַדְתְּךָ
יא וְאֵיטִיבָה עִמָּךְ: קָטֹנְתִּי מִכֹּל הַחֲסָדִים

able to escape while the other is engaged in battle; or that Esau's anger will subside after battling the first camp; or that deliverance will come to them from God in the interim. [Cf. *Rashbam:* The camps were a distance apart, and should danger develop, the other camp would see it and *flee.*]

However, *Ramban* concludes, the correct interpretation, expressed by *Rashi,* citing the *Midrash,* is that Jacob prepared himself also *for war.* Jacob was confident that *all* his posterity could not be destroyed by Esau, and even if one camp fell, the other would certainly escape. This portends the destiny of the Jewish people: Though decrees designed to exterminate the Jewish people will be promulgated in certain countries, Israel will never be exterminated entirely. Should one gentile king decree their destruction, another king will be merciful in *his* country, and offer them refuge.[1]

◆§ Prayer

[Human precautions alone are insufficient; Jacob invokes God's aid in prayer.]

10. אֱלֹהֵי אָבִי אַבְרָהָם וֵאלֹהֵי אָבִי יִצְחָק ה׳ הָאֹמֵר אֵלַי ... – *God of my father Abraham and God of my father Isaac; HASHEM Who said to me ...*

There are two difficulties here: (a) Why does Jacob now use the expression *God* of Isaac, while in 31:42 he avoided this appellation, substituting in its stead פַּחַד יִצְחָק, *the Dread of Isaac;* (b) Why the repetition *'HASHEM* Who said to me'? The passage should have read, *God of my father Abraham and God of my father Isaac, Who said to me ...*

The answer to the first difficulty is that Jacob was not himself *designating* God by the title *God of Isaac,* but alluding to the promise in 28:13 where God referred to Himself as *God of Isaac.* The explanation of the passage, which at the same time resolves the second difficulty, is: Jacob said to the Holy One, Blessed Be He: 'You made me two promises: first, You promised me Your protection when I left Beer Sheba and you appeared to me as *HASHEM, God of Abraham and God of Isaac;* and second, when I left Laban's house You appeared to me as HASHEM and said [31:3]: *Return to the land of your father's and to your relatives and I will be with you.* Now, I appeal for the fulfillment of these *two* promises [and accordingly invoke You with the Names You used in making them: *God of Abraham and God of Isaac* and *HASHEM*] *(Rashi)*

[See *Daas Zekeinim* to *v.* 8 s.v. וַיִּירָא, according to which Esau's aggressive advance against him caused Jacob to think that Isaac was dead, for otherwise, he surmised, Esau would not have come to attack him. This would explain why

1. As *R' Hirsch* writes: Never has Esau's sword reached us all in one swoop. When we bled on the Rhine, our brethren in the Slavic lands were safe, and vice versa. "God acted righteously to Israel by scattering them among the nations" (*Pesachim* 87b). Jacob, during his personal exile, now did the same.

[10] *Then Jacob said, 'God of my father Abraham and
God of my father Isaac; HASHEM Who said to me,
"Return to your land and to your relatives and I will
do good with you"* — [11] *I have been diminished by all*

he used the appellation *God of Isaac*, a title used only of the dead.]

Midrash HaGadol observes that our verse illustrates how the sons of the righteous take pride in their parents. Jacob did not base his petition on his *own* worth, but on the merit of his forefathers Abraham and Isaac.

Sforno notes the similarity between Jacob's introductory words and the beginning of *Shemoneh Esrei*. Both appeal to Hashem as the God of the Patriarchs.

ה׳ הָאֹמֵר אֵלַי שׁוּב לְאַרְצְךָ וּלְמוֹלַדְתְּךָ וְאֵיטִיבָה עִמָּךְ — *HASHEM, Who said to me, 'Return to the land of your fathers and to your relatives and I will do good* [or: *deal bountifully*] *with you.'*

[Jacob thus recalls in a paraphrase of 31:3 that it was God Who had bidden him to return to his native land and promised His protection. As *Ramban* notes, *I will do good with you,* referred to the promise in 31:3: *I will be with you,* for as *Radak* explains, it is God's *intent* that Jacob cites here, not His actual words. (See *v.* 13 אָמַרְתָּ וְאַתָּה). The flow of the prayer, according to *Rashi,* is that Jacob invokes these promises, but he is afraid that he might have forfeited them due to insufficient merit or sinfulness (*v.* 11). Nevertheless in conclusion (*v.* 12), he implores God's graciousness to save him from Esau in any case.]

11. קָטֹנְתִּי מִכֹּל הַחֲסָדִים — *I have been diminished by* [lit. *from*] *all the kindnesses.*[1]

The translation *I have been diminished* follows *Rashi:* My merits have been diminished in the consequence of all the *kindnesses*, which You have already shown me. Therefore I am afraid; perhaps since the

1. The *Talmud* teaches that a Torah scholar should have a שְׁמִינִית שֶׁבִּשְׁמִינִית גַּאֲוָה, *an eighth of an eighth* [one sixty-fourth measure] *of pride (Sotah* 5a). The *Vilna Gaon* comments that this lesson is derived from our verse. Though he feared that he was unworthy of further miracles, Jacob did acknowledge that he had had a prior stock of merit which had earned him God's earlier graciousness. However, a more appropriate show of humility would have been for Jacob to attribute even *those* earlier favors to the merit of Abraham and Isaac, rather to his own.

This teaches a lesson in humility: one should pray for *future* mercy based on the merit of his fathers *(v.* 10), but he should attribute *past* goodness to his *own* meager spiritual merits — which may have become depleted. That Jacob felt justified in taking credit for past mercies proves that although a Torah scholar should be very humble, it should not be to the point of total self-abnegation.

This concept is alluded to by the rather strange expression that a scholar should have an 'eighth of an eighth of pride.' Our *sidrah, Vayishlach*, is the eighth in the Torah, and our verse, קָטֹנְתִּי, *I have become small* is the eighth verse of the *sidrah*. Thus, this form of permissible pride is indicated by this verse *(Vilna Gaon).*

Maharsha (Sotah 5a) explains that a scholar must display a certain measure of pride in honor of the Torah; not to do so would seem to denigrate his learning. He also cites a witty comment on this topic. In that passage, the *Talmud* condemns גַּס רוּחַ, *a person of coarse and arrogant nature.* The word גַּס has the numerical value of sixty-three; thus a scholar who exceeds the permissible extent of pride — 1/64 — puts himself into the category of coarse-natured people.

וּמִכָּל־הָאֱמֶת אֲשֶׁר עָשִׂיתָ אֶת־עַבְדֶּךָ כִּי
בְמַקְלִי עָבַרְתִּי אֶת־הַיַּרְדֵּן הַזֶּה וְעַתָּה

promises were made I have become soiled by sin, and this may cause me to be delivered into Esau's hands.

[The broad aspects of the underlying *hashkafah*/philosophic ramifications of this fundamental concept of יִגְרוֹם הַחֵטְא, *forfeiture by sin,* have been discussed in the *comm.* and *footnote* to *v.* 8.][1]

[Thus *Rashi* renders the מ of מכל not as the comparative *than,* but as meaning מִפְּנֵי, *in consequence of:* I have become unworthy — i.e. I now have less to my credit — in consequence of all the kindnesses, etc.]

Cf. *Onkelos:* 'My merits are less from all the kindnesses, etc.'

Rashi resorts to *both* interpretations: 'my merits have been diminished' *and* 'perhaps ... I have become soiled by sin,' for had Jacob not been apprehensive that he had sinned, certainly that righteous man's merits could not have been so diminished that he would have to fear defeat and death at Esau's hands *(Be'er Mayim Chaim).*

Although [as evident from his commentary to *v.* 13 and to 28:20] *Ramban* agrees that Jacob's *underlying* fear was due to his apprehension that he might have sinned, he disagrees with *Rashi's* interpretation that this fear was *expressed* in the contextual flow of this petition. For, *Ramban* reasons, if Jacob was expressing apprehension that his merits were significantly reduced by God's many favors and, additionally, that he might have forfeited them by sin, what value would there have been in invoking God's promise: *I will surely do good with you, and I will make your offspring like the sand of the sea* [*v.* 13]? It would be contrary to the flow of his petition — perhaps he forfeited *that* promise as well! [*Divrei David* to *v.* 12 answers, in defense of *Rashi,* that it was not Jacob's *own* merit that he was invoking there but the merit of his *forefathers;* such merit he could not forfeit].

Furthermore, *Ramban* reasons, according to *Rashi's* interpretation — what significant showering of kindnesses had Jacob received following God's promise given him only a few weeks earlier in Charan?

— *Ramban* concludes [in consonance with one view in the *Midrash*] *that the phrase* קָטֹנְתִּי מִכֹּל does not mean *I have been diminished in consequence of all...* Rather, Jacob was saying in absolute terms, *I am unworthy* [lit. *too small*] *of all the kindnesses ... You have done for me.* Thus, Jacob was declaring not that his merits had been depleted, but that he was *never* worthy of so many kindnesses.

The חֲסָדִים, *kindnesses,* are those which God did for him without having first promised them, while אֱמֶת, *truth,* refers to the kindnesses performed in fulfillment of earlier promises. [For alternate interpretations of these terms, see below.] Thus, the tenor of Jacob's remark was: I am unworthy both of the kindnesses You did for me in fulfillment of promises, and of the many

1. Compare *Shabbos* 32a: R' Yannai said: A man should never stand in a place of danger and say that a miracle will be performed for him, for perhaps it might not be. And if a miracle *is* performed for him, it is deducted from his merits. [Since the miracle is a reward for some of his merits, he now has less to his credit]. R' Chanin derives this teaching from our verse. [And as the general tenor of the *gemara* there illustrates, when danger is near and one has need of a miracle, his sins are recalled and a determination is made if he is worthy of a miracle.]

the kindnesses and by all the truth that You have done Your servant. For with my staff I crossed this

kindnesses You did without having promised them earlier.

Rashbam interprets like *Ramban*, and adds: You were far more gracious to me than I deserved, for I have not yet fulfilled the vow I made to You twenty years ago. Despite Your promises to me, I know that You judge man according to his deeds — and in these I am deficient.

וּמִכָּל־הָאֱמֶת — *And by all the truth.* [Lit. and] I have been diminished...] *from all the truth* — the truth of Your words, for You have already fulfilled all the promises You made to me *(Rashi).*

Rashi is drawn to this interpretation since *truth* and *falsehood* by definition are possible only in connection with the veracity of statements and the fulfillment of spoken commitments *(Mizrachi).*

[The connotations of the terms חֶסֶד וֶאֱמֶת, *kindness and truth* have been explained in the *comm.* to 24:27 and 24:49. Essentially as noted above, *kindness* is the goodness conferred voluntarily, while *truth* is the fulfillment of an obligation.]

Unlike 24:49 and below 47:29 where *Onkelos* renders the phrase חֶסֶד וֶאֱמֶת as *kindness and truth,* in our verse *Onkelos* renders the phrase *kindness and all the good.* The latter, as *Ramban* explains, refers to the *enduring goodness* which resulted from the promises which *become realized* [=נִתְאַמֵּת] in Jacob, as reflected by his children, by his wealth and by his honor. For, as *Ramban* suggests, the word אֱמֶת, *truth,* derives from אָמֵן ,אֱמוּנָה, *trust,* and refers to *assured existence,* as opposed to something which is fleeting, temporary, and ultimately disappointing. It is analagous to *II Samuel* 7:16: *Your house and your kingdom shall be* נֶאֱמַן, *confirmed* [=existent] *forever.*

Haamek Davar similarly explains אמת as referring to God's promise that from him there would descend the Chosen Nation which would *exist eternally.*

... I was also unworthy of the אֱמֶת, the favors you bestowed upon me for the sake of my forefathers. Just as You have acted beyond the strict requirements of Your promises until now, I beg that You continue to do so, and save me *(Sforno).*

Jacob proceeds to elaborate on the kindnesses God bestowed upon him *(Haamek Davar):*

כִּי בְמַקְלִי עָבַרְתִּי אֶת הַיַּרְדֵּן הַזֶּה — *For with my staff I crossed this Jordan.* — That is, *only* with my staff. I possessed nothing but my staff — neither silver, gold, nor cattle. The *Midrash* explains: When Jacob had reached the river Jordan, he had placed his staff in the Jordan, and the Jordan split for him [allowing him to pass over it *(Rashi).*[1]

According to *Yelamdenu* cited in *Yalkut,* this miracle occurred when Jacob had been enroute to Charan years earlier, while according to the version in *Tanchuma Yashan,* it had just *now* occurred.

Rashi offers both the literal and *Midrashic* interpretations because both are necessary for a proper understanding of the passage. Jacob's former poverty is implicit from the contrast drawn in the subsequent phrase: *And now I have become two camps,* while the inclusion of the otherwise superfluous phrase *this Jordan* demands the *Midrashic*

1. In keeping with the concept that every incident recorded regarding the Patriarchs was a prophetic prognostication of what would befall their descendants, the *Midrashim* observe how the Jordan was destined to divide before Jacob's descendants in the time of Joshua, when they entered the Promised Land; see *Joshua* 3 and 4.

Furthermore, Jacob's staff was the staff later carried by Judah, Moses, Aaron, David, and every king until the destruction of the Temple. It is the staff which will be carried by the Messiah, at the time of the Redemption *(Yalkut* 1:763).

יב הָיִיתִי לִשְׁנֵי מַחֲנוֹת: הַצִּילֵנִי נָא מִיַּד אָחִי
מִיַּד עֵשָׂו כִּי־יָרֵא אָנֹכִי אֹתוֹ פֶּן־יָבוֹא
יג וְהִכַּנִי אֵם עַל־בָּנִים: וְאַתָּה אָמַרְתָּ הֵיטֵב
אֵיטִיב עִמָּךְ וְשַׂמְתִּי אֶת־זַרְעֲךָ כְּחוֹל הַיָּם
°שני יד אֲשֶׁר לֹא־יִסָּפֵר מֵרֹב: °וַיָּלֶן שָׁם בַּלַּיְלָה

interpretation *(Gur Aryeh; Tzeidah laDerech).*

[On Jacob's poverty when he left his father's house, see *'Jacob's Possessions'* in *comm.* to end of 28:10.]

Onkelos perceives *with my staff* to figuratively mean: *I alone.*

The use of the word הַזֶּה, *this* [Jordan], would imply that when Jacob uttered this prayer he was located in the general area of the Jordan *(Hoffman).*

Even according to those who maintain that he was *not* near the Jordan, the phrase can be transposed to mean 'for with *this my staff,* I crossed the Jordan.' Nevertheless, even in the familiar sense it is not unusual for Scripture to employ the word זֶה, *this,* even when not in the presence of the subject, e.g. *Exodus* 32:1 כִּי זֶה מֹשֶׁה הָאִישׁ, *for this man Moses (Tur).*

וְעַתָּה הָיִיתִי לִשְׁנֵי מַחֲנוֹת — *And now I have become* [to] *two camps.*

— So wonderfully had God blessed me! [See 28:15; 31:5, 7, 9, 42] *(Ralbag).*

From Jacob's remark we learn that a person must recall his travail during times of tranquility in order that he may appreciate his advantages and thank God for them *(R' Bachya).*

12. הַצִּילֵנִי נָא מִיַּד אָחִי מִיַּד עֵשָׂו — *Rescue me, please, from the hand of my brother, from the hand of Esau.*

[The contextual flow is either: 'I implore you to rescue me even though my merits have been diminished in consequence of the kindnesses You did on my behalf;' or: 'Though I was never worthy of all the kindnesses You did on my behalf.' Or, the sense is: 'You have been so gracious to me in bestowing Your bountiful blessings; of what use will it all be if Esau prevails and strikes me down? Therefore: *Rescue me from the hand of my brother, from the hand of Esau*']...

— *From the hand of my brother* who does not treat me as a brother, but as a wicked Esau *(Rashi).*[1]

— *From the hand of my brother,* who may have some claim against me as a brother who feels I have wronged him; and save me *from the hand of Esau,* who, in accordance with his violent nature may seek a revenge beyond what I deserve *(R' Hirsch).*

פֶּן יָבוֹא וְהִכַּנִי אֵם עַל־בָּנִים — *Lest he come and strike me down, mother and* [following *Sforno;* lit. *upon*] *children.*

The idiomatic phrase which

1. After having recited God's praise in having showered him with undeserved bounties, Jacob proceeds to pray for his requirements. Jacob's petition is exemplary because he stated it in precise unambiguous terms: He said, *Rescue me, please.* Since this might be interpreted to mean *from Laban* from whom he was already rescued, he added *from the hand of my brother.* Since *brother* might mean *kinsman* in general, he added *from the hand of Esau.* Moreover, lest it be argued that he had no need of such delivery, he continued *for I fear him lest he come and strike me down, mother and children (Zohar).*

Shloh HaKadosh writes in a similar vein: Though the Holy One, Blessed be He, discerns hearts and perceives man's intention, nevertheless one must be very specific when praying. It appears to me that the reason is that the words of prayer are composed of the holy letters, so they rise up and split open the very heavens.

32
12-13

Jordan and now I have become two camps. 12 *Rescue*
me, please, from the hand of my brother, from the
hand of Esau, for I fear him lest he come and strike
me down, mother and children. 13 *And You had said,*
"I will surely do good with you and I will make your
offspring like the sand of the sea which is too
numerous to count."'

figuratively conjures up an image of wholesale, merciless slaughter, is explained by *Ibn Ezra* and others as elliptic: ... *'And will strike me down,* and also strike down *mother and child.'*

— Even if I manage to escape, he will be *striking* at *me* by striking down mother and child, [because my family will be harmed]. The Hebrew expression *mother upon child* means mother *and* child; cf. *Hoshea* 10:14 *(Sforno).*

Jacob's primary fear was that Esau might come and strike down mother and child. As for himself, God's promise of protection came to him when he crossed the Jordan *alone,* with only his staff. He was not certain that this promise would extend even to those in his party — i.e., mother and child *(Daas Zekeinim).* [Cf. *Ramban* to *v.* 9 s.v. וְהָיָה הַמַּחֲנֶה.]

13. וְאַתָּה אָמַרְתָּ הֵיטֵב אֵיטִיב עִמָּךְ — *And You had said, 'I will surely do good* [or: *deal bountifully;* lit. *'good, I will do good'*] *with you.*

[See *v.* 10; a reference to the promise in 31:3.] Though God did not say these exact words, Jacob refers to God's *intent* as expressed in 31:3 *(Haamek Davar; cf. comm.* to end of 24:51).

Rashi, following the *Midrash* comments: The compound form has a dual connotation: הֵיטֵב, *goodness*—in your own merit; אֵיטִיב, *I will do good*—in the merit of your forefathers [since in fact, it was not his *own 'diminished' merit,* but the undiminished זְכוּת אָבוֹת, *merit of his forefathers,* that Jacob was invoking (*Divrei David;* this answers *Ramban's* objection in *v.* 11 s.v. קָטֹנְתִּי)].

Though the compound form may be interpreted as being merely emphatic, *Rashi* cites this interpretation as reflecting the simple sense of the passage since in fact both of God's promises carried distinct connotations and 'wherever it is possible to expound, we expound' *(Gur Aryeh; Mizrachi).* [Comp. *Mizrachi* to 12:1 לֶךְ־לְךָ.]

The continuity of Jacob's prayer is, as noted, variously perceived:

— You have done many *unpromised* kindnesses for me notwithstanding my unworthiness. Surely, You will not withhold from those kindnesses which You *did,* in Your abundant mercy, *promise me* — namely that You would bestow good upon me and increase my offspring *(Ramban).*

Rashbam: 'Though You are not bound to keep Your promise *because I am unworthy* of it, nevertheless rescue me for the sake of Your Name which You make glorious when You keep Your word.' Moses prayed similarly when God wanted to annihilate Israel [*Exodus* 32:12]: *Let not the Egyptian say, 'It was with evil intent that He delivered them ... '* And subsequently [*ibid. v.* 14]: *HASHEM relented regarding the punishment.*

וְשַׂמְתִּי אֶת זַרְעֲךָ כְּחוֹל הַיָּם אֲשֶׁר לֹא יִסָּפֵר מֵרֹב — *And I will make* [lit. *place*] *your offspring like the sand*

הַהוּא וַיִּקַּח מִן־הַבָּא בְיָדוֹ מִנְחָה לְעֵשָׂו
טו אָחִיו: עִזִּים מָאתַיִם וּתְיָשִׁים עֶשְׂרִים
טז רְחֵלִים מָאתַיִם וְאֵילִים עֶשְׂרִים: גְּמַלִּים

of the sea which is too numerous to count [lit. *which is not counted from abundance.*]

Actually God did not promise him this explicitly, but said [28:14]: 'Your offspring shall be as the *dust of the earth.*' Rather, Jacob was referring to God's promise [*ibid. v.* 15] *'I will not forsake you until I have done that which I have spoken* [*to Abraham*] *concerning you,'* — specifically, the promise concerning Jacob, God had made to Abraham [22:17]: *I will greatly increase your offspring like the stars of the heavens and like the sand on the seashore (Rashi).*

Why then did Jacob not invoke the blessing ... *as the dust of the earth* which God had given *him* directly? — Perhaps the blessing given his forefathers was more efficacious, since ancestral merit is not prone to be forfeited by sin. One's own merit can be negated by sin, but God 'recalls the kindnesses of our forefather's' on behalf of the children even when the children are not worthy *(Gur Aryeh).*

☙A tribute is prepared.

Jacob set a pattern for future generations who would be confronted by oppression from Esau's descendants. He sought salvation both by means of דורון, *an attempt to appease the enemy with gifts,* and תְּפִלָּה, *prayer* for God's help *(R' Hirsch).*

14. וַיָּלֶן שָׁם בַּלַּיְלָה הַהוּא — [*And*] *he spent that night there.*

He had hoped for a prophetic dream in response to his prayer. Seeing that he received no such Divine communication, he proceeded to prepare a tribute to send to Esau *(Abarbanel; Alshich; Malbim).*

That God did not, in fact, send an angelic emissary to Jacob until Jacob dispatched the gift to Esau, teaches us an important lesson: Even a righteous person should not rely on miracles, but maintain vigilance and prepare — to his utmost ability — for any eventuality, with prayer, appeasement, and ultimately, battle. Above all, one's heart should be turned toward God with full trust, and He shall do *(Radak).*

According to the *Midrashim* [see *Pirkei d'Rabbi Eliezer* §36], Jacob spent that night soul-searching to uncover the transgression that caused this ordeal to be imposed upon him. He concluded that he must fulfill his earlier vow to separate tithes from that which God had given him [28:22], so first he separated the tithe and then assembled a tribute to Esau from the remaining non-sanctified portion [see *Rashi, below*].

וַיִּקַּח מִן הַבָּא בְיָדוֹ — *Then he took from that what had come in his hand.*

I.e., from that which was in his possession. Compare the use of this term in *Numbers* 21:26: וַיִּקַּח מִיָּדוֹ ..., *and he took ... out of his possession.* Midrashically, 'in his hand' signifies precious stones and jewels which one usually ties in a package and carries in his hand [to guard against loss]. Alternatively, the term refers to those items which

[14] *He spent that night there, then he took, from what had come in his hand, a tribute to Esau his brother:* [15] *Two hundred she-goats and twenty he-goats; two hundred ewes and twenty rams;* [16] *thirty*

a man may keep in his own possession, namely: חוּלִין, *unconsecrated portion* [cattle and produce from which the tithe had already been set aside; until this is done the owner's use of them is limited]. Thus, Jacob had *first* set aside the tithe as he had vowed to [28:22], and only *afterwards* did he prepare a tribute for Esau [from the חוּלִין, *unconsecrated portion,* which legitimately בָּא בְיָדוֹ, *came into his own possession* having been duly tithed] *(Rashi).*

According to *Ramban,* the expression means: *from that which he had with him.* The Torah is telling us that Jacob composed his gift from those possessions which constituted his wealth, namely his flocks [as enumerated in the following verses]. He was en route and had no opportunity to buy silver, gold and garments.

[The idiomatic sense of the term according to *Ramban* would be that Jacob selected the gifts from that which was 'within hand's reach,' i.e., readily available to him — from his livestock.]

— In an effort to send only the *choicest* animals, Jacob selected only those which he kept בְּיָדוֹ, in his *own* charge, and not from those inferior ones which he entrusted בְּיַד עֲבָדָיו, *in his servant's care.* Furthermore, he did not send any wheat or fine fruits since those are items which result from *the dew of the heavens and the fatness of the earth,* and Jacob wished to avoid any suggestion that he had benefitted in a material sense from Isaac's blessing, thus reopening the wound [see *Rashi* to *v.* 5]. The most effective gift would be something that came into Jacob's hand from his *own* toil and labor. That was the livestock he now selected *(Alshich).*

Baal HaTurim notes that the numerical value of מִנְחָה, *tribute; present* [=103], equals that of אֲבָנִים, [precious] *stones* [see *Rashi* above].

מִנְחָה לְעֵשָׂו אָחִיו — *A tribute* [or: *present*] *to Esau his brother.*

That the Torah, which usually economizes on every letter, enumerates in the following verses, the *details* of the gift, implies approval of this method of appeasing Esau *(Radak).*

The word מִנְחָה, *gift, offering,* is generally understood by the commentators to denote a present intended to secure the goodwill of a superior. Cf. *II Kings* 8:9.

15. עִזִּים מָאתַיִם וּתְיָשִׁים עֶשְׂרִים — *Two hundred she-goats and twenty he-goats ...*

Two hundred she-goats need twenty he-goats for breeding. Similarly in the case of the other animals Jacob [who as a skilled shepherd was fully familiar with animals' breeding habits *(Ibn Ezra)*] sent sufficient males for the needs of the females *(Rashi).*

Rashi continues: In the *Midrash* an inference is drawn from here regarding the frequency of conjugal duty required by the Torah [see *Mishnah Kesubos* 5:6]: men of leisure, daily; working men, twice weekly; donkey-drivers, once weekly; camel-drivers, once in thirty days; sailors, once in six months, 'but I do not know *exactly* how to

מֵינִיקוֹת וּבְנֵיהֶם שְׁלֹשִׁים פָּרוֹת אַרְבָּעִים
וּפָרִים עֲשָׂרָה אֲתֹנֹת עֶשְׂרִים וַעְיָרִם
יז עֲשָׂרָה׃ וַיִּתֵּן בְּיַד־עֲבָדָיו עֵדֶר עֵדֶר לְבַדּוֹ
וַיֹּאמֶר אֶל־עֲבָדָיו עִבְרוּ לְפָנַי וְרֶוַח
יח תָּשִׂימוּ בֵּין עֵדֶר וּבֵין עֵדֶר׃ וַיְצַו אֶת־
הָרִאשׁוֹן לֵאמֹר כִּי יִפְגָשְׁךָ עֵשָׂו אָחִי

relate this Midrashic inference [i.e., how the *Midrash* derives these schedules of obligation from Jacob's tribute]. However, it appears to me that we derive from here that the frequency of conjugal duty is not the same for every man, but according to the burden imposed upon him by his occupation [with the frequency decreasing with the amount of physical strain and/or the amount of time his occupation takes away from him]. Thus, he-goats and rams were given ten females each. Since they are free from labor, each can impregnate ten females, and once a female becomes pregnant, it does not receive the male [thus the male is forced to copulate with another female *(Mizrachi)*]. For the oxen that are engaged in labor, he gave but four females for each male; for the donkeys that travel long distances: two females for each male; and for camels that travel even longer distances, one female for each male.'

— The implication is drawn from the fact that the Torah would not list such details did they not contain a moral or *halachic* teaching. Furthermore, we must assume that these numbers were certainly not haphazard, but reflected Jacob's skill as a breeder who intended to provide as acceptable a gift as possible *(Mizrachi; Tzeidah laDerech; Maharsha).*

16. גְּמַלִּים מֵינִיקוֹת וּבְנֵיהֶם שְׁלֹשִׁים — *Thirty nursing camels with* [lit. *and*] *their colts.*

In the *literal* meaning of the phrase, the nursing camels were sent with their colts [and no male adult camels were included in the gift]. According to the *Midrash*, however, the word בְּנֵיהֶם is interpreted *not* as *their colts*, but as בֹּנֵיהֶם, *their builders*, meaning the males who figuratively 'build' the family by impregnating the females. Why are they referred to by allusion as 'builders' rather than directly as male camels? — Because camels are unique in that they cohabit modestly, unlike other animals which do so in the open. In recognition of this moral type of behavior, the Torah does not name them directly *(Rashi* according to *Mizrachi).*

Gur Aryeh explains that the *Midrash* was compelled to offer the alternative interpretation that Jacob sent males rather than colts, so that the set of camels should parallel those of the other animals. Since Jacob sent males and females of all the other animals, we must assume that he did the same with the camels.

The total number of camels is not clear from the verse. The supercommentators to *Rashi* all agree that according to the literal interpretation, there were thirty nursing camels and thirty colts; the word שְׁלֹשִׁים, *thirty*, refers only to the mothers while the colts, since they are dependent upon their mothers, need not to be numbered separately. According to Midrashic the interpretation that males, not colts, were sent, the question arises — were there fifteen males and fifteen females for a *total* of שְׁלֹשִׁים, *thirty*, or were there thirty females accompanied by thirty males for a total of sixty?

Gur Aryeh interprets that there were thirty of *each*. *Levush Ha'Orah*, however, points out that the *Midrash* states that Jacob's tribute consisted of a total of 550 animals, but according to *Gur Aryeh*, there would have been 580! [As mentioned above, if colts were sent, they are not included in the

nursing camels with their colts; forty cows and ten bulls; twenty she-donkeys and ten he-donkeys. [17] *He put in his servants' charge each drove separately and said to his servants, 'Pass on ahead of me and leave a space between drove and drove.'* [18] *He instructed the first one as follows, 'When my brother Esau meets*

total because of their relative insignificance]. *Mizrachi* and *Levush* agree that there were fifteen males and fifteen females. That the ratio was one-to-one is implied, for otherwise the Torah would have specified the respective totals.

אֲתֹנֹת עֶשְׂרִים וַעְיָרִם עֲשָׂרָה — *Twenty she-donkeys and ten he-donkeys.*

[The translation of עְיָרִים as *he-donkeys* follows *Rashi* as distinct from *Targum Yonasan* who renders יְלָדִין דַּקִּין, *small colts.*]

17. עֵדֶר עֵדֶר לְבַדּוֹ — *Each drove separately* [lit. *drove, drove by itself*].

— I.e., every species by itself *(Rashi).*

Jacob wanted each drove to be distinct so that Esau would take note of the proper proportion of males to females. Thereby he would realize that Jacob planned the tribute to yield him maximum productivity. For this reason, Jacob called the tribute בִּרְכָתִי, *my blessing* [33:11], because it was so constituted as to be a source of fertile blessing *(Sforno).*

וַיֹּאמֶר אֶל עֲבָדָיו עִבְרוּ לְפָנַי — *And* [*he*] *said to his servants, 'Pass on ahead of me* [lit. *before me*].'

A day's journey or less, and I will come after you *(Rashi).*

That is, he would not follow *too* closely behind them or all the precautions would have been useless. On the other hand, he would not follow too far behind for he told them to say [*v.* 18] *behold, he is also behind us (Ralbag).*

וְרֶוַח תָּשִׂימוּ בֵּין עֵדֶר וּבֵין עֵדֶר — *And leave* [lit. *put*] *a space between drove and* [*between*] *drove.*

— Place one drove before the other with a distance between them for as far as the eye can see, in order to satisfy the wicked Esau's greed and to amaze him with the sight of so great a gift. [Hardly will he have feasted his eyes on one set of animals than the other will begin to appear. Had all the animals been bunched together, the large number would have been less impressive] *(Rashi).*[1]

Following *Sforno:* So the animals will not wander from drove to drove. By keeping the species separate, Jacob made apparent the the careful forethought that went into calculating the proportion of males to females to assure maximum blessing to Esau.

18. וַיְצַו אֶת הָרִאשׁוֹן לֵאמֹר — [*And*] *he instructed* [lit. *commanded*] *the first one as follows* [lit. *to say; saying.*]

לֵאמֹר, *to say,* that is לֵאמֹר

1. *Ramban* cites the *Midrash* which perceives an allusion to the future, for Jacob thereby implied a prayer to the Almighty: 'Master of the Universe! If troubles come upon my children, do not bring them one after another, but let there be a breathing-space between them!'

וּשְׁאֵלְךָ לֵאמֹר לְמִי־אַתָּה וְאָנָה תֵלֵךְ
יט וּלְמִי אֵלֶּה לְפָנֶיךָ: וְאָמַרְתָּ לְעַבְדְּךָ
לְיַעֲקֹב מִנְחָה הִוא שְׁלוּחָה לַאדֹנִי לְעֵשָׂו
כ וְהִנֵּה גַם־הוּא אַחֲרֵינוּ: וַיְצַו גַּם אֶת־
הַשֵּׁנִי גַּם אֶת־הַשְּׁלִישִׁי גַּם אֶת־כָּל־
הַהֹלְכִים אַחֲרֵי הָעֲדָרִים לֵאמֹר כַּדָּבָר
הַזֶּה תְּדַבְּרוּן אֶל־עֵשָׂו בְּמֹצַאֲכֶם אֹתוֹ:

לְדוֹרוֹת, *with implication for future generations (Lekach Tov;* see *comm.* to *v.* 4). This concept implies that Jacob's descendants, too, were to heed those instructions when encountering Esau's descendants.

לְמִי אַתָּה — *Whose are you?*

— That is, 'Who sent you?' The expression לְמִי אַתָּה, *whose are you?,* means שֶׁל מִי אַתָּה, *whose* [servant *(Rashbam)*] *are you:* The prefix ל is used instead of שֶׁל, *belonging to,* for example in 31:43: שֶׁלִּי הוּא=לִי הוּא, *they are mine; Psalms* 24:1: לַה' הָאָרֶץ, *to* HASHEM *is the earth,* i.e. *the earth belongs to* HASHEM.

Rashi also notes that *Onkelos* should read דְמָאן אַתְּ instead of לְמָן אַתְּ as many editions have it.

וְאָנָה תֵלֵךְ — [*And*] *where are you going?*

— That is, toward where are you headed with such a large drove? *(Or HaChaim).*

וּלְמִי אֵלֶּה לְפָנֶיךָ — *And whose are these that are before you?*[1]

I.e., *to whom* is this tribute being sent? *(Rashi).*

19. וְאָמַרְתָּ — [*And*] *you shall say.*

— In sequential response to the questions in the order he will ask them *(Rashi)*...

לְעַבְדְּךָ לְיַעֲקֹב — *Your servant Jacob's* [lit. *to your servant to Jacob*].

That is, in reply to your his question, 'Whose are you?' — you shall answer: *'I belong to your servant Jacob'* [see note on the prefix שֶׁל=ל above] *(Rashi).*

Rashi also notes that *Onkelos* should read דְעַבְדָּךְ לְיַעֲקֹב instead of לְעַבְדָּךְ לְיַעֲקֹב as most current editions have it.

[On Jacob's demeaning himself by his constant references to himself as 'your *servant* Jacob' see *comm.* to *v.* 5 and *footnote* to 25:23. Regarding God's accusation that Jacob was flattering the wicked, Jacob replied that he was doing it 'to prevent him from killing me' (*Pirkei d'Rabbi Eliezer* 37). The Sages (*Sotah* 41b) consider this reaction legitimate. Cf. 'What sin could Jacob have been apprehensive about?' in *v.* 8.]

מִנְחָה הִוא שְׁלוּחָה לַאדֹנִי לְעֵשָׂו — *It is a tribute sent to my lord, to Esau.*

This is the reply to the question 'Whose are these that are before you?' [implying, as noted, 'To whom is this tribute being sent?'] — *It is a tribute sent to my lord Esau (Rashi).*

— It also answers the question: *Where are you going? (Or HaChaim).*

וְהִנֵּה גַם־הוּא אַחֲרֵינוּ — *And behold he*

1. The *Maggid of Kozhnitz* interprets this in a sarcastic sense as if Esau were chiding them: 'What need has Jacob of all this material wealth? — Did he not choose a spiritual life?'

you and asks you, saying, "Whose are you, where are
you going, and whose are these that are before you?"
— 19 You shall say, "Your servant Jacob's. It is a
tribute sent to my lord, to Esau, and behold he
himself is behind us." '
20 He similarly instructed the second, also the
third, as well as all who followed the droves, saying,
'In this manner shall you speak to Esau when you

himself [lit. *also he*] *is behind us.*

Jacob is the subject *(Rashi).*

The Sages in the *Midrash* derive a lesson from this: If you meet someone on a journey who asks many questions, always answer them, but then add, 'Another caravan is following up close.' [The sense of adding this is that if a stranger asks too many questions he may be a brigand seeking a pretext to rob or harm the defenseless traveler. He may be deterred by being told that others are following close by.]

20. וַיְצַו גַּם אֶת־הַשֵּׁנִי גַּם אֶת הַשְּׁלִישִׁי — *He similarly instructed* [lit. *and he commanded also*] *the second, also the third.*

Although it would be necessary for each of the messengers to identify the origin and destination of the tribute why would each of them be required to repeat that Jacob was following close behind? — Because there was a possibility that Esau would be annoyed that Jacob would not even deign to see him in person. Therefore, Jacob insisted that his messengers stress the point that their master would soon be at hand *(Kli Yakar).*

On a deeper level, the Torah repeats this instruction to four of the groups to indicate that these instructions apply to Israel's relationship with each of the Four Kingdoms under whom it would be exiled *(Pesikta Zutresa; Baal HaTurim).*

גַּם אֶת־כָּל־הַהֹלְכִים אַחֲרֵי הָעֲדָרִים — *As well as* [lit. *also*] *all who followed the droves.*

Following the allusion to the future as cited in the *Midrash* above, *Sechel Tov* notes that this signifies the *Fourth Exile* under Edom/Rome [a general reference to the current Exile under "Western Civilization"] which, by its severity obscured the memory of the three preceding ones.

כַּדָּבָר הַזֶּה תְּדַבְּרוּן אֶל עֵשָׂו — *In this manner shall you speak to Esau.*

Jacob told each of them what to say to Esau, so it would be clear that all the droves formed a single tribute dispatched by Jacob as a token to his older brother *(Sforno).*

בְּמֹצַאֲכֶם אֹתוֹ — *When you find him.*

Following the broader concept that this sequence applies as well to future generations when they have to defend themselves against aggression from Esau's descendants, the implication is: *In this manner shall you speak to Esau whenever you encounter him (R' Munk).*

— When you have no alternative but to humble yourselves to Esau,

כא וְאֲמַרְתֶּ֕ם גַּ֕ם הִנֵּ֛ה עַבְדְּךָ֥ יַעֲקֹ֖ב אַחֲרֵ֑ינוּ
כִּֽי־אָמַ֞ר אֲכַפְּרָ֣ה פָנָ֗יו בַּמִּנְחָה֙ הַהֹלֶ֣כֶת
לְפָנָ֔י וְאַחֲרֵי־כֵן֙ אֶרְאֶ֣ה פָנָ֔יו אוּלַ֖י יִשָּׂ֥א

this is how you shall speak to him (*Ma'or VaShemesh*).

21. וַאֲמַרְתֶּם גַּם הִנֵּה עַבְדְּךָ יַעֲקֹב אַחֲרֵינוּ — *And you shall say* [i.e. be sure to add] *'Moreover, behold your servant Jacob is behind us'.*

Jacob repeated this to emphasize that each of them *must* add this to whatever else they might say, so Esau should understand clearly that Jacob was following them to Seir to greet his brother (*Sforno*).

Even if Esau does *not* ask you any of the above questions, having heard of the tribute from the earlier messengers, nevertheless, you must take the initiative and tell him *'your servant Jacob is behind us,'* so that the constant repetition of the expressions *'servant Jacob'* and *'lord Esau'* will ring in his ears (*Ha'amek Davar*).

Jacob wanted the leader of each drove to prepare Esau for an imminent meeting with him. Esau would prepare himself for an angry outburst at his hated brother — only to be confronted with another generous gift. By such repetitive appeasement, Jacob hoped to fully assuage Esau's wrath (*R' Hirsch*).

The leaders constantly repeated this to emphasize that Jacob was not approaching pompously like a king, but rather, graciously, with appeasement as his goal. Or, the repetition was intended to convince Esau that Jacob was not merely sending gifts and fleeing, but was indeed coming himself (*Minchah Belulah*).

Rashbam suggests that this was really a deception, as Jacob *had* really intended to flee in another direction that night, but the struggle with the angel [*v.* 25] prevented him from doing so.

Following the Midrashic interpretations that this alludes to the future exiles, the message was that Esau's descendants were to be told *'Behold, your servant Jacob is behind us'* — Jacob's merit stands behind us and will endure also for future generations. In the end we will be vindicated.

כִּי אָמַר אֲכַפְּרָה פָנָיו בַּמִּנְחָה הַהֹלֶכֶת לְפָנָי — (*For he* [Jacob] *said, 'I will appease him* [lit. *his face*] *with the tribute that precedes me.'*)

I.e., I will *wipe away* his anger with this gift. As *Rashi* explains, *wipe* away, *remove,* is the meaning of the verb כפר when it occurs in conjunction with sin and figuratively with פָּנִים, [*angry*] *face* (see *comm.* to יִשָּׂא פָנָי below). The meaning of כפר in Aramaic is *to wipe*. Scripturally, too, the bowls in the Sanctuary are called [*Ezra* 1:10] כְּפוֹרֵי זָהָב, *kforim* of gold, because the priest *wiped* his hands on their rims.

[Cf. *Rashi* to *Deut.* 32:43 where he similarly explains the sense of כפר as *appease.*]

According to *Rashi, Rashbam* and *Ibn Ezra,* this phrase was not actually *uttered* by Jacob as part of his instructions to the messengers. Rather, it is a parenthetic third-person explanation of Jacob's motives in sending the tribute. The word *said* should accordingly be understood as *said to himself.*

Ibn Ezra interprets אֲכַפְּרָה פָנָיו as literally: *cover his face,* i.e., cause his face, the barometer of his anger, to be hidden. [Compare the expression כְּסוּת

32 *find him.* 21 *And you shall say, "Moreover — Behold*
21 *your servant Jacob is behind us."' (For he said, 'I*
will appease him with the tribute that precedes me,
and afterwards I will face him; perhaps he will

עֵינַיִם, *eye*-covering, in 20:16 implying *vindication*]. *Radak* similarly explains the literal meaning as *cover*. Cf. וְכִפַּרְתָּ אֹתָהּ, *and you shall cover it*, in 6:14.

Ramban, however, disagrees with *Rashi's* .interpretation of the Hebrew verb כפר as *wiping away*. He interprets it in the sense of a *ransom* to appease someone's anger. It is used in this sense, too, in *Proverbs* 16:14. Thus, in its familiar use as כַּפָּרָה, *atonement for sin*, the sense of the word is that the soul is ransomed from the effects of the sin, not that the sin itself is somehow wiped away or erased [as explained in *Kessef Mezukak*]. The connotation of *wipe away* occurs only in Aramaic, the word *kforim* that *Rashi* cites from *Ezra* is not the Hebrew, but the *Babylonian* name for 'bowls.' In our verse אֲכַפְּרָה פָנָיו figuratively connotes that Jacob was indicating that he was *ransoming* himself against Esau's wrath by means of the gifts he was sending him.

Furthermore, *Ramban* maintains that this phrase *did* form part of Jacob's instructions to the emissaries. They were to tell Esau that Jacob had specifically mentioned that he had sent them ahead to 'ransom' himself by means of these gifts.

וְאַחֲרֵי כֵן אֶרְאֶה פָנָיו — *And afterwards I will face him.*

— Literally, *see his face*, i.e., I will pay him my respects and homage in the sense of *Exodus* 23:17: יֵרָאֶה כָּל־זְכוּרְךָ אֶת פְּנֵי הָאָדֹן ה׳, *All your males shall appear before the face of the Lord HASHEM.*

אוּלַי יִשָּׂא פָנָי — *Perhaps he will forgive me* [lit. *lift up my face*].

By using the metaphor 'lifting up the face,' Jacob suggested that as long as Esau was enraged against him, he was ashamed to raise his face to look directly at Esau. By forgiving, Esau would, in effect, be lifting Jacob's downcast face *(R' Hirsch).*

Face figuratively connotes *anger* since one's facial expression is the barometer of his anger. Cf. *I Samuel* 1:18: וּפָנֶיהָ לֹא הָיוּ לָהּ עוֹד, lit. *and her face was no more to her*, meaning she no longer displayed a vexed countenance *(Ibn Ezra; Radak; Yohel Or).*

[As explained in the comm. to 19:21, the expression *lift up the face* occurs again in the בִּרְכַּת כֹּהֲנִים, *Priestly Blessing*, in *Num.* 6:26 יִשָּׂא ה׳ פָּנָיו אֵלֶיךָ (lit. *'may HASHEM lift up His face unto you,')* which *Rashi* there explains as: *May HASHEM suppress His anger toward you. Ibn Ezra* there elaborates that the connotation is the opposite connotation of *Isaiah* 1:15: אַעְלִים עֵינַי מִכֶּם, *I will avert My eyes from you.* In the Priestly Blessing, the connotation is: Wherever you turn, His face will be lifted up toward you in benevolence (for one who is angry at another averts his face from him — cf. *Deut.* 31:18. (When one *lifts his face* toward someone, it is evident that he bears no ill-will). Compare also the opposite connotation of to *turn back the face* of a supplicant in *I Kings* 2:16.]

R' Hirsch notes that פָּנִים, *face*, from פנה, *to turn*, means the attitude or direction taken by someone; the face is the part of the body expressing that trend. Accordingly, פָּנִים is used to express both a friendly and an unfriendly mood. See both *Proverbs* 16:15 and *Psalms* 34:17.

According to *Ramban* cited above, the connotation is: perhaps *he will accept me* and allow me to be among 'those who see the king's face.'

כב פָּנָֽי: וַתַּעֲבֹר הַמִּנְחָה עַל־פָּנָיו וְהוּא לָן
כג בַּלַּיְלָה־הַהוּא בַּמַּחֲנֶה: וַיָּקָם | בַּלַּיְלָה הוּא
וַיִּקַּח אֶת־שְׁתֵּי נָשָׁיו וְאֶת־שְׁתֵּי שִׁפְחֹתָיו
וְאֶת־אַחַד עָשָׂר יְלָדָיו וַיַּעֲבֹר אֵת מַעֲבַר

22. וַתַּעֲבֹר הַמִּנְחָה עַל־פָּנָיו — *So* [lit. *and*] *the tribute passed on before him* [lit. *upon his face.*]

— Jacob reviewed the procession to make certain that everything was just as he had intended it to be *(Abarbanel; Sforno).*

Our translation follows *Rashi* who cites parallels in *Jeremiah* 6:7 and 65:3 where עַל פָּנָיו, *upon his face,* is synonymous with לְפָנָיו, *before him.*

Rashi cites the *Midrash,* however, that since the verse uses עַל פָּנָיו instead of לְפָנָיו, the term is intended to allude to the word פָּנָיו, [*Esau's angry*] *face,* in the previous verse. The verse suggests that Jacob, too, was angry — the *tribute* passed on before him עַל פָּנָיו, *in his* [Jacob's] *anger* — Jacob was incensed that he needed to do all this.

Shem MiShmuel explains the implication of *Rashi* to be that Jacob's anger was directed at *himself,* since he felt that his action reflected a compromise of his own complete faith. He reasoned that were he to have put his unequivocal trust in God, he would not have found it necessary to resort to all this.

וְהוּא לָן בַּלַּיְלָה־הַהוּא בַּמַּחֲנֶה — *While* [lit. and] *he spent that night in the camp.*

— Not in his *tent,* but in the *camp* together with his servants, dressed for combat, should his brother come at night and attack him *(Ramban).*

According to the *Midrash: And he spent that night in the camp* — supplicating for God's mercy.

The division of the camps [*v.* 8] is not mentioned here. Perhaps, as *Abarbanel* suggests, Jacob slept in the camp where his wives were; or as *Haamek Davar* offers, Jacob had reunited the camps once he saw that Esau had not attacked that day.

[The contrasting sense — *while* he spent — is suggested by the subject + predicate arrangement וְהוּא לָן instead of the conversive וַיָּלֶן הוּא. Comp. *comm.* to 14:18, top of page 494.]

23. Jacob moves his encampment.

וַיָּקָם בַּלַּיְלָה הוּא — *But he got up* [in] *that night.*

— He arose while it was still night, having slept a short while in order to move his encampment under the cover of dark *(Radak).*

R' Hirsch suggests that Jacob's first intention was to stay overnight on that side of the Jabbok, but then his uneasiness gave him no rest.

Most commentators interpret that in crossing the Jabbok, Jacob was proceeding *toward* Esau.

According to *Rashbam,* however, as noted above (*v.* 21) it was Jacob's real intention to *flee* in the dark of night away *from* Esau. We find that David, too, when fleeing from Absalom, crossed the Jordan at night and traversed these same areas [see *II Samuel* 17].

הוּא lacks the definite article ה: הַהוּא. As noted in 19:32 and 30:16 this omission is not grammatically unusual.

Midrashically, however, as noted there, the anomalous form הוּא [lit. *he*] in place of the regular form הַהוּא refers to God — the *He* par excellence. *Midrash Lekach Tov* remarks: The pro-

forgive me.') 22 *So the tribute passed on before him*
while he spent that night in the camp.
23 *But he got up that night and took his two wives,*
his two handmaids and his eleven sons and crossed
the ford of the Jabbok. 24 *And when he took them*

noun הוּא, *He,* indicates that the Holy One, Blessed be He, was with him to assist him.

וַיִּקַּח אֶת שְׁתֵּי נָשָׁיו ... וְאֶת אַחַד עָשָׂר יְלָדָיו — *And* [*he*] *took his two wives,* [*and*] *his two handmaids and his eleven sons.*

— To the edge of the stream *(Radak;* see *Ramban* below).

There is no significance to the order in which Jacob transported them. [Here the wives are mentioned first whereas in 31:17 his *children* are mentioned first, while below in 33:6 the handmaids are mentioned first] *(Ramban).*

That the commentators in 31:17 explain why Jacob gave precedence to his children [see there] is not contradicted by his opposite order of priorities here. *Abarbanel* suggests that Jacob brought the mothers to cross the ford first so his children could watch them and would not be afraid to cross themselves.

Only his *eleven sons* are mentioned; where was his daughter Dinah?

Dinah was included with his wives. She was with Leah, since a daughter stays near her mother *(Radak).*

— *Rashi* cites the *Midrashic* interpretation that Jacob concealed Dinah in a chest and locked it, so Esau should not cast his glance on her [and desire to marry her]. Because Jacob kept her from Esau on whom she might have had a good influence, he was punished by her later abduction by Shechem [see chap. 34].[1]

וַיַּעֲבֹר אֵת מַעֲבַר יַבֹּק — *And* [he] *crossed the ford of the Jabbok.*

The verb *crossed* is in the singular: Jacob gathered his wives and children at the edge of the brook, and *he alone* traversed the ford of Jabbok to see if its waters were high, then he returned and led them across together *(Ramban).*

מַעֲבַר, *ford,* is the shallow place in a stream where it may be crossed. Every stream and river has a commonly known fording place [therefore its precise location is not further identified] *(Radak).*

The river *Jabbok* (today known as Nahr ez-Zerqa, so called because of its blue waters) is a tributary of the Jordan, half way between the Dead Sea and the Sea of Galilee. With its deep banks, the river is a natural boundary. The southwest stretch formed the boundary between Ammon and the Emorites [*Deut.* 3:16; *Josh.* 12:4], and its lower courses formed the boundaries between

1. Comp. the *Midrash:*

The Holy One, Blessed be He, said to Jacob, '... You were unwilling to have her marry one who is circumcised [Esau], she will soon marry one who is uncircumcised; you were unwilling to give her in legitimate marriage; she will soon be wed in a forbidden union.'

[Although a father could hardly be faulted for not wanting his child to marry an Esau, Jacob was punished for seeking to prevent such a marriage. The masters of *Mussar* explain that he should have been saddened that his duty as a father forced him to deprive Esau of the beneficial influence of Dinah. Instead, he hid her without feeling compassion for Esau.]

כד יַבֹּק: וַיִּקָּחֵם וַיַּעֲבִרֵם אֶת־הַנָּחַל וַיַּעֲבֵר
כה אֶת־אֲשֶׁר־לוֹ: וַיִּוָּתֵר יַעֲקֹב לְבַדּוֹ וַיֵּאָבֵק

the kingdoms of Sichon and Og [*Josh.* 11:22]. The lower courses also divided Gilead into two parts [*Deut.* 3:12, 16; *Joshua* 12:2-6] *(R' Hoffmann).*

24. וַיִּקָּחֵם וַיַּעֲבִרֵם אֶת־הַנָּחַל — *And when he took them and had them cross over the stream.*

— Having first tested it and assured himself that the waters were not too high *(Radak).*

[The translation *'and when ... '* is suggested idiomatically by the use of the double conversive verbs.]

וַיַּעֲבֵר אֶת־אֲשֶׁר־לוֹ — [*And,* i.e., *then*] *he sent over all his possessions* [lit. *all that were his*].

— His cattle and movables. Jacob acted as a ferryman [גַּשָּׁר; or according to others: as a *bridge* (גֶּשֶׁר), i.e., he stood in the middle of the water], bringing things from one side of the river to the other *(Rashi* citing *Midrash).*

The commentators note that the current of the Jabbok is very swift. During the greater part of its course, it flows through a deep and narrow valley, with steep precipitous side. Certainly, transporting an entire camp over the river, and that at night, was quite an undertaking.

25. The Struggle with the Angel

וַיִּוָּתֵר יַעֲקֹב לְבַדּוֹ — [*And*] *Jacob was left alone* [lit. *himself*].

According to the literal sense, the previous verse indicates that after Jacob accompanied his family across the river, he returned and ordered the others to cross the brook before him. As this verse informs us, he remained behind *(Ramban).*

He stayed behind to supervise as everyone crossed and to ascertain that nothing had been overlooked *(Ibn Ezra; Sforno).*

Following *Rashbam's* interpretation, this was part of the subterfuge: Jacob purposely stayed behind so he could flee in an opposite direction.

Rashi cites the *Talmudic* interpretation [*Chullin* 91a], that Jacob had forgotten some פַּחִים קְטַנִּים, *small earthenware pitchers,* and returned to fetch them.[1]

The *Talmudic* interpretation is based on a Scriptural allusion, perceiving the Midrashic connotation of לְבַדּוֹ, *himself,* to be לְכַדּוֹ, *for his vessel.* Alternately, לְבַדּוֹ is interpreted to mean: *for his* בֵּית הַבַּד, *vessel in which pressed oil is stored (Da'as Zekeinim).*

Cf. *Da'as Zekeinim* to 45:20: *(Pharaoh said to Joseph) ... Do not mind your belongings* [lit. *vessels*] — Pharaoh knew that Joseph's father had meticulously cared for even unsignificant earthenware jugs at a time of danger. He therefore told Joseph's brothers to inform Jacob that he should not let concern over his belongings delay his trip to Egypt.

R' Bachya offers that these were pitchers used for carrying *water;* Jacob risked his life to fetch them out of concern for his children who might otherwise suffer from thirst on the journey. [Accordingly פַּחִים קְטַנִּים would not mean *small pitchers* but *pitchers of the young children (Toras Chessed).*]

1. The Sages [*Chullin* ibid.] derive from the fact that Jacob risked his life by returning that night for small pitchers, that 'to the righteous, their money is dearer to them than their bodies' — the reason being that they never take anything that is not theirs. [I.e., whatever the righteous acquire is by their toil and honest dealing; accordingly since their money comes to them with great difficulty, it is symbolic of their unflinching adherence to the laws of the Torah. Therefore, they take scrupulous care of their possessions. (See *Overview*).]

and had them cross over the stream, he sent over all
his possessions.
25 *Jacob was left alone and a man wrestled with*

The *Midrash* preserves an opinion that among these pitchers was the jar of oil which Jacob was Providentially provided when he anointed the pillar at Bethel/Luz [see on 28:18]. The jar was endowed with miraculous properties and certainly contained an inexhaustible supply of oil. Jacob foresaw that with the oil from this same cruse, miracles would be performed by Elijah for the woman of Tzarefath [*I Kings* 17:16], and by Elisha [*II Kings* 4:1. Accordingly, Jacob returned for it in the dark of night, though a righteous person usually does not venture out alone at night (*Tanchuma Ki Sisa; Peskita d'Rav Kahana*).

וַיֵּאָבֵק אִישׁ עִמּוֹ — *And a man wrestled with him.*[1]

The Rabbis explained that this 'man' was the Guardian angel of Esau [in the guise of a man] (*Rashi*).

Tanchuma identifies this angel as Samael, generally considered the angel of evil (see *Overview*).

There are other opinions are that this angel was not functioning in an *evil* role, but in a kindly one. *Tanchuma* records an opinion that God, in His mercy, dispatched the angel Michael in the guise of a shepherd, to strive with Jacob, who was afraid of Esau, in order to encourage him. Jacob's victory in the struggle would give him the necessary confidence to face Esau.

R' Bachya perceives this as symbolizing the righteous person's inner struggle against the forces of evil (Cf. *Malbim*).

According to *Rashbam*, the angel's purpose was to prevent Jacob from fleeing so that Jacob would see God keep His promise that Esau would not harm him.

Sforno comments that the angel was undoubtedly dispatched by God to pave the way for Jacob's ultimate salvation. The Patriarch would suffer material losses as a result of the struggle, but he would emerge with an even greater victory and blessing as a result.

While the verb וַיֵּאָבֵק is generally understood to mean *wrestled*, its derivation from the root verb אבק is variously interpreted:

Rashi, quoting Menachem, derives it from אָבָק, *dust*, implying that in combat men cover themselves with the dust which was raised by the vigorous movement of their feet. [Cf. *Ibn Ezra* who interprets similarly, and *Chullin* 91a where it is noted that the dust reached God's Throne of Glory. (See *Chiddushei HaRashba*, and *Maharsha*).]

1. *Rambam* [*Moreh Nevuchim* 2:43] regards this incident as a prophetic vision [just as he regards Abraham's vision of the three angels in *Vayeira*, 18:2ff]. *Ramban* [in *comm.* to 18:1] challenges this vigorously, posing many questions [for example: If Jacob's wrestling was only a vision, why did he limp when he awoke?]

Ramban agrees with *Rambam* to the extent that whenever seeing or hearing an angel is described in the Torah, it refers to a vision, since the human senses cannot perceive an angel. (Such a vision, however, is still below the level of prophecy.) However, wherever the Torah specifically depicts angels garbed in human appearance as *men*, as in our case, then these angels are endowed with what Kabbalists describe as a 'garment', and are thus sensually perceptible to the human vision of the pious and disciples of the prophets even when they are awake. *Ramban* concludes 'I can explain no further.'

Abarbanel cites *Ralbag* who, in defense of *Rambam*, holds that Jacob's hip injury might have been caused by autosuggestion, an aftermath of the prophetic vision.

Radak suggests that God caused Jacob to limp after he awoke from the prophetic vision as a sign of His displeasure that Jacob had 'limped' indecisively in fear of Esau, and failed to place his unequivocal trust in God.

כו אִישׁ עִמּוֹ עַד עֲלוֹת הַשָּׁחַר: וַיַּרְא כִּי לֹא
יָכֹל לוֹ וַיִּגַּע בְּכַף־יְרֵכוֹ וַתֵּקַע כַּף־יֶרֶךְ
כז יַעֲקֹב בְּהֵאָבְקוֹ עִמּוֹ: וַיֹּאמֶר שַׁלְּחֵנִי כִּי

Rashi himself relates the sense of the verb אבק to its Aramaic meaning of *join, intertwine,* figuratively in the manner of wrestlers who *clasp,* and whose arms are *intertwined,* around one another. *Ramban* notes in this context that the Aramaic אבק is equivalent to the Hebrew חבק, *embrace,* the א and ח being interchangeable. However, he interprets the primary sense of the word as does *Menachem,* agreeing with the *Midrash.*

עַד עֲלוֹת הַשָּׁחַר — *Until the break* [lit. *rise*] *of dawn.*[1]

I.e., until the 'departure' of the שַׁחֲרוּת, *blackness,* of night. Alternately, שַׁחַר refers to the appearance of the first rays of daylight through the clouds before sunrise *(Ibn Ezra).*

In the figurative sense, reflecting Israel's destiny in Exile:

The angel — representative of the Edomite Empire — will fight with Jacob's descendants, wrestling with them to lead them astray from God's path *until the break of dawn* — the dawn, Israel's salvation, when the long night of exile will finally end *(Lekach Tov).*

26. וַיַּרְא כִּי לֹא יָכֹל לוֹ — *When* [lit. *and*] *he* [=the *angel*] *perceived that he could not overcome him.*

Though an angel's strength is superior to a human's, he could not overcome Jacob because God restrained him from inflicting permanent damage *(Ramban* according to *Tur).* An angel merely 'fulfills God's Word' [see *Psalms* 103:20], and had been commissioned *only* to strain Jacob's thigh *(Ramban).*

According to *Sforno:* The angel could not overcome him because Jacob cleaved tenaciously to God, in thought and speech.

וַיִּגַּע בְּכַף־יְרֵכוֹ — [*And*] *he struck* [or: *gripped* (lit. *touched*)] *the socket of his hip.*

This caused Jacob to limp. This laming of Jacob was in retribution for his wish to flee and not rely on God's promise of protection. We similarly find of all those who wished to flee against God's will that they were likewise punished: Since Moses was hesitant to go on God's mission, an angel met him on the way with intent to kill him [*Exod.* 4:24]; Jonah who fled from his mission to prophesy against Nineveh, was swallowed by the fish [*Jonah* 2:2]; and Balaam was punished for undertaking his ill-intended journey by being maimed [*Numb.* 22:25] *(Rashbam).*

The angel informed Jacob of the sins of the future leaders of Israel. In his agony, he stopped concentrating on God [see *Sforno,* previous s.v.], thus enabling the angel to hurt him *(Sforno).*

Seeking a sin that would make Jacob vulnerable to harm, the angel saw only one sin that had Jacob committed — that of marrying two sisters. Therefore, the

1. The Sages [*Chullin* 91a] derive from our verse that a scholar should not venture out at night [since in fact, Jacob remained alone at night and was harmed *(Rashi);* and we see (next verse) that the angel was able to exert power over him only at night, not by day *(R' Gershom).*] Others derive it from 22:3: *And Abraham awoke early in the morning* [i.e. waiting until morning rather than venturing out alone at night. See *comm.* there and *Tosafos, Pesachim* 4a].

The parallel citation in *Berachos* 43b and *Pesachim* 112b broaden this prohibition to apply to everyone, not only to scholars.

him until the break of dawn. [26] *When he perceived that he could not overcome him, he struck the socket of his hip. So Jacob's hip-socket was dislocated as he wrestled with him.* [27] *And he said, 'Let me go, for*

angel maimed him at his hip joint — near the organ of cohabitation, by which he had sinned *(R' Bachya).*

According to *Baal HaTurim,* Esau's guardian angel wanted to maim Jacob so as to disqualify him from performing sacrificial services, one of the privileges that went with the birthright he purchased from Esau [see on 25:31].

The *Midrash* understands the angel's act as an attempt to harm Jacob's יוֹצְאֵי יְרֵכוֹ, *descendants* [lit. the *issue of his loins*]. Specifically, this referred to the Jews of the 'generation of religious persecution' during the reign of Hadrian [117-138 C.E.], the Roman Emperor who crushed Bar Kochba's revolt. [The sense of the verse according to the *Midrash* is: The angel perceived that he could not harm Jacob personally, so he inflicted harm on his descendants.][1]

The Sages said of that brutal period: 'Other generations will have to seek favor like a poor man begging charity, but the generation of the persecution [specifically the Hadrianic persecution of 135 C.E.] will be able to ask for it as a laborer demanding his wages' [i.e., they will have suffered so much that they will be entitled to Divine mercy] (*Midrash HaGadol;* comp. *Ramban* in footnote).

The Hebrew for hip-socket is כַּף הַיָּרֵךְ, lit. *spoon of the thigh,* referring to the muscle-structure over the thigh bone that is convex like the ladle [spoon] of a pot *(Rashi).*

The verb נגע essentially means *touching.* Whenever it is followed with the preposition ב [נגע ב-] it denotes an improper touching; frequently also a violent gripping. Thus in *Job* 1:19: וַיִּגַּע בְּאַרְבַּע פִּנּוֹת הַבַּיִת, [the storm] struck the house on all four sides and pulled it down *(Heidenheim; R' Hirsch).*

וַתֵּקַע כַּף־יֶרֶךְ יַעֲקֹב — *So* [lit. *and*] *Jacob's hip socket was dislocated.*

The word וַתֵּקַע means *dislocated.* Cf. *Jeremiah* 6:8 where the word has the sense of *removed,* cf. the *Mishnaic* term קַעְקַע, to *uproot (Rashi).*

27. וַיֹּאמֶר — *And he* [=the angel] *said.*

1. *Ramban* similarly cites *Bereishis Rabbah* (77:4) which interprets the angel's success in injuring Jacob's thigh as an allusion to the Roman persecutions of later years when they nearly succeeded in uprooting the יֹצְאֵי יֶרֶךְ יַעֲקֹב, *future offspring of Jacob.*

Ramban explains that the wound inflicted on Jacob's thigh, which is in the area of the loins, portended a future danger that Esau's offspring, Rome, might come close to mortally wounding Jacob's posterity. This indeed happened during the time of R' Yehudah ben Bava who lived two generations after the destruction of the Second Temple. That was the time when Emperor Hadrian made it a capital offense to spread Torah and Judaism. R' Yehudah himself was murdered for ordaining five of the leading scholars of the period. R' Akiva and others were tortured to death and R' Shimon bar Yochai and others had to flee for their lives and go into hiding. Of this period, R' Chiyya bar Abba commented: 'Were a person to tell me, "Give your life for the Sanctification of God's Name", I would give it, providing only that they slay me immediately. But the דּוֹר הַשְּׁמָד, *generation of religious persecution,* I could not endure!'

Ramban concludes that in other generations, even greater atrocities have been and would be perpetrated against Israel [truly prophetic words in the context of our century!]. But Israel's assurance and consolation, too, is found in the aftermath of the struggle: וַיָּבֹא יַעֲקֹב שָׁלֵם, *and Jacob came intact* (33:18); whatever tribulations Israel will undergo, it will emerge intact and in peace.

עָלָה הַשָּׁחַר וַיֹּאמֶר לֹא אֲשַׁלֵּחֲךָ כִּי אִם־
כח בֵּרַכְתָּנִי: וַיֹּאמֶר אֵלָיו מַה־שְּׁמֶךָ וַיֹּאמֶר
כט יַעֲקֹב: וַיֹּאמֶר לֹא יַעֲקֹב יֵאָמֵר עוֹד שִׁמְךָ
כִּי אִם־יִשְׂרָאֵל כִּי־שָׂרִיתָ עִם־אֱלֹהִים

שַׁלְּחֵנִי כִּי עָלָה הַשָּׁחַר — *Let me go* [lit. *send me*], *for dawn has broken.*

— And I must say praises by day to God *(Rashi).*[1]

Radak suggests that this was the angel's polite way of saying, 'I have fulfilled my mission. Unless you require me any further, I will now depart.' By adding *for dawn has broken,* the angel implied: Do not fear that I am leaving you here alone at night; *dawn is breaking,* it will soon be light.

— *Dawn is breaking* — and you must be on your way [for Esau will be arriving shortly] *(Rashbam; Alshich).*

The angel's plea to be let go illustrates how strong a grip Jacob must have had on him. The angel was unable to loosen it *(Abarbanel),* and under his mandate to wrestle with Jacob, the angel considered himself Jacob's prisoner *(R' Bachya).*

The prophet Hoshea [12:5] evokes the Patriarch's struggle: *So he strove with an angel and he prevailed; he wept and he made supplication to him.* The Sages, in *Chullin* 92a observe that it is not clear from that ambiguous verse *who* prevailed: the angel or Jacob; or whether it was the angel who wept and supplicated or Jacob. They cite our verse to prove that it was the angel who wept and supplicated, and *v.* 29 proves that it was Jacob who prevailed. [In his *comm.* to *v.* 29, s.v. כִּי אִם יִשְׂרָאֵל, *Rashi* explains the nature of the angel's supplication.]

וַיֹּאמֶר לֹא אֲשַׁלֵּחֲךָ — *And he* [=Jacob] *said, 'I will not let you go.'*

This illustrates the Sages' dictum that 'the righteous are greater than the ministering angels' [since Jacob had the power to grant or deny the angel's wish] *(Sforno).*

כִּי אִם־בֵּרַכְתָּנִי — *Unless you bless me.*

— Unless you will acknowledge my right to the blessings which my father has bestowed upon me and which Esau disputes *(Rashi).*

It is not entirely clear how *Rashi* derives this connotation from the passage. Some suggest that he derives it from the past tense בֵּרַכְתָּנִי, rather than תְּבָרְכֵנִי *(Sifsei Chachomim; Bertinoro).* Others suggest that the endorsement of Jacob's right to the blessing is evident from the angel's response; hence, *Rashi* assumes that this was the original intent of Jacob's request *(Mizrachi).*

[It is possible that *Rashi's* exegesis is based on his interpretation that the angel was the Guardian Angel of Esau. What better blessing could Jacob possibly ask of this angel of Esau than an acknowledgment of his right to Isaac's blessings — and hence, a removal of the cause for Esau's hatred?] [2]

1. Cf. *Chullin* 91b:

'Let me go, for dawn has broken.

'Are you a thief or a kidnapper that you are afraid of the morning?' Jacob asked.

'I am an angel,' he replied, 'and from the day that I was created, my time to sing praises [to HASHEM] has not come until now.' [*Yafeh Toar* interprets the angel's remark to be: 'It is now my time to sing before God as I do every day, and if I miss this — regardless of the legitimate excuse I would have — I will never again be allowed to chant before Him.']

According to the *Zohar* [*Tazria* 45a] the powers of the emissaries of evil are restrained when light appears, for then the community of Israel communes with God. Thus this guardian angel of Esau felt that if dawn would come, he would be rendered powerless.

dawn has broken.'
And he said, 'I will not let you go unless you bless me.'
28 *He said to him, 'What is your name?'*
He replied, 'Jacob.'
29 *He said, 'No longer will it be said that your name is Jacob, but Israel, for you have striven with the*

According to *Rashbam:* 'Bless me that I will suffer no further harm from you.' Jacob asked for the blessing now, with daybreak, because he realized that his assailant was an angel.

28. Jacob is informed that his name will be changed to Israel.

וַיֹּאמֶר אֵלָיו מַה־שְּׁמֶךָ — [*And*] *he* [the angel] *said to him, 'What is your name?'*

The question was rhetorical, like God's question to Adam in 3:9: 'Where are you?', designed merely to initiate conversation. Obviously, the angel already knew Jacob's name since he had been sent to Jacob *(Radak).*

29. לֹא יַעֲקֹב יֵאָמֵר עוֹד שִׁמְךָ — *No longer will it be said that your name is Jacob.*

I.e., it will no longer be said that your name *Jacob* [derived from עקב, meaning *heel; outwitting; deceit*] suits you and that you attained the blessings by עָקְבָה, *outwitting and deceit* [as Esau indeed charged in 27:36] *(Rashi)*...

כִּי אִם־יִשְׂרָאֵל — *But Israel* [*=prevailing; superiority*].

Continuing *Rashi* ... But [it will be said] that you attained the blessings through *prevailing* [יִשְׂרָאֵל=שְׂרָרָה] and in an open manner. [It was not, as *Mizrachi* points out, the *angel* who was now *renaming* Jacob; nor was this name-change to be effective immediately, for the angel did not say, 'no longer shall your name *be called* Jacob. The angel was merely revealing to Jacob what *God Himself* would do later. *Jacob* would later be regarded as *Israel* — which would be interpreted as tacit acknowledgment of his *superiority* (from שרר) and his legitimate right to his father's blessings].

As *Rashi* continues the angel's dialogue: '... For later on, the Holy One, Blessed be He, will reveal Himself to you in Bethel [see 35:10]. There, *He* will change your name and bless you. I, too, will be there and acknowledge your right to the blessing. [For it is the angel who, in the following phrase, interprets the significance of the new name: *for you have striven,* etc. That concept is not repeated in 35:10.]

Rashi continues that this angel's response is alluded to in *Hoshea* 12:5, *And he strove with an angel and*

2. *R' David Feinstein* cites in this connection *Taanis* 20a: *Faithful are the wounds of a friend; but the kisses of an enemy are importunate* [*Proverbs* 27:6] — Better is the curse of Ahijah the Shilonite [*I Kings* 14:15] than the blessings with which Balaam the wicked blessed them [*Numbers* 24:6]. Since the angel was the heavenly representative of Esau's destiny, we may assume that Jacob, too, would have shunned a blessing by an adversary; only *confirmation of a previous blessing* would have been an appropriate request under the circumstances.

ל וְעִם־אֲנָשִׁים וַתּוּכָל׃ וַיִּשְׁאַל יַעֲקֹב וַיֹּאמֶר
הַגִּידָה־נָּא שְׁמֶךָ וַיֹּאמֶר לָמָּה זֶּה תִּשְׁאַל
°שלישי לא לִשְׁמִי וַיְבָרֶךְ אֹתוֹ שָׁם׃ °וַיִּקְרָא יַעֲקֹב שֵׁם

prevailed; he [=the angel] *wept and made supplication to him* [=Jacob.] What was the angel's supplication? [As that verse continues]: ... *'At Bethel He will meet us and there He will speak with us'* i.e., implying the supplication: 'Please wait until He will speak with us there [and *there* I will acknowledge your right to the blessings].' Jacob, however, would not agree to this [delay], and against his own wish [the angel] had to acknowledge [Jacob's] right to the blessings. That is the implication of [*v.* 30]: 'And he blessed him *there'* — for the angel had begged Jacob to wait, but he refused to do so. [Jacob did not release the angel until he blessed him].[1]

R' Yanai said: God associated His Name (אֵל) with Israel's. This is like a king who has a small key to open the door of his palace. He says to himself, 'I'll lose the key if I leave it as it is, so I'll attach a string to it in order to find it more easily if it gets lost.' God — if one may use the analogy — did the same for Israel. 'If I leave Israel alone,' He said, 'This people will become lost among the nations. But I shall attach My Name to Israel, so that this people can survive' *(Yerushalmi Taanis* 2:6).

The Talmudic prohibition *(Berachos* 13a) of referring to Abraham as Abram does not apply to Jacob/Israel, whom even the Torah continues to call Jacob in 46:2, showing clearly that he retained that name. [See *comm.* pp. 563-564. In any event, the angel, as noted, did not now *re-name* Jacob, as this was not part of his mission, nor was he authorized to do so. He was merely foretelling that God would later give Jacob his additional name Israel (see 35:10).]

As the Sages in the *Midrash* observe, the prohibition of calling Abraham 'Abram' is not analogous to Jacob/Israel since it was taught: It was not intended that the name 'Jacob' should be abolished, rather Israel was to be the principal name, and 'Jacob' a subsidiary one. According to R' Acha, the verse reads [35:10]: *Your name is Jacob,* however, *Israel shall* [also] *be your name:* Jacob was to remain the principal name, Israel was added as a subsidiary to it.

כִּי שָׂרִיתָ עִם־אֱלֹהִים וְעִם אֲנָשִׁים וַתּוּכָל — *For you have striven with the Divine and with the human* [lit. *men*] *and* [you] *have overcome* [lit. *been able*].

I.e., you have overcome them *(Rashi).*

[Thus the name *Yisrael* is explained as composition of יִשְׂרֶה, *to prevail,* with אֵל, *the divine.* This interpretation of the significance of the name is not repeated later in 35:10.] *Divine* refers not to God, but to the angel *(Midrash).* [This is often the sense of אֱלֹהִים in Scripture; cf. בְּנֵי אֱלֹהִים in 6:2 and *Job* 1:6].

For you have striven with the Divine — i.e. with the angel, inasmuch as you wrestled with me and I could not defeat you; *and with men* — Laban and Esau — who intend to harm you but are unable to. For just as this occurred to you with Laban, it shall happen to you

1. Jacob requested the angel's blessing just as the angels who visited Abraham conferred a blessing on him before they departed [18:10]. The angel responded that those angels were commissioned to bless Abraham; he, however, had no such mission, and he could not bless on his own initiative. Jacob implored him to at least confirm the blessings his father had already given him. In trepidation the angel referred to the case of those angels at the destruction of Sodom who revealed something to Lot on their own initiative and were banished from their Divine abode for a period of 138 years [see 19:13]. Nevertheless, Jacob prevailed and the angel was forced to bless him *(Zohar).*

32 *Divine and with human and have overcome.'*
30 [30] *Then Jacob inquired, and he said: 'Divulge, if*
you please, your name.'
And he said, 'Why then do you inquire of my
name?' And he blessed him there.

with Esau and his chieftains (*Radak*).

[The translation *striven* for שָׂרִיתָ follows the familiar understanding of the verb in the context of this verse, following *B'chor Shor*. The root is perceived by most exegetes to be cognate to שַׂר *superior, noble, prince,* hence *prevail*. Accordingly, several alternate interpretations are offered]:

Ralbag renders: For you are considered a שַׂר, *prince,* [i.e. great], among the angels in recognition of the extent of the Providence exercised over you, and your greater closeness to God.

Onkelos renders שָׂרִיתָ as *have become mighty* and אֱלֹהִים as implying *before God.*

The *Midrash* perceives this as an allusion that Jacob was a prince in God's presence, since his features are inscribed beneath the Heavenly Throne, as it were.

Depending upon the various interpretations of the stich, the word אֱלֹהִים assumes different meanings [*Divine beings* or *God*]. Accordingly, there is a difference of opinion whether the word is sacred [i.e. subject to erasure] or non-sacred (*Minchas Shay*).

30. הַגִּידָה־נָּא שְׁמֶךָ – *Divulge,* [lit. *tell*] *if you please, your name.*

Jacob knew that an angel exists only to perform specific functions assigned by God. As such, his name is temporary and reflects whatever mission he was to perform [see *Rashi* below]. Because the angel had informed Jacob of his new name, Israel, Jacob was curious to know the angel's mission (*Radak; B'chor Shor; Or HaChaim*).

— Tell me your essence and character so I will be able to deduce the transgression for which you were sent to wrestle with me, and I will repent of it and pray (*Sforno*).

וַיֹּאמֶר לָמָּה זֶּה תִּשְׁאַל לִשְׁמִי – *And he* [the angel] *said, 'Why then do you inquire of my name?'*

— We angels have no set names; they change in accordance with the missions entrusted to us (*Midrash; Rashi*).

Following *Radak:* 'You have no need to know my name.' The angel gave a similar answer to Manoach [*Judges* 13:18]: *Why do you ask after my name seeing that it is hidden?* — I do not know my name at any given moment, for it is subject to constant change [cf. *Midrash*] 78:4]. ... Manoach, however, did not know that he was addressing an angel.

— *Sforno:* Our essence is spiritual and cannot be communicated in human terminology for *it is hidden* [ibid.], and its function depends on God's will.

'Of what use could the knowledge of my name be to you? I am powerless except for HASHEM. Should you summon me, I would not respond nor can I help you in your distress.' But the angel blessed him for he had been commissioned to do so (*Ramban; Tur*).

וַיְבָרֶךְ אֹתוֹ שָׁם – *And he blessed him there.*

I.e., he thereby acknowledged Jacob's right to the blessings —

הַמָּקוֹם פְּנִיאֵל כִּי־רָאִיתִי אֱלֹהִים פָּנִים
לב אֶל־פָּנִים וַתִּנָּצֵל נַפְשִׁי: וַיִּזְרַח־לוֹ הַשֶּׁמֶשׁ
כַּאֲשֶׁר עָבַר אֶת־פְּנוּאֵל וְהוּא צֹלֵעַ עַל־
לג יְרֵכוֹ: עַל־כֵּן לֹא־יֹאכְלוּ בְנֵי־יִשְׂרָאֵל אֶת־
גִּיד הַנָּשֶׁה אֲשֶׁר עַל־כַּף הַיָּרֵךְ עַד הַיּוֹם

implicit in the revelation regarding the name change. The angel was forced to give the blessing *then,* since Jacob would not permit him to wait for the later revelation in Bethel *(Rashi v.* 29; *Ramban).*

[The sense of *Rashi,* then, is that this phrase summarizes the *above* incident, the sense being: *Thus, he blessed him there.*]

According to *Radak* and *Alshich* the angel gave him an *additional* [unrecorded] blessing in addition to the name-change. The word שָׁם *there,* is added since this was also in addition to the blessing which would later be conferred upon Jacob in Bethel.

HaKsav V'HaKaballah suggests that the sense of *he blessed* is that he *took leave* of him. Cf. 47:10: *And Jacob blessed Pharaoh* where *Rashi* explains: *he saluted him* and departed. [Comp. *Rashi* to 33:11 s.v. קַח־נָא.]

31. פְּנִיאֵל — *Peniel* [lit. *Face of God*].

In *v.* 32 the name is given as פְּנוּאֵל, *Penuel.* Both names are identical since the letters י, ו, ה, א are interchangeable *(Radak). Or HaChaim* suggests that only Jacob called it Peniel . Everyone else referred to it as Penuel, as it is also called in *Judges* 8:8-17, and in *I Kings* 12:25.

For Jacob, the name פְּנִיאֵל has a first-person connotation — פָּנַי, *my face* (toward) *God.* But for future generations the place name will signify: פְּנוּאֵל, *Turn to God* [פְּנוּ = *turn*] *(R' Munk).*

כִּי רָאִיתִי אֱלֹהִים פָּנִים אֶל פָּנִים — *For I have seen the Divine face to face.*

I.e., *I have seen angels of God face to face (Onkelos).*

The mere sight of an angel would certainly not have inspired this awe in Jacob; he had *seen* angels before. Rather the sense of *seeing face to face* is *to face in combat,* as in *II Kings* 14:11 *(Or HaChaim).*

[Cf. *comm.* to *Deut.* 5:4].

According to *Radak,* Jacob expressed this feeling because it was the first time he had ever had the awesome experience of seeing an angel garbed in a physical appearance.

וַתִּנָּצֵל נַפְשִׁי — *Yet my life* [lit. *soul*] *was saved.*

— Though I have seen a godly being. This is to be understood in light of the awesome prohibition of *Exodus* 33:20: *You cannot see My face, for no man shall see Me and live (Kli Yakar).*

Compare Manoach's apprehension that he and his wife would die after having seen an angel in *Judges* 13:22 *(R' Shmuel ben Chafni Gaon).*

32. וַיִּזְרַח לוֹ הַשֶּׁמֶשׁ כַּאֲשֶׁר עָבַר אֶת פְּנוּאֵל — [*And*] *the sun rose for him as he passed Penuel.*

The term לוֹ, *for him* or *upon him,* is idiomatic; it does not mean

[31] *So Jacob named the place Penuel — 'For I have
seen the Divine face to face, yet my life was saved.'*
[32] *The sun rose for him as he passed Peniel and he
was limping on his hip.* [33] *Therefore the Children of
Israel are not to eat the displaced sinew on the hip-*

to imply that the sun rose *only* for him, but not for others. In the common idiom, people say 'When we arrived there, the sun rose for us.' [I.e., the light of the sun, which had already risen east of him, now *reached him (Chomas Anach).*] *Midrashically*, however, the phrase is interpreted literally: Did the sun rise for Jacob alone? Did it not rise for the whole world? The answer given is that] the sun rose *for him*, i.e., for his needs — to heal his lameness in the manner metaphorically expressed in *Malachi* 3:20: *The sun of righteousness with healing in its wings.* When Jacob left Beersheba, the sun had set *before* its time *on his account* [see on 28:11]; it now made up for that by rising before its time לו, *on his account (Rashi; Chullin* 91b).

וְהוּא צֹלֵעַ עַל יְרֵכוֹ — *And he was limping on his hip.*

— He had already been limping before the sun rose *(Rashi);* i.e, when the sun rose, it found him limping, and its rays healed him *(Sforno).*[1]

33. The prohibition of eating the tendon of an animal's thigh.

עַל כֵּן — *Therefore.*

— In commemoration of Jacob's prowess, and the miracle God wrought to save him from death *(Rashbam)* ...

Sforno: By not eating that part of the thigh, Jews demonstrate that the limb in which Jacob was injured is unessential to us.

Tur: In punishment for having left their father alone and prone to the angel's assault.

לֹא יֹאכְלוּ בְנֵי יִשְׂרָאֵל — *The children of Israel are not to eat.*

The *Talmud* [*Chullin* 101b] observes that as the law is formulated it refers not narrowly to the children of *Jacob* [Reuben, Simeon, Levi, etc.] but to the children of *Israel,* a more general designation by which they were primarily called *after* the Giving of the Torah at Sinai. Accordingly, the Sages note that this law was instituted at Sinai, but was inserted here parenthetically in its present place so that the reason for its prohibition would be known.

R' Yehudah in the *Talmud* (ibid.) differs with the Sages and Jacob's own children were required to observe this prohibition.[2]

אֶת גִּיד הַנָּשֶׁה — *The displaced sinew [R' Hirsch: sinew of weakness.]*

The Hebrew lit. means: *the sinew*

1. The verse alludes to the fact that our suffering appears more difficult to bear when the sun of freedom begins to shine on us. As long as the children of Israel suffer in exile, they bear their misfortunes, injuries, and ordeals in silence. But when the sun of liberation rises and begins to shine, they feel their past suffering more acutely. Israel becomes aware of the fact that it 'limps upon its thigh', and is surprised at the extent of its own endurance *(Zohar* cited by *R'Munk).*

2. In his commentary on the Mishnah, ad. loc., *Rambam* follows the opinion of R' Yehudah,

הַזֶּה כִּי נָגַע בְּכַף־יֶרֶךְ יַעֲקֹב בְּגִיד הַנָּשֶׁה:
א וַיִּשָּׂא יַעֲקֹב עֵינָיו וַיַּרְא וְהִנֵּה עֵשָׂו בָּא
וְעִמּוֹ אַרְבַּע מֵאוֹת אִישׁ וַיַּחַץ אֶת־

that jumped. Why is it so called? Because it *jumped* and was displaced from its proper position. Cf. this meaning of the verb נשה in *Jeremiah* 51:30 and 61:51 *(Rashi* from *Chullin* 91a).

[There are two *primary* tissues which are forbidden in the hind quarter: the consumption of the inner sinew — the sciatic nerve —near the bone, is forbidden by Torah law; the outer sinew — the common peroneal nerve — near the flesh; is forbidden by the restriction of the Sages (*Chullin* 91a). Every last trace of these nerves must be 'porged' i.e. removed. Their fat is technically permitted, but because Jews are scrupulously pious, they treat it as forbidden; accordingly all the fat covering the sciatic nerve must be removed (Baraisa, ibid. 92b). Additionally, the six nerves which appear like strings must be removed as well as certain other veins.

Practically speaking, since 'porging' the hind quarters of the forbidden nerves is a laborious and costly task, kosher slaughterhouses in the United States usually sell the hind quarters of kosher slaughtered animals to non-kosher butchers, and not for kosher trade. In Israel, however, where meat is more expensive, expert butchers porge the hind quarters.

The pertinent *halachos* regarding this prohibition are treated in *Shulchan Aruch, Yoreh Deah* §65.]

עַל כַּף הַיָּרֵךְ — *On the hip socket.*
As explained in *Rashi's comm.* to the term כַּף הַיָּרֵךְ, lit. *spoon of the thigh,* in verse 26, the hip socket is so called since the muscle structure over the thigh bone is convex like the ladle [spoon] of a pot.

Accordingly, the inclusion of this description prohibiting only the displaced nerve *on the spoon of the thigh* is interpreted by the Sages [*Chullin* 89b] to include only the displaced nerve in animals, since their hip structure fits this description. Fowl, however, are excluded from this prohibition since the muscle structure of their hip sockets are not convex, like a spoon, but lay flat against the body [ibid. 96a).

Further, the *Talmudic* Sage Shmuel [ibid.] derives the ruling that *Scripturally* only that part of the nerve *which is on the hip socket* [i.e. only the part of the nerve

and remarks on this point:

Be aware of a fundamental concept that whatever acts we do, or refrain from doing, are the result of God having commanded us concerning them through Moses our Teacher, and not because God had previously related them to any prophets preceding him ... For example, we abstain from eating the displaced sinew on the hip socket not because we intend to observe the prohibition that was laid *on our father Jacob,* but because our intention is to observe the *mitzvah* that was given *to Moses our Teacher* ..., See what the Sages had proclaimed: 613 commandments were conveyed to Moses at Sinai [*Makkos* 23b], this being among the commandments.

[Cf. similar citation regarding the prohibition of eating limbs torn from living animals in footnote to 9:4 (p. 287); and regarding circumcision in comm. to 17:9 (p. 568).]

33
1

socket to this day, because he struck Jacob's hip-socket on the displaced sinew.

1 *Jacob raised his eyes and saw — Behold Esau was coming, accompanied by four hundred men. So*

which runs in these convex shaped muscles at the proximal end of the thigh] is forbidden. [See RaMA, *Yoreh Deah* 100:1].

Though Jacob was wounded on only one of his hips — presumably the right *one* — the prohibition applies to the sinews of *both* hips (cf. Rabbinic controversy in *Chullin* 89b and *Midrash).*

עַד הַיּוֹם הַזֶּה — *To this day.*

This day does not refer to the time when the prohibition was recorded, but to the time it is read: *as long as this will be read,* accordingly, *forever.* Similarly, it is written of Moses' grave [*Deut.* 34:6]: *And no one knows his burial place until this day,* meaning that it will *never* be known *(R' Hirsch).*

[Cf. עַד הַיּוֹם in 19:37, and comm. to עַד הַיּוֹם הַזֶּה in 26:34.]

כִּי נָגַע בְּכַף־יֶרֶךְ יַעֲקֹב בְּגִיד הַנָּשֶׁה — *Because he* [i.e., the angel] struck (or: *gripped;* see above] *Jacob's hip socket on the displaced sinew.*

[I.e., it is in remembrance of that incident that we refrain from eating the aforementioned forbidden nerves. See *comm.* to לָכֵן in the beginning of this verse for additional insights.][1]

XXXIII

1. The encounter between Jacob and Esau.

וַיִּשָּׂא יַעֲקֹב עֵינָיו — [*And*] *Jacob raised his eyes.*

[A common Biblical expression meaning *looked about* — in this case, in anticipation of Esau's arrival.]

וַיַּרְא וְהִנֵּה עֵשָׂו בָּא וְעִמּוֹ אַרְבַּע מֵאוֹת אִישׁ — *And* [*he*] *saw — Behold Esau was coming, accompanied by* [lit. *and with him*] *four hundred men.*

1. The *Sefer HaChinuch* notes that 'at the root of this mitzvah lies the assurance that even though exiled Israel will endure affliction and persecution at the hands of Esau's descendants, it will survive. Israel's progeny and name will endure, and Messiah will redeem it from the hand of its oppressor. The reminder contained in the prohibition against eating the displaced sinew will eternally bolster Israel's faith and righteousness.

R' Hirsch derives גִּיד הַנָּשֶׁה from the root נשה, *creditor,* one who is beholden to someone else. Accordingly, *renders it as sinew of submission,* and perceives in it the idea that one must submit to the power of someone else. Jacob was taught that although Esau could hinder and keep him from total independence, Esau would not be able to defeat him totally and prevent him from 'walking' through history.

For although Jacob's ability to stride forward was hampered, the thigh and its sinew were not *severed,* they were only injured. Even the wounds Esau *can* inflict upon Israel do not last forever.

By the commandment not to eat the sinew, Israel is reminded that Jacob stood almost alone against Esau's army of four hundred — yet he survived with only a minor injury. This was possible because of only one factor — God's help. Thus it stands as an eternal lesson not to feel hopeless in the face of Esau's power.

הַיְלָדִים עַל־לֵאָה וְעַל־רָחֵל וְעַל שְׁתֵּי
ב הַשְּׁפָחוֹת׃ וַיָּשֶׂם אֶת־הַשְּׁפָחוֹת וְאֶת־
יַלְדֵיהֶן רִאשֹׁנָה וְאֶת־לֵאָה וִילָדֶיהָ
אַחֲרֹנִים וְאֶת־רָחֵל וְאֶת־יוֹסֵף אַחֲרֹנִים׃
ג וְהוּא עָבַר לִפְנֵיהֶם וַיִּשְׁתַּחוּ אַרְצָה שֶׁבַע
ד פְּעָמִים עַד־גִּשְׁתּוֹ עַד־אָחִיו׃ וַיָּרָץ עֵשָׂו

[In the Hebrew the collective singular term *man* is used.]

Apparently, the gift had not appeased him *(Sforno).*

וַיַּחַץ אֶת הַיְלָדִים עַל־לֵאָה וְעַל־רָחֵל וְעַל שְׁתֵּי הַשְּׁפָחוֹת — *So* [lit. *and*] *he divided the children among Leah, Rachel, and the two handmaids* [lit. *upon Leah, and upon Rachel and upon the two handmaids.*]

[Jacob did not want to rely on a miracle, and so took every possible precaution. This arrangement of his wives and children is apparently different from his division of his people and cattle in 32:7,8.]

Jacob's reasoning in dividing the children among their own mothers was that a mother naturally has the greatest love for her own children, and would exert herself to the utmost to save them. Should this be impossible she would cry and beg for God's mercy on their behalf *(Radak).*

From Jacob's course of action, we learn that despite our total confidence in God's promises, we still must do everything possible on our own behalf *(R' Hirsch).*

2. וַיָּשֶׂם אֶת הַשְּׁפָחוֹת וְאֶת יַלְדֵיהֶן רִאשֹׁנָה — [*And*] *he put the handmaids and their children first.*

The implication is not that he was actually willing to sacrifice Bilhah, Zilpah and their sons; he placed them first *in his prayers,* as he was less secure regarding *their* safety than he was regarding that of Rachel and Leah *(Targum Yonasan; Sifsei Kohen).*

וְאֶת־לֵאָה וִילָדֶיהָ אַחֲרֹנִים — *Leah and her children next* [lit. *behind*].

In contrast with רִאשׁוֹנִים, *first,* the word אַחֲרֹנִים is usually interpreted *last.* However, as our verse makes evident, the word can also be used in the relative sense of *next in sequence* rather than as the absolute *last (Tosefos Yom Tov, Demai* 7:3).

That is, the term is relative. Compared with the *first,* these are *last,* but there still might be others who will come later. Cf. *Exodus* 4:8: *If they will not heed the first sign, then they will believe the later sign* (הָאַחֲרוֹן)*; and if they will not believe even these two signs, then you shall take ...* etc. Here, too, אַחֲרוֹן does not necessarily mean the *last* one. ... Furthermore, it is interesting that *Tosefos Yom Tov* did not cite the specific *Gemara* in *Nazir* 21a where אַחֲרוֹן is perceived as the intermediate one *(Torah Temimah).*

וְאֶת רָחֵל וְאֶת יוֹסֵף אַחֲרֹנִים — *And Rachel and Joseph last.*

The more precious and beloved, the farther back they were placed [אַחֲרוֹן אַחֲרוֹן חָבִיב] *(Rashi; Ibn Ezra).*

Jacob's hope was that *at worst* Esau's anger would be assuaged with the massacre of those in front, and he would spare those in the rear *(Radak).*

3. וְהוּא עָבַר לִפְנֵיהֶם — *Then* [lit.

he divided the children among Leah, Rachel, and the two handmaids. [2] *He put the handmaids and their children first, Leah and her children next, and Rachel and Joseph last.* [3] *Then he himself went on ahead of them and bowed earthward seven times as he approached his brother.*

and] *he himself went on ahead of them* [lit. *passed before them*].[1]

Saying, 'Should that wicked man intend to attack, let him fight me first!' *(Rashi).*

This is an example of a father's love for his children — should Esau not accept his conciliation, Jacob himself would bear the brunt of the attack so the children might be spared *(Radak).* [Cf. *Sifsei Kohen* above.]

וַיִּשְׁתַּחוּ אַרְצָה שֶׁבַע פְּעָמִים — *And* [he] *bowed earthward seven times.*

— In accordance with the verse [*Prov.* 24:16]: *A righteous man falls seven times, but rises up again (Radak).*

Jacob was quite justified in doing this. Esau was his older brother, and it was incumbent upon Jacob to give him filial-like honor *(Rambam, comm.* to *Esther* 3:2).[2]

The number 'seven' is constantly perceived by the commentators as having great kabbalistic connotations. The *Midrash* interprets 'seven' in this case as indicating *countless times:* R' Chaninah said, Jacob did not cease prostrating himself until the מִדַּת הַדִּין, *God's Aspect of Strict Judgment* gave way to His מִדַּת הָרַחֲמִים, *Aspect of Mercy.*

Similarly, see *R' Bachya* to *Lev.* 26:26 that 'seven' is often to be taken in the figurative sense meaning 'many'.

The *Zohar* suggests that the subject of *He Himself went on ahead of them* is the Divine Presence which preceded Jacob and guarded him. It was accordingly not to *Esau* that Jacob bowed down until he approached his brother, but to the Holy One, Blessed be He, Who passed before him. Esau, however,

1. The *halachah* is that for all precepts a benediction is recited עוֹבֵר לַעֲשִׂיָּתָן, *before* the precepts are performed. Where is it implied that the word עוֹבֵר [lit. *passed*] denotes priority?

— Abaye cites our verse where עָבַר is understood in the sense of *passed before,* i.e. preceded (*Pesachim* 7b).

[The *Rishonim* further qualify this to mean *immediately preceding,* for performance of a precept must follow its blessing with no delay.]

2. When Mordechai, claiming Jews do not bow, refused to prostrate himself in obeisance to Haman [*Esther* 3:2], he was reminded that Jacob prostrated himself before Esau.

'Yes', Mordechai replied. 'But Benjamin was not yet born and did not bow down and I am a *Benjaminite* [ibid. 2:5], a descendant of Benjamin. Therefore, just as my ancestor did not prostrate himself, I too will not bow down' *(Midrash Aggadas Esther* 3; *Torah Sheleimah* §14).

[The commentators similarly observe that Saul — a descendant of Benjamin — rather than someone else from the 'royal' tribe of Judah (see 49:10), was chosen as the first king of Israel. Upon this first king was to fall the obligation to destroy Amalek, Esau's descendants. Judah, as we shall see in *v.* 7, was among those who prostrated themselves to Esau. Only Benjamin, of all the tribes, was spared from witnessing this capitulation, and only a descendant of *his* could be called upon, in good conscience, to obliterate Esau's seed.

Cf. also *Sifre, Deut.* 33:12: 'The Temple in Jerusalem was erected in the territory of Benjamin, for of the twelve sons, he alone did not participate in bowing down before the wicked Esau.']

לִקְרָאתוֹ וַיְחַבְּקֵהוּ וַיִּפֹּל עַל־צַוָּארָו
ה וַיִּשָּׁקֵהוּ וַיִּבְכּוּ׃ וַיִּשָּׂא אֶת־עֵינָיו וַיַּרְא
אֶת־הַנָּשִׁים וְאֶת־הַיְלָדִים וַיֹּאמֶר מִי־

thought that Jacob was bowing down to *him* in great humility; hence his warm response. [See *Overview*.]

עַד־גִּשְׁתּוֹ עַד־אָחִיו — *As* [lit. *until* or *while*] *he approached* [*unto*] *his brother.*

I.e., *while* he approached Esau, he kept bowing. עַד, *until*, in Scripture, often has the sense of עֹד, *while*. Cf. *Job* 1:18 and *Shir HaShirim* 1:12 *(HaKsav V'HaKaballah)*.

4. [Finally, the preliminaries are over and Jacob confronts Esau not knowing whether the result will be bloody battle or brotherly reconciliation.]

וַיָּרָץ עֵשָׂו לִקְרָאתוֹ וַיְחַבְּקֵהוּ — [*And*] *Esau ran toward him,* [*and he*] *embraced him.*

Esau's compassion was aroused at the sight of Jacob's numerous prostrations to him *(Rashi* from *Midrash)*.[1]

Esau thought that Jacob, by his many obeisances, was recognizing his birthright and superiority [see *comm.* to 32:5]. With this he was comforted; for men's hearts belong to God Who directs them wherever He desires *(Ramban* to 32:8).

וַיִּפֹּל עַל־צַוָּארָו וַיִּשָּׁקֵהוּ — [*And*] *fell upon his neck, and* [*he*] *kissed him.*

In Torah Scrolls, the word וַיִּשָּׁקֵהוּ, *and he kissed him,* is dotted over each letter. *Midrashically,* this intimates that the word calls for a special exposition since dotting is one of the methods by which the Torah calls attention to recondite allusions contained within a word [see for example אֵלָיו in 18:9, page 640.]

Rashi notes that the opinions of the Sages in *Sifre* [*B'haalosecha*] differ as to the significance of these dots. Some maintain that it indicates that Esau did not kiss him wholeheartedly. However, R' Shimon bar Yochai maintains that although: הֲלָכָה הִיא בְּיָדוּעַ שֶׁעֵשָׂו שׂוֹנֵא לְיַעֲקֹב, *It is a well-known tradition that Esau hates Jacob,* but at that moment Esau's mercy was aroused and he kissed Jacob with genuine feeling.

The former opinion cited by *Rashi* is also expressed in the *Midrash:*

Said R' Yannai to R' Shimon: If Esau's kiss was sincere why is the word dotted at all? [Left undotted the word would be taken at face value as being sincere; since it is dotted, there must be a *special* significance to the word.] Rather, the dots signify that Esau's intention was not to kiss Jacob but to *bite* him! But Jacob's neck became firm as marble and Esau's teeth were blunted. The following phrase, *and they wept,* accordingly means that both wept — Jacob one wept on account of his hardened neck [which caused him pain *(Sechel Tov)*], and Esau on account of his teeth.

Cf. also *Pirkei d'Rabbi Eliezer* according to which the dots signify that the word is to be read as if it suggested Esau's *intent:* וַיִּשָּׁכֵהוּ, and he *bit* him!

The *Zohar* similarly invokes *Proverbs* 27:6: *But the kisses of an enemy are deceptive.* This is usually applied to Balaam who blessed Israel, but did so

1. The reason Esau's rage was mitigated was because his guardian angel, too, had already yielded to Jacob, and so Esau was forced to follow suit.

Everything in this world depends upon the Upper Realm, and when Esau and Jacob were reconciled previously in the Supernal Realm they were also reconciled below *(Zohar)*.

[4] *Esau ran toward him, embraced him, fell upon his neck and kissed him. Then they wept.* [5] *He raised his eyes and saw the women and children, and he asked, 'Who are these to you?'*

against his will. However, Esau provides another example of this. It is advisable to be more wary of the hypocritical advances and seductive ruses of an enemy than of his overt threats or direct attacks. Jacob was on his guard.

[R' Shimon bar Yochai cited by *Rashi* apparently maintains that the dots point to the *unusual sincerity* in the kiss of an Esau.]

Ibn Ezra asserts that in the simple sense of the narrative Esau's actions were sincere. He cites the similar weeping of Joseph and his brothers [below 45:15] when they reunited. *Ralbag* interprets similarly that Esau was so moved by the abundance of Jacob's gifts and prostrations that he flung himself upon Jacob's neck in warm embrace as is usual for brothers who had not seen one another for many years.

וַיִּבְכּוּ — *Then* [lit. *and*] *they wept.*

Both wept. This informs us that at that moment Jacob, too, felt love for Esau *(Haamek Davar).*[1]

Compare the touching reunion of Joseph and his brothers where there was also much weeping [45:15]; that of Jacob and Joseph [46:29]; and that of Moses and Aaron [*Exodus* 4:27] *(Ralbag).*

That they wept illustrates how Esau was overcome by pure humane feelings. Kisses can be false, but not tears. One cannot cry unless he is genuinely moved, for tears flow from the innermost feelings. Esau's kiss accompanied by tears proved that he, too, was a descendant of Abraham *(R' Hirsch).*

— According to the *Zohar* which views Esau as *insincere:* Jacob wept for fear that he might not escape his brother's onslaught. Esau wept because his father was still alive, so that he was unable to do any harm to Jacob.

— Jacob's weeping was stimulated by memories of his father's house *(Midrash HaGadol).*

5. וַיִּשָּׂא אֶת עֵינָיו וַיַּרְא אֶת הַנָּשִׁים וְאֶת הַיְלָדִים — [*And*] *he* [=Esau] *raised his eyes and saw the women and children.*

They had been standing at a distance to watch how Jacob would fare *(Haamek Davar).*

Even in times of stress the wicked are moved by their own evil inclination [for even now Esau noticed the women] *(Midrash HaBiur* cited by *Torah Sheleimah).*

מִי־אֵלֶּה לָּךְ — *Who are these* [referring to both the women and children *(Ramban)*] *to you?*

The expression is clearly idiomatic:

— *Who are these to be yours?* I.e., how are these yours? *(Rashi);* are

1. This, too, portends an allusion to the future relationship between Jacob's descendants and Esau's. So has it been in all ages: whenever Esau's descendants have been inspired by a spirit of purity to acknowledge Israel's spiritual ascendancy, Israel responded with love and brotherhood. Thus we note the warm and intimate friendship that existed between Rabbi Yehudah the Prince, redacter of the *Mishnah*, and Antoninus, the Roman Emperor *(Haamek Davar).*

[Thus, it is not *Esau's* weeping that the *N'tziv*, author of *Haamek Davar*, finds impressive, but the weeping of Jacob, who, in spite of all that he had suffered at the hand of his brother, was ready to let bygones be bygones, in return for the smallest gesture of friendship.]

אֵלֶּה לָּךְ וַיֹּאמַר הַיְלָדִים אֲשֶׁר־חָנַן
ו אֱלֹהִים אֶת־עַבְדֶּךָ׃ °וַתִּגַּשְׁןָ הַשְּׁפָחוֹת
°רביעי ז הֵנָּה וְיַלְדֵיהֶן וַתִּשְׁתַּחֲוֶיןָ׃ וַתִּגַּשׁ גַּם־לֵאָה
וִילָדֶיהָ וַיִּשְׁתַּחֲווּ וְאַחַר נִגַּשׁ יוֹסֵף וְרָחֵל
ח וַיִּשְׁתַּחֲווּ׃ וַיֹּאמֶר מִי לְךָ כָּל־הַמַּחֲנֶה הַזֶּה

they your children or your servants? *(Sforno).*

— *Who are these with you?* Or: Who are these? Are they yours? *(Ibn Ezra).*

Tosefos HaRosh renders: *Who — these are yours?* I.e., do they all belong to you?

הַיְלָדִים אֲשֶׁר־חָנַן אֱלֹהִים אֶת־עַבְדֶּךָ — [They are] *the children whom God has graciously given your servant.*

— Though Esau had asked about the *women* also, Jacob delicately answered only about the *children.* Esau understood from his answer that the women were his wives, the mothers of the children *(Ramban).*

Esau inquired about the women because he wanted to marry them himself. But when Jacob answered about the children, Esau understood that these women were their mothers *(Haamek Davar).*

The translation of חָנַן, lit. *has been gracious* as meaning *has* [graciously] *given* follows *Ibn Ezra* and *Ibn Janach* [*Shorashim:* חנן] who cites an analagous usage in *Judges* 21:22: חָנּוּנוּ אוֹתָם, *give them to us* [see *Radak* ad loc.]

Rambam in *Moreh Nevuchim* 1:54 notes that חֲנִינָה, *graciousness,* connotes a gift to someone who has no claim to it. For this reason, too, since God brings everything into existence and nourishes beings that have no claim on Him, He is called חַנּוּן, *Gracious.*

6. וַתִּשְׁתַּחֲוֶיןָ — *And* [*they*] *bowed down.*

[Although the handmaids came forward with their children, the verb *bowed down* is in third person *feminine plural* — suggesting that only the *mothers* bowed down. Apparently, their children did not bow]:

As sons of handmaids, Esau would consider them to be of inferior status, and would not even feel honored by their bowing. Alternatively, the sons only *came forward* but refused to *bow* with their mothers. The children reasoned that handmaids could properly bow, but it would be improper for sons of Jacob to do so [comp. action of Rachel and Leah's children, further] *(Chizkuni).*

[*Chizkuni's* second comment, however, does not explain how these children could consider it beneath their dignity to bow down when they had just witnessed Jacob himself bowing down seven times! Furthermore, the inference from the *footnote* to *v.* 3 is that all the children bowed — except Benjamin who was as-yet unborn.]

7. וַתִּגַּשׁ גַּם־לֵאָה וִילָדֶיהָ וַיִּשְׁתַּחֲווּ — [*And*] *Leah, too, came forward* [lit. *approached*] *with her children and they bowed down.*

Here, as well as in the next stich, *bowed down* is in masculine plural encompassing both the mothers and children, for in this case *even the children bowed.* [In Hebrew the masculine plural is used when the collective subject comprises males and females.]

These were the sons of the primary wives, women of standing and aristocracy [as opposed to the handmaids]. When they saw their mothers bow, they followed suit *(Chizkuni).*

He answered, 'The children whom God has graciously given your servant.'
6 *Then the handmaids came forward — they and their children — and they bowed down.*
7 *Leah, too, came forward with her children and they bowed down; and afterwards, Joseph and Rachel came forward and bowed down.*
8 *And he asked, 'What did you intend by that whole camp that I met?'*

וְאַחַר נִגַּשׁ יוֹסֵף וְרָחֵל וַיִּשְׁתַּחֲווּ — *And afterwards, Joseph and Rachel came forward* [lit. *approached*] *and* [*they*] *bowed down.*

In the other groups, the mothers preceded the children; but here it was the reverse: Joseph went in front of his mother because knowing how beautiful she was, he was afraid that the wicked Esau might fix his gaze on her [and desire her]. He therefore stood in front of her and shielded her from Esau's gaze. In reward for this, Joseph merited the blessing associated with the words עֲלֵי עָיִן, lit. *to the eye* [49:22; see *Rashi* there for an explanation of this allusion, and for a slightly different version of the *Midrash*] *(Rashi* from *Midrash).*

Why then did *Jacob* not conceal Rachel from Esau as he did Dinah [above 32:22]? — Possibly Jacob was convinced that a grandson of Abraham would not abduct a married woman. However, Joseph wanted to take every possible precaution *(Chizkuni; Abarbanel).*

According to the literal sense advanced by *Radak,* Joseph was still a child, and Rachel tenderly carried him in her arms in front of her. Therefore he is mentioned first. [Joseph was about six years old at the time (see *comm.* to *v.* 13 below), but it must be remembered that unlike the other wives who had several children, Joseph was Rachel's *only* child.]

8. Esau now inquires about Jacob's intent in sending the immense tribute:

מִי לְךָ כָּל־הַמַּחֲנֶה הַזֶּה אֲשֶׁר פָּגָשְׁתִּי — *What did you intend by that whole camp that I met?*

The Hebrew literally means: *Whom to you is all that camp that I met?* Our translation of the *sense* of the passage follows *Rashi* who explains it to imply, *why did you need it?* [i.e., what was your purpose in sending the gifts to me?]

Rashi continues that in the literal sense [since מִי, *who,* must refer to a person *(Mizrachi)*], the implied subject here is the leaders of the droves: *Who are your* (drove leaders) *that I have met?*

However, as is self-evident from Jacob's reply that the gift was *to gain favor in my lord's eyes,* Esau's question must mean: *Why did you go to the trouble of sending me your whole camp?* And though the word מִי literally means *who* and must refer to a person, Esau had already learned from the leaders of the droves to *whom* they belonged and that the gifts were for *him.* Accordingly, his question could only refer to Jacob's *motives (Maskil l'David).*

— Unlike most commentators *(Ibn Ezra; Radak)* who insist that מִי, *who,* must refer to a *person, Ibn Janach,* explains that מִי could

1. *Rashi* proceeds to cite the Midrashic explanation that Esau's question refers to 'camps' of angels who met and attacked him and his men. The angels asked the men 'Who are you?' 'We are in the service of Esau,' came the reply, and the angels continued their attack. Similarly, the angels took no notice when the men exclaimed to the angels, 'Leave him, he is

אֲשֶׁר פָּגָשְׁתִּי וַיֹּאמֶר לִמְצֹא־חֵן בְּעֵינֵי
ט אֲדֹנִי: וַיֹּאמֶר עֵשָׂו יֶשׁ־לִי רָב אָחִי יְהִי לְךָ
י אֲשֶׁר־לָךְ: וַיֹּאמֶר יַעֲקֹב אַל־נָא אִם־נָא
מָצָאתִי חֵן בְּעֵינֶיךָ וְלָקַחְתָּ מִנְחָתִי מִיָּדִי
כִּי עַל־כֵּן רָאִיתִי פָנֶיךָ כִּרְאֹת פְּנֵי אֱלֹהִים

also take the sense of מָה, *what*, or *how*, as in *Ruth* 3:16: מִי אַתְּ בִּתִּי, *How do things stand with you, my daughter?* [Thus, in our verse the sense would be: '*What is your intent* in having sent this extravagant gift?']

Ramban notes that it is not entirely clear whether or not the drove leaders had been permitted to deliver to Esau the message of 32:8-21. Perhaps he had refused to see them, in which case his question here was sincere for he had never learned the origin of the tribute. Or, perhaps he *had* been told, either by the leaders or by members of his own camp, in which case his question was rhetorical. Nevertheless, *Ramban* maintains that the intent of the question is: מִי זֶה לְךָ=מִי לְךָ, *Who is it to you*, i.e., Whom do you consider important enough for such an immense tribute?

Ralbag perceives the sense to be: Who do you think is able to reciprocate your generosity in return for such a valuable gift?

Sforno assumes that Esau knew that the gift was meant for him. The question meant: The camp whom I met who told me that they were 'a tribute sent to lord Esau' — Did you send me this gift as a mark of honor, or as an act of kindness thinking that I might be in need of it?

לִמְצֹא־חֵן בְּעֵינֵי אֲדֹנִי — [It was] *to gain favor in my lord's eyes.*

[I.e., to appease you and become reconciled with you (following *Rashi's* exegesis).]

Following *Ramban's* interpretation of the question, the sense of the reply is: 'In my opinion *you* are the superior and lord.'

Following *Ralbag's* interpretation: 'It was to *you* that I sent this gift. I expect nothing in return' *(Ralbag)*.

[Following *Sforno*, Jacob's intent was: I sent you this gift as a mark of *honor*, to gain your grace.]

[Comp. *comm.* to this phrase in 32:6.]

9. יֶשׁ לִי רָב — *I have plenty.*[1]

— I have no need for your gifts *(Radak)*.

a son of Isaac!' Nor did the angels release Esau when the men protested that their victim was a grandson of Abraham.

But when they exclaimed, 'He is Jacob's brother!', they said 'If so, you are of with us.'

[This, the *Midrash* concludes, was Esau's intent in asking Jacob who were the camp of angels which he had met (פָּגָשְׁתִּי, connoting *meet in battle)*. Therefore Jacob answered, '*To gain favor in my lord's eyes*,' i.e., 'I sent them to propitiate, not to beat you.']

1. R' Hoshaya related: An elderly scholar once told me, 'I will teach you Midrashic interpretation, but whenever you repeat it, you must say it in my name. Some day Esau will return to Jacob everything he has ever taken from him. As Scripture says [*Psalms* 72:10]: *The kings of Tarshish and of the isles shall return a tribute.* Observe that it says, shall *return* a tribute, and not, shall *bring* a tribute.'

I said to the elderly scholar, 'That is indeed a good thought, and I shall repeat it in your name.'

The scholar went on, 'If Esau will return the gift that Jacob willingly gave him, and even urged him to accept though he was reluctant to accept and said, "*I have enough*" — how much more will Esau return what he has stolen from Israel by *force!*' At that moment I thanked him sincerely (*Tanchuma Yashan*).

He answered, 'To gain favor in my lord's eyes.'
9 *Esau said, 'I have plenty. My brother, let what*
you have remain yours.'
10 *But Jacob said, 'No, I beg of you! If I have after*
all found favor in your eyes, then accept my tribute
from me, inasmuch as I have seen your face, which is
like seeing the face of a Divine being, and you were

[— Your gift, though generous, is unnecessary.]

Note Esau's haughtiness. Jacob constantly attributes his welfare to God: *The children whom God has graciously given your servant* [*v.* 5]; ... *Inasmuch as God has been gracious to me* [*v.* 11]. You will not find Esau ever invoking God's name (*R' Bachya;* comp. *comm.* to 27:21 s.v. גְּשָׁה־נָּא).

[See *footnote* to 32:6 and *Rashi* to *v.* 11 s.v. יֶשׁ־לִי־כֹל.]

אָחִי יְהִי לְךָ אֲשֶׁר לָךְ — *My brother, let what you have remain yours* [lit. *let there be to you what is yours.*]

Since you are my brother, you need not honor me with lavish gifts *(Sforno).*

In effect, by this statement Esau acquiesced to Jacob's possession of Isaac's blessing *(Rashi).*

10. אַל־נָא — *No, I beg of you!*

Do not, I beg you, say such a thing to me *(Rashi).* [I.e., 'hat you have plenty and do not desire my gift. — Jacob referred only to the gift! He was surely not begging Esau to relinquish his acquiescence to Isaac's blessing *(Maharshal).*]

אִם־נָא מָצָאתִי חֵן בְּעֵינֶיךָ — *If I have after all* [lit. *now*] *found favor in your eyes.*

— I.e., if you are now prepared to be well disposed toward me *(Malbim).*

וְלָקַחְתָּ מִנְחָתִי מִיָּדִי — *Then accept* [lit. *and you shall take*] *my tribute from me* [lit. *from my hand*].

— Then forgive me for having sent my tribute to you through servants, which certainly does not reflect my esteem for you. Now accept my gift from *my hand* — for I hereby give it to you *personally (Malbim).*

Jacob begs him to accept the gift as proof of his, Esau's, friendship toward him *(Ralbag).*

כִּי עַל־כֵּן רָאִיתִי פָנֶיךָ כִּרְאֹת פְּנֵי אֱלֹהִים — *Inasmuch as* [lit. *for therefore*] *I have seen your face, which is like seeing the face of a Divine being.*

I.e., [If I have found favor in your eyes] it is entirely appropriate that you accept my gift, inasmuch as the sight of your face is as esteemed to me as seeing the face of your guardian angel whom I saw. Mention of the angel was calculated to instill fear in Esau so that he would conclude that if Jacob could survive seeing an angel, Esau would certainly be unable to prevail over him *(Rashi* from *Midrash).*

Rashi's interpretation is in consonance with his general interpretation of the idiomatic expression כִּי עַל כֵּן. See specifically his *comm.* to 18:5. Accordingly, the sense of our verse is: 'If you view me at all favorably, then please accept my gift כִּי, *for* — it is entirely appropriate that you do so [or according to his exegesis in 18:8: *for,* I ask you this only] — עַל כֵּן, *inasmuch* as I have seen your face which is as esteemed to me as see-

יא וַתִּרְצֵנִי: קַח־נָא אֶת־בִּרְכָתִי אֲשֶׁר הֻבָאת
לָךְ כִּי־חַנַּנִי אֱלֹהִים וְכִי יֶשׁ־לִי־כֹל
יב וַיִּפְצַר־בּוֹ וַיִּקָּח: וַיֹּאמֶר נִסְעָה וְנֵלֵכָה

ing the face of your guardian angel. *Furthermore,* as the verse concludes, you should accept my gift since וַתִּרְצֵנִי, *you have been appeased by me (Mizrachi).*

[See also *R' Hirsch's comm.* to 18:5, the elliptical intent of which is applicable here too: … 'Please accept my gift, *(not because you are in need of it)* but inasmuch as I have seen, etc.']

Sforno renders: Accept it because it is customary to bring a tribute to an honored man.

This follows the *Midrash* which perceives the sense to be: Accept my gift *since I have seen your face* … and just as in respect to the face of God it is written [*Exodus* 23:15]: *None shall appear before My face empty handed,* so in respect to you: None may appear before your face empty handed *(Malbim* renders similarly).

The Talmudic Sage, Resh Lakish [*Sotah* 41b] cites Jacob's comparision of seeing Esau to the esteem of seeing a Divine being as Scriptural proof that one may flatter the wicked in This World.]

That the word אֱלֹהִים in our verse is not sacred and does not refer to *God* [but to an angel or important personage] is stated in *Soferim* 4.

וַתִּרְצֵנִי — *And* [since] *you were appeased by me.*

— I.e., and a further reason you should accept my present is: וַתִּרְצֵנִי, *you were amenable to forgive my offense (Rashi).*

Rashi continues that whenever the root verb רצה [or the noun רצון] occurs in Scripture it denotes *appeasement.* Cf. *Lev.* 22:20 כִּי לֹא לְרָצוֹן יִהְיֶה לָכֶם, *It shall not be conciliatory for you* — for the purpose of the sacrifices is to appease and conciliate. Similarly, *Proverbs* 10:32: שִׂפְתֵי צַדִּיק יֵדְעוּן רָצוֹן, *The lips of the righteous know appeasement* — they know how to appease and conciliate. [Cf. the expression in *Psalms* 19:15 יִהְיוּ לְרָצוֹן אִמְרֵי פִי, which according to *Rashi* should be rendered: *may my utterances be conciliatory* — and bring forgiveness. Thus, in our verse וַתִּרְצֵנִי properly means: *You became appeased* or *reconciled by me.*]

Ramban differs on the meaning of וַתִּרְצֵנִי. He maintains that [it is not an allusion to forgiveness for iniquity as *Rashi* suggests, because] it would have been inadvisable for Jacob to recall past grievances. Rather he maintains that רצה connotes *desire* and *pleasure* in a matter, and he cites verses where it connotes *favorable acceptance.* Accordingly he interprets that in our context Jacob says … *And you would indicate your pleasure with me* by accepting my present, just as God shows His pleasure in those who fear Him (רוֹצֶה ה׳ אֶת יְרֵאָיו) by accepting their offerings [see *Psalms* 147:11].

11. קַח־נָא אֶת־בִּרְכָתִי — *Please accept my gift* [lit. *blessing*].

The translation of בִּרְכָתִי [lit. *my blessing*] as *my gift* follows *Rashi* who explains the term to connote a gift given as a greeting upon seeing someone after a lapse of time. The term *blessing* used in instances of meeting someone, such as below 47:7: *And Jacob 'blessed' Pharaoh* has the sense of *greeted;* in Old French: *saluer* [=salute]. Here, too, the connotation of *my blessing* is *mon salut* (French), my greeting [the figurative name given a gift which is meant as an expression of good wishes. Cf. *HaKsav V'HaKabbalah* to 32:30 s.v. וַיְבָרֶךְ אֹתוֹ שָׁם].

Radak cites the similar use of the term in *II Kings* 5:15.

— In Hebrew a *voluntary* gift is

appeased by me. [11] *Please accept my gift which was*
brought to you, inasmuch as God has been gracious
to me and inasmuch as I have everything.' He urged
him, and he accepted.
[12] *And he said, 'Travel on and let us go — I will*

termed a 'blessing' since one sends it from that with which God has blessed him [see *Deut.* 15:14]. However, an *obligatory* gift due a monarch is called מַס, *tax (Ramban).*

אֲשֶׁר הֻבָאת לָךְ — *Which was been brought to you.*

— By my servants *(Radak).*

— With no exertion on your part. It was I who exerted myself to deliver it to you *(Rashi* from *Midrash).*

This is yet another reason you should accept my gift — I labored greatly to acquire it before it could be brought to you *(Mizrachi).*

כִּי־חַנַּנִי אֱלֹהִים וְכִי יֶשׁ־לִי־כֹל — *Inasmuch as God has been gracious to me, and inasmuch as I have everything.*[1]

I have everything; lit. *I have all* — everything that I require. Jacob spoke modestly, as if to say that whatever he has, constitutes *everything* he needs. Esau, however, spoke boastingly [*v.* 9]: יֶשׁ לִי רָב, *I have plenty* — much, much, more than I need *(Rashi).*

— And though I gave you this extravagant gift, I will lack nothing since I have been endowed with God's blessing. My wealth will not be diminished, since *God's blessing will make me rich* [*Proverbs* 10:22] *(Alshich; Malbim).*

The first נ in חַנַּנִי has a *dagesh* because it serves the purpose of two *nun's.* The root of our word is חנן; and technically it should be conjugated חַנְנַנִי. [That one of the נ's is dropped and replaced with a *dagesh* is to avoid a triple consonant, for ease of pronunciation.] The suffix נִי is not part of the root but serves as the accusative pronominal suffix — meaning *me,* as in עָשָׂנִי, זְבָדַנִי *(Rashi).*

[For connotation of חנן as denoting *unobligated* graciousness, see *Rambam* cited end of *v. 5.*]

וַיִּפְצַר־בּוֹ וַיִּקָּח — [*And*] *he* [Jacob] *urged him, and he* [Esau] *accepted.*

I.e., Jacob showered Esau with appeals until he accepted *(Radak).*

Although Esau *appeared* to have refused Jacob's gift, his hand had been outstretched all along to take it. [I.e., his refusal had been but a formal display of oriental courtesy; Esau throughout had every intention of accepting the gift] *(Midrash).*

Sefer HaYashar notes that in addition to the droves, Jacob also gave Esau gold, silver, and bdellium. Esau divided the cattle, giving half to his mercenaries and half to his sons. The silver, gold, and bdellium he put in the care of his son Eliphaz.

12. וַיֹּאמֶר נִסְעָה וְנֵלֵכָה — *And he said, 'Travel on and let us go'.*

Esau is speaking *(Rashi).* This is evident from the response in *v.* 13 where the expression *my lord* is

1. As noted in the *comm.* to 24:1 and 27:33, the word כֹּל, *all,* has esoteric implications as one of the Attributes of God. The *Talmud, Bava Basra* 16b-17a notes that in connection with each of the Patriarchs, the Torah uses the term כֹּל, *all, everything,* a word which implies *perfection,* a totally unflawed blessing. — With Abraham in 24:1: *HASHEM had blessed Abraham* בַּכֹּל, *with everything;* with Isaac in 27:33: *I partook* מִכֹּל, *from everything;* and with Jacob, our verse is cited. Kabbalistically, this teaches that in life they were given a taste of the World to

יג וְאֵלְכָ֖ה לְנֶגְדֶּֽךָ׃ וַיֹּ֣אמֶר אֵלָ֗יו אֲדֹנִ֤י יֹדֵ֙עַ֙
כִּֽי־הַיְלָדִ֣ים רַכִּ֔ים וְהַצֹּ֥אן וְהַבָּקָ֖ר עָל֣וֹת
עָלָ֑י וּדְפָקוּם֙ י֣וֹם אֶחָ֔ד וָמֵ֖תוּ כָּל־הַצֹּֽאן׃
יד יַעֲבָר־נָ֥א אֲדֹנִ֖י לִפְנֵ֣י עַבְדּ֑וֹ וַאֲנִ֞י אֶתְנָהֲלָ֣ה
לְאִטִּ֗י לְרֶ֨גֶל הַמְּלָאכָ֤ה אֲשֶׁר־לְפָנַי֙ וּלְרֶ֣גֶל

used, an indication that the speaker must be Jacob *(Mizrachi).*

When the verbs הלך and נסע, *travel* and *go,* occur together, the sense of *travel* is rising up from a particular resting place, and *go* is the actual embarking on the journey. Thus, the intent of this suggestion is that they should immediately rise up and without delay set out on the journey *(Malbim).*

This follows *Onkelos* and *Rashi* who similarly interpret the passage. *Rashi* adds that נִסְעָה is the imperative=נְסַע וְנֵלֵךְ, *travel on* [i.e. *rise up*] *and we will go,* the נ of נִסְעָה being part of the root [and not the future-tense prefix, in which case the word would mean *we shall travel on*]. Similar are סְלְחָה and שִׁמְעָה which are the imperative forms of שְׁמַע, סְלַח [the ש and ס of which are also part of the root word *(Mizrachi).*]

[As noted in the *comm.* to 27:19 s.v. וְאָכְלָה, the imperative verb form with a suffix ה (in this case נִסְעָה וְנֵלְכָה instead of נְסַע וְנֵלֵךְ) is used to reflect a connotation of *request* rather than a *command.*]

וְאֵלְכָה לְנֶגְדֶּךָ — [And] *I will proceed at your pace* [following *R' Hirsch;* literally: *And I will go alongside* (or: *opposite) you*].

— I.e., I will do you the favor of slowing down as much as is necessary to keep pace with your slow moving flocks and family. This is the meaning of לְנֶגְדֶּךָ, *alongside of you (Rashi).*

13. [Anxious to part company as quickly as possible, Jacob courteously declines Esau's offer.]

אֲדֹנִי יֹדֵעַ כִּי הַיְלָדִים רַכִּים — *My lord knows* [i.e., it is obvious to you *(Sechel Tov)*] *that the children are tender.*

— The oldest, Reuben, was only little more than twelve years old at the time *(Ibn Ezra).*

[Jacob was in Laban's house a total of 20 years (7+7+6). As noted in the comm. to 29:32, *Seder Olam* maintains that all the children except Benjamin were born during the second seven year period. If so, Reuben, the eldest was born in the eighth year of Jacob's service. The youngest, Joseph, was about six years old — hardly equal to rigorous travel.]

וְהַצֹּאן וְהַבָּקָר עָלוֹת עָלָי — *And the nursing flock*[*s*] *and* [*the*] *herd*[*s*] *are upon me.*

The younger animals, which are עָלוֹת, *giving suck,* are עָלָי, *upon me* — it is my responsibility to drive them slowly *(Rashi).*

[Thus, as the commentators on *Rashi* explain, the word עָלוֹת is not connected with עָלָי, but is an adjective modifying וְהַצֹּאן וְהַבָּקָר, as if the phrase read וְהַצֹּאן וְהַבָּקָר הֶעָלוֹת, *the suckling flocks and herds.* עָלָי, *upon me,* stands by itself, the elliptic connotation being: *their welfare is upon me,* i.e., they are my responsibility.]

Rashi cites words of the same root in Scripture, e.g. *Lam.* 2:11: עוֹלֵל וְיוֹנֵק, *babes and sucklings; Isaiah* 65:20: עוּל יָמִים, *an infant in years; I Samuel* 6:7: פָּרוֹת עָלוֹת, *milch cows.*

Come, that the Evil Incination had no dominion over them, that the Angel of Death had no dominion over them, and that their bodies remained intact after death.

[This, as noted in the *comm.* to ArtScroll *Bircas HaMazon,* is the intent of the blessing in Grace After Meals: 'The compassionate One! May He Bless ... us and all that is ours בַּכֹּל, *with everything,* מִכֹּל *from everything,* כֹּל, *everything.*]

proceed at your pace.'
[13] *But he said to him, 'My lord knows that the*
children are tender, and the nursing flocks and herds
are upon me; if they will be driven hard for a single
day, then all the flocks will die. [14] *Let my lord go*
ahead of his servant; I will make my way at my slow
pace according to the gait of the drove before me and

The sense of the word as perceived by the commentators [see *Radak* to 49:15] is that it refers to infants who are entirely dependent upon their mothers [or, in our case, their shepherd].

[Following the cantillation, however, it would appear that עָלוֹת עָלָי is to be read as a unit, the sense of the passage being: and the flock and the herds עָלוֹת עָלָי, *are dependent upon me* — lit. *take suck from me.*]

וּדְפָקוּם יוֹם אֶחָד — [*And*] *if they will be driven* [lit. *and* (if) *they drive them*] *hard for a single day.*

— And thus weary them on the journey by causing them to run *(Rashi).*

— Should we drive them hard in your honor so as to keep pace with you and not delay you excessively *(Sforno).*

Rashi explains that the verb וּדְפָקוּם means *knock. Cf. Song of Songs* 5:2: קוֹל דּוֹדִי דוֹפֵק, *A sound! My beloved knocks.* [It figuratively applies to whipping animals to make them run faster.]

וּמֵתוּ כָּל־הַצֹּאן — *Then* [lit. and] *all the flocks will die.*

From fatigue *(Rashi).*

Actually, Jacob's primary concern was for his frail children, but delicacy did not permit him to mention death explicitly in their case. 'A covenant is made with the lips' (*Moed Katan* 18a), and even an unintentional implication, much less an explicit statement, may contain a prognostication for the future. Such unintended prognostications often become fulfilled as if by prophecy (see *footnote*, p. 1165, and *comm.* to 31:32).] He did not want to say, 'Then *they* will die,' vaguely omitting the subject of his fear — because it would seem that the children were included by implication ...

It is possible that Jacob mentioned only the צֹאן, *flocks,* [the collective term for sheep, goats and other small ungulates] for it is *they* who would succumb to the fatigue. He omitted בָּקָר, *herds* of cattle because they might suffer injury, but would not die *(Ramban).*

Chizkuni suggests that the children were not mentioned because they traveled on camels and thus were not prone to the mortal danger of the tender sheep which traveled on foot.

14. יַעֲבָר־נָא אֲדֹנִי לִפְנֵי עַבְדּוֹ — *Let my lord go ahead* [lit. *before*] *of his servant.*

— Do not prolong your journey; proceed at your usual speed though you will far outdistance me *(Rashi).*

[Thus *Rashi* clarifies that Jacob's intent was *not* that Esau should *lead the way* with him following close behind, but that Esau should proceed at his own pace, without taking account of Jacob *(Mizrachi).*]

וַאֲנִי אֶתְנַהֲלָה לְאִטִּי — [*And*] *I will make my way at my slow pace.*

— The word לְאַט [*slowness*] like נַחַת, connotes *ease, quietude, tranquility, gentleness.* Cf. use in *Isaiah* 8:6; *II Sam.* 18:5. The ל in לְאִטִּי is a

הַיְלָדִים עַד אֲשֶׁר־אָבֹא אֶל־אֲדֹנִי
טו שֵׂעִירָה: וַיֹּאמֶר עֵשָׂו אַצִּיגָה־נָּא עִמְּךָ
מִן־הָעָם אֲשֶׁר אִתִּי וַיֹּאמֶר לָמָּה זֶּה
טז אֶמְצָא־חֵן בְּעֵינֵי אֲדֹנִי: וַיָּשָׁב בַּיּוֹם הַהוּא

root letter and not a prefix, so that the literal meaning is *I will lead on* לְאַט שֶׁלִּי, *at my own slow pace (Rashi)* [similarly *Ibn Janach.*]

Ibn Ezra in his primary comment perceives the י to be superfluous — [as in גְּנֻבְתִי=גְּנֻבַת (31:39)]— and that the passage means 'I will lead on לְאַט, *slowly.*'

The suffix ה of אֶתְנַהֲלָה is superfluous; it is the equivalent of אֶתְנַהֵל, analagous with אֵרֵד=אֵרְדָה *(Rashi).* [It also implies the more courteous form; see above *v.* 12, נִסְעָה.]

לְרֶגֶל הַמְּלָאכָה אֲשֶׁר לְפָנַי — *According to the gait of the drove* [lit. *work*] [*which is*] *before me.*

Following *Rashi:* לְרֶגֶל, according to the needs *of the feet* of הַמְּלָאכָה, *the drove, which is my duty* [lit. *my work* or *job*] *to lead;* וּלְרֶגֶל הַיְלָדִים, *and according to the gait of the children.*

Thus, *Rashi* interprets לְרֶגֶל as ל, *according to,* the רֶגֶל, *foot*step requirements. מְלָאכָה refers to the *droves,* since it is his *work* [i.e. duty] to lead them from place to place *(Mizrachi).*

Ibn Ezra renders לְרֶגֶל, *for the sake of* (comp. לְרַגְלִי in 30:30) מְלַאכְתִּי, the cattle who are *the object of my occupation.* He writes: 'It seems to me that מְלָאכָה denotes whatever man can produce by his own power and province. Even property may be termed *work,* as in *Exodus* 22:7. The word מַלְאָךְ [*emissary* or *angel*] derives from this root since a מַלְאָךְ is the product of and under the province of the dispatcher.' [*Radak* renders similarly.]

עַד אֲשֶׁר אָבֹא אֶל־אֲדֹנִי שֵׂעִירָה — *Until I come to* [i.e., *catch up with*] *my lord at* [lit. *to*] *Seir.*

— It was not Jacob's intention to go as far as Seir, but only as far as Succoth. He named a place farther than his actual destination because he thought, 'If Esau intends to do me harm, let him wait until I come to him' [i.e., let him be complacent, thinking that he will yet have an opportunity to carry out his contemplated attack when I meet him again; I will, however, not give him that opportunity, and will detour earlier;] and he did not go.[1] When, however, will he go? [i.e., since we do not find in all of Scripture that Jacob ever went to Seir, and he certainly did not intend to utter a blatant falsehood, when indeed did Jacob intend going there? (see *Yerushalmi Avodah Zarah* 2:1)] — He was alluding to the future, in the days of the Messiah, of which it is written [of Jacob's descendants (*Obadiah* 1:21)]: *And saviors* [i.e., the Judges of Israel] *shall come up on Mount Zion to judge the mount of Esau* [=Mount Seir]. There are many Aggadic interpretations on this *Parshah (Rashi).*[2]

1. *Avodah Zarah* 25b gives this bit of advice: If a traveler is approached by a stranger and asked his destination, he should lengthen his journey [i.e., he should answer with a point further along the road than his actual destination. Thus, if the stranger is planning an ambush, he will set his trap in the wrong place, for the traveler will detour earlier *(Rashi)*] as our father Jacob did when confronted by the wicked Esau.

2. Esau said, *'Let us travel on and go* — let us divide between us This World and Next.' Jacob answered, *'The children are frail* — in performance of *mitzvos.* If I choose prosperity

33 *the gait of the children, until I come to my lord at*
15 *Seir.'*
[15] *Then Esau said, 'Let me assign to you some of the people who are with me.'*
And he said, 'To what purpose? Let me just have favor in my lord's eyes!'

Midrash HaChefetz cited in *Torah Sheleimah* records that Jacob's remark was fulfilled when his descendants, upon entering *Eretz Yisrael,* went and annihilated the remnant of Amalek on Mount Seir [see *I Chronicles* 4:42-3].

In the literal sense of the narrative, Seir was one of the routes Jacob could have taken on his journey homeward. Esau had offered on his own initiative to accompany Jacob home as a mark of honor, but Jacob declined and said that he would proceed slowly. However, *should he decide to travel via* Seir — Esau's home — then Esau could escort him from that point onward. Since Esau's effort of escort was not for his benefit, but for Jacob's, the statement that Jacob might meet him in Seir cannot be regarded as an unkept *vow (Ramban).*

Haamek Davar suggests that Jacob *had* initially intended to go to Seir, but changed his mind when he perceived that Esau was peeved at him when they parted [*v.* 16].

15. אַצִּיגָה־נָּא עִמְּךָ מִן־הָעָם אֲשֶׁר אִתִּי — *Let me assign to you* [lit. *make stand up with you*] *some of the people who are with me.*

— This was a further offer on the part of Esau. He would leave a contingent of his men to protect Jacob and be at his service *(Haamek Davar).*

וַיֹּאמֶר לָמָּה זֶּה — *And he* [=Jacob] *said 'To what purpose?'* [lit. *why this?'*]

— I.e., Why should you do me a favor which I do not need? *(Rashi).*

אֶמְצָא־חֵן בְּעֵינֵי אֲדֹנִי — *Let me* [*just*] *have* [lit. *find*] *favor in my lord's eyes.*

— And do not try to pay me any reward now *(Rashi).*

— It was thus Jacob's intention that he did not want them or their company at all, especially since he had no intention of going to Seir *(Ramban).*[1]

Alternatively, both phrases could be read together as a courteous response: לָמָּה זֶּה אֶמְצָא חֵן בְּעֵינֵי אֲדֹנִי, *Why have I*

in This World for their portion, then *they shall be driven hard one day* toward the Day of Judgment. *Then all the flocks* — i.e., Israel — *will die,* and will not be able to withstand the judgments awaiting them in *Gehinnom.*

'Let my lord go ahead of his servant: be the first to take a portion in This World, *while I will lead on at my slow rate,* I will remain behind, exiled and downtrodden.' That is to say, I will not provoke war nor will I grow mighty during my exile; I will endure the yoke of subservience. This is the intent of *following the pace of the drove before me:* How long will the exile last? *Until he shall come* — in the future — *to Seir* [see *Obadiah* 1:21] *(Midrash* cited by *R' Bachya).*

1. The *Midrash* notes that whenever R' Yehudah HaNassi would go to visit the Roman government [the Romans being generally considered the descendants of Esau] he would peruse this episode and not allow any Romans to accompany him on his return journey. Once,

יז עֵשָׂ֛ו לְדַרְכּ֖וֹ שֵׂעִֽירָה׃ וְיַעֲקֹב֙ נָסַ֣ע סֻכֹּ֔תָה וַיִּ֥בֶן ל֖וֹ בָּ֑יִת וּלְמִקְנֵ֙הוּ֙ עָשָׂ֣ה סֻכֹּ֔ת עַל־כֵּ֛ן

found such favor in my lord's eyes? I.e., why am I worthy of such kindness on your part? *(Radak).*

Esau understood the implication that though Jacob acted in a friendly manner toward him *for the moment,* he had no desire to maintain a close *permanent* relationship with him or his people. For in truth, it is Jacob's destiny to dwell alone and secure, as we find further in 46:4 and *Deuteronomy* 33:8. This irritated Esau and he did not speak to Jacob again. However, he could not bring himself to harm him *(Haamek Davar).*

— Jacob's reply is a lesson for all generations not to associate overmuch with government officials. They draw no man next to them except for their own interest *(Tur).*

16. וַיָּשָׁב בַּיּוֹם הַהוּא עֵשָׂו לְדַרְכּוֹ שֵׂעִירָה — *So Esau started back* [lit. *returned*] *that day on his way toward Seir.*

— Esau returned alone; the four hundred men who had accompanied him deserted him one by one. For this they [i.e., their descendants] were rewarded in the days of David, when [*I Samuel* 30:17] David slew a camp of Amalekites [descendants of Esau] four hundred young men escaped *(Rashi* from *Midrash).*

Apparently there was a coolness between Jacob and Esau at the parting. It was not accompanied by the kissing which marked Jacob's departure from Laban [32:1]. Perceiving this coolness, Jacob gave up any thought of going to Seir to receive more honor from Esau *(Haamek Davar).*

The Hebrew literally reads: *So Esau returned that day on his way to Seir,* which *Targum Yonasan* — followed by *Lekach Tov* — interprets to imply that a miracle was performed, and he made the journey in only one day so Jacob would be rid of him that much sooner.

R' Shmuel ben Chafni Gaon, in following the literal sense of the passage, maintains that the verse is informing us that all of the events in this narrative — the meeting and subsequent exchange between Jacob and Esau — took place in one day, and *on that same day* Esau set out on his return journey to Seir.

R' Hirsch perceives that the expression לְדַרְכּוֹ, *on his way,* is not quite clear. Perhaps it signifies that Esau returned to his old life style. This was the last time Jacob and Esau met, and henceforth their ways of life would separate. The brotherly affection of this meeting was but a portent of the ultimate relationship of the two nations in a far-off future.

17. Jacob in Succoth.

וְיַעֲקֹב נָסַע סֻכֹּתָה וַיִּבֶן לוֹ בָּיִת — *But Jacob journeyed to Succoth and built himself a house.*

— Either no city existed there and he had to build a house for himself and shelters for his cattle, or he may have built a large house with

he forgot to pay due attention to the lesson of this verse and took Romans along for company. They had hardly reached Acco when he was forced to sell his cloak to raise money for bribes.

Ramban concludes that the Rabbis attached special significance to this chapter because of the tradition that it was portentious of the future exile, and they perceived in this episode a guide to the nation's conduct under Edomite domination.

Thus, those who later had to conduct communal missions to the Roman rulers would first study this section to draw inspiration from the methods of the wise Patriarch — whom his descendants were to watch and emulate.

33
16-17

[16] *So Esau started back that day on his way toward*
Seir. [17] *But Jacob journeyed to Succoth and built*
himself a house, and for his livestock he made

defense towers should Esau attack him *(Ramban).*

וּלְמִקְנֵהוּ עָשָׂה סֻכֹּת — [*And*] *for his livestock he made shelters* [or: *stalls; booths;* Hebrew: *succoth*].

Rashi, following the traditional Rabbinic chronology in *Megillah* 17a and *Seder Olam* chapt. 2, mentions that Jacob spent eighteen months there: summer, winter and summer. This is exegeted from these three words of our verse: *Succoth* — implying a summer dwelling since it is customary in those warm climates to live outdoors in the summer with a booth-like shelter overhead as protection from the sun; *a house* — implying a winter home; and *succoth* implying a summer dwelling. Thus, two summers and one winter were spent there, a total of eighteen months in all *(Mizrachi)*].[1]

[Jacob then tarried another six months, offering sacrifices at Bethel. Thus the total length of his journey home was two years. See 35:7; *Rashi* to 28:9, and Chart B on p. 1173.]

The commentators differ as to exactly how this eighteen month period is exegetically derived from our verse.

Mizrachi follows the opinion that it is based on the implication of the three references to dwelling places as noted above.

Gur Aryeh, too, holds that the exegesis derives the length of Jacob's stay from the allusion to shelters for three different seasons. Why should Jacob have named the place Succoth to commemorate the shelters he built for the animals, surely, reasonable men are more concerned with the conditions of people than of animals! That being the case, why didn't Jacob name the place to commemorate the houses he built for the people? Furthermore, since he named the place Succoth after the shelters, that fact that he so named it should have been given immediately after the *first* mention that he built animal shelters. According to the *Talmudic* exegesis, however, these questions are easily resolved. He used the name Succoth because shelters had to be put up *twice,* during the two separate summer seasons, while houses were built only once. He chose that name only after the *second* summer, when it became apparent that the prime activity of his stay had been the erection of the shelters.

Gur Aryeh adds further proof that Jacob must have remained in Succoth for a considerable period of time: When Simeon and Levi attacked the people of Shechem to free Dinah, they were described as אִישׁ, *each man* [34:25], a term implying that each had to be at least thirteen years of age. Since Reuben was only slightly over twelve when Jacob left Charan, Levi could not have been over eleven

1. *Mizrachi* questions, however, why *Rashi* has included this Midrashic interpretation here when according to the plain sense of the text the *house* and *shelters* were both made in the same season — the *house* for him and the *shelters* for his livestock.

As *Rashi* specifically mentions in his *comm.* to 3:8: 'Though our Teachers have collected many Midrashic interpretations in their appropriate places ... I, however, am concerned only with פְּשׁוּטוֹ שֶׁל מִקְרָא, *the plain sense of Scripture,* in a manner that is contextually appropriate,' [cf. also below *v.* 20]. If so, why has he not followed the simple meaning here? And furthermore, though Midrashically the first mention of Succoth is exegetically interpreted, in the plain sense of סֻכֹּתָה does not refer to the *construction* of shelters, but that he came to a place later named Succoth.

Kitzur Mizrachi answers that *Rashi* felt that a proper understanding of Jacob's subsequent history requires us to cite this Midrashic interpretation — even though it does not follow the *literal* intent of the text. This information is essential to the comprehension of the chronological calculation which equates the twenty-two year period Jacob stayed away from his parents to the similar period Joseph was in turn away from him, as *Rashi* notes in 37:34 [see also *Haamek Davar*].

יח קָרָ֥א שֵׁם־הַמָּק֖וֹם סֻכּֽוֹת׃ וַיָּבֹא֩ יַעֲקֹ֨ב שָׁלֵ֜ם עִ֣יר שְׁכֶ֗ם אֲשֶׁר֙ בְּאֶ֣רֶץ כְּנַ֔עַן בְּבֹא֖וֹ מִפַּדַּ֣ן אֲרָ֑ם וַיִּ֖חַן אֶת־פְּנֵ֥י הָעִֽיר׃

and a half. For Levi to be thirteen when they left Succoth, an eighteen-month stay was imperative.

Maharsha to *Megillah* 17a submits that the Talmudic source of this interpretation indicates that the first mention of *Succoth* is *not* the catalyst for this exegetical interpretation, since that refers not to *shelters*, but to the name of the town. Rather, the time period is derived from the plural form סֻכּוֹת, *shelters* — implying two summer seasons of shelter-dwelling, while *house* is in the singular, implying a single winter. *Maharsha* observes that although *Rashi* in *Chumash* seems to favor the interpretation as understood by *Mizrachi*, this interpretation avoids many difficulties otherwise inherent.

Haamek Davar suggests that Jacob did not make these shelters for his livestock, but for *himself*. The intent of the phrase וּלְמִקְנֵהוּ עָשָׂה סֻכֹּת, *for his livestock he made shelters*, is that *because of his livestock* — i.e. because he felt that his livestock needed this long period of rest — he set up residence there and built סֻכֹּת, *shelters*, for himself and his family. The plural, as the Sages perceive it, denotes *two* summer seasons when shelters are needed. Although Jacob's intention in delaying his return home was focused on his concern for his livestock, he was nevertheless punished for the delay.

עַל־כֵּן קָרָא שֵׁם־הַמָּקוֹם סֻכּוֹת — *He therefore named the place Succoth.*

— Meaning *shelters*. [See *Gur Aryeh* above for the reason he named the place to commemorate the shelters rather than the houses.]

Or HaChaim suggests that the name commemorated the *shelters*, not the *house*, for this may have been the first time anyone had taken such trouble to preserve animals from the distress of sun and cold.

This site — which was later to become part of the territory of the tribe of Gad — was slightly north of Jabbok in the Transjordan in the kingdom of Sichon. See *Joshua* 13:27; *Judges* 8:5. [It is not to be confused with the Succoth in *Exodus* 12:37, an Egyptian town *(Kesses HaSofer)*.] Conceivably, however, this was yet another Succoth [*I Kings* 7:46], and was nearer to Seir *(Ramban; Abarbanel)*.

18. Jacob in Shechem.

וַיָּבֹא יַעֲקֹב שָׁלֵם — [And] *Jacob arrived intact.*

Literally, שָׁלֵם means *whole; complete; perfect; unimpaired*: The Torah thus intimates that he arrived *intact* in body — having been cured of his limp; *intact* financially — lacking nothing though he had showered a large gift upon Esau [for, as *Midrash Tanchuma* notes, God had replenished everything Jacob spent on that gift]; and *intact* in his learning — having forgotten nothing while in Laban's house *(Rashi* from *Shabbos* 33b).

— He arrived in peace [שָׁלוֹם=שָׁלֵם; *peace*] from his exile, with nothing adverse having happened to him *(Ibn Ezra)*.

The sense is that Jacob now felt secure when he reached Shechem *(Ramban;* see below).

Jacob arrived שָׁלֵם, in total, harmonious *completeness* — physically, materially, morally, and spiritually. This is especially noteworthy in view of the moral dangers always present when a man must struggle strenuously to secure material independence *(R' Hirsch)*.

shelters; he therefore named the place Succoth.

18 Jacob arrived intact at the city of Shechem which is in the land of Canaan, upon arriving from Paddan Aram, and he encamped in view of the city. 19 He

עִיר שְׁכֶם אֲשֶׁר בְּאֶרֶץ כְּנַעַן — *At the city of Shechem [which is] in the land of Canaan.*

Jacob felt secure only when he reached Shechem because, as the Torah emphasizes, *it was in Eretz Yisrael* where he knew that Esau would not molest him since Isaac was nearby, because the inhabitants stood in awe of Isaac and would protect him, or because the merit of *Eretz Yisrael* would protect him. In contrast, during his stay in Succoth, Jacob felt no such security. As the Sages in the *Midrash* point out, as long as he lived in Succoth, Jacob kept sending extravagant gifts to Esau in Seir to appease him *(Ramban).*

[Shechem was an old Canaanite city. It was previously visited by Abraham when he entered Canaan (see *comm.* to 12:6). As we shall see from the tragic events that repeatedly occurred there, it was מָקוֹם מוּכָן לְפוּרְעָנוּת, *a place predestined for misfortunes* (cf. *Rashi* to 37:14).]

Rashbam maintains that שָׁלֵם is not an adjective meaning *intact,* but the name of a locale: Jacob came to *Shalem,* the city where Shechem was chieftain. [I.e., Shechem was the head of a city called *Shalem,* to which Jacob now came. Most commentators disagree inasmuch as the only known city called Shalem was Jerusalem (see on 14:18), which certainly does not fit the above description as the 'city of Shechem'. Although *R' Hoffmann* prefers *Rashi's* interpretation that שָׁלֵם here means *intact,* he notes that even today there is a village named Salaam somewhat north of Shechem.]

בְּבֹאוֹ מִפַּדַּן אֲרָם — *Upon arriving [when he came] from Paddan Aram.*

It is as one says, 'So and so has escaped from between the lion's teeth and arrived whole.' So here we are told וַיָּבֹא ... שָׁלֵם ... מִפַּדַּן אֲרָם, *Jacob arrived intact* [although he was coming] *from Paddan Aram* — from Laban, and from Esau who had encountered him on the way *(Rashi).*

[On Paddan Aram see above 25:20.]

וַיִּחַן אֶת פְּנֵי הָעִיר — *And he encamped in view of the city.*

It was Friday afternoon close to sundown. Jacob was therefore *compelled* to encamp before the city since there was no time left to enter the city, and he established תְּחוּמִין, *Sabbath limits,* while it was yet day. [That is, he established a place where he would spend the Sabbath. (וַיִּחַן is rendered: *he established his* חֲנִיָּה, *resting place).* This permitted him to then go anywhere within a radius of 2,000 cubits from that spot on the Sabbath.] This proves that Jacob kept the Sabbath before it was given *(Midrash;* also cited in some editions of *Rashi* quoting *Sheiltos d'Rav Achai Gaon).*

According to *Ramban* [cited in next verse], Jacob encamped there *intentionally,* since he did not want to be merely a transient lodger in the city, but wanted to buy a piece of land on the outskirts of the city and thus establish a presence in the

יט וַיִּקֶן אֶת־חֶלְקַת הַשָּׂדֶה אֲשֶׁר נָטָה־שָׁם
אָהֳלוֹ מִיַּד בְּנֵי־חֲמוֹר אֲבִי שְׁכֶם בְּמֵאָה
כ קְשִׂיטָה׃ וַיַּצֶּב־שָׁם מִזְבֵּחַ וַיִּקְרָא־לוֹ אֵל

land on his own property [so great was his love of the Land].

Possibly, the city was small, and since Jacob was accompanied by a large entourage he did not want to inconvenience the residents. So he encamped on the outskirts of the city, on the site he planned to purchase *(Radak).*

Midrashically, וַיִּחַן is related to חֵן, *grace,* and פְּנֵי הָעִיר is a reference to the *leading men of the city,* [*cf. Midrash* to 41:56]: ... *and he was gracious to the leaders of the city* — he sent them gifts. This teaches that one must display gratitude to his host community.

Cf. *Shabbos* 33b: *He was gracious* toward the city — he minted coins; he set up market places [where he sold goods cheaply *(Midrash)*]; he provided public baths.

19. וַיִּקֶן אֶת חֶלְקַת הַשָּׂדֶה אֲשֶׁר נָטָה־שָׁם אָהֳלוֹ — [*And*] *he bought the parcel of land upon which he pitched his tent.*

It was Jacob's intention not to be merely a transient lodger, but to establish an inalienable right to the land by means of purchase. That his first purchase was in Shechem was an allusion that this site would be the first one conquered by his family [34:28], almost three hundred years before the inhabitants of the land would be displaced by Israel as noted in the case of Abraham. [See *footnote* to 12:6 (p. 436)] *(Ramban).*

The Torah mentioned the purchase of this *parcel* [lit. *portion*] *of land* in order to inform us of the excellence of *Eretz Yisrael.* Whoever has a *portion* of it, is considered as having a portion in the World to Come *(Ibn Ezra).*

The Sages proclaimed that one who comes to *Eretz Yisrael* with the means to do so must buy himself a portion in the land *(Midrash HaGadol).*

Sforno connects this with the next verse: *He bought the parcel of land ... and set up an altar there.* He cites *Psalms* 137:4: *How shall we sing HASHEM's praise on foreign soil?*

Jacob wanted the altar he was about to erect to be on his own property, and not on land belonging to strangers (*HaKsav V'Ha Kabbalah).*

מִיַּד בְּנֵי חֲמוֹר אֲבִי שְׁכֶם — *From* [*the hand of*] *the children of Chamor, Shechem's father.*

Chamor was the chieftain of the city of Shechem [see 34:2]. As noted in the *comm.* to 12:6 according to *Ibn Ezra,* Chamor had named the city in honor of his son Shechem [cf. *Ramban* there].

Jacob bought the land from the *children* of Chamor rather than from Chamor himself. Perhaps the property had passed on and was now theirs. Chamor is referred to as *Shechem's father,* since Shechem was more honored and well known than his father [as specifically noted in 34:19].

Chamor was infirm, and his interests were handled by his sons, primarily Shechem *(Abarbanel).*

Hoffmann explains בְּנֵי חֲמוֹר as meaning the *clansmen of Chamor.*

33 *bought the parcel of land upon which he pitched his*
20 *tent from the children of Chamor, Shechem's father,*
for one hundred kesitahs. 20 *He set up an altar there*

Some interpret the term *Shechem's father* as meaning: the chieftain [=city father] of the city of Shechem *(Ibn Caspi).*

בְּמֵאָה קְשִׂיטָה — *For one hundred kesitahs.*

The *kesitah* was the equivalent of a *me'ah* [=1/6 of a *dinar*=1/24 of a *shekel* (see *comm.* to *Numb.* 3:47)], both names being used interchangeably in the coastal towns [*Rosh Hashanah* 26b]. *Onkelos* renders it [as an adjective meaning] חוּרְפָן, *good ones,* i.e., *negotiable currency — recognized everywhere,* as in 23:16: עֹבֵר לַסֹּחֵר *(Rashi).*

Among other interpretations of *kesitah* are *precious stones (Targum Yonasan);* and *sheep (Onkelos* as explained by *Midrash HaChefetz* since the Aramaic חוּרְפָן is the same word *Onkelos* uses to translate כְּבָשׂוֹת, *sheep).* Both of these renderings, as well as the familiar interpretation, *coins,* are recorded in the *Midrash.*

[The Sages view this purchase as indicative of the unquestioning faith of the Patriarchs. See citation from *Sanhedrin* 111a in footnote to 28:13.]

The *Midrash* notes that this became the eventual site of Joseph's sepulchre. It is one of the three places where the gentiles cannot besmirch Israel by saying, 'You hold stolen property,' since, as our verse tells us, Jacob bought it with uncontested currency. [See *footnote,* page 882.]

20. וַיַּצֶּב־שָׁם מִזְבֵּחַ — *[And] he set up an altar there.*

Having arrived in safety, Jacob built an altar there in consonance with his twenty-two-year-old vow *(Alshich).*

However, Jacob erred in building his altar in Shechem. Although he had arrived in Canaan safe and sound, in fulfillment of every condition he had requested of God, he still did not fulfill his vow by proceeding directly to *Bethel.* Instead he took up residence in Shechem and set up an altar *there,* hoping thereby to cause the *Shechinah* to descend there. But Providence caused the incident with Dinah to happen in Shechem, so he would be forced to leave that place and keep his vow in Bethel *(Malbim).*

The verb וַיַּצֶּב, *set up,* rather than וַיִּבֶן, *erected* or *built,* would imply that in this instance, it was an altar of a single stone *(Radak).*

According to *Lekach Tov,* 'erect' implies construction with stones of mortar; 'set up' denotes that the altar consisted of stones put together without mortar.[1]

1. *R' Hirsch* perceives in this hybrid expression — וַיַּצֶּב, implying a single-stone *pillar* in association with a multi-stone *altar* — a turning point in man's service to God. [See *footnote* to 28:18.]

The use of a single, natural stone upon which to serve God represents man's acknowledgement that all natural resources and abilities are given us by God. The construction of an altar from many stones implies that man utilizes and regulates his own activity to conform to God's will, and that man thereby shapes the universe. This latter form of service came into play when the Torah and the commandments were given. Jacob's arrival in the future land of the Torah represented the recognition that Israel's philosophy of service would undergo change.

אֱלֹהֵי יִשְׂרָאֵל: א °וַתֵּצֵא דִינָה
°חמישי בַּת־לֵאָה אֲשֶׁר יָלְדָה לְיַעֲקֹב לִרְאוֹת

וַיִּקְרָא־לוֹ אֵל אֱלֹהֵי יִשְׂרָאֵל — *And proclaimed it 'God is the God of Israel.'*

[The Hebrew literally means: *And he called it (or: to it,* or: *to himself): 'God God of Israel.'*]

— This does not mean that the altar was called 'God of Israel' [in the sense that one would think that the altar itself was endowed with Divinity *(Sefer HaZikaron)*]. Rather, Jacob intended that God's praise would be evoked at the mention of the altar's name. 'He Who is *God* — the Holy One, Blessed be He — *is the God* of me whose name is *Israel'*. We find a similar situation in the case of Moses who named the altar *'HASHEM Nissi'* [*Exodus* 17:15]. He did not call the altar HASHEM [as if to imply that the altar itself was the Divinity *(Sefer HaZikaron)*] but that the altar's name was an expression of praise: *'HASHEM is my* (Moses') *banner'*. [*Comp. footnote* on p. 1096] *(Rashi)*.

Ramban quotes *Rashi's* interpretation with approval, and draws attention to similar names which are indicative of God's praises, such as *Zuriel* [=God is my Rock]; *Zurishaddai* [=the Almighty is my Rock]. These names do not imply that one is referring to *that* person as being God Who is his rock. Rather one who calls that name, thereby signifies that *God* is his Rock. Similarly *Immanuel* [=God is with us] ... and the names of angels — *Gavriel* [=God is my strength], *Michael* [=who is like God?] — which proclaim by their very names that power belongs to God and who is comparable to Him.

Ramban proceeds to cite *Onkelos* who renders: *and he worshiped on it before God, the God of Israel.* He then suggests that it is alternatively possible that the passage means: *And he called Him 'God, the God of Israel.'*

Sforno interprets similarly: He invoked God in his prayers as God of Israel, in fulfillment of his vow in 28:21 employing his new name *Israel.*

This is in consonance with *Chizkuni* who additionally explains *Rashi's* intent that not *everyone* called the altar 'God is the God of Israel.' It was Jacob *himself* who referred to it by that designation. This is the intent of וַיִּקְרָא לוֹ, 'he *himself* called.'

Rashi cites the Talmudic interpretation that the subject is *God* Who called *Jacob* אֵל, *mighty.* [Thus the verse would be rendered as if it read: וַיִּקְרָא לוֹ אֱלֹהֵי יִשְׂרָאֵל אֵל, *And the God of Israel called him* [Jacob] *'El' (Megillah* 18a; cf. *Tosafos* s.v. דאי).]

The Midrashic version differs slightly: God said to Jacob: I am the Lord of those on high, while you are the lord of those down below. *Ramban* explains that there is great Kabbalistic significance to this remark — namely the esoteric allusion that the *Shechinah* rests in *Eretz Yisrael;* he concludes that only those immersed in *Kaballah* will understand.

Ramban has yet another version of this *Midrash: Jacob* is describing God as Lord of those on high and himself as the master of those below (see *Gur Aryeh).*

[The commentators remark that Jacob was punished for the haughtiness of this remark with the incident of Dinah, which immediately follows this narrative.]

God called Jacob 'El' on earth — a reference to his new name *Yisra-El* — since he was to be master down below. This also alludes to the merit of the righteous who actually dominate the world, even possessing the power through their prayers to annul decrees that are issued on High *(Me'am Loez).*

Rashi concludes: [Regarding the

34
1

and proclaimed it 'God is the God of Israel.'

1 **N***ow Dinah — the daughter of Leah, whom she*
had borne to Jacob — went out to look over the

various explanations perceived in a Scriptural verse, it may be observed that] 'the words of the Torah admit to many different interpretations, like a hammer splitting the rock into many different pieces. I, however, make it my aim to render the plain sense of Scripture.'

XXXIV

◆§ The abduction of Dinah.

Jacob, who had overcome the terrible trials of the past twenty years and believed that at last he would find tranquility upon his return to *Eretz Yisrael* — as the end of the last chapter seems to indicate — suddenly faces a setback in his destiny. His household is subjected to a succession of calamities: the abduction of his daughter, Rachel's premature death, and Joseph's disappearance. Our Sages, in introducing the following account cite *Psalms* 75:5, *I said to the joyous ones: Cease your rejoicings,* for, as they explain, joy is but transitory.

Nevertheless, this people, which is called on to be a nation of priests and God's standard-bearer on earth, had to experience a moral outrage upon its own flesh and blood right from its beginning. It had to undergo this ordeal so that the world could see in its swift and uncompromising reaction the sacred character of its purity. It had to suffer this outrage so that it could harden the steel of the natural soul for all time *(R' Munk; R' Hirsch).*

1. וַתֵּצֵא דִינָה בַּת לֵאָה — *Now Dinah, the daughter of Leah ... went out.*[1]

— From her abode on the outskirts of the city, into the town of Shechem *(Rashbam; Radak).*

— Dinah is referred to in our verse as *the daughter of Leah.* Was she not the daughter of *Jacob?* [i.e., why is she not identified in the common Scriptural manner, by her father's name rather than her mother's?] But because she *went out* — in violation of the code of modesty becoming a daughter of Jacob — she is called the *daughter of Leah* because Leah, too, was an excessively outgoing person [יַצְאָנִית], as it is written [30:16]: *And Leah went out to meet him.* With her in mind, they formulated the proverb, 'Like mother like daughter' [see *Ezekiel* 16:44-45] *(Rashi* from *Midrash* and *Tanchuma).*

Although, as we shall see below [see *Pirkei d'Rabbi Eliezer*], Shechem took steps to lure Dinah out of the house, she would not have gone had she not inherited her mother's nature as an extrovert *(Or HaChaim).*

1. *R' Bachya* records that the incident of Dinah was in punishment for several sins committed by Jacob:

1) When he told Laban [30:33], *'Let my integrity testify for me in the future'* God said, 'Does anyone know what the future will bring? In the future your daughter will be humbled' [see *comm.* there].

2) For having concealed Dinah in a chest, and not giving Esau the opportunity of marrying him. This was considered wrong since she might have been a good influence on him and inspired him to repent [see *comm.* to 32:23]. Furthermore, he should have had more faith in

ב בִּבְנ֥וֹת הָאָֽרֶץ׃ וַיַּ֨רְא אֹתָ֜הּ שְׁכֶ֧ם בֶּן־חֲמ֛וֹר
הַֽחִוִּ֖י נְשִׂ֣יא הָאָ֑רֶץ וַיִּקַּ֥ח אֹתָ֛הּ וַיִּשְׁכַּ֥ב
ג אֹתָ֖הּ וַיְעַנֶּֽהָ׃ וַתִּדְבַּ֣ק נַפְשׁ֔וֹ בְּדִינָ֖ה בַּֽת־

Dinah paraded about bedecked in jewelry, and thus attracted Shechem's attention; jewelry ought to be worn only inside the house (*Koheles Rabbah; Abarbanel*).

According to *Ramban*, Dinah is referred to as the *daughter of Leah* to allude that she was the full sister of Simeon and Levi, who, as we shall see, avenged her [*v.* 25].

אֲשֶׁר יָלְדָה לְיַעֲקֹב — *Whom she had borne to Jacob.*

Jacob, too, is mentioned, for it was only because she was the daughter of the venerated Jacob that Shechem took notice of her and perpetrated his shameful act upon her, as shall be explained later (*Or HaChaim*).

Even though she was abused, and may even have borne a share of the blame for having entered the society of strangers, she nevertheless deserves respect as one worthy of the title 'daughters of Jacob' (*R' Hirsch*).

According to *Ramban, whom she had borne to Jacob* is added to indicate that even her half-brothers — all of them children of Jacob — were protective of her honor.

לִרְאוֹת בִּבְנוֹת הָאָרֶץ — *To look over the daughters of the land.*

Dinah's motives are not clear. *Targum Yonasan* renders: לְמִיחְזֵי בְּנִימוּס בְּנַת עַמֵּי אַרְעָא, i.e., she went out, as girls do, to see how the girls dressed and what jewelry they wore (*HaKsav V'HaKabbalah*).

She was young and curious (*R' Hirsch*).

Tanchuma Yashan interprets: 'To see and to be seen,' i.e., to display her own beauty; therefore she was punished.

According to *Pirkei d'Rabbi Eliezer* 38, Dinah, as Jacob's daughter, always stayed at home and would not venture into the streets. Shechem became aware that the venerated Jacob had a daughter, and brought girls along to her house to frolic and play the timbrels. When Dinah went out to watch them playing, he seized her and raped her. From this union, Asenath was born [cf. 30:26; Asenath later became Joseph's wife.]

2. וַיַּרְא אֹתָהּ — [*And he*] ... *saw her.*

It would have been far better for the wicked had they been blind. Their gaze brings a curse upon the world! (*Tanchuma Balak* 2).

שְׁכֶם בֶּן־חֲמוֹר הַחִוִּי — *Shechem, son of Chamor the Hivite.*

Was he then a Hivite? He was an Amorite as noted in 48:22 — Rather חִוִּי is an adjective meaning *serpentine* in Aramaic [see *Onkelos* to 3:1]. This describes the serpent-like

God; rather than concealing her in a chest, he should have *prayed to God* that Esau not marry her, just as Leah did when she was regarded as Esau's future bride.

3) Because he was presumptuous in referring to himself as the Lord of the lower world [see *comm.* to 33:20].

Rashi to 35:1 adds that it was in punishment for Jacob delaying in going home [and setting up, instead, his residence in Shechem; see *comm.* there]; and for postponing the fulfillment of his vows (*Midrash*).

Jacob is further criticized for allowing his daughter to venture out alone and bedecked with jewelry, which should only be worn in the house (*Tanchuma; Abarbanel*).

34
2-3

daughters of the land. 2 *Shechem, son of Chamor the*
Hivite, the prince of the region, saw her; he took her,
lay with her, and violated her. 3 *He became deeply at-*

manner in which Shechem acted. King Solomon said [*Eccles.* 10:8]: *He who breaks down a fence* [figuratively set up to inhibit improper behavior] *will be bitten by a snake.* Dinah broke down the fence of propriety and was 'bitten' by a snake. Her parents should have forbidden her to go out *(Midrash).*

נְשִׂיא הָאָרֶץ – *The prince of the region.*

The appellation *prince of the region* refers to Shechem not Chamor. That Shechem was the prince is suggested by *Ibn Janach* and *Ramban* in their commentaries to a similar passage in *Ecclesiastes* 1:1 where the appellation *King of Jerusalem* refers to *Koheles,* not *David;* and *Ibn Ezra* in reference to *Isaiah son of Amotz, the prophet.* It is also suggested by *Ramban* to our verse [see below] who mentions that it was to Dinah's credit that she resisted — though unsuccessfully — the advances of the *prince of the region* — obviously Shechem.

That he was *the prince of the region* explains why, notwithstanding Dinah's screams, no one came to her aid *(Or HaChaim).*

וַיִּקַּח אֹתָהּ – [*And*] *he took her.*

I.e. he seduced her with words *(Lekach Tov).* [See comm. to *took* meaning *persuasion* in 2:15 and 12:5.]

I.e., Shechem *forced* himself upon her; there had been no consent or submission on Dinah's part to his efforts of persuasion at all, not even to his initial advances.]

Thus, *Haamek Davar* interprets: *he* [forcibly] *took her* — to his home.

וַיִּשְׁכַּב אֹתָהּ וַיְעַנֶּהָ – [*And he*] *lay with her, and violated her.*

The use of the double term is perceived by *Rashi* — following the *Midrash* — to denote a double offense: *he lay with her* — naturally, *and violated her* — unnaturally.

According to *Ibn Ezra* there was a single act: *he violated her* naturally — with the heinous act itself — for she had been a maiden.

Ramban maintains that in the literal sense וַיְעַנֶּהָ connotes forcible rape. The Torah emphasizes this to draw our attention to the fact that though Shechem was the *prince of the land,* Dinah did not submit of her own free will, but had to be *forced.*

Ralbag suggests that *Rashi's* Midrashic interpretation is derived from the verb order. Had וַיְעַנֶּהָ meant only that he forcibly violated her as *Ramban* maintains, then the verb order should have been וַיְעַנֶּהָ וַיִּשְׁכַּב אֹתָהּ, *and he forced her and lay with her,* which is the verb order in the case of Amnon and Tamar [*II Samuel* 13:14]. Reading as it does, the verbs suggest an unnatural forced violation subsequent to the initial, natural act.

[Cf. however *Rashi* to *Yoma* 77b s.v. מְבִיאוֹת אֲחֵרוֹת where another interpretation is conjectured; see also *Maharsha* ad. loc., and *Pardes Yosef.*]

[Cf. the force suggested by the indefinite article וַיִּשְׁכַּב אֶת in a similar phrase in 19:33. In this vein, *Haamek Davar* cites *Lev.* 15:35 that unless there is a special exegetical interpretation, the expression וַיִּשְׁכַּב אֶת denotes a *forcible union,* while the expression used for *mutual consent* is וַיִּשְׁכַּב עִם.

יַעֲקֹב וַיֶּאֱהַב אֶת־הַנַּעֲרָ וַיְדַבֵּר עַל־לֵב
ד הַנַּעֲרָ׃ וַיֹּאמֶר שְׁכֶם אֶל־חֲמוֹר אָבִיו
לֵאמֹר קַח־לִי אֶת־הַיַּלְדָּה הַזֹּאת לְאִשָּׁה׃
ה וְיַעֲקֹב שָׁמַע כִּי טִמֵּא אֶת־דִּינָה בִתּוֹ וּבָנָיו
הָיוּ אֶת־מִקְנֵהוּ בַּשָּׂדֶה וְהֶחֱרִשׁ יַעֲקֹב

3. וַתִּדְבַּק נַפְשׁוֹ בְּדִינָה בַּת יַעֲקֹב — [*And*] *he became deeply attached* [lit. *and his soul cleaved*] *to Dinah, daughter of Jacob.*

— Both because of her great beauty, and because she was the daughter of Jacob, an acknowledged great man *(Radak).*

Dinah was indeed beautiful, but the Torah did not mention it — as it did in the case of Sarah, Rebecca and Rachel — since Dinah's beauty was her undoing. The Torah speaks only in praise of righteous women, but not of beauty such as Dinah's which resulted in personal tragedy. [Although Sarah and Rebecca, too, were abducted, they were not physically molested] *(Ramban* to *v.* 12).

The term נַפְשׁוֹ, literally, *his soul,* indicates that Shechem's feelings were profoundly spiritual or intellectual. So deep an attachment on the part of a nobleman can occur only when he views the object as an equal since there can be no 'cleaving of souls' when there are substantial differences in stations of life; the gap in background and culture would preclude it. Shechem could have such strong feelings for Dinah because she, too, was a 'princess' — the *daughter of Jacob* who was a princely man *(Malbim).*

The effect was the reverse in the case of Amnon and Tamor, where once he violated her, he hated her [see *II Samuel* 13:14ff] *(Sforno).*

וַיֶּאֱהַב אֶת הַנַּעֲרָ וַיְדַבֵּר עַל לֵב הַנַּעֲרָ — [*And*] *he loved the maiden, and he appealed to the maiden's emotions* [lit. *spoke upon the girl's heart*].[1]

[He played upon her sensitivities, the heart being considered in Scripture as the seat of the emotions.]

— *He spoke upon the girl's heart:* words that would settle on the heart, i.e., persuadingly: 'See how much money your father squandered on a *small* piece of land; if I marry you, you will acquire the city and *all* its lands!' *(Yoma* 77b; *Rashi).*

The maiden who was imprisoned in his home would constantly protest and cry; this is why he tried to console her (*Ramban v.* 13).

He tried to *console* her over his act, and *appease* her anger while at the same time declaring his wish to make her his wife *(Radak; Ibn Ezra).*

[On the use of the term *speaking upon the heart* to connote *consoling words,* see *Isaiah* 40:2.]

1. [The word נַעֲרָה, *maiden,* is spelled throughout the Torah without the final ה, (נַעֲרָ), as though it were the masculine נַעַר, *lad.* The *Talmud (Kesubos* 40b) notes that only once, in *Deut.* 22:19 is it spelled out fully, and there the full spelling indicates that the maiden is at least twelve years old — a fully developed young lady. Otherwise, Scripture refers to a girl similar to a lad, i.e., one who is not yet, or not necessarily, twelve years old, the age of feminine maturity. Cf. on Rebecca, *comm.* to 24:14.

In our case, following the Rabbinic chronology that all Jacob's children except Benjamin

tached to Dinah daughter of Jacob; he loved the maiden and appealed to the maiden's emotions. [4] *So Shechem said to Chamor, his father, as follows, 'Get me this girl for a wife.'*

[5] *Now Jacob heard that he had defiled his daughter Dinah, while his sons were with his cattle in the field;*

Malbim suggests that it had not *originally* been Shechem's intention to marry Dinah; he had merely wanted to satisfy his lust. It was only *after* he violated her that he gained respect for her as Jacob's daughter. Then he became deeply attached to her, and *loved the maiden* — for the sake of her *own* beauty and virtue. Had he truly loved her earlier, he would never have inflicted on her a disgrace tantamount to murder. It was *now,* after the act, when his animal passion had subsided, that he regretted what he had done and tried to comfort her from her sorrow and grief.

4. **קַח־לִי אֶת־הַיַּלְדָּה הַזֹּאת לְאִשָּׁה** — *Get me this girl* [the Hebrew implies: *young girl* see footnote to *v.* 3] *for a wife.*

קַח, *take,* in Hebrew denotes *pursuasion* [see 2:15 and 12:5] *(Abarbanel).*

5. Jacob's family learns of Dinah's violation.

וְיַעֲקֹב שָׁמַע — *Now* [i.e., in the meanwhile; lit. *and*] *Jacob heard.*

There had been great indignation throughout the town at Shechem's heinous act. The morality of the people had been breached, for Shechem violated the taboo against promiscuous fornication. A member of the nobility had transgressed, and Jacob heard of it *(Lekach Tov; Alshich;* see *Rashi* to *v.* 7 וְכֵן לֹא יֵעָשֶׂה*).*

כִּי טִמֵּא אֶת־דִּינָה בִתּוֹ — *That he had defiled his daughter Dinah.*

That he, i.e., Shechem. The other pronouns in this verse refer to Jacob *(Radak).*

[It must also be conjectured that Jacob's suspicions must have been aroused when Dinah did not return home. As is evident from *v.* 26, she was being held a prisoner in Shechem's home. Jacob might have inquired after her and heard the dastardly news.]

According to *Sefer HaYashar,* Jacob sent two servants to bring Dinah home from Shechem's house, but when they arrived there, Shechem and his men drove them away. The servants observed Shechem making advances to her before their very eyes. When the servants reported back to Jacob, he was convinced that, indeed, Shechem *had defiled his daughter Dinah.*

The term טִמֵּא, *defiled,* reflects the

were born during his second seven-year period of labor, and that Dinah was older than Joseph who was born at the very end of the seven-year period, Dinah was about eight-years old by this time. *R' Bachya* derives this from the fact that Jacob worked an additional six years before he fled, and he had spent, as noted, eighteen months in Succoth. Add the additional half year or so until Dinah's birth — since the Sages calculate that the children were born seven months apart — and Dinah was therefore about a month older than eight by this time.

Thus, as *Lekach Tov* observes, in *v.* 4 Shechem refers to her as a יַלְדָּה, *little girl.*]

ו עַד־בֹּאָם׃ וַיֵּצֵא חֲמוֹר אֲבִי־שְׁכֶם אֶל־
ז יַעֲקֹב לְדַבֵּר אִתּוֹ׃ וּבְנֵי יַעֲקֹב בָּאוּ מִן־
הַשָּׂדֶה כְּשָׁמְעָם וַיִּתְעַצְּבוּ הָאֲנָשִׁים וַיִּחַר
לָהֶם מְאֹד כִּי נְבָלָה עָשָׂה בְיִשְׂרָאֵל
לִשְׁכַּב אֶת־בַּת־יַעֲקֹב וְכֵן לֹא יֵעָשֶׂה׃

status of a woman so violated. She would henceforth live in shame shunned by all (*Ramban* to *v.* 12).

Cf. this term's use in the prohibition of forbidden unions in *Lev.* 18:24 (*R' Shmuel ben Chafni Gaon*).

וְהֶחֱרִשׁ יַעֲקֹב עַד־בֹּאָם — *So* [lit. *and*] *Jacob kept silent until their arrival.*

He avoided any outward expression of grievance until his sons arrived home to learn of the episode and make provision for their own safety (*Sforno*).

Apparently he sent for them and then awaited their arrival (*Or HaChaim*).

Abarbanel suggests the contrary, that Jacob did not summon them lest the sudden shock of the news be too great. Instead, he kept silent and waited for them to arrive at day's end.

The *Midrash* cites *Proverbs* 11:12: *A man of discernment holds his peace.*

The word הֶחֱרִישׁ, *kept silent,* is spelled defectively [without a י (הֶחֱרִשׁ)]. This draws attention to the word and implies that his silence was *total* (*Sechel Tov*).

Jacob maintained his patient silence only, as the verse noted, because he heard that Shechem had *already* violated his daughter. It was a *fait accompli* and there was nothing Jacob could now do to undo it. Had the act *not* yet taken place, Jacob would certainly have sacrificed his very being to prevent her defilement (*Alshich; Malbim*).

6. וַיֵּצֵא חֲמוֹר אֲבִי־שְׁכֶם — [*And*] *Chamor, Shechem's father, went out.*

He noticed that Jacob was maintaining his silence and he grew worried that Jacob was plotting against him (*Sforno*).

R' Meyuchas holds that Jacob maintained his absolute silence even in Chamor's presence and refused to talk with him until his children returned home.

7. וּבְנֵי יַעֲקֹב בָּאוּ מִן הַשָּׂדֶה כְּשָׁמְעָם — [*And*] *Jacob's sons arrived* [home] *from the field, when they heard* [the news].

[Apparently the ugly news reached them out in the fields.]

They arrived at Jacob's tent at about the same time as Chamor, and they did not have the opportunity to consult privately with their father (*Rashbam; Malbim*).

[Our translation follows the punctuation of the Masoretic cantillation. R' Tanchuma in the *Midrash* observes that our verse is ambiguous inasmuch as the syntactic relationship of the word כְּשָׁמְעָם is obscure and the verse *could* also be read to mean: *Jacob's sons came in from the field;* כְּשָׁמְעָם וַיִּתְעַצְּבוּ הָאֲנָשִׁים, *and when they heard it, the men were distressed.* However, the Sages disagree and it is their interpretation that we follow.]

וַיִּתְעַצְּבוּ הָאֲנָשִׁים — [*And*] *the men* [i.e., Jacob's sons] *were distressed.*

At Shechem's outrage (see *Sforno* below).

The term עצב, *distress,* refers to an affront committed against one's own person or ideal. In a real sense

34
6-7
so Jacob kept silent until their arrival.

[6] Chamor, Shechem's father, went out to Jacob to
speak to him. [7] Jacob's sons arrived from the field
when they heard. The men were distressed, and were
fired deeply with indignation, for he had committed
an outrage in Israel by lying with a daughter of Jacob
— such a thing may not be done!

the outrage was committed against *them* since, as they explain in v. 14, it was a disgrace for the children of Israel to be associated with an uncircumcized man. But this *distress* was relatively mild compared with the חָרוֹן, *indignation,* they felt [see below] concerning the breach of the high moral standards of Israel — a code which Shechem could hardly be expected to comprehend *(Abarbanel).*

[On the verb עצב denoting *grief, vexation, sadness,* see comm. to 6:6.]

וַיִּחַר לָהֶם מְאֹד — [*And*] *they were fired deeply with indignation* [lit. *and it seethed them very much*].

[The translation follows *R' Hirsch.* See *comm.* to 32:2 for various connotations of the verb חרה.]

According to *Abarbanel,* the term refers to one whose anger is such that he seeks revenge. Thus, *they were fired with indignation* since he had physically abducted her — a thing not to be done even by heathen standards.

כִּי נְבָלָה עָשָׂה בְיִשְׂרָאֵל לִשְׁכַּב אֶת בַּת יַעֲקֹב — *For he* [Shechem] *had committed an outrage in Israel by lying* [lit. *to lie*] *with a daughter of Jacob.*

— *It was considered an outrage in Israel* — a nation which had high standards of morality and which viewed such dastardly acts with utter contempt *(Levush*; see below).

According to *Ramban*: It was considered an outrage in *Israel* — but not among the heathen nations, who were steeped in such immorality.

[*Rashi* would disagree with this latter interpretation; see below וְכֵן לֹא יֵעָשֶׂה.]

The root נבל in its various contexts refers to: *ruin, withering, weakening of forces, moral degradation.* Therefore, נְבָלָה refers to a disgraceful act demonstrating total moral degeneracy. Furthermore, it demonstrates complete contempt for the victim *(R' Hirsch).*

The term *Israel* is an anachronism since the nation of Israel did not yet exist. It refers to the progeny of Jacob who would later be called Israel *(Lekach Tov).*[1]

וְכֵן לֹא יֵעָשֶׂה — *Such a thing may not be done!*

Such a violation of maidens is intolerable, the heathen nations renounced immorality after the Flood, which had come upon the

1. *R' Munk* observes in this context that this is the first time the descendants of Abraham, Isaac, and Jacob are referred to by this name — and it occurs even before God had conferred the name upon Jacob. They already considered themselves part of the nation which will be a 'priestly people' called on to 'fight for God'. What a lofty concept of duty, virtue, and moral nobility is already connected with this august name! It is particularly significant that the first 'struggle for God' with which the name 'Israel' (ישר־אל) is connected is in defense of the sacred ideal of moral purity. The first mission of the 'children of Israel' is to safeguard this ideal.

ח וַיְדַבֵּר חֲמוֹר אִתָּם לֵאמֹר שְׁכֶם בְּנִי
חָשְׁקָה נַפְשׁוֹ בְּבִתְּכֶם תְּנוּ נָא אֹתָהּ לוֹ
ט לְאִשָּׁה: וְהִתְחַתְּנוּ אֹתָנוּ בְּנֹתֵיכֶם תִּתְּנוּ־
י לָנוּ וְאֶת־בְּנֹתֵינוּ תִּקְחוּ לָכֶם: וְאִתָּנוּ
תֵּשֵׁבוּ וְהָאָרֶץ תִּהְיֶה לִפְנֵיכֶם שְׁבוּ
יא וּסְחָרוּהָ וְהֵאָחֲזוּ בָּהּ: וַיֹּאמֶר שְׁכֶם אֶל־

world as a consequence of this sin *(Rashi* from *Midrash).*

Although the legal status of a maiden is less stringent than other forbidden degrees of unchastity — such as married women or various forms of incest — nevertheless, since he *abducted her* and *forced her,* she is considered a completely forbidden woman (עֶרְוָה), and Shechem was fully liable *(Mizrachi).*

Ramban disagrees with *Rashi's* view that even the heathens of that region would not condone such immoral behavior, on the ground that the Canaanites *were* steeped in immorality and were more corrupt than the other nations. This is explicitly stated in God's later reference to their abominations in *Leviticus* 18:27. Apparently, such was traditional Canaanite behavior. Furthermore, earlier chapters show clearly that even in the days of Abraham and Isaac the Patriarchs were constantly apprehensive that they would be killed and their wives abducted. [See also *comm.* to 12:13 and 20:13 where *Ramban* maintains that it was Abraham's *usual* procedure from the time he left Charan to describe Sarah as his sister wherever they went.]

Thus, *Ramban* concludes, the words *in Israel* in the preceding phrase apply here too, the sense of the passage being: *For he had committed an outrage in Israel ... a thing not to be done — in Israel,* although it might be tolerated by heathen nations.

Mizrachi defends *Rashi* by differing with *Ramban's* interpretation in several respects:

(a) A reading of *Leviticus* 18:27 cited by *Ramban* would tend to imply that the Canaanite abominations were *recent,* not traditional among them. Were they steeped in immorality from Patriarchal times as *Ramban* suggests, the land would have spewed them out even earlier.

(b) That Abraham and Isaac were constantly apprehensive that they would be murdered and their wives abducted proves the contrary. The Canaanites were *very* scrupulous in regard to adultery, but they treated murder lightly [see *comm.* to 12:12]. This is why they would murder the husband to release the wife from her forbidden status. Proof of the importance they attached to the prohibition against adultery is Pharaoh's indignant response to Abraham [12:18]: *What is this you have done to me? Why did you not tell me that she is your wife?;* and Abimelech's angry retort to Isaac [26:10]: *One of the people has nearly lain with your wife, and you would have brought guilt upon us!*

Thus, *Levush* explains that according to *Rashi* the sense of our passage would be: *For he had committed an outrage in Israel* — a nation which had high standards of morality and viewed such dastardly acts with utter contempt, *and furthermore, it was a thing not to be done* — for even among the heathen nations of that time, who had renounced immorality as a consequence of the Flood, such an act was taboo.

According to *Radak: And a thing not to be done* — not even to the daughter of a *commoner,* much less to the daughter of the renowned Jacob.

Sforno perceives the sense of the verse to be: The brothers were distressed *at the outrage which had been perpetrated in Israel,* and furthermore, וְכֵן לֹא יֵעָשֶׂה, *it was something not done* — such an offense had never before been committed against a daughter of a person of renown, therefore *they were fired with indignation* at the un-

[8] *Chamor spoke with them saying, 'My son,
Shechem, longs deeply for your daughter — please
give her to him as a wife,* [9] *and intermarry with us;
give your daughters to us, and take our daughters for
yourselves.* [10] *And among us you shall dwell; the
land will be open before you — settle and trade in it,
and acquire property in it.'*

precedented, contemptuous act.

Furthermore, the future tense implies: *And such* — though done now for the first time — *should not be* done — in the future; the necessary steps must be taken to assure that such a heinous act never again takes place *(Divrei Shaul).*

8. אִתָּם — *With them.*

Since Chamor met the brothers at Jacob's tent, he addressed them all *(Rashbam).*

בְּבִתְּכֶם — *For your daughter.* — [A polite, plural form.]

Consider the conduct of Shechem and Chamor subsequent to their outrage against Dinah. They approach Jacob *as if nothing had happened,* with an impeccably honorable proposal! Chamor suggests an alliance of friendship, commerce, and marriage between the two peoples; he apparently feels that a marriage would legitimize the vile act, and all would be forgiven and forgotten *(R' Hoffmann).*

9. וְהִתְחַתְּנוּ אֹתָנוּ — *And intermarry with us.*

Intermarriage with foreigners was usually forbidden. As *prince of the region* he was granting specific dispensation *(Abarbanel).*

בְּנֹתֵיכֶם תִּתְּנוּ־לָנוּ וְאֶת בְּנֹתֵינוּ תִּקְחוּ לָכֶם — *Give your daughters to us, and take our daughters for yourselves.*

This proposal gave Jacob and his sons the controlling right to exercise the initiative: they would give whomever *they* desired and take whomever *they* pleased. But when he reported it to his townspeople [*v.* 21], he reversed the terms in order to gain their approval; he made it appear as though the Shechemites would have the right to decide *(Rashbam).* [*Rashi* makes this observation in his *comm.* to the parallel phrase in *v.* 16 where Jacob's sons similarly give themselves the initiative.]

10. וְאִתָּנוּ תֵּשֵׁבוּ — *And among us you shall dwell.*

Among us — as our equal *(Haamek Davar).*

Chamor offered the further inducement of permanent domicile within the citizenry. This, too, was usually forbidden to aliens *(Abarbanel).*

שְׁבוּ וּסְחָרוּהָ וְהֵאָחֲזוּ בָּהּ — *Settle and trade in it, and acquire property* [lit. *be grasped*] *in it.*

Here, too, a special license was offered them, because, normally, strangers were not allowed to trade *(Sforno).*

The verb הֵאָחֲזוּ, *be grasped,* is related in this context to אֲחוּזָּה, *real holdings (Ibn Janach).*

It has been observed that the cordiality of Chamor's invitation is in contrast to what he told his townsman in verse 23. To induce them to adopt his suggestion, he promised that it would be profitable to them and they would

אָבִיהָ וְאֶל־אַחֶיהָ אֶמְצָא־חֵן בְּעֵינֵיכֶם
יב וַאֲשֶׁר תֹּאמְרוּ אֵלַי אֶתֵּן: הַרְבּוּ עָלַי מְאֹד
מֹהַר וּמַתָּן וְאֶתְּנָה כַּאֲשֶׁר תֹּאמְרוּ אֵלָי
יג וּתְנוּ־לִי אֶת־הַנַּעֲרָ לְאִשָּׁה: וַיַּעֲנוּ בְנֵי־
יַעֲקֹב אֶת־שְׁכֶם וְאֶת־חֲמוֹר אָבִיו
בְּמִרְמָה וַיְדַבֵּרוּ אֲשֶׁר טִמֵּא אֵת דִּינָה

gradually absorb the rich possessions of Jacob's household *(Heidenheim).*

11. וַיֹּאמֶר שְׁכֶם אֶל אָבִיהָ וְאֶל אַחֶיהָ – *Then Shechem said to her* [i.e., Dinah's] *father and brothers.*

Shechem now mustered up the impudence to speak on his own behalf *(Pesikta Zutresa).*

— He goes into more specific detail regarding his proposal than did his father *(Abarbanel);* and tries to make it more acceptable by offering a huge dowry *(Haamek Davar).*

אֶמְצָא חֵן בְּעֵינֵיכֶם – *Let me gain favor in your eyes.*

Find it in your hearts to forgive me *(Malbim).*

וַאֲשֶׁר תֹּאמְרוּ אֵלַי אֶתֵּן – *And whatever you tell me, I will give.*

In compensation for your humiliation and her diminished value as a result of the loss of her virginity *(Malbim).*

According to *Haamek Davar:* Though the notion of intermarriage with the *others* might be distasteful to you, *let me,* personally, *gain favor in your eyes* by virtue of my proposal to *pay whatever you wish;* you may fix as high a dowry as you like.

12. הַרְבּוּ עָלַי מְאֹד מֹהַר וּמַתָּן – *Inflate exceedingly upon me the marriage settlement* [lit. *dowry*] *and gifts.*

Shechem made this conciliatory offer to induce them to give her willingly in marriage, thereby overcoming Dinah's constant protestations and crying. If her family would agree to let her marry him, she might also consent *(Ramban).*

The translation of מֹהַר as *marriage settlement* follows *Rashi* who [consistent with the Rabbinic interpretation of the term in *Yerushalmi Kesubos* 3:1, and *Bavli* ibid. 10a, and his *comm.* to *Exodus* 22:16] interprets it to refer to the *Kesubah,* the marrige contract which provides for the financial settlement due the wife in case of divorce or death.

The *Midrash,* upon which *Rashi's* comment is based, explains מֹהַר as *Kesubah,* the wife's settlement as provided for by the marriage contract. The *Midrash* defines מַתָּן as פְּרַאפּוּרִין which is variously defined by the commentators: *Rashi* defines it as a voluntary settlement above the standard amount of the marriage contract; *Matnos Kehunah* defines it as נִכְסֵי מְלוֹג, property which belongs to the wife but is managed by the husband, and the proceeds of which go to him for the duration of the marriage; *Maharzu,* citing *Aruch,* defines it as ordinary gifts given to the bride.

Ramban [consistent with his interpretation in *Exod.* 22:16] explains מֹהַר to refer to סִבְלוֹנוֹת the bridal gifts given to the bride; מַתָּן refers to gold and silver gifts given to the father and brother of the bride.

The term מֹהַר, *dowry,* is related to מַהֵר, *quickly,* since these gifts hasten the wedding inasmuch as the groom sends these presents

[11] *Then Shechem said to her father and brothers, 'Let me gain favor in your eyes; and whatever you tell me — I will give.* [12] *Inflate exceedingly upon me the marriage settlement and gifts and I will give whatever you tell me; only give me the maiden for a wife.'*

[13] *Jacob's sons answered Shechem and his father Chamor cleverly and they spoke (because he had*

ahead of him in eager anticipation, and then comes to his father-in-law's house to make the wedding feast *(Heidenheim).*

Thus Shechem was saying: 'Let me marry her; I will legally bind myself to provide her with a very large marriage settlement, in case of divorce or death. I will also give her a large estate' *(Radak).*

וְאֶתְּנָה כַּאֲשֶׁר תֹּאמְרוּ אֵלָי — *And I will give whatever* [lit. *as*] *you tell me.*

Immediately — as soon as you tell me. This was not a vague promise to pay in the distant future, but a firm commitment to produce the amount *immediately upon request.* Compare 12:4 where the phrase כַּאֲשֶׁר דִּבֶּר אֵלָיו ה׳, *as HASHEM had spoken,* also implies that Abraham complied *immediately* and did not linger *(Alshich; Ha'amek Davar).*

13. וַיַּעֲנוּ ... אֶת שְׁכֶם וְאֶת חֲמוֹר — *And Jacob's sons answered Shechem and Chamor.*

Shechem had spoken last, and the response is directed toward him *(R' Hoffmann).*

בְּמִרְמָה — *Cleverly.*

I.e., with wisdom. (*Rashi* following the *Midrash* and *Targum).*

[This negates the other possible translation of בְּמִרְמָה as *deceitfully.* See *comm.* to 27:35 and *comm.* to next stich in this verse.]

The Torah thus bears testimony to the fact that Jacob's sons never seriously considered compromising on the fundamental restriction against intermarriage. From the very beginning of the discussions, their response was cleverly calculated to extricate Dinah *(Haamek Davar).*

Radak — who interprets מִרְמָה in the sense of *deceit* — observes how it was only Jacob's *sons* who spoke; Jacob himself scrupulously refrained from deceitful speech. The sons, however, as the verse proceeds to tell us, permitted themselves this deception since Shechem was the violator of their sister.

The Sages did not criticize the sons of Jacob — as they did Laban (see on 24:50) — for answering before their father. Apparently, as *Ramban* concludes, the sons spoke first as a gesture of respect for their father in order to spare him the humiliation of intervening personally in this disgraceful affair.

But, *Ramban* continues, the question arises: Since Jacob was present it appears that they acted with his consent. He obviously understood their scheme, and it must have had at least his *tacit* approval. Why then was he angry afterwards [see *v.* 30]? His subsequent anger is further perplexing since it is inconceivable that he would have consented to a plan whereby his daughter would be married to a Canaanite who had defiled her. — Therefore, his silence must be construed as knowledge that their offer to Shechem was part of a

יד אֲחֹתָם: וַיֹּאמְרוּ אֲלֵיהֶם לֹא נוּכַל לַעֲשׂוֹת

Or possibly, Jacob was angry because the townsfolk were innocent; the verse implies that it was only to *Shechem and his father Chamor* that they offered this cunning scheme *because of this outrage he committed in defiling their sister Dinah;* but not to the others.[1]

וַיְדַבֵּרוּ אֲשֶׁר טִמֵּא אֵת דִּינָה אֲחֹתָם — *And they spoke (because he had defiled their sister Dinah).*

According to the *Midrash,* these words were interjected parenthetically by the Divine Spirit to justify their 'clever' proposal, and negate any insinuation that בְּמִרְמָה means that they were deceitful: R' Nachman said, Do you think we have a case of *deceit* here? No; for it

clever plan. In any event, since *all* the brothers conspired in this scheme and shared the responsibility for it, why did Jacob chastise only Simeon and Levi who carried it out [see 49:7]?

However, the original intention of the brothers in demanding the circumcision was merely to deter the people of Shechem. The brothers believed that the Shechemites would not accede to the circumcision proposal, or, if they *would* consent, the brothers would wait until the townsmen would be immobilized on the third day, and taking advantage of their weakness, to forcibly rescue Dinah. Simeon and Levi went *beyond* this however; in their *revenge* they acted alone and wiped out every man in the city. Jacob never dreamt that they were planning to commit mass murder.

1. **The collective responsibility of the people of Shechem; the seven Noachide laws.**

In a lengthy fundamental dissertation, *Ramban* discusses the propriety of the righteous sons of Jacob slaughtering all the males of Shechem. Were not the townsfolk innocent? Since he cites opinions affecting the concept of collective guilt within the framework of the Seven Universal Laws, we shall discuss them fully.

Ramban cites *Rambam* [with slight textual changes] who in *Hilchos Melachim* ch. 9 writes of the *Seven Noachide Laws* [שֶׁבַע מִצְוֹת שֶׁל בְּנֵי נֹחַ], the Universal Laws incumbent upon all mankind [see *comm.* to 2:16, p. 101]. The first six of these laws prohibit: (a) עֲבוֹדָה זָרָה, *idolatry;* (b) בִּרְכַּת הַשֵּׁם, *blasphemy;* (c) גִּילוּי עֲרָיוֹת, *incest;* (d) שְׁפִיכוּת דָּמִים, *murder;* (e) גָּזֵל, *robbery;* and (f) אֵבֶר מִן הַחַי וּבָשָׂר מִן הַחַי, *eating of flesh cut from living animals.* The seventh law is entitled דִּינִים, *code of justice.* It requires that they appoint דַּיָּנִים, *judges,* in every district, to enforce compliance with the other six laws, and to caution the people concerning them. A Noachide who transgresses any of the seven laws is subject to death by the sword. Anyone who sees a transgressor and does not bring him to justice is himself liable to the same death penalty, because, by ignoring the crime, he has not fulfilled his personal obligation of דִּינִים, *code of justice.* 'Thus,' *Rambam* concludes, 'the people of Shechem had incurred the penalty of death by the sword, because Shechem [prince of the city] had been guilty of robbery [kidnapping]. They saw it, knew about it, and failed to bring him to justice.'

Ramban, however, disagrees. He maintains that if execution of the population were indeed a meritorious act, Jacob would have been the first to slay them; in any case, he certainly would not have criticized Simeon and Levi for it [49:7]!

Ramban maintains that the classification of דִּינִים, *justice,* among the Seven Noachide Laws does not merely entail the appointment of district דַּיָּנִים, *judges,* to enforce the other six laws. Rather it imposes the obligation to set up a corpus of laws regulating the conduct of society, such as laws concerning theft, overcharge, property damage, loans and debts, rape and seduction, etc. Each society must adopt a fair, reasonable code of laws, although not all societies are required to have the same law. Violation of such laws constitutes a violation of the seventh Noachide Law and, as such, requires the death penalty. Also included in these *'Laws'* is the requirement for heathens to appoint district judges just as Israel was commanded to do [see *Deut.* 16:18], however, the latter is a *positive command,* and failure to perform a positive command does not incur the death penalty. See *Sanhedrin* 58b where it is implicit that only for violation of *admonishments,* i.e., warnings against prohibitions, are they subject to the death penalty; only for a sinful *act,* but not for inaction, is one liable.

Furthermore, the *Yerushalmi* draws a distinction between a Jewish judge who is prohibited

defiled their sister Dinah). 14 *They said to them, 'We*

from refusing to render judgment, by the verse לֹא תָגוּרוּ מִפְּנֵי אִישׁ, *you shall not fear any man* (*Deut.* 1:17), and a heathen judge who cannot be slain for failing to put himself in the precarious position of judging superiors. This is further proof that only *performing* a sinful act makes a Noachide liable to death, not a failure to act.

Ramban concludes that the people of Shechem were, like all the iniquitous Canaanite nations [see *Levit.* 18:27; *Deut.* 18:9], guilty of overall violations of the Seven Noachide Laws, but it was not the responsibility of Jacob and his sons to bring them to justice. However, Simeon and Levi zealously took matters into their own hands and avenged themselves. Had the people of Shechem become proselytes, Simeon and Levi would not have acted against them, but the brothers considered the Shechemite circumcision to be without significance for they did it not to convert, but to flatter their master.

Jacob, however, was angered at their zeal since, he and his children were not required to endanger themselves to punish the Shechemites for failure to observe the Noachide Laws. In addition, Simeon and Levi violated the trust they had gained by the peaceful impression they gave Shechem and Chamor in *v.* 16. Furthermore, who could judge the sincerity of their circumcision? — they might have turned to God. Thus, Simeon and Levi had killed them without justification [see also *comm.* above and to 49:5 where additional reasons for Jacob's anger are offered].

[Accordingly, neither Jacob nor his sons, with the exception of Simeon and Levi, ever contemplated subjecting a whole city to the sword. Their only concern was to rescue Dinah from the clutches of her captors and violators. What transpired afterwards was the work of Simeon and Levi alone.]

[The crux of the disagreement between *Rambam* and *Ramban*, as explained in *Responsa Chasam Sofer* 2:14, lies in whether a heathen incurs the death penalty for failure to act against one who transgresses a Noachide Law. Though both agree that a heathen is responsible to obey whatever code of law is adopted by his country, they differ in classification: *Rambam* classifies these social interdictions under the category of *robbery*, while he classifies the requirement of appointing judges as one of the basic Seven Laws for whose violation Noachides are subject to the death penalty. Because such appointment of judges is the basic requirement of this law, a Noachide who fails to do so is liable to the death penalty. *Ramban* on the other hand, classifies the formulation of a system of justice as the basic requirement for the seventh Noachide Law. Judges must be appointed in order to enforce the laws, but such appointment is not fundamentally *required* by this seventh law.]

Gur Aryeh questions *Rambam's* thesis regarding the responsibility of the *judges*. How could they have been expected to judge the chieftain of the region before whom they stood in mortal fear? Although they were commanded to judge, they could do so only when it was possible; in a case like ours, they would clearly be excused!

In defense of *Rambam*, *Divrei Shaul* cites *Sefer HaYashar* according to which Judah later defended Simeon and Levi to Jacob on the grounds that no one in the city even *questioned* Shechem's wantonness, much less judged him. This proved their collective guilt in the matter (cited by *R' Chavel*).

The *Midrash*, while not condoning their action — since Jacob himself condemned it — points out that savage though it was, it was not the result of mere brutality, but of a desire to safeguard the honor of their sister, as Simeon and Levi put it [*v.* 31]: *Should he treat our sister like a harlot?*

Gur Aryeh offers an entirely different insight into the act of Simeon and Levi. In his view it is unrelated to the Noachide Laws. Only in the case of individual sinners do such laws and the responsibility of the courts come into play. In the case of *nations*, however, the Torah permits a victim of aggression to go to war against its attacker. Since Canaan and Israel were separate nations, and Shechem committed an aggressive act against Israel, Simeon and Levi had the right to declare war. [If so, the questions of how and whether to counterattack were matters of strategy. Simeon and Levi did so under cover of deception, while Jacob held that his family's situation was too precarious to permit *any* violent retaliation.]

However, as *R' Munk* observes, though many commentators justify *Rambam's* opinion that there *is* collective responsibility for a crime committed in a group and not brought before the courts, nevertheless *Or HaChaim* concludes that neither of *those* explanations can justify their action in pillaging the town and taking the spoils [cf. *v.* 27].

הַדָּבָר הַזֶּה לָתֵת אֶת־אֲחֹתֵנוּ לְאִישׁ
טו אֲשֶׁר־לוֹ עָרְלָה כִּי־חֶרְפָּה הִוא לָנוּ: אַךְ־
בְּזֹאת נֵאוֹת לָכֶם אִם תִּהְיוּ כָמֹנוּ לְהִמֹּל
טז לָכֶם כָּל־זָכָר: וְנָתַנּוּ אֶת־בְּנֹתֵינוּ לָכֶם

is the Divine Spirit that states that they spoke in such a manner only *because he had defiled their sister Dinah.*

Rashi similarly observes that the Torah [as the Sacred Historian] mentions this to justify the brothers and testify that their action was not *deceitful* but *clever* — for indeed, Shechem *had defiled their sister Dinah.* [That these words had to be said by God is obvious, because Jacob's sons would surely have wanted to avoid this painful subject *(Mizrachi).*]

[The translation, and commentators like *Rashi* above, who view *because he had defiled* etc. as a parenthetic justification, follow the Masoretic punctuation which places a pause after וַיְדַבֵּרוּ, *and they spoke.*]

Ibn Ezra suggest two alternate renderings: *They answered ... and they spoke* to Shechem *who had defiled,* etc.; or: *speaking as they did because he had defiled their sister Dinah.*

[In any event, this clause, though separated by a pause, serves to modify the first half of the verse. Comp. אֲשֶׁר טִמְּאוּ in *v.* 27 below.]

According to *Sforno,* these words are not parenthetic but *were* uttered by Jacob's sons to Chamor and Shechem, the intent being: Shechem's offer of extravagant gifts is inappropriate *inasmuch as he had already defiled their sister* and for her to accept money would make her seem like a harlot receiving her hire. Nevertheless, Jacob's sons cleverly proceeded to propose circumcision which they thought would be totally unacceptable to Shechem and Chamor, or to their tribesmen — their intention being to use the demand as a ruse to refuse the marriage and thereby get back Dinah.

14. לא נוכל ... לָתֵת אֶת אֲחֹתֵנוּ לְאִישׁ אֲשֶׁר לוֹ עָרְלָה — *We cannot do this thing — to give our sister to a man who is uncircumcised*] [lit. *who has a foreskin*].

I.e. *we cannot do this thing* — i.e., accept an exorbitant monetary settlement — *in order to give our sister,* etc. *(Sechel Tov).*

It is beneath their dignity even to reply directly to Shechem's monetary offer. First a question of principle must be solved; their concern is of a higher nature than money *(Akeidas Yitzchak).*

[The term עָרְלָה, familiarly rendered *foreskin,* has the more literal meaning of *surplusage.* See *comm.* to 17:11. See also 'Purposes of Circumcision' on p. 569.]

כִּי חֶרְפָּה הִוא לָנוּ — *For that would be a disgrace among us.*

— Marriage to an uncircumcised man would disgrace our family for all time *(Ibn Ezra).*

— To us it is a blemish that goes from generation to generation. If one wishes to insult his friend, he would say to him: 'You are uncircumcised,' or: 'You are the son of one who is uncircumcised' *(Rashi)* [See *Joshua* 5:9.]

[Thus, an uncircumcised husband for their sister would cause disgraceful comments for the entire family, and could not be tolerated.][1]

1. Even though the command of circumcision was then still relatively new, it had acquired such religious and national significance that it served to separate Jews from idolators. For a

cannot do this thing, to give our sister to a man who
is uncircumcised, for that would be a disgrace among
us. [15] *Only on this condition will we acquiesce to*
you: If you become like us by letting every male
among you become circumcised. [16] *Then we will give*
our daughters to you, and take your daughters to

— This marriage would give the impression that there was no suitable circumcised man to marry her *(Sforno).*

And were we to intermarry with you while you are still uncircumcised you would eventually mock *us* for being circumcised *(Chizkuni).*

15. אַךְ־בְּזֹאת נֵאוֹת לָכֶם — *Only on this condition* [lit. *only in this*] *will we acquiesce to you.*

נֵאוֹת, *acquiesce,* [root אות, the נ being a first person plural prefix] has the same meaning in *II Kings* 12:9 וַיֵּאֹתוּ, *and they consented (Rashi).*

[Cf. the derivative noun תַּאֲוָה, *desire.*]

אִם תִּהְיוּ כָמֹנוּ לְהִמֹּל לָכֶם כָּל זָכָר — *If you [will] become like us by letting every male among you become circumcised.*

— [*Every* male — so that any difference between our people and yours would disappear, and we can integrate freely with one another].[1]

Further, by specifically stating *if you will become like us* rather than simply, *if you will undergo circumcision* they meant that as part of the circumcision rite, the Shechemites would also have to accept upon themselves the yoke of the Kingdom of Heaven as sincere converts. This, as we shall see, the Shechemites did not accept, despite their agreement to circumcise themselves *(Minchah Belulah).*

Their purpose in choosing circumcision as the scheme by which to render them helpless for the massacre, was to inflict injury on the organ by which Shechem perpetrated his base act *(Sifsei Kohen).*

[The translation of הִמֹּל לָכֶם in the passive *niphal — shall be circumcised —* follows *Rashi* here, and the parallel passage in 17:10.]

16. וְנָתַנּוּ אֶת־בְּנֹתֵינוּ לָכֶם וְאֶת־בְּנֹתֵיכֶם נִקַּח לָנוּ — *Then we will give our daughters to you, and take your daughters to ourselves.*

See *Rashbam* on the parallel phrase in verse 9. *Rashi* makes the observation here that in Jacob's sons' reply they *too* make the initiative rest with themselves — *we* will

Jewish woman to marry an uncircumcised man was shameful — a disgrace. This response sums up in a few telling words the Jewish conception which is still valid to this day: between pure and impure, no union is possible *(R' Munk).*

1. It has been pointed out that Chamor and Shechem are obviously convinced that the refusal to sanction Dinah's marriage is not based on the family's 'social arrogance,' but results from higher necessity. They must be glad that the obstacle is not insurmountable, as differences of 'race' or alien 'blood' would have been. Indeed, differences of race have never been an obstacle to joining Israel, which does not recognize the concept of 'purity of blood.'

The prohibition against marrying Canaanites has a *religious* foundation. (*Ex.* 34:12 ff: *Deut.* 7:3), while that against marrying Ammonites and Moabites has *moral* reasons *(Deut.* 23:4ff). Circumcision, together with acceptance of the Commandments and immersing, turn a man of foreign origin into an Israelite (*Ex.* 12:48) *(Heidenheim).*

וְאֶת־בְּנֹתֵיכֶם נִקַּח־לָנוּ וְיָשַׁבְנוּ אִתְּכֶם
יז וְהָיִינוּ לְעַם אֶחָד׃ וְאִם־לֹא תִשְׁמְעוּ
אֵלֵינוּ לְהִמּוֹל וְלָקַחְנוּ אֶת־בִּתֵּנוּ וְהָלָכְנוּ׃
יח וַיִּיטְבוּ דִבְרֵיהֶם בְּעֵינֵי חֲמוֹר וּבְעֵינֵי שְׁכֶם
יט בֶּן־חֲמוֹר׃ וְלֹא־אֵחַר הַנַּעַר לַעֲשׂוֹת
הַדָּבָר כִּי חָפֵץ בְּבַת־יַעֲקֹב וְהוּא נִכְבָּד
כ מִכֹּל בֵּית אָבִיו׃ וַיָּבֹא חֲמוֹר וּשְׁכֶם בְּנוֹ
אֶל־שַׁעַר עִירָם וַיְדַבְּרוּ אֶל־אַנְשֵׁי עִירָם

give ... and *we* will take ... Compare, however, how Shechem describes the arrangement to his tribesmen in *v.* 21, making the initiative appear to rest with them.

The second נ in וְנָתַנּוּ *has a dagesh* [which grammatically indicates a dropped letter] since it serves the purpose of two נ's; the word should technically be conjugated as וְנָתַנְנוּ from the root נתן and the plural suffix נו. [But when double consonants occur in this way together, one is dropped for ease of pronunciation. Cf. *comm.* to חָנַּנִי in 33:11] *(Rashi).*

וְיָשַׁבְנוּ אִתְּכֶם וְהָיִינוּ לְעַם אֶחָד — [*And*] *we will dwell with you, and become a single people.*

[In *v.* 13 *Ramban* makes the point that it was *this* condition that was the source of Jacob's later agitation when his sons took the lives of the Shechemites. Whatever the evils of the townspeople, his sons had made them a condition — and broken it!]

17. וְאִם לֹא תִשְׁמְעוּ אֵלֵינוּ לְהִמּוֹל — *But if you will not listen to us to be circumcised.*

Jacob's sons also avoided any reference to Shechem's vile deed, or even to the fact that Dinah was incarcerated in his house. They merely made it clear, that should Shechem refuse their proposal they will *take their daughter* [i.e., sister; see below] and go. The implication was clear: In no way will we permit her to be married to one who is uncircumcised; therefore if you do not consent — although she is no longer a maiden and will be entitled to a smaller marriage settlement in consequence — we are not concerned but *we will take our daughter and go (Akeidas Yitzchak).*

וְלָקַחְנוּ אֶת בִּתֵּנוּ וְהָלָכְנוּ — [*Then*] *we will take our daughter and go.*

— Though she is still in your house, *we will take her from you and go* with all our wealth, from which you will derive no benefit *(Sforno).*

They called Dinah their *daughter* not *sister* since they were speaking in behalf of their father *(Tur);* and because she was still a minor *(Ibn Ezra).*

By referring to Dinah as their *daughter,* they emphasized to him that if their terms were not accepted, they would be prepared to jeopardize themselves for her as would a father for his daughter. Cf. *Tanchuma* cited by *Ramban* in *comm.* to 19:8 *(Haamek Davar).*

18. The Shechemites accept.

וַיִּיטְבוּ דִבְרֵיהֶם בְּעֵינֵי חֲמוֹר — *Their proposal* [lit. *words*] *seemed good in the view of Chamor.*

The father was as foolish as the son! *(Lekach Tov).*

ourselves; we will dwell with you, and become a
single people. [17] *But if you will not listen to us to be*
circumcised, we will take our daughter and go.'
[18] *Their proposal seemed good in the view of*
Chamor, and in the view of Shechem, Chamor's son.
[19] *The youth did not delay doing the thing, for he*
wanted Jacob's daughter. Now he was the most
respected of all his father's household.
[20] *Chamor — with his son Shechem — went to the*
gate of their city and spoke to the people of their city,

וּבְעֵינֵי שְׁכֶם בֶּן־חֲמוֹר — *And in the view* [lit. *eyes*] *of Shechem, Chamor's son.*

If it seemed fair to Chamor it *certainly* would have seemed fair to Shechem; why then is it necessary to give *Shechem's* positive reaction? — In making their proposal, the brothers were careful to put it in such a way that it *could* be interpreted that they insisted upon the circumcision *only* of Shechem himself. While they explicitly mentioned the prospective husband (*v.* 14), they did not say *directly* that *all* tribesmen had to be circumcised. This careful omission was to avoid the risk that the very suggestion might so anger the townspeople that they would become violent. As a result, Shechem understood that he might be the *only* one with the 'humiliating mark of circumcision'. It was to this possibility that he had to give his separate assent *(Haamek Davar).*

19. וְלֹא־אֵחַר הַנַּעַר לַעֲשׂוֹת הַדָּבָר — [*And*] *the youth did not delay doing the thing.*

I.e., in presenting the proposal to his townsmen; or alternately, in setting an example by submitting immediately to circumcision even before he revealed the proposal to the others *(Abarbanel).*

— So consumed was he with passion for בְּבַת יַעֲקֹב, *Jacob's daughter (Lekach Tov).*

וְהוּא נִכְבָּד מִכֹּל בֵּית אָבִיו — *Now* [lit. *and*] *he was the most respected of all his father's house*[*hold*].

And he was accordingly confident that the others would consent — so great was his influence upon them as the *most respected of all his father's household (Rashbam; Hoffmann).*

According to *Sforno,* the syntax is: Although he was *the most respected of all his father's household* [and therefore could have waited to circumcise himself last], nevertheless, the youth lost no time [and set himself as the example] ... so strongly did he desire Jacob's daughter.

20. וַיָּבֹא חֲמוֹר וּשְׁכֶם בְּנוֹ אֶל שַׁעַר עִירָם — [*And*] *Chamor—with his son Shechem—went* [lit. *came*] *to the gate of their city.*

[The Hebrew וַיָּבֹא, *went,* is in the singular, indicating that they both came as one — with a common purpose.]

— The gate was where the elders and important citizens would congregate *(Radak).*

כא לֵאמֹר: הָאֲנָשִׁים הָאֵלֶּה שְׁלֵמִים הֵם
אִתָּנוּ וְיֵשְׁבוּ בָאָרֶץ וְיִסְחֲרוּ אֹתָהּ וְהָאָרֶץ
הִנֵּה רַחֲבַת־יָדַיִם לִפְנֵיהֶם אֶת־בְּנֹתָם
נִקַּח־לָנוּ לְנָשִׁים וְאֶת־בְּנֹתֵינוּ נִתֵּן לָהֶם:
כב אַךְ־בְּזֹאת יֵאֹתוּ לָנוּ הָאֲנָשִׁים לָשֶׁבֶת
אִתָּנוּ לִהְיוֹת לְעַם אֶחָד בְּהִמּוֹל לָנוּ כָּל־
כג זָכָר כַּאֲשֶׁר הֵם נִמֹּלִים: מִקְנֵהֶם וְקִנְיָנָם
וְכָל־בְּהֶמְתָּם הֲלוֹא לָנוּ הֵם אַךְ נֵאוֹתָה

[The gates of a city, like the gates around the Old City of Jerusalem today, were fairly large edifices. They were not gathering places for idlers, but for the assembly of the dignitaries of the land. So we find throughout Scripture that the elders and judges stationed themselves at the gate of a city. Boaz, who was a judge, sat at the gate (*Ruth* 4:1); as did Mordechai (who stationed himself at the gate of the King; see *comm.* to *Esther* 2:19). Solomon praises the woman of valor whose *husband* is *known at the gates, where he sits among the elders of the land (Prov.* 31:23). Commercial transactions took place and disputes were settled at the gate of a city.]

Apparently, sufficient time had elapsed since Shechem's circumcision for the wound to heal enough to permit him to go to the city gate *(R' Hoffmann).*

21. Chamor presents the plan in the most glamorous light possible. He tactfully avoids any mention of the *personal* benefit his son sought thereby; the implication is that the town as a *whole* will benefit from this new association, and that Chamor is selflessly interested only in the community's welfare *(R' Hoffmann).*

הָאֲנָשִׁים הָאֵלֶּה שְׁלֵמִים הֵם אִתָּנוּ — *These people are peaceable with us.*

In spite of the wrong perpetrated on them, they are peaceable and whole-hearted [בְּשָׁלוֹם ,וּבְלֵב שָׁלֵם *(Rashi)*] toward us; they have no intention of taking revenge and you need not fear them *(Radak; Sforno).*

Therefore, you need not undertake any security measures to guard yourselves against them *(Ramban).*

וְהָאָרֶץ הִנֵּה רַחֲבַת־יָדַיִם לִפְנֵיהֶם — *For see, there is ample room in the land for them* [lit. *and the land, behold there is breadth of hands before them.*]

— You will lose nothing through their trade, for an abundant amount of merchandise is brought here and there are not enough buyers for it. The metaphor of רַחֲבַת־יָדַיִם, *breadth of hands,* is that of a man whose hand is large and generous; hence it denotes *plentifulness; adequacy (Rashi).*

By their presence they will generate new commerce from which we will all prosper *(Haamek Davar).*

[Shechem added this to justify letting in foreigners who will compete with them.]

אֶת בְּנֹתָם נִקַּח־לָנוּ לְנָשִׁים — *Let us take their daughters for ourselves as wives.*

Here Chamor assigns to his

saying, 21 *'These people are peaceable with us; let*
them settle in the land and trade in it, for see, there is
ample room in the land for them! Let us take their
daughters for ourselves as wives and give our
daughters to them. 22 *Only on this condition will the*
people acquiesce with us to dwell with us to become a
single people: that our males become circumcised as
they themselves are circumcised. 23 *Their livestock,*
their possessions, and all their animals — won't they
be ours? Let us but acquiesce to them and they will
settle with us.'

townspeople the initiative of which daughters to give and take, in order to induce them to cooperate with his proposal (*Rashi;* see *Rashbam* to *v.* 9).

22. אַךְ בְּזֹאת ... בְּהִמּוֹל לָנוּ כָּל־זָכָר כַּאֲשֶׁר הֵם נִמֹּלִים — *Only on this condition* [lit. *on this*] ... *that our males become circumcised as they themselves are circumcised.*

What have we to lose thereby? We can only gain since they are wealthy and there is sufficient pasture for all our herds *(Radak).*

23. And furthermore ...

מִקְנֵהֶם וְקִנְיָנָם וְכָל־בְּהֶמְתָּם — *Their livestock,* [*and*] *their possessions and all their animals.*

— All the riches they have accumulated *(Heidenheim)* ...

Ramban defines the terms מִקְנֶה, *livestock,* and בְּהֵמָה, *animals,* and discusses the difference between them:

מִקְנֶה, literally *possession, acquisition,* refers to cattle which are part of herds in the field [see *Exod.* 9:3] — whether clean or unclean — since they constitute the mainstay of one's substance. בְּהֵמָה, *animals,* includes those domestic animals which do not constitute a herd and cannot be called *cattle.*

Alternatively, *Ramban* suggests that the two terms are synonymous, the repetition being to emphasize the vastness of the herds.

הֲלוֹא לָנוּ הֵם — *Won't they be ours?*

This is how it always ended: The stranger came, toiled, and accumulated wealth which ultimately reverted to his hosts. To induce them to accept his suggestion, Chamor promised that it would be profitable to them and they would gradually absorb the rich possessions of Jacob's household. He showed them that it was worth their pains to accede to the strange condition made by Jacob's sons. Contrast this with the seeming cordiality of Chamor's invitation to Jacob in verse 10! *(Heidenheim).*

The *Midrash* derives from this remark that their circumcision was not undertaken for the sake of Heaven, but out of greed for Israel's possessions. In the end they lost even what they themselves possessed.

אַךְ נֵאוֹתָה לָהֶם וְיֵשְׁבוּ אִתָּנוּ — *Let us but acquiesce to them, and they will settle with us.*

I.e. *Just let us acquiesce to them* — by submitting to circumcision — *and as a result they will settle with us (Rashi,* as explained by *Be'er Mayim Chaim).*

כד לָהֶם וְיֵשְׁבוּ אִתָּנוּ: וַיִּשְׁמְעוּ אֶל־חֲמוֹר
וְאֶל־שְׁכֶם בְּנוֹ כָּל־יֹצְאֵי שַׁעַר עִירוֹ וַיִּמֹּלוּ
כה כָּל־זָכָר כָּל־יֹצְאֵי שַׁעַר עִירוֹ: וַיְהִי בַיּוֹם
הַשְּׁלִישִׁי בִּהְיוֹתָם כֹּאֲבִים וַיִּקְחוּ שְׁנֵי־
בְנֵי־יַעֲקֹב שִׁמְעוֹן וְלֵוִי אֲחֵי דִינָה אִישׁ

24. וַיִּשְׁמְעוּ ... כָּל־יֹצְאֵי שַׁעַר עִירוֹ — *All the people who depart* [through] *the gate of his city, listened.*

I.e., consented (*Onkelos;* see *Rashi* to 37:28).

Radak to 23:10 interprets the expression יֹצְאֵי שַׁעַר, *those who depart through the gate,* as synonymous with בָּאֵי שַׁעַר, *those who enter through the gate,* both idiomatically denoting the *entire population of a city.* He cites *Jeremiah* 17:19 where the two expressions are interchanged.

However, the fact that the entire populace consented to this strange and painful proposal in order to satisfy Shechem and his father calls for a special explanation.

R' Hirsch perceives a clue in the fact that the expression יֹצְאֵי שַׁעַר עִירוֹ, *those who* **depart** *through the gate of his city,* is used twice in our episode, instead of בָּאֵי שַׁעַר עִירוֹ, *those who* **arrive** *through the gate of his city,* the more common expression for city residents. He accordingly suggests that the expression used here seems to indicate that the inhabitants of Shechem's city were, for the greater part, peasants and farmers whose work took them daily out of the city. Chamor and Shechem were apparently the overlords of the district and the people — who regularly departed via the gate of the city — were perhaps their vassals and accustomed to harsh measures; thus, *they listened.*

Meshech Chochmah observes that in 23:10 the expression *those who enter the city gate* included the womenfolk who had come to mourn Sarah, while here the subject is circumcision and the expression *who depart through the city gate* refers to the *men who went out to trade.* Women — especially in Eastern countries — stay at home. [See *Chizkuni* below.]

Tosafos HaRosh offers that the expression used here refers only to those already *in* town at the time of the decree; while in 23:10 the inference is even to transient strangers.

וַיִּמֹּלוּ כָּל־זָכָר כָּל־יֹצְאֵי שַׁעַר עִירוֹ — *And all the males — all those who depart* [through] *the gates of the city — were circumcised.*

The stich implies that all the residents of the city heard Shechem's proposal and wanted to flee from the decree of being circumcised against their will. But no male was allowed to leave the city unless he submitted to circumcision: *all the males — whoever wished to depart the gates of the city — had to submit to circumcision (Chizkuni).*[1]

[The rendering of וַיִּמֹּלוּ in the *niphal,* passive form: *was circumcised,* follows *Rashi* and *Ibn Ezra* to יִמּוֹל in 17:12.]

25. Simeon and Levi decimate Shechem.

וַיְהִי בַיּוֹם הַשְּׁלִישִׁי בִּהְיוֹתָם כֹּאֲבִים —

1. The *Midrash* relates that everyone who passed through the gates of Shechem was asked to be circumcised.

'Why?' asked one of the peasants.

'So that Shechem may marry Jacob's daughter,' they answered.

'Shechem is getting married and the peasant has to get circumcised!'

This became a proverb for a situation where one person suffers for another's decision.

[24] *All the people who depart through the gate of
his city listened to Chamor and his son Shechem, and
all the males — all those who depart through the gates
of the city — were circumcised.*
[25] *And it came to pass on the third day, when they
were in pain, that two of Jacob's sons, Simeon and
Levi, Dinah's brothers, each took his sword and they*

And it came to pass on the third day, when they were in pain.

— Because the third day after circumcision is the most painful *(Ibn Ezra)*.[1]

In another sense, they waited until the third day since it took until then to circumcise all the males; by the third day, *all* of them were circumcised and in pain. Furthermore, the verse does not necessarily mean *physical* pain, but *grief* and *regret* over having submitted to the circumcision *(Daas Zekeinim; Chizkuni)*.

Sefer HaYashar adds that their regret was inspired by the realization that for having undergone circumcision and apparently conversion, the neighboring heathen nations might attack them. Therefore, they decided that once their wounds would heal, they would avenge themselves upon Jacob and his family to regain their status among their fellow heathens and thereby negate the political effects of the circumcision. [See continuation of *Sefer HaYashar* at the end of this verse.]

שְׁנֵי בְנֵי יַעֲקֹב שִׁמְעוֹן וְלֵוִי — *[That] two of Jacob's sons, Simeon and Levi.*

Why is it necessary to identify them as *Jacob's sons?* — Because in spite of being his sons, they did not seek his advice but acted on their own *(Rashi* from *Midrash)*.

Radak observes that although *all* the sons consented to the scheme, as verse 13 implies, only two of the sons, Simeon and Levi, had the courage to *carry out* the plan.

[This differs markedly from *Ramban* ad. loc. who maintains that a wholesale massacre had *never* been the intention of Jacob, or of the brothers in acquiescing to the scheme. They had merely wanted to disable every able-bodied man, and remove Dinah from Shechem's house. Simeon and Levi *alone* wanted to avenge their wickedness violently, and for this Jacob did not forgive them even on his death-bed (see 49:6).]

אֲחֵי דִינָה — *Dinah's brothers.*

Were only Simeon and Levi her brothers, and not the others? — She is called by their name, however, because they risked their lives for her sake *(Midrash)*.

1. The Sages [*Mishnah Shabbos* 86a] derive from the description in this passage of the third day after circumcision being one of great pain, that if there is no hot water available, one may heat water on the Sabbath to bathe a circumcised child on the third day after circumcision. *Yerushalmi Shabbos* 19:3 further clarifies that not just the wound itself, but the baby's entire body may be washed since the expression בִּהְיוֹתָם כֹּאֲבִים denotes that *all* their organs pained them.

Ramban [*Hilchos Shabbos* 2:14] explains that this permissive ruling takes into account that the third day after circumcision is when an infant's life was considered most endangered.

However, nowadays the *halachah* prohibits this, inasmuch as apparently the danger no longer exists, and since it is now not customary — even on weekdays — to bathe a circumcised child on the third day *(Shulchan Aruch, Orach Chaim* 331:9).

חַרְבּוֹ וַיָּבֹאוּ עַל־הָעִיר בֶּטַח וַיַּהַרְגוּ כָּל־
כו זָכָר: וְאֶת־חֲמוֹר וְאֶת־שְׁכֶם בְּנוֹ הָרְגוּ
לְפִי־חָרֶב וַיִּקְחוּ אֶת־דִּינָה מִבֵּית שְׁכֶם

Furthermore, this emphasizes that because they were children of the same mother, they felt the insult more acutely, hence the desire for revenge *(Ralbag)*.

וַיִּקְחוּ ... אִישׁ חַרְבּוֹ — *Each [man] took his sword.*

The *Midrash* notes that Levi was thirteen years old at the time. [Simeon and Levi were born — seven months apart — in the ninth year of Jacob's twenty year stay with Laban; making Levi eleven and a half years old when Jacob fled from Laban. Add the eighteen months of his journeying (*Rashi* 33:17) and we arrive at thirteen years for Levi, and thirteen and seven months (i.e., six months and several days — that is, the seventh month) for Simeon.] Thus, as *Lekach Tov* points out, it is implied in this Midrashic comment that whenever the Torah uses the term אִישׁ, *man*, it refers to an adult over thirteen years old. [Cf. *Rashi* to *Nazir* 29b s.v. ורבי יוסי.]

וַיָּבֹאוּ עַל הָעִיר בֶּטַח — *And they came upon the city confidently.*

Confidently — because the Shechemites were in pain [and incapacitated]. According to the *Midrash* they were confident because they relied on the strength of the 'old one' *(Rashi)*.[1]

Following the *Midrash* [see *footnote*], it was the *physical* strength of their old *father*, Jacob, that they relied on; while many commentators suggest that their confidence was centered on Jacob's *spiritual* merits.

Maharshal and *Kli Yakar* suggest that by the 'old one,' *Rashi* refers to *Abraham*, and their confidence was based on the anticipatory prayers Abraham had offered on their behalf when he had made Shechem his first stop in Canaan [over 180 years earlier!] [see *Rashi* to 12:6.]

Furthermore, *Kli Yakar*, continues, Jacob's sons were confident that the neighboring nations would not come to the Shechemites' aid, reasoning that the Shechemites had read themselves out of Canaanite society by circumcising themselves.[2]

Onkelos perceives that it is the *city* which is described as בֶּטַח, *secure; confident*. The verse tells us that the brothers came upon the city which basked in a feeling of complete security.

Rashbam concurs, and adds that throughout Scripture בֶּטַח, *secure*, refers to the *residents* of a city. *R'Hirsch* similarly renders: ... *and come upon the*

1. The *Midrash* records that although Jacob disapproved of his sons' action, nevertheless he recognized his responsibility to protect them against possible retaliation from vengeful Canaanites.

He took his sword and bow and stood at the entrance to Shechem and exclaimed: 'If the heathens come to attack my sons, I will fight them!' It was to this that Jacob alluded when he said of Shechem [48:22]: *'Which I seized from the hand of the Amorite with my bow and with my sword.'*

Ramban [*v.* 13] cites a version of this Midrash [=*Midrash Vayisu*, in Eisenstein *Otzar Midrashim* p. 157; see *Rashi* to 48:22] that the surrounding nations actually waged three major wars against Jacob's family, and were it not for Jacob who donned his weapons, they would have been in mortal danger.

The Torah, however, does not elaborate about this because it was a hidden miracle, [i.e., a feat which one could erroneously attribute not to a miracle, but to Jacob's natural strength; see *comm.* to 11:28; 17:1; and further 33:5].

34
26 came upon the city confidently. They killed every
male, [26] And Chamor and Shechem his son they killed at the point of the sword. Then they took Dinah
from Shechem's house and left.

city which was resting trustfully. Comp. *Ezekiel* 30:9.

וַיַּהַרְגוּ כָּל־זָכָר — *[And] they killed every male.*

The question of how the righteous sons of Jacob were justified in perpetrating such a massacre against the seemingly innocent townspeople of Shechem, and the question of collective guilt are discussed at length in the footnote to *v.* 13.

Chizkuni suggests that Simeon and Levi acted only after they heard of the insincere and devious manner in which Chamor and Shechem reported their proposal to the people of Shechem [*v.* 23]. Their duplicity made it clear that their circumcision was not sincere.

— It was clear that their primary motive in accepting the plan was to deprive Jacob and his sons of their property *(Sforno).*

According to *Sefer HaYashar,* Dinah had overheard a plot by Chamor's brother Chadakkum, and six other brothers — who had opposed the circumcision plan — to rise up and slay Jacob's family after the Shechemites had recovered from their wounds. Dinah sent word of this to her brothers, and they rose up in this pre-emptive strike, decimating the whole town, except for two young men who escaped and hid in some lime-pits. These two survivors rallied the surrounding nations to attack Jacob's family, as noted in the footnote below.

26. וְאֶת חֲמוֹר וְאֶת שְׁכֶם בְּנוֹ הָרְגוּ לְפִי־חָרֶב — *And they killed Chamor and Shechem his son at the point of the sword.*

— After finally locating them *(Sforno).*

It was only after they had killed every male in town — many of whom had been guarding the palace — that Simeon and Levi were able to slay Chamor and Shechem, who were then left unprotected *(Or HaChaim).*

וַיִּקְחוּ אֶת דִּינָה מִבֵּית שְׁכֶם וַיֵּצֵאוּ — *Then* [lit. *and*] *they took Dinah from Shechem's house and left* [lit. *and went out*].

[*Took* is understood in the *Midrashic* sense of *urging* and *persuading;* comp. וַיִּקַּח in 2:15 and 12:5]:

R' Huna said that she was overcome with shame and argued, 'where shall I go to bear my shame?' and refused to accompany them until Simeon agreed to marry her. He agreed and she became Simeon's *Canaanite* wife mentioned in 46:10, so-called because she had lived with a Canaanite (see *Rashi* and *Mizrachi* there. Cf. also *comm.* to 30:24 and to 37:5 and 38:2).

According to another opinion in

2. This, *R' Yonasan Eyebescheutz* observes, was the reason Jacob's sons chose circumcision as the way to overcome the Shechemites; certainly, the valiant sons of Jacob could have overpowered them even were they not circumcised. However, Jacob's sons knew that had they attacked and defeated uncircumcised heathens, the nations would have clamored in protest. Once the Shechemites circumcised themselves and indentified as Jews, however, the brothers knew that the nations would disassociate themselves from the Shechemites because not a peep is heard when Jewish blood is spilled. This added to their confidence.

כז וַיֵּצֵאוּ: בְּנֵי יַעֲקֹב בָּאוּ עַל־הַחֲלָלִים וַיָּבֹזּוּ
כח הָעִיר אֲשֶׁר טִמְּאוּ אֲחוֹתָם: אֶת־צֹאנָם
וְאֶת־בְּקָרָם וְאֶת־חֲמֹרֵיהֶם וְאֵת אֲשֶׁר־
כט בָּעִיר וְאֶת־אֲשֶׁר בַּשָּׂדֶה לָקָחוּ: וְאֶת־כָּל־
חֵילָם וְאֶת־כָּל־טַפָּם וְאֶת־נְשֵׁיהֶם שָׁבוּ

the *Midrash* — and this is the opinion favored by *Ramban* to *v.* 12 — she lived in Simeon's house [not as his *wife*, but] shut up as a veritable widow. She went down with them to Egypt, and there she died. Simeon — or the children of Israel after the Exodus — compassionately brought her back to Canaan for burial. *Ramban* notes that her grave is in the city of Arbel near the grave of Nitai the Arbelite.

According to *Pirkei d'Rabbi Eliezer* 38, Dinah had borne a daughter from Shechem's assault, whom she named Asenath. The brothers were opposed to keeping the child so that people would not speak of licentiousness in 'Jacob's tents.' To guarantee her safety, Jacob engraved HASHEM's Name on a metal plate, hung it on her neck, and left her in the field under a bush. Providence brought the child to the home of Potiphera, priest of On in Egypt, who was childless. He and his wife adopted her and Joseph later married her [41:45]. *Tosafos HaRosh* mentions that her name *Asenath* was in commemoration of her having been placed under the bush [סְנֶה].

Another tradition recorded in *Bava Basra* 15a, maintains that Dinah married Job and had a most positive influence on him.

27. בְּנֵי יַעֲקֹב בָּאוּ עַל הַחֲלָלִים וַיָּבֹזּוּ הָעִיר — *The sons of Jacob came upon the slain, and they plundered the city.*

Upon the slain — i.e., to strip the corpses *(Rashi).*

[It is not clear from the text whether Simeon and Levi plundered the city *alone*, or whether at this point the other brothers joined in as well.]

According to *Targum Yonasan* (and this is the opinion followed by most commentators), the verse means that the *rest* of the brothers came while Simeon and Levi were departing with Dinah. *R' Hoffmann* offers that this accounts for the past perfect בָּאוּ, lit. *had come*, for they came while Simeon and Levi were still there, but *after* the massacre had been completed. By the time they arrived, no Shechemites were left alive. Thus Scripture testifies that they had no hand in murder; they allowed themselves only to take spoils because of their outrage at Shechem's deed, and to act as a moral deterrent against similar violations in the future.

Or HaChaim maintains that *all* the brothers plundered the city since the property was rightfully theirs as בֹּשֶׁת, *compensation for humiliation*. As *Rambam* notes in *Hilchos Naarah Besulah* chapt. 2, such payments must be assessed on the basis of the status of the man and the girl involved. Thus, considering Dinah's exalted status as

34
27-29 *[27] The sons of Jacob came upon the slain, and they*
plundered the city which had defiled their sister.
[28] Their flocks, their herds, their donkeys, whatever
was in the town and whatever was in the field, they
took. [29] All their wealth, all their children and wives
they took captive and they plundered, as well as

Jacob's daughter, the brothers took *everything* for their father, for in the case of heathens, we do *not* apply the rule: קִים לֵיה בִּדְרַבָּה מִינֵיה, *One is given only the more severe penalty, but is excused from the lesser one.* Therefore, although the Shechemites suffered the supreme penalty of death, they remained culpable for all money payments arising out of the offense.

אֲשֶׁר טִמְּאוּ אֲחוֹתָם — *Which had defiled their sister.*

The translation of the last stich follows *Radak.* Others render: *because they [=the residents] had defiled their sister.*

The verb *defiled* is in the plural. Thereby the Torah bears testimony that *all* the Shechemites were collectively guilty for Shechem's atrocity by allowing it to go unchecked, and by their subsequent insincerity. By their complicity, the Shechemites were guilty of *kidnapping* which comes under the category of the Noachide prohibition against *robbery.* Were this their only crime, Jacob's sons would not have reacted so extremely — it was the emotional outrage by Shechem's rape that caused their vengeful massacre. This also explains their taking of spoils as בֹּשֶׁת, *compensation for the humiliation,* as explained above *(Ibn Caspi; Or HaChaim).*

Additionally, all the townspeople shared responsibility because Shechem would never have committed this evil had it not been tacitly approved by the citizens for the chief to take whomever he lusted after *(Sforno).*

28. אֶת־צֹאנָם וְאֶת־בְּקָרָם וְאֶת־חֲמֹרֵיהֶם — *Their flocks* [of small ungulates: sheep, goats, etc.], [*and*] *their herds* [large cattle], [*and*] *their donkeys.*

Thus by taking their property, Jacob's sons did to the Shechemites what the latter had planned to do to them [*v.* 23] *(Abarbanel).*

וְאֵת אֲשֶׁר־בָּעִיר וְאֶת־אֲשֶׁר בַּשָּׂדֶה לָקָחוּ — [*And*] *whatever was in the town and whatever was in the field, they took.*

— I.e., the stray and domesticated animals *(Radak).*

R' Hirsch explains this stich as further modifying the first part of the passage: *Their flocks, their herds, and their donkeys — both those that were in the city and those that were in the field — they took.*

29. וְאֶת־כָּל־חֵילָם — [*And*] *All their wealth.*

The translation *wealth* follows *Rashi* who cites this meaning of חֵיל [usually *forces* or *strength*] in *Deut.* 8:17; *Numb.* 19:18; *Psalms* 49:11.

וְאֶת־כָּל־טַפָּם וְאֶת־נְשֵׁיהֶם שָׁבוּ וַיָּבֹזּוּ — [*And*] *all their children and* [*their*] *wives, they took captive, and they plundered.*

— To ensure that no one would remain there to foment retaliation by neighboring tribes *(Abarbanel).*

וַיָּבֹזּוּ וְאֵת כָּל־אֲשֶׁר בַּבָּיִת: וַיֹּאמֶר יַעֲקֹב
ל אֶל־שִׁמְעוֹן וְאֶל־לֵוִי עֲכַרְתֶּם אֹתִי
לְהַבְאִישֵׁנִי בְּיֹשֵׁב הָאָרֶץ בַּכְּנַעֲנִי וּבַפְּרִזִּי
וַאֲנִי מְתֵי מִסְפָּר וְנֶאֶסְפוּ עָלַי וְהִכּוּנִי
לא וְנִשְׁמַדְתִּי אֲנִי וּבֵיתִי: וַיֹּאמְרוּ הַכְזוֹנָה
יַעֲשֶׂה אֶת־אֲחוֹתֵנוּ:

The translation of שָׁבוּ as *they took captive* follows *Rashi* who observes that it is accented on the second syllable [and is the third person plural *kal* past tense of the root שבה, *to capture.* Were the accent on the *first* syllable, שָׁבוּ, it would have been the third person plural past tense of the root שוב, meaning *they returned.*]

וְאֵת כָּל־אֲשֶׁר בַּבָּיִת — *As well as everything in the house.*

I.e., the movable property *(Radak),* in Shechem's or Chamor's house *(Ibn Ezra).*

The use of the definite article and singular *the* house indicates the house of the prime subjects of this narrative *(R' Hoffmann).*

30. וַיֹּאמֶר יַעֲקֹב אֶל־שִׁמְעוֹן וְאֶל־לֵוִי — [*And*] *Jacob said to Simeon and to Levi.*

[The double use of וְאֶל, *and to,* implies that he spoke to each of them as a mature *individual,* responsible for his own actions.]

Furthermore, only Simeon and Levi were castigated, for *they* committed murder. The other brothers took spoils as a form of recompense for the humiliation, and the taking of the women and children to avoid repercussions. In the context of what had occurred *their* action was not regarded as evil; perhaps it was the only course they could take under the circumstances *(Akeidas Yitzchak).*

עֲכַרְתֶּם אֹתִי — *You have discomposed me.*

Compare the expression מַיִם עֲכוּרִים, *troubled, unclear, waters.* He meant: My mind is not clear. By their rash violence, Simeon and Levi had disturbed Jacob's composure and placed him in a potentially untenable position should the Canaanites go on the attack. Midrashically, Jacob's intent was: The barrel was clear, but you have made it turbid! *(Rashi).*[1]

— You have clouded me. The family's reputation and honor had been crystal clear, but you have besmirched it *(R' Hirsch).*

לְהַבְאִישֵׁנִי בְּיֹשֵׁב הָאָרֶץ בַּכְּנַעֲנִי וּבַפְּרִיזִּי — *Making me odious among the inhabitants of the land, the Canaanites and Perizzites.*

The Canaanites will despise me and ostracize me, just as one distances himself from a despicable,

1. *Rashi* explains that the Canaanites had a tradition that they would fall by the hands of Jacob's progeny. But they thought that this would be deferred until Jacob's progeny would *numerically increase, and then inherit the land* [*Exod.* 23:30]. Consequently, the Canaanites had maintained their silence until now, not anticipating such an early attack on the part of Jacob's sons. 'Now that you have attacked them, however,' Jacob said, 'they will regard our conquest of Canaan as having begun, and they will band together in alliance against me and I shall be destroyed being so outnumbered.]

everything in the house.
30 *Jacob said to Simeon and to Levi, 'You have dis-*
composed me, making me odious among the inhabi-
tants of the land, the Canaanites and Perizzites. I am
few in number and should they band together and at-
tack me, I will be annihilated — I and my household.'
31 *And they said, 'Should he treat our sister like a*
harlot?'

foul-smelling, putrid object *(Radak).*

You have given my reputation a foul smell. And just as you have been unjust, you have been unwise *(R' Hirsch).*

Sforno: They will say that we broke our word after they became circumcised.

[According to *Rashi* in the *footnote:* They will regard our conquest of the land as having prematurely begun, and though they have been confidently tranquil until now, they will henceforth take steps to counter us.]

[On the *Canaanites and Perizzites,* see above 13:7.]

[It is apparent from Jacob's remark, and from inferences in *Ramban* above, that once the Shechemites had undergone circumcision — which Jacob viewed as possibly signaling a sincere gesture — he was prepared to live among them for at least a while. It is equally clear, however, that he had no intention of permitting the Hivite Shechem — who had defiled Dinah — to marry her. Jacob wanted to incapacitate them enough to gain Dinah's release, and then come to terms with the city.]

וַאֲנִי מְתֵי מִסְפָּר — [And] *I am few in number* [lit. *and I am a numbered people*].

— I.e., I have a meager force of men *(Rashi).*

מִסְפָּר, *number,* idiomatically means: given to be numbered, hence *few.* The singular of מְתֵי [people], מַת, occurs only in names such as מְתוּשֶׁלַח, *Methuselah (R' Hoffmann).*

וְנֶאֶסְפוּ עָלַי וְהִכּוּנִי — *And should they band together and attack me.*

— [To avenge the wrong. According to the *Midrash* cited in the footnote to *v.* 25, this indeed occurred.]

וְנִשְׁמַדְתִּי אֲנִי וּבֵיתִי — [*And*] *I will be annihilated — I and my household.*

[This would have been the case had not Jacob prevailed, and had God not cast His fear upon them (see on 35:5).]

[Note that the Patriarch's reproach refers to the dire *consequence* of his son's misbehavior, not to the iniquity of their acts of violence. See *R' Hirsch* in *footnote* to *v.* 31.]

31. וַיֹּאמְרוּ — *And they said.*

— To the contrary! The 'vessel' you referred to, [i.e., our honor] was made turbid [by Shechem's act], and we cleared it! *(Midrash).*

הַכְזוֹנָה יַעֲשֶׂה אֶת־אֲחוֹתֵנוּ — *Should he treat our sister like a harlot?*

Should he then have been permitted, unchecked and unpunished, to treat our sister like a harlot, like a loose woman who has no avenger? *(Radak).*

— She is *not* a harlot, and her

א וַיֹּאמֶר אֱלֹהִים֙ אֶל־יַעֲקֹב קוּם עֲלֵה בֵית־
אֵל וְשֶׁב־שָׁם וַעֲשֵׂה־שָׁם מִזְבֵּחַ לָאֵל֙

wrong must be avenged! We, as her brothers, had the obligation to avenge her *(Sforno).*

[We were not motivated by brutality, but by a desire to safeguard our honor, and our sister's honor, which must stand above every other consideration.]

Possibly, the sense of יַעֲשֶׂה is not 'shall *he* treat,' but the indefinite 'shall *one* treat': What we did was to make ourselves feared so no one else would ever again dare to commit such a heinous crime against one of our women. Do you then want to keep Dinah and all Jewish daughters locked up in a chest forever, to protect then from the gaze of every lecher? [See on 32:23] *(Ralbag).*

— Is it right that people should say in the congregation of Israel that an uncircumcised idol worshiper defiled a daughter of Jacob and no one came to her aid? Or is it preferable that they hear that because Shechem boastfully abused our sister, treating her like a common harlot, that a whole city was destroyed because of her! *(Zohar; Targum Yonasan).*

Jacob's sons perceived from this experience that they would occasionally have to use to force to defend the ideal of purity and honor *(Alshich).*[1]

[The ז of הַכְּזוֹנָה is traditionally written large in some Torah Scrolls. I have been unable to find a reason for this. *Minchas Shay* cites the

1. *R' Hirsch* finds the entire motive of Simeon and Levi encapsuled in these few words. They were convinced that Shechem would not have dared act as he did were Dinah not a powerless alien, hopelessly outnumbered, Jewess. Precisely because it would continue to march through Canaan — and history — as a tiny nation, Israel had to wield the sword to demonstrate that its women would be protected by whatever necessary means. To do so, they did not care to act prudently; they wanted to be feared.

Had Simeon and Levi stopped at killing Shechem and Chamor, they would not have been blameworthy. But they punished relatively innocent people, and then they looted. For that there was no justification. [See, however, footnote to *v.* 13 for the justifications set forth by *Rambam* and *Ramban.*]

Jacob's death-bed speech to Simeon and Levi reflect this duality: the rightness of their motive, but the wrongness of their excessive means. He cursed their passion and deed, but he implictly recognized the lofty nature of the spirit that moved them. By spreading them throughout the territory of the future Jewish nation, Jacob assured two things: 1) they would not possess the political and military power of decision; and 2) their uncompromising view of justice and national dignity would be disseminated throughout the nation.

Jacob's disapproval of their action was based primarily on the vulnerable position in which it placed the family. He *did* recognize the necessity for armed resistance when called for, but he insisted that each case must be judged individually in terms of its overall effects. Jews are moral and non-violent — not because they are weak, but because their greatest source of strength is the soul, not the sword.

Abarbanel [whose comment should perhaps be viewed from the background of his experience as the leader of Spanish Jewry under the Spanish Inquisition and Expulsion] writes that the act of the brothers demonstrates that there are times when it is worthwhile to risk lives in order to preserve Jewish self-respect. He continues that God apparently ratified their philosophy by causing the Canaanites to fear the family of Jacob.

Most commentators agree that Jacob did not condemn armed resistance *per se*, but insisted that each instance must be calmly and dispassionately evaluated. Although Simeon and Levi can be defended, their course cannot be regarded as a precedent regulating Jewish conduct throughout history.

35 ¹ God said to Jacob, 'Arise — go up to Bethel and
1 remain there, and make an altar there to God

custom but notes that it is not universal.]

Rashi comments on the phrase אֶת אֲחוֹתֵנוּ by simply quoting *Onkelos'* Aramaic translation: *our sister* without further elaboration.

R' Bachya struggles with this, and notes that he fails to grasp what *Rashi* intended in citing the literal translation of an unambiguous word. The commentators provide several possible solutions. *Tosafos HaRosh* suggests that *Rashi* intended to point out that אֶת should be translated as the accusative article יַת and not as עִם, *with*, which would, as *Minchas Yitzchak* notes, imply consent on her part, as if she too, acted the harlot role.

Heidenheim suggests, on the basis of printed texts, that there are three extant versions of *Onkelos'* translation of this phrase: a) יַת אֲחָתָנָא; b) יִתְעֲבֵד לַאֲחָתָנָא; c) יַעֲבִיד לַאֲחָתָנָא, and that *Rashi* wished merely to establish the former as the correct one.

By saying *like a harlot* — but not an *actual* harlot — they emphasized their belief that Dinah had not consented *(Lekach Tov).*

Ibn Caspi maintains that this could also be why in this verse the word אֲחוֹתֵנוּ, *our sister,* is traditionally written 'full' (with a ו) in contrast with the way it is written in verses 13 and 14. For, as the episode draws to a close, the brothers make a point of saying that Dinah remained 'fully' worthy of being their sister.

Jacob does not agree with his sons' contention that their extreme violence was justified, but he maintains his silence; stifling his outrage until he curses their anger on his death bed [49:6] *(R' Hoffmann).*

XXXV

1. Jacob journeys to Bethel.

קוּם עֲלֵה בֵית־אֵל — *Arise — go up to Bethel.*

Nearly twenty-two years earlier, Jacob had vowed that Bethel would be the site of *God's house* [28:22]. The command that he now return there was to imply that Jacob must fulfill the vow without delay; because he had not done so sooner, he was punished by the abduction of Dinah *(Rashi; Radak;* see *footnote* to 34:1).[1]

Cf. *Deut.* 23:22: *When you make a vow to HASHEM your God, do not delay fulfilling it, for HASHEM your God will call you to account, and you will have incurred guilt.*

Bethel is geographically on higher

1. Jacob was held accountable only for his delay in fulfilling the vow *on the way home*, but not for leaving the vow unfulfilled during the years he spent in Laban's house, since the vow was to take effect only after he began his homeward journey — *If I return safely, etc.* [28:21]. Thus, he was blamed only for settling in Succoth, instead of going directly to Bethel and then to his father.

Earlier [32:23], *Rashi* cites only the *Midrash* that Jacob was punished with Dinah's abduction for having withheld Dinah from Esau, but makes no mention that Dinah's abduction was also in punishment for having delayed the fulfillment of his vow. *Gur Aryeh* explains that the sin of procrastination caused God to 'open Jacob's ledger,' as it were, and determine whether he was deserving of punishment. Then, his sin of withholding Dinah was brought to account. Had he fulfilled his vow, the sin of hiding Dinah could have been held in abeyance; meanwhile, Jacob could have atoned for it with repentance and prayer.

Chizkuni and *Mizrachi* explain that his detour to Succoth and the resultant delay in going to Bethel was brought about by Jacob's failure to let Esau marry Dinah. Otherwise, he would have proceeded directly to Bethel. Thus, he *was* punished for his procrastination.

הַנִּרְאֶה אֵלֶיךָ בְּבָרְחֲךָ מִפְּנֵי עֵשָׂו אָחִיךָ׃
ב וַיֹּאמֶר יַעֲקֹב אֶל־בֵּיתוֹ וְאֶל כָּל־אֲשֶׁר
עִמּוֹ הָסִרוּ אֶת־אֱלֹהֵי הַנֵּכָר אֲשֶׁר

terrain than Shechem; hence the term *go up (Abarbanel).*

Interestingly, Abraham's route had also taken him from Shechem to Bethel. See 12:8 *(Hoffmann).*

Basing themselves on the *Midrash* to 28:17-19 that Mount Moriah in Jerusalem had miraculously been moved to Luz/Bethel at the time of Jacob's vision, many commentators explain the implication here, too, that Jacob was to go *up* to *Jerusalem.*

וְשֶׁב־שָׁם — *And remain* [or: *settle*] *there.*

Ramban confesses that he does not know the significance of the command *and remain there.* He conjectures that God commanded him to remain there to enable him to purify his camp from the טֻמְאָה, *defilement,* of idols that had been taken from Shechem or from the defilement the people had incurred by touching corpses. This was similar to the seven-day waiting period outside the camp that was required of the soldiers who returned from the war against the Midianites [*Numb.* 31:19]. Following this, Jacob would make the altar. Alternatively, he was to dwell there for a time before he set up the altar so that his mind could be attuned spiritually to the service of God.[1]

Sforno echoes the latter view, and cites how the pious ones of old used to wait an hour before praying in order that they might focus their thoughts upon their Father in Heaven [*Mishnah Berachos* 5:1].

Possibly the intent was that Jacob and his family become imbued with the spirit which is associated with Bethel and his experience there *(R' Hirsch).*

The command could also mean: Wait there — for the Divine Manifestation *(R' Munk).*

Another implication of *and remain there* is: Do not be concerned with the fact that the Canaanites dwell there; remain there and do not fear them *(Or HaChaim).*

The phrase *remain there* does not imply that Jacob was to settle there *permanently,* for in fact he remained there but a short time. The literal intent is that Jacob should go to Bethel and stay there as long as necessary to prepare himself spiritually, and practically, for fulfilling his vow and making an altar *(Hoffmann).*

וַעֲשֵׂה־שָׁם מִזְבֵּחַ — *And make an altar there.*

After making the necessary spiritual preparations, *make an altar there (Ramban).*

There is an opinion cited in *Chumash Rav Peninim* that Jacob had delayed his vow since he was unsure *where* he was to build the altar. According to the

1. According to the various Rabbinic chronologies, Jacob spent a total of six months in Bethel sacrificing burnt offerings. [Included in that six-month period was the time he spent in Shechem *(Vilna Gaon).*]

Thus, the total duration of Jacob's journey from Paddan Aram to Isaac was two years, and the total time away from his father's service was thirty-six years: fourteen in the Academy of Eber; twenty in Laban's service; eighteen months in Succoth; and six months in Bethel and Shechem. Jacob was held accountable only for the last twenty-two years. His punishment was that Joseph was later absent from him for a like amount of time *(Seder Olam; Megillah* 17a; see *Rashi* further 37:33).

35
2

Who appeared to you when you fled from Esau your
brother.' 2 *So Jacob said to his household and to all*
those who were with him, 'Discard the alien gods

Midrash [see *comm.* to 28:17] Mount Moriah had temporarily moved to Bethel/Luz where Jacob made his vow. Now that Mount Moriah had returned to its location in Jerusalem, Jacob waited for God to tell him whether his vow to build an altar should be fulfilled in Bethel or on Mount Moriah. [Most maintain, however, that Jacob was now in Jerusalem, on Mount Moriah.]

[This altar is perceived by many commentators to be *in addition* to the vow of 28:22. That vow was fulfilled by the reconsecration of the *pillar* in *v. 14.*]

לָאֵל הַנִּרְאֶה אֵלֶיךָ בְּבָרְחֲךָ מִפְּנֵי עֵשָׂו אָחִיךָ — *To* [*the*] *God Who appeared to you when you fled from* [*the presence of*] *Esau your brother.*

As a thanksgiving to God for having fulfilled the promise He made to you there to protect you [28:15ff]. This is akin to the Sages' declaration [*Berachos* 54a] that whenever one passes a place where he was miraculously saved from impending tragedy he must utter the benediction *Blessed be He Who performed a miracle for me in this place (Sforno).*

This was a reminder to Jacob that when he was alone, fleeing from his brother [27:43], God had appeared to him and gave him assurances of safety [28:10-15]. God had fulfilled *His* promise, and now it was Jacob's obligation to reciprocate by fulfilling *his* vow of 28:22 *(Radak).*

The Name *El,* as explained by *Gur Aryeh* to *Exodus* 34:6, indicates a boundless degree of Divine mercy, an outpouring far surpassing that indicated by the Name HASHEM.

Why does God refer to Himself in third person — לָאֵל, *to the God* — rather than in first person — לִי, *to Me?*

Radak answers that it was not God Himself Who spoke to Jacob, but through an angel speaking in His Name. The angel reverently referred to God in third person. Such angelic communications are common in Scripture.

2. אֶל־בֵּיתוֹ וְאֶל כָּל אֲשֶׁר עִמּוֹ — *To his house*[*hold*] *and to all those who were with him.*

בֵּיתוֹ, *his household,* is variously interpreted as referring to his wives *(Abarbanel)* or his sons *(Radak).*

The *Midrash* interprets *all thoser who were with him* to refer to converts whom Jacob had brought under the wings of the *Shechinah.*

Sefer Chassidim [Parma ed.] par. §1765 cites this passage to teach that one should reprove the members of his *own* household first, and *then* reprove others.

הָסִרוּ אֶת־אֱלֹהֵי הַנֵּכָר אֲשֶׁר בְּתֹכְכֶם — *Discard* [or: *remove*] *the alien gods* [lit. *gods of the foreigner*] *that are in your midst.*

— I.e., remove from your possession the idols you have taken from the spoils of Shechem *(Rashi).*

The term אֱלֹהֵי הַנֵּכָר, *gods of the foreigner,* refers to idols worshiped by foreign peoples *(Ralbag).*

R' Hirsch perceives הַנֵּכָר as an abstract noun and renders: *gods of 'strangeness.'* It refers to any characteristics that are foreign to Jews; foreign lands in contrast to the Jewish land, and the gentile character in contrast to Jewry and Judaism.

[Comp. *Rashi* and *Ibn Ezra* to *Deut.* 32:12.]

בְּתֹכְכֶם וְהִטַּהֲרוּ וְהַחֲלִיפוּ שִׂמְלֹתֵיכֶם:
ג וְנָקוּמָה וְנַעֲלֶה בֵּית־אֵל וְאֶעֱשֶׂה־שָּׁם
מִזְבֵּחַ לָאֵל הָעֹנֶה אֹתִי בְּיוֹם צָרָתִי וַיְהִי
ד עִמָּדִי בַּדֶּרֶךְ אֲשֶׁר הָלָכְתִּי: וַיִּתְּנוּ אֶל־
יַעֲקֹב אֵת כָּל־אֱלֹהֵי הַנֵּכָר אֲשֶׁר בְּיָדָם
וְאֶת־הַנְּזָמִים אֲשֶׁר בְּאָזְנֵיהֶם וַיִּטְמֹן אֹתָם

The spoils included silver and gold jewelry engraved with figures that were worshiped as gods. Jacob's household members took them *only* to wear and display, but not for worship. Nevertheless Jacob wanted them to derive no benefit whatever from articles that had been used as idols, but to separate themselves as much as possible from such matters. Similarly, the Torah commanded [*Deut.* 7:25]: *You shall not desire the silver and gold on them,* and [*ibid.* 13:18] *nothing of that which was consigned to condemnation shall remain in your hand (Radak).*

Furthermore, Jacob wanted that their later service HASHEM not even *appear* idolatrous in any way *(Chizkuni).*

R' Hoffmann includes in the category of *alien gods* the *teraphim* which Rachel had stolen from her father [see 31:19], as well as other idolatrous artifacts that his servants might still have had in their possession from Aram Naharaim, a place of idol-worship. Cf. *Josh.* 24:14.

וְהִטַּהֲרוּ – [*And*] *cleanse yourselves.*

— [Spiritually] from idolatry *(Rashi),* since idolatry contaminates *(Radak).*

— By bathing your bodies *(Ibn Ezra).*[1]

וְהַחֲלִיפוּ שִׂמְלֹתֵיכֶם – *And change your clothes.*

— Lest you [inadvertantly *(Yafeh Toar)*] have in your possession a garment that had been used in idolatrous worship *(Rashi).*

— Clothes which have become contaminated along with you, or those clothes which you took off the corpses or from their houses *(Radak).*

R' Hirsch notes the analogy with the order given by Moses before the Revelation at Sinai: *he sanctified the people and they washed their garments* [*Exodus* 19:14]. For the family of Jacob, the ascent to Bethel where God had revealed Himself to the Patriarch had the same significance as the assembly at Mount Sinai for his descendants.

From this verse we learn that when one goes to pray in a place dedicated for prayer, he must be clean in body and in clothing *(Ibn Ezra).*

3. וְנָקוּמָה וְנַעֲלֶה בֵּית־אֵל וְאֶעֱשֶׂה־שָּׁם מִזְבֵּחַ – *Then come, let us go up to Bethel* [lit. *and we shall rise and we shall go up to Bethel*]; [*and*] *I will make there an altar.*

Then, in this cleansed state, we can proceed to Bethel and serve God *(R' Bachya).*

'Though *we* will go up to Bethel,

1. Thus we see that whoever separates himself from idolatry must cleanse himself (see *S'mag* 4:240); this is the reason a convert must undergo immersion *(Torah Temimah).*

Rambam [*Avos HaTum'ah* 6:1] observes that although contamination caused by idolatry is a Soferic enactment, nevertheless we see a Scriptural allusion to it in our verse. [Cf. however *Shabbos* 82b where our verse is not cited.]

that are in your midst; cleanse yourselves and change
your clothes. [3] *Then come, let us go up to Bethel; I*
will make there an altar to God Who answered me in
my time of distress, and was with me on the road that
I have traveled.' [4] *So they gave to Jacob all the alien*
gods that were in their possession, as well as the rings
that were in their ears, and Jacob buried them un-

it is *I* who will build an altar.' Jacob excluded his children from the task of building the altar because they came into the world only *after* his oath and after he suffered the affliction ... Only the one for whom the miracle occurred must render thanks; only he who eats bread at the table must say Grace, not another who has eaten nothing *(Zohar).*

לָאֵל הָעֹנֶה אֹתִי בְּיוֹם צָרָתִי — *To* [*the*] *God Who answered* [lit. *answers*] *me in my time* [lit. *day*] *of distress.*

— When I fled from Esau *(Abarbanel;* cf. *v.* 2).

— Throughout my every dilemma *(Akeidas Yitzchak).*[1]

In relating God's command to his househod, Jacob does not say that God commanded him directly nor does he use God's own description of Himself in verse 1 as *'the God Who appeared to me when I was fleeing from Esau my brother.'* It would have seemed pretentious to say that God had appeared to him, and that the mention of his flight from Esau would have sounded incongruous in view of their public display of peaceful reconciliation *(Alshich; Abarbanel).*

וַיְהִי עִמָּדִי בַּדֶּרֶךְ אֲשֶׁר הָלָכְתִּי — *And was with me on the road that I have traveled.*

[As He promised me in 28:15.]

4. אֲשֶׁר בְּיָדָם — *That were in their possession* [the Hebrew is idiomatically singular: *that were in their 'hand'*].

— [I.e. the idols] in their possession from the artifacts they had taken from the house of idolatry of Shechem *(Targum Yonasan).*

וְאֶת הַנְּזָמִים אֲשֶׁר בְּאָזְנֵיהֶם — *As well as the rings that were in their ears.*

I.e., the ears of the idols *(Chizkuni).*

According to *Targum Yonasan:* '... that had been in the ears *of the inhabitants of Shechem.'* The rings too, were used for idol worship as amulets. They contained images within them *(Pirkei d'Rabbi Eliezer).*

The connection between rings and idolatry is obscure. That the Golden Calf and the *ephod* made by Gideon were both made from such

1. Jacob had been commanded in verse 1 to erect an altar to *God Who had appeared to him when he fled from Esau,* but Jacob wants to pay homage to God not only for the kindnesses of the *past,* but also for those of the present. And so he uses the present tense, saying: *God,* הָעֹנֶה אוֹתִי, *Who answers me in the day of my distress.* Jacob experiences Divine salvation as an uninterrupted, continuing reality. Even at the end of his life, he used the present tense to invoke *the angel who saves me from all harm* [הַמַּלְאָךְ הַגֹּאֵל אֹתִי] (48:16). For Jacob, Divine Providence is *always* present, *always* near to man, *always* merciful. Divine love is infinite and inexhaustible, it knows neither past nor future, but only the eternal present *(R' Munk).*

ה יַעֲקֹב תַּחַת הָאֵלָה אֲשֶׁר עִם־שְׁכֶם: וַיִּסָּעוּ
וַיְהִי | חִתַּת אֱלֹהִים עַל־הֶעָרִים אֲשֶׁר
סְבִיבוֹתֵיהֶם וְלֹא רָדְפוּ אַחֲרֵי בְּנֵי יַעֲקֹב:
ו וַיָּבֹא יַעֲקֹב לוּזָה אֲשֶׁר בְּאֶרֶץ כְּנַעַן הִוא
ז בֵּית־אֵל הוּא וְכָל־הָעָם אֲשֶׁר־עִמּוֹ: וַיִּבֶן

jewelry throws little light on the matter ... It is worth noting that the Aramaic word for נְזָמִים, *earrings*, is קְדָשָׁא [comp. root קדש, *holy*] *(R' Hirsch)*.

וַיִּטְמֹן ... תַּחַת הָאֵלָה אֲשֶׁר עִם שְׁכֶם — *And Jacob buried* [lit. *hid*] *them underneath the terebinth near* [lit. *that was with*, i.e., in the proximity of *(Rashi)*] *Shechem.*[1]

— In a location which will neither be tilled nor sown *(Ramban)*.

— So that others should not come upon them and be led astray *(Radak)*.

☙ Since the law requires that idols be *pulverized* and scattered in the wind, or sunk in the sea where they will be forever inaccessible [*Avodah Zarah* 43b], why did Jacob merely *bury* these idols?

It appears that Jacob's sons did not take the idols or appurtenances until the Shechemites had renounced them as idols, thus making their use permissible to them. For, as we learn [ibid. 52b], a heathen can nullify an idol against its worshiper's will. That Jacob still ordered them to rid themselves of these idols, bathe themselves and change their clothes, was an extra-*halachic* act of piety to add to their spiritual purity in preparation for their service of HASHEM. Accordingly, *burial* in this case was sufficient, since the idols were legally permissible, and Jacob's intention was merely to hide them *(Ramban)*.

Another reason Jacob *buried* the idols there rather than take the time to pulverize them or seek a body of water in which to sink them, was not to delay his execution of God's command to fulfill his vow *(Nachalas Yitzchak)*.

Furthermore, Jacob was afraid that were he to remain there longer to pulverize or burn the idols, the surrounding nations would angrily note the desecration of their gods. Therefore, he took the most expeditious course open to him under the circumstances *(R' Bachya)*.

According to *Midrash HaGadol*, the terror mentioned in the next verse was in consequence of Jacob's act recorded here. The inhabitants of the neighboring cities saw Jacob's mighty feat in picking up the terebinth with his hand, hiding the idols beneath it, and replanting it. The terror of God fell upon them.

אֵלָה is defined by *Rashi* as 'a kind of tree that bears no fruit.'

Jacob purposely chose such a *barren* tree under which to bury them; he would not choose a fruit tree lest its fruit-bearing qualities be adversely affected *(Alshich)*.

The familiar translation *terebinth* or *turpentine tree* follows *Onkelos* who renders it בּוּטְמָא, *Pistacia terebinthus*, which is one of the tallest species of trees in *Eretz Yisrael*.

[*Rashi* in *Joshua* 24:26 mentions a tradition that the terebinth mentioned there is the very tree of our verse.]

1. According to several Talmudic sources, Jacob buried these idols — one of which was in the form of a dove — on Mount Gerizim near Shechem. That the Samaritans revere Mount Gerizim as holy is perceived by R' Yishmael ben R' Yose [*Yer. Avodah Zarah* 5:4] to be not because of the *mountain*, but because of the idols Jacob buried beneath it.

As noted in *Chullin* 6a [see *Tosaf.* ad. loc. s.v. בְּרֹאשׁ] many centuries later the Samaritans found this dove-idol at the top of Mount Gerizim where they built their temple, and venerated it (see *Daas Zekeinim)*.

35 *derneath the terebinth near Shechem.* 5 *They set out,*
5-6 *and there fell a Godly terror on the cities which were*
around them, so that they did not pursue Jacob's
sons.
6 *Thus Jacob came to Luz in the land of Canaan —*
which is Bethel — he, and all the people who were

5. וַיִּסָּעוּ — *And they set out* [lit. *and they traveled*].

וַיְהִי חִתַּת אֱלֹהִים עַל הֶעָרִים אֲשֶׁר סְבִיבוֹתֵיהֶם — *And there fell* [lit. *was*] *a Godly terror on the cities which were around them.*

— A Godly terror was inspired by the military prowess displayed by Jacob and his sons. For, as noted above [*footnote* to 34:25], the surrounding nations had waged three major wars against them, and were it not for Jacob who took up his weapons, they would have been in mortal danger *(Midrash Vayisau).* [See *Rashi* to 48:22.]

Because it was a hidden miracle, however, the Torah did not describe it, referring to it only by allusion in 48:22 and with the passing reference here. [I.e., it was a miracle which man can deny, attributing it to the great natural strength of Jacob and his sons; thus it could appear that their own might saved them.] The Torah is similarly silent regarding Esau's wars with the Horites [see 36:20] *(Ramban* to 34:13).

According to *Midrash Rabbah,* these nations assembled at Chatzor to wage war, but as noted, they were divinely prevented from doing so. For this reason, Joshua burned only Chatzor of all the cities in *Eretz Yisrael* that stood intact after his conquest, (*Joshua* 11:13). This was Chatzor's punishment, for a tradition had been divinely revealed to Moses who in turn transmitted it to Joshua, that it was at Chatzor that they assembled.

וְלֹא רָדְפוּ אַחֲרֵי בְּנֵי יַעֲקֹב — *So that* [lit. *and*] *they did not pursue* [*after*] *Jacob's sons.*

For had God not caused His terror to be upon the Canaanites, they would have fallen upon Jacob's family 'like the sand which is on the seashore in abundance' *(Ramban* to 34:13).

The expression implies that they still bore hatred, but would not dare pursue them *(Ran).*

6. לוּזָה אֲשֶׁר בְּאֶרֶץ כְּנַעַן הִוא בֵּית־אֵל — *To Luz in the land of Canaan — which is Bethel.*

These many descriptions of the site intimate that there was another Luz, not in Canaan and not identified with Bethel *(Chizkuni).* [See *comm.* to 28:19 for the various views on the location of Luz/Bethel.]

It was only now, with his entry into Luz, *in the Land of Canaan* the land of his fathers, that Jacob's journey could be considered as having ended safely: *that is, Bethel* — the holy site which Jacob had sanctified as a 'House of God' when he had departed from the land. God had fulfilled *His* promises, and now Jacob, having been returned safely to his ancestral home, was prepared to fulfill his vow *(Hoffmann).*

הוּא וְכָל־הָעָם אֲשֶׁר עִמּוֹ — *He, and all the people who were with him.*

— This passage informs us that as

שָׁם֙ מִזְבֵּ֔חַ וַיִּקְרָא֙ לַמָּק֔וֹם אֵ֖ל בֵּֽית־אֵ֑ל כִּ֣י
שָׁ֗ם נִגְל֤וּ אֵלָיו֙ הָֽאֱלֹהִ֔ים בְּבָרְח֖וֹ מִפְּנֵ֥י
ח אָחִֽיו׃ וַתָּ֤מָת דְּבֹרָה֙ מֵינֶ֣קֶת רִבְקָ֔ה

a result of the aforementioned *Godly terror* upon the surrounding cities, not one man among Jacob's household or servants was lost in warfare [for *all* his people were with him] *(Ramban* to 34:13); nor did any of them die in Shechem or on the journey *(Radak).*

7. וַיִּבֶן שָׁם מִזְבֵּחַ — *And he built an altar there.*

— On the site where God had revealed Himself to Jacob on his way to Charan; where he had envisioned the angels ascending and descending [28:12-13]; and where he had erected a pillar [28:18] *(Hoffmann).*

Most commentators interpret that the construction of this altar was in specific compliance with God's command in *v.* 1. Jacob's vow in 28:22, however, was accomplished only later, when he rededicated the pillar [*v.* 14].

וַיִּקְרָא לַמָּקוֹם אֵל בֵּית־אֵל — *And [he] named the place El Bethel.*[1]

The phrase is interpreted as if it read אֵל בְּבֵית־אֵל, *the Holy One, Blessed be He, is in Bethel* (the prepositional prefix בְּ, *in*, being implied); He makes His Divine Presence manifest in Bethel. Other passages where the preposition ב, *in*, is implied are: *II Sam.* 9:4: בֵּית מָכִיר= בְּבֵית מָכִיר; above 24:13 בֵּית אָבִיךְ= בְּבֵית אָבִיךְ *(Rashi).*

Jacob had already given it the name *Bethel* in 28:19. He now added the name *El* — an act which had a significance similar to his naming of the altar in Shechem as *El Elohei Yisrael* in 33:20 [i.e., to commemorate the fact that God wrought miracles for him there; see *comm.* there] *(Radak).*

— Jacob thereby intimated that by appearing to him now, God associated His Presence with the site he had named Bethel nearly twenty-two years earlier *(Or HaChaim).*

As *Rashi* explains it, the sense is that Jacob proclaimed to all regarding that place: 'God is in Bethel' *(Abarbanel).*

Rashi to *Exod.* 34:6 cites the *Mechilta* that God's Name *El* depicts Him in His attribute as Dispenser of Divine Mercy [as distinct from *Elohim* which depicts Him as Dispenser of Strict Justice.] See *comm.* end of *v.* 1.

כִּי שָׁם נִגְלוּ אֵלָיו הָאֱלֹהִים — *For it was there that* [*the*] *God* [i.e. in His Aspect of Judge and Lord *(Rashi); R' Hirsch* renders: *the Divine relationship*] *had been revealed to him.*

— This is the specific reason for the altar: it commemorated God's appearance to him. The fulfillment of his vow, however, was accomplished with the rededication of the pillar in *v.* 14 *(Radak).*

[The verb נִגְלוּ, *had been revealed,* is in the plural; while *Elohim* is usually followed by a singular verb, e.g. בָּרָא אֱלֹהִים, *God created.*]

Rashi accordingly notes that Hebrew nouns denoting power or

1. When Abraham and Isaac built altars, Scripture specifies that they *proclaimed God's Name* [וַיִּקְרָא בְּשֵׁם ה׳; see, e.g., 12:8; 26:24]. This mention is unnecessary in the case of Jacob because of his large family and abundant retinue, all of whom served God. Furthermore, God's Name had already been made known by Abraham and Isaac *(Tur* to 13:8).

35 *with him.* [7] *And he built an altar there and named the*
8 *place El Bethel, for it was there that God had been*
revealed to him during his flight from his brother.
[8] *Deborah, the wet-nurse of Rebecca, died, and she*

lordship are often plural, for example 39:20: אֲדוֹנֵי יוֹסֵף [=אֲדוֹן יוֹסֵף], *Joseph's master; Exodus* 22:14: *If its owner* [בַּעְלוֹ=בְּעָלָיו] *is with it.* Similarly, God's Name *Elohim* which describes Him as Judge and Master, occurs in the plural [and may take a plural verb, as in our verse.] But no other Divine Name [e.g., ה׳, שַׁדַּי] ever occurs in the plural.

This follows the Sages, [*Sanhedrin* 38b] who perceived God Himself to be the subject, and the plural verb as merely an idiomatic form. They cite this as one of the verses which prove that 'In all the passages that the heretics have misinterpreted as grounds for their heresy, their refutation is found near at hand. It says (in the plural) *that God had been revealed to him,* while in verse 3 Jacob specifically said that he was building the altar *to the God Who answered* (in the singular) *me in my distress.*' Thus it is clear from verse 3 that there was never a thought ח״ו of a plurality of gods. [Comp. *footnote* to 1:26.]

Onkelos who interprets the *sense* of the phrase renders it in the singular: For it was there that אִתְגְּלִי לֵהּ יְיָ, *God appeared* [singular] *to him;* while *Targum Yonasan* takes the plural to refer to the *angels* whom Jacob envisioned climbing the ladder [28:12] and renders accordingly: אִיתְגְּלִיאוּ לֵיהּ מַלְאֲכַיָּא דַּיְיָ, *that the angels of God had appeared to him.*

בְּבָרְחוֹ מִפְּנֵי אָחִיו — *During his flight from [the presence of] his brother.*

8. The death of Rebecca and Deborah.

This verse interrupts the flow of verse 7 which speaks of Jacob having built an altar in Bethel, and verse 9 which continues with God's blessing which was given at that time in Bethel. As the Sages taught, we are now informed not merely of *Deborah's* death, but of Rebecca's as well. The blessing of verse 9 came to comfort Jacob on his bereavement upon the loss of his mother *(Ramban).*

וַתָּמָת דְּבֹרָה מֵינֶקֶת רִבְקָה — [*And*] *Deborah the wet-nurse of Rebecca died.*

Deborah was the same nurse who had accompanied Rebecca when, as a young girl, she came to marry Isaac. (See 24:59). She is identified as *Rebecca's wet-nurse,* because her name had not been mentioned earlier *(Lekach Tov).*

What was she now doing in Jacob's house? — Rebecca had promised Jacob that she would summon him from Laban's house when it was safe for him to return [27:45]. Accordingly she sent Deborah for him in fulfillment of her promise, but the aged nurse died on the [homeward] journey *(Rashi* citing *R' Moshe HaDarshan).*[1]

Ramban disagrees with *R' Moshe HaDarshan's* view, suggesting that it is highly unlikely that Rebecca

1. [It is not clear *when* Rebecca dispatched Deborah to summon Jacob, and whether or not Jacob left immediately upon Deborah's arrival. Obviously, had Jacob left as soon as Rebecca summoned him, it is difficult to understand why he was punished for staying away from his parents — he stayed away only in obedience to their orders!

We might conjecture that Deborah had been sent to him many years earlier, soon after his

וַתִּקָּבֵר מִתַּחַת לְבֵית־אֵל תַּחַת הָאַלּוֹן וַיִּקְרָא שְׁמוֹ אַלּוֹן בָּכוּת:

would have dispatched an old lady on such a strenuous mission. Instead *Ramban* offers that after accompanying Rebecca to Canaan, Deborah had returned to Paddan Aram. She was now accompanying Jacob home to visit Rebecca. Conceivably, Deborah resided with Jacob in order to care for his children, in deference to Rebecca. Possibly the wet-nurse was different from the wet-nurse mentioned in 24:59, since it was customary for notables to have many nurses. This nurse, Deborah, had remained behind with Laban, and now Jacob was taking her home with him to look after his mother in her old age. Deborah's death was was mentioned, as we shall see, because our verse contains a veiled hint at the death of Rebecca herself.

וַתִּקָּבֵר מִתַּחַת לְבֵית־אֵל – *And she was buried below Bethel.*

– The city lay at the top of a hill and she was buried at the foot of this hill *(Rashi).*

תַּחַת הָאַלּוֹן – *Below the plateau* [or: *the plain*].

As *Onkelos* renders: *On the lower part of the plain.* There was a plateau high on the slope of the hill, and she was buried beneath it. [The word אַלּוֹן does not *mean* plateau or plain *(Mizrachi),* rather] this particular plateau in Bethel bore the name 'Alon' *(Rashi).*

Rashi's interpretation of Alon as a place-name is in consonance with *Rashi's* exegesis to 14:6.

Cf. *Ramban* to 14:6 who disagrees with *Rashi's* view that Alon is a proper noun since the word *Alon* is preceded by the definite article ה, and a definite article is never attached to a proper noun. He maintains, rather, that *alon* is a species of tree – *the oak* as in *Isaiah* 6:13: כָּאֵלָה וְכָאַלּוֹן, *Like the terebinth and like the oak.* In translating it *plain* – called Alon because it was a place containing many oaks – *Onkelos* was conveying the *sense* of the verse rather than a literal translation of *alon.*

Radak draws a distinction between אֵלוֹן [*Ailon*], generally translated by *Onkelos* as *plain,* and אַלּוֹן [*Alon*] in our verse which *Targum Yerushalmi* treats as a different word meaning *oak tree* in Aramaic.

See also *Mizrachi* to 14:6 who observes from the fact that *Targum Onkelos* and *Yerushalmi* disagree as to the meaning of the terms, we must assume that there were two traditions regarding it, and each *Targum* preserved the tradition he had received from his teacher.

וַיִּקְרָא שְׁמוֹ אַלּוֹן בָּכוּת – *And he named it Alon Bachuth.*

According to *Onkelos,* the name is translated as *the Plain of Weeping;* while according to *Rashi,* who renders *Alon* as the name of a particular plateau, it is *'Alon' of Weeping. Targum Yerushalmi, Radak* and *Ramban* render: *'Oak' of Weeping.* According to *Ramban's* interpretation of *Onkelos: 'Grove' of Weeping.*

Rashi cites the *Midrash* that in this verse we have a veiled hint of the death of Rebecca herself for, as the Sages taught, while Jacob was there he was informed that his mother had died. In Greek *alon* means *another.* [Accordingly, the

arrival in Paddan Aram, and he did not return with her, thus making him accountable for his extended absence. Indeed, such a view was cited above in the *footnote* to 30:25. For this reason, we must assume that Deborah died on the journey *back* to Canaan; that would allow for the chronology that she came much earlier but that Jacob did not return home when summoned.]

35 *was buried below Bethel, below the plateau; and he*
8 *named it Alon Bachuth.*

name *Alon Bachuth* would denote: *Another Weeping,* i.e. *weeping for another* (his mother) as well as for Deborah.][1]

Ramban discusses the *Midrashic* tradition that this verse alludes also to Rebecca's death, as implied by the name *Alon Bachuth,* Oak of Weeping, which the *Midrash* perceives to mean *double weeping* [interpreting the word בָּכוּת as if it were the plural בָּכוֹת] — one for Deborah, and the other for Rebecca.

Ramban corroborates this interpretation by observing that it is inconceivable that the grief and weeping solely for the passing of the old wet-nurse could have been of such proportions as to inspire Jacob to name the place after it. Furthermore, it says below [*v.* 27] that *Jacob came to Isaac his father.* Had Rebecca still been alive, she too would have been mentioned since it was she who advised Jacob to go to Paddan Aram and was the cause of all the good which happened to him there; Isaac had merely acted on her advice [see 27:43 ff]. Hence we assume, with Tradition, that this excessive weeping must have been occasioned by Jacob's grief at hearing the news — while attending to the burial of Deborah *(Tanchuma)* — of the death of his righteous mother, who loved him, and who was not privileged to see him when he returned home. This accounts for the name, and for God's appearance in order to bless him, and to comfort him as we shall learn in the next verse.

⤜ Certainly Rebecca's death is a significant event in itself. Why is it merely *alluded* to and not explicitly stated?

— The time of Rebecca's death was kept secret so that people might not curse her as the mother who gave birth to Esau — and therefore the Torah does not mention it *(Rashi* from *Midrash).*[2]

Ramban cites *Rashi's* Midrashic interpretation and notes that the mere fact that Rebecca's death goes unmentioned is, in itself, not remarkable — many deaths, such as Leah's, are not mentioned! The point is, rather, that her death *is* suggested by allusion — if so, why is it revealed only in this *veiled* manner and not explicitly? Furthermore, *Rashi's* argument that the Torah wanted to avoid curses of Rebecca as the 'mother of Esau' is not strong since Esau is mentioned in connection with

1. Cf. *Sefer HaYashar:* Jacob, his sons, and all his people arose and went to Bethel in obedience to God. Jacob was then ninety-nine years of age. They stayed in Bethel for six months, during which time Deborah, the daughter of Uz and the wet-nurse of Rebecca, who was with Jacob's party, died. Jacob buried her below Bethel under an oak that was there.

At about the same time, there died in Hebron, which is Kiryath Arba, Rebecca, the daughter of Bethuel and mother of Jacob. She was buried in the cave of Machpelah, bought by Abraham from the children of Heth. Rebecca was a hundred and thirty-three years old when she died.

Jacob wept exceedingly for his mother, and indulged in grievous lamentation for her and her wet-nurse Deborah under an oak that was afterwards called *Alon-Bachuth, the Oak of Weeping.* Laban the Aramean also died about this time.

2. **Rebecca's age at her death.**

[According to the traditional *Seder Olam Chronology* Rebecca was three years old and Isaac was forty [25:20] when they were married. She remained barren for the first twenty years of her marriage, making her twenty-three years old when she bore Jacob.

Jacob was now ninety-nine years old when he reentered the land. Rebecca died then, making her one-hundred and twenty-two (99+23=122) at the time of her death.

(That Jacob was ninety-nine at this time is a simple calculation: Jacob was sixty-three when he received the blessings and fled [see *footnote* to 25:17]; he spent fourteen years in the

ט וַיֵּרָא אֱלֹהִים אֶל־יַעֲקֹב עוֹד בְּבֹאוֹ מִפַּדַּן
י אֲרָם וַיְבָרֶךְ אֹתוֹ׃ וַיֹּאמֶר־לוֹ אֱלֹהִים
שִׁמְךָ יַעֲקֹב לֹא־יִקָּרֵא שִׁמְךָ עוֹד יַעֲקֹב כִּי
אִם־יִשְׂרָאֵל יִהְיֶה שְׁמֶךָ וַיִּקְרָא אֶת־שְׁמוֹ

Isaac's death *(v.* 29), without concern that Isaac would be cursed.

However, the reason for the veiled reference is because very little honor could have been paid to her at the funeral in view of Isaac's blindness which confined him to the house so he could not attend; Esau's known hatred for her; and Jacob's absence. Cf. the *Midrash* [*Tanchuma Ki Teitzei* 4]: 'Since Esau was the *only one* of her family able to be present at the funeral, there was apprehension that people would curse Rebecca as the mother who bore him. Therefore, they took out her bier at night. Accordingly, since she was buried in this manner by Hittites, the Torah does not explicitly state her death, but also alludes to it only in a veiled manner. [However, in the case of Isaac's death, Esau was not the only member of the family in attendance; Jacob was there too.]

Sifsei Chachomim suggests that the intent is that Rebecca's death was hidden even from Esau *himself,* so he would not participate. Were he to be the only child present, the other participants would particularly notice him and curse Rebecca for bearing him.

It must be remembered that Rebecca was the only one of all the Matriarchs who gave birth to someone wicked [Ishmael was *Hagar's* son, not Sarah's.] Hence the apprehension that she would be cursed.

Sefer HaParshiyos comments that the mother would tend to be blamed more for the wickedness of a child than the father. A father's primary role is to teach Torah and to educate his child. If the child develops badly, people shrug it off saying that the child refused to accept the teachings of his righteous father. But a mother raises and nurtures her child. Her imprint is there in his very being. People will tend to blame *her* for his evil characteristics for they indicate her failure in the day-to-day task of raising him.

Gur Aryeh cites the Talmudic teaching that a mother contributes flesh, blood, and sinew to the infant. These are the parts of a human that symbolize base instincts. Thus, she is blamed if he follows his animal cravings.

9. God consoles Jacob.

וַיֵּרָא ... עוֹד בְּבֹאוֹ מִפַּדַּן אֲרָם — *And God appeared to Jacob again when he came from Paddan Aram.*

This appearance occurred *after* the weeping had ceased, since the *Shechinah* does not reside where there is sadness *(Sforno).*

עוֹד, *again:* i.e., the second time at the same place, the first having been when he left home on his journey to Paddan Aram *(Rashi).*

Academy of Eber; twenty years in Laban's house, and two years traveling [eighteen months in Succoth and six months in Bethel]. Thus 63+14+20+2=99).

However, there is a different opinion based on the *Sifri* which states that Rebecca's life span equaled that of Kehath (which, as recorded in *Exod.* 6:18, was 133 years). According to this chronology, Rebecca was 133 years old when Jacob was ninety-nine, and she was fourteen when she was married.

Tosafos (Yevamos 61a s.v. וְכֵן) concludes that the above *Midrashim* are indeed conflicting. *Mizrachi* in his dissertation to 25:20 and here concludes similarly but adds that the primary Rabbinic chronology agrees that Rebecca was three at her marriage, and hence 122 at her death, not 133.]

[9] And God appeared to Jacob again when he came
from Paddan Aram, and He blessed him.
[10] Then God said to him, 'Your name is Jacob. You
shall not always be named Jacob, but Israel shall be

In Paddan Aram, however, God never appeared to him except when He communicated with him through an angel *(Sforno).*

[Cf. the angel's communication in 31:11-13 where even God's command of 31:3 appears in retrospect to have been part of the *angel's* message; however see other opinions cited there.]

וַיְבָרֶךְ אֹתוֹ — *And He blessed him.*

— With the blessing [of consolation] given to mourners [in this case upon the death of Jacob's mother] *(Rashi).*

[Comp. 25:11 where *Rashi* similarly explains that God 'blessed' Isaac by consoling him during his mourning for Abraham.]

10. Jacob is formally named Israel.

וַיֹּאמֶר לוֹ אֱלֹהִים — *Then* [lit. *and*] *God said to him.*

According to *Radak* this verse gives the content of the blessing mentioned in the previous verse.

[However, following *Rashi's Midrashic* interpretation that the blessing in verse 9 was a consolation upon Rebecca's death, the construction of our verse implies that this is a *new* blessing, unrelated to that of *v.* 9. Were this to be nothing more than a *continuation,* reading the *content* of the earlier blessing, as *Radak* maintains, the verse would not mention God as the subject, but would use the pronoun: ... And *He* said to him. However, one difficulty does remain: If, as *Rashi's* Midrashic interpretation maintains, *v.* 9 is a blessing of consolation for the tragedies of *v.* 8, then the two verses are closely related. However, the Masoretic division begins a new paragraph with *v.* 9, indicating that it is not connected to the events of *v.* 8. This may be the reason that *Radak* associates *v.* 9 with our verse rather than with *v.* 8.]

שִׁמְךָ יַעֲקֹב — *Your name is Jacob.*

Despite the fact 'the lord of Esau' [the angel who struggled with Jacob in 32:29] changed your name, you are still named Jacob, for it was not his mission to do so *(Ramban).*

[Thus, God was saying, as noted in the *comm.* to 32:29, that the angel had only *informed* Jacob — under *great duress* — that God would eventually change his name. It was not the angel's mission to have actually effected the change then.]

— Your name Jacob is not being taken away from you even now; it will still remain one of your names *(Alshich;* see below).

לֹא יִקָּרֵא שִׁמְךָ עוֹד יַעֲקֹב — *You shall not always be named Jacob* [lit. *your name shall not be called more Jacob*].

You shall no longer be called *only* [or: primarily] Jacob *(Ibn Ezra.* See *Berachos* 13a cited below where it is clear that the name Jacob was not henceforth to be obliterated).

You shall no longer be known by a name which implies deceiver and supplanter *(Rashi;* cf. 32:28).

The word עוֹד [*more*] in this context does not have the connotation of *never again,* but of *continuously,* as in 8:22 עֹד כָּל־יְמֵי הָאָרֶץ. The connotation then is: *You shall not continuously be known as Jacob;* you will be known by another name also *(R' Hoffmann).*

כִּי אִם יִשְׂרָאֵל יִהְיֶה שְׁמֶךָ — *But* [(idiomatic) lit. *but if; for but)*] *Israel shall be your name.*

I.e., Israel shall *also* be your name *(Ibn Ezra).*

יא יִשְׂרָאֵל: וַיֹּאמֶר לוֹ אֱלֹהִים אֲנִי אֵל שַׁדַּי
פְּרֵה וּרְבֵה גּוֹי וּקְהַל גּוֹיִם יִהְיֶה מִמֶּךָּ
ששי° יב וּמְלָכִים מֵחֲלָצֶיךָ יֵצֵאוּ: °וְאֶת־הָאָרֶץ

— A name which signifies Prince and Chief *(Israel).*

וַיִּקְרָא אֶת שְׁמוֹ יִשְׂרָאֵל — *Thus* [lit. *and*] *He named him Israel.*

— In *addition* to his name Jacob. This does not suggest that it became *forbidden* to call him Jacob *(Radak; Ramban).*

Since God Himself later refers to him as Jacob [46:2] it is obvious that the name Jacob was not to be abolished, but made subsidiary to his new name Israel. Thus, according to the Sages in *Berachos* 13a, Israel would henceforth be his *principal* name, with Jacob *subsidiary* to it. This is different from the case of Abraham whose name-change was absolute, and regarding which the *halachah* is that whoever refers to him by his former name Abram transgresses a negative command. See *comm.* on pp. 563-564, and *comm.* to 32:39.

This [as noted above] is the force of the opening phrase שִׁמְךָ יַעֲקֹב, *your name is Jacob*, i.e., your subsidiary name will always remain Jacob, notwithstanding the fact that a new principle name is now being added to it. This phrase does not occur in the case of Abraham; therefore, his name change was absolute *(R' David Feinstein).*

The name Jacob continued to be used in matters pertaining to the physical and mundane, while Israel was used in matters reflecting the spiritual role of the Patriarch and his descendants *(R' Bachya).*

[A difficulty arises from *Rashi's* interpretation to 25:26 that *God* named Jacob at birth, if the name was God-given, how could it now have been deemed inadequate? See *comm.* there, p. 1061. (Perhaps the Divine origin of the name Jacob explains why it was not abolished as was Abram's, after the same change, but remained at least the secondary name).]

According to *Sforno*, God conferred upon Jacob the implication of sovereignty upon the gentile nations contained in the name *Yisrael.* Its effect was that he would be able to withstand his enemies, and his progeny would be sole survivors in the End of Days.

11. God ratifies the earlier blessings.

[In the following blessing, God confers on Jacob the blessings of fruitful abundance and the land which He — as El Shaddai — had given to Abraham upon changing *his* name [17:1ff]. This is also a confirmation of the Abrahamitic blessings which Isaac had conferred upon Jacob when he ordered him to go to Paddan Aram [28:3ff]. Then, Isaac had blessed Jacob that God would indeed bless him after his return from Paddan Aram, and that a community of people would descend from him. The following is God's confirmation of that blessing.

In the commentary, citations will be drawn from the parallel expressions in the earlier blessings.]

אֲנִי אֵל שַׁדַּי — *I am El Shaddai.*

— I am sufficient [שַׁדַּי=שֶׁאֲנִי דַּי] to bless, for the blessings are Mine *(Rashi).*

[Comp. *comm.* to this Name on 17:1; 28:3. See also 43:14 where *Rashi* interprets: 'God שַׁ־דַּי, *Who is sufficient* in granting His Mercies (אֵל reflects God's attribute as Dispenser of Mercy [*Rashi, Exodus* 34:6]), and in Whose hand is sufficient (דַּי) power to give. This is the real meaning.']

According to *Sforno*, this expression denotes a divine Oath: *I swear by My Name.* This is the only place we find that God swore in His Name to Jacob. [See *Exod.* 32:13.]

35 *your name.' Thus He named him Israel.* 11 *And God*
11 *said to him, 'I am El Shaddai. Be fruitful and multi-*
ply; a nation and a congregation of nations shall
descend from you, and kings shall issue from your

פְּרֵה וּרְבֵה — *Be fruitful and multiply* [or: *and be numerous*].

— This was a blessing [not a *command*], as at the Creation *(Ibn Ezra)*. [This differs from the view in *Yevamos* 65b cited in *footnote* below.][1]

— The allusion was to Benjamin who had not yet been born, though Rachel was already pregnant with him *(Rashi)*.

Sforno perceives this as an exhortation: Do not be dismayed even if your children's behavior does not please you. Continue to have children nevertheless; then your family will survive even when the other nations are destroyed.

[Comp. God's blessing to Abraham in 17:6: וְהִפְרֵתִי אֹתְךָ בִּמְאֹד מְאֹד, *I will make you most exceedingly fruitful;* and Isaac's blessing to Jacob in 28:3: וְיַפְרְךָ וְיַרְבֶּךָ, *May He make you fruitful and make you numerous.*]

גּוֹי וּקְהַל גּוֹיִם יִהְיֶה מִמֶּךָּ — *A nation and a congregation of nations shall descend* [lit. *shall be*] *from you.*

Rashi offers three interpretations:

(a) [There are two blessings here]: *Yet to descend from Jacob are a nation* — i.e., Benjamin; *and a congregation of nations* — i.e., Menashe and Ephraim, who would descend from Joseph and would be given the status of tribes.

(b) [The phrases form one unit, meaning: A nation — one that may be regarded as one of the world's congregation of nations — will descend from him.] This means that his descendants who would descend to Egypt with him (*Exodus* 1:1) will number seventy, corresponding to the existing seventy nations [see *comm.* to 10:1 (p. 309)]. Furthermore, the Sanhedrin, too, would consist of seventy (ibid).

(c) [A nation — one that will conduct itself like the other congregations of nations — will descend from him.] This signifies that later, in the days of Elijah, Jacob's descendants would sacrifice on בָּמוֹת, *high places,* like all the other nations, at a time when this practice was forbidden to Israel.

[Compare God's parallel blessing to Abraham in 17:6: וּנְתַתִּיךָ לְגוֹיִם, *And I will make nations of you.* Isaac to Jacob in 28:3: וְהָיִיתָ לִקְהַל עַמִּים, *And may you be a congregation of peoples.*]

Targum Yonasan renders: A holy people, and a congregation of priests shall descend from the sons you have begotten.

וּמְלָכִים מֵחֲלָצֶיךָ יֵצֵאוּ — *And kings*

1. R' Yosef in *Yevamos* 65b derives from the use of the singular masculine expression פְּרֵה וּרְבֵה, instead of the plural, genderless פְּרוּ וּרְבוּ, that the *mitzvah* of procreation is incumbent on man, not on woman.

That in 1:28 and 9:1, the similar phrases to Adam and Noah are in *plural* is no contradiction, since those expressions are preceded by *'and God blessed them'*; thus they are not understood as commands, but as Divine *blessings* — that they will have abundant offspring, as *Tosafos* ad. loc. observes.

The *mitzvah* of procreation, however, is primarily derived from 9:7, where as *Maharsha* counters, the commandment is given in the plural. There it also applies only to men, however, notwithstanding the plural, since, the context makes clear, it was addressed to Noah and his *sons (Torah Temimah).*

אֲשֶׁר נָתַתִּי לְאַבְרָהָם וּלְיִצְחָק לְךָ אֶתְּנֶנָּה
יג וּלְזַרְעֲךָ אַחֲרֶיךָ אֶתֵּן אֶת־הָאָרֶץ׃ וַיַּעַל
מֵעָלָיו אֱלֹהִים בַּמָּקוֹם אֲשֶׁר־דִּבֶּר אִתּוֹ׃

shall issue from your loins.

— Saul and Ishbosheth who were of the tribe of Benjamin *(Rashi).*[1]

[And although they were born hundreds of years later, they were still regarded in a loose sense as descending from Jacob's loins.]

According to *Sforno*, the blessing was that men fit to be kings will descend from him; Israel will not require strangers for her kings.

[Comp. God's blessing to Abraham in 17:6: וּמְלָכִים מִמְּךָ יֵצֵאוּ, *Kings shall issue from you.* There is no parallel, however, in Isaac's blessing to Jacob.]

12. As part of this pledge of abundant progeny, God reiterates the Promise of the Land with which this pledge is always associated *(Malbim).*

וְאֶת הָאָרֶץ אֲשֶׁר נָתַתִּי לְאַבְרָהָם וּלְיִצְחָק לְךָ אֶתְּנֶנָּה — *[And] the land that I gave to Abraham and to Isaac, I will give to you.*

I.e., just as I have given the land to Abraham and Isaac with the strength of an oath — a grant not subject to forfeiture by sin — I will similarly give it to you with an oath. This is Scripture's intent in saying [*Exod.* 33:1]: *The land of which I swore to Abraham, to Isaac and to Jacob.* [Though we find nowhere that God *swore* explicitly to Jacob, the oath is implied in this passage]. For originally [in 28:13] Jacob was promised the land without an oath, but perhaps the repetition of that prophecy here constitutes an oath *(Ramban).* [Cf. 26:3. The concept that a repeated phrase constitutes an oath is from *Shevuos* 36a; cf. *Rashi* to 8:21 on the repetition of לֹא אֹסִף. See also *Sforno* to *v.* 11.]

וּלְזַרְעֲךָ אַחֲרֶיךָ אֶתֵּן אֶת־הָאָרֶץ — *And to your offspring after you I will give the land* [lit. *earth*].

— I.e., in the End of Days I will give your offspring the *entire* אֶרֶץ, *earth,* not only *Eretz Yisrael,* as He said [28:14]: *Your offspring shall spread powerfully westward, eastward, northward, and southward* (uncensored ed. of *Sforno).*

This assurance was specifically reiterated to Jacob to emphasize that it was in his offspring that the covenant would be fulfilled and not in Esau's *(Ramban* to 26:3).

13. וַיַּעַל מֵעָלָיו אֱלֹהִים — *Then* [lit. *and*] *God ascended from upon him.*

This is similar to the case of Abraham [17:22] where it is likewise said: *God ascended from upon*

1. Abner explained this verse as referring to Saul and Ishbosheth when he made Ishbosheth king after the death of Saul, instead of David. [The idea is that Abner justified his support of Ishbosheth by noting that the intent of this verse is that *kings* in plural, denoting a minimum of two, would descend from the as yet unborn child of Jacob. Benjamin was the only unborn child, although, as noted, he was already conceived. The Rabbis in the *Midrash* maintain, however, that *this* application of the interpretation was misguided.]

The tribes of Israel interpreted this verse to imply Benjamin's continued existence among the tribes. On this basis, they reconciled with the tribe of Benjamin after the affair of the Concubine of Gibeah, and allowed their daughters to marry with Benjaminites [thus, in effect assuring Benjamin's continual existence within the tribes of Israel and the eventual accession to the throne by descendants of that tribe] (Old text of *Rashi* from *Midrash).*

loins. 12 *The land that I gave to Abraham and to Isaac, I will give to you; and to your offspring after you I will give the land.'* 13 *Then God ascended from upon him in the place where He had spoken with him.*

Abraham. The literal sense of the expression indicates that it was not merely a vision or dream, but that the *Shechinah* [if one can so perceive It] actually rested upon him where he stood. Kabbalistically, [as noted in the *comm.* to 17:22] the expression intimates that the Patriarchs are the 'chariot' of the Omnipresent [i.e. His vehicle, the direct bearers of His Glory on earth; see *Overview* to *Lech Lecha: The Patriarchs* — page 357 *(Ramban).*

Abarbanel maintains that this expression denotes an abrupt cessation of the Divine communication. Having just been promised abundant progeny and the land, Jacob was naturally anxious to ask more details: What was the significance of his wrestling bout with Esau's guardian angel? What effect would Esau's descendants have upon his descendants? What tribulations would they endure? What assurances were there that the promise would not be forfeited? But suddenly — *God ascended from upon him!* God had no intention of revealing to Jacob anything beyond what He had just done, and so *He removed the prophetic inspiration from upon him,* and Jacob perceived no more. This is akin to the case of Abraham where it says [17:21]: *And when He had finished speaking with him, God ascended from upon Abraham.*

בַּמָּקוֹם אֲשֶׁר־דִּבֶּר אִתּוֹ — *In the place where He had spoken with him.*

— I.e., when he had left home for Charan. It was at this very site that God had now appeared to him again and then ascended *(Sforno).*

[This expression occurs three times in the following verses.] *Rashi* comments without further elaboration: 'I do not know what this [expression] is intended to teach us.'

— That is, although the *Midrash* derives from the earlier part of this verse, as it does from the parallel expression in the case of Abraham [17:22], that 'the Patriarchs are the chariot of the Omnipresent,' nevertheless the phrase *In the place where He had spoken to him* does not occur in the case of Abraham. Therefore, *Rashi* feels that its inclusion here is inexplicably superfluous.

Furthermore, as noted, the expression is repeated *three* times in these verses. Perhaps it is the *repetition* of this phrase that *Rashi* finds difficult *(Akeidas Yitzchak).*

[*Rashi* makes a similar comment in 28:5. *Kitzur Mizrachi* there observes that '*Rashi* was indeed aware of *possible* interpretations, but he knows of none *that he considers to fit the literal flow of the narrative.*']

In the kabbalistic sense, *Ramban* explains its inclusion by interpreting, as noted, that the *Shechinah* had actually rested upon *the place where he stood,* and now It ascended *from that place.* The sense of the *Shechinah* esoterically being in a 'place' must be understood in the context of *Ezekiel* 3:12: *Blessed be the Glory of HASHEM from His place.*

Kli Yakar adds that this expression supports and further amplifies the Midrashic interpretation of 28:17. Jacob was now standing at Luz/Bethel which he had described as the *gate of heaven* since Mount Moriah had been transported there [see *comm.* ibid.] Thus this phrase, stating that the *Shechinah* rose up directly from that very spot, in-

יד וַיַּצֵּב יַעֲקֹב מַצֵּבָה בַּמָּקוֹם אֲשֶׁר־דִּבֶּר
אִתּוֹ מַצֶּבֶת אָבֶן וַיַּסֵּךְ עָלֶיהָ נֶסֶךְ וַיִּצֹק
טו עָלֶיהָ שָׁמֶן׃ וַיִּקְרָא יַעֲקֹב אֶת־שֵׁם הַמָּקוֹם
אֲשֶׁר דִּבֶּר אִתּוֹ שָׁם אֱלֹהִים בֵּית־אֵל׃
טז וַיִּסְעוּ מִבֵּית אֵל וַיְהִי־עוֹד כִּבְרַת־הָאָרֶץ
לָבוֹא אֶפְרָתָה וַתֵּלֶד רָחֵל וַתְּקַשׁ

timates that the Earthly Temple corresponds to the Heavenly one. Jacob remained on earth while the *Shechinah* rose up to the corresponding holy spot in heaven.

Furthermore, the *Zohar* perceives an implication from this phrase that Mount Moriah was again uprooted and merged with Luz/Bethel for the occasion of this sanctification, as it had been before.

14. Jacob fulfills his vow.

וַיַּצֵּב יַעֲקֹב מַצֵּבָה בַּמָּקוֹם אֲשֶׁר־דִּבֶּר אִתּוֹ — [*And*] *Jacob had set up a pillar at the place where God had spoken with him.*

— The translation in past-perfect follows *Ibn Ezra* and *Ramban:* Jacob *had* erected such a pillar when God first spoke to him at Bethel [28:18]. Thus, this verse does not describe a *new* pillar, but refers to the original one. Jacob now *rededicated* it in fulfillment of his vow of 28:22.

Ibn Ezra adds that, alternatively, this verse could be describing a *new* pillar, but he prefers the former interpretation. *Ramban* concurs, and writes: 'This is the correct view.'

The Torah mentions that Jacob set up the pillar *at the place where God had spoken to him* to emphasize that Jacob fully perceived the sanctity of that very site — now even more so than before — as a result of all the Divine Revelations he experienced there (*Radak;* see *Ramban* above).

The question of how Jacob could have set up a pillar, an erection which the Torah later forbade and ordered destroyed, is discussed in the *comm.* to 28:18 s.v. וַיָּשֶׂם.

מַצֶּבֶת אָבֶן — *A pillar of stone.*

— The stone on which he had slept, and which had miraculously coalesced [28:18; 22 (*Midrash*). See *Ramban* there who distinguishes between a *pillar* which consists of *one* standing stone, and an *altar* which is constructed of many stones.]

וַיַּסֵּךְ עָלֶיהָ נֶסֶךְ — *And he poured a libation upon it.*

— This, Jacob did *now* (*Ramban*).

According to *Ibn Ezra,* this pouring of water or wine was to cleanse the pillar in preparation for the ritual pouring of *oil* which was to follow. Most commentators however, perceive this act of libation to be a ritual act in itself, symbolic of future libations that Jacob's descendants would make as part of their sacrificial service in the Temple.

Cf. *Targum Yonasan:* '... and he poured upon it a libation of wine and a libation of water because this is [symbolic of] what would be done [by his descendants] at the feast of Succos.'

In this vein, *Sforno* [who apparently interprets that this Luz/Bethel site was identical with

[14] *Jacob had set up a pillar at the place where God had spoken with him — a pillar of stone — and he poured a libation upon it, and poured oil upon it.*
[15] *Then Jacob named the place where God had spoken with him Bethel.*
[16] *They journeyed from Bethel and there was still a stretch of land to go to Ephrath, when Rachel went*

Mount Moriah, as noted in the *comm.* to 28:19] maintains that Jacob thereby fulfilled his vow [28:22]: *Then this stone which I have set up as a pillar shall become a House of God.* The libation served to dedicate the place in preparation for that ultimate purpose.

[*Rashi* to 28:22 similarly comments that this verse describes the fulfillment of Jacob's vow.]

וַיִּצֹק עָלֶיהָ שָׁמֶן — *And* [*he*] *poured oil upon it.*

[Thereby anointing it and consecrating it as an altar. (See *Rashbam* to 28:18 and *Rashi* to 31:13).]

In 28:18, Jacob had but a meager amount of oil, so he poured oil only עַל רֹאשָׁהּ, *on its top* [see *Radal* there]; now he had oil in abundance, so he poured oil עָלֶיהָ, *upon its entire surface.*

It is self-evident that while in Bethel, Jacob also fulfilled the portion of his vow concerning tithes [28:22], and gave the tithes to 'one in that generation worthy of receiving it' *(Ibn Ezra).* [According to *Rashi* on 32:22, Jacob had already set aside the tithes before he sent his tribute to Esau.]

15. וַיִּקְרָא יַעֲקֹב אֶת שֵׁם הַמָּקוֹם אֲשֶׁר דִּבֶּר אִתּוֹ שָׁם אֱלֹהִים בֵּית־אֵל — *Then Jacob named the place where God had spoken with him* [there] *Bethel.*

He had named it Bethel previously [28:19], but he reiterated that name several times to confirm that it was indeed a suitable place for a בֵּית אֵל, lit. *House of God*, and that the Divine Presence would always be manifest there *(Ramban).*

Or HaChaim [following *Radak*] suggests that Jacob had originally named the entire city Bethel. This verse informs us that now he bestowed that name also on the immediate area surrounding the pillar *where God had spoken to him.*

According to the *Vilna Gaon's comm.* to *Joshua* 16:12, there were three different locations that Jacob named Bethel: In 28:16; *El Bethel* [35:7]; and *Elohim Bethel* in our verse. [Apparently, he translates our verse to mean: *And Jacob named the* place where He had spoken to him: *Elohim Bethel.* Cf. on *El Bethel* in *v.* 7.]

⚜ The birth of Benjamin and death of Rachel.

16. וַיְהִי־עוֹד כִּבְרַת־הָאָרֶץ לָבוֹא אֶפְרָתָה — *And there was still a stretch of land* [i.e. a short distance (see *Rashi* below)] *to go* [lit. *to come*] *to Ephrath.*

[Identified in *v.* 19 with Bethlehem.]

The phrase כִּבְרַת הָאָרֶץ is discussed by *Rashi.* He cites *Menachem* who relates the word כִּבְרָה to כְּבָרַת, *much,* and accordingly explains the phrase to mean: *a great distance. Rashi* also cites the *Midrashic* interpretation that it is related to כְּבָרָה, *sieve,* referring to the time of year when the earth is riddled with holes like a sieve — a time when the land is plowed. This *follows* the winter

יז בְּלִדְתָּהּ: וַיְהִי בְהַקְשֹׁתָהּ בְּלִדְתָּהּ וַתֹּאמֶר
לָהּ הַמְיַלֶּדֶת אַל־תִּירְאִי כִּי־גַם־זֶה לָךְ בֵּן:
יח וַיְהִי בְּצֵאת נַפְשָׁהּ כִּי מֵתָה וַתִּקְרָא שְׁמוֹ

rainy reason, and precedes the intense summer heat. [Unlike the roads *during* the rainy season, they are then fully passable. (See *Rashi* to 48:7 where this is definitely the implication).]

Rashi discounts the above as incorrect. As proof, he cites *II Kings* 5:19 where it is related that Naaman departed כִּבְרַת הָאָרֶץ. [There it could not mean *a great distance* as Menachem interprets, since the context implies that he went only a *short* distance when Gehazi ran after him; nor is the Midrashic interpretation that the land was passable relevant to the context there.]

Accordingly *Rashi* concludes that the expression כִּבְרַת הָאָרֶץ means a כִּבְרָה, *'certain measure of land'* which is called a כִּבְרָה [*kivrah*]. This is similar to such expressions as *acres* (צִמְדֵּי) *of vineyard; a portion* (חֶלְקַת) *of the field*. In measuring *walking distance*, the term *'kivrah of land'* is used to denote a certain distance [the exact length of which is now unknown to us].

From *Rashi's* commentary to the parallel expression in 48:7, it becomes clear that a *short distance* is meant equal to about 2,000 cubits [about ¾ of a mile] — the distance outside of a city permitted to be covered on the Sabbath [תְּחוּם שַׁבָּת]. The Midrashic interpretation takes כִּבְרַת אֶרֶץ as a description of the terrain, showing that the road was not impassable; were it not for the Divine command to bury Rachel there by the roadside, Jacob could have borne her to Bethlehem.]

Ramban writes that while he lived in Spain he agreed with *Radak* [*Shorashim* s.v. ברה] that the root word was ברה, *to take food*, and the כ is not a root letter of the word, but the כ of comparison. The expression כִּבְרַת accordingly would mean: *like* the distance of בְּרַת, i.e. the distance one journeys from the morning until the first meal is taken [probably equal to several miles], for travelers measure distance in this manner.

When *Ramban* arrived in *Eretz Yisrael*, however, and saw that Rachel's Tomb was less than a mile from Bethlehem, he realized that both *Menachem* and *Radak's* interpretation [that it denotes a *great* distance] must be rejected.

Rather, *Ramban* concludes along with *Rashi* that the term denotes a measure of land, but that the כ is a prefix meaning *approximately*, indicating that it was not an *exact* measure [rendering: 'there was still *about* a (certain measure) of land to Ephrath.'] Alternatively, the word is an adjective derived from בַּת=בְּרַת, *a daughter* of land signifying a short distance, about a *mil*, the 'daughter' [i.e. a smaller measure than] of the larger *parasang* or some other ancient measure of distance.[1]

Ibn Ezra renders similarly. *Ibn Janach* renders 'about a *mil*' as does *Radak* in his *comm.* to *II Kings* 5:19 (in an obvious change from his opinion cited by *Ramban* from *Shorashim*). *Onkelos* translates כְּרוּבַת אַרְעָא, which *Rashi* in 48:7 interprets to denote an amount of land equal to a full day's plowing.

Ralbag here and in *II Kings ibid.*, ex-

1. *Ramban* adds from personal observation the insight that Rachel's Tomb is not in Ramah or near it as would seem to be the plain meaning of the verse in *Jeremiah* 31:15: *A voice is heard in Ramah ... Rachel weeping for her children.* It is about four parasangs from the Ramah of Benjamin and more than two days' journey from the Ramah of Ephraim. The verse in *Jeremiah* must therefore be a hyperbole: So loud was her weeping that it could be heard as far as Ramah, on top of a mountain in the territory of her son Benjamin. Or as *Targum Yonasan* renders, the phrase means *a voice was heard On High*... Therefore the verse does not read *in Ramah, Rachel weeps for her children,* instead it reads, *a voice was heard* בָּרָמָה, *On High.*

35 *into labor and had difficulty in her childbirth.* 17 *And*
17-18 *it was when her labor was at its most difficult, that*
the midwife said to her, 'Have no fear, for this one,
too, is a son for you.' 18 *And it came to pass, as her*
soul was departing — for she died — that she named

plains our expression to denote a measure of land equal to those cultivated fields and vineyards which surround a city. Thus, the verse notes how only a small stretch of cultivated land separated the spot of Rachel's death from Bethlehem.

וַתֵּלֶד רָחֵל וַתְּקַשׁ בְּלִדְתָּהּ — *When* [lit. *and*] *Rachel went into labor* [lit. *gave birth*] *and* [*she*] *had difficulty in her childbirth.*

The *Midrash* records that Rachel was one of three women in Scripture who had hard labor and died shortly afterwards. The others are the wife of Phineas [*II Samuel* 4:19-22] and Michal, the daughter of Saul [Midrashically derived from *II Samuel* 6:23].

The Sages observe that a woman's account is examined in heaven primarily when she is in labor. For we have learned in *Mishnah Shabbos* 2:6 that for three transgressions do women die in childbirth. And though our mother Rachel was not guilty of any of these three, nevertheless, because Jacob said, *'With whomever you find your gods, he shall not live'* (31:32), she was punished, and her judgment was not carried out until she was in childbirth. Thus people say, 'When the ox is fallen the knife is sharpened' *(Midrash Lekach Tov).*

17. אַל־תִּירְאִי — *Have no fear.*

— 'That your hard labor will result in your death.' The midwife said this to cheer her in her travail *(Rashbam).*

According to *Sforno:*

— That your hard labor indicates that it might be a girl. (The Sages in *Niddah* 31a say that the travail is much harder when it is a girl).

[The idea is that Rachel had greatly longed for another son (see 30:24), and seeing that her labor was so difficult, Rachel grew apprehensive that she was giving birth to a daughter. Therefore the midwife comforted her this way *(Torah Temimah).*]

כִּי־גַם־זֶה לָךְ בֵּן — *For this one, too, is a son for you.*

גַּם, *too,* — i.e., in addition to Joseph. According to the *Midrash* with each of Jacob's other sons [except Joseph (*Gur Aryeh;* see *Pirkei d'Rabbi Eliezer* cited at the end of 30:23)] a twin sister was born, while with Benjamin an *additional* sister was born and the word גַּם, *too,* serves to include this second sister as well *(Rashi).*

[The *Midrashic* implication is that when Rachel discovered that two girls emerged she grew apprehensive and was reassured that *in addition to this (second) one, there is a son for you.*]

— As you prayed when Joseph was born [30:24] saying: *May* HASHEM *add on for me another son (Rashbam).*

Following *Sforno: For this one, too, is a son for you* — although the labor is so hard.

18. וַיְהִי בְּצֵאת נַפְשָׁהּ כִּי מֵתָה — *And it came to pass, as her soul was departing — for she died* [past tense as indicated by the cantillation accent on the first syllable of מֵתָה].

יט בֶּן־אוֹנִי וְאָבִיו קָרָא־לוֹ בִנְיָמִין: וַתָּמָת רָחֵל וַתִּקָּבֵר בְּדֶרֶךְ אֶפְרָתָה הִוא בֵּית

— The *sense* is: *For she was dying,* but not yet dead *(Midrash Shmuel).*

Tur notes that the literal implication of the verse is that she named him *after* she died. He comments that she seemed to die and then was unexpectedly revived. She named her newborn son and 'died' again.

[See *Zohar* where the implication is the reverse: 'This verse makes it clear that when Rachel's soul departed, it did not return and so she died.']

Tosefes Brachah renders כִּי מֵתָה as a parenthetic interpolation: ... *As her soul was departing — when she died —.*

בֶּן־אוֹנִי —*Ben Oni.*

— Son of my sorrow *(Rashi; Onkelos).*

— Son of my mourning [as if to say: His birth caused my death]. Cf. the expression לֶחֶם אוֹנִים, *bread of mourners* in *Hoshea* 9:4; בְאֹנִי, *my mourning,* in *Deut.* 26:14 *(Ibn Ezra; Ramban).*

וְאָבִיו קָרָא לוֹ בִנְיָמִין — *But his father called him Benjamin.*

Rashi offers two interpretations: (a) The name means בֶּן יָמִין, *son of the right,* that is, *son of the south* [for in Hebrew thinking, the primary orientation is toward the *east,* hence *right*=south. Cf. *Onkelos* to 13:9 where *right* refers to the south, and *Psalms* 89:13 צָפוֹן וְיָמִין, *north and south.*]

This name accordingly commemorates how Benjamin alone of all Jacob's children was born in Canaan which lay *south* of Paddan Aram [cf. *Numb.* 33:40; and above, 12:9]. This is the reason the name is spelled out in full here [i.e. with the י after the מ=בִנְיָמִין, thus suggesting the derivation of the name (בֶּן־יָמִין. In most other passages in Scripture, however, the second י is omitted (בִּנְיָמִן) since there is no point in continually emphasizing the derivation of the name (cf. *Sota* 32b). Furthermore, the vocalization (which is a *chirik)* allows this letter to be dropped without danger of mispronunciation *(Torah Temimah).*]

(b) The word יָמִים, [*yamim*] *days* can be spelled יָמִין [*yamin*] as it is in *Daniel* 12:13, לְקֵץ הַיָּמִין, *at the End of Days.* Thus, Jacob named him 'son of my days' as if to say that he was born in his father's advanced years. *Rashbam* interprets similarly.

Ramban differs on geographical grounds with *Rashi's* primary interpretation that Benjamin's name means 'son of the south.' He cites various verses which would indicate that Aram was *south*east of *Eretz Yisroel* which accordingly lay to its *north;* hence a name meaning 'son of the south' to commemorate the child's birth in Canaan would be incorrect. [*Mizrachi* however, in his dissertation to 32:2 defends *Rashi's* (and most commentators') contention that Aram was to the *northwest* of Canaan and hence the appellation was quite appropriate.]

Ramban concludes that Rachel, near death, called him *Ben Oni,* meaning 'son of my mourning.' Jacob wished to preserve the *form* of the name given by the child's mother, but wished to give it an optimistic connotation. So, reinterpreting *oni* to mean 'strength' [see 49:19: רֵאשִׁית אוֹנִי], he named the child *ben yamin,* [lit. *son of the right*] i.e., 'son of power' or 'son of strength,' since the right hand is a symbol of strength and success [cf. *Eccles.* 10:2; *Psalms* 21:9].

him Ben Oni, but his father called him Benjamin.
19 *Thus Rachel died, and was buried on the road to*
Ephrath, which is Bethlehem. 20 *Jacob set up a monu-*

[The construction of the subject+predicate וְאָבִיו קָרָא instead of וַיִּקְרָא אָבִיו indicates a contrast to the previous statement, hence '*but* his father called him.' Cf. *comm.* top of p. 494 to 14:8 ...וּמַלְכִּי־צֶדֶק הוֹצִיא, and to 31:47: וְיַעֲקֹב קָרָא לוֹ.]

[Jacob was 99 years old at Benjamin's birth.]

19. וַתָּמָת רָחֵל – *Thus,* [lit. *and*] *Rachel died.*[1]

And as the verse continues *she was buried* — immediately, for the law requires that one be buried near the time of death *(Midrash)* — especially in the case of a woman who died in childbirth *(Radal;* cf. *Moed Katan* 27a).

The Sages [*Rosh HaShanah* 6a] note that 'whoever leaves a vow unfulfilled, his wife dies.' Hence, because Jacob delayed so long in fulfilling the vow he made upon his departure, his wife died. (See *Meshech Chochmah* to 31:13).

That it was *Rachel* rather than Leah who now died is variously explained. [See *Overview* to *Vayeitzei* for other implications of Rachel's death at this time and in this place.]

The *Midrash* to 31:14 cites an opinion that since Rachel presumptuously spoke up before her older sister she died first. According to another opinion [cited also by *Rashi* ibid. *v.* 32], Rachel died first because of the curse implied in Jacob's statement to Laban [ibid.]: *Anyone with whom you find your gods shall not remain alive,* which was a fatal prognostication.

Since, as noted, a woman's 'account in heaven' is examined primarily while she is in childbirth, Rachel's judgment was carried out now *(Lekach Tov).*

According to *Seder Olam* there was a tradition that Rachel was born on the day Jacob received his father's blessings. Jacob was sixty-three years old when he received the blessings, and was ninety-nine years old when he entered the land [see *footnote* end of *v.* 8]. Therefore Rachel was thirty-six years old when she died [99-63=36].

וַתִּקָּבֵר בְּדֶרֶךְ אֶפְרָתָה הִוא בֵּית לָחֶם – *And* [*she*] *was buried on the road to Ephrath, which is Bethlehem.*

I.e., which is *now* known as Bethlehem; a city in Judah located five miles south of Jerusalem. Its names: *Ephrath* [from פָּרָה, *parah, fruitfulness*] and Bethelehem [lit. *house of bread*] both reflect the abundance of its crops. This Bethlehem is often referred to in Scripture as *Bethlehem of Judah* to distinguish it from another city by that name in the western Galilee in

1. In a major pronouncement on the sanctity of *Eretz Yisrael, Ramban* to *Deut.* 18:25 notes that Jacob would never have married two sisters in *Eretz Yisrael,* a liaison the Torah would later forbid. Therefore, *Ramban* concludes, God caused the death of Rachel — the sister married second and therefore the forbidden one — on the way, shortly after entering the land. Because of Rachel's merit she did not die *before* she entered the sacred environs of the land; and because of *Jacob's* merit, he did not remain married to two sisters after having settled in the Land; the sanctity of the land would not bear it.

[See *comm.* to 26:5 (p. 1083); 29:28; 32:15; *Leviticus* 18:18. Regarding the judgment of Sodom being so severe because *Eretz Yisrael* would not tolerate abomination in its environs, see *Ramban* to 19:5, and *Overview* to *Vayeira: 'Eretz Yisrael* — The Supremacy of the Land' (p. 400).]

כ לָֽחֶם: וַיַּצֵּ֧ב יַעֲקֹ֛ב מַצֵּבָ֖ה עַל־קְבֻרָתָ֑הּ הִ֗וא
כא מַצֶּ֥בֶת קְבֻרַת־רָחֵ֖ל עַד־הַיּֽוֹם: וַיִּסַּ֖ע
יִשְׂרָאֵ֑ל וַיֵּ֣ט אָהֳלֹ֔ה מֵהָ֖לְאָה לְמִגְדַּל־
כב עֵֽדֶר: וַֽיְהִ֗י בִּשְׁכֹּ֤ן יִשְׂרָאֵל֙ בָּאָ֣רֶץ הַהִ֔וא

the lower Zebulun region (*Joshua* 19:15) [somewhat south of today's Haifa]. In *Yerushalmi Megillah* 1, the latter Bethlehem is called *Beth-lehem Tzeriyah (Otzar Yisrael* s.v. *Bethlehem).*

Jacob's intention in choosing this site in the middle of the road, rather than bringing her the short distance to Bethlehem was that he prophetically foresaw that his descendants going into exile would pass that way. He buried Rachel there so she should pray for them as it is said [*Jeremiah* 31:15]: *Rachel weeping for her children (Midrash).*

Comp. *Rashi* to 48:7 where Jacob further justifies his action and states that he buried her there by the command of God.

Rachel died in territory which would later be the portion of Benjamin [*Sifre, Deut.* 33:12]. *Ramban* to *v.* 16 accordingly writes that Jacob buried her on that very site, on the wayside, and did not bring her into nearby Bethlehem because he foresaw that Bethlehem would belong to the tribe of Judah. He wanted her body to lie in the portion of her son, Benjamin, on whose border her tomb is. [See *footnote* to *v.* 16.]

[See *Rashi* and *Mizrachi* cited above to 30:15 regarding why *Rachel* of the two sisters was the one who forfeited the right to be buried with Jacob in the Cave of Machpelah.]

Furthermore, in his *comm.* to 48:7 *Ramban* notes that since his marriage to Rachel — as the second sister — would have been prohibited by Torah Law [see *footnote*], Jacob could not bury her in the Cave of Machpelah 'for he would be embarrassed before his ancestors.'

It has been noted that in yet another display of the reserve of the Scriptural narrative, nothing is said of Jacob's grief over the death of the woman for whom he patiently worked for fourteen years. It is only alluded to later on in the pathetic reference in 48:7 *(R' Hoffmann).*

20. The Tomb of Rachel.

וַיַּצֵּב יַעֲקֹב מַצֵּבָה עַל־קְבֻרָתָהּ — [*And*] *Jacob set up a monument over her grave.*

— To serve as a memorial *(R' Hirsch),* and to assure that since her grave was on a public thoroughfare, it could be identified as such and not be defaced *(Sforno).*

He wanted the site of her grave to be known until the day of Resurrection of the Dead *(Zohar).*

Though the righteous have enough of a memorial through their good deeds, Jacob knew that his descendants would pass that way. He wanted her grave to be recognizable, so that his children would stop to pray there in time of trouble, and Rachel would intercede on their behalf *(Midrash; Yafeh Toar).*

The word קְבֻרָתָהּ, *her grave,* is synonymous with קְבֻרָה *(Ibn Ezra).*

הִוא מַצֶּבֶת קְבֻרַת־רָחֵל עַד הַיּוֹם — *It is the monument of Rachel's grave*

*ment over her grave; it is the monument of Rachel's
grave until today.*
[21] *Israel journeyed on, and he pitched his tent
beyond Migdal Eder.* [22] *And it came to pass, while*

until today.

— I.e. until the time of Moses, when the Torah was committed to writing *(Radak).*

[Cf. the expression in 19:37, 38; 26:33; 32:33.]

R' Meyuchas explains the intent to be: As long as the world endures.

— It serves as a place for prayer until today *(Me'am Loez).*

According to *R' Saadiah Gaon:* This is the site known as the 'Tomb of Rachel' until today.

21. וַיִּסַּע יִשְׂרָאֵל — [*And*] *Israel journeyed on.*

— Toward his father's house in Hebron *(Radak).*

He could not bear the grief of remaining near his beloved wife's tomb. He journeyed on to assuage his grief, but he was not yet ready to meet his father; he encamped temporarily at Migdal-Eder *(Emunas Chachomim).*

וַיֵּט אָהֳלֹה מֵהָלְאָה לְמִגְדַּל־עֵדֶר — *And* [*he*] *pitched his tent beyond Migdal Eder* [lit. *Tower of the Flock*].

The name of an area near Bethlehem, as is evident from the context of *Micah* 4:8 *(Rashbam).*

While the above reflects the view of the commentators on *our verse,* they perceive the term מִגְדַּל־עֵדֶר lit. *'Tower of the Flock',* as it appears in *Micah* 4:8 differently. There they do not interpret it as a proper noun, but as an adjective alluding variously in that context to: 'the anointed one of the flock of Israel' *(Targum);* 'the Temple' *(Rashi);* 'the Tower of David, and more correctly: Jerusalem itself which is a *tower* to the *flock,* i.e. Israel' which congregated like flocks in Jerusalem during the thrice-yearly pilgrimage festivals *(Ibn Ezra; Radak).*

22. Reuben's incident with Bilhah.

[After Rachel's death, Jacob established his primary residence in the tent of Bilhah, Rachel's maidservant. Reuben took it upon himself to defend his mother's honor, so he moved Jacob's bed to Leah's tent. This is all that actually transpired, as explained by the *Talmud* (see *comm.* below). Nevertheless Scripture describes it in such stark terms as if Reuben had sinned grievously. This is in line with the dictum that even minor transgressions of great people are judged with the utmost gravity because the personal conduct of the holy ancients was measured by infinitely higher standards than ours. For a person of Reuben's stature to tamper with Jacob's marriage bed was a coarse act, and the Torah so labels it. This concept is explained at length in the *Overview* to *Ruth.*

Nevertheless in *Megillah* 25b it is ruled that out of respect for Reuben's memory, the incident of Reuben is read in the Synagogue but not translated (into the vernacular by the *Meturgeman* when the Reader read from the Torah as was the custom in ancient times). As *Rashi* explains there, however, the prohibition applies only to a brief literal translation that easily lends itself to misunderstanding.]

וַיֵּלֶךְ רְאוּבֵן וַיִּשְׁכַּב אֶת־בִּלְהָה פִּילֶגֶשׁ אָבִיו וַיִּשְׁמַע יִשְׂרָאֵל

That this incident is recorded at all in the Torah, is to explain Jacob's later reference to it in 49:4 *(Rashbam).*

וַיְהִי בִּשְׁכֹּן יִשְׂרָאֵל בָּאָרֶץ הַהִוא — *And it came to pass, while Israel dwelt* [lit. *was dwelling*] *in that land.*

I.e., all this happened before Jacob returned to his father in Hebron *(Rashi)* It was a punishment, for he delayed on the way and did not proceed immediately to Isaac *(Mizrachi).*

Thus, the intent of this passage is not merely to inform us where the incident occurred, but to stress that this misfortune, too, resulted from Jacob's delay in returning home. Instead of traveling as quickly as he could, he *dwelt* in that land *(Gur Aryeh; Tzeidah LaDerech).*

Radak interprets differently. Jacob did not actually *dwell* there, rather his party was so large and journeyed so slowly, that they *seemed* to be dwelling in the land *(Radak).*

On the connotation of שכן, *dwell,* in contrast to ישב, *settle,* see *R' Hirsch* to 14:13.

וַיֵּלֶךְ רְאוּבֵן — *That* [lit. *and*] *Reuben went.*

This is the same expression used of Reuben in 30:14 when he 'went' to gather *dudaim* for Leah. All Reuben's 'goings' were for the sake of his mother *(Emunas Chachomim).*

Here, too, as in the case of the *dudaim,* it was selflessness that prompted Reuben to act *(Or HaChaim* to 30:14).

וַיִּשְׁכַּב אֶת־בִּלְהָה פִּילֶגֶשׁ אָבִיו — *And* [*he*] *lay with Bilhah, his father's concubine.*

Rashi explains that this is not to be understood literally. Rather, Reuben *tampered with his father's couch* [by removing it from Bilhah's tent (see below)], but the Torah charges him for this as if he had actually lain with her.[1] What caused Reuben to disarrange and *'defile his father's bed'* [cf. reference to this in *I Chron.* 5:1]?:

— During Rachel's lifetime, Jacob's couch [i.e., primary residence] was always in Rachel's tent [see 29:31 s.v. וְרָחֵל עֲקָרָה]; upon her death he removed it to Bilhah's tent. Reuben resented this insult to his mother [Leah], saying, 'If my mother's sister Rachel was my mother's rival, is that any reason that the *handmaid* of my mother's sister must now become my mother's rival?' He therefore acted in order to right matters *(Rashi).*

[This interpretation that 'lay with his father's wife' means that he tampered with his father's couch is based on *Shabbos* 55b where the Sages emphatically declare that Reuben did *not* commit the sin of adultery. They proclaim that מִי שֶׁאָמַר רְאוּבֵן חָטָא אֵינוֹ אֶלָּא טוֹעֶה, *Whoever says Reuben sinned* (and actually lay with Bilhah) *is mistaken,* and advance the explanation cited by *Rashi* above.

As further proof that Reuben did not

1. Although Reuben did not sin in the literal sense the Torah refers to his act the harshest terms. The sin of adultery involves the talking of a wife from her husband. Reuben interfered with his father's right to conduct his married life as he saw fit. Thus, in a figurative sense, Reuben's deed could be legitimately related to that of an adulterer. Furthermore, the privacy of the marital relationship is a major component of the Jewish concept of morality. The Sages state that adherence to the code of modesty is a prerequisite to holiness. Therefore, Reuben's interference with Jacob's privacy is related, in degree, to an immoral act *(Harav David Feinstein).*

35 *Israel dwelt in that land, that Reuben went and lay*
22 *with Bilhah, his father's concubine, and Israel heard.*

literally commit this sin, the *Talmud* notes that Reuben's descendants would stand one day on Mount Ebal when the curses would be pronounced upon those who did not keep the Torah. Among these curses was [*Deut.* 27:20] *Cursed be he who lays with his father's wife.* Had Reuben been guilty of this cardinal sin, would God have allowed the Reubenites to be among those six tribes chosen to stand on Mount Ebal when those curses would be uttered? [To publicly recall the former sins of a penitent is forbidden *(Torah Temimah).*] Therefore, the incident must be understood as interpreted by the Sages.

Maharsha suggests that the latter may be interpreted in the reverse: Since God knew that Reuben's descendants would one day be chosen to proclaim this curse, would He have allowed Reuben himself to stumble in this matter? He notes that the difficulty of this interpretation is that Providence does not *direct* man's behavior in matters of sinfulness.

Another view in the *Talmud* ibid. is that Reuben transposed *two* couches — one of the *Shechinah,* and the other of his father. [*Rashi* there explains that Jacob had set a couch for the *Shechinah* in the tents of each of his wives, and wherever the *Shechinah* came to 'rest' so to speak, there Jacob spent the night. (See *Rashi* on 49:4).]

Ramban suggests that Reuben tampered with Bilhah's couch for fear that Jacob might have another son by her, as she was still young, and so diminish his heritage. Reuben was accordingly punished measure-for-measure in being deprived of the right of the first born [see *I Chron.* 5:1]. Thus, the phrase *the sons of Jacob were* [i.e., remained] *twelve* would mean literally that Jacob did not beget children after that.

The Kabbalists write that Menashe and Ephraim were destined to be conceived *from Jacob* the night Reuben transposed the couch. Because of his interference, they were not born, and this was accounted to him as if he had lain with his father's wife *(ARIzal).* The explanation of why Jacob considered Menashe and Ephraim as his own sons [48:3] is the fact that they were worthy to have been born of him. When HASHEM blessed Jacob: *Be fruitful and multiply* [*v.* 11], Rachel had already been pregnant with Benjamin, so Jacob assumed that Rachel would yet bear these two other children for him. When Rachel died, Jacob removed his residence to the tent of Bilhah, Rachel's maidservant, so the children could be considered as Rachel's.

Reuben was aware of this [i.e. that there would yet be two children — Menashe and Ephraim — whom Jacob would consider his own, and of Jacob's intention in locating his residence in Bilhah's tent]. However, he wanted his mother to bear those children, and so he transposed his father's couch into her tent, thereby affronting both his father and Bilhah, and preventing the birth of the offspring that were to have descended from her. This invasion of his father's conjugal privacy was tantamount to having sinned with his father's wife *(Malbim).* [See continuation of this comment in the *footnote,* at end of this verse.]

⊷§ Why Jacob moved to Bilhah's tent.

[Attempts have been made to explain why Jacob moved his couch to Bilhah's tent although Leah might feel slighted by his doing so. At the outset, the question must be put in perspective. The actions of the Patriarchs are motivated by considerations beyond our ability to understand — this is axiomatic. Of course, we attempt to derive lessons from their deeds, but we dare not make the mistake of thinking that the reasons we understand are the *only* ones or that they are necessarily correct. This is similar to attempts to find reasons for the commandments of the Torah. Many of the greatest commentators have done so, but always with the stated understanding that while we try to derive lessons from the Torah, we can in no way claim to plumb the depths of the Divine wisdom.

Perhaps we may add that in view of Leah's particular role in the history of Israel (see *Overview: Jacob, Rachel, and*

כג וַיִּהְיוּ בְנֵי־יַעֲקֹב שְׁנֵים עָשָׂר: בְּנֵי לֵאָה
בְּכוֹר יַעֲקֹב רְאוּבֵן וְשִׁמְעוֹן וְלֵוִי וִיהוּדָה

Leah), it need not have been appropriate for her ever to be regarded as the primary wife on *earth*.

Maharsha justifies Jacob's action in moving his primary residence to *Bilhah's* rather than Leah's tent, by noting how Rachel had been the mainstay of his household, and his primary wife. She was the woman for whom he had served Laban a total of fourteen years [whereas Leah had become his wife only by subterfuge, and therefore remained secondary to Rachel.] Accordingly when Rachel died, Jacob honored her memory by moving his primary residence to the tent of her handmaid Bilhah. She was also his legitimate *wife* in the fullest sense of the word, since Rachel had freed her before Jacob married her [see on 30:4-5].

Furthermore, that the Torah here refers to her as a *concubine* is only to allude to Reuben's *misconception* of her as such. He believed that she was not Jacob's full-fledged *wife*, and therefore he became indignant over the slight to his mother's honor. But later in this verse, the Torah goes on to emphasize that *all* twelve sons — including those of Bilhah and Zilpah — were equally full-fledged *sons of Jacob*, and that by implication Bilhah was his legitimate wife. That Reuben erroneously entertained thoughts to the contrary, was tantamount to defiling his father's wife, and the Torah records it as such.

In another sense it might be conjectured that it was only natural for Jacob to select Bilhah's tent. Rachel had died leaving an infant son, and Bilhah, her maidservant, undoubtedly cared for the baby. She also raised Joseph, the next to youngest child, who was about eight years old at the time. Since Benjamin and Joseph were Jacob's youngest, most dependent and — as survivors of Rachel — his best-loved children, he chose Bilhah's tent for his primary residence *(R' Nosson Scherman)*.

[In summary, there are two lines of reasoning, both valid, to explain why Reuben had no right to do what he did even though his intention was honorable:

1) Even assuming that Reuben was correct in deciding that Jacob had erred, he had no right to take it upon himself to interfere with Jacob's privacy.

2) Reuben should have realized that any decision of Jacob could be based on considerations far beyond the obvious. Any action of a Patriarch must be viewed with as much awe as if it had been a גְּזֵרַת הַכָּתוּב, *Scriptural decree*.]

וַיִּשְׁמַע יִשְׂרָאֵל — *And Israel heard.*

— I.e. heard that Reuben tampered with his bed. The Torah tells of Jacob's awareness in order to prepare us for his reference to the defilement in 49:4 *(Chizkuni)*.

— He shuddered and said, 'Woe is to me that there is such unworthiness in a son of mine.' He was informed by God, however, that Reuben had repented [see below] *(Sifre, Devarim* §31).

Cf. *Targum Yonasan's* interpretation of our verse: And Israel heard it and it grieved him, and he said, 'Alas that one so profane should have come forth from me, just as Ishmael came forth from Abraham and Esau from my father!' [See continuation below.]

וַיִּהְיוּ בְנֵי־יַעֲקֹב שְׁנֵים עָשָׂר — [*And*] *the sons of Jacob were twelve.*

Although the *Mesorah* considers this clause to be part of verse 22, it begins a new paragraph which lists all twelve tribes as a unit for the first time since they were born. In Torah scrolls, the two passages are separated by an open space. By combining these two sections

35
23 The sons of Jacob were twelve. 23 The sons of Leah:
Jacob's firstborn, Reuben; Simeon; Levi; Judah;

though one disjointed verse, the Torah portrays the humility of Jacob. Though *Jacob became aware* that his son had profaned his couch, he did not disinherit him or remove him from the genealogy of his sons, but still counted him among them. וַיִּהְיוּ בְנֵי־יַעֲקֹב שְׁנֵים עָשָׂר, *the sons of Jacob were twelve* — Reuben was not rejected; he continued to be listed first among them *(Ramban; Sforno).*

[Again this is a graphic example of Jacob's marvelous reserve. He does not react immediately to Reuben's tactless invasion of his privacy. Jacob restrains himself for now, but his condemnation would be voiced on his death bed 'blessing' to Reuben (49:4), and a certain aspect of his birthright was taken away from him and given to Joseph (*Rashi v.* 23).]

Rashi makes no specific mention that this verse bridges two chapters in the Hebrew. He notes, however, that the parenthetical digression relating to the incident of Reuben abruptly ends, and he explains that the Torah returns to the previous narrative — the birth of Benjamin. When Benjamin was born the destined number of Jacob's sons [twelve] was complete. Accordingly, it was proper that the sons should be enumerated and the Torah proceeds to do so. The Sages interpret the passage as teaching that *all twelve sons* [including Reuben] *were equal in merit and righteous,* for in actuality Reuben had not sinned.

R' Munk observes that the fact that the Torah enumerates the children of Jacob on sixteen different occasions — each time in a different order — can be explained in the light of *Rashi's* comment that 'it wants to teach that all were equal, all were righteous.' [In each of the instances, however, Reuben is listed first.]

[Continuing *Targum Yonasan*]: ... The Divine Spirit answered Jacob and said, 'Fear not, for all are righteous and none of them are profane!'

According to *Sifre* [see above], our passage signifies that Reuben had repented [for the Torah testifies that Jacob's children — notwithstanding what had occurred — were twelve: *all* were equally meritorious and righteous].

BaMidbar Rabbah 13 also derives from this passage that Reuben had repented. The open space between the text of the incident and the genealogy indicates that Reuben caused himself to be separated from the status of his brothers, but because he repented wholeheartedly, he became wholly at peace with his family; as the verse concludes, he was again counted among them. The sacrifice later offered by the Prince of Reuben in *Numb.* 7:34 was to fully atone for the incident of Bilhah.

[See *Maharsha* above that this passage emphasizes — notwithstanding Reuben's slur that Bilhah was a concubine — that *Jacob's sons were twelve* — all twelve of them were equally Jacob's sons, and their mothers equally his wives.]

Others perceive that the first part of the verse is abruptly dropped because the Torah made its point and prepared the reader for the reference to this in Jacob's blessing of Reuben in 49:4; there was no further point in lingering upon so distasteful a theme. This, however, does not explain why a *new* verse does not begin with the phrase *the sons of Jacob,* etc. It is rather as the Sages say: Both paragraphs were

כד וְיִשָּׂשכָר וּזְבֻלוּן׃ בְּנֵי רָחֵל יוֹסֵף וּבִנְיָמִן׃
כה־כו וּבְנֵי בִלְהָה שִׁפְחַת רָחֵל דָּן וְנַפְתָּלִי׃ וּבְנֵי
זִלְפָּה שִׁפְחַת לֵאָה גָּד וְאָשֵׁר אֵלֶּה בְּנֵי
כז יַעֲקֹב אֲשֶׁר יֻלַּד־לוֹ בְּפַדַּן אֲרָם׃ וַיָּבֹא
יַעֲקֹב אֶל־יִצְחָק אָבִיו מַמְרֵא קִרְיַת

combined into a single verse to show that Reuben's action did not cause him to be excluded from the tally of Jacob's sons *(B'chor Shor).*[1]

23. בְּנֵי לֵאָה בְּכוֹר יַעֲקֹב רְאוּבֵן – *The sons of Leah: Jacob's firstborn, Reuben.*

Even when the context of the narrative relates his degradation, he is called *first born* ... He was *firstborn* with respect to:
(a) *inheritance* – he received the firstborn's double portion of Jacob's legacy, and his tribe was the first to get its share of *Eretz Yisrael (Yafeh Toar);*
(b) *service* – [i.e., Reuben's name appeared first on the breastplate which the High Priest wore during his service *(Sifsei Chachomim);* according to *Matnos Kehunah,* Reuben, as firstborn, performed the sacrificial service for the family, a privilege that belonged to the firstborn until the sin of the Golden Calf (cf. *Rashi* to 25:31)]; and
(c) *counting* [i.e., genealogy; when the children of Israel are enumerated, Reuben always comes first].

That the birthright was taken from him and given to Joseph [see *I Chron.* 5:1] was only with respect to *tribes* – for Joseph formed two tribes [just as a firstborn son receives a double share of his father's property, whereas Reuben formed only one] *(Rashi).*

This is based on the *Midrash* which records that 'The Holy One, Blessed be He, is reluctant to uproot a name from its genealogical place.' Thus it is written [*I Chronicles* 5:1]: *The sons of Reuben, Israel's firstborn – for he was the first born. But inasmuch as he defiled is father's couch, his birthright was given to Joseph* [whose sons, Menashe and Ephraim constituted two separate tribes]; *nevertheless he was to be reckoned in the genealogy as first born.'*

Sforno writes that because Reuben repented – and repentance reaches God's Throne of Glory – he did not forfeit his birthright in the scale of Heavenly judgment. Even in This World, the birthright with its privileges remained his. Jacob took it from him as he was legally entitled to do. Similarly, in Talmudic times one guilty of excommunication was not considered excommunicated until a prominent person pronounced him as such. Cf. *Moed Katan* 16a.

25. שִׁפְחַת רָחֵל – *Maidservant of Rachel.*

She had already been freed when

1. Following *Malbim's* kabbalistic interpretation: Jacob understood what had occurred, as a result of which *the sons of Jacob remained but twelve;* having missed that propitious night, Jacob thereby lost the opportunity to have two more children of his own.

It was with this incident in mind that Jacob later told Joseph [48:3]: *El Shaddai appeared to me at Luz in the land of Canaan, and He blessed me, and said to me, 'I will make you fruitful and numerous, making you a community of peoples ... ' Now* [that I lost that promise] *your two sons, who were born to you in the land of Egypt before I came to Egypt, shall be mine; Ephraim and Menashe shall be mine just like Reuben and Simeon.*

35 *Issachar; and Zebulun.* 24 *The sons of Rachel: Joseph*
24-27 *and Benjamin.* 25 *The sons of Bilhah, maidservant of*
Rachel: Dan and Naftali. 26 *And the sons of Zilpah,*
maidservant of Leah: Gad and Asher. — These are the
sons of Jacob, who were born to him in Paddan
Aram.
27 *Jacob came to Isaac his father, at Mamre, Kiriath*

Jacob married her [30:4]. The Torah refers to Bilhah as Rachel's *maidservant* only to indicate that Bilhah still conducted herself with Rachel as a maidservant. The same was true of Zilpah's relationship with Leah (*Haamek Davar;* cf. 30:7 and 12).

26. אֵלֶּה בְּנֵי יַעֲקֹב אֲשֶׁר יֻלַּד־לוֹ בְּפַדַּן אֲרָם — *These are the sons of Jacob who were* [lit. *was;* (the verb is in singular)] *born to him in Paddan Aram.*

Actually only *eleven* of his sons were born in Paddan Aram; Benjamin was born in Canaan. As the Torah often does, it generalizes [see 46:23] *(Ibn Ezra).*

They were listed here to record that Jacob returned to his father with all his twelve sons *(Chizkuni).*

That the verb יֻלַּד, *was born,* is in the singular, indicates that they were all regarded as a single entity *(Lekach Tov).*

27. Jacob reunites with his father.

וַיָּבֹא יַעֲקֹב אֶל־יִצְחָק אָבִיו — [*And*] *Jacob came to Isaac his father.*

That Jacob's beloved mother Rebecca is not mentioned here proves that she had already died earlier. Had Rebecca still been alive she would have been mentioned since it was she who advised Jacob to go to Paddan Aram, and was the cause of all the benefit he acquired there; Isaac had merely acted on her advice (*Ramban* to *v.* 8).

[The reunion was certainly emotional and tearful: Isaac had not seen Jacob — the heir of the Abrahamitic covenant — for twenty-two years (including his fourteen years in the Academy of Eber, it was thirty-six years). Jacob had left empty-handed and now came back with twelve sons — all meritorious and righteous — plus a great camp. But this joy was tempered with sorrow: Rebecca was not there to witness Jacob's return, nor was Rachel ever to meet her parents-in-law.

Jacob resided with Isaac until his death, twenty one years later. But his stay was deeply marred by the sale of Joseph eight years after the return home (see *v.* 29 below).]

מַמְרֵא קִרְיַת הָאַרְבַּע — *At Mamre, Kiriath Arba.*

Mamre is the name of the plain; *Kiriath Arba* [lit. *city of four*] is the name of the city. Hence the phrase מַמְרֵא קִרְיַת הָאַרְבַּע means *to the plain called Mamre of Kiriath Arba (Rashi).*

Mamre was the name of the original owner of the plain *(Rashi* to 13:18). [He was one of the confederates of Abraham. See 14:13; *footnote* to 17:26; 18:1.]

According to *Ramban* in 12:6, however, whenever *Mamre* is mentioned alone, rather than *plains of Mamre* — as in 23:19 and here — it is the name of a *city.*

הָֽאַרְבַּ֔ע הִ֖וא חֶבְר֑וֹן אֲשֶׁר־גָּֽר־שָׁ֥ם
כח אַבְרָהָ֖ם וְיִצְחָֽק׃ וַיִּהְי֖וּ יְמֵ֣י יִצְחָ֑ק מְאַ֥ת
כט שָׁנָ֖ה וּשְׁמֹנִ֥ים שָׁנָֽה׃ וַיִּגְוַ֨ע יִצְחָ֤ק וַיָּ֙מָת֙

The meaning and origins of the name *Kiriath Arba* are fully discussed in the *comm.* and *footnote* to 23:2.

In the Hebrew, the definite article ה, *the*, appears in the name קִרְיַת הָאַרְבַּע, lit. *Kiriah of the Arba. Rashi* explains that the ה precedes the *second* word [*Kiriath* **Ha***Arbah*] and not the first word [**Ha***Kiriath Arba*] for there is a grammatical rule that whenever a name is compounded of two words such as Kiriath-Arba, Beth-Lechem, Avi-Ezer, and Beth-El, the definite article, ה, whenever required, precedes the *second* part of the name. Thus, we find בֵּית הַלַּחְמִי, *the Bethlehemite* [*I Samuel* 16:1]; אֲבִי הָעֶזְרִי, *the Aviezrites* [*Judge* 6:24]; בֵּית הָאֱלִי, *the Bethelite* [*I Kings* 16:34].

הִוא חֶבְרוֹן — *That is Hebron.*

— I.e. which later came to be called Hebron [*Joshua* 14:15 and *Judges* 1:10].

On Hebron, see *comm.* to 13:18; 23:2 and 19.

אֲשֶׁר גָּר שָׁם אַבְרָהָם וְיִצְחָק — *Where Abraham and Isaac sojourned.*

Hebron, a city sacred from ancient times, was the primary residence of the Patriarchs. See *Prefatory Synopsis* to 23:1 (p. 857), and *comm.* to 24:63 s.v. וְהוּא יוֹשֵׁב. As noted often in the *comm.*, the verb גור indicates that they resided there as גֵּרִים, *aliens* — separate and distinct, leading solitary lives, and not intermingling socially with the heathen citizens *(Sh'lah; Haamek Davar).*

The recollection that a citizen had righteous, respected forebears creates good will and friendliness toward him on the part of his neighbors *(Sforno).*

28. The death of Isaac.

וַיִּהְיוּ יְמֵי יִצְחָק — [*And*] *Isaac's days were.*

The Torah does not say of Isaac, as it does of the other Patriarchs, וַיְחִי יִצְחָק, *and Isaac* **lived.** This is because, in certain respects, Isaac cannot be considered to have 'lived' in the full sense of the word: he remained without a destined wife until *the Akeidah,* and 'he who is without a wife is as one who is without life.' Also, after the *Akeidah* his eyesight was diminished; and since a blind man is considered as dead,' the Torah does not refer to him as having 'lived' *(Or HaChaim).*

מְאַת שָׁנָה וּשְׁמֹנִים שָׁנָה — *One hundred* [*years*] *and eighty years.*

Abraham, too, was to have lived to that age, but God caused him to die five years earlier, at 175, so that he would not witness the beginning of Esau's evil conduct (see *comm.* to 15:15 and *footnote* to 25:8, p. 975).

29. וַיִּגְוַע יִצְחָק וַיָּמָת וַיֵּאָסֶף אֶל־עַמָּיו — *And Isaac expired and died, and he was gathered to his people.*

[The expressions *expired, died* and *gathered to his people* are discussed in the *comm.* to 25:7-8. These terms occur together only in the case of a righteous person's death.]

The Torah does not follow a chronological order [אֵין מוּקְדָּם וּמְאוּחָר בַּתּוֹרָה] in recording Isaac's death here. The sale of Joseph actually *preceded* Isaac's death by twelve years *(Rashi).*[1]

[As can be calculated from the *footnote,* Jacob was 108 years old when Joseph was sold and 120 years old when Isaac died. Jacob was in his hundredth year when he returned

35 *Arba; that is Hebron where Abraham and Isaac so-*
28-29 *journed.* 28 *Isaac's days were one-hundred and eighty*
years. 29 *And Isaac expired and died, and he was*

to his father. Accordingly, Isaac lived twenty-one years after this point in the narrative and did not die until twelve years after Joseph had been sold. This anachronism prompted *Rashi's* citation of the Rabbinic dictum that the Torah does not concern itself with strict chronological order.]

Ramban maintains [referring to his *comm.* to the death of Terach in 11:32] that it is in accordance with the Torah's usual practice to complete the story of one person with his death and then go on to the next generation, even though events recorded later might have preceded the death.

Thus, as noted in the *comm.* to 25:7, the Torah bids farewell, so to speak, to a person when there is nothing further of his life that it must recount. Then, the Torah can proceed uninterrupted to the central figure of the succeeding narrative. Accordingly, Noah's death is recorded in 9:29 before the history of his sons although Noah lived well into the days of Abraham [see vol. I p. xii:

1. *Rashi's* chronology is based upon the following calculations:

[A]

Isaac's age when he died	180
Isaac's age at Jacob's birth (see 25:26)	- 60
Jacob's age at Isaac's death	**120**

[B]

Jacob's age when he received the blessings and left his father's house [see p. 1173]	63
Years engaged in study at Academy of Eber	+ 14
Years he served Laban until Joseph was born	+ 14
Jacob's age when Joseph was born	**91**
Joseph's age when he was separated from his father and sold [see 37:2]	+ 17
Jacob's age when Joseph was sold	**108**

[C]

Jacob's age at Isaac's death [see "A" above]	120
Jacob's age when Joseph was sold ["B" above]	-108
Number of years Isaac lived after the sale of Joseph	**12**

[D]

Alternate calculation — more directly supported by Biblical texts — to arrive at the same conclusion.

Joseph's age when he stood before Pharaoh [41:46]	30
Joseph's age when he was sold [37:2]	-17
Total years Joseph had been in Egypt before the famine	**13**
Seven years of plenty and two years of famine before Jacob came to Egypt [45:6]	+ 9
Total years Joseph was in Egypt until Jacob's arrival	**22**
Jacob's age, as given to Pharoah when he came to Egypt [47:9]	130
Years elapsed since Joseph had been sold	- 22
Jacob's age when Joseph was sold	**108**

[continue with "C" above to arrive at conclusion.]

וַיִּגְוַע יִצְחָק וַיָּמָת וַיֵּאָסֶף אֶל־עַמָּיו זָקֵן וּשְׂבַע יָמִים וַיִּקְבְּרוּ אֹתוֹ עֵשָׂו וְיַעֲקֹב בָּנָיו׃

Chronology/Time Line]; the passing of Terach (11:32) is recorded before the story of Abraham, although Terach lived another 60 years (in that case the *Midrash* offers a special interpretation; see *Rashi* and *Ramban* there); and the death of Abraham (25:7) is recorded before the birth of his grandson Jacob (25:26) though Abraham lived until Jacob was fifteen years old. The same is true of the narrative here recording Isaac's death who was still alive when his grandson Joseph was sold into slavery.]

Ramban concludes that the above being so, we might have expected Isaac's death to have been recorded earlier, prior to the narrative of Jacob's experiences, just as we find of Abraham and the earlier generations [whose deaths were recorded before the experiences of their offspring were related.] — Perhaps, it was left for this point to emphasize that Isaac died in *a good old age ad content of years* [as it says of Abraham], for he lived to see the return of Jacob his spiritual heir, and had the privilege of having both his sons — Jacob and Esau — attend to his burial.

However, it is observed that when Isaac died, twelve years after Joseph was sold, they were still under the impression that Joseph was dead. And so we can see why the words בְּשֵׂיבָה טוֹבָה, *in a good old age,* used in recording Abraham's death [25:8] are explicitly missing in the account of Isaac's death *(Pesikta).*

[But cf. *Rashi* to 37:33 that Isaac prophetically knew that Joseph was alive, but since God did not reveal it to Jacob, Isaac also maintained a profile of being ignorant of the fact and instead pretend to mourn along with his son.]

זָקֵן וּשְׂבַע יָמִים — *Old and fulfilled of days.*

[Compare the expression used in the case of Abraham (25:8): בְּשֵׂיבָה טוֹבָה זָקֵן וְשָׂבֵעַ, *at a good old age, mature* (lit. *old) and content.* See *comm.* there for meaning of the expressions which are applicable here. Cf. expression used regarding David in *I Chron.* 29:28: *And he died in a good old age, full of days, riches and honor.* See also *Pesikta* cited above as to why the expression *at a good old age* is omitted here.]

In the case of Abraham the expression *fulfilled of days* does not occur because his 'days' were not full — five years were deducted from his life *(Lekach Tov).* [See *Rashi* to 15:15 and *footnote* to p.975.]

Ramban in 25:8 explains this expression *fulfilled of days* to mean that Isaac's soul was satisfied with his days; he was fully content with whatever each day brought him and he had no desire that the future days should bring him something new. This is a further example of God's mercy toward the righteous, in that they are content with their lot and desire no luxuries.

Furthermore, as the *Midrash* records, the expression *old and fulfilled of days* implies that he foresaw his share in the Garden of Eden.

[Cf. *Midrash Rabbah* 62:3: The Holy One, Blessed be He, shows the righteous in This World the reward He is accumulating for them in the World to Come. Their souls become contented and they fall asleep; i.e., they die as if falling asleep after a

35 *gathered to his people, old and fulfilled of days. His*
29 *son Esau and Jacob buried him.*

satisfying, relaxing experience.]

Chasam Sofer suggests that like the expression בָּא בַּיָּמִים, *came with the days* [see on 24:1], שְׂבַע יָמִים, *fulfilled of days,* represents one whose life was full and meaningful in every aspect. Not one moment of Isaac's life was wasted or spent on anything but service to his Creator.

וַיִּקְבְּרוּ אֹתוֹ עֵשָׂו וְיַעֲקֹב בָּנָיו — *And his sons, Esau and Jacob, buried him.*

— In the Cave of Machpelah. It was unnecessary to specify this was the burial site since Isaac resided in Hebron [*v.* 27] where the cave was located, and it was obvious that they would not have buried him anywhere but in his father's gravesite *(Ramban).*

Esau and Jacob are mentioned here in order of birth. [Esau was the firstborn and Jacob gave him precedence; the Torah therefore mentions him first *(Rashbam).*] In the case of Abraham's burial [25:8], though both of his sons jointly attended to his burial, Isaac is mentioned before the older son Ishmael, because Isaac was the son of Sarah, and clearly had precedence over Ishmael who was the son of the maidservant, Hagar *(Ibn Ezra; Akeidah).*

[Cf. *Rashi* and *comm.* to 25:8 according to which the prior mention of Ishmael in that verse indicates that it was Ishmael himself who, because he had repented, took a secondary role and gave precedence to Isaac. Esau, however, maintained his arrogant wickedness and refused to stand aside for Jacob. (See *Mizrachi* and *Gur Aryeh* cited there).]

Midrash Or HaAfeilah [cited by *Torah Sheleimah*] suggests that Esau is mentioned first because he had always honored his father to an extraordinary degree.

Oznaim LaTorah explains why Jacob deferred to Esau. Jacob knew that Esau had vowed to kill him. He also knew, as the prophet says [*Amos* 1:11], that Esau nursed his grudge forever. Therefore, Jacob recognized that the day of Isaac's burial could be more dangerous to him than even the confrontation at the Ford of Jabbok. In order not to give Esau a pretext for an angry attack, Jacob honored him by allowing Esau to hold first rank at the burial.

XXXVI

1. The Chronicles of Esau.

[As has been emphasized constantly throughout this commentary, the Torah is not merely a history book. It records only facts from which we can derive halachic or moral lessons.

Although many important principles of the Torah (גּוּפֵי תוֹרָה) are derived only from *brief textual allusions* (בִּרְמִיזָה), in this case the Torah devotes an *entire chapter* to the seemingly unimportant genealogies of Seir-Edom!

It is clear, that the Torah would not have devoted so much space to this topic unless it contained many sublime mysteries. Though much of such esoteric knowledge eludes us, the kabbalists have dwelt heavily upon it. A profoundly mystical part of the *Zohar,* (part 3, pp. 127-145), known as the *Idra Rabbah,* is devoted to its exposition.

Even in the literal sense of the verses, several factors surface.

From the earlier mention of Esau's

א-ב וְאֵלֶּה תֹּלְדוֹת עֵשָׂו הוּא אֱדוֹם: עֵשָׂו לָקַח
אֶת־נָשָׁיו מִבְּנוֹת כְּנָעַן אֶת־עָדָה בַּת־
אֵילוֹן הַחִתִּי וְאֶת־אָהֳלִיבָמָה בַּת־עֲנָה
ג בַּת־צִבְעוֹן הַחִוִּי: וְאֶת־בָּשְׂמַת בַּת־

wives in 26:34 and 28:9, from certain discrepancies within the genealogical listing that follows, and from the parallel genealogies in the Book of *Chronicles* it emerges that many of Esau's descendants were of incestuous or illegitimate birth. This, as well as the halachic and moral lessons that are perceived from other discrepancies in the listing — for example that a man's sins are forgiven on the day of his marriage and that *Amalek* is excluded from the general designation of Edomite — are dealt with fully by the *Rishonim* (early commentators) and shall be presented below.

Mizrachi (to verse 12) points out that this entire genealogy was recorded only to emphasize the depravity of Esau's family; therefore, any suggestion of their illegitimacy and immorality that can be gleaned from the allusions in the various verses (although not readily discernible from the literal meaning of the Text) should be encouraged (הֵיכָא דְאִיכָּא לְמִידְרַשׁ דָּרְשִׁינָן). The *Midrash* emphasizes this purpose of the chapter by recalling *Jeremiah* 49:10: *I have made Esau bare, I have uncovered his secrets, he can no longer hide himself.*

Furthermore we learn of the honor that came to Esau only by virtue of his being of Abraham's seed.

As *R' Hoffmann* notes in his *comm.* to 24:34, it is common for the Torah to repeat a halachic or narrative passage בִּשְׁבִיל דָּבָר שֶׁנִּתְחַדֵּשׁ בָּהּ, *because of substantive detail that is added in the second version (Sotah* 3a). As we shall note, this genealogy contains many such instructive nuances and additions.]

וְאֵלֶּה תֹּלְדוֹת עֵשָׂו — *And these are the genealogies of Esau.*

The conjunctive *and* connects this with the foregoing. Having concluded the story of Isaac, Scripture proceeds to narrate that of his children. It begins with Esau's line, listing his genealogy and mentioning their military and political ascendancy. With chapter 37, the Torah will return to deal in greater detail with Jacob's progeny, Isaac's primary offspring *(Abarbanel).*

Sforno renders: *These are the histories* [chronicles] *of Esau* — that which time brings forth (יָלַד). [For various interpretations of תּוֹלְדוֹת as referring to *offspring, descendants, genealogies, products, chronicles, history,* cf. *comm.* to 2:4; 6:9; 11:27; 25:12, 19.]

הוּא אֱדוֹם — *Who* [lit. he] *is Edom.*

I.e., he acquired the name Edom at an early age [see 25:30] and continued to be so called. The nation that later descended from him was also called by that name and was so known in the time of Moses *(Radak; Ibn Ezra).*

The description of Esau as Edom is meant to provide an insight into his character. He was given the name Edom when he greedily demanded beans from Jacob; so consumed was he by desire for food that he described it by color, not even recognizing its name. This sort of gluttonous, acquisitive greed characterized him all through life (*Sforno;* cf. also *comm.* to verses 7 and 19).

2. עֵשָׂו לָקַח אֶת־נָשָׁיו מִבְּנוֹת כְּנָעַן — *Esau had taken his wives from among the Canaanite women.*

36
1-3

¹ And these are the genealogies of Esau who is
Edom. ² Esau had taken his wives from among
the Canaanite women: Adah, daughter of Elon the
Hittite; Oholibamah, daughter of Anah, daughter of
Zibeon the Hivite; ³ and Basemath, daughter of

— [Much to the consternation of Isaac and Rebecca (see 26:35). These wives were actually *Hittites;* the Torah refers to them by the broader designation *Canaanites* since the Hittites (from Heth) were descendants of Canaan (25:16).]

This passage does not refer to *new* wives, but to the women Esau had already married [26:34 and 28:9]. Hence the past-perfect construction עֵשָׂו לָקַח, Esau *had* taken, rather than the conversive וַיִּקַּח עֵשָׂו, *Esau took (Hoffmann).*

אֶת־עָדָה בַּת־אֵילוֹן הַחִתִּי (1) — *Adah daughter of Elon the Hittite.*[1]

— She is *Basemath* daughter of Elon already mentioned in 26:34. She was known as Basemath because she burned incense *(besamim)* to idols *(Rashi).*

We do not say that this verse refers to wives *other* than those previously mentioned since, as noted, the verse says לָקַח אֶת נָשָׁיו, *'had taken' his wives,* meaning that he had previously taken them. Therefore, the discrepancy of names is exegetically instructive and must be interpreted *(Mizrachi).*

R' Hirsch comments that the discrepancy of names should not be considered disturbing. Even in the comparatively small circle of the Abrahamitic family, several people had two names: Abram, Abraham; Sarai, Sarah; Esau, Edom; Jacob, Israel; Benjamin, Benoni. It should not be surprising, therefore, that Adah and Basemath are one and the same, or that Oholibamah was also called Judith.

[But cf. *Ramban* below who, pursuing the literal sense, suggests that she may be a sister whom Esau married because Basemath was childless.]

וְאֶת־אָהֳלִיבָמָה (2) ... — *[And] Oholibamah, daughter of Anah, daughter of Zibeon.*

— She is identical with *Judith daughter of Beeri* (26:34) [both she and her father having two names]. Esau had given her the name Judith in order to deceive his father into believing that she had abandoned idol worship *(Rashi).*[2]

Ramban disagrees with *Rashi's* interpretation, maintaining that *Rashi* does not account for the change in her *father's* name from Be'eri to Anah. Furthermore, consistency would require that our chapter should use either real names in all cases, or descriptive names in all cases. *Rashi* does not explain why, in the case of Adah he considers Basemath to be only a descriptive name and her real name to be Adah, while in the case of Basemath, daughter of Ishmael, (*v.*

1. [The names in the following genealogies are numbered in the sequence in which they appear in the Torah to correspond with the Genealogical Table on page 1535].

2. The name Judith has come to mean 'Jewess' but that would be an anachronism and it is clearly not its implication here. Also, the name has no relationship to Judah who was not yet born at the time.

R' David Feinstein notes that Esau chose the name יְהוּדִית with which to deceive his father since it contains the four letters of HASHEM's Ineffable Name. Similarly in *Megillah* 13a the words יְהוּדָה and יְהוּדִיָה are interpreted to refer to anyone who has repudiated idolatry.

3), he considers Basemath to be the real name and Mahalath a descriptive name ...

He offers that, possibly, the wives in this verse are *different* ones, and in the literal sense the original wives mentioned in 26:34 — Judith and Basemath — may have died childless, perhaps in punishment for their rebelliousness to Isaac and Rebecca [26:35]. Esau then married *Adah*, the sister of Basemath and another woman by the name of *Oholibamah, daughter of Anah.* [See on Basemath, next verse.]

[As we shall see in *Rashi's comm.* to *v.* 4, s.v. *Korach;* Oholibamah [herself the illegitimate child of an adulterous union (see below)] adulterously cohabited with Eliphaz. *Midrash Shocher Tov* perceives her name to imply: She made her tent *(Oholah)* like an illegitimate alter *(bamah)* upon which to act adulterously.]

(3-4) בַּת־עֲנָה בַּת־צִבְעוֹן הַחִוִּי — *Daughter of Anah, daughter of Zibeon the Hivvite.*

[Anah was a man's name, so the phrase cannot mean: *daughter of Anah* who was the *daughter of Zibeon.* The phrase implies, rather, that Oholibamah was the daughter of two fathers!] Clearly the verse cannot mean that Oholibamah literally had two fathers, an obvious impossibility! Furthermore, Anah himself is mentioned in verse 24 as the *son of Zibeon.* The phraseology of our verse accordingly teaches that Zibeon adulterously cohabited with his daughter-in-law, Anah's wife (who is unidentified), resulting in the birth of Oholibamah. [I.e., Oholibamah is called the *daughter of Anah* because Anah's wife bore her; she was publicly known as Anah's daughter because she was raised in his home, but the Torah reveals that she was actually fathered by her adulterous grandfather, Zibeon. Accordingly all their descendants were בְּנֵי מַמְזֵרוּת, *children of illegitimate birth (Rashi).*

There is an additional discrepancy inasmuch as in *v.* 20 Anah is identified as Zibeon's brother, while further in *v.* 24 we find that he was Zibeon's *son!* This indicates, as *Rashi* explains there, that Zibeon committed incest with his own mother [Seir's wife], fathering Anah [who is thus described as Zibeon's putative *brother* since he was born of the same mother, while the Torah also reveals to us that in truth he was Zibeon's *son* since Zibeon fathered him incestuously.]

Mizrachi observes that the Sages assume Zibeon to have been the adulterer although the following interpretation would seem to be just as acceptable: Seir committed adultery with Zibeon's wife. Their child, Anah, could be described both as Zibeon's son, since Zibeon's wife bore him, and Zibeon's brother since his father, Seir, begot him.

— We do not make this suggestion, since the Sages assume that תָּלִינָן קִלְקוּל בִּמְקוּלְקָל *we may assume that a wicked deed was done by a wicked person;* and if two wicked acts took place, he presumably committed them both. We already know from the case of Oholibamah that Zibeon adulterously cohabited with his daughter-in-law, Anah's wife, but we have no evidence that Seir ever committed such an abomination. Therefore, we assume that Anah was born of Zibeon's incestuous act, not Seir's. Similarly, in the case of the illegitimate birth of Oholibamah, the Sages assume that the known adulterer, Zibeon, committed adultery with his daughter-in-law, Anah's wife, but not that Anah committed incest with his mother, Zibeon's wife. They do not conjecture otherwise since most other people — presumably including Seir, regarding whom we have no external evidence to the contrary — are virtuous in this respect, and there is less reason to assume that *two* people acted adulterously rather than to assume that *one* person did so twice.

[Cf. *Tosafos, Bava Basra* 115b s.v. מְלַמֵּד.]

In *v.* 20 Zibeon and Anah are described as *Horites.* The *Talmud* [*Shabbos* 85a] explains the term *Hivvite* here to refer not to the proper noun but

The Edomite/Seirite Genealogies

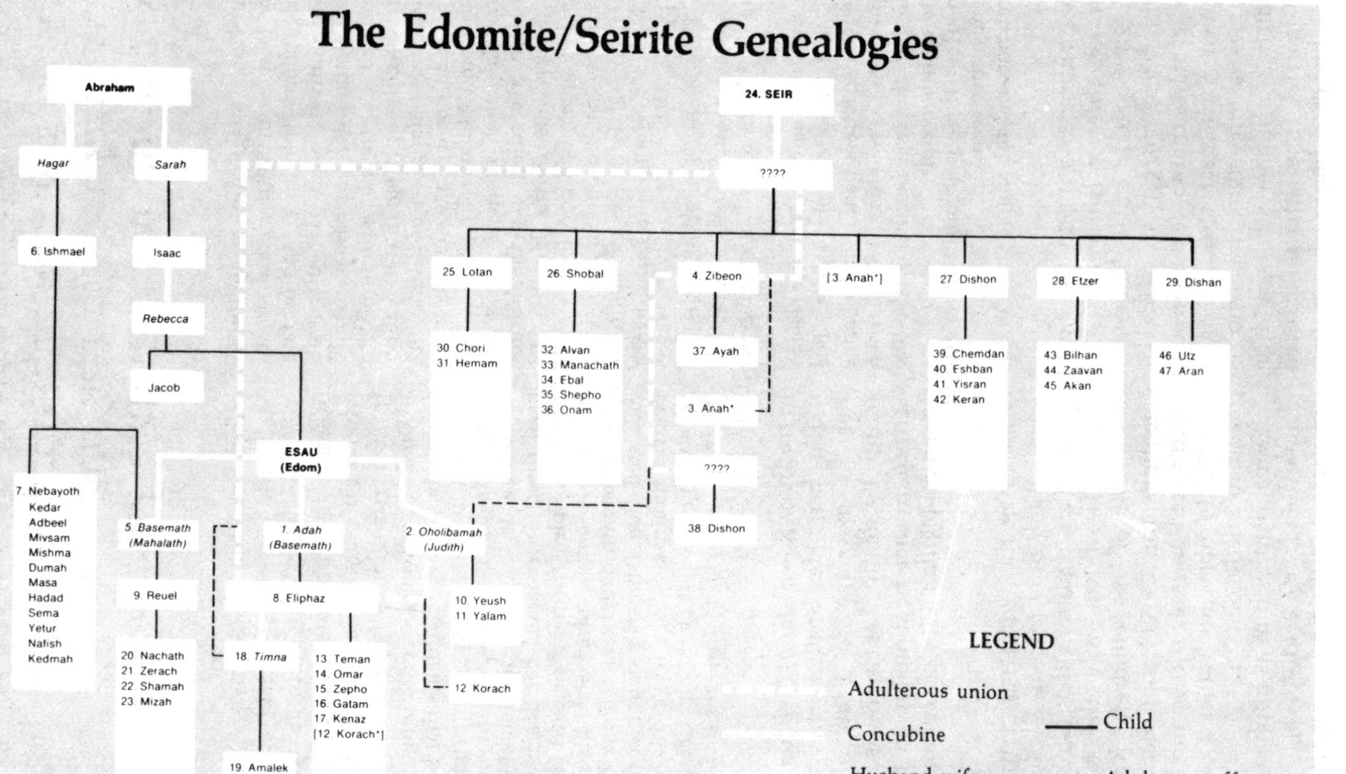

The numbers on this chart refer to the sequence in which these names appear in the Torah, and correspond with the parenthesized numbers in the commentary headings

ד יִשְׁמָעֵאל אֲחוֹת נְבָיוֹת: וַתֵּלֶד עָדָה לְעֵשָׂו
אֶת־אֱלִיפָז וּבָשְׂמַת יָלְדָה אֶת־רְעוּאֵל:
ה °יְעוּשׁ וְאָהֳלִיבָמָה יָלְדָה אֶת־°יעיש וְאֶת־יַעְלָם
וְאֶת־קֹרַח אֵלֶּה בְּנֵי עֵשָׂו אֲשֶׁר יֻלְּדוּ־לוֹ
ו בְּאֶרֶץ כְּנָעַן: וַיִּקַּח עֵשָׂו אֶת־נָשָׁיו וְאֶת־

to the Horite's agricultural ability to merely taste earth כְּחִוְיָא, *like a snake*, and determine the most appropriate crop to cultivate on a particular soil. [Thus Talmudically, our passage would be rendered: '... (publicly presumed to be) *the daughter of Anah* (but in reality, the illegitimate) *daughter of Zibeon, the serpentine soil taster.* See *Tosafos* there s.v. הַחִוִּי, and *Maharsha.*]

Sefer HaYashar reconciles many difficulties by recording that the Horites were descendants of the Hivvites. *R' Hoffmann* notes, additionally, that the term Hittite — as it occurs in *Joshua* 1:4 — is a general term for *Canaanite* — embracing also the Hivvites, and hence the Horites.

Cf. *Ramban* to *Deut.* 2:10 who maintains — citing our verses — that the Horite is identical with the Hivvite, Canaanite nation. *Horite* is derived from חור, *the* [*hole of*] *the asp (Isaiah* 11:8) and *Hivvite* from *snake.* The terms [whose letters ו and ר interchange but preserve the meaning] were chosen to suggest the treacherous, snake-like nature of this people.

[In effect, there is accordingly no discrepancy between the Rabbinic interpretation and the simple sense of the text.]

3. (5-6) בָּשְׂמַת בַּת־יִשְׁמָעֵאל — *Basemath, daughter of Ishmael.*

In 28:9 she is called Mahalath (from מחל, *forgive). Midrash Shmuel* states that three persons are forgiven their past sins: he who becomes a proselyte, he who is elevated to a higher status, and he who marries. The latter is deduced from this case inasmuch she was called [by the descriptive name] Mahalath [lit., forgiveness] at the time she and Esau were married (*Rashi;* see *footnote* to p. 1171 where the same thought is cited from *Yerushalmi Bikkurim* 3:3).

Ramban however, continuing his commentary above, maintains that both were her *proper* names. Her original name, Mahalath, was repugnant since in Hebrew it suggests *choli,* sickness. Esau therefore renamed her Basemath, which is a pleasant name derived from the word *besamim,* spices, after his first wife, Basemath daughter of Elon. This indicated that Ishmael's daughter was beloved to him since she was of his own family and was *not* of the the Canaanites who were *evil in the eyes of Isaac his father* [28:8].

(7) אֲחוֹת נְבָיוֹת — *Sister of Nebayoth.*

[As her older brother], he gave her in marriage to Esau after Ishmael's death; hence she is described by her relationship to him *(Rashi; Megillah* 17a; cf. *comm.* to 28:9).

4. (8) וַתֵּלֶד עָדָה לְעֵשָׂו אֶת־אֱלִיפָז — [*And*] *Adah bore to Esau Eliphaz.*

There are traditions that Eliphaz, Esau's firstborn, was the most deserving of his children. *Rashi* mentions [on 29:11] that 'he had been raised on Isaac's knee and had refused to obey his father's command to kill Jacob.'

Some identify him as Eliphaz the Temanite [*Job* 2:11, 4:1] who prophesied in the time of his friend

Ishmael, sister of Nebayoth.
4 *Adah bore to Esau Eliphaz; Basemath bore Reuel;*
5 *and Oholibamah bore Yeush, Yalom, and Korach.*
These are Esau's sons who were born to him in the
land of Canaan.
6 *Esau took his wives, his sons, his daughters, and*

Job (*Sechel Tov;* see *comm.* to *Job* ad. loc.).

וּבָשְׂמַת יָלְדָה אֶת רְעוּאֵל (9) — [*And*] *Basemath bore Reuel.*

5. וְאָהֳלִיבָמָה יָלְדָה אֶת יְעוּשׁ (10-12) וְאֶת יַעְלָם וְאֶת קֹרַח — *And Oholibamah bore Yeush,* [*and*] *Yalam, and Korach.*

This Korach was later [*v.* 16] included among the chiefs of *Eliphaz* [son of *Adah,* while here he is listed as a son of Esau through *Oholibamah!*] This alludes to the fact that this Korach was really the illegitimate child of Eliphaz, Esau's son, through an adulterous union with Oholibamah, his father's wife (*Rashi* from *Midrash*).

[In effect, then, as *Rashi* notes in *v.* 2 all Oholibamah's children were tainted by illegitimacy (בְּנֵי מַמְזֵרוּת).]

The Sages do *not* suggest that there were *two* Korachs referred to in this generation — the one mentioned here and the Eliphazite Chief in *v.* 16. Korach is absent from the list of Eliphaz's children in *v.* 11 which the Sages perceive as implying that Korach was not generally known to be Eliphaz's son since he was not borne by Eliphaz's wife as were Eliphaz's other children. Since, however, we find Korach among Oholibamah's children in this verse, and inexplicably among the chiefs of Eliphaz later in *v.* 16, we assume he was one and the same, and that accordingly he was the illegitimate offspring of an incestuous union between Eliphaz and his father's wife Oholibamah.

Although *Rashi* in *Sotah* 13a s.v. ל״ו כְּתָרִים *does* suggest that there were *two* Korachs in apparent contradiction to his commentary here, *Rashi* is really not contradicting himself. Rather, he cites two differing Midrashic traditions. In *Sotah, Rashi* explains the Talmudic opinion cited there that a total of thirty-six crowns were hung on Jacob's coffin [see on 50:10]. *Rashi's* interpretation to our verse — that there was one Korach who was illegitimate — is based on *Midrash* reflecting another tradition (*Mizrachi*).

[Note: This Edomite Korach is not to be confused with Levi's great-grandson Korach — antagonist of Moses — in *Numbers* 16.]

Ibn Ezra maintains that there was but one Korach, and that in the literal sense there was no adultery implied in the repetition of his name here and in *v.* 16. He suggests that Korach was the youngest of Oholibamah's children [as indicated by the fact that he is here mentioned last]. Upon his mother's death, Adah raised him, which according to *Ibn Ezra* explains why he is mentioned among Adah's children in *v.* 16.

אֵלֶּה בְּנֵי עֵשָׂו אֲשֶׁר יֻלְּדוּ־לוֹ בְּאֶרֶץ כְּנָעַן— *These* [i.e., the aforementioned] *are Esau's sons who were born to him in the land of Canaan.*

In the following verses, by contrast, we shall be told of the descendants who were born to him later in the land of Seir (*Hoffmann*).

6. Esau separates himself from Jacob.

וַיִּקַּח עֵשָׂו אֶת־נָשָׁיו וְאֶת־בָּנָיו וְאֶת בְּנֹתָיו — [*And*] *Esau took his wives,* [*and*] *his sons,* [*and*] *his daughters.*

This journey was undertaken after Jacob returned from Charan and settled in Canaan; possibly also after the death of their father (*Ramban*).

[Chronologically this second

בָּנָיו וְאֶת־בְּנֹתָיו וְאֶל־כָּל־נַפְשׁוֹת בֵּיתוֹ
וְאֶת־מִקְנֵהוּ וְאֶת־כָּל־בְּהֶמְתּוֹ וְאֵת כָּל־
קִנְיָנוֹ אֲשֶׁר רָכַשׁ בְּאֶרֶץ כְּנָעַן וַיֵּלֶךְ אֶל־
ז אֶרֶץ מִפְּנֵי יַעֲקֹב אָחִיו: כִּי־הָיָה רְכוּשָׁם
רָב מִשֶּׁבֶת יַחְדָּו וְלֹא יָכְלָה אֶרֶץ
מְגוּרֵיהֶם לָשֵׂאת אֹתָם מִפְּנֵי מִקְנֵיהֶם:

view would imply that about twenty-one years passed before Esau departed! (see *comm.* to 35:29).][1]

That Esau licentiously thought more of women than of children is demonstrated by his giving precedence to his females. This is alluded to in that his wives are here mentioned before his sons and daughters. Jacob, by contrast, gave precedence to the children [see *Rashi* to 31:17]. The commentators cite this to illustrate a basic difference in attitude between the righteous and the wicked: The righteous marry in order to produce righteous offspring; they cherish their children as the purpose of marriage. Immoral people marry for physical pleasure; their children are secondary by-products [see also *comm.* to 32:17.

וְאֶת־כָּל־נַפְשׁוֹת בֵּיתוֹ — *And all the members of his household* [lit. *and all the souls of his house*].

Although Esau's family consisted only of six [himself and his five sons] the Torah uses the plural term נַפְשׁוֹת, *souls*, of his house, since they each worshiped different gods, and were not unified. When Jacob's family came to Egypt, it consisted of seventy, yet the Torah [in 46:27] uses the singular term נֶפֶשׁ, *soul*, since they all served one God *(Rashi* to 46:27 citing *Vayikra Rabbah).*

וַיֵּלֶךְ אֶל־אֶרֶץ — *And [he] went to a land.*

— To another land *(Onkelos).*

— [An unspecified land]; to wherever he found a suitable spot to dwell *(Rashi).* [Ultimately, as we see in the next verse, he settled in Mount Seir *(Ramban* explaining *Rashi).*]

According to *Ramban's* own interpretation the phrase itself is elliptic, and connotes: into the land *of Seir.* The name of the place need not be mentioned since it has already been said that he dwelled in Seir [32:4], and because Seir is mentioned in the very next verse as his destination.

1. It is evident from previous Scriptural references associating Esau with Seir that Esau had moved to Seir earlier. Because of its excellent hunting grounds, he had gone there with a force of four hundred men [32:7] *before* Jacob's return, and dwelt in the *plain* referred to in 32:4 as the *field* of Edom. Apparently the inhabitants of the fortified mountain of Seir would not let him dwell higher up.

Esau's children and wives, however, remained behind in Canaan and Esau commuted between residences to honor his father and supply his needs. After Jacob returned to Canaan — and presumably after Isaac's death — Esau vacated the land *permanently* because he knew that Canaan was the inheritance of his brother.

He therefore moved his family to his original dwelling place in the field of Edom, and eventually conquered the whole region from the Horites — including Mount Seir — making it his principal residence. This remained Esau's possession by Divine sanction [see *Deut.* 2:5] *(Ramban).*

36 *all the members of his household — his livestock and*
7 *all his animals, and all the wealth he had acquired in*
the land of Canaan — and went to a land because of
his brother Jacob. [7] *For their wealth was too abun-*
dant for them to dwell together, and the land of their
sojourns could not support them because of their

מִפְּנֵי יַעֲקֹב אָחִיו — *Because of his brother Jacob.*[1]

This phrase informs us that Esau's journey took place *after* Jacob's return from Charan *(Ramban).*

[The next verse tells us the apparent reason, *why,* in fact, they could not both live side by side in the same land: — the land was unable to support them because of their abundant livestock. However, the commentators infer an *underlying* reason for the fact that Esau, rather than Jacob, was the one who sought a new land]:

Because of his brother Jacob, i.e., because Esau feared Jacob, his brother, having heard of the military strength displayed by the family in Shechem *(Targum Yonasan; Midrash HaGadol).*

Since Jacob had purchased the birthright, he was Isaac's heir. Therefore *he* remained in the ancestral land, while Esau sought another country *(Rashbam).*

The *Midrash* explains that Esau left on account of the obligation involved in the decree [15:13] that there would be a long, hard exile as strangers in a foreign land before Isaac's descendants would inherit Canaan. Esau reasoned: 'I will leave here. I want no part either of the gift of this land or the payment of the obligation of going into exile for it.' Another reason *Esau* left was because he was ashamed of having sold his birthright *(Rashi).*

In reward for having cleared out his utensils [i.e. departing from the land] *because of his brother Jacob,* God granted Esau one hundred provinces from Seir to Magdiel; and Magdiel is Rome *(Pirkei d'Rabbi Eliezer* 38; cf. *comm.* to *v.* 43).

7. כִּי הָיָה רְכוּשָׁם רָב מִשֶּׁבֶת יַחְדָּו — *For their wealth was too abundant for them to dwell together.*

Therefore, in light of the above, Esau felt compelled to vacate in the favor of Jacob. He knew that Isaac had bequeathed the land to Jacob, and perhaps he also knew that he himself was to inherit Mount Seir [see *Deut.* 2:5] *(Radak).*

וְלֹא יָכְלָה אֶרֶץ מְגוּרֵיהֶם לָשֵׂאת אֹתָם מִפְּנֵי מִקְנֵיהֶם — *And the land of their sojourns could not support them because of their livestock.*

The land could not supply sufficient pasture for their cattle *(Rashi).*

1. The use of the word אָחִיו, *his brother,* indicates that Esau and Jacob lived as 'brothers', having wiped away the animosity of the past. But the spiritual and moral gulf between them was such that Esau could not feel comfortable living near Jacob. Still, had economic conditions been better in Canaan, Esau would not have left. But their flocks were so abundant that the land could not support them both.

That the Torah describes Esau as going אֶל אֶרֶץ, *to* [an unnamed] *country,* מִפְּנֵי יַעֲקֹב אָחִיו, to rid himself of the spiritual and moral influence of his brother indicates that Esau's intention was simply to put distance between himself and Jacob *(R' Hirsch).*

ח וַיֵּשֶׁב עֵשָׂו בְּהַר שֵׂעִיר עֵשָׂו הוּא אֱדוֹם:
ט וְאֵלֶּה תֹּלְדוֹת עֵשָׂו אֲבִי אֱדוֹם בְּהַר
י שֵׂעִיר: אֵלֶּה שְׁמוֹת בְּנֵי־עֵשָׂו אֱלִיפַז בֶּן־
עָדָה אֵשֶׁת עֵשָׂו רְעוּאֵל בֶּן־בָּשְׂמַת אֵשֶׁת
יא עֵשָׂו: וַיִּהְיוּ בְּנֵי אֱלִיפָז תֵּימָן אוֹמָר צְפוֹ
יב וְגַעְתָּם וּקְנַז: וְתִמְנַע | הָיְתָה פִילֶגֶשׁ
לֶאֱלִיפַז בֶּן־עֵשָׂו וַתֵּלֶד לֶאֱלִיפַז אֶת־

According to *Ramban, land of their sojourns* refers to the *'city* of their sojourns' — Hebron — where Abraham and Isaac sojourned [35:27]. Canaan as a whole could certainly support a thousand times more than them. But when Esau realized he could no longer stay in his native city, he decided to leave the whole country to his brother and go his own way.

8. וַיֵּשֶׁב עֵשָׂו בְּהַר שֵׂעִיר — *So* [lit. *and*] *Esau settled on Mount Seir.*

— He successfully captured the fortified mountain from the original inhabitants, the Horites, descendants of Seir. Esau gained the territory by Divine sanction, as it is written [*Deut.* 2:22]: *as He did for the children of Esau that dwell in Seir when He destroyed the Horites from before them;* and [*Deut.* 2:5]: *Because I have given Mount Seir to Esau for a possession (Ramban v.* 6; see *footnote* there).

In his *comm.* to 34:13, *Ramban* mentions that the Torah did not explicitly mention Esau's wars with the Horites because his victory was a 'hidden miracle'. [I.e., one could deny the miraculous nature of the event, attributing it not to the clear intervention of God, but to one's own military prowess.]

Sforno [to *v.* 2 and 32:4] observes that Oholibamah was a descendant of Seir the Horite, and offers that Esau had obtained the site as a dowry when he married her. Thus, Esau went to Seir and dwelt on the mountain because of her.

[See also on 14:6.]

עֵשָׂו הוּא אֱדוֹם — *Esau who is Edom.*

Until this point only Esau *himself* was called Edom. Only when he established himself in Seir [next verse] and had grandchildren born there, were his offspring considered as a nation named Edom. In the next verse, therefore, he is called אֲבִי אֱדוֹם, *ancestor of Edom (Haamek Davar).*

The fact that Esau is Edom is repeated three times in this chapter. Some take this repetition as a message that this significant group of nations stretching from East to West was descended from Esau, a son of Isaac and a grandson of Abraham. It was inevitable that ideas concerning the existence of God and certain Abrahamitic moral principles were spread among these nations, thanks to the heritage of their founder. This is true despite the fact that these principles were surely watered down to make them popular and acceptable. Accordingly, this chapter intends to outline a vast historical picture of the cultural evolution within humanity *(R' Munk).*

Other sages maintain, to the contrary, that the Torah is emphasizing hereby that Esau's abundant progeny — notwithstanding their apparent superiority in this world — comprise these na-

36
8-12

livestock. [8] *So Esau settled on Mount Seir; Esau who*
is Edom.
[9] *And these are the progeny of Esau, ancestor of*
Edom, on Mount Seir. [10] *These are the names of*
Esau's sons: Eliphaz, son of Adah, Esau's wife;
Reuel, son of Basemath, Esau's wife.
[11] *The sons of Eliphaz were: Teman; Omar;*
Zepho; Gatam; and Kenaz. [12] *And Timna was a con-*
cubine of Eliphaz, son of Esau, and she bore Amalek

tions making up the kingdom of Edom who are destined to ultimately disappear in Messianic times (cf. *Or HaChaim; Abarbanel*). [Cf. *v.* 19.]

9. Esau's descendants in Seir.

וְאֵלֶּה תֹּלְדוֹת עֵשָׂו אֲבִי אֱדוֹם בְּהַר שֵׂעִיר — *And these are the progeny of Esau, ancestor of Edom, on Mount Seir.*

I.e. the [following are the] progeny (תֹּלְדוֹת) which Esau's *children* begot after he went to Seir *(Rashi).* [The children born to Esau while still in Canaan were listed in verses 2-5. The following were his *grandchildren (Abarbanel).*]

Esau's descendants born in Seir are listed here because it was *they* who vanquished the Horites and established Edom's sovereignty over Mount Seir. See *Deut.* 2:22 *(Sforno).*

10. אֵלֶּה שְׁמוֹת בְּנֵי עֵשָׂו — *These are the names of Esau's sons.*

First the sons already born to Esau in Canaan are again mentioned. Then the offspring whom his sons begot while in Seir are enumerated, for Esau himself begot no more offspring while in Seir. The listing then reverts to his children by Oholibamah [*v.* 14], however, none of her grandchildren are named. This is because only the chiefs are listed, and while Oholibamah's *children* were chiefs, apparently her grandchildren were not *(Radak).*

[*Radak* apparently pursues this interpretation since it is only reasonable to assume that Oholibamah *had* grandchildren through at least some of her three sons, but that they were not, for some reason, counted as chiefs.]

Abarbanel suggests that it is conceivable that no grandchildren were *yet* born to her at that time, or that they were all girls.

11. Esau' genealogy through Eliphaz son of Adah:

תֵּימָן אוֹמָר צְפוֹ וְגַעְתָּם וּקְנַז (13-17) — *Teman, Omar, Zepho, Gatam and Kenaz.*

12. Amalek: Eliphaz's son by his concubine.

וְתִמְנַע הָיְתָה פִילֶגֶשׁ לֶאֱלִיפַז בֶּן־עֵשָׂו (18) — [*And*] *Timna was a concubine of Eliphaz, son of Esau.*

This is stated [although the women of Esau's other sons are not mentioned *(Ramban)*] to emphasize that Abraham was held in such esteem that people were eager to attach themselves to his descendants. As we see in *v.* 22, Timna was a descendant of chiefs; she was the sister of Lotan who was one of the chiefs of Seir [Lotan was a son of Seir himself (*v.* 20)], a Horite who lived there from ancient times. Yet she was so anxious to marry a descendant of Abraham that she

יג עֲמָלֵק אֵלֶּה בְּנֵי עָדָה אֵשֶׁת עֵשָׂו: וְאֵלֶּה
בְּנֵי רְעוּאֵל נַחַת וָזֶרַח שַׁמָּה וּמִזָּה אֵלֶּה
יד הָיוּ בְּנֵי בָשְׂמַת אֵשֶׁת עֵשָׂו: וְאֵלֶּה הָיוּ בְּנֵי

said to Eliphaz: 'If I am unworthy to become your wife, let me at least be your concubine!' *(Rashi).*

Cf. *Sanhedrin* 99b: Timna was a royal princess, being the sister of Lotan, an uncrowned prince. She desired to convert to Judaism. She went to Abraham, Isaac, and Jacob but they would not accept her. So she went and became the concubine of Eliphaz, Esau's son, saying: 'I would rather be a servant to one of this people than a noblewoman of another nation.' From her descended Amalek who afflicted Israel. Why so? — Because they [i.e. the Patriarchs] should not have rejected her.[1]

[This was one of the passages that Manassah, son of King Hezekiah, would expound in a mocking fashion. See *footnote* to *v.* 22; s.v. וַאֲחוֹת לוֹטָן תִּמְנָע.]

Rashi [from *Tanchuma*] continues that in *I Chronicles* 1:36 Timna is counted as one of Eliphaz's *children!* This intimates that Eliphaz cohabited adulterously with Seir's wife and from this union Timna was born. When she grew up she became Eliphaz's concubine. We are therefore told that *Lotan's sister was Timna* [*v.* 22], Lotan being the son of Seir, thus intimating in a veiled manner that Timna was Seir's daughter. She is not more explicitly listed among the children of Seir because she was Lotan's *maternal*, but not *paternal* sister. [I.e., she was only Seir's putative daughter through the adulterous act of his wife.]

[It is not clear, however, why Oholibamah (see *v.* 2) *is* explicitly called Anah's *daughter*, although the circumstances were similar and she was Anah's 'daughter' only in the sense that his wife bore her but from another man. In the case of Timna, the circumstances were the same, yet the Torah refrains from specifically calling her Seir's 'daughter', but nevertheless alludes to these circumstances by referring to her as 'Lotan's sister.' The reason *Rashi* advances appears difficult in this context וצ"ע.]

Ramban suggests that Timna is specifically mentioned here as Amalek's mother to draw attention to the fact that Amalek — as the child of a concubine — was of lowly birth, not a true heir of Esau, and did not dwell with the other offspring of Esau on Mount Seir. Only the sons of the *true* wives were called Esau's seed, not those of the concubines. In this, Esau followed the practice of his grandfather, Abraham [see 21:10).[2]

In a long exegetical dissertation — not within the scope of inclusion in this commentary — *Ramban* proceeds to expound on the verses in *Chronicles* cited by *Rashi* and on the discrepancies

1. In discussing this Talmudic tradition, *R' Munk* observes that once before, *Abraham* had been blamed for a failure to seek converts. *Nedarim* 32a records R' Yochanan as stating that Abraham was blameworthy for not insisting on his right to keep the captives whom he had freed and for not bringing them to a belief in God (cf. *comm.* to 14:22).

Although Abraham is the very model of the Jew who spread faith in God, he wanted to win people solely with truth, not by force and not because they saw some personal advantage in joining him. Therefore, he refused Timna's wish to convert, because she wanted only to join the prestigious family of Abraham, not to convert sincerely (*Rashi* to *v.* 20). For a similar reason, he refused to keep the prisoners of war and convert them. He felt that such a conversion would be carried out under duress, and would be lacking in religious conviction.

In both cases, however, he erred. He should have realized that the truth of his faith could conquer even reluctant minds. And so, Israel paid the consequences. Amalek, son of the rejected Timna, became the arch enemy of the Jews.

to Eliphaz. — These are the children of Adah, Esau's
wife.
13 And these are the sons of Reuel: Nachath;
Zerach; Shamah; and Mizah. — These are the
children of Basemath, Esau's wife.

between the listings. Seeking to avoid *Rashi's* approach of attributing to them adulterous relationships and illegitimate births, *Ramban* advances several possible alternative interpretations to reconcile divergencies in the chronologies. Among these suggested conclusions are (a) that Eliphaz consorted with Seir's wife *after* the death of Seir, making Timna in effect a legitimate child; when she grew up Eliphaz took her as a concubine, this being permissible to a gentile (see *Sanhedrin* 55b). [This view, which looks upon Eliphaz more favorably, fits in well with some other traditions regarding Eliphaz, Esau's firstborn, who, as *Rashi* to 29:11 observes, 'had been raised on Isaac's knee and had refused to obey his father's command to kill Jacob.' He was, according to the Sages, the friend of Job whose idealogical discussions are recorded in that Book (see *Rashi* on *Job* 4:1).]; (b) there are two Timna's — one male and one female; (c) Korach was the youngest (legitimate) son of Oholibamah; upon his mother's death Adah raised him [following *Ibn Ezra;* cf. *v.* 5].

[However, cf. *Mizrachi* cited in *v.* 1 who defends *Rashi's* Talmudic approach of emphasizing whatever suggestions of the illegitimacy and immorality within Esau's family, though not readily discernable from the literal meaning of the Text.]

(19) וַתֵּלֶד לֶאֱלִיפַז אֶת־עֲמָלֵק — *And she bore Amalek to Eliphaz.*

— Who later afflicted Israel [see *Exod.* 18:8]. This was in punishment for the Patriarchs having rejected his mother from converting (*Sanhedrin* 99b; see *comm.* and *footnote* above).

אֵלֶּה בְּנֵי עָדָה אֵשֶׁת עֵשָׂו — *These are the children* [i.e. grandchildren] *of Adah, Esau's wife.*

13. Esau's genealogy through Reuel son of Basemath.

(20-23) נַחַת וָזֶרַח שַׁמָּה וּמִזָּה — *Nachath, Zerach, Shamah and Mizah.*

14. Esau's sons through Oholibamah.

According to *Ramban* [*v.* 9] the justification for mentioning the birth of Esau's sons Eliphaz and Reuel in verse 10, was in order to list the offspring born to them in Seir, which is the primary reason for this genealogy. Although Oholibamah's children had no offspring in Seir, they are gratuitously included in order to complete the list of Esau's children. Furthermore, they became chiefs, and all the

2. *Ramban* continues that in general, we have been commanded not to abhor descendants of Esau, nor to take their land [see *Deut.* 23:8 and 2:5]. This applies to those who dwelt in Seir and are known as Edomites.

However, our verse comes to specially exclude *Amalek's* line from this interdiction. He was a son of a concubine, and not part of Esau's inheritance. In fact, regarding Amalek we *have* been commanded to abhor him and utterly blot out his name (*Deut.* 25:19).

According to *Abarbanel,* Amalek as an Edomite-relative, was initially *included* in the designation of Edomites who were not to be abhorred. It was only after his dastardly, cruel attack against the Israelites that he was singled out for extermination. [See *Rambam, Moreh Nevuchim* cited in *footnote* to *v.* 20, and *Ikkarim* 2:25.]

אָהֳלִיבָמָה בַת־עֲנָה בַּת־צִבְעוֹן אֵשֶׁת
°יְעוּשׁ עֵשָׂו וַתֵּלֶד לְעֵשָׂו אֶת־°יעיש וְאֶת־יַעְלָם
טו וְאֶת־קֹרַח: אֵלֶּה אַלּוּפֵי בְנֵי־עֵשָׂו בְּנֵי
אֱלִיפַז בְּכוֹר עֵשָׂו אַלּוּף תֵּימָן אַלּוּף
טז אוֹמָר אַלּוּף צְפוֹ אַלּוּף קְנַז: אַלּוּף־קֹרַח
אַלּוּף גַּעְתָּם אַלּוּף עֲמָלֵק אֵלֶּה אַלּוּפֵי
יז אֱלִיפַז בְּאֶרֶץ אֱדוֹם אֵלֶּה בְּנֵי עָדָה: וְאֵלֶּה
בְּנֵי רְעוּאֵל בֶּן־עֵשָׂו אַלּוּף נַחַת אַלּוּף
זֶרַח אַלּוּף שַׁמָּה אַלּוּף מִזָּה אֵלֶּה אַלּוּפֵי
רְעוּאֵל בְּאֶרֶץ אֱדוֹם אֵלֶּה בְּנֵי בָשְׂמַת
יח אֵשֶׁת עֵשָׂו: וְאֵלֶּה בְּנֵי אָהֳלִיבָמָה אֵשֶׁת
עֵשָׂו אַלּוּף יְעוּשׁ אַלּוּף יַעְלָם אַלּוּף קֹרַח
אֵלֶּה אַלּוּפֵי אָהֳלִיבָמָה בַּת־עֲנָה אֵשֶׁת
יט עֵשָׂו: אֵלֶּה בְנֵי־עֵשָׂו וְאֵלֶּה אַלּוּפֵיהֶם
°שביעי כ הוּא אֱדוֹם: °אֵלֶּה בְנֵי־שֵׂעִיר

chiefs — even those not born in Seir — are enumerated.

[Contextually perhaps this verse should have followed immediately after verse 10 where Esau's sons through his other wives Adah and Basemath respectively had been listed. However as noted there, in each of the former cases the verses went on to list Esau's grandchildren through those sons, while in the case of Oholibamah no grandchildren are enumerated, and so the listing of Esau's children through those were left for last. Possibly also, Oholibamah's children were tainted by illegitimacy (בְּנֵי מַמְזֵרוּת), and Korach himself was additionally illegitimate having been the offspring of an adulterous relationship between Oholibamah and Eliphaz.]

15. The chiefs among Esau's descendants:

The chiefs of Eliphaz; Adah's descendants.

אֵלֶּה אַלּוּפֵי בְנֵי־עֵשָׂו — *These are the chiefs of the children of Esau.*

The translation *chief* follows *Rashi* who explains אַלּוּף to mean *head of a clan.* [*Cf. Sanhedrin* 99b: an *'alluf'* is an uncrowned ruler. Cf. *Ramban v.* 40. See also *comm.* to *Num.* 20:14].

16. אַלּוּף קֹרַח — *Chief Korach.*

Although Korach is originally listed in verse 5 as *Oholibamah's* son, he is listed here among the chiefs of *Eliphaz* since Korach was Eliphaz's illegitimate child through Oholibamah (*Rashi* to *v.* 5).

[In *v.* 18 Korach is listed again among the chiefs of Oholibamah. As noted in the *comm.* to verse 5, according to the *Midrash* there

14 *And these were the sons of Oholibamah,
daughter of Anah, daughter of Zibeon, Esau's wife:
She bore to Esau Jeush, Jalom, and Korach.*
15 *These are the chiefs of the children of Esau. The
descendants of Esau's firstborn Eliphaz: Chief
Teman, Chief Omar, Chief Zepho, Chief Kenaz.*
16 *Chief Korach, Chief Gatam, and Chief Amalek;
these are the chiefs of Eliphaz in the land of Edom —
These are the descendants of Adah.*
17 *And these are the descendants of Reuel, Esau's
son: Chief Nahath, Chief Zerah, Chief Shammah,
and Chief Mizah; these are the chiefs of Reuel in the
land of Edom. — These are the descendants of
Basemath, Esau's wife.*
18 *And these are the descendants of Oholibamah,
Esau's wife: Chief Jeush, Chief Jalam, and Chief
Korach. — These are the chiefs of Oholibamah,
daughter of Anah, Esau's wife.* 19 *These are the
children of Esau, and these are their chiefs; he is
Edom.*
20 *These are the sons of Seir, the Horites, who were*

was only one Korach; according to an opinion in *Sotah* 13a, there were indeed two Korachs.]

אַלּוּף עֲמָלֵק — *Chief Amalek.*

— [By his concubine Timna; see *v.* 12.]

17. The chiefs of Reuel; Basemath's descendants.

18. The chiefs of Oholibamah.

אַלּוּף קֹרַח — *Chief Korach.*

[See *comm.* to *v.* 16.]

19. אֵלֶּה בְנֵי עֵשָׂו וְאֵלֶּה אַלּוּפֵיהֶם הוּא אֱדוֹם — *These are the children of Esau, and these are their chiefs; he is Edom.*

— In this genealogy lay the roots of Edom, which evolved into Rome, the perpetual enemy of Israel (*Lekach Tov;* cf. *v.* 8).

20. The Seirite Genealogy.

(24) אֵלֶּה בְנֵי־שֵׂעִיר — *These are the sons of Seir.*

The word אֵלֶּה, *these,* is not preceded with a conjunctive ו, *and,* since the next part of the genealogy does not *add* to the preceding, but *contrasts* with it *(R' Hoffmann).*

We do not know Seir's ancestry. His genealogy is included in order to distinguish between his descendants and Esau's, for the Israelites would later be commanded concerning Esau's descendants [not to abhor them or take their land. Therefore it would be necessary to know the origins of the Seirite — Edomite families] *(Ibn Ezra;* see

הַחֹרִ֔י יֹשְׁבֵ֖י הָאָ֑רֶץ לוֹטָ֥ן וְשׁוֹבָ֖ל וְצִבְע֥וֹן
כא וַעֲנָֽה׃ וְדִשׁ֥וֹן וְאֵ֖צֶר וְדִישָׁ֑ן אֵ֣לֶּה אַלּוּפֵ֧י
כב הַחֹרִ֛י בְּנֵ֥י שֵׂעִ֖יר בְּאֶ֥רֶץ אֱדֽוֹם׃ וַיִּהְי֥וּ בְנֵֽי־
לוֹטָ֖ן חֹרִ֣י וְהֵימָ֑ם וַאֲח֥וֹת לוֹטָ֖ן תִּמְנָֽע׃

Rambam in *footnote* below).[1]

According to *Rashi* [*v.* 24], it would have been unnecessary to list the genealogy of the Horites had the Torah not wished to mention Timna, thereby demonstrating the esteem in which Abraham was held [as *Rashi* explains in *v.* 12].

The Seirites were an ancient, populous nation who were the original inhabitants of the land of Seir [see 14:16]. The children of Esau succeeded them and dwelt in their stead by a miraculous event, for in effect God gave it to Esau's descendants as a heritage, just as He gave the other portions of the land to Israel. [See *Deut.* 2:5; *Ramban* to *Deut.* 2:10; and also *comm.* above, end of *v.* 2].

הַחֹרִי — *The Horites.*

The word חֹרִי is familiarly translated *Horite,* by which name Seir's tribe was known. *Ibn Ezra,* citing its use as an adjective in *Jeremiah* 27:20, defines the word as signifying *nobility.* This is derived from the root חור as in *Isaiah* 19:9 where it means *white* — figuratively denoting nobility, in the same sense that black figuratively denotes soiled people, hence peasantry.

R' Hoffmann explains the derivation of חֹרִי to be from חוּר, *hole,* indicating that they were *cave-dwellers.* According to *Sefer HaYashar* the Horites were descendants of the Hivvites. [In this context cf. *Ramban* to *Deut.* 2:10 cited above, end of *v.* 2.]

The Sages in *Shabbos* 85a Aggadically interpret the word חֹרִי [*Horite*] — by rearranging the letters — to allude to the Horites' agricultural expertise: they could determine which were the best plants for a particular plot by merely *sniffing* [מְרִיחִין] the earth. The word חִוִּי [*Hivvite*] refers to their ability to *taste* the soil like a serpent [חִוְיָא] for the same purpose. [It is in this adjectival sense that Zibeon and Anah are referred to in *v.* 2 as 'Hivvites.' See *comm.* there.] Another view derives Horite from חוֹרִין, *free men,* denoting that they were 'freed' from their possessions [because Esau's descendants took it away from them.]

According to *Rambam,* however, 'Seir' in this context is not a name of a Horite, at all. Rather, it refers to the *land,* which was called the land of Seir. It was named after Esau, who was אִישׁ שָׂעִיר, [*Seir*] *a hairy man* [27:11]. Esau was referred to as Seir, and the land he conquered took his name from the time of his arrival. Even the native Horites then came to be identified as the people of Seir. The Torah, distinguishes between the *Horites* who lived in Seir and Esau's descendants who were the *Edomites* who lived in Seir [*vs.* 1-19].

1. *Rambam* writes in *Moreh Nevuchim* 3:50 that the Torah elaborates on Seir's genealogy because of one particular commandment. God commanded the Israelites to erase Amalek's name (*Deut.* 25:17-19), but the commandment applied to no other part of Esau's family. From the time Esau conquered the land of Seir, the Seirites were ruled by him, intermarried with his offspring; and eventually came to be given the name of Esau's strongest family — the Amalekites.

Had the families of Seir not been identified as *non*-Amalekites, they would have been killed along with Amalek. For this reason, the merciful Torah clarifies their genealogy and status. [See *Ramban* in *footnote* to *v.* 13 above.]

settled in the land: Lotan; Shobal; Zibeon; and Anah.
21 *Dishon; Etzer; and Dishan. — These are the chiefs of the Horites, the descendants of Seir in the land of Edom.*
22 *The sons of Lotan were: Chori and Hemam; Lotan's sister was Timna.*

According to *Ramban,* the phrase would be rendered: *This is the Horite lineage of the land Seir.*

יֹשְׁבֵי הָאָרֶץ — *Who were settled in* [or, *inhabitants of*] *the land.*

— Before Esau came there. The Rabbis [*Shabbos* 85b] interpret the term יוֹשְׁבֵי הָאָרֶץ, *inhabitants of the land,* to denote that they were expert in יְשׁוּבָהּ שֶׁל אֶרֶץ, *making the land habitable* [by skillful cultivation]. By just tasting the soil they could determine what crop should be planted in each area *(Rashi;* cf. *Shabbos* 85a cited above, s.v. הַחֹרִי).

The Torah mentions this to emphasize that God is the Master of the Land, and He bequeaths the earth to whomever He desires. The Seirites were *the original inhabitants of Seir,* and yet God caused them to surrender it to the descendants of Esau, for such was His will *(Radak).*

לוֹטָן וְשׁוֹבָל (25-26) וְצִבְעוֹן וַעֲנָה (3-4) — *Lotan* [*and*] *Shobal* [*and*] *Zibeon and Anah.*

[In *v.* 2 Zibeon and Anah are referred to as 'Hivvites.' See above, and *comm.* to *v.* 2 which also reconciles the Rabbinic view that Anah is identified with Beeri the *Hittite* in 26:34. See also *comm.* to *v.* 24 where Anah is listed among *Zibeon's sons.*]

21. וְדִשׁוֹן וְאֵצֶר וְדִישָׁן (27-29) — [*And*] *Dishon,* [*and*] *Etzer and Dishan.*

בְּאֶרֶץ אֱדוֹם — *In the land of Edom.*

I.e., in the land [of Seir] which would later be called the land of Edom. Midrashically, because of the redness of the soil, the land was named Edom [*red*] even then *(Haamek Davar).*

22. Lotan's sons.

חֹרִי וְהֵימָם (30-31) — *Chori and Hemam.*

וַאֲחוֹת לוֹטָן תִּמְנָע — *And Lotan's sister is Timna.*

— The concubine of Eliphaz, mentioned in *v.* 12. *Rashi* writes in *v.* 24 that this entire Horite genealogy was recorded only to emphasize that Timna was of noble birth [her brother was a chief]. This demonstrates the esteem in which Abraham's descendants were held in that rulers sought to ally themselves in marriage to his descendants; notwithstanding her noble status, she was satisfied to become merely a concubine of Esau's sons. [See *Sanhedrin* 99b cited in *v.* 12.][1]

In the *literal* sense, it is common

1. [This *Talmudic* explanation for the inclusion of this detail regarding Timna is noteworthy.]
The *Talmud* [ibid.] records that Manasseh son of King Hezekiah would take pleasure in blasphemously expounding on the Torah to mock it. He once, remarked: 'Did Moses have nothing more important to put into the Torah than that *Lotan's sister was Timna* and that *Timna was the concubine of Eliphaz?'* ... A heavenly voice replied: *'You sit and speak against your brother; you slander your mother's son!'* [*Psalms* 50:20]. The Sages proceeded to justify the inclusion of these facts by pointing out the esteem in which Abraham's grandson, Esau,

כג וְאֵ֛לֶּה בְּנֵ֥י שׁוֹבָ֖ל עַלְוָ֣ן וּמָנַ֑חַת וְעֵיבָ֖ל שְׁפ֥וֹ
כד וְאוֹנָֽם׃ וְאֵ֥לֶּה בְנֵֽי־צִבְע֖וֹן וְאַיָּ֣ה וַעֲנָ֑ה ה֣וּא
עֲנָ֗ה אֲשֶׁ֨ר מָצָ֤א אֶת־הַיֵּמִם֙ בַּמִּדְבָּ֔ר
בִּרְעֹת֥וֹ אֶת־הַחֲמֹרִ֖ים לְצִבְע֥וֹן אָבִֽיו׃

for the Torah to link daughters with their [eldest *(Rashbam)*] brothers. Comp.: *The sister of Tuval-Cain was Naamah* [4:22]; *sister of Laban* [25:20]; *sister of Nebayoth* [28:29]; *sister of Aaron* [*Exod.* 15:20]; *sister of Nachshon* [ibid. 6:23] *(Rashbam; Ibn Ezra; Radak; Ramban).*

[In each of the above cases, however, the commentators also perceive a deeper *exegetical* intent for the inclusion of such identifications in the Torah. See *comm.* to each case.]

In our case — as *Ramban* notes — Timna was identified as Lotan's sister rather than as Seir's daughter because in truth, although she was only Lotan's *maternal* sister, she was not Seir's daughter at all [but the illegitimate daughter of Seir's wife as explained in *v.* 12].

23. Shobal's sons.

עַלְוָן וּמָנַחַת וְעֵיבָל שְׁפוֹ וְאוֹנָם (32-36) — *Alvan,* [*and*] *Manachath,* [*and*] *Ebal, Shepho and Onam.*

24. Zibeon's sons.

וְאַיָּה (37) וַעֲנָה (3) — [*And*] *Ayah, and Anah.*

The Hebrew reads וְאַיָּה, *'and' Ayah. Rashi* comments that the ו in this case is superfluous and the phrase is equivalent to אַיָּה וַעֲנָה. Similar cases in Scripture where a ו occurs as a superfluous prefix are *Daniel* 8:13: (וְ)קֹדֶשׁ וְצָבָא [and] *holy and the host; Psalms* 86:7 (וְ)רֶכֶב וָסוּס [and] *rider and horse.*

Ramban concurs and adds other examples such as *II Sam.* 15:34 (וַ)אֲנִי [and] *I; I Chron.* 5:24: *And these were the heads of their father's houses:* (וְ)עֵפֶר וְיִשְׁעִי [and] *Epher and Ishi.*

[Some translators attempt to account for the superfluous ו in passages such as ours by rendering: *'both* Ayah and Anah', but this is apparently not *Rashi's* view.]

הוּא עֲנָה — *The same* [lit. *he is*] *Anah.*

— He is the Anah mentioned above in verse 20. There is an apparent contradiction between the two verses: there he appears as Zibeon's *brother* [the putative son of Seir], while here he is called Zibeon's *son!* This teaches that Zibeon committed incest with his own mother and fathered Anah [see *comm.* to *v.* 2 s.v. בַּת עֲנָה] *(Rashi).*

[According to this view, since Zibeon committed incest with his mother, the wife of Seir the Horite, the Torah lists

was held. They also record other lessons to be learned from the genealogies listed here, for nothing in the Torah is superfluous or unnecessary.

[See also *Rambam* cited in *footnote* to previous verse, who offers that by telling us that Timna was but a concubine the Torah thereby differentiates Timna's offspring — Amalek — from the rest of Edom's descendants.]

Furthermore, as *Rambam* writes in his introduction to *Chelek*, Fundamental §7: 'There is no difference between verses such as *And Timna was the concubine*, etc., ... *Lotan's sister was Timna,* and *I am* HASHEM *your God* or the *Shema:* ... All proceeded from the Almighty and all are God's perfect Torah — pure, holy and true.'

23 *These are the sons of Shobal: Alvan; Manachath; Ebal; Shepho; and Onam.*
24 *These are the sons of Zibeon: Ayah and Anah —
the same Anah who discovered the mules in the
desert while he was pasturing the sheep for Zibeon,
his father.*

him in *v.* 20 among Seir's (putative) sons. Since he grew up in Seir's house, among Seir's other children, people would refer to him as 'Anah son of Seir', and Seir himself also thought Anah was his son. The Torah proceeds to refer to him a second time, here, as *Zibeon's* son to reveal to us the true fact.]

Although the flow of the passage is: *The same Anah who discovered etc.*, nevertheless the literal phrase *he is Anah* implies that Anah was *previously described* elsewhere as the one who discovered the mules, etc. Yet we find no such reference any place else in Scripture. Therefore *Rashi* pursues his interpretation that the phrase means: *he was the Anah* — mentioned above in *v.* 20 as Zibeon's brother and — *who* [we are *now* told] *discovered the mules in the desert.* The phrase *he was the Ahasuerus* in *Esther* 1:1 similarly implies: *he was the Ahasuerus* — mentioned elsewhere as a great king *(Gur Aryeh).*

Ramban, however, maintains that in the literal sense, there were *two* Anahs. The Torah identifies *this* Anah as *the same one who discovered the mules,* in order to differentiate him from the Anah in *v.* 20 who was his uncle the brother of his father Zibeon. The Anah in our verse was Ishmael's father-in-law mentioned in *v.* 2. *Ramban* accordingly maintains that the opinion in *Pesachim* 54a [followed by *Rashi*] that there was only one [illegitimate] Anah, is an Aggadic interpretation which does not reflect the *plain* meaning of Scripture.

[However, see *Mizrachi* cited in *v.* 1 who encourages such derogatory interpretations of this genealogical table. Cf. *Haamek Davar.*]

...אֲשֶׁר מָצָא אֶת הַיֵּמִם בַּמִּדְבָּר — *Who discovered* [lit. *found*] *the mules in the desert while he was pasturing the sheep for Zibeon, his father.*

— I.e., he crossbred a donkey and a female horse and the result was a mule. Being himself born of an illegitimate union [between Zibeon and Zibeon's mother], he introduced a 'tainted' animal [i.e. born of a heterogeneous breeding] into the world [thus intimating that 'evil begets evil'] *(Rashi; Midrash; Pesachim* 54a).

The idea is that Anah was the first to discover that a donkey and a mare could be crossbred though they were dissimilar [heterogeneous]. Anah made this discovery while he was pasturing his father's donkeys in the desert. Many of the donkeys were in heat, seeking females. He mated them with female horses, and they bore mules. This discovery was considered so wise by his contemporaries that Anah came to be famous because of it. The Torah therefore so described him *(Ramban).*

Another view in the *Midrash* suggests that he mated a *male horse* with a *female donkey.*

According to an alternative Talmudic opinion [*Pesachim* 54a], mules already existed at the time of Adam when a kind of Divine instinct entered into Adam and he mated two heterogeneous animals. The implication is that this art was forgotten. Though *wild* mules existed, and were often domesticated, no one knew how to *breed* them until Anah made this discovery *(Emek Yehoshua).*

The above also answers the implication in *Rashi* 26:13 that mules already existed in the time of Isaac.

Such crossbred offspring remain

כה וְאֵלֶּה בְנֵי־עֲנָה דִּשֹׁן וְאָהֳלִיבָמָה בַּת־
כו עֲנָה: וְאֵלֶּה בְּנֵי דִישָׁן חֶמְדָּן וְאֶשְׁבָּן וְיִתְרָן
כז וּכְרָן: אֵלֶּה בְּנֵי־אֵצֶר בִּלְהָן וְזַעֲוָן וַעֲקָן:
כח-כט אֵלֶּה בְנֵי־דִישָׁן עוּץ וַאֲרָן: אֵלֶּה אַלּוּפֵי
הַחֹרִי אַלּוּף לוֹטָן אַלּוּף שׁוֹבָל אַלּוּף
ל צִבְעוֹן אַלּוּף עֲנָה: אַלּוּף דִּשֹׁן אַלּוּף אֵצֶר
אַלּוּף דִּישָׁן אֵלֶּה אַלּוּפֵי הַחֹרִי לְאַלֻּפֵיהֶם
בְּאֶרֶץ שֵׂעִיר:

sterile, however, since God is not pleased with this effort. They can only be produced by crossbreeding a horse and a donkey. Also, crossbred animals were not included in the blessing of פְּרוּ וּרְבוּ, *be fruitful and multiply* pronounced on those who left the Ark; they therefore are incapable of bearing young *(Chizkuni)*. [See also *Rambam, Hilchos Melachim* 10:6.]

Ramban proceeds to note that *Onkelos* translates יֵמִים as [*mighty*] *men*. He explains that once, when Anah was pasturing his father's donkeys in the desert, he was attacked by marauders from a giant-like nation called Eimim [see *Deut.* 2:10] who wanted to steal his father's donkeys. But Anah overcame them single-handedly. Accordingly, the word מָצָא [*found*] in this verse would have the sense of *overtake*, as in *Psalms* 21:9; *II Sam.* 38. Or, it means *found* in the usual sense and refers to how *he came upon these warriors in the desert* ... and nevertheless, was saved. He later became famous for his prowess.

Thus, *Yemim* would be synonymous with *Eimim*, the א and י being interchangeable letters as in *Isaiah* 61:6 where תִּתְאַמָּרוּ=תִּתְיַמָּרוּ *(R'Bachya)*.

The reason mules are called יֵמִים [phonetically associated with אֵמִים, *dreaded ones*], is because of the dread associated with the fear of injury of a white mule, the wound from which is incurable *(Rashi* from *Chullin* 7b).

25. Anah's children.

דִּשֹׁן (38) וְאָהֳלִיבָמָה (2) בַּת־עֲנָה — *Dishon and Oholibamah daughter of Anah.*

The same Anah mentioned above *Ramban* who maintains that there were two Anahs *(Haamek Davar).*

26. Dishon's sons.

וְאֵלֶּה בְּנֵי דִישָׁן — [*And*] *these are the sons of Dishan* [i.e., *Dishon*].

Dishan is identical with *Dishon* (27) *Seir's fifth son mentioned in v.* 21. Both spellings are interchangeable; it is of no consequence how the name is spelled, except when they both appear in one verse and a distinction between the two is necessary. That the Torah spells his name *Dishan* here is to differentiate him from *Dishon son of Anah* (38) mentioned in *v.* 25, for it would have otherwise appeared that the latter's children are being listed here, which is not the case *(Ramban).*

[*Ramban's* interpretation is supported by the parallel genealogy in *I Chron.* 1:41 where the father of these sons is given as *Dishon*.]

25 *These are the sons of Anah: Dishon and
Oholibamah, daughter of Anah.*
26 *These are the sons of Dishan: Chemdan;
Eshban; Yisran; and Keran.*
27 *These are the sons of Etzer: Bilhan; Zaavan; and
Akan.*
28 *These are the sons of Dishan: Utz and Aran.*
29 *These are the chiefs of the Horites: Chief Lotan;
Chief Shobal; Chief Zibeon; Chief Anah;* 30 *Chief
Dishon; Chief Etzer; and Chief Dishan. — These are
the chiefs of the Horites, chief by chief, in the land of
Seir.*

חֶמְדָּן וְאֶשְׁבָּן וְיִתְרָן וּכְרָן (39-42) — *Chemdan, [and] Eshban, [and] Yisran and Keran.*

[Incidentally, in the parallel genealogy in *I Chron.* 1:41, חֶמְדָּן, *Chemdan,* appears as חַמְרָן, *Chamran.* In the literal sense, the letters ד and ר are interchangeable. Cf. *Reuel* and *Deuel* in *Numb.* 1:14-2:14. *Rashi* in *I Chronicles* ibid. offers a Midrashic interpretation that originally they were חֲמוּדִים וְנֶחֱמָדִים, *beloved and desireable,* like righteous people, but ultimately they became ugly like חֲמוֹרִים, *donkeys.*]

27. Etzer's sons.

בִּלְהָן וְזַעֲוָן וַעֲקָן (43-45) — *Bilhan, Zaavan and Akan.*

28. Dishan's sons.

עוּץ וַאֲרָן (46-47) — *Utz and Aran.*

29. The Horite Chiefs.

אֵלֶּה אַלּוּפֵי הַחֹרִי לְאַלֻּפֵיהֶם בְּאֶרֶץ שֵׂעִיר — *These are the chiefs of the Horites, chief by chief* [lit. *to their chiefs*] *in the land of Seir.*

The apparently superfluous listing of the Horite chiefs is given by the Torah in order to show that God conferred great honor upon Isaac. Even to Esau, God gave a heritage that had been the choice of great and powerful chiefs *(Radak).*

31. The Edomite Kings.

The following illustrates the fulfillment of Isaac's blessing to Esau: *by your sword you shall live* [27:40]. Esau's descendants were victorious over the descendants of Seir the Horite and even established their own kings in the Horite land ... At the same time, however, from the genealogies of the Edomite kings and the fact that various cities of origin are listed, we see that the Edomite crown did not go from father to son as was the case later with the Israelite crown *(Ramban).*

[However, see the alternate view in 35:11 where it is noted that the blessing to Jacob *kings shall descend from you* intimates that men fit to be kings will descend from Jacob; Israel will not require strangers to become her kings nor does Torah law permit them to designate a stranger to reign over them (see *Deut.* 17:15). By contrast, the monarchy of Edom *depended* on foreigners. It was *elective* or dependent upon a particular individual to acquire supremacy over the rest.]

Rambam, in *Moreh Nevuchim* 3:50

לא וְאֵ֗לֶּה הַמְּלָכִ֔ים אֲשֶׁ֥ר מָלְכ֖וּ בְּאֶ֣רֶץ אֱד֑וֹם
לב לִפְנֵ֥י מְלָךְ־מֶ֖לֶךְ לִבְנֵ֥י יִשְׂרָאֵֽל׃ וַיִּמְלֹ֣ךְ
בֶּֽאֱד֔וֹם בֶּ֖לַע בֶּן־בְּע֑וֹר וְשֵׁ֥ם עִיר֖וֹ דִּנְהָֽבָה׃

maintains accordingly, that this listing of Edomite kings was recorded in the Torah as a reminder, in a sense, to Israel that they strictly adhere to the *mitzvah* of choosing only an Israelite as their monarch. It is as if they were being told to take warning from their brothers the descendants of Esau, whose kings were all foreigners; for never has a foreigner reigned over a nation without exercising a more or less tyrannical rule.

וְאֵלֶּה הַמְּלָכִים אֲשֶׁר מָלְכוּ בְּאֶרֶץ אֱדוֹם לִפְנֵי מְלָךְ מֶלֶךְ לִבְנֵי יִשְׂרָאֵל — *Now* [lit. *and*] *these are the kings who reigned in the land of Edom, before a king reigned over* [lit. *to*] *the children of Israel.*

The chapter goes on to list eight Edomite kings who reigned before the first Jewish king. The commentators offer two acceptable interpretations of the period under discussion, both of which are cited by *Ibn Ezra*: The eight Edomite kings reigned up to the time of Moses, in which case, this passage is a historical rendering of events that occurred before the Torah was given. The second view is that the passage is prophetic. It gives the names of eight Edomite kings who were destined to reign in *future* years, prior to Saul, the first Jewish king. In addition, *Ibn Ezra* cites and dismisses a blasphemous interpretation that was given currency in his time.

Ibn Ezra gives the view that the first Jewish king referred to by our verse is Moses, who is described in *Deuteronomy* 33:5 as 'king' of Israel [see *Ibn Ezra* there]. Most commentators follow this interpretation. It is based on the principle that Moses, as the savior and leader of Israel, had the status of a king. Thus, the verse states that Edom had eight kings before the time of *Moses* when the Torah was committed to writing.[1]

Others subscribe to the view that this verse was a prophetic prognostication of Israel's later kingship which would begin with Saul and David.

Rashi apparently adopts to this view, for he comments — following the *Midrash* — that just as our chapter lists eight Edomite kings, so eight of Jacob's descendants emerged to suppress the Edomite monarchy. The eight Jewish kings were: Saul, his son Ish-bosheth, David, his son Solomon, his son Rehoboam, his son Abijah, his son Asa, and his son Jehoshaphat. Concerning Saul's time, it was written [*ibid.* 22:48]: *There was no king in Edom; a deputy* [appointed by the Jewish monarchs] *was king.* However, in the reign of Joram, Jehoshaphat's son, Edom rebelled, regained its independence, and crowned a new king over itself [*II Kings* 8:20].

Before Jacob and Esau were born, the prophecy was given that

1. Esau's destiny developed rapidly in accordance with the natural effects of the 'power of the sword'. While Jacob's descendants were still enslaved and leaderless in Egypt, Edom had already developed into a state with a line of royal dynasties. Joshua refers to this contrast (*Josh.* 24:4): *I gave Esau Mount Seir to possess it; but Jacob and his children went down to Egypt (R' Hirsch).*

[31] Now these are the kings who reigned in the land of Edom before a king reigned over the children of Israel: [32] Bela, son of Beor, reigned in Edom, and the name of his city was Dinhabah.

[25:23]: לְאֹם מִלְאֹם יֶאֱמָץ, *The might shall pass from one regime to the other*, meaning that the two of them would never be mighty simultaneously. The *Midrashim* and commentators emphasize accordingly, that Edom's kings ceased to reign when Israel's monarchy was on the ascendancy.

Ibn Ezra quotes the false interpretation of *Yitzchaki* [the Spanish exegete Yitzchak ben Yashush] who maintained that this chapter was added to the Torah after the reign of Yehoshafat, when the names of the Edomite kings were known. But this interpretation is clearly unacceptable [since it is based on the blasphemous idea that our Torah was as yet incomplete ח"ו in Moses' time] *(Yohel Or)*. 'Furthermore, *Yitzchaki* is wrong also on historical grounds. Whoever hears him will laugh at him [a play on *Yitzchaki's* name יִצְחָק, *he will laugh*]. God forbid even to suggest such an approach! For expressing such an opinion, his book should be burned!' [*Ibn Ezra*].

That Esau's descendants produced eight kings before Israel had even one is viewed in the *Midrash* as Jacob's punishment for having abased himself eight times in chapter 32 by calling Esau 'my lord' (*Baal HaTurim*; see comm. to 32:5 s.v. עַבְדְּךָ יַעֲקֹב).

The phrase does not necessarily imply that the Edomite monarchy existed until the kingdom of Israel was established. The last of these Edomite kings probably died before the Torah was given. [This explains how Moses was able to list the names of these kings. Apparently the Torah would not have listed the name of kings who were not yet born since the Torah does not interfere this way with the natural order (*Ramban* end of *v.* 40).] Furthermore, they were old when they were crowned and did not live long *(Ramban)*.

Rashbam adds that according to genealogical accounts in *Josephus* there were more than *forty* Edomite kings from Esau until David's time. [This confirms the interpretation that the *eight* kings listed here lived before Moses' time.]

32. בֶּלַע בֶּן־בְּעוֹר — *Bela, son of Beor.*

According to *Targum Yonasan*, this was Balaam son of Beor. *Ibn Ezra* disagrees, pointing out that Balaam was an Aramean [see *Numbers* 23:7], while it is apparent from our context that Bela was an Edomite. [Apparently, *Targum Yonasan* follows the opinion echoed in *Shemos Rabbah* 37:1 (see *footnote* below) that the Edomites chose foreigners as kings. Therefore, Bela was not necessarily an Edomite and could be identified with Balaam.]

Furthermore, the identification of Bela with Balaam would intimate that Balaam, who was alive in the days of Moses, enjoyed great longevity. Indeed, there is a Talmudic view [*Sotah* 11a], that Balaam was among the three who participated in Pharaoh's deliberations leading to the enslavement of the Jews *(R' David Feinstein)*.

וְשֵׁם עִירוֹ דִּנְהָבָה — *And the name of his city was Dinhabah.*

— Dinhabah was his native city *(Rashi)*. According to *Ramban*, these places were all Edomite cities [and all these kings were Edomite], but as the names indicate, the

לג וַיָּ֖מָת בָּ֑לַע וַיִּמְלֹ֣ךְ תַּחְתָּ֔יו יוֹבָ֥ב בֶּן־זֶ֖רַח
לד מִבָּצְרָֽה׃ וַיָּ֖מָת יוֹבָ֑ב וַיִּמְלֹ֣ךְ תַּחְתָּ֔יו חֻשָׁ֖ם
לה מֵאֶ֥רֶץ הַתֵּֽימָנִֽי׃ וַיָּ֖מָת חֻשָׁ֑ם וַיִּמְלֹ֨ךְ
תַּחְתָּ֜יו הֲדַ֣ד בֶּן־בְּדַ֗ד הַמַּכֶּ֤ה אֶת־מִדְיָן֙
לו בִּשְׂדֵ֣ה מוֹאָ֔ב וְשֵׁ֥ם עִיר֖וֹ עֲוִֽית׃ וַיָּ֖מָת הֲדָ֑ד
לז וַיִּמְלֹ֣ךְ תַּחְתָּ֔יו שַׂמְלָ֖ה מִמַּשְׂרֵקָֽה׃ וַיָּ֖מָת
שַׂמְלָ֑ה וַיִּמְלֹ֣ךְ תַּחְתָּ֔יו שָׁא֖וּל מֵרְחֹב֥וֹת
לח הַנָּהָֽר׃ וַיָּ֖מָת שָׁא֑וּל וַיִּמְלֹ֣ךְ תַּחְתָּ֔יו בַּ֥עַל
לט חָנָ֖ן בֶּן־עַכְבּֽוֹר׃ וַיָּ֗מָת בַּ֣עַל חָנָן֮ בֶּן־עַכְבּוֹר֒
וַיִּמְלֹ֤ךְ תַּחְתָּיו֙ הֲדַ֔ר וְשֵׁ֥ם עִיר֖וֹ פָּ֑עוּ וְשֵׁ֣ם
אִשְׁתּ֞וֹ מְהֵֽיטַבְאֵ֛ל בַּת־מַטְרֵ֔ד בַּ֖ת מֵ֥י זָהָֽב׃

Edomite crown did not pass from father to son.

33. וַיָּמָת בָּלַע — *And Bela died.*

[That all these kings are recorded as having *died* would tend to intimate that they died a natural death, and that the succession of kings was orderly and not the result of assassination.]

מִבָּצְרָה — *From Bozrah.*

According to *Rashi* following *Pesikta,* Bozrah was a Moabite city [cf. *Jeremiah* 43:24]. For producing a king of Edom it was destined to be punished along with that land [cf. *Isaiah* 34:6].

Ramban, consistent with his view, interprets that same verse in *Isaiah* 34:6 to denote that Bozrah itself was an *Edomite* city as were all the places mentioned here.

34. הַתֵּימָנִי — *The Temanites.*

Ramban citing *Obadiah* 1:9: *And your mighty men of Teman shall be dismayed that every one may be cut off from the Mount of Seir,* maintains that Teman was an Edomite [it was called *Teman (=south) since Mount Seir lay to the south*[*=west*] *of Eretz Yisrael (Radak* ad.loc.).]

Onkelos renders: מֵאַרְעָא דָרוֹמָא, *from the land of the south.*

Rashi is silent on our verse. However, from his comm. to *Obadiah* ibid. it is clear that he holds Teman was an *Ishmaelite* location. He interprets that verse to imply that out of fear of being massacred in Mount Seir, the mighty men of that region will attempt to flee to Teman, an Ishmaelite region, free from Edomite terror.

[Many identify *Teman* with the modern Yemen.]

35. הַמַּכֶּה אֶת־מִדְיָן בִּשְׂדֵה מוֹאָב — *Who defeated* [lit. *strikes*] *the Midianites* [lit. *Midian*] *in the field of Moab.*

This describes Hadad's military prowess *(Ramban)* ...

When Midian attacked Moab, this Edomite king came to Moab's aid and defeated Midian. From this we learn that Midian and Moab were enemies, but in the time of

36
33-39

[33] *And Bela died, and Jobab son of Zerah, from*
Bozrah, succeeded him as king. [34] *And Jobab died*
and Husham, of the land of the Temanites, succeeded
him as king. [35] *And Husham died, and Hadad son of*
Bedad, who defeated the Midianites in the field of
Moab, succeeded him as king, and the name of his
city was Avith. [36] *And Hadad died, and Samlah of*
Masrekah succeeded him as king. [37] *Samlah died, and*
Saul of Rechovos Nahar succeeded him as king.
[38] *And Saul died, and Baal Hanan, son of Achbor,*
succeeded him as king. [39] *Baal Hanan, son of Achbor,*
died, and Hadar succeeded him as king. The name of
his city was Pau and his wife's name was Mehetabel,
daughter of Matred, daughter of Me-zahab.

Balaam they made peace in order to combine against Israel *(Rashi).*

[See *Rashi* to *Numb.* 22:4.]

37. מֵרְחֹבוֹת־הַנָּהָר — *Of* [lit. *from*] *Rechovos Nahar* [lit. *Rechovos the river*].

From Rechovos on the Euphrates River *(Targum)* [as distinct from the Rechovos associated with Isaac 26:22].

38. בַּעַל חָנָן — *Baal Hanan.*

His place of origin is not mentioned. Either he came from the same place as his predecessor, Saul of Rechovos Nahar, or possibly he came from a place called Chanan, and as his name signifies he had been בַּעַל חָנָן, *the master of Chanan;* subsequently he became king *(Ramban).*

39. הֲדַר — *Hadar.*

In *I Chron.* 1:50 he is called Hadad, the ר and ד being interchangeable as noted above regarding *Chemran — Chemdan* in *v.* 26.

וְשֵׁם אִשְׁתּוֹ מְהֵיטַבְאֵל — *And his wife's name was Mehetabel.*

'We do not know why in this case the wife is mentioned' *(Radak).*

— His wife is mentioned for it was due to her that he became a chief, inasmuch as she was the daughter of illustrious and wealthy parents [see below on *Me-zahab*] *(Baal HaTurim).*

[*Radak* apparently does not pursue this exegesis because, in following the literal sense, he does not interpret the name *Mezahab* as signifying that he was wealthy.]

בַּת מַטְרֵד בַּת מֵי־זָהָב — *Daughter of Matred daughter of Me-zahab.*

This phraseology is similar to [*v.* 2] *daughter of Anah, daughter of Zibeon* [where the Sages interpret that the mention of two fathers suggests that the child was born of an adulterous relationship. Hence the Torah lists two 'fathers' — the putative father in whose home the child was raised, and the individual whom the Torah identifies as the biological father]. Or [since in our verse] the Torah might be naming both her father and mother [unlike the case of *v.* 2 where from parallel

מ °וְאֵ֗לֶּה שְׁמוֹת֙ אַלּוּפֵ֣י עֵשָׂ֔ו לְמִשְׁפְּחֹתָ֔ם
°מפטיר לִמְקֹמֹתָ֖ם בִּשְׁמֹתָ֑ם אַלּ֥וּף תִּמְנָ֛ע אַלּ֥וּף
מא עַלְוָ֖ה אַלּ֥וּף יְתֵֽת׃ אַלּ֧וּף אָהֳלִֽיבָמָ֛ה אַלּ֥וּף
מב אֵלָ֖ה אַלּ֥וּף פִּינֹֽן׃ אַלּ֥וּף קְנַ֛ז אַלּ֥וּף תֵּימָ֖ן
מג אַלּ֥וּף מִבְצָֽר׃ אַלּ֣וּף מַגְדִּיאֵ֔ל אַלּ֖וּף עִירָ֑ם

genealogies, we know both names were those of *men*] (*Ibn Ezra*).

Radak agrees with the latter, but writes that it is not known why the names of both parents should be mentioned only in this case.

Possibly, Matred was the name of her *mother*, who in turn was the daughter of a woman named Me-zahab. Or Matred was her *father* who died young, and another man named Me-zahab raised her. Perhaps Scripture is noting that Mehetabal was Matred's daughter, and, therefore, was also the descendant ['daughter'] of the renowned personage Me-zahab (*Ralbag*).

Rashi explains the name Me-zahab to mean: מַהוּ זָהָב, *what is gold?* — He was so wealthy that gold had no value to him.

— Matred was originally a pauper who became so wealthy that he would go about boasting: 'What is gold, what is silver?' — it had no value to him (*Targum Yonasan*).

— He was so wealthy that gold flowed in his house like water [מֵי זָהָב may be rendered literally as *waters of gold*] (*Abarbanel*).

According to *Onkelos*, the name denotes that he was a *goldsmith*.

Rashbam remarks that in pursuing the literal sense, he does not attach much importance to names. [Cf. *Radak* above.]

However, as the *Zohar* declares: 'The ways of the Torah are the ways of HASHEM, and the slightest word within it leaves its mark in the supernal spheres of higher wisdom. Thus each word, each incident, each name in the Torah contains profound mysteries and should be expounded.'

40-41. The chiefs following the Edomite monarchy.

וְאֵלֶּה שְׁמוֹת אַלּוּפֵי עֵשָׂו לְמִשְׁפְּחֹתָם לִמְקֹמֹתָם בִּשְׁמֹתָם — *Now* [lit. *and*] *these are the names of the chiefs of Esau, by their families, by their regions, by their names.*

The phrase *by their regions by their names* indicates a change in the manner of naming the chiefs. The earlier group of kings [*v.* 15ff] used their own names. After Hadad's death and the end of the Edomite monarchy, the kingship ceased and the ensuing leaders were known as 'chieftains' of their respective regions. This new procedure is evident from *I Chronicles* 1:52: *And Hadad (=Hadar) died and the chiefs of Edom were: The chief of Timna, etc. (Rashi).*

Ramban asserts that in earlier times all the Edomite brothers ruled simultaneously as a group. Those who are named from verse 40 onward ruled as individual chieftains *by their families, by their regions;* during each respective reign, each had absolute sovereignty over *all* the clans and regions. In effect they were kings, but were not formally known as such.

Some of those listed here were mentioned in the earlier list of

36
40-43

[40] *Now these are the names of the chiefs of Esau,*
by their families, by their regions, by their names:
The chief of Timna; the chief of Alvah; the chief of
Jetheth. [41] *the chief of Oholibamah; the chief of Elah;*
the chief of Pinon; [42] *the chief of Kenaz; the chief of*
Teman; the chief of Mivtzar; [43] *the chief of Magdiel*
and the chief of Iram.

chiefs [*v.* 15ff]. In time, apparently, *they* became the primary chiefs of the regions, for only they — and not other members of the earlier group — are enumerated in *I Chron.* ibid. *(Rashbam).*

Ibn Ezra maintains that these were the actual names of the chiefs. He explains that the chiefs enumerated here were the *offspring* of the chiefs enumerated above.

Only those famous personages who ruled in a particular region identifiable in Moses' days are mentioned here *(Ralbag).*

אַלּוּף תִּמְנָע ... אַלּוּף אָהֳלִיבָמָה — *The chief of Timna ... the chief of Oholibamah.*

[The translation *'chief* of *Timna'* rather than *'Chief Timna'* follows the implication of *Rashi* above where he explains that unlike the listing of chiefs in *v.* 15ff, the following are not personal appellations. Rather, after the dissolution of the monarchy following Hadad's death, the chiefs were referred to by their regions. (Apparently, some of these regions took their names from earlier chieftains who ruled there, or from the matriarchs of the Edomite nation such as Timna and Oholibamah). Accordingly, our passage refers to the *chief of the region known as Timna,* etc.]

According to *Ibn Ezra* who holds that these are the actual names of the chiefs, this Timna and Oholibamah are *men;* they are not the *women* of those names mentioned in verses 12 and 2. Or, they may refer respectively to Eliphaz's concubine and Esau's wife Oholibamah, mentioned above, the intent being: *the chiefs of Timna,* i.e., the chiefs who descended from Timna Eliphaz's concubine, were: *Chief Alvah, Chief Yatheth,* who were Amalekite chiefs. Similarly in the case of Oholibamah, the chiefs of her clan were those seven enumerated in verses 41-43, contemporaries with Moses.

42. אַלּוּף תֵּימָן אַלּוּף מִבְצָר — *The chief of Teman, the chief of Mivtzar.*

43. מַגְדִּיאֵל — *Magdiel.*

According to *Rashi* following *Pirkei d'Rabbi Eliezer* and the *Midrash,* the place Magdiel [lit. *raised by God*] is to be identified with Rome. This is in line with the frequently expressed tradition of the Sages that Rome evolved from Esau.

Ramban differs with this identification maintaining that even if it is a prophetic prognostication of the future, this particular indentification of Magdiel as Rome is unclear, since Rome was not merely a *chieftaincy,* but the greatest empire that ever existed! Furthermore, Rome had many emperors; why should only Magdiel be mentioned? Rather, the reference in *Pirkei d'Rabbi Eliezer* to Magdiel being Rome

אֵ֣לֶּה ׀ אַלּוּפֵ֣י אֱד֗וֹם לְמֹֽשְׁבֹתָם֙ בְּאֶ֣רֶץ אֲחֻזָּתָ֔ם ה֥וּא עֵשָׂ֖ו אֲבִ֥י אֱדֽוֹם׃

is not meant as an identification of this particular chieftain, but as a symbolic allusion of the development of history, just as so much of the Book of Genesis depicts events in the lives of the parents that are portentious for future generations of their children. The ten latter Edomite chiefs — including Magdiel — intimate that there will be ten Edomite rulers during the Fourth Kingdom [i.e. the fourth great world power] who will in succession subjugate Israel until such time as Israel's final and complete deliverance will be effected by the Messiah. [The sovereignty of the Fourth Kingdom — Rome — still holds sway (see comm. to 28:12).]

The tenth of these rulers, Magdiel, ruled over Persia and as his name implies he will be raised above every power (מַגְדִּיאֵל=יִתְגַּדֵּל עַל כָּל אֵל, see *Daniel* 11:36) in that his influence will extend throughout the world. As the *Midrash* explains, his successor, *the chief of Iram,* was so called because he was destined to *heap up* [*l'arom*] treasures for the king Messiah — may he speedily reveal himself.

Gur Aryeh defends *Rashi's* identification of Magdiel as Rome against *Ramban's* objections. He notes that the Roman Empire at its zenith was certainly the world's greatest monarchy as *Ramban* claims, but it was not always to remain so, while its status as the tormentor of Israel until the coming of Messiah remains intact. Therefore, it is called a 'chieftain,' reflecting on its entire history. Furthermore, the name Magdiel was not intended to identify a single emperor; rather it is a generic term referring to all Roman rulers as 'he whom God made great.'

Others explain that the Rome was founded by the descendants of Magdiel.

אֵלֶּה אַלּוּפֵי אֱדוֹם לְמשְׁבֹתָם בְּאֶרֶץ אֲחֻזָּתָם — *These* [enumerated above] *are the chiefs of Edom by their settlements in the land of their possession.*

In its concluding comment to this *Sidrah,* the *Midrash* cites the following parable:

The wheat, the straw, and the stubble engaged in a controversy. The wheat said: 'For my sake has the field been sown'; and the stubble maintained: 'For my sake was the field sown.'

Said the wheat to them: 'When the time comes, you will see.'

When harvest time came, the farmer took the stubble and burnt it, scattered the straw, and piled up the wheat into a stack, which everyone kissed.

Similarly, Israel and the nations have a controversy, each asserting: 'For our sake was the world created.' Says Israel: 'The hour will come in the Messianic future and

36
43 These are the chiefs of Edom by their settlements,
in the land of their possession.— That is Esau, father
of Edom.

you will see how *You shall fan them, and the wind shall carry them away (Isa.* 41:16); but as for Israel — *And you shall rejoice in HASHEM you shall glory in the Holy One of Israel' (ibid.).*

הוּא עֵשָׂו אֲבִי אֱדוֹם — *That is Esau, father of Edom.*

— This is Esau [who remained] in his wickedness from beginning to end [he never repented *(Torah Temimah)*] *(Megillah* 11a).[1]

According to the Masoretic note appearing at the end of the *Sidrah* there are 154 verses in the *Sidrah* numerically corresponding to the mnemonic קְלִיטָ״ה [related to מִקְלָט, *refuge, asylum*]. This alludes to the theme of our *Sidrah* which, as expressed by *Ramban* in his introduction to 32:4, is to teach us how to survive in Exile among Esau's descendants. The *Haftorah* begins with *Obadiah* 1:1 חֲזוֹן עוֹבַדְיָה.

נשלם סדר וישלח
ונשלם כרך ד מספר בראשית בעזרת האל

Meir Zlotowitz
Rosh Chodesh Tammuz, 5739/July, 1979
Brooklyn, New York

1. Esau remained the mortal enemy of Jacob from the time his birthright changed hands for a bowl of lentils, and Esau earned the name Edom as a constant reminder of his greed and gluttony [25:30]. This hatred went down the generations to this very day. The closing words of our Sidrah proclaim to us that Edom — the kingdom that developed into Rome — remains *Esau.* No matter what its outer veneer, it still despises its brother Jacob. This is a constant in history that Esau despises his brother Jacob (cf. *Megillah* 11a).

But the response to this eternal hatred is found in the fourth verse of the *Haftarah.* The prophet *Obadiah* (1:4) predicted of Edom: *Though you make your nest as high as the eagle and set it among the stars, I will bring you down from there, says HASHEM.* They are our hope in the face of Esau/Edom/Rome's implacable hatred *(R' Munk).*

◈ סדר וישב

◈ Sidrah Vayeishev

— The Overviews

An Overview —
Joseph and His Brothers*

הָיָה רָאוּי יוֹסֵף לָצֵאת מִמֶּנּוּ שְׁנֵים עָשָׂר שְׁבָטִים כְּדֶרֶךְ שֶׁיָּצָא מִיַּעֲקֹב אָבִינוּ

Joseph was worthy that twelve tribes should emerge from him just as they emerged from our father Jacob.

דְמוּתוֹ דוֹמֶה לְשֶׁל אָבִיו

[*Joseph's*] *appearance was like his father's* (*Bereishis Rabbah* 84:7).

הָיָה יַעֲקֹב אָבִינוּ רָאוּי לֵירֵד לְמִצְרַיִם בְּשַׁלְשְׁלָאוֹת וּבְקוֹלָרִין. אָמַר הקב״ה בְּנִי בְכוֹרִי וַאֲנִי מוֹרִידוֹ בְבִזָּיוֹן ... אֶלָּא הֲרֵינִי מוֹשֵׁךְ אֶת בְּנוֹ לְפָנָיו וְהוּא יוֹרֵד אַחֲרָיו בְּעַל כָּרְחוֹ

Our father Jacob would have had to descend to Egypt in chains and a collar. Said the Holy One, Blessed be He, 'He is My firstborn son, shall I bring him down there in disgrace? ... Rather I will lead his son before him and he will be forced to descend after him' (*Bereishis Rabbah* 86:2).

To a child, the story is one of the most exciting and suspenseful in all of Scripture; to an adult it is one of the most perplexing and mystifying.

To a child, the story of Joseph and his brothers is one of the most exciting and suspenseful in all of Scripture; to an adult it is one of the most perplexing and mystifying. Why did Jacob favor Joseph over all his other sons? The child might accept the superficial explanation that the elderly father reserved his tenderest feeling for the youngster born in his old age — but the adult knows that "blatant favoritism" is inexcusable even on the part of *ordinary* parents, surely we cannot attribute such an elementary error to Jacob. Why did Joseph flaunt his dreams with their obvious implications that he would dominate his brothers? The child may wish that he too had something to hold over his brothers and sisters — but

* This Overview is based on the thesis of *Sh'loh HaKadosh* in his commentary on *Vayeishev*. Much of the material is drawn from there.

the adult expects more maturity from any seventeen-year-old, certainly from one great enough to be granted prophetic visions. How could the brothers have been so influenced by their jealousy as to consider the murder of their own flesh and blood, and finally to sell him into slavery — this is incomprehensible even to a child!

How could the brothers have been so influenced by their jealousy as to consider the murder of their own flesh and blood?

Clearly, this episode demands the insight of the Sages. And, indeed, the Sages and commentators have given us a wealth of perception and clarification; with it we can sketch outlines of the personalities and events that represent the transition between the family of the Patriarchs and the nation of Israel.

I. Joseph's Appearance

Jacob's Special Love

The very beginning of the narrative stresses the overriding importance of Joseph in the development of Jacob's family ... אֵלֶּה תֹּלְדוֹת יַעֲקֹב יוֹסֵף, *These are the offspring of Jacob — Joseph* ... (37:2). Jacob had twelve sons and a daughter, but in telling the experiences of his children, the Torah mentions only Joseph. Citing the Midrash, *Rashi* writes that Joseph is considered the foremost of Jacob's offspring, so much so that the others are secondary to him. *Rashi* gives three reasons:

Joseph is considered the foremost of Jacob's offspring, so much so that the others are secondary to him.

1) With all his being, Jacob worked for Laban *only* for the sake of marrying Rachel, Joseph's mother;

2) Joseph's features resembled Jacob's;

3) Whatever happened to Jacob, happened to Joseph: one was hated and the other was hated, one had a brother who tried to kill him and the other had brothers who tried to kill him. The Midrash cites a score of other similarities between Joseph and Jacob. The accumulation of them all demonstrates that Joseph, more than any of his brothers, was his father's heir.

Joseph was *the* offspring, *par excellence.* As such, it was natural and proper that he enjoyed the special attention of his father, just as God decreed that Isaac be Abraham's favored son and Jacob be Isaac's.

In the next verse, (37:3) the Torah tells us why Jacob loved Joseph so much

וְיִשְׂרָאֵל אָהַב אֶת־יוֹסֵף מִכָּל בָּנָיו כִּי־בֶן־זְקֻנִים הוּא לוֹ

Now Israel loved Joseph more than all his sons since he was a child of his old age.

Here, too, *Rashi* cites three reasons:

1) The simple meaning of the verse is that Jacob felt a special affection for the son who was born to him in his old age, after nearly all the others [see commentary to that verse];

2) *Onkelos* derives the word זְקֻנִים not from the word זָקֵן in the sense of *old man,* but from the word's other connotation of a *wise man.* Jacob loved Joseph because he was the outstanding scholar among the brothers;

Jacob loved Joseph because he was the outstanding scholar among the brothers.

3) The word זְקֻנִים is a contraction of זִיו אִיקוּנִים, *facial features;* because Joseph's features resembled his more closely than any of the others, Jacob loved him the most.

We *begin* the process of understanding, but these three reasons, taken superficially, still leave us far short of our goal.

Of all the reasons none seems stranger than this: Jacob loved the son whose features most closely resembled his own.

Of all the reasons given both for Joseph's primacy and for the special affection in which Jacob held him, none seems stranger than this: Jacob loved the son whose features most closely resembled his own. Can it be that among twelve sons only *one* looked like the father? And even if he did, can the judgment of a Jacob have been so warped that nothing weighed more heavily on his scales than the accident of eye color or nose length? No! Precisely because this reason as stated is so bizarre, logic forbids us to take it literally. Let us investigate this statement of our Sages, and when we understand it, we will be on the way to a comprehension of Joseph's unique position in Jacob's family.

Joseph's Face

It is true — there *was* something unique about Joseph's appearance, but it was not something that could be captured in a photograph.

R' Yitzchak Ze'ev Soloveitchik, the *Brisker Rav*, noted that Joseph's face had a uniqueness that only Jacob could discern. When Jacob was told, after twenty-two years of mourning, that Joseph was still alive, the Patriarch exclaimed: אֵלְכָה וְאֶרְאֶנּוּ בְּטֶרֶם אָמוּת, *I shall go and* **see** *him before I die* (45:28). When they finally met, Jacob said, אָמוּתָה הַפָּעַם אַחֲרֵי רְאוֹתִי אֶת־פָּנֶיךָ, *at this time I am ready to die after having* **seen** *your* **face** (46:30). And when Jacob lay near death, he told Joseph רְאֹה פָנֶיךָ לֹא פִלָּלְתִּי, *I dared not think I would* **see** *your* **face** (48:11). Three times Jacob emphasizes the need to *see* Joseph, and the Torah considers these statements important enough to quote. Clearly, there was something about Joseph's face that Jacob had to see, and having seen it he stated openly that he was content to die.

Joseph's face had a uniqueness that only Jacob could discern.

What was it about Joseph's face that meant so much to Jacob? Why could not his eleven other sons describe it to him, whatever it was? And why does Jacob imply that his life's purpose is fulfilled — that he is prepared to die — after having seen what he wanted in Joseph's 'face'?

Wise people know of a beauty that radiates from within. Character, goodness, integrity, and wisdom have their own way of stamping their inner beauty on a face that never had picture-book features. The Torah scholar and *tzaddik* have a beauty of a soul that pierces the limitations of its bodily host. Adam, God's Own handiwork, had that beauty when he was created; Jacob had it, too:

Character, goodness, integrity, and wisdom have their own way of stamping their inner beauty on a face that never had picture-book features.

שׁוּפְרֵיהּ דְיַעֲקֹב מֵעֵין שׁוּפְרֵיהּ דְאָדָם
Jacob's beauty resembled Adam's beauty (Bava Metzia 84a).

To a significant degree, Jacob's spiritual grandeur was even greater, because Adam's beauty was not earned; he had it by virtue of the fact of his creation by God's hand. But Jacob acquired his greatness by dint of his struggles at self-perfection. Adam's beauty was given; Jacob's was earned. In speaking of Jacob as the embodiment of the ideal human being — the sort of person because of whom God said, *Let us create man!* — the Sages teach that Jacob's image was engraved upon God's throne of glory [see *Bereishis Rabbah* 82:2 and *Chullin* 91b).

If Adam and Jacob could stand side by side, would an onlooker say they were twin brothers? Certainly not.

Is there an engraving on God's throne? Is God ח״ו a physical being Who sits on an ornate throne? If Adam and Jacob could stand side by side, would an onlooker say they were twin brothers? Certainly not. To speak of a human image as constantly before God is to express figuratively how high mortal man can rise; the 'resemblance to Adam' is a metaphor for the spiritual height climbed by Jacob.

The Resemblance Remains

In *this* sense Joseph resembled Jacob. Perhaps Joseph looked like his father; perhaps he was the image of his mother. Perhaps all eleven of his brothers looked more like Jacob. All that is immaterial. But if someone could look at Joseph and say, 'He has a beauty like that of the man whose essence is engraved in God's plan of creation' — then Joseph was truly a cut above his brothers, a son worthy of his father's attention.

That sort of beauty is not visible to everyone. Only a spiritual person can appreciate spiritual beauty. And the more attuned someone is to holiness, the more he can discern nuances and varying levels in holiness, just as experts in any field can identify differences in quality where laymen recognize nothing. As we shall see below in detail, Joseph's greatness made him the spiritual heir of his father and this eminence found outward expression in a facial beauty like Jacob's and Adam's. If the brothers' perception had not been clouded by their resentment of Joseph, they could have seen it. After he revealed himself in Egypt and made peace with them, they surely recognized that he was more than just brother number eleven, and they must have reported that back to Jacob. When they said that Joseph still 'lives,' they meant a *quality* of life far above animal functioning. That is all true, but only Jacob could perceive from Joseph's face how great he was, how much of his Adam-like beauty had remained.

Only Jacob could perceive from Joseph's face how great he was, how much of his Adam-like beauty had remained.

Jealousy? It was there, of course; the Torah tells us

so — although, as we shall see below, it was not the base, corroding, evil sort that one might infer from a casual reading of Scripture. Nevertheless, as we continue to gain a better perception of what Joseph represented, our question changes. Rather than ask why Jacob by his actions and Joseph by his words incited the jealousy and hatred of the brothers, we should ask why the brothers did not recognize that there was no more reason for them to feel ill toward Joseph than toward Jacob or Isaac. For in judging Jacob's family, we must put aside the notions which we impute to ordinary human beings. As we have seen in exploring the relationship of Jacob, Rachel, and Leah *(Overview* to *Vayeitzei)*, one who explains their story as a triangle tottering on envy, physical attraction, and deception tells more about himself than about them. Surely we would find it incomprehensible for one of the brothers to have declared himself more worthy than *Jacob*. They knew that Jacob was not only their father, but a Patriarch of Israel, and as such was the model for them to emulate. Similarly, if Joseph was truly the 'image of Jacob', they should have followed, not rejected, his lead. Let us first explore his role in the family and then explore their antipathy toward him.

If Joseph was truly the 'image of Jacob,' they should have followed, not rejected, his lead.

II. The Transition

Extension of Jacob

Though of a lesser stature than Abraham, Isaac and Jacob, Joseph was a 'patriarch' of the entire nation, rather than the forerunner of a single tribe.

Sh'loh HaKadosh explains that Joseph represented the transitionary stage between the concept of Patriarchs and that of nationhood. Though of a lesser stature than Abraham, Isaac and Jacob, Joseph was a 'patriarch' of the entire nation, rather than the forerunner of a single tribe. For this reason, only he could be the father of two tribes, Ephraim and Menasseh, who were granted equal status with Reuben, Simeon and all the others (48:5). Judah and Levi, too, had outstanding sons. From one would come monarchy and from the other priesthood, but Peretz, the ancestor of the Davidic dynasty, and Kehath, the ancestor of the *Kohanim*, are parts of their respective tribes of Judah and Levi; they are not separate tribes like Ephraim and Menasseh.

Joseph was an extension of Jacob in a more fundamental sense as well. Jacob's primary attribute is אֱמֶת, Truth.

Joseph was an extension of Jacob in a more fundamental sense as well. Jacob's primary attribute is אֱמֶת, *Truth*, or as it is also known, תִּפְאֶרֶת, *Splendor*. Both terms represent the concept of uniting all traits and talents in the proper measure so that the end product does justice to each and the whole becomes more effective — and truer — than any of its parts. For example, kindness is exemplary, but too much kindness can lead to a lack of discipline that can degenerate into self-indulgence, corruption, and debauchery. Strict justice, on the other hand, is exemplary, but carried to an extreme it can lead to harshness, callousness, and cruelty. Similarly, anger is a vice and forbearance is a virtue, but anger is a virtue when it must be directed against evil, and forbearance is a vice when it encourages the wicked. But the proper blend of kindness and strictness brings man to the ideal, it produces the 'splendor of truth.' When to shout and when to smile, when to suffer and when to enjoy, when to act and when to withdraw, finding the proper time and measure for each emotion and deed — this is the function of *Truth*, its proper exercise is *Splendor*. [These concepts are discussed at length in *'The Patriarchs,'* an Overview to *Lech-Lecha*.]

Joseph's Test

It is illustrative that Joseph, the symbol of peace, was the center of so much controversy. This should not surprise us.

The Zohar sums up Joseph's essence as בְּרִית שָׁלוֹם, *the covenant of peace*, for the ideal 'peace' is the proper harmonizing of all needs, interests, and desires so that all are fairly satisfied. It is illustrative that Joseph, the symbol of peace, was the center of so much controversy. If anything threatened to destroy the peace of Israel, it was the nearly fatal dispute between Joseph and his brothers and it was *he* who was accused of disrupting the harmony of the family. This should not surprise us. As we have seen in earlier Overviews, each Patriarch was tested with ordeals to which the proper response ran counter to his basic instinct. Abraham, the symbol of goodness, was faced with a series of challenges that called upon him to act harshly and alienate people whom he wanted to draw closer to God. For the kind Abraham to send Hagar and Ishmael into the desert or to bind Isaac on an altar was agonizing. Could he act harshly against his nature if that was God's will? Jacob, the symbol of truth, was forced into situation after situation where deception was required. Could he deal deceptively with Esau and Laban without his basic truthfulness being affected?

Could he suffer jealousy, hatred, accusation, assault, and loss of freedom at the hands of his brothers, yet remain the seeker of peace and harmony?

Joseph was the symbol of peace, so he was tested in predicaments involving strife and alienation. Could he suffer jealousy, hatred, accusation, assault, and loss of freedom at the hands of his brothers, yet remain the seeker of peace and harmony? Only through such excruciating tests can greatness be established.

Joseph is described as the *tzaddik* and his attribute is יְסוֹד, *Foundation.* To be truly 'righteous', one must assign each function its proper place, time, and degree. Wherever Joseph went, he won the trust of his master, whether it was Jacob, Potiphar, the head of his prison, or Pharaoh. Joseph mastered his drives and temptations as well (see below *Joseph's Test).* For this reason he was the *tzaddik* of his family and became the 'foundation' upon which Israel, and therefore the world, could be established. Therefore, Joseph represents the One Name of God, because his life revealed the harmony and balance in earthly terms that reflect the essence of God's perfection.

Coal and Flame

This intimate relationship between Jacob and Joseph is expressed in *Ovadiah* (1:18):

וְהָיָה בֵית יַעֲקֹב אֵשׁ וּבֵית יוֹסֵף לֶהָבָה וּבֵית עֵשָׂו לְקַשׁ

The family of Jacob will be a fire and the family of Joseph will be a flame; and the family of Esau will be like straw.

Jacob will be like a glowing coal, but a coal cannot consume unless a flame leaps from it.

Jacob will be like a glowing coal, but a coal cannot consume unless a flame leaps from it. The coal *is* fire, but it lacks the power to go further; the flame can destroy its enemies, but without the coal it cannot come into existence. Similarly, Jacob and Joseph are one of a piece, Jacob is the source and Joseph his continuation.

The word אֵשׁ, *fire,* has the initials of אֱמֶת and שָׁלוֹם, *truth* and *peace,* the attributes of Jacob and Joseph, while the word that represents Esau, קַשׁ, *straw,*has the initials of קִנְאָה and שִׂנְאָה, *jealousy* and *hatred,* the two traits of Esau, which are the opposites of truth and peace. For when one seeks truth there is no room for jealousy; if property, privilege or status *truly* belong to someone, honesty forbids anyone else to be jealous. Even if superior power or clever chicanery could enable an envious opponent to rob them, the usurper can be only occupier, never an owner, for they are not legitimately his. And obviously, peace and hatred are incompatible. Therefore, when Joseph was born, Jacob was ready to leave Laban's employ and, if necessary, to do battle with Esau; Jacob's truth combined with Joseph's peace were the spiritual armaments that could negate Esau's jealousy and hatred (see *Rashi* to 30:25).

Jacob's truth combined with Joseph's peace were the spiritual armaments that could negate Esau's jealousy and hatred.

It was an enduring tragedy of Jewish history that in misunderstanding Jacob's feelings toward Joseph and Joseph's feelings toward them, the brothers gave way to emotions that belonged to Esau, but that had no place in the family of Jacob: they felt hatred for Joseph (37:4) and they were jealous of him (37:11). When Israel assimilates Esau's characteristics it has been defeated, because the true arena of Israel's struggle with Esau is not the battlefield but the soul. After a spiritual defeat, physical subjugation becomes inevitable, though centuries may pass before it happens. Because the brothers felt toward Joseph as an Esau might; the result was that under the oppression of Edom — Rome, the descendants of Esau — ten of the Mishnah's great sages were chosen by Rome for barbaric execution in perverse 'punishment' for the sin of the ten brothers who were responsible for the sale of Joseph.

Because the brothers felt toward Joseph as an Esau might, ten of the Mishnah's great sages were chosen by Rome for barbaric execution.

Before going further, let us emphasize that Jacob's righteous children at their worst are not to be compared to Esau at his best; when we speak of them hating and envying we do so only in terms relative to their righteousness, as we do regarding all the base-sounding sins that Scripture records of the spiritual giants of the past (see *Overview* to *Ruth).*

Inheritance The process of inheritance has spiritual connotations in addition to its utility in law as a method of allocating property. Every person has his own mission on earth as does every family and every community. So that he can fulfill his individual role, a person is granted the necessary combination of talent, health, money, property, friends, relatives, country — everything that goes along with life in organized society. As a general rule, children, despite their independent existence, share in the mission of their parents and can be expected to carry it forward when the parents leave the scene. If they share the mission, it stands to reason that they share the tools to fulfill it. So children tend to resemble their parents in looks, lifespan, and intelligence. We call it the natural process of heredity, as indeed it is, but God created the genes and their function only as the means to bring about His desired goal, not vice-versa. We inherit our parent's traits because God wants us to; the genes are there only to give effect to His will. Similarly, if fulfillment of a mission of a family requires this amount of money and that many acres of property, then the estate should rightly go to the heirs whose duty it is to continue the tasks assigned their parents, brothers, or other relatives.

We call it the natural process of heredity, as indeed it is, but God created the genes and their function only as the means to bring about His desired goal.

Isn't it possible that children have a role unrelated or different from that of their parents? Of course. So wealthy heirs can lose their fortune and the children of paupers can become wealthy. The child of wise parents may be a fool and the child of ordinary people may be a genius. What we call aberrations may be God's premeditated way of preparing for the fulfillment of His will — and leaving it to man to carry out his assigned task.

The Torah tells us that Joseph was Jacob's heir, the flame emanating from his coal.

Seen in this perspective, Joseph's similarity to Jacob takes on new significance. The Torah tells us that Joseph was Jacob's heir, the flame emanating from his coal. Of course the other eleven tribes were

Jacob's heirs as well, but Joseph was his primary heir: *These are the offspring of Jacob — Joseph ...* (37:2). Three reasons for so understanding Joseph's status are given by *Rashi:*

Jacob worked for Laban with his entire being [שֶׁכָּל עַצְמוֹ שֶׁל יַעֲקֹב] for the sake of Rachel. As discussed at length in the Overview to *Vayeitzei,* the name 'Jacob' represents one aspect of Jacob's service, and the name 'Israel' another. In his role of Jacob, he was required to elevate the world of external beauty and physical demands, to recognize that what we call the 'real world' is a means of attaining the eternal world. In this stage of his service, Rachel was his helpmeet, and it was her whom he wanted to marry first.

In his role of Jacob, he was required to elevate the world of external beauty and physical demands.

Many commentators note that because Joseph had been deceived into thinking he had married Rachel, Joseph was the *intended* product of his first cohabition as a married man, and Jacob therefore regarded him as the firstborn, which he *would* have been if not for Laban's dishonesty. The comment is valid, but it goes deeper. Let us not think that Joseph's status was a product only of Jacob's ignorance. Had Jacob known that the woman with him was Leah, Joseph would *still* have been what he was, because the *Jacob*-mission could be successfully realized only by an offspring of Jacob and Rachel. *Rashi* chose his words carefully: the entire being of *Jacob,* not Israel, labored for Rachel, and our portion tells us that Jacob's essential offspring was Joseph.

Had Jacob known that the woman with him was Leah, Joseph would still have been what he was.

Rashi continues that Joseph resembled Jacob, and, as we have already seen, this resemblance was of a profound spiritual nature. Akin to this is *Onkelos'* rendering in the next verse that Joseph was the greatest Torah scholar of the family.

Finally, Jacob and Joseph shared similar experiences. Of twenty-three mentioned by the Midrash, *Rashi* cites the two that are probably most indicative of their common greatness: each was hated and each was the target of murderous intentions on the part of his brother(s). *Maharal (Gur Aryeh)* explains that Jacob and Joseph were both the victims of

We can understand why someone hates an enemy, but why should someone hate a person who means him no harm?

baseless hatred. We can understand why someone hates an enemy, but why should someone hate a person who means him no harm? — It is an unpleasant part of human nature that we can sometimes dislike a person who is obviously better than we are; he makes us look bad, he makes us suffer by comparison with him, he makes our desires look petty and our excuses seem foolish. Such a person, especially if he exercises his obligation to lead, becomes a nuisance, an enemy of the people. And he is hated. Of such hatred, both Jacob and Joseph were victims because each was a superior person. This was the common denominator of their lives *(Michtav MeEliyahu)*.

III. The Brothers' Hatred

A Usurper

Though we may understand the brothers' antipathy for Joseph, however, how are we to understand, much less justify, their treatment of him? Esau kills whomever he hates; that is what makes him Esau — but Jacob's sons?

[As noted above, our treatment of this major question follows the thesis of *Sh'loh*. Several other views are offered in the commentary.]

His task was to initiate the roles that would eventually be taken over by other tribes.

We return again to Joseph's special role as the transition between Patriarch and People. His task was to initiate the roles that would eventually be taken over by other tribes. Aside from the *mitzvos* and spiritual greatness that are common to all Jews, there are three special positions of leadership: monarchy is the province of Judah, priestly service belongs to the *Kohanim* of Levi, and the tribe of Yissachar traditionally produced the largest proportion of the great scholars. In all these areas, Joseph was the forerunner of his eventual successors.

As *Onkelos* teaches, Joseph was the premier scholar of the family. Was there jealousy of that? Perhaps, but Torah is the property of all, and none of the brothers could condemn him for excelling in an area where they were free to match him. In the area of priestly service, the future territory of Joseph would be chosen to introduce the concept that *Eretz Yisrael* would have a sanctuary as the central resting place of God's Presence. Before there was a Temple in Jerusalem, there was a permanent Tabernacle in Shiloh, in the land of Ephraim. But Joseph's offspring never replaced the *Kohanim* as the performers of the service, so that could not have been an issue between the brothers.

The crux of their dispute was the monarchy. The brothers knew that whenever a permanent kingship would be established in Israel, the dynasty would come from the tribe of Judah.

The crux of their dispute was the monarchy. The brothers knew that whenever a permanent kingship would be established in Israel, the dynasty would come from the tribe of Judah. This was not a mere accident of history; it was a requirement, and it was strictly forbidden to tamper with Judah's monarchial status. According to *Zohar,* the duty of a king to submerge his personal interests to the will of God was implicit in the name Leah gave Judah, יְהוּדָה, for it contains the Four-Letter Name of God [see Overview to *Ruth*].

In his commentary *Ramban* speaks movingly of the Hasmoneans, the great priestly family that led the battle against the Syrian-Greeks that resulted in the miracle of Chanukah: 'They were devout men of lofty stature, and if not for them the Torah and commandments would have been forgotten from Israel.' Nevertheless, the sons of Mattisyahu the Chashmonai died violent deaths and after several generations the entire family was assassinated without a survivor — because, *Ramban* maintains, by taking over the kingship and not returning it to the Davidic family to whom it belonged, they violated Jacob's final testament.

לֹא־יָסוּר שֵׁבֶט מִיהוּדָה וּמְחֹקֵק מִבֵּין רַגְלָיו
The scepter [*of monarchy*] *shall not depart from Judah nor scholars from among his descendants* (49:10).

All hold that an attempt to usurp the monarchy constitutes the ultimate attempt at מוֹרֵד בְּמַלְכוּת, *rebellion against the monarchy.*

Although not all commentators agree with *Ramban's* interpretation of the sin of the Hasmoneans, all hold that an attempt to usurp the monarchy constitutes the ultimate attempt at מוֹרֵד בְּמַלְכוּת, *rebellion against the monarchy,* a crime for which the king has the right to order the execution of the rebel *(Rambam, Hil. Melachim* 3:5). If it was true, as his dreams seemed to indicate, that Joseph truly wanted to become king over his brothers against their will (see *comm.* to 37:8), then he was a rebel against the monarchy of Judah and liable to the death penalty.

Let us not minimize the deliberations of the brothers. They were not engaged in a power struggle.

Let us not minimize the deliberations of the brothers. They were not engaged in a power struggle. They, too, knew that the Jewish nation was in its formative stage. They had seen how destructive to the nation Esau could have been. They had heard how destructive Ishmael could have been. It was a known fact in the Abrahamitic family that the first two generations of Patriarchs produced some offspring who were unworthy of inclusion in the family of Israel. Ishmael was ready to kill Isaac. Jacob was ready to defend himself to the death, if need be, against Esau's intended attack. In the perspective of those times, it should not strike us as outlandish if the brothers had to be alert to a threat against the integrity of the family. And a traitor within — if that was what Joseph was — is more dangerous than an enemy without. Yet Jacob considered Joseph his primary heir! Shouldn't the *Patriarch* know what was injurious to the Patriarchal ideal? True, but hadn't Isaac thought the same of Esau? *(R' Gedalya Schorr).*

Shouldn't the Patriarch know what was injurious to the Patriarchal ideal? True, but hadn't Isaac thought the same of Esau?

The brothers knew, however, that there had to be twelve tribes; if they did away with Joseph they would be destroying the integrity of the family, whatever his real or imagined shortcomings.This problem, too, had a resolution. As far as the brothers knew, it could have meant that Jacob could have another son in place of Joseph or that one of his grandsons — perhaps Peretz, the ancestor of monarchs, or Kehath, the ancestor of priests — would be elevated to the status of tribes (see 35:11 and *comm.*). Be that as it may, what would happen to the promised number of twelve tribes was not for the brothers to decide. They had a responsibility to deal with the immediate problem in consonance with the exigencies of the hour and in accord with the law of the Torah *(Be'er Moshe).*

They felt remorse over what they did to Joseph — but not over their judgment against him! *Nowhere do we find them regretting their legal judgment.*

Had Joseph truly been a usurper, they would have been right to treat him as they did. Let us note that during their ordeal before the Egyptian viceroy, they felt remorse over what they did to Joseph (42:21) — but *not over their judgment against him!* 'He begged us for pity and we ignored his pleas,' they said. Nowhere do we find them regretting their *legal* judgment against him. In fact, according to one Midrashic view cited by *Sh'loh*, when Joseph finally identified himself to his brothers, they converged on him to kill him then and there! God had to dispatch an angel to disperse them so that Joseph could explain himself. Throughout their travail before the viceroy, they made no effort to resist, but when they learned that he was Joseph and that he had indeed become tantamount to a king, they moved against him, because they were convinced they were carrying out the law of the Torah.

That explains how they could include even God in their ban against revealing to Jacob what they had done [see *Rashi*, 37:33]. Murderers and criminals can hardly invoke God's cooperation; they considered themselves neither.

Where They Erred

Where did they err?

He even tried to insinuate himself to power by including in his interpretation of Pharaoh's dream that the king should confer absolute power upon a 'wise and understanding man.'

In kingship, too, Joseph was to prepare the way for the future; that was his mission. He became viceroy of Egypt. He even tried to insinuate himself to power by including in his interpretation of Pharaoh's dream that the king should confer absolute power upon a 'wise and understanding man,' an obvious reference to himself. Pharaoh had not asked him for advice, by what right did he go beyond the interpretation of the dreams? He *had* to — since he knew it was his duty to reign, he seized the opportunity to gain power. His assigned task was to so dominate Egypt — the nation below and its heavenly angel above — that the way would be paved for Israel's later domination of Egypt at the time of the Exodus. His dealings with the hungry Egyptian people whom he subjugated economically and physically were in the manner of a prophecy that is reinforced by means of a tangible act, like Abraham's Covenant Between the Parts and the many prophecies in Scripture that were accompanied by symbolic acts. By rendering the Egyptians powerless and forcing them to surrender their wealth to Pharaoh, Joseph prepared the way for Egypt's later surrender to Israel.

Without doubt, kings of Israel must come from Judah, and Joseph knew that as well as his brothers. But without Joseph's ascendancy in Egypt there would have been no Exodus and no Davidic dynasty. In speaking of the Exodus, the Psalmist says הָיְתָה יְהוּדָה לְקָדְשׁוֹ, *Judah became His sanctuary* (*Psalms* 114:2). He does not single out Joseph, for the tribe of Joseph sought no dominance for itself; having performed its mission with the viceroyship of Joseph, it relinquished the scepter for eventual assumption by its rightful owner, Judah. Indeed, the leading tribe in the encampments in the Wilderness was Judah, and Judah led Israel in the conquest of *Eretz Yisrael*.

The tribe of Joseph sought no dominance for itself; having performed its mission with the viceroyship of Joseph, it relinquished the scepter.

In the future, too, it will be necessary for Joseph to lead in order to introduce the era of the Judean king.

In the future, too, it will be necessary for Joseph to lead in order to introduce the era of the Judean king. In Messianic times, the redemption will be inaugurated by a Messiah descended from Joseph. He will die and be succeeded by the Messiah from the house of David (*Succah* 52a). Then, too, Joseph will be the necessary transition to make possible the eventual reign of Judah.

The spiritual greatness of the brothers was such that they quite likely would have recognized in Joseph's desire for monarchy nothing but a sincere desire to clear the obstacles from Judah's way — if Joseph were to rule only in Egypt and in his inauguration of the Messianic era. But there would be another episode in the history of Israel.

Rehoboam, successor to King Solomon, was not in the tradition of his father and grandfather. To chastise him and help lead the family of David back to the spiritual heights of David, God designated

Jeroboam ben Nebat, a great warrior and *tzaddik*, to lead a competitive kingdom. Jeroboam, from the tribe of Joseph's son Ephraim, led a secession of ten tribes, but instead of remaining righteous and eventually reuniting with the kingdom of Jerusalem, Jeroboam was blinded by his new power and prestige. To prop up his throne and act as a counterweight to the Temple in Jerusalem, Jeroboam established idol worship in his kingdom. [See *I Kings* chap. 11-14.] Eventually, this idolatry infiltrated the kingdom of Judah. It resulted in the early dispersion and virtual disappearance of the Ten Tribes, and later, the inner corruption of Judah and the destruction of the Temple.

Joseph was pure, but in him was the seed of a Jeroboam and his successors who would seize kingship, hold it, and drag the nation down.

Joseph was pure, but in him was the seed of a Jeroboam and his successors who would seize kingship, hold it, and drag the nation down to destruction. When the brothers heard Joseph's dreams, they perceived in the dreamer the one who would reign until he dragged his people down to ruin — and they judged him as a usurper who would destroy the nation if he were permitted to live.

The Sages teach כָּל הַחוֹלֵק עַל מַלְכוּת בֵּית דָּוִד כְּחוֹלֵק עַל הַשְּׁכִינָה, *whoever disputes the dynasty of the House of David is like one who disputes the authority of God's Presence* (so it is cited by *Sh'loh*, but see *Sanhedrin* 110a). Because Joseph, as his brothers understood his intentions, rebelled against the authority of Judah, he was a rebel against the *Shechinah*. In judging him as they did, therefore, the brothers considered that they had the right to include God Himself, as it were, in their plot.

IV. Why the Brothers?

Predestined Event

So we find a rationale for what they did, and a powerful rationale it was. They were wrong, it is true, but let us not think that the events they set in motion should not have occurred, and took place *only* because of their mistake. That Joseph was taken to Egypt and that Jacob and his family followed, *had* to happen. The question was only how God would bring it about.

The place from which Jacob sent Joseph to visit his brothers is described in the Torah as עֵמֶק חֶבְרוֹן, *the valley of Hebron (37:14). But, Rashi* asks, Hebron is in a mountain range, not a valley!

> אֶלָּא מֵעֵצָה עֲמוּקָה שֶׁל אוֹתוֹ צַדִּיק הַקָּבוּר בְּחֶבְרוֹן לְקַיֵּם מַה שֶּׁנֶּאֱמַר לְאַבְרָהָם בֵּין הַבְּתָרִים כִּי גֵר יִהְיֶה זַרְעֲךָ
>
> [*Joseph was sent*] *as a result of the profound* [עֲמוּקָה=עֵמֶק] *scheme of the tzaddik* [*Abraham*] *who is buried in Hebron, to fulfill what was said to Abraham* [*at the Covenant*] *between the Parts (15:16), 'Your offspring will be a stranger ...'*

The time had come to begin the long, painful, but necessary process of sojourn and servitude that would prepare the family of Jacob for nationhood and the giving of the Torah. None of the principal actors — Jacob, Joseph, nor the brothers — knew what process was about to begin, but it was part of God's design.

None of the principal actors — Jacob, Joseph, nor the brothers — knew what process was about to begin, but it was part of God's design.

The brothers were determined to give the lie to Joseph's dreams, to shatter his ambitions of dominion over them. "The dreamer," they called him contemptuously (37:19). They would sit as a court and condemn him to death as a rebel, and then: וְנִרְאֶה מַה־יִּהְיוּ חֲלֹמֹתָיו, *'we shall see what will become of his dreams* (37:20). But as they confidently predicted an end to their tormentor, God was saying the same words: 'Yes, We shall see ... whose wish will be fulfilled, Mine or yours.' Their sale of Joseph to slavery in Egypt was part of God's scenario.

The hand of Heaven was at work. They thought they would kill him, and a dead man cannot reign. They made him a slave, and a slave can never be king. But God thought otherwise. Joseph *would* be king. Wherever he went, he ruled. As a slave of Potiphar, he was placed in charge of the household; as a disgraced prisoner, he was placed in charge of the prison; as a despised Hebrew, rushed to the

They made him a slave, and a slave can never be king. But God thought otherwise. Joseph would be king.

palace to interpret Pharaoh's dream, he was placed in charge of the entire country; and then all the surrounding countries had to come to him abjectly pleading for the privilege of buying food. And finally his entire family bowed to him. Indeed, what had become of his dreams!

Finally his entire family bowed to him. Indeed, what had become of his dreams!

There is more:

> הָיָה יַעֲקֹב אָבִינוּ רָאוּי לֵירֵד לְמִצְרַיִם בְּשַׁלְשְׁלָאוֹת וּבְקוֹלָרִין. אָמַר הקב״ה בְּנִי בְכוֹרִי וַאֲנִי מוֹרִידוֹ בְבִזָּיוֹן ... אֶלָּא הֲרֵינִי מוֹשֵׁךְ אֶת־בְּנוֹ לְפָנָיו וְהוּא יוֹרֵד אַחֲרָיו בְּעַל כָּרְחוֹ
>
> *Our father Jacob would have had to descend to Egypt in chains and a collar. Said the Holy One, Blessed be He, 'He is My firstborn son, shall I bring him down there in disgrace? ... Rather I will lead his son before him and he will be forced to descend after him' (Bereishis Rabbah 86:2; cf. Shabbos 89b).*

So the outcome of the scenario was predetermined. Jacob and his family *would* come to Egypt; the only question was how. God chose to mix mercy into His decree by preparing circumstances that would bring Jacob to his unavoidable Egyptian destination in comfort and honor — just as Joseph's slave-journey to Egypt was eased by a series of sales that placed him in a caravan bearing sweet-smelling spices rather than malodorous pitch and tar (see *comm.* to 37:25).

But if the fate of Joseph was inevitable, why should his righteous brothers have been the agency of his suffering?

But if the fate of Joseph was inevitable, why should his righteous brothers have been the agency of his suffering? And if God only used them to effect His will, why were they punished for what they did?

When the Lofty Fall

No one is forced to act, for good or for bad. God does not tamper with man's free will; this is a cardinal tenet of our belief, though man's intelligence is too limited to let him understand how he remains free in the face of inexorable forces that seem to propel him onto one course or another. What does often happen is that God gives opportunities for constructive action to those whose previous deeds have earned them the privilege, and He brings opportunities for evil to those who have conditioned themselves to do wrong. As the Sages describe it:

מְגַלְגְּלִים זְכוּת עַל יְדֵי זַכַּאי וְחוֹבָה עַל יְדֵי חַיָּב
They cause merit to come through deserving people and harm through bad people (Shabbos 32a).

That a righteous person is put in a position to do good is not unearned patronage.

That a righteous person is put in a position to do good is not unearned patronage; by making himself a meritorious person he has earned the right to be the agent of further good, just as — in material terms — we do not question why the hard-working, determined businessman 'somehow finds' opportunities for further profitable ventures. We are conditioned to think that talented people 'make their own breaks.' Similarly, when harm must be done and God seeks the person who will bring it about, He tends to select someone who has made *himself* prone to wrong others. By choosing to be perverse, such people fashioned themselves into instruments of harm.

The judgment of who is righteous and who is not is far from easy. As we find constantly in the study of Scripture, the most righteous people are judged far more strictly than are others. What could easily pass as a *mitzvah* for others can be considered an unpardonable laxity for them. We know in our personal experience that we *do* maintain double standards. We expect higher standards of conduct from superior people, and well we should. The average man should be commended if he devotes 'as much as' a few hours a day to Torah study; the great scholar would be justly criticized if he considered 'only' a few hours to be sufficient.

God had no shortage of means to bring Joseph to Egypt. Midianite or Ishmaelite slave traders could have kidnapped him directly.

God had no shortage of means to bring Joseph to Egypt. Midianite or Ishmaelite slave traders could have kidnapped him directly instead of buying him from the brothers. Why should the brothers, who were trying to preserve the integrity of Israel, have been permitted to make the grievous error of so misjudging and nearly killing the one who stood only a little lower than the Patriarchs?

— Because they were so great that they were

judged by only the strictest standards, and in such scales they were found wanting. *They hated him* ... (37:4), *his brothers were jealous of him* ... (37:11). Dislike and jealousy are not uncommon, not even — sometimes especially — among siblings. Undoubtedly, their negative reactions to him were trivial at the start, evidenced by nothing more than a shrug of the shoulder, an edge in the voice. But such feelings were unworthy of Jacob's children, the founders of the tribes of God. The brothers were placed in God's scale of justice and found to be wanting. For even a twinge of ill feeling toward their younger, but superior brother, men of such stature were stamped in God's eyes as people who had earned the dubious right to be placed in situations where their dislike would ripen into virulent hatred, and who would be substituted for the iron chains that would drag Jacob down to Egypt to commence the agony that had been foretold to Abraham.

Their negative reactions to him were trivial at the start, evidenced by nothing more than a shrug of the shoulder, an edge in the voice. But such feelings were unworthy of Jacob's children.

The story of Joseph and his brothers is one of the most perplexing in the Torah. We have not answered all the questions it raises, but perhaps we have succeeded somewhat in showing the depth with which the deeds of our ancestors must be examined and the lessons they hold for anyone who would be worthy of being called their offspring.

An Overview —
Joseph and Potiphar's Wife*

אָמַר [יוֹסֵף] אַבָּא נִתְנַסָּה זְקֵינִי נִתְנַסָּה וַאֲנִי אֵינִי נִתְנַסֶּה. א״ל הקב״ה חַיֶּיךָ שֶׁאֲנִי מְנַסֶּה אוֹתְךָ יוֹתֵר מֵהֶם

[*Joseph*] *said, 'My father was tested, my grandfather was tested, but I have not been tested.' The Holy One, Blessed be He, said to him, 'By your life I will test you more than them' (Bereishis Rabbah* 87:4).

יוֹסֵף מְחַיֵּב אֶת הָרְשָׁעִים

Joseph obligates the wicked (Yoma 35b).

דְיוּקְנוֹ שֶׁל אָבִיו נִרְאֲתָה לוֹ בְחַלּוֹן

The image of his father appeared to him in the window (Sotah 36b).

Was It a Test?

Joseph was tempted over and over by his master's wife, so much so that the Sages describe the temptation as greater than any of the tests faced by Jacob or Isaac, and his triumph is held up as the example that proves even to the wicked that man can be strong. As we have seen in earlier Overviews, a נִסָּיוֹן, *test,* in God's terms is an ordeal precisely calculated to stretch a person's will to the very limits of his endurance.

Were it not for the superlatives with which the Sages and commentators describe the gravity of Joseph's test and his greatness in surmounting it, we would hardly assign such status to either.

Every human being faces some degree of temptation many times in an average week, or even day. But not every seductive chocolate, profit, or pleasure constitutes a 'test' in classic terms. Were it not for the superlatives with which the Sages and commentators describe the gravity of Joseph's test and his greatness in surmounting it, we would hardly assign such status to either. On the one hand, Joseph was asked to commit an act of immorality that would have been a sin to God and an act of ingratitude to Potiphar, his benefactor. Granted that his temptress made his life

* This Overview is based on *Be'er Moshe.*

an unremitting ordeal of threats and blandishments, it is hard to see how such a test could be called superior to those of the Patriarchs. Joseph was asked to commit a blatant, undeniable sin. He was not the first nor the last to resist such temptations. Why should his response be accounted great enough to earn him the title יוֹסֵף הַצַּדִּיק, *Joseph the Righteous?*

Joseph's strength was not his own; there was a miraculous intervention at his moment of weakness.

Furthermore, Joseph did not persevere on his own. Joseph's strength was not his own; there was a miraculous intervention at his moment of weakness. His father's image appeared to him by the window just as he was about to submit to the advances of Potiphar's wife. How can such an event serve as a lesson to the wicked who are not given inspirational assistance at their point of failure? *(Pri HaAretz).*

Like Tamar and Ruth

The comments of the Sages compel us to recognize that the test was of an awesome degree, and that Joseph's response was worthy of Jacob's greatest heir. Consequently, the sudden appearance of his father's image could not have been unrelated to Joseph's own stature, otherwise his ultimate refusal to sin could not be considered such a mark of personal exaltation.

Let us understand clearly that the intensity of Joseph's test was not related to the woman's promises of pleasure or her threats of death. Lesser Jews have withstood worse.

Let us understand clearly that the intensity of Joseph's test was not related to the woman's promises of pleasure or her threats of death. Lesser Jews than Joseph have withstood worse. Rather, the siren call of the Egyptian woman struck a spiritual chord in him and very nearly convinced him that God wished him to live with her.

Two other women in Scripture made advances to men. The first was Tamar who deceived Judah into living with her, and conceived Peretz and Zerach, two-thirds of Israel's leading tribe, one of them the ancestor of David. The second woman was Ruth who came to Boaz secretly and asked him to marry her, a marriage that produced Oved, the grandfather of David. The Sages compare Potiphar's wife with Tamar and Ruth. She fell short of them, it is true, but not by very far.

אָמַר ר׳ יְהוֹשֻׁעַ בֶּן לֵוִי, רָאֲתָה בְּאִצְטְרוֹלוֹגִין שֶׁלָּהּ

שֶׁעֲתִידָה לְהַעֲמִיד בָּנִים מִמֶּנּוּ וְאֵינָה יוֹדַעַת אִם מִמֶּנָּה אִם מִבִּתָּהּ

R' Yehoshua ben Levi said: She saw through her astrology that she was destined to establish descendants from him, but she did not know whether it would be from her or from her daughter (Bereishis Rabbah 85:2).

Both she and Tamar acted as they did for the sake of Heaven. Tamar was right, Potiphar's wife was nearly right.

Both she and Tamar acted as they did for the sake of Heaven because each was convinced that noble offspring would be the product of the respective unions. Tamar was right, Potiphar's wife was nearly right — and she was close enough to the truth to put Joseph to one of the severest of all tests *(Bereishis Rabbah* 85:2).

In comparing her with Ruth, the Sages describe her in unusually harsh terms, but it is remarkable to note the particular aspect of her behavior that they criticize:

> Accursed are the wicked! Later [in the case of Ruth we find her saying]: 'Spread your robe over her handmaid' [as a symbol of marriage], but this one spoke like an animal: 'Lay with me!'

Tamar and Ruth are among the most outstandingly righteous women in Jewish history. The sincerity of Potiphar's wife is placed on a par with Tamar's: 'Just as one's intent was for the sake of Heaven, so the other's intent was for the sake of Heaven.' She is denigrated in comparision with Ruth only regarding the coarseness of her speech. It would seem that, though she erred in wanting to live with Joseph, there was justification for it, so much so that Joseph was tested and proved his greatness by not being ensnared.

Duty to Sin?

As is plain from numerous passages in the Torah and Talmudic literature, the ancients knew how to foretell events through astrology. Potiphar's wife could see that she was destined to be the ancestress of Joseph's children and she coveted the privilege, just as Tamar before her had coveted the privilege of giving birth to Judah's children. Whatever she knew through her occult powers, Joseph surely knew. He was fully aware that he was Jacob's primary heir and the prophetic dreams that antagonized his brothers never left his consciousness (see *Ramban* 42:9 and *comm.* throughout the narrative). He knew his responsibility to the future of Israel, and if his master's wife was truly sincere — 'for the sake of Heaven' — in wishing to unite with him, then he had to consider that he might be duty-bound to accept her entreaties. Two tribes, Manasseh and Ephraim, were destined to be born to him, Messiah ben Joseph, the forerunner of the Davidic Messiah would descend from him, the destiny of Israel depended on him and his progeny. And the ancestress of all this was to be the woman who did everything in her power to incite him. Had he the right to refuse her? *(Ramchal).*

The ancestress of all this was to be the woman who did everything in her power to incite him. Had he the right to refuse her?

According to R' Yochanan and Shmuel *(Sotah* 36b), Joseph had finally decided to go along with her wishes when he had his final encounter with her (39:11ff). [However, Rav (ibid.) disagrees, maintaining that he intended only to carry out the household duties assigned him by Potiphar.] It would be an injustice to Joseph to assume that he was weakened by her urgings and finally overcome by his lust. Joseph was surely able to control his desires. He had already been shown prophetic dreams, had come to 'resemble' the holiness of Jacob and Adam, had emerged as the greatest scholar among the brothers, and had been acknowledged as Jacob's paramount son. Even the greatest people can sin, but in understanding the sins of the holiest, we must attempt to find the source in miscalculation rather than uncontrollable passion. Joseph made a judgment. He knew that Potiphar's wife was an essential component of his future, and therefore he decided to join her.

The greatest people can sin, but in understanding the sins of the holiest, we must attempt to find the source in miscalculation rather than uncontrollable passion.

In this light, Joseph's earlier protestations seem more plausible. The Torah tells us that he spoke to the woman of sin, ingratitude, and betraying Potiphar's trust. The Talmud (*Sotah* 36b) states that Joseph argued God might appear to him in the evening and he had to maintain himself in a condition of טַהֲרָה, *purity,* and that he had to remain worthy to have his name engraved with those of his brothers on the sacred garments of the *Kohen Gadol.* How strange that his arguments emphasized ethics, morality, and piety. If one were urged to murder and he expressed such tepid demurrals — it isn't nice, the victim was kind to me, what will the neighbors say? — instead of protesting vehemently that he would rather be killed than kill, we would regard him as failing to comprehend the enormity of murder. There was a good reason why Joseph spoke as he did. He *could not* label this act as a grotesque sin — because it might not have been a sin at all! Finally, he concluded that, indeed, the *mitzvah* of building his share of Israel required him to live with Potiphar's wife. And he came to the house to do what he was required to do.

How strange that his arguments emphasized ethics, morality, and piety.

Jacob's Image

Then he saw Jacob's image before him and he recoiled. All his life, Joseph's goal had been to resemble his father more closely.

Then he saw Jacob's image before him and he recoiled. The image was no miracle. One of the proofs of Joseph's pre-eminence had been his spiritual resemblance to Jacob. All his life, Joseph's goal had been to resemble his father more closely to be worthy of bridging the eras of the Patriarchs and nation.

As *Chiddushei HaRim* commented on Abraham's test at the *Akeidah,* in a time of extreme crisis, a person becomes incapable of calm, reasoned analysis. His greatest strength at such a moment is the instinct he has developed through all his years of living and striving. People who have failed to develop their spiritual resources before crisis strikes them will not have the reserves to conquer it. This is true in all areas. The businessman who failed to develop his integrity in routine times will not have it when the price of honesty seems to be a lifetime of effort crashing down around him. The political leader who failed to develop a general philosophy of life, governance, and statecraft will lack instincts of consistent decision-making when all hangs on his judgment. The scholar who failed to develop his concentration and to stoke his desire in ordinary times will fail to muster the intensity and recall needed when complex and knotty problems challenge his intellect.

Joseph had absorbed his father's attribute. Jacob was the Patriarch of אֱמֶת and תִּפְאֶרֶת, *truth* and *splendor.* As discussed above, these attributes represent a weighing and apportioning of all values and components to produce a perfect balance. Jacob was present within Joseph. At the moment when presence of mind should have deserted Joseph, he recalled the prime influence on his life — Jacob's unforgiving quest for truth. At the moment when Joseph's resistance to sin had been eroded by the persuasive insistence that he was about to do a *mitzvah,* the training of a lifetime passed before him.

When presence of mind should have deserted Joseph, he recalled the prime influence of his life — Jacob's unforgiving quest for truth.

Truth allows no compromise. Might have beens are not good enough. Potiphar's wife had seen her stars and Joseph had seen his רוּחַ קֹדֶשׁ, *holy spirit* — but neither one knew that the mother of Menasseh and Ephraim had to be *this particular* woman, or that the *possibility* of performing a *mitzvah* could override all the arguments to the contrary, including the brazenness and coarseness with which she expressed her desire to act for the sake of heaven. *R' Simcha Bunim* of *P'schis'cha* taught that even one's deeds done for the sake of Heaven must be done in a manner befitting Heaven. It is all too easy to delude oneself into thinking that he may take every form of license as long as he is convinced he is doing the right thing with honorable intentions.

According to the *Zohar,* Joseph earned the appellation *Tzaddik* only by virtue of his resistance to Potiphar's wife. He was ready to sin with the woman. Day after day he had refused her and kept a tight rein over his passion, but once he had made the determination that *her* vision of their joint destiny was correct, he allowed human feelings to run unbridled. Passion unleashed is as hard to restrain as a runaway team of horses going downhill. Nevertheless, when Joseph's vision of truth reasserted itself, he regained full control over all his faculties, even the lust that normally drags man along with it until it is

Passion unleashed is as hard to restrain as a runaway team of horses going downhill.

At the hardest of all moments, Joseph summoned up the vision of Jacob — and thereby became the personification of a righteousness that dominates even man's most animalistic drives.

sated. At the hardest of all moments, Joseph summoned up the vision of Jacob — and thereby became the personification of a righteousness that embraces, purifies, and dominates even man's most animalistic drives.

In a deeper sense, this vision, too, represents an overpowering passion — a passion for truth that becomes the strongest factor in a person's life, not a negative passion, but a positive one that does not compromise with the allures of the moment. As the *Maggid of Mezritch (Or Torah)* commented, Joseph's vision of an 'image of Jacob' symbolized his dedication to the particular value best represented by Jacob: *Tiferes,* the splendor of perfect harmony. She utilized every wile and device to create settings of perfect beauty to tempt and entice the young, lonely Hebrew slave. *Midrash Tanchuma* teaches that she even wore different outfits morning and evening so that beautiful physical surroundings would aid her enticing mirage of a spiritual destiny together. But at the crucial moment, Joseph would not be blinded. Instead of accepting *her* image of splendor, he saw the splendor of *Jacob's* world view, that of defining every act and desire in terms of a harmonious picture of Godly service through absolute truth and honesty.

The *Zohar* to *Vayechi* makes it unmistakably clear that the appearance to Joseph of Jacob's image was an indication of Joseph's own victory over himself rather than a miraculous intervention to rescue him from sin:

> [As Jacob lay on his deathbed] *He called to his son Joseph* (47:29) — were the other tribes not his sons? Rather, Joseph was more his son than any of the others ... Come and see what is written [of Joseph] וַיְמָאֵן וַיֹּאמֶר אֶל־אֵשֶׁת אֲדֹנָיו, *but he adamantly refused. He said to his master's wife* ... (39:8). The Holy One, Blessed be He, said of him, 'Of you is written the words וַיְמָאֵן וַיֹּאמֶר, *he refused and said;* by your life, the same phrase will come as [the introduction to] the blessing for your children and they will be blessed with it, as it is written [וַיְמָאֵן] *and he* [Jacob]

Of you is written, 'he refused and said'; by your life, the same phrase will come as [the introduction to] the blessing for your children.

refused [to give preference to Menasseh over Ephraim] ... וַיֹּאמֶר, *and he said* ... (48:19). [Jacob said of Joseph's refusal to comply with her wishes] at that time you proved with your own body that you are my son, when you saw my image and remained firm in your bodily covenant ... Joseph was truly *his* son, for they both had the same image; whoever saw Joseph testified that he was Jacob's son.

[Control over] the body and the covenant are identical, for our father Jacob symbolizes the concept of truth, and Joseph [who overcame passion] symbolizes the *tzaddik*.

Joseph's Legacy

The Talmud describes vividly the excruciating torment with which he forced himself away from the deed he had contemplated.

Let us not think that Joseph's last-second decision to flee from his temptress was easy. Desire, once unleashed, is not like a faucet that can be turned off easily. The Talmud *(Sotah* 36b) describes vividly the excruciating torment with which he forced himself away from the deed he had contemplated. That is why his accomplishment had significance for the entire nation.

As we have seen often in the Torah's narration of the lives of the Patriarchs, their deeds had eternal repercussions because they embodied all generations of Israel within themselves. *Ramban* writes that because Abraham went to Egypt to escape the Canaanite famine and because he exposed Sarah to danger by saying that she was his sister, his descendants would be forced to go to Egypt and live under Egyptian domination. *Nefesh HaChaim* writes that Jewish love of *Eretz Yisrael* throughout all exiles and Jewish readiness to sacrifice life and even children for the sake of God are legacies of Abraham's devotion to the Land and his binding of Isaac on the altar. The Sages teach that Abraham's hospitality to the angels (18:2-8) was reciprocated by God Who provided for Israel in the Wilderness. As the bearer of the Patriarchal tradition, Joseph's deeds, too, were not private affairs.

As the bearer of the Patriarchal tradition, Joseph's deeds, too, were not private affairs.

Indeed, R' Shimon ben Yochai *(Bereishis Rabbah* 71:2) teaches that the entire nation is regarded as if it descended from Joseph, because it inherited the holiness of Joseph. Jewish tenacity to preserve its morality is his legacy *(Vayikra Rabbah* 32). The Midrash *(Bereishis Rabbah* 87:8) teaches that the Sea of Reeds split to permit Israel to pass through because they carried with them the coffin containing Joseph's remains:

> Because Joseph [וַיָּנָס] 'fled' from Potiphar's wife [39:12], הַיָּם רָאָה וַיָּנֹס, *the sea saw* [his remains] *and fled (Psalms* 114:3).

Therefore, the Sages taught, Joseph's example obligates even the wicked to subdue their passions *(Yoma* 35b). He was no eunuch. Once he made his decision to come to her, his desire was as powerful as any lesser man's — no! it was *more* powerful because he thought he was performing a *mitzvah* — but he was able to subdue it because he recognized the truth as paramount. So his triumph is all the greater.

So, too, anyone who departs from sin because of the Holy One, Blessed be He, like Joseph who restrained himself from his master's wife, has sanctified God's Name.

'So, too, anyone who departs from sin or who performs a commandment not because of any consideration whatever — not dread, not fear, not to seek honor — but only because of the Holy One, Blessed be He, like Joseph who restrained himself from his master's wife, has sanctified God's Name *(Rambam, Yesodei HaTorah* 5:10).

An Overview —
Dreams — Prophetic and Pointless

דִּבְרֵי חֲלוֹמוֹת לֹא מַעֲלִין וְלֹא מוֹרִידִין
Contents of dreams have no validity (Sanhedrin 30a)

רָבָא רָמֵי, כְּתִיב בַּחֲלוֹם אֲדַבֶּר בּוֹ וּכְתִיב וַחֲלֹמוֹת הַשָּׁוְא יְדַבֵּרוּ? לֹא קַשְׁיָא כָּאן עַל יְדֵי מַלְאָךְ כָּאן עַל יְדֵי שֵׁד
Rava noted a contradiction: It is written, 'I [God] speak to him [a prophet] through a dream' (Numbers 12:6) and it is written 'and the dreamers speak vanity (Zechariah 10:2)? — This is not difficult, here [the dream] is through an angel and there it is through a demon (Berachos 55b).

חֲלוֹמוֹת הוֹלְכִים אַחַר הַפֶּה
[The realizations of] dreams follow the words [of the interpreter] (Berachos 55b).

Dreams form an essential part of Joseph's story. His long travail was set in motion by the dreams he told his brothers and he was recommended to Pharaoh because of the dreams of the two imprisoned chamberlains. Finally, he became viceroy of Egypt, fed the world, and brought his family to Egypt as a result of Pharaoh's dreams. These dreams seem to be prophetic, although the Talmud derives from Scripture that such dreams as those of the chamberlains are fulfilled only in accordance with the words of their interpreter *(Berachos* 55b).

Sometimes the Talmud derides the validity of dreams and other times it lends them credence.

Sometimes the Talmud derides the validity of dreams and other times it lends them credence. A person who has a disturbing dream may fast even on the Sabbath to annul its evil portent, and during the Priestly Blessings we recite a prayer asking God to fulfill good dreams and nullify bad ones *(Berachos* 55b). If one dreams that he has been placed under a חֵרֶם, *ban,* he must assume it to be a heavenly message and assemble ten people to release him (*Nedarim* 8a; see also *She'iltos d'Rav Achai Gaon, Miketz; Tashbetz,* part 2:128, 129).

When the Soul Rises

A general outline of man's ability to assimilate heavenly messages in his dreams is given by *Derech Hashem* (3:1). Sometimes God conveys a prophecy in a dream. Such prophecies come directly from God and are not to be confused with the dreams discussed by the Talmudic passages cited here. There are forms of metaphysical communication, however, that are received in dreams.

Man has a higher soul. Its function is to provide a bridge between man's animal nature and the wholly spiritual forces above him.

In addition to the soul that gives man the ability to live — a soul that is more or less similar to the life-force of all animals — man has a higher soul. Its function is to provide a bridge between man's animal nature and the wholly spiritual forces above him. Naturally, this soul becomes substantially limited as long as it is connected to its human host, but certain facets of it retain the power to soar above the body, so to speak, and absorb spiritual messages that ordinarily would be beyond a person's ability to comprehend. An illustration of this is found in *Megillah* 3a, which tells of Daniel who was shown a vision. His companions did not see the vision but they became frightened nonetheless. Why did they fear something of which they were unaware? asks the Talmud. אִינְהוּ לֹא חָזֵי מַזְלַיְהוּ חָזֵי, *they could not see but their 'mazal' saw.* This *mazal, Derech Hashem* explains, refers to a facet of their higher soul that was capable of knowing, and fearing, what its human body could not perceive.

Night time, when a person sleeps, provides freedom for the imagination from the discipline man imposes on it while he is awake.

Night time, when a person sleeps, provides freedom for the imagination from the discipline man imposes on it while he is awake and in need of all his faculties. Then people dream. They may dream of many things, most of them outgrowths of their experiences and ambitions of the day. Whatever absorbs a person's consciousness during the day — his activities or what he wishes his activities to be — will tend to form the subject matter of his dreams.

Another thing happens during those sleeping

A portion of the higher soul leaves the body and associates with spiritual beings that are unencumbered by a body.

hours. A portion of the higher soul leaves the body and associates with spiritual beings that are unencumbered by a body. It can be told things by them, sometimes by holy angels and sometimes by evil demons. If the soul transmits these messages and revelations to man's lower intelligence, they may take the form of dreams.

Thus, dreams are of various origins. Sometimes they are pure fantasies affected by a person's health, strivings, or preoccupations; such dreams have no meaning or value, except to the extent that they reveal what goes on in the individual dreamer's fantasy. If a dream reflects the message of a demon, it, too, is false. But if its origin is the teaching of a higher spiritual being, then its message is true and it is God's way of communicating knowledge of the future or insight into the present.

Since man has an active imagination, however, all dreams, even those that originate from higher sources, become intermixed with his personal images. As a result, there is no dream without some meaningless portions, and even the dreams that are essentially true will not be accurate in every detail; the parts that are realized were supplied to the higher soul by spiritual forces, while the parts that never happen were products of the dreamer's personal fantasy (*Berachos* 55a). *R' Bachya (Bereishis* 41:1) describes this form of revelation with the figure of speech נְבוּאָה קְטַנָּה, *minor prophecy;* it is what the Sages describe as חֲלוֹם אֶחָד מִשִּׁשִּׁים בִּנְבוּאָה, *a dream is one sixtieth of a prophecy (Berachos* 57a).

The Talmud states that fools and children are more prone than others to prophecy. The Talmud does not mean that God reveals Himself to them.

Since this limited degree of revelation is diluted and obscured by the personal fantasies of the dreamer, it stands to reason that the less active his imagination, the less diluted his dream will be by external factors. This is why the Talmud *(Bava Basra* 12b) states that fools and children are more prone than others to prophecy. The Talmud does not mean that God reveals Himself to them as He did to the prophets of Scripture; such revelation could only be experienced by people who had attained a level of spiritual greatness far beyond that of even people of high caliber, much less fools and children. Additionally, true prophecy disappeared after the Babylonian exile. What the Talmud describes as the 'prophecies accessible to fools and children' are the fragments of revelation brought by the higher soul from the angels. When conveyed to people with highly active minds, such revelations will find their way into dreams where they will be overwhelmed by so many other images that the heavenly message will be unrecognizable. But if they are incorporated into the dreams of those who bring less personal stimuli into their dreams, the bits of revelation will remain relatively undiluted. Such dreams can come to the wicked as well as the righteous, for even the wicked are endowed with a soul that can reach the very heavens; what must be done is to retrieve the substance of the dream from the chaff (see also *Tashbatz,* part 2:128).

When conveyed to people with highly active minds, such revelations will find their way into dreams where they will be overwhelmed by many other images.

Indeed, *Or HaChaim* stresses that an indication of a dream's validity is that it be clear and vivid *(Bereishis* 28:12, 37:7), and that its content not be an obvious outgrowth of the dreamer's daily preoccupations (41:1).

Kinds of Messages

As the soul makes its way through the spiritual spheres, it can receive a wide variety of messages from many angels and demons. When they are filtered into the sleeping psyche, they are garbed in the images that we see in dreams. For example, revelations of abundant rainfall, flowing Torah knowledge, or a damaging flood may all take the form of a dream about a well. Plentiful fruit, several generations of offspring, many branches of a family, or the healthy and rapid growth of children may all be portrayed in a dream-image of a growing vine with many full bunches of grapes.

Many different messages may be translated into a single dream-image.

Furthermore, many different messages may be translated into a single dream-image. This is why the Talmud states that the twenty-four acknowledged interpreters of dreams in Jerusalem once gave different intepretations of a single dream, *all* of which came true. There is neither magic nor contradiction in this. *All* the messages were garbed in the same set of images, but each interpreter perceived only one aspect of the dream. Because each interpretation was valid, however, all came true. Had the interpretations been contradictory, it would have been obvious that some were purely the imagination of the interpreter. This is why the Talmud teaches that a dream will be fulfilled according to the formula pronounced by a reliable interpreter — provided his interpretation fits the content of the dream and provided it is not contradicted by other interpreters. In other words, it is not that an interpreter has the power to control a person's destiny; rather he has the ability to discern the truth that may be buried in a welter of fantasies. But if his view is not consonant with the dream itself, or if equally competent analysts dispute him, his view may be invalid *(Abarbanel; Maharsha).*

Because each interpretation was valid, however, all came true. Had the interpretations been contradictory, it would have been obvious that some were purely the imagination of the interpreter.

Maharsha and *Or HaChaim* (in *Chofetz Hashem* to *Berachos* 56a) hold that sometimes even the flawed revelation of a demon can come true. This sort of dream, as noted above, is of the sort that has no validity. As *Berachos* 55a puts it, it is like an 'unread letter' whose contents are meaningless to someone who ignores them. But if the dreamer takes the dream seriously enough to seek an interpreter, he has given it credence and subjected himself to the power of its message, even though it may come from a demon. The key to this concept is that the dream in question was not the product of daytime preoccupations, but of a spiritual force that seeks to influence the dreamer.

If the dreamer takes the dream seriously enough to seek an interpreter, he has given it credence and subjected himself to the power of its message.

A truly prophetic dream, such as those of Jacob in *Vayeitzei* and countless others described throughout Scripture, is fulfilled whatever would-be interpreters say of it. As the classic commentators explain, only Moses was able to perceive prophetic revelation while in control of all his human faculties. Because Godly revelation is too much for the human body to endure, no other prophet could accept God's word while in full control of his body. Depending on the spiritual perfection of the individual prophet, one might only fall into a trance, while another could accept revelation only in a dream. But such dreams are as much prophecies as the Face-to-face revelations given Moses, and they *must* come true.

The Dreams of Bereishis

Joseph's dreams were prophetic and would have come true whether or not they were interpreted.

In the light of the above, we can better understand the dreams of our narrative. Joseph's dreams were prophetic and would have come true whether or not they were interpreted. The Sages differ only on one point: Were the dreams prophetic in their entirety or were they, too, invaded by an element of external fantasy? As the Commentary notes, the problem arises regarding the 'moon' that he dreamt would bow to him. The moon was obviously symbolic of his mother, Rachel, who was not living. According to one view of the Sages, that part of his dream had no significance, according to the other view it referred to Bilhah who raised him after Rachel's death.

The dreams of the two chamberlains are cited by the Talmud as examples of the sort whose fulfillment depends on the word of the interpreter. There were many implications in those dreams in addition to ones quoted by Scripture, that the cupbearer would live and the baker die. According to *Chullin* 92a, there were references to Jewish history, and, quite likely, there were others as well. Had Joseph interpreted some of the symbolisms in a manner that did not contradict the symbolism of the dream or God's will, his interpretation would have been fulfilled.

Pharaoh's dream cannot be regarded as a prophecy in the sense of a personal revelation from God, for he was surely not worthy of prophecy. Nevertheless, as Joseph made clear to Pharaoh, the dream was given him to forewarn him of future events. Theoretically, it, too, could have been open to more than one correct interpretation, like the one interpreted by the twenty-four wise men of Jerusalem. Had the speculations of Pharaoh's wizards been faithful to the context of the dream and had they been competent to interpret dreams, their interpretations might have been just as valid as Joseph's but Pharaoh would not accept their versions for the reasons given in the Com-

Had the speculations of Pharaoh's wizards been faithful to the context of the dream, their interpretations might have been valid.

mentary. In addition to those reasons, however, part of the Divine plan was, as *R' Bachya* writes:

God wished to make Pharaoh dream and to perplex his spirit through a dream in order to promote Joseph.

> God wished to make Pharaoh dream and to perplex his spirit through a dream, and to make the advice of his necromancers and wise men seem foolish in order to promote Joseph to that eminence.

[The above is but a brief outline of the Talmudic sources and the views of the commentators on the subject of dreams. It includes only information deemed helpful in providing a perspective on our chapters of *Bereishis*. For a fuller understanding, the reader should consult the sources cited in this presentation.]

An Overview —
And He Was a Youth*

„וְהוּא נַעַר" שֶׁהָיָה עוֹשֶׂה מַעֲשֶׂה נַעֲרוּת, מְתַקֵּן בִּשְׂעָרוֹ מְמַשְׁמֵשׁ בְּעֵינָיו כְּדֵי שֶׁיִּהְיֶה נִרְאֶה יָפֶה

'And he [Joseph] was a youth': he acted like an adolescent, dressing his hair, and adorning his eyes to look handsome (Rashi from *Bereishis Rabbah* 84:7).

ג׳ מִדּוֹת הָיוּ בוֹ, בֶּן תּוֹרָה וְנָבִיא וְאֶת אֶחָיו הוּא מְכַלְכֵּל ... וּמִנַּיִן שֶׁהוּא נָבִיא שֶׁנֶּאֱמַר וְהוּא נַעַר ... וּכְתִיב וּמְשָׁרְתוֹ יְהוֹשֻׁעַ בִּן נוּן נַעַר ... וּכְתִיב וַיִּגְדַּל הַנַּעַר שְׁמוּאֵל

[Joseph] had three attributes: he was a Torah scholar, a prophet, and he supported his brothers ... How do we know he was a prophet? For it says (37:2), *'He was a* **youth** *... and it says (Exodus* 33:11), *'and [Moses'] servant Joshua ben Nun was a* **youth** *... and it says (I Samuel* 2:21), *'and the* **youth** *Samuel grew up (Tanchuma Yashan).*

Contradictory Interpretations

The seventeen-year old Joseph was described as נַעַר, *a youth* (37:2), to which *Rashi* quotes the Midrashic interpretation cited above. Without doubt, the words must be taken literally: surely Joseph *did* those things and none of the commentators to the Midrash or *Rashi* suggests otherwise. But the unadorned words of *Rashi* do violence to our comprehension of a Joseph's greatness — even at the age of seventeen. We expect more from a mature seventeen year old today, what are we to say of one who was already established as Jacob's primary son and heir, who was already receiving prophetic dreams, who had acquired enough wisdom and maturity to survive a twenty-two year exile in the ordeals of slavery and monarchy! In the words of

The unadorned words of Rashi do violence to our comprehension of a Joseph's greatness — even at the age of seventeen.

* This Overview is based on *Michtav MeEliyahu.*

Chiddushei HaRim, 'Who is fool enough to believe that these words are to be taken only at face value?'

Of course, Joseph did all those things, and that is one of the reasons his brothers lost their regard for him. The question is, why did he do it?

Of course, Joseph did all those things, and that is one of the reasons his brothers lost their regard for him. The question is, why did he do it? Certainly Joseph should have known that such preening could gain him nothing and cost him much.

Among the writings of the Sages and commentators, we find six interpretations of the phrase *'he was a youth'*; two understanding it in its demeaning literal sense and the other four in a diametrically opposed manner:

1) *Rashi's* interpretation that he constantly preened himself.

2) He was too immature to foresee the consequences of such behavior *(Gur Aryeh).*

3) According to the Kabbalah, both Jacob and Joseph were considered like כְּרוּבִים, *the cherubim,* atop the Holy Ark. Each of them was called נַעַר: Joseph as we find here and Jacob as we find כִּי נַעַר יִשְׂרָאֵל וָאֹהֲבֵהוּ, *for Israel* [i.e., Jacob] *is a youth and I* [God] *love him (Hoshea* 11:1) ... In the literal sense, the opening phrase of the verse teaches that Joseph was the primary son of Jacob, meaning, as our Sages say, that he combined within himself all the attributes of his brothers *(R' Bachya).*

He had three attributes: he was a Torah scholar, a prophet, and he supported his brothers.

4) He had three attributes: he was a Torah scholar, a prophet, and he supported his brothers. The word נַעַר, *youth,* indicates he was a prophet as quoted above *(Tanchuma Yashan).*

5) His brothers demeaned the sons of Bilhah and Zilpah, but Joseph served them like a slave *(Yelamdeinu).*

6) He was a נַעַר, *youth,* in the sense that the great angel, Matatron, is called a נַעַר, literally *youth.* Just as Matatron is described by the Sages as a means by which God reveals His goodness on earth, so Joseph brought about revelation of God's majesty on earth. Additionally, Joseph was the fulfillment of the Jacob-mission (as opposed to the Israel-mission) of his father [as described at length in the first *Overview*] *(Sh'loh; Megaleh Amukos).*

It is axiomatic in studying the sacred writings of the Sages and commentators that such differing perceptions of people or subjects do not represent conflicting opinions. Rather they express different facets and levels of the same whole. The sun may be described as yellow, bright, hot, a star, the center of the solar system, huge beyond comprehension, an insignificant part of our galaxy, a gravitational force, and so on and so on. Each description is true and all taken together give a rounded impression, but for someone completely unfamiliar with the sun, they seem like a contradictory jumble. Similiarly, while Joseph acted like a child, he was too great to be so small; therefore, we must find the key to his personality that lends validity to all the interpretations.

While Joseph acted like a child, he was too great to be so small; therefore, we must find the key to his personality that lends validity to all the interpretations.

Correct, but Ill-timed

On the one hand, Joseph knew that he was foremost among the brothers and that the task of insuring the first step in Israel's development was up to him. His dreams added a dimension to his role: he would reign over his brothers and they would gather around him to bow. He understood his dreams to be tantamount to a command that he must act like a king. Furthermore, as Jacob's primary heir, he bore even a greater responsibility for the conduct of the family.

The honor of the nation requires its king to be well-groomed at all times. *Rambam* rules: The king must cut his hair every day, groom himself, and dress well in beautiful, glorious clothes *(Hilchos Melachim* 2:5). A leader cannot lead unless the people respect him, and people expect their leader to look the part. In modern times, the majesty of many an important office has suffered because its occupant has chosen to dress and act like a follower rather than a leader. So Joseph, who was destined to *be* a king, preened himself like a king.

A leader cannot lead unless the people respect him, and people expect their leader to look the part. So Joseph preened himself like a king.

That this was his motive is indicated by *Rashi* to 39:6. There, after Joseph became a slave in Egypt, the verse tells us that he was physically attractive. *Rashi* comments that [כֵּיוָן שֶׁרָאָה עַצְמוֹ מוֹשֵׁל], *once he saw himself as a ruler,* having been appointed overseer of Potiphar's household, he began grooming and preening himself as he had back in *Eretz Yisrael.* Thus, God punished him for his impertinence, but his motive emerges with a clarity we had not had earlier: he considered himself a ruler and felt he should act the part.

Similarly, because his personal status was midway between his father and his brothers, Joseph took upon himself the responsiblity to oversee his brothers. When he thought they had sinned he went straight to Jacob, and when he felt that Bilhah and Zilpah's sons were slighted, he befriended them. The results of his deeds, as chapter 37 makes clear, were disastrous — at least until the outlines of God's master plan emerged.

What was Joseph's mistake? Despite his greatness and sincere motives, he should have realized his place.

What was Joseph's mistake? Despite his greatness and sincere motives, he should have realized his place and given consideration to whether his actions were ill-timed, even if they had logic on their side. A future king he might be, but in Canaan he was still only seventeen, and the eleventh of twelve sons. In Potiphar's house he was only a slave and he should have considered the grief his father still felt at his loss. As *Gur Aryeh* says of Joseph's behavior, he failed to foresee the consequences of his behavior.

But why didn't he? Surely a Joseph could be expected to recognize the need for elementary tact! Surely he must have known the effect he was having on his brothers, and understood that it was unwise to antagonize them further! At the very least, if he was erring innocently, should not God have protected him in the manner of the famous Talmudic exclamation, 'If God saves even the animals of the righteous from mishaps, surely he saves the righteous themselves!'

But God did not want Joseph protected. The Divine plan called for him to lose his brothers' love.

But God did not want Joseph protected. The Divine plan called for him to lose his brothers' love, become a slave and then a king, and become the instrument to bring his family to Egypt. So God allowed his judgment to be clouded, and he acted untactfully. Knowing that he was destined to be a king, he decided to *act* like a king. So Joseph groomed himself like a king, ignoring the fact that to do so was ludicrous for a seventeen-year old who was the eleventh son in his family *(Michtav MeEliyahu).*

Chiddushei HaRim, as explained by *S'fas Emes*, gives a different interpretation of the Scriptural use of נַעַר, *youth*, to describe Joseph. Righteousness has no absolute definition. The service of a *tzaddik* must grow and change as he becomes older and wiser. No one may remain static; he must always advance and build new structures of service on his previous accomplishments. In his youth, for example, he is expected to perfect his character and behavior; as he gradually grows older, his spiritual development becomes more compassionate and seeks to help others.

Righteousness has no absolute definition. The service of a tzaddik *must grow and change as he becomes older and wiser.*

In Joseph's youth, when he was engaged in perfecting the external characteristics of his spiritual nature, he was intolerant of what he perceived as his brothers' shortcomings. In his later years, when he became *Joseph the Tzaddik*, he looked differently at his brothers. Then he calmed them, forgave them and promised to provide for them and their families as long as breath was in him. Compared to the greatness expected of him as he grew and developed into one of the foremost *tzaddikim* in history, his great achievements at the age of seventeen were like a *youth* compared to a mature adult.

◆ סדר וישב

◆ Sidrah Vayeishev

א וַיֵּשֶׁב יַעֲקֹב בְּאֶרֶץ מְגוּרֵי אָבִיו בְּאֶרֶץ

XXXVII

SIDRA VAYEISHEV

1. The chronicles of Jacob and his offspring.

The Torah dealt with the story of Esau only very briefly. [Although it was given an entire chapter, none but the barest facts of genealogical names and places were cited.] The Torah deemed Esau's line too insignificant for a detailed recording of their settlements, wars, victories over the Horites, etc. [see *Deut.* 2:12], and so on; it limited itself to mere glosses.

Now that we come to Jacob, the Torah proceeds to relate at length and in great detail his full history and that of his progeny because God regards them as prominent and deserving of such detailed attention.

Similarly, the ten generations from Adam to Noah [5:1ff], and again those from Noah to Abraham [11:10ff], are reported in a summary manner merely listing their respective genealogies. However, when the Torah reaches Noah and Abraham, it relates their experiences in detail.

This may be compared to the case of a pearl which fell into the sand. One searches and sifts the sand in a sieve until he finds the pearl. After finding it, he discards the pebbles and retains only the pearl (*Rashi* drawing from *Tanchuma).*

וַיֵּשֶׁב יַעֲקֹב בְּאֶרֶץ מְגוּרֵי אָבִיו — [*And*] *Jacob settled in the land where his father had sojourned.*

Esau had gone to a different land to be away from his brother [as mentioned in 36:6], but Jacob, in contrast, *remained* in the land of his father because he had the rights of the firstborn *(Rashbam).*

Though, as the previous chapter concludes, the chiefs of Esau dwelt as *masters* in *the land of their possessions* [36:43] — i.e. the land that was *their* eternal possession — Jacob, like his father, dwelt as an *alien* in Canaan, the land of *his* heritage. God's prophecy that Abraham's progeny would be *aliens* [15:13], and consequently the concomitant promise of the ultimate ownership of the land, was fulfilled only through Jacob and his progeny, but not through Esau *(Ramban).*

[This interpretation however does not account for the use of וַיֵּשֶׁב, *settled,* instead of וַיָּגָר, *sojourned,* a word that is much more reflective of *alien status,* as discussed below. Hence the comments that follow.]

Our passage is perceived in the *Midrash* to connote how Jacob, after his life-long struggles wished finally לֵישֵׁב בְּשַׁלְוָה, *to settle down in tranquility,* but the anguish of the Joseph affair sprang upon him. For when the righteous look forward to tranquility, the Holy One, Blessed be He* says, 'Are the righteous not satisfied with what is stored up for them in the World to Come that they expect to live at ease in This World too!' *(Rashi).*[1]

*In the *Midrash* the reading is: *'The Satan* says.' The latter reading follows the majority of parallel *Midrashim* which comment similarly that wherever one finds settling and tranquility, there the *Satan* accuses. Cf. *Sanhedrin* 106a: 'The term וַיֵּשֶׁב, *settled,* always foreshadows grief.' (Cf. *Torah Temimah).* In *Tanchuma Yashan* and *R' Bachya* however, the reading is as *Rashi* cites it.] Cf. *Torah Sheleimah* notes 1, 6 and 9.]

1. Certain old texts of *Rashi* add the following parable from the *Midrash:*
The camels of a flax dealer once came into a city laden with flax (this follows the reading in *Tanchuma; Rabbah* reads: thorns). A blacksmith asked in wonder where all that flax could possibly be stored.

37
1 Jacob settled in the land where his father had sojourned, in the land of Canaan. 2 These are the

[The commentators explain that the Midrashic interpretation is inspired by the fact that the verb ישב, *settle*, generally denotes a permanent, tranquil state of dwelling, whereas גור, *sojourn*, denotes the insecure גֵרוּת, *alien-status*, experienced by Abraham and Isaac. Abraham had been told in 15:13 that his *offspring would be aliens. Rashi* there explains that they would experience this alien status even while living in Canaan. Abraham is accordingly described as having only וַיָּגָר, *sojourned* [20:1 and 21:34]; Isaac was similarly commanded to *sojourn (*גור*) in the land* [26:3]. But as this verse intimates, Jacob wished to לֵישֵׁב, *settle down*, permanently and tranquilly in the land where his father had experienced only temporary *sojourning* (מְגוּרֵי). The opening verse of this portion is intended to emphasize this contrast. But as the narrative proceeds to tell us, the affair of Joseph shattered this tranquility. Apparently God did not wish Jacob to enjoy tranquility in This World; his tranquility would be enjoyed in the World to Come.

[The Divine Plan decreed that Abraham's offspring could not live in Canaan on a permanent footing until the fulfillment of the prophecy that they would be enslaved 400 years ... and that the fourth generation would return (see 15:13ff). Therefore, the affair with Joseph occurred which, as *Rashi* explains below, was the catalyst leading to the family's migration to Egypt and, eventually, Israel's enslavement.]

As *R' David Feinstein* explains, Jacob's desire לֵישֵׁב, *to settle down* was premature, since the decree of גֵרוּת, *temporary sojourning*, was still in force. Therefore, as soon as Jacob sought a permanent status, the events leading to his Egyptian exile were set in motion.

בְּאֶרֶץ כְּנָעַן — *In the land of Canaan.* Since 35:27 has already related that Jacob arrived safely at the home of Isaac, this is added to emphasize how, although Esau went on to inherit Mount Seir, Jacob remained behind in *Canaan*. Though the land had been promised him as an eternal heritage — and he was now *in effect but an alien* — he accepted his status in complete faith. This was the case until, as the narrative continues, events led to the Egyptian bondage and their eventual conquest of *Eretz Yisrael (Or HaChaim).*

[The implication of *Or HaChaim* seems to put Jacob in the position of a conscious exile while yet in Canaan. This differs somewhat from the implication of *Rashi* above that Jacob attempted to alter his status to that of an indigenous inhabitant. *Or HaChaim* may be interpreted as observing how *in effect* — notwithstanding Jacob's desires or plans — he was but an alien on alien soil in contrast with Esau who was already master of his territory.]

This detail also serves to inform us why Jacob did not follow his past custom of courteously submitting to Esau by moving elsewhere and allowing Esau to remain in 'the land where his

'Don't worry,' one clever man answered. 'One spark from your smithy, and all of it will go up in flames!'

Similarly, when Jacob heard of the multitude of Esau's chieftains enumerated above, he was struck with fear: 'Who could ever hope to conquer them?' he asked.

[God reassured him: 'You fear them? One spark from Joseph, and they will go up in flames!' *Midrash).*]

Thus, the list of Edomite rulers is followed by: *These are the offspring of Jacob — Joseph.* And it is written (*Obadiah* 1:18): *The house of Jacob shall be a fire, and the house of Joseph a flame, and the house of Esau stubble; they shall burn them and consume them.*

As *Rashi* says above (30:25), with the birth of Joseph, Jacob felt confident enough to leave Laban and return to Canaan without fear of Esau.

ב כְּנָעַן: אֵלֶּה | תֹּלְדוֹת יַעֲקֹב יוֹסֵף בֶּן־שְׁבַע־

father had sojourned.' Jacob insisted on remaining there because *it was Canaan,* and inherent in his remaining there was the *mitzvah* of יִשּׁוּב הָאָרֶץ, *settling Eretz Yisrael.* Furthermore, Canaan is more suited to the development of holiness than any other land *(Haamek Davar).*

2. Joseph and his relations with his brothers. The seeds of the Egyptian bondage.

אֵלֶּה תֹּלְדוֹת יַעֲקֹב־יוֹסֵף — *These are the chronicles of Jacob—Joseph,* etc.

[The primary meaning of תולדות, as *Rashi* interprets it throughout Scripture, is *genealogy; generations; offspring; progeny; products* (cf. 2:4; 5:1; 6:9; 10:1; 11:10; 11:27; 25:12; 25:19; 36:1; 36:9). Since Joseph is the only one enumerated from among Jacob's many children, it is impossible in this context to interpret it as a listing of Jacob's offspring. Had this verse been genealogical, it should have read, as the *Midrash* notes: *These are the progeny of Jacob: Reuben, Simon, Levi, etc.*]

Therefore, pursuing what he feels to be 'the most literal meaning of the text within the context of the narrative,' *Rashi* explains that our passage implies אֵלֶּה שֶׁל תּוֹלְדוֹת יַעֲקֹב *these are the chronicles* **pertaining to** *the offspring of Jacob.* [I.e., having recorded Jacob's settlement in Canaan, the Torah proceeds to relate]: This is the story of the settlements and wanderings of Jacob's *sons* until they were permanently settled in the Holy Land by Joshua. The primary factor in this odyssey was the narrative beginning: *Joseph was seventeen years old* etc. This incident resulted in the descent to Egypt [and the foretold bondage, setting the stage for the return and permanent settlement of *Eretz Yisrael.*]

[Thus, *Rashi* regards our verse as the introduction to the entire remainder of the Torah. As he explains above, upon completion of the brief outline of Esau's progeny and their settlements, the Torah goes on to trace Jacob's wanderings and the history of his progeny until *they* were permanently settled in Canaan, an event which, as foretold to Abraham at the Covenant Between the Parts [see 15:13], could occur only after they were enslaved. That the Torah attaches this entire narrative to *Joseph* is because he is the primary protagonist of this initial part of the family's history (cf. *Mizrachi; Tzeidah laDerech; Gur Aryeh; Levush).*][1]

Our translation: *these are the*

1. In the *Midrashic* sense, *Rashi* continues that our passage, *These are the progeny of Jacob*—**Joseph,** [instead of *Reuben* who was the firstborn] implies that Joseph was Jacob's primary son and all of Jacob's other sons were secondary to him. This was because:

(a) Jacob served Laban for no other reason than to marry Rachel [Joseph's mother, and so it may be said that Joseph, Rachel's oldest son, was the *primary* son while the others — though they preceded him — were born only in consequence of Jacob's desired marriage to Rachel. As we clearly see in 30:25 it was only after Joseph was born that Jacob desired to return home. Who brought them down to Egypt? — Joseph. Who sustained them in Egypt? — Joseph. It was for Joseph's sake alone that the Red Sea parted [see *Psalms* 78:17 *(Midrash)*];

(b) Joseph's facial features bore a 'striking resemblance to Jacob's [see below *v.* 3 on בֶּן־זְקֻנִים; also see *Overview*];

(c) The destinies of both were similar: both were hated; both had brothers who wished to kill them; [the *Midrash* adds: both were born circumcised; both were born of mothers who were barren by nature; both were shepherds ... both left the Holy Land; both married and begot children outside the Holy Land; both attained greatness through dreams; both brought blessings to the homes of their fathers-in-law ... both died in Egypt and were embalmed; the bones of both were carried back to *Eretz Yisrael* for burial.]

chronicles of Jacob is but an attempt to capture *Rashi's* sense as succinctly as possible. *Rashi's* interpretation as understood by *Mizrachi* — in context with the previous verse — is: וַיֵּשֶׁב יַעֲקֹב...בְּאֶרֶץ כְּנָעַן, *Jacob's* **[own]** *settlement was in Canaan,* while אֵלֶּה, *these are [the settlements of]* תֹּלְדֹת יַעֲקֹב, *the* **progeny** *of Jacob,* i.e. the events that occurred to them until the Israelites achieved permanency in *Eretz Yisrael.*

Apparently, most of the early commentators [such as *Ramban* below] understood *Rashi* to imply that the word תֹּלְדֹת itself refers to *settlements.* This is erroneous, as *Mizrachi* points out. Rather *Rashi* finds *settlements* implicit in אֵלֶּה, *these,* a pronoun which has as its antecedent the *settlements* of Jacob which is mentioned in the previous verse. Thus, the flow of the verse is: having just spoken of Jacob's settlement, we now go on to speak of those [i.e., the settlements] of his offspring.

Ibn Ezra — consistent with his interpretation of the word תּוֹלְדוֹת throughout Scripture — renders: *these are the histories of Jacob:* the events which befell him and the occurrences which befell him. The sense of the word תּוֹלְדוֹת is: *that which time* יֵלֵד, *brings forth* [*Prov.* 27:1], i.e. the events which evolved in his lifetime.

Rashbam disagrees with the above interpretations and delivers a lengthy dissertation on the principle that the interpretation of Torah must always be approached on more than one level. There is a responsibility to interpret a verse in its plain, literal sense whenever possible. Simultaneously, however, one must not forget that the *essence* of Torah learning — its laws and precepts — must be elicited by the various hermeneutic rules from allusions in the text. He writes that 'the early ones, because of their piety, involved themselves in leaning toward the primary task of Talmudic interpretation which, as the Sages taught, is the most laudable pursuit. Therefore they did not accustom themselves to pursue the depth of the *literal* interpretation of Scripture.' Nevertheless he maintains that not to be overlooked is the Rabbinic dictum [*Yev.* 11b]: אֵין הַמִּקְרָא יוֹצֵא מִידֵי פְשׁוּטוֹ, *a Scriptural text* [though it is subject to *Midrashic* interpretation] *is never deprived of its 'literal'* meaning. *Rashbam* states that *Rashi,* his grandfather, had conceded to him that if he had had the time he would have composed another commentary incorporating the literal interpretations that were constantly being discovered.

Going to the exposition of our verse, *Rashbam* continues that in the literal sense תּוֹלְדוֹת never means *events* [as *Ibn Ezra* interprets], but *offspring* or *descendants.* In the case of Esau, his *children* born in Canaan are listed in 36:1. The תּוֹלְדוֹת listed in 36:9 refer to Esau's children in the *broader* sense — the generations (kings, chiefs, etc.) which *eventually* descended from him in Seir [up to the time the Torah was

Similarly, in accordance with our verse which counts Joseph as the most prominent son, the Sages note that the firstborn should have issued from Rachel, but Leah earned the privilege through her supplications [or: through God's mercy]. Yet, in reward for Rachel's modesty [in disclosing the secret sign to Leah on her wedding night (see on 29:21)] God restored the privilege to her [by conferring the status of tribes on Menashe and Ephraim, thus, in effect, giving Joseph the double portion of the firstborn (see 48:5; 35:22 ff; cf. also 49:3ff; *I Chronicles* 5:1)] *(Bava Basra* 123a).

Actually *all* of Jacob's children should be enumerated here. That the verse reads: *These are Jacob's progeny: Joseph,* intimates that Joseph personified the qualities of all the tribes.

Similarly, did the Sages expound: The qualities of the tribes were represented in Joseph:

The firstborn status of Reuben [which was transferred to him *(I Chron.* 5:3)];
The prophetic powers of Levi [as an interpreter of dreams (41:13)];
The sovereignty of Judah [as a ruler of Egypt (42:6)];
The wisdom of Issachar [ibid. *v.* 40] *(R'Bachya).*

עֶשְׂרֵה שָׁנָה הָיָה רֹעֶה אֶת־אֶחָיו בַּצֹּאן
וְהוּא נַעַר אֶת־בְּנֵי בִלְהָה וְאֶת־בְּנֵי זִלְפָּה

given *(Ramban)*]. In the case of Jacob, too, the Torah first named the children born to him in Paddan Aram in 35:22. Now the Torah similarly proceeds to enumerate his תולדות in the broader sense — *his line of descendants* (children and grandchildren) who numbered seventy when they descended to Egypt. Accordingly, the Torah begins with Joseph to relate how it came about that they descended to Egypt.

Ramban disagrees with *Rashi's* interpretation because, he maintains, *settlements* is simply not a proper translation of תּוֹלְדוֹת. He also disputes *Ibn Ezra's* interpretation of *events*, because it is idiomatically incorrect to speak of a man as (יָלַד) *begetting*, events; in the Hebrew, the begetting of events can be ascribed only to *days*, as the verse in *Proverbs* intimates. *Ramban* conjectures that according to *Ibn Ezra* the verse may mean: *these are the events which* [*the 'days' of*] *Jacob begot.* [*Sforno* interprets similarly. Accordingly, the word *days* would be unstated but clearly implied].

Ramban suggests that the passage is elliptic and means: *'These are the offspring of Jacob: Joseph* and his brothers,' but 'and his brothers' is omitted since they were mentioned earlier [35:23-26. Joseph however, *is* mentioned because he is the *main* subject of the narrative that immediately follows.] Alternatively, *Ramban* offers an interpretation similar to *Rashbam's*, that אֵלֶּה, *these are*, refers to all those mentioned in the rest of this Book: the seventy souls who went down to Egypt, and the תולדות, *offspring* of Jacob beginning with Joseph who was the prime mover of the events that led to their descent to Egypt.

When Jacob left his father's home to live with Laban, the events that occurred to him foreshadowed the history of his descendants at the first exile. After his return home, his experiences symbolized their history during the Second Temple, its destruction, the long exile, and the ultimate redemption *(Sforno)*.

יוֹסֵף בֶּן־שְׁבַע־עֶשְׂרֵה שָׁנָה — *Joseph, at the age of seventeen.*

From this chronological detail we can calculate that Jacob was 108 at the time, since he was ninety-one when Joseph was born. Isaac — who as noted in the *comm.* to 35:29 was still to live twelve years beyond Joseph's sale, and who was sixty at the time of Jacob's birth — was then 168 years old. This incident occurred nine years after Jacob was reunited with his father. Following the traditional dating, Leah died at about this time (see *Seder Olam* 2).

We also deduce from this that Joseph was absent from his father for a total of twenty-two years. He was thirty years old when he stood before Pharaoh [41:46], following which came seven prosperous years and two years at which time his father came to Egypt. Deduct Joseph's age at the sale (17) from his age when he was reunited with his father (39), and we arrrive at twenty-two *(Rashbam*; see 'Chronological Deductions' on p. 1173).

הָיָה רֹעֶה אֶת־אֶחָיו בַּצֹּאן — [*He*] *was a shepherd with his brothers by the sheep.*

— I.e., *he was a shepherd*, and as such, was *with his brothers by the sheep.* Thus, only at work was he together with his brothers, the sons of Leah *(R' Hirsch)*.

Only the sons of Leah, who like Rachel was a primary wife, are described as Joseph's *brothers,* in contrast with the sons of the ser-

was a shepherd with his brothers by the sheep, but he was a youth with the sons of Bilhah and the sons of

vants [Bilhah and Zilpah] *(Rashbam).*

The translation of אֶת אֶחָיו as עִם אֶחָיו, *with his brothers* [cf. אִתּוֹ=עִמּוֹ] follows *Onkelos* and most commentators.

The translation *he was a shepherd* ... by *the sheep* attempts to account for the preposition בְּ preceding צֹאן, *sheep*, rather than the more common form רֹעֶה אֶת הַצֹּאן, *tended the sheep.* In the latter form, *sheep* is the object of the verb *tended*, [רֹעֶה]; if so, the flow would have been: *he tended the sheep with his brothers.* Most commentators, based on the preposition בְּ, maintain that רֹעֶה is a noun meaning *shepherd*, and the flow is *he was a shepherd along with his brothers*, therefore he would tend to be found בַּצֹּאן, *'by' the sheep.*

Others perceive the connotation to be that he was too young to shepherd the sheep himself, but הָיָה רֹעֶה אֶת אֶחָיו, *he shepherded* [אֶת=the accusative] *his brothers* בַּצֹּאן *by the sheep.* That is, he assisted his brothers as they tended the sheep *(Chizkuni; Alshich;* similarly *Abarbanel).*

וְהוּא נַעַר אֶת־בְּנֵי בִלְהָה וְאֶת־בְּנֵי זִלְפָּה — *But he was a youth with the sons of Bilhah and the sons of Zilpah.*

— I.e. but [in contrast with his *work* time when he associated with Leah's sons], his youthful *recreation time — his youth* — was spent associating with the sons of Bilhah and Zilpah, his father's wives. He kept aloof *socially* from Leah's sons and this caused them to hate him *(Rashbam).*

Joseph associated with the sons of Bilhah and Zilpah because Leah's children always slighted them [as being sons of the maidservants]; he therefore made it a point to befriend them *(Rashi).*

These sons of the maidservants are called here not his 'brothers', but *the sons of his father's wives.* So the picture presented to us is of a *motherless and brotherless youth.* All the others grew up in company with brothers and under the wing and influence of mother-love. Joseph stood alone. He had lost his mother early in life, and Benjamin was still too young to be a companion for him. With his step-brothers [from Leah] he did not feel comfortable; he felt more drawn towards the sons of the maidservants *(R'Hirsch).*

Joseph is called נַעַר, *a youth* [even though at seventeen one is considered a man] to imply that *he acted like an adolescent* — dressing his hair and adorning his eyes to look handsome *(Rashi* from *Midrash;* see *Overview).*

Ramban maintains that although Joseph was seventeen years old at the time, he was called נַעַר, *youth*, in the relative sense, for he was the youngest and frailest of the brothers [with the exception of Benjamin who was still a child], and therefore he sought the company of the sons of Bilhah and Zilpah. It was *their* sons, not those of Leah, whom Jacob charged with the responsibility of raising Joseph [and presumably Benjamin too] after the death of Rachel. This interpretation is confirmed by the authoritative translation of *Onkelos* who renders the sense of our passage as: וְהוּא מְרַבֵּי, *and he grew up*, with the sons of Bilhah and the sons of Zilpah. The Torah thus informs us that since he was a youth he stayed in their company.

According to *Ibn Ezra* the term indicates that the sons of the maidservants made him serve them because he was young [thus rendering: and *he was a 'boy' of the sons of Bilhah*, etc. A servant is therefore called נַעַר, *'boy,'* since a young person is generally servile to an older one *(Yohel Or).*] Had Joseph served his brothers from Leah — the matron — it would not have been wrong. This [degrading treatment from the sons of the maidservants] was the subject of the evil report Joseph later brought to his father.

Sforno suggests that the Torah mentions Joseph's youthfulness to illustrate that it was precisely *because he was young* and did not foresee the consequences that he sinned by telling tales about his brothers. Though Joseph was brilliant, the Sages observed that in general לֹא בְּדַרְדְּקֵי עֵצָה, *there is no wise counsel in children* [*Shabbos* 89b].

נְשֵׁי אָבִיו — His father's wives.

They were indeed Jacob's full-fledged *wives* [not concubines]. He married them as such [see on 30:4]. The Torah refers to them as *maidservants* only when they are mentioned together with Rachel and Leah to whom Bilhah and Zilpah were originally presented as servants. Likewise, in 35:22 when we are told that Reuben slighted Bilhah his father's *concubine,* the intent of the rather uncomplimentary reference was to indicate that *Reuben* considered her but a concubine unworthy of esteem; had she not been a maidservant, the incident would not have occurred [see *comm.* there] ...

Alternatively, while Rachel and Leah were alive, the Torah calls Bilhah and Zilpah *maidservants* and *concubines.* But now that Rachel and Leah were dead [see *Seder Olam* cited above] Jacob gave Bilhah and Zilpah the status of wives *(Ramban).*

See *comm.* to 30:7 where *Haamek Davar* makes the observation that although Rachel had freed Bilhah, the Torah still refers to her as שִׁפְחַת רָחֵל, *Rachel's maidservant,* to intimate that after having given birth Bilhah had continued to treat her still childless mistress with respect, unlike Hagar who treated the childless Sarah with lowered esteem after having given birth to Ishmael.

וַיָּבֵא יוֹסֵף אֶת־דִּבָּתָם רָעָה אֶל־אֲבִיהֶם — [*And*] *Joseph would bring*] *evil reports about them to their father.*

Whatever evil Joseph noticed in the sons of Leah, he reported to his father. He accused them of eating limbs torn from living animals, of treating the sons of the maidservants contemptuously by calling them slaves, and of suspicion of immoral behavior. Joseph was punished measure for measure [and in effect the Torah later vindicates the brothers as having been guiltless in his allegations *(Yerushalmi Peah* 1:1)]. When the brothers sold Joseph [*v.* 31] the Torah tells us that they *slaughtered* a he-goat and did not eat it live [intimating that they were not to be suspect of eating limbs torn from living animals, since 'even in the very act of wrongdoing they slaughtered ritually' *(Midrash)*]; in punishment for Joseph's 'gossip' that they called the sons of the maidservants *slaves,* Joseph himself was sold for a slave; and because he accused them of immorality, he himself was accused of immorality by Potiphar's wife [39:7] *(Rashi* from *Tanchuma).*[1]

1. Nearly all commentators agree that Joseph truthfully reported what he saw and that he was not slandering his brothers. Two obvious questions arise: (a) Why was Joseph punished for telling the truth? (b) How could the sons of Jacob be guilty of such charges? The consensus of the commentators is as follows:

— The brothers acted according to their understanding of the laws, but Joseph considered them to have acted improperly because he interpreted the law differently. He would then bring evil reports concerning them back to his father — based on his own assumptions. This is the intent of וַיָּבֵא ... אֶת דִּבָּתָם רָעָה, [*he*] *brought evil reports about them to their father.* The verse emphasizes the evil manner of the *reports* rather than of the *deeds,* as if to imply that

Zilpah, his father's wives. And Joseph would bring evil reports about them to their father.

[For alternate interpretations of what these evil report consisted, see below s.v. דִּבָּתָם רָעָה.]

Ramban **disagrees with** ***Rashi's*** interpretation that the evil reports were about the sons of Leah. He maintains that the evil reports concerned the *last*-mentioned subject of our verse: the sons of Bilhah and Zilpah whom he always associated with. *Ramban* argues that according to *Rashi*, the sons of Leah may well have hated Joseph but the others, the sons of Bilhah and Zilpah whom he befriended and defended, should have been loyal to him and protected him when Leah's sons conspired to kill or sell him. But as the narrative below makes clear, *all* the brothers [except Reuben and Benjamin *(R'Bachya)*] consented to Joseph's sale — the sons of Leah because they were jealous of him as a result of their father's love for him [next verse], and the sons of Bilhah and Zilpah because of his slanderous reports. Furthermore, it appears from *Bereishis Rabbah* [84:7] that Joseph's slander involved *all* the brothers.

Accordingly, *Ramban* suggests that Joseph spent all his leisure time with the sons of Bilhah and Zilpah and brought evil reports about *them* to his father, thus incurring *their* hatred. When the sons of Leah saw the favoritism their father showed Joseph [next verse], they too hated him. He was accordingly hated by *all* his brothers: by the sons of the maidservants because of his evil reports, and by the sons of Leah out of jealousy [and, as we shall see later, also for his dreams].

Mizrachi defends *Rashi* by maintaining that the reason the sons of the maidservants did not protect him from being sold was because of Joseph's dreams, but not because he slandered them. As the sons of maidservants they did not expect of Jacob to show them the same love as the son of Jacob's favorite wife, and therefore were not jealous of Jacob's favoritism, however, they were incensed at the implication of Joseph's dream — which affected them all — that they would have to be *subservient* to Joseph who would rule over them.

דִּבָּתָם רָעָה — ***Evil reports about them*** [lit. *their gossip* (which was) *evil*].

Rashi interprets the noun דִּבָּה as *gossip.* It is related to the same root

their *actions* were *not* intrinsically evil, but Joseph's *reports about them* [דִּבָּתָם] — which reflected the way he perceived their actions — were brought רָעָה, *in an evil manner.* He could have interpreted their actions *favorably,* but he did not. Whatever he could interpret as evil, he did, and he conveyed the facts to Jacob according to his own interpretation. He was therefore punished for all three reports:

a) **The charge that they ate limbs from living animals.** The brothers would slaughter an animal and, בְּעוֹדָהּ מְפַרְכֶּסֶת, *while the animal was still having spasmodic movements,* they would cut off a piece of flesh and prepare it for eating. They did this because as the Talmud observes [*Chullin* 33a] such meat is healthy [presumably because it is then freshest]. Of course, as the Talmud ibid. notes, one must first ritually salt and soak the meat before eating it, and, as is further noted in *Sanhedrin* 63a, it may not be eaten until the animal 'dies,' i.e., its spasmodic movements have ended.

Such action is permitted to *Jews only* since the criterion for Jews is that an animal be kosher-slaughtered. Once that has been accomplished, and though it still might make spasmodic movements it is no longer considered אֵבֶר מִן הַחַי, *flesh* [lit. *a limb*] *from a living animal,* and one may — even while it is still moving — cut a limb from it. However, the meat may not be *eaten* as long as the animal shows signs of life [because of the prohibition in *Lev.* 19:26 *you shall not eat with the blood;* see comm. there; cf. *Sanhedrin* 63a; *Yoreh Deah* 27:1].

Gentiles, too, are charged with the prohibition of tearing limbs from a living animal [see 9:4], but there is a basic difference: Gentiles may kill an animal in any manner they see fit, but they are enjoined that the animal be *completely dead and not show any signs of life* before a

ג אֶל־אֲבִיהֶם: וְיִשְׂרָאֵל אָהַב אֶת־יוֹסֵף

about them was רָעָה, *evil*. Whenever the Torah uses the expression מֵבִיא דִבָּה, lit. *brings gossip,* it refers to *truthful* reporting [and perhaps even suggests the 'bringing' of proof *(Akeidas Yitzchak)*] *of what one has actually seen* as in our case [where Joseph told the truth as he perceived it, even though he misinterpreted the facts; see footnote], as דובב, *causing to speak*, in *Song of Songs* 7:10. Our passage denotes that whatever ill Joseph could speak regarding them, he told his father.

Ramban explains that according to *Rashi's* interpretation דִבָּה, *gossip,* can refer either to good or evil reports; hence the Torah adds that the report

limb may even be torn from it [see *Chullin* 33a]. In their case it is not dependent upon *slaughter,* but upon death. Accordingly while the slaughtered animal is moving, its meat is forbidden to gentiles but permitted to Jews. In any case, as noted above, even a Jew may not *eat* the torn-off limb until it is soaked and salted, and the animal has died.

The Talmud cites another opinion, the prevailing one, that in the cases of kosher animals, gentiles too may tear the flesh immediately after a kosher-slaughter in accord with the principle that לית מידי דלְיִשְׂרָאֵל שָׁרֵי וּלְנָכְרִי אָסוּר, *there is nothing which is permitted to Israel, but is forbidden to a gentile.* Therefore, since Israelites may cut off flesh from kosher animals immediately after slaughter, it would be incongruous to forbid gentiles to engage in that very practice.

Joseph's evil report resulted from confusion over the above halachah. Following his own opinion, Joseph considered the brothers to be in violation of the law when he observed them cutting flesh from a just-slaughtered animal, before it had stopped moving. In accord with his own view, he told Jacob that the brothers were eating the flesh of living animals. He was wrong, either because Jacob's family had voluntarily obligated itself to observe the laws of kosher slaughter and thus had the status of Jews; or because even gentiles are not forbidden in the case of kosher animals.

The report was in effect malicious since Joseph should have judged them in a more favorable light and reported all the facts. For not doing so, he was punished *(Mizrachi; Gur Aryeh; Levush;* cf. *Tzeidah LaDerech* and *Yafeh Toar).*

[There is also an opinion that he considered them to still have the status of gentiles since the Torah was not yet given. Though they practiced kosher-slaughtering voluntarily, he erroneously thought they were still bound by restrictions incumbent upon gentiles and were not permitted to tear off a limb of an animal until all spasmodic movement stopped]

There is a further opinion [cf. *Tzeidah laDerech; Sifsei Chachamim*] that the 'living animals from which the brothers tore limbs' were בְּנֵי פְּקִיעָה, lit. *plucked out* children — a designation for fully grown calves — dead or alive — found inside a kosher-slaughtered animal. Even if such a calf survives its mother's slaughter and grows to maturity, it may be eaten without slaughter — as long as its mother was kosher-slaughtered. [The Sages later prohibited this practice because of מַרְאִית עַיִן, *it would appear* as though a transgression had been committed (see *Yoreh Deah* §13:2)]. Joseph, however, was under the impression that such animals required kosher-slaughter, and when he saw his brothers — who were following Torah law tearing their flesh without slaughtering them, he reported the 'sin' to their father without specifying the nature of the circumstances.

b) **The charge that they referred to the sons of the maidservants as 'slaves.'** What actually occurred was that they would taunt the sons of Bilhah and Zilpah by reminding them that their mothers had been servants of Rachel and Leah before Jacob freed and married them *(Mizrachi).*

Or the insult was in the figurative sense: By not socializing with them it was as if the other brothers were designating them as slave children *(Gur Aryeh).*

c) **The charge of immorality.** Joseph was super-righteous; he subscribed to the view [see *Kiddushin* 70a] that one may not associate at all with women. Therefore it irked him to see his brothers conduct trade with women. However the Halachah permits such commerce and non-personal association [see *Yoreh Deah Even HaEzer* 21:6]. A righteous person, however, does not even glance at women, and he might tend to suspect those who are lax in this regard. Joseph assumed the worst of his brothers and would paint a black picture of their behavior to their father *(Mizrachi; Gur Aryeh).*

3 *Now Israel loved Joseph more than all his sons*

whereas when the expression is מוֹצִיא דִבָּה, lit. *'extracts* gossip' [as in the case of the Spies (see *Numbers* 13:32)] it refers to a fabrication of *false* gossip.

Ramban, however, maintains that דִבָּה in *itself* refers to *evil* gossip. The Torah adds the redundant term רָעָה, *evil,* as a superlative to magnify the evil nature of the report.

According to *Radak,* the intent is that Joseph reported the evil that all his brothers spoke about *him* [Joseph]. He reported that they hated him and berated him, for as the next verse proceeds to tell us, Joseph was Jacob's favorite child.

Only *Ibn Ezra* of all the commentators interprets that the evil report is explicit in the Torah. As noted above, he maintains that the evil report was the fact that he was made a נַעַר, *servant,* to the sons of Bilhah and Zilpah.

It was, in a sense, to Joseph's credit that he reported these infractions *to their father only* but did not spread them about. He refrained, as the younger brother, from rebuking them directly, but instead reported them to his father in the hope that he would reprimand them *(Akeidas Yitzchak; Abarbanel).*

Hoffmann elicits this interpretation of Joseph's sincerity from the fact that the verse does not say that he brought evil reports to *his* father, but to *their* father — the father of them all — so that Jacob would reprimand his children and correct their misconduct.

[This follows the primary view that Joseph *truthfully* reported what he believed to have been their actions as he interpreted them. See footnote.]

3. The Torah now details for us the additional cause for the brothers' hatred of Joseph: jealousy over Jacob's obvious favoritism for him *(Radak).*

וְיִשְׂרָאֵל אָהַב אֶת־יוֹסֵף מִכָּל־בָּנָיו — *Now* [lit. *and*] *Israel loved Joseph more than all his sons.*

It emerges that Joseph's talebearing would not have been sufficient cause for the brothers to despise him to such a degree. Rather it was the combination of his talebearing coupled with their jealousy of Jacob's blatant favoritism that caused all the brothers to unite against him (*Alshich; Or HaChaim;* see *Ramban* above).

Midrashically, Joseph is considered a prototype presaging the destiny of the Jewish nation. His father's excessive love caused him to be hated by his brothers. They drove him from his father's house and, eventually, this led to the exile of the whole family. In the same way, all the heathen nations hate the people of Israel because God loves them and has associated Himself with them *(Tanchuma Yashan).*[1]

By referring to Jacob as *Israel* — [the name used to reflect Jacob's *spiritual*

1. Although Jacob is generally held to have erred in showing partiality to Joseph [see footnote end of next verse], the *Zohar* differs. The *Zohar* recalls that God Himself openly proclaims His affection for Jacob/Israel and His hatred of Esau and declares it formally through the prophet Malachi [1:2, 3] and others. Similarly, the three Patriarchs did not hesitate to demonstrate their love for one child, even though this might arouse feelings of hostility among the other children. When true love is the product of goodness and justice, it excludes everything which stands in its way; if the expression of love is inhibited, it is diminished and, to that extent, it becomes less true. When the Patriarchs showered greater love on one of their children, it was because they recognized that child as the true guardian of their spiritual heritage. Jacob knew full well that love for one could provoke the hatred of others, but he gave Joseph his love without reservation, even though it might cause fierce hostility on the part of the brothers. So too, God never concealed His love for His 'chosen people,' although it called forth the rancor and hatred of the nations.

Thus the struggle between the rival brothers of the Patriarchal family, as well as of the vast

מִכָּל־בָּנָיו כִּי־בֶן־זְקֻנִים הוּא לוֹ וְעָשָׂה
ד לוֹ כְּתֹנֶת פַּסִּים: וַיִּרְאוּ אֶחָיו כִּי־אֹתוֹ

role *(R' Bachya)*] — the verse emphasizes that this love had a *spiritual* origin, because Jacob saw in Joseph the making of an exceptional man.

However, as noted in the footnote to the end of this verse, it was an error for Jacob to *openly display* this love.

כִּי־בֶן־זְקֻנִים הוּא לוֹ — *Since he was a child of his old age* [lit. *for a son of old age was he to him*].

The translation follows *Rashi* who comments: *For he was born to him in his old age. Rashi* cites the alternative interpretation of *Onkelos* who renders: he was a *wise son* to him. [This interpretation follows the *Talmudic* dictum that זָקֵן, *old*, refers to זֶה שֶׁקָּנָה חָכְמָה, *one who acquired wisdom.*] Whatever Jacob learned in the Academy of Shem and Eber [during his fourteen years there (see 28:10 s.v. וַיֵּלֶךְ חָרָנָה)], he transmitted to Joseph.[1]

Alternatively, [following the *Midrash*, the word זְקֻנִים, *old age*, alludes to a contraction of זִיו אִיקוּנִין, *facial features*] — Joseph's facial features resembled Jacob's. [Cf. on 21:3 s.v. לִזְקֻנָיו where a similar Midrashic interpretation is given regarding Isaac's physical resemblance to Abraham.]

Ibn Ezra, like *Rashi*, explains that Joseph was referred to as *a child of his old age* since Jacob begot him in his old age when he was ninety-one years old [see calculation "B' in footnote to 35:29. Jacob was born in the year 2108 from Creation, and Joseph in 2199]. They likewise referred to his brother Benjamin *a little son of his old age* [44:20].

Ramban disagrees with this interpretation which singles out Joseph as the child *born in Jacob's old age*, since *all* Jacob's children were born to him in his old age, Issachar and Zevulun being but a year or two older than Joseph! (cf. *comm.* end of 30:24). [Additionally, the implied difficulty is that if the term refers to the *youngest* child born in old age, then it should apply only to Benjamin, not Joseph.]

Ramban maintains that the term בֶּן זְקֻנִים [lit. *son of old age*] refers to the custom of old men to choose one of their children to attend to their personal needs. Joseph was the son chosen by the aged Jacob *to look after him in his old age* and to remain at his side constantly. That is why Joseph did not accompany his brothers when they went to pasture the flocks in distant places. Joseph's constant attendance naturally increased Jacob's affection for him, especially since, as the Sages note, Joseph had the understanding of an elder, and Jacob imparted to him his knowledge of Torah. In the case of Benjamin, however, [see 44:20] the term is to be understood literally *as son of his old age*. This is supported by *Onkelos*, too,

'family of nations,' finds a fertile breeding-ground in the choice of the privilege of love. Apparently this struggle is necessary for the conquest of moral perfection and for the ultimate triumph of good. Without such struggle, mankind would lapse into stagnation and indolence *(R' Munk)*.

1. That Jacob chose to teach Joseph what he had learned at the Academy was prophetic. Eber, who headed the Academy after Shem's death, was surely not superior to Isaac in his knowledge of Torah, nevertheless Jacob chose to spend fourteen years studying at the Academy although he was already sixty-three years old and an accomplished student of Isaac. Jacob had to prepare for a long exile with Laban, and he had to equip himself with the spiritual tools that would enable him to remain strong even when he was away from the environment of Isaac and Rebecca. To do that, he went to Eber. Those were the teachings Jacob conveyed to Joseph, for Joseph, like his father, would be forced to endure a personal exile of twenty-two years *(Sh'lah)*.

4 *since he was a child of his old age, and he made him a*
fine woolen tunic. 4 *His brothers saw that it was he*

for in the case of Benjamin *Onkelos* renders the term as בַּר סַבְתִּין, *son of old age,* while here he renders it as בַּר חַכִּים, *a wise son.* Therefore, unlike its description of Benjamin, the Torah does not limit itself to the observation that Joseph was merely a בֶּן זְקוּנִים, but qualifies it by adding the possessive הוּא לוֹ, *to him,* i.e., Joseph was considered by *Jacob* as *his* son, to whom he would impart his Torah learning, and who would look after him in his old age.

Mizrachi and *Gur Aryeh* defend the interpretation of *Rashi* [and *Ibn Ezra*] against *Ramban's* criticism by noting that Jacob begot no children after Joseph for a period of about eight years before Benjamin was born. Throughout this period, Joseph was the youngest child, and he quite naturally acquired the nickname בֶּן זְקוּנִים, *a child of old age.* Furthermore, Joseph was the only child of the beloved Rachel, and Jacob may well have despaired of having more children after the passage of so many years. By the time Benjamin was born eight years later, Jacob's love of Joseph as the 'ben zekunim' had become so firmly rooted, that it could not be displaced by the birth of Benjamin. Furthermore, Joseph proved to be the wisest of them all, and Benjamin was but a child at the time.

Onkelos [who renders the term here as meaning *wise son*] does not accept the interpretation that Jacob loved Joseph as a son of his old age because, if so, the brothers would not have despised Joseph since it is only natural for an elderly father to love such a child. *Onkelos* therefore adopts the interpretation that Jacob loved Joseph since he perceived him to have superior wisdom; this could be a cause of jealousy *(Gur Aryeh).*

Abarbanel suggests that while Joseph acted childishly (וְהוּא נַעַר, *and he was a youth)* when he was with his brothers, his behavior toward Jacob, in contrast, was different. With him, Joseph acted as a בֶּן זְקֻנִים, *a person of maturity;* thereby he won Jacob's love.

Chizkuni suggests that *Benjamin* never quite captured Jacob's heart the way Joseph did because Jacob always associated Benjamin's birth with the death of his beloved wife, Rachel, who died while giving birth to him.

R'Hirsch in 21:3 explains זְקֻנִים, *old age,* as the time when a person reflects upon the accomplishments and experiences of his life, and looks forward to passing them on to a child who can take his place and carry on. The son who is best suited to succeed his father is called his בֶּן זְקֻנִים, *the child of his old age,* i.e., the heir to his fund of experience. This is the implication of the Sages' teachings that Joseph resembled Jacob's זִיו אִיקוּנִים, literally *'splendor' of his image.* The word *splendor* suggests more than facial resemblance — Jacob's splendor was his role and accomplishment. It was this aspect of Jacob's spiritual image that Joseph resembled as his בֶּן זְקוּנִים.

וְעָשָׂה לוֹ כְּתֹנֶת פַּסִּים — *[And] he made [for] him a fine woolen tunic.*

The translation follows *Rashi:* A garment of *fine wool.* The word is similar to כַּרְפַּס in *Esther* 1:6 [which is explained in *Megillah* 12a as a compound word: כַּר, *cushion,* of פַּס, *fine wool.* We find the same sort of garment mentioned in the story of David's children Amnon and Tamar [which would imply that it was a very fine garment, suitable for members of a royal family; see *II Samuel* 13:18ff (*Mizrachi;* see *Gur Aryeh* and *Tzeidah l'Derech)*] *(Rashi).*[1]

Rashi adds that Midrashically, the word פַּסִּים may be interpreted as an acronym an-

1. Based on the unbridled hatred that ensued from the favoritism Jacob showed Joseph, the

אָהַב אֲבִיהֶם מִכָּל־אֶחָיו וַיִּשְׂנְאוּ אֹתוֹ
ה וְלֹא יָכְלוּ דַּבְּרוֹ לְשָׁלֹם: וַיַּחֲלֹם יוֹסֵף

ticipating the troubles that were to befall Joseph as a result of the כְּתֹנֶת פַּסִּים, as he was soon to be sold from one owner to another: the פ represents Potiphar; the ס, the סוֹחֲרִים, *merchants;* the י, the יִשְׁמְעֵאלִים, *Ishmaelites;* and the מ, the *Midianites (Rashi).*

Other interpretations are:

— A *long-sleeved* garment which reached to פַּס יָדוֹ, *the palms of his hands (Midrash)* [(or according to *Pesikta Zutresa: the soles of his feet)*], in contrast with the shorter tunics generally worn at the time. Such long sleeved garments which reached over the wrists as well as long garments which reached the soles of the feet were a symbol of nobility inasmuch as they indicated that the wearer was not meant for manual labor *(Maharzu).* With fatherly love, Jacob saw that Rachel's first-born son would become master of the family, but as the Sages observe, it was a mistake for Jacob to show it [see *footnote*].

— An embroidered robe *(Targum Yonasan).*

Yafeh Toar emphasizes that the above interpretations are not mutually exclusive: It was a long-sleeved embroidered tunic, made of variously colored strips of fine wool.

— The tunic which designated him for leadership *(Sforno).*

It would appear that after Reuben 'disarranged his father's bed' and the birthright was transferred to Joseph [see above 35:22 and *I Chron.* 5:1], Jacob made the special garment to distinguish Joseph as the new possessor of 'first-born' status, who was now qualified to perform the sacrificial service. This might also be the connotation of בֶּן זְקֻנִים, the son whom he now considered the 'eldest' — the 'firstborn' — of all the children *(Kli Yakar).*

Me'am Loez mentions a tradition that the tunic was the garment that Jacob received from Esau when the latter sold him his birthright. This garment originally belonged to Adam; it would fit only a firstborn

Sages proclaimed that: "A man should never single out one child among his other sons, for on account of two *sela's* weight of the fine woolen [garment] which Jacob gave Joseph in excess of his other sons, his brothers became jealous of him, and the matter resulted in our forefathers' descent into Egypt" (*Shabbos* 10b; see *Rambam,* Laws of Inheritance 6:13, and *Choshen Mishpat* 282). [Cf. *Zohar* cited in the footnote above.]

Actually, as *Tosafos* observes, the Egyptian servitude had already been decreed since Abraham's time at the Covenant Between the Parts [15:13ff (nearly 200 years earlier)], but without this unjustified hatred perhaps the oppression would not have been so severe.

Maharsha explains alternatively that were it not for these events the immediate cause of the decreed descent to Egypt would not have been a family tragedy whereby the brothers sold their own flesh and blood into slavery. Instead the cause would have been one that would not disgrace the righteous sons of Jacob. According to *Torah Temimah,* the Covenant Between the Parts did not specify Egypt as the country of oppression; it was as a result of the sequence of events evolving from the jealousy that Egypt became the place. [See also *footnote* on page 455.]

* * *

Why does the *Talmudic* ruling above read 'A man should **never** [לְעוֹלָם אַל יְשַׁנֶּה אָדָם] single out ... '? It would have sufficed to read: אַל יְשַׁנֶּה אָדָם, *'A man should not single out ...* ' What is the significance of *never?*

Apparently Jacob, too, was quite aware what jealousy among children could cause. But he was under the false impression that in the case of *his* righteous children it would be different. As the Sages observe, even Jacob miscalculated in this matter. From Jacob's bitter experience, the Sages derive that a man should *never* single out one of his children — not even in a situation where he is is convinced that *his* children are better and would be unaffected by such distinction *(Harav David Feinstein).*

whom their father loved most of all his brothers so they hated him; and they could not speak to him peaceably.

son. Since the birthright had been taken away from Reuben because of the incident with Bilhah, the garment was now given to Joseph. [According to this tradition the phrase *he had made him* would have to be understood in the sense of *provided him.*]

According to *Malbim* Jacob presented Joseph with this tunic because, unlike the other brothers who tended the sheep, Joseph was always in attendance on Jacob [see *Ramban* above on בֶּן זְקֻנִים]. It was only fitting that Joseph be garbed beautifully when performing the *mitzvah* of serving his father. Similarly, Esau, who was renowned for his great filial devotion, wore special garments while waiting upon his father [27:15].

4. וַיִּרְאוּ אֶחָיו כִּי־אֹתוֹ אָהַב אֲבִיהֶם ... וַיִּשְׂנְאוּ אֹתוֹ — *[And] his brothers saw that it was he whom their father loved ... so* [lit. *and*] *they hated him.*

They saw — i.e., they perceived from the tunic that what they hitherto only *suspected* was obviously true *(Hoffmann).*

The construction of the verse stresses the word אתו, *he.* The most galling thing to the brothers was that of all the members of the family, Jacob's affections were centered on *him* — the one who had no friendly relations with them and who drew the reproaches of their father on them *(R'Hirsch).*

Our verse describes hatred that resulted from Jacob's affection. Accordingly, 'brothers' here refers to the sons of Leah; *they* were jealous of Joseph because they felt equally entitled to Jacob's love. The sons of the *maidservants*, however, were not jealous of Jacob's partiality for Joseph — they knew that they could not expect to equal the favor shown the son of Jacob's favorite wife; *they* hated Joseph for his evil talebearing. Additionally, as we shall see, *all* of the brothers hated him for the implication of his dreams: that he would reign over them and they would be subservient to him *(Ramban; Mizrachi).*

Abarbanel suggests that all the brothers hated Joseph because they interpreted Jacob's preference for him to mean that Jacob planned to disinherit them. Just as Abraham disinherited Ishmael and the sons of Keturah in favor of Isaac [25:5ff], and Isaac disinherited Esau in favor of Jacob, they feared that Jacob was grooming Joseph at their expense to be the sole heir to the blessings and the land.

וְלֹא יָכְלוּ דַּבְּרוֹ לְשָׁלֹם — *And they could not speak to him peaceably.*

— I.e., *even* peaceably. They could not speak *at all* with him: certainly not regarding matters of contention, but not even regarding general, peaceful matters *(Ibn Ezra; Yohel Or).*

Abarbanel [based on *Tanchuma Yashan*] interprets: *They could not respond to his greetings of 'Shalom.'* He would come and ask after their welfare and they would not answer him.

Cf. *R' Hirsch: They could not bear his speaking for peace.* They took nothing from him in a friendly spirit; interpreted everything he said in a bad way, and, most of all, misunderstood any friendly advances.

חֲלוֹם וַיַּגֵּד לְאֶחָיו וַיּוֹסִפוּ עוֹד שְׂנֹא
ו אֹתוֹ: וַיֹּאמֶר אֲלֵיהֶם שִׁמְעוּ־נָא הַחֲלוֹם

According to *Radak:* They could not converse with him peaceably, but constantly quarrelled.

Though they *had* to speak with him regarding household matters and shepherding with which he was involved at Jacob's command, they could not do so peaceably as brothers *(Sforno)*.

That the brothers openly expressed their bitter feelings to Joseph and did not suppress their hatred follows the following *Midrash* cited by *Rashi*:

From [what is written here about] the disgrace [of the Tribal Ancestors] you may learn their virtues: They did not pretend what they did not feel [lit. 'they did not speak one thing in their mouth having another in their hearts'].

5. Joseph's dream.

Dreams of which Scripture speaks are generally interpreted to be vehicles of prophecy. See *comm.* to 28:12. Dreams play a significant role in Joseph's life as will be discussed in the commentary and *Overview.*

Our Sages in *Berachos* 55a leave as an open question whether dreams have any meaning. To be sure, Joseph's dreams, and those of Pharaoh and his officials contain revelations of future events which can originate only from a transcendent Source. That Providence uses this half-conscious state to prophetically introduce thoughts in people's minds and thereby to cause whole series of events to happen, and that God uses peoples' belief in dreams to achieve this end we see repeatedly from Jacob's and Joseph's history, as well as from the prophetic dreams of Pharaoh, Nebuchadnezzar and Gideon. All were prognostications and fulfilled according to their interpretations.

The commentors grapple with a difficult philosophic question: In view of the fact that God determines the sequence of events in advance, why should any responsibility fall upon the actors who carry out God's plan? Are they not mere puppets?

This problem, which touches the very core of the relationship between predestination and man's free will, is approached through various perspectives. In the final analysis, however, as *Rambam* [*Hilchos Teshuvah* 5:5] states, this eternal problem cannot be resolved in terms of human thought processes which are fundamentally different from Divine Thought. Although it is incumbent upon us to understand as much as we can, we must not forget that human analysis is totally inadequate to comprehend fully the interplay of human deeds and Providential acts *(Radak; R'Hirsch; R'Munk)*.

וַיַּחֲלֹם יוֹסֵף חֲלוֹם — [*And*] *Joseph dreamt a dream.*

The Torah itself tells us that Joseph truly had a dream. This negates any possible suspicion on our part that Joseph *fabricated* the dream to gain superiority over them *(Or HaChaim)*.

It is not clear, however, whether the dream mentioned in this verse is the one described in the next verse.

Most commentators maintain that this *was* the dream described below. Our verse, stating that Joseph became even more hated by his brothers because of his dreams, is a general introduction to the ensuing narrative. The next verse proceeds to *detail* the exchange that led to this intensified hatred.

However, *Chizkuni* is of the opinion that the dream of our verse is not recorded because it was not fulfilled.

R'Hirsch perceives the continuity of verses 5 and 6 to be that Joseph had a dream [*v.* 5] and *started* telling it to his brothers in a general way: 'I had a

[5] *Joseph dreamt a dream which he told to his brothers, and they hated him even more.* [6] *He said to them, 'Hear, if you please, this dream which I*

dream ... ' but as soon as he innocently started speaking, they cut him off. He persisted, however [*v.* 6], insisting that the dream was too important for them to ignore.

Kli Chemdah similarly offers that the phraseology of the verses suggests that Joseph had a dream not recorded in the Torah. וַיַּגֵּד לְאֶחָיו, *and he told his brothers* (not: וַיַּגֵּד אֹתוֹ לְאֶחָיו, and he told *it* to his brothers) — i.e., he merely told them he had a dream, but they did not give him the opportunity to describe it. When he had the dream described in the next verse however he urged them to listen to it since it affected them greatly. [Comp. *Haamek Davar* below.]

וַיַּגֵּד לְאֶחָיו — *Which* [lit. *and*] *he told to his brothers.*

If Joseph knew that relating the dream would provoke their hatred, why, indeed, did he relate it to them?

The commentators grapple with this and the opinions vary.

— *Sforno* suggests that this was an example of the young Joseph's immaturity.

— Perhaps Joseph wanted to justify Jacob's excessive love for him by emphasizing that his future greatness was decreed by Providence [and would not come as a result of Jacob's preferential treatment *(Chizkuni)*]. Thereby he hoped to remove their hatred.

— Alternatively, he wanted to end their hatred by making them realize that he would yet rise up to greatness and they would some day need him and have to bow down to him. Becoming aware of this they might stop hating him, being afraid of possible later retribution *(Or HaChaim).*

— *Lekach Tov* observes that Joseph implored them to listen to the dream because as the Sages said [*Berachos* 55b]: 'An uninterpreted dream is like an unread letter.' To be effective it must be communicated and interpreted.

— *Vilna Gaon* notes that since Joseph understood the dreams to be prophetic in nature, he was required to reveal them lest he be guilty of the grievous sin of withholding a prophecy [כּוֹבֵשׁ נְבוּאָתוֹ] from those for whom it was intended.

וַיּוֹסִפוּ עוֹד שְׂנֹא אֹתוֹ — *And they hated him even more* [lit. *and they increased more to hate him*].[1]

Since they understood him to be claiming that he was their superior *(Or HaChaim).*

Abarbanel interprets that their hatred increased as soon as he *started* telling the dream to them [see *R'Hirsch* above] because they assumed he was fabricating the matter. But he pressed on and insisted on telling it to them.

6. According to most commentators, as noted, after having introduced this topic in the previous verse, the Torah now proceeds to detail their conversation.

שִׁמְעוּ־נָא הַחֲלוֹם הַזֶּה אֲשֶׁר חָלָמְתִּי — *Hear, if you please, this dream which I dreamt.*

He urged them to listen to it.

1. *Midrash HaGadol* observes that Joseph fell because of a dream, and achieved greatness because of a dream: He fell because of a dream as evidenced by the hatred of his brothers which resulted from this dream; he owed his prodigious rise to Pharaoh's dream [chapt. 42].

ז הַזֶּה אֲשֶׁר חָלָמְתִּי: וְהִנֵּה אֲנַחְנוּ
מְאַלְּמִים אֲלֻמִּים בְּתוֹךְ הַשָּׂדֶה וְהִנֵּה
קָמָה אֲלֻמָּתִי וְגַם־נִצָּבָה וְהִנֵּה תְסֻבֶּינָה
ח אֲלֻמֹּתֵיכֶם וַתִּשְׁתַּחֲוֶיןָ לַאֲלֻמָּתִי: וַיֹּאמְרוּ
לוֹ אֶחָיו הֲמָלֹךְ תִּמְלֹךְ עָלֵינוּ אִם־
מָשׁוֹל תִּמְשֹׁל בָּנוּ וַיּוֹסִפוּ עוֹד שְׂנֹא

Haamek Davar explains the flow of verses 5 and 6 as follows: Having dreamt, Joseph hastened to tell his brothers about the dream as if they were his trusted confidantes. In view of the strained relations between them, the brothers regarded his friendliness as hypocritical and insincere, and hated him for it. Nevertheless, since he urged them to listen, they indulged him, not realizing that the dream related directly to them.

Not only did he *relate* the dream to them but he pressed them to *hear* it, i.e. to understand its significance. This resulted only in arousing their hatred even further *(Sforno).*

The definite article **הַחֲלוֹם הַזֶּה, this** ***dream,*** **is stressed.** Earlier, he told them only that he had a dream. Now he was more specific and implored: Listen to this dream that I told you about before *(Or HaChaim).*

7. וְהִנֵּה — [*And*] *behold!*

Joseph used the word וְהִנֵּה, *behold,* three times in his account of the dream. [As observed in the comm. to 28:13 and 31:10] it emphasizes that Joseph's vision was more than a mere fantastic dream: הִנֵּה, *behold,* [in the colloquial sense of *look!; see!*] is used in Scripture to introduce something of *substance (Ramban).*[1]

It is axiomatic that when a dream is perceived as vividly as though one were awake, it attests to the Providential truthfulness of the vision. Therefore Joseph kept emphasizing that such was the case: every facet of the dream was vivid and hence true *(Or HaChaim).*

אֲנַחְנוּ מְאַלְּמִים אֲלֻמִּים בְּתוֹךְ הַשָּׂדֶה — *We were* [lit. *are*] *binding sheaves in the middle of the field.*

The theme of this dream was sheaves of wheat. It was in fulfillment of the dream that Joseph's rise to greatness was in conjunction with grain [see *Ramban* below] *(Daas Zekeinim; Radak).*

וְהִנֵּה קָמָה אֲלֻמָּתִי וְגַם־נִצָּבָה — *When, behold! my sheaf arose and remained standing.*

My sheaf *arose* — by itself. This intimated that Joseph's rise to greatness would come about without apparent cause — through Providence — and not because they would promote him to it *(Abarbanel).*

That it *remained standing* implied that his rule would endure a long time, as it did. In fact, he was viceroy of Egypt for eighty years — the longest reign recorded in Scripture *(Sforno).*

The rendering of the nearly synonymous terms קום and נצב follows *Rashi:* קָמָה אֲלֻמָּתִי

1. *R' Bachya* writes that the three times Joseph affirmed his dream alluded to the three times that his brothers would have to come to Egypt: (1) when the famine began; (2) when Jacob told them to return [43:2] during which time Joseph revealed himself; (3) when they finally returned with Jacob.

dreamt: 7 Behold — we were binding sheaves in the
middle of the field when, behold! — my sheaf arose
and remained standing; then behold! — your sheaves
gathered around and bowed down to my sheaf.'
8 His brothers answered, 'Would you then reign
over us? Would you then dominate us?' And they

— *my sheaf arose* [active voice] *erect,* וְגַם נִצָּבָה, *and remained standing* [passive voice] *in its place.*

Malbim perceives the verb נצב to imply *resistance.* His sheaf remained standing despite attempts to overthrow it.

וְהִנֵּה תְסֻבֶּינָה אֲלֻמֹּתֵיכֶם וַתִּשְׁתַּחֲוֶיןָ לַאֲלֻמָּתִי — *Then* [lit. *and*] *behold! — your sheaves gathered around* [lit. *surrounded*] *and bowed down to my sheaf.*

The symbolism of the 'sheaves' intimated to Joseph that they would come to bow down to him because of grain. That they *gathered around* indicated that they would surround him like subjects around a king *(Ramban).*

Though initially they would try to resist him, they would eventually come around and accept him of their own volition *(Abarbanel).*

8. The brothers' response.

[The meaning of the dream could not be misunderstood, especially in connection with the fine woolen tunic which singled him out for leadership. It humiliated the brothers]:

הֲמָלֹךְ תִּמְלֹךְ עָלֵינוּ אִם־מָשׁוֹל תִּמְשֹׁל בָּנוּ — *Would you then reign* [lit. *reign will you reign*] *over us? Would you then dominate* [lit. *rule shall you rule*] *us?*

A מֶלֶךְ, *king,* rules with the consent of the people, while a מוֹשֵׁל, *ruler,* rules despotically. Our passage accordingly means:

Do you imagine that we will *voluntarily* accept you as king [הֲמָלֹךְ תִּמְלֹךְ] over us or that you will rule [אִם מָשֹׁל תִּמְשֹׁל] over us *forcibly? (Ibn Ezra* as explained by *Yohel Or).*[1]

Onkelos renders: *Do you imagine that you will be a king over us or do you expect to impose yourself as an authority over us?* — since people bow down before both kings and others in positions of authority. [According to this interpretation, the word מֶלֶךְ, *king,* makes no distinction between one who rules by *consent* or *despotically;* rather it refers to the extent of the power he exercises. The word מוֹשֵׁל *ruler,* from the root meaning *dominion,* implies degree of authority which is lower than that of a king]. The verse accordingly means: Not only will you never be *king* over us, you will never exercise *any* authority over us *(Ramban).*

1. The literal translation of their response: *reign will you reign over us, if rule shall you rule us?* implies a prognostication that he would indeed rule over them, and the repetitive phraseology implies that he would become the ancestor of two kings — Jeroboam and Jehu, and of two judges — Joshua and Gideon. [This is an example of what the Sages term as 'he prophecied without realizing what he prophecied.'] It is as the Sages observe [*Berachos* 55a]: The significance of all dreams depends on their interpretation *(Midrash; Lekach Tov; Zohar)* [See footnote to 41:13.]

ט אֹתוֹ עַל־חֲלֹמֹתָיו וְעַל־דְּבָרָיו: וַיַּחֲלֹם
עוֹד חֲלוֹם אַחֵר וַיְסַפֵּר אֹתוֹ לְאֶחָיו
וַיֹּאמֶר הִנֵּה חָלַמְתִּי חֲלוֹם עוֹד וְהִנֵּה
הַשֶּׁמֶשׁ וְהַיָּרֵחַ וְאַחַד עָשָׂר כּוֹכָבִים
י מִשְׁתַּחֲוִים לִי: וַיְסַפֵּר אֶל־אָבִיו וְאֶל־
אֶחָיו וַיִּגְעַר־בּוֹ אָבִיו וַיֹּאמֶר לוֹ מָה

וַיּוֹסִפוּ עוֹד שְׂנֹא אֹתוֹ עַל־חֲלֹמֹתָיו וְעַל־דְּבָרָיו — *And they hated him even more—because of his dreams and because of his talk* [lit. *words*].

I.e. for the dreams themselves and for his temerity in relating them, as well as the boastful manner in which he did so *(Ramban).*

In his brother's eyes, Joseph's visions of lordship betrayed his true aspirations, for, even if it were true that he was having such deams, it is fair to assume that dreams reflect the fantasies of the dreamer. Moreover, his visions contained the very real potential of fulfillment. That is why they could arouse hostility so intense as to culminate in a conspiracy to murder *(Alshich.* See also *Ramban, v.* 10).

Rashi explains *his talk* as a reference to his *evil reports* about them [*v.* 2].

Dreams is in the plural to imply that they hated him not only because of this particular dream but because they assumed that he was *always* dreaming of ruling over them *(Abarbanel),* or it refers to other dreams of his which are unrecorded by Scripture, or it anticipates any dreams he was yet to have *(Radak).*

9. Joseph's second dream: *The bowing heavenly spheres.*

The message of this dream — although employing a different metaphor — is essentially the same as that of the first. The repetition was meant to provide evidence that God is the ultimate Source of the message being conveyed. A dream repeated indicates the certainty of the fulfillment, as we find in 41:32: *As for ... having had the same dream twice, it signifies that the matter has been determined by God and that God will soon carry it out (Akeidas Yitzchak).*

וַיְסַפֵּר אֹתוֹ לְאֶחָיו — *And he related it to his brothers.*

In *v.* 5, the verb וַיַּגֵּד, *and he told,* is used, while our verse employs the verb וַיְסַפֵּר, *and he related.* In general the root נגד, *told,* denotes a comprehensive and detailed communication of a *new* experience or observation [see *Isaiah* 42:9], while ספר, *relate,* implies a recapitulation of something previously said, and is used often of dreams *(Radak* shoresh נגד; see *Ibn Ezra* to *Exod.* 19:9. But cf. *Kli Chemdah* regarding the omission of the word אֹתוֹ, *it).*

וַיֹּאמֶר — *And he said.*

Whereas in *v.* 6 Joseph *asked* his brothers to listen to his story, here he simply waited for an opportune time and started telling it to them. He knew that if he would *ask* them to listen this time, they would surely refuse *(Haamek Davar).*

hated him even more — because of his dreams and
because of his talk.
9 *He dreamt another dream, and related it to his*
brothers. And he said, 'Look, I dreamt another
dream: Behold! the sun, the moon, and eleven stars
were bowing down to me.'
10 *And he related it to his father and to his*
brothers. His father scolded him, and said to him,

הִנֵּה חָלַמְתִּי חֲלוֹם עוֹד — *Look* [or: *behold*] *I dreamt another dream.*

— And a recurrent dream indicates the certainty of fulfillment (see *Akeidas Yitzchak* above).

[The word הִנֵּה, *behold,* introduces again that what he was about to reveal was a matter of substance. See *v.* 7].

וְהִנֵּה הַשֶּׁמֶשׁ וְהַיָּרֵחַ וְאַחַד עָשָׂר כּוֹכָבִים מִשְׁתַּחֲוִים לִי — [*And*] *Behold! the sun,* [*and*] *the moon, and eleven stars were bowing down to me.*

'Joseph was standing in the east, and the sun, moon and stars were traveling west in their normal orbits; then they turned back on their orbits and went east, dipping low in the heavens so they appeared to bow down' (*B'chor Shor* cited by *Torah Sheleimah*).

[The symbolism of the dream (as apparently understood by *Rashi* following *Berachos* 55b; cf. *Ramban* below) was: *The sun* represented his father, *the moon,* his mother (actually Bilhah who raised him after Rachel's death, see below); *the eleven stars,* his brothers who later bowed down to him in Egypt.]

The first dream, as noted, represented their motive in bowing to Joseph — not in recognition of his personal greatness — but because he was the dispenser of *grain.* When they first bowed, they were unaware that the all-powerful viceroy of Egypt was their brother. This dream however represented obeisance to Joseph *personally,* in recognition of the stature, and position he had attained (*Abarbanel*).

10. וַיְסַפֵּר אֶל־אָבִיו וְאֶל־אֶחָיו — *And he related* [it] *to his father and to his brothers.*

After having told it to his brothers [*v.* 9], he repeated it to his father in their presence (*Rashi*).

Joseph did not tell his father the first dream concerning the sheaves because it referred only to the brothers. However, he did tell him this dream, because he understood that the *sun* in this dream symbolized Jacob (*Ramban*).

His brothers did not interpret the dream and, as noted, 'an uninterpreted dream is like an unread letter.' He therefore repeated the dream to his father in their presence (*Haamek Davar*).

וַיִּגְעַר־בּוֹ אָבִיו — [*And*] *his father scolded him.*

For arousing their hatred [by relating the dream] ... and also to appease the furious brothers (*Rashi; Ramban*).

— But Jacob's purpose in scolding him was *not* because Jacob considered the matter to be impossible (*Mizrachi*).

הַחֲלוֹם הַזֶּה אֲשֶׁר חָלָמְתָּ הֲבוֹא נָבוֹא אֲנִי
וְאִמְּךָ וְאַחֶיךָ לְהִשְׁתַּחֲוֹת לְךָ אָרְצָה:
יא וַיְקַנְאוּ־בוֹ אֶחָיו וְאָבִיו שָׁמַר אֶת־הַדָּבָר:

מָה הַחֲלוֹם הַזֶּה אֲשֶׁר חָלָמְתָּ — *What is this dream that you have dreamt!*

— This is not to be understood as a *question,* but as a rhetorical outburst like [*Psalms* 144:3]: *'What is man that You should take cognizance of him!'* The intent here is: 'What kind of dream is that? You should not even have repeated such nonsense.' Or the meaning is: 'How dare you dream such a dream! It is nothing but a symptom of the conceit and ambitions that cause you to have such thoughts.' Cf. *Daniel* 2:29 where the verse intimates that dreams are composed of thoughts entertained during the day; cf. also ibid. 4:2 *(Ramban).*

[Jacob immediately understood the *sun* to refer to himself and *moon* to refer to Joseph's mother]:

הֲבוֹא נָבוֹא אֲנִי וְאִמְּךָ וְאַחֶיךָ לְהִשְׁתַּחֲוֹת לְךָ אָרְצָה — *Are we to come* [lit. *come, should we come*] — *I and your mother and your brothers — to bow down to you to the ground?*

— Your mother [Rachel] is long dead [so fulfillment of your dream is impossible]! He [Jacob; or according to *Be'er Mayim Chaim:* Joseph] did not realize that the 'moon' of Joseph's dream referred to Bilhah who reared him like a mother. [The above follows the *Midrash* (cf. *Ibn Ezra)*]. The Rabbis [in the *Talmud, Berachos* 55a], hold that the moon did, indeed, refer to Rachel. Since this part of the dream was obviously not possible of fulfilment, they derive from this portion of Joseph's vision that even a prophetic dream is bound to contain a portion that will not come true. [Although Jacob surely knew of the tradition concerning unfulfillable portions of dreams *(Mizrachi),* and, as the next verse shows, he *did* take the dreams seriously *(Sefer HaZikaron),* Jacob's purpose in speaking out strongly against Joseph was to remove the jealousy and resentment of the brothers. He therefore attempted to reassure them by intimating that just as the dream was absurd with respect to *Rachel,* so it had no validity with regard to *them (Rashi).*

Had Joseph's mother been alive, Jacob would still have rebuked him in this way *(Rashbam).*

Ramban maintains that the 'moon' in the dream does not refer to Bilhah since according to him *all* Jacob's wives had died before Jacob went down to Egypt. *Ramban* derives this opinion from the omission of any reference to Jacob's wives in the genealogy in 46:26. Accordingly, *Ramban* cannot accept *Rashi's* view that the 'moon' symbolized Bilhah.

Ramban theorizes that the *moon* symbolized the household in general — the seventy souls who would prostrate themselves before Joseph. The *stars* symbolized the brothers in particular who are singled out because they bowed down to Joseph separately before Jacob and the entire family arrived [see 43:26].

11. וַיְקַנְאוּ־בוֹ אֶחָיו — *So* [lit. *and*] *his brothers were jealous of him.*

Earlier, they *hated* him for the notion of his dream and his temerity

37 *'What is this dream that you have dreamt! Are we to*
11 *come — I and your mother and your brothers — to*
bow down to you to the ground?' 11 *So his brothers*
were jealous of him, but his father kept the matter in
mind.

at urging them to hear it. But now they were sure that his dreams of grandeur were not merely products of egotistical fantasies; he would certainly not have an ambition to rule over his father! Obviously, therefore, the dreams were a Providential revelation that he would some day attain greatness, and this inspired *jealousy* within them *(Alshich; Or HaChaim).*[1]

וְאָבִיו שָׁמַר אֶת הַדָּבָר — *But his father kept the matter in mind* [lit. *safeguarded the matter*].

I.e., he waited for its fulfillment *(Rashi).*

Though he scolded Joseph for the reason noted, Jacob respected the dream's reliability, and kept the matter in mind *(Radak).*

The notion of his having to bow before his son did not disturb him as it did his sons, for "of everyone a man is jealous, except his son and disciple" [*Sanhedrin* 105b] *(Haamek Davar).*

Though Jacob initially thought the dream referred to Rachel who was dead and could not possibly bow down before Jacob, he thought that תְּחִיַּית הַמֵּתִים, *Resurrection of the Dead,* would take place in his days, and regarded the dream as possible ... According to Rav Chiyyah the passage implies: *But his Father* [i.e. Jacob's heavenly Father], the Divine Spirit, bade him: *keep the matter in mind* — it will be fulfilled! *(Midrash).*[2]

Although we find later that many steps were taken to make Jacob believe that Joseph had died, it was only because Jacob kept his belief in the substance of the dream that he did not assimilate the 'fact' of Joseph's death. This underlying faith in Joseph's survival enabled him to accept and believe the seemingly impossible report that Joseph was alive and had attained greatness [45:28] *(Rashbam).*

1. *R' Bachya* points out that since hatred [especially among people who are close] is generally coupled with jealousy, we already know from the earlier revelations of their hatred [*v.* 4, 8] that they must have been jealous of him. That our verse speaks of jealousy must, therefore, imply a new kind of emotion. *R' Bachya* explains that one feels jealous of his competitor in a competitive field: a wise man resents a greater scholar, but he has no feelings against a muscular giant. The earlier hatred was an outgrowth of jealousy resulting from Jacob's favoritism for all the sons felt equally entitled to his love — but the brothers still considered themselves superior to the lad who was many years their junior. Now, however, they perceived from his dreams — which, as wise and great people in their own right, they understood — that Joseph was destined to rule over them. This created the conditions of a *new* form of jealousy; now they viewed him as a peer in wisdom and authority, who was about to surpass them.

2. The *Midrash* continues: Jacob *safeguarded* the matter: He took a pen and wrote down the dream, recording its precise time and place, and awaiting its fulfillment. He attributed to his own sins the travail of the brothers in Egypt before the dream would be fulfilled and the fact that he would have to bow down to Joseph: 'If my ledger has been scrutinized,' [i.e., if this is punishment for my deeds]', Jacob exclaimed, 'what can I do?'

°וַיֵּלְכוּ אֶחָיו לִרְעוֹת אֶת־צֹאן אֲבִיהֶם
יג בִּשְׁכֶם: וַיֹּאמֶר יִשְׂרָאֵל אֶל־יוֹסֵף הֲלוֹא

12. The sale of Joseph.

Following the precedent of *Sforno,* we think it our duty to look, if not for a *justification,* then at least for an *explanation* for the event which now follows. After all, we are not dealing with a band of robbers and murderers who would lightly murder for the sake of a coat. *Sforno* refers us to the time when the brothers considered themselves to be in mortal danger and they examined their deeds to find the reason God had punished them (42:21). They found no cause for remorse in the sale of Joseph, but they *did* condemn themselves for hard-heartedly ignoring his pleas for mercy. Clearly they considered the act to have been harsh but not wrong. Accordingly, we must remain alert for any indication which could help make the affair psychologically explainable. This theme will be followed throughout the commentary *(R'Hirsch).* [See *Overview.*]

וַיֵּלְכוּ אֶחָיו – *Now* [lit. *and*], *his brothers went.*

This phrase is separated by the disjunctive *esnachta* from לִרְעוֹת, *to pasture.* The implication is that the true purpose of their trip was not to pasture the sheep, but simply to get away. They were convinced that their rights were threatened by Joseph, and this is why they took advantage of an opportunity to go very far away from his abrasive presence. Shechem is about fifty miles from Hebron. [See continuation below] *(R' Hirsch).*

לִרְעוֹת אֶת־צֹאן אֲבִיהֶם – *To pasture their father's flock.*

The word אֶת is an untranslated accusative particle. Its function is to indicate that the noun following it receives the action of the preceding verb. In our verse, this would mean that the *sheep* were the subjects of the *pasturing.* In our verse, however, the letters of אֶת have dots above them in the Torah's text. [Such dots are meant to indicate that a word is not to be understood in its general meaning *(Mizrachi; Gur Aryeh).*] Thus, we are shown that the *sheep* were not the object of the pasturing as would normally be understood from the word אֶת. Rather they went to *pasture themselves,* that is, to indulge themselves *(Rashi* from *Midrash;* see *Mizrachi).*

With the particle אֶת omitted, the verse would be homiletically rendered: *Now his brothers went to feed* [themselves]; *their father's flock was in Shechem (Tzeidah laDerech; Sifsei Chachomim).*

It was only ostensibly for the sake of the sheep that they went. In reality, however, their purpose was to "pasture themselves," to preserve their independence which they believed to be jeopardized by Jacob's ideas of Joseph's future *(R' Hirsch).*

Hadar Zekeinim perceives the Hand of Providence in the motive for their trip to Shechem. From that journey, events evolved which made it possible for them eventually to *sustain themselves* in famine. For through the events whose providential roots were in Shechem, Joseph became ruler of Egypt and was enabled to assure sustenance to the flocks of Jacob.

In this context we can better understand Joseph's later comforting statement to his brothers [45:5] *Look! God has sent me before you as a source of*

[12] *Now, his brothers went to pasture their father's flock in Shechem.* [13] *And Israel said to Joseph, 'Your*

life. The dotted אֶת in our verse — rather than the omission of the particle entirely (see above) — signals this dual connotation: As far as the brothers were concerned, they had gone *to shepherd their father's flock;* the dots, however, draw attention to the Hand of Providence in the matter: they were actually laying the groundwork for sustaining *themselves* — the 'flock of their father' Jacob *(Divrei David).*[1]

בִּשְׁכֶם — *In Shechem.*

— Known for its fertile grazing land *(Akeidas Yitzchak).*

They had chosen a spot far from home because they could not bear to witness the favoritism shown Joseph; and possibly they already harbored plans of taking revenge on Joseph, a task that would be easier at a distance. As the Sages observe, Shechem was a spot foredestined to be the scene of misfortunes [see *Rashi* next verse] *(Abarbanel;* comp. *Ramban* below).

They reasoned that Jacob would probably not send his beloved Joseph to such a treacherous place, and *should* he send him, Jacob would always blame his death on the vengeful inhabitants of Shechem who acted in hatred of Jacob *(Malbim).*

In view of the massacre they had perpetrated against Shechem [ch. 34], it would have seemed foolhardy for the brothers to venture into that city. Nevertheless, the brothers were fearless. They placed their trust in God, Who, as we are told in 35:5, inspired His fear in the surrounding nations soon after the incident occurred, enabling Jacob's family to remain unmolested. Now, with the passage of time, the matter was as much as forgotten *(Radak).*[2]

13. Jacob feels the breach between

1. Similarly the matter may be explained as follows: אֶת is usually perceived Midrashically as signalling a רִבּוּי, *exegetical amplification* [see comm. to 1:1], in this case alluding to themselves: *His brothers went to pasture* אֶת, themselves, in addition to צֹאן אֲבִיהֶם, *their father's flock.* The dots over אֶת accentuate that within the Divine Scheme, the Hidden רִבּוּי, *amplification* of the particle — *themselves* — was more important than their own motive, *the flock.*

They had ostensibly gone to *pasture the flock,* but in reality they were actively responsible for the events that caused *themselves* to be 'pastured' during the later years of famine. True, these events were already pre-ordained at the Covenant Between the Parts when it was foretold to Abraham that his descendants would be enslaved, and the Hand of Providence was guiding throughout. But God's goal, though incontrovertible, could have been achieved by other means. That the brothers were chosen to become God's agents in carrying out His Will by their malicious scheme is because מְגַלְגְלִין חוֹבָה עַל יְדֵי חַיָּיב, *evil is brought about through the guilty (R' David Feinstein;* see *Overview* and footnote to *v.* 15).

[A similar concept is expressed of Pharaoh in *Semachos* 8: Even had no Pharaoh arisen, Israel was destined to servitude as God specifically foretold. But Pharaoh was chosen for this mission because he was wicked and deserved punishment. See *comm.* to 15:14, p. 528: *'Egypt as God's Agent; Free-Will and Foreknowledge.'*]

1. *R'Hirsch* finds great significance in their choice of Shechem. That was the place where family unity and a sense of responsibility for one another were forged. There Simeon and Levi had made the memorable declaration: הַכְזוֹנָה יַעֲשֶׂה אֶת אֲחוֹתֵנוּ, *should he treat our sister like a harlot?* [34:31]. Then, when Dinah had been defiled, the entire family stood together for the sake of *one* of its members who was threatened from without, how much more must they unite when the honor and independence of the *whole* is threatened from within by one member. This could have been their intention. Therefore, they went to Shechem, where the memory of the great deed of fraternity could encourage them to do what seemed to them imperative. For if their fears concerning Joseph's future were justified, they could have cause to feel threatened.

אַחֶיךָ רֹעִים בִּשְׁכֶם לְכָה וְאֶשְׁלָחֲךָ
יד אֲלֵיהֶם וַיֹּאמֶר לוֹ הִנֵּנִי: וַיֹּאמֶר לוֹ לֶךְ־נָא
רְאֵה אֶת־שְׁלוֹם אַחֶיךָ וְאֶת־שְׁלוֹם הַצֹּאן
וַהֲשִׁבֵנִי דָּבָר וַיִּשְׁלָחֵהוּ מֵעֵמֶק חֶבְרוֹן

Joseph and his brethren, and does not want it to grow. At the same time, he wants to test Joseph's feelings towards his brothers, so at first he gives him no special errand, but simply says: 'I think it would be better to send you out to the flocks, to be with the others.' Joseph is at once ready to go. His conscience is quite clear; he has no ambition to be king or dictator *(Ralbag).*

וַיֹּאמֶר יִשְׂרָאֵל אֶל־יוֹסֵף — *And Israel said to Joseph.*

Joseph had remained home in his father's service and did not accompany the flocks when they went to pasture in distant places *(Ramban* on *v.* 3 s.v. בֶּן זְקֻנִים).

In dispatching Joseph on this fateful mission — preparatory to the Egyptian exile — the Patriarch is referred to here as *Israel* denoting his spiritual aspect as architect of the destiny of his descendants *(R' Bachya).*

הֲלוֹא אַחֶיךָ רֹעִים בִּשְׁכֶם — *Your brothers are pasturing in Shechem, are they not?*

I.e., you certainly are aware that your brothers are pasturing in Shechem *(Radak)* ...

... A place wrought with danger for them since they had slain all its inhabitants *(Rashbam* quoting *R' Yosef Kara).*

[Thus, though the brothers themselves feared no revenge from the Shechemites, Jacob's fatherly compassion and fear for his children's welfare and safety overwhelmed him.]

לְכָה וְאֶשְׁלָחֲךָ אֲלֵיהֶם — *Come* [lit. *go* (idiomatic)], [*and*] *I will send you to them.*

Jacob never suspected that there would be foul play, or he would never have sent Joseph *(Radak).*

The verb form לְכָה, *go,* with a suffix ה [as distinct from the usual imperative לֵךְ] denotes a courteous request: *go, if you please.* It was not a *demand* since Jacob understood that Joseph might be hesitant to go under the circumstances. When Joseph agreed to go, however, Jacob used [in the next verse] the usual imperative form לֵךְ, *go,* in specifying the mission *(Abarbanel; Malbim).* [Cf. שְׁבָה and אָכְלָה in 27:19.]

וַיֹּאמֶר לוֹ הִנֵּנִי — [*And*] *he said to him, 'I am ready'* [lit. *here I am*].'

In this one-word response Joseph was not merely acknowledging his physical presence or responding to the call of his name — the contexts in which this reply usually occurs in the Torah. [Cf. 22:1 and 27:1]. In this case the reply is more significant because Joseph already knew what he was being asked to do. Thus, the commentators explain the response as indicating *total preparedness and obedience.*

— It is an expression denoting humility and readiness to do his father's bidding, though he was well aware that his brothers hated him [and that it was dangerous to place himself at their mercy] *(Rashi).*

He obediently strengthened himself to comply with his father's bidding; he did not offer the excuse 'How can I undertake such a mission — they hate me! *(Ramban).*[1]

Joseph had hoped that reverence

brothers are pasturing in Shechem, are they not?
Come, I will send you to them.' He said to him: 'I am
ready.' 14 And he said to him, 'Go now, look into the
welfare of your brothers and the welfare of the flock,
and bring me back word.' So he sent him from the
depth of Hebron, and he arrived at Shechem.

for their father would prevent them from harming him despite their hatred of him *(Radak).*

14. לֶךְ־נָא־רְאֵה אֶת־שְׁלוֹם אַחֶיךָ וְאֶת־שְׁלוֹם הַצֹּאן וַהֲשִׁבֵנִי דָּבָר — *Go now, look into the welfare of your brothers and the welfare of the flock* [lit. *see the peace of your brothers and the peace of the flock*], *and bring me back word.*[2]

Look into the welfare, etc. — i.e. make an intelligent evaluation of whatever needs improvement and correct it. Obviously if Jacob wanted only a *report,* he could have sent one of his servants *(Sforno).*

Jacob made Joseph a שְׁלִיחַ מִצְוָה, *an agent to perform a mitzvah,* inasmuch as he was heeding the command of his father. By asking him to *bring back word,* Jacob was also, in effect, causing Joseph to be his agent on the *return* journey as well, thus making that a meritorious mission as well. It is a rabbinic dictum that שְׁלוּחֵי מִצְוָה אֵינָם נִיזוֹקִים, *those on a meritorious mission are not harmed (Alshich; Or HaChaim; Malbim).*

[Despite his long ordeal, Joseph was not *physically* harmed; to the contrary, he eventually became ruler of Egypt and the source of sustenance for his family during the famine.

That Joseph suffered at all might be because, as *Rashi* observes below, Shechem was 'a place pre-destined to be the scene of misfortunes,' and, as the *Talmud* notes in *Chullin* 142b and elsewhere, the special protection afforded agents of a *mitzvah* does not extend to places of unusual danger *(Torah Temimah).* [See *Or HaChaim* cited below, *v.* 5 s.v. וְהִנֵּה תֹעֶה who suggests that Joseph forfeited his invioable status as שְׁלִיחַ מִצְוָה when he ventured further than Shechem.]

It is quite natural for one to inquire after his *children;* but why after the *flock?* — This proves that one must inquire after the well-being of anything from which he benefits *(Midrash).*

... For R'Aibu said: A man must pray on behalf of the provider of his needs. Therefore, because he benefited from his sheep, drinking their milk and wearing their wool, he had to inquire after their well-being *(Tanchuma Yashan).*

וַיִּשְׁלָחֵהוּ מֵעֵמֶק חֶבְרוֹן — *So he sent him from the depth* [or: *valley*] *of Hebron.*

Jacob escorted him [cf. this meaning of the verb שלח in 12:20 and 24:59] to that point, and dispatched him from there on his mission *(Malbim).*

The Torah mentions the place

1. The *Midrash* praises Joseph for immediately expressing his absolute filial devotion notwithstanding his brothers' hatred for him:

R' Chama bar R' Chaninah said, 'Our father Jacob later remembered these words and grieved to his innermost depths: "I [other versions read: You] knew that your brothers hated you, and yet you answered me 'Here I am?'!"

2. Some Sages in *Chullin* 91b derive the dictum that a scholar should not venture out alone at night from our verse. Jacob said 'Go now, *see* how your brothers are.' The word *see* implies that he go at a time when he can *see,* namely, by day. [Others deduce it from 32:25; 23:3; 32:32; and *Ruth* 3:2.]

טו וַיָּבֹא שְׁכֶמָה׃ וַיִּמְצָאֵהוּ אִישׁ וְהִנֵּה תֹעֶה
בַּשָּׂדֶה וַיִּשְׁאָלֵהוּ הָאִישׁ לֵאמֹר מַה־

from which Joseph was dispatched to emphasize that Jacob was a great distance from his sons. Therefore, they had the temerity to act as they did *(Ramban* cf. *Abarbanel v.* 1).

[The translation *depth of Hebron* instead of *valley of Hebron* reflects the insight of the Sages in the *Midrash* who perceive in this passage an allusion to the workings of Divine Providence. This interpretation is cited by *Rashi* and nearly every major commentator. The concept reappears frequently and in various forms in the reflections of the Midrashic Sages in their exegesis to this episode]:

— **מֵעֵמֶק** חֶבְרוֹן, *from the* valley of Hebron. But Hebron was situated on a *mountain,* as it is said [*Numbers* 13:22]: *And they went up into the Negev and came to Hebron!** [Rather, the term מֵעֵמֶק חֶבְרוֹן, *from the 'valley' of Hebron* is to be understood in the *figurative* sense]: Jacob's decision to send Joseph to what appeared to be his potential doom was in fulfillment of **עֵצָה עֲמוּקָה**, the *profound* [lit. *deep*] *design* which had been confided to Abraham who is here called חֶבְרוֹן a contraction of the words חָבֵר נָאֶה, *pleasant companion* of God, who was buried in Hebron. The chain of events beginning with Joseph's trip would fulfill God's prophecy to Abraham at the Covenant Between the Parts [15:13]: *Your offspring shall be aliens in a land not their own (Midrash; Rashi; Targum Yonasan).*[1]

The *Zohar* records that Jacob took Joseph to Abraham's grave in the 'depth of Hebron,' and from there he dispatched him on his mission.

וַיָּבֹא שְׁכֶמָה — *And he arrived at Shechem.*

— A place pre-destined to be the scene of misfortunes [מָקוֹם מוּכָן לְפוּרְעָנִיּוֹת]. It was there that the sons of Jacob sinned [by selling

*[*Torah Temimah* cites *Joshua* 14:12 where Hebron is even more explicitly described as a mountain, and wonders why *Rashi* did not cite that verse.]

1. [Abraham had been informed at the Covenant Between the Parts that his offspring would be aliens in a strange land for 400 years where they would be subjugated and enslaved [15:13]. As noted in the commentary there, the 400 years of 'alienation' would begin with the birth of Isaac, while the period of *servitude* would not begin until Jacob's sons emigrated to Egypt. This story of Joseph and his brothers — who appear as agents of Providence — is perceived as the catalyst of the process culminating in the Egyptian Exile.

Thus, the second portion of the prophecy began finding expression in Joseph's mission. Underlying that mission were the hidden workings of Providence: God was sending the descendants of Abraham to Egypt, a land not their own. Jacob and Joseph were unwittingly fulfilling this prophecy — the father in sending, and the son in going to seek his brothers, though neither knew where Joseph's steps would lead him.]

The *Zohar* perceives this by observing that Jacob, who knew how much his sons hated Joseph, should not have exposed his son to such danger; he could have sent others instead. That he nevertheless sent his favorite son against his every natural instinct illustrates the Hand of Providence as the Prime Mover (cf. *Malbim).*

As *R' Munk* writes: 'The people involved in this episode appear as agents of Providence. The Universal plans for the realization of the Messianic goals of history are carried out amidst the comings and goings, the dreams and grudges, the ambitions and vindictiveness of the children of the family of Abraham. And here the Torah gives us an example of the story of a family in which each person remains totally responsible for his acts although in historical

37
15 [15] *A man discovered him, and behold — he was blundering in the field. The man asked him, saying,*

Joseph]; that Dinah was ravished; and that the House of David was later divided [see *I Kings* 12:1] (*Rashi* from Sanhedrin 102a).

Although Joseph's sale took place in *Dothan*, that was but a hamlet in the general area of the large city of Shechem. Furthermore, according to the Midrashic interpretation [cited in *v.* 17 s.v. כִּי שָׁמַעְתִּי], Dothan was not a place name at all (see *Rashi Sotah* 13b s.v. מִשְּׁכֶם גְּנָבוּהוּ; and *Rashi Sanhedrin* 102a s.v. בִּשְׁכֶם מְכָרוּ. Cf. *Torah Temimah* §17).

15. וַיִּמְצָאֵהוּ אִישׁ — *[And] a man discovered him.*

This 'man' was the angel Gabriel. Cf. *Daniel* 10:21 where he is also called 'man' (*Rashi*). He was in the likeness of a man (*Targum Yonasan*).

— He was sent by God to Providentially lead him to his brothers in the ultimate fulfillment of His Plan [see below] (*Ramban*).[1]

Rashi's exegesis [from *Midrash Tanchuma* and concurred with by most *Midrashim*] that the 'man' was really an angel is based on the fact that in the ensuing exchange, Joseph simply asked about his brothers as though he had not the slightest doubt that the 'man' knew his brother and where to find them. This would not have been the case had he been a mortal. Having established that he was an angel, the Sages further identified him — on the basis of the appellation 'man' — as Gabriel (*Mizrachi*).

There is another view in the *Midrash* that since *'man'* is mentioned here three times there were a total of *three* angels — each 'man' being understood to refer to someone else. *Midrash HaChefetz* cited by *Torah Sheleimah* suggests that these angels were the same three who appeared to Abraham [18:2].

Ibn Ezra, however, interprets that the man was indeed a *mortal* wayfarer. Thus, when Joseph inquired about his brothers, he meant: Tell me, if you know. [This does not negate the interpretation that this 'man' was sent by Providence to lead Joseph to his brothers in fulfillment of the Divine scheme.]

וְהִנֵּה תֹעֶה בַּשָּׂדֶה — *And behold — he [Joseph] was blundering in the field.*

I.e., having come to Shechem, Joseph did not find his brothers in the fields. He proceeded to search the area for them, blundering about from field to field — since he was looking for them in pasture lands — when he stumbled into the 'man' (*Radak*).

This episode is to Joseph's credit. When he did not find his brothers, he

perspective they were acting as שְׁלוּחִים לַמָּקוֹם, agents of the Divine Providence.'

R' David Feinstein explains the above *Zohar* in the light of *Gittin* 56b. There, the Sages teach that God sometimes causes wise men to make seemingly unwise decisions in order that they be instrumental in bringing about the Divine end. This is based on מֵשִׁיב חֲכָמִים אָחוֹר וְדַעְתָּם יְסַכֵּל, *God turns wise men backward and makes their knowledge foolish* [*Isaiah* 44:25]. Here, too, Jacob's 'error' was part of God's plan.

1. How distressing that a heavenly angel had to be dispatched to create the encounter which placed the brothers in a spiritual dilemma they could not overcome! Would it not have been sufficient to have the Midianites capture and sell Joseph without involving his brothers in the shocking crime?

Were this story to unfold that way, however, we might have ח״ו questioned God's judgment. We would have said, as did Moses before he understood why Israel deserved such suffering, "Why is this family worse than any other that it suffers such misfortune?" Therefore we must be shown that the brothers resentment of Joseph's ambitions was so great that they could contemplate such extreme measures against him. That being the case, we can understand why the family had to undergo a purging exile that would purify them sufficiently for spiritual freedom and to receive the Torah (*Oznaim LaTorah*). [See also *footnote* to *vs.* 3, 12.]

טז תְּבַקֵּשׁ: וַיֹּאמֶר אֶת־אַחַי אָנֹכִי מְבַקֵּשׁ
יז הַגִּידָה־נָּא לִי אֵיפֹה הֵם רֹעִים: וַיֹּאמֶר
הָאִישׁ נָסְעוּ מִזֶּה כִּי שָׁמַעְתִּי אֹמְרִים
נֵלְכָה דֹּתָיְנָה וַיֵּלֶךְ יוֹסֵף אַחַר אֶחָיו

did not give up his quest and return home even though he had technically obeyed his father by going as far as Shechem. In spite of the danger posed by his brothers' hatred of him, he persisted in his search until he found them. He patiently endured the many difficulties for his father's honor, and in respect of his father's wish that he bring back word. Moreover, this serves to demonstrate that nothing can thwart the Divine purpose nothwithstanding man's intentions. The angel was therefore sent to direct him to his brothers, for *it is the counsel of HASHEM that will stand (Rashbam; Ramban).*

The definite article, *the* **field**, indicates that it was some previously known field. According to *Alshich* it was the field which Jacob had once bought from the Shechemites [33:19].

According to *Or HaChaim* Joseph *technically* lost his protected status as שְׁלִיחַ מִצְוָה, *emissary for a mitzvah,* when he exceeded the literal bounds of the mission and ventured beyond Shechem, contrary to his father's specific instruction. From that point on — however lofty his intentions — he was on his own initiative and he was vulnerable.

מַה־תְּבַקֵּשׁ — *What do you seek?*

The angel knew what Joseph was seeking. The question was rhetorical — a means of engaging Joseph into conversation *(Oznaim LaTorah).*

[Cf. God's question to Adam: 'Where are you' in 3:9.]

16. אֶת אַחַי אָנֹכִי מְבַקֵּשׁ — *My brothers do I seek.*

[Joseph did not say who his brothers were. Either he realized the 'man' was an angel and took it for granted that he knew them, or perhaps there was additional conversation not recorded in the Torah. If the 'man' were a human, it is quite likely that the conversation was more extensive. From *Alshich* it may be inferred that since this was the field Jacob had once bought from the Shechemites (see above), Jacob's sons were familiar and well-known in the area.]

הַגִּידָה־נָּא לִי אֵיפֹה הֵם רֹעִים — *Tell me, please, where* [i.e., in what part of this region *(Sforno)*] *they are pasturing?*

As an angel, he would certainly know *(Mizrachi);* or following *Ibn Ezra* according to whom he was a *human* wayfarer, the intent is: *tell me* — if you know.

17. נָסְעוּ מִזֶּה — *They have journeyed on from here* [lit. *from this,* i.e. *from this place;* cf. בָּזֶה in 38:21.]

They are no longer in this pasture and it is pointless to search for them in this vicinity and further *(Sforno).*

[The *Midrash* takes this phrase to be superfluous — he could have answered simply, *I heard them saying, let us go to Dothan.* The *Midrash* also perceives in Joseph's statement that he was seeking אַחַי, *my brothers,* a feeling on his part that he and they were united by feelings of loving *brotherhood (Sifsei Chachomim).* Accordingly, the inner intent of the angel's reply is understood to be:] *'They have departed from* [i.e., *discarded*] *any*

37
16-17 'What do you seek?' 16 And he said, 'My brothers do
I seek. Tell me, please, where they are pasturing.'
17 The man said: 'They have journeyed on from here
for I heard them saying, 'Let us go to Dothan.' So
Joseph went after his brothers and found them at
Dothan.

feeling of brotherhood toward you' (*Rashi;* see *Ramban* below).

כִּי שָׁמַעְתִּי אֹמְרִים נֵלְכָה דֹּתָיְנָה — *For I heard them* [or *I heard people* (who might be your brothers) *(Ramban)*] *saying, 'Let us go to Dothan.'*

I told you that *they journeyed from here* not because I actually saw them leaving, but *because I heard them saying, 'Let us go to Dothan'* (*Sforno*).

In accordance with the *Midrashic* view that the angel reported that the brothers 'departed from all feelings of brotherhood,' the *Midrash* — followed by *Rashi* — interprets: '[I know that they no longer have brotherly feelings to you] *For I heard them saying* נֵלְכָה דֹּתָיְנָה, *let us go seek legal pretexts* [*dothan* being homiletically interpreted as a *noun* meaning דָּתוֹת, *laws*], with which to put Joseph to death.' According to the literal sense, however, *Rashi* acknowledges that *Dothan* is a place, וְאֵין מִקְרָא יוֹצֵא מִידֵי פְּשׁוּטוֹ, *and the verse does not shed its literal sense.*

The above Midrashic interpretation does not imply that the 'man' *expressly* told Joseph that his brothers had no more love for him and, moreover, were planning to kill him. Had that been the case, Joseph would not have endangered himself by going there. The intent of the exegesis is that the angel spoke to Joseph in words that had a double connotation — each of them true. Joseph however, understood only the obvious meaning and followed his brothers to Dothan (*Ramban*).[1]

Or HaChaim further clarifies that Joseph understood only the obvious meaning since he did not know the 'man' was an angel.

That Dothan is literally the name of a place is, as noted, the common interpretation of this passage.

The expression דֹּתָיְנָה means *to* דֹּתַיִן *(Hoffmann).* Here it is spelled with a *yud:* דֹּתַיִן, while later in the verse the *yud* is omitted: דֹּתָן. In either case, it refers to the same place *(Ibn Ezra).*

Dothan, also mentioned in *II Kings* 6:13-15, was located about fifteen miles north of Shechem. It was known for its broad plains, and its pasturage was reputed to be finer than Shechem's. The name is still preserved in *Tel Dothan.* The gully of Dothan was a main artery in the trade-route connecting Syria to Egypt via the Sharon Valley *(Hoffmann).*

[*Rashi* apparently cites the Midrashic interpretation that Dothan is not the name of a place in consonance with the Talmudic interpretation (*Sotah* 13b and *Sanhedrin* 102a) that Joseph was sold in *Shechem;* accordingly, Shechem refers to the *place* while Dothan refers to the *mood.* See *v.* 14 s.v. וַיָּבֹא שְׁכֶמָה. In the literal sense that Dothan was the name of a place, the Talmudic statement is reconciled by suggesting that Dothan was a hamlet in the general area of Shechem.]

Targum Yonasan renders that the angel said: 'They left here, for I have heard from

1. *Baal HaTurim* observes that since it was in Dothan that Judah sought to find merit for Joseph [*v.* 26], he in turn merited that his descendants ruled a period numerically equivalent to the Hebrew word *Dothan* [דתן=454 years] from David until Zedekiah. [David reigned 40 years + 4 years of Solomon's reign until he began construction of the Temple + 410 years during which the Temple stood until the Destruction at the end of Zedekiah's reign=454.]

יח וַיִּמְצָאֵם בְּדֹתָן: וַיִּרְאוּ אֹתוֹ מֵרָחֹק
וּבְטֶרֶם יִקְרַב אֲלֵיהֶם וַיִּתְנַכְּלוּ אֹתוֹ
יט לַהֲמִיתוֹ: וַיֹּאמְרוּ אִישׁ אֶל־אָחִיו הִנֵּה
כ בַּעַל הַחֲלֹמוֹת הַלָּזֶה בָּא: וְעַתָּה | לְכוּ

behind the Heavenly Curtain of Mystery that the Egyptian exile will begin today, and they were told prophetically that the Hivvites [kinsmen of the Shechemites] are preparing to do battle against them.'

וַיֵּלֶךְ יוֹסֵף אַחַר אֶחָיו וַיִּמְצָאֵם בְּדֹתָן — *So Joseph went after his brothers and found them at Dothan.*

This further emphasizes how Joseph exerted himself in every way — journeying even beyond Shechem to find his brothers — to fulfill his father's mission *(Sforno).*

18. The brothers plot to kill Joseph.

וַיִּרְאוּ אֹתוֹ מֵרָחֹק — *[And] they* [the brothers] *saw him from afar.*

— They recognized him by his special tunic *(Ralbag).*

[And they seized what they believed to be a Divinely afforded opportunity] ...

וּבְטֶרֶם יִקְרַב אֲלֵיהֶם וַיִּתְנַכְּלוּ אֹתוֹ לַהֲמִיתוֹ — *And before he got near them they conspired against him to kill him.*

— I.e. they attempted to kill him before he reached them [by shooting arrows at him *(Tur)*] so they would not have to shed his blood with their own hands. Similarly, the *Midrash* asserts, they incited [sheep-]dogs against him. When they saw that these efforts failed as well, they resolved to kill him themselves [verses 19-20] *(Ramban).*

They reasoned that the incitement of dogs is not considered direct murder. See *Sanhedrin* 76b and *Ramban* to *v.* 26 s.v. כִּי נַהֲרֹג]. *Rokeach* suggests that they considered inciting dogs against Joseph an appropriate punishment for Joseph's tale-bearing activities against them. The Talmud [*Pesachim* 118a] mentions that 'whoever relates slander ... deserves to be cast to dogs,' for it is written [*Exod.* 22:30]: *You shall cast to the dogs,* which is followed by *you must not carry false reports* [ibid. 23:1]. [This would also explain why they shot arrows, since tale-bearing is likened to shooting arrows.]

The reflexive form וַיִּתְנַכְּלוּ denotes that they became filled with נְכָלִים, *crafty plots;* אֹתוֹ, like אִתּוֹ, *with him,* means that these designs were aimed *at him (Rashi).*[1]

Thus, the verb נכל refers to a *conspiracy to do evil. R' Hirsch,* citing analagous verses, defines it as an attempt to do harm in a secret and conspiratorial manner to the noblest interests of others.

They reasoned that their plans would be a supreme test of the truthfulness of his 'dreams'. — If they succeeded in harming him it would prove that his dreams were not Divinely and prophetically inspired [see *v.* 20] *(Akeidas Yitzchak).*

1. According to *Sforno* [and *R' Hirsch*], the construction וַיִּתְנַכְּלוּ אֹתוֹ instead of וַיִּתְנַכְּלוּ בּוֹ changes the meaning from *they conspired against him* to *they regarded him as one who was conspiring against them.* This is analagous to וְהִתְנַחַלְתֶּם אוֹתָם which does not mean: you shall inherit yourselves with them, but: you shall cause them to be inherited to yourselves ... (*Lev.* 25:46).

They concluded that he was coming to them only to find fault which he could then use to incite Jacob against them. Or possibly he would provoke them to sin, for which they would be punished by God. They would suffer death in this world or punishment in the next, and he alone would inherit the Patriarchal blessings.

Because they were convinced that he was intriguing against them, they felt that whatever

[18] *They saw him from afar. And before he got near*
them they conspired against him to kill him. [19] *And*
they said to one another 'Look! That Dreamer is com-

19. וַיֹּאמְרוּ אִישׁ אֶל־אָחִיו — *And they said to one another* [lit. *man to his brother*].

According to the *Zohar, man to his brother* refers to Simeon and Levi who were truly brothers in all respects. Their anger was the sort that causes death in the world, and Jacob later cursed it when he said [49:5]: *Cursed be their anger for it was fierce, and their wrath for it was cruel.* [See 34:25 where Simeon and Levi were similarly those who collaborated as *brothers* in the massacre of the people of Shechem.]

Cf. *Rashi* to 49:5 citing *Tanchuma: Simeon and Levi are brothers* — harboring the same thoughts in the cases of both Shechem and Joseph. For when the Torah states [here]: *And they said man to his brother,* it can only refer to Simeon and Levi. It could not refer to Reuben and Judah since they were opposed to it [verses 21-26]; it could not have been the sons of the handmaids [Dan, Naftali, Gad or Asher] since Joseph associated himself with them [*v.* 2] and their hatred for him was not so great; Issachar and Zevulon [Leah's youngest sons] are ruled out because they would not have spoken presumptuously before their elders. Consequently it was Simeon and Levi whom their father also referred to as 'brothers'.

R' Zalman Sorotzkin [in *Oznaim LaTorah*] finds it noteworthy that Simeon and Levi should have been more jealous of Joseph having attained the birthright than Reuben the firstborn, who tried to save Joseph from their hands! They may have felt that their prowess at the massacre at Shechem entitled them to exercise authority over the family.

הִנֵּה בַּעַל הַחֲלֹמוֹת הַלָּזֶה בָּא — *Look!* [or: *behold*] *that Dreamer* [lit. *this master of dreams*] *is coming!*

The remark was contemptuous: Look at him — all wrapped up in his dreams! *(Midrash);* this one who skillfully fabricates dreams to his liking! *(Alshich);* is he coming to tell us yet more of his dreams; does he still think of ways to become our master? *(Abarbanel).*

Sforno — continuing the interpretation cited in the *footnote* to *v.* 18 — interprets: 'He purposely told us his dreams to provoke us into taking revenge, thereby making us sin to God and our father so that we would perish.' [And, as noted in the footnote, feeling that Joseph's visit now was a further attempt at entrapment, they rationalized that they had to do away with him to prevent him from harming them.]

The expression בַּעַל הַחֲלוֹמוֹת, lit. *master of dreams* idiomatically refers to one who dreams excessively: a dreamer. Compare the expressions: בַּעַל כְּנָפַיִם, *a winged creature;* בַּעַל עֲבֵירָה, *one who sins excessively;* בַּעַל מוֹפֵת, *a miracle worker;* בַּעַל קְרִיאָה, *a skilled reader.*

Abarbanel, as noted, perceives בַּעַל הַחֲלוֹמוֹת to also imply that Joseph was *master* — in the

course they took would be self-defense. They agreed that it was permissible לַהֲמִיתוֹ, *to kill him* — moreover, it seemed morally *right* to do so, for הַבָּא לְהָרְגְךָ הַשְׁכֵּם וְהָרְגוֹ, *if one comes to murder you, arise and kill him!*

This verse accordingly explains how the righteous sons of Jacob — whose names were later engraved on the High Priest's חֹשֶׁן, *breastplate* [which was known as חֹשֶׁן מִשְׁפָּט, *Breastplate of 'Justice'*] as a remembrance before God — could unanimously have resolved to kill or sell their brother, an act for which they never expressed regret. For though they later admitted [42:21] *'we are indeed guilty concerning our brother',* that was, as they made clear, only over their callousness in ignoring his pleas for mercy, not for the sale or the plan to kill. They thought their act completely justified.

וְנַהַרְגֵהוּ וְנַשְׁלִכֵהוּ בְּאַחַד הַבֹּרוֹת
וְאָמַרְנוּ חַיָּה רָעָה אֲכָלָתְהוּ וְנִרְאֶה מַה־
כא יִּהְיוּ חֲלֹמֹתָיו: וַיִּשְׁמַע רְאוּבֵן וַיַּצִּלֵהוּ
כב מִיָּדָם וַיֹּאמֶר לֹא נַכֶּנּוּ נָפֶשׁ: וַיֹּאמֶר

sense of 'fabricator' — of his dreams; the dreams did not *come* to him, he invented them.

The word הַלָּזֶה is synonymous with הַזֶּה, *this.* The former expression is used when speaking of someone at a distance, as in our case and the case of Isaac in 24:65; when somene is *near*, as in *Esther* 7:6, הַזֶּה, *this*, is used *(Rashbam* to 24:65).

20. וְעַתָּה לְכוּ וְנַהַרְגֵהוּ — *So, now, come* [idiomatic; lit. *go*] *and let us kill him.*

Now — before he rises to power over us *(Malbim).*

As noted above, they reasoned that killing him to prevent the coordination of his misdeeds against them was an act of self-defense *(Sforno).*

The term לְכוּ, *go* [here rendered: *come*] has the idiomatic connotation of inviting comrades to participate in an act. Similarly in *v.* 27: *come* [לְכוּ] *let us sell him to the Ishmaelites.* Compare the analogous expression [*Exodus* 1:10]: הָבָה נִתְחַכְּמָה, *come, let us deal shrewdly (Rashbam).*

וְנַשְׁלִכֵהוּ בְּאַחַד הַבֹּרוֹת — *And* [*we will*] *throw him into one of the pits.*

— And he will not even get a proper burial! *(Oznaim LaTorah).*

[The brothers were not specific about which pit into which to throw him; Reuben, however, was more specific in his suggestion in *v.* 22. See *Oznaim LaTorah* cited there s.v. הַשְׁלִיכוּ אוֹתוֹ.]

וְאָמַרְנוּ חַיָּה רָעָה אֲכָלָתְהוּ — *And we will say 'A wild beast devoured him.'*

— To project the blame away from ourselves and thereby prevent the possibility of Father cursing us *(Sforno).*

Since, as the story unfolds, they planned to bring his bloody tunic to Jacob as proof that he was dead, they had to devise this story to account for his death. Had a robber rather than a beast slain Joseph, he would certainly have taken the fine woolen tunic! *(Abarbanel).*

וְנִרְאֶה מַה־יִּהְיוּ חֲלֹמֹתָיו — *Then we shall see what will become of his dreams* [lit. *and we will see what his dreams will be.*]

Rashi cites the Midrashic interpretation offered in *Bereishis Rabbah* by Rav Yitzchak [who does not understand these words as rhetoric of the conspiring brothers]:

— It is [not Joseph's brothers but] the Holy Spirit that interjects and says the latter part of this sentence. 'You say, *Let us slay him,* but I say, *Then we shall see what will become of his dreams* — i.e. then we will see whose will shall prevail, yours or Mine.' It is impossible that the brothers should have said these words [and use his dreams as a criteria], for as soon as they would kill him his dreams would *obviously* be ineffective!

Of course, the brothers did not hear this Divine pronouncement or else they would never have proceeded to do what they did. [Cf. וַיִּשְׁמַע רְאוּבֵן next verse] *(Alshich).*

Ramban cites this *Midrash,* but maintains that in the *literal* sense the remark was said by the brothers and intended derisively: *Then we shall see what will become of his dreams!* Or they reasoned that their plan would be a test: If he is rescued from our hands [it will prove his dreams were prophetic] and we will

ing! 20 So, now, come and let us kill him, and throw
him into one of the pits; and we will say, "A wild
beast devoured him." Then we shall see what will
become of his dreams.'
21 Reuben heard, and he rescued him from their
hand. He said, 'We will not strike him mortally!'

indeed see the fulfillment of his dreams — for he will then reign over us.

Let us kill him ... for if the plan to kill him succeeds, it will be obvious that his dreams of ruling over us were nothing but lies *(Sforno)*.

21. Reuben reacts.

וַיִּשְׁמַע רְאוּבֵן וַיַּצִּלֵהוּ מִיָּדָם — *[And] Reuben heard, and he rescued him from their hand.*

— Although Joseph's ordeal was far from over, Reuben is praised in past tense: *and he rescued him from their hand* as if the rescue were *a fait accompli* and he was already successful in having delivered him *(Akeidas Yitzchak)*. [See *Malbim* below and *Ramban* to *v.* 26 s.v. כִּי נַהֲרֹג].[1]

He took the initiative here because he reasoned that as the oldest he alone would be held responsible for the crime *(Midrash*; see *Rashi v.* 22 s.v. לְמַעַן הַצִּיל and *comm.* to *v.* 30).

Although of all the brothers Reuben was the most injured by Joseph inasmuch as Joseph was to assume some of Reuben's rights as first born [see 35:22 and *I Chron.* 5:1], nevertheless he was opposed to his brothers taking the law into their own hands. Still, he could not protect Joseph openly so he used the subterfuge of suggesting a 'cleaner' way of putting their brother to death in the hope, as we see below, that he would be able to save him *(Daas Soferim)*.

The expression *Reuben heard* would seem to imply that Reuben had been with them just by chance as he must have soon left and was not present at the actual development of the drama. Whether as firstborn he did not have to take part in the ordinary daily work, or whether in general he differed from their ideas about Joseph and therefore took no part in the plans regarding him, is doubtful. We shall come back to this question again in *v.* 30 *(R' Hirsch)*.

According to the *Midrash*, it had been Reuben's turn to attend his father. He had been on the way to care for Jacob when his brothers conspired against Joseph. Thus the verse tells us that *when Reuben heard* of their plan he rushed back and was determined to stop them.

Alshich suggests that of all the brothers it was only Reuben who *heard* the Divine pronouncement cited by *Rashi* in the previous verse: 'We shall see whose will shall prevail — yours or Mine.' Reuben took this as a personal charge to thwart the plan.

The Sages [*Makkos* 10a] note that when the Cities of Refuge are listed in *Deut.* 4:43, the one in the territory of Reuben was privileged to be mentioned first 'because it was Reuben who spoke first in delivering [Joseph out of the pit]' (see *Torah Temimah*).

וַיֹּאמֶר לֹא נַכֶּנּוּ נָפֶשׁ — *[And] he said, 'We will not strike him mortally.'*

— I, as the oldest brother, will not

1. The Sages observe that we learn from this incident [where we find that though Reuben's intentions of saving were good they went unfulfilled] that when a man performs a *mitzvah* he must carry it out joyously and completely [and not only partially].

'For,' said R' Yitzchak, 'had Reuben known that the Torah was recording for eternity these

אֲלֵהֶ֗ם | רְאוּבֵן֮ אַל־תִּשְׁפְּכוּ־דָם֒ הַשְׁלִ֣יכוּ
אֹת֗וֹ אֶל־הַבּ֤וֹר הַזֶּה֙ אֲשֶׁ֣ר בַּמִּדְבָּ֔ר וְיָ֖ד
אַל־תִּשְׁלְחוּ־ב֑וֹ לְמַ֗עַן הַצִּ֤יל אֹתוֹ֙ מִיָּדָ֔ם
לַהֲשִׁיב֖וֹ אֶל־אָבִֽיו׃ °וַיְהִ֕י כַּאֲשֶׁר־בָּ֥א יוֹסֵ֖ף °שלישי כג

tolerate that *(R' Hirsch).*

Reuben tried — as noted earlier in the verse — to save Joseph from *any* harm by them, but his efforts were unsuccessful. He now attempted at least to prevent them from perpetrating an act of wanton *murder* against him, by suggesting that they punish him in some other way *(Abarbanel; Malbim).*

[It is also possible that this verse is informing us that Reuben had *resolved* to save Joseph by determining to himself that they would not murder their brother. Only in the following verse did he actually *verbalize* his determination to his brothers. Therefore it does not say here **וַיֹּאמֶר אֲלֵהֶם**, he said *to them* but merely *he said,* i.e., resolved. Only in the next verse did he *verbalize* his intention **אֲלֵהֶם**, *to them.*]

[*Hoffmann* interprets similarly. This differs from *Ramban* next verse who maintains that the double וַיֹּאמֶר, *he said,* here and in *v.* 22, implies that after Reuben made this pronouncement much discussion ensued — not recorded by the Torah but evident from 42:22. Hence the second וַיֹּאמֶר in *v.* 22 to indicate there was a lapse in the unrecorded conversation. Our interpretation would assume that this unrecorded converstion took place within the parameters of *v.* 22, i.e., after he actually said to them *'shed no blood.'*]

The Hebrew reads: *We will not strike his soul.* The translation follows *Rashi* who explains that the phrase is elliptic and means *We will not strike him* מַכַּת נֶפֶשׁ, *a striking of the soul,* i.e. mortally.

22. וַיֹּאמֶר אֲלֵהֶם רְאוּבֵן — *And Reuben said to them.*

Apparently there was much discussion on the matter as evidenced by Reuben's later recrimination [cf. 42:22] when he accused his brothers of not listening to him when he tried to deter them from harming Joseph. When his arguments failed, he *was* successful with the following proposal. The Torah records only *this* argument because it yielded positive results *(Ramban).*

אַל־תִּשְׁפְּכוּ־דָם — *Shed no blood!*

Reuben made as general a pronouncement as possible. He did not say, 'do not shed *his* blood' — rather his point was that they should not shed *any* blood, that they should not stoop to the crime of murder. He wanted to sound dispassionate, and not want it to appear that he had any special love for Joseph *(Ramban).*

If you want to rid yourselves of him there is a 'clean' way whereby you don't have to *personally* commit murder *(Hoffmann)...*

הַשְׁלִיכוּ אֹתוֹ אֶל־הַבּוֹר הַזֶּה אֲשֶׁר בַּמִּדְבָּר — *Throw him into this pit* [*which is*] *in the wilderness.*

I.e., *'shed no blood,* for he does not deserve death. If he has pained you with his dreams and taunts, then make him suffer by throwing him in a pit; but lay no hand on him to kill him.' This, too, was suggested only as a deterrent *(Radak).*

The pit is deep and he will not be

verses about his attempted rescue of Joseph, he would have carried Joseph on his shoulders and brought him back to his father [instead of allowing him to be cast into the pit].'

Similarly, the Sages observe: Had Boaz known that Scripture was recording of him that he was taking the trouble to provide food for Ruth, instead of giving her only *parched grain* [*Ruth* 2:14], he would have fed her fatted calves *(Vayikra Rabbah* 34:8).

37
22

[22] *And Reuben said to them: 'Shed no blood! Throw him into this pit in the wilderness, but lay no hand on him!' — intending to rescue him from their hand, to return him to his father.*

able to escape. Moreover, it is in the *wilderness* — his cries for help will go unheard for there will be no passersby to rescue him *(Ramban).*

Thus he will die without your committing murder *(Rashbam).*

The brothers planned to throw Joseph בְּאַחַד הַבּוֹרוֹת, *into one of the pits* [*v.* 20] — without distinction as to which one, since any pit would serve their morbid purpose. However, since Reuben's purpose was not murder but to save Joseph, he carefully specified a particular pit — one which, as we shall see, had no water *(Oznaim LaTorah).*

וְיָד אַל־תִּשְׁלְחוּ בוֹ — *But lay no hand on him* [lit. *and a hand do not send forth in him*].

— 'I would have been tolerant had you tried to kill him by intrigue — through others — because I, too, hate him. But far be it from you to kill him with your *own* hands!' This was another of Reuben's arguments. He was teaching them that the punishment for one who *indirectly* causes death is less than that of one who kills [for the former is punished only by the hands of Heaven, not by human courts. Cf. *Sanhedrin* 77a] *(Ramban).*

A similar expression occurs in 22:12 ... וְאַל תִּשְׁלַח יָדְךָ אֶל, *Do not stretch out your hand to ... (Hoffmann).*

לְמַעַן הַצִּיל אֹתוֹ מִיָּדָם לַהֲשִׁיבוֹ אֶל־אָבִיו — *Intending* [lit. *in order*] *to rescue him* [Joseph] *from their hand, to return him to his father.*

The Divine Spirit [i.e. Scripture *(Rashbam)*] thus bears witness that Reuben advised his brothers to cast him into a pit only to rescue him, his intention being to return later and pull him out. As the eldest son, and their leader, he knew he would be held responsible *(Rashi).*[1]

That Reuben's suggestion to cast Joseph into a pit was intended to save Joseph's life is predicated on the assumption that Reuben thought the pit contained neither serpents nor scorpions. Had he known that (as *Rashi* comments in *v.* 24) the pit *was* infested, Reuben would not have been saving him by his suggestion since, as noted in *Yevamos* 121a, one who has fallen into a snake pit is assumed to have died. Moreover, had the brothers seen Joseph survive such an ordeal they never would have sold him; they would have considered his survival as miraculous as Abraham's safe departure from the furnace of Ur Kasdim or Daniel's escape from the lions' pit. They would then have certainly believed in the truthfulness of his dreams *(Mizrachi).*

Why does *Rashi* suggest that Reuben acted to save Joseph out of fear of being blamed rather than out of a spirit of righteousness and aversion to bloodshed?

— Reuben could not have acted out of love for the Torah makes it clear that the brothers hated him excessively *(Mizrachi).*

— In his final blessings to his sons, Jacob singled out Judah for praise as the one who desisted from the plan to kill Joseph [49:9]: If Reuben's intentions had been truly sincere, Jacob should have mentioned him as the one who planned to save Joseph even from slavery. We deduce, therefore, that Reuben's motive was selfish in part *(Sifsei Chachomim).*

1. From the fact that the Torah publicly acknowledges Reuben's noble intention in attempting to save Joseph, we deduce that it is proper to publicly acknowledge and record one who performs a *mitzvah (Rashba, Responsa* 981).

Similarly, *Rama* in *Yoreh Deah* 249:13 rules that one who donated an article for charity may inscribe his name upon it and the community may not protest it.

אֶל־אֶחָיו וַיַּפְשִׁטוּ אֶת־יוֹסֵף אֶת־כֻּתָּנְתּוֹ
כד אֶת־כְּתֹנֶת הַפַּסִּים אֲשֶׁר עָלָיו: וַיִּקָּחֻהוּ
וַיַּשְׁלִכוּ אֹתוֹ הַבֹּרָה וְהַבּוֹר רֵק אֵין בּוֹ

23. The brothers execute judgment.

וַיְהִי כַּאֲשֶׁר־בָּא יוֹסֵף אֶל אֶחָיו — *And so it was, when Joseph came to his brothers.*

[For all of the above transpired before he reached them.]

Midrashically, Joseph's approach is mentioned — though we already know from *v.* 19 that he was coming — to inform us that his coming was noteworthy: he came with praises [either with self-praise about his own superiority, or with praise of his brothers, that is, in friendship *(Yafeh Toar)*].

וַיַּפְשִׁיטוּ אֶת יוֹסֵף אֶת כֻּתָּנְתּוֹ — *They stripped Joseph of his tunic.*

I.e., *they stripped Joseph bare (Akeidah) of his tunic.* — The word כֻּתֹּנֶת, in Biblical Hebrew, refers to an *undershirt (Rashi).*

Ibn Ezra interprets וַיַּפְשִׁיטוּ אֶת [in the הִפְעִיל, *causative* form, with the particle אֶת which indicates a transitive verb with an object] to imply that *they ordered Joseph to remove his own tunic by himself.*

Possibly they persuaded him to do so under some pretext. It was only *after* the tunic was removed that they revealed their sinister intentions by forcibly casting him into the pit *(Ralbag).*

אֶת־כְּתֹנֶת הַפַּסִּים אֲשֶׁר עָלָיו — *The fine woolen tunic which he had on* [lit. *which was upon it* (or: *him*)].

[In addition to stripping Joseph of his *undershirt,* they also stripped him of] *the fine woolen tunic* — which his father had given him to wear as a second garment, one more than the single shirt worn by his brothers [*v.* 3] *(Rashi).*

Thus, they stripped him of the *two* garments he was wearing — an undershirt and the fine woolen tunic אֲשֶׁר עָלָיו, which was upon *it* [*the undershirt*], which he wore against his body to protect the fine woolen tunic from perspiration. The Torah does not connect these two tunics with the conjunction (וְ)אֶת *and,* to intimate that in the brothers' anger they stripped him of both garments *together (Or HaChaim),* also demonstrating to him thereby that it was not the tunic given him by their father that they were after *(Maharshal; cf. Mizrachi).*[1]

According to *Abarbanel,* both *tunics* refer to the *fine woolen tunic,* the second phrase modifying the first: *they stripped Joseph of his tunic,* which was *the fine woolen tunic which he had on him.* It is understood that they did not leave him bare, however, since he probably was wearing some other shirt, [חָלוּק] beneath that tunic.

The *fine woolen tunic* is emphatically mentioned because it was this garment which had initially stirred up their envy. The mention also prepares us for the fact that they

1. The mention of Joseph's *tunic* [an undergarment] before his כְּתֹנֶת פַּסִּים, *fine woolen tunic* is apparently out of sequence since the woolen one was the outer garment which would have been removed first. What occurred was that in order not to antagonize his brothers, Joseph wore his outer *fine woolen tunic* — a prime source of their envy — *beneath* the tunic which he usually wore against his body. Thus, in effect they first removed his *tunic* and then *his fine woolen tunic (Meleches Machsheves; Kli Yakar).*

[23] *And so it was, when Joseph came to his brothers
they stripped Joseph of his tunic, the fine woolen
tunic which he had on.* [24] *Then they took him, and
cast him into the pit. The pit was empty; no water
was in it.*

later dipped it in blood and sent it back to Jacob as proof that Joseph was dead [*v.* 31ff] *(Rashbam).*

24. וַיִּקָּחֻהוּ וַיַּשְׁלִכוּ אֹתוֹ הַבֹּרָה — *Then they took him, and cast him into the pit.*

[The Hebrew verb *took* always implies physical or persuasive force.]

From the brothers' later recriminations recalling that when they had thrown Jacob into the pit *'we looked at his anguish yet paid no heed when he pleaded with us'* [42:21], we know that Joseph pleaded and prostrated himself before them. He seems not to have offered *physical* resistance [since he was hopelessly outnumbered], but only *said* whatever was possible to save himself. However, they were callous to his entreaties *(Radak).*

Ramban comments there that the Torah did not mention his entreaties in our narrative either because it is self-evident that there would be a struggle and entreaties in such a situation; or because the Torah wanted to gloss over as many details of their sin as possible; or because it is characteristic for the Torah to economize on details of a matter in one place and elaborate on them in another.

The Torah is written unvowelized allowing for exegical interpretations beyond the obvious meaning of the text. The word וַיִּקָּחוּהוּ, *they took him,* is spelled וַיִּקָּחֻהוּ. As it is spelled, it can also be read as וַיִּקָּחֵהוּ, and *he* took him. This alludes to the fact that it was primarily one of the brothers — acting on behalf of all the others — who took and cast him into the pit. It was Simeon. He was later punished when Joseph singled him out for detention in 42:24 *(Midrash).*

וְהַבּוֹר רֵק אֵין בּוֹ מָיִם — [*And*] *the pit was empty; no water was in it.*

— Why the repetition? Since it states that *the pit was empty,* isn't it obvious that *no water was in it?* — The redundancy intimates: there was no *water* in it but there *were* serpents and scorpions in it *(Rashi* from *Shabbos* 22a).

I.e., the added phrase *there was no water in it* implies that the *emptiness* was not total; the pit was empty *only of water,* as well as shrubbery, stones, and the like, but *not* of serpents and scorpions which constantly crawl in and out of crevices. Although they are intermittently present, such a pit can be called 'empty' in this qualified sense. This too appears to be based on the Rabbinic exegesis found in *Sanhedrin* 15a אֵין מִיעוּט אַחַר מִיעוּט אֶלָּא לְרַבּוֹת, 'one exclusion [in our case: *the pit was empty*] following another exclusion [in our case: *there was no water in it*] does not imply a limitation but an extension [that is, the first limitation is not total, but is circumscribed by the second one]. In our case, the emptiness of the pit did not include a lack of serpents and scorpions in it (cf. *Mizrachi; Sefer Zikaron).*

That this rabbinic exegesis indicates only the presence of *serpents and scorpions,* rather than other dangerous creatures, is understood by the commentators to be a *gezerah shavah,* teaching derived from a similarity of the phrases. Our verse has אֵין בּוֹ מָיִם, *there is no water in it;* a similar phrase which occurs in *Deut.* 8:15 where the passage reads: ... *serpents and scorpions a parched land* אֲשֶׁר אֵין מָיִם, *which has no water.* Just as there the phrase is used in a situation where there were serpents and scorpions, in our case, too, the pit was waterless but it contained serpents and scorpions.

Ramban maintains that in the literal sense, the Torah accentuates that they had no intention of drowning him in the pit. Had it contained water they would not have cast him into it, for Joseph would have drowned and it would have

כה מָיִם: וַיֵּשְׁבוּ לֶאֱכָל־לֶחֶם וַיִּשְׂאוּ עֵינֵיהֶם
וַיִּרְאוּ וְהִנֵּה אֹרְחַת יִשְׁמְעֵאלִים בָּאָה

been regarded as the direct murder which they wished to avoid. If so, the intent is that the pit was completely empty.

Ramban maintains that according to the Rabbinic interpretation advanced by *Rashi,* the poisonous creatures must have been hidden in the deep crevices of the pit. Had the brothers seen that the pit was infested with deadly reptiles, they would have realized that only Joseph's righteousness could account for the miracle of his survival in the pit. Knowing that, they would have saved him from all harm and vindicated him in their eyes.

The consensus of commentators similarly agrees that Reuben, too, was unaware that the pit was infested. Since he meant to deter them from killing Joseph, he certainly could not have hoped to rescue him and bring him back to his father by casting him into mortal danger in an infested pit! Moreover [as noted by *Ramban*], the brothers would never have sold Joseph had they seen Joseph miraculously survive in an infested pit. Even the evil Nebuchadnezzar was moved to repentance when he saw Hananiah, Mishael and Azariah survive the fiery furnace; surely the righteous sons of Jacob! ...

Torah Temimah notes the Rabbinic dictum that the term הַשְׁלָכָה, *casting,* is used only to denote throwing from a height of at least twenty cubits. [See *comm.* to *Tamid* 28b]. Accordingly, the use of the verb *cast* in our verse implies that Joseph's pit was twenty cubits deep. This would explain why the brothers were unaware that poisonous creatures were in the pit; they could not see clearly to such a depth. For, as the Sages explain in connection with a Chanukah *menorah* or סְכָךְ, *succah covering,* they may not be placed at a height of over twenty cubits because they would not be seen clearly from below *(Shabbos* 22a).[1]

25. וַיֵּשְׁבוּ לֶאֱכָל לֶחֶם — *[And] they sat to eat food* [lit. *bread*].[2]

— At a distance from the pit, so as not to eat brazenly at the scene of potential bloodshed (*Rashbam v.* 28).

The expression וַיִּשְׂאוּ עֵינֵיהֶם, *they*

1. The *Zohar,* however, assumes that Reuben *was* aware that the pit was infested. How then, the *Zohar* asks, could Reuben have advised casting Joseph into the pit — was he not concerned about the fatal bites of the deadly creatures?

The answer offered is that Reuben was quite aware of the intense enmity which his brothers — led by Simeon and Levi — felt for Joseph. He reasoned that if an entire city could not escape these two brothers at Shechem, then if Joseph should fall into their hands they would not leave any evidence: not a single trace of his corpse would remain to provide Jacob at least the consolation of burial. Reuben therefore decided it was preferable to cast him into a reptile-infested pit than to let him fall into the hands of avowed, ruthless enemies.

The rationale is that if one is deserving, God may perform a miracle to save him *from beasts.* But Providence will very rarely interfere with *man's* exercise of his Free Will, even when they seek to harm their enemies. That would require a much greater miracle.

This is the intent of the phrase: *Intending to rescue Joseph from their hand to return him to his father.* Reuben's primary aim was to keep Joseph away from Simeon and Levi's ruthless clutches, opting to expose him to vicious reptiles as the lesser of the evils, so at the very worst — even if Providence did not interfere and save Joseph — at least there was glimmer of a chance that his corpse could possibly be returned to Jacob for burial.

R' Munk concludes that Reuben was hoping for divine mercy, like King David when he said to the prophet Gad [II *Samuel* 24:14]: *Let us fall into the hands of HASHEM for His compassion is great, but let me not fall into the hand of men.*

2. As they were casting him into the pit they said, 'Let us eat and drink and then we shall raise him up and slay him.'

After they ate and drank and were about to say the Grace After Meals, Judah said to them: 'We are about to slay and yet we would say Grace to the Holy One, Blessed be He! We are nothing but blasphemers!'

This was Judah's intent in exclaiming [*v.* 26] ... מַה, בֶּצַע, *'What! An act of plunder* [or

37 [25] *They sat to eat food. Raising their eyes they saw,*
25 *behold! — a caravan of Ishmaelites was coming from*

looked up [lit. *lifted up their eyes*] never intimates a *casual* looking around, but always an *intentional* one. Throughout their meal, they felt uneasy. They kept looking toward the pit *(R' Hirsch).*

That the brothers were able to sit down to a meal while the piercing cries of their doomed brother were still ringing in their ears proves that they had a clear conscience. They considered themselves wholly justified to have acted in self-defense [see on *v.* 20 above] *(Sforno).*

Midrashically, too, the Sages perceive how the Providential effects of their sinister action were ultimately favorable and for the benefit of mankind: In sitting down to eat and planning to sell Joseph, the tribal ancestors ultimately benefited the entire world. For Joseph was sold into Egypt to provide sustenance to the entire world during the years of famine. Accordingly, the passage *they sat down to eat food* should be understood retrospectively: they made it possible for the entire world to eat bread *(Pesikta Rabbosi* 10:31).

Nevertheless, in the Upper Realms, though God is long-suffering, no sin is overlooked. He eventually exacts punishment. 'You sold your brother, then sat down to eat,' the Holy One, Blessed be He, said of the Tribal Ancestors. 'There will yet come a time that your descendants will be sold in the midst of a feast!' And so it was many centuries later in Shushan, when the King and Haman sat down to drink [*Esther* 3:15], that the extermination of the Jews was plotted. R' Yissachar observed that this eventual retribution hung over them although Joseph forgave them [45:8]; how much more so when one does not forgive! *(Midrash Tehillim* 10).

It appears from *v.* 29: *And Reuben returned,* that Reuben was not present throughout this time. [Thus a total of nine brothers sat down to eat; Joseph and Benjamin were also not present *(Ibn Ezra).*] According to the *Midrash* cited by *Rashi* in *v.* 29, Reuben was not present since it was his day to look after Jacob. According to another Midrashic interpretation: [Reuben did not dine nor otherwise associate with them on mundane matters] since he was occupied with his sackcloth and fasting in penitence for his having disturbed his father's couch [see 35:22].

B'chor Shor is sensitive to the difficulty of suggesting that Reuben had gone the long distance from Dothan to Hebron to look after his father for one day. He comments that Reuben was not present because shepherds cannot all sit together to eat; some must be available to look after the flocks while the others eat. Thus, Judah was eating with *some* of the brothers while Reuben was tending the sheep with the rest. This was why Reuben was not present, and Judah suggested the sale in his absence.

אֹרְחַת יִשְׁמְעֵאלִים בָּאָה מִגִּלְעָד — *A caravan of Ishmaelites was coming from Gilead.*

From the appearance of the camels, they recognized the caravan to be Ishmaelite. Since it was com-

employing the other meaning of **בצע**, the technical term for *break bread: What! Shall there be breaking of bread*] *and Grace if we then slay our brother!'* He alluded to the verse in *Psalms* 10:3: וּבֹצֵעַ בֵּרֵךְ נִאֵץ ה', [Midrashically rendered: *He who despoils and then says Grace, blasphemes* HASHEM] — He therefore went on to say, *Come, let us sell him to the Ishmaelites* (*Pesikta Rabbosi* 10:13. See *footnote* next verse where this exegesis is explained in more detail).

מִגִּלְעָד וּגְמַלֵּיהֶם נֹשְׂאִים נְכֹאת וּצְרִי
כו וָלֹט הוֹלְכִים לְהוֹרִיד מִצְרָיְמָה: וַיֹּאמֶר
יְהוּדָה אֶל־אֶחָיו מַה־בֶּצַע כִּי נַהֲרֹג אֶת־
כז אָחִינוּ וְכִסִּינוּ אֶת־דָּמוֹ: לְכוּ וְנִמְכְּרֶנּוּ

ing from Gilead, a source of spices, they surmised that it was plying the trade route, bringing spices to Egypt *(Ramban).*

[On Gilead see 31:21-25.]

According to the implication of *Rashi* [see below] this description of the caravan's load was *not* assumed by the brothers; instead, Scripture gives us these facts. The brothers could not have known what the camels were carrying until the caravan drew near. From the mere knowledge that the merchants were Ishmaelites, the brothers originally assumed that they carried their *usual* wares, evil-smelling commodities like naphtha.

A caravan is termed אֹרְחָה in Hebrew, referring as it does to הוֹלְכֵי אוֹרַח, *wayfarers* [lit. 'travelers of the road'] *(Rashi).*

It has been noted that in the clear air of *Eretz Yisrael,* such a caravan could be discerned several miles away. It could take several hours before it reached the brothers *(Hoffmann).*

וּגְמַלֵּיהֶם נֹשְׂאִים נְכֹאת – [*And*] *their camels* [*were*] *bearing spicery.*

The Torah informs us of their load to emphasize how Providence arranges for the reward of the righteous: Arabs generally traded in naphtha and tar which have a foul odor, but on this occasion it was providentially arranged that they carry fragrant spicery so that Joseph would be spared from enduring an offensive odor *(Rashi* from *Midrash).*

Also, spicery is carried in small vials and there would be room for Joseph to ride on the camels. Had the camels been loaded with bulkier commodities, Joseph would have been forced to make the long journey on foot *(Haamek Davar).*

The translation of נְכֹאת as a collective term for *spicery* follows *Rashi* who cites *II Kings* 20:13 where the cognate term בֵּית נְכֹתֹה refers to the house where spices were mixed [i.e., a perfumery.] *Onkelos* renders it as a kind of *wax* [probably an aromatic gum], while *Ibn Janach* [*Shorashim* s.v. נכת] explains it as referring to the essence of the carob tree. Interestingly, further in 43:11 *Rashi,* too, renders the term in that context as meaning wax.

וּצְרִי – [*And*] *balsam.*

— I.e., the fragrant resin [=balm] that exudes from the wood of the balsam tree *(Rashi;* see *Shabbos* 26a and *Kerisos* 6a where this balm is listed as one of the ingredients of the compound of קְטֹרֶת, *incense).*

In *Jeremiah* 8:22 and 46:11 it is intimated that this was a product of Gilead *(Hoffmann).*

וָלֹט – *And Lotus.*

This translation follows *Rashi* who cites the analagous Mishnaic term לוֹטִיתָא [see *Sheviis* 7:6]. He notes that the Sages explain it as a vegetable root which bears the name *aristolochia* [=birthwart]; cf. *Niddah* 8a *(Rashi).*

In the *Midrash,* the term is rendered as מַסְטִיכִי, *gum mastic,* while others render it as labdanum, a fragrant gum of rockroses of the *Cistus genus,* used in the manufacture of perfume.

הוֹלְכִים לְהוֹרִיד מִצְרָיְמָה – *On their way to bring* [them] *down to Egypt.*

While the caravan was still at a

Gilead, their camels bearing spicery, balsam, and
lotus — on their way to bring them down to Egypt.
26 Judah said to his brothers, 'What gain will there be
if we kill our brother and cover up his blood? 27 Come

distance, the brothers surmised that it was headed toward Egypt, that being the usual destination of spices from Gilead *(Ramban).*

[As noted in the *comm.* to *v.* 18, the plain north and west of Dothan was crossed by the trade route from Gilead past Beth Shean and Jezreel, on through the Sharon Valley, and Lydda to Egypt.]

We find that Jacob later sent a gift of such spices to Joseph [see 43:11]; apparently these were considered precious in Egypt where these resins would be used medicinally, as incense, and in embalming *(Abarbanel; Malbim).*

26. Judah's proposal.

וַיֹּאמֶר יְהוּדָה אֶל אֶחָיו — *Then* [lit. *and*] *Judah said to his brothers.*

Judah is named because he was responsible for the decision that saved Joseph's life, just as Reuben was named [*v.* 21-22] because he initiated Joseph's salvation. However, the Torah concealed the identity of the brothers who conspired against Joseph and delicately referred to them only as **אִישׁ אֶל אָחִיו**, *one to another (Oznaim LaTorah* following *Midrash).*

מַה בֶּצַע — *What gain* [will there be].

[This is an idiomatic expression meaning: what benefit could we possibly derive ...?] Literally, as *Onkelos* renders it: *What moneys will we have (Rashi).*[1]

This interpretation is based on the fact that the verb בצע as used in Scripture contextually refers to greed, avariciousness, unjust gain cf. *Exod.* 18:21 *(Ibn Janach; Heidenheim).*

HaKsav V'HaKabbalah relates it to the verb בצע in *Lamentations* 2:17 where it has the sense of *execute judgment. 'Is this the right way to execute judgment against Joseph for his misdeed?'* Judah then went on to show how this course of action was undesirable.

Midrashically, *Pesikta Rabbosi* [cited in the footnote to *v.* 25] interprets בצע as the technical term for breaking bread: *What! Shall there be a breaking of bread* [*i.e. shall you sit down to dine*] *when we are about to kill our brother!*

כִּי נַהֲרֹג אֶת־אָחִינוּ וְכִסִּינוּ אֶת־דָּמוֹ — *If we kill our brother and* [*we*] *cover up his blood?*

The commentators differ on the connotation of his argument:

— *Ramban:* In convincing them that by throwing Joseph into the pit

1. [*Rashi's* explanation of Judah's suggestion as a mercenary one: what *monetary gain* could we reap by killing Joseph, seems to follow the Talmudic interpretation in *Sanhedrin* 6a.

In expounding upon the verse in *Psalms* 10:3 וּבֹצֵעַ בֵּרֵךְ נִאֵץ ה׳ [lit. *he who blesses one who is avaricious has blasphemed HASHEM,*] the Sages explain this as a derogatory reference to Judah and proclaim: כָּל־הַמְבָרֵךְ אֶת־יְהוּדָה [שֶׁאָמַר ,,מַה־בֶּצַע כִּי נַהֲרֹג אֶת־אָחִינוּ״] הֲרֵי זֶה מְנַאֵץ, וְעַל זֶה נֶאֱמַר: ,,וּבֹצֵעַ בֵּרֵךְ נִאֵץ ה׳.״, Whoever praises Judah [who said to his brothers *'What gain* (בֶּצַע) *has will there be if we kill our brother and cover up his blood?'*] is but a blasphemer, as it is written *'He who praises the one who is avaricious* (בֹּצֵעַ) *blasphemed HASHEM.*

The intent of this exposition is that since Judah's advice was heeded by his brothers, he should have insisted that they return him to Jacob, rather than suggesting that they sell him.

Maharsha explains the intent to be: Whoever praises Judah for having suggested that money be a consideration in determining Joseph's fate, thereby blasphemes HASHEM since Judah should have invoked fear of committing murder as a deterrent, not considerations of profit.

Alternatively, *Maharsha* offers that since Judah's advice *did* result in Joseph's being *spared,* the Talmud might have meant an opposite interpretation. This is based on the frequent prac-

לַיִּשְׁמְעֵאלִים וְיָדֵנוּ אַל־תְּהִי־בוֹ כִּי־אָחִינוּ
כח בְשָׂרֵנוּ הוּא וַיִּשְׁמְעוּ אֶחָיו: וַיַּעַבְרוּ

they would not be guilty of murder [see *comm.* to *v.* 22], Reuben had already persuaded the brothers not to kill Joseph. Now Judah said: 'Surely even by sending him to his death in this *indirect* way we will be considered murderers, and we will have thereby covered his blood (see below) like common killers.'

Ramban continues that one who causes murder is indeed considered a murderer. This is evidenced in *II Sam.* 12:9 where the prophet Nathan accused King David of murdering Uriah though David had only ordered Uriah placed in a situation that resulted in his death. The only difference between the two forms of murder is that the punishment is greater for one who *personally* murders than for one who *indirectly* causes death [for as noted above in *v.* 22, the latter is punished only by the hands of Heaven and not by human courts]. Thus both Reuben and Judah were correct.

Sforno: What benefit will accrue from killing him? If we seek the satisfaction of revenge, the deed will recoil on our own heads since we will come to grieve over our brutality. If, however, we intend the killing as a warning to other potential enemies, that cannot be achieved since we will have to conceal his blood and none will know. [Similarly, *Abarbanel* and *Malbim.*]

... We will not even have the satisfaction of boasting about our revenge since we will have to hide our act from Father. Human nature is such that revenge is not truly sweet unless one can boast of it *(Chizkuni).*

— *R' Hirsch:* How would the death of our brother serve our pur-

tice of Scripture and the Sages to use a euphemism in place of particularly unpleasant word. Thus a blind person is called סַגֵּי נְהוֹר, *one with much light* or *enhanced vision.* Similarly, instead of קלל, *curse,* the Sages frequently substitute the euphemistic expression ברך, *bless.* In connection with Judah, the Sages would be saying: Whoever *curses* [מְבָרֵךְ lit. *blesses*=a euphemism for מְקַלֵּל, *curses*] *Judah* for using absence of profit as the reason for not killing Joseph, thereby blasphemes HASHEM since Judah's motive was entirely for the sake of Heaven. He felt that his brothers would not listen to him had he suggested that they release Joseph for a pure motive. He therefore advanced the suggestion that they rid themselves of Joseph by selling him; it was his only hope of sparing Joseph's life. This is termed 'blasphemy to HASHEM' because the Hebrew name יְהוּדָה [*Yehudah*], *Judah,* contains all the letters of HASHEM's Four-Letter-name, with the addition of a ד, *dalet* [see *Overview* to *Ruth*].

See also *Torah Temimah* who supports this interpretation inasmuch as Jacob, in the blessings before his death, also praised Judah's efforts [but cf. *Tosafos* ad. loc. sv. אֶלָּא and footnote to previous verse.]

In *Midrash Rabbah* cited in the *comm.*, the implication is also that in recording Judah's suggestion the Torah praises him. It should not be thought that Judah was mercenary, for he saw no other way of saving him.

[Comp. *Mechilta Beshallach* §5, however, where Judah is praised only moderately for his feeble but sincere efforts — he should have taken a firmer stand and advised that they restore him to Jacob. See also *Sotah* 13 (cited in footnote to 38:7 and *comm.* to 38:11) where Judah is criticized for abandoning his good deed of trying to rescue Joseph, leaving it unfinished. One who leaves a good deed uncompleted, the Sages teach, will eventually bury his wife and children, as indeed happened to Judah. (Reuben is not castigated in this way since he *had*, in fact saved Joseph from murder by his brothers. That they sold Joseph before Reuben could rescue him from the pit and return him to Jacob was no fault of Reuben).]

37
27 *let us sell him to the Ishmaelites — but let our hand not be upon him, for he is our brother, our own flesh.' His brothers agreed.*

pose better than sending him far away from us?

It is noted that Judah's apprehension was not based on knowledge that the pit contained snakes and scorpions, but on the fear that Joseph would die of thirst and hunger (*Mizrachi* to *v.* 22 s.v. רוּחַ הַקֹּדֶשׁ).

[Thus, Judah directed his appeal not to emotion but to reason: Leaving Joseph in the pit also means to kill him.]

וְכִסִּינוּ אֶת־דָּמוֹ — *And* [*we*] *cover up his blood.*

— Figuratively: *Conceal the fact of his death* (*Rashi; Radak* and most commentators).

Rashi pursues a figurative interpretation since, in the literal sense, no blood had been spilled (*Mizrachi*).

Ramban interprets the phrase in its literal sense since murderers generally do away with their victim by burying the corpse and 'concealing his blood.' In this case, the inference was that by letting Joseph languish and die in the pit, they would in effect be murdering him and covering his blood with dust.

HaKsav V'HaKabbalah interprets this in the figurative sense: ' ... *And garb ourselves with* [the moral stain of having shed] *his blood.*

27. לְכוּ וְנִמְכְּרֶנּוּ לַיִּשְׁמְעֵאלִים — *Come* [idiomatic; lit. *go*] *let us sell him to the Ishmaelites.*

— They are traveling to a distant country; the matter will never be discovered (*Ramban, v.* 25).

— By selling him, we will be punishing him measure for measure: He wished to become our master, now he will be a slave (*Sforno*).

וְיָדֵנוּ אַל־תְּהִי־בוֹ כִּי אָחִינוּ בְשָׂרֵנוּ הוּא — *But* [lit. *and*] *let our hand not be upon him, for he is our brother, our own flesh.*

But let our hand not be upon him. Even though he will die in the pit, and our involvement in it will be only indirect, nevertheless we will have been instrumental in his death. *Let our hand* not have even that involvement — if we sell him he will not die (*Radak*).

He is our *brother* from one father, and our *flesh* inasmuch as our mothers were sisters and it is the mother who supplies the flesh [*Niddah* 31a] (*Haamek Davar*).

[Comp. Laban's remark to Jacob (29:14): *You are my flesh and bones.* Cf. also *Meshech Chochmah* and *Maharsha Niddah ad.loc.*]

[On the expression *flesh* denoting one familial entity, cf. also on 2:24 וְהָיוּ לְבָשָׂר אֶחָד, *And they shall become one flesh.*]

וַיִּשְׁמְעוּ אֶחָיו — [*And*] *his brothers agreed.*

The brothers reasoned: It has already been decreed at the Covenant Between the Parts [15:13] that the descendants of our ancestor Abraham are to be enslaved. We are all his descendants. If we sell Joseph as a slave, perhaps the decree will be fulfilled in him alone (*Chizkuni*).

The translation of וַיִּשְׁמְעוּ [lit. ...*heard*] as *agreed* [in the sense of *heeded*] follows *Rashi* who notes that whenever the verb שמע has the contextual sense of *heeding, agreeing with* or *obeying, Onkelos* uses the Aramaic root קבל. Examples are our verse; 28:7: *And Jacob obeyed his father; Exod.* 24:7:

אֲנָשִׁים מִדְיָנִים סֹחֲרִים וַיִּמְשְׁכוּ וַיַּעֲלוּ אֶת־יוֹסֵף מִן־הַבּוֹר וַיִּמְכְּרוּ אֶת־יוֹסֵף

נַעֲשֶׂה וְנִשְׁמָע: *We will do and we will obey* [cf. also 34:24]. — However, where the word literally means *hear* with the auditory sense, *Onkelos* employs the root שמע, *hear*, which is used in Aramaic as well as Hebrew. Examples are 3:8: *They heard the sound of HASHEM God manifesting Itself in the garden*; 27:5; 31:1; *Exod.* 16:12.

[*Rashi* pursues this interpretation since the Torah could not mean the obvious fact that the brothers *heard with their ears* what Judah had spoken.

28. וַיַּעַבְרוּ אֲנָשִׁים מִדְיָנִים סֹחֲרִים — *Then* [lit. *and*] *Midianite men, traders, passed by.*

[The appearance of a Midianite caravan surprises us, as we have previously been informed only of an *Ishmaelite* caravan]:

This was another caravan. The Torah thus indicates that he was sold several times *(Rashi)* ...

וַיִּמְשְׁכוּ וַיַּעֲלוּ אֶת יוֹסֵף מִן הַבּוֹר — [*And*] *they drew Joseph up and lifted him out of the pit and sold Joseph to the Ishmaelites.*

They drew refers to the sons of Jacob — they took him out of the pit and sold him to the Ishmaelites; in turn, the Ishmaelites sold him to the Midianites, and the Midianites to the Egyptians *(Rashi).*

That the brothers, acting on Judah's advice, sold Joseph to the Ishmaelites is basic to *Rashi's* exegesis which is based on the Talmud and Midrash. Though the Torah does not explicitly mention that the Ishmaelites sold Joseph to the Midianites, *Rashi* relies on *v.* 36 which states that the *Medanites* [whom *Rashi* apparently identifies with their brother-clan the Midianites; see *comm.* there] *had sold Joseph to Egypt.* Obviously they had to have *purchased* Joseph before they had *sold* him *(Mizrachi).*

☙ Who sold Joseph?
— *The alternate views.*

This passage constitutes the turning point in the history of Joseph; it marks the descent of the Israelites into Egypt. The subject of the passage has been a matter of much controversy among the commentators. It should be noted that a reading of *v.* 28, *in isolation*, would strongly intimate that the *Midianites* were the ones who pulled Joseph from the pit and sold him.

Rashi, following the Talmudic exegesis, postulates that the subject of this latter passage — *they drew Joseph up ... and sold Joseph to the Ishmaelites* — reverts to *the brothers* who are the subject of the previous *verse* and not to the Midianites who are the subject of the immediately preceding *phrase.* This identification is followed by many commentators. In fact, *Ramban* to 24:32 cites our passage as an example of a subject changing within the same verse, in this case from the Midianites to the sons of Jacob.

That Jacob's sons, the tribal ancestors, sold their brother is the basis of much Rabbinic exegesis, and its *Hashkafah* (philosophic) implications are discussed in the *Overview* to this *Sidrah* [see also *footnote* to *v.* 15]. In general, as *R' Bachya* notes, the later imperial decree against the Ten Martyrs who were slain during the Roman Persecutions was on account of the sin of the sale of Joseph by the ten brothers. [See *Midrash Mishlei* s.v. כל הון. The martyrs are generally identified as: R' Shimon ben Gamliel; R' Yishmael the High Priest; R' Akiva; R' Yehudah ben Bava; R' Chaninah ben Teradion; R' Yeshovav the Scribe; R' Elazar ben Dama; R' Chaninah ben Chachinai; R' Chutzpis the *Meturgeman* and R' Elazar ben Shamua.] It is unclear how we arrive at the total of *ten* brothers, since Reuben was not involved in the sale, and Benjamin, who was only about nine years old, had been at home during the

28 *Midianite men, traders, passed by. They drew Joseph up and lifted him out of the pit and sold*

entire episode. However, *R' Bachya* includes Reuben in the number and maintains that by his participation in the *formulation* of the plot against Joseph, he shared responsibility for the sale as well).]

As we shall see, however, not *all* commentators agree that it was the brothers who lifted Joseph out of the pit and sold him, nor do they all agree with the identity of the caravans and the sequence of transferences by which Joseph eventually ended up in Egypt.

Among the various difficulties that inspire the various interpretations is the contextual flow of the narrative itself, and the surprise introduction of Midianite merchants in the midst of the account of the sale.

In *v.* 27 we are told that the brothers agreed to Judah's suggestion that they sell Joseph to the caravan of Ishmaelites. Then, in *v.* 28, in apparent compliance with this suggestion, we are told that *they* [=presumably the brothers] *drew Joseph up ... and sold Joseph to the Ishmaelites for twenty pieces of silver.* However, prior to this narrative, previously unmentioned *Midianite* merchants are inexplicably introduced to us. Who were they and what was their role?

Rashi, as noted above, advances the Talmudic exegesis that the mention of the Midianite merchants at this point prepares us for *v.* 36 where they are implicitly recorded as Joseph's owners; thereby we are shown that a three-fold sale had taken place: The brothers sold Joseph to the Ishmaelites, who sold him to the Midianites, who sold him to Potiphar in Egypt. [This is inferred from *v.* 36 which states the Midianites sold him; obviously, then, they must have bought him.]

[It appears that *Rashi* identifies the Midianites with their brother-clan the Medanites mentioned in *v.* 36.]

The seemingly left unanswered question is what we are to make of 39:1 where Potiphar is described as having bought Joseph 'from the hand of the *Ishmaelites who brought him down there.*' Even *Mizrachi,* writes: 'I do not know what *Rashi* would make of that verse.'

The *Daas Zekeinim* basically share *Rashi's* view that the brothers sold Joseph. In reconciling some of the Scriptural difficulties, however, they differ drastically in the sequence of the sale and the identity of the various purchasers. According to them there were *four* sales, not three.

They postulate that the brothers had agreed to sell Joseph to the approaching Ishmaelite caravan. But while they were discussing the matter, a group of Midianite merchants passed by and the brothers sold Joseph to *them* while he was still in the pit. The Midianites hauled him out of the pit and in turn sold him to the Ishmaelites who had arrived in the interim. The Ishmaelites sold him to the Medanites who sold him to the Egyptians. That in 39:1 we are told that Potiphar bought him *from the hand of the Ishmaelites* is no contradiction. Potiphar's suspicions were aroused by Joseph's handsome and commanding appearance. He could not believe that the dark-skinned Medanites could have owned a 'white slave,' especially a white boy of such carriage and ability; usually the situation was reversed. The Ishmaelites were therefore brought to give their 'hand' — i.e., the necessary guarantee, that the Medanites were indeed the legitimate owners. This then is the force of 39:1: *Potiphar bought him from the hand* [i.e. as a result of the surety of the hand — the guarantee] *of the Ishmaelites* — though the Medanites were actually his owners.

Ramban follows *Rashi's* view that the brothers lifted Joseph out of the pit and sold him, but he proposes a different solution to the identity of the caravans and hence the nature of the sale.

He cites *Ibn Ezra* who maintains that

the Midianites are referred to by the designation Ishmaelites. [*Radak* in *Judges* 8:24 interprets similarly on the basis that Midian was the son of Keturah who is traditionally identified with Hagar, mother of Ishmael.][1] *Ramban* disgrees with this identification on various contextual grounds and maintains that the Ishmaelites and Midianites were distinct peoples who together formed one caravan. For when the caravan, which had seemed from afar to be Ishmaelite, drew closer, they discovered that it was composed of Ishmaelite camel drivers who hired themselves and their camels to Midianite merchants — traders — but who were not themselves engaged in trade.

Thus, according to *Ramban*, the brothers planned to sell Joseph to Ishmaelites, but they actually sold him to Midianites.

Accordingly, the verse which states: *They sold Joseph to the Ishmaelites* implies that the Midianites purchasers turned him over to their Ishmaelite haulers who would transport him to Egypt. This is also the implication of the verse [39:1]: *from the hand of the Ishmaelites who brought him down there*, for Joseph was in their care — but the Midianites were his owners. This is the force of the verse: *And the Medanites* [=Midianites] *sold him to Egypt*.

Ramban proceeds to defend his exegesis by demonstrating that the Torah often employs this narrative method. Sometimes it attributes a deed to its primary author, and at other times to the ultimate commissioner of the deed, or intermediary. Thus, *God* is sometimes credited with an act as in *Deut.* 11:7: *All the marvelous deeds that HASHEM performed* in Egypt and in the Wilderness; while at other times Moses is credited with the same deeds, as in *(ibid.* 34:12): ... *that Moses performed in the sight of all Israel.* Similarly, Solomon is credited with the work in the Temple [*I Kings* 7:51] which was actually executed by Hiram [ibid. *v.* 14].

[Thus, following *Ramban's* thesis the Torah alternately refers to Joseph's captors as Ishmaelites and Midianites, because the Torah sometimes attributes a deed to its *immediate* cause, in our context the Midianites, and at others to its more *indirect* one, in our context the Ishmaelites.]

Sforno pursues a somewhat similar interpretation, maintaining however, that it was with the *Ishmaelites* — who were acting as intermediaries for the Midianites — that the brothers negotiated. The brothers did not wish to deal directly with the Midianites, who, as merchants, traveled to many towns and might recognize them at some later time. They did not have this apprehension about dealing with the Ishmaelites who, as caravan leaders, took circuitous routes. The Midianites were the actual purchasers, however. A parallel to this sale of a brother by brothers occurred during the wars with the Romans — especially during the period of tyrranical Hasmoneans — when Jews sold their own kinfolk to the Romans.

1. *Ibn Ezra's* view that Midianites and Ishmaelites are designations for one people, is followed by many commentators — among them *Abarbanel* and *Ralbag* — *Ramban's* criticism notwithstanding.

Among its foremost proponents is *R' Yosef B'chor Schor.* He explains that the ancestors of the Midianites, Medanites and Ishmaelites were brothers — children of Abraham's concubines. Though the Torah refers to them interchangeably by different names, they are really one and the same, just as Jews are interchangeably called Jews, Hebrews, and Israelites. There is according to this view no discrepancy in the narrative.

Interestingly even *Rashi's* supercommentary, *Gur Aryeh*, subscribes to *Ibn Ezra's* interpretation. He maintains that the Torah refers to the Midianites as Ishmaelites since the latter were the primary clan [much as we would refer to Middle Eastern Semites by the common designation Arab]. From the way the Midianites were dressed, the brothers and Potiphar assumed them to be Ishmaelites, but the Torah informs us that they were really Midianites. Possibly it was a caravan composed of several peoples — including Midianites — and the whole of which was referred to by the general term Ishmaelite.

Not all commentators, however, agree that the brothers sold Joseph. Based on the context of the verse which begins with the approach of the Midianites, these commentators maintain that the Midianites, not the brothers, drew Joseph out of the pit. Furthermore, according to this thesis, these Midianites sold him without the brothers' knowledge or consent.

One of the earliest proponents of this approach, which has its roots in *Tanchuma Yashan,* is *Rashbam.* [He is followed (with many important changes) by *Chizkuni, R'Bachya, R'Hirsch, Malbim* and *Netziv.* (The latter maintains however that the brothers observed how the Midianite — drawn to the pit by Joseph's cries — hauled him out and were joyous that their desired goal was being executed by others without their own *active* participation).

We cite *Rashbam* fully:

'*And Midianite merchants passed by.* This occurred while they were sitting down partaking of their meal. They [the brothers] had positioned themselves at some distance from the pit so as to avoid [callously] 'eating on the blood', and they waited for the Ishmaelites they had seen. Before the Ishmaelites arrived, another group — Midianites — passed, saw Joseph in the pit, lifted him out, and sold him to the Ishmaelites. It may be that the brothers were unaware of it [until Reuben discovered his absence from the pit]. Though the Torah later states [Joseph's charge when he revealed himself to his brothers (45:4)]: *I am Joseph your brother*] *whom* **you sold to Egypt,** this was meant only in the sense of their primary responsibility for the sale [by having thrown him into the pit in the first place]. This appears to me correct on the basis of profound interpretation of the plain meaning of Scripture. For the expression *then Midianite men, traders, passed by* implies that they passed by quite *coincidentally* and *they* [not the brothers] sold him to the Ishmaelites.'

He continues, that 'even if one wishes to say [as *Rashi* does] that the phrase *they sold Joseph to the Ishmaelites* means that the *brothers* sold him, then we would have to say that the brothers asked the Midianites to draw Joseph out of the pit, and afterwards they [the brothers] sold him to the Ishmaelites.'

According to those who follow the primary interpretation advanced by *Rashbam* that Joseph was sold without the knowledge of the brothers [clearly not the *traditional* Rabbinic interpretation], it would appear that the brothers thought he had died. Reuben discovered his disappearance and was convinced that a wild animal had killed him. They, too, were convinced that this was the case, and they devised the scheme of dipping his tunic in blood to protect themselves and convince their father that Joseph had indeed been devoured by a wild beast. Several texts are answered by this premise, including Judah's vehement insistence that Joseph was dead [44:20] as well as the intent of Joseph's later remark [40:15] *I was stolen* — not sold — *from the land of the Hebrews.* It also explains why — after the brothers suffered complete remorse for their act [42:22] — they did not go to all ends to find him and relieve their father's unconsolable anguish over Joseph's absence. [The Talmudic interpretation of these passages is dealt with in the commentary to the respective verses.]

בְּעֶשְׂרִים כָּסֶף — *For twenty* [pieces of] *silver..*[1]

— Two pieces of silver for each, which they used to buy shoes [see *Amos* 2:6]. Thus they heaped

1. **The solemn ban against divulging what had occurred.**

It is at this point that the brothers proposed to proclaim a חֵרֶם, *solemn ban,* forbidding anyone from divulging to Jacob what had occurred.

[It is noteworthy that according to *Sefer Chassidim,* ed. Mekitzei Nirdamim §1562, Joseph too was adjured by this dreaded oath. He was prohibited from attempting to return to Jacob,

כט יוֹסֵף מִצְרָיְמָה: וַיָּשָׁב רְאוּבֵן אֶל־הַבּוֹר
וְהִנֵּה אֵין־יוֹסֵף בַּבּוֹר וַיִּקְרַע אֶת־בְּגָדָיו:

further indignity upon Joseph by buying shoes with the money. They said, We will tread upon him symbolically and we will see what will become of his dreams [*v.* 20]! *(Tanchuma; Pirkei d'Rabbi Eliezer).*

They settled for such a paltry sum since they were eager to be rid

or even notifying his father by word of mouth or letter of his whereabouts without their consent. This accounts for Joseph's failure to contact Jacob throughout his twenty-two year period in Egypt. Even had Joseph not consented to this dread oath, he was bound by it. Such is the law; when a quorum of ten adult males invoke a solemn ban, the entire community becomes bound by it.]

Judah said to them: 'Reuben is not here, and a ban by less than ten people is not valid' [Benjamin was absent, too]. What did they do? — They associated the Almighty with them so that He should not reveal the matter of Jacob.

Because of the ban, the Holy One, Blessed be He, did not tell Jacob what had occurred. Though it is written [*Psalms* 147:19]: מַגִּיד דְּבָרָו לְיַעֲקֹב, *He declares His word to Jacob,* He did not reveal *this* matter to him, and Jacob remained ignorant of what had occurred.

Isaac was still alive at this time. [As noted in the *comm.* to 35:29, he was to live another twelve years beyond Joseph's sale; cf. *v.* 2 s.v. יוֹסֵף]. He *did* know [prophetically] that Joseph was living, but seeing that God Himself did not reveal it, he did not dare reveal it *(Tanchuma; Pirkei d'Rabbi Eliezer; Rashi v.* 33 from *Midrash).* [When the brothers eventually told Jacob that Joseph was alive in Egypt, their decision to tell him was a *de facto* annulment of the ban. See also comm. to 41:51.]

For this same reason Isaac did not pray that God annul the decree and inform Jacob of Joseph's whereabouts, although it was certainly within his province as a *tzaddik* to do so. He realized that Jacob's ignorance of the event was essential to the Divine workings of Providence. That God informed Isaac at all of what had occurred was so that Isaac should not spend his last years grieving the 'death' of a grandson. Only Jacob deserved such grief because it was punishment for the grief he had caused his parents during his twenty-two years of absence. Furthermore, had Isaac — who died before Joseph's rise to eminence in Egypt was revealed — not been informed, he would have remained ignorant until his dying day that Joseph was indeed alive; Jacob, on the other hand, lived to see Joseph as a supreme regent of all Egypt *(Yafeh Toar).*

* * *

That God allowed Himself to be associated in this ban does not infer that He associates Himself with evil-doers ח״ו. He participated for several reasons:

(a) To prevent Jacob from pronouncing an eternal curse upon his progeny which would have had disastrous results for all time. If only his *tears* resulted in the death of the Ten Martyrs (see comm. above), how much more of an effect would his curse have had! *(Chemdas Yamim).*

(b) It was also part of the Divine Will that the family destiny unfold according to the Providential plan. The ultimate goal was that events should evolve into Jacob's honorable descent to Egypt. Had it been otherwise, he would never have left the sacred environs of *Eretz Yisrael* to go to the immoral Egypt; instead he would have sent emissaries to purchase Joseph's freedom *(Sifsei Kohen);*

(c) God desired that Joseph's twenty-two years of isolated absence during which Jacob was unaware of his welfare should be an atonement for the like period during which Jacob had been with Laban and had not fulfilled the *mitzvah* of honoring his parents [see on 29:18] *(Sefer Chassidim* ed. *Mekeitzei Nirdamim* §1562).

R' Bachya observes additionally that the notion of God associating Himself with man to make a quorum is not unprecendented. Abraham, too, had asked God to include His Majesty with the righteous of Sodom in order to make up the necessary quorum of ten to save the inhabitants [see on 18:28, s.v. הֲתַשְׁחִית]. The brothers rationalized that it was justifiable to associate God with their oath in order to spare Jacob even greater grief and to prevent the eternal repercussions of his curse on his progeny.

Then they brought Joseph to Egypt.
[29] Reuben returned to the pit — and behold, Joseph
was not in the pit! So he rent his garments. [30] Return-

of him at any price *(Ralbag).*

But couldn't the sale of the handsome Joseph have commanded a much higher price? — Perhaps it means twenty pieces of silver *for each brother.* Or according to *Pirkei d'Rabbi Eliezer,* since Joseph's face had a ghastly pallor from his fear of the serpents and scorpions, he looked sickly and they could not demand more for him *(Da'as Zekeinim).*

The Sages in *Yerushalmi Shekalim* 2:3 remark that because they sold Rachel's firstborn for twenty *dinarim* [a *shekel*=four *dinarim*] of silver, therefore we redeem our firstborns for twenty *dinarim* of silver (=five *shekalim)* [as an atonement for the misdeed of our ancestors *(R' Bachya).* See *Numbers* 18:15-6.]

Mechech Chochma [to *Exod.* 13 s.v. וְכָל פֶּטֶר] finds this puzzling. Why, he asks, should even descendants of Joseph have to redeem their firstborn by paying a sum to the *Kohanim,* descendants of Levi, when Levi [as noted in comm. to *v.* 19] was one of the prime instigators of the sale! He suggests, therefore, that *Yerushalmi's* intent is: In selling Joseph, Rachel's firstborn, Levi agreed that he was worth no more than five *shekalim.* Consequently Levi's descendants must also be content with accepting no more than that amount for the redemption of Israel's firstborn.

Furthermore, *Yerushalmi Shekalim* (ibid.) continues, since each brother's share of these twenty pieces of silver was two pieces of silver, equaling a half-shekel, we give a half-shekel annually for the Temple upkeep.

וַיָּבִיאוּ אֶת יוֹסֵף מִצְרָיְמָה — *Then* [lit. *and*] *they* [=the Midianites/Medanites *(Rashi; Mizrachi)*] *brought Joseph to Egypt.*

29. Reuben discovers Joseph's absence.

וַיָּשָׁב רְאוּבֵן אֶל־הַבּוֹר — [Lit. *and*] *Reuben returned to the pit.*

— In order to rescue him and return him to Jacob [see comm. to *v.* 22].

Reuben was not present at Joseph's sale, it having been his turn to attend Jacob. Alternatively, he did not participate in the meal and was not present at the sale because he was occupied with fasting and sackcloth in penitence for having disarranged his father's couch [in the incident with Bilhah; see 35:22] *(Rashi* from *Midrash).*

Following the latter interpretation, the expression 'returned to the pit' has the metaphoric connotation of 'repented [=returned] to the original source of purity and sinlessness' *(Yafeh Toar).*

According to *Rashi's* first interpretation, the implication is that Reuben's absence was unavoidable; he had to leave Joseph in the pit at such a crucial time in order to perform the *mitzvah* of tending to his father's needs.

Following the second interpretation we must assume that Reuben's penitence was done in private. This would reconcile with the tradition cited by *Rashi* to *Deut.* 33:7 s.v. וְזֹאת לִיהוּדָה that Reuben repented the matter with Bilhah *after* Judah's penitence for his affair with Tamar. [See 38:26]. Apparently, since the episode of Tamar had not yet occurred, we must surmise that Reuben's penitence now was still private; after Judah repented, Reuben repented *publicly (Mizrachi; Tzeidah LaDerech).*

B'chor Shor differs in the literal sense with the suggestion that Reuben journeyed the long distance from Dothan to Hebron to look after his father for one day. See *comm.* to *v.* 25 end of s.v. וַיֵּשְׁבוּ.

According to *Pirkei d'Rabbi Eliezer,*

ל וַיָּשָׁב אֶל־אֶחָיו וַיֹּאמַר הַיֶּלֶד אֵינֶנּוּ וַאֲנִי
לא אָנָה אֲנִי־בָא: וַיִּקְחוּ אֶת־כְּתֹנֶת יוֹסֵף
וַיִּשְׁחֲטוּ שְׂעִיר עִזִּים וַיִּטְבְּלוּ אֶת־הַכֻּתֹּנֶת

Reuben had slipped away, awaiting an opportunity to rescue Joseph; therefore he was not present at the sale.[1]

וַיִּקְרַע אֶת־בְּגָדָיו — *So* [lit. *and*] *he rent his garments.*

[In a manifestation of his grief.]

[Cf. Jacob's rending in *v.* 34.]

30. הַיֶּלֶד אֵינֶנּוּ — *The boy is gone* [lit. *is not*]*!*

— I do not even have his remains to bring back to Father! *(Zohar).*

וַאֲנִי אָנָה אֲנִי־בָא — *And I — where can I go?* [lit. *and I, where shall I come?*].

Where can I flee from my father's grief? *(Rashi).*

The sense is: The boy is missing and I [as the eldest son who will bear the greatest responsibility for the matter] must flee because of the grief this will cause Father. But where can I flee? *(Maharshal).*

Reuben despaired at the prospect of seeing Jacob's grief. By ignoring the terrible effect their deed would have on their father, the brothers acted more callously than Esau who resolved to murder Jacob only *after* the death of their father. But until Reuben proclaimed this consideration, the brothers ignored it. That these righteous people could do so is further proof that they were helpless pawns in executing God's plan to bring Joseph to Egypt *(Oznaim laTorah).*

Another reason Reuben felt more responsible than the others was that it would be said that he was jealous of Joseph to whom Jacob had awarded the birthright after the incident of Bilhah [See I *Chron.* 5:1 and *comm.* to 35:23] *(Chizkuni).*

Also, Judah had made the proposal to *sell* Joseph, while Reuben had initially proposed throwing Joseph into the pit (ibid.).

Ralbag perceives the sense to be: 'How can I appear before Father without even a trace of Joseph's corpse to prove he is dead. Jacob will sustain a hope that Joseph was kidnapped and make me search for him to the end of the world.'

The term בא usually refers to returning home: How can I possibly return home [to father]! *(HaRechasim leBik'ah).*[2]

[We have preserved the idiomatic double use of the pronoun וַאֲנִי ... אֲנִי. *Ibn Ezra* comments that this is but Hebrew style and that a single אֲנִי would have sufficed. However, our translation attempts to reproduce the nuances of the Hebrew text whenever possible.]

1. Many disturbing questions arise regarding Reuben's handling of the situation:

Why didn't Reuben — who spent his time in penitence — take his portion of food and cast it to the starving Joseph in the pit? Why did he not save him while the brothers were eating; wouldn't that have been more appropriate than occupying himself with fasting and sackcloth while his brother was in mortal danger?

Only one response adequately answers all such questions: It was the absolute Will of Heaven that Joseph be brought down to Egypt! *(Oznaim laTorah).*

Asking the same question, *Tzror HaMor* concludes that Reuben had been waiting for an auspicious time to save Joseph. In the interim he isolated himself and engaged in acts of penitence, but Providence did not allow him to execute his intended rescue. His brothers sold Joseph before Reuben returned to the pit.

2. *R' Hirsch* notes that Reuben did not say *where shall* אֵלֵךְ, *I go;* instead he used the word בָּא, *come.* This word has the connotation of *coming home,* or some other place where one has a feeling of belonging. Thus, Reuben's words should be understood as expressing a feeling of shame, as if to say. 'There is no place where I can hold up my head without feeling that

ing to his brothers he said, 'The boy is gone! And I — where can I go?'

31 *They took Joseph's tunic, slaughtered a goatling, and dipped the tunic in the blood.* 32 *They dis-*

31. The brothers prepare an alibi.

[The Torah does not record the brothers' response to Reuben's outburst, and it is not entirely clear whether he learned what had really occurred. How their subsequent decision to dip Joseph's tunic in blood was a suitable response to Reuben's outburst similarly needs clarification]:

According to *Pirkei d'Rabbi Eliezer* and *Tanchuma Yashan,* they told Reuben what they had done and their ban against revealing it [see footnote *v.* 28]. When he heard the ban, he kept his peace.

According to the *Zohar,* they did not reveal the sale even to Reuben. Accordingly he believed that Joseph was dead until Joseph revealed himself to his brothers in Egypt.

The commentators who maintain that the brothers, too, were unaware that Midianites had snatched up Joseph from the pit and sold him, maintain that when Reuben informed them that Joseph was missing they *all* sincerely believed that Joseph had been devoured by a wild beast. Thus, they were not intentionally lying to their father. They brought the bloody tunic to assure him that indeed such was the case and that the matter was beyond their control and responsibility *(see Chizkuni).*

In any case, the dipping of Joseph's tunic in blood was a response to Reuben's outburst inasmuch as it provided him with the 'evidence' to convince Jacob that Joseph was indeed dead and not just missing. Otherwise, as mentioned above, Reuben was apprehensive that Jacob would have sent him, as the firstborn, to the very ends of the earth to find his still-living son *(Or HaChaim).*

At the same time it removed the culpability from all of the brothers. They knew that if they were to remain silent, Jacob would suspect them, for he knew of their hatred for Joseph *(Ramban v.* 32).

וַיִּקְחוּ אֶת־כְּתֹנֶת יוֹסֵף — *[And] they took Joseph's tunic.*

The commentators differ as to whether the word *tunic* here refers to his כְּתֹנֶת פַּסִּים, *fine-woolen tunic,* or merely to his *undershirt* [lit. *under-tunic*] [cf. *v.* 23]. *Meleches Machsheves* in the next verse interprets that it was *his undershirt* that they dipped and sent to Jacob. The majority of commentators maintain, however, that they used his *fine woolen tunic.*

וַיִּשְׁחֲטוּ שְׂעִיר עִזִּים — *[And they] slaughtered a goatling.*

They chose a goatling because its blood resembles human blood *(Rashi).*

The term שחט denotes ritual slaughter.

The *Midrash* notes that this passage vindicates the brothers against Joseph's earlier charges of eating flesh from living animals. Even in their degradation, they ritually slaughtered the goatling and would not eat its flesh while it was still alive [see *Rashi* to *v.* 2 s.v. אֶת דִּבָּתָם רָעָה].

Torah Sheleimah §181 cites a *Midrash* that even in this matter God was repaying Jacob measure for measure. Jacob had deceived his father with *skins of goat-kids* [27:16]; therefore his sons now deceived him with a goat. [See also 38:25.]

וַיִּטְבְּלוּ אֶת הַכֻּתֹּנֶת בַּדָּם — *And [they] dipped the tunic in the blood.*

Rashi makes the grammatical

everyone will avoid me and hold recriminations against me — there is no place where I can "come home."'

Why should only Reuben — and none of the others — have felt so responsible? He possibly

לב בַּדָּם: וַיְשַׁלְּחוּ אֶת־כְּתֹנֶת הַפַּסִּים וַיָּבִיאוּ
אֶל־אֲבִיהֶם וַיֹּאמְרוּ זֹאת מָצָאנוּ הַכֶּר־נָא
לג הַכְּתֹנֶת בִּנְךָ הִוא אִם־לֹא: וַיַּכִּירָהּ וַיֹּאמֶר
כְּתֹנֶת בְּנִי חַיָּה רָעָה אֲכָלָתְהוּ טָרֹף טֹרַף

note that the noun כתנת in its absolute state is vowelized כְּתֹנֶת. When it occurs in the construct state, it is vowelized כְּתֹנֶת as in כְּתֹנֶת יוֹסֵף, כְּתֹנֶת פַּסִּים, כְּתֹנֶת בַּד.

32. וַיְשַׁלְּחוּ ... וַיָּבִיאוּ אֶל אֲבִיהֶם – [*And*] *they dispatched ... and they brought it to their father.*

The expression *they dispatched* implies that they sent the information through messengers; and they — the messengers — *brought it to their father.* [The brothers did not want to be the ones to tell Jacob since their well-known dislike of Joseph might arouse Jacob's suspicion *(Chizkuni).* Additionally they did not want to be the 'foolish bearers of evil tidings' *(Gur Aryeh),* nor could they bear to witness Jacob's grief or lie to his face *(Oznaim leTorah).*] Possibly, they sent the tunic ahead to Hebron to await their own arrival, and later brought it to their father themselves, and told him they found it. They realized that silence would only have aroused Jacob's suspicion *(Ramban).*

According to *Targum Yonasan,* the brothers sent the tunic with the sons of Bilhah and Zilpah. Since they were known to be Joseph's friends [see comm. to *v.* 2 s.v. וְהוּא נַעַר], Jacob would not suspect them of foul play.

R' Bachya cites a *Midrash* that the brothers cast lots to determine who should bring the tunic, and Judah was chosen [comp. *Sotah* 10b cited below].

Ramban cites another translation [mentioned in *Radak*] of וַיְשַׁלְּחוּ, according to which the verb, in our context means *and they pierced;* cf. בְּשֶׁלַח, *by the sword,* in Job 36:12. The intent is that they pierced the tunic with a sword in many places to give it the appearance of having been gnashed by a wild beast's fangs and claws. [Cf. *Gur Aryeh*].

וַיֹּאמְרוּ זֹאת מָצָאנוּ – *And* [*they said,* '*We found this.*'

As noted above, the brothers took turns coming back to Hebron to attend to Jacob's personal needs. When Joseph failed to return, Jacob asked each newly arrived son whether he had seen Joseph. Each, of course, answered in the negative whereupon Jacob instructed them all to search for him. This command gave them the pretext to bring home the bloody tunic which they claimed to have "found." Had there been no such contact between Jacob and his sons, they would have no justifiable

blamed himself for not having acted more vigorously to prevent what had happened. He had started the *mitzvah* and then dropped it. His conscience bothered him — perhaps he had neglected his responsibility to save Joseph because in his subconscious he was as guilty as they of wanting to do away with Joseph.

There could have been another reason too. The fear that had driven the brothers was that Joseph would take away their independence. None of them had more to fear than Jacob's firstborn, Reuben. After all, Joseph was the firstborn of Jacob's intended wife. [In addition, Jacob had already conferred the double-portion of the firstborn upon Joseph.] Suspicion therefore would inevitably fall on Reuben.

37 *patched the fine woolen tunic and they brought it to*
33 *their father, and said, 'We found this. Recognize, if*
you please: is it your son's tunic or not?' 33 *He*
recognized it and he said, 'My son's tunic! A savage
beast devoured him! Joseph has surely been torn to

reason for bringing him a tunic that they "happened to find" *(Oznaim laTorah).*

הַכֶּר־נָא הַכְּתֹנֶת בִּנְךָ הִוא אִם־לֹא — *Recognize* [cf. 31:32] *if you please: Is it your son's tunic or not?*[1]

[According to the opinion that this was said by the brothers' messengers, it is obvious why they used the expression 'your son's tunic' rather than mentioned Joseph by name. If the brothers themselves said these words, we can perceive the extent of their hatred: even at this juncture they could not refer to him by name. Their words also carried the connotation of: *Is this the fine woolen tunic you gave to your darling son?* According to *Sotah* 10b it was Judah — their leader — who said this. He was later punished measure for measure when Tamar confronted him with these same words. See 38:25.]

Here, too, God was repaying Jacob measure for measure for the terror he inflicted on his father. Because Jacob deceived Isaac and caused him to ask in anguish [27:21]: הַאַתָּה זֶה בְּנִי עֵשָׂו אִם־לֹא, *Are you indeed my son Esau or not?* God now caused Jacob's children to ask him [a question reflecting a similar phraseology]: הַכְּתֹנֶת בִּנְךָ הִוא אִם־לֹא, *Is it your son's tunic or not? (Tzror HaMor).*

33. כְּתֹנֶת בְּנִי — *My son's tunic!*

The phrase is elliptic and should be understood as if it read: כְּתֹנֶת בְּנִי הִיא זוּ, *this is my son's tunic (Rashi).*

חַיָּה רָעָה אֲכָלָתְהוּ — *A savage* [lit. *evil*] *beast devoured him!*[2]

Had robbers attacked him, they would not have left the tunic *(Chizkuni).*

A prophetic spirit was instilled within Jacob. His words contained the hidden meaning that Potiphar's wife — a bestial person — would attempt to devour him *(Rashi;* cf. *Targum Yonasan).*

Rashi cites the *Midrash* discussed in the footnote to *v.* 28 that God did not reveal the truth to Jacob because He had associated Himself with the brothers' ban prohibiting such disclosure. [See *footnote* to *v.* 28.]

טָרֹף טֹרַף יוֹסֵף — *Joseph has surely been torn to bits!*

[The translation attempts to con-

1. *Meleches Machsheves* suggests that the two 'distinct' designations in our narrative [*fine woolen tunic* and *tunic*] refer to two different garments: Jacob's special gift and Joseph's ordinary under-tunic. The brothers shrewdly did not dip the *fine woolen tunic* since a defacement of this symbol of their hatred for Joseph would have aroused Jacob's suspicion.

Therefore, *Joseph's tunic* mentioned in *v.* 31 was his ordinary tunic worn near his body — his undershirt. It was this they dipped in blood. Then they *sent the fine woolen tunic* away and hid it; it was the bloodstained *undershirt* — 'your son's tunic' — which they brought to Jacob and asked him to identify.

[The above differs with *Ramban* and most commentators who maintain that it was the כְּתֹנֶת פַּסִּים, *fine woolen tunic,* that they sent him so that he might recognize it by its uniqueness.]

2. The Sages [*Yevamos* 120b] rule that proof of a corpse's identity cannot be established from his clothing inasmuch as people are liable to lend their clothes. How then could Jacob have es-

לד יוֹסֵף: וַיִּקְרַע יַעֲקֹב שִׂמְלֹתָיו וַיָּשֶׂם שַׂק
בְּמָתְנָיו וַיִּתְאַבֵּל עַל־בְּנוֹ יָמִים רַבִּים:
לה וַיָּקֻמוּ כָל־בָּנָיו וְכָל־בְּנֹתָיו לְנַחֲמוֹ וַיְמָאֵן

vey the emphatic idiomatic force of the compound infinitive verbs. In Hebrew the passage literally reads: *Tear* (infin. absolute) *is torn Joseph!*]

R' Hirsch accounts for the double verbs by rendering: *'Torn to pieces; Joseph has been torn to pieces!'* Jacob visualizes the horror of the event — his dear son, his beloved child in the flower of developing manhood, ripped by the snarling teeth of a beast of prey.

[Jacob suspected Judah of foul play in this matter. See *Rashi* on 49:9 מִטֶּרֶף בְּנִי עָלִיתָ.]

34. וַיִּקְרַע יַעֲקֹב שִׂמְלֹתָיו וַיָּשֶׂם שַׂק בְּמָתְנָיו — *Then* [lit. *and*] *Jacob rent his garments and* [*he*] *placed sackcloth on his loins.*

— In grievous mourning for his favorite son, and also because he felt responsible for having sent him to his death *(Radak).*

He *rent his garments* because of mourning; *he placed the sackcloth on his loins* as an act of penitence. For, as *Mahari Weil* writes in his Responsa: If one dispatched an emissary to a dangerous area and that emissary is killed, the sender must undertake acts of penitence *(Malbim).*

The law of rending garments as a part of the mourning rites is not derived from our verse, since a binding *halachah* is not derived from events which preceded the giving of the Torah at Sinai. The Sages in *Moed Katan* 24a derive it as an *Asmachta* [Scriptural allusion] from *Lev.* 10:6 [see *Tosafos* there].

There is a noteworthy distinction between Reuben's rending in *v.* 29, and Jacob's. Reuben rent his בְּגָדִים, *outer* garments; Jacob rent שִׂמְלוֹתָיו, more specifically *his shirt* i.e. even his undergarments *(Tur).*[1]

וַיִּתְאַבֵּל עַל־בְּנוֹ יָמִים רַבִּים — [*And*] *he mourned for* [lit. *upon*] *his son many days.*

Rashi (based on *Megillah* 17a) explains *many days* as referring to *twenty-two years,* corresponding to the period that Jacob had been away from his parents' home. During that period Jacob had neglected to honor his parents and did not attend to their needs.

tablished by this bloodstained tunic that Joseph had definitely been devoured and torn to pieces?

— Possibly, since this fine woolen tunic had been given to Joseph by his father as a special mark of his esteem, he would have treasured it too much to lend it out. And the rule [ibid.] is that articles which are not generally lent may be used for identification *(Oznaim laTorah).*

1. *R' Hirsch* notes that the expression is usually קָרַע בֶּגֶד not קָרַע שִׂמְלָה. בֶּגֶד is the outer garment by which people project their outward appearance (hence a בּוֹגֵד, *traitor,* is the בֶּגֶד of a man; by having cast himself beyond the moral pale; he becomes a 'man' only in his outward appearance). Pain, grief, and shame are signified by tearing a garment, just as the outward relations of the people involved have been rent. Hence, mourning, too, is expressed by קְרִיעָה, *rending, tearing.* It is the opposite of שָׁלוֹם, *peace,* related to שָׁלֵם, *whole;* thus, the torn condition which causes grief is the opposite of wholeness. To express the extent of his grief, Jacob tore even his שִׂמְלָה, generally worn next to the skin, and replaced his soft, comfortable undergarment with a שַׂק, *sackcloth.* (Sackcloth is made of goat-hair, and is often called a hair-shirt). The nature of the material made every movement an uncomfortable reminder of his grief, as if to remind him that he had not right to feel comfortable. Hence, also וַיִּתְאַבֵּל, *he kept himself in his grief.*

bits!' 34 *Then Jacob rent his garments and placed*
sackcloth on his loins. He mourned for his son many
days. 35 *All his sons and all his daughters tried to*
comfort him, but he refused to comfort himself, and

The chronology is as follows: Joseph was seventeen years old when this occurred [*v.* 2], and was thirty years old when he stood before Pharaoh [see 41:46], an interim of thirteen years. Add the seven years of plenty and two years of famine which elapsed before Jacob came to Egypt and we arrive at the total of twenty-two years that Joseph was away from his father. Jacob, too, was away twenty-two years: twenty in Laban's house, one and a half in Succoth and half year in Bethel.

Jacob alluded to this when he told Laban [31:41]: זֶה לִּי עֶשְׂרִים שָׁנָה בְּבֵיתֶךָ, *this twenty years in your home is to me,* i.e., the responsibility for them lies *upon me,* and at some time in the future I will be punished for an equal period.

[See *Chronological Deductions* on page 1173, and *footnote* to 35:1 where it is explained why Jacob was punished for his stay in Laban's house when he had initially gone there at the command of his parents. (See also *comm.* to 30:25.)]

According to *Torah Temimah* [next verse] *many days* refers to *twelve months.*

35. וַיָּקֻמוּ כָל־בָּנָיו וְכָל בְּנֹתָיו לְנַחֲמוֹ — *[And] all his sons and all his daughters tried* [lit. *arose*] *to comfort him.*

In the classical sense, they offered him the traditional Cup of Consolation and mourner's meal. Jacob had done similarly for Isaac when he cooked the lentils on the day Abraham died [see 25:29] *(Sechel Tov).*

According to *Or HaChaim,* the phraseology: *All his sons and all his daughters arose to comfort him* suggests that their effort was planned: they all came together; the sight of his many other children was meant to console him.

◆§ The identity of Jacob's daughters-in-law

The plural *daughters* inspires a controversy in the Midrash inasmuch as Scripture specifically mentions only Dinah as a daughter of Jacob. R' Yehudah maintains that a twin daughter was born with each son, and the siblings married one another (see below). Thus Jacob had many daughters, all of whom tried to comfort him. R' Nechemiah maintains that the brothers were married to Canaanite women. The term *daughters* in our verse refers to Jacob's daughters-in-law, since it is quite common for one to refer to his son-in-law as his son, and to his daughter-in-law as his daughter *(Rashi).* [See 'Jacob's children' on p. 1313.]

Following the tradition cited by R' Yehudah that twin-sisters were born with each of the sons and that Jacob's sons and daughters married one another, we must presume that Leah's daughters married the sons of the maidservants. In that case they were brother and sister only *by their father,* and such marriage was not considered incestuous for a Noachide [i.e. for universal man, and before the Torah was given]. Although Abraham's progeny scrupulously observed the *mitzvos* before the Torah was given [see p. 1083], in this case it was deemed preferable to marry a sister by their father — which was permissible at the time — than to marry a Canaanite. After all, one must recall Abraham's intense efforts to assure that Isaac would not marry a Canaanite [see 24:3] and Isaac's similar charge to Jacob [28:1].

Presumably, R' Nechemiah would follow the tradition given in *Pesachim* 50a which discusses the account of Judah marrying בַּת אִישׁ כְּנַעֲנִי, *the daughter of a Canaanite man* (38:2). Raising the question of how Judah could have violated the family tradition not to marry Canaanites, the Talmud there notes that in *Hosea* 12:8 [and also in *Proverbs* 31:24] the word כְּנַעֲנִי means *merchant*. Consequently, Judah married not the daughter of a *Canaanite*, but the daughter of a *merchant*. Assuming that R' Nechemiah follows this interpretation, he would maintain that the brothers married the daughters of foreign merchants. These daughters-in-law are the 'daughters' who comforted Jacob; his only *true* daughter was Dinah. Or Jacob may have had other daughters, the twins of his sons, who were not married to his sons. (See *Ramban* to 38:2; *Mizrachi; Ralbag; Akeidas Yitzchak; Maskil l'David;* cf. *Rashi* 46:26 and *Ramban* ibid *v.* 15).

According to *Ramban*, the plural *daughters* refers to Jacob's *daughter*, Dinah, and his *granddaughter* [Serach, the daughter of Asher (mentioned in *Numbers* 26:46)] (*R' Bachya*).]

[The only other granddaughter of Jacob recorded in the Torah is Yocheved daughter of Levi. But she was not yet born at this time.]

The Rabbinic interpretation that *daughters* here refers either literally to the twin sisters of Jacob's sons whom the Torah had no need to mention until now, or is a term of endearment for Jacob's daughters-in-law, is based also on the tradition cited by *Onkelos* [see *Ramban* to *Numbers* 26:46] that Serach was not Jacob's natural granddaughter. According to that interpretation [not shared by all commentators] the term *daughter* could not apply to her.

וַיְמָאֵן לְהִתְנַחֵם — *But* [lit. *and*] *he refused to comfort himself.*

There had never been a case of a child's death in the house of the Patriarchs because the race of the righteous is blessed. This is why Jacob mourned for his son so long and refused to allow himself to be comforted. In addition to his great love for Joseph he considered this to be a severe punishment intended for him *(Ramban* to 38:7).

Thus, in addition to the fact that Joseph was his favorite son by his favorite wife and he found his loss unbearable *(Alshich),* Jacob constantly recriminated over his past actions and blamed himself for having sent Joseph on his ill-fated mission *(Chizkuni; Sforno).* He also would constantly recall Joseph's faithfulness. Though Joseph knew the mission was dangerous, he undertook it unquestioningly. Jacob could not be consoled over the loss of such a faithful child *(Alshich).*

Furthermore, Jacob continued to nurse the hope that Joseph's remains might some day be discovered so that he could be given a proper burial *(Gur Aryeh).*

R' Hirsch notes the use of the reflexive לְהִתְנַחֵם, lit. *to comfort himself* [rather than the passive לְהִנָּחֵם, *to be comforted*]. He explains that consolation can never be imposed by an outsider. One can only offer a mourner reasons for consolation and hope he will accept them emotionally and intellectually. Jacob, however, would not permit himself to be influenced by such arguments; *he refused to comfort himself*.

Their words of consolation are not recorded in the Torah. What could they possibly have said under the circumstances! Their vain attempts fell upon deaf ears; their empty words could not move their venerable father from his tragic sense of loss of the son in whom he saw the personification of his own destiny; the son to whom he imparted the Torah he had learned in the Academy of Eber, and the son to whom the forfeited birthright of Reuben had passed after the incident with Bilhah *(Chiddushei HaRim)*.[1]

וַיֹּאמֶר כִּי אֵרֵד אֶל־בְּנִי אָבֵל שְׁאֹלָה — *And [he] said, For I will go down to the grave mourning for my son* [lit. *because I will go down to my son as a mourner to the grave*].

— Literally שְׁאֹל means *grave*, the sense of the passage being: I will be buried while still in mourning — i.e., I will mourn for my son even to the day of my own burial, and shall never be consoled for him all my life. Midrashically, שְׁאֹל refers to *Gehinnom*. "I was given this omen by God: If none of my sons die during my lifetime I may be assured that I will not see *Gehinnom*." [The Midrashic sense of the passage would then be: 'Because of my son's death, I am convinced that I will descend as a mourner to *Gehinnom*'] *(Rashi)*.[2]

1. *Rashi* cites the Rabbinic insight that no one can be consoled for the loss of a person who is actually alive. It is a Divine decree that the *dead* be forgotten — but not the living. This is adduced from *Psalms* 31:13: *I am forgotten as a dead man out of mind* [*Soferim* 21].

Even psychologically the known death of a loved one carries with it a certain finality since it is reversible only by תְּחִיַּת הַמֵּתִים, *Resurrection*. However, one never gives up hope for a person who is only *presumed* to be dead. Such a person is never forgotten. When the dead person is buried, the decree is that he is forgotten after twelve months; hence King David in *Psalms* [88:13] writes of the *earth of forgetfulness*. But if one is still alive, constant inquiries are made as to his whereabouts in the hope that he might be found *(Akeidah Yitzchak)*.

In view of the teaching of the Sages that one does not accept consolation for a person who is still alive, why did Jacob not realize from his own disconsolate state that Jacob was not dead?

— As *Rashi* notes, it had been revealed to Jacob that if any of his children predeceased him, it would be a portent that he, Jacob, would suffer the judgment of Gehinnom. Hence, while it is true that one forgets a dear one who is dead and forever gone, Jacob could not be oblivious to a terrible fate that he 'knew' awaited him *(Gur Aryeh)*.

— After so much time went by without his grief being diminished, Jacob *did* realize that Joseph must be alive. But he reasoned that the bloody tunic indicated that a beast had attacked Joseph and, although he escaped with his life, he must have been badly hurt. To make matters worse, his continued absence indicated that he must have been enslaved. So Jacob's beloved son was living as a maimed, brutally treated slave — surely an adequate cause for intense grief *(Levush)*.

— Although Jacob realized that Joseph had survived the initial attack, he might have died at any time during the succeeding years. Therefore, Jacob constantly felt as though he might *just* have lost his son *(Divrei David)*.

2. When Jacob had gone to Laban, the Divine Presence said to him, 'Jacob my son, lift up your eyes heavenward and see the twelve signs of the zodiac. There are twelve hours in the day and twelve in the night. They correspond to the twelve tribes who will rise from you.'

Now, upon discovering Joseph's loss, Jacob wept and said, 'Now the covenant of the tribes

לו שְׁאֹלָה וַיֵּבְךְּ אֹתוֹ אָבִיו: וְהַמְּדָנִים מָכְרוּ
אֹתוֹ אֶל־מִצְרָיִם לְפוֹטִיפַר סְרִיס פַּרְעֹה

[On *She'ol* see also 42:37.]

Because of my negligence in sending my son to a place I knew to be wrought with mortal danger I will go to my own grave still in mourning *(Chizkuni)*.

Kli Chemdah uniquely interprets this as an incredulous question: *Can I go down to my son as a mourner to* [*his*] *grave?* I.e., do I then know where my son is buried so I can go to weep at his grave and gain some consolation thereby? This not being the case, I am inconsolable.

[My father, Harav Aron Zlotowitz שליט״א once similarly explained homiletically that Rachel's 'lamentation and bitter weeping' for her children described by Jeremiah [31:14] was for the same reason. As the Prophet writes: *She refused to be comforted for her children* כִּי אֵינֶנּוּ, *because they were not* — i.e. because they were not in her proximity. They were dying in Exile and did not leave even a grave where their mothers could shed a tear.]

The phrase אֶל־בְּנִי [lit. *to my son*] in this passage has the sense of עַל בְּנִי *on account of* [lit. *upon*] *my son.* אֶל often means עַל in Scripture, e.g. *II Sam.* 4:21: אֶל שָׁאוּל וְאֶל בֵּית הַדָּמִים; *I Sam.* 4:21: ... אֶל הִלָּקַח אֲרוֹן הָאֱלֹהִים *(Rashi)*.

According to *Radak: I will go to my son* and *be gathered to his people* [see on 25:8].

וַיֵּבְךְּ אֹתוֹ אָבִיו — *And his father bewailed him.*

Jacob is already the subject of this verse. Therefore *his father* refers to *Jacob's* father, the sense being: *Isaac bewailed Jacob (Riva).*

Isaac *wept* for Jacob's sorrow, but he did not actually *observe mourning* along with him [see *v.* 33] because he knew that Joseph was alive *(Rashi)*.

That is, while in Jacob's presence Isaac would display his empathy and pretend to mourn. For indeed such is required by etiquette: כָּל הַמִּתְאַבֵּל עָלָיו מִתְאַבֵּל עִמּוֹ לְפָנָיו, 'when in the presence of a mourner for whom one himself must mourn [such as a father in the presence of his bereaved son or a husband in the presence of his bereaved wife] one must *outwardly* mourn too.' But when Isaac was not in Jacob's presence, he did not mourn because he knew Joseph was alive *(Chizkuni* from *Midrash)*.

[See *footnote* to *v.* 28 regarding why Isaac did not reveal this knowledge to his son.]

According to *Sforno*, Isaac bewailed that Jacob had assumed life-long mourning, for such a posture of grief would keep the Divine Presence away from him [since It does not descend on one who is sad] *(Sforno)*.

[And so it was. For the Divine Spirit which had left him did not return to Jacob until he heard the news that Joseph was still alive; then his spirit revived. See *Rashi* to 45:27].

Or HaChaim [following *Ralbag*] maintains that our verse refers to *Joseph's* father, Jacob, the sense be-

has been broken! How many struggles have I endured raising these twelve children. Now that there are no longer twelve, the covenant has been abrogated since these twelve tribes paralleled the twelve signs of the zodiac, the twelve months of the year, the twelve hours of the day and of the night and the twelve precious stones that the High Priest will one day wear in his breastplate. It is all now gone!' ... *(Seder Eliyahu Rabbah; Tanchuma Yashan)*.

The Zohar observes that Jacob maintained a state of celibacy during this mourning period, for all his wives had already died by that time. He also did not remarry in order to have another son to take Joseph's place because of the oath he had made to Laban not to take any other wives [see 31:50].

37
36

my son.' And his father bewailed him.
[36] *Now the Medanites had sold him to Egypt, for Potiphar, a courtier of Pharaoh, the Chamberlain of*

ing: *Thus Jacob bewailed Joseph.* The Torah refers to Jacob as *his,* i.e., Joseph's *father,* who bewailed Joseph so intensely; not the others who hated him [see below 42:36 s.v. עָלָי].[1]

Significantly, Jacob's weeping is mentioned last in the narrative. The term **בָּכָה אֶת**, unlike בָּכָה עַל, denotes an *inner* grief that is manifested outwardly only by an occasional tear that could not be restrained. The stray tear is but proof of the constant grief that is stifled within. Thus, our final phrase tells us that Jacob still *bewailed* Joseph even after all the others had stopped consoling him and had forgotten his misfortune *(R' Hirsch).*

36. וְהַמְּדָנִים מָכְרוּ אֹתוֹ אֶל מִצְרָיִם — *Now* [lit. *and;* i.e., in the interim] *the Medanites had sold him to Egypt.*

The word אֶל, *to,* in this context has the sense of *in:* they sold him *in* Egypt. Cf. *Exod.* 25:21: אֶל הָאָרֹן, *in* the ark; *Num.* 19:17: אֶל כְּלִי, *in* the vessel *(Chizkuni).*

According to *Midrash Tanchuma,* the Medanites sold him to the public trustee [דְּמוּסְיָא שֶׁל מְדִינָה] who in turn — after verification by the Ishmaelites that he was rightfully theirs to sell — sold him to Potiphar.

On the identity of the Midianites/Medanites, see controversy expounded in the commentary to *v.* 28. The prevalent view followed by most commentators is that they were brother tribes — both Midian and Medan being listed in 25:2 as sons of Abraham by Keturah. The Torah therefore refers to them alternately by either name. Others interpret that in introducing the new name Medanites, the Torah is alluding to an additional unrecorded sale.

לְפוֹטִיפַר סְרִיס פַּרְעֹה — *For* [or: *to*] *Potiphar, a courtier of Pharaoh.*

The term סָרִיס, often translated *eunuch,* has two meanings. Sometimes it describes one who had been made incapable of reproduction; sometimes it means a court official. In Potiphar's case, the latter interpretation is indicated since he was married and Asenath was presumably his daughter. Hence most commentators render it in the general sense of *court official.* [Cf. *Onkelos:* לְפוֹטִיפַר רַבָּא דְפַרְעֹה.]

The *Midrash* [86:3] understands סָרִיס in its familar sense of *eunuch; castrate,* and explains that Potiphar had purchased Joseph for purposes of sodomy, whereupon the Holy One, Blessed be He emasculated him, making him an eunuch [see 39:1].

[The Midrashic interpretation is not necessarily at variance with the literal sense. Potiphar could have been emasculated *after* his daughter was born. See comm. to 39:1, 6 and 19 where this interpretation is postulated.]

[Pharaoh was not the *personal* name of the king, but the royal *title* of the Egyptian monarchs. See on 12:15.]

1. After such a terrible occurrence one criticizes himself very sharply and does not forgive himself the slightest slip. Jacob's weeping was inspired also by remorse over his own misdeeds [interpreting: וַיֵּבְךְּ אֹתוֹ=and he bewailed *himself*]: 'Perhaps I am being punished,' he exclaimed, 'for having married two sisters; or possibly for having derived benefit from Laban's money or from Shechem's money, and the Covenant God made with me has been annulled.' God's mercy was immediately aroused, and He granted Jacob seventeen good years in his old age *(Seder Eliyahu Rabbah).*

שַׂר הַטַּבָּחִים׃
א °וַיְהִי בָּעֵת הַהִוא וַיֵּרֶד יְהוּדָה מֵאֵת אֶחָיו
ב וַיֵּט עַד־אִישׁ עֲדֻלָּמִי וּשְׁמוֹ חִירָה׃ וַיַּרְא־

°רביעי

שַׂר הַטַּבָּחִים — *The Chamberlain of the Butchers.*

The Hebrew literally means *the chamberlain of the slaughterers.* The translation follows *Rashi* who explains טַבָּחִים to refer to the chief of 'the slaughterers of the king's animals.'

Ramban following *Onkelos* renders it as: *the chief executioner.*

Radak in *Shorashim* notes that the term טבח, *slaughter*, can refer equally to animals or people, the latter being the probable interpretation here.

[Comp. *comm.* to 39:1.]

Rashi prefers the rendering of *butcher* since he finds it distasteful to assume that God would allow Joseph — who was spared even the foul odor of Ishmaelites' regular wares (see *Rashi v.* 25) — to be sold to one as detestable as an executioner. However, following *Onkelos* who *did* render it as *executioner* we must assume that Potiphar did not execute criminals personally, but was in charge of those criminals sentenced to death and delegated the killing to others *(Gur Aryeh).*

— Therefore, we later [40:3] find him also in charge of the prison *(Ralbag).*

Some cite in support of *Onkelos* the interpretation that the Egyptians — who considered sheep to be sacred [cf. 43:34; *Exod.* 8:22] — did not eat meat. Therefore, why would Pharaoh require a butcher? — *Mizrachi* maintains, however, that the Egyptians refrained from eating only *sheep*, but *did* eat beef and flesh of other animals. To imply this, *Rashi* says בְּהֵמוֹת, *animals* [i.e., cattle], not צֹאן, *sheep* (see *Tzeidah laDerech; Maskil l'David).*

Divrei David finds it unusual however, that *Rashi* in this case differs with *Onkelos* without even citing his opinion. He suggests that it would appear that *Rashi* understands even *Onkelos* who renders the term in Aramaic רַב קְטוֹלַיָּא as referring to *butchering* since in translating the passage [*Lev.* 24:18] וּמַכֵּה נֶפֶשׁ בְּהֵמָה, *He that kills a beast, Onkelos* uses the same term וְדִי קְטוֹל.

The end of the chapter emphasizes that Joseph was sold several times and to several people. And so the brothers completely lost track of him and he could not be found. The end of the chapter takes us then right to the heart of tragedy. The brothers probably shared the vague feeling that Joseph was not gone forever. Therefore, they could bear their father's suffering because they were convinced that sooner or later his suffering would give way to the joy of finding his lost son. But for the moment, the Patriarchal family was plunged into despair *(R' Munk).*

XXXVIII

1. Judah and Tamar: The roots of the Messiah and the Israelite monarchy.

וַיְהִי בָּעֵת הַהִוא וַיֵּרֶד יְהוּדָה מֵאֵת אֶחָיו — [*And*] *it was at that time that* [lit. *and*] *Judah went down from his brothers.*

Judah 'went down' in the sense that he was *deposed* by his brothers from his position of leadership. This narrative is placed here interrupting the story of Joseph to teach how Judah was lowered in esteem by his brothers as a result of the incident with Joseph. [That is, although this espisode did indeed occur after the sale of Joseph, the Torah — which axiomatically does not concern itself with strict chronological order — would not have inserted it in the middle of the ongoing narrative of Joseph unless there were some connection

the Butchers.

It was at that time that Judah went down from his brothers and turned away towards an Adullamite man whose name was Hirah. 2 *There Judah saw the*

between Joseph's sale and Judah's fall *(Mizrachi).*][1] For when the brothers saw their father's intense grief, they blamed Judah for it and deposed him from his leadership over them. 'You told us to sell him,' they complained. 'Had you advised us to send him back to Father, we would have listened!' *(Rashi* from *Midrash;* See also *footnote* to *v.* 2).

The *Tanchuma* continues: They pronounced a ban on him and accordingly *he went down from his brothers* ... i.e., he was *censured* by them and they demoted him from his position of authority. [Cf. *Sotah* 13b where Judah is castigated for having dropped his efforts to save Joseph.] Nevertheless of all Jacob's sons, the Holy One Blessed be He chose Judah to rule His people, as it says [49:10]: *The scepter shall not depart from Judah.*

Rashi's exegesis that Judah's 'descent' occurred after the sale of Joseph follows the Rabbinic tradition echoed in *Midrash Rabbah; Tanchuma; Tanchuma Yashan; Midrash Aggadah* and specifically in *Seder Olam* [see below] that these events transpired in the twenty-two year period between Joseph's sale and Jacob's descent with his family to Egypt. The twenty-two year interval is calculated by *Rashi* in his comm. to 37:24 s.v. וַיִּתְאַבֵּל עַל בְּנוֹ יָמִים רַבִּים. Briefly, Joseph was seventeen years old when he was sold, and thirty when he stood before Pharaoh — a lapse of thirteen years. Add the seven years of plenty and two of famine at which time Jacob and his family descended to Egypt — the aggregate total is twenty-two years.

Ibn Ezra differs and maintains that *at that time* is an indefinite phrase used concerning events which occurred either several years earlier or later. Cf. *Deut.* 10:7, 8. In our verse *Ibn Ezra* interprets that the incident *preceded* the sale of Joseph since he finds it difficult to interpret that all the events narrated in this chapter could have been compressed in the twenty-two aggregate period between Joseph's sale and Jacob's descent to Egypt. He notes that the Torah tells us that Onan, Judah's second son, reached the age when he was capable of begetting children, which means that he must have been at least twelve years old. Additionally, after a considerable interval — presumably at least two years — Peretz was born. The latter had grown up and had two sons, Chetzron and Chamul, by the time Jacob's family descended to Egypt. Accordingly, he postulates that this narrative must have spanned a total of more than twenty-two years.

He suggests, therefore, that the Torah's purpose in breaking into the natural sequence and narrating the incident at *this* point rather than *earlier* when Judah had actually separated from his brothers and married the daughter of Shua, was to draw a contrast between Joseph's conduct in connection with Potiphar's wife and Judah's in connection with Tamar. [Cf. *Ibn Ezra* to *Deut.* 10:7, 8 and *Numb.* 3:1.]

Ralbag concurs. He suggests that Judah went off on his own because he had considerable flocks of his own, possibly acquired in the plunder of Shechem. Nevertheless, he regularly commuted back to his family to help tend Jacob's flocks and those of his brothers. That explains why he was present at the sale of Joseph.

Mizrachi defends the traditional Rabbinic chronology that all these events occurred within the twenty-two year period of Joseph's absence. He notes that the Sages [*Sanhedrin* 69b referring to Caleb begetting Chur] record that in those days people of *eight* were capable of becoming fathers.

1. According to R' Leazar's view in the *Midrash,* the narrative of Judah and Tamar was inserted here in order to bring the two passages of 'descent' together [כְּדֵי לִסְמוֹךְ יְרִידָה לִירִידָה] — [Judah's *descent* from his brothers, and Joseph's *descent* to Egypt; also Judah's spiritual decline, and Joseph's enslavement]; according to R' Yochanan: In order to couple the two passages הַכֶּר־נָא, *Identify, if you please* [37:23, and below, *v.* 25. — The sons said this to Jacob and Tamar said it to Judah; this was regarded as measure for measure].

Hence, all the events in this episode transpired quite comfortably within the twenty-two year period following the sale of Joseph. [For details of this chronology, see *Seder Olam* §2.] That Er and Onan were subject to the death penalty at so tender an age is no more difficult than their culpability at age thirteen. In either case this poses a problem since the Heavenly Court does not inflict punishment under the age of twenty. See *Oznaim l'Torah* cited in *v.* 7.

[That the incident of Judah followed the sale of Joseph is maintained also by *Radak, Chizkuni, Abarbanel* and *Sforno*.]

Sforno comments that Judah's ordeal occurred after Joseph's sale, and that it was in punishment for Judah's role in causing Jacob to be bereaved. Judah's culpability was great and he was now repaid according to the fruit of his action by being bereaved of *his* two sons. Now he would personally experience the sort of cruel suffering he caused his father. [Cf. *Ramban* to *v.* 7.]

Cf. *Sanhedrin* 102a where the phrase בָּעֵת הַהִיא, *at that time*, is interpreted to allude to the fact that it was 'a time predestined for tribulation' [a reference to the tribulations recounted in this chapter; see *Torah Temimah*].

According to R' David Feinstein, this 'time of tribulation' was the punishment noted below in the comm. to *v.* 7 that one who leaves a *mitzvah* unfinished runs the danger of losing his wife and children.

As noted above, the phrase Judah *went down* is interpreted homiletically in the Talmud to imply the *spiritual decline* of Judah's loss of position of leadership within the family. However, following the *literal* interpretation, the term *went down* implies: from the rocky hills around Hebron to Adullam, in the foothill district southwest of Jerusalem. [See below] *(Heidenheim;* cf. *Radak)*.

Ibn Ezra accordingly observes that when one travels from the north to the south he is said to 'descend.'

Among other interpretations regarding Judah's descent from his brothers are:

Targum: His fortunes took a turn for the worse and he lost his influence; he therefore sought solitude (cf. *Oznaim l'Torah).*

Chizkuni: He could not bear to witness his father's inconsolable grief at Joseph's absence, and he therefore separated himself from his family.

However, his separation from them was not *total* — we see that he was present when his father dispatched the brothers to Egypt *(Abarbanel;* see *Ralbag* above).

וַיֵּט עַד־אִישׁ עֲדֻלָּמִי — *And turned away* [from the root נטה; *Targum Yonasan: and inclined*] *towards* [lit. *until*] *an Adullamite man.*

I.e. he *turned away* from his brothers and became partners with a certain Adullamite man *(Rashi)*.

According to *Radak*, the sense of the passage is: he camped [in the elliptic sense of וַיֵּט אָהֳלוֹ] with his flocks from place to place until he came to Adullam where he became associated with this man.

[The term *Adullamite* refers to one from the region of Adullam in the Shefelah (see *Joshua* 37:14; 15:35). *Ramban* mentions that it was a Canaanite region. In *Joshua* 12:15 the king of Adullam is listed among the kings of Canaan. Although Scripturally its exact location cannot be ascertained, some identify Adullam with the modern Aid el-ma, seventeen miles southwest of Jerusalem.]

וּשְׁמוֹ חִירָה — *Whose name* [lit. *and his name*] *was Hirah.*

Some Sages in the *Midrash* identify him with Hiram of King David's time, of whom there is a further tradition that he lived to the time of Ezekiel. According to the various traditions, then, he would have enjoyed the exceptional longevity of between 1100 and 1500 years!

Many commentators, however, maintain that Hirah was not necessarily Hiram, but the ancestor of Hiram's family. [*Gur Aryeh* to 14:13 offers a similar interpretation in discussing the exceptional longevity attributed to Og.] His family apparently lived near Hebron. Later we find them in Tyre, to the north of *Eretz Yisrael.* Judah's friendship with this ancestor of the Tyres is perceived as another example of the Patriarchal family portending the destiny of its descendants. In the days of the Israelite Monarchy, the Tyres were traditionally Israel's friendliest neighbor, and Hiram, King of Tyre, was always a friend of King David [*I Kings* 5:15]. He supplied much of the material for the Temple, and entered into a treaty with Solomon. Because Judah's warm friendship with Hirah was the seed of this later development, his name is recorded in the Torah *(Akeidas Yitzchak; Maharal;* see *Da'as Soferim).*

2. **וַיַּרְא שָׁם יְהוּדָה בַּת־אִישׁ כְּנַעֲנִי וּשְׁמוֹ שׁוּעַ** — [*And*] *there* [i.e., in Adullam] *Judah saw the daughter of a prominent* [אִישׁ] *merchant* [כְּנַעֲנִי] *whose name was Shua.*[1]

The translation *prominent* is based on the word אִישׁ, literally *man,* which has the connotation of a distinguished, repected person *(Abarbanel).*

Judah particularly noticed her because she was not of the regular Canaanite community *(Ramban;* see below).

Her own name is not given; only that of her father. The reason for this anonymity is uncertain *(Radak).*

— Perhaps she was not outstanding; Judah married her on account of her father's importance *(Ramban).*

In addition to being the daughter of Shua, it may be that her name was *Bath Shua.* Compare the name Bath Sheba *(Abarbanel).*

The Hebrew literally reads: *the daughter of a Canaanite.* The translation of כְּנַעֲנִי as *merchant* follows *Onkelos, Rashi, Ibn Ezra's* first interpretation, *Radak, Ramban, Ralbag* and *Abarbanel.*

This interpretation is based on *Pesachim* 50a where it is remarked: Is it possible that Abraham exhorted Isaac, and Isaac Jacob [not to marry a Canaanite woman] and yet Judah went and married one! — Rather, the term 'daughter of a *Canaanite'* in this context denotes daughter of a *merchant.* This is the meaning of the term *Canaanite* in *Hoshea* 12:8 and *Isaiah* 23:8.

— She was a daughter of one of the foreign traders who trafficked through Canaan selling their wares, for all Jacob's sons guarded themselves — as did their fathers before them — from marrying the accursed Canaanites [see 9:25]. Simeon was the only one among them who did marry a Canaanite woman, and he is derided for it when his son is called *Shaul, son of the Canaanite woman* [46:10]. Even in that case

1. The *Midrash* penetratingly perceives the Providential Hand of God at work in this narrative and at the same time accounts for its placement here:

The tribes were occupied with the sale of Joseph; Joseph was occupied with his sackcloth and fast [doing penitence because of the trouble that had befallen him]; Reuben was occupied with his sackcloth and fast [over the incident with Bilhah]; Jacob was occupied with his sackcloth and fast [unconsolably mourning the loss of his son]; and Judah was occupied with taking a wife. And the Holy One, Blessed be He, was occupied with creating the light of the King Messiah.

[Thus before subjecting His people to their first exile, God had already prepared the light of the future Redeemer. For "God creates the healing before the illness" *(Meg.* 13b)] *(Midrash;* see *Overview* to ArtScroll *Ruth* p. xix).

ג וַיִּקָּחֶהָ וַיָּבֹא אֵלֶיהָ: וַתַּהַר וַתֵּלֶד בֵּן
ד וַיִּקְרָא אֶת־שְׁמוֹ עֵר: וַתַּהַר עוֹד וַתֵּלֶד בֵּן
ה וַתִּקְרָא אֶת־שְׁמוֹ אוֹנָן: וַתֹּסֶף עוֹד וַתֵּלֶד

the Sages expounded that *Canaanite woman* was a reference to Dinah who had been forced to live with the Canaanite Shechem [and whom Simeon later married; see *comm.* to 34:26 s.v. וַיִּקְחוּ] *(Radak; Ramban).*

Why, then is Shua described by the ambiguous term *'Canaanite'* which is only *rarely* used in this sense of 'merchant'? Apparently the Torah wishes to stress that although Judah's wife was of foreign descent, she and her family were adversely affected by their association with the tainted Canaanite people *(Alshich).*

Ramban proceeds to discuss the differing Midrashic opinion of R' Nechemiah [already cited above in the *comm.* to 37:35; see there] who maintains that the brothers married Canaanite women.

Ramban explains this to mean that the tribal ancestors married foreign women whose fathers were passing through Canaan at the time, for it is illogical to assume that they all married women who were descended from the accursed servile Canaanite nation. Had this been the case, then Abraham's descendants would share their claim to *Eretz Yisrael* with the descendants of Canaan whom the former had been commanded to replace and destroy until neither remnant nor survivor remained.

That *Canaanite* here has its other meaning of 'merchant' or 'trader' follows from the context. Everyone in that area including the Perizzites, Jebusites and their brother clans as well as those of Adullam [whose king is mentioned in *Josh.* 12:15 among the kings of Canaan] was assumed to be of Canaanite descent. Had the term Canaanite therefore merely referred to Shua's genealogy, it would have been superfluous to mention it. Therefore the term has its other meaning of merchant. Shua was a foreigner whom Judah met in Canaan, and whose daughter he married. Although in *I Chronicles* 2:3 Judah's wife herself is referred to as the *Canaanitess* [which certainly would seem to indicate that she was of Canaanite stock], there too the word means 'merchant'. Because her father was known as the כְּנַעֲנִי=*'merchant' par excellence,* she, too, came to be referred to by this designation, being his daughter.

Tamar, too, was not of Canaanite descent but the daughter of one of the aliens in the land. 'Far be it that our lord David [who descended from Judah and Tamar (see *Ruth* 4:15-22)], and righteous Messiah who will speedily reveal himself to us, be a descendant of the accursed Canaan!' *(Ramban).*

[There are, however, conflicting Midrashim on the matter. *Midrash HaGadol* cites *Malachi* 2:11: *Judah has dealt treacherously,* which it interprets as a reference to Judah's [spiritual] 'descent' due to his marriage to a Canaanite: '...He married what even Esau eventually rejected. For even Esau saw how displeasing Canaanite women were to Isaac his father and married an Ishmaelite instead, yet Judah went and married a Canaanite!' Cf. also *Aggadas Bereishis* §64.]

וַיִּקָּחֶהָ וַיָּבֹא אֵלֶיהָ — *[And] he married* [lit. *took*] *her and consorted with her.*

The translation of וַיִּקָּחֶהָ as *he married* follows *Onkelos* who renders: וְנַסְבַהּ.

— First he *married* her and then consorted; his relations with her were not illicit *(Radak).*

The *Midrash* understands *took* in the sense of: *he spoke persuasively to her* in order to consort with her:

38
3-5

Shua. He married her and consorted with her 3 *She*
conceived and bore a son and he named him Er. 4 *She*
conceived again and bore a son and she named him
Onan. 5 *And yet again and she bore a son; and named*

'You are fortunate' he said, 'for the opportunity to unite with the offspring of Abraham, Isaac and Jacob and come under the wings of the Shechinah.' She consented, and she became a proselyte. He then married her. [Comp. this use of וַיִּקָּח meaning *persuaded with soothing words* in 12:5].

3. Er.

This birth, according to *Seder Olam,* took place one year after the sale of Joseph.

וַיִּקְרָא אֶת־שְׁמוֹ עֵר — *And he named him Er.*

I.e., *Judah* gave him this name which, in the literal sense, means: *Awaken! (Ramban).*

Midrashically, the name indicates that this child would be prematurely *wiped out* [הוּעַר from the root ערה] from the world. According to *Targum Yonasan* the name indicates that he was destined to die childless [עֲרִירִי; see on *Levit.* 20:20]. Of course, this was not Judah's intent when he gave this name to the child. It is an exposition of the Sages who maintain that names contain prophetic prognostications of the future *(Ramban).*

That is, our ancestors were endowed with a prophetic spirit, and in naming their children they were unconsciously prophesying future events without always realizing the significance of the words they were uttering (*Sechel Tov*).

4. Onan.

וַתַּהַר עוֹד וַתֵּלֶד בֵּן — *She conceived again and bore a son.*

This occurred in the second year after the sale of Joseph *(Seder Olam).*

וַתִּקְרָא אֶת שְׁמוֹ אוֹנָן — *And she named him Onan.*

Judah had named the firstborn son and his wife named their second child. The word אנן has the connotation of *complaining* [*Numb.* 11:1 and *Lamen.* 3:39] and *sorrow,* as in the case of Rachel who named her child *Ben Oni* [lit. son of my sorrow; mourning] (see *comm.* to 35:18). Perhaps Judah's wife experienced difficult labor pains and named him accordingly. The mother of Yaavetz [from עצב *pain*] so named him because of her labor pains [*I Chronicles* 4:9], as did Atarah the mother of Onam [ibid. 2:26]. For a similar reason Rachel called her second son Ben Oni. Although Jacob changed the tragic name Ben Oni to Benjamin, Judah did not feel it was necessary for him to change Onan's name [to one with a more optimistic connotation] *(Ramban).*

According to the *Midrash,* the name — connoting *grief* and *mourning* — refers prophetically to the grief he would bring himself and the mourning he would cause his father [by his premature death].

Cf. *Targum Yonasan: ' ... and she called his name Onan because his father would have to mourn for him.'*

בֵּן וַתִּקְרָא אֶת־שְׁמוֹ שֵׁלָה וְהָיָה בִכְזִיב
ו בְּלִדְתָּהּ אֹתוֹ: וַיִּקַּח יְהוּדָה אִשָּׁה לְעֵר
ז בְּכוֹרוֹ וּשְׁמָהּ תָּמָר: וַיְהִי עֵר בְּכוֹר

5. Shelah.

וַתֹּסֶף עוֹד וַתֵּלֶד בֵּן — *And yet again* [lit. *and she yet added and*], *and she bore a son.*

שֵׁלָה — *Shelah.*

[Meaning *deceit* or *disappointment;* see below].

וְהָיָה בִכְזִיב בְּלִדְתָּהּ אֹתוֹ — *And it was in Chezib when she bore him.*

The translation follows *Rambam. Rashbam* renders *and he* [i.e., Judah] *was in Chezib when she bore him.*

Chezib was the name of a place [possibly to be identified with the Judean city Achzib mentioned in *Joshua* 15:44 and *Michah* 1:10, or the Achzib in the territory of Asher (*Judges* 21:31) mentioned frequently in the *Talmud (Demai* 1:3; *Sheviis* 6:1; *Gittin* 7b *(Yohel Or)*] *(Rashi).*

Rashi finds it difficult, in terms of the simple meaning, that the Torah — which economizes on every word — should, for no apparent reason, tell us the name of the place where this child was born. He therefore suggests that it [i.e. the city] was named Chezib — from כזב *false,* to *fail* [in the sense of *cease* (cf. *Jer.* 15:18; *Isaiah* 58:2)] — because she ceased bearing. [That is, since Judah's wife was a prominent woman and it was there that she ceased bearing, the site was named Chezib commemorating the *failing* of her ability to bear further children *(Maskil l'David).*]

Rashi draws support for his interpretation from the *Midrash* which comments: 'And *she named him Shelah,* etc. — she ceased [to bear after this].'

Comp. *Targum Yonasan: And she was in cessation when she bore him.*

According to *Radak:* It was customary for the father to name the firstborn, and the mother the second one. Therefore the Torah records that *he* named the firstborn Er, and *she* named the second child Onan. The naming of the third child should have been the prerogative of the *father,* yet the Torah tells us *she* named him Shelah and explains that this was because *he* [Judah] *was in Chezib when she gave birth to him,* and was not present to name him. [Similarly, *Da'as Zekeinim; B'chor Shor. Ramban* disagrees; see below.]

Ramban questions *Rashi's* interpretation that the name Chezib commemorated her ceasing to bear children; having already given birth to three children, her failure to have more was not so tragic that the place had to be named in its memory. Furthermore, how could she have known at the time that she would never have children in the future? [*Mizrachi* defends *Rashi* by offering that with the birth of this third child her physiognomy changed and she ceased ovulating; after having borne three children in rapid succession this was so significant that the place was named to commemorate the event. *Gur Aryeh* suggests that she might have named the place years later after it became apparent that she could no longer give birth.]

Ramban proceeds to cite the view of *Radak* and *Daas Zekeinim* cited above, which he dismisses as being 'without taste or fragrance' [presumably because there is no Biblical support for a father naming a first child and a mother the second. To the contrary, we see that Rachel and Leah named their children

him Shelah; and it was in Chezib when she bore him.
[6] Judah took a wife for Er his firstborn. Her name was Tamar. [7] But *Er, Judah's firstborn was evil in the*

and those of their maidservants (*Oznaim l'Torah*)]. He offers that in his opinion the name *Shelah,* like the name *Chezib,* denotes *deceit.* The intent of the passage is that *she named him Shelah* (a name suggested to her by the place where her child was born), וְהָיָה, *because* **it** [not *he,* but the event] *was in Chezib that she bore him.*

According to *Sforno,* the name Shelah has a negative connotation and denotes *disappointment.* The passage informs us that she gave him this name *since Judah was in Chezib when the child was born,* and she thereby expressed her disappointment at her husband's absence when she gave birth. Judah would not have agreed to a name with this unpleasant connotation had he returned in time to prevent it.

6. Er marries Tamar.

וַיִּקַּח יְהוּדָה אִשָּׁה לְעֵר בְּכוֹרוֹ — [*And*] *Judah took a wife for Er his firstborn.*

Er was very young [about seven years old, according to the chronology in *Seder Olam*] when he married, for all the events related in this chapter transpired, as noted, in the twenty-two years between the sale of Joseph and Jacob's descent to Egypt *(Seder Olam).*

Possibly this is the intent of the phraseology: *Judah took a wife for Er* rather than the usual expression *and he* [himself] *married* [see *v.* 2]. Er was still too young to take a woman on his own, so Judah arranged the marriage for him, in keeping with the contemporary custom to marry very young. Apparently when the opportunity arose to marry his son to someone so noble and pure as Tamar [the daughter of Shem; see below] Judah did not procrastinate, but arranged it immediately *(Daas Soferim).*

וּשְׁמָהּ תָּמָר — *And her name was Tamar.*

As noted, she was not a Canaanitess by descent, but the daughter of one of the alien-merchants then living in the land. Far be it that King David [a descendant of Tamar through Peretz (see *Ruth* 4:15-22)] and the Messiah be of the seed of the accursed Canaan! According to the Sages, Tamar was the daughter of Noah's son Shem, who was a *priest of the most high God* [see *comm.* to 14:18 and *Mizrachi* to 38:24] (*Ramban, v.* 2).

According to the view that Tamar was Shem's daughter, she had to be at least sixty-seven years old when she married the young Er since Shem died in 2158 and Er married in 2225-6. There is another view recorded by *Rashi* to *Sotah* 10a s.v. יְתוֹמָה that she was not Shem's daughter. *Sefer HaYashar* records a tradition that she was the daughter of Elam, son of Shem. *Mizrachi* to *v.* 24 similarly cites a view that *daughter* of Shem could mean *granddaughter.*

Judah was intent on assuring abundant progeny for his son, and therefore married him to an older woman. Cf. *Sanhedrin* 104 and *Eicha Rabbosi* that in Jerusalem it was customary to wed a young boy to an older woman to assure many children *(Haamek Davar).*

In *Midrash Lekach Tov* Tamar is praised for her steadfastness in desiring to become associated with the House of Judah.

Tamar's name is mentioned since she was reputed to have been virtuous and righteous. She plays an important role in the narrative that follows and deserves to be identified. Her name in-

יְהוּדָה רַע בְּעֵינֵי יהוה וַיְמִתֵהוּ יהוה:
ח וַיֹּאמֶר יְהוּדָה לְאוֹנָן בֹּא אֶל־אֵשֶׁת אָחִיךָ
ט וְיַבֵּם אֹתָהּ וְהָקֵם זֶרַע לְאָחִיךָ: וַיֵּדַע אוֹנָן

dicates that she was as graceful as a *tamar* [*palm tree*], and extraordinarily beautiful. Her father's name is omitted to emphasize that Judah chose her because of her *own* worth. She was well worthy that the seeds of Israel's later monarchy should sprout from her (*Midrash Hagadol; Alshich; Akeidas Yitzchak*).

7. Er dies.

עֵר בְּכוֹר יְהוּדָה — *Er, Judah's firstborn.*

That he was Judah's *firstborn* is repeated to emphasize that Er's sin was judged so severely because he was a potential ancestor of the royal seed. Another, not of Judah's seed, might not have been punished so severely for this level of sinfulness (*Haamek Davar*).

[Comp. *footnote* next page.]

רַע בְּעֵינֵי ה׳ — *Was evil in the eyes of HASHEM.*

The nature of Er's evil-doing is not explicitly indicated, unlike the case of his brother [*v.* 9].

Rashi explains that Er's sin was the same as Onan's [see *v.* 9] — he wasted his semen. This is deduced from the statement [*v.* 10] that God *caused him* [Onan] *to die* **also** — the last word implying *for the same reason* [as Er]. Why did Er destroy his semen? — Tamar was exceedingly beautiful, and he did not want her beauty to be marred by pregnancy. [Cf. *Oznaim l'Torah.*]

Radak deduces this from the phrase *evil in the eyes of HASHEM* — i.e., only in matters revealed to God — viz. in his conjugal relations, destroying his semen so that Tamar should not conceive.

Ramban does not discuss the nature of Er's sin, but states that the intent of the verse is to inform us that Er's death was in punishment for his *own* sinfulness, not as a punishment for Judah. Judah's efforts to save Joseph's life absolved him for his role in the sale. The righteousness of the Patriarchal family of Jacob was such that none of its members had ever died prematurely due to sin, until the death of Er. This is why Jacob mourned so inconsolably for Joseph [37:34ff] since, besides his love for him, he considered his 'death' to be a punishment intended for him. [Nevertheless, it emerges from the *Talmud* and commentators that though Judah's sons died as a result of their own wickedness, all of these travails befell Judah (i.e. that he had to bury his wife and his children in his lifetime) as a measure of punishment for the anguish he caused his father by his complicity in Joseph's sale. See *footnote.*]

The *Midrash* notes that names influence man's destiny. Thus, the name עֵר, *Er*, is the anagram of רַע, *evil*, and presages his character. Similarly, נֹחַ, *Noah*, read backward is חֵן, *grace*. See *Zohar* cited to 6:8, p. 194.

וַיְמִתֵהוּ ה׳ — *And HASHEM caused him to die.*

This was the Divine punishment for Onan's destroying his seed and killing the offspring who were to descend from him. This is similar to 4:10 where the phrase *Hark! The bloods* [literal translation] *of your brother cry out to Me* is interpreted to refer both to his blood and the

38 *eyes of HASHEM, and HASHEM caused him to die.*
8 [8] *Then Judah said to Onan. 'Consort with your*
brother's wife and enter into levirate marriage with
her, and establish offspring for your brother.'

blood of his potential descendants *(Pesikta).*[1]

Er was accordingly unworthy to found the royal house of Israel *(Alshich).*

8. וַיֹּאמֶר יְהוּדָה לְאוֹנָן — *Then* [lit. *and*] *Judah said to Onan.*

בֹּא אֶל־אֵשֶׁת אָחִיךָ וְיַבֵּם אֹתָהּ — *Consort with your brother's wife and enter into levirate marriage with her.*

This is a reference to יִבּוּם [*yibum*], *levirate marriage* [the term *levirate* derives from the Latin *levir* meaning 'brother-in-law'] the details of which are given in *Deut.* 25:5 ff. Briefly, when a man died without offspring, Torah law obliged his brother to marry the widow, and the son of this union was considered the spiritual son of the deceased. One who refused to perform *yibum* was considered to be derelict in his duty to the deceased brother. The widow was to loosen his shoe off his foot, spit in front of him, and say, *'So shall be done to the man who does not build up his brother's house'* [ibid. *v.* 9].[2]

וְהָקֵם זֶרַע לְאָחִיךָ — *And establish offspring for your brother.*

For the son [born of such a union] will be called by the name of the deceased *(Rashi).*

Ramban disagrees, observing that the seemingly literal implication of *Deut.* 25:6 notwithstanding, the brother-in-law is not commanded by Halachah to name the offspring of the levirate marriage after his deceased brother [*Yevamos* 24a]. He cites the example of Boaz's marriage to Ruth, Machlon's widow, which was specifically intended *to perpetuate the name of the deceased upon his inheritance, that the name of the deceased be not cut off from among his brethren* [*Ruth* 4:10] — yet she named the child Obed [*ibid., v.* 21] not Machlon. The intent, rather, as noted above, is that the offspring of the *yibum* union would be spiritually accounted as having been born to the deceased. This is what Naomi's neighbors meant when they exclaimed [ibid. 4:17]: *There is a son born to* **Naomi,**

1. The commentators grapple with the problem of how Er and Onan were punished with death for their wickedness at the tender age of seven or eight when it is known that the Heavenly Court does not inflict punishment for sins committed under the age of twenty [see *Mizrachi v.* 1].

Oznaim l'Torah conjectures that since the tribal ancestors were so wise [לִפְלַגּוֹת רְאוּבֵן] they became subject to Divine punishment at an earlier age. However, he prefers the view in *Sotah* 13a [see *v.* 12] that Judah's wife and sons died because of his participation in Joseph's sale in which he left his rescue attempt unfinished.

As *Maharsha* there explains, though Scripture attributes Er and Onan's deaths to *their* sinfulness, in view of their youth the sinfulness was but a *contributing* factor; if it had not been for *Judah's* sin, they would not have been punished.

This is a further reason the Torah emphasizes that Er was Judah's firstborn, as if to imply that it was because of the latter's sinfulness that they died.

2. *Ramban* notes that the subject of levirate marriage is one of the great mystical doctrines of Torah. [He does not go into detail here, but from *Ramban's* writing in other areas, the commentators glean that he is referring to the doctrine of the transmigration of souls whereby the

כִּי לֹּא לוֹ יִהְיֶה הַזָּרַע וְהָיָה אִם־בָּא אֶל־
אֵשֶׁת אָחִיו וְשִׁחֵת אַרְצָה לְבִלְתִּי נְתָן־
י זֶרַע לְאָחִיו: וַיֵּרַע בְּעֵינֵי יהוה אֲשֶׁר עָשָׂה
יא וַיָּמֶת גַּם־אֹתוֹ: וַיֹּאמֶר יְהוּדָה לְתָמָר

meaning that she was thereby given back the son Machlon whom she had lost; it explains why they did not say, 'There is a son born to *Ruth* or *Boaz.*' This knowledge that the offspring would not be considered his — and not the mere designation of a name — is what troubled Onan to the point that he refused to impregnate her. Furthermore, the mere choice of a name could hardly be enough to deter a sensible person from honoring the memory of his dead brother.

Mizrachi responds to *Rambam's* arguments. *Rashi* never meant to say that the new-born child *must* be named after the dead brother; in *Deuteronomy* 25:6, *Rashi* says clearly that the Torah's reference to 'name' refers to the disposition of the deceased's *property,* not merely his *appellation.* Rather *Rashi's* intent in our verse is to explain that ancient *custom* called for naming the newborn son after the dead brother. That such was the common practice is implied by *v.* 9: *Onan knew that the seed would not be* [*considered*] *his* — unless the child were to be named after Er, in what way would it not be considered Onan's? However, once the Torah prescribed the law of *yibum* (which omits mention of names), the ancient customs lost their validity.

As to *Rambam's* amazement that so trivial a matter as the giving of a name could have turned Onan to such a sinful course, *Mizrachi* makes a distinction. When a name is given *voluntarily* in memory of someone, the gesture shows generosity on the part of the parent. But when a father is *forced* to use the name of his dead brother, it becomes a public symbol that the child is not considered his.

HaKsav V'haKabbalah agrees that *Rashi* refers not to the literal bestowal of a name, but he interprets *Rashi* differently. *Rashi* says that the child would be called עַל שֵׁם הַמֵּת, which means 'he will be dedicated to the memory of the deceased.' Were *Rashi* to mean that the child had to be *named* after the

soul of the dead brother would become reincarnated in the child born of the levirate union (see *R' Chavel* and *R' Eisenstadt*)].

Even before the giving of the Torah, ancient wise men understood that there was great significance in such a union. The brother of the deceased would take precedence in marrying his widow, and upon his failure to do so it could be performed by his father or any close relation. According to the *Midrash,* Judah was the first one to be involved in the commandment of levirate marriage, the mystical implications of which he learned from his ancestors. Although the ancient custom extended the obligation of levirate marriage to relatives other than the brother of the deceased, under Torah law this was not the case. Only a brother was obligated; other relatives were not. Furthermore, a father-in-law remained forbidden to marry his widowed daughter-in-law even if she was childless.

Only a *brother* could perform *yibum* since the mystical benefits thereof are more inherent in the case of brothers with whom the soul of the deceased finds closer identification than with other relatives.

In ancient Israel, the people perceived the benefits of this union, and established the custom of the closest kin marrying the childless widow of the deceased — providing there was no prohibition against the marriage. Such a marriage could not be termed *yibum* because it did not fall under the command of the Torah; it was given the name גְּאוּלָּה, *redemption,* as in the case of Boaz who married Ruth, the widow of his cousin [see *Ruth* 4:7].

[9] *But Onan knew that the seed would not be his.
So it was, whenever he would consort with his
brother's wife, he would let it go to waste on the
ground so as not to provide offspring for his brother.*
[10] *What he did was evil in the eyes of HASHEM, and
He caused him to die also.*
[11] *Then Judah said to Tamar, his daughter-in-law,*

deceased, the proper expression would have been בְּשֵׁם הַמֵּת.

9. וַיֵּדַע אוֹנָן כִּי לֹּא לוֹ יִהְיֶה הַזָּרַע — *But* [lit. *and*] *Onan knew that the seed would not be* [*considered*] *his.*

He had some kind of definite knowledge of the mystical significance of *yibum* and he was aware that the resulting offspring of his union — regardless of the actual *name* given the child — would be an incarnation of his brother's soul. The wicked Onan had no desire of raising a child he did not consider his own *(Ramban v. 8,* as explained by commentators).

Onan knew that the *mitzvah* of having children would not be his alone, because he was marrying Tamar as an outcome of Tamar's prior betrothal to Er. Thus, it was as if he was sharing his marriage and offspring with Er *(Sforno).*

וְהָיָה אִם־בָּא אֶל־אֵשֶׁת אָחִיו וְשִׁחֵת אַרְצָה — *So it was, whenever he would consort with his brother's wife,* [*and*] *he would let it go to waste on the ground.*

He practised *coitus interruptus* — cohabiting naturally but scattering his semen without *(Midrash; Rashi).*

There is, however, an opinion in *Yevamos* 34b that Tamar was still a maiden when Judah later consorted with her and that she conceived from Judah's first intimacy. As the *Gemara* ad. loc. concludes, this opinion would maintain that Er and Onan practised only *unnatural* intimacies [שֶׁלֹּא כְּדַרְכָּהּ] with her. [See *Maharsha.*]

The Torah describes Tamar as אֵשֶׁת אָחִיו, *his brother's wife,* although his act of *yibum* made her *his* legal wife, to emphasize that this was the very reason Onan acted as selfishly as he did *(R' Sheah Brander).*

לְבִלְתִּי נְתָן־זֶרַע לְאָחִיו — *So as not to provide offspring for his brother.*

He begrudged Er the posthumous fulfillment through his *yibum* of the purpose of marriage — begetting children *(Sforno).*

According to *B'chor Shor:* he wanted to avoid the responsibility of raising another's child.

10. וַיֵּרַע בְּעֵינֵי ה׳ אֲשֶׁר עָשָׂה — [*And*] *what he did was evil in the eyes of HASHEM.*

He misused the organs God gave him for propagating the race to unnaturally satisfy his own lust, and he was therefore deserving of death *(Alshich;* see *Nidah* 13b).

וַיָּמֶת גַּם־אֹתוֹ — *And He caused him to die also.*

[The connotation of גַּם, *also,* is explained by *Rashi* in *v. 7* s.v. רַע as implying that both Er and Onan died for a similar sin.]

11. Judah rebuffs Tamar.

וַיֹּאמֶר יְהוּדָה לְתָמָר כַּלָּתוֹ — *Then* [lit. *and*] *Judah said to Tamar, his daughter-in-law.*

כַּלָּתוֹ שְׁבִי אַלְמָנָה בֵית־אָבִיךְ עַד־יִגְדַּל
שֵׁלָה בְנִי כִּי אָמַר פֶּן־יָמוּת גַּם־הוּא
כְּאֶחָיו וַתֵּלֶךְ תָּמָר וַתֵּשֶׁב בֵּית אָבִיהָ:
יב וַיִּרְבּוּ הַיָּמִים וַתָּמָת בַּת־שׁוּעַ אֵשֶׁת־
יְהוּדָה וַיִּנָּחֶם יְהוּדָה וַיַּעַל עַל־גֹּזְזֵי צֹאנוֹ

שְׁבִי אַלְמָנָה בֵית אָבִיךְ — *Remain a widow in your father's house.*

'Continue conducting yourself as a widow by wearing mourner's garb and not anointing yourself until Shelah grows up. By so doing you will indicate that you do not intend to marry another'. For it was the custom that a widow would indicate her readiness to marry a stranger by removing her mourning garb and arraying herself in scarlet to display that she was no longer in mourning *(Ramban).*

According to the traditional chronology, Shem, Tamar's father, had died many years earlier [see *comm.* to *v.* 5 s.v. וּשְׁמָהּ]. Nevertheless the term *father's house* extends even to his heirs (*Tosafos, Eruvin* 15b cited by *Gur Aryeh* to *v.* 24).

עַד יִגְדַּל שֵׁלָה בְנִי— *Until my son Shelah grows up.*

— I.e., until he reaches thirteen years and a day *(Sechel Tov)* [see *Ramban* below].

כִּי אָמַר פֶּן יָמוּת גַּם הוּא כְּאֶחָיו — *For he thought* [lit. *said* (to himself)], *Lest he also die like his brothers.*

I.e., when Judah made his suggestion that Tamar remain a widow until Shelah grew up he was diplomatically rebuffing her, for as this passage makes clear, he never intended for her to marry his son. He feared that she had established herself as a woman whose husbands die young [*'katlanis'* (see *Kesubos* 43b)] and he was apprehensive that Shelah might die prematurely like his brothers *(Rashi).*

Thus *Rashi* interprets כִּי אָמַר, *for he thought,* as the excuse for asking her to stay as a widow in her father's house, which was merely his way of rebuffing her indefinitely; when Shelah came of age, Judah would have found some other excuse to put off the marriage. The verse should not be understood to mean that Judah *did* want the marriage to take place when Shelah was older but that he wanted a delay of a few years, for if Judah truly thought marriage to her would result in Shelah's death, he had no reason to think that the situation would change in a few years *(Mizrachi).*

Ramban differs and maintains that had Judah been apprehensive that Tamar was a *katlanis* (one whose husbands presumably die young), he would not have found it necessary to resort to putting her off with a feigned promise, but would have forthrightly told her, 'Go in peace from my house since marriage to such a woman would be prohibited to Shelah' [see *Kesubos* 43b. (The *Poskim* discuss whether the prohibition of *katlanis* applies to cases of *yibum.* See *HaKsav V'HaKabbalah* who distinguishes between the case of Tamar and cases after the giving of the Torah)]. To the contrary, *Ramban* continues, Judah must have known [as Tamar herself knew from their conjugal behavior] that his sons died through their *own* sins and not because the guiltless Tamar was a *katlanis.* That Judah wanted Tamar to remarry in his family is evident from the fact that he was angered by Tamar's harlotry to the extent of condemning her to be burned [which presumably would not have been his attitude had he intended to be rid of her].

Rather, Judah consented in principle to the marriage, but he was afraid that if

38 *'Remain a widow in your father's house until my son*
12 *Shelah grows up' — for he thought, 'Lest he also die*
like his brothers.' — So Tamar went and lived in her
father's house.
12 *Many days passed and Shua's daughter, the wife*
of Judah, died. When Judah was consoled, he went
up to oversee his sheepshearers — he and his Adul-

Shelah married her while he was so young he might have the tendency to sin with her as had his brothers. Therefore, he wanted her to wait until Shelah would mature and be receptive to his father's influence as a deterrent against sin [comp. *Sforno*].

[Conceivably, then, according to *Ramban*, Judah might have even *verbalized* to Tamar the phrase *lest he also die like his brothers*, which according to *Ramban* was Judah's reason for asking her to wait until Shelah grows up, and not merely *thought* it to himself.]

Gur Aryeh defends *Rashi's* interpretation that Judah was merely rebuffing Tamar and had no intention of allowing Tamar — whom he feared was a *katlanis* — to become married to Shelah. That Judah wanted her to remain a widow in her father's house, and was so incensed at her later infidelity, was because — in deference to his sons' memory — he did not want her to become married to anyone else.

וַתֵּלֶךְ תָּמָר וַתֵּשֶׁב בֵּית אָבִיהָ — *So Tamar went and lived* [lit. *settled*] *in her father's house.*

— In a display of her loyalty to the tradition and her desire to remain associated with the sacred race. She waited patiently for Shelah to come of age and marry her, and thereby perpetuate her husband's seed *(Ralbag).*

12. וַיִּרְבּוּ הַיָּמִים — *Many days passed* [lit. *and the days increased*].

Following the Rabbinic chronology in *Seder Olam* (discussed in *v.* 1), according to which all the events in this chapter transpired in a twenty-two year period, the phrase *many days passed* is interpreted to indicate the passing of *twelve months.*

וַתָּמָת בַּת־שׁוּעַ אֵשֶׁת־יְהוּדָה — *And Shua's daughter, the wife of Judah, died.*

That Judah's wife and sons died prematurely is, as noted in the comm. and footnote to *v.* 7, perceived in *Sotah* 13a as punishment for Judah's complicity in the sale of Joseph. He *began* a good deed of telling his brothers not to kill Joseph, but neglected to follow through. One who abandons a good deed without completing it, the Sages teach, will eventually bury his wife and children, as happened to Judah.

וַיִּנָּחֶם יְהוּדָה — *When* [lit. *and*] *Judah was consoled.*

The translation follows *Onkelos* and *Ibn Ezra* who interpret that after Judah was consoled of his wife's death he went up, etc.

According to *Ramban*, the phrase implies: *And Judah sought consoliation* by going up to his sheepshearers.

וַיַּעַל עַל־גֹּזְזֵי צֹאנוֹ — [*And*] *he went up to oversee* [lit. *upon*] *his sheepshearers.*

I.e., he went up to Timnah to 'stand upon' [i.e., supervise] his sheep-shearers (*Rashi;* see below).

Thus, *Rashi* connects וַיַּעַל, *went up*, with תִּמְנָתָה, *to Timnah (Mizrachi).*

יג הוּא וְחִירָה רֵעֵהוּ הָעֲדֻלָּמִי תִּמְנָתָה: וַיֻּגַּד
לְתָמָר לֵאמֹר הִנֵּה חָמִיךְ עֹלֶה תִמְנָתָה
יד לָגֹז צֹאנוֹ: וַתָּסַר בִּגְדֵי אַלְמְנוּתָהּ מֵעָלֶיהָ
וַתְּכַס בַּצָּעִיף וַתִּתְעַלָּף וַתֵּשֶׁב בְּפֶתַח

Judah would go there regularly in search of consolation; by busying himself with the sheep he would forget his grief. Or possibly since Judah was a prominent man, the shearing of his sheep was a festive occasion accompanied by a public feast for the poor *(Ramban).*

[Comp. *Haamek Davar* cited to 31:19.]

That sheep-shearing was a festive occasion may be seen from the feast Absalom made on such an event [*II Samuel* 13:23], and from the story of Nabal [*I Samuel* 25:2] (*R' Avraham ben HaRambam).*[1]

The translation of עַל גֹּזְזֵי צֹאנוֹ, lit. *upon his sheep-shearers,* as connoting 'to *stand* upon,' i.e. *oversee,* follows *Rashi.* [Comp. also *Rashi* to 24:30 s.v. עַל הַגְּמַלִּים.]

Ibn Ezra interprets עַל, *upon,* as synonymous in this case with אֶל, *to.* [Comp. *I Samuel* 1:10 וַתִּתְפַּלֵּל עַל ה׳ *(Yohel Or).*]

HaKsav V'HaKabbalah interprets עַל as meaning *concerning* — Judah went up to attend to matters concerning the sheep shearing.

הוּא וְחִירָה רֵעֵהוּ הָעֲדֻלָּמִי — *He and his Adullamite friend, Hirah.*

It is with his friend and partner that Judah seeks this consolation as he travels the distance to Timnah *(Abarbanel).*

תִּמְנָתָה — *To Timnah.*

Presumably this is the *Timnah* mentioned in *Joshua* 15:57, a town several miles south of Hebron. It is logical that Judah remained in the same general area of *Eretz Yisrael* as the rest of Jacob's family, even though he found it necessary to move away from his brothers.

[It is noteworthy that *Onkelos* here and *Targum* to *Judges* 14:1 renders the name of the town as *Timnas,* while in *Joshua, Targum* renders *Timnah.* This apparent inconsistency may be related to the controversy cited below.]

The Talmud [*Sotah* 10a] and *Midrash* note a dispute concerning the identity of the town. According to one view, there were two towns named Timnah, one where Judah settled and the other, mentioned in Judges, where Samson married. Samson's Timnah has been located by some as near Beth Shemesh on the northern border of Judah.

The second view is that there was only one Timnah in *Eretz Yisrael.* If so, the Talmud inquiries, how is it that Judah is described as going *up* to Timnah, [indicating it was on a mountain while Samson is described as *descending* to Timnah indicating it was in a valley]? The Talmud gives two responses:

— The 'ascent' and 'descent' are meant figuratively. Judah was 'elevated' in Timnah because it was there that Tamar conceived from him, giving birth to Peretz, the forerunner of the Davidic

1. The *Midrash* observes how every case of sheep shearing in Scripture left its mark [i.e., it had evil consequences].

We find this in the case of Nabal, Laban, and Absalom. [Jacob fled from Laban while the latter was shearing his sheep (30:19); this ultimately led to Laban's pursuit and confrontation with Jacob, a confrontation which lead to Jacob's curse (31:32) to which Rachel's death is directly ascribed. Nabal's death followed his sheep shearing (*I Samuel* 25:4-8). Absalom's sheep shearing was the scene of Amnon's assassination (*II Sam.* 13:23 ff).]

lamite friend, Hirah — to Timnah.
[13] *And Tamar was told as follows, 'Behold, your father-in-law is coming up to Timnah for the sheepshearing.'* [14] *So she removed her widow's garb from upon her, covered herself with a veil, and wrapped herself up. She then sat by the crossroad*

dynasty. Samson, on the other hand, 'descended' in Timnah because there he suffered the disgrace of marrying a Philistine woman.

— Timnah was situated on a mountainside between Samson's home in the mountainous north and Judah's home in low-lying Hebron. Thus, Judah's route to Timnah was uphill while Samson's was downhill. *Rashi* to *v.* 13 cites this view.

According to *Abarbanel,* the term *went up* is used here because Timnah is to the north of Adullam, and one is therefore said to 'go up' from Adullam to Timnah.

13. וַיֻּגַּד לְתָמָר — *And Tamar was told* [lit. *and it was told to Tamar*].

— Through a prophetic spirit *(Midrash HaGadol).*

Cf. *Alshich:* A prophetic message from the Academy of Shem and Eber was revealed to her: חָמִיךְ עוֹלֶה, *your father-in-law is 'going up'* — his time has come to 'ascend' great heights and beget the Messiah.

According to the simple sense it was not necessarily through a prophetic vision. Since Judah was such an important personage, his travel plans — especially to something as festive as a sheep-shearing — would be common knowledge and she was told of it by one of the townsfolk *(Ibn Caspi).*

She was told either that Judah went to Timnah *regularly,* and she waited for him on one of those days; or as noted, that he *would* be going there for some specific occasion, and she made plans to await him on that particular day *(Ramban v.* 12).

14. Tamar disguises herself. It is her intention to force Judah himself to perform the levirate duty.

וַתָּסַר בִּגְדֵי אַלְמְנוּתָהּ מֵעָלֶיהָ — *So* [lit. *and*] *she removed her widow's garb from upon her.*

וַתְּכַס בַּצָּעִיף וַתִּתְעַלָּף — [*And*] *covered herself with a veil, and wrapped herself up.*

In addition to wearing a veil, she covered her face so well that he would be unable to recognize her. [That she did so is indicated by *v.* 15 which says clearly that he could not recognize her for that reason *(Mizrachi)*] *(Rashi).*

According to *Ramban,* she acted in the manner of harlots who *partially* wrap themselves in a veil, leaving portions of their hair and face — eyes, mouth, and neck — uncovered, to allow them to entice passersby.

The sense of וַתִּתְעַלָּף [lit. *and wrapped herself up*] as meaning hid her face with a garment, follows *Rashi. Ibn Ezra* interprets the verb similarly, which agrees with his rendering of the word וַיִּתְעַלָּף in *Jonah* 4:8. Most others render the term in *Jonah* ibid. as *swoon; faint,* which is how *Ibn Caspi* perceives the word in our passage: i.e. she covered herself with a veil, and when she saw Judah approaching pretended to *swoon* in a feminine manner to draw his attention.

Tzror HaMor also interprets the word as *swoon,* but writes that Tamar indeed felt *faint* at the overwhelming implications of what she was about to do. But it was a matter of survival and she proceeded with the task at hand.

עֵינַ֖יִם אֲשֶׁ֣ר עַל־דֶּ֣רֶךְ תִּמְנָ֑תָה כִּ֤י רָאֲתָה֙
כִּֽי־גָדַ֣ל שֵׁלָ֔ה וְהִ֕וא לֹֽא־נִתְּנָ֥ה ל֖וֹ לְאִשָּֽׁה׃
טו וַיִּרְאֶ֣הָ יְהוּדָ֔ה וַיַּחְשְׁבֶ֖הָ לְזוֹנָ֑ה כִּ֥י כִסְּתָ֖ה
טז פָּנֶֽיהָ׃ וַיֵּ֨ט אֵלֶ֜יהָ אֶל־הַדֶּ֗רֶךְ וַיֹּ֙אמֶר֙ הָֽבָה־נָּא֙

וַתֵּשֶׁב בְּפֶתַח עֵינַיִם אֲשֶׁר עַל־דֶּרֶךְ תִּמְנָתָה — *She then sat by the crossroad which is on the road toward Timnah.*

— It was the practise of harlots to sit at a crossroad where they would be seen by many people *(Ramban).*

The term בְּפֶתַח עֵינַיִם literally means *at the opening of eyes.* It refers to a *crossroad* — the juncture where travelers *'open their eyes'* to determine in which direction to proceed. According to the Sages [*Sotah* 10b], the term refers figuratively to the *entrance* [פֶּתַח] of Abraham's home [or sepulchre *(Mizrachi);* or *Eishel (Chem'as HaChemdah)*] — a place to which all *eyes* turned. [She sat there because everyone traveling along that road visited Abraham's residence, and Judah, too, was certain to do so] *(Rashi).*[1]

Ralbag interprets it as open area which provided an unobstructed view of all travelers. According to *Ibn Ezra* עֵינַיִם is the plural of עַיִן, *fountain.* There were two fountains on the road which formed a gate, as it were, through which Judah had to pass.

According to another view in *Sotah* ibid., the phrase means *the entrance of Enayim,* Enayim being the name of a place, identical with Enam mentioned in *Joshua* 15:34. *Yohel Or* elaborates that Enam was located near Tzar'ah [ibid. *v.* 33] which in turn was near Timnah [ibid. 19:41-43]. Enam was similarly near Adullam, Hirah's home.

According to the dialogue recorded in *Sotah* 10a [cited in *v.* 15 s.v. וַיֵּט], the expression פֶּתַח עֵינַיִם figuratively alludes to the manner in which Tamar 'gave eyes to her words' [i.e. gave an 'opening' (=credibility) to her response *(Daas Zekeinim)*], by offering convincing replies to Judah's questions regarding her status.

כִּי רָאֲתָה כִּי־גָדַל שֵׁלָה וְהִוא לֹא־נִתְּנָה לוֹ לְאִשָּׁה — *For she saw that Shelah had grown, and she had not been given to him as a wife.*

The Torah thus explains why Tamar took so undignified an initiative in offering herself to Judah. She was determined to have children from him. [Since it could not be through Shelah, she had no alternative but that it be from Judah himself *(Gur Aryeh)*] *(Rashi).*[2]

Following *Rashi's* implication in *v.* 11: She realized that Judah had merely been rebuffing her and had no real intention of ever allowing Shelah to marry her.

Ramban ibid.: It *was* Judah's intention for Shelah to marry Tamar after he grew up; however, in Judah's eyes Shelah was still achild since he was not yet ten years old and Judah was determined to have him wait longer. To Tamar it appeared that Shelah was already old

1. The phraseology of this passage implies a deeper insight: When Tamar set herself there for her noble purpose, it was בְּעֵינַיִם פְּתוּחוֹת, *with open eyes* — she fully perceived the Providential chain of events that would proceed from her action: that she would become the ancestress of the royal House of David *(Chiddushei HaRim).*

2. The Talmud (*Nazir* 23b) teaches: Ulla said, Tamar [*v.* 18] and Zimri [*Numb.* 25:14] both lived with people outside of wedlock. From Tamar's harlotry kings and prophets descended [because she had lofty moral intentions, acting for the Sake of Heaven to raise up righteous progeny (*Rashi* ad. loc. and to *Horayos* 10b)], while Zimri's immorality resulted in the downfall of myriads of Israel [ibid. *v.* 9]. R' Nachman bar Yitzchak [referring to Tamar] said, Greater is a transgression committed for the sake of Heaven [לִשְׁמָהּ] than a *mitzvah* committed with an ulterior motive [see *Overview*].

which is on the road toward Timnah, for she saw that Shelah had grown, and she had not been given to him as a wife.

15 When Judah saw her, he thought her to be a harlot since she had covered her face. 16 So he detoured to her by the road and said, 'Come, if you

enough [her first husbands, as noted, were but seven years old at marriage.] She craved greatly to give birth from the sacred famly, and hurried to do this deed.

Her initial intent had been that Judah would see her without her widow's garb and question her motive. She would then tell him that he had bidden her to wear her mourning clothes only until Shelah grew up; now that he was old enough, she no longer had to remain a widow. But the dialogue did not occur that way for he did not recognize her *(Sforno)*.

As *B'chor Shor* explains, Tamar was justified in contriving to have Judah perform the levirate marriage for [as *Ramban* writes in *v.* 8] before the Torah was given levirate marriage was performed by *any* close relative — even the father of the deceased. Since Shelah had not done so, it was Judah's responsibility to do so.

15. וַיִּרְאֶהָ יְהוּדָה וַיַּחְשְׁבֶהָ לְזוֹנָה — *When* [lit. *and*] *Judah saw her,* [*and*] *he thought her to be a harlot.*

— Because she was sitting at the crossroads *(Rashi).*

[Harlotry was not prohibited before the Torah was given; see *footnote* next verse.]

According to the *Midrash* [see next verse] when Judah initially saw her he reasoned: 'She is a harlot;' he paid her no attention, and proceeded on his way.

כִּי כִסְּתָה פָּנֶיהָ — *Since she had covered her face.*

— And he could not recognize her. [This phrase anticipates why — as the next verse states — Judah did not recognize Tamar *(Tzeidah LaDerech)*]. The Rabbis [in *Sotah* 10a, who interpret a covered face as a sign of modesty — not harlotry] explain that our phrase is to be rendered in the past-perfect: *Since she had covered her face* all the while she had lived in her father-in-law's home, Tamar had earned a reputation as a modest woman, above suspicion. Therefore, Judah never thought to connect her with this 'harlot' *(Rashi).*

16. וַיֵּט אֵלֶיהָ אֶל־הַדֶּרֶךְ — *So* [lit. *and*] *he detoured to her by the road.*

— I.e. he left his path to go to her. In old French: *detourner (Rashi).*

According to the *Midrash* [see *v.* 15], Providence *forced* Judah to detour to her:

Judah had ignored her and proceeded on his way, but Tamar prayed: 'Sovereign of the Universe: Shall I be deprived of offspring from this righteous man?' Then God sent the Angel of Desire to appear before Judah and say to him: 'Where are you going Judah? If you flee, from where will kings arise? From where else will redeemers arise?' So Judah *detoured to her by the road* — despite himself

נָא אָבוֹא אֵלַיִךְ כִּי לֹא יָדַע כִּי כַלָּתוֹ הִוא וַתֹּאמֶר מַה־תִּתֶּן־לִי כִּי תָבוֹא אֵלָי:
יז וַיֹּאמֶר אָנֹכִי אֲשַׁלַּח גְּדִי־עִזִּים מִן־הַצֹּאן וַתֹּאמֶר אִם־תִּתֵּן עֵרָבוֹן עַד שָׁלְחֶךָ:

and against his wish *(Tanchuma Yashan; Midrash;* see *Moreh Nevuchim* 2:6).[1]

הָבָה־נָּא אָבוֹא אֵלַיִךְ – *Come, if you please, let me* [lit. *and I will*] *consort with you.*[2]

The term הָבָה [*come*], signifies an invitation to another to *prepare oneself and one's mind for something.* It always has this meaning unless the context requires the translation *give.* Indeed, even in contexts where the term means *prepare* the word is closely related to the

1. The Talmud [*Sotah* 10a] records the following dialogue between Judah and Tamar:
'Are you perhaps a pagan?' Judah asked her.
'I am a proselyte,' she answered, [and do not worship idols' *(Rashi* in *Sotah* ad. loc.)].
'Are you married?'
'I am unmarried' [and permissible to any man *(Rashi, ibid.)*].
'Perhaps your father accepted betrothals on your behalf?'
'No. I am an orphan [and have no father. My mother and brothers married me off as a minor *(Rashi, ibid.)*.]

[The Rabbis provided that a girl with no father could be betrothed by her mother and brothers while she is still a minor. However, she retains the right to renounce the marriage until she attains her majority. By her statements to Judah, she expressed her opposition to the marriages — מיאון, *refusal.* As a result, her marriages to Er and Onan were invalid retroactively and she was not prohibited to Judah as his daughter-in-law. This interpretation, that Tamar was a *minor* when she was married to Er and Onan would differ from the Midrashic tradition (cited by *Rashi* in *v.* 24) that Tamar was the daughter of Shem, since, as noted in *v.* 6, Shem had died at least sixty-seven years before Tamar married Er *(Rashi, ibid.)*.]

[*Maharsha* differs with *Rashi* and reconciles the tradition that Tamar was Shem's daughter. Since Judah was unaware that Tamar was his daughter-in-law, his innocent intent in his question was 'Perhaps your father accepted betrothals on your behalf — while you were still a minor and without your knowledge. If so, are you not free to marry any man?' To which Tamar replied, 'I am an orphan. My father [Shem] died while my mother was pregnant, and he could certainly not have accepted betrothal on my behalf before I was born.'

The Talmudic dialogue continues: 'Perhaps you are [menstrually] unclean?' Judah asked. — 'I am clean.'

2. **The moral perspective of Judah's action.**

Judah's action must be viewed in the moral perspective of ancient times — before the Torah was given — when harlotry was not yet forbidden. All morality depends on the Torah. Had the Torah not forbade certain forbidden foods, we would be able to enjoy them guiltlessly. The same is true of harlotry; before the Torah was given it was simply not prohibited.

As *Rambam* writes in *Ishus* 1:4: 'Before the Torah was given, if a man met a woman in the market place and desired her, if she consented he would pay her hire and consort with her at the crossroads, and go his way. [The incident of Judah and Tamar corroborates this *(Maggid Mishnah)*.] She is what is known as a קְדֵשָׁה, *prostitute.* When the Torah was given, prostitution was prohibited, [see *comm.* to *Deut.* 23-18]. See also *Moreh Nevuchim* 3:49].

That the Patriarchs — and presumably their families — observed the Torah before it was given is no contradiction. They observed it *voluntarily* and Judah was not obligated to go beyond what was absolutely *required* of him. [Cf. the case of Jacob marrying two sisters which later Torah law absolutely forbade (see *comm.* to 26:5; 32:5; *footnote* to 35:19).]

Also, the direct hand of Providence must not be ignored in this case, as discussed in the *Overview,* and the *Overview to Ruth.* For as the *Midrash* notes, Providence caused Judah to be virtually coerced by an angel [i.e. caused Judah's passions to be enflamed *(Rambam)*. See also *Or HaChaim* to 49:9.]

38 *please, let me consort with you,' for he did not know*
17 *that she was his daughter-in-law. And she said, 'What will you give me if you consort with me?'*

[17] *He replied, 'I will send you a kid of the goats from the flock.'*

And she said, 'Provided you leave a pledge until you send it.'

meaning of *give (Rashi).*

כִּי לֹא יָדַע כִּי כַלָּתוֹ הִוא — *For he did not know that she was his daughter-in-law.*

— Even after he approached her; otherwise he would have spoken with her on behalf of Shelah. That Judah could not recognize her was part of the Divine plan. God wanted the seed of the Messianic dynasty to come directly from Judah — who was more righteous and pure than Shelah — and Tamar *(Sforno).*

Once Judah concluded that she was a harlot, he did not recognize her by her voice, since it never occurred to him that his highly prominent daughter-in-law, Tamar, could be a harlot, God forbid. Thus her voice did not arouse his suspicions just as Jacob's voice did not arouse Isaac's suspicions once the Patriarch felt Jacob's 'hairy arms' and concluded he was Esau *(Haamek Davar).*

מַה־תִּתֶּן־לִי כִּי תָבוֹא אֵלָי — *What will you give me if you consort with me?*

Tamar initiated the conversation with the intention that Judah would recognize her by her voice. She certainly did not seek any harlot's *fee,* it being her intention to establish offspring from Judah. Therefore, she wanted a *pledge,* not for personal gain, but as proof of her real intentions. Had he given her a *fee* she would not have taken it, for then she would have no proof of her righteous intention *(Sforno).*

17. אָנֹכִי אֲשַׁלַּח גְּדִי־עִזִּים מִן־הַצֹּאן — *I will send you a kid of the goats from the flock.*

In general, a gift of a kid was considered quite honorable. Jesse sent a kid with David to Saul [*I Sam.* 16:20], and Samson brought a kid when he visited his wife [*Judges* 15:1] *(HaRechasim leBik'ah).*

From the specific qualification that it would be a 'kid *of the goats,*' the Sages [*Chullin* 113a] derive that whenever the term גְּדִי, *kid,* occurs without the limitation הָעִזִּים, *of the goats,* it halachically includes the young of the cow and ewe. [See *Torah Temimah*].

The pronoun אָנֹכִי, as distinct from אֲנִי has an emphatic connotation. In this case it implies *'As for me* — i.e. a man of my worth — it is sufficient that I send you a kid from the flocks.' For a harlot's fee is often established by a man's prominence — the lowly usually paying a higher fee while the mere interest of an important person has independent value to a harlot. Tamar agreed that for a man of Judah's prominence a kid would suffice, but cleverly requested a pledge *(Haamek Davar).*

וַתֹּאמֶר אִם־תִּתֵּן עֵרָבוֹן עַד שָׁלְחֶךָ — *And she said, 'Provided* [lit. *if*] *you leave* [lit. *give*] *a pledge until you send it.*

As noted earlier, Tamar was not interested in the harlot's fee, but in securing something she could use as later proof of her intention. She

יח וַיֹּאמֶר מָה הָעֵרָבוֹן אֲשֶׁר אֶתֶּן־לָּךְ
וַתֹּאמֶר חֹתָמְךָ וּפְתִילֶךָ וּמַטְּךָ אֲשֶׁר
בְּיָדֶךָ וַיִּתֶּן־לָהּ וַיָּבֹא אֵלֶיהָ וַתַּהַר לוֹ׃
יט וַתָּקָם וַתֵּלֶךְ וַתָּסַר צְעִיפָהּ מֵעָלֶיהָ
כ וַתִּלְבַּשׁ בִּגְדֵי אַלְמְנוּתָהּ׃ וַיִּשְׁלַח יְהוּדָה
אֶת־גְּדִי הָעִזִּים בְּיַד רֵעֵהוּ הָעֲדֻלָּמִי
לָקַחַת הָעֵרָבוֹן מִיַּד הָאִשָּׁה וְלֹא מְצָאָהּ׃
כא וַיִּשְׁאַל אֶת־אַנְשֵׁי מְקֹמָהּ לֵאמֹר אַיֵּה
הַקְּדֵשָׁה הִוא בָעֵינַיִם עַל־הַדָּרֶךְ וַיֹּאמְרוּ

therefore consented to consort with Judah only on condition that he leave her a pledge *(Sforno).*

18. חֹתָמְךָ וּפְתִילֶךָ וּמַטְּךָ אֲשֶׁר בְּיָדֶךָ — *'Your signet, your wrap, and your staff that is in your hand.*

She selected the three articles which most distinguished him as a ruler or lord *(Ramban),* in order to inspire her to contemplate about Judah's greatness [thereby elevating her spiritual level while she carried the child] *(Sforno).* Furthermore, such distinctive articles would provide indisputable proof of the identity of the child's father.

The translation *your signet and your wrap* follows *Onkelos:* עִזְקְתָךְ וְשׁוֹשִׁיפָךְ; the ring which you use as a seal and the garment with which you cover yourself *(Rashi).*

Ramban differs with *Rashi's* suggestion that Judah would have left Tamar his *wrap* and gone from Tamar in a state of partial undress. Rather, *Ramban* maintains that by the Aramaic שׁוֹשִׁיפָא, *Onkelos* referred to a small shawl which distinguished persons would spread over their headcoverings. It was called פְּתִיל, [literally *fringe* as in *Numbers* 15:38], because it was as short as a fringe. For in only one instance [*Deut.* 22:17] does *Onkelos* render the Hebrew שִׂמְלָה, [*cloak*], as שׁוֹשִׁיפָא, and in that case it means the scarf known in the Talmud as *sudar.*

Alternately *Ramban* suggests that Judah possessed a signet impressed with the form of a lion, as rulers do; fringed cords woven into the same design as his signet; and a rod symbolic of a royal sceptre. It was these that he gave to Tamar.

Rashbam renders פְּתִיל as *belt,* while *Ralbag* perceives it as an ornamental braided cord worn by distinguished personages on their outer garments, or as an adornment on their head-dress [cf. *Haamek Davar*]. Others suggest that the signet was suspended from a פְּתִיל, *fringed cord. According to Abarbanel,* it referred to Judah's fringed handkerchief.

The signet ring was engraved with the Ineffable Four Letter Name — HASHEM ... The staff was the one which Jacob carried when he left home [see 32:11] *(Yalkut Shimoni).*

... Moreover, this rod was the one with which Moses would later split the Sea and perform all the miracles *(Baal HaTurim).*

וַיִּתֶּן לָהּ — [*And*] *he gave* [them] *to her.*

So great was the passion burning within him [as a result of the Providential intervention *(Abarbanel)*] that Judah gave these three valuable items as a pledge for a single goat *(Ibn Ezra).*

Rashbam interprets to the contrary. Judah gladly parted with these items since they were *not* indispensable articles of clothing.

וַתַּהַר לוֹ — *And she conceived by* [lit. *to*] *him.*

From the first intimacy. Although it is axiomatic that a

[18] *And he said, 'What pledge shall I give you?'
She replied, 'Your signet, your wrap, and your
staff that is in your hand.' And he gave them to her.
He consorted with her and she conceived by him.*
[19] *Then she arose, left, and removed her veil from
upon her. She put on her widow's garb.*
[20] *Judah sent the kid of the goats through his
friend the Adullamite to retrieve the pledge from the
woman. But he did not find her.* [21] *He inquired of the
people of her place, 'Where is the prostitute, the one
at the crossroads by the road?' And they said, 'There*

maiden does not conceive from the first intimacy, Tamar had made special preparations rendering it possible (*Yevamos* 34b; comp. the cases of Lot's daughters in 19:36, Hagar in 16:4, and Leah in 29:32 and 49:2).

[This follows the view in *Yevamos* ibid. (cited in *v.* 9) that Tamar was still a maiden when Judah consorted with her, for Er and Onan had indulged only in unnatural intimacies with her. *Rashi*, in his exposition to *v.* 9 does not follow this view, following instead the Midrash that Er and Onan had practised *coitus interruptus* and Tamar was no longer a maiden. He therefore does not find it noteworthy that she conceived from this union. It was not her first natural intimacy with a man.]

The phraseology וַתַּהַר לוֹ, and she conceived *to him* [rather than simply וַתַּהַר or וַתַּהַר מִמֶּנּוּ *(Mizrachi)*] connotes that she conceived progeny who were *similar in stature to him:* strong and righteous like Judah *(Rashi).*

19. וַתָּקָם וַתֵּלֶךְ — *Then she arose and left* [lit. *and went*].

She arose — spiritually, for kings and prophets were to result from this union *(Lekach Tov;* comp. *Rashi* to 23:17 s.v. וַיָּקָם שְׂדֵה עֶפְרוֹן).

וַתִּלְבַּשׁ בִּגְדֵי אַלְמְנוּתָהּ — *And she put on her widow's garb.*

For now that she had acquired the longed-for seed she had no more desire to marry *(Sforno).*

20. Judah dispatches his Adullamite friend to redeem the pledge.

בְּיַד רֵעֵהוּ הָעֲדֻלָּמִי — *Through* [lit. *in the hand of*] *his friend the Adullamite.*

— There is a difference of opinion recorded in *Bereishis Rabbosi* regarding why the Adullamite's name is not recorded here. According to one view, his anonymity was preserved in deference to his selflessness in performing this shameful mission out of love and friendship for the righteous Judah. According to another view, his name is omitted as token of rebuke, because he undertook to participate in this disgraceful affair.

לָקַחַת הָעֵרָבוֹן — *To retrieve* [lit. *take*] *the pledge.*

— And thereby keep his promise regarding the kid *(Malbim).*

וְלֹא מְצָאָהּ — *But he* [i.e. his friend] *did not find her.*

21. אַיֵּה הַקְּדֵשָׁה — *Where is the prostitute?*[1]

1. *R' Shmelke of Nicholsburg* commented homiletically:
אַיֵּה קְדֵשָׁה, where does harlotry originate? הִיא בָעֵינַיִם, it is in the eyes! *(Peninei Torah).*

כב לֹא־הָיְתָה בָזֶה קְדֵשָׁה: וַיָּשָׁב אֶל־יְהוּדָה
וַיֹּאמֶר לֹא מְצָאתִיהָ וְגַם אַנְשֵׁי הַמָּקוֹם
כג אָמְרוּ לֹא־הָיְתָה בָזֶה קְדֵשָׁה: וַיֹּאמֶר
יְהוּדָה תִּקַּח־לָהּ פֶּן נִהְיֶה לָבוּז הִנֵּה
שָׁלַחְתִּי הַגְּדִי הַזֶּה וְאַתָּה לֹא מְצָאתָהּ:

[The term קְדֵשָׁה derives from the root קדש which in its most literal sense denotes *dedication to a specific purpose;* it refers to a woman who *by profession* acts licentiously and is dedicated [מְקוּדֶשֶׁת] and known to be available for prostitution (see *Rashi* here, *Ibn Ezra* to *Deut.* 23:18, and *Ibn Ezra* to *Haggai* 2:12. Comp. also *R' Hirsch* to 2:30 who distinguishes between the spellings קָדוֹשׁ which refers to the 'unresisting acquiescence to everything noble,' and קָדֵשׁ, the opposite, 'complete acquiescence in sensuality'; cf. כָּבוֹד denoting spiritual contentment, and כָּבֹד, the material [see 31:1]; שָׁלוֹם, spiritual harmony, and שָׁלֵם material totality). As *Rambam* notes in *Ishus* 1:4] (cited above in the footnote to *v.* 16) in pre-Mosaic times there was absolutely no prohibition in harlotry; it first became prohibited when the Torah was given, as set forth in *Deut.* 23:18.]

[The terms זוֹנָה and קְדֵשָׁה, meaning *harlot* or *prostitute* are used interchangeably. They do not represent two different categories nor is there any Halachic distinction between the two. Although the modern secularist Bible exegetes distinguish between the Hebrew terms for harlot זוֹנָה and קְדֵשָׁה by interpreting that the latter term refers to 'cult' prostitutes who, according to them, used to minister in Canaanite heathen temples, this interpretation has no basis in classical Biblical exegesis and certainly is not halachically valid. Halachically, it is clear that the prohibition of harlotry *in general* (not just of some supposed cult prostitution!) derives from *Deut.* 23:18, and the *Poskim* use the terms זוֹנָה and קְדֵשָׁה interchangeably. See specifically *Midrash Tannaim* cited in *Torah Sheleimah* 888.]

הוא בָעֵינַיִם עַל הַדָּרֶךְ — *The one* [lit. *she*] *at the crossroads* [*lit. by the eyes*] *by the road?*

[What had probably occurred was that Judah had originally asked Tamar where in that area she lived so he could send her the kid and redeem his pledge. When he sent the Adullamite to the place she told him, and could not find a prostitute there, he inquired of the local residents: 'The prostitute — the one who was stationed yesterday at the crossroads and who supposedly lives in this neighborhood. — Do you know where she is?']

וַיֹּאמְרוּ לֹא הָיְתָה בָזֶה קְדֵשָׁה — *And they said, 'There was no prostitute here'* [lit. *in this,* Cf. מִזֶּה in 37:17].

— There has *never* been a harlot here; in this place we are scrupulous regarding immorality *(Shochar Tov).*

The deeper intent of their reply was: 'There was no act of harlotry committed here.' They prophesied and knew not what they prophesied *(Minchah Belulah).*

22. וְגַם אַנְשֵׁי הַמָּקוֹם אָמְרוּ — [*And*] *even the local men* [lit. *men of the place*] *said.*

— In derision; ridiculing your honor *(Sforno).*

23. תִּקַּח לָהּ פֶּן נִהְיֶה לָבוּז — *Let her keep them* [lit. *let her take to herself*], *lest we become a laughing stock.*

38
22-23 *was no prostitute here.'* 22 *So he returned to Judah*
and said, 'I did not find her; even the local men said,
"There was no prostitute here."' 23 So Judah said,
'Let her keep them, lest we become a laughing stock. I
really sent her this kid, but you could not find her.'

Let her keep the signet, wrap, and staff she is holding as a pledge. If you continue searching for her, the matter [of our being taken in by this woman who fled with my pledge *(Nachalas Yitzchak)*] will become generally known, much to our disgrace. What more must I do to verify my word [that I would redeem my pledge by sending her the kid]? *(Rashi).*

According to *Ibn Ezra: lest we become a laughing stock* — for having pledged things as valuable as a signet, wrap and staff for such a trifle.

Or, according to *Abarbanel:* for inquiring about harlots.

Judah's fear was not that he would be ridiculed for purchasing the services of a harlot. Were that his concern, Hirah would not have made public inquiries about her whereabouts *(Nachlas Yitzchak).*

We will be a laughing stock — since matters of sexual intimacy, even those of a permitted nature, are a cause of embarrassment to distinguished people when they become a subject of public discussion *(R' Avraham ben HaRambam* in *Rambam's* name).[1]

הִנֵּה שָׁלַחְתִּי הַגְּדִי הַזֶּה וְאַתָּה לֹא מְצָאתָהּ — *I really* [idiomatically: *behold I*] *sent her this kid, but you could not find her.*

I.e. I scrupulously fulfilled my commitment to her and sent her the kid. That you could not find her is a sign that she should keep the pledge *(Ibn Ezra).* [See footnote].

The *Midrash* notes that because Judah deceived his father by means of a kid — having dipped Joseph's tunic in its blood [37:31] — he was himself deceived through one *(Rashi).*

Rambam (Moreh Nevuchim 3:49) derives an important lesson in ethics from Judah's remark. By stressing that he sent her **this** *kid,* he was displaying his gift as if to say the he had sent her a choice animal and made a sincere attempt to keep his word. Although he had made no promise regarding the quality of the kid, he was careful not to defraud her. [See footnote.]

1. Judah's decision to forfeit his pledge rather than engage in further discussion of the Tamar matter provides a lesson in moral conduct.

As stated above, harlotry was not forbidden prior to the giving of the Torah. Furthermore, it is obvious that the personal articles Judah had left Tamar as a pledge were far more valuable than the kid he had promised to send her and which Hirah had brought in order to redeem this signet, wrap, and staff. Nevertheless, to discuss sexual matters in public — even if they involve no forbidden conduct — is shameful and should be avoided. Judah was ready to forfeit his important pledge rather than become involved in further public discussion of the topic *(Rambam, Moreh Nevuchim* 3:49).

◆§ Judah said *'we'* will be a laughing stock, in the plural, as if to include Hirah the Adullamite who had no part in the escapade with Tamar. As the saying goes, 'If you show me someone's friends, I will tell you what he is like.' Were Judah to become the butt of ridicule, his friend Hirah would become a laughing stock, too *(Midrash).*

כד וַיְהִי | כְּמִשְׁלֹשׁ חֳדָשִׁים וַיֻּגַּד לִיהוּדָה לֵאמֹר זָנְתָה תָּמָר כַּלָּתֶךָ וְגַם הִנֵּה הָרָה לִזְנוּנִים וַיֹּאמֶר יְהוּדָה הוֹצִיאוּהָ וְתִשָּׂרֵף:

24. Judah is informed of Tamar's 'trespass.'

וַיְהִי כְּמִשְׁלֹשׁ חֳדָשִׁים — [*And*] *about three months passed.*

And her pregnancy became recognizable *(Abarbanel).*

[Not three *full* months, but] the greater parts of the first and third, and the entire middle [second] one (*Rashi* from *Yevamos* 43a).

In interpreting that Tamar's pregnancy became noticeable in *about,* but not after a full, three months, *Rashi* bases himself on *Niddah* 8a and the Midrash which state that in the case of a full-term, nine-month pregnancy, the presence of the fetus becomes recognizeable after three months [a trimester]. Since Tamar's twins were born after only *seven* months [see *Rashi* to *v.* 27] her pregnancy would be noticeable after a third of *her abbreviated term,* as *Rashi* puts it, the full second month and most of the first and third (*Mizrachi;* cf. *Levush; Sanhedrin* 69a).[1]

Rashi could have simplified his comment by saying 'two and a third months' instead of the more cumbersome 'greater parts of the first and third and all of the second months.' He based his interpretation on the Torah's term כְּמִשְׁלֹשׁ, literally *at the tripling,* or *trimester* [see below]. The expression implies that the three months were of roughly equal length, a phenomenon that occurred since the majority of a month can be regarded as a full month (*Mizrachi* cf. *Gur Aryeh).*

An illustration of *Rashi's* interpretation would be that Tamar conceived on the tenth of Nissan. Thus, the major part of Nissan passed; the whole of Iyar, and the major part of Sivan — when Judah was informed on the twentieth of Sivan *(Sefer Zikaron).*

The translation *'about three months passed'* captures the *sense* of the passage. *Rashi* [as explained by *Mizrachi* and *Dikdukei Rashi*] takes the word כְּמִשְׁלֹשׁ in the infinite sense with the temporal כ prefixed: *And it came to pass at the tripling of the months,* i.e., when the months became three, or when the months were about equally tripled [=trimester]. *Onkelos* renders similarly with the word כְּתַלְתוּת which is the infinitive of the verb תְּלַת. *Rashi* regards the word מִשְׁלֹחַ, *sending* [*Esther* 9:19] as another example of an infinitive construction with a מ preformative.

וַיֻּגַּד לִיהוּדָה — *And Judah was told* [lit. *and it was told to Judah*].

The word וַיֻּגַּד, *was told,* is spelled defectively [instead of וַיּוּגַּד]. According to *Midrash Sechel Tov* this intimates that the information was given 'defectively' — with malice and spite.

Tamar's pregnancy was a subject of boasting by Tamar herself. The *Midrash* records that she would go to the bathhouse and boast: 'Prophets and Redeemers will descend from me!'

וְגַם הִנֵּה הָרָה לִזְנוּנִים — *And moreover, she has conceived by harlotry.*

The fact that she is pregnant is conclusive proof that she indeed played the harlot *(Rashbam).*

— And what is more, she didn't even attempt to hide her shame to protect your honor! *(Sforno).*

1. [When halachic considerations are involved, we follow the marjority of women who carry a full nine-month term, and whose pregnancy can be ascertained conclusively three months after conception. This halachah applies to widows or divorcees who may not remarry until a total of ninety-one days have elapsed and it can be definitely established that they are not pregnant from their first husbands *(Toah Temimah).*]

38
24

24 *About three months passed, and Judah was told, 'Your daughter-in-law has committed harlotry, and moreover she has conceived by harlotry.' Judah said, 'Take her out and let her be burned!'*

The word לִזְנוּנִים, *by harlotry,* is in the plural intimating that the rumor was that Tamar's pregnancy was the result of repeated immorality. Those who engage in harlotry usually take precautions against conception; it was considered highly unlikely, therefore that Tamar could have become pregnant through an isolated incident *(Haamek Davar).*

Daas Zekeinim discusses why they made *two* charges: that Tamar had been guilty of immoral behavior and that 'furthermore *she was pregnant by harlotry.'* Possibly, acts of immorality were not punished in those times unless they resulted in pregnancy; and possibly [as the plural term זְנוּנִים denotes] they were punished only when harlotry was committed with more than one person.

The word הָרָה [with the accent on the second syllable, as in our passage] is an adjective, as in *Exod.* 21:22: אִשָּׁה הָרָה, *pregnant woman.* [Had the accent been on the first syllable, it would be a verb: she has conceived] *(Rashi).*

וַיֹּאמֶר יְהוּדָה — *[And] Judah said.*

According to *Tanchuma Yashan* a tribunal consisting of Isaac, Jacob and Judah sat in judgment on Tamar. The verdict was stated in the name of the junior member, Judah, since it was an erroneous [or *condemnatory;* Hebrew קַלְקָלָה (see *Torah Shelemiah* §98)] judgment.

R' David Cohen notes that the attribution of the judgment to Judah could be in consonance with the Talmudic dictum that the discussion of capital cases always begins with the youngest member of the court (*Sanhedrin* 36a). [This was done to avoid a situation where a senior member would rule for conviction and younger judges would be reluctant to disagree out of respect for his superior wisdom.]

הוֹצִיאוּהָ וְתִשָּׂרֵף — *Take her out and let her be burned!*

Rashi cites the *Midrash:* "Ephraim *'maksha'ah'* [so called because he was a scholar with great ability to debate (מַקְשֶׁה הֲלָכוֹת); or because he was a watchman of a cucumber (קִישּׁוּאִין) field *(Rashi* in *Midrash)*], a disciple of R' Meir, said in the name of R' Meir: Tamar was the daughter of Shem who was a priest [see *comm.* to 14:18 where Malchizedek, the priest, is identified with Shem]. Therefore they sentenced her to be burnt.

[Cf. *Lev.* 21:9: *The daughter of any priest who shall profane herself by playing the harlot* (i.e. who is unchaste after betrothal or marriage — (*Sanhedrin* 51b; see *Rashi* there); *she has thereby profaned her father: she shall be burned by fire.*]

Ramban differs with *Rashi's* Midrashic interpretation inasmuch as the halachah, as formulated in *Sanhedrin* 50b, is clear that the punishment of burning stated in *Leviticus* 21:9 [cited above] applies only to a priest's daughter who committed adultery while she was betrothed or married. The death penalty certainly does not apply to a woman who acted the harlot while, as in Tamar's case, she was waiting to be married by the *yabam* [cf. also *Sanhedrin* 58a].

Rather, *Ramban* continues, the intent is that Judah condemned her to this punishment not on legal grounds, but because he was a great chief, and his daughter-in-law's harlotry was an affront to his status, just as a priest's

כה הִוא מוּצֵאת וְהִיא שָׁלְחָה אֶל־חָמִיהָ
לֵאמֹר לְאִישׁ אֲשֶׁר־אֵלֶּה לּוֹ אָנֹכִי הָרָה
וַתֹּאמֶר הַכֶּר־נָא לְמִי הַחֹתֶמֶת
כו וְהַפְּתִילִים וְהַמַּטֶּה הָאֵלֶּה: וַיַּכֵּר יְהוּדָה

daughter who committed harlotry is condemned for having 'thereby profaned her father.' This judgment would not have been meted out to a commoner.

Alternatively, *Ramban* suggests that it is possible that their law was similar to the law current in Spain in *Ramban's* own time: That the punishment of an unfaithful woman was wholly at her husband's discretion. Since Tamar had been designated for Shelah, she was considered a married woman and Judah had the right to mete out punishment on his son's behalf.

Mizrachi defends *Rashi's* Midrashic citation by offering that the intent of the Midrash was only to explain why — once it was decided that Tamar was to be executed — the *form* of death decided upon was burning; that was because she was a daughter of Shem the priest. The reason that Judah ordered the death penalty at all may have been one of the following: (a) By committing an immoral act, she betrayed and defamed the aristocratic Judah. She deserved the death penalty much as one who transgressed against a king could be punished by death sentence through the crime itself, in other circumstances might not be a mortal one; (b) sexual immorality was rampant at the time, and the contingencies demanded that an example be made of Tamar to deter others from sinning [see cases cited in *Sanhedrin* 46a].

Gur Aryeh suggests that Tamar was given the death sentence because, after the Flood, Shem had legislated that immorality, even by an unmarried woman, is punishable by death. This tradition had come down to Judah from the Court of Shem [see *Avodah Zarah* 36b]. Because adultery by a married daughter of a priest is punishable by *burning* [*Leviticus* ibid.], Judah selected this punishment for Tamar as well.

[On the chronology of Tamar's being the daughter of Shem, see *comm.* to *v.* 6 s.v. וּשְׁמָהּ תָּמָר. See also footnote to *v.* 16.]

According to *R' Yehudah HaChassid* cited by *Baal HaTurim*, it was not Judah's intent to sentence her to death, but to *brand* her. *Rosh*, in *Responsa* §18:13 mentions that the custom of branding harlots was current even in his time.

What caused *R' Yehudah HaChassid* to deviate from the traditional interpretation?

Torah Temimah conjectures that his point of view is possibly based on the fact that whenever the Torah refers to death by burning, for example *Lev.* 20:14; 21:9, the term *burn* is always qualified by the term בָּאֵשׁ, *in fire*. Here that qualifying word is absent, and hence he interprets that the term *burn* connotes *disfiguring*, much as in the manner of *Ezekiel* 23:25. Once it was established however, that it was with Judah that she had consorted, the punishment was dropped.

25. הִוא מוּצֵאת — *As she was taken out.*

To be burnt *(Rashi)*.

[The word for *she*, הִיא, in our passage is spelled הוא meaning *he*, but vowelized הִוא, *she*.] R' Huna remarked: *'She* was being taken out' — She *and he* should have been taken out! [i.e., by the dual she/he spelling, the Torah intimates that they both shared the guilt; it was only due to Tamar's reluctance to shame Judah publicly (as noted below) that *she* was condemned to be burned and not he *(Rashi* in *Midrash)*] *(Midrash)*.

וְהִיא שָׁלְחָה אֶל חָמִיהָ — [*And*] *she sent* [word] *to her father-in-law.*

— Through those who were taking her out to be burned. What she sent was the following message to be transmitted *verbatim (R' Bachya)*.

לְאִישׁ אֲשֶׁר אֵלֶּה לוֹ אָנֹכִי הָרָה — *By the man to whom these belong I am with child.*

[25] *As she was taken out, she sent word to her*
father-in-law, as follows, 'By the man to whom these
belong I am with child.' And she said, 'Identify, if
you please, whose are this seal, this wrap, and this
staff.'
[26] *Judah recognized; and he said, 'She is right; it is*

Tamar did not shame Judah publicly by naming him as the father. She reasoned: 'If he admits it voluntarily, well and good; if not let them burn me, but let me not publicly disgrace him.' From this incident, the Sages taught [*Sotah* 10b]: 'One should rather let himself be thrown into a fiery furnace [as Tamar was ready to do] than expose his neighbor to public shame' *(Rashi).*[1]

[Comp. the behavior of Potiphar's wife discussed in footnote to 39:1.]

וַתֹּאמֶר הַכֶּר־נָא — *And she said, 'Recognize if you please'.*

The expression נָא [if you please] denotes a request [as distinct from *Onkelos* who renders the term as meaning *now*] *(Rashi).*

With the expression הַכֶּר־נָא [*recognize if you please* — is it your son's tunic or not? (37:32)] Judah had caused his father untold anguish. Now God repaid him 'measure for measure.' Tamar now made her accusation with that same expression, and its impact registered solidly upon Judah *(Sotah 10b; Midrash;* see *Maharsha* ad. loc. Cf. footnote next verse).

The inner intent of her request was: *'Recognize* — i.e. *acknowledge* your Creator. [Even if you would be tempted to feign ignorance of the pledges and your involvement with me because no witnesses were present — acknowledge your Creator Who is All knowing, and hide not your eyes from me *(Maharsha)*], and do not destroy three lives [— mine and the two children I am carrying, by consigning me to be burned]' *(Rashi* based on *Sotah* 10b).

Apparently, though others did not discover that Tamar was carrying twins until the time of her childbirth [*v.* 27], Tamar herself *was* prophetically aware even *then* that she was carrying twins. In fact according to the *Midrash* cited in *v.* 24, Tamar was even aware she was carrying children from whom royalty would descend! *(Maskil leDavid).*

26. 'She is more righteous than I!'

וַיַּכֵּר יְהוּדָה — *Judah recognized.*[2]

The measure-for-measure aspect

1. If the Torah makes a special point of telling us that Tamar sent back his pledges only at the last moment, when "she was brought forth" to be executed, then there was good reason for it, notes R' Eleazar in the *Midrash* [see also *Sotah* 10b]: She had mislaid the pledges and could not find them. This was the work of Satan who did his utmost to impede the entry of the Messianic dynasty into the world for he understood it as his most dangerous enemy. Tamar implored Divine Mercy with all her soul and just as she was being led to the stake she found the objects as if by miracle. Thus, historical destinies sometimes hang by a thread and their happy outcome is dependent on a miracle *(R' Munk).*

2. Now when Judah saw the pledges, he recognized them and thought: 'It is better for me to be ashamed in This transient World, than be ashamed before my righteous fathers in the

וַיֹּאמֶר צָדְקָה מִמֶּנִּי כִּי־עַל־כֵּן לֹא־
נְתַתִּיהָ לְשֵׁלָה בְנִי וְלֹא־יָסַף עוֹד
כז לְדַעְתָּהּ: וַיְהִי בְּעֵת לִדְתָּהּ וְהִנֵּה תְאוֹמִים

of Tamar's words הַכֶּר־נָא rang loudly in Judah's ears. See footnote.

צָדְקָה מִמֶּנִּי — *She is right; [it is] from me!*

The translation follows *Rashi* who renders: צָדְקָה, *she is right* in what she said; מִמֶּנִּי, *it is from me* that she is with child! [Cf. *Targum Yonasan:* 'Tamar is innocent; she is with child by me!']

Alternatively, *Rashi* cites the Sages that a *bas kol* [heavenly voice] came forth and said מִמֶּנִּי, i.e. 'From Me and My agency did these events unfold! [i.e., that these two people who are destined to be the ancestors of kings should have united in this manner]. Because Tamar was modest in her father-in-law's house [see *comm.* to *v.* 15], I have ordained that kings descend from her; and I have already ordained that I would make kings descend from the tribe of Judah.' [See *Overview*].

In citing the latter interpretation, *Rashi* follows: (a) The opinion in *Sotah* 10a that Judah could not have known that he was the father since she could have been intimate with others as well; (b) The opinion in *Makkos* 23b which cites this as one of the three tribunals where the Divine voice was heard.

According to *Rashbam* and *Ramban* [in an interpretation which more closely follows the traditional cantillation punctuation] צָדְקָה מִמֶּנִּי is to be interpreted in the *comparative* sense similar to *I Samuel* 24:18: *And Saul said to David: You are more righteous than I, for you have treated me well whereas I have treated you badly.* In our case, Judah said: *she is more righteous* [in this matter] *than I* — for she acted righteously in obeying My order to wait until Shelah grew up, but I did not keep my implied promise to let her marry Shelah when he was older. Since Shelah did not marry her as her brother-in-law, I was next in line to redeem her as her father-in-law [see *Ramban v.* 8].

'Her act of seducing me was ostensibly immoral, while my act in sending her the stipulated kid was ostensibly ethical — nevertheless, she was more righteous than I. For her intention was not for personal pleasure but only to bear children, while my intention was to recover my pledge and spare myself possible embarrassment.' As the Sages teach, a sin for the sake of heaven is greater than a selfish *mitzvah (Sforno).*

She is more righteous than I — My intention was an act of harlotry, when her intention was to fulfill the *mitzvah* of *yibum (R' Bachya).*

כִּי־עַל־כֵּן לֹא נְתַתִּיהָ לְשֵׁלָה בְנִי — *Inasmuch as* [lit. *for therefore*] *I did not give her to Shelah my son.*

The elliptical intent is: כִּי, *for* she has acted rightly, עַל־כֵּן=עַל־אֲשֶׁר *inasmuch as* I did not give her to Shelah my son *(Rashi).*

[Cf. *Rashi's* interpretation of the idiomatic expression כִּי־עַל־כֵּן in 18:5 and 33:10.]

... I acknowledge that Tamar is innocent. She is pregnant from me not because she yielded to any illicit passion, but because I did not give her my son Shelah.' A Divine voice then rang out and proclaimed, 'You are both innocent, for it was by My will that this has come to pass!' *(Targum Yerushalmi).*

When the Divine Voice forgave Judah, the

World to Come; it is better that I burn in this world with extinguishable fire, than burn in the World to Come with ever-consuming fire. For measure is set against measure. I used the same expression to my father when I asked him to identify his son's tunic and I am now constrained to hear at my judgment that I identify my signet, wrap and staff ...' *(Targum Yonasan).*

from me, inasmuch as I did not give her to Shelah my son.' And he was not intimate with her anymore.
27 And it came to pass at the time she gave birth
that behold! There were twins in her womb. 28 And it

Ministering Angels began chanting: בָּרוּךְ אַתָּה ה׳ חַנּוּן הַמַּרְבֶּה לִסְלוֹחַ, *Blessed are You* HASHEM, *the Compassionate One, Who forgives abundantly (Midrash* of the *Shemoneh Esrei Prayer* [*Beth HaMidrash* 5:54a; *Torah Sheleimah* §115).

According to a view in *Mechilta Beshallach* §5, when Reuben heard Judah confess, he too arose and [for the first time *publicly*] confessed regarding his desecration of his father's couch [see above 35:22 and comm. to 37:29 s.v. וַיָּשָׁב רְאוּבֵן. See also *Rashi* to *Deut.* 33:7 s.v. וְזֹאת לִיהוּדָה].

The *Talmud* [*Sotah* 10b] notes that when Judah made this admission, his name יְהוּדָה — containing the dual meaning of the verb הדה, *thank* (29:35) and *admit* — finally acquired its full significance. HASHEM fully associated His Name, הוי״ה, with יהודה, thereby showing His affection for the one who has the moral courage to confess his sins publicly *(R' Munk).*

וְלֹא יָסַף עוֹד לְדַעְתָּהּ — *And he was not intimate with her any more* [lit. *and he did not continue to know her more;* as noted in 4:1 ידע is used throughout Scripture as a delicate term for marital intimacy.]

[The translation follows the primary view of *Rashi, Onkelos,* and most commentators]:

Some understand לֹא יָסַף as *he did not continue,* while others explain the verb to mean *he did not cease* to be intimate with her thenceforth. A similar case is in *Numbers* 11:25 where וְלֹא יָסָפוּ [*and they did not continue to prophesy*] is rendered by *Onkelos* 'and they did not *cease* to prophesy' *(Rashi;* cf. *Sotah* 10b; see also *Rashi* to *Numbers* 11:25 and *Deut.* 5:19).

The view that he was *not* intimate with her any more is based on the explanation that once Judah established progeny — that being his primary goal — it was his wish not to be intimate with her any further, even though a *yebamah* is considered a legitimate wife to the one who performs *yibum.* The fact that she *was* permitted to him was the very reason the other Sage explains our passage to infer that *he did not cease* being intimate with her. See *Deut.* 5:19 *(Ramban).*

Rashi in *Sotah* 10b explains the latter view by commenting that once the Divine Voice established that Tamar was righteous and had acted with the loftiest motives, Judah did not cease conducting himself with her as his full wife in every respect.

Possibly he did not continue to be intimate with her because the sight of her evoked memories of the sordid circumstances by which he first consorted with her. She was certainly prohibited to Shelah because she was now Judah's full wife in every sense *(Oznaim l'Torah).*

27. Tamar bears twins.

וַיְהִי בְּעֵת לִדְתָּהּ — *And it came to pass at the time she gave birth* [lit. *at the time of her childbearing*].

The *Midrash* draws a distinction between the phraseology here and the similar phraseology in regard to Rebecca's birth of Jacob and Esau [28:25:24]:

In the case of Rebecca the verse reads וַיִּמְלְאוּ יָמֶיהָ לָלֶדֶת, *when her term to bear grew full,* because her term of pregnancy was complete; Tamar, however, did not carry a full term [she bore in the seventh month as noted above in *v.* 24] *(Rashi).*

וְהִנֵּה תְאוֹמִים בְּבִטְנָהּ — *That behold! There were twins in her womb.*

כח בְּבִטְנָהּ: וַיְהִי בְלִדְתָּהּ וַיִּתֶּן־יָד וַתִּקַּח
הַמְיַלֶּדֶת וַתִּקְשֹׁר עַל־יָדוֹ שָׁנִי לֵאמֹר
כט זֶה יָצָא רִאשֹׁנָה: וַיְהִי | כְּמֵשִׁיב יָדוֹ
וְהִנֵּה יָצָא אָחִיו וַתֹּאמֶר מַה־פָּרַצְתָּ
ל עָלֶיךָ פָּרֶץ וַיִּקְרָא שְׁמוֹ פָּרֶץ: וְאַחַר

They recognized this before the first child emerged, therefore, as the narrative continues, they tied the thread on the hand of the first *(Sforno)*.

[Continuing the comparison with 25:24]: In our case the word for twins, תְּאוֹמִים, is spelled 'full,' while in the case of Esau and Jacob it is spelled 'defectively': תוֹמִם. In the latter case, one of them [i.e., Esau] was wicked [and therefore their similarity as twins was incomplete], while in the case of Tamar both were righteous [and they were תְּאוֹמִים, *twins*, in the fullest sense of the word] *(Rashi)*.

That she bore twins is significant: Tamar's two sons took the place of her two husbands who died: Peretz took Er's place, while Zerach replaced Onan *(Alshich)*.

28. וַיִּתֶּן־יָד — *One* [lit. *and he*] *put out* [lit. *gave*] *a hand.*

I.e. one of them stretched forth his hand outside *(Rashi)*.

Since they were as yet unnamed the Torah writes abstractly: *he* (unnamed) *stuck out his hand (Ibn Ezra).*

Because our passage associates *giving birth* with the one sticking out his hand, R' Huna ruled that the ritual uncleanness associated with giving birth [*Lev.* 12:2] technically begins with the moment part of the embryo begins to emerge, even though he might subsequently draw back *(Niddah* 28a).

וַתִּקְשֹׁר עַל יָדוֹ שָׁנִי לֵאמֹר — *And* [*she*] *tied a crimson* [thread] *on his hand, saying* [i.e., as if to signify].

It was her intent to be able to identify this as the first born *(Sforno)*.

זֶה יָצָא רִאשֹׁנָה — *This one emerged first.*

From this verse *Yerushalmi Bava Basra* 3:1 derives that the testimony of a midwife is accepted, provided it is given immediately after birth [cf. *Bavli Kiddushin* 74a].

29. 'Peretz.

וַיְהִי כְּמֵשִׁיב יָדוֹ — *And it was, as he drew back* [lit. *returned*] *his hand.*

For after the midwife tied the scarlet thread on his hand he drew it back *(Rashi v.* 28).

Cf. *Ramban* to 40:10 who explains that this usage of the כ is temporal and denotes immediacy: *As soon as he drew back his hand.*

According to *Sforno*, he was **כְּמֵשִׁיב יָד**, *like* one who drew back his hand — for he did not really draw it back of his own *independent* power; it was the pressure of the second emerging child that forced his hand back.

וְהִנֵּה יָצָא אָחִיו — *That* [lit. *and*] *behold! his brother emerged.*

— By his own power; without the midwife's assistance *(Abarbanel)*.

This was part of the Divine plan. For Zerach desired to emerge first but God declared: Messiah is destined to descend from Peretz; is it right, then, that Zerach should emerge first? Let Zerach return to his mother's womb, and Peretz shall be born first! *(Aggadas Bereishis* 64, *Torah Sheleimah* §128).

מַה־פָּרַצְתָּ עָלֶיךָ פָּרֶץ — [*With*] *what strength* [Hebrew: *peretz*] *you as-*

38 *happened that as she gave birth, one put out a hand;*
29 *the midwife took a crimson thread and tied it on his*
hand saying, 'This one emerged first!' 29 *And it was,*
as he drew back his hand, that behold! his brother
emerged. And she said, 'With what strength you as-
serted yourself!' And he named him Peretz.

serted yourself! [lit. *you were strong*].

— [As demonstrated by your emerging first, notwithstanding the fact that your brother had already stuck his hand out.]

The translation of פרץ as denoting *strength* follows *Rashi,* and is consistent with his interpretation of the verb וּפָרַצְתָּ in 28:14.

According to *Ramban,* the verb literally denotes the *breaching* of a fence, while more generally it refers to anything that oversteps its normal boundary. The latter is its meaning in 28:14 [referring to the conquest of land] and in 30:43 [where it refers to increase in wealth to the extent that one metaphorically *burst through barriers* until the region could not contain him; see *Radak* there]. In our context, her intent was: "What a great breach you have made in the 'fence' restraining you by hurrying out before your brother!"[1]

According to *Ibn Ezra* and *Radak,* the intent is, "Oh, how you have made a breach, and now the responsibility for the breach is upon you!" [That is, had your brother died because of your hurried breach, you would have been held responsible just as a thief who breaches a wall is held accountable for the damage he causes thereby. See *HaKsav V'HaKaballah.*] *Ramban* disagrees with this interpretation.

וַיִּקְרָא שְׁמוֹ פָּרֶץ — *And he named him Peretz.*[1]

I.e., *Judah* named the child *Peretz* [meaning *strength (Rashi)* or: *breaking forth (Ramban)*] because of what the midwife had said *(Radak).*

[Peretz was the ancestor of the House of David from whom the Messsiah would descend. His line of descendants were: Chetzron, Ram, Aminadab, Nachshon, Shalmon, Boaz, Obed, Jesse and David (see *Ruth* 4:18-22).]

Peretz's action in 'breaking forth' is an indication of the royal privilege which will subsequently be held by his descendants. For the king 'has a right to open a breach for himself [מֶלֶךְ פּוֹרֵץ גָּדֵר, lit. *a king may breach fences blocking his direct path*]; without anyone having the authority to stop him' [*Sanhedrin* 20b] *(R' Munk).*

1. Kabbalistically, the names Peretz and Zerach have great mystical significance.

Zerach [shining] was so called on account of the sun which always shines, and *Peretz* [breach] on account of the moon which is sometimes breached [i.e. its light is sometimes hidden (at the end of a month) and sometimes completely intact. But Peretz [symbolizing the moon] was the first born, although the sun is greater than the moon? [I.e. why should the firstborn be symbolized by the smaller orb?] — In a sense Zerach, who stuck out his hand first, *was* to be the firstborn; but Peretz, the ancestor of the House of David, was given the Divine privilege of actually being the first born. The Davidic dynasty is likened to the moon because it underwent various stages of ascendancy and descendancy.

Since the Davidic dynasty evolved from Peretz who was likened to the moon, the Talmudic Sages [see *Rosh HaShanah* 25a], — when wishing to inform the Jews in other countries that the New Moon had appeared and been sanctified, would use the message 'David King of Israel lives and exists' *(Ramban* citing *Sefer HaBahir;* see *comm.* ad. loc. of *R' Chavel).*

יָצָא אָחִיו אֲשֶׁר עַל־יָדוֹ הַשָּׁנִי וַיִּקְרָא שְׁמוֹ זָרַח: °חמישי א °וְיוֹסֵף הוּרַד מִצְרָיְמָה וַיִּקְנֵהוּ פּוֹטִיפַר סְרִיס

30. Zerach.

אֲשֶׁר עַל־יָדוֹ הַשָּׁנִי — *On whose hand was the crimson* [*thread*].

Citing the *Midrash, Rashi* records that the word יַד, *hand,* occurs four times in this narrative, alluding to the four times that Achan, a descendant of Zerach, 'stretched forth his hand' to violate prohibitions (some by Moses and some by Joshua) against enjoying the spoils of various victories over the enemies of Israel. Thus, the four 'hands' signify four separate crimes.

Alternatively, the four references to *hand* allude only to the four items Achan took [from the spoils of Jericho; see *Joshua* ibid. *v.* 21]: A mantle from Shinar; two pieces of silver weighing two hundred *shekel*-weights; and a wedge of gold.

The commentators raise the problem that the Talmud and *Midrash* enumerate a total of *five* such infractions committed by Achan — four in Moses' time and the fifth, at Jericho, in Joshua's time. *Gur Aryeh* suggests that there are two sets of four violations each: four separate occasions against Moses' order and the theft at Jericho when Achan took four individual items.

זָרַח — *Zerach.*

— *Brightness.* Alluding to the brightness of the crimson thread *(Rashi).*

The name Zerach also alludes to how he shone forth [זָרַח] by appearing, at least momentarily, before his brother *(Midrash HaGadol).*

Malbim notes that from Zerach there descended prophets and men who acquired רוּחַ הַקֹּדֶשׁ, the Divine Spirit — [Ethan the Ezrachite, Heiman, Kalkol and Darda [see *I Kings* 5:11] upon whom were the 'hand of God'. Since Peretz was to be the ancestor of *kings,* he had precedence in being the first born.

XXXIX

1. Joseph in Egypt.

The Torah takes up the thread temporarily dropped because of the Judah/Tamar interlude. As noted in 38:1, Judah's degradation had been interpolated at this point because it was his role in the sale of Joseph that caused the brothers to lower him from his leadership status. Furthermore, the close proximity of the narratives of Tamar and Potiphar's wife indicates that both women had pure motives [both of them desiring to found a family in Israel.] For Potiphar's wife had foreseen by astrological signs that she was destined to be the ancestress of children by Joseph — but she did not know whether *she* or her daughter would have the children. [According to tradition, Joseph married her daughter. See *Rashi* to 41:45] *(Rashi).*[1]

וְיוֹסֵף הוּרַד מִצְרָיְמָה — [*And*] *Joseph*

1. If both of them acted with equal sincerity, why has Tamar entered Jewish history as a woman of great virtue while Potiphar's wife is remembered as a symbol of infidelity and treachery?

The difference lies not in their commendable ambitions but in their reaction to adversity.

38 [30] *Afterwards his brother on whose hand was the*
30 *crimson thread came out. And he named him Zerach.*

39 [1] *And Joseph had been brought down to Egypt.*
1 *Potiphar, a courtier of Pharaoh, the Chamberlain*

had been brought down to Egypt.

[The verb הוּרַד, *had been brought down*, is in past perfect indicating that this had already taken place in the distant past — not at this moment in the narrative. The sense of our passage is accordingly]:

During the interim — when Judah separated from his brothers and the episode of Tamar occurred — *Joseph had been brought down to Egypt (Sforno).*

Before Joseph's descent into Egypt — marking the beginning of the first Exile — Judah had already produced the ancestor of the Final Redeemer, the King Messiah who will descend from Peretz *(Daas Zekeinim).*[2]

That Joseph was brought into Egypt was already mentioned in 37:36. It is now repeated in order to resume the narrative of Joseph from the point it was left off *(Radak.* [See *Abarbanel* below.]

פּוֹטִיפַר סְרִיס פַּרְעֹה שַׂר הַטַּבָּחִים — *Potiphar, a courtier of Pharaoh, the Chamberlain of the Butchers.*

This is repeated from 37:36 to emphasize the Providential Hand in this matter. Joseph could have been carried off to a far-away land and made to do menial slave-work. Instead he was brought to Egypt,

Tamar accepts the death sentence in silence rather than humiliate Judah. But, in contrast, when the wife of Potiphar sees her incessant blandishments resisted by Joseph [see *v.* 10 below] she publicly slanders and effects the disgrace and imprisonment of an innocent man *(R' Munk)* [cf. footnote to 40:1].

2. **Prelude to Exile.**

Joseph's descent into Egypt was, as the Sages perceive, the prelude to the Egyptian exile foretold to Abraham at the Covenant Between the Parts [15:13].

The phrase וְיוֹסֵף הוּרַד מִצְרָיְמָה, *Joseph had been brought down to Egypt,* has, according to *Tanchuma Yashan,* the deeper implication that 'Joseph *brought down* [הוֹרִיד] his father and the tribal ancestors to Egypt. That is, God engineered Joseph's descent into Egypt in order to implement His decree that Jacob would be exiled, but to spare him harshness of a *forced descent* into hostile conditions.

As R' Yitzchak is quoted in Shabbos 89b: רָאוּי הָיָה יַעֲקֹב אָבִינוּ לֵירֵד לְמִצְרַיִם בְּשַׁלְשְׁלָאוֹת שֶׁל בַּרְזֶל אֶלָּא שֶׁזְּכוּתוֹ גָּרְמָה לוֹ, *It would have been fitting for our father Jacob to go down to Egypt in iron chains* [in the manner of all exiles, since it was by God's Decree that he went there (*Rashi* ad. loc.)], *but his merit availed him* [that he should go instead as Joseph's honored guest], *for it is written* [*Hoshea* 11:4]: *I drew them with human ties, with cords of love.*

Midrash Tanchuma elaborates: *Joseph was brought down to Egypt* — this is the intent of the verse in *Hoshea* [cited above]; for Joseph's earlier descent to Egypt caused Jacob to follow him honorably and begin the exile. The matter may be compared to a cow refusing to be dragged to its work. Rather than dragging her in chains, her calf was taken away from her and led to the field. When the cow heard her calf bleating, she went there willingly, for the sake of the calf.

Thus, Joseph's descent to Egypt was divinely orchestrated so Jacob and his sons should eventually follow in honor [see *Oznaim l'Torah* cited in footnote to 37:15, and *Overview*].

According to *Hadar Zekeinim,* Joseph was not brought down to Egypt alone: The Divine Presence, as it were, descended with him.

פַּרְעֹה שַׂר הַטַּבָּחִים אִישׁ מִצְרִי מִיַּד
ב הַיִּשְׁמְעֵאלִים אֲשֶׁר הוֹרִדֻהוּ שָׁמָּה: וַיְהִי
יהוה אֶת־יוֹסֵף וַיְהִי אִישׁ מַצְלִיחַ וַיְהִי

the greatest metropolis of the time, to the home of one of Pharaoh's courtiers, a man who, as we see later, was in charge of the prison where Joseph was eventually incarcerated.

The translation of of סָרִיס as *courtier* follows *Onkelos.* See *comm.* to 37:36. The translation of שַׂר הַטַּבָּחִים as *chamberlain of the butchers* follows *Rashi* in 37:36. Most others translate הַטַּבָּחִים as *executioner,* which is how *R' Bachya* to our verse also interprets the term, citing parallel meanings in *Jeremiah* 39:13; *II Kings* 25:11; *Daniel* 2:14. *Rashbam* interprets the term as referring to the officer in charge of condemned criminals and other prisoners.

The *Midrash* notes that Potiphar is identical with Potiphera [whose daughter Joseph later married (41:45).] He was called *Potiphar* because he fattened bulls [מְפַטֵּם פָּרִים, *m'fatem parim*] for idolatrous purposes.

The Sages in *Sotah* 13b [who understand סָרִיס in the familiar sense of *eunuch, castrate*] maintain that Potiphar purchased Joseph for purposes of sodomy, but Gabriel was dispatched to castrate and then mutilate him [פרע, *Phera,* referring to the removal of the *membrum*]; hence he was later called *Potiphera.*

Rashi in *Sanhedrin* 92b mentions that it was the custom of ancient kings to castrate their court officials so they would not marry and instead be devoted entirely to the service of the monarch.

According to *Ramban* below [*v.* 19], Potiphar had married as a youth, and later fell victim to a disease which made him impotent and lack desire for conjugal relations.

אִישׁ מִצְרִי — *A prominent Egyptian* [lit. *an Egyptian man*].

[The term *prominent* is suggested by the superfluous appellation אִישׁ, *man,* which in Scriptural usage is usually reserved for an important personage.]

According to the *Midrash,* the term is descriptive: A man who possessed the proverbial wisdom of the Egyptian.

Maharil Diskin interprets: *An Egyptian resident* — and hence entitled to own a slave.

R' Hirsch notes the repeated mention that Potiphar was an *Egyptian.* That such was his nationality was self-evident from the mere fact that he was a high official in Pharaoh's court. Rather the word must be understood to reflect his attitude and morals. The 'elite' Egyptians looked with contempt upon the nomads of Canaan, and Joseph's moral code could hardly have differed more sharply from that of the lecherous Egyptians. That Joseph could have succeeded to such a degree in an 'Egyptian' society is the best testimony to his unusual ability and intelligence.

וַיִּקְנֵהוּ ... מִיַּד הַיִּשְׁמְעֵאלִים אֲשֶׁר הוֹרִדֻהוּ שָׁמָּה — [*And he*] *purchased him from* [*the hand of*] *the Ishmaelites who had brought him down there.*

In 37:27, the *Medanites,* rather than the Ishmaelites, are described as having sold Joseph into Egypt. This discrepancy and the various reconciliations of the sequence of the sale have been fully dealt with in 37:27: "Who sold Joseph?" But a brief summary — as the discrepancy directly relates to our verse — is in order.

To recapitulate:

It is not clear how *Rashi* — who main-

39 *of the Butchers, a prominent Egyptian, purchased*
2 *him from the Ishmaelites who had brought him down*
there. 2 *HASHEM was with Joseph, and he became a*

tains that the Medanites/Midianites bought Joseph from the Ishmaelites and then sold him into Egypt — reconciles with our verse. *Daas Zekeinim* postulates that our verse intimates that Potiphar agreed to purchase Joseph only after the Ishmaelites gave their *hand* to guarantee that Joseph had indeed become the property of the Medanites. [Comp. *Midrash Tanchuma* in 37:36.]

Ramban maintains that the Ishmaelite caravan owners hauled Joseph to Egypt on behalf of the Midianites; hence the sale was attributed *indirectly* to them since they were the ones *who had brought him down there,* and the Torah refers to them alternately as Ishmaelites and Midianites.

Ibn Ezra maintains that the Torah refers to the Midianites and Ishmaelites interchangeably because they are kinsmen. *Gur Aryeh* elaborates and explains that the term *Ishmaelite* was the common designation for the clan which included the Midianites. Our verse intimates that Potiphar assumed by their dress that they were Ishmaelites, but the Torah, in 37:28, informed us that they were really Midianites.

The *Midrash* notes the proverbial irony and obvious Hand of Providence in this sale:

R' Levi remarked: A slave buys, the son of a slave woman sells, and a free man is slave to both! [That is, the purchaser was Potiphar — a descendant of Ham whom Noah had cursed that he should be a 'slave's slave to his brothers' (9:25), and who was now a slave to Pharaoh; the sellers were the Ishmaelites, descendants of Abraham's slave Hagar; and the slave of such people was Joseph, the firstborn son of Jacob's favorite wife.]

Although Joseph was urged to answer questions about his origin, he admitted only that he was an Ivri [Hebrew]. He divulged no more, and kept the oath of secrecy that was imposed upon him against attempting to return to his father, or revealing his identity *(Midrash HaGadol)* [see footnote to 37:28; *Ramban* to 42:9 below; *Rashi* to 45:27].

2. וַיְהִי ה׳ אֶת יוֹסֵף — *[And] HASHEM was with Joseph.*

— Enabling him to withstand spiritual absorption by his heathen captors *(Chizkuni).*

— Protecting him from his enemies *(Sforno).*

The connotation of God being 'with' someone, an expression occurring often in Scripture [usually עִם rather than אֶת occurs], refers to Providence watching over the details of man's various activities according to the degree of man's perfection *(Rambam: Moreh Nevuchim* 3:18, see comm. to 28:15).[1]

The word אֶת denotes an exegetical amplification [רִבּוּי]: Not only was HASHEM with Joseph, but with everyone with whom he came in contact. Compare the case of Lot who accumulated great wealth merely by virtue of accompanying Abraham [see 13:5] *(Vayaged Yaakov).*

Abarbanel comments that each of the three stiches in this verse is introduced by the word וַיְהִי. God's special Providential beneficence was present in

1. According to *R' Hirsch* the triple mention of וַיְהִי in this verse evokes the Rabbinic observation that the other brothers required no special Divine care because they were together in the company of Jacob and their families. Joseph, however, was an isolated outcast from his family, thrown into the most incongenial circumstances. He needed God to be always near and 'with' him. But conversely, if *God was with Joseph,* that could only have been because Joseph

ג בְּבֵית אֲדֹנָיו הַמִּצְרִי׃ וַיַּרְא אֲדֹנָיו כִּי
יְהוָה אִתּוֹ וְכֹל אֲשֶׁר־הוּא עֹשֶׂה יְהוָה
ד מַצְלִיחַ בְּיָדוֹ׃ וַיִּמְצָא יוֹסֵף חֵן בְּעֵינָיו
וַיְשָׁרֶת אֹתוֹ וַיַּפְקִדֵהוּ עַל־בֵּיתוֹ וְכָל־יֶשׁ־

each happening. The stich *HASHEM was with Joseph* alludes to the fact that he was divinely inspired to interpret dreams with *absolute* accuracy, an impossible feat had he relied merely on human wisdom.

— He enjoyed a special Providential success, transcending the natural *(Malbim).*

וַיְהִי אִישׁ מַצְלִיחַ — *And he became a successful man.*

In accomplishing whatever was required of him *(Sforno; Abarbanel).*

— Joseph's success was especially striking in view of the adverse factors facing him. *He was in the house of his master* — and natural success usually comes to one who is his own master; otherwise, his success is not considered his but his master's. Furthermore his master was *Egyptian*, a further negative factor in the view of Divine Providence *(Malbim).*

Ksav Sofer notes that מַצְלִיחַ is in the causative form: his mere presence *caused others* as well to prosper.

וַיְהִי בְּבֵית אֲדֹנָיו הַמִּצְרִי — [*And*] *he remained* [lit. *was*] *in the house of his Egyptian master.*

— This is yet another manifestation of God's beneficent Providence: Although most slaves are consigned to strenuous labor in the *field*, Joseph was given a relatively easy job *inside* the Egyptian's house *(Abarbanel).*

Furthermore, Providence caused him to work near his master and mistress at jobs in which he could distinguish himself. Indeed that soon became the case *(Ibn Caspi).*

Here the title of distinction אִישׁ is omitted because, as noted above, Potiphar's lewd designs on Joseph resulted in his castration by the angel Gabriel *(R' Shea Brander).*

3. וַיַּרְא אֲדֹנָיו כִּי ה׳ אִתּוֹ — [*And*] *his master perceived* [lit. *saw*] *that HASHEM was with him.*[1]

I.e., God's Name was always in his mouth *(Rashi* from *Midrash).*

[The sense is that Joseph would invoke God's Name whenever he undertook a task.]

According to *Ramban*, the phrase intimates that Potiphar concluded from Joseph's unusual success in all his endeavors, that he was aided by God. The phrase is similar to 26:28: *We have indeed seen that HASHEM has been with you* — which indicates a perception of Divinely granted success.

Rashi, however, disagrees with *Ramban's*

was with God. If man's own aspirations coincide with God's purpose, then He arranges circumstances conducive to their achievement.

Midrashically — as has been often noted in this commentary — the word וַיְהִי introduces a sad event. An objection was raised on the basis of our verse: *HASHEM was with* [וַיְהִי] *Joseph and he became* [וַיְהִי] *a successful man* — which would certainly imply an occasion for rejoicing?

R' Shmuel replied: This instance, too, is not a cause for joy; it was because of Joseph's success that Potiphar's wife assailed him *(Vayikra Rabbah* 11:7).

1. The first rays of the Divine light penetrated the spiritual darkness of Egypt only thanks to Joseph's presence. As the Sages teach, the *Shechinah* had 'accompanied' him there, and it hovered over him so plainly that even Potiphar could 'see' it *(R' Hirsch; R' Munk).*

39 *successful man; he remained in the house of his*
3-4 *Egyptian master.* [3] *His master perceived that*
HASHEM was with him, and whatever he did
HASHEM made succeed through him. [4] *Joseph found*
favor in his eyes, and he attended him. He appointed
him over his household, and whatever he had he

interpretation since the very next phrase of our verse explicitly mentions Joseph's success. Therefore, *Rashi* prefers the Midrashic interpretation that this stich speaks of Joseph's constant invocation of God's Name *(Gur Aryeh).*

According to another view in the *Midrash* [cited by *Ramban* in *v.* 4], because Joseph was always whispering HASHEM's Name, Potiphar accused him of sorcery, until, as this verse tells us, *His master perceived* — i.e., in a dream or some other form of vision — that HASHEM was with him. Potiphar was shown the Divine Presence standing over Joseph; only then did *Joseph find favor in his sight,* and Potiphar realized that Joseph's success was God-given.

[This view, that the wicked Potiphar could have perceived — even in a dream — the Divine Presence, is disputed by the former Midrashic view (cited in part by *Rashi*) that *HASHEM is with him* means that God's Name never left Joseph's lips, a phenomenon that convinced Potiphar of Joseph's Godliness.]

The noun אָדוֹן, *master,* often occurs in the plural form, as do other nouns denoting power or lordship, for example בַּעְלוֹ=בְּעָלָיו *(Rashi* to 35:8). In our passage the plural form אֲדֹנָיו has a singular connotation — *his master,* and takes a singular verb וַיַּרְא.]

וְכֹל אֲשֶׁר הוּא עֹשֶׂה ה׳ מַצְלִיחַ בְּיָדוֹ — *And* [*that*] *whatever he did* [lit. *does*] *HASHEM made succeed through him* [lit. *in his hand*].

— Even those undertakings that would have failed had they been undertaken by someone else *(Malbim).*

In his hand idiomatically denotes immediacy — whatever he undertook succeeded immediately *(Minchah Belulah).*

The *Midrash* takes *in his hand* literally: If Potiphar would bid Joseph, 'Mix me a hot drink,' he would obey immediately; likewise if he would say, 'Mix me a cold drink'; 'Give me strong wine'; or 'Give me diluted wine.' In every case Joseph would serve it immediately for it miraculously changed of itself in his hand. For *whatever he did, HASHEM made succeed in his hand.*

[It is not clear how *Ramban* would interpret the apparent redundancy in this verse except to maintain that it clarifies the earlier stich by explaining that Potiphar was able to perceive Joseph's unusual success as God-given since it was obvious in everything he undertook.]

4. As a result of his perception that Joseph was Divinely assisted, Potiphar took a special liking to him. First he made him his personal attendant, and afterwards appointed him over his house.

וַיְשָׁרֶת אֹתוֹ — *And he attended him.*

I.e., Joseph became his *personal* attendant, and was freed from all other tasks *(Sforno; Hirsch; Haamek Davar).*

He served אֹתוֹ, his master, exclusively, and none other *(Malbim).*

וְכָל־יֶשׁ־לוֹ נָתַן בְּיָדוֹ — *And whatever* [lit. *all*] *he had he placed in his custody* [*lit. hand*].[1]

1. Following the *Midrash* cited above that everything Joseph took into his hands prospered, this verse intimates that Potiphar would bring Joseph all merchandise he planned to sell. Joseph would merely touch it and he could command the highest profit *(Tzeidah LaDerech).*

ה לוֹ נָתַן בְּיָדוֹ: וַיְהִי מֵאָז הִפְקִיד אֹתוֹ
בְּבֵיתוֹ וְעַל כָּל־אֲשֶׁר יֶשׁ־לוֹ וַיְבָרֶךְ
יהוה אֶת־בֵּית הַמִּצְרִי בִּגְלַל יוֹסֵף וַיְהִי
בִּרְכַּת יהוה בְּכָל־אֲשֶׁר יֶשׁ־לוֹ בַּבַּיִת
ו וּבַשָּׂדֶה: וַיַּעֲזֹב כָּל־אֲשֶׁר־לוֹ בְּיַד־יוֹסֵף
וְלֹא־יָדַע אִתּוֹ מְאוּמָה כִּי אִם־הַלֶּחֶם
אֲשֶׁר־הוּא אוֹכֵל וַיְהִי יוֹסֵף יְפֵה־תֹאַר

— Potiphar appointed him overseer of all his possessions, both in his house and in his fields *(Ramban).*

He had Potiphar's fullest confidence in every domestic matter *(R' Bachya).*

The phrase וְכָל־יֶשׁ־לוֹ is elliptic and should be interpreted as if it read וְכָל־אֲשֶׁר־יֶשׁ־לוֹ *(Rashi).*

5. וַיְבָרֶךְ ה׳ אֶת בֵּית הַמִּצְרִי בִּגְלַל יוֹסֵף — *That* [lit. *and*] *HASHEM blessed the Egyptian's house on Joseph's account.*

— I.e. in his merit, since he was righteous *(Ramban* to a parallel expression in 30:27).

Although the Egyptian house should not have been worthy of any special Providential grace, it was blessed because of Joseph *(Malbim).*

The *Shechinah* accompanies the righteous and causes their environs to prosper. Isaac brought prosperity to Gerar [26:12], Jacob to Laban [30:30], and Joseph to Potiphar *(Midrash).*

Cf. *Berachos* 42a: תֵּיכֶף לת״ח בְּרָכָה, *a blessing promptly follows a scholar.* Our verse is cited.

בַּבַּיִת וּבַשָּׂדֶה — *In the house and* [*in*] *the field.*

Of the total of twelve months that Joseph spent in Potiphar's house [*Seder Olam*] six were *in the house* [intimating the cold, rainy season — when Joseph was in charge of domestic affairs] and six *in the field* [intimating the warm season when Joseph was in charge of the field work] *(Midrash).*

When he was in the fields, the fields were blessed; when in the house, the house was blessed *(Tanchuma).*

6. וְלֹא יָדַע אִתּוֹ מְאוּמָה — *And with him [present] he concerned himself with nothing.*

As long as Joseph was in attendance over his person and supervised his affairs, Potiphar felt secure that all was in good hands. Literally, the verse reads: *And he did not know with him anything.* The translation follows *Rashi.*

כִּי אִם־הַלֶּחֶם אֲשֶׁר הוּא אוֹכֵל — *Except for the bread he ate.*

This is a delicate expression; *bread* here refers to his wife *(Rashi).*

[The sense is that Potiphar unquestioningly entrusted to Joseph everything except for his own wife.]

Bread is a familiar euphemism for 'wife', and *eat* for conjugal intimacy. *Rashi* pursues this interpretation [following the *Midrash*], rather than *food* in the literal sense, because in *v.* 9 Joseph himself says that only Potiphar's wife was withheld from him in the house.

That Potiphar was, according to the Sages, a castrate [see *v.* 1] does not contradict this

placed in his custody.
5 And it happened, that from the time he appointed
him in his house and over whatever he had, HASHEM
blessed the Egyptian's house on Joseph's account, so
that HASHEM's blessing was in whatever he owned,
in the house and in the field. 6 He left all that he had
in Joseph's custody and with him present he con-
cerned himself with nothing except for the bread he
ate. Now Joseph was handsome of form and hand-
some of appearance.

passage which implies: except for the wife *with whom he consorted.* For the phrase does not imply present tense but past: *with whom he used to consort* before he was castrated as punishment for his lewd designs on Joseph. Furthermore there are varying degrees of 'castration' some affecting only the degree of desire *(Mizrachi; Gur Aryeh;* cf. *Daas Zekeinim* to *v.* 19).

According to *Ibn Ezra, bread* has the sense of 'food': Joseph was in charge of everything except the bread which Potiphar ate. This, Joseph was not even allowed to touch since Egyptians regarded it as an abomination for Hebrews to touch their food [see 43:22].

Ramban offers an alternative interpretation: Servants habitually steal from their masters, but Joseph was different; for himself, he took only the food to which he was entitled. Thus, Potiphar did not know of Joseph taking anything from him *except for the bread he* (Joseph) *ate.*

Tur interprets: Potiphar would not interfere at all in household matters; Joseph would have free reign of the house. Potiphar would give orders only regarding the kind of food he wanted each day.

וַיְהִי יוֹסֵף יְפֵה תֹאַר וִיפֵה מַרְאֶה — *Now Joseph was handsome of form and handsome of appearance.*

— Possessing handsome features and a radiant appearance [complexion] *(Rashi* to parallel expression in 29:17).

[See comm. to יְפַת מַרְאֶה in 12:11 and טֹבַת מַרְאֶה in 24:16.]

— In this Joseph resembled his mother [see 29:17] *(Ibn Ezra).*

As the *Midrash* observes: 'Throw a stick into the air and it falls back to its source.' Rachel was beautiful and so was Joseph.

This stich serves as an introduction to the following episode. It was on account of his good looks that his master's wife cast her gaze upon him *(Ramban).*

Citing the *Midrash, Rashi* explains the contextual placement of this passage here as it affects the continuity of the narrative:

When Joseph was given this important position, he began to eat, drink, and curl his hair. God said of him: 'Your father is mourning [for you] and you curl your hair! I will incite the bear [Potiphar's wife] against you.' Immediately [as implied by the expression אַחַר הַדְּבָרִים הָאֵלֶּה, *after these things* (see *Rashi* next verse)] ... *his master's wife cast her eyes upon Joseph.*[1]

1. The Midrashic metaphor of symbolically referring to Potiphar's wife as a 'bear' is not entirely clear.

Maharzu [*Bereishis Rabbah* 84:7] discusses this and cites an interpretation that the bear is shameless, as was Potiphar's wife.

R' David Feinstein conjectures that the metaphor reflects how Potiphar's wife was persis-

° ששי ז וִיפֵה מַרְאֶה: וַיְהִי אַחַר הַדְּבָרִים הָאֵלֶּה
וַתִּשָּׂא אֵשֶׁת־אֲדֹנָיו אֶת־עֵינֶיהָ אֶל־יוֹסֵף
ח וַתֹּאמֶר שִׁכְבָה עִמִּי: וַיְמָאֵן | וַיֹּאמֶר אֶל־
אֵשֶׁת אֲדֹנָיו הֵן אֲדֹנִי לֹא־יָדַע אִתִּי מַה־

Another view offered by the *Midrash* [see *Rashi* to 37:2] is that the temptation of his mistress was brought upon Joseph in retribution for his accusation against the brothers. He told Jacob that they cast their eyes on other women; as punishment, a woman cast her covetous eyes on him.

R' Hirsch notes the remarkable placement of the Torah's description of Joseph's good looks. Instead of mentioning them first, the Torah first lists all of Joseph's spiritual virtues and his successful management of Potiphar's affairs. Those virtues, not his handsome appearance, led to his speedy promotions. Potiphar's wife, too, was drawn to him primarily because of his outstanding character and achievement. His good looks were but the crowning feature in attracting here passionate attention.

This supports the Midrashic interpretation which maintains that Potiphar's wife's intentions were as pure as Tamar's [see *Rashi v.* 1] *(HaKsav V'HaKabbalah; Yalkut Yehudah).*

7. Potiphar's wife makes unwelcome advances to Joseph which he repels.

אַחַר הַדְּבָרִים הָאֵלֶּה — *After these things.*

As the Sages note in *Sotah* 33a, and as *Rashi* comments in 15:1, 22:1, 22:20, and here, the expression אַחַר הַדְּבָרִים הָאֵלֶּה signifies a *short* lapse of time from the preceding, or that the new event is dependent upon, and the direct result of the preceding one. The expression אַחֲרֵי הַדְּבָרִים הָאֵלֶּה in contrast, signifies a *long* lapse of time from the preceding, or that the narratives are not inherently unified. [See *Mizrachi* and *Gur Aryeh* cited in comm. to 22:20.]

In continuity with *Rashi's* comment to *v.* 6 above, the intent is that the advances of Potiphar's wife *immediately followed,* and were a *direct result* of, Joseph's aforementioned beauty [and his other qualities, as *R' Hirsch* observes]. According to *Rashi's* Midrashic interpretation, her seductions were a cause-and-effect result of Joseph's vain reaction to his new-found fortune and environment. He was overconfident, and God was testing his mettle.

Cf. *Alshich; Malbim:* The following events happened only *after these things* — i.e. only after she observed the handsome and exceptionally talented Joseph's dramatic rise to power in her husband's house. Before then, she would never have dreamt of consorting with a lowly slave.

וַתִּשָּׂא ... אֵשֶׁת־אֲדֹנָיו אֶת עֵינֶיהָ אֶל־יוֹסֵף — *His master's wife cast her eyes upon Joseph* [lit. *lifted up her eyes to Joseph*].

I.e., she became inflamed by his beauty. The expression *casting eyes* throughout Scripture denotes longing and desire. Cf. *Psalms* 123:1; *Ezekiel* 18:12.

The righteous are exalted through their eyes, but the wicked fall through their eyes *(Midrash).*

tant and relentless in her evil designs against Joseph. She was like the bear which the Talmud [*Kiddushin* 72a] describes as אֵין לָהֶם מְנוּחָה, *they have no rest.* The bear is restless and persistent in pursuing his desires. So, too, Potiphar's wife — she was dogged in her pursuit of Joseph. [Cf. also the metaphor of a bear in *Proverbs* 17:12.]

[7] *After these things, his master's wife cast her eyes upon Joseph and she said, 'Lie with me.'* [8] *But he adamantly refused. He said to his master's wife, 'Look — with me here, my master concerns himself*

The *Midrash* relates that Joseph was so exceptionally handsome [which was even more conspicuous in Egypt where, as *Rashi* notes in 12:11, the people were ugly], that the Egyptian women would come to gaze upon him. Once, Potiphar's wife gave them each an ethrog and a knife [to peel it with]. They became so overcome by Joseph's beauty that the knives slipped and they cut their hands.

'This is how you are affected when you see him only a moment,' she said to them. 'How much more so I who see him all day long!' She ceaselessly attempted to entice him, but he resisted temptation.

שִׁכְבָה עִמִּי — *Lie with me.*

Accursed are the wicked! Elsewhere we find Ruth delicately saying: *Spread your robe over your handmaid* [*Ruth* 3:9], but this one [Potiphar's wife] spoke like an animal, *Lie with me (Midrash).*

8. וַיְמָאֵ֓ן ׀ — *But* [lit. *and*] *he* [*adamantly*] *refused.*

[The adverb *adamantly* is suggested by the stacatto and emphatic cantillation by which this word is punctuated: the *shalsheles,* followed by the disjunctive *psik,* both of which set off the word and enhance the absoluteness of its implication. It indicates that Joseph's refusal was constant, categorical, and definitive. Joseph repulsed her with absolute firmness.]

Cf. *Haamek Davar:* The Torah thus attests to the fact that Joseph's refusal [further in this verse] was unequalized. The reason he later gives for his refusal was wrangled out of him by Potiphar's wife, but he himself had no need to rationalize it.[1]

There is a Talmudic view, however, that Joseph's resolve once weakened, but he saw the image of his father who admonished him: 'Joseph, Joseph! Your brothers' names will one day be inscribed in the High Priest's breastplate; would you want to be left out as a consort of an adulteress?' Thus he was inspired to resist her *(Sotah* 36b; see *Rashi* to *v.* 11 and to 49:22).

[The *Zohar* observes how Joseph was later rewarded with the same expression וַיְמָאֵן וַיֹּאמֶר, *but he refused and said*]: The Holy One, Blessed be He, declared, "Joseph! By your life these very words will some day be used on an occasion when your sons are to be blessed." Thus we read [48:19]: His father *refused* [to change his intended order of blessing Ephraim and Menashe] *and said,* 'I know, my son; I know.'

וַיֹּאמֶר אֶל אֵשֶׁת אֲדֹנָיו — [*And*] *he said to his master's wife.*

She is referred to as *his master's wife* to emphasize that as such, Joseph had reason to fear antagonizing her, but he feared God even more, and refused her advances *(Ramban).*

הֵן אֲדֹנִי לֹא יָדַע אִתִּי מַה בַּבָּיִת — *Look — with me here, my master con-*

1. In this regard, *Sfas Emes* makes a key point concerning human behavior. One must have a firm resolve concerning what he will or will not do; then he may seek to find a rationale that will make it palatable to himself and others. If he first seeks to rationalize what is right and what is wrong, he can easily fall prey to man's capacity for self-delusion.

Joseph began with a firm principle! He would not sin! Only then did he attempt to show that decency, etiquette, gratitude, or other considerations dictated the same course of conduct.

ט בַּבַּיִת וְכֹל אֲשֶׁר־יֶשׁ־לוֹ נָתַן בְּיָדִי: אֵינֶנּוּ
גָּדוֹל בַּבַּיִת הַזֶּה מִמֶּנִּי וְלֹא־חָשַׂךְ מִמֶּנִּי
מְאוּמָה כִּי אִם־אוֹתָךְ בַּאֲשֶׁר אַתְּ־אִשְׁתּוֹ
וְאֵיךְ אֶעֱשֶׂה הָרָעָה הַגְּדֹלָה הַזֹּאת
י וְחָטָאתִי לֵאלֹהִים: וַיְהִי כְּדַבְּרָהּ אֶל־יוֹסֵף
יוֹם | יוֹם וְלֹא־שָׁמַע אֵלֶיהָ לִשְׁכַּב אֶצְלָהּ

cerns himself about nothing in the house.

He has unbounded confidence in my capabilities ... and in my honesty *(R' Hirsch).*

How can I so ungratefully betray his confidence? *(Malbim; Haamek Davar).*

[Although, as noted, Joseph had no need to rationalize his refusal, and could have bluntly stated, 'How can you expect me to sin to God? He nevertheless tried to pacify her in terms she could understand so as not to incur the wrath of his master's wife, a person who had the power to harm him].

'I am mortally afraid of my master,' Joseph said. 'Then I will kill him,' she proposed.

'Is it not enough that you want to make me into an adulterer?' Joseph countered. 'Now you also want me to become an accomplice to murder!' *(Midrash).*

9. [Joseph presses further with the human aspect of his refusal. How can he be such an ingrate to the master who entrusted him with every one of his possessions except his wife?]

אֵינֶנּוּ גָּדוֹל בַּבַּיִת הַזֶּה מִמֶּנִּי — *There is no one greater in this house than I.*

The translation of אֵינֶנּוּ, as לֵית, *there is no one,* follows most editions of *Onkelos.*

Others render **אֵינֶנּוּ**, *he is not.* [Thus the antecedent of the pronoun *he* is Potiphar.] Joseph told her, *He* [i.e. Potiphar] *is not greater in this house than I* [i.e., even Potiphar himself wields no more authority in this house than he has bestowed upon me *(HaKsav VHaKabbalah)*].

— The honor he bestowed upon me is that he is not greater than I *(Malbim; Abarbanel).*

The latter interpretation is followed by many commentators and is apparently based on a different version of *Onkelos* which instead of לֵית [=אֵין, *there is not*] reads לֵיתוֹהִי [=אֵינֶנּוּ, *he is not*]. This version appears in many *Chumashim,* e.g. *Chorev, Malbim, Haamek Davar, Mechokekei Yehudah, Torah Temimah.*

The early commentary on *Onkelos, Ya'er,* defends the former version of *Onkelos.* He maintains that *Onkelos* subtly elicited the intent of the passage by translating the nuance as *there is no one greater,* rather than *he* [i.e. Potiphar] *is not greater.* This is a matter of etiquette because in fact the servant can never equal the higher status of his master, who appointed him and can dismiss him at will. [The Hebrew אֵינֶנּוּ is accordingly taken idiomatically: *One is not greater* in this house than I.]

כִּי אִם אוֹתָךְ בַּאֲשֶׁר אַתְּ אִשְׁתּוֹ — *But* [lit. *other than*] *you, since you are his wife.*

It was only in matters of conjugal relationship that he forbade us to be involved with one another. [In ordinary business or household matters I was in your service] *(Sforno).*

It is possible, also, that Potiphar once specifically warned Joseph

about nothing in the house, and whatever he has he placed in my custody. [9] *There is no one greater in this house than I, and he has denied me nothing but you, since you are his wife. How then can I perpetrate this great evil? I will have sinned against God!'*

[10] *And so it was — just as she coaxed Joseph day after day, so he would not listen to her to lie beside*

regarding his wife, for she was beautiful *(Radak).*

וְחָטָאתִי לֵאלֹהִים — *[And] I will have sinned against* [lit. *to*] *God!*

Apart from the wrong I would be doing against your husband, it would also be — as is all immorality — a sin against God *(Mizrachi).*

— Incest and adultery were forbidden to the descendants of Noah ['Noachides' — a term denoting all mankind prior to the Giving of the Torah on Mount Sinai, and all Non-Israelites after the Giving of the Torah] *(Rashi; Sanhedrin* 56b [see *comm.* to 2:16]).[1]

Now, I might be able to conceal my act from man, but never from Him! *(Chizkuni).*

Ramban agrees with *Rashi's* comment that Joseph's reference was to the sin of immorality. *Ramban* adds that Joseph first emphasized the disloyalty and betrayal to his master because she would understand that better. Only then did he add that it would also constitute a sin to God.

Alternatively, *Ramban* suggests that Joseph was intimating that betrayal of his master would in itself be considered as a sin against God Who concerns Himself with man's rights. According to this interpretation, Joseph made no reference to the prohibition of adultery, since he wanted to address her in terms suitable to her.

10. וַיְהִי כְּדַבְּרָהּ אֶל־יוֹסֵף יוֹם יוֹם — *And so it was — just as she coaxed* [lit. *spoke to*] *Joseph day* [*after*] *day.*

According to a Midrashic view in *Daas Zekeinim* (by analogy with *Esther* 3:7), the expression יוֹם יוֹם means *twelve months.*

She tried to entice him in every way possible: with words; by varying her dress; by threats of imprisonment, humiliation and physical harm; by offering him huge amounts of money *(Yoma* 35b).

It is based on this verse that the Sages proclaimed [*Avos* 1:4, *Nedarim* 20a]: 'He who speaks too much to a woman is eventually seduced by her to sin' *(Midrash HaGadol).*

וְלֹא שָׁמַע אֵלֶיהָ — *So* [lit. *and*] *he would not listen to her.*[2]

'Why don't you listen to me?' she urged. 'I am married and no one would be the wiser.'

1. Potiphar's wife too was included in the designation 'Noachide,' and she too would have sinned by this act. Why then did Joseph not use the plural וְחָטָאנוּ, *and we will have sinned against God?*

However, this righteous Joseph did not want to associate with a wicked person even as the co-subject of a sentence *(R' Heshel — Chanukas HaTorah).*

2. The *Midrash* relates that a matron once asked the Talmudic Sage R' Yose:

'Could it really be true that Joseph, a seventeen-year old youth in all his passion, rejected

יא לִהְיוֹת עִמָּהּ: וַיְהִי כְּהַיּוֹם הַזֶּה וַיָּבֹא
הַבַּיְתָה לַעֲשׂוֹת מְלַאכְתּוֹ וְאֵין אִישׁ
יב מֵאַנְשֵׁי הַבַּיִת שָׁם בַּבָּיִת: וַתִּתְפְּשֵׂהוּ

'Even your *un*married women are forbidden to us,' Joseph replied; 'all the more you who are married!' In this way, Joseph rebuffed her.

R' Yehudah bar Nachman compared the above to the case of a non-Jew who offered a delicacy to a Jew.

'What is it?' the Jew asked.

'It is pork,' came the reply.

'Fool!' the Jew angrily retorted. 'Even the flesh of a kosher animal slaughtered by a non-Jew is forbidden us; how much more so pork!' *(Tanchuma)*.

According to the *Yalkut*, Joseph also told her that he was afraid of his father in Canaan. 'When Reuben committed an infraction by tampering with my father's bedroom [see *comm.* to 35:22] it was considered adultery and as a result of it his birthright was taken from him and given to me. If I listen to you, I might forfeit my birthright as well.'

לִשְׁכַּב אֶצְלָהּ — *To lie beside her.*

— Even without sexual intimacy *(Rashi)*.

— Even while fully clothed, or to simply be near her for conversation *(Ibn Ezra)*.

This is derived from the expression לִשְׁכַּב אֶצְלָהּ to lie *beside her* rather than the usual expression for conjugal relations לִשְׁכַּב עִמָּהּ or לִשְׁכַּב אִתָּהּ lie *with* her *(Ramban)*.

לִהְיוֹת עִמָּהּ — *To be with her.*

— Alone *(Rashbam)*.

— To consort with her *(Ibn Ezra)*.

According to *Rashi* [following R' Eleazar in *Sotah* 3b and *Avodah Zarah* 5a] the intent is that Joseph did not want to be with her in the World to Come.

— That is, he did not want his sin with her to 'attach itself to him like a dog' and accompany him in the Hereafter *(Gemara* ibid. as explained by *Maharsha* [cf. *Yoma* 35b]; or according to the *Midrash* he wanted neither to sinfully associate with her in this World or to accompany her to *Gehinom* which would be her portion in the World to Come.

11. וַיְהִי כְּהַיּוֹם הַזֶּה — *Then there was an opportune day* [lit. *and it was like this day*].

This translation follows *Rashi* (from *Sotah* 36b and *Tanchuma)*. That is, on a certain famous, important, day — a festival when they all went to their temple. She, however, pleaded illness and stayed home, for she reasoned: I will never have such an opportunity to seduce Joseph כְּהַיּוֹם הַזֶּה, *as this day.*

The intent, then, of the expression כְּהַיּוֹם הַזֶּה [lit. *like this day*] is: on a day particularly suited for this purpose *(Mizrachi)*; a day of which Potiphar's wife could say, 'Everyone is in the temple and I can be absolutely alone with him.' [See below s.v. וְאֵין אִישׁ].

Radak: On a day like the one as that mentioned in *v.* 10 when she importuned him excessively.[1]

the seductions of that woman [or is the Torah actually trying to conceal his sin with her]?'

R' Yose took the Book of Genesis and read her the story of Reuben and Bilhah (35:22) and Judah and Tamar (chapt. 38).

'If the Torah did not conceal the sins of these — who were still under parental authority,' R' Yose said, 'how much the more would the Torah not conceal the sins of one who was but a slave in his master's house, and not subject to any parental control!'

'You are right, and your Torah is true!' she exclaimed *(Midrash HaGadol)*.

1. *R' Hirsch* similarly explains that contextually, the expression *like this day* refers back to the phrase 'day by day' in the preceding verse; *this day* was like any other, when she pursued

her, to be with her. 11 *Then there was an opportune*
day when he entered the house to do his work — no
man of the household staff being there in the house

According to *Ibn Ezra* and *Ralbag:* On the anniversary of the first time — or the same day of the week or month — that she first began imploring him.

וַיָּבֹא הַבַּיְתָה לַעֲשׂוֹת מְלַאכְתּוֹ — *When* [lit. *and*] *he entered the house to do his work.*

The Talmudic sages Rav and Shmuel differ: One maintains that Joseph entered the house with only the [innocent] intent of performing his household *work,* while the other maintains that [as a result of her ceaseless importunities, Joseph's resolve weakened and] his intended 'work' was to yield to her and satisfy his own desires. But when *she caught hold of him by his garment* [*v.* 12], his father's image appeared before him and immediately his desire left him *(Rashi; Sotah* 36b; see *comm.* to *v.* 8 above and to 49:22).[1]

The sage who interprets that Joseph came to the house for immoral purposes apparently infers it from the expression *to do* **his** *work* — i.e., to satisfy his *own* lust and not to serve his master. The other opinion would, following *Tanchuma,* interpret *his work* literally, referring to a review of the account books *(Maharsha, Sotah* 36b).

Cf. *Onkelos* and *Targum Yonasan:* It was on a certain day that he entered the house to examine the tablets of his accounts.

It is not clear why the one who interprets Joseph's motive as lustful chose to reveal what the Torah, by use of the innocent term 'work', chose to conceal, especially since he could have interpreted the term literally.

Torah Temimah conjectures that possibly this interpretation is to Joseph's merit inasmuch as it emphasizes the full extent of Joseph's righteousness. He had come to the house ready to sin, yet was able to overpower his Evil Inclination and flee.

[Another reason for the interpretation might be the need to reconcile the *tradition* that Joseph was about to sin, with the simple flow of the narrative where Joseph's weakness is nowhere indicated. Apparently the only allusion to this in the text is the euphemistic use of the term *'his' work.* See below for the source of the tradition that Jacob's image appeared and that Joseph's desire left him.]

[See *Shabbos* 49b where the Sages differ on whether or not the word מְלָאכָה in our verse denotes *work* and is to be counted among the thirty-nine times that forms of the word occur in the Torah.]

וְאֵין אִישׁ מֵאַנְשֵׁי הַבַּיִת שָׁם בַּבָּיִת — [*And*] *no man of the household staff* [lit. *men of the house*] *being there in the house.*

How could it be that in such a large house there was not a single

him incessantly. Nevertheless though Joseph knew he would be alone with her and what to expect of her, Joseph still ventured into the house. The implication of this expression, therefore, would be one of reproach for Joseph. He voluntarily placed himself in a trying predicament for which he paid dearly. No man should depend too much on his moral strength and power of resistance.

1. The goal of a Jewish upbringing can be no better expressed than in the Midrashic account of Joseph's inner struggle against the temptation of Potiphar's wife. Joseph's will weakens and he is about to sin; his temptress is convinced she has finally seduced him. Just then, the sudden vision of his father gives him the strength to overcome his weakness and reassert his nature, now at the breaking point after months of heroic resistance. Such is the test of a child's upbringing. When his father's influence still guides him long after he has been separated from the family home and cast alone into a licentious society — then the training of his Jewish home has been fully vindicated *(R'Munk).* [See *Overview.*]

☙ This concept is illustrated by a story involving R' Yehoshua Trunk, the famous gaon of

בְּבִגְדוֹ לֵאמֹר שִׁכְבָה עִמִּי וַיַּעֲזֹב בִּגְדוֹ
יג בְּיָדָהּ וַיָּנָס וַיֵּצֵא הַחוּצָה: וַיְהִי כִּרְאוֹתָהּ
יד כִּי־עָזַב בִּגְדוֹ בְּיָדָהּ וַיָּנָס הַחוּצָה: וַתִּקְרָא

man? — It was, as noted, a festival and all were in their idolatrous temple (*Sotah* 36b cited by *Rashi* above).

According to the *Midrash*, the Nile overflowed its banks that day irrigating the land of Egypt and all except Joseph flocked to witness it and render homage to their gods. Alternately, there was a performance at the theater that day, and everyone flocked to see it.

As noted above, Potiphar's wife feigned illness on that particular day so she could remain home alone with Joseph who, she knew, had work to do.

According to *Sforno*, the passage means that no man was present in that particular *room.*

The expression *there was no man ... in the house* is also perceived in the *Midrash* to connote Joseph's realization that if he sinned with her, he would be like an animal, not a man. Immediately his desire left him, as if he lacked normal human impulses — so there was *'no man inside.'*

Furthermore, the phrase *of the men of the household* is a limitation: There was no one there *of the household* but there *was* someone present who was *not* of the household. This is the basis of the Talmudic exegesis [*Sotah* 36b cited by *Rashi* above] that Jacob's image appeared to Joseph *(Tur).*

12. וַתִּתְפְּשֵׂהוּ בְּבִגְדוֹ לֵאמֹר — *That* [lit. *and*] *she caught hold of him by his garment, saying 'Lie with me.'*

She did not actually say so, but this was the clear implication of her seizure of his garment *(Or HaChaim; see Likutei Anshei Shem* in *Chumash Rav Peninim).*

It is on *this* passage that the Talmud, *Sotah* 36b, cited by *Rashi* in the previous verse [and in the comm. to *v.* 8] remarks that Joseph resisted temptation when his father's countenance appeared through the window and admonished him that if he consorted with an adultress, his name would be omitted from the High Priest's breastplate. [See *Oznaim laTorah.*]

Rabbi David Feinstein notes homiletically that בְּבִגְדוֹ, *his garment,* can be vocalized בְּבָגְדוֹ, ***his rebellion.*** Following the opinion in *Sotah* 36b that Joseph's resolve weakened and he was about to sin, our verse alludes to the fact that she made use of the opportunity: ***she caught hold of him*** **בְּבָגְדוֹ*, in his*** [moment of] ***rebellion.***

The verb תפש denotes a more forceful, protracted grasp than אחז *(HaRechasim leBik'ah).*

וַיַּעֲזֹב בִּגְדוֹ בְּיָדָהּ — *But* [lit. *and*] *he*

Kutna. Once while he was riding in a train, his neighbor was a non-observant young Jew who seemed to go out of his way to provoke the rabbi with his rude behavior. When R' Yehoshua chastised him, he replied,

"I don't need you to teach me how to behave," and to strengthen his point, he revealed that he was the descendant of distinguished rabbis.

R' Yehoshua replied, "King David had a son named Adoniyahu who was insolent and arrogant, and who came to a bad end when he tried to usurp the throne while his father lay on his death bed. Of Adoniyahu, Scripture says [I *Kings* 1:6] וְלֹא עֲצָבוֹ אָבִיו מִיָּמָיו [lit. *and his father never caused him to feel sad*]. This has a deeper meaning: the identity of his great and righteous father *never saddened* the wayward son; Adoniyahu was never saddened by the thought that his behavior would cause David intense humiliation. Because he failed to consider the obligations imposed by his august ancestry, Adoniyahu never relented from the behavior that led him to his doom. Joseph was different. Even after he had decided to let himself be seduced by Potiphar's wife, he did not forget that he was Jacob's son. When Joseph saw his father's image before him, he reconsidered immediately and fled fron sin."

— [12] *that she caught hold of him by his garment saying, 'Lie with me!' But he left his garment in her hand, and he fled, going outside.*

[13] *When she saw that he had left his garment in her hand and fled outside,* [14] *she called out to the men of*

left his garment in her hand.

Out of courtesy to her as the wife of his master he did not overpower her and tear his garment from her. Instead he slipped out of it to elude her while she was still grasping it *(Ramban).*

וַיָּנָס וַיֵּצֵא הַחוּצָה — *And he fled, going* [lit. *and went*] *outside.*

He fled the room — lest his passions overcome him — *and went outside.* Once outside he slowed down and resumed his normal gait to avoid arousing curiosity *(Sforno).* [Comp. the phrase וַיָּנָס הַחוּצָה, *and he fled outside* in *verses* 13 and 18.]

R' Munk observes how, in choosing to flee rather than to remain and resist, Joseph teaches us an excellent lesson: To overcome a powerful temptation, it is best not to fight it but to flee from it.[1]

[See *comm.* to 14:11 for the distinction between the verbs נוס and ברח.]

The verb וַיָּנֹס, *flee,* occurs here, and in reference to the sea in *Psalms* 114:3: *The sea saw and fled* [וַיָּנֹס]. *Midrash Tanchuma* [*Naso* 30] and *Daas Zekeinim* record: The Holy One, Blessed be He said, 'In reward for your having fled, I promise that when your descendants leave Egypt the sea will flee because of your coffin [when your remains are brought back to *Eretz Yisrael*].' Thus, the verse reads *The sea saw and fled* — what did it see? It saw Joseph's remains, for God had declared that He would divide the sea for Joseph's sake.

13. Joseph is slandered.

When Potiphar's wife saw that he had left his garment and fled, she was afraid that he might expose her to the members of the household or to her husband. Anticipating this, she hurried to them first. She made a scene and accused him of having removed his garment to violate her, 'but when he saw that I screamed he fled in confusion' *(Ramban).*

According to *B'chor Shor,* she vindictively slandered him with the intent of gaining revenge and at the same time ridding herself of him. She realized she could not seduce him, but she could not control her passions in his presence. [See footnote to *v.* 1].

וַיָּנָס הַחוּצָה — *And he fled outside.*

Verse 12 reads: *He fled, going outside,* to intimate that when he

1. For Joseph's exemplary virtue and purity of conduct in the face of overwhelming temptation, the Sages consider him to have 'Sanctified the Name of Heaven in private' in reward for which R' Chanin observes [*Sotah* 10b and 36b] that one letter [a ה, *he*] from the Name of the Holy One, Blessed be He was added to Joseph's name [see *Psalms* 81:6 where Joseph is spelled יהוסף, *Yehoseph.*]

Joseph's piety rightfully earned him the appellation יוֹסֵף הַצַּדִּיק, *Joseph the righteous,* a designation by which he is known throughout Rabbinic literature. On the Day of Judgment, Joseph's example of piety will refuse the excuse of the sensuous. For when the sensuous come before the Heavenly Court to be condemned for abandoning the Torah, they would justify themselves by saying: 'We were overcome by our beauty and were led astray by our passion.' — 'And were you more beautiful than Joseph who was subjected to every possible attempt by Potiphar's wife to seduce him yet controlled his passions?' The Court would retort.

Kabbalistically Joseph the righteous is enumerated as one of the seven 'pillars' who, if it may be so expressed, 'support' the Divine Presence on earth [מֶרְכָּבָה לַשְּׁכִינָה].

לְאַנְשֵׁי בֵיתָהּ וַתֹּאמֶר לָהֶם לֵאמֹר רְאוּ
הֵבִיא לָנוּ אִישׁ עִבְרִי לְצַחֶק בָּנוּ בָּא אֵלַי

14. וַתִּקְרָא לְאַנְשֵׁי בֵיתָהּ — [*And*] *she called out to the men* [or *people*] *of her household.*

[Who by this time had returned from wherever they had been.]

It is not clear whether she spoke to them in the courtyard, or whether she summoned them into her chamber where the alleged assault was to have occurred. Most sources appear to favor the latter view.

Cf. *Radak: She called out to the men* — But there were no men in the

got outside he slowed down to avoid arousing curiosity. However, from *her* vantage point at this moment, she presumed that he kept running even while outside. She was apprehensive that the household people would ask him whom he was escaping and what had occurred, and that he might have told them. So she quickly took the following steps to counter him *(Sforno).*[1]

Were it not for this apprehension she might otherwise have kept the matter secret *(Haamek Davar).*

1. The following chart compares the subtle differences in the account as it actually occured and how Potiphar's wife reported it to the men of the household and subsequently to her husband.

The commentary deals with these nuances and their meaning.

Biblical Account *(v. 14,12)*	**Potiphar's wife's Perception** *(v. 13)*	**Potiphar's wife to the men of the household** *(v. 14-15)*	**Potiphar's wife to Potiphar** *(v. 17-18)*
		הֵבִיא לָנוּ אִישׁ עִבְרִי לְצַחֶק בָּנוּ בָּא אֵלַי לִשְׁכַּב עִמִּי *He brought us a Hebrew man to sport with us; he came to me to lie with me*	בָּא אֵלַי הָעֶבֶד הָעִבְרִי אֲשֶׁר־הֵבֵאתָ לָנוּ לְצַחֶק בִּי *came to me* the Hebrew slave whom you brought to us to sport with me*
וַתִּקְרָא לְאַנְשֵׁי בֵיתָהּ *and she called to the men of her household*		וָאֶקְרָא בְּקוֹל גָּדוֹל *but I called out with a loud scream*	כַּהֲרִימִי קוֹלִי וָאֶקְרָא *as I raised my voice and called*
וַיַּעֲזֹב בִּגְדוֹ בְּיָדָהּ *and he left his garment in her hand*	כִּי עָזַב בִּגְדוֹ בְּיָדָהּ *that he left his garment in her hand*	וַיַּעֲזֹב בִּגְדוֹ אֶצְלִי *and he left his garment beside me*	וַיַּעֲזֹב בִּגְדוֹ אֶצְלִי *and he left his garment beside me*
וַיָּנָס וַיֵּצֵא הַחוּצָה *and he fled and went outside*	וַיָּנָס הַחוּצָה *and he fled outside*	וַיָּנָס וַיֵּצֵא הַחוּצָה *and he fled and went outside*	וַיָּנָס הַחוּצָה *and he fled outside*

* (literal translation for purposes of comparison)

39 her household and said to them as follows, 'Look! He
14 brought us a Hebrew man to sport with us! He came

house? — She called out loudly, and when those outside heard her, they came into the house. It was to this calling that she referred in verses **15** and **18**.

וַתֹּאמֶר לָהֶם לֵאמֹר — *And said to them as follows* [לֵאמֹר lit. *to say.*]

I.e., she knew that her husband might not believe her story so she summoned them that they too might rally behind her against this stranger; and as the superfluous word לֵאמֹר, *to say,* intimates, they in turn were to tell her husband when he would return *(Rashi; Or HaChaim).*

רְאוּ — *Look!* [lit. *see!*]

In the most simple sense, *Look* is meant idiomatically, not that she actually pointed at Joseph *(Akeidah).*

According to *Lekach Tov,* it is meant literally: she had Joseph brought before them and put on display that they might all attack him; according to *Abarbanel,* she held up his garment for all to see and thus verify her slander.

According to *Targum Yonasan* and *Zohar,* she tried to make it seem as though Joseph had succeeded in a forcible assault.

[Although *Ramban* does not cite the above opinion, the implication of his *comm.* to *v.* 19 is that Potiphar's wife would not have made such a claim, since her participation in an adultress act — even under duress — would have been loathsome in the eyes of her husband. Therefore, we see that she was careful to say that *he came to lie with me,* i.e. with the *intention* of violating her, but her screams caused him to flee.]

הֵבִיא לָנוּ אִישׁ עִבְרִי — *He brought us a Hebrew* [*Ivri*] *man.*

Apparently Joseph had told them he was a Hebrew since he did not want to be taken for a Canaanite *(Ramban* to 40:15).

We see from 43:32 the Egyptians abhorred the Hebrews and would not even eat with them. The Hebrews were given only field work and were never brought into the house. Therefore, Potiphar's wife charged that her husband's having brought a Hebrew slave into the house and appointing him to a position of trust was an affront to them. 'No wonder he took advantage of it and saw fit to exploit his position and trifle with our sensibilities!' *(Ramban).*

The phrase is elliptical. **He** *brought us* clearly refers to her husband although she does not mention him specifically by name *(Rashi).* [See *Rashi* to 41:13.]

She did not mention *her husband* explicitly either out of respect, or because it was self-evident that it was he who brought Joseph into the house *(Ramban).*

The term עִבְרִי, *Ivri* [=Hebrew] refers to one who hailed from the 'other side' [עֵבֶר *('ever')*] of the River [Euphrates]. It also designates a descendant of Eber *(Rashi).*

Mizrachi explains that both of the above criteria are necessary for one to be called an *Ivri,* and as such only the Abrahamatic family was so identified. The family of Nachor, Abraham's brother, was descended from Eber, but they never crossed the River; Ishmael and the children of Keturah are not termed *Ivri* — though they are of Abraham's family — because only Isaac is referred to as Abraham's offspring [21:13]. Similarly, though Esau was the child of Isaac, he was not called *Ivri* since the exegesis of 21:33 excluded him from being considered Abraham's offspring.

[See *comm.* to 14:13, *Ramban* to 40:15, and *comm.* to 43:32.]

לְצַחֶק בָּנוּ — *To sport with us.*

The verb לְצַחֶק, to *sport,* in this

טו לִשְׁכַּב עִמִּי וָאֶקְרָא בְּקוֹל גָּדוֹל: וַיְהִי
כְשָׁמְעוֹ כִּי־הֲרִימֹתִי קוֹלִי וָאֶקְרָא וַיַּעֲזֹב
טז בִּגְדוֹ אֶצְלִי וַיָּנָס וַיֵּצֵא הַחוּצָה: וַתַּנַּח
בִּגְדוֹ אֶצְלָהּ עַד־בּוֹא אֲדֹנָיו אֶל־בֵּיתוֹ:
יז וַתְּדַבֵּר אֵלָיו כַּדְּבָרִים הָאֵלֶּה לֵאמֹר בָּא
אֵלַי הָעֶבֶד הָעִבְרִי אֲשֶׁר־הֵבֵאתָ לָּנוּ

context denotes *adultery*, as *Rashi* explains the various meanings of the word in 21:9.

The connotation of the verb according to *Ramban*, is to *assume airs* or *to mock*, while *Sforno* interprets it as *'playing'* in a manner that made his immoral intentions obvious.

She used the plural *us*, as the plural of majesty *(Radak)*, while according to *Yalkut*, the plural refers also to the other women of the household whom she coached to testify that Joseph tried to seduce them as well.[1]

וָאֶקְרָא בְּקוֹל גָּדוֹל — *But* [lit. *and*] *I cried out with a loud scream.*

You were far away from me and I had to scream *aloud;* had I not done so, he would have forcibly violated me *(Rashbam).*

But, as noted in *Ramban* to *v.* 19, she was careful to stress that Joseph only *attempted* to lie with her, but that her screams caused him to flee. She carefully avoided any suggestion that Joseph had been successful in his attempts, for her participation — even under duress — in an act of adultery would have been too loathsome in her husband's eyes. In any case, there was no need to carry her fabrication so far, since even Joseph's *attempt* to violate her was sufficient to earn him the death penalty.

[Her calling out to summon the men of the household *after* Joseph had fled (*v.* 14) is the only calling out recorded in this incident (see *Radak* ibid). In order to absolve herself from suspicion of complicity, she emphasizes both to her slaves and subsequently to her husband (*v.* 18) that she did indeed cry out — implicitly *during* the attack (cf. *Deut.* 22:24).]

15. וַיַּעֲזֹב בִּגְדוֹ אֶצְלִי — *[And] he left his garment beside me.*

Note the subtle change: She did not say, 'he left his garment *in my hand'* [as had actually occurred (*v.*

1. According to *Alshich* and *Abarbanel* — echoed by *Malbim* — she used the plural *us* to arouse their hostility against Joseph, the stranger, a Hebrew, and conjure up an image of him as the common enemy of them all. 'The Hebrew stranger has mocked not only *me*, but *all of us* — the whole Egyptian nation!'

Note that she was addressing her slaves when she stated this. When she repeated the incident to her husband [*v.* 15], she refers to Joseph as a Hebrew *slave*, but in addressing the other slaves, she wants to avoid their feeling a sense of solidarity with Joseph as one of them. Were they to think of him as one of them, it would be natural for downtrodden slaves to side with a fellow sufferer. So she sublty cleverly described Joseph as the Hebrew *man* — an overlord over them, and hence their common enemy — who arrogantly mocked *them* by his attempted seduction of her, for although *she* was his intended victim this time, he would treat them *all* the same way should the opportunity present itself.

So throughout history have anti-Semites furthered their own self-interest by arousing the citizenry's ire against their 'common enemy — the Jew, the stranger in their midst — by slander and lies that led to the shedding of innocent blood.

to lie with me but I called out with a loud scream.
15 And when he heard that I raised my voice and
screamed, he left his garment beside me, fled, and
went outside!'
16 She kept his garment beside her until his master
came home. 17 Then she told him a similar account
saying, 'The Hebrew slave whom you brought to us

12), since that would implicate her as having seized him]. Instead she told the people of her household and her husband that Joseph left his garment *beside* her [intimating that he left it in the midst of disrobing], when he fled upon being panicked by her screams *(Ramban).*

וַיָּנָס וַיֵּצֵא הַחוּצָה — [*And*] *he fled, and went outside.*

In *v.* 12, the passage reads similarly. *Sforno* explains that Joseph ran only until he was out of the room; then he slowed down to a normal walk. She probably realized that Joseph had not run to report the incident to his fellow servants. Therefore she reported — accurately — to the bystanders that he had run for only a short while. But when she repeated her account to Potiphar who had not been there [*v.* 18] she said וַיָּנָס הַחוּצָה, *he fled outside,* — implying that he kept running when he was outside too [to arouse the curiosity of bystanders and slander her].

16. וַתַּנַּח בִּגְדוֹ אֶצְלָהּ — [*And*] *she kept his garment beside her.*

— As evidence *(Abarbanel).*

— Kissing and fondling it all the while *(Midrash).*

עַד בּוֹא אֲדֹנָיו אֶל־בֵּיתוֹ — *Until his master* [*i.e. Joseph's master (Rashi)*] *came home* [lit. *to his house*].

17. Potiphar's wife proceeds to repeat her vindictive slander to her husband, repeating the accusation to him in great detail.

בָּא אֵלַי ... לְצַחֶק בִּי — *Came to me to sport with me.*

The Hebrew literally reads, *came to me the Hebrew slave whom you brought to us to sport with me. Rashi* wishes to negate the false inference that she suggested that Potiphar purposely brought the *Hebrew slave to sport with her.* Therefore, for the purpose of clearer understanding, *Rashi* interprets the syntax, and our translation follows him: *The Hebrew slave whom you brought to us came to me to sport with me.*

Why, then, did the Torah construct the phrase in so ambiguous a manner?

Potiphar's wife was suggesting to her husband that by placing such an attractive slave boy in the household, he had created a situation filled with unbearable temptation. Indeed, it was truly as if Potiphar had brought Joseph *to sport* with her *(Rabbi David Feinstein).*

הָעֶבֶד הָעִבְרִי — *The Hebrew slave.*

[In her account to the her slaves she did not refer to Joseph as a *slave* but simply as *the Hebrew* **man.** See *comm.* to *v.* 14 s.v. הֵבִיא.]

She intimated to her husband that as a mere slave, Joseph should have displayed the utmost respect for her *(Haamek Davar).*

אֲשֶׁר הֵבֵאתָ לָּנוּ — *Whom you brought to us.*

Your very act of bringing such a

יח לִצְחֶק בִּי: וַיְהִי כַּהֲרִימִי קוֹלִי וָאֶקְרָא
יט וַיַּעֲזֹב בִּגְדוֹ אֶצְלִי וַיָּנָס הַחוּצָה: וַיְהִי
כִּשְׁמֹעַ אֲדֹנָיו אֶת־דִּבְרֵי אִשְׁתּוֹ אֲשֶׁר
דִּבְּרָה אֵלָיו לֵאמֹר כַּדְּבָרִים הָאֵלֶּה עָשָׂה
כ לִי עַבְדֶּךָ וַיִּחַר אַפּוֹ: וַיִּקַּח אֲדֹנֵי יוֹסֵף
אֹתוֹ וַיִּתְּנֵהוּ אֶל־בֵּית הַסֹּהַר מְקוֹם אֲשֶׁר־
°אסורי הַמֶּלֶךְ אֲסוּרִים וַיְהִי־שָׁם בְּבֵית

°אֲסִירֵי ק׳

person into our house was abhorrent! (*Ramban v.* 14).

18. וַיָּנָס הַחוּצָה — *And ran outside.*

[I.e. he did not even have the decency to slow down when he got outside, but kept running to arouse the curiosity of the servants and cast aspersions upon me.]

(See *Sforno* to *v.* 12 and 15).

19. וַיְהִי כִּשְׁמֹעַ אֲדֹנָיו אֶת דִּבְרֵי אִשְׁתּוֹ — *And it was, when his master heard his wife's words.*

— Emphasizing the gravity of Joseph's affront (*Ralbag*).

כַּדְּבָרִים הָאֵלֶּה עָשָׂה לִי עַבְדֶּךָ — *Your slave did things like these to me.*

She told this to Potiphar at the time of conjugal intimacy. Therefore she specifically stated, 'your servant did the kind of things you are doing right now!' (*Rashi*).

Although the Rabbinic view is that Potiphar was a castrate (see *vss.* 1 and 6), this did not preclude his ability to be intimate in some ways with his wife (*Mizrachi*).

Ramban maintains that *Rashi's* Midrashic exegesis is inspired by the expression כַּדְּבָרִים הָאֵלֶּה, *things like these*, i.e., matters of intimacy as they themselves were then engaged in.

Ramban maintains however that in the literal sense all of this is academic since the prefix כ in כַּדְּבָרִים הָאֵלֶּה does not denote an *exact comparison* i.e., *these very things*, but merely indicates an approximation, being the idiomatic equivalent of הַדְּבָרִים הָאֵלֶּה, *similar* [lit. *these*] *things*. Or the כ indicates *exaggeration*, i.e. *things as terrible as these.*

וַיִּחַר אַפּוֹ — *And his anger flared up.*

— At Joseph. However, Potiphar did not have Joseph killed either because of his great love for him; or it was a miracle; or because he doubted her story in view of Joseph's righteousness. The Sages in the *Midrash* similarly interpreted this matter [see *Midrash* next verse] (*Ibn Ezra; Ramban*).

There is an opinion in the *Yalkut* that Potiphar *was* ready to kill Joseph, but his daughter Asenath came to him and swore that Joseph was innocent. She told her father the entire story as it actually happened. It was in the merit of this that she was eventually privileged to marry him [see 41:50].

According to *Sforno*, Potiphar's anger was directed at *his wife* for having publicly complained about his bringing a Hebrew slave into the house to sport with her. The accusation itself, however, he disbelieved.

— He was angry at the turn of events that mandated that he could no longer retain Joseph in his household service (*Malbim*).

The expression וַיִּחַר אַפּוֹ idiomatically describes *fierce anger*. It metaphorically means: *and his nostrils flared*. See *comm.* to 30:2.

20. וַיִּקַּח אֲדֹנֵי יוֹסֵף אֹתוֹ — *Then* [lit. *and*] *Joseph's master took him.*

came to me to sport with me. 18 *But it happened that*
when I raised my voice and screamed, he left his gar-
ment beside me, and ran outside.'
19 *And it was, when his master heard his wife's*
words which she spoke to him saying, 'Your slave
did things like these to me,' and his anger flared up.
20 *Then Joseph's master took him and placed him in*
the prison — the place where the king's prisoners
were confined. And he remained there in the prison.

This, too, was a display of Potiphar's love for Joseph: Potiphar *himself* took Joseph and did not summon the prison officials *(Abarbanel; Malbim).*

'I know the charge against you is false,' Potiphar said to Joseph, 'but I must imprison you lest a stigma fall on my children' [i.e., 'I must punish you to demonstrate that I believe my wife's assertion that you seduced her and not *vice-versa* or else people will say that she acted the same way with others, and our children are not mine.' Had Potiphar believed Joseph to be guilty he would certainly have put him to death *(Yafeh Toar)*] *(Midrash; Ramban).*[1]

On the *plural* construct form for *master* אֲדֹנֵי rather than the singular אָדוֹן, see *Rashi* to 35:7 and above *v.* 2.

וַיִּתְּנֵהוּ אֶל־בֵּית הַסֹּהַר מְקוֹם אֲשֶׁר אֲסוּרֵי הַמֶּלֶךְ אֲסוּרִים — *And he placed* [lit. *gave*] *him in* [lit. *to*] *the prison* [Herbrew: *beth hasohar*] — *the place where the king's prisoners were confined* [*lit. bound*].

The word *sohar* is an Egyptian word and therefore the Torah itself goes on to define that a *beth hasohar* is the *place where the king's prisoners were confined.* This is in keeping with the Scriptural style of defining foreign words, as in *Esther* 3:7: *They cast 'pur,' that is the lot (Ibn Ezra).*

Ramban disagrees and maintains that *sohar* is a dungeon [see below], and the reason the Torah provides us with the qualifying phrase *the place where the king's prisoners were confined* is to demonstrate how this was yet another example of God's graciousness toward Joseph: Because of Potiphar's Divinely inspired love for Joseph, he did not imprison him with common criminals, but with the *king's prisoners,* i.e., officials who sinned against the king. By telling us this, the Torah also prepares us for the

1. By presenting us in detail with a revolting injustice arising from the accusation of a slanderer, the Torah portrays for coming generations the destiny of the people of Israel. But Joseph accepts this new ordeal just as calmly as he had accepted the fierce hatred of his brothers and his descent to slavery. He did not indulge in useless protestations of innocence nor did he cry out in rebellion. He accepted the unjust imprisonment for twelve years.

However, even during this long period of incarceration, his exemplary conduct would gain him high honors. All would regard him as entirely cleansed of the false and shameful accusations; this former slave, thrown into a dungeon, would ultimately rise to glory.

Such is the reaction of the just and pious man who can overcome all hardships, whatever the circumstances. Joseph's attitude serves as an inspiration to future generations facing similar situations *(R' Munk).*

כא הַסֹּהַר: וַיְהִ֤י יהוה֙ אֶת־יוֹסֵ֔ף וַיֵּ֥ט אֵלָ֖יו
חָ֑סֶד וַיִּתֵּ֣ן חִנּ֔וֹ בְּעֵינֵ֖י שַׂ֥ר בֵּית־הַסֹּֽהַר:
כב וַיִּתֵּ֞ן שַׂ֣ר בֵּית־הַסֹּ֗הַר בְּיַד־יוֹסֵ֔ף אֵ֚ת כָּל־
הָאֲסִירִ֔ם אֲשֶׁ֖ר בְּבֵ֣ית הַסֹּ֑הַר וְאֵ֨ת כָּל־
כג אֲשֶׁ֤ר עֹשִׂים֙ שָׁ֔ם ה֖וּא הָיָ֥ה עֹשֶֽׂה: אֵ֣ין |
שַׂ֣ר בֵּית־הַסֹּ֗הַר רֹאֶ֤ה אֶת־כָּל־מְא֙וּמָה֙

fact that the royal butler and baker were imprisoned with him. [See *Meshech Chochmah.*]

Since Potiphar was the שַׂר הַטַּבָּחִים, *chief executioner* [see *comm.* to *v.* 1 and 37:36], he was in full charge of this prison and had the authority to incarcerate Joseph there. [See 40:3] *(Haamek Davar).*

Radak in *Shorashim* relates the word סהר to *Song of Songs* 7:3 where it has the meaning of *roundness,* and explains that בֵּית הַסֹּהַר lit. *house of roundness* refers to a circular tower which they used as prisons.

Ramban explains it as an underground *dungeon* with an overhead opening through which they lowered the prisoners and through which the prisoners had light. The word סהר is related to the Aramaic סִיהֲרָא, *dim light.* [*Onkelos* renders 'moon' with the word סִיהֲרָא], and is related etymologically to the Hebrew term צֹהַר, *light,* from צָהֳרַיִם, *midday,* when light reaches its zenith. However, by distinction, סֹהַר denotes the *faint light* that percolated into the dungeon.

R' Hirsch notes that the Traditional spelling [כְּתִיב] is אֲסוּרֵי while the pronunciation [קְרִי] is אֲסִירֵי. The two words have different connotations. The first, אֲסוּרֵי is a verb, the *imprisoned,* implying that although the people were confined in jail, they could not be called 'prisoners' for they had not been convicted of a crime; they were being held for trial. The latter word אֲסִירֵי, however, is a noun; *prisoners,* implying that they had already been convicted of the crime for which they were imprisoned. The dual nature of the word indicates that both categories of people were there: convicts like Joseph and people like the chamberlain of the cupbearers and the baker whose acquaintance Joseph was to make in the next chapter.

The passage literally reads *and gave* [*or placed*] *him to, the prison.* The expression *to* the prison is synonymous with *in* the prison. Cf. *Exodus* 25:21 *to* the ark=*in* the ark *(Radak).*

וַיְהִי שָׁם בְּבֵית הַסֹּהַר — *And he remained* [lit. *was*] *there in the prison.*

— Potiphar would not change his mind and liberate him *(Radak).*

Joseph was incarcerated there a total of twelve years: Ten years — one for each of the ten brothers about whom he had brought evil reports [37:2] — plus two more in punishment for having placed his trust in the chamberlain of the cupbearers instead of in God alone [see *comm.* to 40:14 and 41:1] (*Seder Olam; Tanchuma; Shmos Rabbah* 7:1).

21. וַיְהִי ה׳ אֶת יוֹסֵף — [*And*] *HASHEM was with Joseph.*

— Even in prison. This was yet a further manifestation of God's grace, for whenever an individual of Israel suffers bondage, the Shechinah accompanies him, if one may so express it, as it is written: [*Psalms* 91:15] *I* [*God*] *will be with him in trouble (Mechilta).*

וַיֵּט אֵלָיו חָסֶד — *And He endowed him with charisma* [lit. *and He extended charm to him*].

God caused Joseph to be liked by

[21] *HASHEM was with Joseph, and He endowed him with charisma; He made the prison warden view him favorably.* [22] *The prison warden placed all inmates of the prison in Joseph's custody, and everything that was done there, he would accomplish.* [23] *The prison warden did not scrutinize anything that was in his*

all who saw him. We find the word חֶסֶד [in this sense of *charisma*] in the Talmudic expression [*Kesubos* 17a] כַּלָּה נָאָה וַחֲסוּדָה, 'a handsome bride liked by all' *(Rashi).*

Normally, prisoners are the dregs of society, and the whole concept of emotion or affection is absent among them. In Joseph's case, however, Providence specifically ordained that all the prisoners took a special liking for him *(Haamek Davar).*

— HASHEM endowed Joseph with an aura of innocence *(Malbim).*

וַיִּתֵּן חִנּוֹ בְּעֵינֵי שַׂר בֵּית־הַסֹּהַר — [*And*] *He made the prison warden view him favorably* [lit. *and He gave his grace in the eyes of the official of the prison*].

I.e. this was the *specific* way in which God extended *grace* or *charisma* to him *(Akeidah).*

22. וְאֵת כָּל־אֲשֶׁר עֹשִׂים שָׁם הוּא הָיָה עֹשֶׂה — *And everything that was done* [lit. *that they do*] *there, he would accomplish* [lit. *he was the doer*].

[I.e. he was in authority to have it accomplished;] as *Onkelos* renders: it was done at his command *(Rashi).*

Although the literal meaning of the phrase indicates that Joseph was the *doer* of all the work, the context of the verse makes this interpretation impossible. If the warden liked Joseph enough to put him in charge of all the prisoners, he could hardly have expected Joseph to do all the work. Instead, Rashi interprets 'doer' in the sense of God's command to Moses: וְעָשִׂיתָ מְנֹרַת זָהָב, *you are to make a golden menorah;* the physical work was to be done by Bezalel, but Moses had responsibility for it *(Mizrachi).*

Tur cites an opinion that this phrase intimates how Joseph supported himself by plying a trade as did the other prisoners.

R' Hirsch offers an alternate interpretation: what previously a number of prisoners had to do, Joseph did himself.

Haamek Davar notes how the verb עשה denotes putting an object into its final form [see *Ramban* to 1:7]. Hence this passage informs us that Joseph was the one to arrange for the sale of the crafts that the prisoners fashioned in prison, this being the ultimate purpose of their labor.

23. אֵין שַׂר בֵּית־הַסֹּהַר רֹאֶה אֶת־כָּל־מְאוּמָה בְּיָדוֹ — *The prison warden did not scrutinize anything that was in his* [Joseph's] *charge* [lit. *the warden of the prison does not see anything at all in his hand*].

The translation of *supervise* for רֹאֶה, *see,* follows *Ralbag.*

The warden of the prison never demanded an accounting of Joseph nor did he guard him. He realized that Joseph was innocent, that HASHEM was with him, and that HASHEM made him succeed in everything he undertook *(Targum Yonasan).*

According to *Haamek Davar,* the intimation is that the warden scrutinized Joseph carefully since he felt that it was not for naught that his master had incarcerated such an apparently capable servant. But this verse informs us, that

בְּיָדוֹ בַּאֲשֶׁר יהוָה אִתּוֹ וַאֲשֶׁר־הוּא עֹשֶׂה
יהוָה מַצְלִיחַ׃
°שביעי א °וַיְהִי אַחַר הַדְּבָרִים הָאֵלֶּה חָטְאוּ מַשְׁקֵה
מֶלֶךְ־מִצְרַיִם וְהָאֹפֶה לַאֲדֹנֵיהֶם לְמֶלֶךְ

the warden was unable to detect anything adverse in Joseph. He therefore concluded, as the verse proceeds to inform us, that Joseph's perfection was בַּאֲשֶׁר ה׳ אִתּוֹ, *Inasmuch as HASHEM was with him,* i.e., due to God's assistance.

בַּאֲשֶׁר ה׳ אִתּוֹ — *Inasmuch as HASHEM was with him.*

The translation of בַּאֲשֶׁר as *inasmuch* follows *Rashi.*

וַאֲשֶׁר הוּא עֹשֶׂה ה׳ מַצְלִיחַ — *And whatever he did HASHEM made successful.*

Joseph's success was extraordinary. Accordingly, it was obvious that HASHEM was with him because of his righteousness *(Haamek Davar).*

This is a general statement. Not only in prison, but at *all* times — even when he later rose to greatness and prosperity — HASHEM was with him and made him prosper *(Midrash).*

XL

1. Joseph interprets dreams in prison.

וַיְהִי אַחַר הַדְּבָרִים הָאֵלֶּה — *And it happened after these things.*

[This expression, as distinct from the expression **וַיְהִי אַחֲרֵי** כו׳, signifies that an occurrence about to be related followed soon after the preceding event, or resulted directly from it. (See *Rashi* to 39:7 and *Mizrachi* cited in comm. to 22:20). Since this expression is used to introduce the imprisonment of Pharaoh's two courtiers, the imprisonment is accordingly perceived as a direct result of the incident just related — the scandal maliciously engineered by Potiphar's wife]:

— Because Potiphar's accursed wife[1] had made Joseph the subject of general gossip, God now arranged for a new scandal: He brought about the offenses of these men [prominent officials of the royal palace] so that people's attention should be diverted to them and

1. Although in 39:1 *Rashi* refers to the 'purity' of Potiphar's wife's intention, nevertheless here he calls her אֲרוּרָה, *accursed.*

Perhaps, like Tamar, her *intentions* were noble, but, unlike Tamar, her method was misguided. Tamar acted within the law in seeking to have a child by the righteous Judah, for, as noted in the *comm.* to 38:8, Judah was the next of kin upon whom it was incumbent to 'redeem' Tamar in levirate marriage; her method, though it seemed to be an act of prostitution, was not adulterous.

Potiphar's wife, on the other hand, allowed her noble intentions to justify any means, no matter how forbidden. She, too, wanted a child by a righteous man, Joseph, but she followed her evil inclination to entice Joseph into depraved adultery. It was only by Joseph's exemplary resistance that her evil plans did not come to fruition. Thus, *Rashi's* designation of her, as 'accursed' is in the light of her deeds, not her aspirations — it portrays the Rabbinic perspective of that evil woman, and is not inconsistent with his earlier evaluation of her motives. [Cf. *footnote* to 39:1]

40
1 *charge inasmuch as HASHEM was with him. And whatever he did HASHEM made successful.*

And it happened after these things that the cupbearer of the king of Egypt and the baker transgressed against their master, against the king of

away from Joseph. God's other purpose [in causing the officials' offense and imprisonment] was to make Joseph's relief [and ultimate elevation to a high position] occur through them *(Rashi).*

Rashi is drawn to the latter reason because the imprisonment of only *one* royal official would have sufficed if God's intention had been to divert attention from Joseph. That *two* officials were imprisoned is perceived as setting the stage of Joseph's rise to prominence. Two people were needed because Joseph's diametrically opposed interpretations of their dreams proved his veracity beyond doubt *(Gur Aryeh;* comp. *Malbim).* [Furthermore, *Rashi* might have been drawn to the second interpretation because there was a lapse of many years between the two events.]

חָטְאוּ מַשְׁקֵה מֶלֶךְ מִצְרַיִם וְהָאֹפֶה — *That the cupbearer of the king of Egypt and the baker transgressed.*

[By performing their duties unsatisfactorily]:

In the case of one, a fly was found in his goblet of wine, while in the case of the other, a pebble was discovered in his bread *(Rashi* from *Midrash).*[1]

This Rabbinic tradition cited by *Rashi* explains why the cupbearer was ultimately restored to his former position [*v.* 21] while the baker was put to death. The cupbearer's offense was less serious than that of the baker, since a fly could have fallen in at any time, and presumably was not in the goblet when the cupbearer originally prepared and served it. The baker, however, was guilty of negligence since a pebble must have been in the dough or oven all along *(Mizrachi; Gur Aryeh.* See *Gittin* 6b for an analogy).

Furthermore, the presence of a pebble was a more serious offense since it could have choked Pharaoh, whereas the presence of a dead fly, while repulsive, is harmless *(Radal).*

In general, the Rabbinic tradition that these offenses involved the respective foods of which they were in charge is inspired by the fact that the Torah — which economizes on its every word — found it necessary to mention the occupation of these two officers, thus intimating that this was relevant to their offense *(Akeidas Yitzchak).*

Rashi notes that the noun אוֹפֶה, *baker,* refers specifically to the baker of *bread* since Scripture uses the root אפה, *bake,* only in that sense.

According to *Sforno* and many other commentators, the respective offenses were committed by *underlings* of the two chamberlains, but the chamberlains themselves were held responsible for not exercising proper supervision. [See *Malbim* cited in footnote next page.]

לַאֲדֹנֵיהֶם לְמֶלֶךְ מִצְרָיִם — *Against* [lit. *to*] *their master, against* [lit. *to*] *the king of Egypt.*

1. There is another Midrashic opinion that these officials were accused of plotting to poison Pharaoh. They allegedly conspired to place a fatal dose in his wine and in his bread *(Targum Yonasan).* According to *Yafeh Toar* the king was saved only because Providence caused him to discover a fly in his wine and pebble in his bread.

According to another view in the *Midrash,* they planned to seduce the king's daughter. This is suggested by analogy with 39:9 where the same term חֵטְא, *sin,* is used to denote a sexual offense.

The prevalent Rabbinic opinion, however, is that there was no conspiracy. Providence merely arranged the fly in the wine and the pebble in the bread to precipitate the chain of events which led to Joseph's elevation to greatness.

ב מִצְרָיִם: וַיִּקְצֹף פַּרְעֹה עַל שְׁנֵי סָרִיסָיו
ג עַל שַׂר הַמַּשְׁקִים וְעַל שַׂר הָאוֹפִים: וַיִּתֵּן
אֹתָם בְּמִשְׁמַר בֵּית שַׂר הַטַּבָּחִים אֶל־בֵּית
הַסֹּהַר מְקוֹם אֲשֶׁר יוֹסֵף אָסוּר שָׁם:

— I.e., in their duties to their master *(Midrash).*

The redundant terms are used to emphasize that their offense was all the more serious because it affected the king of Egypt *(Malbim).*

Some commentators hold that *their master* is *not* identical with *the king of Egypt.* Instead, the verse divides the offense into two steps: the servants of the Chamberlain of the Cupbearers and of the Chamberlain of the Bakers were guilty of malfeasance to their masters, the respective chamberlains. These misdeeds, in turn, constituted crimes against *the king of Egypt.* Therefore, although ordinary servants were responsible, the *Chamberlain* of the Cupbearers and *Chamberlain* of the Bakers were jailed *(v.* 2); they were held responsible for not supervising their subordinates properly. [Cf. *Sforno* cited above].[1]

2. וַיִּקְצֹף פַּרְעֹה עַל שְׁנֵי סָרִיסָיו — [And] *Pharaoh was enraged at his two courtiers.*

This was part of the Divine plan. God caused Pharaoh to be incensed at his two courtiers in order to engineer the rise of Joseph to greatness. Similarly, the Sages perceive that God engineered the rise of Mordechai through Ahasuerus's *wrath* (קֶצֶף) at Bigsan and Teresh [*Esther* 2:21] *(Midrash; Lekach Tov;* cf. *Megillah* 13b).

The translation of סָרִיסָיו as *his courtiers* follows the rendering of *Onkelos* [רַבְרְבָנוֹהִי]. The term is discussed in the *comm.* to 37:36 and 39:1.

Ramban maintains that these officials were called סָרִיסִים which literally means *eunuchs,* since their duties required them to go into the women's quarters of the royal palace, and the kings would customarily castrate them.

עַל שַׂר הַמַּשְׁקִים וְעַל שַׂר הָאוֹפִים — [*Upon*] *the Chamberlain of the Cupbearers and* [*upon*] *the Chamberlain of the Bakers.*

— For having improperly supervised their subordinates (see *Sforno*

1. *Malbim* pursues this interpretation, but goes a step further. It is true that in terms of their supervisory obligations, the cupbearer was less delinquent than the baker because the presence of a fly is accidental. However, from a different viewpoint, the cupbearer was the *more* guilty party. For [as is clear from *v.* 13] the *Chamberlain of the Cupbearers* was the courtier who actually handed the cup to Pharaoh — he should have noticed at the last moment that something had fallen into Pharaoh's drink, something that was impossible for the *Chamberlain of the Bakers* who could not know that a loaf contained a pebble. Therefore, the *personal* guilt of the cupbearer was the greater of the two. Accordingly, in *v.* 2, the king's wrath was first primarily on the Chamberlain of the Cupbearers and secondarily upon the Chamberlain of the Bakers.

Viewed from this perspective, Pharaoh would have been more likely to show mercy to the baker, whose guilt was indirect. Had Joseph interpreted the dreams that way and such been Pharaoh's decision, no one would have taken Joseph's role seriously, because his interpretation of the dreams would have demonstrated simple common sense rather than great incisiveness or supernatural powers. That events followed a different course is further proof that Providence ordered history so that Joseph would be elevated to greatness.

Egypt. [2] Pharaoh was enraged at his two courtiers,
the Chamberlain of the Cupbearers and the
Chamberlain of the Bakers. [3] And he placed them in
the ward of the house of the Chamberlain of the
Butchers, into the prison, the place where Joseph

above, *v.* 1 and *footnote* there).

However, most commentators maintain that the people designated simply as *cupbearer* and *baker* in verses 1 and 5 are identical with those designated as *chamberlain* in this verse. They *themselves* sinned and were now incarcerated.

R' Hirsch explains that the difference in the Torah's designation of them first simply by their respective designations as *cupbearer* and *baker* and then as *chamberlains.* To the masses they were שָׂרִים, *chamberlains,* whom the king honored with his favor, while to the king [as reflected in this verse] they were nothing more than סָרִיסָיו, *courtiers* [literally *castrates*]. Like the most inconsequential slave, they were his powerless chattels whom he could have thrown into a dungeon at his slightest whim. [Comp. *Kli Yakar*].

3. וַיִּתֵּן אֹתָם — *And he placed them.*

I.e., ordered them placed *(Ralbag).*

R' Hirsch [to *v.* 7] observes how in imprisoning his offensive chamberlains Pharaoh acted differently from his later Persian counterpart, Ahasuerus, who *executed* offending officials [cf. *Esther* 2:23]. Pharaoh's less impetuous behavior was an integral stitch in the intricate Providential fabric being woven.

בְּמִשְׁמַר בֵּית שַׂר הַטַּבָּחִים אֶל־בֵּית הַסֹּהַר — *In the ward of the house of the Chamberlain of the Butchers* [or *Chamberlain of the Executioners* (see above)], *into the prison.*

In the ward — i.e., a place where they could be guarded from escaping *(Ibn Ezra).*

Their incarceration was for the purpose of detaining them pending sentence. This is derived from the case of the blasphemer [*Leviticus* 24:12] and the man who gathered wood on the Sabbath [ibid. 15:34] both of whom were held — in the case of the former, so that his punishment *might be declared to them by the mouth of* HASHEM [*Lev.* 24:12], and in the case of the latter, *because it had not been declared what should be done to him* [*Numbers* 15:34] *(Bereishis Rabbosi).*

As this verse makes plain, Potiphar was in charge of this ward, as it was in part of his home *(Ibn Ezra; Akeidah).*

This passage would tend to strengthen *Onkelos* and *Ramban's* interpretation that שַׂר הַטַּבָּחִים means *Chamberlain of the Executioners* who was also in charge of the prisoners awaiting sentencing. But according to *Rashi's* interpretation in 37:36 and 39:1 that it means *Chamberlain of the Butchers,* it seems difficult that he would have anything to do with condemned prisoners *(Ibn Caspi).*

מְקוֹם אֲשֶׁר יוֹסֵף אָסוּר שָׁם — *The place where Joseph was confined* [see above].

We are given this information to prepare us for the narrative which follows *(Radak).*

It was a further manifestation of God's Providence that these prisoners were guided to the very ward

ד וַיִּפְקֹד שַׂר הַטַּבָּחִים אֶת־יוֹסֵף אִתָּם
וַיְשָׁרֶת אֹתָם וַיִּהְיוּ יָמִים בְּמִשְׁמָר׃
ה וַיַּחַלְמוּ חֲלוֹם שְׁנֵיהֶם אִישׁ חֲלֹמוֹ בְּלַיְלָה
אֶחָד אִישׁ כְּפִתְרוֹן חֲלֹמוֹ הַמַּשְׁקֶה

of the prison where Joseph, too, was confined *(Malbim).*

All of these circumloculations took place in order to cause Jacob's eventual descent into Egypt and begin the foretold exile *(R' Bachya).*

4. וַיִּפְקֹד שַׂר הַטַּבָּחִים אֶת יוֹסֵף אִתָּם — *The Chamberlain of the Butchers* [or: *Executioners*] *appointed Joseph* [*to be*] *with them.*

The translation *appointed* follows *Rashi:* Joseph was appointed to serve them. As a gesture of courtesy on Potiphar's part to his fallen colleagues, he selected his foremost servant to be their attendant *(Gur Aryeh; Tzeidah laDerech;* cf. *Ibn Ezra).*

וַיְשָׁרֶת אֹתָם — *And he attended them.*

That Joseph was brought into *personal* contact with the individuals through whom he would ultimately be liberated, was yet another facet of the guiding hand of Providence *(Abarbanel; Malbim).*

וַיִּהְיוּ יָמִים בְּמִשְׁמָר — *And they remained in the ward* [for a period of] *days.*

Twelve months *(Rashi).*[1]

Joseph's long period of incarceration together with political prisoners during which time he had the opportunity of gaining their trust and learning about the intimate workings of government was also part of the Divine scheme. Joseph's association with them benefited him in later years when he controlled the government of Egypt *(Abarbanel).*

5. The dreams of the chamberlains.

[On the veracity of dreams in Scripture as prognostications of the future and a determining influence, see *comm.* to 28:12; 37:5 and *Overview.*]

וַיַּחַלְמוּ חֲלוֹם שְׁנֵיהֶם — *The two of them had dreamt a dream.*

— This translation based upon *Rashi* follows the simple sense of the Hebrew which literally reads: *and they dreamt a dream the two of them* [i.e., that the *two of them* is the subject of *they dreamt;* see *Ramban* below s.v. הַמַּשְׁקֶה.]

Midrashically [the word חֲלוֹם is interpreted in the construct state and] the phrase is rendered: *They dreamt the dream of both of them,* i.e., each of them dreamt his own

1. This interpretation of *days* as meaning *one year* is derived by analogy [*gezerah shavah*] from *Lev.* 25:29: יָמִים תִּהְיֶה גְאֻלָּתוֹ, *for a 'full year'* [יָמִים] *shall he have the right of redemption.* In that passage, as explained in *Kesubos* 57b, יָמִים, *days,* has the meaning of *year.* As the *Gemara* ibid. explains, we do not compare our verse to *Numbers* 11:20 חֹדֶשׁ יָמִים lit. *a month of days,* since we may draw an analogy only from a parallel verse where יָמִים is left undefined, not from a passage which specifies its meaning as a *month (Mizrachi; Gur Aryeh.* See *Rashi* above 24:55).

The implication is that within three days — at Pharaoh's birthday — they will have been imprisoned for a *total* period of one year — a full cycle of days. It emerges that they were imprisoned a year earlier on Pharaoh's birthday, and their fate determined a full year later to the day *(R' David Feinstein).*

was confined. 4 *The Chamberlain of the Butchers ap-*
pointed Joseph to be with them, and he attended
them and they remained in the ward for a period of
days.
5 *The two of them dreamt a dream, each one had*
his dream on the same night, each one according to
the interpretation of his dream — the cupbearer and

dream as well as the interpretation of the other's dream. This is the meaning of *v.* 16 which states that *the Chamberlain of the Bakers saw that he* [Joseph] *had interpreted well.* [Unless the baker had dreamt that the cupbearer would indeed be reappointed to serve Pharaoh, how could he have known that Joseph's interpretation was correct? *(Mizrachi; Gur Aryeh).*] [Cf. *Midrash* and *Berachos* 55b.]

Abarbanel observes that sometimes Scripture refers to the dreams in the singular, as in our phrase, חֲלוֹם, as if they were one dream. This is because the symbolism of the two dreams was so similar that they both seemed to have the same meaning although it was only natural that each dreamt in terms of his own occupation. Only when Joseph enlightened them did they realize that the dreams were distinct.

אִישׁ חֲלֹמוֹ בְּלַיְלָה אֶחָד — *Each one had his dream on the same night* [lit. *man his dream on one night*].

— A further omen that their dreams were not coincidence or mere fantasy *(Malbim).*

As *R' Hirsch* explains, there was nothing extraordinary in a prisoner dreaming that he had been freed and was back at the occupation he had been performing for many years. Rather they were struck by the similarity of both dreams *on the same night.* [See continuation of this comment below.]

Oznaim l'Torah mentions that that evening was the first of Tishrei, Rosh HaShanah. Since the fate of men and nations is determined on that day (a fact apparently recognized even by the gentiles in those times), they gave special emphasis to the omens contained in their dreams as portents of the fates awaiting them in the coming year. [See his *comm.* to 41:1; cf. *Rosh HaShanah* 10a; comp. also *Maharsha to Berachos* 55b that dreams dreamt on Rosh HaShanah are auspicious.]

אִישׁ כְּפִתְרוֹן חֲלֹמוֹ — *Each one* [lit. *man*] *according to the interpretation of his dream.*

Each dream was consistent with the interpretation which foretold what would befall the dreamer *(Rashi).*

That is, the Chamberlain of the Cupbearers dreamed of wine, the symbol of joy, while the Chamberlain of the Bakers dreamed of a bird snatching the food he was bringing to the king, an event portending grief *(Tur).*

This does not suggest that they were aware of the respective interpretations at the time. Rather, the Torah is thus informing us that in retrospect it would become apparent that each dream was consistent with what the future held — as later interpreted by Joseph *(Sefer HaZikoron; Devek Tov).*

As *Ibn Ezra* (explained by *Ramban)* and *Radak* interpret, each dream contained an accurate vision of the future, verifying that it was a true dream — not the kind which one fantasizes as the result of anxiety and of which only a part is fulfilled. Cf. *Rashbam:* Each dreamed a dream worthy of interpreta-

וְהָאֹפֶה אֲשֶׁר לְמֶלֶךְ מִצְרַיִם אֲשֶׁר
ו אֲסוּרִים בְּבֵית הַסֹּהַר: וַיָּבֹא אֲלֵיהֶם יוֹסֵף
ז בַּבֹּקֶר וַיַּרְא אֹתָם וְהִנָּם זֹעֲפִים: וַיִּשְׁאַל
אֶת־סְרִיסֵי פַרְעֹה אֲשֶׁר אִתּוֹ בְמִשְׁמַר
בֵּית אֲדֹנָיו לֵאמֹר מַדּוּעַ פְּנֵיכֶם רָעִים
ח הַיּוֹם: וַיֹּאמְרוּ אֵלָיו חֲלוֹם חָלַמְנוּ וּפֹתֵר
אֵין אֹתוֹ וַיֹּאמֶר אֲלֵהֶם יוֹסֵף הֲלוֹא

tion; they were significant and not mere fantasies.

The dreams were so indicative of their true meaning that they hardly seemed to be dreams at all. They were so clear that they seemed to lack only a minor point to make their meaning so apparent that an interpreter would be unnecessary *(R' Hirsch).*

According to *Rashi's* Midrashic interpretation cited above: Each dreamed of the interpretation of the other's dream: The cupbearer saw an image of the baker being hanged, while the baker saw the cup-bearer being restored to his former position. Cf. also *Targum Yonasan.*

Minchah Belulah understands the Midrash to intimate that each envisioned one man promoted to honor and one hung but they did not know which was which.

הַמַּשְׁקֶה וְהָאֹפֶה אֲשֶׁר לְמֶלֶךְ מִצְרַיִם — *The Cupbearer and the Baker of* [lit. *that were to*] *the king of Egypt.*

— This is repeated because their duties to the king were central in the theme of their respective dreams *(Rashi).*

They are designated without their title שַׂר, *chamberlain,* to intimate that each dreamt of himself as nothing more than a *cupbearer* or *a baker,* not as men of great rank in charge of underlings. Being incarcerated, their spirits were broken and they gave no thought to lordship *(Sforno).*

In the contextual flow of the verse, the following phrases modify the earlier subject שְׁנֵיהֶם, *the two of them.* For clarity of interpretation of the verse should be perceived as if the phrases were transposed to read: *The two of them — the cupbearer and baker of the king of Egypt who were confined in the prison — dreamt a dream; each one had his dream on the same night, each one according to the interpretation of his dream.* There are many similar verses which require transposition of the stiches for better comprehension *(Ramban* to 37:2).

6. וַיָּבֹא אֲלֵיהֶם יוֹסֵף בַּבֹּקֶר — [*And*] *Joseph came to them in the morning.*

To attend to their needs as was his practice *(Abarbanel).*[1]

וַיַּרְא אֹתָם וְהִנָּם זֹעֲפִים — [*And*] *he saw them — Behold! they were aggrieved.*

The translation *aggrieved* follows *Rashi.* Comp. this meaning of the verb זעף, in *I Kings* 20:23 and *Micah* 7:9. *Radak* interprets similarly.

Ibn Ezra interprets the verb as נִתְרַעֵשׁ, *agitated, distraught,* citing this meaning in *Jonah* 1:15: *The sea stopped* מִזַּעְפּוֹ, *its raging; agitation.*

1. Where did he come from? — Possibly he slept in the lower dungeon while they, as illustrious officials, stayed in the more spacious מִשְׁמָר, *ward,* mentioned often in this narrative. According to the *Midrash,* Joseph would go every day to attend to Potiphar's household needs [the house was attached to the prison; perhaps Potiphar wanted Joseph's Divine blessing to continue resting on the house] and he now came to serve these two prisoners as was his daily responsibility *(Oznaim l'Torah).*

*the baker of the king of Egypt who were confined in
the prison.*
*[6] Joseph came to them in the morning. He saw
them — Behold! they were aggrieved. [7] And he asked
Pharaoh's courtiers who were with him in the ward
of his master's house, saying, 'Why do you appear
downcast today?' [8] And they said to him, 'We dreamt
a dream, but there is no interpreter for it.' So Joseph*

R' Hirsch renders: *And behold they were overcast.* He explains that זעף is related to צעף and hence צעיף, *veil* — an external covering of the face. Similarly זעף refers to a veiling of the countenance from within a perplexed face — shielding one's ordinary expression of liveliness with an appearance of a troubled face.

7. וַיִּשְׁאַל אֶת סְרִיסֵי פַרְעֹה אֲשֶׁר אִתּוֹ בְמִשְׁמַר בֵּית אֲדֹנָיו — *And he asked Pharaoh's courtiers who were with him in the ward of his master's house.*

The passage could simply have read 'And he asked *them*' without this circumlocution! Scripture's purpose in detailing this at length was to demonstrate that Joseph had serene confidence in himself. Though they regarded him as a despised, foreign slave and lowly prisoner, he nevertheless questioned these important *courtiers of Pharaoh,* offering to interpret their dreams at great personal risk, though he knew full well that if he were wrong and the baker were restored to his former position by Pharaoh, the baker would have hanged Joseph for his false interpretation *(Ramban).*

Sforno offers that it was only because Joseph had been appointed to minister to their personal needs that he had the temerity to question them. Otherwise it would have been presumptuous on his part.

Haamek Davar suggests that Joseph was unafraid of them because, as the verse tells us, they were *with him,* his fellow prisoners in the ward of his master's house.

מַדּוּעַ פְּנֵיכֶם רָעִים הַיּוֹם — *Why do you appear downcast today?* [lit. *why are your faces bad today?*]

— Joseph recognized that the presence of Pharaoh's two officers in prison with him was Providential and had meaning regarding his own future destiny. Their sad and worried appearance, therefore, made him personally interested in their plight *(R' Munk).*

8. חֲלוֹם חָלַמְנוּ וּפֹתֵר אֵין אֹתוֹ — *We* [i.e. *each of us (Abarbanel)*] *dreamt a dream, but there is no interpreter for it.*

I.e., there is no one who can explain the prophetic portentions of the dream. Apparently they had sent for interpreters, or perhaps there were people with them in prison, but none could interpret it. Or the implication of their remark could be: 'No one in the world could, in our opinion, interpret these dreams, so difficult are they' *(Ramban).*

According to *Or HaChaim,* the sense is that there was absolutely no one who could offer *any interpretation whatsoever.* This was different from the case of Pharaoh where the implication is that interpretations were offered, but none which would satisfy Pharaoh [see 41:8].

Haamek Davar [contrary to *Ramban*

ט לֵאלֹהִים פִּתְרֹנִים סַפְּרוּ־נָא לִי: וַיְסַפֵּר
שַׂר־הַמַּשְׁקִים אֶת־חֲלֹמוֹ לְיוֹסֵף וַיֹּאמֶר
י לוֹ בַּחֲלוֹמִי וְהִנֵּה־גֶפֶן לְפָנָי: וּבַגֶּפֶן
שְׁלֹשָׁה שָׂרִיגִם וְהִוא כְפֹרַחַת עָלְתָה נִצָּהּ

above] maintains that the implication is that *here in jail there is no one to interpret it,* since no one is allowed in [presumably, had they been free they would have consulted one of the professional interpreters or soothsayers common in ancient Egypt who *could* have offered an acceptable interpretation].

הֲלוֹא לֵאלֹהִים פִּתְרֹנִים סַפְּרוּ־נָא לִי — *Do not interpretations belong to God?* [or: *Behold!* (הֲלוֹא being understood as synonymous with הִנֵּה) *Interpretations belong to God (alone)! (Ramban).*] *Relate* [*it*] *to me, if you please.*

— Just as God sends the dream, so He grants man the wisdom to interpret it; otherwise, the dream would have been in vain. Therefore *tell it to me* — perhaps God will endow me with the wisdom to interpret it *(Radak).*

— The portentous interpretations of dreams belong only to God since He knows the future and it is He Who sends dreams to foreshadow events to whomever He wishes. Therefore you may tell it to me without fear — if my interpretation is untrue it will have no effect whatsoever since the meaning and fulfillment of dreams belong exclusively to God' *(Ibn Ezra;* see *Akeidas Yitzchak;* cf. *comm.* to *v.* 16 and *Or HaChaim* cited in *v.* 18).

Ramban cites *Ibn Ezra* and adds that Joseph intimated this so they should not punish him should evil befall them as a result of his prognostication.

According to *Ramban's* own opinion [which is similar to *Radak's*], the interpretation is: 'Do not the interpretations of all obscure dreams belong to God? He reveals it to whomever He wishes. Now, please relate your mysterious dream to me; perhaps He will reveal its interpretation to me.'

Sforno: Man has wisdom to interpret dreams only because he was formed in the image of God; therefore I too, though now only a slave in prison, may possess this wisdom. Accordingly, you might not have been correct in saying that there is no one to interpret it.

— If dreams have meaning, then God must have caused them and arranged for them to be understood. He can convey understanding through anyone *(R' Hirsch).*

It is not the magician's art that will explain the dream. Dreams are revelation, so one has to be Divinely inspired to comprehend their significance *(Zohar).*

סַפְּרוּ־נָא לִי — *Relate it to me, if you please.*

I.e., in detail. See difference between the Hebrew terms ספר and הגד in comm. to 37:9-10.

The translation of נָא as *please* follows *Rashi's* interpretation of this word throughout Scripture [see for example 38:25 and *v.* 14 below]. *Onkelos* — except for a few isolated instances — regularly renders the word as כְּעַן, *now.*

Or HaChaim in this instance also interprets it as *now,* rendering: *relate it to me now.* There two reasons for this. He explains that an interpretation of a dream is valid only if offered on the very next day; not later. Therefore Joseph insisted on being told the dream immediately, before it was too late. Secondly, according to the view that dreams follow the interpretation given them, Joseph was apprehensive that the chamberlains might seek another's interpretation first, and the other's might

said to them, 'Do not interpretations belong to God?
Relate it to me, if you please.'
9 *Then the Chamberlain of the Cupbearers*
recounted his dream to Joseph and said to him, 'In
my dream — Behold! there was a grapevine in front
of me! 10 *On the grapevine were three tendrils.*
And it was as though it budded — its blossoms

materialize before his. Although the Talmud records an incident where twenty-four interpretations were given to a dream and they all materialized, *Or HaChaim* insists that this is so only where the interpretations do not oppose one another; otherwise, only the first one has veracity, and Joseph did not wish to forfeit the opportunity.

9. בַּחֲלוֹמִי וְהִנֵּה־גֶפֶן לְפָנָי — *In my dream* [i.e., I saw in my dream *(Radak)*] — *Behold! there was a grapevine in front of me.*

The term הִנֵּה, *behold,* in the context of dreams, denotes that it was not merely a fantasy. The term [which has the colloquial sense of *look!; see!*] is used only to introduce something clearly of substance *(Akeidas Yitzchak;* see *comm.* to 28:13 p. 1228; 31:10; 37:7).

According to *Ramban,* the term in this context denotes comparison: 'In my dream *it was as if* there was a grape vine in front of me.'

Ibn Ezra in *v.* 15 mentions that all physical objects in dreams are comparisons rather than realities since all dreams are visual representations and not physically tangible.

10. וּבַגֶּפֶן שְׁלֹשָׁה שָׂרִיגִם — [*And*] *on the grapevine were three tendrils.*

— Long branches known in Old French as *vitis (Rashi).*

There are usually many more than three tendrils on a vine. Joseph accordingly perceived a special significance in this number *(Daas Soferim).* [See *comm.* to *v.* 12].

וְהִוא כְפֹרַחַת עָלְתָה נִצָּהּ — *And it was as though it budded — its blossoms bloomed;* [lit. *and it, as budding its blossom arose*].

[The translation follows *Rashi* who interprets that the prefix כ is the כ of comparison *as though*]:

— It appeared to me in my dream *as though it budded,* and after the bud *its blossom sprang up,* i.e. it began to flower. The נֵץ [*blossom*], is a later stage of development than פֶּרַח [*bud*] as is evident from *Isaiah* 18:5; *Numbers* 17:23 *(Rashi).*

[*Rashi* makes an additional observation that *Onkelos'* rendering: וְהִיא כַּד אַפְרַחַת אַפֵּקַת לַבְלְבִין, *and it, when it budded, brought forth blossoms* is his translation only of the word כְּפֹרַחַת. *Ramban* differs with this opinion maintaining that אַפֵּקַת לַבְלְבִין is *Onkelos'* Aramaic equivalent of the term עָלְתָה. See *Ramban* and *R' Chavel's* notes for a full understanding of their respective opinions regarding which Aramaic words correspond to the Hebrew.]

According to *Ramban,* the prefix כ is temporal: *as; when,* and denotes immediacy. *At the very moment that it budded its blossoms shot up and its clusters ripened into grapes.* From this rapid development of the three tendrils, Joseph deduced that the dream would be fulfilled in three *days* rather than three months or years. [This differs with the view of *Ibn Ezra* below in *v.* 12]. The usage of כ to denote im-

יא הִבְשִׁילוּ אַשְׁכְּלֹתֶיהָ עֲנָבִים: וְכוֹס פַּרְעֹה
בְּיָדִי וָאֶקַּח אֶת־הָעֲנָבִים וָאֶשְׂחַט אֹתָם
אֶל־כּוֹס פַּרְעֹה וָאֶתֵּן אֶת־הַכּוֹס עַל־כַּף
יב פַּרְעֹה: וַיֹּאמֶר לוֹ יוֹסֵף זֶה פִּתְרֹנוֹ שְׁלֹשֶׁת
יג הַשָּׂרִגִים שְׁלֹשֶׁת יָמִים הֵם: בְּעוֹד |
שְׁלֹשֶׁת יָמִים יִשָּׂא פַרְעֹה אֶת־רֹאשֶׁךָ

mediacy occurs often. Cf. 12:14, כְּבוֹא אַבְרָהָם and 38:2, כְּמֵשִׁיב יָד.

הִבְשִׁילוּ אַשְׁכְּלֹתֶיהָ עֲנָבִים — *And its clusters ripened* [into] *grapes.*

All in rapid succession following its blossoming *(Ramban).*

11. וְכוֹס פַּרְעֹה בְּיָדִי — *[And] Pharaoh's cup was in my hand.*

[There is an opinion in *Yerushalmi Pesachim* 10:1 that four cups are drunk at the Seder on Passover evening in allusion to the four times the word 'cup' is mentioned in these verses.]

וָאֶשְׂחַט אֹתָם אֶל כּוֹס פַּרְעֹה — *[And I] pressed them* [i.e. the grapes] *into* [following *Radak;* lit. *to*] *Pharaoh's cup.*

The verb שחט appears nowhere else in Scripture. The translation *pressed* follows *Rashi* who cites *Onkelos:* וְעָצְרִית, and relates it to the Mishnaic term סחט, *press.*

וָאֶתֵּן אֶת הַכּוֹס עַל־כַּף פַּרְעֹה — *And I placed* [lit. *gave*] *the cup on Pharaoh's palm.*

— Pharaoh stretched out his hand to receive the cup from me *(R' Hirsch).*

12. The interpretation.

זֶה פִּתְרֹנוֹ — *This is its interpretation.*

I.e., this is the interpretation of the details; the *general* significance of the dream is obvious *(Haamek Davar).*

'You have given me good tidings,' said Joseph to him [for, as noted in the footnote below, Joseph perceived the dream as alluding to the future Redemption]; 'therefore I too give you good tidings' *(Midrash).*

Ibn Ezra remarks that the term פִּתְרוֹן, *interpretation,* occurs only in connection with dreams.

שְׁלֹשֶׁת הַשָּׂרִגִים שְׁלֹשֶׁת יָמִים הֵם — *The three tendrils are three days.*

I.e., they are meant to signify to you three days. There are many Midrashic interpretations of these words [cf. *Chullin* 92a] *(Rashi).*[1]

According to *Ibn Ezra,* Joseph

1. The vine is Kabbalistically perceived as the symbol of Israel [see *Hoshea* 10:1]. The *Zohar* observes how Joseph was convinced that his Providential meeting with these chamberlains of the royal court was related to the destiny of the Abrahamitic line. He was overjoyed at hearing the Egyptian describe the miraculous fruition of the vine — its symbolic three tendrils budding, blossoming, and bringing forth succulent grapes in rapid succession. Beneath the immediate significance of the dream as it affected the cupbearer, Joseph connected it with the future flowering of his people. As the Midrash notes, when Joseph heard the prognostications of the dream, he said, 'You have given me good tidings, I too, will give you good tidings.'

With this introduction, we begin to appreciate the dream's deeper symbolisms as perceived by the Sages in *Chullin* 92a. Among these interpretations [the full understanding of which eludes our grasp] are:

— *The three branches* represent the three men of excellence who arrive in every generation ... or the three celestial princes of the heathen nations who plead on behalf of Israel in every generation;

bloomed and its clusters ripened into grapes. [11] *And*
Pharaoh's cup was in my hand and I took the grapes,
pressed them into Pharaoh's cup, and I placed the
cup on Pharaoh's palm.
[12] *Joseph said to him, 'This is its interpretation:*
The three tendrils are three days. [13] *In another three*
days Pharaoh will lift up your head and will restore

knew that the three branches represented three *days* rather than months or years, since he knew that Pharaoh's birthday would be in three days' time — a day when Pharaoh would make a great feast and summon all his courtiers.

Radak, Ramban [see above *v.* 10 s.v. הִוא כְפֹרַחַת] and *Ralbag* maintain that Joseph knew from the rapid budding, blossoming, and maturing of the grapes in the dream that the dream would be fulfilled soon; hence he chose the shortest duration of time and interpreted the allusion of the tendrils as three *days* rather than months or years.

Abarbanel emphasizes however, that such speculation is academic. Joseph successfully interpreted the dream because of the agency of the Divine inspiration which provided him with the correct interpretation; not because he arrived at this interpretation by his own wisdom.

HaKsav V'HaKabbalah makes the grammatical observation that both the cupbearer and baker used the Hebrew term שְׁלֹשָׁה [*v.* 10, 16] while Joseph, in both his interpretations employed the term שְׁלֹשֶׁת. The nuance suggests the difference between the speakers. The dreamers perceived three tendrils or baskets *individually* as unrelated units, a concept implied by the term שְׁלֹשָׁה. Joseph, on the other hand, understood them as a *set* of three, therefore, he uses the term שְׁלֹשֶׁת, suggesting a *group of three.*

13. **בְּעוֹד שְׁלֹשֶׁת יָמִים יִשָּׂא פַרְעֹה אֶת רֹאשֶׁךָ** — *In another three days Pharaoh will lift up your head.*

I.e., he will take account of you. The idiom *lift up the head* means *to count* [cf. *Exod.* 30:12]. The sense here is that when Pharaoh will assemble his other servants to wait upon him during the meal *he will count you among them (Rashi).*

[Compare the use of this expression in verses 19 and 20 below.]

R' Hirsch [to *v.* 20] explains that the counting of people is expressed by this idiom probably because a large number of people crowded together look like a solid compact mass which cannot be counted; only their protruding heads can be counted.

Ibn Ezra agrees with *Rashi's* interpretation citing *v.* 20 where the chamberlains were *counted among Pharaoh's servants.* He also cites a

— The *vine*=the world; the *three branches*=the Patriarchs Abraham, Isaac and Jacob; *the budding blossoms*=the Matriarchs; *the clusters bringing forth grapes*=the tribes;

— *The vine*=the Torah; the *three branches*=Moses, Aaron, and Miriam; *the budding blossoms*=the members of the Sanhedrin; *the clusters bringing forth grapes*=the righteous people of every generation.

One Talmudic Sage interprets the passage as referring to Jerusalem:

— *The vine*=Jerusalem; the *three branches*=the Temple, the king, and the High Priest; *the budding blossoms*=the budding young priests; *the clusters bringing forth grapes*=the drink-offerings;

Another opinion is that it symbolized God's gifts to Israel:

— *The vine*=the Torah; *the three branches*=the well [see *Numb.* 21:16-20], the pillar of smoke [*Exod.* 40:36], and the Manna [*ibid.* 16:4]; *the budding blossoms*=[the fertile land

וְהֱשִׁיבְךָ עַל־כַּנֶּךָ וְנָתַתָּ כוֹס־פַּרְעֹה בְּיָדוֹ
יד כַּמִּשְׁפָּט הָרִאשׁוֹן אֲשֶׁר הָיִיתָ מַשְׁקֵהוּ: כִּי
אִם־זְכַרְתַּנִי אִתְּךָ כַּאֲשֶׁר יִיטַב לָךְ
וְעָשִׂיתָ־נָּא עִמָּדִי חָסֶד וְהִזְכַּרְתַּנִי אֶל־
טו פַּרְעֹה וְהוֹצֵאתַנִי מִן־הַבַּיִת הַזֶּה: כִּי־גֻנֹּב

figurative interpretation, shared by *Radak*, that *his head would be lifted up* from its present lowly status.

According to *Abarbanel*, the verb יִשָּׂא denotes *forgiveness* [comp. 32:21 יִשָּׂא פָנָי, *forgive me.*] Accordingly, the expression here denotes: *Pharaoh will forgive you.*

וֶהֱשִׁיבְךָ עַל־כַּנֶּךָ – *And* [he] *will restore you to your post.*

The translation of כַּנֶּךָ as *your post; place*, follows *Rashi.*

Ibn Ezra relates it to the words מָכוֹן, *base* [see *Rashi* to *Zechariah* 5:11]; מְתֻכֹּנֶת, *former condition* [see *II Chron.* 24:13]. He suggests that it is possibly related to כן [root כון; cf. *Numb.* 27:7 כֵּן בְּנוֹת צְלָפְחָד דֹּבְרֹת, *the daughters of Zelaphachad speak correctly,* i.e. with *basis (Yohel Or)*]; comp. *Daniel* 11:20 וְעָמַד עַל כַּנּוֹ, *shall stand on his place.*

וְנָתַתָּ כוֹס־פַּרְעֹה בְּיָדוֹ – *And you will place Pharaoh's cup in his hand.*

Pharaoh's former trust in you will be fully restored; he will unquestioningly take his cup directly from your hand without demanding that you taste it first *(Meshech Chochmah).*

14. Joseph asks the cupbearer to intercede on his behalf.

כִּי אִם־זְכַרְתַּנִי אִתְּךָ כַּאֲשֶׁר יִיטַב לָךְ – *If only* [lit. *for if*] *you would think of me with yourself when he* [i.e., Pharaoh] *benefits you.*

The contextual flow is: You will be restored to your former post (and achieve such influence) ... that if you would keep me in mind along with yourself after it will go well with you as I predicted in my interpretation, *and you will do me a personal kindness, and mention me to Pharaoh — then you would* [thereby] *get me out of this place. (Rashi* as explained by *Mizrachi).*

I.e., your rise to prominence, in accordance with my interpretation will be so profound, that you will merely need mention me to Pharaoh in order to free me from prison, for he will certainly listen to you *(Rashbam).*

This interpretation bases itself on the phrase כִּי אִם being the idiomatic equivalent of אֲשֶׁר אִם, that if; cf. *Rashi* to 24:33 עַד אִם is equivalent to עַד אֲשֶׁר. Furthermore, the hoped-for consequence, according to *Mizrachi*, commences at וְהוֹצֵאתָנִי, **then** *you will thereby get me out.*

According to *Ramban* the contextual flow is: 'If you plan to remember me

which produced abundant] First Fruits [*ibid.* 23:16]; *the clusters bringing forth grapes*=the drink offerings.

— *The vine*=Israel (see *Psalms* 80:9); *the three branches*=the Three Festivals, Pesach, Shavuos, Succos; *the budding*=the abundant fertility of Israel (*Exod.* 1:7); *its blossoms bloomed*=its time for Redemption is at hand; *the clusters bringing forth grapes*=the time has come for Egypt to drink the cup of staggering [i.e. of disaster; see *Jeremiah* 46:2, 13].

R' Shimon ben Lakish said, The people of Israel is like a vine: Its branches are the aristocracy, its clusters the scholars, its leaves the common people, its twigs those in Israel who are void of learning. This was the intent of the message once sent from *Eretz Yisrael* to the community in Babylon: 'Let the clusters pray for the leaves, for were it not for the leaves the clusters could not exist' [i.e., every class is essential to the well-being of the community] *(Chullin* 92a).

you to your post, and you will place Pharaoh's cup in his hand as was the former practise when you were his cupbearer. 14 *If only you would think of me with yourself when he benefits you, and you will do me a kindness, if you please, and mention me to Pharaoh, then you would get me out of this building.* 15 *For in-*

when things go well for you, then I *now* [נָא] ask you to do me the favor of making mention of me to Pharaoh in order to secure my release.' Or, if [as *Rashi* maintains] נָא denotes *supplication,* then the syntax is: 'If you plan to remember me and would like to do me a kindness, then mention me to Pharaoh, etc.'

Chizkuni renders: 'If only you would keep me in mind, you would be doing me a great service since you would secure my release from this house.'

It is only reasonable to assume that you will bear me in mind to do me a kindness inasmuch as through my interpretation you realized some joy and I gladdened you in your misery. It is proper that you deal kindly with me when my interpretation will materialize *(Radak).*

Joseph asked the cupbearer two favors: That he himself *remember* him; and that he *recall* him to Pharaoh.' This accounts for the dual phraseology of *v.* 23: *The Chamberlain of the Cupbearers did not remember Joseph; and he forgot him* — i.e. he forgot to mention him to Pharaoh *(Daas Zekainim; R' Bachya).*

The force of the word אִתְּךָ, *along with you,* is either: remember to show me mercy in the same way that it will be shown you when you will have been released from prison; or: think of me as if I were with you *(Ramban).*

וְעָשִׂיתָ־נָּא עִמָּדִי חָסֶד — *And you will do me a kindness, if you please.*

נָא always denotes a personal supplication *(Rashi).*

According to one interpretation in *Ramban,* above, it could also mean *now.*

וְהִזְכַּרְתַּנִי אֶל־פַּרְעֹה — *And mention* [lit. *recall*] *me to Pharaoh.*

I.e., intercede on my behalf with Pharaoh. He will weigh your words heavily inasmuch as you are an important official *(Radak).*

Praise me by saying that in the house of the Chamberlain of the Butchers there is a servant worthy of serving kings. Or: once you are returned to your former exalted position, do me the favor of praising me as the lad who served you well in prison and ask that Pharaoh release me from prison to become your personal servant. Or the sense might be: Pharaoh already knows me from my excellent service in Potiphar's house. All you need do is mention my name to him and protest my innocence; that will be enough to secure my release from here *(Ramban; Tur; Sforno).*

וְהוֹצֵאתַנִי מִן־הַבַּיִת הַזֶּה — *Then* [lit. *and*] *you would* [thereby] *get me out of this building* [lit. *house*].

I.e., secure my freedom. Not only from this prison, but from this entire house where I am enslaved *(Haamek Davar).*

That the desired outcome of Joseph's request commences with this phrase [if you do all the above **then** *you would thereby be getting me out of this house*] follows *Mizrachi's* interpretation of *Rashi.*

According to the various interpretations offered by *Ramban,* the desired outcome commenced either with וְעָשִׂיתָ־נָּא עִמָּדִי חָסֶד, **then** *do me now a kindness, and mention me,* etc., or וְהִזְכַּרְתַּנִי אֶל פַּרְעֹה, **then** *mention me to Pharaoh.*

As mentioned in the *comm.* to 39:20, because Joseph placed his trust in the Chamberlain of the

גֻּנַּבְתִּי מֵאֶרֶץ הָעִבְרִים וְגַם־פֹּה לֹא־
טז עָשִׂיתִי מְאוּמָה כִּֽי־שָׂמוּ אֹתִי בַּבּוֹר: וַיַּרְא
שַׂר־הָאֹפִים כִּי טוֹב פָּתָר וַיֹּאמֶר אֶל־

Cupbearers instead of in God Himself, he was punished by having his prison sentence — which would otherwise have totaled ten years: one for each of the ten brothers about whom he had brought evil reports — increase by an additional two years (*Seder Olam; Tanchuma; Shmos Rabbah* 7:1. [Cited by *Rashi* in *v.* 23 below.][1]

15. 'Do not think you would be committing an injustice by praising me and being instrumental in securing my release from jail, for I am not a slave by birth. I am really innocent and should not have been here in the first place!' (*Rashbam; Ramban*).

כִּי גֻנֹּב גֻּנַּבְתִּי מֵאֶרֶץ הָעִבְרִים — *For indeed I was kidnaped* [idiomatic; literally the Hebrew is in the infinitive compound for emphasis: *steal I was stolen*] *from the land of the Hebrews.*[2]

Land of the Hebrews [*Ivrim*] is a reference to the territory of Hebron where Abraham, Isaac and Jacob dwelt. Abraham — the illustrious patriarch of the family in whom the blessing of *I will make your name great* [12:1] was exemplified — was called the *Ivri* [above 14:13] since he came מֵעֵבֶר, *from* [*ever*] *'across',*

1. *R' Bachya* comments that we dare not think that a *tzaddik* of Joseph's stature would place his trust in a human being rather than in God. That Joseph asked for the chamberlain's assistance was only because he assumed that Providence had placed the deposed courtier in prison so that he would become the vehicle to bring about the miracle. Joseph knew that God customarily assists the righteous through seemingly natural means. In this, he was right, but it was sinful for so great a man to seek natural means of salvation; he should have allowed God to work His way as He saw fit.

Most of our Sages find nothing reprehensible in an ordinary person resorting to the intervention of a human being, with the idea that he may serve as an instrument of Divine Providence. But "God is exacting to a hairsbreadth with those closest to Him" (*Yevamos* 121b) — and Joseph was surely among the closest. Throughout his long series of misfortunes, Joseph's confidence in God was absolute; never did he utter a word of recrimination, complaint, or self-justification. Then, suddenly, he meets Pharaoh's deposed chamberlain and his faith in God wavers ever so slightly! For a man of Joseph's stature, this is a major shortcoming (*R' Munk*). [See *Bais HaLevi* and the *Overview* to *Mikeitz*.]

'Had the cupbearer mentioned Joseph to Pharaoh', *Midrash HaGadol* [to 41:1] asks, 'what could Joseph have done when he was freed — open a shop for the interpretation of dreams? Therefore Providence caused him to be incarcerated another two years until *Pharaoh* would dream and he could achieve greatness.'

[However, even these additional two years of imprisonment imposed upon him was a manifestation of God's grace. The commentators perceive that Joseph's excessively long stay in prison was a way of preparing him for the workings of government and the monarchy. For he was, as 39:20 records, incarcerated together with political prisoners, and he learned from them about politics and the power interplay of the royal palace.]

2. The *Midrash* [*Devarim Rabbah* 2:5] records that God refused Moses' request to be buried in *Eretz Yisrael*, saying: 'One who acknowledged it as his land is buried in his land, one who did not acknowledge it as his land is not buried there.'

Joseph was described contemptuously by Potiphar's wife as אִישׁ עִבְרִי, *a Hebrew man* (39:14), yet he did not deny the fact; even in prison he proclaimed himself to be a native of *the land of the Hebrews.* Therefore he earned the right to be buried in *Eretz Yisrael.* But Moses heard himself described by Jethro's daughters as *an Egyptian man* (*Exodus* 2:19), and he ac-

40
16

deed I was kidnaped from the land of the Hebrews,
and even here I have done nothing for them to have
put me in the pit.'
16 *The Chamberlain of the Bakers saw that he had*
interpreted well. He said to Joseph, 'I, too! In my

the River Euphrates. His offspring assumed the distinguishing name *Ivri* [=Hebrew] in order not to intermingle with the various Canaanite people, and this name has remained Israel's name ever since. When Joseph came to Potiphar's house he apparently told them he was a Hebrew [39:14]. The territory around Hebron, where they resided, was referred to as the land of the *Ivrim,* not because the Canaanites acknowledged it as theirs, but because of the prominence achieved by the descendants of Abraham, who was acknowledged by the inhabitants as a *prince of God* [23:6] *(Ramban).*

The *Midrash* finds in the dual expression *steal I was stolen* an allusion to the several times Joseph's captors changed hands when he had been sold [see *comm.* to 37:35].

וְגַם־פֹּה לֹא־עָשִׂיתִי מְאוּמָה כִּי־שָׂמוּ אֹתִי בַּבּוֹר — *And even here I have done nothing for them to have put me in the pit.*

I am confident, therefore, that Pharaoh would be disposed to heed your recommendation and release me *(Sforno).*

[It is noteworthy that this is the very first time throughout all Joseph's trials that he breaks his silence and protests his innocence.]

[Possibly Joseph's use of the word בּוֹר, *pit,* subtly alluded to the pit into which his brothers had thrown him into before they sold him (37:24), the intimation being: I was innocent then just as I was here in Egypt. I did nothing to deserve being thrown into the pit in either of the cases.]

16. The baker's dream.

וַיַּרְא שַׂר הָאֹפִים כִּי טוֹב פָּתָר — [*And*] *the Chamberlain of the Bakers saw that he* [=Joseph] *had interpreted well* [lit. *good*].

— Accounting for every detail *(Haamek Davar).*

The word טוֹב can be interpreted as an adverb: *well, accurately,* or as an adjective: *favorably, good.*

I.e., that he had interpreted it accurately, as *Onkelos* renders. The sense of the passage is that the Chamberlain of the Bakers had no confidence in Joseph and did not intend to tell him his dream. [He

quiesced silently and did not identify himself as a Hebrew. Therefore, he did not merit burial in *Eretz Yisrael.*

The question is raised, however, that Joseph was truly a native of the *land of the Hebrews,* while Moses had never even seen *Eretz Yisrael.* Why should Moses be expected to describe himself as other than an Egyptian?

— The unfavorable Midrashic comparison of Moses with Joseph teaches that from the time when *Eretz Yisrael* was promised to Abraham, a Jew is duty-bound to consider himself a native of the Holy Land, no matter what his origin *(R' Meir Yechiel of Ostrovtza).*

— Furthermore, Moses came to Jethro as the hero who had saved his daughters; he had no reason not to declare proudly 'I am a Jew!' But Joseph was a slave imprisoned for a shameful crime, and instead of currying the favor of the powerful by denying that he was a Hebrew, he was proud of his origin and awaited the day when his innocence would be acknowledged and lend credit to his native land *(R' Munk).*

יוֹסֵף אַף־אֲנִי֙ בַּחֲלוֹמִ֔י וְהִנֵּ֗ה שְׁלֹשָׁ֛ה סַלֵּ֥י
יז חֹרִ֖י עַל־רֹאשִֽׁי׃ וּבַסַּ֣ל הָֽעֶלְי֔וֹן מִכֹּ֛ל
מַאֲכַ֥ל פַּרְעֹ֖ה מַעֲשֵׂ֣ה אֹפֶ֑ה וְהָע֗וֹף אֹכֵ֥ל
יח אֹתָ֛ם מִן־הַסַּ֖ל מֵעַ֥ל רֹאשִֽׁי׃ וַיַּ֤עַן יוֹסֵף֙

viewed Joseph as a mere slave — certainly not vested with the art of interpreting dreams *(Abarbanel).*] But when he saw that Joseph had interpreted his comrade's dream in a fair and proper manner, he changed his mind and told Joseph his dream as well. Or, the sense of the passage is that when he saw that Joseph gave a *favorable* interpretation to his comrade's dream he rejoiced and proceeded to relate his own dream also, expecting a cheerful report *(Ramban).*

— He hoped that Joseph would give him a similar favorable interpretation of his dream, because as the Sages declared, the fulfillment of a dream depends on how it is interpreted; similarly, verse 22 states that the fate of the chamberlains was just as Joseph had interpreted to them *(Sforno;* see *Ibn Ezra* to *v.* 8 above).

The Talmud asks: How did the baker know that Joseph had interpreted the dream well [i.e., accurately]? — This teaches that each of them dreamt his own dream and the interpretation of his companion's dream [see *comm.* to *v.* 5] *(Berachos* 55b).

— And when he perceived that Joseph's interpretation coincided with the interpretation as he had dreamt it [but which he did not comprehend until Joseph gave it meaning] he realized that Joseph was right *(Or HaChaim).*[1]

According to *Rashbam,* he knew the interpretation was correct because 'the truth speaks for itself.' [Although the baker had no objective proof that Joseph was right, he was convinced of it for the very reason that it *was* the truth. The expression 'the truth speaks for itself' (נִיכָּרִין דִּבְרֵי אֱמֶת) is taken from *Sotah* 9b where in interpreting *Judges* 16:18 Rava explains that the perfidious Delilah could tell when Samson had opened his heart to her completely since 'the truth speaks for itself'. Such is the power of truth.

אַף־אֲנִי בַּחֲלוֹמִי — *I, too! In my dream—*

I.e., I too had a dream. In it I perceived the following *(Ralbag).*

R' Hirsch renders: *I, too, was in my dream* — I too had a dream in which I was the main character.

The Hebrew word אַף, here translated in the contextual, literal, sense of *too,* also has the meaning of *anger.* The Sages in the *Midrash* observe that a description of his dream with this inauspicious word augured evil for the baker. This is similar to the fate of three others in Scripture "who commenced with אַף and subsequently perished with אַף, *anger*: The serpent [3:1]; the assembly of Korach [*Numbers* 16:14]; Haman [*Esther* 5:12]."

וְהִנֵּה — *Behold!*

I.e., in my dream I envisioned, in a concrete, non-fantastic vision, what appeared to be ... (see *Ibn Ezra* and *Ramban* to *v.* 9).

1. When God uses dreams as a vehicle to reveal His plans, the structure of the message must be such that upon hearing the interpretation the dreamer should exclaim, 'Of course! — it is so obvious I should have thought of it myself!' Once Joseph had added the new insight that the three tendrils represented three days, the dream seemed almost self-explanatory so the cupbearer could correctly say, *'he has interpreted well.'* When God conveys a message through a vision, the explanation must flow naturally from the vision once the key to its interpretation has been provided *(R' Hirsch).*

40
17

dream — Behold! three wicker baskets were on my head. [17] *And in the uppermost basket were all kinds of Pharaoh's food — baker's handiwork — and the birds were eating them from the basket above my head.'*

שְׁלֹשָׁה סַלֵּי חֹרִי עַל־רֹאשִׁי — *Three wicker* [lit. *open-work*] *baskets* [were] *on my head.*

The translation *wicker baskets* follows *Rashi* who derives the word חֹרִי from חוֹר, *hole.* He explains that the reference is to 'baskets made of peeled willow, made so that they have many holes' i.e., the plaited wicker baskets commonly used in *Rashi's* time by merchants of fancy rolls to hold their goods.

Ramban, following *R' Saadiah Gaon* [cited by *Ibn Ezra*] interprets חור as *white* (cf. *Isaiah* 29:22 and the Aramaic חיור, *white,* and Mishnah *Beitzah* 2:6 חֲיוּרֵי, *white cakes.* Cf. also *Yerushalmi* ibid. where it is derived from our passage that the term חורי refers to extra fine, large loaves of white bread). *Ramban* accordingly interprets our phrase as *baskets* of *white bread,* the kind of bread that befits a king. He maintains that this is the correct interpretation inasmuch as the baskets in the dream contained the king's bread and in the uppermost basket there were all manner of baked goods for Pharaoh.

Ralbag renders: White baskets.

The three baskets are Midrashically perceived to foreshadow the later Powers who would subjugate Israel in its exiles.

17. וּבַסַּל הָעֶלְיוֹן מִכֹּל מַאֲכַל פַּרְעֹה מַעֲשֵׂה אֹפֶה — *And in the uppermost basket were* [of] *all kinds of Pharaoh's food — baker's handiwork.*

The sense is that all the food in the baskets were fit for a Pharaoh *(R' Hirsch)* ...

The *Midrash* perceives this to prophetically symbolize the insatiable greed of Rome, the uppermost enemy of Israel who extorted tribute from all the nations of the earth.

וְהָעוֹף אֹכֵל אֹתָם מִן־הַסַּל מֵעַל רֹאשִׁי — *And the birds were eating them* [i.e. these baked goods] *from the basket above my head.*

[The noun עוֹף, *bird,* is in the singular. In the Hebrew idiom, the singular form is used to designate an indefinite number of a particular species].

[Continuing *R' Hirsch* above]: ... Yet the baker saw birds, not Pharaoh, eating his goods. Not only did they eat Pharaoh's own food, they had the impudence to eat it right off the basket on the baker's head, and he was powerless to stop them! No bird would have the temerity to do that to a living person.

Birds generally symbolize Israel's enemies, Israel itself being metaphorically compared to bread. Thus the inner meaning of the birds eating the baked goods was perceived by Joseph to be a prognostication of the suffering inflicted on Israel by its preying enemies. Joseph was constantly aware of omens unfavorable to Israel's destiny. He perceived that these birds were symbolically swooping down to attack and scatter Israel [as in Abraham's vision 15:11] whenever Israel tried to shake off the yoke of Torah and refuse to uphold the crown of the Heavenly King placed on its forehead [as represented here by the baskets] *(Tanchuma; Zohar;* cf. *Or HaChaim).*

וַיֹּאמֶר זֶה פִּתְרֹנוֹ שְׁלֹשֶׁת הַסַּלִּים שְׁלֹשֶׁת
יט יָמִים הֵם: בְּעוֹד | שְׁלֹשֶׁת יָמִים יִשָּׂא
פַרְעֹה אֶת־רֹאשְׁךָ מֵעָלֶיךָ וְתָלָה אוֹתְךָ
עַל־עֵץ וְאָכַל הָעוֹף אֶת־בְּשָׂרְךָ מֵעָלֶיךָ:
°מפטיר כ °וַיְהִי | בַּיּוֹם הַשְּׁלִישִׁי יוֹם הֻלֶּדֶת אֶת־
פַּרְעֹה וַיַּעַשׂ מִשְׁתֶּה לְכָל־עֲבָדָיו וַיִּשָּׂא

18. וַיַּעַן יוֹסֵף וַיֹּאמֶר — [*And*] *Joseph responded and said.*

Oznaim LaTorah notes that Joseph's response to the baker is prefaced by the word וַיַּעַן *and he answered,* while his reply to the cupbearer has no such introduction. This alludes to the rule that while one should avoid being the bearer of evil tidings, if one is questioned directly, he should not lie in order to avoid announcing the unpleasant news [*Yoreh De'ah* 402:12]. Therefore, Joseph did not hesitate in his interpretation of the cupbearers dream. Since its meaning was favorable, Joseph had no compunctions about expressing it, and he even *initiated* the interpretation. The baker's dream, however, presaged the baker's death. Therefore, Joseph did not *offer* to tell its meaning, but when the baker pressed him to do so — וַיַּעַן, *he responded.*

זֶה פִּתְרֹנוֹ — *This is its interpretation.*

I.e., the dream is its own interpretation. The general symbolism is obvious, only the details require interpretation [comp. *v.* 12] *(Haamek Davar).*

'You have brought *me* evil tidings,' Joseph told him [since as noted, Joseph perceived inauspicious symbolisms for Israel in the dream], 'I, too, bring *you* evil tidings regarding your fate ... *(Midrash).*

Joseph used these same words to introduce his interpretation of the cupbearer's dream [*v.* 12]. By stressing *this is its interpretation,* he asserted his authority, making clear that the dream would come true only according to *his* interpretation. This was in consonance with the Talmudic dictum that the fulfillment of a dream follows its interpretation [i.e., if one articulated a favorable interpretation, his words would force events to shape themselves favorably, even if they had been destined to take an evil turn *(Alshich)*]. With this principle in mind, Joseph made a similar declaration before interpreting Pharaoh's dream [see *comm.* to 41:16] *(Or HaChaim).*

Actually, both dreams could have lent themselves to the same interpretation since the bird eating the food from atop the baker's head could have been taken as symbolizing Pharaoh having a change of heart and restoring the baker to his post [see *Ezekiel* 17]. But Joseph was influenced by the histories of the dreamers — their status at the royal court and the difference between the crimes for which they had been sentenced, the one for forgivable carelessness and the other for gross negligence [see *Rashi* and *Malbim* to *v.* 1-2] *(Akeidas Yitzchak).*[1]

Cf. *Abarbanel* cited to *v.* 12,

18 *Joseph responded and said, 'This is its interpretation: The three baskets are three days.* 19 *In
three days Pharaoh will lift your head from you and
hang you on a tree. Birds will eat your flesh from
you.'*

20 *And it was on the third day, Pharaoh's birthday,
that he made a feast for all his servants and he*

however, who objects to such explanations and maintains that *Divine inspiration* guided Joseph in his interpretation, not his own wisdom alone.

שְׁלֹשֶׁת הַסַּלִּים שְׁלֹשֶׁת יָמִים הֵם — *The three baskets are* [i.e., represent] *three days.*

Haamek Davar maintains that Joseph perceived this short span from the closeness to one another of the three baskets in the dream. [But cf. *Abarbanel* above to *v.* 12] *(Haamek Davar).*

R' Bachya notes that the *gematria* [numerical equivalent] of שְׁלֹשֶׁת הַסַּלִּים equals that of שְׁלֹשֶׁת יָמִים־הֵם.

19. יִשָּׂא פַרְעֹה אֶת רֹאשְׁךָ מֵעָלֶיךָ — *Pharaoh will lift your head from* [*upon*] *you.*

This term יִשָּׂא רֹאשׁ, *lift off the head,* is used here in the literal sense meaning: *he will behead you.* As a play on words, the same expression is used in the figurative sense of to *count* in verses 13 and 20.

20. Pharaoh's birthday feast. The fulfillment of the interpretation.

יוֹם הֻלֶּדֶת אֶת־פַּרְעֹה — *Pharaoh's birthday* [lit. *the day Pharaoh was caused to be born*].

— His birthday; the day referred to in the Talmud [*Avodah Zarah* 10a] as יוֹם גִּינוּסְיָא, *the birthday festival.* The verb הֻלֶּדֶת [lit. *caused to be born*] is in the causative *hifil* form [and takes the particle אֶת before the subject] because the birth of a child is assisted by others, such as the midwife helping the mother to give birth. Thus the midwife is called מְיַלֶּדֶת, *one who* causes to be born. Comp. *Ezekiel* 16:4; *Lev.* 13:55 *(Rashi).*

R' Bachya, following *Radak,* offers an alternative interpretation: It was the birthday of a *new* Pharaoh. On that day a son was born to Pharaoh. As crown prince, the baby was named Pharaoh because he would eventually ascend the throne. To celebrate the event, the king made a great feast.

וַיַּעַשׂ מִשְׁתֶּה לְכָל־עֲבָדָיו — *That* [lit. *and*] *he made a feast for all his servants.*

The word מִשְׁתֶּה, from שתה, *drink,* refers throughout Scripture

1. It was necessary that there be different fates for the cupbearer and the baker. Had both the favorable dreams, they would have assumed that the Hebrew slave had fabricated favorable interpretations in order to flatter them for his own self-advancement. Joseph's veracity was established only by the fact that he put his life in mortal danger by predicting the baker's doom, for had Joseph been wrong, and had the baker been restored to his former power, he would certainly have had Joseph executed for the anguish caused by his terrifying interpretation.

Because this proved to the cupbearer that Joseph was Divinely inspired, he eventually praised him to Pharaoh *(Abarbanel).*

אֶת־רֹאשׁ | שַׂר הַמַּשְׁקִים וְאֶת־רֹאשׁ שַׂר
כא הָאֹפִים בְּתוֹךְ עֲבָדָיו: וַיָּשֶׁב אֶת־שַׂר
הַמַּשְׁקִים עַל־מַשְׁקֵהוּ וַיִּתֵּן הַכּוֹס עַל־כַּף
כב פַּרְעֹה: וְאֵת שַׂר הָאֹפִים תָּלָה כַּאֲשֶׁר
כג פָּתַר לָהֶם יוֹסֵף: וְלֹא־זָכַר שַׂר־הַמַּשְׁקִים
אֶת־יוֹסֵף וַיִּשְׁכָּחֵהוּ:

to a *wine feast (Sforno;* cf. 19:3; 26:30; 21:8).

וַיִּשָּׂא אֶת רֹאשׁ ... בְּתוֹךְ עֲבָדָיו — *And he counted* (see *v.* 13)] *the* [*head of the*] *Chamberlain of the Cupbearers and* [*the head of*] *the Chamberlain of the Bakers among his servants.*

The translation follows *Rashi* here and in *v.* 13. Pharaoh included them among the other servants whom he expected to serve him at his feast, and he took special notice of them *(Rashi).*

21. וַיָּשֶׁב אֶת־שַׂר הַמַּשְׁקִים עַל מַשְׁקֵהוּ — [*And*] *He restored the Chamberlain of the Cupbearers to his cupbearing* [lit. *to his beverage*].

— His offense was found to be less serious than that of the baker's, and therefore pardonable [see *Mizrachi* to *v.* 1 s.v. חָטְאוּ].

22. וְאֵת שַׂר הָאֹפִים תָּלָה — *But the Chamberlain of the Bakers he* [Pharaoh] *hanged.*

Because his offense displayed gross negligence of his duties towards the monarch [*ibid.*].

According to *Malbim* [see his *comm.* here and to verses 1 and 2], the reverse would have been true justice since the baker had less *personal* responsibility in his offense than the cupbearer in his. Nevertheless, this was the fate of each — not because it was just — but, as the verse proceeds to inform us, *because this was how Joseph interpreted it to them.*

כַּאֲשֶׁר פָּתַר לָהֶם יוֹסֵף — *Just as Joseph had interpreted to them.*

Each met the fate which Joseph had predicted *(Midrash).*

— This proved that the manner in which each dream was fulfilled was *due* to its interpretation *(Sforno; Yafeh Toar).*

Providence ordained their respective fates in order to prove Joseph's veracity and prepare the circumstances for his rise to greatness *(Abarbanel; Malbim).*

23. וְלֹא זָכַר שַׂר הַמַּשְׁקִים אֶת יוֹסֵף וַיִּשְׁכָּחֵהוּ — *But the Chamberlain of the Cupbearers did not remember Joseph, and he forgot him.*

The passage is apparently redundant and the commentators explain the nuances of the two similar phrases.

— *The Chamberlain of the Cupbearers did not remember Joseph* on the day he was freed; *and*

counted the Chamberlain of the Cupbearers and the
Chamberlain of the Bakers among his servants. 21 *He*
restored the Chamberlain of the Cupbearers to his
cupbearing and he placed the cup on Pharaoh's palm.
22 *But the Chamberlain of the Bakers he hung just as*
Joseph had interpreted to them.
23 *Yet the Chamberlain of the Cupbearers did not*
remember Joseph, and he forgot him.

he forgot him in the future *(Rashi).*[1]

It was not that the cupbearer had no opportunity to recall Joseph — he deliberately *forgot him,* by putting him out of his mind *(Haamek Davar).*

Ibn Ezra interprets — He did not make mention of him to Pharaoh, and he forgot him in his heart.

The *Midrash* perceives another intent of this verse: True, the Chamberlain of the Cupbearers forgot Joseph, but the Holy One Blessed be He did not, as the events in the next *Sidrah* will graphically portray.

According to the Masoretic note appearing at the end of the *Sidrah* there are 112 verses in *Vayeshev,* numerically corresponding to the mnemonic יבק. The root of the word is בקק, *emptying out.* The allusion is that this *Sidrah* contains the beginning of the process which was to culminate in Israel's first exile, the process by which Jacob and his family were *emptied out* of their native land and forced to spend 210 years in Egypt.

The *Haftorah* begins with *Amos* 2:6 כֹּה אָמַר ה'.

נשלם סדרה וישב בעזרת האל

1. Rashi continues that [the cupbearer's forgetting of Joseph was a Providentially inspired punishment.] Joseph placed his trust in the cupbearer, [rather than in God], depending on the cupbearer to remember him and secure his release. Joseph was therefore condemned to remain in prison for another two years. [See *Seder Olam* cited in *v.* 14.] There is a Midrashic tradition [*Shemos Rabbah* 7:1] that Joseph deserved to be imprisoned only ten years — one year for each of his ten brothers about whom he had brought evil reports [above 37:2] — but since he placed his trust in the human agencies of the cupbearer, imploring him twice to remember him — זְכַרְתַּנִי, *remember me,* and וְהִזְכַּרְתַּנִי, *recall me,* — he was punished with two more years in prison *(Tanchuma).* As we learn in 41:1, it was not for another two years that Joseph was to have the opportunity of being freed.

[Furthermore, as *R' Bachya* writes, since Joseph used the dual expression of *remembering,* the Torah uses coresponding dual terms to record how the cupbearer *did not remember him and forgot him.*]

Rashi concludes: Thus is it written [*Psalms* 40:5]: *Praises to the man who made* H*ASHEM his trust and turned not to the* רְהָבִים, *'arrogant'* — a reference to the Egyptians whom *Isaiah* (30:7) calls רַהַב, *arrogant.* [For explanations of Joseph's motive in so placing his trust, see footnote to *v.* 14 above, and the *Overview* to *Mikeitz.*]

◆§ סדר מקץ ◆§
◆§ Sidrah Mikeitz

— The Overviews

An Overview —
Faith and Trust

,,אַשְׁרֵי־הַגֶּבֶר אֲשֶׁר־שָׂם ה׳ מִבְטַחוֹ״ זֶה יוֹסֵף ,,וְלֹא־פָנָה אֶל־רְהָבִים״ ע״י שֶׁאָמַר לְשַׂר הַמַּשְׁקִים ,,זְכַרְתַּנִי ... וְהִזְכַּרְתַּנִי״ נִיתּוֹסֵף לוֹ שְׁתֵּי שָׁנִים

'Praises to the man who made HASHEM His trust,' this refers to Joseph, 'and turned not to the arrogant' (Psalms 40:5) — because he said to the chamberlain of the cupbearers, 'Remember me ... and mention me [to Pharaoh]' (40:14), *two years were added to his [term in prison] (Bereishis Rabbah* 89:3).

Wavering Trust

These Midrashic descriptions of Joseph seem to be contradictory. The Midrash cites a verse that praises one who maintains his trust in HASHEM but without disapproves of the one who seeks the aid of the arrogant, yet both descriptions are applied to Joseph. He is described as the one of perfect trust while in the same breath he is dubbed the person who was punished with two years in prison for wrongly soliciting the aid of Pharaoh's cupbearer. If he epitomizes the one who trusts, then why did he 'turn to the arrogant,' and if he was so callous in his trust as to seek out the arrogant why is he praised as 'the man who made HASHEM his trust'?

Joseph was severely punished — two years in prison! — for doing nothing more than any normal human being would consider his minimum obligation.

Aside from the contradiction, the verse shocks us. Its implication, especially as interpreted by the Midrash, is that no one is permitted to seek natural means to further his own ends. Joseph was severely punished — two years in prison! — for doing nothing more than any normal human being would consider his minimum obligation. He had already been jailed ten years for a crime he did not commit. Without family or friends he had languished in the Egyptian dungeon for the best years of his young adulthood. Now for the first time he had the ear and a claim upon the assistance of a member of Pharaoh's inner circle. Should he not take the opportunity to get his message to those who could help him?

To a man of Joseph's stature, the strange phenomenon of the two dreams that enabled him to prove his unusual skill could be nothing less than a Divine intervention.

Even more, Joseph surely understood the presence in his jail of the two deposed officials and their subsequent dreams as a Heaven-sent means of effecting his release. To a man of Joseph's stature, the strange phenomenon of the two dreams that enabled him to prove his unusual skill could be nothing less than a Divine intervention. All he did in urging his innocence upon the cupbearer was to seek a means by which God's will could be carried out — what was his crime? How was he different from the farmer who plows, sows, and reaps? The Torah assures Israel וּבֵרַכְךָ ה׳ אֱלֹהֶיךָ בְּכֹל אֲשֶׁר תַּעֲשֶׂה, *and HASHEM your God will bless you in all that you do (Deut.* 15:18), and וְאָסַפְתָּ דְגָנֶךָ, *you are to gather in your grain (Deut.* 11:15). The implication is clear that one *may* — indeed, *should,* — work for a livelihood, and that God will bless him, not punish him, for doing so. As R' Yishmael taught in *Berachos* 35b, one should live a normal life of working for his sustenance at appropriate times and in appropriate ways. Surely Joseph had the right, if not the duty, to seek his freedom! *(Bais HaLevi).*

Similar but Different

Every Jew has two commandments that seem identical but are different. He must have faith in God's existence and he must place his trust in Him. *Rambam (Sefer HaMitzvos),* lists Faith in God as the primary commandment, for it is a logical imperative that there can be no commandments unless there is a Being Who has the authority to command. In the temporal sense, legislation cannot be binding unless the law-making body represents a sovereign state or city that has the authority to make laws. An American is not bound by the laws of Great Britain unless he is on British territory. Similarly, organizational by-laws are binding only on members of that organization. The Torah's commandments are

Legislation cannot be binding unless the law-making body represents a sovereign state or city that has the authority to make laws.

binding because they are the laws of God Who introduced Himself to Israel at the start of the Ten Commandments with the words אָנֹכִי ה׳ אֱלֹהֶיךָ, *I am* HASHEM *Your God (Exodus* 20:2). As the commentators explain, that statement constitutes the *mitzvah* לְהַאֲמִין, *to believe,* in HASHEM as the God Who is Master of all — and Who therefore has the absolute right to command obedience to His Torah.

Chazon Ish (Emunah u'Bitachon ch. 2) explains that Faith — or belief — in God has infinite degrees. Like all commandments involving intellect, emotions and character, it is fundamentally different from *mitzvos* relating to tangible matters. A *mezuzah,* for example, is either valid or it is not. A portion of meat is either kosher or it is not. If a *mezuzah* has missing letters, one cannot attach it to his doorpost with the declaration that he is in *partial* compliance with the *mitzvah* — an invalid *mezuzah* is no *mezuzah* at all. If an animal was slaughtered with an improper knife, it is just as non-kosher as if it were killed on a guillotine; by definition one cannot eat partly kosher meat.

If an animal was slaughtered with an improper knife, it is just as non-kosher as if it were killed on a guillotine; by definition one cannot eat partly kosher meat.

Faith, however, is different; it can have degrees. Of course, a Jew is required to display total faith in God in every area of his life. There may be a *mitzvah,* or even a detail in the *halachah* of a particular commandment, that may seem incomprehensible according to currently fashionable social mores or according to science as it is currently known to man. Nevertheless, the Jew believes that the God Who created heaven and earth and Who brought Israel out of Egypt is the Supreme Authority with the right to command, whether or not man is capable of understanding the reasons for His doing so. Similarly, we must believe that God's hand is everywhere even if we cannot account for what He does. A study of history leaves us full of questions: Why should this have happened? Why didn't God show His mercy? Why did the wicked triumph? The questions can go on and on, but we have faith in God's wisdom and omnipotence despite His unwillingness to share His reasons with us.

A study of history leaves us full of questions. The questions can go on and on, but we have faith in God's wisdom.

Clearly, the Jew who does not consider himself bound by the *mitzvos* of the Torah or who denies that the entire Torah was given at Sinai ח״ו is not in compliance with the commandment to believe. But he may not be a non-believer, either. *Chazon Ish* maintains that even someone whose belief in God goes only so far as to prevent him from ignoring the most widely accepted *mitzvos* — he will circumcise his sons or attend the synagogue on Yom Kippur — cannot be labeled a non-believer. True, his faith is so weak that it hangs by the slenderest hair, but it exists. Just as no two people are alike in their compliance with the commandments to be merciful, humble, or honest, no two people are alike in the degree of their belief. The absolute is everyone's goal, but there are infinite stations along the way.

Even someone whose belief in God goes only so far as to prevent him from ignoring the most widely accepted mitzvos *cannot be labled a non-believer.*

The commandment to have בִּטָחוֹן, *trust,* in God, is similar, but different. *R' Bachya* writes:

יָדוּעַ כִּי כָּל הַבּוֹטֵחַ הוּא מַאֲמִין, שֶׁאֵין אָדָם בּוֹטֵחַ אֶלָּא בְּמִי שֶׁמַּאֲמִין בּוֹ שֶׁהַיְכוֹלֶת בְּיָדוֹ לְמַלֵּא אֶת שְׁאֵלָתוֹ, וְהַמַּאֲמִין יִתָּכֵן שֶׁלֹּא יִהְיֶה בּוֹטֵחַ

It is obvious that everyone who trusts is a believer, for one can trust only in Someone Whom he believes to have the power to fulfill his request, but it is possible for a believer not to trust (Kad HaKemach, Bitachon).

Although faith in God and trust in God are closely related, they are not synonymous. As R' Bachya points out, one may have a perfect belief in God's existence, power, and authority, yet fail to translate it into trust, for 'trust in God' involves one's thoughts and deeds in a specific instance.

Although faith in God and trust in God are closely related, they are not synonymous.

What happens when someone is confronted with a 'completely hopeless' situation? A dear one is terminally ill. One's business is deeply in debt and dependent on an obsolete product. A city is surrounded by a vastly superior army. Is there a God? Of course, one has total faith in that! Does his power extend over every conceivable situation? Surely! In that case, why the hopelessness? If the believer in the abstract existence of God can translate his belief into a perfect, calm, unruffled trust that whatever his predicament, it is God's will, and further, that it is within God's power to effect whatever outcome He desires, then that person can be described as a בַּעַל בִּטָּחוֹן, *a person with trust.*

Trust involves that a person place his confidence in God alone and remember Him in every detail of his activities.

'Trust involves that a person place his confidence in God alone and remember Him in every detail of his activities, that he bear in mind that any situation is not in his own control, but that it depends on God's will. For there are many people who trust in God only in a general way, and who believe with a perfect faith that everything is in His blessed hands, but they fail to take to heart this essential of trust — namely, that He controls everything they do and every direction in which they turn' *(Kad HaKemach).*

As *Chazon Ish* succinctly puts it:

> Faith and trust are [virtually] identical, except that 'faith' involves the general world view of a person while 'trust' involves his perspective on himself; faith is theoretical, while trust is practical. It is simple to have trust when trust is not truly required — but it is *so* difficult to trust when trust is truly required!

A further definition of trust is given by the commentators. There is a popular *mis*conception that a devout Jew must have faith that whatever alternatives face him, only the good will occur. As a corrolary to this, anyone who plans for the worst is regarded as lacking in faith. It is clear from *R' Bachya* that this is not so. Our duty is to recognize that only God controls results and only His will determines whether our efforts, reasoned or frantic, will succeed. Again, *Chazon Ish* expresses the concept concisely:

Unless the future has been clarified by prophecy, the future is not definite, for who can know God's judgment or His deeds?

> Unless the future has been clarified by prophecy, the future is not definite, for who can know God's judgment or His deeds? Rather trust involves the faith that there is no coincidence in the world and that every occurrence under the sun was by His proclamation.

Degrees of Trust

Trust in God, like other personal matters, is not an absolute concept. Its variations are infinite. *Meshech Chochmah (Deuteronomy* 10:20) comments that the Torah refers to this *mitzvah* only by allusion because it is impossible to be specific. Its degrees are so great that the individual Jew must struggle for a lifetime to climb the ladder of trust. The closer one comes to identify with God in all aspects of his life, the more he will trust Him. By recognizing that it is incumbent upon him to seek closeness to God's will and His example, as it were, in his every activity, a Jew learns to impregnate every aspect of his life with awareness of God's majesty. Such a person will naturally turn to God at times of illness and disaster. The *mitzvah* to trust, therefore, is subsumed under the general category of וּבוֹ תִדְבָּק, *cleave to Him.* The Sages interpret this commandment as a call to imitate God's mercy, compassion, truthfulness, and so on. It involves a general and constant striving to approximate our behavior to His. There are no absolutes in such a *mitzvah* for today's maximum always becomes the springboard for tomorrow's greater achievement. So, too, with trust. When one cleaves to God, one trusts; and the closer one cleaves, the more he trusts.

There are no absolutes in such a mitzvah *for today's maximum always becomes the springboard for tomorrow's greater achievement.*

Chovos HaLevavos' Spectrum

In the progress of the person of trust from infant to saint *Chovos HaLevavos (Shaar HaBitachon)* lists ten stations on the spectrum of trust:

1) The newborn baby instinctively trusts in its mother's breast.

2) As an infant grows, it learns to rely on its mother not only for nursing, but for all its physical needs.

3) A child learns that the family's livelihood is dependent on its father. In infancy, the father was a distant, almost anonymous, figure, but with maturity a child recognizes his major role.

In infancy, the father was a distant, almost anonymous, figure, but with maturity a child recognizes his major role.

4) The young adult comes to rely on his own strong right arm or business sense as an avenue to success. The new self-confidence and self-reliance eventually replace the earlier dependence on parents.

5) As one becomes aware of the interdependence of all members of the community, he comes to depend on the cooperation and support of fellow citizens.

6) The individual is strong and collective society is even stronger, but none of them can make the sun shine, the rains fall, or prevent drought and epidemic. The maturing person turns to God to do what he cannot do for himself.

7) As one's perception of God grows, one begins to realize that some forms of labor are too dangerous or too difficult to be worthy of man's effort — unless there is no other way for him to survive. If man has no choice he *must* take the risk. But now that he believes in God, he will forgo such risky pursuits in favor of a trust that God will provide for him in some other way.

If a man has no choice, he must take the risk. But now that he believes in God, he will forgo such risky pursuits.

8) If God can provide a better way than the risk of life and limb for the sake of bread, then He can also provide for everyone in every occupation. That being the case, one should devote himself to business or labor only because the Torah instructs us not to rely on miracles. At bottom, however, profits come not from labor or shrewdness, but from God, and every resource in life should be utilized for His service.

At bottom, however, profits come not from labor or shrewdness but from God.

9) Recognition of God's concern for His creatures becomes so all pervasive and trust becomes so total that the person gives up all personal desires in favor of the wish to serve God. It is no longer a matter of seeking success in order to serve God. Instead, this person is happy to endure success or failure, prosperity or poverty, health or illness, life or death — whatever God chooses to mete out.

10) The highest stage available to man is a recognition that nothing matters but the spiritual life of the World to Come. Though he must remain here as long as his body lives, his mind and heart are in another, spiritual world. Clearly, only a tiny number of the most sublime saints fall into this final category.

Joseph's Place

All human beings fall somewhere within this spectrum of trust.

All human beings fall somewhere within this spectrum of trust. While all mature people would look disdainfully on people who never advance past the bottom rungs of the scale, we can scarcely comprehend the holiness of those who make it to the top. Whatever one's level happens to be at any given point in his life, he must consolidate himself on that level and strive to go higher, but to drop is unforgiveable.

Let us depart a moment from spiritual considerations. Let us imagine someone whose awareness of God is limited or even non-existent, but he stands at level 5, that of appreciating his need to rely on others and to reciprocate by being a reliable, cooperative member of society. Suddenly, he drops back to level 4, where he becomes not only self-reliant, but selfish and indifferent to his comrades. On whatever grounds, religious, moral, or practical, such a reversion would be condemned and the person would deserve severe criticism. We are not, and should not be, tolerant of people who lapse toward a less civilized level of conduct. Similarly, a person who has developed an awareness of God's role in his life has no right to regress into total reliance on his neighbors or himself, even if he still acknowledges the need to pray for things like rain, which even self-delusion places beyond his control.

We are not, and should not be, tolerant of people who lapse toward a less civilized level of conduct.

Joseph knew that human agencies were powerless. He had attained the very highest stages in developing trust in God. He knew full well that Pharaoh's and cupbearers were as meaningless to him as a newborn ant on the other side of the planet. His level of trust was such that he relied on God alone and found his joy in accepting what God apportioned to him. Why should he have taken notice of the cupbearer's potential influence with Pharaoh; even Pharaoh's *own* power was insignificant to Joseph. Why then did he seek the cupbearer's help? Joseph perceived that God had placed the deposed official in prison only to set in motion the events that would rescue him. So Joseph took the initiative in broaching to the

He knew full well that Pharaohs and cupbearers were as meaningless to him as a newborn ant on the other side of the planet.

cupbearer that he tell Pharaoh of the young, kidnapped, victimized Hebrew who deserved to be set free.

For another person, such an act would be commendable. More — it would be required! Just as we must plow, seek employment, and inquire after the best doctors, so we must utilize every available means of rescue. If we do so with the realization that plows, jobs, medicines, and influence are among the infinite means at God's disposal, such efforts place us high on *Chovos HaLevavos'* scale of trust in God.

In enlisting the cupbearer in God's army of tools, Joseph was lowering himself.

But this was *Joseph*. In enlisting the cupbearer in God's army of tools, Joseph was lowering himself — and for that he was punished with two additional years in prison, years during which he relearned the lesson of trust he had momentarily forgotten *(R' Bachya* 40:14; *Bais HaLevi).*

This, *Bais HaLevi* explains, is why the Midrash uses the very same verse to depict Joseph both as a man of trust and as one who was punished for relying on the arrogant. No one would be faulted; much less punished for what Joseph did — unless that person had reached Joseph's level of trust in God.

We would never have realized how great Joseph was had we not been shown the amazingly high standard of conduct that God expected of him.

We would never have realized how great Joseph was had we not been shown the amazingly high standard of conduct that God expected of him.

Chazon Ish offers a different explanation of Joseph's error, one that provides a scale of measurement for people like us, who can hardly imagine the spiritual grandeur of a Joseph. In the view of *Chazon Ish,* Joseph may well have been *required* to make efforts to obtain his release. The requirement to trust in God does not absolve us from seeking natural means instead of relying on miracles. Simultaneously, however, we must beware of wildly clutching at any straw, even if it holds no reasonable chance of success.

To flounder and foolishly enlist unreliable allies and concoct illogical schemes for the sake of 'doing something' is wrong and sinful.

To flounder and foolishly enlist unreliable allies and concoct illogical schemes for the sake of 'doing something' is wrong and sinful. It is tantamount to a declaration that God cannot help and that it makes more sense to hope to fools than to trust God. The Midrash implies the essence of Joseph's error by the description it assigns to the cupbearer: רְהָבִים, *the ar-*

rogant. It is the nature of people like him to be selfish. They are users. When he was the humble prisoner and Joseph was the overseer, when he was the perplexed dreamer and Joseph the brilliant interpreter, he obsequiously fawned upon Joseph, seeking his favor. Such people forget their benefactors immediately when the wheel of fortune turns, and Joseph should have realized it. That he failed to do so was indicative of a desperation that was unworthy of him and suggested a lapse in his trust in God.

Portion of Trust

Rabbi David Feinstein has made a practice of analizing the *masoretic* code words [mnemonics] at the end of each *sidrah.* These mnemonics are a device to assist in remembering the number of verses in the respective portions. The numerical value of each such mnemonic equals the number of verses in the portion. It is axiomatic that the mnemonics were carefully chosen to reflect the theme of each *sidrah.* Therefore, the fact that the mnemonic words of *Mikeitz* are the same as those for *Bereishis* — *'Yechizkiyah'* and *'Amatziah'* [יְחִזְקִיָּהוּ, אֲמַצְיָה] — should give us pause. What theme do the two *sidros* share? Both words mean *power is God's.* That theme is quite apropos to *Bereishis,* which begins with the account of how God created the universe from nothing, and closes with the prelude to the Deluge, in which God reduced the failed world to virtual nothingness. But what does *Mikeitz* tell us about God's power?

The message is indeed there.

Then God showed all of Egypt that the strength was His — *not Pharaoh's, not the Nile's.*

Egypt was the garden spot of the earth (13:11), the place that was so well irrigated by its god, the Nile, that a farmer could virtually drop seeds in the ground and be assured of lush growth *(Deuteronomy* 11:10). And Pharaoh stood above even the Nile , at least in his own mind [see *comm.* to 41:1]. Then God showed all of Egypt that the strength was *His* — not Pharaoh's, not the Nile's. Pharoah's dreams and Joseph's interpretations proved that only God determines the cycles of abundance and famine. He was still as much the Master as He had been during Creation.

Joseph's brothers found themselves at the mercy of a seemingly paranoid viceroy. They sought a reason for their plight and they found it: God was punishing them for their lack of pity twenty-two years earlier (42:21-22). Later, after apparently proving their innocence, they were arrested on another fabricated charge, and again they proclaimed their recognition that the affairs of men are not haphazard: the power is God's though He may exercise it through an Egyptian viceroy. So Judah spoke for his brothers in announcing that they could only remain speechless in the face of the Divine will that had chosen to seek retribution for their sin (44:16).

It is more than a coincidence that *Mikeitz* is always read during the Chanukah. The jug of oil was sufficient to burn for one day, but even *that* day is celebrated as part of the miracle because Jews recognize that *every* flame is a miracle, even when it seems to burn naturally.

This theme of *Mikeitz* first appears with mention of righteous Joseph who was to languish in prison for two years, because he had failed momentarily to realize that only God could decide whether or not He would unlock Joseph's chains with a key called 'chamberlain of the cupbearers.'

Yes. Mikeitz *is indeed parallel to* Bereishis. *Both declare:* the power is God's!

Yes, *Mikeitz* is indeed parallel to *Bereishis.* Both declare 'the power is God's!'

Rabbi Nosson Scherman

סדר מקץ

Sidrah Mikeitz

א וַיְהִי מִקֵּץ שְׁנָתַיִם יָמִים וּפַרְעֹה חֹלֵם
ב וְהִנֵּה עֹמֵד עַל־הַיְאֹר: וְהִנֵּה מִן־הַיְאֹר

XLI

SIDRA MIKEITZ

1. Pharaoh's dream.

וַיְהִי מִקֵּץ שְׁנָתַיִם יָמִים — *[And] it happened at the end of two years to the day* [lit. *two years of days*].

— After the release of the Chamberlain of the Cupbearers — a total of twelve years since Joseph's imprisonment (Rabbinic Chronology based upon *Seder Olam;* see *comm.* to 39:20; 40:14). At this point, Joseph was almost thirty years old, Jacob 120, and Isaac 180. Isaac died about this time. (See footnote to 35:29, p. 1529).

Joseph should have, according to Heavenly decree, been sentenced to be imprisoned for ten years, but as noted in the commentary to the previous *Sidrah* [see 40:14 and 23], because he placed his trust in the dual 'remembrance' of the cupbearer, he was punished with two extra years in prison. As noted there, the *Midrash* applies to Joseph the verse [*Psalms* 40:5]: *Praises to the man who made HASHEM his trust and turned not to the 'arrogant'* — a reference to the Egyptians who are so described in *Isaiah* 30:7. [See *Overview*].

Baal HaTurim finds a homiletic allusion to these ten years in the phraseology itself; A similar expression occurs in 16;3: *at the end* [מִקֵּץ] *of ten years.* Just as there the term is related to *ten years,* in our passage, too, it alludes to ten years, to which the additional שְׁנָתַיִם, *two years,* are added.

Midrash Sechel Tov observes that the term וַיְהִי [*it was*] can denote both joy and grief [for only in conjunction with בִּימֵי does וַיְהִי denote *only* grief]. It is used in this introductory phrase to allude to both the grief of Isaac's passing and the joy of Joseph's impending release from prison.

The translation of מִקֵּץ is as *Onkelos* renders it: מִסּוֹף, *at the end.* This is the interpretation of the word throughout Scripture *(Rashi).*[1]

It is not unusual that *Rashi* offers his interpretation of מִקֵּץ here, but not the previous times the word appears in Scripture [e.g. 4:3, 8l:6, 16:3] *(Mizrachi).* Perhaps *Rashi* felt the particular necessity to comment here because the presence of the word יָמִים, which also denotes *completeness,* renders our passage more prone to ambiguity *(Tzeidah laDerech).*

Our translation *two years to the day* follows the interpretation of *Ibn Ezra* and other commentators [see e.g. *Rashi* to 24:55 and *comm.* above to 40:4] who perceive יָמִים, *days,* to denote a *complete cycle of days* — i.e., a cycle of time, a year, when the same date recurs; hence in our context *two years to the day.* Comp. *Lev.* 25:9 and the expression חֹדֶשׁ יָמִים, *a month* of days [*Numbers* 11:21] where the sense is *a full month* — the recurrence of the same date within the full cycle of a month.

וּפַרְעֹה חֹלֵם — *That* [lit. *and*] *Pharaoh was dreaming* [following *Ibn Ezra;* comp. 27:5.]

1. *Rashi* cites *Onkelos* to make clear that מִקֵּץ in our verse is to be translated as *at the end,* and should not be confused with the cognate word קָצֶה, *edge.* Were we to render מִקֵּץ as *from the edge,* it could be understood to refer either to the *beginning* [i.e., 'the cutting edge,' so to speak] of the two-year period, or to its *end.*

Cf. *comm.* to *Deut.* 15:1 regarding the cancellation of financial debts at the end of the Sabbatical year [*Shmittah*]: מִקֵּץ שֶׁבַע שָׁנִים, *at the end of seven years.* There, some grammarians (see *Ibn Ezra)* interpret the literal sense of the passage as the *beginning* of the seventh year. Not only would that rendering contradict *Rashi* to our verse, it is also contrary to the Talmudic, halachically adopted interpretation of קֵץ as *end.* [*See Ramban* there who defends the halachic interpretation. Cf. also *Rashbam* here who maintains that were it not for the qualifying word יָמִים, *days,* in our passage which clearly denotes *full* years [see below], one would be justified in interpreting מִקֵּץ as the *beginning* of the second year.]

It happened at the end of two years to the day:
Pharaoh was dreaming that behold! he was
standing over the River, 2 *when behold! out of the*

The present tense, *was dreaming,* may indicate that the dream was a *recurring* one that Pharaoh kept dreaming throughout the two years, but that he always forgot in the morning. That night, however, it made an indelible impression on him *(Midrash HaGadol).*

Sforno renders: *While Pharaoh was dreaming,* meaning that while the king was dreaming of typical fantasies that absorbed his mind, *he also had the following dream,* about the cows that, unlike the others, had significance. As the Sages observed [*Berachos* 55a], in every dream there must be meaningless elements.

Pharaoh was not the name of an individual but the royal title of the Egyptian kings, just as Abimelech was the royal title of Philistine monarchs.[1]

Ordinarily the passage should have read in the conversive, predicate+subject: וַיַּחֲלֹם פַּרְעֹה. That the subject precedes the verb in our verse is the Scriptural method of emphasizing the uniqueness of the subject: this was *Pharaoh* — no private citizen — who was dreaming. This was a dream which affected a whole nation, not merely an individual, and it must be perceived and interpreted as such. In this light the Sages in the *Midrash* expounded: *'Pharaoh was dreaming.* Do not *all* people dream? — True, but a king's dream affects the whole nation.' It was this universal aspect of the dream that eluded the Egyptian necromancers who could not interpret the dream *vis a vis* Pharaoh [see *comm.* to *v.* 8] *(Malbim).*

It is noted that dreams were at the root of Joseph's misfortunes; and now dreams bring about his salvation. This is reminiscent of *Jeremiah* 30:17: *I will heal you with your own wounds (Zohar).*

וְהִנֵּה עֹמֵד עַל הַיְאֹר — *That* [lit. *and*] *behold! he was standing over* [lit. *upon*] *the River.*

The expression עֹמֵד עַל, literally *standing upon,* can refer to the place *next* to which someone stands, as well as figuratively to the place where one's mind and thoughts are directed [cf. *Exod.* 18:13; *Daniel* 12:1; see also *comm.* to 28:13 above]. Accordingly, the implication is that Pharaoh, King of Egypt, was standing next to the river, reflecting upon it. His thoughts focused in the Nile, upon whose overflow depended the agricultural productivity of Egypt *(R' Hirsch).*

The Nile was venerated as a god of Egypt. Midrashically, therefore, Pharaoh's position *'over'* the Nile suggests that he haughtily imagined himself superior to his god; Pharaoh was protecting it, like a god looking down on his river. Cf. *Ezekiel* 29:3 where Pharaoh is exhorted for having boasted *My river is mine and I have made it.* As noted earlier, the present tense *Pharaoh dreams* implies that Pharaoh *constantly* had such grandiose dreams. He believed himself to be a god, the all-powerful creator of Egyptian prosperity due to *'his river'* the Nile.

Further, the *Midrash* derives from this expression that 'the wicked stand over their gods; however, as for the

1. *R' Munk* observes that Pharaoh's ultimate decline, foretold in *Ezekiel* 29:3, was connected to his fancying himself as god of the Nile [see *comm.*]. This was forseen right from the start, and the Torah alludes to it throughout this episode by omitting the title 'king of Egypt' from Pharaoh's name. The sole exception is the solemn announcement of Joseph's accession to power: *Joseph was thirty years old when he stood before Pharaoh, king of Egypt* [*v.* 46].

עֹלֹת שֶׁבַע פָּרוֹת יְפוֹת מַרְאֶה וּבְרִיאֹת
ג בָּשָׂר וַתִּרְעֶינָה בָּאָחוּ: וְהִנֵּה שֶׁבַע פָּרוֹת
אֲחֵרוֹת עֹלוֹת אַחֲרֵיהֶן מִן־הַיְאֹר רָעוֹת
מַרְאֶה וְדַקּוֹת בָּשָׂר וַתַּעֲמֹדְנָה אֵצֶל

righteous, God stands over them, as it is written of Jacob [28:13]: *Behold! HASHEM was standing over him.*

[Comp. *v.* 17 where in Pharaoh's repetition of the dream he delicately changes the implication by saying instead that he was standing upon *the bank* of the river.]

Rashi notes that our verse avoids the use of נָהָר, the word Scripture invariably employs for *river.* This is because יְאֹר means *canal,* and Egypt, while depending on the Nile for virtually all its irrigation, was criss-crossed with a network of canals drawing water from overflow of the Nile. Therefore, the word יְאֹר is used exclusively for the Nile, because it was not only a river, but the center of the entire series of canals.

[In the translation we have capitalized the word River, because in Egypt the Nile was *the* river *par excellence.*]

[The Nile's annual overflow — a time of great rejoicing in Egypt — is the product of the spring rains in the Abyssinian highlands, and the melting of the mountain snow.]

Ramban, citing *Daniel* 10:4-5 and 12:5-6 where the Tigris is referred to both as נָהָר and יְאוֹר, maintains that the term יְאוֹר can apply to any river, whether or not it is part of a network of canals. Large rivers are referred to by both terms, while canals are referred to exclusively as יְאוֹר.

Basing himself on *Onkelos* who translates יְאֹר as נַהֲרָא — [from the Hebrew נָהָר, *river*], *Ramban* suggests that both terms are derived from אוֹר, *light.* In *Job,* the rain is referred to as *light* [see ibid. 36:30; 37:11; *Bereishis Rabbah* 26:18], perhaps because the rains are influenced by the luminaries; accordingly, the rivers, products of these rains, are related to the luminaries, their first cause.

In defense of *Rashi's* interpretation, the supercommentators urge that , one should not conclude that *Rashi* overlooked the verse in *Daniel* where the Tigris is called יְאוֹר. Rather, the implication of *Rashi's* comment here is that only the Nile is referred to simply as הַיְאֹר, **the** *river,* with the definite article ה, without the need for any other identification. In Egypt, the Nile was the river/canal *par excellence.* While it is true that the word הַיְאֹר, *the river,* with the definite article ה occurs in *Daniel* 12:5 to designate the Tigris, that is only because the Tigris had already been named earlier [10:4] and this word referred to the earlier verse (see *Gur Aryeh; Tzeidah l'Derech; Maskil l'David).*

[On the implication of the term וְהִנֵּה in dreams denoting *perceptive substance* rather than fantasy, see *comm.* to 28:13 (p. 1228). Its interpretation, as noted by *Ibn Ezra* and *Ramban* (see *comm.* to 40:9) is: *It was as if.*]

2. וְהִנֵּה מִן הַיְאֹר עֹלֹת שֶׁבַע פָּרוֹת — *When* [lit. *and*] *behold! out of the River there emerged* [lit. *came up*] *seven cows.*

The symbolism is clear: Since famine and abundance in Egypt depend on the overflow of the Nile, Pharaoh saw the cows — which symbolize plowing [since oxen are usually harnessed for this purpose] — coming up from the river *(Ramban).*

The order of the phrase should have been *there emerged seven cows from the river.* That the river is mentioned first emphasizes that in the symbolism of the dream, the cows *originated* in the river — the Source of Egypt's sustenance; they were not ordinary cows that had gone from dry land into the river and were now leaving it *(Or HaChaim).*

The Nile overflows and dispenses

River there emerged seven cows, beautiful, and
robust, and they were grazing in the marshland.
3 *Then behold! seven other cows emerged after them*
out of the River — ugly and gaunt; and they stood

its gifts only once a year. Accordingly, the seven cows emerging from the Nile indicated seven years; this applied also to the seven ears of grain, each representing one annual crop *(R' Hirsch).*

יְפוֹת מַרְאֶה וּבְרִיאוֹת בָּשָׂר — *Beautiful [of appearance] and robust* [following *Ralbag;* [lit. *healthy in flesh*].

I.e., fattened [indicating well-fed] *(Rambam, comm.* to Mishnah *Shabbos* 20:4).

That the cows were *beautiful* alludes to years of plenty when people look favorably upon one another *(Rashi).*

It is not *Rashi's* intent to interpret the dream. He explains this segment of the dream here only because Joseph does not account for it in his interpretation in *v.* 26 below *(Gur Aryeh).* Joseph's omission was because Pharaoh himself in repeating the dream did not use the term יְפַת מַרְאֶה which denotes, as *Rashi* writes in 29:17 a beautiful *complexion,* a term which is clearly unsuitable for animals. Pharaoh substituted the more suitable term יְפוֹת תֹּאַר, *handsome of form.* Therefore *Rashi* offered his comment here to explain why the Torah used this term to denote the period of plenty *(Maskil l'David).*

וַתִּרְעֶינָה בָּאָחוּ — *And they were grazing in the marshland.*

They remained there in Egypt — on the banks of the Nile — indicating that the years of plenty would be only in Egypt [see verses 29-30]. Accordingly, the other lands would have been unable to store up food even had they heard about the impending famine. That the famine was universal is foreshadowed in the dream by the fact that after the lean ones consumed the fat ones they did not remain there [i.e., in Egypt], but dispersed as Pharaoh awoke *(Ramban).*

The translation *in the marshland* follows *Rashi* who also cites the word in *Job* 8:11.

Ramban, however, disagrees. Citing the same verse in *Job,* he maintains that the word אָחוּ refers not to a *marshland* but to *reed grass* and other vegetation that grow on river banks. He suggests that *Rashi* may hold that the word is used interchangeably for both reed grass and marshland. Furthermore, in this context the preposition ב, *in,* should be understood as meaning *of,* i.e., and they fed of the reed grass which was on the bank of the river. A similar use of this preposition occurs in *Proverbs* 9:5: *come eat* בְּלַחְמִי, of *my bread and drink* בְּיַיִן, of *the wine which I have mingled.* Possibly, אָחוּ might be derived from אַחֲוָה, *brotherhood,* indicating a place where many varieties of grass grow together.

The Midrash, similarly interpreting אָחוּ as denoting *brotherhood,* perceives the symbolism of the grazing area as figuratively portraying the love and brotherliness men feel toward one another in prosperous times.

3. וְהִנֵּה שֶׁבַע פָּרוֹת אֲחֵרוֹת — *Then* [lit. *and*] *behold — seven other cows.*

Symbolic of another season of plowing *(Ralbag)* ...

עֹלוֹת אַחֲרֵיהֶן מִן הַיְאֹר — *Emerged* [lit. *came up*] *after them out of the River.*

— I.e., immediately after them *(Abarbanel).*

Thus intimating that famine would follow on the heels of the plenty *(Haamek Davar).*

[In recapitulating the dream in *v.* 19, Pharaoh omitted the phrase מִן הַיְאֹר, *out of the river.* See *comm.* there.]

רָעוֹת מַרְאֶה וְדַקּוֹת בָּשָׂר — *Ugly* [lit. *bad in appearance*] *and gaunt* [lit. *of lean flesh*].

An unusual sight in Egypt [see *v.* 19].

ד הַפָּרוֹת עַל־שְׂפַת הַיְאֹר: וַתֹּאכַלְנָה
הַפָּרוֹת רָעוֹת הַמַּרְאֶה וְדַקֹּת הַבָּשָׂר אֵת
שֶׁבַע הַפָּרוֹת יְפֹת הַמַּרְאֶה וְהַבְּרִיאֹת
ה וַיִּיקַץ פַּרְעֹה: וַיִּישָׁן וַיַּחֲלֹם שֵׁנִית וְהִנֵּה |
שֶׁבַע שִׁבֳּלִים עֹלוֹת בְּקָנֶה אֶחָד בְּרִיאוֹת

וַתַּעֲמֹדְנָה אֵצֶל הַפָּרוֹת עַל שְׂפַת הַיְאֹר — *And they stood next to the cows on the bank of the River.*

They did not *graze*, but merely *stood* near the first cows *(Radak).*[1]

This [sequence of the fat cows followed by the lean cows that stood beside them] indicated that the years of famine would immediately follow the years of plenty with no lapse of time between them *(Ramban).*

When he related his dream to Joseph in *v.* 23, Pharaoh did not mention this detail *(Ramban).* [See "Pharaoh's Dream: Variations and Nuances" in the *comm.* to *v.* 17, and chart there.]

According to *Sforno,* that the lean cows stood alongside the fat ones for some time before consuming them, symbolized that for a period of time there would be *both* famine and plenty, as it is written [*v.* 54 below]: *there was famine in all the lands, but in all the land of Egypt there was bread.*

4. ... וַתֹּאכַלְנָה — *The ugly gaunt cows then ate up the seven beautiful [and] robust cows.*

This symbolized that all the joy of the years of plenty would be forgotten during the famine *(Rashi).*

[*Rashi* alludes to Joseph's prediction in *v.* 30: *And all the abundance in the land of Egypt will be forgotten.*]

According to *Ramban,* the symbolism of the emaciated cows 'eating' the fat ones was that the years of famine *would consume the years of abundance* in the sense that the abundant years would have to provide food for the years of famine. This vision prompted Joseph to advise Pharaoh that they should store food as a reserve against the famine [verses 35-36]. Ordinarily Joseph would not have dared offer the king unsolicited counsel; only because this was an integral part of the interpretation of the dream itself did he presume to offer the proposition. [Comp. *R' Hirsch* in footnote to previous verse.][2]

וַיִּיקַץ פַּרְעֹה — *And Pharaoh awoke.*

The appearance of the bad cows gave him such a shock that he woke up *(R' Hirsch).*

Radak explains that Pharaoh's

1. *R' Hirsch* makes a similar observation. Apparently, by the time the lean cows emerged, the fat cows had consumed all the available grass. Cows are not cannibalistic. Hunger would never have made the lean cows eat the others had food been left in the meadow. Clearly, therefore, the dream taught symbolically that the Egyptians should not consume the entire produce in the years of plenty.

2. The commentators to *Rashi* defend his interpretation by explaining that the difference between *Rashi* and *Ramban* lies chiefly in their understanding of the metaphorical implications of the term אכל, *eating up* or *devouring.* As *Mizrachi* observes, *eating* can imply the destruction of the food and its disappearance. According to *Rashi,* the fact that the lean cows

41
4-5

next to the cows on the bank of the River. [4] *The ugly, gaunt cows then ate up the seven beautiful, robust cows. And Pharaoh awoke.* [5] *He fell asleep and dreamt a second time, and behold! seven ears of grain were sprouting on a single stalk — healthy and good.*

awakening between dreams was necessary. The break and repetition made it clear that these were not *additional* but parallel symbolisms, and that they would materialize quickly [see *v.* 32].

Akeidas Yitzchak cites an opinion that Pharaoh did not really wake up at this point, but that this was part of the dream: he saw himself awaken and fall back to sleep.

5. But Pharaoh was not fully awake, so before he could be aware that it was only a dream, he went to sleep again and went on dreaming *(Rashbam; R' Hirsch).*

וַיִּישָׁן וַיַּחֲלֹם שֵׁנִית — *[And] he fell asleep and [he] dreamt a second time.*

The passage does not read *and he dreamt* עוֹד, *more,* but *he dreamt* שֵׁנִית, *a second time* to intimate that it was essentially a single dream which was being repeated *(Kli Yakar).*

Midrash HaGadol perceives שֵׁנִית as implying that this dream was *incredible* (from מְשׁוּנֶה, *different, out of the ordinary).* The first dream showed animals devouring each other, which is within the realm of the imagination — but how can inanimate ears of grain swallow one another? Hence, the *second* 'incredible' dream, not the first, troubled Pharaoh's spirit.

וְהִנֵּה שֶׁבַע שִׁבֳּלִים עֹלוֹת בְּקָנֶה אֶחָד בְּרִיאוֹת וְטֹבוֹת — *And behold! seven ears of grain were sprouting up* [lit. going up] *on a single stalk — healthy and good.*

devoured the fat ones without any visible improvement in their own state, expresses the eating in terms of *the destruction of the object eaten,* rather than the beneficial effect *on the eater.* Consequently *Rashi* perceives the eating of the fat cows by the lean ones as symbolizing the forgetting of the period of plenty during the days of famine.

Rashi's basis for this understanding is the dream of the stalks where Pharaoh was shown that the thin stalks 'swallowed' the healthy ones [*v.* 8]. Now certainly such 'swallowing' had no beneficial effect on the swallowing stalks; it only symbolized that the swallowed object is destroyed and out of sight. Therefore, in *v.* 30, s.v. *and all the abundance in the land of Egypt will be forgotten, Rashi* writes that it is the interpretation of the 'swallowing' [of the stalks] and does not mention the 'eating' of the cows, for it was on that basis that he gained his understanding of the fact that the eating of the cows metaphorically implied the destruction of the object eaten and not its beneficial effect on the eater.

Ramban, on the other hand, maintains that Joseph — the stranger, slave, and prisoner summoned from the dungeon only to interpret the dream — would never have dared volunteer his own advice to the king. That he did so can be comprehended only if his words were part of the interpretation. According to *Ramban,* then, the lean eating the fat symbolized the lean years living on the surplus of the fat ones. The eating is conceived in terms of its *nutritious efect on the consumer* [i.e., during the years of famine, Egypt would be sustained by the surplus of the good years — hence Joseph's 'advice' was an integral part of the interpretation]. *Rashi's* and *Ramban's* differing conceptions of the eating stem from conflicting views of Joseph's 'advice', with *Rashi* apparently maintaining that Joseph, perceiving the guiding Hand of Providence in this audience with Pharaoh, seized the opportunity of offering his unsolicited advice — Joseph assumed that Pharaoh would not have been shown this portentous dream unless he, as head of state, was expected to take constructive measures to prepare for the famine. For as *Ramban* himself makes clear in *v.* 36, the dream itself indicated that the land would not perish in the famine, for the lean cows, though remaining emaciated even after having eaten the seven fat cows, nevertheless did not die of hunger (see *Mizrachi; Gur Aryeh; Maharshal).*

ו וְטֹבוֹת: וְהִנֵּה שֶׁבַע שִׁבֳּלִים דַּקּוֹת
וּשְׁדוּפֹת קָדִים צֹמְחוֹת אַחֲרֵיהֶן:
ז וַתִּבְלַעְנָה הַשִּׁבֳּלִים הַדַּקּוֹת אֵת שֶׁבַע
הַשִּׁבֳּלִים הַבְּרִיאוֹת וְהַמְּלֵאוֹת וַיִּיקַץ
ח פַּרְעֹה וְהִנֵּה חֲלוֹם: וַיְהִי בַבֹּקֶר וַתִּפָּעֶם

Grain is a symbol of harvest (*Ramban v.* 2); that one stalk had seven ears indicated abundance (*Rashbam*).

The seven ears of grain sprouting on a single stalk also indicated that the prosperity would be centralized in one area, Egypt [see verses 29-30]. The thin and scorched ears, by contrast, were on separate stalks (*v.* 6) presaging that the famine would be widespread throughout all the lands (*Haamek Davar*).

Furthermore, *healthy and good* ears sprouting on one stalk also reflected the cooperative, sharing disposition of people in times of abundant prosperity (*Oznaim l'Torah*).

Rashi makes the etymological note that בְּרִיאוֹת [*healthy*] (an adjective generally used only to modify a human being) is synonymous with *sains* [healthy] in Old French [and hence, like the French, is occasionally used to describe an inanimate object (*Mizrachi*).] See *Ibn Ezra* and *Haamek Davar* cited in *v.* 22 s.v. מְלֵאוֹת.

[The description *healthy and good* modifies the *seven ears of grain* as the plural of the Hebrew בְּרִיאוֹת וְטֹבוֹת makes clear. The sense of the syntax may best be captured by rendering: *And behold — seven healthy and good ears of grain were sprouting up on one stalk.*]

6. דַּקּוֹת וּשְׁדוּפֹת קָדִים — *Thin and scorched by the east wind.*

This intimated that any attempt to harvest [symbolized, as noted, by the ears of grain], would be unsuccessful. All the new crops would be *scorched* by the east wind (*Ramban*).

In explaining the term שְׁדוּפֹת, *Rashi* cites the Old French word *heiles* meaning scorched. He notes also that *Onkelos* renders it שְׁקִיפָן, *beaten,* related to the noun מַשְׁקוֹף, *a lintel,* which is beaten continually by the door knocking against it. קָדִים, lit. *easterly,* refers to the *east wind* [*wind* being implicit in the elliptic expression] (*Rashi*).

[The scorching eastern wind, the *sirocco,* referred to today as *chamsin,* is noted for its oppressive severity. Cf. *Ezekiel* 19:12: *the east wind withered its fruit.* In *Jonah* 4:8 it is a *stifling east wind* that caused Jonah extreme discomfort. These burning winds often spring up suddenly with great violence from the desert. They so parch and wither vegetation that the it becomes completely inedible.

[*Rashi* to *Exodus* 14:21 observes that the east wind is the most powerful of all winds. It is the wind by which the Holy One Blessed be He exacts punishment from the wicked. See *Jeremiah* 18:17; *Isaiah* 27:8. In *Hoshea* 12 *the wind blowing from the east* is portrayed as *a wind from* HASHEM.]

צֹמְחוֹת אַחֲרֵיהֶן — *Were growing after them.*

Although the verb is technically in present tense it does not imply that Pharaoh saw them in the process of *growing.* Rather he saw them *fully grown,* as if the phrase read: [the scorched stalks] *grew after them.* The connotation of this verb form is that as soon as he saw the good stalks, he saw the bad ones. Every facet of the dream included such portents of immediacy (*Ramban*).

7. וַתִּבְלַעְנָה — *Then the seven thin ears swallowed up the seven healthy and full ears.*

[On the symbolism, see *v.* 4 s.v. וַתֹּאכַלְנָה.]

The translation of וַתִּבְלַעְנָה as *swallowed* follows *Onkelos:*

41
6-8

[6] *And suddenly! seven ears, thin and scorched by the east wind, were growing after them.* [7] *Then the seven thin ears swallowed up the seven healthy and full ears. Pharaoh awoke and behold! it had been a dream.*

[8] *And it was in the morning: his spirit was agitated*

The verb וַתֹּאכַלְנָה, *ate,* is not used here as it is in connection with the cows [*v.* 4] for it would be inappropriate to describe plant-life as 'eating' *(R' Avraham ben HaRambam).*

Chizkuni maintains that the thin ears outgrew and *covered up* the full ears. The verb בלע should thus be interpreted *covered* as in *Numbers* 4:20. One should not interpret that the thin ears literally *swallowed up* the full ears since prophetic dreams do not contain the utterly impossible, such as an elephant going through the eye of a needle [comp. *Berachos* 55b].

הַבְּרִיאוֹת וְהַמְּלֵאוֹת — *Healthy and full.*

The Torah emphasizes further that though the seven ears were growing from one stalk, they had not robbed nourishment from one another, but each ear of grain was *healthy* as well as *full (Chizkuni).*

וַיִּיקַץ פַּרְעֹה וְהִנֵּה חֲלוֹם — *[And] Pharaoh awoke and behold! it had been a dream.*

I.e., behold — what was evidently a complete dream ended, and he was in need of interpreters *(Rashi).*

That is, since he did not fall asleep again — it being almost morning — he knew that the dream was completed *(Nachalas Yaakov).*

According to *R' Hirsch: He woke up and lo! it was a dream!* The impact of the dream had been so strong that Pharaoh thought he had seen a real event. Only when he was fully awake did he realize that it had been only a dream. [*Rashbam* and *Malbim* interpret similarly.]

According to *Ramban:* When Pharaoh got up he understood that it was but *one dream.* Therefore when relating it to Joseph he constantly referred to it as his *dream* — not dreams. Pharaoh's wise men, however, perceived it as two different dreams and tried to interpret it accordingly. See *comm.* to *v.* 8 s.v. וַיְסַפֵּר.

8. וַיְהִי בַבֹּקֶר וַתִּפָּעֶם רוּחוֹ — *And it was in the morning:* [*and*] *his spirit was agitated.*

And it was in the morning — the morning that Providence had ordained for Joseph's release *(Midrash HaGadol).*

Following *Onkelos: his spirit rang within him like a bell* [פַּעֲמוֹן=פַּעַם]. In describing Nebuchadnezzar's similar reaction to a dream, however, the word is spelled [*Daniel* 2:1]: וַתִּתְפָּעֶם רוּחוֹ [with two ת's, to imply that there were *two* sources of agitation *(Mizrachi;* cf. *Gur Aryeh)*]. This is because Nebuchadnezzar had *two* reasons to be agitated: [like Pharaoh] he sought an interpretation, but additionally, he had forgotten the dream *(Rashi;* see *comm.* to ArtScroll *Daniel ibid.).*

R' David Feinstein notes that וַתִּתְפָּעֶם in Nebuchadnezzar's case is in the *his'pael* [reflexive] form. This implies that his agitation was so great because he 'worked himself into a frenzy.'

Radak renders: His spirit was *knocked, beaten* over the anxiety caused by the dream. *Ibn Ezra*

רוּחוֹ וַיִּשְׁלַח וַיִּקְרָא אֶת־כָּל־חַרְטֻמֵּי
מִצְרַיִם וְאֶת־כָּל־חֲכָמֶיהָ וַיְסַפֵּר פַּרְעֹה
לָהֶם אֶת־חֲלֹמוֹ וְאֵין־פּוֹתֵר אוֹתָם
ט לְפַרְעֹה: וַיְדַבֵּר שַׂר הַמַּשְׁקִים אֶת־פַּרְעֹה
לֵאמֹר אֶת־חֲטָאַי אֲנִי מַזְכִּיר הַיּוֹם:

renders similarly; see verb פעם in *Psalms* 77:5; *Isaiah* 41:7.

He was especially agitated because וַיְהִי בַבֹּקֶר this dream had occurred near morning, and what one dreams in the morning has substance *(Alshich;* see *Maharsha* to *Berachos* 55b).

וַיִּשְׁלַח וַיִּקְרָא אֶת־כָּל־חַרְטֻמֵּי מִצְרַיִם — *So he sent and summoned* [lit. *called*] *all the necromancers of Egypt.*

He sent and summoned — i.e., he dispatched emissaries to summon them *(Radak).*

The term חַרְטֻמִּים has the general connotation of *magician* or *soothsayer.* The translation *necromancer* follows *Rashi* who perceives the term as a composite of חַר טֻם — referring to הַנִּחָרִים בְּטִימֵי מֵתִים, those who 'excite' themselves by the bones of the dead — i.e., *who inquire of the dead.*

R' Hirsch explains the term — which he perceives as derived from חרט, *chisel; engrave* — to refer to those versed in hieroglyphics. As people who devoted themselves to the meaning of symbols, they were the best qualified to explain a dream.

Abarbanel and *Malbim* render: *wizards; fortune tellers.*

וְאֶת־כָּל־חֲכָמֶיהָ — *And all its wise men.*

— Astrologers *(Malbim).*

וַיְסַפֵּר ... אֶת חֲלֹמוֹ וְאֵין־פּוֹתֵר אוֹתָם לְפַרְעֹה — *Pharaoh related his dream to them but none [could] interpret them for* [lit. *to*] *Pharaoh* [lit. *but there was no interpreter of them to Pharaoh*].

There *were* interpreters, but no one who could interpret it suitably *for Pharaoh* — i.e., in reference to Pharaoh, for none of their interpretations satisfied him. [They offered interpretations applicable to him as an *individual,* but not as *a Pharaoh;* they failed to realize that the dream of a king must have nationalistic implications for the nation as a whole (see *Malbim* to *v.* 1)]. An example of their interpretations was: Pharaoh will beget seven daughters and bury seven daughters [he will conquer seven provinces and seven provinces will rebel against him] *(Rashi;* bracketed addition is from the *Midrash)* [cf. 40:8].[1]

According to *Haamek Davar,* the Egyptian wizards could not formulate a correct interpretation since they could not conceive how a king could be affected personally by hunger; therefore they sought far-fetched solutions.

Pharaoh referred to his dream in singular, but the wise men regarded it as *two* dreams and tried to interpret accordingly. That is why our passage reads: Pharaoh related them his *dream* but none could interpret

1. If, as noted in *Berachos* 55b and cited in the footnote to *v.* 13, 'the outcome of every dream depends on its interpretation' why then were the interpretations of the wise men not effective in determining the meaning of Pharaoh's dream?

— Essentially, as Rava cautions in the Talmud *(ibid.),* the outcome of a dream depends on its

41
9

so he sent and summoned all the necromancers of
Egypt and all its wise men. Pharaoh related his dream
to them but none could interpret them for Pharaoh.
9 *Then the Chamberlain of the Cupbearers spoke*
up before Pharaoh, "My transgressions do I mention

them for Pharaoh *(Ramban v. 7).*

Their erroneous explanations stemmed from a failure to perceive that the dreams were but the two halves of one message: the first dream alluded to the physical phenomenon of animals plowing fields, while the second dream alluded to the prosperity and hunger of the respective seven-year periods. By failing to connect these two parts of the message, the necromancers could not understand the dreams properly *(Sforno).*

According to *Ashtruc* in *Midrashei HaTorah,* some of the wizards *did* perceive the essential significance of the dream, but none of them could verbalize the calamities that the dreams portended.

9. The chamberlain of the cupbearers 'remembers' Joseph.

וַיְדַבֵּר שַׂר הַמַּשְׁקִים אֶת פַּרְעֹה — *Then* [lit. *and*] *the Chamberlain of the Cupbearers spoke up before* [lit. *with*] *Pharaoh.*

Seeing Pharaoh's anguished state, the chamberlain realized that he was putting himself in great danger by withholding his personal knowledge of someone who could interpret Pharaoh's dream correctly. He saw that Pharaoh was ready to expire, and he reasoned to himself: 'If this Pharaoh dies and another succeeds him, I have no way of being certain whether the new king will retain me in office or not; therefore I had better enhance my position with this Pharaoh and tell him about Joseph before he dies of grief' *(Midrash).*

The cupbearer's own experience had shown that a dreamer can instinctively recognize the correctness of a valid interpretation. He therefore spoke up, 'I can understand why none of these explanations satisfy you; I was once in the same position' *(R' Hirsch).*

Haamek Davar notes the lack of the preposition אֶל, *to.* Furthermore the word וַיְדַבֵּר, *and he spoke,* implies a harshness as opposed to וַיֹּאמֶר, *and he said,* which suggests normal conversation. He comments, therefore, that the chamberlain spoke harshly to *himself,* reproaching himself for not having told Pharaoh about Joseph, the one person who could set his mind to ease.

R' David Feinstein similarly detects a *harshness* in the phraseology, as if the Chamberlain was bitter at the very fact that he now had to evoke memories of an incident he would rather forget.

According to *Moshav Zekeinim* the sense of this phraseology אֶת (וַיְדַבֵּר) is that the cupbearer spoke *in the presence* of Pharaoh, i.e., addressing his courtiers, while referring to the king in respectful third person.

אֶת חֲטָאַי אֲנִי מַזְכִּיר הַיּוֹם — *My transgressions do I mention today.*

I.e., even though I will have to recall my sins to make this revela-

interpretation *only when the interpretation is in conformity with the dream.* In this case the Egyptian wizards entirely missed the significance of the dream — perceiving it as affecting Pharaoh the *individual* and interpreting both dreams separately rather than as one repeated entity; hence their interpretations were meaningless. Furthermore, Joseph stipulated that in Pharaoh's case it is *God Who will respond to Pharaoh's welfare* [*v.* 16], and the interpretation of such dreams are in God's exclusive Province — He and *only* He — determines who shall be His emissary in interpreting it (see *comm.* to 40:8). (Cf. *Maharsha* to *Berachos ibid.).*

י פַּרְעֹה קָצַף עַל־עֲבָדָיו וַיִּתֵּן אֹתִי בְּמִשְׁמַר
בֵּית שַׂר הַטַּבָּחִים אֹתִי וְאֵת שַׂר הָאֹפִים׃
יא וַנַּחַלְמָה חֲלוֹם בְּלַיְלָה אֶחָד אֲנִי וָהוּא
יב אִישׁ כְּפִתְרוֹן חֲלֹמוֹ חָלָמְנוּ׃ וְשָׁם אִתָּנוּ
נַעַר עִבְרִי עֶבֶד לְשַׂר הַטַּבָּחִים וַנְּסַפֶּר־לוֹ

tion, I will do it for the sake of your majesty — to tell you of my personal knowledge of an interpreter *(Radak; Ibn Ezra).*

Although I am about to mention my incarceration, I do not complain nor do I impugne Pharaoh's justice; for it was in punishment for *my sins* that I was imprisoned *(Alshich; Sforno).*

My offenses (in plural) — my sin against Pharaoh, and my sin against Joseph in forgetting my promise to him *(Chizkuni).*

— I am doubly guilty: firstly, by not having shown Joseph kindness by mentioning him to you; and secondly, in watching you suffer without telling you that he will know its meaning *(Midrash).*

10. פַּרְעֹה קָצַף עַל עֲבָדָיו — *Pharaoh had* [once] *become incensed* [see above] *at his servants.*

It is clear from this verse that Pharaoh was the royal title, not a personal name, for it would have otherwise been presumptuous for the cupbearer — or Joseph in *v.* 15 — to have addressed the king as 'Pharaoh' if that were his own name. Cf. Pharaoh-Necho in *Jeremiah* 46:2 where Pharaoh is the royal title and Necho his personal name *(Ibn Ezra; Rashbam; Lekach Tov).*

אֹתִי וְאֵת שַׂר הָאֹפִים — *Me and the Chamberlain of the Bakers.*

Both of us were equally charged with the same crime — offending the king. Nothing about our crime or treatment could have suggested our ultimate fate so that Joseph could tailor his interpretations to fit the situation *(Abarbanel).*

The double use of אֹתִי in this verse is not redundant but stylistic. Cf. double use of אֲנִי above 37:30 *(Ibn Ezra).*

11. וַנַּחַלְמָה חֲלוֹם בְּלַיְלָה אֶחָד אֲנִי וָהוּא — [*And*] *we dreamt a dream on the same* [lit. *one*] *night — I and he.*

Both our dreams appeared alike. They were so similar that they would have misled any but the most Divinely inspired interpreter. Moreover, since both dreams occurred on one night, the interpreter could have assumed that the same astrological influences would cause both our fates to be the same *(Abarbanel; Akeidah).*

אִישׁ כְּפִתְרוֹן חֲלֹמוֹ חָלָמְנוּ — *Each of us dreamt according to the interpretation of his dream.*

— I.e., each dream corresponded *exactly* with the interpretation that was given us [unlike the irrelevant interpretations offered you by your savants] *(Rashi).*

— Every detail of each dream was relevant to its interpretation; there was nothing extraneous in them *(Akeidah).*

According to *Ramban* and *Ibn Ezra* to 40:5: Each dream faithfully prognosticated the future indicating that it was a true prophetic dream, not the kind which comes as a result of anxiety.

41
10-12

today. [10] *Pharaoh had once become incensed at his*
servants and placed me in the ward of the house of
the Chamberlain of the Butchers — me and the
Chamberlain of the Bakers. [11] *We dreamt a dream on*
the same night, I and he; each of us dreamt according
to the interpretation of his dream. [12] *And there, with*
us, was a Hebrew youth, a slave of the Chamberlain
of the Butchers. We related it to him, and he in-

12. וְשָׁם אִתָּנוּ נַעַר עִבְרִי עֶבֶד לְשַׂר הַטַּבָּחִים — *And there with us was a Hebrew youth, a slave of the Chamberlain of the Butchers* [or: *Executioners*].

Cursed are the wicked because even their favors are incomplete! The chamberlain recalled Joseph in the most disparaging terms [i.e. in terms which would by their very nature negate Joseph's worthiness of recognition and rise to power in Egyptian society. The cupbearer intended only to introduce Joseph to Pharaoh for the limited purpose of interpreting the dream and nothing more. The chamberlain feared that if Joseph achieved a position of power, he would avenge himself against the ingrate who had let two years go by before mentioning him to Pharaoh]. He called Joseph נַעַר, *a youth* — ignorant and unfit for distinction; עִבְרִי, *a Hebrew* — a foreigner who does not even understand our language [and the laws of Egypt prohibit anyone holding high office unless he is fluent in seventy languages *(Nachalas Yaakov)*; furthermore, the Hebrews were detested by the Egyptians. See *comm.* to 39:6 and *Ramban* to 41:36; cf. also derogatory connotation in 40:14]; עֶבֶד, *a slave* — and it is written in the laws of Egypt that a slave can neither be ruler nor wear the robes of a noble *(Rashi)*.

[However, as we shall see, the Hand of Providence prevailed and Pharaoh perceived exceptional greatness in Joseph. He circumvened these laws and promoted Joseph to the highest ranks of authority nevertheless — without regard to his background. See *Ramban v.* 38 s.v. הֲנִמְצָא].

Others perceive less sinister motives in these designations.

According to *Radak:* Since Joseph attended to their needs in prison [40:4] the Chamberlain referred to him as נַעַר [lit. *youth*] which is a term for *attendant,* regardless of age. [Cf. *Exodus* 33:11; *Moreh Nevuchim* 2:32.] He mentioned that Joseph had been Potiphar's slave for identification purposes, since Joseph had been well known in that role.

Haamek Davar similarly suggests that the implication of these designations was that the person whom the cupbearer was about to recommend to Pharaoh was certainly Divinely inspired in interpreting dreams inasmuch as he was but a נַעַר, *youth,* who had no formal education in such matters; עִבְרִי, *a Hebrew,* and as such did not use witchcraft; עֶבֶד, *a slave,* and as such was certainly untutored [*Abarbanel* and *Ralbag* interpret similarly].

These commentators emphasize that the cupbearer purposely used these derogatory terms so Pharaoh would not suspect that the cupbearer had an ulterior motive in

וַיִּפְתָּר־לָנוּ אֶת־חֲלֹמֹתֵינוּ אִישׁ כַּחֲלֹמוֹ
יג פָּתָר: וַיְהִי כַּאֲשֶׁר פָּתַר־לָנוּ כֵּן הָיָה אֹתִי
יד הֵשִׁיב עַל־כַּנִּי וְאֹתוֹ תָלָה: וַיִּשְׁלַח פַּרְעֹה
וַיִּקְרָא אֶת־יוֹסֵף וַיְרִיצֻהוּ מִן־הַבּוֹר
וַיְגַלַּח וַיְחַלֵּף שִׂמְלֹתָיו וַיָּבֹא אֶל־פַּרְעֹה:

recommending a man who, if he succeeded in interpreting Pharaoh's dream, could rise to prominence.

Rashi rejects the interpretation that the cupbearer meant well, because, by stigmatizing Joseph as *a slave,* the cupbearer doomed him to insignificance since, as *Rashi* notes, it was contrary to Egyptian law for a slave to rise to power *(Be'er Mayim Chaim).*

Oznaim l'Torah similarly observes that since these words were uttered by a wicked man the terms could not be interpreted favorably since it is an established axiom that the favors of the wicked are incomplete.

וַיִּפְתָּר־לָנוּ אֶת־חֲלֹמֹתֵינוּ — *And he interpreted our dreams for us.*

These were different dreams and his interpretations drew the proper distinction between them *(Ramban).*

אִישׁ כַּחֲלֹמוֹ פָּתָר — *He interpreted for each in accordance with his dream* [lit. *man, according to his dream, did he interpret*].

— In accordance with the dream and consistent with its contents *(Rashi; Berachos* 55b — see next verse); — as it was destined to befall each of us *(Ramban).*

— He allowed no facet of the dream to go uninterpreted *(Haamek Davar).*

13. כַּאֲשֶׁר פָּתַר לָנוּ כֵּן הָיָה — *Just as he interpreted for us so did it happen.*[1]

I.e., he perceived the truth of the dreams, and as he interpreted each one, so it befell us. Cf. the expression: *every man according to his blessing he blessed him* [49:28] — according to the blessing destined to befall him; he did not bless all with a common blessing, but gave each a unique one *(Ramban).*

אֹתִי הֵשִׁיב עַל כַּנִּי וְאֹתוֹ תָלָה — *Me he restored to my post and him he hanged.*

The unnamed subject of the verbs, *restored* and *hanged,* clearly is Pharaoh, the primary subject of this entire episode beginning with v. 10: *Pharaoh once became incensed at his servants.* The passage does not say *who* restored him since it was obviously the one with the power to do so — Pharaoh. This is

1. The Talmud [*Berachos* 55b] derives from this passage that: כָּל הַחֲלוֹמוֹת הוֹלְכִין אַחַר הַפֶּה [=הַפִּתְרוֹן (עַיֵּין ירוש׳ מַעֲשֵׂר־שֵׁנִי ד:ו)], *the outcome of every dream depends on its interpretation* (lit. mouth) — i.e., the interpretation *determines* its meaning. However, Rava cautioned, the interpretation must conform with the dream, as it is written [*v.* 12] *he interpreted for each in accordance with his dream.* [Cf. footnote to *v.* 8; *Akeidah* §29; *Ein Yaakov; Yafeh Toar* 89:8; *footnote* to 37:8; *Ibn Ezra* to 40:8.]

In this connection, the Talmud (ibid.) mentions that there were twenty-four interpreters of dreams in Jerusalem. One Sage recorded that he once had a dream and he went to consult them all, but each interpretation differed from all the others. Nevertheless all the interpretations were fulfilled.

Maharsha explains that the understanding of this esoteric concept — that one's speech can affect the outcome of a dream — lies in the cosmic influence our Sages attribute to speech: in blessings and curses, prayers and blessings, and in such concepts as the casting of a 'good' or

terpreted our dreams for us; he interpreted for each in accordance with his dream. 13 *And it was that just as he interpreted for us so did it happen: me he restored to my post and him he hanged."*

14 *So Pharaoh sent and summoned Joseph, and he was rushed from the dungeon. He shaved and changed his clothes, and he came to Pharaoh.* 15 *And*

the case with all elliptic passages which omit the obvious subjects of the verb *(Rashi).*

It is proper etiquette to address royalty in third person *(Abarbanel).*

Ibn Ezra [the *Zohar* interprets similarly] adds that following the Talmudic dictum [see footnote] that the outcome of every dream depends on its interpretation [a concept he discusses in 40:8], the subject of this passage is *Joseph* — the implicit subject of the immediately preceding passages. By his positive interpretation of the dream, *he* [*Joseph*], in effect, restored the one to his post and caused the other to be hanged.

14. וַיִּשְׁלַח פַּרְעֹה וַיִּקְרָא אֶת־יוֹסֵף — *So* [lit. *and*] *Pharaoh sent and summoned* [lit. *called*] *Joseph.*

According to the traditional chronology [see *Rosh Hashanah* 10b] Joseph was released from prison on Rosh Hashanah [in the year 2230 from Creation].

In *Torah Anthology, R' Aryeh Kaplan* [note 21] calculates accordingly that 'the King of Egypt in the time of Joseph was most probably Amenhotep I of the eighteenth dynasty who ruled 1545-1525 B.C.E.' [2217-2237 from Creation].

וַיְרִיצֻהוּ מִן הַבּוֹר — *And he was rushed* [lit. *and they made him run*] *from the dungeon* [lit. *pit*].

He was rushed — in the manner of every case of Divine salvation which comes hastily and unexpectedly. Similarly, the coming of the Messiah will be sudden and hasty [see *Malachi* 3:1] *(Sforno).*

— Every Providential act which leads to the miraculous rescue of the downtrodden comes by surprise at the moment one least expects it, בְּהֶסַּח הַדַּעַת, *in a moment of inattention* [*Sanhedrin* 97a] *(R' Munk).*

The term בּוֹר [*pit*] refers to the prison which was made like a hole [dungeon]. Throughout Scripture, the term בּוֹר similarly signifies *hole*, whether or not it contains water *(Rashi).*

וַיְגַלַּח וַיְחַלֵּף שִׂמְלֹתָיו — [*And*] *he shaved and changed his clothes.*

— Out of respect for royalty *(Rashi; Midrash).*

Rashi wishes to clarify that Joseph did not shave and change his clothes to celebrate his release, for Joseph did not yet know whether he was indeed freed permanently; it was rather specifically out of respect for the king *(Mizrachi* et al).

Sforno cites *Esther* 4:2: *it was forbidden to enter the King's gate* clothed with sackcloth.

'evil' eye. [Cf. also the Rabbinic dictum (*Moed Katan* 18a; see comm. to 2:6): בְּרִית כְּרוּתָה לַשְּׂפָתַיִם, *a covenant has been made with the lips*, i.e., the spoken word, even if unintentional, may contain a portent for the future, and often becomes fulfilled as if by prophecy.]

Accordingly, the Sages caution [*Berachos* 56b] that since the effect of a dream is dependent upon its interpretation, it is important to think of an auspicious verse in conjunction with the symbolism of the dream — and generally seek a favorable interpretation — before one with a less favorable meaning comes to mind.

* * *

The Midrash records that a woman once told R' Eliezer, 'I dreamed that the upper chamber

°שני טו °וַיֹּאמֶר פַּרְעֹה֙ אֶל־יוֹסֵ֔ף חֲל֣וֹם חָלַ֔מְתִּי
וּפֹתֵ֖ר אֵ֣ין אֹת֑וֹ וַאֲנִ֗י שָׁמַ֤עְתִּי עָלֶ֙יךָ֙ לֵאמֹ֔ר
טז תִּשְׁמַ֥ע חֲל֖וֹם לִפְתֹּ֥ר אֹתֽוֹ׃ וַיַּ֨עַן יוֹסֵ֧ף אֶת־
פַּרְעֹ֛ה לֵאמֹ֖ר בִּלְעָדָ֑י אֱלֹהִ֕ים יַעֲנֶ֖ה אֶת־
יז שְׁל֥וֹם פַּרְעֹֽה׃ וַיְדַבֵּ֥ר פַּרְעֹ֖ה אֶל־יוֹסֵ֑ף

15. Pharaoh relates his dream to Joseph.

חֲלוֹם חָלַמְתִּי וּפֹתֵר אֵין אֹתוֹ — *I dreamt a dream, but no one can interpret it.*

— There were interpreters, but none who could do the dream justice *(Or HaChaim)*. [Cf 40:8.]

וַאֲנִי שָׁמַעְתִּי עָלֶיךָ לֵאמֹר — *Now I heard it said of you* [lit. *and I heard about you saying*].

The אֲנִי, *I*, is emphatic, the implication being: *I*, the King of Egypt — to whom no one would dare lie — have heard about your talent in interpreting dreams. Therefore you need not go through the motions of modestly denying it; time is of the essence. Hear me out and interpret my dream *(Chumash R' Peninim)*.

תִּשְׁמַע חֲלוֹם לִפְתֹּר אֹתוֹ — [*That*] *you comprehend* [lit. *hear*] *a dream to interpret it.*

I.e., that you hear — listen and understand — a dream to interpret it. The verb שמע [*hear*] refers both to comprehension and listening. Cf. 42:23 שֹׁמֵעַ יוֹסֵף, *Joseph understood; Deut.* 28:49: *A people whose language you shall not understand* [תִּשְׁמַע] *(Rashi).*

Cf. *Deut.* 6:7 שְׁמַע יִשְׂרָאֵל, *hear* — i.e. comprehend — *O Israel.* King Belshazzar similarly told Daniel [*Dan.* 5:16]: *I have heard about you that you are able to interpret interpretations and to loosen knots (R' Bachya).*

— I am informed that you listen to a dream so well that you decipher it from its very context. Finding solutions depends on listening properly. Of ten people who listen to a speech or a story, each one may hear it differently and only one correctly *(R' Hirsch).*

16. בִּלְעָדָי — [*That is*] *beyond me* [lit. *without me (Ibn Janach);* see 14:24].

— The wisdom [to interpret dreams] is not my own *(Rashi)* ...

Rashi thus perceives the word to be a combination of בַּל, *not,* עָדַי, *unto me* — i.e., the power is not my own. It does not mean: *Not I* — i.e., I refuse to interpret it, for Joseph *does* proceed to interpret the dream for Pharaoh. The intent is that Joseph humbly gave credit to Whom credit was due, and acknowledged that the powers ascribed to him were not his own. Cf. comm. to 40:8 *(Mizrachi; Tzeidah laDerech).*

in the second story of my house was split open.'

'This indicates that you will conceive and bear a son,' R' Eliezer assured her.

She left, and so it happened.

She had the same dream again at some later date. R' Eliezer repeated the interpretation and again it was fulfilled.

Some time later, she had the same dream a third time. Again she went to R' Eliezer but he was away. So she related the dream to his disciples who interpreted it to mean that she would bury her husband.

And this is exactly what occurred.

When R' Eliezer returned and heard her cries of grief, he inquired what had happened. They told him about her dream and their interpretation, and R' Eliezer sternly rebuked them, 'You have killed a man! The Torah explicitly intimates [in our verse] that dreams follow the mouth of the interpreter!'

Pharaoh said to Joseph, "I dreamt a dream, but no
one can interpret it. Now I heard it said of you that
you comprehend a dream to interpret it."
16 *Joseph answered Pharaoh saying, "That is*
beyond me. It is God Who will respond with
Pharaoh's welfare."
17 *Then Pharaoh said to Joseph, "In my dream,*

אֱלֹהִים יַעֲנֶה אֶת שְׁלוֹם פַּרְעֹה — *It is God Who will respond with Pharaoh's welfare.*

— I.e., it is *God* Who will place in my mouth an answer that will be for Pharaoh's welfare *(Rashi).*

Ralbag interprets this as a prayer: 'It is not my prerogative to interpret a dream as I wish, but as I am inspired from Heaven.' Accordingly, Joseph prayed: *May God respond with an interpretation favorable to Pharaoh.*

Because Joseph did not claim greatness himself and attributed whatever wisdom he had to God, the Sages in *Midrash Tanchuma* maintain that he was rewarded by rising to greatness and sovereignty.

Daniel similarly ascribed his powers to God when he was about to interpret Nebuchadnezzar's dream [*Daniel* 2:30]: *This secret was revealed to me not because I possess more wisdom than any other being, but rather to make the interpretation known to the king.* Daniel was rewarded by being *clothed in purple, with a gold chain around his neck, and it was proclaimed about him that he would rule one third of the kingdom* [*ibid.* 5:30].

Concerning such men Scripture writes [*I Samuel* 2:30]: *Those that honor Me I will honor (Midrash HaGadol).*

According to *Ibn Ezra* the word יַעֲנֶה [*respond*] has the connotation of *provide* [מַעֲנֶה] *him with the joy of his heart. Ibn Janach* interprets it as referring to Providence, while *Radak* maintains that the literal interpretation *respond* connotes in this context the granting of His beneficence as if in response to prayer.

17-24. Pharaoh's recapitulation of his dream.

A comparison of Pharaoh's account of the dream in the following verses with the Torah's narrative of it in verses 1-8 yields astonishing variations, omissions and additions. This parallel representation is graphically portrayed on the chart on the following pages: "Pharaoh's Dream: Variations and nuances."

The commentators approach these nuances in different ways:

Radak and *Ramban* do not elicit any special significance to these changes. Consistent with his commentary to the nuances in Eliezer's account to Laban in chapt. 24, *Radak* maintains that 'in reported speech a person always varies his wording — adding or substracting as he sees fit, but always preserving the essential content ... It is useless to look for any special reason for Pharaoh's omissions and additions; these are characteristic of any repetition or paraphrase; the words change but not the content.'

See also *Ibn Ezra* to *Exodus* 20:1 for a similar interpretation.

Along similar lines, *Ramban* [to *v.* 3] suggests that both accounts might really have been identical, but that the Torah may not have been concerned with matching all the details.

Midrash Tanchuma, Zohar, and many of the later commentators however, e.g. *Kli Yakar, Paaneach Raza, HaKsav V'HaKabbalah, Haamek Davar, R' Hirsch,* perceive great significance in the subtle variations, additions and omissions. This is especially so since the Torah usually economizes on its every word, and could have avoided the repetition entirely unless the differences were intentional.

As *Haamek Davar* observes, 'The Torah did not have to make any changes in the account, but could simply have said, *Then Pharaoh told Joseph his dream.* The fact that the Torah did not do so indicates that there are details which were not explained earlier, for special significance must be attached to every variation in the wording, and these we shall duly explain.'

In general, the commentators who attribute significance to the variations maintain either that Pharaoh did not grasp the implication of the symbolisms and therefore did not always lay due emphasis upon the essential key points of the dream when reporting it to Joseph, or that Pharaoh purposely disguised these essential points to *test Joseph's veracity.* Joseph passed the test; he was undaunted by Pharaoh's attempts and interpreted — to Pharaoh's satisfaction — the essence of the *actual* dream.

Midrash Tanchuma records that each time Pharaoh deliberately changed the dream to confuse and test Joseph, Joseph would correct him saying, 'That is not what you dreamed.' Pharaoh was amazed and asked 'Were you eavesdropping on my dreams?'

According to the latter interpretations, Joseph's remark in *v.* 32: וְעַל הִשָּׁנוֹת הַחֲלוֹם has two connotations: it alludes to Joseph's corrections of Pharaoh's intentional שִׁינוּי, *alteration,* of the dream, as well as the repetition of the vision. Both were indicative that *the matter stands ready before God and God is hastening to acommplish it* [*v.* 32]. (See *Paaneach Raza; HaKsav V'HaKabbalah).*

The various perceptions of these nuances will be treated in the commentary to the subsequent verses.

PHARAOH'S DREAM / Variations and Nuances

JOSEPH'S REITERATION *(verses 26–27)*	PHARAOH'S ACCOUNT *(verses 17–24)*	THE SCRIPTURAL NARRATIVE *(verses 1–8)*
	... בַּחֲלֹמִי *In my dream,*	... וּפַרְעֹה חֹלֵם *And Pharoah dreamt*
	הִנְנִי עֹמֵד עַל שְׂפַת הַיְאֹר *behold! I was standing by the bank of the River—*	וְהִנֵּה עֹמֵד עַל הַיְאֹר *and behold! he was standing by the River—*
שֶׁבַע פָּרֹת *seven cows*	וְהִנֵּה מִן הַיְאֹר עֹלֹת שֶׁבַע פָּרוֹת *when behold! out of the River there emerged seven cows,*	וְהִנֵּה מִן הַיְאֹר עֹלֹת שֶׁבַע פָּרוֹת *when behold! out of the River there emerged seven cows,*
הַטֹּבֹת *the good ones*	בְּרִיאוֹת בָּשָׂר וִיפֹת תֹּאַר *physically healthy and beautiful of form,*	יְפוֹת מַרְאֶה וּבְרִיאֹת בָּשָׂר *beautiful of appearance and physically healthy,*
	וַתִּרְעֶינָה בָּאָחוּ *and they grazed in the marshland.*	וַתִּרְעֶינָה בָּאָחוּ *and they grazed in the marshland.*
וְשֶׁבַע הַפָּרוֹת *and the seven cows*	וְהִנֵּה שֶׁבַע פָּרוֹת אֲחֵרוֹת עֹלוֹת אַחֲרֵיהֶן *Then behold! seven other cows emerged after them,*	וְהִנֵּה שֶׁבַע פָּרוֹת אֲחֵרוֹת עֹלוֹת אַחֲרֵיהֶן *Then behold! seven other cows emerged after them*
		מִן הַיְאֹר *out of the River,*
	דַּלּוֹת *scrawny,*	
הָרַקּוֹת וְהָרָעֹת *emaciated and inferior*	וְרָעוֹת תֹּאַר מְאֹד *and of very inferior form*	רָעוֹת מַרְאֶה *inferior of appearance*
	וְרַקּוֹת בָּשָׂר *and of emaciated flesh.*	וְדַקּוֹת בָּשָׂר *and of lean flesh;*

JOSEPH'S REITERATION	PHARAOH'S ACCOUNT	THE SCRIPTURAL NARRATIVE
הָעֹלֹת אַחֲרֵיהֶן *who emerged after them*		
	לֹא רָאִיתִי כָהֵנָּה בְּכָל אֶרֶץ מִצְרַיִם לָרֹעַ *I have never seen the likes of them in all the land of Egypt for inferiority.*	
		וַתַּעֲמֹדְנָה אֵצֶל הַפָּרוֹת עַל שְׂפַת הַיְאֹר *they stood next to the cows on the bank of the River.*
	וַתֹּאכַלְנָה הַפָּרוֹת הָרַקּוֹת וְהָרָעוֹת *Then the cows, emaciated and inferior, ate up*	וַתֹּאכַלְנָה הַפָּרוֹת רָעוֹת הַמַּרְאֶה וְדַקֹּת הַבָּשָׂר *Then the cows, inferior of appearance and of thin flesh, ate up*
	אֵת שֶׁבַע הַפָּרוֹת *the seven cows,*	אֵת שֶׁבַע הַפָּרוֹת *the seven cows,*
	הָרִאשֹׁנוֹת *the first ones,*	
		יְפֹת הַמַּרְאֶה *handsome of appearance*
	הַבְּרִיאֹת *the healthy ones;*	וְהַבְּרִיאֹת *and the healthy ones.*
	וַתָּבֹאנָה אֶל קִרְבֶּנָה וְלֹא נוֹדַע כִּי בָאוּ אֶל קִרְבֶּנָה וּמַרְאֵיהֶן רַע כַּאֲשֶׁר בַּתְּחִלָּה *thus they came inside them but it was not apparent that they had come inside them for their appearance remained as inferior as at first.*	
	וָאִיקָץ *Then I awoke.*	וַיִּיקַץ פַּרְעֹה *Then Pharaoh awoke.*
	וָאֵרֶא בַּחֲלֹמִי *Then I saw in my dream*	וַיִּישָׁן וַיַּחֲלֹם שֵׁנִית *He fell asleep and dreamt a second time—*
וְשֶׁבַע הַשִּׁבֳּלִים *and the seven ears of grain*	וְהִנֵּה שֶׁבַע שִׁבֳּלִים עֹלֹת בְּקָנֶה אֶחָד *and behold! seven ears of grain were sprouting on a single stalk,*	וְהִנֵּה שֶׁבַע שִׁבֳּלִים עֹלוֹת בְּקָנֶה אֶחָד *and behold! seven ears of grain were sprouting on a single stalk,*
הַטֹּבֹת *the good ones*	מְלֵאֹת וְטֹבוֹת *full and good.*	בְּרִיאוֹת וְטֹבוֹת *healthy and good.*
וְשֶׁבַע הַשִּׁבֳּלִים *and the seven ears of grain*	וְהִנֵּה שֶׁבַע שִׁבֳּלִים *And behold! seven ears of grain,*	וְהִנֵּה שֶׁבַע שִׁבֳּלִים *And behold! seven ears of grain,*
הָרֵקוֹת *the empty ones*	צְנֻמוֹת דַּקּוֹת *shriveled, thin,*	דַּקּוֹת *thin*
שְׁדֻפוֹת הַקָּדִים *scorched by the east wind*	שְׁדֻפוֹת קָדִים *scorched by the east wind,*	וּשְׁדוּפֹת קָדִים *and scorched by the east wind,*
	צֹמְחוֹת אַחֲרֵיהֶם *were growing after them.*	צֹמְחוֹת אַחֲרֵיהֶן *were growing after them.*
	וַתִּבְלַעְןָ הַשִּׁבֳּלִים הַדַּקֹּת *Then the seven thin ears of grain swallowed up*	וַתִּבְלַעְנָה הַשִּׁבֳּלִים הַדַּקּוֹת *Then the seven thin ears of grain swallowed up*
	אֵת שֶׁבַע הַשִּׁבֳּלִים הַטֹּבוֹת *the seven good ears of grain.*	אֵת שֶׁבַע הַשִּׁבֳּלִים הַבְּרִיאוֹת וְהַמְּלֵאוֹת *the seven healthy and full ears of grain.*
		וַיִּיקַץ פַּרְעֹה וְהִנֵּה חֲלוֹם *Pharaoh awoke and behold! it had been a dream.*

יח בַּחֲלֹמִי הִנְנִי עֹמֵד עַל־שְׂפַת הַיְאֹר: וְהִנֵּה
מִן־הַיְאֹר עֹלֹת שֶׁבַע פָּרוֹת בְּרִיאוֹת בָּשָׂר
יט וִיפֹת תֹּאַר וַתִּרְעֶינָה בָּאָחוּ: וְהִנֵּה שֶׁבַע
פָּרוֹת אֲחֵרוֹת עֹלוֹת אַחֲרֵיהֶן דַּלּוֹת
וְרָעוֹת תֹּאַר מְאֹד וְרַקּוֹת בָּשָׂר לֹא־
רָאִיתִי כָהֵנָּה בְּכָל־אֶרֶץ מִצְרַיִם לָרֹעַ:

JOSEPH'S REITERATION	PHARAOH'S ACCOUNT	THE SCRIPTURAL NARRATIVE
	וָאֹמַר אֶל הַחַרְטֻמִּים *And I said [this] to the necromancers—*	וַיְהִי בַבֹּקֶר וַתִּפָּעֶם רוּחוֹ וַיִּשְׁלַח וַיִּקְרָא אֶת כָּל חַרְטֻמֵּי מִצְרַיִם וְאֶת כָּל חֲכָמֶיהָ וַיְסַפֵּר פַּרְעֹה לָהֶם אֶת חֲלֹמוֹ *And it was in the morning: his spirit was agitated, so he sent and summoned all the necromancers of Egypt and all its wise men. And Pharaoh related his dream to them—*
	וְאֵין מַגִּיד לִי *but no one could explain [it] to me.*	וְאֵין פּוֹתֵר אוֹתָם לְפַרְעֹה *but none could interpret them for Pharaoh.*

17. בַּחֲלֹמִי הִנְנִי עֹמֵד עַל־שְׂפַת הַיְאֹר — *In my dream, behold! I was standing onthe bank of the River.*

Since the Nile was venerated as a god of Egypt (see *comm.* to *v.* 1), Pharaoh delicately avoided mention that he stood *on the river,* which would connote a feeling of superiority over his god. Instead he said that he stood *on* **the bank** *of the River (Kli Yakar).*

18. בְּרִיאוֹת בָּשָׂר וִיפֹת תֹּאַר — *Robust* [lit. *healthy of flesh*] *and handsome* [lit. *beautiful of form*].

In his dream these terms are in the reverse order [*v.* 2], indicating that his initial perception of them was in that order. Furthermore, *v.* 2 used the expression יְפוֹת מַרְאֶה, lit. *beautiful of appearance. Radak* maintains that such minor reversals of order and detail are insignificant as long as the essence of the description remains unchanged.

Haamek Davar, however, notes a significance even in this seemingly minor change of detail. The initial account of the dream *(v.* 2) first described the cows as יְפוֹת מַרְאֶה, *beautiful of appearance,* a characteristic which refers to the healthy, attractive sheen of their hide. Then they were described as בְּרִיאוֹת בָּשָׂר, lit. *healthy of flesh* [i.e., *robust*]. The implication is that their attractive external appearance is emphasized. This indicated that during the good years, Egypt would be a center of commerce that would be a magnet to other nations. In our verse, however, the emphasis is on the בָּשָׂר, *flesh.* In this context, וִיפֹת תֹּאַר, literally *beautiful of form,* means that the animals looked *extremely* fat and meaty, like pregnant cows. This was to indicate that Egypt would supply sustenance to other countries — like a pregnant cow that would give birth and nurse its young. Cf. *Kli Yakar* who infers from Pharaoh's use of these two terms — and the order in which he reported them — that he wished to emphasize to Joseph that the health and beauty of the cows was a gift of the god Nile from which

behold! I was standing upon the bank of the River.
[18] When out of the River there emerged seven cows,
robust and handsome, and they were grazing in the
marshland. [19] Suddenly, seven other cows emerged
after them — scrawny and of very inferior form and
of emaciated flesh; I have never seen inferiority like

they emerged. That the animals were בְּרִיאוֹת בָּשָׂר, *robust* [lit. *healthy of flesh*], and fat could be taken as a natural consequence of their well-watered, fertile habitat; any animal could be expected to be well fed and robust if it grew up in a land of abundance. But these cows had a further characteristic — they were יְפַת תֹּאַר, *handsome of form*, and with beautifully formed features. That sort of beauty is God-given; water and pasture land cannot affect an animal's features. The presence of even this second characteristic showed that the "divine" Nile was responsible.

19-21. *R' Hirsch* infers from Pharaoh's elaborate description of the bad cows that they made a far stronger impression on him than did the good ones. He stresses bad qualities in order to emphasize the impression they made on him.

19. שֶׁבַע־פָּרוֹת אֲחֵרוֹת עוֹלוֹת אַחֲרֵיהֶן — *Seven other cows emerged* [lit. *went up*] *after them.*

In repeating the dream, Pharaoh fails to mention that the emaciated cows emerged מִן הַיְאוֹר, *from the River* (see *v.* 3). This was because the Nile, as noted, was venerated as a god, and Pharaoh delicately wished to avoid the connotation that something ugly and auguring misfortune could emanate from the gods *(Kli Yakar; Akeidah; Bereishis Rabbosi).*

דַּלּוֹת וְרָעוֹת תֹּאַר מְאֹד — *Scrawny, and of very inferior* [lit. *bad*] *form.*

Pharaoh added that they were דַּלּוֹת, *scrawny;* and he substituted רָעוֹת תֹּאַר מְאֹד, *of very inferior form,* for רָעוֹת מַרְאֶה, *of inferior appearance.* According to *Ibn Ezra,* the implication of both terms is generally the same, while according to the *Midrash,* as mentioned in the Prefatory Comment above, this was yet another illustration of how Pharaoh deliberately changed the dream to test Joseph, but in every case — much to Pharaoh's astonishment — Joseph brought the discrepancy to his attention.

The translation *scrawny* follows *Rashi* who explains דַּלּוֹת as *lean,* citing *II Samuel* 13:4: *Why are you becoming* דַּל, *lean?*

R' Hirsch relates דַּל to its meaning of *poor* — hence *needy, miserable.*

וְרַקּוֹת בָּשָׂר — *And of emaciated flesh.*

Throughout Scripture the term רַקּוֹת means lacking flesh *(Rashi).*

That is, the word רַק [*but; only*] from the root רקק always denotes a limitation. — Hence whenever, the term רַקּוֹת occurs in Scripture it contextually means: *limited in flesh.* It is thus to be distinguished from the words רֵיק and רֵיקוֹת which means *empty (Mizrachi; Gur Aryeh).*

[See *comm.* to רַקּוֹת in *v.* 27.]

They were so emaciated that they had absolutely no flesh between their skin and bones, in contrast to the fat cows that were so full they appeared to be pregnant *(Haamek Davar).*

When Pharaoh described these cows as רַקּוֹת בָּשָׂר, *of emaciated flesh,* Joseph interjected 'you did not see them so, but דַּקּוֹת בָּשָׂר, *gaunt* [*of lean flesh*]' *(Tanchuma).*

לֹא רָאִיתִי כָהֵנָּה בְּכָל־אֶרֶץ מִצְרַיִם לָרֹעַ — *I have never seen inferiority like theirs in all the land of Egypt.*

כ וַתֹּאכַלְנָה הַפָּרוֹת הָרַקּוֹת וְהָרָעוֹת אֵת
שֶׁבַע הַפָּרוֹת הָרִאשֹׁנוֹת הַבְּרִיאֹת׃
כא וַתָּבֹאנָה אֶל־קִרְבֶּנָה וְלֹא נוֹדַע כִּי־בָאוּ
אֶל־קִרְבֶּנָה וּמַרְאֵיהֶן רַע כַּאֲשֶׁר בַּתְּחִלָּה
כב וָאִיקָץ׃ וָאֵרֶא בַּחֲלֹמִי וְהִנֵּה | שֶׁבַע
שִׁבֳּלִים עֹלֹת בְּקָנֶה אֶחָד מְלֵאֹת וְטֹבוֹת׃
כג וְהִנֵּה שֶׁבַע שִׁבֳּלִים צְנֻמוֹת דַּקּוֹת שְׁדֻפוֹת
כד קָדִים צֹמְחוֹת אַחֲרֵיהֶם׃ וַתִּבְלַעְןָ

This phrase does not occur in the original account of the dream in *v.* 3.

[In the most literal sense, it would have been out of context for the Torah to interrupt a report of the dream with Pharaoh's personal impression that he had never before seen such inferior cows. (Comp. *Rashbam* to *v.* 21 s.v. וּמַרְאֵיהֶן).] Accordingly, *Kli Yakar* suggests that Pharaoh purposely added this fact for a specific reason: Sometimes dreams are the product of what one has seen or fantasized during the day. Pharaoh wanted to emphasize that the inferior cows of his dream were not merely the product of his imagination, for he had never before seen such inferior cows.

Furthermore, it is noted that Pharaoh omitted in this account that *these cows stood next to the cows* on the bank of the river [see *comm.* above, *v.* 2].

20. וַתֹּאכַלְנָה הַפָּרוֹת הָרַקּוֹת וְהָרָעוֹת אֵת שֶׁבַע הַפָּרוֹת הָרִאשֹׁנוֹת הַבְּרִיאֹת — *And the emaciated and inferior cows ate up the first seven healthy cows.*

Joseph perceived this as a sign that surplus food from the seven abundant years would nourish the Egyptians during the seven years of famine, and that accordingly, they should set aside a reserve for those years *(Ramban v.* 4).

21. וַתָּבֹאנָה אֶל קִרְבֶּנָה — *Thus, they came inside them.*

— I.e. the fat cows entered the bodies of the emaciated cows. The phrase suggests that they were swallowed *whole (Sechel Tov).*

וְלֹא נוֹדַע כִּי־בָאוּ אֶל־קִרְבֶּנָה — *But it was not apparent* [lit. *and it was not known*] *that they had come inside them.*

I.e. it remained unrecognizable that they consumed them ...

וּמַרְאֵיהֶן רַע כַּאֲשֶׁר בַּתְּחִלָּה — *For their appearance remained as inferior as at first.*

Their appearance — i.e., the appearance of each of them. This explains why the adjective רַע, *inferior*, is in the singular *(Ibn Ezra).*

This observation is not mentioned in the earlier account of the dream [see *v.* 4]. Pharaoh added it now because he realized while reporting the dream that he had not noticed any difference in the emaciated cows. In the original narrative of the dream, however, it would have been inappropriate for the Torah to embellish the facts with Pharaoh's personal impressions *(Rashbam).*

theirs in all the land of Egypt. [20] *And the emaciated and inferior cows ate up the first seven healthy cows.*
[21] *Thus they came inside them. But it was not apparent that they had come inside them, for their appearance remained as inferior as at first. Then I awoke.* [22] *I then saw in my dream: Behold! seven ears of grain were sprouting on a single stalk — full and good.* [23] *And suddenly! seven ears of grain, withered, thin and scorched by the east wind were growing*

[See *comm.* of *Ramban* cited in *v.* 31 below.]

22. וָאֵרֶא בַּחֲלֹמִי — *I then saw in my dream.*

וְהִנֵּה שֶׁבַע שִׁבֳּלִים עֹלֹת בְּקָנֶה אֶחָד — *Behold — seven ears of grain were sprouting* [lit. going up] *on a single stalk.*

מְלֵאֹת וְטֹבוֹת — *Full and good.*

Full — i.e., full of kernels *(Ralbag).*

In verse 5 the expression used is בְּרִיאוֹת וְטֹבוֹת, *healthy and good. Ibn Ezra* (ad. loc.) comments that regarding plant life the terms *full* and *healthy* are synonymous. *Avi Ezer* maintains, however, that there is a distinction between the terms: *healthy* implies that something is free of insect ravages, while *full* means full of kernels. Since in Hebrew the term בָּרִיא, *healthy,* is not commonly used of non-humans, *Ibn Ezra* is merely observing that it is a borrowed term to denote fullness.

According to *Haamek Davar,* the connotation of *fullness* is that there would be grain enough even to export from Egypt, while the term *healthy* suggests that the grain would last a long time.

23. וְהִנֵּה שֶׁבַע שִׁבֳּלִים צְנֻמוֹת דַּקּוֹת שְׁדֻפוֹת קָדִים — *And suddenly! seven ears of grain, withered, thin,* [and] *scorched by the east wind.*

The translation of צְנֻמוֹת as *withered* follows *Rashi* who explains that the word is related to the cognate Aramaic term צוּנְמָא, *stone.* Accordingly, in our passage these ears lacked moisture and became as hard as wood or stone. [Some versions of *Rashi* read: and as *dry* as stone.]

Rashi also cites *Onkelos* who renders: נָצָן לָקְיָן, *whose blossoms were stricken* — i.e., they were *void* of everything but their [withered] blossoms, for they were *emptied of their grain.*

Thus *Rashi* is of the opinion that *Onkelos* takes צְנֻמוֹת in the sense of *empty,* while in his own opinion it means *hard (Be'er Yitzchak).*

On linguistic grounds, *Ramban* denies that this has anything to do with the blossoms. Citing the Talmudic use of the word צוּנְמָא in *Berachos* 39a, he maintains that צְנֻמוֹת essentially means *separated* [fragmented; *(Rashi* there interprets the word as 'dry' consistent with his commentary here)]. The interpretation according to *Onkelos'* use of the term נָצָן is accordingly: *cut; deficient.*

Essentially, *Ramban* explains that there were portions on the ears void of kernels while higher up on the stalks the ears were scorched and entirely empty.

In interpreting the dream [*v.* 27], Joseph did not repeat this term, because he knew that Pharaoh had added it merely to test him and it was not part of his actual dream *(Sifsei Chachomim).* As the *Midrash* notes: Joseph said, 'It is not צְנוּמוֹת, *withered ones,* that you saw, but דַּקּוֹת, *thin ones.*' According to *Ramban,* however, in Joseph's interpretation [*v.* 27] he substituted it with the word רֵקוֹת which *Ramban* interprets as *empty* [but which *Rashi,* consistent with his interpretation in v. 19, interprets as *lean*]. See *comm.* to *v.* 27.

הַשִּׁבֳּלִים הַדַּקֹּת אֵת שֶׁבַע הַשִּׁבֳּלִים
הַטֹּבוֹת וָאֹמַר אֶל־הַחַרְטֻמִּים וְאֵין מַגִּיד
כה לִי׃ וַיֹּאמֶר יוֹסֵף אֶל־פַּרְעֹה חֲלוֹם פַּרְעֹה
אֶחָד הוּא אֵת אֲשֶׁר הָאֱלֹהִים עֹשֶׂה הִגִּיד
כו לְפַרְעֹה׃ שֶׁבַע פָּרֹת הַטֹּבֹת שֶׁבַע שָׁנִים
הֵנָּה וְשֶׁבַע הַשִּׁבֳּלִים הַטֹּבֹת שֶׁבַע שָׁנִים
כז הֵנָּה חֲלוֹם אֶחָד הוּא׃ וְשֶׁבַע הַפָּרוֹת
הָרַקּוֹת וְהָרָעֹת הָעֹלֹת אַחֲרֵיהֶן שֶׁבַע
שָׁנִים הֵנָּה וְשֶׁבַע הַשִּׁבֳּלִים הָרֵקוֹת

24. וַתִּבְלַעְןָ ... אֵת שֶׁבַע הַשִּׁבֳּלִים הַטֹּבוֹת — *Then* [lit. *and*] *the thin ears of grain swallowed up the seven good ears.*

[In *v.* 7 the adjectives are הַבְּרִיאוֹת וְהַמְּלֵאוֹת *healthy and full.*]

וָאֹמַר אֶל־הַחַרְטֻמִּים וְאֵין מַגִּיד לִי — [*And*] *I said this to the necromancers* (see *v.* 8) *but no one could explain* [lit. *tell*] *it to me.*

Pharaoh did not mention that he had summoned the *wise men* as well. Pharaoh had apparently not been so astonished that the wise men — who rely on logic — could not fathom the inner symbolisms of his dream. He was dismayed, rather, that the necromancers — who could use *'magic'* to decipher the dream — were also unable to interpret it *(Haamek Davar).*

[Furthermore, Pharaoh apparently finds it beneath his dignity to mention that when he awoke (*v.* 8): וַתִּפָּעֶם רוּחוֹ, *his spirit was agitated.*]

25. Joseph's interpretation.

חֲלוֹם פַּרְעֹה אֶחָד הוּא — *The dream of Pharaoh is a single one.*

Both dreams complement each other: they are two components of a cogent whole. The cows represent plowing, and the ears of grain represent reaping *(Abarbanel.*

אֵת אֲשֶׁר הָאֱלֹהִים עֹשֶׂה הִגִּיד לְפַרְעֹה — *What God is about to do* [lit. *that which God does*] *He has told to Pharaoh.*

— This has been revealed to Pharaoh because only he can take the necessary measures to deal with the situation *(Rashbam).*

Because the dream concerns matters of State, God sent it directly to Pharaoh. God wished to communicate with Pharaoh only through His *own* agent who can translate the Divine language clearly; that is why Pharaoh's wizards cannot interpret the dream *(Alshich).*[1]

Cf. the Talmudic dictum [*Berachos*

1. Joseph placed heavy emphasis on the fact that God was communicating His intentions directly to Pharaoh; not only did Joseph make the point in this verse, he repeated it in *v.* 28. There were two reasons for this insistence: The dreams occurred on the night of Rosh Hashanah [*Rosh Hashanah* 10b; see *comm.* to *v.* 14], a time when dreams are particularly auspicious since a country's destiny, including its fertility and drought, are decided then. [Cf. *Ein Yaakov* ad. loc.] Furthermore, the dreams were communicated to the ruler of the nation. R' Yitzchak teaches that the more prominent a person, the more significant a revelation

41
24-27

after them. 24 Then the thin ears of grain swallowed
up the seven good ears. I said this to the necromancers, but no one could explain it to me."
25 Joseph said to Pharaoh, "The dream of Pharaoh
is a single one. What God is about to do, He has told
to Pharaoh: 26 The seven good cows are seven years,
and the good ears are seven years. it is one dream.
27 Now, the seven emaciated and bad cows who
emerged after them are seven years as are the seven
emaciated ears scorched by the east wind. There shall

55a]: 'There are three things which the Holy One Blessed be He, proclaims Himself, namely: famine, plenty, and a good provider' [Scriptural verses are cited for each]. *Or HaChaim* comments that all three proclamations were inherent in Joseph's interpretation: The *famine* in *v.* 27; the *plenty* in *v.* 29; and the *good provider* in verses 33-34.

In referring to the case of the seven good years, Joseph used the expression God 'has **told** [הִגִּיד] to *Pharaoh,'* since it alluded to a period that was near at hand; but with reference to the famine he said [*v.* 28], *'what God is about to do He has* **shown** [הֶרְאָה] to Pharaoh,' because that was to take place in the distant future and *show* is a more appropriate term in such a case *(Rashi).*

26. שֶׁבַע פָּרוֹת הַטֹּבֹת שֶׁבַע שָׁנִים הֵנָּה וְשֶׁבַע הַשִּׁבֳּלִים הַטֹּבֹת שֶׁבַע שָׁנִים הֵנָּה — *The seven good cows are seven years and the good ears are seven years.*

I.e., they represent the *same* seven years [not a total of fourteen). — This is the implication in this verse of חֲלוֹם אֶחָד הוּא, *it is one dream (Mizrachi)*]. The reason the dream was repeated was not to suggest that there would be *fourteen* years of plenty, but because the matter has been set in motion and is about to happen, as Joseph expressly told him in *v.* 32 *(Rashi).*

Joseph understood that the units referred to *years* [rather than *months* or *days*] because famine and abundance run in yearly cycles *(B'chor Shor).*

27. וְשֶׁבַע הַפָּרוֹת ... שֶׁבַע שָׁנִים הֵנָּה — *Now the seven emaciated and bad* [i.e., ugly] *cows who emerged after them are seven years.*

וְשֶׁבַע הַשִּׁבֳּלִים הָרֵקוֹת שְׁדֻפוֹת הַקָּדִים — *As are* [lit. and] *the seven emaciated ears scorched by the east wind.*

According to the implication of *Rashi* in *v.* 19, the meaning of רַקּוֹת throughout Scripture means *emaciated* while *Ramban* in *v.* 23 appears to render it *empty. Onkelos* translates it לְקִיתָא, *stricken.*

Beer Yitzchak to *v.* 19, interprets *Rashi* to agree that the word in our verse means *empty* because it is vowelized רֵקוֹת (from רֵיק, *empty)* rather than רַקּוֹת as in *v.* 19. Most commentators to *Rashi* disagree, however, maintaining that only if the word is spelled with a *yud* [רֵיק] would *Rashi* render it as *empty.*

[To the Torah's description of the inferior ears *(v.* 6), Pharaoh added the ad-

granted him. Pharaoh's Rosh Hashanah dream, therefore, was vital to all of Egypt *(Zohar).*

In the same vein, *R' Bachya* cites *Proverbs* 21:1: *Like streams of water is the king's heart in the hand of HASHEM.* Knowing that God exercises such intimate control over rulers, he realized that a revelation to the king of the world's greatest power was important to the entire nation. Coming on the night of judgment, Rosh Hashanah, the dream could only be a revelation of God's imminent intentions.

כח שְׁדֻפוֹת הַקָּדִים יִהְיוּ שֶׁבַע שְׁנֵי רָעָב: הוּא
הַדָּבָר אֲשֶׁר דִּבַּרְתִּי אֶל־פַּרְעֹה אֲשֶׁר
כט הָאֱלֹהִים עֹשֶׂה הֶרְאָה אֶת־פַּרְעֹה: הִנֵּה
שֶׁבַע שָׁנִים בָּאוֹת שָׂבָע גָּדוֹל בְּכָל־אֶרֶץ
ל מִצְרָיִם: וְקָמוּ שֶׁבַע שְׁנֵי רָעָב אַחֲרֵיהֶן
וְנִשְׁכַּח כָּל־הַשָּׂבָע בְּאֶרֶץ מִצְרָיִם וְכִלָּה
לא הָרָעָב אֶת־הָאָרֶץ: וְלֹא־יִוָּדַע הַשָּׂבָע

jective צְנֻמוֹת, *shriveled.* Reacting to Pharaoh's obvious emphasis on their inferiority, Joseph referred to them by the even stronger term רֵקוֹת, *emaciated* [or *empty*].

יִהְיוּ שֶׁבַע שְׁנֵי רָעָב — *There shall be seven years of famine.*

Although the dream began with visions of the seven years of abundance, Joseph began his interpretation with the prediction of the famine because only thereby could he attract Pharaoh's serious attention. Egypt was such a fertile, wealthy country — Scripture (13:10) calls it *a garden of HASHEM* — that prosperity was taken for granted. Even the seven years of abundance was not considered conclusive proof of Joseph's wisdom; accordingly, only when the famine arrived do we read [*v.* 54]: 'The seven years of famine began approaching *just as Joseph had foretold,*' for the truth of Joseph's prediction was not realized until the famine began. By singling out the famine, Joseph made the point that God had forewarned Pharaoh of impending disaster to assure the country's survival *(Ramban).*

Furthermore, he mentioned the famine first because knowledge of the abundance was necessary only because it made it possible to plan for the following famine *(Or HaChaim).*

28. הוּא הַדָּבָר ... הֶרְאָה אֶת־פַּרְעֹה — *It is the matter that I have spoken to Pharaoh: What God is about to do He has shown to Pharaoh.*

Thereby allowing the king to make provisions for saving his subjects in the future *(Sforno).*

[On the use here of *shown* instead of *told* see *comm.* to *v.* 25.]

29. [Having outlined the general interpretation of the dream, Joseph now proceeds to interpret it in detail.]

הִנֵּה שֶׁבַע שָׁנִים בָּאוֹת — *Behold! seven years are coming.*

הִנֵּה, *behold,* in this context denotes immediacy *(Ralbag).*

שָׂבָע גָּדוֹל בְּכָל־אֶרֶץ מִצְרָיִם — *A great abundance throughout all the land of Egypt.*

— An abundance even greater than usual. Moreover, this abundance will be throughout *all the land of Egypt* not only in the areas adjoining the Nile itself where the land is irrigated by its overflow *(Abarbanel).*

This passage implies that the *abundance* was only *in the land of Egypt,* whereas no such limitation is made regarding the *famine* predicted in the following verse. That the famine would extend to other lands may be indicated by Pharaoh's vision that the good cows

be seven years of famine. 28 *It is the matter that I have*
spoken to Pharaoh: What God is about to do He has
shown to Pharaoh.
29 *"Behold! seven years are coming — a great abun-*
dance throughout all the land of Egypt. 30 *Then seven*
years of famine will arise after them; and all the
abundance in the land of Egypt will be forgotten. The
famine will ravage the land. 31 *And the abundance*

remained in the reed grass near the river *in Egypt* [*v.* 2], whereas the inferior cows wandered away — Pharaoh knew not where — implying that the famine would spread beyond the borders of Egypt *(Ramban v.* 2).

30. וְקָמוּ שֶׁבַע שְׁנֵי רָעָב אַחֲרֵיהֶן — *Then seven years of famine will arise after them.*

— They will 'arise' as if they had until this point been restrained involuntarily and are now coming to collect their due *(Zohar).*

I.e., though the good years will *come* [*v.* 29] as a friend, the seven years of famine will *rise up* — a term used for violence as above 4:8; *Deut.* 19:11 *(Oznaim l'Torah).*

וְנִשְׁכַּח כָּל־הַשָּׂבָע בְּאֶרֶץ מִצְרָיִם — *And all the abundance in the land of Egypt will be forgotten.*

Even healthy, strong people will become enfeebled during the famine as if there had never been abundance at all *(Haamek Davar).*

— That people will 'forget' the abundance is not ingratitude. Someone who is tormented by hunger forgets that he was ever satisfied *(Alshich).*

According to *Rashi,* this constituted Joseph's interpretation of the בְּלִיעָה, *the 'swallowing'* [of the healthy stalks by the thin stalks (*v.* 7).]

[In v. 4, however, *Rashi* writes that it was the vision of the fat cows devouring the emaciated cows that inspired Joseph's interpretation in this verse. See footnote there for an explanation of why *Rashi* changes metaphors.]

According to *Ramban* [ibid.], however, Joseph's interpretation in this verse as well as the next was inspired by *v.* 21: *But it was not apparent that they had come inside them for their appearance remained as inferior as at first.*

וְכִלָּה הָרָעָב אֶת־הָאָרֶץ — [*And*] *the famine will ravage* [lit. *consume*] *the land.*

— Unless previous precautions and taken *(Akeidas Yitzchak).*

— The *whole* region, not just the land *of Egypt;* for the famine would be universal. However, since the abundance would be limited to Egypt, other countries would be unable to store up food although they undoubtedly heard about the impending famine, since the matter was well known *(Ramban v.* 2).

This 'ravaging' refers to areas [even in Egypt] which will lack the foresight or ability to prepare against the famine — they will be utterly consumed. This was symbolized in the dream by the inferior stalks which were devoid of kernels *(Haamek Davar).*

Targum Yonasan renders: *The famine will consume* the inhabitants *of the land* [comp. *v.* 47].

בָּאָרֶץ מִפְּנֵי הָרָעָב הַהוּא אַחֲרֵי־כֵן כִּי־
לב כָבֵד הוּא מְאֹד׃ וְעַל הִשָּׁנוֹת הַחֲלוֹם אֶל־
פַּרְעֹה פַּעֲמָיִם כִּי־נָכוֹן הַדָּבָר מֵעִם
הָאֱלֹהִים וּמְמַהֵר הָאֱלֹהִים לַעֲשֹׂתוֹ׃

31. וְלֹא יִוָּדַע הַשָּׂבָע בָּאָרֶץ מִפְּנֵי הָרָעָב הַהוּא אַחֲרֵי־כֵן כִּי כָבֵד הוּא מְאֹד — *And the abundance will be unknown in the land in the face of that subsequent famine — for it will be terribly severe.*

I.e., the surplus that the land enjoyed will not be recognizable because of the terrible famine that will follow it.

According to *Ramban* [*v.* 4] and *Rashi* to our verse this constituted Joseph's interpretation of 'thus they [the fat cows] came inside them [the emaciated cows] *but* it was not *apparent that they had come inside them'* [*v.* 21]. The fact that the emaciated cows did not themselves become fattened even after having consumed the fat cows, indicated to Joseph that the stores of the seven abundant years would barely suffice to support life, but nothing more. [Though people would find sustenance in the famine from the hoarded abundance of the preceding seven years, they would not become 'fattened' by it — it would supply only their basic needs. This is what motivated Joseph's advice in the following verses.]

[Where *Ramban* and *Rashi* differ is that *Ramban* maintains that Joseph's interpretation in both this and the previous verse was inspired by *v.* 21, while *Rashi* maintains that the previous verse was based on the interpretation of the 'eating' and 'swallowing' described in verses 4 and 24 respectively.]

Haamek Davar maintains that this is an independent statement not referring to the famine: Even during the years of abundance themselves, the abundance will not be apparent, because so much of the grain will have to be hoarded for the impending famine.

Abarbanel interprets: *The* [former] *abundance will be unknown* **in the land** — i.e., during the subsequent years of famine the soil will become so arid that it will be unrecognizable *in the soil itself* [בָּאָרֶץ] that the ground was ever fertile and abundant.

32. וְעַל הִשָּׁנוֹת הַחֲלוֹם אֶל־פַּרְעֹה פַּעֲמָיִם — *As for the repetition of the dream to Pharaoh twice.*

Although the dreams were not truly identical, Joseph used the word *repetition* with reference to the identical themes of the two dreams: the cows and the ears of grain. By *twice* he refers to the fact that both dreams occurred on the same night. The repetition attested to the fact that *the matter is set and established by God,* while the fact that both dreams occurred in the same night attested to the fact that *God is hastening to* make it materialize *(Ibn Ezra).*

According to *Ramban,* however, the repeated symbolism was not intended to prove that God's plan was complete, but was an integral part of the message — the cows representing plowing and the stalks representing harvesting [see *comm.* to *v.* 2]. Thus, the *repetition* mentioned by Joseph is the unusual fact that these symbolisms were shown to Pharaoh in two separate dreams on the same night, instead of combining both plowing and harvesting in a single dream. That the two symbolisms were shown in separate dreams indicated both that the mat-

41
32 *will be unknown in the land in the face of the subse-*
quent famine — for it will be terribly severe. [32] *As for*
the repetition of the dream to Pharaoh twice, it is because the matter stands ready before God and God is hastening to accomplish it.

ter was determined by God and that He is rushing to make it materialize.

The observation has been made that Joseph's statement is important for the understanding of Biblical style. Repetition and parallelism indicate determination and emphasis. Comp. also such Scriptural idioms as אָכֹל תֹּאכֵל, you shall *surely* eat, מוֹת תָּמוּת, you shall *surely* die.

[Some perceive in the word הִשָּׁנוֹת a suggestion of Pharaoh's having constantly *changed* the dream to confuse Joseph and test his veracity. See *Prefatory Comment* to *v.* 17.]

כִּי נָכוֹן הַדָּבָר מֵעִם הָאֱלֹהִים — *It is because the matter stands ready before* [lit. *from*] *God.*

The term נָכוֹן in this context means *prepared; ready (Rashi).*

Thus it is synonymous with *Exodus* 19:11 וְהָיוּ נְכֹנִים, *let them be 'ready.'* It is different from נָכוֹן, *correct,* in *Deut.* 13:15: אֱמֶת נָכוֹן הַדָּבָר, *the matter is true and 'correct' (Mizrachi).*

Onkelos renders: *It is a confirmed thing before God.*

— And accordingly it is irrevocable *(Malbim).*

[This apparently is based on *Berachos* 55b which cites our verse as proof that repetitive dreams are fulfilled.]

וּמְמַהֵר הָאֱלֹהִים לַעֲשֹׂתוֹ — *And God is hastening to accomplish it.*[1]

[Lit. *to do it.* The connotation of the verb עשה, *do,* in this context is to *put something into its ultimate condition;* to cause it to materialize (see *Ramban* to 1:7).]

Rashbam observes that although the symbolism of Joseph's own dream had also been repeated — in the form of sheaves and stars respectively [37:7, 9] — they were not dreamt on the same night. Therefore there could be a long delay before their fulfillment.

33. Joseph's plan.

The following was not mere *counsel,* for was Joseph asked to be Pharaoh's counselor? — Joseph dared to offer the following plan only because he perceived it to be *part of the interpretation* of the dream itself. As noted in the *comm.* to *v.* 4, the vision of the fat cows absorbed by the lean ones was an absolute sign to Joseph that the plenty of the abundant years would be used during the famine, indicating that food from the abundant years should be set aside for the famine.

1. According to the rules of syntax Joseph should not have repeated God's Name in this phrase; since God is the subject of the previous phrase, Joseph should have used the pronoun *He.* However, throughout these verses we see Joseph emphasizing to Pharaoh that it is God Who is the *Doer* and *Teller* [*v.* 25], the *Shower* [*v.* 28], and the One Who is *hastening to accomplish it.* Thus God is mentioned twice in this verse to accentuate the central role of Divine Providence.

Joseph achieves this proclamation of God's omnipotence in the midst of an idolatrous world not by a lecture or a discourse, but by the rhetoric device of repeating His Name.

Pharaoh responded to this device by himself proclaiming Joseph as a *man in whom is the spirit of God* [*v.* 38], and instead of describing Joseph as merely an expert as he did in *v.* 15, he acknowledges that *'God* has informed you of all this' [*v.* 39].

Thus, as a result of Joseph's daring, Pharaoh, king of Egypt, defers for the first time to the supreme King of Kings *(Akeidas Yitzchak; Alshich).*

לג וְעַתָּה יֵרֶא פַרְעֹה אִישׁ נָבוֹן וְחָכָם
לד וִישִׁיתֵהוּ עַל־אֶרֶץ מִצְרָיִם׃ יַעֲשֶׂה פַרְעֹה
וְיַפְקֵד פְּקִדִים עַל־הָאָרֶץ וְחִמֵּשׁ אֶת־

Joseph felt compelled to offer this proposal in the context of the interpretation *(Ramban).*

[According to the implication of *Rashi* and others, Joseph's advice was not part of the interpretation. Rather, encouraged by the successful climate of his royal audience Joseph trusted in the Divine Presence that obviously guided his actions and ventured to offer the proposal on his own — confident of God's Protection. (Cf. footnote to *v.* 4 s.v. וַתֹּאכַלְנָה).] See also *R' Munk* below s.v. אִישׁ נָבוֹן וְחָכָם.

Sforno maintains that the advice flowed naturally from the interpretation. Since God's purpose in letting Pharaoh know all this was to enable him to provide against the famine, it followed that Pharaoh should undertake the following preventative steps.

R' Avraham ben HaRambam cites his father that Joseph offered this unsolicited advice to demonstrate to Pharaoh that his interpretation was not merely the result of his own speculation, but was definitive and absolute, and therefore it was only natural that the monarch would want to implement certain procedures to forestall disaster. For as maintained by *R' Avraham HaChassid,* whom he also cites, Joseph offered the advice as an act of compassion so that *the land will not perish in the famine* [*v.* 36]. He was apprehensive that Pharaoh and his courtiers might otherwise not be stirred to action.

The *Zohar* states that Joseph was told the interpretation of Pharaoh's dream by prophetic inspiration and was also informed at that time that Pharaoh would appoint *a discerning and wise man* whose plan would save the populace from starvation. Joseph therefore felt compelled to relate every facet of his prophetic vision since [as noted in *Sanhedrin* 89a] 'one who suppresses his prophecy [הַכּוֹבֵשׁ אֶת נְבוּאָתוֹ] is liable to the death penalty at the hands of heaven.'

וְעַתָּה — *Now.*

I.e., immediately; time is a major factor in its fulfillment *(Ibn Caspi).*

יֵרֶא פַּרְעֹה — *Let Pharaoh seek out* [lit. *look*].

I.e. *choose, select,* as in 22:8: *God will seek out* [יִרְאֶה] *for Himself the lamb for the offering, my son. ...* It is Pharaoh *himself* who must do this since the dream was revealed to him *(HaKsav V' HaKabbalah).*

אִישׁ נָבוֹן וְחָכָם — *A discerning* [lit. *understanding*] *and wise man.*

Discerning — who will understand how much food to leave for the needs of the people in accordance with their individual family requirements, and then sell the surplus to other countries to accumulate wealth for Pharaoh's treasury; and *wise* — in the science of preserving grain, by mixing it with salty substances and raw silver dust so it would not rot [following the advice recorded in the *Talmud;* see *Shabbos* 31a; *Machshirin* 6:1; *Rashi* Shabbos 88b; *Midrash* 90:50] *(Ramban).*[1]

1. *Rashi,* in *Deut.* 1:13 explains *discerning* as 'one who understands one thing from another.'

He cites the *Sifre* where it is recorded that: Arios asked R' Yose, What is the distinction between חֲכָמִים, *wise men,* and נְבוֹנִים, *discerning men?*

— A *wise man* resembles a *wealthy* money-changer. When people bring him money to consider he does so, but when they do not bring him any he merely sits and gazes.

A *discerning man* resembles an *industrious* money-changer. When people bring him money

[33] *"Now let Pharaoh seek out a discerning and wise man and set him over the land of Egypt.* [34] *Let Pharaoh proceed and let him appoint overseers on the land, and he shall prepare the land of Egypt during*

Ramban further suggests that Joseph said this with himself in mind.

Surely Joseph must have viewed as providential the sudden and dramatic manner in which he was brought before Pharaoh. He still had faith in the fulfillment of his adolescent dreams [37:5-9] and felt that the long-awaited turning-point in his destiny had finally arrived. If so, he had to utilize this unique opportunity. He did so decisively by offering his unsolicited counsel. His advice was so relevant and wise that Pharaoh was enormously impressed *(R' Munk).*

According to *Abarbanel,* 'the discernment and the wisdom' of which Joseph spoke was the business acumen to buy grain cheaply without driving up prices during the prosperity and to prevent inflation during the famine.

Obviously, God showed Pharaoh the extraordinary abundance of the next seven years so that the surplus could be set aside for the famine. Unless plans were made to remove the additional food from the market, farmers, seeing bumper crops and low prices in the first year, would plant very little in the second year and so on. The result would be no surplus for the years of the famine. It would be an integral part of this scheme to encourage additional planting despite the surplus *(Or HaChaim).*

וישתהו על־ארץ מצרים — *And set him over the land of Egypt.*

— To administer this program throughout the entire land *(Ramban).*

— As the king's regent vested with his authority over all the inhabitants of the land *(Akeidas Yitzchak; R' Bachya).*

34. יַעֲשֶׂה פַרְעֹה — *Let Pharaoh proceed* [lit. *make; do*].

Let him carry out this advice [i.e., bring it to fruition (cf. *Ramban* to 1:7). Or in the sense of עשה meaning *acquire* [grain] in *Deut.* 8:17 — *let Pharaoh acquire* through the overseers he will appoint, etc. *(Ibn Ezra).*

The sense is: Let Pharaoh himself be active in this matter and motivate others *(Or HaChaim).*

וְיַפְקֵד פְּקִדִים עַל־הָאָרֶץ — *And let him appoint overseers* [lit. *commanders; appointees*] *on the land.*

These appointees are to act under the *discerning and wise man* entrusted with the overall supervision of the scheme; since that individual could not possibly carry out the task by himself *(Ramban).*

Onkelos renders פְּקִדִים *trustworthy men.*

— Men who have the confidence of the local residents, to insure harmonious collaboration *(Akeidas Yitzchak).*

The commentators differ over *who* should appoint these overseers.

R' Bachya, Alshich and *Sforno* explain that Pharaoh was to empower the

to consider he does so, but when they do not bring him any, he goes about soliciting and brings his own business.'

[Similarly, a *wise man* can grasp what is told him but cannot think a matter out for himself; a *discerning man* is an original thinker — not dependent upon what he has been taught him by others.]

לה אֶרֶץ מִצְרָיִם בְּשֶׁבַע שְׁנֵי הַשָּׂבָע: וְיִקְבְּצוּ
אֶת־כָּל־אֹכֶל הַשָּׁנִים הַטֹּבֹות הַבָּאֹת
הָאֵלֶּה וְיִצְבְּרוּ־בָר תַּחַת יַד־פַּרְעֹה אֹכֶל
לו בֶּעָרִים וְשָׁמָרוּ: וְהָיָה הָאֹכֶל לְפִקָּדוֹן

discerning and wise man to appoint regional supervisors so his supreme authority over them would be consolidated and unquestioned. Thus, the verse is interpreted to mean: יַעֲשֶׂה פַרְעֹה, *let Pharaoh act* — i.e., grant the authority, *and let him* — i.e., *the wise and discerning man,* appoint overseers, etc.

Ralbag and *Abarbanel* suggest that although the *wise and discerning man* would have autonomy in administering the program, the subject of this verse is Pharaoh — let Pharaoh *himself* act and appoint overseers.

וְחִמֵּשׁ אֶת אֶרֶץ מִצְרַיִם בְּשֶׁבַע שְׁנֵי הַשָּׂבָע — *And he shall prepare the land of Egypt during the seven years of abundance.*

The translation of וְחִמֵּשׁ as *prepare* follows *Rashi* who quotes *Onkelos:* וִיזָרְזוּן [*make active and ready*], and cites *Exodus* 13:18 where חֲמֻשִׁים means *prepared; equipped* [in the contextual sense of *prepared for warfare;* see *Rashi* there]. The implication here is: and let Pharaoh 'arm' the land with provisions during the period of abundance.

According to *Ibn Ezra* and many commentators, the word חִמֵּשׁ derives from the Hebrew word חָמֵשׁ, *five,* and the verse means that Pharaoh should buy a *fifth* of the land of Egypt during the seven years of abundance.

Along similar lines, *Rashbam* and *Radak* observe that this was a proposal that Pharaoh double the usual one-tenth tax on grain, and have his overseers collect a *fifth* of all the produce for the royal granary during that period. Joseph ultimately instituted such a concept when he purchased the land and demanded a fifth of all the produce for Pharaoh [see 47:24-26].

R' Hirsch emphasizes that it is not the *overseers* who are to impose this tax of twenty percent of all produce, but Pharaoh himself, and it is to be collected by the permanent tax officials. By freeing the overseers from the onerous and unpopular tasks of imposing and collecting taxes, they would be permitted to develop the harmonious relationship with the farmers that is indispensable to their tax. They could not achieve the planning of maximum harvests unless they would exert moral influence over the people, something that would be impossible if they became villainous tax collectors.[1]

Rashi follows *Onkelos'* interpretation of *prepare,* and does not subscribe to the interpretations of a *fifth* because the narrative which follows mentions only the *storing up*

1. *R' Hirsch* observes that Joseph's advice to separate a fifth of the annual produce during the years of plenty for distribution in the years of famine was quite calculated to supply the basic needs of existence.

'Let us assume,' he writes, 'that in years of plenty one uses twice as much as in ordinary years, and, in contrast, in years of scarcity one makes do with half the ordinary quantity. Hence, in a year of abundance one would use four times as much as in a year of famine. If this is so, then it is quite simple that in any case, one fifth of what is produced in a year of superfluity must suffice to feed one famine year even if everything else, the remaining four fifths are completely consumed.'

41
35-36 the seven years of abundance. 35 And let them gather all the food of those approaching good years; let them amass fine grain under Pharaoh's authority for food in the cities, and safeguard it. 36 The food will be a reserve for the land against the seven years of

of reserves (verses 48 and 49) and says nothing about acquisition of land or produce *(Mizrachi).*

[The verses *Rashbam* cites in 47:24-26 are not really parallel inasmuch as they reflect a special arrangement made later during the famine and according to *Rashi*, were not part of the scheme Joseph proposed here. *Rashbam* and the other commentators would presumably counter that there *was* such a program in effect during the abundance but the Torah did not specifically record it since it was already alluded to. Cf. *Karnei Or* on *Ibn Ezra.*]

Haamek Davar renders: Let the country be divided into five districts.

35. וְיִקְבְּצוּ אֶת־כָּל־אֹכֶל הַשָּׁנִים הַטֹּבֹת הַבָּאֹת הָאֵלֶּה — *And let them* [i.e. the overseers] *gather all the food of those approaching good years.*

— As a levy from the landowners. These were exacted from them even against their will *(Rashbam).*

All the food — i.e., whatever can be stored of the surplus crops in years of unnatural abundance *(Chizkuni; Abarbanel).*

According to *Ramban* in *v.* 48 below, it was literally *all* the food that Joseph suggested gathering. It would then be doled out to the Egyptians commensurate with their needs so they should not squander it. The balance would be hoarded for use during the famine. According to those who interpret חמש as a *fifth,* our verse refers only to the ingathering of the aforementioned double tithe.

Rashi makes the grammatical note that the word אֹכֶל, *food,* is a noun and therefore the accent is on the first syllable, the א, and it is punctuated with a *patach katan* [a name *Rashi* uses for our *segol*] under the כ; while the word אוכל, which is a participle, *who eats,* has the accent on the last syllable, the כ, and is punctuated with a *kametz katan* [=*tzeire*].

וְיִצְבְּרוּ־בָר תַּחַת יַד־פַּרְעֹה אֹכֶל בֶּעָרִים וְשָׁמָרוּ — *And let them amass fine grain under Pharaoh's authority* [lit. hand] *for food in the cities, and* [*let them*] *safeguard it.*

As culled from the commentators, this passage is telling us that the regional overseers should store up the winnowed and sifted fine grain [from the root ברר, *sift*] *(Ibn Ezra);* grain that could be stored without rotting *(Haamek Davar* [see *Ramban* to *v.* 48 below]; and this should be placed directly under Pharaoh's own 'hand' — i.e. under his personal control and stored in his granaries *(Rashi).* This should be done in every city: every city will have its own royal granaries where food will be collected to save transport charges and will serve to reassure the citizens that their food is not being taken for the benefit of others *(Tur; Ralbag; R' Bachya).*

And let them guard the food from harm *(Malbim).*

[See *v.* 48 for further elucidation of this plan and its operation.]

36. וְהָיָה הָאֹכֶל לְפִקָּדוֹן לָאָרֶץ — [*And*] *the food will be a reserve for the land against* [lit. *for*] *the seven years of famine which will befall* [lit. *be in*] *the land of Egypt.*

I.e., the food thus stored shall be treated like any other פִּקָּדוֹן, [*deposit entrusted to another's care until required*] — it shall be for the maintenance of [the inhabitants of

לָאָרֶץ לְשֶׁבַע שְׁנֵי הָרָעָב אֲשֶׁר תִּהְיֶיןָ
בְּאֶרֶץ מִצְרָיִם וְלֹא־תִכָּרֵת הָאָרֶץ בָּרָעָב:
לז וַיִּיטַב הַדָּבָר בְּעֵינֵי פַרְעֹה וּבְעֵינֵי כָּל־
לח עֲבָדָיו: וַיֹּאמֶר פַּרְעֹה אֶל־עֲבָדָיו הֲנִמְצָא
°שלישי לט כָזֶה אִישׁ אֲשֶׁר רוּחַ אֱלֹהִים בּוֹ:°וַיֹּאמֶר

(Onkelos)] the land against the seven years of famine which shall befall the land of Egypt *(Rashi).*

— It may not be used for any other purpose *(Ramban).*

וְלֹא־תִכָּרֵת הָאָרֶץ בָּרָעָב — *So that* [lit. *and*] *the land will not perish in the famine.*

That the land would not perish [if proper steps were taken] was indicated in the dream: the lean cows, though still emaciated even after having eaten the seven fat cows, nevertheless did not die of hunger *(Ramban).*

37. The interpretation is well received.

וַיִּיטַב הַדָּבָר בְּעֵינֵי פַרְעֹה וּבְעֵינֵי כָּל־עֲבָדָיו — *The matter appeared good to Pharaoh and to all his servants.*

The matter — i.e. the interpretation and Joseph's general demeanor *(Sforno).*

⌘ What caused Pharaoh and his courtiers to believe Joseph's interpretation, when he did not believe that of his own wise men? Why did Pharaoh promote him to high office before the truth of his interpretation could be proven?

Many reasons are offered in the *Midrashim* and by the commentators.

The interpretation pleased Pharaoh himself, *Sechel Tov* records, because Pharaoh had also dreamed of the interpretation but he had forgotten what it was. Now that he heard Joseph's words, he remembered that this was the very interpretation about which he had dreamt![1]

Sechel Tov continues that Joseph's counsel pleased Pharaoh's servants because it would save the lives of all the inhabitants of the country. This is the intent of *Proverbs* 16:7: *When a man's ways please HASHEM He makes even his enemies be at peace with him* — for even the cupbearer and the wizards admitted that Joseph was right.

Following *Midrash Tanchuma* and *Zohar,* Pharaoh had a particular reason for acknowledging Joseph's wisdom. The king had intentionally altered many details of his dream when relating it to Joseph [see Pref. comm. to *v.* 17], but Joseph constantly corrected Pharaoh and refused to be swayed from dealing with the *true* symbolisms as Pharaoh had actually dreamt them. Pharaoh was assured, therefore, that Joseph had interpreted correctly. As the *Tanchuma* notes, Pharaoh was amazed at the accuracy of Joseph's perception and asked him, 'Were you eavesdropping on my dreams?

Additionally, as the *Midrash* notes, all of Pharaoh's wizards interpreted

1. *Abarbanel* makes the following similar observation: One who has been entrusted with an authentic dream has been given a glimpse of matters directed by Divine Providence, but in his imaginative perception this relevation was translated into pictures and symbols. Upon awakening, the dreamer will tend to remember only the empty symbols — the pictures and the parable — but he forgets the dream's significance; the object of the symbol remains hidden in the folds of his dream fanatasies, just as a kernel is hidden in the husk.

As soon as the interpreter discovers the dream's true and accurate meaning, the dreamer will immediately sense that this is what he saw. This is how human memory functions, particularly where a considerable time has not elapsed since the event; as soon as someone is reminded of it, he will recall that this is what he forgot.

*famine which will befall the land of Egypt, so that the
land will not perish in the famine."*

37 *The matter appeared good to Pharaoh and to all
his servants.* 38 *Pharaoh said to his servants, "Could
we find another like him — a man in whom is the
spirit of God?"*

them as *two distinct dreams,* contrary to Pharaoh's understanding, but Joseph perceived both as one and interpreted them accordingly. Furthermore of them all, only Joseph perceived Pharaoh's dream as affecting the State, not Pharaoh the individual [see comm. to *v.* 8 s.v. וַיְסַפֵּר.

Cf. also *Rashbam* to 40:16 who emphasizes that one knows the truth when one hears it because 'the truth speaks for itself.'

According to *Radak: It appeared good to them* because they understood that he had given good advice. They also believed his interpretation because: (a) it fit in well with the dream, and (b) because the cupbearer had already told them that *just as Joseph had interpreted for them, so did it happen* [*v.* 13], and finally (c) because Joseph did not refer it to the distant future [when its veracity could not be established until after a long delay], but predicted that its fulfillment was imminent: *Behold seven years are coming* [*v.* 29].

38. Joseph is appointed viceroy of Egypt.

[As noted earlier, Egyptian law specified that a slave could not be appointed to a position of aristocracy. But, because Pharaoh realized that only Joseph could properly implement and administer the master plan for national salvation, he recognized that Joseph would require a prestigious governmental post. Therefore, he sought means to make an exception to the law.]

וַיֹּאמֶר פַּרְעֹה אֶל עֲבָדָיו — *And Pharaoh said to his servants.*

He 'consulted' with his servants because he wanted them to concede Joseph's superiority over themselves *(Abarbanel).*

הֲנִמְצָא כָזֶה — *Could we find another like him.*

[I.e., with his qualifications?] — If we were to go out and seek it, could we expect to find anyone like him? *(Rashi).*

We must now appoint a wise and discerning man over the land of Egypt. Now, where can we possibly find one like him? — For Joseph's wisdom far exceeds that of any of our magicians! *(Radak).*

As pointed out by *Rashi* in *v.* 12, there were several reasons why Egyptian law should have disqualified Joseph from rising in the governmental hierarchy of that country. *Ramban* accordingly observes that since the Hebrews were detested by the Egyptians who considered them untouchables [see *comm.* to 39:6 and 43:32], Pharaoh preferred not to confer quasi-royal powers upon Joseph without first ensuring the approval and consent of his advisers. Therefore he emphasized that they would find no Egyptian equally qualified for the post for *the spirit of God is within him.*[1]

The translation of הֲנִמְצָא in first person plural imperfect *kal* as: *can we find?* follows

1. The Talmud [*Sotah* 36b] records that when Pharaoh proposed elevating Joseph to this high position, the royal astrologers exclaimed, "Will you set over us a slave whom his master bought for twenty pieces of silver?"

פַּרְעֹה֙ אֶל־יוֹסֵ֔ף אַֽחֲרֵ֨י הוֹדִ֧יעַ אֱלֹהִ֛ים
אוֹתְךָ֖ אֶת־כָּל־זֹ֑את אֵין־נָב֥וֹן וְחָכָ֖ם
מ כָּמ֑וֹךָ: אַתָּה֙ תִּהְיֶ֣ה עַל־בֵּיתִ֔י וְעַל־פִּ֖יךָ

Rashi. He quotes *Onkelos* who also interprets it this way by rendering: הֲנִשְׁכַּח.

Ibn Ezra cites this as an alternate interpretation, and is followed by *Radak* and *Ramban.* In his primary opinion, however, *Ibn Ezra* interprets the word in third person masculine perfect *niphal* [passive] as meaning: *Can there be found?* [Had *Onkelos* taken it as *niphal,* he would have translated it by אִשְׁתְּכַח, as in *Exod.* 21:16 where he thus translates the Hebrew word וְנִמְצָא.]

Ibn Janach renders: *Has there ever been found?*

Rashi's interpretation is also supported by the Sages in the Midrash: Pharaoh said to them, 'Were we to traverse the world from one end to the other we could not find one like him.' [*Rashi* rejects the *niphal* interpretation on contextual grounds. See *Gur Aryeh* and *Levush.*]

Rashi makes the additional grammatical observation that the word הֲנִמְצָא is a question, as is every word prefixed by a ה vowelized with a *chataph-patach.* [Cf. *Rashi* to הֲשֹׁפֵט in 18:25. (If the ה were the definite article, and our word in *niphal,* it would be vowelized: הַנִּמְצָא).]

[Were the ה to be taken as a definite article, the word הֲנִמְצָא would have to be translated, *anyone found who is like him* (is a man in whom...). To avoid this erroneous interpretation *Rashi* repeats the grammatical rule regarding the prefix ה, although it has already been cited in 18:25 to הֲשֹׁפֵט.]

אִישׁ אֲשֶׁר רוּחַ אֱלֹהִים בּוֹ — ***A man in whom is the spirit of God?***

As evidenced by his interpretation of dreams and certainly in respect to general wisdom *(Rashbam).*

— [Joseph specifically maintained throughout that it was not him, but *God* Who would respond with Pharaoh's welfare (*v.* 16). After such a meaning-

"I discern in him royal characteristics," Pharaoh said [i.e., he is of noble stock and was wrongly sold as a slave *(Maharsha).*].

"But for him to be elevated to a royal position he must know all seventy languages."

God sent the angel Gabriel to teach Joseph these languages, but he could not learn them. So He added to Joseph's name a letter from the Ineffable Name of HASHEM — a ה — calling him יְהוֹסֵף, *Yehoseph,* and with this additional spiritual power he was able to learn all seventy languages that night. Thus is it written [*Psalms* 81:6: עֵדוּת בִּיהוֹסֵף שָׂמוֹ בְּצֵאתוֹ עַל־אֶרֶץ מִצְרָיִם שְׂפַת לֹא יָדַעְתִּי אֶשְׁמָע, *He imposed by 'Yehoseph' a sign of testimony, when he went out over the land of Egypt — a language unknown to me* [Joseph] *I heard.*

[As noted in *Sotah* 10a, the addition of this letter also attested to Joseph's having sanctified HASHEM's Name when he resisted Potiphar's wife's attempts at seducing him. Furthermore, *Yalkut Shimoni* §831 notes that the above quoted verse in *Psalms* begins and ends with an ע, which has the numerical value of 70. This alludes to the seventy languages; Joseph began his audience with Pharaoh in ignorance of them and then, thanks to the miracle, knew them all (see *comm.* to *ArtScroll Tehillim* ad. loc.).]

The following morning, Pharaoh tested Joseph by speaking with him in many languages, and Joseph replied fluently in every language. But when Joseph addressed Pharaoh in the Holy Tongue [Hebrew], Pharaoh did not understand what he said, nor *could* he learn it notwithstanding Joseph's attempts to teach it to him.

So Pharaoh asked Joseph to swear that he would not reveal his ignorance to anyone [because a king was supposed to know all existing languages], and Joseph agreed.

[This oath played an important role when Joseph used it to enforce one he later made to Jacob. See *Rashi* on 50:6.]

41 [39] *Then Pharaoh said to Joseph, "Since God has in-*
40 *formed you of all this, there can be no one so discern-*
ing and wise as you. [40] *You shall be in charge of my*

ful interpretation and advice, Pharaoh concluded that it could only be that Joseph speaks in the name of God Who endowed him with His Spirit.]

This is yet another instance where even the mighty Pharaoh who considered himself a god responded in acknowledgment of the Supreme King of Kings (see footnote to *v.* 32).

The *Kuzari* [4:15] mentions that the Egyptians had no knowledge of the Ineffable Name of God — *HASHEM* — as Pharaoh was to say to Moses [*Exodus* 5:2]: *I know not HASHEM.* All they had was a vague notion of the existence of a Supreme Divinity named *Elohim,* whom Pharaoh mentioned several times in this episode.

By describing someone as possessing the *spirit of God,* one implies that he is endowed with the ultimate degree of natural wisdom and understanding *(Malbim).*

— Godliness is *within* him, it is part of him *(R' Bunem of Ps'his'cha).*

Oznaim laTorah offers that Pharaoh did not want to affront his own wizards, who, in ancient times, were renowned for their wisdom [cf. *I Kings* 5:10]. He therefore made it a note to emphasize that this foreigner whom he was 'importing' as viceroy of Egypt was wise not because of his personal ability — as were the wizards — but because the spirit of God was within him, an external factor. Therefore his selection should not impugn the honor of the wizards of Egypt.

39. וַיֹּאמֶר פַּרְעֹה אֶל־יוֹסֵף — *Then Pharaoh said to Joseph.*

After his courtiers acknowledged that Joseph was indeed endowed with God-given talents, Pharaoh turned to Joseph and addressed him directly *(Akeidah; Abarbanel).*

אַחֲרֵי הוֹדִיעַ אֱלֹהִים אוֹתְךָ אֶת כָּל־זֹאת — *Since* [lit. *after*] *God has informed you of all this* [i.e., the interpretation and the advice *(Rashbam).*]

'All this' is a reference also to Joseph's correct interpretation of the *cupbearer's* dream,as well as to the current situation about to be experienced in Egypt. Although Joseph's interpretation of *Pharaoh's* dream could not yet be verified absolutely until the famine began (see *v.* 54), nevertheless, since his interpretation met with the unanimous approval of Pharaoh and his courtiers, they regarded the prediction as if it had been fulfilled *(Ramban v.* 38).

[Other interpretations regarding how Pharaoh knew even at this premature time that Joseph's interpretation was correct have been discussed in the *comm.* to *v.* 37.]

אֵין נָבוֹן וְחָכָם כָּמוֹךָ — *There can be no one so discerning and wise as you.*

Discerning — in foreseeing the future, and *wise* in perceiving lessons from what you have seen and heard *(Rashbam).*

[Pharaoh was not merely complimenting Joseph; rather, this is the response to Joseph's suggestion in *v.* 33 that Pharaoh seek a '**discerning** *and* **wise** *man*']:

'In following your suggestion to seek out a "discerning and wise man," we are certain that we would be unable to find anyone to fit this description as well as you do' [since you have so amply demonstrated your God-given wisdom] *(Rashi; R' Meyuchas).*[1]

1. In so saying, Pharaoh unknowingly alluded to a basic tenet of prophecy. If a man has merited receiving from God extraordinary wisdom, it is certain that his natural wisdom too is

יִשַּׁק כָּל־עַמִּי רַק הַכִּסֵּא אֶגְדַּל מִמֶּךָּ׃
מא וַיֹּאמֶר פַּרְעֹה אֶל־יוֹסֵף רְאֵה נָתַתִּי אֹתְךָ
מב עַל כָּל־אֶרֶץ מִצְרָיִם׃ וַיָּסַר פַּרְעֹה אֶת־
טַבַּעְתּוֹ מֵעַל יָדוֹ וַיִּתֵּן אֹתָהּ עַל־יַד יוֹסֵף

40. Pharaoh, like Potiphar [39:4-6] and the prison warden [39:22], perceives Joseph's greatness and appoints him virtual master over his court, granting him complete autonomy over matters of sustenance.

אַתָּה תִּהְיֶה עַל־בֵּיתִי — *You* [personally *(Abarbanel)*] *shall be in charge of my palace* [lit. *house*].

I.e., shall have full charge in all affairs of State *(Haamek Davar)*.

The Hebrew phrase which literally reads *you shall be upon my house,* is elliptic. The meaning is: *You shall be* the officer *over my house (Ibn Ezra). HaKsav V'HaKabbalah* maintains that it is not elliptic, but the word עַל in itself is a noun meaning *the uppermost* as in *Hoshea* 11:7. Accordingly the phrase עַל־בֵּיתִי is in the construct state and means *the supreme* [authority] *of my house.*

וְעַל פִּיךָ יִשַּׁק כָּל־עַמִּי — *And by your command* [lit. *and upon your* mouth] *shall all my people be sustained.*

The verb יִשַּׁק is to be understood as *Onkelos* renders it יִתְּזַן, i.e. *sustained.* That is, *all my people's needs shall be provided through you.* Comp. 15:2 בֶּן מֶשֶׁק, *steward,* [the man by whose authority the needs of the household are dispensed]; and *Psalms* 2:12: נַשְּׁקוּ בַר, *stimulate* [*sustain*] *yourselves in purity (Rashi).*

Rashbam relates the word to נֶשֶׁק, *arms* [see *I Kings* 10:2], and interprets: you shall supervise the arming of my people against the enemy; *Ibn Ezra* interprets somewhat similarly, as does *Chizkuni.*

Radak in his comm. to Torah also interprets the sense to be that the people will *equip themselves with arms* by Joseph's command. He draws support from *Oneklos'* rendering of יִתְּזַן, which, unlike *Rashi,* he does not interpret to mean *sustain* but *arm.*

Ibn Ezra offers an alternative interpretation that the word is related to נְשִׁיקָה, *kiss,* in the sense that all will kiss [i.e. pay homage to] Joseph in loving obeisance to his every command. Cf. the *Midrash. Radak* in *Shorashim* s.v. נשק cites both views — that of *arms* and of *kissing.* He interprets the latter in the figurative sense of the cleaving of two kissing people and explains our passage to metaphorically describe how all the

at the highest level since God does not confer His wisdom on man until he has achieved his own maximum potential [see *Nedarim* 38a]. Therefore, if God endowed Joseph with secrets of the future, it is certain that *there is none so discerning and wise as him* in matters concerning the present *(Daas Soferim).*

The *Dubna Maggid* explains the intent of our verse with a parable:

Once a merchant opened a store carrying a large selection of very expensive items. The municipal authorities assessed a large tax on his inventory, upon which he protested, 'I am not a wealthy man, as you seem to think. All my merchandise is given to me on consignment; *none* of it belongs to me!'

The authorities replied, 'Nevertheless you *must* be a rich man, or your wholesalers would not give you so much credit.'

Similarly in the discussion between Pharaoh and Joseph, when Pharaoh said that the interpretation showed phenomenal wisdom, Joseph protested that the solution to Pharaoh's dilemma came not from him, but from God. Pharaoh responded, 'Nevertheless, God would not have given you this wisdom unless you were a wise a wise and understanding man in your own right.'

palace and by your command shall all my people be
sustained. Only by the throne shall I outrank you."
41 *Then Pharaoh said to Joseph, "See — I have*
placed you in charge of all the land of Egypt." 42 *And*
Pharaoh removed his ring from his hand and put it
on Joseph's hand. He then had him dressed in gar-

Egyptians will 'cleave to the mouth of Joseph' — i.e., adhere to his every command.

רַק הַכִּסֵּא אֶגְדַּל מִמֶּךָּ — *Only* [by] *the throne shall I outrank you.*

I.e., only by virtue of the fact that they refer to me as 'king', for which 'throne' is a metaphor. Cf. *I Kings* 1:37 *(Rashi).*

— Only in matters relating to the throne [i.e., the royal lineage] shall I outrank you *(Radak).*

According to *Onkelos* the implication of the definite article הַכִּסֵּא, *the throne,* is that Pharaoh pointed to his throne and said: 'Only by this royal throne shall I be greater than you.'

41. וַיֹּאמֶר פַּרְעֹה אֶל־יוֹסֵף — *Then* [lit. *and*] *Pharaoh said to Joseph.*

After his first pronouncement, Pharaoh proceeded to inform Joseph that he was promoting him to a still higher post *(Malbim).*

[The formula *and Pharaoh said* recurs throughout these verses since these various pronouncements were uttered successively.]

רְאֵה נָתַתִּי אֹתְךָ עַל כָּל אֶרֶץ מִצְרָיִם — *See, I have placed* [lit. *given*] *you in charge of* [lit. *over; upon*] *all the land of Egypt.*

See and consider that you take good care to lead well, for it is a great thing that I have entrusted to you *(Sforno).*

Rashbam understands this in the present tense: *See, I hereby appoint you* etc. Pharaoh said this as he placed the signet ring on Joseph's finger [next verse].

[Cf. 1:29 הִנֵּה נָתַתִּי לָכֶם, and 23:11 לְךָ נְתַתִּיהָ where the sense is *I hereby give to you (Rashbam);* I have decided to give it to you *(Abarbanel);* it is as if I have already given it to you *(Rashi).*]

Possibly Joseph was abashed at the lofty appointment and was uncertain whether it was meant seriously or whether it was in mockery of his own statement 'Now therefore let Pharaoh seek out a wise and discerning man.' For this reason Pharaoh reiterated, 'See I have placed you in charge of all the land of Egypt.' This is indicated by the repetition here of *and Pharaoh said to Joseph,* although in the previous verse it was also Pharaoh speaking to Joseph *(Midrashei Torah).*

Rashi explains that although the expression *I have given you* idiomatically means, as *Onkelos* interprets it, I have *appointed* you, nevertheless term נתן, *give,* expresses the concept of placing someone in a changed status, either in the context of *raising* to a high rank as in *Deut.* 26:19: וּלְתִתְּךָ עֶלְיוֹן or of *degrading,* as in *Malachi*: 2:9: נָתַתִּי אֶתְכֶם נִבְזִים וּשְׁפָלִים, *I have made you contemptible and base.*

42. ...וַיָּסַר פַּרְעֹה אֶת טַבַּעְתּוֹ מֵעַל יָדוֹ — *And Pharaoh removed his ring from* [*upon*] *his hand and put* [lit. *gave*] *it on Joseph's hand.*

This signified that the recipient had become second to the king in rank *(Rashi).*

Ramban explains that the king's ring contained his royal seal [cf. *Esther* 8:8]. The giving of the ring to Joseph symbolized that he would henceforth be the leader of the entire government and would have the authority to seal decrees with the king's seal decreee, as he desired (cf. *R' Bachya).*

וַיַּלְבֵּ֤שׁ אֹתוֹ֙ בִּגְדֵי־שֵׁ֔שׁ וַיָּ֛שֶׂם רְבִ֥ד הַזָּהָ֖ב
מג עַל־צַוָּארֽוֹ: וַיַּרְכֵּ֣ב אֹת֗וֹ בְּמִרְכֶּ֤בֶת
הַמִּשְׁנֶה֙ אֲשֶׁר־ל֔וֹ וַיִּקְרְא֥וּ לְפָנָ֖יו אַבְרֵ֑ךְ
מד וְנָת֣וֹן אֹת֔וֹ עַ֖ל כָּל־אֶ֥רֶץ מִצְרָֽיִם: וַיֹּ֧אמֶר

וַיַּלְבֵּשׁ אֹתוֹ בִּגְדֵי־שֵׁשׁ — *He then had him dressed in garments of fine linen.*

— This was highly valued in Egypt *(Rashi).*

The term שֵׁשׁ refers to an exceptionally fine white linen made of flax found only in Egypt (*Ibn Ezra* to *Exod.* 24:4). Cf. *Ezekiel* 29:7.

In later Books of Scripture this linen it is referred to by the term בּוּץ. Cf. *Esther* 1:6; 8:15 *(Karnei Or).*

Garments of this material were worn only by the aristocracy and nobility *(Ralbag).*

וַיָּשֶׂם רְבִד הַזָּהָב עַל צַוָּארוֹ — *And he placed the gold chain upon his neck.*

I.e., the particular gold chain worn by the Grand Vizier. The placing of this chain *by the king himself* was an ancient symbol of investiture to high office *(Abarbanel).*

R' Shimon ben Gamliel said, Joseph well deserved the honors bestowed upon him because of his virtuous life. The hands, neck, and body which had refused to sin [with Potiphar's wife] were now adorned with the glorious signs of royalty *(Midrash).*

Rashi explains that רבד is synonymous with רצף both of which mean *row.* A chain is called a רְבִד because it is made up of links placed in a row. Cf. *Proverbs* 7:16 מַרְבַדִּים רָבַדְתִּי עַרְשִׂי, *I have decked my bed with coverings* — i.e., I have placed on my couch *rows* of rugs.

According to *Radak* it refers to a type of *scarf.*

43. וַיַּרְכֵּב אֹתוֹ בְּמִרְכֶּבֶת הַמִּשְׁנֶה אֲשֶׁר־לוֹ — *[And] he also had him ride in his second royal chariot [lit. in the second chariot that was his].*

I.e., the chariot second in rank to his chariot — that which drove alongside Pharaoh's own *(Rashi).*

Ramban explains that according to *Rashi's* interpretation the word הַמִּשְׁנֶה, *the second,* modifies the noun מֶרְכֶּבֶת, *chariot,* meaning that this was the *second-rank chariot.* Cf. similar construction in *II Kings* 23:4: כֹּהֲנֵי הַמִּשְׁנֶה, *the second-rank priests.*

According to his own opinion however, *Ramban* maintains that in this context the term מִשְׁנֶה refers to the *person* who was second in command to the king, as in the case of *Mordechai* who was the מִשְׁנֶה, *viceroy,* to King Ahasuerus [*Esther* 10:3]. Cf. also the expression כֶּסֶף מִשְׁנֶה which does not mean 'second-rank money' but *the money of the 'second' purchase.*

Accordingly, *Ramban* maintains that our passage refers to the *chariot of the second-in-command.* For Pharaoh had a chariot for his own exclusive use, as well as another chariot reserved for his viceroy, and another one for the third in rank. [Comp. also *Radak Shorashim* s.v. רכב and *Abarbanel.*]

It is not clear why *Rashi* adopts his interpretation rather than that of most other commentators such as *Ramban.* Perhaps *Rashi* was influenced by the qualifying phrase אֲשֶׁר לוֹ, *that was his:* If מִשְׁנֶה meant *viceroy,* the passage should have read: בְּמִרְכֶּבֶת מִשְׁנֵהוּ, *the chariot of his viceroy* [lit. *of his second-in-command*] *(Sefer HaZikaron).*

The translation *chariot* follows *Ibn Ezra* who explains that the term מֶרְכָּבָה refers to a palanquin drawn by four horses. Comp. *Radak* to *I Kings* 10:29 and *Shorashim* s.v. רכב.

According to *Rashbam,* [as explained by *Michlol Yofi*] the spelling מִרְכָּבָה [with a *chirik,* under the מ in our verse instead of מֶרְכָּבָה with a *segol*] refers not to the chariot itself but to the *horse* or *mule* which in this case was ridden by the viceroy.

וַיִּקְרְאוּ לְפָנָיו אַבְרֵךְ — *And they proclaimed before him: 'Avrech!'*

I.e. as they rode him on the

ments of fine linen and he placed the gold chain upon his neck. [43] *He also had him ride in his second royal chariot and they proclaimed before him: "Avrech!" Thus, he placed him in charge of all the land of Egypt.*

chariot the servants called out before him 'Avrech!' *(Ralbag).*

Avrech is a composite of two words: *Father* [i.e. counselor; mentor] to the *rech,* which means *king* in Aramaic [some editions of *Rashi* read 'in Roman' (i.e. in Latin=rex)]. Comp. the term רֵיכָא in *Bava Basra* 4a *(Rashi; Onkelos).*

Rashbam follows this interpretation and cites 45:8: *He has made me a father to Pharaoh.*

Rashi proceeds to cite the view of the Sages in the *Midrash* and *Sifre* [cf. also *Targum Yonasan*]: R' Yehudah expounded, *Avrech* is an appellation for Joseph who was an *av* (father) in wisdom though *rach* (tender) in years. R' Yose ben Dormaskis said to him, How much longer will you distort Biblical texts for us? [The reason R' Yose considers this interpretation to be a 'distortion' is not clear.][1] — Rather, R' Yose continued, the word *avrech* is connected with *berech* (knee) [i.e. everyone presented to Joseph declared אַבְרֵךְ, *I will bend my knee,* in obeisence to Joseph *(Ibn Ezra; Radak)*]— signifying that all came and went forth only by his permission as the verse proceeds to tell us: *he placed him in charge of all the land of Egypt.*

Sforno [following *Ibn Janach* s.v. הברך] adopts a similar interpretation: This is like the imperative: הַבְרֵךְ, *kneel!* I.e., they announced: 'Everyone must kneel before him.' [Cf. *Radak* to הַשְׁכֵּם=אַשְׁכִּים, *Jeremiah* 25:3; the letters אהח״ע frequently interchange *(R' Bachya).*] This was like the announcement that was usually made before the king [as his chariot was passing *(Machberes Menachem)*] to instruct all subjects to bow down before him.

This was a special distinction, because such homage was usually reserved for the king alone, unless he specially decreed it, as here. We know this to be the case also from *Esther* 3:2 where Ahasuerus had to issue a special decree that everyone must bow down to Haman *(Abarbanel).*

וְנָתוֹן אֹתוֹ עַל כָּל־אֶרֶץ מִצְרָיִם — *Thus he placed* [lit. *gave*] *him in charge of* [lit. *over; upon*] *all the land of Egypt.*

HaKsav V'haKabbalah maintains that the phrase means: *In order to popularize him throughout the entire land of Egypt,* i.e. Pharaoh did all the above — gave him his ring, the special garments, the gold chain, and had them ride Joseph in the royal chariot and call out *'Avrech'* before him *in order to make it manifestly clear* that it was in-

1. *Menachem Zion* homiletically explains the dispute between R' Yehudah and R' Yose ben Dormaskis as follows:

R' Yehudah interprets the name *Avrech* as a tribute to Joseph's mature wisdom. So impressed were the Egyptians with the brilliance of the young Hebrew that they named him in its honor. To this R' Yose retorted angrily that such an interpretation is a 'distortion' because history demonstrates that gentiles do not respect Jewish wisdom unless it is backed by power. The Egyptian regard for Joseph was based on the simple fact that they were forced by royal edict to approach him on bended knees!

פַּרְעֹה אֶל־יוֹסֵף אֲנִי פַרְעֹה וּבִלְעָדֶיךָ
לֹא־יָרִים אִישׁ אֶת־יָדוֹ וְאֶת־רַגְלוֹ בְּכָל־
מה אֶרֶץ מִצְרָיִם: וַיִּקְרָא פַרְעֹה שֵׁם־יוֹסֵף
צָפְנַת פַּעְנֵחַ וַיִּתֶּן־לוֹ אֶת־אָסְנַת בַּת־פּוֹטִי

deed true that the king himself had appointed this former slave and prisoner the viceroy of Egypt. In this context, the term *give* connotes *popularizing*.

According to *R' Bachya, Abarbanel* and many others [comp. *Or HaChaim*] this phrase formed part of the proclamation: as he approached they cried, *'Kneel! He is the one whom Pharaoh placed in charge of all of the land of Egypt* — these ceremonies are all undertaken in compliance with Pharaoh's dream and accordingly no one may contest Joseph's authority.'

[Compare "the honor bestowed upon the man whom the king especially wants to honor" in *Esther* 6:8ff.]

Akeidas Yitzchak interprets the subject of אתו to be not Joseph, but the proclamation: ' ... *And this* [i.e., the proclamation] *was issued throughout the land of Egypt*.

44. וַיֹּאמֶר פַּרְעֹה אֶל־יוֹסֵף — [*And*] *Pharaoh said to Joseph.*

— Probably on his return from the public installation procession through the city *(R' Hirsch)*.

אֲנִי פַּרְעֹה — *I am Pharaoh.*[1]

I.e., I have the authority as king to issue decrees for my kingdom and therefore I decree that: *Without you no one may lift*, etc. Alternatively: *I remain the king, but without your permission no one shall lift*, etc. It is exactly similar in meaning to [*v.* 40]: *Only by the throne shall I outrank you*. But Pharaoh felt it necessary to reiterate it as he gave Joseph the ring *(Rashi)*.

Cf. *Radak*: Only the royal title 'Pharaoh' will remain mine — in every other respect all power will be vested in you.

[Possibly Pharaoh was also intimating a warning to Joseph: Notwithstanding the powers I am granting you, *I am still king*. Never be tempted to usurp my throne as some people might be tempted to do after appointment to such a lofty position.]

According to *Abarbanel* [following *Rashi's* primary interpretation] Pharaoh was assuring Joseph: *I am Pharaoh:* have no fear of the jealousy of the masses — I will protect you.

The Sages in the *Midrash* offer the following exegesis: — 'Lest you think you will be as great as I,' Pharaoh said, 'I now specify *"I am Pharaoh"* — i.e., my greatness remains above yours.'

וּבִלְעָדֶיךָ לֹא יָרִים אִישׁ אֶת־יָדוֹ וְאֶת רַגְלוֹ — *And without you no man may lift up his hand or his foot in all the land of Egypt.*[2]

Without you — i.e. without your

1. R' Acha said, From the 'I' spoken by a mortal you may learn the force of the 'I' spoken by the Holy One Blessed be He. If Joseph attained all this greatness because Pharaoh said to him, *I am Pharaoh*, how much more so when the 'I' of the Holy One Blessed be He comes to pass — viz. *I have made and I will bear; and I will carry and rescue you* [*Isaiah* 46:4] *(Midrash)*.

2. The exegetes perceive significance and the Hand of Providence in every passage and narrative in the Torah:

Because Joseph minimized his own greatness and humbled himself by saying [*v.* 16] בִּלְעָדַי, *it is beyond me*, thereby ascribing greatness to God, he was rewarded now when greatness was bestowed upon him with that same word בִּלְעָדֶיךָ, *without you* [it is the same word except for the necessary change of suffix] *(Tzror HaMor; Torah Sheleimah* §104).

[44] *Pharaoh said to Joseph, "I am Pharaoh. And
without you no man may lift up his hand or foot in
all the land of Egypt."* [45] *Pharaoh named Joseph
Tzafnas Pane'ach, and he gave him Asenath*

permission. The metaphor of *lifting up the hand or foot* should be understood as *Onkelos* understands it ['no man shall raise his hand to gird on a sword or raise his foot to mount a horse'] *(Rashi).*

According to *Abarbanel* the expression is figurative: No one shall do anything or go anywhere throughout all the land of Egypt without your specific consent.

45. וַיִּקְרָא פַרְעֹה שֵׁם יוֹסֵף – [*And*] *Pharaoh named Joseph.*

Appointees to a high position were customarily assigned a name commensurate with their new eminence. Similarly, when Hoshea became Moses' servant, Moses changed his name to Joshua [*Numbers* 13:16], and Nebuchadnezzar changed Daniel's name to Belteshazzar [*Daniel* 1:6] *(Rashbam* and *Radak).*

It is noted that the Providential importance of Joseph's change of name lies in the fact that it helped conceal the identity of the young Egyptian viceroy from his family until the time came for him to reveal himself. People referred to him as Tzafnas Pane'ach — no one knew him as Joseph *(Zohar).*

צָפְנַת פַּעְנֵחַ – *Tzafnas Pane'ach.*

Rashi and *Rashbam* [following *Onkelos*] interpret: מְפָרֵשׁ הַצְּפוּנוֹת 'he who explains what is hidden.' There is no other example of the word *Pane'ach* in Scripture. [*Radak* interprets similarly in *Shorashim* s.v. פענח.]

Rashbam and *Radak* maintain that this name was not Hebrew, but Egyptian.

Ibn Ezra adds that if the name is Egyptian, "We do not know its meaning; and if it is an Egyptian translation of the Hebrew name of Joseph, then we do not know the meaning of the name *Yoseph*" [i.e., the aspect of the Hebrew name that lends itself to this translation *(R' Chavel;* cf. *Yohel Or).*] The correct interpretation is as *Onkelos* renders it [see above].

Ramban [as explained by *R' Eisenstadt*] notes that since the expression הַמְפַעְנֵחַ נֶעֱלָמִים, *explainer of secrets,* has become part of the liturgy [in the *Nusach Sfard* version of the Hebrew prayer *Nishmas*], it is apparent that the early scholars considered פַּעְנֵחַ a Hebrew word. Possibly, Pharaoh wished to do Joseph the courtesy of assigning him a name in his native tongue, and asked him how to say 'one who reveals secrets,' and Joseph told him *'tzafnas pane'ach.'* Or possibly, Pharaoh knew the Canaanite language himself, Canaan being near Egypt. [Cf. *Sotah* 36b cited in *footnote* to *v.* 38 above, according to which Pharaoh did *not* know Hebrew.] Compare the case of Pharaoh's daughter who also gave Moses a name in the language of his people, Hebrew [see *Exod.* 2:10]. Although it is recorded that the Egyptian writers referred to Moses as Munyos, that is because they used the Egyptian equivalent of the Hebrew, just as *Onkelos* sometimes substitutes Aramaic names for the Hebrew as in the case of *Kadesh and Shur* [above 20:1] which he translated as *Rekem and Chigra.*

R' Hirsch draws an analogy for the meaning of the word פַּעְנֵחַ from the Rabbinic term פנח in *Yevamos* 115b [לפנחיא שבקיא, which *Rashi* interprets in the sense of *safeguard.*] Accordingly, the name might mean: 'he with whom the most secret things are safeguarded' — who holds the key to the most hidden secrets.

פֶּ֥רַע כֹּהֵ֖ן אֹ֣ן לְאִשָּׁ֑ה וַיֵּצֵ֥א יוֹסֵ֖ף עַל־אֶ֥רֶץ
מו מִצְרָֽיִם׃ וְיוֹסֵף֙ בֶּן־שְׁלֹשִׁ֣ים שָׁנָ֔ה בְּעָמְד֕וֹ
לִפְנֵ֖י פַּרְעֹ֣ה מֶֽלֶךְ־מִצְרָ֑יִם וַיֵּצֵ֤א יוֹסֵף֙

וַיִּתֵּן לוֹ — *And he gave him.*

As part of this effort to enhance Joseph's prestige, Pharaoh even arranged an aristocratic marriage for him. Possibly, Pharaoh took all these steps in order to accelerate Joseph's acceptance among the Egyptian aristocracy. Although the marriage is mentioned now — as part of all of these elevations — it did not occur until a bit later *(Akeidas Yitzchak).*[1]

אָסְנַת בַּת־פּוֹטִי פֶרַע כֹּהֵן אֹן — *Asenath daughter of Poti Phera, Chief* [following *Rashi* to 47:22; *Ramban* (see below) renders: *priest*] *of On.*

Poti Phera, the Chief of On, is identical with Potiphar [see above 37:36]. Midrashically the word *Phera* is derived from פרע, *uncover, pull down,* and it has the figurative sense of *unman, emasculate.* Potiphar was given that name because he had been emasculated in punishment for having purchased Joseph for sodomy *(Rashi; Sotah* 13b; *Bereishis Rabbah* 86:3). [See *comm.* to 37:36; 39:1; *Ramban* to 39:19 s.v. כַּדְּבָרִים הָאֵלֶּה.][2]

Ramban asserts that the Midrashic identificaton of Poti Phera with Potiphar, Pharaoh's courtier, compelled *Rashi* [in his comm. to 47:22] to give a novel interpretation to the word *kohen.* Although other uses of the word *kohen* in Scripture generally refer to one who ministers to a deity, *Rashi* regards our passage and 47:22 as exceptions, since Potiphar/Poti Phera was chief of the butchers, and clearly not a *priest.* In this context, therefore, *kohen* must be rendered *chief* or *governor.*

Ramban suggests, however, that even according to the above-cited Midrash, we can render *kohen* in its usual sense of *priest.* When Potiphar's debility became public knowledge people began ridiculing him with the nickname *Poti Phera,* whereupon he resigned his post in shame and became a priest in the temple of On. It was customary among retired Egyptian nobility to devote themselves to such "godly" service.

Notwithstanding the above, *Ramban*

1. Pharaoh also arranged the marriage with Potiphar's daughter to ensure that Potiphar would not meet Joseph and blurt out: 'You are my slave!' Once Joseph was married to his daughter, Potiphar would never do this.

Secondly, this marriage was tacit proof to all that Potiphar had not really believed his wife's accusation against Joseph; otherwise, he would never have consented to a marriage that would bring Joseph in close association with his wife. The Rabbinic directive [*Yevamos* 26a] that 'one suspected of illicit intimacy with a woman is forbidden to marry her daughter,' is a course dictated by ordinary good sense *(Oznaim laTorah).*

2. In the opinion of many commentators, Poti Phera fathered Asenath before he was emasculated.

According to *Pirkei d'Rabbi Eliezer* 38 and other Midrashic sources [cited in the comm. to 34:26 (p. 1492)], however, she was only Poti Phera's *adopted* daughter, born to Dinah from Shechem's assault. She came to Poti Phera in the following way: The sons of Jacob could not bear the presence of this child in their home, so Jacob made her an amulet engraved with HASHEM's Name in order to indicate that she was the daughter of Dinah, daughter of Jacob, grandson of Abraham. He attached the amulet to a chain which he placed around her neck. The child was then cast out of Jacob's house and placed under a bush [Hebrew: *s'neh* — hence her name Asenath]. Providence eventually brought her to the house of Poti Phera whose wife, being childless, raised the child as her own. Since Asenath grew up in Poti Phera's home, Scripture refers to her as his *daughter.* As culled from the various parallel Midrashic accounts,

41 *daughter of Poti Phera, Chief of On, for a wife. Thus*
46 *Joseph emerged in charge of the land of Egypt.*
46 Now Joseph was thirty years old when he stood
before Pharaoh king of Egypt. Joseph left Pharaoh's

concludes that the word *kohen* is a general term denoting 'ministry' [or *'servitor' (Ibn Ezra)*], not exclusively in religious matters. Accordingly, *II Samuel* 8:18 refers to David's sons as *kohanim* [rendered: *chief ministers*], although David's sons could not have been *kohanim* in the sense of priests since David hailed from the tribe of Judah, not Levi, while in the parallel verse in *I Chron.* 18:17 they are referred to as the *foremost ones about the king.* Cf. also *Job* 12:19 and *Isaiah* 61:10.

Cf. *Rashbam* who, following *Targum,* interprets *kohen On* as the *governor of On.* [He maintains, however, that in the plain sense Poti Phera is not to be identified with Potiphar.]

On — from the Egyptian word for sun — is identified by many with the later Heliopolis, the 'Sun City,' near today's Cairo. *R' Saadiah Gaon* identifies it with Alexandria in Egypt.

Ramban suggests that On may have been the name of Poti Phera's deity.

וַיֵּצֵא יוֹסֵף עַל־אֶרֶץ מִצְרָיִם — *Thus Joseph emerged* [lit. *and Joseph went out*] *in charge of* [lit. *over; upon*] *the land of Egypt.*

He emerged from Pharaoh in such a manner that it was evident to all that he was the ruler of Egypt *(Sforno).*

— His *name* went out; he became famous throughout the land of Egypt. Or, in the more literal sense, he traveled throughout the land of Egypt and announcements were made about him so that he would become known *(Ibn Ezra).*

46. וְיוֹסֵף בֶּן־שְׁלשִׁים שָׁנָה בְּעָמְדוֹ לִפְנֵי פַּרְעֹה מֶלֶךְ מִצְרָיִם — *Now Joseph was thirty years old when he stood* [lit. *as he was standing*] *before Pharaoh king of Egypt.*[1]

— And was accordingly fit to rule *(Rashbam).*

According to *Abarbanel,* the knowledge of Joseph's age at this juncture points to the hand of Pro-

it emerges that Joseph met her in Potiphar's house but never suspected her origins.

When Potiphar's wife slanderously accused Joseph of attempting to violate her, Asenath came on her own initiative to her father and convinced him of Joseph's innocence [as noted in 39:19 s.v. וַיִּחַר אַפּוֹ]. The Sages mention that it was in this merit that she married Joseph.

This marriage was predestined, for as *Rashi* mentions in 39:1, Potiphar's wife had foreseen by astrology that she would be the ancestress of Joseph's children — but she did not know that their mother would be her 'daughter' rather than she.

The Midrashim record that when Joseph became viceroy and rode through the town on the royal chariot, *the daughters stepped on to the wall* [49:22] to gaze upon him as he passed by. Each of them threw him something precious , and since Asenath had nothing else, she threw her amulet. When Joseph examined it, he realized that she was Jacob's granddaughter. [See *comm.* to 48:9].

In any case, as *Alshich* observes, Joseph's marriage to Potiphar's own daughter vindicated him in the eyes of the Egyptians from the accusations of his master's wife.

1. The parenthetic detail of Joseph's age provides us with an important chronological focus. It informs us that Joseph — who was seventeen years old when he was sold [37:2] — served in Potiphar's house for one year [see 39:5 s.v. בַּבַּיִת וּבַשָּׂדֶה *(Seder Olam)*] and spent the following twelve years in prison until he was brought before Pharaoh at the age of thirty [see 39:20 and 40:14, 23].

Joseph's age at this juncture also forms a basic link in *Rashi's* calculations of the total

מִלִּפְנֵי פַרְעֹה וַיַּעֲבֹר בְּכָל־אֶרֶץ מִצְרָיִם׃
מז וַתַּעַשׂ הָאָרֶץ בְּשֶׁבַע שְׁנֵי הַשָּׂבָע
מח לִקְמָצִים׃ וַיִּקְבֹּץ אֶת־כָּל־אֹכֶל | שֶׁבַע
שָׁנִים אֲשֶׁר הָיוּ בְּאֶרֶץ מִצְרַיִם וַיִּתֶּן־אֹכֶל
בֶּעָרִים אֹכֶל שְׂדֵה־הָעִיר אֲשֶׁר סְבִיבֹתֶיהָ

vidence. Ordinarily, one so young could never have risen to the highest position in a great land were it not for his God-given wisdom and grace.

This is the first time the monarch is referred to by his full title as 'Pharaoh, King of Egypt.' He was worthy of this auspicious title only because Joseph stood before him.

This title is subsequently suppressed, not to be used again until Moses appeared with the Divine request that Pharaoh — as king of Egypt — allow the Israelites to leave his land [*Exodus* 6:11ff]. Then, too, [when Pharaoh was given the opportunity to take part in the destiny of Israel], the Torah shows him respect by using his full title *(Tanchuma Yashan).*

וַיֵּצֵא יוֹסֵף מִלִּפְנֵי פַרְעֹה וַיַּעֲבֹר בְּכָל־אֶרֶץ מִצְרָיִם — [*And*] *Joseph left* [*from*] *Pharaoh's presence and he passed through the entire land of Egypt.*

The previous verse also speaks of Joseph's 'going out' over the land of Egypt. There, as noted, it is in the figurative sense: Joseph *emerged* as the ruler; his fame went throughout the land *(Ibn Ezra).* Here, as *Sforno* comments, the intent is that Joseph literally *toured* the length and breadth of the land to attend to its affairs.

— He made himself known to the populace, learned about the countryside, warned the populace of the impending famine, and commissioned the construction of royal granaries in every city *(Akeidah).*

Furthermore the additional nuance here implies a departure beyond that of the previous verse: Joseph now left מִלִּפְנֵי פַרְעֹה, *Pharaoh's presence,* thus intimating that the earlier travels were chiefly ceremonial and under Pharaoh's direction; now Joseph traveled *independent* of the king's direct supervision, and began to perform duties of State in his position of viceroy *(Alshich).*

Haamek Davar perceives that the contextual flow of the verse informs us that Joseph's appearance before Pharaoh, his promotion, and his trip through Egypt all took place in one year — when Joseph was thirty years old. [Thus the verse would be rendered: *And Joseph was thirty years old when he stood before Pharaoh and when Joseph left Pharaoh's presence and passed through the entire land of Egypt.*]

47. The seven years of abundance. Joseph's plan is implemented.

וַתַּעַשׂ הָאָרֶץ בְּשֶׁבַע שְׁנֵי הַשָּׂבָע — [*And*] *the earth produced* [lit. *made*] *during the seven years of abundance.*

The connotation of this passage is as *Onkelos* paraphrased it: And the *inhabitants* of the land gathered; thus the word *earth* refers to the earth's inhabitants [cf. *Ezek.* 14:12]. Nevertheless, the word וַתַּעַשׂ [which *Onkelos* renders figuratively as *gathered*] does not real-

number of years Joseph was separated from his father, and in determining that Jacob spent fourteen years in the Academy of Eber [see 28:9 and chart on p. 1173]. Among other things, it is also a factor in determining that the sale of Joseph preceded Isaac's death by twelve years [see chart on p. 1529].

presence and he passed through the entire land of Egypt.

[47] *The earth produced during the seven years of abundance by the handfuls.* [48] *He gathered all food of the seven years that came to pass in Egypt, and he placed foods in the cities — the food of the field*

ly lose its primary meaning of *made.* [The literal intent is that the earth itself — not its inhabitants — yielded crops in such abundance that the grain could be scooped up by the handful] *(Rashi* as explained by *Levush;* comp. *Targum Yonasan; Rashbam).*

לִקְמָצִים — *By the handfuls.*

I.e., the grain was collected *handful by handful, fist upon fist (Rashi).*

This can be understood to mean that the abundance was so great that food was accumulated 'hand over fist.' *R' David Feinstein,* however, explains that the intent is that such scrupulous care was taken in carrying out Joseph's requisition policy, that not even a single handful was overlooked.

Each ear produced a handful of grain *(Rashbam).*

Ramban following *Onkelos* renders: *Into store houses* [i.e., the people gathered the abundant produce and heaped it into store houses, or: the earth produced enough surplus for storage]. He maintains that the term קמץ is synonymous with גמץ, *a pit,* and refers to storehouses excavated in the earth.

48-49. The execution of the plan outlined in verses 35-36.

וַיִּקְבֹּץ אֶת־כָּל־אֹכֶל שֶׁבַע שָׁנִים אֲשֶׁר הָיוּ בְּאֶרֶץ מִצְרַיִם — *[And] he gathered all food of the seven years that came to pass in Egypt.*

'He' refers to Joseph who is the last named subject [in *v.* 46] *(Ramban).*

Egypt is specified because only this abundance and surplus was experienced in no other country. This explains why other countries did not store food, although they undoubtedly heard about the famine *(Ramban v.* 2).

'All' the food is certainly not to be understood literally, or else they would have died of starvation [cf. *v.* 57 below]. It means that he gathered as much he could *(Ibn Ezra).* Cf. *Ralbag:* He gathered whatever he could after first leaving the people their requirements for food and planting.

Ramban maintains however, that the passage is to be taken literally: Joseph gathered the *entire crop* — either at a low price or by force [see below, 47:14] — and released each year only as much as the people required for their sustenance. His purpose was to prevent waste of food, and this was the intent of the plan he outlined in *v.* 35. *Ramban* further draws a distinction between אֹכֶל, *food,* and בָּר, *grain,* [verses 35-36; our verse, and verse 49]: *food* refers to *all* edibles — even dried fruit — which Joseph stored up in the cities to provide the essential minimum for the preservation of life, while *grain* refers to the balance of the crops, which he kept in storehouses. He observes, however, that *Onkelos* drew no distinction between the terms.

According to *Or HaChaim,* following the interpretation that חִמֵּשׁ in *v.* 34 refers to a tax of a *fifth* of all produce, the gathering of 'all' the food mentioned in this verse refers to that levy; or it refers to whatever surplus he could buy in addition to the fifth that was levied [the latter follows *Abarbanel*].

וַיִּתֶּן־אֹכֶל בֶּעָרִים — *And he placed* [lit. *gave*] *food in the cities.*

I.e., in royal granaries which were

מט נָתַן בְּתוֹכָהּ׃ וַיִּצְבֹּר יוֹסֵף בָּר כְּחוֹל הַיָּם
הַרְבֵּה מְאֹד עַד כִּי־חָדַל לִסְפֹּר כִּי־אֵין
נ מִסְפָּר׃ וּלְיוֹסֵף יֻלַּד שְׁנֵי בָנִים בְּטֶרֶם
תָּבוֹא שְׁנַת הָרָעָב אֲשֶׁר יָלְדָה־לּוֹ אָסְנַת

built by Joseph's order in every city *(Pirkei d'Rabbi Eliezer).*

— This too was an example of Joseph's wisdom: he did not build the granaries in the fields where their contents could be stolen, but in the more secure cities *(Abarbanel).*

אֹכֶל שְׂדֵה־הָעִיר אֲשֶׁר סְבִיבֹתֶיהָ נָתַן בְּתוֹכָהּ — *The food of the fields around each city he placed* [lit. *gave*] *within it.*

— For each type of soil preserves its own produce. [Consequently], people add to grain some local soil and this inhibits it from decaying *(Rashi;* the latter view follows R' Nechemiah in the *Midrash;* [*Levush* interprets differently]).

Joseph did this as a measure of justice: He did not take produce from one city and store it elsewhere. Only the produce of fields far away from cities were taken to royal granaries in central locations to be stored for eventual export *(Abarbanel).*

— At the same time, as noted above, this local storage saved freight charges from city to city *(Chizkuni).*

49. וַיִּצְבֹּר יוֹסֵף בָּר כְּחוֹל הַיָּם הַרְבֵּה מְאֹד — [*And*] *Joseph amassed* [see *v.* 35] *grain like the sand of the sea — in great abundance.*

The expression *like the sand of the sea* is hyperbolic *(Radak).*

עַד כִּי חָדַל לִסְפֹּר — *Until he ceased taking stock* [lit. *to count*].

The antecedent of *he* is not identified. The verse means: Until *whoever was numbering* stopped numbering *(Rashi;* see above *v.* 13 s.v. הֵשִׁיב).

According to *Ramban 'he'* refers to Joseph who is the subject of the previous verses as well.

כִּי־אֵין מִסְפָּר — *For there was no number.*

I.e., the quantity of grain grew beyond the capacity of the person in charge of counting to compute it *(Rashi).*

The calculations were so intricate that they had to be abandoned *(Alshich; Or HaChaim);* the quantities were beyond human imagination *(Sforno).*[1]

Ralbag interprets this as a hyperbole.

R' David Feinstein explains that such a policy of accumulation generally has a goal of gathering a predetermined minimum amount. Once that goal has been reached, it is no longer necessary to be as scrupulous in counting future accumulations. This, then, is the intent of our verse: the stores of grain became so huge that it was no longer necessary to keep count; there would surely be more than enough for every conceivable exigency.

1. Cf. *R' Hirsch* who refutes the foolish notion that the ancients were simply unable to count large numbers. The verse does not mean that such numbers did not exist, but that the quantities of food grew to be meaningless. In modern times, for example, we are accustomed to speaking of sums of money or capacities for destruction that go beyond the mind's capacity to grasp them meaningfully.

around each city he placed within it. 49 *Joseph*
amassed grain like the sand of the sea in great abun-
dance until he ceased taking stock, for there was no
number.
50 *Now to Joseph were born two sons — before the*
year of famine was to set in — whom Asenath

— They no longer calculated quantities of *grain;* they now began numbering the *storage places (R' Bachya).*

50. Joseph's children: Manasseh and Ephraim.

וּלְיוֹסֵף יֻלַּד שְׁנֵי בָנִים — *Now to Joseph was born two sons.*

The Hebrew verb יֻלַּד, *was born,* is in singular. The term is either to be construed collectively, or perhaps they were twins and the singular verb denotes that they were both born as the result of a single childbirth *(Radak).*

⸎ Abstention from conjugal relations in time of famine.

בְּטֶרֶם תָּבוֹא שְׁנַת הָרָעָב — *Before the year of famine was to set in* [lit. *would come (kal* imperfect).][1]

[From the emphasis that Joseph's children were born *before* the onset of the famine], the Sages (*Taanis* 11a) derive that one must abstain from conjugal relations in a time of famine *(Rashi).*

The *Talmud* ibid. adds: It was taught that those who are childless are permitted.[2]

When the world is suffering tribulation and destruction a man may not indulge in procreating, lest it be that while the Holy One Blessed be He is engaged in destroying the world this man would be building. Cf. *Job* 30:3 where Job said: בְּחֶסֶר וּבְכָפָן גַּלְמוּד, *solitary in want and famine,* i.e., when the world is in want and famine-stricken, be *galmud* [solitary] — exile yourself [*galeh*] from the conjugal bed! *(Tanchuma Noach* 11; cf. *Yerushalmi Taanis* 1:6).

[According to the above, then, con-

1. That this exegesis presumes the famine to have raged in Egypt as well is not contradicted by *v.* 54 below which mentions that Egypt had bread. What they had was the wheat they had stored in the abundant years, but the land itself was not yielding new crops and the Torah therefore emphasizes that Joseph's children were born *before* the onset of the famine *(Mizrachi; Tzeidah laDerech).*

2. This Talmudic exegesis is cited as halachah in *Shulchan Aruch Orach Chaim* §574:4: "It is a *mitzvah* for one to hunger oneself [i.e. eat restrictedly *(Mishneh Berurah)*] during a year of famine, and it is prohibited to have conjugal relations therein except for the evening of *tevillah* [i.e., the evening of a woman's ritual immersion in a *mikvah* when the obligation of fulfilling one's conjugal duty is greatest]; and for 'childless people' it is permitted" [to have relations at any permissible time — even not on the evening of *tevillah* — until such time as one's wife conceives *(Beis Yosef)*].

The halachic authority *Magen Avraham* prohibits relations for couples with children in such times even on the evening of *tevillah,* but the consensus of Rabbinic opinion differ. They appear to be lenient regarding the evening of *tevillah,* relying on the opinion of *Tosafos* in *Taanis* 11a cited in the commentary above that such abstinence is not *obligatory* but a מִנְהַג חֲסִידוּת, *custom of exceptional piety.*

As *Ritva* to *Megillah* 28a observes; 'We often find that the Sages in the Talmud will describe something as אָסוּר, *prohibited,* when in reality it is nothing more than a pious custom.'

The *Poskim* also express varying opinions regarding whether the permissive category חֲשׂוּכֵי בָנִים, *'childless people'* [lit. *denied children*] mentioned in the *Talmud* refers to those who have

jugal relations would be prohibited not only in times of famine but in times of calamity as well, and the dispensation mentioned in *Shulchan Aruch* permitting relations on the evening of *tevillah* [immersion; see footnote] would not apply. However, this extension of the prohibitions to times of calamity has not become the accepted *halachah*. See footnote and *Magen Avraham* to *Orach Chaim* 574:4]).

Tosafos in *Taanis ibid.* s.v. אָסוּר notes that this rule is apparently contradicted by the tradition that Yocheved, youngest child of Levi, was born as he entered Egypt [see *Rashi* to 46:26; *Numb.* 26:59; *Bava Basra* 120a] — a time when the famine still raged. It would therefore follow that Levi had conjugal relations during the famine [and since he had previously begotten Gershon, Kehath, and Merari (46:11), he could not rely on the dispensation permitted childless couples.]

— In answer, *Tosafos* suggests that this was not *forbidden* except to someone who wished to conduct himself with an extra measure of piety [לִנְהוֹג עַצְמוֹ בַּחֲסִידוּת]. Joseph chose to abstain for this reason, but other people [including Levi] did not.

Tosafos' comment regarding Levi evokes much comment by later exegetes who are discomfited by the implication that Levi — ancestor of the tribes who would minister to HASHEM and to whom Moses in his blessings would refer to as pious [see *Deut.* 33:8] — conducted himself less piously than Joseph. They offer several additional solutions to defend Levi's action.

Tosefos HaRosh Hadar Zekeinim proposes that Joseph and Levi differed in whether one has fulfilled the *mitzvah* of procreation if all his children are sons [see footnote]. Apparently maintaining that one *has* thereby fulfilled it, Joseph abstained, while Levi maintained that one does not fulfill the *mitzvah* until he has also begotten a daughter. Not having a daughter as yet, Levi did not abstain.

In a similar manner and citing *Mizrachi, Maharsha* defends *Tosafos'* opinion and maintains that since Joseph still had no daughter he would have been permitted to procreate, but he abstained *as an act of piety*. Levi, however, chose the obligation of cohabiting in order to beget a daughter and fulfill the *mitzvah* of procreation. Alternatively, this conception might have taken place on the evening of *tevillah*, when, according to *Yerushalmi*, cohabitation is permitted even at times of famine [see *Orach Chaim* §574:4].

Or HaChaim emphasizes that immediately after deriving from our verse that one should refrain from cohabitation in time of famine, the Talmud states clearly that childless people *are* permitted to cohabit. Accordingly, both Joseph and Levi — who lacked daughters and consequently had not fulfilled the *mitzvah* of procreation — were exempted from any prohibition against cohabitation during the famine. Furthermore, since Moses describes Levi as the epitome of חֲסִידוּת, *devout piety* (see *Deut.* 33:8), *Or HaChaim* finds it difficult to accept *Tosafos'* contention that Levi failed to match Joseph's piety.

no children at all, or if it applies also to those who are 'childless' in the sense that they have not yet fulfilled the *mitzvah* of procreation [פְּרִיָּה וְרִבְיָה] by having begotten both a son and daughter. In *Rashi's* interpretation of the term in the Talmud (ad. loc.), he adopts the latter sense. Many *Acharonim* [later commentators] as well apparently adopt this view [with the notable exception of the *Magen Avraham*] and they permit relations on the evening of *tevillah* [see *Rambam, Hilchos Taanis* 2]. Accordingly many *Poskim* are lenient in cases such as a marriage where either partner has not begotten a son and daughter or where there are other extenuating circumstances. This leniency basically follows the view of *Taz* in *Divrei David* as cited by *Eliyahu Rabbah*, which maintains: [only] "conjugal relations *for pleasure* come under this prohibited category, since it is proper to share in distress with the rest of the population. But to propagate the species or when one's urge overpowers him and [to deny] it might lead to other sins, there is no prohibition, and this falls under the permitted category of 'childlessness' which was the term used because it is clear [i.e., the term *childless* was not meant literally]; the

Therefore, he contends that neither brother was required to abstain. The Scriptural allusion to such abstention in Joseph's case is an instance of אִם אֵינוֹ עִנְיָן, the hermeneutical principle that sometimes Scripture teaches a law even though it does not apply to the person or case where it is stated. Thus, the law of abstention is binding upon people who have sons and daughters only, even though it is taught with regard to Joseph, to whom it did not apply.

Ran and *Chizkuni* [similarly *Pa'aneach Raza* cited by *Maharsha*] suggest that the criteria for the abstention is when Israelites, rather than the gentile world at large, are beset by famine. Consequently, although Joseph was not *personally* affected by the famine, he was required to abstain because, as far as he knew his family in Canaan was experiencing hunger. On the other hand, because Levi and his brothers knew that they were faring well in that stage of the famine and had sufficient sustenance [see *Rashi* 42:1 s.v. לָמָּה תִּתְרָאוּ], they were not obligated to abstain. Furthermore, they did not have to abstain out of concern for Joseph — who, for all they knew, might have been suffering from the famine — since he was but an individual.

Citing the above, *Divrei David* adds that in any event it was only conjugal relations for *pleasure* that were proscribed — not cohabitation to propagate the species [see *Taz* in footnote].

Riva suggests that Levi may, indeed, have abstained until he learned that Joseph was well and the ruler of Egypt. Only then did his wife conceive.

It is additionally noted by *Mizrachi* that none of this is contradicted by Isaac who indulged in marital intimacy during a famine [see *Rashi* to 26:8], because — as *Mizrachi* explains — there was no famine in that country. [Or according to *Maharsha* the famine had ended before that incident.]

According to *Rashbam,* we are now told that these sons were born to Joseph before the onset of the famine to prepare us for a later verse. Jacob came to Egypt during the second year of the famine and seventeen years later on his death-bed announced that Joseph's two sons born before his arrival would be accounted as his own [48:5], while *the progeny born to him after them,* i.e. those born to Joseph after Jacob's arrival, would be Joseph's [48:6]. Therefore Ephraim and Manasseh are identified as the sons born to Joseph before the famine and before Jacob arrived. However, children born to Joseph after Jacob's arrival were to be reckoned as part of the tribes of Ephraim and Manasseh for purposes of the division of the Land in *Eretz Yisrael.*

אֲשֶׁר יָלְדָה־לּוֹ אָסְנַת בַּת־פּוֹטִי פֶרַע כֹּהֵן אוֹן — *Whom Asenath daughter of Poti Phera Chief of On* [see *v.* 45 on translation of כֹּהֵן as chief] bore to him.

This is mentioned to clarify that these were not children of another wife *(R' Shmuel ben Chafni).*

[After stating that Joseph had two sons, the verse concludes with the apparently superfluous statement that Asenath bore them to him.]

— The verse stresses that Joseph's *only* wife was Asenath *(Radak);* it

Sages used it because they preferred to use an unconditional term (מילתא דפסיקא נקט).

However, in his commentary to *Orach Chaim, Taz* (574:2) takes a different view. There he says that only people with no children *at all* were permitted to cohabit because the Sages perceived that the Scriptural prohibition could not have encompassed even those who felt the anguish of being completely childless. People with children, however — even if they had not fulfilled the *mitzvah* of procreation because they did not have a son *and* a daughter — are surely not the objects of pity and should not be absolved of the obligation to share in the suffering of the masses.

Furthermore the definition of what degree of scarcity would qualify as a 'famine' is in itself somewhat vague in Rabbinic literature since 'famines' in the severe Scriptural sense were apparently rare occurrences. Together with the other variables mentioned above, this might account for the lack of a definitive ruling on this topic in the halachic codes. [See *Shaarei Teshuvah; Eliyahu Rabbah; Shiyurei Knesses HaGedolah; Pri Megadim*].

אֶת־שֵׁם הַבְּכוֹר מְנַשֶּׁה כִּֽי־נַשַּׁנִי אֱלֹהִים
נב אֶת־כָּל־עֲמָלִי וְאֵת כָּל־בֵּית אָבִי: וְאֵת

was important to Joseph that only Asenath be his wife because that was public proof that he had not sinned with her mother *(Chizkuni)*.

— *R' Hirsch* perceives a different stress in the phrase: *Asenath ... bore to* **him**; the children she conceived, bore, and raised were dedicated to the ideals of Joseph; not those in which *she* had been raised. She was an aristocratic, cultured Egyptian, while he was 'merely' an enslaved, imprisoned Hebrew raised to prominence only by whim of the king. It would not have been surprising for her to dominate the home. Had that happened, the children would have been hers, not his. Therefore the verse tells us that Asenath adopted Joseph's spiritual and moral outlook. She bore children to *him*.

To be the only Jew in Egypt, and to be married to the daughter of an idolatrous priest, yet to raise children who remain the model after whom Jewish parents bless their children — *may God make you like Ephraim* and *Manasseh* (48:20) — is no small זְכִיָּה, *privilege*.

— *R' Munk*, citing *Radak*, notes a different significance in this phrase: Despite the greatness of Joseph and the sincerity of Asenath, the unsavory influences of Egypt insinuated themselves into the character of Joseph's children. This accounts for some of the evil deeds performed centuries later by the tribes of Manasseh and Ephraim. Even Jacob was apprehensive in this regard as *Rashi* points out in 48:8.

51. מְנַשֶּׁה — *Manasseh.* [Hebrew: *Menasheh*].

— Lit. He Who causes to forget [=הַמַּשְׁכִּיחַ] *(R' Shmuel ben Chofni Gaon)*.

כִּי נַשַּׁנִי אֱלֹהִים אֶת־כָּל־עֲמָלִי — *For* [*he said (Ibn Ezra)*] *"God has made me forget* [Hebrew: *nashah,* in assonance with *Menasheh*] *all my hardship"* [lit. *toil*].

— I.e. which I endured since I was sold *(Radak)*.

Upon seeing the end-result of all his travail, Joseph thanked God for allowing him to forget the hardships imposed upon him; he fully recognized their purpose and harbored no malice toward anyone *(HaKsav V'HaKabbalah)*.

The verb נַשַּׁנִי, *caused me to forget,* is related to נשה, *displaced,* as in גִּיד הַנָּשֶׁה, *the displaced nerve.* It implies forgetfulness in the sense that God displaces one thought from the forefront of one's mind and replaces it with other thoughts. Cf. *Lamentations* 3:17: נָשִׁיתִי טוֹבָה, *I have forgotten goodness (Karnei Or)*.

[Cf. *Rashbam* who maintains that in distinction with נָשִׁיתִי whose root is נשה, the root of נַשַּׁנִי is נשש, the vowelization being similar to חַנֵּנִי from חנן. He holds that if the root were נשה, then our word would be vowelized נַשָּׁנִי, similar to רִמָּנִי from רמה; כִּלָּנוּ from כלה. *Ibn Ezra* cites both views including that which maintains that the vowels נַ and נָ are interchangeable. (It is interesting however that neither *Ibn Janach* nor *Radak* in *Shorashim* list נשש as a root; nor do they include נַשַּׁנִי among the words in נשה).]

The Talmudic term בֵּי נַשָּׁא, lit. *forgotten house,* is used by the Sages [*Bava Basra* 12b] in reference to the paternal home of a married woman since a woman — like a man — upon marriage 'forgets' her parents' home and clings instead to her spouse [see 2:24] *(R' Bachya)*.

וְאֵת כָּל־בֵּית אָבִי — *And all my father's household.*

I.e., God made me 'forget' the hardships to which my brothers subjected me in my paternal home. He imbued me with a prophetic spirit to recognize that the Hand of Providence engineered my tribulations during those years, thereby causing me not to harbor hatred toward my brothers for their

[51] *Joseph named the firstborn Manasseh for, "God*
has made me forget all my hardship and all my
father's household." [52] *And the second son he named*

maltreatment of me [see 45:7, 8] *(Akeidah).*

The commentators agree that the implication is certainly *not* that Joseph — Jacob's favorite child — was so crass as to have named a child in grateful commemoration of having *forgotten* his paternal home. It has been noted that the very fact that he evokes his paternal home in this pronouncement in the very moment of his rejoicing at the birth proves that Joseph did not forget it! Furthermore, an obvious question arises:

⌁§Why, indeed, did Joseph 'forget' his father at all; why did he not now, as viceroy of Egypt, seize the opportunity to visit his aged father whom he had not seen for about twenty years and who certainly must have thought him to be dead?

Even if a personal visit would prove impossible at this very busy juncture in his new executive position, Joseph could have dispatched a personal emissary with a letter telling Jacob of his whereabouts. Also, in view of the impending famine, why didn't Joseph inform Jacob that grain would be available through him?

As discussed in the *footnote* to 37:28, it is the traditional view of the Sages that when the brothers sold Joseph they proclaimed a *cherem* [solemn ban] against anyone who divulged what had been done with Joseph. According to some opinions noted there, Joseph, too, was bound by this *cherem* — against his will — from contacting his father, or disclosing his whereabouts, which accounts for Joseph's failure to contact Jacob throughout his twenty-two years in Egypt. Some reasons are noted in that footnote as to why the Providential plan necessitated Jacob's ignorance of Joseph's whereabouts — so that the family destiny and Jacob's descent into Egypt could develop according to the Providential plan, and also so that this absence be an atonement for the similar period that Jacob was away from Isaac.

Thus, Joseph was bound by a solemn oath against contacting his father. Accordingly, his reason for giving the name Manasseh must be perceived as a painful display of gratitude to God for making his ordeal and solitude less painful by having granted him the fortitude to 'forget' his father's house in the sense that he was not constantly obsessed by the need to contact Jacob. (See *HaKsav V'HaKabbalah* [also *Akeidas Yitzchak*] where the verb נַשַּׁנִי, as noted above, means *displaced for me* — i.e., caused thoughts of home to be 'displaced' from my thoughts by the heavy responsibilities assigned him).[1]

Haamek Davar interprets similarly and adds that the real reason Joseph did not take steps to contact his father was that he considered his dreams, in which first his brothers and then his father as well bowed to him (see 37:7ff), as a form of prophecy. He considered it his duty not to negate the dreams so as not to be guilty of suppressing prophecy [which the Sages *(Sanhedrin* 89a) consider a capital offense].

This essentially follows the interpretation of *Ramban* in 42:9 who maintains that had Joseph's where-

1. *R' David Feinstein* suggests that Joseph gratefully viewed this child as a Divine gift whereby he could now refocus his orientation — as every new father does — from his parental roots to this new link in the eternal chain of human destiny. The child would help Joseph 'forget' his former misery and look to the future rather than to the past. This concept is embodied in the Torah's teaching above, [2:24] that upon marriage *a man shall leave his father and his mother and cling to his wife.* With a new child, a father's priority goes to his child. This concept Joseph wished to preserve in naming the child Manasseh.

שֵׁם הַשֵּׁנִי קָרָא אֶפְרָיִם כִּי־הִפְרַנִי אֱלֹהִים
נג בְּאֶרֶץ עָנְיִי: °וַתִּכְלֶינָה שֶׁבַע שְׁנֵי הַשָּׂבָע
נד אֲשֶׁר הָיָה בְּאֶרֶץ מִצְרָיִם: וַתְּחִלֶּינָה שֶׁבַע
שְׁנֵי הָרָעָב לָבוֹא כַּאֲשֶׁר אָמַר יוֹסֵף וַיְהִי

abouts been known, Jacob would have redeemed him regardless of how extravagant his ransom might have been. [For, as noted above, Jacob would never have left the sacred environs of *Eretz Yisrael* to go to Egypt unless circumstances made it absolutely necessary.] Joseph perceived that the fulfillment of his dreams — that his family would bow to him — could not possibly be accomplished in *Eretz Yisrael* [where Jacob was considered a prince of God *(R' Eisenstadt)*] and he was hoping that it would be effected in Egypt as a result of his, Joseph's, new power there. This feeling was enhanced when Pharaoh's dreams made clear that the famine could bring them all to Egypt where the dreams would be fulfilled.

Thus, in effect, Manasseh's name was an acknowledgment that God had given Joseph the fortitude to ignore Jacob and allow Providence to take its course. For although Joseph was obligated by the *mitzvah* of honoring his father to contact him, nevertheless the Will of God as evidenced by the prophetic dream inspired him to subordinate his own wishes to those of his Creator, and God replaced Joseph's constant thoughts of his father with other thoughts.

Malbim following *Alshich* suggests that Joseph gave his child that name as a constant reminder that he should not now in prosperous time forget his former hardships and father's house. This is similar in concept to eating bitter foods on Passover to remind us — in times of freedom — of former exile. Thus, Joseph named the child Manasseh to keep alive the memory that God Providentially engineered a series of events resulting in Joseph's lengthy absence from home and thrusting him into a position of compelled 'forgetfulness' of his paternal home. This condition grieved him greatly.

R' Hirsch offers that the verb נשה signifies not only *to forget*, but also to be a *creditor* so that נַשַּׁנִי can be rendered: "God has turned my misfortunes and my family *into my creditors.*" It was as if Joseph said: I feel indebted to my sufferings and my mistreatment at the hands of my family, because God has made them the vehicles to bring me abundant happiness.

52. אֶפְרָיִם — *Ephraim* [i.e., fruitful, from the Hebrew *pri.*]

כִּי־הִפְרַנִי אֱלֹהִים — *For* [he said *(Ibn Ezra)*] *God has made me fruitful* [Hebrew: *hifrani* from פְּרִי, *fruit*, in assonance with *Ephraim*].

— With children, wealth, and honor *(Radak)*.

בְּאֶרֶץ עָנְיִי — *In the land of my suffering.*

I.e., in the land where I had suffered so much until now *(Radak)*.

With all the greatness, splendor, and honor Joseph now enjoyed, along with the wealth and grain that he controlled, he nevertheless viewed Egypt as 'the land of his suffering' inasmuch as it was far away from his father's home and from the Holy Land *(Abarbanel)*.

— There could be no greater proof of Joseph's heartfelt loyalty to his origins and his determination to refuse assimilation into the Egyptian culture than the names he gave his children. They were constant reminders of his duty to be faithful to his family and to *Eretz Yisrael* *(R' Hirsch)*.

Ephraim for, "God has made me fruitful in the land of my suffering."

[53] *The seven years of abundance that came to pass in the land of Egypt ended.* [54] *And the seven years of famine began approaching just as Joseph had said.*

Torah Sheleimah cites *Chemdas Yamim* that the phrase is to be rendered: *In the land of my poverty.* Joseph's intent was that he had been privileged to rise to such heights *not* within the environs of *Eretz Yisrael,* but only in a spiritually poor land outside it; similar to a poor man who is given something from the king's table on the condition that he eat it outside.

According to *Tzror HaMor,* Joseph was commemorating the greatness of the miracle: He rose to such heights in the very place where they knew he had been a slave. Cf. *Psalms* 113:7-8: *He raises the poor from the dust ... to set them with the great men.*

The name *Ephraim* — which is composed of letters of the word *epher (ashes)* in the plural form — contains an allusion to Abraham and Isaac who are associated with *epher.* Of Abraham it is written [18:27]: אָנֹכִי עָפָר וָאֵפֶר, *I am but dust and ashes,* and Isaac is considered as having had his ashes on the altar [at the *Akeidah*]. Thus the descendants of Israel are referred to by the designation Ephraim as it is written [*Jeremiah* 31:19]: *Truly, Ephraim* [a general designation for the Ten Tribes *(Metzudos ibid. v.* 17)] *is a dear son to me (Daas Zekeinim).*

53. The onset of the famine.

וַתִּכְלֶינָה שֶׁבַע שְׁנֵי הַשָּׂבָע אֲשֶׁר הָיָה בְּאֶרֶץ מִצְרָיִם — *[And] the seven-years of abundande that came to pass* [lit. *that was*] *in the land of Egypt ended.*

The singular אֲשֶׁר הָיָה, *that was,* is used in the collective sense since the seven years were viewed as one entity *(Radak).*

In the land of Egypt is specified because it was only there that this abundance was experienced, not elsewhere [see *v.* 48].

The *Midrash* perceives וַתִּכְלֶינָה, [...*ended*] to be homiletically related to כלל, *beauty, perfection.* The verse connotes that the years of abundance were perfectly beautiful, and that the people, too, were handsome amid all the abundance [comp. *footnote* to next verse].

54. וַתְּחִלֶּינָה שֶׁבַע שְׁנֵי הָרָעָב לָבוֹא — *And the seven years of famine began approaching.*

Their onset was particularly noticeable since famine was rare in Egypt. Moreover, the famine came suddenly and with great force, as Joseph had predicted [*v.* 30]: *The seven years of famine will arise after them* — violently, as if they forcibly had been restrained up to that time *(Tz'ror HaMor).*[1]

Normally, a famine begins slowly as the supplies begin to dwindle. In this case, however, it struck with horrible suddenness. There was no transition period. For seven consecutive years the Nile rose and irrigated the land causing abundant crops. Then, without warning, in the following year the Nile did not overflow, causing drought and the rotting of subsequent crops. Already with the first year of the

1. According to the *Midrash* the word וַתְּחִלֶּינָה is homiletically derived from חלה, *sickness:* The seven years of famine brought sickness [i.e. sickly crops *(Sifsei Kohen)* or disease from hunger *(Baalei HaTosafos)*] with them. It reached a point that people sought even a coarse loaf of bread and could not find one. Then they exclaimed: Is this not כַּאֲשֶׁר אָמַר יוֹסֵף, *just as Joseph had said*?!

רָעָב֙ בְּכָל־הָ֣אֲרָצ֔וֹת וּבְכָל־אֶ֥רֶץ מִצְרַ֖יִם
נה הָ֥יָה לָֽחֶם׃ וַתִּרְעַב֙ כָּל־אֶ֣רֶץ מִצְרַ֔יִם
וַיִּצְעַ֥ק הָעָ֛ם אֶל־פַּרְעֹ֖ה לַלָּ֑חֶם וַיֹּ֨אמֶר
פַּרְעֹ֤ה לְכָל־מִצְרַ֙יִם֙ לְכ֣וּ אֶל־יוֹסֵ֔ף אֲשֶׁר־
נו יֹאמַ֥ר לָכֶ֖ם תַּעֲשֽׂוּ׃ וְהָרָעָ֣ב הָיָ֔ה עַ֖ל כָּל־

famine there was neither sowing nor harvest. It was as if people were sitting and eating and the next moment thee was no food to be had. Even the most common bread suddenly became unavailable *(Abarbanel; Ralbag;* based upon *Tanchuma).*

כַּאֲשֶׁר אָמַר יוֹסֵף – *Just as Joseph had said* [i.e. *foretold*].

Although Pharaoh regarded Joseph's interpretation of his dream as already having been fulfilled *(Ramban v.* 36), nevertheless, since abundance was not a novelty in fertile Egypt, it was only with the advent of the famine that Joseph's interpretation of the dream was absolutely verified *(Ramban v.* 27).

וַיְהִי רָעָב בְּכָל־הָאֲרָצוֹת וּבְכָל־אֶרֶץ מִצְרַיִם הָיָה לָחֶם – *There was famine in all the lands, but in all the land of Egypt there was bread.*

— From their stored-up food, for Joseph had prepared them for the impending famine *(Rashbam; R' Bachya; Abarbanel).*

Unlike the other lands which had not experienced abundance and, accordingly, could not store up surplus crops, in Egypt *there was bread* from the grain that Joseph had stored away. However, the land itself was not yielding new crops even in Egypt *(Mizrachi* to *v.* 50).

Sforno in *v.* 3 interprets that this period of both famine and plenty — hunger in other countries and food in Egypt — was symbolized in Pharaoh's dream by the lean cows standing alongside the fat cows for a while.

There was famine in the all the lands — that is, only in the lands *adjacent to Egypt;* other lands, however, were unaffected — otherwise how could faraway countries have survived? Thus have the Sages said in the *Midrash,* 'The famine raged in three lands: Phoenicia, Arabia and Palestine' *(Ramban).*

[The Sages in the *Talmud,* however, interpret that the famine was worldwide. See *v.* 57.]

55. וַתִּרְעַב כָּל־אֶרֶץ מִצְרַיִם – *When* [lit. *and*] *all the land of Egypt hungered.*

— For all the stored grain rotted except that which Joseph had stored up *(Rashi).*

Cf. *Tanchuma:* All the grain they had at home rotted — even the bread in their baskets became moldy;and even those individuals who stored up food went hungry *(Oznaim LaTorah).*

According to *Lekach Tov,* they felt the shortage so acutely, 'Because the very knowledge that there is famine whets the appetite; a man who normally eats one measure of bread, eats three measures.'

This occurred in the second year of the famine when even Egypt itself felt the hunger of the famine *(R' Bachya).*

וַיִּצְעַק הָעָם אֶל־פַּרְעֹה לַלָּחֶם – [*And*] *the people cried out to Pharaoh for bread.*

Complaining to the monarch that Joseph was making an unreasonable demand upon them [see below].

וַיֹּאמֶר פַּרְעֹה לְכָל־מִצְרַיִם לְכוּ אֶל יוֹסֵף אֲשֶׁר יֹאמַר לָכֶם תַּעֲשׂוּ – *So Pharaoh said to all of Egypt, 'Go to Joseph.*

There was famine in all the lands, but in all the land of Egypt there was bread.
55 *When all the land of Egypt hungered, the people cried out to Pharaoh for bread. So Pharaoh said to all of Egypt, "Go to Joseph. Whatever he tells you, do."*

Whatever he tells you [you shall] do.'

— He is in full charge over all matters; his word is final *(R' Bachya; Abarbanel).*

⌂§ Joseph demands that the Egyptians be circumcised.

[Pharaoh had to give them this firm order because] Joseph demanded of them to [first] be circumcised [or else he would not provide them with grain]. When they came to Pharaoh and told him what Joseph demanded, he asked them, 'Why did you yourselves not store up grain? Did he not constantly resound the warning that years of famine were coming?' [If you were neglectful, why do you now cry to me?]

'We gathered in a lot,' they answered, 'but it rotted.'

'If so,' Pharaoh retorted, 'then go to Joseph; whatever he orders you, do. See, he decreed about the produce [that it rot] and it rotted, what if he decrees about us and we will all die?' (*Rashi;* bracketed additions are from *Tanchuma;* see *comm.* to 45:1).[1]

⌂§ What was Joseph's purpose in demanding that the Egyptian masses undergo circumcision?

□ As *Yafeh Toar* observes, the difficulty is compounded by the following: (a) circumcision is not among the commandments incumbent upon non-Jews; (b) since the Egyptians still served idols, their circumcision would have no efficacy (see *Nedarim* 41a); (c) circumcision of a gentile without ritual immersion is of no value.

Yafeh Toar answers that Joseph's intent was not to convert the Egyptians or to have them perform a *mitzvah.* Rather, in his prophetic wisdom, Joseph was preparing for the eventual descent of his brothers to Egypt. He knew that gentiles mock Jews because they are circumcised. By making the Egyptians circumcise themselves, he made it impossible for them to ridicule the circumcised Jews.

My father שליט"א compares this with Joseph's scheme in 47:21 whereby Joseph ordered the Egyptians to relocate *en masse,* for the specific purpose of removing the possible reproach that might be leveled against his brothers, viz. that they were aliens, since the Egyptians themselves now became strangers and aliens in their own land.

□ According to *Rambam* [*Melachim* 10:8], the descendants of Keturah — [who intermingled with the Egyptians *(Tosefos HaRosh)*] — were obligated to circumcise themselves. Perhaps it was to include this segment of the population that Joseph ordered everyone to undergo circumcision. (See *Torah Sheleimah* note §138).

□ Another suggestion advanced is that circumcision reduces the libido and causes one to exercise more moderation especially in times of famine (see *Kli Yakar).*

□ In a Kabbalistic vein, *R' Munk* explains that Joseph's demand is related to the phenomenon that wheat stored by him remained edible, while that of the

1. *Meam Loez* cites *Bircas Avraham* to the effect that the Egyptians responded to Joseph's demand with such reluctance because they were familiar with Joseph's background. They knew that Simeon and Levi had tricked the city of Shechem into submitting to circumcision, and on the third day, when the Shechemites were weak and sick from the operation, the brothers at-

פְּנֵי הָאָרֶץ וַיִּפְתַּח יוֹסֵף אֶת־כָּל־אֲשֶׁר בָּהֶם וַיִּשְׁבֹּר לְמִצְרַיִם וַיֶּחֱזַק הָרָעָב

Egyptians rotted. Some commentators, such as *R' Bachya* and *Maharal,* explain that Joseph attributed this to the benefits of the Covenant of circumcision. Indeed, as the history of Israel demonstrates, this Covenant confers enduring life and possessions on its adherents. Accordingly, Joseph held that performing the sign of the Covenant would be an antidote against degeneration and a guarantee of longevity and survival. (The usual Aramaic translation for the word בְּרִית is קְיָמָא, as in *Onkelos* on 17:11. It means *conservation, permanent existence).* The *Shelah* holds that in the depravity of Egyptian morals Joseph saw the initial cause of the Divine punishments which were to be inflicted on the land of Egypt. The Torah itself confirms this view in Chap. 18 of *Leviticus* where it warns Israel against bringing about its own destruction by imitating the immorality of Egypt. Right from his accession to power, Joseph wanted to strike at the root of this evil and to lead the Egyptians to a healthier, purer moral life. He hoped to do so by having them undergo circumcision, which has the effect [as noted above] of diminishing the sexual drive. The Egyptians obeyed Joseph as long as he ruled over them, but they abandoned the practice very shortly after his death *(Aruch* s.v. מל).

56. וְהָרָעָב הָיָה עַל כָּל־פְּנֵי הָאָרֶץ — *When* [*lit. and*] *the famine spread* [lit. *was*] *over all the face of the earth.*

The phrase literally reads: *And the famine was upon all the face(s) of the earth. Rashi* explains that in this context, 'faces' (or *prominent)* of the earth refers to the well-to-do people. [Cf. פְּנֵי הָעִיר in 33:18].

— The famine spread and struck the wealthy with particular force *(R' Meyuchas).*

This follows the *Midrash* which explains that the famine commenced with the wealthy who are called the פְּנֵי 'faces' of the earth. When a man is wealthy he has a happy disposition [lit. 'face'] for seeking out his friends; but when he is impoverished he does not show himself to his neighbors for he is embarrassed.

According to *R' Bachya,* wealthy people are called פְּנֵי הָאָרֶץ, *the 'faces' of the earth,* 'since everyone's face is directed thoward them.'

Divrei David explains that *Rashi* departs from the simple meaning — *and the famine raged throughout the entire land* — because were that the intended meaning, the verse should have read: וְהָרָעָב הָיָה עַל פְּנֵי כָל הָאָרֶץ, *and the famine was upon the face* [i.e. surface] *of all the land.* Since the verse reads עַל כָּל פְּנֵי הָאָרֶץ, *upon all the face of the earth, Rashi* pursues the Midrashic interpretation.

Additionally, this exegesis that *the 'face' of all the land* refers to the *wealthy* whom the famine affected, rather than to the *surface* of the land itself, is inspired by the fact that following the latter interpretation this verse would be superfluous. We already know from verses 44 and 55 that the famine raged throughout the land *(Devek Tov).*

The famine is said to have affected the wealthy because poor people are accustomed to hunger, and take the suffering in stride. For the wealthy, however, it is different — they are unfamiliar with hunger, and they suffer from it most *(Yalkut Yehudah).*

The poor people did not suffer so much at first because they ate the moldy bread. The wealthy people who are accustomed to dine on delicacies felt the

tacked the city and massacred its inhabitants (34:25). The Egyptians were afraid that Joseph was demanding that they submit to circumcision because he had a similar plan in mind.

"Foolish people" laughed Pharaoh. "You think that Joseph has to resort to such tricks? Who do you think made all our private stores of grain rot? You have no idea of this man's power. If he wishes, he can decree that we all die. You have no other choice but to do as he bids!"

56 *When the famine spread over all the face of the earth, Joseph opened all the containers and sold provisions to Egypt. And the famine became severe*

deprivation most acutely *(Oznaim laTorah).*

Akeidas Yitzchak suggests, to the contrary, that in the literal sense the verse is telling us that the famine reached such proportions that the whole 'face of the earth' was dry and parched; even the cattle had no pasture.

Ramban similarly maintains that this verse magnifies the severity of the famine. He explains that contextually the implication of the verse is that Joseph did not open his storehouses until those of the people were completely deleted. When they first complained to Pharaoh *(v.* 55), however, he ignored them, because people tend to cry out as soon as there is the least shortage.

וַיִּפְתַּח יוֹסֵף אֶת־כָּל־אֲשֶׁר בָּהֶם — *[And] Joseph opened all the containers.*

The passage literally reads: *And Joseph opened all that had within them.* The commentators agree that the phrase is clearly elliptic [מִקְרָא קָצֵר, *a 'shortened' passage,* i.e., a passage in which omitted words are to be understood] and the words *storehouses* and *grain* are implied. The translation follows *Rashi* who explains that the verse should be understood as *Onkelos* paraphrases it: *Joseph opened all the storehouses in which there was grain.*

[It may also be that the implied object of Joseph's opening was storehouses which contained the לֶחֶם, *bread,* that the Egyptians requested in *v.* 55].

According to *Sforno,* Joseph opened the granaries in order to reassure the populace that he had ample supplies for them and there was no cause for alarm.

It is obvious that Joseph did not open all the granaries simultaneously, or else he would have lost personal control of them and a great loss would have resulted. Rather, the intent is that he ordered them opened as needed *(R' Shmuel ben Chofni Gaon).*

וַיִּשְׁבֹּר לְמִצְרַיִם — *And [he] sold [provisions] to Egypt* [i.e. *to the Egyptians (Targum Yonasan; R' Saadiah Gaon)*].

I.e., he sold to Egyptians before selling to others *(Tur).*

The verb שבר can denote either selling or buying. Here it signifies *selling* while in 42:2 it signifies *buying.* The term is not used *exclusively* of trading in *grain* [as the noun form שֶׁבֶר, *grain,* would lead one to believe] for we find the term used also of trading in wine and milk [*Isaiah* 55:1] *(Rashi).*

Rashi thus teaches us that although the verb שבר almost invariably occurs in reference to the trading of *grain* — as in our verse where the word שֶׁבֶר or בָּר, *grain,* is the implied object being sold; it by no means is used exclusively for that. It is not a denominative verb formed from שֶׁבֶר, *grain,* but its meaning is extended to apply to trading in any food, or as its use in *Isaiah* makes clear, to such specific articles of food as wine and milk *(Rashbam; Tzeidah laDerech).*

Radak explains that food is called *shever* [lit. 'break'] because it 'breaks' hunger. Hence the verb *shavar* refers to trading in food.

Haamek Davar maintains that the verb *shavar* [lit. *break*] refers to selling food in small ['broken'] quantities — rationing.[1]

1. Cf. *R' Hirsch* who also explains the verb as referring to sales in measured quantities.

He explains that Joseph would sell only quantities sufficient for the immediate requirements of each family. Only in this way could he prevent speculative buying and hoarding. As our Sages remark, people had to present themselves personally; nothing was sold to slaves, or

נז בְּאֶרֶץ מִצְרָיִם: וְכָל־הָאָרֶץ בָּאוּ מִצְרַיְמָה
לִשְׁבֹּר אֶל־יוֹסֵף כִּי־חָזַק הָרָעָב בְּכָל־
א הָאָרֶץ: וַיַּרְא יַעֲקֹב כִּי יֶשׁ־שֶׁבֶר בְּמִצְרָיִם

וַיֶּחֱזַק הָרָעָב בְּאֶרֶץ מִצְרָיִם — [*And*] *the famine became severe in the land of Egypt.*

— Even in all kinds of food, in addition to bread (*Sforno*).

They ate, but were not satiated (*R' Bachya*).

57. וְכָל הָאָרֶץ בָּאוּ מִצְרַיְמָה לִשְׁבֹּר אֶל יוֹסֵף — *And all* [*inhabitants of*] *the earth came to Egypt unto Joseph to buy provisions.*

And all the earth refers specifically to the people of the three countries *adjacent to* Egypt (*Ramban v.* 54 following the *Midrash*).

According to the Sages in *Pesachim* 119a, however, the implication is that people of all the countries of the *whole world* came to buy grain in Egypt. Joseph accordingly amassed all the silver and gold of the world and stored it in Egypt. This formed the treasure that the Israelites later took with them when they left Egypt.[1] *Pirkei d'Rabbi Eliezer* 11 derives from this verse that Joseph was one of the ten kings who, in effect, reigned throughout the entire world.

The Hebrew of this verse literally reads: *And all the land* (or: *earth*) *came to Egypt to buy to Joseph. Rashi* maintains that for comprehension the word order must be transposed [as in our translation] as if it read: *to Egypt to Joseph to buy.* For if one were to explain the passage in the order the words are written, it should have stated: לִשְׁבֹּר מִן יוֹסֵף, to buy *from* [rather than *to*] Joseph.

In its simplest sense, the verse — structured as it is — sequentially informs us first that *all the earth came to Egypt* after which it states their reason for coming — *to buy provisions,* and for this purpose their destination was specifically to *Joseph* (*Ibn Caspi*).

כִּי חָזַק הָרָעָב בְּכָל הָאָרֶץ — *For the famine had become severe in all the earth.*

— I.e. in the lands adjacent to

a man could send fifty slaves; each person was allowed to bring only one beast of burden with him, and everybody had to come to Joseph. He attended the sales personally, not depending on subordinate officials, but coming into direct contact with the hungry householders who came to buy. That is why the following chapter says in *v.* 6: יוֹסֵף הוּא הַשַּׁלִּיט הוּא הַמַּשְׁבִּיר, *Joseph, he was the viceroy over the land, he was the provider.* Although he was the שַׁלִּיט, *the viceroy,* he himself was the מַשְׁבִּיר, *the provider.*

These necessary and wise methods brought about all that ensued. Only because each purchaser had to meet Joseph did it happen that he *himself* came into contact with his brothers. The repeated description of the famine's severity gives the cause for all these precautions.

1. That Egypt was to amass all this wealth is perceived in the *Zohar* and Kabbalistic literature as one of the Providential reasons that Egypt was subjected to this famine.

In addition to the fact that the sale of Joseph and ensuing famine were the vehicles whereby Jacob and his family were brought down to Egypt to begin the exile foretold to Abraham in chapter 15, the famine itself was God's way, in a sense, of providing the cure before the disease.

When God decreed to Abraham that his offspring would be enslaved, He promised him that *afterward they will leave with great wealth* [15:14]. At the time Joseph arrived in Egypt, however, it was a poor country and had very little wealth. Providence therefore arranged for a wide-spread famine in which everyone would have to come to Egypt to purchase grain. As a result of this, Egypt would become fabulously wealthy in anticipation of the Israelites' descent.

41 *in the land of Egypt.* [57] *All the earth came to Egypt*
57 *unto Joseph to buy provisions, for the famine had*
become severe in all the earth.

42
1 [1] *Jacob perceived that there were provisions in*

Egypt [see *v.* 4] *(Midrash; Ramban);* or the whole world (the Sages in the *Talmud).*

It was only after Joseph ascertained that the famine had become severe in the other lands as well that he allowed non-Egyptians to come and purchase grain. Until them, as noted, he restricted sales to Egyptians *(Akediah;* cf. *Tur).*

XLII

1. The brothers in Egypt.

It is now in the second year of the famine *(Seder Olam).* Although his family still has a supply of provisions, Jacob is concerned. He dispatches his sons to Egypt.

וַיַּרְא יַעֲקֹב כִּי יֶשׁ־שֶׁבֶר בְּמִצְרָיִם — *[And] Jacob perceived* [lit. *saw*] *that there were provisions* [lit. *purchase*] *in Egypt.*

The commentators discuss the connotation of the verb *saw* in this context:

— He literally *saw* travelers bearing wheat. When he asked them whence they were coming they replied from Egypt. This is what he meant by saying [next verse], Behold I have *heard,* etc. (*Radak;* however, comp. *Rashi* in footnote who maintains that prophetic perception is meant).[1]

According to *Ibn Ezra* the expression *saw* is synonymous with *heard.* Since the five senses originate in the brain the verb describing the perception made by one sense is often substituted for another.Compare, for example [27:27]: רְאֵה רֵיחַ בְּנִי, *See* the fragrance of my son [where *see* figuratively means *smell*]; *Ecclesiastes* 11:7: *sweet is the light* [where 'sweet' must be allegorical because sweetness cannot refer to light]. [Cf. also *Exodus* 20:15: *'Saw* (i.e. *heard)* the thunderings.'] Here, too, *saw* is to be understood to mean *heard* as in *v.* 2. [Comp. *Rambam, Moreh Nevuchim* 1:46.]

'See' in this context does not refer to *visual,* but *mental* perception [lit. 'see-

1. *Rashi* pursues what appears to be the Midrashic interpretation:

"Where did Jacob 'see' [that there were provisions]? Surely he did not 'see' it but he *heard* it [from travelers returning from Egypt], as he said [*v.* 27]: *'Behold I have heard ...'*

What then is meant by *and Jacob saw?* It means that he saw in a holy *ispaklaria** that there was *shever* (provisions) [or *sever* (hope) (see below)] for him in Egypt. However, it was not a literal prophecy informing him specifically that it was Joseph."

According to the view of most commentators *Rashi* refers to the Midrash that in-

* [Aramaic אִסְפַּקְלַרְיָא, lit. *glass* — 'mirror' or 'lens'. The Sages use this simile to describe prophecy. Since the human mind does not have the faculty directly to perceive the Divine, the prophet's perception is likened to having been seen through a dull mirror or lens. Figuratively the clarity of a prophecy varies with the quality and cleanliness of the *ispaklaria* [sometimes vowelized *aspaklaria*]. Of all the prophets only Moses is said to have prophesied as if through a perfectly clear *ispaklaria.* See *Yevamos* 49b and *comm.* there. See also *Rashi* and *comm.* to *Numbers* 12:6.]

ב וַיֹּאמֶר יַעֲקֹב לְבָנָיו לָמָּה תִּתְרָאוּ: וַיֹּאמֶר

ing of the heart']. Proof of this is that Jacob said [*v.* 2], Behold I *heard* rather than, Behold I *saw (R' Bachya).*

שֶׁבֶר – *Provisions.*

This translation reflects the contextual sense of the word. The term *shever* is explained at length in 40:56.

Midrashically [see footnote] the word *shever* is equated with *sever*, hope. Kabbalistically, the word *shever* is used in this context to denote *provisions*, instead of the more common terms אֹכֶל, *food*, or בָּר, *grain*, because *shever* also has the connotation of *ruin; exile* [see *Isaiah* 51:19]. This latter interpretation also alludes to Jacob's foresight in recognizing that their descent into Egypt would fulfill the exile foretold to Abraham. Thus through the ambiguity of the term, Jacob was referring both to the *hope* of obtaining *provisions*, as well as to the *calamity* awaiting him and his family in Egypt *(R' Bachya)*. There is also an opinion that *shever* means *in-*

terprets שֶׁבֶר as *sever*, hope and the meaning of *Rashi* is that Jacob saw that there was 'hope' for him in Egypt. A verbatim translation of *Bereishis Rabbah* 91:6 from which *Rashi* presumably derives this interpretation follows:

> Now Jacob saw that there was *shever* in Egypt. Was then Jacob in Egypt that Scripture says that he **saw** that there was *shever* in Egypt? Did he not say to his sons, 'Behold I have **heard** that there is *shever* in Egypt?' Since the day that Joseph was stolen, however, the Holy Spirit departed from Joseph so that he saw yet did not see, heard yet did not hear [i.e. his prophetic perception was imperfect]. Now, why does it not say 'Jacob saw there was בָּר, *grain*,' or 'there was אֹכֶל, *food*,' but there was *'shever'* [*provisions; rations*]? — Read not *shever* but *sever* [hope]:
>
> "Jacob saw in the *ispaklaria* that his *hope* was in Egypt. — Who was this? — Joseph."

Thus, the commentators explain, since the verses are inconsistent in their use of *seeing* and *hearing*, and the term *shever* rather than *grain* is used, *Rashi* follows the Midrashic interpretation that Jacob was privy to a *quasi-prophetic revelation* by which he 'saw' that *hope* awaited him in Egypt. Unknown to Jacob, the revelation referred to Joseph.

[Since the vision was somewhat unclear and since Jacob would not boast about matters of prophecy, when relating it to his sons in *v.* 2, he described his perception as 'hearing' rather than 'seeing' — and at the same time shielded this prophetic intimation from his children who probably understood his remark in the literal sense (see *Yafeh Toar* and *Bereishis Rabbah* 91:1).]

[What is difficult, however, according to the commentators mentioned above, is why *Rashi* — who is usually so clear in his comments — does not state clearly that his exegesis is based on the premise that the *Midrash* interprets the unvocalized word שבר, *shever* as if it were to be read *sever*, 'hope', rather than in its contextual sense of *the sale of the provisions.*

[Possibly *Rashi* prefers not to depart from the literal, contextual,meaning of *shever* (spelled with a *shin*) meaning *provisions*, omitting the reference to the reading of *sever*, hope. He utilizes the Midrash only to explain the surprising term 'saw' instead of 'heard,' but he blends the Midrashic exegesis into the plain meaning of the verse. Thus he interprets that Jacob *saw* in an *ispaklaria* that there were *provisions* in Egypt.]

[In any case, *Rashi* is providing us with a very fundamental premise in the workings of prophecy. A prophet does not always comprehend the *whole* message of his prophecy; he is allowed to perceive only that portion of the Divine message which God wishes to reveal to him. In this case, though Jacob was granted the quasi-prophetic insight that there was *shever* for him in Egypt, he was not granted the knowledge that this would involve Joseph.]

Egypt. So Jacob said to his sons, "Why do you make yourselves conspicuous?" 2 *And he said, "Behold, I*

terpretation [see *Judges* 7:15], and that the connotation is that Jacob perceived that the *interpretation of Joseph's dream* would be fulfilled in Egypt *(Shaarei Aharon).*

וַיֹּאמֶר יַעֲקֹב לְבָנָיו – *So* [lit. *and*] *Jacob said to his sons.*

All his sons were married by this time, and no longer at Jacob's table, as we can infer from the case of Judah who left home shortly after the sale of Joseph [38:1]. Cf. also the reference to their *households* in *v.* 19 below. It is to the brothers' credit that they all responded obediently to their father's call *(Abarbanel).*

לָמָּה תִּתְרָאוּ – *Why do you make yourselves conspicuous?* [lit. make yourselves seen]

Rashi offers several explanations:

Although we are not yet short of food, why do you show yourselves in the eyes of the children of Ishmael and Esau as having plenty [to eat]? [Such behavior will bring their envy and ill will *(Taanis* 10b, upon which this interpretation is based)].[1]

The commentators wonder why the Talmud speaks of envy on the part of the families of Ishmael and Esau, but not of the Canaanite neighbors of Jacob.

— *Ramban* suggests that people from Ishmael and Esau might pass through Canaan on their way to Egypt and, seeing that Jacob had food, they would avail themselves of Jacob's hospitality coming to him for free meals. The result would be that his resources would be depleted quickly. Jacob therefore cautioned that they be more prudent with the provisions they had.

— *Mizrachi* postulates that the land of Canaan *did* have food; the shortage had affected only the southern lands of Ishmael and Esau who would seek to take advantage of Jacob's apparent wealth and generosity.

Maharsha (Taanis 10b) offers that many Canaanites, too, lacked food, but relatives are more likely than strangers to feel envy. The children of Ishmael and Esau, as Jacob's cousins and nephews, fit into this category.

— Thus, *'why'* in this context is not a question, but an exclamation of incredulity: How can you make yourselves conspicuous at such a time! Furthermore, that Jacob's family still had grain at that time is evident from the fact that the brothers did not go on their own volition until Jacob exhorted them. This occurred in the second year of the famine as indicated by 45:6 *(Mizrachi).*

Rashi continues: It appears to me however that the expression simply means [*why should you cause yourselves to be looked upon? (Divrei David)*] — *why should*

1. The context of *Taanis* 10b from which *Rashi* cites this interpretation is a discussion of how one should conduct himself when going to a place where the local residents are fasting on account of some calamity:

'The Rabbis have taught: ... If one journeys from a place where they do not fast to a place where they do, he should fast with them ... If he forgot and ate and drank, let him not make it obvious in public [and appear like a groom among mourners, thereby arousing their envy *(Rashi* ad. loc.)], nor may he indulge in delicacies [and reason that since he already ate something insignificant he might as well eat more *(ibid.)*], as it is written: *Why do you make yourselves conspicuous?* Jacob conveyed thereby to his sons, 'When you are fully sated do not show yourselves [that you have much of grain (*ibid.*)] either before Esau or Ishmael so that they should not envy you.' "

[Accordingly, the brothers went to Egypt only to avoid being conspicuous before the descendants of Esau and Ishmael who were starving at the time (ibid.).]

הִנֵּה שָׁמַעְתִּי כִּי יֶשׁ־שֶׁבֶר בְּמִצְרָיִם רְדוּ־
שָׁמָּה וְשִׁבְרוּ־לָנוּ מִשָּׁם וְנִחְיֶה וְלֹא נָמוּת׃

everyone look at you and wonder why you do not seek food before your stock is depleted? From others I heard [*Tosafos* ad. loc. s.v. למה cites the following interpretation in the name of a *Midrash*] that it has the meaning of *weakness:* Why should you become weakened through hunger? Similar to this is *Proverbs* 11:25 וּמַרְוֶה גַּם הוּא יוֹרֶא, *he that satiates* [others] *will himself also be satiated.*[1]

Sforno renders: *Why do you look at one another — each one waiting for the other to go?* Cf. the Talmudic proverb [*Eruvin* 3a]: קְדֵירָה דְשׁוּתָּפֵי לֹא חֲמִימָא וְלֹא קְרִירָא, 'A pot supervised by two chefs is neither hot nor cold' [for each relies upon the other].

R' Hirsch renders similarly. He explains that Jacob correctly assumed that only individual householders could purchase rations in Egypt — one could not buy on behalf of another; everyone had to appear personally. The sons apparently believed otherwise, and looked at one another, each waiting for one to go on behalf of them all. But Jacob deduced the truth of the rumor from the urgency of the conditions and said, 'Why are you looking at each other? You must all go down yourselves.'

Heidenheim rejects the above interpretations, maintaining that the *hispael* [reflexive] form תִּתְרָאוּ does not refer to one person looking at another, but to each person observing his own appearance as in *Rashi's* interpretation.

Tur cites an interpretation similar to *Sforno's*, but explains תִּתְרָאוּ as alluding to *contention; warfare;* as in *II Kings* 14:8. They argued with one another regarding who should go to Egypt, so Jacob reprimanded them: *Why do you contend with one another?* (So *Ibn Ezra).*

Targum Yonasan relates it to the root ירא meaning *fear*, and renders: 'Why do you *fear* going down to Egypt?' [*Karnei Or* notes, however, that according to this interpretation the Hebrew should have read תִּירְאוּ or תִּתְיָרְאוּ.] [2]

According to the Midrash, Jacob's admonition was: Do not travel with food in your hands lest you cause ill

1. The commentators on *Rashi* differ as to which of the interpretations the proof verse from *Proverbs* supports. According to some views, most notably *Mizrachi,* it appears to support the *first* explanation: *Rashi* cited the proof verse after mentioning the alternate interpretation to emphasize the contrast between them. Thus,Rashi seemingly takes תִּתְרָאוּ [lit. *make yourselves seen*] to be of the root רוה [*satiate*] as if it were written תִּתְרָוּ [*why do you make yourselves appear satiated?*]. *The letters* א and ו frequently interchange [cf. for example *Psalms* 91:16: וְאַרְאֵהוּ=וְאַרְוֵהוּ; *Job 10:16* וּרְאֵה=וּרְוֵא]. A similar form of the root רוה occurring with an א is the word יורא is *Prov. 11:25* as quoted by *Rashi.*

According to others [see *Chizkuni*], a proof verse must be taken to support the immediately preceding interpretation — *why should you become weakened?* Therefore in *Proverbs* רוה means *satiated* while in our verse it means *weakened by hunger,* since the word is among those that have opposite meanings depending upon the context. Comp. דשן*: to fatten/to remove ashes;* שרש*: root/uproot;* שבר*: buy/sell.*

See also *Maharsha ad. loc.* s.v. א״ל יעקב who defends the latter view against *Mizrachi* and maintains that יוֹרֶא with an א means *weaken,* and explains the verse in *Proverbs* accordingly.

R' David Feinstein contends that the very structure of the verses in *Proverbs* strongly favors the interpretation that this stich means the *opposite* of sated. In *Proverbs,* half of each verse contrasts with the connotation of the other half. Therefore, since the verse begins with a reference to satiety, the word מַרְוֶה in its second stich can only mean the opposite. He wonders why the commentators ad. loc. — including *Rashi* — do not mention this. [See *Sefer HaZikaron and Bertinoro* who indeed maintain that the verse in *Proverbs* must be interpreted according to the third interpretation cited by *Rashi.*]

42 *have heard that there are provisions in Egypt. Go*
2 *down there and purchase for us from there, that we*

feeling, and [as you enter Egypt] do not all enter through one gate for fear of the evil eye [which someone might cast through envy that one man should be blessed with ten such sons.]

2. וַיֹּאמֶר — *And he said.*

[The repetition of *and he said* implies a renewed plea. Apparently Jacob's sons did not take his hint. He found it necessary to instruct them explicitly.]

הִנֵּה שָׁמַעְתִּי כִּי יֶשׁ־שֶׁבֶר בְּמִצְרָיִם — *Behold I have heard that there are provisions for sale in Egypt.*

[See above *v.* 1 s.v. וַיַּרְא.]

רְדוּ שָׁמָּה — *Go down there.*

Jacob did not use the verb לְכוּ, *go,* but רְדוּ [*go down*] thereby hinting at the 210 years [the numerical value of the word רְדוּ (ר=200; ד=4; ו=6)] they would be enslaved in Egypt *(Rashi).*

[God informed Abraham at the Covenant Between the Parts (15:13) that his descendants would be exiled for 400 years. The 400 year duration of the exile was reckoned from Isaac's birth. The actual period they were *enslaved in Egypt,* however, from Jacob's arrival there until the Exodus, was 210 years, corresponding to the numerical equivalent of רְדוּ. (See calculations in *Rashi* to 15:13 s.v. אַרְבַּע מֵאוֹת שָׁנָה, p. 527).]

The Sages derive this exegesis from the fact that telling one to 'descend' is an expression with demeaning spiritual connotations, and one which Jacob would have avoided unless he had a specific intention in using it. Even though Scriptural narrative frequently uses 'descent' to describe one who journeys from *Eretz Yisrael* — the 'highest of all the lands' [see 13:1] — to Egypt [see 12:10] as in *v.* 3 below, it should be avoided in direct speech since it is demeaning to the one being addressed. Accordingly Jacob would never have used the expression had he not been alluding to the 210 years of bondage *(Gur Aryeh; Bertinoro).*

Since one's own field supplied one's needs in ancient times, it was regarded a misfortune to purchase grain from another. The Midrash derived this from Jacob's charge to his sons: '*Go down* to Egypt' — implying that one who must purchase grain from the market has gone down in status.

On two successive occasions, here and in 43:2, Jacob insisted that his sons go to Egypt. He who had so much hoped to live peacefully in Canaan — see *comm.* to וַיֵּשֶׁב יַעֲקֹב (37:1) — was now compelled by necessity to indicate descent into the land of Exile. Thus, the Divine Will progressively comes to be realized despite the reluctance of people *(R' Munk).*

וְשִׁבְרוּ לָנוּ מִשָּׁם — *And purchase for us from there.*

Here the verb שבר means *purchase (Rashi* 41:56).

From there — rather than from the local traders who charge exorbitant prices *(Malbim).*

Jacob did not specify that they

2. Cf. *R' Munk* who writes that Jacob noticed his sons' apprehension about making this journey. They looked at one another with worry and embarrassment. When Abraham traveled to Egypt to escape famine, he went through severe anguish. In Isaac's time of famine, God forbade him to go to Egypt. And as for themselves, the very thought of going to Egypt reminded them that they had sold Joseph into a slavery that had Egypt as its final destination. Were *they* now to go there, would not Egypt again become a scene of adversity for the patriarchal family? Furthermore, they had a premonition that Egypt would become the land of exile announced long before to Abraham. Jacob sought to calm their fears by telling them (*v.* 2): *Behold I have heard that* [*despite everything*] *there* is *hope in Egypt;* go down there. [As noted in *v.* 2, רְדוּ, *go down,* has the numerical value of 210 and portends that the actual enslavement in Egypt was to last 210 years instead of the 400 years announced to Abraham]. Despite the trials and persecutions of the exile, we shall survive.''

ג וַיֵּרְדוּ אֲחֵי־יוֹסֵף עֲשָׂרָה לִשְׁבֹּר בָּר
ד מִמִּצְרָיִם: וְאֶת־בִּנְיָמִין אֲחִי יוֹסֵף לֹא־
שָׁלַח יַעֲקֹב אֶת־אֶחָיו כִּי אָמַר פֶּן־יִקְרָאֶנּוּ

purchase *grain* but used the more ambiguous term *shever* since, as noted in *v.* 1, the term *shever* carried an additional connotation of the calamity [lit. *breaking*] — exile — that he knew they would experience with their descent there. This is also the connotation of *and we will live and not die,* for despite the numerous future exiles the children of Israel were to endure, Jacob knew they would not be annihilated, but would thrive *(R' Bachya).*

וְנִחְיֶה וְלֹא נָמוּת — That [lit. *and*] *we may live and* [*we may*] *not die.*

— When our present supplies are depleted. As noted, at that time they still had provisions *(Maharsha, Taanis 10b s.v.* לֹא בִּפְנֵי עֵשָׂו; see *Rashi in footnote* to *v.* 1).

Jacob was cautioning them to be frugal with the meager amount they had left, and purchase additional supplies lest they die when their stock became depleted ... The correct interpretation appears to be, however, that their provisions had by this time been nearly exhausted and they were in mortal danger unless they quickly replenished their supplies *(Ramban v.* 1).

That we may *live* — not luxuriously, but that we may buy enough food to keep alive *and not die* of hunger *(Sforno).*

3. וַיֵּרְדוּ אֲחֵי יוֹסֵף עֲשָׂרָה — *So* [lit. *and*] *Joseph's brothers — ten (of them) — went down.*

— Not because they were in dire need at that time, but to avoid appearing conspicuous before the descendants of Esau who were distressed and hungry *(Rashi Sotah* 10b s.v. אַל תִּרְאוּ לָמָּה תִּתְרָאוּ; see *Rashi* and *Ramban* above).

Why did all ten brothers have to go?

All had to go because the Egyptians would not sell any one more food than was needed for a single household lest the purchaser trade in grain as often happens during a famine *(Sforno).*[1]

And as *Abarbanel* explains, by this time each of the sons was married [so each had to go individually to acquire sufficient rations for his own household.]

The phraseology of this passage — *the brothers of Joseph—ten* is somewhat redundant and *Rashi,* basing his comment on *Midrash Tanchuma,* elicits the implication of the expressions:

— They are described as *Joseph's brothers* rather than as Jacob's sons, to imply that they regretted having sold him and were resolved to act as brothers

1. The Midrashim record that Joseph had promulgated several decrees in anticipation of his brothers' arrival:

a) No slave may enter Egypt to buy grain. [This was in order to ensure that the brothers *themselves* would come]; b) no one might come with two donkeys. [This was to avoid hoarding by individuals and assure that *all* of the brothers would have to come]; c) no one may enter without registering his own name, his father's and his grandfather's. Furthermore Joseph ordered that the lists of everyone who entered the gates of Egypt be brought to him daily.

Now when Joseph's brothers came to Egypt, they did not all enter through the same gate [see *Midrash* cited end of *v.* 1, and *Rashi* to *v.* 12 s.v. כִּי עֶרְוַת]. When Joseph saw the names 'Reuben son of Jacob, son of Isaac,' 'Simeon son of Jacob, son of Isaac', etc. listed on the various gatekeepers' lists, he realized that his brothers had arrived. So he sent his son Menasseh to watch where they were going, and he found them walking about the various markets

may live and not die." 3 *So Joseph's brothers — ten of them — went down to buy grain from Egypt.* 4 *But Benjamin, Joseph's brother, Jacob did not send along with his brothers, for he said, "Lest disaster befall*

toward him and secure his freedom from slavery at any cost.

— Inasmuch as it is stated [*v.* 4] that Benjamin stayed behind, we know that ten brothers went; why is the number mentioned? It implies that in regard to their feelings of brotherhood [i.e., their role as אֲחֵי יוֹסֵף, *brothers of Joseph*] they were עֲשָׂרָה, *ten* different individuals, inasmuch as they did not have the same degree of love or hate for him; they *were* unanimous, however, in their purpose of לִשְׁבֹּר בָּר מִמִּצְרָיִם, *to buy grain from Egypt (Rashi;* cf. *Midrash).*

4. וְאֶת בִּנְיָמִין אֲחִי יוֹסֵף וכו׳ — *But* [lit. *and*] *Benjamin, Joseph's brother, Jacob did not send along with his brothers.* [Or: *But Jacob did not send Joseph's brother Benjamin along with his brothers.*]

Joseph's brother, i.e., his *full* brother from the same mother and father. Because of what had happened to Joseph, Jacob was afraid to send Benjamin with them *(Radak).*

It was destined from Above that Benjamin — who had not participated in the sale of Joseph — not accompany them so that he would be spared their tribulations in Egypt. Although admittedly he suffered along with them when he joined them on their second trip, he was compensated for this by having the intense joy of meeting Joseph *(Oznaim l'Torah).*

פֶּן־יִקְרָאֶנּוּ אָסוֹן — *'Lest disaster befall him'.*

— But could not disaster befall him at home? R' Eliezer ben Yaakov said, We may infer from this that הַשָּׂטָן מְקַטְרֵג בִּשְׁעַת הַסַּכָּנָה, *the Satan accuses in a time of danger* [i.e., there is generally a greater danger on the road than at home, and the Satan maliciously capitalizes upon the traveler's vulnerability to danger by seizing the opportunity to lay his sins before God so that misfortune should readily befall him while en route] *(Rashi).*

Jacob's feared possible consequences of a journey because such dangers as wild beasts and brigands are more prevalent on the road than near home where one can protect himself from the elements. In general, one must avoid places of danger. Even a righteous man should not rely on his righteousness and hope for a possible miracle, for even if a miracle is wrought for him, it will be deducted from his merits [*Shabbos* 32a; cf. footnote to 32:11 (p. 1422)]. This was the reason for Jacob's apprehension *(Radak).*

Why should Jacob have been more apprehensive about Benjamin than any

and streets, Joseph had them brought before him and immediately he recognized them, but they did not recognize him.

According to another Midrash, when Joseph learned that his brothers were in Egypt, he ordered all the granaries closed except for one, and he left orders that he be notified when his brothers appear.

Several days passed and they did not come. So he sent for them and they were found in a street of prostitutes where they had gone to search for Joseph, fearing, because he was so handsome, that he might have been forcefully placed in a brothel.

It was in this way that they were apprehended, and the stage was set for them to be brought to Joseph.

אָסוֹן: וַיָּבֹאוּ בְּנֵי יִשְׂרָאֵל לִשְׁבֹּר בְּתוֹךְ ה
הַבָּאִים כִּי־הָיָה הָרָעָב בְּאֶרֶץ כְּנָעַן:
ו וְיוֹסֵף הוּא הַשַּׁלִּיט עַל־הָאָרֶץ הוּא
הַמַּשְׁבִּיר לְכָל־עַם הָאָרֶץ וַיָּבֹאוּ אֲחֵי

other of his children? Benjamin was no child at this time; he must have already been about thirty years old.

— He was the only remaining child of Rachel, and was therefore irreplaceable *(B'chor Shor).*

[Cf. *Rashi* to 44:29 who quotes Jacob as saying: While Benjamin is with me I find comfort in him for the loss of his mother and his brother; if he should die it will seem to me as though the three of them died on the same day.]

According to *Midrash HaChefetz* cited in *Torah Sheleimah,* Jacob reasoned: It may have been decreed that the sons of Rachel should perish on the road. I sent Joseph on a journey and he did not return; the same might happen to Benjamin if I send him, for their mother, too, died on the road [48:7; comp. *Rashi* to 44:22]. [1]

The term פֶּן, *lest,* implies a fear that an *undesired event* will take place, while אוּלַי, *perhaps,* implies a hope that an event *will* occur *(HaKsav V'HaKabbalah* to 24:39; 27:12).

אָסוֹן — *Disaster.*

I.e., death *(Ibn Ezra).*

The Talmud [*Kesubos* 30a] defines the term in this context as a general reference to all possible misfortunes, whether acts of God or human violence. As examples, the Sages give attacks by lions and thieves, and cold and heat [see *Proverbs* 22:5 and *comm.* there].

5. וַיָּבֹאוּ בְּנֵי יִשְׂרָאֵל לִשְׁבֹּר בְּתוֹךְ הַבָּאִים — *[And] the sons of Israel came to buy provisions, among the arrivals.*

— They kept themselves inconspicuous by mingling among the many other arriving purchasers, for Jacob had instructed them to enter the city individually by separate entrances so that the 'evil eye' might not harm them [if they attracted envy] for they were all handsome, strong men *(Rashi; Tanchuma).*

According to *Sforno,* the implication of *among the arrivals* is that they traveled in large groups as protection against bandits who would be particularly rampant at a time of famine.

That they are referred to here as *the sons of Israel* in contrast with *v.* 3 where they were called *Joseph's brothers* is perceived in *Bereishis Rabbosi* to indicate that their father's merit accompanied them, for they were heeding his instructions.

R' Hirsch observes that this is the first time they are described as בְּנֵי יִשְׂרָאֵל, *the children of Israel.* This introduction of the new concept of Jewish nationhood is of major significance to the future of mankind,

1. *R' Hirsch* makes the emphatic point that יִקְרָאֶנּוּ [*befall*] in our context means *will 'call' him.* Jacob feared that Benjamin might be going in one direction, but something might occur which would figuratively 'call' him away from that direction.

But if קרא, is a *call,* there must be a 'Caller'. The common translation of the related expression מִקְרֶה as *happening,* is heathenish. Nothing 'happens' by chance; everything is engineered. Of all the creatures in the universe, only Man has the power of moral free will to decide his actions.

All influences, happy or otherwise, that deflect an object or person from its natural or chosen direction are called מִקְרֶה, *chance.* But to God, the Cause, there is no chance. To the Great Master of Plans it was not 'chance,' but destiny. [Comp. *R' Hirsch's comm.* to 24:12.]

him." [5] *So the sons of Israel come to buy provisions among the arrivals, for the famine prevailed in the land of Canaan.*

[6] *Now Joseph, he was the viceroy over the land, he was the provider to all the populace. Joseph's*

but they were unconscious of it. They saw themselves merely as בְּתוֹךְ הַבָּאִים, *part of the overall crowd.*[2]

— However, though they came like other people, they enter Egypt as the moral unit of 'sons of Israel'. In the same role they will later move there, and as 'sons of Israel' they will be redeemed from there *(Akeidah).*

The historic name בְּנֵי יִשְׂרָאֵל, *children of Israel,* has already been used in 33:33 to designate the future nation. The title of honor is used at this ignominious juncture because the descent of the brothers into Egypt was of crucial importance for the future of the nation. It comes to remind us that their historic vocation is never lost in the miseries of exile, but it remains preserved in its entirety for the future *(R' Bachya* on 45:28).

כִּי־הָיָה הָרָעָב בְּאֶרֶץ כְּנָעַן — *For the famine prevailed in the land of Canaan.*

— Forcing many people to come from Canaan to Egypt to buy provisions *(Radak).*

[I.e., this phrase clarifies the earlier word הַבָּאִים, *the arrivals,* by explaining that it refers to the many Canaanites who traveled to Egypt because of the famine.

[It must be remembered that since Egypt was fertile and had never been affected by earlier famines, it was common for people to seek food in Egypt during times of hunger in their own lands. Abraham and Isaac also looked to Egypt when there were hungers in Canaan. Thus many Canaanites must have flocked to Egypt at this time, and the brothers entered its gates among them (see *Ramban* below).]

6. וְיוֹסֵף הוּא הַשַּׁלִּיט עַל הָאָרֶץ הוּא הַמַּשְׁבִּיר לְכָל־עַם הָאָרֶץ— *Now* [lit. *and*] *Joseph he was the viceroy over the land; he was the provider to all the populace* [lit. *to the people of the land*].

The verse implies that Joseph personally negotiated every transaction, but surely it was beneath his dignity as regent to handle every petty purchase. Therefore the Rabbis in the *Midrash* explain that Joseph ordered all the storehouses except one to be closed temporarily, so he would be sure to meet his brothers when they arrived there [see footnote to *v. 3*] *(Ramban).*

Ramban continues that the plain meaning of our passage is probably that people [i.e., representatives] from all lands came before Joseph. He would question them and then instruct his officials regarding how much to sell each locale and city. It was therefore necessary for the Canaanites, including the brothers, to appear before Joseph so he could

2. *Talmud Yerushalmi* [*Berachos* 7:3] derives from our verse that matters of holiness [e.g. *Kaddish, Kedushah, Barchu,* Reading of the Torah, Priestly Benediction, etc.] may not be recited in a quorum of less than ten men:

It is written here: *The sons* [lit. *children*] *of Israel,* and in *Levit.* 22:32 it is written *And I will be hallowed among the children of Israel.* Just as *children of Israel* written here refers to ten, so does *children of Israel* written there refer to ten. From this analogy we learn that matters of holiness may not be recited in a group of less than ten.

[In the Babylonian Talmud *(Megillah* 23b), this law is derived from other verses. See comm. to *Levit.* ibid. and *Torah Temimah.*]

ז יוֹסֵף וַיִּשְׁתַּחֲווּ־לוֹ אַפַּיִם אָרְצָה: וַיַּרְא
יוֹסֵף אֶת־אֶחָיו וַיַּכִּרֵם וַיִּתְנַכֵּר אֲלֵיהֶם
וַיְדַבֵּר אִתָּם קָשׁוֹת וַיֹּאמֶר אֲלֵהֶם מֵאַיִן
בָּאתֶם וַיֹּאמְרוּ מֵאֶרֶץ כְּנַעַן לִשְׁבָּר־אֹכֶל:

determine the amounts he would allocate to their country. This group was the first to arrive from Canaan [see *Ramban* to *v.* 9] and represented the entire country. *Ramban* to *v.* 9 surmises that the brothers may have been the very first arrivals from Canaan.

This follows *Radak* who adds that the term מַשְׁבִּיר is causative — he did not *personally* sell, but instructed his officials to sell, after personally interviewing each purchaser. Joseph insisted on this arrangement since he knew that his brothers would inevitably be forced to come to Egypt in search of grain because of the severe famine in Canaan.

Others maintain that the emphasis of this verse is to the contrary. Notwithstanding the fact that Joseph was the regent, he was involved in every sale, as the verse informs us. Inasmuch as the royal coffers derived a vast cash income from these sales [see 47:14, 15], he made it a firm rule that no sale could be made without his own seal or written authorization (cf. *Ralbag; Sforno).*

Pesikta Zutressa and *Or HaChaim* appear to suggest an even more personal participation by Joseph in each transaction, his purpose being, as noted, to assure that he did not miss seeing his brothers.

וַיִּשְׁתַּחֲווּ־לוֹ אַפַּיִם אָרְצָה — *And they bowed to him, faces to the ground.*

I.e., in total prostration upon their faces. The term הִשְׁתַּחֲוָאָה implies the stretching out of hands and feet *(Rashi;* from *Berachos* 34b *Megillah* 22b; *Shevuos* 16b).

[Cf. also *comm.* to 19:1.]

7. Joseph recognizes his brothers.

וַיַּרְא יוֹסֵף אֶת אֶחָיו וַיַּכִּרֵם — [And] *Joseph saw his brothers and he recognized them.*

I.e., as soon as he saw his brothers he recognized them *(Ramban).*

According to *Tz'ror HaMor* the phraseology suggests: At first he was not sure, so he carefully *looked at his brothers,* i.e. scrutinized them, and then he was sure.

At this point he recognized them *collectively* as his brothers, but could not yet distinguish them individually [see next verse] *(Ibn Ezra; Sforno).*

וַיִּתְנַכֵּר אֲלֵיהֶם וַיְדַבֵּר אִתָּם קָשׁוֹת — But [lit. and] *he acted like a stranger* [lit. *he made himself a stranger*] *toward them and spoke with them harshly.*

— Fearing that they might recognize him *(Ramban).*

The translation *acted like a stranger* by speaking harshly with them follows *Rashi,* who bases himself upon the Midrash.

— By speaking this way he hoped to confuse them and lessen the chance of their recognizing him. Normally, he spoke softly, but he was afraid they might recognize his voice *(Akeidah; Sforno).*

According to *Ramban,* the intent of וַיִּתְנַכֵּר is not *made himself a stranger* [נָכְרִי] as *Rashi* interprets, but that he *made himself unrecognizable* [see *Cur Zahav* cited by *R' Chavel*]. Fearing that his brothers might recognize him, Joseph concealed his identity perhaps

brothers came and they bowed to him, faces to the ground.

[7] Joseph saw his brothers and he recognized them, but he acted like a stranger toward them and spoke with them harshly. He asked them, "From where do you come?" And they said, "From the land of Ca-

by lowering his mitre to partially cover his face thereby disguising himself as Jeroboam's wife did [see *I Kings* 14:1, 5]. Or it means that he *disguised himself* by changing his voice and speaking to them in a gruff manner.

☙ Why did Joseph not reveal his identity to his brothers?

As discussed below in the comm. to *v.* 9, the commentators generally agree that Joseph's conduct toward his brothers was not a malicious attempt at vengeance. Rather he was motivated by the conviction that he had to secure the fulfillment of the prophetic dreams of his youth, something that was now made possible by his new eminence. He had never stopped believing his dreams. His special destiny, his astonishing rise to power, were they not all connected with dreams? He was apprehensive that if he were to reveal himself *now,* the brothers would:

(a) remind him that the dreaded oath of secrecy imposed upon him was still in force [see footnote to 37:28], for they would certainly not want their crime revealed to their father. He therefore devised a means to cause *them* to rescind the oath and reveal his whereabouts to Jacob *(B'chor Shor);* (b) they would insist that Jacob be sent for immediately — but Joseph knew that the fulfillment of his *second* dream called for Jacob to bow to him. First it was necessary to bring Benjamin before him so that all eleven brothers would bow in fulfillment of his *first* dream (see *Ramban* and comm. to *v.* 9).

Furthermore, as *R' Hirsch* makes clear below, virtually every action of Joseph was designed to test whether the brothers had changed — in filial devotion to Jacob, their love for Benjamin, and their sincere contrition for their crime against Joseph himself. [Perhaps they bore a hatred for all of Rachel's children, and had done away with Benjamin, too! *(Ralbag).*] Had he revealed himself to them now, these facts could not be established. It would merely have resulted in a reunion of a family where bitterness and enmity — perhaps worse than before — might have prevailed.

Abarbanel accordingly emphasizes that Joseph put his brothers to the test until he was convinced of all the above. At that point, however, he forgave them unreservedly, with all his love, because as Joseph later made clear, his mission was a Divine one [see 45:5]. However, though his heart overflowed with love, and he was moved to weeping while subjecting his brothers to this ordeal, he felt that he had to control himself and pretend to be a stranger, while he awakened their guilty conscience and brought about their repentence.

Onkelos renders the sense to be: וְחַשִׁיב מָה דְמַלִּיל לְהוֹן, *and he considered what he should say to them.*

The commentary to *Onkelos, HaMarpei,* writes that this interpretation is analogous with *Onkelos'* rendering of וַיִּתְנַכְּלוּ אוֹתוֹ [*they conspired against him*] in 37:18 as וְחַשִׁיבוּ עֲלוֹהִי, *they considered about him.* Following this opinion, it emerges that the Hebrew words וַיִּתְנַכְּלוּ and וַיִּתְנַכְּרוּ are synonyms, the letters ר and ל being interchangeable, as in the words מַזָּל and מַזָּר both synonymous for *constellation.* Accordingly, the connotation of *Onkelos* would be that Joseph was now repaying them measure for measure: because they *conspired* against him, he now feigned *strangeness* toward them. [In *I Kings* 14:5 the *Targum* renders מִתְנַכֵּרָה as מִשְׁתַּנְּיָא].

מֵאַיִן בָּאתֶם — *From where did you come?*

— Thus indicating that he did not recognize them *(Rashbam).*

ח וַיַּכֵּר יוֹסֵף אֶת־אֶחָיו וְהֵם לֹא הִכִּרֻהוּ׃
ט וַיִּזְכֹּר יוֹסֵף אֵת הַחֲלֹמוֹת אֲשֶׁר חָלַם

He asked the question angrily, as if it were unusual for strangers to come before him. It was also apparently a way of verifying that they were really his brothers *(Ramban)*.

מֵאֶרֶץ כְּנַעַן לִשְׁבָּר־אֹכֶל — *From the land of Canaan to buy food.*

Their overdone response to Joseph's inquiry gave ground for his accusation that they were spies. They should have replied simply, 'From the land of Canaan.' That they unnecessarily added 'to buy food,' implied that they were going out of their way to provide an excuse for their presence and avert suspicion *(Abarbanel; Malbim)*.[1]

8. וַיַּכֵּר יוֹסֵף אֶת־אֶחָיו — *Thus, Joseph recognized his brothers.*

Although *v.* 7 has told us that Joseph recognized his brothers, our verse reiterates the fact to emphasize that it was no mere coincidence that he had recognized them immediately, but not vice versa. Were that the case, Joseph could not have proceeded as he did, because of the danger that they might realize who he was. Therefore, the Torah stresses that he could easily recognize them, since, as *Rashi* observes [see below], they were bearded when he had last seen them and their appearance had not greatly changed. He, however, was then a beardless youth who had changed considerably in the intervening years. That being so, he was confident that he could proceed undetected *(Gur Aryeh)*.

That Joseph recognized Isaachar and Zevulon who were only a little older than he, and who were also presumably beardless when he last saw them, is no contradiction to the above. As *Ramban* observes, once he recognized the older brothers, he recognized each of them *(Divrei David)*.

According to *Ibn Ezra* the repetition intimates that while at first Joseph recognized them as his brothers only collectively as a group [*v.* 7], now, after additional scrutiny, he distinguished each one individually.

Ramban comments that after the brothers said they came from Canaan, Joseph had an additional sense of recognition regarding them. While his earlier recognition was somewhat vague, now he knew with absolute certainty that they were his brothers [*Akeidas Yitzchak*].

He recognized them with certainty by now because in the course of conversation they referred to each other by name *(Chizkuni)*.

וְהֵם לֹא הִכִּרֻהוּ — *But* [lit. *and*] *they did not recognize him.*

[I.e., his ruse was effective — they did not recognize him.]

The reason they did not recognize him was because he was now bearded while when they had last seen him [twenty-two years earlier when he was but a boy of seventeen years old] he had been beardless [*Kesubos* 27b] *(Rashi)*.[2]

Moreover, Joseph recognized them because he knew they would eventually come, but they did not recognize him because it never occurred to them that this great regent

1. They felt an inner compulsion to justify themselves for leaving the holy environs of *Eretz Yisrael*, a deed that is ordinarily sinful *(Bava Basra* 91a), unless it is absolutely necessary. Although they were standing before a 'gentile' ruler to whom such considerations would not apply, they wished to make clear that they left *Eretz Yisrael* only because of the severity of the famine *(Oznayim l'Torah)*.

naan to buy food." 8 *Thus, Joseph recognized his*
brothers but they did not recognize him.
9 *Joseph recalled the dreams that he dreamed about*

of Egypt before whom they now stood in trepidation could possibly be the young brother whom they had once sold into slavery *(Ramban;* comp. *Or HaChaim).*

And, as noted above, his identity was even further concealed by the fact that he was not referred to as Joseph, but as Tzafenas Paane'ach [41:45].

9. וַיִּזְכֹּר יוֹסֵף אֵת הַחֲלֹמוֹת אֲשֶׁר חָלַם לָהֶם — [*And*] *Joseph recalled the dreams that he had dreamed about them* [lit. *to them;* the translation *about them* (עֲלֵיהֶם=לָהֶם) follows *Rashi*].

[I.e., the dreams recorded in 37:7-9.]

He knew the dreams were fulfilled inasmuch as his brothers bowed down to him *(Rashi).*

☙ Joseph's motivation for the ordeal to which he subjected his brothers. [See also comm. to *v.* 7 above.]

Ramban disagrees with *Rashi's* comment that the dreams were now fulfilled. In a dissertation fundamental to a proper understanding of the narrative, *Ramban* maintains that when Joseph saw his brothers bowing down to him, he recalled the dreams and realized that *neither* of them had yet been completely fulfilled. He knew that the first dream required all *eleven* brothers to bow down to him, as indicated by the fact that he said [37:7], *'Behold, we were binding sheaves'* — 'we' referring to all eleven of his brothers. This was to be followed later by his father paying him homage as indicated by his second dream [see 37:9-10].

[Joseph perceived the dreams to be prophecies, therefore for him not to labor toward their fulfillment would be tantamount to "withholding prophecy" *(Haamek Davar).*] Accordingly, *Ramban* maintains since Benjamin was absent at this first meeting, Joseph arranged a scheme to bring him to Egypt so the first dream could be fulfilled. Only then could he reveal his true identity to them and bid them to summon Jacob so the second dream could be fulfilled.

Ramban emphasizes that were it not for such considerations, Joseph would have been guilty of a serious sin in inflicting anxiety on Jacob, first by sending his brothers home without Simeon and then by demanding that Benjamin be brought to him. He would surely have identified himself immediately and spared his father pain and worry. — Similarly, the anxiety Joseph later inflicted upon them by hiding the goblet in Benjamin's sack was for the sole purpose of testing their love for Benjamin before allowing him to travel with them.

Ramban continues that the above explains why Joseph, in all his years in Egypt, did not send a single letter to Jacob; even as a slave he could have done so since Egypt is only six days from Canaan. Even if it were a year's journey, Jacob would have spared nothing to

2. According to the Midrash, the deeper connotation of this verse is that the Torah provides us with a glimpse into the comparative brotherly attitudes of Joseph and his brothers:

Joseph recognized his brothers — now that they were in his power he [nevertheless] recognized them *as his brothers* and was merciful to them; *but they had not recognized him* — when he had fallen into their hands they failed to act toward him in a brotherly manner *(Rashi).*

The above exegesis is based upon the repetition in this verse of *his brothers,* the verse could have used a pronoun and said, *Joseph recognized 'them.'* Accordingly the Sages understood the repetition of *his brothers* to intimate that despite their helplessness, he recognized them *as brothers,* i.e., with brotherly feelings *(Gur Aryeh).*

לָהֶ֑ם וַיֹּ֤אמֶר אֲלֵהֶם֙ מְרַגְּלִ֣ים אַתֶּ֔ם
י לִרְא֛וֹת אֶת־עֶרְוַ֥ת הָאָ֖רֶץ בָּאתֶֽם׃ וַיֹּאמְר֥וּ

ransom him. But Joseph realized that the fulfillment of his dreams — the bowing, respectively, of his eleven brothers, and then of his father — could not possibly be accomplished in Canaan, and he hoped that it could be fulfilled now that he had attained eminence. The matter became even clearer to Joseph when he heard Pharaoh's dreams; he understood from them that his family was destined to come to Egypt in quest of grain and his dreams would be fulfilled. [Other reasons for Joseph's failure to contact Jacob throughout their twenty-two year separation — among them the ban of silence that had been imposed upon Joseph, and the fact that it was the Divine Will that Jacob be punished for the like amount of years he had been absent without communication from Isaac — have been discussed in the *comm.* to 41:51.] (Comp. *Aderes Eliyahu).*

R' Hirsch offers an entirely different rationale for Joseph's behavior: That Joseph wanted to be reunited with the House of Jacob is plain from the way he maintained his Jewishness in Egypt, the way he raised his children, and his wish to be buried in *Eretz Yisrael.* But he could not be reunited with his brothers unless they had purged themselves of their animosity toward him. Otherwise, even if the family had superficially come together, the gulf between him and his brothers would have remained. He would have been lost to them, and they to him.

To remove the old feelings of bitterness from his mind, two tests were needed:

1) Twenty-two years earlier, the brothers had not hesitated to deprive Jacob of his beloved son Joseph. What would they do now if circumstance was about to deprive Jacob of Benjamin as well? If they were prepared to risk personal sacrifice to prevent that tragedy from repeating itself, Joseph could forgive the past, knowing that they had changed.

b) Joseph remembered their violent reaction to his dreams that showed him to be king over them. How much more malevolent could their attitude now be when he was *really* a king with absolute power over them! He had to show them that despite his enormous power, he would use it only to benefit them, without rancor or revenge. Then they would realize that their resentment and jealousy of him had been without basis, and then he could reveal himself to them hoping confidently that all the ill-will on both sides would be removed — with the result that the family would be united and Joseph would be restored as Jacob's son and his siblings' brother.

מְרַגְּלִים אַתֶּם — *You are spies!*

Why did Joseph fabricate *this* particular accusation against them rather than some other one?

— This detail, too, demonstrates Joseph's wisdom. He suspected that once in Egypt, his brothers would try to seek him out since they knew that the Ishmaelite caravan to which they had sold him had been headed toward Egypt. He was concerned that if they inquired and investigated long enough, they might discover his true identity....

But if he denounced them as spies, they would not dare travel about making personal inquires of strangers lest they thereby appear to substantiate Joseph's charge that they were spies seeking sensitive information *(Kli Yakar).*

Many people from every country came to Joseph to buy provisions and Joseph's brothers were among the multitudes. It is obvious therefore, that there must have been something about

42 *them, so he said to them, "You are spies! To see the*
10 *nakedness of the land have you come!"*
10 *They answered him, "Not so, my lord. But your*

them that made the accusation plausible.

— They had aroused suspicion by making inquiries of malefactors on the street of prostitutes [see *Midrash* cited end of *v.* 3] *(Tanchuma);*

— They had entered through separate gates *(Rashi v.* 11 from *Midrash).* [That the Torah did not specifically mention this is inconsequential *(Ramban v.* 11).]

—While entering the country they tried to conceal themselves by mingling with the crowds [see *v.* 5] *(Kli Yakar);*

— They stayed together constantly *(Rashbam);*

— Possibly they came richly dressed as noblemen, thus giving Joseph a pretext for charging that such prominent people do not come in person to buy food but send their servants. [This apparently differs with the Midrash cited above which maintains that Joseph had issued a decree that each householder must personally come to buy grain; otherwise a wealthy slaveowner might send countless numbers of his slaves to purchase food for him.] It might also be that as noted in *v.* 6, s.v. ויוסף, they were the first ones to come from Canaan to buy grain. He therefore seized upon their reply — that they were from Canaan — as a pretext for accusing them of being spies since no one else had come from there. Joseph had this ruse in mind when he asked them where they were from *(Ramban).*

[Each of the above commentators understand the brothers' reply in *v.* 11 as an attempt to justify the act that aroused Joseph's 'suspicions'.]

לִרְאוֹת אֶת־עֶרְוַת הָאָרֶץ בָּאתֶם — *To see the nakedness of the land* have *you come.*

The nakedness of the land, i.e., the exposed part of the land — where it is [not protected by a wall and therefore] most vulnerable to attack. Compare other uses of this word connoting *exposure* and *vulnerability* in *Lev.* 20:18 and *Ezekiel* 16:7. Indeed, all forms of the verb ערה signify *exposing. Onkelos* renders בִּדְקָא דְעַרְעָא, *the breach of the land* (cf. *II Kings* 12:6); however, that is not meant as a literal translation *(Rashi).*

I.e., its secret places, called 'naked' in a figurative sense since these parts are usually concealed *(Ibn Ezra).*

— *Rashbam* comments: the breaches in its walls and its vulnerability to conquest. Interpreting the sense of the verb as *exposure to destruction,* he cites parallel forms in *Habakuk* 3:13; *Psalms* 137:7.

According to *Sforno,* the implication of Joseph's accusation is: 'You have not come to buy, because innocent purchasers do not stay in groups of ten. You have come to investigate whether we have sufficient food supply for our country.'

Implicit in this accusation is also the fact recorded in the Midrash above, that the brothers were discovered in the street of the prostitutes where they had gone in search of Joseph. 'You went there first,' Joseph charged, 'to literally gaze upon the nakedness of the earth. Why were you not afraid of congregating *there* and inciting the evil eye? Surely, you have come to spy!' 'Not so', they countered, 'we lost something [our brother] and were looking for it — we felt that this overrode every other consideration' *(Sechel Tov).*

אֵלָ֑יו לֹ֣א אֲדֹנִ֔י וַעֲבָדֶ֥יךָ בָּ֖אוּ לִשְׁבָּר־אֹֽכֶל׃
יא כֻּלָּ֕נוּ בְּנֵ֥י אִישׁ־אֶחָ֖ד נָ֑חְנוּ כֵּנִ֣ים אֲנַ֔חְנוּ
יב לֹא־הָי֥וּ עֲבָדֶ֖יךָ מְרַגְּלִֽים׃ וַיֹּ֖אמֶר אֲלֵהֶ֑ם
לֹ֕א כִּֽי־עֶרְוַ֥ת הָאָ֖רֶץ בָּאתֶ֥ם לִרְאֽוֹת׃
יג וַיֹּאמְר֗וּ שְׁנֵ֣ים עָשָׂ֣ר עֲבָדֶ֡יךָ אַחִ֣ים ׀ אֲנַ֧חְנוּ

10. לֹא אֲדֹנִי — *Not so, my lord.*

— Do not say this [i.e. that we are spies] *(Rashi).*

וַעֲבָדֶיךָ בָּאוּ לִשְׁבָּר־אֹכֶל — *But* [i.e. *truly;* lit. *and*] *Your servants have come to buy food.*

— The syntax follows *Rashi:* Do not accuse us of spying, *for your servants' purpose in coming was merely to buy food.*

The propositional prefix ו of this phrase means *but,* i.e., *no my lord,* not as you maintain [that we are spies], *but we have come to buy food (Radak).*

11. כֻּלָּנוּ בְּנֵי אִישׁ אֶחָד נָחְנוּ — *All of us — sons of one man are we.*

The Divine Spirit was enkindled within them and they unwittingly included Joseph in their statement by saying נָחְנוּ, *are we* — including him; *all* of us are sons of one father *(Midrash; Rashi).*

The Hebrew word for *we,* אֲנַחְנוּ, is spelled here without an א [numerically equalling 1], as נַחְנוּ. Midrashically this indicates that one of the brothers was missing in the 'we' *(Baal HaTurim).* The various sources differ whether Benjamin or Joseph is alluded to. [See *Torah Sheleimah*].

Each of the above-cited commentators perceives in this answer a direct reply to Joseph's charge, paralleling the various interpretations of what prompted the accusation in *v.* 9:

— [We were on the street of prostitutes] — Because *we are all sons of one father* — the word נַחְנוּ, *we,* spelled without an א indicating that one of them was missing — and we were looking for our missing brother who was very handsome and might have been sold as a slave in a brothel *(Midrash;* see *v.* 13);

— [We entered through separate gates, inconspicuously mingling with the crowds] because *we are sons of one man,* and we were thereby complying with our father's wishes *(Midrash);*

— We stayed together constantly — not because we are spies but because *we are all sons of one man (Rashbam);*

— 'We have all come in person instead of having one of us come with servants for the rest of us since it is our father's will that we remain inseparable.' The implication of this is that servants could not be entrusted to properly guard precious grain on the journey against robbery, since the famine was severe. A further implication of their reply was: *All of us — sons of one man are we;* You can investigate him for he is known in the gates by the vastness of his wealth and multitude of his children *(Ramban).*

— How could you suspect us of all being spies? *We are all the sons of one man.* Ten men fit for such dangerous work could not be found in one family. Furthermore, a father would not send all his sons on such a mission *(Akeidas Yitchak; Daas Zekeinim;* comp. *Or HaChaim).*

כֵּנִים אֲנַחְנוּ — *We are truthful people.*

This is a continuation of the previous argument: *We are all sons of one man* — about whom you can inquire. You can therefore easily ascertain that we are trustworthy, righteous men, sons of a righteous man — we are certainly not spies *(Ramban).*

servants have come to buy food." 11 *All of us — sons
of, one man are we. We are truthful people; your servants have never been spies."*
12 *And he said to them, "No! but to see the land in
its nakedness you have come."*
13 *And they replied, "We, your servants, are
twelve brothers, the sons of one man in the land of*

The word כֵּנִים means *truthful.* Cf. the similar meaning of כֵּן meaning *true; right,* in *Exod.* 20:29, and *Numbers* 28:7: *The daughters of Zelaphechad speak* right [כֵּן]; comp. also *Isaiah* 16:6 where לֹא־כֵן means *untruthful (Rashi).*

לֹא־הָיוּ עֲבָדֶיךָ מְרַגְּלִים — *Your servants have never* [lit. *not*] *been spies.*

I.e., there are absolutely no grounds for such suspicions.

The translation follows *Ramban:* we have been trustworthy in all our affairs from our youth on. *We have never been spies all our lives.*

12. לֹא כִּי־עֶרְוַת הָאָרֶץ בָּאתֶם לִרְאוֹת — *No! but to see the land in its nakedness you have come.*

— 'It cannot be as you say. If you are brothers traveling together you should have entered the country together and not by ten different gates [cf. footnote *v.* 3]. Therefore, since you entered by different gates you must be involved in some conspiracy' *(Rashi; Ramban).*

Rashi cites the Midrashic interpretation regarding their entering via different gates here, rather than above in *v.* 9, since it fits in better with the context of their reply in the next verse *(Mizrachi).*

Ramban defends the Midrashic thread of the narrative and mentions that the Torah did not record every detail of what was obviously a longer exchange since it did not care to prolong the discussion.

— 'If you did not come here to spy [and you are all the sons of one man], how is it that not even one of you remained behind with your [evidently aged] father?' He asked them this to ascertain whether Benjamin was still alive [for, as noted above, Joseph was concerned that they might have hated all of Rachel's children and have done away with Benjamin, too *(Ralbag)*]. They accordingly replied [next verse] *that there were twelve* brothers, and while one of them was missing, the youngest was indeed at home with their father. That Joseph did in fact question them about the family [although the Torah did not record that part of the dialogue] follows from what they later told their father [see 43:7] *(Rashbam).*

According to *Sforno: 'No,* it is not true that you are brothers. You are strangers and only pretending to be brothers to mask your spying!'

13. שְׁנֵים עָשָׂר עֲבָדֶיךָ אַחִים אֲנַחְנוּ — *We, your servants, are twelve brothers* [lit. *twelve, your servants, brothers are we*].

[I.e., It is not as you charge that our entry through separate gates tends to indicate that we are not really brothers, and that we are conspirators. The converse is true, for we are not only *ten,* but *twelve* brothers, and since *one of our brothers is no more,* we had a special reason for entering separately. (See *Rashi* below s.v. *and one is no more.*) [*See Rashbam* cited end of *v.* 12.]

בְּנֵי אִישׁ־אֶחָד בְּאֶרֶץ כְּנָעַן וְהִנֵּה הַקָּטֹן
יד אֶת־אָבִינוּ הַיּוֹם וְהָאֶחָד אֵינֶנּוּ: וַיֹּאמֶר
אֲלֵהֶם יוֹסֵף הוּא אֲשֶׁר דִּבַּרְתִּי אֲלֵכֶם
טו לֵאמֹר מְרַגְּלִים אַתֶּם: בְּזֹאת תִּבָּחֵנוּ חֵי
פַרְעֹה אִם־תֵּצְאוּ מִזֶּה כִּי אִם־בְּבוֹא

Sforno maintains that by this response, the brothers attempted to prove their innocence by providing easily verifiable details about themselves and their family.

According to *R' Avraham ben HaRambam* [citing his grandfather, R' Maimon], their response in this verse did not really counter the charge of spying, but was in answer to an unrecorded question Joseph must have asked about their family. Such additional dialogue is alluded to by the brothers in their recapitulation of their adventures to Jacob, later in 43:7. However except for this answer, the Torah, in usual Scriptural style, did not elaborate on the dialogue here.

בְּנֵי אִישׁ אֶחָד בְּאֶרֶץ כְּנָעַן — *The sons of one man in the land of Canaan.*

— A land which is on friendly terms with Egypt. It is nearby, and even should it desire to attack, has no need to send spies *(Haamek Davar).*

הַקָּטֹן אֶת־אָבִינוּ הַיּוֹם — *The youngest is now* [lit. *today*] *with our father.*

According to *Rashbam* in the previous verse, this was their reply to Joseph's objection that they would not *all* have left home without leaving a brother home to care for their father and household. They emphasized that they were *twelve* brothers, and indeed, the youngest remained at home to attend to their father [also, *Radak*].

Maasei Hashem explains the intent to be: the brother whom we left at home will testify that we are brothers. No man would falsely claim kinship with people who are charged with such a grave offense [see *Torah Sheleimah*].

[In any event, it must be noted that as a by-product of this remark, Joseph learned that his aged father was still alive.]

וְהָאֶחָד אֵינֶנּוּ — *And one is gone.*

I.e., we do not know where he is *(Targum Yonasan).*

— And it was to find him that we scattered (*Rashi,* see above).

The expression אֵינֶנּוּ, *is gone,* may be taken in the sense of *dead* as in the case of Chanoch (above 5:24) or *missing,* since they really had no idea what his true condition was; they knew only that they had sold him to a caravan headed toward Egypt *(Radak).* [Comp. comm. below to 44:20 where they specifically refer to Joseph as being *dead.*]

14. [Joseph repeats the accusation. He pretends to find their protests of innocence unconvincing, and now emphasizes his firm belief in their guilt. He is the supreme viceroy of Egypt, and as such he knows that he does not have to justify his accusations; rationally it suffices that such is his whim. The brothers are totally in his power, and Joseph uses this to his full advantage and proceeds with his well-planned scheme.]

הוּא אֲשֶׁר דִּבַּרְתִּי אֲלֵכֶם לֵאמֹר מְרַגְּלִים אַתֶּם — *It is just as I have declared to*

Canaan. The youngest is now with our father and
one is gone."
14 But Joseph said to them, "It is just as I have
declared to you: 'You are spies!' 15 By this shall you
be tested: By Pharaoh's life you will not leave here

you: [*saying*] *'You are spies!'*

The plain meaning is that Joseph reiterated his accusation: *The statement that I made that you are spies is true and certain.* According to the Midrash, however, the following exchange took place:

'If you found your missing brother', Joseph asked, 'and a large sum were demanded for his release, would you pay it?'

'Yes', they replied.

'And what if they refused to release him at any price?'

'That was our purpose in coming here — to kill or be killed' [in liberating him], they retorted.

'Then,' Joseph countered, *'it is just as I have said to you:* you have come to slay the people of this city, for I have seen in my divining cup that two of you destroyed the city of Shechem!' *(Rashi).*

According to *Radak:* If ten brothers came, why did you not already bring the youngest who you claim you left with your father? Your wives and children could have stayed behind to look after the old man! Therefore, it is as I said ... you are spies!

That your youngest brother stayed behind proves my contention. Because your father knew you were on a dangerous errand he would not allow the youngster to go with you! *(R' Hirsch).*

You said nothing before about another brother! — Your whole story must be a lie! *(Akeidas Yitzchak).*

— Even if there are eleven of you, surely no father would send out ten and allow only the youngest to remain behind in full charge of the household and flocks! This proves that my charge is true! *(Abarbanel; Malbim).*

15. בְּזֹאת תִּבָּחֵנוּ—*By this shall you be tested.*

If your statement regarding a youngest brother can be verified, I will believe everything else you said as well *(B'chor Shor).*

— For if you are not brothers, you will not find a youngster to risk his life coming with you to lie and put himself into the same danger of death as you now are *(Sforno).*

חֵי פַרְעֹה — [*By*] *Pharaoh's life.*

Lit. *the life of Pharaoh,* i.e., if Pharaoh shall live. [This was a formula for a kind of oath or strong assertion, as if to say, 'I swear by Pharaoh's life' *(Gur Aryeh);* i.e., 'Just as I wish the king to live so do I wish that the following occur' *(Divrei David).*] Whenever Joseph swore falsely [as he did now when his oath was not intended seriously for he *did* release them before they brought their younger brother to Egypt (see *v.* 19)], he swore by Pharaoh's life *(Rashi).*

Actually, as *R' Bachya* insists, Joseph did not swear falsely in this case, for he did not release them *all* from prison; Simeon remained behind.

[The Scriptural *Hebrew* forms of oath were חַי ה', *the Living God,* חֵי נַפְשְׁךָ, *, as your soul lives,* cf. *I Sam.* 14:39; 17:55.][1]

1. *Rambam* [*Hilchos Yesodei HaTorah* 2:10] notes that when an oath is made on a human, the word is punctuated חֵי, but when it refers to God it is punctuated חַי. In the former, the proper

טז אֲחִיכֶם הַקָּטֹן הֵנָּה: שִׁלְחוּ מִכֶּם אֶחָד
וְיִקַּח אֶת־אֲחִיכֶם וְאַתֶּם הֵאָסְרוּ וְיִבָּחֲנוּ
דִּבְרֵיכֶם הַאֱמֶת אִתְּכֶם וְאִם־לֹא חֵי
יז פַרְעֹה כִּי מְרַגְּלִים אַתֶּם: וַיֶּאֱסֹף אֹתָם
יח אֶל־מִשְׁמָר שְׁלֹשֶׁת יָמִים: וַיֹּאמֶר אֲלֵהֶם

אִם־תֵּצְאוּ מִזֶּה כִּי אִם־בְּבוֹא אֲחִיכֶם הַקָּטֹן הֵנָּה — *You will not leave from here* [lit. *from this* i.e., from this place *(Rashi)*] *unless your youngest brother comes here.*

[Joseph's real motive in wanting them to bring Benjamin has been analyzed in the footnote and comm. to verses 7 and 9 respectively.]

— *Ostensibly,* he wanted to interrogate their youngest brother who — because of his age — would probably provide the most revealing information *(Alshich; Akeidas Yitzchak).*

It must have remained unclear to the brothers, however, why the presence of Benjamin would suffice to absolve them from this regent's capricious charge that they were spies. But they knew that they were powerless against his demands; a ruler's whims are not always rational *(Daas Soferim).*

The Hebrew literally reads אִם if *you will leave* ... The translation of this phrase in the context of an oath as meaning *you shall not* leave ... follows the rule expounded in the comm. to 14:23 s.v. וְאִם אֶקַּח. Comp. also *Rambam* cited to 21:23 s.v. אִם תִּשְׁקֹר.

16. שִׁלְחוּ מִכֶּם אֶחָד וְיִקַּח אֶת־אֲחִיכֶם וְאַתֶּם הֵאָסְרוּ — *Send one of you, and let him fetch your brother while you shall remain* [lit. *be*] *imprisoned.*

But the brothers, as we shall see, did not voluntarily select one of their number to go. They knew the effort would be futile, and they were concerned about their father's grief when he would learn from one brother that the others had been imprisoned in Egypt *(Alshich; Or HaChaim).*

Later, when Joseph heard their expressions of remorse at having callously sold him (*v.* 22 ff.), he freed all except one of them, it having been his purpose that they acknowledge their sinfulness for having sold him. When he now suggested that they choose one of them to go, he was certain they would select Reuben, since as firstborn, the right of freedom was due him. Furthermore, he assumed they would acknowledge that Reuben was least responsible for the sale and was thereby most deservant to be freed. For, although Simeon and Levi bore primary responsibility for the sale, even Judah was involved and, as *Rashi* comments in 38:1, the brothers held him responsible for it and deposed him from his leadership as a result *(Kli Yakar).*

According to *Malbim,* Joseph did not intend that one of the brothers go to fetch Benjamin; that would defeat the overt purpose of establishing their veracity since the one fetching him could coach him on the way. Rather Joseph wanted them to select *a stranger* who would go *on their behalf* to fetch Benjamin. The interpretation, then, of שִׁלְחוּ מִכֶּם אֶחָד, would be *send from*

translation is [*by*] *Pharaoh's life,* and in the latter *the Living God* — for in contrast to human beings and their lives, God and His life are one and the same *(R' Munk).*

unless your youngest brother comes here. 16 *Send one*
of you, and let him fetch your brother while you shall
remain imprisoned, so that your words may be tested
whether truth is with you. But if not, by Pharaoh's
life — surely you are spies!" 17 *Then he herded them*
into a ward for three days.

you [i.e., on your behalf] *one.*

וְאַתֶּם הֵאָסְרוּ — *While* [lit. *and*] *you shall remain* [lit. *be*] *imprisoned.*

Although the word הֵאָסְרוּ *be imprisoned* is in the imperative form, *Ibn Ezra* explains that it is not a *command* [since one does not imprison himself; others imprison him *(Karnei Or)*] but like תֵּאָסְרוּ is a statement of fact: *and you shall be imprisoned.* It is similar to God's command to Moses [*Deut.* 32:50] וּמוּת בָּהָר, which is not to be rendered in the imperative: *and die on the mountain,* but as a statement of fact: *and you will die on the mountain.* [Comp. *Ibn Ezra* to 1:22 פְּרוּ וּרְבוּ.]

Abarbanel explains the imperative sense to be: *While you willfully submit yourselves to imprisonment.*

וְיִבָּחֲנוּ דִּבְרֵיכֶם הַאֱמֶת אִתְּכֶם — *That* [lit. *and*] *your words may be tested whether truth is with you.*

Although the one who brings him might coach him en route, I will still be able to determine the truthfulness of your claims *(Abarbanel).*

The ה of הַאֱמֶת is punctuated with a *patach* to indicate that it is an interrogative participle and the word forms a kind of question, *Is there truth?* [Had the word been punctuated with a *kametz,* הָאֱמֶת, the ה would indicate the definite article and the word would mean *the truth*] *(Rashi).*

וְאִם לֹא — *But* [lit. *and*] *if not.*

I.e., but if you do not bring your younger brother back here [and thereby verify your claims] *(Rashi).*

חֵי פַרְעֹה כִּי מְרַגְּלִים אַתֶּם — [*By*] *Pharaoh's life surely you are spies.*

— And you will never leave here *(Ralbag).*

By making this assertion, Joseph wished to convince them that it was futile to offer any further arguments *(Abarbanel).*

17. וַיֶּאֱסֹף אֹתָם אֶל־מִשְׁמָר שְׁלֹשֶׁת יָמִים — *Then* [lit. *and*] *he herded them into a ward for three days.*

— He did this to frighten them and make them more submissive *(Ramban).*

[Perhaps Joseph had expected his brothers to consent readily to his proposal that they select one of them to return home and fetch Benjamin. When none of them volunteered, he feigned anger and ordered them imprisoned until he decided how to proceed.]

This period of incarceration would enable them to realize the gravity of their predicament and to allow the urgency of it to work its effect on them *(R' Hirsch).*

— *Three days* — corresponding to their three acts against him: removing his tunic; throwing him into the pit; and selling him *(Baal HaTurim).*

According to a view in the *Zohar,* the three days corresponded to the three days the people of Shechem were in pain as a result of the brothers' scheme [34:25].

The number three is significant. The Midrash enumerates many instances of important events in the history of Jewish salvation which occurred on the third day, among them that Joseph freed his brothers on the third day and the Torah was given on the third day [*Exodus* 19:16]. See also *Esther* 5:1 and *Jonah* 2:1. The Sages accordingly

יוֹסֵף בַּיּוֹם הַשְּׁלִישִׁי זֹאת עֲשׂוּ וִחְיוּ אֶת־
יט הָאֱלֹהִים אֲנִי יָרֵא: אִם־כֵּנִים אַתֶּם
°חמישי אֲחִיכֶם אֶחָד יֵאָסֵר בְּבֵית מִשְׁמַרְכֶם
וְאַתֶּם לְכוּ הָבִיאוּ שֶׁבֶר רַעֲבוֹן בָּתֵּיכֶם:

observed that 'God does not allow His righteous to remain in dire straits for more than three days.'

The term מִשְׁמָר [*ward*] refers to a prison (*Rashi*).

Rashi does not make this comment above in 40:3 where the term first appears, because the context of that verse makes the definition self-evident (*Mizrachi*).

18. Realizing that — their incarceration notwithstanding — his earlier suggestion that one of the brothers volunteer to return home and fetch Benjamin would not be accepted, Joseph makes a different proposal.

וַיֹּאמֶר אֲלֵהֶם יוֹסֵף בַּיּוֹם הַשְּׁלִישִׁי — [*And*] *Joseph said to them on the third day.*

— He did not detain them longer; he was afraid of the grief their extended absence would cause Jacob (*Abarbanel*).

זֹאת עֲשׂוּ וִחְיוּ — *Do this and live.*

I.e., follow the advice I offer you and you will be spared (*Abarbanel*).

אֶת הָאֱלֹהִים אֲנִי יָרֵא — *I fear God.*[1]

— And accordingly, I will not keep *all* of you imprisoned while your families are starving. I will release *most* of you to allow you to bring provisions home while I detain only one of you to establish your veracity (*Radak; Ramban; Sforno*).

— It is improper that I, as a religious man, detain you all on mere suspicion (*Abarbanel*).

— I am a religious man, and I find no pleasure in harming you or keeping you detained. I merely want to establish your truthfulness, and therefore offer you the following plan (*Ibn Caspi*).

[When the Divine Name is preceded by the definite article הָאֱלֹהִים, lit. **the** *God* it designates Him in the midst of His celestial tribunal.

[References to אֱלֹהִים, *God*, uttered

1. Many people fear God in poverty, but when they become wealthy they place their trust in their money and lose their piety, but Joseph was different. He feared God as a slave, as he said, *'How can I do this great wickedness and sin against God?'* [39:9]. His piety was even greater when he became a ruler, as he specifically proclaimed *I fear God!* (*Tanchuma Naso*).

The *Midrash* [*Sh'mos Rabbah* 26:3] maintains that when Amalek attacked Israel it was Joshua — a descendant of Joseph — who was instructed by Moses to select warriors to battle Amalek. Moses said to him, "Your ancestor [Joseph] said, *'I fear God'*, while of Amalek it is written: *He did not fear God* [*Deut.* 25:18]. Let the descendant of the former inflict retribution on the latter."

R' Munk records that the fear of God which Joseph felt was of the same kind as Abraham's (*Avos d'Rabbi Nosson 10:13*), meaning that it was a product of his *love* of God [יִרְאָה מֵאַהֲבָה] (*Sotah* 31b). This form of יִרְאַת ה׳, *'fear' of God*, is far loftier than a primitive fear of Divine punishment [יִרְאַת הָעוֹנֶשׁ]; it is a form of reverence based on a tripod of love, worship and fear [יִרְאַת הָרוֹמְמוּת, *awe of the Divine majesty*]. It is, as it were, the crowning glory of an all-encompassing love.

However, the *Zohar* points out that for Joseph, the reference to the fear of God implied first and foremost that he had resolved not to pay back evil with evil. He wanted to follow the maxim given in *Proverbs* (20:22): *Say not I will pay back the evil! Have confidence in* HASHEM. *He will help you.*

[18] *Joseph said to them on the third day, "Do this
and live; I fear God:* [19] *If you are truthful people let
one of your brothers be imprisoned in your place of
confinement while the rest of you go and bring
provisions for the hunger of your households.*

by gentiles — as Joseph here pretended to be — addressing Hebrews are not uncommon in Scripture. Joseph's remark should accordingly *not* be construed as an implicit admission by Joseph to his brothers of his true identity. Abimelech referred to *God* in conversation with Isaac (21:22), as did Pharaoh in conversation with Joseph (41:38, 39). Accordingly, his profession of faith in *God* did not arouse their suspicions.]

19. אִם כֵּנִים אַתֶּם — *If you are truthful* [*people*].

[I.e., if you wish to prove to me that you are truthful people.]...

אֲחִיכֶם אֶחָד יֵאָסֵר בְּבֵית מִשְׁמַרְכֶם — *Let one of your brothers be imprisoned, in your place of confinement* [lit. *guardhouse*][1]

I.e., in the building where you have been confined until now (*Rashi*).

וְאַתֶּם לְכוּ הָבִיאוּ שֶׁבֶר רַעֲבוֹן בָּתֵּיכֶם — *While* [lit. *and*] [the rest of you] *go and bring provisions for the hunger of your households.*

I.e., bring home what you have purchased [שֶׁבֶר according to *Rashi* in 41:56 is a noun referring to *purchased* provisions] to feed the hungry members of your household (*Rashi*).

The Hebrew which literally reads "...and bring שֶׁבֶר, a 'break', for the hunger of your households," homiletically intimates the moderation one must exercise during times of famine — the amount consumed should be sufficient only to 'break' the hunger; indulgence should be avoided (*R' Bachya*).

The expression שֶׁבֶר רַעֲבוֹן בָּתֵּיכֶם literally refers to that which will 'break' the hunger i.e., *wheat.* Therefore, wheat is referred to as שֶׁבֶר, as we have explained earlier (*Radak*).

Joseph purposely emphasized that his reason for releasing them was to allow them to take provisions to their starving households. He was certain that otherwise they would never have voluntarily agreed to leave one behind (*Ramban v.* 17) [see *v.* 24].

1. The deeper implication of this verse may be understood on the basis of *Yerushalmi Terumos* 8:4, which states that if gentile brigands confront a group of Jews and say to them, 'Give us one of your group that we may kill him or else we will kill all of you', then even if all of them would be killed they may not surrender a single person in Israel. However, if they demand that a specific individual be given them, [the Jews] should surrender him, and not let all of them be killed. Comp. the case of Sheva son of Bichri as related in *II Samuel* chapt. 20.

This was Joseph's intent when he said, *'If you are truthful people,'* i.e. since you know whether you are truly innocent, you should have no qualms about letting *one* — [without specifying which one] — *of your brothers be imprisoned,* for you certainly believe that he will be in no danger of being killed [since once you return with your younger brother your truthfulness will be proven and Simeon will be released]. The converse implication is also true; if their innocence was at all doubtful they would have no right to offer up one of their own for a seemingly certain death.

That we find later that Joseph selected Simeon — which is tantamount to specifying one of them — is no contradiction. Possibly, *they* chose him first, or after they decided to choose one brother, Joseph anticipated them by selecting Simeon, in order to separate him from his cohort, Levi (*Or HaChaim*).

[See *comm.* to *v.* 24 where contrasting views are cited to the effect that Joseph selected Simeon *after* the brothers — though consenting in *principle* to Joseph's plan — refused to make the selection of which brother to surrender.]

כ וְאֶת־אֲחִיכֶם הַקָּטֹן תָּבִיאוּ אֵלַי וְיֵאָמְנוּ
כא דִבְרֵיכֶם וְלֹא תָמוּתוּ וַיַּעֲשׂוּ־כֵן: וַיֹּאמְרוּ
אִישׁ אֶל־אָחִיו אֲבָל אֲשֵׁמִים | אֲנַחְנוּ עַל־
אָחִינוּ אֲשֶׁר רָאִינוּ צָרַת נַפְשׁוֹ בְּהִתְחַנְנוֹ

20. וְיֵאָמְנוּ דִבְרֵיכֶם — *So your words will be verified.*

For as soon as you produce your youngest brother I will believe all your other statements as well *(Alshich).*

וְלֹא תָמוּתוּ — *And you will not die.*

— For I can have you put to death even in Canaan if you do not return *(Sforno).*

— From the famine, for if your words are verified you will be free to buy as much grain as your households will require *(Akeidas Yitzchak).*

The verb יֵאָמְנוּ [from the root אמן related to אֱמֶת, *truth*] means *verified* and *confirmed.* Compare *Numbers* 5:22 and *I Kings* 8:26 *(Rashi).*

Rashi offers this comment to avoid misinterpreting the word as *be believed* [from אֱמוּנָה, *faith*] *(Mizrachi).*

וַיַּעֲשׂוּ־כֵן — *And they consented* [lit. *and they did so;* comp. this meaning of the verb עשה in 29:28].

They consented to leave one brother behind, and promised to fetch their youngest brother *(R' Avraham ben HaRambam).*

— They said: 'We are under your authority: Take whomever you wish!' *(R' Bachya).*

21. The brothers become introspective regarding their lot and recognize what has befallen them as a Divine punishment for their cruel treatment of Joseph. 'Happy are the righteous,' declares *Midrash HaGadol,* 'who submit to retribution with joy and declare the Almighty just in whatever way He acts.'

וַיֹּאמְרוּ אִישׁ אֶל־אָחִיו — *They then said to one another* [lit. *man to his brother*].

Simeon said this to Levi. They are discreetly described with the same expression *man to his brother* when they conspired against Joseph in 37:19: *They said man to his brother, 'See, this dreamer comes!'* [see *comm.* there]. Simeon [as the elder of the two, and presumably the speaker] was now penitent over what he had done, and remorsefully cried out to Levi, *'Indeed we are guilty ...' (Zohar).*

An interpreter had been present throughout Joseph's communication with them [see *v.* 23] because Joseph feigned ignorance of Hebrew lest they realize his true identity. When Joseph had finished addressing them the interpreter stepped out so the brothers felt free to converse without fear that the interpreter would repeat their discussion to Joseph *(Radak; Akeidah).*

אֲבָל אֲשֵׁמִים אֲנַחְנוּ עַל אָחִינוּ — *Indeed we are guilty concerning our brother.*

They examined their pasts and concluded that the only sin which they had committed was the mistreatment of their own flesh and blood, for which retribution was now being meted out to them *(Bamidbar Rabbah* 13:18).

B'chor Shor interprets our passage to mean: Indeed אֲשֵׁמִים אֲנַחְנוּ, *we are being punished,* concerning our brother [אָשָׁם as חֵטְא means *penalty, sin,* well as *guilt (HaKsav V'HaKabbalah)*]. They realized that the sin of selling their brother was the only trespass for which they could be held *collectively* responsi-

42
20-21

20 *Then bring your youngest brother to me so your words will be verified and you will not die." And they consented.*
21 *They then said to one another, "Indeed we are guilty concerning our brother inasmuch as we saw his heartfelt anguish when he pleaded with us and we*

ble and for which they were now being punished *as a group*. [See *Or HaChaim* below.]

The translation of אֲבָל [usually rendered *but*] as *indeed, in truth*, follows *Onkelos* cited by *Rashi, Ibn Janach* and *Ibn Ezra*. Comp. 17:19 above אֲבָל שָׂרָה אִשְׁתְּךָ. *Rashi* mentions that in the *Midrash* it is noted that in the Roman language [דְּרוֹמָאָה lit. *'of Roma'* (i.e. Latin), or *'Southern'*, possibly a reference to the dialect of the inhabitants of south *Eretz Yisrael*] the word אֲבָל is used in the sense of בְּרַם [=verum], *true; indeed*.[1]

R' Hirsch perceives אֲבָל even in our context as similar to *but*, in that it expresses a contrast to a previous assumption. For more than twenty years they were convinced that their action against Joseph was a justifiable act of self-defense ... But now, in analyzing the possible reason for the misfortune now befalling them, they realize that unatoned wrongs have come to the fore: 'אֲבָל! *After all*, whatever we have been telling ourselves is not true; we *are* guilty concerning our brother!' It is noteworthy, however, that, as they go on to say, they recognize having sinned ***only in not showing compassion when Joseph pleaded***, but they are still convinced that they did the right thing in selling him.

Or HaChaim [in a comment similar to *B'chor Shor's* above] maintains that the brothers had searched for a sin they had *all* committed which could be the cause of their present common suffering. They ruled out the *sale* itself since Reuben had not participated in it. Therefore, they said אֲבָל, *but*, we are *all* guilty over having witnessed our brother's supplications. That is, while we bear no *collective* guilt for the sale, and our *collective* troubles could not be in retribution for that, אֲבָל, *nevertheless* we bear common guilt over the suffering we inflicted on Joseph when we cast him into the pit and turned a deaf ear to his supplications — for in this act Reuben also participated. This, too, is the sense of: *that is why this distress has come upon us* — i.e. *all* of us, collectively.

[Additionally, those commentators who maintain that it was not the brothers who actually sold Joseph (see *comm.* to 37:27, "Who sold Joseph?") cite our verse in which the brothers express remorse only over their callousness and not over the sale itself, as support for their view.]

אֲשֶׁר רָאִינוּ צָרַת נַפְשׁוֹ בְּהִתְחַנְנוֹ אֵלֵינוּ וְלֹא שָׁמָעְנוּ — *Inasmuch as we saw his heartfelt anguish* [*lit.* *anguish of his soul*] *when he had pleaded with* [lit. *at*] *us and we paid no heed.*

They regarded this callousness

1. Indeed, the term אֲבָל in the sense of *Alas*, is still used to express a feeling of contrition. It has been adopted by the siddur as an introduction to the confession of sins: אֲבָל אֲנַחְנוּ חָטָאנוּ, *Alas we have sinned*.

The brothers react to this misfortune in an authentically Jewish manner. Rather than blaming the hard-hearted viceroy and indulging in self-pity, they seek the *real* cause of their adversity in themselves. As we say in the liturgical confession... שֶׁאֵין אָנוּ עַזֵּי פָנִים, *We are not so insolent nor so stubborn that we consider ourselves as righteous people who have never sinned*, אֲבָל אֲנַחְנוּ חָטָאנוּ *but alas, we have sinned* [Prayer Book]. Only in his own moral or religious conduct does the Jew search for the source of the trials that destiny inflicts upon him *(R' Munk)*.

אֵלֵינוּ וְלֹא שָׁמָעְנוּ עַל־כֵּן בָּאָה אֵלֵינוּ
כב הַצָּרָה הַזֹּאת: וַיַּעַן רְאוּבֵן אֹתָם לֵאמֹר
הֲלוֹא אָמַרְתִּי אֲלֵיכֶם | לֵאמֹר אַל־
תֶּחֶטְאוּ בַיֶּלֶד וְלֹא שְׁמַעְתֶּם וְגַם־דָּמוֹ
כג הִנֵּה נִדְרָשׁ: וְהֵם לֹא יָדְעוּ כִּי שֹׁמֵעַ יוֹסֵף

toward the entreaties of their blood brother as deserving even greater punishment than the actual sale. That Joseph implored them is not related in the story of the sale [chapt. 37], since it is obvious that he must have invoked every possible plea to save himself from death. Possibly, the Torah preferred not to list their sin in all its details, or the omission is characteristic of the Torah's practice of intentionally shortening a narrative in one place and elaborating on the details elsewhere *(Ramban)*. [*See commentary to 37:24.*]

Torn by their stricken conscience, they drew a contrast between the Egyptian viceroy's compassionate attitude toward their starving families — although the families were aliens and he would not *personally* witness their suffering — and the cruelty they had long ago displayed to their own brother. Joseph was their flesh and blood. They personally witnessed his suffering and heard his impassioned pleas, yet they remained callous to him *(Yafeh Toar)*.

Although they did not consider as sinful their death sentence against Joseph, for they had rationalized it as a legitimate act of self-defense [see comm. to 37:18], in retrospect they now felt that they should nevertheless have shown compassion for his cries. Accordingly, they surmised that it was in retribution for their own callousness that the Egyptian ruler was subjecting them to this suffering *(Sforno; Malbim)*.

עַל־כֵּן בָּאָה אֵלֵינוּ הַצָּרָה הַזֹּאת — *That is why this distress has come upon* [lit. *to*] *us.*

— Measure for measure. We threw him in a pit; therefore we have been thrown into this prison *(Rashbam)*.

We learn from this account that when a person is beset by trouble he should search out his deeds and establish what sin he has committed. He should express his regret for it, confess to the Almighty and beg for atonement *(Radak)*.

R' Bachya interpret עַל כֵּן in this context to mean עַל הַנָּכוֹן, *quite properly* and justly has this distress come upon us. כֵּן in this sense means *true, correct* as in *Numbers* 28:7. [Comp. כֵּנִים above in *v.* 11.]

Rashi offers the grammatical observation that the word בָּאָה is accented on the first syllable בָּ because it is the past perfect tense — *has come* — for the distress had already come upon them. *Onkelos* also rendered it in the perfect tense אֲתַת.

[Comp. comm. to 29:6 where בָּאָה is accented on the second syllable אָ and *Rashi* notes that it indicates present tense, *is coming*, as does *Onkelos* who renders אָתְיָא. However, in ibid. *v.* 9 the accent is on the first syllable בָּ and *Onkelos* renders as in our verse אֲתַת. Cf. also *Rashi* to בָּאָה in 16:17 and שָׁבָה in *Ruth* 1:15.]

22. וַיַּעַן רְאוּבֵן אֹתָם לֵאמֹר — [*And*] *Reuben retorted to them as follows* [lit. *saying*].

His *retort* was inspired by their statement that they were אֲשֵׁמִים, *guilty*, a term which denotes sin through *inadvertence*. He refuted them, saying that there was no excuse for of their offense since he had attempted to dissuade them, but

paid no heed. That is why this distress has come
upon us."
22 *Reuben retorted to them as follows, "Did I not*
say to you in effect, 'Do not sin against the boy' but
you would not listen! And his blood as well — see! it
is being avenged." 23 *Now they did not know that*

they refused to listen [see 37:21,22] *(Akeidas Yitzchak).*

הֲלוֹא אָמַרְתִּי אֲלֵיכֶם לֵאמֹר אַל־תֶּחֶטְאוּ בַיֶּלֶד — *Did I not say to you, in effect* [lit. *saying*], *'Do not sin against the boy.'*

— I.e. for he was only a boy. It was only because of his youth that he wronged you, and you should have overlooked his trespasses for that reason *(Ramban).*

Although Reuben had not specifically said [in Chap. 37] the words 'Do not sin against the boy,' he had urged his brothers *'we will not take his life...shed no blood'* [37:21, 22]. When he suggested that they throw Joseph into the pit [ibid.], his intention, as the Torah attests in that verse, was that they not even harm Joseph. Reuben now maintains that he had been stalling for time, intending that they do *nothing* to the boy — certainly not sell him to brigands who might harm him! — but that they restore him unharmed to their father. He could not, however, specifically say so at the time since, as noted there, he was afraid of them and knew such direct efforts would be futile *(Akeidas Yitzchak; Or HaChaim).*

[Our translation of לֵאמֹר as *in effect* rather than the more common, *saying*, is based on the above comments of *Akeidas Yitzchak* and *Or HaChaim.* As they note, Reuben did not actually *say* these exact words; they were implied *in his urging* that Joseph not be put to death. However, see *Ramban* to 37:22 who maintains that Reuben probably did tell them these words at the time, but the Torah did not record it there. Comp. also *Ramban* in *v.* 21 above who maintains that it is characteristic of the Torah to shorten a narrative in one place and elaborate on the details elsewhere.]

וְלֹא שְׁמַעְתֶּם — *But you would not listen?!*

— I.e., you pretended not to understand that I wanted you to not harm him at all *(Ralbag; Akeidah;* cf. *Or HaChaim* above).

וְגַם־דָּמוֹ הִנֵּה נִדְרָשׁ — *And his blood as well — see! it is being avenged.*

In addition to the display of cruelty to which you admit, *his blood* is being avenged. Possibly the intent of the phrase is: Though you did not kill Joseph with your own hands, you sold him into a life of hard labor as a slave. Unaccustomed to such work, he must have died by now because of what you did. God considers *you* his murderers and He will avenge Joseph's blood of you (*Ramban*).

Rashi follows the Rabbinical rule that particles such as אֶת and גַּם indicate a רִבּוּי, *extension,* beyond the literal scope of the clause (cf. 1:1, *Deut.* 10:20; *Exod.* 20:12). In our case, therefore the phrase *his blood* **also** *is being avenged* implies *his blood in addition* to the blood of some other person involved with him. The implication is that Joseph's blood — *as well as the blood of our father,* who suffers intense grief because of you — [see

כד כִּי הַמֵּלִיץ בֵּינֹתָם: וַיִּסֹּב מֵעֲלֵיהֶם וַיֵּבְךְּ
וַיָּשָׁב אֲלֵהֶם וַיְדַבֵּר אֲלֵהֶם וַיִּקַּח מֵאִתָּם
כה אֶת־שִׁמְעוֹן וַיֶּאֱסֹר אֹתוֹ לְעֵינֵיהֶם: וַיְצַו
יוֹסֵף וַיְמַלְאוּ אֶת־כְּלֵיהֶם בָּר וּלְהָשִׁיב
כַּסְפֵּיהֶם אִישׁ אֶל־שַׂקּוֹ וְלָתֵת לָהֶם צֵדָה

37:35] — now cries out for retribution. [1]

23. וְהֵם לֹא יָדְעוּ כִּי שֹׁמֵעַ יוֹסֵף כִּי הַמֵּלִיץ בֵּינֹתָם — *Now they did not know that Joseph understood* [lit. *was hearing* (see above 41:15)], *for an interpreter was between them.*

When they had spoken to Joseph earlier, an interpreter translated their Hebrew and his Egyptian. Consequently, they assumed that Joseph did not understand their language. [Therefore, now that the interpreter had left — for it is obvious that they would not have spoken these incriminating words had he still been present *(Radak; Mizrachi)*], they spoke freely among themselves in Joseph's presence. According to the *Midrash*, the interpreter was Menasseh, Joseph's first born son *(Rashi)*.

24. וַיִּסֹּב מֵעֲלֵיהֶם — *Then he* [Joseph] *turned away from them.*

— And stayed at a distance so they would not see him crying *(Rashi)*.

וַיֵּבְךְּ — *And* [*he*] *wept.*

Over having heard their expressions of remorse for their past conduct toward him *(Rashi)*.

His feelings of compassion for them were aroused *(Sechel Tov)*; and he wept at witnessing their distress *(Sforno)*.

Bereishis Rabbossi maintains that Joseph was moved to tears at the implication of the phrase *and his blood also* which reminded him of the grief of his aged father.

However, he could not yet reveal himself to them for his prophetic dreams were not yet fulfilled, and by revealing himself to them prematurely he would have defeated the very purpose of his scheme, as outlined in the *comm.* to *v.* 9.

וַיָּשָׁב אֲלֵהֶם וַיְדַבֵּר אֲלֵהֶם — [*And*] *he returned to them and spoke to them.*

The ensuing conversation is not recorded. According to *R' Avraham ben HaRambam*, Joseph reassured them that his intent was not malicious. The implication of *R' Bachya* is that Joseph wanted them to designate which brother should remain behind, but when they refused, he selected Simeon for the reasons given below. [See footnote to *v.* 19, and cf. *Rambam, Yesodei HaTorah* 5:5 where it is derived that Jews are forbidden to designate one of their number to be handed over to Gentile marauders, even to save the entire group from death.]

וַיִּקַּח מֵאִתָּם אֶת־שִׁמְעוֹן — *And he took Simeon from them.*

Why did Joseph choose Simeon?

— It was Simeon who had thrown

1. See *Sefer Chassidim* §131: 'Know and understand that whoever commits murder or harms another person is not punished only for that individual, but also for everyone who grieves over that individual, as derived from the phrase וְגַם דָּמוֹ, *also his blood,* which extends the retribution for his father's grief as well as that of everyone else associated with his loss.'

Joseph understood for an interpreter was between them.

[24] *He turned away from them and wept. He returned to them and spoke to them; he took Simeon from them and imprisoned him before their eyes*
[25] *Joseph commanded that they fill their vessels with grain, and to return each one's money to his sack and*

Joseph into the pit, and who had said to Levi, *Look! That dreamer is coming* [37:19]. Alternatively, he wished to separate Simeon from Levi lest the two of them conspire to kill him *(Rashi).*

[The latter interpretation follows a Midrashic explanation of why, if both Simeon and Levi instigated the plot against Joseph, (37:19), Joseph did not imprison *both* of them.]

— And lest the two of them form some conspiracy as they did in Shechem *(Rashbam).*

In reality, Reuben should have been selected because, as the first born, he was accountable for the deeds of his younger siblings. However, [as Joseph knew either from witnessing it at the time of the sale, or from overhearing Reuben's retort now in *v.* 22] Reuben had attempted to protect Joseph when his brothers wanted to kill him, so Joseph spared him and selected Simeon who was next in seniority *(Ibn Ezra; Tur).*

וַיֶּאֱסֹר אֹתוֹ לְעֵינֵיהֶם — *And* [*he*] *imprisoned him before their eyes.*

— To cause them to realize the seriousness of their plight. When they would see him interned, they would not procrastinate but would hasten back all the more quickly with their younger brother in order to free Simeon *(R' Avraham ben HaRambam).*

However, it was only *before their eyes* that Joseph kept him imprisoned. As soon as they left Joseph freed him and gave him food and drink *(Midrash; Rashi).*

— Simeon was not to know, however, that Joseph was aware of this *(Meam Loez).*

Midrash Tanchuma records that only Menasseh could restrain and bind Simeon; the soldiers of the guard were not able to subdue him. When Menasseh subdued him with only a single blow, Simeon remarked, 'Such a blow is [like that] of my father's household!'

25. וַיְצַו יוֹסֵף וַיְמַלְאוּ אֶת־כְּלֵיהֶם בָּר — *Then Joseph commanded that they* [i.e. those in charge of dispensing grain] *fill* [lit. *and they filled*] *their vessels with grain.*

— [Presumably the reference is to the grain which the brothers had purchased for their households.]

Since Joseph did not want Simeon's family to go hungry while he was in prison, he ordered that Simeon's sack should also be filled. His brothers were to bring it to his family. Simeon's money, however, was not placed in *his* sack, but in Levi's *(Kesef Mezukak* cited in *Meam Loez).*

וּלְהָשִׁיב כַּסְפֵּיהֶם אִישׁ אֶל־שַׂקּוֹ — [*And*] [=he gave orders *(Radak)*] *to return each one's money* [lit. *silver*] *to his sack.*

While the previous command was carried out by the officials in charge of the grain, this command

כו לַדָּרֶךְ וַיַּעַשׂ לָהֶם כֵּן: וַיִּשְׂאוּ אֶת־שִׁבְרָם
כז עַל־חֲמֹרֵיהֶם וַיֵּלְכוּ מִשָּׁם: וַיִּפְתַּח הָאֶחָד
אֶת־שַׂקּוֹ לָתֵת מִסְפּוֹא לַחֲמֹרוֹ בַּמָּלוֹן
וַיַּרְא אֶת־כַּסְפּוֹ וְהִנֵּה־הוּא בְּפִי

was directed *secretly* to Menasseh who carried it out personally *(Midrash).*

Joseph intended thereby to provide atonement — measure for measure — for their having sold him. When they would discover their money they would worry that they would be arrested as thieves and sold as slaves. This was also one of the reasons he later used the goblet to fabricate evidence against him (*Kli Yakar; Abarbanel).*

The names of precious metals — gold, silver, etc. — never occur in the plural. The plural in our verse כַּסְפֵּיהֶם, lit. *their silvers,* refers not to the metal but to the coins *(Sforno; Karnei Or).*

וְלָתֵת לָהֶם צֵדָה לַדָּרֶךְ — *And to give them provisions for the journey.*

So during their journey they would not have to eat what they had bought for their households. Joseph told them that he was graciously giving them provisions for the journey [and did not conceal it as he did the restoration of their monies *(R' Eisenstadt)*] because he wanted to demonstrate that he had no evil intentions, but merely wanted them to return with Benjamin so their claims could be verified *(Ramban).*

וַיַּעַשׂ לָהֶם כֵּן — *And so he* [i.e. the person in charge *of so doing*] *did for them.*

[The phrase is elliptic and, in usual Scriptural style, refers to an implied subject — the obvious one in charge of performing the act described. See *Rashi* to 41:13 s.v. הֵשִׁיב.]

According to the Midrash, as noted, Menasseh did this and he is the subject of the phrase.

This phrase refers to the replacement of the money and the supplying of provisions for the journey. The filling of their vessels with grain was already described in the beginning of this verse *(Radak).*

26. וַיִּשְׂאוּ אֶת־שִׁבְרָם עַל חֲמֹרֵיהֶם — *Then they loaded their purchases onto their donkeys.*

The subject of this phrase is ambiguous. The *brothers* may have loaded the sacks that had been filled by Joseph's officials (*v.* 25) — in which case the brothers are the subject of both verbs in this verse (*loading* and *departing*). *Maasei Hashem* suggests that the loading was done by *Joseph's workers* to avoid the possibility that the brothers might notice the money were they to load the sacks themselves. The subject of the *departure,* of course, is the brothers.

וַיֵּלְכוּ מִשָּׁם — *And* [*they*] *departed from there.*

They left without delay after their donkeys were loaded. Were this not the implication of the quick succession of phrases, there would be no need for the Torah to report the obvious fact that they loaded their donkeys *(Or HaChaim).*

27. וַיִּפְתַּח הָאֶחָד אֶת־שַׂקּוֹ — *When the one of them opened his sack.*

The one of them — Levi. Now that he was separated from his companion Simeon, he was *the one (Rashi).*

This interpretation is based upon the

*to give them provisions for the journey. And so he
did for them.* [26] *Then they loaded their purchase onto
their donkeys and departed from there.*
[27] *When the one of them opened his sack to give
feed to his donkey at the inn, he saw his money right
there in the mouth if his sack.* [28] *So he said to his*

definite article הָאֶחָד, *the* one, indicating that the individual was in this case distinctive as being only *one,* a reference to Levi who was usually paired with Simeon *(Mizrachi; Tzeidah LaDerech).*

According to *Ibn Ezra,* it was probably the *foremost* [lit. *one*] among them — Reuben, the first born.

לָתֵת מִסְפּוֹא לַחֲמֹרוֹ בַּמָּלוֹן — *To give feed to his donkey at the inn.*

Ramban offers several interpretations of how it occurred that only one of the brothers discovered his money, while the others did not discover theirs until later [*v.* 25]:

— Possibly, the others took along תֶּבֶן, *straw* [which is an inferior feed not affected by the famine] for their donkeys, and they therefore had no need to open their packs to feed them, while this brother had a weaker donkey which required מִסְפּוֹא, *feed* [i.e. a better mixture including *grain* (see *Radak* to 24:25)]. When he opened the sack to feed it, he found the money in the mouth of his pack.

— According to the implication of *Onkelos* who interprets אַמְתַּחְתּוֹ as *his load* [see below], *Ramban* suggests that each donkey was loaded with several sacks to balance its load. Though several of the men may each have opened one of their sacks, only this one happened to find money in the particular sack he opened. His brothers then emptied their other sacks and found the rest of the money.

— Alternately, *Ramban* offers that each load consisted of a double-sided large sack, and that one brother happened to open that particular side where the money lay, while the others did not.

Rosh, cited by his son, the *Tur,* maintains, like *Rashi,* that it was Levi. He was the first to discover the money because he led Simeon's donkey too, and since he had to feed both donkeys, he reached the bottom of his pack before the other brothers.

According to *Abarbanel* and *Malbim,* Joseph ordered that in the case of all the brothers except for Levi, the money be placed near the *bottom* of their packs. He purposely had *Levi's* money left closer to the mouth, so he would be the first to discover the money and be distressed even during the journey. The reason was that of the nine brothers, Levi was the most guilty for the sale [and this would provide atonement measure for measure].

This essentially follows the view of *Radak* who explains that Joseph did not make the monies in *all* their packs readily visible for fear that if all of them discovered the money during the journey they would have immediately returned to Egypt to restore the money and protest their innocence. He therefore ordered that the money of *one* of them be placed near the mouth in order to frighten them. He knew, however, that they would not return to Egypt because of a single discovery.

וַיַּרְא אֶת־כַּסְפּוֹ וְהִנֵּה־הוּא בְּפִי אַמְתַּחְתּוֹ — [Then] *he saw his money right there* [lit. *and behold it was*] *in the mouth of his sack.*

He knew it was *his own money* — the money with which he had paid for his provisions — because it was tied up in his own bundle *(R' Avraham ben HaRambam).*

Rashi interprets אַמְתַּחַת as synonymous with the *sack* just mentioned.

Ramban explains it as referring to a large, double-sided sack, called מְטַרְתָּא in Aramaic

כח אַמְתַּחְתּוֹ: וַיֹּאמֶר אֶל־אֶחָיו הוּשַׁב כַּסְפִּי
וְגַם הִנֵּה בְאַמְתַּחְתִּי וַיֵּצֵא לִבָּם וַיֶּחֶרְדוּ
אִישׁ אֶל־אָחִיו לֵאמֹר מַה זֹּאת עָשָׂה
כט אֱלֹהִים לָנוּ: וַיָּבֹאוּ אֶל־יַעֲקֹב אֲבִיהֶם
אַרְצָה כְּנָעַן וַיַּגִּידוּ לוֹ אֵת כָּל־הַקֹּרֹת
ל אֹתָם לֵאמֹר: דִּבֶּר הָאִישׁ אֲדֹנֵי הָאָרֶץ
אִתָּנוּ קָשׁוֹת וַיִּתֵּן אֹתָנוּ כִּמְרַגְּלִים אֶת־

[see *Kesubos* 110a and *Rashi* there]. Because it stretches [יִמְתַּח] at the sides while it is being filled, it is also called אַמְתַּחַת.

Onkelos renders it *load,* referring to the total numbers of sacks loaded on each animal to equalize the weight.

According to *Malbim,* the term refers to a smaller pouch into which personal articles are kept, while שַׂק refers to the large bags where wheat and feed are kept.

28. הוּשַׁב כַּסְפִּי וְגַם הִנֵּה בְאַמְתַּחְתִּי — *My money has been returned and look! it, too, is in my sack!*

His fright was greatest when he recognized the money as *his own* — so that he was vulnerable to a personal accusation. This was part of Joseph's scheme. He wanted the brothers to realize how fully they were in his power and that he could do as he pleased with them *(R' Hirsch).*

The word גַּם, *too,* is somewhat superfluous in this verse. *Rashi* explains that it refers to the money in the sack *in addition to the grain.*

According to *Tzror HaMor,* גַּם, *too,* [which indicates a רִבּוּי, *extension,* beyond the literal scope of the clause (see *v.* 22 (וְגַם דָּמוֹ)] intimates that he [Levi, see *Rashi v.* 27] found *Simeon's* money there too.

וַיֵּצֵא לִבָּם — [And] *their hearts sank* [lit. *departed*].[1]

[I.e., they felt faint at the prospect that this returned money might imply some sinister plot on the part of Joseph; see below.]

According to an early commentator cited in *Torah Sheleimah* §91, they were afraid that Joseph intended to keep Simeon as a slave and the money was the price he had paid.

[The heart is figuratively depicted throughout Scripture as the seat of the intellect. Accordingly, *Onkelos* renders: *And the knowledge of their hearts departed,* and they became confounded. Cf. the metaphor in *Deut.* 29:3.]

וַיֶּחֶרְדוּ אִישׁ אֶל־אָחִיו לֵאמֹר — *And they turned trembling one to another, saying* [lit. *and they trembled, man to his brother, to say*].

[On the verb חרד *tremble,* cf. 27:33.]

מַה־זֹּאת עָשָׂה אֱלֹהִים לָנוּ — *What is this that God has done to us?*[2]

The Divine Name used here, *Elohim,* refers to God in His Aspect as Dispenser of Strict Justice [see on 1:1]. *What is this that God,* in a display of His Aspect of Justice, *has done to us?* They knew — even in this moment of their distress — that this was no mere accident, but a calculated act of Providence *(Akei-*

1. In a touching aside, the Midrash records that when the Talmudic Sage R' Shimon ben R' Zavdi died, R' Levi was called upon to deliver the eulogy:

'Our Tribal Ancestors *found* an article [the money in their sacks], yet their hearts sank,' he lamented. 'How much greater should our anguish be at having *lost* R' Shimon ben R' Zavdi!'

42
29-30

*brothers, "My money has been returned and look! it,
too, is in my sack!" Their hearts sank and they
turned trembling one to another saying, "What is
this that God has done to us?"*
*29 They came to Jacob their father in the land of
Canaan and they told him of all their experiences as
follows, 30 "The man, the lord of the land, spoke
harshly to us and considerred us as if we were spying*

das Yitzchak; R' Bachya). [See *R' Munk* cited in footnote to *v.* 19 above.]

— What is this that God has done to us—by bringing us into a situation of suspicion? For the money was returned only to furnish a pretext for a plot against us *(Rashi).*

— By inspiring this self-portrayed 'God-fearing' man to treat us in a way that will provide him with a fresh pretext on account of which he will be able to sell us as slaves. In this way we would be punished measure for measure for having sold Joseph. But this would not be a true measure for measure. We acted justifiably in self-defense [see comm. to 37:18] — and the fact that we sold rather than executed him was an act of compassion on our part *(Sforno).*

29. Their report to their father.

וַיָּבֹאוּ אֶל־יַעֲקֹב אֲבִיהֶם אַרְצָה כְּנָעַן — *[And] they came to Jacob their father in* [lit. *to*] *the land of Canaan.*

The *land of Canaan* is mentioned here because the locale of the narrative has changed; all the preceding had happened in Egypt *(Michlol Yofi).*

וַיַּגִּידוּ לוֹ אֵת כָּל הַקֹּרֹת אֹתָם לֵאמֹר — *And they told him of all their experiences* [lit. *all that had happened to them*], *as follows* [lit. *saying*].

I.e., the following is exactly how the brothers related their experiences to Jacob. A comparison of the following *verbatim* recapitulation with the narrative above, however, will show they concealed certain things, minimizing the gravity of their dilemma as will be pointed out in the commentary *(Akeidah; Ralbag).*

This is further alluded to by the fact that the Torah spells the word הַקֹּרֹת, *experiences,* deficiently, without the ו, *vav* [instead of הַקּוֹרוֹת], to indicate that the brother's narrative of these events was also deficient. They did not tell Jacob *everything* that happened. They initially minimized the harshness of Joseph's ultimatums to spare him grief. They also knew that had Jacob heard how harshly Joseph had dealt with them, he would never, under any circumstances, have allowed Benjamin to return with them *(Alshich; Ralbag).*

30. דִּבֶּר הָאִישׁ אֲדֹנֵי הָאָרֶץ אִתָּנוּ קָשׁוֹת — *The man, the lord of the land, spoke harshly to us.*

[The noun אֲדֹנֵי, *lord,* [lit. *lords*], is in the plural, but takes a singular

2. Commenting upon how, in their great distress, the brothers blamed God for a situation which they had brought upon themselves by selling Joseph, the Talmud *(Taanis* 9a) records the following:

R' Yochanan happened to come across Resh Lakish's young son reciting the verse in

לא הָאָרֶץ: וַנֹּאמֶר אֵלָיו כֵּנִים אֲנָחְנוּ לֹא
לב הָיִינוּ מְרַגְּלִים: שְׁנֵים־עָשָׂר אֲנַחְנוּ אַחִים
בְּנֵי אָבִינוּ הָאֶחָד אֵינֶנּוּ וְהַקָּטֹן הַיּוֹם אֶת־
לג אָבִינוּ בְּאֶרֶץ כְּנָעַן: וַיֹּאמֶר אֵלֵינוּ הָאִישׁ
אֲדֹנֵי הָאָרֶץ בְּזֹאת אֵדַע כִּי כֵנִים אַתֶּם
אֲחִיכֶם הָאֶחָד הַנִּיחוּ אִתִּי וְאֶת־רַעֲבוֹן
לד בָּתֵּיכֶם קְחוּ וָלֵכוּ: וְהָבִיאוּ אֶת־אֲחִיכֶם
הַקָּטֹן אֵלַי וְאֵדְעָה כִּי לֹא מְרַגְּלִים אַתֶּם
כִּי כֵנִים אַתֶּם אֶת־אֲחִיכֶם אֶתֵּן לָכֶם
לה וְאֶת־הָאָרֶץ תִּסְחָרוּ: וַיְהִי הֵם מְרִיקִים

verb דִּבֶּר, *spoke*. See *Rashi* to 35:8 who explains that nouns denoting power or lordship often occur in plural. Cf. also 39:2.]

Sifre [*Numbers* 99] cites our verse to prove that the Hebrew verb for *speak* [דבר] always denotes harsh words. See *Numbers* 12:1.

וַיִּתֵּן אֹתָנוּ כִּמְרַגְּלִים אֶת הָאָרֶץ — *And considered* [lit. *gave*] *us as if* [*we were*] *spying out the land.*

The language they used to their aged father — כִּמְרַגְּלִים, *as if we were spying* [i.e., implying that he merely *suspected* them of being spies] — subtly concealed the true fact that the Egyptian was quite *definite* in his accusation *(Abarbanel).*

32. שְׁנֵים־עָשָׂר אֲנַחְנוּ אַחִים בְּנֵי אָבִינוּ — *We are twelve brothers, sons of our father.*]

הָאֶחָד אֵינֶנּוּ וְהַקָּטֹן הַיּוֹם אֶת אָבִינוּ בְּאֶרֶץ כְּנָעַן — *One is gone and the youngest is now* [lit. *today*] *with our father in the land of Canaan.*

In this recapitulation they reversed the order of *v.* 13 where the youngest was mentioned first and the missing one second. The subtle implication here to their father is that they were *forced* in the course of the dialogue to reveal that they had a younger brother — something they ordinarily would not have offered of their own volition, being sensitive to the probable consequences, and something they tried to keep secret as long as possible *(Tur; Akeidah).*

33. בְּזֹאת אֵדַע כִּי כֵנִים אַתֶּם — *By this I will ascertain whether you are truthful people.*

[Joseph's words were much harsher: *By this you shall be tested* (*v.* 15) ... *Do this and live* [*v.* 18]. The brothers tactfully omitted all references and suggestions that their very lives depended on their acquiescence.]

אֲחִיכֶם הָאֶחָד הַנִּיחוּ אִתִּי — *One of your brothers — leave with me.*

Proverbs 19:3: *Man's foolishness perverts his way, yet his heart frets against* HASHEM [i.e., yet he blames God]. This inspired Resh Lakish to inquire where such a concept is intimated in the *Chumash* itself.

"Surely it is intimated," the child said to him, "in the verse, *And they turned trembling one to another saying 'What is this that God has done to us?'*"

42
31-34 out the land. 31 But we said to him, 'We are truthful
men: we have never been spies! 32 We are twelve
brothers, sons of our father. One is gone and the
youngest is now with our father in the land of Canaan.' 33 Then the man, the lord of the land, said to
us, 'By this I will ascertain whether you are truthful
people: One of your brothers leave with me, and
what is needed for the hunger of your households
take and go. 34 And bring your youngest brother to
me so I will know that you are not spies, but truthful
people. I will restore your brother to you and you will
be free to circulate about the land.' "

[Again, fearful of their father's reaction they concealed the harsh aspects of their encounter with the Egyptian ruler: The ordeal of their three days' imprisonment; that Joseph's actual words were, 'let one of your brothers *be imprisoned in your place of confinement;* and the fact that he bound Simeon before their eyes. It was, as noted above, their intention throughout to minimize the gravity of the situation, so Jacob would be less reluctant to send Benjamin.]

וְאֶת־רַעֲבוֹן בָּתֵּיכֶם קְחוּ וָלֵכוּ — *And* [whatever is needed for] *the hunger of your household — take and go.*

The phrase רַעֲבוֹן בָּתֵּיכֶם, *the hunger of your households,* is clearly elliptical. The implication that the intended phrase is *whatever is needed* follows *Ibn Janach* and *Ibn Ezra.*

Targum renders this passage, as he did verse 19 above: 'and take *the grain* which is lacking in your households'.

34. וְהָבִיאוּ אֶת־אֲחִיכֶם הַקָּטֹן אֵלַי וְאֵדְעָה כִּי לֹא מְרַגְּלִים אַתֶּם כִּי כֵנִים אַתֶּם — *And bring your youngest brother to me, so* [lit. *and*] *I will know that you are not spies, but* [*you are*] *truthful people.*

[They make this sound almost like a conciliatory request, omitting Joseph's implicit ultimatum, *'So your words will be verified and you will not die' (v.* 20).]

אֶת־אֲחִיכֶם אֶתֵּן לָכֶם וְאֶת־הָאָרֶץ תִּסְחָרוּ — *I will restore* [lit. *give*] *your brother* [i.e., Simeon, whom you have left behind with me] *to you, and you will* [be free to] *circulate about the land.*

The translation of תִּסְחָרוּ as *to circulate about* rather than the familiar translation *to engage in trade* follows *Rashi* who offers that all expressions of סְחוֹרָה, *merchandise,* and סוֹחֲרִים, *merchants,* are derived from the verb סחר which essentially means *going about,* because merchants *circulate,* looking for merchandise.

With this interpretation, *Rashi* avoids an obvious difficulty, for we do not find anywhere that Joseph had told the brothers that they would be free *to trade* in the land. Therefore, *Rashi* explains that Joseph promised them the right to circulate about the land and buy grain without hindrance. [We must assume that the brothers did not lie to Jacob. The implication of freedom to circulate

שַׂקֵּיהֶם וְהִנֵּה־אִישׁ צְרוֹר־כַּסְפּוֹ בְּשַׂקּוֹ
וַיִּרְאוּ אֶת־צְרֹרוֹת כַּסְפֵּיהֶם הֵמָּה
לו וַאֲבִיהֶם וַיִּירָאוּ: וַיֹּאמֶר אֲלֵהֶם יַעֲקֹב
אֲבִיהֶם אֹתִי שִׁכַּלְתֶּם יוֹסֵף אֵינֶנּוּ וְשִׁמְעוֹן
אֵינֶנּוּ וְאֶת־בִּנְיָמִן תִּקָּחוּ עָלַי הָיוּ כֻלָּנָה:

through the land to buy grain unhindered was implicit in Joseph's promise of exoneration when they established their innocence]. However, above in the story of Shechem *Rashi* did not offer his interpretation that the word וְיִסְחֲרוּהָ in 34:21 means *circulate,* for there the subject of the discussion is actual *trade;* they were being offered a special dispensation not regularly offered to foreigners (see *comm.* there). Here, however, only freedom to *travel* the land is meant; therefore he offers his interpretation here and not above *(Ramban).*

Ramban maintains, however [as does *Onkelos* to our verse], that *trading* is the correct sense, although we do not find that Joseph had actually told this to the brothers. Accordingly he postulates that they altered Joseph's assurance 'for the sake of peace' by presenting a somewhat more optimistic picture to make Jacob more amenable towards allowing Benjamin to return with them. Possibly, Joseph *had* intimated that if they established their innocence, he would compensate for their embarrassment by granting them special trading privileges not normally granted foreigners [see 34:10]. However, just as there might have been other details of their dialogue which remained unrecorded, the Torah did not record this particular detail either, for as noted in *v.* 21, the Torah characteristically shortens a narrative in one place and elaborates on the details in another.

35. וַיְהִי הֵם מְרִיקִים שַׂקֵּיהֶם — *Then* [lit. *and*] *as they were emptying their sacks.*

This refers to the rest of the brothers; one of the brothers had already opened his sack at the inn and made the discovery earlier [*v.* 27] *(Radak).*

וְהִנֵּה־אִישׁ צְרוֹר־כַּסְפּוֹ בְּשַׂקּוֹ — *That behold! Every man's bundle of money was in his sack!*

It was unmistakeably the very same bundles of money with which they had paid for the rations of grain that had now been *(Ralbag).*

וַיִּרְאוּ אֶת־צְרֹרוֹת כַּסְפֵּיהֶם הֵמָּה וַאֲבִיהֶם וַיִּירָאוּ — *And when they and their father saw their bundles of money, they were terrified.*[1]

They knew that the money in *all* their sacks could not possibly be an oversight. It was obvious that a plot was being implemented against them and they were terrified at its implications *(Alshich).*

Targum Yonasan interprets: And they were terrified on account of Simeon whom they had left behind.

36. אֹתִי שִׁכַּלְתֶּם — *I am the one whom you bereaved!*

The term שְׁכוֹל [*bereft*] refers to one who has lost his children *(Rashi;* cf. on 27:45).

1. In a deeper, Kabbalistic sense, this verse intimates that the brothers prophetically foresaw the destiny of the ten martyred Sages of Israel [עֲשָׂרָה הֲרוּגֵי מַלְכוּת] who would be killed centuries later in atonement for the ten brothers' sale of Joseph [see comm. to 37:28]. Thus, *they and their father perceived the* צְרוֹת, *troubles,* that would befall their descendants — as a result of כַּסְפֵּיהֶם, *their monies* [in the plural] alluding both to this returned money and the money they received when they sold Joseph — *and they were terrified (Paane'ach Raza).*

42
35-36

35 *Then, as they were emptying their sacks, behold! every man's bundle of money was in his sack. When they and their father saw their bundles of money they were terrified.* 36 *Their father Jacob said to them, "I am the one whom you bereaved! Joseph is gone, Simeon is gone, and now you would take away Benjamin? Upon me has it all befallen!"*

We derive from Jacob's remark that he suspected them of having slain or sold Simeon and that they may have done the same to Joseph (*Rashi* according to *Gur Aryeh*).

[That the unexpected wealth in their sacks aroused Jacob's suspicions that they had *sold* Simeon for the grain, and possibly led him to suspect that they had sold Joseph too, has basis in *Bereishis Rabbah* 91:9. However, *Rashi's* suggestion that Jacob suspected that they had *slain* Joseph needs clarification, especially in light of Jacob's later statement regarding Joseph (44:28): אַךְ טָרֹף טֹרָף, *surely he is torn in pieces* (a Hebrew expression used *exclusively* of one *mangled by wild beasts;* not one murdered by human agency)].

[Actually, as *Tzeidah laDerech* points out, it is not Jacob speaking in 44:28; rather, the speaker is Judah quoting Jacob. He postulates that just as in 44:20 *Rashi* suggests that Judah mistated a fact out of fear, the expression *surely he is torn in pieces* might also be an example of such a misquote, and in fact, while Jacob did not *explicitly* mention it, he did indeed harbor an inner suspicion that both Joseph and Simeon were victims of foul play. (Cf. *Gur Aryeh; Be'er Yitzchak.* See, for example, *v.* 38 below where Jacob uses the expression *for his brother is dead.)*

יוֹסֵף אֵינֶנּוּ וְשִׁמְעוֹן אֵינֶנּוּ וְאֶת־בִּנְיָמִין תִּקָּחוּ — *Joseph is gone* [lit. *is not*], [*and*] *Simeon is gone* [lit. *is not*], *and* [now] *you would take away Benjamin!*

— Who knows what misfortune will befall him? (*R' Bachya*).

— The Egyptian might accuse him also of spying! (*Abarbanel*).

Although the expression אֵינֶנּוּ, *is gone,* is used for both Joseph and Simeon, the connotations are not the same. *Onkelos* accordingly renders: *Joseph is not and Simeon is not here.*

Targum Yonasan paraphrases the sense: 'Of Joseph you said, An evil beast has devoured him; of Simeon you said, The king of the land has bound him; and Benjamin you seek to take away!'

According to the Talmud [*Chullin* 95b], Jacob was worried that should anything happen to Benjamin, this third misfortune would portend that endless calamities awaited him henceforth. [Cf. *Rashi* and *R'Gershom* there.]

As *R' Hirsch* explains Jacob's response: 'You cannot hold my refusal against me. Though I do not know what happened to them, *I* am the one now bereft of Joseph and Simeon. And since both suffered misfortune under similar curcumstance — when they were among you — I have no right to place a third son in such jeopardy. For (as the Sages teach in *Chullin* 95b) although we may not be superstitious, we may take note of 'signs' regarding houses, children, and wives'.

עָלַי הָיוּ כֻלָּנָה — *Upon me has it all befallen.*

— *All,* i.e. all of these disasters (*Ibn Ezra*).[1]

1. When Rebecca instructed Jacob to deceive Isaac into giving him the blessings, Jacob expressed the fear that he would be discovered and incur Isaac's curse. To this, Rebecca responded עָלַי קִלְלָתְךָ בְּנִי, *your curse be on me, my son* [27:13].

The word עָלַי is interpreted homiletically as the initials of the three names עֵשָׂו, לָבָן, יוֹסֵף, *Esau, Laban, Joseph.* Rebecca was intimating that Jacob would suffer only in connection with those three. Remembering that promise, Jacob now bemoaned his plight: Joseph and Simeon

לז וַיֹּאמֶר רְאוּבֵן אֶל־אָבִיו לֵאמֹר אֶת־שְׁנֵי
בָנַי תָּמִית אִם־לֹא אֲבִיאֶנּוּ אֵלֶיךָ תְּנָה
לח אֹתוֹ עַל־יָדִי וַאֲנִי אֲשִׁיבֶנּוּ אֵלֶיךָ: וַיֹּאמֶר
לֹא־יֵרֵד בְּנִי עִמָּכֶם כִּי־אָחִיו מֵת וְהוּא

Not necessarily these in particular, but in general: I have experienced all kinds of disasters in my lifetime *(Heidenheim).*

— *Upon me has it all befallen,* i.e., the tragedy of the loss of children affected primarily *me,* the father. This sense of עָלַי, *upon me,* as meaning *primarily affecting me,* is similar to 48:7: מֵתָה עָלַי רָחֵל, *Rachel died 'upon' me,* i.e., her death affected primarily me [Jacob], for as the Sages teach, 'a woman dies for none but her husband' *(Sechel Tov).*

Thus, your grief as brothers, cannot compare with mine as a father! *(Akeidah).*

— Such tragedies have not happened to *your* children, but to mine. Undoubtedly, the cause is your quarrels with each other, and I regard you as the indirect cause of my bereavement *(Sforno).*

According to *Malbim,* the meaning is different: The blame for all of their misfortune is upon me. I caused Joseph's death by sending him into danger, and I will be similarly held accountable for Simeon's and Benjamin's deaths for allowing them to go to a place of danger, and I dread the punishment in store for me in consequence of this.

The *Midrash* interprets: Upon me has devolved the duty of begetting the Twelve Tribes, and I have reared them; but now that their number is diminished I am as one utterly bereft *(Lekach Tov).*

37. Reuben's Proposal.

וַיֹּאמֶר רְאוּבֵן אֶל אָבִיו לֵאמֹר — *Then Reuben said to his father as follows* [lit. *saying*].

As the firstborn, he felt it his duty to speak up *(Abarbanel).*

אֶת־שְׁנֵי בָנַי תָּמִית אִם־לֹא אֲבִיאֶנּוּ אֵלֶיךָ — *You may slay my two sons if I fail to bring him* [Benjamin] *back to you* [lit. *if I do not take him to you.*]

The commentators agree that this was not meant literally:

Reuben spoke figuratively, in the sense of obligating himself under the penalty of a curse *(Ramban).*

— You may slay my two sons with a curse *(Targum Yonasan). Onkelos,* too, uses the verb תְּמִית which he employs throughout Scripture only when the sense is *death at the hands of Heaven* [the meaning here accordingly being: *Bring about his death by cursing him*]. When *Onkelos* speaks of *murder,* he uses the verb קְטִיל *(Nesinah l'Ger).*

Reuben thereby uttered a curse that his two sons should die if he should fail to return Benjamin. See incident of Rav and Shmuel related in *Shabbos* 108a *(Sforno).*

According to *Tosafos HaRosh* the implication was: *May you consider them as dead and disinherited if I fail (HaKsav V'Hakabbalah).*

Ibn Ezra cites two interpretations: (a) *slay,* i.e. punish [by excommunication *(Karnei Or)*]; (b) this was not said *to*

were already gone; Benjamin might be endangered, too — what had happened to Rebecca's promise that Jacob's only misfortune would be those represented by the word עָלַי? *(Vilna Gaon).*

37 *Then Reuben said to his father as follows, "You
may slay my two sons if I fail to bring him back to
you. Put him in my care and I will return him to
you."*
38 *But he said, "My son shall not go down with*

Jacob, but in Jacob's presence *as a prayer to God* [that *He* take the children's life away] if Reuben does not bring Benjamin back.

Avos d'Rabbi Nosson [quoted in *Torah Sheleimah* §102] cites Reuben as an example of 'a fool who asks improperly.' For was Jacob our Father a murderer? Reuben's crass suggestion did not even deserve an answer from Jacob.

Following *Malbim* [end of last verse] according to whom Jacob was expressing fear of the consequences to himself should he expose Benjamin to danger, Reuben now answered: 'The sin shall devolve upon me; *let this sin take the lives of my two sons* [תָּמִית being here interpreted in the third pers. fem. passive — *let* **her** (the sin) *kill*] — *if I do not,* etc.

אֶת שְׁנֵי בָנַי — *My two sons.*

I.e., *two of my sons,* for he had a total of *four* [Chanoch, Phalu, Chetzron, Carmi (see 46:9] *(Radak).*

He mentioned *two* in the sense of *double:* In retribution for harm that may come to *one* of your sons, punishment may befall *two* of my sons if I fail to bring Benjamin back *(Ramban).*

Sifsei Kohen maintains that Reuben's offer of two was the *quid pro quo* for Jacob's *two* sons: *Simeon and Benjamin,* for Reuben obligated himself to return with both of them.

תְּנָה אֹתוֹ עַל־יָדִי וַאֲנִי אֲשִׁיבֶנּוּ אֵלֶיךָ — *Put him in my care* [lit. *upon my hand*] *and I will return him to you.*

Reuben had this confidence in himself because he knew he was guiltless in the affair of selling Joseph, and of all the brothers he would be the most likely to succeed in this mission *(Or HaChaim).*

38. Jacob does not respond to Reuben's offer directly. Instead, he addressed his rejection to his sons as a group.

לֹא־יֵרֵד בְּנִי עִמָּכֶם — *My son shall not go down with you* ['you' is in plural].

Thus, Jacob summarily rejected Reuben's offer. 'He is a fool, this eldest son of mine,' Jacob declared. 'He suggests that I should kill his sons. Are not his sons also my sons!' *(Rashi).*

Although Jacob refused Reuben's offer, he later entrusted Judah with the mission (43:9-13) because he was confident that Judah's great influence with his brothers would assure their cooperation in bringing back Benjamin no matter how great the difficulty. Moreover, Reuben had already sinned against Jacob [in the matter of Bilhah (35:22)] and Jacob would no longer rely on him. Furthermore, the timing of Judah's offer was better conceived; he left his father alone until there was no more food in the house [see below 43:8] *(Ramban).*

[The reasons Jacob gave here for refusing Reuben's offer were sincere, quite valid, and applied equally to Judah's. Nevertheless Jacob acceded to Judah's request because he had more confidence in him and because the timing of his offer was more propitious.]

Sforno notes how Jacob referred to Benjamin as *my son* — the only one left of his mother who had been the cornerstone of the household.

לְבַדּוֹ נִשְׁאָר וּקְרָאָהוּ אָסוֹן בַּדֶּרֶךְ אֲשֶׁר
תֵּלְכוּ־בָהּ וְהוֹרַדְתֶּם אֶת־שֵׂיבָתִי בְּיָגוֹן
א־ב שְׁאוֹלָה: וְהָרָעָב כָּבֵד בָּאָרֶץ: וַיְהִי כַּאֲשֶׁר
כִּלּוּ לֶאֱכֹל אֶת־הַשֶּׁבֶר אֲשֶׁר הֵבִיאוּ
מִמִּצְרָיִם וַיֹּאמֶר אֲלֵיהֶם אֲבִיהֶם שֻׁבוּ
ג שִׁבְרוּ־לָנוּ מְעַט־אֹכֶל: וַיֹּאמֶר אֵלָיו

כִּי־אָחִיו מֵת וְהוּא לְבַדּוֹ נִשְׁאָר — *For his brother is dead* [or: *has died*] *and he alone is left.*

For his brother, i.e. his *full* brother, Joseph, from the same mother, *is dead, and he alone* — of that mother — is left *(Ralbag).*

Jacob thus expressed his rationale for showing greater concern for Benjamin, whom danger *might* befall, than for Simeon, who was languishing in an Egyptian prison and whose life would *certainly* be in danger if all his brothers did not return to Egypt to redeem him. Accordingly, Jacob emphasized Benjamin's uniqueness: He is the only one whose full brother had died, and his loss would, in a sense, be greater than that of Simeon, since Benjamin was the only survivor of his mother while Simeon had five brothers *(Or HaChaim).*

וּקְרָאָהוּ אָסוֹן בַּדֶּרֶךְ אֲשֶׁר תֵּלְכוּ־בָהּ — *And should disaster befall* [lit. *call;* see *v.* 4] him on the journey which you shall take [lit. *on the road that you shall walk on it*].

... Which is highly likely since 'the Satan accuses in time of danger,' i.e., there is greater danger on a hazardous road than at home (see *Rashi v.* 4 s.v. פֶּן).

The Hebrew literally reads: *And disaster* **will** *call him on the journey,* etc. Jacob was agonizing: I am *certain* he will be harmed on the way; how will you be able to save him from sudden danger? *(Akeidah).*

וְהוֹרַדְתֶּם אֶת־שֵׂיבָתִי בְּיָגוֹן שְׁאוֹלָה — *Then you will have brought down my hoariness* [*lit. white hair, white head;* metaphorically *old age*] *in sorrow to the grave* [Hebrew: *she'ol*].

—Since I will never cease mourning. Benjamin is Rachel's only survivor; while he is with me I find consolation for the loss of his mother and brother; if he should die it will seem to me as though the three of them died on the same day (see *Rashi* 44:29).

Comp. also *Rashi* to 37:35 where the Midrashic implication is that שְׁאוֹל refers to *Gehinnom,* and Jacob was bemoaning that by the loss of his son he will experience Divine punishment in the afterlife. For Jacob had a tradition that as long as none of his sons died during his lifetime, he was assured that he would never experience such punishment.

The word שְׁאוֹל, *lower-world* refers to the depths of the earth, the opposite of the heavens which are the *heights (Ibn Ezra* to *Jonah* 2:3). Metaphorically, as *Rashi* notes in 37:35 it refers to the depths of the grave, the place of the dead. According to the *Zohar* [III:285] *She'ol* is one of the levels of Gehinnom. It is often used figuratively to indicate spiritual distress [for example, *Psalms* 18:5].

you, for his brother is dead and he alone is left.
Should disaster befall him on the journey which you
shall take, then you will have brought down my
hoariness in sorrow to the grave."

The famine was severe in the land. [2] *When they had*
finished eating the provisions which they had
brought from Egypt their father said to them, "Go
back, buy us some food." [3] *But Judah said to him as*

XLIII

1. The brothers return to Egypt

וְהָרָעָב כָּבֵד בָּאָרֶץ — [*And*] *the famine was severe in the land.*

I.e. it grew more severe *(Ralbag).*

The land in this context, refers to the land *par excellence* — Eretz Yisrael *(Akeidah).*

According to *Midrash HaGadol, earth* in our verse refers to the *whole world,* and this passage is cited among nine others proof verses to indicate that famine had gripped the whole world ten times.

2. כַּאֲשֶׁר כִּלּוּ לֶאֱכֹל אֶת־הַשֶּׁבֶר — *When they* [i.e., Jacob's family] *had finished eating the provisions* [lit. *purchase*].

— Depleting whatever they had left *(Rashi).* Possibly they remained with only enough to last until they could make a trip to Egypt and back *(Or HaChaim).*

Judah had advised his brothers to wait and leave the Patriarch alone until the household ran out of food — for then he would be more disposed to consent to Benjamin's going *(Rashi; Ramban* 42:37).

— That is why Judah did not speak immediately after Jacob rejected Reuben's offer. Out of respect to their aged father, they did not press him, but they made do with a little and waited until the famine became more severe and their survival would *demand* that Jacob allow Benjamin to go with them *(Gur Aryeh; Tzeidah laDerech).*

Rashi notes that *Onkelos* renders כַּאֲשֶׁר כִּלּוּ as כַּד שֵׁיצִיאוּ [*when they had finished,* i.e., completely depleted their supplies, no more food being left]. Some Temanite manuscripts preserve a version in *Onkelos* where this phrase is rendered כַּד סַפִּיקוּ [i.e., *when they had enough* (intimating, contrary to the above, that they ate sufficiently for their needs, and *not* that they were lacking in remaining supplies)]. *Rashi* maintains that the latter version is incorrect. He explains that in 24:22, *when the camels had finished* [כַּאֲשֶׁר כִּלּוּ] *drinking, Onkelos* rightly renders כַּד סַפִּיקוּ since the context implies that the camels had drunk sufficiently for their thirst. Here, however, the reference is to *total* consumption, and the correct Aramaic for this connotation is כַּד שֵׁיצִיאוּ.

אֲשֶׁר הֵבִיאוּ מִמִּצְרָיִם — *Which they had brought from Egypt.*

It is conceivable that this otherwise superfluous phrase intimates that only the food they had brought from Egypt was now depleted; they were now dependent upon whatever reserves Jacob had put away against the famine *(Or HaChaim).*

שֻׁבוּ שִׁבְרוּ לָנוּ מְעַט אֹכֶל — *Go back, buy us some food.*

How could Jacob tell them to do this after having been apprised of the Egyptian viceroy's condition that they dare not return without Benjamin?

יְהוּדָה לֵאמֹר הָעֵד הֵעִד בָּנוּ הָאִישׁ
לֵאמֹר לֹא־תִרְאוּ פָנַי בִּלְתִּי אֲחִיכֶם
ד אִתְּכֶם: אִם־יֶשְׁךָ מְשַׁלֵּחַ אֶת־אָחִינוּ אִתָּנוּ
ה נֵרְדָה וְנִשְׁבְּרָה לְךָ אֹכֶל: וְאִם־אֵינְךָ
מְשַׁלֵּחַ לֹא נֵרֵד כִּי־הָאִישׁ אָמַר אֵלֵינוּ
לֹא־תִרְאוּ פָנַי בִּלְתִּי אֲחִיכֶם אִתְּכֶם:
ו וַיֹּאמֶר יִשְׂרָאֵל לָמָה הֲרֵעֹתֶם לִי לְהַגִּיד
ז לָאִישׁ הַעוֹד לָכֶם אָח: וַיֹּאמְרוּ שָׁאוֹל

Jacob's emphasis is on **מְעַט אֹכֶל, a little** *food:* He reasoned that perhaps if they returned to purchase only a *small* amount of food, the viceroy would not notice them (*Sechel Tov*).

Sforno suggests that Jacob did not believe their story. He suspected that they only wanted an opportunity to take Benjamin in order to do away with him like Joseph. Jacob implied his suspicions when he said, *I am the one whom you bereaved* [42:37; see *Rashi* there].

3. וַיֹּאמֶר אֵלָיו יְהוּדָה לֵאמֹר — *But* [lit. *and*] *Judah said to him as follows* [lit. *saying*].

[Again it is Judah, as in 37:26 ff, who speaks the decisive word after a futile suggestion from Reuben.]

הָעֵד הֵעִד בָּנוּ הָאִישׁ — *The man sternly* [or: *repeatedly*] *warned us* [the Hebrew idiom is in the emphatic infinitive compound: *warn he has warned us*].

The reference is to the solemn oath that Joseph had taken in 42:15ff, threatening them with death (ibid. verses 18, 20).

In this context, the word העד [derived from the verb עוד, *to bear witness*] denotes *warning,* since a warning is generally given in the presence of witnesses. Comp. *Jeremiah* 11:7 הַעִדֹתִי בַּאֲבוֹתֵיכֶם, *I have persistently warned your fathers; Exodus* 19:21: רֵד הָעֵד בָּעָם, *go down warn the people (Rashi).*

In addition to giving testimony, Jewish witnesses have the additional responsibility of warning someone before he commits a crime and making him aware of the law. Thus, the expression העיד ב can refer either to giving evidence against someone *after* the deed, or warning him *before* the deed. Here it is the latter. The doubled verb הָעֵד הֵעִד implies that Joseph had warned them at the outset and again when they left that they should not dare to return without Benjamin *(R' Hirsch).*

לֹא־תִרְאוּ פָנַי בִּלְתִּי אֲחִיכֶם אִתְּכֶם — *You dare not see my face unless your brother is with you.*

— He will not allow us to see him at all; he is in charge of the food and it will be impossible to buy even a *little* grain *(Sechel Tov).*

[Judah now quoted the Egyptian viceroy in stronger terms than the brothers used earlier in their recapitulation (42:34). Originally, they minimized the harshness of their predicament in order to spare Jacob grief, and to give him less reason to oppose Benjamin's return with them. Now, however, they realized that only extreme urgency would make Jacob consent; the situation demanded unabashed candor.]

The term בִּלְתִּי means either *except* as above in 21:26, or *unless,* as in our verse. *Rashi* notes that *Onkelos* renders our pas-

follows, "The man sternly warned us saying, 'You dare not see my face unless your brother is with you.'
4 *If you are ready to send our brother with us we will go down and buy you food. But if you do not send, we will not go down for the man said to us, 'You dare not see my face unless your brother is with you.' "*
6 *Then Israel said, "Why did you treat me so ill by telling the man that you had another brother?"*

sage אֱלָהֵין כַּד אֲחוּכוֹן עִמְּכוֹן, *except when your brother is with you* [adding the word כַּד, *when*, to which there is no corresponding word in the Hebrew.] Accordingly, *Rashi* offers that while *Onkelos* correctly interpreted the *sense* of the matter, he was not particular to translate it literally [as *unless*, a translation which would not require additional words. See *Mizrachi; Divrei David*].

4. אִם יֶשְׁךָ מְשַׁלֵּחַ אֶת אָחִינוּ אִתָּנוּ — *If you are ready* [lit. *if you have it* (i.e. if you have it within you; intend) see comm. to 24:42] *to send* [lit. *sending*] *our brother with us.*

נֵרְדָה וְנִשְׁבְּרָה לְךָ אֹכֶל — *We will go down and buy* [*for*] *you food.*

— I.e. *for you*, as the Patriarch upon whom the entire household depends *(Ralbag).*

The suffix ה in נֵרְדָה וְנִשְׁבְּרָה rather than נֵרֵד וְנִשְׁבֹּר [in addition to being a polite form (see on 27:19)] denotes frequency of action: If you are ready to send our brother with us *we will go down and buy you food* — even many times. But [next verse] if you do not send him, *we will not go down even once* — [רֵד occurs without the suffix ה] *(Tur).*

5. וְאִם־אֵינְךָ מְשַׁלֵּחַ לֹא נֵרֵד — *But if you do not send* [lit. *but if you are not sending*], *we will not go down.*

כִּי הָאִישׁ אָמַר אֵלֵינוּ וְכוּ׳ — *For the man said to us, 'You dare not see my face unless your brother is with you.'*

Judah repeated this [from *v.* 3] to *emphasize* the gravity of the threat. It was not simply a matter of a *warning* which they dare ignore, out of honor to their father, by returning without Benjamin. The man made it clear that their returning without Benjamin would be futile; they would not be able to see him, nor would they be able to procure food. Therefore, Judah maintained, it was purposeless to return (cf. *Malbim; Haamek Davar).*

6. וַיֹּאמֶר יִשְׂרָאֵל — *Then* [lit. *and*] *Israel said.*

As noted, Israel is the name used to depict Jacob in his spiritual role as Patriarch of the Jewish nation.

In this case, he is referred to as Israel, because he offered them a teaching for future generations. Whenever Jews are forced to appear before hostile rulers, they should not offer more information than the question requires (*Haamek Davar).*

לָמָה הֲרֵעֹתֶם לִי לְהַגִּיד לָאִישׁ הַעוֹד לָכֶם אָח — *Why did you treat me so ill by telling* [lit. *to tell*] *the man that you had another brother?*

— You spoke unnecessarily by telling him things he did not ask, things which had nothing to do with the charge of spying. Your mentioning that you had a younger brother at home was superfluous and is causing me anguish *(Abarbanel; Alshich).*

The prefix ה of הַעוֹד [lit. *the another*] does

שָׁאַל־הָאִישׁ לָנוּ וּלְמוֹלַדְתֵּנוּ לֵאמֹר
הַעוֹד אֲבִיכֶם חַי הֲיֵשׁ לָכֶם אָח וַנַּגֶּד־לוֹ
עַל־פִּי הַדְּבָרִים הָאֵלֶּה הֲיָדוֹעַ נֵדַע כִּי
ח יֹאמַר הוֹרִידוּ אֶת־אֲחִיכֶם: וַיֹּאמֶר
יְהוּדָה אֶל־יִשְׂרָאֵל אָבִיו שִׁלְחָה הַנַּעַר
אִתִּי וְנָקוּמָה וְנֵלֵכָה וְנִחְיֶה וְלֹא נָמוּת

not indicate a question here as it does in the next verse. Here it is the definite article introducing a statement *(Haamek Davar).*

7. וַיֹּאמְרוּ — [*And*] *they said.*

— Speaking as a group, they defended themselves against Jacob's charge that they had loose tongues *(Akeidah).*

שָׁאוֹל שָׁאַל הָאִישׁ — *The man* [*persistently*] *asked* [the Hebrew is in the emphatic infinitive compound; literally: *the man ask, asked*].

We did not *offer* him unnecessary information. His investigation was exhaustive and he demanded information about the minutest details of our lives. We *had* to tell him that we are all sons of the same father in order to escape the charge of being spies. As a result, he asked if we had another brother. He implied nothing sinister. That we innocently told him about Benjamin was in reply to a direct question (*Abarbanel*). These particular questions were not asked harshly, like his other accusations, but in a spirit of friendship. Such questions deserve a forthright reply, especially since there was nothing suspicious about them *(Haamek Davar).*

לָנוּ וּלְמוֹלַדְתֵּנוּ — *About us and* [*about*] *our relatives.*

— I.e., *about our family* [as distinct from other contexts where the term מוֹלֶדֶת, means *birthplace,* a meaning it could not have here since they had immediately told Joseph they were from Canaan.] Midrashically [the ambiguous term מוֹלֶדֶת (connoting *birth; childhood)* instead of מִשְׁפָּחָה, *family, (Gur Aryeh)*] denotes that he even told us what kind of wood our cradles [we slept on as יְלָדִים, *children*] were made of *(Rashi).*

[The sense of the Midrash is that the man kept asking questions about the most intimate details of our lives: even of what wood our cradles were made. Or the sense is: The viceroy had mystical powers. He was able to describe our house to the minutest detail, and even told us what kind of wood was used to make the cradles we slept on as children! In asking about our father and brother he was merely testing us to see if we would tell him the truth; we therefore *had* to tell him! (see *Yafeh Toar).*]

הַעוֹד אֲבִיכֶם חַי הֲיֵשׁ לָכֶם אָח — *Is your father still alive? have you a brother?*

These questions are not recorded in the original account in chapt. 42.

Ramban [42:34] postulates that: (a) this constituted an excuse to Jacob [and did not entirely reflect the actual exchange with Joseph]; or more likely (b) when they told Joseph [42:11] *all of us, sons of one man are we,* and he countered with [*v.* 12], *No, but to see the land in its nakedness you have come,* he then proceeded to ask them about their

[7] *And they said, "The man persistently asked
about us and our relatives, saying, 'Is your father still
alive? have you a brother?' and we responded to him
according to these words. Could we possibly have
known that he would say, 'Bring your brother
down'?"*
[8] *Then Judah said to Israel his father, "Send the
lad with me, and let us arise and go, so we will live*

father and brother, threatening to send back investigators to test their truthfulness. It was then that they gave the information about their father and brother [ibid. *v.* 13]. Judah made reference to such interrogation when he later said to Joseph [44:19], *My lord asked his servants, Have you a father or a brother?* That the Torah left this unrecorded above is in keeping with Scriptural style which is concise in one place regarding a narrative, and expansive in another. [See also *Ramban* to 42:21 and *Rashbam* ibid *v.* 12].

וַנַּגֶּד־לוֹ עַל־פִּי הַדְּבָרִים הָאֵלֶּה — *And we responded* [lit. *told*] *to him according to these words.*

I.e., *and we responded* — that we had a father and a brother; *according to these words,* i.e. to the questions he asked, by which it was mandatory that we give the information *(Rashi).*

[Or, according to the implication of *Yafeh Toar* above: *By the way he asked* — displaying such intimate mystical knowledge of our lives, and intimating that he knew the answers but was asking us merely to test our truthfulness — *we had to answer him.*]

According to *Haamek Davar: According to these words* — which were so friendly and seemingly sincere.

הֲיָדוֹעַ נֵדַע כִּי יֹאמַר הוֹרִידוּ אֶת אֲחִיכֶם — *Could we possibly have known* [idiomatic; the Hebrew is in the compound infinitive: *know, could we have known*] *that he would say, 'Bring your brother down'?*

According to the Sages in *Rosh Hashanah* 3a (see footnote to 28:15), the word כִּי has four meanings: *if; perhaps; but; because.* Here, however, *Rashi* renders it as אֲשֶׁר, *that,* explaining that one of the four basic meanings of כִּי is אִם, [*if*], which, as noted in 24:33, is also synonymous with אֲשֶׁר, *when.* Accordingly, כִּי, in certain contexts such as ours, has the meaning of *when* [כִּי=אִם=אֲשֶׁר],but this as *Rashi* insists, is not to be construed as a fifth meaning of the word.

8. וַיֹּאמֶר יְהוּדָה אֶל יִשְׂרָאֵל אָבִיו — *Then* [lit. *and*] *Judah said to Israel his father.*[1]

— [I.e., as a son talking to his father.]

שִׁלְחָה הַנַּעַר אִתִּי וְנָקוּמָה וְנֵלֵכָה — *Send the lad with me, and let us arise*

1. [The name Israel, here as above, emphasizes the eternal spiritual aspect of Jacob as Patriarch of the "Children of Israel." On the threshold of the Egyptian Exile, Judah spoke with a vision of Jewish eternity which would survive all the rigors of future persecution and exile.

Judah's assurance to Jacob can be understood to have very broad implications: "I will be responsible for your progeny in all their millennia of exile; and we will endure every travail and not die!" For the primary survivors of Jewish nationhood after the dispersion of the Ten Tribes were the descendants of Judah, Benjamin and the priestly tribe of Levi.]

ט גַּם־אֲנַחְנוּ גַּם־אַתָּה גַּם־טַפֵּנוּ: אָנֹכִי
אֶעֶרְבֶנּוּ מִיָּדִי תְּבַקְשֶׁנּוּ אִם־לֹא הֲבִיאֹתִיו
אֵלֶיךָ וְהִצַּגְתִּיו לְפָנֶיךָ וְחָטָאתִי לְךָ כָּל־
י הַיָּמִים: כִּי לוּלֵא הִתְמַהְמָהְנוּ כִּי־עַתָּה

[idiomatic for *set out*], *and go.*

The imperative suffix ה in שִׁלְחָה, *send*, in place of the usual imperative form שְׁלַח, denotes a polite request rather than an order (*HaKsav VeHakabbalah*; cf. *comm.* to שְׁבָה in 27:19).

וְנִחְיֶה — *So* [lit. *and*] *we will live.*

In the literal sense: by having food (*Sforno*).

Rashi offers a Midrashic interpretation: The Divine Spirit was enkindled within him, and he unconsciously prophesied: 'As a sequel of this journey, תְּחִי רוּחֲךָ, *your own spirit will be revived.*' Indeed such was the case, as it is said [45:27], *And the spirit of Jacob their father was revived.*

וְלֹא נָמוּת — *And* [we will] *not die.*

— Of hunger. [The essence of Judah's argument was]: If Benjamin does go with us it is doubtful whether or not he will be seized; but as for us, we will all *certainly* die of hunger if we do not go. It is better that you disregard the doubtful and come to grips with the certainty (*Rashi* from *Tanchuma*).

Comp. *Bereishis Rabbah:* Better that one life be *risked* than that all *certainly* die.

According to *Sforno: If we take Benjamin to Egypt, our trip will be a success and we will not die* at the hands of the viceroy who warned us [42:20]: *So your words will be verified and you will not die.*

גַּם אֲנַחְנוּ גַּם אַתָּה גַּם טַפֵּנוּ — *We as well as you as well as our children* [lit. *also we, also you, also our children*].

It is usual for Scripture to precede even the first noun of a comparative phrase with גַּם, *also*, for emphasis. Comp. *Judges* 8:22 (*Radak; Ibn Ezra;* see *Neter*).

Exegetically, גַּם, *also*, is considered a רִבּוּי, a particle which *extends* the meaning of a passage beyond the things specified in the text. In this case, *Midrash HaGadol* comments that the implied extensions are: *also we* — including our wives; *also you* — including your wives; *also our children* — including our flocks.

9. אָנֹכִי אֶעֶרְבֶנּוּ מִיָּדִי תְּבַקְשֶׁנּוּ — *I will personally* [implied by the emphatic form אָנֹכִי, lit. *it is I who will,* etc.] *guarantee him; of my own hand you can demand him.*

I will do everything humanly possible to guard him from heat, cold, evil beasts, and brigands. I will offer my life for his and muster up whatever means to assure his absolute safety. I *alone* will be responsible for him; if you charged us all with joint responsibility, each may leave it to the other. Furthermore, do not worry that he may suffer from a libelous charge that may arise from the monies returned in our sacks; Benjamin was not with us at the time (*B'chor Shor*).

I *personally* will be security. I offer *myself*, not my children, as security (*Abarbanel*).

Judah's guarantee was not necessarily

and not die, we as well as you as well as our children.
[9] *— I will personally guarantee him; of my own hand you can demand him. If I do not bring him back to you and stand him before you, then I will have sinned to you for all time. —* [10] *For had we not delayed*

that he would be able to *physically* overcome any natural danger and bring Benjamin home safely. The sense of his obligation was, 'I will bear responsibility to accept Divine punishment in his stead in the event of danger' *(Haamek Davar).*

According to *R' Hirsch,* Judah's intent was: 'The lingering suspicion that you have against all of us [regarding Joseph's disappearance], will rest solely on me with regard to Benjamin'.

Bava Basra 173b rules that עָרֵב קַבְּלָן, *a guarantor who accepted unconditional obligation,* is responsible for the debt he has guaranteed [merely by virtue of his verbal undertaking, though he had not made a *kinyan* (a formal act legally concluding the obligation; Rashi ad. loc)]. The Talmud derives the law from our passage, and cites 42:37. According to others, a guarantor's responsibility is derived from *Proverbs* 20:16. [See *Maharsha;* cf. *Torah Temimah.*]

אִם לֹא הֲבִיאֹתִיו אֵלֶיךָ וְהִצַּגְתִּיו לְפָנֶיךָ — *If* [through my negligence *(B'chor Shor)*] *I do not bring him back to you and stand him before you.*

I.e., alive. I will not bring him back to you dead but alive *(Rashi).*

[The verb נצג means *stand,* or *set up,* as above, 30:38.] *Rashi's* comment is based on the fact that only the living can be 'stood up' *(Mizrachi).*

וְחָטָאתִי לְךָ כָּל הַיָּמִים — *Then* [lit. *and*] *I will have sinned to you for all time* [lit. *all the days*].

— Even in the World to Come [which is wholly 'day' *(Midrash)*] *(Rashi).*

I will regard myself as a sinner and under a ban all my life *(Radak).*[1]

10. כִּי לוּלֵא הִתְמַהְמָהְנוּ — *For had we not delayed.*

— Because of you *(Rashi).*

Although Judah did not mention Jacob as being responsible for the delay, that was the implication of his remark; otherwise, what was the purpose of making this complaint? *(Mizrachi).*

The term לוּלֵא is a composite of לוּ לֹא *if only not.* Cf. לוּלֵי in 31:42. The *Midrash* notes that this term is used to introduce prayers for God's protection and care accorded through the merit of the Patriarchs. In our context, too, their merit was being invoked, since without it the brothers would not have left Egypt safely.

1. The Sages [*Makkos* 11b] teach that a ban — even if only conditional and self-imposed — requires formal abrogation. This is known from the fate of Judah who imposed this conditional ban upon himself and he remained subject to it throughout all his life — [and even after his death] — because no one ever formally absolved him of it.

On this theme, R' Shmuel bar Nachmeni cited R' Yochanan who said, What is implicit in Moses' words [*Deut.* 33:6-7] *Hear HASHEM the voice of Judah and bring him to his people?* ... During the entire forty years in the wilderness, Judah's bones rolled about in their coffin until Moses arose and supplicated for mercy on his behalf [the prayer, in effect finally absolving him of the ban].

Tosafos ad. loc. asks why indeed, Judah's ban needed abrogation, when other bans are automatically abrogated upon fulfillment of the condition. The answer given is that the fulfillment of the condition was not in Judah's control since it depended upon Joseph or upon no accident befalling Benjamin. In such a case the ban remains in effect until formally absolved; if, however, the fulfillment of the condition is in the power of the one who imposed it, the ban is nullified upon fulfillment of the condition.

יא שַׁבְנוּ זֶה פַעֲמָיִם: וַיֹּאמֶר אֲלֵהֶם יִשְׂרָאֵל אֲבִיהֶם אִם־כֵּן | אֵפוֹא זֹאת עֲשׂוּ קְחוּ מִזִּמְרַת הָאָרֶץ בִּכְלֵיכֶם וְהוֹרִידוּ לָאִישׁ מִנְחָה מְעַט צֳרִי וּמְעַט דְּבַשׁ נְכֹאת וָלֹט

כִּי־עַתָּה שַׁבְנוּ זֶה פַעֲמָיִם — *We could have by now returned twice.*

I.e., we could have been there and back twice by this time *(Ralbag).*

I.e., we would since have long returned with Simeon and you would not have had such anxiety all this time *(Rashi).*

11. Jacob acquiesces.[1]

יִשְׂרָאֵל אֲבִיהֶם — *Israel their father.*

He is referred to here as *their father,* for were it not for the fact that he was the father of *all* of them and his mercies were aroused he would never have consented to Judah's proposal *(Midrash).*

אִם־כֵּן | אֵפוֹא זֹאת עֲשׂוּ — *If it must be so then do this.*

I.e., if such is the case and I cannot detain Benjamin any longer, then at least do the following to appease the lord of the land *(Radak).*

Jacob sought to appease the Egyptian viceroy with tributes, much as he had tried to appease Esau before confronting him [32:14 ff] *(Akeidah).*

In this context, the word אֵפוֹא is a redundant particle used for stylistic purposes. Idiomatically it means *therefore, then.* Contextually, the word is a composite of אַיֵּה *where, and* פֹּה, *here,* and the connotation of the full phrase is: אִם כֵּן, *if it must be so* that I shall be forced to send him with you — then I must look around and seek אַיֵּה, *where,* there is פֹּה, *here,* a plan and counsel to offer you. Accordingly, I say, *Do this! (Rashi).*[2]

[Thus the intent of the verse according to *Rashi's* latter interpretation is: If it must be so — 'where is there' a remedy? — by doing this, etc.]

[See comm. to מִי־אֵפוֹא in 27:33 and *Sforno* there.]

מִזִּמְרַת הָאָרֶץ — *Of the land's glory* (Hebrew: *Zimras).*

— *Onkelos* renders: *Of that*

1. *Why was Judah's offer more acceptable to Jacob than that of Reuben which he had refused?*

[In addition to the reasons recorded above and in the comm. to 42:37-38, there might be another possibility:

When Jacob said, 'Upon *me* has it all befallen' (42:36), he implied, as mentioned by the commentators, that only *he* as their father could realize the magnitude of the loss of two of his children; they as brothers could never appreciate his grief, and they could therefore never convince him to risk sending Benjamin.

Thus of all the brothers only Judah could step forward and convince Jacob otherwise. Judah, too, had been bereaved of two children (38:7, 10) and could appreciate his father's grief. Therefore, when *he* accepted responsibility for Benjamin's welfare, Jacob acquiesced.]

2. When Jacob said אֵפוֹא, his conscience smote him and he exclaimed, 'I am now being punished for the grief I caused my father when I instead of Esau received his blessings.

When Esau came in after me, Father trembled and cried out מִי־אֵפוֹא, *who — where — is the one ... ?* [27:33]. Providence is therefore causing me this grief now! *(Midrash; Yafeh Toar).*

[This *Midrash* is based on the fact that, as *Rashi* notes, the word אֵפוֹא is essentially

43
11

we could have by now returned twice."
[11] *Israel their father said to them, "If it must be so
then do this: take of the land's glory in your baggage
and bring it down to the man as a tribute — a bit of
balsam, a bit of honey, wax, lotus, pistachios and al-*

which is praised in the land — take every product that inspires people to sing *(m'zamrim)* its praises when it comes into being in the world *(Rashi; Midrash).*

— Products by which the land is praised *(Radak).*

בִּכְלֵיכֶם — *In your baggage* [lit. *utensils*].

וְהוֹרִידוּ לָאִישׁ מִנְחָה — *And bring* [it] *down to the man as a tribute.*

See to it that he gets it before you actually have an audience with him. Then, by his response to the gift, you will be able to gauge his disposition toward you *(Sforno).*

מְעַט צֳרִי וּמְעַט דְּבַשׁ — *A bit of balsam* [and] *a bit of honey.*

The choice of gifts was wisely considered. A tribute directed to someone as barbarically materialistic as Esau, an outdoorsman, had to be eye-dazzling in quantity and in form of presentation; therefore Jacob had selected the large tribute enumerated in 32:15 ff. This occasion, however, called for a different kind of gift: it was being sent to the fabulously wealthy 'civilized' ruler of Egypt to whom money and cattle meant little. A gift to such a man must consist of quality not quantity. Jacob selected bits of *Eretz Yisrael's* rarest and choicest delicacies. Some of the items listed here were mentioned above in 37:25 as items brought by Ishmaelite caravans to Egypt. Apparently, they were not readily available in Egypt (cf. *Sforno; Chizkuni).*

According to *Tur,* Jacob instructed them to take only a *little* of each so they should not show themselves off as being wealthy.

צֳרִי, *balsam,* as noted in 37:25, refers to the fragrant resin [=balm] that exudes from the wood of the balsam tree.

When *Eretz Yisrael* is called *a land flowing with milk and honey* [*Exodus* 3:8], the *honey* refers to the honey exuded from sweet *fruit,* such as dates. See *Ramban* ibid. and *Rashi* to *Lev.* 2:11.

נְכֹאת וָלֹט — *Wax* [*and*] *lotus.*

The translation of נְכֹאת as *wax* [either beeswax or an aromatic gum] follows *Onkelos, Rashi,* and the Midrash. In the context of 37:25, above, *Rashi* interprets the word as a collective term for *spicery,* citing a cognate term in *II Kings* 20:13.

Rashi agrees that the word has *both* meanings. In the context of ch. 37, where it heads a detailed list of spices, *Rashi* interprets it as a collective term for spicery. Here, however, where it appears in the *middle* of the list, *Rashi* follows the context in rendering *wax* as do *Onkelos* and the Midrash (Divrei David).

On the translation of לט as *lotus* see comm. to 37:25. According to the Midrash, here it refers to firmly kneaded gum mastic — scarce in Egypt.

superfluous and the verse would be quite intelligible even were it omitted. Hence its inclusion is interpreted as evoking a memory of another occasion when the same unusual word was used. Accordingly, in the Midrashic sense, the verse means: If it is so then it is due to the time I aggravated my father, causing him to exclaim אֵיפֹה. Nevertheless, do this.]

יב בָּטְנִים וּשְׁקֵדִים: וְכֶסֶף מִשְׁנֶה קְחוּ
בְיֶדְכֶם וְאֶת־הַכֶּסֶף הַמּוּשָׁב בְּפִי
אַמְתְּחֹתֵיכֶם תָּשִׁיבוּ בְיֶדְכֶם אוּלַי מִשְׁגֶּה
יג הוּא: וְאֶת־אֲחִיכֶם קָחוּ וְקוּמוּ שׁוּבוּ אֶל־
יד הָאִישׁ: וְאֵל שַׁדַּי יִתֵּן לָכֶם רַחֲמִים לִפְנֵי

בָּטְנִים וּשְׁקֵדִים — *Pistachios and almonds.*[1]

— Kinds of nuts found in abundance today, but apparently scarce delicacies in ancient times *(Ralbag).*

According to the *Midrash,* the *oil extract* of these nuts is referred to. [See *footnote*].

The familiar translation of בָּטְנִים as *pistachios* is conjectural. *Rashi* comments: 'I do not know what they [בָּטְנִים] are, but in the dictionary of R' Machir [11th century grammarian, younger brother of R' Gershom Meor haGolah; who compiled a now-lost but oft-quoted Talmudic-French dictionary] I saw that it refers to *pistachios.* It seems to me that they are *peaches.'*

Onkelos renders it as בוּטְמִין, which *Passhegen* maintains is synonymous with בוּטְמָא, *Onkelos'* Aramaic rendering of אֵלָה, *terebinth* [*Pistacia terebinthus*] above in 25:4.

[I have been unable to find a basis for *Rashi's* suggestion — in the face of sources who interpret otherwise — that the term refers to peaches. Perhaps, he feels that pistachios were too insignificant a product to send to the Egyptian viceroy.]

The Midrash adds to the above items: wine and *chilazon* — the rare worm from which תְּכֵלֶת, *purple die,* was made.

12. וְכֶסֶף מִשְׁנֶה קְחוּ בְיֶדְכֶם — *And take with you* [lit. *in your hands*] *double the money.*

I.e., to buy food take twice as much money as you had on your first trip; perhaps the price of grain has risen *(Rashi).*

... Or perhaps he wanted them to buy a double ration to spare themselves the difficulty of an early return to Egypt for more provisions *(R' Avraham ben HaRambam).*

The Hebrew phrase כֶּסֶף מִשְׁנֶה, literally means *money twice.* The translation as *double the money,* i.e. a larger amount of money for a more expensive purchase, follows *Rashi,* Midrash, *Targum* and most commentators. *Ramban* to 41:43 renders: The *money* for *the second purchase. Ibn Ezra* interprets: *second monies,* i.e. money with which to buy new grain — in addition to the returned monies from the first purchase.

The commentators on *Rashi* explain that the adjective מִשְׁנֶה occurs in Scripture either as *the second,* as above 41:43, or in the sense of *double,* as in *Exod.* 16:22: לֶחֶם מִשְׁנֶה, *double loaf.* In the former cases *Onkelos* renders תִּנְיָתָא, while in the latter he renders עַל חַד תְּרֵין, as he does here.

וְאֶת הַכֶּסֶף הַמּוּשָׁב ... תָּשִׁיבוּ בְיֶדְכֶם — *And the money that was returned ... return in your hands.*

Return in your hands — literally. Do not leave it in your sacks, nor wait until you are asked for it, but *carry it in your hands* to demonstrate immediately on your return that you are honest men and intend to return any money not rightfully yours (Alshich).

— You must make an obvious point of returning with the money

1. Why did Jacob send nothing of the שִׁבְעָה מִינִים, *the seven kinds of produce,* which *really* constitute the 'glory of the land'? — Simply because the famine was severe and nothing was growing. Jacob could send only products that keep a long time, and were left from previous seasons. That is why the Midrash takes 'pistachios and almonds' to refer to the *oil* of these nuts rather than the nuts themselves, which would long ago have been eaten *(R' Hirsch).*

43
12-14

monds [12] *And take with you double the money, and*
the money that was returned in the mouth of your
sacks return in your hands; perhaps it was an over-
sight. [13] *Take your brother, too, and arise, return to*
the man. [14] *And may El Shaddai grant you mercy*

in your hand, since this will be a *Kiddush HASHEM,* a public sanctification of God's Name *(R' Bachya; Alshich).* [See *Me'am Loez* in footnote below].

According to most commentators, this was *in addition* to the double amount of money they were to take to buy grain.

According to *Haamek Davar,* however, since the returned money is not explicitly mentioned in *v.* 15 [see *comm.* there], the sense of כֶּסֶף מִשְׁנֶה, *double the money* in our verse is: money sufficient for a new purchase as well as for the return, the latter being *included* in the double amount. Accordingly, he postulates that the interpretation of our verse is: *And take with you double the money* [i.e. the money that was returned as well as money for a new purchase]; *but the money that was returned in the mouth of your sacks you should hold in your hands* — open for all to see.

אולַי מִשְׁגֶּה הוּא — *Perhaps it was an oversight.*

The Egyptian official might have forgotten it inadvertently *(Rashi).*

Because of the great confusion resulting from the many buyers thronging throughout Egypt, the following sales procedure was followed: Purchasers would put money in their sacks and give them to the official. He would weigh grain for them according to the amount of money he found in the sacks, and the purchasers would take their closed sacks *(Ramban* to 44:1; *Radak).*

Jacob reasoned that the officials may have put the payments on top of the sacks to help them identify the owners of the sacks, and then, due to the confusion, forgotten to take the money when delivering the filled sacks to the customers *(Rashbam; Radak).*

13. וְאֶת־אֲחִיכֶם קָחוּ — *Take your brother too.*

The verb *take* is in plural. Although it was only to Judah that he entrusted Benjamin, Jacob addressed *all* his sons, so they should feel a sense of collective responsibility *(Sechel Tov).*

14. 'Now, [that you have the money, the gift, and your brother Benjamin' *(Midrash)*] Jacob said, 'you lack nothing except prayer. And therefore I pray for you' *(Rashi).*

As the Sages declared [*Sanhedrin* 44b]: One should always offer up prayer before misfortune comes *(R' Bachya).*

וְאֵל שַׁדַּי — *And may El Shaddai.*

[The Divine Attributes designated by this Name were discussed in the comm. to 17:1.]

Rashi here explains: *El Shaddai — God* שֶׁ־דַּי, *Who is sufficient* in granting His mercies, and in Whose hand is sufficient [דַּי] power to give, *may He give you mercy,* etc. This is the real meaning of the Name.[1]

Further, Jacob said, 'My father blessed me with these words *May El Shaddai bless you* [28:2], and no mis-

1. *Rashi* proceeds to cite the Midrashic interpretation that the Name *El Shaddai* refers to Him as *God Who said to the World* [during Creation] דַּי, *Enough!* [For the heavens and earth, once

הָאִישׁ וְשִׁלַּח לָכֶם אֶת־אֲחִיכֶם אַחֵר
וְאֶת־בִּנְיָמִין וַאֲנִי כַּאֲשֶׁר שָׁכֹלְתִּי

hap befell me on the road. In the same way do I bless you: *May El Shaddai grant you mercy' (Midrash Or HaAfeilah* cited in *Torah Sheleimah* §43).

— Since it is as *El Shaddai* that God revealed himself to my forefathers Abraham and Isaac [as well as to me (in 35:11)], I invoke that Name now when praying to Him on behalf of my sons *(Midrash HaGadol).*

יִתֵּן לָכֶם רַחֲמִים לִפְנֵי הָאִישׁ — *Grant you mercy before the man* [Joseph].

— I.e., make him well-disposed and compassionate toward you *(Abarbanel).*

וְשִׁלַּח לָכֶם — *That* [lit. and] *he may release* [lit. *send*] *to you.*

— The translation *release* in the sense of release from captivity follows *Onkelos.* Comp. *Exodus* 21:26 where the verb יְשַׁלְּחֶנּוּ, lit. *send* also has the connotation of *release.* It would be inappropriate to translate the verb here as *may he 'send' to you* since the brothers were going to him *(Rashi).*

אֶת אֲחִיכֶם אַחֵר — *Your other brother.*

In the literal sense this refers to Simeon. Apparently, Simeon was in disfavor with Jacob because of the Shechem incident [see 34:25-30], and Jacob avoided even mentioning him by name. It is for this very reason that he left him in Egypt so long. Indeed, had his household not run out of provisions, Jacob would not yet have allowed Benjamin to go, but would have left Simeon in Egypt *(Ramban).*

Rashi [apparently drawn by the unusual Hebrew phraseology אֲחִיכֶם אַחֵר which literally means: *your brother another*] cites a Midrashic interpretation that Jacob was enkindled with a prophetic inspiration: When he said אַחֵר, *other,* he implied that Joseph, as well as Simeon, would be redeemed.

Ramban approvingly mentions this interpretation and writes: 'This is correct. For at the moment of prayer Jacob directed his intentions to pray in a general manner for the other one [Joseph] as well, for perhaps he was still alive.'[1]

וַאֲנִי כַּאֲשֶׁר שָׁכֹלְתִּי שָׁכָלְתִּי — *And as*

created, kept on expanding until God decreed 'Enough!' (see *Overview* to *Bereishis* p. 5).]

— 'May He Who said to the world 'Enough!' now declare 'Enough' to my troubles. I have had no rest since my youth:

— Trouble through Laban; trouble through Esau; trouble of Rachel; trouble of Dinah; trouble of Joseph; trouble of Simeon; and trouble of Benjamin *(Rashi).*

— Whenever I finally sought tranquility, a new trouble always befell me *(R' Bachya;* see *Rashi* to 37:1).

Cf. *Tanchuma:* He Who will one day say to the righteous, 'Your sufferings are enough!' and to the wicked, 'Your ease has endured long enough!' may He grant you mercy before the man.

1. The Midrash perceives this prayer as connoting even a deeper, prophetic matter.

R' Yehoshua ben Levi expounded the verse as alluding to the Exiles:

May El Shaddai grant you mercy — corresponding to *He made all their captors kindly disposed toward them* [*Psalms* 106:46];

Before the 'man' alludes to the Holy One Blessed be He, Who is referred to as a *'man' of war* [*Exodus* 15:3];

That he may release to you your brother — alluding to the Ten Tribes;

43
14

before the man that he may release to you your other brother as well as Benjamin. And as for me, as I have been bereaved, so I am bereaved."

for me, as I have been bereaved so I am bereaved.

— And as for me — [in contrast with you] — until you return, I will be in constant suspense, not knowing if I am to be even more bereaved than I already have been. As I consider myself bereft of Joseph and of Simeon, so I will now feel bereft of Benjamin [a feeling I will continue to have until you return safely] *(Rashi).*

Radak interprets: What can I do? If God decrees that a mishap befalls one of you, then the bereavement I suffered with Joseph will be repeated again.

Bereishis Zuta interprets this in the sense of utter resignation: Since I am already bereaved of my Joseph, I need not worry about further bereavement [i.e., no future bereavement can match that which I already endured by losing Joseph.] Compare Esther's cry [*Esther* 4:17] כַּאֲשֶׁר אָבַדְתִּי אָבָדְתִּי, *What I have lost, I have lost,* i.e., my sacrifice has already been great; I have nothing more to lose.

Comp. *Ibn Ezra:* When I was bereaved of Joseph I felt that I was entirely bereft [i.e. of *all* of you *(Ralbag).*]

— 'You can no longer add to my bereavement, for I am already bereaved.' Jacob consoled himself in this way for every tribulation that came upon him, comparing everything to his bereavement of Joseph. Similarly, Esther's cry is to be interpreted: I am already lost [by being separated from my people *(Ibn Ezra* to *Esther* ibid.)], and if the king will slay me he will not add to my destruction' *(Ramban).*

Acccording to *R' Hirsch,* Jacob meant, 'Unlike the journey you are about to begin, for which I pray that God will show you mercy, אֲנִי, *and I,* meanwhile, will prepare myself for the ordeal I may have to face. *If I am to be bereft of my*

Your other brothers as well as Benjamin — referring symbolically to the exile of Judah and Benjamin;

And as for me — as I have been bereaved, by the First Destruction [brought about by the Babylonians], *so I am bereaved* by the *Second Destruction* [caused by the Romans]; but I will be bereaved no more.

[That is, following the Redemption from the 'Roman' (or: 'Edomite') exile (which according to Rabbinic tradition is still in force today) there will no longer be a destruction. This is derived from the phraseology of our passage which the *Midrash* perceives to mean: *As I have been bereaved, I have been bereaved,* i.e., I will suffer two destructions, but I will experience no more bereavement beyond those.]

In his commentary to the beginning of *Vayechi* (below 47:28), *Ramban* expounds upon this Midrashic interpretation that the descent into Egypt foreshadowed the Edomite Exile. Jacob prophetically perceived this symbolism, and therefore prayed in a general manner that applied to the future as well as to the immediate situation. [On the fundamental principle that every event that befell the Patriarchs foreshadowed the future destiny of their children, see *Ramban* to 12:6 (*footnote,* p. 436). On the Four Exiles, see *Overview* to *Lech Lecha* (p. 417).]

Ramban observes additionally that this passage has profound Kabbalistic implications. By invoking God as *El Shaddai* — a Name representing Him in His Divine Aspect of Strict *Justice* — and praying that He grant *mercy,* Jacob meant that God should raise Israel from the Divine attribute of Justice to that of Mercy. 'The student of Kabbalah will understand.'

טו שָׁכָלְתִּי: וַיִּקְחוּ הָאֲנָשִׁים אֶת־הַמִּנְחָה
הַזֹּאת וּמִשְׁנֶה־כֶּסֶף לָקְחוּ בְיָדָם וְאֶת־
בִּנְיָמִן וַיָּקֻמוּ וַיֵּרְדוּ מִצְרַיִם וַיַּעַמְדוּ לִפְנֵי
°ששי טז יוֹסֵף: וַיַּרְא יוֹסֵף אִתָּם אֶת־בִּנְיָמִין וַיֹּאמֶר

children as a result of your departure, I will be prepared for it.[1]

15. וַיִּקְחוּ הָאֲנָשִׁים אֶת־הַמִּנְחָה הַזֹּאת — *So* [lit. *and*] *the men took this tribute.*

They are described as *'men'* rather than 'brothers' to indicate that they embarked on their mission as 'men'; also, because they were in great fear and when they entered the gates of Egypt they did so not as brothers but disguised as ordinary men who 'coincidentally' came together *(R' Bachya).*

וּמִשְׁנֶה כֶסֶף לָקְחוּ בְיָדָם — *And they took double money in their hand.*

The 'money that was returned in the mouth of their sacks' [*v.* 12] which Jacob instructed them to take back is not mentioned here. Following *Rashi* and most commentators, our verse discusses only the money they brought for their new purchases, as directed by Jacob. Of course, they also took the money they had found in their sacks! *(Etz Yosef).*

According to *Haamek Davar,* as noted, the failure to mention the returned money indicates that the latter was *included* in the term כֶּסֶף מִשְׁנָה, *double amount of money.*

וְאֶת בִּנְיָמִן — *As well as Benjamin.*

— I.e., *and they took* Benjamin as well. Although the verse uses the single verb לָקְחוּ, *they took,* for both the money and Benjamin, *Onkelos* uses *two* verbs: וּנְסִיבוּ for the money, and וּדְבָרוּ for Benjamin. This is because Aramaic uses different verbs for objects and for people. When something *inanimate* is taken literally by the hand, the

1. **Jacob's letter to the viceroy of Egypt.**

Sefer HaYashar records that Jacob wrote a message to the viceroy of Egypt, and he gave it to his sons.

It read: "From your servant Jacob, son of Isaac the son of Abraham the Hebrew, prince of God, to the mighty and wise viceroy Tzafenas-Paane'ach, ruler of Egypt: Greetings of peace! May it be known to my lord, the ruler of Egypt, that the famine has become severe for us in Canaan, and therefore I sent my sons to you to buy some food for our sustenance. My children surround me — seventy people — and alas, I am very old, and cannot see with my eyes, for they are dimmed with age and with constant weeping for my son Joseph, who was taken from me. I charged my sons not to pass all together through the gates of the city when the came to Egypt, on account of the inhabitants of the land [so that they not be conspicuous to the people.] I also bade them go about the land of Egypt and seek my son Joseph: perhaps they would find him there.

"This they did, but as a result you considered them to be spies. Have we not heard of you as wise and understanding? How can you look upon their faces and declare them to be spies? We heard how you interpreted Pharaoh's dream, foretold the coming of the famine, and told him the truth; in your discernment, how can you fail to know whether or not my sons are spies?

"And now, my lord viceroy, I send you my son Benjamin, as you demanded of

[15] *So the men took this tribute and they took double money in their hand, as well as Benjamin. They set out and went down to Egypt and stood before Joseph.*

[16] *Joseph saw Benjamin with them. He said to the*

Targum renders *take* by the verb וּנְסֵיב [e.g. 34:25], while something which is 'taken' by persuasion [see also e.g. 2:15; 34:26] is rendered by the verb וּדְבַר [lit. *led*] *(Rashi).*

וַיַּעַמְדוּ לִפְנֵי יוֹסֵף — *And* [*they*] *stood before Joseph.*

— In the official area where he supervised sales of grain. At this point they had not yet exchanged any words with him, nor had they the opportunity of presenting their gift to him. Joseph had noticed them, but said nothing. Not knowing how to interpret his silence, they grew frightened, and stood in fear when they were brought to his house *(Chizkuni; Sforno; Akeidah).*

16. Joseph sees Benjamin and tests his brothers' sincerity

That Joseph was deeply moved by the sight of Benjamin is clear from the next several verses. Nevertheless, he still refrained from revealing his identity because he had vital questions that had to be answered. Had the brothers lost their jealousy of Rachel's children? How would they react when be showed favoritism to Benjamin? What would they do when he announced his intention to detain Benjamin — who 'stole' the goblet — as a slave? Had they kidnapped Benjamin from Jacob? *(Akeidah; R' Hirsch)*

וַיֹּאמֶר לַאֲשֶׁר עַל־בֵּיתוֹ — [*And*] *he said to the one in charge* [lit. *upon*] *of his house.*

— His son, Menasseh *(Midrash; Targum Yonasan).*

my other sons. I only beg you, protect him until you send him back to me in peace with his brothers. Surely you know, or have heard, what our God did to Pharaoh when he took Sarah our mother to himself, or what He did to Abimelech, king of the Philistines, on her account; and what Abraham our father did to the four kings of Elam — how he defeated them all with his few men; and also what my two sons Simeon and Levi did to the city of Shechem, which they destroyed for the sake of their sister Dinah? What will they do for the sake of their brother Benjamin, who consoled them over Joseph, if they see a viceroy raise a strong hand against them on his account?

"Surely you know, O viceroy of Egypt, that our God's strength is with us, that He always listens to our prayers, and never forsakes us. As God lives, had I called upon God to rise up against you, when my sons told me how you treated them, you and your people all would have been destroyed before my son Benjamin ever appeared before you. But I reflected that Simeon my son was in your house and perhaps you were treating him kindly; therefore I did not act in this manner toward you. Now my son Benjamin comes to you with my other sons. Be careful and protect him, and God will stand guard for you over all your dominion.

"Now I have told you all that is in my heart. My sons come to you with their brother; rule the entire land well for their sake and send them all back to me in peace."

לַאֲשֶׁר עַל־בֵּיתוֹ הָבֵא אֶת־הָאֲנָשִׁים
הַבָּיְתָה וּטְבֹחַ טֶבַח וְהָכֵן כִּי אִתִּי יֹאכְלוּ
יז הָאֲנָשִׁים בַּצָּהֳרָיִם: וַיַּעַשׂ הָאִישׁ כַּאֲשֶׁר
אָמַר יוֹסֵף וַיָּבֵא הָאִישׁ אֶת־הָאֲנָשִׁים
יח בֵּיתָה יוֹסֵף: וַיִּירְאוּ הָאֲנָשִׁים כִּי הוּבְאוּ

הָבֵא אֶת־הָאֲנָשִׁים הַבָּיְתָה — *Bring the men into the house.*

I.e., into my private residence. Joseph was then standing at the palace gate or at the place where he judged the people *(Sforno).*

וּטְבֹחַ טֶבַח וְהָכֵן — [*And*] *have meat slaughtered, and prepare it.*

According to the Sages in *Chullin* 91a, the expression וּטְבֹחַ טֶבַח implies Menasseh was to expose the slaughter-incision [so the brothers could see for themselves that the meat had been properly slaughtered according to Halachah. Although the Torah had not yet been given, Jacob's sons observed the commandments according to the tradition of their forefathers *(Rashi* there; see comm. to 26:5, p. 1083]. The Sages continue that וְהָכֵן, *and prepare,* means remove the גִּיד הַנָּשֶׁה, *displaced sinew,* in their presence. This latter interpretation follows the view that the displaced sinew was forbidden to Noachides [i.e. to the sons of Jacob before the Torah was given. (See *Tosafos* there s.v. כְּמַאן; *Maharsha;* and comm. to 32:33).] See also *Targum Yonasan.*

Following another view in the Midrash, since the term וְהָכֵן, *prepare,* is used in connection with the Sabbath [see *Exodus* 16:5], the Sages exegetically derived that the brothers had come to Joseph on a Friday and by הָכֵן, *prepare,* Joseph ordered his steward to prepare for the Sabbath. This is regarded as a Biblical allusion for the Rabbinic tradition that Joseph observed the Sabbath before it was ordained. (See also *R' Bachya).*

[The translation follows the syntax.] The phrase *literally* has an infinitive sense: וְלִטְבֹּחַ טֶבַח וּלְהָכִין, *and to slaughter something slaughterable and to prepare.* Technically, were the word וּטְבֹחַ to be a command, it would be vowelized וּטְבַח [just as the imperative form of שלח, *send,* is שְׁלַח *(Mizrachi)*] *(Rashi).*

Maharsha to *Chullin* 91a interprets Rashi's comment here— the וּטְבֹחַ is not an imperative — in consonance with the Talmudic interpretation cited above: Joseph told his steward to allow the brothers to slaughter the animals themselves, since the Halacha forbids ritual slaughter by a heathen. The word וְהָכֵן, *prepare,* however, is in the imperative, indicating that the steward *himself* should remove the forbidden nerve — but in their presence.

כִּי אִתִּי יֹאכְלוּ הָאֲנָשִׁים בַּצָּהֳרָיִם — *For it is with me that these men will dine at noon.*

I.e. the first meal of the day. *Onkelos* renders צָהֳרַיִם [lit. *noon*] *in this context as* שֵׁירוּתָא, an Aramaic term denoting *the first meal* [of the day]. This term often occurs in the Talmud in this sense; e.g. *Taanis* 11b; *Berachos* 39b. Wherever צָהֳרַיִם means *noon* rather than a *meal, Onkelos* renders it טִיהֲרָא *(Rashi).*

The idea is that *Onkelos* rendered the term צָהֳרַיִם here by its contextual connotation of *first* [main] *meal* rather than by its literal interpretation of *noon.* That the Torah calls this meal 'noon' is because, as the Sages in *Shabbos* 10a observe, governmental officials do not eat a large meal early in the morning —

one in charge of his house, "Bring the men into the
house; have meat slaughtered, and prepare it, for it is
with me that these men will dine at noon." 17 *The*
man did as Joseph said, and the man brought the men
to Joseph's house. 18 *But the men became frightened*
when they were brought to Joseph's house, and they

a time they reserve for judging the people — but at mid-day or early evening (see *Be'er Yitzchak).*

Joseph meant this as a test. He wished to observe how they behaved toward Benjamin during the meal, and whether they would display envy when Benjamin was given larger portions than the rest *(Sforno).*

Joseph had them dine at his table to lay the groundwork for the charge that they stole his goblet *(Ibn Caspi).*

17. וַיַּעַשׂ הָאִישׁ כַּאֲשֶׁר אָמַר יוֹסֵף — *[And] the man did as Joseph said.*

Da'as Zekeinim cites the tradition that it is Menasseh, Joseph's son, who is referrred to here as אִישׁ *man.* However, he wonders, Menasseh could not have been more that nine years old at the time [since Joseph was married at the beginning of the seven years of plenty and this was the second year of the famine (45:11; 47:18)]. It is difficult to reconcile this with *Rashi's* Midrashic interpretation [on 34:25] that the word אִישׁ, *man,* means someone over the age of thirteen. He leaves the matter unresolved.

Riva discusses this and citing *R' Yehudah HaChassid* compares it to the case of Er and Onan who, according to *Seder Olam* were but eight years old when they sinned [see *Mizrachi* cited in 38:1], yet were subject to the Divine death penalty although it is axiomatic that Divine punishment is not inflicted on someone younger than twenty. R' Yehudah resolves the difficulty by maintaining that everything depends upon one's *maturity,* not necessarily his chronological age. In our case too, the reference to Menasseh as *man* was a reflection of his maturity, not his age.

וַיָּבֵא הָאִישׁ אֶת־הָאֲנָשִׁים בֵּיתָה יוֹסֵף — *And the man brought the men to Joseph's house.*

I.e., he *meant to* bring them in, but did not succeed since they stopped him at the entrance [see verses 19 and 24]. This style is similar to 28:10 וַיֵּלֶךְ חָרָנָה [lit. *and he went to Charan*] where the sense is that he *headed* for Charan, not that he actually *arrived* there as yet *(Or HaChaim v.* 24).

[Cf. *Rashi* to *v.* 24 where the Midrashic implication is that *after* he brought them inside they edged him back outside toward the doorway to talk with him.]

18. וַיִּירְאוּ הָאֲנָשִׁים כִּי הוּבְאוּ בֵּית יוֹסֵף — *But* [lit. *and*] *the men became frightened when they were brought to Joseph's house.*[1]

1. The *Zohar* notes that the powerful brothers were terrified in the presence of the young steward who led them because they still felt guilt for having sold Joseph, and their courage failed them. Had it not been for this sin, they would not have feared at all.

The *Zohar* quotes Rabbi Yosi: "Woe to people who do not observe the Torah's commandments. Woe to them when God calls them for judgment and to account for their deeds. We know that Jacob's ten sons were very powerful, but when a young steward summoned them to Joseph's house they were terrified. How then must one feel when God summons him on the awesome Day of Judgment. Everyone should consider how he will answer before God his actions!"

בֵּ֣ית יוֹסֵ֑ף וַיֹּֽאמְר֗וּ עַל־דְּבַ֤ר הַכֶּ֙סֶף֙ הַשָּׁ֤ב
בְּאַמְתְּחֹתֵ֙ינוּ֙ בַּתְּחִלָּ֔ה אֲנַ֖חְנוּ מֽוּבָאִ֑ים
לְהִתְגֹּלֵ֤ל עָלֵ֙ינוּ֙ וּלְהִתְנַפֵּ֣ל עָלֵ֔ינוּ וְלָקַ֧חַת
יט אֹתָ֛נוּ לַעֲבָדִ֖ים וְאֶת־חֲמֹרֵֽינוּ׃ וַֽיִּגְּשׁוּ֙ אֶל־
הָאִ֗ישׁ אֲשֶׁר֙ עַל־בֵּ֣ית יוֹסֵ֔ף וַיְדַבְּר֥וּ אֵלָ֖יו
כ פֶּ֥תַח הַבָּֽיִת׃ וַיֹּאמְר֖וּ בִּ֣י אֲדֹנִ֑י יָרֹ֥ד יָרַ֖דְנוּ

— And it was unusual for grain customers to lodge in Joseph's home; they usually stayed in the city's inns. Therefore the brothers assumed that this surprising visit was preliminary to imprisonment *(Rashi).*

Furthermore, they feared that in the relative seclusion and privacy of Joseph's home an act of injustice could be committed against them with impunity, whereas Joseph would be deterred from harming them publicly *(Akeidah).*

Rashi makes the linguistic observation that the word וַיִּירְאוּ, spelled as it is with two י's [rather than וַיִּרְאוּ, with one י (from the root ראה) meaning *and they saw*], means *and they were afraid* (from the root ירא). *Onkelos* accordingly renders it by the Aramaic term for *fear,* וּדְחִילוּ.

וַיֹּאמְרוּ — *And they said.*

I.e., one to another *(Ralbag).*

אֲנַחְנוּ מוּבָאִים — *Are we being brought.*

I.e., inside this house *(Rashi).*

לְהִתְגֹּלֵל עָלֵינוּ — *So that a charge can be fabricated against us* [lit. *in order to roll itself on us*].

I.e., in order that an accusation regarding the money be 'rolled' [=devolved] upon us. *Onkelos,* taking גלל in the symbolic sense of *royal rank* — as he does in *Eccles.* 12:6; *Nech.* 2:8 — renders: לְאִתְרַבְרְבָא, *to play the lord over us (Rashi).*

Onkelos apparently perceives the phrase as a metaphor: He will elevate himself above us as the Sea raises its waves [relating *hisgolel* to *gal,* the Hebrew word for wave]. Actually, the sense of the word is to *roll,* as one who turns from side to side against his fellow *(Ramban).*

— 'To turn himself against us', i.e. to oppress us *(R' Hirsch).*

וּלְהִתְנַפֵּל עָלֵינוּ — *[And] that it crash down on us* [lit. *and to fall itself down upon us*].

I.e., and in order that this accusation of [having stolen] the money should fall upon us. *Onkelos,* who rendered *this* phrase by וּלְאִסְתַּקָּפָא עֲלָנָא, *to seek a pretext against us,* did not translate it literally *(Rashi).*

R' Hirsch renders: To pounce down upon us.

וְלָקַחַת אֹתָנוּ לַעֲבָדִים וְאֶת־חֲמֹרֵינוּ — *And that we be taken* [lit. *and to take us*] *as slaves along with our donkeys.*

I.e., because of his false pretext that we stole from him he will take *us* as slaves, while to redeem the loss of his money he will appropriate *our donkeys (Haamek Davar).*

Why did they mention their donkeys?

In *Moreh Nevuchim* 3:40, *Rambam* discusses the compassion people have for their possessions. He notes that, 'People fear the loss of

said "Because of the money replaced in our sacks
originally are we being brought so that a charge can
be fabricated against us, that it crash down on us, and
that we be taken as slaves along with our donkeys."
19 They approached the man who was in charge of
Joseph's house and spoke to him at the entrance of
the house. 20 And they said, "If you please, my lord:

their property as much as that of their own lives, some even more; but most people hold both in the same esteem.' He cites our passage as proof. [Cf. *Abarbanel*].

According to *Ramban* their concern for their donkeys was due to their apprehension of the consequences of their donkeys' loss: 'He will rob even our donkeys with our sacks; we will not be able to send grain home and our families will die of hunger!'

R' Bachya maintains that their animals were so important to them because one's animal is his sole means of survival in the desert. Comp. the murmurings of the Israelites against Moses in *Exod.* 17:3: *'Why is it that you have brought us up out of Egypt to kill us, our children, and our livestock with thirst?'*

19. וַיִּגְּשׁוּ אֶל־הָאִישׁ אֲשֶׁר עַל־בֵּית יוֹסֵף — [*And*] *they approached the man who was in charge of* [lit. *upon*] *Joseph's house.*

The implication of the verb וַיִּגְּשׁוּ [*approached*] is *pushed up,* i.e., 'somewhat forcibly. Cf. the verb in 19:9 *(Sechel Tov;* see *Rashi* below).

וַיְדַבְּרוּ אֵלָיו פֶּתַח הַבָּיִת — *And* [they] *spoke to him at the entrance of the house.*

I.e., before they entered *(Rashbam),* it being their intention that the members of the household not overhear them *(Radak).*

According to *Rashi* in *v.* 24, however, they had already entered [*v.* 17] but they gradually pushed him back towards the outside until they were talking with him at the doorway.

They wanted to discuss the matter of the money and ascertain why they had been brought there *(Or HaChaim).*

Malbim suggests that by talking with the steward at the doorway, they wished to demonstrate that they did not want to enter until they had returned the money.

20. וַיֹּאמְרוּ — *And they said.*

— I.e., Judah spoke on their behalf. This accounts for *they said* being in plural, while *my lord* is in singular *(Ibn Caspi; Sechel Tov).*

בִּי אֲדֹנִי — *If you please, my lord.*

Rashi understands בִּי [*bi*] as an expression of *petition* (בָּעְיָא) and *supplication,* related to the Aramaic term *biya.*

Ramban disagrees on several counts: a) the Hebrew בִּי cannot be cognate to the Aramaic בְּיָיא; b) as the Aramaic word *biya* is used in the Talmud and Midrash, it never connotes *entreaty;* to the contrary it connotes *woe* and distress. [He goes on to cite many such examples. However, see *Mizrachi* who defends *Rashi* on every count.]

Ramban continues that *Onkelos,* who translated the phrase בְּבָעוּ רִבּוֹנִי, *please my lord,* did not intend to suggest that *bi* is a derivative of *b'va'u* but merely rendered the phrase in accordance with the context, since *bi* always contextually connotes supplication.

כא בַּתְּחִלָּה לִשְׁבָּר־אֹכֶל: וַיְהִי כִּי־בָאנוּ אֶל־
הַמָּלוֹן וַנִּפְתְּחָה אֶת־אַמְתְּחֹתֵינוּ וְהִנֵּה
כֶסֶף־אִישׁ בְּפִי אַמְתַּחְתּוֹ כַּסְפֵּנוּ בְּמִשְׁקָלוֹ
כב וַנָּשֶׁב אֹתוֹ בְּיָדֵנוּ: וְכֶסֶף אַחֵר הוֹרַדְנוּ
בְיָדֵנוּ לִשְׁבָּר־אֹכֶל לֹא יָדַעְנוּ מִי־שָׂם
כג כַּסְפֵּנוּ בְּאַמְתְּחֹתֵינוּ: וַיֹּאמֶר שָׁלוֹם לָכֶם
אַל־תִּירָאוּ אֱלֹהֵיכֶם וֵאלֹהֵי אֲבִיכֶם נָתַן

... Similarly *Ramban* maintains that *Ibn Ezra's* interpretation is difficult. *Ibn Ezra* renders בִּי, *upon me*; it implies the elliptical declaration 'the iniquity is *upon me*; do with me as you wish, but hear me out.' [The basis for this is *I Samuel* 25:24.] *Ramban* finds this difficult since we find the term *bi* used only in conjunction with אֲדֹנִי, *my lord* or *master*. According to *Ibn Ezra*, it should be used in other ways, such as '*bi*, my brother', or '*bi*, listen to me.'

Accordingly *Ramban* postulates that the expression is one of submission to a superior person: בִּי אֲדֹנִי, *over me, you are my lord* — the double pronoun *me* and *my* being used for emphasis.

יָרֹד יָרַדְנוּ בַּתְּחִלָּה לִשְׁבָּר־אֹכֶל — *We had indeed come down* [lit. *come we came down*] *originally* [lit. *at the first*] *to buy food.*

[The verb is in the compound infinitive to lend emphasis.]

I.e., when we came down to Egypt at the very beginning of the famine to buy food we had sufficient funds for grain; we had no need to steal the purchase money *(Meshech Chochmah).*

Rashi follows the Midrashic interpretation based upon the dual emphasis of *come we came down:* "It was indeed a 'come-down' for us to descend here for grain; in our own country we supported others, and now we are dependent on your support!"

Although in the literal sense it would be quite proper to use the verb *go down* when speaking of the journey from the higher terrain of *Eretz Yisrael* to Egypt [cf. 12:10], nevertheless *Rashi* pursues the Midrashic interpretation, this being a case of הֵיכָא דְאִיכָּא לְמִידְרַשׁ דָּרְשִׁינַן, *whereas it is possible to expound we expound* [see *Mizrachi* to 12:1 (p. 425)] *(Sechel Tov).*

21. אֶל הַמָּלוֹן — *At* [lit. *to*] *the inn.*

— From where it was too distant for us to return with the money *(Akeidah).*

Or suggesting: There was no way we could return the money then without putting our lives in jeopardy, because the viceroy had warned us not to come to Egypt again without our younger brother *(HaKsav V 'HaKabbalah).*

They modified the actual account for brevity, for in reality only Levi had opened his sack at the inn [42:27,35]; the rest of them did not discover their money until they reached their father's house *(Sechel Tov).*

HaKsav V' HaKabbalah maintains that the word מָלוֹן, *inn*, is used in many contexts for a *permanent dwelling place* (the Temple-site of the *Shechinah's* 'dwelling' is called מָלוֹן). Thus the brothers' account was accurate; they used a term referring to both the inn and their home.

כַּסְפֵּנוּ בְּמִשְׁקָלוֹ — *It was our own money in full* [lit. *by its weight*].

— The coins were those we used to pay for our purchase; there wasn't even the slightest possibility

We had indeed come down originally to buy food.
[21] But it happened, when we arrived at the inn, that
behold! each one's money was in the mouth of his
sack; it was our own money in full; so we have
brought it back in our hand. [22] We have also brought
other money down in our hand to buy food. We do
not know who put our money in our sacks."
[23] He replied, "All is peaceful with you; fear not.
Your God and the God of your father must have put

that someone else's monies fell into our sacks by mistake *(Sforno).*

— It was clearly a plot to ensnare us; it could not be merely a coincidence *(Ralbag).*

וַנָּשֶׁב אֹתוֹ בְּיָדֵנוּ — *So* [lit. *and*] *we have brought it back in our hand.*

— With the obvious intention of returning it immediately *(Abarbanel).*

[See *Malbim* next verse.]

22. וְכֶסֶף אַחֵר הוֹרַדְנוּ בְיָדֵנוּ לִשְׁבָּר־אֹכֶל — *We have also brought other money down in our hand to buy food.*

This proves the honesty and sincerity of our intentions *(B'chor Shor).*

Do not think that we are confessing out of fear and that the money we are claiming to 'return' is really the money we brought to purchase grain. To the contrary! — we brought *other* money to buy food *(Malbim).*

לֹא יָדַעְנוּ מִי־שָׂם כַּסְפֵּנוּ בְּאַמְתְּחֹתֵינוּ — *We do not know who put our money in our sacks.*

The matter remains a mystery and a concern to us *(Alshich).*

[It is not clear why this phrase — which would appear to fit better contextually at the end of *v.* 21 — is placed here.]

23. The steward reassures them.

שָׁלוֹם לָכֶם אַל־תִּירָאוּ — *All is peaceful with you* [lit. *peace is to you*], *fear not.*

— It was not to charge you with a crime that I brought you here, but merely as guests to dine with my master *(Abarbanel; Malbim).*

They were so obviously afraid [*v.* 18] that the steward felt compelled to offer this calming assurance *(Or HaChaim).*

אֱלֹהֵיכֶם וֵאלֹהֵי אֲבִיכֶם — *Your God and the God of your father.*

— *Your God:* for He rewarded you in your own merit, but in the event your merit is not sufficient, then He rewarded you in your father's merit, as *the God of your father (Rashi).*

— Everyone knew that Jacob's family was accustomed to miracles *(Rashbam).*

נָתַן לָכֶם מַטְמוֹן בְּאַמְתְּחֹתֵיכֶם — *Must have put a treasure* [following *Onkelos;* lit. *something hidden (Ramban)*] *in your sacks.*

God caused it to be placed there. Rest assured that it was not a ploy to fabricate some charge against you *(Ralbag).*

— Perhaps someone hid a treasure in his granary and it was lost among the grain collected during the years of

לָכֶם מַטְמוֹן בְּאַמְתְּחֹתֵיכֶם כַּסְפְּכֶם בָּא
כד אֵלָי וַיּוֹצֵא אֲלֵהֶם אֶת־שִׁמְעוֹן: וַיָּבֵא
הָאִישׁ אֶת־הָאֲנָשִׁים בֵּיתָה יוֹסֵף וַיִּתֶּן־
מַיִם וַיִּרְחֲצוּ רַגְלֵיהֶם וַיִּתֵּן מִסְפּוֹא
כה לַחֲמֹרֵיהֶם: וַיָּכִינוּ אֶת־הַמִּנְחָה עַד־בּוֹא
יוֹסֵף בַּצָּהֳרָיִם כִּי שָׁמְעוּ כִּי־שָׁם יֹאכְלוּ
כו לָחֶם: וַיָּבֹא יוֹסֵף הַבַּיְתָה וַיָּבִיאוּ לוֹ אֶת־
הַמִּנְחָה אֲשֶׁר־בְּיָדָם הַבָּיְתָה וַיִּשְׁתַּחֲווּ־לוֹ

plenty. By some lucky chance it got into your sacks. It does not belong to the treasury — for I have received your payment *(Ibn Ezra).*

That is, someone must have left a hidden treasure in his sacks and despaired of its recovery and God caused you to have it. Now, Noachides who find a lost object are not commanded to seek its owner *(Or HaChaim).*

Ramban dismisses *Ibn Ezra's* interpretation of the Egyptian's explanation as mere words of consolation, that could not have been meant seriously — for how could it happen that each of the brothers 'happened' to receive *precisely* his own money?

He therefore postulates a more plausible explanation. In busy grain markets, the customers place their payment in empty sacks which they give to the attendant. Then the attendant empties the money from the sack, fills it with an equivalent value of grain, and has the donkeys loaded. In the case of the ten brothers, the marketplace was so hectic that day that their money was inadvertently left in the sack since the one who filled the order was in a great rush. Or perhaps the one who filled the sacks was not the one in charge of removing the money, and the two workers failed to coordinate their tasks. Thus it happened that each found his own money still in his sack [see above *v.* 13; below 44:1].

According to *Ramban's* interpretation that money was left in the sacks, how could Joseph have said, *'Your payment reached me'*? — Presumably, Joseph told them that since his ledgers showed that the brothers had paid in full, he had no claim against them. It could only be that God had wanted them to have the money *(R' David Feinstein).*

[In reply to *Ramban's* criticism, perhaps *Ibn Ezra* means to account for the Egyptian's insistence that the money was a gift from God. The very fact that it was virtually impossible for each to find his exact amount of money purely by coincidence was the best proof that *their God* had performed a miracle. *Ramban* may hold that even miracles should be seen to happen through a natural agency.]

כַּסְפְּכֶם בָּא אֵלָי — *Your payment had reached me* [lit. *your money had come to me*].[1]

The money you found was a Divine blessing; *your money,* however, was duly received by me — have no fears about that! *(Radak).*

That your money found its way

1. As noted in the footnote to 41:57, the reason God caused Egypt to enjoy plenty while the rest of the lands suffered famine was in order to render possible the fulfillment of the promise to Abraham that his descendants would be enslaved and then leave with great wealth [see 15:14]. At the time, Egypt was a poor country, and God orchestrated all of these events so that she would benefit from an influx of the gold and silver from other lands who were forced to

a treasure in your sacks. Your payment had reached
me." And he brought Simeon out to them.

24 Then the man brought the men into Joseph's
house. He provided water and they washed their feet,
and he gave feed to their donkeys. 25 They prepared
the tribute for when Joseph would come at noon, for
they had heard that they were to dine there.

26 When Joseph came home they brought the
tribute that was in their hands to him into the house,

back into your sacks after I received it must have been the result of a miracle — it was certainly not placed in your sacks to implicate you in some sinister plot. I specifically recall and acknowledge that I received your payment; no one is accusing you of foul play *(Akeidah).*

וַיּוֹצֵא אֲלֵהֶם אֶת־שִׁמְעוֹן — *And he brought Simeon out to them.*

— To reassure them that they had nothing to fear *(Or HaChaim),* and to show that he no longer required a hostage *(B'chor Shor).*

24. וַיָּבֵא הָאִישׁ אֶת־הָאֲנָשִׁים בֵּיתָה יוֹסֵף — *Then the man brought the men into Joseph's house.*

Though *v.* 17 stated that he brought them to the house, it was only at this point — after he reassured them by saying [*v.* 23] *all is well with you* — that they followed him and actually *entered* the house. The whole previous conversation had, as noted, taken place at the entrance. Earlier, as noted above, they had been unwilling to remain there — they edged him towards the entrance where they conversed with him *(Rashi).*

וַיִּתֵּן מִסְפּוֹא לַחֲמֹרֵיהֶם — *And he gave feed to their donkeys.*

[On מִסְפּוֹא, *feed,* see 24:25.]

25. וַיָּכִינוּ אֶת הַמִּנְחָה — [*And*] *they prepared the tribute.*

— I.e., they arranged it beautifully, adorning it in fine vessels *(Midrash; Rashi).*

עַד־בּוֹא יוֹסֵף בַּצָּהֳרָיִם — *For* [lit. *until*] *Joseph would arrive at noon.*

The 'full' spelling of בּוֹא, *arrival* [instead of the usual spelling בֹּא] exegetically implies an extension [intimating that his arrival would be a 'full' one]: on this occasion he would arrive with his attendants *(Sechel Tov).*

כִּי שָׁמְעוּ כִּי־שָׁם יֹאכְלוּ לָחֶם — *For they had heard that they were to dine there* [lit. *that there they would eat bread*].

They had heard — from the steward and from the members of the household who were preparing the meal. *Bread* is a general term for *food (Radak).*

26. וַיָּבֹא יוֹסֵף הַבַּיְתָה — *When* [lit. *and*] *Joseph came home* [lit. *to the house*].

וַיָּבִיאוּ לוֹ אֶת הַמִּנְחָה אֲשֶׁר בְּיָדָם הַבָּיְתָה — [*And*] *they brought the tribute that was in their hands to him into the house.*

buy Egyptian grain. Thus, Egypt would amass fortunes that the Israelites would eventually take with them at the Exodus.

Though Joseph's steward did not realize it, his words contained a prophetic implication: *'your' money came to me:* all the money that has come to me from everywhere is *your money,* i.e., it is ready for you to take *(Malbim).*

כז אָֽרְצָה: וַיִּשְׁאַל לָהֶם֙ לְשָׁל֔וֹם וַיֹּ֕אמֶר
הֲשָׁל֛וֹם אֲבִיכֶ֥ם הַזָּקֵ֖ן אֲשֶׁ֣ר אֲמַרְתֶּ֑ם
כח הַעוֹדֶ֖נּוּ חָֽי: וַיֹּאמְר֗וּ שָׁל֛וֹם לְעַבְדְּךָ֥
כט לְאָבִ֖ינוּ עוֹדֶ֣נּוּ חָ֑י וַֽיִּקְּד֖וּ וַיִּשְׁתַּחֲוֻֽ: וַיִּשָּׂ֣א
עֵינָ֗יו וַיַּ֞רְא אֶת־בִּנְיָמִ֣ין אָחִיו֮ בֶּן־אִמּוֹ֒

They were already inside the building — but the sense of *into the house* is that they were ushered from the ante-room where they had been waiting into his private inner chamber (*Rashi; Radak*).

Bereishis Rabbosi observes that they waited until he came into the house and did not go *outside* to meet him with the gift because outsiders might have suspected them of attempting to bribe him.

וַיִּשְׁתַּחֲווּ־לוֹ אָרְצָה — *And they prostrated themselves to him toward the ground.*

This is the first time *all* Joseph's brothers — including Benjamin — bowed down to him. This is perceived by many commentators as the fulfillment of Joseph's first dream [37:7]. (See *Ramban* to 42:9).

27. וַיִּשְׁאַל לָהֶם לְשָׁלוֹם — [*And*] *he inquired after their welfare* [lit. *and he asked them about peace*].

Etiquette dictates that one ask first after the welfare of those present, and only afterwards about those not present. Therefore, Joseph inquired first about them and then about Jacob (*Or HaChaim*).

הֲשָׁלוֹם אֲבִיכֶם הַזָּקֵן אֲשֶׁר אֲמַרְתֶּם — *Is your aged father of whom you spoke at peace?*

[That they had mentioned their aged father is evident from 44:20.]

This is more than a general question concerning their father's external relationships with his neighbors and surroundings. Were that Joseph's intention, he would have *said* הֲשָׁלוֹם לַאֲבִיכֶם, the usual idiomatic inquiry. Instead his question related to Jacob's *emotional* and *spiritual* well-being: Is he at peace with himself; free of worry and harassment? (*R' Hirsch*).

הַעוֹדֶנּוּ חָי — *Does he still live?*

The sequence of Joseph's questions seems strange; first he asked about Jacob's health and *then* whether he was still alive. *R' Hirsch* comments that this order reveals Joseph's anxiety about his father. He asked after his father's welfare as would be expected — but then he had a frightening thought: perhaps my father has died in the interim! Quickly he adds, 'He is still alive, is he not?' "

Other commentators resolve the sequence of the questions by suggesting that the second question

1. According to the Midrash, Joseph asked about *two* people: *Is your father well?* referring to *Jacob; the old man of whom you spoke* referring to Isaac — *is he still alive?*

In their reply, however, they mentioned only that their *father* was well and alive, but they said nothing about Isaac who was already dead [he had died about ten years earlier], since they did not wish to be the bearers of evil tidings.

Hadar Zekeinim simplifies the chronology: Isaac was sixty years older than Jacob [25:26]. Thus, when Isaac died at 180 [35:28] Jacob was 120. As Jacob told Pharaoh shortly after this narrative [47:9], he was 130 years old at this time. Accordingly, thus, Isaac had died ten years earlier.

and they prostrated themselves to him toward the
ground. 27 *He inquired after their welfare, and he*
said, "Is your aged father of whom you spoke at
peace? Does he still live?"
28 *They replied, "Your servant our father is at*
peace; he still lives." And they bowed and prostrated
themselves.
29 *Then he lifted up his eyes and saw his brother*
Benjamin, his mother's son, so he said, "Is this your

does not mean Is he still *alive?* but, is he still *vigorous?* Cf. this sense of the word in *Josh.* 5:8 and *Rashi* to *Psalms* 58:10. Thus, Joseph first inquired after Jacob's general welfare, then after the state of his health.

28. שָׁלוֹם לְעַבְדְּךָ לְאָבִינוּ — *Your servant our father is at peace* [lit. *peace is to your servant to our father*].[1]

[In continuation of *R' Hirsch's* comment to the previous verse] '...They could answer only שָׁלוֹם לְאָבִינוּ [intimating that he was at peace only *externally*, but not, as Joseph had asked, that he *was* שָׁלוֹם, *internally* at peace, since he was fearful about Joseph, Simeon and Benjamin.']

וַיִּקְּדוּ וַיִּשְׁתַּחֲוֻ — *And they bowed and prostrated themselves.*

— In gratitude for his concern about their welfare *(Rashi).*

— At the mention of their father *(Radak).*

According to *Alshich,* it was not in deference to Joseph that they bowed, but in gratitude to *HASHEM* for the warm reception they had received.

The verb קדד denotes bowing the head [קָדְקֹד], and הִשְׁתַּחֲוָאָה denotes prostration upon the ground *(Rashi).*

Ralbag renders similarly: First they bowed their heads in deference to him as demanded by etiquette, and then they paid him further obeisance by prostrating themselves. See *Radak Shorashim* s.v. קדד, and cf. *Ibn Ezra* to 23:8 above.

Rashi's interpretation follows the Sages in *Berachos* 34b; *Shevuos* 16b; *Megillah* 22b (see *Maharsha* there) that "קִידָּה means falling on the face; כְּרִיעָה means going down upon the knees, and הִשְׁתַּחֲוָאָה is spreading out of the hands and feet."

Rashi in *Sukkah* 53a explains in more detail that *kidah* as mentioned in Scripture consists of bending *only* the face down to the ground. The Talmud notes there that no one in the Temple could perform this feat except,R' Shimon ben Gamliel. When Levi attempted a *kidah* in the presence of R' [Yehudah HaNassi], he became lame [due to the tremendous strain which dislocated his thigh].

29. וַיִּשָּׂא עֵינָיו — *Then he lifted up his eyes.*

In the sense that he focused his gaze on the members of the group before him *(Radak).*

וַיַּרְא אֶת בִּנְיָמִין אָחִיו בֶּן־אִמּוֹ — *And [he] saw* [i.e., singled out] *(Ralbag)] his brother Benjamin, his mother's son.*

That he had already *seen* Benjamin is mentioned in *v.* 16.

1. Joseph is criticized by the Sages in *Sotah* 13b for having remained silent when his brothers referred to his father as *your servant* and not protesting this slight to his father's honor. [Cf. 50:25].

According to R' Yishmael in *Pirkei d'Rabbi Eliezer,* in punishment for each of the ten times

וַיֹּאמֶר הֲזֶה אֲחִיכֶם הַקָּטֹן אֲשֶׁר אֲמַרְתֶּם
ל אֵלָי וַיֹּאמַר אֱלֹהִים יָחְנְךָ בְּנִי׃ °וַיְמַהֵר
°שביעי יוֹסֵף כִּֽי־נִכְמְרוּ רַחֲמָיו אֶל־אָחִיו וַיְבַקֵּשׁ
לא לִבְכּוֹת וַיָּבֹא הַחַדְרָה וַיֵּבְךְּ שָׁמָּה׃ וַיִּרְחַץ

The intent is that his eyes now singled out Benjamin, and he saw him as *his brother, his mother's son.* Benjamin's features resembled Rachel's and in him Joseph saw his mother who died when he was but an eight year old child. Furthermore, this passage prepares us for his desire to weep *(Zohar; Ashtruc; Haamek Davar).*

הֲזֶה אֲחִיכֶם הַקָּטֹן אֲשֶׁר אֲמַרְתֶּם אֵלָי — *Is this your 'little'brother of whom you spoke to me?*

The question directed about the thirty-one year old Benjamin was both humorous and sarcastic: Is this the one you call 'little,' the one you were afraid to bring here on acount of his tender years? Is this the 'young child' from whom we are to learn the truth? He is a grown man! *(Abarbanel; Haamek Davar).*

וַיֹּאמַר — *And he* [Joseph] *said.*

[I.e., turning to Benjamin and addressing him directly] ...

אֱלֹהִים יָחְנְךָ בְּנִי — *God be gracious to you, my son.*

Since you are the survivor of your mother, may God grant you grace that your brothers and others will befriend you *(Sforno).*

By adding the words *my son* Joseph was also emphasizing his pretended surprise and sarcasm over seeing this grown man — himself the father of ten children — who had been presented to him as their 'little' brother *(Ashtruc).*

According to the *Midrash,* Joseph's choice of blessing him with an expession of חֵן, *grace,* is significant:

The other brothers had already been blessed with God's *grace,* as we find Jacob referring to his children as 'the children whom God has *graciously given* [חָנַן] your servant.' [33:5]. Benjamin had not yet been born [and was therefore not included among the children mentioned in that blessing] — therefore, Joseph now blessed him with God's grace *(Rashi).*

In *Bereishis Zuta* this benediction is credited with benefitting Benjamin's descendants: 'Were it not for this prayer, the tribe of Benjamin would have been left without a survivor in the incident of the Con-

Joseph silently listened to the epithets *servant* used of his father [five times directly from the brothers and five times as repeated by the translator who stood between them *(Radal* ad. loc.)], a year was deducted from his life-span [which traditionally should have been the usual 120 years for the righteous]; he died at the age of 110 [50:26].

This punishment was consistent with the Commandment [*Exodus* 20:12], *Honor your father and your mother that your days may be prolonged,* where *Rashi* explains, '... but if you do not honor them your days will be shortened.'

In this connection, *R' Yehudah HaChassid* notes that even Jacob's being called 'servants' was not without Providential significance. According to one opinion, Jacob was called 'servant' five times in retribution for the five times he had described himself as a servant of his brother Esau [32:5; cf. footnote to 25:23 (p. 1057)]. Another opinion maintains, to the contrary, that Jacob's humility in his confrontation with Esau entitled him to be described five times in Scripture as the 'servant' of God. [Cf. *Eruvin* 13b.]

'little' brother of whom you spoke to me?" And he
said, "God be gracious to you, my son."
[30] *Then Joseph rushed because his compassion for*
his brother had been stirred and he wanted to weep.
So he went into the room and wept there. [31] *He*

cubine of Gibeah; cf. *Judges* 21:22 חָנּוּנוּ אוֹתָם, we have acted *graciously* with them.

30. וַיְמַהֵר יוֹסֵף — *Then* [lit. *and*] *Joseph rushed.*

I.e. he hastily completed his business in order to get to his room for he was overcome with emotion and wanted to weep *(Sifsei Kohen).*

כִּי נִכְמְרוּ רַחֲמָיו אֶל־אָחִיו — *Because his compassion for his brother had been stirred.*

— [Lit. *his compassion became enkindled toward Benjamin.*] The verb כמר means *enkindled; heated.* In Mishnaitic Hebrew [*Bava Metzia* 74a] we find the term כּוֹמֶר זֵיתִים, *a heated mass of olives;* in Aramaic [*Pesachim* 58a]: מִכְמָר, *drying up;* in Scripture [*Lam.* 5:10]: עוֹרֵנוּ כְּתַנּוּר נִכְמָרוּ, *Our skin was scorched like an oven (Rashi).*[1]

וַיְבַקֵּשׁ לִבְכּוֹת — *And he wanted to weep.*

Joseph became so emotional because he could still not reveal his true identity to Benjamin, and because he knew that he would still be inflicting further suffering on him in the matter of the goblet [chapt. 44] *(Haamek Davar).*

וַיָּבֹא הַחַדְרָה וַיֵּבְךְּ שָׁמָּה — *So* [lit. *and*] *he went into the room and wept there.*

The room, i.e., his private inner chamber, which only he was allowed to enter *(Haamek Davar).*

— There he could weep without being overheard *(Midrashei HaTorah).*

And wept — at the grief of his father and brothers *(Sforno).*

According to *Midrash HaChefetz* [*Torah Sheleimah* §82], Joseph wept also for his grandfather Isaac, for he learned from the brothers that the Patriarch had died [see comm. to *v.* 28] and he, Joseph, had not been able to pay him final honor.

From the fact that his weeping enabled Joseph to regain his com-

1. *Rashi* cites the Midrashic account of the dialogue that brought Joseph to tears.

Joseph asked Benjamin 'Have you a maternal brother?'

'I had a brother,' Benjamin replied, 'but I do not know where he is.'

'Do you have sons?'

'I have ten.'

'What are their names?'

'Bela, and Becher,' etc. [see 46:21].

'What is the significance of these names?'

Benjamin replied, 'They all have some reference to my brother and the troubles that have befallen him: Bela — because he was swallowed up *(nivla)* among alien nations; Becher — because he was the first born *(bechor)* of his mother; Ashbel — because God sent him into captivity *(sh'va'o El);* Gera — because he became an alien *(ger)* in a strange land; Na'aman — because he was very pleasant *(na'im);* Achi and Rosh — because he was my brother *(achi)* and my superior *(rosh);* Muppim — because he learned from the mouth *(mepi)* of my father; Chuppim — because he did not witness my marriage canopy *(chuppah)* nor I his; and Ard — because he went down *(yarad)* among the nations [see *Sotah* 36b].

When Joseph heard this his *feelings became stirred up* for his brother.

פָּנָיו וַיֵּצֵא וַיִּתְאַפַּק וַיֹּאמֶר שִׂימוּ לָחֶם׃
לב וַיָּשִׂימוּ לוֹ לְבַדּוֹ וְלָהֶם לְבַדָּם וְלַמִּצְרִים
הָאֹכְלִים אִתּוֹ לְבַדָּם כִּי לֹא יוּכְלוּן
הַמִּצְרִים לֶאֱכֹל אֶת־הָעִבְרִים לֶחֶם כִּי־
לג תוֹעֵבָה הִוא לְמִצְרָיִם׃ וַיֵּשְׁבוּ לְפָנָיו
הַבְּכֹר כִּבְכֹרָתוֹ וְהַצָּעִיר כִּצְעִרָתוֹ

posure, *Sechel Tov* observes that 'tears extinguish the coals of the heart.'

31. The meal with Joseph.

וַיִּרְחַץ פָּנָיו — [*And*] *he washed his face.*

— To wash away his tears and conceal the fact that he had been crying *(Sechel Tov).*

The first time Joseph cried [above 42:24] the verse does not mention that he washed his face. Perhaps then he was not planning to spend much time with them and did not fear that they could tell he had been crying, while now he was to remain in their intimate company for an entire meal, and he wanted to avoid detection *(Chizkuni).*

וַיִּתְאַפַּק וַיֹּאמֶר שִׂימוּ לָחֶם — [*And he*] *fortified* [lit. *strengthened*] *himself and* [*he*] *said, 'Serve* [lit. *place*] *food* [lit. *bread*]*!'*

He fortified himself — i.e., he controlled his emotions *(Sechel Tov).*

The rendering *fortified* in the sense of *made a strong effort* [to contain himself] follows *Rashi* who cites the meaning of *strong* in the verb אפק in *Job* 12:21 and *ibid.* 41:7.

32. וַיָּשִׂימוּ לוֹ לְבַדּוֹ וְלָהֶם לְבַדָּם וְלַמִּצְרִים הָאֹכְלִים אִתּוֹ לְבַדָּם — [*And*] *they served* [lit. *placed*] *him* [Joseph] *separately, and them* [=the brothers] *separately, and the Egyptians who ate with him by separately.*

They served Joseph by himself — in deference to his royal rank *(B'chor Shor; Radak);* furthermore, since Egyptians and Hebrews did not, as noted further in this verse, dine together, Joseph did not dine with his brothers, nor did he and his brothers dine together with the Egyptians *(Sforno).* From the fact that Joseph did not dine with the Egyptians, *R' Hirsch* infers that he did not disown his Jewish heritage, even after so many years in Egypt.

Haamek Davar emphasizes that Joseph's practice of dining privately was not because he was a Hebrew and the Egyptians refused to eat with him. To the contrary, the Egyptians accorded him the highest honors and were in awe of his royal position. They would certainly not have shunned him. Rather he ate alone because it was not proper for someone of his royal status to sit with servants. The statement that *the Egyptians could not bear to eat with the Hebrews* is meant to explain why the Egyptians would not eat with the brothers.

Furthermore, had Joseph dined with his brothers — a practice the Egyptians found abhorrent — brothers might have suspected that he was not an Egyptian.He did not dine with the Egyptians out of respect to his brothers, and the Egyptians did not dine with the brothers because of the reason given by the verse. Thus, each group dined separately *(Ibn Caspi).*

כִּי לֹא יוּכְלוּן הַמִּצְרִים לֶאֱכֹל אֶת הָעִבְרִים לֶחֶם — *For the Egyptians could not*

washed his face and went out, fortified himself and
said, "Serve food." 32 *They served him separately*
and them separately and the Egyptians who ate with
him separately, for the Egyptians could not bear to
eat food with the Hebrews it being loathsome to
Egypt. 33 *They were seated before him, the firstborn*
according to his seniority and the youngest according

bear to eat food [lit. *bread*, a general term for *food*] *with the Hebrews.*

The term עִבְרִים, *Hebrews,* was used for no other group but the descendants of Abraham. It is remarkable, therefore, that even then, when the famiy consisted of less than seventy people, they were prominent enough to have a special national name. Even earlier [40:15], in describing his background to the Chamberlain of the Cupbearers, Joseph could call the land of Canaan אֶרֶץ הָעִבְרִיִּים, *land of the Hebrews (R' Hirsch).*

Most commentators agree, however, that the Egyptians despised *all* foreigners, avoiding social intercourse with members of *any* national group that ate foods the Egyptians abhorred. That our verse specifies 'Hebrews' is simply because the brothers happened to be Hebrews.

Rashbam accordingly interprets that *Ivrim* in this context refers to *all* foreigners from עֵבֶר הַנָּהָר, *the other side of the river,* whom the Egyptians, as a haughty and arrogant people, held in contempt [see *Isaiah* 30:7].

כִּי תוֹעֵבָה הוּא לְמִצְרָיִם — *It being loathsome to Egypt.*

I.e., it was a *hateful* thing to the Egyptians to eat together with the Hebrews [and other foreigners]. *Onkelos* states the reason for this *(Rashi).* [*Comp. Rashi, Exodus* 8:22].

The reason offered by *Onkelos* and *Targum Yonasan* is that 'the Hebrews would eat flesh of the sheep which the Egyptians worshipped.' Comp. 46:34: *For every shepherd is loathsome to the Egyptians;* furthermore in *Exod.* 8:22 it is written: *We shall sacrifice what is loathsome in Egypt to HASHEM our God.*

That they ate meat at this meal is evident from Joseph's instructions to his steward that an animal be slaughtered and prepared [*v.* 16]. Some are of the opinion that the Egyptians worshipped the constellation טָלֶה, *lamb* [Aries] and therefore refrained from eating meat. Whatever sheep the Egyptians raised were for milk and wool *(Radak).* [see *Mizrachi,* cited in 37:36 s.v. שַׂר הַטַּבָּחִים, however, who suggests that the Egyptians refrained only from eating sheep but *did* eat beef and flesh of other animals.]

Tzror HaMor observes that Joseph's eating and serving sheep to his guests was eloquent testimony to his repudiation of this form of idolatry.

33. וַיֵּשְׁבוּ לְפָנָיו הַבְּכֹר כִּבְכֹרָתוֹ וְהַצָּעִיר כִּצְעִרָתוֹ — *And they were seated* [*lit. they sat*] *before him — the firstborn according to his seniority, and the young*[est] *according to his youth.*

The translation *were seated* follows *Rashi's* Midrashic interpreta-

לד וַיִּתְמְהוּ הָאֲנָשִׁים אִישׁ אֶל־רֵעֵהוּ׃ וַיִּשָּׂא
מַשְׂאֹת מֵאֵת פָּנָיו אֲלֵהֶם וַתֵּרֶב מַשְׂאַת
בִּנְיָמִן מִמַּשְׂאֹת כֻּלָּם חָמֵשׁ יָדוֹת וַיִּשְׁתּוּ

א וַיִּשְׁכְּרוּ עִמּוֹ׃ וַיְצַו אֶת־אֲשֶׁר עַל־בֵּיתוֹ

tion according to which *they sat* means that they did so *in compliance with Joseph's instructions:*

'He tapped the goblet [as though divining] and called out: "Reuben, Simeon, Levi, Judah, Issachar and Zevulun, sons of one mother, be seated in that order," and similarly with the others. When he came to Benjamin he said, "He has no mother, and neither do I — let him sit beside me" [i.e. at the next table, nearest in position to Joseph; from *Tanchuma*].

[Apparently, the Midrash presumes that Joseph thought that Jacob's other wives were still alive. Actually, all his wives (except according to some views, Bilhah) had died by this time; see *Seder Olam* §2 *(Chizkuni).*]

By making this public display of divining with the goblet, Joseph was preparing them for the test that followed *(Ibn Caspi). Rashbam* interprets similarly; see below.

According to *Chizkuni's* own interpretation of the passage, the literal sense of the phraseology וַיֵּשְׁבוּ *and they sat,* indicates that they sat down in the order of their seniority *of their own accord* as they usually did on such occasions.

Some find Scriptural support for the Rabbinic interpretation that the seating arrangement was dictated by Joseph. The expression וַיֵּשְׁבוּ לְפָנָיו, [literally *and they sat* **before him**] implies strongly that they took their seats by his command and *in accordance with his will.* This stands to reason since one does not simply seat himself before a high official without being instructed to do so. Comp. 10:9: like Nimrod a mighty hunter *before HASHEM,* where the connotation of לִפְנֵי ה׳ could similarly be: *by HASHEM's grace.* Cf. also 27:7 where *Rashi* explicitly explains and 'I will bless you *before HASHEM'* to mean by His permission; with His approval.

According to *Yafeh Toar,* the seating order is as *Rashi* comments: the brothers were separated according to their mothers, and within each group they were seated chronologically.

The implication of *Onkelos* and *Bereishis Rabbah,* however, is that they were seated chronologically without regard to their mothers.

וַיִּתְמְהוּ הָאֲנָשִׁים אִישׁ אֶל רֵעֵהוּ — *The men looked at one another in astonishment* [lit. *and the men were astonished man to his comrade*].

Following *Rashi's* Midrashic interpretation:

— They were astonished at the knowledge displayed by Joseph's seating instructions in which he knew the order of their birth. They had all been born in the span of seven years so he could not have guessed their ages merely from their appearance *(Akeidah; Rashbam).*

According to *Chizkuni* [following *Daas Zekeinim*], their astonishment does not refer to the seating, but to Joseph's decision to dine

to his youth. The men looked at one another in astonishment.

34 *He had portions that had been set before him served to them, and Benjamin's portion was five times as much as the portion of any of them. They drank and became intoxicated with him.*

separately — neither with the Egyptians nor with them, thus confusing them as to his real identity.

Minchah Belulah maintains that the passage refers to the *Egyptians* who were astonished at the unprecedented special treatment Joseph accorded the brothers.

Torah Sheleimah cites *Midrash HaBiur* that the brothers were astonished and fearful lest Joseph's goblet reveal to him that they had sold Joseph.

34. וַיִּשָּׂא מַשְׂאֹת מֵאֵת פָּנָיו אֲלֵהֶם — *[And] he had portions that had been set before him served to them* [lit. *and he* (i.e. the steward in charge [*Radak*]) *carried the portions from his* (Joseph's) *face to them*].

It was customary for monarchs and dignitaries during meals to send selections of their own portions to certain special guests as a mark of honor *(R' Avraham ben HaRambam).*

The term מַשָּׂא refers to portions of *food (Rashi;* following *Midrash* and *Pesachim* 36b).

According to *Ibn Ezra* and *Radak* the term מַשְׂאֹת refers not to portions of *food*, but to *gifts*, which Joseph gave them during the meal. The expression מֵאֵת פָּנָיו, lit. *from his face*, means that were first brought before him for his personal inspection and prior approval.

וַתֵּרֶב מַשְׂאַת בִּנְיָמִן מִמַּשְׂאֹת כֻּלָּם חָמֵשׁ יָדוֹת — *[And] Benjamin's portion was five times as much as the portion of any of them* [lit. *but Benjamin's portion was increased from the portions of all of them five 'hands.'*]

Joseph gave Benjamin a portion five times as large as that of the other individuals; it was not five times as much as *the sum total* of all the portions *(R' Avraham ben HaRambam).*

Rashi follows the Midrash: In addition to the regular portion presented to Benjamin, Joseph gave him additional [four] portions, from himself, his wife, and his two sons.

The brothers surmised that Joseph was befriending them in this way in order to assuage his conscience over the maltreatment to which he had subjected them. They also assumed that Joseph was giving Benjamin favorable treatment to compensate for having torn him away from his aged father because of suspicions that were proven baseless *(Radak).*

According to most commentators, however, [e.g. *Ramban; Akeidah; Bchor Shor; Sforno*] Joseph's behavior toward them was a test to see whether they would be jealous of Benjamin. This theme will be discussed in more detail below.

וַיִּשְׁתּוּ וַיִּשְׁכְּרוּ עִמּוֹ — [And] *they drank and became intoxicated with him.*

[The Torah informs us of this because it was an unusual event]: From the day Joseph was sold until that moment neither the brothers

לֵאמֹר מַלֵּא אֶת־אַמְתְּחֹת הָאֲנָשִׁים אֹכֶל
כַּאֲשֶׁר יוּכְלוּן שְׂאֵת וְשִׂים כֶּסֶף־אִישׁ בְּפִי
ב אַמְתַּחְתּוֹ: וְאֶת־גְּבִיעִי גְּבִיעַ הַכֶּסֶף תָּשִׂים
בְּפִי אַמְתַּחַת הַקָּטֹן וְאֵת כֶּסֶף שִׁבְרוֹ
ג וַיַּעַשׂ כִּדְבַר יוֹסֵף אֲשֶׁר דִּבֵּר: הַבֹּקֶר אוֹר

nor he had drunk wine (*Rashi* from Midrash).[1]

This exegesis is alluded to in the qualifying word עִמּוֹ, *with him* — i.e., it was only *with him* that they now drank; without him they had not. Similarly, that Joseph had refrained from drinking all these years is alluded to by the reference to him in 49:26 as the *'Nazarite of his brothers'* (*Shabbos* 139a).

Chizkuni explains why the brothers, who observed the laws of the Torah before it was given, were permitted to drink the wine of non-Jews. The prohibition against such wine falls under two categories: יֵין נֶסֶךְ, *wine used for idolatry*, and סְתָם יֵינָם, *their ordinary wine*. The first category is forbidden by the Torah, and the brothers would have avoided drinking it. The second category, ordinary wine, was prohibited only by the Sages. Since it was a Rabbinic enactment, the brothers were not required to observe it, just as no Jews were required to do so prior to this enactment.

The term וַיִּשְׁכְּרוּ [*and they became intoxicated*] implies that they drank to excess, not being accustomed to drink with royalty (*Sforno*).

According to *R' Shmuel ben Chafni*, the term does not necessarily imply *intoxication* but drinking in excess of one's personal capacity to a point of becoming lightheaded and merry.

Tur maintains that Joseph's true intention in trying to intoxicate them was so that when they left they would not think of looking in their sacks and thereby discover the goblet he planned to hide there.

XLIV

1. The final test. Benjamin is accused of thievery.

The brothers' attitude toward the privileged treatment afforded Benjamin convinced Joseph that they were no longer spiteful, but not all his doubts had been resolved. Would they be ready to fight and sacrifice for the sake of a child of Rachel? If so, he could pardon them (*R' Munk*).[2]

1. The obvious questions arises: That Joseph drank is understandable since he was finally reunited with his brothers. However, the brothers did not recognize *him*; why did they drink after so many years of mournful abstinence? It is not sufficient to suggest that they did so out of respect for the Egyptian's royal position; some excuse could have been offered.

More probably, the brothers were puzzled by Joseph's vacillating behavior toward them. "Only yesterday he condemned us as spies," they reasoned, "and now he drinks with us! Perhaps he still thinks we are spies and he is trying to intoxicate us to find out our secrets and establish our veracity. As people say, 'when wine enters secrets leave.' If we refuse to drink with him he will definitely accuse us of having something sinister to hide. No, we will drink and become intoxicated and thereby *prove* we are innocent." So, they drank and became intoxicated with him (*Tzeidah LaDerech; Gur Aryeh*).

2. *Or HaChaim* offers three reasons for Joseph's subjecting them to this tribulaton:

a) By exposing them to shame for thievery, he intended this charge of stealing to atone for their sin of having stolen [i.e. kidnapped and sold] him;

b) to test their love for Benjamin and provide atonement for their hatred of himself;

c) to give them the apprehension that just as he knew other intimate things about them — ostensibly by divination — perhaps he was aware of their crime against him.

[1] *Then he instructed the one in charge of his*
house saying, "Fill the men's sacks with as much
food as they can carry and put each man's money in
the mouth of his sack. [2] *And my goblet — my silver*
goblet — place in the mouth of the youngest one's
sack along with the money of his purchase." And he
followed Joseph's word exactly.

As *Ramban* explains in 42:9, it was not Joseph's intention merely to cause them further anguish. He was afraid that they were as jealous of Benjamin — Jacob's favorite — as they had been of him. Possibly, there was strife between them and Benjamin because Benjamin knew or sensed that they had done away with Joseph. If such was the case, it would be dangerous to let Benjamin travel with them. To test them, he arranged for Benjamin to be charged with theft and arrested.

וַיְצַו אֶת־אֲשֶׁר עַל־בֵּיתוֹ — *Then* [lit. *and*] *he* [Joseph] *instructed the one in charge of his house.*

— His son, Menasseh (*Midrash*; see 43:16, 17).

מַלֵּא אֶת־אַמְתְּחֹת הָאֲנָשִׁים אֹכֶל כַּאֲשֶׁר יוּכְלוּן שְׂאֵת — *Fill the men's sacks with as much food as they can carry.*

— More than their money's worth (*Ramban*).

Joseph's extravagant heaping up of food and the return of their money was intended to point up by contrast their apparent baseness in 'repaying with evil' by stealing the goblet (*Alshich*).

וְשִׂים כֶּסֶף־אִישׁ בְּפִי אַמְתַּחְתּוֹ — *And put each man's money in the mouth of his sack.*

This placing of each man's money in his sack was to be done with the brothers' knowledge, ostensibly in reparation for Joseph's earlier harsh treatment. As noted, the official who filled the grain sacks would close and seal them, therefore the brothers did not open their sacks and discover the silver goblet that had been slipped into Benjamin's sack (*Ramban*).

According to *Abarbanel,* the steward was to return *all* their money — even what they returned from the first visit.

2. וְאֶת־גְּבִיעִי גְּבִיעַ הַכֶּסֶף — *And my goblet — my silver goblet.*

— He stipulated the *silver* one, since he had others (*Ralbag*).

— The reference was to the silver *royal* goblet [see *v.* 5] (*Tz'ror HaMor*).

In Egypt silver was scarcer, and hence more valuable, than gold (*Paaneach Raza*).

תָּשִׂים בְּפִי אַמְתַּחַת הַקָּטֹן וְאֵת כֶּסֶף שִׁבְרוֹ — *Place in the mouth of the youngest* [lit. *little*] *one's pouch along with the money of his purchase.*

I.e., 'when you put his money in his bags, slip in the silver goblet at the same time.' Benjamin is referred to as הַקָּטֹן, *the 'little'* one, as a term of endearment (*Sechel Tov*).

וַיַּעַשׂ כִּדְבַר יוֹסֵף אֲשֶׁר דִּבֵּר — *And he followed Joseph's word exactly* [lit. *and he did as Joseph's word that he had spoken.*]

ד וְהָאֲנָשִׁים שֻׁלְּחוּ הֵמָּה וַחֲמֹרֵיהֶם: הֵם
יָצְאוּ אֶת־הָעִיר לֹא הִרְחִיקוּ וְיוֹסֵף אָמַר
לַאֲשֶׁר עַל־בֵּיתוֹ קוּם רְדֹף אַחֲרֵי
הָאֲנָשִׁים וְהִשַּׂגְתָּם וְאָמַרְתָּ אֲלֵהֶם לָמָּה
ה שִׁלַּמְתֶּם רָעָה תַּחַת טוֹבָה: הֲלוֹא זֶה
אֲשֶׁר יִשְׁתֶּה אֲדֹנִי בּוֹ וְהוּא נַחֵשׁ יְנַחֵשׁ בּוֹ

3. הַבֹּקֶר אוֹר — *The day* [lit. *morning*] *dawned* [lit. *was light*].

I.e., as soon as day dawned. On one hand, Joseph wanted them to leave as soon as possible lest they dally and discover the goblet. On the other hand, he did not send them off at night since he was afraid that, under darkness, they would kill the man he sent after them *(Akeidah; Chizkuni).*

Rav, in *Pesachim* 29 derives from our verse that one should always set out on a journey when it is light, and enter a town while it is still light.

The interpretation of אור as a verb meaning that it grew light follows one view in the Talmud, *Pesachim* 2a. According to the other view, אור is another name for daybreak. [In Talmudic usage, however, אור is used for evening. Thus, אור לְאַרְבָּעָה עָשָׂר means the *night of the fourteenth* (ad loc).

וְהָאֲנָשִׁים שֻׁלְּחוּ — *And the men were sent off.*

— I.e. honorably escorted. See *Rashi* to 12:20; 18:16; and comm. to 24:59.

הֵמָּה וַחֲמֹרֵיהֶם — *They and their donkeys.*

— I.e. their fully laden donkeys. This is mentioned to emphasize how their fears that Joseph would detain them and confiscate their donkeys [43:18] were thus far unfounded *(Zohar).*

Tz'ror HaMor postulates that we infer from this passage that no one was permitted to leave Egypt and take his animals with him except by special permission of the government.

4. הֵם יָצְאוּ אֶת־הָעִיר לֹא הִרְחִיקוּ — *They had left the city* — [*they*] *had not gone far.*

— Less than 1 *mil* [2,000 cubits] away. Joseph was apprehensive that if he let them go away further, they would have been unafraid of his orders and he would not have been able to get them back *(Yalkut Shimoni).*

Furthermore, he wanted to spare them the additional strain of a long trip back *(R' Bachya).*

The term אֶת הָעִיר is equivalent to מִן הָעִיר. Cf. *Exod.* 9:29 *(Lekach Tov).*

The term אֶת הָעִיר, lit. *with the city,* Midrashically intimates that they were still within the boundaries of the city which extend 2,000 cubits [תְּחוּם שַׁבָּת] in each direction. Hence the *Yalkut's* interpretation above *(R' David Feinstein).*

קוּם רְדֹף אַחֲרֵי הָאֲנָשִׁים — *Get up, chase after the men.*

— While the fear of the city is still upon them *(Tanchuma).*

וְהִשַּׂגְתָּם וְאָמַרְתָּ אֲלֵהֶם — *When you overtake them* [*and*] *you are to say to them.*

I.e. only after you overtake them are you to tell them this; speak to them privately and do not make a scene *(Abarbanel).*

לָמָּה שִׁלַּמְתֶּם רָעָה תַּחַת טוֹבָה — *Why did you repay evil for good?* [lit.

44
3-5

[3] *The day dawned and the men were sent off, they*
and their donkeys. [4] *They had left the city, had not*
gone far, when Joseph said to his steward, "Get up,
chase after the men. When you overtake them, you
are to say to them, 'Why do you repay evil for good?
[5] *It is the one from which my master drinks, and he*
regularly divines with it. You have behaved badly in

why have you repaid evil in place of good?]

Before directly accusing them of stealing the goblet, he accused them of ingratitude, a charge sometimes worse than theft. The assumption was that these words of reproof would crush their courage and put them on the defensive. 'My master invited you to a feast, gave you food and drink at no cost — and you went ahead and rewarded him by stealing his personal utensil!' *(Sechel Tov).*

5. הֲלוֹא זֶה אֲשֶׁר יִשְׁתֶּה אֲדֹנִי בּוֹ — *It is the one from which my master drinks* [lit. *is this not the one from which my master drinks* (see *Ramban* to 40:8 that הֲלוֹא is idiomatically equivalent to הִנֵּה).]

— This charge magnified the enormity of the accusation against them. Someone who would dare steal the royal cup from which a monarch drinks demonstrates disdain for royalty — any bribe or ransom is inadequate to pardon him *(Ramban).*

According to the laws of Egypt, no one but a royal official was permitted to drink out of a silver goblet *(Tz'ror HaMor).*

The steward did not mention the goblet specifically, but spoke generally as if it was quite obvious that they had taken it. It is obvious from their answers in verses 8 and 9 where they mention only silver or gold, that they did not know what he wanted *(Ramban).*

וְהוּא נַחֵשׁ יְנַחֵשׁ בּוֹ — *And he regularly divines with it* [the Hebrew is literally in the compound infinitive; *and he divines, he divines in it*].

— Thus emphasizing even more the enormity of their crime; they had the temerity to steal his personal divining cup! *(Akeidah; R' Avraham ben HaRambam).*

[See *Rashi* above 43:33 for an example of how Joseph pretended to divine with his goblet.]

Ramban renders: [*It is the one from which my master drinks* ... *and* it is obvious that] *he would certainly make divination on its account.* That is, it was his personal cup and surely you should have known that he would not take its loss lightly, but would ask other diviners who had stolen it — which he in fact did. That is how he knows you are the culprits.

On this form of occult art, see *comm.* to 30:27 s.v. נִחַשְׁתִּי. The commentators explain further that there was a certain art of divination by which one foretold events by the surface motion of wine in a special cup *(Eisenstein).* All such forms of soothsaying were prohibited by Torah law [cf. *Deut.* 28:10-11].

— Since he divines with it he considers it a bad omen to have lost the cup he usually uses *(Radak; Abarbanel).*

According to *Ibn Ezra* — consistent with his comm. to 30:27 that נחש basically connotes *testing* — the sense

ו הֲרֵעֹתֶם אֲשֶׁר עֲשִׂיתֶם: וַיַּשִּׂגֵם וַיְדַבֵּר
ז אֲלֵהֶם אֶת־הַדְּבָרִים הָאֵלֶּה: וַיֹּאמְרוּ
אֵלָיו לָמָּה יְדַבֵּר אֲדֹנִי כַּדְּבָרִים הָאֵלֶּה
ח חָלִילָה לַעֲבָדֶיךָ מֵעֲשׂוֹת כַּדָּבָר הַזֶּה: הֵן
כֶּסֶף אֲשֶׁר מָצָאנוּ בְּפִי אַמְתְּחֹתֵינוּ
הֱשִׁיבֹנוּ אֵלֶיךָ מֵאֶרֶץ כְּנָעַן וְאֵיךְ נִגְנֹב
ט מִבֵּית אֲדֹנֶיךָ כֶּסֶף אוֹ זָהָב: אֲשֶׁר יִמָּצֵא

is: ' and this is the goblet whereby he indeed *tested* you,' by intentionally placing the goblet in front of you to see whether you would take it. [See *HaKsav V'HaKabbalah.*]

הֲרֵעֹתֶם אֲשֶׁר עֲשִׂיתֶם – *You have behaved badly in what you have done!*

I.e., by taking the cup, you have destroyed the honest reputation you regained with the return of the money *(Or HaChaim).*

According to *Abarbanel:* You committed this deed badly; because you executed the theft so crudely you were caught.

Since the Generation of the Flood, all great people have been scrupulous against stealing. You, who claim to come from a most prominent home, have trampled the prohibition! *(Sechel Tov).*

— You have acted foolishly and immaturely in three ways:

1. You stole something that is in constant use and would be sorely missed; its absence was immediately noticed.

2. The stolen article belongs to a royal official, who has unlimited power to recover it;

3. The cup is extremely valuable and its owner will not rest until it is returned *(Meam Loez* citing *Toledos Yitzchak).*

7. וַיֹּאמְרוּ אֵלָיו – *And they said to him.*

Through a spokesman. Therefore, the next phrase has the expression *my* lord in singular *(Radak).*

לָמָּה יְדַבֵּר אֲדֹנִי כַּדְּבָרִים הָאֵלֶּה – *Why does my lord say such things?*

— Hurling accusations at all of us? *(Sforno).*

You yourself admitted earlier that we were honest men [33:23] *(Ralbag).*

[On the phrase כַּדְּבָרִים הָאֵלֶּה being synonymous with הַדְּבָרִים הָאֵלֶּה, see *Ramban* to 39:19.]

חָלִילָה לַעֲבָדֶיךָ מֵעֲשׂוֹת כַּדָּבָר הַזֶּה – *It would be sacrilegious* [lit. *a sacrilege*] *for your servants to do* [lit. *from doing*] *such a thing!*

— Or anything similar to it *(Sechel Tov).*

Have we not demonstrated that we do not care for money? *(Abarbanel).*

— I.e., it would be a 'profanation' [חוּלִין] for us; we would be ashamed to do such a thing! *Onkelos* interpretively translated חָלִילָה as חַס [lit. *merciful protection*]. Thus, according to him the expression idiomatically means: 'God mercifully protect us from such an act!' Cf. the frequently quoted Talmudic expression חַס וְשָׁלוֹם [*'Chas V'Shalom!'*] [lit. *merciful protection and peace,* in the sense of *Heaven forfend!*].

[See *comm.* to 18:25 s.v. חָלִלָה לְּךָ.]

what you have done!' "
[6] *He overtook them and spoke those words to*
them. [7] *And they said to him, "Why does my lord say*
such things? It would be sacrilegious for your ser-
vants to do such a thing! [8] *Here, look: the money that*
we found in the mouth of our sacks we brought back
to you from the land of Canaan. How then could we
have stolen from your master's house any silver or

R' Hirsch perceives חָלִילָה to be related to חָלָל, *corpse,* and renders accordingly: 'We would regard the commission of such an act as a deathblow to our moral character.'

8. הֵן — *Look* [lit. *here*].

Synonymous with the idiomatic הִנֵּה, *behold (Ramban).*

כֶּסֶף...הֱשִׁיבֹנוּ אֵלֶיךָ מֵאֶרֶץ כְּנָעַן — *The money that we found in the mouth of our sacks we brought back to you from the land of Canaan.*

I.e. all the way from the land of Canaan — a great distance away where it might never have been discovered, and after so long a lapse of time *(Akeidah).*

וְאֵיךְ נִגְנֹב מִבֵּית אֲדֹנֶיךָ כֶּסֶף אוֹ זָהָב — *How then could we have stolen from your master's house any silver or gold?*[1]

Their argument, known in Talmudic literature as *kal va'chomer,* (*a fortiori,* deduction from 'minor to major') was based on simple logic: If they proved their honesty by bringing all the way back from Canaan money that they had not even taken, how could they now be accused of having gone on to steal?[2]

They displayed their ignorance of what he sought by not referring specifically to a *goblet* but vaguely to *silver* or *gold (Ramban).*

Furthermore, by this vagueness they were trying to fortify their claim of innocence by implying that since they were not familiar with the occult art of divination — such practises being fobidden to them — it was merely an object of silver or gold; to them it had no worth besides its intrinsic value *(Ralbag; Or HaChaim).*

By the above they were also anticipating a possible refutation of their *kal va'chomer* [*a fortiori*] argument. For

1. *Rashi* mentions that this is one of the ten *a fortiori* arguments mentioned in the Torah. They are all enumerated in *Bereishis Rabbah.*

The other nine listed in the *Midrash are: Exod.* 6:12; *Numb.* 12:14; *Deut.* 31:27; *I Samuel* 23:3; *Jeremiah* 12:5; loc. cit.; *Prov.* 11:31; *Esther* 9:12; *Ezekiel* 15:5 (some editions substitute the last with *Gen.* 4:24).

Although *Rashi* uses the term 'Torah' [usually limited to the first Five Books], he obviously refers to all of *Tanach,* [i.e. the twenty-four Books of Prophets and Writings]. The Talmud often uses 'Torah' in this broader designation *(Sefer HaZikaron).*

2. *Alshich* and *Malbim* explain the significance of their carefully chosen words:

The money — coins have no distinctive סִימָן, *mark* proving of ownership. *That we found* — the emphasis is on *found;* we did not steal it; *in the mouth of our sacks* — that something is found in a person's personal property gives him a presumption of ownership; *we brought back to you* — we returned it of our own volition, without anyone even telling us it was missed; *from the land of Canaan* — i.e., we brought it back from our own domain. Therefore *how could we have stolen?* — stealing is quite different from 'finding' something; *from your master's house* — finding something in the viceroy's house is far different from seeing it in the mouth of our sacks; *silver or gold* — a silver object quite identifiably its owners! *(Alshich; Malbim).*

אִתּוֹ מֵעֲבָדֶיךָ וָמֵת וְגַם־אֲנַחְנוּ נִהְיֶה
י לַאדֹנִי לַעֲבָדִים: וַיֹּאמֶר גַּם־עַתָּה
כְדִבְרֵיכֶם כֶּן־הוּא אֲשֶׁר יִמָּצֵא אִתּוֹ
יא יִהְיֶה־לִּי עָבֶד וְאַתֶּם תִּהְיוּ נְקִיִּם: וַיְמַהֲרוּ

the steward could have retorted, 'You returned the money because you are wealthy and the sum was not so great, or because you wanted to gain our trust so you could steal something more precious; this does not necessarily prove your innocence in this case where a *priceless* object, such as my master's goblet, was stolen.' This is why they claimed that to them it was nothing more than a piece of silver — whereas the money they returned was far more valuable *(Sifsei Kohen;* cf. *Or HaChaim).*

[It is unclear, however, why the steward could not have refuted their *a fortiori* argument by saying: 'Your return of the money proves nothing. We were holding your brother as a hostage and you were convinced that the money had been planted on you to implicate you in a plot; you returned the money only to ingratiate yourselves, and because you feared the consequences of not returning it. Now, however, all of you were leaving the land and you had no such restraints on you; you certainly stole it, as will proceed to prove.' וצ״ע.]

9. [Although the brothers vehemently denied the charge, they went even further. So certain were they that none of them was guilty that they agreed to accept an unusually harsh punishment if the cup was found among them]:

אֲשֶׁר יִמָּצֵא אִתּוֹ מֵעֲבָדֶיךָ וָמֵת — *Anyone among your servants with whom it is found shall die* [lit. *that it shall be found with him of your servants, and he shall die*].

— Since he is the thief *(Ramban).*

In so saying they emulated their father Jacob who protested the innocence of his retinue by telling Laban [31:32]: *With whomever you find your gods, he shall not live (Bereishis Rabbosi).*[1]

Their intention, in proposing a penalty severer than the law demanded was to demonstrate their certainty in their innocence *(Ralbag).*

וְגַם־אֲנַחְנוּ נִהְיֶה לַאדֹנִי לַעֲבָדִים — *And we, also, will become slaves to my lord.*

They were so convinced that *all were* innocent that if any one of them were found guilty, they were all ready to offer themselves as slaves since they were suspected of conspiring with the thief *(Bereishis Rabbosi).*

Comp. the Midrash: 'If one of a company of ten is convicted of theft, are they not all indeed liable to imprisonment?'

Ramban disagrees and maintains that such was not the law, since only if they conceived and executed the theft with mutual consent and

1. Why did Benjamin not die prematurely as a result of that curse as did Rachel as a result of Jacob's curse [see *comm.* to 31:32]?

— Unlike Rachel who, despite her noble motive, committed a theft, Benjamin was *completely* innocent, since the steward had placed the goblet in his sack.

However, how did the brothers utter this imprecation, knowing as they did that someone could have planted the goblet in their packs and their words might come back to haunt them?

— They carefully chose their words. By saying lit. 'that it shall be found אִתּוֹ, *with him'* they specifically meant *on* his *person,* but not in his pack. Nevertheless, since the purpose of the charge was to ensnare them, not to establish the truth, their protestations were ineffective *(Moshav Zekeinim).*

gold? 9 Anyone among your servants with whom it is
found shall die, and we also will become slaves to my
lord."
10 He replied, "Although what you say now is also
correct, nevertheless, with whomever it is found shall
be my slave, but the rest of you shall be exonerated."

knowledge is the entire group guilty. He postulates that they were pleading that since they knew nothing about the crime, they could *not* all be held responsible for the sin of one. It was only as a form of voluntary punishment that they offered to become slaves. They made this gesture to demonstrate complete faith in their innocence.

10. The steward agrees but not to their exaggerated proposal.

גַּם־עַתָּה כְדִבְרֵיכֶם כֶּן־הוּא — *Although what you say now is also correct* [lit. *also now as per your words it is so*].

[Following the Midrashic interpretation]: The law is indeed as you say. A whole group is liable to imprisonment for the act of one of its members *(Rashi)* ...

Following *Ramban:*

גַּם־עַתָּה, *also now,* the fact that you are now all found together, is presumptive evidence that *as your word it is so,* i.e. that you all participated in the theft and are guilty.

Alternately [in an interpretation more closely related to *Rashi's*], *Ramban* interprets: Although you suggest that your offering to become slaves is merely voluntary, you are wrong since there is a suspicion on all of you, and you should be arrested until the matter is clarified. Nevertheless, *as per your words* — that you are innocent of the theft and unaware that it even happened — *so shall it be.* I will free all but the culprit.

Chizkuni perceives the tenor of the dialogue to be: Although, by your own admission, the thief would be worthy of the death penalty, nevertheless I will not be so harsh ...

Sforno: Because the stolen article belongs to the viceroy, your proposed punishment is not sufficiently excessive, nevertheless I will be lenient and not exact the full measure of justice.

אֲשֶׁר יִמָּצֵא אִתּוֹ יִהְיֶה לִּי עָבֶד — [*Nevertheless*], *with whomever it is found shall be my slave.* [The steward speaks on behalf of Joseph; therefore he uses the expression *'my' slave.*]

Rashi: [Though by law you are guilty] ... I will be magnanimous and *only* the thief will be punished with slavery.

The judgment will be clear-cut. There will be no discussion of how the crime was committed or how the goblet came into Benjamin's pack *(Yafeh Toar).*

Ramban: Though you are not legally responsible for the crimes of an individual, the presumption of guilt is upon you because of your association. I should keep you imprisoned until your innocence is established; nevertheless, I will accept your plea of innocence. Even if one of you is proven guilty, I will not accept your offer to become slaves, but will hold only the thief. Furthermore, even his punishment will be less than you propose. I will make him my slave, since I desire his services more than his death.

Daas Zekeinim: Now, too, it is as you said: You claimed all along that

וַיּוֹרִדוּ אִישׁ אֶת־אַמְתַּחְתּוֹ אָרְצָה
יב וַיִּפְתְּחוּ אִישׁ אַמְתַּחְתּוֹ: וַיְחַפֵּשׂ בַּגָּדוֹל
הֵחֵל וּבַקָּטֹן כִּלָּה וַיִּמָּצֵא הַגָּבִיעַ
יג בְּאַמְתַּחַת בִּנְיָמִן: וַיִּקְרְעוּ שִׂמְלֹתָם
וַיַּעֲמֹס אִישׁ עַל־חֲמֹרוֹ וַיָּשֻׁבוּ הָעִירָה:
°מפטיר יד °וַיָּבֹא יְהוּדָה וְאֶחָיו בֵּיתָה יוֹסֵף וְהוּא

you were honest people, and you proved it by returning the money. However, your younger brother whom I never saw until now has not established his honesty and he might have stolen it without your knowledge. Therefore I say: *the one with whom it is found shall be my slave, but the rest of you shall be exonerated.*

— Of course, the steward knew all along in whose sack the goblet had been hidden *(R' Hirsch).*

וְאַתֶּם תִּהְיוּ נְקִיִּם — *But* [the rest of] *you shall be exonerated* [lit. *clean*].

For perhaps, as you claim, you did not collaborate together in stealing the goblet *(Ramban).*

You will be free to return home. This too was a test to see whether they would willingly leave Benjamin behind *(Haamek Davar).*

11. ... וַיְמַהֲרוּ — *Hurriedly* [*lit. and they made haste*].

— Anxious to prove their innocence *(Zohar).*

וַיִּפְתְּחוּ אִישׁ אַמְתַּחְתּוֹ — *And each one opened* [lit. *and they opened* (each) *man*] *his sack.*

This was further demonstration of their eagerness to exonerate themselves as quickly as possible. They did not wait for him to open their sacks; each one opened his own and offered to be searched first *(Bereishis Rabbosi).*

12. וַיְחַפֵּשׂ — [*And*] *he searched.*

I.e., he went through the motions of searching *(Midrash).*

בַּגָּדוֹל הֵחֵל וּבַקָּטֹן כִּלָּה — *He began with the oldest and ended with the youngest.*

So they should not suspect that he actually knew where it had been hidden *(Rashi; Alshich).*

וַיִּמָּצֵא הַגָּבִיעַ בְּאַמְתַּחַת בִּנְיָמִן — *And the goblet was found in Benjamin's sack.*

The *Midrash* relates that when the goblet was found in Benjamin's sack, the disgraced brothers began pouncing upon him and taunting him: 'Woe, thief! Son of a thieving woman! You have disgraced us by stealing, just as your mother disgraced Father by stealing the *teraphim'* [31:34]. Benjamin countered by calling them thieves who had orchestrated the sale of their own brother. [The tenor of Benjamin's reply was that he was suspicious that *they* might have stolen the goblet and planted it in his pack to incriminate him, and thereby create a pretext to rid themselves of him just as they had disposed of Joseph *(Beis HaLevi)*].

According to another view, they kept beating him until he swore by the life of his father that he had committed no crime and was innocent. It was only after they heard him take this oath that they believed him and ceased taunting him.

The Sages maintain that in com-

[11] *Hurriedly, each one lowered his sack to the*
ground and each one opened his sack [12] *He searched;*
he began with the oldest and ended with the
youngest. And the goblet was found in Benjamin's
sack. [13] *They rent their garments. Each one reloaded*
his donkey and they returned to the city.
[14] *When Judah arrived with his brothers to*

pensation for the undeserved blows, he merited the privilege of the Divine Presence 'dwelling between his shoulders' [a metaphoric allusion to the Temple which would later be built in Benjamin's territory. See *Deut.* 33:12 *Midrash; Tanchuma Yashan; Zohar*]. It is with such a thought in mind that R' Yose declared [*Moed Katan* 18b]: 'May my share be with him whom they suspect of something of which he is innocent.'

13. וַיִּקְרְעוּ שִׂמְלֹתָם – [*And*] *they rent their garments.*

— In grief *(Ibn Caspi).*

Their distress was magnified by the fact that it happened to be Benjamin, and they agonized over the potential fatal grief it would cause Jacob when he would learn of it *(Ralbag; Abarbanel).*

The *Midrash* — noting that no act ever goes unrewarded or unpunished — records that the brothers were put into a position of rending their garments in grief in retribution for having caused Jacob to rend his garments when they sent him Joseph's blood-stained tunic [37:34].[1]

Benjamin, too, was not unscathed. Innocent though he may have been, the very fact that his plight was what caused the brothers to tear their garments meant that he must have had some share of guilt; otherwise God would not have made him the cause of their grief. In retribution for this, according to *Yalkut Shimoni* to *Esther*, Benjamin's descendant Mordechai tore his cloithes in Shushan in response to Haman's decree of annihilation against the Jews.

וַיַּעֲמֹס אִישׁ עַל חֲמֹרוֹ – [*And*] *each one reloaded* [singular] *his donkey.*

They were strong, and did not need each other's assistance to do so *(Rashi).*

Sechel Tov asserts that it usually requires two men to lift a donkey's load.

וַיָּשֻׁבוּ הָעִירָה – *And they returned to the city.*

It was a metropolis, yet Scripture refers to it as עִיר, an ordinary *city!* This intimates that it ranked no higher in their eyes than a township of ten should they have to wage war against it *(Rashi).*

14. וַיָּבֹא יְהוּדָה וְאֶחָיו בֵּיתָה יוֹסֵף – *When Judah arrived with his brothers to Joseph's house.*

They were directed to go to

1. Additionally, since Menasseh was the agent who caused the brothers to tear their garments, he, too, suffered retribution: his territory in *Eretz Yisrael* was 'torn', in the sense that it was bisected by the Jordan River *(Tanchuma).*

This might be the reason Menasseh is not identified as the steward. The Torah wanted to avoid later hatred of him by the tribes for his role in their tribulation, and also prevent an accusation that he was chosen for this mission since he himself was guilty of some misdeed and 'evil is brought through the guilty' [cf. footnote p. 529] *(Yalkut Yehudah).*

עוֹדֶנּוּ שָׁם וַיִּפְּלוּ לְפָנָיו אָרְצָה: וַיֹּאמֶר טו
לָהֶם יוֹסֵף מָה־הַמַּעֲשֶׂה הַזֶּה אֲשֶׁר
עֲשִׂיתֶם הֲלוֹא יְדַעְתֶּם כִּי־נַחֵשׁ יְנַחֵשׁ
טז אִישׁ אֲשֶׁר כָּמֹנִי: וַיֹּאמֶר יְהוּדָה מַה־
נֹּאמַר לַאדֹנִי מַה־נְּדַבֵּר וּמַה־נִּצְטַדָּק
הָאֱלֹהִים מָצָא אֶת־עֲוֹן עֲבָדֶיךָ הִנֶּנּוּ

Joseph's house because he wanted to spare them the shame of appearing before other Egyptians *(Midrash HaGadol).*

Only Judah is specifically mentioned since he had assumed responsibility for Benjamin's safe return, and he therefore assumed the leading role *(Ralbag).*

וְהוּא עוֹדֶנּוּ שָׁם — [*And*] *he was still there.*

— Waiting for them *(Rashi).*

I.e., he did not leave his house that day to judge the people, but waited for them at home so he could meet them in private *(Tanchuma).*

וַיִּפְּלוּ לְפָנָיו אָרְצָה — [And] *they fell* [i.e. *threw themselves*] *to the ground before him.*

In obeisance. According to *Tanchuma,* it was now that Joseph's dream of the eleven bowing stars [37:9] was fulfilled.

15. With affected indignation, Joseph reproaches them for what they have done.

מָה־הַמַּעֲשֶׂה הַזֶּה אֲשֶׁר עֲשִׂיתֶם — *What is this deed that you have perpetrated?*

— It was both wicked and foolish, for you should have known that you could not succeed *(Sforno).*

הֲלוֹא יְדַעְתֶּם כִּי־נַחֵשׁ יְנַחֵשׁ אִישׁ אֲשֶׁר כָּמֹנִי — *Do you not realize that a man like me practices divination?*

Don't you realize that a noble man like me knows how to divine, and [though now deprived of my goblet] that I would be able to determine by my own logic and reason that it was you who stole the goblet? *(Rashi).*

Joseph did not chide them about their ingratitude, as Menasseh had done earlier, because it would have been beneath his dignity to invoke the kindness he had shown them *(Alshich; Haamek Davar).*

16. וַיֹּאמֶר יְהוּדָה — *So Judah said.*

Judah speaks on their behalf [see *v.* 14] and attempts no excuse, for the facts seem to allow none *(Abarbanel).*

מַה נֹּאמַר לַאדֹנִי מַה נְּדַבֵּר וּמַה־נִּצְטַדָּק — *What can we say to my lord? How can we speak? And how can we justify ourselves?*

What can we say to my lord in answer to your question, 'What is this deed that you have done?' Realistically, *How can we speak?* i.e., in denial of the charge, although we are innocent, for *how can we justify ourselves?* — to establish unequivocally that the charge was fabricated? *(Sforno).*[1]

— Since Benjamin is the 'culprit,' we cannot even invoke the *a fortiori* argument of *v.* 8 since Benjamin had not participated in the return of

1. Judah used three forms of expression: נֹּאמַר: what can we say to touch your heart and gain your compassion; נְדַבֵּר: on what grounds can we **speak** strongly and insist on our rights; נִצְטַדָּק: how can we **justify** ourselves. Of one thing we are certain; though we know we

Joseph's house, he was still there. They fell to the
ground before him. 15 *Joseph said to them, "What is*
this deed that you have perpetrated? Do you not
realize that a man like me practices divination!"
16 *So Judah said, "What can we say to my lord?*
How can we speak? And how can we justify
ourselves? God has uncovered the sin of your ser-
vants. Here we are: we are ready to be slaves to my

the money *(Or HaChaim).*

What can we say to my lord in our defense? *How can we speak* to my father to whom I assured Benjamin's safety? *And how can we justify ourselves* before the Divine Presence? *(Tanchuma Yashan).*

Rashi provides an instructive grammatical insight to explain the form of the word נִצְטַדָּק, *justify ourselves,* which, he notes, is a form of the word צדק, *righteous.*

He cites the following regarding the conjungation of the *His'pael* and *Nis'pael* forms: every word whose first root letter is a צ takes a prefix ט instead of the usual ת; furthermore the ט does not precede the first root-letter as is usual in *His'pael-Nis'pael* forms [such as, נתרצה from the root רצה] but between the first two letters of the root as follows צדק=נצטדק; *Daniel* 4:13: צבע= ויצטבע; *Joshua* 9:4: ציר=ויצטירו. Similarly, in the case of a word whose first root-letter is a ס or ש, the prefix ת is placed between the first two root-letters, e.g. *Eccles.* 12:5: סבל=ויסתבל; *Micah* 6:16: שמר=ישתמרו; *Exod.* 9:17 סלולה=מסתולל.

הָאֱלֹהִים מָצָא אֶת עֲוֹן עֲבָדֶיךָ – *God has uncovered* [lit. *found*] *the sin of your servants.*

[*Elohim* is introduced with the definite article ה: **The** *God,* as if to say that this is a pronounced instance of God's exercise of Strict Justice.]

"We know we committed no wrong in this matter. Rather it emanates from God, Who caused all of this to befall us because He wishes to seize this opportunity to punish us for an earlier sin. It is as if the previous misdeed had lain in abeyance, but now it is *uncovered* — *found,* as it were — to be dealt with. 'The Creditor has found an opportunity to collect His debt'" *(Rashi* from *Midrash).*[1]

The sense is: *'God has found* [the opportunity for exacting retribution for] *the sin of your servants.'* They referred are innocent of *this* charge, we must have sinned on some other occasion for which we are being punished now. The punishment was ironic, indeed. Benjamin had been summoned to establish *their* integrity, and now *he* is found to be a thief. They must have been convinced that the old charge of spying would again be hurled at them and, as before, they would be sentenced to slavery.

Only after Joseph proclaimed that Benjamin alone would be punished did Judah dare make the argument that begins in *v.* 18 *(R' Hirsch).*

1. R' Levi said: This is comparable to a man who lent money to ten people in partnership. While they were dispersed, he could not make his claim against them; but when they came together, he had the chance to exact his debt.

R' Isaac interpreted: 'The Creditor has now found the occasion to exact his debt.' We shared in the sin of selling [Joseph], but up to now we were not together, for *Judah went down from his brothers* [38:1]. Now, however, we are all together — so God uncovered *that* iniquity, not the 'crime' of the theft [of which we are now accused].

Joseph said to him [Judah], "If what you say is true, how is it that this brother of yours [Benjamin] has come to sin?"

Judah answered, "Whoever is caught with a thief is punished with him; he has been seized

עֲבָדִים לַֽאדֹנִי גַּם־אֲנַחְנוּ גַּם אֲשֶׁר־נִמְצָא
יז הַגָּבִיעַ בְּיָדוֹ: וַיֹּאמֶר חָלִילָה לִּי מֵעֲשׂוֹת
זֹאת הָאִישׁ אֲשֶׁר נִמְצָא הַגָּבִיעַ בְּיָדוֹ הוּא
יִהְיֶה־לִּי עָבֶד וְאַתֶּם עֲלוּ לְשָׁלוֹם אֶל־
אֲבִיכֶם:

not to the sin of stealing the goblet of which they were innocent, but to the sin of selling Joseph, which they committed long ago, but which God was now repaying through the instrumentality of the Egyptian viceroy *(Tzeidah laDerech; Sforno).*

It is not to *you* that we are guilty, but to *God* for an old sin that seemed to be forgotten and is now disclosed. Alternatively: עָוֹן, *iniquity,* in this context refers to the *punishment* for wrongdoing [cf. 4:13], and God is now punishing us for a sin *(Ibn Ezra).*

הִנֶּנּוּ עֲבָדִים לַאדֹנִי — *We are ready to be* [*lit.* here we are].

[The translation follows *Rashi* to 22:1 who explains הִנֵּנִי as an expression of submission and readiness to accept an assignment.]

We are, as I tried to convince you, all innocent in this matter, and therefore we *all* deserve nothing more harsh than becoming slaves to you *(Abarbanel).*

Judah, as the brother responsible for Benjamin could not bring himself to allow the others to depart without Benjamin. He proposed that they all remain as slaves in the hope that by staying together — even as slaves — they would eventually find a way to escape *(Akeidah).*

גַּם־אֲנַחְנוּ גַּם אֲשֶׁר נִמְצָא הַגָּבִיעַ בְּיָדוֹ — *Both we* [lit. *also we*] *and the one in whose hand the goblet was found.*

Because we are *all* equally innocent, are being punished by God for an entirely different sin, therefore — although earlier we advocated *death* for the *one* in whose hand the goblet was found [*v.* 9] — we now ask that we *all* become your *slaves* instead *(Akeidah.).*

17. Joseph presses his advantage home, and in order to make them realize more keenly their precarious position, he declares that he will retain Benjamin alone.

חָלִילָה לִי מֵעֲשׂוֹת זֹאת — *It would be sacrilegious* [lit. *a sacrilege*] *for me to do* [lit. *from doing*] *this.*

It would be sacrilegious for *me* to punish you for a former sin and thereby be like a 'wicked person from whom there proceeds wickedness' *(Sforno).*

Following *Ramban* in *v.* 10: *Far be it for me* to keep you all as slaves and thus deal with you more harshly than the assurance of my steward who said that you would be exonerated [*v.* 10]; no — I am the judge of the whole land; far be it from me to do you wrong.

הָאִישׁ — *The man.*

— Benjamin, the thief, is a *man,*

for *our* [old] crime, not for the theft of the goblet"

Said Joseph to him: "I have no interest in this. He against Whom you sinned will exact retribution from you, but I will not be His tool. I will act according to the law that a thief is imprisoned. As for you, you may go in peace to your father' " *(Midrash* in *Tzror HaMor,* cited in *Torah Sheleimah* §38).

44 *lord — both we and the one in whose hand the goblet*
17 *was found."*
17 *But he replied, "It would be sacrilegious for me to do this. The man in whose possession the goblet was found, only he shall be my slave, and as for you — go up in peace to your father."*

and fully responsible for his actions. He is not the קָטֹן, *innocent 'little one'* as you choose to call him *(Alshich).*

הוּא יִהְיֶה לִי עָבֶד — [*Only*] *he shall be my slave.*

Only *he* — the perpetrator of *this* crime — will be punished by me *(Sforno).*

Meshech Chochmah observes that Joseph's judgment intimated to the brothers that he knew Benjamin to be innocent, otherwise he would never have allowed a thief to be a servant in the house. He was fabricating the charge to detain an innocent man as his servant. This gave Judah the courage to offer himself as a substitute. [Cf. *Midrash HaChefetz* in *Torah Sheleimah* §43.]

Tur notes that the unusual vocalization עָבֶד instead of עֶבֶד — in this case where such a spelling is not mandated by a disjunctive punctuation — implies an insinuation that Joseph would keep him as a special kind of slave.

וְאַתֶּם עֲלוּ לְשָׁלוֹם אֶל אֲבִיכֶם — *And as for you — go up in peace to your father.*

It now became apparent to Judah that this was not a Divine punishment for their former sins or else *all* of them would have been enslaved. It was either the viceroy's capriciousness, or the result of some sin of Benjamin. Therefore, from this point on, Judah began exercising his responsibility to do whatever he could for Benjamin *(Haamek Davar).*

The precariousness of their position, and the ensuing consequences, inspires Judah in the following verses, to step forward and offer an eloquent personal appeal on Benjamin's behalf. But it is at this suspenseful point that the *Sidrah* closes.[1]

According to the Masoretic note appearing at the end of the *Sidrah,* there are 146 verses in the *Sidrah* numerically coresponding to the mnemonics יְחִזְקִיָּה״וּ, [*Yechizkiyahu*], אֲמַצְיָ״ה, [*Amatzyah*], יִהְיֶה לִי עֶבֶ״ד, [*he shall be My slave*]. The *Sidrah* contains 2,025 letters. The *Haftorah* begins with *I Kings* 3:1 וַיִּקַץ שְׁלֹמֹה.

The names *Yechizkiyahu* and *Amatzyah* are the same as the mnemonics used for the *Sidrah Bereishis,* implying that the two portions have common themes. *Bereishis,* the portion of Creation, proclaims God's all-powerful majesty; as Creator of the universe, only He sustains it and determines its course, whatever pretensions man may have to the contrary. In *Parshas Mikeitz,* we find Pharaoh considering himself a god and Egypt worshipping the Nile as its deity. Through the devices of abundance and famine, God displays beyond doubt that only *His* is the

1. What could Joseph have done if the brothers had accepted his judgment that only Benjamin stay behind — would he have subjected Jacob to such an awful blow? Undoubtedly Joseph would have revealed himself immediately.

But he would have invited only Jacob and Benjamin to come live near him in Egypt, for it would have been proven, tragically, that the brothers still harbored their jealous hatred for Rachel's children. But now that they showed themselves ready to sacrifice for Benjamin's sake, he could reveal himself in loving brotherhood, and begin the process of fulfilling God's prophecy to Abraham of the Egyptian exile *(Oznaim LaTorah).*

power. Pharaoh and his people are forced to acknowledge that they are subservient to Joseph whose distinction is in the fact that whatever his position — slave or viceroy — he remains but a servant of God: יִהְיֶה לִי עָבֶד, *He shall be My slave.*

R' Baruch Epstein [*Torah Temimah*] notes that this is the only portion in the Torah where a mnemonic is provided for the number of *words*, in this case 2025. He finds in this an allusion to Chanukah, which falls in the week of *Parshas Mikeitz*. On Chanukah, we light a new נֵר, *lamp*, for each of the eight nights. The numerical value of נֵר is 250; accordingly the eight lights of Chanukah give a total of 2000. Chanukah begins on the *twenty-fifth* of Kislev. Thus, 2025 is an allusion to the lights and the date of Chanukah.

The theme of Chanukah is especially appropriate to *Mikeitz*. On Chanukah we commemorate even the first day's burning, even though the jug of oil was big enough to burn for a day without miraculous intervention. By doing so we testify to our belief, that even the seemingly 'natural' process of burning oil is in essence a miracle because it is a manifestation of God's will (see *Overview*).

נשלם סדר מקץ

נשלם כרך ה מספר בראשית בעזרת האל

Meir Zlotowitz
Iyar, 5740/May, 1980
Brooklyn, New York

סדר ויגש

Sidrah Vayigash

— The Overviews

*An Overview/ Judah and Joseph**

וְאֶת יְהוּדָה שָׁלַח לְפָנָיו, זֶה שֶׁאָמַר הַכָּתוּב הַמְשֵׁל וָפַחַד עִמּוֹ עֹשֶׂה שָׁלוֹם בִּמְרוֹמָיו. הַמְשֵׁל, זֶה מִיכָאֵל; וָפַחַד, זֶה גַבְרִיאֵל. מִיכָאֵל מִן הַמַּיִם וְגַבְרִיאֵל מִן הָאֵשׁ. וְהֵן עוֹמְדִין לִפְנֵי הַשְּׁכִינָה וְאֵינָן מַזִּיקִין זֶה אֶת זֶה. הֱוֵי אוֹמֵר עֹשֶׂה שָׁלוֹם בִּמְרוֹמָיו ... יְהוּדָה וְיוֹסֵף ... אֶתְמוֹל מִתְנַגְּחִין זֶה עִם זֶה, וְעַכְשָׁיו הוּא מְשַׁלְּחוֹ אֶצְלוֹ! שֶׁנֶּאֱמַר וְאֶת יְהוּדָה שָׁלַח לְפָנָיו. הֱוֵי, עֹשֶׂה שָׁלוֹם בִּמְרוֹמָיו.

And he [Jacob] sent Judah before him (46:28). Scripture alludes to this: Dominion and fear are with him, He who makes peace in His heights (Job 25:2). Dominion refers to Michael and fear refers to Gabriel. Michael is of water and Gabriel of fire, but they stand before God's Presence and do not harm one another. Say [about this] He Who makes peace in His heights ...

Judah and Joseph ... yesterday they clashed with one another and now [Jacob] sends [Judah] to [Joseph]! Say [about this], He Who makes peace in His heights (Tanchuma Vayigash).

I. Unity in Diversity

Spokes of a Wheel

During World War I, the eastern battlefront cut through much of the most intensely Jewish parts of Poland and Russia and many hundreds of thousands of Jews — among them some of the great yeshivos and leading rabbinic leaders — were forced to flee and become wandering refugees. One of them was Rabbi Yisrael Meir Kagan, the Chofetz Chaim, who took part of his yeshiva with him deeper into

*Most of the Overview is drawn from the thought of *Harav* Gedaliah Schorr זצ״ל, much of which is collected in *Ohr Gedaliahu.*

Russia. By the time the war had ended, the Bolshevik Revolution had taken place, not only making it nearly impossible for them to return to Poland, but putting them at the mercy of Communist commissars for food at a time when Russia was near famine. Obviously the country's new Communist masters put 'parasitic' Talmudists at the very bottom of their list, and the yeshivah students suffered from severe deprivation.

Obviously the country's new Communist masters put 'parasitic' Talmudists at the very bottom of their list.

One Sabbath the distraught Chofetz Chaim took a walk, deep in thought, wondering how he could get food for his students. The larder was empty and the suffering was great. Ahead of him he noticed the Russian official in charge of distributing food. He was a former yeshiva student who had become a Communist and, like many converts, took extra pains to convince his colleagues that his conversion was real. The man's Hebrew name was Aaron and he had once been called 'Archik.'

As they met, the Chofetz Chaim said, *'Gut Shabbos, Reb Archik.'*

Archik replied roughly, 'For me today is no different from any other day.'

The Chofetz Chaim said, 'Let me tell you a *vort* (a thought) on today's Torah portion.'

'You know I don't believe in the Torah any more.'

'Just the same, everyone likes to hear a clever idea. The Torah specifies that God placed the Tree of Life in the *center* of the Garden of Eden [*Genesis* 2:9]. Why did He put it in the center and why was it necessary for Him to inform us where He put it? He wanted everyone to have equal access to it. There are many ways for someone to reach the Tree of Spiritual Life. Some people do it through Torah study, some through *mitzvos,* and some through kindness to other people. You no longer study the Torah, Reb Archik, and you no longer believe in Sabbath or the other *mitzvos.* But you are a good-hearted man. I want you to know that my students are starving! *Gut Shabbos,* Reb Archik.' The Chofetz Chaim nodded his head and walked on.

There are many ways for someone to reach the Tree of Spiritual Life.

You are a good-hearted man. I want you to know that my students are starving!

That night just after the Sabbath ended, a

wagonload of food was delivered to the yeshiva.

The Chofetz Chaim's unpretentious nature and gift for simplicity often obscured the depth of even his casual conversation.

The Chofetz Chaim's unpretentious nature and gift for simplicity often obscured the depth of even his casual conversation. Although his *vort* was calculated to soften Reb Archik's animosity toward committed Jews, his observation regarding the Tree of Life was true and profound: the Torah provides the Jew many ways to perceive his mission on earth, many ways to reach his goal.

While this concept is found in the differing roles of the Patriarchs [see Overview to *Lech Lecha*], it received greatest expression in the phenomenon of the Twelve Tribes. Each of Jacob's sons, the ancestors of the tribes, was unique in that each was assigned a particular mode of service, a special role in fulfilling the national mission of Israel. The nation is a mosaic of these parts, or, in the Chofetz Chaim's analogy to Archik, Israel is like a wheel with the Tree of Life at its center and twelve tribal spokes flaring out from it. The spokes are important individually, but their greatest significance lies in their interaction. Both Jacob and Moses blessed the tribes *(Genesis* ch. 49; *Deuteronomy* ch. 33) and, as the blessings make clear, each tribe had a unique role to play in the national destiny: Judah had monarchy; Issachar, Torah; Zebulun, commerce; and so on [see comm. to the respective blessings in chapter 49]. Of course, the specific blessing conferred upon one tribe did not exclude it from sharing those of the others. Jacob concluded his testament by giving all his sons a joint blessing, declaring that each would share in the gifts of his brothers (49:28, see comm.). This meant that all the tribes would enjoy the regal nature of a Judah and the agricultural success of a Naftali, and so on — nevertheless each tribe would be distinguished especially by the particular characteristics mentioned in its own blessing.

Jacob concluded his testament by giving all his sons a joint blessing, nevertheless each tribe would be distinguished.

Oneness of Israel

Sfas Emes likens Abraham, Isaac, and Jacob to the written, revealed Torah, in the sense that they formed the spiritual basis of the nation. Though they differed from one another, the three formed a unit, not only as an epoch in Israel's history, but as the foundation of their people's very existence. It is as if a new creation began with the Patriarchs; we are not described as בְּנֵי נֹחַ, *descendants of Noah,* as is the rest of the human race — we are called the descendants of Abraham, Isaac, and Jacob. After the Patriarchs, a new epoch began, that of the Twelve Tribes, each of which had its own role within the guidelines of the Torah. *Sfas Emes* likens the Tribes to the י״ג מִדּוֹת שֶׁהַתּוֹרָה נִדְרֶשֶׁת בָּהֵן, *the thirteen hermeneutic principles of Scriptural interpretation.* Each principle has its function, but if a scholar attempted to interpret the Torah by using only two or three — or even eleven or twelve — of the principles, he would have a flawed, false picture of the Torah. Each principle has its specific rules and applications, but it cannot be seen in isolation from the others. The principles complement each other to provide a complete, accurate understanding of the Law.

If a scholar attempted to interpret the Torah by using only two or three — or even eleven or twelve — of the principles, he would have a flawed, false picture of the Torah.

Similarly, when the tribes complement one another, joining their disparate natures to make a united nation, they parallel the many facets of the Oral Law, all deriving from the Written Torah to form a unified whole. The parallel goes further: when the Tribes act in concert, they are likened on earth to the Oneness of God Himself, as it were.

Every day the Jew accepts upon himself the yoke of God's sovereignty [קַבָּלַת עוֹל מַלְכוּת שָׁמַיִם] by reciting the *Shema: Hear, O Israel, HASHEM Who is our God is* ה׳ אֶחָד*, the One and Only God.* As many commentators note, the letters of אֶחָד, *One,* allude to the all-encompassing power that makes God unique. The letter א, with the value of one, alludes of course to His absolute indivisibility and Oneness. The letter ח, with the numerical value of eight, refers to the seven heavens — representing different levels of spirituality — and the earth; the letter ד, with the value of four, refers to all four directions of the compass, meaning that God's sovereignty is everywhere. Thus the full word represents the concept that God is One, as expressed by his absolute power in all twelve areas and directions: the seven heavens above, the

The full word represents the concept that God is One, as expressed by his absolute power in all twelve areas and directions.

earth below, and all four directions.

The same word אֶחָד *one,* describes Israel, for it is said of us וּמִי כְּעַמְּךָ יִשְׂרָאֵל גּוֹי אֶחָד בָּאָרֶץ, *who is like Your nation Israel, a unique* [lit. *one*] *nation in the world (I Chronicles* 17:21). Indeed the Midrash draws parallels between Israel's uniqueness and God's, as it were. In the case of Israel, too, the letters of אֶחָד describe the nation. Its last two letters equal twelve, the twelve tribes, and the letter א, *one,* refers to the national entity of a *united* nation. Its tribes are separate and distinct — as they must be if each is to carry out its individual function — but when they work together as a united nation, they merge into a single unit. It is as if Israel is described as a single nation composed of twelve parts; indeed, the whole is greater than the sum of its parts for a united Israel is the bearer of God's glory on earth, while a factionalized Israel brings discredit to the One Who made it His chosen people.

The Midrash draws parallels between Israel's uniqueness and God's, as it were.

The whole is greater than the sum of its parts for a united Israel is the bearer of God's glory on earth, while a factionalized Israel brings discredit to the One.

The Stones Unite

Jacob had in mind this indispensable need for national unity in diversity when he summoned his children to receive his death-bed blessings and when he wished to reveal the secret of the End of Days. He emphasized and repeated that they must 'gather together' (49:1-2), for Israel can rise to its greatest moments only when it is united, and he specifically warned them against discord *(Bereishis Rabbah* 98:2). The Sages report that God did not wish Jacob to disclose the time when the Messiah would herald the end of all exiles, so knowledge of this event was withdrawn from him *(Pesachim* 56a; *Bereishis Rabbah* 98:3; see footnote to 49:1). Jacob feared that this withdrawal of the Divine Presence might have been caused by unworthiness on the part of one or more of his sons:

Jacob feared that this withdrawal of the Divine Presence might have been caused by unworthiness on the part of his sons.

> אָמַר שֶׁמָּא חַס וְשָׁלוֹם יֵשׁ בְּמִטָּתִי פְּסוּל כְּאַבְרָהָם שֶׁיָּצָא מִמֶּנּוּ יִשְׁמָעֵאל, וְאָבִי יִצְחָק שֶׁיָּצָא מִמֶּנּוּ עֵשָׂו?
>
> [*Jacob*] *said, 'Perhaps, God forbid, there is a disqualification among my offspring, like Abraham from whom Ishmael was*

born and my father Isaac from whom Esau was born' (Pesachim 56a)?

Jacob's fearful question suggests that he had no fear that all his sons were unrighteous; he feared only that *one* of them had become unworthy — that he had produced an Ishmael or an Esau. We may well wonder — what if his suspicion were correct? Could anyone find serious fault with a family that produced one laggard among twelve sons who were among the great *tzaddikim* of all time?

What if his suspicion were correct? Could anyone find serious fault?

In the case of Jacob's family, the answer is yes.

In the case of *Jacob's* family, the answer is yes. Jacob was the last of the Patriarchs; from him issued the twelve tribal ancestors and it was required that he produce and raise the family that would become the *nation* of Israel. When the Sages praise Jacob as מִטָּתוֹ שְׁלֵמָה, *his bed* [i.e., offspring] *was perfect,* they refer to the prerequisite for Jacob's fulfillment of his mission on earth. *He* knew he would have twelve sons, his wives knew it, and his children knew the heavy responsibility that lay upon them. Jacob's offspring were the intertwined genesis of the *nation* of Israel. They had to be perfect, every one of them, or the national structure would be stillborn. Abraham and Isaac were to have purged the unworthiness represented by Ishmael and Esau so that the Patriarchal role could culminate with Jacob, a culmination that would result in a family of unblemished righteousness. If Jacob, too, had produced an unworthy son, the nation could not have begun then either, and the Patriarchal task would not have been accomplished.

This need for unity in perfection was revealed to Jacob at the time he was shown his vision of the ladder and heard God's promise to return him unharmed for his soon-to-begin personal exile in the home of Laban (28:13-15). As he lay down to sleep there on Mount Moriah, he had arranged stones around his head (28:11). The Sages teach that Jacob took twelve stones; if they coalesced to form a single one, he would know that his family, unlike that of Abraham and Isaac, would be united and therefore capable of being Israel's forerunner *(Pirkei d'Rabbi*

The Sages teach that Jacob took twelve stones; if they coalesced to form a single one he would know that his family, would be united.

Eliezer; Bereishis Rabbah 68:11). So it was: the stones cleaved and Jacob knew. The nation *would* begin with his children — but there had to be twelve, they had to be united, and they all had to be worthy of becoming part of אֶבֶן יִשְׂרָאֵל, *the* [single] *rock of Israel.*

This was no parochial fright, and his sons understood him well. They responded by reciting the verse of Shema.

Consequently, we can well understand Jacob's alarm at the suggestion that one of his sons might be unworthy. Not only was he a loving father concerned over the shortcoming of *one* beloved child, he feared that the 'twelve-part stone' of Israel might be crumbling, jeopardizing the entire national destiny. This was no parochial fright, and his sons understood him well when he voiced it to them. They responded by reciting the verse of *Shema,* proclaiming their total faith in and allegiance to God. And they concluded by saying:

> כְּשֵׁם שֶׁאֵין בְּלִבְּךָ אֶלָּא אֶחָד, כַּךְ אֵין בְּלִבֵּנוּ אֶלָּא אֶחָד
>
> *Just as there is only One* [*God*] *in your heart so there is only one in our heart* (*Pesachim* 56a).

As Jacob's corporeal life came to an end, he exhorted his sons to gather together in brotherly unity.

Implied in their answer was another facet of oneness. God is One and Israel is one. Our expression of His Oneness is less than complete if Israel is splintered. On Mount Moriah Jacob was shown that the twelve separate parts of his family would have to become one national unit for him to succeed in spawning the nation of Israel. Now, as his corporeal life came to an end, he exhorted his sons to gather together in brotherly unity and support so that he could bless them and reveal the glories of the future. The knowledge of the End of Days was denied them [see comm. for reasons why God would not allow Jacob to reveal it], but his children reassured him that *their* oneness, and thus their ability fully to proclaim *God's* Oneness, was not impaired.

II. The King as Unifier

עַל הֲסָרַת לִבּוֹ הִקְפִּידָה תּוֹרָה ... שֶׁלִּבּוֹ הוּא לֵב כָּל קְהַל יִשְׂרָאֵל לְפִיכָךְ דִּבְּקוֹ הַכָּתוּב בַּתּוֹרָה יֶתֶר מִשְּׁאָר הָעָם ...

The Torah objected to [forces that would lead the king's] heart astray. For his heart is the heart of the entire Jewish community, therefore Scripture [commands] him to cleave to the Torah more than it does the rest of the nation (Rambam, Hil. Melachim 3:6).

Conduit from Above

The two main unifying factors are the Temple, and the nation's leader.

Since unity is so essential to Israel's destiny, it is clear that the forces that unify the nation must be cherished and nurtured. In the normal order of things, the two main unifying factors are the Temple, which focuses Israel's devotion upon the site of the *Shechinah* [God's Presence], and the nation's leader — whether he is a judge or prophet — whose primary responsibility it is to guide Israel to the path of God and prevent it from straying.

After Joseph revealed himself to his brothers and assured them that he bore them no ill will, he and Benjamin fell upon one another's necks and wept (45:14). As *Rashi* explains, 'neck' is a metaphor for the Temples. Benjamin wept over the future destruction of the Tabernacle of Shiloh, which would stand in Joseph's territory, and Joseph wept over the destruction of both Temples, parts of which would stand in Benjamin's territory.

For these supreme resting places of *Shechinah,* the Torah uses the metaphor of 'neck,' *Sfas Emes* explains, because the neck serves as the conduit from the brain to the body. Both the Temple and the neck carry messages from above to the national and individual bodies. Just as man's spiritual success depends on how well his mind guides him and controls his animal impulses, so Israel's stature as a nation depends on how well it assimilates the charge of its Heavenly wisdom. The Temples were built by the

The Temples were built by the nation as a whole because they served national functions.

nation as a whole because they served national functions. Although the Temple would stand within its borders, no single tribe could claim a proprietary interest in it because, as the centerpiece of all Israel, it was essential to all the tribes. The Temple was no more the private property of Joseph or Benjamin than the neck is the property of the shoulders that bear it, the hands that protect it or the heart that nourishes it. The Temple is the nation's and the neck is the body's.

The Torah imposed added restrictions on a king to prevent him from being led astray by his ready access to power.

The king, too, as leader and guide of the nation is essential to the unified national well-being. There were kings like David, Solomon, and Hezekiah who drew Israel together and made it great. And there were kings like Jeroboam, Ahab, and Manasseh who splintered it and led to its downfall. The Torah imposed added restrictions on a king to prevent him from being led astray by his ready access to power, temptation, and wealth, and the Torah imposed upon him a special responsibility to study the Torah constantly and to have a Torah scroll accompany him wherever he went.

Judah the Leader

If the king is so crucial to national unity — if he is the 'heart' of the nation — then the *identity* of the king is equally crucial. From the youth of Jacob's family, it was known among them that Judah was the leader. Jacob was to bless him with sole right to reign (49:8) and no permanent dynasty had standing except the Judean line of David. Only a prophet speaking on behalf of God had the right to appoint a king from another tribe, and even then the kingship could be in his family only temporarily, and he could not be anointed with the holy oil used for Judean kings *(Rambam, Melachim* 1:8-10). Indeed, the hopes and prophecies for the future center around the coming Messiah, a scion of David, the first and quintessential Judean king.

With their prophetic insight, the brothers knew that they must follow Judah; he was their leader.

With their prophetic insight, the brothers knew that they must follow Judah; he was their leader, their king, their heart. In contrast to Reuben who is praised as Joseph's savior even though he dared not suggest that Joseph be returned to Jacob (37:21-22), Judah — who proposed that Joseph be sold rather than killed — is criticized by the Sages. He should have insisted that Joseph be returned to his loving father. Reuben, the firstborn, could not command his brothers' obedience, but Judah the 'king' could. Why didn't he? For this lapse the Sages criticized him (*Bereishis Rabbah* 85:3).

Seeds of Dissidence

As discussed in detail in the Overview to *Vayeishev*, the question of kingship was at the crux of the brothers' bitter dispute with Joseph. By his dreams and his behavior, Joseph indicated that he considered himself entitled to reign over his family. As the brothers understood him — erroneously, as we know — Joseph's motives were selfish; if not checked, he would destroy the family's unity and bring Israel's potential to a stillborn end. The brothers feared that they had in their midst another Ishmael or Esau, and it was their duty to keep him from destroying the family [see Overview to *Vayeishev*].

The prophetically endowed brothers perceived in Joseph the seed of his descendant Jeroboam.

They had another reason to distrust his protestations of innocence. The prophetically endowed brothers perceived in Joseph the seed of his descendant Jeroboam, who led the Ten Tribes to secede from the Davidic monarchy (*I Kings* ch. 11-14; see pp. 1578-79). Jeroboam began as a truly great sage and *tzaddik*, so much so that after he began to sin, God appeared to him, pleading that he repent:

אָמַר לוֹ, חֲזוֹר בָּךְ, וַאֲנִי וְאַתָּה וּבֶן יִשַׁי נְטַיֵּל בְּגַן עֵדֶן! אָמַר לוֹ, מִי בָּרֹאשׁ? אָמַר לוֹ, בֶּן יִשַׁי בָּרֹאשׁ. אִם כֵּן אֵינֶנִּי רוֹצֶה.

[God] said to him, 'Repent, then I and you and [David] son of Jesse, will stroll together in the Garden of Eden.'

[Jeroboam] answered Him, 'Who will be in the lead?'

[God] said to him, 'The son of Jesse will be in the lead.'

'If so,' [Jeroboam replied] 'I refuse' (*Sanhedrin* 102a).

Jeroboam's secession had been ordained by God

through the prophet Achiyah the Shilonite. God ordered Jeroboam to assume the throne because Rehoboam, Solomon's son and successor, was unworthy of the mantle of David and Solomon. But God's command to Jeroboam concluded with the admonition that his reign was not to be permanent — אַךְ לֹא כָּל הַיָּמִים, *but not for all time* — only the Davidic dynasty was to be eternal (*I Kings* 11:29-39). Nevertheless, the once righteous Jeroboam could not resist the newfound taste of power. Once he became king he enjoyed the throne and his perquisites. He realized that as long as his subjects continued to go to the Temple in Jerusalem, the capital of Rehoboam's shrunken kingdom, they would never shake loose the conviction that the Holy City was the true center of the Jewish people.

The once righteous Jeroboam could not resist the newfound taste of power.

Despite the seemingly well-founded suspicion of the brothers, God *had* designated Joseph as the transitionary leader of the twelve brothers; he was the 'neck,' the conduit from the Patriarchal Era to the Tribal Era. Although the monarchy would fall to Judah later on, for the present only Joseph could bridge the gap between the Patriarchs and the brothers. Undoubtedly Joseph protested that he had no intention of usurping what was rightly Judah's, but his brothers would not believe him.

Undoubtedly Joseph protested that he had no intention of usurping what was rightly Judah's, but his brothers would not believe him.

Even twenty-two years later when they were tormented and accused by a hard-hearted 'Egyptian viceroy,' and they attributed their travail to their treatment of Joseph, they did not retract their earlier judgment that he must be removed from the family's midst through death or servitude. They recognized in their travail the Divine hand of punishment for their ill treatment of Joseph, but they acknowledged only the sin of hardhearted lack of compassion when he begged for mercy: 'Indeed we are guilty concerning our brother inasmuch as we saw his heartfelt anguish when he pleaded with us and we paid no heed' (42:21).

At this point the question becomes difficult beyond belief: the brothers were wise and righteous people; if they could realize that they were being

If they could realize that they were being punished for what they did to Joseph, why couldn't they realize that they had misjudged his intentions?

punished for what they did to Joseph, why couldn't they realize that they had misjudged his intentions? Why did they not recognize the true Joseph even when they saw themselves being punished for what they had done to him?

Harav Gedaliah Schorr finds the answer suggested subtly in the narrative of the brothers' growing antagonism toward him. When they saw Jacob's partiality toward Joseph, they hated him; when he first began to dream of mastery over them, their hatred increased (37:4,5,8). As he continued to dream, the Torah no longer speaks of hatred; it says they were *jealous* of him (37:11). *R' Bachya, Alshich,* and *Or HaChaim* explain that they gradually perceived that his dreams were not the product of ambitious fantasy, but prophetic indications that he would indeed surpass and wield authority over them. Knowing that this was so, they should have come to terms with Joseph's spiritual majesty — but jealousy prevented them from doing so. Had they remained objective they would have realized that he had no base, selfish designs on anyone, but even a tinge of jealousy — and such great people could not have felt more than a tinge — warps the judgment of the most august and righteous. It affected their judgment enough so that they saw in Joseph the worst excesses of Jeroboam, and did not consider that Joseph's true character was better reflected by such descendants as Joshua. Joseph should no more be seen as an earlier Jeroboam than Judah should be seen as an earlier King Manasseh the Davidic king whose idolatrous excess led to the destruction of the First Temple.

They should have come to terms with Joseph's spiritual majesty — but jealousy prevented them from doing so.

One on Behalf of Many

This jealousy may well have had a more far-reaching effect than anyone could have realized.

This jealousy may well have had a more far-reaching effect than anyone could have realized. Although God had decreed upon Abraham's descendants a four-hundred year period that would include three conditions: alien-status, servitude, and suffering (15:13), it was not known at the time how these years would be reckoned and how many years each of the three conditions would exist (see comm. to 15:13 and ArtScroll Elias *Haggadah* pp. 95-97). Certainly, not every member of the Jewish people need suffer all the pangs of exile equally. In Egypt the Levites were not enslaved, but they were included in the national exile suffered with such intensity by their brethren. As the current exile plays itself out in modern times, we see clearly that not all Jewish communities fare equally. Somehow, however, in the Divine scales all Jewish fortunes and ordeals have their place in God's total plan. *Rashi* to 15:13 tells us that the count of four hundred years began with the birth of Isaac; even *one* man, apparently, can act out the travail decreed upon an entire people — if he represents the entire people.

The four hundred years began with the birth of Isaac; even one man, apparently, can act out the travail decreed upon an entire people — if he represents the entire people.

The Sages teach that Jacob felt entitled to live out his life in tranquility after his return to *Eretz Yisrael* from Charan (see *Rashi* and ArtScroll comm. to 37:1). *Pri Tzaddik* maintains that Jacob's desire was based on a conviction that his multiple ordeals of the previous twenty-two years had been of sufficient intensity to comply with the conditions of servitude and affliction foretold to Abraham. When he could no longer endure Laban's suspicions and presumptuous attempts to dominate the founding family of Israel, Jacob lashed out with a brief, but eloquent, recitation of the conditions under which he had labored for him (31:36-42). His tale could well qualify as one of 'servitude and affliction' and Jacob considered that he had fulfilled those parts of the four-hundred-year decree. If so, he reasoned, he could ask to live in tranquility from then on. Similarly, we find commentators who hold that the sojourn in Egypt was shortened from 400 years to 210 because the Egyptians imposed as much hardship in a relatively short time as had been ordained for the full 400 year period. God reckoned otherwise, of course. But the reckoning of a Jacob cannot be dismissed as frivolous. Undoubtedly his ordeal *did* weigh in God's scales.

Jacob lashed out with a brief, but eloquent, recitation of the conditions under which he had labored.

Joseph, too, spent years in Egyptian exile and slavery. Had his brothers accepted him as their leader, those years, too, could have been sufficient to defray some of the suffering decreed upon the family

Joseph, too, spent years in Egyptian exile and slavery; those years, too, could have been sufficient to defray some of the suffering.

because a king, like a Patriarch, is the heart and embodiment of his people. Had they not been blinded by a trace of jealousy, they would have acknowledged him as their head — their temporary king — and his agony could have represented them all. But jealousy displaced unity, so Joseph suffered as an individual, not as the representative of the entire nation. It was not until almost nine years after Joseph became viceroy of Egypt and provider for the world that his brothers were forced to bend their knees to him in fulfillment of the dreams they had once scorned.

But jealousy displaced unity, so Joseph suffered as an individual.

III. Uses of Diversity

From Master to King

Different approaches and strong differences of opinion among people seeking the same goal are not only unsurprising, they are part of the order of creation. The Talmud *(Rosh Hashanah* 31a) explains the bases on which the Sages selected the various daily psalms sung in the Levite Temple service and in our liturgy. For Monday they chose Psalm 48, a composition of the sons of Korach:

> בַּשֵּׁנִי מַה הָיוּ אוֹמְרִים? גָּדוֹל ה׳ וּמְהֻלָּל מְאֹד ... עַל שֵׁם שֶׁחִילֵּק מַעֲשָׂיו וּמָלַךְ עֲלֵיהֶם
>
> *Which [psalm] did they say on the second day of the week? 'Great is HASHEM and much praised ... [in the city of our God, Mount of His Holiness]' (Psalm 48), because [on the second day of creation] He separated His creations and reigned over them (Rosh Hashanah* 31a).

Rashi there explains simply that on the second day God spread out the רָקִיעַ, *firmament,* to separate the lower from the higher waters *(Genesis* 1:7). At that time He was likened to an earthly king in that He ascended to reign over His newly recognizable Heavenly sphere, just as His human counterpart would one day reign in Jerusalem.

He ascended to reign over His newly recognizable Heavenly sphere, just as His human counterpart would one day reign in Jerusalem.

R' Tzadok HaKohen (Resisei Laylah ch. 47) explains in far more detail. The Talmud uses two terms to express God's mastery over creation. In speaking of the first day, before the upper and lower spheres were separated from one another, the Talmud calls God a שַׁלִּיט, *Ruler* or *Master.* Only after the separation, on the second day, is He called מֶלֶךְ, *King.* What is the difference between the two terms and why does one better describe God on the first day and the other on the second day?

Someone can be a 'master' in the privacy of his home, to be a king involves having a kingdom with all its trappings.

As the Sages use these words, the difference between the terms is not in the degree of dominion they imply, but in the way it is exercised. Someone can be a 'master' in the privacy of his home, as long as there is no one to oppose him and no conflicting people to reconcile. The Hebrew word מֶלֶךְ, *king,* on the other hand, implies more than mere domination. Almost by definition, to be a king involves having a kingdom with all its trappings of local governments, armies and police, relations with other powers, and countless citizens, each insisting — vocally or inwardly — on his needs and rights. In the famous saying of *Kad HaKemach,* אֵין מֶלֶךְ בְּלֹא עָם, *there is no king without a nation.* In Aramaic, the word מְלַךְ means *counsel* or *advice (Daniel* 4:24), and it is no coincidence that the words for king and counsel are almost identical. To exercise the art of statecraft, a king must know how to reconcile conflicting interests and disharmonious ideas. For him to survive and to make his reign successful, he must be able to maneuver the many people with whom he must deal.

On the second day, God separated the heavenly from the earthly. That act of separation set in motion the infinite distinctions of the future.

On the first day of creation, God was a שַׁלִּיט, *Master,* for different levels of intelligence and spiritual greatness did not yet exist. But on the second day, God separated the heavenly from the earthly. That act of separation set in motion the infinite distinctions of the future, for by that act of dividing the waters into two levels of holiness, God showed that He wanted His universe to contain different kinds of beings. Just as there would be angels and people, sacred and profane, spiritual and material, there would be people with infinitely varying combinations of ability and ideas. They would see, understand, and react to things differently. This is healthy for it is God's glory that diverse people serve him in a variety of ways, each in his own mode — as long as they function within the guidelines of the Torah — just as the celestial and terrestrial waters of primeval creation were both legitimate expressions of God's will.

God is a 'King,' for He creates conditions that make it possible for all things to serve him in their diversity.

Over such a universe, God is a *'King,'* for He creates conditions that make it possible for all things to serve him in their diversity. Or, as the Chofetz Chaim put it to Reb Archik, during their meeting on that Sabbath in Russia, there are many paths to the Tree of Life, and all lead to the same goal even though they start from different points of the circle's periphery.

From Diversity to Strife

But by introducing diversity, God also introduced the possibility of acrimonious dispute when people devise points of view in order to further their own selfish ends. When differing parties search for the truth and disagree violently over how to come by or how to recognize it, the disputants are deserving of honor and, indeed, despite their conflicting views, all may well have perceived a measure of truth, though from different perspectives.

Of such disputes as those of Beis Hillel and Beis Shammai or Rava and Abaye, who disagree dozens of times in the Mishnah and Gemara, the Sages say אֵלּוּ וְאֵלּוּ דִבְרֵי אֱלֹקִים חַיִּים, *both this view and that view are the words of the living God (Eruvin* 13b; *Gittin* 6b).

But of such a dispute as that of Korach against Moses, there is no such praise, only contempt. Korach *spoke* in valid terms; he insisted upon the holiness of *all* Jews — and, indeed, every Jew stood at Sinai, heard the word of God, descended from the Patriarchs, witnessed daily miracles, absorbed an enormous degree of holiness. But Korach's argument stemmed not from love of Israel but from love of *Korach.* Had he sincerely sought ways to intensify the nation's service of God, Moses would have debated him and been able to convince him that the *Kehunah Gedolah* [High Priesthood] was not a

Korach's argument stemmed not from love of Israel but from love of Korach.

plaything that could be made available to anyone who lusted after moments of religious ecstasy. Indeed, when Korach first broached his complaint, Moses attempted to answer and dissuade him. Only when he recognized Korach's insincerity did he dismiss him contemptuously and pray for God's miraculous intervention [see *R' Hirsch* to *Numbers* 16:1-11].

Korach's sons, however, survived. When they joined their father in arguing for the holiness of the people, their words were not an eloquent disguise for hatred, jealousy, and ambition, they sincerely accepted the argument that all Jews were equally holy and Moses and Aaron were unjustly keeping glory and power. Because Korach's sons were sincere, they repented and withdrew when they saw that God was intervening on the side of Moses. They were not so blinded by selfish motives that they could not see the truth when it stared them in the face.

Because Korach's sons were sincere, they were not so blinded by selfish motives that they could not see the truth when it stared them in the face.

Therefore the psalm of the second day, fittingly, was one composed by the sons of Korach. The Sages chose wisely. On the day when diversity was created, we sing a hymn composed by those who proved that diversity is truly a virtue if it derives from a sincere search for truth and a desire to serve God according to one's ability to discern how best to do it. Others had searched sincerely, to be sure, but none had been more sorely challenged than Korach's sons — who followed a potentially great father when he seemed to be right, and left him when he was proven wrong.

The dispute between Joseph and his brothers is another case in point. It should never have occurred. Instead the relationship within the family should have been one of twelve brothers branching out within the Patriarchal heritage to beat twelve different paths to the same Tree of Life. God chose Joseph, an aristocrat of personal merit, to lead them so that their diverse marches would complement, not clash with, one another. But instead of respect the brothers felt jealousy, and instead of accepting Joseph they conspired against him.

Instead of accepting Joseph they conspired against him. Like Korach's sons, however, Joseph's brothers drew back from the brink.

Like Korach's sons, however, Joseph's brothers

drew back from the brink. When he revealed himself to them in Egypt, they recognized their error and accepted him as the premier among them. Not that they suddenly surrendered their separate modes of Divine service. To do so would have been as great a mistake, perhaps, as a continued denial of Joseph's superiority, for each was required to serve God according to the unique potential with which he had been endowed. Jacob's and Moses' blessings proved that, if any proof was necessary.

What the brothers did not do was demonstrate that their essence had remained pure and righteous. They had erred, but not become corrupt.

What the brothers *did* do was demonstrate that their essence had remained pure and righteous. They had erred, but not become corrupt; they had come to hate the ambition and danger they perceived in Joseph, but not the human being. With the error recognized and the perception corrected, the brotherly feelings took control and Jacob's family became what it had been intended to be when twelve different stones united.

IV. Judah's Triumph

Healing the Spirit

There were two majestic, royal figures among the brothers: Joseph and Judah.

Another element was necessary. There were two majestic, royal figures among the brothers: Joseph and Judah. Both were kingly leaders and the ancestors of kings, and each embodied an essential characteristic of the Jewish people. Simultaneously, however, they represented a cleavage that could cause inestimable damage to the people. In broad historical terms, this danger would seem to have been starkest during the period of the first Temple when Jeroboam's secession caused a permanent split in the nation and led to the eventual exile into oblivion of the Ten Tribes. It should not be forgotten, however, that this split first occurred in Jacob's lifetime when the brothers rallied to Judah's leadership and repulsed Joseph.

The split had taken place when the brothers' rejected Joseph's dreams and his claim to leadership — even his claim to brotherhood. The rift endured for twenty-two years during which the family of Israel was in spiritual limbo, as Jacob received no prophetic vision and the Torah did not refer to him by his exalted name Israel. Before the tribes could coalesce again, their leaders had to approach one another and melt the icy barrier of suspicion. As we shall see, the reunion of Joseph and Judah brought about the redemption of their family from the exile of antagonism and isolation and paved the way for the growth of Israel into a great and mighty nation.

Before the tribes could coalesce again, their leaders had to approach one another and melt the icy barrier of suspicion.

Not only that, but the Midrash also implies that the redemption from the current, last exile is foreshadowed in the Egyptian experience. Joseph's personal exile from his family is likened to the national history of the last nineteen centuries: if the renewed love of those brothers is duplicated by their modern-day descendants, our redemption will come, as did theirs. Nor is this surprising. The Sages teach that the current exile was caused by שִׂנְאַת חִנָּם, *baseless hatred.* Clearly Joseph, too, was the victim of such hatred, and the entire family of Israel suffered, too. Their ordeal was ended thanks to a reconciliation, as ours would be if its cause were similarly removed.

The current exile was caused by baseless hatred. Clearly, Joseph, too, was the victim of such hatred.

When Benjamin was 'exposed' as the thief who stole Joseph's silver goblet, the brothers were at a complete loss for words. They resigned themselves to whatever fate the viceroy's sense of justice or mercy would decree. Judah said despairingly, *"What can we say to my lord? How can we speak? And how can we justify ourselves? God has uncovered the sin of your servants. Here we are: we are ready to be slaves to my lord ..."* (44:16). Yet only two verses later, at the beginning of *Vayigash,* we find the same Judah approaching Joseph to argue against Joseph's even more lenient judgment that no one except for the 'thief' need be enslaved. Judah had been speechless and resigned; suddenly he became belligerent and argumentative. What had happened?

Judah had been speechless and resigned; suddenly he became belligerent and argumentative. What had happened?

Two things.

Judah's Approach

Pri Tzaddik, citing *R' Menachem Azariah of Fano,* explains that Judah's appeal to Joseph was in reality a prayer for God's help. Only a Divine punishment could have heaped such harshness against them, so only God's help could spare them. Judah's words were directed to Joseph, but in his heart he was speaking to God. [This concept of inner prayer is discussed in the Overview to the ArtScroll *Siddur*.]

In addition to his prayer, Judah undertook to penetrate to the heart of the implacable viceroy.

In addition to his prayer, Judah undertook to penetrate to the heart of the implacable viceroy. The Torah devotes fully seventeen verses to Judah's speech, and, in the Torah's terms, this is an exceptionally lengthy amount of space. Even with the Midrashic expositions, what he said may not strike *us* as being especially new or compelling. Whether or not Judah knew how to reach Joseph's inner feelings is beyond dispute — he succeeded. We all know from personal experience that sound arguments will not necessarily convince someone who, like Joseph, wishes *not* to be convinced. Even when persuasion seems to be effective, more often than not the listener will be hearing our words as *he* wishes to hear them, not as we wish them to be heard. Nevertheless, though all the odds were against him, Judah penetrated. He succeeded. And the Sages are lavish in their praise of his feat.

Though all the odds were against him, Judah penetrated. He succeeded.

The *Zohar* and Midrash *(Bereishis Rabbah* 93:4) interpret וַיִּגַּשׁ אֵלָיו יְהוּדָה, *And Judah approached him* (44:18), to mean that Judah approached Joseph's innermost depths; the word אֵלָיו implies the most intimate sort of association *(D'rashos HaRan, Matnos Kehunah).* The *Zohar* writes:

תקרובתא דעלמא בעלמא, לאתאחדא דא בדא, למיהוי כולא חד, בגין דיהודה איהו מלך ויוסף מלך אתקריבו דא בדא ואתאחידו דא בדא ... בגין דקורבא דלהון דאתקריבו כחדא גרם כמה טבין לעלמא גרם שלמא לכולהו שבטין, גרם שלמא בינייהו גרם דאתקיים רוחא דיליה, כד״א ותחי רוח יעקב אביהם

[*The approach of Judah to Joseph was like*] *the approach of one world to another, uniting one with the other so that all would become like one. Because Judah who was king and Joseph, a king, came close to one another ... As a result of their closeness, for they came together as one, many benefits were caused for the world: it caused peace for all of the tribes and peace among [the brothers], and it caused the [prophetic] spirit [of Jacob] to be reestablished, as it says, then the spirit of their father Jacob was revived* (45:27).

In describing Judah's successful attempt to influence Joseph, the Midrash (ibid.) likens him to someone who came across a well of clear, cool water, but had no way to draw the water up. Then a wise man came along. He tied one rope to another until he had made a rope long enough to lower a bucket into the well — and then the delicious water became accessible to everyone. In a similar vein, the Midrash cites *Proverbs* (20:5): מַיִם עֲמֻקִּים עֵצָה בְלֶב אִישׁ וְאִישׁ תְּבוּנָה יִדְלֶנָּה, *Counsel is like deep waters in a man's heart, but an understanding man can draw it up.* Buried in Joseph's heart was a plan to conceal his identity until the appropriate moment when he would tell them that he was their brother — but Judah tied together argument, narrative, and appeal until he drew the secret from Joseph, and then the refreshing news that not only had Joseph been found but that he was still *their brother* burst forth to refresh the entire family.

Counsel is like deep waters in a man's heart, but an understanding man can draw it up.

Regal Judah

It was a confrontation that ended with all the brothers acknowledging that Joseph was their 'king,' at least for that period of Jewish history — but how magnificently regal Judah proved himself to be in those tense moments! As noted above, the special grace of a king — as opposed to a שַׁלִּיט, *master* — is that he can coordinate the behavior of so many different people to achieve a harmony between them; and the very word מֶלֶךְ [king] is related to the Aramaic word [מְלָךְ] for עֵצָה, *counsel.* How deep are the pristine waters of counsel that are buried deep down in the human psyche! *God created man upright* [i.e. simple, honest, and upright], *but they sought many intrigues,* says Koheles (7:29). Man too often deceives himself and builds dream castles of perverted logic, but God did not create him that way.

How deep are the pristine waters of counsel that are buried deep down in the human psyche!

Within every man is a pool of clear, refreshing honesty, although sometimes it seems to be hopelessly beyond reach.

Deep down within every man is a pool of clear, refreshing honesty, although sometimes it seems to be hopelessly beyond reach. Then, sometimes, a Judah comes along — an אִישׁ תְּבוּנָה, *man of understanding* — and finds ways to bring it to the surface.

This Judah did to Joseph, exercising the wisdom and tact of the most profound king. The Torah implies unmistakably that Joseph did not wish to reveal his identity as yet. As *Ramban* explains (see comm.), Joseph considered it his obligation to bring about the fulfillment of his dreams; they were a prophecy and he was the prophet to whom they were addressed. As such, he was charged with doing everything necessary to bring his entire family — including Jacob — to Egypt to bow to him. This was one reason why he continued his harsh demeanor for so long and why he had Benjamin brought to Egypt. Judah succeeded so well in breaking down Joseph's resistance that וְלֹא יָכֹל יוֹסֵף לְהִתְאַפֵּק, *Joseph could not restrain himself* (45:1) — Joseph *wanted to* restrain himself, but he could not. Judah had stripped away his harsh exterior and exposed him as a loving brother and son.

Joseph wanted to restrain himself, but he could not. Judah had stripped away his harsh exterior.

V. Plower and Harvester

וַיִּגַּשׁ אֵלָיו יְהוּדָה: הִנֵּה יָמִים בָּאִים נְאֻם ה׳ וְנִגַּשׁ חוֹרֵשׁ בַּקֹּצֵר. חוֹרֵשׁ זֶה יְהוּדָה, בַּקֹּצֵר זֶה יוֹסֵף.
Judah approached him: Behold days are coming — the words of HASHEM — when the plower will approach the harvester (Amos 9:13). The 'plower' is Judah. The 'harvester' is Joseph (Bereishis Rabbah 93:5).

Two Ways to Sanctify

The verse selected by the Midrash describes the future redemption. After a long and discouraging litany of Israel's shortcomings and its agonizing descent into the throes of exile, Amos proclaimed that redemption would come and there would be such prosperity that by the time one year's harvest was over it would be time for the next year's plowing. The joining together of harvest and plowing would

The Midrash describes the meeting of the two brotherly 'kings,' likening Judah to the plower and Joseph to the harvester.

be a symbol of joy and deliverance, and it is in the same terms that the Midrash describes the meeting of the two brotherly 'kings,' likening Judah to the plower and Joseph to the harvester. Why? If we can understand this, we will have come a long way in understanding the destiny and goals of Israel.

יוסֵף שֶׁקִּדֵּשׁ שֵׁם שָׁמַיִם בְּסֵתֶר זָכָה וְהוֹסִיפוּ לוֹ אוֹת אַחַת מִשְּׁמוֹ שֶׁל הקב״ה. יְהוּדָה שֶׁקִּדֵּשׁ שֵׁם שָׁמַיִם בְּפַרְהֶסְיָא זָכָה וְנִקְרָא כֻּלּוֹ עַל שְׁמוֹ שֶׁל הקב״ה.

Joseph, who sanctified God's Name in privacy, merited that one letter of the Name of the Holy One, Blessed is He, would be added to his name. Judah, who sanctified God's Name publicly, merited that he would be called entirely by the Name of the Holy One, Blessed is He (Sotah 36b).

Though he sanctified the Name by his steadfastness and courage, he did it in privacy, not making an impact on broad masses.

Joseph was sorely tempted by the seductive wife of Potiphar, his master, but despite her near success, Joseph remained strong and spurned her (see ch. 39 and Overview to *Vayeishev).* In recognition of his merit, the letter ה from God's Four-Letter Name was added to Joseph's name, as we find in *Psalms* 81:6 that that he is called Yehoseph [יְהוֹסֵף]. Though he sanctified the Name by his steadfastness and courage, he did it in privacy, not making an impact on broad masses of people, so he was rewarded with only one letter of the Divine Name; it was inserted into his name in a hardly noticeable manner, and only one time in Scripture is it found.

Harav Gedaliah Schorr notes that the name Yehoseph, which already had the letters י and ו, thus contained three letters of the Name: י, ה, ו. The last ה of the Four-Letter Name is lacking, quite appropriately, because, in Kabbalistic terms, that letter allludes to the attribute of מַלְכוּת, God's *Kingship,* the attribute that signifies *public* awareness of His power, just as a human king's authority is acknowledged throughout his realm. Joseph did not bring God's power to public awareness, so the final letter of the Name could not be awarded to him.

Judah's characteristic was different. He sanctified God's Name publicly.

Judah's characteristic was different. He sanctified God's Name publicly, the Talmud explains, when Nachshon ben Aminadav, the leader of Judah, set an example for the entire Jewish nation by being the first to plunge into the Sea of Reeds. When Israel found itself pinned against the sea by Pharaoh's pursuing army, the Jews, understandably, were afraid. If they advanced they would drown, if they turned back they would face the full armed might of Egypt. The people were gripped by indecision, but Nachshon walked directly into the water and kept going until it nearly covered him — then the sea split. Nachshon of Judah was instrumental in one of history's greatest sanctifications of God's Name. Because God was so exalted by a member of Judah, all four letters of the Name are found in Yehudah [יְהוּדָה], with only the letter ד inserted in the middle.

Spiritual Heritage

When he was born, his mother, Leah, felt a special surge of gratitude to God.

The matter of Judah's name is instructive, for the Talmud explains the presence of four of its letters by referring to an event that occurred more than 250 years after he was born. Furthermore, the Torah gives a different reason for his name. When he was born, his mother, Leah, felt a special surge of gratitude to God. Jacob's family knew that he was destined to have twelve sons; since he would have four wives, each of them could be expected to bear three sons. When Leah had her fourth, she exulted: הַפַּעַם אוֹדֶה אֶת ה׳ עַל כֵּן קָרְאָה שְׁמוֹ יְהוּדָה, *'This time, let me gratefully praise HASHEM.' Therefore she named him Judah* (29:35; see comm. and footnote). [The Hebrew name Yehudah is related to הוֹדָאָה, *praiseful thanks.*] Having a fourth son meant that she had been granted a greater than expected share in the building of the Jewish people and she used her baby's name as a vehicle to express her thanks.

If so, why does the Talmud say that Judah bears God's Name because of the example his descendant set at the sea?

The principle illustrated by this incident is applicable to many of the lessons the Sages teach us about Scriptural and post-Scriptural events. Often

Often we find that characteristics of a nation or ruler are attributed to its ancestor.

we find that characteristics of a nation or ruler are attributed to its ancestor. The Syrian-Greeks who attempted to impose their will upon Israel at the time of Chanukah are said to be carrying on, though in a perverse way, the heritage of their ancestor Yapheth [see Overviews to *Noach* and *Chanukah*]. The Roman Empire, which descended from Esau-Edom, is seen by the Sages as carrying on its ancestor's hatred for Israel. Must we assume, however, that the Syrian officer who set up a Greek gymnasium and idols in the area of the Temple was aware of the heritage of Yapheth — or that he even knew he was Yapheth's descendant? Did every Roman soldier, or even his commander, know the story of Esau and Jacob? Surely the Sages meant no such thing.

Did every Roman soldier, or even his commander, know the story of Esau and Jacob? Surely the Sages meant no such thing.

Harav Schorr explains that the Sages, who received the God-given tradition of Scriptural interpretation, taught us that certain characteristics are endemic to a people, rather than merely products of a changeable environment or temporary conditions. For example, a blind or deaf couple will give birth to children who can see and hear. An amputee or someone born without a limb will give birth to healthy children. This proves that the blindness, deafness, or limblessness of parents is not a genetic condition. But parents *will* transfer their color and other racial characteristics to their children.

Some characteristics are hereditary while others are not; some spiritual traits remain with a nation.

Obviously, some characteristics are hereditary while others are not. Similarly, some spiritual traits, the Sages teach, remain with a nation. Not all the nations descended from Yapheth were equal heirs of his love of beauty and culture, but Yavan, the ancestor of Greece, was, and this legacy showed itself in Greece and in the Syrian-Greek's insistence on replacing the life of Torah with the "torah" of Greece. Rome inherited Esau's hatred of Jacob and became the nemesis of Israel. Similarly, Jacob's blessings of his sons revealed what characteristics would be innate in them. We cannot take it upon ourselves to say that every person mentioned in the Torah would pass on his nature to his descendants a thousand years into the future; but the Sages knew when this was the case and they revealed this knowledge when they considered it appropriate. In a sense, this is similar to contemporary analyses of events based on historical trends and biases of individual nations. For example, a conflict between Russia and China would be explained in terms of ancient antagonisms rather than current conditions alone; or Latin attitudes might be explained in terms of national temperament rather than issues.

When the Sages say that Judah bore God's Name because of Nachshon's act, they are revealing to us that Judah, the person and the tribe, had the mission of sanctifying God's Name in public. Thus, another Jew who sanctified the Name might have done so as an outgrowth of his personal development and greatness, but when Nachshon rose to the occasion he did so as a scion of Judah.

Judah's Essence

What is the essence of Judah, the inner source of his exalted mission? That we can see from the story of his birth. Leah named him as a symbol of her gratitude. As *Rashi* (29:35) puts it, she said נָטַלְתִּי יוֹתֵר מֵחֶלְקִי מֵעַתָּה יֵשׁ לִי לְהוֹדוֹת, *Since I have taken more than my share, it is incumbent upon me to give grateful praise.* As *Chiddushei HaRim* so beautifully put it, that declaration of Leah expressed Judah's essence — *'I have taken more than my share.'* Judah would be numerous, powerful, prestigious, regal, wealthy. Judah would have a Nachshon, a David, a Solomon, a Hezekiah; Judah would have a Messiah and bring about the final redemption of all mankind. Nevertheless, Judah would always say, 'I have taken more than my share.' He would never ascribe his greatness to himself, nor would he insist on the prerogatives that might be due him. Judah, the man and the tribe, had one goal in his life: to sanctify God's Name. His very birth caused an expression of overpowering gratitude based on Leah's feeling that she had received more than she deserved. But let us go a layer deeper. Leah only *expressed* gratitude, but the newborn Judah was the *cause* of her realization — he was the very essence of ascribing everything to

That declaration of Leah expressed Judah's essence — 'I have taken more than my share.'

Leah only expressed gratitude, but the newborn Judah was the very essence of ascribing everything to God's will.

God's will, God's generosity, God's mercy.

It was not enough for Judah *privately* to acknowledge that everything came from God. His mission was to be *king* — and a monarch must proclaim and infiltrate his beliefs and principles throughout the realm, he must inculcate different kinds of people with them in order to create unity within diversity. Nachshon's act was the most public sanctification of the Name that had taken place up to that point, but even there Judah had shown the way. His moment came after Tamar proved that he — Judah — was the father of her unborn twins (38:6-26). It is interesting to note that Judah's test was not whether or not he would live with the woman who, unknown to him, was really Tamar; that he *had* to do. She awaited him at a crossroads and tried to tempt him, but:

> *Rabbi Yochanan said, Judah sought to pass by Tamar. The Holy One, Blessed is He, dispatched the angel of lust to waylay him. The angel said to Judah, 'Where are you going? [If you pass this woman by] from where will kings arise, from where will great men arise?' Then he [Judah] turned to her by the way — he was coerced, against his good sense (Bereishis Rabbah* 85:8).

Unlike Joseph whose test was whether he could resist his master's wife, there was no question that Judah was required to marry Tamar.

Unlike Joseph whose test was whether he could *resist* the blandishments of his master's wife, there was no question that Judah was required to marry Tamar. Because he would not have done it on his own, an angel was dispatched to remove his resolve and force him to act. Obviously then, he was not expected to ignore Tamar — what then was his test?

Judah's Challenge

When Tamar was being taken to her public execution as penalty for her presumed 'adultery,' she presented proof that no adultery had taken place — that the man was Judah himself. Picture the scene. She had been adjudged in the court established by Shem. Among the judges were Isaac, Jacob, and Judah. Multitudes came to see the judgment carried out upon the 'immoral' woman who dared besmirch the name of Abraham's sacred family. *And there she confronted Judah!* Why hadn't she told him the truth privately, before the trial and the death penalty? No one knew, perhaps not even Judah, that an angel had intervened — was it fair to humiliate him so, *now,* in so large a forum? Couldn't Judah find some way to save her life without acknowledging his guilt? Surely, some pretext could have been found to show last minute mercy. Surely Judah could have confided in Isaac and Jacob, who would have saved Tamar without disgracing him.

Why hadn't she told him the truth privately, before the trial and the death penalty?

Judah recognized that his moment of challenge had come and, presumably, that Tamar's earlier reticence was a necessary step in constructing the test that he must now confront. Remember — Judah's primary mission was not to do good and refrain from sin. His mission was to proclaim that every achievement was God's gift and that God's Name must be sanctified publicly whatever the cost.

Nachshon was ready to display his faith even if it might cost him his life — Judah went further. He admitted the truth even though it could cost him his dignity, his self-respect, his reputation. Many a kingdom has been lost, many rivers of blood have been spilled for the sake of honor. Not Judah. Judah stood up before everyone and let it be known that a Jew will not permit a wrong to be done or a person to be hurt because of his error or to salvage his dignity. *Yes* — he could have found a way to save her without disgracing himself, but that would have forfeited the opportunity to sanctify God's Name publicly. Instead, Judah made the admission that proved him worthy of leadership in God's eyes, if not in the eyes of the stunned onlookers of Canaan.

Many a kingdom has been lost, many rivers of blood have been spilled for the sake of honor. Not Judah.

The strength of Judah lay in his readiness to be a willing receptacle of God's talent, blessing, and responsibility while ascribing nothing to himself. His very name indicates this quality. The Hebrew spelling of Judah's name, יְהוּדָה, contains the sacred four-letter name of God — plus one more letter, a ד, *dalet.* The word דַל, *dal,* in Hebrew means a pauper. Judah

Judah has within himself the majesty of his Creator, in his own eyes, however, Judah remains דַל, a pauper.

has within himself the majesty of his Creator; his kingship is no less than the Kingship, in a mortal guise, of God Himself, — in his own eyes, however, Judah remains דַל, a pauper. No matter how exalted his position, whatever he has is an undeserved gift of God.

David, first of the Judean kings and model for all his successors, embodies the same concept in his name. It begins with *dalet* and ends with *dalet*. For all his grandeur and achievement, for all the love his Maker bore for him and the holiness that made even the blood of his war victims seem like holy offerings before the altar of God, David, from beginning to end, considered himself a pauper, an impoverished mortal who carried only the gifts of God, but nothing of his own. The future *Mashiach* is described by Zechariah as עָנִי וְרוֹכֵב עַל חֲמוֹר, *a poor man riding a donkey*. He will finally fulfill the purpose of creation by bringing the Kingdom of Heaven to earth and by crowning God as King of all mankind — but he is a pauper riding the humblest of domestic beasts of burden.

The future Mashiach will finally fulfill the purpose of creation, but he is a pauper riding the humblest of domestic beasts.

Such kings represent the final stage of revelation. They are themselves but an embodiment of God's will on earth.

When Leah gave birth to her fourth son, she gave special thanks because God had given her more than her share. That is why Jews are called *Yehudim* (implying that they are descended from Judah) no matter what tribe they belong to. Even Mordechai, a Benjaminite, is referred to in *Megillas Esther* as *Mordechai haYehudi*. We are Yehudim because we always thank God for giving us more than our share, more than we deserve. The Jew is ever conscious of the graciousness and mercy of God. To him, health, prosperity — life itself — are never his by right; he thanks God for everything, for it is all an undeserved gift *(Chidushei HaRim* in *Sefer haZechus;* see Overview to *Ruth).*

The prophet alludes to Judah with the term חוֹרֵשׁ, *plower*. In discussing the forbidden labors of Sabbath, the Talmud defines the purpose of plowing as

לְרַכֵּךְ אַרְעָא, *to soften the earth* so that it is suited to receive seeds. Judah's mission was a public one: to soften the hearts of his fellow Jews so that they would be receptive to the word of God and the teachings of the Torah. Judah and his tribe 'plowed' through their personal example of negating themselves, ascribing nothing to themselves, working for their people, and sanctifying their Maker.

Judah's mission was a public one: to soften the hearts of his fellow Jews so that they would be receptive to the word of God.

Some of *R' Bachya's* comments on Jacob's blessings of Judah (49:12) are illustrative of this concept:

— He notes that the letter *zayin* is not found in the five verses of the blessing. The word זַיִן [*zayin*] means *armament,* and the prime expression of Judah's blessing is that God's Presence be so obviously with him that he would require no army to conquer his foes. In the time of Hezekiah, for example, prayer and repentance were sufficient, for God responded by causing the massive, terrifying army of Sennacherib to die in their camp overnight. Can there be a better example of a *plower* making the world receptive to God's word and able to see His hand?

— Aside from the four letters of the Name, Judah's name contains a ד, which has the numerical value of four. This is a reminder that he was the fourth son of Leah — and his birth provoked her to exclaim with joy and gratitude, 'I have taken more than my share!'

Abundant wine, an allusion to Kiddush, our testimony that God created heaven and earth in six days and rested on the seventh.

— Judah was blessed with abundant wine, an allusion to the *Kiddush* of Sabbath. *Kiddush* is our testimony that God created heaven and earth in six days and rested on the seventh. Its recitation is an extension of Judah's mission that God's greatness be proclaimed and His Name sanctified.

David's humiliation with BathSheba was caused from Above so that he would become the model of repentance for every Jew ever since.

Judah's quintessential heir was David who, despite his personal greatness and achievement, proclaimed אָנֹכִי תוֹלַעַת וְלֹא אִישׁ, *I am but a worm, not a man,* and who became Israel's teacher *par excellence* in the art of self-effacing prayer and repentance. Just as Judah was forced into his predicament with Tamar so that he would proclaim publicly that she was right and he was wrong, so David's humiliation with BathSheba was caused from Above so that he would repent for the rest of his life and thereby become the model of repentance for every Jew ever since *(Avodah Zarah* 5b).

Joseph's Challenge

Joseph's role was different. He was exemplified by one who harvests, discarding everything except what is absolutely useful. As the bridge between the Patriarchs and his brothers, Joseph stood on a higher level of perception and service. His was the intimate communion with God, the higher wisdom that would not permit sin. Therefore his challenge was different from Judah's. When he was tempted, he would have been accounted a failure had he succumbed and then tried to sanctify the Name by a public acknowledgment. Joseph *was* more so he had to do more.

Joseph was the son who was most like Jacob and was therefore his spiritual heir.

As described at length in the Overview to *Vayeishev,* Joseph was the son who was most like Jacob and was therefore his spiritual heir. His greatness was such that only the great Jacob could fully perceive it, and it was for this reason that he was charged with the leadership of the family, to be the surrogate Jacob, so to speak. The Jewish nation was moving from the level of Patriarchs — triumvirate whose every act and gesture was a guidepost for the future history of Israel — to the august but lower level of the tribal ancestors.

Despite the greatness of Jacob's twelve sons, they were not Abrahams, Isaacs, nor Jacobs, and they needed someone who could 'cushion the descent,' as it were, from the lofty spiritual world of the Patriarchs. Joseph was the one; he was on a plane between that of his father and that of his brothers and it was for that reason that he could give birth to tribal ancestors, a privilege denied any of his brothers. That his sons Ephraim and Manasseh were named to the status of tribes (48:5) is no mean tribute to Joseph. However one understands Jacob's motives in so honoring Ephraim and Manasseh, one fact must remain clear — the Three Patriarchs and the Twelve Tribal Ancestors represent two distinct levels in the strata of Jewish history. Just as no one could aspire to join the triumvirate of the Patriarchs, no one of a later generation could climb to parity with the twelve brothers — except for Ephraim and Manasseh. If only a Jacob could be the father of the tribal ancestors, then only someone approaching him could be the father of two who were the equal of Jacob's sons. Indeed, the Talmudic Sages teach that Joseph was worthy to be the father of twelve sons who would be the equals of the tribal ancestors (*Sotah* 36b).

If only a Jacob could be the father of the tribal ancestors, then only someone approaching him could be the father of two who were the equal of Jacob's sons.

In this sense, the Kabbalists refer to Joseph as the possessor of חָכְמָה עִלָּאָה, *higher wisdom,* while Judah, the other leader of the brothers, was the possessor of חָכְמָה תַּתָּאָה, *lower wisdom.* Joseph, the monarch with heavenly wisdom, sanctifies God's Name in privacy, for he dares not permit sin to tarnish him. God's higher wisdom does not consort with sin, even to serve as the vehicle for repentance and self-negation.

This wisdom represents God, the Source of life, and because it does, Joseph's challenge took the form of sexual passion. Man's strongest drive is also his most sublime for it is the source of life itself. God commands Israel to affix the seal of בְּרִית קֹדֶשׁ, *His holy covenant,* on the organ that produces life, thereby signifying that the Jew harnesses his most animal-like passions to the service of God, to produce the sort of life *He* desires. Joseph epitomized this goal, and for that reason he was uniquely honored with the title Joseph the *Tzaddik*. That title was given him not merely for maintaining his saintliness in Egypt — though that was no small achievement — but for the *manner* in which he did so.

Man's strongest drive is also his most sublime for it is the source of life itself.

The person who exemplifies such wisdom and behavior is fittingly called קוֹצֵר, *the harvester,* because he discards all the unavoidable trivia of life on earth and cuts through to the essence and purpose of existence.

The harvester discards all the unavoidable trivia of life and cuts through to the essence and purpose of existence.

Two Redemptions

As we have seen above, the Sages liken the climactic meeting between Joseph and Judah, the harvester and the plower, to Amos' prophecy regarding the End of Days. There are times when Israel must look to the plower and there are times when it must look to the harvester, times when its primary duty is to proclaim God's Name to the multitudes and times when it must draw itself in and sanctify his Name within the privacy of its own four cubits and its most intimate behavior.

The redemption of Jacob's family from inner turmoil and its loss of the spirit of prophecy began when Judah approached the innermost recesses of Joseph's being and wrenched from him the admission that he was Joseph and had remained their brother throughout the ordeal that had required him to display rage rather than love. It was a confrontation that began in anger and ended in embrace — and only then could the process go forward that would unite Jacob's family and prepare it for nationhood and the acceptance of the Torah. So it will be on that long awaited day when Israel's inner wounds and schisms will heal and — in the prophecy so aptly chosen for the *Haftarah* of *Vayigash* — *Ephraim shall not envy Judah and Judah shall not oppress Ephraim* (*Isaiah* 11:13). When the plower and the harvester approach one another with good will and understanding, when they recognize that Israel at peace with itself has much to learn from each of its members, then Redemption will be upon us.

When the plower and the harvester approach one another with good will and understanding, then Redemption will be upon us.

Travail and Birth

Earlier we noted that the Sages assigned Psalm 48 as the song of Monday because the second day of creation was the time when God put into motion the diversity that could lead to healthy tension or destructive discord. Very fittingly, the Midrash (*Bereishis Rabbah* 93:2) applies part of the psalm to the confrontation of Judah and Joseph. The psalm says (vs. 5-7): *For behold the kings* [i.e., Judah and Joseph] *assembled, they raged together* [i.e., Judah and Joseph were enraged at each other]. *They* [i.e., the other brothers] *saw and were forthwith astounded, they were terrified and fled in haste. Trembling gripped them there ...*

The Midrash expounds that the other ten brothers said:

מְלָכִים מְדַיְּנִים אֵלוּ עִם אֵלוּ, אָנוּ מָה אִיכְפַּת לָנוּ.
יָאֵי לְמֶלֶךְ מְדַיֵּן עִם מֶלֶךְ.

Kings [i.e., Judah and Joseph] are contesting with one another, what affair is it of ours? It is proper for a king to contest with a king.

The psalm's eloquent depiction of commoners gripped with terror helps us visualize the electric tension that gripped the palace as Judah advanced.

The psalm's eloquent depiction of commoners gripped with terror as their monarchs rage at one another helps us visualize the electric tension that gripped the palace as Judah advanced upon the facade of hostility and majesty that Joseph had thrown up to shield his identity from his brothers. But the Midrash does not tell us how the same psalm foreshadows the happy outcome. *Harav Schorr* was fond of finding a postscript to the Midrash in an anecdote told about Rabbi Akiva Eiger, of eighteenth and nineteenth century Posen.

At a wedding in the company of distinguished rabbis, Rabbi Eiger and the others became embroiled in a Talmudic discussion, grew animated and heated; this led to raised voices and high emotions. Such is the nature of Talmudic disputation, which the Sages praise saying that when scholars seek the truth and argue in its pursuit the end result of their clash is love and companionship [אֶת וָהֵב בְּסוּפָה]. But the laymen, unacquainted with the world of Talmudic debate, stood aghast as they watched the great rabbis 'shouting disrespectfully at one another.' Rabbi Eiger noticed their discomfort and lightheartedly explained with the words of Psalm 48:

The laymen, unacquainted with the world of Talmudic debate, stood aghast as they watched the great rabbis shouting disrespectfully.

'*The kings assembled and rage together* — for, as the Talmud explains, מַאן מַלְכֵי? רַבָּנָן, *who are the true kings? — the Torah scholars.* But they, the onlookers, are astounded and terrified at this spectacle. They flee from what they think is a lack of courtesy and they tremble in the presence of such conduct. But they fail to realize that the outcome of the noisy discussion is, as the verse concludes, חִיל כַּיּוֹלֵדָה, *convulsions like a woman in birth travail.*

'Do not be put off by the shouting and convulsions,' Rabbi Eiger told the people. 'It is like a mother in labor. The result of her shocking agony and

The struggles and debates of scholars create new life in the form of a better understanding of God's Torah.

frightful cries of pain is a new life. Similarly, the struggles and debates of scholars create new life in the form of a better understanding of God's Torah.'

Harav Schorr would say that Rabbi Akiva Eiger's witty soothing of perplexed townspeople should be understood as if it were one of his Talmudic glosses. He is giving us the conclusion that the Midrash implies, perhaps, but does not say: the brothers withdrew in fear and perplexity as the two kings, Judah and Joseph, engaged in a tournament that seemed as if it could destroy them both. What was the result? It ended like the labor pains of a mother — with the joy of renewed life. A plower and a harvester came together, joy and prophecy returned to Jacob, and a journey began that would end at Sinai and Jerusalem.

A plower and a harvester came together, joy and prophecy returned to Jacob.

VI. Survival in Exile

Jacob's Trepidation

We can only imagine the foreboding that mingled with Jacob's joy as he heard that Joseph was still alive and — more important — that his favorite son had remained the same Joseph even thought he had risen to power in the midst of a country notorious for its debauchery [see comm. to 45:26-27]. True the brothers had told him the good news that his favorite son had not changed, but Jacob had to wonder. Joseph's role was to embody חָכְמָה עִלָּאָה, *higher wisdom,* to resist temptation, to maintain his bond with the source of life, and to be but a step below the Patriarchs. In all these roles, he had been superior to his brothers, but if they had not perceived his stature when he lived in Canaan and studied at Jacob's feet, how could they be expected to perceive it throught the royal robes of Egypt? Just as they had been blinded before by jealousy, so they might be blinded now by the happiness of their discovery. People have a way of seeing what they want to, and the brothers could be pardoned if they wanted to see a Joseph unaffected by the wrong they had done him. But most important, Joseph's spiritual

True the brothers had told him the good news that his favorite son had not changed, but Jacob had to wonder.

stature was such that even in the best of circumstances, only a Jacob was qualified to be its true judge.

Let us imagine that after a disappearance of over twenty years, the son of a great tzaddik has become the prime minister of the Soviet Union.

Let us imagine that after a disappearance of over twenty years, the son of a great *tzaddik* is discovered — he has become the prime minister of the Soviet Union. Would not his father's happiness be dampened by fears that the son's scholarship, righteousness, and fear of God could not have remained untainted by his environment and position? The standards at the peak of government, especially in an atheistic or idolatrous country are not the same as those of the academy.

Nevertheless, there was enough meaningful comfort in the brothers' news to rejuvenate Jacob's spirits sufficiently to bring a return of his prophetic spirit even before he saw Joseph with his own eyes (45:27). As *Rashi* notes, Joseph had transmitted through his brothers the last Torah teaching he had learned from Jacob, as proof that he had retained the knowledge that set him above the rest of the family. Surely there is more to this than appears on the surface. It would not be unreasonable to expect that a son torn from his loving father would make a special effort not to forget his father's last words. Many a child who drifted far from his parents' way of life can repeat their last words verbatim, especially if the circumstances of their separation, like Joseph's from Jacob, were so sudden and tragic.

It would not be unreasonable to expect that a son torn from his loving father would make a special effort not to forget his father's last words.

Harav Yaakov Kaminetzky שליט״א notes the apparent strangeness of Jacob's decision to spend fourteen years at the Academy of Shem and Eber before going on to Laban (see comm. to 26:10). His parents had sent him to Paddan Aram to escape Esau's wrath and seek a mate, but, at the age of sixty-three, he made a lengthy detour for the sole purpose of studying Torah. Already when he was a child the Torah describes Jacob as a studious boy who spent his time in the halls of Torah (25:27). All his life he had had Isaac as a teacher — what could he learn from Eber that Isaac could not teach him?

What could he learn from Eber that Isaac could not teach him?

Torah of Exile *Sh'lah* and *Alshich* explain that apparently Jacob's scholarship needed an embellishment beyond what he had received from Isaac, one that he could not be without if he were to survive his exile with Laban. In the home of Isaac, Jacob had studied in the holiest possible atmosphere, the sort of rarefied environment that could hardly be compromised by the deleterious influences of exile.

The exile endured by Isaac was an external thing — expressed by an occasional sneer or contention over wells.

True, all of Isaac's life was included in the four hundred years of exile foretold to Abraham, but that was true only as concerned the attitude displayed toward him by his neighbors: sometimes it was hostile, more often it consisted of bare tolerance with a touch of disdain, but it fell short of the respectful reverence shown Abraham throughout his tenure in Canaan. So the exile endured by Isaac was an external thing — expressed more by an occasional sneer or contention over wells, but it never included hostility of a dangerous sort or the plight of being a total foreigner in a strange land. Most important, it never affected the quality of his life. In and around Isaac's home there was never an exile: his tent was a sanctuary, his study the chariot of the *Shechinah,* his family a miniature Temple, insulated and secure from the idolatrous, immoral surroundings.

That was exile! An exile not defined by subtleties, like Isaac's, but one that the most unsophisticated observer could recognize only too well.

Jacob, however, was called upon to endure exile — not figurative nor symbolic — stark, real, hostile, dangerous exile in a foreign land, under the sway of a conniving, swindling Laban, who did not hesitate to voice barely veiled threats when his ire was aroused (31:28) or to state flatly that only at his pleasure could Jacob marry and raise a family — and expect to keep it (29:25-28; 31:43). Jacob would spend over twenty years of his life with the knowledge that his brutish, violent brother had vowed to kill him, and when he was finally returning to *Eretz Yisrael* with his large family and huge flocks of livestock and servants — Jacob would learn that Esau was marching at the head of a sizable army to exact his vengeance.

That was exile! An exile not defined by subtleties, like Isaac's, but one that the most unsophisticated observer could recognize only too well. To face an exile in such inhospitable surroundings and among such unsavory people, Jacob needed preparations of a sort that Isaac and Rebeccah could not afford. Life among saints does not prepare one to cope with barbarians. Jacob had grown up in the holiness of *Eretz Yisrael* with a father who had never left the Holy Land — the Land Jacob was now forced to leave, completely on his own. For such an ordeal Jacob needed new spiritual underpinnings. For that he went to the Academy of Eber, there to study Torah for fourteen uninterrupted years in preparation for an exile harsher than any Isaac ever knew. From Isaac he learned the Torah of *Eretz Yisrael;* from Eber he learned the Torah of exile.

From Isaac he learned the Torah of Eretz Yisrael; from Eber he learned the Torah of exile.

That Jacob taught the Torah to Joseph, we know; the Sages tell us that Joseph was his father's premier student and this was one of the reasons Jacob loved him so (see comm. to 37:3). In describing what Jacob had taught Joseph, the Sages say: כָּל הֲלָכוֹת שֶׁמָּסְרוּ שֵׁם וְעֵבֶר לְיַעֲקֹב מָסְרָן לוֹ, *all the laws that* [the Academy of] *Shem and Eber transmitted to Jacob, he transmitted to* [*Joseph*] *(Bereishis Rabbah* 84:8; *Rashi* to 37:3). In one of those prophetic insights by which God sprinkled meaning into every act of the Patriarchs, He influenced Jacob to teach the Torah of Shem and Eber to Joseph. Jacob did not know that Joseph would need the Torah of exile even more than he had, but when the seventeen-year old leader of Israel's next epoch was dispatched to his own twenty-two year exile, the 'harvester' had amassed the stories of spiritual food he would need during the agonizing years while he prepared for the task of nourishing a famine-stricken world.

When Joseph sent back word that he was still alive, he knew that Jacob would want to know what *kind* of Joseph was still alive — had Joseph's *soul* survived with his body? So Joseph's message was a recitation of the last law Jacob had taught him. Perhaps even the choice of that law was Divinely inspired. The subject was עֶגְלָה עֲרוּפָה *(Deuteronomy* 21:1-9), the ritual symbolizing that the elders of a city bear responsibility to provide lodging, food, and safe passage for wayfarers. By signaling his brothers to tell Jacob that he still remembered, Joseph was declaring, in effect, that the teachings of Eber had succeeded in preparing a second Jew for the rigors of exile, and that Jacob had not fallen short in carrying out his duty to Joseph, his son who had been a lonely wayfarer for so long.

The teachings of Eber had succeeded in preparing a second Jew for the rigors of exile.

True, Jacob could not be satisfied until he saw Joseph with his own eyes, but that message went far enough toward removing his anxiety that he could again receive prophecy after a twenty-two year lapse.

When Doubts Disappear

The episode of Joseph's revelation to his brothers contains another portent for the future Redemption. Familiarity has dulled our perception of the anguish Joseph's brothers felt before Joseph's uttered those electrifying words: אֲנִי יוֹסֵף, *I am Joseph.*

The brothers had seen Jacob's unrelieved suffering for twenty-two years. They were responsible for Joseph's disappearace — perhaps death — and now they were being punished for it. They had taken Benjamin, too, from his father — would Jacob survive another loss? Even if Judah were to take Benjamin's place, they would lose their leader. How could they, the heirs of Abraham, Isaac, and Jacob become the playthings of a paranoid, sadistic viceroy? Was Benjamin truly a thief? Jacob had been told by God that the destiny of Israel depended on twelve righteous tribal ancestors, and now it was all crumbling. So many thoughts tortured them. So many questions without answers.

How could they become the playthings of a paranoid, sadistic viceroy?

Then the Egyptian viceroy said 'I am Joseph' — *and the questions disappeared!* In a flash of lightning, God's plan took shape before their eyes and twenty-two years of trauma became the framework upon which nationhood, growth, and redemption were being built. There was *no* stolen cup, *no* lost brother, *no* crumbled destiny, *no* fratricide. There was unity, recognition that Joseph had been right all along, and there was still time for them to accept him in the role in which God had cast him.

Then the Egyptian viceroy said 'I am Joseph' — and the questions disappeared!

More important, Harvester and Plower had met,

had joined, had forged a brotherhood of redemption. It was true — the destiny of Israel depended on twelve sons united in an impregnable rock, and now the pieces had come together again. It is doubtful whether the spiritual integrity of Israel could have survived an Egyptian exile if the tribal ancestors had remained fractious — even under the best conditions of unity, their descendants slid to almost the lowest level of contamination before they were finally redeemed — but now they *were* united in both mission and love. So it was that וַיִּשְׂאוּ בְנֵי יִשְׂרָאֵל אֶת יַעֲקֹב אֲבִיהֶם, *and the Children of Israel transported Jacob their father* (46:5); Jacob could go into yet another exile without foreboding because his children, *all* his children, shared in carrying the burden of Jewish destiny.

Someday, perhaps even today, God will reveal Himself and His plan, as Joseph did then.

After nineteen centuries of exile, Israel has questions at least as perplexing as those that tormented the brothers. But someday, perhaps even today, *God* will reveal Himself and His plan, as Joseph did then. He will interrupt our agonies with an electrifying call of His own:

רְאוּ עַתָּה כִּי אֲנִי אֲנִי הוּא וְאֵין אֱלֹהִים עִמָּדִי אֲנִי אָמִית וַאֲחַיֶּה מָחַצְתִּי וַאֲנִי אֶרְפָּא

See now — it is I, I am He! — and there is no god with me. I kill and give life. I wound and I heal (Deuteronomy 32:39).

Can this be? Surely. It happened in Egypt — when a plower broke through the icy reserve of a harvester, the edifice of doubt crumbled like a house of cards.

At the climactic moment that God reveals Himself in the history of man, every incomprehensible happening will take on meaning, every unanswerable question will become part of the answer. Can this be? Surely. It happened in Egypt — when a plower broke through the icy reserve of a harvester, the edifice of doubt crumbled like a house of cards and the temple of future greatness rose in its place. May the prophecy of Amos be fulfilled again, speedily in our days, so that doubt disappear when a Ruler can repress His mercy no longer and He proclaims: 'See now, it is I, I am He! ... I have wounded and I will heal!'

סדר ויגש

Sidrah Vayigash

יח וַיִּגַּשׁ אֵלָיו יְהוּדָה וַיֹּאמֶר בִּי אֲדֹנִי יְדַבֶּר־
נָא עַבְדְּךָ דָבָר בְּאָזְנֵי אֲדֹנִי וְאַל־יִחַר אַפְּךָ
בְּעַבְדֶּךָ כִּי כָמוֹךָ כְּפַרְעֹה: יט אֲדֹנִי שָׁאַל

SIDRAH VAYIGASH

18. Judah Intercedes.

[As we learned in the conclusion of the last Sidrah, Benjamin had been caught with the viceroy's goblet, and Joseph ruled that Benjamin would have to remain in Egypt as a slave while the other brothers must return to their father. The brothers were dumbfounded. Only Judah risked his life to intercede.

[His speech was eloquent. As the exegetes remark, it was controlled yet emotion-filled; respectful yet firm and daring. He petitioned without humiliating himself. He could not protest the fairness of the verdict, because the goblet *was* found in Benjamin's sack! Instead he offered himself as slave — unknowingly to the very brother whom he had once sold as slave to Egypt ...]

וַיִּגַּשׁ אֵלָיו יְהוּדָה — *Then* [lit. *and*] *Judah approached* [to] *him.*

— At first they had all been standing at a respectful distance from the viceroy; now Judah stepped forward. It was not his intent to plead for *justice,* but to appeal to the viceroy's compassion *(Malbim).*

The Midrash records three interpretations of the verb נגש, *approach.* It can often connote *drawing near for the purpose of engaging in battle as in II Samuel* 10:13. Another view maintains that it implies a *conciliatory* approach as in *Joshua* 14:6. The Rabbis maintain that it implies that *coming near for prayer;* see *I Kings* 18:36 [comp *Rashi* to 18:23].

R' Elazar combines the three views and interprets that Judah approached Joseph with all of the above in mind: He was prepared for *battle* [see below for Midrashic interpretation cited by *Rashi*]; for *conciliation* [as is indicated by the text of his plea]; and for *prayer* [i.e. that Judah would transfer his claim to God and beg for Heavenly justice *(Tanchuma)*].

בִּי אֲדֹנִי — *If you please, my lord.*

The translation follows *Rashi* to 43:20, but *Ramban* differs. See *comm.* there.

Sechel Tov interprets: בִּי, *me:* Benjamin's fate affects *me,* primarily, my lord, since I guaranteed his safety to my father; therefore, *let your servant speak a word,* etc.

יְדַבֶּר־נָא עַבְדְּךָ דָבָר בְּאָזְנֵי אֲדֹנִי — *May your servant speak a word in my lord's ears.*

I.e. may my words penetrate into your ears [that is, may my request convince you] *(Rashi).*

Rashi rejects the literal interpretation that Judah whispered in Joseph's ear, since it would be highly improper for a commoner to dare speak to a monarch that way. Furthermore the plural *ears* rules out literal whispering — which would be done into *one* ear. Moreover, as noted in 42:23, they always spoke through an interpreter, so Judah could not have wanted to whisper directly to the viceroy, since he had every reason to think Joseph did not understand Hebrew *(Mizrachi; Gur Aryeh; Sifsei Chachomim).*

Targum Yonasan renders the idiom: In the *hearing* of my lord.

— You emphasized [*v.* 17] that it would be 'sacrilegious' for you to let even the guilty suffer. Therefore, *let your servant speak a word in my lord's ears* to apprise you of the harm that will come to our innocent father if you keep Benjamin as a slave [i.e. that he will die of grief] *(Sforno).*

44
18-19

[18] Then Judah approached him and said: "If you
please, my lord, may your servant speak a word
in my lord's ears and let not your anger flare up at
your servant — For you are like Pharaoh. [19] My lord

Specifically, the 'word' Judah requested was the plea *(v.* 33) that Joseph substitute him for his brother Benjamin; everything else Judah said was to introduce that conciliatory appeal *(Ramban).*

Permit me to speak but one thing to my lord: I do not make a *legal* argument for exoneration; it is *mercy* that I beseech of you. Therefore let it be *in my lord's ears* — that is, directed *personally* to you and not to your servants, since they lack the authority to exonerate *(Abarbanel; Malbim).*

וְאַל יִחַר אַפְּךָ בְּעַבְדֶּךָ — *And let not your anger flare up at your servant.*

'We derive from this that he spoke harshly to him' *(Rashi).*

That is, Judah knew that in the course of his emotional appeal he would inevitably speak harshly, and he wanted Joseph to anticipate it and not be angry. Had Judah not expected to speak antagonistically, there would have been no need for him to mention this *(Mizrachi; Be'er Yitzchak).*

R' Avraham ben HaRambam maintains that Judah was afraid that he might infuriate Joseph by his temerity in making a lengthy address to the monarch in his time of anger; he therefore begged his indulgence in advance. *Ramban* similarly writes that Judah was asking the viceroy not to be angry at him for speaking up.

Sforno: Do not be angry when I imply that you *forced* us into this position.

[The expression חֲרוֹן אַף, *flaring anger,* referring to outwardly displayed vexation is discussed in the *comm.* to 30:2.]

כִּי כָמוֹךָ כְּפַרְעֹה — *For you are like Pharaoh* [lit. *for like you like Pharaoh*].

That is, I consider you as important as the King. This is the plain sense of the phrase. The Midrash [which, as noted above, perceives that Judah spoke harshly and was prepared even for battle] interprets the inner connotation of the phrase to imply: You will be smitten with leprosy for detaining Benjamin, just as Pharaoh was smitten for detaining my great-grandmother, Sarah, for only one night [above 12:17]. Another [Midrashic] interpretation: You are like Pharaoh in that neither of you keeps promises — is this what you call 'setting eyes on him'? [*v.* 21 below; see comm. there and *Ramban* below].[1] Another [Midrashic] interpretation: *You shall become like Pharaoh* — if you provoke me I will slay both of you [therefore I beseech you not to provoke me by *flaring up your anger* at me *(Midrash HaGadol)*] *(Rashi).*

1. *Ramban* does not agree that Judah could have reasonably argued, "Is this the 'setting your eyes upon him' to which you referred when you said, *'and I will set my eye on him'* [*v.* 21]?" To the contrary, Joseph displayed unusual courtesy to Benjamin when he first met him: he blessed him [43:29], made a banquet, and gave him presents! [*ibid. v.* 34]. Obviously, when a monarch commands that a person be brought before him he does not imply immunity from the consequences of crimes he may commit, especially when the crime is the theft of the monarch's own goblet! What else should Joseph have done under the circumstances?

Accordingly *Ramban* suggests that Judah's appeal was directed not to *reason,* but to Joseph's *compassion* as a man who claimed that he feared God [42:18], and who demonstrated his piety by consoling them for having caused them trouble [43:23]. The thrust of Judah's appeal, then, was that they brought Benjamin to Egypt only at Joseph's insistence, and that

אֶת־עֲבָדָיו לֵאמֹר הֲיֵשׁ־לָכֶם אָב אוֹ־אָח׃
כ וַנֹּאמֶר אֶל־אֲדֹנִי יֶשׁ־לָנוּ אָב זָקֵן וְיֶלֶד
זְקֻנִים קָטָן וְאָחִיו מֵת וַיִּוָּתֵר הוּא לְבַדּוֹ

Following *Rashi's* plain interpretation that Judah meant 'because I consider you as important as Pharaoh,' this phrase modifies the foregoing and the verse means: *'Let not your anger flare up at your servant* — even though my anxiety may prompt me to speak to you harshly — because, indeed, *I consider you as important as Pharaoh,* and my impertinence is motivated not by disrespect or rebelliousness, but by the bitterness of my heart' *(Maskil l'David).*

The double use of the comparative prefix [כְּ *like*] preceding both pronouns indicates that the two are completely similar — You are like Pharaoh and Pharaoh is like you *(Ibn Ezra).* [See comm. to 18:25 כַּצַּדִּיק כָּרָשָׁע; and 13:10 כְּגַן ה׳ כְּאֶרֶץ מִצְרָיִם.]

Rashi mentions only the comparison of Joseph to Pharaoh since that is the essence of the context *(Mizrachi).*

Ramban interprets: I stand speaking before you with the same trepidation I would feel were I speaking to Pharaoh.

Furthermore, as *Ramban* writes in *v.* 19: Since you are comparable to the monarch, it is befitting that you stand by your word to treat Benjamin well. It was only on account of you and under great duress that we brought him to you [see footnote].

For you are like Pharaoh — and who then am I to address you? *(Ralbag).*

19-34. Variations in the Recapitulation.

[Judah skillfully proceeds to recapitulate the dialogues and interrogations between the viceroy and the brothers. Although there are minor variances between Judah's recapitulation and the Torah's earlier accounts of the conversations — and the commentators perceive nuances in many of the variances — it is clear that Judah could not be misrepresenting the truth to Joseph, who was a participant in those conversations. Clearly, Judah artfully passed over whatever minor details might irritate Joseph as well as any that would not support his petition that *he* and not Benjamin be held behind. Furthermore, as *Radak* often notes (see also *Ramban* to 41:3 and 17): 'In reported speech, a person always varies his wording — adding or subtracting as he sees fit, while preserving the essential content ... these are characteristic of any repetition or paraphrase; the words change but not the content.' *Ramban,* too, notes that the Torah characteristically varies the report of an event according to the situation, so that the complete facts must be ascertained by combining the differing accounts.

Judah undoubtedly perceived a sinister conspiracy in the matter of the goblet — although he could not fathom its purpose — so he knew it would be futile to argue for Benjamin's innocence. Instead, as *Ramban* writes, Judah's appeal was designed to evoke Joseph's compassion as a self-proclaimed God-fearing man [42:18]. Accordingly, at great personal risk, he presented an emotional argument, that was compelled by his pledge and love of his father: If only one of us is to remain as a slave let it be me, so that our aged and anxious father may again see his beloved youngest son. I, who guaranteed Benjamin's safety, could not

Jacob consented with the greatest reluctance, only because they were in dire need of food. Therefore, Judah implied, it behooved Joseph to be compassionate toward the aged father, and to substitute Judah for Benjamin.

In defense of the Rabbinic interpretation of "is this what you meant by *I will set my eyes upon him?,*" *Ramban* comments Judah knew that the goblet affair was a hoax orchestrated by

44
20

had asked his servants as follows: 'Have you a father or brother?'

20 *And we said to my lord, 'We have an old father and a young child of his old age; his brother is dead,*

return home without him, 'lest I witness the ill fate that would overtake my father.'

19. אֲדֹנִי שָׁאַל אֶת־עֲבָדָיו לֵאמֹר הֲיֵשׁ לָכֶם אָב אוֹ אָח — *My lord had asked his servants as follows* [lit. *saying*], *'Have you a father or brother?'*

— You sought a pretext against us from the very beginning. What need was there to ask us all these questions? Were we seeking your daughter in marriage or were you seeking our sister [that such intimate interrogation would be justified]? *(Rashi).*

[The implication is that although every purchaser of provisions was screened to determine how large his ration should be, none was interrogated so intimately by Joseph as they were.]

Although 42:13 indicates that they had *volunteered* this information, 43:7 implies clearly that they mentioned Benjamin only in response to Joseph's pressing question. *Ramban* [43:7] explains that Joseph had interrogated them and they gave the information about their father and brother only in response to his threatening inquiries. That the Torah did not record this part of the dialogue in chapt. 42 is in keeping with Scriptural style, which is concise in one place and expansive in another.

Oznaim L'Torah conjectures that Joseph had shrewdly avoided family questions at first since he was apprehensive that they might recognize him. But when they voluntarily offered information about the family, saying [42:11] *'All of us — sons of one man are we,'* he quite naturally inquired, 'Have you a father or a brother?'

Abarbanel and *Malbim* maintain that Joseph had not initially asked them about their family. Rather our passage is a rhetorical question: *Had, then, my lord asked his servants whether we have a father or brother ?* — No, you did *not* ask, but [*v.* 20] *we said* [voluntarily] *to my lord, 'we have an old father and a young child of his old age'.* We had no ulterior motive other than to emphasize how much our father frets over him.

20. וַנֹּאמֶר אֶל־אֲדֹנִי יֶשׁ־לָנוּ אָב זָקֵן וְיֶלֶד זְקֻנִים קָטָן — *And we said to my lord, 'We have an old father and a young* [lit. *little*] *child of* [his] *old age.'*

[The intimation was:] Although we resented your inquisitiveness, we concealed nothing from you *(Rashi).*

Judah's emphasis on their *old* father was intended to stir Joseph's compassion. Since Reuben, the oldest brother, was only forty-five, the viceroy may not have realized that Jacob was so old — 130 years (47:9) — at the time *(Ibn Ezra).*

The implication is that an *old father* worries more over a child than a young one, and he is especially protective of *a child of his old age (Malbim).*

[The term בֶּן זְקֻנִים has been discussed in the *comm.* to 37:3.]

וְאָחִיו מֵת — [*And*] *his brother is dead* — And this causes his father to be excessively concerned over him *(Malbim).*

Judah spoke an untruth [by stating categorically that Joseph was *dead,*

Joseph to create a pretext against them. Similarly, the Midrash records [see *Rashi,* next verse] that Judah said, 'Have you interrogated anyone else who came to buy provisions as thoroughly as you interrogated us? Were we asking for your daughter in marriage or were you seeking to marry our sister?' Arguments such as these were suggested in his words.

כא לְאִמּוֹ וְאָבִיו אֲהֵבוֹ: וַתֹּאמֶר אֶל־עֲבָדֶיךָ
כב הוֹרִדֻהוּ אֵלָי וְאָשִׂימָה עֵינִי עָלָיו: וַנֹּאמֶר
אֶל־אֲדֹנִי לֹא־יוּכַל הַנַּעַר לַעֲזֹב אֶת־אָבִיו
כג וְעָזַב אֶת־אָבִיו וָמֵת: וַתֹּאמֶר אֶל־עֲבָדֶיךָ
אִם־לֹא יֵרֵד אֲחִיכֶם הַקָּטֹן אִתְּכֶם לֹא
כד תֹסִפוּן לִרְאוֹת פָּנָי: וַיְהִי כִּי עָלִינוּ אֶל־

rather than אֵינֶנּוּ, *he is gone,* as he said in 42:13] because he was afraid that if he said Joseph was alive [or if he left it ambiguous], the viceroy might say, 'Bring him to me!' *(Rashi).*

Judah meant: Since we have not known his whereabouts for so long, we assume he is dead; or: he is dead to *us.* This is what we meant in saying 'he is gone' [42:13] *(Tzeidah LaDerech; Gur Aryeh).*

[According to the commentators who hold that the brothers did not sell Joseph and that he was taken from the pit without their knowledge, this verse should be understood literally, because the brothers truly thought Joseph had been devoured by wild beasts. (This is clearly *not* the traditional Rabbinic interpretation; see *comm.* to p. 1650 "Who Sold Joseph?", specifically p. 1653).]

וַיִּוָּתֵר הוּא לְבַדּוֹ לְאִמּוֹ — [And] *he alone is left of* [lit. *to*] *his mother.*

That is, he is the only surviving child from that mother *(Rashi).*

And there is no substitute for him *(B'chor Shor).*

Accordingly, his father is even more anxious over him *(Malbim).*

The phraseology *'left* **to** *his mother'* would imply that his mother Rachel was still alive, which she was not. Therefore, *Rashi* comments that *'to* his mother' in this context means *'from/of* his mother.' According to *Lekach Tov* the implication of the expression is that only Benjamin was left as a reminder of his dead mother, and whoever saw him exclaimed, "This is Rachel's son!"

וְאָבִיו אֲהֵבוֹ — *And his father loves him.*

His father loves him the most, and *that* is why he did not let him accompany us at first — not, as you charged, because he had sent us to spy *(Sforno).*

And his father loves him — because through him our father recalls Rachel whom he loved so dearly *(Pesikta).*

21. וְאָשִׂימָה עֵינִי עָלָיו — *And I will set my eye on him.*

I.e., my 'eye' will be gracious to him *(Targum Yerushalmi).*

— And therefore his father need not be apprehensive about sending him *(Sforno).*

The implication is not, as *Ibn Ezra* would have it, merely 'I will *see* him,' [to establish that the brothers did not lie in describing their family], but that Joseph would treat him well and be protective of him. (Comp. the same use of this idiom in *Jeremiah* 39:12 where Nebuchadnezzar commanded Nebuzaradan to 'look at' Jeremiah when he took him into custody, meaning that the king wanted his officers to treat Jeremiah well). — 'Therefore,' Judah implied, 'it behooves you to keep your word and allow Benjamin to return to his father, and keep me instead.' Joseph said this in the narrative of the original confrontation; but the

he alone is left of his mother, and his father loves
him.'
[21] *Then you said to your servants, 'Bring him*
down to me, and I will set my eye on him.'
[22] *We said to my lord, 'The youth cannot leave his*
father, for should he leave his father he will die.'
[23] *But you said to your servants, 'If your youngest*
brother does not come down with you, you will not
see my face again!'

Torah did not record it there; however it is common for Scripture to be brief in one narrative and provide details elsewhere. What Joseph probably said was: 'Do not fear that I have evil intentions regarding your brother, I want only to be convinced of your truthfulness. Bring him to me and I shall keep an eye on him' *(Ramban; Malbim; Abarbanel).*

[Furthermore, as noted in the Prefatory Comment to *v.* 19, Judah's references to the earlier dialogues with Joseph had to be accurate, since he was reporting them to Joseph. See *comm.* and footnote to *v.* 18.]

— Even if Benjamin has committed a crime, you should let him go, since you assured us that you would protect him and it is beneath the dignity of a leader to go back on his word *(B'chor Shor).*

22. לֹא־יוּכַל הַנַּעַר לַעֲזֹב אֶת־אָבִיו — *The youth cannot leave his father* ... For all the reasons stated above *(Akeidah).*

And furthermore, having been so pampered all his life, the youth would not be able to withstand the rigors of travel *(Lekach Tov).*

וְעָזַב אֶת אָבִיו וָמֵת — *For should he leave his father* [*then*] *he will die.*

That is, should he leave his father we are apprehensive that he — *Benjamin* — would die on the journey — just as his mother died during a journey *(Rashi).*

Comp. *Midrash HaChefetz* cited in *comm.* to 42:4 (p. 1824): 'Jacob reasoned, It may have been decreed that the sons of Rachel should perish on the road. I sent Joseph on a journey and he did not return; the same might happen to Benjamin if I send him, for their mother, too, died on the road.'

Thus, *Rashi* interprets the subject of וָמֵת, *then 'he' would die,* to be Benjamin, who is the subject of the rest of this passage. According to *Rashbam,* the subject is *his father: For should he leave his father then he* [his father] *would die. Ramban* agrees with *Rashi* that the context of the passage indicates that Benjamin is the subject.

23. אִם־לֹא יֵרֵד ... לֹא תֹסִפוּן לִרְאוֹת פָּנָי — *But you said to your servants, 'If your youngest brother does not come down with you, you will not see my face again!'*

You paid no attention to our fears, and instead you capriciously demanded that we bring him, notwithstanding our just pleas *(Alshich; Sforno).*

... In retrospect, however, was it really so important for us to have brought him here? *(B'chor Shor).*

עַבְדְּךָ אָבִי וַנַּגֶּד־לוֹ אֵת דִּבְרֵי אֲדֹנִי:
כה וַיֹּאמֶר אָבִינוּ שֻׁבוּ שִׁבְרוּ־לָנוּ מְעַט־אֹכֶל:
כו וַנֹּאמֶר לֹא נוּכַל לָרֶדֶת אִם־יֵשׁ אָחִינוּ
הַקָּטֹן אִתָּנוּ וְיָרַדְנוּ כִּי־לֹא נוּכַל לִרְאוֹת
פְּנֵי הָאִישׁ וְאָחִינוּ הַקָּטֹן אֵינֶנּוּ אִתָּנוּ:
כז וַיֹּאמֶר עַבְדְּךָ אָבִי אֵלֵינוּ אַתֶּם יְדַעְתֶּם כִּי
כח שְׁנַיִם יָלְדָה־לִּי אִשְׁתִּי: וַיֵּצֵא הָאֶחָד
מֵאִתִּי וָאֹמַר אַךְ טָרֹף טֹרָף וְלֹא רְאִיתִיו
כט עַד־הֵנָּה: וּלְקַחְתֶּם גַּם־אֶת־זֶה מֵעִם פָּנַי
וְקָרָהוּ אָסוֹן וְהוֹרַדְתֶּם אֶת־שֵׂיבָתִי

24. וַיְהִי כִּי עָלִינוּ אֶל־עַבְדְּךָ אָבִי ... — *And it was, when we went up to your servant my father* [and] *we told him my lord's words.*

We immediately told our father of your insistence that Benjamin return with us, but even though it meant leaving Simeon in prison he would not let Benjamin go with us until he was *forced* to do so by the famine [next verse] *(Ramban).*

[Joseph was criticized by the Sages for his disrespect in remaining silent when his brothers referred to his father as *your* servant. In punishment for it he died prematurely. See footnote on p. 1881 and comm. to 50:2.]

25. שֻׁבוּ שִׁבְרוּ־לָנוּ מְעַט־אֹכֶל — *'Go back, buy us some food.'*

— Because he realized full well the consequence of his request, Jacob did not make it until he was forced to do so because of the severity of the famine *(Ramban).*

26. וַנֹּאמֶר לֹא נוּכַל לָרֶדֶת — [Then] *we said, We cannot go down.*

That is, it would be futile *(Alshich).*

אִם יֵשׁ אָחִינוּ הַקָּטֹן אִתָּנוּ וְיָרַדְנוּ ... — *Only if our youngest brother is with us, then will we go down, for we cannot see the man's face if our youngest brother is not with us.*

[The nuances of this dialogue have been treated in the *comm.* to 43:3-5.]

27. Although the pangs of famine *forced* our father to consent that Benjamin go with us, he still warned us that if we did not bring Benjamin back, he would die from grief *(Sforno v.* 24).

[The following passage was not recorded in the original account of the dialogue, in keeping with *Ramban's* rule that the Torah is brief in one place and expansive in another, reserving details for wherever they would be more pertinent.]

אַתֶּם יְדַעְתֶּם כִּי שְׁנַיִם יָלְדָה־לִּי אִשְׁתִּי — *You know that my wife* [Rachel] *bore* [*to*] *me two sons* ['sons' is not in the Hebrew but it is implicit in the masculine number שְׁנַיִם, *two*].

My wife, that is, the only woman that I originally wanted as a wife — Rachel — bore me but two sons. Upon them I bestowed all my love — as though they were my only children *(Ramban).*

[24] *And it was, when we went up to your servant
my father we told him my lord's words.* [25] *And our
father said, 'Go back buy us some food,'* [26] *we said,
'We cannot go down. Only if our youngest brother is
with us, then will we go down, for we cannot see the
man's face if our youngest brother is not with us.'*
[27] *Then your servant my father said to us, 'You
know that my wife bore me two [sons].* [28] *One has
left me and I presumed: Alas, he has surely been torn
to pieces! for I have not seen him since.* [29] *So should
you take this one, too, from my presence, and disaster befall him, then you will have brought down
my hoariness in evil to the grave.'*

יָלְדָה לִּי, *bore to* **me**, i.e. closely resembling me *(Or HaAfeilah — Torah Sheleimah* §86).

28. וַיֵּצֵא הָאֶחָד מֵאִתִּי — *One* [lit. *the one*] *has left me* [lit. *has gone forth from me*].

הָאֶחָד, *the one,* i.e. the more outstanding of the two *(Lekach Tov; Haamek Davar).*

[From me — i.e. by my command. By associating himself with Joseph's absence, the Patriarch still criticizes himself as if he were responsible for Joseph's disappearance.]

[Furthermore, it was *me* he left — I alone was affected by his loss. Comp. 42:36 עָלַי הָיוּ כֻלָּנָה, *'Upon me has it all befallen!'*]

וָאֹמַר אַךְ טָרֹף טֹרָף — *And I presumed: Alas, he has surely been torn to pieces!*

[See 37:33.]

וְלֹא רְאִיתִיו עַד־הֵנָּה — *For* [lit. *and*] *I have not seen him since* [lit. *until now*].

This is the proof that he must have been mangled by wild beasts, for I have never seen him since *(Ibn Ezra),* and there was no other source of danger to him but wild beasts *(Abarbanel).*

[Actually, however, Jacob harbored a suspicion that his sons had slain or sold Joseph. See *Rashi* and commentators cited in 42:36.]

29. וּלְקַחְתֶּם גַּם־אֶת־זֶה מֵעִם פָּנַי — *So* [lit. *and*] *should you take this one, too, from my presence* [lit. *from my face*].

I.e., from my protective care *(Haamek Davar)* ...

וְקָרָהוּ אָסוֹן — *And* [should] *disaster befall him.*

— As it did to his brother Joseph, since Benjamin was young and unaccustomed to travel *(Ramban).*

— A disaster on the way is highly likely since 'the Satan accuses in time of danger.' That is, there is greater danger on a hazardous journey than at home *(Rashi;* see *comm.* to 43:4).

The term אָסוֹן [disaster] refers to unnatural or unexpected death, for example by bandits, wild beasts, or change of climate *(Ramban;* see *Kesubos* 30a cited in the *comm.* to 42:4).

וְהוֹרַדְתֶּם אֶת־שֵׂיבָתִי בְּרָעָה שְׁאֹלָה — *Then you will* [thereby *(Rambam)*] *have brought down my hoariness*

ל בְּרָעָה שְׁאֹלָה: וְעַתָּה כְּבֹאִי֙ אֶל־עַבְדְּךָ
אָבִי וְהַנַּעַר אֵינֶנּוּ אִתָּנוּ וְנַפְשׁוֹ קְשׁוּרָה
°שני לא בְנַפְשׁוֹ: °וְהָיָה כִּרְאוֹתוֹ כִּי־אֵין הַנַּעַר
וָמֵת וְהוֹרִידוּ עֲבָדֶיךָ אֶת־שֵׂיבַת עַבְדְּךָ
לב אָבִינוּ בְּיָגוֹן שְׁאֹלָה: כִּי עַבְדְּךָ עָרַב אֶת־

[i.e., *grey hairs*] *in evil to the grave.*

[Since I will be left bereft of all of those I love and I will be, in effect, devoid of all *goodness (Maharshal).*]

Benjamin is Rachel's only survivor; while he is with me I find consolation through him for the loss of his mother and brother. If he should die it will seem to me as though the three of them died on the same day *(Rashi).*[1]

[See *comm.* to 43:38, and *Rashi* to 37:35.]

In 42:38, and below *v.* 31 the expression used is **בְּיָגוֹן שְׁאֹלָה**, *in* **sorrow** [lit. *grief*] *to the grave,* while here the expression used is **בְּרָעָה שְׁאֹלָה**, *in* **evil** *to the grave. Yalkut Or HaAfeilah* [cited in *Torah Sheleimah* §907] suggests that *grief* refers to This World; *evil* to the Next World. [The allusion is unclear, however. See footnote.]

30. **וְעַתָּה כְּבֹאִי אֶל־עַבְדְּךָ אָבִי וְהַנַּעַר אֵינֶנּוּ אִתָּנוּ** — *And now, if I come to your servant my father and the youth is not with us.*

And now — especially now that our father had forewarned us so emphatically that he would not attribute Benjamin's absence to happenstance but would consider it as if we deliberately brought this misfortune upon him *(Sforno).*

וְנַפְשׁוֹ קְשׁוּרָה בְנַפְשׁוֹ — *Since his soul is so bound up with his* [i.e., Benjamin's] *soul!*

I.e., his soul is as dear to him as his own [i.e., he loves him as much as himself] *(Onkelos).*

[This is a subordinate clause bridging this verse and the next.]

[The same phrase is used of the intertwined souls of David and Jonathan in *I Samuel* 18:1.]

Moreover, the yearning Jacob would have for Benjamin while he is away would be even greater than when he sees him constantly *(Alshich).*

31. **וְהָיָה כִּרְאוֹתוֹ כִּי־אֵין הַנַּעַר וָמֵת** —

1. *Rashi's* comment that Benjamin's death would be tantamount to all three having died on the same day is based upon the Midrash. As Jacob mentioned before, his primary wife bore him two sons. When she died he derived some consolation from Joseph — upon whose presumed 'death' Jacob also exclaimed [37:35]: *'For I will go down to the grave mourning for my son!'* However, as the Midrash records, Jacob was somewhat consoled by Benjamin for the deaths of Rachel and Joseph. Should Benjamin die, Jacob would be left without *any* consolation, for he would feel as if all three of them had died on the same day.

Though Jacob did not mention Rachel's death, he alluded to it with the term **בְּרָעָה שְׁאֹלָה**, *in* **evil** *to the grave,* instead of saying **בְּיָגוֹן שְׁאֹלָה**, in **grief** *to the grave,* as he did in 42:38 and *v.* 31 below.

He was implying the dictum that he who lives without a wife is in *'evil', for the Sages* [*Yevamos* 62b] proclaimed [based on *Genesis* 2:18], "He who has no wife dwells without 'good' "— hence, in evil.

Accordingly, the flow of Jacob's argument, was: I had found consolation over my wife's and son's deaths from her sole survivor, Benjamin. But should he die, I will be devoid of *any* consolation and in effect, will be going down to my grave *in evil,* that is, bereft even of my wife *(Mizrachi; Gur Aryeh; Tzeidah laDerech).*

30 And now, if I come to your servant my father
and the youth is not with us — since his soul is so
bound up with his soul! — 31 it will happen that when
he sees the youth is missing he will die, and your servants will have brought down the hoariness of your servant our father, in sorrow to the grave.
32 For your servant took responsibility for the

It will happen, that when he sees the youth is missing [and] *he will die.*

I.e., the very instant Jacob sees that Benjamin is not with us *(Ralbag)*...

He, i.e., our father, *will die* — of grief *(Rashi).*[1]

We will not even have a chance to explain what happened to Benjamin. The instant he will see that the youth did not return with us, Father will fall dead in grief *(Abarbanel).*

Conceivably, if we would tell Father that Benjamin stole, he would suppress his instincts and agree that Benjamin deserves this punishment, for Father is righteous and a man of truth. However, we will not even have the opportunity of telling him; he will die immediately *(Dubno Maggid).*

The question arises: Benjamin had ten children at home; why didn't Judah mention the grief Benjamin's *children* would experience at their father's absence?

R' Menachem Mendel of Kotzk used this as an example of how parents have more compassion for their children's misfortunes, than children for their parents.

וְהוֹרִידוּ עֲבָדֶיךָ אֶת־שֵׂיבַת עַבְדְּךָ אָבִינוּ בְּיָגוֹן שְׁאֹלָה — *And your servants will have brought down the hoariness of your servant our father in sorrow* [lit. *grief*] *to the grave.*

— An idiom meaning to cause one to die of grief *(R' Saadiah Gaon).*

In the literal sense, *we* refers to the brothers *(Ramban v. 32)*; however, it is possible that Judah *really* meant: *And* **you** [Joseph] *will thereby have brought the hoariness of your servant our father in sorrow to the grave.* Out of respect for the viceroy, Judah used the euphemism *we (Ramban v. 19).*

32. Judah proceeds to explain why of all the brothers only he has taken the initiative to plead Benjamin's cause ...

כִּי עַבְדְּךָ עָרַב אֶת הַנַּעַר מֵעִם אָבִי — *For your servant* [i.e., I, Judah] *took responsibility for* [lit. *guaranteed*] *the youth from my father.*

1. Kabbalistically, there is an interpretation that the one who would die in our passage is *Benjamin!* Since Jacob will assume that because Benjamin did not return he must have died — and indeed Jacob's words will *cause* Benjamin to die: the power of the righteous is so great that even their inadvertent statements come true and then your servants will be culpable for this grief caused to our father. [See *comm.* to 31:32 and the incident recorded in *Kesubos* 62b from the verse *Like an error proceeding from a dictator (Eccles.* 10:5)] *(R' Moshe ibn Chabib* cited in *Me'am Loez).*

☙ In a homiletical paraphrase of this verse *R' Meir of Prymishlan* once remarked:

"How can we have the audacity to one day ascend and stand before our Father in heaven [i.e. after death, when our souls must account for our deeds on earth] at a time when *'the youth is not with me'* — when our *young people* are not walking in their parents' ways; *for your servant appointed the youth as the guarantor,* that is, we promised at Mt. Sinai that our children will guarantee the eternal observance of the commmandments!"

הַנַּעַר מֵעִם אָבִי לֵאמֹר אִם־לֹא אֲבִיאֶנּוּ
לג אֵלֶיךָ וְחָטָאתִי לְאָבִי כָּל־הַיָּמִים: וְעַתָּה
יֵשֶׁב־נָא עַבְדְּךָ תַּחַת הַנַּעַר עֶבֶד לַאדֹנִי
לד וְהַנַּעַר יַעַל עִם־אֶחָיו: כִּי־אֵיךְ אֶעֱלֶה אֶל־
אָבִי וְהַנַּעַר אֵינֶנּוּ אִתִּי פֶּן אֶרְאֶה בָרָע
מה/א א אֲשֶׁר יִמְצָא אֶת־אָבִי: וְלֹא־יָכֹל יוֹסֵף

Should you ask why *I* am speaking and not my brothers, it is because they are less involved; the responsibility for the youth rests with *me* since I have placed myself under a firm bond to be an outcast in both worlds if I fail to bring him home *(Midrash; Rashi).*

Ramban suggests that Judah was emphasizing that even after the food shortage became acute, Jacob was still unwilling to let Benjamin go until Judah took personal responsibility for his safety. This would explain why Judah was so afraid that Jacob would die if Benjamin were detained and also why Judah — who had guaranteed the youth's safety — was ready to offer himself as a slave to save Benjamin.

According to *Sforno,* Judah said this to explain why his father would die as soon as he saw Benjamin did not return with them — without even inquiring after the youth: Since I became the personal guarantor for the youth, if I do not bring him back Father will assume he was surely lost, otherwise, I would surely have brought him back.

Targum Yonasan explains כִּי as *therefore: Therefore,* i.e. because my father was so reluctant to send the youth, *your servant undertook responsibility for the youth.* I felt I had no alternative but to reassure Jacob and accept full responsibility.

וְחָטָאתִי לְאָבִי כָּל־הַיָּמִים ... — *Then I will be sinning to my father for all time* [lit. *all the days*].

— Judah said this to impress Joseph with the fact that the oath was not an idle insignificant promise, but one that carried a great imprecation ... The connotation of *all the days* is either all of *Jacob's* days if Judah would survive him, or all of *Judah's* days, if Jacob would be the survivor *(R' Shmuel ben Chofni).*

33. וְעַתָּה יֵשֶׁב־נָא עַבְדְּךָ תַּחַת הַנַּעַר עֶבֶד לַאדֹנִי — *Now, therefore* [lit. *and now*] *please let your servant remain instead of the youth as a servant to my lord.*[1]

— I.e., if you will not pardon him *(Radak).*

I am more suited than he for every purpose: in strength, for battle and for personal service *(Rashi).*

Comp. *Tanchuma Yashan:* One who buys a slave and discovers that he is a thief sends him back, yet you would force a thief to be your servant! You must have some sinister

1. Judah's self-sacrifice for Benjamin had significant consequences for the future history of the Jewish people, and Benjamin was to have an opportunity to do the same for Judah. When the Ten Tribes of Israel seceded from the Davidic dynasty, only Benjamin remained loyal to the Judean kingdom. This made it possible for Judah to survive as an independent nation despite its repudiation by the majority of the people *(Yalkut Yehudah).*

youth from my father saying, 'If I do not bring him back to you then I will be sinning to my father for all time.'

33 *Now, therefore, please let your servant remain instead of the youth as a servant to my lord, and let the youth go up with his brothers.* 34 *For how can I go up to my father if the youth is not with me lest I see the evil that would befall my father!"*

design. If you want him as a personal attendant, I am more skilled than he; if you require him as a fighter, I can fight better than he. Therefore please let your servant remain as a slave to my lord instead of the youth.

וְהַנַּעַר יַעַל עִם אֶחָיו — *And let the youth go up with his brothers.*

Our law says that only if a thief has nothing with which to make restitution shall he be sold as a slave [see *Exodus* 22:2]; but this one [Benjamin] *does* have enough possessions and *can* make restitution; why, then, do you wish to hold him as a slave? *(Tanchuma).* [The implication is that even according to *your* laws, why would you want a slave whom you indicted as a *professional* thief — since he obviously did not steal out of *need?* Therefore, let him make restitution and release him. But if you wish, out of principle, to retain someone as a slave, choose me *(Dubno Maggid).*]

34. כִּי אֵיךְ אֶעֱלֶה אֶל־אָבִי וְהַנַּעַר אֵינֶנּוּ אִתִּי — *For how can I go up to my father if the youth is not with me.*

I.e., *how* — in the name of compassion — could I do such a thing? Compare Esther's similar outburst [*Esth.* 8:6] *How can I bear to witness the destruction of my relatives! (R' Avraham ben HaRambam).*

How could I go back to Father under such circumstances? I would rather remain a permanent servant than go up to Father without the youth. Judah mentioned this so the viceroy would not suspect that Judah's offer was a deception, knowing he could more easily escape than Benjamin *(Rambam).*[1]

According to *Akeidas Yitzchak* Judah meant: 'You told us [*v.* 17] *"As for you — go up in peace to your father."* But how can I do so, seeing the inconsolable grief it will cause him!'

פֶּן אֶרְאֶה בָרָע אֲשֶׁר יִמְצָא אֶת־אָבִי — *Lest I see the evil that would befall* my *father!*

— Since he would constantly weep and mourn for him all day *(Ramban).*

1. Judah's oath to Jacob *If I do not bring him back to you* — [*v.* 32] — could not be fulfilled if Benjamin returned on his own, but only if Judah would *personally* bring him back. The implication was that even if Benjamin returned without Judah, the dread oath would still be in effect and Judah would be considered as having sinned to his father all the days.

Nevertheless, Judah emphasized that he was ready to sacrifice himself and remain a slave — even though the imprecation of the oath would in any case remain in force.It was as if to say, 'What have I to lose? If I am to face the penalty of the oath in any event, I would rather remain a servant here than to return without Benjamin and — in addition to the oath — face the grief my father would suffer at the loss of Benjamin!' *(Alshich; Maasei Hashem; Haamek Davar).*

לְהִתְאַפֵּק לְכֹל הַנִּצָּבִים עָלָיו וַיִּקְרָא הוֹצִיאוּ כָל־אִישׁ מֵעָלָי וְלֹא־עָמַד אִישׁ

XLV

1. Joseph identifies himself.

With Judah's selfless offer of himself as a substitute for Benjamin, Joseph finally had the irrefutable proof of the change in his brothers' old attitude, as exemplified by their filial devotion to Jacob, their love for Benjamin, and their sincere contrition for their crime against Joseph himself. It was to ascertain this that he subjected them to all these tribulations to begin with [see *R' Hirsch* to 42:7, 9, and 43:16]. Moreover, his brothers had had their share of the expiatory humiliation they deserved. Joseph felt, therefore, that the time of reconciliation had at last arrived *(Akeidah; Abarbanel; R' Hirsch; R' Munk).*

וְלֹא יָכֹל יוֹסֵף לְהִתְאַפֵּק לְכֹל הַנִּצָּבִים עָלָיו — *Now Joseph could not restrain himself in the presence of all who attended him.*

The flow of this verse is difficult — especially the inclusion of the phrase *in the presence of all who attended him* in this context — and the commentators vary in their interpretations.

According to *Rashi* the sense is: He could not *bear* [לִסְבֹּל, lit. *suffer; endure*] for the Egyptian bystanders to witness the shame his brothers would feel when he made himself known to them. [The meaning, then, of the verse is: *He could not restrain himself* (to witness their shame) *in the presence of all* (the Egyptians) *who attended him.*]

Levush insists that *Rashi* is explaining the *general context* rather than the *individual words,* because it is clear from *Rashi's* interpretation of the word הִתְאַפֵּק in 43:31 that the word means *fortify* [lit. *strengthen*], in the sense of controlling one's emotions, and not *bear.* In harmony with this interpretation, *Levush* interprets *Rashi* that Joseph had been fortifying himself all along in the sense that he overcome his emotional inclination to reveal himself — for, had he done so, his brothers would have been humiliated in the face of the Egyptian bystanders. Now, however, that he could no longer control the need to identify himself, he ordered that everyone but his brothers leave his presence.

Ibn Ezra: He could not bear to wait until all the bystanders would leave of their own accord; he ordered that they leave immediately.

Until this point, Joseph conducted himself with great self-control, but now he could no longer do so. Rather than lose his composure in the company of so many Egyptians, he ordered that they leave *(Rashbam).*

[It would appear, according to this view, that Joseph had not planned as yet to divulge his identity, but he could no longer restrain himself.]

Targum Yonasan interprets the object of Joseph's restraint to be *his tears:* He could no longer restrain his tears despite the importance of not crying in front of all those who stood before him. [*Onkelos* may have interpreted the phrase the same way.]

Ralbag interprets similarly that Joseph was afraid that his welled-up tears [over hearing Judah's repeated description of Jacob's grief *(Radak)*] would burst forth while the Egyptian bystanders were still present, and it is unseemly for a ruler to display strong emotion before his subjects.

45
1 [1] *Now Joseph could not restrain himself in the presence of all who attended him, so he called out, 'Make everyone withdraw from me!' Thus no one*

On two previous occasions, Joseph was able to stifle his tears long enough to leave the room and weep [see 42:24 and 43:30], but now — because of the great throng of people milling about — he could not comfortably make his way to his private chambers. This is implied by the phrase *of all who attended him.* Therefore, unable to restrain himself further because of their presence he ordered them to clear the room *(Abarbanel).*

Ramban suggests that many Egyptians joined in the plea for Benjamin's release since they were deeply stirred by Judah's presentation, and Joseph was not strong enough to resist them all. He therefore ordered, 'Let every stranger leave me and I will converse with them [i.e. the brothers].'

Abarbanel disagrees with the above implication that Joseph's revelation was motivated by outsiders' pleas. *HaKsav V'haKabbalah* defends *Ramban,* noting that Joseph had refrained all along from revealing himself — not maliciously — but only to bring about the fulfillment of the prophetic dreams of his youth [37:6*ff;* see *comm.* to 42:9]. Up to this point, the dreams had been *partially* fulfilled — only the 'stars' [his brothers] had bowed to him — and it is conceivable that if not for the pleas of the Egyptians, Joseph would have waited still longer, until *all* of his dreams were fulfilled.

According to the *Midrash,* Joseph's inability to restrain himself was not out of compassion, but because Judah threatened to destroy Egypt. See footnote verse 3, s.v. הַעוֹד אָבִי חָי.

The translation of נִצָּבִים עָלָיו, *standing upon* (i.e. before) *him* as referring to those who stood before him — in his attendance — follows the context. Comp. *Rashi* to 18:2 that נִצָּבִים לְפָנָיו=נִצָּבִים עָלָיו, and *ibid.* 18:8 that עמד על, *stand upon,* means to *stand in attendance. Ramban* interprets similarly.

וַיִּקְרָא הוֹצִיאוּ כָל־אִישׁ מֵעָלָי — *So* [lit. *and*] *he called out, 'Make everyone withdraw from me!'*

He called out angrily [to his son, Manasseh *(Sechel Tov)*], *Make everyone,* except these men, *withdraw from me,* and I will converse with them personally!" In addition to the reason offered by *Rashi* in the beginning of this verse, it may be that Joseph expelled the Egyptians to prevent them from learning that his brothers had sold him. Had the Egyptians known, they might refuse permission to the brothers to settle in Egypt on the ground that they were treacherous people. If they acted that way to their own brother and father, how would they act toward Pharaoh and the Egyptians! Moreover, the Egyptians might, as a result, lose faith even in Joseph *(Ramban).*

Tanchuma Yashan mentions yet another reason why Joseph wanted no outsiders present when he revealed himself to his brothers: The ban his brothers had imposed upon him against revealing what had occurred [see footnote p. 1653] was still in effect, and under its terms he might not disclose it to any outsider. [Presumably once the following dialogue took place and the brothers agreed to reveal Joseph's whereabouts to their father, the ban was *de facto* annulled. See *comm.* to *v.* 9, below.]

The *Midrash* records that Joseph risked great danger by remaining alone with his brothers. If the brothers, put to shame by his revelation, had attacked him, he would have had no one to defend him. Though aware of this danger, Joseph thought: "It is better that I die than humiliate my brothers in front of the Egyptians!" This is the opinion of R' Chama ben Chanina. But the son of R' Nachman disagrees: "Joseph had no

ב אִתּוֹ בְּהִתְוַדַּע יוֹסֵף אֶל־אֶחָיו: וַיִּתֵּן אֶת־
קֹלוֹ בִּבְכִי וַיִּשְׁמְעוּ מִצְרַיִם וַיִּשְׁמַע בֵּית
ג פַּרְעֹה: וַיֹּאמֶר יוֹסֵף אֶל־אֶחָיו אֲנִי יוֹסֵף
הַעוֹד אָבִי חָי וְלֹא־יָכְלוּ אֶחָיו לַעֲנוֹת

reason for fear. He was aware of his brothers' piety and knew they were not murderers."

וְלֹא־עָמַד אִישׁ אִתּוֹ בְּהִתְוַדַּע יוֹסֵף אֶל־אֶחָיו — *Thus no one* [lit. *no man*] *remained* [lit. *stood*] *with him when Joseph made himself known to his brothers.*

Although the wording of the command would imply that Joseph ordered his attendants to expel every *outsider,* and he did not specifically order his attendants to leave, they understood that even they were to go. As a result, no one but his brothers remained *(Haamek Davar).*

2. וַיִּתֵּן אֶת־קֹלוֹ בִּבְכִי — *He cried uncontrollably* [lit. *and he gave his voice in weeping*].

— He gave his voice free rein, and kept it back no longer. ... Such an uncontrolled sobbing is a manifestation of deep feeling, of great sincerity *(R' Hirsch).* [*See footnote 2 on page 1260*].

וַיִּשְׁמְעוּ מִצְרַיִם — [*And*] *Egypt heard.*

The reference is to the townsfolk *(Rashbam).*

The courtiers who had been expelled from Joseph's presence heard it for they were still in the outer courtyard *(Ramban v.* 1).

They heard Joseph's loud weeping, but they did not know why he was crying *(Malbim).*

וַיִּשְׁמַע בֵּית פַּרְעֹה — *And* [then] *Pharaoh's house*[hold] *heard.*

The passage is telling us that first the *townsfolk* and then the *members of Pharaoh's household* — his ministers and courtiers — heard it *(Rashbam).*

Egypt heard it, and the royal household heard it. This is indicative of Joseph's high position. The entire land and the entire court were concerned over Joseph's emotional outburst, even though they had no idea why he was weeping *(R' Hirsch).*

The Hebrew phrase literally reads *And Pharaoh's house heard it. Rashi* explains that *house* refers to the servants and members of the *household.* In this context בֵּית does not mean *house* [as it does in *v.* 16 where the verb שמע is used in the *niphal* and the sense is that it was heard *in* Pharaoh's *house*], but it has a similar meaning to בֵּית יִשְׂרָאֵל, *House of Israel* and בֵּית יְהוּדָה, *House of Judah* where the reference is to the *people* of Israel and Judah.

3. 'I am Joseph! Does my father still live?'

אֲנִי יוֹסֵף — *I am Joseph.*[1]

He did not say 'your brother' or add 'whom you sold to Egypt' as he did later [*v.* 4], since he knew that some Egyptians were still outside. Even if he had been overheard, the

1. When Joseph said these two words אֲנִי יוֹסֵף, *'I am Joseph,'* God's master plan in all that had transpired became clear to them. They had no more questions, *I am Joseph* made everything crystal clear in their disconcertion notwithstanding.

So, too, will it be in the Time to Come when the Holy One, Blessed is He, will reveal Himself and announce 'I am HASHEM!' The mask will roll off of our eyes and we will fully comprehend everything that transpired throughout history *(Chofetz Chaim).*

45
2-3

remained with him when Joseph made himself known to his brothers.

[2] He cried uncontrollably. Egypt heard, and Pharaoh's household heard.

[3] And Joseph said to his brothers, "I am Joseph. Does my father still live?" But his brothers could not

listening Egyptians would surmise that he was sold only by Ishmaelites, as had been thought heretofore *(Abarbanel; Haamek Davar).*

הַעוֹד אָבִי חָי — *Does my father still live?* [see 43:27]

Joseph's primary concern was about his father *(R' Bachya).*

[The brothers mentioned several times that their father was alive, so the question obviously has a deeper connotation.]

— Is it indeed possible that he survived all these sorrows? *(Sforno).*

As noted in the commentary to 43:27 the word חָי, *alive,* also means *vigorous,* and it is possible that the intent of the question was: Is Father still vigorous; is he healthy? *(Tur).*

According to *Abarbanel,* Joseph now asked them this directly — although he had already heard through the interpreter that his father was alive — in order to draw them into conversation and show them that he was friendly toward them. He intended to continue this line of conversation and ask them about their wives and children, but since they were so startled at his revelation that they did not answer

1. **The dialogue that led up to the revelation.**

According to the *Midrashim* as noted, a bitter denunciatory dialogue between Judah and Joseph accompanied Judah's speech. Some excerpts:

Judah: 'I took responsibility for the safety of my brother.'

Joseph: 'Why didn't you take responsibility for your other brother when you sold him to the Ishmaelites for twenty pieces of silver and grieved your old father, who did you no wrong? Regarding this one who *did* wrong and stole the goblet, tell your father: "The rope has followed the bucket." '

* * *

Judah called to his brother Naftali: 'Go and see how many markets there are in Egypt,' whereupon he leapt forth, returned and told him: ' Twelve.' Judah said: 'I will destroy three of them; the rest of you, take one market each and spare no one.' His brothers answered him: 'Judah, Egypt is not Shechem! Should you destroy Egypt, you thereby destroy the whole world [since the whole world depends upon Egypt for food' *(Matnas Kehunah).*]

* * *

Judah was determined, however. He said, 'The fire of Shechem burns within me.'

'It is not the fire of Shechem,' Joseph replied, 'but the fire that burned when you wanted to burn your daughter-in-law Tamar [despite her innocence]. — I will douse it.'

Judah said, 'Now I will go forth and dye all the markets of Egypt in blood!'

'You were dyers even before, when you dyed your brother's tunic and told your father he was mangled by wild beasts!' Joseph countered.

* * *

Joseph could no longer restrain himself and resolved to reveal himself. He saw that a full battle was about to rage and he wanted to avoid that.

Joseph said, 'Did you not say that the brother of this one [Benjamin, referring to himself] is dead? I purchased him. I am going to call him and he will come to you.' He began to call: 'Joseph the son of Jacob, come to me! Joseph the son of Jacob come to me! Speak with your brothers who sold you.' The brothers looked to the four corners of the house. Said Joseph to them: 'Why do you look here and there? *I am Joseph!'* whereupon their souls flew out and they could not answer him *(Midrash Rabbah; Tanchuma; Tanchuma Yashan).*

אִתּוֹ כִּי נִבְהֲלוּ מִפָּנָיו: ד וַיֹּאמֶר יוֹסֵף אֶל־אֶחָיו גְּשׁוּ־נָא אֵלַי וַיִּגָּשׁוּ וַיֹּאמֶר אֲנִי יוֹסֵף אֲחִיכֶם אֲשֶׁר־מְכַרְתֶּם אֹתִי מִצְרָיְמָה:

this question, he proceeded to be more specific and defend his statement that he was indeed the brother they had sold.

Ralbag suggests that Joseph meant the question seriously. He was concerned that Judah might have been harping on an 'aged father' merely to gain sympathy, when in reality Jacob was no longer alive. [Judah had spoken inaccurately about his brother's 'death' — which *Rashi* justifies (see 44:20) — and Joseph wanted to be sure that now that he revealed himself, they were entirely truthful; so he repeated the question *(Torah Temimah).*]

Many commentators perceive an implication of bitter rebuke in these words, as if Joseph were saying to Judah and his brothers: What have you all done! How did you expect my father to survive all of the suffering and grief you heaped upon him!' [See footnote next verse.]

וְלֹא־יָכְלוּ אֶחָיו לַעֲנוֹת אֹתוֹ כִּי נִבְהֲלוּ מִפָּנָיו — *But his brothers could not answer him because they felt disconcerted before him.*

— They were overwhelmed by shame *(Rashi).*[1]

That is, they perceived the full implication of this revelation and they were remorseful and ashamed of what they had done to him *(Chizkuni; Bchor Shor).*

They were confused and frightened over his revelation, and they were concerned that he might seek revenge *(Malbim).*

— They vacillated between belief and utter disbelief. On the one hand, he mentioned the name Joseph, while on the other hand, they could not bring themselves to

1. The Talmud [*Chagigah* 4b] records that when R' Eleazar came to our passage, *But the brothers could not answer him because they felt disconcerted before him,* he wept. 'If such is the result of a rebuke by a flesh and blood human being,' R' Eleazar exclaimed, 'how much more so must it be when someone is rebuked by the Holy One Blessed is He!'

The Midrash similarly records: R' Yochanan said, Woe to us for fear of the Day of Judgment! Woe to us for fear of the Day of Retribution! [וַי לָנוּ מִיּוֹם הַדִּין, וַי לָנוּ מִיּוֹם הַתּוֹכָחָה]. In the case of Joseph who said to his brothers *I am Joseph your brother,* their souls flew out, how much more so when the Holy One Blessed is He will stand in judgment, as it is written [*Malachi* 3:2]: *Who will survive the day of His coming?* And if his own brothers were frightened of him, how much more so when the Holy One Blessed is He comes to judge us for neglect of His commands and the violation of the Torah!

The commentators ponder: What rebuke did Joseph give them to inspire such fear? According to the Torah's narrative, he said nothing about the sale!

Maharsha suggests that they cowered in expectation that Joseph might rebuke them for everything they perpetrated upon him.

Bais HaLevi explains that Joseph's question — *does my father still live?* — was an implied reply to Judah's plea for compassion for Jacob, as if to say: *'You plead for mercy for your father? How is it that you yourselves showed no mercy for his life when you callously sold me — his beloved son?' His brothers could not answer him, so startled were they by him.*

Kli Yakar perceives Joseph's rebuke to be intimated by his use of the word my, rather than **our,** *father,* as if to imply that after the way they mistreated Jacob they could not consider him *their* father.

[According to the Midrash cited in the previous footnote, however, there is no doubt that Joseph's declaration was associated with bitter reproof. This accounts for the brothers' fright which inspired R' Eleazar and R' Yochanan's outbursts.]

answer him because they felt disconcerted before him.

4 Then Joseph said to his brothers, "Come close to
me, if you please," and they came close. And he said,
"I am Joseph your brother — it is me, whom you sold

believe that the young brother they had once sold, shackled as a slave, was now the supreme ruler of Egypt *(R' Yosef Kara; Daas Zekeinim).*

Others translate the phrase: ' ... *because they shrank away from his presence.'*

4. Joseph's question, as noted, was primarily an expression of astonishment; therefore, he did not wait for an answer *(R' Munk).*

גְּשׁוּ־נָא אֵלַי — *Come close to me, if you please.*

Seeing that they were recoiling from him, Joseph thought 'My brothers now feel ashamed.' He therefore beckoned them in a mild and gentle language [saying נָא, *if you please*], and then he showed them that he was circumcised [as proof that he was indeed Joseph] *(Rashi* from *Midrash).*

Actually, as we have seen earlier, Joseph had forced all the Egyptians to submit to circumcision [see *comm.* to 41:55]. Presumably he told them this as well since that was the greatest possible proof that he was Joseph *(Gur Aryeh; Yad Yosef).*

Futhermore, only the populace — who came for rations — were subject to the circumcision decree; Joseph, as the supreme ruler, was not required to undergo circumcision. That he *was* circumcised proved he was Joseph *(Chizkuni).*

Many commentators suggest that the Midrash cited by *Rashi* is not to be taken literally, as it would have been immodest for Joseph to have exposed himself even to his own brothers. Rather, the intent is that he *told* them he had been circumcised.

According to *Sforno, Abarbanel,* and most others, Joseph's purpose in asking them to come near him was that those who overheard his weeping should not hear him speak of the sale, which was a topic of great embarrassment to them.[1]

וַיֹּאמֶר אֲנִי יוֹסֵף אֲחִיכֶם אֲשֶׁר מְכַרְתֶּם אֹתִי מִצְרָיְמָה — *And he said, 'I am Joseph your brother — it is me whom you sold into Egypt.'* [lit. *that you sold me to Egypt.*][2]

Even while you were selling me, I retained brotherly feelings towards you *(Abarbanel;* see *Or HaChaim).* — And I still consider myself your brother — retaining even now

1. We will learn later in the Book of Exodus how the Israelites deserved redemption from Egypt in the merit of four things: a) they did not change their names [to non-Hebrew names]; b) they did not change their language; c) they separated themselves from immorality; d) they did not indulge in לְשׁוֹן הָרָע, *evil gossip.*

In his revelation to his brothers, Joseph intimated that though he was in a strange land, he too was scrupulous about these four things. By stating *I am Joseph* he indicated that though Pharaoh had given him a foreign name *Tzafenas Paane'ach,* his name was still Joseph; by stating [*v.* 12] *it is my mouth that is speaking to you* he intimated that he still spoke Hebrew; by showing them that he was circumcised he intimated that he had kept away from immorality; by saying *come close to me* he intimated that he did not want Benjamin to hear their discussion of the sale, thus avoiding the sin of evil gossip *(Kli Yakar).*

2. *Sfas Emes* comments that Joseph's choice of words — אֲשֶׁר מְכַרְתֶּם, lit., *whom you sold* — carried with it an implication of consolation for his brothers. The word אֲשֶׁר is sometimes interpreted by the Sages to be related to אִישּׁוּר, *approval.* In this sense, they expound that God expressed approval of Moses' decision to smash the first Tablets of the Ten Commandments

ה וְעַתָּה אַל־תֵּעָצְבוּ וְאַל־יִחַר בְּעֵינֵיכֶם כִּי־
מְכַרְתֶּם אֹתִי הֵנָּה כִּי לְמִחְיָה שְׁלָחַנִי
ו אֱלֹהִים לִפְנֵיכֶם: כִּי־זֶה שְׁנָתַיִם הָרָעָב

these feelings of brotherhood *(Ibn Caspi).*

The only reason I mention this unpleasant event is because it is the best proof that I am Joseph. No one but us knows that you sold me or that I am your brother; even those who purchased me from you did not know we were brothers *(Sforno).*

He whispered this to them quietly so that even Benjamin would not hear. He also promised not to tell Jacob what they had done *(Tz'ror HaMor).*

According to *Rashbam* and others cited in the *comm.* to 37:28 [''Who Sold Joseph?''] who interpret that Midianites passed Joseph's pit, hauled him out and sold him *without the knowledge of the brothers* to the Ishmaelites who were passing by, Joseph charged: *whom* **you** *sold to Egypt,* only in the sense that his brothers were *responsible* for the sale because they threw him into the pit in the first place.

5. וְעַתָּה אַל־תֵּעָצְבוּ וְאַל־יִחַר בְּעֵינֵיכֶם כִּי־מְכַרְתֶּם אֹתִי הֵנָּה — *And now, be not distressed, nor reproach yourselves* [lit. *and do not be angry in your eyes*] *for having* [or: *that you have*] *sold me here.*

— For one should grieve only for having done evil, but, as you shall see, your act resulted in great good *(Abarbanel).*[1]

Joseph had observed that they were distressed and angry with themselves for having sold him because he had heard them say [42:21], *Indeed we are guilty concerning our brother,* etc. *(Akeidah; Or HaChaim).*

[... And, following *Rashi's* Midrashic comment above, Joseph knew they were remorseful because they cowered away in shame when he revealed himself.]

Do not be angry with yourselves for having sold me here — after all, it is you to whom I owe the exalted position I now hold here in Egypt *(R' Hirsch).*

The word *now* is emphatic, as if to say that they should not be distressed *now* — but *later* there would indeed be cause for distress. The Kabbalists perceive the prophetic implication of the passage to be one of intimated punishment at a future time: 'Be not grieved, for your generation will not suffer for what you did, but an outgrowth of your sale will be the cruelty of the Egyptian exile, and eventually you will be punished through your descendants with the imperial decree against the Ten Martyrs' [who were slain during the Roman Persecutions on account of the sale of Joseph by the ten

upon seeing the Jews worshiping the Golden Calf. God said to Moses [*Exod.* 34:1]: אֲשֶׁר שִׁבַּרְתָּ [lit. *which you broke*], which the Sages interpret as implying יְיַשַׁר כֹּחֲךָ שֶׁשִּׁבַּרְתָּ, *more power to you* [an expression of thanks and approval *(Rashi)*] for having broken the Tablets *(Shabbos* 87a).

Similarly Joseph comforted his brothers by saying אֲשֶׁר מְכַרְתֶּם, as if to say 'Thank you for selling me, because my presence in Egypt made it possible for me to save the world, and especially our family, from famine. In 50:20 Joseph explicitly expressed the same thought to his brothers.

1. **Joseph's reconciliation vs. the brother's moral responsibility**

[Although Joseph attributed his ordeal to God's providential preparation for the eventual growth of Israel into a great nation, this was not to imply that the brothers were guiltless of any wrong-doing. They sold him without knowledge of God's plan, and surely had to re-

45
5-6

into Egypt. [5] *And now, be not distressed, nor*
reproach yourselves for having sold me here, for it
was to be a provider that God sent me ahead of you.
[6] *For this has been two of the hunger years in the*

brothers; see *comm.* to p. 1650] *(Ashtruc, Midrashei HaTorah).*

[Comp. *comm.* to 50:17 s.v. וְעַתָּה שָׂא־נָא.]

In the Midrash [*Bereishis Rabbah* 21:6] the word וְעַתָּה is said always to be associated with repentance.

כִּי לְמִחְיָה שְׁלָחַנִי אֱלֹהִים לִפְנֵיכֶם — *For it was to be a provider* [to serve you as a source of sustenance *(Rashi)*], *that God sent me ahead of you.*

God, not you, sent me here. His purpose was to implant me here to preserve life; therefore you need not be distressed. Obviously, you were chosen only to be His instrument for accomplishing this goal. All of us were destined to descend to Egypt in fulfillment of God's decree that Abraham's descendants would be aliens in a foreign land [15:13]. Normally we should have gone to Egypt in iron fetters [in the manner of all enslaved exiles], but the Holy One Blessed is He chose to orchestrate events so that Father and the rest of you would be spared the harshness of a *forced descent* into hostile conditions, and instead sent me down here to prepare the way and provide for you so you could follow in honor (gathered from *Tanchuma; Lekach Tov; Sechel Tov*). [*See footnotes to 37:12, 15 and especially to 32:1.*]

Midrash HaGadol records: Our Sages accordingly observed that even the wrongs committed by the righteous are of service to the world; how much more so their righteous deeds!

Rambam, in *Moreh Nevuchim* 2:48, cites our verse as an example of how the Torah attributes to God, as the First Cause, an act that is accomplished by a human agency. Although the brothers are the ones who 'sent' Joseph, the act is attributed to God as Prime Mover of all events. As *Abarbanel* writes, although the brothers had Free Will, God Himself guided their judgment so that they acted in accord with the Divine Plan [see footnote previous verse].

The word מִחְיָה, from חַי, *life,* means *sustenance. Rashi* accordingly interprets that the literal expression כִּי לְמִחְיָה, *for to* [or: *as*] *sustenance* really means: *for to be for you a* (source of) *sustenance.* As *R' Meyuchas* explains it: *To prepare sustenance for you.*

6. Joseph proceeds to elaborate on the extent of what he means by *'for a provider.'* He repeats that he considers the chain of events and his own extraordinary destiny to be part of the Master Plan that was to save Jacob's family from a famine *(R'Hirsch).*

כִּי זֶה שְׁנָתַיִם הָרָעָב בְּקֶרֶב הָאָרֶץ — *For this has been two of the hunger years in the midst of the land* [lit. *for this is two years of the famine in the midst of the land.*]

Following *Rashi: For two years*

pent their deed. Rather, Joseph's conciliatory words should be understood as an expression of faith that whatever happened to him was God's will. Had it not been brought about by the brothers, it would have happened some other way. Therefore, he felt no *personal* animosity toward them, since he looked only at the outcome: God's purpose was obviously that Joseph be raised to power and prominence and that he be the one to provide for his family and many countries in time of hunger.

As for the brothers, that they had been the instruments in causing him to lose his freedom and suffer for so many years must demonstrate that they were not innocent parties. As the

בְּקֶרֶב הָאָרֶץ וְעוֹד חָמֵשׁ שָׁנִים אֲשֶׁר אֵין־
ז חָרִישׁ וְקָצִיר: וַיִּשְׁלָחֵנִי אֱלֹהִים לִפְנֵיכֶם
לָשׂוּם לָכֶם שְׁאֵרִית בָּאָרֶץ וּלְהַחֲיוֹת
°שלישי ח לָכֶם לִפְלֵיטָה גְּדֹלָה: °וְעַתָּה לֹא־אַתֶּם
שְׁלַחְתֶּם אֹתִי הֵנָּה כִּי הָאֱלֹהִים וַיְשִׂימֵנִי
לְאָב לְפַרְעֹה וּלְאָדוֹן לְכָל־בֵּיתוֹ וּמֹשֵׁל

have passed of *the* [seven-year] *famine that is to befall the land.*

וְעוֹד חָמֵשׁ שָׁנִים אֲשֶׁר אֵין חָרִישׁ וְקָצִיר — *And there are yet five years in which there shall be neither plowing nor harvest.*

If there is no plowing there will certainly be no harvest. Why, then, the redundancy? — The connotation is that although the first two years possibly yielded a small residual harvest, in the subsequent five years there would be none at all — not even a spontaneous growth. Accordingly, it would appear that people did not even work the land during the later years of the famine. It was so noticeably parched that planting would have been futile *(Akeidas Yitzchak).*

Joseph mentioned the impending years of famine (although it was common knowledge) to stress, as noted, that a land which had endured two years of famine — during which the people had consumed most of their reserves causing prices to soar, and which was destined to experience yet another five years — could offer them no sustenance whatever, had God not dispatched him to provide for their sustenance *(Ramban).*

[This is one of the rare instances where *Onkelos* renders חָרִישׁ *(plowing)* as זְרוּעָה, *planting.* See *Shaarei Aharon.*]

7. וַיִּשְׁלָחֵנִי אֱלֹהִים לִפְנֵיכֶם לָשׂוּם לָכֶם שְׁאֵרִית בָּאָרֶץ — *Thus* [lit. *and*] *God has sent me ahead of you to insure your survival in the land* [lit. *to place for you a remnant in the land*].

— God thereby "provided the cure before the blow" by not inflicting famine on the Tribal Ancestors until He first sent Joseph to provide for them and assure their survival *(Abarbanel).*

That He sent *me* was not for my

Sages teach מְגַלְגְּלִין חוֹבָה עַל יְדֵי חַיָּב, *guilt* [i.e., an evil deed] *is brought about through a guilty party (Shabbos* 32a), meaning that God does not cause completely righteous people to carry out an unrighteous act, even if the act is necessary.

R' Hirsch writes that Joseph repeatedly emphasized to his brothers that the extraordinary sequence of events that brought him from the pit to the throne was undeniably a plan prearranged by God in order to save Jacob's family and set the stage for its development into a nation. This saga provided an insight into God's directing Hand in universal history. In the case of Joseph, retrospect showed how everything fit into His plan; it should be understood as a lesson that all other events are equally in accordance with His will, though they are not so easily understood.

The promise made to Abraham at the בְּרִית בֵּין הַבְּתָרִים, *Covenant between the Parts* (Chapter 15) came true because, as our Sages expressed it, of 'the fine woolen cloak, worth two *selas,* which Jacob had given to Joseph.' To preserve its integrity, this family of Jacob had to be formed into a nation in the midst of surroundings so hostile, both from a national and a cultural point of view, that assimilation would be impossible. No country complied better with these conditions than Egypt, which thus became the crucible, the 'iron furnace' *(Deut.* 4:20) wherein the Jewish people was forged.

midst of the land, and there are yet five years in which there shall be neither plowing nor harvest. 7 *Thus God has sent me ahead of you to insure your survival in the land and to sustain you for a momentous deliverance.* 8 *And now: It was not you who sent me here, but God. He has made me father to Pharoah, master of his entire household, and ruler throughout*

benefit, for my merit is no greater than yours. His purpose was to insure your survival in the land *(Lekach Tov).*

This passage is reminiscent of Ezra's statement [*Ezra* 9:8]: *And now for a little moment grace has been shown by HASHEM our God to leave us a remnant to escape ... and give us a little reviving* in our bondage *(R' Shmuel ben Chofni Gaon).*

וּלְהַחֲיוֹת לָכֶם לִפְלֵיטָה גְּדֹלָה — *And to sustain you for a momentous* [lit. *large*] *deliverance.*

God sent me here so that there would be a refuge for you in Egypt by virtue of the fact that I am the ruler of Egypt and will arrange for you to be received with lavish hopitality *(Haamek Davar).*

The deliverance must indeed be a *momentous* [lit. *large*] one since you number seventy souls and possess much livestock *(Abarbanel; Malbim).*

Alternatively, the essence of the phrase is: ... *And to keep you alive so you may develop into a large remnant.* Although at this time, they were still a relatively small extended family, Joseph perceived that God had lain the groundwork for the emergence of the House of Israel as a great nation *(R' David Feinstein).*

R' Hirsch conjectures that the verse may mean **וּלְהַחֲיוֹת לָכֶם**, *to sustain* [the land] *for your benefit* **לִפְלֵיטָה גְּדֹלָה** [so that its riches will serve to provide] *a momentous deliverance* [for you]. Egypt's prosperity was Divinely ordained for your sake.

HaK'sav V'HaKabbalah maintains that had the phrase meant *to sustain you*, as *Abarbanel* and many others interpret it, the Hebrew would have read **לְהַחֲיוֹת אֶתְכֶם**. Reading as it does, the word **לָכֶם** [lit. *to you*] connotes, as it often does, **שֶׁלָּכֶם**, *that which is yours* — in this case: [*to sustain*] *your household.* Compare this use of the prefix **ל** indicating **שֶׁל**, *of*, as in the phrases שֶׁלִי הֵם=לִי הֵם; שֶׁל מִי=לְמִי; שֶׁל ה׳=לַה׳.

8. **וְעַתָּה לֹא־אַתֶּם שְׁלַחְתֶּם אֹתִי הֵנָּה כִּי הָאֱלֹהִים** — *And now: It was not you who sent me here, but God* [lit. **the** God; i.e., God in His Aspect of *ELOHIM*, representing the Attribute of Divine Justice (see on 1:2).]

The *now* is emphatic, and Joseph was stressing that he bore no hatred for them: When you first sold me, it was inexplicable to me how brothers could act this way towards one another. *Now,* however, that God's plan has become apparent, it becomes clear *in retrospect* that *it was not you who sent me here but God.* You were acting only as His instruments and accordingly I harbor absolutely no hatred toward you *(Akeidah; Or HaChaim).*

וַיְשִׂימֵנִי לְאָב לְפַרְעֹה — *And He has made me father to Pharaoh.*

'Father' has the figurative meaning of colleague and patron *(Rashi).*

According to *Ibn Ezra* 'father' in this context means *mentor.*

[Comp. the designation of Joseph

ט בְּכָל־אֶרֶץ מִצְרָיִם: מַהֲרוּ וַעֲלוּ אֶל־אָבִי
וַאֲמַרְתֶּם אֵלָיו כֹּה אָמַר בִּנְךָ יוֹסֵף שָׂמַנִי
אֱלֹהִים לְאָדוֹן לְכָל־מִצְרָיִם רְדָה אֵלַי
י אַל־תַּעֲמֹד: וְיָשַׁבְתָּ בְאֶרֶץ־גֹּשֶׁן וְהָיִיתָ
קָרוֹב אֵלַי אַתָּה וּבָנֶיךָ וּבְנֵי בָנֶיךָ וְצֹאנְךָ
יא וּבְקָרְךָ וְכָל־אֲשֶׁר־לָךְ: וְכִלְכַּלְתִּי אֹתְךָ

as 'Avrech'=*father of the king,* in 41:43.]

וּלְאָדוֹן לְכָל־בֵּיתוֹ — [*And*] *master of his entire house*[*hold*].

— Everyone in his household calls me 'master' *(Sechel Tov).*

In Hebrew the term אָדוֹן denotes lordship over servants. Thus, the connotation of our phrase is that everyone in Pharaoh's household was considered Joseph's servant *(HaRechasim LeBik'ah).*

וּמֹשֵׁל בְּכָל־אֶרֶץ מִצְרָיִם — *And ruler throughout the entire land of Egypt.*

I decree and they fulfill *(Sechel Tov).*

Joseph stressed his exalted postion to allude to the tradition that God forgives all the sins of one who gains high position. Consequently, they all could assume that God had forgiven him for his sin of slandering them to Jacob [37:2] *(Tz'ror HaMor).*

9. מַהֲרוּ וַעֲלוּ אֶל־אָבִי — *Hurry* — [and] *go up to my father.*

Hurry — So he will stop worrying *(Sforno).*

Hurry! Do not fail to take advantage of this propitious hour! *(Midrash).*

He used the verb *go up* since *Eretz Yisrael* is the highest of all the [neighboring] countries. [See *comm.* to 12:10; 13:1] *(Rashi).*

וַאֲמַרְתֶּם אֵלָיו — *And say to him.*

[By *your* informing Father of my whereabouts you will in effect annul the solemn ban you imposed against telling him, which has prevented me from contacting him until now. See footnote on p. 1653, and *comm.* to end of *v. 1* above.]

כֹּה אָמַר בִּנְךָ יוֹסֵף — *So said your son Joseph.*

— *Your son* — the son you love most *(Lekach Tov).*

The expression כֹּה אָמַר, *So said,* is the formula used to introduce prophecy. By using this expression, he was intimating that his request was prophetically inspired *(Lekach Tov).*

שָׂמַנִי אֱלֹהִים לְאָדוֹן לְכָל־מִצְרָיִם — *God has made me master of all Egypt.*

Accordingly, it is in my power to assure you a secluded dwelling place, not among the Egyptians, since I know you would want to live apart from them *(Alshich; Haamek Davar).*

And the cares of State imposed upon me by my position do not permit me to come to you; therefore *please come down to me (Abarbanel).*

1. "As I mentioned before," Joseph said, "Father and the rest of his family should have been brought down to Egypt in iron chains to begin the predestined servitude, but God in His compassion spared us all the harshness of a *forced descent.* However, this is the predestined time and you must hurry and summon Father now! Who knows what the morrow will bring? Should you neglect this propitious moment, then you might forfeit that grace and you might all yet have to be brought down in chains"*(Agra d'Kallah).*

the entire land of Egypt. [9] *Hurry — go up to my*
father and say to him, 'So said your son Joseph:
"God has made me master of all Egypt. Come down
to me please; do not delay. [10] *You will reside in the*
land of Goshen and you will be near to me — you,
your sons, your grandchildren, your flock and herd
and all that is yours. [11] *And I will provide for you*

רְדָה אֵלַי אַל־תַּעֲמֹד — *Come down to me, please; do not delay.*

["As I emphasized before, my responsibilities here make it *impossible* for me to leave. The Divine scheme — so apparent in what has occurred — makes it imperative that I remain here, and that you join me. *Therefore, come down to me, please, do not delay."*]

Come with your entire family and possessions, as enumerated in the next verse *(Ramban).*

Do not delay. Do not let time wait for you *(Midrash).*

[The word 'please' is not in the Hebrew; it is suggested by the courteous form רְדָה instead of the usual imperative רֵד. See *comm.* to שְׁבָה in 27:19.]

10. וְיָשַׁבְתָּ בְאֶרֶץ־גֹּשֶׁן — [And] *You will reside in the land* [i.e. region] *of Goshen.*

— Away from the idolatrous Egyptians *(Malbim),* for Joseph knew that Jacob would not want to live in the land of Egypt where the royal palace was [with the resultant swirl of social and political activity] *(Ramban).*

Goshen.

Goshen was a fertile region in the Northeast of Egypt, east of the Nile delta. The Israelites lived there throughout their stay in Egypt, their primary residence being in Ramses, its major city. Goshen contained Egypt's most fertile soil and in 47:6 it is described as *the best of the land.*

Joseph purposely assigned this region to his family to keep them segregated from the mainstream of Egypt's idolatrous, immoral life, and to allow them to freely pursue their shepherding which was hateful to the Egyptians.

That Goshen was selected for their residence was not haphazard. According to *Pirkei d'Rabbi Eliezer* cited in the footnote to 12:16, an earlier Pharaoh had given the region of Goshen to Sarah, and it was appropriate that her descendants settle there.

The territory in Judah by the name of Goshen [*Josh.* 10:41] is not to be confused with the Goshen in Egypt *(Radak).*

The Arabs identify Goshen as Wadi Tumeilat, but Egyptians Jews believe that Goshen is Fayum, the later residence of R' Saadia Gaon. R' Saadia himself, in his translation of the Torah, renders Goshen as Al-Sadir. [See also 46:28].

וְהָיִיתָ קָרוֹב אֵלַי — *And you will be near to me.*

Though my position forces me to live in the metropolis, at least you will be relatively near to me; I will be able to visit and look after you *(Abarbanel; Alshich).*

אַתָּה וּבָנֶיךָ וּבְנֵי בָנֶיךָ וְצֹאנְךָ וּבְקָרְךָ וְכָל־אֲשֶׁר־לָךְ — *You,* [and] *your sons,* [and] *your grandchildren,* [and] *your flock and* [*your*] *herd and all that is yours.*

— This phrase reverts to modify the end of the previous verse: *Please come down to me; do not delay ... you, your children, your children's children,* etc. *(Ramban).*

He mentioned the flocks and

שָׁם כִּי־עוֹד חָמֵשׁ שָׁנִים רָעָב פֶּן־תִּוָּרֵשׁ
יב אַתָּה וּבֵיתְךָ וְכָל־אֲשֶׁר־לָךְ׃ וְהִנֵּה עֵינֵיכֶם
רֹאוֹת וְעֵינֵי אָחִי בִנְיָמִין כִּי־פִי הַמְדַבֵּר

herds as well because in Canaan Jacob had to graze his cattle in faraway Shechem, and now because of the famine there were no longer any grazing lands available there *(Abarbanel).*

11. וְכִלְכַּלְתִּי אֹתְךָ שָׁם — *And I will provide for you there.*

I.e., in Goshen. However, I cannot provide for if you remain in Canaan since I will be charged with sending money out of the country *(Malbim;* see *Ramban below).*

The Midrash [*Koheles Zuta*] invokes this passage to illustrate how *there are no riches to the intelligent* [*Eccles.* 9:11]: Only a short while earlier, *the man* [Jacob] *increased exceedingly* [above 30:43] indicating that he grew immensely wealthy — and now he required Joseph's promise of support.

כִּי־עוֹד חָמֵשׁ שָׁנִים רָעָב — *For there* [will be] *five more years of famine.*

— This famine will not end soon. Whatever hesitations you may have about coming here must be set aside — you *must* come soon *(Abarbanel).*

פֶּן תִּוָּרֵשׁ אַתָּה וּבֵיתְךָ וְכָל־אֲשֶׁר־לָךְ — *So you do not become destitute, you,* [and] *your house*[*hold*] *and all that is yours.*

The translation of תִּוָּרֵשׁ as *destitute* follows *Rashi.* He cites *Onkelos* who renders תִּתְמַסְכֵּן [*you will (not) become poor*]; it is similar to the word of the same root [רש or ריש] in *I Sam.* 2:7 where we find the expression מוֹרִישׁ וּמַעֲשִׁיר, *God impoverishes and enriches.* [*See Ohev Ger; Ya'er; Lechem V'Simlah; Mizrachi; Karnei Or.*]

According to *Ibn Ezra* the term is related to the root ירש, *cut off; dispossessed,* as in *Deut.* 4:38: לְהוֹרִישׁ גוֹיִם. [The continuity of the verses, according to this interpretation, is: *God sent me ahead of you to assure survival for you in the land* [*v.* 7] ... *Therefore come down to me* [*v.* 9] ... *And I will provide for you* [*v.* 11] ... *lest you be* **utterly cut off** *from the land (Abarbanel).*]

Rashbam similarly interprets *lest you be driven out of the land* — by the force of the famine.[1]

Ramban agrees with the interpretation *impoverished.* To his brothers Joseph had implied that they would die unless they came to him, saying [*v.* 5]: *for it was to serve you as a source of sustenance* that God has sent me ahead of you; [*v.* 7]: *to provide refuge for you ... and to save your lives* ... But out of respect to Jacob, he expressed himself much more mildly to him, saying only that they would become *impoverished* if they remained in Canaan. Joseph could not be expected to send large supplies of food from the royal storehouses to Canaan lest the Egyptians suspect him of privately trading in food and accumulating a personal fortune with the intention of returning to his homeland. However, were his family to come to Egypt the king would surely grant permission to sustain them.

— The apprehension that they might become impoverished proves that they had been wealthy *(Lekach Tov).*

12. [The brothers had been standing dumbfounded before him all this time; Joseph was apprehensive

1. Figuratively, the connotation was: *Lest you become impoverished of your Torah studies.* Joseph suggested to Jacob: Better that you come down here even though it means leaving *Eretz Yisrael,* than you become impoverished of Torah, for you will not be able to study there because of the famine *(Tur).*

45
12

there — for there will be five more years of famine —
so you do not become destitute, you, your household,
and all that is yours."
12 *"Behold! Your eyes see as do the eyes of my*
brother Benjamin that it is my mouth that is speaking

that they still might be doubtful about his true identity, so he proceeds to reassure them again that he is really Joseph.]

וְהִנֵּה עֵינֵיכֶם רֹאוֹת וְעֵינֵי אָחִי בִנְיָמִין — *And behold! Your eyes see as do* [lit. *and*] *the eyes of my brother, Benjamin.*

I.e., *your eyes see* my glory, and that I am your brother, for I am circumcised as you are [see *comm.* to *v.* 4 above] *(Rashi)* ...

As do the eyes of my brother Benjamin who did not know I was sold [but thought me to be dead; even *he* would admit I am Joseph *(Chizkuni)*] *(Sforno).*

Rashi [basing himself on *Megillah* 16b] notes that Joseph made a point of singling out Benjamin and equating him with the other brothers, as if to say: Just as I do not hate him, for he was not implicated in my sale, so I do not hate you.

כִּי־פִי הַמְדַבֵּר אֲלֵיכֶם — *That it is my mouth that is speaking to you.*

— In the Holy Tongue (Hebrew) [i.e., without my interpreter. When you relate this to Father he will believe that I am indeed Joseph.] *(Rashi; Tanchuma; Targum Yonasan)*

Ramban cites the above-quoted opinion of most commentators that Joseph was invoking his knowledge of Hebrew as uncontestable proof of his identity. *Ramban,* maintains, however, that this must have been intended merely as an additional assurance, but surely not as conclusive proof. The viceroy's ability to speak Hebrew could not prove he was Joseph, for, as *Ramban* suggests, many Egyptians — particularly officials — must have spoken Hebrew since it was the native language of the neighboring Canaanite nation. We find similarly that Nebuchadnezzer spoke Hebrew and all his courtiers understood him [see *Daniel* 2:2,3]. In *Ramban's* opinion, Abraham did not bring the Hebrew language with him from Ur or Haran, for they spoke Aramaic there. This is evidenced by Laban's use of the Aramaic term *yegar* for 'heap.'[1]

Furthermore, just as Joseph had come from Canaan, there must have been others from there. Besides, the brothers' best proof that the viceroy was Joseph was his familiarity with the sale [which only Joseph could have known] and his knowledge of the name Joseph, saying, *I am Joseph your brother — he whom you sold to Egypt* [*v.* 4].

Rather, *Ramban* maintains, *it is my mouth that is speaking to you* means: I — who, as you have all seen, have the authority to do so — promise to sustain you. Therefore go summon my father ...

— I did not assure you through an intermediary of my support, *but it was my own mouth that spoke to you,* and you need not fear that I will deny it

1. *Oznaim L'Torah* suggests that the intent of 'Holy Tongue' is not so much that they ascertained his identity from his speaking Hebrew, for as noted the interpreter also spoke Hebrew! Rather the meaning is that Joseph was emphasizing how he spoke in a holy *manner* — the Name of Heaven was ever-present in his mouth; he always invoked God in his expressions: *For to save life God has sent me ahead of you; ... it was not you who sent me here but God; ... God has made me master of all Egypt.* Isaac also recognized קוֹל יַעֲקֹב, *the 'voice' of Jacob* by the fact that he always invoked the Name of Heaven [see *comm.* to 27:22].

יג אֲלֵיכֶם: וְהִגַּדְתֶּם לְאָבִי אֶת־כָּל־כְּבוֹדִי
בְּמִצְרַיִם וְאֵת כָּל־אֲשֶׁר רְאִיתֶם וּמִהַרְתֶּם
יד וְהוֹרַדְתֶּם אֶת־אָבִי הֵנָּה: וַיִּפֹּל עַל־צַוְּארֵי
בִנְיָמִן־אָחִיו וַיֵּבְךְּ וּבִנְיָמִן בָּכָה עַל־

afterward *(Hadar Zekeinim).*

According to *Or HaChaim,* the 'proof' Joseph was invoking was not his knowledge of the Hebrew language. Rather he meant that his brothers could recognize his voice when he spoke in Hebrew, which they could not do when he spoke in the unfamiliar Egyptian.

— Furthermore Joseph was emphasizing how his pronunciation and accent were entirely like his brothers; no Egyptian could possibly speak Hebrew with such a native accent *(Nesinah laGer).*

'When you sold me, no one but us was present who spoke Hebrew, for the traders were Ishmaelites' [thus, if I am quoting your discussion of the sale in Hebrew, I can only be Joseph] *(Sforno).*

The primary interpretation is: The news you are to tell my father was not heard from others as hearsay. With your own eyes, you have seen and recognize that I — Joseph your brother — am speaking to you. Therefore [*v.* 13]: *Tell my father of all my glory* etc. *(Rashbam).*

What you have seen here proves that I predicted these events correctly when I related my dreams to you as a youth [37:7] *(Ashtruc).*

The Sages in *Megillah* 16b expound the passage to imply: כְּפִי, *As my mouth* [speaks] *so my heart* [feels] [i.e., what I am saying to you reflects my innermost feelings].

Compare *R' Shmuel ben Chofni* who interprets the syntactical flow of the verse to be: What you have seen here with your own eyes attests to the fact that I, with my own mouth, am speaking to you.

Others explain that Joseph was now explaining that modesty prevented him from describing the full extent of his privileged position in Egypt. *Since it is my own mouth that is speaking to you* it would be unseemly for me to boast about myself. [יְהַלֶּלְךָ זָר וְלֹא פִיךָ *(Prov.* 27:2).] But I rely on you to help induce Father to come by telling him what you have seen here in Egypt *(Abarbanel; Malbim; HaKsav V'HaKabalah).*

13. וְהִגַּדְתֶּם לְאָבִי אֶת־כָּל־כְּבוֹדִי בְּמִצְרַיִם — *Therefore, tell my father of all my glory in Egypt.*

Knowing that it would not be an easy task to persuade Jacob to leave the Holy Land, Joseph again emphasizes the importance of convincing him of Joseph's position in Egypt and the urgency that the family reunite there *(Ralbag).*

וְאֵת כָּל־אֲשֶׁר רְאִיתֶם — *And all that you saw.*

— I.e., even that which out of modesty I declined to mention. Do not tell Father only what I told you to say, but add to it from your own experiences and observations. Convince him that I can provide well for him, and persuade him to come *(Ralbag; Akeidah).*

וּמִהַרְתֶּם וְהוֹרַדְתֶּם אֶת אָבִי הֵנָּה — *But you must hurry, and bring my father down here.*

Hurry — so he may experience joy at seeing all of this *(Sforno).*

[What joy could Joseph have expected his righteous father Jacob to experience upon seeing him as viceroy of Egypt? True, the reunion after twenty-two years would bring the aged Patriarch boundless joy. But how this joy would be tempered with anxiety! For Jacob would certainly be apprehensive about how Joseph's posterity could have possibly maintained his spirituality in the pagan, im-

45 13-15 *to you.* [13] *Therefore, tell my father of all my glory in*
Egypt and all that you saw. But you must hurry, and
bring my father down here."
[14] *Then he fell upon his brother Benjamin's neck*
and wept; and Benjamin wept upon his neck. [15] *He*

moral culture of Egypt. This why Jacob had the burning desire to gaze upon Joseph's face. See *comm.* to 46:30, and Overview].

14. Joseph had cried when he revealed himself to his brothers, but those were tears of joy. Now, new tears are brought on by sadness and a premonition of suffering. He had just invited Jacob to Egypt, with all his family, to begin a national existence in exile. Though Joseph had to do as he did, still he clearly foresaw that this Egyptian exile would not be the last in the history of his people. As he embraced his brothers, he had the vision that Providence had many other trials and hardships in store for them. This combination of joy and sadness is typical of the Jewish people; even while thanking God for His infinite mercy — הוֹדוּ לַה׳ כִּי טוֹב, *give praise to HASHEM for He is good* — we tremble at the thought of the future. Thereupon, we beseech God's help, אָנָּא ה׳ הוֹשִׁיעָה נָּא, *please HASHEM bring salvation now (R' Munk).*

וַיִּפֹּל עַל־צַוְּארֵי בִנְיָמִן־אָחִיו וַיֵּבְךְּ — *Then he fell upon his brother Benjamin's neck* [lit. *necks*] *and wept.*

In the literal sense: Since they were brothers from the same father and mother their love for each other was very strong; therefore each wept on the other's neck *(Radak).*

The implication of the plural is that he wept on both sides of his neck *(Chizkuni).*

Midrashically, Joseph wept for the two Temples that would be in Benjamin's territory [the Temple Mount was in his portion; see footnote 2 on page 1449] and would suffer destruction *(Rashi).*[1]

וּבִנְיָמִן בָּכָה עַל צַוָּארָיו — *And Benjamin wept upon his neck.*

For the Tabernacle of Shiloh which was destined to be in Joseph's territory and would likewise be destroyed *(Rashi).*

1. **Rashi's basis for the exegesis**

The commentators explain *Rashi's* exegesis to be based upon *Midrash Rabbah* §93:12 and *Megillah* 16b. The Midrash reads: *"And he fell upon his brother Benjamin's* [צַוְּארֵי] *necks and wept.* [The word צַוְּארֵי is plural]. Did Benjamin have two necks? — In fact, said R' Eleazar, Joseph foresaw through Divine Inspiration that two Temples based in Benjamin's territory, would be destroyed. *And Benjamin wept upon his neck,* for Benjamin saw that the Tabernacle of Shiloh would be built in Joseph's territory and would be destroyed." [The connection between neck and the Temple is discussed below.]

The commentators grapple with why צַוְּארֵי, the plural *necks* in the first phrase should allude to *two* Temples, while the word צַוָּארָיו, — which is also plural — when used with Joseph should allude to but *one* Tabernacle. [See *Mizrachi;* cf. also Heidenheim].

Actually, however, *Rashi's* view on the matter is made quite clear in his commentary to *Megillah* 16b. There *Rashi* comments that no inference is to be drawn from the plural of צַוָּאר, because Scripture commonly uses the plural structure of the word. For, as *R' David Feinstein* notes, *Rashi* maintains in *Proverbs* 1:9 that צַוָּאר, *neck,* usually takes the plural form in Hebrew since the trachea is composed of many rings [accordingly, no significance can be derived from the use of the plural form].

Rather, the exposition is based on the fact that this is one of the rare places in Scripture that

טו צַוָּארָיו: וַיְנַשֵּׁק לְכָל־אֶחָיו וַיֵּבְךְּ עֲלֵהֶם
טז וְאַחֲרֵי כֵן דִּבְּרוּ אֶחָיו אִתּוֹ: וְהַקֹּל נִשְׁמַע
בֵּית פַּרְעֹה לֵאמֹר בָּאוּ אֲחֵי יוֹסֵף וַיִּיטַב
יז בְּעֵינֵי פַרְעֹה וּבְעֵינֵי עֲבָדָיו: וַיֹּאמֶר

⥈ Why was this particular moment of their reconciliation chosen to weep over the destruction of the future Temples?

The mutual joy of Joseph and Benjamin was so great that they could have died of ecstasy. In order to temper their joy, they were shown the destructions of the Holy Temples. Similarly, a goblet is smashed at a wedding ceremony to temper the joy of the guests and evoke the memory of the Destruction of the Temple *(Yad Yosef; Meam Loez)*.

Yafeh Toar suggests that this entire Midrashic interpretation that *neck* is a metaphor for *Temples* is based on the fact that they cried only after Joseph told them to bring his father down rather than immediately after he revealed himself to them. Upon realizing that Jacob's descent to Egypt was symbolic of all future Jewish Exiles [see *Ramban* beginning of *Vayechi*], Joseph was reminded also of the Destructions [see *Yalkut Yehudah.*]

15. וַיְנַשֵּׁק לְכָל־אֶחָיו וַיֵּבְךְּ עֲלֵהֶם — *He then kissed all his brothers and wept upon them.*

— To reassure all of them that he harbored no evil against them *(Ralbag)*.

Kabbalistically: Because he prophetically foresaw that the Ten Tribes would be exiled and scattered among the nations *(Zohar)*.

mentions weeping *on the neck*. Since the Torah economizes on every letter, it would not have mentioned that the weeping took place on the neck unless an allusion was intended. That allusion is the homiletical connection between neck and Temple [see below].

That Joseph wept over two destructions and Benjamin over one is based, not on exegesis, but on the historical fact that there were *two* Temples in Benjamin's territory and *one* Tabernacle in Joseph's (see *Mizrachi; Sifsei Chachamim)*.

[*Torah Temimah* observes, however, that although צואר *usually* occurs in plural, there are instances that it appears in singular, as for example צַוָּארֶךָ in 27:40, and צַוָּארוֹ in 41:42. This would tend to possibly support the Midrashic question 'how many necks did Benjamin have?' Since in this case it occurs in the plural, a usage that is not universal, it is therefore suggestive of a homiletic interpretation. But as noted, *Rashi*, did not base his exposition on this fact, and wrote that the question should be omitted from the Talmud, as indeed it is in old manuscripts of the Talmud.]

⥈ The homiletical metaphor of neck alluding to the Temple

This metaphor is borrowed from the Talmudic interpretation of *Songs of Songs* 4:4, — כְּמִגְדַּל דָּוִיד צַוָּארֵךְ, *Your neck is like the Tower of David* — in *Berachos* 30a which perceives in *neck* an allusion to the Temple.

Maharsha there [s.v. כְּמִגְדַּל] explains: The Temple is compared to the neck which is at the top of man's body; similarly the Temple is the summit and splendor of Israel.

Shir HaShirim Rabbah 4:9 homiletically elaborates on the connection of Temple and neck:

a) As long as the Temple stood Israel was prosperous and at ease and could walk with an erect head and 'straight neck'. When the Temple was destroyed, Israel became degraded and persecuted. The neck of the Jews became 'bent'; they can no longer raise their heads among the nations;

b) Unlike other parts of the body, if the neck is cut a person can die. The neck is a human being's lifeline. The Temple is, similarly the life channel of Israel;

c) Just as a man's neck is the highest part of him, so was the Temple in the highest part of the world; and

d) Just as most ornaments are hung around the neck, so were the 'ornaments' of Israel — the Priests and Levites — attached to the Temple.

45
16-17

then kissed all his brothers and wept upon them, and
afterwards his brothers conversed with him.
16 *The news was heard in Pharaoh's palace saying,*
"Joseph's brothers have come!" And it pleased
Pharaoh and his servants. 17 *Pharaoh said to Joseph,*

— But *they* did not weep, as they stood ashamed before him *(Radak).*

Or according to the *Zohar* because they had not been granted a prophetic spirit, as were Joseph and Benjamin, informing them of future disasters.

The verb נשק, *kiss* is found both in the simple *kal* form וַיִּשַּׁק, and in the intensive form וַיְנַשֵּׁק, as in our passage. The latter form connotes total absorption and deep emotion in this display of affection *(Heidenheim).*

וְאַחֲרֵי כֵן דִּבְּרוּ אֶחָיו אִתּוֹ — *And afterwards his brothers conversed with him.*

I.e. after they saw that Joseph wept and realized that he was peaceably inclined towards them — *his brothers conversed with him.* Until then they felt ashamed before him *(Rashi).*

Although Joseph had wept before, the brothers thought his earlier weeping may have been caused by his memories of his troubles *(Or HaChaim).*

His brothers conversed with him — asking him about everything that had happened to him since he was separated from them, and how he had achieved his lofty status *(Radak).*

16. Pharaoh echoes Joseph's invitation and orders wagons to be sent for Jacob and his family.

וְהַקֹּל נִשְׁמַע בֵּית פַּרְעֹה לֵאמֹר — *[And] the news* [lit. *voice; sound*] *was heard* [*in*] *Pharaoh's palace* [lit. *house*] *saying.*

Pharaoh's people inquired about the abundant weeping which, as noted in *v.* 2, was heard in Pharaoh's house, and it was learned that Joseph's brothers had come *(Or HaChaim).*

According to *Midrash Tanchuma* the 'voice' that was heard in Paraoh's house was that of Judah who, on hearing Joseph's revelation, 'cried out with such a terrible voice that all the walls of Egypt fell down, every beast was cowed, Joseph fell from his throne and Pharaoh too descended from his throne.'

The word *in* is not in the Hebrew but *Rashi* maintains that it is implied in the phraseology which should be interpreted as if it read בְּבֵית פַּרְעֹה. Furthermore, in our passage בֵּית, *house,* is to be taken literally [unlike in *v.* 2 where it means *household*].

בָּאוּ אֲחֵי יוֹסֵף — *Joseph's brothers have come.*

— I.e., the honorable brothers that Joseph always claimed to have in Canaan from where he had been kidnapped. [As noted in 40:15, Joseph had always boasted that he was a Hebrew from a distinguished family, since he did not want to be taken as a Canaanite]. Now Joseph's story was confirmed by their arrival *(Ramban).*

However, only this was heard, but nothing about how they had sold him *(Alshich).*

וַיִּיטַב בְּעֵינֵי פַרְעֹה וּבְעֵינֵי עֲבָדָיו — *And it pleased Pharaoh and his servants* [lit. *and it was good in the eyes of Pharaoh and in the eyes of his servants*].

It had been a disgrace for Egypt to be ruled by a stranger, a slave released from prison. Now when Pharaoh and his courtiers saw that

פַּרְעֹה אֶל־יוֹסֵף אֱמֹר אֶל־אַחֶיךָ זֹאת
עֲשׂוּ טַעֲנוּ אֶת־בְּעִירְכֶם וּלְכוּ־בֹאוּ אַרְצָה
יח כְּנָעַן: וּקְחוּ אֶת־אֲבִיכֶם וְאֶת־בָּתֵּיכֶם
וּבֹאוּ אֵלָי וְאֶתְּנָה לָכֶם אֶת־טוּב אֶרֶץ
°רביעי יט מִצְרַיִם וְאִכְלוּ אֶת־חֵלֶב הָאָרֶץ: °וְאַתָּה
צֻוֵּיתָה זֹאת עֲשׂוּ קְחוּ־לָכֶם° מֵאֶרֶץ

Joseph had important brothers [who were descended from Abraham, the renowned 'prince of God' of whom Pharaoh himself had heard *(Lekach Tov)*] and was indeed worthy of having a royal position, they were naturally very pleased *(Ramban).*[1]

According to *Sforno,* they rejoiced at the news of his brothers' arrival since henceforth Joseph would regard himself and his children as permanent residents of the country. No longer would he consider himself an alien; henceforth he would turn his full attention to the long-term best interests of the country.

17. וַיֹּאמֶר פַּרְעֹה אֶל־יוֹסֵף — *[And] Pharaoh said to Joseph.*

Pharaoh's invitation that Joseph have his brothers return to Canaan to bring his family to Egypt was selfishly motivated. He was afraid that now that Joseph was reunited with his illustrious brothers, he might display a desire to return home with them, and leave Egypt without anyone competent to run the government *(Yalkut Reuveni; Meam Loez).*

אֱמֹר אֶל־אַחֶיךָ זֹאת עֲשׂוּ — *Say to your brothers, 'Do this'.*

I.e., *'Say to your brothers* — in my name and by my authority as Pharaoh — *Do the following.'* They needed special royal permission to take along the wagons, since in those days wagons and chariots were used only by kings and in time of war; no one else could use them without the king's personal permission *(Abarbanel; Or HaChaim).*

טַעֲנוּ אֶת בְּעִירְכֶם — *Load up your animals.*

— With grain *(Rashi).*

The translation of טַעֲנוּ *as load up* follows *Rashi, Onkelos,* and general Talmudic usage; *Ibn Janach* and *Ralbag* concur. *Radak* in *Shorashim* cites this as his primary interpretation, but in an alternate translation [followed by *Tur,* and similar to *R' Saadia Gaon*] relates it to the cognate term מְטֹעֲנֵי in *Isaiah* 14:19 where it means *thrust through,* the sense here being that Joseph wanted the brothers to goad [lit. *stab*] the animals [as with spurs] to make them hurry to the land of Canaan. [Cf. *Ibn Ezra* in *Isaiah* 14:19].

The term בְּעִיר meaning *cattle, animal, beast* is derived from the verb בער, *destroy,* since beasts utterly consume and destroy vegetation and verdure. Comp. the term in *Exodus* 22:4 and *Numbers* 20:4 *(Ibn Caspi;* see *R' Hirsch).*

וּלְכוּ־בֹאוּ אַרְצָה כְּנָעַן — *And go directly* [lit. *and go, come*] *to the land of Canaan.*

— Without delay *(Lekach Tov).*

The word בֹאוּ, *come,* is superfluous,

1. *Midrash HaGadol* offers the following:

'... *And in the eyes of his servants'* — but not of *all* his servants. They said, 'If this one [Joseph], who is but an individual, displaced us from our highest status, how much more so will these ten!' This is inferred in *Psalms* 105:38: *Rejoice, O Egypt, in their departure.* The Egyptians rejoiced in their departure, but not at their entrance.

"Say to your brothers, 'Do this: Load up your ani-
mals and go directly to the land of Canaan. 18 *Bring*
your father and your households and come to me. I
will give you the best of the land of Egypt and you
will eat the fat of the land.' 19 *And you are com-*
manded [*to say*]*: 'Do this: Take yourselves from the*

as it would have sufficed to write וּלְכוּ אַרְצָה כְּנָעַן, *and go to the land of Canaan.* Most commentators perceive לְכוּ בֹאוּ, *go come,* to be an idiomatic expression meaning *go directly,* without delay. *Onkelos* renders לְכוּ as synonymous with the transitive verb — הָבִיאוּ, *bring.* Joseph ordered them to *go* and *bring* grain to the land of Canaan. (See *HaKsav V' HaKabalah).*

18. וּקְחוּ אֶת־אֲבִיכֶם וְאֶת־בָּתֵּיכֶם וּבֹאוּ אֵלָי — [*And*] *bring* [lit. *take*] *your father and your households and come to me.*

Pharaoh was thus instructing Joseph to emphasize the personal aspect of his family's descent to Egypt: *'To me,* Joseph' (and not *'to the land'),* for the primary reason you are to bring the family to this country is to be with me (*Alshich).*

Possibly, by the words *and come to me,* Pharaoh meant himself, as if Joseph were to suggest to Jacob, 'Come to Pharaoh, for he will give you the best of the land of Egypt' *(Akeidah; Abarbanel).*

וְאֶתְּנָה לָכֶם אֶת־טוּב אֶרֶץ מִצְרַיִם — *And I will give you the best of the land of Egypt.*

— The land of Goshen *(Rashi).*

Rashi continues that in saying *I will give you the best of the land of Egypt* "Pharaoh was prophesying but he did not know the significance of what he was saying. For ultimately [the Israelites] would make [Egypt] like a deep sea void of fish" [מְצוּלָה, i.e. *despoiled;* see *comm.* to וַיְנַצְּלוּ in *Exodus* 12:36.]

[That is, Pharaoh unknowingly prophesied that the Egyptians would indeed some day give the Israelites the best of the land of Egypt. For at the end of their long Exile in Egypt, the Israelites would go out with all the best the land had to offer, and would literally empty out the nation's treasuries. This would be in fulfillment of God's promise to Abraham [15:14] *Afterwards they shall leave with great possessions (Meam Loez).*]

וְאִכְלוּ אֶת־חֵלֶב הָאָרֶץ — *And you will eat the fat of the land.*

The word *fat* always denotes "the choicest" *(Rashi).*

19. וְאַתָּה צֻוֵּיתָה זֹאת עֲשׂוּ — *And you are commanded* [to say]: *'Do this.'*

The phrase is elliptical. It means: And you [Joseph] are commanded *by me* [Pharaoh] *to tell them:* 'Do this.' — for it is with my permission *(Rashi).*

Rashi thus tells us by *whom* Joseph was commanded [i.e. Pharaoh], and that עֲשׂוּ *do,* is in plural, since it was not Pharaoh's instructions to Joseph, but to relay to his brothers *(Mizrachi).*

Pharaoh issued this as a royal *decree* because Joseph's integrity and honesty were such that Pharaoh knew Joseph would never abuse his high office for personal advantage [especially in this case since, as noted, the export of wagons from Egypt was prohibited], and that he therefore might not send his father anything. Therefore Pharaoh specifically *commanded* him to do the following *(Ramban).*

מִצְרַ֫יִם עֲגָלוֹת לְטַפְּכֶם֙ וְלִנְשֵׁיכֶ֔ם
כ וּנְשָׂאתֶ֥ם אֶת־אֲבִיכֶ֖ם וּבָאתֶֽם׃ וְעֵ֣ינְכֶ֔ם
אַל־תָּחֹ֖ס עַל־כְּלֵיכֶ֑ם כִּי־ט֛וּב כָּל־אֶ֥רֶץ
כא מִצְרַ֖יִם לָכֶ֥ם הֽוּא׃ וַיַּֽעֲשׂוּ־כֵן֙ בְּנֵ֣י יִשְׂרָאֵ֔ל

On the other hand, the *Zohar* [as explained by the commentators (see specifically *HaKsav V' HaKabalah)*] holds that the initiative to send wagons came from Joseph [as is implied from *v.* 27 below], and Pharaoh accomodated him by granting the needed royal decree. This is derived from the fact that the word צֻוֵּיתָה *you are commanded* ends with a ה (not צֻוֵּיתָ, the usual imperative form). This spelling implies that the phrase be interpreted *what* **you have commanded,** *they should do.*

As *R' David Feinstein* offers, Joseph arranged for the dispatch of the wagons to be done at his personal direction. The brothers would notice this and convey it to their father when they returned home. Hearing that *Joseph* sent the wagons, Jacob would understand the desired sign Joseph wished to convey by means of the wagons, as we shall learn in *v.* 27.

Targum Yonasan paraphrases: 'And you, Joseph, are commanded to honor your father. Therefore, tell your brothers, Do this ... ' [That is, Pharaoh was apprehensive, now that the brothers were reunited, that out of filial devotion Joseph might want to go *personally* to his father. In order to prevent this, Pharaoh acknowledged Joseph's desire to honor his father, but he advised him that by personally telling his brothers to take wagons the idea will be attributed to him, and it will be considered as if he personally performed the good deed *(Yayin HaTov).*]

קְחוּ לָכֶם מֵאֶרֶץ מִצְרַיִם עֲגָלוֹת לְטַפְּכֶם וְלִנְשֵׁיכֶם — *Take yourselves from the land of Egypt wagons for your small children and for your wives.*

The use and export of wagons was generally forbidden, and, as noted, was a limited privilege which could be granted only by Pharaoh himself — especially since the famine. Therefore Pharaoh prefaced this instruction by the formula *And you are commanded (Lekach Tov; Malbim).*

Comp. *Rashbam:* 'Now I am commanding you to take wagons and beasts to pull [them].' For no one was permitted to take a wagon out of the kingdom without Pharaoh's authority. An analogy to this law is found in the Talmud [*Mishnah Bechoros* 4:4; *Sanhedrin* 33a; 93a]: No cow or sow was permitted to leave Egypt without her womb being first removed [to ensure that she would not calve].

[The most common interpretation of the analogy is that just as fertile cows and sows could not be exported from Egypt, so could wagons not be exported. There are some, however, who suggest that *Rashbam* is interpreting עֲגָלוֹת (plural of עֲגָלָה, *wagon)* in this passage as the plural of עֶגְלָה, *heifer,* as if Pharaoh were granting Joseph's brothers permission to take *heifers* out of Egypt — something usually forbidden — and the analogy from the Talmud is cited in support for this interpretation. The former, more common interpretation, however, is the traditional and more acceptable one. See *Torah Sheleimah* 45 note 72, and *comm.* to *v.* 27.]

Chizkuni synthesizes both views and

*land of Egypt wagons for your small children and for
your wives; transport your father and come.* 20 *And
do not be concerned with your belongings for the
best of all the land of Egypt shall be yours.' "*
21 *The sons of Israel consented, and Joseph gave*

postulates that *heifers* were to be harnessed to these *wagons* and it was for this reason that Pharaoh had to give his personal permission, for as noted, cows could not be exported from Egypt unless their wombs were removed; however, Pharaoh ordered that these heifers be whole.

[Pharaoh felt that if Jacob saw that wagons were sent for his use, he would have no excuse for delaying or refusing to come. And so, indeed, it happened. The sight of the wagons convinced Jacob to acquiesce [*v.* 27 below).]

וּנְשָׂאתֶם אֶת־אֲבִיכֶם וּבָאתֶם — [*And*] *transport* [lit. *raise; carry*] *your father and come.*

To dwell here permanently (*Malbim*).

The verb נשא literally means *carry*. The implication of the verse is: *Take wagons ... for your small children and for your wives, but carry your father* — on your shoulders [as befits his honor; the wagons are not intended for him] — *and come* (*Daas Zekeinim*).

According to most commentators, however, it was clear that the wagons were intended in honor of Jacob (*Abarbanel; Akeidah*). [However, the Midrash maintains that the brothers *did* carry their father. See further 46:5.]

20. וְעֵינְכֶם אַל־תָּחֹס עַל־כְּלֵיכֶם — *And do not be concerned with your belongings* [lit. *and your eye be not compassionate upon your utensils*].

I.e., do not be concerned about the belongings that you will have to leave behind in the land of Canaan, since you will be able to transport only part of your movable property (*Ralbag*) ...

Joseph knew that Jacob was very particular about his possessions, for as the Sages note in 32:25, Jacob had been concerned in a time of danger even for some earthenware jugs that he had left behind. He therefore cautioned that Jacob not let concern over his belongings delay his descent to Egypt (*Daas Zekeinim*).

When people move far away they usually beging selling their household goods half a year in advance in order to receive a good price. I am advising you, however, not to procrastinate in Canaan awaiting buyers for your property. You do not have to do this, *since the best of the land of Egypt shall be yours* (*Me'am Loez*).

— *Do not delay because of your belongings*; if you delay, many of your cattle [*your belongings*] will die of famine (*Sforno*).

כִּי טוּב כָּל־אֶרֶץ מִצְרַיִם לָכֶם הוּא — *For the best of all the land of Egypt shall be yours.* [See on *v.* 18].

[It has been noted that Jacob and his family came to Egypt at the express invitation of the king. There was even a promise of good treatment to the immigrants as guests of the State, which one of their family had saved. This good treatment was not to last, however. The Providential Plan would later require a different course of events.]

21. וַיַּעֲשׂוּ־כֵן בְּנֵי יִשְׂרָאֵל — *The sons of Israel consented* [lit. *did so*; comp. this meaning in 29:28 and 42:21].

They agreed to return with their

וַיִּתֵּן לָהֶם יוֹסֵף עֲגָלוֹת עַל־פִּי פַרְעֹה
כב וַיִּתֵּן לָהֶם צֵדָה לַדָּרֶךְ׃ לְכֻלָּם נָתַן לָאִישׁ
חֲלִפוֹת שְׂמָלֹת וּלְבִנְיָמִן נָתַן שְׁלֹשׁ מֵאוֹת
כג כֶּסֶף וְחָמֵשׁ חֲלִפֹת שְׂמָלֹת׃ וּלְאָבִיו שָׁלַח

father as soon as possible *(Malbim)*.

Or: *And they did so*, i.e., they loaded their animals as they were instructed *(Radak)*.

וַיִּתֵּן לָהֶם יוֹסֵף עֲגָלוֹת עַל־פִּי פַרְעֹה — *And he* [Joseph] *gave them wagons by Pharaoh's word* [lit. *mouth*].

This is emphasized because, as noted several times above, without Pharaoh's permission no wagons could be exported from Egypt *(Or HaChaim)*.

וַיִּתֵּן לָהֶם צֵדָה לַדָּרֶךְ — [*And*] *he also gave them provisions for the journey*.

Apparently in addition to the grain which they were to load onto their beasts *(Akeidah)*.

22. לְכֻלָּם נָתַן לָאִישׁ חֲלִפוֹת שְׂמָלֹת — *To each of them he gave changes of clothing*. [The translation follows *Radak*. The Hebrew literally reads: *To all of them he gave to the man changes of clothing*.]

I.e., two sets of clothing — *two* being the minimum of the plural term *(Ibn Ezra)*. He gave them very elegant garments, the intention being that everyone should realize that they were distinguished people, and brothers of the viceroy *(R' Avraham b. HaRambam)*.

Since they had rent their garments in grief when they were accused of having stolen Joseph's goblet [44:13], Joseph now gave them *changes of garments (Riva* citing *R' Tam)*.

According to *HaKsav V'HaKabalah* the term חֲלִפוֹת refers to braided or finely woven garments which were an Egyptian specialty. Since they were very expensive only the nobility wore them. See the term מַחְלְפוֹת in *Judges* 16:19; cf. also the textile skills of the Egyptians, alluded to in *Proverbs* 7:16; *Isaiah* 19:9.

וּלְבִנְיָמִן נָתַן שְׁלֹשׁ מֵאוֹת כֶּסֶף וְחָמֵשׁ חֲלִפֹת שְׂמָלֹת — *But to Benjamin he gave three hundred* [pieces of] *silver and five changes of clothing*.

The Sages in the *Talmud* [*Megillah* 16b] ask: How could Joseph have fallen into the same snare that caused his father so much grief, by giving Benjamin such preferential treatment that his brothers would be jealous? It was just this kind of jealousy over 'two ounces of fine wool' [alluding to the fine woolen garment Jacob had given to Joseph] that provoked his brothers to sell him, thereby triggering the chain of events that culminated in the family's descent into Egypt and the Egyptian Exile.

The *Gemara* answers that Joseph's motive was prophetically inspired. Joseph intimated thereby that one of Benjamin's descendants, Mordechai, would one day go forth from the royal palace attired *in five* kingly garments [see *Esther* 8:15].[1]

Maharsha notes that the *Gemara*

1. The *Vilna Gaon* in *Sh'nos Eliyahu* poses the obvious question: since the brothers did not know that the gift of clothing was a prophetic allusion to Mordechai, how did this minimize the envy of his brothers? He suggests that each of the garments given Benjamin was worth only a fifth of those given the other brothers; therefore, his five were equal to each of theirs in

*them wagons by Pharaoh's word. He also gave them
provisions for the journey.* [22] *To each of them he
gave changes of clothing; but to Benjamin he gave
three hundred pieces of silver and five changes of
clothing.* [23] *And to his father he sent the following:*

focuses this interpretation specifically on the *garments,* but not on Joseph's substantial gifts of money to Benjamin. Since garments are worn publicly, every time Benjamin wore them it would be an implied rebuke to the brothers, as if to say that Joseph loved Benjamin but hated the brothers who sold him. But they had no objection to a gift of money, because Joseph was entitled to show special affection to his only maternal brother in a *private* manner.[1]

23. וּלְאָבִיו שָׁלַח כְּזֹאת – *And to his father he sent the following.*

[The Hebrew literally reads: *And to his father he sent like this.* The word כְּזֹאת, *like this,* appears on the surface to be somewhat superfluous since the passage could have read: *And to his father he sent ten he-donkeys* etc. without the word כְּזֹאת.]

Rashi suggests that the implication of the passage is elliptic: 'And to his father he sent *according to this amount'* [כְּזֹאת=כְּחֶשְׁבּוֹן הַזֶּה].

Ramban disagrees that the feminine form זאת could allude to the masculine noun חֶשְׁבּוֹן *amount;* had that been the allusion, the masculine form כָּזֶה would have been used. [*Mizrachi* defends *Rashi* by stating that *Rashi* was concerned only with the phrase's *general* implication. *Rashi's* point is that Joseph's gift to Jacob was independent of his above-mentioned gifts to the brothers. Thus the word כְּזֹאת is under-

value and gave no cause for envy since this made it apparent that Joseph's gift was symbolic [see also *Eitz Yosef; Iyun Yaakov*].

Torah Temimah finds homiletical Scriptural support for this thesis in the verse. In the case of the brothers the word חֲלִפוֹת [changes] is spelled 'fully,' while in the case of Benjamin it is spelled 'defectively' — חֲלִפֹת — thus alluding to the 'inferior' worth of each of Benjamin's garments.

Regarding pieces of silver, however, *Torah Temimah* cites *R' Bachya* that the three hundred silver pieces Joseph gave Benjamin were equal to the sum that the brothers were liable to for having sold him. That is, the average value of a slave is deemed to be thirty shekels [see *Exodus* 21:32], and the Talmud [*Gittin* 449] rules that one who sells his slave to a heathen [thereby removing him from performance of *mitzvos*] can be penalized and forced to redeem him for as much as ten times his value, that is, ten times thirty shekels = 300 pieces of silver.

Torah Temimah elaborates: By law each of the brothers should have given Joseph 300 pieces of silver. Joseph however did not take it from them, and instead gave Benjamin — who was not present at the sale and was not obligated for this amount — a like sum.

Thus it emerges that by forfeiting the penalty from each of the ten brothers, it is as if he gave them *each* 300 pieces of silver; therefore, they were not envious when Benjamin received that sum, since it equalized the compensation granted all of them. [Cf. *Chizkuni,* and *Chidah* in *Nachal Kedumim.*]

As for additional reasons for the choice of the number five, *R' Munk* writes, the *Midrashim* explain it in the way *Rashi* quoted on 43:34 explained the five portions Joseph had set in front of Benjamin: "Benjamin was given his own portion, equal to that of his brothers, but in addition, he was given portions by Joseph, Asenath, Manasseh and Ephraim" *(Midrash HaChefetz).* The *Midrash Sechel Tov* notes that five was Joseph's favorite number: *Let the country be divided into five parts* (41:34): *You will give one fifth to Pharaoh* (47:24). *R' Bachya* (on 46:4) explains at length Joseph's preference for the number five and relates it to the letter ה (with a numerical value of five), which is the sign of the Divine Name.

כְּזֹאת עֲשָׂרָה חֲמֹרִים נֹשְׂאִים מִטּוּב
מִצְרָיִם וְעֶשֶׂר אֲתֹנֹת נֹשְׂאֹת בָּר וָלֶחֶם
וּמָזוֹן לְאָבִיו לַדָּרֶךְ׃ כד וַיְשַׁלַּח אֶת־אֶחָיו
וַיֵּלֵכוּ וַיֹּאמֶר אֲלֵהֶם אַל־תִּרְגְּזוּ בַּדָּרֶךְ׃

stood in the sense of 'as follows:'; *Rashi* used the term חֶשְׁבּוֹן only to illustrate his explanation.]

Ramban suggests that the elliptic meaning is: *And to his father he sent according to this gift* [כְּזֹאת הַמִּנְחָה], i.e., *he sent the following gift: ten he-donkeys,* etc., the word כְּזֹאת being understood as if it read זֹאת *this,* the כ being superfluous, as in the phrase כַּדְּבָרִים הָאֵלֶּה [24:28; *Daniel* 10:15; see *Ramban* to 39:17-19].

Ramban continues that the term כְּזֹאת may mean 'the same thing,' implying that just as Joseph gave each of his brothers a generous gift of provisions for the way, he sent the same gift to his father. Then the verse lists the *additional gifts* he sent Jacob.

According to *Maharshal, Rashi's* intent in his comment כְּחֶשְׁבּוֹן הַזֶּה, 'according to this amount,' is that the expression כְּזֹאת, *like this,* means *the equivalent of.* That is, Joseph loaded the wagons with the *equivalent* of the loads of ten he- and she-donkeys, not the animals themselves, for we do not find these animals mentioned later, only the wagons.

According to *Ibn Ezra:* He sent *like this* — i.e., the finest garments obtainable in Egypt, similar to the clothing he gave his brothers.

Sforno likewise interprets: And to his father he sent 'like this,' i.e. a gift similar to the aforementioned gift given Benjamin. In *addition* to this he also sent *ten he-donkeys ... and ten she-donkeys.* Thus, our passage would have the same meaning as if it read: And to his father he sent gifts similar to those he gave the brothers, [and he also sent him] ten he-donkeys ... and ten she-donkeys ... *Abarbanel* interprets similarly. [Although one would therefore expect the phrase *ten he-donkeys* to be preceded by the conjunction ו, *and,* this presents no problem, for] it is usual for a conjunction to occur at the *end* of a group of clauses, as for example יִשָּׂשכָר זְבוּלֻן וּבִנְיָמִן, Issachar, Zevulun *and* Benjamin [*Exodus* 1:2].

עֲשָׂרָה חֲמֹרִים נֹשְׂאִים מִטּוּב מִצְרָיִם — *Ten he-donkeys laden with the best of Egypt.*

According to the Talmud [*Megillah* 16b] Joseph sent old wine, which pleases the aged [as it warms their blood and stimulates circulation *(Maharsha)*]. The *Midrash* mentions that he sent him split peas [which were unique to Egypt, and as implied in *Yerushalmi Yoma* I:39a were also supposed to exercise a soothing effect on people (Joseph's intention being to soothe his aged father from the shock he would experience at learning that Joseph was still alive)] *(Rashi).*

Joseph chose the number *ten* because it was known that Jacob had once made a vow to dedicate to God a tenth of whatever came into his possession [28:22] and Joseph therefore wanted to simplify the calculations: All Jacob need do is dedicate one of the ten *(Rosh).*

וְעֶשֶׂר אֲתֹנֹת נֹשְׂאֹת בָּר וָלֶחֶם וּמָזוֹן לְאָבִיו לַדָּרֶךְ — *And ten she-donkeys laden with grain,* [*and*] *bread, and food for his father for the journey.*

The Torah mentions that he sent both males and females as was the custom. Jacob had done the same in his gift to Esau [32:16] *(Ramban).*

בָּר refers to the five species of grain *(Onkelos; R' Bachya; Ibn Ezra).* In 41:35 the commentators explain that it is derived from ברר,

ten he-donkeys laden with the best of Egypt and ten
she-donkeys laden with grain, bread, and food for his
father for the journey. 24 *And he sent off his*
brothers, and they went. He said to them, "Do not
become agitated on the way."

sift, and refers to winnowed and sifted fine grain. According to *Radak,* however, it refers to fodder, while לֶחֶם — which *Rashi* and most commentators interpret literally as *bread* — refers, to sifted grain fit for humans.

[When it occurs by itself, the term מָזוֹן (lit. *nourishment)* refers specifically to the five species of grain (wheat, barley, rye, oats and spelt), which both nourish and sustain *(Rashi* to *Eruvin* 30a s.v. בְּאוֹמֵר; comp. *Gemara* there and *Torah Temimah).*] In our verse [since בָּר, *grain* (following *Onkelos)* and לֶחֶם, *bread* have already been mentioned], *Rashi* explains the term to refer to לִפְתָּן, foods that are eaten together with bread. *Ralbag* interprets similarly.

According to *Radak,* מָזוֹן refers to any human food, such as dates and other delicacies, besides wheat. Similarly, *Ibn Ezra* interprets that מָזוֹן in our verse refers to peas, white beans, lentils, millet, spelt, figs, raisins and dates. Except for grain and barley [which have already been mentioned] these are the only foods referred to as מָזוֹן [nutrients].

24. וַיְשַׁלַּח אֶת־אֶחָיו וַיֵּלֵכוּ — *And he sent off his brothers, and they went.*

The term וַיְשַׁלַּח, *sent off,* denotes that he *escorted* them a short distance, as is the etiquette of a host to his departing guests *(Akeidah; Rashbam;* comp. this meaning of שלח in 12:20; 18:16; 24:59; 37:14).

According to *Sefer HaYashar,* Joseph accompanied them all the way to the Egyptian border to see them off.

Sforno interprets: He dismissed them and granted them leave. Compare 32:27: *Let me go* [שַׁלְּחֵנִי] *for dawn has broken;* 24:56: *Send me* [שַׁלְּחוּנִי] *and I will go to my master.*

The consensus of commentators maintain that all eleven brothers — including Benjamin — returned to Jacob, and Judah thereby fulfilled his vow to bring back Benjamin — although as noted in the footnote to 43:9 [p. 1863] his vow was never *formally* abrogated, and technically remained in force.

There are opinions in the Midrash, however [see for example *Pesikta Zutresa*], that Benjamin stayed behind with Joseph. That is the reason Joseph sent *ten* laden animals — one with each of the ten brothers. Following this view, had all the brothers returned, Joseph would presumably have sent *eleven* animals. [Cf. *Rosh,* however.]

According to those who maintain that Benjamin *did* return, Joseph did not want to burden him with the care of pack animals.

Or HaChaim defends the view that Joseph sent Benjamin back by noting how in *v.* 12, in urging them to report to Jacob on his great status in Egypt, Joseph said, *'Behold, your eyes see as well as the eyes of my brother Benjamin',* thus relying on Benjamin's testimony to convince Jacob.

וַיֹּאמֶר אֲלֵהֶם אַל־תִּרְגְּזוּ בַּדָּרֶךְ — *He said to them, "Do not become agitated on the way."*

Rashi interprets the word רגז as *quarrel; anger; agitation,* and offers three interpretations of our passage,

כה וַיַּעֲלוּ מִמִּצְרָיִם וַיָּבֹאוּ אֶרֶץ כְּנַעַן אֶל־
כו יַעֲקֹב אֲבִיהֶם: וַיַּגִּדוּ לוֹ לֵאמֹר עוֹד יוֹסֵף

the first two being based on *Taanis* 10b and the last being his interpretation of the simple meaning of the passage:

a) Do not become involved in halachic discussion [matter] lest the road become 'angry' at you [a figurative expression, meaning: lest you become so engrossed that you lose your way].[1]

[According to this interpretation the phrase would be rendered homiletically: *Do not be angered by the road,* i.e., do not become so 'agitated' in intense halachic dispute that the road will 'anger' you, in the sense that you will lose your way, making the trip take longer than necessary; see *Mizrachi* and commentators].

Rashi's comment, as noted, is based on the Talmudic text in *Taanis* 10b. The implication, following *all* commentators, is certainly not that Joseph was cautioning them against discussing Torah study along the way, since it is clear from *Deut.* 6:7 [וְדִבַּרְתָּ בָּם ... וּבְלֶכְתְּךָ בַדֶּרֶךְ] that it is a *mitzvah* to discuss Torah at all times — even on the road, and the *Gemara* there severely condemns scholars who do not discuss Torah while they travel. [Comp. also the Mishnah in *Avos* 3:9 which indicates that one must not interrupt his studies on a journey]. Rather, as is evident from the phraseology in the Talmud, *Rashi* explains that Joseph was cautioning them not to engage in deep, difficult concepts which can provoke disagreement and cause them to lose their way but should rather focus on simple subjects, which would not provoke dissension.

This might be the implication of *Midrash Rabbah's* parallel interpretation of our passage which reads differently: 'Do not *refrain* from words of Torah.' The intent, as explained by the commentators, is that Joseph was cautioning them not to neglect Torah study — even though they were rushing to Canaan at his request — since they would be endangering themselves by such neglect, as is evident from the Talmudic citations above. At the same time, however, he warned them against intensive study, which leads to debate and could cause them to lose their way entirely. [See *Maharsha* to *Gemara; Matnas Kehunah* and *Maharzu* to Midrash, and *Divrei David*].

b) Do not take long strides [i.e., although you are in a great haste to return with this news to Father, it is unhealthy to rush too much. As the Sages proclaimed, long strides decrease a man's eyesight by one five-hundredth part]. Moreover, enter the town where you will lodge

1. **The Halachic dilemma.**

What inspired, according to the Talmudic interpretation cited by *Rashi,* Joseph's worry at this juncture in particular that his brothers might become so involved in Halachic dispute as to affect their very safety during the journey? If such a problem was to be expected, why didn't Jacob caution them about such a thing when they left Canaan?

Joseph apparently realized that he had presented them with a profound Halachic dilemma: Do they have a right to abandon *Eretz Yisrael* because of the famine? On one hand, they could have reasoned [as the Halachah is cited in *Bava Basra* 91a] that it is permissible to leave *Eretz Yisrael* during a famine only when produce is unobtainable, but Jacob's family could make arrangements to obtain provisions from Joseph. On the other hand, they might be required to remain only if food is obtainable within *Eretz Yisrael,* but if produce is available only from abroad, they are permitted to leave.

Moreover, the very notion of leaving *Eretz Yisrael* confronted them with a quandary of the most serious dimensions. As *Ramban* [2:10] observes, Abraham sinned by leaving *Eretz Yisrael* in the face of famine; he should have trusted that God would provide for him. In punishment for this act, according to *Ramban,* since Abraham sinned by going to Egypt, the Egyptian Exile was decreed upon his descendants. Possibly, it was for this very reason that Jacob did not descend to Egypt until expressly directed by God to do so. This was the sort of halachic discussion that could have caused intense contention among the brothers and against which Joseph cautioned them *(Yalkut Yehudah).*

[25] *They went up from Egypt and came to the land of Canaan to Jacob their father.* [26] *And they told him,*

overnight while the sun is still shining [i.e., despite your haste, do not travel late into the night, since this would expose you to robbers].

According to the latter, which follows the Talmud and Midrash, the passage is understood in the following sense: *Do not become agitated on account of the journey.* That is, do not regard the journey as a cause of annoyance, so that, in order to reach our father as soon as possible with the good news, you proceed too quickly or travel into the night before resting. [There is no need to hurry; everything has its destined moment from Heaven, and is not to be delayed or hurried *(R' Menachem Mendel of Kotzk).*]

Moreover, Joseph's instruction that they enter the town before sunset follows the dictum of R' Yehudah citing Rav: A man should always set out on a journey in daylight and enter a town while it is still light [see *comm.* to 44:3].

Gur Aryeh emphasizes that these Midrashic interpretations are inspired by the use of the term רגז *anger, agitation,* instead of the term ריב, *strife,* which would be used if only explanation "c" were intended. The former term intimates many kinds of agitations — including those provoked by intellectual disagreement or unpleasant travel conditions, and therefore *Rashi* cites these Talmudic-Midrashic interpretations not as homiletical, but as reflecting also the simple meaning *(p'shat)* of the passage.

c) According to the 'plain' sense of the passage, however, Joseph feared that the brothers would quarrel with each other about responsibilities for his sale and engage in mutual recrimination. One would accuse the other saying, 'It was because of *you* that he was sold'; and the other would respond, 'It was *you* who made slanderous statements about him and caused us to hate him!' He therefore cautioned them against quarreling on the way. [*Ibn Ezra* and most commentators follow this latter interpretation.]

Ramban interprets רגז to mean *fear,* as in the expression לֵב רַגָּז, *a trembling heart* [*Deut.* 28:65]; וְרָגְזוּ [*Habakkuk* 3:16]; בְּרָגְזָה [*Ezekiel* 12:18]. He renders: *Do not fear on the road.* Joseph meant to reassure them that they could travel without fear even though they were heavily laden with 'grain, bread and food' and the best of Egypt. In times of famine they could be expected to fear attack by robbers on their way to Canaan and certainly on their return to Egypt with all their possessions. As a result they might delay their move. Joseph assured them that such fears are unfounded because they would be traveling under his aegis. Since he was the ruler of Egypt, and the entire region was dependent on him and in awe of him, the brothers could expect to travel and arrive in peace. [*Rashbam* and *Daas Zekeinim* interpret similarly.]

25. The brothers tell Jacob that Joseph is alive.

וַיַּעֲלוּ מִמִּצְרָיִם — *They went up from Egypt.*

Because *Eretz Yisrael* is more elevated than other countries, it says *They 'went up' from Egypt.*

Many perceive the implication to refer to the higher *spiritual* degree of *Eretz Yisrael.* See *Zohar* cited in footnote to 13:1.

וַיָּבֹאוּ אֶרֶץ כְּנַעַן אֶל־יַעֲקֹב אֲבִיהֶם — *And* [*they*] *came to the land of Canaan, to Jacob their father.*

The land of Canaan is mentioned

חַ֑י וְכִֽי־ה֖וּא מֹשֵׁ֣ל בְּכָל־אֶ֣רֶץ מִצְרָ֑יִם וַיָּ֣פָג
כז לִבּ֔וֹ כִּ֥י לֹא־הֶאֱמִ֖ין לָהֶֽם׃ וַיְדַבְּר֣וּ אֵלָ֗יו
אֵ֣ת כָּל־דִּבְרֵ֤י יוֹסֵף֙ אֲשֶׁ֣ר דִּבֶּ֣ר אֲלֵהֶ֔ם

first. Since they knew they would soon be separated from the Holy Land, they yearned greatly for it. Under these circumstances, the *land of Canaan* was their primary destination, and Jacob was in a sense secondary. Compare above 42:29 where the reverse was the case *(Haamek Davar).*

26. וַיַּגִּדוּ לוֹ לֵאמֹר — *And they told him, saying.*

The word וַיַּגִּדוּ is written defectively (without the letter י). This implies a 'defect' in the telling: the brothers did not tell him themselves but had the wonderful news announced by someone else: לֵאמֹר, in the sense of *to have it said.* They were apprehensive that suddenly announcing so extraordinary a surprise would affect the health of their aged father *(Midrash; Zohar).*[1]

עוֹד יוֹסֵף חַי — *"Joseph is still alive."*

Possibly, to break the news to Jacob gently and gradually, the brothers [or their emissary] first said that Simeon and Benjamin returned safely, and then told him that Joseph was alive and well. In this case עוֹד [*still*] would have its other meaning of *moreover,* as if they said, ' ... *moreover* [i.e. not only are Simeon and Benjamin safe, but] Joseph is alive!' *(Or HaChaim).*

וְכִי הוּא מֹשֵׁל בְּכָל־אֶרֶץ מִצְרָיִם — *Also that he was ruler over all the land of Egypt.*

— So Jacob should not have qualms about going to him *(Ramban).*

Following the implication of *Rashi,* this is not part of the direct quote 'Joseph is still alive.' The verse now tells us what else they said to Jacob.

וַיָּפָג לִבּוֹ כִּי לֹא־הֶאֱמִין לָהֶם — *But* [lit. *and*] *his heart rejected* [*it*] *for he could not believe them.*

This is the fate of a liar: He is disbelieved even when he tells the truth! Jacob originally believed them when they came and showed him Joseph's blood-stained tunic, suggesting thereby that a wild beast had devoured him; but now he did not believe them even though they were telling the truth *(Avos d'Rabbi Nosson; Midrash).*

According to the above, *for he did not believe them* is not limited to this instance. Rather, the implication of the passage is that he had not believed them for a long time.

1. **Serach daughter of Asher breaks the news to Jacob.**

Sefer HaYashar relates that as the brothers were nearing home and discussing the problem, they saw Serach, the daughter of Asher. Full of spiritual charm, she played the harp beautifully. They greeted her and asked her to go and play for their father Jacob and to sing the words that they would tell her. So she went and sat before her grandfather Jacob and sang the following refrain to beautiful music accompanied by the soothing melody of her harp: עוֹד יוֹסֵף חַי, 'Joseph, my uncle, is still alive. He rules the whole of Egypt for he is not dead.'

As she repeated this refrain over and over again, Jacob began to listen to it and became deeply moved. He felt an intense joy and little by little his spirits began to revive. Since being separated from Joseph he had lived in sadness, and prophetic inspiration had departed from him. But with Serach's touching words, his heart overflowed with immense happiness and he asked her to sing her song again.

'You have truly comforted me, dear Serach,' Jacob told her. 'As your reward, I pray that

45
27

saying, "Joseph is still alive," also that he was ruler
over all the land of Egypt. But his heart rejected it for
he could not believe them. 27 *However, when they*
related to him all the words that Joseph had spoken

They had lost their credibility with him and therefore his heart rejected them now, too *(Maharzu).*

The translation of **וַיָּפָג** as *rejected* follows *Rashi* who interprets the phrase to mean: his heart 'changed' and he ceased to believe, i.e., he took no notice of their words. *Rashi* cites several Biblical and Talmudic passages to support this interpretation *(Beitzah* 14a; *Lamentations* 3:49; *Targum* to *Jeremiah* 48:11). [*Onkelos; Rashbam; Akeidas Yitzchak* and *Abarbanel* interpret similarly.]

Ramban cites these and other passages *(Lamentations* 2:18; *Habakuk* 1:4), but he maintains that the meaning [even in those passages] is *ceased,* the implication here being that Jacob's heart momentarily stopped beating.

In *Ramban's* words, ' ... The books of medicine mention that old or feeble people cannot withstand the shock of sudden joy, for many of them faint when joy comes to them suddenly ... their body temperature lowers and they fall in a swoon ... Jacob fainted and lay in this state much of the day because he did not believe them. They eventually revived him by shouting in his ear what Joseph had said to accustom him to the joy and they brought the wagons before him, until he revived and accepted the news calmly ...' [*Rambam* in *comm.* to *Mishnah Yoma* 1:7 similarly interprets וְהָפֵג to mean *dispel coolness*].

Akeidas Yitzchak and *Abarbanel* disagree with *Ramban's* interpretation on several counts; see *Kesef Mezukak* cited by *R' Chavel,* and *Shaarei Aharon.*

Other interpretations include:

Targum Yonasan: His heart *was divided,* because he did not believe them;

Radak: His heart became *weakened* at the memory of his son Joseph;

When they mentioned his beloved son Joseph over whom he agonized all these years, his yearning and grief resurfaced and his heart *turned within him* as his grief was renewed, draining him of all his strength *(Akeidas Yitzchak);*

Chizkuni: His heart *became numb* and he did not react because he did not believe them until he saw the wagons [cf. *Ibn Ezra*].

27. וַיְדַבְּרוּ אֵלָיו אֵת כָּל־דִּבְרֵי יוֹסֵף אֲשֶׁר דִּבֶּר אֲלֵהֶם — *However, when* [lit. *and;* the translation *however when* is suggested by the syntax and the compound conversive verbs וַיְדַבְּרוּ and וַיַּרְא] *they related* [lit. *spoke*] *to him all the words that Joseph had spoken to them* [lit. *all Joseph's words that he had spoken to them*].

By *'all* the words' the intent is

death never conquer you.' And this blessing came true. Serach never knew death. She was still alive in King David's time. She was one of the righteous individuals who entered alive into Paradise [*Pirkei d'Rabbi Eliezer; Targum Yonasan* on 47:17; *Rashi* on *II Samuel* 20:19; *R' Munk*]. While Jacob was speaking with her, the brothers entered the room. They stood before him in their magnificent garments and exclaimed: 'There is wonderful news! Our brother Joseph is still alive and he is governor over the land of Egypt!' Even though Jacob had been prepared emotionally for the news, the news was so unexpected that Jacob still could not believe it.

According to other Midrashic sources, see *comm.* to 49:21, the brothers had dispatched the fleet-footed Naftali to tell their aged father the good news. [However, as R' Kaplan points out in his translation of *Me'am Loez,* Naftali apparently did not go in to see Jacob until his brothers arrived and transmitted the message through Serach.]

[This was the *de-facto* annulment by the brothers of their *cherem* (ban) against revealing Joseph's whereabouts to their father Jacob. See footnote to 37:28.]

that they repeated Joseph's verbatim message in verses 9-11, *So said your son Joseph: God has made me master of all Egypt. Come down to me please; do not delay ... so you become impoverished, you, your household and all that is yours.* However, they did *not* repeat that it was they who sold him *(R' Bachya)* [see footnote].[1]

They also reported on their meeting with Joseph: their weeping and how he identified himself beyond doubt *(Ibn Caspi; Rashbam).*

Following *Ramban:* They kept shouting Joseph's message to accustom him to its happy import ... until he could accept it with a tranquil heart ...

⧫§ The sign of the Eglah Arufah

Moreover, to convince their disbelieving father that it was Joseph who sent these messages, they presented further evidence, repeating that Joseph had given them a special directive to bring wagons, since Joseph had given them a sign which would provide Jacob with certain proof of his identity: When Joseph had left Jacob, they had been studying the topic of *eglah arufah* [the heifer whose neck was broken in expiation of an unsolved murder (see *Deut.* 21:1-9 and *Tanchuma Yashan/Daas Zekeinim* cited below)]. Therefore it is written [further in this verse], *And he saw the wagons that Joseph had sent,* and it does not say, ...that *Pharaoh* had sent [see *comm.* below] *(Rashi).*

This exposition is based on the fact that the Hebrew word for wagon, עֲגָלָה, is similar to the word עֶגְלָה meaning *heifer* (both words are spelled the same in Hebrew). Joseph's sign was that the brothers were to emphasize that he had sent *agalos,* wagons, the mention of which would evoke in Jacob the memory of *'eglah arufah'* — the topic he was studying with Joseph when they last saw each other — a fact only Joseph could have known.

The above is the view of the commentators on *Rashi.* According to the Midrash, however, Joseph told the brothers specifically to verbally remind Jacob that they had been learning the halachah of *eglah arufah,* and the wagons would constitute a symbolic 'proof' of this. In the words of the Midrash: Joseph said, "If Father believes you, fine; but if not, tell him in my name: 'When I left you, was I not engaged in studying with you the chapter of *eglah arufah?'* " Therefore it says, *and he saw the wagons that Joseph had sent* ... " [i.e., he perceived the significance of the wagons that Joseph had sent].

1. **Did the brothers ever tell Jacob that they had sold Joseph?**

In relating Joseph's messages of verses 9-13, the brothers make no reference to having sold him as a slave or to the sequence of events that brought him to Egypt. *Ramban* maintains that Jacob was never told that the brothers had sold Joseph. Instead, he thought that Joseph had lost his way in the countryside and was abducted by strangers who sold him into Egypt. The brothers scrupulously kept their crime secret, afraid that if Jacob became aware of it he would angrily curse them as he did Reuben, Simeon and Levi [see further 49:3-7]. Joseph, too, maintained his high ethical standard by remaining silent to spare his father and brothers grief.

It would appear from several inferences in *Rashi,* however, following the Talmud and Midrash, that Jacob was aware of the truth and suspected some of the brothers. See *Rashi* to 49:9 and 50:16.

There is also a view that Joseph did not communicate privately with his father all 17 of his father's last years in Egypt lest his father discover how he got to Egypt. [See comm. to 48:1-2.]

Tanchuma Yashan and *Daas Zekeinim* record that when Jacob sent Joseph to his brothers [37:15], Jacob escorted him part of the way. Joseph told Jacob to return home, but he refused, saying, "My son, it is important to accompany someone who is taking leave, as an entire section in the Torah is devoted to it [*Deut.* 21:1-9]. For, if a slain man is found in the open country and the murderer is unknown, the law requires the elders of the nearest town to slay a young heifer in an uncultivated valley by breaking its neck. Then they are to testify that they neither shed the victim's blood nor saw it shed, and pray for forgiveness. But could it ever occur to anyone to suspect the elders of murder? No! By this avowal the elders of the town declare, 'He did not come to us hungry and we let him go unfed ... he did not come to us friendless and we let him go unescorted.' For, had they indeed not escorted him, Scripture would have equated it with shedding blood." Jacob therefore insisted on escorting Joseph and took this opportunity to teach him the lesson of *eglah arufah*, the memory of which Joseph recalled by sending the *agalos*.

[The commentators delve extensively into the connection Jacob was supposed to make between the *wagons* he saw and the assonance of the Hebrew words *agalos* and *eglos*. Opinions vary widely. At one extreme, Joseph sent *only* wagons; at the other, the word in our narrative does not mean *wagons* but actual *heifers*, or that the wagons were drawn by *heifers* and that the heifers constituted the appropriate sign. For further research in this topic, see *Gur Aryeh; Yafeh Toar; Rosh; Minchas Yitzchak; Hadar Zekeinim;* see also note to *Torah Sheleimah* §91; and *Rashbam* and *Chizkuni* cited above *v.* 19 s.v. קְחוּ לָכֶם.]

[My brother-in-law, R' Yaakov Kiffel, reports hearing that Jacob's teaching about *eglah arufah* at that very juncture was prophetic, although Jacob did not realize it at the time. The law of *eglah arufah* presupposes a moral responsibility that elders and leaders have for each of their subjects. When a foul deed is perpetrated it is symbolic of a laxity on the part of the elders of the closest town, and the leaders must therefore symbolically disavow the community's guilt. This was the lesson that the future viceroy of Egypt was taught during his last moments with his father. However, cf. the account recorded in the *Zohar*.]

וַיַּרְא אֶת־הָעֲגָלוֹת אֲשֶׁר־שָׁלַח יוֹסֵף לָשֵׂאת אֹתוֹ — ***And he saw the wagons that Joseph had sent to transport him.***

Following the Midrashic interpretation cited by *Rashi:* he perceived the symbolism of the *wagons* [*agalos*] as alluding to the *eglah arufah*. The word וַיַּרְא, *saw*, denoting [prophetic] perception occurs also above in 42:1: "Jacob *perceived* that there was 'provision' in Egypt" [see *comm.* there] (*Mizrachi; Tzeidah laDerech*).

It was then, as the verse proceeds to tell us, that Jacob believed them and his soul was revived.

In a non-Midrashic sense, *Tur* explains that Jacob believed them only after seeing the wagons because how else could they possibly have come back with wagons loaded with Egypt's best were it not by special royal command? For, as *Akeidas Yitzchak* emphasizes, it was well-known that wagons could not be exported from Egypt without royal authority. Thus, the wagons were absolute proof that they must have been telling the truth — especially since, as the Sages record, they transmitted certain 'signs' from Joseph.

Obvious questions arise: Was it not *Pharaoh* who ordered the wagons to be sent [*v.* 21]? Why does this verse attribute the wagons to Joseph?

According to the *Zohar*, Pharaoh gave the command only in response to

לָשֵׂאת אֹתוֹ וַתְּחִי רוּחַ יַעֲקֹב אֲבִיהֶם׃
כח °וַיֹּאמֶר יִשְׂרָאֵל רַב עוֹד־יוֹסֵף בְּנִי חָי

°חמישי

Joseph's request. [Therefore, our verse attributes the act to Joseph to allude to his special purpose in sending these wagons. Later, in 46:5, *Pharaoh* is mentioned once again as the 'sender' since it was exclusively by his authority that the wagons could be exported from Egypt, and the variance of 'senders' in the two passages draw our attention to this exposition *(Yafeh Toar).*]

According to the Midrash, however, the reason Joseph is mentioned here as the sender is that these particular wagons were not the same ones Pharaoh had sent. As recorded in the Midrash, Pharaoh's wagons had an idol engraved on them — and Judah arose and burnt them. Joseph replaced them and therefore he is mentioned as the sender. [That *Pharaoh* is mentioned later as the sender is, as *Yafeh Toar* notes above, because it was by his royal decree that special permission to export wagons during the famine was obtained; he was the prime 'sender'.]

[*To transport him* is the contextual meaning of the phrase לָשֵׂאת אֹתוֹ (lit. *to lift him up).* It is possible, that in the Midrashic context of these verses, the phrase might imply: Jacob perceived the significance of the wagons Joseph had sent *to lift him up* — i.e. to raise his spirits by the message they conveyed that Joseph was still alive. And so it was, for when Jacob perceived the implication of the gift, *Jacob's spirit was revived.*]

וַתְּחִי רוּחַ יַעֲקֹב אֲבִיהֶם — *Then the spirit of their father Jacob was revived.*

I.e., [he believed the joyous news, and] the Divine, prophetic, spirit which had left him during his grief, rested upon him again in his joy *(Rashi; Onkelos; Midrash).*

See *comm.* to וַיֵּבְךְּ in 37:35. See also *Rambam, Moreh Nevuchim* 2:36, who discusses the Talmudic dictum that prophecy (i.e. the Divine Presence) comes neither during sadness nor gloom *(Shabbos* 30b), and observes that Jacob did not receive any revelation during this period since his mind was occupied with Joseph's loss and it affected his prophetic faculty. [Only after Jacob ceased his mourning and resumed his joy do we see that God communicated with him again (46:2).] Similarly, *Rambam ibid.* adds Moses did not receive any Divine revelation following the evil report of the Spies until the death of the entire generation of the desert *(Taanis* 30b), for he was in a state of depression, totally grieved by the enormity of their sin and the gravity of their punishment.

Ramban agrees with [*Rashi* and] *Onkelos'* interpretation of the passage [that *spirit* refers to the Divine Spirit], He maintains that it reflects even the *literal* meaning, since the verse includes the word רוּחַ, *spirit.* For had the verse referred only to the fact that Jacob's depression was lifted, it would have been sufficient to say, וַיְחִי יַעֲקֹב אֲבִיהֶם, *Jacob their father was revived.* Instead the verse tells us that his [*prophetic*] *spirit,* רוּחַ, was revived.

Rashbam comments that Jacob believed the brothers now because he had always kept faith in the prophetic nature of Joseph's dreams. Then the spirit of their father Jacob was revived, for after hearing Joseph's youthful dreams Jacob 'kept the matter in mind' [37:11], believing that Joseph would eventually become a ruler, and because [such wagons] could not have left Egypt except by a ruler's decree as already explained [37:11; above v. 19].

[In his *comm.* on 37:11, *Rashbam* ex-

45
28

to transport him, then the spirit of their father Jacob was revived.

[28] *And Israel said, "How great! My son Joseph still*

plained that because of his faith in Joseph's dreams, Jacob did not fully assimilate the 'fact' of Joseph's death even though the blood-soaked tunic was powerful circumstantial evidence. This underlying faith in Joseph's survival enabled him to believe the seemingly impossible report that Joseph was alive and had attained greatness.]

According to the *Zohar*, the Divine Presence had departed from Jacob when the brothers made It a party to the oath of secrecy against revealing Joseph's whereabouts [see footnote to 37:28 (p. 1653-4)]. Now that the brothers, in effect, annulled the ban by revealing Joseph's whereabouts themselves, the Divine Presence was no longer 'bound' by their oath [if one may use such an expression], and It again rested on Jacob.

28. וַיֹּאמֶר יִשְׂרָאֵל — And *Israel said.*

During the period that the Divine Presence did not rest upon the Patriarch, he was referred to by his less exalted name, Jacob. But now that the Divine Presence rested upon him again, he is referred to as Israel, his title of spiritual nobility, grandeur, and power [see *comm.* to 32:29 and 35:10*ff*]. *(Zohar).*

[See *comm.* to 46:2 s.v. *Jacob, Jacob.*]

רַב עוֹד יוֹסֵף בְּנִי חָי — *How great! My son Joseph still lives!*[1]

I.e., much joy and pleasure is still in store for me since my son Joseph is still alive! *(Rashi).*

Rashi is apparently referring to Jacob's apprehension [37:35] because he had been given an omen by God that if none of his sons died during his lifetime he may be assured that he would not see *Gehinnom;* and with Joseph thought to be dead, Jacob believed that he forfeited this assurance. Now however that he learned Joseph was alive, Jacob knew that much joy awaited him in the Hereafter. As the *Midrash* comments: I was foolish in losing hope, but now I am again confident that I have a portion רַב טוּבְךָ, *Your abundant goodness* [see *Psalms* 31:20] *(Tzeidah LaDerech).*

Targum Yonasan, interpretively paraphrases Jacob's thought in this way: "Many are the blessings which God has bestowed upon me. He saved me from Esau, Laban, and the Canaanites who were persecuting me. I have had many joys and I hope to experience still others. But I had given up hope of ever setting eyes on Joseph again. Now I want to go and see him before I die."

Rashbam interprets רַב as *enough: Enough! Joseph my son is still alive! —*

1. A unique interpretation is offered in *Hadar Zekeinim.* Esau is described as רַב, *the leader,* in relation to Jacob, his younger brother: וְרַב יַעֲבֹד צָעִיר, *and the leader shall serve the younger* (25:23). Although Jacob had received the Patriarchal blessings and although Rebecca had been given the prophecy that Jacob would be superior to Esau, Jacob could confront his powerful brother with confidence only if Joseph was present as the leading figure among the brothers.

As Scripture describes it, Joseph was like a flame that would consume the straw-like Esau *(Obadiah v.* 18). It was for this reason that Jacob first expressed his readiness to leave the safety of Laban's home only after Joseph was born (see *Rashi* to 30:25). With the disappearance and presumed death of Joseph, therefore, Esau surely gloated and Jacob must have feared for the future. But now Joseph was alive!

Hearing this, Jacob exulted as if he were directly addressing his sworn foe, Esau: רַב, *O elder [brother] — Joseph my son is still alive!* — The 'flame' that will one day consume you still burns bright. Do not rejoice, thinking that it has been extinguished! [See *Overview* to *Vayeishev.*]

א אֱלְכָה וְאֶרְאֶנּוּ בְּטֶרֶם אָמוּת: וַיִּסַּע
יִשְׂרָאֵל וְכָל־אֲשֶׁר־לוֹ וַיָּבֹא בְּאֵרָה שָּׁבַע
ב וַיִּזְבַּח זְבָחִים לֵאלֹהֵי אָבִיו יִצְחָק: וַיֹּאמֶר

My disbelief in the truth of this wonderful news has lasted long enough! I am now truly convinced that indeed my son Joseph is alive! [Another interpretation is preserved in a marginal note in early manuscripts of *Rashbam*: *It is enough that my son Joseph is still alive.* Your news that he is the *ruler of Egypt* is unimportant to me; the fact that he is alive is sufficient, even without his being a ruler. *(Chizkuni* interprets similarly, as do *Malbim* and *Kli Yakar).*]

The *Midrash* perceives חַי, *alive,* to connote *alive in righteousness* [for 'only the righeous are truly "alive" *(Berachos* 18a)] and interprets: רַב, *great is the strength of my son; he experienced so many misfortunes and yet he has retained his righteousness.*

It was only after the Prophetic Spirit again rested on Jacob that he was able to make this pronouncement and entertain no further doubts *(Tiferes Shlomo-Radomsk; Haamek Davar).*

אֵלְכָה וְאֶרְאֶנּוּ בְּטֶרֶם אָמוּת — *I must go and see him before I die.*

I have no intention of *remaining* there; I am going neither to witness his greatness nor to have him support me; my sole purpose is to *see* him. The very connotation of the expression going to *see* someone, implies for but a short visit [cf. on *Exodus* 4:18] *(Sforno; Abarbanel; Malbim; Haamek Davar).*

It is a natural phenomenon that a person wishes to see his beloved and that he feels calmed and contented when he does so *(R' Shmuel b. Chofni).*[1]

Furthermore, by gazing at him, Jacob in his wisdom could ascertain for himself the extent of Joseph's righteousness *(Yalkut Reuveni).* [See *Overview* to *Vayeishev*].

As *Alshich* explains, although Jacob prophetically *sensed* that Joseph had retained his righteousness in the most immoral country of that time, he could not rest until he had seen Joseph's face for himself. The Patriarchs could gaze upon the face of an individual and know — from the extent that he manifested the image of God — if he were righteous or not. Therefore, after meeting Joseph and seeing his face, Jacob could acclaim with certainty [46:30]: *for you are still* חַי, *alive* — you have indeed retained your righteousness! *(Alshich).*

[In another sense, Joseph's beauty and charisma were so profound that Jacob expresses a desire to *see* him. After finally meeting him after twenty-two years, Jacob's first words are (46:30): 'Now I can die; I have already *seen your face* for you are still alive.' That Joseph was an object of people's *gazing* also forms a basic theme in the Jacob's blessing in 49:22: בֵּן פֹּרָת יוֹסֵף, בֵּן פֹּרָת עֲלֵי עָיִן, *Joseph is a charming son, a charming son to the eye* — his charisma was so great that everyone wanted to *look* at him, yet the evil eye had no effect on him. Even in later times, the Talmud (*Zevachim* 118b) notes that the Tabernacle of Shiloh, in Joseph's territory, had the unique characteristic that offerings could be eaten even far away, as long as Shilo could be seen, unlike Jerusalem where the city walls were the

1. *Sefer HaYashar* records that when the inhabitants of Canaan heard that Joseph was still alive they came and rejoiced with Jacob, sharing his joy.

"Jacob made a three-day feast for them, and all the kings of Canaan and nobles of the land ate, drank, and rejoiced in the house of Jacob."

46
1
lives! I must go and see him before I die."

1 *So Israel set out with all that he had and he came
to Beer Sheba. He slaughtered sacrifices to the
God of his father Isaac.*

boundary. This was a reward to Joseph for his behavior with Potiphar's wife when his eye would not enjoy what did not belong to him (see comm. to 49:22).]

XLVI

1. Jacob undertakes the journey to Joseph.

וַיִּסַּע יִשְׂרָאֵל וְכָל־אֲשֶׁר־לוֹ — *So* [lit. *and*] *Israel set out* [lit. *journeyed*] [from Hebron *(R' Shmuel ben Chofni)*] *with all that he had.*

— With his entire household. Everyone wished to accompany him to see Joseph *(Abarbanel).*

[Jacob's sons were all grown men with their own families, so this cohesiveness is to the family's credit. The verse emphasizes that when the aged Patriarch set out for Egypt, every one of his descendants went with him.]

וַיָּבֹא בְּאֵרָה שָּׁבַע — *And he came to Beer Sheba.*

Beer Sheba [28 miles southwest of Hebron] was the southernmost city on the border of *Eretz Yisrael en-route* to Egypt *(Radak; Akeidah).*[1]

1. **The Prominence of Beer Sheba.**

[Beer Sheba was prominent in the lives of all the Patriarchs. As noted in the commentary to 22:19, Abraham resided there for twenty-six years following the destruction of Sodom. There, he made a treaty with Abimelech, gave the city its name (21:29), and located his *eshel* (21:33).

[Beer Sheba was Isaac's birthplace and it was the site of the great feast held to celebrate his weaning. Abraham had returned to his *eshel* in Beer Sheba to offer thanks for the miracle of the *akeidah,* even though Sarah resided in Hebron at the time. It was in Beer Sheba that he heard the news of Sarah's demise (see *Ramban* 23:3).

[When famine ravaged *Eretz Yisrael* (ch. 26), Isaac sought God's permission in Beer Sheba to leave the Land. God commanded him not to leave Holy Land, but to move to Gerar. After some bad relations between Isaac and the Philistines, Isaac returned to Beer Sheba where God appeared to him at night to bless and reassure him. Then Isaac built an altar and invoked HASHEM.

[In Isaac's time, Beer Sheba, in the Gerar Valley, belonged to Philistia, as pointed out in the footnotes on pp., 736 and 1100 (following *Rambam's comm.* to 21:32 and the accepted Rabbinic view). When the land was apportioned among the Tribes, it became part of Judah's territory. As *Sforno* and others write on 26:3, even in Isaac's time Gerar — and certainly Beer Sheba — was considered part of the Land that would be inherited by the children of Israel. The description of *Eretz Yisrael's* borders as extending "from Dan (in the north) to Beer Sheba (in the south)" is almost proverbial and occurs numerous times in Scripture. Thus, Beer Sheba was both in *Eretz Yisrael* and in Philistia. Consequently, by living in Beer Sheba (see 26:33), Isaac satisfied both of God's commands that (a) being an עוֹלָה תְּמִימָה, an 'unblemished offering,' he not reside outside of *Eretz Yisrael (Rashi* 26:2); and (b) that he sojourn in Philistia (*ibid, v.* 3).

[The site was prominent in Jacob's life as well, for it was from there that he embarked on his journey to Laban in Charan. He had gone to Beer Sheba — to the site of his grandfather's *eshel,* and his father's altar — to ascertain whether it was indeed God's Will that he forsake *Eretz Yisrael.* On his way to Charan, he slept at Mt. Moriah and had his prophetic dream, which included a ladder upon which angels went up and down. The ladder was standing in Beer Sheba (see comm. to 28:17, p. 128), and it was in that dream that he was promised Divine protection.

[It is to Beer Sheba, also, that Jacob now came again, as he began his journey to Egypt — a journey which would mark the beginning of the foretold Egyptian Exile.]

Although Beer Sheba was on the way to Egypt, the Torah would not have mentioned that Jacob stopped there unless he had some reason for doing so. The commentators give several reasons why Jacob made Beer Sheba his major way station:

a) As noted in the footnote, Jacob stopped there, as he did once before, to seek Divine inspiration and permission to leave the Holy Land — especially since God had forbidden Isaac to leave the Land. *R' Munk* writes that Jacob's desire to receive the Divine blessing before his descent to Egypt is all the more understandable since he and his sons were still very apprehensive at the prospect of leaving the Promised Land for a country where new hardships might await them. As noted in our commentary to 42:1, this was the reason the brothers hesitated when they were first going down into Egypt to buy provisions.

Furthermore, he was apprehensive since he foresaw the beginning of the presaged Exile *(Ramban;* see below). At the same time he had the dual fear that his children would intermarry with the Egyptians and that his remains would not be interred in the Cave of Machpelah. It was about these fears that God reassured him in the next verse *(Akeidas Yitzchak).*

b) According to the Midrash, Jacob's further purpose in going to Beer Sheba was to cut down Abraham's *eshel* [the grove of trees] (21:33). He took the trees to Egypt, knowing prophetically that they would provide the *shittim* (cedar) wood for the Tabernacle that his descendants would be commanded to build in the desert after the Exodus.

[*Rashi* cites this in *Exodus* 25:5, and writes that Jacob replanted the trees in Egypt and ordered his children to take them along when they would leave there, for use in the Tabernacle. According to *Yafeh Toar*, these trees grew straight up without knots for thirty cubits (45-60 feet).]

The expression בְּאֵרָה שָׁבַע is synonymous with לִבְאֵר שָׁבַע; the suffix ה replaces the prefix ל, *to* [Cf. לָאָרֶץ=אַרְצָה] *(Rashi).*

וַיִּזְבַּח זְבָחִים לֵאלֹהֵי אָבִיו יִצְחָק — *And he slaughtered sacrifices to the God of his father Isaac.*

[Several reasons are offered below for Jacob's offer of a sacrifice at this juncture — many of which are connected with the very purpose of his coming to Beer Sheba and which form the basis for the revelation of reassurance God was about to give him. Other comments focus on **זְבָחִים** — the unusual term describing the sacrifices — while still others focus on the phrase *to the God of his father Isaac* instead of the more general *God of his forefathers*, or *God of Abraham*. Let us cite each in turn and the syntactical implications of the passage will become clear.]

Rashi comments:

... *To the God of his father Isaac:* [Isaac is particularly mentioned because] a man owes more honor to his father than to his grandfather. Therefore, Jacob associated [the sacrifice] with Isaac rather than Abraham. [This follows the view of *R' Yochanan* in the Midrash.]

Ramban counters that *Rashi's* comment does not suffice. Jacob should have associated the sacrifices with *both* Abraham and Isaac, as he did in his prayer for help (32:10) and his expression of gratitude (48:15). Or the verse could have said simply *He slaughtered sacrifices to God* without specifying either Patriarch.

To this objection *Mizrachi* replies that *Rashi* is not trying to explain why Jacob preferred Isaac to Abraham: if such were the case, *Rambam* would be right in arguing that either both or neither should have been associated. Instead, *Rashi* means to explain an entirely different point. Since Abraham was the first mortal to proclaim God's greatness on earth, it stands to reason that God should be described *only* as Abraham's God; if so it would seem to be wrong for Jacob to omit Abraham's name completely. *Rashi* explains, therefore, that a son is justified in ascribing honor to his father, consequently Jacob need not have been required to use the plural, 'my fathers' to associate the sacrifice with both Abraham and Isaac. Nevertheless, the omission did not exclude Abraham, because the honor ascribed to Isaac also reflected upon Abraham, the one who proclaimed God's glory to Isaac as well as to all humanity. And since, as *Rashi* points out, someone owes more honor to his father than to his grandfather, Jacob was justified in mentioning only Isaac.

Ramban continues that the emphasis on *Isaac* is intended to imply a kabbalistic secret alluded to by the Sages: Jacob was fearful of the grave consequences the Egyptian exile might have for his descendants. Such an exile was indicative of the Attribute of Justice, for we find God, in His relationship to Isaac, described as פַּחַד יִצְחָק, *the Dread of Isaac* — this appellation denoting the purest form of Awe, which inspired Isaac to submit himself to the *Akeidah*, [see 31:42]. In directing his prayers to the 'God of Isaac,' Jacob wished to seek a softening of this harsh manifestation of God in order that Divine judgment not be directed at him. [He chose the appellation God *of Isaac* rather than *of Abraham* — since it was Isaac whom God had warned not to go down to Egypt *(Racanati).*] — Jacob accompanied his supplications with peace offerings, because they symbolize harmony between God and Israel. Jacob prayed at the same place where Isaac had requested Divine permission to leave *Eretz Yisrael,* and where he himself had received such permission [53 years earlier] when he went to Laban's home in Paddan Aram [see footnote].

The Midrash explains the prominence given Isaac here: "When a Rabbi and his disciples are walking on a road, you first greet the disciples and afterward you greet the Rabbi." [That is, since the disciples travel in advance of the Rabbi, a person coming from the opposite direction would first meet the disciples and then the Rabbi. Similarly, Isaac is the 'disciple' and Abraham the 'Rabbi'. Therefore, Jacob offered sacrifices to the God of his father Isaac.]

R' Bachya understands this Midrash in a kabbalistic sense and in a vein similar to that of the Midrash cited by *Rashi:* that the duty of honoring one's father is more imperative than that of honoring one's grandfather. In consonance with *Ramban's* exegesis above, *R' Bachya* writes that *'his father'* alludes to God's title 'the Dread of Isaac,' a description denoting the strictest sense of God's judgment, in contrast to the Godly Attribute of Mercy associated with Abraham. Jacob's personal attribute was a combination of Mercy and Judgment, resulting in רַחֲמִים, the compassion that comes when judgment is tempered. [This concept is discussed in *'Three Prayers,'* an Overview to the ArtScroll *Siddur.*] Since Jacob was closer to Isaac's attribute — because Isaac was the 'discipline' and the father who raised him — Jacob directed his offering toward the attribute he was attempting to soften, that of Isaac.

Kedushas Levi derives from the above that Jacob was reluctant to descend to Egypt, knowing the consequences of his descent. Therefore, he directed his sacrifices to the *God of his father Isaac,* in the hope that God would deny him permission to leave Canaan just as He had instructed Isaac to remain in the Land.[1]

R' Shlomo Ashtruc in *Midrashei HaTorah* writes that without doubt Jacob was aware of the vision at the Covenant

1. The commentators note that the sacrifices offered by Noah, Abraham and Isaac were 'burnt offerings' [עוֹלָה], the only type of sacrifices known to the Noachides [*Zevachim* 116a]. But now, as both thankfulness and apprehension fill Jacob's heart and he prepares to go to his

אֱלֹהִים׀ לְיִשְׂרָאֵל בְּמַרְאֹת הַלַּיְלָה וַיֹּאמֶר
ג יַעֲקֹב׀ יַעֲקֹב וַיֹּאמֶר הִנֵּנִי: וַיֹּאמֶר אָנֹכִי
הָאֵל אֱלֹהֵי אָבִיךָ אַל־תִּירָא מֵרְדָה

Between the Parts that Abraham's descendants would be aliens and slaves in a strange land, and he was fearful that the exile and servitude would begin with him. He therefore prayed to *the God of his father Isaac,* for Isaac was spared the travails of physical exile and servitude even though the four hundred years of alien status commenced with his birth. Jacob prayed for the same dispensation. Accordingly he offered these sacrifices imploring God to spare him these travails just as He spared Isaac. God granted his prayer, as we shall learn below.

2. God appears to Jacob in a nocturnal prophetic revelation and grants him permission to migrate to Egypt.

וַיֹּאמֶר אֱלֹהִים לְיִשְׂרָאֵל בְּמַרְאֹת הַלַּיְלָה — *And God spoke to Israel in night visions.*

Night visions, i.e. the perception of a Divine revelation at night, is one of the levels of prophecy. In *Moreh Nevuchim* 2:41, *Rambam* holds that while *all* prophetic revelations (excluding those of Moses) come only in dreams or visions, there is a great distinction between prophetic 'vision' and that which comes in a *'dream' of the night.* The latter may come even to impious persons, as in the cases of Abimelech [20:3] and Laban [31:24], but when they awake, they are conscious only of having dreamt. In the case of Jacob, however, it was apparent to him when he arose that God had communicated with him prophetically, and he did not have the misimpression that it was merely a dream. In 2:45 *Rambam* further analyzes the eleven levels of prophecy and writes that the seventh level of prophecy is a dream in which a prophet perceives that he is being addressed by God.

Ramban writes that God's revelation in a night-vision alludes to nighttime's importance as a period of דִּין רָפֶה, *clemency in Judgment.* It was with the mercy-tempered Divine attribute of Justice that God now appeared to Jacob

long-lost son, he is the first one to offer זְבָחִים — which connote sacrifices in the category of *shelamim* [see further]. (That in 31:54 Jacob also had slaughtered a זֶבַח is no contradiction. There, as *Rashi* notes, the term has a secular sense, and does not denote a sacrifice to God. Our passage is the first time the term appears in a ritualistic sacrificial sense.)

The Sages expound [*Toras Kohanim Vayikra* 16:1] that the name *'shelamim'* sacrifice derives from *shalom,* peace. The sacrifice is so called because it brings peace into the world. Therefore, at this juncture when Jacob feared the consequences his descent into Egypt would have on his descendants, he wanted to pave the way for peace and conciliation. In the kabbalistic sense explained by *R' Bachya,* he directed the sacrifice to God's Attribute of Power [מִדַּת הַגְּבוּרָה] which was nearer to Isaac, because he wanted to soften God's judgment with sacrifices of peace.

[Comp. *Rashi* to *Leviticus* 3:1 that *shelamim* are so called because "they bring peace to the altar, the priests, and the owners — all who participate."]

R' Hirsch perceives the connotation of 'completeness' [שָׁלֵם] in *shelamim* — the sacrifice that is not burnt completely upon the altar but becomes a meal sanctified by God, a family meal that consecrates all its participants. He suggests that Jacob/Israel brought this sacrifice now because, for the first time, he felt himself happy, joyful, and 'complete' in his family circle.

Another connotation of זְבָחִים is its association with the תּוֹדָה [thanksgiving] sacrifice. Several commentators [see *Tur*] accordingly suggest that Jacob offered these sacrifices in thanksgiving for a safe journey, or in gratitude that Joseph was still alive *(RI of Vienna).*

[2] *God spoke to Israel in night visions and He said,
"Jacob, Jacob," and he said, "Here I am."*
[3] *And He said, "I am the God — God of your*

and assured him that he should have no fear in Egypt for he would be found righteous in Divine Judgment and be redeemed after the prescribed period of affliction.

God revealed himself to Jacob — whose own painful life corresponded to the period of night — precisely when the 'night of exile' was about to commence. He solemnly announced then that the 'night' would be followed by the dawn of freedom, for if God 'goes down' with him into Egypt [see below], He will also 'go up' with him from Egypt *(R' Munk).*

וַיֹּאמֶר יַעֲקֹב יַעֲקֹב — *And He said, "Jacob, Jacob."* The repetition expresses love *(Rashi).*

[*Rashi* makes a similar comment on the repetition *"Abraham, Abraham"* in 22:11. According to the *Zohar* cited there, the repetition of his name was intended to animate his spirit and spur him on.]

Radak offers that since Jacob had not received prophetic communication for many years, God now called his name *twice* so that he should truly understand that it was a Prophetic Spirit that was summoning him [and the sound of his name was not something that he imagined].

God had given Jacob the name *Israel* denoting triumph [see 35:10] and that name is used three times in this section [in verses 1, 2, and 5], but, in addressing him now, God calls him *Jacob* [the name indicating subservience]. This implies that during his forthcoming stay in Egypt he would not "contend with God and man and triumph", as the name Israel intimates, rather he would be in a house of bondage until God will bring him [i.e., his remains or his descendants] back. In verse 8, below, Jacob's family is called the *Children of Israel* although the Patriarch is called "Jacob" in that verse "since the progeny would multiply there and their glory extend." Therefore, the *family* is given a name alluding to their future growth in Egypt, but the father, who would not live to share that happy fate, is called Jacob *(Ramban).* [See also *v.* 5 below.]

The Talmud [*Berachos* 13b] cites our passage as proof that although God changed Jacob's name to Israel, one is permitted to refer to him by his old name since the Torah itself calls him Jacob in our verse, thus clearly showing that he retained that name. This is unlike the case of Abraham, where one who refers to him as "Abram" transgresses. [See *comm.* to 17:5 p. 563-4.]

וַיֹּאמֶר הִנֵּנִי — *And he said, "Here I am."*

Such is the answer of the pious, the expression denoting both humility and readiness *(Rashi* to 22:1).

3. אָנֹכִי הָאֵל אֱלֹהֵי אָבִיךָ — *I am the God — God of your father.*[1]

[The definite article, *'the'* God,

1. Following *R' Shlomo Ashtruc* in *Midrashei HaTorah* cited at the end of last verse: " ... *I am the God of your father Isaac.* — Just as I watched over him, and spared him the travails of servitude during his lifetime, so will I spare you. *Do not be afraid of going down to Egypt ... for I myself will go down with you to Egypt* and protect you."

This is the sense of the Sages' observation [*Shabbos* 89b; see footnote p. 1699]: "It would have been fitting for our father Jacob to go down to Egypt in iron chains [in the manner of all exiles, since it was by God's decree that he went there *(Rashi ad loc.)*] but his merit availed him." That is, it would have been fitting for the actual servitude to have begun with Jacob, but his merit availed him, and God delayed, thereby shortening the duration of the period.

מִצְרַ֫יְמָה כִּֽי־לְג֥וֹי גָּד֖וֹל אֲשִֽׂימְךָ֥ שָֽׁם׃
ד אָנֹכִ֗י אֵרֵ֤ד עִמְּךָ֙ מִצְרַ֔יְמָה וְאָנֹכִ֖י אַֽעַלְךָ֣

intimates that God introduced Himself to Jacob in the same manifestation as that to which Jacob had just directed his sacrifice. In other words, the perception of God that Jacob held when he offered his sacrifice, is the same one that came to him in this vision. Or, as *Ramban* notes kabbalistically, by calling Himself, *"the* God," God is designating Himself as *the God of Bethel where you anointed a Pillar (31:13)* and *the God of your father.*

— I, the God Who told your father [26:2], *'Do not descend to Egypt,'* I am the One Who now tells *you* not to fear going to Egypt, for I shall make of you a great nation there. For were your children to remain here [in Canaan] they would intermarry with the Canaanites and assimilate, but this will not happen in Egypt 'for the Egyptians could not bear to eat food with the Hebrews' [43:32 (see *comm.* there). Thus, the Hebrews will be a nation set-apart in Egypt], as our Sages stated [*Sifre Devarim,* cited also in the Passover Haggadah (see *ArtScroll-Elias* ed. p. 105f)]: וַיְהִי שָׁם לְגוֹי, *and he became there a nation* — this teaches you that the Israelites were מְצוּיָנִים שָׁם, *prominent and set apart there* [the emphasis being on the word שָׁם, *there* — in Egypt (*R' David Feinstein*)] (*Sforno; Radak*).

Haamek Davar similarly interprets that Jacob was apprehensive that his descendants would be absorbed by the Egyptian nation, but God assured him to the contrary; see below.

אַל תִּירָא מֵרְדָה מִצְרַיְמָה — *Have no fear of descending to Egypt.*

[That God was now telling Jacob not to fear going down to Egypt proves, as noted above, that the Patriarch had previously entertained such a fear. Although no previous explicit indication is given in the text that Jacob was afraid of the descent — and to the contrary, as *Abarbanel* observes, Jacob had wanted to see Joseph (45:28) and had begun the journey (*v.* 1) — nevertheless we are taught that nothing is hidden from God Who penetrates the innermost thoughts of man. The reassurance אַל תִּירָא, *Fear not!* was uttered by God to each of the Patriarchs (15:1 and 26:24), to Moses, and to almost every important personage in Scripture. In each case the commentators seek to uncover the fear which prompted the Divine reassurance. We have recorded some of the fears attributed to Jacob. They range from Jacob's knowledge that this descent would begin the Egyptian bondage, to his fear that the nation might forget its spiritual destiny amid the plenty of Egypt, and that it might choose assimilation with the Egyptians instead of a return to the land of Canaan, which had been promised to his forefathers. To all of these misgivings — and those recorded below — the Divine reassurance alluded.][1]

Rashi states simply that God told this to Jacob 'because he [Jacob] was grieved that he was compelled to

1. *R' Hirsch* treats the underlying sequence of events as follows:

As 45:27-28 and 46:1 indicate, Jacob was exultant. What was it that prompted God to tell him *'Fear not ...'*? Verse 2 suggests what happened. First, the term *vision of the night* implies that the future held gloom; second, God's use of the name Jacob, instead of Israel, showed that triumph was not to be part of the Jewish future in Egypt. Thus prepared for the worst, Jacob answered הִנֵּנִי, as if to say, 'I am ready for whatever You decide for me.'

To this, God responded, *'Have no fear, Jacob* — I am the God to Whom you have dedicated your joyous family offering, and the ultimate purpose of your descent to Egypt, too, is joyous

46
4

father. Have no fear of descending to Egypt, for I shall establish you as a great nation there. [4] *I shall descend with you to Egypt, and I shall also surely*

leave the Land' [i.e. *Eretz Yisrael*].

[Although *Rashi* is not more explicit, it is clear that he is summing up in this brief comment all of the multiple fears implicit in leaving the Land enumerated by the other commentators.]

Comp. the *Zohar:* When asked why he was afraid to go to Egypt, Jacob replied, "I am afraid that my family will succumb there, that the *Shechinah* will no longer dwell among us, that I will not be buried with my ancestors, and that I will not see the redemption of my children."

God reassured him on each of these accounts: *"I will establish you as a great nation there; I will go down with you to Egypt and I will also bring you up from there, and Joseph will place his hand over your eyes."*

Furthermore, Jacob feared that if he abandoned *Eretz Yisrael,* God's promise to give the Land to his descendants might be withdrawn. God, therefore, assured him to the contrary *(Akeidah;* cf. *Alshich).*

כִּי לְגוֹי־גָּדוֹל אֲשִׂימְךָ שָׁם — *For I shall establish you as a great nation there.*

There specifically. For your sojourn in Egypt will provide the necessary prerequisite to becoming a great nation. This can happen only there; in Canaan you could not maintain the separateness needed to form you into a unique nation (see *Sforno* above).

As *R' Hirsch* expresses it in his *comm.* to 45:11: ... In Canaan, where the family of Jacob was accepted as a neighbor, Israel could hardly have developed into a nation. As it became more populous, its members would have been scattered among the inhabitants. To become a nation without assimilation, they had to live among a nation that was opposed to the very nature of the Jews as a matter of principle. Egypt was that nation.

In this connection *Harav David Feinstein* notes that the word מִצְרַיִם, *Egypt,* is spelled with the letters (but not the vowels) of מְצָרִים, *straits* or *confines.* This refers to the ghetto existence of Egypt and many other countries where Jews lived. Despite the suffering and oppression endured in such places, the ghettoes had the positive result of binding the Jews together.

Have no fear about going to Egypt. Just as I forbade your father to go there, I am assuring you that just as the Exile and servitude foretold to Abraham is imminent, so is the blessing I bestowed upon him when I said [12:2]: וְאֶעֶשְׂךָ לְגוֹי גָּדוֹל, *I will make of you a great nation.* This will be fulfilled there *(Chizkuni; Tzeidah laDerech).*

God thus also intimated to Jacob that notwithstanding Jacob's earlier thoughts, he would not return to Canaan after seeing Joseph, but would remain in Egypt until his descendants became a great nation *(Abarbanel).*

4. אָנֹכִי אֵרֵד עִמְּךָ מִצְרַיְמָה — *I* [*the Hebrew* אָנֹכִי has an emphatic connotation: *I personally*] *shall descend with you to Egypt.*

In the figurative sense: My protection will extend to you even

greatness, for in Egypt your family will become a great nation, as I promised you and your ancestors. I will accompany your family there and, at the proper time, when they have become a nation, I will lead them back to *Eretz Yisrael.* As for you personally — you will not be separated from Joseph again.'

ה גַּם־עָלֹה וְיוֹסֵף יָשִׁית יָדוֹ עַל־עֵינֶיךָ׃ וַיָּקָם

there. In the *Kabbalistic* sense this passage forms the basis of the Rabbinic concept of שְׁכִינְתָּא בְגָלוּתָא, *'The Shechinah* [*Divine Presence*] *in Exile,'* for as the *Mechilta* notes: This passage teaches us that when the Israelites descended to Egypt the Divine Presence descended along with them. This concept occurs often in the Talmud. See specifically *Megillah* 29a: 'Wherever Israel was exiled, the Divine Presence was exiled with them ...' This concept is also discussed in the *Overview.* [See footnote].[1]

The commentators maintain that the *Shechinah* associated Itself with the Israelites descending to Egypt and even joined their number. For according to *v.* 27 below, the total number of Jacob's descendants was seventy, yet a count of the individual names yields only sixty-nine. According to one view in *Daas Zekeinim* the *Shechinah* is to be counted among the descendants, bringing the total to seventy.

According to *Michtav MeEliyahu,* these words contained the assurance that God would protect Jacob's family from any permanent spiritually harmful effects, and prevent their total assimilation. In accordance with His promise, God redeemed the Israelites before they became altogether submerged in Egyptian idolatry and lost forever.

וְאָנֹכִי אַעַלְךָ גַם־עָלֹה — *And I shall also surely bring you up* [lit. *and I shall bring you up, also bring up*].

Directed as it is in the singular to Jacob individually who, as we know, died in Exile, this Divine promise refers to the fact that Jacob's body would be buried in his ancestors' sepulchre in the Cave of Machpelah *(Rashi; Rashbam; Ibn Ezra).*

The expression וְאָנֹכִי אַעַלְךָ גַם־עָלֹה is in-

1. **Onkelos' principles of translating terms that might imply corporeality.**

Rambam [*Moreh,* 1:27] comments on this verse as follows: "*Onkelos* the proselyte, who knew the Hebrew and Syriac languages perfectly, made every effort to avoid anthropomorphisms (attributions of human form to God). Whenever the Torah (speaking of God) employs a term that might impute corporeality, *Onkelos* paraphrases it according to its contextual non-anthropomorphic, sense. Whenever he finds such a term implying one of the various forms of *movement,* he interprets the movement in the sense of manifestation or 'appearance.' ... However, to the words *I shall go down with you to Egypt,* he gives a literal translation: אֲנָא אֵחוֹת עִמָּךְ לְמִצְרַיִם" [instead of rendering *'I shall appear ...'*].

"That is very noteworthy and it demonstrates the unusual talent of this master and the superlative nature of his interpretation, since, by means of this translation, he lets us perceive one principle of prophecy. The beginning of this narrative says that God spoke to Israel in night visions, etc. Since it is clear from the beginning of the episode that this occurred in night visions, *Onkelos* does not object to a literal rendering of what had been said in these night visons. And he is right to do so, for he is relating something which had been *said,* rather than an actual happening, as for example when God came down upon Sinai *(Exodus* 19:20)."

After quoting these views of *Rambam, Ramban* gives his own analysis of *Onkelos'* principles of translation and he reaches a somewhat different conclusion. He holds that *Onkelos'* reason for not translating literally is not to avoid anthropomorphism, but is rather based on Kabbalistic grounds. Thus, when *Onkelos* translated the phrase *I shall go down with you to Egypt* in a *literal* sense, he alluded to the Talmudic statement that the *Shechinah* accompanies Jewry in its wanderings among the nations *(Shabbos* 89b and *Megillah* 29a). *Onkelos* regards this Divine solicitude for exiled Israel so supremely important that he refuses to paraphrase the verse.

A similar opinion is expressed by such commentators as *Akeidas Yitzchak, R' Bachya* and *Or HaChaim.* (See *R' Munk.)*

46 *bring you up; and Joseph shall place his hand on*
4 *your eyes."*

terpreted as if it read וְאָנֹכִי גַּם עָלֹה אַעַלְךָ, *I will also surely bring you up (Karnei Or;* cf. *Rashbam).*

The particle גַּם, *also,* usually indicates a רִבּוּי, *extension,* beyond the simple meaning of the phrase. In this case, it is interpreted to include also the *bones of Joseph,* which, God promised, would also be brought back to *Eretz Yisrael* for burial *(Akeidah);* also to the bones of all the Tribal Ancestors, for there is a tradition that each tribe brought up the remains of its ancestor (see *Yerushalmi Sotah* 1:10). According to the *Midrash* it signifies: I will bring up not only you, but all those who are righteous like you.

Radak and *Ralbag* maintain that the reference is not to Jacob as an *individual,* but to his descendants: And I will lead your descendants out of Egypt to take possession of the Promised Land. The great nation being formed in Egypt will also be brought home by Me.[1]

— And when they come up from Exile, My *Shechinah* which accompanied them will come up along with them *(Pesikta).*

— I will bring you [i.e. your descendants] out of this Exile and I will also bring your children out of future Exiles *(Yafeh Toar).*

According to *Tur,* this is a subtle allusion to the Rabbinic dictum: "Jacob our father did not die" [*Taanis* 5b; see on 49:33].

Sforno explains the phraseology: After I bring you up from Egypt, אַעַלְךָ, *I will raise you* [i.e. your progeny], גַּם־עָלֹה, *even higher,* than you were before you went there.

— The double phraseology Kabbilistically alludes to the ultimate ascendancy they will achieve: The spiritual rise to the heights of the World to Come *(R' Bachya).*

וְיוֹסֵף יָשִׁית יָדוֹ עַל־עֵינֶיךָ — *And Joseph shall place his hand on your eyes.*

The expression *place his hand on your eyes* is idiomatic; literally it refers to closing the eyes of the deceased, but in practice it denotes taking care of burial arrangements, a duty and privilege devolving primarily on the firstborn. For reasons which will be discussed in the *comm.* to 49:3-4, certain rights of the firsborn passed from Reuben to Joseph. Jacob was now informed that Joseph will retain his exalted position and the privilege of "closing his father's eyes" would be

1. *Oznaim l'Torah* synthesizes the expositions:

אָנֹכִי אַעַלְךָ, *And I will bring you up,* that is, God assured Jacob that he would be buried in *Eretz Yisrael;* גַּם עָלֹה, *also bring up* — that He would bring up out of Egypt the 'great nation' which Jacob's descendants will become in Egypt. Without such an assurance that Israel would not assimilate among the Egyptians, there would be no value to the promise of establishing of his great nation!

In fulfillment of the promise *I shall go down with you to Egypt and I will also surely bring you up,* God Himself would later descend to Egypt to redeem the children of Israel.

As the author of the Passover Haggadah records the exegesis: *'HASHEM brought us out of Egypt* — not through an angel ... but the Holy One Blessed is He alone in His Glory' [see *ArtScroll Haggadah* p. 120ff]. This appears difficult, however, — why indeed He did not do it through the agency of an angel? ... It was because in this passage God 'obligated Himself' to take them out personally [this being the connotation of the more emphatic אָנֹכִי denoting exclusiveness, instead of אֲנִי].

Similarly we recite in Hallel [*Psalms* 114:5]: מַה לְּךָ הַיָּם כִּי תָנוּס? ... מִלִּפְנֵי אֱלוֹהַּ יַעֲקֹב, *What ails you, O sea, that you flee? ... Before the God of Jacob.* The Sea fled before the God of Jacob; in describing the Exodus, the Psalmist relates God to Jacob, because He came Himself, as it were, to liberate the Israelites as He had promised Jacob.

ויגש
מו/ה

יַעֲקֹב מִבְּאֵר שָׁבַע וַיִּשְׂאוּ בְנֵי־יִשְׂרָאֵל אֶת־יַעֲקֹב אֲבִיהֶם וְאֶת־טַפָּם וְאֶת־ נְשֵׁיהֶם בָּעֲגָלוֹת אֲשֶׁר־שָׁלַח פַּרְעֹה

given him *(Zohar).* [See *Me'am Loez*].

The blessing implicit in this promise was that Jacob's children would not die before him, but that his son — and not strangers — would personally attend to his burial (see *Rashbam*, bottom of *Bava Basra* 108a).

God specifically assured Jacob that Joseph would survive him since on many occasions Jacob had expressed apprehension that Joseph would die before him and he would descend to the grave as a mourner. Furthermore, God intimated that Jacob would not leave Egypt alive, but would die there *(Or HaChaim).*

Rashbam [in *Chumash*], *Radak* and others render the passage figuratively: Joseph, who will survive you, will look after your affairs [עִנְיָן=עַיִן] and provide for your family when you are gone.

5. Jacob and his family set out for Egypt.

וַיָּקָם יַעֲקֹב מִבְּאֵר שָׁבַע — *So Jacob arose from Beer Sheba.*

The term 'arose' implies in the literal sense that Jacob had been kneeling, thankful for the past and praying for the future. Now he 'arose' and set out on the journey. Furthermore, it was truly a 'rising' for he had been informed that the *Shechinah* would accompany him and redeem his descendants *(Tz'ror HaMor).*

The expression וַיָּקָם, *he arose* [in the sense of *prevailed upon himself*], is significant. It implies that the matter was difficult for Jacob because he knew he was going into bondage. With great effort he had to muster up all his energy to continue. Compare a similar meaning of this verb in 19:34: *And the younger got up* [וַתָּקָם, *arose*], where the connotation is also that the matter was difficult for her *(Haamek Davar; R' Hirsch).*[1]

Abarbanel maintains that this is what the Passover *Haggadah* means when it describes Jacob as going down to Egypt אָנוּס עַל פִּי הַדִּבּוּר, *'compelled' by the Divine decree* [ArtScroll *Haggadah* p. 103], while the surface narrative would imply to the contrary: rather than being coerced, Jacob was merely being reassured by God not to fear going down to Egypt. However, as we have noted, God was responding to Jacob's deep-seated fear against going to Egypt, and as this 'informal reassurance' came from God, Jacob went as if he were "compelled" by direct command. [See *Overview.*]

וַיִּשְׂאוּ בְנֵי־יִשְׂרָאֵל אֶת יַעֲקֹב אֲבִיהֶם וְאֶת־טַפָּם וְאֶת־נְשֵׁיהֶם — [*And*] *the sons of Israel transported* [lit. *carried*] *Jacob their father as well as their small children and* [*their*] *wives.*

The change of names in this clause between *Israel* and *Jacob* is instructive. Jacob's sons did not

1. On the verse *And Jacob lifted his feet* [29:1] *Rashi* comments that, 'At the good tidings which Jacob had received assuring him of God's protection, his heart "lifted his feet" and he felt very light as he continued his journey.'

But here, too, Jacob had heard good tidings that Joseph was still alive, and he was on his way to see him. Why is there no allusion here of his heart 'lifting his feet' and feeling very 'light'?

The answer is that now Jacob was going down to Egypt, to a long Exile. The verse therefore

[5] *So Jacob arose from Beer Sheba. The sons of*
Israel transported Jacob their father, as well as their
small children and wives, in the wagons which
Pharaoh had sent to transport him. [6] *They took their*

realize what a sad future lay ahead in Egypt; they thought they were on a triumphant journey [as the name *Israel* implies (see *Ramban* above *v.* 2, s.v., יַעֲקֹב יַעֲקֹב).] Their brother was viceroy in Egypt, and they proudly considered themselves children of *Israel.* Jacob, however, knew that they were beginning a new era of *'Galus'* during which he would have to assume the subservient role represented by his name *Jacob.* The Torah alludes to this by calling him Jacob. Therefore it says: The sons of *'Israel'* led their father *'Jacob' (R' Hirsch; Yalkut Yehoshua).*

See also *Sforno* who maintains that as they set out on their journey to Exile they are referred to as children of *Israel,* since henceforth they would have to be a people who will 'strive with God and man' [see 32:29]. The name *Jacob* is also mentioned as an allusion to the 'destiny' [connected with עָקֵב, *heel,* from which the name Jacob is derived] that awaited him. The Patriarch was now going to his ultimate joy, which would not be followed for him by any sorrow, his troubles over at last. This presaged the destiny of his progeny who, after all their troubles, will experience joy. Thus, it is written [*Jeremiah* 31:7]: *Sing with gladness for Jacob.*

Sechel Tov notes the order of priority as reflective of their levels of love: *their father, children, and wives.* See *comm.* to 31:17 where Jacob gave priority to his children, whereas the lecherous Esau gave priority [in 36:6] to the women.

According to *Midrash HaGadol,* the meaning of the passage is that the brothers literally *carried* their father in their arms, and transported their children and wives in the wagons. [The verse would accordingly be translated: *And the children of Israel carried Jacob their father; and their small children and their wives* (they transported) *in the wagons which Pharaoh had sent to transport him.*]

Tur interprets similarly, and, noting how no act goes unrewarded, suggests that now they were repaying Jacob for his earlier kindness when they were young children and he carried them across the stream [32:24].

The *Midrash* notes the irony in Jacob's now being carried, and applies to him the verse in *Ecclesiastes* 9:11: *The race is not to the swift nor the battle to the strong* ... "It was [figuratively] only 'yesterday' that Jacob was so mighty that he singlehandedly rolled off the boulder from the well's mouth [see 29:8-10], yet when his own time came he was so frail that he had to be carried bodily."

בָּעֲגָלוֹת אֲשֶׁר־שָׁלַח פַּרְעֹה לָשֵׂאת אֹתוֹ — *In the wagons which Pharaoh had sent to transport* [lit. *to carry*] *him.*

Pharaoh, not Joseph, is mentioned as the sender, because it was by his royal authority that the wagons were permitted to be exported from Egypt. Furthermore, this is repeated with a view of

intimates that it was against his will, and not joyously. He had to muster up all his strength to raise himself up from that spot. Therefore, we see later that his sons had to transport him in the wagons: Even his legs became enfeebled and reluctant to trudge into exile. He therefore had to be transported *(Itturei Torah).*

ו לָשֵׂאת אֹתוֹ: וַיִּקְחוּ אֶת־מִקְנֵיהֶם וְאֶת־
רְכוּשָׁם אֲשֶׁר רָכְשׁוּ בְּאֶרֶץ כְּנַעַן וַיָּבֹאוּ
ז מִצְרָיְמָה יַעֲקֹב וְכָל־זַרְעוֹ אִתּוֹ: בָּנָיו וּבְנֵי
בָנָיו אִתּוֹ בְּנֹתָיו וּבְנוֹת בָּנָיו וְכָל־זַרְעוֹ

showing how Pharaoh had invited the family of Jacob to come to Egypt *(Akeidah).*

To transport *him,* i.e. Jacob, primarily. The others were secondary *(Lekach Tov).*

6. וַיִּקְחוּ אֶת־מִקְנֵיהֶם וְאֶת־רְכוּשָׁם אֲשֶׁר רָכְשׁוּ בְּאֶרֶץ כְּנַעַן וַיָּבֹאוּ מִצְרָיְמָה — *They took their livestock and their wealth which they had amassed in the land of Canaan and they came to Egypt.*

Now that Jacob resolved to settle in Egypt for as long as God willed him to remain, he took all his wealth and cattle with him. The Torah does not mention this when telling that he set out for Beer Sheba. Perhaps Jacob's family had intended merely to accompany him and see Joseph, but when God's approval for their descent and sojourn in Egypt was revealed to them, they consented to bring all their wealth and cattle. Alternately, the Torah also informs us to their credit that even though Jacob's family knew about the impending Exile, not one of them hesitated to fulfill the debt of the foretold Exile, but they took their small children, etc., and went to Egypt *(Or HaChaim; Alshich).* [This differs from some of the views mentioned above that the brothers were then unaware of the long stay that awaited them in Egypt.]

[That the Torah specifically mentions *the wealth he amassed* **in the land of Canaan** intimates that the immense wealth he amassed while working for Laban *in Paddan Aram* (31:18) is excluded]:

The fortune Jacob acquired in Paddan Aram he gave to Esau in payment for a burial place in the Cave of Machpelah. He said, 'The possessions of countries [outside of *Eretz Yisrael*] are worthless to me.' [See below, 50:5] *(Rashi; Tanchuma).*

[On the translation of מִקְנֶה, lit. *possessions,* as *livestock,* see *comm.* to 31:18.]

יַעֲקֹב וְכָל זַרְעוֹ אִתּוֹ — *Jacob and all his offspring with him.*

Not one of his descendants stayed behind *(Abarbanel).*

7. [The Torah characteristically proceeds to specify who are included in the general designation זַרְעוֹ, *his offspring*]:

בָּנָיו וּבְנֵי בָנָיו אִתּוֹ — *His sons and grandsons with him.*

I.e., these went freely and eagerly with him. As the verse proceeds to imply, however, he had to *force his daughters and grand-daughters* as well as the rest of *his offspring* — meaning his great grandchildren — to come with him; these הֵבִיא אִתּוֹ מִצְרָיְמָה, *he* **brought** [i.e. forcibly] *with him to Egypt.* Support for this interpretation may be derived from the Rabbinic dictum that the actual *bondage* did not begin while any of those who originally descended was still alive, as it says [*Exodus* 1:6] *And Joseph died ... and all that generation* [i.e. who descended to Egypt; cf. *comm.* there]; only then did the bondage begin. Perhaps, being spared bondage was their reward for willingly submitting to the Divine Decree of descending to Egypt. ... The proof of this is that Yocheved and Serach were among these that originally went down to Egypt, yet the bondage began during their lifetimes. We must accordingly maintain that they did not

46 livestock and their wealth which they had amassed in
7 the land of Canaan and they came to Egypt — Jacob
and all his offspring with him. 7 His sons and
grandsons with him, his daughters and grand-

earn a reward because Jacob *brought* them, and it was not of their own will that they came *(Or HaChaim).*

On the other hand, *R' Hirsch* perceives it greatly significant and a tribute to the Patriarchal family that every member of the family went with Jacob: "They were *all* with him, and united with him. Jacob did not share his fathers' grief, of seeing estrangement among his children; and although they had already formed many families, they all grouped themselves in unity about their Father Jacob. They trusted him, and everyone went along to Egypt."

בְּנֹתָיו וּבְנוֹת בָּנָיו — *His daughters and granddaughters* [lit. *and the daughters of his sons.*]

Exactly who is referred to by the plural *daughters* is unclear inasmuch as Scripture mentions only Dinah as a daughter of Jacob. The Midrashic controversy in this matter has been treated in the *comm.* to 37:35 where the plural *daughters* also occurs. Briefly, as noted there, R' Yehudah maintains that a twin sister was born with each of Jacob's sons, thus Jacob had many daughters; while R' Nechemiah maintains that the term *daughters* refers to Jacob's daughters-in-law since 'it is quite common for one to refer to his daughter-in-law as his "daughter".'

Rashi does not comment on the word *daughters* in our verse but focuses instead on the phrase *daughters of his sons,* which he interprets as referring to 'Serach daughter of Asher and Yocheved the daughter of Levi.'

Ramban cites this interpretation and observes that *Rashi* leaves the plural of *his daughters* unexplained. [It is certain that *Rashi* could not be suggesting that it refers to twin sisters as he does in 37:35 since, in *v.* 26 below, he specifically writes that according to R' Yehudah's view that twin sisters were born with Jacob's sons, they must have died before Jacob and his family went down to Egypt since they are not enumerated. Nor can our verse refer to Canaanite daughters-in-law, as R' Nechemiah interprets 37:35, since our verse explicitly mentions Jacob's זֶרַע, *offspring (Nimukei Shmuel;* cf. *Mizrachi; Maharsha* to *Bava Basra* 123b).]

Ramban accordingly suggests that in genealogical lists it is common for Scripture to use the plural form for an individual. For example in *v.* 23 below: *And the* **sons** *of Dan: Chushim* [see *comm.* there]; and *Numbers* 26:8: *And the* **sons** *of Pallu: Eliab.* Therefore, in our verse too, though *daughters* is in plural it refers to only Dinah. Moreover, only Serach who was already born is meant by *daughters of his sons,* but Yocheved whose name is not mentioned was not [since according to tradition she was not born until they actually entered the walls of Egypt] although in the opinion of the Sages [*Bava Basra* 123a] she is alluded to [see *comm.* to *v.* 15].

Daas Zekeinim maintains that by the plural *daughters,* Jacob's *grand-*

ח הֵבִיא אִתּוֹ מִצְרָיְמָה: וְאֵלֶּה
שְׁמוֹת בְּנֵי־יִשְׂרָאֵל הַבָּאִים מִצְרַיְמָה
ט יַעֲקֹב וּבָנָיו בְּכֹר יַעֲקֹב רְאוּבֵן: וּבְנֵי
י רְאוּבֵן חֲנוֹךְ וּפַלּוּא וְחֶצְרֹן וְכַרְמִי: וּבְנֵי
שִׁמְעוֹן יְמוּאֵל וְיָמִין וְאֹהַד וְיָכִין וְצֹחַר

daughter, Jochebed, is included, as 'grandchildren are like children.' [The difficulty with this, as later commentators note, is that Jochebed is already included in the designation *daughters of his son.*]

According to *Ibn Ezra,* perhaps Dinah and Serach had young personal attendants who grew up with them and who were regarded as his daughters. [Hence the allusion in the plural term. However, they are not reckoned among the seventy souls since they were not Jacob's biological offspring.]

The *Midrash* observes that *daughters of his sons* are mentioned but not *sons of his daughters.* R' Yehudah bar Ilai said, *Sons' daughters rank as sons while daughters' sons* do not rank as sons. [Halachically, however, this does not apply in matters of inheritance, where daughters' sons share in the inheritance. See *Yafeh Toar; Radal* to *Pirkei d'Rabbi Eliezer* 36; Cf. *Bava Basra* 143b.]

וְכָל זַרְעוֹ — *And all his offspring.*

Including his great grandchildren, for example: Chetzron and Chamul the sons of Judah's son Peretz [enumerated below] *(Sechel Tov; Or HaChaim).*

הֵבִיא אִתּוֹ מִצְרָיְמָה — *He brought h him to Egypt.*

He made certain that none stayed behind *(Akeidah).*

The last-mentioned group had to be *forced* to accompany him (see *Or HaChaim* cited in the beginning of this verse).

✤ List of the Descendants:

8.-14. Descendants through Leah

8. וְאֵלֶּה שְׁמוֹת בְּנֵי־יִשְׂרָאֵל הַבָּאִים מִצְרַיְמָה יַעֲקֹב וּבָנָיו — *Now these are the names of the Children of Israel who were coming* [lit. *the comers*] *to Egypt — Jacob and his children.*

The Torah speaks of them — in the context of the time-frame of the narrative — as בָּאִים, *coming,* in the present tense. "Therefore, one need not be surprised that it does not state אֲשֶׁר בָּאוּ, *who came"* [in past tense] *(Rashi).*

The intent of *Rashi's* comment is to explain why, though the Torah was committed to writing about two and a half centuries later, the present rather than the past tense was used. He answers that in correct literary style the narrative was placed in the perspective of the time in which the event actually occurred, not when it was reported, and therefore the present tense was used *(Mizrachi; Be'er Yitzchak).*

The Jewish nation is based on chaste, pure family life, just as its census counts in the Wilderness were always reckoned according to its families. In the same way, at the moment of their entry into Egypt they are all enumerated according to their genealogy — יַעֲקֹב וּבָנָיו, *Jacob and his children.* They were so united that Jacob himself is counted as one of them [see *Rashbam* below] *(R' Hirsch).*

[On their being referred to here as 'children of *Israel'* while the Patriarch himself is referred to as *Jacob,* see *Ramban* above *v.* 2 s.v. *Jacob, Jacob.*]

R' Bachya makes the observation "all of the Patriarchs were called 'Israel' [in the sense that 'Israel' alludes to triumph over all opposing forces]. Here Isaac is called Israel, since *Jacob and his sons* are called children of *Israel.* Abraham is also referred to as Israel inasmuch as it is written [*Exodus* 12:40]: *Now the sojourning of the children of 'Israel' who dwelt in Egypt was four hundred and*

*daughters and all his offspring he brought with him
to Egypt.*
[8] *Now these are the names of the children of Israel
who were coming to Egypt — Jacob and his children:
Jacob's first-born, Reuben.*
[9] *Reuben's sons: Chanoch, Pallu, Chetzron and
Carmi.*
[10] *Simeon's Sons: Yemuel, Yamin, Ohad, Yachin,*

thirty years, whereas it is known that the computation of the sojourning began from Isaac; accordingly children of *Israel* in that verse refers to the children of Abraham." [See *comm.* 15:14.]

The phrase *Jacob and his sons* implies that Jacob is included in the count of seventy [verses 26-27 below] *(Rashbam).* [This is not the universal opinion, however; see *comm.* to *v.* 15 below.]

בְּכֹר יַעֲקֹב רְאוּבֵן — *Jacob's firstborn Reuben.*

Since his infraction with Bilhah, the birthright was taken from Reuben and given to Joseph [see 35:22]. Nevertheless, he was called 'firstborn' here only with regard to the division of the territory in *Eretz Yisrael.* The reason the Torah specifically designated him here as 'firstborn,' when the title could have been avoided entirely, is because Reuben acted like a firstborn when he attempted to save Joseph [37:21] *(Zohar; Lekach Tov).*

9. בְּנֵי רְאוּבֵן — Reuben's sons:

חֲנוֹךְ וּפַלּוּא וְחֶצְרֹן וְכַרְמִי — *Chanoch, [and] Pallu [and] Chetzron, and Carmi.*

The Sages derive exegetical significance in Scriptural names, and explain that these names were Divinely inspired to allude to the destinies of the respective people. We shall cite a representative sampling of such interpretations. Most are taken from *Midrash Sechel Tov,* whose author, according to *Torah Sheleimah,* apparently had before him a no-longer-extant Midrash on the subject of Biblical names and their meanings.

Chanoch: He was so called because he was involved in the *chinuch* [education] of his sons; and he was named after the righteous Chanoch [5:21-24].

Pallu: Signifies *destruction* [see *Onkelos* to *Deut.* 13:6 who renders *destroy* as וּתְפַלֵּי] inasmuch as his descendants were removed from the world. He had only one son, Eliab, who in turn begot Nemuel, Dathan and Abiram. Dathan and Abiram later perished in punishment for participating in the revolt of Korach, and only Nemuel survived.

Chetzron and *Carmi* were both born after the incident with Bilhah, when aspects of Reuben's birthright were taken from him. Thus *Chetzron* [*deprivation*], alludes to the forfeiture of these rights. Similarly *Carmi,* from the word כרם meaning shame, intimates how Reuben's face paled with shame at that incident *(Sechel Tov).*

10. וּבְנֵי שִׁמְעוֹן—Simeon's sons:

יְמוּאֵל וְיָמִין וְאֹהַד וְיָכִין וְצֹחַר — *Yemuel, [and] Yamin, [and] Ohad, [and] Yachin, [and] Tzochar.*

[The reader interested in the Midrashic allusions of these names

יא וְשָׁאוּל בֶּן־הַכְּנַעֲנִית: וּבְנֵי לֵוִי גֵּרְשׁוֹן
יב קְהָת וּמְרָרִי: וּבְנֵי יְהוּדָה עֵר וְאוֹנָן וְשֵׁלָה
וָפֶרֶץ וָזָרַח וַיָּמָת עֵר וְאוֹנָן בְּאֶרֶץ כְּנַעַן

is directed to *Torah Sheleimah* 46:§ 55-58 and notes thereon.]

[In the parallel lists in *Exodus* 6:15 *ff*, *Numbers* 26, and *I Chronicles* 2-8 several of the names listed here occur with slightly different spellings. We will indicate them as they are encountered. Some of the nuances of these differences are treated by the commentators in *Numbers*, and especially in *I Chronicles*, and will אי״ה be cited there. *Radak* in *Chronicles* 4:24 comments, 'You will see that regarding most Hebrew names of people or cities there is no concern over the substitution of a letter or two. Just as in the case of nations who are referred to by two names which bear no resemblance to one another, and one calls them in one place by one name and in another by another name.']

Yemuel is identical with the Yemuel listed in *Exodus* 6:15, and with Nemuel in *Numbers* 26:12. (See *R' Shmuel b. Chofni*).

Tzochar is identical with *Zerach* in *Numbers* 26:13, both names meaning 'light.' (*Rashi* to *Numbers* 26:13).

Both Ohad and Yachin are mentioned in *Exodus*, but not in *Numbers*. *Rashi* in *Numbers* 26:13 mentions that certain Simeonite tribes became extinct either after the death of Aaron or after the sin at Baal Peor. In *Chronicles* Yariv is substituted for Ohad and Yachin. There is an opinion that the remnants of these two sub-tribes united to form a new group.

וְשָׁאוּל בֶּן־הַכְּנַעֲנִית — *And Saul son of the Canaanite woman* [or: *Canaanitess*].

In the most literal sense, this verse is tacit proof that only Simeon, of all the brothers, married a woman of Canaanite descent, and the Torah therefore singles him out for it as he did wrong in taking a Canaanite wife. [The Canaanites were an accursed race, and one must recall Abraham's intense efforts to assure that Isaac would not marry a Canaanite woman (see 24:3), and Isaac's similar charge to Jacob (28:1)] (*Ibn Ezra*).

Ramban interprets similarly in 38:2. See also *Rashi* to 50:13 and *comm.* there.

According to the predominant Rabbinic view advanced by *Rashi*, 'Canaanitess' refers to Dinah. He explains that Saul was actually the son of Dinah who is here called a Canaanitess because she had been ravished by the Canaanite Shechem. When her brothers killed Shechem, Dinah refused to accompany them until Simeon agreed to marry her, which he did (*Rashi; Midrash*).[1]

[See *comm.* to 34:26; 37:35; *Ramban* to 38:2; *Mizrachi* and *Gur Aryeh* who discuss the identification with Dinah and the halachic aspects of this marriage; *Tiferes Zion* to the *Midrash; Maskil l'David* and *Divrei David*. [*See also Rashi* to 50:13.]

According to one view in the Midrash [*Bereishis Rabbah* 80:10] Dinah is here called a Canaanitess [not to evoke her shame, as the Torah is careful about the honor of every creature (*Tiferes Zion*)] but because Simeon brought her [re-

1. According to the Talmud [*Sanhedrin* 82b; see also *Targum Yonasan*] *'son' of a Canaanite* means: "one who acted like a Canaanite." This 'son' is identified with Zimri who later com-

Tzochar, and Saul, son of the Canaanite woman.
11 *Levi's sons: Gershon, Kehas, and Merari.*
12 *Judah's sons: Er, Onan, Shelah, Peretz and*
Zerach; but Er and Onan had died in the land of Ca-

mains from Egypt] and buried her in Canaan.

11. וּבְנֵי לֵוִי — Levi's sons:

גֵּרְשׁוֹן קְהָת וּמְרָרִי — *Gershon, Kehas, and Merari.*

Kehas [or Kehath] was the grandfather of Moses.

Midrash HaGadol notes that the mention of Kehas as one of the emigres to Egypt corroborates the promise made to Abraham in 15:16 that *the fourth generation shall return here.* For according to one computation, the four generations were: Kehas, who entered Egypt, Amram, Moses, and Moses' sons, the latter who entered the Land. [See *Ramban* cited in 15:16.]

12. וּבְנֵי יְהוּדָה — Judah's sons:

עֵר וְאוֹנָן וְשֵׁלָה וָפֶרֶץ וָזָרַח — *Er, [and] Onan, [and] Shelah, [and] Peretz, and Zerach.*

[The first three were born to Judah's first wife, the daughter of Shua, while the last two were born to Tamar.]

וַיָּמָת עֵר וְאוֹנָן בְּאֶרֶץ כְּנַעַן — *But* [lit. *and*] *Er and Onan had died in the land of Canaan.*

Since it is known that Er and Onan had died and are not included in the number of those who descended, why did the Torah deem it important to enumerate them at all in this verse among Judah's children?

— *Ramban* in *v.* 2 poses the question and answers it mystically by noting that "... it is due to a secret which can be known from the words we have already written. The learned student [of Kabbalah] will understand this as well as the meaning of the entire verse."

The commentators explain that *Ramban* is alluding to the mystical doctrine of transmigration of souls to which he refers in 38:8 [see footnote 2 on p. 1675]. In a mystical sense, according to *Alshich* (38:27), the souls of Er and Onan were reincarnated in the bodies of Peretz and Zerach after Judah performed the levirate union with Tamar. Thus, Er and Onan were still to be listed among Judah's children though they had died.

In a similar manner, *Or HaChaim* maintains that the souls of Er and Onan transmigrated into the bodies of Peretz's sons, Chetzron and Chamul. This accounts for the unusual phraseology **וַיִּהְיוּ** בְנֵי־פֶרֶץ חֶצְרֹן וְחָמוּל, *and they* — i.e., Er and Onan, who had died — **became** *the sons of Peretz Chetzron and Chamul,* rather than simply וּבְנֵי פֶרֶץ חֶצְרֹן וְחָמוּל, *and the sons of Peretz: Chetzron and Chamul* [without the word וַיִּהְיוּ. Apparently *Sechel Tov* interprets similarly; see below.]

According to *Ibn Ezra* in *v.* 10 who interprets that both Simeon and Judah married *Canaanite* wives in the literal sense, the Torah mentioned the names of Er and Onan to draw attention to the fact that these children begotten from a Canaanite wife were evil and subsequently died. [See *Yohel Or*].

R' Hirsch emphasizes that whenever the Torah mentions Er and Onan, it always stresses that they had died.

mitted the heinous act of brazen immorality in Shittim [see *Numbers* 25]. Indeed, the Talmud records that, "he had five names: 1. Zimri; 2. ben Salu [ibid 25:14]; 3. Saul; 4. *ben Canaanis;* 5. Shelumiel son of Tzurishaddai" [see *Maharsha*].

יג וַיִּהְיוּ בְּנֵי־פֶרֶץ חֶצְרֹן וְחָמוּל׃ וּבְנֵי
יד יִשָּׂשכָר תּוֹלָע וּפֻוָּה וְיוֹב וְשִׁמְרֹן׃ וּבְנֵי
טו זְבֻלוּן סֶרֶד וְאֵלוֹן וְיַחְלְאֵל׃ אֵלֶּה בְּנֵי לֵאָה
אֲשֶׁר יָלְדָה לְיַעֲקֹב בְּפַדַּן אֲרָם וְאֵת דִּינָה
בִתּוֹ כָּל־נֶפֶשׁ בָּנָיו וּבְנוֹתָיו שְׁלֹשִׁים

Belonging to the Godly family is not simply a matter of Jewish parentage. It carries the responsibility to live a pure and moral life, and failure to do so is not without consequence. The fate of Er and Onan recalls this lesson.

וַיִּהְיוּ בְנֵי־פֶרֶץ חֶצְרֹן וְחָמוּל — *And Peretz's sons were Chetzron and Chamul.*

Their grandfather Judah named the elder, declaring: 'May *Chetzron* be named in memory of the loss [*Chesron*] of my sons Er and Onan.' When the second was born he declared, 'Now God has had compassion [*Chamal*] on me and recompensed me with these, for my sons Er and Onan' *(Sechel Tov).*

[See *Or HaChaim above.*]

According to the traditional Rabbinic chronology presented on p. 1667, a total of twenty-two years elapsed between the sale of Joseph and Jacob's descent to Egypt. During this relatively short period the following transpired: Judah married the daughter of Shua [ch. 38]; Er, Onan and Shelah were born; he gave Er in marriage to Tamar, and Er died; Onan was then given to Tamar, and Onan also died. Tamar remained a widow for one year, after which Judah consorted with her and she gave birth to Peretz and Zerach. Peretz grew up, married, and had Chetzron and Chamul — Judah's grandchildren — who were among those who entered Egypt.

Thus, three generations spanned this twenty-two year period, and careful analysis will yield that Er, Onan, and Peretz could not have been older than 8 years when each of them married, a fact most noteworthy, but not unusual in Biblical times. See *Seder Olam* ch. 2, and cf. *Ibn Ezra* to 38:1.

13. וּבְנֵי יִשָּׂשְכָר—Issachar's sons:

תּוֹלָע וּפֻוָּה וְיוֹב וְשִׁמְרֹן — *Tola* [*and*] *Puvah,* [*and*] *Yov and Shimron.*

Yov is identified with Yashuv in *Numbers* 26:24 and *I Chronicles* 7:1. [See *comm.* there.] As an illustrious member of the Tribe known for its spiritual pursuits [see *comm.* to 49:14-15] the name Yashuv signifies that הֵשִׁיב, *he brought Israel back* to their Father in Heaven since he devoted his life to Torah study, while Yov signifies how, when he studied Torah, his voice quavered [יָבוּב] with trepidation *(Sechel Tov).*

According to one view, Issachar later realized that his son's name Yov was disgraceful inasmuch as it was the name of a heathen god. Issachar gave a letter (ש) of his own name to Yov and renamed him Yashuv. [This accounts for the silent *'shin'* in יִשָּׂשְכָר which is pronounced *Yissachar* rather than *Yissas'char; see Daas Zekeinim* to 30:18, p. 1308.]

14. וּבְנֵי זְבֻלוּן—Zebulun's sons:

סֶרֶד וְאֵלֹן וְיַחְלְאֵל — *Sered* [*and*] *Elon and Yachleel.*

"They were merchants, masters

*naan — and Peretz's sons were Chetzron and
Chamul.*
13 *Issachar's sons: Tola, Puvah, Yov and Shimron.*
14 *Zebulun's sons: Sered, Elon and Yachleel.*
15 *These are the sons of Leah whom she bore to Jacob
in Paddon Aram, in addition to Dinah his daughter.
All the persons — his sons and daughters —
numbered thirty-three.*

of commerce, nourishing their brothers ... " [see 49:14] *(Targum Yonasan).*

15. אֵלֶּה בְּנֵי לֵאָה אֲשֶׁר יָלְדָה לְיַעֲקֹב בְּפַדַּן אֲרָם — *These* [i.e., the aforementioned] *were the sons of Leah whom she bore to Jacob in Paddan Aram.*

The *sons* were born in Paddan Aram; the *grandchildren* were born in Canaan *(Sechel Tov).*

וְאֵת דִּינָה בִתּוֹ — *In addition to Dinah his daughter.*

The males are associated with Leah ['these are the sons of *Leah*'] and the female with Jacob [*'his* daughter'], to teach you that when the woman emits seed first she bears a male, but when the male is the first to emit seed she bears a female *(Rashi* from *Niddah* 31a).

[The exact connotation of this dictum in contemporary medical terms is unclear. The inference is either that the time relationship of ovulation to conception affects the sex of the fetus, or that female glandular secretions affect in some way the sex determining chromosomes of the male seed.]

Possibly the Torah emphasizes that Dinah was *his daughter* to stress that though she was defiled by Shechem, Jacob did not alienate her but still considered her *his daughter* in every respect *(R' Sheah Brander).*

⁂ The birth of Yocheved; the unnamed descendant.

כָּל־נֶפֶשׁ בָּנָיו וּבְנוֹתָיו שְׁלֹשִׁים וְשָׁלֹשׁ — *All the persons—his sons and daughters, numbered* [lit. *were*] *thirty-three.*

— A detailed count, however, yields only thirty-two! The thirty-third one is Yocheved who was born [as they entered the gateway] between the walls [or according to the reading in the Midrash: *at the gates of Egypt*] on the way into the city, as it is written [*Numbers* 26:59]: [*Yocheved* ...] who was *born to Levi in Egypt.* — [This is interpreted to imply:] she was *born* in Egypt, but she had not been *conceived* in Egypt *(Rashi).*

[Therefore, since she was still unborn when they set out, the Torah did not name her; but because she would be born by the time they reached the inner walls of Egypt, the Torah included her in the total count.]

[This is based on *Bava Basra* 123a and the Midrash. However, in both of these sources the interpretation is inspired by the fact that the aggregate total is given in *v.* 26 below as seventy whereas only sixty-nine names are enumerated. In providing a running commentary to Scripture, however, *Rashi* attaches his comment here, instead of *v.* 26, since it is in our verse that the discrepancy is first encountered.

[Yocheved's birth at this time — when the famine still raged — raises the question of how Levi indulged in procreation in violation of the rule that one must abstain from conjugal relations in time of famine. This has been discussed at length in the *comm.* to 41:50.]

Ibn Ezra's approach.

Characteristic of his literal approach to Scriptural interpretation, *Ibn Ezra (v.* 23) finds great difficulty in the Midrashic interpretation that Yocheved was born as they entered Egypt. [To preserve the flavor, there follows an almost literal translation:]

"... It is surprising why Scripture did not mention the miracle wrought for her, for [if she was born as they entered Egypt, it follows that] she gave birth to Moses when she was 130 years old! [The duration of the Israelite stay in Egypt was 210 years. Moses was 80 years old when he stood before Pharaoh shortly before the Exodus; accordingly he was born 130 years after the Israelites arrived in Egypt. If his mother Yocheved was indeed born as Jacob's family entered the gates, she would have been 130 years old when Moses was born. According to Rabbinic tradition cited by *Rashi* in *Exodus* 2:1, Yocheved *was* truly 130 years old when Moses was born.]

"And why *did* the Torah publicize the case of Sarah, who gave birth when she was ninety years old [i.e., if the miracle of Yocheved's giving birth at a much older age was even greater]? And as if this 'distress' was not enough, the liturgical poets *(payyatanim)* composed a *piyut* for Simchas Torah wherein Moses is poetically quoted as saying, יוֹכֶבֶד אִמִּי אַחֲרַי הִתְנַחֲמִי, *Yocheved my mother, be comforted after my death* [implying that Yocheved outlived Moses]. Accordingly, Yocheved would have been 250 years old [when Moses died, adding 130 to Moses' lifespan of 120]. Now, that Ahijah the Shilonite [*I Kings* 11:29] lived a life of long duration is an Aggadic exposition or the opinion of an individual." [According to *Seder Olam* and *Bava Basra* 121b, Ahijah the Shilonite was one of those who enjoyed exceptional longevity. He was among those who left Egypt and was still alive in the days of Jeroboam I, king of Israel — a period of about 550 years. *Ibn Ezra* maintains that if this Aggadic tradition of Ahijah's exceptional longevity of close to 550 years was the basis for the *payyatan's* assertion that Yocheved could have been alive when Moses died, this conclusion has no bearing on *the exposition of Scripture in its literal sense,* inasmuch as the *Seder Olam* exegesis is the opinion of an individual (see *Ibn Ezra's* comment to *Exodus* 19:17; however cf. *Rambam,* intro. to *Yad; Ra'avad* there; and intro. of *Kessef Mishnah).*

Instead, *Ibn Ezra* [as does *Rashbam, Lekach Tov, Ralbag, Abarbanel,* and *Radal* to *Pirkei d' Rabbi Eliezer* §39] goes on to maintain that in the *p'shat* — simple sense of Scripture — Jacob himself is included in the count. He explains that, "the verse should be interpreted as if it read, *All the persons — his sons and daughters* [including himself] — *were thirty-three.* Proof of this is that it said above [*v.* 8]: *These are the names of the children of Israel coming to Egypt,* **Jacob and his sons** ... Jacob thus being included in the count. The fact that several verses seem to imply that only Jacob's *descendants* are included in the count [see *v.* 26; *Exodus* 1:5] is no contradiction inasmuch as the Torah often includes an individual in a general context. An example of this occurs in 35:26, which lists Jacob's sons *who were born to him in Paddan Aram.* Benjamin is included although he was born in Canaan, since the Torah generalizes ... And this is the primary interpretation." [This opinion, that Jacob was included in the count also follows one view in the *Midrash. R' David Feinstein* queries, however, why if Jacob is included in the total count, he is enumerated specifically here among Leah's children, rather than with the total in verses 26-27 below. רצ״ע.]

[Nevertheless, *Ibn Ezra's* opinion that Jacob is to be included in the total count of descendants, a view shared by many commentators — and even by one Sage in the Midrash — does not *necessarily* conflict with the Rabbinic tradition that Yocheved was born at the precise moment they entered Egypt. The difference lies only in whether she is to be included in the count of thirty-three, and later in the total count of the seventy souls who descended to Egypt. Those who expound the literal sense of the passage suggest that the number includes Jacob, while others — citing the tradition that Yocheved was born as they entered Egypt — include her in the account. There is even the view, advanced by *Daas Zekeinim* above that it is the *Shechinah* (Divine Presence), that promised to 'descend' with them, that is included in the count.

[It is because *Ibn Ezra* attempts to rationally disprove the notion of Yocheved's exceptional longevity, however, that *Ramban* enunciates his lengthy refutation which follows.]

Ramban's defense of the Rabbinic tradition.

Ramban cites *Ibn Ezra's* disagreement with the tradition of Yocheved's longevity and his question of why, if she actually lived so long, the Torah does not mention the miracle of her giving birth to Moses at such an advanced age. In an expression of 'open rebuke and hidden love' (as *Ramban,* in his introduction to *Bereishis* describes the mixture of criticism and admiration with which he reacted to *Ibn Ezra's* sometimes controversial comments), *Ramban* takes exception to *Ibn Ezra's* stance.

In a discourse fundamental to the correct understanding of Biblical narratives, *Ramban* maintains that Yocheved's advanced age at the time of Moses' birth is indeed a miracle, but of the category of 'hidden' miracles, which constitute the foundation of the Torah. [See *Ramban* to 27:1 where he explains that 'hidden' miracles are occurrences that do not clearly show Divine intervention, but appear to be merely part of the 'natural' order, while 'obvious' miracles are those which incontrovertibly defy the 'laws of nature', and clearly and undeniably are recognized as direct Divine intervention. See also *Exodus* 6:2; *Levit.* 26:11.] Even according to *Ibn Ezra's* thesis that Yocheved could not have been born at the gateway to Egypt, we cannot escape the fact that unusual longevity existed in Moses' family. For Yocheved was clearly Levi's daughter, and Levi was 43 years old when the family went down to Egypt. [Jacob was 87 years old when Levi was born; since Jacob describes himself as 130 when he stood before Pharaoh (further 47:9) it follows that Levi was 43 at the time.]

Now, there is no doubt that Moses was born 130 years after the descent into Egypt, since he was 80 at the time of the Exodus. Therefore, if we were to presume that Levi did not beget Yocheved for many years after they arrived in Egypt — say, for example, 57 years — then [following *Ibn Ezra's* rationale] there would be *two* miracles here: a) that Levi begot a child at the age of 100 [the age at which Abraham had Isaac], and b) Yocheved would still have been an elderly woman of 73 when Moses was born! And should we postpone Yocheved's birth to an even later time [as *Ibn Ezra* would have it] then the wonder of Levi's begetting her at such an advanced age increases dramatically![1]

1. *Ramban* proceeds to enunciate the principle that 'The Torah mentions [only] miracles performed through a prophet and which he previously prophesied, or performed by an angel who is revealed in the course of a Divine mission. However, those "hidden" miracles effected "naturally" in order to help the righteous or destroy the wicked are not mentioned in the Torah or in the books of the Prophets ...

'For why should Scripture mention "hidden" miracles when all the foundations of the Torah are hidden miracles! Every assurance in the Torah is truly a sign and wonder, since the concept of heavenly death for one who has transgressed the prohibition of forbidden unions is not natural, nor is it "natural" that the "heavens should become like iron" [*Levit.* 26:19] because we sowed our fields in a Sabbatical [שְׁמִיטָּה] year.

'Similarly, all of the Torah's assurances of blessings that will result from observance of the *mitzvos* and all the good fortune enjoyed by the righteous ... as well as all our prayers, are predicated on miracles and wonders, except that there is no heralded change in the nature of the world, as I have already explained [see above 17:1] and I will yet explain further [*Lev.* 26:11] with the help of God.'

טז וְשָׁלֹשׁ: וּבְנֵי גָד צִפְיוֹן וְחַגִּי שׁוּנִי וְאֶצְבֹּן
יז עֵרִי וַאֲרוֹדִי וְאַרְאֵלִי: וּבְנֵי אָשֵׁר יִמְנָה
וְיִשְׁוָה וְיִשְׁוִי וּבְרִיעָה וְשֶׂרַח אֲחֹתָם וּבְנֵי
יח בְרִיעָה חֶבֶר וּמַלְכִּיאֵל: אֵלֶּה בְּנֵי זִלְפָּה
אֲשֶׁר־נָתַן לָבָן לְלֵאָה בִתּוֹ וַתֵּלֶד אֶת־
יט אֵלֶּה לְיַעֲקֹב שֵׁשׁ עֶשְׂרֵה נָפֶשׁ: בְּנֵי רָחֵל

Ramban proceeds to draw support from the case of Obed [Boaz's son, and grandfather of King David] who, according to the Sages, lived more than 400 years, and Ruth who, according to tradition, was still alive in the days of King Solomon.

He maintains that it was not Abraham's age alone at the birth of Isaac that was miraculous, for old age does not affect someone until three-quarters of his life has passed, and Abraham, who lived to be 175, begot Isaac twenty-five years prior to the completion of two-thirds of his lifespan. Moreover, Abraham had children forty years after the birth of Isaac [see 25:1*ff*] — something far more noteworthy.

Rather, the real miracle in the case of Abraham and Sarah [which puts it into the category of an 'open' miracle that is worthy of mention in the Torah] was that they could not have children together in their younger years, and now, at relatively advanced ages, they begot a child. Moreover, in Sarah's case the additional wonder was that she no longer menstruated [see 18:11] and so was incapable of giving birth.

Accordingly, *Ramban* concludes, "if Yocheved's lifespan reached her father's age [of 137 years (*Exodus* 6:16)] and her vitality remained with her near her old age, as is the case, it is not an obvious miracle that she gave birth at the age recorded by the Sages [i.e. 130 years]. It is because God wanted to redeem Israel through the brothers [Moses and Aaron], and since the time of the redemption had not yet come, He delayed their births many years until their mother was old. Nothing is too difficult for HASHEM!"

16-17 Descendants through Zilpah.

[See *Ramban* v. 18].

16. וּבְנֵי גָד — Gad's sons:

צִפְיוֹן וְחַגִּי שׁוּנִי וְאֶצְבֹּן עֵרִי וַאֲרוֹדִי וְאַרְאֵלִי — *Tziphion,* [*and*] *Chaggi,* [*and*] *Shuni,* [*and*] *Etzbon, Eri,* [*and*] *Arodi and Areli.*

[In *Numbers* 26:15-16, *Tziphion* occurs as *Tzephon,* and *Etzbon* occurs as *Ozni.* The Midrash derives exegetical significance in these changes.]

17. וּבְנֵי אָשֵׁר — Asher's sons:

וְשֶׂרַח אֲחֹתָם — *And their sister Serach.*

Tur writes: "Some interpret [see *Ramban* to *Numb.* 26:46] that inasmuch as it does not say *Serach his daughter,* the implication is that she was not Asher's daughter but was the daughter of his wife [i.e. from a previous marriage]. And so does *Onkelos* translate *Numbers* 26:46, *Serach the daughter of Asher* as: "Serach the daughter of Asher's *wife*" [our versions of *Onkelos* do not read this way; but see *Sefer HaYashar* where this tradition is recorded]. However, I do not understand this," *Tur* continues, "'because our Scriptural narrative is enumerating only those who were Jacob's biological descendants 'that

[16] *Gad's sons: Tziphion, Chaggi, Shuni, Etzbon,
Eri, Arodi, and Areli.*
[17] *Asher's sons: Yimnah, Yishvah, Yishvi, Beriah,
and their sister Serach; Beriah's sons, Cheber and
Malkiel* [18] *These were the descendants of Zilpah
whom Laban had given to Leah his daughter. These
she bore to Jacob: sixteen persons.*
[19] *The sons of Rachel, Jacob's wife: Joseph and
Benjamin.*

came out of his loins' [*v.* 26; accordingly, that she was Asher's daughter is immaterial to the listing of Jacob's descendants]. Rather, that she is identified in keeping with the Scriptural style to identify women through their brothers. For example [36:22]: *Lotan's sister was Timna"* [*also 4:22; 25:20; 28:29; Exod.* 6:23; 15:20].

[Serach had played a special role in gently informing Jacob that Joseph was still alive. For her comforting mannerism, Jacob blessed her with exceptional longevity and following the tradition cited in the *comm.* to 45:26, she was one of the righteous people who never experienced death and entered live into the Garden of Eden.]

Comp. *Targum Yonasan: "And Serach their sister* — who was carried away while yet alive into the Garden of Eden because she had announced to Jacob that Joseph was still alive. It was she who saved the inhabitants of the city of Abel from death in the days of Joab."[1]

18. אֵלֶּה בְּנֵי זִלְפָּה אֲשֶׁר נָתַן לָבָן לְלֵאָה בִתּוֹ — *These* [enumerated above] *were the descendants of Zilpah, whom Laban had given to Leah his daughter.*

As a servant, and Rachel freed her (*Sechel Tov*).

The Torah generally lists Leah's children first, then Rachel's, and then the servants. In this case, however, the four mothers are enumerated in descending order according to the number of their children, because the purpose is to show how the total of seventy was composed. Therefore Zilpah's more numerous descendants are listed before Rachel's (*Ramban*).

וַתֵּלֶד אֶת־אֵלֶּה לְיַעֲקֹב שֵׁשׁ עֶשְׂרֵה נָפֶשׁ — *These she bore to Jacob: sixteen persons* [lit. *soul(s)*].

The *Vilna Gaon* observes that in this genealogy the descendants of the matriarchs [Rachel and Leah] were double those of their respective servants [Bilhah and Zilpah]. Leah's descendants totaled 32 [the number 33, as noted, includes Yocheved or Jacob], while those of Zilpah, her servant, numbered 16;

1. The incident of Joab, King David's commanding general and the city of Abel is formed in *II Samuel* 20:14-22 and expanded upon in *Bereishis Rabbah* 94:9. Sheva ben Bichri was a traitor who followed Absalom's rebellion against David. As a rebel, Sheva was liable to the death penalty and Joab was dispatched with a troop of soldiers to carry it out. Sheva took refuge in Abel whereupon Joab laid seige to the city. Since the townspeople refused to surrender Sheva, Joab was prepared to fight them to the last man. Scripture relates that אִשָּׁה חֲכָמָה מִן הָעִיר, *a wise woman of the city,* spoke to Joab and convinced him to leave the city alone if they would give up Sheva. Then, as explained by the Midrash, she shrewdly convinced the townspeople to execute Sheva, whereupon Joab lifted the seige.

כ אֵ֥שֶׁת יַעֲקֹ֖ב יוֹסֵ֥ף וּבִנְיָמִֽן: וַיִּוָּלֵ֣ד לְיוֹסֵף֮
בְּאֶ֣רֶץ מִצְרַיִם֒ אֲשֶׁ֤ר יָֽלְדָה־לּוֹ֙ אָֽסְנַ֔ת בַּת
פּ֥וֹטִי פֶ֖רַע כֹּהֵ֣ן אֹ֑ן אֶת־מְנַשֶּׁ֖ה וְאֶת־
כא אֶפְרָֽיִם: וּבְנֵ֣י בִנְיָמִ֗ן בֶּ֤לַע וָבֶ֙כֶר֙ וְאַשְׁבֵּ֔ל
גֵּרָ֖א וְנַעֲמָ֑ן אֵחִ֣י וָרֹ֔אשׁ מֻפִּ֥ים וְחֻפִּ֖ים
כב וָאָֽרְדְּ: אֵ֚לֶּה בְּנֵ֣י רָחֵ֔ל אֲשֶׁ֥ר יֻלַּ֖ד לְיַעֲקֹ֑ב
כג כָּל־נֶ֖פֶשׁ אַרְבָּעָ֥ה עָשָֽׂר: וּבְנֵי־דָ֖ן חֻשִֽׁים:

Rachel's descendants numbered 14, while those of Bilhah, her servant, numbered 7 *(HaKsav V'Hakabbalah).*

19.-20. Descendants through Rachel.

19. בְּנֵי רָחֵל אֵשֶׁת יַעֲקֹב יוֹסֵף וּבִנְיָמִן — *The sons of Rachel, Jacob's wife: Joseph and Benjamin.*

Since for the reason mentioned above [v. 18], Rachel was preceded in this chapter by Zilpah, special honor is now paid to her by designating her as Jacob's wife *(Ramban).*

None of the other wives are described as *Jacob's wife;* Rachel however, was the עֲקֶרֶת הַבַּיִת, *mainstay of the household* [i.e. his principal wife, since it was for her that he initially had agreed to work for Laban] *(Rashi;* see *Rashi* to 31:4;31:33, and Midrash to 29:31 s.v. רָחֵל עֲקָרָה).

[See also 44:27 where even Judah quotes his father as referring to Rachel by the designation אִשְׁתִּי, *my wife (par excellence).*]

Though Rachel was the primary wife she was not blessed with abundant progeny as was Leah. But she surpassed Leah in the quality of her children. This is why, as *Sforno* notes, the Torah assigns a special honor to her: In the case of the other three wives, we are not told that, for example, the children of Leah were Reuben, Simeon, etc. Only in Rachel's case does the Torah say *The sons of Rachel* ... However, she earned special mention because her sons were the most outstanding, as the Talmud *(Sotah* 36b) teaches, Joseph was worthy to be the father of twelve tribes, and *(Shabbos* 55b) Benjamin never sinned.

20. אֲשֶׁר יָלְדָה־לוֹ אָסְנַת בַּת־פּוֹטִי פֶרַע כֹּהֵן אֹן — *Whom Asenath daughter of Poti Phera chief of On bore to him.*

She bore them to him in the sense that she converted to Joseph's faith and raised the children in a manner dedicated to his ideals *(Midrash Tadshe* cited in *Torah Sheleimah* §105; comp. *comm.* 41:50).

It says, *These are the generations of Jacob — Joseph* [37:2] because Joseph was like Jacob in every way [see commentary there]. For this reason the Torah mentions the name of Joseph's wife and her father [which it does not do in the case of the other sons], just as the names of Jacob's wives and their father Laban are mentioned when Jacob's genealogies are listed *(Tz'ror HaMor).*

[The translation of כֹּהֵן as *chief* follows *Rashi* to 47:22. *Ramban* to 41:46 interprets

[20] To Joseph were born in the land of Egypt —
whom Asenath daughter of Poti Phera Chief of On
bore to him — Manasseh and Ephraim.
[21] Benjamin's sons: Bela, Becher, Ashbel, Gera,
Naaman, Echi, Rosh, Mupim, Chupim, and Ard.
[22] These were the descendants of Rachel who were
born to Jacob, fourteen persons in all.
[23] Dan's sons: Chushim.

the word in its usual sense of *priest*.

[On the identity of Poti Phera with Potiphar see *comm.* to 41:46. On Asenath, see footnote there (p. 1800).]

אֶת מְנַשֶּׁה וְאֶת אֶפְרָיִם — *Manasseh and Ephraim.*

The particle אֶת is often exegetically interpreted as connoting a רִבּוּי, extension, beyond the literal scope of the noun it precedes, as if it implied *'along with ...'*. In this case, the אֶת preceding the names of *Manasseh* and *Ephraim* implies: *and all who were descended from them.* For just as Jacob's own children were to develop into subdivisions and families, so were the families of Manasseh and Ephraim [who themselves were the heads of tribes] destined to develop into subdivisions *(Tz'ror HaMor).*

21. וּבְנֵי בִנְיָמִן—Benjamin's sons:

בֶּלַע וָבֶכֶר וְאַשְׁבֵּל גֵּרָא וְנַעֲמָן אֵחִי וָרֹאשׁ מֻפִּים וְחֻפִּים וָאָרְדְּ — *Bela, [and] Becher, [and] Ashbel, Gera, [and] Naaman, Echi, [and] Rosh, Mupim, [and] Chupim, and Ard.*

[The names appear differently in *Numbers* 26:38 and in *I Chronicles* 7:6, 8:1. See *Rashi* and comm. to *Numbers* 26:24 and *Malbim* to *I Chron.* 7:6.]

[Benjamin had his 'lost' brother, Joseph, in mind when he named his children. For as *Rashi* notes in 43:34 each one of these names referred to Joseph and signified in some way the troubles that had befallen him. See footnote p. 1883.]

22. אֵלֶּה בְּנֵי רָחֵל אֲשֶׁר יֻלַּד לְיַעֲקֹב — *These were the descendants of Rachel who were born to Jacob.*

[The Hebrew verb יֻלַּד, *was born,* is in singular. In Scriptural style the singular is often to be construed collectively. Comp. 41:50 וּלְיוֹסֵף יֻלַּד שְׁנֵי בָנִים.]

כָּל־נֶפֶשׁ אַרְבָּעָה עָשָׂר — *Fourteen persons in all* [lit. *all soul(s): fourteen*].

Counting children and grandchildren *(Tz'ror HaMor).*

23.-24. Descendants through Bilhah.

23. וּבְנֵי דָן—Dan's sons:

חֻשִׁים — *Chushim.*

The plural *sons* is used even though only the name of one son is given.

Ibn Ezra conjectures that the phraseology implies that Dan might have originally had two sons, one of whom died and is therefore not named.

Radak, R' Shmuel b. Chofni, and most other commentators, however, maintain that Dan's only son was Chushim. The plural *sons* is used with the following meaning: *All of Dan's sons were only Chushim.* Similarly do we find in *Numbers* 26:8: *And the sons of Pallu: Eliab.* The form occurs frequently in

כד וּבְנֵי נַפְתָּלִי יַחְצְאֵל וְגוּנִי וְיֵצֶר וְשִׁלֵּם׃
כה אֵלֶּה בְּנֵי בִלְהָה אֲשֶׁר־נָתַן לָבָן לְרָחֵל
בִּתּוֹ וַתֵּלֶד אֶת־אֵלֶּה לְיַעֲקֹב כָּל־נֶפֶשׁ
כו שִׁבְעָה׃ כָּל־הַנֶּפֶשׁ הַבָּאָה לְיַעֲקֹב
מִצְרַיְמָה יֹצְאֵי יְרֵכוֹ מִלְּבַד נְשֵׁי בְנֵי־
כז יַעֲקֹב כָּל־נֶפֶשׁ שִׁשִּׁים וָשֵׁשׁ׃ וּבְנֵי יוֹסֵף
אֲשֶׁר־יֻלַּד־לוֹ בְמִצְרַיִם נֶפֶשׁ שְׁנָיִם כָּל־
הַנֶּפֶשׁ לְבֵית־יַעֲקֹב הַבָּאָה מִצְרַיְמָה
°ששי כח שִׁבְעִים׃ °וְאֶת־יְהוּדָה שָׁלַח

Scripture. [See also *I Chron.* 2:8. *R' Shmuel b. Chofni* lists eleven instances where the plural *sons* is used and only one son is listed].

In *v.* 7 above, too, as *Ramban* there notes, the plural *daughters* is used although only Dinah is meant. He cites our verse and explains that in genealogical lists it is common for Scripture to use the plural form for an individual.

From our passage the Talmud [*Bava Basra* 143b] derives a law of inheritance. If a dying man, with a son and a daughter, said נְכָסַי לְבָנַי, *my property should go to my sons* (in the plural), do we say that the plural form was intended to include his daughter [in which case, the word לְבָנַי would be understood to mean *my children*], or do we say that he meant only his *son*, but people sometimes refer to a single son in the plural? Our verse is cited as proof, since Dan's only son is described as וּבְנֵי דָן, the **sons** of Dan.

Although this is the settled law, as proven from other verses, the Talmud cites a different interpretation of our verse, as taught by the Academy of Chizkiah. The name Chushim may not have been his proper name. Instead, *Chushim* may mean fast-growing leaves of a reed and denotes how [in later generations (*Tosafos* s.v. שֶׁהָיוּ)] Dan's offspring — though descending from an only son — would become חֲשִׁים, as numerous as the leaves of a reed just as undergrowth develops from only a single root.

The implication, as *Tosafos* writes, is that at this point Dan had only one son who was named *Chushim* in anticipation of Dan's future progeny *(Meam Loez).* [In Numbers 26:42 he is called Shucham.]

Comp. *Targum Yonasan:* "The sons of Dan — prolific men and merchants of whose numbers there is no end."

According to the tradition cited in *Sotah* 13a Chushim was deaf and very powerful. It was he who killed Esau [see *Commentary* to 49:21 and 50:13].

24. וּבְנֵי נַפְתָּלִי—Naftali's sons:

יַחְצְאֵל וְגוּנִי וְיֵצֶר וְשִׁלֵּם — *Jahzeel, [and] Guni, [and] Jezer and Shilem.*

25. אֵלֶּה בְּנֵי בִלְהָה אֲשֶׁר נָתַן לָבָן לְרָחֵל בִּתּוֹ — *These were the descendants of Bilhah, whom Laban had given to Rachel his daughter.*

— As a servant, and Rachel freed her *(Sechel Tov).*

וַתֵּלֶד אֶת־אֵלֶּה לְיַעֲקֹב כָּל נֶפֶשׁ שִׁבְעָה — *[And] she bore these to Jacob — seven persons in all* [lit. *all soul(s): seven*].

She bore in the sense that those mentioned descended from her, and

[24] *Naftali's sons: Yahzeel, Guni, Yezer and Shilem.*
[25] *These were the descendants of Bilhah whom Laban had given to Rachel his daughter. She bore these to Jacob: seven persons in all.*
[26] *All the persons coming with Jacob to Egypt — his own descendants aside from the wives of Jacob's sons — sixty-six persons in all.*
[27] *And Joseph's sons who were born to him in Egypt numbered two persons. All the persons of Jacob's household who came to Egypt [totaled] seventy.*

'grandchildren are like children' *(R' Shmuel b. Chofni).*

26. The totals:

כָּל הַנֶּפֶשׁ הַבָּאָה לְיַעֲקֹב מִצְרַיְמָה ... כָּל נֶפֶשׁ שִׁשִּׁים וָשֵׁשׁ — *All the persons* [lit. *soul*] *coming with* [lit. *to*] *Jacob to Egypt ... sixty-six persons in all* [lit. *all the soul: sixty-six*].

That is, all the persons who set out on the journey from Canaan to Egypt numbered 66, thus excluding Joseph and his sons, who were awaiting them in Egypt. [Leah's listed descendants: 32; Zilpah's: 16; Rachel's: 11; Bilhah's: 7=66.] The word בָּאָה, accented as it is on the second syllable, אָה, is in the present (imperfect) tense *were coming*, as in 29:6: בָּאָה עִם הַצֹּאן, *Rachel ... was coming with the sheep,* meaning that *those who were accompanying Jacob* to Egypt numbered sixty-six. [See next verse] *(Rashi).*

יֹצְאֵי יְרֵכוֹ מִלְּבַד נְשֵׁי בְנֵי־יַעֲקֹב — *His own descendants* [lit. *who emanated from his loins*], *aside from the wives of Jacob's sons.*

I.e., the total included only blood descendants of Jacob, exclusive of his daughters-in-law.

[The Midrashic controversy regarding the identity of Jacob's daughters-in-law is given in 37:35 and 38:2. Briefly, R' Yehudah maintains that twin sisters were born together with each of Jacob's sons, and the siblings married one another (see *comm.* there and to *v.* 10 above). R' Nechemiah maintains that the brothers married Canaanite women. Following R' Nechemiah, Canaanite daughters-in-law are not mentioned, because, as the verse tells us, they were not Jacob's biological descendants.]

Following R' Yehudah's view that twin sisters were born with each of Jacob's sons [and accordingly, as Jacob's biological descendants, they should have been enumerated as was Serach], *Rashi* maintains that it must be assumed that they died before this. [And the fact that it says *aside from the wives of Jacob's sons* implies that the sons remarrried, and these wives, not being Jacob's biological descendants, are not numbered among the seventy *(Divrei David;* see *Gur Aryeh).*]

Ramban cites *Rashi* and disagrees with his conclusion that the twin sisters died. Since they were married to the brothers, the Torah alludes to them in the phrase: *aside from the wives of*

Jacob's sons. They need not be counted separately since a man and his wife are one with regard to raising a family.

[*Ramban* in 37:10 derives from the absence of any mention of Jacob's wives in this genealogy that they had all died by this time. It is unclear how this reconciles with the view advanced here that wives are not counted separately since husband and wife are one.]

27. וּבְנֵי יוֹסֵף — Joseph's sons:

אֲשֶׁר יֻלַּד־לוֹ מִצְרַיִם נֶפֶשׁ שְׁנָיִם — *Who were* [lit. *was*] *born to him in Egypt were two persons* [lit., *two soul(s)*].

The singular יֻלַּד, *was born*, possibly indicates that Manasseh and Ephraim were twins and born in one childbirth (*Radak* to 41:50).

◆§ The 70 Descendants

כָּל הַנֶּפֶשׁ לְבֵית־יַעֲקֹב הַבָּאָה מִצְרַיְמָה שִׁבְעִים — *All the persons* [lit. *soul*] *of Jacob's household who had come to Egypt* [totaled] *seventy.*[1]

Unlike *v.* 26 above, here the accent on the word בָּאָה is on the first syllable, בָּ, to indicate the past tense: The number of people who had actually *come* to Egypt was 70. The 66 immigrants found Joseph and his two sons there [so they are also included in the number who arrived there], and Yocheved was added to their number at that point because, as noted, she was born 'between the walls' (*Rashi*).

As discussed at length in the *comm.* to *v.* 15, if one were to count the individual names enumerated in this chapter, one would find a total of only 69, not 70, names. *Rashi* thus follows the traditional Rabbinic tradition that the unnamed seventieth person is Yocheved.

◆§ Other views of who completed the total number of 70:

- ☐ The Patriarch Jacob himself is to be counted among the group as the expression *Jacob and his children* in *v.* 8 might imply [see *Ibn Ezra v.* 15].
- ☐ The Divine Presence was the seventieth, for He joined their group, as it were, in fulfillment of His promise to Jacob [in *v.* 4]: *I will go down with you.*[2]
- ☐ Furthermore, *Rosh* at the end of *Pesachim* advances the view that in the simple sense, no one is 'missing', since it is reflective of Biblical usage for the Torah to round off a number when just one unit is missing (e.g. 69 to 70).[3]

1. Although when he left Canaan, Esau's family consisted only of six members [himself and his five sons], the Torah, in 36:6, uses the plural term נְפָשׁוֹת, '*souls* of his house,' since they each worshipped different gods [and were not unified, each of them being, different personalities, and each displaying, as it were, different 'souls']. In the case of Jacob's family, however, although it consisted of seventy members, the Torah uses the singular term נֶפֶשׁ, *soul,* since they all served one God [and displayed a single 'soul'. Thus, the souls the Jewish people are joined in their collective closeness to God, for as they affirm their bond with God, they form one organism.] (*Rashi* citing *Vayikra Rabbah*).

2. The tradition of the Divine Presence 'associating' Itself, as it were, with the righteous, has precedent. Abraham had asked God to include His Majesty with the righteous of Sodom in order to make up the necessary quorum of ten to save the inhabitants [see on 18:28, s.v. הֲתַשְׁחִית]. Joseph's brothers, too, when selling Joseph, associated the Divine Majesty in order to complete a quorum to effectuate their solemn ban against divulging what they had done [see footnote p. 1653]. Similarly, according to *Midrash HaGadol,* when the Israelites left Egypt they numbered 599,999 and the Divine Presence associated with them to bring the total up to the sacred mystical number 600,000.

3. [*Torah Temimah* questions the latter interpretation inasmuch as the discrepancy leading to the need to identify a 'missing' person does not originate with this verse where the number 69 might merely have been rounded off to 70, but originates in *v.* 15 where the number of Leah's descendants is given as 33 although a name-by-name count yields only 32.]

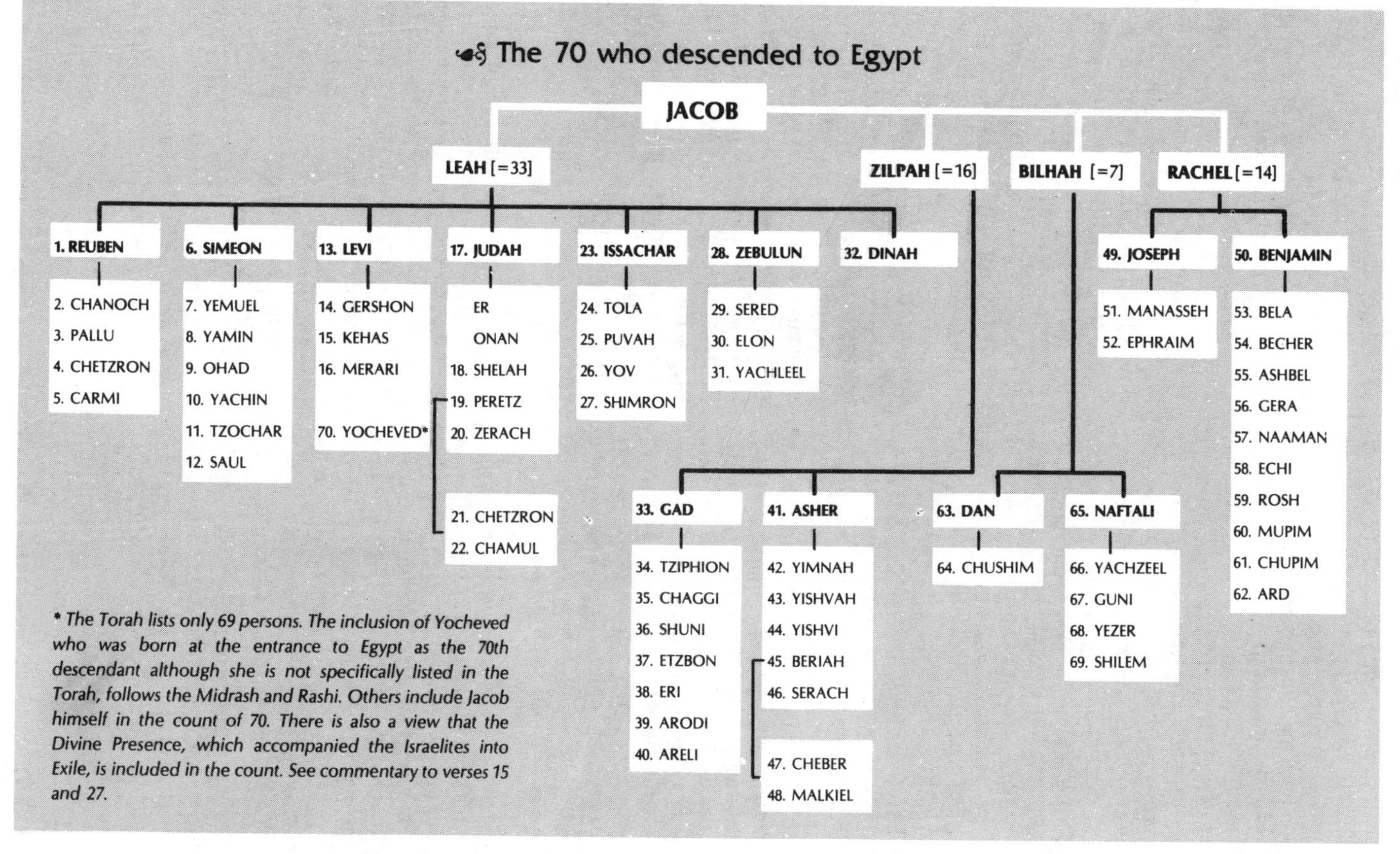

** The Torah lists only 69 persons. The inclusion of Yocheved who was born at the entrance to Egypt as the 70th descendant although she is not specifically listed in the Torah, follows the Midrash and Rashi. Others include Jacob himself in the count of 70. There is also a view that the Divine Presence, which accompanied the Israelites into Exile, is included in the count. See commentary to verses 15 and 27.*

The Torah's purpose in stating their number was to accentuate the miraculous increase they enjoyed in Egypt. For at this juncture they numbered but 70 persons, and at the Exodus they numbered 600,000 males of fighting age! *(Ramban).*

Thus, in the Passover Haggadah we repeat the verse [*Deut.* 10:22]: *With seventy souls your fathers went down to Egypt, but now God has made you as numerous as the stars of the heavens.*

Sfas Emes and others elaborate on the connection between Jacob's seventy descendants and the seventy primary nations of whom the Sages frequently speak. *Deuteronomy* 32:8 teaches יַצֵּב גְּבוּלוֹת עַמִּים לְמִסְפַּר בְּנֵי יִשְׂרָאֵל, [God] *set the boundaries of the nations according to the number of the Children of Israel.* Just as each nation has its own unique role to play on the stage of history, so each member of Jacob's family made his own special contribution to the development of the national destiny. The seventy souls also correspond to the 'seventy aspects of the Torah,' because each Jew has his own share in understanding and embodying the Torah's teachings. [See *R' David Feinstein's* explanation of the significance of the many parallels to the seventy nations in the footnote on p. 309.]

28. Jacob dispatches Judah

Joseph had informed Jacob that he would be dwelling in Goshen [45:10]. Now that Jacob neared the Egyptian border, he sent Judah ahead [*Rashi* explains לְפָנָיו as: *before his arrival*] to Joseph to alert him of their arrival so that the necessary preparations could be authorized and carried out.

וְאֶת־יְהוּדָה שָׁלַח לְפָנָיו אֶל יוֹסֵף – [*And*] *he* [Jacob] *sent Judah ahead of him to Joseph.*

The subject is Jacob. The Torah often omits the subject when it is evident from the context *(Radak).*

[The Torah emphasizes that he sent him *to Joseph.* All necessary preparations had to be authorized by Joseph.]

Jacob chose Judah for this since he was the sovereign over his brothers, as will become clear when Jacob blesses his sons on his deathbed [see 49:5*ff*]. Reuben forfeited his primary position following the incident with Bilhah; Simeon and Levi were likewise passed over because of their impetuosity in the matter of Shechem.

By his many deeds, Judah had consistently demonstrated himself to be the most accomplished and competent of Jacob's older sons. It was only Judah to whom Jacob entrusted Benjamin, and he had proven to be reliable. Jacob therefore chose him for this mission as they drew near the Egyptian border *(Akeidah; R' Bachya).*

During the years that Joseph was missing, Jacob had suspected Judah of foul play in that deed [see *Rashi* to 49:9 *s.v.* מִטֶּרֶף]. But when it became known how loyally Judah had offered himself to the viceroy of Egypt in Benjamin's place [see 44:33], Judah was cleared of all further suspicion. Therefore, Jacob now sent Judah *(Tanchuma).*

28 **H**e sent Judah ahead of him to Joseph to prepare ahead of him in Goshen. And they arrived

Moreover, Jacob had been informed how greatly *Joseph* was impressed with Judah for risking his life to secure Benjamin's freedom and how this self-sacrifice caused Joseph to become very fond of Judah. Jacob therefore chose Judah *(Yafeh Toar).*

Furthermore, since it was Judah who started this good deed by initially approaching Jacob [44:18], Jacob now gave him the opportunity of completing it. Indeed we learn that whoever starts a good deed should complete it [see *comm.* to *Exod.* 40:33] *(Midrash HaGadol).*

According to *Koheles Rabbah* 9:15, God rewarded Judah by inspiring Jacob to choose him since he was so instrumental in protecting Benjamin. [According to this exposition, the implied subject of this passage is *God* Who — by so inspiring Jacob — in effect *sent Judah.*]

לְהוֹרֹת לְפָנָיו גֹּשְׁנָה — *To prepare ahead of him* [lit. *before him*] i.e., in advance of his arrival *(Rashi)*] *in* [lit. *to*] *Goshen.*

The commentators differ regarding Judah's exact mission.

Rashi following Onkelos, interprets: 'To prepare a place for him [Jacob] and show him [לְהוֹרֹת=לְהַרְאוֹת] how to settle there.'

There is an opinion [see *R' Munk*] that the subject of this clause is Joseph. That is, Jacob sent Judah ahead to Joseph so that *Joseph* could make the still necessary preparations for the family in Goshen.

According to *Radak, Chizkuni* and *Akeidah:* To ask Joseph to provide them with a guide to take them directly to Goshen so that they could avoid the metropolis of Egypt entirely.

Jacob did not want to give the impression that he unilaterally moved into Goshen with all his family. He realized that the Egyptians would judge him by their own petty standards. For this reason, he wanted Joseph to appoint a guide to lead them to Goshen *(R' Hirsch).*

Rashi cites an alternate interpretation from the *Midrash* [which understands לְהוֹרֹת in its other sense of *to teach* (from the root ירה, the same word from which *Torah* derives)]: 'To establish for him a House of Study [בֵּית תַּלְמוּד] from which teaching [הוֹרָאָה] could go forth.'

That is, 'To prepare a study house from which Jacob would teach Torah, and where the Tribal Ancestors would read the Torah, ... for it is known that the Patriarchs studied the Torah before it was given' *(Midrash; Tanchuma).*[1]

There is an opinion (see *Midrash* cited by *Radak* on *Joshua* 11:16) that Goshen was originally a region in Egypt, but it became part of *Eretz Yisrael* when Canaan was distributed among the tribes (see 45:10). In reward for undertaking this mission on his father's behalf, Judah earned the privilege that this very fertile region fall in his territory. That the following verse describes Joseph as going *up* toward his father indicates that Goshen was on the ascent toward *Eretz Yisrael.* [In the literal sense, however, *Radak* and other commentators do not agree that the Egyptian Goshen is the same as the Goshen mentioned in Joshua.]

1. This interpretation reveals the insight of the Sages that not a moment is to be wasted of study; Jacob dispatched Judah so that as soon as he arrived in Goshen he could resume his studies without need for further preparation *(Vayaged Yaakov).*

Jacob was also setting an example for his descendants: The primary building in any new Jewish settlement is a Torah center. One cannot survive even a moment without Torah, and it is inconceivable that there be a Jewish settlement without a House of Torah from which teaching can emanate *(Itturei Torah).* [*See footnote end of v.* 29.]

כט וַיָּבֹאוּ אַרְצָה גֹּשֶׁן׃ וַיֶּאְסֹר יוֹסֵף מֶרְכַּבְתּוֹ
וַיַּעַל לִקְרַאת־יִשְׂרָאֵל אָבִיו גֹּשְׁנָה וַיֵּרָא
אֵלָיו וַיִּפֹּל עַל־צַוָּארָיו וַיֵּבְךְּ עַל־צַוָּארָיו

וַיָּבֹאוּ אַרְצָה גֹּשֶׁן — *And they arrived in the region of Goshen.*

The syntax would imply that the subjects are Jacob and his family. According to *Alshich,* the subjects are Joseph and Judah who went together to Goshen to make the necessary preparations, after which Joseph went to meet his father.

29. Joseph reunites with Jacob.

וַיֶּאְסֹר יוֹסֵף מֶרְכַּבְתּוֹ — [*And*] *Joseph harnessed his chariot.*

— Joseph *personally* harnessed the horses to the chariot in a display of eagerness to honor his father *(Rashi* from *Mechilta Beshallach).*

The Talmud [*Sanhedrin* 105b] cites the case of Abraham who also, in a display of love [in that case, love of God], did not order one of his servants to saddle his donkey — an act normally beneath the dignity of a great man — but eagerly saddled his donkey *personally* [22:3]. This is because, הָאַהֲבָה מְקַלְקֶלֶת אֶת הַשּׁוּרָה, *'love causes disregard of normal conduct.'* [Conversely, the *Gemara* adds that 'hate, likewise, causes disregard of normal conduct,' as is deduced from Balaam who, in his hatred for Israel, also ignored his own dignity and saddled his own donkey *(Numbers* 22:21). See footnote on p. 790.]

According to *Ibn Ezra,* the literal implication of the phraseology is that Joseph ordered his chariot to be harnessed: *Joseph harnessed* — by command — *his chariot.* Comp. *I Kings* 6:4: *Solomon built* [i.e. not with his own hands, but ordered others to build] *the house.* The Torah often ascribes an act not to the one who performed the labor, but to the one who was its primary originator.

[*Rashi* cites the Midrashic interpretation as being contextually more reflective of the literal meaning of our passage since the Torah — which economizes on its every word — would not have informed us of the obvious fact that Joseph's wagons were harnessed unless it intended to suggest that Joseph did it personally out of filial love.]

וַיַּעַל לִקְרַאת־יִשְׂרָאֵל אָבִיו גֹּשְׁנָה — *And went up to meet* [lit. *toward*] *Israel his father in* [lit. *to*] *Goshen.*

According to *Tur,* the singular וַיַּעַל indicates that Joseph went up *alone.* Just as Joseph harnessed his chariot *personally* in a display of filial piety, so did he ascend it [this being the connotation here of *went up*] unaided, in his anxiety to greet Jacob, unlike nobles, who wait for their servants to help them up. Furthermore, according to the opinion that Goshen is on the border of *Eretz Yisrael,* Joseph is described as *going up* since *Eretz Yisrael* is higher than other countries; while acording to the more literal view that Goshen is in Egypt proper, then the term *went up* is used since Goshen was on higher terrain that the rest of the country [see previous verse, and *v.* 31 s.v. אֶעֱלֶה].

Daas Zekeinim interprets *went up* in the spiritual sense, noting that Joseph experienced a spiritual elevation by going to his father to honor him.

וַיֵּרָא אֵלָיו — *He appeared before him.*

[Joseph is still the subject:] Joseph appeared [i.e. presented himself] before his father *(Rashi).*[1]

The significance of this seeming-

1. Jacob had said [45:28], *I shall go and see him before I die.* He also said [further *v.* 30], *Now, I can die after having seen your face.* Although the inner connotation of this emphasis on *see-*

46 *in the region of Goshen*
29 [29] ***Joseph harnessed his chariot and went up to***
meet Israel his father in Goshen. He appeared before
him, fell on his neck, and he wept on his neck ex-

ly superfluous detail is explained by the commentators:

Either Israel's eyes were dim with age, or Joseph came in his royal chariot wearing a mitre on his head as is the custom of Egyptian kings: Therefore Jacob did not recognize him — just as the brothers had not recognized him when they had first seen him [42:8]. Therefore, the Torah mentions that *he appeared before his father,* who looked at him closely and only then recognized him *(Ramban).*

Sforno explains the term as: *he presented himself* from among his retinue, and did not wait for his father to approach the chariot.

The deeper implication of the phrase is that Joseph had nothing to hide when he saw his father. He was not like the wicked who, ashamed of his evil deeds, cringes in the presence of the righteous. Joseph maintained his righteousness throughout his years in Egypt and proudly presented himself to his father *(Alshich).*

According to *Targum Yonasan,* before Jacob recognized that the imposing regal figure approaching him was his son, Joseph, Jacob prostrated himself before him. In liability for allowing this to take place, Joseph's lifespan was shortened [he lived only 110 years and though he was the youngest of the brothers, he died first; see 50:26].

[Other opinions regarding Joseph's premature death are recorded in the *footnote* to 50:2; see also *Sechel Tov* ibid. *v.* 21 s.v. אָנֹכִי אֲכַלְכֵּל.]

וַיִּפֹּל עַל צַוָּארָיו וַיֵּבְךְּ עַל־צַוָּארָיו עוֹד — *[And he] fell on his neck and he wept on his neck excessively.*

[The subject here, too, is Joseph:] He wept greatly and continuously — more than is usual, the word עוֹד meaning in this context *very much,* as it does in *Job* 34:23. Jacob, however, did not fall upon Joseph's neck, nor did he kiss him for, as the Sages [see below] say, Jacob was occupied with reciting the *Shema* at that moment *(Rashi).*[1]

The source of this Aggadah is *Midrash Aggadah; Teshuvos HaGeonim* [Lyck ed.] §45 resp. 38. The Sages consistently give examples of how the Patriarchs prophetically fulfilled the Torah before it was given. See comm. to 26:5, p. 1083.

See also *Yoma* 19b: ... Concerning someone who, while reading the *Shema,* winks his eyes [in order to communicate with

ing is beyond our understanding, it is certain that Jacob had a special purpose and reason for it. That the Torah here mentions that Joseph *appeared* before Jacob, that is, was *seen* by him, indicates that this was the *seeing* that Jacob longed for before his death, *(Brisker Rav).* [See *Commentary* end of 45:28 and *Overview* to *Vayeishev* pp 15 64-67.]

Although Joseph longed to see Jacob as much as Jacob longed to see him, Joseph stifled his own desire and thought only of honoring his father's wish. Therefore *Rashi* comments that 'Joseph appeared before his father' — the purpose of his going was to please Jacob, not to satisfy his own longing *(Rav Avraham Trop).*

1. The concept of Jacob's reciting the *Shema* at that very moment reflects the Patriarch's supreme submission to HASHEM when a lesser person might have been overwhelmed with more mundane thoughts. He diverted the ecstatic love and joy which he experienced at his reunion with his long-lost favorite son — a love that enveloped him almost to the exclusion of all else — and instead directed them to the supreme object of his love: The Creator, blessed is He.

As *Maharal* in *Gur Aryeh* explains it: When the opportunity arises for the righteous to ex-

ל עוֹד: וַיֹּאמֶר יִשְׂרָאֵל אֶל־יוֹסֵף אָמוּתָה
הַפָּעַם אַחֲרֵי רְאוֹתִי אֶת־פָּנֶיךָ כִּי עוֹדְךָ

someone], gesticulates with his lips, or points with his fingers, Scripture has said, *Not upon Me have you called, O Jacob* [*Isaiah* 43:22]. *Maharsha* explains the allusion to be based on our Midrash and refers to Jacob who did not interrupt his recitation of the *Shema.* [See *Overview*].

Thus, following *Rashi,* the term עוד means *unremittingly.* Joseph wept copiously, and, when Jacob did not acknowledge him, he wept even more *(Akeidah; B'chor Shor).*

Ramban disagrees with *Rashi* and maintains that in the literal sense the subject of the phrase is not Joseph but the antecedent of the preceding pronoun אֵלָיו, *to him,* i.e., *Jacob* — Jacob being the one who wept. He accordingly interprets: *And he* [Jacob] *fell on* [Joseph's] *neck and he* [Jacob] *wept* ...

He bases this on two considerations: a) according to *Rashi's* interpretation that the subject throughout is Joseph why does the Torah have to mention that *Joseph appeared to him* when it is obvious? b) It would not have been respectful for Joseph to fall on his father's neck, rather he should have bowed to him as he does later in 48:12, or kiss his hands. Moreover, *Ramban* maintains that the word עוד in this context [which *Rashi* interprets as *excessively*] means *more; additionally.*

According to *Ramban,* therefore the verse is to be understood: ... *When he* [Joseph] *appeared to his father* — whose eyesight was already failing — and his father, upon close scrutiny recognized him, *then* [his father] *fell upon his* [Joseph's] *neck and wept on his neck* עוד, *more,* i.e., in addition to the constant weeping of all the years they had been separated.

Ramban sums up his interpretation by writing: 'It is quite well known whose tears are more present, the aged parent who finds his long-lost son alive after having despaired and mourned for him, or the young son who rules?'

press their sentiments of love, they do not want to keep these feelings of joy just for their own personal happiness, but they utilize them to pay tribute to God. Such was the case with Jacob. Just when he had the immense joy of finding the son whom he had believed lost, just as he sensed the flame of paternal love blaze up in his heart, he controlled his feelings and recited *Shema,* offering all his love to God. At this, the happiest hour of his life, he wanted to have but one thought: וְאָהַבְתָּ אֵת ה׳ אֱלֹקֶיךָ, *You shall love HASHEM, your God* ...

My father, *Harav Aharon Zlotowitz* שליט״א, notes that the Sages tell us of two people who recited *Shema* in pivotal moments in their lives: Jacob expressed his love for God at a moment of spiritual rebirth, when twenty-two years of uninterrupted mourning came to an end. R' Akiva recited *Shema* as he was being tortured to death by the Roman's to express his total love and dedication to God even as his life was being taken [*Berachos* 61b]. These two incidents symbolize the times when the Torah ordains that *Shema* be recited: in the morning when a new day begins, and at night when darkness encloses man and brings an end to his productive activity.

In a similar vein, *Harav David Cohen* notes that the Torah commands the recitation of *Shema* in the morning and evening. These periods represent the ending of a period or stage in life and beginning of a new one. At such times, *Shema* is recited to symbolize our acceptance and dedication of our lot and mission. Similarly, one recites the *Shema* with the approach of death to symbolize this concept.

The Sages in *Berachos* 5b advise that in order to conquer the Evil Inclination one should: a) study Torah; b) recite the *Shema;* c) recall the inevitable day of death. The Chortkover Rebbe once remarked that when entering the defiled land of Egypt Jacob availed himself of all three 'remedies': a) he sent Judah ahead to prepare a Torah center; b) he recited the *Shema;* and c) he recalled his day of death by saying *Now I can die*...

cessively. 30 *Then Israel said to Joseph, "Now I can die, after my having seen your face, because you are still alive."*

The commentators vigorously defend *Rashi's* Rabbinic interpretation against *Ramban's* criticism, maintaining that it was quite properly a display of filial honor and devotion for Joseph, the viceroy in Egypt, to have fallen on his father's neck and wept. [See *Mizrachi*].

Regarding *Ramban's* comment that it is more natural to assume that the father would be weeping for his son than the reverse, *R' David Feinstein* notes how Joseph wept many times during the episode with his brothers, and it was quite in character for him, when he finally saw his beloved father from whom he had been forcefully separated these past twenty-two years, to burst into tears just as he did when he revealed himself to Benjamin.

The Hebrew word *neck* is in plural: he fell on both sides of his neck (*Sechel Tov;* see above 45:14).

30. וַיֹּאמֶר יִשְׂרָאֵל אֶל־יוֹסֵף — *Then Israel said to Joseph.*

According to *Rashi's* interpretation that the subject of the previous verse is Joseph, it is quite understandable that the Torah begins this verse by naming the new subject, *Israel.* According to *Ramban,* that the subject of the previous verse, too, is Israel, why shouldn't our verse begin *he,* without naming him again?

Ramban dismisses this objection by citing Scriptural cases where a subject is named again although he was the subject of the preceding passage. An example is 41:48 where Joseph is clearly the subject, yet 41:50 names him again. 'There are constantly many similar cases in the Torah and in other books of Scripture.'

אָמוּתָה הַפָּעַם אַחֲרֵי רְאוֹתִי אֶת־פָּנֶיךָ כִּי עוֹדְךָ חָי — *Now* [lit. *this time*] *I can die, after my having seen your face, because you are still alive.*

The Hebrew literally reads, *Now I will die* ... However, it is obvious that Jacob could not be wishing his own death!

Accordingly, our translation follows the implication of *Rashi* who writes that in the literal sense the passage is to be understood as *Onkelos* interprets it: *If I were to die now, I would die with the comforting knowledge that you are still alive.*

Alternatively *Rashi* cites the Midrash, which perceives the Hebrew to mean *I will die* [but] *one time.* Jacob said: "I had thought that I would die two deaths — both in this world and in the next — because the Divine Presence departed from me and I accordingly thought that God would hold me responsible for your death." [Jacob's apprehension was inspired by the fact that it was his favoritism to Joseph that caused his brothers to be jealous of him, and it was Jacob who sent Joseph on the ill-fated visit to his brothers in Shechem, notwithstanding the inherent danger such a mission involved (see *Sforno* 37:35).] "Now that you are alive, *I will die only one death* [i.e. a physical death — in this world — but not a spiritual death in the Hereafter since I can no longer be held responsible for anyone's death" (*Mizrachi*)].

Furthermore, by this declaration Jacob was retracting his earlier fear. For when he had been told that Joseph was dead, he had cried out: *"I will go down to Sh'eol* [*the grave,* i.e., *Gehinnom*] *mourning for my son"* (37:35). As *Rashi* records there, Jacob had been given a Divine omen that if none of his

לא חָי: וַיֹּאמֶר יוֹסֵף אֶל־אֶחָיו וְאֶל־בֵּית אָבִיו
אֶעֱלֶה וְאַגִּידָה לְפַרְעֹה וְאֹמְרָה אֵלָיו
אַחַי וּבֵית־אָבִי אֲשֶׁר בְּאֶרֶץ־כְּנַעַן בָּאוּ
לב אֵלָי: וְהָאֲנָשִׁים רֹעֵי צֹאן כִּי־אַנְשֵׁי מִקְנֶה

sons died during his lifetime, he may be assured that he would not see *Gehinnom.* As long as he thought Joseph was dead, Jacob was convinced that he would descend as a mourner to *Gehinnom,* and this apprehension haunted him all the years that he mourned Joseph's 'death.' But now, however, that Jacob saw with his own eyes that his son was alive, he no longer feared punishment in *Gehinnom,* and therefore, exclaimed, 'Inasmuch as I have seen that you are still alive, I no longer fear *Gehinnom.* Now I can die knowing that punishment does not await me in the Hereafter!'

Maskil l'David cites this interpretation and offers that *Rashi* does not mention it here since Jacob still had no assurance that none of his sons would die before him, thereby removing his assurance against *Gehinnom. Rashi* therefore focuses his interpretation on the aspect of Jacob's apprehension that God will hold him accountable for Joseph's 'death', a fear that was no longer applicable.

Sforno suggests that Jacob was praying that he die before any fresh sorrows come upon him, for his earlier salvation had always been followed by more sorrows.

Many commentators interpret חָי [*alive*] to imply *spiritually vigorous,* in the same sense that the righteous are called חַיִּים, *'alive.'* They maintain Kabbalistically that from merely *looking* at Joseph's face the Patriarch was able to discern that his son still maintained his righteousness, untainted by the depravities of Egypt. Jacob therefore used the word הַפָּעַם, *this time,* to imply that he could feel such confidence only after having *seen* Joseph, not earlier when he was merely *informed* verbally that Joseph was still alive.

As *Or HaChaim* elaborates, though Jacob's joy was great at this moment, his happiness remained incomplete as long as he had not assured himself of one fact: that Joseph had maintained a high standard of piety, both as a slave and as a viceroy. How can one rejoice at rediscovering a son who has abandoned his faith and his fear of God? But Jacob could recognize the spiritual state of an individual by looking at his features, so it was sufficient for him 'to see Joseph's face' in order to assure himself that he had remained pure and pious. 'Now,' he exclaimed, 'I can die in peace, since I have seen your face [and know] that you are yet alive,' in the sense that 'only the righteous are truly alive' [*Berachos* 18a; see *commentary* to 45:28, and footnote above, *v.* 29].

Others see this outburst of emotion as implying: 'I could die this moment from the excessive joy I am experiencing from seeing you! The emotion is more than I can bear!' *(Akeidah).*

[Though the reader naturally wonders what Joseph said during the reunion, the Torah omits it. As we know the Torah records historical facts only if they have eternal significance. We can only assume that the further conversation between Jacob and Joseph did not fit into this category.]

31. Joseph ensures his family's settlement in Goshen.

Although Pharaoh had offered Joseph's family the choicest part of Egypt — a reference, apparently to Goshen, as is evident from 45:13 (see *Rashi)* and 47:6 — he had not *specifically* designated Goshen. Accordingly, Joseph takes leave of his family, explaining that he must go to Pharaoh to arrange their settlement in Goshen *(R' Shmuel b. Chofni; R' Avraham b. HaRambam; Tzror HaMor).*

וַיֹּאמֶר יוֹסֵף אֶל־אֶחָיו וְאֶל־בֵּית אָבִיו — *And Joseph said to his brothers and*

³¹ *And Joseph said to his brothers and to his brothers' household, "I will go up and tell Pharaoh, and I will say to him, 'My brothers and my father's household who were in the land of Canaan have come to me.* ³² *The men are shepherds, for they have*

to his father's household.

His *brothers* are specifically mentioned, because they were directly concerned; it was they whom Pharaoh would summon *(Radak).*

Although transient shepherds were permitted to graze their herds wherever they wished, people wishing permanent residence required Pharaoh's permission. Now, Joseph was apprehensive that Pharaoh might insist that Joseph's family live in the metropolis and become public officials [something clearly undesirable as far as Joseph was concerned (see *comm.* to *v.* 32 below)]. Joseph therefore took the initiative of informing Pharaoh that his brothers were shepherds, so that he would have them settle in the out-of-the-way region of Goshen *since all shepherds are abhorrent to Egyptians.* Joseph chose his words carefully to achieve this desired goal of obtaining an isolated province for their home *(Malbim).*

Chiddushei HaRim remarks that Joseph was thereby establishing a pattern for his descendants to follow in every generation: Do not seek the grace of gentile rulers; neither emulate their ways nor mingle with them socially. Joseph knew that shepherds were detested by Egypt, yet he openly told Pharaoh that his brothers were shepherds in order to separate them from the Egyptians and in order that they should be settled in a separate region.

אֶעֱלֶה וְאַגִּידָה לְפַרְעֹה — *I will go up and tell Pharaoh.*

I.e., I will offer this information to Pharaoh before he requests it *(Sforno).*

'Go up' is here to be understood in the sense of ascending the chariot. He was humbly asking their leave *(Daas Zekenim; Tur v.* 29).

[These interpretations are based on *v.* 29 where the implication is that Goshen was on higher terrain than the rest of Egypt. Therefore, the expression *go up* in our passage cannot imply *from Goshen to Egypt.*]

According to *Haamek Davar,* by *go up,* Joseph meant that he would go to Pharaoh's private upper chamber — where only Joseph could visit the king.

According to *HaRechesim LeBik'ah,* a mountain range separated Goshen from the rest of Egypt. Therefore, the term *go up* applies when traveling in either direction.

וְאֹמְרָה אֵלָיו אַחַי וּבֵית־אָבִי אֲשֶׁר בְּאֶרֶץ־כְּנַעַן בָּאוּ אֵלָי — *And I will say to him, 'My brothers and my father's household, who were in the land of Canaan, have come to me.*

— To settle permanently, for which Pharaoh's permission was necessary *(Abrabanel).*

Joseph would not mention, however, that they were already in Goshen *(Ralbag).*

32. וְהָאֲנָשִׁים רֹעֵי צֹאן כִּי אַנְשֵׁי מִקְנֶה הָיוּ — *And the men are shepherds, for they have been cattlemen.*

That is, their wealth consists of cattle. Joseph thereby described them in an honorable way and emphasized that they were shepherds — not merely in the menial sense that they tended the cattle of others [as was Jacob when he shepherded

הָיוּ וְצֹאנָם וּבְקָרָם וְכָל־אֲשֶׁר לָהֶם
לג הֵבִיאוּ: וְהָיָה כִּי־יִקְרָא לָכֶם פַּרְעֹה וְאָמַר
לד מַה־מַּעֲשֵׂיכֶם: וַאֲמַרְתֶּם אַנְשֵׁי מִקְנֶה הָיוּ
עֲבָדֶיךָ מִנְּעוּרֵינוּ וְעַד־עַתָּה גַּם־אֲנַחְנוּ
גַּם־אֲבֹתֵינוּ בַּעֲבוּר תֵּשְׁבוּ בְּאֶרֶץ גֹּשֶׁן כִּי־
מז/א א תוֹעֲבַת מִצְרַיִם כָּל־רֹעֵה צֹאן: וַיָּבֹא יוֹסֵף

Laban's sheep] — but that they owned many herds of their own, and even with respect to their own cattle, they had servants and attendants to pasture them. They were men of esteem and means *(Ramban)*.[1]

This verse is not a paranthetical Scriptural insertion to clarify the narrative, but is part of what Joseph would tell Pharaoh *(Rashi; Rashbam)*.

וְצֹאנָם וּבְקָרָם וְכָל אֲשֶׁר לָהֶם הֵבִיאוּ — *And their sheep and cattle — and everything they own* [lit. *that is theirs*] *— they have brought.*

Thus they are independently wealthy and will not require support from the royal treasury *(Malbim)*.

That they brought all their flocks and cattle proves that they came to reside here permanently and serve the monarch *(R' Avraham b. HaRambam; Sechel Tov)*.

33. וְהָיָה כִּי יִקְרָא לָכֶם פַּרְעֹה וְאָמַר מַה־מַּעֲשֵׂיכֶם — *And it shall be, when Pharaoh summons you* [or: *if Pharaoh should summon you*] *and says, 'What is your occupation?'*

— His intention being to ascertain for which governmental post you are suited *(Malbim)*.

As *R' Hirsch* explains, in a state like Egypt, where men were irrevocably locked into the trade or profession of their fathers, the first question would naturally be about their profession.

34. וַאֲמַרְתֶּם אַנְשֵׁי מִקְנֶה וכו׳ — *Then you are to say, 'Your servants have been cattlemen from our youth till now.'*

It is the family occupation *(Sechel Tov)*.

— And we know no other *(Malbim)*.

Joseph thus cautioned them that the general tenor of their response must correspond to his, and he rehearsed their answer so they would not flounder. It was obvious that they could not categorically refuse to enter Pharaoh's service, but their response was calculated to make them seem unqualified for his needs *(Akeidah)*.

To Pharaoh's question they were to acknowledge immediately and unashamedly that they were shep-

1. **The Patriarchal occupation.**

According to *R' Bachya,* two reasons prompted Jacob's children and the most illustrious people of the Bible to become shepherds. First, this profession is healthy and profitable. Secondly, it minimizes association with idolaters who, because they worship sheep, consider herdsmen to be loathesome *(Rashi, v.* 34). Thus, shepherds live in relative isolation, close to pasture-land and far from large settlements.

This has two advantages: being alone, the shepherd can better safeguard his spiritual and religious heritage, and can better avoid the many vices of the sophisticated social life of big

46
33-34 been cattlemen. Their sheep and cattle — and
everything they own — they have brought.' 33 And it
shall be, when Pharaoh summons you, and says,
'What is your occupation?' 34 Then you are to say,
'Your servants have been cattlemen from our youth
till now, both we and our forefathers,' so that you
may be able to stay on the region of Goshen, since all
shepherds are abhorrent to Egyptians."

herds, a profession the Egyptians held in undisguised contempt. Pharaoh's resultant wish to isolate them in a faraway province would be a significant means of preserving the nation that was destined to flourish in isolation throughout its history *(R' Hirsch)*.

They were not to apply to themselves the more demeaning term רוֹעֵי צֹאן, *shepherds*, since Pharaoh would already know this from Joseph's words. They were merely to say אַנְשֵׁי מִקְנֶה, *cattlemen*, stressing the business, rather than the menial, nature of the profession *(Haamek Davar)*.

[They did not precisely follow this advice however. See *comm.* to 47:1-3.]

גַּם־אֲנַחְנוּ גַּם־אֲבוֹתֵינוּ — *Both we and our forefathers.*

They were to mention their forefathers, who were widely known by then, and held in high esteem. Witness Abraham who was renowned as a 'Prince of God' [23:6] *(Akeidas Yitzchak)*.

[The Hebrew literally reads *also we, also our fathers*. This double use of גַּם, *also*, is idiomatic. See, for example, 24:19; 32:19; 43:8; 44:10.]

בַּעֲבוּר תֵּשְׁבוּ בְּאֶרֶץ גֹּשֶׁן — *So that you may be able to stay in the region of Goshen.*

I.e., giving Pharaoh the response that your sole occupation for generations has been trading in cattle will assure that Pharaoh will settle you in Goshen *(Malbim)*.

— Away from the mainstream of the immoral Egyptians. It was this separateness that would help preserve them from assimilation in Egypt *(Akeidah)*.

This is the area that you require since it is grazing land. And when you say that you are not versed in any other work, he will send you far away from himself and settle you there *(Rashi)*.

כִּי־תוֹעֲבַת מִצְרַיִם כָּל־רֹעֵה צֹאן — *Since all shepherds are abhorrent to Egyptians* [lit. *for the abomination of Egypt is every shepherd*].

And since you are shepherds,

cities — gossip, slander, depravity, thievery, hypocrisy, and falsehood. Being a shepherd allows one to be alone, far from men and their evil ways — and for this, the righteous and the prophets have always searched. It answers their wish to devote themselves to a meditative, austere, and holy way of life which would elevate them until they reached to the Source of divine inspiration *(R' Munk)*.

As *R' Hirsch* [4:2] writes, pastoral life has many advantages. The fact that shepherds are involved with dependent living creatures calls for the exercise of humane feelings and constant care. The unstable nature of a shepherd's property is a safeguard against placing too much value on both the property and its owner. Less physical exertion is required than in agriculture; the mind is less occupied by the work and is free to think Godliness and goodness. Thus we find that our Patriarchs were shepherds, and Moses and David tended flocks.

The Egyptians hated pastoral people. Their civilization was based on agriculture and

וַיַּגֵּד לְפַרְעֹה וַיֹּאמֶר אָבִי וְאַחַי וְצֹאנָם וּבְקָרָם וְכָל־אֲשֶׁר לָהֶם בָּאוּ מֵאֶרֶץ כְּנָעַן

Pharaoh will not settle you in the urban centers. In this way Joseph contrived to achieve the goal that they should dwell apart, though it involved degrading the family in Pharaoh's eyes. Everything was worth sacrificing in order to ensure the preservation of Israel's sanctity *(Haamek Davar)*.

Shepherds were abhorrent to Egyptians — because the Egyptians worshipped sheep *(Rashi)*, and would therefore not tolerate slaughtering sheep or deriving benefit from them *(Abarbanel)*.

It is apparent, however, from 47:6 and *Exodus* 9:3 that the Egyptians had flocks of their own. It seems probable that they would raise them only in consecrated fields. They would never strike them, or dare slaughter them except on the rarest occasions. Egyptians therefore hated [foreign] shepherds who recognize so clearly that sheep, which the Egyptians worshiped, are not gods *(Akeidah; Alshich; Sechel Tov;* cf. *Radak)*.

R' Abraham ben HaRambam cites with approval *R' Shmuel b. Chofni's* comment that the Egyptians did not despise shepherds *per se*, but only those who slaughtered the sheep in their care.

As *Ibn Ezra* explains, the Egyptians in those days were not meat-eaters, and would not permit anyone to kill sheep. This is still the custom in India. All shepherds were held in contempt because they drank sheep's milk. To this day, the Hindus of India do not drink or eat anything derived from living creatures. [Indians believed they are descended from Ham, as are the Egyptians; in those days they shared common beliefs *(Yohel Or)*].

Rashbam, in an opposing view, holds that the Egyptians did *not* venerate sheep. He maintains that they found shepherds contemptible since Egyptians *despised* sheep, both as food and for sacrifices, as it is written [*Exodus* 8:22]: *For we will sacrifice that which is loathed by the Egyptians.*

There is yet another opinion. The Torah frequently refers to idols with the derogatory word תּוֹעֵבָה [*abomination; abhorrence*]. According to this opinion, Joseph's intent was that Egyptians should *honor* his brothers since they cared for the animals that Egypt worshiped. Pharaoh, accordingly, would want them to dwell in a fertile region like Goshen [see 45:18]. Those who hold this opinion find it inconceivable that Joseph should present his brothers as objects of contempt *(Zohar; B'chor Shor)*.

manifested many base symptoms — from slavery and polytheism to total disregard for human dignity. Only in our ancestors, that tribe of shepherds, were faith in God, freedom, and man's likeness to his Creator to be found. The Egyptian leaders had good reason to cultivate in their subjects an overwhelming aversion to pastoral peoples.

It is true that agricultural life is more natural to man than pastoral life, and, indeed, the Torah's many commandments regarding agriculture indicate that this applies to Israel as well. But by its commandments regarding the Sabbath, the Sabbatical year, the laws of tithing, and similar laws, the Torah protects Jewry against the excesses that lead to the worship of property. As a result of these laws, the Torah creates the basis of an agricultural state that serves God, of a nation united in fraternity and freedom. Without the Torah, the very existence of these ideals is threatened.

47
1 ¹ *Then Joseph came and told Pharaoh, and he said,*
"My father and my brothers, their sheep, their cattle,
and everything they own, have arrived from the land

XLVII

1-4. Joseph's report to Pharaoh — variations in the dialogue.

In the previous chapter [46:31-34] Joseph told his brothers how he would announce their arrival and how they should describe themselves to Pharaoh. In the next four verses, however, we find that both Joseph and his brothers made slight changes when they actually spoke to the king. Is there any significance in these variations?

A similar question arose in several earlier cases where the Torah recapitulated dialogue. Among these cases are: Eliezer's recapitulation to Rebecca's family of his experiences at the well [24:34-39; see chart on pp. 986-7]; when Hamor, father of Shechem, reported on the proposal to intermarry and unite with Jacob's family, he deliberately misled his own subjects to make the arrangements palatable [34:21-33]; Potiphar's wife falsified to Joseph's disadvantage her account of their confrontation [see chart on p. 1714]; and Pharaoh's account to Joseph of his dreams differed from the Torah's account [41:17-24; see chart on pp. 1774-6].

As noted in the commentaries to the above narratives, there are two schools of thought among the commentators. Such commentators as *Ibn Ezra, Radak,* and occasionally *Ramban,* find little if no new significance in such minor variations. As *Radak* puts it, when a person reports an event or conversation, he invariably varies the wording, adding or subtracting as he sees fit, but preserving the essential content. Since such changes are characteristic of narrative, there is no point in seeking specific reasons for such changes provided they do not affect the content.

However, the Midrash, *Zohar* and most later commentators, such as *Or HaChaim, Abarbanel,* and *Haamek Davar* perceive great significance in such variations, even minor ones. In their view, it is axiomatic that the Torah would not have repeated a narrative unless the recapitulation contained a new teaching. In the case of Joseph and Pharaoh, for example, unless there was significance in the variations in dialogue, the Torah should have told us simply in a few words that Joseph and his brothers spoke to Pharaoh as planned. That it did not do so — and especially since there are differences between the plan and the execution — requires us to make careful comparisons and seek reasons for any changes.

The commentary below shall point out these interpretations.

1. וַיָּבֹא יוֹסֵף וַיַּגֵּד לְפַרְעֹה — *Then Joseph came and told Pharaoh.*

It does not say *he went up* to Pharaoh's private, upper-level chamber [see 46:31], for Providence arranged it that when Joseph arrived he found Pharaoh below, with his officials. That he was not addressing Pharaoh privately, but in the presence of the court officials, accounts in part for changes in Joseph's planned dialogue *(Haamek Davar).*

וַיֹּאמֶר אָבִי וְאַחַי וְצֹאנָם וּבְקָרָם וְכָל אֲשֶׁר לָהֶם בָּאוּ מֵאֶרֶץ כְּנָעַן — *[And] he said, My father and my brothers, and their sheep, [and] their cattle, and everything they own* [lit. *that is theirs*], *have arrived from the land of Canaan.*

As you commanded them *(Or HaChaim;* see below).

In speaking to Pharaoh, Joseph did not say 'have come *to me*' as he proposed [46:31] lest Pharaoh suspect that they expected Joseph to support them out of the royal treasury. To further disabuse Pharaoh of the notion that the new arrivals were poor and would

ב וְהִנָּם בְּאֶרֶץ גֹּשֶׁן: וּמִקְצֵה אֶחָיו לָקַח
חֲמִשָּׁה אֲנָשִׁים וַיַּצִּגֵם לִפְנֵי פַרְעֹה:
ג וַיֹּאמֶר פַּרְעֹה אֶל־אֶחָיו מַה מַּעֲשֵׂיכֶם

become public charges, he added *and their sheep, their cattle, and everything they own, have arrived,* to emphasize that they were wealthy. Joseph thus changed the wording according to his perception at that moment of what would be most effective *(Akeidah; Abarbanel).*

וְהִנָּם בְּאֶרֶץ גֹּשֶׁן — *And they are now in the region of Goshen.*

Joseph added this fact — though he did not mention it to his brothers [46:31] — in order to prompt Pharaoh in the right direction. As *Or HaChaim* explains: *'And they are in the region of Goshen,* as you (Pharaoh) commanded when you said [45:18]: *"And I shall give you the best of the land of Egypt"* — the region of Goshen, which possesses the best pasture land of the country.'

Joseph did not say explicitly that they were shepherds or cattlemen, letting Pharaoh infer this for himself; furthermore, the courtiers who were present did not know that Joseph's brothers were shepherds and, since this occupation was despised in Egypt, Joseph avoided describing them as such *(Abarbanel; Haamek Davar).*

2. וּמִקְצֵה אֶחָיו לָקַח חֲמִשָּׁה אֲנָשִׁים — *From the least of his brothers he took five men.*

From the weakest of them — from those who did not *look* robust; because if Pharaoh saw powerful men, he would have enlisted them as soldiers *(Rashi).*

That he selected the weaker brothers is implied by the term מִקְצֵה, literally *and from the 'end'* [i.e., *least* (physically) *significant, (Midrash)*] *of his brothers.* Otherwise, the Torah would have said simply וּמֵאֶחָיו לָקַח וכו׳, *and from his brothers he took,* etc. *(Be'er Yitzchak; Beer Mayim Chaim; Shaarei Aharon).*

Rashi continues that there is a difference of opinion among the Sages regarding the identity of these five. According to the *Midrash Rabbah* 'which is the *Aggadah* of *Eretz Yisrael'* [it was compiled by the third century Palestinian amora R' Hoshaiah], the 'weaker' brothers chosen were: Reuben, Simeon, Levi, Issachar, and Benjamin. [We know that these were not the mighty brothers, because, as the Midrash explains,] these were the brothers whose names Moses did *not* repeat when he blessed the Tribes before his death [*Deut.* 33], whereas Moses *did* repeat the names of the more *powerful* brothers: [*Deut.* 33:7] *And this is for Judah ... hear,* HASHEM, *the voice of Judah;* [ibid. *v.* 20] *And of Gad he said ... Blessed be He Who extended Gad;* [ibid. *v.* 25] *And of Naftali he said, Naftali ... ;* [ibid. *v.* 22] *And of Dan he said, Dan ... ;* similarly he repeated the names of Zebulun [ibid. *v.* 18] and of Asher [ibid. *v.* 24].

"According to our Babylonian Talmud, however [*Bava Kamma* 92a]," *Rashi* continues, "those whose names Moses *did* mention twice were the *weaker* of the brothers and it was *they* whom Joseph brought before Pharaoh." [The difference in both interpretations involves only one point: The

47 *of Canaan and they are now in the region of Goshen."*
2-3 *2 From the least of his brothers he took five men and*
presented them to Pharaoh. 3 Pharaoh said to his
brothers, "What is your occupation?" They answered

Midrash and Talmud both agree that repetition alludes to strength. However, the Midrash maintains that Moses repeated certain names to attest that these were *already* strong, while the Talmud maintains that Moses' repetition was really a supplication that henceforth these (weaker) brothers should become strong *(Divrei David).*]

According to the latter interpretations that the 'weaker' brothers taken by Joseph were the ones whose names were repeated, there is a difficulty since Moses repeated the names of *six* brothers, whereas Joseph took only five with him. — The answer given is that Judah was not brought to Pharaoh; Moses doubled Judah's name not because he was weak but because he required a special blessing as the Talmud explains in *Makkos* 11b and *Bava Kamma* 92a *(Rashi).*

[As the Talmud explains, Judah's bones knew no rest nor did his soul find a place of honor in the Heavenly Academy because he had placed himself under a ban when he promised to return Benjamin to Jacob — a ban which still was technically in force (see footnote to 43:9). Therefore Moses repeated Judah's name in supplication.]

In summation, it is clear that both the Midrash and Talmud agree that Joseph brought the weaker brothers to Pharaoh; however, their identity is in dispute. According to the Midrash, the Tribes whose names Moses did *not* repeat (Reuben, Simeon, Levi, Issachar and Benjamin) were the weaker ones, and hence [except for Manasseh and Ephraim whose names also were not repeated] they were the five brothers whom Joseph brought; while according to the Talmud, those whose names Moses *did* repeat (Judah, Dan, Zebulun, Gad, Asher, and Naftali) were the weaker brothers — except for Judah, as the Gemara explains.

Tur, however, interprets that, to the contrary, the word מִקְצֵה is related to קָצִין, *leader;* Joseph took five of his most *prominent* brothers. *Radak* records a similar view as does *Tz'ror HaMor.*

The implication of *Onkelos* is that the literal sense of the word וּמִקְצֵה has nothing to do with strength or weakness, but is simply synonymous with וּמִקְצָת, *some,* the meaning of our passage being: *And he* took *some* of his brothers, five men, etc. [Cf. also *R' Shmuel ben Chofni Gaon; Raabam.*]

וַיַּצִּגֵם לִפְנֵי פַרְעֹה — *And [he] presented them to Pharaoh.*

Joseph wanted Pharaoh to see for himself, from their words and general demeanor, that they were suitable only for shepherding *(Sforno).*

The phrase literally reads, *and he stood them up before Pharaoh.* The verb וַיַּצִּגֵם from נצג, as above in 43:10 means *stand* or *set up.* The term suggests physical support; its use here, as *Sechel Tov* observes, implies that Joseph had them stand in a humble manner, showing no sign of strength, so that Pharaoh would not enlist them as soldiers. *R' Hirsch* perceives that the verb connotes that *he placed them at Pharaoh's disposal,* which is similar to the meaning of the verb אַצִּיגָה, *let me assign,* in 33:15.

3. וַיֹּאמֶר פַּרְעֹה אֶל־אֶחָיו מַה מַּעֲשֵׂיכֶם — *[And] Pharaoh said to his brothers, "What is your occupation?"*

[See 46:33.]

וַיֹּאמְרוּ אֶל־פַּרְעֹה רֹעֵה צֹאן עֲבָדֶיךָ גַּם־
ד אֲנַחְנוּ גַּם־אֲבוֹתֵינוּ: וַיֹּאמְרוּ אֶל־פַּרְעֹה
לָגוּר בָּאָרֶץ בָּאנוּ כִּי־אֵין מִרְעֶה לַצֹּאן
אֲשֶׁר לַעֲבָדֶיךָ כִּי־כָבֵד הָרָעָב בְּאֶרֶץ כְּנָעַן
וְעַתָּה יֵשְׁבוּ־נָא עֲבָדֶיךָ בְּאֶרֶץ גֹּשֶׁן:
ה וַיֹּאמֶר פַּרְעֹה אֶל־יוֹסֵף לֵאמֹר אָבִיךָ
ו וְאַחֶיךָ בָּאוּ אֵלֶיךָ: אֶרֶץ מִצְרַיִם לְפָנֶיךָ

רֹעֵה צֹאן עֲבָדֶיךָ גַּם־אֲנַחְנוּ גַּם־אֲבוֹתֵינוּ — *Your servants are shepherds, we as well as our* [lit. *also we also our*] *forefathers.*

There is a significant variation here as well. Joseph had instructed them to emphasize that they were אַנְשֵׁי מִקְנֶה, *cattlemen,* emphasizing, as *Ramban* observes there, that they did not work for others, but owned their own flocks. But the brothers omitted this and said simply, *your servants are* **shepherds.**

As *R' Hirsch* points out, רֹעֵה צֹאן [lit. *shepherd*] is in the singular: We, your servants, belong to the shepherd class. Notwithstanding what Joseph had told them to say, they were not ashamed of their profession and said straight out: shepherds.

4. וַיֹּאמְרוּ אֶל־פַּרְעֹה — *And they said to Pharaoh.*

I.e., sensing that Pharaoh was unresponsive, they added ... *(Abarbanel; Malbim).*

לָגוּר בָּאָרֶץ בָּאנוּ — *We have come to sojourn in this* [lit. *the*] *land.*

I.e., to live here temporarily as גֵּרִים, *aliens; sojourners* [see below]. The brothers thereby presented themselves as humbly seeking Pharaoh's good will, not as if they were claiming any privileges by virtue of his promise to Joseph [in 45:18] *(Or HaChaim).*

They had left *Eretz Yisrael* most reluctantly, perceiving their departure as a form of גֵּרוּת, *exile (Chidah).*

The implication was that as temporary residents, they could not be expected to change their occupation *(Akeidah).*

כִּי אֵין מִרְעֶה לַצֹּאן אֲשֶׁר לַעֲבָדֶיךָ וכו׳ — *Since there is no grazing* [pasture] *for your servants' sheep, for the famine is severe in the land of Canaan.*

This had forced them to leave Canaan temporarily, but they would return home when the famine was over *(Ramban v. 11; Abarbanel).*

Comp. the Passover Haggadah: " ... *Then my father* [Jacob] *descended to Egypt and sojourned there* ... [*Deut.* 26:5]. — This teaches that our father Jacob did not descend to Egypt to settle, but only to sojourn temporarily, as it says, *They said to Pharaoh: 'We have come to sojourn in this land since there is no pasture for your servants' sheep, for the famine is severe in the land of Canaan.'* "

Ramban questions the rationale of their telling Pharaoh that they had come to Egypt for the duration of the famine since the famine was severe in Canaan, inasmuch as the famine was equally severe in Egypt, or possibly even more severe since the brunt of the decree was on Egypt.

He explains that they intended to

47
4-6

Pharaoh, "Your servants are shepherds — we as well as
our forefathers." [4] *And they said to Pharaoh, "We*
have come to sojourn in this land, since there is no grazing for your servants' sheep, for the famine is severe in the land of Canaan. Now, if you please, allow your servants to dwell in the region of Goshen."
[5] *And Pharaoh said to Joseph as follows, "Your*
father and your brothers have come to you. [6] *The land*
of Egypt is before you — in the best part of the land

imply that in Canaan people were forced to eat even the grass of the fields leaving virtually no sustenance for livestock, so severe was the famine, but in Egypt there was still some grass in the pastures because the people subsisted on Joseph's stores of grain. It is also possible that in Egypt there was some pasture in the marshes because of the canals and ponds, whereas Canaan was totally dependent upon rain and there was no verdure. [See also *Deut.* 11:10].

וְעַתָּה יֵשְׁבוּ־נָא עֲבָדֶיךָ בְּאֶרֶץ גֹּשֶׁן — [*And*] *now, if you please, allow your servants to dwell in the region of Goshen.*

Now, until the famine will end by Divine grace — for then we will return home *(Alshich; Chizkuni).*

Therefore, under the circumstances, let your servants *dwell,* that is *remain,* in the region of Goshen where we have already taken up temporary residence, and where the land is suitable for grazing *(Akeidah).*

5. וַיֹּאמֶר פַּרְעֹה אֶל־יוֹסֵף לֵאמֹר — [*And*] *Pharaoh said to Joseph as follows* [lit. *saying*].

Pharaoh did not respond directly to the brothers' request, but turned and directed his remarks to Joseph, his viceroy *(Abarbanel;* see *Or HaChaim* below).

אָבִיךָ וְאַחֶיךָ בָּאוּ אֵלֶיךָ — *Your father and your brothers have come to you.*

The statement is introductory, as if to say, 'I have now learned that your family has arrived here.' The implication of the words *to you* is that it is apparent that they have come *to you,* depending on you because of your lofty position. Therefore, see that you treat them well since it is entirely within your power to do so *(Ramban).*

Joseph had not said, 'have come *to me'* as he originally intended, [see 46:31, 47:1] because he wanted to give Pharaoh the impression that his family had come in response to the royal invitation [45:17ff]. Pharaoh, however, wished to intimate that Joseph's family had come to *him,* Joseph, and that he should allot them land. Among Pharaoh's reasons for this was that according to Egyptian custom had Pharaoh bestowed the gift it would have been irrevocable, while if it were bestowed by Joseph — although at the king's pleasure — it could be revoked at some future date by the throne *(Or HaChaim).*

6. אֶרֶץ מִצְרַיִם לְפָנֶיךָ הִוא — *The land of Egypt is before you.*

I.e., is open before you. You can act with full authority to do as you please without seeking my further

הִ֗וא בְּמֵיטַ֣ב הָאָ֔רֶץ הוֹשֵׁ֥ב אֶת־אָבִ֖יךָ
וְאֶת־אַחֶ֑יךָ יֵשְׁבוּ֙ בְּאֶ֣רֶץ גֹּ֔שֶׁן וְאִם־יָדַ֗עְתָּ
וְיֶשׁ־בָּם֙ אַנְשֵׁי־חַ֔יִל וְשַׂמְתָּ֛ם שָׂרֵ֥י מִקְנֶ֖ה
ז עַל־אֲשֶׁר־לִֽי׃ וַיָּבֵ֤א יוֹסֵף֙ אֶת־יַעֲקֹ֣ב אָבִ֔יו
וַיַּֽעֲמִדֵ֖הוּ לִפְנֵ֣י פַרְעֹ֑ה וַיְבָ֥רֶךְ יַעֲקֹ֖ב אֶת־

permission *(Akeidah; Haamek Davar).*

This was Pharaoh's way of displaying his gratitude for Joseph's loyal and devoted service *(Ibn Caspi).*

בְּמֵיטַב הָאָרֶץ הוֹשֵׁב אֶת־אָבִיךָ וְאֶת־אַחֶיךָ — *In the best part of the land settle your father and your brothers.*

'The king's heart is in the hands of HASHEM' [*Prov.* 21:1]. Joseph's fear that Pharaoh would find his brothers detestable as shepherds was unfounded. Providence inspired Pharaoh to offer them the very best part of Egypt, notwithstanding other interests of the State which might have dictated that he take advantage of their reduced status *(Tz'ror HaMor; Haamek Davar).*

By הוֹשֵׁב, *settle,* Pharaoh meant: Provide them with everything they could possibly need — houses, fields, vineyards, etc. — in the manner of Egyptian citizens who reside in Goshen *(Ramban v.* 11).

יֵשְׁבוּ בְּאֶרֶץ גֹּשֶׁן — *Let them settle in the region of Goshen.*

— In accordance with their wishes. 'Whatever one wishes for himself, is his honor and benefit' *(Haamek Davar).*

— I consider Goshen *the choicest region in Egypt (Or HaChaim).*[1]

וְאִם־יָדַעְתָּ וְיֶשׁ־בָּם אַנְשֵׁי־חַיִל — *And if you know that there are capable men among them.*

And if you know. That is, if you *wish* to know it. You may prefer to ignore your brothers' talents because you would rather that they not become government officials. Thus, Pharaoh himself gives Joseph an excuse to free his brothers from royal service *(R' Hirsch).*

The translation of אַנְשֵׁי חַיִל as *capable* [or: *accomplished*] *men,* follows *Rashi,* who interprets: 'skilled in their profession of feeding sheep.'

The term literally means *men of strength* and usually refers to *soldiers* — a connotation it cannot have here inasmuch as it would contradict *Rashi's* earlier contention that Joseph brought his weaker brothers. Moreover, Pharaoh proceeds to suggest that such persons become chamberlains of his livestock, not soldiers — but if Pharaoh meant *men* of *strength,* they would have been better suited to the military than shepherdry. This meaning of *capable* also occurs in *Proverbs* 31:10 where Solomon describes the proverbial

1. *Moshav Zekeinim* notes that the Talmud [*Kesubos* 112a] describes Zoan, not Goshen, as the choicest part of Egypt [see *Rashi* to *Numbers* 13:22]; he leaves the question unresolved.

[Possibly, Pharaoh intimated that he would prefer that they settle in the choicest part of Egypt — presumably Zoan — but since the brothers specifically requested Goshen, they may remain there. (They specified Goshen because as the Midrash records, the Pharaoh of Abraham's time had presented Goshen to Sarah.) This might also be *Haamek Davar's* understanding of the text as well.

[Moreover, there are some commentators who suggest that Zoan is to be identified with Raameses; see *comm.* to *Numb.* 13:22].

47
7

settle your father and your brothers. Let them settle in
the region of Goshen, and if you know that there are
capable men among them, appoint them as
chamberlains over the livestock that belongs to me."
7 Then Joseph brought Jacob, his father, and
presented him to Pharaoh, and Jacob blessed Pharaoh.

אֵשֶׁת חַיִל, *accomplished* woman; in that context, too, it certainly does not refer to a *military* or *powerful* woman *(Shaarei Aharon).*

According to *Chizkuni,* אַנְשֵׁי חַיִל does mean, even in our context, *powerful men,* since shepherds must be powerful to ward off wild beasts and robbers.

וְשַׂמְתָּם שָׂרֵי מִקְנֶה עַל־אֲשֶׁר־לִי — *[And] appoint them [as] chamberlains over the livestock that belongs to me.*

I.e., over my sheep *(Rashi).*

[As noted above, sheep was raised in Egypt, but not for food. See 46:34 for this and other opinions.]

According to *Ibn Ezra* מִקְנֶה, *livestock,* refers to the royal herds of horses and mules [used for military purposes.]

Ibn Caspi suggests that the meaning of שָׂרֵי מִקְנֶה is *livestock chamberlains,* that is, chamberlains over the shepherds — certainly a position reflecting the dignity of Joseph's brothers.

Cf. *Rashbam:* People worthy of power and authority.

The Torah does not record whether or not they accepted this duty. It is probable that they did not inasmuch as they were trying to maintain a humble posture *(Sechel Tov).*

7. Joseph presents Jacob to Pharaoh.

וַיָּבֵא יוֹסֵף אֶת־יַעֲקֹב אָבִיו — *Then Joseph brought Jacob his father.*

Joseph meant to reflect honor on himself by his venerable father's obvious distinction *(Sechel Tov).*

Note the use of the more honorable term וַיָּבֵא, *brought,* used here, rather than לָקַח, *took,* used in the case of his brothers in *v.* 2 *(R' Hirsch).*

וַיַּעֲמִדֵהוּ לִפְנֵי פַרְעֹה — *And presented him to Pharaoh.*

Here, too, as in *v.* 2 above, the passage literally reads *and he stood him up before Pharaoh.* While the idiomatic meaning in both verses is *he presented,* different Hebrew verbs for *stood up* are used. In *v.* 2 the verb נצג is used, while here the verb is עמד.

R' Hirsch perceives the verb עמד in our passage to denote a dignified standing "on equal footing" before Pharaoh. Jacob is a spiritual prince on earth and meets Pharaoh as an equal by blessing him in greeting.

Following the Mesorah, [traditional spelling as found in Torah Scrolls], according to which וַיַּעֲמִדֵהוּ is spelled 'defectively' [without the י after the מ], *Baal HaTurim* perceives to the contrary that Jacob's standing here was 'defective.' He was extremely old and Joseph had to support him.

וַיְבָרֶךְ יַעֲקֹב אֶת־פַּרְעֹה — *And Jacob blessed Pharaoh.*

'Blessed' here denotes a greeting of peace as is customary with all who occasionally present themselves before kings *(Rashi).*

Rashi pursues this interpretation because Jacob is described as blessing Pharaoh twice — here and in *v.* 10. Therefore he construes the 'blessing' in the first instance to denote greeting, whereas in the second instance he

ח פַּרְעֹה: וַיֹּאמֶר פַּרְעֹה אֶל־יַעֲקֹב כַּמָּה יְמֵי
ט שְׁנֵי חַיֶּיךָ: וַיֹּאמֶר יַעֲקֹב אֶל־פַּרְעֹה יְמֵי
שְׁנֵי מְגוּרַי שְׁלֹשִׁים וּמְאַת שָׁנָה מְעַט
וְרָעִים הָיוּ יְמֵי שְׁנֵי חַיַּי וְלֹא הִשִּׂיגוּ אֶת־
י יְמֵי שְׁנֵי חַיֵּי אֲבֹתַי בִּימֵי מְגוּרֵיהֶם: וַיְבָרֶךְ

interprets it in its usual sense of blessing *(Divrei David).*

Comp. 33:11 where *Rashi* explains that the term *blessing* used in instances of meeting someone has the sense of *greeted* [and he cites our passage]; in old French: *saluer* [=salute]. See also *Haksav V'HaKabbalah* to 32:30. *Radak* interprets similarly, citing *II Kings* 4:29 where ברך also means *greet* rather than *bless.*

Ramban disagrees with *Rashi* that 'blessing' in this passage refers to salutation, inasmuch as it is not royal protocol for a commoner to greet a king, as the Sages have said [*Shabbos* 89a]: 'May a servant greet his master?' Rather, it refers to an actual blessing, since it is customary for the old and the pious, when they appear before kings, to bless them with wealth and a glorious reign. Similarly we find [*I Kings* 1:31]: *Let my lord king David reign forever.* Upon departing, Jacob blessed him again [*v.* 10] in order to take permission to leave.

The commentators respond to *Ramban's* criticism by emphasizing that *Rashi* does not suggest that Jacob greeted Pharaoh the way one would greet his comrade, but the way one greets royalty. That is why *Rashi* was careful to write 'as is customary with all who occasionally present themselves *before kings'* rather than *'before comrades' (Mizrachi; Gur Aryeh).*

8. כַּמָּה יְמֵי שְׁנֵי חַיֶּיךָ — *How many years have you lived?* [lit. *How many are the days of the years of your life?*][1]

The manner in which Pharaoh phrased the question reflects the very deep impression that Jacob made on him, for Pharaoh spoke of both *days* and *years.* Pharaoh understood that every single day in the life of a great man is important and productive — and Jacob was obviously a very great man *(R' Hirsch)*

What prompted Pharaoh to ask Jacob this question is discussed by *Ramban* in *v.* 9 below.[1]

9. In his reply Jacob draws a distinction. 'You ask about the days of the years of my *life.* My *life* has not been significant; I have *sojourned* on earth 130 years' *(R' Hirsch).*

יְמֵי שְׁנֵי מְגוּרַי שְׁלֹשִׁים וּמְאַת שָׁנָה — *The years* [lit. *the days of the years*] *of my sojourns have been a hundred and thirty years.*[2]

The days that I have lived as a גֵּר, *stranger, alien* have totalled 130 years, for I have been a stranger in other people's lands all my life *(Rashi).*

As *R' Bachya* notes, Jacob did not

1. The *Midrash* records that Og, who was Pharaoh's friend, was present when Jacob was presented to Pharaoh. [According to tradition, Og was Abraham's contemporary and enjoyed exceptional longevity. He fell in battle against the Israelites in the last days of Moses' life.] Pharaoh turned to Og and said, 'Had you not once told me that Abraham was a sterile mule who could not bear offspring? Yet, here is his grandson with 70 other descendants!'

'It is impossible!' Og answered. 'This man is very old; it must be Abraham himself.'

It was then that Pharaoh asked Jacob his age and his reply established that he was indeed Jacob.

Og tried to cast an Evil Eye upon them, but the Holy One Blessed is He, rebuked him and informed him that for having this desire, Og would one day be slain by a descendant of Jacob.

2. From the chronological detail of Jacob's age at this juncture the Sages in *Megillah* 17a deduce that Jacob had spent fourteen years in the Academy of Eber before proceeding to

[8] *Pharoah said to Jacob, "How many years have you lived?"* [9] *Jacob answered Pharaoh, "The years of my sojourns have been a hundred and thirty years. Few and bad have been the years of my life, and they have not attained the lifespans of my forefathers in the days*

echo Pharaoh and say 'the years of *my life*' but 'the years of *my sojourns*,' that is, the days that I was a stranger on this earthly world were 130 years. Such is the way of the righteous who regard themselves merely as transient strangers in this world.

מְעַט וְרָעִים הָיוּ יְמֵי שְׁנֵי חַיַּי — *Few and bad have been the years* [lit. *days of the years*] *of my life.*

The times that I can really call my *life*, the days when I really *accomplished* all that I should have, were *few* and they were רָעִים, bitter and full of anxiety. I had to carry out my life's mission in unhappiness *(R' Hirsch).*

Even the few 'happy' years I experienced were marred by evil and misfortune *(Abarbanel; Malbim).*

As *Sforno* observes, years of suffering are not termed years of *living*. Therefore Jacob emphasized that the days of the years of his *sojourns* totaled a hundred-thirty.

Thus, most commentators perceive *few* in the *qualitative* sense to intimate the years Jacob truly *lived*, rather than existed.

Radak takes it in the *quantitative* sense referring to the total number of years of Jacob's life, and asks: How could he call his years few; did he then know how long he would live? — Rather, because of all he suffered he felt feeble and knew he could not expect to live too much longer. [He lived to the age of 147.]

⇐§ What prompted Pharaoh to ask Jacob his age, and why was Jacob's response a complaining one?

Jacob had white hair and appeared very old to Pharaoh. Pharaoh therefore asked Jacob's age implying that he had never seen so old-looking a man in his entire kingdom.

Then Jacob answered that he was 130 years old — which was young in comparison with the ages his ancestors had attained — but he aged prematurely because he had experienced much trouble and vicissitude during his life. Thus, he did not mean to complain but to explain his premature aging *(Rashbam; Ramban).*

[However, see another view in the footnote on next page that Jacob was reprimanded for complaining to Pharaoh.]

וְלֹא הִשִּׂיגוּ אֶת־יְמֵי שְׁנֵי חַיֵּי אֲבֹתַי בִּימֵי מְגוּרֵיהֶם— *And they have not attained the lifespans* [lit. *the days of*

Laban. See 'Chronological Deductions' on p. 1173.

Briefly, according to the relevant data, Jacob should have been 116 years old at this point. (Jacob was 63 years old when he received the blessings and fled + 14 years spent with Laban until Joseph was born + 30 years, Joseph's age when he became ruler of Egypt + 7 years of abundance + 2 years of famine=116) yet Jacob, by his own admission, was now 130 years!

— The 14 year discrepancy was those unrecorded years that Jacob spent in the Academy of Eber after leaving his father *en route* to Laban.

Accordingly, although it emerges that Jacob was away from his father a total of thirty-six years (14 years of study and 22 years with Laban), the fourteen years of Torah study were meritorious, and Jacob was punished only for the 22 years with Laban. His punishment was the absence of Joseph for a similar period of twenty-two years.

יַעֲקֹב אֶת־פַּרְעֹה וַיֵּצֵא מִלִּפְנֵי פַרְעֹה:
יא °וַיּוֹשֵׁב יוֹסֵף אֶת־אָבִיו וְאֶת־אֶחָיו וַיִּתֵּן
°שביעי לָהֶם אֲחֻזָּה בְּאֶרֶץ מִצְרַיִם בְּמֵיטַב הָאָרֶץ
בְּאֶרֶץ רַעְמְסֵס כַּאֲשֶׁר צִוָּה פַרְעֹה:
יב וַיְכַלְכֵּל יוֹסֵף אֶת־אָבִיו וְאֶת־אֶחָיו וְאֵת
יג כָּל־בֵּית אָבִיו לֶחֶם לְפִי הַטָּף: וְלֶחֶם אֵין

the years of the lives] *of my forefathers in the days of their sojourns.*[1]

How could Jacob have said this? He could still equal their longevity and might even outlive them! Rather, Jacob was intimating, as noted above, that regardless of how old he appeared, he still had not reached their lifespans [Abraham had lived to 175; Isaac to 180]; his suffering aged him prematurely *(Ramban;* see above).

Most commentators, however, perceive the *qualitative* rather than *quantitative* implication of this statement:

And they have not attained — in happiness *(Rashi).*

— My life is not comparable to the lives of my fathers. They lived *more* in the sense that every day of their existence was *living,* and they were able to carry out their missions under cheerful conditions. Jacob was modestly assessing the qualitative paucity of his life *(R' Hirsch).*

Although my forefathers, too, were strangers in foreign lands, they nevertheless enjoyed many years of trouble-free living, even in exile, but my years as a stranger were not comparably free of travail.

10. וַיְבָרֶךְ יַעֲקֹב אֶת פַּרְעֹה וַיֵּצֵא מִלִּפְנֵי פַרְעֹה — *Then Jacob blessed Pharaoh, and left Pharaoh's presence.*

Jacob blessed him and asked permission to depart, as is the custom of all who take their leave of high officials *(Rashi; Ramban* similarly).

[Comp. *I Kings* 8:66: *On the eighth day he* [Solomon] *sent the people away; they blessed the king and went to their tents,* etc.]

Rashi continues, citing *Tanchuma Naso:* What was the blessing with which he blessed him? — That the Nile should rise at his approach [lit. *at his feet*] — the overflowing Nile being the symbol of Egypt's fertility, for Egypt is not irrigated by rain, but by the Nile. [It was because the Nile did not overflow and irrigate the land for two years that there was a famine in Egypt *(Maskil l'David).*] Jacob's blessing was fulfilled, and from that moment

1. **Jacob is punished for his complaint.**

The Sages maintain that the Holy One Blessed is He is much more exacting when judging the righteous and demands a scrupulous accounting for their actions. Accordingly, Jacob was held to account for bemoaning his lot to Pharoah.

Thus, when Jacob complained how 'few and bad' his days were, God upbraided him and said, 'I saved you from Esau and Laban, and returned Dinah and Joseph to you, yet you complain about My Ways!'

'By your life! Your years will indeed not number those of your forefathers, just as you have said. Your father Isaac lived 180 years; 33 years will be deducted from your years corresponding to the 33 words in those two verses' *(Daas Zekeinim; Midrash; Chizkuni).*

[Another reason for Jacob's "premature" death is offered in *v.* 28 below.]

47
11-12

of their sojourns." [10] *Then Jacob blessed Pharaoh, and*
left Pharaoh's presence.
[11] *So Joseph settled his father and his brothers and*
he gave them a possession in the land of Egypt in the
best part of the land, in the region of Rameses, as
Pharaoh had commanded. [12] *Joseph sustained his*
father and his brothers and all of his father's
household with food according to the children.

whenever Pharaoh approached the Nile it overflowed and irrigated the land [as it used to before the onset of the famine (*Maskil l'David*).]

[Thus, as a result of Jacob's blessing, the famine came to an end after only two years, instead of the seven years foretold by Joseph. (See comm. to v. 18 below).]

11. Joseph settles his family in Rameses.

וַיִּתֵּן לָהֶם אֲחֻזָּה בְּאֶרֶץ מִצְרַיִם — [And] *he gave them a possession in the land of Egypt.*

He settled them as full-fledged citizens, providing them with houses, fields, vineyards, and permanent property *(Ramban).*

בְּמֵיטַב הָאָרֶץ בְּאֶרֶץ רַעְמְסֵס — *In the best part of the land, in the region of Rameses.*

Rameses was part of Goshen *(Rashi).*

[This city, according to some, is the same as רַעְמְסֵס, *Raamses* mentioned in *Exodus* 1:11.(Note the vocalization under the ע; in our verse, it is עְ, whereas in *Exodus* it is עַ.) It was first named later, during the reign of Rameses II, who is considered by some to have been the Pharaoh of the oppression, but the Torah uses that name now for the sake of clarity. Others such as *Ibn Ezra* maintain that inasmuch as Rameses here is vowelized differently from the city in *Exodus* it is not to be identified with it. See *comm.* to *Exod.* 1:22. *Targum Yonasan* identifies both names with Pelusium, a city at the extreme northeast of the Nile delta.]

כַּאֲשֶׁר צִוָּה פַרְעֹה — *As Pharaoh had commanded.*

— In *v.* 6 above *(Ramban).*

Akeidas Yitzchak observes that the Torah purposely mentions this to emphasize that the settling of Joseph's family as full-fledged property-holders, was specifically by royal command. Therefore, their subsequent oppression and enslavement was criminal, since a royal decree conferring rights cannot be annulled.

12. לֶחֶם לְפִי הַטָּף — *Food* [lit. *bread*] *according to the children.*

That is, according to the individual needs of all the members of their households *(Rashi).*

I.e., in sufficient quantity for their needs. The phrase *'according to the children'* is employed because children scatter and waste; thus the passage implies that Joseph supplied them with enough bread even to compensate for the wastefulness of their little ones. *Rashi* capsulizes this thought in his comment by referring to the 'needs of *all* the members of their households' *(Mizrachi).*

Sforno maintains, however, that the implication of our passage is that although Joseph could have provided them with an abundant amount of rations, this verse em-

בְּכָל־הָאָ֔רֶץ כִּֽי־כָבֵ֥ד הָרָעָ֖ב מְאֹ֑ד וַתֵּ֜לַהּ
אֶ֤רֶץ מִצְרַ֙יִם֙ וְאֶ֣רֶץ כְּנַ֔עַן מִפְּנֵ֖י הָרָעָֽב׃
יד וַיְלַקֵּ֣ט יוֹסֵ֗ף אֶת־כָּל־הַכֶּ֙סֶף֙ הַנִּמְצָ֤א
בְאֶֽרֶץ־מִצְרַ֙יִם֙ וּבְאֶ֣רֶץ כְּנַ֔עַן בַּשֶּׁ֖בֶר
אֲשֶׁר־הֵ֣ם שֹׁבְרִ֑ים וַיָּבֵ֥א יוֹסֵ֛ף אֶת־הַכֶּ֖סֶף

phasizes that he gave them only the amount required for their minimum needs, since it would have been insensitive to act otherwise when the rest of the land was suffering famine. Cf. *Taanis* 11a: "When the community is in trouble let not a man say, 'I will go to my house and I will eat and drink and all will be well with me.' "

According to various interpretations advanced by *Ramban* in his *comm.* to *v.* 18 below, this passage is describing either how Joseph sustained his family during the remainder of the famine, or more generally throughout all the following years of his life — even after Jacob's death, as indicated in 50:21 below.

13. Joseph's agrarian policy.

According to *Rashi,* the following narrative occurred before Jacob arrived in Egypt. The Torah now resume its narrative of the beginning of the famine.

[As emphasized often, the Torah is not a history book and it need not necessarily describe events in the chronological order of their occurrence. The following verses are a case in point. Following the Midrashic chronology, the famine ended when Jacob blessed Pharaoh (*v.* 10; see *v.* 19 below). Since it is clear that Jacob arrived in the second year of the famine, the following account which, as is evident from *v.* 18, spans two years, must have preceded his arrival, and happened in the first year of the famine. Sequentially, therefore, it follows chapter 41, and parallels the events in chapter 42.]

Ibn Ezra and *Ramban* view the chronology differently, and their opinions will be cited in the commentary below.

וְלֶחֶם אֵין בְּכָל־הָאָרֶץ כִּי־כָבֵד הָרָעָב מְאֹד — *Now there was no bread in all the earth for the famine was very severe.*

[Whether the term הָאָרֶץ means *earth* or *land* is discussed above in 41:57. It refers either to the three countries adjacent to Egypt, as *Ramban* following the *Midrash* interprets it, or, according to the Talmud, *Pesachim* 119a, the reference is to the whole *world.*]

The reference here is to the market places and private homes, which lacked bread; there was an abundance of grain, however, in Pharaoh's royal granaries which had been stored away by Joseph during the preceding seven years of abundance *(R' Shmuel ben Chofni).*

וַתֵּלַהּ אֶרֶץ מִצְרַיִם וְאֶרֶץ כְּנַעַן מִפְּנֵי הָרָעָב— *And the land of Egypt and the land of Canaan became weary from the hunger.*

Egypt and Canaan are mentioned because they are central to the narrative (*Ramban*).

The translation *became weary* follows *Rashi* who explains that this is the meaning of the term וַתֵּלַהּ which is synonymous with וַתִּלְאֶה [although both are from different roots: להה and לאה respectively]; this is as *Onkelos* renders it. Related to this word is

[13] *Now there was no bread in all the earth for the*
famine was very severe. The land of Egypt and the
land of Canaan became weary from hunger. [14] *Joseph*
gathered all the money that was to be found in the land
of Egypt and in the land of Canaan through the provi-
sions which they were purchasing, and Joseph brought
the money into Pharaoh's palace. [15] *And when the*

Proverbs 26:18: כְּמִתְלַהְלֵהַּ הַיֹּרֶה זִקִּים [which *Rashi* renders: *like a fatigued person who throws firebrands*].

[*Radak* and *R' Saadiah* render similarly. See also *comm.* to וַיִּלְאוּ, *and they became wearied,* above 19:11.]

According to *Menachem ben Seruk,* this word, as well as the word in *Proverbs,* signifies *madness,* and our passage depicts how the Egyptians *became insane* from the deprivation caused by the famine.

Historical descriptions of similar famines in Egypt give an idea of the frightening suffering from which Joseph spared the country. A witness to a Middle Eastern famine wrote, 'The consumption of human flesh became so commonplace that it no longer astonished anyone. The route from Syria to Egypt resembled a vast field strewn with corpses' *(R' Munk).*

14. וַיְלַקֵּט יוֹסֵף ... וּבְאֶרֶץ כְּנַעַן — [And] *Joseph gathered all the money that was to be found in the land of Egypt and in the land of Canaan.*

But the inhabitants of other more distant lands did not come to Egypt, either because the distance was too great or perhaps the famine was not so severe there *(Rashbam).*

Since only a little money was left by then, the appropriate verb is לקט, which denotes gleaning in small quantities *(HaRechasim leBik'ah).*

בַּשֶּׁבֶר אֲשֶׁר־הֵם שֹׁבְרִים — *Through the provisions which they were purchasing.*

I.e., for which they were paying him money *(Rashi).* [*Rashi* is thus clarifying that שֹׁבְרִים is a verb meaning *purchasing;* comp. 41:56.]

Actually, the farmers themselves had contributed the grain during the years of plenty when Joseph stored it in royal granaries [41:48-49]. Why, then, were they now forced to *pay* for it?

Ramban in 41:48 suggests two possibilities: Joseph *bought* the grain from them when market prices were low due to the abundance and *sold* it back when prices were high due to the famine. Or possibly Pharaoh had originally taken it from them by force and now charged them for it by claiming that the food was preserved only by his foresight, as otherwise it would have been squandered or become rotten.

וַיָּבֵא יוֹסֵף אֶת־הַכֶּסֶף בֵּיתָה פַּרְעֹה — *And Joseph brought the money into Pharaoh's palace* [i.e., treasury *(Targum Yonasan)*].

In a monarchy such as Egypt's, the king was synonymous with the State and the money was held by him personally *(Alshich).*

This is recorded to show how loyally Joseph served in his role. He faithfully gave all the proceeds to the king who trusted him, and did not exploit his position to enrich

1. As noted in the footnote on p. 1816, the Providential Master Plan called for Egypt to amass all this wealth. This constituted the foretold 'great wealth' [15:14] which the Israelites would take along — more than two centuries later — when they left Egypt. Thanks to these riches, *R' Munk* points out, the Tabernacle (מִשְׁכָּן) with its sumptuous interior, could be constructed in the middle of the desert.

בֵּיתָה פַּרְעֹה: וַיִּתֹּם הַכֶּסֶף מֵאֶרֶץ מִצְרַיִם
טו וּמֵאֶרֶץ כְּנַעַן וַיָּבֹאוּ כָל־מִצְרַיִם אֶל־יוֹסֵף
לֵאמֹר הָבָה־לָּנוּ לֶחֶם וְלָמָּה נָמוּת נֶגְדֶּךָ
טז כִּי אָפֵס כָּסֶף: וַיֹּאמֶר יוֹסֵף הָבוּ מִקְנֵיכֶם
וְאֶתְּנָה לָכֶם בְּמִקְנֵיכֶם אִם־אָפֵס כָּסֶף:
יז וַיָּבִיאוּ אֶת־מִקְנֵיהֶם אֶל־יוֹסֵף וַיִּתֵּן לָהֶם
יוֹסֵף לֶחֶם בַּסּוּסִים וּבְמִקְנֵה הַצֹּאן
וּבְמִקְנֵה הַבָּקָר וּבַחֲמֹרִים וַיְנַהֲלֵם בַּלֶּחֶם
יח בְּכָל־מִקְנֵהֶם בַּשָּׁנָה הַהִוא: וַתִּתֹּם הַשָּׁנָה

himself by secretly hoarding money for himself by sending it to Canaan. As the narrative teaches us, Joseph even purchased all the farm land of Egypt for the monarch, and even the bodies of the Egyptians. Through his efforts, he was esteemed even by the populace "for it is God Who causes those who fear Him to prosper" *(Ramban).*

15. וַיִּתֹּם הַכֶּסֶף מֵאֶרֶץ מִצְרַיִם וּמֵאֶרֶץ כְּנַעַן — *And when the money was exhausted from the land of Egypt and from the land of Canaan.*

All the money was not used up at the same time. The poor obviously used up their money before the rich. Our passage accordingly speaks of the time when even the money of the rich was depleted *(Tur).*

According to the Midrash, however, Joseph was endowed with a prophetic spirit whereby he knew how much money each applicant had. He charged the rich high prices, and the poor low prices. The result was that both the rich and poor ran out of money at the same time.

The Torah specifically adds that the money was also used up in Canaan, because this was the basis of the Egyptians' argument to Joseph in the following verses. When they came to Joseph they argued that since there was no more money left even in Canaan, there was no purpose in hoarding the grain since no other buyers could possibly apply for it. Therefore, *'why should we die in your presence?* The money has been used up, and by withholding the grain you will cause our death in vain, inasmuch as the food will remain in your hands and no one else has the means to buy it' *(Ramban).*

וַיָּבֹאוּ כָל־מִצְרַיִם אֶל־יוֹסֵף לֵאמֹר — *All the Egyptians* [lit. *and all of Egypt*] *came to Joseph saying.*

הָבָה־לָּנוּ לֶחֶם וְלָמָּה נָמוּת נֶגְדֶּךָ — *Give us bread;* [*and*] *why should we die in your presence.*

Give us bread — do not insist on *selling* it. Why should you be the cause of our dying right in your presence? What benefit would the country have if we die and the food remains! *(Alshich).*

כִּי אָפֵס כָּסֶף — *For the money is gone.*

— And if you do not make food available it will remain in your possession unsold, since no one has the money to buy it *(Ramban).*

money was exhausted from the land of Egypt and from the land of Canaan, all the Egyptians came to Joseph saying "Give us bread; why should we die in your presence? — forthe money is gone!" 16 *And Joseph said, "Bring your livestock and I will provide for you in return for your livestock if the money is gone."* 17 *So they brought their livestock to Joseph, and Joseph gave them bread in return for the horses, for the flocks of sheep, for the herds of cattle, and for the donkeys; thus he provided them with bread for all their livestock during that year.*

[The implication is: Why should we be forced to die of starvation just because we have used up all of our *money;* we have *possessions* which we can barter!]

16. Joseph's proposal to barter livestock for food.

... וְאֶתְּנָה־לָכֶם בְּמִקְנֵיכֶם אִם־אָפֵס כָּסֶף — *Bring your livestock, and I will provide for you in return for your livestock if the money is gone.*

[This was all part of Joseph's master plan — to impoverish the Egyptians, and make them totally dependent upon the king. His argument was: To *give* you bread is not within my power. However, if it is indeed as you say that the money is used up, then bring me your cattle and I will barter them for food. If you still have livestock you have no right to ask for charity.]

Joseph used the expression, *'If the money is gone,'* because he doubted it and therefore asked for their cattle; a man will give up his money sooner then his livestock *(Haamek Davar).*

The translation of מִקְנֶה as *livestock* follows the familiar understanding of the term. Literally, it means *possessions* [from קנה, *possess* or *acquire*] in general, but it is usually applied to livestock and real property, and in certain contexts, to domestic animals *(Ralbag; Haamek Davar).*

17. וַיִּתֵּן לָהֶם יוֹסֵף לֶחֶם בַּסּוּסִים וכו׳ — *And Joseph gave them bread* [in return] *for the horses,* [*and*] *for the flocks of sheep,* [and] *for the herds of cattle, and for the donkeys.*

Joseph took horses first since they were the most valuable animals; Egypt was renowned for its horses *(R' Hirsch).*

וַיְנַהֲלֵם בַּלֶּחֶם בְּכָל־מִקְנֵהֶם בַּשָּׁנָה הַהִוא — *Thus he provided* [lit. *led*] *them with bread* [in exchange] *for all their livestock during that year.*

He provided, literally *he led them little by little.* He gave them just enough to sustain them, as is right in time of famine. As the Sages say [*Taanis* 11a]: 'He who starves himself in years of famine escapes unnatural death.' Furthermore, as physicians note, excessive indulgence after a period of hunger leads to fatal consequences *(Sforno).*

בַּשָּׁנָה הַהִוא — *During that year.* — Following *Rashi* and the Midrash [according to whom this narrative reverts to the beginning of the famine (see prefatory *comm.* to *v.* 13)], the reference is to the first year of the famine.

הַהוּא וַיָּבֹאוּ אֵלָיו בַּשָּׁנָה הַשֵּׁנִית וַיֹּאמְרוּ לוֹ לֹא־נְכַחֵד מֵאֲדֹנִי כִּי אִם־תַּם הַכֶּסֶף

According to *Sforno* [essentially following *Ramban* and others — see below — the narrative is sequentially in order, and] the reference is to the *sixth* year of the famine.

[The above views are discussed in the following verse.]

18. Joseph sustains the Egyptians in exchange for their land.

בַּשָּׁנָה הַשֵּׁנִית — *In the next* [lit. *second*] *year.*

The second year of the famine [see prefatory comm. to *v.* 13].

☙ The end of the famine

Although Joseph had said to his brothers [45:6]: *There will yet be five years when there will be no plowing or sowing,* as soon as Jacob came to Egypt a blessing came with him; they began to sow, and the famine came to an end [see *v.* 10 above]. This is derived from *Tosefta Sotah* 10:9. [This reference to the *second year* refers to the second year of the famine, which coincided with the arrival of Jacob, who came to Egypt in the famine's second year (above 45:6). Since the famine had ended as a result of Jacob's blessing, the populace begged Joseph for *seed* with which to sow the land again (*v.* 19).] *(Rashi* here and to *v.* 19 s.v. וְתֶן זֶרַע, Cf. *Bereishis Rabbah* 89:9).

Ramban elaborates on the interpretation that the famine ended after only two years. He explains that this premature ending of the famine did not cause people to doubt the wisdom or veracity of Joseph who had interpreted Pharaoh's dream as an omen of *seven* years of famine. Possibly the famine continued in Canaan for the full seven years, but in Egypt, Jacob went down to the Nile in the presence of Pharaoh and all the Egyptians and everyone saw the Nile rise as soon as he approached it. They all attributed the premature ending of the famine to Jacob's blessing and merit, not as an adverse reflection on Joseph's wisdom.

However, another difficulty remains. If the famine lasted only two years, it emerges that Pharaoh's dream was not true since it only revealed the seven-year *decree* to him, but not what would actually happen during those years!

To this, *Ramban* cites the continuation of the *Tosefta* in *Sotah* [mentioned in part by *Rashi*] that as soon as Jacob died the famine resumed. Similarly we find in *Sifre Eikev* §38 that in the view of *R' Yose,* Jacob's blessing to Pharaoh was that the famine should cease — which indeed happened — and it resumed after Jacob died [to complete the last five of the pre-ordained seven years]. This was why it was necessary for Joseph to assure his brothers again after his father's death that he would sustain them (50:21). Since the famine had resumed, Joseph used the term *sustenance* in the sense that he used it in 45:11: providing nourishment in times of famine.[1] Thus, the remaining five years were completed. [See 50:21.]

Ibn Ezra mentions the Midrashic interpretation that the famine ended in the

1. The *Sifre* continues its discussion of R' Yosei's statement that as soon as Jacob died the famine — which had ceased — resumed again for five more years.

R' Shimon says: It is not a sanctification of God's Name for the words of the righteous to be effective only as long as they lived and then be removed after their death. [Accordingly, Jacob's blessing of plenty should have survived him, and the famine should not have resumed after his death.]

R' Eleazar the son of R' Shimon said: I accept the opinion of R' Yosei rather than that of my father, for it is *indeed* a sanctification of God's Name for there to be a blessing in the world for as long as the righteous are alive, and for the blessing to be removed from it upon their departure!

47 18 *And when that year ended, they came to him in*
18 *the next year and said to him, "We will not withhold*
from my lord that with the money and flocks of cattle

merit of Jacob. However, in line with the literal implication of the narrative he suggests that the two years of barter recounted in these verses occurred *after* Jacob's arrival. Since Jacob arrived after two years of the famine, a total of four years are now accounted for, leaving three more years of famine. As evidenced by the fact that the Egyptians requested seed for sowing — something they would not have requested had the famine still been raging in full strength — we can assume that the last three years of the total of seven, were not as severe as the first four. Presumably, there was *some* vegetation as a result of their sowing during the following three years.

Ramban dismisses this interpretation inasmuch as Pharaoh's dream gave no hint of different degrees in the severity of the famine; had there been such a difference, the Torah would have mentioned it.

Ramban concludes by discussing the *literal* sense [*p'shat*] of the narrative [i.e., the meaning indicated by the words of the Text itself — which does not specify that the famine ended after its second year]. Verse 14, which describes Joseph's collecting all the money in the region, refers to a period spanning the first five years of the famine, for how is it possible for all the money and cattle to have been exhausted in one year? Rather, their money lasted for five years and since nothing exceptional occurred during this period, the Torah treats it in one sweep by summarily relating how Joseph gathered up the money and brought it to Pharaoh. [It was, of course, during this period — in the second year of the famine as indicated in 45:6 — that Jacob came to Egypt.] Verses 15-17 refer to the *sixth* year of the famine when Joseph bartered food for cattle. Accordingly, the reference in our verse to שָׁנָה הַשֵּׁנִית; *the 'second' year,* refers to the year following the sixth year — the year under discussion — that is, the seventh year, when the Egyptians begged Joseph to buy their bodies and land in exchange for feeding them during that seventh year. Because the land would belong to Pharaoh, they argued, Joseph should give them seed so the land would not be desolate, for they knew that the seven years of famine were about to end and they would again plant and reap.

[*Maasei Hashem* disagrees with *Ramban's* argument that the money would not have been depleted in only one year, but would have lasted five years. He observes that most small farmers are poor and would not have had the resources to last beyond that one year.]

Chizkuni also interprets that the events are sequentially related and the chronology is as follows:

Year 1 and 2: Beginning of Famine;
End of year 2: Jacob arrives;
Year 3: Joseph collects all the money [*v.* 14];
Year 4: Joseph sustains the Egyptians in exchange for their livestock [*v.* 17];
Year 5: Joseph sustains them in exchange for their land [*vs.* 18-20];
Year 6: Joseph sustains them in exchange for their bodies [*v.* 25];
Year 7: Joseph provides them with seed for sowing. The famine then ended and they reaped a harvest for the first time since the famine began. (Comp. *Radak; Abarbanel; Malbim*).

Sforno, as noted, similarly interprets that the *'second year'* mentioned in this verse refers to the year following the one in which the money was depleted, that is, the seventh and final year of the famine.

לֹא־נְכַחֵד מֵאֲדֹנִי כִּי אִם־תַּם הַכֶּסֶף וּמִקְנֵה הַבְּהֵמָה אֶל־אֲדֹנִי — *We will not withhold from my lord* [i.e., *our lord;* the collective singular is used here], *that with the money and flocks of cattle having been exhausted to my lord.*

וּמִקְנֵה הַבְּהֵמָה אֶל־אֲדֹנִי לֹא נִשְׁאַר
לִפְנֵי אֲדֹנִי בִּלְתִּי אִם־גְּוִיָּתֵנוּ וְאַדְמָתֵנוּ:
יט לָמָּה נָמוּת לְעֵינֶיךָ גַּם־אֲנַחְנוּ גַּם־
אַדְמָתֵנוּ קְנֵה־אֹתָנוּ וְאֶת־אַדְמָתֵנוּ
בַּלָּחֶם וְנִהְיֶה אֲנַחְנוּ וְאַדְמָתֵנוּ עֲבָדִים
לְפַרְעֹה וְתֶן־זֶרַע וְנִחְיֶה וְלֹא נָמוּת

The idiomatic implication of לֹא נִכְחַד is: We would not dare withhold anything from you; there is simply nothing left to hide and the following proposal is made out of sincere desperation *(Akeidah; Chizkuni; Abarbanel).*

Rashi comments that the idiomatic expression כִּי־אִם is synonymous with כִּי אֲשֶׁר. [See *Rashi* to 24:33 where he similarly notes that עַד אִם is synonymous with עַד אֲשֶׁר. See also *footnote* 18:15 where it is noted that in certain contexts the word כִּי is also synonymous with אֲשֶׁר. *Mizrachi* is uncomfortable with the fact that following this interpretation the word אֲשֶׁר is superfluous, and the phrase could just as well have read כִּי תַּם. Our translation *that with* follows the comment of *Gur Aryeh* who implicitly renders the sense to be כִּי כַּאֲשֶׁר (Cf. *Levush). Gur Aryeh, R' Shmuel ben Chofni* and *Ibn Janach* suggest that the thrust of most commentators is to emphasize that the use of אִם in such contexts does not mean *if* but is idiomatic. See *Ribag* Shoresh אִם*; Machberes Menachem* s.v. אִם. Comp. also כִּי אִם in 40:14 where the context causes *Rashi* to offer another interpretation of the phrase.

Alternatively, some interpret the phrase כִּי אִם, following as it does the word לֹא, *not,* to mean *but indeed.* It implies: We would not insist that we used up our money if it were not true — *but indeed* the money and cattle had been consigned to my lord. Compare the similar usage above in 15:4; 32:27; 32:29. *Shaarei Aharon* suggests that since this interpretation in our context would require that too many words be elliptically added to our verse, *Rashi* preferred the translation he advanced.

However, *Sforno* perceives the meaning of אִם more literally as *if.* He explains the passage as implying: We are not withholding from my lord the fact that indeed we have more cattle, but even *if* it were true that everything was depleted it would be improper for you to let us die ...

The latter part of the phrase literally reads: ... *there has been used up the money and the flocks of cattle to my lord.* The passage is clearly ellipt**ic**. *Rashi* takes both *the money* and *the flocks of cattle* as the subjects of *have been used up* and explains the elliptic connotation of the passage to mean: *'The money and the flocks of cattle have been used up* and everything has now come *into my lord's hands.'* [That the verb תַּם, *used up,* is in the singular —instead of the plural תַּמּוּ — is no contradiction inasmuch as Hebrew verbs often employ the singular in the collective sense.] Our translation *have been exhausted* follows *Rashi's* exegesis.

Others divide the subjects and interpret: ... *that the money has been used up, and the flocks of cattle have come into my lord's possession.*

לֹא נִשְׁאַר לִפְנֵי אֲדֹנִי בִּלְתִּי אִם־גְּוִיָּתֵנוּ וְאַדְמָתֵנוּ — *Nothing is left before my lord but our bodies and our land.*

I.e., nothing is left that we could offer our lord ... *(Sechel Tov).*

The expression בִּלְתִּי אִם [lit. *except if*] is idiomatic. The word בִּלְתִּי sometimes means לֹא, *not.* בִּלְתִּי אִם therefore means לֹא אִם which according to *Rashi* is an inversion of

47
19 *having been exhausted to my lord, nothing is left*
before my lord but our bodies and our land. [19] *Why*
should we die before your eyes, both we and our land?
Acquire us and our land for bread; and we — with our
land — will become serfs to Pharaoh; and provide seed
so that we may live and not die, and the land will not

אִם לֹא, *if not.* The meaning of the passage accordingly is: *nothing remains if not* [i.e., except for] *our bodies.* The commentators to *Rashi* note that the thrust of his commentary, here, as above [s.v. כִּי־אִם], is to negate mistranslating אִם in its other sense of *if.*

19. לָמָּה נָמוּת לְעֵינֶיךָ גַּם־אֲנַחְנוּ גַּם־אַדְמָתֵנוּ — *Why should we die before your eyes, both we and our land?*

What possible benefit could you gain from seeing us die? *(Sechel Tov).*

Do not wonder that the term *death* is used in connection with land; comp. the opposite connotation in *Nehemiah* 9:6: *and You give "life" to them all* [i.e. to the heavens, earth and seas mentioned in that verse] *(Ibn Ezra).*

Radak, B'chor Shor, R' Meyuchas and *Ralbag* similarly observe that land 'dies' when it is laid waste and neither plowed nor worked to yield produce.

קְנֵה־אוֹתָנוּ וְאֶת־אַדְמָתֵנוּ בַּלָּחֶם — *Acquire us and our land* [in exchange] *for bread.*

Then we will become your serfs, and you will be responsible to feed us in return for our labor *(Haamek Davar).*

Acquire us as serfs, *and our land* to become tax-yielding royal property *(Chizkuni; Ralbag).*

וְנִהְיֶה אֲנַחְנוּ וְאַדְמָתֵנוּ עֲבָדִים לְפַרְעֹה — *And we — with our land — will become serfs to Pharaoh* [lit. *let us and our land become servants to Pharaoh*].

Technically it is only the people ['we'] who will become 'servants' to Pharaoh; servitude does not apply to land, although in Talmudic usage we find the term שִׁעְבּוּד [*subjection* (in the sense of pledge or security)] applied to קַרְקַע, land. The sense of the passage, then, as I interpret it is: *We will be slaves, and our land* — possessions. Comp. the Talmud's [*Sanhedrin* 44a] interpretation of *Joshua* 7:24 where the subjects in the verse are not treated as a group, but individually *(R' Shmuel b. Chofni;* see also *R' Saadiah).*

Cf. *Sifra* to *Lev.* 10:14 and *Rashi* there. See also R' Yishmael's Hermeneutic rule No. 20 (printed in beginning of Mossad Harav Kook ed. of *Midrash HaGadol, Bereishis).* This concept is discussed fully in Greenbaum's note on this passage in his ed. of R' Shmuel b. Chofni.

וְתֶן־זֶרַע — [And] *provide seed* [*grain*].

With which to sow the land, for, as noted above, they had seen that the Nile again overflowed as a result of Jacob's blessing. If they could begin planting the famine would be over [see *Rashi* above].

According to *Ramban* and *Sforno,* this occurred in the seventh year when it was common knowledge that the famine would end, and they were acting in anticipation of this.

וְנִחְיֶה וְלֹא נָמוּת — *So that we may live and not die.*

With the end of the famine at

כ וְהָאֲדָמָה לֹא תֵשָׁם: וַיִּקֶן יוֹסֵף אֶת־כָּל־
אַדְמַת מִצְרַיִם לְפַרְעֹה כִּי־מָכְרוּ מִצְרַיִם
אִישׁ שָׂדֵהוּ כִּי־חָזַק עֲלֵהֶם הָרָעָב וַתְּהִי
כא הָאָרֶץ לְפַרְעֹה: וְאֶת־הָעָם הֶעֱבִיר אֹתוֹ
לֶעָרִים מִקְצֵה גְבוּל־מִצְרַיִם וְעַד־קָצֵהוּ:

hand, the seed would assure their survival since the following season would yield crops if they planted now.

Life in the sense of physical survival was the most they could now hope for; since their freedom had been forfeited they could no longer live a full, satisfaction-filled life. The implication then of the dual phraseology is: "That we may live in the sense of not dying," even though a life of servitude is not called *truly* living *(Haamek Davar; Shaarei Aharon).*

וְהָאֲדָמָה לֹא תֵשָׁם — *And the* [farm] *land will not become desolate.*

[Through lack of cultivation.]

The Egyptians apparently were unaware of the full efficacy of Jacob's blessing and they were apprehensive that their 'land would become desolate.' The prophet Ezekiel paints a very bleak picture of what such desolation would mean for Egypt [29:8-12] *(R' Munk).*

The rendering *desolate* (=שְׁמָמָה) follows *Rashi* who cites *Onkelos'* rendering לָא תְבוּר, *shall not be uncultivated,* the word תְבוּר being related to the Mishnaic term שְׂדֵה בוּר, *an unploughed field.*

Alternatively: that it not become desolate in the sense of losing its inhabitants from starvation. Comp. *Ezekiel* 12:19 *(R' Shmuel b. Chofni).*

They thus vowed that if Joseph agreed to sustain them and provide them with seed, they would cultivate it and it would *never* bcome desolate *(Ramban).*

20. **וַיִּקֶן יוֹסֵף אֶת־כָּל־אַדְמַת מִצְרַיִם לְפַרְעֹה** — *Thus Joseph acquired all the* [farm] *land of Egypt for Pharaoh.*

He acquired *all* the land, even courtyards, etc. that were not useful for farming *(Haamek Davar).*

Although in *v.* 19 they offered to sell *themselves* also as slaves to Pharaoh, we now find that Joseph bought only their *land,* stipulating in the following verses that they should work it forever as sharecroppers, and pay part of the produce to Pharaoh as rent *(Ramban).*

According to *Haamek Davar,* the reason Joseph did not make slaves of them was out of concern for the welfare of the State. He wanted them to remain self-sustaining and not become State wards. And as *Malbim* emphasizes, a ruler must always feel responsible for the sustenance of his subjects; and it would have been wrong for him to have bought them as slaves in return for bread.[1]

1. *Meshech Chochmah* similarly observes that as a former slave Joseph could not tolerate the notion of one person enslaving another. Therefore, notwithstanding their offer, he did not buy them as slaves. He bought only their land, and engaged them as tenants — day workers, as it were — earning their bread. Therefore, Joseph says: [*v.* 23]: *Behold I have bought you this day, and your land for Pharaoh;* he meant, *I have bought you this day* — i.e. to work for me temporarily, as 'day workers', as it were, for the duration of the famine; *and your land* — per-

become desolate."

[20] *Thus Joseph acquired all the land of Egypt for Pharaoh, for every Egyptian sold his field because the famine had overwhelmed them. And the land became Pharaoh's.* [21] *As for the nation, he resettled it by cities, from one end of Egypt's borders to the other.* [22] *Only*

כִּי־מָכְרוּ מִצְרַיִם אִישׁ שָׂדֵהוּ כִּי חָזַק עֲלֵהֶם הָרָעָב — *For every Egyptian sold his field because the famine had overwhelmed them.*

Every Egyptian executed a deed of sale for his land and presented it to Joseph *(Midrash HaGadol).*

וַתְּהִי הָאָרֶץ לְפַרְעֹה — *And the land became Pharaoh's.*

I.e., acquired by him *(Rashi).* Not only did he *reign* over the land — that was the case even before this arrangement — now the land was legally *owned* by him *(Mizrachi).*

21. וְאֶת־הָעָם הֶעֱבִיר אֹתוֹ לֶעָרִים — *And as for the nation, he resettled it by cities* [i.e., from city to city].

That is, Joseph transferred the population from one city to the other to establish the monarchy's undisputed ownership of the land, and commemorate that individuals no longer had claim to any property they formerly owned. Joseph was concerned that each would cling tenaciously to his former property, and he wanted it absolutely apparent that anyone's association with a certain piece of State property was at the king's pleasure exclusively *(Rashi; Radak; Chizkuni; Meshech Chochmah).*[1]

Rashbam cites the parallel action of Sennacherib [portrayed in *Isaiah* 36:16*f*]. In both instances the purpose was to prevent the people from claiming ownership on the ground of possession.

R' Hirsch adds that even in carrying out this general evacuation, Joseph executed it wisely. He did not move about people haphazardly, for that would have broken down the social and community structure with harmful effects to the nation. Instead, Joseph arranged for the residents who had always lived together in a region to be moved *en masse* so that they found themselves still together with their friends in their new environment.

The translation of לֶעָרִים as *by cities,* meaning *from city to city,* follows *Rashi.* [To express the idea of a transfer *to the cities* would have grammatically required the expression אֶל הֶעָרִים *(Akeidah).*]

מִקְצֵה גְבוּל־מִצְרַיִם וְעַד־קָצֵהוּ — *From one end of Egypt's borders to the other* [lit. *from the end of Egypt's border and until its end*].

manently, for Pharaoh. Thus, the obligation upon the *people* was only *temporary,* while the acquisition of the *land* was *permanent.*

Similarly, it was to assure that they would not cling to their property that Joseph transferred from city to city [next verse], for since they remained free men, there was no other way to make it obvious that Pharaoh now owned their land.

1. *Rashi* notes further — citing *Chullin* 60b — that the Torah had no need to mention this except to suggest to us Joseph's lofty purpose in transposing them: He intended to prevent the Egyptians from jeering at his Jewish brothers because they were aliens. [That is, since the Egyptians themselves now became aliens in different parts of the country — none of them remaining as 'old inhabitants' on their own ancestral lands — they could henceforth not look down with disdain on Joseph's family as 'newcomers.']

כב רַק אַדְמַת הַכֹּהֲנִים לֹא קָנָה כִּי חֹק
לַכֹּהֲנִים מֵאֵת פַּרְעֹה וְאָכְלוּ אֶת־חֻקָּם
אֲשֶׁר נָתַן לָהֶם פַּרְעֹה עַל־כֵּן לֹא מָכְרוּ
כג אֶת־אַדְמָתָם: וַיֹּאמֶר יוֹסֵף אֶל־הָעָם הֵן
קָנִיתִי אֶתְכֶם הַיּוֹם וְאֶת־אַדְמַתְכֶם
לְפַרְעֹה הֵא־לָכֶם זֶרַע וּזְרַעְתֶּם אֶת־
כד הָאֲדָמָה: וְהָיָה בַּתְּבוּאֹת וּנְתַתֶּם
חֲמִישִׁית לְפַרְעֹה וְאַרְבַּע הַיָּדֹת יִהְיֶה

I.e., Joseph carried out the above-mentioned policy of displacement in all the cities of the Egyptian kingdom from one end of Egypt's borders to the other *(Rashi).* [Not that Joseph caused individual people to be *transferred* from one end of Egypt to the other.]

22. רַק אַדְמַת הַכֹּהֲנִים לֹא קָנָה — *Only the land of the priests he did not buy.*

[For the reason that the verse proceeds to tell us. Joseph's rationale for this display of reverence for idolatrous priests by granting them this dispensation is discussed in the *comm.* to the end of *v.* 26 below.]

The term *kohen* [*priest*] refers to one who ministers to a deity. There are exceptions to this, such as 47:22 above (*kohen of On),* and *Exodus* 2:16 (*kohen of Midian)* where the context denotes that the term refers to one of high rank [— *chief* or *governor*] *(Rashi;* see *Ramban* to 47:22).

According to *Chizkuni* the term *kohen* in our verse, too, refers to the high officers. Joseph did not acquire their lands as he was afraid they might rebel.

כִּי חֹק לַכֹּהֲנִים מֵאֵת פַּרְעֹה — *Since the priests had a stipend from Pharaoh.*[1]

The translation of חק as *stipend* follows *Rashi* who explains the term — in this context — to mean "an assigned ration of bread daily." [This is apparently to avoid mistranslating חק in its other meaning of *statute* as below in *v.* 26.]

עַל־כֵּן לֹא מָכְרוּ אֶת־אַדְמָתָם — *Therefore they did not sell their land.*

I.e. therefore they did not *have* to sell their land for bread *(R' Saadiah Gaon).*

1. *R' Yehudah HaChassid* asked: Why is this detail recorded in the Torah?

— It was recorded so that the children of Israel should not be miserly in giving the *terumah* and tithes even though it would total a fifth [i.e. a negligible gift to the *Kohen,* a tenth to the Levite, and another tenth to be eaten in Jerusalem or, in the third and sixth years of the Seven-year cycle, to be given to the poor]. 'See what Pharaoh did on behalf of his idol-serving priests by not acquiring their land, and freeing them from paying him a fifth of their produce,' says God. 'But to you, My Children, I give *Eretz Yisrael* as an outright gift — surely you, who are children of the Living God, should give a fifth graciously' *(Moshav Zekeinim).*

Similarly, does the *Midrash* note: Pharaoh owned nothing of the world, yet he demanded a fifth of the crop [next verse] ... But the Holy One, Blessed is He, owns everything, and He demands that the children of Israel separate for Him only a [bit more than a] tenth for his servants the *Kohanim* and Levites.

the land of the priests he did not buy, since the priests
had a stipend from Pharaoh, and they lived off their
stipend that Pharaoh had given them, therefore they
did not sell their land.
23 *Joseph said to the people, "Look — I have acquired*
you this day with your land for Pharaoh; here is seed
for you — sow the land. 24 *At the ingathering of the*
harvests you will give a fifth to Pharaoh; the [other]

23. Joseph demands a fifth of all produce for the king.

הֵן קָנִיתִי אֶתְכֶם הַיּוֹם וְאֶת אַדְמַתְכֶם לְפַרְעֹה — *Look — I have acquired you this day with your land, for Pharaoh.*

I have bought *you* — not as you offered, to be slaves performing whatever tasks Pharaoh imposes upon you — but only in the sense that I have now acquired you along with the land. You must therefore remain on the land as permanent tenants to cultivate it. And I have the following lenient proposal to make to you [next verse] *(Ramban).*

[*Meshech Chochmah* in *v.* 20 distinguishes between the 'acquisition' of the *people* themselves הַיּוֹם, only *today* — i.e. the obligation upon the *people* was only temporary, to work for their bread for the duration of the famine, but the *land* was different — Pharaoh's acquisition of that was permanent.]

הֵא־לָכֶם זֶרַע וּזְרַעְתֶּם אֶת־הָאֲדָמָה — *Here is seed for you* — [and] *sow the land.*

That they were to sow the land was their obligation to Pharaoh under the conditions of the agreement they had made in exchange for food *(Ramban).*

Therefore Joseph said, *Look I have acquired you this day with your land for Pharaoh. You are his serfs and obligated to work his land and he is obligated to supply you with food and seed for planting.* Accordingly, the arrangement that all the harvests would belong to Pharaoh was quite legal, and they were required to sow the land *(Sforno).*

The word הֵא is synonymous with הִנֵּה, *here, behold.* Compare *Ezekiel* 16:43 *(Rashi).*

24. The following is the sharecropping arrangement as it would apply in the future when their planting — from Joseph's seed and on State property — would yield produce.

וְהָיָה בַּתְּבוּאֹת וּנְתַתֶּם חֲמִישִׁית לְפַרְעֹה — [*And*] *at the ingathering of the harvests* [when the crops come up] *you will give a fifth to Pharaoh.*

Under our arrangement, it would have been proper for the king, who is now lord of the land, to take *four* fifths of the harvest and leave only the remaining fifth for you. However, I will deal generously with you: *You* will take the portion due the owner of the land — four-fifths — and Pharaoh will receive only the portion due the tenant — one-fifth. The one restriction will be that you must remain to work the fields and cannot leave them *(Ramban).*

Some see in this a permanent extension of the scheme which Joseph instituted during the years of plenty when [according to their interpreta-

לָכֶם לְזֶרַע הַשָּׂדֶה וּלְאָכְלְכֶם וְלַאֲשֶׁר
כה בְּבָתֵּיכֶם וְלֶאֱכֹל לְטַפְּכֶם: °וַיֹּאמְרוּ
°מפטיר הֶחֱיִתָנוּ נִמְצָא־חֵן בְּעֵינֵי אֲדֹנִי וְהָיִינוּ
כו עֲבָדִים לְפַרְעֹה: וַיָּשֶׂם אֹתָהּ יוֹסֵף לְחֹק
עַד־הַיּוֹם הַזֶּה עַל־אַדְמַת מִצְרַיִם לְפַרְעֹה
לַחֹמֶשׁ רַק אַדְמַת הַכֹּהֲנִים לְבַדָּם לֹא

tion of וְחִמֵּשׁ in 41:34] Joseph collected a fifth of all the produce grown in Egypt to be stored for use during the famine.[1] [*Rashi* does not subscribe to that view, interpreting חִמֵּשׁ in that context to mean *prepare.* See *comm.* there.]

The translation of בַּתְּבוּאֹת as **ingathering** *of the harvests,* rather than the more literal and common *at the harvest,* follows *Onkelos.* His reason for this deviation is that tithes are not customarily separated until after the crops are gathered, as recorded in *Berachos* 35. *(Marpei Lashon; Sechel Tov* renders similarly).

וְאַרְבַּע הַיָּדֹת יִהְיֶה לָכֶם לְזֶרַע הַשָּׂדֶה וּלְאָכְלְכֶם — *And the* [*other*] *four parts shall remain yours—as seed for the field and as food for yourselves.*

To be divided among the four categories enumerated later in the verse *(Chizkuni).*

As seed for the field — i.e., with which to plant in future years *(Rashi).* [He thus made it clear that in the future seed would not be provided them from Pharaoh's share, but from the generous four-fifths which Pharaoh allowed them.]

וְלַאֲשֶׁר בְּבָתֵּיכֶם — [*And*] *for those in your household.*

I.e., the slaves and maidservants of your households *(Rashi).* [It cannot mean the *children* of the household since they are mentioned separately at the end of the verse *(Sifsei Chachamim).*]

Radak adds the livestock as well to this category.

וְלֶאֱכֹל לְטַפְּכֶם — *And to feed* [lit. *and to eat for*] *your little ones.*

Your share of four-fifths will be adequate to satisfy all of these needs as the soil will be very fertile *(Radak).*

25. וַיֹּאמְרוּ הֶחֱיִתָנוּ — *And they said, 'You have saved our lives!'* [lit. *you have given us life*].

— By having provided us with food throughout the famine, and with seed for the future *(Sechel Tov).*

According to *Ramban* [*v.* 19]: You have given us life by generously allowing us to take four-fifths of the harvest.

The Rabbis in the Midrash perceive in the long form of this word הֶחֱיִתָנוּ (instead of חִיִּתָנוּ) a homiletical extension implying gratitude not only for life in this world, but for life in the Hereafter as well. They were acknowledging their gratitude that Joseph had forced them to undergo circumcision [see *Rashi* to 41:55].

נִמְצָא־חֵן בְּעֵינֵי אֲדֹנִי — *May we find favor in your eyes, my lord.*

1. Why did Joseph institute specifically this levy of a *fifth?*

There is an allusion here to the fact that everything was in Jacob's merit. Jacob had vowed to partake only of the four-fifths of whatever came into his possession, while the other fifth [=double tithe] was to be separated for sacred purposes [see עַשֵּׂר אֲעַשְּׂרֶנּוּ in 28:22].

Accordingly, since the Egyptians now had food as a result of Jacob's blessing [for it was in

47
25-26

four parts shall remain yours — as seed for the field,
food for yourselves and for those in your household,
and to feed your little ones."

25 *And they said, "You have saved our lives; may we find favor in your eyes, my lord, and we will be serfs to Pharaoh."*

26 *So Joseph imposed it as a statute till this day regarding the land of Egypt: it was Pharaoh's for the fifth; only the priests' land alone did not become Pharaoh's.*

[I.e., may you continue to find us worthy.]

— To be treated as you have said (*Rashi*).

According to *R' Meyuchas,* the expression is idiomatic. It means: We are gratefully indebted to you.

וְהָיִינוּ עֲבָדִים לְפַרְעֹה — *And we will be serfs to Pharaoh.*

— And will pay this tax annually *(Rashi).*

Rashi is emphasizing that the Egyptians did not repeat their earlier offer that they would be slaves to Pharaoh, as Joseph had already rejected that offer. Rather, they agreed to be serfs, in the sense of paying the annual tax Joseph was imposing *(Mizrachi).*

Ramban interprets: *We will be serfs to Pharaoh* as we have vowed, in the sense that we will work the land in accordance with his will.

26. וַיָּשֶׂם אֹתָהּ יוֹסֵף לְחֹק עַד הַיּוֹם הַזֶּה — *So Joseph imposed it as a statute till this day.*

As a statute — an irrevocable law *(Rashi).*

Till this day — until the days of Moses when the Torah was given. [That is, the statute mentioned in this verse was still in force in the days of Moses.] Throughout Scripture *until this day* means until the time of the Scribe who recorded the matter *(Rashbam* to 19:37).

עַל־אַדְמַת מִצְרַיִם לְפַרְעֹה לַחֹמֶשׁ — *Regarding the* [farm] *land of Egypt: it was Pharaoh's for the fifth.*

The phraseology לְפַרְעֹה לַחֹמֶשׁ, literally *to Pharaoh for the fifth,* rather than חֹמֶשׁ לְפַרְעֹה, *a fifth for Pharaoh,* is significant. The land was Pharaoh's property to guarantee that he would receive payment of a fifth of the produce, for the State could take everything if a farmer failed to make his payment. This was meant to establish the principle that Pharaoh was not merely a one-fifth partner — as would be implied by חֹמֶשׁ לְפַרְעֹה — but that he was the complete owner, to guarantee the fifth *(R' Hirsch).*

רַק אַדְמַת הַכֹּהֲנִים לְבַדָּם לֹא הָיְתָה לְפַרְעֹה — *Only the priests' land alone did not become Pharaoh's.*

☙ Why did Joseph not oppose this special dispensation to the idolatrous clergy?

Tur explains that he remained grateful to Potiphera the priest of On whose daughter he had married,

his merit that the famine ended] Joseph imposed upon all the Egyptians a similar double tithe as their levy to the State *(Kli Yakar).*

כז הָיְתָה לְפַרְעֹה: וַיֵּשֶׁב יִשְׂרָאֵל בְּאֶרֶץ
מִצְרַיִם בְּאֶרֶץ גֹּשֶׁן וַיֵּאָחֲזוּ בָהּ וַיִּפְרוּ
וַיִּרְבּוּ מְאֹד:

and to the Egyptian priests who had spoken up in his defense against the accusations of his master's wife. They had saved him from being condemned to death as *Targum Yonasan* tells us in 39:20.

R' Yaakov Kaminetzky, שליט״א, explains that Joseph prophetically established a precedent that would later benefit Israel. By giving a privileged status to the clergy, Joseph made it possible for the tribe of Levi — who were the 'clerics' in Israel — to be exempt from the servitude to which the Egyptians later subjected the other tribes.

[See also footnote end of *v.* 22.]

27. According to *Rashbam* [*v.* 29] this verse would have been a natural place for the next Sidrah to have begun, but *v.* 26 did not provide a suitable ending for this Sidrah.

וַיֵּשֶׁב יִשְׂרָאֵל בְּאֶרֶץ מִצְרַיִם בְּאֶרֶץ גֹּשֶׁן — *Thus Israel settled in the land of Egypt in the region of Goshen.*

The region of Goshen explains where in *the land of Egypt* they dwelt *(Rashi).*

According to *Malbim,* they originally lived in Raamses [*v.* 11], but when Joseph resettled the Egyptians by cities [*v.* 21] he gave all of Goshen to the Israelites who were fruitful and needed a larger territory.

The Talmud [*Sanhedrin* 106a] records: 'The term וַיֵּשֶׁב, *settled,* always foreshadows grief.' Thus in our verse, *Israel settled in the land of Egypt* ... is closely followed by *the time approached for Israel to die* [*v.* 29].

וַיֵּאָחֲזוּ בָהּ — [And] *they acquired property in it.*

I.e., they purchased property in Goshen beyond what Joseph had given them *(Radak; Ibn Ezra; Chizkuni).*

This verse is a condemnation of the children of Israel. Notwithstanding God's decree to Abraham in ch. 15 that his descendants would be *aliens* in a foreign land, they

47
27 [27] *Thus Israel settled in the land of Egypt in the
region of Goshen; they acquired property in it and
they were fruitful and multiplied greatly.*

sought to be settlers and property holders in a land not rightfully theirs *(Kli Yakar).*[1]

וַיִּפְרוּ וַיִּרְבּוּ מְאֹד — *And they were fruitful and* [*they*] *multiplied greatly.*

They were fruitful — in children; and *multiplied greatly* — in wealth, both because they were not required to give a fifth of their crops to Pharaoh, and because Heaven aided them *(Sechel Tov).*

[See *Ramban* to *Numbers* 3:14.]

Thus was fulfilled God's promise made to Jacob upon his departure to Egypt [46:3]: *For I shall establish you as a great nation there (Chizkuni).*

According to the Masoretic note appearing at the end of the *Sidrah* there are 106 verses in *Vayigash* numerically corresponding to the mnemonic יהללא״ל, literally *praised be God.* This is a reference to the many praises due the Almighty for having spared Joseph and reunited the unblemished Patriarchal family. Furthermore, the Divine appellation אֵל designates, according to many opinions, the continuation of God's Aspect of Mercy with Strict Justice, and the mnemonic alludes to the praise due Him even for orchestrating the events that led to the Egyptian bondage. For just as the Jew is obligated to praise God for the goodness He bestows, so must we praise Him for that which appears evil.

The *Haftarah* begins with *Ezekiel* 37:15: וְאַתָּה בֶן־אָדָם קַח לְךָ עֵץ.

נשלם סדרה ויגש בעזרת האל

1. The phrase is literally in the passive: *And they were possessed by it.* According to the Midrash, the expression denotes how *the land took possession of them,* as it were, to make sure that they would fulfill their bond of servitude foretold to Abraham at the Covenant Between the Parts [15:13]. The land gripped them firmly, and had they desired to leave it they would not be free to leave it until the predetermined end of the bondage.

R' Hirsch, however, perceives in the nuances of our verse a contrast between Jacob and his family. While the Patriarch only *settled* in the land, his descendants let themselves 'be gripped' by the land. This attachment of the Israelites to the land of Egypt was attacked by the prophet Ezekiel *(Ezekiel* 20:67).

◆§ סדר ויחי

◆§ Sidrah Vayechi

— The Overviews

*An Overview/ In Egypt and for All Time**

אָמַר ר׳ סִימוֹן בְּשָׁעָה שֶׁבָּא הקב״ה לִבְרֹא אֶת אָדָם הָרִאשׁוֹן ... אֱמֶת אוֹמֵר, אַל יִבְרָא שֶׁכֻּלּוֹ שְׁקָרִים ... מֶה עָשָׂה הקב״ה? נָטַל אֱמֶת וְהִשְׁלִיכוֹ לָאָרֶץ. הֲדָא הוּא דִכְתִיב, וְתַשְׁלֵךְ אֱמֶת אַרְצָה.

Rabbi Simon said: At the time that the Holy One, Blessed is He, came to create the first man ... Truth said, 'He should not create [man] because he is filled with falsehoods' ... What did the Holy One, Blessed is He, do? He took truth and threw it to the earth. This is alluded to in the verse (Daniel 8:12): *He will throw truth to the earth (Bereishis Rabbah* 8:5).

לָמָּה פָּרָשָׁה זוֹ סְתוּמָה? לְפִי שֶׁכֵּיוָן שֶׁנִּפְטַר יַעֲקֹב אָבִינוּ נִסְתְּמוּ עֵינֵיהֶם וְלִבָּם שֶׁל יִשְׂרָאֵל מִצָּרַת הַשִּׁעְבּוּד שֶׁהִתְחִילוּ לְשַׁעְבְּדָם. דָּבָר אַחֵר שֶׁבִּקֵּשׁ יַעֲקֹב לְגַלּוֹת אֶת הַקֵּץ לְבָנָיו וְנִסְתַּם מִמֶּנּוּ.

Why is this sidrah closed [*i.e., without the space that customarily appears in a Torah scroll to separate a new sidrah from the previous one*]? *Because as soon as our father Jacob died, the eyes and heart of Israel were closed as a result of the oppression of the servitude, for they* [*Egyptians*] *began to enslave them. Another reason: because Jacob wished to reveal the prescribed time for the end of all exiles*], *but it was sealed from him (Rashi* to 47:28).

*The Overview is drawn primarily from the thought of *Harav HaGaon Gedaliah Schorr,* זצ״ל, much of which is recorded in *Ohr Gedaliahu.*

I. Jacob's Life in Egypt

Truth on Earth

Jacob is epitomized by the attribute of 'Truth,' as the prophet says תִּתֵּן אֱמֶת לְיַעֲקֹב, *grant truth to Jacob (Micah* 7:20). The man of truth takes all other values and traits and subjects them to the scrutiny of truth. Kindness is an exemplary characteristic, but there are times when kindness is destructive: generosity to thieves, murderers, and adulterers may well be a camouflaged form of cruelty that makes society its victim. Strictness can be a virtue, but there are times when it can inflict unnecessary harm. To give everything and everyone the proper regard and put them to their proper use is a sublime exercise of truth. It makes possible individual and societal behavior of the highest sort. By his judicious exercise of discriminating judgment, the man of truth blends extremes to create a symphony of the diverse voices of nature and people.

To give everything and everyone the proper regard and put them to their proper use is a sublime exercise of truth.

Small wonder that the literature of Kabbalah refers to the attribute of אֱמֶת, *truth,* as תִּפְאֶרֶת, *splendor.* When a course does justice to the potential of the individual, the demands of the environment, and the wishes of God, there is nothing truer and nothing more splendrous. As the one who combined and found the proper balance between Abraham's attribute of חֶסֶד, *kindness,* and Isaac's attribute of גְּבוּרָה, *strength,* Jacob represents אֱמֶת, *truth,* and therefore, he is described by the Sages as the finest of the Patriarchs, the culmination of the Patriarchal ideal (see Overview to *Lech Lecha,* pp. 361-374).

Truth is one of the most fragile attributes, as modern man has proven.

Truth is one of the most fragile attributes, as modern man has proven to the distressed satisfaction of all but the most unobjective observer. We see falsehood handsomely dressed in the garb of truth in all areas — commercial, political, social, ethical, moral. Language has been turned on its head to laud monsters as angels — and vice versa. Small wonder that the attribute of Truth argued that man should not be created because he would be saturated with falsehood. But, having decided that His plan required the creation of the universe despite its potential for major flaws, God flung Truth to the earth, so to speak, and created man.

The Best Years

Sfas Emes comments homiletically that God 'cast Truth down to earth in the sense that it *could* find a home in a man. Despite all the pressures and temptations of life, man is not compelled to surrender to falsehood.

As a symbol of truth, Jacob is the one whose life and legacy best illustrate that man need not succumb.

As the symbol of truth, Jacob is the one whose life and legacy best illustrate that man need not succumb. The Torah introduces our *sidrah* by telling us that Jacob — the very epitome of truth — *lived in Egypt.* The Torah uses the word 'life' advisedly; we are not told that Jacob settled [וַיֵּשֶׁב] or sojourned [וַיָּגָר], the customary Scriptural terms for habitation. Unlike English, idiomatic Scriptural Hebrew does not use וַיְחִי — from חַיִּים, *life* — to refer to dwelling. If we are told that Jacob *lived* in Egypt, it can only mean to indicate that his life there was wholesome, spiritual, complete — that it was a true, meaningful life — according to the definition of the Patriarch.

Tanna d'Bei Eliyahu derives from the use of the expression וַיְחִי, [Jacob] *lived,* that his seventeen years in Egypt were of the highest possible form of life: it was מֵעֵין עוֹלָם הַבָּא, *a semblance of the World to Come. Baal HaTurim* notes that he lived there for seventeen years, the numerical equivalent of טוֹב, *good* [טוֹב=17], meaning that his years in Egypt epitomized the best in life.

Egypt was not only the world's leading power at the time, it was a hotbed of sorcery, idolatry, and immorality.

This seems shockingly incongruous. Egypt was not only the world's leading power at the time, it was a hotbed of sorcery, idolatry, and immorality, as both Scripture and the writings of the Sages make unmistakably clear. We are not surprised that a great man like Jacob could maintain his spiritual standing in Egypt — if Joseph could do it as a lonely, helpless lad, surely Jacob could do so as a mature man surrounded by his family and living in the relative isolation of Goshen. But how can it be that Jacob's years in Egypt could be more akin to the sanctity of the World to Come than even his years in the Holy Land itself?

Straits and Egypt

Jacob's years of spiritual exaltation in Egypt were the triumphant climax of his task of nation building. He had taught his children many things and ingrained many traits in the people of Israel. Our existence and survival is based on the foundation of the Patriarchs and the tradition extending from them, but the final touch was provided by Jacob in Egypt. It was he, let us remember, who had demonstrated that one must prepare himself for exile with particular care: after leaving the greatest people of the age, Isaac and Rebeccah, with whom he had spent the first sixty-three years of his life, Jacob found himself unready to go to Laban until he had spent fourteen years studying the 'Torah of Exile' in the Academy of Shem and Eber [see Overview to *Vayigash*].

It was he, let us remember, who had demonstrated that one must prepare himself for exile with particular care.

Now, in Egypt, he had another lesson to teach about exile. How does one keep from drifting or declining in Egypt? The Hebrew word for Egypt has the identical spelling as the word for *'straits'* [מִצְרַיִם=מְצָרִים]; like all such phenomena in the Holy Tongue, the similarity is not coincidental. As the first national exile decreed by the Torah, Israel's Egyptian sojourn is symbolic of all the later exiles, and the tactics of survival practiced in Egypt are illustrative of those needed in the future. For exile consists primarily of the Jew finding his existence 'straitened' and under inhospitable pressure from his surroundings.

Exile consists primarily of the Jew finding his existence 'straitened' and under inhospitable pressure.

What are these 'straits'? They can take many forms: the 'new' moralities, business competition, the price of acceptance by the non-Jewish or non-observant world, the homogenizing effects of a free society, and so on. O yes, persecution and intolerance qualify fully as 'straits,' but history has shown, unfortunately, that freedom and prosperity can be even more damaging to Jewishness. By telling us that Jacob, the embodiment of Truth, experienced a flowering of life particularly in Egypt the Torah tells us that a passion for truth as defined by Jacob is the key to flourishing survival in every human condition, no matter how straitened it may be. Truth for the Jew is Torah, for God created the universe in consonance with the dictates and precepts of the Torah. The Torah is our lifeline in Egypt and everywhere, in Jacob's final years and for all time.

II. Torah and Reality

Blueprint of Events

The *Zohar* teaches אִסְתַּכֵּל בְּאוֹרַיְתָא וּבָרָא עָלְמָא, [God] *looked into the Torah and created the universe.* Every part of creation was made and exists because, in one way or another, it serves the needs outlined in the Torah. [This concept is explained in the Overview to *Bereishis,* pp. xxix-xxxi.] Nothing is haphazard in creation; just as God imposes so-called natural laws governing the regular, unchanging functions of nature, so there is an order to so-called miracles, the more obvious manifestations of God's hand. But whether an event is natural or miraculous, it flows from the system contained in the 'blueprint' of creation — the Torah — which God translated into the flesh-and-blood, sticks-and-stones, mountain-and-valley world we live in.

Commentators note that there is a close relationship between the power the Torah gives qualified Sages to suspend temporarily certain laws (under carefully defined and strictly limited rules) and their power to work miracles, as R' Pinchas ben Yair and R' Chaninah ben Dosa did (*Chullin* 7a). Given the fact that the Sages can 'amend the blueprint,' so to speak, by suspending a law, it stands to reason that they can suspend nature, which is but the translation of such laws into physical phenomena. For example, if Rosh Hashanah fell on the Sabbath, the Sages ordained that the shofar not be blown; if they had that power, why could they not have the power to split a river, as R' Pinchas did (ibid.), by temporarily suspending the law of nature

Given the fact that the Sages can 'amend the blueprint,' so to speak, by suspending a law, it stands to reason that they can suspend nature.

The commandments and narratives of the Torah are reflected in events as well as in law and observance.

that water must flow downstream? Clearly, the commandments and narratives, and even the allusions and implications of the Torah, are reflected in events as well as in law and observance.

There are chapters of redemption and chapters of exile, and these chapters, when applicable, control the events they foreshadow in the history of Israel. Our *sidrah* contains at least a suggestion of redemption. Before his death, Jacob wished to reveal to his children when the End of Time, the culmination of all suffering and exile, would come. He summoned his children to gather around him so that he could tell them אֵת אֲשֶׁר יִקְרָא אֶתְכֶם בְּאַחֲרִית הַיָּמִים — *what will befall you in the End of Days* (49:1). It is noteworthy that the verse uses the word יִקְרָא, from קרא, *call,* instead of the seemingly more appropriate יִקְרֶה, from קרה, *happen.* [See *Daniel* 10:14 where on almost identical phrase *does* use יִקְרֶה.] The Torah thereby stresses that the events of that longed-for time of fulfillment will not be mere 'happenings,' as if they were coincidental or caused by the impersonal and inexorable grinding of the wheels of history. Instead, those events will be in the nature of God *calling* [יִקְרָא אֶתְכֶם, lit. *He will* **call** *you*] upon us to discard the physical and spiritual fetters of exile; calling us in love to come join Him, to become again the resting place of His Presence. In attempting to relate what the future would hold — information that God did not permit him to transmit — Jacob made it plain that Jews would not be the pawns of history, but that their ordeals and their deliverance would result from God's attention and conscious concern. God will *call* us when the time comes — and then the exile will end.

In attempting to relate what the future would hold, Jacob made it plain that Jews would not be the pawns of history.

Function of Spaces

In this light the Sages understand the unusual manner in which our *sidrah, Vayechi,* is printed in the Torah scroll. Always, the Torah leaves a space between one *sidrah* and the next. Usually a *sidrah* will begin on a new line, but never is there less than a blank space the width of nine normal letters. The only exception is *Vayechi,* which begins with no extra separation at all. The Sages recogniezed that this phenomenon indicates an added dimension of the narrative.

The 'spaces' in the Torah have a function aside from the aesthetic purpose of indicating that a new subject is about to begin.

The 'spaces' in the Torah have a function aside from the aesthetic purpose of indicating that a new subject is about to begin. Every chapter and subject in the Torah contains an infinite degree of intellectual and spiritual illumination. The Midrash relates that whenever R' Yehudah the Prince [according to some versions, R' Yannai] went to Rome to intercede on behalf of his Jewish brethren, he would immerse himself in the narrative of Jacob's confrontation with Esau *(Genesis* ch. 32-33). Once R' Yehudah failed to study these chapters and his mission was a failure. The Sages perceived that narrative to be Jacob/Israel's guide in all its future dealings with a more powerful Esau/Edom/Rome *(Bereishis Rabbah* 78:15; *Ramban* 33:15). We would surely not see in those chapters what R' Yehudah saw, but to his perceptive eyes, they provided illumination in the most delicate negotiations and interventions. Similarly every verse of the Torah has its own teachings and unique degree of enlightenment — witness the many tomes of halachic and aggadic literature that elucidate seemingly obscure references in the Torah.

The Sages teach in *Toras Kohanim* that the separations between subjects in the Torah Scroll indicate that God paused at those spots to allow Moses an opportunity to reflect on what he had just been taught and absorb its full meaning. The implication is that an open space in the Torah implies an 'openness' of meaning, a degree of accessibility to the student who wishes to extract the meaning of the verses.

An open space in the Torah implies an 'openness' of meaning, a degree of accessibility to the student.

Whenever the Torah records prophetic songs that were ecstatically sung in gratitude for God's miraculous interventions on behalf of Israel — such as the Song at the Sea *(Exodus* 15:1-19) or the Song of Deborah *(Judges* 5:1-31) — there is a broad open space after every phrase. The use of such spaces alludes to the special nature of the experiences and events commemorated by such songs.

In our human terms, the difference between music

and noise is that music is 'the art of organizing sound so as to elicit an aesthetic response in a listener,' while noise is 'a sound or sounds, especially when unexpected or disagreeable.' When people recognize the harmony in creation — that all of its parts respond to the will of God, each in its own ordained way — they have 'heard the song of the universe.' [The concept of song is discussed at length in the Overview to *Song of Songs.*] It is not often that ordinary humans are privileged to perceive such harmony in the service of God; it is a rare degree of open revelation of God's controlling hand. It is as if God had opened a window and allowed us to see how the most dissimilar, even contradictory, forces mesh their efforts to carry out his will. The open spaces in Scriptural song symbolize this 'openness' of understanding. When such a phenomenon of harmonious people and nature stimulates man to his own voice to join the song of the universe, Scripture reflects man's insight into the workings of God by means of the wide spaces between the phrases of the prophetic song.

When people recognize the harmony in creation they have heard the song of the universe.

Conversely, when Jacob's life ended, his offspring lost their capacity to perceive. What it was that they could not see will be discussed below, but as *Rashi* tells us, their eyes and heart were sealed with Jacob's death, as the shadows of servitude closed in upon them and Jacob was not permitted to tell them when the exiles would end. The Torah's text suggests this sense of unending, unrelieved gloom by omitting the customary space between the *sidros.* A space would imply understanding and illumination, but Jacob's family felt none.

The shadows of servitude closed in upon them and Jacob was not permitted to tell them when the exiles would end.

III. Human Tabernacle

Book of Creation

As noted above, Jacob's seventeen years in Egypt brought him to a spiritual zenith. Nor was this greatness limited to him. By demonstrating to what a great extent someone could 'live,' if he allowed himself to be guided by the truth of Torah, Jacob provided precedent and inspiration to every generation of Jews in whatever 'Egypt' they might find themselves. His was a life so saturated with holiness and meaning that it should have remained a beacon for all time. Indeed, the lives of the Patriarchs have a significance far beyond that of any other individual, no matter how great he might be.

His was a life so saturated with holiness and meaning that it should have remained as a beacon for all time.

Ramban (Introduction to *Exodus)* calls *Genesis* סֵפֶר הַיְצִירָה, *the Book of Creation,* in two respects. Obviously it tells how the universe was created, but it is also the tale of another Creation:

וּבְמִקְרֵי הָאָבוֹת שֶׁהֵם כְּעִנְיַן יְצִירָה לְזַרְעָם מִפְּנֵי שֶׁכָּל מִקְרֵיהֶם צִיּוּרֵי דְבָרִים לִרְמוֹז וּלְהוֹדִיעַ כָּל עָתִיד לָבֹא לָהֶם

The experiences of the Patriarchs are like a creation to their children, because all their experiences are symbolic occurrences, alluding to and foretelling everything that would happen to them [*i.e., the descendants of the Patriarchs*] *in the future.*

As we have frequently seen throughout the Book of *Genesis,* the experiences of the Patriarchs are the signposts of Jewish history. Since God created the universe as a vehicle where Israel could accept and carry out the precepts of the Torah, the development of the Jewish nation is not merely a minor cog in creation. *Midrash Tanchuma (Bereishis* 1) teaches that God made a condition with the universe that it would remain in existence only if Israel agreed to accept the Torah. The creation of Israel, therefore, is as exalted and essential an act of creation as any of the acts described in the first chapter of Genesis. The *entire* book is the story of creation, because the lives of the Patriarchs, until Jacob's last breath, were portentous and cast shadows on eternity.

The creation of Israel is as exalted and essential an act of creation as any of the acts described in the first chapter of Genesis.

The True Redemption

The Book of Exodus, *Ramban* continues, is the book of the first exile and redemption, but those events do not end with the story of the exodus from Egypt, despite the fact that the physical exile ended when Israel crossed through the Sea of Reeds and left their former oppressors behind them forever:

הַגָּלוּת אֵינֶנּוּ נִשְׁלָם עַד יוֹם שׁוּבָם אֶל מְקוֹמָם וְאֶל מַעֲלַת אֲבוֹתָם יָשׁוּבוּ ... וְלָכֵן נִשְׁלַם הַסֵּפֶר הַזֶּה בְּהַשְׁלִימוֹ עִנְיַן הַמִּשְׁכָּן וּבִהְיוֹת כְּבוֹד ה׳ מָלֵא אוֹתוֹ תָּמִיד.

The exile was not completed until the day they returned to their place and were restored to the status of their forefathers ... Therefore this book ends with the conclusion of the subject of the Tabernacle and when 'the glory of HASHEM filled it' (Exodus 40:35) constantly.

The exile had begun when creation ended; redemption did not come until the nation succeeded in returning to the place and exalted status of its forefathers.

Ramban's definition of redemption is truly electrifying. The exile had begun when creation ended; redemption did not come until the nation succeeded in returning to the *place* and exalted *status of its forefathers. Ramban* implies clearly that the tents of the Patriarchs were equivalent to the Tabernacle and Temple; all were the home of the *Shechinah. Bereishis Rabbah* (60:16) describes the similarity between the tent of Sarah and the Tabernacle. A cloud of holiness hung by the entrance of Sarah's tent, like the pillar of holiness that was suspended over the Tabernacle; her dough remained fresh and tasty so that guests could always satisfy their hunger, like the לֶחֶם הַפָּנִים, *show bread,* that was placed in the Tabernacle only once a week but was always fresh; her lamp would remain lit from Sabbath eve until Sabbath eve, like the נֵר מַעֲרָבִי, *western light* of the Temple, that stayed aflame until it was time to light the Menorah the next day.

As long as Jacob was alive, his descendants had a human Tabernacle in their midst; when he was gone they were plunged into an exile that would not end until they could erect a Tabernacle.

When Solomon erected the First Temple he prayed that God would heed the prayers and favor the sacrifices that would be offered there.

Centuries later when Solomon erected the First Temple, he made a lavish and soulful dedication ceremony and prayed that God would heed the prayers and favor the sacrifices that would be offered there. God replied that he had heard and accepted Solomon's prayers, that the Temple would remain sacred forever, and that *(I Kings* 9:3): וְהָיוּ עֵינַי וְלִבִּי שָׁם כָּל הַיָּמִים, *My eyes and My heart will be there for all time.* God's *'eyes'* symbolize His Providential concern for each Jew and His *'heart'* symbolizes His love for all Jews. God sees His children and, each according to what he deserves, provides his needs and cares for him; and He loves them with a love that survives despite their apathy and sin. God promised Jacob that He would accompany him to Egypt and, the Sages derive, the same promise applied to every Jewish exile, even those caused by Jewish iniquity. 'Beloved is Israel; the *Shechinah* is with them. When they were exiled to Egypt the *Shechinah* was with them, when they were exiled to Babylon the *Shechinah* was with them' *(Megillah* 29a). God does not wait for Israel to repent; He shares their agony. There can be no greater expression of His love.

God promised Jacob that He would accompany Him to Egypt and the same promise applied to every Jewish exile.

Sins of Eye and Heart

Jacob himself was equivalent to a Tabernacle; after the exodus, all his descendants contributed to the construction of a Tabernacle so that the nation as a whole stood in place of its Patriarch. But each individual Jew is a miniature sanctuary with the potential to serve as the chariot for at least some degree of God's Presence. The Talmud *(Berachos* 6a) teaches that God wears *tefillin,* as it were, to symbolize His dedication to Israel just as Israel's *tefillin* symbolizes its dedication to Him. God's eye is upon the Jew and His heart throbs for him, and it is incumbent upon the Jew to reciprocate by dedicating his own eyes to perceive Godliness and his heart to love God.

The eyes and heart are the two agents that bring man to transgress; the eye sees and the heart is tempted.

The eyes and heart are particularly susceptible to temptation. They are described as the two agents that bring man to transgress; the eye sees and the heart is tempted — then the body acts *(Yerushalmi Berachos* 1:5). The heart and eyes of Israel were sorely tested in Egypt. The Talmud *(Berachos* 12b) interprets the sin of the heart as idolatry, which comes when one discards his love of God and transfers it to some other being. In Egypt, sorcery had become a well-developed art: the art of denial that God is the ruling force of creation. The sin of the eye is immorality *(ibid.),* for people are drawn to beauty when they see it; man's imagination can lead him far enough astray, but his eyes are far more dangerous. Egypt was a licentious country as the bitter experiences of Sarah and Joseph demonstrate. A land of sorcery and immorality by its very nature wages war against the special holiness expected of Jewish eyes and hearts.

A land of sorcery and immorality by its very nature wages war against the special holiness expected of Jewish eyes and hearts.

As long as Jacob was alive, the eyes and heart of God were directed toward the Patriarchal sanctuary in Egypt. The growing, thriving young Jewish nation drew its own spiritual sustenance from Jacob; he was a life-force for them, a moral buffer protecting them from the deleterious influences of Egypt. Throughout the long exile, Jews have groaned that their personal lives would be better if only they could see the Temple, if only they could be warmed and draw inspiration from the *Shechinah*. In Egypt it happened. Jacob was their Temple. God's eyes and heart were perceptibly directed at him and were reflected from him to his children.

IV. Exile Closes In

Subtle Servitude Information Imparted

When Jacob died, the *'eyes and heart of Israel were closed.'* The Temple, the chariot of the *Shechinah*, was no longer present. God's scrutiny and love were no longer apparent though they were still there, just as they remain with Israel in the darkest, gloomiest depths of every exile.

But Israel could no longer see Him.

When Jacob was gone, Egypt's appeal to Jewish eyes and heart was incessant, enticing; it was a matter of the senses, while God's providence and love was a matter of faith.

This is not to say that Israel lost its faith in God as soon as Jacob died, certainly not for as long as the tribal ancestors were alive. The process of change is slow and subtle. One sees the Tabernacle, one remembers it well, then more faintly, finally it recedes to a corner of the mind. The process is not sudden at all and is often unnoticed by all but the most perceptive people. Someone once said of the Chofetz Chaim, 'You and I believe in the World to

One sees the Tabernacle, one remembers it well, then more faintly, finally it recedes to a corner of the mind.

To him the World, was as real as the room next door, while to us it is an abstract concept.

Come just as he did, but to him the World to Come was as real as the room next door, while to us it is an abstract concept, like our knowledge that there are salt mines in Siberia.' While Jacob was alive, his family 'saw' the Tabernacle, but when he died, the vision changed to an ever fainter memory.

The Sages say that Israel's 'eyes and heart were closed' because of the servitude. This seems strange because we know that Joseph served as viceroy until his own death, fifty-four years after Jacob's passing, surely there was no servitude then. Furthermore, the servitude did not begin until the death of Levi, the last surviving tribal ancestor (see *Rashi* to *Exodus* 6:16), who outlived Joseph by nearly twenty-five years. It seems incongruous, therefore, for the Midrash to speak of Egyptian subjugation at the death of Jacob, when it did not begin until nearly eighty years later. To understand this we must reorient our thinking. We are accustomed to describe an Egyptian experience as one of bricks, work quotas, back-breaking labor, murder of infants, whips, and tears. They were all present, of course, later on. But there are other forms of servitude.

On the simplest level, Jews began feeling like aliens after Jacob died. The citizens of Egypt may have begun showing resentment against the 'foreign interlopers' in subtle ways — the lack of a smile; the pointed remarks about the 'pushy Jews' who were too numerous, too successful, too well entrenched; the feeling that the Patriarch had been a holy man who brought an end to the famine, but that his son, the viceroy, had bled the people dry and robbed them of their land and funds before giving them a piece of bread. Poor people don't feel servitude until the lash stings their back; aristocrats feel it when their privileges are threatened.

Poor people don't feel servitude until the lash stings their back; aristocrats feel it when their privileges are threatened.

On a deeper and truer level, the bondage of the Jewish soul began before that of the Jewish body. Israel's eye began losing its glow and its heart began beating to the wrong cadence long before Pisom and Ramesses were planned and the first brick baked. While they were still comfortably ensconced in

Goshen, prospering and multiplying, their spiritual selves realized that subjugation to the culture of Egypt was creeping up on them — their eyes and heart were closing.

Jacob wished to reveal the End to his children, but it was closed from him (see comm. to 47:28 and 49:1). The commentators inquire, if Jacob did not reveal the End, why was it necessary for the Torah to imply that he wished to do so? Surely there must be some reason for telling us of his frustrated intention. The *Zohar* emphasizes that the Torah would not have alluded to Jacob's attempt if it had been a total failure. Rather, 'He accomplished whatever he wished to reveal — he revealed it and then it was concealed.'

The Torah would not have alluded to Jacob's attempt if it had been a total failure.

Let us try to understand the profound words of the *Zohar*.

What was to be gained by informing the tribal ancestors of the date when the exile would end? Simply understood, an exile is easier to bear if one knows when it will be over. A prisoner who can count down the days — or even years — to his release is fortunate compared to someone serving an indefinite sentence.

Jacob's intention can be understood in a different, deeper sense. The expression קֵץ, *End* [*of Days*], has a meaning beyond the calendrical *date* when Moses or the Messiah will arrive. The End of Days is a concept; it refers to the condition that will prevail when the Messiah arrives. It expresses the ideal of human perfection and a world where everyone recognizes God's greatness, a world where nothing obscures the truth of His Presence. This is what Jacob wanted to reveal to his children. He wanted to teach them how they could live in alien surroundings, but not be part of them; how they could draw inward and live in a world of mind and heart that is bounded and informed by the Torah and God's Presence.

The End of Days is a concept; it refers to the condition that will prevail when the Messiah arrives.

That, God would not permit him to do, because the Divine Plan called for a *true* exile; had Jacob carried out his intention the exile would have been only one of form, not substance.

This may be strange to a twentieth century mind. To those who live in luxury, the 'spiritual life' can seem like something out of a fable, to those who endure true suffering, the exile is only too real. In one of Jacob's last 'acts of creation,' however, he implanted with the Jewish nation the capacity to build Tabernacles wherever they were, for that was the *personal* world in which he spent his last seventeen years. Geographically, he was in Goshen, but spiritually he was in *Eretz Yisrael* on the Temple Mount — for did he not embody the very Temple where God's eyes and heart are always directed? This, too, is part of Jacob's legacy — that someone who always perceives the *Shechinah* and God's guiding hand never suffers exile whether he is in an Egypt or a dungeon. In this sense, the commentators differentiate between *personal* redemption and *general* redemption. True, the entire nation of Israel lacks its Temple and suffers exile, but there are degrees in the exile as it is felt by *individuals* — some suffer from it more than others.

Geographically, he was in Goshen, but spiritually he was in Eretz Yisrael on the Temple Mount.

In the physical sense we understand this most clearly, for Jewish suffering has always varied from community to community and generation to generation. *Ramban* derives this familiar historical phenomenon from the Torah itself. When Jacob prepared to wage war to save his family from Esau, he divided his people into two camps, saying that if Esau succeeded in striking one, the other group would be able to escape. This portends Jacob's plan of coping with the future exile of Esau/Rome. Never would *all* Jews be in danger of extermination, חלילה, at the same time. If one Jewish community is in physical danger, another will be secure; if one is poor, another will be growing stronger. Many times this has enabled a community to be a physical refuge or a source of support for its less fortunate brethren. Obviously, then, the distress of the exile is not distributed evenly. Nor do all the prophesied ravages of God's wrath come at once or in close succession. History demonstrates that so-called golden eras have been interspersed among the crusades, pogroms, ex-

If one Jewish community is in physical danger, another will be secure; if one is poor, another will be growing stronger.

pulsions, and discriminations, so that Israel could 'catch its breath' so to speak, develop new communities, strengthen its spiritual resources, and muster up the strength to survive.

There are variations as well in the levels of exile among individuals. Rare people are always in communion with God, recognizing even travails as part of His ultimately merciful purpose. A famous American journalist once insisted on seeing the Chofetz Chaim. Though an interview was out of the question, she managed to watch him through the window of his modest little home in Radun, Poland. Never a robust physical specimen, he was frail and in his nineties. She watched silently and as she left, she said reverently, 'I have seen the Jewish God.'

She watched silently and as she left, she said reverently, 'I have seen the Jewish God.'

By twentieth century terms, the Chofetz Chaim's 'exile' was surely minimal compared to that of others, and his bearing was so obviously saintly that it was apparent even to someone who shared no part of his world with him. Such spiritual strength has made *tzaddikim* joyous when others despaired. When the great Gaon of Rogatchov, Rabbi Yosef Rosen, was suffering terribly in his final illness, he found relief from pain only when he was engaged in Talmudic discussion. For him, immersion in the Sea of the Talmud drowned the agony of illness. One contemporary *rosh yeshivah* was surprised that his students demanded air-conditioning in the middle of the summer: how could they even feel the heat when they were studying Torah? Another would ask, 'How can a student yawn while he is studying Torah; how can someone be bored or tired while he is learning?' Such people are not part of *our* exile. This attitude — and rescue — was what Jacob wished to instill, but he was not permitted to succeed.

Did he fail? No. The spiritual illumination of a Jacob is not lost. In the words of the *Zohar,* לְלִבִּי גַּלִּיתִי וּלְאֵבָרַי לֹא גִּלִּיתִי, *I revealed it to my heart, but to my limbs I did not reveal it.* A 'revelation to the heart' is an inner conviction, a 'revelation to the limbs' is public knowledge. Jacob could not reveal to everyone his secret of escaping the most lethal effect

A 'revelation to the heart' is an inner conviction, a 'revelation to the limbs' is public knowledge.

of exile, but the revelation is concealed in the Torah where it remains available to anyone who will draw it forth. The allusion to Jacob's unsuccessful attempt is contained in the first verse of *Vayechi* (by the omission of the customary space between *sidros*). rather than later in 49:1 where the event took place. But the first verse speaks of Jacob's greatest success, his ultimate 'life' in Egypt. God used that verse to show us what Jacob tried but was not permitted to do — simultaneously, however, God showed us Jacob's secret. *He found life in Egypt* — so can we. He illuminated an exile to such an extent that it was hardly felt while he lived — and that is our legacy. We need not suffer from exile if we open our eyes to see the Hand that inflicts it, the truth it contains, the Torah that illuminates it.

God showed us Jacob's secret. He found life in Egypt — so can we.

V. Rabbi and Jacob

רַבִּי הֲוָה יָתִיב לֵיהּ בְּצִפּוֹרִין שִׁבְעָה עֲשַׂר שְׁנִין וְקָרָא עַל גַּרְמֵיהּ, וַיְחִי יַעֲקֹב בְּאֶרֶץ מִצְרַיִם שְׁבַע עֶשְׂרֵה שָׁנָה. וַיְחִי יְהוּדָה בְּצִפּוֹרִין שְׁבַע עֶשְׂרֵה שְׁנִין

Rabbi [R' Yehudah the Prince] lived in Zipori for seventeen years and proclaimed of himself: 'Jacob lived in Egypt for seventeen years. Judah lived in Zipori for seventeen years *(Yerushalmi Kesubos* 12:3, *Bereishis Rabbah* 96:9).

Rabbi's comparison of his tenure in Zipori to Jacob's in Egypt must be understood as a statement of purpose: there was a similarity between the accomplishments of those two periods. Unless he meant to impart a lofty concept, it would have been out of character for Rabbi — of whom the Talmud says, 'When Rabbi died, humility ceased to exist' *(Sotah* 49a) — to liken himself to Jacob.

Both Jacob and Rabbi lived on the threshhold of bitter exiles.

Both Jacob and Rabbi lived on the threshhold of bitter exiles. Jacob came to Egypt with his family to inaugurate a sojourn of 210 years by the end of which the bulk of his offspring would have fallen to a level of degradation barely above that of the Egyptians and of whom it would be said, 'These [the Israelites] are idol worshipers and these [the Egyptians] are idol worshipers — why should the sea split to save the Jews and then collapse upon the Egyptians?' *(Tanchuma, Beshallach).* Rabbi lived not long after the destruction of the Second Temple, at a time when Jewish life in *Eretz Yisrael* had been virtually decimated by Roman persecution and ruthless suppression of Torah study.

Both Jacob and Rabbi enjoyed the respect of their rulers: Pharaoh revered Jacob as the holy man whose arrival and blessing had ended the famine and Rabbi won the friendship and deep respect of the Roman emperor Antony. Each undertook the responsibility to prepare his people for survival in the impending exile, and each did it in a similar way during the last seventeen years of his life.

Each undertook the responsibility to prepare his people for survival and each did it during the last seventeen years of his life.

Jacob symbolizes Truth as embodied in the Torah. He studied the Torah of exile with Joseph, he dispatched Yehudah ahead of him to Egypt to establish an academy for Torah study, he designated the tribe of Levi to devote itself exclusively to Torah study and the service of God even when the other tribes entered the service of Egypt. In so doing, Jacob was planting the seed that came to fruition at Sinai. The brutal melting pot of Egypt became the crucible that prepared Israel to be the Nation of Torah [this concept will be discussed in the commentary and Overview to *Shemos).* And Jacob buried within the nation the possibility of transcending exiles. He represents, therefore, תּוֹרָה שֶׁבִּכְתָב, *the Written Torah.*

Rabbi, too, confronted an impending disaster and devised an identical solution. Successive generations of Roman persecution had brought Torah scholarship to a relatively low ebb. Such great men as R' Akiva and R' Chanina ben Teradion had been tortured to death for daring to teach their students. Though there were still many to whom Torah was life and who would not commit spiritual suicide to satisfy Roman paranoia, conditions made it virtually impossible for them to study enough to memorize all

There were still many to whom Torah was life and who would not commit spiritual suicide to satisfy Roman paranoia.

the laws and their explanations. And this was still the period of תּוֹרָה שֶׁבְּעַל פֶּה, *the Oral Law,* when it was forbidden to record any Torah except for the books of Scripture. As *Nassi* [prince], Rabbi had not only the responsibility, but the authority to act. As the friend of Antony, he could secure governmental sanction.

He propounded the doctrine that the only way to preserve the knowledge of the Torah was to commit the Oral Law to writing.

He propounded the doctrine that the only way to preserve the knowledge of the Torah was to commit the Oral Law to writing. He called an assembly of the Sages to collect the laws and decide most matters in dispute. Then he recorded the major laws and principles in the Mishnah — the foundation of the Talmud and the vast body of halachic literature. His seventeen years in Zipori were a time of monumental accomplishment, a time that, in its way, could stand together with Jacob's seventeen years in Egypt as a true golden era of Jewish survival.

Wisely have the Sages said:

> לֹא מְאַסְתִּים וְלֹא גְעַלְתִּים לְכַלּוֹתָם׳, — שֶׁהֶעֱמַדְתִּי לָהֶם בֵּית רַבִּי וְחַכְמֵי הַדּוֹרוֹת
>
> [*God said of Israel in its exile*] *I have not despised them nor have I abhorred them to exterminate them (Leviticus 26:44) — for I will have established on their behalf the House of Rabbi and the wise men of the ages (Megillah* 11a).

The Book of *Genesis* is one of creation. It begins with the creation of heaven and earth for the sake of Torah and Israel (see comm. to 1:1) and it ends with Jacob's 'creation' of the conditions that would enable Israel to survive in order to receive the Torah. Rabbi, the great and holy teacher of Israel, looked into Jacob's seventeen years of life and perceived the secret hidden within them. He translated the secret into a new source of life, the Mishnah, that remains the source and guarantor of Israel's national survival.'

Rabbi, the great and holy teacher of Israel, looked into Jacob's seventeen years of life and perceived the secret hidden within them.

Rabbi Nosson Scherman
Kislev 14, 5742

May the Overviews in this volume
be a source of merit for the soul of
the author's uncle

החבר ר׳ יצחק גדליה ב״ר מרדכי ע״ה

Mr. Julius Loeb ע״ה

נפטר ב׳ סכות, תשמ״ב

A patriarch of his community,
an inspiration and joy to his family;
he was one of the select leaders who transplanted
Frankfurt to Washington Heights

ת נ צ ב ה

סדר ויחי

Sidrah Vayechi

כח וַיְחִ֤י יַעֲקֹב֙ בְּאֶ֣רֶץ מִצְרַ֔יִם שְׁבַ֥ע עֶשְׂרֵ֖ה
שָׁנָ֑ה וַיְהִ֤י יְמֵֽי־יַעֲקֹב֙ שְׁנֵ֣י חַיָּ֔יו שֶׁ֣בַע שָׁנִ֔ים
כט וְאַרְבָּעִ֥ים וּמְאַ֖ת שָׁנָֽה׃ וַיִּקְרְב֣וּ יְמֵֽי־

SIDRAH VAYECHI

◆§ Vayechi — the "closed' section.

[Following tradition, this verse begins a new *sidrah.* As a general rule, all *parshiyos* [paragraph divisions] are separated from one another in a Torah scroll by a space of at least nine letters. Our *parshah,* however, is unique in that it follows the preceding with only a one-letter division between them. *Rashi* therefore calls it סְתוּמָה, *closed:*]

Why is this section 'closed'? — [Because this Sidrah comprises the account of Jacob's death, and] as soon as Jacob our father departed this life, the hearts of the children of Israel were 'closed' due to the suffering and despair of the bondage which was then imposed on them. [That is, the *initial* stages of the spiritual bondage began to materialize immediately after Jacob's death, even though the actual travails of *enslavement* did not commence until all the Tribal Ancestors had died *(Tur).*] Another reason: Jacob had desired to reveal to his children the 'End' [i.e., the Messianic age when Israel's exiles would finally end], but his prophetic vision was 'closed' [i.e. concealed] from him *(Rashi* from Midrash and *Zohar).* [On Jacob's desire to reveal the 'End', see *Rashi* to 49:1.][1]

R' Hirsch, however, advances an entirely different view. The superficial observer would assume that Jacob's seventeen peaceful years surrounded by his family comprised the golden era of his life, and as such, should be separated from the narrative of his earlier, anxiety-filled years. The Torah shows us the contrary, however. Jacob's 'golden' years are given no special prominence, they are not even set off from his years of hardship, because it was during his lifetime of struggle that he rose to the status of 'Israel' and prepared his family for its future Messianic calling. From the vantage point of the *nation,* Jacob's earlier years were more productive than his years in Egypt; only as an *individual* did he experience greater happiness in Egypt.

28. וַיְחִי יַעֲקֹב ... שְׁבַע עֶשְׂרֵה שָׁנָה — [And] *Jacob lived in the land of Egypt seventeen years.*

The Torah tells us this to inform us how Jacob — though initially intending to remain in Egypt but a short time until God commanded him to the contrary [46:3*f*] — established his home permanently in Egypt. He did not return to Canaan after seeing Joseph, but remained in Egypt for the last seventeen years of his life *(Abarbanel).*

◆§ Significance of the term וַיְחִי, 'lived.'

[The unusual use of the term וַיְחִי, *lived,* in this context inspires comment

1. *Ramban* prefaces this *sidrah* with a theme consistent with his view in 43:14, that Jacob's descent into the Egyptian exile is a forerunner of the Jewish nation's descent into the exile of Edom/Rome [which traditionally refers to the current lingering exile amid Western Civilization; see above on 15:2; footnote to 14:1 p. 474; comm. to 28:12 p. 1225].

The analogy extends to a series of circumstances. Both exiles were brought about by causeless hatred between brothers. Like Jacob, who thought he would be going to a friendly king, so Agrippa, the last Jewish king during the Second Temple, went to the Roman court, to

47
28-29

[28] *Jacob lived in the land of Egypt seventeen years. And the days of Jacob — the years of his life — were one hundred and forty seven years.* [29] *The time ap-*

inasmuch as the Torah usually employs such terms as וַיֵּשֶׁב, *settled,* or וַיָּגָר, *dwelt,* to describe the years one spent in a particular place.]

It was primarily during these latter seventeen years of his life that Jacob — who endured so much suffering throughout his life — can be described as having *'lived.'* He was finally united with *all* his children, and he enjoyed the tranquility and harmony he had always longed for. Hence, the saying 'If one's end is good, all is good' *(Akeidah; Chizkuni).*

The Zohar similarly expounds *Lamentations* 3:27, *It is good for a man that he bear a yoke in his youth:* happy is a man who is subjected to suffering in his youth, for he will ultimately enjoy tranquility. So it was with Jacob: he suffered from Esau who pursued him; from Laban who subjected him to slave-like conditions in return for his wives; from the shameful incident of Dinah and Shechem; and from Joseph who was sold and mourned for so many years. Yet, after it all, Jacob finally enjoyed tranquility.

According to *Tosafos HaRosh,* however, Jacob had really 'lived,' in the sense of happiness and fulfillment, for a total of thirty-four years, equivalent to the numerical value of the word וַיְחִי, *he lived,* in our verse: Seventeen years from Joseph's birth until he was sold, and seventeen years of living with Joseph in Egypt. All his other years were not really 'living,' spent as they were in grief and suffering.

Daas Zekeinim records that these seventeen years correspond to the seventeen which Joseph lived in Jacob's house before he was sold. Just as Jacob sustained Joseph for seventeen years, so did Joseph now sustain his father for a like period.

R' Munk observes that the *sidrah* which records the death of Jacob is entitled *Jacob 'lived'*. Similarly, the one recounting the death of Sarah is called חַיֵּי שָׂרָה, *the 'life' of Sarah.* As the Sages tell us *(Berachos* 18b), the righteous continue to live on after death, because of the example which they have given and the spiritual heritage which they have bequeathed to posterity. So 'our father Jacob did not die,' as *Rashi* notes on 49:33.

There is an opinion that the name used here is the less spiritual one, *Jacob,* rather than *Israel,* because he did not strive to return to *Eretz Yisrael* during his lifetime *(Maggid Mesharim;* comp. footnote to *v.* 29).

וַיְהִי יְמֵי יַעֲקֹב שְׁנֵי חַיָּיו — *And the days of Jacob — the years of his life — were.*

[On this phraseology, see *comm.* above 47:8 s.v. כַּמָּה.]

Baal HaTurim observes that anyone of whom it is said וַיְהִי יְמֵי, *his days were,* did not attain the age of his father — e.g. Chanoch and Lemech. The same is true of the expression 'drew near' with regard to death. See *Rashi* next verse.

שֶׁבַע שָׁנִים וְאַרְבָּעִים וּמְאַת שָׁנָה — *One hundred and forty seven years* [lit. *seven years and forty and one*

Gaius Caligula, whom he considered his intimate friend, and he thereby caused Israel to fall into Roman clutches.

As for the inhabitants of besieged Jerusalem, they were made captives because of famine, just as the family of Jacob had been compelled to leave *Eretz Yisrael* because of a famine.

Nevertheless the day is coming when *they shall bring all your brethren out of all the nations ... upon horses and in chariots ... to My holy mountain, Jerusalem (Isaiah* 66:20), even as the Egyptians ultimately accompanied Jacob's remains with great honors to the Holy Land.

The nations will be in deep sorrow when they perceive the vengeance of HASHEM. *May He raise us that we may live in His presence* [*Hoshea* 6:2].

hundred year(s)].

Since Jacob's life was short and wrought with trouble the Torah mentions his years beginning with the smaller number first, unlike the case of Abraham and Isaac where the usual order is followed *(Baal HaTurim)*.

According to *R' Munk,* the smaller number is given before the larger one so that the number forty-seven will be in proximity to the words שְׁנֵי חַיָּיו, *the years of his life.* That is to say, there were forty-seven years when Jacob really 'lived.' As *Or HaChaim* points out, that was the number of years when he was in the company of either Rachel or Joseph.

R' Hirsch notes, as he explained above [see 47:8], that *days* of life indicates the worthwhile, productive days in which someone lived. Consequently our verse stresses that all the years of Jacob's life were filled with important 'days.'

29. וַיִּקְרְבוּ יְמֵי יִשְׂרָאֵל לָמוּת — *The time approached for Israel to die* [lit. *and Israel's days to die approached*].[1]

How did Jacob know that his life was drawing to a close? [After all, he should have expected his lifespan to approximate that of his father. He was now thirty-three years younger than his father had been when he died, and as *Rashi* notes in 27:2, one should fear death only during the *five* year period before and after the age at which one's parents had died.]

— He was not really sick, but he was getting increasingly weaker and realized he would not live much longer. He therefore summoned Joseph to give him instructions about his burial wishes *(Ramban).*

Or HaChaim notes in this context that the onset of physical weakness is far from proving that death is approaching. But the righteous perceive certain symptoms thirty days before the end, when death is decreed in the celestial spheres. [See *comm.* to 50:1.] From that moment the image of God which is reflected in the human face becomes obscured.

According to *Haamek Davar* the use of the spiritual name *Israel* in this passage intimates that it was by *prophetic* inspiration — which is symbolized by the name *Israel* — that he was aware that he would shortly die.

Rashi notes that everyone of whom it is said that death *drew near* did not attain the age of his fathers; in this case, Isaac lived 180 years, while Jacob lived only 147. Similarly it is said of David that *his days to die drew near* [*I Kings* 2:1], and he lived to 70 while his father reached the age of 80. [The Midrash adds the case of Moses of whom *drawing near* is also used (*Deut.* 31:14). He lived 120 years compared with his father's 137.][2]

The Midrash discusses the concept of the literal phrase: *the days of Jacob drew near to die* (which appears to say that the days

1. R' Yose in the *Zohar* notes that in the previous verse which speaks of his *life,* he is called Jacob, whereas here, he is called Israel when his *death* is imminent. This appears inconsistent with the usual usage, for the Torah generally calls him 'Jacob' when he appears in a state of weakness, and 'Israel' in the opposite context. R' Yose explains that as Jacob's life drew to a close, all his days appeared, encircled with an aura of glory, implied by the name 'Israel.' This phenomenon proclaimed that the Patriarch would appear before the Celestial Judge at the time of his death with his supreme title of earned nobility *(R' Munk;* comp. *R' Bachya).*

2. The reason Jacob lived thirty-three years less than his father was, as noted in 47:8-9, in

themselves seemed to die. When someone's time comes, the very day [i.e. *sun*] refuses to go on its course and demands that person's death. Thus, the day itself is said to 'draw near' — an expression idiomatically denoting attack for battle (cf. *Deut.* 20:10) — to inexorably demand death.

According to R' Shmuel bar Nachmeni in *Midrash Tanchuma,* the meaning is: In the case of the death of the righteous their 'days' cease [i.e., they are physically lost to the world] while they themselves continue to exist ... for the righteous — even when dead — are described as living.

וַיִּקְרָא לִבְנוֹ לְיוֹסֵף — *[So] he called for his son, for Joseph.*

Jacob summoned Joseph to ask that he, as viceroy with the power to carry out his wishes, take responsibility to bury him in the Cave of Machpelah.

Jacob did not want to postpone the request until he was sick and on his deathbed. At that time, when he would give his final blessing to his children, he planned to formally confer Reuben's birthright on Joseph. He was concerned, therefore, that if he delayed his request to Joseph until then, it would seem as though he were giving Joseph the birthright only to elicit his promise regarding the burial, in which case it would seem as though the transfer of the birthrights was not Divinely ordained. Therefore, Jacob summoned him now, before Joseph had even an inkling of the birthright *(Haamek Davar).*

He called for לִבְנוֹ, *his son,* because it is a son's duty to bury his father [24:9; 35:29] *(Alshich);* and he chose יוֹסֵף, *Joseph* [rather than any of his other sons], because only he had the power to do so *(Rashi).*

Cf. *Tanchuma:* Why did Jacob summon neither Reuben, the eldest, nor Judah, who was destined for royalty, but instead summoned Joseph? This teaches that 'everyone honors the one who at the moment is on the ascendancy' [lit. to whom the hours stands], also because he had the capacity to fulfill his request.

Furthermore Joseph was the son whom God had promised would 'put his hand on Jacob's eye' [46:4; i.e. look after his burial] *(Abarbanel).*

The Midrash adds that Jacob summoned Joseph because he loved him more than all his other children. Furthermore, Jacob intimated that since he had come to Egypt on Joseph's account, the primary obligation was upon Joseph to arrange for the return of his remains to Canaan for burial.

According to *Abarbanel,* Jacob foresaw prophetically that Joseph's bones would remain in Egypt until the Exodus when the Tribal descendants would take his remains to Canaan. Jacob was apprehensive that unless he commanded Joseph to the contrary, Joseph would allow Jacob's remains as well to stay in Egypt until the Exodus. He therefore considered it necessary to adjure Joseph that he arrange burial in *Eretz Yisrael* for him as soon as possible after his death and not wait for the Redemption.

Paane'ach Raza explains that this is why Jacob found it necessary to have

punishment for having complained to Pharaoh about the suffering he endured throughout his life. Those verses contain thirty-three words.

Another reason is that Jacob's 'premature' death was an example of how 'a causeless curse comes home to roost' [see *Proverbs* 26:2]. Jacob had cursed Rachel causelessly by saying to Laban [31:32]: *with whomever you find your god,* לֹא יִחְיֶה, *he shall not live.* As a result Jacob's own years were diminished by thirty-three, the numerical equivalent of the word יִחְיֶה, *live (Baal HaTurim).*

וַיֹּאמֶר לוֹ אִם־נָא מָצָאתִי חֵן בְּעֵינֶיךָ שִׂים־נָא יָדְךָ תַּחַת יְרֵכִי וְעָשִׂיתָ עִמָּדִי חֶסֶד וֶאֱמֶת אַל־נָא תִקְבְּרֵנִי בְּמִצְרָיִם׃

Joseph take an oath to this effect, instead of relying on God's promise *and I will surely bring you back* [46:4], which implied that God Himself guaranteed Jacob's interment in *Eretz Yisrael.* Rather, as *Tiferes Y'honasan* explains, Jacob was concerned that, like Joseph, only his *bones* would eventually be brought to *Eretz Yisrael* for burial; he therefore demanded an oath that Joseph would personally see to it that his *body* would be buried there soon after his demise.

אִם־נָא מָצָאתִי חֵן בְּעֵינֶיךָ — *Please — if I have found favor in your eyes.*

I.e., if you really wish to fulfill the *mitzvah* of filial honor toward me ... *(Sechel Tov).*

'There is no power in the day of death' [*Eccles.* 8:8], observes the Midrash '... Approaching death, Jacob must humble himself before his son and *plead* with him [rather than *command* him with paternal authority. This accounts for the triple use of the word נָא, *please,* in this verse.]

שִׂים - נָא יָדְךָ תַּחַת יְרֵכִי — *Please place your hand under my thigh.*

— And take an oath *(Rashi).*

[*Thigh* is here a euphemism for the circumcised organ. On this form of oath, see *Rashi* and *comm.* to 24:6. At the time of the Patriarchs, this *mitzvah* represented their sole sacred object; it was upon this that they swore until the day of the giving of the Torah *(Pirkei d' Rabbi Eliezer* 39). However, the feeling of modesty held the son back from complying and taking the oath 'under Jacob's thigh.' Instead, he promised him: *'I will do as you have said'* [*v.* 30] *(Targum Yonasan).*

As *Rashbam* notes in 24:2, Jacob used this form of oath because it is the form used when a superior adjures an inferior, such as a master his servant or a father his son. When *equals* are parties to a covenant, however, כַּף אֶל כַּף, *clasping of hand to hand,* was used [see *Ezek.* 17:18]. Sometimes a treaty was made binding by dividing an animal and passing between its parts [see *comm.* to 15:15].

The word נָא usually means *please,* the connotation here being: do not resent that I am asking you to take an oath *(Tosafos HaRosh).* According to *Or HaChaim* the connotation is: Take an oath *now* [this is how *Onkelos* translates נָא]; do not delay making the promise until my actual day of death.

וְעָשִׂיתָ עִמָּדִי חֶסֶד וֶאֱמֶת — *And do kindness and truth with me.*

As noted in 24:49, *kindness* is goodness conferred *voluntarily,* while *truth* is the fulfillment of an *obligation (Ralbag).* [Since both elements were present in this case, Jacob phrased his request accordingly.]

Comp. *Maayan Ganim* cited in *Torah Sheleimah* §107: My burial will be an act of *truth* [since as my son you have the *obligation* of burying my remains] whereas carrying me to *Eretz Yisrael* will be a *kindness* [inasmuch as that exceeds the normal obligation]. *(Radak* interprets similarly.)

Yalkut Shimoni adds that Jacob also informed Joseph that the חֶסֶד, *kindness,* of burying him was especially incumbent upon Joseph, since God had specifically promised him, 'Joseph will put his hand on

47
30

Joseph and said to him, "Please — if I have found favor
in your eyes, please place your hand under my thigh
and do kindness and truth with me — please do not
bury me in Egypt. 30 *For I will lie down with my fathers*

your eyes' [46:4].

— The kindness shown to the dead is the true חֶסֶד שֶׁל אֱמֶת, *kindness of truth* [i.e., sincere altruistic kindness] in that there can be no expectation that the beneficiary will return the favor (*Rashi*).

אַל־נָא תִקְבְּרֵנִי בְּמִצְרָיִם — *Please do not bury me in Egypt.*

— Even for a short time; as soon as I die transport me to Canaan. Unlike Joseph, Jacob could not be content with a pledge that his remains would be taken to *Eretz Yisrael* only *after* the Exodus [see above s.v. וַיִּקְרָא] (*Abarbanel*).

[See also citation of *R' David Cohen* in *comm.* to 28:13 s.v. הָאָרֶץ to the effect that God's promise to give Jacob the land 'whereon you lie' was contingent upon his actually returning to 'lie' in it. Comp. *Tanchuma*.]

Do not even put me into a coffin temporarily, as is the Egyptian practice. If you do so the Egyptians might maintain that this is adequate and not allow you to carry my body away (*Sforno*).

According to *Rashi*, Jacob insisted on not being buried in Egypt for several reasons:

(a) Jacob knew that the soil of Egypt would one day be plagued with כִּנִּים, *vermin* [*Exod.* 8:12] which would swarm beneath his body [if he were to be buried there. Although the plagues did not affect *Goshen*, Jacob feared that the Egyptians would want to inter him in an honorable sepulchre somewhere in Egypt *itself*. (However, see *Avnei Shoham; Rambam* to *Avos* 5:4; *Oznaim l'Torah*)];

(b) those who are buried outside of *Eretz Yisrael* will not come to life at Resurrection until they roll through the earth to *Eretz Yisrael*. [This Midrashic-Talmudic interpretation (*Kesubos* 111a) is based on *Ezekiel* 37:12-14];

(c) to prevent the Egyptians from making his body [or tomb] a shrine of idol worship. [That is, since the Egyptians were all aware that the famine ended on his account, Jacob was afraid that the Egyptians would deify him after his death and venerate him. He was very concerned about this because he knew that retribution would be taken against Egypt's gods, as it says [*Exodus* 12:12]: *And against all the gods of Egypt I will execute judgments* (*Midrash*).]

Furthermore, Jacob was concerned that if he were indeed buried in Egypt, in his merit the Egyptians might be spared the Ten Plagues (*R' Tam*); additionally, he was afraid that if he allowed his remains to be buried there the Tribes would always assert that Egypt, too, was a Holy Land (*Midrash HaGadol*).

As *R' Munk* — drawing from *R' Hirsch* — explains, Jacob also wanted to establish in his posterity for all time the principle that only *Eretz Yisrael* is their heritage. The most effective means to do so would be to have his tomb there. He knew that his burial there would create an indestructible link between the country where the ancestors were buried and their descendants, wherever they were. They would feel the need to pray there and never give up the land to

ל וְשָׁכַבְתִּי֙ עִם־אֲבֹתַ֔י וּנְשָׂאתַ֙נִי֙ מִמִּצְרַ֔יִם
וּקְבַרְתַּ֖נִי בִּקְבֻרָתָ֑ם וַיֹּאמַ֕ר אָנֹכִ֖י

their enemies. Jacob's decision was all the more imperative because he knew that his children had begun to "let themselves be possessed by the land of Goshen," as was pointed out previously (cf. our commentary to verse 27). Life in Egypt threatened to have a profound influence on them. Soon they might substitute the Nile for the Jordan and what began as a 'temporary' sojourn in Egypt would no longer seem to them an exile.

As *R' Hirsch* concludes, this provided sufficient motive for him to press with such ceremonious solemnity that they should not bury him in Egypt, but that they should carry him to their true homeland. This was reason enough for him to say: 'Though you may wish to live in Egypt, I refuse even to be *buried* here!' This is also why he used the name Israel in expressing his wish — he spoke as Israel, the bearer of the national mission.

The Midrash notes that the Patriarchs were anxious to be buried in *Eretz Yisrael* because those buried there will be the first to enjoy resurrection in the Messianic era. This is deduced from *Isaiah* 42:5: *He gives breath* [i.e., restores life] *to the people upon it* [*Eretz Yisrael*].

Furthermore, the soil of Israel itself acts as atonement for one's sins, as it is written *Deut.* 32:43: *And His land shall make atonement for His people (Tanchuma).* [See *Torah Temimah*].

There are many more reasons offered for Jacob's wish to be buried not in Egypt but in *Eretz Yisrael,* and, as the *Zohar* concludes, it is important to reflect on these reasons, for without them it would have been more in keeping with the Patriarch's feelings to leave his tomb near his children and descendants. For them it would have been an object of comfort and protection amid the sufferings and calamities which Egyptian exile would inflict upon them.

However, it must be recalled that when Jacob came to Egypt he was concerned that the Divine Presence would abandon him for leaving *Eretz Yisrael* and his children would become assimilated among the nations. God, therefore, reassured him and said, "Do not be afraid to go down to Egypt ... I will go down with you to Egypt *and I will also bring you up*" [46:3, 4]. Jacob therefore realized that there was no need for him to be buried in Egypt and he therefore made it absolutely clear that he wanted to be buried in *Eretz Yisrael (Akeidah).*

30. וְשָׁכַבְתִּי אִם־אֲבֹתַי — *For I will lie down with my fathers.*

Rashi comments: This phrase connects with the previous thought, the contextual flow being: *Take this oath ... for I will eventually lie down with my fathers* [i.e., *die*] and you shall transport me out of Egypt and bury me in their sepulchre. Furthermore, *Rashi* emphasizes that we must avoid possibly mistranslating וְשָׁכַבְתִּי, *lie down,* as referring to *burial,* in the sense of laying Jacob to rest in burial. This translation is obviously incorrect, since burial is specifically mentioned later in the verse. As a rule, whenever the idiom *lying with one's fathers* occurs, it refers to death, not burial. See, for example, *I Kings* 2:10: *and David lay with his fathers,* and afterwards it specifically states, *and he was buried with his fathers.* [*See Ibn Ezra.*]

Jacob's assertive statement carried within it the prophetic knowlege that indeed he *would* repose with his fathers *(Midrash HaGadol).*

The Talmud [*Bava Basra* 116a] notes that wherever the expression *lie down* is used in connection with one's death it indicates that he left children like himself ... Similarly,

47 *and you shall transport me out of Egypt and bury me*
30 *in their sepulchre." He said, "I personally will do as*

because Jacob left twelve righteous and worthy sons like himself, his death is described as lying down. [The idea is that one who leaves a child like himself to take his place cannot be said to have really 'died'; he is rather like one who has merely 'lain down' *(Maharsha).*]

In the literal sense, *Sforno* explains that this expression refers to the custom of placing the departed on a bier where the lamentations and eulogies are held and the mourners file around it. This expression is therefore used of all the kings mentioned in the Books of Kings — righteous and wicked — who died on their beds [i.e., of natural causes].

Kabbalistically, the connotation of death referred to by the expression וְשָׁכַבְתִּי, *lie down,* refers to the spiritual repose of the soul and its reunion with that of its righteous ancestors (see *R' Bachya; Tz'ror HaMor).*

וּנְשָׂאתַנִי מִמִּצְרַיִם וּקְבַרְתַּנִי בִּקְבֻרָתָם — *And you shall transport me out of Egypt and* [*you shall*] *bury me in their sepulchre.*[1]

You *personally* shall see to this; *and bury me in their sepulchre* — the Cave of Machpelah, where there are buried the four couples [Adam and Eve, Abraham and Sarah, Isaac and Rebecca, Jacob and Leah] I am destined to complete *(Midrash HaGadol).*

Following *Sforno:* If you follow the procedure of this שְׁכִיבָה, *laying* my body in Egypt for the customary period of eulogy and mourning, the immediate and intense grief over my death will be assuaged and the Egyptians will not hinder you from transporting me to another country.

1. The Talmud [*Nazir* 64b-65a] uses this phrase as a Scriptural support [אַסְמַכְתָּא] for a law relating to the removal and burial of a body. The Mishnah there [*Nazir* 9:3] teaches that if a Jewish corpse is found in an area not otherwise known to be burial ground, the body may be removed to a Jewish cemetery so that the place where it was found need not be declared ritually contaminated [טָמֵא] and off-limits to Nazirites and *Kohanim* who who must maintain their ritual purity. The Mishnah rules that when the body is removed three-fingerbreadths of the adjacent soil must be removed with it, since fluids from the corpse may have seeped into the soil.

This law that adjacent soil must be removed is supported by our verse. The phrase וּנְשָׂאתַנִי מִמִּצְרַיִם, *you shall transport me out of Egypt,* may be considered superfluous since it was obvious that Jacob's burial in Canaan required his removal from Egypt. The Sages, therefore, draw a new teaching from it: it is interpreted as if it meant transport me מִמִּצְרַיִם, *with part of Egypt.* That is, with my remains take along the Egyptian soil on which my body will have rested.

Rambam notes that this is only an *asmachta,* a support verse, rather than a direct teaching, because we have no indication that Jacob was buried even temporarily in Egypt.

The commentators [see *Nazir* 14b *Tos.* s.v. נוטלו and *Sanhedrin* 47b] explain that the body discussed in *Nazir* 64b is regarded as one that was buried temporarily with the intention that it would be removed to a more suitable grave, but was subsequently forgotten. If it were intended as a permanent grave, its removal would be forbidden. Similarly, if it were a מֵת מִצְוָה, an abandoned body with no relatives to take responsibility for it, it would have to be buried — and remain buried — wherever it was found. For if the body discussed in *Nazir* were of the sort that could not be moved — such as a מֵת מִצְוָה — we assume that the earlier burial would have become public knowledge, and not have come to light *unexpectedly* during random digging in a field.

[On the question of whether Jacob was buried even temporarily in Egypt, see *Chizkuni; Rvid HaZahav; Tzafnas Paane'ach; VaYosef Avraham,* and the synopsis of this topic in Nachshoni's *Hagus B'Parshiyos HaTorah.*]

לא אֶעֱשֶׂה כִדְבָרֶךָ: וַיֹּאמֶר הִשָּׁבְעָה לִי
וַיִּשָּׁבַע לוֹ וַיִּשְׁתַּחוּ יִשְׂרָאֵל עַל־רֹאשׁ
הַמִּטָּה:

וַיֹּאמַר אָנֹכִי אֶעֱשֶׂה כִדְבָרֶךָ — *[And] he* [=Joseph] *said, I personally will do as you have said.* [The word *personally* is intimated by the use of the emphatic pronoun אָנֹכִי rather than אֲנִי.]

— Insofar as I am able, I will do as you have said with all my power *(Sforno).*

Since Jacob had requested an oath and (see next verse), Joseph *did* swear, why was it necessary for Joseph to verbalize this seemingly superfluous reassurance? In a similar case, when Abraham adjured Eliezer with an oath, we read that *Eliezer placed his hand beneath Abraham's thigh and swore to him regarding this matter* [24:9] without first verbalizing any reassurance.

— Apparently Joseph wanted to emphasize that he was quite ready to fulfill his father's wishes of his own free will and an *oath* to that effect was unnecessary. Jacob insisted on the oath, however, as we learn in the next verse *(Or HaChaim).*

As noted above, *Targum Yonasan* similarly observes that feelings of modesty prevented Joseph from placing his hand under his father's 'thigh' so he just promised him: 'I will do as you have said.'

According to *Daas Zekeinim,* the connotation of Joseph's reply was, *I, too, will do as you say, i.e., I will follow your suggestion and when I am dying I, too, will urge my brothers to take me from here* [see *50:25*].

31. הִשָּׁבְעָה לִי וַיִּשָּׁבַע לוֹ — *'Swear to me,' and he swore to him.*

Following the opinion that Joseph wanted to avoid placing his hand under his father's 'thigh,' Jacob now suggested instead that Joseph take an oath by God's Name, which Joseph proceeded to do *(Akeidah; Ralbag; Radak; Targum Yonasan).*

The commentators emphasize that Jacob's insistence that Joseph take a formal vow did not imply any suspicion on his part that Joseph might renege on his promise unless he swore. But Jacob knew that his unwillingness to be buried in Egypt constituted an insult to the land that had given him hospitality, and accordingly Pharaoh might forbid Joseph to go to *Eretz Yisrael.* It was Jacob's intention to make the promise more binding, for Jacob knew it would not be proper for Pharaoh to force Joseph to violate an *oath,* and Joseph himself would feel more obligated to withstand adverse pressure and fulfill his father's wish if there was an oath to which he could make reference. This indeed is what occurred, for when Pharaoh granted permission to Joseph he emphasized that he was acceding solely because Jacob had imposed an oath [see *Rashi* 50:6] *(Ramban; Sforno; Kli Yakar).*

Furthermore, Jacob did not say, as did Abraham to Eliezer, וְאַשְׁבִּיעֲךָ, *and I will have you swear* [24:3], since Jacob did not want any implication that Joseph had been *forced* against his will to swear. He therefore asked Joseph to undertake the oath himself — as if he were proceeding of his own free volition *(Malbim).*

וַיִּשְׁתַּחוּ יִשְׂרָאֵל עַל־רֹאשׁ הַמִּטָּה —

47 *you have said."*

31 [31] *He replied, "Swear to me," and he swore to him.*
Then Israel prostrated himself towards the head of the
bed.

Then Israel prostrated himself towards [lit. *upon*] *the head of the bed.*

Rashi explains: *Then Israel prostrated himself* [to Joseph]. As the proverb says, תַּעֲלָא בְּעִידָּנֵיהּ סְגִיד לֵיהּ, "When the fox has his hour bow down to him."

[I.e. although the lion is king, nevertheless, should the insignificant fox assume rulership, then even the regal lion should show him the proper reverence.

By Joseph's acceptance of the obligation to fulfill Jacob's burial wishes — an obligation by which Joseph risked putting himself in disgrace before Pharaoh — Jacob felt the desire to display his gratitude. Ordinarily it would have been improper for him to bow to his son, but since Joseph was a reigning, royal figure, Jacob bowed to him in keeping with the proverb quoted by *Rashi.* Jacob, therefore, paid him this gesture in supreme tribute *(Mizrachi; Gur Aryeh).*

The allusion, according to this interpretation, of עַל רֹאשׁ הַמִּטָּה, *at the head of the bed,* is explained by *Maharsha* ibid. as alluding to Joseph who was now 'at the head' of Jacob's descendants — *bed* being a metaphor for *descendants.*

According to one view in *Midrash Tanchuma,* this bowing to Joseph finally constituted the fulfillment of Joseph's early dream in which the sun (his father) bowed to him.

Rashbam renders: *Jacob prostrated himself* **towards Joseph,** *from where he* [Jacob] *was, at the head of the bed.*

Rashi continues that, as implied by the expression עַל רֹאשׁ הַמִּטָּה, *upon* [i.e. *toward* or *at*] *the head of the bed,* Jacob — [while bowing in gratitude to Joseph] — turned himself toward the *Shechinah* (Divine Presence). The Rabbis [see *Shabbos* 12a and *Nedarim* 40a] derive from this that the *Shechinah* is above the head of a sick person.

Ordinarily, in bowing toward Joseph, Jacob would have, in effect, placed his back toward the *Shechinah* which was above his head — a mark of disrespect. To avoid this, he inclined himself *toward* (עַל having the meaning of אֶל) the head of the bed so his bowing would be *towards* the *Shechinah* — in a display of both gratitude to Joseph and respect to the *Shechinah.* That Jacob is here called 'sick' although he had not yet become ill, is explained by *Gur Aryeh.* Jacob is called sick because of the general decline of his strength and vigor. The Rabbis in *Nedarim* 40a actually derive that the Shechinah hovers above the *bed* of a sick person from *Psalms* 41:4. That it hovers above the *head* of the bed is, according to *Rashi,* derived from our passage.

Alternatively, *Rashi* interprets: *Jacob bowed* [in thanks to God] *regarding the excellence of his bed* [i.e. of his progeny — רֹאשׁ, *head,* referring to *choicest quality* (as in *Exodus* 30:23 בְּשָׂמִים רֹאשׁ, *choicest spices*), and מִטָּה, *bed,* being a metaphor for children], for Jacob's 'bed' was 'whole' [שֶׁהָיְתָה מִטָּתוֹ שְׁלֵמָה. That is, his progeny were all whole-hearted with God] and none of them was wicked. For although Joseph was a viceroy, and although he had been a captive among heathens, he adhered to righteousness. [It was at this juncture, when the thought of his death inspired Jacob to elicit the oath from Joseph, that Jacob showed gratitude to God for having granted him the merit of unblemished progeny. He had been particularly concerned because Abraham had had his Ishmael, and Isaac his Esau, and Jacob — for the reasons noted — was always worried that Joseph had become blemished in Egypt. But as he now perceived, Joseph had remained good and virtuous.] (The bracketed explanations are culled

א וַיְהִי אַחֲרֵי הַדְּבָרִים הָאֵלֶּה וַיֹּאמֶר לְיוֹסֵף
הִנֵּה אָבִיךָ חֹלֶה וַיִּקַּח אֶת־שְׁנֵי בָנָיו עִמּוֹ
ב אֶת־מְנַשֶּׁה וְאֶת־אֶפְרָיִם: וַיַּגֵּד לְיַעֲקֹב

from *Mizrachi; Zohar; Tzeidah laDerech* and *Akeidah).*[1]

Sforno interprets: Jacob prostrated himself in gratitude to his Creator for having graciously allowed him to achieve this [promise of burial] from his son. Similar to this is 24:52 where it is recorded that when Eliezer heard Rebecca's family consent to his proposal that she accompany him home to marry his master, *he prostrated himself to the ground unto HASHEM* in gratitude and joy.

XLVIII

1. Jacob's illness.

After Joseph returned from visiting his father in Goshen, Jacob became ill. When Joseph was informed, he brought his two sons so that Jacob would bless them *(Ramban* 47:29).

וַיְהִי אַחֲרֵי הַדְּבָרִים הָאֵלֶּה – *And it came to pass after these things.*

I.e., after Jacob had arranged to be buried in *Eretz Yisrael (Oznaim L'Torah).*

According to the Rabbinic chronology, several months elapsed since the preceding.

[As explained in the *comm.* to 22:20 the use of the Hebrew term for *after* – אַחֲרֵי – denotes either that some time has elapsed since the preceding event (in this case less than a year), or it denotes that the following episode occurred after 'deep reflection' on the part of the main subject.]

According to *Midrash HaGadol,* in our context the phrase refers to thoughts that had disturbed the Patriarch since his coming down to Egypt: Was he going to die and be buried in Egypt, and would his children then settle down in this land, and lose themselves in the Egyptian population? These grave sources of anxiety had just been dispelled by Joseph's oath, and the Patriarch felt fully confident that the promise he had received from God would be carried out to the letter: *"I shall also bring you up from there* (from Egypt), *and Joseph will place his hand over your eyes* [46:4]." It was after these reassuring thoughts that an illness made Jacob aware that his time was drawing near.

וַיֹּאמֶר לְיוֹסֵף – *That someone said to Joseph.*

The Hebrew literally reads *And he said to Joseph.* The subject in this elliptic phrase is unidentified; it was told to Joseph by whomever it was. This is a common Biblical style *(Rashi; Ibn Ezra).*

Rashi continues that according to

1. Joseph lived a total of 110 years. By this time Joseph was 56 years old and had already lived the majority of his life. The accounting is as follows: He was 30 when he stood before Pharaoh; add to this the 7 years of plenty and 2 years of famine at which time his father came to Egypt, plus the 17 years that Jacob had dwelt in Egypt.

Thus, since Joseph attained more than half his lifespan without sinning, Jacob now felt assured that Joseph would not sin for the duration of his life. As the Talmud [*Yoma* 38b] notes: 'When the majority of a man's years have passed without sin, he will not sin any more' *(Meshech Chochmah).*

48
1

1 And it came to pass after these things that someone said to Joseph, "Behold! your father is ill." So he took his two sons, Ephraim and Manasseh, with him.

הִנֵּה אָבִיךָ חֹלֶה — *Behold! your father is ill.*[1]

The term הִנֵּה, *behold,* denotes in many contexts, the unexpected and unusual.

וַיִּקַּח אֶת־שְׁנֵי בָנָיו עִמּוֹ אֶת־מְנַשֶּׁה וְאֶת אֶפְרָיִם — *So he took his two sons, Ephraim and Manasseh, with him.*

That Jacob might bless them before he died *(Rashi).*

The naming of the sons seems to be redundant since we know that they were Joseph's only *two sons.* The names are given to signify that they were worthy of receiving the Patriarch's blessing both because they were Joseph's sons, and because of their personal merit as Ephraim and Manasseh — each a worthy personage in his own right. This is further intimated by the indefinite article אֶת preceding each name, giving each one individual significance *(Akeidah; Or HaChaim).*

2. וַיַּגֵּד לְיַעֲקֹב — *Jacob was told.*

The Hebrew literally reads *he* [i.e., *someone*] *told Jacob.* Here, too, the Torah does not identify who

the Midrash it was Ephraim who informed Joseph. Ephraim frequently studied under Jacob and when the latter became ill in Goshen, Ephraim rushed to his father in Egypt and brought him the news.

Other versions in *Midrash Rabbah* read: Who told him? Some say, Benjamin; others, the Divine Spirit.

From the fact that Joseph had to be informed of his father's illness, it would appear that Joseph did not spend much time with him.

This points to Joseph's noble character. He avoided being alone with his father since he feared that Jacob would inquire regarding the circumstances of how he got to Egypt, and the conversation might lead to a revelation of the sale and the behavior of his brothers. He feared that he would thereby provoke his father's wrath against his brothers and this would result in a great upheaval. Witness the effects of Jacob's unwitting curse which resulted in Rachel's death on the road to Ephrath [35:17]. How much more devastating would the effects of Jacob's *purposeful* wrath be! *(Tosafos HaRosh).*

1. **Jacob, the first to experience fatal illness.**

Until Jacob, no person ever experienced illness. Instead one would suddenly sneeze and his soul would depart through his nostrils. [At Creation, God *blew into Adam's nostrils the soul of life* (2:7); therefore, by sneezing, the soul, in a sense, is expelled through that very same passage and it returns to its abode *(Radal).*] But Jacob prayed that God grant people a short period of illness prior to death. One would thereby have a warning that he was about to die, thus providing him the opportunity to settle his worldly affairs and give final instructions to his children and household who would have the opportunity to be present at the time of his death. Jacob's prayer was granted [and the illness recorded in our verse was the first illness ever experienced.] ... We therefore have the custom when one sneezes to say 'to life!' [or 'to health!'] since sneezing was once a moment of mortal danger *(Pirkei d'Rabbi Eliezer* 52; *Bereishis Rabbah; Bava Metzia* 87a; *Maharsha* ibid.; *Sanhedrin* 107b; *Rashi* ibid.; cf. *Yalkut HaMachiri Proverbs* 20:28; *Berachos* 53a).

In *Bava Basra* 16b [see *comm.* to 24:1 (footnote p. 892)] we learn that Abraham had a precious stone suspended from his neck, which brought an immediate cure to any 'sick' person who gazed upon it. *Tosafos* s.v. שֶׁבַּל explains that this is no contradiction to the citation above that there was no illness until Jacob requested it. In Abraham's case, the word sick means 'wounded,' while in Jacob's the reference is to fatal illness.

וַיֹּ֕אמֶר הִנֵּ֛ה בִּנְךָ֥ יוֹסֵ֖ף בָּ֣א אֵלֶ֑יךָ וַיִּתְחַזֵּק֙
ג יִשְׂרָאֵ֔ל וַיֵּ֖שֶׁב עַל־הַמִּטָּֽה׃ וַיֹּ֤אמֶר יַעֲקֹב֙
אֶל־יוֹסֵ֔ף אֵ֥ל שַׁדַּ֛י נִרְאָֽה־אֵלַ֥י בְּל֖וּז בְּאֶ֣רֶץ
ד כְּנָ֑עַן וַיְבָ֖רֶךְ אֹתִֽי׃ וַיֹּ֣אמֶר אֵלַ֗י הִנְנִ֤י מַפְרְךָ֙
וְהִרְבִּיתִ֔ךָ וּנְתַתִּ֖יךָ לִקְהַ֣ל עַמִּ֑ים וְנָ֨תַתִּ֜י

told him. There are many such elliptical verses *(Rashi).*

The Midrash derives a standard of etiquette from this passage telling that someone went to announce Joseph's arrival. One should not walk in unexpectedly on a sick person, lest he shame him, but wait to be announced.

הִנֵּה בִּנְךָ יוֹסֵף בָּא אֵלֶיךָ — *Behold! your son Joseph has come to you.*

Such visits, as noted in *v.* 1, were unusual. Therefore the use of the term הִנֵּה, *behold,* which in many contexts denotes the unexpected *(Ralbag).*

וַיִּתְחַזֵּק יִשְׂרָאֵל וַיֵּשֶׁב עַל הַמִּטָּה — *So Israel exerted himself and sat up on the bed.*

Jacob said, 'Though he is my son he is of royal rank; therefore I must pay him honor!' From this we learn that honor must be paid to royalty [see *Menachos* 98a]. Similarly Moses honored Pharaoh [see *Rashi* to *Exodus* 11:8], as did Elijah who ran before Ahab [I *Kings* 18:46] *(Rashi).*

In this case although it was Joseph who was coming for a favor, Jacob paid him honor, because, as *Rashi* explains, Joseph was of royal rank. The context here is different from 47:31 where Jacob was requesting a favor from Joseph. This explains why *Rashi* offers differing insights in both cases [see comm. above] *(Sifsei Chachomim).*

The phrase implies that Jacob sat with his feet upon the ground, as implicit in *v.* 12 where we are told that *Joseph then removed them from his* [Jacob's] *knees.* The Torah tells us this to inform us of Jacob's extraordinary strength; his entire last will and testament was transmitted while he sat on the bed with his feet upon the ground. Only when he finished *did he draw his feet into the bed* [49:33], and then he immediately expired *(Rashbam).*

Daas Zekeinim explains that Jacob did not want to bless his children while lying in bed lest it appear that he was making a death-bed gift and was not really in full possession of his senses. He, therefore, mustered up all his strength to remain seated on his bed throughout, to show that he was in full control of his faculties.

3. The birthright is transferred to Joseph.

Jacob formally makes Ephraim and Manasseh equal to any of his other sons — in effect adopting them as his own — thereby transferring to Joseph a double portion of the inheritance.

אֵל שַׁדַּי נִרְאָה אֵלַי בְּלוּז בְּאֶרֶץ כְּנָעַן — *El Shaddai had appeared to me in Luz in the land of Canaan.*

The reference is to the revelation in 35:9*ff* on Jacob's return from Paddan Aram, when God — in His Aspect of El Shaddai — said to him: *I am El Shaddai; be fruitful and multiply ... (Rashbam; Radak).*

[Comp. also the revelation in 28:13, and the blessing Isaac conferred upon Jacob in 28:3.]

*[2] Jacob was told, "Behold! your son Joseph has come
to you." So Israel exerted himself and sat up on the
bed. [3] Jacob said to Joseph, "El Shaddai had appeared
to me in Luz in the land of Canaan and He blessed me.
[4] He said to me 'Behold: I will make you fruitful and
numerous; I will make you a congregation of peoples,*

Luz is the original name of the site; Jacob renamed it Beth El [see 28:19; 35:6].

וַיְבָרֶךְ אֹתִי – *And He blessed me.*

— With a blessing sufficient even for my grandchildren. He promised me the Land as an eternal inheritance for my descendants; now I am conferring the firstborn privileges of that inheritance upon your two sons *(Radak; Abarbanel).*

4. הִנְנִי מַפְרְךָ וְהִרְבִּיתִךָ וּנְתַתִּיךָ לִקְהַל עַמִּים – *Behold: I will make you fruitful and numerous* [lit. *I am fructifying you and I will make you numerous*]; *and I will make you a congregation of peoples.*

— "He informed me that there will yet descend from me a congregation of peoples [i.e., additional progeny besides the eleven sons I had at that time. (This rendering of *Rashi* follows *Maskil l'David* who notes that the printed versions which read קְהַל וְעַמִּים, 'a congregation *and* peoples' are in error.)] Although God had promised that *a nation and a congregation of nations would descend from me* [I do not refer now to His promise of a new *nation,* since] by *nation* God alluded to Benjamin [who was born after the promise was made]. By *a congregation of nations,* God intimated that two more *besides* Benjamin would descend from me to become nations. Consequently, since no more sons were born to me, I assume that one of my sons was intended to branch out into two tribes, and it is that blessing that I now confer upon you *(Rashi* from *Pesikta;* comp. *Rashi* to 35:11).[1]

[The passage to which Jacob alludes literally reads: *Be fruitful and multiply; a nation and a congregation of nations* (גּוֹי וּקְהַל גּוֹיִם) *shall descend from you.* The commentators perceive גּוֹיִם, *nations,* and עַמִּים, *peoples,* to be essentially synonymous in this context except, as *R' Kitov* observes, the original blessing was uttered in *Eretz Yisrael* and therefore the word גּוֹי, *nation,* was used, since Israel can be called a *nation* only when in *Eretz Yisrael.* (See also Israel's blessing to Jacob in 28:3. See also *Ramban* to 17:6 וּנְתַתִּיךָ לְגוֹיִם). *Onkelos* renders: ... *a congregation of tribes.*]

1. That the birthright was taken from Reuben is discussed in the comm. to 35:22 and 49:4. That it was transferred to Joseph is explicitly stated in *I Chronicles* 5:1.

However, why was Joseph chosen above Jacob's other sons?

Chizkuni cites the Talmud that Joseph earned the birthright because he sustained the family during the famine. Alternately, he suggests that Joseph was the firstborn of Jacob's primary wife, Rachel. Additionally, Jacob wanted Rachel to have more than the concubines [Bilhah and Zilpah, each of whom had two tribes].

According to the Arizal, Ephraim and Manasseh would have been begotten by Jacob had Reuben not transposed his couch in the matter of Bilhah. See comm. to 35:22 [footnote to page 1523]. Jacob therefore bestowed this tribal right on them since he considered them his own.

אֶת־הָאָרֶץ הַזֹּאת לְזַרְעֲךָ אַחֲרֶיךָ אֲחֻזַּת
ה עוֹלָם: וְעַתָּה שְׁנֵי־בָנֶיךָ הַנּוֹלָדִים לְךָ
בְּאֶרֶץ מִצְרַיִם עַד־בֹּאִי אֵלֶיךָ מִצְרַיְמָה
לִי־הֵם אֶפְרַיִם וּמְנַשֶּׁה כִּרְאוּבֵן וְשִׁמְעוֹן
ו יִהְיוּ־לִי: וּמוֹלַדְתְּךָ אֲשֶׁר־הוֹלַדְתָּ
אַחֲרֵיהֶם לְךָ יִהְיוּ עַל שֵׁם אֲחֵיהֶם יִקָּרְאוּ

וְנָתַתִּי אֶת־הָאָרֶץ הַזֹּאת לְזַרְעֲךָ אַחֲרֶיךָ אֲחֻזַּת עוֹלָם — *And I will give this land to your offspring after you as a permanent possession.*

Even when Israel's descendants are temporarily exiled from their Land, their inalienable right to it is not diminished *(Akeidah).*

5. וְעַתָּה — *And now.*

I.e., since God has promised me the land I am entitled to give it to whomever I wish, and I accordingly pronounce you to be my firstborn in this regard so you can receive the inheritance of two tribes *(Rashbam).*

שְׁנֵי־בָנֶיךָ הַנּוֹלָדִים לְךָ בְּאֶרֶץ מִצְרַיִם עַד־בֹּאִי אֵלֶיךָ מִצְרַיְמָה — *Your two sons who were born to you in Egypt before* [lit. *until*] *my coming to you in* [lit. *to*] *Egypt.*

I.e., who were born to you between the time you left me and the time I came to you in Egypt *(Rashi).*

— A reference to Ephraim and Manasseh; *(Rashbam).*

In the Talmud, *Nedarim* 30b, there is a controversy affecting the connotation of oaths. If someone makes an oath affecting נוֹלָדִים, does he mean living children or children who will be born in the future? That is, does the word נוֹלָדִים [lit. *are born*] have a past-tense implication: *have been born,* or future: *shall be born?* Our passage is cited to prove that the former is the case, while *I Kings* 13:2 is cited to prove the latter. The conclusion is that the word can have either meaning, and in Biblical usage its definition depends on the context.

לִי הֵם — *Shall be mine.*

They shall be counted among my other sons [not like my grandsons], each to have his own territory exactly like each of my other sons *(Rashi).*

On the Kabbalistic reason that Jacob considered Manasseh and Ephraim as his own sons, see *Arizal* and *Malbim* cited on p. 1523.

Sforno renders: *Shall be mine* — for it was only them that God granted me to see together with you. Comp. v. 11 below: *I never expected to see your face again, and here God has allowed me to see your children as well.*

אֶפְרַיִם וּמְנַשֶּׁה כִּרְאוּבֵן וְשִׁמְעוֹן יִהְיוּ־לִי — *Ephraim and Manasseh shall be mine like Reuben and Simeon.*

Just as Reuben and Simeon — my own sons — will be tribes, so will they *(Midrash).*

[That Jacob mentioned the younger son Ephraim before the firstborn Manasseh was quite intentional and he later gives him precedence in his blessing as well. Jacob's justification is given in *v.* 19 below.]

The Talmud (*Kesubos* 72a) cites our passage as an illustration that 'grandchildren are considered as children' [see also *Pirkei d' Rabbi Eliezer* §36], and rules that a man has the right to divorce his wife — and she forfeits her *kesubah,* marriage settlement — if she curses her husband's parents either to his face, or in the presence of his children, because this is tantamount to cursing her husband, an offense for which he is

and I will give this land to your offspring after you as a
permanent possession.' [5] *And now, your two sons who were born to you in Egypt before my coming to you in Egypt shall be mine; Ephraim and Manasseh shall be mine like Reuben and Simeon.* [6] *But progeny born to you after them shall be yours; they will be included*

permitted to divorce her (*Tosafos Rid;* cf. *Ritva).*

6. **וּמוֹלַדְתְּךָ אֲשֶׁר הוֹלַדְתָּ אַחֲרֵיהֶם לְךָ** [lit. *whom you shall beget*][1] *after them shall be yours.*

◆§ The territorial effects of Manasseh and Ephraim's elevation to the status of tribes.

[According to *Rashi,* Manasseh and Ephraim's elevation to the status of tribes was primarily prestigious in nature, meaning that each bore the title of a separate tribe, had its own banner and encampment in the Wilderness, and cast lots for the division of territory in *Eretz Yisrael.* However, whether or not they were separate tribes had no bearing on the *amount* of territory they would receive in *Eretz Yisrael* since each eligible Jew received an equal piece of land; thus, two tribes totaling 70,000 people would receive the same territory as a single tribe of equal population.]

— If you beget any more children, they will not be included among my sons. Instead, they will be included in the tribes of Ephraim and Manasseh, and they will not bear the title of separate tribes regarding the division of *Eretz Yisrael (Rashi).*

Rashi continues: Now even though *Eretz Yisrael* was divided on a *per capita* basis, as it is written [*Numbers* 26:54]: *To the more numerous you shall give a larger inheritance,* so that each person received an equal share — except for firstborns who received double shares — nevertheless only Manasseh and Ephraim of Joseph's sons would be separate tribes with respect to casting lots by tribe for the division of the land [ibid. *v.* 55], and the right to have their own prince and flag *(Rashi).* [See also *Rashi* to *Numbers* 26:56].

The intent of *Rashi's* comment is as follows: Although the land was divided among the twelve tribes, the sizes of their respective territories were unequal and dependent upon their population. A tribe with many members received a larger territory than one with less members. When Scripture says that the land was divided by lots [*Numbers* 26:55], it means that a tribe's *general* location — north or south, mountain or plain, and so on — would be determined by lots, but the *size* of the respective

1. *Rashi* interprets הוֹלַדְתָּ in the imperfect future: *whom you shall beget,* rather than past tense: *whom you have begotten.* This is necessitated by the fact that it is nowhere recorded that children other than Ephraim and Manasseh had been born to Joseph up to that time.

Ramban [*v.* 15 below] citing *Onkelos* — also interprets הוֹלַדְתָּ as future tense, but maintains that Joseph must have had more children after this blessing, since Jacob's words would not be in vain. That is why Jacob took pains to be so specific in these two verses instead of saying simply, *And now your sons, Ephraim and Manasseh,who were born to you, shall be mine, like Reuben and Simeon.* However, the Torah does not identify these additional children [since they were absorbed into the tribes of Ephraim and Manasseh].

Akeidah concurs that no other sons had been born as *yet,* but he, like *Ramban,* emphasizes that the prophet [Jacob] would not have spoken in vain, and it is to be presumed that other children were subsequently born to Joseph. [Comp. *Rashbam* to 41:50.]

ז בְּנַחֲלָתָם: וַאֲנִי בְּבֹאִי מִפַּדָּן מֵתָה עָלַי

portions would depend on the population of the individual tribes. Thus, Jacob declared: Let Manasseh and Ephraim come and claim separate territories like my other sons, with the *size* of their portions — like those of the other tribes — based upon their populations. They will not be like my *grandchildren,* Chanoch and Pallu, sons of Reuben, who could claim land only secondarily, as members of their father's tribe. However, other children born to Joseph will be considered part of Manasseh or Ephraim and receive portions within their territories.

By the phrase, "Now even though *Eretz Yisrael* was divided on a *per capita* basis," *Rashi* meant: Since in any event all individuals received *equal amounts of territory,* what difference did it make if Joseph's other sons were or were not considered separate tribes? *Rashi* acknowledges that subsequent sons of Joseph were not inferior to Ephraim and Manasseh in terms of allotment of territory; but they would not have the status of separate tribes and would therefore not have their own princes or tribal banners as did Ephraim and Manasseh [nor would they be included in the lots to determine the part of *Eretz Yisrael* where they would receive their portions] *(Sefer Zikaron).*

Ramban disagrees.

Ramban disagrees with *Rashi's* thesis that Jacob's granting of the birthright to Joseph meant only that his sons would have tribes named after them — and did not affect the size of each individual's territory. *Ramban* cites the end of our verse, 'they will be included under the names of their brothers with *regard to their inheritance,'* which, he maintains, intimates that Joseph would enjoy a *territorial* advantage as well by virtue of Manasseh and Ephraim's designation as tribes. He also cites the Talmud, *Horayos* 6b and *Bava Basra* 123, to the effect that Joseph's right of the firstborn involved the firstborn's right of double territorial inheritance for his tribe (as will be explained below), which contradicts *Rashi's* assertion that no territorial advantage was involved.

Rather — *Ramban* continues — the land was not divided merely by total population, the more populous tribes taking a larger share *per capita* than the less populous, for in that case there would be no territorial advantage to Joseph's being granted the rights of the firstborn. Additionally, it is nowhere suggested in Scripture that *individual descendants* of Joseph received a double portion of territory — only that the gift of the birthright meant that *Joseph's sons* would be considered *'like Reuben and Simeon'* meaning that Ephraim and Manasseh would form separate tribes, with the associated territorial benefits this would accrue to them.

For, as *Ramban* maintains, the Land was divided into *twelve equal parts,* irrespective of the number of members of each tribe — with for example, Simeon, the least populous tribe, receiving a territory equal in size to Judah's. Thus, Joseph's birthright entitled him to a double territorial share inasmuch as two of his children formed full-fledged tribes, each receiving an equal portion of land. The verse in *Numbers* cited by *Rashi, to the numerous you shall give a large inheritance,* refers to the fact that each tribal portion was internally divided equally among the members of the clans of paternal families [בָּתֵּי אָבוֹת] within each tribe, and the more

under the name of their brothers with regard to their
inheritance. [7] *But as for me — when I came from Pad-*

populous clans received larger sections of the tribe's territory than the less populous ones. [See *Sifre Pinchas* §132, and *comm.* to *Numbers* 26:54.]

[In effect, then, each member of Judah, the largest tribe, received a much smaller portion than each member of Simeon, the smallest tribe; Judah's portion was divided among many more people than was Simeon's.]

Ramban concludes that even if we were to admit that the Land was divided *per capita* according to the number of *individuals* — as the passage in *Numbers* 26:54 seems to indicate [and which *Rashi,* following one view in the Talmud, interprets accordingly] — we must assume that Joseph received a territorial advantage. Accordingly, if the Land was divided *per capita,* we must suggest that each descendant of Joseph received an ordinary portion equal to members of other tribes, plus an additional portion representing the added share of firstborn. Whatever the interpretation, however, Jacob's gift of the birthright to Joseph — via his children Ephraim and Manasseh — was more than merely nominal.

As the commentators note, the controversy between *Rashi* and *Ramban* reflects differing views found in *Bava Basra* 121b. *Rashi* chose the exegesis that he perceives to more closely reflect the literal meaning of the text in *Numbers,* as *Ramban* himself appears to admit in the latter part of his comment regarding the question of how the Land was divided. It is regarding the question of whether Joseph's 'birthright' was merely nominal or resulted in more territory for his descendants that *Rashi* and *Ramban* differ. See *Mizrachi; Gur Aryeh* and *Levush.*

Sforno interprets that *'your progeny'* refers to Joseph's *grandchildren,* not *future sons.* Joseph was told that they ... *shall be yours* in the sense that they would be called the House of Joseph and would be blessed as a result of Jacob's blessing to Joseph.

עַל שֵׁם אֲחֵיהֶם יִקָּרְאוּ בְּנַחֲלָתָם — *They will be included under* [lit. *they will be called by*] *the name of their brothers with regard to their inheritance.*

Following *Rashi:* No tribes will be *named* after such subsequent children; they will be part of Ephraim and Manasseh's tribes.

Following *Ramban:* There will be no further independent *tribal allotment of territories* for such children; they will inherit portions in the territories of Ephraim and Manasseh.

Rashbam: They —i.e. the sons or grandsons subsequently born — will not form independent *tribes* but will form בָּתֵּי אָבוֹת, *clans of paternal families,* among whom the Land was eventually apportioned as noted in *Bava Basra* 118b and Scripturally in *Numbers* 26:53-55.

7. וַאֲנִי בְּבֹאִי מִפַּדָּן — *But as for me, when I came from Paddan ...*

[How this statement fits in the context of the chapter is unclear. *Rashi* connects it with Jacob's earlier request that Joseph inter him in Canaan, and perceives this statement as Jacob's anticipation of Joseph's unspoken complaint. In fairness, how could Jacob ask to be taken for burial to the Cave of Machpelah when he did not do the same for Rachel, who died on the way home from Paddan? Apparently Jacob sensed that Joseph harbored resentment about this, and he seized this opportunity to justify his action]:

But as for me — although I trou-

רָחֵל בְּאֶרֶץ כְּנַעַן בַּדֶּרֶךְ בְּעוֹד כִּבְרַת־
אֶרֶץ לָבֹא אֶפְרָתָה וָאֶקְבְּרֶהָ שָּׁם בְּדֶרֶךְ
ח אֶפְרָת הִוא בֵּית לָחֶם: וַיַּרְא יִשְׂרָאֵל אֶת־

ble you to transport me for burial in the land of Canaan, while I did not do this for your mother [i.e., I buried her by the roadside where she died] even though she died but a short distance from Bethlehem; nevertheless be aware that I did so by the command of God (*Rashi;* see continuation, and other views below).

According to *Rashbam,* the continuity is different. Having related in *v.* 3 that God blessed him on his return from Paddan Aram, Jacob now continued that it was after those blessings on that same road that Rachel had died. Following this view, many commentators interpret Jacob's statement to imply: The fact that Rachel died soon after God promised me a congregation of peoples made it clear that this promise would be realized through *grandchildren* from her whom I would consider as my own sons. It is accordingly *your* sons, Ephraim and Manasseh, whom I so consider and upon whom I bestow the birthright.

מֵתָה עָלַי רָחֵל — *Rachel died on me.*[1]

I.e., suddenly. Comp. *Numbers* 6:9 where *on* is also used in this sense (*Ibn Ezra; HaRechasim le-Bik'ah).*

בְּעוֹד כִּבְרַת־אֶרֶץ לָבֹא אֶפְרָתָה — *While there was still a stretch of land to go* [lit. *to come*] *to Ephrath* [identified below with Bethlehem].

I.e. it was but a short distance to Bethlehem. The term *"kivrah* of land," refers to a measure equal to 2,000 cubits [about ¾ of a mile] — the distance outside a city one is permitted to walk on the Sabbath [תְּחוּם שַׁבָּת]. This follows the view of R' Moshe HaDarshan. According to the Midrash, Jacob used the word *kivrah,* related to *kvarah,* a sieve, to describe the terrain. He was telling Joseph: *The land on the way to Ephrath was still sieve-like,* i.e., "Do not imagine that rains and

1. The *Talmud* [*Sanhedrin* 22b] derives from the superfluous word עָלַי, *on me,* that אֵין אִשָּׁה מֵתָה אֶלָּא לְבַעְלָהּ, *a woman dies only to her husband* [i.e., it is the husband who primarily feels her loss; hence Jacob emphasized: Rachel died *on me*]. That, conversely, *a man dies only to his wife* is inferred from the verse *And Elimelech* **Naomi's husband** *died* [*Ruth* 1:3], implying that it was primarily as *Naomi's husband* that he died; others did not feel his loss as much as she.

[Comp. 42:36 עָלַי הָיוּ כֻלָּנָה, *upon me has it all fallen,* where עָלַי, *upon me,* similarly means: it has primarily affected me. *Radak* cites 33:13, וְהַצֹּאן וְהַבָּקָר עָלוֹת עָלָי, *and the nursing flocks and the herds are upon me*].

— Of all the tribulations I had ever experienced, her death befell me the hardest *(Midrash HaGadol).*

A further implication of the expression *died on me,* is that it was a lament on Jacob's part that Rachel had died *through him,* i.e., as a result of the curse he had uttered when confronted by Laban about the stolen *teraphim* [31:32 or because Jacob had delayed in fulfilling his vow, as a result of which his wife died prematurely (*Rosh Hashanah* 6a; see *comm.* to 35:19 and *Meshech Chochmah* to 35:19)] (*Or HaChaim; Lekach Tov;* see footnote on p. 1359). — [The accountability for her death remains mine (*R' David Feinstein).*]

Meshech Chochmah to our verse accordingly comments that Jacob was concerned that Joseph might delay fulfillment of his vow to bury him in *Eretz Yisrael.* He therefore intimated that Rachel died *through him* because he had delayed a vow.

48 dan, Rachel died on me in the land of Canaan on the
7 road, while there was still a stretch of land to go to
Ephrath; and I buried her there on the road to Ephrath,
which is Bethlehem."

mud prevented me from bringing her to Hebron for burial; it was the dry season [following the rainy season], when the earth is [very dry, and] riddled with holes like a sieve" — a time when the land is easily passable. [Following either interpretation, Jacob told Joseph that although it had been possible for him to bring Rachel's body to Hebron for burial in the cave, he buried her by the roadside — as *Rashi* continues below — at the Divine command] *(Rashi;* see also *Rashi* to 35:16 and other *comm.* there).

Rashi continues that *Onkelos* rendered the expression כִּבְרַת אֶרֶץ as כְּרוּב אַרְעָא, i.e., an area of land that can be plowed in a full day. 'And I maintain,' notes *Rashi,* 'that they had a definite measure of land which they referred to as 'one full furrow.' Comp. the Talmudic terms for plowing, כָּרִיב, and כַּרְבָּא, in *Bava Metzia* 107a and *Yoma* 43b respectively.

According to *Rashbam* the implication was that it was a *long* distance to Bethlehem, and Jacob thereby explained the impossibility of bringing Rachel to Machpelah.

וָאֶקְבְּרֶהָ שָּׁם בְּדֶרֶךְ אֶפְרָת הִוא בֵּית לָחֶם — *And I buried her there on the road to Ephrath, which is Bethlehem* [see 35:19].

Rashi continues: ' ... And I did not carry her even the short distance to Bethlehem to bring her into the Land.[1] I know that in your heart you bear a grievance against me. Know, however, that it was by the command of God that I buried her there so that she might be of help to her children, when Nebuzaradan [the chief general of Nebuchadnezzar, king of Babylon (see *II Kings* 25:8*ff*)] would lead Israel into captivity [after the destruction of the First Temple]. For we find that when the Jews were passing

1. *Ramban* writes that he does not comprehend why *Rashi* says: 'And I did not carry her even the short distance to Bethlehem to bring her *into the Land'* [which would appear to imply that Jacob was apologizing for having not buried her within *Eretz Yisrael,* which is not the case as the area of Bethlehem *is* part of *Eretz Yisrael,* as *Ramban* proceeds to emphasize].

'Was she then buried outside the Land?' *Ramban* queries. 'Heaven forbid! She died within the Land and was buried there, as it is explicitly written in our verse *Rachel died on me in the land of Canaan.* And in the narrative of her death it is stated even more clearly that her death occurred after Jacob departed from Luz/Bethel *in the land of Canaan* [35:6] and she died in the region between Bethel and the Ephrathite Bethlehem in *Eretz Yisrael.'*

Mizrachi defends *Rashi* by suggesting that *Rashi* used the term הָאָרֶץ, *the land,* in the sense of not having brought Rachel לְאֶרֶץ נוֹשֶׁבֶת, *to populated territory,* i.e., the city, but instead buried her on the then-desolate roadside.

Chasam Sofer offers a novel interpretation: Although *Eretz Yisrael* was established as a heritage from our Forefathers, it was not sanctified until Joshua sanctified it at the time of his conquest. Prior to its sanctification it had the status of land outside of *Eretz Yisrael* except for the Cave of Machpelah which Abraham had purchased and the site of the altar which Jacob had purchased in Shechem. Theoretically had Jacob brought Rachel into Bethlehem and purchased a burial site there, that site too would have achieved the sanctity of *Eretz Yisrael.* But having buried her on the roadside in ownerless property, the area remained unsanctified until the conquest by Joshua, and *Rashi* alludes to this in his comment.

ט בְּנַי יוֹסֵף וַיֹּאמֶר מִי־אֵלֶּה: וַיֹּאמֶר יוֹסֵף
אֶל־אָבִיו בָּנַי הֵם אֲשֶׁר־נָתַן־לִי אֱלֹהִים

along that road, Rachel ascended over her grave, and wept, beseeching mercy upon them, as it is said [*Jeremiah* 31:15*ff*]: *A voice is heard on high, the sound of lamentation ... Rachel weeping for her children ... The Holy One, Blessed is He, replied to her: Withhold your voice from weeping and your eyes from tears, for your work shall be rewarded, says* HASHEM *... and your children will return to their own border.* [Based upon the *Midrash.*]

Ramban cites this Midrashic interpretation cited by *Rashi* that Rachel was buried on the roadside so she could later plead for her descendants. He suggests that the Midrash finds a Scriptural allusion to this interpretation in this verse's dual usage of the word בַּדֶּרֶךְ, *on the road,* as if to emphasize the significance of her dying *on the road,* for she died on the road her descendants would some day pass. He observes that Scripture does not fully explain future events but alludes to them in a general manner.

However, in pursuing the literal sense of the verse [i.e. without the Midrashic interpretation that Jacob was Divinely inspired to bury Rachel there on the road so she could later plead for her children], *Ramban* maintains that Jacob was *apologizing* to Joseph for not having buried Rachel in the Cave of Machpelah, where he buried Leah. Jacob emphasized that at least Rachel was buried in *Eretz Yisrael,* in contrast to himself, for Jacob was about to die in Egypt and was anxious for assurance that he would be buried in *Eretz Yisrael,* notwithstanding Joseph's possible grievance. Furthermore, the implication of עָלַי, *on me,* was that Rachel died on the road *suddenly,* and though it was but a relatively short distance to Hebron, it was impossible for him to leave his children and flocks on the road and hurry on to Machpelah, nor could he find any doctors to embalm her for a journey which, burdened as he was with his family, would take at least several days. The Sages [*Moed Katan* 27a] also taught that a woman's bier may not be set down, delaying her burial, out of respect for her body. The Talmud there cites the case of Miriam who was buried near where she died *(Numbers* 20:1).]

Ramban concludes, however, that within the non-Midrashic interpretation, the real reason Jacob had not transported her to the Cave of Machpelah was that he was ashamed before his ancestors to bury two sisters there, since marriage to two sisters was later forbidden by the Torah [*Leviticus* 18:18]. Since Leah was the one he married first, her marriage was permissible; it was the subsequent marriage to Rachel that would have been forbidden, and her burial could not be in the Cave of Machpelah.

[On the justification for Jacob's marriage to two sisters, see *Gur Aryeh* cited on p. 1084, *Chizkuni* and *Pesachim* 119b cited in the *footnote* on p. 1279 and *Ramban* to *Deut.* 18:25, cited in footnote above, p. 1519.

[See also *comm.* to 35:19, and *Rashi* and *Gur Aryeh* to 30:15ff (p. 1304) that Rachel forfeited the privilege of being buried with Jacob in the Cave of Machpelah because she made light of Jacob's companionship (see *Overview* to *Vayeitzei*).

[See also *Ramban* to 35:16 cited in 35:19 s.v. וַתִּקָּבֵר who suggests that Jacob buried her on that very site, on the wayside, and did not bring her into nearby Bethlehem because he foresaw that Bethlehem would belong to the tribe of Judah. He wanted her body to lie in the portion of her son, Benjamin, on whose border her tomb is.]

A reminder of the site.

Oznaim L'Torah writes that in the simplest sense, Jacob specified where he buried Rachel lest Joseph had forgotten it, since he was only a child when she died. After Jacob's death there would be no one to ask. The children of Leah and of the maidservants would not be visiting Rachel's

[8] *Then Israel saw Joseph's sons and he said, "Who are these?"* [9] *And Joseph said to his father, "They are my sons whom God has given me here." He said,*

sepulchre. Benjamin never knew his mother and would certainly not know her burial site.

8. Jacob perceives Joseph's sons.

וַיַּרְא יִשְׂרָאֵל אֶת־בְּנֵי יוֹסֵף וַיֹּאמֶר מִי אֵלֶּה — *Then Israel saw Joseph's sons and he said, 'Who are these?'*

That Jacob is described here as seeing is difficult inasmuch as we are told below [*v.* 10] that Jacob's eyes were heavy with age and he could not see. Furthermore, his inquiring about the identity of Ephraim and Manasseh at this point is puzzling especially since he spoke about them earlier [*v.* 5-6] and the fact above that Ephraim regularly studied with Jacob, as *Rashi* notes in *v.* 1.

Commentators who advance the most simple, literal sense of Scripture (e.g. *Radak; Bchor Shor; Rashbam; Sforno* and others) maintain that Jacob could perceive figures but could not distinguish individuals. In this sense, Jacob is described in our verse as 'seeing' Joseph's sons, i.e., apprehending that the two people were present and asking which was which [see also *Malbim*].

Rashi follows the Midrash. He explains that Jacob wished to bless the children, but the Divine Spirit departed from him because Jacob *saw* [i.e., prophetically perceived (comp., 42:1)] that wicked kings would descend from Joseph's sons — Jeroboam and Ahab from Ephraim, and Jehu and his sons from Manasseh. He therefore said to Joseph, *'Who are these?'* meaning: Where did these sons, who are apparently unworthy of a blessing, come from?

As the *Midrash Aggadah* explains, Jacob meant to ask, 'From what marriage were they born that they should be unworthy of blessing?' [Thus Jacob implied that Joseph's marriage may not have been halachically valid.]

Or HaChaim and *Haamek Davar* cite the Midrashic interpretation, but suggest that Jacob's desire to have his grandchildren discussed and named was to enhance the blessing he was about to confer by intensifying his love for Joseph, his favorite son, and the two grandsons. Similarly, Joseph's response — invoking God's beneficence, and Jacob's hugging and kissing the boys was calculated to bring about the same spiritual joy and ecstasy. See *comm.* to *v.* 10.

Or HaChaim adds that this is the mystical intent of *Jeremiah* 31:19: *Is Ephraim my dear son? ... for whenever I speak of him, I remember him still ... therefore My innards are stirred for him ... I will surely have mercy on him.*

9. בָּנַי הֵם אֲשֶׁר־נָתַן־לִי אֱלֹהִים בָּזֶה — *'They are my sons, whom God has given me here'* [lit; *by this* see *Rashi* below].

Following the simple, literal intimation, Joseph was merely responding to his blind father's query: 'They are my sons whom God has given me בָּזֶה, *in this place'* [the translation follows *Onkelos*].

According to *Ramban,* בָּזֶה denotes: *in line with your earlier statement.* That is, they are the ones you described earlier [*v.* 5] as the sons who were given me by God before you came to Egypt, and whom you are considering as your own. Compare the similar connotation

בָּזֶה וַיֹּאמַר קָחֶם־נָא אֵלַי וַאֲבָרְכֵם:
שני י ○וְעֵינֵי יִשְׂרָאֵל כָּבְדוּ מִזֹּקֶן לֹא יוּכַל
לִרְאוֹת וַיַּגֵּשׁ אֹתָם אֵלָיו וַיִּשַּׁק לָהֶם
יא וַיְחַבֵּק לָהֶם: וַיֹּאמֶר יִשְׂרָאֵל אֶל־יוֹסֵף

of בָּזֶה in *Esther* 2:13: *In this way* (וּבָזֶה, i.e., in the manner described above) *the maiden would come to the king.*

That Joseph was so lengthy in his response, instead of saying merely *'They are my sons,'* is because the righteous are so careful to attribute all goodness to God and praise Him as the Prime Giver. Jacob had similarly introduced his sons to Esau by mentioning that they were *the children whom God has graciously given your servant* [33:5]. Joseph's intent, too,was one of gratitude that even in exile God graciously provided him with these fine children (*Ramban).*

[Following *Rashi's* Midrashic interpretation that Jacob inquired about the origin of the children and the legitimacy of Joseph's marriage, Joseph responded with an assurance that the children were begotten from a marriage of holiness, and worthy of being blessed (notwithstanding the fact that they — not unlike the other brothers — would be the ancestors of certain wicked descendants):]

Rashi accordingly translates בָּזֶה to mean *by this,* i.e., *by means of this document,* and interprets: Joseph showed his father his betrothal and marriage contracts [evidence that Asenath was his wife and not a concubine; that she embraced his Jewish faith since *kiddushin* (halachic betrothal) does not apply to gentiles. This was evidence that these offspring of the marriage were accordingly of the faith of Israel *(Mizrachi; Levush; Zikaron).* However, when Jacob still did not bless the children, Joseph perceived that the Divine Spirit was still absent.] Joseph then prayed to God and the Divine Spirit again rested upon Jacob.

Levush adds that Joseph invoked God in this connection to emphasize that his marriage to Potiphar's daughter was Providentially arranged and undertaken with utmost religious concern and sensitivity.[1]

Pesikta Rabbosi perceives בָּנַי הֵם, *they are my sons,* to imply: They are as righteous as I, and worthy to be mine.

— It connotes that they were legitimate and fit to be blessed *(Sechel Tov).*

Comp. *Ramban:* It means, God has performed miracles for me, so much so that the king gave me this wife, and I have these children from her.

קָחֶם־נָא אֵלַי וַאֲבָרְכֵם — *Bring them to me, if you please, and I will bless them.*

1. The *Midrashim* add that Joseph showed Jacob the amulet engraved with HASHEM's Name that his wife, Asenath, wore around her neck since childhood. The amulet indicated that she was the daughter of Dinah, daughter of Jacob [see footnote, p. 1800].

Thus, when Joseph mentioned God in the context of his reply, he was suggesting that only direct Divine Providence could have arranged for the mother of his children to be a member of his father's family, notwithstanding some unworthy people who would descend from them. Therefore, they were worthy of the Partriarch's blessing.

At this, the Divine Spirit again rested upon Jacob and he blessed the children.

*"Bring them to me, if you please, and I will bless
them."*
10 *Now Israel's eyes were heavy with age; he could
not see. So he brought them near him and he kissed
them and hugged them.* 11 *Israel said to Joseph, "I*

— Having thus been satisfactorily apprised of their identity, and, according to *Rashi,* the Divine Spirit having again alighted upon him.

(According to other Midrashim — e.g. *Pesikta Rabbosi, Midrash Aggadah* — the Divine Spirit did not return to Jacob until he again became joyous from kissing the children and Joseph specifically beseeched God's mercy).

Rashi cites an allusion to this entire episode in the prophecy of *Hoshea* [11:3]: וְאָנֹכִי תִרְגַּלְתִּי לְאֶפְרַיִם קָחָם עַל־זְרוֹעֹתָיו [literally: *And I* (God) *was familiar towards Ephraim, taking them by his arms*] which *Midrash Tanchuma* homiletically renders: I made My spirit once again alight familiarly upon Jacob for Ephraim's sake, until he (Jacob) took them (Ephraim and Manasseh) upon his arms. [See also *Rashi* to *Hoshea* ibid.]

The translation of נָא, *if you please,* follows *Rashi's* general interpretation of the term throughout Scripture. *R' Avraham b. HaRambam* follows *Onkelos* and suggests that in this context the word means *now.*

10. וְעֵינֵי יִשְׂרָאֵל כָּבְדוּ מִזֹּקֶן לֹא יוּכַל לִרְאוֹת — *Now Israel's eyes were heavy with age; he could not see.*

— I.e., he could not see well enough for his blessing to be effective, for we derive from many Scriptural passages that for one's blessing [or curse] to take effect, it is preferable for him to see whom he blesses [or curses]. See for example *Numbers* 23:13: *Come with me to another place from which you can see them; Deut.* 34:1: *And HASHEM showed him* (Moses) *the whole land* prior to blessing it; similarly of Elisha [*II Kings* 2:24]: *He turned around and looked at them and cursed them (Sforno;* see also *Sforno* to *Numbers* 22:41).

[*Sforno* thus explains why this detail of Jacob's failing eyesight is recorded here. He knew who Manasseh and Ephraim were, but there had to be personal contact for his blessing to be efficacious; since he could not see them, he was about to draw them close, to hug and kiss them in preparation for his blessing (see below).]

The Talmud [*Yoma* 28b] perceives the spiritual implication of this passage to be that Jacob's eyes had grown weak from Torah-study and the pursuit of wisdom, the connotation of זֹקֶן, *old age* being a *notarikon* [abbreviation] for זֶה קָנָה חָכְמָה, *he who has acquired wisdom.*

וַיַּגֵּשׁ אֹתָם אֵלָיו — [*So*] *he* [Joseph, or perhaps, Jacob] *brought them* [his sons] *near him.*

וַיִּשַּׁק לָהֶם וַיְחַבֵּק לָהֶם — *And he* [Jacob] *kissed them and hugged them.*

Since Jacob had experienced some difficulties, as noted, in arousing the spiritual feelings requisite for blessing them, he kissed and hugged them to arouse his love preparatory to the blessing. In this way, the blessing would be more efficacious *(Tzror HaMor; Sforno).*

For, as noted *ibid.*, a kiss Kabbalistically brings about deep spiritual intimacy. Furthermore, the Divine Presence alights only where there is joy; kissing his grandsons heightened Jacob's feeling of joy prior to conferring the blessing [see *comm.* ibid. *v.* 27].

רְאֹה פָנֶיךָ לֹא פִלָּלְתִּי וְהִנֵּה הֶרְאָה אֹתִי
יב אֱלֹהִים גַּם אֶת־זַרְעֶךָ: וַיּוֹצֵא יוֹסֵף אֹתָם
יג מֵעִם בִּרְכָּיו וַיִּשְׁתַּחוּ לְאַפָּיו אָרְצָה: וַיִּקַּח
יוֹסֵף אֶת־שְׁנֵיהֶם אֶת־אֶפְרַיִם בִּימִינוֹ
מִשְּׂמֹאל יִשְׂרָאֵל וְאֶת־מְנַשֶּׁה בִשְׂמֹאלוֹ

In so doing, Jacob emulated his father Isaac who similarly kissed him before he blessed him [27:26] *(Tur).*

11. רְאֹה פָנֶיךָ לֹא פִלָּלְתִּי — *I dared not accept the thought that I would see your face.*

Preliminary to invoking the blessing, Jacob makes yet a further acknowledgment of God's beneficence in order to intensify his love and heighten the spiritual efficacy of the blessing *(Abarbanel).*

After mentioning Rachel's death, Jacob became saddened. It is known that the Divine Spirit does not rest amid sadness. That is why Jacob chose this moment to cheer himself by reflecting on God's graciousness *vis-a-vis* Joseph and his grandchildren *(Divrei Yirmiyah).*

The translation of לֹא פִלָּלְתִּי follows *Rashi* who interprets: I never dared think that I would see your face again. פִּלָּלְתִּי is an expression for *thinking;* comp. the noun פְּלִילָה, *counsel,* in *Isaiah* 16:3.

Onkelos renders: סְבָרִית, *hoped,* while *Lekach Tov* interprets: *I never even prayed* [הִתְפַּלַּלְתִּי] *to see your face.* I have utterly resigned myself to the thought that you were torn to pieces by wild beasts, and one never prays for what he thinks to be non-existent. [See Rabbi Scherman's *Overview* to ArtScroll *Siddur* regarding why prayer is referred to as *tefillah.*]

Ibn Ezra [similarly *Radak, Ralbag,* one view in *Chizkuni*] interprets the term to denote *judgment* (cf. פְּלִילִים, *judges,* in *Deut.* 32:31). The nuance here is: I never judged in my heart that I would ever see you again.

וְהִנֵּה הֶרְאָה אֹתִי אֱלֹהִים גַּם אֶת זַרְעֶךָ — *And here God has shown me even your offspring!*[1]

The term גַּם, *even,* or *as well,* always denotes a רִבּוּי, exegetical extension implying something additional to the simple meaning of the subject. In this case the word גַּם is perceived by *Meshech Chochmah* to include Joseph's *grandchildren* whom Jacob lived to see. For, as we learn in *Bava Basra* 121b, there is a Rabbinic tradition — without direct Biblical support — that Machir and Yair, sons of Manasseh, were born during Jacob's lifetime.

12. וַיּוֹצֵא יוֹסֵף אֹתָם מֵעִם בִּרְכָּיו — *Joseph then removed them from his knees.*

I.e., from the knees of his father who had been hugging them *(Sforno).*

1. [I once heard from my father שליט״א that the inner implication of Jacob's expression הֶרְאָה אותי, *showed me,* rather than the expected הֶרְאָה לִי, *showed to me,* was that Jacob was displaying his gratitude to God that notwithstanding the fact that Joseph's children were born and reared in Egypt among immoral influences, they have retained their righteousness to such an extent that *"God has shown* אותי, **me** (in) *your offspring as well"* — i.e., I can see myself in your offspring; the chain of tradition remains unbroken. This is the greatest compliment a grandfather can pay: that his children follow in his footsteps and that he can see in them a continuity of himself.]

dared not accept the thought that I would see your face, and here God has shown me even your offspring!"

12 *Joseph then removed them from his knees and he prostrated himself with his face toward the ground.*

13 *Joseph took the two of them — Ephraim with his right hand, to Israel's left, and Manasseh with his left*

After Jacob kissed them, Joseph took them in order to position them — one to the right and the other to the left — so that Jacob might lay his hands on them and bless them *(Rashi).*

[*Rashi* thus explains the contextual flow of the narrative. *Ibn Ezra* maintains, however, that this detail is not in strict chronological order, and that *v.* 12 occurred after the blessing and sequentially follows *v.* 20. *Radak* and most commentators (see *Abarbanel* below) follow *Rashi's* view however.]

As noted above [see *Rashbam v.* 2], Jacob was sitting on his bed and his feet were on the ground. Thus, his grandchildren had been standing between his knees as he hugged and kissed them. We find, accordingly, that when Jacob concluded all his blessings, he gathered his feet into the bed [49:33] *(Paane'ach Raza;* cf. *Ibn Ezra).*

Abarbanel [who agrees with *Rashi* that this verse reflects the sequence of events] suggests that the boys were seated *on* Jacob's knees. Joseph was concerned that they were too heavy for his father so he removed them from his lap, bowed in filial obeisance, and presented them to Jacob — properly positioned for his blessing.

וַיִּשְׁתַּחוּ לְאַפָּיו אָרְצָה — *And he prostrated himself with* [lit. *to*] *his face toward the ground.*

— While he stepped backward from before his father *(Rashi).*

13. Jacob blesses Ephraim and Manasseh.

[One traditionally blesses another by laying his hand on the person's head, thereby concentrating the supernal blessing upon him (see *R' Bachya* cited end of *v.* 14). The right hand is the preferred one for the performance of *mitzvos* and, accordingly, has spiritual primacy. Therefore if both children are blessed at the same time, the right hand should be placed on the head of the older one. Joseph has the children stand so that Manasseh is opposite Jacob's right hand, but the Patriarch has other intentions.]

וַיִּקַּח יוֹסֵף אֶת־שְׁנֵיהֶם — *Joseph took the two of them.*

According to *Ibn Ezra,* this verse chronologically precedes *v.* 8 and is in the past perfect: Joseph *had taken* the two of them.

The translation follows *Rashi* and most commentators, however, who perceive this verse to be in correct chronological sequence.

אֶת־אֶפְרַיִם בִּימִינוֹ מִשְּׂמֹאל יִשְׂרָאֵל — *Ephraim with his right hand, to Israel's left.*

If one faces another, his right hand is opposite the other's left. [Since Ephraim was the younger, Joseph positioned him on his own right side, facing Jacob's left hand] *(Rashi).*

In effect, by positioning Ephraim with his right hand [and presenting him first] Joseph was unwittingly affirming Ephraim's supremacy *(R' David Feinstein)*

יד מִימִין יִשְׂרָאֵל וַיַּגֵּשׁ אֵלָיו: וַיִּשְׁלַח
יִשְׂרָאֵל אֶת־יְמִינוֹ וַיָּשֶׁת עַל־רֹאשׁ
אֶפְרַיִם וְהוּא הַצָּעִיר וְאֶת־שְׂמֹאלוֹ עַל־
רֹאשׁ מְנַשֶּׁה שִׂכֵּל אֶת־יָדָיו כִּי מְנַשֶּׁה
טו הַבְּכוֹר: וַיְבָרֶךְ אֶת־יוֹסֵף וַיֹּאמַר

וְאֶת־מְנַשֶּׁה בִשְׂמֹאלוֹ מִימִין יִשְׂרָאֵל — *And Manasseh with his left hand, to Israel's right.*

— Thus appointing Manasseh, the first born, for the primary blessing *(Rashi).*

According to *Midrash Aggadah,* since Joseph heard Jacob mention Ephraim first — *Ephraim and Manasseh shall be mine* [*v.* 5] — he became apprehensive that Manasseh was to be degraded from his birthright. Therefore he now presented them in a manner that emphasized Manasseh as the firstborn.

14. וַיִּשְׁלַח יִשְׂרָאֵל אֶת־יְמִינוֹ וַיָּשֶׁת עַל־רֹאשׁ אֶפְרַיִם — *But Israel extended his right hand and laid it on Ephraim's head.*

Jacob extended his right hand diagonally toward Ephraim, who was on his left side *(Akeidah).*

The hand is the organ *par excellence* for carrying out the wishes of the brain, but it is also through it that the Divine Spirit is transmitted at the time of ordination [*Numbers* 27:18], of consecration [*Leviticus* 1:4] and of blessing [*ibid.* 9:22]. (*R' Munk; see R' Bachya* cited end of next verse and *Rashi* to *Exodus* 15:6).

[Apparently, as they came closer, Jacob was able to recognize them and distinguish between them. Otherwise, as offered below, he knew by prophetic inspiration which was Ephraim.]

וְהוּא הַצָּעִיר — *Though* [lit. *and*] *he was the younger.*

Jacob's reason for preferring the younger son is stated clearly in *v.*19 below.

וְאֶת־שְׂמֹאלוֹ עַל־רֹאשׁ מְנַשֶּׁה — *And his left hand on Manasseh's head.*

[See *Malbim* below.]

שִׂכֵּל אֶת־יָדָיו — *He maneuvered his hands.*

The verb שִׂכֵּל [related to the noun שֶׂכֶל, *intelligence*] is to be understood as *Onkelos* renders it: אַחְכִּימִנּוּן, *he put wisdom into them* (his hands). That is, with full knowledge of how he wanted to confer the blessing, Jacob wisely directed his hands for this purpose *(Rashi).*

[Other interpretations of his phrase are recorded below.]

כִּי מְנַשֶּׁה הַבְּכוֹר — *For Manasseh was the firstborn.*

I.e. that Jacob had to resort to this skillful crossing of his hands instead of extending his hands straight ahead was *because* Manasseh was the firstborn, but Jacob did not wish to bless him with the right hand *(Rashi).*

Some [e.g. *Ibn Ezra; R' Bachya; Chizkuni*] interpret the preposition כִּי in this context as meaning *although* — i.e., Jacob *wisely directed his hands* (and placed his right hand on Ephraim) **although** *Manasseh was the first born.* They draw support from such passages as *Exodus* 13:17: וְלֹא נָחָם ... כִּי קָרוֹב הוּא; *Psalms* 41:5 רְפָא נַפְשִׁי כִּי חָטָאתִי לָךְ; the daily *Amidah:* סְלַח לָנוּ אָבִינוּ כִּי חָטָאנוּ; which respectively they interpret to mean: *God did not lead them the way of the land of the Philistines* **although** *that was near; heal my soul* **although** *I have sinned to You; forgive us, our Father* **although** *we have sinned.*

hand, to Israel's right — and he drew close to him.
14 *But Israel extended his right hand and laid it on Ephraim's head though he was the younger and his left hand on Manasseh's head. He maneuvered his hands, for Manasseh was the firstborn.* 15 *And he blessed*

Rashi does not subscribe to this view [and would accordingly interpret each of the passages: *God did not lead them ...* **because** *it was near* (see *Rashi's comm.* ibid.); *heal ...* **because** *I have sinned to You; forgive ...* **because** *we have sinned,* since *although* is not among the four Talmudic translations of כִּי listed by *Rashi* in his comm. to 18:15. Rather, he maintains that our phrase *modifies* rather than *negates* the previous clause and views the passage as somewhat elliptic.

Other commentators also interpret this phrase as explaining the previous clause, but perceive the continuity as follows:

— שִׂכֵּל אֶת יָדָיו, he thus perceived through feeling with his hands כִּי מְנַשֶּׁה הַבְּכוֹר, *that Manasseh was the firstborn.* [That is, the nearly blind Patriarch was able, as described in the beginning of this verse, to direct his hands onto the desired grandson — though he could not see him — because he intelligently perceived through his sense of touch that the one on his right was Manasseh, the firstborn] *(Sforno).*

Daas Zekeinim interprets: שִׂכֵּל אֶת יָדָיו — Jacob intelligently deduced from *his* [i.e. **Joseph's**] *hands,* כִּי מְנַשֶּׁה הַבְּכוֹר, *that Manasseh was the firstborn.* That is, since Joseph positioned one son opposite Jacob's right, Jacob realized that Joseph wanted him to receive the blessing of the right hand. Consequently, Jacob understood that Manasseh was the firstborn; *nevertheless* he placed his right hand on Ephraim's head. [Cf. *Or HaChaim*].[1]

— *He directed his hands with wisdom,* and for this reason he merely crossed his hands because he did not want to slight Manasseh who was the firstborn by *physically* moving *him* to the left. Had Jacob not felt that as firstborn Manasseh merited some honor, he would have repositioned *them* instead of maneuvering his hands *(Chizkuni).*

Malbim maintains that the wisdom of this crossing of the hands was further demonstrated by the fact that Jacob first laid his right hand on Ephraim and then his left on Manasseh; his left hand was therefore above his right, to show that he was aware that Manasseh was the firstborn.

R' Bachya continues that, "The blessing was effected by this laying of the hands [סְמִיכָה] as occurred when Moses laid his hands on Joshua [*Numbers* 27:23] so that the Divine Spirit should be imparted to him. This was also the manner of the *Semichah* — laying of the hands for ordination in the time of the Talmudic Sages — and of the raising of the hands by the *Kohanim* for the priestly benedictions. It is impossible for the *Kohen* to actually lay his hands upon each Israelite; he therefore raises his hands high in order to impart the blessing below from the source of all blessing above. This is the intent of שִׂכֵּל אֶת יָדָיו, *he maneuvered his hands,* for he intended, by means of his ten fingers, to draw the blessings from their source of Wisdom and Intelligence ... Ponder this."

15. וַיְבָרֶךְ אֶת־יוֹסֵף — *And he blessed Joseph.*

We do not find, however, in these verses a blessing directed to *Joseph*

1. *R' Joseph Breuer* זצ"ל would frequently cite the *Ksav Sofer's* understanding of Jacob's intention. Manasseh was the man of affairs who assisted Joseph in governing Egypt while Ephraim was the scholar who devoted himself totally to the study of Torah. By conferring the

הָאֱלֹהִים אֲשֶׁר הִתְהַלְּכוּ אֲבֹתַי לְפָנָיו
אַבְרָהָם וְיִצְחָק הָאֱלֹהִים הָרֹעֶה אֹתִי
טז מֵעוֹדִי עַד־הַיּוֹם הַזֶּה: הַמַּלְאָךְ הַגֹּאֵל
אֹתִי מִכָּל־רָע יְבָרֵךְ אֶת־הַנְּעָרִים וְיִקָּרֵא

personally; the blessing in *v.* 16 is directed to his children.

Ramban resolves this difficulty. By blessing Joseph's children, Jacob was, in effect, blessing Joseph. These were Joseph's only children, and his entire blessing was concentrated upon them. Even if he did have other children, they would be included in the blessing of these two.

This follows the *Zohar:* "The blessing of a man's sons is his own blessing." [*Rashbam* and *Radak* interpret similarly.]

[That Jacob addressed the blessing toward Joseph rather than toward Manasseh and Ephraim directly is apparent from the third-person phraseology in the next verse ' ... *bless the lads'* rather than ' ... *bless you.'* By conferring a blessing that Joseph's progeny will be such that his ancestors would be proud to be associated with them (see *comm.* below to וְיִקָּרֵא בָהֶם שְׁמִי), the blessing was on Joseph, the father of such children.]

According to *Sforno,* Jacob *did* bless Joseph as this phrase relates, but the blessing itself is not recorded. This *unrecorded* blessing is now followed with one for the children. [*Or HaChaim* interprets similarly and adds that in Joseph's case Jacob did not require the preparatory spiritual stimulation of hugging and kissing.]

הָאֱלֹהִים אֲשֶׁר הִתְהַלְּכוּ אֲבֹתַי לְפָנָיו אַבְרָהָם וְיִצְחָק — *O God before Whom my forefathers Abraham and Isaac walked.* [1]

— I.e. Whom my forefathers Abraham and Isaac served in heart and deed *(Radak).*

[As explained in the comm. to 24:40, the expression figuratively refers to one whose righteousness is so strong that he can *'walk before Him,'* that is, alone and unsupported. Comp. 6:9.]

As *Rashi* writes in his *comm.* to a parallel expression in 17:1, the phrase is to be understood as *Targum* renders it: before Whom my fathers worshipped [פָּלְחוּ] — i.e., to Whose service they cleaved. [This avoids the anthropomorphic connotation of 'walking' in relation to God (*Levush* ibid.).]

Comp. *Ramban ibid.* who interprets that the connotation of 'walking before God' is: To follow His ways, to fear Him alone, and to do whatever He commands.

According to *Sforno,* the implication of Jacob's invocation is that God should act in the merit of his forefathers

main blessing on Ephraim, Jacob wished to demonstrate for all time that Israel reserves its highest regard for the Torah scholar, no matter what the qualifications of any others [see footnote further, *v.* 19].

1. The Midrash offers two figurative illustrations of our forefathers 'walking before God': R' Yochanan said: It was like a shepherd standing and watching his flock [i.e., our forefathers were like sheep preceding their Shepherd who cared for them, since all depend on God's sustenance]; Resh Lakish said: Like a prince who walks and elders precede him [in an entourage heralding, as it were, his arrival and presence; so did the Patriarchs, God's 'chariot,' herald His Presence on Earth]. The Midrash concludes that R' Yochanan's view demonstrates how we need His honor [i.e., how we rely on His Providential care] while Resh Lakish's view emphasizes how He requires us to glorify him [that is, since He created all for His honor (*Isaiah* 43:7) He demands that His creatures pay Him due honor *(Yafeh Toar* ch. 30].

48 *Joseph saying, "O God before Whom my forefathers*
16 *Abraham and Isaac walked — God Who shepherds me*
from my inception until this day: [16] *May the angel who*
redeems me from all evil bless the lads, and may my

Abraham and Isaac who walked before Him.

[On the propriety of Jacob's referring to his father by name, see footnote to 49:31.]

Jacob did not include himself with his forefathers, although he also 'walked before God,' because he did not want to consider himself in their category of absolute righteousness *(Radak; Kli Yakar).*

The translation of אֱלֹהִים as *O God* — i.e. *You, O God* — the הֵא being a הֵא הַקְּרִיאָה, *interjectional particle* (as in the exclamation הוֹשִׁיעָה הַמֶּלֶךְ), rather than a הֵא הַיְדִיעָה, *definite article,* follows *Sforno* who perceives this passage as introductory to the following verse.

הָאֱלֹהִים הָרֹעֶה אֹתִי מֵעוֹדִי עַד־הַיּוֹם הַזֶּה — *God Who shepherds me from my inception until this day.*[1]

Who shepherds me like a shepherd. That is, who graciously sustained me from the moment I breathed my first breath unto this very day *(Radak;* comp. *Onkelos).*

Jacob introduced his blessing by invoking the love of the ancients [i.e., his forebears, Abraham and Isaac] just as we do in our daily *Shemoneh Esrei* prayers, beginning first with the remembrance of the Patriarchs. He then modestly added his own merit by mentioning God Who shepherded him, thereby implying that he had followed in God's path like a sheep following its shepherd. When he finished invoking the merit of the ancestors, he began the prayer recorded in the following verse *(Or HaChaim).*

According to *Ramban,* the word רוֹעֶה, shepherd, in this context might be connected with the word רֵיעַ, *friend,* Kabbalistically denoting the attribute of peace and friendship. [The passage would thus be translated: *The God Who manifested His attribute of Friendship to me ...*]

16. הַמַּלְאָךְ הַגֹּאֵל אֹתִי מִכָּל רָע יְבָרֵךְ אֶת הַנְּעָרִים — *May the angel who redeems me from all evil bless the lads.*

[This is the essence of the prayer Jacob began with the previous verse: May You, O God, cause Your 'emissary' — the angel whom You always dispatched to redeem me from all evil — to bless the lads, etc. The prayer-blessing in this verse was certainly not addressed to the angel himself, who clearly has no power to act except as an agent of the Holy One, Blessed is He [see *Rashi* to 18:10]; it was directed to the One Who dispatches the angel, and to Whom Jacob referred in the introductory invocation in the previous verse. The syntax of this translation follows *R' Avraham ben HaRambam* and avoids many difficulties encountered by other translations.

Comp. also *Targum Yonasan: 'God before Whom ... God Who sustained me ...* **May it be pleasing to You that** *the angel whom You assigned to me to redeem me from all evil shall bless the lads.'*]

God performs His will through angels whom He dispatches to act as

1. The *gematria* [numerical equivalent] of the letters of the word מֵעוֹדִי, *from my inception,* equals 130 — Jacob's years before he came to Egypt; עַד הַיּוֹם הַזֶּה, *until this day:* the *gematria* of הַזֶּה, *this* equals 17 — all the years Jacob was in Egypt *(Kedushas Levi).*

guardians of His loyal, righteous servants, and to benefit them, as it is written [*Psalms* 34:8]: *The angel of HASHEM encamps round those who fear Him, and he delivers them (Radak).*

As *Rashi* notes, the expression refers to: The angel whom God *usually dispatches* to help me in my distress. [— May God grant him the authority to *bless the lads (Radak).*] This is similar to 21:11-12: *The angel of God said to me in a dream ... I am the God of Bethel* [where the connotation is *I am* **the emissary of** *the God of Bethel.* See *Moreh Nevuchim* 1:27].[1]

Who redeems me from all evil. — On every occasion of misfortune *(Rashi,* see above);

— From the hands of Laban and in the incident of Shechem [ch. 34] *(Radak);*

— Who saved me from being assigned an evil wife, of whom it is written that she is more bitter than death. As a result my progeny are all perfect *(Zohar).*

The present tense הַגֹּאֵל, *who redeems,* is poignant. For Jacob, Divine Providence is present eternally, always near to man, always merciful ... God's love is inexhaustible; it knows neither past nor future — only the present *(R' Munk* to 35:3).

יְבָרֵךְ אֶת־הַנְּעָרִים — *Bless the lads.* — Manasseh and Ephraim *(Rashi).*

[Why *Rashi* found it necessary to make this comment is unclear, inasmuch as it is self-evident from the context that Manasseh and Ephraim are the subjects. The commentators on *Rashi* struggle with this problem.]

Rosh appears to suggest that this first blessing was directed primarily to Joseph, rather than to his sons who were not mentioned until *v.* 20. Consequently, in his blessing to Joseph himself, Jacob did not tamper with the order of his childrens' birth; and *Rashi* alludes to this by mentioning Manasseh first. Later, when Jacob turned his attention to the children, he named Ephraim before Manasseh.

Perhaps by emphasizing Manasseh and Ephraim's names, *Rashi* implies that it was Jacob's intention that the children merit the blessing not only because they were sons of Joseph but in their own individual merit — as Manasseh and Ephraim. By their own achievements they will earn the privilege of having their forefathers' names invoked, as people will proudly point and say: These are descendants of Abraham, Isaac and Jacob! Comp. the converse case of Ishmael who was worthy of being blessed only by virtue of the fact that he was Abraham's offspring [21:13: כִּי זַרְעֲךָ הוּא] *(R' David Feinstein).*

— Just as this angel had always been dispatched to redeem me, so may he be given the mission to *bless the lads (Radak).*

Sforno perceives the connotation: *O God,* even if [as *Rashi* records in *v.* 8, Jacob originally feared] they are not worthy of Your personal blessing, at least bless them through an intermediary — *command the angel who always redeems me to bless the lads.*

וְיִקָּרֵא בָהֶם שְׁמִי וְשֵׁם אֲבֹתַי אַבְרָהָם וְיִצְחָק — *And may my name be declared upon* [lit. *in*] *them, and the*

1. The Talmud [*Pesachim* 118a] observes that man's sustenance is more difficult [other versions: greater] to achieve than the redemption. Of redemption it is written: The *angel* who redeems me from all evil — a mere angel. Of sustenance, however, it is written *God* Who sustained [lit. *shepherded*] *me.* [Comp. versions in *Midrash Tehillim* 80:2; 89:2; *Bereishis Rabbah* 97; *Pesikta Rabbasi* 33.]

name be declared upon them, and the names of my forefathers Abraham and Isaac, and may they prolif-

names of my forefathers Abraham and Isaac. [1]

May they constantly strive to such heights that they will be worthy of having their names coupled with those of their ancestors, the Patriarchs. We find that whenever the Jews strayed they were identified not with their forefathers, but with those whose evil ways they emulated, as it is written [*Isaiah* 1:10]: *Hear the word of HASHEM, O rulers of Sodom* [i.e. Jewish rulers who conduct themselves like Sodomites *(Rashi; Radak* ad loc.)] *(R' Avraham ben HaRambam* citing his grandfather *R' Maimon).*

It is in this general vein that Jacob mentioned himself before his fathers — first *'my name'* and then *the name of my forefathers Abraham and Isaac.* It is as if he were implying: May my progeny be so righteous that not only I will proudly associate my name with them, but even my more illustrious forefathers will be proud of them and want to associate their names with them. Or in another sense, May they act so righteously that all will couple their names not only with mine, but with my illustrious forebears as well *(R' David Feinstein).*

B'chor Shor interprets: May it be evident from their deeds and behavior that they are my progeny and the progeny of my forefathers. For the Holy One, Blessed is He, blessed our progeny, and when they are prolific and blessed, the world will say of them, 'These are certainly the descendants of Abraham, Isaac and Jacob whom God has blessed,' as it is written [*Isaiah* 61:9]: *And their progeny shall be known among the nations, and their offspring among the peoples; all that see them shall acknowledge them that they are the progeny which HASHEM has blessed.*

Ibn Ezra [in the version available to *Ramban;* see *Karnei Or*] interprets that the phrase means that the entire Jewish nation will be called by the name Ephraim [see, for example, *Jeremiah* 31:19] just as they are referred to as the children of Abraham, Isaac and Jacob.

Ramban disagrees, noting that Jacob said 'upon *them,*' referring to both Manasseh and Ephraim, whereas we never find the people of Israel called Manasseh! However, *Ibn Ezra's* comment may be defended since *Zechariah* 10:6 refers to all Israel as *the house,* a designation that includes both Manasseh and Ephraim. The more probable meaning of the blessing, *Ramban* maintains, is that their line should exist forever, and Abraham, Isaac and Jacob be recalled in them forever.

... *And the names of my forefathers Abraham and Isaac* — but not Terach or Nachor, because righteous men are not called by their father's names if the latter are wicked, nor *vice versa,* as in the Talmudic dictum [*Sanhedrin* 52a]: 'A wicked man is called by his wicked ancestor even if he is the son of a

1. Many *Mussar* writers perceive in this passage an intimation that the true blessing will come when Israelites retain their Hebrew names. They homiletically interpret the verse as follows: Let them be called by my name and the names of my forefathers Abraham and Isaac — and let them not be called by foreign names; and *then* they will merit multiplying like fish within the land.

Indeed, *Mechilta Bo* [*Pis'cha* §5] cites our verse in support of the Rabbinic tradition that one of the reasons the Israelites merited redemption from Egypt was because they retained their Hebrew names.

°שלישי יז וְיִדְגּוּ לָרֹב בְּקֶרֶב הָאָרֶץ: °וַיַּרְא יוֹסֵף כִּי־
יָשִׁית אָבִיו יַד־יְמִינוֹ עַל־רֹאשׁ אֶפְרַיִם

righteous man,' that is, a wicked man should not be associated with his righteous father but rather with one of his wicked ancestors. Thus, this blessing was a prayer that they might be righteous and worthy enough to be associated with the memories of Abraham and Isaac. [For though everything is in the hands of Heaven except whether an individual will fear Heaven (*Berachos* 33b), Jacob prayed that God should assist his grandsons to conquer their evil inclinations, as the Sages proclaimed (*Sucah* 52a): 'Were it not for God's help, one would never be able to conquer' (his inclination)]. David prayed similarly [*Psalms* 86:11], *Unify my heart to fear Your Name (Sforno).*

We find conversely that when Jacob prophetically perceived that some of his descendants were conducting themselves sinfully, he exclaimed [49:6]: *Into their conspiracy, may my soul not enter! With their congregation do not join, O my honor!* [i.e. let me not be associated with those evildoers]. We accordingly find in both the cases of Zimri and Korach — to whom, as noted in the *footnote* to 49:6, these disclaimers refer — that when the Torah traces their genealogies, it does not mention Jacob among their ancestors, thus not associating them with Jacob, whose name would have been tarnished by their actions.

Haamek Davar comments that the invocation of the three Patriarchs was intended to invoke God's blessing in three areas: military security, livelihood, and internal peace and harmony.

[On the propriety of Jacob mentioning his father by name see footnote to 49:31.]

וְיִדְגּוּ לָרֹב בְּקֶרֶב הָאָרֶץ — *And may they multiply like fish within the land.*

Like fish — which are fruitful and which multiply, and which the Evil Eye cannot affect [since fish live in an element apart, in calm, and in unseen depths. Mankind, inhabitants of another element, remain unaware of this carefree aquatic existence, and so do not cast an evil eye upon them. And in any event, the Evil Eye has no effect over what is hidden from sight (see *Berachos* 20a)]. So will Joseph's descendants multiply and be unharmed by the Evil Eye (*Rashi;* see also on עֲלֵי עָיִן further 49:22).[1]

As *R' Hirsch* explains in his *Siddur* (p. 726), just as fish enjoy a quiet but contented and cheerful life beyond the conception of human beings, so Jews who live in the sphere assigned them by God will have a degree of serenity and happiness far beyond the comprehension of those around them.

The *Gemara* ibid. explains that Joseph was worthy of this blessing of immunity against the Evil Eye, since 'The Evil Eye has no power over the eye which refused to feed itself on what did not belong to it' [a reference to Joseph

1. The phrase *within the land* is taken to imply that this great fruitfulness will occur specifically in *Eretz Yisrael* — when they settle the Land *par excellence* — not before. For in the census counts taken in the Wilderness, we do not find that the tribes of Manasseh and Ephraim were more numerous than the others. By the time they arrived in *Eretz Yisrael,* however, the sons of Joseph had become numerous and they required large tracts of land. But since the land was apportioned according to the number of people who lived at the time of the Exodus, the portions allotted were too small for the newly populous tribes of Manasseh and Ephraim.

And so, as theTalmud *Bava Basra* 118a records, Joseph's descendants complained to Joshua [*Joshua* 17:14]: *'Why have you assigned as our portion a single allotment and a single district, seeing that we are a numerous people whom HASHEM has blessed so greatly?'* [*So greatly ...*

48
17

erate abundantly like fish within the land."
[17] Joseph saw that his father was placing his right hand on Ephraim's head and it displeased him; so he

who 'closed his eye' against the advances of Potiphar's wife.]

Onkelos renders: And like the fish of the sea may they multiply among the children of men on earth.

Abarbanel perceives the nuance to be: Although the names of Abraham and Isaac would be proclaimed upon Joseph's descendants, let them not be barren as these Patriarchs were initially, but let them multiply as prolifically on earth as fish do in the sea.

In a homiletical vein, the *Chasam Sofer* once remarked that the survival of the Jews is as unnatural as our verse's depiction of fish flourishing *within the land.*

The literal translation of וְיִדְגּוּ [a verb derived from the noun דָּג, *fish*] as *may they multiply like fish* follows *Rashi.*

Similarly, *Rashi* in *Yoma* 75a comments that דְּגָה refers to *procreation.* Comp. also *Menachem, shoresh* דג, but cf. *Donash* who maintains that even in its meaning of *procreation* the word essentially denotes fish. See also *R' Avraham ben HaRambam* and *R' Shmuel ben Chofni.*

17. **וַיַּרְא יוֹסֵף כִּי־יָשִׁית אָבִיו יַד יְמִינוֹ עַל־רֹאשׁ אֶפְרַיִם** — *Joseph saw that his father was placing* [or: *was about to place* (see footnote)] *his right hand on Ephraim's head.*[1]

עַד כֹּה, lit. *until now* — our members have increased dramatically in the short period from our arrival in *Eretz Yisrael,* עַד כֹּה, *until now (Vilna Gaon).*]

Joshua was concerned that by speaking so openly about their numbers, they were inviting the Evil Eye. He therefore gave them the advice in the following verse [ibid. *v.* 15]: *'If you are such a numerous people, go up to the forest country ...'* His intention was, 'Go and hide in the wooded areas so you will be shielded from the Evil Eye.' But they refused his suggestion pointing out, 'We are descendants of Joseph over whom the Evil Eye has no power.'

Or HaChaim observes that in this regard the children of Joseph are superior to fish in their immunity against the Evil Eye. Fish enjoy their immunity because, as noted, they are covered by waters; Joseph's descendants will be protected against the Evil Eye even when they are **בְּקֶרֶב הָאָרֶץ, in the midst** of the land.

The commentators to *Numbers* 26:54 explain that many children had been born to Ephraim and Manasseh in the years shortly before the division of the land. Since they were not yet twenty years old when the land was divided, they were not eligible to receive plots in *Eretz Yisrael,* but within a few years they would be landless adults. This was the reason for the complaint to Joshua, not that they received less than they were entitled to according to the laws regulating distribution of *Eretz Yisrael.* Joshua's response was that they should conquer land in their *own* portion that was still occupied by the indigenous Canaanites.

1. The Torah does not always necessarily record events in the exact sequence they occurred [אֵין מוּקְדָּם וּמְאוּחָר בַּתּוֹרָה]. There is a difference of opinion among the commentators as to when the incident in this verse took place.

The most common interpretation is that the verses reflect the true chronological sequence, and the attempted removal of Jacob's hand occurred between the blessings of *v.* 5. 15-16 and *v. 20.*

Radak records the possibility that this occurred even before Jacob began the first blessing, but he favors the view that it occurred after Jacob completed the first blessing, and the Scriptural narrative is in chronological order.

R' Avraham ben HaRambam maintains that this verse reverts to describe what had occurred after *v.* 14 when Jacob was about to utter the blessing in *v.* 15. After relating how Jacob crossed his hands, the Torah records the beginning of blessing, and then reverts to relate what had occurred in the interim. According to this interpretation our passage would be rendered in past perfect: 'Now when Joseph *had seen* that his father *was about to place* [יָשִׁית thus having a future connotation] his right hand on Ephraim's head.' [*Rashbam* also appears to follow this view.]

וַיֵּרַע בְּעֵינָיו וַיִּתְמֹךְ יַד־אָבִיו לְהָסִיר
אֹתָהּ מֵעַל רֹאשׁ־אֶפְרַיִם עַל־רֹאשׁ
יח מְנַשֶּׁה: וַיֹּאמֶר יוֹסֵף אֶל־אָבִיו לֹא־כֵן אָבִי
כִּי־זֶה הַבְּכֹר שִׂים יְמִינְךָ עַל־רֹאשׁוֹ:
יט וַיְמָאֵן אָבִיו וַיֹּאמֶר יָדַעְתִּי בְנִי יָדַעְתִּי גַּם־

— The right hand being more honored than the left, and more powerful *(Ibn Ezra;* see verses 13 and 14).

וַיֵּרַע בְּעֵינָיו — *And it displeased him* [lit. *and it was bad in his eyes*].

'Father must think I am a fool and did not position them properly,' Joseph thought, 'whereas the reverse is true: I was quite calculated in how I positioned them' *(Daas Zekeinim).*

Joseph feared that by maneuvering his hands in this manner, Jacob was unwittingly establishing a pattern for all time granting Ephraim permanent precedence [which indeed was Jacob's intention] and this displeased him *(M'leches Machsheves).*

Perhaps Joseph loved Manasseh more because he was the firstborn, and therefore Jacob's action displeased him. More probably he was concerned that his father was making an error, and if he blessed them without knowing upon which son he had placed his right hand, his blessing would be ineffective as it would be without proper Divine inspiration. When, however, Jacob said, *'I know my son, I know'* [v. 19], Joseph was reassured *(Ramban).*

Minchah Belulah explains why Joseph did not react earlier to Jacob's maneuver: At first Joseph thought that Jacob crossed his hands to compensate the younger Ephraim for a lesser blessing. However, when he saw that Jacob was blessing them equally, and that Ephraim would obtain the greater benefit of the right hand, Joseph reacted.

[*Rosh* cited above maintains that since the original blessing was directed primarily to *Joseph (v.* 15), he did not mind; the following blessing was to be directed to the children themselves so Joseph was concerned that the placement of the hands should reflect their true status.]

וַיִּתְמֹךְ יַד־אָבִיו לְהָסִיר אֹתָהּ מֵעַל רֹאשׁ־אֶפְרַיִם עַל רֹאשׁ מְנַשֶּׁה — *So he supported his father's hand to remove it from Ephraim's head to Manasseh's* [i.e., *in order to place it upon Manassah's;* the phrase is elliptic *(R' Meyuchas; Menachem* Shoresh ה*; Sechel Tov; R' Shmuel b. Chofni)*].

That is, he lifted it from his son's head holding it up with his own hand *(Rashi).*

Rashi thereby resolves the ambiguity of the phraseology *supported ... to remove.* It emphasizes that Joseph did not disrespectfully take his father's hand from Ephraim's head and *place* it on Manasseh's head; were that the case the phrase would have read וַיָּשֶׂם ... וַיָּסַר ... וַיִּתְמֹךְ, *he supported and removed ... and placed.* Rather, *Rashi* explains, Joseph thought his nearly blind father had erred. So he gently lifted up Jacob's hand and held it in his own as if to intimate thereby that *his father* should remove his hand from Ephraim's head and place it on Manasseh's (Be'er Yitzchak).

18. לֹא־כֵן אָבִי כִּי־זֶה הַבְּכֹר — *Not so, Father* [lit. *my father*], *for this is*

48
18-19
supported his father's hand to remove it from
Ephraim's head to Manasseh's. 18 *And Joseph said to*
his father, "Not so, Father, for this is the firstborn;
place your right hand on his head."
19 *But his father refused, saying, "I know, my son, I*

the firstborn.

This does not signify that Joseph told Jacob he was doing wrong, for that would have been disrespectful. What he meant was, I did not position the children, as you seem to have assumed, with the firstborn to *my* right and therefore to your left. *Not so, Father* — I placed the firstborn to *my* left and hence to your right, *for this one is the firstborn* — the one standing to *your* right *(Rashbam).*

According to *Paane'ach Raza* this was a politely worded question: *Not so, Father?* — Did I not act correctly in so positioning them? *This one* — to your right — *is the firstborn.*

שִׂים יְמִינְךָ עַל־רֹאשׁוֹ—*Place your right hand on his head.*

Joseph asked Jacob to place his right hand on Manasseh's head because that hand is the conduit through which the greater degree of spiritual power is conveyed to the person being blessed. [Since Manasseh was the firstborn, Joseph felt that he, rather than Ephraim, was entitled to the more potent blessing] *(Sforno).* [See *Pesikta* cited in the footnote to next verse.]

19. וַיְמָאֵן אָבִיו — *But his father refused.*

He refused to remove his right hand from Ephraim's head *(Or HaChaim).*

"The hand," Jacob said, "that — by Divine Power — repelled even an angel, you seek to thrust away!" *(Midrash* as explained by *comm.).*

[See the *Zohar's* comment on the same expression וַיְמָאֵן וַיֹּאמֶר cited in the *comm.* to 39:8.]

יָדַעְתִּי בְנִי יָדַעְתִּי — *I know, my son, I know.*

— That he is the firstborn *(Rashi).*

Thus, according to *Rashi,* this phrase forms Jacob's reply to Joseph's statement that Manasseh is the firstborn. The phrase should not be read in conjunction with the following phrase as if the entire passage means *I know, my son, I know, that he too will become a people (Mizrachi).*

The phrase literally reads in past tense: *I have known my son, I have known;* it implies: I have always known and I am fully aware *(Alshich).*

The repetition of the phrase is for emphasis *(Mizrachi).*

According to *Rashbam:* I did not err. I know that you are wise and that you positioned them correctly with the firstborn to your left, assuming that I would naturally place my right hand on the firstborn. However I acted *intentionally* in placing my right hand on the younger one.[1]

1. According to the Midrash, Jacob was somewhat taken aback by the suggestion implicit in Joseph's words that he had been unaware which of Joseph's sons was the firstborn. His dual response *I know my son, I know,* intimated a knowledge of many incidents: 'I know [by Prophetic inspiration] about the incidents of Reuben and Bilhah, and of Judah and Tamar [i.e., I knew about their motives during these incidents *(Yafeh Toar)*]. If things unrevealed to you were revealed to me, how much more the things revealed to you! [I.e. and you thought I did not know which of your sons is the firstborn! (see *Tiferes Zion).*]

According to the *Pesikta,* the contextual flow is that Joseph feared that Jacob was unaware

הוּא יִהְיֶה־לְּעָם וְגַם־הוּא יִגְדָּל וְאוּלָם אָחִיו הַקָּטֹן יִגְדַּל מִמֶּנּוּ וְזַרְעוֹ יִהְיֶה מְלֹא־

גַּם־הוּא יִהְיֶה לְעָם וְגַם־הוּא יִגְדָּל — *He, too, will become a people, and he, too, will become great.*

I perceive that he [Manasseh] too will become a great people and he too will become great *(Targum Yonasan).*

The phrase is elliptic and intimates: לְעָם רָב, a *large* nation *(R' Avraham b. HaRambam).*

He too will become a people — i.e. his offspring will be numerous enough to be termed a 'people,' *and he, too, will become great* — qualitatively *(Radak).*

And he too will become great, for from him will descend Gideon through whom God will perform a miracle *(Rashi* from *Tanchuma).*

וְאוּלָם אָחִיו הַקָּטֹן יִגְדַּל מִמֶּנּוּ — *Yet his younger brother shall become greater than he.*

Ephraim's descendant will be Joshua who will lead Israel into the Promised Land and teach them Torah *(Rashi* from *Tanchuma).*

In saying that Ephraim would be *greater* than Manasseh, Jacob meant superiority in prestige and spiritual greatness. He could not have meant numerical superiority because the tribe of Manasseh was 60% larger than Ephraim when Israel entered *Eretz Yisrael* (see *Numbers* 26:34, 37). In the *spiritual* sense, however, Ephraim was preeminent because Joshua, the leader of Israel, and Jeroboam, the first king of the Ten Tribes, were Ephraimites. Similarly, when the Tabernacle was inaugurated, Ephraim's offering came before Manasseh's *(Numbers* 7:45, 54), and when the tribes were divided into formations, Manasseh was assigned to the camp led by Ephraim *(Numbers* 2:18, 20). Because of Ephraim's pre-eminence we find *(Isaiah* 11:13) that the entire kingdom of the Ten Tribes was called Ephraim *(Radak).*

Cause, not result.

Haamek Davar maintains that Ephraim's pre-eminence was not the *result* of Jacob's blessing; to the contrary, it was because Ephraim was destined for more greatness that Jacob blessed him. Jacob explained that since Ephraim would be greater, he required a more intensive blessing. Whoever plays a more prominent role needs more of a blessing so that he can carry out his mission successfully.[1]

וְזַרְעוֹ יִהְיֶה מְלֹא־הַגּוֹיִם — *And his offspring['s fame] will fill the nations.*

In its literal sense the expression

of the grave consequences that result from favoritism. He therefore tried to see that his father put his more important hand on the firstborn's head so as to avoid jealousy.

When Jacob said *"I know my son, I know,"* he meant: I am fully aware: I know which of them is the firstborn, and I also know of your sale by your jealous brothers. Nevertheless, I perceive more greatness emanating from the younger Ephraim, and it is upon him that I bestow the primary blessing. Having thus been reassured that his father was acting with full purpose and direction, Joseph acquiesced.

1. **Ephraim's pre-eminence; Torah prominence takes priority over worldliness.**

In our verse, Jacob states the reason for preferring the younger grandson, and attributes the pre-eminence of the younger brother to his future destiny and not to the effect of his blessing.

One may, however, safely assume that this distinction was earned. For seventeen years Ephraim devoted himself to sacred studies with his grandfather [see *Rashi* to *v.* 1], while Manasseh, the supervisor in Joseph's palace, was involved in temporal matters [according to

48
19 *know; he too will become a people, and he too will become great; yet his younger brother shall become greater then he, and his offspring['s fame] will fill the*

filling of the nations is somewhat ambiguous. *Rashi* [following *Avodah Zarah* 25a] explains that it alludes to the *fame* of his descendant Joshua. The whole world will be filled with Joshua's fame and awesome renown when he will make the sun stand still at Gibeon and the moon in the valley of Ajilon [see *Joshua* 10:22*ff* and *Rashi* to *Avodah Zarah* 25a s.v. וְהֵיכָא רְמִיזָא].

Other interpretations of the phrase are:

Ibn Ezra: Many nations will descend from him. [I.e., the word מְלֹא, *fullness,* connotes *abundance,* the phrase meaning: And his seed will become the abundance of the nations *(Neter; Karnei Or).*]

R' Avraham b. HaRambam somewhat similarly: The expression denotes abundant profligacy to a point that they will have to inhabit lands of other nations. It is an allusion to Ephraim's expansive territory.

Radak: This refers to the Exile when the lands of others will be filled with his scattered descendants. [See *Ibn Ezra* to *Numbers* 22:18 s.v. מְלֹא בֵיתוֹ.] See also *Hoshea* 7:8: *Ephraim shall be mingled among the nations.*

☙ What kind of *blessing* was this prediction that one day his descendants — the Ten Tribes — would be scattered among the nations?

R' Munk explains: while it is true that the dispersion was caused by the unfaithfulness and sinfulness of Ephraim's descendants [*Hoshea* 7:8*ff*], Jacob's blessing was not in vain for 'they will return to God' and will have their share in the world to come *(Sanhedrin* 110b). And R' Eliezer adds: 'Even the darkness in which the Ten Tribes were lost will one day become as radiant as the day' [according to the version of *Avos d'Rabbi Nosson* 36]. And in the perspective of history, did not these exiled children of the Patriarchs enlighten the nations among whom they were scattered? They did so by teaching their conquerors the fundamental ideals of the knowledge and love of God, ideals they had never forsaken. Hence they too have a messianic vocation and their Messiah, the מָשִׁיחַ בֶּן יוֹסֵף *Messiah son of Joseph* [*Succah* 52a], also called מָשִׁיחַ בֶּן אֶפְרַיִם, *Messiah son of Ephraim (Targum Yonasan* on *Exodus* 40:11), will play an essential role in humanity's redemption, for he will be the precursor of מָשִׁיחַ בֶּן דָּוִד, the *Messiah son of David.* It is therefore not surprising to find that the prophet Jeremiah [3:12] speaks af-

Rashi in 42:23 Manasseh was Joseph's interpreter]. In this contrast between the brothers, Jacob saw a repetition of other historical phenomena when the moral and spiritual calling was better safeguarded by a younger brother than by an elder. [*R' Hirsch* points to Abel's spiritual superiority over Cain; Shem's over his probably older brothers; Isaac's over Ishmael; Jacob's over Esau; Joseph's over Reuben.]

And so Jacob acted accordingly, with his thoughts on the future of the two tribes of Ephraim and Manasseh which he had just glimpsed in his prophetic vision. His benediction was accordingly aimed at assuring his grandsons זְכוּת אָבוֹת, *the merit of the Patriarchs,* and Divine protection.

Essentially then, we find that despite the privileges due the firstborn, Ephraim earned primacy because of his Torah study.

Thus, *Haamek Davar* observes, the Torah teaches us that Torah prominence takes priority over worldliness. This is an essential component of כְּבוֹד הַתּוֹרָה, *honor due to the Torah,* and the preservation of Israel's spiritual mission. This is not comparable with the case of Zebulun and Issachar where Zebulun, who engaged in commerce, is mentioned before Issachar, who devoted his life to Torah study [see 49:13]. In their case, Issachar's spiritual accomplishments were made possible only by virtue of Zebulun's support, while Ephraim received no help from Manasseh; Ephraim therefore deserved pre-eminence. And such is the rule in every generation.

כ הַגּוֹיִם: וַיְבָרְכֵם בַּיּוֹם הַהוּא לֵאמוֹר בְּךָ יְבָרֵךְ יִשְׂרָאֵל לֵאמֹר יְשִׂמְךָ אֱלֹהִים כְּאֶפְרַיִם וְכִמְנַשֶּׁה וַיָּשֶׂם אֶת־אֶפְרַיִם

fectionately of Ephraim. In this light, Jacob's words, *his offspring's fame will fill the nations* nations,' assume the significance of a blessing.

Onkelos: His descendants will become rulers of nations. [Exactly how *Onkelos* derives this interpretation is unclear. See *Nesinah LaGer; Nefesh HaGer* and note to *Torah Sheleimah* §120. *Lekach Tov explains that* מְלֹא in certain contexts means *defeat* (see *Psalms* 118:10 אֲמִילַם) hence our passage alludes to Joshua who defeated thirty-one kings: *His descendant shall be the conqueror of the nations.*

20. וַיְבָרְכֵם בַּיּוֹם הַהוּא — *So he blessed them that day.*

He gave them an additional blessing that day *(Radak).*

— On that same day that Joseph brought them to him *(R' Avraham ben HaRambam).*

— On the very same day that he conferred the first blessings, he conferred the following blessing *(Sechel Tov).*

He blessed them *on that day* — i.e., according to what they deserved on *that day.* Although Jacob knew that some of their descendants would be infamous villains, he also knew that Ephraim and Manasseh *themselves* in that order, were virtuous and deservant of the blessing *(Kessef Nivchar; Meam Loez).*

According to *Ramban* the connotation is that *on the very same day* that Joseph had urged Jacob to place his right hand on Manasseh's head, Jacob insistently kept his right hand on Ephraim's head and blessed them, putting Ephraim before Manasseh.

It may be inferred from *Rashi* that the term *on that day* refers to the day, whenever it is, that Jewish parents would wish to bless their children. Whenever such days arrive, they will use the text of Jacob's blessing. *Targum Yonason* explains the reference as alluding to the day when a newborn child is circumcised. Sephardic communities have adopted the custom of pronouncing the blessing recorded below on such occasions.

In many Jewish rites, it is still customary on the eve of the Sabbath for every pious Jewish father to place his hand over the head of his son and to bless him with the formula: *May God make you like Ephraim and like Manasseh.*

The *Zohar* remarks that Jacob blessed Joseph's sons before his own because a man loves his grandchildren more than his own children.

לֵאמוֹר — *Saying.*

The word is written "full," as לֵאמוֹר rather than לֵאמֹר. It implies, as is so often the case, לֵאמֹר לְדוֹרוֹת, to repeat it in coming generations; i.e., to have it "fully" affirmed *(R' Munk).*

According to *Midrash HaBiur* and *Midrash HaGadol* the 'full' spelling intimates that he blessed them with a 'full' blessing.

בְּךָ יְבָרֵךְ יִשְׂרָאֵל לֵאמֹר — *By you shall Israel invoke blessing, saying.*

Israel in this context is not a personal reference to Jacob, but a collective designation for his descendants, 'the children of Israel' *(Ibn Ezra).*

When one wishes to bless his sons he will bless them by invoking this blessing, and a man will say to

48
20 *nations."* [20] *So he blessed them that day saying, "By you shall Israel invoke blessing, saying, 'May God make you like Ephraim and like Manasseh' " — thus he*

his son: *May God make you like Ephraim and Manasseh (Rashi).*

Rashi seeks to avoid the misapprehension that Jacob *commanded* all Jewish fathers to bless their children this way. Rather it reflects the esteem in which Ephraim and Manasseh will be held. Ephraim and Manasseh will be so prominent in people's minds, that when one wishes, of his own volition, to bless his sons he will cite Joseph's sons as the model for his children to emulate *(Gur Aryeh).*

You are so pregnant with abundant blessings, that all will acclaim: 'By you is it proper for all Israelites to invoke blessings ...' *(Or HaChaim; Alshich).*

⸎ The Hebrew word בְּךָ, *by you,* is in singular, whereas the plural בָּכֶם would be expected since Jacob was presumably addressing Ephraim and Manasseh.

Ramban explains that the phrase *by you* was addressed to *Joseph,* i.e., *by your children,* the meaning being that the nation of Israel will bless itself with Joseph's children and say to those being blessed, "May God make you like Ephraim and like Manasseh."[1]

Thus *Joseph* will be the model for every *father* in Israel, Ephraim and Manasseh for all *sons.* The highest blessing that can be wished upon a person is that he may be like someone who is generally recognized as a blessed man. The happiest father is one who can serve as a model for all fathers — and that is Joseph. By blessing the sons in the father, and the father in the sons, the natural relation of father and sons is preserved. Jacob says that every family should hope for a good fortune like Joseph's — that a father will lead his children to their grandfather for a blessing, and that the blessing should apply to both generations simultaneously. (See *Akeidah; Alshich).*

According to *Radak,* the singular *by you* was addressed to Ephraim; Manasseh was included secondarily.

Oznaim LaTorah perceives a deeper significance. By speaking to the brothers in the singular, Jacob was implying that the blessing would be effective only if there were unity and harmony between them.

יְשִׂמְךָ אֱלֹהִים כְּאֶפְרַיִם וְכִמְנַשֶּׁה — *"May God make you like Ephraim and like Manasseh."*

Why were Ephraim and Manasseh specifically chosen to serve as models for parents to cite in blessing their own children?

The commentators explain that Ephraim and Manasseh were the first Jews to be born and educated in the highest echelons of an exile-society who remained loyal to their religion, despite the foreign influences and daily temptations of an alien culture. They had never thought of exchanging their Judaism for high social standing or the brilliant political careers that Egypt offered them. On the contrary, they abandoned their positions in the Egyptian aristocracy to join their "foreign" relatives, who were viewed as contemptible immigrant shepherds. In so doing, they

1. In the Kabbalistic sense, the word בְּךָ is to be perceived as denoting the Twenty-two Letter Name of God, corresponding to the twenty-two letters of the Hebrew alphabet with which the Torah is written [the numerical value of the letters ב״ך is 22].

Israel is blessed by this Name בך, as we read [*Exod.* 32:13]: Remember Abraham, Isaac, and Israel Your servants, to whom You swore בָּךְ, *by Your own self* [i.e. by Your designation בָּךְ]. That, too, is the inner implication of [*Song of Songs* 1:4]: We will be glad and rejoice בָּךְ, *In You,* i.e. in the Twenty-two Letter Name by which You are designated *(Zohar; Zohar Chadash Shir HaShirim).* [*For an exposition on the Twenty-two letter Name of God, see ArtScroll Bircas Kohanim* p. 45.]

כא לִפְנֵי מְנַשֶּׁה: וַיֹּאמֶר יִשְׂרָאֵל אֶל־יוֹסֵף
הִנֵּה אָנֹכִי מֵת וְהָיָה אֱלֹהִים עִמָּכֶם
וְהֵשִׁיב אֶתְכֶם אֶל־אֶרֶץ אֲבֹתֵיכֶם:
כב וַאֲנִי נָתַתִּי לְךָ שְׁכֶם אַחַד עַל־אַחֶיךָ

set the example of an upbringing based entirely on an ideal of life, based on strong direction by a father conscious of his duty. They therefore serve as perpetual models for all children to emulate in maintaining their Torah-standards throughout life.

As *R' Hirsch* writes in 41:50, To be the only Jew in Egypt ... and still to raise children who remain for all time the model of Jewish aspiration and blessing is an achievement worthy of emphasis.

וַיָּשֶׂם אֶת־אֶפְרַיִם לִפְנֵי מְנַשֶּׁה — *Thus he put Ephraim before Manasseh.*

— In this blessing thereby giving Ephraim precedence in determining the standard-bearers in the Wilderness — where Ephraim was the leader of the three-tribe group to which Manasseh was assigned — and in the inauguration offering at the dedication of the Tabernacle, when Ephraim's offering preceded Manasseh's. See *Numbers* 2:18, 20; *ibid.* 7:48; 54. [In each of these cases, the tribe of Ephraim is mentioned before Manasseh] *(Rashi* from *Midrash).*[1]

Ibn Ezra, Rashbam, and *Ramban* interpret that the 'putting' of Ephraim before Manasseh was in specific regards to *this* blessing, where Ephraim is mentioned first.

— Jacob thus set the stage for the proper reverence due to Torah Sages. An Ephraim, who engages in Torah study, must precede one who devotes his life primarily to worldly pursuits *(Akeidah; Haamek Davar.* See footnote previous verse, s.v. "Ephraim's Preeminence").

Abarbanel maintains however that the Torah would not have mentioned this obvious fact were it only to be understood in the sense of precedence in the phraseology of the blessing. He suggests, therefore, that the phrase has a more *literal* connotation, depicting how Jacob *physically* moved Ephraim to the forefront, giving him precedence.

21. וַיֹּאמֶר יִשְׂרָאֵל אֶל־יוֹסֵף — *Then Israel said to Joseph.*

Having blessed Joseph's sons and made them two tribes, Jacob once again turns to Joseph and informs him that his descendants will be heir to an additional portion of *Eretz Yisrael,* which Jacob was now bequeathing to him *(Ramban; Akeidah; Haamek Davar).*

1. *R' Shmuel ben Chofni* draws from the various Midrashim and lists seven areas in which we find Ephraim given priority or superiority over Manasseh:
   1. In the Scriptural listing of genealogies where Ephraim is mentioned first [see *Numb.* 1:32];
   2. In the territorial division of *Eretz Yisrael* [see *Joshua* 16:5; 17:1];
   3. In the listing of the standards (דְּגָלִים) [see *Numbers* :2:18, 20];
   4. In the order of the princely sacrifices [see *ibid.* 7:48, 54];
   5. In the fact that Joshua descended from Ephraim. Although Gideon descended from Manasseh, nevertheless Joshua was the acknowledged superior [see *Judges* 8:2];
   6. In the fact that the more prominent kings descended from Ephraim. Jeroboam was an Ephraimite while Jehu was a descendant of Manasseh [see verses cited by *R' Shmuel b. Chofni* in support of this thesis; see also *Mossad Harav Kook* ed. note §105];
   7. In the blessing herein stated where Ephraim's name precedes Manasseh's.

put Ephraim before Manasseh.
[21] *Then Israel said to Joseph, "Behold I am about to*
die; God will be with you and will bring you back to
the land of your fathers. [22] *And as for me, I have given*
you Shechem — one portion more than your brothers,

הִנֵּה אָנֹכִי מֵת — *Behold I am about to die* [lit. *I am dying;* the translation follows *Radak; Targum Yonasan: My time to die* has drawn near].

— And I know that *God will be with you ... (Rashbam).*

I.e., do not think that with my death the Divine Presence will depart from among you; even when I die God will be with you *(Or HaChaim).*

I am confirming my gift to you before my death *(Sforno).*

וְהָיָה אֱלֹהִים עִמָּכֶם — [*And*] *God will be with you.*

— In your exile to save you from all travail; and you will increase and multiply greatly (*Ramban*)

These words were said as Jacob's death neared, and this gave them a prophetic meaning. They assured Joseph with absolute certainty that God would remain with the Jews in their exile and that He would redeem them and return them to the land of their ancestors. And so, these words became an unending source of confidence in God, strengthening and inspiring Jewry throughout the centuries of exile and hardship. Joseph repeats them almost word for word to his brothers before his own death (50:24), adding some allusions Jacob had taught him regarding the signs that will herald the redemption [סִימָנֵי גְאוּלָּה]. And, as *Rashi* points out [*Deut.* 33:28], Moses' last words, too, refer to Jacob's deathbed promise of deliverance for the Jewish people *(R' Munk).*

וְהֵשִׁיב אֶתְכֶם אֶל־אֶרֶץ אֲבֹתֵיכֶם — *And* [*He*] *will bring you back to the land of your fathers.*

— After the four hundred years foretold to Abraham [15:13-16] *(Rashbam).*

... To inherit it *(Ramban).*

Joseph was careful to mention that the land was *of the fathers.* For it was to the Patriarchs, and not to those who would leave Egypt, that God had bequeathed the land. Therefore, Jacob had the legal right to grant Joseph an additional portion in it; this is what he meant by saying, *And as for me, I have given to you ... (Or HaChaim).*

22. וַאֲנִי נָתַתִּי לְךָ שְׁכֶם אַחַד עַל־אַחֶיךָ — *And as for me, I have given you* [in that land of your fathers *(Rashbam)*] *Shechem — one portion more than your brothers.*

☐ I.e., since you are undertaking responsibility for my burial, in return I have bequeathed to you [already, so it does not interfere with the blessing that I will soon bestow on my other children *(Maharshal)*] an inheritance for *your* burial — Shechem. (Cf. *Joshua* 24:32: *And Joseph's bones, which the children of Israel brought up out of Egypt, they buried in Shechem.)* The word *shechem* means literally the city of Shechem: I give you the city of Shechem as your own portion beyond that of your brothers *(Rashi).*[1]

1. The choice of Shechem for this gift is noteworthy.

First, as pointed out by *Maharzu,* in his commentary to the Midrash, Jacob had once purchased from Chamor the parcel of land around Shechem where he pitched his tent [see 33:19]. It was legally his to dispose of as he saw fit, and he now bequeathed it to Joseph. That

אֲשֶׁר לָקַחְתִּי מִיַּד הָאֱמֹרִי בְּחַרְבִּי וּבְקַשְׁתִּי׃

[The Hebrew passage literally reads: *I have given to you one 'shechem' upon your brothers.* The word *shechem* has two meanings: (a) the actual city of Shechem; and (b) a *portion* [see references cited below]. In our passage it shares both meanings. *Rashi* initially follows the Midrash that it means the city of Shechem, citing support from the verse in *Joshua* that Joseph's remains were eventually buried in Shechem. However, that interpretation leaves the word אחד, *one*, unexplained. *Rashi* [see below] therefore weaves in the second meaning of *portion* intimating that Shechem will be the *one portion* that Joseph will receive in addition to the portion he will receive in conjunction with his brothers. Our translation attempts to capture this dual connotation.]

Comp. *Targum Yonasan:* "Behold I have given to you the city of Shechem, one portion, for a gift above your brothers."

☐ Alternately, *Rashi* offers the other meaning of *shechem,* as *portion:*

I have given you one portion more than your brothers — this refers to the *birthright:* [having been bestowed with the rights of the firstborn] Joseph's children would receive two portions [when *Eretz Yisrael* would later be apportioned]. The word *shechem* means *portion* as in *Psalms* 21:13; *ibid.* 60:8; *Hoshea* 6:9; *Zephaniah* 3:9.

[In the most literal sense, *shechem* means *shoulder.* The figurative expression implies that Joseph was bequeathed a 'shoulder,' as it were, over his brethren.]

Ramban follows the latter interpretation, and explains Jacob's comment: 'I have already given you the one thing I could confer — namely, the double portion of the birthright by which you will become two tribes in many respects — to be yours above that of your brothers.' Jacob's intent was conciliatory and he wanted to display his love for Joseph by emphasizing that he had given him as much as he could. The only thing Jacob could confer in the land was the birthright, as he had no power to deprive any of his other sons of their due heritage, and it was to Joseph that he bequeathed it.

⁂ Why was Jacob not concerned that by granting Joseph an extra portion he was provoking the jealousy of his other sons? Did he not witness the unbridled jealousy he once caused by the 'two *sela* measures of fine wool' [i.e., the tunic he had given Joseph, 37:3-4] he had once given Joseph, an act which resulted in the family's descent to Egypt?

The commentators emphasize, however, that in every family, one brother — the firstborn — is entitled to a double portion, a condition that does not in-

site became the eventual location of Joseph's tomb, and according to the Midrash, is one of the three sites in *Eretz Yisrael* whose Jewish ownership cannot be contested since the Torah itself documents their legal acquisition. (The other two places are the Cave of Machpelah, Abraham's purchase of which is precisely documented in 23:16*ff*, and the Temple site in Jerusalem as recorded in *I Chronicles* 21:25).

Second, as noted in the Midrash cited by *Ramban*, Shechem had been in effect conquered by Jacob with his 'sword' and his 'bow' when the Emorite kings gathered to make war on the family in retaliation for the destructive attack made by two of his sons; and Jacob now exercised his prerogative of bequeathing it to his beloved son.

Jacob chose this city as his gift because Joseph's heroic chastity in Potiphar's house had wiped away the degradation suffered in Shechem, where Dinah had been violated by a stranger. The family's reputation for perfect morality, blemished for the first time at Shechem, had thus been re-established due to Joseph's exemplary conduct.

Furthermore, Shechem was the place where Joseph had previously gone to look for his

48 *which I took from the hand of the Emorite with my sword and with my bow."*

herently involve favoritism. Consequently when Reuben's forfeited birthright was transferred to Joseph, the latter was *entitled* to a double portion, without provoking the jealousy of the others.

Da'as Zekeinim adds that only Jacob's display of special favor to Joseph when the latter was still a child, and not obviously superior to the others, could inspire jealousy. Now that Joseph was a king, all recognized that special honor was due him. Moreover, they now perceived that Joseph's dreams had indeed been prophetic and their fulfillment was God's will, and furthermore, from a very practical viewpoint, they were beholden to Joseph, and there was no room for jealousy.

☐ *Targum Yerushalmi* alternatively interprets that the one portion Jacob was giving Joseph was the special garment originally made for Adam, which had been passed on to Nimrod, and eventually came into Esau's possession (27:15) [see footnote to 25:27 (p. 1063)]. It was this garment that Jacob wore when he received the blessings, and which he acquired from his brother Esau 'not with my sword nor with my bow, but through my righteousness and my good works' [see *BaMidbar Rabbah* 4:6; *Pirkei d'Rabbi Eliezer* 24; and *Rashi* below who interprets these as spiritual weapons].

This garment, originally fashioned by God, had passed through various hands, as noted above. It was later used in the investiture of those firstborn who were the primary servants of God in their generations (*Bamidbar Rabbah,* 4). Hence Jacob bequeathed it to Joseph when he gave him the *extra portion* deriving from the right of the firstborn. One may assume that there is a connection between this garment and the 'fine woolen garment' that had been given to Joseph as a youth; it too is called a כְּתֹנֶת (37:3), and ancient Midrashic sources identify it as one of the garments coming from Paradise. The jealousy it caused resulted in a nearly permanent split in Jacob's family and it was brought to him bloodstained as proof of Joseph's death. Now, on the eve of his death, Jacob gives it again to his dearly beloved son, thus confirming that Joseph had always been his choice, a choice Joseph had by now justified to everyone's satisfaction (*R' Munk*).

אֲשֶׁר לָקַחְתִּי מִיַּד הָאֱמֹרִי בְּחַרְבִּי וּבְקַשְׁתִּי — *Which I took from the hand of the Emorite with my sword and with my bow.*

☐ [The translation follows *Rashi's* primary interpretation that the city of Shechem is the subject. He explains that this passage in which Jacob himself claims to have taken Shechem "from the hand of the Emorite with my sword and with my bow" is based on a Midrash]:

brothers and where his deportation to Egypt began to unfold [37:13]. Now, Jacob asserted his legal rights over Shechem and transferred them to Joseph, for as the Midrash notes, justice demanded that when the tribes would be redeemed in Egyptian slavery, they should bring Joseph's remains back to the place where their ancestors had sold Joseph into Egyptian slavery. [Cf. *Rashi* to *Joshua* 24:32: מִשְּׁכֶם גְּנָבוּהוּ לִשְׁכֶם הַחֲזִירוּהוּ.]

In this connection, the Midrash cites the parable of thieves who stole a barrel of wine. When the owner found them, he said, 'When you have drunk the wine, kindly return the barrel to its place.' Similarly, Joseph was stolen from Shechem, and to Shechem he had to be returned.

Indeed, Shechem lord of the city, had offered it to Dinah as a gift [as the Midrash notes on the verse, *'Inflate excessively upon me the marriage settlement and gifts and I will give whatever you tell me'* (34:12)]. Since Dinah's daughter Asenath had married Joseph (cf. *comm.* to 41:45), he obtained his right to Shechem as part of his wife's estate. [Cf. *Tzror HaMor; R' Munk.*]

— When Simeon and Levi slew the inhabitants of Shechem all the surrounding nations gathered together against them, and Jacob took up arms to do battle with them *(Rashi).*

[This Midrashic tradition has been cited in the footnote to 34:25 (p. 1490). There are several versions of it: *Ramban ibid. v.* 13 cites the version in *Midrash Vayisa'u* (see Eisenstein *Otzar Midrashim* p. 157). He explains that the Torah did not explicitly record this incident — referring to it only by the allusion in our verse — because it was a 'hidden miracle,' that is, a miracle which man could deny, attributing it not to God but to Jacob's great natural strength. (See *Ramban* to 17:1).]

That only the *Emorite* are mentioned in this context, though they were not the only Canaanite nation to participate in this war, is because they were the most powerful nation in Canaan and hence most representative of them all *(Ibn Ezra* to 15:16 כִּי־לֹא שָׁלֵם עֲוֹן הָאֱמֹרִי, and *Ramban* to our verse; see below).

The 'Emorite' from whom Jacob wrested the city of Shechem was Chamor son of Shechem. As the Midrash [to 34:2] queries: Was he an Emorite? He was a Hivvite! [as stated in 34:2; see *comm.* there]. — The Midrash answers: He was indeed an Emorite; *Hivvite* [חִוִּי] in his case is an Aramaic adjective meaning *serpentine*. It describes Shechem's serpent-like behavior in the matter of Dinah. [In its exegesis to *our* verse, however, the parallel Midrash reads: *"Hivvite* is included within the category of *Emorite.'"*]

Maharzu notes that לָקַחְתִּי, *I have taken,* might have the legal connotation of *have acquired,* i.e., *bought,* since as noted in the *comm.* to 33:19, Jacob purchased from the sons of Chamor the parcel of land where he pitched his tent. It was the one site in *Eretz Yisrael* that Jacob legally owned and could dispose of as he saw fit; it was there that Joseph was to be later buried as the Midrash points out. [See *Abarbanel.*]

☐ Following *Rashi's* alternative interpretation that the subject of our verse is the *birthright,* the 'Emorite' from whom Jacob wrested this birthright is Esau, who is so called (a) because he acted like an Emorite; and (b) he used to ensnare his father by the words (אִמְרֵי, *imrei)* of his mouth. [See *Rashi* to 25:7.]

[In consonance with the above, it is obvious that *by my 'sword' and by my 'bow'* must have a figurative meaning, since Jacob did not use force to wrest the birthright from the 'Emorite' Esau.] *Rashi* therefore interprets the terms to denote Jacob's *spiritual* weapons — *his* kind of 'sword', and *his* kind of 'bow', the weapons of the righteous: *by my 'wisdom'* [which was sharp as חֶרֶב, *a sword*] *(Mizrachi) and my prayer* [which, like a well-aimed קֶשֶׁת, *bow, sends its messages to its 'target' on High*].[1]

Ramban, Radak, Ibn Ezra and *Rashbam* take the words *sword*

1. **By my prayer and by my supplication.**

Onkelos figuratively renders *my sword and my bow* as בִּצְלוֹתִי וּבְבָעוּתִי, *by my prayer and by my supplication.*

This is based on the *Mechilta* [*Beshallach* §2] and the Talmud *Bava Basra* 123a: " ... Did Jacob take it with his sword and with his bow? Surely as it has already been said [*Psalms* 44:7]: *For I trust not in my bow, nor can my sword save me!* However, *my sword* means 'prayer' and *my bow* means 'supplication' "[i.e. spiritual weapons; *prayer* protects the righteous like a *sword* in the hand of the mighty, and vocalized differently, בְּקַשְׁתִּי, *my bow,* reads בְּקָשָׁתִי, *my petition (R' Bachya).*]

As *Rashbam* in his comm. to the Talmud there explains, the reference is to the prayers which Jacob uttered on behalf of his children, and as a result of which he successfully obtained the birthright from Esau.

The connotation is that Jacob was able to accomplish more with his prayers than Esau with his sword [cf. 27:40] and Ishmael with his bow [cf 21:20], as it says [27:22]: *The voice is the voice of Jacob ... (Maharsha* ad loc.).

and bow literally and interpret them to refer to the *future* conquest of the Land by Joshua, Joseph's descendant, as follows: *Which I* — i.e. my descendants — *will take,* the past tense being often used for the future, particularly in prophecy [...'prophetic past'; in this case, since God had promised the land to Abraham, Jacob regarded it as though it was a *fait accompli* and already conquered]; the *Emorite* is mentioned because it was the strongest of the seven nations, and because, as *Ramban* notes, Sichon and Og were Emorite kings, and the Emorite was the first nation the Israelites battled and with whom the conquest really commenced. [See *Joshua* 10:12; *Numbers* 32:39; *Judges* 1:35].

Comp. *Amos* 2:9: *Yet I destroyed the Emorite before them, whose height was like the height of the cedars, and he was strong as the oaks.*

Ramban continues that *my sword* and *my bow* indicate that the Israelites had to fight for everything they captured, as it is written [*Joshua* 11:19, see

As the commentators note, the metaphor of *sword* meaning *prayer* is similar to that in *Psalms* 149:5,6: *let the faithful exult in glory ... two-edged swords in their hands,* which is also Rabbinically interpreted as a metaphor for prayer. As noted, the Hebrew word וּבְקַשְׁתִּי, and *with my bow* is composed of the same letters as the word וּבַקָּשָׁתִי, and my supplication. The Rabbis in the Talmud prefer this figurative interpretation (a) in consonance with the verse cited from *Psalms* 44:7; and (b) since it is nowhere explicitly mentioned in the Torah that Jacob ever resorted to actual weapons.

According to *Gur Aryeh,* the prayer of the righteous is figuratively called 'sword' since it pierces Above and Below. Prayer is like a bow because he concentrates intensely [מִתְקַשֶּׁה מְאֹד בִּתְפִלָּתוֹ] and to the degree that he does, the prayer is more far-reaching, like an arrow whose flight depends on the pressure exerted on the bow.

[*Meshech Chochmah* notes the distinction between צְלוֹתִי, *my prayer* and בְּבָעוּתִי, *my petition:* The former refers to the structured order of prayers ordained by the Great Assembly, while the latter refers to spontaneous individual supplication. The distinction between the two is that *prayer* — i.e., the *Shemoneh Esrei* prayer, is a prescribed sanctified, service and as such is not rendered ineffective by lack of *kavanah* [devoted concentration]; however, *personal petition* in which one composes his own supplications, is entirely dependent on the degree of one's *kavanah.* Cf. *Taanis 86.* In this manner, *Shemonah Esrei* is like a very sharp sword that can cause injury even if it is not wielded with great force, but private prayers are like a bow-and-arrow — their effectiveness is in direct proportion to the degree of spiritual exertion with which one 'propels' them.]

[See *Harchev Davar* on this verse].

Midrash Rabbah to our verse, however, interprets the metaphor to mean: with *pious acts* and *noble deeds* [for it was by merit of these 'weapons' wielded by Jacob that the Holy One, Blessed is He, granted Jacob the privilege of acquiring the birthright from Esau (*Yafeh Toar).*]

The commentators offer several homiletical interpretations of why *Rashi* interpreted the metaphor to mean *by my wisdom* and *by my prayer.* [Perhaps by 'wisdom' he meant the cunning by which Jacob acquired the firstborn's blessings from Isaac.] But *Maharsha* to *Bava Basra* ibid. sums up the consensus when he writes: 'We do not know why *Rashi* embarked on a different path and put aside the words of the Talmud and Midrash. The matter calls for further contemplation.'

* * *

☙ Joseph left his father looking radiant. When the other brothers discovered that Jacob had blessed him, they became quite jealous. There were two reasons for this. First, Jacob made Joseph's two sons into two new tribes. Second, Jacob had blessed Joseph's sons, while he had not done so for any of his other grandchildren.

The other brothers said: "We can understand why Father made Joseph's sons into two additional tribes; after all Joseph is ruler of Egypt. But why did he bless Joseph's sons and not ours? Just because Joseph has high status, does that mean that Father should increase his status and at the same time give us nothing?"

Jacob replied, *'Fear God, you holy ones.* I promise you that *those who fear Him will lack nothing.* You will lack nothing, because God watches over those who fear Him' *(Midrash; Me'am Loez).*

°רביעי א °וַיִּקְרָא יַעֲקֹב אֶל־בָּנָיו וַיֹּאמֶר הֵאָסְפוּ
וְאַגִּידָה לָכֶם אֵת אֲשֶׁר־יִקְרָא אֶתְכֶם
ב בְּאַחֲרִית הַיָּמִים: הִקָּבְצוּ וְשִׁמְעוּ בְּנֵי

comm. there]: '... *Not a single city made peace with the Israelites; all were taken in battle. For it was* HASHEM'*s doing to stiffen their hearts ... so that they might be utterly wiped out.*'

The first-person *my* sword ... *my* bow implies: By the help of God — Who is figuratively my 'sword' and my 'bow' [see *Deut.* 33:29; *Psalms* 18:3; *II Samuel* 22:3] *(Ibn Ezra; Radak; Ralbag).*

Ramban adds that Jacob used the first-person to imply that it was in his merit that they were victorious; not by their own power, as it is written [Psalms 44:4]: *For not by their own sword did they acquire the Land, neither did their own arm save them; rather Your right hand and Your arm and the light of Your countenance, because You were favorable to them.* Kabbalistically, this refers to the merit of the Patriarchs, *Your right hand* alluding to the merit of Abraham, *Your arm* to that of Isaac, and *the light of Your countenance* to that of Jacob.

Ramban suggests the possibility that Jacob symbolically stretched out his sword toward the land of the Emorites and shot arrows in that direction as a sign that the land would be captured by his children. The later prophets did similar things; compare Elisha's act in *II Kings* 13:16-17. This might be the allusion intended by the past tense *which I took,* for as soon as Jacob did so he regarded the Land as already taken. [*Ramban* elaborates on this theme in his comm. to 12:6.]

XLIX

1. Jacob blesses his children.

Blessings occupy a prominent place throughout the Torah and particularly in the book of *Genesis.* From the time Abraham was given the power to 'bless whomever he wanted' (*Rashi* on 12:2), the concept of blessing played an increasingly important role. That the righteous can confer a blessing is a privilege conferred by God and He provides the metaphysical force that makes the blessing efficacious ...

At this moment in Egypt, Jacob's progeny were embarking on the historic task of constituting an independent nation. Before he died, the Patriarch wished to confer upon them the Divine blessing for success in this undertaking of universal importance (*R' Munk).*

וַיִּקְרָא יַעֲקֹב אֶל־בָּנָיו — *Then* [lit. *and*] *Jacob called for* [lit. *to*] *his sons.*

— I.e., he summoned them *(Rashbam).*

The reference here is literally to his *sons,* i.e. the tribal ancestors *(Haamek Davar).* [*Comp. v.* 2 where *Haamek Davar* interprets that Jacob's blessing was meant for his descendants in general.]

According to a view in the *Midrash,* the inner sense of *called for his sons* is that Jacob *invoked* [God] *on behalf of his sons,* beseeching Him to hearken to them.

הֵאָסְפוּ — *Assemble yourselves.*

— I.e. come from your various residences, and surround my bedside *(Tzror HaMor).*

Rashbam notes that the seventy souls who came to Egypt [46:27] had multiplied greatly during the seventeen years since their arrival. Hence, the term *assemble,* [which implies that a large number of people was involved]. According to *Haamek Davar,* as noted, this was a call to his *sons* only, the verb אסף,

49
1

1 Then Jacob called for his sons and said, "Assemble yourselves and I will tell you what will befall you in the End of Days.

assemble referring to a selective gathering of individuals for a specified purpose, rather than a *general* assemblage of many people.

Compare *Kli Yakar* who draws a distinction between the verb אסף [*assemble*] which in Hebrew denotes gathering from outdoors to the privacy of the indoors (see for example *Deut.* 22:2; *Judg.* 19:18), and the verb קבץ [*gather*] used in *v.* 2 which is used in reference to the assemblage of scattered people to one, not necessarily private, place. He suggests that since, as the Sages maintain [see below], Jacob initially wanted to reveal the secret of the End of Days to his children, he used the verb הֵאָסְפוּ, *assemble,* to intimate that they came into the privacy of his home to hear these secrets; when the spirit of prophecy left him, however, he used the term הִקָּבְצוּ, *gather,* which implies a public gathering, because since he could no longer reveal secrets to them privacy was not necessary. [See *HaKsav V'HaKabbalah.*]

Midrashically, the intimation was that Jacob was warning them against dissension, bidding them to *assemble* and *gather* together, i.e., to remain united even after his death. Only in this way could the true Redemption come about. [See Overview to *Vayigash.*]

The past had shown how much harm could come from disunity, hatred, and envy. When Jacob thought of the family's future after his death, when they would no longer have him as a unifying force, he realized the indispensable importance of unshakable family solidarity. Jewry would face many attacks in the future and its most vital defense would be an impregnable spirit of brotherhood. Jacob requested this unity — then he was ready to deliver his last will and testament (*R' Munk*).

וְאַגִּידָה לָכֶם — *And I will tell you.*

Jacob wanted them to believe that his intention in summoning them was not to rebuke them, but to reveal the future. Since the future is hidden, everyone desires to know it (*Abarbanel*).

[See *Rashi* below.]

אֵת אֲשֶׁר יִקְרָא אֶתְכֶם — *What will befall you.*

Literally, what will 'call to you' ... if there is a *call,* there must be a *Caller;* all events must be understood as messages from God. To translate the related word מִקְרֶה, [coincidental] *happening,* smacks of a heathen belief that history is haphazard. Nothing happens by chance; everything is designed (*R' Hirsch* to 42:4).

בְּאַחֲרִית הַיָּמִים — *In the End of Days.*

I.e. in the Messianic era (*Ramban* and almost all commentators).

This follows the Midrashic view that the expression *End of Days* has this meaning in *Ezekiel* 38:16 where the defeat of Gog is prophesied. (See the *Overview* to ArtScroll *Daniel* and ibid. 12:13.)

Rashi — following the above Midrash — writes that: Jacob intended to reveal the קֵץ, *End,* but the Divine Presence departed from him and he began to say other things [as evidenced by Jacob's ensuing blessings, which, although prophetic, do *not* reveal when the epoch of the Messiah would come to be].[1]

Presumably, Jacob desired to reveal the End of Days in order to

1. The Midrash records that the End was revealed to two men — Jacob and Daniel — but was subsequently hidden from them. Daniel was told [*Dan.* 12:4]: *Obscure the matters and seal the Book,* while in Jacob's case, though he intended to reveal the End of Days to his sons, the Divine Presence left him and everything was hidden from him. Jacob therefore proceeded to speak of other things.

comfort and encourage his children as they stood on the threshold of a long period of exile and slavery. The 'End of Days' is a concept that emphasizes the assurance that good will triumph — a concept that Jacob wanted his children to believe in during their imminent ordeal.

But, as noted in the footnote below, the Divine Presence withdrew, signifying to Jacob that knowledge of the time of the End must remain hidden. However, the Jewish people have another source of consolation, one that substitutes for precise knowledge of the timetable of Redemption. As the footnote states in detail, the brothers assured Jacob of their absolute faith in God, making a declaration of faith in the Oneness of God and in His mission for Israel. If such a faith is truly strong, it is a better defense against hopelessness than the knowledge of when the trials will end; belief in one's cause is more important than knowledge of when he will find relief. When Jacob heard this expression of faith, he gratefully cried out, "בָּרוּךְ שֵׁם כְּבוֹד מַלְכוּתוֹ לְעֹלָם וָעֶד, *Blessed be the Name of His glorious kingdom for ever and ever" (R' Munk).*[1]

According to *Rashbam* and *Radak,*

1. **The origin of the Shema and of the passage, בָּרוּךְ שֵׁם כְּבוֹד מַלְכוּתוֹ לְעוֹלָם וָעֶד.**

In a discussion about the origins of the first verses of *Shema,* the Sages [*Pesachim* 56a] record the following tradition:

When Jacob wished to reveal the End of Days to his sons, the *Shechinah* [Divine Presence] departed from him. Jacob grew frightened and mused: "Perhaps, Heaven forbid, there is someone unworthy among my children [lit. 'in my bed'], like Abraham who begot Ishmael, or like my father Isaac who begot Esau [and this is why the *Shechinah* left me when my children arrived]?"

Thereupon his sons reassured him: "שְׁמַע יִשְׂרָאֵל ה׳ אֱלֹהֵינוּ ה׳ אֶחָד, *Hear O Israel* [i.e. our father] *HASHEM is our God, HASHEM is One!* Just as there is only One in your heart, so is there in only One in our heart."

At that moment Jacob, in relief that God's reason for denying them knowledge of the future was not because they lacked faith in Him ח״ו even to the slightest degree], exclaimed: "בָּרוּךְ שֵׁם כְּבוֹד מַלְכוּתוֹ לְעוֹלָם וָעֶד , *Blessed be the name of His glorious kingdom for ever and ever."* [See *Maharsha.*]

[*Me'am Loez* writes that although it is normally forbidden to address one's father by name, in this case it was permitted, since the name Israel denotes greatness and authority (see 32:29), and as such it was more a title than a name. It was as if they said, "Listen Master." See also footnote to *v.* 31 below.]

The Talmudic discussion continues: The Sages pondered, Shall we say it? [I.e. shall we include the phrase בָּרוּךְ שֵׁם, *Blessed be the name,* etc., during our daily recitations of *Shema*]? Moses our Teacher did not. [That is, Moses did not include that phrase in the chapter of the *Shema (Deut.* 6:4-9). If Jacob's response were said in our *Shema,* we would be inserting something not written in the Torah.] However, Jacob *did* say it. [Therefore, if we exclude it, we would be ignoring Jacob's original response to the first declaration of the *Shema.*] Accordingly the Sages established that the phrase בָּרוּךְ שֵׁם, *Blessed be the Name,* etc., be recited silently [to make it apparent that it is not part of the *Shema* as written in the Torah but that it was uttered by Jacob *(Mishnah Berurah* §61:30 s.v. בְּחַשָּׁאִי)].

Indeed, the Halachah, as codified in *Shulchan Aruch* [ibid.], is that when reciting the *Shema* throughout the year we whisper the phrase *Blessed be* etc. The only time this phrase is said aloud is on Yom Kippur. This custom is based on an alternate version of the declaration's origin. As *Tur* writes in *Hilchos Yom Kippur* §619:

> It is the custom in Ashkenaz [i.e. Germany and the Eastern European countries] to recite בָּרוּךְ שֵׁם כְּבוֹד מַלְכוּתוֹ לְעוֹלָם וָעֶד in a loud voice on Yom Kippur. Support for this is in the Midrash, *Devarim Rabbah (Sidrah Va'eschanan),* where it is written that when

²*Gather yourselves and listen, O sons of Jacob and listen to Israel your father.*

the sense is that Jacob's expression, *what will befall you ...*, was referring to the time they would enter *Eretz Yisrael.* He was alluding to their wars, conquests, and territories.

Haamek Davar similarly observes that in the literal sense, the expression אַחֲרִית הַיָּמִים, *End of the Days* does not *necessarily* refer to the Messianic Age. He cites many references in Scripture where the term is not applicable to events in the days of the Messiah. Accordingly, he postulates, that the expression refers to the *end of the particular era in which the speaker finds himself.* In Jacob's case it refers to the end of his Exile which would culminate in its entirety when his descendants achieved security under the Davidic and Solomonic monarchies. When the Prophets spoke of the *End of Days,* it was, from their vantage point, the end of the post-Destruction Exile which will culminate with the coming of the Messiah.

2. הִקָּבְצוּ וְשִׁמְעוּ בְּנֵי יַעֲקֹב — *Gather yourselves and listen, O sons of Jacob.*

— To my words of retort and chastisement *(Kli Yakar).*

Sechel Tov — following the Talmudic-Midrashic interpretation in the footnote to *v.* 1 — maintains that when Jacob's children realized that he would not reveal the 'End', they began to depart. Then, with the words of this verse Jacob summoned them to remain and hear his words of chastisement and blessing.

According to *Haamek Davar,* the call of *v.* 1 was limited to Jacob's twelve sons, while this verse was directed to all his descendants — who are called *the 'sons' of Jacob* just as they are called *'sons' of Israel.* Since it would have been impossible for such a large group to assemble around his bed, in effect Jacob was inviting them to assemble in some spacious area and hear from the Tribal Ancestors what Jacob was about to tell them.

וְשִׁמְעוּ אֶל־יִשְׂרָאֵל אֲבִיכֶם — *And listen to Israel your father.*[2]

I.e., to the prophecies reflecting the destiny of his descendants he

Moses ascended to heaven he heard the Ministering Angels praising God, "Blessed be the name of His glorious kingdom for ever and ever," and Moses brought this declaration back to Israel. This may be compared to a man who stole jewelry from the royal palace [i.e., Moses 'stole' the declaration of the angels, as it were], which he gave to his wife, telling her, "Do not wear these in public, but only in the house."

Therefore, the *Midrash,* teaches, throughout the year we recite the declaration in a whisper, but on Yom Kippur when we are as pure as the Ministering Angels we recite it publicly [i.e. in a loud voice].

[Comp. also *Devarim Rabbah* 2:31, according to which "Blessed be, etc." was *Moses'* response at Sinai to *HASHEM's* exhortation: *"Hear O Israel, I am HASHEM your God..."* See also *Magen Avraham* 619 §8.]

R' Levi in *Devarim Rabbah* 2:35 cites the view that Jacob's children reassured him of their faith by saying *Shema* as quoted above from *Pesachim* 56a. He remarks that when a Jew recites *Shema* nowadays, it is as if he says: "Hear our father Israel: your command to our ancestors is still observed by us: HASHEM is our God, HASHEM is One!"

[Interestingly, in the Aramaic *Targum Yerushalmi* to our verse, Jacob's response to his sons' recitation of the *Shema* is given as: יְהֵא שְׁמֵהּ רַבָּא מְבָרַךְ לְעָלַם וּלְעָלְמֵי עָלְמַיִן, 'May His Great Name be Blessed forever and ever.' This response has been preserved as the primary response in the *Kaddish* prayer. See Overview to *ArtScroll Kaddish.*]

2. *Malbim,* following *Alshich,* mentions that while writing his commentary to Scripture it became apparent to him that "wherever a verse speaks of the ten tribes in contrast with the tribe of Judah and Benjamin, which remained loyal to the Davidic dynasty and the Temple after the ten tribes seceded to form their own nation, the two tribes are [metaphorically] referred to as *Israel,* in contrast with the other ten tribes who are called *Jacob."* Thus, in terms of the future history of the nation, Jacob's message was: O ten tribes, gather around and obey the teachings of Judah and Benjamin, for they are on a higher spiritual level than you.

בְּכֹרִי אַתָּה כֹּחִי וְרֵאשִׁית אוֹנִי יֶתֶר
ד שְׂאֵת וְיֶתֶר עָז: פַּחַז כַּמַּיִם אַל־תּוֹתַר כִּי

was about to tell some of them. This is intimated by the use of the name *Israel*, which, in contrast with *Jacob*, carries a spiritual connotation *(Kli Yakar; Alshich)*.

Onkelos renders: '... And receive instruction from Israel your father.'

Compare *Sforno: Listen to Israel your father* — accept the way he has taught you all his life. If you do so, you will be sons of 'Israel' and he will be your father, because then you, like him, will be able to overcome angel and man, and you will not lose the benefits destined for you. [See 32:29].

... And accept my words inasmuch as: a) I address you as *Israel* — [the name symbolizing my spiritual and prophetic qualities] indicating that I speak with Divine Inspiration; and b) *I am your father* — so it is only proper that you accept my decree and advice *(Haamek Davar)*.

The Midrash interprets the phrase as if it read וְשִׁמְעוּ אֵל יִשְׂרָאֵל אֲבִיכֶם, *And obey* **the God of** Israel your father.

3. Reuben.

Jacob rebuked his older sons, and the younger ones, by extension, felt rebuked as well. He did not rebuke them, however, until shortly before his death, because, as *Sifre Devarim* §2 records, Jacob said to Reuben: 'Reuben, my son, I did not rebuke you all these years so that you would not leave me and stay with my brother, Esau.'

רְאוּבֵן בְּכֹרִי אַתָּה — *Reuben, you are my firstborn.*

Jacob begins by giving tribute to Reuben's position, recounting what he should have achieved as firstborn, then he explains why Reuben lost those privileges. The contextual flow, as *Rashbam* explains it, is: *Reuben, you are my firstborn,* and as such you are *my strength,* etc.

כֹּחִי — *My strength.*

I.e., with your birth, my potential strength began to be realized *(Ibn Ezra)*.

Unlike Jacob himself who acquired his birthright by purchase from Esau, Reuben was the *biological* firstborn, and as such should have been Jacob's *spiritual* heir, since the firstborn can be expected to acquire more of his father's spirituality than the other sons *(Haamek Davar)*.

וְרֵאשִׁית אוֹנִי — *And my initial vigor.*

The term און refers to *strength* [see *Hosh.* 12:9; *Isaiah* 40:26, 29] *(Rashi)*.

In the literal sense this stich rephrases the previous stich, in the usual style of Scriptural poetry *(Rashbam)*.

[*Rashi* follows the Rabbinic interpretation that since nothing in Scripture is superfluous, each stich has quite a distinct meaning of its own:]

My initial vigor — that is, you were born of the first drop of my semen, for Jacob had never experienced a seminal discharge in his life *(Rashi; Tanchuma Yashan)*.

Thus, Reuben was conceived from Jacob's first intimacy with Leah. Though it is axiomatic in Rabbinic literature [*Yevamos* 34a] that 'a woman does not conceive from the first intimacy,' *Tosafos (ibid.* 76a s.v. שֶׁלֹּא) offers that in this case, as in the case of Tamar [38:18] special preparations were made [מִיעֲכָה בְּאֶצְבָּעָהּ] to facilitate conception. [See *Torah Sheleimah, Addendum* to 49:3 for a full discussion of this topic].

3 Reuben, you are my firstborn,
my strength and my initial vigor,
foremost in rank and foremost in power.
4 Water-like impetuousity — you cannot be foremost,

יֶתֶר שְׂאֵת וְיֶתֶר עָז — *Foremost* [lit. *excess*] *in rank* [lit. *elevation; uplifting*] *and foremost in power.*

Since you were the firstborn, you should have been superior to your brothers in two major areas: priesthood [שְׂאֵת, *rank*] and kingship [עָז, *power*]. The term שְׂאֵת, lit. *uplifting,* alludes to priesthood because the *kohanim* 'lift their hands' to confer the Priestly Blessing [*Lev.* 29:22]; the term עָז, *power,* refers to kingship, the meaning it has in *I Samuel* 2:10 (*Rashi;* comp. *Onkelos).*

In defining שְׂאֵת as *eminence, R' Hirsch* cites this meaning of the word in *Job* 12:11 and *Psalms* 62:5. As the firstborn you have the responsibility to be נָשִׂיא [prince: the 'elevated one'] of your brothers, the leader of the entire family ... a leader must bear the greatest burden; commensurately he must have greater power than his followers. Consequently, it may be that the word נָשִׂיא comes from the root נשא, *to bear.*

4. However, you have forfeited all these privileges.

What was responsible for this forfeiture? *(Rashi)*...

פַּחַז כַּמַּיִם אַל־תּוֹתַר — *Water-like impetuosity* [see *Rashi* below] — *you cannot be foremost.*

Because of the פַּחַז, *impetuosity* and haste with which you rushed to vent your anger [in the incident with Bilhah; see below], a hasty recklessness *like that of fast-flowing waters* — therefore אַל־תּוֹתַר *you cannot be foremost,* you do not deserve to partake of the abundant superiorities that were designated for you *(Rashi).*

As noted in the comm. to 35:22, Reuben had repented. Although his repentance restored him to his status as a righteous individual, he was nevertheless disqualified from leadership of the family *(R' Munk).*

Actually, this forfeiture of special status applied only in later times. While in Egypt Reuben *did* exercise certain superiority over the other tribes as mentioned in *Bamidbar Rabbah* §13 *(Haamek Davar v.* 2).

Targum Yonasan [following the Midrash] interpretively comments: But because you sinned, my son, the birthright is given to Joseph[1], the kingship to Judah, and the priesthood to Levi. [Comp. *Rashi* to 35:23].

The Midrash notes that, Reuben's sin notwithstanding, Jacob did not reject him *entirely.* 'I am not alienating you outright, nor am I drawing you closer. I will leave the question of your status for the future. One day there will arise a leader of Israel by the name of Moses; he will deal with you as he sees fit.' Indeed, Moses prayed for Reuben and rehabilitated him morally when he began his blessing of the tribe by say-

1. The birthright [i.e., the distinction of being considered *two* tribes] was transferred to Joseph [with the result that his sons, Ephraim and Menasseh, became separate tribes *(Rashi* from *Berachos* 7b; *Rashi* to 35:22)]. This is clearly stated in *I Chronicles* 5:1: *But since he* [Reuben] *desecrated his father's couch, his birthright was given to the sons of Joseph the son of Israel.*

The *Zohar* explains why it was granted to Joseph. When Jacob married Leah he thought he was marrying Rachel [29:25], in which case Rachel's oldest, Joseph, would have been the first born. Therefore, when the birthright was taken from Reuben, it was given to Joseph since it was originally destined to be his.

עָלִיתָ מִשְׁכְּבֵי אָבִיךָ אָז חִלַּלְתָּ יְצוּעִי עָלָה:

ing, *May Reuben live and not die!* [*Deut.* 33:6].

Rashi translates פַּחַז as a [segolate] noun, observing that it is similar to שַׁעַר, נַעַר (*Dikdukei Rashi*). It is therefore accented [with its cantillation] on the first syllable [פַּ] and the entire word is vowelized with *patachs.* Were it a verb in the past tense [meaning: *he was* impetuous], it would have been vowelized פָּחַז, with a *kametz* and a *patach,* and with the accent on the last syllable [חַז].

Ramban similarly renders it as a noun, explaining the term as *hastiness, impulsiveness,* drawing a parallel from *Judges* 9:4 and from the Aramaic expression פְּחִיזָא, *reckless.* He also postulates that the term פַּחַז might be a permutation of חִפָּזוֹן, *haste. Ralbag* and *Radak,* too, render it as referring to people who lack stability and act impulsively and impetuously.

According to the above comments, Jacob was telling Reuben: In your impetuous haste you ascended my couch like a rising and gushing torrent of water. (Compare the Scriptural description of uncontrollably gushing water in *Isaiah* 8:7f.)

— Through your haste and rash temper you irreversibly forfeited your pre-eminence; your action cannot be corrected any more than spilled water can be regathered *(Akeidas Yitzchak).*

— As water is poured from place to place, so have your privileges been poured away *(Midrash).*

— You were afraid that if I lived with Bilhah, I would have more children, with whom you and your brothers would have to share my estate. By recklessly and impetuously tampering with Bilhah's bed, you sought to prevent the growth of my family and avoid a diminution of your inheritance. You will be punished measure for measure; instead of safeguarding your inheritance, you will lose your firstborn portion [see *Ramban* 35:22]; אַל תּוֹתַר, *you will have no gain from it,* only loss *(Ramban).*

Ibn Ezra cites several interpretations: — פָּחַז כַּמַּיִם, *O You who acted impetuously, like water that is spilled out with nothing left behind,* consequently אַל תּוֹתַר, *you will not have pre-eminence. Ibn Ezra* rejects this interpretation on the grounds that the second phrase should have been vowelized אַל תּוּתַר according to this view.

— Others say: *You who acted like someone who poured out water and* [אַל תּוֹתַר] *left nothing behind in the vessel. Ibn Ezra* rejects this because אַל must be understood in the imperative sense, not as a simple statement of fact.

Ibn Ezra concludes by citing *R' Saadiah Gaon:* פַּחַז כַּמַּיִם, *Even in as trivial a thing as water,* אַל תּוֹתַר, *do not aspire to pre-eminence. Ibn Ezra* concurs, noting that *pachaz* means *empty, trivial* [see his comm. to *Judges* 9:4] and is not a permutation of פחז *hurry.*

In the Talmud [*Shabbos* 55b] the word *pachaz* is homiletically interpreted as an acronym, combining the initial letters of several words. Among the several interpretatons of the acronym is: פַּזְתָּ, חַבְתָּ, זַלְתָּ, **pa**z*tah* [you were hasty], **cha**v*tah* [you were guilty], **za**l*tah* [you acted disgracefully].

And what was the unstable act committed by Reuben? *(Rashi)* ...

כִּי עָלִיתָ מִשְׁכְּבֵי אָבִיךָ — *Because you mounted your father's bed.*

Onkelos renders, *because you went up to your father's bedroom.*

As discussed in *Shabbos* 55b, Jacob's reference was to the incident after Rachel's death, which is delicately alluded to in 35:22. In an attempt to move Jacob's primary residence from Bilhah's tent into that of his mother Leah, Reuben tampered with his father's bed. Scripturally, Reuben's interfering with his father's conjugal bed is considered as such a moral offense, that the Torah [35:22] charges him as if he had actually sinned with Bilhah [see commentary there].

From all this it is evident that the incident referred to could not have been one in which Reuben had *actually* sinned with Bilhah as is implied by the blunt expression וַיִּשְׁכַּב אֶת בִּלְהָה, *Reuben 'lay' with Bilhah* [35:22]. To a son who was the strength and first of his father's vigor, one to whom superiority in rank and power belonged, an offense which otherwise would be considered quite lightly, is taken most seriously. Had Reuben actually committed a *real* sin, surely Jacob would not have used so mild and gentle an epithet as פַּחַז כַּמַּיִם, *water-like impetuosity (R' Hirsch).*

According to another view in the Midrash [cf. also *Daas Zekeinim*], the reference is to the episode of the *dudaim* that Reuben gathered for his mother [30:14ff]. As a result of Reuben's gift, Jacob spent the night with Leah rather than Rachel [ibid. *v.* 16]. Jacob resentfully considered this as tampering with his beds, and now castigated Reuben for that invasion of his conjugal privacy.

אָז חִלַּלְתָּ יְצוּעִי עָלָה — *Then* [or: *thus*] *you desecrated Him Who ascended my couch* [lit. *then you desecrated — my couch He ascended!*].

— I.e., by interfering with my bed you desecrated the Name of the Divine Presence that used to ascend [i.e. hover above] my couch *(Rashi).*

Rashi's interpretation of this phrase follows the Talmud (*Shabbos* 55b), according to which Reuben — in the incident with Bilhah [35:22; see above] — had, in effect, transposed *two* couches, that of the Divine Presence and that of Jacob. Thus, by his vile act, Reuben desecrated the Name of the Divine Presence, as well as the honor of his father.

Rashi there explains that this interpretation is based upon the use of the third person עָלָה, *He* [*i.e., God*] *ascended*, rather than the second person עָלִיתָ, *you* ascended. Furthermore, *Rashi* writes, before the Tent of Meeting ['dwelling place' of God's Presence in the Tabernacle] was constructed, God's Presence rested in the tents of the righteous. Jacob placed a couch for the Divine Presence in the tents of each of his wives, and wherever the Divine Presence came to 'rest' so to speak, there Jacob spent the night.

Ramban cites the Talmudic interpretation that the object of the 'desecration' was the Divine Presence, which abided above Jacob's couch. He points to *I Chronicles* 5:1, however, which clearly states that it was *his father's couch* that Reuben defiled, and not that of the Divine Presence. *Ramban* resolves this difficulty by suggesting that it was indeed the Divine Presence that was defiled, but out of respect for God, Scripture avoids explicitly stating that Reuben desecrated the *Shechinah; I Chronicles,* therefore, speaks euphemistically of Jacob's couch.

Ramban proceeds to suggest that Jacob might have been referring only to the desecration of his personal honor, the tenor of his charge being: 'Then you defiled *me.'* In deference to his own self-respect, however, Jacob spoke in third person: *then you desecrated my couch* which **'he,'** i.e., I, your father used to *ascend.* Similarly, the passage in *I Chronicles* 5:1: *inasmuch as he desecrated his father's couch,* is also a Scriptural euphemism meaning that Reuben desecrated Jacob whose couch it was.

According to *Chizkuni,* Jacob addressed to Reuben only the first words of this phrase: אָז חִלַּלְתָּ, *then you desecrated.* He then turned to his other sons, and incredulously

5 שִׁמְעוֹן וְלֵוִי אַחִים כְּלֵי חָמָס מְכֵרֹתֵיהֶם:

exclaimed, 'Do not wonder why I speak so harshly to him; יְצוּעִי עָלָה, *he ascended my couch!'*

B'chor Shor interprets: *Then you desecrated the one* [i.e. yourself] *who ascended my couch!* That is, by your act of *'climbing up' to your father's bed,* you — the one who perpetrated this invasion of my privacy — desecrated *yourself* by forfeiting thereby many of the privileges that would otherwise have been yours as firstborn. Thus the verse reads in *I Chronicles* 5: *And when he desecrated his father's couch, his birthright was given to Joseph.*

... *My* couch, however, remained עָלָה, *lofty* and inviolable *(R' Saadiah Gaon).* Your impetuous indiscretion is all the more serious because of my couch's unusual degree of sanctity. Since not one of my children was unfit — like Ishmael or Esau in the case of my grandfather and father respectively — to be a member of the chosen people יְצוּעִי עָלָה, *my couch was loftier* than that of my forefathers. How could you desecrate such a couch! *(Tosafos HaRosh).*

Radak renders עָלָה as *removed* [see *Psalms* 102:25], interpreting: 'From the very day on which you perpetrated that desecration, יְצוּעִי עָלָה, *my couch was removed from me,'* for ever since that day Jacob never consorted with Bilhah.

The word יָצוּעַ means *couch; bed.* It is so called because it is *spread* [root יצע] with pads and linens. The term occurs frequently in Scripture; see for example *Psalms* 3:7, 132:3 *(Rashi).*

5. Simeon and Levi.

Having explained why Reuben forfeited the prerogatives of the birthright, Jacob proceeds to explain why Simeon and Levi, the next oldest, were also unworthy of kingship. Men of the sword are unworthy of being 'the king who by *justice* establishes the land' [*Proverbs* 29:4] *(Sforno; Abarbanel; Malbim).*

שִׁמְעוֹן וְלֵוִי אַחִים — *Simeon and Levi are comrades* [lit. *brothers*].

[The word אַחִים cannot be taken in its literal, biological sense, for *all* of Jacob's sons were *brothers.* Rather, as the commentators explain, the sense is they are a *pair* and *acted* like one:]

That is, they are *real* brothers in the sense that they unite in fraternity and brotherhood in counsel and deed *(Ramban;* see below).

— They harbored the same thoughts in the conspiracies against Shechem and Joseph. [Although the Torah does not specifically mention that Simeon and Levi instigated the plot against Joseph] it is clear that the passage [37:19]: *And they said man to his brother ... "So, now, come and let us kill him,"* can refer only to them. It could not refer to Reuben and Judah, since they were opposed to slaying Joseph [37:21-26]; it could not refer to the sons of Bilhah and Zilpah [Dan, Naftali, Gad or Asher], since Joseph befriended them [37:2] and their hatred for him was not so great; Issachar and Zevulun [Leah's youngest sons] are ruled out because they would not have presumptuously suggested such a serious course before their elders. Consequently, the reference there must be to Simeon and Levi whom their father now described as *comrades (Rashi* from *Tanchuma).*

Actually, one could refute *Rashi's* argument. If Issachar and Zevulun are ruled out because they would not have spoken presumptuously before their elders, Simeon and Levi too should be ruled out since their older brother, Reuben, was present at the time. However, because they were capable of taking strong initiatives, as demonstrated by their activity in Shechem, it could be expected that they *would* speak up even in the presence of an older brother. Furthermore,

5 **S**imeon and Levi are comrades,
their weaponry is a stolen craft.

this is a classic example of the Rabbinic axiom [*Bereishis Rabbah* 36:11] of תוֹלִין הַקַּלְקָלָה בִּמְקוּלְקָל, *we may assume that an improper deed was done by a person who acts improperly* [i.e., if two unacceptable acts were committed, we presume that someone already known to have to committed such an act committed the new one as well.] This concept is discussed in the comm. to 36:2 (p. 1534). [Cf. *Pesachim* 9b.] *(Divrei David).*

The Midrash interprets: *Simeon and Levi are brothers.* — You acted as 'brothers' when you avenged your sister Dinah in the matter of Shechem [the Midrash cites 34:25 where Simeon and Levi are referred to in that context as *brothers of Dinah* because they had come to her defense]; but you were not 'brothers' to Joseph whom you sold.

Ramban suggests that in this blessing Jacob might have been defending their behavior in the matter of Shechem, for they had acted with *brotherly zeal* in defense of their wronged sister. Jacob was implying that were it not for this extenuating circumstance, Simeon and Levi would have deserved great punishment since the citizens of Shechem were innocent and not liable to the death penalty. [This is consistent with *Ramban's* interpretation in 34:14. It differs substantially from *Rambam.* See dissertation: "The collective responsibility of the people of Shechem" on p. 1480.]

כְּלֵי חָמָס מְכֵרֹתֵיהֶם — *Their weaponry is a stolen craft.*

The Sages understand Scripture's use of the term חָמָס to be essentially synonymous with גֶּזֶל, *robbery*, the distinction being merely in degree and magnitude of the crime: חָמָס referring to petty robbery and cases where one takes by force but gives money in return (see *comm.* and Midrash to 6:11; *Bava Kamma* 62a; and *comm.* ad loc.). [Some commentators to 6:11 broaden the connotation to include other forms of social *violence* as well.] In the figurative sense, however, the term חָמָס may refer to the imitation of someone else's form of behavior. It is in this latter sense that *Rashi* perceives it here in his primary interpretation.

— Your preoccupation with murder [that is, the wielding of מְכֵרֹת, *weaponry* (see below), as illustrated by your participation in murderous plots] is not a Jewish trait; you have *usurped* this behavior from Esau whose blessings included [27:40]: *By your sword you shall live.* Such preoccupations should be *his,* and you usurped it from him. The term מְכֵרֹת denotes *weaponry.* In Greek the word for *sword* is *machaira (Rashi* from *Midrash).*

Drawing from an alternate interpretation in the Midrash, *Rashi* records an opinion that the term מְכֵרֹתֵיהֶם means their *dwelling place* [=מְגֻרֹתֵיהֶם, the letters ג and כ being interchangeable]. He renders: [*They introduced*] כְּלֵי חָמָס, *instruments of plunder* (lit. *robbery),* מְכֵרֹתֵיהֶם, [*in*] *their habitations,* i.e., they accustomed themselves to the use of weaponry even in *Eretz Yisrael,* the land meant for the habitation of Israel. Comp. the term מְכֹרֹתַיִךְ in *Ezekiel* 16:3. *Rashi* concludes that 'this is how *Onkelos* renders the passage.'

Onkelos literally reads: 'Mighty men — in the land of their dwelling they did mightily,' [*Onkelos* is thus metaphorically referring to Simeon and Levi themselves as כְּלֵי חָמָס, *weapons of plunder,* just as in *II Sam.* 1:27 Saul and Jonathan are referred to as כְּלֵי מִלְחָמָה, *weapons of war (*see *Rashi* there).]

Ibn Ezra and *Radak* render similarly, explaining that מְכֵרֹתֵיהֶם, *their dwelling place,* is to be interpreted as if it read **בִּמְכֵרֹתֵיהֶם, in** *their dwelling place.* Scripture often uses such elliptic constructions. See, for example, *II Kings* 16:8 בֵּית ה׳=בְּבֵית ה׳; *I Samuel* 2:29

בִּמְעוֹן=מָעוֹן. The sense here accordingly is: *They wielded weapons of plunder in the land of their dwelling* with their neighbors with whom they dwelt peaceably and had no reason to go to war.

According to *Ramban*, the intimation of מְגֻרֹתַיִךְ=מְכֹרֹתַיִךְ, *their dwelling places*, in our context is that *the essence of their lives*, i.e. the means by which they sustain themselves, is *their instrument of plunder*. Comp. מְגוּרֵיהֶם above 47:9.

Rashbam also relates מְכֵרֹתֵיהֶם to מְכֹרֹתַיִךְ in *Ezekiel* 16:3, but he interprets it as *kinship*. He suggests that this stich parallels the first, the contextual flow being: 'Simeon and Levi are comrades, *weapons of plunder are their kinship*,' [i.e. their kinship is based on violence]. *B'chor Shor* interprets similarly, relating מְכֹרֹתַיִךְ to מַכָּרוֹ, *his acquaintance*, in *II Kings* 12:6, the sense here being: *their affinity for one another is based upon the sword of plunder;* much plunder resulted from their scheming. *Sechel Tov* similarly relates the term to *recognize:* They are *recognized* as men of plunder.

6. בְּסֹדָם אַל־תָּבֹא נַפְשִׁי — *Into their conspiracy, may my soul not enter!*

Jacob was disclaiming any knowledge of their plot when they answered Shechem and his father Chamor *'cleverly'* [see 34:13]. As mentioned earlier, Jacob was angry with them lest people think that their evil scheme was suggested by him, a charge which might result in the profanation of God's Name (*Ramban*).

Thus, in the literal sense, Jacob is pronouncing a denial, emphasizing that Simeon and Levi's murders in Shechem were not in Jacob's behalf or with his consent. The future [imperfect] tense, *may not enter*, is used here in place of the past tense, *had not entered* (*Akeidah; Ralbag*).

This follows *Radak* and many other 'literal' commentators who maintain that both this stich and the next are examples of 'parallelism' — that Jacob expressed the same thought in different ways, referring in both cases to the incident of Shechem.

According to the Midrash, however [see *Rashi* in footnote below], since nothing in the Torah is superfluous, both stiches must be allusions to *different* incidents. The use of the future tense תֵּחַד ... תָּבֹא, *shall come ... shall join*, indicates that they refer prophetically to incidents that would occur in the lives of Simeon and Levi's *descendants*. The end of the passage, which employs past tense verbs, refers to incidents perpetrated by Simeon and Levi themselves. Jacob does not want his name connected with any wrong the two have done in the past, or will do in the future.[1]

The term בְּסוֹדָם, *into their conspiracy*,

1. Following the Midrash [which apparently bases itself on the future tense of Jacob's disclaimer], *Rashi* interprets the parallel stiches in this passage as prophetic allusions to *future revolts* involving descendants of Simeon and Levi— Zimri [*Number* 25:6ff] and Korach [ibid. 16:1] respectively. Jacob now exclaimed that he did not wish to be associated with either incident:

Into their conspiracy, may my soul not enter! This alludes to the incident of Zimri, when members of the tribe of Simeon assembled to ask Moses, 'May Zimri, our leader, marry this Midianite woman? Should you forbid it, who permitted you to marry a Midianite woman?' [See *Sanhedrin* 82b]. With regard to this provocation, Jacob exclaimed, 'Let not my name be associated with that event!' And accordingly, when the Torah later traces Zimri's genealogy, it reads [*Numbers* 25:14]: *Zimri, the son of Salu, prince of a father's house among the Simeonites* — but it does not trace his genealogy back to Jacob by stating 'son of Jacob.'

6 *Into their conspiracy, may my soul not enter!*
With their congregation, do not join,
O my honor!

derives from the verb סוד, *secret,* and refers in this context to secret deliberations: hence, *conspiracy* or *plot.* According to *Ralbag,* בְּסוֹדָם parallels בִּקְהָלָם; it derives from יסד and is synonymous with בְּהִוָּסְדָם, *in their establishment.* It refers to the time when they gathered to hatch a secret plot *(Ibn Ezra; Rashbam).*

R' Munk cites the *Zohar* that after his initial hesitation at granting a blessing to tribes that had engaged in such savage behavior, Jacob decided that they should be blessed, but he left the text of the blessing to Moses, who would bless the tribes just before his death. When that time came, however, a rift had developed between Simeon and Levi; they were no longer indistinguishable from one another. The tribe of Levi had redeemed their ancestor's atrocity at Shechem. After the sin of the Golden Calf, when Moses called out מִי לַה׳ אֵלָי, *Whoever is loyal to HASHEM, come to me (Exodus* 32:26), only Levi stood to him unanimously. And when Zimri, the Simeonite leader, sinned brazenly, it was Phineas, a descendant of Levi, who courageously and gloriously redeemed the honor of God and saved Israel from the Divine wrath (*Numbers* ch. 25). Thus, Simeon remained sinful, but Levi emerged as the spiritual elite of Israel. The Midrash likens Levi to a man who borrowed from the king, but later not only repaid him but was able to extend loans to him. Simeon, on the other hand, was like someone who borrowed and never repaid — but kept going further into debt. Moses blessed Levi abundantly, but he avoided mentioning Simeon by name. Just as Simeon's inheritance in *Eretz Yisrael* was sprinkled through the territory of Judah, so his blessing was included in that of Judah. (See *Joshua* 19:1,9.)

בִּקְהָלָם אַל־תֵּחַד כְּבֹדִי — *With* [lit. *in*] *their congregation, do not join* [lit. *unite*], *O my honor.*

... This was a further disclaimer regarding their behavior in Shechem. Earlier, Jacob had denied complicity in their deceitful reply to Shechem. Now he denied that he was associated with them when they gathered upon the Shechemites and slew them *(Ramban).*

According to the Rabbinic interpretation cited by *Rashi* [see footnote], this referred prophetically to the time when Levi's descendant Korach, would assemble his band to make a schism in the nation. Jacob refused to be mentioned among Korach's ancestors in that connection.

The word תֵּחַד is used for both third person *feminine* imperfect: [*she*] *shall not be united,* or second person *masculine*

With their congregation, do not join, O my honor! This alludes to the time when Korach will assemble a congregation against Moses and Aaron. Regarding this occasion, too, Jacob exclaimed, 'Let my name not be associated with them!' And so it was, for Korach's genealogy is listed [*Numb.* 16:1]: *Korach, son of Itzhar the son of Kehath, the son of Levi* — but it does not say, 'the son of Jacob.' However, in *I Chronicles* 6:22f — where Korach's genealogy is traced in connection with the Levitical Temple service — the passage reads, 'The son of Kehath, the son of Levi, *the son of Israel'* [*Tanchuma*].

[According to a view in *Sanhedrin* 109b, the first stich in our passage alludes to the מְרַגְּלִים, *Spies* (who slandered *Eretz Yisrael,* maintaining that it was unconquerable [see *Numbers* 13:4]). *Rashi* in *Sanhedrin* ad. loc. explains that there too, none of the Spies are traced back to Jacob. However, the obvious question arises: What special role did Simeon or Levi play in the episode of the Spies; the tribe of Levi was not even represented among the Spies, nor is the tribe of Simeon mentioned as having played an especially prominent role in that episode?

Maharsha suggests that possibly there was a tradition that the Simeonite among them was the spokesman for the Spies.]

כְּבֹדִ֑י כִּ֤י בְאַפָּם֙ הָ֣רְגוּ אִ֔ישׁ וּבִרְצֹנָ֖ם
7 עִקְּרוּ־שֽׁוֹר׃ אָר֤וּר אַפָּם֙ כִּ֣י עָ֔ז וְעֶבְרָתָ֖ם

imperative: *you are not to be united.* The translation that it is the masculine imperative follows *Rashi,* who explains that this rendering is required by the word כָּבוֹד, *honor,* which is a masculine noun. Thus, as *Rashi* explains, the syntax requires that the phrase be interpreted as if Jacob were speaking to his honor, saying: *O you, my honor, do not unite with their gathering!* [In the first stich the phrase אַל־תָּבֹא נַפְשִׁי, must be rendered in third person feminine imperfect, *may my soul not enter,* rather than *O, my soul, do not enter,* since נֶפֶשׁ, *soul,* is feminine and cannot take a masculine verb.]

כִּי בְאַפָּם הָרְגוּ אִישׁ — *For in their anger* [or: *fury*] *they murdered people* [lit. *a man*].

A reference to Chamor and the people of Shechem [34:25]. Midrashically, they are spoken of in the singular as אִישׁ, [*one*] *man,* since Simeon and Levi had as little fear as if the entire populace was only one man [i.e., the fact that Simeon and Levi were faced with attacking *many* men was no deterrent to them]. A similar expression appears in the episode of Gideon [*Judges* 6:16]: *And you shall slay the Midianites as one man;* similarly concerning Egypt [*Exodus* 15:1]: *the horse and its rider He has thrown into the sea* [a reference to the whole army which was as insignificant in God's view as if it consisted of but a single horse and rider] *(Rashi* citing the *Midrash).*

In the literal sense however, *Rashi* explains that the singular term *man* is a collective noun referring to people in general, the connotation being: *they killed every man with whom they were angry.* [*Ramban* renders similarly.]

וּבִרְצֹנָם עִקְּרוּ־שׁוֹר — *And at their whim they maimed an ox.*

— I.e., they sought to disable Joseph who is figuratively likened to an *ox;* see *Deut.* 33:17. The word עִקְּרוּ, in Old French, *essarter,* means *hamstring; disable; lame.* Comp. תְּעַקֵּר in *Joshua* 11:6 *(Rashi).*[1]

Rashi's interpretation that עִקְּרוּ denotes their *intention* to disable Joseph is based on the fact that they were not successful in carrying out their design; to the contrary, Joseph was still thriving as absolute ruler of Egypt! That the Torah labels their *intention* to disable Joseph as if it were a *fait accompli* is significant, since it is axiomatic that God does not consider evil *intent* as tantamount to the deed. Possibly, since Simeon and Levi had actually *begun* the evil act designed to disable Joseph — by throwing him into an infested pit — they are considered as having committed a *fait accompli.* Additionally, perhaps the phraseology וּבִרְצֹנָם, *and at their whim,* indicates in itself that it was only their *desire* to *lame,* but not that they did so *(Maskil l'David; Tzeidah laDerech;* see *Mizrachi).*

Ramban interprets *ox* in the literal collective sense as denoting the cattle of Shechem. He explains the flow of the passage: *In their fury they killed men,* i.e., every man of Shechem; וּבִרְצֹנָם, *and by their whim,* i.e., premeditatedly, when their fury had subsided, *they proceeded to destroy the cattle.* Jacob specifically mentioned this now to formally disassociate himself from *every* aspect of their plot — even in their subsequent plunder of the cattle and property of Shechem.

1. In *Megillah* 9a our verse is listed among the several in Scripture which the seventy-two Elders of Israel were inspired to subtly emend in their Greek translation of Scripture, undertaken at the command of King Ptolemy [Philadelphus]. To soften the denunciation of the Tribal Ancestors, each one of the Sages, sequestered in separate cubicles, produced the same Divinely inspired translation of this passage, which read: *For in their fury they killed an ox, and in their capriciousness uprooted the manger.* See also 1:1; 1:26.

49
7

For in their anger they murdered people
and at their whim they maimed an ox.
7 *Accursed is their rage for it is fierce,*
and their wrath for it was harsh;

It is similar to one who sees his acquaintance committing a transgression and prayerfully exclaims, 'May I not be associated with this act!' thereby publicly announcing his disassociation with that deed *(Marpei Lashon).*

According to *Onkelos,* the word שׁוֹר, *ox,* should be interpreted as if it were vowelized שׁוּר, *wall,* as in v. 22 below; cf. also בְּשׁוּרָי in *Psalms* 92:12. The intent of our passage would be: and in their capriciousness *they uprooted a* [city fortified by a] *wall.* In this sense, *Ramban* explains, the verb עִקְּרוּ means *uprooted* as in *Zephaniah* 2:4.

According to an opinion cited in *Radak,* the metaphor of *ox,* largest animal of the cattle families, figuratively alludes to Chamor, the ruler of Shechem, and his son Shechem, the prince [above 34:2]. Scripture commonly describes the strong and powerful as אֵילִים, *rams* [see *Exodus* 15:15] and עַתּוּדִים, *he-goats* [see *Isaiah* 14:9].

7. אָרוּר אַפָּם כִּי עָז — *Accursed is their rage for it is fierce.*

Rashi explains: Even when Jacob was chastising them he did not curse *them* but their *anger.* The wicked Balaam similarly observed [*Numb.* 23:8]: *How can I curse* [Israel] *whom God* [*El*] *has not cursed?* — [if even in fury he did not curse *them* but only their *anger,* shall *I* curse them? *(Midrash)*].

[Actually, Balaam said that אֵל *(El)* lit. *God,* did not curse Israel, but the Midrash interprets this as a reference to Jacob who pronounced his curse against only their anger in consonance with God's will; or the word *El* may be a reference to Jacob himself, whom God called *El* (see *comm.* to 33:20).]

As the Sages note in *Berachos* 10a, the righteous pray for the destruction of *sin,* but not of sinners. Let the sinners repent so that they will survive while their sins will no longer exist.

This was either a prayer or a prophetic prognostication. The sense is: *May their anger diminish, for it is fierce.* For just as *blessed* often implies increase, so does *cursed* denote the reverse *(Ibn Ezra; Radak; Tur).*

Lekach Tov similarly interprets אָרוּר in our passage as related to the term אָרוּהָ *plucked,* in *Psalms* 80:13, the sense being: *May their anger subside.*

Comp. *Chizkuni:* This was not a curse but a blessing, as if to say: May they not succeed in their wrathful ways, so that they not accustom themselves to be bad-tempered. [See *Moed Katan* 9a where it is recorded that even statements that appeared to be curses were actually blessings.]

The term אַף, *rage* [lit. *nose*] metaphorically alludes to the flaring of the nostrils during one's anger *(Rashi Exodus* 15:8; see above 27:45; 30:2).

Haamek Davar explains that אַף refers to uncontrollable fury one feels when he loses his temper, while עֶבְרָה [wrath] in the next stich refers to *residual anger* that one continues to feel even after the initial fury has subsided. The differing manifestations of *rage* and *residual anger* can be seen earlier in *v.* 6. In describing the result of their rage, that verse says that they killed people, but after the rage was spent — and they still harbored inner anger — they destroyed cattle, but not human life.

וְעֶבְרָתָם כִּי קָשָׁתָה — *And their wrath for it was harsh.*

This parallels the previous stich. Jacob repeats essentially the same thought in different words for emphasis *(Ibn Ezra; Radak).*

כִּי קָשָׁתָה אֲחַלְּקֵם בְּיַעֲקֹב וַאֲפִיצֵם בְּיִשְׂרָאֵל׃

ח יְהוּדָה אַתָּה יוֹדוּךָ אַחֶיךָ יָדְךָ בְּעֹרֶף

The Midrash homiletically reads this passage as if the word were vowelized וַעֲבֵירָתָם *and their sin for it was harsh.*

When they are together, they are a destructive force, therefore ...

אֲחַלְּקֵם בְּיַעֲקֹב וַאֲפִיצֵם בְּיִשְׂרָאֵל — *I will separate them within Jacob, and I will disperse them in Israel.*

(a) I will separate them *from one another* in that Levi shall not be numbered among the tribes [see *Numbers* 26:62; this difference in status between the two would diminish their feelings of equality and closeness]. (b) Each of these tribes will be dispersed throughout Israel. You will find that most poor people, scribes and elementary grade teachers were of the tribe of Simeon. This was so in order that the tribe be dispersed [since such people were required by their professions to seek their livelihood among others]. Regarding the tribe of Levi, God caused them to roam from one threshing floor to another to collect the priestly offerings [תְּרוּמוֹת] and tithes, in effect causing them to be 'dispersed'. Their dispersion, however, was more respectable than Simeon's [since Levi had the status of a tribe especially dedicated to the service of God] *(Rashi* from *Midrash* and *Tanchuma).* [See also *Rashi* to *I Chron.* 4:27.]

According to another opinion in the Midrash, Jacob's prophetic pronouncement was fulfilled when twenty-four thousand Simeonites, followers of Zimri, perished [see *Numbers* 25:9; *Sanhedrin* 82a], and their widows were scattered among all the other tribes [see also Midrash cited in *Tz'ror HaMor*].

By dividing and scattering these two tribes, Jacob intended to neutralize the destructiveness caused by their unity. Indeed, when the tribes received their portions in *Eretz Yisrael,* Simeon and Levi were separated geographically. Simeon's cities were sprinkled throughout the southern part of Judah's portion [see *Joshua* 19:1]. Levi did not receive a territory *per se,* but the Levites were given forty-eight cities (among which were the six עָרֵי מִקְלָט, *Cities of Refuge)* [see *Numbers* 35:1*ff*] which were scattered throughout the territories of all the tribes [see *Joshua* 21] *(Ramban).*

Cf. *Aggadas Bereishis:* Jacob said, If these two tribes dwell in proximity to one another, they will destroy the whole world; I will therefore scatter them — *I will separate them within Jacob and disperse them in Israel.*

This, then, is the contextual flow: אָרוּר אַפָּם, *may their rage be lessened,* by their lowly state and the hard life caused by their being dispersed and scattered *(Sforno).*

According to many commentators there is a very positive implication in these words. Occasions arise where zealousness is a necessary trait, as it was in the case of Phineas. Too much zealousness concentrated in one place, however, is dangerous. For that reason *I will separate them within Jacob,* so there will be only a few of them in any one place, *and disperse them in Israel.* In this way, *all* of the tribes will be able to benefit from their trait of zealousness, but because of their dispersion they will be more restrained than if they were geo-

49
8 *I will separate them within Jacob,*
and I will disperse them in Israel.

8 *Judah — you, your brothers shall acknowledge;*
your hand will be at your enemies' nape.

graphically united. Thus neutralized, theirs will not be a *cursed* trait but an effective one in avenging Evil *(R' Yosef Kimchi; Haamek Davar; Malbim).*

[The parallelism of *Jacob* and *Israel* in this context is not clear. The name Jacob, as often noted in the commentary, represents the more *materialistic* side of the Patriarch and his descendants, while the name Israel represents their *spiritual* aspect. Possibly this duality is the basis of the many Midrashic interpretations [see *Bereishis Rabbah* 97:5] which refer the first clause, *I will separate them within* **Jacob** to Simeon and the second clause *and disperse them in* **Israel,** to Levi, the more 'spiritual' of the two. Comp. Moses' charge to Levi [*Deut.* 32:10]: *They shall teach Your judgments to Jacob; Your Torah to Israel.*][1]

8. Judah.

When Judah heard Jacob rebuking his brothers this way, his face blanched and he began drawing back into a corner of the room, afraid that Jacob might chastise him over the affair of Tamar. So Jacob called him soothingly, "Judah — *you* [the 'you' is emphatic] are not like them [I am not about to rebuke you as I did them]! *You* your brothers shall acknowledge!" *(Midrash; Rashi).*

יְהוּדָה אַתָּה יוֹדוּךָ אַחֶיךָ — *Judah — you, your brothers shall acknowledge.*

The translation of יודוך as *acknowledge* follows *Radak* in *Shorashim,* s.v. ידה who explains it as: they shall ascribe majesty to you.

Rashbam similarly explains the word [from הוד, majesty] as: *they will ascribe majesty to you.* After

1. *R' Hirsch* maintains that *Jacob* refers to the oppressed *Galus* aspect of the Jewish people, while *Israel* refers to them when they are triumphant, as was Israel when he defeated the angel of Esau. In a flourishing *Eretz Yisrael,* the impetuosity of these two tribes would be a divisive force, detrimental to the general harmony. The verb used for *dispersed,* נפץ, connotes the breaking of the whole into the smallest possible pieces. This was the case in *Eretz Yisrael,* where, as noted by *Rashi,* the Levites received no province and were forced to depend on the good will of land owners for their tithes; and the Simeonites had small enclaves, completely dependent upon the surrounding Judeans. Thus, when Israel was a flourishing state, Simeon and Levi's political influence was nullified — crushed and scattered into the smallest pieces.

In the Jacob-state of exile, however, the strength and zeal of Simeon and Levi are essential to the morale and pride of the people; the nation could not afford to let their energies be dissipated. The exilic separation of Simeon and Levi is expressed by the verb חלק, which implies a portion of value from which people can benefit. In exile, the professions of teacher, scribe, and synagogue functionary would cause the people of Simeon and Levi to be found everywhere. With their fiery, proud dispositions they would keep alive the nation's courage, fire and pride in the Jewish spirit, outliving the loss of the state.

As *R' Munk* concludes, their physical drive would be redirected and would find a happier and more productive outlet when transformed into spiritual strength. Then the generosity and vigor of the two brothers will serve the common good. The initial harm thereby transformed itself into a source of benefit and blessing in the service of God.

ט אֹיְבֶיךָ יִשְׁתַּחֲווּ לְךָ בְּנֵי אָבִיךָ: גּוּר אַרְיֵה

censuring the older sons, stripping Reuben of his privileges and scattering Simeon and Levi, Jacob turned to Judah. 'To 'you,' he said, 'your brothers will concede the kingship.'

This is evidenced by the end of the passage, *your father's sons will prostrate themselves before you.*

Chizkuni interprets in the sense of *praise: You, your brothers will praise and respect* [since their success will come through you *(Alshich).*]

— Your brothers shall acknowledge your primacy because *you confessed* your relationship with Tamar [see 38:26. This is a play on words based on the fact that the Hebrew for *acknowledge, confess, praise, pay homage* is the same] *(Tanchuma).*[1]

Your brothers praise you; your mother rendered praise when you were born [see 29:35]; and I, too, herewith praise you *(Midrash).*

R' Shimon bar Yochai said, the essence of this 'acknowledgment' is that all Judah's brothers will be called by his name. A man does not say, 'I am a Reubenite or a Simeonite' but 'I am a Yehudi' [Judahite; Jew] *(Midrash).*

According to *Sechel Tov* the intimation is: יְהוּדָה אַתָּה, *You are* [truly what is implied by your name] *Judah.* That is, your very name denotes acknowledgment; confession; praise. Your mother was the first to offer praise [29:35]; therefore you too confessed over the matter of Tamar [... and for this very reason your brothers will acknowledge you as their superior (*Toldos Yitzchak)*].

As a reward for his acknowledgment, the Messiah will descend from him and save Israel, as it is written [*Isaiah* 11:10]: *In that day shall nations seek the root of Jesse, that stands for an ensign of the peoples (Yalkut).*

According to *Abarbanel,* after disqualifying the three older brothers as future leaders, Jacob recognized in his fourth son, Judah, the necessary virtues of leadership. *Abarbanel* elicits from the succeeding verses four reasons which prompted this choice: (a) Judah's brothers respected his natural authority without feeling jealousy towards him as they did toward Joseph; (b) he had emerged victorious from all his undertakings; (c) he had succeeded in establishing harmony among his brothers; (d) he was not impetuous like Reuben, nor did he have violent tendencies like Simeon and Levi. Instead, he possessed the majestic calm that comes from confidence in one's own powers.

יָדְךָ בְּעֹרֶף אֹיְבֶיךָ — *Your hand will be at your enemies' nape.*

A metaphor meaning, You will be victorious. Your enemies will turn

1. In *Makkos* 11b we learn that [by setting the precedent of acknowledging wrong in the incident with Tamar] Judah, in effect, was instrumental in Reuben's public confession of wrongdoing in the matter of Bilhah [see *comm.* to 37:29].

Tosafos ad loc. [s.v. מִי גָרַם] mentions that we find a Scriptural allusion for this in our passage, which the *Targum* interprets as: אַתְּ הוֹדֵיתָ כַּךְ הוֹדִית אַחִיךְ, *you acknowledged* [i.e., publicly confessed] *so will your brothers acknowledge,* i.e., just as you were not ashamed to confess, so did your brother, Reuben, come forward and confess. [Current editions of *Targum Onkelos* read differently. Apparently the *Tosafist* is referring to another version then extant. Cf. *Targum Yonasan.* See *Overview* to *Vayigash.*]

49
9 *Your father's sons will prostrate themselves before you.*

[9] *A lion cub is Judah;*

their backs and flee you *(Sforno; Akeidah; Ralbag).*

This prophecy was fulfilled in the days of David [Judah's descendant]. See *II Samuel* 22:41: וְאֹיְבַי תַּתָּה לִּי עֹרֶף, *You have given me the nape of my enemies (Rashi).*

Ibn Ezra connects this with the following phrase: Because you will be victorious in war, your father's sons will prostrate themselves to you — as before a monarch.

יִשְׁתַּחֲווּ לְךָ בְּנֵי אָבִיךָ — *Your father's sons will prostrate themselves before you.*

— In deference to you as their monarch *(Sforno).*

Some leaders are great warriors but are ineffective when it comes to leading their own countrymen at home. With others, the reverse is true. Judah possessed both qualities: not only will his *hand be at his enemies' nape,* but *his father's sons,* i.e. his own countrymen, *will prostrate themselves before him,* acknowledging him as a king who can lead in peace and justice *(Haamek Davar).*

Isaac had blessed Jacob with the expression *your mother's sons* [27:29], but since Jacob had four wives, he used the all-inclusive expression *your father's* sons *(Rashi).*

Had Jacob said your *mother's* sons, the implication would have been that only Judah's brothers from *Leah* would prostrate themselves. Additionally, as *Mizrachi* in 27:29 points out, the reason Isaac preferred to use the expression *mother's sons* was that he did not want to associate himself directly [by saying *your father's sons*] with making one of his children subservient; Jacob, however, had no choice but to say *your father's sons.*

9. Jacob introduces the metaphor of a lion cub for Judah in order to heighten the impression of majesty and power that was manifest in Judah's personality *(Abarbanel).*

גּוּר אַרְיֵה יְהוּדָה — *A lion cub is Judah.*

The addition of *cub* is significant since the metaphor *lion* would have sufficed to imply majesty and power *(Maskil l'David; Tzeidah laDerech).*

Rashbam interprets that Jacob specifically likened Judah to a lion *cub,* since it is stronger and swifter than an old lion.

— Although Judah was not yet a 'lion' inasmuch as he had not attained kingship, nevertheless he was a lion *cub* [with the *potential* to become a lion], prevailing over his brothers, and destined to reign *(Sforno).*

— You combine the courage of *youth* with the prudence of *age.* You have no lust for fighting and plunder for their own sake; as a lion you are above low robbery and murder *(R' Hirsch).*

Onkelos interpretively paraphrases our passage: 'The dominion shall be in the beginning, and in the end the kingdom shall be increased from the House of Judah ...'

According to *Rashi, Onkelos* means that the dual expression *lion* and *cub* alluded to two periods in the life of Judah's descendant King David. When he was still a 'cub' under Saul, he *began* to lead Israel [*II Samuel* 5:2] and then he became a 'lion' when they proclaimed him king over them. [Accordingly, *Onkelos* rendered the verse: first David will be a *ruler,* and later he will be anointed *king.*]

Cf. *R' Shmuel ben Chofni:* The Davidic

יְהוּדָה מִטֶּרֶף בְּנִי עָלִיתָ כָּרַע רָבַץ
י כְּאַרְיֵה וּכְלָבִיא מִי יְקִימֶנּוּ: לֹא־יָסוּר

dynasty is compared to a lion to reflect its majestic stature and strength. See *II Samuel* 17:10. Jacob called Judah a lion, mightiest of the beasts [*Proverbs* 30:30], since Judah was the mightiest of the tribes [*I Chron.* 5:2]. Possibly, Jacob used the metaphor of a *cub* to allude to David's rise to prominence when he was still weak, for only later did he become powerful [*II Samuel* 5:10; *I Chron.* 11:9].

HaKsav V'HaKabbalah offers a novel interpretation that גור is related to the verb גרה, *provoked,* the sense being: *Judah is a provoked lion* — potentially the most dangerous kind.

מִטֶּרֶף בְּנִי עָלִיתָ — *From* [*the*] *prey* [lit. *from the tearing apart*], *my son, you elevated yourself* [lit. *you have risen*].

The translation follows *Rashi:*

Jacob had suspected Judah of being responsible for the murder of Joseph, a deed he described with the word טֶרֶף, *tearing apart:* as Jacob said טָרֹף טֹרַף יוֹסֵף, *Joseph has surely been torn to bits!* [37:33]. In assigning responsibility for that crime, Jacob said חַיָּה רָעָה אֲכָלָתְהוּ, *a savage beast devoured him!* [ibid], an allusion to Judah, whom Jacob suspected of responsibility, for the word *beast* refers to Judah who is described as a *lion.* Now Jacob declares that Judah is vindicated: not only had he not been the one who 'tore Joseph to bits' — he *elevated* himself above such a crime by being the one who saved Joseph's life. It was Judah who said [ibid. v. 26]: *'What gain will there be if we kill our brother and cover up his blood!'* You also rose above the situation when, in the incident of Tamar, you spared her from death by admitting your responsibility [see *comm.* to 38:26 s.v. צָדְקָה מִמֶּנִּי] (*Rashi*). [See *Overview*].

Thus, *Rashi* perceives our passage to say: *You my son, had risen above the act of 'tearing',* of which I had suspected you; to the contrary, it was you who were instrumental in *sparing* him.

Gur Aryeh explains that Jacob had suspected Judah of foul play since he knew that Judah, as the tribe that would one day possess the kingship, would feel the most threatened by Joseph's dreams, in which he seemed to aspire to sovereignty over the brothers.

Kli Yakar interprets similarly: Although your temperament is that of a *lion cub,* you kept aloof from the incident when Joseph was his brother's prey. That Judah removed himself from his brother's intention may be inferred from the fact that Judah 'descended' from among his brothers [38:1] as he did not wish to be associated with them after their act.

It is clear from the commentators to *Rashi* [*Mizrachi; Tzeidah laDerech; Be'er Yitzchak*] that בְּנִי is not to be connected with מִטֶּרֶף (reading: מִטֶּרֶף בְּנִי, *from the tearing of my son)* but that בְּנִי *is to be connected with* עָלִיתָ [lit. *you ascended,* reading: בְּנִי עָלִיתָ, *my son, you elevated yourself*]. This is supported by the cantillation under מִטֶּרֶף, a disjunctive *tipcha,* which separates it from the word בְּנִי. Since *Rashi* divided the opening words of his comment on this passage into two phrases, מִטֶּרֶף and בְּנִי עָלִיתָ, it is clear that he too understood the phrase that way.

There is a view in *Sechel Tov,* however, that בְּנִי *is* to be connected in the construct state with מִטֶּרֶף, rendering: מִטֶּרֶף בְּנִי, *from the act of preying upon my son (Joseph)* עָלִיתָ, *you kept aloof.* This is based on a differing tradition [not mentioned by *Minchas Shay*] that the cantillation under מִטֶּרֶף is a *t'vir,* which would connect it with בְּנִי.

According to a Midrashic interpretation, the word עָלִיתָ [*have risen*] has the connotation of: *You have become exalted:* By your conduct *vis-a-vis* the טֶרֶף, *the prey* — in the cases of Joseph and Tamar — עָלִיתָ, *you have become exalted.*

Many commentators — e.g. *Rashbam; Radak; Chizkuni; Ibn Ezra* — do not interpret *'prey'* as al-

49 *from the prey, my son, you elevated yourself.*
10 *He crouches, lies down like a lion,*
and like an awesome lion
who dares rouse him?
10 *The scepter shall not depart from Judah*

luding to Joseph. They see the entire context of the verse as the development of Judah's power. He begins his career as a vigorous, strong cub, then he goes out to attack and defeat his *prey*. After he succeeds, he rises from the fray and settles down in the security of his cities like a crouching, relaxing adult lion with the metaphor of *lion cub* as alluding to Judah's general prowess.

Tur refers this to Judah's descendant David who first demonstrated his prowess by killing a lion and a bear [*I Samuel* 17:34 *ff*]. It was this act that imbued him with the courage to battle Goliath, as a result of which David rose to preeminence. Thus: *through prey* [the lion and bear] *you* [i.e. your descendant David] *will rise to preeminence.*

כָּרַע רָבַץ כְּאַרְיֵה וּכְלָבִיא מִי יְקִימֶנּוּ — *He crouches, lies down like a lion; and like an awesome lion, who* [dares] *rouse him?*

[The translation of רבץ as *lies down* (peacefully) follows *R' Hirsch* on 4:7; see *comm.* there.]

[*Rashi*, continuing his interpretation of the syntax, follows the Midrash and interprets this phrase as Judah's reward for having held himself aloof from the prey: Your descendants will enjoy the tranquility that only a crouching lion, king of beasts, can experience for it fears no other creature. No man will be able to budge Judah from his secure position.]

We are told that such was the case in the days of King Solomon [I Kings 5:5]: *And Judah and Israel dwelt in security, every man under his vine and under his fig tree, from Dan to Beersheba, all the days of Solomon.*

The Hebrew terms for lion, לָבִיא and אַרְיֵה, are essentially synonymous, but the former has a more mature, majestic and awesome connotation. According to *Avos d'Rabbi Nosson Version B* end of chapt. 43, לָבִיא, from לֵב, *heart*, implies the fear a lion's roar stikes in the 'hearts' of other animals.

Targum Yonasan renders: 'He dwells quietly and in strength like a lion; and, like an old lion when he reposes — who may stir him up?'

Malbim punctuates the phrase differently, interpreting: כָּרַע רָבַץ כְּאַרְיֵה וּכְלָבִיא, *he kneels, rests, like a lion and like a mature lion* — the *kneeling* refers to *lion* and *resting* to *mature lion,* — מִי יְקִימֶנּוּ, *who will dare rouse him?* No one would place himself in mortal danger by daring to rouse him. Similarly, your enemies will not dare provoke you.

10. לֹא־יָסוּר שֵׁבֶט מִיהוּדָה — *The scepter shall not depart from Judah.*

I.e., the privilege of providing Israel's sovereign ruler, who is symbolized by his possession of the royal scepter, shall not pass from the House of Judah *(Onkelos).*[1]

[Reconciling this prophecy with

1. The Talmud [*Yoma* 53b] records that on Yom Kippur the High Priest uttered a short prayer, which, according to one opinion ended with the Aramaic equivalent of our passage: 'May a ruler not depart from the House of Judah.'

the historical facts that Saul, a Benjaminite, reigned before Judah's first king, David, assumed the throne, and that the Davidic dynasty ceased to reign after the destruction of the Temple, *Rashi* comments:] — This refers to the period from the ascension of the House of David [and thenceforth — even when the Jews would be in Exile *(Mizrachi)*]. It is an allusion to [not only kings *per se* but to whomever exercises dominion over Israel. Specifically, it alludes to Judah's descendants] the רָאשֵׁי, גָלֻיּוֹת *Exilarchs* in Babylon, appointed by the civil authorities, who ruled the people with the 'rod,' meaning that they could use force, if necessary, to secure obedience [the word שֵׁבֶט means both *rod* and *scepter*]. [See *Sanhedrin* 5a; *Horayos* 11b].

Gur Aryeh gives two answers to the question of how Jacob's prophetic blessing could have become nullified in the many centuries when there has been no Jewish monarchy:

— The Patriarchal blessing meant that whenever Israel merits a legally constituted monarchy, the king will come from Judah, but Jacob never said that there would always be a Judean king.

— There have been periods in history when there was no king from Judah, as during the time of the Judges and under Saul, but these were temporary aberrations that were followed by a Davidic dynasty. Similarly, the current Exile will culminate in the Davidic reign of Messiah. The fact that the kingship always returns to Judah means that Jacob's testament is still binding. Only if the monarchy were to revert permanently from Judah could it be said that the tribe lost its hereditary right to the throne.

The intimation is that Jacob's promise applied even to periods when Israel had no king. Moreover, during the Second Commonwealth when the priestly Levite family of Hasmoneans occupied the throne, a descendant of David always held a position of leadership as head of the Sanhedrin, in fulfillment of this verse, as Yosef ben Gurion writes *(Abarbanel)*. [See ArtScroll *"Chanukah,"* history sect. p. 33*ff.*]

Compare *Rambam's Commentary to the Mishnah, Bechoros* 4:4:

The Exilarch was appointed in Babylon. He need not be a scholar and yeshiva head who was appointed in *Eretz Yisrael*, but it is proper that he be very great in Torah wisdom, so much so that when he is appointed there be none greater than him in any way in *Eretz Yisrael* ... The authority of the Exilarch over all of Israel is the same as the authority of the monarchy, which can compel and enforce, as implied by the fact that the Torah calls him שֵׁבֶט, *rod*, and the Sages state: *The scepter* [i.e. rod] *shall not depart from Judah*, this refers to the Exilarchs of Babylon, who rule Israel with the 'rod,' i.e., with force and power. You should note that we do not require him to possess wisdom [although, as stated above, it is desirable that he be the leading scholar of the generation] but he must have the proper lineage [from the Davidic dynasty] ... But the Heads of the Yeshivos of *Eretz Yisrael* [רָאשֵׁי יְשִׁיבוֹת אֶרֶץ יִשְׂרָאֵל] are [i.e., must be] scholars as it is written [in our verse] וּמְחֹקֵק מִבֵּין רַגְלָיו, *a scholar from among his descendants.*

Although, as *Radak* notes, the שֵׁבֶט, *rod* or *scepter*, is technically symbolic of the monarchy since a king has the absolute power to punish his subjects as if with a rod, and kings held a scepter to symbolize this power, *R' Avraham ben HaRambam* maintains that not only *royalty* is meant by the figurative expression *scepter*, but *dominion* in general, as was wielded by the Exilarchs even after the monarchy ceased to exist [as *Rashi* and *Abarbanel* note above].

According to *Ibn Ezra*, *scepter* refers to greatness and pre-eminence in general, of the kind enjoyed by the tribe of Judah even *before* David reigned when it traveled at the head of the nation in the desert [see *Numbers* 2:9] and after Joshua's death when Judah was ordered to lead the campaign to conquer *Eretz Yisrael* [*Judges* 1:2].

Ramban differs.

Ramban differs strongly, maintaining that *scepter* refers exclusively to *royalty* as evidenced by *Psalms* 45:7 and *Isaiah* 14:5, and does not refer to pre-eminence of the kind mentioned by *Ibn Ezra*.

Ramban emphasizes that the implication of Jacob's pronouncement is not that Judah's descendants would never be subjugated by other nations or that Judah would never lose the kingship, for indeed the nation *would* eventually go into exile, as foretold in *Deut.* 28:36, and be devoid of monarchy.

Rather, the intent is that as long as there is a monarchy in Israel, the king will be from Judah and none of his brothers will rule him. In this way Jacob bequeathed sovereignty to Judah, as David mentions in *I Chronicles* 28:4.

Ramban continues that by the expression לֹא יָסוּר, *shall not depart,* Jacob was alluding to the fact that another tribe [Benjamin, tribe of Saul the first king of Israel] would initially rule over Israel; but once the scepter of monarchy passed to Judah's line [i.e., to David, Judah's descendant] it was not to *depart* to any other tribe.[1] The kings from other tribes who ruled Israel after David violated Jacob's testament and were punished accordingly [see *Hoshea* 8:4].

Similarly, the Hasmoneans who ruled in the time of the Second Temple were punished and fell by their enemies' swords. Though they were very pious, and were it not for them Torah and the observance of the Commandments would have been forgotten in Israel, they sinned by assuming the monarchy though they were not of the tribe of Judah [they were Priests of the tribe of Levi] and were thereby guilty of causing the 'scepter' to depart from Judah. Additionally, they were punished since, as *Kohanim* who should be wholly devoted to the Service of God, there was an extra stricture against their reign [see *Numbers* 18:7]. Even in cases where it might be necessary for Israel to appoint a king over itself from the other tribes, such a person should not be anointed as royal monarch, but should function merely as a judge or official [see *Yerushalmi Horayos* 3:2].

Rambam [*Hil. Melachim* 1:9] similarly maintains that this verse was not merely a *foretelling of future developments by the Patriarch,* but *a command* which vested the tribe of Judah with royalty; accordingly sovereignty from any tribe other than Judah was considered an act of usurpation.

1. **Saul — temporary monarch.**

In a dissertation fundamental to an understanding of the concept of the monarchy in Israel, *Ramban* discusses why Saul was appointed first king of Israel.

Briefly, *Ramban* asserts that the people's request for a monarchy was unpleasing to God at that time since Samuel was their judge and prophet and was effectively leading them according to God's Word and winning their battles. Accordingly, the people's request for a king was perceived as a rejection of God Himself [see *I Samuel* 8:7].

For this reason, though God acquiesced to their request for a king, He granted them only a temporary monarchy, which He later removed in His wrath. [See the allusion in *Hoshea* 13:11]. He did not wish to appoint a king over them from the tribe of Judah to whom royalty belonged and from whom it was never to depart. Had Saul not sinned, he would have retained sovereignty over *part* of Israel, perhaps over the tribes that were descended from his mother [Rachel, namely Benjamin, Ephraim and Manasseh], or he might have been a vassal king, subject to the king of Judah.

שֵׁ֣בֶט מִֽיהוּדָ֔ה וּמְחֹקֵ֖ק מִבֵּ֣ין רַגְלָ֑יו עַ֚ד כִּֽי־
יא יָבֹ֣א שִׁילֹ֔ה וְל֖וֹ יִקְּהַ֥ת עַמִּֽים׃ אֹסְרִ֤י לַגֶּ֙פֶן֙

According to *Tosafos, Yoma* 26a, this passage was intended as a *blessing*, and its effects were only partially achieved because of the unworthiness of certain descendants of the Davidic line [see *II Samuel* 7; *Drashos HaRan* §7; *Abarbanel*].

R' Ashtruc in *Midrashei HaTorah* maintains that 'although his kingship will depart as a result of his sins, it will not be a *permanent* departure, for kingship will return to his line with the coming of the Messiah.'

וּמְחֹקֵק מִבֵּין רַגְלָיו — *Nor* [lit. *and*] *scholars from among his descendants* [lit. *between his feet;* compare the metaphor in *Deut.* 28:57 *(Radak)*].

Following *Rashi:* A reference to the Torah scholars [מְחֹקֵק being derived from חוק, *law,* an allusion to the Torah *(Be'er Yitzchak)*] — the *Nesi'im,* princes, of *Eretz Yisrael* [who descended from the line of Judah].

This is derived from *Sanhedrin* 5a, which explains this phrase as alluding to 'Hillel's descendants [in *Eretz Yisrael*] who teach Torah to the multitudes.' Thanks to their descent from the Davidic dynasty, they enjoyed immense prestige both at home and abroad.

Ibn Ezra interprets מְחֹקֵק [from חקק, *inscribe*] as *scribe* [i.e., a disciple who inscribes the Law], while *Radak* explains the term as a reference to *rulers* who are *legislators.*

The metaphor of *between his feet,* according to *Ibn Ezra,* depicts the scribe who sits at the feet of the ruler.

Radak in *Shorashim* interprets like *Ibn Ezra,* and explains our passage: *'The rule shall not depart from Judah nor the scribe sitting at his feet.'* [Thus, the scribes are not descendants of Judah, but are other Jews who are subservient to Judah.]

Radak, in his commentary to *Genesis,* however, explains *from between his feet* as a metaphor for *descendants.*

Comp. *Onkelos:* ' ... Nor scribes from his children's children forever.'

— Whoever will have position and power will come from the tribe of Judah. He will give rise to the heads of the academies, and to rabbis who have authority in questions of law, and most members of the Sanhedrin will be from Judah. In every generation there will be people who have access to kings and who are respected by governments. These people will generally descend from Judah. In every generaton there will be someone from the tribe of Judah exercising power and authority *(Sh'lah; R' Bachya;* cf. *Me'am Loez; Abarbanel).*

עַד כִּי־יָבֹא שִׁילֹה — *Until Shiloh arrives* [lit. *until when Shiloh shall come*].

⬥§ Torah source for the belief in the Messiah.

The general consensus [with few exceptions] of Rabbinic interpretation is that this phrase refers to the coming of the Messiah. This passage accordingly constitutes the primary Torah source for the belief that the Messiah will come. In the Middle Ages the wisest dignitaries of Jewish communities always made reference to this passage when they had to engage in debates with the ecclesiastics of the other religions.

Onkelos renders: Until the Messiah comes, to whom the kingdom belongs.

Rashi concurs and similarly comments: Until the King Messiah will come — שֶׁהַמְּלוּכָה שֶׁלוֹ, *to whom the kingdom belongs.* According to the

49
10

nor a scholar from among his descendants,
until Shiloh arrives
and his will be an assemblage of nations.

Midrash, שִׁילֹה is a composite of שַׁי לוֹ, *a gift to him* — a reference to King Messiah to whom all peoples will bring gifts. See *Isaiah* 18:7; *Psalms* 76:12.

Sforno relates the etymology of this word to שלה, the root of שַׁלְוָה and שָׁלוֹם, *happiness* and *peace,* depicting the definitive character of the Messiah's mission which will usher in an era of peace and universal harmony. He would render: *Until [the final] tranquility arrives.*

Midrash Tanchuma preserves an opinion that שִׁילֹה is derived from שִׁלְיָה, *little child* [lit. *the amniotic sac* in which the fetus is formed; comp. *Deut.* 28:57]. Thus, the passage means: *Until his scion* [i.e. Messiah] *comes.* [The intimation is that the Messiah will not be a Divine being, but will be one who will be born into the world normally like mortal men.]

It is manifestly clear that the Rabbis who interpret the allusion in this passage as referring to the Messiah do *not* imply that the word עַד, **until** [*the coming of the Messiah*] intimates that Judah's sovereignty will end when the Messiah arrives. Rather, the Messiah — who will be a descendant of Judah through the line of David — is perceived as the *pinnacle* of Judah's sovereignty, one in whom the sovereignty will reach its greatest glory, the culmination of Jacob's blessing to Judah. [See Overview to ArtScroll *Ruth.*]

Thus, the phraseology of the blessing: עַד כִּי יָבֹא שִׁילֹה *'until' Shiloh comes,* has the sense of *'peaking'* with the coming of the Messiah. The meaning is that the scepter will *never* depart from Judah, but will be fully realized when the Messiah comes. This is similar to God's promise to Jacob in 28:15, *I will not forsake you 'until' I have done what I have spoken about you,* which was an assurance that God would *never* forsake him *(Shlah; Teshuvos HaRashba* 4:187; *Abarbanel).*

Another interpretation of the passage is that of *Rashbam:* Judah's privilege of sovereignty over his eleven brothers will last only עַד כִּי יָבֹא שִׁילֹה, *until he comes to* [the city of] *Shiloh.* That is, until the King of Judah, Rehoboam, son of Solomon, will come to establish the monarchy at Shiloh — which is near Shechem, as is evident from I *Kings* 12:1; II *Chron.* 10:1 (comp. context of *Joshua* chapt. 24). It was then that the Ten Tribes seceded and crowned Jeroboam, leaving Rehoboam with only the tribes of Judah and Benjamin. וְלוֹ יִקְּהַת עַמִּים, *and to him* [i.e., Rehoboam] *shall belong the assemblage of nations,* the nations that remained loyal to the memory of Rehoboam's father, Solomon. [See *Torah Sheleimah* for many other Midrashic interpretations; also *R' Bachya* who refers this to the Egyptian Redemption through Moses; *Chizkuni* who refers it to Ahijah the Shilonite; *Ralbag* — to David. Nevertheless, the overwhelming consensus of Rabbinic commentary interprets the verse to allude to the Messiah.]

וְלוֹ יִקְּהַת עַמִּים — *And his will be an assemblage of nations.*

The translation of יִקְּהַת as a noun — *assemblage* — follows *Rashi,* the reference being to all the people who will assemble to pay him [the Messiah] homage. Cf. *Isaiah* 11:10: *Unto him shall all the nations seek* [see below].

— Until the Messiah's coming

Judah will hold the royal scepter in the midst of his own nation, but the Messiah, descendant of David, will reign over the *gathered* nations *(R' Munk).*

Rashi explains that the word יִקְהַת could not be a third person future *verb* of the root קהה, with the meaning of *'he will ...,'* for if so the verb should have agreed with the plural subject עַמִּים, *nations,* and the phrase should have read וְלוֹ יִקְהֲתוּ עַמִּים, *'and to him the* nations (plural) *will ...'*. Rather, the term is a noun of the root יקה, which *Rashi* interprets as meaning *assemble,* the י being part of the root. A word of similar construction is יִפְעָתֶךָ *[Ezekiel* 28:17] which is also not a verb but a noun, (from the root יפע) meaning *your brightness.*

In a grammatical note, *Rashi* continues that the root letter י of יקה is sometimes omitted, and therefore our passage could also have read קְהַיַּת instead of יִקְהַת while retaining the same meaning. Many root letters are subject to this grammatical rule, technically known as עיקר נופל, *'Root letters that are omitted.'* Examples are the נ of נגף and נשך [which in future tense are יִגֹּף and יִשֹּׁךְ], and the א in אסף [which sometimes is conjugated as הסםך and נסך].

Ramban agrees that יִקְהַת is to be interpreted as a noun, but maintains that it derives from the root קהה meaning *weaken, collapse,* the י being similar to the function of the י in the word יִצְהָר, *oil* [which indicates it as the noun form of צהר]. He renders: *'And his* [i.e. Messiah's] *shall be the weakening of peoples'* — that is, he shall vanquish them and reign supreme. Following this interpretation, the sense would be that the rod of the oppressors shall not be removed from Judah until the coming of his descendant, the Messiah — who will bring about the weakness of peoples and their collapse — since he will subjugate them. Comp. the expression in the Passover *Haggadah* [from *Mechilta Bo*] הַקְהֵה אֶת שִׁנָּיו, *'weaken* [i.e. blunt] *his teeth'* by your sharp response.

According to *Radak,* the root יקה means *obedience* and *acceptance of authority,* denoting that, *To him will be the obedience of the nations,* for they will be subservient to him. 'Such was the case with David; how much more so with the King Messiah.'

Onkelos similarly renders: Unto whom shall be the obedience of the nations.

11. אֹסְרִי לַגֶּפֶן עִירֹה וְלַשֹּׂרֵקָה בְּנִי אֲתֹנוֹ — *He will tie* [lit. = אֹסֵר, *ties*] *his donkey to the vine; to the vine-branch his donkey's foal.*

In early Biblical times the donkey was the usual animal for riding — even for persons of rank. See above 22:3, *Judges* 5:10; 10:4 *(Ibn Caspi).*

Having prophesied about Judah's *personal greatness* and that of his offspring, Jacob now turns to prophesy about Judah's *territory.* [Though Jacob could not reveal the 'End' to his sons, he did provide them with tiny glimpses of what the Messianic era would hold in store *(Abarbanel).*]

He draws an idyllic picture of how Judah's district would be productive and flow with wine like a fountain. Its vines would be so productive that a man would tie a donkey to a vine since a single vine will require a donkey to carry its grapes; similarly from the vintage of only a single branch of a vine one will load up a foal *(Rashi; Rashbam; R' Avraham ben HaRambam).*

Ibn Ezra explains that the vintage will be so abundant that one will bind his donkey to a vine, unconcerned whether it eats the grapes.

There is the further connotation that the vines will be so sturdy that one would be able to securely tether a donkey to them *(Haamek Davar).*

11 *He will tie his donkey to the vine;*
to the vine branch his donkey's foal.

Onkelos also refers our passage to the Era of the Messiah, but interpretively renders the passage as a metaphor. He offers dual symbolisms: (a): Israel shall pass round about in his [i.e. the Messiah's] city; the people shall build his Temple; (b) they will be righteous all around him, and fulfill the Torah through his teachings.

Rashi explains *Onkelos'* symbolisms as follows: in the first interpretation, גֶּפֶן, *the vine*, symbolizes Israel, see *Psalms* 80:9: *You have caused a 'vine' to journey out of Israel;* עירֹה [in the literal context from the root עַיִר, *donkey*, but metaphorically derived from עִיר, *city*] alludes to Jerusalem; שׂורֵקָה, *vine branch*, alludes to Israel [cf. *Jeremiah* 2:21]: *I had planted you a vine branch;* בְּנִי אֲתֹנוֹ is an allusion to the *building* [בֹּנֵי=בְּנִי , *builders* (cf. *Berachos* 64a אַל תִּקְרֵי בָּנַיִךְ אֶלָּא בֹּנָיִךְ, read not *your sons* but *your builders)*] of his [the Messiah's] Temple, the term אֵיתָן being symbolically related to the term שַׁעַר הָאֵיתָן, *Entry Gate* of the Temple mentioned in *Ezekiel* 40:15. Furthermore, *Onkelos* interprets אֹסְרִי *(bind; tether)* in the sense of the Aramaic *go round about.*

In *Onkelos'* second interpretation the *vine* alludes to the *righteous;* בְּנִי אֲתֹנוֹ to those who — riding on white donkeys (See *Judges* 5:10) — occupy themselves with the dissemination of Torah [this follows the exegesis in *Eruvin* 54b where that verse from *Judges* is interpreted to refer to the scholars who ride from city to city and from district to district to teach the Torah, thus making the explanation of Torah 'shining-white' as the light at noon].

Sforno follows the interpretation that the allusion in the verse is to the Messiah, and perceives in this blessing signs by which he will be recognized: He will be revealed on a donkey as the Prophet [*Zechariah* 9:9] writes: *humble, riding on a donkey; on a donkey foaled by a she-donkey.* That the Messiah is not depicted as arriving upon a horse ready for battle is because the wars against the gentile nations and the downfall of their kingdoms will already have been accomplished by God Almighty, and the Messiah will reign in peace. Secondly, the donkey tethered to the vine symbolizes how his kingdom of peace will dwell amidst Israel, a nation compared by the Rabbis to a vine [*Chullin* 92a]: *For the vineyard of HASHEM of Legions is the House of Israel.*[1]

The words אֹסְרִי and בְּנִי have a superfluous י and are to be interpreted as if they were spelled אֹסֵר and בֶּן respectively. Similar forms are מְקִימִי [=מֵקִים] and הַיּוֹשְׁבִי [=הַיּוֹשֵׁב] in Psalm 113. [Cf. also רַבָּתִי (=רַבַּת) in *Lament.* 1:1] *(Rashi).*[2]

The translation of שֹׂרֵקָה follows *Rashi* who interprets it as a *long branch; runner; coriere* in Old French.

1. *R' Hirsch* similarly observes how Jacob visualizes the Messiah, conqueror of humanity, not on a steed, but on a young donkey. The donkey is the beast of burden that always represents peace, well-being, and national greatness, whereas the steed represents military might. Accordingly, the Jewish conception of royal power is not represented by the number of horses, and it is forbidden for the king to accumulate many horses [*Deut.* 17:16].

Consequently the future Redeemer of Jewry and humanity appears here in connection with the donkey, symbolizing the twofold vision of peace and material well-being. For to tie up his animal and especially עַיִר, a donkey's frisky colt, to the vine, implies a greatly increased development of nature (the vine being as strong as a tree) and extraordinary abundance. This is how the prophet Zachariah visualized the coming of the Messiah: *Rejoice greatly O daughter of Zion, shout with joy O daughter of Jerusalem! Look how your king comes to you, righteous and victorious, humbly riding upon a donkey upon the colt of a donkey* (9:9).

2. Citing the *Zohar,* R' Munk writes that the name of God is alluded to twice in this verse. The letter י as a suffix to the verb אסר, and the letter ה, written in place of a modifier of the word עיר, form the Name י־ה. And this name is constituted once more by the letter י, the suffix on the word בן, with the letter ה, suffix of שרק (the usual form, as in *Jeremiah* 2:21). This double allusion is to remind us that the mission of the true Messiah will be accomplished only 'when God is recognized as King over all the earth.'

יב לְבֻשׁוֹ וּבְדַם־עֲנָבִים סוּתֹה: חַכְלִילִי
עֵינַיִם מִיָּיִן וּלְבֶן־שִׁנַּיִם מֵחָלָב:

Ibn Janach and *Radak* in *Shorashim* s.v. שרק explain the term as referring to *the choicest kind of grape vines,* known in Arabic as *s'rik,* while *Ibn Ghayyat* refers it to a choice vine that bears seedless grapes. *Targum* and *Rashi* to *Isaiah* 5:2 and *Jeremiah* 2:21 also interpret it as a *choice vine.*

כִּבֵּס בַּיַּיִן לְבֻשׁוֹ וּבְדַם עֲנָבִים סוּתֹה — *He will launder* [lit. *has laundered* (this is known as "prophetic past tense" in which a future event is depicted as if it had already occurred)] *his garment in wine and his robe in the blood of grapes.*

These phrases continue the hyperbole of the abundance of wine *(Rashi).* So productive will Judah's vineyards be that he will figuratively be able to use wine even for washing his garments. [Comp. the hyperbole in *Job* 29:6.]

— Grapes will be so abundant that wine will figuratively run down the hillsides and garments will become soaked with wine *(Ralbag).*

— This continues the poetic metaphor in the previous phrase: After treading the abundant vintage of grapes, his garments will be stained. Comp. *Isaiah* 63:2: *Why is your clothing red, and your garment like one who treads in a winepress?* He will then have to wash them of the wine *(Rashbam).*

Onkelos interpretively renders: His garments will be of fine purple, as though washed in wine.

Following the prophetic interpretation of this verse as alluding to the Messianic Era, *Sforno* perceives this verse as depicting how the Messiah will figuratively wash his garment in the blood of his enemies.

— The Messiah will do battle with those who oppose him, and slaughter those who come to attack him. The mountains will run red with the blood of the dead, and the uniforms of the Messiah's troops will be drenched as if soaked in red wine *(Zohar; Targum Yonasan).*[1]

Comp. *Lekach Tov:* This alludes to the retribution which the Holy One, Blessed be He, will bring on Edom [i.e. Rome; a reference to the Fourth Kingdom under whom Israel will be in Exile prior to the Messianic redemption], as it says *(Isaiah* 63:1): *Who is this coming from Edom in crimsoned garments from Bozrah? ... Why is your clothing so red, your garments like his who treads grapes? ... I trod them down in My anger ... their life-blood bespattered My garments and all My clothing was stained, for I had planned a day of vengeance, and My year of redemption arrived.*

In accordance with the Messianic allusions in this verse, the Talmud [*Berachos* 57a] records that he who sees a vine stem in a dream may look forward to the Messiah.

The translation of סותה [=סותו] as *robe* follows *Rashi* who explains that it refers to a kind of garment; this is the only place the term appears throughout Scripture.

Rashi writes further that *Onkelos* renders

1. However, *R' Bachya* notes that in Judah's blessing one finds every letter of the *aleph beth* except for the letter *zayin.* The word *zayin* means *weapon,* and the absence of this letter indicates that the the Judaic kingdom will win its ultimate victory not with weapons, or through natural means, but by the merit of the Word of God. This is further indicated by Judah's name יְהוּדָה, which contains the Four-Letter Name of God, indicating that the foundation of Judah's reign is in compliance with the will of God, not physical force or weaponry.

49
12 *He will launder his garments in wine*
and his robe in the blood of grapes.
12 *Red-eyed from wine,*
and white-toothed from milk.

the term as *colored* garments, basing himself on the fact that such garments are worn to *allure* and *entice*, from the root סות, as in the word מֵסִית, *one who entices to idolatry*. Comp. this interpretation of the root in *Kesubos* 111b.

R' Shmuel ben Chofni Gaon [whose opinion is cited anonymously by *Ibn Ezra*] suggests that the definition of *garment* intimates that the word סות is an elliptic form of the word for garment, כְּסוּת.

סותה is synonymous with סותו. That it is spelled with a ה [the numerical equivalent of which is 5] alludes to the five garments which Judah wore [see *Bereishis Rabbah* 93:7] *(Midrash* cited in Torah *comm.* of *R' Yitzchak of Vienna)*. [See Zohar cited in footnote.]

12. חַכְלִילִי עֵינַיִם מִיָּיִן וּלְבֶן־שִׁנַּיִם מֵחָלָב — *Red-eyed from wine, and white-toothed from milk.*

This verse continues the metaphor of the abundant vintage and grazing land in Judah's region:

— There will be redness of eyes from the abundance of wine and there will be whiteness of teeth from the abundance of milk. The expression 'redness of eyes' is associated with the drinking of wine because one who drinks wine gets red eyes. [The מ of מִיָּיִן is not the comparative prefix meaning reddereyed *than* wine, but indicates redeyed *from* wine.] That milk will be abundant is proof that Judah will have sufficient pasture land to support large flocks *(Rashi)*.

Rashi continues that *Onkelos* interprets the verse figuratively in two ways: (a) *His mountains* ['eyes' metaphorically referring to lofty mountains from which one can gaze from afar] *red with wine*, (b) *his fountains* [taking עֵינַיִם in the sense of מַעְיָן, *wellspring*] i.e., his winepress and vats *flowing with wine;* his *valleys* [שִׁנַּיִם; see *Rashi* to *Exod.* 14:2] *white with grain and with flocks of sheep.*[1]

Radak interprets עֵינַיִם as *appearance* [comp. *Rashi* to *Exod.* 10:5]: His appearance will be ruddy from wine. The entire verse is a hyperbole.

R' Saadia Gaon also renders עֵינַיִם as *appearance*, but perceives the מ of מִיָּיִן as comparative. He accordingly renders: *Ruddier* [more robust; sparkling] *in appearance than wine, and teeth whiter than milk.*

— I.e., he is a man of regal appearance and suitable for royalty, as it says of David [*I Samuel* 16:12]: *Now he was ruddy, with fine eyes and good looking (B'chor Shor)*.

— The generation of the Messiah will be brilliant, glowing with vitality — with sparkling eyes and physical vigor, and teeth whiter than milk *(Akeidas Yitzchak)*.

The translation of חַכְלִילִי as denoting *redness* follows *Rashi* who cites the similar word חַכְלִלוּת in *Proverbs* 23:29.

[Apparently *Rashi* interprets the word as an adjectivial noun in the construct form, synonymous with חַכְלִיל, the suffix י being superfluous like the י in the words אֹסְרִי and בְּנִי in *v.* 11 above.]

The root is חכל, *red*. The double ל emphasizes the intensity of the redness *(Yohel Or)*.

1. The Sages in *Kesubos* 111b perceive the homiletical inference of this passage to refer to Israel's plea for God's graciousness. Israel says: A friendly look in God's 'eyes' [an anthropomorphic expression denoting God's beneficence] is more pleasant than wine, and His 'smile' is more pleasant than milk.

R' Yochanan said, 'The person who "makes his teeth white" [by smiling affectionately] to his friend is better than one who gives him milk to drink. Do not read וּלְבֶן שִׁנַּיִם מֵחָלָב, *and teeth white from milk*, but וּלְבוּן שִׁנַּיִם מֵחָלָב, [showing] *the whiteness of teeth* [is better] *than milk*.

יג זְבוּלֻן לְחוֹף יַמִּים יִשְׁכֹּן וְהוּא לְחוֹף אֳנִיֹּת
וְיַרְכָתוֹ עַל־צִידֹן:

Ramban also cites the word in Proverbs. He suggests, however, that contextually חַכְלִילִי, has the same meaning as כחלילי, *paint*, the letters חכ and כח being transposed. Thus, he renders: *His eyes shall be as though rouged with wine.*

13. Zebulun.

Having given a glimpse of the Messianic era and finding in Judah a fitting leader of the future house of Jewry, the Patriarch turns to his other children. He bestows his blessings, assigning to each according to his particular aptitudes his role in the harmony of the twelve tribes *(Abarbanel).*

Until this point, the Patriarch mentioned the children in the order of their birth. Now, although Dan, Naftali, and Gad were next in seniority, Jacob skipped to Issachar and Zebulun because they were sons of Leah, like the four oldest. He wished to conclude them as a unit before continuing with the sons of the maidservants *(Moshav Zekeinim).*

☙ Zebulun precedes Issachar.

Issachar was older than Zebulun, yet Jacob gave the latter precedence, because [as *Rashi* notes below], Zebulun engaged in commerce, and supported Issachar who studied Torah. Issachar's Torah-learning was made possible by Zebulun, and Zebulun was therefore accorded honor as if he were the elder, and blessed first *(Tanchuma;* cf. *Ibn Ezra).*

זְבוּלֻן לְחוֹף יַמִּים יִשְׁכֹּן — *Zebulun shall settle* [dwell] *by the seashore.*

I.e., his territory shall be by the 'border' of the sea. The term לְחוֹף [lit. **to** *the border* (i.e. *shore)*] is synonymous with עַל חוֹף, **upon** [or *by*] *the border (Rashi).*

And so it was when the land of Canaan was later divided among the tribes, Zebulun's territory was between the Sea of Kineret and the Mediterranean *(Akeidas Yitzchak).*

Zebulun's exact territory is delineated in *Joshua* 19:10ff. See *comm.* to ArtScroll ed.

The Talmud [*Megillah* 6a] records that Zebulun complained to the Holy One, Blessed is He, that his territory consisting of seashore and hills was inferior to the fertile fields of his brothers. Therefore God reassured him with the knowledge that in his waters will be found the *chilazon* [a much sought-after small, rare fish from which the purple *t'cheles* dye for the *tzitzis* was extracted], and the popular *taris* [*Rashi:* tunny fish]; and furthermore, Zebulun was assured that from his sands would be made the colorless glass [which was a source of wealth in ancient times].

Zebulun was thus blessed that he would live near seaports and engage in transporting his merchandise by ships to distant seaports where he would sell it at great profit.

וְהוּא לְחוֹף אֳנִיֹּת — *And he shall be at the ships' harbor* [lit. *shore*].

I.e., [since his territory will border the seashore] he [i.e., Zebulun] will constantly be at the port, where the ships bring merchandise. Moses alluded to the Issachar-Zebulun partnership when he said [*Deut.* 33:18]: *Rejoice Zebulun in your going out, and Issachar in your tents.* Zebulun went forth to trade, while Issachar studied Torah in the tents *(Rashi* from *Tanchuma;* see *Rashi* to יֹשֵׁב אֹהָלִים 25:27).

— Accordingly, Zebulun was accorded priority over Issachar who was older because גָּדוֹל הַמַּעֲשֶׂה

13 Zebulun shall settle by the seashore.
He shall be at the ships' harbor,
and his last border will reach Zidon.

יוֹתֵר מִן הָעוֹשֶׂה, *one who motivates others to accomplish is greater than one who accomplishes (Tanchuma; Mizrachi).*[1]

Nachalas Yitzchak perceives Zebulun's *territory* rather than Zebulun *himself* to be the subject of this phrase. He renders: *Zebulun shall settle by the seashore, and* **it** — i.e., his territory — *shall become a haven for ships, with its extreme province at Zidon.*

וְיַרְכָתוֹ עַל־צִידֹן — *And his last border* [lit. *flank; thigh*] *will reach* [lit. *is upon*] *Zidon.*

I.e., it will extend close to Zidon *(Rashi).*

Zidon was famed for its commerce. Cf. *Isaiah* 23:2 *(Rashbam).*

Zidon [now Saida] was a city between Tyre and Beirut, bordering the Mediterranean. It was the northwest boundary of Canaan. (See above 10:19) At one time it was apparently the dominant Phoenician city, but its hegemony later passed over to Tyre.

Since the well-known Zidon was actually in Asher's territory the Sages in the *Midrash* variously identify the Zidon in this verse with other lesser-known cities by similar names.

The *Vilna Gaon* maintains, however, that the Zidon in Asher's territory is referred to. In his comm. to *Joshua* 19:14, he explains that the implication of our verse is that Zebulun's territory bisected that of Asher to the north of him, and he had a land corridor, in the shape of a thigh-bone as it were, hugging the Mediterranean coast and extending to Zidon.

According to *Yafeh Toar* the implication is that Zebulun's extreme border will be near Zidon. However, Zidon itself will be in Asher's portion.

The translation of יַרְכָתוֹ [lit. *flank; hind part*] as *last* border follows *Rashi* who explains that in this context the term denotes *end*, as in *Exod.* 26:22 וּלְיַרְכְּתֵי הַמִּשְׁכָּן, *and for the ends of the Tabernacle.* Thus *Rashi* avoids the possible misinterpretation that *flank* in the literal sense refers *physically* to Zebulun's body *(Devek Tov).*

The term is derived from the root יְרֵכָה, *hindmost part, extremity,* not from the cognate root יָרֵךְ, *thigh (Ibn Caspi).*

Kli Yakar suggests that *thigh* connotes *commerce* which supports a person as a thigh supports the torso; he renders: *his commerce will extend to Zidon.*

14. Issachar.

[The Patriarch proceeds to bless the last of Leah's sons, Issachar. Although the simile of *strong-boned donkey* and the references to *land* seem to denote an allusion to *agricultural* pursuit — a view indeed expressed by one Sage in the Midrash and followed by several commentators — *Rashi* favors the traditional

1. *Sforno* elaborates: Jacob gave Zebulun the merchant precedence over Issachar the scholar and Moses did the same in his blessing *(Deut.* 33:18). It is impossible to engage in Torah study unless one first has his material necessities, as the Sages said, 'If there is no flour there is no Torah.' Wheneve someone assists his friend by providing his needs so that he can study Torah as Zebulun did, the service of God performed through the efforts of the scholar will be attributed to both of them. This is why the Torah instructed Israel to give gifts to *Kohanim* and *Levites,* so that the entire nation could have a share in those who uphold the Torah — for the *Kohanim* and Levites have the responsibility to study and teach Torah. Thereby all Jews will earn a share of the World to Come, as it is taught, All Israel has a share in the World to Come.

יד יִשָּׂשכָר חֲמֹר גָּרֶם רֹבֵץ בֵּין הַמִּשְׁפְּתָיִם:

Rabbinic interpretation that Jacob's blessing reflects Issachar's *spiritual* role as *bearer of the yoke of Torah* and cultivator of the spiritual treasures of the People. As noted above, Issachar devoted his time to Torah study and was supported by his brother Zebulun. Moses, too, alluded to this in his blessing (*Deut.* 33:28): *Rejoice, Zebulun, in your going out* (i.e. in your commerce), *and Issachar in your tents* (i.e. in your pursuit of Torah-study).

[A Biblical reference to Issachar's later emergence in a major role in the spiritual life of the People occurs in *I Chron.* 12:32 where the descendants of Issachar are described as *understanding the times to know what Israel must do; their leaders numbered two hundred, and all their brothers were at their pronouncement.* The Midrash (*Bereishis Rabbah* §72:5) expounds this verse:

Understanding the times — means that the scholars of Issachar had either an understanding of the seasons or of the science of intercalation (i.e. the adding of a month during lunar leap years];

their leaders numbered two hundred — denotes that the tribe of Issachar produced two hundred heads of the Sanhedrin;

all their brothers were at their pronouncement — means that Issachar's rulings were accepted as authoritative, the other tribes agreed to the *halachah* as pronounced by Issachar and he instructed them as though his words were a *halachah* given to Moses at Sinai.

[The esteem in which the tribe of Issachar was held for its proficiency in Torah, according to the Midrash, is further demonstated by the fact that although Issachar was Jacob's ninth son, his tribal prince was the *second* to bring an offering for the dedication of the altar (*Num.* 7:18-23). *Esther Rabbah* 4 records that the wise men consulted by Ahasuerus [Esther 1:13] were people of Issachar.

[Furthermore, the greatness of Issachar in matters of Torah law was so profound that the Talmudic Sage Rava (in *Yoma* 26a) declared that there was not to be found a rabbinic scholar who decided halachic matters who was not a descendant of Levi or Issachar. (The intent, according to *Yafeh Toar,* is that though the tribe of *Judah* was numerically predominant in the Sanhedrin in Jerusalem, the members of Levi and Issachar were the most prominent in interpreting individual questions of halachah for their brethren).

[Jacob's allusions to the *land* are perceived in the Midrash and *Zohar* to refer to the Torah of which it says: The *measure thereof is longer than the earth (Job* 11:9). Following a more literal interpretation of the allusion to *land,* however, some views in the Midrash and commentators infer from our verse that at least some people from Issachar worked the land in addition to their Torah study — a combination of Torah being combined with a wordly pursuit (see *Avos* 2:2). These various views will be synthesized in the commentary that follows.]

יִשָּׂשכָר חֲמֹר גָּרֶם — ***Issachar is a strong-boned donkey.***

Like a sturdy donkey capable of bearing a heavy load, Issachar can bear the heavy burden of Torah study *(Rashi* from *Tanchuma).*[1] [2]

1. As noted in the *comm.* to 30:16, the Sages [*Niddah* 31a and Midrash to our verse] perceive another implication of this passage to be: *As for Issachar, a donkey was instrumental* [as if vowelized גָּרַם, *caused*]. The reference is to the episode in chapt. 30 when Rachel gave Leah the right to spend the evening with Jacob in exchange for the *dudaim.* When Jacob rode home from the field, Leah knew of his arrival only because his donkey brayed loudly and headed toward her tent where she intercepted him and told him of her arrangement with Rachel. As a result of this encounter, Jacob spent that night with Leah, and Issachar was conceived.

14 **Issachar is a strong-boned donkey;
he rests between the boundaries.**

גָּרֶם is an Aramaic term meaning *bone*, hence the connotation of *strong-boned, sturdy (Ibn Caspi).*

The phrase is elliptic and should be understood as if it read חֲמוֹר בַּעַל גָּרֶם *(Mizrachi).*

R' Hirsch distinguishes between the terms גָּרֶם and עֶצֶם. He explains the latter to mean *bone* in general, the גָּרֶם of our verse means *limb* and *joint*, the bones that perform the moving, working function of a lever.

רֹבֵץ בֵּין הַמִּשְׁפְּתָיִם — *He rests* [lit. *crouches*] *between the boundaries.*

— Like a donkey roaming day and night that cannot rest in its stable, but has to lie down on the road between the boundaries of the cities to which it carries merchandise *(Rashi).*

The allusion is to the Torah Sages who toil day and night in their studies and know no formal rest, but are spiritually tranquil *(Shaarei Aharon).*

The Sages in the Midrash interpret this as a poetic description of the disciples who sit on the ground before the Sages, imbibing Torah-learning.

Sforno translates מִשְׁפְּתָיִם as *dual burdens* and interprets the reference to the strong-boned donkey which takes its rest 'between its packs,' i.e., while its burden and saddlebags are still upon it. Similarly, Issachar will toil restlessly, simultaneously bearing the burdens of Torah study, an occupation, and communal service, as befits a wise man who is well-rounded in intellect and character.

The above views follow the familiar Rabbinic interpretation, whereby the tribe of Issachar — supported by Zebulun — was noted for its role as Torah scholar and cultivator of the spiritual treasures of the nation [see below]. There are views in the Midrash — followed by many commentators who stress the simple sense of Scripture — that our passage implies that Issachar spent at least some of his time working the land. As *R' Hirsch* notes [see footnote next verse], Issachar's study of Torah — his primary goal — was combined in a worldly pursuit.

B'chor Shor [similarly, *Rashbam*], following this 'literal' sense, interprets our verse and contrasts the 'strong-boned' Issachar — who was physically endowed for agricultural work — with Zebulun who engaged in maritime trade. The metaphor reflects how Issachar, the farmer, would spend even his leisure time between the boundaries of his properties, guarding his fields.

— Between city boundaries tilling his fields *(Rashbam).*

Or, according to *Abarbanel:* between the furrows of the soil, tilling it.

2. When Moses blessed Zebulun and Issachar he added [*Deut.* 33:10]: עַמִּים הַר יִקְרָאוּ, *they shall call people to the Mountain.*

Rashi, based on the Midrash, explains the phrase in these terms: To trade with Zebulun, merchants from many parts of the world will come into his territory while he remains at the border. Then they will say, 'having come this far, let us continue to Jerusalem [i.e., the Temple Mount] to see how the God of Israel is worshipped, and what He has done.' When they will see all Jewry worshipping one God and following the same kashruth laws — unlike heathen nations, each of which worships a different diety — they will be inspired to say, 'There is no people as pure as this,' and they will become converts there, as it is written [*ibid.*]: שָׁם יִזְבְּחוּ זִבְחֵי צֶדֶק, *there they shall offer sacrifices of righteousness.*

According to R' Acha in the Midrash, the conversion of these foreigners will be a direct result of their admiration for the tribe of Issachar, which prospered though it devoted itself to the spiritual life of Torah. Accordingly, the intimation of יִשָּׂשכָר חֲמֹר גָּרֶם is that *Issachar is a donkey for 'gerim,'* proselytes [i.e. in the sense that, like a donkey delivering his load, Issachar is a proselyte-bearing donkey, bringing them to Judaism. *(Gerim* in this Midrashic context is a play on words of the Hebrew verb *garem.)*]

טו וַיַּרְא מְנֻחָה כִּי טוֹב וְאֶת־הָאָרֶץ כִּי
נָעֵמָה וַיֵּט שִׁכְמוֹ לִסְבֹּל וַיְהִי לְמַס
טז עֹבֵד: דָּן יָדִין עַמּוֹ כְּאַחַד

15. וַיַּרְא מְנֻחָה כִּי טוב — *[And] he saw tranquility that it was good.*

He realized that his territory was a blessed land. [The word מְנֻחָה, (lit. *rest)* alludes to the *land* where he found *tranquility;* comp. the connotation of the term מְנֻחָה as *land* in *Deut.* 12:9 אֶל־הַמְּנוּחָה וְאֶל־הַנַּחֲלָה, to the *'tranquility'* and to the *inheritance (Rashbam)*] *(Rashi; Onkelos).*

He saw that the tranquility of living on his land was better than travel to far-off places *(Rashbam).*

[This verse — like the others in this chapter — is phrased in the 'prophetic past' tense, which depicts the future as if it had already occurred.]

According to the Midrash, tranquility is an allusion to Torah doctrine, which is also described as טוב, *good* [*Prov.* 4:2]. [See *Radak* below.]

וְאֶת־הָאָרֶץ כִּי נָעֵמָה — *And the land that it was pleasant.*

— I.e., suitable for bearing fruit *(Rashi; Onkelos).*

According to the Midrash, *land* alludes to Torah 'whose ways are ways of נֹעַם, *pleasantness'* [*Prov.* 4:3], and 'whose measure is longer than the earth' [*Job* 11:9].

In an alternate rendering, *Radak* cites a Rabbinic interpretation, writing: The passage *he saw tranquility that it was good and the land that it was pleasant* is a metaphor depicting how Issachar's Torah will be pleasant and fulfilling, and his toil in Torah will be his repose; therefore *he bent his shoulder to bear* the toil of Torah and wisdom.

וַיֵּט שִׁכְמוֹ לִסְבֹּל — *Yet* [lit. *and*] *he bent his shoulder* [i.e., devoted his essence] *to bear.*

— The burden of Torah *(Rashi; Midrash; Targum Yonasan).*

The translation of the conjunctive ו as *yet* follows the interpretation of *Rashi* as understood by *R' Munk* and other commentators: Though Issachar perceived that his territory was blessed, etc., he had little interest in material wealth. Instead, *he bent his shoulder to bear* the burden of Torah, and he became a servant of the Jewish people, accepting the burden of deciding the rulings of the Torah for them and answering their questions. In other words, he became their 'spiritual servant,' as it were.

B'chor Shor, Rashbam and others: *When he saw that tranquility* — of remaining at home and working the land instead of traveling afar and engaging in maritime trade — *was good, and that the land was pleasant,* and able to provide his needs without the toil of commerce, *he bent his shoulder to the burden* of cultivating the land [or according to *Rashbam: to bear the burden* of kings (i.e. paying a portion of his crops as tax)].

Similarly, according to one Sage in the Midrash, the implication is that *he bent his shoulder to bear* — the burden of *Eretz Yisrael.* That is, he set himself to the labor required by the land.

In a different sense, within the expression *he bent his shoulder to bear* is the implication that he *humbled himself.* We derive from this that every Torah scholar should have the trait of humility *(R' Bachya).*

49 [15] *He saw tranquility that it was good,*
15 *and the land that it was pleasant,*
yet he bent his shoulder to bear
and he became an indentured laborer.

וַיְהִי לְמַס-עֹבֵד — *And he became an indentured laborer.*

[In the spiritual sense: as a result of Issachar's bearing the burden of Torah] *he, in effect, became* — to all his Israelite brothers — like an *indentured worker,* totally dedicated to his role of rendering decisions in matters of Torah and teaching the regulations concerning the fixing of the leap-years [סִדְרֵי עִיבּוּרִין]. This point is specifically mentioned in *I Chron.* 12:32: *The children of Issachar who knew the understanding of times, to know what Israel must do* [in observing the seasons *(Radak* ad loc.)]; *their leaders numbered two hundred* — Issachar provided two hundred heads of Sanhedrin — *and all their brothers followed their pronouncement* [i.e. their halachic rulings were accepted as authoritative] *(Rashi* from *Midrash).*

As mentioned in the introduction to *v.* 14, the tribe of Zebulun later played such a prominent role in the intellectual and religious life of the people that the Talmud [*Yoma* 26a] observes that there was hardly a decisor of halachic matters who was not from Levi or Issachar.

The sense of the idiomatic phrase לְמַס-עֹבֵד is to be interpreted as if it read עֹבֵד לְמַס or לְמַס-עֲבָדוּת, lit. *laborer for tribute* or *tributary of labor,* the sense being that the laborer in question had become obligated to perform work for the community. The term מַס has the familiar connotation of a monetary *tax,* but here [especially since it is qualified by עֹבֵד, *laborer*] it contextually refers to taxation paid by labor and physical task. According to the Rabbinic exegesis cited by *Rashi,* it refers to Issachar's service to the nation. Comp. *Exodus* 1:11 where שָׂרֵי מִסִּים lit. *taskmasters* refers to those whose job it was *to afflict them with their burdens* [ibid.], and *I Kings* 5:27 where King Solomon is recorded as having raised a מַס [levy; tribute] where the tribute consisted of thirty thousand laborers *(R' David Feinstein).*

Thus, in the figurative sense, as interpreted by *Rashi,* the obligatory burden was in their round-the-clock role as halachic *poskim* [decisors] to their brethren.

Although *Rashi* agreed with *Onkelos'* interpretation of the beginning of this verse, he notes that *Onkelos'* interpretation of this part differs.

Onkelos renders, *and he bowed his shoulder to bear* — i.e., to bear wars and conquer regions, for the tribe of Issachar dwelled near the border; *and he* — i.e., the enemy conquered by Issachar — *became a laboring payer of tribute.*

Many commentators maintain, to the contrary, that Issachar *avoided* military combat. *Ibn Ezra* writes that [although we find that during the time of the early Judges Issachar produced valiant warriors whom Deborah praised in *Judges* 5:15 *(Yohel Or)*], the tribe of Issachar appreciated the tranquility of agriculture and deeply loved the land. They preferred to pay levies to the King of Israel rather than furnish soldiers [similarly *Radak* in his primary interpretation], or to pay a levy to foreign nations so they would not attack them, becoming in effect tribute-paying vassals.

Rashbam somewhat similarly interprets that Issachar paid the kings a tithe of their crops as royal tax.

16. Dan.

The Patriarch now turns to Dan since he was the oldest son of Bilhah, Rachel's maidservant *(Abarbanel).*

יז שִׁבְטֵי יִשְׂרָאֵל׃ יְהִי־דָן נָחָשׁ עֲלֵי־דֶרֶךְ

דָּן יָדִין עַמּוֹ — *Dan will avenge* [lit. *judge*] *his people.*

He will take vengeance for all his people from the Philistines. The prophetic allusion is to Dan's descendant, Samson [one of the Judges of Israel, who single-handedly fought the Philistines (*Judges* 13:24 — 16-31)] (*Rashi* from *Midrash*).

— This is in keeping with the interpretation that Jacob's blessings of the Tribes were allusions to prominent *descendants* of the Tribal Ancestors (*Maharzu*).

Rashi explains that the word יָדִין, familiarly interpreted *judge*, means *avenge* in this context. It has the same meaning in *Deut.* 32:36: כִּי יָדִין ה׳ עַמּוֹ, *for HASHEM will avenge His people.*

Ramban interprets similarly, explaining that the term יָדִין [*judge*] is used to denote the vengeance instead of the more exact term for vengeance, יִקּוֹם [from נְקָמָה, *revenge*], since Samson the 'avenger' bore the title of Judge, rather than King.

The familiar term for revenge is נְקָמָה, but that term includes even cases where the vengeance is unlawful. The term used in our verse, יָדִין, applies only to lawful vengeance (*Be'er Yitzchak*).

Other early commentators — e.g. *R' Shmuel ben Chofni, B'chor Shor, R' Meyuchas* [also the *Midrash*; see next verse] — interpret יָדִין in the literal sense of *judge* and note that this is a reference to the Judge who will descend from Dan — Samson — and will actually judge the entire nation.[1]

כְּאַחַד־שִׁבְטֵי יִשְׂרָאֵל — *The tribes of Israel* [*will be*] *united as one.*

The Hebrew idiomatically reads *as one of the tribes of Israel.* The translation follows *Rashi's* primary interpretation [as if the phrase read שִׁבְטֵי יִשְׂרָאֵל כְּאֶחָד (*Mizrachi*)]. Alternatively, *Rashi* adds, one could interpret the verse to refer to the *'unique one'* (הַמְיוּחָד) from among the tribes — a reference to David, a member of Judah [the most distinguished of the tribes.][2]

According to the latter interpreta-

1. In *Pesachim* 4a, the further intimation of the Patriarch's testament is that the Danites were a very litigious tribe — they would continually argue over money matters and go to the courts. "There was a certain man who would always say, 'Let us go to litigate.' It was inferred from this habit that he was a Danite, as the verse says *Dan will judge his people.*"

✥§ It is the custom from Rosh Chodesh Nissan until the twelfth of that month to read, at morning services, verses from the chapter of the *Nesi'im*, tribal Princes [*Numbers* chapt. 7] — a selection dealing with a different *Nasi* each day.

Interestingly, the day of the week that the verses dealing with the *Nasi* of the tribe of Dan are read always coincides with the day of the week on which the next Rosh Hashanah will fall. *R' Shlomo Zalman* [brother of R' Chaim of Volozhin] once remarked homiletically that an allusion for this association occurs in our verse: *Dan will judge his people* — that is, on the day of the week that the portion of Dan is read, *God will judge His People*, i.e., Rosh Hashanah.

2. The Midrash observes: Had Dan not been linked with this outstanding tribe [Judah], Dan would not have produced the one judge that he did produce — Samson the son of Manoah.

Sefer Chassidim ed. *Mekitzei Nirdamim*, p.18, records that implicit in the Patriarch's prophetic linkage of Dan with Judah, was that Chushim, Dan's only son, would join Judah to slay Esau and thus Dan *avenged his people like the distinguished one among the tribes.*

In another Midrashic exegesis, כְּאַחַד alludes to יְחִידוֹ שֶׁל עוֹלָם, *the Unique One of the universe*, the Holy One, Blessed is He. "R' Yochanan said, Samson judged Israel like the Unique One of the tribes of Israel. Just as God needs no help in battle, Samson, too, required no assistance but slew his enemies with only the jawbone of a donkey" [*Judges* 15:15].

[16] *Dan will avenge his people,*
the tribes of Israel will be united as one.
[17] *Dan will be a serpent on the highway,*

tion, the verse would mean: (Samson, the noted descendant of) *Dan will avenge his people like the 'unique one' of the tribes of Israel* (i.e., like David, of the distinguished tribe of Judah, who would slay Goliath and cut off the foreskins of a hundred Philistines [*I Sam.* 18:27 *Be'er Mayim Chaim*).

Comp. *Onkelos:* "From the house of Dan there will be chosen and will arise a man in whose days his people shall be delivered and in whose years the tribes of Israel will have tranquility together." Targum Yonasan renders: " ... All the tribes of Israel will heed him together."

Rashbam denies vigorously that in the literal sense of the passage the Patriarch would have focused his blessing on Samson — an individual who fell to the Philistines, was blinded by them, and died ignominiously together with them. Rather, he maintains that the prophetic reference is to the *tribe of Dan* who in the days of both Moses [see *Num.* 2:31; 10:25] and later Joshua [see *Josh.* 6:9] formed the rear-guard of the camps warding off the enemy and avenging attacks made on the stragglers.

Ibn Ezra maintains that the implication is a Patriarchal assurance that: Although Dan was the son of a maidservant, he would have his own standard *like the tribes of Israel* who descended from the other wives, and moreover would be a ruler [during Samson's judgeship] over others. [*Radak* comments similarly.]

17. יְהִי־דָן נָחָשׁ עֲלֵי־דֶרֶךְ — *Dan will be a serpent on the highway.*

Following *Rashi* and *Ramban,* the words apply to Samson whose single-handed tactics in battle against the Philistines corresponded closely to Jacob's description. *Ramban* suggests that he is compared to a serpent because he did not wage open war against his enemies as did the other judges and kings, but instead went out alone to strike against them, like the serpent that leaves his lair to attack travelers on the road and then recoils into its hiding place, or like the small species of serpent that is entirely imperceptible to travelers. Similarly, using guerilla tactics, Samson struck alone without an army, and then retired into hiding.

According to *Rashbam,* as noted, the reference is to the *tribe* of Dan. [His was the northernmost tribe; the first one whom marauding invaders from the north would encounter.] The blessing was that Dan be like a serpent on the way and kill the heathens.

R' Hirsch observes that it does not say דָּן נָחָשׁ, Dan *is* a serpent, as it says Issachar *is* a strong-boned donkey, or Naftali *is* a hind. Rather, the characteristic with which Jacob blessed Dan is not an essential part of him. Rather it is a distasteful, *un-*Jewish characteristic that he will adapt of necessity and discard as soon as he can. Dan will not have the strength of Judah. Not having the force with which to repel enemies, Dan will resort to cunning, doing with clever tactics what he cannot do with brute force; like a treacherous snake biting a steed's hoof so that its rider will topple backward. But Jacob did not say דָּן נָחָשׁ, *Dan 'is'* a serpent — rather ... יְהִי דָן, *Dan will be* cunning when forced to defend the nation, but when the danger is over, he will revert to Israel-like honestly and wholesome conduct.

שְׁפִיפֹן עֲלֵי־אֹרַח הַנֹּשֵׁךְ עִקְּבֵי־סוּס
יח וַיִּפֹּל רֹכְבוֹ אָחוֹר: לִישׁוּעָתְךָ קִוִּיתִי

Primarily it is related to נשף, as in *Isaiah* 40:24 where it means *hiss; blow.* He comments further in 3:15 that, 'when a serpent comes to bite it blows with a kind of hissing sound.'

According to *Ramban*, the term refers to a snake that bites [יָשׁוּף] at the heel. It derives from שפה but its second root-letter is doubled in this form. [*Radak* in *Shorashim* interprets similarly.] *Rambam* goes on to cite *Yerushalmi Terumos* 8:3 that *sh'fifon* is a small specie of serpent that seems as thin as a hair, almost imperceptible to unsuspecting travelers.

[*R' Eisenstadt* in his comm. to *Ramban* suggests that this serpent's thinness is alluded to by the very diminutive ון suffix of his name. Comp. such words as אִישׁוֹן, פַּעֲמוֹן.]

הַנֹּשֵׁךְ עִקְּבֵי־סוּס — *That bites a horse's heels.*

— Such being the manner of the serpent. The Torah thus continues the analogy comparing Samson with the serpent that bites the horse's heel *(Rashi)* ...

[*Rashi* makes this comment to emphasize that the subject of this phrase is the figurative serpent and not Dan himself.]

Continuing *Onkelos:* " ... He will weaken the horses and chariots and throw their riders backward." *Targum Yonasan* paraphrases:" ... that bites the horse on his heel, and the terrified horse throws his rider. In this way will Samson, son of Manoach, slay all the Philistine heroes, the horsemen and infantry; he will hamstring their horses and hurl their riders backwards."

וַיִּפֹּל רֹכְבוֹ אָחוֹר — *So its rider falls backward.*

— The rider falls although the serpent had not even touched him directly. Similarly, Samson caused the death of many Philistines without touching them by breaking the two middle pillars of their temple, causing the roof to collapse upon them [*Judges* 16:29] *(Rashi).*

Ramban agrees, explaining that *biting the horse's heel* alludes to how Samson pushed down the twin pillars upon which the temple of the idol Dagan rested, and the three thousand people on the roof — figuratively, *the rider falling backward* — were killed. The simile depicts how a horse, when bitten, raises its head and forefeet, causing the rider to fall backward.

Onkelos translates נָחָשׁ [serpent] by כְּחִיוִי חוּרְמָן, *like the serpent called churman,* a species whose bite is incurable; it is [also called in Hebrew] צִפְעוֹנִי, *tzifoni.* It is called a *churman* because it renders everything devastated [*cherem*]. *(Rashi).*

Comp. *Targum Yonasan* to *Isaiah* 11:8 who renders צִפְעוֹנִי as חִוֵי חוּרְמָן. Cf. also *Jeremiah* 8:17: *Behold I will send against you 'tzifoni,' serpents which cannot be charmed,* i.e. they are not responsive even to a charmer and cannot be warded off.

שְׁפִיפֹן עֲלֵי־אֹרַח — *A viper by the path.*[1]

This parallels the description of the deadly serpent in the previous stich: "... Moreover when the circumstances warrant it, he will be like a viper who lurks by the path and venomously attacks the unsuspecting passersby" *(Ibn Caspi).*

Cf. *Onkelos:* "A unique man will

1. In the Talmud [*Sanhedrin* 105a and *Sotah* 10a] *shfifon* is related to שְׁפִי, *haltingly* [i.e., as if *lame* on one foot; cf. *comm.* to *Numb.* 23:3]. The double consonant is homiletically rendered as denoting *double lameness* and depicting a *slithering movement,* as if the word were an adjective, the phrase meaning: *slithering along the path.*

Since this blessing is Talmudically interpreted as referring to Samson, the view is recorded that Samson — here compared with a *slithering serpent* — was lame in both feet, and had to 'slither' along. [See *Maharsha* there.]

*a viper by the path
that bites a horse's heels
so its rider falls backward.*
18 *For your salvation do I long, HASHEM!*

arise from the house of Dan, whose terror will fall upon the peoples; one who will smite the Philistines with strength as does the serpent *churman* [=devoted to destruction (see *Rashi* above)]. Lurking by the way he will slay the mighty of the Philistine host ...''

The translation of *shfifon* as *viper* is conjectural.

Rashi explains the term as meaning נָחָשׁ [serpent]. 'I am of the opinion,' writes *Rashi*, 'that it is so called because it hisses [*noshef*] [when biting].' Cf. 3:15 וְאַתָּה תְּשׁוּפֶנּוּ עָקֵב. *Rashi*, in his comm. to that verse, explains that the term תְּשׁוּפֶנּוּ [which in the context of that verse means: *bite*] has several meanings.

18. לִישׁוּעָתְךָ קִוִּיתִי ה׳ — *For Your salvation do I long, HASHEM!*

[According to *Rashi* these words were not Jacob's prayer for himself. Rather with these words he was intimating that *Samson* would one day utter a heartfelt plea to God for salvation:]

Jacob prophesied that Samson, blinded by the Philistines, would finally pray *to God, 'Remember me, please, and strengthen me,please, only this once ...' (Rashi).*[1]

[Thus, according to *Rashi* the first-person in this verse is a prophetic quote of Samson's prayer. *R' Saadia Gaon* and *R' Bachya* interpret similarly.]

R' Bachya explains that even though Samson himself died together with the Philistines, his prayer was answered by God. He prayed that he be granted the strength to demolish the Temple and cause its collapse upon himself as well; he said תָּמוֹת נַפְשִׁי עִם פְּלִשְׁתִּים, *may I die together with the Philistines.*[2]

According to *Ramban*, however, this is *Jacob's* own outburst of prayer to God:

When Jacob foresaw that the salvation brought about by Samson would cease with the judge's capture and death, Jacob exclaimed, ''*For* **Your** *salvation do I hope, HASHEM* — I do not rely on temporary salvation through a 'serpent' or a judge, but I await *Your* salvation — which will be for all eternity!''

Comp. the *Midrash:* Jacob prophetically saw Samson and thought that the Redemption would come in his days. But when he saw him dead he exclaimed 'He, too, is dead! Then *I wait for Your salvation, HASHEM!'* — It is not *he* who will herald the Redemption, but one who will descend from Gad — Elijah. [See footnote end of next verse.] *Targum Yonasan* interprets similarly.

Da'as Zekeinim explains that when Jacob foresaw Samson's phenomenal power he said, 'Even though he is victoriously powerful it is wrong to revel in his strength' ... Jacob therefore emphasized that the real Source of strength is only the Almighty. The flow of the blessing, then, is: *Dan will be a*

2. *R' Bachya* writes that the Kabbalists find in this three-word prayer mystical combinations of letters that spell the Divine Name that provides salvation against enemies. This fact is alluded to in the story of Samson, for Scripture says of him, וַיֵּט בְּכֹחַ, *he turned with strength* [*Judges* 16:30]; the verse does not say Samson used כֹּחוֹ, *his own strength*, for the strength making his feat possible was granted him by God, in response to this invocation of the Name that provides help against enemies.

In order to arrive at the combination of letters that yields this Name, the three words of this prayer must be recited in different orders. The common custom is to recite it in the *Krias Shema* before going to sleep as follows: לִישׁוּעָתְךָ קִוִּיתִי ה׳, קִוִּיתִי ה׳ לִישׁוּעָתְךָ, ה׳ לִישׁוּעָתְךָ קִוִּיתִי. However, some infer that *R' Bachya* prefers a different order (see *Chavel* ed.), and *Sh'lah* requires *six* variations of the verse.

serpent, etc., but nevertheless, the real Victor is the Holy One, Blessed is He, as I acknowledge by stating, *For Your salvation do I hope, HASHEM.*

Rashbam interprets: I pray, Dan, that God grant you His salvation and strengthen you in the task of fighting the nations. He renders, *That you be granted* [*Divine*] *salvation,* [*O Dan*], *do I pray to HASHEM.*

Ibn Ezra interprets similarly, that upon prophetically seeing his son as a serpent biting a horse's heel, he grew apprehensive that the 'serpent' would be in mortal danger that the rider would crush its head. Jacob therefore interjected, *For your Godly salvation,* O Dan, *do I hope.* The prayer לִישׁוּעָתְךָ קִוִּיתִי ה׳ either means: *I have hoped that HASHEM will be your salvation,* or: *that HASHEM will save you.*[1]

Ibn Ezra goes on to cite R' Yitzchak who postulates that when Jacob envisioned his son Dan as a serpent [possibly intimating cunning wickedness] Jacob grew frightened and prayed that God save him [Jacob from evil descendants].

An interpretation has been advanced that at that moment Jacob's sickness grew sharply worse, so he prayed that God save him and grant him the strength to bless his other sons. Most commentators, however [see e.g. *HaKsav V'HaKaballah; Yohel Or*], dismiss this as being 'without rhyme or reason,' and as entirely conjectural and out of context with the Scriptural narrative, which does not even hint at such a possibility. Furthermore, a brief remission from sickness is not the connotation of the term יְשׁוּעָה, *salvation,* which has a more permanent, long lasting connotation.

19. Gad.

Jacob now blesses Gad, the eldest son of Leah's maidservant Zilpah *(Abarbanel).*

גָּד גְּדוּד יְגוּדֶנּוּ — *Gad will recruit a regiment* [lit. *a troop will troop from Gad.* The Hebrew verbs *g'dud y'gudenu* were chosen for this context because they are plays on the name Gad].

I.e., the tribe of Gad will recruit regiments of troops from its citizens. The reference is to the time when the Israelites crossed the Jordan to conquer *Eretz Yisrael.* Although the Gadites' territory was on the east of the Jordan, and they had no personal interest in the conquest, they nobly sent armed troops across the Jordan to assist their brothers in waging war. The Gadites valiantly fought the Canaanite nations together with the other tribes and remained until the Land was conquered *(Rashi; Midrash).*

The translation of יְגוּדֶנּוּ as יָגוּד, literally: *shall troop forth,* הֵימֶנּוּ, **from** *him,* rather than in the reflexive: *troops shall troop* **against** *him,* follows *Rashi* who compares the verb form with יְצָאוּנִי in *Jeremiah* 10:20 which means *have gone forth from me* [i.e., have left me] rather than have gone out *toward* me. [Cf. *Rashi* on תִּמְלָאֵמוֹ, *Exod.* 15:9].

1. *R' Munk* makes the incisive observation that Jacob had need to pray for the entire tribe of Dan, for it faced physical and spiritual dangers greater than that of the other tribes. Physically, as the extreme northernmost tribe in *Eretz Yisrael* proper, Dan was more exposed to attack than any other tribe on the western side of the Jordan. Spiritually, there was even greater cause for foreboding. It seems that idolatry had a greater lure for Dan than for any other tribe; it became the haven of Michah's idol [*Judges* ch. 18], and it was the tribe that worshiped the golden calves set up by King Jeroboam in its territory [*I Kings* 12:30]. Jacob feared that the entire tribe would suffer the fate of its illustrious son, Samson, whose tragic fate was partly caused by his marriage to a Philistine woman. Knowing this prophetically, Jacob prayed for God's salvation for Dan.

19 **G***ad will recruit a regiment*
and it will retreat in its tracks.

Rashi explains further — citing the grammarian Menachem ben Seruk — that all of the words in this verse containing the letters גד are to be classified under the cognate noun גדד. The two-letter root is גד, but as is the rule with all such roots, the second root-letter is doubled when the word occurs as a noun; hence גְּדוּד. Cf. שָׁד/נְדוּדִים/לָנוּד/נָד; שָׁדוּד/יָשׁוּד. In the *kal*, future tense [as in our verse], the root letter is not doubled; hence: יָגוּד; יָנוּד; יָרוּם. [Thus יָגוּד=יְגוּדֶנּוּ, *shall troop forth*, הֵימֶנּוּ, *from him*.] However, when the verb is reflexive or causative [which is not the case here according to *Rashi*] the second root letter is doubled: יְעוֹדֵד; יִתְעוֹדֵד; יִתְרוֹמֵם; יִתְגוֹדֵד; מְשׁוֹבֵב.

[For differing interpretations of this phrase by *Ramban* and others, see below.]

וְהוּא יָגֻד עָקֵב — *And it will retreat in its tracks* [lit. *it shall troop, heel*].

Following *Rashi:* And after the conquest, Gad's regiment will return safely to their territory on the east of the Jordan עָקֵב, *in its tracks,* i.e. by the same roads and paths upon which they had initially traveled — and not one of the troops will be missing. The expression עָקֵב [lit. *heel*] has the meaning of *footpaths; tracks;* comp. *Psalms* 128:20; *Song of Songs* 1:8. [Thus, the term עָקֵב in this context idiomatically means: *shall retrace their footsteps.*]

Ramban is in apparent disagreement with *Rashi's* grammatical analysis of the word יְגוּדֶנּוּ [see above] and following the interpretation in *Yerushalmi Sotah* 8:10, explains the passage as follows: גָּד גְּדוּד יְגוּדֶנּוּ, *Gad: troops shall constantly raid him,* וְהוּא יָגוּד עָקֵב, *but he* [the word וְהוּא, lit. *and he* being emphatic in this syntax] *shall raid at their heel.* That is, since Gad had a large area east of the Jordan, his land would be surrounded by enemies and subject to constant attack by neighboring Ammon and Moab. Jacob praised the valor and courage of Gad, stating that the Gadites would not be dismayed by these invading troops but would follow the enemy in his tracks, pursue him, and be victorious over him 'returning on the heel of those who tried to shame him.' The connotation is similar to Moses' later blessing [*Deut.* 33:20]: *Blessed be He that enlarges Gad; he dwells like a lioness,* i.e. he lurks like a lioness over the 'prey' of the foreign troops that always attempted to invade his enlarged territory. Gad would be undaunted by them, and would always be victorious.

Ramban suggests further that this passage might be a prophetic allusion to the wars of the Ammonites against Jephtah the Gileadite [see *Judges* 11:33]. Troops from Ammon would always raid Gilead, and the reference is to the occasion when Jephtah, after they refused his overtures of peace, won a smashing victory over them and their cities. *Ramban* explains that the conflict of Ammon with Gad was because the Gadites inherited all the cities of Gilead and half the cities of Ammon. [Gilead was a city of Gad. See *Joshua* 13:25.] Jacob prophetically alluded to this specific event in his testament to Gad since it was a great miracle, just as he alluded specifically to Samson's miraculous slaughter of the Philistines in his testament to Dan.

Onkelos interprets עָקֵב as denoting *wealth; substance* [comp. עֵקֶב in *Deut.* 7:5 which *Ibn Ezra* interprets as *reward*]. He renders our passage: From the house of Gad armed legions will go over the Jordan before their brothers in battle; *and with much substance will they return to their land.*

According to *Rashbam,* the reference is to the war of Joshua when the Gadite troops would march in the forefront [see *Josh.* 6:9 and comp. there] as the Israelites went out to conquer the Land;

כ עָקֵב׃ מֵאָשֵׁר שְׁמֵנָה לַחְמוֹ וְהוּא יִתֵּן
כא מַעֲדַנֵּי־מֶלֶךְ׃ נַפְתָּלִי אַיָּלָה שְׁלֻחָה

and on their victorious return from battle, they would bring up the rear to defend against possible attacks from the defeated enemy.

Sforno explains the implication to be: *Gad shall go forward and attack* [in contrast with Dan who will use guerrilla tactics] *and he will battle his enemies at the heel,* that is, his enemies will flee from his superior forces.

The Midrash interprets similarly, rendering יְגוּדֶנּוּ from גדד meaning *cut; destroy; despoil: Battalions shall come to despoil Gad, but Gad will cut them down at their heel,* i.e. as they flee him. [*R' Shmuel ben Chofni* and *Tur,* similarly.]

According to *Ibn Ezra,* Jacob was prophesying that a troop will pounce upon Gad but Gad will be victorious עָקֵב, *in the end* [the *heel* being so called because it is at the *extremity* of the body — i.e., he will have the final victory.] *Ibn Ezra* writes [that it is unknown to us exactly which event Jacob meant since] 'we cannot know today all the tribulations that befell our ancestors.'[1]

Another possible translation is: *Good fortune will pursue Gad, and he will have good fortune in the end.* See 30:10 (*Akeidah*).

20. Asher.

Having blessed Gad, Zilpah's older son, Jacob now continues with her younger son. *Daas Zekeinim* [cited below] advances an explanation for the continuity between Gad and Asher in this connection.

מֵאָשֵׁר שְׁמֵנָה לַחְמוֹ — *From Asher — his bread* [*will have*] *richness* [lit. *oil*].

I.e., the food [referred to here, as is common in Scripture, as *bread*] that will come *from* [the territory of] *Asher* will be 'oily' in the sense that Asher's land will be so rich in olive groves that it will flow with oil like a fountain. Moses blessed Asher similarly [*Deut.* 33:24]: וְטֹבֵל בַּשֶּׁמֶן רַגְלוֹ, *he shall dip his foot in oil.* As we find related in the Talmud [*Menachos* 85b]: Once the people of Laodicia were in need of oil. Only at a city in Asher was their agent able to obtain the very large quantity they needed, after having failed at Jerusalem and other cities (*Rashi*).

Rashi thus interprets the prefix מ of מֵאָשֵׁר [lit. *from Asher*] as denoting *from* **the territory of** *Asher. Ibn Ezra* interprets similarly, contrary to the view of *R' Avraham ben HaRambam* who suggests that the מ is poetically superfluous, much like the last י in הַיּוֹשְׁבִי, a word which is synonymous with הַיּוֹשֵׁב. The sense according to the latter view is that our passage is constructed like *v.* 19, the syntactical sense being: [As for] *Asher: his food shall be rich.*

Rashbam explains that the Israelites used to dip their food in oil supplied from Asher [thus: *from Asher: the oil for its* (i.e. the Israelite nation's) *food*].

Rashi's interpretation of *bread* as a general

1. The Sages in the Midrash perceive a Messianic allusion in this verse. As noted in the comm. to *v.* 18, Jacob originally thought that Samson, a descendant of Dan, would herald the redemption of Israel. But when he prophetically saw him dead, he foresaw that the Redemption would be heralded by a descendant of Gad — Elijah.

Accordingly, the passage, *but Gad ... will troop at the End* [עָקֵב, *heel,* referring to the *End;* see *Ibn Ezra* above], Midrashically refers to Elijah, a descendant of Gad, who in the End of Days will be the precursor of the Messiah, as it says [*Malachi* 3:23]: *Behold I send you Elijah the prophet before the coming of the great and awesome day of HASHEM.*

[Cf. also *Bereishis Rabbah* 71:9. Elijah hailed from Gilead (see *I Kings* 17:1), and as *Ramban* notes above, s.v. וְהוּא יָגֻד, Gilead is associated with Gad. There are differing Midrashic opinions on this matter, however. Some say Elijah was a *Kohen* and others say he was a Benjaminite.]

49
20

20 **F**rom Asher — his bread will have richness, and he will provide kingly delicacies.

term for *food* is consistent with his interpretation of the word in 31:54.

Radak suggests that the prefix מ, *of Asher,* might indicate that only a *portion* of Asher's territory would be *rich.* He further interprets that *bread* is a metaphor for *soil,* since it is the soil that yields bread. In general, however, the term embraces all food.

According to *Midrash Tanchuma, bread* is a metaphor for women, the sense being that the women of Asher were beautiful.

Daas Zekeinim followed by *Tur* interprets this verse as reverting to Gad: If Gad will be so involved in military pursuits, when will he have the time to cultivate his own Land? The answer given is: *From Asher shall his* [Gad's] *food be rich, and he* [i.e. Asher] *will provide him* [i.e. Gad] *with royal dainties.* Included in this verse, then, is Asher's blessing as well, since by implication he learns that his territory will be fertile and abundant.

After saying that Dan and Gad will defend Israel against external foes, Jacob turned to two tribes, Asher and Naftali, who would advance the nation's internal prosperity. Asher would provide choice food; apparently his soil was better suited to growing luxuries than ordinary necessities *(Daas Zekeinim).*

According to *Chizkuni,* since Jacob did not really bless Gad, he now blessed his territory by implication: *More than* [this being the meaning of the prefix מ] *Asher's shall his,* that is, Gad's, *bread be rich,* for his territory shall be fertile. This does not imply, however, that Asher's own territory would be in any way deficient, since *he — Asher — too, shall provide royal dainties,* but nevertheless, Gad's territory shall be superior.

Ibn Ezra observes that our verse uses לֶחֶם as a *feminine* noun as it is modified by a *feminine* adjective, שְׁמֵנָה. In other places, however, the word occurs as a *masculine* noun. He concludes therefore, that לֶחֶם is among those words, such as אֵשׁ and רוּחַ, which can occur either in the masculine or feminine forms.

וְהוּא יִתֵּן מַעֲדַנֵּי מֶלֶךְ — *And he will provide* [lit. *give*] *kingly delicacies.*

His rich produce will be worthy of royal tables and will be sought by kings *(Radak; R' Meyuchas).*

The term מַעֲדַן is thus derived from עדן, *pleasure;* when applied to food it means *delicacy.*

Rashbam interprets מַעֲדָן from עדן as *emollient; ointment.* Comp. עֶדְנָה, *delicate skin,* in 18:12. The meaning here is: *And he will provide royal emollients.* That is, kings will use his oil to make softening ointments for their skin. The Talmud [*Menachos* 86a] speaks of *anfakinon,* which is the oil of not-yet-ripe olives. It was used for smearing as it removes hair and softens the skin.

Following *Tanchuma* that 'bread' is a metaphor for women [see comm. to 39:6, *'Except for the bread*], the intimation here is that the kings of Israel would take their queens from the tribe of Asher. Furthermore, the Midrash notes, whenever the kings were angry at the Asherites, they forgave them for the sake of these queens.

Midrash Rabbah, homiletically reading the unvowelized word שמנה [rich; oily] as if it were also vowelized שְׁמֹנָה, *eight,* interprets: *His land shall be rich, his bread shall be rich, and he shall be the ancestor of those who wear eight garments* [for his tribe will provide wives for High Priests, who, in the course of their service, wore eight vestments].

There is a further view in the Midrash that the blessing alludes to the capacity of Asher's soil to yield fine oil and that his tribe would furnish the sacred olive oil for the Temple.

21. Naftali.

Having blessed Zilpah's son, Jacob now reverts to bless Bilhah's younger son, and thus conclude the sons of the maidservants.

נַפְתָּלִי אַיָּלָה שְׁלֻחָה — *Naftali is a hind let loose.*

Rashi offers three interpretations based on different Midrashim:

☐ 1. This is a figurative reference to Naftali's *territory,* specifically to the Plain of Gennesar [a district near the Sea of Kinnereth, which, as noted in *Joshua* 19:25, was located in Naftali's district; see *Onkelos* to *Deut.* 3:17 who renders Kinnereth as *Gennesar*] where the crops ripen swiftly, like a running hind. The expression *hind let loose* means let loose to run free.

The metaphor of hind שְׁלוּחָה, *sent forth,* refers to a hind that had been captured and was then released, so that it runs all the faster to escape *(Daas Zekeinim).*

☐ 2. This alludes to the war against Sisera [during the time of Deborah the prophetess, a descendant of Naftali, when Barak from Kadesh-Naftali led Israelite forces in a war against the Canaanite forces led by their general, Sisera *(Judges 4ff)*]. The valiant and swift warriors of Naftali played a leading role in this battle. Scripture *ibid.* relates that Deborah told Barak, *Take with you ten thousand men of the tribe of Naftali,* and they deployed there most swiftly. The term שָׁלַח, in the sense of *run quickly* is used there describing the incident [*ibid.* 5:15]. [*Rashbam* renders somewhat similarly that the reference is to the warriors of Naftali who were nimble as hinds.]

The Midrash records that while other tribes were compared to animals [see *Sotah* 11b], only Naftali is compared to a *female* animal, an אַיָּלָה, *hind.* This was to allude to his female descendant, the prophetess Deborah.

☐ 3. It is a reference to the Talmudic tradition that on the day Jacob was buried, Naftali's swiftness afoot was instrumental in establishing the Patriarch's right to burial in the family sepulchre (see below).

As related in the Talmud [*Sotah* 13a], when Jacob's sons desired to bury him in the Cave of Machpelah, Esau [according to the *Midrash* 98:17 and *Pirkei d'Rabbi Eliezer* 9, the Hittites] tried to stop them claiming that he, as firstborn had the right to burial in the cave. Esau challenged, 'Produce your deed of title to this cave.'

'It is in Egypt,' they replied.

'Who shall go for it?' they pondered. — 'Naftali, who is swift as a hind.' And they dispatched Naftali who brought it back swiftly *like a hind let loose.*

R' Hirsch observes that if hind could be used as messengers, one could be sure that they would carry out their missions swiftly. Accordingly, Jacob's implication was that Naftali, although he does not do things on his own initiative, can be trusted to execute swiftly whatever has been entrusted to him by those responsible for the benefit of the community.[1]

1. Ancient rulers used to send hinds as message-bearers [much in the manner that homing pigeons were used for this task]. Hinds born in one country would be brought to another. When the king of the latter country wished to dispatch a message to the king of the former country, he would select a hind from there, attach a message to its horns, and release it to run quickly to its original habitat where the king would receive the message. The phrase *who delivers beautiful sayings* [*v.* 21] alludes to this mission of the swift hind.

This practice is mentioned in *Yerushalmi Shevi'is* 9:2, where an incident is recorded that a

49
21

21 **N***aftali is a hind let loose*
who delivers beautiful sayings.

Abarbanel — consistent with his interpretation that in his blessings to each of the tribes Jacob was insinuating why none of the tribes were suitable for royalty except Judah — explains that Jacob was implying that Naftali possessed qualities fit for royal *servitors*, but not for kings themselves.

הַנֹּתֵן אִמְרֵי שָׁפֶר — *Who delivers* [lit. *gives*] *beautiful sayings.*

Generally, this refers to the tribe's reputation for eloquence *(Abarbanel).* According to the *Targumim,* the name Naftali is a composite of נוֹפֶת לוֹ, *the honey which flows from him,* as in *Proverbs* 24:13.

Following *Rashi's* three interpretations cited above:

□ 1. [That the first half of the verse figuratively refers to the swiftness of the ripening of the fruit, and its excellence] ... *Who delivers beautiful sayings*: They [i.e. the people of Naftali] will, with beautiful words, give thanks and praise God for them [i.e., for the fruits] *(Onkelos* renders similarly).

□ 2. [That the blessing is a prophetic allusion to Deborah and the swift prowess of Barak and the valiant ten thousand men of the tribe of Naftali in the war against Sisera:] A reference to the beautiful song Deborah and Barak would sing in honor of their valiant struggle [*Judges,* chapt. 5].

□ 3. [That the blessing is an allusion to what occurred on the day of Jacob's burial when Naftali fetched the title deed to the Cave of Machpelah]: The Talmud [*Sotah* 13a], to which *Rashi* refers, continues: " ... Instead of 'who delivers *imrei shefer'* [beautiful sayings], interpretively reads the phrase 'who delivers *imrei sefer'* [words of the *document;* i.e. the ownership deed]."

Moreover, according to some Midrashic sources Naftali was the one who first announced to Jacob that Joseph was still alive. [See on 45:26.]

B'chor Shor perceives the allusion to be that whenever the Israelites were victorious in a battle, it was the fleet-footed tribe of Naftali that always brought the good tidings.

R' Hirsch observes that the subject of the masculine form הַנֹּתֵן, *who gives,* cannot be the feminine, אַיָּלָה, *hind,* but must be *Naftali.* [Hence we translated *'who* gives' rather than *'which* gives.'] שָׁפֶר — unlike יפה which designates radiant, external beauty as perceived by the beholder — designates a graceful conformation of the separate parts of an object. Referring to speech, the word denotes elegant articulation. Thus, Naftali is not original in deed or thought but he is skillful at taking the thoughts of

hind born in *Eretz Yisrael* was brought to Africa and kept in captivity there for thirteen years. Then its horns were covered with silver [to provide a means of identifying the animal] and it was released from captivity. It returned shortly to its original habitat in *Eretz Yisrael.*

The figurative allusion here is that Naftali, *satisfied with favor and full* [as Moses was later to bless him in *Deut.* 33:23], would go forth to all of Israel with tidings that his land had produced abundant fruit as our Rabbis have mentioned concerning the fruit of Gennesar *(Ramban).*

[*Ramban* is referring to *Berachos* 44a where it is recorded that the unusual fruit of Genessar in Naftali's territory was considered more nourishing than bread. This had halachic ramifications as well, for the Sages ruled that if one ate these particular fruits together with bread, one recited the Blessing over the fruit since they were the primary food (see *Rashi ad loc.).*]

others and articulating and executing them beautifully and speedily.

According to *Ibn Ezra,* שְׁלֻחָה means *sent as a gift* [comp. *Micah* 1:14], the sense being that [the produce of] *Naftali is like a hind sent as a gift,* [the recipients of] *which will give* [i.e., express their gratitude with] *eloquent words.*

Chizkuni takes אַיָּלָה to be related to אִילָן, *terebinth tree;* שְׁלוּחָה to mean *planted* — as in *Isaiah* 16:8, שְׁלוּחֹתֶיהָ, *her offshoots;* and אִמְרֵי to mean *bough* — as in *Isaiah* 17:6: אָמִיר — the fine uppermost bough. Accordingly, he suggests the following possible interpretation: *Naftali's plains will be densely planted with trees, yielding boughs of beautiful produce.*

Malbim similarly interprets: Naftali's territory which extended so far that it touched the territory of several other tribes is like a tree whose fine foliage extends in all directions, and yields fine boughs.

[See *Ramban's* interpretation of this stich in the *footnote* on previous page.]

22. Joseph.

בֵּן פֹּרָת יוֹסֵף — *A charming son is Joseph.*

The translation of פֹּרָת [*poras*] as *charming, graceful, charismatic* follows *Rashi* according to whom the word is related to the Aramaic אַפִּרְיוֹן of similar meaning. Comp. the Talmudic expression *apirion namtayei* — let us be charming to ... [see *Bava Metzia* 119a].

Onkelos relates פֹּרָת to פְּרִי, *fruit, fruitfulness* [לָשׁוֹן פְּרִיָּה וְרִבְיָּה] and renders: *Joseph is a thriving son.*

Rashbam similarly renders: a prolific son is Joseph.

In a grammatical note, *Rashi* writes that the ת of פֹּרָת [is not indicative of the feminine form, but] is for stylistic purposes, similar to the ת in דִּבְרַת in *Eccles.* 3:18 which is synonymous with דְּבַר.

Ramban disagrees with: a) *Rashi's* basing Scriptural interpretation upon the use of a foreign word like the Aramaic expression *apirion;* b) *Rashi's* connection of *poras* with *apirion,* since the נ of *apirion* is part of the root [whereas *poras* has no נ]; c) *Rashi's* definition of *apirion* as *charming; which Ramban* suggests it does not mean. [*Mizrachi* defends *Rashi* against each of these objections.]

Ramban, therefore, suggests that the phrase could be translated *a fruitful son,* like *Onkelos* who interprets *poras* as related to פְּרִי, *fruit;* or, as the grammarians [see *Radak, Shorashim* s.v. בנה] interpret it, *poras* could mean *branch* (cf. the word פֹּארֹת, *branch,* in *Ezekiel* 31:5) and בֵּן [usually translated *son*] could be *branch* or *bough,* a meaning the word has in *Psalms* 80:16 [since a bough is a 'son' i.e., offshoot, of the tree (*Radak*)]. According to the latter view, our verse means: *Joseph is a* בֵּן פֹּרָת, *multi-twigged bough.*

Ramban concurs that *poras* means *multi-branched* but maintains that בֵּן, vowelized as it is with a *tzeirei* rather than a *segol,* is not in the construct mode with the word פֹּרָת, in which case בֵּן would refer to the *'son'* or *twig* of פֹּרָת, a larger branch]. Rather, בֵּן is an *independent* word retaining its usual primary meaning of *son.* Consequently, *Rambam* renders: *Joseph is a son like a multi-branched sapling,* or more literally, *'son, a multi-branched sapling is Joseph.'* Jacob used the term *son* parenthetically to display affection, as he did in the case of Judah [above *v.* 9]: From the prey, *my son,* you have elevated yourself.

Abarbanel renders: A son of [הַמְּפוֹאֶרֶת], the most beautiful of women [Rachel], is Joseph.

Targum Yonasan interpretively paraphrases: Joseph, my son, you have become great; Joseph my son, you have

22 A *charming son is Joseph*
a charming son to the eye;
each of the girls climbed heights to gaze.

become great and mighty; your destiny was to become mighty because you subdued your Inclination in the matter of your matron [i.e, Potiphar's wife].

The Midrash homiletically relates *poras* to פָּרוֹת, *cows*, and renders: *A son* [made great] *through cows is Joseph* [alluding to Joseph's rise to prominence as a result of the cows of Pharaoh's dream].

In the case of the other sons Jacob mentioned their names before their blessing [e.g. *Reuben — you are my firstborn; Simeon and Levi are comrades; Judah — you your brothers shall acknowledge; Issachar is a strong-boned donkey*] while in the case of Joseph he did not begin with his name. Jacob acted this way in order to confer honor to him by treating him like a monarch whom one does not address by name *(Hadar Zekeinim).*

בֵּן פֹּרָת עֲלֵי עָיִן — *A charming son to the eye.*

The phrase allows for various interpretations:

□ His charm attracts the eye of the beholder. The Sages [*Berachos* 20a] perceive a further implication: He is עֲלֵי עָיִן, *raised above the eye,* in the sense that the Evil Eye will be ineffective against his children. So, too, when Jacob blessed Ephraim and Manasseh [above 48:16] he blessed them that they be like fish which the Evil Eye cannot affect *(Rashi).*[1]

□ The word עָיִן [*eye*] in this context means *spring; fountain* [as in 24:42]. The implication is: He is like a many-branched sapling *planted by a fountain whose waters never dry up (Ramban).*

Comp. *Onkelos:* Joseph is my son who shall thrive, my son who shall be blessed, like a vine planted by a fountain of waters.— Such plants planted by fountains of water will thrive and their leaves will not wither. Comp. *Psalms* 1:3: *He shall be like a tree planted by streams of water that yields its fruit in due season, and whose leaf never withers and everything he does will succeed.* Similarly, Joseph's progeny through his sons Ephraim and Menasseh will flourish and be numerous *(Radak).*

□ The stich is poetically repeated as is usual in Scripture. In such cases the second stich complements and amplifies the first. Compare, for example, *Psalms* 93:3: *like rivers they raised, O HASHEM, like rivers they raised their voice* [the second stich explains *what* they *raised*]; *ibid.* 92:10; *ibid.* 94:3; *Eccles.* 1:1: *'Futility of futilities' said Koheles, 'futility of futilities, all is futile!'* In this case, too, our stich amplifies Joseph's fruitfulness: He is a prolific son *over the eye,* i.e., so tall in stature that all must look up to regard him *(Rashbam; Bchor Shor).*

Radak maintains, however, that there is a definite reason why the phrase is doubled in this blessing: It is an allusion to the two tribes that will branch out from Joseph — Ephraim and Menasseh. [See *Ramban* in footnote and *Onkelos* further.]

□ *Abarbanel:* The son of a woman beautiful in the eyes of all who saw her.

בָּנוֹת צָעֲדָה עֲלֵי שׁוּר *Each of the girls climbed heights* [lit. *daughters — she stepped*] *to gaze.*

□ A reference to how the Egyptian

1. *Rashi* cites a Midrashic interpretation of this passage which, according to him, 'fits in with the text.' [He alluded to it in his commentary to 33:7 s.v. אַחַר נִגַּשׁ, in slightly different form:]

When Esau came to meet Jacob [and each of Jacob's wives with their children came forward

girls used to climb [atop the wall[1]] to catch a glimpse of his beauty when he passed by [see footnote on p. 1801]. The term עֲלֵי שׁוּר is to be interpreted [*in order*] *to gaze* [see below]. 'There are many Midrashic expositions, but this inclines nearest to the literal sense of the verse' *(Rashi).*

Rashi notes further that the word בָּנוֹת, *girls,* is in plural while the verb צָעֲדָה is in singular. He offers that the verb is to be perceived as emphasizing that every single one of the young woman tried to find herself the best vantage point from which to catch a glimpse of him. [*Ibn Ezra* and others cite many examples of how Scripture poetically changes forms from singular to plural in mid-verse.]

Furthermore, *Rashi* explains that the verb שׁוּר, *gaze,* is similar to אֲשׁוּרֶנּוּ, *I behold him,* in *Num.* 24:17; the form שׁוּר is in the infinitive, synonymous with לָשׁוּר, *to see.* עֲלֵי is the poetical form of עַל, which in our context means *for the purpose of.* Consequently, the phrase עֲלֵי שׁוּר means *in order to gaze.*

Rashbam similarly interprets this stich as referring to how the Egyptian women used to gaze upon him, as did Potiphar's wife and her companions. He offers that the stich עֲלֵי שׁוּר poetically

to present themselves to Esau], Leah, Bilhah, and Zilpah preceded their children [see 3:6 and 7]. However, in the case of Rachel it was the reverse. There, as the verse states [ibid. *v.* 7]: *Afterwards,* [first] *Joseph* [and then] *Rachel came forward.* Joseph reasoned, 'This wicked man [Esau] is haughty. He may fix his gaze upon my mother [and desire her].' He stepped in front of her and drew himself up to his full height in order to shield her [from Esau's gaze].

Alluding to this incident, his father called him בֵּן פֹּרָת, *a son who grew in stature* (by protecting his mother) עֲלֵי עָיִן, *against the 'eye'* [i.e, *gaze*] of Esau.

In reward for this Joseph was blessed with 'greatness' [i.e., a distinguished position in Egypt], inasmuch as the Egyptian women climbed up to look at him (see next stich) when he went forth [as Viceroy] over Egypt *(Pirkei d'Rabbi Eliezer* 12).

☙ Another exegesis — with halachic ramifications — is elicited from our verse. During most of the time until the Temple was erected in Jerusalem, offerings were brought in מִשְׁכַּן שִׁלֹה, *the Tabernacle of Shiloh,* a city in the territory of Joseph's son Ephraim. The Mishnah [*Zevachim* 112b] records several laws that applied only to Shiloh. One of them was that קָדָשִׁים קַלִּים, *offerings of a lesser degree of holiness,* such as peace offerings, may be eaten throughout the vicinity of Shiloh, as far as the Tabernacle can be seen. [In contrast, when the Temple stood, such offerings could be eaten only within the walls of Jerusalem.]

The Gemara [ibid. 119b] derives this exegetically from our verse: *Joseph is a fruitful son* [i.e., his territory, as regards eating certain sacrifices, will be abundant (see *Rashi* there)] — *fruitful* עֲלֵי־עָיִן *through the eye.* That is, let him, whose eye would not enjoy what did not belong to it [an allusion to Joseph who avoided the advances of Potiphar's wife], be privileged [in his territory] to consume sacrifices as far as the eye can see.

1. [The words עַל הַחוֹמָה, *atop the wall,* do not occur in every edition of *Rashi,* and where they do occur they are usually enclosed within parentheses. As is evident from *Mizrachi, Rashi* does not subscribe to the view of many other commentators (see below) that עֲלֵי שׁוּר means *upon the wall.* Accordingly *Rashi's* citation here of the Midrash cited in the footnote on p. 1801 that the Egyptian girls would climb *atop walls* to catch a glimpse of Joseph's beauty, is not taken as a translation of the Scriptural phrase עֲלֵי שׁוּר.

Rather *Rashi* interprets the phrase to mean: [*daughters climbed*] *to gaze.* In order to explain *where* they climbed, *Rashi* adds that they *climbed walls* to get a better look at him. *Sefer HaZikaron* and *Be'er Yitzchak* therefore do not include the words *atop the wall* in their text of *Rashi.*

Maskil l'David, however, suggests that *Rashi* is offering *two* interpretations of שׁוּר: a) it means *wall* and the verse tells us that the Egyptian girls would climb *atop walls* to gaze upon him; and alternatively b) שׁוּר means *gaze* and tells us that they longed to *gaze* upon him. Following this view of *Maskil l'David,* several printed editions of *Rashi* contain a parenthetical printer's notation that the abbreviation ד״א [דָּבָר אַחֵר], *another interpretation* should precede *Rashi's* statement that שׁוּר means *gaze.*]

parallels עֲלֵי עָיִן, *for the eye,* in the previous stich.

☐ *Ramban* interprets בָּנוֹת as *boughs* — i.e. offshoots, of the branches פֹּארֹת=פֹּרָת, earlier in the verse — and שׁוּר as חוֹמָה, *wall.* Thus, having compared Joseph to a multi-branched tree that is planted beside a live fountain, Jacob mentions that the *boughs,* i.e., his offspring, will climb over the sky-high walls. [That is, his progeny will be so abundant that they will figuratively 'run over the wall' *(Ibn Ezra* interprets similarly).] Furthermore, the metaphor is one of great fertility: his branches [i.e., offspring] will be so long and so heavily laden with fruit that they will have to rest upon a wall.[2]

☐ *Onkelos* interpretively paraphrases: Two tribes [בָּנוֹת in the sense of *descendants*] will descend from his sons. They will receive a portion and inheritance.

Thus, *Onkelos'* figurative interpretation is similar to *Ramban's* that Joseph's 'branches' will 'run over the wall'. They will be prolific, and receive much territory.

According to *Onkelos'* rendition, one would expect the masculine בָּנִים, *sons,* instead of the feminine בָּנוֹת, *daughters.* The allusion, however, is specifically to the *daughters of Zelafechad* — of the tribe of Manasseh — who inherited territory on both sides of the Jordan *(Rashi* from *Tanchuma, Pinchas).* [*See Numbers* 27:1; *Joshua* 17:6.]

That is, they 'straddled the wall' — alluding to the Jordan that was as formidable a barrier to Moses as a *'wall',* preventing his entry into the Land — and they overran this wall and inherited territory on both sides of it *(Bertinoro).*

Or following the latter, the verse could be rendered: *Daughters will walk the boundaries* [of their lands; women will be among the foremost of Joseph's descendants who will inherit the land].

Ramban in 48:6 maintains, however, that the reference is to the tribes of Ephraim and Manasseh. He explains that the connotation is that each of them will inherit a share of the land equal to that of Jacob's sons. 'Portion' refers to the extra share of the firstborn, and 'inheritance' refers to the ordinary inheritance; Joseph was treated as the firstborn in the sense that two portions of the land went to his progeny.

☐ *Sforno* perceives a different connotation. He interprets that the verse compares Joseph to a flourishing vine. He notes that a vine is not noticed beyond its immediate vicinity until its branches grow over the vineyard wall that encloses it. Only then is it revealed unexpectedly on the other side to people who did not even know of its existence. So did Joseph suddenly make himself known to his family when they thought he no longer existed.

☐ *Abarbanel:* The praises of his mother's [i.e., Rachel's] beauty surpassed that of all other women; [וְעַל כָּל הַבָּנוֹת צָעֲדָה בְּיָפְיָהּ ע״ד רָאוּהָ בָנוֹת וַיְאַשְּׁרוּהָ].

2. Jacob's blessing of Joseph clearly alludes to the two tribes that descended from him — Ephraim and Manasseh. This is based upon the connotation of the term *poras* [branches] as well as *banos* [boughs]. Jacob spoke of them as offspring of a single tree rather than as completely separate tribes. Knowing that the destined number of tribes was twelve, Jacob did not wish to designate them explicitly as two separate tribes because he wished not to exceed the number twelve.

[As a general rule in the Torah, the number of tribes is twelve: when Manasseh and Ephraim are counted separately in place of Joseph, as they are regarding the inheritance of territory in *Eretz Yisrael,* Levi is also omitted because Levi did not receive a tribal portion, only far-flung cities of residence. Where Levi is counted, Ephraim and Manasseh are considered to be branches of the tribe of Joseph, as in Jacob's blessings. See *Sforno v.* 28.]

Moses also alluded to the dual 'horns' that would branch forth from Joseph [33:17], but he made a specific reference to Ephraim and Manasseh since he omitted the name of Simeon as the commentators note there *(Ramban).*

כג וַיְמָרֲרֻהוּ וָרֹבּוּ וַיִּשְׂטְמֻהוּ בַּעֲלֵי חִצִּים:
כד וַתֵּשֶׁב בְּאֵיתָן קַשְׁתּוֹ וַיָּפֹזּוּ זְרֹעֵי יָדָיו

23. וַיְמָרֲרֻהוּ וָרֹבּוּ — *They embittered him and [they] became antagonists.*

The reference is to Joseph's brothers, as well as Potiphar and his wife, all of whom dealt bitterly with him. In *Exodus* 1:14, too, וַיְמָרֲרוּ has the meaning of *dealing bitterly.* The subject of וָרֹבּוּ, *they became antagonists,* is Joseph's brothers, whose relationship with him deteriorated to a point where [37:4] *they hated him; and they could not speak to him personally (Rashi).*

[According to *Rashi* (as understood by the commentators) this verse begins a new thought to be linked with the next verse, tracing Joseph's rise to prominence notwithstanding the hatred and slander to which he had been exposed.]

Rashbam, however, links our verse with the *previous* one: Because Joseph was so handsome that girls jumped on walls to gaze upon him, Potiphar's wife desired him; but because he spurned her she viciously slandered him and made life bitter for him, but finally he rose to prominence despite her.

In a long grammatical dissertion, *Rashi* justifies his translations of רֹבּוּ in the passive sense meaning that they *'became' antagonists.* He explains that the word cannot be interpreted in the *kal* form as meaning *they antagonized* or *aggrieved,* for if so the word would be וְרָבוּ [from the root ריב] as it is in *Numbers* 20:13 where it has that meaning. Nor could it mean [as some commentators interpret] *and they shot arrows* [from the root רבה] for in that case, too, it would be vowelized רָבוּ. Vowelized as it is, רֹבּוּ is to be interpreted in the passive [*pu'al*] form like the word שֹׁמּוּ in *Jeremiah* 2:12 meaning *become astonished* — lit. *astonish yourselves;* רֹמּוּ in *Job* 24:24 meaning *become exalted* — lit. *exalt yourselves;* דֹּמּוּ in *Isaiah* 23:2 meaning *be silent* — lit. *silence yourselves.* In all these cases these words have essentially the same meaning as in their *hoph'al* counterpart forms except that the connotation of *hoph'al* is that the action is caused or forced by others, while in the *pu'al* form of our verse the connotation is that the action arose out of the people themselves; hence וָרֹבּוּ denotes how they became men of contention in regard to Joseph. *Onkelos* similarly renders the sense: וְנַקְמוּהִי, *and they avenged themselves against him.*

Rashbam differs and maintains that vowelized as it is, וָרֹבּוּ is derived from the root רבב, *to shoot,* just as the root סבב is conjugated סֹבּוּ, and רנן is conjugated רֹנִּי. He explains that the allusion is to the *'archers'* mentioned further in the verse. Joseph's enemies hurled accusations at him like *archers shooting arrows,* the expression alluding to Potiphar's wife who slandered him. *Ibn Ezra* interprets similarly, but suggests that וַיְמָרֲרֻהוּ is from the word מְרֵרָה, *gall;* they were like archers aiming for the gall bladder and liver, intending to destroy their victim permanently.

וַיִּשְׂטְמֻהוּ בַּעֲלֵי חִצִּים — *The arrow-tongued men* [lit. *men of arrows*] *hated him.*

[A further allusion to his afore-referenced brothers, as well as Potiphar and his wife, who hated him.] They are called בַּעֲלֵי חִצִּים, *men of arrows,* because their tongues were sharp as arrows. *Onkelos,* taking חִצִּים to be related to the term מֶחֱצָה [*Num.* 31:36] meaning *half; division,* renders: מָרֵי פַּלְגּוּתָא, alluding to the hatred shown him by *those who were designated to divide the inheritance with him* [i.e., his brothers] *(Rashi).*[1]

1. *Abarbanel* perceives in this verse the essence of why Joseph — noble though he was — could not aspire to be the leader of the family. Unlike Judah, whom the brothers recognized as their uncontested leader and who enjoyed undisputed popularity, Joseph provoked jealousy

23 *They embittered him and became antagonists;*
the arrow-tongued men hated him.
24 *But his bow was firmly emplaced*
and his arms were gilded,

Radak insists that the context of this chapter precludes the notion that Jacob meant to include the evil deeds of his children in this phrase [as *Onkelos* interprets]. That Jacob spoke in such a castigating way in the case of Reuben was only to explain why he was unfit for the firstborn's birthright; and, in the case of Simeon and Levi, to explain why he divided them. In our verse, accordingly, the reference must be to Potiphar and his wife [not to the brothers].

Targum Yonasan explains this stich to refer to the Egyptians who opposed Joseph's rise to power and slandered him to Pharaoh. They were jealous and tried to convince Pharaoh to dismiss him from his high post [see *comm.* to 41:21], but God watched over him, and protected him from their plots.

The Torah likens slander to arrows, as in the verse [*Jeremiah* 9:7]: *Their tongue is a sharpened arrow;* and *ibid. v.* 2: *They flee their tongues, their bow of falsehood (Rashbam).*

[The verb שטם has been discussed in 27:41.]

24. But, by the grace of God, he prevailed and rose to prominence...

וַתֵּשֶׁב בְּאֵיתָן קַשְׁתּוֹ — *But his bow was firmly* [lit. *in firmness*] *emplaced.*

Metaphorically: [notwithstanding the above], Joseph's power [as regent of Egypt] was firmly established. קַשְׁתּוֹ, *his bow,* alludes to *his power (Rashi).*

Rashbam explains the metaphor to depict how notwithstanding the 'bitter arrows of slander' to which the Egyptians subjected Joseph, he nevertheless rose to prominence because 'his bow was stronger than theirs.'

Onkelos, as explained by *Rashi,* interpretively paraphrases: Joseph's prophecy [i.e., the dreams he dreamt about his brothers] was fulfilled because he was faithful to the precepts of the Torah in secret. [*Rashi* remarks that the foregoing is not a literal rendering of any words in the Hebrew text but is *Onkelos'* elaboration of the implication. *Rashi* fits in the words as follows] ... The dreams were fulfilled [וַתֵּשֶׁב, *established*] because the might of the Holy One, Blessed is He, [שֶׁאֵיתָנוֹ שֶׁל הקב״ה] was his bow and his stronghold.

וַיָּפֹזּוּ זְרֹעֵי יָדָיו — *And his arms* [lit. *arms of his hands*] *were gilded* [from פָּז, *fine gold (Rashi)*].

— An allusion to the golden signet ring Pharaoh placed on Joseph's hand [41:42] *(Rashi).*[2]

Following *Rashbam* who continues the metaphor that Joseph's bow was strong: ... *And his arms were supple as he mightily drew the bow to its fullest extent.* The word וַיָּפֹזּוּ in this context means: *supple, pliant* from the root פזז as in *II Samuel* 6:16 מְפַזֵּז, *agile dancing.*

and could not be expected to effectively lead his brothers.

And yet, as *R' Munk* observes, in grandeur of soul and in moral worth, Joseph was superior to Judah. It was he, not Judah,who is honored in Jewish tradition with the title of צַדִּיק, *righteous one* [*Yoma* 35b; see *Overview* to *Vayeishev-Mikeitz*]. His father calls him here the *crown among his brothers,* the one who wears the diadem of moral perfection. This exceptional tribute from the dying Patriarch was earned by Joseph's strength of character and nobleness of heart, which he had demonstrated on two decisive occasions. Jacob discreetly recalls them through the euphemistic words he addresses next to Joseph.

2. *Rashi* proceeds to briefly cite the Rabbinic interpretation of this verse as it appears in the Talmud, *Sotah* 36b, and with some minor differences in the Midrash [§87:7]. According to

מִידֵי אֲבִיר יַעֲקֹב מִשָּׁם רֹעֶה אֶבֶן
כה יִשְׂרָאֵל: מֵאֵל אָבִיךָ וְיַעְזְרֶךָּ וְאֵת שַׁדַּי

מִידֵי אֲבִיר יַעֲקֹב — *From the hands of the Mighty Power of Jacob.*

The above happened to him [*from the hands*] through the instrumentality of the Holy One, Blessed is He, who is the 'Mighty One' of Jacob *(Rashi).*

A shepherd, too, is called אֲבִיר. The continuity of the passage is: "Who bestowed all this upon you? — The Holy One, Who is אֲבִיר יַעֲקֹב, *the Shepherd of Israel* — the 'God Who has been my [i.e. Jacob's] Shepherd all my life until this day' [48:15]; — He has, through your greatness, sustained me in Egypt" *(Rashbam).*

מִשָּׁם רֹעֶה אֶבֶן יִשְׂרָאֵל — *From there, he shepherded the stone of Israel.*[1]

From there, [i.e., from Joseph's God-given position as viceroy, or from his earlier status of hated and slandered person (see below)], Joseph rose to become *the shepherd* who cared for and provided sus-

that interpretation, this verse refers to the incident when Joseph controlled his urge for Potiphar's wife.

When she finally entrapped him alone in her house, as related in 39:12, Joseph's temptation grew great. As we learned there, his father's image appeared to him through the window and warned him against sinning with the evil woman.

Immediately וַתֵּשֶׁב בְּאֵיתָן קַשְׁתּוֹ, *his 'bow' was relaxed in vigor,* which according to R' Yochanan metaphorically depicts how Joseph's self control forced his passion to subside. וַיָּפֹזּוּ זְרֹעֵי יָדָיו, *and the seeds of his hands were scattered* — he struck his hands into the ground so that his virility [lit. seed] was channeled forth between his fingernails [i.e., he bore all his weight on his fingers so his thoughts would focus on the excruciating pain, and his ardor would leave him *(Rashi* ad loc.)].

This cooling of Joseph's ardor occurred מִידֵי אֲבִיר יַעֲקֹב, *at the hands of* [i.e. due to the effect of] *the mighty one, Jacob,* since, as noted, the image of Jacob appeared to Joseph and exhorted him, and thus, Joseph's demonstration of supreme inner strength was directly caused *from afar* by the Patriarch, the Rock of Israel, who influenced his son like a *shepherd.*

According to another interpretation in the Talmud, the contextual flow of this interpretation is: מִשָּׁם, *from there,* i.e. — by virtue of this incident, Joseph merited to become *the Shepherd,* i.e., provider; *a stone of Israel.* That is, his father's exhortation warned him that if he succumbed to her seduction he would forfeit the privilege of having his name inscribed with those of his brothers on the stones of the High Priest's breastplate [see *comm.* to 39:8, 12]. However, now that he controlled his passion, he merited a place among his brethren to become *a stone among the stones of Israel (Rif* in *Ein Yaakov).*

Comp. *Targum Yonasan:* " ... And accordingly he became worthy of being a ruler, and of being associated in the engraving of the names upon the stones of Israel."

The *Midrash* relates *v.* 25 to this theme by interpreting: The strength to accomplish all of this [i.e. withstanding the enticements of Potiphar's wife] was *from the God of your father Who helped you.*

The Talmud [ibid.] concludes:

It has been taught that Joseph was worthy that twelve tribes should issue from him as they issued from his father Jacob, since the two were compared in many ways [see *comm.* to 37:2], but because his ardor [lit. seed] emerged from between his [ten] fingernails [his power to beget was diminished and he had only two children]. Nevertheless, [ten sons, who, added to Joseph's two, made the total of twelve] emerged from his brother Benjamin. All of these sons of Benjamin bore names which were associated with Joseph [as *Rashi* records in the *comm.* to 43:30 s.v. כִּי נִכְמְרוּ]. (See *Overview* to *Vayigash).*

1. *R' Hirsch* juxtaposes this verse with the previous verse which depicts the brothers, the hating archers who shot their arrows at Joseph, and emphasizes how Joseph did not exploit the opportunity to take revenge against the guilty. Though a viceroy in Egypt with almost un-

49
25

from the hands of the Mighty Power of Jacob —
from there, he shepherded the stone of Israel.
25 *[That was] from the God of your father*
and He will help you,
and with Shaddai — and He will bless you

tenance for **Jacob,** *the stone of Israel.* The word אֶבֶן, *stone,* denotes kingship, the primary personage of the nation, as it does in *Zechariah* 4:7 *(Rashi).* [*Comp. Psalms* 118:22 where *stone* in that context metaphorically refers to David. See also footnote to previous verse.]

The sense is that Providence orchestrated events so that Joseph steadily rose in stature to finally become the one who 'shepherded the Stone of Israel'; that is, he became the one who provided for Jacob who is considered the primogenitor of Israel inasmuch as the twelve tribes descended from him *(Tzeidah laDerech; Be'er Yitzchak).*

Or following certain Midrashim, *Joseph* is called the 'Stone of Israel,' the sense being that Joseph rose from the lowly status of hated brother to be the *shepherd,* that is the provider and the cornerstone of the Israelite family.

Rashi writes that אֶבֶן is a contraction [*notarikon*] of the words אָב וּבֵן, *father and son* [an allusion, according to *Midrash HaGadol,* of how Joseph became the provider for both father and son] — Jacob and his sons. *Onkelos* interprets similarly [but according to him the subject of this phrase is God, *the Mighty One of Jacob,* referred to in the previous phrase, by Whose Will fathers and sons are nourished].

Continuing *Rashbam:* From there, i.e., your position of greatness in Egypt, God has caused you to be the shepherd — that is, provider — for the *'even' of Israel,* the family of Israel, for Joseph had sustained his father and brothers. The term *'even'* refers to *'av'* [father] and family. The *nun* is paragogic [=liguistically superfluous] as is the *mem* of רֵיקָם.

According to *Radak* and *Sforno,* אֶבֶן, *stone,* is a metaphor for the permanence of Israel, who survive like a stone, whether esteemed by the nations like a precious stone, or held in contempt by them like a common stone.

25. מֵאֵל אָבִיךָ וְיַעְזְרֶךָּ — *[That was] from the God of your father and He will help you.*

All the foregoing blessings came to you from the God of your father — *and He will help you* [in the future as well *(Midrash)*] *(Rashi).*

R' Shmuel ben Chofni Gaon interprets this verse as a prayer with the following bracketed words implied: [I beseech] *from the God of your father* [*that*] *He help you.*

וְאֵת שַׁדַּי וִיבָרְכֶךָּ — *And with Shaddai, and He will bless you.*

— *Rashi* takes וְאֵת as a preposition meaning *and with.* He in-

limited powers, he was still able to forgive. Instead of aiming his bow against his brothers, וַתֵּשֶׁב בְּאֵיתָן קַשְׁתּוֹ, *his bow remained in imperturbable rest,* וַיָּפֹזּוּ זְרֹעֵי יָדָיו even though *his arms were ornamented with the gold of royalty* and his brothers were at his mercy. Joseph was able to do this because he perceived that his fate was guided *by the Mighty One of* his father *Jacob, the Shepherd* Who bestowed His solicitude upon the *stone of Israel.*

R' Hirsch continues that this stone was the one upon which Jacob had rested his head on the lonely mountain when he was fleeing from Esau, the same stone that he consecrated to become Beth-El, the cornerstone of the family dedicated to the service of God וְהָאֶבֶן הזאת כו' (28:22).

Since then Jacob had never ceased to look upon it as the symbol not only of his deepest misery, but also of the marvelous Divine blessing which he had received in the dream. The blessing had been completely fulfilled and now, in the evening of his life, Yaakov gratefully recalled this "stone of Israel".

וִיבָרְכֶךָּ בִּרְכֹת שָׁמַיִם מֵעָל בִּרְכֹת תְּהוֹם
כו רֹבֶצֶת תָּחַת בִּרְכֹת שָׁדַיִם וָרָחַם׃ בִּרְכֹת
אָבִיךָ גָּבְרוּ עַל־בִּרְכֹת הוֹרַי עַד־תַּאֲוַת

terprets, 'When you were tempted by Potiphar's wife, your heart *was with Shaddai*, and therefore — *He will bless you.*'

[The Name *Shaddai* depicts God in His Aspect of God Who is *sufficient* [דַּי = *sufficient*] in granting His Mercies, and who has *sufficient* power to give (see *Rashi* to 43:14 and *comm.* to 17:1; 28:3 and 35:11).] The Name here, following *Rashi,* would accordingly imply: You were *with Shaddai, and He,* with His boundless sufficiency to grant mercy to every creature, *will bless you.*

— *Targum Yonasan* takes אֵת as the indefinite article and interprets: ... *And He Who is called Shaddai* [All Sufficient] *shall bless you.*

In Joseph the Patriarch recognized the one son who had understood more deeply than the others the meaning of the moral mission of mankind. He is the true heir; the 'crown of his brothers.' His noble character and exceptional talents combine to make him the truly 'righteous one.' He merits the great title of *tzaddik* because at moments of great temptation Joseph mastered himself and remained faithful to his beliefs and to the God of his father. Accordingly, Jacob prays to the God of his father [מֵאֵל אָבִיךָ], asking that He continue to watch over Joseph *(R' Munk).*

The blessings He will grant you will be composed of:

בִּרְכֹת שָׁמַיִם מֵעָל — [With] *blessings of heaven from above.*

That is, with blessings of dew and rain in their proper times *(Radak; Onkelos* interprets similarly).

The expression *blessings of heaven from above* also carries a connotation of those blessings which are beyond Nature, a supernatural increase of strength and personal worth *(Zohar).*

בִּרְכֹת תְּהוֹם רֹבֶצֶת תָּחַת — *Blessings of the deep crouching below.*

The reference is to the subterranean fountains deep beneath the earth, which crouch, so to speak, as if they are waiting for the opportunity to gush forth and irrigate the land. The blessing was that Joseph's territory would be irrigated by these subterranean waters so that his vegetation and trees would lack no moisture even in times of little rainfall, and his land would be fertile *(Radak).*

[On תְּהוֹם, *deep* or *abyss,* see 1:2. At the time of the Flood, these waters are described in 7:11 as having 'burst forth' to inundate the land.]

Targum Yonasan renders: ... And with the good blessing of the fountains of the Deep, which ascend and clothe the herbage from below.

Following the *Zohar*: these refer to blessings of 'natural' abundance. He blessed him that the whole of Nature — unto the very core of the Deep, so to speak — would benefit him and his descendants.

בִּרְכֹת שָׁדַיִם וָרָחַם — *Blessings of the bosom and womb.*

[The blessing of *bosom* is that all mothers will be able to provide their infants with sufficient nourishment; and the blessing of *womb* is that all pregnant woman will be able to carry their fetuses to full term and give birth without mishap.]

Onkelos renders: *blessings of fatherhood and motherhood,* meaning that the men and women of Joseph will be blessed so that none

[with] blessings of heaven from above,
26 *blessings of the deep crouching below,*
blessings of the bosom and womb.
26 *The blessings of your father surpassed*
the blessings of my fathers,

will be sterile or barren (*Rashi*).

Rashi explains how *Onkelos* sees an allusion to 'fatherhood' in the word שָׁדַיִם, which invariably means *bosom* or *breasts*. The *Targum* of the root יָרָה, *to throw with force*, is שְׁדִי (see *Exodus* 15:4). Accordingly, שָׁדַיִם can be understood as an allusion to male semen, which must move with velocity in order to fertilize the female ovum and cause conception.

Gur Aryeh offers a different explanation of *Onkelos*. The word שָׁדַיִם, meaning *bosom*, symbolizes the concept of 'giving' to someone else, just as a mother nurses her baby. Consequently, this word can be used to allude to the father's contribution to the process of conception.

R' Munk records that Joseph's sinful descendants eventually forfeited this blessing of bosom and womb. Into such depravity had the people of Ephraim fallen that the prophet Hoshea exclaimed — using a similar but contrary metaphor: *'Give them, HASHEM whatever You will give; give them a barren womb and dry bosom!' (Hoshea* 9:14).

Targum Yonasan interprets this as referring to Rachel: ... *The bosom at which you were nursed is blessed, and the womb in which you have lain.*

This follows the *Midrash* which interprets that this blessing was aimed specifically at Rachel whom Jacob loved greatly. For even when Jacob blessed Joseph he treated him as but secondary to her, saying, *Blessed be the bosom that suckled you, and the womb from which you were nursed.*

26. בִּרְכֹת אָבִיךָ גָּבְרוּ עַל־בִּרְכֹת הוֹרַי — *The blessings of your father surpassed the blessings of my fathers.*

That is, the blessings with which God blessed me were greater in their extent and efficacy than those with which He blessed my father and grandfather *(Rashi).*

Rashi thus interprets *blessings of your father* to refer to the blessings which God had bestowed upon Jacob; *the blessings of my fathers* refer to the blessings which God bestowed upon Abraham and Isaac, and גָּבְרוּ, *surpassed*, is in the past tense, meaning that Jacob had *already* been given more than the other Patriarchs.

Radak however, interprets the sense differently: *'The blessings of your father*, i.e., those blessings which I [Jacob] now bestow upon you, *will surpass my forefathers' blessings*, i.e. the blessings which my forefathers bequeathed me.'

Comp. *Onkelos:* The blessing of your father [which I now bestow upon you] shall be added to the blessing with which my fathers blessed me.

The word הוֹרַי [lit. *my conceivers*] from the term הֵרָיוֹן, *conception*, denotes those who caused one to be conceived in the mother's womb. Both parents are referred to by this term since they share in the conception *(Rashi; Radak).*

Rashbam interprets הוֹרַי [parents] in this context as related to הַר, *mountain,*

1. R' Hirsch rejects the views that Jacob would say that his blessings far *surpass* those of his forebears; such a statement would imply a conceit unbecoming of Jacob.

Rather, the sense would be: 'The blessings that I, your father, give you are powerful only because they are based upon the cumulative blessings my parents gave me. Because of *their* blessings, mine has strength. Do not be indifferent to parental blessings; that I can bless you now is due to the purity of my parents.

גִּבְעֹת עוֹלָם תִּהְיֶיןָ לְרֹאשׁ יוֹסֵף וּלְקָדְקֹד נְזִיר אֶחָיו:

and it parallels the phrase *eternal hills* that follows in the next stich. The implication is: The blessing God bestowed upon me — that I will *spread out powerfully westward, eastward, northward and southward* (28:19), is a blessing *that exceeds the boundaries of mountains,* more, indeed, than all the mountains of the world. Moses' later blessing supports this view of the passage, because he, too, drew a parallel between mountains and hills. Moses declared [*Deut. 33:14*]: וּמֵרֹאשׁ הַרְרֵי קֶדֶם וּמִמֶּגֶד גִּבְעוֹת עוֹלָם, *for the chief things of the ancient mountains for the precious things of the eternal hills.* Jacob concluded, too, with a similar formula: תָּבוֹאתָה לְרֹאשׁ יוֹסֵף וּלְקָדְקֹד נְזִיר אֶחָיו, *Let them* [*i.e. these blessings*] *come upon Joseph's head, and on the head of one who was separated from his brothers* [*ibid. v.* 16].

עַד־תַּאֲוַת גִּבְעֹת עוֹלָם — *To the endless bounds of the world's hills.*

— I.e., the blessings I received were unlimited, figuratively expanding to the furthest hills in the world. As it is written in the blessing God gave Jacob [28:14]: *And you shall spread out powerfully westward, eastward, northward and southward* — an unbounded blessing which was given to neither Abraham nor Isaac. Abraham was promised only the Land of Israel, as it is said [13:14]: *'Raise now your eyes and look out from where you are: northward, southward, eastward and westward. For all the land* **that you see,** *to you will I give it ...'* but God showed Abraham only *Eretz Yisrael.* To Isaac He said [26:23]: *For to you and your offspring will I give all* **these lands** *and establish the oath that I swore to Abraham your father.* This was Isaiah's intent when he said [*Isaiah* 48:14]: *'I will feed you with the inheritance of* **Jacob** your father [i.e. a boundless inheritance]', and he did not say, 'the inheritance of *Abrahum'* [which was less extensive] *(Rashi).*

The translation of תַּאֲוַת as *bounds, ends,* follows *Rashi* who relates it to the verbs וְהִתְאַוִּיתֶם and תְּתָאוּ meaning *mark off boundaries,* in *Numbers* 34:8, 10.

Onkelos interpretively paraphrases: '... [May your father's blessings be added to those with which my fathers blessed me] of which the great ones of the world were desirous.' The Matriarchs are described figuratively as גִּבְעֹת עוֹלָם, *the towering hills of the world,* because they overshadowed lesser people. Jacob's mother, Rebecca, *desired* Isaac's blessings so much that she compelled Jacob to resort to devious means to obtain him *(Rashi).*

Rashi explains that *Onkelos* derived this interpretation by rendering תַּאֲוַת as *desire* and גִּבְעֹת עוֹלָם [lit. the world's hills] as figuratively referring to the *great* [i.e. *'lofty'*] *ones of the world.* [*Onkelos* would render the Hebrew syntax: *Until the desire of the great ones of the world.*]

According to *Targum Yonasan* the implication is: ... 'May the blessings of your father be added to the blessings given me by my fathers Abraham and Isaac *and which the great ones of the world, Ishmael, Esau and all the sons of Keturah, have desired.'*

[Thus, *Targum Yonasan* figuratively refers גִּבְעֹת עוֹלָם, 'great ones of the world' to Ishamel and Esau who coveted these blessings, while *Rashi* interprets the reference in *Onkelos* to allude to Rebecca who encouraged Jacob to get the blessings. *Shaarei Aharon* records that this is in keeping with *Rashi's* interpretation throughout Scripture that גְּבָעוֹת, *hills,* is a metaphor for the Matriarchs. See, for example, *Rashi's comm.* to *Numbers* 23:9; *Micah* 6:1. See also *Rosh Hashanah* 11a. *Paane'ach Raza* interprets similarly, and adds that therefore the word גִּבְעֹת is spelled 'defectively' (without the

to the endless bounds of the world's hills.
Let them be upon Joseph's head
and upon the head of the exile from his brothers.

plural ו), to give it the connotation of the singular as a reference to Rebecca.]

Radak renders: 'May the blessings of your father in conjunction with the blessings my forefathers bestowed upon me be yours and your descendants until the boundaries of the eternal hills,' i.e., for all time. עוֹלָם here has the meaning not of the physical *world* but of timeless *eternity*. Jacob chose hills and mountains for this metaphor since they have an aura of timelessness about them. Accordingly, Jacob's blessing was one which knew no bounds in either geography or duration.'

תִּהְיֶיןָ לְרֹאשׁ יוֹסֵף — *Let them* [i.e. all (the aforementioned blessings) *(Rashi)*] *be upon Joseph's head.*

Targum Yonasan: 'May all these blessings form a diadem of majesty for the head of Joseph ... '

The contextual flow is: Many great people have desired these blessings. But I am now declaring that all of them — mine and my forebears' blessings — devolve upon Joseph's head since he was the most consecrated of his brothers and was separated from them for so long *(Akeidas Yitzchak)*.

וּלְקָדְקֹד נְזִיר אֶחָיו — [*And*] *upon the head of the exile from his brothers.*

The translation of נְזִיר אֶחָיו as *the exile from his brothers* refers to Joseph as the one who was separated from his family [first during his twenty two years of isolation and then by virtue of his duties in the palace]. This rendering follows *Onkelos* [פְּרִישָׁא דַאֲחוֹהִי] as explained by *Rashi*, who cites similar meanings of the root נזר, *separate*, in *Leviticus* 22:2 and *Isaiah* 1:4.[1]

Targum Yonasan apparently interprets the word נְזִיר as related to זהר and renders: ' ... [let the blessings be a diadem] for the brow of the man who became chief and ruler in Egypt, *and the brightness* [וְזָהִיר] *of the glory of his brothers.'*

Rashbam interprets: *The king* [metaphorically: *the crown* from the cognate noun נֵזֶר] *over his brothers.*

Ralbag perceives the meaning to be: *the most abstinent* of his brothers, that is, the brother who exercised the greatest control over his emotions, and abstained from sin under the most trying circumstances.

[*R' Avraham ben HaRambam* mentions that the comparative aspect of this description is indicated by the construct [סְמִיכוּת] state of the words. Jacob does not refer to him as נָזִיר, *an abstinent person;* instead Jacob compares him with the rest of the family, describing him as נְזִיר אֶחָיו, *the most abstinent of his brothers.* The implication is that his brothers, too, experienced self-control, but he was the most abstinent of all.]

Jacob, as noted, thus alludes to Joseph as the one who wears, unseen by others, the diadem of moral perfection. Only Joseph, not his brothers, earned the title צַדִּיק, *righteous one* [see *Yoma* 35b; Overview to *Vayeishev*].

As *R' Munk* notes, Joseph's primary moral victory over himself was in maintaining his unblemished morality in Egypt, despite the daily temptations from all sides. 'Each day,' exclaims R' Yochanan, 'God Himself praises the virtue of the bachelor who lives in a large

1. The Talmud, [*Shabbos* 139a] derives from the description of Joseph here as *nazir* [which in other contexts refers to one who has vowed to abstain from wine and strong drink], that for the entire twenty-two years that Jacob was separated from his brothers he did not taste any wine [to symbolize his grief]. [See *comm.* to end of 43:34 where it is indicated that the brothers, too, refrained from wine during this period.]

°ששי כז °בִּנְיָמִין זְאֵב יִטְרָף בַּבֹּקֶר יֹאכַל עַד
כח וְלָעֶרֶב יְחַלֵּק שָׁלָל: כָּל־אֵלֶּה שִׁבְטֵי
יִשְׂרָאֵל שְׁנֵים עָשָׂר וְזֹאת אֲשֶׁר־דִּבֶּר

town without yielding to sin' *(Pesachim* 113a). Egypt was the land where moral perversion and sexual license were practiced in their lowest form, as the Torah itself attests (*Leviticus* 18:3). But Joseph remained supremely unaffected by the debauchery surrounding him. He was able to resist the constant temptations of his master's wife even though she threatened him with death.

קָדְקֹד refers to the *cranium,* the vertex — the top — of the head. Figuratively it means the 'crown' of the head *(Ibn Janach; Radak).*

27. Benjamin.

בִּנְיָמִין זְאֵב יִטְרָף — *Benjamin is a predatory wolf* [lit. *a wolf who tears* (its prey)].

The metaphor of a ravenous wolf that seizes prey is a prophetic allusion to two incidents in the life of Benjamin's descendants:

a) On the aftermath of the incident of the Concubine at Gibeah, the young men of Benjamin had to seize wives in a 'wolf-like' manner [see *Judges* 21];

b) King Saul [Benjamin's descendant] conquered his enemies on all sides: As recorded in *I Samuel* 14:48, he consolidated his reign, fought against Moab and against Edom, and wherever he went he wrought havoc [like a ravenous wolf] *(Rashi).*

The tribe of Benjamin will be like a wolf, which preys on other animals and beasts and which is the most fearless of animals to enter human habitations. Benjamin's descendants were mighty, fearless warriors, and so they are depicted in the affair of the Concubine at Gibeah [*Judges* chapts. 19-20] *(Radak).*

Midrash HaGadol perceives this ascription of rapacity to be a reference to the warlike Ehud, a descendant of Benjamin, who 'snatched the soul' of Eglon and killed him [i.e., by a subterfuge (see *Judges* 3:20)].

The phrase which literally reads: *Benjamin a wolf will tear* could be interpreted with *wolf* as the object to mean *Benjamin shall tear a wolf,** or: *Benjamin shall be torn by a wolf. Rashi* therefore makes the comment that the word אֲשֶׁר is elliptically understood before יִטְרָף, and the phrase should be interpreted as if it read בִּנְיָמִין זְאֵב אֲשֶׁר יִטְרָף, *Benjamin is a wolf that shall tear,* or *Benjamin* is a wolf inasmuch as he [Benjamin] *preys* like a wolf *(Mizrachi; Gur Aryeh; Maharshal).*

In consonance with his theme that each testament alluded to the trait that disqualified that particular tribe from disputing Judah's rights to the throne, *Abarbanel* notes that Benjamin's characteristic of relative rapacity was contrary to the quality needed to rule the nation. Even the great and righteous Joseph was disqualified because he was hated by the others. Of all the brothers, only Judah was fit to rule.

בַּבֹּקֶר יֹאכַל עַד — *In the morning he will devour prey.*

He is always ready to fight and will be successful in his wars ...

This is a further reference to Saul who rose as Israel's champion during the 'morning' of national existence — when Israel began to flourish and shine *(Rashi* from *Tanchuma).*

In this respect Benjamin even exceeded the wolf. The wolf, as noted

---

* *R' Hirsch* indeed interprets the verse to mean *Benjamin will tear the 'wolf' to pieces.* He explains this as a reference to the tradition that at the end of the final exile, Amalek will be overcome by a descendant of Rachel. Thus, Benjamin will be the one to tear the Amalekite 'wolf' and bring about the Redemption of Israel.

27 Benjamin is a predatory wolf;
in the morning he will devour prey
and in the evening he will distribute spoils."
28 All these are the tribes of Israel — twelve — and

in *Zephaniah* 3:3, tears its prey in the evening while Benjamin will devour the spoil of his enemies in the 'morning,' a reference to Saul's wars against Amalek and the other nations — as well as in the 'evening,' a reference to Mordechai's triumph over Haman *(Radak).*

עַד is synonymous with שָׁלָל, *spoils,* and בִּזָּה, *booty. Onkelos* renders it עַדְאָה. It occurs in *Isaiah* 33:23 אָז חֻלַּק עַד שָׁלָל, *Then the prey of the spoils was divided (Rashi).*

וְלָעֶרֶב יְחַלֵּק שָׁלָל — *And in the evening he will distribute spoils.*

Even in the dark *evening* of Israel's history, when Nebuchadnezzar will have exiled them to Babylon, *he* [i.e. the descendants of Benjamin] *will still divide the spoils,* of victory. This is an allusion to Mordechai and Esther, of the tribe of Benjamin, who divided the spoils of Haman [see *Esther* 3:7] *(Rashi).*

Radak also interprets this prophecy as an allusion to the triumph of Mordechai. He explains that the period is called 'evening' because exile is likened to the evening darkness.

Comp. the view of R' Pinchas in the Midrash who interprets that the metaphor alludes to the altar [in the Temple, which was in Benjamin's territory]. As the wolf seizes its prey, so did the altar 'seize' the sacrifices which were offered on it. *In the morning he* [i.e. *it*=the altar] *devours the prey,* alludes to the lamb that was offered in the morning [*Num.* 28:4]; *in the evening it divides the spoils,* alludes to the other lamb that was offered at dusk [*ibid.*].

Rashi continues that *Onkelos* interpretively perceives the metaphor as a reference to the 'booty' — the Priestly portion — which the *Kohanim* received from the holy sacrifices in the Temple [which was situated in the territory of Benjamin].

The following is *Onkelos'* full interpretive rendering of Benjamin's benediction: 'Benjamin: In his land will dwell the Divine Presence; in his territory will the Temple [other versions read: *Altar*] be built. In the morning and evening will the Priests offer the oblations and in the evening divide the remaining portions of the residue of the sacred things.'

Actually, *Onkelos* is offering two interpretations: that the Divine Presence will be located in Benjamin's territory, and that the Temple Altar will be there; see Midrash below. The basic metaphor in consonance with that Midrash alludes to the consumption of the sacrifices on the altar in the Temple; the Divine Presence refers to the Heavenly Fire which consumed the sacrifices. [For a clearer understanding of *Onkelos'* interpretation see the controversy of Rav and Levi in *Zevachim* 54a; see also *Rashi* ibid. 53b s.v. טורף, and *Nesinah LaGer.*]

28. כָּל־אֵלֶּה שִׁבְטֵי יִשְׂרָאֵל שְׁנֵים־עָשָׂר — *All these are the tribes of Israel — twelve.*

The Torah makes a point of reaffirming the number twelve, already established in 35:22, since the tribe of Joseph had since been divided into two. The connotation of the passage is:

Only the aforementioned — [and not Ephraim and Manasseh] — are truly accounted as the 'twelve full-fledged tribes of Israel.' *These* are the twelve whose names were later inscribed on the High Priest's breastplate; *these* participated in the

לָהֶם אֲבִיהֶם וַיְבָרֶךְ אוֹתָם אִישׁ אֲשֶׁר
כט כְּבִרְכָתוֹ בֵּרַךְ אֹתָם: וַיְצַו אוֹתָם וַיֹּאמֶר

covenant of the blessings and curses at Mount Gerizim and Mount Ebal, and it was corresponding to *these* twelve tribes that twelve stones were set up by Moses on the east of the Jordan, by Joshua in the dry bed of the Jordan and later at Gilgal, and by Elijah on Mount Carmel. Manasseh and Ephraim, however, did not rank among the tribes except with respect to the division of the Land and the separate tribal encampments in the Wilderness. In these two instances, Levi was not counted among the tribes because the Levites, as the servants of God, had no territorial allotment in *Eretz Yisrael;* see *Deut.* 18:1. In such cases, the tribe of Joseph was counted as two — Manasseh and Ephraim — so that the number of tribes would remain at twelve *(Sforno).*

What is the connotation of כָּל אֵלֶּה, *all these,* when the Torah could have simply written אֵלֶּה, *these?* Possibly the expression *all these, the twelve tribes of Israel* conveys the intimation that *all things* that exist in the world exist by the merit of the twelve tribes. The expression *all these* alludes to the expression in *Isaiah* 66:2: *All these things* [i.e. Heaven, earth, and all Creation] *has My hand made (R' Bachya).*

וְזֹאת אֲשֶׁר־דִּבֶּר לָהֶם אֲבִיהֶם וַיְבָרֶךְ אוֹתָם — *And this*[1] *is what their father spoke to them when* [lit. *and*] *he blessed them.*

But surely [as appears evident from some of the preceding verses] Jacob did not *bless* some of his sons but to the contrary scolded them! Actually, the Torah could have summed up this narrative by merely stating, *And this* — i.e., what we have just read in the preceding narrative — *is what their father spoke to them.* If such were the case, however, we might conclude that Jacob gave no blessing at all to Reuben, Simeon, and Levi. To prevent such a misapprehension, the Torah specifically added: *When* [lit. *and*] *he blessed them,* to emphasize that he indeed blessed *all* of them *(Rashi).*

This needs clarification. For how are we to take the earlier rebukes to Reuben, Simeon, and Levi as *blessings?*

— *Or HaChaim* explains that even Jacob's rebukes were truly blessings. By addressing Reuben as his *firstborn,* Jacob gave him the implied assurance that in Messianic times, when the firstborn would share the sacred service with the Levites, Reuben would regain part of his privileges. As for Simeon and Levi, Jacob cursed only their excessive anger, but they would remain like all the others. Even the dispersion Jacob decreed upon Simeon and Levi was designed only to rid them of their aggressiveness.

1. The word זאת *this,* is not very common in Scripture, and the Sages in the Midrash expound upon its use here in the summation of Jacob's blessing:

Moses' later blessing of the Children of Israel is introduced with the words וְזֹאת הַבְּרָכָה, *and this is the blessing which Moses the man of God blessed the children of Israel.* The Torah's use of the word זאת at the conclusion of Jacob's blessings implies that Moses commenced his blessing where Jacob left off [thus emphasizing the continuity and progressive aspects of the blessings; they were not separate and unrelated, but parts of the continuing development of Israel] *(Tanchuma Yashan).*

בְּזֹאת יָבֹא אַהֲרֹן אֶל־הַקֹּדֶשׁ — *With 'this' shall Aaron come to the Sanctuary* [*Lev.* 16:3]. R' Yitzchak said: the word זאת, *this,* is an allusion to the twelve Tribes of Israel [our verse is cited]. The passage in *Leviticus* alludes to the merit of the twelve Tribal Ancestors, which accompanied Aaron when he ministered in the Temple *(Pesikta Rabbosi* 47).

this is what their father spoke to them when he blessed them. He blessed each according to his appropriate blessing.

— *Sechel Tov* explains that the three rebuked sons understood the underlying blessing implicit in Jacob's words. They could have expected him to expel them from the nation of Israel; instead, he took away privileges that might have been due them — but this included the implied blessing that they remain part of Israel.

According to other commentators, [e.g. *Ibn Ezra* to *v.* 1, *Sforno* here], Reuben, Simeon and Levi were *not* blessed in the foregoing testament. Rather, the implication of our verse is that the foregoing is what their father 'spoke' to them — the Hebrew verb for spoke, דִּבֶּר, denoting sternness — וַיְבָרֶךְ אוֹתָם, and *then he blessed them* with an unrecorded blessing, apart from what was written in this chapter.

אִישׁ אֲשֶׁר כְּבִרְכָתוֹ בֵּרַךְ אֹתָם — *He blessed each according to his appropriate blessing* [lit. *man according to his blessing he blessed them*].

He blessed each according to the blessing destined to befall him. He did not bless all with a common blessing, but gave each a unique one. The future would prove the prophetic veracity of his benedictions *(Ramban* to 41:12).

— He blessed each according to his unique requirements. For example, Judah's blessing was related to the monarchy, Issachar's to Torah-study, etc. *(Sforno).*

As *R' Munk* writes, Jacob did not give a single, uniform blessing to all families of Israel. Though the nation must be unified, each of its component tribes has its separate function; thus, Israel is a pluralistic people with each tribe having a mission suited to its particular character and location. Reuben, Gad, and Manasseh specialized in cattle-raising and grazing [*Numbers* 32:1-4], Simeon provided scribes and teachers, Levi provided clergy, Judah royalty, Ephraim and Benjamin had the best soldiers [*Psalms* 80:3], Zebulun specialized in commerce and supported the scholarly tribe of Issachar, Asher and Naftali excelled in agriculture and the latter produced orators as well. Finally, Dan [*Pesachim* 4a] was known for its judicial competence.

Rashi observes: We would normally have expected the verse to read אִישׁ אֲשֶׁר כְּבִרְכָתוֹ בֵּרַךְ **אֹתוֹ**, lit. *each according to his blessing he blessed* **him.** Phrased as it is ... *he blessed* **them,** the intimation is: Included in the personal blessing he bestowed upon each of them individually — for example, ascribing to Judah the strength of the lion, to Benjamin the rapacity of the wolf, to Naftali the fleetness of a deer — he included them all in a *general* blessing. [That is, every *individual* blessing applied to them *all,* extending all the blessings to each and every one of them, so that each of them benefited by and possessed the combined qualities of all the blessings. While each individual tribe excelled in its particular quality, all the tribes shared in *all* the national blessings.]

The *Midrash* elaborates: ... Jacob in effect declared them *all* strong as lions, rapacious as wolves, fleet as deer. That each of the Tribal Ancestors was endowed with the others' unique characteristics is corroborated by Moses' later blessing, in which, for example, he referred to Dan as a lion while Jacob had referred to him as a serpent. ...

אֲלֵהֶם֮ אֲנִי֮ נֶאֱסָ֣ף אֶל־עַמִּ֔י קִבְר֥וּ אֹתִ֖י
אֶל־אֲבֹתָ֑י אֶ֨ל־הַמְּעָרָ֔ה אֲשֶׁ֥ר בִּשְׂדֵ֖ה
ל עֶפְרֹ֥ן הַחִתִּֽי׃ בַּמְּעָרָ֞ה אֲשֶׁ֨ר בִּשְׂדֵ֧ה
הַמַּכְפֵּלָ֛ה אֲשֶׁר־עַל־פְּנֵ֥י מַמְרֵ֖א בְּאֶ֣רֶץ
כְּנָ֑עַן אֲשֶׁ֨ר קָנָ֜ה אַבְרָהָ֗ם אֶת־הַשָּׂדֶ֛ה
לא מֵאֵ֛ת עֶפְרֹ֥ן הַחִתִּ֖י לַאֲחֻזַּת־קָֽבֶר׃ שָׁ֣מָּה

29. Jacob's final command.

וַיְצַו אוֹתָם — *Then he instructed them.*

According to *Malbim* and others, this phrase does not introduce the following subject, in which Jacob gave instructions regarding his burial. Rather, this phrase connotes that he gave them general instructions — which the Torah did not record — on how they should conduct themselves. Among these instructions was his command regarding the burial. [Therefore the next phrase starts independently with וַיֹּאמֶר, *and he said;* to indicate that it is separate.]

אֲנִי נֶאֱסָף אֶל־עַמִּי — *I am about to be gathered to my people.*

This expression is used to denote death because then the souls are 'gathered' into their place of concealment *(Rashi).*

The verb אסף, *gather,* often connotes the ingathering of an object to its proper place. See *Judges* 19:15; *Deut.* 22:2. *Lev.* 23:39. Whenever it is stated in reference to death it connotes this ingathering of souls *(Rashi).*

[See also *comm.* to וַיֵּאָסֶף אֶל עַמָּיו above 25:8, where many interpretations are cited. Among them: the deceased joins his ancestors in death; the reunification of the soul with the Upper Worlds; the classification of the departed with others of like character; the gathering into the 'bond of eternal life' with the righteous of all generations who are referred to as עַם, *people,* because they are similar to him.]

קִבְרוּ אֹתִי אֶל־אֲבֹתָי — *Bury me with my fathers.*

So that in addition to my *soul* being united with them, my body, too, will be with them *(Malbim).*

[The word קִבְרוּ, *bury,* is in plural.] Although Jacob had already imposed an oath upon Joseph about this matter, he now gave them *all* the duty of burying him in the Cave of Machpelah, because he was apprehensive that Pharaoh might forbid Joseph to leave the country. Jacob's apprehension was quite justified for we see that Joseph had to plead with the royal courtiers to intercede with Pharaoh for permission to go. Pharaoh consented only because Jacob had imposed an oath *(Ramban;* see further 50:4).

The translation of אֶל, lit. *to,* as *with* follows *Rashi.* In an alternate interpretation, *Ramban* concurs citing *Levit.* 8:18: אִשָּׁה אֶל אֲחוֹתָהּ, *a woman with her sister,* where אֶל similarly means *with* [see below].

אֶל־הַמְּעָרָה אֲשֶׁר בִּשְׂדֵה עֶפְרוֹן הַחִתִּי — *In the cave that is in the field of Ephron the Hittite.*

[That is, in the field that had once belonged to Ephron the Hittite.]

The translation of אֶל [lit. *to*] in this phrase as *in* follows *Ramban* who cites the similar idiomatic usage above in 23:19. Compare also *Exodus* 25:21 וְאֶל־הָאָרוֹן, *'in* the ark.'

In his primary interpretation however, *Ramban* suggests that the

[29] *Then he instructed them; and he said to them, "I am about to be gathered to my people. Bury me with my fathers in the cave that is in the field of Ephron the Hittite.* [30] *In the cave that is in the field of Machpelah, which faces Mamre, in the land of Canaan, which Abraham bought with the field from Ephron the Hittite as an estate for a burial site.*

dual usage of אֶל in this verse is elliptic and should be understood to mean: *Bury me* [i.e., inter me in a casket] *and carry me to my fathers to the cave.*

30. בַּמְּעָרָה אֲשֶׁר בִּשְׂדֵה הַמַּכְפֵּלָה אֲשֶׁר עַל־פְּנֵי מַמְרֵא בְּאֶרֶץ כְּנָעַן — *In the cave that is in the field of Machpelah which faces Mamre, in the land of Canaan.*

[The terms in this verse have been fully explained in the commentary to 23:17-20.

[Jacob proceeds to go into great detail about the burial site. Seventeen years had elapsed since the family had left the land of Canaan, so he was very specific in informing his sons about its location and his rights to the property.

[As culled from the commentators, Jacob was apprehensive that in the course of the years since they left Canaan, someone might have seized the cave (as happened to the Shunammite woman whose house had been seized during her absence; see *II Kings* 8:2), or that its precise location would be forgotten. He said, *in the cave*, but they might not have understood which cave he meant, so he added *which was in the field of Machpelah*, thus defining its location. To identify the region he added *which faces Mamre*, i.e. the city — another name for Hebron, and more specifically (as *Rashi* writes in 35:27) it is the name of the *plain* which lay before the city. To complete the geographic description, Jacob mentions *in the land of Canaan.*]

אֲשֶׁר קָנָה אַבְרָהָם אֶת הַשָּׂדֶה מֵאֵת עֶפְרֹן הַחִתִּי לַאֲחֻזַּת־קָבֶר — *Which Abraham bought with the field from Ephron the Hittite as an estate for a burial site.*

Therefore my right to be buried there cannot be disputed *(Rashbam).*

Jacob's intention in mentioning all of this about the site was to impress them with its importance. He wanted them to understand that Abraham had purchased the cave for a specific reason, and that he had commanded that it be their burial ground as an everlasting possession *(Ramban).* [See further, 50:13.]

The details in this verse were in anticipation of their possible apprehension: Should you fear that someone will contest your right to the site, be aware it is the cave *which Abraham bought, together with the field;* furthermore, it was not bought from an unauthorized person, but from *Ephron the Hittite,* who was the chief and had every right to sell it. Have no fear that Abraham bought it for farming; he purchased it specifically *as an estate for a burial site* and designated that it be used exclusively for this purpose *(Hadar Zekeinim; Abarbanel; Malbim).*

קָבְרוּ אֶת־אַבְרָהָם וְאֵת שָׂרָה אִשְׁתּוֹ
שָׁמָּה קָבְרוּ אֶת־יִצְחָק וְאֵת רִבְקָה אִשְׁתּוֹ
לב וְשָׁמָּה קָבַרְתִּי אֶת־לֵאָה: מִקְנֵה הַשָּׂדֶה
לג וְהַמְּעָרָה אֲשֶׁר־בּוֹ מֵאֵת בְּנֵי־חֵת: וַיְכַל

31. שָׁמָּה קָבְרוּ אַבְרָהָם וְאֵת שָׂרָה אִשְׁתּוֹ — *There they buried Abraham and Sarah his wife.*

Thus, demonstrating that the sale had been confirmed in *practice,* actual possession was taken of the cave *(Hadar Zekeinim),* and its use confirmed its intended purpose *(Alshich).*

By evoking this memory of those interred there, Jacob hoped to inspire his sons with the significance of the place and make them even more zealous in carrying out his command to bury him there. Jacob also wanted it understood that only the three couples were to be buried there — beginning with Abraham and Sarah and terminating with Jacob himself. [See below and further 50:5] *(Ramban).*

Sechel Tov notes that although Sarah and Rebecca died before their respective husbands, Jacob mentioned the males first to accord them honor.

[The subject of this phrase is not mentioned. Who buried them? As *Rashi* notes in his *comm.* to 41:13 s.v. אֹתִי הֵשִׁיב, the unnamed subjects in an elliptic Scriptural verse are always the ones with the power to perform that particular action, or to those who are described earlier as having performed that action. In this case the inferred subjects are Abraham who buried Sarah (23:19), and Isaac and Ishmael who buried Abraham (25:9).]

שָׁמָּה קָבְרוּ אֶת יִצְחָק וְאֵת רִבְקָה אִשְׁתּוֹ — *There they buried Isaac and Rebecca his wife.*[1]

Jacob mentioned this as proof that possession of the cave passed on to Isaac and his children; it was meant to preclude any possible claims by the descendants of Ishmael that the cave was *their* inheritance from Abraham *(Hadar Zekeinim; Abarbanel).*

'Furthermore, it is only proper that I should wish to be buried near my parents' *(Haamek Davar).*

Jacob used the abstract expression *they* buried rather than *I buried* [as in the case of Leah] because Esau had par-

1. **Why did Jacob mention his parents by name?**

The prohibition of calling a parent by name even after their death [*Kiddushin* 41b] applies only to cases where one simply mentions them by name, without a title. But if their name is preceded by 'father' or 'mother' it is not considered an impropriety and is permitted, as in the case of the Talmudic usage of Abba ['father'] Chalafta, Yannai Abba [see GRA to *Yoreh Deah* 242 § 34.] Therefore, having prefaced his statement by saying *Bury me with my 'fathers'* [v. 29], Jacob could now name them without impropriety.

However Joseph's mention of Jacob by name [further, 50:24] and Isaac, of Abraham in 28:4, needs clarification. Perhaps the rule does not apply to the Patriarchs since their names in themselves are exalted and God Himself assigned their names, which undoubtedly attest to their spiritual superiority. It is accordingly an honor for their ancestors to refer to them by such august, Divinely sanctioned names. [See also *Me'am Loez* cited in footnote to *v.* 1.]

Support for this may be adduced from the Talmud, [*Yoma* 38] where we learn that one should not give a child the name of a wicked person. *Ritva* rules we may use the name of Ishmael since even God referred to him by name. [Therefore, it is certainly proper to refer to the Patriarchs by name] *(HaKsav V'HaKaballah).*

[31]*There they buried Abraham and Sarah his wife; there they buried Isaac and Rebecca his wife; and there I buried Leah.* [32] *Purchase of the field and the cave within it was from the sons of Heth."*

ticipated in the burial of Isaac [35:29], and Jacob did not want to mention Esau's name. Moreover, he did not say '*we* buried' since he would then have had to elaborate by clarifying: 'there *we* buried Isaac, and there *they* buried Rebecca,' since Jacob was on his way home from Laban when his mother was buried. [Presumably Esau and other members of the household buried her; as *Ramban* writes in 35:8, the blind Isaac could not even participate.]

וְשָׁמָּה קָבַרְתִּי אֶת־לֵאָה — *And there I buried Leah.*

— 'Accordingly I have already established possession of it' [and it would not be fitting for anyone but me, her husband, to be buried there with her *(Tz'ror HaMor)*]. Jacob said this with Esau in mind, lest Esau and his children claim the cave and maintain that it was his right as firstborn that *he* be the only son buried there with his ancestors. Moreover, it was clear that *both* could not be buried there. This apprehension was also the purport of Jacob's words [cited by Joseph in 50:5]: *In my grave which I have hewn for myself,* meaning that he had already prepared his own sepulchre there (*Ramban).*

[Jacob's apprehension was well-founded, for indeed, the Rabbis in *Sotah* 13a record that there was a quarrel with Esau at the cave prior to Jacob's burial. See *Rashi* to *v.* 21 above, and footnote to 50:13.]

32. מִקְנֵה הַשָּׂדֶה וְהַמְּעָרָה אֲשֶׁר בּוֹ מֵאֵת בְּנֵי חֵת — *Purchase of the field and the cave within it was from the sons of Heth.*

Jacob mentioned this last point to put his sons' minds at ease on one final matter: Ephron had been the chief of the city when he sold the site to Abraham. The brothers might have been apprehensive that the townsfolk possibly were unhap-

1. **When did Leah die? Why didn't Esau quarrel when Leah was buried?**

This is the first and only reference in the Torah to Leah's death. The Torah is not, as has often been emphasized, a history book. It recorded only those events God deemed necessary for us to know; apparently the time and circumstances of Leah's death did not fit into this category.

According to the authoritative *Seder Olam,* Leah died at the age of 45, at the time Joseph was sold. This was yet another one of the misfortunes Jacob experienced during that period.

[Several interesting chronological details emerge from the fact that Leah's death coincided with Joseph's sale:

1. The year was 2216 from Creation.
2. Leah survived Rachel, who died in 2207 as Jacob returned to Canaan, by only 9 years.
3. Leah died twelve years before Isaac, who, as noted in the *comm.* to 37:29 and 37:2, lived twelve years after Joseph's sale.
4. Jacob, who died at the age of 147 in the year 2255, outlived Leah by 39 years, and Rachel by 48 years.
5. The sequence of the deaths of the Patriarchs and Matriarchs were:

Sarah, Abraham, Rebecca, Rachel, Leah, Isaac, Jacob.

[When I mentioned the above chronology to *R' David Feinstein,* he suggested that point 3, that Isaac was still alive when Jacob buried Leah, would account for why Esau did not try to stop Jacob from burying her in the Cave. As long as either of his parents was alive, Esau was solicitous of their feelings and would not defy Isaac's wishes regarding the cave. It was only at Jacob's burial, after their father was dead, that Esau dared show his true colors.]

יַעֲקֹב֙ לְצַוֺּ֣ת אֶת־בָּנָ֔יו וַיֶּאֱסֹ֥ף רַגְלָ֖יו אֶל־
א הַמִּטָּ֑ה וַיִּגְוַ֖ע וַיֵּאָ֥סֶף אֶל־עַמָּֽיו׃ וַיִּפֹּ֥ל יוֹסֵ֖ף

py with the sale of a Hittite property to a foreigner as a gravesite, but could not resist because Ephron was their leader. Now that Ephron was dead they might contest the sale and try to prevent Jacob's burial. Jacob therefore assured them that the sale was *from the sons of Heth* — they *all* consented to the sale unequivocally *(Hadar Zekeinim; Abarbanel; Chizkuni).* [See *comm.* to מֵאֵת בְּנֵי חֵת in 23:20.]

According to the Talmud [*Sotah* 13a] Jacob even possessed a deed for the property. [See footnote to 50:13.]

33. Jacob dies.

וַיְכַל יַעֲקֹב לְצַוֺּת אֶת־בָּנָיו — *When Jacob finished instructing* [lit. *to command*] *his sons.*

He is likened to one about to embark on a journey and who first sets his house in order and instructs his family how to act in his absence *(Pesikta; Malbim).*[1]

'Fortunate are the righteous,' proclaim the Sages in the Midrash, 'who do not depart from the world until they have charged their sons!'

The syntax makes it clear that only *after* Jacob finished his charge to his sons did he draw his feet into the bed and return his soul to his Maker. This indicates that death had no power over Jacob; and he was entirely in control of his body. This is the implication of the Sages' statement [see *Rashi* below]: 'Jacob our father did not die,' for had death had power over him he would not have been able to delay his demise until the moment he concluded his final instructions and willfully drew his feet onto the bed *(Alshich; Or HaChaim).*[2]

וַיֶּאֱסֹף רַגְלָיו אֶל־הַמִּטָּה — *[And] he drew* [lit. *gathered*] *his feet into the bed.*

The sense of the expression is that he *drew* his legs onto the bed, this being the meaning in this context of אסף [usually translated *gathered;* see on *v.* 29] *(Rashi).*

Until this point Jacob had been sitting up on the bed with his feet on the ground. He now raised his feet and lay down *(Ibn Ezra; Rashbam).*

[Continuing *Malbim's* simile of a man embarking upon a journey]:

1. The Midrashim preserve some of the additional instructions Jacob gave his sons at the time:

"When you carry me up, do so reverently and respectfully; no one who is uncircumcised may touch my bier so as not to drive away the Divine Presence. Also, let no one of my descendants who married a Canaanite woman touch my bier. Let Judah, Issachar, and Zebulun be its bearers on the east; Reuben, Simeon, and Gad on the south; Ephraim, Manasseh, and Benjamin on the west; and Dan, Asher, and Naftali on the north. In a similar order will your tribes be grouped some time in the future under four standards in the desert with the Divine Presence in the center."

Jacob insisted that Joseph not carry his bier since he was a monarch; also that it would be improper for Levi — whose descendants were destined to carry the Holy Ark — to carry Jacob's remains.

2. **'One dies only from inactivity.'**

R' Tarfon in *Avos d'Rabbi Nosson* interprets our verse to teach that 'One dies only from inactivity.'

Yalkut Yehudah explains R' Tarfon's comment to mean that as long as Jacob still had the task of instructing his children before him, he stayed alive; when he finished charging them and was left idle — only then could death overtake him.

49
33

[33] *When Jacob finished instructing his sons, he drew his feet into the bed. He expired and was gathered to his people.*

Jacob placed his feet on his sickbed, which was like a vehicle that would take him to his destination.

וַיִּגְוַע וַיֵּאָסֶף אֶל־עַמָּיו — *He expired and was gathered to his people.*

[As explained at length in the *comm.* to 25:8, this expression refers to quick death without prolonged sickness or pain; this is the death enjoyed by the righteous. It is a death that, according to some, comes unexpectedly, while one is even alert enough to carry on a conversation. According to others it refers to a state of unconsciousness preceding death, hence the term וַיִּגְוַע, *expired,* lit. *shriveled* (like something deflated), which colloquially has the connotation of 'he breathed his last'].

— It depicts the moment that the soul leaves the body *(Malbim).*

⇐§ Jacob lives on.

[In recording the passing of Abraham (25:8) and Isaac (35:29), the Torah uses a similar expression with the addition of the word וַיָּמָת, *and he died.*] However, the term 'death' *per se* is not mentioned in this case. Our Rabbis [*Taanis* 5b] accordingly, said, 'Jacob our father is not dead' *(Rashi).*

The full text of this Rabbinic interpretation in *Taanis* 5b follows:

"R' Yochanan said: Our Father Jacob did not die.' R' Nachman retorted to R' Yitzchak: 'Was it for nothing that the mourners mourned, the embalmers embalmed and the grave-diggers buried?' He replied, 'It is a Biblical verse which I expound [*Jeremiah* 30:10]: *'Therefore, do not fear O Jacob My servant,' said HASHEM 'and do not be dismayed, O Israel: for I will save you from afar, and your descendants from captivity.'* Jacob is thus equated with his descendants: Just as his descendants live on so does he.

Rashi there explains that the intimation of Jeremiah's prophecy was that Jacob would be 'brought' into Exile in order to witness the redemption of his descendants. This was indeed the case in Egypt where the Sages expound that the passage וַיַּרְא יִשְׂרָאֵל *"Israel" saw,* in *Exodus* 14:31, refers personally to the Patriarch Israel.

Tosafos derives the Rabbinic concept that Jacob did not die from the fact that any direct reference to 'death' is missing from the Biblical narrative in these verses.

Interestingly, the Sages in *Sotah* 13b where the episode of Esau's interference with Jacob's burial is related [see footnote to 50:13], apparently understand that Jacob lived on even in the *literal,* physical sense. The Talmud there records that when Chushim son of Dan angrily struck Esau on the head with a club, causing his eyes to fall out and roll to Jacob's feet. 'Jacob opened his eyes and laughed.'

However, most later commentators, perceive a purely spiritual connotation in the statement that Jacob did not die to imply that he lives on spiritually through the heritage he passed on to his descendants — the Children of Israel.

Concluding his commentary to Genesis with an interpretation of this statement, *Ramban* notes the apparent incongruity in this context of the fact that Jacob had applied the term 'death' to himself, above in 48:21. *Ramban* postulates that Jacob did so either because he did not know he would live on or did not want to reveal it. That his sons *'saw'* that their father was dead [50:15] indicates that to *them* he was dead, or, as *R' Bachya* explains, that

ב עַל־פְּנֵי אָבִיו וַיֵּבְךְּ עָלָיו וַיִּשַּׁק־לוֹ: וַיְצַו
יוֹסֵף אֶת־עֲבָדָיו אֶת־הָרֹפְאִים לַחֲנֹט

Jacob did not experience the *taste* of death.

Furthermore, *R' Bachya,* in elaborating upon *Ramban,* interprets the statement 'Jacob did not die' to mean that Jacob's soul always remained hovering over his body, whereas the souls of other righteous men who do not reach that degree of holiness return to their source and have no attachment to their bodies. But Jacob's soul ascended and descended, a power confined only to those who achieved the highest degree of holiness.[1]

R' Nosson Scherman writes in the Overview to *Eichah* [p. xxxix]: "*'Our father Jacob did not die' (Taanis* 5b) because he had so perfected his body that it was no contradiction whatever to his soul. 'Death' is a wrenching, painful concept only because — and to the extent that — it involves the removal of the soul from a material existence it has come to crave. The more materially lustful a person is, the less he can bear to part from this life for the holier one awaiting him. And the more spiritual his life on earth has become, the less he cares to be encumbered by his body with its demands and animal instincts. Jacob had perfected himself to the point where leaving earthly life meant no more to him than removing a coat means to us. His soul simply discarded its earthly raiment — his body — and continued essentially unchanged. 'Death' in the deeper sense simply did not exist for Jacob — hence he did not 'die' "*(Resisei Layalah).*

Jacob was 147 years old when he passed on. [He was 130 when he presented himself to Pharaoh upon his arrival to Egypt, and he lived 17 years beyond that.] He died in the year 2255 from Creation *(Seder Olam).*

L

1. Jacob is embalmed and mourned.

וַיִּפֹּל יוֹסֵף עַל־פְּנֵי אָבִיו — *Then Joseph fell upon his father's face.*

He threw himself on his father's face and wept unrestrainedly. When he could weep no more, he gave him a parting kiss *(R' Hirsch).*

This does not imply that the other children of Jacob did not do as much. Joseph is mentioned specifically because his presence at Jacob's final moment was in fulfillment of God's promise to Jacob [46:4], *Joseph will place his hand over your eyes (Sechel Tov).* The Torah does not have to mention that Joseph placed his hand over his father's eyes; it is self-understood *(Ralbag).*

Haamek Davar suggests that

1. It is recorded [*Kesubos* 108b] that after his death Rabbeinu HaKodesh ['our Holy Rabbi' — R' Judah the Prince, compiler of the Mishnah] would return home every Sabbath evening to recite the *Kiddush.* Rabbeinu HaKodesh eventually stopped the practice lest it reflect on earlier righteous men who did not enjoy this privilege. [See also story of R' Achai in *Shabbos* 152b.]

R' Bachya writes that Jacob would certainly have had this power since he possessed holiness from three sources: From Abraham, who was sanctified with the command to circumcise himself before begetting Isaac; from Isaac, who was sanctified as a sacrifice without blemish; and his own, for he was the third of the Patriarchs and completed the Divine Chariot [the Patriarchs are mystically regarded as the Chariot that bears God's Presence — see *comm.* to 17:22]. Moreover, unlike the other Patriarchs, Jacob had no wicked children. That is why the Almighty is called 'The Holy One *of Jacob' (Isaiah* 29:23), but never the Holy One *of Abraham* or *of Isaac.*

[1] Then Joseph fell upon his father's face. He wept
over him and kissed him. [2] Joseph ordered his
servants, the physicians, to embalm his father; so the

Joseph is mentioned because he was nearest to Jacob at the last moment of his life, listening to his final whispered instructions in which Jacob presumably revealed to him certain Divine secrets not known to his brothers. It was because Joseph was privy to such prophetic information while Jacob experienced a final surge of the Divine Presence that Joseph could allude to signs of redemption when he later addressed his brothers [*v.* 25].

וַיֵּבְךְּ עָלָיו וַיִּשַּׁק־לוֹ — *He wept over him and* [he] *kissed him.*

It was a farewell kiss; the kiss at death *(Midrash HaGadol).*

While some *Midrashim* note that from this verse it is implicit that one is permitted to kiss the dead before burial, the *halachah* nowadays frowns upon the practice since a corpse imparts defilement that can adversely affect the soul of one who kisses it. The commentators maintain further that no permissive ruling may be derived from Joseph's example since the Patriarch's body was wholly sacred and did not become ritually defiled by death, in the sense that we learned above [49:33]: 'Jacob our father did not die.' [See *Pischei Teshuvah* to *Yoreh Deah* §394 who is permissive regarding parents, and the Testament of R' Yehudah HaChassid §4 in *Sefer Chassidim* Mossad Harav Kook ed., and notes thereon by R' Reuven Margulioth.]

2. וַיְצַו יוֹסֵף ... לַחֲנֹט אֶת אָבִיו — [*And*] *Joseph ordered his servants, the physicians, to embalm his father.*

Embalming involves the use of a mixture of aromatic spices *(Rashi).*

Embalming was an Egyptian custom. It was believed that the soul would eventually return to its body after death and pains were therefore taken to preserve the body from dissolution in the grave. Numerous mummies have been found in a state of preservation that testifies to the skill of the ancient embalmers. Jewish law, however, forbids embalming; it mandates an unimpeded physical return to the elements by burial in the earth so that the body will decompose naturally. The soul rises to God; but the physical shelter, the chemical elements that clothed the soul, sink into the vast reservoir of nature. God's words to Adam were, *For you are dust, and unto dust you shall return* [3:10].

Malbim explains why Jewish law requires burial of a sort that will not delay the natural decomposition of the body. A living person has a higher, Godly soul [נְשָׁמָה הָאֱלֹהִית] that cannot be degraded by sin and that leaves the body when death takes place. But there is also a lower spirit [רוח] in a living person. A man has the obligation to serve God in such a manner that he elevates even this lower spirit until it is completely holy. If he does so, the spirit leaves the dead body together with the soul, for both are uncontaminated by man's animal nature. But to the extent that man sins he utilizes this life-giving spirit to feed the desires of his body, that it remains with it even in the grave. Only as the body decomposes does the spirit become free to return to its heavenly home. Embalming, therefore, is a disservice to the deceased because by preserving the body it entraps the spirit. In Jacob's case, however, his life was so righteous and holy that his spirit had been totally freed of any bodily attachment. This being the case, embalming served the positive purpose of preserving the body that had been a host, during his lifetime, to so much sanctity.

As gleaned from the commentators, the embalming was limited to royalty and consisted of: a) anointing and washing the body with mixtures of aromatic spices and oils to keep the

אֶת־אָבִיו וַיַּחַנְטוּ הָרֹפְאִים אֶת־יִשְׂרָאֵל׃
ג וַיִּמְלְאוּ־לוֹ אַרְבָּעִים יוֹם כִּי כֵּן יִמְלְאוּ יְמֵי
הַחֲנֻטִים וַיִּבְכּוּ אֹתוֹ מִצְרַיִם שִׁבְעִים יוֹם׃

body fragrant and delay putrefaction [comp. the case of Assa in *II Chronicles* 16:14]. The internal organs were infused with the fluids via the navel. The solution was changed daily and the body massaged daily for forty days, as *v.* 3 records. Eventually the body would become dehydrated and rigid and no repugnant odor would remain; b) the removal by chemical means of the putrefying elements so as to inhibit decomposition. Physicians performed this process because it required knowledge of anatomy and of the drugs necessary for the preservation of bodies (see *Abarbanel; R' Shmuel b. Chofni; Zohar; Michlol Yofi).*

☙ Joseph's purpose in embalming Jacob.

It appears that Joseph's intention had nothing to do with the pagan *religious* significance attached to the rite by the Egyptians, *viz.* to preserve the body after death and keep it ready for reoccupation by the soul. Joseph's purpose was only to respectfully preserve his father's body from putrefaction during the long journey to the Sepulchre at Machpelah. [See footnote.][1]

Or HaChaim maintains to the contrary. Since the body of as righteous a person as Jacob never putrefies [as noted in the footnote below], Joseph purposely ordered Jacob embalmed lest the Egyptians venerate him as a god when they realized that his body did not decompose. [See the third interpretation offered by *Rashi* 47:29 s.v. אַל־נָא.]

וַיַּחַנְטוּ הָרֹפְאִים אֶת־יִשְׂרָאֵל — *So the physicians embalmed Israel.*

As noted below [see inference in *Rashi* to *v.* 13], Jacob had left instructions that his corpse not be attended by any but his sons. That Joseph commanded the court physicians to embalm his father does not contradict this. The embalming process was done only by Jacob's sons; the physicians merely supervised and instructed them on the embalming procedure, but did not touch his body themselves *(R' Bachya; R' Shmuel b. Chofni; Sefer Chassidim* ed. Mekitzei Nirdamim §1563).

[The act is attributed to the physicians because they, as experts,

1. The Rabbis in the Midrash debate the propriety of Joseph's order that his father be embalmed.

R' Yehudah HaNassi and the Sages disagree. The former maintains that Joseph erred, and the Holy One rebuked him for taking such measures to artificially protect his father, saying, 'Could *I* not have protected My righteous? Did I not assure him not to fear the worm?' [see *Isaiah* 41:14]. In punishment for this Joseph died in his brothers' lifetime. [Joseph was next to [illegible] youngest brother; that he died before all his older brothers is because he did not display [illegible]er filial honor. Just as the reward for honoring parents is a long life, the converse is also true (see *Exodus* 20:12).]

According to the Sages, however, Joseph acted properly since Jacob himself asked that he be embalmed, as is apparent from what the Torah informs us in *v.* 12 below: *His sons did for him as he had instructed them* [which implies that even in embalming him Joseph was merely following instructions]. The Sages accordingly attribute Joseph's early death not to this, but to the fact that he listened without protest when Jacob was slighted five times by Judah who said, *your servant, my father,* five times. [This was not considered a sin on Judah's part, because he thought he was speaking to an Egyptian viceroy before whom such an expression was proper.]

[Cf. also *Berachos* 55a where the opinion is recorded that Joseph died prematurely because he assumed airs of authority (or because "public responsibility shortens the life"); see also

physicians embalmed Israel.
[3] *Its forty-day term was completed, for such is the term of the embalmed; and Egypt bewailed him for seventy days.* [4] *When his bewailing period passed,*

were responsible to oversee its proper execution. Sometimes the Torah attributes a deed to the one who performed it, and sometimes to the one who ordered or supervised it. See discussion in 37:28 "Who sold Joseph?"]

The spiritual name *Israel* is used here to imply that all this honor was bestowed upon Jacob not only because of Joseph's royal status and in compliance with his command, but because he was *Israel* [denoting שְׂרָרָה, *authority; dominion* (see *comm.* to 35:29) and hence himself worthy of royal treatment *(Sforno).*

— The physicians embalmed "Israel" — i.e., in accordance with his status *(R' Hirsch).*

3. וַיִּמְלְאוּ־לוֹ אַרְבָּעִים יוֹם — *[And] its forty-day term was completed* [lit. *and forty days were filled for him*].

They were involved in the embalming day after day until forty days were completed for it *(Rashi).*

כִּי כֵּן יִמְלְאוּ יְמֵי הַחֲנֻטִים — *For such is the term of the embalmed* [lit. *for such are filled the days of those embalmed*].

This is the period of time required for the spices and chemicals to be absorbed into the body to achieve their purpose of retarding decomposition *(Sechel Tov; Alshich).*

וַיִּבְכּוּ אֹתוֹ מִצְרַיִם שִׁבְעִים יוֹם — *And Egypt bewailed him for seventy days.*

[Not *in addition* to the aforementioned forty days, but inclusive of them:] These seventy days consisted of the forty for embalming plus [an additional] thirty for weeping. [The Egyptians bewailed Jacob so intensely and long] because they had been blessed on his account: with his arrival the famine had ceased [see on 47:19], and the Nile was blessed *(Rashi).*

— *All* of Egypt bewailed him. Jacob's descendants are not specifically mentioned as having also bewailed him as it is self-evident that they did. Although the Jewish period of mourning is seven days [see *v.* 15], Joseph mourned for the full seventy days, in com-

footnote on p. 1881, and comm. to *v.* 21 below where the opinion is recorded that Joseph died prematurely because he presumptuously told his brothers that *he* would sustain them rather than attributing their sustenance to God. See also *Targum Yonasan* to 46:29 s.v. וַיֵּרָא that Joseph's life was shortened because he permitted Jacob to prostrate himself before him when they first met upon Jacob's arrival from Canaan.]

[Jacob's reason for requesting embalming (and Joseph's own rationalization for it, according to the first opinion in the Midrash) would have been simply to avoid putrefaction of the body because it was known that burial would have to be delayed a considerable amount of time due to: a) the unusually long national mourning period the Egyptians would observe for him; b) the long journey back to Canaan. Furthermore, in *Sanhedrin* 47b the purpose of burial is discussed, and the view is recorded that the decomposition of the body in the ground is a means of atonement for the sins that the dead committed in his lifetime, a reason that did not apply to Jacob (see comm. to *Ramban* 23:8 where a similar thought is expressed regarding Sarah's burial). In the case of the wholly righteous Patriarch, coupled with these overriding considerations, it was thought that embalming was appropriate. However, the first Sage in the Midrash disagreed, maintaining that embalming implied a certain lack of trust.]

ד וַיַּעַבְרוּ֙ יְמֵ֣י בְכִית֔וֹ וַיְדַבֵּ֣ר יוֹסֵ֔ף אֶל־בֵּ֥ית פַּרְעֹ֖ה לֵאמֹ֑ר אִם־נָ֨א מָצָ֤אתִי חֵן֙ בְּעֵ֣ינֵיכֶ֔ם דַּבְּרוּ־נָ֕א בְּאָזְנֵ֥י פַרְעֹ֖ה לֵאמֹֽר׃

pliance with this national mourning period *(R' Shmuel b. Chofni).*[1]

Several Midrashim [see *Torah Sheleimah*] perceive in the number seventy an allusion to the seventy souls who descended with Jacob to Egypt, each of whom had by now grown into a household and each of whom bewailed him a different day.

4. **וַיַּעַבְרוּ יְמֵי בְכִיתוֹ** — *When his bewailing period* [lit. *days*] *passed.*

Concerning the death of Moses the Torah uses the expression: *the days of bewailing were* **ended** **[וַיִּתְּמוּ]** *(Deut.* 34:8), implying finality, while our verse says that the bewailing *passed,* [וַיַּעַבְרוּ], implying a gradual process. This difference in wording is explained by the fact that Moses died on the threshhold of the Promised Land. Then the Jews were living with the joyful prospect of the imminent occupation of their own land. Consequently after the prescribed period of thirty days, the mourning ended. Jacob's passing, though, was felt as a more far-reaching calamity. The last representative of the glorious Patriarchal epoch was gone. His descendants felt deprived of their protector, and they knew that their position as aliens in Egypt would become more precarious. This is why "the bewailing days" *passed* without ever being formally *ended* as in Moses' case *(R' Munk* from the *Midrash).*

וַיְדַבֵּר יוֹסֵף אֶל בֵּית פַּרְעֹה — *Joseph spoke to Pharaoh's household.*

Not to Pharaoh *himself,* but to members of the royal court, asking them to deliver the following message to Pharaoh and intercede on his behalf *(Ralbag).*

According to the Midrash, Joseph feared that the courtiers might oppose his request to Pharaoh. So he acted according to the proverb: 'Win the accuser over to your cause if you want him not to act against you.' Joseph was obliged to speak first with the lady-in-waiting to the queen: she influenced her mistress, who in her turn persuaded Pharaoh on Joseph's behalf.

☙ Why did the all-powerful viceroy of Egypt require the members of the royal household to intercede with Pharaoh, rather than entering the king's presence himself? Why

1. Under normal circumstances, the Talmud makes it clear, excessive weeping for the dead is forbidden 'lest we appear to be more merciful than God Himself' [see *Moed Kattan* 27b]. *A. Greenbaum* in his notes to the above comment of *R' Shmuel b. Chofni* [Mossad HaRav Kook ed. Jerusalem 1979 §313] cites the case of *R' Yehudah HaNassi* in *Kesubos* 103b for whom the Sages considered instituting twelve months of mourning; cf. also *Rambam, Avel* 13:10. By quoting other sources as well, he defends R' Shmuel's view that in the case of the Patriarch, Joseph was permitted to extend his personal mourning period to coincide with that of the rest of the country.

There is also the view in *Midrash* HaChefetz that the mourning period extended until Jacob was buried.

See *R' Bachya,* however, who derives from our verse that it is not permitted to mourn for even a great personage in Israel longer than thirty days [since the thirty-day mourning period did not *begin* until the embalming procedure ended]. Cf. the case of Moses for whom the Israelites ended their mourning after thirty days [see comm. to *Deut.* 34:8].

50
5

Joseph spoke to Pharaoh's household saying, "If you
please — if I have found favor in your eyes, speak
now in the ears of Pharaoh as follows. 5 *My father*

did he require Pharaoh's permission in the first place?

— He was a mourner wearing rent clothing and sackcloth, and a mourner was not permitted to enter the royal palace, for *one may not enter the king's gate wearing sackcloth* [see *Esther* 4:2] *(Moshav Zekeinim; Midrash; Sforno).*

— Etiquette demanded that when even the highest official wished to make a personal request of the king, that he do so through one of the king's officers *(R' Avraham ben HaRambam).*

That Joseph needed permission at all to leave the land is quite understandable. Firstly, Joseph was the sole ruler and administrator of the land [see 41:44], and his absence — even temporarily — would cause a strain on the government. Furthermore, Pharaoh might have been apprehensive that Joseph would want to remain in Canaan; therefore, Joseph had to convince him to the contrary *(Chizkuni).* [See *Ramban* to 49:29.]

According to *Or HaAfeilah* [*Torah Sheleimah* §15], when Pharaoh had entrusted the kingdom to Joseph he extracted an oath that Joseph would never leave Egypt without his permission. Joseph now demonstrated his allegiance to that oath by seeking permission.

Minchah Belulah notes that Joseph might have needed royal permission because the journey would require horses and chariots; and these [as noted in 45:19, 27] were not allowed out of the country without Pharaoh's personal permission.

According to many commentators this need for permission demonstrated that certain forms of the Egyptian bondage had begun to take effect although it would not become official policy until after the last of the brothers was dead. Already with Jacob's death Joseph's prominence was somewhat diminished.

In his Notes to *Me'am Loez/Torah Anthology* [chapt. 11, note 28 (p. 665)] the translator, R' Aryeh Kaplan, offers that "Jacob's death in 2255 [1506 B.C.E.] came two years after the beginning of the reign of Thutmose II, who ruled from 1508 to 1490 B.C.E. Thutmose II was the son of Thutmose I, and is generally considered to have been a weak ruler. Some say that his father was still alive during his reign, and ruled jointly with him. Apparently, seeing the death of Jacob, whom he considered a miracle man, Thutmose was emboldened to diminish Joseph's authority."

אִם־נָא מָצָאתִי חֵן בְּעֵינֵיכֶם דַּבְּרוּ־נָא בְּאָזְנֵי פַרְעֹה לֵאמֹר — *If you please — if I have found favor in your eyes, speak now in the ears of Pharaoh as follows.*

The word נָא is used in Scripture both for *please* and for *now.* In our verse, it combines both connotations: the only way they could do him a favor was by expediting his request without delay, because he was afraid to postpone fulfillment of his oath to Jacob *(Or HaChaim).*

As a statesman, Joseph used אִם־נָא, *if you please,* the courteous form required by protocol, even though he knew that Pharaoh's courtiers would not dare refuse him, and would be pleased to perform a service for the viceroy of the land *(R' Hirsch).*

[The idiom of *speaking in the ears* denoting *personally* occurs in 44:18. See also 23:10.]

ה אָבִי הִשְׁבִּיעַנִי לֵאמֹר הִנֵּה אָנֹכִי מֵת
בְּקִבְרִי אֲשֶׁר כָּרִיתִי לִי בְּאֶרֶץ כְּנַעַן שָׁמָּה
תִּקְבְּרֵנִי וְעַתָּה אֶעֱלֶה־נָּא וְאֶקְבְּרָה אֶת־
ו אָבִי וְאָשׁוּבָה: וַיֹּאמֶר פַּרְעֹה עֲלֵה וּקְבֹר
ז אֶת־אָבִיךָ כַּאֲשֶׁר הִשְׁבִּיעֶךָ: וַיַּעַל יוֹסֵף
לִקְבֹּר אֶת־אָבִיו וַיַּעֲלוּ אִתּוֹ כָּל־עַבְדֵי

5. אָבִי הִשְׁבִּיעַנִי לֵאמֹר — *My father had adjured me* [bound me by an oath], *saying.*

Joseph was careful to stress that his father had insisted on an oath. This emphasized that in addition to filial *duty*, an *oath* was involved, which he was bound under every circumstance to fulfill. Joseph knew that this latter detail would be the determining factor in Pharaoh's grant of permission. See *v.* 6 *(Abarbanel; Malbim; Akeidah).*

הִנֵּה אָנֹכִי מֵת — *Behold, I am about to die.* [*See 48:21.*]

— Jacob wanted to give his request the greater power of a deathbed charge *(Malbim).*

בְּקִבְרִי אֲשֶׁר כָּרִיתִי לִי בְּאֶרֶץ כְּנַעַן שָׁמָּה תִּקְבְּרֵנִי — *In my grave, which I have hewn for myself in the land of Canaan — there you are to bury me.*

This does not quite parallel the reason Jacob himself gave in 47:30 where his emphasis was on being buried with his ancestors. Joseph may have thought that Pharaoh would be more impressed by Jacob's desire to be buried in a duly-acquired grave than by his desire to be buried with his ancestors *(R' Munk).*

Rashi interprets that in its most literal sense the verb כָּרִיתִי [*hewn*] means *dug,* as in *Exodus* 21:33 כִּי יִכְרֶה אִישׁ, *if a man shall dig.* He continues that in the Midrash there is an interpretation which fits the contextual meaning of the word — viz. אֲשֶׁר כָּרִיתִי means *which I have bought.* In coastal cities they use the term כִּירָה to signify מְכִירָה, *purchase.* [*Midrash;* see also *Sotah* 13a; *Chullin* 92a. See also *Rashi* to *Deut.* 2:6 s.v. תִּכְרוּ].

Rashi cites another Midrashic interpretation that כָּרִיתִי is a verbal form of כְּרִי, *heap,* denoting that Jacob had *heaped up* all the silver and gold which he had brought from the house of Laban and said to Esau, 'Take this for your share in the Cave.' (See *Rashi* to 46:6.) [Following the latter, the passage would be rendered: *In my grave for which I made a heap* — i.e., which I acquired from Esau by heaping up my possessions.]

[All the above interpretations emphasize how Joseph was trying to impress Pharaoh with the fact that Jacob's stake in the Cave of Machpelah was not merely an emotional one: Jacob had actually carved out the grave himself, or bought it, or acquired it by heaping up a vast fortune for it.]

Ramban [who interprets the word as *dug*] writes in his comm. to 49:31 that Jacob emphasized that he had already dug his grave in order to emphasize that he had taken personal possession of it. He said this with reference to his fear that Esau — or his children — might lay claim to the gravesite in the ancestral Cave of Machpelah. Jacob longed to

50
6-7

had adjured me, saying, 'Behold, I am about to die. In
my grave, which I have hewn for myself in the land
of Canaan — there you are to bury me. 'Now, I will
go up if you please, and bury my father; then I will
return.'' 6 *And Pharaoh said, ''Go up and bury your*
father as he adjured you.''
7 *So Joseph went up to bury his father, and with*

be united in burial with his sacred ancestors. If Esau was buried there, Jacob could not be buried there for one burial place does not serve two families. As noted in *Mechilta,* no one would be permitted to be buried there except the three Patriarchs and Matriarchs. Therefore Jacob was determined to establish his claim to the site during his lifetime by digging a grave for himself ... thereby indicating that with him terminated the group of people who was to be buried there.

Onkelos — followed by many commentators — renders the phrase אֲשֶׁר כָּרִיתִי לִי, *which I 'prepared' for myself.* [*Nefesh HaGer* notes that the expression 'prepare a grave' is used by *Onkelos'* teacher, R' Eliezer, in *Taanis* 25b.]

וְעַתָּה אֶעֱלֶה־נָּא וְאֶקְבְּרָה אֶת־אָבִי וְאָשׁוּבָה — *Now, I will go up, if you please, and* [*I will*] *bury my father; then I will return.*

It is only *now* that I wish to go there, and only for the express purpose of burying my father and returning immediately thereafter. You need not be concerned that I will want to remain there *(Abarbanel; Malbim).*

Now — in fulfillment of my personal obligation under the terms of the oath — *I will go up,* etc. *(Haamek Davar).*

The word וְאֶקְבְּרָה is synonymous with וְאֶקְבֹּר. The addition of the suffix ה is courteous form of expression and denotes humility by the speaker [comp. וְאָכְלָה in 27:19] *(Sechel Tov).*

6. **וַיֹּאמֶר פַּרְעֹה** — *And Pharaoh said.*

I.e., to the courtiers who acted on Joseph's behalf and relayed his request to Pharaoh. Pharaoh spoke to them in second person as if to imply: ''Tell Joseph: *'Go up and bury your father,' ''* etc. *(Sechel Tov).*

כַּאֲשֶׁר הִשְׁבִּיעֶךָ — *As he adjured you.*

'Were it not for that oath I would not permit you to go.' Pharaoh did not dare to tell Joseph to violate the oath, for he was afraid Joseph might answer him, 'If that is your attitude, I have the right to violate the oath I once made to you. I once swore not to divulge that [although the king of Egypt is required to know all the existing languages] you do not possess a knowledge of the Hebrew language while I do.' [Accordingly I am more fit to be king than you *(Gur Aryeh)*] *(Rashi* citing *Sotah* 36b). [The entire incident *Rashi* is referring to is recorded in the footnote to 41:38 (p. 1791-2).]

7. The burial procession.

וַיַּעַל יוֹסֵף לִקְבֹּר אֶת־אָבִיו — *So Joseph went up to bury his father.*

Joseph is specifically mentioned here to allude to the fact that though he was the greatest man of his time, he still personally attended to his father's burial. In reward for this — measure for measure —

פַּרְעֹה֙ זִקְנֵ֣י בֵיתוֹ֔ וְכֹ֖ל זִקְנֵ֥י אֶֽרֶץ־מִצְרָֽיִם׃
ח וְכֹל֙ בֵּ֣ית יוֹסֵ֔ף וְאֶחָ֖יו וּבֵ֣ית אָבִ֑יו רַ֗ק טַפָּם֙
ט וְצֹאנָ֣ם וּבְקָרָ֔ם עָזְב֖וּ בְּאֶ֥רֶץ גֹּֽשֶׁן׃ וַיַּ֣עַל
עִמּ֔וֹ גַּם־רֶ֖כֶב גַּם־פָּרָשִׁ֑ים וַיְהִ֥י הַֽמַּחֲנֶ֖ה
י כָּבֵ֥ד מְאֹֽד׃ וַיָּבֹ֜אוּ עַד־גֹּ֣רֶן הָאָטָ֗ד אֲשֶׁר֙

Moses, the greatest of all, personally attended to Joseph's remains (*Sotah* 9b).

וַיַּעֲלוּ אִתּוֹ כָּל־עַבְדֵי פַרְעֹה זִקְנֵי בֵיתוֹ — *And with him went up all of Pharaoh's servants, the elders of his household.*

According to some commentators, these dignitaries accompanied Joseph of their own accord in a display of honor to Joseph and to show their respect for Jacob who was acknowledged as great and wise even by the wise men of his time and the one in whose merit the famine had ended prematurely (cf. *Sforno*).

Abarbanel maintains, however, that Pharaoh sent this group of Egyptians to accompany the burial party because he feared that Joseph and his brothers might be influenced to remain in Canaan by Jacob's attachment to the land:

The expression *all Pharaoh's servants* refers to ordinary Egyptians, as everyone in Egypt, except Joseph, was termed *Pharaoh's servant* [i.e. *subject*] *(Ibn Ezra).*

As noted in the *comm.* to 23:3, עִמּוֹ, *with him,* denotes *equality,* while the synonym אִתּוֹ denotes accompaniment by one of *secondary stature.* Here the latter term is used to denote that those who accompanied Joseph were of lower status and Joseph remained aloof from them throughout the journey since he was in grief *(Haamek Davar).*

וְכֹל זִקְנֵי אֶרֶץ מִצְרָיִם — *And all the elders of the land of Egypt.*

Elders denotes *wise men.* They paid Jacob this honor because he was regarded as a wise man by the wise of that generation *(Sforno).*

8. רַק טַפָּם וְצֹאנָם וּבְקָרָם עָזְבוּ בְּאֶרֶץ גֹּשֶׁן — *Only their little ones,* [*and*] *their sheep,and their cattle did they leave in the land of Goshen.*

Since Joseph intended to return, there was no need to take along the children and cattle. However, many commentators follow the view that with Jacob's death subtle aspects of the Egyptian bondage began, although they did not take on serious proportions until Joseph and that entire generation died. These commentators maintain that the brothers wanted to take along everyone — including their children and belongings — but Pharaoh would not permit it. Because of this, Joseph found it unnecessary to reassure his brothers [*v.* 24 below] that God would surely remember them and bring them out of Egypt, for they were not permitted to leave of their own accord *(Malbim).*

In any event, this leaving behind of the children and cattle may have formed a precedent. When Moses asked Pharaoh to permit the Jews to leave for three days to worship God, Pharaoh insisted that only the men go, and the children and others remain in Egypt [see *Exodus* 10:11] *(R' Sheah Brander).*

9. וַיַּעַל עִמּוֹ גַּם־רֶכֶב גַּם־פָּרָשִׁים — *And he brought up with him both chariots and horsemen* [lit. *also chariot(s) also horsemen*].

50
8-10

him went up all of Pharaoh's servants, the elders of
his household, all the elders of the land of Egypt,
8 *and all of Jacob's household — his brothers, and his*
father's household; only their little ones, their sheep,
and their cattle did they leave in the land of Goshen.
9 *And he brought up with him both chariots and*
horsemen; and the camp was very imposing.
10 *They came to Goren HaAtad, which is across the*

That horsemen accompanied him was a tribute to Jacob whom the military chiefs regarded as a great warrior *(Sforno).*

The translation of וַיַּעַל עִמּוֹ as a transitive verb: *brought up with him,* rather than intransitive: *there went up with him,* follows *Rashbam.*

This is based on the singular וַיַּעַל *(Haamek Davar).*

According to the Midrash, these were not part of the mourning cortege, but were for battle [in the event Esau would dispute their right to bury Jacob in the Cave of Machpelah].

Ramban [*com.* 49:31], too, interprets that Joseph had these chariots and horsemen accompany him since he knew the presumptuousness of Esau and his sons, and he feared an attack. And his fear was justified. An encounter between Esau and Jacob's sons indeed occurred. See footnote to *v.* 13.

Following *Haamek Davar's* distinction betwen עִמּוֹ and אִתּוֹ in *v.* 7, the use of עִמּוֹ here suggests a certain equality, since Joseph, too, shared with them their responsibility in overseeing the safety of the cortege. [But cf. *HaKsav V'HaKabbalah.*]

It is common for Scripture to repeat the adverb גַּם, *also,* to idiomatically denote *'this as well as that'* as in 24:25: גַּם תֶּבֶן גַּם מִסְפּוֹא; 47:3: גַּם אֲנַחְנוּ גַּם אֲבוֹתֵינוּ; 47:19: גַּם אֲנַחְנוּ גַּם אַדְמָתֵנוּ.

Nevertheless, the word גַּם usually denotes a רִיבּוּי, an implied extension beyond what is specifically mentioned in the text. In this case it alludes to *armed warriors* who accompanied them to provide additional protection in case the circumstances would demand it. Moreover, angels also guarded him [see below] *(R' Bachya).*

וַיְהִי הַמַּחֲנֶה כָּבֵד מְאֹד — *And the camp was very imposing.*

Besides the literal meaning, this might also allude to a *celestial camp* [of angels] who came to guard Jacob in death as they had in life. Perhaps this camp was composed of that same camp of angels who encountered him when he was *en-route* to Laban and whom on his return journey he had later referred to as a *Godly camp* [32:3]. (They had also been sent from on high at that time to protect Jacob from Esau.) Kabbalistically there is an esoteric allusion in the words כָּבֵד מְאֹד to the Sacred Names of God *(R' Bachya;* see *HaEzrach b'Yisrael* cited by *R' Chavel).*

10. וַיָּבֹאוּ עַד־גֹּרֶן הָאָטָד — *[And] they came to Goren HaAtad.*

[The exact site is unknown.]

The Hebrew name means: *the field* [or: *threshing floor*] *of thorns. Rashi* explains that in the most literal sense, the site was so named because it was *surrounded by thorns* [and from afar it appeared like a field of thorns].

Rashi proceeds to cite the Talmudic tradition of how this previously obscure place came to be so designated when so many other fields and threshing floors are surrounded by thorns: The Rabbis in *Sotah* 13a record that the sons of Esau, of Ishmael, and of Keturah [this is the version in the *Gemara; Rashi* in *Chumash* reads: all the kings of Canaan and the princes of Ishmael] came to wage war against them [i.e., against the sons of Jacob and prevent his burial]. But when they saw Joseph's crown hanging upon Jacob's coffin, they all took their crowns as well and hung them on his coffin. Thus, at that place they wreathed his coffin with their own crowns [which, by comparison to Joseph's crown, were nothing more than 'thorns']. The scene figuratively resembled a 'field surrounded by thorns' [and the Torah commemorated that event by giving the place a name alluding to that incident].

[The *Gemara* concludes that there were thirty-six crowns in all, which *Rashi* there enumerates as belonging to twelve princes of Ishmael; twenty-three chiefs of Esau ... plus the one crown of Joseph (see *Mizrachi* to 36:5)].

[Homiletically, the figurative comparison of the heathen *crowns* to *thorns* intimates that even the goodness wrought by the wicked is but a 'thorn' to the truly righteous (see *Rashi* to 31:24 and 41:10)].

[The Talmud records that notwithstanding this tribute by the chiefs of Esau at Goren HaAtad, there were hostilities at Machpelah as Esau tried to prevent Jacob's burial in the cave. See footnote to *v.* 13.]

אֲשֶׁר בְּעֵבֶר הַיַּרְדֵּן — *Which is across the Jordan.*

This phrase is somewhat confusing. The term *across the Jordan* in relation to Canaan usually refers to the territory on the east bank of the Jordan [i.e., the twentieth century country of Jordan]. It is difficult to assume that this is its meaning here since it leaves unexplained why the cortege was so far from the normal route from Egypt to Hebron; for them to travel via Jordan would have lengthened the trip considerably [see map next page].

Chizkuni maintains that the passage refers to the *west* bank of the Jordan, in Canaan proper. [*Rashbam* refers to such an interpretation of the term in *Deut.* 1:1 where he explains that from the vantage point of the desert, *the land of Canaan* is the *'other* [i.e. western] *side' of the Jordan.* See also *ibid.* 11:30].

In his *comm.* to *v.* 11 below, *Chizkuni* writes that *all the Canaanite inhabitants of the land saw ... which is across the Jordan* -- i.e., the inhabitants of the *east bank* saw what was happening across the river *in Canaan.* The inhabitants of Sichon and Og, who lived to the east of the Jordan and were considered Canaanites [see *Numbers* 21:22ff; see *Rashi* to *Deut.* 18:2] saw the mourning in Goren HaAtad in Canaan proper, which they — from their territory — referred to as *'across the Jordan.'* Similarly, in *Numbers* 32:19 [where Reuben and Gad are speaking to Moses from the east, the desert-side of the Jordan] they said: *For we will not inherit with them* [the other tribes] *on the other side* [i.e., Canaan] *of the Jordan.*

[Comp. also *Kaftor VaFerach* chapt. 48 who ascertains from *Rambam* and other sources that the Mishnaic reference to 'across the Jordan' in *Shevi'is* 9:2 refers to the west side of the Jordan. There the, Mishnah speaks of three territories in *Eretz Yisrael* regarding the Sabbatical Year: Judah; across the Jordan; and Galilee." *Sechel Tov* appears to interpret similarly by stating: 'Goren HaAtad was located on the other side of the Jordan — i.e., between the Jordan River and Egypt,' i.e. in *Eretz Yisrael* proper].

What remains difficult, as *Shaarei Aharon* observes, is why the Torah here calls it *across the Jordan* instead of *Canaan* as it does elsewhere in Genesis. In *v.* 11, following *Chizkuni's* view cited above, the reference is quite correct since the description refers to the vantage point of Sichon and Og who lived on the east bank. However, in *v.* 10, which does not quote onlookers, the Torah should have stated: *And they came to Goren HaAtad in the land of Canaan.*

Shaarei Aharon postulates that by this designation the Torah alludes to Joseph's circuitous route. He maintains that the only part of *Eretz Yisrael* designated as 'across the Jordan' is the territory north of Judah directly adjacent to the Jordan River. The territory of Judah — where Hebron and the Cave of Machpelah are situated — is not called 'across the Jordan' since it borders on the Dead Sea, not the Jordan River [see map]. This is further evidenced by the wording in the Mishnah *Shevi'is* cited above where Judah is distinct from 'across the Jordan.'

Now, had Joseph taken the direct route from Egypt to Hebron in Judah, he would have been south of the Jordan, and not in the territory called 'across the Jordan.' The fact that the Torah uses

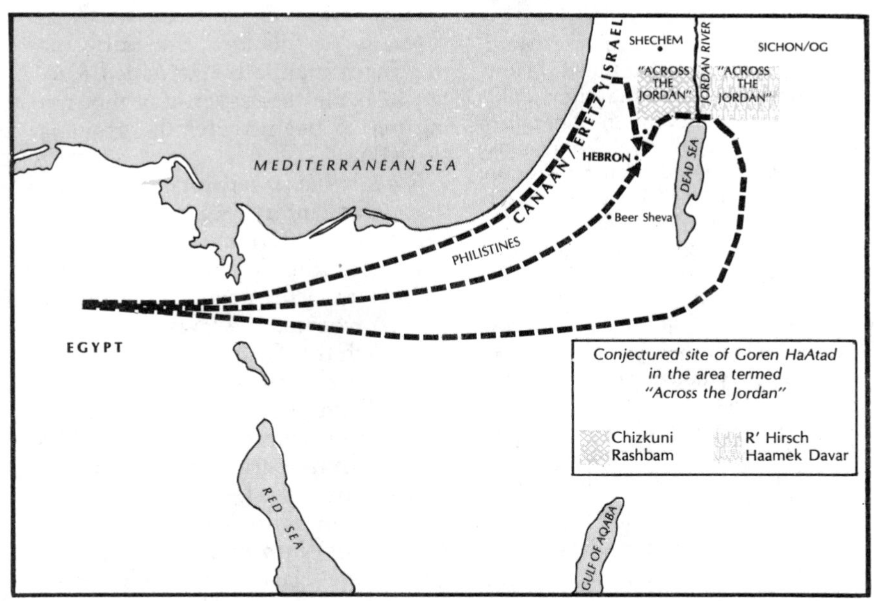

Possible routes of the burial procession

ויחי
נ/יא

וְכָבֵד מְאֹד וַיַּעַשׂ לְאָבִיו אֵבֶל שִׁבְעַת
יא יָמִים׃ וַיַּרְא יוֹשֵׁב הָאָרֶץ הַכְּנַעֲנִי אֶת־
הָאֵבֶל בְּגֹרֶן הָאָטָד וַיֹּאמְרוּ אֵבֶל־כָּבֵד זֶה

this term is to indicate that Joseph took a longer roundabout route around the Dead Sea and approached Hebron from the north so that many peoples would join the funeral cortege and pay their final respects to the venerable Patriarch whose ancestors were renowned among the Canaanite nations as princes of God.

Haamek Davar interprets similarly and draws support from Mishnah *Kelim* 1:7 that it is customary to transport a corpse from place to place until the burial site is reached, in order to honor the deceased.

Cf. note to *Torah Sheleimah* that Joseph might have been *forced* to take a roundabout route to Hebron since some of the Canaanite inhabitants were hostile to Egypt and refused passage to the armed cortege. In fact, *R' Meyuchas* suggests that the cortege traversed the same desert route east of the Jordan that the Israelites would later take at the Exodus, and entered Canaan westward, across the Jordan. [As noted below, some Midrashim record that they took a roundabout route even on the *return* journey, passing through Shechem.] Goren HaAtad would then be literally located on the 'other,' i.e. eastern, side of the Jordan in relation to *Eretz Yisrael.*

R' Hirsch to *v.* 12 also maintains that they took the roundabout route via the Jordan for the sake of the Egyptians who wished to avoid the land of the Philistines, which they would have had to cross had they taken the direct route.

For, as *Akeidas Yitzchak* explains, the Egyptian sphere of influence included the territory east of the Jordan, but not Canaan proper or the land of the Philistines.

וַיִּסְפְּדוּ־שָׁם מִסְפֵּד גָּדוֹל וְכָבֵד מְאֹד — *And there they held a very great and imposing eulogy.*

גָּדוֹל, *great,* means that they spent several hours eulogizing their profound loss; וְכָבֵד, *and imposing* [lit. *heavy*], means that they spoke words that penetrate the inner recesses of the heart *(Haamek Davar).*

— The eulogy was more imposing than any ever held before it *(Sechel Tov).*

According to the Talmud [*Sotah* 13a] even the horses and donkeys took part in the mourning [i.e., their owners draped garments of mourning on them *(Maharshal)*].

[The varied meanings of הֶסְפֵּד, *eulogy or lamentation,* have been discussed in the *comm.* to 23:2 (p. 864).]

וַיַּעַשׂ לְאָבִיו אֵבֶל שִׁבְעַת יָמִים — *And he observed a seven-day mourning period for his father.*

According to *Ibn Ezra,* these seven days *followed* the burial as the Sages mandated [in *Moed Kattan* 27a, that the seven-day mourning period begins after the grave is closed].

R' Bachya interprets, however, that this mourning took place *before* the interment and the sequence of the Scriptural narrative reflects the chronological order of events, whereas the laws of mourning which the Torah commanded *us* are to be observed after interment. In the Talmud, *Moed Katan* 20a, we find: 'From where is it derived that the mourning period is seven days? — From the verse [*Amos* 8:10]: *And I shall turn your feasts* (Passover and Succos) *into mourning.* Just as the "feasts" last seven days, so is the period for mourning also seven days.'[1]

50 *eulogy. And he observed a seven-day mourning*
11 *period for his father.* [11] *When the Canaanite inhabi-*
tants of the land saw the mourning in Goren HaAtad,
they said, "This is a grievous mourning for Egypt.'

11. וַיַּרְא יוֹשֵׁב הָאָרֶץ הַכְּנַעֲנִי אֶת הָאֵבֶל בְּגֹרֶן הָאָטָד — *When the Canaanite inhabitants of the land* [lit. *and the inhabitant of the land, the Canaanite* (the singular has the collective sense)] *saw the mourning in Goren HaAtad.*

The Canaanite inhabitants of the land refers, according to *Chizkuni* cited in the previous verse, to Sichon and Og who lived in the Emorite territory east of the Jordan, and who are referred to as Canaanites [see *Rashi* to *Deut.* 18:2]. Others interpret conversely that the Canaanites referred to here lived west of the River — in Canaan proper — and the *east* bank is referred to as 'across the Jordan.'

וַיֹּאמְרוּ אֵבֶל־כָּבֵד זֶה לְמִצְרָיִם — [And] *they said, 'This is a grievous* [*severe*] *mourning for Eygpt.'*

The Canaanites realized why the Egyptians were mourning even more intensely now than they had previously. As the party neared Jacob's burial place and saw how even the Canaanite kings paid tribute to Jacob by putting their crowns on his coffin, the Egyptians felt the full impact of their great loss. Then they lamented that they could not have the privilege of burying Jacob in their own country, where his presence, even in death, would be a lasting source of merit for them. Therefore the Torah refers to it as a grievous mourning *for Egypt* since they perceived how greatly Jacob's absence would affect *Egypt,* for a righteous person's presence brings benefit, even after his death [see *Sotah* 36a].[2]

Furthermore, several commentators subscribe to the view that they were now leaving the periphery of the Egyptian sphere of influence. About to enter the foreign soil of Canaan, they sensed

1. **Seven-day mourning period.**

Tosafos ibid. s.v. מַה writes that we cannot derive the seven-days of mourning from our passage — *and he observed a seven day mourning period for his father* [as the *Yerushalmi Moed Katan* 3:5 indeed attempts to do] — since our passage speaks of mourning *before* burial. Furthermore, as the *Yerushalmi* concludes, we cannot derive a law from a practice observed before the Torah was given. [See *Torah Temimah*].

In any event, we see that the custom of having a seven-day period of mourning dates back to the time of the Patriarchs [see *Ramban* to 29:27].

Rambam [*Hilchos Avel* 1:1] writes in this regard: According to Torah law, the mourning period is only on the first day — the day of death and of burial; the seven days, however, are not Scripturally mandated, although the Torah does mention: *he observed a seven-day mourning period for his father.* When the Torah was given, the law was established anew [and the *Scriptural* mandate was established as *one* day] while the Rabbis established the law at seven days based upon the exegetical interpretation of *Amos* 8:10 cited above. The *halachah* has so been codified, and a seven-day mourning period has been universally adopted.

[See note to *Torah Sheleimah* §33-34.]

2. R' Menachem Mendel of Lubavitch [*Or HaTorah*] perceives a prophetic connotation in the fact that *Egypt* is portrayed as the prime mourner in this event. Jacob's stay in Egypt resulted in the land being blessed with abundance, and this blessing would have resulted in both the spiritual and material elevation of Egypt for untold generations, and in the development of

לְמִצְרַ֫יִם עַל־כֵּ֗ן קָרָ֤א שְׁמָהּ֙ אָבֵ֣ל מִצְרַ֔יִם
יב אֲשֶׁ֖ר בְּעֵ֥בֶר הַיַּרְדֵּֽן: וַיַּֽעֲשׂ֥וּ בָנָ֖יו ל֑וֹ כֵּ֖ן
יג כַּאֲשֶׁ֥ר צִוָּֽם: וַיִּשְׂא֨וּ אֹת֤וֹ בָנָיו֙ אַ֣רְצָה

their loss even more profoundly *(Kesef Nivchar; Akeidah; Me'am Loez; Malbim).*

According to *Abarbanel,* the emphasis on *Egypt* might imply that the Canaanites were fearful that the great mourning augured evil for their land. They therefore said, 'This is a grievous mourning *for Egypt,*' that is, 'May any evil consequences befall *them,* not us!' and therefore they gave it this name.

עַל־כֵּן קָרָא שְׁמָהּ אָבֵל מִצְרַיִם אֲשֶׁר בְּעֵבֶר הַיַּרְדֵּן — *Therefore it was named* [lit. *he called its name*] *Avel Mitzraim* [lit. *the mourning of Egypt*] *which is across the Jordan.*

The local populace was so impressed by the unprecedented national mourning of the great Egyptian state that their ruler chose this place-name to memorialize a foreign nation's love and respect for a Jewish Patriarch *(R' Munk).*

[That *Jacob's* descendants bewailed Jacob's loss was only natural and would not inspire onlookers to name a place after it; it was the massive outpouring of grief by the *Egyptian* cortege that was so inspiring.]

The Torah mentions again that it was "across the Jordan" to identify it, for there were other places named Avel. [Comp. Avel haShittim in *Numbers* 33:49 where Moses was mourned.] It also alludes to the roundabout route the cortege took in honor of Jacob as noted in the previous verse.

12. The burial.

וַיַּעֲשׂוּ בָנָיו לוֹ כֵּן כַּאֲשֶׁר צִוָּם — [*And*] *his sons did for him as he had instructed them:*

What they did is explained in the following verse *(Rashi).*

[*Rashi* thus accounts for the apparent superfluity of this passage by explaining that this verse introduces the next one. The import of the statement is that even the way the sons carried Jacob's bier, as recorded in the following verse, was in strict conformity with the instructions he had given before he died. (See footnote to 49:33).]

According to the Midrash cited in *v.* 1 this passage refers to Jacob's instruction that they embalm him.

R' Hirsch writes that the continuity of the verses suggests that the Egyptians accompanied them only to this point, but not further. From there on the children *alone* took the body and buried it in accordance with Jacob's wishes, while the rest of the retinue awaited their return and then accompanied them back to Egypt.

כֵּן has also the meaning of *with sincerity,* as in *Proverbs* 11:19. Jacob's sons acted *sincerely,* that is to say, without trying to discover the reasons

Israel as well. Instead, after Jacob's burial, Egypt began to despise Israel and eventually enslaved them. The result was the utter destruction of Egypt through the plagues and Splitting of the Sea. Though the Egyptians themselves were unaware of this outcome of Jacob's death, in retrospect it was truly a grievous event for their nation.

... Thus as *Oznaim LaTorah* concludes, they prophesied and knew not what they prophesied. Jacob's death resulted in great mourning *for Egypt,* for with it the bondage began, and Israel had long before been promised [15:14]: *But also upon the nation which they shall serve will I execute judgment* — the ten plagues and the drowning of Pharaoh's host in the Sea of Reeds.

Therefore it was named Avel Mitzraim, which is across the Jordan.

[12] *His sons did for him as he had instructed them:*
[13] *His sons carried him to the land of Canaan and*

which had prompted their father to arrange them in the order mentioned below. They acted with sincerity, simply because *he had commanded them.*

13. וַיִּשְׂאוּ אֹתוֹ בָנָיו אַרְצָה כְּנַעַן — *His sons carried him to the land of Canaan.*

I.e., from Avel Mitzraim onward they carried the casket on their shoulders *(Abarbanel).*

His *sons,* not his grandsons. For Jacob had commanded them: My bier should not be carried by an Egyptian or by one of your sons because they are children of Canaanite women; you yourselves shall carry it *(Rashi).*

This follows the opinion of R' Nechemiah in the Midrash [cited in the comm. to 37:35, 38:2, and 46:9] who maintains that Jacob's children married Canaanites [see *Ramban* to 38:2 who, drawing from *Pesachim* 50a, explains Canaanites in this context to refer to "*foreign* women, whose fathers were merchants passing through Canaan (the word כְּנַעֲנִי sometimes means *merchant,* as in *Proverbs* 31:24), for it is illogical to assume that they all married women who were from the accursed, servile Canaanite nation."]

According to R' Yehudah in the Midrash, who maintains that twin sisters were born with each of Jacob's sons and the sons and daughters of different mothers married one another, it is not clear why Jacob did not permit his grandchildren from these marriages to carry his bier.

Possibly, as *R' David Feinstein* suggests, R' Yehudah draws a different exegetical inference from the phrase *his 'sons' carried him,* inferring not that it excluded grandchildren but that it alludes to the formation of his sons as they carried his bier. Their position formed the precedent for the tribes in the Wilderness, who stationed themselves around the Tabernacle just as the sons stood around Jacob's bier, as *Rashi* proceeds to record further in his comment.

[See *Chizkuni* who postulates that R' Yehudah would maintain that the half-sister wives of the sons died childless and then they married Canaanites. It was the offspring of these marriages Jacob then forbade to carry his bier. Now, although the children of Simeon, whose 'Canaanite' wife is Midrashically identified as Dinah, should not have been disqualified along with the others, Jacob did not want to promote jealousy by permitting only part of his grandchildren to participate. Ephraim and Manasseh did accompany the bier, but this would not have caused jealousy since they were of royalty and had been raised to the level of full-fledged tribes.]

[The question of whether the twin sisters had died by the time Jacob went down to Egypt is the subject of controversy between *Rashi* and *Ramban*. See comm. to 46:26.]

Rashi continues: ... Jacob had also assigned his sons their positions: three on the east [i.e. front] side and three on each of the other three sides of the bier, establishing the precedent for the arrangement they would follow later in the desert when each tribe encamped under its own standard. [The Midrash depicts the order as follows: *East:* Judah, Issachar, Zebulun; *South:* Reuben, Simeon, Gad; *West:* Ephraim, Manasseh, Benjamin; *North:* Dan, Asher, Naftali.]

	Dan/Asher/Naftali	
Benjamin		**Judah**
Manasseh	**BIER**	**Issachar**
Ephraim		**Zebulun**
	Gad/Simeon/Reuben	

However, *Rashi* continues, the twelve tribes that formed these four divisions did not include Levi or Joseph. 'Levi shall not carry my bier,' Jacob had said, 'since his descendants are destined to carry the holy Ark [and it is therefore not proper for him to carry a bier containing human remains]. Joseph shall not carry it because he is a

כְּנַעַן וַיִּקְבְּרוּ אֹתוֹ בִּמְעָרַת שְׂדֵה
הַמַּכְפֵּלָה אֲשֶׁר קָנָה אַבְרָהָם אֶת־הַשָּׂדֶה
לַאֲחֻזַּת־קֶבֶר מֵאֵת עֶפְרֹן הַחִתִּי עַל־פְּנֵי
יד מַמְרֵא׃ וַיָּשָׁב יוֹסֵף מִצְרַיְמָה הוּא וְאֶחָיו
וְכָל־הָעֹלִים אִתּוֹ לִקְבֹּר אֶת־אָבִיו אַחֲרֵי

ruler [and must be given respect]. Manasseh and Ephraim shall take their places.' This is what the Torah refers to when it says [*Numbers* 2:2]: *Every man shall encamp by his own banner according to the 'signs'* — meaning: according to the *signs* [i.e., symbolic precedent] which their father had given them individually for carrying his coffin [see *Tanchuma* ad loc.].

וַיִּקְבְּרוּ אֹתוֹ בִּמְעָרַת שְׂדֵה הַמַּכְפֵּלָה — *And they buried him in the Cave of the Machpelah field.*[1]

— Precisely following Jacob's detailed instructions *(Ralbag)* ...

אֲשֶׁר קָנָה אַבְרָהָם ... עַל־פְּנֵי מַמְרֵא — *The field that Abraham had bought as a burial estate from Ephron the Hittite, facing Mamre.*

The reason the verse mentions

1. **The War at the Burial.**

Ramban cites Yosef HaKohen ben Gorion, the presumed author of the chronicles called *Yossifon* [ch. 2] 'and other books of ancient history' that Zepho the son of Eliphaz the son of Esau [see above 36:11] came and waged war with Jacob's children concerning the burial. But Joseph's might prevailed and Zepho and his army were vanquished and brought back to Egypt.

Zepho remained in prison for the rest of Joseph's life. After Joseph's death Zepho escaped and fled to Compagna in Italy. He became ruler of the Caetheans in Rome and eventually was crowned ruler of Italy. He was the first sovereign ruler of Rome and it was he who built the first and foremost palace there.

The death of Esau at the Cave of Machpelah.

The Talmud and several Midrashim record another incident at the burial which resulted in the death of Esau:

In *Sotah* 13a [already cited in the comm. to Naftali's blessing in 49:21] we learn that when Jacob's sons attempted to bury Jacob in the Machpelah Cave, Esau [who according to some Midrashim accompanied the cortege from Goren HaAtad where he had paid his respects to his brother along with the other Canaanite kings (*v.* 10)] protested. He claimed that of the two graves that had remained in the cave, Jacob used his share for Leah's burial, and the remaining grave was therefore Esau's.

When Jacob's sons countered that Jacob had purchased the rights to burial in the Cave from Esau, Esau protested that he had sold only Jacob the double share of the firstborn, but not his simple burial right as Isaac's son in the family sepulchre.

When the sons persisted that Esau had sold everything and retained no rights in the Cave, Esau demanded that they produce a document.

The brothers had left the document in Egypt. They pondered what to do and they decided to send Naftali since he could run swiftly as a deer.

As they waited for Naftali to return, among those present was Chushim son of Dan, who was deaf. When he understood the debate and that they were waiting for Naftali to return, he became angry and shouted: 'It is a disgrace! Is my grandfather

50
14

they buried him in the cave of the Machpelah field,
the field that Abraham had bought as a burial estate
from Ephron the Hittite, facing Mamre.
14 *Joseph returned to Egypt — he and his brothers,*
and all who had gone up with him to bury his father
— after he buried his father.

that this was *the field that Abraham had bought as a burial estate* is to allude to the fact that Abraham's intention was completely fulfilled with Jacob's burial since he bought the sepulchre for the three Patriarchs and Matriarchs, and no other person was to be buried there. This is the reason Joseph did not ask that he be buried in the cave with his father since, as noted in *Mechilta,* no one else may be buried there *(Ramban* to 49:30).

[On the phraseology and detailed description of the site, see comm. to parallel passages in 23:17-19 and 49:30.]

14. וַיָּשָׁב יוֹסֵף ... וְאֶחָיו וְכָל הָעֹלִים אִתּוֹ ... אַחֲרֵי קָבְרוֹ אֶת אָבִיו — *Joseph returned to Egypt — he, [and] his brothers, and all who had gone up with him to bury his father — after he buried his father.*

On the outward journey [*v.* 7] the Egyptians took precedence over the brothers and are mentioned first. But when they saw the honor

to lie there in contempt until Naftali returns from Egypt?' With that he took a club and struck Esau on the head so hard that Esau's eyes fell out and rolled to Jacob's feet. Jacob [who according to the Talmud 'did not die'] opened his eyes and smiled. This is what the Psalmist alluded to in *Psalms* 58:11, *The righteous shall rejoice when he sees vengeance; he shall wash his feet in the blood of the wicked.* [See *Maharsha* who notes that this entire psalm speaks of Esau.]

This incident fulfilled Rebecca's unwitting prognostication when she said [27:45]: *Why should I be bereaved of both of you on the same day?* For though the *death* of the two of them did not occur on the same day [since at least seventy-seven days had already passed since Jacob's demise], still their *burial* took place on the same day.

According to *Tosafos* in *Gittin* 55b s.v. בִּיהוּדָה, there was a tradition that *Judah* killed Esau, as it says (49:8): *Your hand is on your enemy's neck,* and as *Sifre Zos HaBrachah* maintains, Moses later intimated this in his blessing of Judah: *his hands are sufficient for him* — when he slew Esau. *Tosafos* reconciles that tradition with the one in *Sotah* by suggesting that Esau did not die from Chushim's blow, and it was Judah who delivered the *coup de grace* [cf. *Yerushalmi Kesubos* 1:5; *Yerushalmi Gittin* 5:7].

Parallel Midrashic accounts [e.g. *Pirkei d'Rabbi Eliezer* 36] record that Esau was decapitated and his head rolled into the cave, at Jacob's feet. Esau's head was thus buried in the Cave of Machpelah, and his body on Mount Seir. [Cf. however *Yalkut Shimoni* drawing from *Midrash Tehillim* §18 for an opinion that Judah killed Esau on the day that *Isaac* died. Esau and Jacob had been left alone in the cave to bewail their father; Judah's suspicions that Esau would resort to treachery against Jacob proved correct. When Esau began to attack Jacob, Judah decapitated him.]

Midrash Rabbah §98 records an opinion that it was the *Hittites* who disrupted the burial and contested Jacob's ownership of the cave. They waited until Naftali returned from Egypt with the deed of sale that confirmed Jacob's rights.

קָבְרוֹ אֶת־אָבִיו׃ 15 וַיִּרְאוּ אֲחֵי־יוֹסֵף כִּי־מֵת
אֲבִיהֶם וַיֹּאמְרוּ לוּ יִשְׂטְמֵנוּ יוֹסֵף וְהָשֵׁב

bestowed on Jacob in *Goren Ha-Atad* [*v.* 11] they gave precedence to his sons, and so here the brothers are mentioned first *(Rashi* from *Sotah* 13a).

In the literal sense the phraseology denotes that on their return the mourners went first and the others followed. This is our custom today as well *(Abarbanel).*

That the Torah specificies *all* who had gone up with him intimates that despite the battles which Esau's sons had waged against them, no mishap befell any one of the cortege, and *everyone* who went returned. This was because the merit of Jacob, to whom they were paying homage, stood by those who went up with him *(Ramban* to 49:31; *R' Bachya; Midrash; Midrash HaChefetz).* The seemingly superfluous phrase *after he had buried his father* emphasizes that not a single person returned *before* the burial *(Malbim; Haamek Davar).*

Joseph is especially designated as the subject of this verse, and the burial is ascribed to him to stress that he conscientiously fulfilled his oath to the last detail: it was primarily Joseph who attended to the burial; everyone else was merely secondary *(R' Bachya).*

In *Sotah* 13a the brothers are cited as saying, 'Let it be ascribed to Joseph. It is a greater honor for Father that kings, rather than commoners, should engage in his burial.'

That is, though the previous verse uses the plural: *they* buried him, the intent is that they *began* the interment, but decided among themselves to let Joseph personally carry it through, deeming it a greater honor for their father that one of Joseph's stature be personally involved in his burial; see *Sotah* 9b *(Torah Temimah).*

15. Joseph's brothers fear his retribution.

וַיִּרְאוּ אֲחֵי־יוֹסֵף כִּי־מֵת אֲבִיהֶם — *[And] Joseph's brothers perceived* [lit. *saw*] *that their father was dead.*

Through Joseph's changed conduct they perceived the effect of their father's death. During Jacob's lifetime, they used to dine at Joseph's table and he would receive them with open arms out of deference to his father. After Jacob's death, however, he ceased to invite them *(Rashi* from *Midrash).*

The commentators explain Joseph's change of behavior, maintaining that his intentions were pure. During Jacob's lifetime he had given Joseph prominence over Judah the leader, and Reuben the firstborn, and seated Joseph ahead of them. With his father's demise, however, Joseph felt uncomfortable sitting at the head of the table and he felt it unbecoming that he do so; on the other hand, his royal position mandated that he not relinquish his primary position. To avoid the problem he decreased his invitations to them. The brothers, however, thought he was acting out of hatred for them *(Tanchuma).*

Gur Aryeh suggests that as long as Jacob was alive, Joseph was excessively close to his family, having them as his guests almost constantly. After Jacob died, Joseph still invited them but not as often. The brothers saw something ominous in this.

Alternatively, *Gur Aryeh* comments that he may have ceased *all* invitations, but not out of antagonism. Joseph knew that as long as Jacob lived, neither he nor his family would suffer persecution in Egypt, but after his death, the oppression could begin. The first symptom of the impending slavery would be that the Egyptians would suspect the Jews of seeking power. If Joseph continued his invitations, the Egyptians would say that the Jews are too close to the throne, and attack them in the palace. Therefore,

50
15 [15] *Joseph's brothers perceived that their father was dead, and they said, "Perhaps Joseph will nurse*

Joseph slighted his brothers to avoid grounds for such suspicion.

Another reason for their apprehension offered in *Tanchuma* was that on the return journey, Joseph had them detour to the pit where they had once cast him as a youth before they had sold him to the Ishmaelites. The brothers assumed Joseph's intention was to revive old grudges whereas Joseph sincerely meant to pay tribute to God and recite the blessing בָּרוּךְ שֶׁעָשָׂה לִי נֵס בַּמָּקוֹם הַזֶּה, *Blessed is He Who performed a miracle for me in this place.*

The Midrash learns from this incident that one should always make his intentions clear. Since Joseph did not explain his actions to his brothers they thought he was acting out of malice and he thereby caused them much needless anxiety.

R' Hirsch observes that after the death of parents, the familial bond holding the children together becomes loosened; with their parents as a focal point, they meet less often and tend to become estranged from one another. That this happened in the case of Joseph and the brothers was quite natural, but the brothers perceived it as a symptom of Jacob's absence and feared that Joseph would recall past grievances.

According to *Abarbanel* these fears began while they were still in Canaan. The brothers wanted to determine Joseph's intentions; had they ascertained that he intended punitive steps against them, they might have considered remaining in Canaan *(Akeidah; Abarbanel).*

לוּ יִשְׂטְמֵנוּ יוֹסֵף — *Perhaps Joseph will nurse hatred against us.*

The verb שטם denotes *repressed hatred.* [See *comm.* to 27:41 and 49:23].

The simplest syntactical interpretation following *Rashi* [see below] is that seeing Joseph's changed demeanor toward them since Jacob's death, the brothers' bad conscience caused them to grow apprehensive that Joseph held a grudge against them and might avenge himself for the evil they had perpetrated against him.

The implications of their father's death dawned on them. The brothers feared that Joseph might act according to popular morality and retaliate. Affection for Jacob might have restrained his revenge as long as the aged father was alive, but now they were completely in his power *(Ibn Caspi).*

The translation of לו as *may be, perhaps* — שֶׁמָּא — synonymous with אוּלַי follows *Rashi.*

As *Rashi* explains, the word לו has several meanings depending upon the context. Sometimes לו denotes a petition, synonymous with הַלְוַאי, *if only* [in the sense of *may it so be,* as for example 30:34; *If only it would remain as you say!* [23:13]; *If only you would heed me* [*Joshua* 7:7 *Numbers* 14:2]. In other contexts לו means *if* and אוּלַי, as e.g. *Deut.* 32:29: לוּ חָכְמוּ, *if they were wise they would understand;* [*Isaiah* 48:18; *II Samuel* 18:12]. The meaning of לו in our verse is synonymous with that of אוּלַי, *perhaps,* and this is the only place in Scripture where לו has this meaning. The word אוּלַי has this meaning in 24:5: *perhaps the woman will not wish to follow me.*

Since, as *Rashi* asserts, this is the only place in Scripture where לו is synonymous with אוּלַי meaning *perhaps,* why indeed is this term used here instead of the more familiar אוּלַי or פֶּן? Possibly the Torah wishes to inform us that in the deeper sense it is the familiar meaning of לו — הַלְוַאי, *if only* — that is alluded to here in the brothers' words. Their inner thought was: *If only Joseph would detest us and pay us back for all the harm which we have caused him!* Then there would no longer be any trace of our sin and we would not fear that it might rebound against our children and

יָשִׁיב לָנוּ אֵת כָּל־הָרָעָה אֲשֶׁר גָּמַלְנוּ
טז אֹתוֹ: וַיְצַוּוּ אֶל־יוֹסֵף לֵאמֹר אָבִיךָ צִוָּה
יז לִפְנֵי מוֹתוֹ לֵאמֹר: כֹּה־תֹאמְרוּ לְיוֹסֵף

our descendants. For as noted in the comm. on p. 1650, the brothers' sin did not go unpunished. Divine justice was meted out centuries later at the time of the Ten Martyrs *(Or HaChaim).*

Interpreting that יִשְׂטְמֵנוּ denotes *inner, stifled hatred,* and that לו is synonymous with הַלְוַאי, *if only, B'Chor Shor* renders: *If only Joseph would keep his anger stifled and* not *reveal it to repay us in deed for all the evil we did him!*

According to *Akeidas Yitzchak,* the brothers initially were apprehensive that with their father gone Joseph might seek vengeance against them. But upon further consideration they decided that, to the contrary, they were instrumental in his rise to greatness! They therefore concluded: May he repay us for all the 'evil' we caused him! [See continuation of this in *v.* 13 s.v. וְעַתָּה.]

Baal HaTurim similarly interprets: May Joseph stifle his anger. However, if he does desire to repay us, then let him repay the so-called 'evil' we did him; for our selling him was instrumental in his eventually becoming a monarch; may he repay us accordingly!

Malbim likewise interprets לו as *if only* and יִשְׂטְמֵנוּ as *hate us;* he renders: If only Joseph would hate us [openly] and repay us in kind for all the evil we caused him. The brothers wished that Joseph would stop showering them with undeserved kindnesses. They understood full well that the sweetest revenge is to treat one's enemies with great generosity, because that serves as a constant reminder of the evil they had conspired to do. As King Solomon taught *(Proverbs* 25:21), *If your foe is hungry feed him bread, for you will be pouring coals upon his head.*

According to *Haamek Davar,* לו has the meaning of *if* as it does in *Deut.* 32:29, and יִשְׂטְמֵנוּ denotes scheming about revenge as it does in 49:23. While they were certain that Joseph would not sell his brothers into slavery, nevertheless: לוּ יִשְׂטְמֵנוּ יוסף, *if Joseph is scheming to gain revenge against us* וְהָשֵׁב יָשִׁיב לָנוּ וכו׳, *then he will certainly find a way to repay us,* etc. [*R' Hirsch* interprets similarly.]

וְהָשֵׁב יָשִׁיב לָנוּ אֵת כָּל־הָרָעָה אֲשֶׁר גָּמַלְנוּ אֹתוֹ — *And then he will surely repay* [lit. *return*] *us all the evil that we did him.*

The Hebrew reads *and return he will return,* etc. The compound verb implies emphasis, hence: *surely repay.* According to *Sechel Tov* the double verb signifies: he will repay us through our children as well as through ourselves.

— *All the evil,* our having thrown him into the pit and having sold him as a slave, *that we caused him* because of his dreams *(Sechel Tov).*

16. וַיְצַוּוּ אֶל־יוֹסֵף לֵאמֹר — *So they instructed that Joseph be told.*

The passage literally reads: *And they instructed to Joseph saying.* The expression **וַיְצַוּוּ אֶל** [lit. *they instructed* **to**] has the same meaning as *Exodus* 6:13: וַיְצַוֵּם **אֶל** בְּנֵי יִשְׂרָאֵל [lit. *he instructed them* **to** *the children of Israel*] which signifies: [God] commanded Moses and Aaron to act as emissaries to the children of Israel. Here too it signifies that *they instructed* their emissary *to Joseph* regarding the message he was *to speak* to him. Who was it they sent? — The sons of Bilhah with whom Joseph had been most accustomed to associate, as it says [37:2]: *He was a youth*

50 *hatred against us and then he will surely repay us all*
16-17 *the evil that we did him."* 16 *So they instructed that*
Joseph be told, "Your father gave orders before his
death, saying: 17 *'Thus shall you say to Joseph: "O*

with the sons of Bilhah [i.e., as *Rambam* explains there: Joseph's youthful recreation time was spent associating with the sons of Bilhah and Zilpah] *(Rashi* from *Tanchuma).*

According to *Tanchuma Yashan* it was Bilhah herself — who had raised Joseph after Rachel's death — with whom they entrusted this message.

אָבִיךָ צִוָּה לִפְנֵי מוֹתוֹ לֵאמֹר — *Your father gave orders before his death, saying:*

They altered the facts [by stating an untruth] for the sake of peace. Jacob had never given such a command since he did not suspect Joseph of seeking vengeance *(Rashi).*

Comp. *Yevamos* 65b: A person may tamper with the truth for the sake of peace as it is written *Your father instructed,* etc. [which was untrue]. [See also *Bava Metzia* 87a cited in comm. to 18:13 s.v. וַאֲנִי זָקַנְתִּי.]

The brothers never dared reveal to Jacob that Joseph had been sold. They were mortally afraid that if told of their sin Jacob would curse them as he did Reuben, Simeon, and Levi [49:3]. Joseph, too, did not tell him for ethical reasons. It is because Jacob remained ignorant of the true facts that they had to fabricate Jacob's instructions. Had he known the truth, his sons would certainly have asked him to instruct Joseph to act kindly toward them after his death, rather than resort to this fabrication *(Ramban* to 46:1).[1]

[However, cf. *Peskikta* cited in 48:19 where Jacob intimates that he was aware that his jealous sons sold Joseph.]

According to *Sforno,* the emissaries were instructed to say *Your father ordered before his death, to say;* that is, he commanded us to say the entire following statement to you in our own name, not in his, for he never suspected you of anything. He rather indicated that if we had any fears we should tell you the following.

The brothers phrase the message as *your* father, not *our* father; in their contrition they felt unworthy to call themselves Jacob's sons *(R' Hirsch).*

By emphasizing that Jacob had said this *before his death* they implied that it was incumbent upon Joseph to fulfill a deathbed command *(Abarbanel).*

17. כֹּה תֹאמְרוּ לְיוֹסֵף — *Thus shall you say to Joseph:*

Should you ever become apprehensive ... *(Sforno).*

1. Some commentators suggest, however, that since Joseph did not leave his father's bedside for a moment before his demise, their story must have been based on an instruction Jacob *had* given — at least by implication — before his death that the brothers preserve their unity; by implication he had as much as commanded that Joseph not be angry with them.

Yalkut Yehudah cites in this connection the Midrashic interpretation of Jacob's deathbed summons to his sons in 49:1: הֵאָסְפוּ, i.e., let there be no quarreling among you ... gather yourselves together in brotherly unity.

Haamek Davar derives this from Jacob's blessing [49:24] in which he praised Joseph for not being vengeful against those who had treated him bitterly. [Thus by implication Jacob was hinting that even after his death Joseph should maintain peaceful relations with his brothers.]

אָנָּ֡א שָׂ֣א נָ֠א פֶּ֣שַׁע אַחֶ֤יךָ וְחַטָּאתָם֙ כִּֽי־
רָעָ֣ה גְמָל֔וּךָ וְעַתָּה֙ שָׂ֣א נָ֔א לְפֶ֥שַׁע עַבְדֵ֖י
אֱלֹהֵ֣י אָבִ֑יךָ וַיֵּ֥בְךְּ יוֹסֵ֖ף בְּדַבְּרָ֥ם אֵלָֽיו׃
יח וַיֵּֽלְכוּ֙ גַּם־אֶחָ֔יו וַֽיִּפְּל֖וּ לְפָנָ֑יו וַיֹּ֣אמְר֔וּ הִנֶּ֥נּוּ

אָנָּא שָׂא־נָא פֶּשַׁע אַחֶיךָ וְחַטָּאתָם — *O please, kindly forgive* [lit. *bear if you please*] *the spiteful deed of your brothers and their sin.*

[פֶּשַׁע, *spiteful deed* or *transgression,* signifies a worse offense than חֵטְא, *sin,* in that the former is committed in a spirit of *rebellion,* while the latter denotes an *inadvertent* trespass. (See *comm.* to *Exodus* 34:7 where the various terms for *sin* are defined.)]

Their act of selling Joseph comprised both פֶּשַׁע, *intentional transgression* and חֵטְא, *unintentional trespass.* Since they were his brothers, their act was ruthless, and is therefore referred to as פֶּשַׁע אַחֶיךָ, *the intentional transgression of your brothers.* However, since at the same time they acted out of sincere conviction that Joseph was persecuting them they were acting in self-defense [see footnote to 37:18], and accordingly, theirs was a חֵטְא, *unintentional sin (Alshich;* cf. *Malbim.* See *Overview* to *Vayeishev).*

Sechel Tov interprets that *spiteful deed* refers to their having cast him into the pit, and *sin* to their having sold him.

The Sages in the Talmud [*Yoma* 87a] derive from the thrice-repeated word נָא [(once as אָנָּא, twice as נָא) — signifying entreaty *(Rashi* ad loc.) —] that when one seeks his neighbor's pardon he need not beseech him more than three times [see *Maharsha*].

[The 'trop' musical cantillation on the word אָנָּא, *O please,* is a *pazer,* one of the more intense and sustained of the cantillations. This emphasizes the intensity of their plea.]

The verb שָׂא, *forgive,* literally means *carry* since by forgiving one 'lifts up' the transgression from the sinner and lightens his burden, figuratively 'bearing' it for him. See *Ibn Caspi* to 4:13, and comm. to 32:21.

כִּי־רָעָה גְמָלוּךָ — *For they have done you evil.*

The Hebrew expression [lit. *for they have "recompensed" you evil*] denotes undeserved evil *(HaRechasim leBikah).*

An integral part of asking forgiveness is that one acknowledge wrongdoing *(R' Shmuel ben Chofni).*

וְעַתָּה שָׂא נָא לְפֶשַׁע עַבְדֵי אֱלֹהֵי אָבִיךָ — *So now, please forgive the spiteful deed of the servants of your father's God.*

This was to be added by the emissary as if it were a personal plea *(Chizkuni; Akeidah).*

— Even though your father is dead, his God is living and they are His servants *(Rashi).*

— In the final analysis, though they acted with sinful intention, they were God's 'servants' inasmuch as they were instruments He employed to exalt you to this lofty position *(Abarbanel).*

[See comm. of Ashtruc: *Midrashei HaTorah* cited in comm. to 45:5.]

— Even if they were not your brothers, they are of your father's faith. You have a spiritual fraternity

50
18 please, kindly forgive the spiteful deed of your brothers and their sin for they have done you evil; so now, please forgive the spiteful deed of the servants of your father's God.' " And Joseph wept when they spoke to him.

[18] His brothers themselves also went and flung themselves before him and said, "We are ready to be

and should be forgiving *(Michlol Yofi).*

וַיֵּבְךְּ יוֹסֵף בְּדַבְּרָם אֵלָיו — *And Joseph wept when they spoke to him.*

— Because he was suspected of evil intent *(Pesikta Zutresa).*

If one is suspected of impropriety it is proper for him to weep over it. So do we find in *Yoma* 19b that when the elders would adjure the High Priest not to act in the manner of the Sadducees when performing the Yom Kippur service, he would weep that they suspected him of considering such sacrilege *(Yalkut Yehudah; Haamek Davar).*

— As soon as they mentioned his father, he wept out of sheer love, and his compassion was aroused. However, we find it nowhere specifically mentioned that Joseph formally forgave them. They technically remained unforgiven until their dying day. Their sin was eventually atoned for with the death of the Ten Martyrs centuries later. Thus their punishment was postponed until centuries later. This is consistent with the principle that God visits the sin of the father on the children *(R' Bachya).* [See *comm.* to p. 1650.]

Other opinions regarding whether Joseph had forgiven his brothers include that of *R' Yehudah HaChassid* [*Sefer Chassidim* ed. *Mekitzei Nirdamim* p. 437] who maintains that since Joseph attributed to Divine Providence that their bad deeds ultimately resulted in good, they were absolved as far as *Joseph* was concerned, but not with respect to God. [See also *B'chor Shor, OrHaChaim* and *Zohar.*]

According to *Sforno* [in continuation of his *comm.* above, end of *v.* 16], *Joseph wept* sentimentally at their mention of the beloved Jacob and that he had refused to suspect Joseph of scheming against his brothers.

Tz'ror HaMor maintains that Joseph wept because this message made it apparent that they had told Jacob of the sale, while Joseph had always taken pains to spare his father the grief of learning of it.

18. וַיֵּלְכוּ גַּם־אֶחָיו וַיִּפְּלוּ לְפָנָיו — [And] *his brothers themselves also went and flung themselves before him.*

I.e., in addition to their emissaries, the brothers themselves also went ... *(Rashi).*

The syntax seems to imply that the emissaries returned to the brothers and reported that Joseph did not answer them but merely wept. *B'chor Shor* writes that the brothers took this as a sign that Joseph bore them no malice and they felt it was safe to go to him and fling themselves down before him in obeisance and gratitude. [*Sechel Tov* derives from this that proper etiquette requires that even if one's trespass is forgiven through an emissary, the trespasser should still appear personally before the other.]

Or, as *Haamek Davar* suggests, the brothers did not know how to interpret Joseph's weeping. They were concerned that he wept because the emissaries reminded him of the tribulations he had suffered at their hands. If so, they might be in greater danger and they decided to beseech him on their own behalf.

The word **גַּם**, *also,* could refer to the *bowing down* as well: The brothers

לְךָ לַעֲבָדִים: יט וַיֹּאמֶר אֲלֵהֶם יוֹסֵף אַל־
כ תִּירָאוּ כִּי הֲתַחַת אֱלֹהִים אָנִי: וְאַתֶּם
חֲשַׁבְתֶּם עָלַי רָעָה אֱלֹהִים חֲשָׁבָהּ לְטֹבָה

went and bowed, just as the emissary had done. According to the view cited above that the emissary was Bilhah [cf. also *Targum Yonasan*], these events might have been in fulfillment of Joseph's dream wherein the 'moon' and the eleven 'stars' prostrated themselves before him *(Oznaim L'Torah)*.

הִנֶּנּוּ לְךָ לַעֲבָדִים — *We are ready to be your slaves.*

— Because we once sold you into slavery. Enslave us and let that be our punishment — measure for measure — and not some other punishment *(R' Avraham b. HaRambam)*.

According to *Haamek Davar*, the brothers were, as noted above, fearful that Joseph had wept at the memory of his earlier tribulations and would now repay them by selling them as slaves. So they anticipated him by saying, 'You need not think of measures to requite us for having sold you; we are quite ready to be your slaves!'

19. Joseph reassures them.

אַל־תִּירָאוּ — *Fear not.*

Of what you suspect I might be thinking *(Haamek Davar)*.

כִּי הֲתַחַת אֱלֹהִים אָנִי — *For am I instead* [following *Rashi* in 30:2; lit. *beneath*] *of God?*

— Have I the power to harm you even if I wanted to? [As Joseph continues in the next verse:] You all devised harm for me [and I am but an individual], yet [you did not succeed because] God turned it to good; how then could *I alone* [without God's consent; not being in His stead] harm you all? [Therefore: Fear not] *(Rashi)*.

B'Chor Shor interprets: Am I in God's stead that I have the authority to harm you? I do not even have a valid claim against you since your evil intentions were turned to good. Moreover, people would accuse me of betrayal, saying that I brought you here under my trust and now I harmed you.

[Many of the consoling statements Joseph now makes echo those he made when he first identified himself to his brothers. See specifically 45:5-9.]

Sforno: Am I then a judge in His stead that I should analyze His decrees and punish those who acted as His agents, as though I were presiding over a court that had authority to annul His decrees? You certainly acted merely as His agents as I once told you [45:8]: *It was not you who sent me here but God.*[1]

Cf. *Malbim:* Having witnessed the Providential effects of the matter, how can I purport to analyze God's ways; can I thwart His obvious will? Moreover, since you have not harmed me, I have no right to inflict 'evil' on you unless it results in goodness, like the 'evil' you did to me — but *am I in God's stead* that I can know if the evil I do you would indeed result in your benefit?

According to *Ibn Ezra: Am I then in God's stead* — that you flung yourselves before me and offered

1. [The moral implications of their having to account for being the tools with which the Divine Plan was executed have been discussed in the footnote to 45:5.]

50
19-20

your slaves." [19] But Joseph said to them, "Fear not,
for am I instead of God? [20] Although you intended
me harm God intended it for good: in order to ac-

yourselves as my slaves!

Akeidah interprets differently: You certainly need neither my forgiveness nor my reassurance; nor, on the other hand, are you worthy of receiving a reward from me. *For am I in God's stead* that I should thank you for having been instrumental in realizing His plan, since when in reality [next verse:] your intentions were evil and designed to harm me; it was God Who intended for good, not only for me personally but for the general welfare to sustain an entire populace ... Nevertheless, [*v.* 21]: *Fear not* ...

— God can judge thoughts and intentions. I, as a human being, can only consider the result. As a result of your deed I owe you deep gratitude! *(R' Hirsch).*

The interpretation of this phrase as an incredulous rhetorical question follows *Rashi* and most commentators. [The ה of הֲתַחַת punctuated as it is with a *chataf patach* indicates a question =ה הַשְּׁאֵלָה, interrogative particle; see *Rashi* to הֲשֹׁפֵט in 15:25].

Sechel Tov, however, perceives the prefix ה to be a ה הַקְרִיאָה, *interjectional particle,* and interprets the statement in an affirmative sense: *Fear not for I am indeed in God's stead!* — That is, I emulate His ways. Just as He overlooks transgressions, so do I.

Divrei Shaul interprets homiletically: "Am only *I* beneath God?" Is it only *I* who is beneath His Providential care and not you? Of course not! His care encompasses all of you. Therefore, *Fear not!*[2]

This was the same response an angry Jacob had once given the barren Rachel when she had demanded children of him [30:2]. As *Ramban* there notes, the Sages took Jacob to task, stating in the Midrash: The Holy One, Blessed is He, said to Jacob, 'Is this the way to answer an aggrieved person? By your life! Your children [by your other wives] are destined to stand humbly before her son Joseph [i.e., they will be brought to such despair that they will need this assurance].

20. וְאַתֶּם חֲשַׁבְתֶּם עָלַי רָעָה וכו׳ — *Although you intended me harm* [lit. *and you thought evil onto me*] *God intended it for good.*

[As *Rashi* explains the continuity above: How then could you fear reprisals by me! When *all* of you intended to do me harm God thwarted you and turned it to good, so how could God permit me — as an individual — to do harm to all of you?]

— Accordingly, you did not sin; God providentially guided you, for He intended it for your good *(Rashbam).*

You are like a person who intended to pass someone a cup of poison, but inadvertently gave him wine instead: he is free and guiltless even of Heavenly judgment *(Or HaChaim).*

Bais Yitzchak objects to *Or HaChaim's* thesis that there is no sin involved in the switch from poison to wine. The Sages [*Kiddushim* 81b] teach

1. *Torah Sheleimah* cites the following Midrash from *Tz'ror HaMor:*

'Am I in God's stead to harm you; you who personify the purpose of the entire universe!' As our Sages observed: There are twelve hours in the day; twelve hours in the night; twelve constellations; twelve months in the year; and Aaron's breastplate consisted of twelve stones corresponding to the Tribes. Am I then God, that I should presume to be capable to overthrow the order of the universe?" [Comp. the *Midrash*].

לְמַעַן עֲשֹׂה כַּיּוֹם הַזֶּה לְהַחֲיֹת עַם־רָב׃
°שביעי כא °וְעַתָּה אַל־תִּירָאוּ אָנֹכִי אֲכַלְכֵּל אֶתְכֶם
וְאֶת־טַפְּכֶם וַיְנַחֵם אוֹתָם וַיְדַבֵּר עַל־

that if someone meant to eat pork but picked up beef by mistake he must repent. *Bais Yitzchak* explains that the Sages refer only to a case where someone intended to sin, but if he had intended to use the pork for something that he considered to be a *mitzvah* [עֲבֵרָה לִשְׁמָהּ], no repentance is required; neither in thought nor in deed was there a sin. Since the brothers were convinced that they acted properly in the case of Joseph, *Or HaChaim* maintains that they were completely blameless.

[See *Akeidah's* interpretation, end of last verse.]

Sforno interprets: Your action was motivated by error: You thought that I was persecuting you [interpreting: *you attributed wickedness to me*]; had this been true, you would have been justified *to act in self-defense against me. But God intended it for good* — He guided your deed to create a beneficial outcome.

לְמַעַן עֲשֹׂה כַּיּוֹם הַזֶּה לְהַחֲיֹת עַם־רָב — *In order to accomplish — it is as clear as this day — that a vast people be kept alive* [lit. *in order to do like this day to keep alive a vast people.*]

The reference to *vast people* obviously included the general populace who Joseph sustained. However, the intention of God's Providence in engineering all these events was, as noted in 45:6, primarily directed at the preservation of Jacob's family — who would multiply miraculously in Egypt and become a great people. Compare Joseph's earlier statement in 45:7 *God has sent me ahead of you to insure your survival in the land and to sustain you for a momentous deliverance.*

According to *R' Shmuel b. Chofni*, the term *vast* people refers to the offspring of the Tribes. Joseph's descendants, the tribes of Manasseh and Ephraim, used a similar expression to Joshua [*Joshua* 17:4]: וַאֲנִי עַם רָב, *and I am a vast or great people.*

The expression כַּיּוֹם הַזֶּה [lit. *like this day*] is ambiguous.

The translation follows *R' Saadiah Gaon* who renders: In order to accomplish what you are witnessing today, i.e., what is, in retrospect, now clear as this day.

[The expression denotes exceptional clarity. Comp. *Rashi* to 25:31.]

21. וְעַתָּה אַל־תִּירָאוּ — *[And] so now, fear not.*

Joseph found it necessary to reiterate that they need not entertain any fears although he had said it to them earlier in *v.* 19. For they still could have been fearful that, despite his assurance that he had no plans to take *revenge* on them, it did not necessarily mean that he would continue supporting them.

Minchah Belulah perceives the prophetic connotation to be: *Now* you need not fear; but in the days of the Ten Martyrs [when your descendants will be punished for your evil deed (see comm. to p. 1650)] there *will* be cause for fear.

אָנֹכִי אֲכַלְכֵּל אֶתְכֶם וְאֶת טַפְּכֶם — *I* [the pronoun is emphatic: *I personally*] *will sustain you and your little ones.*

— Since it is clear that that was God's reason for sending me here [see 45:7] *(Alshich).*

— *I will provide for you* — during the duration of the renewed famine. For according to *Tosefta Sotah,*

50
21 *complish — it is as clear as this day — that a vast peo-*
ple be kept alive. [21] *So now, fear not — I will sustain*
you and your little ones." Thus he comforted them
and appealed to their emotions.

after Jacob died, the famine — which had ceased with Jacob's arrival in the second year of the hunger — resumed [and lasted for another five years to complete the foretold total of seven years]. According to *Sifre Eikev* §38 this resumption of the famine is inferred from our verse. This is derived from the fact that the verb אֲכַלְכֵּל, *provide/sustain* is used both here and above in 45:11, implying that the same conditions prevailed in both instances. 'Now just as the term *provide* above refers to years of famine, so does that term in our verse refer to the renewed years of famine.' [See *Ramban* 47:18].

Sechel Tov observes that for presumptuously saying that *he* would provide for his brothers, rather than attributing sustenance to God Who provides for all life, Joseph was punished and he died before all his brothers [see footnote to *v.* 2 above for other opinions regarding Joseph's premature death].

The term כלכל refers to providing for one's individualized needs *(Radak).*

וַיְנַחֵם אוֹתָם וַיְדַבֵּר עַל־לִבָּם — *Thus he comforted them and appealed to their emotions.*

Literally: *And he spoke upon their hearts* — i.e., persuasive words that settle upon [lit. *are received upon*] the heart [the heart being considered in Scripture as the seat of the emotions and reason]: "Before you came, people spread rumors that I was a slave; your coming showed I was born free. If I kill you people will say: 'They were not his brothers at all! He saw a group of fine young men and passed them off as his brothers, but when he had no further need for them, he killed them. Have you ever heard of a man killing his brothers!?' " *(Midrash; Rashi).*[1]

Rashi cites from *Megillah* 16b an alternative sample of the reassuring words he addressed to them: 'If ten lights could not extinguish one light, how could one light extinguish ten?' [I.e., obviously it cannot, for it is not within the nature of a light to *extinguish* another light; to the contrary one *kindles* a light from another. Such, too, is the expected relationship of brothers (see *Maharsha*)].

The Midrashim record many other arguments used by Joseph to convince them that, as absolute ruler of Egypt, he could have done

1. The question arises: Having already assured his brothers countless times that he meant them no harm, why did he still have to 'appeal to their emotions'?

However [as observed by *Malbim* at the end of *v.* 15] it is uncomfortable for someone to be showered with kindness by a person he has wronged. They therefore needed the intellectual and emotional consolation Joseph gave them in order to be absolutely convinced that their relationship was beneficial to Joseph as well, and it was important to him for all to know they were his brothers *(Beer Yitzchak).*

Furthermore, according to *HaKsav V'Hakabbalah* and *Alshich* it was necessary for him to console them at this point so that they would not feel humiliated at being dependent upon his support, especially in view of their guilt feelings. Joseph went out of his way to soothe their emotions and convince them of his sincerity, so they would regard themselves as if self-sustaining.

כב לִבָּם: וַיֵּשֶׁב יוֹסֵף בְּמִצְרַיִם הוּא וּבֵית
כג אָבִיו וַיְחִי יוֹסֵף מֵאָה וָעֶשֶׂר שָׁנִים: °וַיַּרְא
°מפטיר יוֹסֵף לְאֶפְרַיִם בְּנֵי שִׁלֵּשִׁים גַּם בְּנֵי מָכִיר
כד בֶּן־מְנַשֶּׁה יֻלְּדוּ עַל־בִּרְכֵּי יוֹסֵף: וַיֹּאמֶר
יוֹסֵף אֶל־אֶחָיו אָנֹכִי מֵת וֵאלֹהִים פָּקֹד

away with them easily, had he wanted to. The fact was that he had no evil designs against them. The brothers finally recognized his sincerity. He removed their last doubts and they were comforted.

[On the use of the idiom *speaking upon the heart* to connote *consoling words,* see *Isaiah* 40:2 and *Ruth* 2:13].

22. Joseph in Egypt.

The narrative now reverts to Joseph and sums up his life after his father's demise *(Abarbanel).*

וַיֵּשֶׁב יוֹסֵף בְּמִצְרַיִם הוּא וּבֵית אָבִיו — *[And] Joseph dwelt in Egypt — he and his father's household.*

The continuity is: Having established a full fraternal harmony with his brothers that was greater in many respects than it had ever been before, *Joseph dwelt in Egypt* — in peace and contentment — *together with his brothers (Tzror HaMor).*

That Joseph *dwelt* (וַיֵּשֶׁב) in Egypt is obvious. *Lekach Tov* perceives it to mean: *He created settlements* [יִשּׁוּבִים] in Egypt — erecting houses and other structures.

וַיֵּשֶׁב frequently implies: *he settled.* Joseph settled down in exile, remembering the Divine words addressed to his father: *'Do not be afraid to go down to Egypt, for I shall make you into a great nation there'* (46:3). None of Jacob's descendants looked for ways of leaving Egypt. They resolved to trust in God's words and to wait for the End that He had promised. Joseph felt that this End could not be too far off, since the "fourth generation" was approaching, and God had announced to return that generation to Canaan (15:16). Joseph was satisfied to tell his brothers how the arrival of the future Redemption could be recognized. It was his last act before his death [verse 24] *(R' Munk* from *Zohar).*

According to *Abarbanel's* view that the preceding occurred while the family was still in Canaan and the brothers were entertaining the notion that if Joseph was indeed ill-disposed toward them they would not return to Egypt, this verse describes how they all returned together to Egypt after Joseph succeeded in reassuring them. (Cf. *Abarbanel; Oznaim L'Torah).*

וַיְחִי יוֹסֵף מֵאָה וָעֶשֶׂר שָׁנִים — *And Joseph lived one hundred and ten years.*

Every one of the years were truly 'lived' — he enjoyed vigorous health *(Zohar;* cf. *R' Shmuel b. Chofni).*

Since Joseph ascended to rulership at the age of 30 [see 41:46], he ruled for a total of 80 years — longer than anyone before him, and rarely duplicated *(Abarbanel; Malbim).*

However, Joseph's lifespan was the shortest of his brothers, and though he was among the youngest, he died first. See footnote to *v.* 2 above, and comm. to *Exodus.* 1:6.

23. וַיַּרְא יוֹסֵף לְאֶפְרַיִם בְּנֵי שִׁלֵּשִׁים — *Joseph saw* [i.e., *lived to see*] *three generations* [lit. *children of the third*] *through Ephraim.*

That is, although Joseph died before any of his brothers, he lived to see Ephraim's children, grandchildren and great-grandchildren. (Cf. *Ibn Ezra; Radak*

22 *Joseph dwelt in Egypt — he and his father's household — and Joseph lived one hundred and ten years.*

23 *Joseph saw three generations through Ephraim; even the sons of Machir son of Manasseh were raised on Joseph's knees.*

24 *Joseph said to his brothers, 'I am about to die,*

to *II Kings* 10:30; *Shaarei Aharon; Karnei Or; R' Shmuel b. Chofni; R' Bachya; Rivash; Moshav Zekeinim.)*

In some *Chumashim* the final *mem* of the word שִׁלֵּשִׁים is enlarged; *Minchas Shay* disapproves and maintains that in correctly written Torah Scrolls the letter is of normal size.

גַּם בְּנֵי מָכִיר בֶּן־מְנַשֶּׁה יֻלְּדוּ עַל־בִּרְכֵּי יוֹסֵף — *Even the sons of Machir son of Manasseh were raised* [lit. *born*] *on Joseph's knees.*

The idiomatic expression יֻלְּדוּ עַל־בִּרְכֵּי יוֹסֵף [lit. *were born upon Joseph's knees*] is to be interpreted as *Onkelos* renders it: *were* **raised** *between his knees* [a figurative expression meaning: *grew up during his lifetime* and raised under his spiritual guidance] *(Rashi).*

According to *Targum Yonasan,* it alludes to the circumcision of his grandchildren, which was carried out by Joseph himself. *Sechel Tov* suggests that the idiom *on Joseph's knees* implies that Joseph was the *sandek* at the circumcision of his grandchildren. [See note loc. cit. in *Yayin HaTov.*]

Thus, in the case of Manasseh, Joseph lived to see Manasseh's grandchildren — [in Scriptural terms: בָּנִים שְׁנִיִּים, lit. children of the second generation *(Rashbam)*] — a reference to Gilead, Machir's son *(Numbers* 26:29). Though Manasseh was the elder of the brothers, we see that Joseph saw an additional generation from Ephraim. Already in Joseph's lifetime we see evidence of Jacob's prognostication that Ephraim would surpass Manasseh (48:19) *(Rashbam; R' Bachya;* cf. sources cited above).

The term גַּם, *also,* denotes that Ephraim's offspring as well as Manasseh's were brought up in Joseph's house. Only Manasseh's offspring are specifically mentioned as having been raised on Joseph's knees because of Joseph's love for him as the firstborn. The phrase "sons of Machir" refers primarily to Gilead, the grandfather of the daughters of Zelophechad [*Numbers* 27:1]; this indicates that the righteous Joseph raised wholly righteous descendants in his house from whom descended these women who were wise and pious in their generation [see *Bamidbar Rabbah* 21:11] *(R' Bachya).*

The beautiful point has been made that the sons of Machir were contemporaries of Moses [*Numbers* 26:29*ff*], the foretold fourth generation [15:16] which was to be liberated from Egypt. As children they had seen Joseph, the pride and glory of their people in Egypt; they would live to see the redemption and the Promised Land.

24. Joseph imparts signs of the Redemption to his brothers and adjures them to bury his remains in Eretz Yisrael.

אָנֹכִי מֵת — *I am about to die.*

This teaches that he gathered

יִפְקֹד אֶתְכֶם וְהֶעֱלָה אֶתְכֶם מִן־הָאָרֶץ הַזֹּאת אֶל־הָאָרֶץ אֲשֶׁר נִשְׁבַּע לְאַבְרָהָם

them all at the time of his death and charged them as a father charges his children *(Sechel Tov).*

[The year was 2309; fifty-four years since Jacob's death in 2255.]

His brothers were all alive for they survived him [as implied by the fact that the Torah tells us in this verse that he addressed *his brothers;* and that in *Exodus* 1:6 Joseph's death is mentioned before his brothers. Joseph died prematurely as noted in footnote to *v.* 2 above.] He wanted to be sure that his bones would be taken to Canaan but he knew that this could not be done until the Exodus, [as explained in comm. to *v.* 25]. Therefore, he wanted to assure himself that the departing Jews would take his remains with them. Seeing that his brothers were old [Reuben, the oldest, was 116] and realizing that they would not survive until the Exodus, Joseph administered an oath to them that they would transmit to their descendants *(Ramban).*

וֵאלֹהִים פָּקֹד יִפְקֹד אֶתְכֶם — *But God will surely remember you.* [The verb is repeated for emphasis, literally, *remember He will remember you.*]

The continuity is: Joseph knew from his father that future generations would remain enslaved in Egypt. Therefore, he now comforted them: *I will die* and will be unable to help you any longer, but do not despair — *God will surely remember you,* etc. *(Abarbanel).*

⧫ The words "Pakod Yifkod," identify the Redeemer.

During the last moments of his life, Jacob had imparted to Joseph some secret signs of the future redemption from Egypt, which Joseph now transmitted to his brothers. The words in our verse [although not recorded above in Jacob's name] were a direct quotation from Jacob. As noted with reference to Noah in 8:3 and the barren Sarah in 20:1, the term פקד like זכר usually announces the appearance of Divine Providence. The figurative implication is that God will manifest His Providence as if He 'remembered' to carry out an earlier plan or promise. Since a long span of time elapses between the promise and the event, God is spoken of as 'remembering,' as if He were a human being who forgot a promise and then, after a lapse, remembered to carry it out. Obviously, however, such an expression cannot be taken literally since God cannot forget.

As we will אי״ה see in *Exodus* 3:16, the words פָּקֹד פָּקַדְתִּי, *I have indeed remembered* were pivotal in the acceptance by the Israelites of Moses' announcement of the impending redemption.

For, when Moses was given the mission to go and deliver the Jews from bondage, God promised him: *'They will listen to you.' Rashi* explains: As soon as you address them with the words פָּקֹד פָּקַדְתִּי, *I have indeed remembered you,* they will listen to your voice, for this sign has been passed on to them from the time of Jacob and Joseph. They know that these are the words that will herald the redemption. For both Jacob and Joseph said פָּקֹד יִפְקֹד, *God will surely remember you.* [The first time Joseph says it in *v.* 24, he

50 *but God will surely remember you and bring you up out of this land to the land which He promised on oath to Abraham, to Isaac, and to Jacob."*

is quoting his father; when he repeats it in *v.* 25 it is in the context of his own request *(Mizrachi;* see *Ramban* to *Exodus* 3:19).]

Pirkei d'Rabbi Eliezer 48 maintains that this proof of the "authentic language of Redemption" had originally been revealed to Abraham and then transmitted successively to Isaac, Jacob, and Joseph, who entrusted it to his brothers. It ultimately reached Serach, daughter of Asher. She enjoyed exceptional longevity [as noted in the *comm.* to 45:26] and was the only one of Jacob's grandchildren still alive in the time of Moses. When Moses came to the Israelite elders, they asked Serach to verify whether Moses' words corresponded to the secret tradition that she had received. When she replied affirmatively, the elders believed him.[1]

The double phraseology *pakod yifkod* implies a "double remembrance." God would remember them twice — in the days of Moses and throughout their many Exiles culminating in the days of the Messiah. Moreover, He would remember them in Tishrei and Nissan: their servitude ended in the months of Tishrei and they were liberated in Nissan *(Midrash HaGadol).*

וְהֶעֱלָה אֶתְכֶם מִן הָאָרֶץ הַזֹּאת — *And [He will] bring you up out of this land.*

[This promise that God will one day bring them up out of the land is yet another indication that some form of bondage had already begun although, as the Sages maintain, it was not severe until all the Tribal Ancestors died.]

By the expression *and bring you up* Joseph intimated to his brothers that their physical remains too would eventually be brought up from Egypt. Indeed, this occurred. At the Exodus, each tribe took along the remains of its ancestor *(Sechel Tov).* [*R' Bachya* to *v.* 25 citing *Peskita* derives this exegesis from the word אִתְּכֶם in *Exodus* 13:19; see *Rashi* there.]

אֶל הָאָרֶץ אֲשֶׁר נִשְׁבַּע לְאַבְרָהָם לְיִצְחָק וּלְיַעֲקֹב — *To the land which He promised on oath to Abraham, to Isaac, and to Jacob.*

1. The numerical value of the word פָּקוֹד spelled 'full' equals 190; יִפְקֹד can be translated *shall cause to be missed,* as in *Numbers* 31:49: וְלֹא נִפְקַד מִמֶּנּוּ אִישׁ *and not one man of us is missing.* Thus, these two words prophetically imply that God will surely 'remember' the enslaved Jews and shorten their bondage ["cause it to be missed"] by 190 years (i.e., פָּקֹד יִפְקֹד=*He will "reduce" by 190),* for at the Covenant Between the Parts it was foretold to Abraham that his descendants would be enslaved 400 years. This calculation began from the birth of Isaac. God subtracted 190 years from the period and He liberated them after only 210 years (see *comm.* to רְדוּ in 42:2).

This premature redemption by God is also celebrated in allegorical terms in *Song of Songs* 2:8: *Hark! The sound of my Beloved! Behold He comes! Leaping upon the mountains, skipping upon the hills* [see *comm.* to ArtScroll *Shir Hashirim*] *(Tanchuma; Midrash Aggadah).*

The Midrashim also elicit from this a warning that the Jews should not seek to liberate themselves prematurely from Egypt, but wait until God would remember and redeem them — not like the Ephraimites who attempted to liberate themselves prematurely before the Providential End [cf. *Rashi Exod.* 15:14] (see *Baal HaTurim; Meshech Chochmah).*

[For a further discussion of the 'shortening' of the Exile, see ArtScroll *Haggadah* pp 95-98; *Haggadah Treasury* pp. 65-67. This will be dealt with in depth in the comm. and Overview to *Exodus.*]

כה לְיִצְחָק וּלְיַעֲקֹב: וַיַּשְׁבַּע יוֹסֵף אֶת־בְּנֵי
יִשְׂרָאֵל לֵאמֹר פָּקֹד יִפְקֹד אֱלֹהִים אֶתְכֶם
כו וְהַעֲלִתֶם אֶת־עַצְמֹתַי מִזֶּה: וַיָּמָת יוֹסֵף

— Each of them individually on various repetitive occasions *(Akeidah)*.

If any 'prophet' ever arises claiming that he will redeem you and lead you to a country other than *Eretz Yisrael*, do not believe him *(Tanchuma)*.

[On the use of a father's first name by his son see *comm.* to 49:31. Briefly, as *Ritva* maintains, the Patriarchs bore names given them by God and this allowed the sons to mention them.]

25. וַיַּשְׁבַּע יוֹסֵף אֶת־בְּנֵי יִשְׂרָאֵל לֵאמֹר — *Then Joseph adjured the children of Israel saying.*

He had them vow that they would administer the oath from generation to generation [לֵאמֹר לְדורות] until it could be fulfilled. He said: "Just as Father made me swear, and I kept that oath, so do I adjure you and your offspring and expect you to fulfill *your* oath." And so it was: *Moses took the bones of Joseph with him for he had strongly adjured* [הַשְׁבֵּעַ הִשְׁבִּיעַ] *the children of Israel saying, God will surely remember you and you shall carry my bones up from here with you* [*Exodus.* 13:19; as *Rashi* explains there, the double phraseology implies: 'He made them swear to in turn make their children swear.'] *(Midrash HaGadol; Sechel Tov)*.

פָּקֹד יִפְקֹד אֱלֹהִים אֶתְכֶם — *When God will indeed remember you.*

[The syntax of the translation: *when ... then ...* follows *R' Avraham b. HaRambam; R' Saadia Gaon* and *R' Shmuel b. Chofni* (comp. also *Daas Zekeinim*). It avoids the difficulty that this phrase seems to be repeated from the previous verse. In *v.* 24 Joseph transmitted his father's prophetic promise that God would certainly 'remember' their plight and free them from bondage in Egypt. In this verse he continues: "When He does so, please be sure to take my remains out of here with you." For as *Mizrachi* cited above mentions, in *v.* 24 Joseph cited his father's prophetic words, now he repeats it as his own statement of fact.]

וְהַעֲלִתֶם אֶת־עַצְמֹתַי מִזֶּה — *Then you must bring my bones up out of here.*

By using the term *my bones* instead of *my body* it was clear that Joseph — unlike his father — was not requesting that they bury him in *Eretz Yisrael* immediately after his death.

But why *didn't* Joseph make his sons swear that they would take him to Canaan *immediately*, as Jacob had done? Joseph said: "I am a ruler in Egypt and I had sufficient authority to fulfill my father's wish to bring his body to Canaan. But the Egyptians would not let my sons do this for me after I die." He therefore made his brothers take an oath that when they were liberated his remains would accompany them *(Rashi* to *Exod.* 13:19; *Mechilta)*.

As *Ramban* to 49:31 explains, Pharaoh's courtiers would never have allowed Joseph's body to be removed for burial to Canaan since Joseph was a source of pride to them. Furthermore, if all his kin were to accompany him, the Egyptian populace would pillage what-

[25] *Then Joseph adjured the children of Israel saying "When God will indeed remember you, then you must bring my bones up out of here."*

[26] *Joseph died at the age of one hundred and ten*

ever they had left at home [since the Egyptians would no longer fear retribution as they did when Joseph was alive]. As for possibly having others transport him there, it would not have been proper for him to be buried by strangers *(Ramban* 49:31).

The reason Joseph did not adjure his own sons exclusively was because he knew that a portion of his descendants — half the tribe of Manasseh — would inherit territory across the Jordan and they might want to bury him near them instead of bringing him to *Eretz Yisrael* proper. He therefore addressed his oath to *the children of Israel* that *they* bury him. And so it was; *Moses* took responsibility for his bones *(Meshech Chochmah).*

Joseph did not ask to be buried in the Cave of Machpelah because he knew by tradition that no one but the three Patriarchs and three Matriarchs were to be buried there. He requested only that his bones be brought up for burial in the Holy Land, but did not specify a site. They were to bury him wherever they wished *(Mechilta d'Rabbi Shimon b. Yochai* cited by *Ramban* in 49:31).

[We find in *Joshua* that Joseph's bones were finally buried in Shechem. Either, as implied in *Rashi* to 48:22, it was a tradition that Jacob gave Joseph the city of Shechem — שְׁכֶם אַחַד עַל אַחֶיךָ — as a burial site, or as the Talmud [*Sotah* 13b] suggests, the tribes wanted to make amends, at least in part, by burying him with full honors at the very place where they had betrayed him (see *Rashi* to *Joshua* 24:32).]

The reason Joseph adjured his brothers to go to the trouble of transporting his remains to *Eretz Yisrael* though he knew that the righteous will *in any event* become transported and resurrected there, was because he wished to avoid the pain of rolling through the underground cavities to reach *Eretz Yisrael* for the Resurrection *(Yalkut Shimoni;* cf. *Kesubos* 111a; see *comm.* to 47:30).

In any event, it has been emphasized above that all the Patriarchs and the great Sages longed for burial in the Holy Land.

Rambam in *Hilchos Melachim* 5:11 writes that whoever is buried in *Eretz Yisrael* is granted absolution, as it says וְכִפֶּר אַדְמָתוֹ עַמּוֹ, *His land makes expiation for His people* [*Deut.* 32:43]. Although one who is buried there after death cannot be compared to one who lived there, many Sages arranged for their bodies to be taken to the Holy Land, following the examples of Joseph and Jacob *(R' Munk).*

26. The death of Joseph.

וַיָּמָת יוֹסֵף בֶּן־מֵאָה וָעֶשֶׂר שָׁנִים — [*And*] *Joseph died at the age of one hundred and ten years.*

Joseph's age is mentioned again to emphasize that his reign lasted for the unusually long, uninterrupted period of eighty years. *(R' Shmuel b. Chofni).*

In *v.* 22 his lifespan was mentioned in relating the years of his *life;* here it is repeated in the context of his *death (Abarbanel).*

As *R' Munk* writes, the Torah

בֶּן־מֵאָה וָעֶשֶׂר שָׁנִים וַיַּחַנְטוּ אֹתוֹ וַיִּישֶׂם בָּאָרוֹן בְּמִצְרָיִם׃

frequently provides details of this kind that help us put Biblical events in historical perspective. Joseph survived his father by fifty-four years. As viceroy, he had presided over the destiny of Egypt for 80 consecutive years [he had been 30 years old when he appeared before Pharaoh (41:46)]. Joseph's death was 71 years after Jacob's arrival in Egypt, and during this time Jacob's family had led a peaceful existence, which was to continue for another 23 years until the death of Levi, Jacob's last surviving son. The 116 years of slavery and servitude began only after this happy period of 94 years *(Rashi* on *Exodus* 6:16). The period of slavery and oppression, which was to have lasted 400 years (15:13), was, as noted earlier, shortened to 210 years.

Some commentators perceive the phrase וַיָּמָת יוֹסֵף as a homiletical praise: *He died as 'Joseph'*. Although he ruled for eighty years and Pharaoh had changed his name to *Tzafenas Paan'each,* Joseph still retained his Hebrew name. Thereby he set an example to his brethren to retain their Hebrew identity. The Sages maintain that the Israelite resolve not to drop their Hebrew names throughout the Egyptian servitude was one of the merits for which they deserved Redemption (see *Pardes Yosef).*

וַיַּחַנְטוּ אֹתוֹ — [*And*] *they embalmed him.*

There is a difference of opinion in the Midrash regarding who embalmed Joseph: the court physicians or the brothers.

That he was embalmed at all was probably demanded by the royal court out of respect for the illustrious Joseph who had governed the land for as long as most people could remember.

In punishment for Joseph's having embalmed Jacob, however, the embalming was ineffective. By the time Moses retrieved Joseph's remains, only his bones were left *(Pesikta Rabbosi).*

וַיִּישֶׂם בָּאָרוֹן בְּמִצְרָיִם — *And he was placed in a coffin in Egypt.*

The Hebrew literally reads: "... and he was put in *the* coffin," that is, in the coffin Joseph had prepared for himself *(Ibn Ezra).*

— It was *the* coffin in which they embalmed him. The coffin was left above-ground so its identity would remain known to future generations. That is how Moses recognized it and took it out of Egypt at the Exodus [*Exod.* 13:19] *(Sforno; Ralbag).*[1]

אָרוֹן, *ark; container* is a delicate word for *coffin.* The word is used elsewhere only to describe the container holding the Tablets of the

1. Since the Torah mentions only that the coffin was in *Egypt* but does not speak of the *burial* of the coffin, the Sages in *Sotah* 13a deduce that the Egyptians lowered it into the depths of the Nile so that its waters might be blessed. (According to another opinion in the Talmud, he was buried in the royal tombs).

The Midrash cites the view that originally Joseph's coffin was buried in a field — and the field immediately became blessed. When others heard of it they stole his remains and buried it

50 *years; they embalmed him and he was placed in a coffin in Egypt.*

Law, and for the collection-boxes for holy purposes (*II Kings* 12:10). In all these cases, it is not used for burial, but for receiving and safeguarding for others — the Tablets for Israel and the contribution for the Temple. Accordingly, the use of this word for 'coffin' would signify a container in which the physical casing of a human being is — temporarily — kept *(R' Hirsch).*

As *Tz'ror HaMor* notes, the use of the term *ark* for his *coffin* indicates Joseph's greatness in that he was like the Ark of the Covenant, lord over the land. As the Sages said, Two arks led the Israelites in the desert: the ark containing the bones of Joseph, and the Ark containing the Tables of the Covenant [the Ten Commandments]. When people questioned the propriety of a coffin near the Ark of the Covenant, the response would be: 'He whose remains are preserved in the one ark, loyally obeyed the Divine commands enshrined in the other.'

It would appear that they did not bury him, but concealed him in a coffin. Apparently they did this for one or all of the following three reasons: a) they did not think it permissible to exhume a body [even for the purpose of reburying it] once it had been buried in the ground; b) they were afraid that if it were buried, its whereabouts would be forgotten with the passing of time; c) embalming and interment in a sarcophagus better preserves the remains than natural burial in the ground where it is a natural process for the body to disintegrate and merge with the ground from which the first human body was created. As we are taught, *For the dust returns to the ground as it was and the spirit returns to God Who gave it* [*Ecclesiastes* 12:7] *(R' Avraham b. HaRambam).*

The translation of וַיִּישֶׂם [root שום], *and he was placed,* follows *Radak* and most commentators who perceive the word to be synonymous with וַיּוּשַׂם. *Ibn Ezra* suggests the root is ישם and the form וַיִּישֶׂם is in the *kal* form meaning *and he* [i.e., whoever was in charge] *placed.* Similar to this is וַיִּיצֶר, *He formed* [root: יצר] in 2:7. [*Onkelos* renders similarly].

וַיִּישֶׂם is an obscure form. Above, with Laban (24:33) it is קְרִי and כְּתִיב and we took that to indicate Laban's vacillating behavior. Perhaps here it points to the unusual procedure — which Joseph himself had ordered for the reasons given above — of keeping a body unburied in a sarcophagus. "It was as if Joseph *had himself placed* in a coffin in Egypt "*(R' Hirsch).*

The mention of *in Egypt* seems

in their fields so that they might be blessed. When Pharaoh heard of this, he ordered that the coffin be lowered into the Nile, the primary source of irrigation in Egypt, so that *all* the fields might be thereby blessed.

Another opinion [*Bereishis Rabbosi*] has it that the Egyptian sorcerers knew that because of their oath to Joseph, the children of Israel could not leave Egypt without Joseph's remains. It was they who ordered the coffin lowered into the Nile so the Israelites would never find it. When the Israelites saw this they despaired of ever being redeemed. That is why they cried וַיִּישֶׂם [*and he was placed*] which is homiletically to be interpreted as two words: "וַי, *Woe,* יָשָׂם, *that he was placed into that coffin!"*

Still another view is that the brothers themselves lowered Joseph's coffin into the Nile so that the Egyptians would not deify his tomb.

In any event, as we learn in *Sotah* 13a, at the Exodus Moses had to pray for a miracle to locate Joseph's remains. This will be cited אי״ה in the *comm.* to *Exod.* 13:19.

superfluous. Perhaps it points to the contrast to his father's burial. His father had himself brought to Canaan immediately after his death. Joseph had no alternative [see *v.* 25 s.v. וְהַעֲלִיתֶם] but to be kept in a coffin until he could be brought to Canaan *(R' Hirsch).*

... The presence in Egypt of Joseph's coffin symbolized that his spirit would remain with his children during the hardships awaiting them *in Egypt.* On this note of moral comfort, *Genesis* comes to an end ... The end of the Patriarchal epoch is not a conclusion, but a beginning. The nucleus of the future "nation of Priests" has been created and firmly established. Though a period of suffering and trial is about to begin, the nation will emerge from it with its spiritual strength formed to endure for all time *(R' Munk).*

According to the Masoretic note appearing at the end of the *Sidrah,* there are 85 verses in the *Sidrah,* numerically corresponding to the mnemonic פֶּ״ה אֶל פֶּ״ה [literally *'mouth to mouth'* (each word פֶּה equals 85)]. This alludes to the theme of our *Sidrah,* in which Jacob spoke to his children, relating to them the blessings that would form the core of their mission for all time. In the mnemonic of our *Sidrah, Harav David Feinstein,* who interprets these Masoretic notes, finds support for his contention that they are meant not only as convenient memory devices but to encapsulate the message of the *Sidrah.* If nothing were intended except a reminder that there are 85 verses, it would have been sufficient to use only the word פֹּה, *mouth* or פֹּה, *here* — but this would tell us nothing about the *sidrah* itself, therefore it was expanded to פֶּה אֶל פֶּה, *mouth to mouth.*

The *Haftarah* begins with *I Kings* 2:1 וַיִּקְרְבוּ יְמֵי דָוִד.

Most Chumashim conclude with the following note:

The Book of Bereishis contains 1,534 verses. The mnemonic is א״ך ל״ד [the א with a dot over it=1,000; the final ך =500; ל=30; ד=4];

The phrase וְעַל חַרְבְּךָ תִחְיֶה, *and by your sword you shall live* [27:40] marks the midpoint of the Book;

It contains 12 *Parshiyos* [weekly portions], the mnemonic being **זֶ״ה** שְׁמִי לְעֹלָם [*Exod.* 3:15]: *This is My name forever/for concealment;*

Its *Sidros* [smaller Masoretic divisions according to the Triennial cycle once in use in *Eretz Yisrael*] number 43, the mnemonic being: **גַּ״ם** בָּרוּךְ יִהְיֶה [27:33]: *He too, shall be blessed;*

Its chapters number 50, the mnemonic being: ה׳ חָנֵּנוּ **לְ״ךָ** קִוִּינוּ [*Isaiah* 33:2]: *O HASHEM be gracious to us, in You we have hoped;*

The total number of פְּתוּחוֹת, traditional 'open' line divisions between Masoretic chapters in Torah Scrolls, is 43; while the סְתוּמוֹת, 'closed' smaller spaced divisions, number 48, totaling 91 chapters. The mnemonic is **צֵ״א** אַתָּה וְכָל הָעָם אֲשֶׁר בְּרַגְלֶיךָ [*Exod.* 11:8]: *Go out, you and all the people who follow you.*

נשלם סדר ויחי
ונשלם ספר בראשית בעזרת האל
חזק

Meir Zlotowitz
Sivan, 5741/June 1981
Brooklyn, New York

ArtScroll Tanach Series®

A traditional commentary on the Books of the Bible

Rabbi Nosson Scherman/Rabbi Meir Zlotowitz
General Editors

Bereishis

VOL. I(a)

בראשית	BEREISHIS
נח	NOACH
לך לך	LECH LECHA
וירא	VAYEIRA
חיי שרה	CHAYEI SARAH
תולדות	TOLDOS

Foreword / דברי פתיחה

HaGaon HaRav Mordechai Gifter

Telshe Rosh HaYeshivah

BEREISHIS

GENESIS / A NEW TRANSLATION WITH A COMMENTARY ANTHOLOGIZED FROM TALMUDIC, MIDRASHIC AND RABBINIC SOURCES.

Published by

Mesorah Publications, Ltd.

Translation and commentary by
Rabbi Meir Zlotowitz

Overviews by
Rabbi Nosson Scherman

FIRST EDITION — SIX VOLUMES
Two Impressions . . . June, 1977 - November, 1982

SECOND EDITION — COMPLETE IN TWO VOLUMES
First Impression . . . June, 1986
Second Impression . . . April, 1988
Third Impression . . . May, 1989
Fourth Impression . . . July, 1991
Fifth Impression . . . September, 1995

Published and Distributed by
MESORAH PUBLICATIONS, Ltd.
4401 Second Avenue
Brooklyn, New York 11232

Distributed in Europe by
J. LEHMANN HEBREW BOOKSELLERS
20 Cambridge Terrace
Gateshead, Tyne and Wear
England NE8 1RP

Distributed in Australia & New Zealand by
GOLDS BOOK & GIFT CO.
36 William Street
Balaclava 3183, Vic., Australia

Distributed in Israel by
SIFRIATI / A. GITLER — BOOKS
4 Bilu Street
P.O.B. 14075
Tel Aviv 61140

Distributed in South Africa by
KOLLEL BOOKSHOP
22 Muller Street
Yeoville 2198, Johannesburg, South Africa

THE ARTSCROLL TANACH SERIES®
BEREISHIS / GENESIS SECTION I

ISBN
Two Volume Set 0-89906-362-4 (hard cover

Typography by CompuScribe at ArtScroll Studios, Ltd.
1969 Coney Island Avenue / Brooklyn, N.Y. 11223 / (718) 339-1700

Printed in the United States of America by Moriah Offset
Bound by Sefercraft, Inc., Brooklyn, N.Y.

This work on Sefer Bereishis
is lovingly dedicated by the author
to the memory of his mother

הרבנית פרומא בת ר׳ חיים צבי ע״ה

Rebetzin Fannie Zlotowitz ע״ה

נפ׳ יב טבת תשמ״ה

Like multitudes of Jews, she and her husband came to America
in the days of steerage and tenements, over half a century ago.
But unlike most, they held fast to their roots.
Her pride was her husband, the gaon, שליט״א
who plumbed undisturbed the depths of Talmudic wisdom.
She inspired him in his learning and his commitment
to maintain the highest standards of rabbinical service.
Together they helped prepare the American soil
for today's lush crop of Torah scholars and communities.
Her ambition was that her children grow up
to bring pride to her forebears.
Her duty was to help the institutions and individuals who depended
on her warm heart and respected leadership.
She succeeded as did few others.
Wise, devoted, noble and kind;
she was the quintessential Jewish matriarch.
And the vineyard she planted will honor her memory
for generations to come.

תנצב״ה

Table of Contents

סדר בראשית/Sidrah Bereishis

◆§ סדר נח/Sidrah Noach

◆§ סדר לך-לך / Sidrah Lech-Lecha

◆§ סדר וירא / Sidrah Vayeira

◆§ סדר חיי־שרה/Sidrah Chayei-Sarah

* *Lot and his daughters are discussed in the Overview to Ruth.*

סדר תולדת / Sidrah Toldos

הסכמת הגאון האמיתי שר התורה ועמוד ההוראה
מורנו ורבנו מרן ר׳ משה פיינשטיין זצוקללה״ה

RABBI MOSES FEINSTEIN
455 F. D. R. DRIVE
NEW YORK, N. Y. 10002
OREGON 7.1222

משה פיינשטיין
ר״מ תפארת ירושלים
בנוא יארק

בע״ה

הנה ידידי הרב הנכבד מאד **מוהר״ר מאיר בן ידידי הרב הגאון ר׳ אהרן זלאטאוויץ** שליט״א אשר כבר נתפרסם בספריו על חמש המגילות בשפה האנגלית המדוברים ביותר במדינה זו אשר קבץ דברים יקרים ופנינים נחמדים מספרי רבותינו נ״ע אשר הם מעוררים לאהבת התורה וקיום המצות וחזוק האמונה בהשי״ת ויש מזה תועלת לקרב לב הרחוקים לאבינו שבשמים ולקיים מצותיו, ונשא לבו לחבר ספר כעין זה שהוא ביאור חשוב על התורה וכבר ראה אותו בני הרה״ג ר׳ דוד שליט״א ושבחוהו מאד, אשר על כן דבר טוב הוא שמדפיסו ומוציאו לאור עולם להגדיל אהבת השי״ת ותורתו הקדושה ואמונתנו הטהורה וקיום מצותיו.

וגם אני מברך את ידידי הנכבד **מוהר״ר נתן שערמאן** שליט״א אשר הוסיף נופך בפתיחת הספר בדברים המושכין את הלב לתורה ויראת השי״ת שיצליח מאד בכל מעשיו בפרט בעבודת החינוך אשר עוסק בזה בכל כחו לקדש שם שמים. ועל זה באתי על החתום ביום א׳ לסדר בהעלתך את הנרות י״ב סיון תשל״ז.

נאום משה פיינשטיין

מכתב ברכה מאאמו"ר
הרב הגאון ר' אהרן זלאטאוויץ שליט"א

בעזהשי"ת

הרב אהרן זלאטאוויץ

Rabbi Aron Zlotowitz

CONGREGATION ETZ CHAIM ANSHEI LUBIN
EXECUTIVE DIRECTOR: BOARD OF ORTHODOX RABBIS OF BROOKLYN

RESIDENCE:
1134 EAST 9 STREET
BROOKLYN, N.Y. 11230
(212) 252-9188

RABBI A. ZLOTOWITZ of Brooklyn N.Y.

מכתב ברכה
ממרן הגאון ר׳ גדלי׳ הלוי שארר זצוקלה״ה

גדלי׳ הלוי שארר
מתיבתא תורה ודעת

בס"ד, ט"ז סיון תשל"ז לפ"ק

לכבוד ידידי המפורסם בפעולותיו
בשדה החינוך ובהפצת אור התורה,
הרה"ג ר׳ נתן שערמאן שליט"א

אחרי דרך מבוא השלום,

מאד שמחתי להתבשר אשר כבודו קבל על עצמו לסייע בידי המוציאים לאור את החמשה חומשי תורה מתורגם בשפה אנגלית. כמעשהו בראשון, בהחמש מגילות אשר הם תהלה בפי כל, כך מעשהו בשני. ואמינא יישר חילו להרה"ג ר׳ מאיר יעקב זלאטאוויץ שליט"א אשר הפליא לעשות בתרגומו לבאר את המקראות עפ"י המסורה שמסרו לנו חז"ל וללקט מכל ספרי המפרשים, ראשונים ואחרונים המצויים ובלתי מצויים, הכל כלשון צח וקל.

במיוחד יש לציין עבודת כבודו אשר חיבר הקדמה ארוכה לכל מגילה ומגילה לבאר את תוכנה ולגלות את האורות הגנוזים בה עפ"י גדולי חכמינו ז"ל, כן עתה עומד לתת הקדמות לכל פרשיות התורה, אשר בודאי יהי׳ זה לתועלת גדולה לכל הלומדים להבנת הענין עפ"י השקפת חז"ל.

בזה קאמינא לפעלא טבא: יישר! יצליחהו ה׳ בכל מעשיו לזכות את הרבים, וכיון "דנבט נבט" (תענית ד ת"ח כיון שיצא שמו הולך וגדל למעלה (רש"י),
כעתירת ידי"נ הדו"ש ואשרו כל הימים החותם בברכה והוקרה

גדלי׳ הלוי שארר

מכתב ברכה
ממרן הגאון ר׳ מרדכי גיפטער שליט״א

בעה״י — ו׳ עש״ק במדבר, מ״ז למטמונים, תשל״ז — פה ירושלים עיה״ק, תוב״ב

מע״כ ידינ״ע הרב הנעלה **ר׳ מאיר**, נ״י, שלום וברכה נצח!

באתי בזה להביע ברכתי מקרב ולב למפעלו החדש בסדרת ספרי קדש של ארט-סקרול, תרגום וביאור החומש, תורה שבכתב, לשפה המדבורת. כבר הגדיל ידידי לקדש שם שמים בעבודתו על המגילות, וקשה היא כמה עבודה זו על החומש, אבל כפי מדת הקושי כן יגדל שכרו, ושכר כל הצוות שעמו בעבודת הקדש.

מן המעט היה לפני מעלי ההגהה הנני דן על הכלל כולו, שידידי מוציא מתח״י דבר נאה ומתוקן, וכן בנוגע לסקירה הכללות בפתיחת הספר, פרי מחשבתו של ידידנו **הרב ר׳ נתן**, נ״י, שהשקיע בדבריו מאדני יסוד האמונה של רבותינו הרמח״ל ומהר״ל זצ״ל, דברים שהם קילורין לעינים כהות לאור באור אמונה טהורה. ועיקר הכל, שזהו המפעל הראשון המביא לקהל את תרגום ובאור התוה״ק לפי המסורה בשפה האנגלית, וזה מכלל ה,,באר היטב״.

יתברכו ידידי וכל הצוות אשר אתו בעבודה גדולה זו, ותרבה החכמה והדעת למען נזכה לאותו היעוד של ,,ומלאה הארץ דעה את ה׳ כמים לים מכסים״.

בברכת קבלת תורה באהבה בחג שבועות שמח,

אוהבו מלונ״ח,
מרדכי

Chronology / Time Line: *Adam to Jacob*

Name	Years	Born	Died
Adam	930	1	930
Seth	912	130	1042
Enosh	905	235	1140
Kenan	910	325	1235
Mehalalel	895	395	1290
Yered	962	460	1422
Chanoch	365	622	987
Methuselah	969	687	1656
Lemech	777	874	1651
Noah	950	1056	2006
Shem	600	1558	2158
Arpachshad	438	1658	2096
Shelach	433	1693	2126
Eber	464	1723	2187
Peleg	239	1757	1996
Reu	239	1787	2026
Serug	230	1819	2049
Nachor	148	1849	1997
Terach	205	1878	2083
Abraham	175	1948	2123
Isaac	180	2048	2228
Jacob	147	2108	2255

1656 The Flood

1996 The Dispersion

◆§ Preface to the Two-Volume Edition

This compact two-volume edition of Sefer Bereishis *contains every word of the original six-volume* Bereishis. *It represents six years of intensive research, of days and nights poring through classic and little-known commentaries, and countless consultations with human repositories of Hashem's Torah, many of whom have since been called to the* Yeshivah shel Maalah. *It is in response to many requests that this work is now being published in a form that will make it accessible to a broader public.*

Although several years have passed since the last ArtScroll Chumash volume, this hiatus will soon end אי״ה. *My esteemed colleague Reb Hershel Goldwurm and I have been writing commentaries on the balance of Chumash, and they will be published over the course of the next few years.*

❦ ❦ ❦

The decade has witnessed the loss of some of the Torah giants of the American Torah community: Maranan v'rabbanan, the geonim and tzaddikim HARAV MOSHE FEINSTEIN, HARAV YAAKOV KAMENETZKY, HARAV GEDALIAH SCHORR *and* HARAV SHNEUR KOTLER זצ״ל. *They guided and inspired the ArtScroll Series since its inception. The burgeoning Torah communities on this continent are the monuments to their greatness and vision. Part of this monument is the ArtScroll Series, now well over a hundred titles, spanning Tanach, Mishnah liturgy, biography, history, and youth literature. Their vision remains before us always and we pray that we may approach their goals and standards.*

The last year has also seen the loss of my mother ע״ה, *and it is as a* z'chus *to her memory that this work is being published. She was a woman of rare nobility, grace, and* yiras shamayim. *She was the quintessential Jewish mother, an* isha k'sheirah osah r'tzon baalah — *a woman who inspired my father* שליט״א *to excel in his learning and service to the* klal, *and who always tried to imbue her children with the richness of Torah values. Her passing was a greivous loss to our family and all who knew her; it was a microcosm of the loss felt by* klal Yisrael *at the recent passing of the* gedolei Torah.

May their memory and the Harbotzas Torah *they have inspired be a* z'chus *for our family: my dear wife, Rachel, my children Gedaliah, Estie, Faigie, Dvorah, Tziviah, Yisroel, Boruch and Chaim, and for my father, HaGaon Harav Aron Zlotowitz* שליט״א*, and mother-in-law Mrs. Chaya Schulman* תחי׳*. We have been fortunate in having an older generation to serve as our model of* ahavas Torah *and* yiras shamayim. *May that example be the prime focus of our lives and we be worthy of the blessing of the prophet Isaiah:* My spirit that is upon you and My words that I have placed in your mouth shall not be withdrawn from your mouth, nor from the mouth of your offspring, nor from the mouth of you offspring's offspring [Isaiah *59:20-21*].

Our revered mentor, the Telshe Rosh Yeshiva, HAGAON HARAV MORDECHAI GIFTER שליט״א *refers to Mesorah Publications as "Yeshivas ArtScroll." Indeed it is. The "Kollel" of authors and editors that has enriched our people with so much Torah is a source of constant inspiration. In particular, I must mention the dear friends with whom I have the privilege of working on a daily basis: Reb Nosson Scherman, Reb Shea Brander, Reb Avi Gold, Reb Hershel Goldwurm, Reb Yehezkel Danzinger, Reb Shimon Golding, Reb Eli Kroen, Reb Yussie Timinsky, Michael Zivitz and our office staff, Lea Freier, Estie Zlotowitz, Malkie Helfgott, and Simie Gluck; and Stephen Blitz and his family who are about to move to* Eretz Yisrael *but who will remain close from afar.* Hashem Yisborach *has permitted us to be a conduit of His word. May we continue to merit that supreme blessing and privilege.*

Meir Zlotowitz

Iyar 5746
Brooklyn, NY

AUTHORS' PREFACE TO VOLUME I OF THE ORIGINAL SIX VOLUME EDITION

וְכָתַבְתָּ עַל הָאֲבָנִים
אֶת כׇּל דִּבְרֵי הַתּוֹרָה הַזֹּאת
בַּאֵר הֵיטֵב (דברים כז:ח) —
— בְּשִׁבְעִים לָשׁוֹן (סוטה לב.)

And you shall inscribe upon the stones
all the words of this Torah
to be well understood (*Deut.* 27:8)
— In seventy languages (*Sotah* 32a).

In beginning a commentary on the Torah, we are siezed by awe and trepidation. Our minds turn to the words with which Ramban prefaced his commentary, one of the revered classics of Torah literature:

> *I shall begin to write ... with terror, fear, trembling, sweat, and dread ... knowing clearly that the egg of an ant is not as puny compared to the loftiest sphere as my wisdom is small and my knowledge stunted compared to the mysteries of the Torah, hidden in her home, concealed in her chamber ...*

If such were the thoughts of Ramban, then what are we to say?

Nevertheless the work was begun, encouraged by Roshei HaYeshivah and Torah scholars, and buoyed by the good wishes and appreciation of thousands of readers who have felt that, in the ArtScroll editions of the Five Megillos, a genuine need was perceived and filled. The work was undertaken in the hope that it would provide a new dimension of understanding for English readers from the entire spectrum of Torah knowledge, from rank beginners to accomplished scholars.

Translations of Torah and some of the classic commentaries are available, to be sure, but no single work brings together so wide a range of authors spanning two thousand years of Torah literature as does this one.

THE TRANSLATION

Following our approach in the previous volumes of the Five Megillos, a new translation was prepared which, in contemporary, lucid English attempts to render the Text in a manner faithful to the exegesis of the Sages. The wealth of Targumim and commentaries with their varying interpretations raised the serious question of how to decide upon a definitive translation. Upon the guidance of the Roshei Hayeshivah, the commentary of Rashi has been followed in all instances because he is the 'Father of Commentators' and because for nine centuries, the study of Chumash has been synonymous with Chumash-Rashi. As Ramban says in his introduction, לוֹ מִשְׁפַּט הַבְּכוֹרָה*, to him [Rashi] belongs the right of the firstborn.*

As a result, there are cases where our translation differs from that familiar to most readers. For example, the first verse in Bereishis, commonly rendered 'In the beginning God created the heavens and the earth', *now becomes, following Rashi*: 'In the beginning of God's creating the heavens and the earth.' *The familiar* 'And the earth was without form and void' *of verse 2, now becomes:* 'when the earth was astonishingly empty.'

The translation sometimes deviates slighty from the literal in the interest of English syntax or idiom. When this occurs,the literal translation is always given in brackets in the commentary.

HASHEM'S NAME

Wherever the Hebrew Four Letter Name of God appears, it is translated: "HASHEM," i.e. 'THE Name' — the Holy Name of God. Where the Hebrew has Elokim, the more general and less 'personal' Name of the Deity — it is translated 'God' [see comm. to 1:1, 2:4.] Although the name of the Creator is generally written 'G-d' and not spelled out in its entirety, this Book is a portion of the Holy Scriptures and the full Four Letter Name of HASHEM appears in the Hebrew; it would have been ludicrous to abbreviate the spelling of the Name in English. אֶרֶץ יִשְׂרָאֵל*, was translated* Eretz Yisrael *(Land of Israel). Where the word 'Israel' is found, it refers to the Jewish people in general, not always specifically in distinction with the Tribes of Judah.*

TRANSLITERATION

A cross between the Sephardi and Ashkenazi transliteration of Hebrew words was used: Ashkenazi consonants, so to speak, with Sephardi vowels. Thus: Akeidas Yitzchak, *not* Akeidas Yitzchok; Bereishis *not* Bereishit, *etc.*

Proper names from Scripture that have become generally accepted have been retained. Thus, for example: Adam, Abel, Noah, Methuselah, and Abraham, were retained and not changed to conform to our method of transliteration. However, when these names appear in Talmudic or Midrashic citations we have conformed to our method by using: Yitzchak, Yehudah, Yaakov, etc. Although there are several inconsistencies, the style has generally been held throughout the work.

THE COMMENTARY

The commentary attempts to explain each verse with its varied meanings and nuances as they were understood by the Sages and commentators from the days of the Talmud and Midrash down to contemporary times. At all times the primary goal was to remove surface difficulties and thereby enable the reader to study a verse with the feeling that he understands it clearly. Thus, several redundancies were left in the commentary when it was felt that the reader would benefit from seeing a similar comment keyed to different verses, thereby not burdening him to search through myriad cross-references.

The pithy, meaning-laden words of Rashi, Ibn Ezra, Ramban *and others are often illuminated by references from other parts of the sea of Torah. They have been assembled to create a tapestry rich in insight and suggestive of further areas of research for the interested reader.*

The commentary is an anthology in the sense that it draws upon scores of sources, but it is also original in its blend of material and its frequent presentation of the author's bracketed comments. 'There are seventy facets to Torah' and myriad wisdom in its every verse. The commentary offers a wide range of such diverse insights for all of them are like the many sparks flashing from the impact of hammer against rock — the lightning flashes that are produced when great minds are honed against the words of the Torah (see Shabbos 88b).

Thus, the commentary is designed to fill several needs. First, when necessary, it explains the derivation of the translation. This is followed by Rashi's *interpretation. Where there are surface difficulties in Rashi, they are resolved by citing the Talmudic and Midrashic sources upon which he based himself, or by citing the standard commentaries to Rashi: Mizrachi; Gur Aryeh; Levush; Tzeidah LaDerech; Rav Ovadiah Bertinoro, or others.*

The major commentators were then consulted for interpretations close to פְּשַׁט*, the plain meaning of the Text. In general chronological order, they are primarily: Machberes Menachem; Ibn Janach; Rav Saadiah Gaon; Rashbam; Ibn Ezra; Rambam (who elucidates the early part of Bereishis in Moreh Nevuchim); B'chor Shor; Radak; Ramban; R' Meyuchas; Chizkuni; R' Bachya; Abarbanel; Akeidas Yitzchak; Sforno; Alshich; Or HaChaim; Vilna Gaon, Kli Yakar, on to the later commentaries of Hirsch; HaRechasim L'Bikah; HaK'sav V'Hakaballah; Malbim; Imrei Shefer; N'tziv; and Rav David Zvi Hoffmann.*

Much use was also made of The Seven Days of the Beginning, *(Feldheim Pub.), a brilliant study of the Creation Chapter by Harav Dr. Eli Munk, presently residing in Eretz Yisrael.*

Of invaluable assistance were Torah Sheleimah, *the encyclopedic masterpiece of Harav Menachem Kasher;* P'shutto Shel Mikra *by Harav Shimon Kasher; Harav Chaim Dov Chavel's annotated edition of* Ramban *(Mossad Harav Kook; Shilo Pub.); and Dr. Isaac Levi's translation of* Hirsch *(Judaica Press), from which selections were adapted.*

A comprehensive bibliography of all commentaries consulted as well as biographical sketches of the commentators will appear א״יה *after* Deuteronomy *along with exhaustive Subject, Scriptural, and Rabbinic Indices embracing the commentary to all Five Books of the Torah.*

The interpretations attributed to Harav Mordechai Gifter, Harav David Feinstein, and Harav David Cohen were the product of preliminary discussions with the author or of verbal or written comments on the manuscript.

All bracketed comments not specifically attributed are those of Rabbi Meir Zlotowitz.

Care was also taken not to lose sight of another dimension of Torah: The Aggadic, philosophical, and homiletical expositions of the Sages and commentators.

Obviously, the commentary to Torah had to be far more extensive than that of the previously published works in the Series. Every word, every letter of the Torah is laden with law and meaning and there is a limitless wealth of Talmudic and rabbinic commentary. While we have barely scratched the surface, we feel that a representative and valuable anthologized commentary has been offered.

FORMAT OF THE COMMENTARY

In order to simplify for the reader the task of choosing between commentary necessary for an understanding of the text and other, more complex material, we have adopted the graphic format of the Haggadah by Harav Joseph Elias, published as part of the ArtScroll Mesorah Series.

The more analytic, homiletical, and philologically complex comments not crucial to the simple understanding and exposition of the flow of the narrative have been set in smaller type within the commentary.

Material culled from Aggadic, Hashkafah, and mussar-ethical writings are found as footnotes.

The need for such a tri-level division of the commentary was nowhere more keenly felt or necessary than in the first chapter — and especially the first verse — of Bereishis — which is replete *with varying degrees of complexity and interpretation.*

OVERVIEWS

It was felt that in order to make the work complete, an attempt should be made to present each Sidra and major topic in a broad Hashkafah — philosophical persepective. The Overviews draw on a wide range of Talmudic and rabbinic sources in presenting a broad and deep understanding that would not be possible from merely a verse-by-verse study, even one as thorough as that offered in the commentary. Thus, for example, this book is introduced with in-depth perspectives of the role of Torah, the purpose of creation, and the sin of Adam.

WORDS OF CAUTION

While we have endeavored to make this work one deserving the attention of even accomplished scholars, we urge all readers to bear in mind that it is not a substitute for in-depth study of the original source. The ARTSCROLL TANACH SERIES *offers readers an unprecedented taste of the richness of the wide range of Torah literature; those capable of pursuing their own research should utilize the series as a springboard to broaden and deepen their own learning. In addition, the commentary cannot possibly offer every word and nuance of those upon whom it draws. In many cases, study of the original sources will lead a reader to different interpretations and additional insights. This is as it should be for the Torah greats of earlier generations were, in the expression of the Sages, 'like angels compared to men or like men compared to donkeys.'*

IN CONCLUSION

Many of the leading Torah personalities of this generation — most prominently, MARAN HAGAON HARAV MOSHE FEINSTEIN שליט״א *and* MARAN HAGAON HARAV YAAKOV KAMINETZKY שליט״א *— have offered warm encouragement.* MARAN HAGAON HARAV MORDECHAI GIFTER שליט״א*, Rosh HaYeshivah of Telshe Yeshivah has been a tower of support and a fountain of wisdom. Although his every moment is precious, he has graciously allowed us to visit with him in New York and in his home in Wickliffe to offer guidance and advice. Moreover, he has read major portions of the Commentary and Overview and offered copious, sagacious comments by mail and phone. Although his comments are frequently quoted in both, his influence pervades the entire work far out of proportion to the times he is mentioned by name. Moreover, he has graciously written a Hebrew foreword for the work which it is our privilege to provide to the Torah public. Without the gracious support of these Gedolei Hatorah—*אשר מפיהם אנו חיין*—we would not have undertaken the awesome mission of attempting to render the Word of Hashem.*

HARAV DAVID FEINSTEIN שליט״א*, a self-effacing gaon of encyclopedic knowledge, has given unstintingly of himself to encourage and inspire, to criticize and perfect. He read every selection, noting discrepancies, clarifying difficulties, and pointing out new material. His frequently quoted insights are but a small indication of his contribution. His warm concern and encouragement have pervaded this entire undertaking.*

HARAV DAVID COHEN שליט״א*, a rare blend of phenomenal breadth of knowledge and clarity of thought, made himself available far beyond the bounds of friendship. He read, advised, clarified, corrected, and gave generously and freely from the spring of his original thought and wide scholarship. He has left his mark on this work far in excess of the comments attributed to him in this volume.*

Before us is the first volume in an undertaking that will consume years and require a degree of dedication worthy to merit סייעתא דשמיא *needed to achieve success. We are grateful to Hashem Yisborach that He has enabled us to become a vehicle for dissemination of Torah to so great an extent. The acceptance of the* ARTSCROLL TANACH SERIES *on the part of gedolei Torah, bnei hayeshivah, and the broader Torah public has been heartening and inspiring beyond description. But every privilege brings with it a responsibility. If one is granted the ability to accomplish for Torah then it becomes an obligation to do so. The responsibility is awesome for the universe rests upon it.* ישראל ואורייתא וקב״ה חד הוא *— Israel, the Torah, and the Holy One, Blessed be He are one. We pray that we may be granted the strength and ability to utilize the printed word to continue bringing the three closer together* להגדיל תורה ולהאדירה.

In the זכות *of these efforts may our children ascend ever upward on the heights of Torah and* יראת שמים.

Rabbi Nosson Scherman / Meir Zlotowitz

This work is further dedicated to the memory of the author's father:

הגאון ר׳ אהרן זלוטוביץ זצוקלל״ה

HaGaon Rav Aron Zlotowitz זצוקלל״ה

נפטר ג׳ טבת תש״נ

He came to the United States as a young man in 1924 rich in the Torah and tradition of the yeshiva world and high in the esteem of his rebbe, the Lomza Rosh Yeshiva זצ״ל. *The obstacles of his era broke many, but not him, thanks to his own strength and that of his beloved rebbetzin* ע״ה.

He had Shas and poskim at his fingertips, page by page and line by line — and they were his road map at every difficult crossroads. An accomplished mohel, he battled for the integrity of milah against those who sought to dilute its requirements to satisfy the public whim. He was one of those who fought the lonely struggle to elevate the standards of Kashrus supervision. His family rose and retired to the sound of his "blatt Gemara," and lived with his conversation that was always flavored with the wisdom of Chazal. A leader of Agudas HaRabbanim in its most fruitful years and author of Nachalas Aharon, his memory lives in his Torah legacy and the generations of Torah families that survive him.

תנצב״ה

Acknowledgements

The duty is pleasantly mine to express my deepest feelings of gratitude to those who did not allow me to stumble over my own ignorance, and who have graciously given of their time to encourage, inspire, read, and comment upon this work in its various stages:

My father HARAV HAGAON ARON ZLOTOWITZ שליט״א *has given of his paternal guidance and phenomenal storehouse of Torah-scholarship. Many of the selections were discussed with him, and I benefited greatly from his sagely comments. May he and my dear mother be blessed with longevity and* נחת *from their children, grandchildren and greatgrandchildren;*

HARAV JOSEPH ELIAS, *has been intimately involved in the ArtScroll Tanach Series since its inception. His cooperation and incisive comments are deeply appreciated.*

I must likewise express my appreciation to the long-time friends who encouraged me to undertake this work, read the manuscript, and offered suggestions: MR. DAVID H. SCHWARTZ, RABBI BORUCH B. BORCHARDT, RABBI ELI MUNK, RABBI NISSON WOLPIN, RABBI YOSEF WEINBAUM, MR. CHARLES GRANDOVSKY, RABBI BURTON JAFFA, MR. JOSHUA GROSSMAN, *my brother-in-law,* RABBI JACOB KIFFEL, *and my nephew,* REB MEIR PLATNICK. *The finished product is the best testimony to their sincere and productive contribution.*

The staff of ARTSCROLL PRINTING CORP. *under the direction of my friend* ELLIOT SCHWARTZ *has kindly assisted under great pressure to the technical needs of this project. They have my gratitude.*

To REB MEIR (MARTIN) YAROSLAWITZ *of Ziontalis Mfg. Co., a man of rare integrity and competence, goes a very special expression of gratitude. In assuming the role of distributor, he demonstrated a keen sense of responsibility to provide the public with a series of Torah works ambitious in scope and important beyond any yet attempted in English. His dedication to the needs of the project goes far to assure works of maximum quality and beauty.*

The efforts of my friend, ZUNDEL BERMAN, *in disseminating this work to the b'nai hayeshivah for whom it is primarily intended are deeply appreciated.*

A special note of thanks is due my long-time friend RABBI AVIE GOLD *who undertook to meticulously proofread and check the source references. Additionally, he made valuable comments, many of which were incorporated into the final text.* REB BINYAMIN GIFTER *generously volunteered to assist in the proofreading. His assistance has been invaluable and is gratefully acknowledged.*

MRS. JUDY GROSSMAN, *too, has not only given of her personal time to proofread the galleys and help assure the accuracy of the printed page, but has shouldered much of the responsibility of running ArtScroll Studios during my absence while I was compiling this volume. She has our profound gratitude.* MISS RIVA ALPER *has also kindly given of her personal time to proofread the final pages. I am grateful for her efforts.*

Any remaining errors are due to technical reasons beyond their control.

MRS. PEARL EIDLIS *and* MISS ESTHER HARTMAN *have given selfless devotion in preparing the manuscript for the computer. Working under great stress, and from my very complicated manuscript, they responded with much dedication to the project. I am indebted to them.*

There is one person who has remained in the background but whose presence is crucial to the quality of the project. REB SHEA BRANDER'S *mastery of graphics has been highly praised by all who have noted the esthetic beauty of the books in the* ARTSCROLL SERIES. *But that is only a part of the story. He has read and discussed, criticized and recommended. He has thrown himself into the work with an idealistic and boundless passion, submerging all else to its needs, contributing unbelievable hours and concentration. The finished product is the most eloquent testimony to what he has done. No words can express my gratitude.*

In closing, I would again like to share with the readers my profound recognition that the ARTSCROLL TANACH SERIES *would not have achieved its widespread acceptance were it not for the involvement of my* יְדִיד נֶכְבָּד, HARAV NOSSON SCHERMAN, *who continues to distinguish himself as a master of eloquence and clarity, presenting the most abstract Torah concepts in a manner that inspires every level of readership. By enlightening me on methodology of translating obscure phrases and concepts, he has lent the manuscript the benefit of his erudition sensitivity and flowing style.*

My deepest appreciation goes to my wife מנב״ת, RACHEL, *for her constant good cheer, guidance, and astute insights. The work could not have proceeded at such a pace — amidst the duties of* גדול־בָּנִים *and domestic responsibilities — were it not for her constant encouragement. She has created an atmosphere conducive for Torah-study and turned our home into a* בֵּית וַעַד לַחֲכָמִים, *a forum for Torah scholars. May her sincere efforts for Harbatzas Torah be amply rewarded with the blessing most precious to her: that our children may dwell in the 'tent of Torah'.*

I humbly thank the רבש״ע *for giving me the inspiration and strength to begin the task of expounding His holy Torah. May His blessings continue, that His word may be placed* לְעֵינֵי כָּל יִשְׂרָאֵל *in every Jewish heart and home. May we merit to continue this work.*

Meir Zlotowitz

Brooklyn, New York
16 Sivan, 5737

⊰ Foreword / דברי פתיחה ⊱

⊰ Overview

דברי פתיחה
(לתרגום וביאור התורה)

מאת מרן הגאון ר׳ מרדכי גיפטער שליט״א

ר״מ ישיבת טעלז

בן בג בג אומר הפך בה והפך בה דכולא בה ומינה לא תזוע שאין לך מדה טובה הימנה (אבות פ״ה, כ״ב)

א. למדנו התנא שאין לך דבר בעולם, ממה שכונן וברא הקב״ה שאין שרשו ועיקרו בתורת ה׳, ולכן כל החכמות כלולים בה — כדברי הרמב״ן ז״ל בהקדמת פירושו על התורה — ולו חכמנו והשכלנו היינו עומדים על סודות הבריאה מתוך עיון התורה, שהיא ביסודה שמותיו של הקב״ה (הרמב״ן שם) ורק בה תחזה ותראה את האמת (רמב״ם), ובהיות כן הרי טבע הדברים מחייב שיקדיש האדם כל ימי חייו עד לנשימה אחרונה ללמוד התורה, ויהא כל כולו מסור אלי׳ לבל לזוז ממנה אף זיז כל שהוא, שכל עניני החיים נמדדים אך ורק בה ואין היא טעונה השלמה ממקום אחר (מדרש שמואל).

אין פלא איפה שדבר ה׳ בתורתו מתפרש לכמה גוונים — כפטיש יפוצץ סלע, וע׳ פנים לתורה, ואף בחלק המצוה שבתורה — תרי״ג מצוות — המכוון להנהגה המעשית של בן ישראל עלי אדמות שלא ניתן לפוצצו לגוונים שונים, וחיוב המצוה למעשה מסוייג ומוגבל הוא, היינו רק ביחס להמוטל על האדם שמוגבל ומסוייג הוא, וקבעה החכמה העליונה המעשה כפי הנאות להגבלת האדם וכחותיו. אבל זו המצוה עצמה בשרשה שלמעלה ג״כ ע׳ פנים לה, אשר קצת מן האור הנפלא הזה מתגלה לנו בטעמי המצוות.

ולכן מסר לנו הקב״ה בתורתו לא רק תרי״ג מצוות המוטלות עלינו אלא גם „תורה״ ללמדנו גישה לעולם ומלואו, לראות בכל גילוי שכינתו, בין מבחינת הנמצא בין מבחינת פעולת הנמצא, שהכל אך ורק ממנו ית׳, והורה לנו בתורתו התפתחות עולם והתפתחות האנושיות בכלל, ויצירת עם ישראל והתפתחותו, במשימתנו הנשגבה כמובחר

שבעמים, להעיד בעצם ישותנו על הבורא ברוך הוא כאדון עולם ומלכו של עולם — אתם עדי נאום ה׳

אי לזאת א״א לגשת ללימודה של תורה אלא מתוך רוב עמל ויגיעה — אם בחקותי תלכו — שתהיו עמלים בתורה — שלא ככל החכמות חכמת התורה, שאם בכל החכמות ששרשם ממנו ית׳ נתנן הקב״ה לבשר ודם לגשת אליהם כנטולות משרשן, הנה בחכמת התורה כל מציאותה כפי מה שהיא חלק ממנו ית׳ (ט״ז סי׳ רכ״ד) ולכן על האדם להיות עמל ומתיגע להחלץ מכבלי החומר וחשך הטבע להתקרב אליו, ומתוך כך לזכות לאותה מתנת אלקים, הברקה משמים בהבנת שכל העליון של תורה, (הרמב״ם בהקדמה להמורה). ולכן לא יגעתי ומצאתי אל תאמין, שהכל בסופו של דבר רק מציאה הבאה כשכר היגיעה והעמל.

אכן יתכן שאדם ילמוד תורה כדרך למוד כל החכמות וגם אז יראה רב חכמה, אבל לא תורה היא זו אלא חכמה, ועל זה אמרו רז״ל: ,,תורתו מן השפה ולחוץ״ — והלומד תורה באופן זה הוא שאמרו רז״ל: למשמאילים בה סמא דמותא.

ב. תורת ה׳ ניתנה למשה בסיני בכתב ובעל פה, שנתפרש לו בעל פה פירושה של תורה, ולכן כל סטי׳ מתורה שבעל פה היא סתירת התורה, וזו היא בכלל כפירה המונעת מקור חיים, ואין לו לזה הכופר חלק לעולם הבא (רמב״ם בהקדמתו לי״ד, ובה׳ תשובה פ״ג, ה״ח)

ומכלל יסוד תורה שבעל פה לבל ישלטו ידי זרים בתורת ה׳, וטהרתה של תורה נשמרת בתורה שבעל פה — תוס׳ גיטין ס׳, ב׳, ד״ה אתמוהי קא מתמה.

בכלל למוד המקרא — המתחיל מהיות הבן בן חמש — הוא למוד תורה שבכתב כפי שהיא מתפרשת בתורה שבעל פה, שאין זה מכלל בן עשר למשנה, אלא הוא מכלל למוד המקרא עצמו. לא יתכן ללמוד עין תחת עין מבלי לפרשו — ממון, לא יתכן ללמוד פרי עץ הדר מבלי לפרשו אתרוג, וכן בכל המצוות. וכן גם בחלק התורה שאין בה ממצות מעשיות יש בה הרבה שהתורה שבכתב א״א לצאת בה תורת למוד מקרא מבלי לפרשה ע״פ תורה שבע״פ ולכן קבעו לנו רז״ל ללמוד שנים מקרא ואחד תרגום, וקדמונינו ז״ל קבעו הלימוד בפירוש רש״י כתרגום, אשר זוהי צורת למוד המקרא בקרב ישראל.

ג. תורת ה׳ כחלק ממנו יתברך אינה ניתנת להתפרש אלא מתוך אור תורה וכפי מה שיתרומם אדם להדבק בו ית׳ כן יזכהו למתנת ה׳ בהבנת תורתו. כשדבר ה׳ דברו במעמד הר סיני ונתן לעמו עשרת הדברים,

אשר הם שרש כל תרי״ג מצוות, דבר דברים אשר לכאורה נתפסים בשכל אנוש, ואינם בגדר חקים, כגון איסור רציחה, ניאוף, גזל, שביתת השבת, ואף גם מצות האמונה בבורא והשגחתו. ושמעתי מאדמו״ר הגאון אב״ד ור״מ דטלז ז״ל הי״ד למה זה לא דבר ה׳ דברים שאינם נתפסים בשכל אדם כגון פרה אדומה, שעטנז, מאכלות אסורות. והיתה תשובתו, כי נהפוך הוא, דבר שאין נתפס בשכל אנוש, אם מקבלם האדם כציווי ה׳ יעשם כפי מה שנצטוה, לא כן בדברים הנתפסים בשכלו, והרי כל העמים יש להם חק האוסר ניאוף, אבל גירוי תאות הניאוף קרוי אצלם אומנות. כולם יש להם חק האוסר את הרציחה, אבל הקומניזם חקק צו של רציחה לצורך העמדת הקומניזם, וכן בכל חוקי אנוש. אכן כששמעו ישראל הדברים מפי ה׳ שמעו באיסור רציחה שהמלבין פני חבירו ברבים הרי זו רציחה, וכששמעו איסור הניאוף שמעו שהמטמא אשת חבירו — זה היורד לאומנותו של חבירו. פירושה של תורה לאמתתה דורשת מהאדם שמיעת קול ה׳.

שמענו בזה ציור מהגאון המופלא בתורתו וצדקתו ר׳ מרדכי פוגרמנסקי ז״ל. הכניסו פעם לאדם לתוך מרתף חשוך ושם ציור נפלא מאד מאחד מגדולי הציירים, ויסתכל בו ויאמר,וכי מעשה אומנות היא זו. ויעלו את הציור לחדר מואר, ויקרינו עליו קרן אור באופן מסויים שהבליט את כל קוי הציור, קו לקו, ויתפעל המסתכל מעומק חכמת הציור. רק בהקרנת אור תורה אפשר לראות שלמות התורה הקדושה לכל קוי׳, אבל אם בשכל אנוש יסתכל אדם, הרי הוא מוריד לתורה למרתף חשוך.

אם זוהי גישת בן ישראל לתורת ה׳ אז יזכה לאותו נועם עליון של ערבות התורה אשר עלי׳ נתפלל בברכת ,,והערב נא ה׳ אלקינו את דברי תורתך בפינו״ וכו׳. וראה האיך הבינו בזה רבותינו הראשונים ז״ל. ,,אבל מצות לימוד שהוא ענין ציור הלב וידיעת האמת, עיקר הציווי הוא כדי לצייר האמת ולהתענג וליהנות במדע לשמח לבבו ושכלו, כדכתיב פקודי ה׳ ישרים משמחי לב, וכו׳. הילכך לא שייך למימר במצות תלמוד דלא ניתן ליהנות, שעיקר מצותו הוא ההנאה והתענוג במה שמשיג ומבין בלימודו״. (רבינו אברהם מן ההר ז״ל בפי׳ לנדרים מ״ח, א׳.)

יעמידנו ה׳ בקרן אורה למען התענג עליו ית׳.

An Overview— Torah — Written and Oral

בנוהג שבעולם מלך בשר ודם בונה פלטין אינו בונה מדעת עצמו אלא מדעת אומן, והאומן אינו בונה מדעת עצמו אלא דיפתראות ופנקסאות יש לו לדעת האיך הוא עושה חדרים האיך הוא עושה פשפשין. כך היה הקב״ה מביט בתורה ובורא את העולם (בראשית רבה)

It is customary that when a human being builds a palace, he does not build it according to his own wisdom, but according to the wisdom of a craftsman. And the craftsman does not build according to his own wisdom, rather he has plans and records in order to know how to make rooms and corridors. The Holy One, blessed be He, did the same. He looked into the Torah and created the world (Midrash).

I. Master Plan of Creation

The Blueprint

The architect begins with an idea, and from that idea his plan emerges.

The well-planned building is built around a concept. The architect begins with an idea, and from that idea his plan emerges. The intricacies of construction may involve scores of contractors, hundreds of subcontractors, thousands of suppliers, tens of thousands of workers, millions of tools and parts and nails and screws. There may be piping enough to stretch for miles, wiring enough to span a continent. But everything unfolds from that single concept.

How many people will recognize the central idea in the finished construction? Very few. Most will know the location of elevators and corridors — the ones they need for their own particular purposes. They come to work every day for years and never know where the pillars are that keep thousands of tons of rubble from crashing down upon them. Architects may visit the structure and marvel at it; but laymen will wonder what there is to admire. The graceful strength of a classic suspension bridge can be an inspiration to engineers and designers, but the thousands of people who cross it daily will mutter about delays, strain to gain an extra few seconds, and never stop to think that they ride on a tribute to the human intellect.

To thoroughly understand a structure one must know its plan, but it takes much training and uncommon brilliance to look through thousands of pages of blueprint and decipher the single unifying concept out of which they all grew and which gives them all meaning. But even without the ability to find the architect's purpose, every intelligent person knows that there is a purpose to the plan, and that the voluminous material in the blueprints is there only to make it possible for the plan to take shape.

First and Last

The Sabbath was the crowning feature of creation, but it was not created first.

In praising the holy Sabbath, Rav Shlomo Alkabetz says in his classic *L'cha Dodi*, סוֹף מַעֲשֶׂה בְּמַחֲשָׁבָה תְּחִלָּה, *the end of deed, is first in thought.* The Sabbath was the crowning feature of creation, but it was not created first. A home is built to provide living quarters for a family, but furnishings and interior decoration are the last things that go into it. A yeshiva is built to provide a study hall where the sounds of eternity will reverberate day and night, but bookstacks, desks, chairs, and students will enter only after the bulldozers and bricklayers have long since left.

Bookstacks, desks, chairs, and students will enter only after the bulldozers and bricklayers have long since left.

The first thought of parents planning a home for their family is of a comfortable and wholesome apartment; and the first thought of the *rosh hayeshiva* seeking to perpetuate the study of Torah is of the study hall where his students can forge themselves onto the eternal chain. Nevertheless, before that final goal can be realized, there is a long list of tasks that seemingly have no relationship to the goal, but they are indispensable to its attainment: obtaining the land, engaging an architect, formulating a concept, reducing it to a blueprint, finding a builder, obtaining financing, and so on and so on. Finally, when all the work is done, that original dream — a home, a study hall — has taken shape.

The more accomplished the person, the more ambitious the goal; and the more difficult and complex the road to its attainment.

'End of deed, first in thought' — all intelligent people live their lives this way: they decide upon a goal and then work their way toward its fulfillment. The more accomplished the person, the more ambitious the goal; and the more difficult and complex the road to its attainment. In human experience, however, it is all too common that, in the struggle to achieve their goals, people forget the end and throw themselves so mindlessly into the means that they become ends unto themselves. They may acquire a home in order to live a more comfortable life only to enslave themselves and their substance to the maintenance and never-ending beautification of the home which has become their master. Or people attempt to gain power in order to help others, and descend to a continuous pursuit of ever more power and glory built upon the hapless shoulders of the erstwhile beneficiaries.

God's Blueprint

God, too, created the world from a plan and for a purpose. His plan was the Torah which preceded the world *(Shabbos* 88b), and His purpose was that man find the meaning and the goal of creation in the Torah: *'He looked into the Torah and created the world' (Midrash).*

Torah was the blueprint of creation.

Torah was the blueprint of creation. It is commonly thought that, following the failure of the human race and the emergence of Abraham and his descendants as people worthy of bearing the privilege of becoming God's chosen people, God decided upon the commandments which he transmitted to the Jews through Moses. Nothing could be more wrong. The Torah and its commandments were not designed in response to the demands and needs of earthly life. The Torah pre-existed earth; and the universe as we know it was designed to conform to the requirements of the Torah.

The Torah pre-existed earth; and the universe as we know it was designed to conform to the requirements of the Torah

Matzah is a food that, by its nature, is prepared and baked in haste, without the slightest delay — therefore, God tailored the history of His people to conform to the nature of *matzah*. They were exiled to Egypt and emerged only through a chain of circumstances that required them to leave the land of their captivity in such haste that their dough had no time to rise and form bread instead of *matzah*. True, we say that *matzah* is זכר ליציאת מצרים, a remembrance of the Exodus from Egypt. But that, too, is ordained in the Torah which preceded not only the exile, but the very creation. The events of the Egyptian exile and its aftermath are themselves nothing more than the physical translation of the spiritual content of the Torah *(Bais Halevi)*.

The events of the Egyptian exile and its aftermath are themselves nothing more than the physical translation of the spiritual content of the Torah.

It was this very argument which Moses advanced to the heavenly angels when they angrily contended that man was too lowly and degraded to be given the holy gift of Torah. Moses answered that the Torah says, *'Thou shalt not steal'* — but the angels have no need or temptation to steal. The Torah commands, *'Honor your father and your mother'* — but the angels have no parents.

Surely Moses could not have meant that the Torah had no place in the higher spiritual spheres that we refer to as heaven — the Torah existed before the creation and is surely not dependent on man's puny efforts or his earthbound intellect. Indeed, it is clear that the angels study Torah on a level far beyond that of human beings. Instead Moses was pointing to earth and man as the instruments selected by the Divine Architect for the fulfillment of the Torah's demands. If God looked into the Torah and created the universe in consonance with its requirements, then the conclusion was inescapable that Torah had to descend to earth to enable man to fulfill the will of his Creator.

Had God wanted 'Thou shall not steal' *to refer only to its spiritual meaning, then he would not have created a physical world with the temptations of wealth and the larcenous instincts to which human beings are prey.*

Had God wanted *'Thou shalt not steal'* to refer only to its spiritual meaning, then he would not have created a physical world with the temptations of wealth and the larcenous instinct to which human beings are prey. Had He wanted only angelic concepts of honor to parents, then He would not have brought into being, flesh and blood parents and children with the blend of friction and dependence, resentment and love that makes the relationship at once difficult and beautiful and that makes the commandment *'Honor thy father and thy mother'* a constant challenge to children and parent. Precisely because the universe was a translation of Torah into a material manifestation of God's will, Moses was able to convince the angels that man, God's handiwork, could not carry out his Creator's will without the Torah which was not only the plan, but also the purpose of creation.

Repository of Light

Indicative of the august role of the Torah in enabling man to find and realize his higher purpose is this interpretation of *Rabbi Dov Ber* of Mezritch, successor of the Ba'al Shem Tov and seminal figure in the spread of the Chassidic movement:

ראה הקב״ה האור שאינו כדאי להשתמש בו וגנזו לצדיקים לעתיד לבא.

The Holy One, blessed be He perceived that it was improper for [the wicked] to make use of the [primeval] light, so He hid it for the benefit of the righteous in the time to come (Rashi). [See comm. 1:4].

'Where did He hide the light'? The light is there. It is available between the lines and letters and wisdom of the Torah.

'Where did He hide the light'? asked Rabbi Dov Ber. He answered: The great light of creation was the light of Torah. At first, the light was available to all, but God saw that few people are worthy of enjoying it, so He clothed it in the Torah, and there it remains hidden.

We bemoan the lack of that primeval light that

made the sun pale by its spiritual brilliance, and long for the promised day when it will glow for us again. But it is not gone. The light is there. It is available. It awaits the diligent, indefatigable efforts of the righteous to unearth it from between the lines and letters and wisdom of the Ṭorah. The righteous of the future — *all ages of man* — can find the light in Torah, for Torah is its embodiment.

II. Gates of Understanding

Source of all Secrets

Indeed it is true that Torah is the blueprint of creation, but that is only a small part of the total truth: Torah remains the key to all the secrets and resources of creation. When Adam was created, God placed him in the Garden of Eden לְעָבְדָהּ וּלְשָׁמְרָהּ, *to work it and guard it (Genesis* 2:15), upon which the *Midrash* comments לעבדה במצות עשה ולשמרה במצות לא תעשה, *to work it* through the performance of positive commandments, and *to guard it* through the observance of negative commandments. The garden was real and so were its trees and their fruits. But there are tools better than plows and rakes, protection safer than fences and shotguns. Man in his most exalted form can grasp that the true essence of all his earthly endeavor is the extent of his service to God. Plows and fences are the tools of blindness, the implementation of a curse that robs him of his spirituality and blinds him to the truth of his mission. Let us attempt to understand — at least imperfectly — how Torah permeates every molecule of the universe. If we succeed, we will have found the first marker on the road to fulfillment as the Creator intended it.

The garden was real and so were its trees and their fruits.

Plows and fences are the tools of blindness, the implementation of a curse that robs him of his spirituality and blinds him to the truth of his mission.

חמשים שערי בינה נבראו בעולם וכולן נתנו למשה חסר אחד

Fifty gates of understanding were created and all were transmitted to Moses save for one (Rosh Hashana 21b).

What were these 'gates of understanding?' *Ramban* (Introduction to Torah) explains that each order of the universe was created according to a plan, and its content, growth, function, and all other of its aspects are determined according to it. To enter into the mysteries of this plan and to comprehend it is to be admitted into its 'gate of understanding'. The lowest order of creation is דוֹמֵם, the inanimate objects like rocks, sand, water. Above it comes צוֹמֵחַ, simple plant life, trees; חַי, the various living creatures until, as one goes higher and higher on the ladder of the universe, he reaches מְדַבֵּר, man — the only creature possessing the power of intelligent speech, and a human soul. The knowledge of man is the forty-ninth gate of understanding, the ability to know the complexities of the human mind and personality.

To enter into mysteries of this plan and to comprehend it is to be admitted into its 'gate of understanding'.

The Fifty Gates

Above that gate is the fiftieth — the knowledge of God. Forty-nine gates were presented to Moses; the fiftieth was denied even him, for no mortal being can attain the understanding of God. Thus, in the truest sense, *Ramban* continues, the fiftieth gate was never 'created', for the term creation implies that it was part of heaven and earth — part of the handiwork of the Six Days of Creation that is within the realm of human dominion and understanding. But that gate, the ability to comprehend and understand the essence of God, was never *created* in the normal sense, because it is beyond the scope of man.

The ability to comprehend and under stand the essence of God, is beyond the scope of man.

[*Chidushei HaRim*, in a piercing insight, suggests that not only was the 'fiftieth gate' *created*, as implied by the above Talmudic text, but it was even *transmitted* to Moses! The very fact that a human being can conceive God's greatness to the extent that he can say 'if all the seas were ink and all the heavens parchment and all the trees quills I could not begin to write Your greatness' — this in itself is a glimmer of the glories within the fiftieth gate of understanding. This barest breath of the last gate was transmitted to man; otherwise how could he ever imagine that the unimaginable exists, how could his soul soar in futile

This barest breath of the last gate was transmitted to man; otherwise how could he ever imagine that the unimaginable exists, how could his soul soar in futile yet fruitful quest of the infinite riches of God's wisdom and spirituality?

yet fruitful quest of the infinite riches of God's wisdom and spirituality?]

With mastery of the forty-nine gates, Moses could understand the complexities of every aspect of creation and the workings of every human mind. He could look at a person and perceive his sins and merits, his flaws and virtues. Indeed, as *Ramban* comments in *Numbers,* when the Jews were counted, each would pass before Moses and Aaron so that those two spiritual giants could gaze upon him and, perceiving his deepest needs, bless him according to what was truly best for him.

Thus the wisdom of the forty-nine gates was more than theoretical. It enabled its possessor to know all the secrets of any aspect of creation to whose 'gate of understanding' he was privy. He could unlock the hidden recesses of the human mind as Moses could, he could even know the workings of animal life and the earth. The master of terrestrial understanding could know without Geiger counters and divining rods where mineral deposits were located and what veins of land were suited to the production of exotic plants. He could know the 'speech' and behavior of animals and the secrets of human healing.

The master of terrestrial understanding could know without Geiger counters and divining rods where mineral deposits were located.

Mastery of Time

It is illustrative that *Rashi,* in his first comment on *Genesis,* asks why the Torah did not begin with the commandment that Israel proclaim the New Moon (see *comm.* 1:1). That the first commandment concerned Israel's ability to inject sanctity into the calendar is no accident!

Mortal man is subject to many self-imposed pressures and tyrannies, but probably none is more universally pervasive than the tyranny of the clock. Time controls man's life, time is symbolic of the unyielding sway of nature over man. Its requirements, its limitations, its animal desires, its denial of spirituality — all combine to overwhelm him.

Time controls man's life, time is symbolic of the unyielding sway of nature over man.

But the Torah has a different standard. God gave sanctity to the Sabbath from the seventh day of creation and He continues to sanctify it every week. But

Israel alone sanctifies the New Moon, and through it the festivals. Without the New Moon, there is no calendar and there are no festivals. That these 'meeting places in time' provide annual, seasonal rendezvous between God and Israel is the eternal testimony to the fact that God did not mean man to be enslaved by time, but to breathe holiness into time — to be its master *(Pri Tzaddik, Harav Gifter).*

Through this mastery over time — the unforgiving, unyielding symbol of nature's power — Israel has the power to assert its freedom from, even its domination over nature. Thus it was that the Mishnaic Sage Rabbi Chanina ben Dosa overcame magical opponents. The ancient sorcerors practiced a magic called כישוף, a word which, our Sages taught, came from a contraction of מכחישים פמליא של מעלה, they denied the power of the heavenly *famalia.* To the great people of Israel whose very being was a proclamation of אֵין עוֹד מִלְבַדּוֹ, *there is nothing except for Him,* opposing forces vanished and lost all power and validity *(Maharil Bloch).*

To the great people of Israel whose very being was a proclamation of אֵין עוֹד מִלְבַדּוֹ, there is nothing except for Him, opposing forces vanished and lost all power and validity.

Solomon's Request

According to the Sages, King Solomon was the possessor of all wisdom, but the wise king did not request encyclopedic knowledge — he asked only for the wisdom of Torah so that he could judge his people wisely and justly! [See Overview, ArtScroll edition of Koheles]

True. He wanted knowledge of the Torah and it was knowledge of the Torah and nothing more that God gave him. For the forty-nine gates of understanding are *all in the Torah.* The man who can decipher the depths of the Torah's wisdom knows the secrets of agriculture, mining, music, mathematics, healing, law — everything! — because nothing was built into heaven and earth unless it was found in the Torah. The question is not whether Torah is the source of all wisdom, the question is only how one interprets the Torah to unseal its riches. The man who cannot find the key to a treasure chest and comforts himself in his frustration by proclaiming that

It was knowledge of the Torah and nothing more that God gave him.

The man who cannot find the key to a treasure chest and comforts himself in his frustration by proclaiming that the ancient chest contains nothing but useless curiosities and moldy rags, goes away not only foolish but poor.

the ancient chest contains nothing but useless curiosities and moldy rags, goes away not only foolish but poor. Every aspect of the wisdom transmitted to Moses and presented to Solomon — and shared by the great figures of ancient Israel — is contained in the Torah. One need only know how to find it.

We might survey an unappealing natural setting and not find the diamonds, platinum, gold, or petroleum locked beneath its surface.

Yet we peruse the verses and study the commentaries and do not find the wisdom of Solomon, just as we might survey an unappealing natural setting and not find the diamonds, platinum, gold, or petroleum locked beneath its surface. This is because we, in our spiritual poverty, lack the keys to the gates of understanding. The Torah commands us in laws of agriculture — but how does this tell us how to make farms more productive? We are permitted to seek medical help — but how does this teach us to conquer disease? We are commanded to seek the benefit of our fellow men — but how does this show us the way to peace in a jealous, fractious, selfish world?

III. Treasures Within Torah

Laws Within Crowns

The answers to all these questions could be found in the Torah if only we knew how to read it. The ancients knew.

גַּל עֵינַי וְאַבִּיטָה נִפְלָאוֹת מִתּוֹרָתֶךָ

Uncover my eyes that I may behold wonders from Your Torah (Psalms 119:18*).*

The wonders are there, it is we who fail to see them.

The wonders are there, it is we who fail to see them. The eyes of the ancients were free of the material veils that so becloud our vision.

The Talmud tells us that when Moses ascended to heaven to be taught the Torah and receive the Tablets of the Law; he saw God writing the תגין, the small crowns, on top of the letters in the heavenly Torah. Moses wondered why they were necessary, and God answered,

אדם א׳ יש שעתיד להיות בסוף כמה דורות

ועקיבא בן יוסף שמו שעתיד לדרוש על כל קוץ וקוץ תילין תילין של הלכות

There is a man named Akiba ben Joseph who will live many generations in the future who will derive mounds and mounds of laws from each crown (Menachos 29b).

The myriad laws studied in Rabbi Akiba's academy were all found in the Torah, many of them in the crowns of letters that appear to us to be no more than scribal flourishes.

The myriad laws studied in Rabbi Akiba's academy were all found in the Torah, many of them in the crowns of letters that appear to us to be no more than scribal flourishes. An extra letter here, a missing letter there, an enlarged letter, a miniature letter — all of these seeming aberrations in a Torah scroll are meticulously preserved guideposts to law, nature, and untold mysteries of the universe. This explains why Jews down the ages have taken scrupulous care that all Torah scrolls remain faithful to the ancient texts. Ezra the Scribe, who led the Jews back from the Babylonian exile, wrote a Torah scroll which remained the authoritative one for centuries and which was the standard against which all others were checked for accuracy. Therefore, too, a Torah scroll with an extra letter — even a silent vowel like *vav* or *yud* — is halachically unfit for use. This knowledge has resulted in such careful preservation of the masoretic tradition that the Torahs of Yemen and Poland — communities that had been isolated from one another for over a thousand years — remained virtually identical. More recent generations no longer perceive the infinite shades of meaning and volumes of law that the holy parchments reveal to those who know how to read them, but the holy scrolls still contain them.

The entire Torah can be read as Names of God — different combinations of letters, numerical values, exegeses. It was such wisdom that Solomon used until, slowly and tragically, the art became forgotten.

In addition, the entire Torah can be read as Names of God *(Zohar),* names that have the miraculous powers of creation and sustenance. Different combinations of letters can be made to form new words, numerical values of the words contain meanings, exegeses forms the basis of much of the Oral Law — all of these are derived from and implicit in the Torah. It was such wisdom of Torah interpretation that

Solomon used to reveal the mysteries of creation, and that great men used for centuries until, slowly and tragically, the art became forgotten.

The Translation to Life

It existed, written in black fire upon white fire. But somehow, in a manner beyond our capacity to grasp, Torah did exist.

The sum total of human knowledge, therefore, derives from the Torah, for the very universe itself is a product of Torah. We cannot begin to fathom what Torah was before the creation. It existed, as the *Midrash* tells us, כתובה אש שחורה על גבי אש לבנה, *written in black fire upon white fire.* We can have no conception of what it truly was because, before the creation, fire in earthly terms did not exist.. But somehow, in a manner beyond our capacity to grasp, Torah did exist.

Then, בִּדְבַר ה׳ שָׁמַיִם נַעֲשׂוּ, *through the words of HASHEM were the heavens made (Psalms* 33:6). God's ineffable word took physical form. Heaven and earth and all their fullness became the clothing for the word of God which infuses creation, and without which creation could not continue its existence. The black and white fire of Torah became clothed in ink and parchment, and the Godly wisdom which is the essence of Torah, remained hidden in its words and letters. The very wisdom which dictated the creation remains imbedded in Torah and reveals itself to those chosen few who are capable of peering beneath its material camouflage.

When the ancient Romans apprehended the Mishnaic sage Rabbi Chanina ben Teradion for bravely committing the 'crime' of teaching the Torah to his students, they condemned him to death. They wrapped him in a Torah scroll and set him aflame. As his agony reached its climax, his students asked him, 'Rabbi, what do you see?'

He answered,

גוילין נשרפין ואותיות פורחות

The parchments are consumed, and the letters fly up [*to heaven*] *(Avodah Zarah* 18a).

The great Rabbi Chanina ben Teradion could see what his students couldn't. Flames could burn parchment and ink, but the letters of the Torah are eternal,

The scroll is not their essence, but their abode.

for the scroll is not their essence but their abode. They find a temporary home in the artistry of the scribe, but hidden in his handiwork is the wisdom of the scribe Who preceded him — Who composed and wrote the first Torah in black fire upon white fire. Let the earthly scroll be burned and its letters — those eternal letters that preceded earth and define its destiny — rise up to their Author. The Roman executioners could exult as did barbarians in every century down to our own as they vented their hatred on the symbol of all they despised: God's Torah. But they could no more destroy it than they could override the law of gravity. The letters are eternal for they are the will of the Eternal.

But they could no more destroy it than they could overrule the law of gravity. The letters are eternal for they are the will of the Eternal.

Thus it was that when the young Rabbi Meir announced to the Sage, Rabbi Ishmael, that he was a scribe, the great man cautioned him:

בני הוי זהיר במלאכתך שמלאכתך מלאכת שמים היא שמא אתה מחסר אות אחת או מייתר אות אחת נמצאת מחריב את כל העולם כולו

My son, be careful in your work, for your work is heavenly. In case you delete even one letter or add even one letter, you may destroy the entire world (Eruvin 13a*).*

IV The Oral Law

Its Obvious Existence

Even a cursory study of the Torah proves that there must be an unwritten law, that there is much more to Torah than the Five Books of Moses, the *Chumash;* much more even than the entire twenty-four books of *Tanach.*

— Following the war with Amalek, God told Moses:

כְּתוֹב זֹאת זִכָּרוֹן בַּסֵּפֶר וְשִׂים בְּאָזְנֵי יְהוֹשֻׁעַ

Write this as a remembrance in a book and place it in the ears of Joshua ... (Exodus 17:14).

It is plain that, in addition to the written verses of the Torah, something else had to be told to Joshua.

— The Torah prescribes that one who assaults his fellow must pay עַיִן תַּחַת עַיִן, *an eye for an eye (Exodus* 21:24), yet never in Jewish history was physical punishment meted out for an assault. Instead, the verse was always interpreted to require monetary compensation. Who gave Moses and his successors the sanction to tamper with the 'plain' meaning of the text?

— On the threshold of *Eretz Yisrael,* the Jews were told that they would be permitted to eat meat without the requirement of bringing the animal as an offering to the Tabernacle. How should animals be slaughtered? וְזָבַחְתָּ מִבְּקָרְךָ וּמִצֹּאנְךָ אֲשֶׁר נָתַן ה׳ לְךָ כַּאֲשֶׁר צִוִּיתִךָ, *You may slaughter from your herd and your flock which HASHEM has given you as I have commanded you (Deut.* 12:21). Moses says clearly that he had 'commanded' his people concerning *shechitah,* halachic slaughter, yet we find nowhere in the written text of the Torah even one of the intricate and demanding rules of kosher slaughter.

There is a second Torah, an Oral Law, without which the first Torah is not only a closed book, but without which the written Torah can be twisted ana misinterpreted beyond recognition, as indeed it has been down the centuries.

Countless similar questions could be raised. The implication of them all is clear beyond a doubt: there is a *second* Torah, an Oral Law, without which the first Torah is not only a closed book, but without which the written Torah can be twisted and misinterpreted beyond recognition, as indeed it has been down the centuries.

The responsibility to transmit the Oral Law faithfully and for a chosen few of Israel's greatest scholars to be responsible for its maintenance and interpretation in each generation began with Moses' own successors. As *Rambam* says in his Introduction, Moses had three primary disciples: Joshua, Eleazar and Pinchas, but it was to Joshua 'who was Moses' disciple' that he transmitted the Oral Law and whom he commanded in it. This is further indicated by the very first *Mishnah* in *Avos* which states clearly that Moses passed on the Torah to Joshua.

It may be that *Rambam's* source for his assertion that responsibility for the *Oral Law* was placed particularly in the hands of Joshua, is *Sifre (Pinchas).*

There we are told that when Moses was commanded to designate Joshua as his successor, he was commanded: צוהו על דברי תלמוד, instruct him concerning the 'Talmud'. This *Rambam* interprets as a clear reference to the Oral Law. This would explain why Israel was so incensed when Joshua forgot three hundred laws following the death of Moses, that there were some who threatened to kill him (*Temurah* 16a)! Why the wrath against Joshua alone when there were myriad other scholars and elders in the nation who were equally guilty? Because, as leader of the people, Joshua had been made responsible for the preservation of the Oral Law *(Harav Yitzchok Zev Soloveitchick)*.

Indivisibility of Torah

The Oral Law was taught in its entirety to Moses during his forty days and forty nights in heaven.

אפילו מה שתלמיד ותיק עתיד להורות לפני רבו
כבר נאמר למשה בסיני

> *Even what a faithful disciple will in the future expound in front of his master was already disclosed to Moses at Sinai* (*Yerushalmi Peah* 6:2).

Not only the basic exegetic laws and interpretations, but every possible nuance and logical extension of existing principles, even those that will be expounded in academies of the future, were all included in the Oral Torah that Moses accepted at Sinai.

In essence, Torah is the wisdom of God, the ultimate in spiritual greatness. The performance of any deed prescribed in Shulchan Aruch becomes a spiritual act because it is a physical embodiment of the divine will

When one considers the origin of the hundreds of thousands of volumes that constitute only a fraction of the total body of knowledge that we refer to with the all inclusive name Torah, the phenomenon of Moses knowing it all is not surprising. In essence, Torah is the wisdom of God, the ultimate in spiritual greatness. Unlike material things, spirituality is indivisible. A car, a house, a space satellite, a pair of shoes — these are all separate objects bearing no conceivable relation to one another. But the performance of any deed prescribed in *Shulchan Aruch (A Table Prepared* — the compendium of Jewish Law) whether it is fasting on *Yom Kippur* or donning *tefillin* daily

— the sort of act commonly called a 'religious observance' — or determining who is liable for the damage caused by a cracked pavement or refraining from gossip — both very 'mundane' tasks — becomes a spiritual act because it is a physical embodiment of the divine will.

They are like the spokes of a wheel — its source, the Torah is God's wisdom, His own thought.

Spirituality is indivisible because, ultimately, all spirituality derives from God Himself. People may walk different paths in the service of God, but as long as they are all seeking His closeness in ways hallowed by the Torah, they are all united in a single pursuit of the same goal. They are like the spokes of a wheel — but in a very real sense they are even more unified than that, because, at its source, the Torah is God's wisdom, His own thought.

But we proclaim that God is one, because the changes are not in Him, but in our perceptions of Him.

The ultimate unity is God Himself. Jews accept His sovereignty upon themselves daily by proclaiming this unity, saying שְׁמַע יִשְׂרָאֵל ה׳ אֱלֹהֵינוּ ה׳ אֶחָד *Hear, O Israel HASHEM, our God, HASHEM is One (Deut* 6:4). God has numerous manifestations. He appears to us as HASHEM, the Source of mercy, and as אלהים, the God of Judgment. He is patient and jealous, the Giver of reward and the Exactor of punishment, He gives life and takes it away, heals and afflicts, enriches and impoverishes. Ancient idolators were convinced that one God was incapable of so many modes of behavior; there had to be a different deity for each, ר״ל. But we proclaim that God is *one,* because the changes are not in Him, but in our perceptions of Him.

God's manifestations are like a spectrum. Spectators seeing isolated slivers of a spectrum would be convinced that they are looking at different, variously colored rays of light.

God's manifestations are like a spectrum. Light enters it and is bent into its component colors. There are the seven major colors and infinite shades as one goes from the brightest to the darkest end. Spectators seeing isolated slivers of a spectrum would be convinced that they are looking at different, variously colored rays of light. Someone seeing the full picture would know that there is only one ray of light and that the many onlookers are strengthened in their convictions by a shared ignorance. So, too, must we understand God in His wisdom: whether human behavior requires that He smile benevolently or punish wrathfully, *He is One (Harav Gedaliah Schorr).*

Torah, too, is one. Whatever it was in its purely spiritual state before the universe was created, with the event of creation the Torah assumed physical garb just as the soul clothes itself in a human body to assume earthly life. The wisdom of God took the form of six hundred and thirteen commandments, so much so, that Torah was obviously intended for human beings with all their frailties, and not for angels. But the precepts are not isolated phenomena; they are all interrelated aspects of a single Torah, like the organs and vessels of a single human body to which the totality of the commandments are likened. Indeed, the six hundred thirteen commandments give spiritual life and nourishment to the organs and vessels of the individual human being just as they provide continued existence to all of creation.

But the precepts are not isolated phenomena; they are all interrelated aspects of a single Torah.

Rav Saadiah Gaon shows how all six hundred and thirteen are derivatives of the Ten Commandments. It is as if the Ten Commandments expanded to become the entire Torah and then, with the necessity to commit the Oral Law to writing, expanded to include Mishna, Talmud, and the countless holy books. Each commandment, law, and insight illuminates and warms Jewish minds and hearts no less than rays of the sun illuminate and warm the earth. But just as all the rays originate from the sun, all these parts of Torah are rays of a single spiritual splendor — the Oneness of God *(Sfas Emes).*

It is as if the Ten Commandments expanded to become the entire Torah.

כל העוסק בתורת חטאת ... כאילו הקריב חטאת

Whoever studies the laws of the Chatos offering, is considered as if he had actually offered a Chatos (Menachos 110a).

On earth, the *Korban* is an animal which is sanctified and brought to the Temple, and offered upon the altar where it is burned. What was the offering before the creation, when its laws were written in white and black fire? Then there were no animals and no altars — but the Torah *did* exist. Now, when the Temple is in ruins and the commandment of an offering cannot be carried out, one may perform it, in a sense, by studying its laws. In so doing, one unites with the divine wisdom from which the physical offering was created. The essence of *Chatos* is its laws for it is them which the offering embodies; when the commandment cannot be performed, one may still derive a closeness to its holiness by studying its laws *(Iglei Tal)*.

Now, when the Temple is in ruins and the commandment of an offering cannot be carried out, one may perform it, in a sense, by studying its laws.

V. Survival of Torah

Torah Embodied

The study of Torah is exalted above all other commandments. It is written כִּי נֵר מִצְוָה וְתוֹרָה אוֹר, *For a commandment is a lamp and Torah is light (Proverbs* 6:23). The lamp is the bearer of light. Without a lamp, the light could not endure, but a lamp without any light is cold and useless. On earth after creation, Torah became embodied in *matzos, tefillin,* money, offerings, *mezuzos,* food, and countless other things that are used in the performance of God's will. His wisdom dictated that in our human existence, the way to ascend the spiritual ladder is through — and only through — the commandments of the Torah, just as a lamp is the means to attain light. But the lamp's greatest glory is in the flame it bears. Man's highest privilege and loftiest attainment is in the study of Torah itself. The performance of commandments involves the use of the material accoutrements of creation to serve God, but the study of Torah enables mortal man to unite with the thought and wisdom of God.

But the lamp's greatest glory is in the flame it bears.

Surely it is true that every original thought of every diligent student is a part of the Torah which Moses received at Sinai, and no matter how voluminous the library, its contents were part of the spiritual treasure transmitted to Israel through Moses. But this is not to say that Moses was drilled

No matter how how voluminous the library, its contents were part of the spiritual treasure transmitted to Israel.

line by line in every part of Torah literature and thought.

The Principles

Every human being makes scores of decisions every day; responsible people make more decisions of greater consequence. Yet if each person had to consider the alternatives of every decision, little would ever be accomplished: What time to wake up? Whether to wash one's face? What to have for breakfast? Whether to work conscientiously? The list would be endless. These are, in a sense, decisions that one must make, but one does not think about them at all.

Most questions that arise during the day are answered intuitively because they fit into each individual's own personal pattern.

The choices are unconscious and obvious, according to the taste and mode of living each individual has developed. Everyone has a philosophy of life, a set of priorities, a scale of values. Most questions that arise during the day are answered intuitively because they fit into each individual's own personal pattern. It is only a rare problem that demands a thought-out response — that is the question that tests a person and demands his attention.

The struggling student memorizes individual facts, questions and answers; the sage knows broad principles.

Moses was taught the unity of Torah, the essential principles and laws with a clarity that implicitly contained the response to every question. The great sage can easily answer questions he has never heard because his knowledge is so thorough and his understanding so clear that there are no difficulties for him. The struggling student memorizes individual facts, questions and answers; the sage knows broad principles. This clear knowledge added to an indefatigable intensity of study and single-minded desire to master every nuance of every law became the firm basis of an unbroken oral tradition that transmitted Moses' teachings intact from generation to generation with flawless accuracy until the period of the Second Commonwealth. This was a time when the only written Torah was the Five Books of the Chumash and the Prophets. The entire Oral Torah remained oral.

When difficult questions arose, they were decided

by the Great Sanhedrin whose authority was binding. Indeed, the Torah commanded that the decision be heeded even when the judgment appeared to be erroneous.

עַל פִּי הַתּוֹרָה אֲשֶׁר יוֹרוּךָ וְעַל הַמִּשְׁפָּט אֲשֶׁר יֹאמְרוּ לְךָ תַּעֲשֶׂה לֹא תָסוּר מִן הַדָּבָר אֲשֶׁר יַגִּידוּ לְךָ יָמִין וּשְׂמֹאל

According to the Torah which they shall teach you and upon the judgment which they shall tell you shall you do. Do not swerve from the word which they shall tell you right or left (Deut. 17:11)

אפילו נראים בעיניך על שמאל שהוא ימין ועל ימין שהוא שמאל שמע להם

Even if it seems to you that [their judgment is as if they had said that] left is right and right is left, you must obey them (Sifre).

Unless the Torah had insisted so strictly on total obedience to the vested bearers of the halachic tradition, all dissenters, frivolous or otherwise, would have felt free to challenge its authority with the result that there would have developed *many* Torahs, each one suiting the needs and predilections of this or that community or scholar (*Ramban, Chinuch,* and others.)

The Oral Law Blossoms

The blossoming of the Oral Law in all its intellectual brilliance and glory did not begin until the period of the Second Temple.

The chain of tradition during those centuries of Jewish history was transmitted intact from teacher to student, generation after generation. The blossoming of the Oral Law in all its intellectual brilliance and glory as we find it recorded in the Talmud and other books, did not begin until the period of the Second Temple. The Shechinah, the Divine Presence, was not to rest upon the Second Temple as it had upon the first, a loss that caused the people enormous distress. The אנשי כנסת הגדולה, Men of the Great Assembly, an august assemblage of one hundred and twenty great men that included many prophets and such leaders as Ezra, Mordechai, Daniel and others, beseeched God for a divine gift to compensate for the losses.

אע״פ שלא שרתה שכינה בבית שני, מ״מ עיקר התורה וזיוה והדרה לא היה אלא בבית ב׳ שלא רצו לבנות עד שהבטיחם השי״ת לגלות להם רזי תורה.

Even though the Divine Presence did not rest on the Second Temple, nevertheless the main part of Torah, its splendor and its glory, was only in the period of the Second Temple, for they did not wish to build it until Hashem, blessed be He, promised that He would reveal to them the secrets of the Torah (Pirkei Heichalos 27).

Heaven forbid that anyone suggest that the Rabbinic Era which began during the Second Commonwealth produced a new or reinterpreted Torah. The glories of Torah that they articulated were always there, but it was never necessary to make use of them. During the entire period from the Giving of the Law at Sinai until the opening generations of the Second Commonwealth, the Oral Law was handed down intact and free of dispute. We find no record of halachic disagreement during the entire period. Undoubtedly, there were halachic questions that engendered doubt and disagreement, but these were settled by the Sanhedrin. During the Second Commonwealth, however, the historic intensity of study began to decline ever so slightly, with the result that disputes began to arise among the Sages (*Sanhedrin* 88b; see *Rambam's* Introduction to *Mishnah).*

During the entire period from the Giving of the Law at Sinai until the opening generations of the Second Commonwealth, the Oral Law was handed down intact and free of dispute.

Although only one halachic dispute arose during the first three centuries of the period, and an additional three disputes arose between Hillel and Shammai, there are numerous disputes recorded among their students. In addition, during the long and cruel period of harsh Roman persecution, Torah study became virtually impossible except with the most extreme self-sacrifice. The result was a further tragic decline in knowledge and an impairment in the transmission of the oral tradition. Without the totally reliable teacher-to-student chain of Oral Law, ways had to be employed to regain what was being lost.

Without the totally reliable teacher-to-student chain of Oral Law, ways had to be employed to regain what was being lost.

The Old-New Methods

These ways were not new. The principles of Biblical interpretation were taught to Moses at Sinai together with the rest of the Oral Law. The Talmud teaches us the י״ג מדות שהתורה נדרשת בהם, the Thirteen Hermeneutic Principles through which the Torah is interpreted *(Sifra).* The *Talmud* makes extensive use of these principles, in fact they form its heart. Through their use, it was possible to find within the Torah, laws from the oral tradition which had become forgotten or confused.

> אלף ושבע מאות קלין וחמורין וגזירות שוות ודקדוקי סופרים נשתכחו בימי אבלו של משה . . . החזירן עתניאל בן קנז מתוך פלפולו
>
> *Seventeen hundred* [*laws*] *were forgotten during the mourning period for Moses. Asniel ben Kenaz retrieved them through his exegesis (Temurah* 16a).

Asniel, applied the principles of Biblical exegesis and restored the lost knowledge.

Following the death of Moses, a substantial body of orally transmitted law was forgotten as a result of the people's grief over the loss of their teacher. The leader and sage, Asniel, applied the principles of Biblical exegesis and restored the lost knowledge to Israel. How did he do it? The laws were not concoctions of Moses. They were taught him by God as part of the Oral Law which, in turn, is the authentic interpretation of the Torah. During Moses' lifetime, the people found no need to derive the laws from Scripture itself, because the oral tradition was intact.

It may be likened to the well-educated person who speaks and writes a language flawlessly although he may never have learned — and surely does not remember — the rules of grammar. He may never have any need to study the grammatical principles — as long as he makes no errors or runs into no questions of judgment. When that happens, however, he will need a grammarian to right his errant language pattern.

Asniel made use of established principles to regain knowledge that had been forgotten. During the Mishnaic and Talmudic periods, the Sages of Israel employed the same devices. In this sense, God promised the men of the Great Assembly that He would reveal to them the secrets of the Torah (above). They took the eternal tools of exegesis and used them to reveal the secrets that had always been locked within the words of the Torah, secrets that Moses had taught Israel and that, in turn, had been transmitted orally for over a thousand years until the oral tradition began to crumble due to a lack of diligence and outside persecution. They did nothing new and certainly made no changes in the Torah; they merely made use of hermeneutic principles that had not been needed while the tradition of study was still at its zenith.

They took the eternal tools of exegesis and used them to reveal the secrets that had always been locked within the words of the Torah. They did nothing new and certainly made no changes in the Torah.

The Torah of Holiness

This may be understood more deeply. Earlier generations perceived the spiritual essence of Torah so clearly that the detailed laws flowed from that perception. The highest levels of spirituality attained by human beings were those of the Patriarchs, Abraham, Isaac, and Jacob. They obeyed the laws of the Torah before it was given. Who told them the laws? No one. Their own spiritual greatness combined with the holy emanations of Eretz Israel to create within them the instincts that dictated which deeds had to be performed and which were forbidden. An attainment of holiness contains its own laws, for it carries with it the realization of what enhances that holiness and what profanes it. As said above, God and Torah form one unity; when the Patriarchs attained the lofty heights that brought them as close to God as human beings can become, they simultaneously became human manifestations of Torah and understood how it was to be clothed in human deed *(Ramban).*

Their own spiritual greatness combined with the holy emanations of Eretz Israel to create within them instincts that dictated which deeds had to be performed and which were forbidden.

Following the giving of the Torah, the Oral Law enabled the greatest people among Jews to see the total concept of a commandment. When the tradition began to crumble, it became necessary to interpret the Written Torah to derive from it the individual laws. That human intellect is capable of divining even some degree of God's wisdom is one of His greatest gifts to man. As *Rabbeinu Tam* put it, that man can sometimes give a logical explanation of one law or the other of the Torah is no proof whatever of the validity of Torah; rather it is a tribute to the brilliance of human intellect that it is capable of understanding an aspect of God's wisdom.

It is a tribute to the brilliance of human intellect that it is capable of understanding an aspect of God's wisdom.

The Torah of Wisdom

When Moses was told that Rabbi Akiba would derive laws from the crowns of the letters, he was astounded that a human could reach such a level of greatness.

אמר לפניו, רבש״ע הראהו לי א״ל חזור לאחורך. הלך וישב בסוף י״ח שורות ולא היה יודע מה הן אומרים. תשש כחו. כיון שהגיע לדבר אחד, אמרו לו תלמידיו, רבי מנין לך? אמר להן: הלכה למשה מסיני. נתיישבה דעתו

Moses said before Him, 'Master of the Universe, show [*Rabbi Akiba*] *to me.' He said, 'Move backwards.' He went and sat at the end of the eighteenth row* [*of students*] *and he* [*Moses*] *did not understand what they were saying. He grew weak* [*from the realization of his inferior knowledge*]. *As soon as they came to a particular law,* [*Rabbi Akiba's*] *students said to him, 'My master, how do you know this?' He said to them 'It is a law transmitted to Moses at Sinai.* [*Moses'*] *feelings were set at ease. (Menachos* 29b).

Maharal explains this cryptic passage. Moses understood the root of every commandment. His depth of understanding was such that he intuitively knew every individual law associated with the commandment. He did not perceive them as separate parts, but as aspects of one whole just as a skilled and experienced diagnostician will not think of an illness in terms of pulse, blood pressure, swelling, pain, or any of a hundred other symptoms. To the skilled doctor, all the symptoms flow out of the illness; they are inseparable and entirely predictable. The raw prac-

He did not perceive them as separate parts, but as aspects of one whole. Rabbi Akiba had to make use of the exegetical principles to find the separate laws in the letters and logic and even crowns of the Torah.

titioner, on the other hand, will find it necessary to make a score of tests and measurements to arrive at the same result. Similarly, the spiritual descent of the generations from Moses to Rabbi Akiba resulted in the loss of the all-embracing perception that was the essence of Moses' understanding of Torah. Rabbi Akiba had to make use of the exegetical principles to find the separate laws in the letters and logic and even crowns of the Torah.

This sort of Torah study was a symptom of a diminished generation and, to attempt an understanding of it, Moses had to descend from his august pinnacle of Torah greatness — a descent symbolized by going to the rear of Rabbi Akiba's academy. Moses was bewildered by this unfamiliar method of uncovering the laws, until he heard Rabbi Akiba say that the source of all his knowledge remained the law that Moses received at Sinai.

Prophet and Sage

The prophet sees with a dazzling clarity, but he is limited to what God reveals to him.

This incident illustrates the fundamental difference between the vision of a prophet and the wisdom of a sage. The prophet sees with a dazzling clarity, but he is limited to what God reveals to him. The sage may lack the clarity of the prophet, but by means of his Torah wisdom he is able to delve more deeply and develop a breadth of knowledge beyond what the prophet has been shown. The prophet's knowledge is far clearer and he attains a degree of closeness to God that was lost to the great men of the Second Temple, but the sage's knowledge can be broader and more embracing.

The Talmud expresses it as חכם עדיף מנביא, a wise man is superior to a prophet *(Bava Basra* 12a). His superiority lies in his ability to use his wisdom to explore and discover and uncover the infinite mysteries buried in the Torah that are ready to be revealed to those who know how to find them (see *Ramban ibid).* Rabbi Akiba's knowledge bore no comparison to Moses' — indeed, in the final analysis, it was based upon the teaching of Moses. But Moses had never needed to make use of the hermeneutic princi-

Rabbi Akiba was able to embody the splendor of Torah promised to the men of the Great Assembly in a manner that Moses could not duplicate, although he uncovered no laws that were unknown to Moses.

ples he had bequeathed to his people. Thus, Rabbi Akiba was able to embody the splendor of Torah promised to the men of the Great Assembly in a manner that Moses could not duplicate, although he uncovered no laws that were unknown to Moses *(Resisei Layla).*

This ability of man to use his human intellect to add to the store of Torah knowledge — *and to have his novellae achieve the status of the Torah transmitted to Moses* — is surely one of God's greatest gifts to man *(ibid.).* Indeed, it has been said that the entire narrative of the Patriarchs and Joseph and his brothers are included in the book of Genesis in order to demonstrate that the word and deed of holy people can achieve the status of God's Torah itself *(Sfas Emes).*

> יפה שיחתן של עבדי אבות לפני הקב״ה מתורתן של בנים
>
> *The conversation of the servants of the Patriarchs is more beautiful before God than the Torah law given to* [*their*] *descendants (Bereishis Rabba* 60:11).

Again, God gave man the opportunity to become so great that his very conversation can become sacred.

Considerable space is given to the conversation of Eliezer, servant of Abraham, while many laws of the Torah are given through allusion and exegesis. Again, God gave man the opportunity to become so great that his very conversation can become sacred.

VI. Divisions of the Oral Law*

Five Categories

Rambam, in his *Introduction* divides the *Mishnah* into five categories:

1. פֵּירוּשִׁים מְקוּבָּלִים עַל פְּסוּקֵי הַתַּנַ״ךְ — The traditional

* The scope of the Oral Law and the exact status of laws derived through the hermeneutic principles are subjects of intricate discussion and, in certain areas, controversy among the classic commentaries. Prominent among them are *Rambam* and *Ramban*. There are similarly differing views concerning the derivation of Rabbinic authority to impose new laws. This *Overview* makes no attempt to cite all views. The reader seeking to achieve an understanding of the authorative opinions might best begin with *Sefer HaMitzvos, Shoresh* 2 and proceed from there.

explanation of the Torah's text. This includes such verses as *'an eye for an eye'* which, as we have seen refers to monetary compensation only, and not physical mutilation. Countless verses in *Tanach* cannot be understood properly in the light of the simple translation, but only as our Sages received the interpretation in the chain of tradition extending from Moses. [For further elucidation, see Overview, ArtScroll edition of *Shir HaShirim*.]

2. הֲלָכָה לְמֹשֶׁה מִסִּינַי — *Halacha l'Moshe mi'Sinai,* laws given to Moses at Sinai which are not specifically rooted in the Written Law, such as the detailed laws of *tefillin* .

3. דִּינִים שֶׁחִידְּשׁוּ עַל פִּי סְבָרָא — Laws derived through logic. A compelling logical inference has the status of a written law. [For example, it is forbidden for someone to kill another human being in order to save his own life. As the Talmud puts it: Why do you think your blood is redder than his? *(Sanhedrin* 74a) . It must be made absolutely clear, however, that 'logic' in order to have any validity in Torah terms, must be firmly and unquestionably rooted in the tradition stretching from Sinai.]

4. גְּזֵירוֹת — Rabbinic decrees. By saying, וּשְׁמַרְתֶּם אֶת מִשְׁמַרְתִּי, *you shall guard My ordinance (Lev* 18:30), the Torah placed upon the Sages the responsibility to act whenever there appeared to be a danger of laxity in the observance the Torah's laws *(Yevamos* 21a). In observance of this Scriptural injunction, the Sages enacted such decrees as prohibitions against the marriage of close relatives who were permitted by the Torah to marry one another.

5. דִּינִים וְתַקָּנוֹת עַל פִּי הַסְכָּמָה — General laws, ordinances, and customs that are enacted based on a rabbinic judgment of the need for them. Included among this category are Moses' ordinance that the laws of Passover be studied during the festival *(Megillah* 4a), Hillel's enactment of *prozbul (Sh'vi'is* 10:3) and countless others.

The Rabbinic authority to enact and enforce

observance of their laws is conferred by the Torah itself.

> כִּי יִפָּלֵא מִמְּךָ דָבָר לַמִּשְׁפָּט . . . וּבָאתָ אֶל־הַכֹּהֲנִים הַלְוִיִּם וְאֶל הַשֹּׁפֵט אֲשֶׁר יִהְיֶה בַּיָּמִים הָהֵם וְדָרַשְׁתָּ וְהִגִּידוּ לְךָ אֵת דְּבַר הַמִּשְׁפָּט. וְעָשִׂיתָ עַל פִּי הַדָּבָר אֲשֶׁר יַגִּידוּ לְךָ . . . וְשָׁמַרְתָּ לַעֲשׂוֹת כְּכֹל אֲשֶׁר יוֹרוּךָ . . . לֹא תָסוּר מִן הַדָּבָר אֲשֶׁר יַגִּידוּ לְךָ יָמִין וּשְׂמֹאל
>
> *If a matter arises for judgment that is too difficult for you . . . Then you shall come to the priests, the Levites, and the judge that shall be in those days, and you shall inquire; and they shall tell you the word of judgment. And you shall do according to the word that they shall tell you . . . and you shall observe to do according to all that they shall inform you . . . you shall not swerve from the word which they shall tell you to the right or to the left (Deut.* 17:8-11).

Asmachta

There is a particular type of Rabbinic ordinance, that provides an enlightening glimpse of the all-embracing nature of the Torah.

There is a particular type of Rabbinic ordinance, one that is much misunderstood, that provides an enlightening glimpse of the all-embracing nature of the Torah. It is called אַסְמַכְתָּא, *asmachta,* a Rabbinic law which is supported by a Biblical text. For example, the Sages decreed that it is forbidden, under normal circumstances to have a non-Jew perform prohibited forms of labor on festivals. Although the prohibition is Rabbinic in nature, they found support for it in a Scriptural verse: כָּל מְלָאכָה לֹא יֵעָשֶׂה, *no work 'may be done.'* The phrase *may be done* indicates that the act is forbidden even if not done by a Jew.

One might be tempted to hold that the reliance on a Scriptural verse for a purely Rabbinic law is a rhetorical flourish or a device to make the law easier to remember or more carefully observed. (There are some authorities who do subscribe to these views.) Strangely, *Rashi* interprets the above verse in line with the *asmachta,* an explanation that, as *Ramban* notes, is patently not the intent of the verse. *Rashi* follows this same practice, in each case disputed by *Ramban*, of reading an *asmachta* into the text in many other places as well (see *Exodus* 22:15; *Exodus* 21:10; *Exodus* 23:11; *Leviticus* 21:24; *Numbers* 10:10). Obviously, it is beyond the realm of possibility that *Rashi*; "father of commentators", erred in his simple interpretation of so many verses. Rather we must see in this a conscious pattern and a deeper understanding of the true intent of the verses. True, the specific ordinance referred to by *Rashi* is Rabbinic, but it is no stranger to the Torah.

Obviously, it is beyond the realm of possibility that Rashi; "father of commentators", erred in his simple interpretation of so many verses.

Ritva (Rosh Hashanah 16a) explains the concept of *asmachta* in connection with the requirement that Biblical verses be recited in conjunction with the blowing of the *shofar* on *Rosh Hashanah*. Although Rabbinic in origin, the Sages find support for the ordinance in *Numbers* 10:10 (see *Rashi* and *Ramban* there). *Ritva* says:

> In referring to the verses that must be recited, Rabbi Akiba says, 'The Holy One, blessed be He said: Say the verses citing My majesty etc., because whenever a certain ordinance has support *(asmachta)* in Scripture, the Holy One, blessed be He prompts us that it is proper to do so except that He has not required it, but left it to the Sages to do so. . . . The Torah suggested [the ordinance] and left it to the Sages to determine whether they wish to impose it as it says *'and you shall do according to the word which they shall tell you' (Deut.* 17:10). Therefore, you find that the Sages everywhere give a proof or an allusion or a support to their words from the Torah, as if to say that they do not originate anything on their own; and the entire Oral Torah is alluded to in the Written Torah which is complete. Heaven forbid that it is lacking in anything.

The Torah is, indeed, complete and perfect.

The Torah is, indeed, complete and perfect.

Solomon found all knowledge and science in it, the Sages found forgotten laws between its lines and among its crowns — and even their own ordinances foreshadowed in its verses.

Every Destiny

It is said that *Ramban* told his students that every man's name and destiny are hinted by the Torah. He had a student named Avner, who turned heretic and came to taunt his former teacher, asking 'Where is *my* name found in the Torah?' *Ramban* answered that the third letters of the words of the following verse contain both his name and his fate: אַפְאֵיהֶם אַשְׁבִּיתָה מֵאֱנוֹשׁ זִכְרָם, [God said of those who defy Him] *I will scatter them to the far corners of the earth, I will make their remembrance cease from among men (Deut.* 32:26).

Avner blanched. His master had found in the Torah punishment for his heresy — or, perhaps, a message to repent.

Avner blanched. His master had found in the Torah punishment for his heresy — or, perhaps, a message to repent. Avner, indeed, repented and spent the rest of his life in self-imposed exile.

The *Vilna Gaon* could not find all knowledge in the Torah as Solomon did — that depth of wisdom did not make its way through generations of steadily decreasing spiritual stature. But *the Gaon* studied whatever sciences he deemed necessary for an understanding of Torah, and then he understood where in Torah each could have been found. He was able to show where every law in the voluminous Oral Torah had its basis in Scripture *(Harav Aharon Kotler).*

The Gaon was able to show where every law in the voluminous Oral Torah had its basis in Scripture.

In more recent times, when blasphemers dared raise their heads against the sanctity of the Oral Torah, such commentaries as *Malbim, Harav Samson Raphael Hirsch, Netziv,* and *Ha'Ksav V'haKabbalah* were written to demonstrate clearly how the Written Torah and the Oral Torah are indivisible halves of a sacred whole.

The written Torah and the Oral Torah are indivisible halves of a sacred whole.

Torah is the beginning of creation — אסתכל באוריתא וברא עלמא, He looked into the Torah and created the world *(Midrash)* — and its purpose — אִם־לֹא בְרִיתִי יוֹמָם וָלָיְלָה חֻקּוֹת שָׁמַיִם וָאָרֶץ לֹא שָׂמְתִּי, *were it not for My covenant day and night, I would not have appointed the ordinances of heaven and earth (Jeremiah* 33:25). The privilege of accepting the Torah from God, for carrying out its precepts, and for finding its sacred sparks in the darkest corners of earthly existence, belongs to Israel. Torah and Israel — the twin purposes of creation. The very first verse in the Torah alludes to them: בְּרֵאשִׁית בָּרָא א׳ אֵת הַשָּׁמַיִם וְאֵת הָאָרֶץ, For the sake of Torah and Israel, both of which are called רֵאשִׁית, the primary cause and purpose, did God create heaven and earth *(Midrash,* see *comm.* 1:1).

The privilege of accepting the Torah from God, for carrying out its precepts, and for finding its sacred sparks in the darkest corners of earthly existence belongs to Israel.

To embody Torah in a physical garb and to enable Israel to elevate the spiritual from the morass of the mundane, were heaven and earth created.

Rabbi Nosson Scherman

לזכר נשמת אנשים נאמנים לה׳ ולתורתו
שנדדו לפה וזכו להרבות האור ולדחות החשך
אבי מורי **ר׳ אברהם דוב ב״ר שמואל נטע שערמאן ע״ה**
א׳ דשבועות תשכ״א
ורעיתו הכבודה
אמי מורתי **ליבא בת ר׳ זאב ע״ה**
ו׳ שבט תשכ״ט
מורי חמי **החבר אפרים בן הר״ר רפאל גוגענהיים ע״ה**
א׳ דר״ח תמוז תש״ך
תנצב״ה.

סדר בראשית
Sidra Bereishis

The Overviews

*An Overview— Creation**

I. Before the Beginning

Prior to creation there was nothing save the glory of God.

Prior to creation there was nothing save the glory of God. Nothing — it is a concept that we, creatures in a physical world, cannot even begin to comprehend, just as the blind cannot comprehend the sunset and the deaf a symphony. Can we conceive of a world without time or space? We can speak of it, think of it, but the truth is that we cannot really imagine phenomena so foreign to our experience. It is illustrative that the most vividly imaginative fictional conceptions of creatures from another planet do not really leave the experience of Mother Earth — they portray beings that are a montage of living things and laboratory experiments, but there is nothing that is truly beyond experiences of man.

Existence prior to creation is unfathomable. There was no sun nor moon — they were created on the fourth day. There were no angels — they were created on the second day. There was not even light or darkness — they were created on the first day. That seems like a contradiction in terms; if there was no light then there was automatically darkness, for is not darkness the absence of light? No, for even that seemingly basic concept is a product of our earthbound experience.

There was only God, incorporeal, omnipresent, without beginning and without end. But God wanted to do good to beings apart from Himself, and in order to make it possible for Him to do so, He created a uni-

*This treatment of Creation is based primarily on *Derech Hashem*

Because God is absolutely perfect, he wanted the good that He would confer upon others to be equally perfect.

verse with human life. Because God is absolutely perfect, he wanted the good that He would confer upon others to be equally perfect. This could be possible only if the beneficiaries of His goodness would be enabled to share in the perfection of His Glory.

To Confer Good

His wisdom decreed that simply to create a being and lavish upon him the blessings of his Maker would not be enough, because the person who has not earned reward feels no satisfaction in undeserved gifts. They are נהמא דכיסופא, *the bread of shame,* because, rather than make the recipient feel proud that he has been found deserving, he feels humiliated that he is showered with blessings that are not truly his. Thus in order for the intended goodness to be worthy of the Source of all good, it would have to be of a nature that could be earned by the beneficiary and thus be the greatest possible source of satisfaction, fulfillment, and happiness to him.

In order for the intended goodness to be worthy of the Source of all good, it would have to be of a nature that could be earned by the beneficiary.

In order to achieve this goal, God desired these conditions: man, His intended creature, had to have free choice; he had to be placed in a setting where he would be required to choose between good and evil; and the choice could not be obvious — if it were then it would be ludicrous to reward man for choosing well. After all, one does not reward a child for not putting his hand into a fiery oven.

The choice could not be obvious. One does not reward a child for not putting his hand into a fiery oven.

If the superiority of good over evil were too manifest, the choice would become an automatic, instinctive decision; one unworthy of the sort of reward God wanted to bestow. The goal could be achieved only if the holiness of God were so concealed that it would be possible to err. If man could live in an atmosphere of conflict between good and evil, an atmosphere where evil was not only plausible but tempting, not only tempting but rewarding, then the successful struggle against seduction would steadily elevate him. At every stage of his existence he would face new challenges, always struggling against the desires of the flesh and the titillation of the temptation that shouted to him, 'In hedonism

In hedonism there is pleasure, in wealth there is comfort, in culture there is fulfillment.

there is pleasure, in wealth there is comfort, in culture there is fulfillment.' If he could then surmount the 'obvious' and cleave to the way of God, recognizing that the alluring impediments were nothing more than a mirage, his spiritual growth would be constant, and eventually he would be worthy of the reward which God created the universe in order to bestow.

II. Good and Evil

Existence of Evil

But if God is everywhere, and nothing can exist unless He makes it so — הַמְחַדֵּשׁ בְּטוּבוֹ בְּכָל יוֹם תָּמִיד מַעֲשֵׂה בְרֵאשִׁית, *In His goodness He constantly renews the acts of creation every day* — how then can we associate Him with the existence of evil?

In order to understand this, we must redefine good and evil. We think of 'good' as whatever gives us satisfaction. To a child, good is ice cream and a bicycle. To an adult, good can be anything from an undisturbed hour with a tractate of the Talmud to — as we move toward the other extreme of the human spectrum — a symphony concert, accumulation of wealth, sensual gratification, sadistic subjugation of others. Always, one man's good is another's foolishness or evil.

'Good' is the presence of God; evil is not His absence— for He is everywhere — but His hiddenness, the lack of awareness that He is present.

The Torah defines 'good' differently. 'Good' is the presence of God; evil is not His *absence* — for He is everywhere — but His hiddenness, the lack of awareness that He is present.

The cardinal principles of Jewish belief are that God exists and that He is One. His Oneness implies that לית אתר פנוי מיניה, *there is no place free from Him.* The more one is aware of His Presence, the more that place or situation is good. A crowded study hall reverberating with the crescendo of Torah study, a synagogue filled with children speaking to their Father, a poor threshold hallowed with a food package that will gladden a hungry family — all these

The more one is aware of His Presence, the more that place or situation is good. A crowded study hall, a synagogue, a poor threshold hallowed with a food package.

are good, because they are manifestations of His existence in the minds and hearts of people. But scenes of suffering and tragedy can also be good if we could but realize that all is part of His master plan. It is when we do not perceive His Presence, when we fail to see purpose and direction in earthly affairs that we live with evil. In short, evil is a condition where God is not seen.

It is when we do not perceive His Presence, when we fail to see purpose and direction in earthly affairs that we live with evil.

There are situations in life that seem inherently evil: surely the ugliness of man at his worst cannot be described as good, or even neutral. But even they can serve as a vehicle for elevating man. If he surmounts the challenge that they present, then he has become a better, stronger person. The person who lives in a cruel society as Abraham did and remains kind and compassionate, has grown. The one who travels through a deceitful land and remains honest and upright as Jacob did, has grown. Thus, the evil around him served the beneficial purpose of elevating him to further greatness.

'It Is Enough'

In order to create the conditions for this type of choice, God created a world where His Presence would be obscure enough to enable man not to see it, if he so chose. He subjected his all-pervasive holiness to צמצום אחר צמצום, limitation upon limitation, as layer after layer of material existence built up to disguise and conceal His Presence. This process was set in motion by God and continued until He, in His Supreme Wisdom, determined that it had reached its desired extent.

He subjected His all-pervasive holiness to limitation upon limitation to disguise and conceal His Presence.

God's name שדי, *Shaddai,* is derived from the phrase מי שאמר לעולמו די, He Who said to His עולם, world, 'it is enough' *(Zohar, Pesikta, Tanchuma).* In its plain meaning, it refers to the physical expansion of the earth. Creation began with a single point on earth, the אבן שתיה, *Even Sh'siah,* the rock in the Holy of Holies in the Temple upon which the Holy Ark rested. It was given that name שממנו הושתת העולם, for from it the earth 'sprang forth.' It continued to expand until God said, 'It is enough.' Had He said

It continued to expand until God said 'It is enough'.

it sooner, the planet would have been smaller; had He said it later, the planet would have continued to grow. He allowed the process to continue until the mass of earth achieved the proper size and balance of forces it needed to support the quality and extent of life that He desired for it *(Zohar).*

Every physical phenomenon has its spiritual counterpart.

This is the purely material sense of Shaddai. But every physical phenomenon has its spiritual counterpart. The name *Olam,* earth has a spiritual connotation, and God's command 'it is enough' applies to this other aspect as well.

The most vital element in creation is spirituality. It is obscured by the material, interlaced with evil, disguised by statistics, logic, and data. But it is man's task on earth to cut away the earthly insulation that prevents the rays of spirituality from warming his soul. The Torah says זֶה שְּׁמִי לְעֹלָם וְזֶה זִכְרִי לְדֹר דֹּר, *This is My Name forever and this is My memorial for all generations (Exodus* 3:15). The Talmud notes that the word לְעֹלָם, *forever,* is spelled the same way as לְעָלֵם, *to be hidden.* From this spelling with its implication that God's Name would be 'hidden', the Sages derive that לא כשאני נכתב אני נקרא, 'I [My Name] am not to be pronounced as I am written.' Hence the law that it is forbidden to pronounce the Four-Letter Name of God as it is written. There was one exception to the rule that God's Name may not be properly pronounced — *the Holy Temple.* There, because His Presence was apparent, His Name could be said. *Because He was not hidden, His Name need not be hidden (Ritva).*

Because He was not hidden, His Name need not be hidden.

The Measure of Hiddenness

God's Name is hidden — *His very Presence* is hidden within the universe He created. This is the meaning of צמצום אחר צמצום, the one limitation after another by means of which He steadily diminished the perceptibility of His holiness, by means of which he made the עָלַם-עוֹלָם world an instrument to hide Himself from His creatures. This increasing extent of hiddenness had to continue until it reached the right state — the state at which man could be deceived into

This increasing extent of hiddenness had to continue until it reached the right state.

thinking that there is חס וחלילה no God save for the dictates of his senses and his lust for power and license, but also the state at which sincere, seeking men could find God's presence on earth and in every aspect of life. When that point was reached אמר לעולמו די, God said to His *Olam,* His process of hiding the Godly Presence, that it was enough.

Indeed, we may perhaps be permitted to say that the creation of חשך, the primeval 'darkness,' constituted this very process. As mentioned above, darkness was a creation, not merely the absence of light. Rashi quotes the Sages, that during the first day, אור וחשך משתמשים בערבוביא, light and darkness were intermixed *(Gen.* 1:4). Surely if light were present then darkness could not have existed — unless it was a specific creation that was not subject to the light. It may well be that, in the spiritual sense, the 'darkness' of that first day was the very limitation that obscured God's Presence. It was when the extent of material obscurity had adequately veiled the clarity of spiritual vision that God declared an end to the process of ever-expanding darkness.

The 'darkness' of the first day was the very limitation that obscured God's Presence.

III. Man's Role

To See the Truth

That task accomplished, the world was ready for man. To see the light through the mists would not be easy, but it could be done if man were honest in seeking the truth rather than satisfying his animal desires. Because it could be done, man was required to do it. Because it was not an easy task, he would be amply deserving of reward if he achieved it. Thus, God satisfied the motive of creation: He would be able to confer good upon man, but it would not be a cheap, undeserved good. Man could attain it only by elevating the spiritual in himself and by uniting it with the spiritual in creation. He would see the uni-

Because it could be done, man was required to do it. Because it was not an easy task, he would be amply deserving of reward if he achieved it.

verse for what it was, a camouflage disguising what was truly meaningful and eternal. He would realize that in total immersion in Torah even amid poverty, hunger, and thirst, lay a degree of happiness and contentment *in this world* that was infinitely greater than any to be found in wealth, luxury, and self-indulgence (see *Avos* 6:1).

To whatever extent he is able to accomplish that, man attains a degree of perfection that is somewhat akin to that of His Maker. By uniting his intellect with that of God through the study of Torah and by perfecting his deeds through the performance of the commandments, man earns the degree of perfection that it is possible for him to attain, and the degree of reward that God seeks to give.

Israel — People and Land

In all of creation, only man has unlimited freedom of choice.

In all of creation, only man has unlimited freedom of choice. The forces of nature have no such freedom. The natural forces are under the control of angels who serve as the intermediaries in carrying out God's will. Thus we find references in the words of the Sages to the angels of the sea, the angels of individual nations, even the angels of blades of grass. These angelic ministers carry out God's dictates throughout the universe. The only exceptions are the people of Israel and Eretz Israel, both of which have greater holiness and are, therefore, guided only by God Himself.

Until the time of the Patriarchs, all men were equal both in their calling and in their opportunity to achieve the heavenly goal set for them.

The Jewish people began to attain this degree of holiness through the deeds of Abraham, Isaac, and Jacob. Until the time of the Patriarchs, all men were equal both in their calling and in their opportunity to achieve the heavenly goal set for them. But the ten generations up to Noah, failed to achieve their mission, and the ten generations from Noah to Abraham failed again, (see *Overview* to Noah) until Abraham founded the nation that would become God's chosen one. Eretz Israel, because creation began from the *'even sh'siah'* on the holy mountain — is the 'center of creation' in the material sense, and it is the center of holiness on earth, as well *(Ramban).*

The Higher Power

Despite the laws of nature and the angels who carry them out, there is a power higher then them — man.

Despite the laws of nature and the angels who carry them out, there is a power higher than them — man. For it was given to him through his free choice, to make nature yield to him. Throughout the Torah are sprinkled blessings that will come to man if he makes the Torah his love and the commandments his pursuit.

Indeed, as *Ramban* explains, this is one of the great miracles of creation. It is not at all surprising that man can sanctify himself and earn the blessings of holiness through immersion in spiritual pursuit. That souls can cleave to God after they leave their bodies, or that righteous human beings can be rewarded with the superhuman height of prophecy is not at all surprising: spiritual attainment is deserving of spiritual reward. But rain, prosperity, security, triumph over enemies? Why should the study of Torah or the performance of commandments affect crops, bank accounts, and battles? That is one of the great miracles of creation. For that reason the Torah declines to promise spiritual rewards instead of material ones; the first are understood, the second could never be fathomed had not the Torah made them plain.

Why should the study of Torah or the performance of the commandments affect crops, bank accounts, and battles?

It is clear, therefore, that man's deeds are not statistics in a personal ledger. They can split the sea and stop the sun, water the desert and silence a cannon, because the world's existence is founded in the spirit of God. It is covered and camouflaged, but without it there is no universe, for without God's Presence — open or concealed — nothing can exist. Man can unite himself in thought and deed with that Presence. When he does so he has fulfilled the purpose of creation, and creation bends to his needs.

Man's deeds can split the sea and stop the sun, water the desert and silence a cannon, because the world's existence is founded in the spirit of God.

IV. More Worlds Than One

What is a World?

Do the intellectual and the aborigine live in the same world? A person's world consists of far more than sand and sea.

Even in this world of obscurity and hiddenness, there are still many levels of existence — many *worlds.* Can one say that the great and holy sage and the avaricious criminal inhabit the same world in any save the physical sense? Do the intellectual and the aborigine live in the same world? A person's world consists of far more than sand and sea — in essence the physical peculiarities of his existence are no more important than the brown paper bag in which a treasure may be wrapped.

In these terms, we can catch the merest glimpse of the vast difference between essence and appurtenance. Some people do indeed believe that clothes make the man, while others know that worth makes him. Some judge a person by his cover, others by his content. Is it merely figurative to say that the Chofetz Chaim and the Gerer Rebbi did not inhabit the same world as Hitler and Stalin?

Is it merely figurative to say that the Chofetz Chaim and the Gerer Rebbe did not inhabit the same world as Hitler and Stalin?

Just as there are parallel lines of existence between righteous and wicked, so, too, there are higher worlds than any we can conceive of. The Sages tell us that there is a Holy Temple in heaven that awaits the final redemption of Israel when it will descend to earth. It is not a building of brick and mortar. There is a spiritual Temple which will one day become clothed in physical form and take shape on earth just as the Torah of black fire on white fire took the form of parchment and ink and earthly commandments. There was a physical Garden of Eden and there is a heavenly paradise — the first is the physical manifestation of the second. When Jacob returned to the land of Canaan he saw a company of angels and named the place *Machanaim,* twin camps. *Ramban* explains that there were *two* camps — one, a company of angels on high; the other, Jacob's company below. The one below was the human complement of the one above — except that it was greater, because

The one below was the human complement of the one above — except that it was greater, because creation came into being to serve it and to be influenced by it.

creation came into being to serve it and to be influenced by it.

Two Suns

Even familiar sights exist on levels beyond our perception. With this concept *Rav Moshe Chaim Luzzatto,* in *Adir BaMarom* explains many seemingly difficult Talmudic passages concerning the sun.

'The sun should have set in the middle of the sky' *(Sanhedrin* 91b) — how is this possible? He splits the windows of the firmament and removes the sun from its place' *(Siddur)* — but the earth is round and it circles the sun continuously; from what 'place' is the sun removed?

Although the sun, the moon, and the stars are physical things, they are also the garb of metaphysical properties and emanations by which God infuses spiritual life to creation.

The fact is, however, that although the sun, the moon, and the stars are physical things, they are also the garb of metaphysical properties and emanations by which God infuses spiritual life to creation. Whenever the Sages refer to astronomical phenomena that contradict observable facts, they are referring to this spiritual aspect — the *higher world* — of those heavenly bodies. It is certainly true that, because the earth is round, there is no factual basis for saying that any point on the globe is 'the east' — wherever one stands on earth, there is always a point further east as one continues to go round and round, nor does the world have a top or center. But in a higher sense, it has.

There are other holy places on earth: synagogues, study halls, Eretz Yisrael, homes that are founded upon and guided by the dictates of Torah. It is upon such places that God smiles in the benevolent glow of His Presence.

The *Even Sh'siah* is the top, the center, because it was the beginning of creation and remained forever the point of utmost holiness on earth. There are other holy places on earth: synagogues, study halls, *Eretz Yisrael,* homes that are founded upon and guided by the dictates of Torah. It is upon such places that God smiles in the benevolent glow of His Presence with emanations that are dispatched to earth by means of the sun. When the sun moves above a place that is deserving of these spiritual rays, God removes the higher sun from its place in heaven. It proceeds through the 'windows' of the firmament and unperceptibly melds with the ball of gas that astronomers call the sun. When the sun goes by the repositories of spirituality on earth, it is indeed fitting that 'it should set in the midst of the sky': the *spiritual* manifestation should cease to radiate, not the gaseous mass that provides light, heat, and energy — that physical body rotates endlessly, serving its planetary satellites everywhere on earth.

That, too, is part of the sun's task, just as it is part of a teacher's job to apply band-aids and care for bloody noses.

That, too, is part of the sun's task, just as it is part of a teacher's job to apply band-aids and care for bloody noses. But his main task is to inspire a child with a love of Torah and an unquenchable desire to make it his. The sun does all the things that scientists say it does, but their vision fails them before they can see the sun's greatest tasks, before they can bask in its spiritual rays.

The sun does all the things that scientists say it does, but their vision fails them before they can see the sun's greatest tasks, before they can bask in its spiritual rays.

Each person can be buffeted by the angelic enforcers of the law of nature, or he can rise above them and bend them to his greatness.

All of this is part of the creation in which we live: limitation upon limitation, level after level. Each person lives in his own world with the responsibility to climb to a higher one and the danger that he will stumble and fall to a lower one. Each person can be buffeted by the angelic enforcers of the laws of nature, or he can rise above them and bend them to his greatness. He can be one more earthly creature, hardly rising above animal life, or he can become the fulfillment of God's wish when He created heaven and earth and said נַעֲשֶׂה אָדָם, *Let us make man.*

*An Overview— Adam – And Sin**

I. The Greatness of Adam

Unimaginable Stature

In order to understand a sin, one must understand the sinner. Moses — master of all prophets, most trusted in God's universe, most humble of men — was denied the cherished goal of entering *Eretz Israel* because he hit the stone and chastised the people (*Numbers* 20:7-13). There are many differing explanations of the sin; the commentators themselves find it hard to explain how Moses' deed and words were serious enough to merit so severe a punishment. Any understanding of the sin of Moses, as of any of the ancients, requires a realization that they were so great that their actions were measured by standards far above our own (see Overview, ArtScroll edition of Ruth).

Who was Adam whose sin played such a pivotal role in the history and destiny of man?

Who was Adam whose sin played such a pivotal role in the history and destiny of man?

כשנברא טעו מלאכי השרת ובקשו לומר לפניו קדוש

> *When he was created the angels erred* [thinking he was a divine being] *and wished to sing 'Holy' before him (Midrash).*

The very angels thought that Adam was a deity. They had no concept of what he really was. We cannot even imagine how exalted was his greatness — for, if the angels didn't know, can we mortals hope to know?

If the angels didn't know, can we mortals hope to know?

* The following treatment is based primarily on *Michtav me'Eliyahu*

אדם הראשון מן הארץ עד לרקיע ... מסוף העולם ועד סופו היה

Adam extended from the earth to the firmament ... from one end of the earth to the other (Chagigah 12a)

There was no facet of creation, from the most mundane to the most sublime, that Adam did not encompass.

This statement of the Sages has a profound spiritual dimension. There was no facet of creation, from the most mundane to the most sublime, that Adam did not encompass. Nothing was hidden from him. More — no one ever comprehended better than Adam how each of his actions could determine the course of creation. The angels knew that, ultimately, it was not they who controlled him, but he who controlled them, for the Divine Will made the functioning of earth dependent upon the deeds of man (see *Overview* of Creation above).

שני עקביו דומין לשני גלגלי החמה

[*After Adam's death*] *his two heels were like two suns (Bava Basra* 58a).

Even after his sin and after death, the holiness of Adam was so awesome that the least significant part of his body, his heel, was as brilliant as the sun.

Having these barest insights into the greatness of Adam, we still know nothing of his awesome nature.

Having these barest insights into the greatness of Adam, we still know nothing of his awesome nature; it is sufficient to know that the distance between his loftiness and ourselves is like the distance between heaven and earth. Only in these terms can we hope to have a faint understanding of his sin. Surely, however, we cannot either understand it or learn from it to perfect our own puny selves unless we banish from our minds the foolish myth of 'apples in Eden'.

Adam's World

Adam's 'world' was much different from our own. He tilled and planted without tools: he was placed in the Garden of Eden לעבדה במצות עשה ולשמרה במצות לא תעשה, he was conscious in his everyday life that he worked the Garden of Eden through the performance of positive commandments and he protected it by means of avoiding transgression. We, too, 'know' this, but only in an abstract sense. As

As believers we know that our deeds matter; but as part of a physical, cause-and-effect world, we find ourselves seeing *and* feeling *the efficacy of medicines and surgeons, of bulldozers and bricklayers, of bombs and physicists*

believers, we *know* that our deeds matter; but as part of a physical, cause-and-effect world, we find ourselves *seeing* and *feeling* the efficacy of medicines and surgeons, of bulldozers and bricklayers, of bombs and physicists. True, the Talmud says, אין ערוד ממית אלא חטא ממית, it is not the poisonous snake that kills, but the sin that kills *(Berachos* 33a). The snake, the bullet, the runaway auto, the disease — these are but the messengers that carry out a decree sealed by human misdeed. They are no more the cause of death than the white sheet pulled over the face of the expired patient.

We may find it so hard to believe that spiritual causes brought about physical effects that most of us are quick to point to impressive lists of external factors that caused them to be so. But this is nothing more than a sympton of God's concealment in this Olam-world of hiddenness. The great Jewish believers knew it to be so.

> בָּרוּךְ הַגֶּבֶר אֲשֶׁר יִבְטַח בַּה׳ וְהָיָה ה׳ מִבְטַחוֹ
> *Blessed is the man who trusts in God and who makes God the source of his trust (Jeremiah* 17:7).

Chidushei HaRim explains that the two halves of the verse are dependent upon one another: the more one trusts in God, the more God justifies his trust with the result that his trust in God continues to increase. Our greatest people found no difficulty in casting their lots for service of God without knowing where the next morning's breakfast would come from. Indeed, לא ניתנה תורה אלא לאוכלי המן, Torah was given only to the generation that ate the manna *(Mechilta).* They learned in their everyday lives that they could live in a barren wilderness without fear, in secure confidence that God's promise was their assurance of the next days sustenance. Only after developing such faith was Israel worthy of receiving the Torah.

Our greatest people found no difficulty in casting their lots for service of God without knowing where the next morning's breakfast would come from.

As the *Kotzker* said, Torah greatness can be attained only when there is indifference to need for financial security. Torah is the wisdom of God; the

Torah sage unites his own mind with the intelligence of the Creator. To the extent that he is concerned with his needs in this world, he cannot escape its snares to ascend to a higher one.

For us, mired in our work ethic and forty hour week, faith is a fringe benefit we can afford only after having attained bogus 'security.' After telling an inspiring story of a great *tzaddik's* perfect faith, we return our shoulders to the wheel. Adam not only knew but *saw* that his service of God was the determining factor in his success. And he saw it to a greater extent than any man who ever lived — until he sinned!

II. Adam's Sin

Foreign Temptation

What was the difference between Adam before the sin and Adam after the sin?

Each of us is subject to his own temptations — some to money, some to lust, some to glory, some to power. Whatever our spiritual station, there are some sins that tempt us sorely, others that have conquered us, and still others that we never even consider. Which of us, imperfect though we are, would attempt to commit a barbaric atrocity? We know that human beings have, do, and will commit such acts — even people who love their families, assist helpless old people across the street, and consider themselves civilized. Nevertheless, we don't consider ourselves prey to this pathology. There may be gossip on our tongues and larceny (in varying degrees) in our hearts; but some transgressions are beyond the pale, are so unjustifiably evil that in no way could we conceive of ourselves ever commiting them. They are beyond our thought processes. Even modern terminology reflects this conviction: certain behavior is called the law of the jungle — but that behavior is beneath us, because we live in 'civilization', not the jungle.

Which of us, imperfect though we are, would attempt to commit a barbaric atrocitty?

Certain behavior is called the law of the jungle — but that behavior is beneath us, because we live in 'civilization', not the jungle.

This can help us understand, in small measure, the

greatness of Adam before his sin. *Ramban* explains, and *Rav Chaim of Volozhin* in *Nefesh HaChaim* elaborates, that when Adam was created, his nature was to do good. He was not the mixture of good and evil inclinations that human beings are today. We have lusts and desires that are part of our very humanity. The desire for wealth, comfort, and pleasure is not whispered in our ears by some outside agency seeking to lead us astray. We *want* them, our psyche demands them. We are born as selfish beings who would grow up to be totally avaricious and hedonistic were it not for the strictures of society and the strength of developing conscience. Adam was different: his innate nature was good and it sought to perform nothing but the will of his Maker.

Adam was not the mixture of good and evil inclinations.

We have lusts and desires. We want them, our psyche demands them.

Of course, he had free will, for, as we have seen above, without man's free-willed struggle to choose good over evil, the purpose of creation could not be fulfilled. But the temptation to evil was not a part of him; it came from without and it was against his nature. He was free to heed its blandishments just as we are free to place ourselves in great danger or even to commit suicide, but such courses are as alien to our nature as evil was to Adam's. When the call to sin came to Adam, it came not from within himself, but from the serpent who served as the embodiment of the Satanic evil inclination. But after the sin, man changed. The urge to sin was no longer dangled in front of him by a seductive serpent; it had become part of him. Now the desire for forbidden fruits comes from within man; when we sin, we respond not to the urging of an outside force, but to our own desires. It is *we* — not *it* or *they* — who urge transgression upon us.

But after the sin, man changed. The urge to sin was no longer dangled in front of him by a seductive serpent; it had become part of him.

How could it happen?

If Adam was so great how could he sin? If he has so clear a perception of God's holiness, and was himself a person of such exalted spirituality, how could any outside temptation have swayed him?

Even at his rarefied level, there was still a challenge. Temptation came from outside, but Adam was

It was his mission to elevate himself to a level where the urge to sin was so patently false and senseless that it made no more impact on him that the buzzing of a fly.

capable of hearing and understanding it: it was his mission to elevate himself to a level where the urge to sin was so patently false and senseless that it made no more impact on him than the buzzing of a fly. Holy though he was by virtue of being the handiwork of God and the subject of angelic awe and praise, he was still created in partnership with the earth. His animal flesh was the agent of *Olam-earth* to conceal even greater levels of holiness: it was his mission to elevate even the fleshly, the earthly, until the very veils shone with the splendor of their Creator.

To us — intertwined and interlocked as we are in contradiction, doubt, and temptation — Adam's challenge seems like simplicity itself. But it was a real challenge, nevertheless. Had he persevered during the few hours between his creation and the onset of the first Sabbath, the purpose of creation would have been achieved and the rest of history would have been a tale of perfection and sublime enjoyment of God's rewards. His immediate challenge was to resist the inclination to disobey represented by the serpent, and to cleave ever closer to God despite the barrier of flesh that removed him from the ultimate heavenly glory. That the challenge was indeed worthy of even so great a creature as Adam is plain from the reward in store. The purpose of creation was God's wish to bestow well-deserved, hard-earned reward — and that purpose would have been achieved in just a few hours had not Adam succumbed. In the heavenly scale, mighty rewards are not earned by puny achievements. No matter how convinced we are that we would have done better had we had the opportunity, we must realize that our lack of comprehension does not minimize Adam's challenge. Just as we have no conception of his greatness, we have no conception of the seeds of his failure.

His immediate challenge was to resist the inclination to disobey.

In the heavenly scale, mighty rewards are not earned by puny achievements.

His Mission

Adam's mission was to create a *Kiddush Hashem,* Sanctification of the Name, by overcoming the temptation to sin. But because the temptation came from without, the *Kiddush Hashem* could never be as great as it would have been had he been able to overcome an internal urge to do wrong. Had the falsehood of evil been less plain to him; had he been forced to choose between pleasant and ugly instead of between truth and falsehood, then the potential sanctification would have been much greater. The businessman sanctifies the Name far more by not cheating his competitors than by not murdering them. The Torah scholar sanctifies the Name far more by not wasting a precious moment than by not burning his books. Because it is man's mission to glorify God's name — כֹּל הַנִּקְרָא בִשְׁמִי וְלִכְבוֹדִי בְּרָאתִיו, *everyone that is called by My Name, and I have created him for My Glory (Isaiah 43:7)* — Adam hoped to accomplish greater glory for God by subjecting himself to and persevering against a greater challenge.

Had the falsehood of evil been less plain to him; had he been forced to choose between pleasant and ugly instead of between truth and falsehood, then the potential sanctification would have been much greater.

The Tree of the Knowledge of Good and Evil, עֵץ הַדַּעַת טוֹב וָרָע, contained more than luscious, attractive fruit. It represented the mixture of good and evil, a conflict between desire and conscience. The commentators explain that when he ate of the tree, Adam changed. No longer was temptation a serpent that sought to attract his interest from a distance. No longer was sin like a fire beckoning him to jump into its consuming flame. Temptation entered inside him and became part of him. Lust was no longer the message of a glib serpent, it was the desire of pleasure-seeking man. Until then, Adam and Eve wore no clothing — for why should they? All of their organs were tools in the service of God. There was no difference between mind and heart, between hands and other parts of the body. There was no need for shame, for animal lust was not a human attribute.

Until then, Adam and Eve wore no clothing — for why Should they? All of their organs were tools in the service of God.

His Failure

After eating the fruit of the tree, however, 'knowledge' entered man. It was not a new dimension in the knowledge of good — Adam's knowledge of the good was intimate and awesome before then. It was an awareness that good and evil are intertwined and that his limbs and organs, divinely bestowed instruments of good, could also be the tools of lust. Mating had been exclusively the means of fulfilling God's injunction to be fruitful and multiply, to produce new bearers of God's mission, new creatures to whom the angels would sing and pay obeisance. After his sin and his attainment of a new 'knowledge' of desire, it became a means toward gratifying man's most powerful urge and transforming human beings into two-legged animals. Therefore, the immediate product of the forbidden meal was shame and the need for clothing. Man knew the anguish of his new knowledge, for it was a knowledge that brought lust and impurity inside him and sullied the organs that had once existed only for good.

Man knew the anguish of his new knowledge, for it was a knowledge that brought lust and impurity inside him and sullied the organs that had once existed only for good.

For a human being to face such a challenge and surmount it is indeed a task of enormous difficulty. Success constitutes a high degree of *Kiddush Hashem.* That was what Adam wanted. By making his task harder, he was hoping to serve his Maker better. To find one's way in darkness is a greater feat than finding it in sunlight. Adam thought he could please God by plunging into darkness. The hiddenness of creation itself was not enough for him; he thought he could serve God more if he served Him in new ways. He was wrong. He changed his mission, changed his essence, drew more veils of obscurity between himself and God, exchanged Eden for thistles and thorns, diminished his labor from positive and negative commandments to plow and scythe, changed from a target of the serpent to its host.

To find one's way in darkness is a greater feat than finding it in the sunlight. Adam thought he could please God by plunging into darkness.

The Effect of Sin

Had Adam not sinned, his life would have been an upward spiral of spiritual elevation. But he did. By doing so he caused a basic change in his make-up, and, therefore, in his mission. Up to then evil had been an outside temptation, a clear-cut falsehood with no claim on the credence of man; by eating the fruit that held the knowledge of combined good and evil, Adam took evil into himself. It became part of

From then on, his evil inclination became 'I want, I desire, I need. . .'

his nature and from then on, his evil inclination became 'I want, I desire, I need. . . .'

Perfection would require millenia and the combined efforts of countless millions of human beings down the generations.

The perfection of newly fallen man required a new, laborious, seemingly endless process. It would require millenia and the combined efforts of countless millions of human beings down the generations. We cannot understand why this particular course was necessary, but so the divine wisdom decreed. Man's emergence from evil to good became infinitely more difficult because his perception of good and evil became clouded. Lust and temptation became part of him and he began to see evil as unpleasant, ugly, 'not nice' — or enticing. Since that day, man's history has been an unending effort to raise himself out of that morass and to return to that original realization when good and evil were distinct and clear cut.

In his present form, man cannot return to his original state. Only through death and resuscitation could he be born once again as man before the sin. For this reason, the sin brought death upon the human race. It was not a vindictive punishment; had that been the case, succeeding generations would not have fallen victim to the decree. Death became the only road to renewed perfection; by means of it, man left the life and earth that had become imperfect and, when the proper moment in God's design arrived, his soul would return to a new life in a world of renewed perfection. During this interval and again in its new life, the soul would reap the reward it had earned by its degree of success in the struggle to wrest good from its concealment on earth *(Derech Hashem).*

During this interval and again in its new life, the soul would reap the reward it had earned by its degree of success in the struggle to wrest good from its concealment on earth.

The state of creation following the sin was confusion. From the state of clear-cut division between good and evil, there emerged desire for evil and revulsion for good, impaired recognition of which was which, and a blurring of values. Man's mission on earth became הבדלה, separation. He had to find the good both within himself and in the world around him, and he had to identify the evil masquerading as good. The most dangerous result of his

Man's mission on earth became הבדלה, separation. He had to find the good both within himself and in the world around him.

sin was the confusion. In a sense, earth returned to its primeval state when light and darkness reigned in an ill-defined mixture until God separated them. Now man had created a new mixture within himself and it became his mission to define the ingredients once again *(Sfas Emes)*.

With that task accomplished man can once again see creation as it truly is. The Sages say:

. . . . בַּיּוֹם הַהוּא יִהְיֶה ה׳ אֶחָד . . . . אטו האידנא לאו אחד הוא? אמר ר׳ אחא בר חנינא . . . . העולם הזה על בשורות טובות אומר ברוך הטוב והמטיב ועל בשורות רעות אומר ברוך דיין האמת. לעולם הבא כולו הטוב והמטיב

On that day Hashem will be one (Zecharia 14:9).

Isn't He one now as well? Rabbi Acha bar Chanina said, The World to Come is not like this world. In this world, for good news one says, 'Blessed is the Good One Who does good'. For bad news one says, 'Blessed is the Judge of truth'. In the world to come, for everything one will bless 'the Good One Who does good' (Pesachim 50a).

At his best, he recognizes God as the true Judge, but he is inadequate to recognize the ultimate goodness in apparent tragedy. That will have to wait.

No matter how high man rises in this world, he is still limited by his material nature and by the evil that is internalized within him. At his best, he recognizes God as the true Judge, but he is inadequate to recognize the ultimate goodness in apparent tragedy. That will have to wait.

The purpose of creation is man. It was made to test him, elevate him and to be the vehicle for bringing God's mercy upon him. And only he could fulfill it. For that reason, the Torah does not say וירא אלקים כי טוב, *'and God saw that it was good'* after the creations of the second day even though the angels were created on that day. The creation of angels, holy though they were, was not designated with a divine seal of approval because they are not essential to the fulfillment of God's purpose as is man *(Rabbeinu Bachya)*. And of man, it does not say כי טוב, *it was good,* because man is never complete. After more than fifty-seven centuries, his task still goes on *(Sefer HaIkkarim).*

III. The Earth is Man's

Lessons and Challenges

הַשָּׁמַיִם שָׁמַיִם לה׳ וְהָאָרֶץ נָתַן לִבְנֵי אָדָם

The heavens are the heavens of Hashem, but He has given the earth to the children of man (Psalms 115:16).

Chidushei HaRim gives us a truly dazzling insight into this familiar verse. God needs no assistance from man to make the heavens 'heavenly.' They are holy by virtue of His Presence and the hosts that serve and glorify His Name. But the earth — to make the earth heavenly He gave it to man so that he, by the performance of good and the avoidance of evil can transform the cloak concealing His holiness and even His very existence into a slice of heaven.

To make the world heavenly He gave it to man so that he, by his performance of good and the avoidance of evil can transform the cloak concealing His holiness and even His very existence into a slice of heaven.

The earth is man's to perfect and he must learn from it. Its phenomena were set in place to challenge him or to teach him. So strange an occurrence as a sin of the dead, silent earth is incomprehensible without this perception. Yet, at the beginning of creation the earth itself did not carry out God's will:

וַיֹּאמֶר אֱלֹקִים תַּדְשֵׁא הָאָרֶץ דֶּשֶׁא עֵשֶׂב מַזְרִיעַ זֶרַע עֵץ פְּרִי עֹשֶׂה פְּרִי לְמִינוֹ

God said, 'Let the earth sprout vegetation: herbage yielding seed, fruit trees yielding fruit each after its kind (Genesis 1:11).

HASHEM commanded the earth to produce trees whose bark would taste the same as their fruit. The earth did not comply. Therefore, when Adam was cursed for his sin, the earth, too, was cursed *(Rashi,* see comm. 1:11).

How did the earth have the temerity to disobey? The earth, through its controlling angel, knew that God would store away the brilliant primeval light because the wicked people of the future were unworthy of it *(Midrash).* It reasoned that if the original plan of creation was altered to prevent the wicked from enjoying a spiritual light that they did not deserve, then the richness of earth's produce, too, was more than the wicked should be given. Therefore, earth diminished the pleasures available to them and defied God's order that it produce trees that would be edible and tasty throughout. This failure of the earth contributed to Adam's later sin, because the serpent strengthened his argument by pointing to the earth which had ignored God's command with impunity. For contributing to man's downfall, the earth was cursed along with him (*Shaloh HaKadosh*).

This failure of the earth contributed to Adam's later sin, because the serpent strengthened his argument by pointing to the earth which had ignored God's command with impunity.

His Mysteries

But the earth's intention was honorable, its logic faultless. It intended only to follow the example of God Himself — why was it punished?

Its behavior and future punishment were meant to be lessons to man. Otherwise earth would not have been given the power to sin and the Torah would not have found it necessary to record the sin for eternity. The earth had been given a command yet it was presumptuous enough to arrogate to itself the authority to overrule the word of God. Its reason? — logical. Its precedent? — God Himself. Where had it erred?

A very great man in the future — a man who was deemed worthy of becoming *Mashiach* — also took it upon himself to contravene a commandment. King Chizkiyahu was shown that wicked people would descend from him, so he decided not to beget children. It would be better to have no children than to have idolatrous children, he reasoned. But the prophet Isaiah came to him and proclaimed angrily:

בהדי כבשי דרחמנא למה לך? מאי דמפקדת איבעי לך למעבד, ומאי דניחא קמי קוב״ה לעביד

Why do you meddle in God's mysteries? You must do what you are commanded to do, and the Holy One blessed be He will do what pleases him (Berachos 10a).

The earth presumed to meddle in God's mysteries. It was forbidden to do so and was punished for having dared.

The earth presumed to meddle in God's mysteries. It was forbidden to do so and punished for having dared. This, too, is Torah and we must learn from it. No lesson of Torah should ever be lost upon us. Its every commandment, every incident, every conversation was included to educate and elevate man.

To Forget — and to Die

To ignore or forget is to lose a portion of life. The Sages teach that when Israel accepted the Ten Commandments, it approached the exaltation of Adam before the sin. Had the Golden Calf not been built, they would have entered *Eretz Israel,* built an eternal Temple, and the entire world would have received all the prophetic blessings of the world to come. Like Adam, they sinned (see Overview, ArtScroll edition, The Book of Ruth) and fell from their greatness. They received the Ten Commandments anew and the Second Tablets of the Law, but it was not the same. Had they retained the first Tablets they would have learned and never forgotten; with the second Tablets, we learn and *do* forget *(Midrash).* Adam sinned and became subject to death; Israel sinned and became subject to forgetfulness. When a man studies and learns, he makes Torah a part of himself. When he forgets his learning, a part of himself has left him — he has suffered a degree of death *(Harav Gedalyah Schorr).*

When he forgets his learning, a part of himself has left him — he has suffered a degree of death.

Adam sinned and humanity changed forever. But the antidote to the serpent's poison is forever available, even though forgetfulness is our lot. We can succeed in isolating light from darkness, and holiness from profanity even though confusion is the legacy of that tempting but lethal fruit.

We can control the levers of creation by our study of Torah and performance of its precepts, even though a montage of men and machines blocks our view of the power of our deeds.

אַהֲבַת עוֹלָם בֵּית יִשְׂרָאֵל עַמְּךָ אָהַבְתָּ. תּוֹרָה
וּמִצְוֹת חֻקִּים וּמִשְׁפָּטִים אוֹתָנוּ לִמַּדְתָּ. . . . . כִּי הֵם
חַיֵּינוּ וְאֹרֶךְ יָמֵינוּ וּבָהֶם נֶהְגֶּה יוֹמָם וָלָיְלָה

With eternal love, you have loved the House of Israel, your people; Torah and commandments, statutes and ordinances you have taught us . . . . for they are our life and the length of our days and upon them we will meditate day and night.

God made the universe and presented us with its blueprint. Let us turn the page and begin to read it.

סדר בראשית
Sidra Bereishis

א
א־ב

א בְּרֵאשִׁ֖ית בָּרָ֣א אֱלֹהִ֑ים אֵ֥ת הַשָּׁמַ֖יִם וְאֵ֥ת
ב הָאָֽרֶץ׃ וְהָאָ֗רֶץ הָיְתָ֥ה תֹ֙הוּ֙ וָבֹ֔הוּ וְחֹ֖שֶׁךְ

Rav Yitzchak said: Since the Torah is the book of laws, it should have begun with *'This month shall be to you the first of the months' (Exodus* 12:2), for that was the first commandment given to all Israel. Why, then, did it begin with the narrative of creation?

The reason is in order to establish the sovereignty of God over the earth. כֹּחַ מַעֲשָׂיו הִגִּיד לְעַמּוֹ לָתֵת לָהֶם נַחֲלַת גּוֹיִם, *He declared to His people the power of His works in order to give them the heritage of the nations (Psalms* 111:6). If the nations accuse Israel of banditry for seizing the lands of the seven nations of Canaan, Israel will tell them: 'The entire universe belongs to God. He created it and He granted it to whomever was deemed fit in His eyes. It was His desire to give it to them and it was then His desire to take it from them and cede it to us.' *(Adapted from Rashi's introductory comment).*

1. בְּרֵאשִׁית — *In the beginning of.* [Although the first word of the Torah is familiarly translated *'In the beginning'*, many commentators disagree, on grammatical grounds: (1) — Had the Torah meant the isolated phrase *in the beginning,* the proper word would have been בָּרִאשׁוֹנָה. The word בְּרֵאשִׁית, however, implies סְמִיכוּת, the *construct* state (a word which is attached to the next: in the beginning 'of'); (2) — *In the beginning* implies that a chronological order of creation is being given, but this interpretation is belied by the following verse which mentions the existence of water but does not explain when it was created.]

Rashi therefore rejects the interpretation that the verse describes the *sequence* of creation i.e. that heaven and earth were created before anything else. He maintains that the verse demands the *Midrashic* explanation of the Sages who note that Scripture entitles two things as רֵאשִׁית, *beginning,* implying that they are of paramount importance: *Torah* which is called רֵאשִׁית דַּרְכּוֹ, *the beginning of His way (Proverbs* 8:22), and *Israel* which is called רֵאשִׁית תְּבוּאָתֹה, *the beginning of His crops (Jeremiah* 2:3). The Sages therefore interpret בְּרֵאשִׁית in our verse as a contraction of בִּשְׁבִיל רֵאשִׁית, *for the sake of,* the things which are called רֵאשִׁית, *beginning.* Thus, the verse should be rendered: *For the sake of 'the beginning'* [Torah and Israel] *did God create the heavens and the earth.*

Rashi explains that in the plain sense, however, the verse should be interpreted in סְמִיכוּת, the construct state: *In the beginning of God's creating the heavens and the earth, when the earth was astonishingly empty with darkness upon the face*

[Please note: The source for every excerpt has been documented. All bracketed comments, unless otherwise attributed, are those of the author.]

The first chapter of *Breishis* — and especially the first verse — by virtue of the difficulty of the text and the abundance of commentaries, requires lengthy and complex treatment.
The use of small type in the commentary indicates material that is especially analytical or not expository of the simple meaning of the text.

I In the beginning of God's creating the heavens and
1-2 the earth — 2 when the earth was astonishingly
empty, with darkness upon the surface of the deep,

of the deep, then God said: 'Let there be light'.

As explained above, *Rashi* rejects the idea that the Torah discusses the chronological sequence of creation, for, if so, it would have begun בָּרִאשׁוֹנָה, since the word בְּרֵאשִׁית is used only in the construct state as, for example [*Jeremiah* 26:1] בְּרֵאשִׁית מַמְלְכוּת יְהוֹיָקִים *'in the beginning of the reign of Yehoiakim'* ... [cf. also *Gen.* 10:10; *Deut.* 18:4.] Thus, *Rashi* renders that verses 1 and 2 set the stage for verse 3, the creation of light.

Therefore, *Rashi* continues, this verse should be expounded as if it said בְּרֵאשִׁית בְּרֹא אֱלֹהִים *in the beginning of God's creating* ... (This is grammatically similar to [*Hosea* 1:2] תְּחִלַּת דִּבֶּר־ה׳ בְּהוֹשֵׁעַ, *'At the beginning of* HASHEM*'s speaking to Hosea, —* i.e. when HASHEM began to speak to Hosea — then וַיֹּאמֶר ה׳ אֶל־הוֹשֵׁעַ *'*HASHEM *said to Hosea'* etc.) . . .

Rashi comments further that the word בְּרֵאשִׁית cannot be interpreted as being in construct form attached to an implied noun, translating: בְּרֵאשִׁית (הַכֹּל) בָּרָא, *in the beginning* (of all things) *God created the heaven and the earth,* a translation that would indicate the sequence of creation. If one were to accept such an interpretation, then 'you should be astonished at yourself because the waters, indeed, preceded them, for the next verse says *"and the spirit of God hovered over the face of the waters"*, proving that the creation of waters preceded that of earth, while Scripture had not as yet disclosed when the creation of the waters took place. Additionally, the heaven, שָׁמַיִם, was created from אֵשׁ, fire, and מַיִם, water [see *Rashi* to verse 8], which proves that waters pre-existed the heaven and that the verse teaches *nothing about the sequence* of creation.'

Ibn Ezra agrees with this contruct-form rendering. He adds that had the ב, *beth,* been punctuated with a *kametz* reading בָּרֵאשִׁית, it would have implied the definite article [for the prefix בָּ is equivilant to בְּהַ, *in the*] and allowed for the translation: *'in the beginning.'* However, since it is punctuated with a *sh'va:* בְּרֵאשִׁית, it grammatically requires translation in the construct form: *'in the beginning of.'*

Ramban emphasizes that 'the work of creation is a deep secret which cannot be comprehended from the verses, nor can it be definitively known except through the tradition going back to Moses our teacher [who heard it] from the mouth of the Almighty. Those who *do* know it are enjoined to conceal it.' [As the *Talmud, Chagigah* 11b, exhorts: 'The Works of Creation may not be expounded before two.' (see *Overview*).]

Ramban disagrees with the construct form interpretation of *Rashi* and *Ibn Ezra: In the beginning of God's creating* ... He holds that in its literal sense בְּרֵאשִׁית should be rendered as if connected to an implied noun: *In the beginning of 'all things'* (הַכֹּל), *God created* ... . The first stage was God's creation, from utter and complete nothingness, of the raw material which He later molded and fashioned into the specific parts of the universe. The terms *'Heaven and earth'* designate the potentials for the later stages of creation — *'heaven'* encompassing the heavenly bodies, and *'earth'* encompassing the earth and its fullness.

The flow of the verses is: (1) At first God created, from absolute nothingness, the heaven and the earth including the potent of the four elements [fire, wind, water, and dust]; (2) after this stage of creation, the earth was תֹהוּ, [which *Ramban* explains as 'matter without substance', (see below on verse 2)], and it became בֹהוּ when God clothed it with form; which, the Torah goes on to explain, includes the form of the four essential elements: fire, wind, water, and dust [see below on verse 2.]

Rabbeinu Bachya concludes that בְּרֵאשִׁית should be rendered as an independent, rather than a construct ['סְמוּכָה'] word. The best proof for this is the accented punctuation of the word' [which is a *'tipcha'*, (similar to the English comma)], indicating that it is not joined with the following phrase. Hence בְּרֵאשִׁית must be read independently: *'In the beginning, God created.'*

The *Vilna Gaon*, too, holds that: 'the word רֵאשִׁית was chosen to indicate a definite beginning, before which one cannot imagine any form of existence ... *At the beginning.* It cannot be a construct phrase, but must stand alone because it designates the very first state of existence, preceding all of Creation and preceded by nothing except for God' *(Aderes Eliyahu).*

Accordingly, the intent of the narrative is that heaven and earth — including all their potential for future creation — were created on the first day from absolute nothingness [*'creatio ex nihilo'*] as evidenced by the use of the verb בָּרָא, *created* [see below].

This interpretation is in consonance with the opinion of Rav Nechemiah, as recorded in the *Midrash* [*Tanchuma* (Buber) *Gen.* 1, *Yalkut Shimoni* 6], who maintains that the entire world was created on the first day: 'Rav Yehudah and Rav Nechemiah differ. Rav Yehudah maintains that the world was created in six days, for it is written after the work of each day וַיְהִי כֵן, *and it was so.* Rav Nechemiah maintains that the [potential of the] whole world was created on the first day. Note the use [in verse 24] of תּוֹצֵא הָאָרֶץ, *'Let the earth bring forth'* — implying that nothing new was to be created, but that the earth was merely to yield what had already been prepared and arranged from the Beginning ...

'This is comparable to one who planted six seeds at one time: One sprouted forth on the first day, another on the second, and so on.'

Rabbeinu Bachya sums up that Rav Nechemiah applies this parable to show that the prime matter from which everything else originated was created on the first day. Subsequently, on the following days the rest of Creation was created from portions of this matter — each on its own day. This is the explanation of the verse in *Psalms* 33:9: כִּי הוּא אָמַר וַיֶּהִי *'For He spoke and it was'* i.e. everything instantaneously came into being with one divine call. Thereafter, הוּא־צִוָּה וַיַּעֲמֹד, *He commanded and it arose* — i.e. He commanded them individually each day and brought them into being.]

Rambam (Moreh Nevuchim II:30) in discussing Creation, demonstrates that prior to Creation nothing existed. In addition, there was no concept of time, because there were no rotating spheres; the very concept of time is a part of the Creation.

Accordingly, בְּרֵאשִׁית is derived from רֹאשׁ, *head*, the principal part. He suggests that the true explanation of the verse is: *'In the origin* God created the beings above and the things below,' i.e. God created the origin of all existence, both the heaven and earth. God created the heaven and the earth in their origin, or together with their origin — i.e. He created the entire Universe from absolute nothing. Accordingly everything was created simultaneously, then [as explained in the comment of *Rabbeinu Bachya* above] all things became differentiated.

As *S'forno* interprets: בְּרֵאשִׁית, *at the beginning of time,* the very first moment. Since time did not exist prior to creation, the verse cannot mean to separate a point in time from what came previously; rather it describes the instant when creation began, as the first instant.

There was no sequence of time in Creation — nothing was created earlier or later. The use of the word בְּרֵאשִׁית teaches us that the potential for all creation happened at רֵאשִׁית, at the first instance of what, in our limited intellect, we term *'Beginning' (Or HaChaim).*

[**In summation**, then, it would appear that there are two distinct lines of interpretation:

a. *Rashi* and *Ibn Ezra:* The verses do not deal with the *sequence* of Creation. The intent of the verses is to declare that God, alone, as Master of the World is the Source of all Creation, and gave the land to whom He pleased, and according to His will later took the land from the Canaanites and gave it to Israel;

b. *Most others:* The verse begins with a general statement: *At the very first moment* (time itself being one of the objects of creation) *God created* — from absolute nothing — *the heaven and the earth,* i.e. the upper matter and the lower matter, with all their inherent potential including the principal elements — light (fire), darkness, water and air — which He developed separately as expounded in the following verses. This process reaches its ultimate meaning and essence in the creation of Man — the prime goal of Creation.

The narrative thus dispels any notion that the world always existed. It was created מֵאַיִן, *ex nihilo,* and the Torah which is essentially a Book of Law begins with the narrative of Creation rather than with the Laws in order to confirm our realization of this fundamental principle of belief. Furthermore God commanded us in the Ten Commandments to rest on the Seventh day, in testimony that the World was created by Him in six days and He 'rested' on the seventh.]

בָּרָא — *Creating.* The verb [which is used in Scriptures exclusively with reference to Divine activity] is explained by the commentators as referring to producing something out of nothing — יֵשׁ מֵאַיִן [*creatio ex nihilo*].

There is no expression in Hebrew for producing something from nothing other than the word ברא, *created (Ramban).*

Ibn Ezra notes that in the word בָּרָא there are implicit profound and esoteric implications which only 'those with understanding can perceive ...'[1]

Abarbanel, however, notes that the verb ברא, *created,* is sometimes used in verses where *creation out of nothingness* is not explicit and which would seem to imply creation from some pre-existing matter — e.g. verse 21: וַיִּבְרָא אֱלֹהִים אֶת הַתַּנִּינִם הַגְּדֹלִים, *and God created the great fish* [where the verse later states אֲשֶׁר שָׁרְצוּ הַמַּיִם לְמִינֵהֶם, lit. *'which the water swarmed for their species'* possibly implying that they were formed from the water *(Yohel Ohr)*]; three times in verse 27 regarding the creation of man [although man was formed from elements into which God breathed the breath of life *(ibid)*]; and in other places in Scripture...

He goes on to explain that whatever formation occurs through drastic change of the established laws of nature is termed *'creation'* because something fundamentally new without prior existence has come into being. Therefore the term *'created'* in v. 21 stresses the magnitude of the fishes' size which

1. [As *Rambam* prefaces to Part III of the *Moreh:* 'The Account of the Beginning belongs to those matters which are סִתְרֵי תוֹרָה, mysteries of the Torah, [see *Overview*]... not to be divulged and which may not be explained except orally to one man having certain stated qualities, and even to that one only the chapter headings may be mentioned. Therefore has the knowledge of this matter ceased to exist in the entire religious community. This was inevitable, because this knowledge was transmitted only from one principal to another and was never committed to writing ...']

[The verse of *Ben Sira* is quoted in *Chagigah* 13a with approval: 'Seek not out the things that are too hard for you, and into the things that are hidden from you inquire not. In what is permitted to you instruct yourself — you have no business with secret things.'

[Similarly, to the question, Why does the story of Creation begin with the letter ב, *beth,* (the second letter, instead of the first letter א, *aleph*), the *Talmud Yerushalmi Chagigah* 2:1 answers: 'Just as the letter *beth* is closed on all sides and open only in front, similarly you are not permitted to inquire what is before or what is behind, but only from the actual time of creation.']

⊱ בְּרֵאשִׁית בָּרָא אֱלֹהִים, In the beginning God created. The final letters of the first three words of the Torah are אֱמֶת, *truth.* It is customary for a liturgical poet to fit the initials of his name into the stanzas of his work; God did the same. The Sages say חותמו של הקב״ה אמת, the seal of the Holy One, blessed be He is Truth. Therefore he placed His seal upon the first words of the Torah *(Rabbi Bunam).*

was unprecedented. *'Created'* regarding man [in verse 27] refers not to his *physical* formation but to man's creation — from nothingness — as a being endowed, in God's 'image,' with reason and intellect; the first such creature in the Universe. And similarly, wherever else the verb appears it is to be so interpreted.

The *Vilna Gaon* explains that 'the word בָּרָא, *created,* specifically designates the origination of substance — a creative process which is beyond the human power, 'such as the inorganic, the organic, and the metallic' *(Aderes Eliyahu).*

Hirsch explains בָּרָא to mean bringing something into reality which hitherto had existed inwardly, in the mind. It is used only for creation by God because the verb implies creating something purely out of one's mind and will without utilizing anything else. Before Creation, the world existed — to express it in human terms — only as a thought in the mind of God. Thus Creation is nothing but a materialized thought of God, by which He imparted to this thought an external concrete existence.

[The Sages proclaimed *(Avos* 5:1) that 'with ten sayings was the world created'. In *Meg.* 21b the creative sentence בְּרֵאשִׁית בָּרָא is reckoned as one saying, plus the following nine creative sayings of וַיֹּאמֶר, *He said* (see *Overview).*]

אֱלֹהִים — *God.* The Sages explain that אֱלֹהִים denotes God in His Attribute of Justice, מִדַּת הַדִּין — as Ruler, Director, Law-giver, and Judge of the world, while יהוה [read reverently as *'Adonoy'* and referred to in common usage as HASHEM, (The Name)], denotes Him in His compassionate Attribute of Mercy, מִדַּת הָרַחֲמִים[1]

Ibn Ezra suggests that the name אֱלֹהִים is derived from אֵל [literally meaning 'strength'.] It appears in the plural form 'as a matter of reverence, for every language has its reverent form of address [as in

1. The source for this concept of the Names of God referring to His Attributes appears to be the *Sifri* to *Deut.* 3:24: "Wherever God is referred to as ה׳, HASHEM, it designates His Attribute of Mercy, as it is written *(Exodus* 34:6) ה׳ ה׳ אֵל רַחוּם, *'HASHEM, HASHEM, merciful God';* and wherever He is referred to as אֱלֹהִים, *God,* it designates His Attribute of Justice, as it is written *(ibid* 22:8): עַד הָאֱלֹהִים יָבֹא דְּבַר שְׁנֵיהֶם, *unto the Judges ('Elohim') shall the cause of both parties come* [Thus a court is called *'Elohim,'* denoting judgment.]

Furthermore, the *Talmud, Rosh Hashanah* 17b comments on *Exodus* 34:6: *'HASHEM, HASHEM'* — I am He [i.e. merciful as designated by My Name, HASHEM *(Rashi)*] before a man sins, and I am He [i.e. merciful *(Rashi)*] after a man sins, if he repents.

... As *Tosafos* explains: *'HASHEM'* designates the Attribute of Mercy unlike *'Elohim'* which designates the Attribute of Justice.'

Rambam [*Moreh* I:61] elaborates and explains: 'All the names of God occurring in Scripture are derived from His actions except the Four lettered Name which consists of the letters *yod, he, vav, he,* and which is applied exclusively to God and is called שֵׁם הַמְּפֹרָשׁ [lit. *'the clarified Name;* or: *the separated Name.'*] See also *Song of Songs,* ArtScroll ed. footnote to page 73.

'Throughout this section the name אֱלֹהִים alone is used — *Elohim* denoting one who has the power to produce all things — to show that the only purpose of the whole narrative is to teach the existence of a Being who made all existing things, which is the first principle' [see also on 2:1] *(Ikkarim* 1:11).

⸎ The Torah's first chapter uses the Name אֱלֹהִים indicating the God of Judgment. This teaches that at first God wanted the universe to survive only if it proved to be worthy in His scales of justice. Seeing that the world could not exist, He added His divine mercy.

Why must we know the original intention since, now that He exercises His mercy, the original plan does not affect us? To show man that his ideal state is one that is worthy of even God's judgment untempered by mercy. To attain that goal should be man's ambition *(Maharal).*

the 'plural of majesty'], but no idea of plurality is to be inferred from this form as evidenced by the fact that the verb בָּרָא, *created*, is in the singular.'[1]

The primary explanations of *'Elohim'* are:

☙ A name which throughout Scriptures signifies מָרוּת, authority *(Rashi* on 6:2);

☙ It denotes God as 'chief' *(Rambam);*

☙ It is a term signifying 'Proprietor' or 'Governor' of the world in broad terms; or in narrower terms, to a human judge (see *Kuzari* 4);

☙ It denotes God as the Eternal and Everlasting. Human judges are referred to as *Elohim* because they judge 'in the image of God' *(S'forno);*

☙ It describes God as 'the Mighty One who wields authority over the beings Above and Below' *(Tur Orach Chaim* 5);

☙ It describes God as בַּעַל הַיְכוֹלֶת, the omnipotent, the all-powerful (*Shulchan Aruch;* ibid);

☙ In the plural form it signifies the many forces which spread throughout Creation. All these forces emanate from the One God, and in Him are found the sources of all forces in complete unity *(Malbim).*

☙ [It indicates the sum total of His attributes and powers united in Him (see *Overview).*]

Hirsch comments that the Sages note that it does not say אֱלֹהִים בָּרָא בְּרֵאשִׁית, *God created in the beginning,* but בְּרֵאשִׁית בָּרָא אֱלֹהִים, *In the beginning God created.* He explains that אֱלֹהִים — in reference to God — is derived from אֵלֶּה, the demonstrative plural 'these' which views the plurality of things in the world as being joined together to form a unit. — Accordingly He can be called אֱלֹהִים only *after* the creation of the world, as the name refers to His relation to the world. Hence the word אֱלֹהִים follows בְּרֵאשִׁית בָּרָא.[2]

In the sequence of these words, the *Midrash* perceives evidence of God's modesty 'for only *after* creating the requirements of the universe did He deign to record His own Name. First בְּרֵאשִׁית בָּרָא, and then אֱלֹהִים.'

Me'am Loez, citing the fact that God's Name is not mentioned until the end of the verse, derives that man must not begin a statement by invoking God's Name — as in the *Talmudic* prohibition [*Nedarim* 10b]: One must not undertake a vow saying *'laAdonai Korban'* — 'Unto HASHEM a sacrifice', lest he [not complete the statement] and be left having uttered *'Adonai'* without *'korban'* with the result that the Name was said in vain. Thus, even in cases where it is permissible to utter the Name, it should be done only if the complete statement is made, not if the Name might be uttered in isolation.

אֵת הַשָּׁמַיִם וְאֵת הָאָרֶץ — *The heavens and the earth.*

[The words *'heaven and earth'* preceded by the prepositions אֶת

1. See *Yerushalmi Berachos* 9:1:

Heretics asked Rav Simlai: 'How many Gods created the world?'

He answered: 'Go, seek your answer from Adam' [i.e. examine the verses in *Genesis* and derive a response *(Torah Temimah)*].

It is written, *In the beginning Elohim* [i.e. plural] *created',* they said.

'Yes,' he answered, 'but בָּרָא, *created,* is singular and not plural!'

2. God is undefinable because He is beyond the perception of our physical senses. *Rambam* explains that Moses, when he asked God *'Show me, please, Your Glory,'* [*Exodus* 33:18], requested that the 'existence' of God should be distinguished in his mind from other beings so that he would become aware of the true existence of God, as it is. God replied that it is beyond the mental capacity of a living man, composed of body and soul, to attain a clear understanding of this truth. But the Holy One imparted to him an awareness of what no man knew before him, and no man will know after him *(Hilchos Yesodei HaTorah* 1:10).

and the definite articles ה, *the,* are to be understood as all-embracing terms including the entire universe and cosmogony as we now know it (see comm. below).]

שָׁמַיִם, *heavens,* is a plural form of שָׁם, *there,* indicating a great distance from our point of perspective. The plural form indicating that many equidistant points are suggested, is a reference to the revolving orbits *(Sforno).*

According to *haKsav V'haKaballah,* שָׁמַיִם denotes height ... it is related to the word הִשְׁתּוֹמְמוּת, awe, bewilderment, for when one contemplates the vastness of the heavenly bodies one becomes bewildered and overawed, as explained in the *Midrash.*

The *Talmud* [*Chagigah* 12a] esoterically explains שָׁמַיִם as a compound of שָׁם מַיִם, 'the waters are there'. [1] It is also interpreted as a compound of אֵשׁ וּמַיִם, fire, and water: 'This teaches that the Holy One, blessed be He, brought them and mixed them with one another and made from them the רָקִיעַ, firmament'.

Although by definition it is singular, שָׁמַיִם always appears in the plural form, akin to words like חַיִּים, life, מַיִם, water, פָּנִים, face, etc. Its simple meaning is 'height' while אֶרֶץ, *earth,* denotes lowliness *(Chizkuni).*

Harav Mordechai Gifter explains that the above words appear in plural because the are inherently not singular: פָּנִים, *face,* has a duality of two profiles; מַיִם, *water,* has no single drop which is indivisible; חַיִּים, *life,* has no singular situation; שָׁמַיִם, *heaven,* is considered plural because of its vast expanse.

אֶרֶץ, *earth,* is derived from the root רָץ, run, for all 'run' to and fro upon it — from cradle to grave *(Lekach Tov);* it also alludes to the 'running of the orbiting spheres which circle it' *(Radak)* or to the earth's swift race in orbit around the sun *(Hirsch).* Or, it refers to the entire cosmos because it is not static but in perpetual motion *(Harav Gifter).* It is also derived from רצץ, which means 'that which is compressed' [a reference to earth's density as compared to the atmosphere] *(Ibn Caspi).*

'Earth', thus implies all that is below the sphere of the moon ... it designates the four basic elements: fire, wind, water and dust *(Moreh Nevuchim* 2:30; *Ramban).*

[The *Midrash* perceives that since these were new, previously unknown creations, the definite article הַ, *the,* before heaven and earth is not applicable. Hence the inclusion of the article evokes the following interpretation]:

When man builds a structure, he makes later modifications if the finished product does not suit his intentions. The Holy One, blessed be He, is different. He built *the* heaven and *the* earth — as He originally contemplated them [i.e. He had no need to modify His original designs for His work is perfect.]

The definite article הַ, *the,* preceding heaven and earth indicates that the heaven and earth created on the first day are *the* heaven and *the* earth in their pre-

1. [I.e., that simultaneously with the heaven, water was created. The merging of two words with the same ending and beginning consonant — known as 'haplography' — is not unusual in Scriptures; in this case שָׁם מַיִם becoming שָׁמַיִם *(Torah Temimah).* According to *Ramban,* however, the Talmudic interpretation is to be vocalized שֵׁם מַיִם, 'the name is water', because it assumed the name of the substance from which it was created.]

sent forms — the heavens with their constellations (although they did not give light until the fourth day), and the earth with its fruit-yielding potential *(Malbim).*

[The Sages, in their profound perception of the language find a significant difference if an object is termed simply by its name or if it is preceded by the indefinite article אֶת. Some regard the article אֶת as being related to אות, *a sign*, presenting an object in all the phases by which its nature is to be recognized; and others regard it as being related to אתת, *join*. Hence it has the implied meaning *with* giving rise to an exegetical amplification seeking an implied extension wherever אֶת occurs in the Bible — especially in verses dealing with laws. Thus, for example, in *Pes.* 22b the word אֶת '[*with*] *HASHEM your God shall you fear' (Deut.* 10:20) [implying that the same awe one feels for God should be extended to another] which is interpreted by Rabbi Akiva to require that we display reverence for Torah scholars. Also in *Kesubos* 103a on *Exodus* 20:12: *'Honor* אֶת [*with*] *your father and* אֶת [*with*] *your mother:* the אֶת in both cases is seen as an amplification extending parental honor to those in whom the personality of the father and mother are represented — the stepfather and stepmother. Similarly in our verse the אֶת preceding *heaven* is a רִבּוּי, an amplification, which extends the conception of heaven to include all the heavenly bodies and constellations; the אֶת preceding *earth* includes all that is on earth: the trees, herbage, and Garden of Eden (see *comm.* to word בְּרֵאשִׁית; cf. *Midrash; v. Chagigah* 12a).]

Malbim comments that the description of the creation of heaven and earth is not preceded, as is the rest of creation, with the words, *'And God said'*. This is because *'and God said'* is a command, implying that an object of the order existed. Prior to heaven and earth, however, there was only nothingness, a condition toward which no command could be addressed. Also, the verb אמר, *say,* — unlike דבר, *speak,* — must have an object; *'saying'* must be directed toward something.[1] Subsequent to the creation of heaven and earth, however, commands could be directed, because heaven and earth included the potential of all future creation [see *Ramban* cited above.].

2. This verse specifically dispels any possible notion of the eternity of the universe. Let no one think that the world with all its goodness existed forever. Rather, the world which was created by God was then *'formless and void' ... (Rashbam).*

וְהָאָרֶץ הָיְתָה — *When the earth was.*

[The translation continues according to *Rashi's* interpretation which views this and the preceding verse as introductory and circumstantial to verse 3. Accordingly, the prefix ו is rendered as a conjunction, *'when'*.]

Therefore, according to most commentators, the verse is a parenthetic clause meaning: *'the earth being then ... '* for had the verse meant to begin a new thought it would have begun with וַתְּהִי הָאָרֶץ instead of וְהָאָרֶץ הָיְתָה [see *Hirsch.*]

Others render the *vav* as the connective *'and'*, translating: *'And the earth was.'*

[The commentators differ as to whether the verse is describing the state of *'earth'* prior to Creation (see *Ramban*, v. 1), or subsequent to the initial Creation but before God's work was completed]:

Rav Saadiah Gaon [*Emunos V'Deos* 1] states that any interpretation implying that the air and water mentioned in this verse existed prior to Creation 'is sheer nonsense because it is only *after* having first stated: *"In the beginning God created"* that the Torah says *"and the earth was,* etc." Only subsequent to its creation did the earth [i.e. the world (see below)] consist of the elements of earth, water and air.'

1. [Nevertheless, note that the *Talmud, Megillah* 21b considers the words בְּרֵאשִׁית בָּרָא a creative utterance [מַאֲמַר] bringing about heaven and earth. The verse cited is *Psalms* 33:6: בִּדְבַר ה׳ שָׁמַיִם נַעֲשׂוּ וּבְרוּחַ פִּיו כָּל־צְבָאָם *'by the word* (דבר, not אמר in keeping with *Malbim's* comm.) *of HASHEM the heavens were made, and the host of them by the breath of His mouth.'*]

Harav Gifter explains that מַאֲמַר, creative utterance, refers to an expression of God's will. Therefore [*Psalms* 148:5]: הוּא צִוָּה וְנִבְרָאוּ, *for He commanded and they were created:* God's very desire is His command.

א
ב

עַל־פְּנֵי תְהוֹם וְרוּחַ אֱלֹהִים מְרַחֶפֶת עַל־

However, the phrase may also be taken to mean: Before heaven and earth were created, the place where earth was subsequently to stand was *tohu* and *bohu*. Similarly, עַל־פְּנֵי תְהוֹם is to be understood: *'upon that place where the abyss was to be'*; and מְרַחֶפֶת עַל־פְּנֵי הַמָּיִם: *hovering over the place where 'the water was to flow'* — for none of these things were yet created. (Additionally, only 'earth' [habitat of man] is spoken of as being *tohu* and *bohu*; 'heaven' is not mentioned in this degrading context because of the glory of the Shechinah which abides in the heavens, nor is the water so described because the Divine Presence hovered over it during the prelude to Creation [*Chizkuni*]).

Many view אָרֶץ, as a general term referring in this context to the entire Universe, because the 'land' was not given the name אֶרֶץ, *earth*, until the third day — verse 10 *(Karnei Ohr)*. Render, therefore, *'when the world was' (Radak)*.

That *'earth'* and *'universe'* are interchangeable may be discerned from such parallel phrases as כְּבוֹדוֹ מָלֵא עוֹלָם, 'His glory fills the universe' *(Siddur)*, while the verse in Scripture reads מְלֹא כָל־הָאָרֶץ כְּבוֹדוֹ, *the whole earth is full of His glory'* [*Isaiah* 6:3] *(Karnei Ohr)*.[1]

תֹהוּ וָבֹהוּ — *Astonishingly empty.* [or: *'desolate and void'*]

[The terms are difficult and laden with esoteric connotations. Our translation which takes the phrase as a hendiadys, follows *Rashi* who explains תֹהוּ as meaning 'astonishment and amazement', — which as he explains, is the reaction one would have at its בֹהוּ, emptiness and state of being void.][2]

Targum Yonasan renders: 'And the earth was emptiness and desolation, solitary of the sons of men, and void of every animal.'

[The phrase refers to the chaotic and confused terrestrial state]:

—There was nothing. As Jeremiah writes referring to the period following the Destruction [Jeremiah 4:23,25]: *'I behold, and lo, it was* תֹהוּ וָבֹהוּ, *desolate and empty; and to the heavens, and they had no light ... I beheld, and lo, there was no man, and all the birds of the sky had fled.'* This then, is the meaning of *'tohu'* and *'bohu'*: desolate from all habitation *(Rashbam)* ... As the *Kuzari* explains: 'the absence of form and order is called darkness and תֹהוּ וָבֹהוּ.'

The desolation was absolute: There was neither tree, nor grass, man nor beast, bird, nor fish nor insect; neither darkness nor light, wind [spirit] nor water — an utter vacuum *(B'chor Shor)*.

Ramban mystically interprets תֹהוּ as being the very thin substance — entirely devoid of form but having potential — which was the primary matter created from absolute nothing by God, and known as חוֹמֶר הַהִיוּלִי from the Greek *hyly* [matter]. It was from this *hyly* that He then formed and brought everything else into existence, clothing the forms, putting them into finished condition ... The form which this substance finally took on is called in Hebrew בֹהוּ, a composite of two words בּוֹ הוּא, 'in it there is (substance)'.

... It is this תֹהוּ, which took on form and

1. The *Vilna Gaon* finds it unusual that אָרֶץ in the beginning of our verse is vocalized with a *'Kametz'*, reading אָרֶץ, a grammatical form usually reserved for words appearing at the *end* of a stich. He concludes that wherever the word is vocalized אָרֶץ, as in our verse, it encompasses all the elements and refers to the universe as a whole. Where it is vocalized אֶרֶץ throughout Scripture it refers to the land, the earth and specifically to *Eretz Yisrael.*

2. As the *Midrash* comments 'The earth sat bewildered and astonished, saying: "The heavenly and earthly beings were created at the same time: why do the former live eternally whereas the latter are mortal?" Therefore, וְהָאָרֶץ הָיְתָה תֹהוּ וָבֹהוּ, *the earth was bewildered and astonished'*.

became בֹּהוּ, and is, according to *Ramban,* what the Sages [*Yoma* 54b] call אֶבֶן שְׁתִיָּה 'the Rock of Foundation', from which the world was founded'.

The *Vilna Gaon* notes that the traditional punctuation specifically calls for a pause after בֹּהוּ indicating that unlike the *'darkness'* of the next phrase, *tohu,* and *bohu* were not *upon the face of the deep.'*

וְחֹשֶׁךְ — [*And*] *darkness.* [i.e. the utter darkness which enveloped all.]

The Talmud comments that *'darkness'* is one of the things created on the first day.[1] [In fact the creation of darkness preceded the creation of light, as evidenced by the sequence of the narrative (*Tamid* 32a).]

[Therefore, the commentators point out, *darkness* is not merely the absence of light, but it is a specific object of God's creation. That this is so is clearly stated in *Isaiah* 45:7 where God describes Himself as יוֹצֵר אוֹר וּבוֹרֵא חֹשֶׁךְ, *'He who forms the light and creates darkness.'*]

[The *Midrash* relates that a philosopher said to Raban Gamliel: Your God is a great craftsman, but He found good materials from which to fashion His work of Creation — *tohu, bohu,* darkness, wind, water, and the deep. ...

The Rabbi rebuked him: 'In connection with every one of them Scripture says that they were indeed created!' (The *Midrash* proceeds to cite proof verses for each.)

According to *Rambam* and *Ramban,* חֹשֶׁךְ, *darkness,* refers to the elemental fire which is dark, 'for were it red, it would redden the night for us.'

— The phrase וְחֹשֶׁךְ עַל־פְּנֵי תְהוֹם, lit. *and darkness upon the face of the abyss,* refers to the elemental fire which is still deep underground, even today *(Ha'amek Davar).*

Rav E. Munk, in rendering: *'the opaque matter',* sums up well the Sages' intent in explanation of the original חֹשֶׁךְ.

The mention of *'darkness'* in this verse introduces the need for the creation of light in the following verse. Had there not been darkness, He would not have commanded that there be light *(Mizrachi).*

עַל־פְּנֵי תְהוֹם — *Upon the surface* [lit. *'face'*] *of the deep.* — i.e. upon the surface of the waters which were on the earth *(Rashi).*

[Although *Rashi* to *Psalms* 104:6 translates תְּהוֹם as 'the sea', the word cannot be synonymous with *'sea'* in the context of this verse. The sea, as we know it, was not created until the third day (verse 9). Therefore, תְּהוֹם in this verse must refer to the great mass of undivided waters which covered the earth. (See comm. to *'water'* cited below from *Moreh Nevuchim* 2:30).]

'Any great mass of water is referred to as תְּהוֹם' *(Radak).*

Hirsch denies that תְּהוֹם means the *abyss,* the deep. He relates it rather, to המם, ebullition, effervescence, and, hence, the billowing of the waves. The confused state of the earth mass, as the end of the verse shows, encompassed water, too ... *'Darkness* lay upon the turmoil, there was no light to penetrate the mass and awaken the germs slumbering in this mass to individual, separate development.'

וְרוּחַ אֱלֹהִים מְרַחֶפֶת — *And the Divine Presence hovered.*

The commentators, here, too,

1. 'Ten things were created the first day: heaven and earth, *tohu* and *bohu,* light and darkness, wind and water, the measure of day, and the measure of night' [i.e. night and day comprising together twenty-four hours *(Rashi)*] *(Chagigah* 12a).

ג פְּנֵי הַמָּיִם: וַיֹּאמֶר אֱלֹהִים יְהִי־אוֹר וַיְהִי־

perceive different meanings in this phrase. Especially difficult is רוּחַ which has been translated *'spirit'*, *'wind'*, or *'breath'*.[1]

Onkelos seems to translate 'a wind from before God blew on the face of the waters', while *Yonasan* renders: 'and spirit of mercies from before God breathed upon the face of the waters.'

Onkelos' rendering agrees with the Talmudic interpretation *(Chagigah* 12a) which explains רוּחַ here as denoting an actual wind — moving air — which was created on the first day.

'Elohim' in this context has the significance of 'might' — i.e., *'a mighty wind'*. Similarly when one wants to enhance the greatness of something he associates it with God as in עִיר־גְּדוֹלָה לֵאלֹהִים, *'a great city unto God'* [*Jonah* 3:3; cf. הַרְרֵי אֵל, אַרְזֵי אֵל] *(Rashbam; Hak'sav V'hakaballah; Harekasim L'Bik'ah).*

[Our translation, however, follows *Rashi* who maintains that if 'wind' were meant, the verb מְנַשֶּׁבֶת, *blew,* would have been used instead of מְרַחֶפֶת, *hovered (Mizrachi; Maharal);* and therefore esoterically explains this phrase as referrring to the כִּסֵּא הַכָּבוֹד, 'Throne of Divine Glory, which stood suspended in the air hovering above the surface of the waters by the *'breath'* of the mouth of the Holy One, Blessed be He, and by His command — as a dove *hovers* over its nest.' [v. also *Chag.* 15a].

[The word מְרַחֶפֶת, *hovers,* is related to the word, יְרַחֵף, in *Deut.* 32:11 where it speaks of an eagle caring for its young and protecting them.]

[*Ha'amek Davar* agrees with the translation *'wind'* and justifies the use of the verb מְרַחֶפֶת]:

It did not [מְנַשֵּׁף] *blow strongly* enough to dry the land as do other gusts which are referred to as רוּחַ אֱלֹהִים, *wind of God,* a title implying great power. Rather, this wind hovered, i.e. blew [מְרַחֵף] gently. [But see, in contrast, *Ibn Ezra* above.]

עַל פְּנֵי הַמָּיִם — *Upon the surface* [lit. *'face'*] *of the waters'* [which fully covered the earth.]

According to *Hirsch* ... 'The Breath of God which now penetrates earthly matter and produces life, [was then] only *hovering over the waters.*

The *'water'* mentioned in this verse is not the water that is in the 'seas' [verse 10]. It is clear that there was a certain common matter which was called 'water.' Afterwards, it was divided into three forms; a part of it became 'seas', another part of it became 'firmament'; a third part became that which is above the 'firmament' — entirely beyond the earth *(Moreh Nevuchim 2:30).*

Perhaps this is why מַיִם, *water,* is invariably in the plural form — suggestive of this pluralistic division *(Radak).*

[We will follow *Munk* therefore, 'and render מַיִם, *waters,* until we reach the third day when the oceans as we know them today developed from the primeval water.]

3. Light.

[From this point onward, we are given a detailed chronology of Creation *(Me'am Loez)*]:

וַיֹּאמֶר אֱלֹהִים — *Then* [or: *'and'*] *God*

1. *Rambam* — in *Moreh* 1:40 and 2:30 — emphasizes that רוּחַ is an equivocal term that has many definitions: 1. the meaning which it has in our verse, *'air'* one of the four elements. Additionally, according to its context, the word can denote: 2. *'blowing wind'* [*Exodus* 10:13, 19], a sense in which the word occurs frequently; 3. *'breath'* [*Psalms* 78:39; *Gen.* 7:15]; 4. the part of man that remains indestructible even after death [in the sense of 'soul' — *Ecclesiastes* 12:7]; 5. it also frequently denotes the divine inspiration that overflows to the prophets and by virtue of which they prophecy [*Num.* 11:17, 25; II *Sam.* 23:2]; 6. it signifies also *'intention'*, *'will'* [*Prov.* 29:11; *Isaiah* 19:3; 40:13].

The meaning of the word must therefore, be gathered from the context.

Ramban, too, translates רוּחַ as 'the element air,' as does *Rav Saadiah Gaon.*

said. According to *Ibn Ezra,* this should be understood literally, as in the verse [*Psalms* 33:6]: בִּדְבַר ה׳ שָׁמַיִם נַעֲשׂוּ, *'By the word of HASHEM the heavens were made'*; and [ibid. 148:5]: כִּי הוּא צִוָּה וְנִבְרָאוּ, *'For He gave a command and they were created.'* The verb indicates effortless activity, as a king who utters commands to his subjects.

[See *Midrash Tehilim* 18:26: 'An artist can make nothing except by hard work, but God makes things by the mere breath of a word, as when *"God said: 'Let there be light.' "*]

Many commentators [*Rav Saadiah Gaon; Ramban; Rambam; Kuzari*] interpret וַיֹּאמֶר as: *'He willed'*, the intention being to signify that the world came into existence through His purposive will.[1]

The intent is that creation was thought out: there is a rationale for each part of it — creation was not a manifestation of purposeless Will alone *(Ramban).*

According to those [e.g. *Ibn Ezra*] who interpret *light* as being the first act of Creation, וַיֹּאמֶר, *He said,* must be understood as *'He said to Himself'* for nothing else yet existed for Him to address. Cf. 6:6 *(Chizkuni;* but see comm. of *Malbim* cited at end of verse 1).

יְהִי־אוֹר — *'Let there be light!'*

It is the heavens — and all their potentials — that are here being addressed by God. He willed that from their substance there should come forth a shining matter called אוֹר, *'light' (Ramban).*[2]

The *Talmud (Chagigah* 12a), states that the light created on the first day is identical with the luminaries [verse 14], for the luminaries were created on the first day but were not suspended [in the firmament] until the fourth day. [Cf. comm. of *Rashi* to verse 14; cf. also comm. to end of verse 1 that the article אֶת *('with')* preceding *'the heavens'* is an amplification which extends the conception of heaven to include all the heavenly bodies and constellations which were created on the first day.]

The Sages state that the luminaries were *'suspended'* [נִתְלוּ] on the fourth day. Note that they did not use the verb 'created' but 'suspended'. *'Light'* in our verse designates the sun, moon, and stars which were created on the first day along with the heaven, earth, light, darkness, air, and water. God thus prepared the potential for everything on the first day ... Note that from the first until the fifth day you will not find either the words

1. As *Rambam* makes clear, the terms אמר, *say,* and דבר, *speak,* as applied to God can only signify will, desire, or thought. It makes no difference whether this divine intention becomes known to man by means of a supernatural voice created for the purpose, or through one of the ways of prophecy, for they are all manifestations of the divine will. The terms never signify that He actually spoke using the sounds of letters and a voice *(Moreh Nevuchim* 1:65).

[The Torah has been given for the use of man, and has thus been worded in terms that man can comprehend. Even the spiritual is expressed in physical terms, as the *Talmud (Berachos* 31b) comments: דִּבְּרָה תּוֹרָה כִּלְשׁוֹן בְּנֵי אָדָם 'the Torah expressed itself in the language of man.']

2. *Rav Yehudah* and *Rav Nechemiah* disagree. *Rav Yehudah* maintains: The light was created first, this being comparable to a king who wished to build a palace, but the site was dark. So he lit lamps to know where to lay the foundations; similarly was light created first.

Rav Nechemiah said: The world was created first, this being comparable to a king who first builds a palace and then adorns it with light.

אוֹר: וַיַּרְא אֱלֹהִים אֶת־הָאוֹר כִּי־טוֹב
וַיַּבְדֵּל אֱלֹהִים בֵּין הָאוֹר וּבֵין הַחֹשֶׁךְ:

'created' or *'formed'* *(B'chor Shor).*[1]

Kli Yakar explains that the light of the first day was indeed special and was reserved. [See *Rashi* beginning of next verse.] Nevertheless, the emanations of its potentials provided the illumination that was embodied in the luminaries of the fourth day. Because they are not the true light, they are not referred to as אוֹר, light, but as מָאוֹר, *luminaries.*

Munk thus renders: *'Matter shall radiate.'*

[It is one of the mysteries of creation beyond human comprehension, that although everything was created *simultaneously* — at one instant with one Word — on the first day, there was nevertheless a 'sequence', with the creation of darkness preceding the creation of light and so on.]

The darkness was all-pervading, then the light of the first day was all-pervading, filling the entire universe. The luminaries created on the fourth day served as receptacles to contain and harness the primal light — which, in its pure state, had now been reserved for the righteous *(Malbim).*

וַיְהִי אוֹר — *And there was light.* i.e. 'and at once there was light' *(Targum Yonasan).*

The Decree became a reality. 'And radiation developed.' *(Munk).*

'The light that was created that day was so exceedingly intense that no human being could gaze upon it; God stored it away for the righteous in the Hereafter' *(Sefer HaBahir)...*

Me'am Loez [citing the *Midrash* and *Tos. Shabbos* 22] comments that this light was so strong that it may be compared to a small house which is abundantly illuminated with large candles ... a light by which one could gaze from one end of the world to another and see even minute, usually invisible, particles.

The verse does not read וַיְהִי כֵן, *and it was so,* [in the sense of: 'it eternally remained so'] as it does on the other days, because this light did not always remain in that unchanged state as did the other creations *(Ramban).*

Rabbeinu Bachya, kabbalistically citing *Zohar* and *Sefer HaBahir,* notes that light did not come into existence with this saying; it already existed with the first act of creation, בְּרֵאשִׁית, which as noted above [*Rosh Hashanah* 32a] was itself a creative utterance. Initially the light was concealed, but with this Utterance He revealed it. This is implicit in the phrase *'and there was light'* — i.e. the light that already existed from the Work of Creation.

4. וַיַּרְא אֱלֹהִים אֶת־הָאוֹר כִּי־טוֹב — *God saw that the light was good.*

1. *Radak* explains: 'Although the luminaries were not suspended in the firmament until the fourth day, they were created with the spheres on the first day. Everything was created simultaneously but each of their individual potentials was not manifested until the respectively designated day. Even the light did not dispense its rays causing the earth to sprout forth its vegetation until God commanded that there be luminaries in the firmament to give light upon the earth [verse 15] and to perform their function in the terrestrial world.'

I *was light.* 4 *God saw that the light was good, and God*
4-5 *separated between the light and the darkness.* 5 *God*

[lit. *'And God saw the light that it was good.'*]

Rashi comments, 'here, too, we must depend upon the statement of Aggadah[1]: He saw that the wicked were unworthy of utilizing this light, and he therefore divided it, reserving it for the righteous in the hereafter.* But in the literal sense, explain the verse thus: He saw that it was good, but it was not proper that light and darkness should function together in a confused manner. He established the daytime as the limit of the former's sphere of activity, and the nighttime, as the latter's.

*The commentators [*Mizrachi; Gur Aryeh*] explain that *Rashi* perceived several difficulties in the text which led him to this *Midrashic* interpretation: (a) Light and darkness are opposites — one being the absence of the other — it is implicit in their very existence that they function at separate times for there is no darkness when it is light: what, then, was this new separation? (b) In the other acts of Creation the words *'and God saw that it was good'* are written at the end of the act, while here the sequence *'and God saw ... that it was good and God divided'* implies that *as a result* of seeing that it was good He *therefore* divided.

[Thus, both difficulties are Aggadically resolved: (a) The need for division was not a natural one, but one necessitated by God's desire to reserve this light for the righteous; (b) the implication is correct. As a result of seeing that the light was *'too* good' for the wicked, He divided it and stored it away.]

Ramban disagrees. He suggests that just as in the previous verse the verb אמר, *say,* when applied to God refers to the creative process of bringing things into existence, similarly, the permanence of those things already created is referred to here by the verb ראה, *see,* implying that their continued existence is at His pleasure. The phrase וַיַּרְא אֱלֹהִים אֶת־הָאוֹר כִּי־טוֹב *'and God saw the light that it was good'* means: He desired that it exist eternally. The verse specifies *'the light'* for were it to say simply *'and God saw that it was good'* it would refer to heaven and earth, but their permanence was not yet decreed because they required further development until the dry land appeared on the third day. Only then did He decree their permanence and say [verse 10] וַיַּרְא אֱלֹהִים כִּי טוֹב, *'and God saw that it was good.'*

There are two implications in the phrase *'it is good'*: (a) that an object is functionally good in that it is compatible with its intended purpose; and (b) that it is intrinsically good. God created certain things whose goodness is not evident, but which were nevertheless deemed by God to be necessary to fulfill the purpose of Creation. Light, however, was seen by God to be intrinsically *'good' (Ha'amek Davar).*

This follows the commentary of the *Vilna Gaon: 'Good'* designates that its usefulness is obvious, but it does not imply that other things are not good — for even 'evil' was created for a purpose, but its benefits are not revealed to us. 'Good', therefore, is not associated with 'darkness' at this point because its benefits have not yet been revealed to us. [See *Overview.*]

וַיַּבְדֵּל אֱלֹהִים — *And God separated* — by reserving one for the righteous (according to *Rashi's Midrashic* interpretation; see above).

[According to his literal interpretation: 'by separating their respective spheres of activity.']

Chizkuni explains away several

1. *Rashi's* interpretation follows the *Talmud, Chagigah* 12a:

'The light the Holy One, blessed be He, created on the first day, one could see thereby from one end of the world to the other, but as soon as He saw the corrupt actions of the wicked, He

א ה וַיִּקְרָא אֱלֹהִים | לָאוֹר יוֹם וְלַחֹשֶׁךְ קָרָא
ה לָיְלָה וַיְהִי־עֶרֶב וַיְהִי־בֹקֶר יוֹם אֶחָד׃

difficulties by suggesting that the *'division'* here refers to that which happened later, on the fourth day when light was clothed in the luminaries. However, since the creation of light was begun on the first day, Scripture notes that the light was divided, for that was its ultimate destiny.

Ibn Ezra however, suggests that the 'separation' here refers to God's differentiation of light and darkness by assigning them different names as detailed in the following verse.

The verb בדל does not mean simply *'divide'*. It carries with it, at the same time, 'a positive allocation, a separate existence, a separate purpose.' Light thus awakens, and darkness gives the opportunities to relax from stimulation, and it is God who arranged and limited these two most important contrasts ... Light is not to work unceasingly ... we cannot bear constant light ... we must sink back, after twelve hours of using all our forces, into the old darkness and imbibe fresh forces ...' *(Hirsch).*

A *halachah* is derived from this verse: A blessing may not be recited over a light on Saturday evening [at the הַבְדָּלָה ('separation') service] unless one can derive some benefit from that light. [Similarly this applies to a blind person who cannot *see* that light and is, therefore, exempt from the blessing *(Torah Temimah)*]. This is derived from the sequence: וַיַּרְא, *He saw* (He perceived its benefits) ... *and* (only then) וַיַּבְדֵּל *he separated* [i.e. pronounced a division — *('havdalah')*. First one must *'see'*, i.e. enjoy, and only then *'separate'*.] *(Yerushalmi Berachos* 8:6).

5. וַיִּקְרָא אֱלֹהִים לָאוֹר יוֹם [*And*] *God called to the light: Day!*

[The term *'called'* in this context is difficult because, in fact, as the commentators perceive, the terms 'light' and 'day' are by no means synonymous, in common usage.]

[The *Talmud* renders וַיִּקְרָא, not *'He called'*, but rather *'He summoned'*, and interprets]: 'God summoned the light and appointed it for duty by day, and He summoned the darkness and appointed it for duty by night' *(Pesachim* 2a).[1] I.e., *'calling'* does not refer here to giving a name but rather to *'summoning'* as a king who summons his subject *(Rashi,* ad. loc.).

arose and hid it from them and reserved it for the righteous in the time to come.'

As *Harav Gifter* points out, this primal light was hidden in the holy Torah and reveals itself to its Sages (see *Overview).*

The Chidushei HaRim once remarked: 'We are indeed fortunte that God hid away this first light. He knew that the wicked are capable of blemishing even that!'

The light-day refers to the deeds of the righteous, and the darkness-night refers to the deeds of the wicked *(Midrash).* There are times when the entire afternoon is considered ערב evening [i.e. the 'evening' *Tamid* offering] and when the hours following midnight are considered morning. This shows us how careful one must be in evaluation: the darkest night may contain elements of day and the brightest day may contain elements of night. So, too, we should carefully evaluate our own deeds and those of others. Even the apparent 'darkness' of the deeds of the wicked may contain sufficient merit in the eyes of God to be considered 'day' *(Harav Nosson Zvi Finkel).*

1. [It must be noted that here again, the Torah — given to man — speaks in human terms and views everything from his perspective. In reality, the terms light and darkness, designating

I *called to the light: 'Day', and to the darkness He*
5 *called: 'Night.' And there was evening and there was*
morning, one day.

'It is comparable to a king who had two servants, both of whom wanted to serve during the day. He summoned one of them and said 'the day will be your domain,' and to the other he said 'the night will be yours.' Similarly, here: *and to the light He called day* — i.e. to the light He said 'the day will be your domain', *and to the darkness He called night* — i.e. to the darkness He said, 'the night will be your domain' *(Yerushalmi Berachos* 8:6).

Hirsch similarly explains that when God calls something by a name, it always expresses a mission ... He directed both to their separate provinces, as in the Talmudic interpretation, above.

The intent of this verse is not that God changed the name of *'light'* to *'day'*. Additionally the name 'day' does not refer to light itself, but to the duration of its radiance. Similarly, night is not a title of darkness, but the term that defines its duration. Hence,the verse does not say 'וַיִּקְרָא אֶת הָאוֹר' *'And He called the light'*, but rather ... וַיִּקְרָא לָאוֹר, *'and He called to* (the function of) *the light' (HaK'sav v'Hakaballah).*

The above follows *Targum Yonasan:* 'And God called the light Day and He made it that the inhabitants of the world might labor by it; and the darkness He called Night, and He made it that in it the creatures might have rest.'

Ramban, following *Ibn Ezra,* interprets the phrase more literally, and explains that just as Adam later gave names to the beasts and fowl, this verse tells us that God Himself named those creations which preceded man's existence [light, darkness, heaven, earth, seas.]

[*Sforno* emphasizes that *'day'* in our verse does not refer to the effect of the sun on earth, for it did not give forth its radiation until the fourth day]: 'At that time when the original light functioned, the periods of light and darkness were not determined by rotating spheres but by the Will of God who separated the time of light from the time of darkness'.

[This primal light, then, is quite distinct from the luminaries, and in other Scriptural verses we note that light and darkness have their own distinct dwelling places. See, for example, *Job* 38:19 *'Where is the way where light dwells? And darkness, where is its place?'*]

וְלַחֹשֶׁךְ קָרָא לָיְלָה — *And to the darkness He called: Night!*

The *Midrash* comments that the Holy One, blessed be He, does not link His name with evil but only with good. Thus, it is not written here 'and God called to the light day and to the darkness *'God'* called

day and night, are valid only in human terms. When we perceive a certain period to be *'day'* this is true only in terms of our geographical location: others experience *'night'* at this very same time. In divine terms, therefore, as we imagine Him peering down from His heavenly abode, there is no one 'time' that is truly night nor one time that is truly day. דִּבְּרָה תוֹרָה כִּלְשׁוֹן בְּנֵי אָדָם, 'the Torah speaks like the language (i.e. from the viewpoint) of man.']

Harav Gifter points out that the *Talmud (Pesachim* 2a) comments: 'God appointed it [light] over the commandments of the day and [darkness] over the commandments of the night.' *Tosafos Rabbeinu Peretz* explains that there are commandments like *tzitzis* and *tefillin* that are applicable only by day, and others, like the counting of the *Omer,* that are applicable only by night. Performance of the commandments by man is the purpose of creation [see *Overview*]. God created day and night primarily so that the conditions would exist for the precepts which are dependent upon them.

night,' but 'and to the darkness *He* called night.'[1]

Citing the *Talmud, Tamid* 32a that darkness was created before light, *Torah Temimah* suggests that the intent of the *Midrash* is as follows: Since darkness was created first, it would have been more logical for the verse to say, *'and God called the darkness night and to the light He called day.'* The order was reversed because God does not wish to associate His name with a force which man perceives as evil, although, as mentioned earlier, darkness is 'evil' only in man's limited understanding.

Ksav Sofer, in this vein, cites a *Midrash*: 'It is known to God what is hidden in the darkness — the purpose and deeper meaning of all trouble which is, in reality, only good and light.'

וַיְהִי עֶרֶב וַיְהִי בֹקֶר — *And there was evening and there was morning.**

[The cycle of the day is complete. In the *halachic* reckoning of time, the day begins with the preceding evening (see *Mishnah Chulin* 5:5). Thus the Sabbaths and festivals begin in the evening — *'from evening unto evening' (Lev.* 23:32). The exception to this rule is the eating of *Kadashim,* the flesh of offerings (*Leviticus* 7:15) where the day begins with morning and concludes with the following night.]

Ibn Ezra explains that etymologically, עֶרֶב, *evening,* is so called because it refers to the time when forms mingle [from ערב, to mingle] and become indistinct. בֹּקֶר, *morning,* [from בקר, to examine] is the reverse of עֶרֶב: it refers to the time when one can 'examine' [i.e. distinguish] forms.

The intent of the verse, which can be inferred to mean that morning and evening are simultaneously present, is: When there is evening in one part of the globe there is morning in another part ... *(Ha'amek Davar* citing *Baal HaMaor, Rosh Hashanah* 20b).

... The above is inferred from the dual use of וַיְהִי, *'and there was'*, in the verse, as if to render: *'There was constant evening, and there was constant morning'* — but not at the same place *(R'vid Hazahav).*

Ramban cites the above view that *'one day'* refers to a twenty-four hour rotation of the sphere upon the earth during which there is light and darkness in opposite places. He concludes, however, that if that interpretation is correct then it must allude to what would not take place until after the luminaries were suspended in the heavens.

יוֹם אֶחָד — *One day.* Here Scripture uses the cardinal number אֶחָד, *one,* instead of the ordinal number רִאשׁוֹן, *first,* — unlike the other days where it uses the ordinal numbers *'second', 'third', etc.* — to indicate that on this day He was Alone, the angels not having been created until the second day *(Rashi)* ...

[According to *Rashi,* therefore, יוֹם אֶחָד, would be understood: *'on*

1. *Harav David Cohen,* extending this *Midrashic* explanation also to *v.* 7 where he notes that the verse does not read וַיַּבְדֵּל אֱלֹהִים, 'and *God* separated', suggests that His name is absent there also because God similarly does not associate His name with that 'separation' which indicates strife [see *comm.* and footnote to *v.* 7, s.v. כִּי־טוֹב.]

**Rav Tzadok HaCohen* sees in this verse a lesson on man's earthly striving. All material pursuits begin in 'darkness', for man is mired in his material existence and is charged with the mission of escaping from it. After striving toward perfection, he emerges into the 'dawn' of a higher, spiritual existence.

⁶ God said, 'Let there be a firmament in the midst

the day of אֶחָד, *the Solitary One'*]

Ramban, however, explains that the use in our verse of the *cardinal* number אֶחָד, *one,* instead of the *ordinal* number רִאשׁוֹן, first, is correct because the use of *'first'* implies the presence of a 'second' while here the second had not yet come into existence. [1]

This follows *Ibn Ezra* who adds that *'One'* here indicates one completed cycle of the revolution of the spheres *(Iggeres HaShabbos).*

6. [Second day. Creation of the firmament.]

יְהִי רָקִיעַ — *Let there be a firmament* (or: *'expanse'*) — i.e. let the expanse (firmament; heaven) solidify. Although the heavens were created on the first day, they were still in a state of flux, solidifying on the second day at God's command [lit. 'rebuke]: יְהִי רָקִיעַ, *'Let there be firmament!' (Rashi; Midrash).*

[The usual translation for רָקִיעַ, *firmament,* the expanse of the heavens, best follows *Rashi.* It is derived from *firmare,* to make firm = solidify.]

Other commentators, however, differ on the meaning of רָקִיעַ, the root of which is related to that of וַיְרַקְּעוּ, 'and they *hammered out'* [*Exodus* 39:3]; and רֹקַע, *spread out* [*Isaiah* 42:5]:

Ibn Ezra states that רָקִיַע means something that is stretched out, and that in our verse it refers specifically to the אֲוִיר, atmosphere. He esoterically explains that when the primal light intensified upon the earth, and the [moisture-laden] wind evaporated, the primal flame changed and became the *firmament.*

Hirsch explains that if it is derived from רקע, extending, stretching, then רָקִיַע could characterize the gaseous expansion of the air, in contrast to the denser water and earth — hence the atmosphere which fills the space between the waters below and those above. The vapor of the lower waters rises to its upper stratum where it forms clouds and dispenses rain — the atmosphere thus rests on the water upon earth and bears the 'water' of clouds. But *Hirsch* suggests that this is only a secondary meaning of רקע. It has rather the meaning of 'beating thin', by which, in the case of metals, an extension is achieved. Accordingly, רָקִיַע refers to the lower surface of the heaven which has the appearance of a dome or vault over and about the earth.

The 'dome' however is merely an optical illusion. *Malbim* explains that the heavenly bodies, as we now understand them, are suspended in air and there is no such thing as a physical 'dome' girdling the earth. The term רָקִיַע is therefore to be understood as referring to the area of the clouds. The vaporous mist ascends until that area where it becomes water in the form of rain and returns to earth.

Pirkei d'Rabbi Eliezer states that the firmament and the angels were created on the second day. The *'firmament'* is not the same as the *'heaven'* of the first day — it refers to the 'firmament' stretched forth over the heads of the *Chayyos* which Ezekiel saw in his vision [*Ezekiel* 1:22] ... The *Midrash* continues that were it not for that firmament, the earth would be engulfed by the waters above and below it.

The interpretation, then, of the verse is: 'Let the sky which was created on the first day be stretched forth amidst the waters which engulfed the earth' *(B'chor Shor).*

בְּתוֹךְ הַמָּיִם — *'In the midst of the waters.'* i.e. in the [exact] center, the separation between the upper waters and the firmament being equal to the separation between the firmament and the waters on the earth. Thus we learn that the upper waters remain suspended by divine edict *(Rashi).*

א ז וַיְהִ֣י מַבְדִּ֔יל בֵּ֥ין מַ֖יִם לָמָֽיִם׃ וַיַּ֣עַשׂ אֱלֹהִים֮
ז אֶת־הָרָקִיעַ֒ וַיַּבְדֵּ֗ל בֵּ֤ין הַמַּ֙יִם֙ אֲשֶׁר֙
מִתַּ֣חַת לָרָקִ֔יעַ וּבֵ֥ין הַמַּ֖יִם אֲשֶׁ֣ר מֵעַ֣ל

וַיְהִי מַבְדִּיל בֵּין מַיִם לָמָיִם – *'And let it separate* [or: *'let it serve as a means of separating'*] *between water and water* – i.e. between the waters above and the waters below *(Targum Yonasan* [as elaborated upon in the following verse]), leaving half above and half below *(Rashbam).*

It is noted that the Hebrew וַיְהִי מַבְדִּיל, [lit. *'let it be a divider'*] denotes that the division is to be permanent *(B'chor Shor).*

[Our translation follows *HaRechasim leBik'ah* who stresses that מַבְדִּיל [*divider, separation*] must, in this case, be translated as a verb with *'firmament'* the implied subject, and not as a noun as erroneously translated by some: *'and let there be a separation.'*]

Perceiving that these verses touch upon the innermost mysteries of Creation [which those who comprehend it are obliged to conceal *(Chavel*], *Ramban* states: 'Do not expect me to write anything about it since Scripture itself did not elaborate upon it ... The verses in their literal sense do not require such an explanation ...'

7. וַיַּעַשׂ אֱלֹהִים אֶת־הָרָקִיַע – *So* [lit. *'and'*] *God made the firmament.* i.e. He set it in its ordained position *(Rashi).*

... Thus the term עשה always means putting an object into its ultimate condition *(Ramban)* i.e. God *'completed'* the expansion. He let it proceed to a certain state and there He stopped further expansion *(Munk).*

The *Midrash* notes, however, that this is one of the verses which Ben Zoma found extraordinary: וַיַּעַשׂ, *He made* – how remarkable! Surely it came into existence at His *word,* as it is written [*Psalms* 33:6]: 'By the *word* of HASHEM were the heavens made; all the host of them by the breath of His mouth'.[Thus, the expression *'made'* is misleading.]

[*Rashi's* interpretation, which explains *'made'* as setting into ordained position, an act not inconsistent with creation by the mere Word of His mouth, seems to resolve Ben Zoma's difficulty. (See also *Ramban's* explanation of this *Midrash* cited at the end of this verse).]

וַיַּבְדֵּל בֵּין הַמַּיִם אֲשֶׁר מִתַּחַת לָרָקִיעַ – *And He separated between the waters which were beneath the firmament* – i.e. he separated between the waters and the firmament with the atmoshere *(HaRechasim leBik'ah).*

וּבֵין הַמַּיִם אֲשֶׁר מֵעַל לָרָקִיעַ – *And* [*between*] *the waters which were above the firmament.* The verse does not say עַל הָרָקִיַע, *'on'* [i.e. directly upon] *the firmament,* but מֵעַל לָרָקִיַע *'above' the firmament,* because the waters above the firmament were suspended in mid-air *(Rashi).*

Me'am Loez states that though the water above the firmament is of a spiritual nature, we are nevertheless obliged to believe that there is, indeed, water there, as King David said: [*Psalms* 148:4]: *'Praise Him, heavens of heavens, and you waters that are above the heavens.'*

Ibn Ezra notes the difference in usage between בֵּין מַיִם לָמָיִם, *between waters and waters* [without the definite article 'ה', *'the'*, and

I
7

of the waters, and let it separate between water and
water.' 7 So God made the firmament, and separated
between the waters which were beneath the firmament and the waters which were above the firma-

without repeating the word 'between' before each noun] as used in the previous verse; and בֵּין הַמַּיִם וּבֵין הַמָּיִם ... *between 'the' waters ... and between 'the' waters* [repeating the word *'between'* each time] as used in this verse ...

Malbim explains that the former 'denotes a barrier between two similar substances' — the water above possibly being the same as the water below. Here the division was made not only in space, but in kind: the water below was literally a liquid, while the water above was vapor.

וַיְהִי כֵן — *And it was so.* — And so it became! *(Hirsch).*

I.e., 'This state of expanse became firmly established. There was to be no further development of the רָקִיעַ [firmament] which had formed between the waters' *(Munk).*

Ibn Ezra suggests that this phrase should be connected as introductory to the next verse and rendered: וַיְהִי כֵן, *when it was so* — then — *God called the firmament Heaven.*

If the verse has already explicitly said *'And God made'* [as a *fait accompli*], why must it repeat *'and it was so'*? — The phrase implies absolute perpetuity and eternity in an unchanging state from the day of its creation *(Lekach Tov).*

[Nevertheless, it must be understood that God renews the Creation daily — מְחַדֵּשׁ בְּכָל יוֹם תָּמִיד מַעֲשֵׂה בְרֵאשִׁית] otherwise it could not continue to exist. Hence, there is no *self-sustaining* permanence in Creation. When we speak of the 'permanence' of the universe, we mean that it is His will that creation be renewed constantly.]

It would seem that consistent with the other days of creation, the phrase *'and it was so'* should appear at the end of the previous verse and then begin the new verse *'And God made'* to demonstrate how God carried out the utterance in the previous verse [see verses 9-10 and 15-16] *(Ibn Janach)* ...

'But had the phrase been placed above I would have thought that — like its use on the other days — the phrase implies the completion of the water's creation. However, that did not really happen until the third day when the waters were gathered in one place *(Chizkuni).*

HaRechasim leBik'ah explains that this is the proper place for the phrase because this verse does *not* merely elaborate on the act mentioned in the previous verse — it is a vital part of it: It implies that He made a *wide barrier* between the two previously-connected levels of water — not merely a 'separation' but a distant division.

Ramban notes that וַיְהִי כֵן *'and it was so'* is written after וַיַּעַשׂ, *'and He made,'* to indicate that the making of the firmament as a division between the upper and the lower waters would remain permanent and eternal. The *Midrash* [cited in our comm. at the beginning of this verse] comments that this is one of the verses which caused Ben Zoma so much difficulty that 'he caused the earth to shake.' He questioned why, after God expressed his intention in v. 6, it was necessary to say in v. 7 that *'He made,'* as though His wish were insufficient. *Ramban* suggests that Ben Zoma was aware of some mystical interpretation of this verse which he did not want to disclose, and it was for this reason that 'he caused the earth to shake'.

Rashi notes that the Torah does not conclude this verse with the phrase כִּי טוֹב *'that it was good'* as it does on the other days of Creation, because the task of creating the waters, although begun on the second day, was not completed until the following day [when they were gathered and became seas]. Incomplete work is still imperfect [i.e. because having not yet attained its intended state, it could not be described as 'good']. However, on the third day, when the work of the waters was completed, the expression *'that it was good'* is said twice — once for the completion of the second day's creation, and once for the new creation of the third day [plant life].

Other reasons are offered for the omission of כִּי טוֹב, *'that it was good'* on the second day:

— Because the fire of Gehinnom was created thereon (*Peschim* 54a);

— Because on it division [מַחְלוֹקֶת = schism; strife] was created because the waters were divided against their 'will', so to speak *(Midrash);* [1]

— Because the Angel of Death was created thereon *(Midrash; Zohar);*

— Because from the very beginning of Creation, God foresaw the existence of Moses who was referred to as טוֹב, *'good'* [*Exodus* 2:2] and that he was destined to be punished through water [i.e. his sin at the waters of Meribah (*Num.* 20:12f)];

— Because the heavens were not yet completed, the stars not having yet been created *(Ralbag);*

Therefore, the use of כִּי טוֹב, *that it was good,* was inappropriate in the above connections.

Rabbeinu Bachya notes that these were momentous achievements on the second day — the creation of the angels and the firmament — and for those feats alone *'good'* should have been applied to that day. Nevertheless, this is the best proof that the 'lower world' is the primary purpose of Creation. The world was created for man — and until the next day when the dry land was visible and thus a habitat for man began to take shape, "good" did not apply. Only when man's interests were served did the heavens attain a purpose in their existence: 'the righteous are greater than the ministering angels' *(Sanhedrin* 93a; see Overview).

Rambam [*Moreh* II:30] notes the *Midrashic* explanation [cited by *Rashi,* above] and states that in each case where the Torah mentions something which is durable and perpetual it says in reference to it *'that it was good'*. Here, however, the matter of firmament and that which is above it, called 'water', is of a profoundly mysterious nature and very remote and incomprehensible. This mystique was necessary in order to prevent the vulgar from knowing it. What good, therefore, can people find in things whose apparent nature is hidden? How then could it be proper to say of such a thing *'that it is good'*? For the meaning of 'good' is that something is of *obvious* utility. [And everything in the Torah, as pointed out previously, is seen from the vantage point of man. Since this part of creation is incomprehensible to man, it cannot be called *'good'* in human terms.]

8. וַיִּקְרָא אֱלֹהִים לָרָקִיעַ שָׁמָיִם — *[And] God called to the firmament*

1. This schism, which started on the second day, *Rabbeinu Bachya* explains, *was the beginning of all later strife as will be noted from the defiance of the creations on subsequent days* (e.g. the trees, verse 11; moon, verse 16). [Thus, the *Talmud* Shabbos 156a comments: 'he who is born on the second day will be bad-tempered, because the waters were divided thereon (and so, through his temper will he be 'divided' — estranged — from other people — *Rashi* — *Chavel*] See footnote to verse 9.

Resisei Layla points out that because strife began with the second day, the song which the Levites sang during the Temple service on Mondays was one composed by Korach, instigator of strife against Moses and Aaron in the desert.

I
8 *ment. And it was so.* [8] *God called to the firmament:*

'Heaven'. i.e. [a compound of two words] שָׂא מַיִם, *'carry water'*; שָׁם מַיִם, *'the waters are there'*; אֵשׁ וּמַיִם, *'fire and water,'* — which He mixed together and from which He made heaven *(Rashi;* see *comm.* to שָׁמַיִם, *heavens,* end of verse 1; see also comm. to וַיִּקְרָא, *He called,* verse 5).

According to *Ramban,* by this name [which is a composite of its component parts] He revealed the mystery of their creation... The composite form is שֵׁם מַיִם, 'the [new] name of water' — i.e. that *'heaven'* is the name given to the waters when they assumed their new form ... However, Scripture related nothing *specific* concerning their creation, just as it did not mention the creation of the angels or other incorporeal beings. It only mentioned in general terms that heaven was created and that on the second day the firmament should separate the waters and assume the name שָׁמַיִם, *heaven.* This is not the heavens mentioned in the first verse for those heavens encompass all extra-terrestrial, spiritual aspects of creation *(Ramban).*

Just as God named the light *'Day'* [verse 5] and thereby assigned to it its mission for the earth, so did He name the רָקִיעַ *Heaven;* thereby giving it its meaning for the earth. Though שָׁמַיִם designates the whole extra-terrestrial universe surrounding the earth in space (just as יוֹם designates *day* in general, but more specifically that part of day [the light] when its most essential function occurs). רָקִיעַ thus designates the real 'heaven', because through it comes everything the earth receives from the heights of heaven. Even light does not come direct and pure to earth, but only through the רָקִיעַ where it is refracted and filtered to be prepared and made ready for its work on earth. Thus, it is the container and transmitter of all the gifts and forces of the extra-terrestrial world *(Hirsch).*[1]

Furthermore, the designation of firmament now means: From this point in the atmosphere [רָקִיעַ] begins the heavenly realm [שָׁמַיִם] where human existence is not possible. *'Called'* means that *He instilled it with this nature* that it should be *'heaven'* and not fit for earthlings *(Malbim).*

[Cf. *Psalms* 115:16: *'The heavens are the heavens of HASHEM, but He has given the earth to the children of man.'*]

According to *Rashbam,* the intent of the verse is that it [i.e. the רָקִיעַ, *firmament*], will henceforth be called שָׁמַיִם, *Heaven,* throughout the Torah.

§ An object should be named for its purpose rather than for the raw material from which it was made. Why, then, were the heavens called שמים indicating that they were made from water? They should have been named רקיע. The reason is that the purpose of the רקיע, heaven, was division — separation between the waters above and the waters below. Separation, the opposite of unity, is nothing to be proud of; therefore God did not wish to insult the heavens by using a name symbolic of division *(Yismach Moshe).*

1. [*Additionally* there are profoundly sublime mysteries in the word שָׁמַיִם, *heaven* for it is sometimes used synonymously with God. See, e.g. *Sefer HaBahir* 100: How do we know that *'heaven'* is identified with the Holy One, blessed be He? — From the verse (*I Kings* 8:32) וְאַתָּה תִּשְׁמַע הַשָּׁמַיִם (lit. *'and you, hear O heaven'*). Did, then, Solomon pray that the heavens should hear their prayers? It refers to Him whose name is associated with the heavens.]

שָׁמָ֑יִם וַֽיְהִי־עֶ֥רֶב וַֽיְהִי־בֹ֖קֶר י֥וֹם שֵׁנִֽי׃
ט וַיֹּ֣אמֶר אֱלֹהִ֗ים יִקָּו֨וּ הַמַּ֜יִם מִתַּ֤חַת
הַשָּׁמַ֙יִם֙ אֶל־מָק֣וֹם אֶחָ֔ד וְתֵרָאֶ֖ה הַיַּבָּשָׁ֑ה
י וַֽיְהִי־כֵֽן׃ וַיִּקְרָ֨א אֱלֹהִ֤ים ׀ לַיַּבָּשָׁה֙ אֶ֔רֶץ
וּלְמִקְוֵ֥ה הַמַּ֖יִם קָרָ֣א יַמִּ֑ים וַיַּ֥רְא אֱלֹהִ֖ים

וַיְהִי עֶרֶב וַיְהִי בֹקֶר יוֹם שֵׁנִי — *And there was evening and there was morning a second day.* Although the work of the second day was not sufficiently complete to describe it as כִּי טוֹב, *that it was good,* nevertheless, since the act of *separating* the upper from the lower waters was finished giving the appearance of completion, the Torah culminates the day's activity like the other days, with the summation *'and there was evening and there was morning', ... (Chizkuni).*

9. The Third day.

[God decrees boundaries for the water, making way for the development of land, vegetation, and ultimately man]:

וַיֹּאמֶר אֱלֹהִים — *[And] God said.* According to *Ibn Ezra* this phrase should be attached to the previous verse describing the firmament and be rendered *'now God had already said.'* Both the heaven and the dry land were created on the same day, as written in verse (2:4) *'in the day that HASHEM God made heaven and earth.'* [Thus the Biblical account of the third day begins with a summary of the second day's activity, and the pronouncement *'that it was good.'*] The account of the third day's new creation — the vegetation — begins with verse 11.

יִקָּווּ הַמַּיִם מִתַּחַת הַשָּׁמַיִם אֶל מָקוֹם אֶחָד — *Let the waters beneath the heaven be gathered into one area.*

The waters were scattered over the surface of the whole earth and He gathered them into one place: אוֹקְיָינוּס, the Ocean, largest of all seas *(Rashi).*

Munk renders: 'The waters below the sky shall be confined into one area.'

[Esoterically יִקָּווּ is related to קָו]: 'Just as an architect lays down a line [קָו] to define the boundaries of his structure, so did God lay down a line to contain the waters and define their boundaries as expressed in *Job* 38:8,11 '[*God*] ... *who enclosed the sea ... and said: "Until here shall you come, but no further" (Midrash HaNe'elam).*

Until then the earth was a plain, entirely submerged under water. Scarcely had God's words: *'Let the waters be gathered'* been uttered, when mountains and hills appeared all over and the waters collected in the deep-lying valleys. But the water threatened to overflow the earth until God forced it back into the sea, encircling the sea with sand. Whenever the sea is tempted to transgress its bounds, it beholds the sand and recoils *(Pirkei d'Rabbi Eliezer; Zohar).*[1]

1. [That God created within the water, earth and those creatures not endowed with Free Will the imperative to seemingly rebel and be subsequently punished must be perceived in the context of its moral lesson to man. (See *Overview*)]

I 'Heaven.' And there was evening and there was
9-10 morning, a second day.

9 God said, 'Let the waters beneath the heaven be
gathered into one area, that the dry land may appear.'
And it was so. 10 God called to the dry land: 'Earth',
and to the gathering of waters He called: 'Seas.' And

וְתֵרָאֶה הַיַּבָּשָׁה — *'that the dry land may appear* [or: *'and let the dry land appear.'*] This refers to the earth which was created on the first day but which had been neither visible nor dry until the waters were commanded to assemble *(Lekach Tov; Rashbam).*

Zohar Chadash mystically states that while the earth was still submerged beneath the water, it dried up in anticipation of God's directive. The mention in our verse that the *'dry land'* should *appear* implies that dry land already existed but could not appear until the water receded. This is one of the reasons the earth is named אֶרֶץ [from רץ *run, rush*] because it rushed to do the will of the Creator in anticipation of His word *(Me'am Loez).* [cf *comm.* to הָאָרֶץ in v. 1.]

וַיְהִי כֵן — *And it was so.* [i.e. the position of water in relation to dry land became firmly established as a 'natural' fact in God's daily re-creation of the world forever.] 'At God's command, accordingly, did it become so' *(Hirsch)* ...

10. וַיִּקְרָא אֱלֹהִים לַיַּבָּשָׁה אֶרֶץ –[*And*] *God called to the dry land: Earth!* — [Earth here signifies the terrestrial surface which was to be the scene of man's activity.]

According to *Ramban,* God gave them names when they assumed the forms described, for initially both the waters and the dry land were referred to collectively as תְּהוֹם, *the deep.*

Initially, at the Creation, שָׁמַיִם, *heaven,* was an all-embracing term for everything above the orbit of the moon, while everything below it was referred to as אֶרֶץ, *earth.* However, as creation was refined and molded toward its ultimate purpose, the general names began to refer to specific functions. *'Earth'* referred to that which was below the firmament — the area which He reserved for human habitation. When the ultimate Purpose drew yet closer, and He gathered the waters of the earth into seas, then the connotation of 'earth' became even more specific: only the dry land — the dwelling place of man — is referred to as אֶרֶץ, *earth (Malbim).*

וּלְמִקְוֵה הַמַּיִם קָרָא יַמִּים — *And to the gathering of water He called: Seas.* i.e. "Be seas!" Do not remain a single gathering of waters but diversify throughout the dry land and form separate seas. This division of the land by the seas into separate countries became the foundation of all the development of nations *(Hirsch).*

Although all the waters really form only one great sea, *'seas'* is in the plural, because fish caught at Acco do not have the same taste as fish caught in Aspamia [Spain?] *(Rashi).*

יא כִּי־טוֹב: וַיֹּאמֶר אֱלֹהִים תַּדְשֵׁא הָאָרֶץ
דֶּשֶׁא עֵשֶׂב מַזְרִיעַ זֶרַע עֵץ פְּרִי עֹשֶׂה פְּרִי
לְמִינוֹ אֲשֶׁר זַרְעוֹ־בוֹ עַל־הָאָרֶץ וַיְהִי־כֵן:
יב וַתּוֹצֵא הָאָרֶץ דֶּשֶׁא עֵשֶׂב מַזְרִיעַ זֶרַע

... And also because there is no one ocean that encircles the whole globe *(Ibn Ezra).*

וַיַּרְא אֱלֹהִים כִּי טוֹב – *And God saw that it was good.* – that their continued existence was by His will, and their existence was thus established in the form desired by Him *(Ramban).*[1]

This phrase brings the division between the upper and lower waters to a conclusion. *'God saw that this division was good'* – it was in accordance with His plan and continues so now in its wonderous pristine power as the water rises from the ocean to the clouds above and thence pours down again; and hurries back to the sea ... to restart the cycle ... This is not only so because He had once created it so, but because He still finds it in accordance with His purposes *(Hirsch).*

11. Organic life

תַּדְשֵׁא הָאָרֶץ דֶּשֶׁא – *Let the earth sprout vegetation* – i.e. let it be filled and covered with a garment of grasses *(Rashi).* And with this command, God implanted within the earth the eternal power to produce vegetation *(Ibn Ezra).*

The verb תַּדְשֵׁא, *sprout,* has the same meaning as תַּצְמִיחַ, *let grow.* The words *vegetation, herbs,* and *fruit trees* are all objects of the verb 'let sprout' (Ramban).

The earth was granted the power to sprout forth new vegetation forever, but man must first sow – only then will the ground yield up its produce. The exception to this rule was the original vegetation which sprouted solely at God's command *(Aderes Eliyahu).*

עֵשֶׂב מַזְרִיעַ זֶרַע – *Herbage yielding seed,* i.e. it should grow its own seed within itself so that it may be planted somewhere else *(Rashi).*

– This refers to wheat and vegetables which do not grow wild, but only as a result of seeding and tending *(Akeidas Yitzchak).*

Rashi explains that דֶּשֶׁא is a general term for vegetation, while each particular species is called עֵשֶׂב;

Rambam and *Radak* explain that דֶּשֶׁא refers to a young plant, while a mature plant is referred to as עֵשֶׂב;

Sforno suggests that vegetation fit for animals is called דֶּשֶׁא, while herbage eaten by man is called עֵשֶׂב.

עֵץ פְּרִי עֹשֶׂה פְּרִי לְמִינוֹ – *Fruit trees yielding fruit each after its kind.* [lit. (in singular): *fruit tree yielding fruit after its kind.* The singular in Hebrew contextually infers fruit trees in general.] God commanded that it be עֵץ פְּרִי, *a fruit tree:* that the taste of the tree be the same as its fruit. The earth, however, dis-

1. The word ראה [see] which denotes 'to perceive with the eye' is also used in the sense of intellectual perception ... When applied to God, it is to be understood only in the figurative sense, for God does not require organs or modes of perception (*Rambam, Moreh* 1:4).

I
11-12

God saw that it was good. ¹¹ *God said, 'Let the earth*
sprout vegetation: herbage yielding seed, fruit trees
yielding fruit each after its kind, containing its own
seed on the earth.' And it was so. ¹² *And the earth*
brought forth vegetation: herbage yielding seed after

obeyed and *brought forth* עֵץ עֹשֶׂה פְּרִי, *'tree yielding fruit,'* but the tree itself was not a fruit. Therefore, when Adam was cursed for his sin, the earth, too, was remembered and punished [3:17] *(Rashi; Midrash).* [See *footnote* to *verse* 9, and *Overview.*]

Ramban notes that the creation of *barren* trees is not mentioned here. He suggests that originally all trees bore fruit, but barren trees came into existence when the earth was cursed [3:17] due to the sin of Adam. Alternately, he suggests that in this verse, *'sprout vegetation'* is a general term that includes barren trees, after which He specified herbs which yield seeds and fruit bearing trees.

The *Vilna Gaon* explains that לְמִינוֹ, *after its kind,* means that it will not change its character: an apple-tree will not produce pomegranates.

אֲשֶׁר זַרְעוֹ־בוֹ עַל־הָאָרֶץ — *Containing its own seed* [lit. *'Whose seed is in it'* i.e. *yielding their own species*] *on the earth.*

— This refers to the kernels of each fruit from which the tree grows so that the species is self-perpetuating *(Rashi).*

Additionally, the tree cannot reproduce unless its seed is placed עַל הָאָרֶץ, *upon the land* through planting, then the fruit will produce another fruit similar to it *(Abarbanel).*

Thus, from this potential seed bearing force in the earth, all vegetation emanated . . . from this force the grass and trees in the Garden of Eden and in the world originated.' For as the Sages have said: 'On the third day He created three things: trees, grass, and the Garden of Eden' *(Ramban).*

וַיְהִי־כֵן — *And it was so* — i.e. the earth was granted this unique productive power forever *(Aderes Eliyahu).*

12. וַתּוֹצֵא הָאָרֶץ — *And the earth brought forth.* [The herbs emerged, but did not yet sprout forth fully as the *Talmud* notes]:

Rav Assi perceived an apparent inconsistency between this verse where it says *'and the earth brought forth vegetation'*, and later, referring to the sixth day, where the verse says *'no shrub of the field was yet in the earth.'* This teaches, that the herbs commenced to grow [on the third day] but stopped just as they were about to break through the soil, until Adam came and prayed for them, and rain fell and they grew. This teaches you that the Holy One, blessed be He, longs for the prayers of the righteous. Rav Nachman bar Papa had a garden and he planted in it seeds but they did not grow. He prayed; immediately rain came and they began to grow. 'That,' he exclaimed, 'is what Rav Assi had taught.' *(Chullin* 60b). [Cf. *Comm.* to 2:5, and *Overview.*]

לְמִינֵהוּ וְעֵץ עֹשֶׂה־פְּרִי אֲשֶׁר זַרְעוֹ־בוֹ
יג לְמִינֵהוּ וַיַּרְא אֱלֹהִים כִּי־טוֹב: וַיְהִי־עֶרֶב
וַיְהִי־בֹקֶר יוֹם שְׁלִישִׁי:
יד וַיֹּאמֶר אֱלֹהִים יְהִי מְאֹרֹת בִּרְקִיעַ
הַשָּׁמַיִם לְהַבְדִּיל בֵּין הַיּוֹם וּבֵין הַלָּיְלָה

עֵשֶׂב מַזְרִיעַ זֶרַע לְמִינֵהוּ — *Herbage yielding seed after its kind.*

Although only the *trees* were bidden to produce fruit לְמִינוֹ, *after its kind*, the herbs applied this to themselves also and did likewise *(Rashi; Chullin* 60a).

Radak, however, suggests that since לְמִינוֹ, *after its kind*, occurs at the *end* of the previous verse, it applies to the *herbs* as well as to the *trees*.

וְעֵץ עֹשֶׂה פְּרִי — *And trees yielding fruit.* [*Rashi*, in the previous verse, notes the difference between God's decree and its faulty execution by the trees. See above.]

The *Midrash* continues, however, that according to Rav Pinchas the earth, thinking to do His will, exceeded His command, for עֵץ עֹשֶׂה פְּרִי, *trees yielding fruit* implies that even non-fruit bearing trees yielded fruit ... Then why was she later cursed [3:17]? It is in fact as one might say 'Cursed be the bosom that suckled such a one as this!' [i.e. the sinful Adam and Eve.]

וַיַּרְא אֱלֹהִים כִּי טוֹב — *And God saw that it was good.* [i.e. that its goodness was manifest] and the various species will exist forever *(Ramban)*.

[See *comm.* to verse 7 where *Rashi* explains why כִּי טוֹב *that it was good* is said twice in connection with the third day: once for the completion of the work of the water begun on the second day, and once for the work of the third day.]

Akeidas Yitzchak comments that the earth progressed toward its purpose and perfection with these two utterances of the day; therefore, *'that it was good'* was pronounced for each of them. With the appearance of dry land the earth emerged from its state of תֹּהוּ, *tohu* [desolation; see *comm.* to *verse* 2]; and with the appearance of vegetation it emerged from its state of בֹּהוּ, *bohu* [void; *ibid.*]. Thus its latent potential reached its mature state of being on the third day.

14. The fourth day

יְהִי מְאֹרֹת — *Let there be luminaries.* — They had already been created on the first day but were not suspended in the firmament until the fourth day *(Chagigah* 12a). Indeed (as pointed out above, end of verse 1 on the words אֵת הַשָּׁמַיִם וְאֵת הָאָרֶץ), all the potentials of heaven and earth were created on the first day but each was established on the day when it was so commanded *(Rashi)*.

[The commentators note the use of the singular form יְהִי instead of the plural יְהִיוּ which would be consonant with the plural object מְאֹרֹת, *luminaries.*]:

Rashbam, Ibn Ezra and *Radak* note that it is not unusual for Scripture to intermix number and

its kind, and trees yielding fruit, each containing its
seed after its kind. And God saw that it was good.
13 And there was evening and there was morning, a
third day.
14 God said, 'Let there be luminaries in the firma-
ment of the heaven to separate between the day and

gender, and several proof verses are quoted.

According to *Rabbeinu Bachya,* the singular form is used because only the sun, of the two luminaries, gives forth its own light [the moon being only reflective.]

The origin of the word מְאֹרֹת, *luminaries,* is derived from מָאוֹר, *from the light,* indicating that they possessed no independent light; they were like 'windows' that transmitted a portion of the primeval light which had been hidden from view by the firmament *(Aderes Eliyahu).*

This follows *Ramban* who elaborates that the firmament created on the second day obscured the primeval light, and thus, on the third day the earth was dark, until the luminaries in the firmament illuminated the earth on the fourth day. This is the meaning of the phrase [verse 17] בִּרְקִיעַ הַשָּׁמַיִם לְהָאִיר עַל הָאָרֶץ, *'in the firmament of the heaven to give light upon the the earth'* — for light did exist *above* the firmament but it did not illuminate the earth.

בִּרְקִיעַ הַשָּׁמַיִם — *In the firmament of the heaven.* Or, as *Munk* renders: 'in the expanse of the sky.'

I.e., the firmament, which is spread out beneath the heavens *(Rashbam).*

The *Vilna Gaon* explains the phrase: *'the firmament which is called Heaven.'*

[Cf. *comm.* to same phrase in v. 17.]

לְהַבְדִּיל בֵּין הַיּוֹם וּבֵין הַלָּיְלָה — *To separate between the day and [between] the night.*

Rashi explains that this [division] happened only after the primeval light was hidden for the future benefit of the righteous in the World to Come, because during the seven days of Creation, the primeval light and darkness functioned together, in a mixture, both by day and by night. [According to *Ramban's* text of *Rashi* read: 'functioned one by day and one by night.']

[*Rashi's* interpretation (following the alternate *Talmudic* view in *Chagigah* 12a) is in consonance with his *Midrashic* interpretation of verses 4 and 5 according to which the 'division' mentioned there was allegorical (referring to the setting aside of the light for the future benefit of the righteous); and in consonance with his 'simple' interpretation there according to which the 'division' did not occur until the fourth day when the luminaries were suspended.]

Gur Aryeh explains that according to this opinion, the primeval light was concealed until after the first Sabbath. Consequently, as *Levush HaOrah* elaborates, the luminaries did not begin to render light until the primeval light was concealed.

Ramban, however, comments that the primeval light functioned for *three* days, and on the fourth day the two luminaries were formed.

[Thus, the luminaries served as the permanent regulators of the dis-

וְהָיוּ לְאֹתֹת וּלְמוֹעֲדִים וּלְיָמִים וְשָׁנִים׃
טו וְהָיוּ לִמְאוֹרֹת בִּרְקִיעַ הַשָּׁמַיִם לְהָאִיר
טז עַל־הָאָרֶץ וַיְהִי־כֵן׃ וַיַּעַשׂ אֱלֹהִים אֶת־
שְׁנֵי הַמְּאֹרֹת הַגְּדֹלִים אֶת־הַמָּאוֹר הַגָּדֹל
לְמֶמְשֶׁלֶת הַיּוֹם וְאֶת־הַמָּאוֹר הַקָּטֹן

tinction between day and night that is laid down in verses 4 and 5.]

For until now [in the absense of sun and moon] there was light during the day and darkness at night. Now He decreed that there be a luminary for each of them: the greater luminary to serve during the day, and the smaller one at night. This, then, is meant by *'separation'* *(Radak).*

וְהָיוּ לְאֹתֹת — *And they shall serve as* [lit. *'be for'*] *signs,* i.e. as omens, for when the luminaries are eclipsed, it is an ill-omen for the world, as in the verse [*Jeremiah* 10:2] *'Be not dismayed at the signs of heaven'* — but when you comply with the will of God, you need not worry about punishment *(Rashi).*

... There are many such verses in Scripture alluding to the heavenly bodies as omens, for example, in reference to Hezekiah [*II Kings* 20:9] *'this sign shall you have ... the shadow shall go back ten degrees'* — thus the moon was the sign; *Joel* 3:3 *'and I will exhibit wonders in the heavens and the earth' (Rashbam).*

According to many, אֹתֹת, *signs,* refers to the luminaries function as man's *guide* [i.e. compass] as navigational aids.

HaRechasim leBik'ah comments: They are *'signs'* of God's greatness in two ways: (1) they are constant signs and symbols of His omnipotence, as in the verse [*Isaiah* 40:26]: *'Lift up your eyes on high and behold Who has created these things';* (2) that they sometimes diverge from their natural course to comply with His will as when the sun stopped for Joshua.

[And as a guide to determining the festivals]:

וּלְמוֹעֲדִים — *And for festivals.* This translation follows *Rashi* who interprets מוֹעֲדִים here as a reference to the *'Festivals':* 'This is in anticipation of the future when Israel would be commanded to regulate the festivals by lunar calculation.'

[The translation also agrees with *Targum Yonasan* and with the *Midrash* which specifically renders]: 'This refers to the three pilgrimage festivals.'

[Many commentator, however, interpret מוֹעֲדִים as *seasons,* referring to the function of the luminaries in determining the seasons]:

— This refers to *'seedtime and harvest, cold and heat, summer and winter'* [*Gen.* 8:22] *(Ibn Janach; Ramban).*

According to *Ibn Ezra,* however, מוֹעֲדִים means *'hours'* [and the verse ascends from the shorter time-span to the longer ones.]

[And for the division of time, and counting days and cycles]:

וּלְיָמִים וְשָׁנִים — *And for days and years.*

'And for days': the sun and moon each functioning half a day — together a full day;

I
15-16 *the night; and they shall serve as signs, and for festivals, and for days and years;* [15] *and they shall serve as luminaries in the firmament of the heaven to shine upon the earth.' And it was so.* [16] *And God made the two great luminaries, the greater luminary to dominate the day and the lesser luminary to*

'And years': at the end of 365¼ days they complete their course ... making one year, and then begin a renewed cycle *(Rashi);* for without the orbiting luminaries we could never reckon the days or years *(Lekach Tov; Ha'amek Davar).*

... The luminaries complete their orbit ... thus making the solar year consist of 365 days, and the lunar year consist of (lunar cycles, each approximately) thirty days *(Ramban* [*Chavel* transl.]*).*

... For from one appearance of the stars until the next appearance of the stars, one day has elapsed, while the passing of four seasons constitutes one year *(Rashbam).*

[And in addition to the functions above] ...

15. וְהָיוּ לִמְאוֹרֹת ... לְהָאִיר עַל הָאָרֶץ — *And they shall serve as* [lit. *'and they shall be'*] *luminaries ... to shine upon the earth.'*

I.e., in addition to the above they would illuminate the world *(Rashi).*

They were thus directed to shine upon earth because it is possible for light to perform all the [regulatory] functions mentioned without illuminating the earth. Hence He specifically decreed that the light be directed toward earth to illuminate it *(Ramban).*

וַיְהִי כֵן — *And it was so.*[1]

The luminaries, which had the inherent direction to develop themselves for their purposes, were developed *(Munk).*

... But they were still not hung in the firmament; that will be described in v. 17 *(Ha'amek Davar).*

16. [The following verses proceed to describe in detail how God caused each of them to shine according to its allotted time *(Radak)*]:

וַיַּעַשׂ אֱלֹהִים אֶת שְׁנֵי הַמְּאֹרֹת הַגְּדֹלִים — *And God made the two great luminaries.* They were originally created of equal size, but the moon was diminished because it complained and said, 'It is impossible for two kings to make use of the same crown'. [It thus demanded more power than the sun, and was punished by being made smaller] *(Chullin* 60b; *Rashi);* see *Overview.*

Ibn Ezra suggests that they were referred to as גְּדֹלִים, *great* [lit. *large*] in comparison with the size of the stars [as viewed from man's vantage point on earth.]

[On וַיַּעַשׂ, *and He made,* see *comm.* to *verse* 7]

אֶת הַמָּאוֹר הַגָּדֹל ... וְאֶת הַמָּאוֹר הַקָּטֹן — *The greater* [lit. *'large'*] *luminary to dominate* [lit. *'for the domination of'*] *the day, and the lesser* [lit.

1. I.e. *It was so* — then, and it remained so established forever.

Their orbits and cycles will never deviate as evidenced by two-thousand year old astronomical charts from ancient Egypt and China which were discovered showing that none of the stars changed its basic orbit throughout all this time by even a hair's-breadth *(Malbim).*

יז לְמֶמְשֶׁלֶת הַלַּיְלָה וְאֵת הַכּוֹכָבִים: וַיִּתֵּן
אֹתָם אֱלֹהִים בִּרְקִיעַ הַשָּׁמָיִם לְהָאִיר
יח עַל־הָאָרֶץ: וְלִמְשֹׁל בַּיּוֹם וּבַלַּיְלָה
וּֽלֲהַבְדִּיל בֵּין הָאוֹר וּבֵין הַחֹשֶׁךְ וַיַּרְא
יט אֱלֹהִים כִּי־טוֹב: וַיְהִי־עֶרֶב וַיְהִי־בֹקֶר יוֹם
רְבִיעִי:

'small'] luminary to dominate [lit. *for the domination of*] *the night.*

'Great' does not refer to their size for the stars are larger than the moon as has been ascertained by astronomers. The intent, rather, is 'great' in the visible intensity of their illumination, the moon's light being stronger than that of the other stars, except the sun, because it is closer to the earth *(Radak; Malbim).*

קָטֹן *'small'*, accordingly means: 'lesser of the two great luminaries' *(Rashbam).*

וְאֵת הַכּוֹכָבִים — *And the stars.* The *Midrash* comments that the stars were created as 'attendants' [of the moon], to mollify it for being diminished in size *(Rashi).*[1]

[Here, again, the Torah presents creation from man's perspective on earth. The stars are much greater in size and intensity than the moon, and many of them dwarf even the sun, but since they are mere 'specks' from man's vantage point and play a subordinate part in his life when compared to these two bodies, they are mentioned last, and without elaboration.]

17-18. וַיִּתֵּן אֹתָם אֱלֹהִים — *And God set them,* i.e. He put them into fixed orbits *(Munk).*

And appointed them for their fixed roles *(Malbim).*

בִּרְקִיעַ הַשָּׁמָיִם — *In the firmament of the heaven.* The *Midrash* comments that these concepts are beyond man's grasp. 'It is an exceedingly difficult matter and no mortal can fathom it'.

וְלִמְשֹׁל בַּיּוֹם וּבַלַּיְלָה — [*And*] *to dominate by* [or: *'during the'*] *day and by* [or *'during the'*] *night* — each in its respective realm *(Lekach Tov)*: one during the day and the other during the night; for though the moon is sometimes visible during the day it is like 'a candle in the afternoon' [shedding no light] *(B'chor Shor).*

The concept of domination differs from the function of illumination ... This 'domination' refers to the sun's power, by its rule during the day, to cause sprouting, etc. ... while the moon by its domination at night affects the tides of the oceans. ...Included, also, are the astrological

1. Rav Acha said: Imagine a king who had two governors, one ruling in the city and the other in a province. The king said: Since the former has humbled himself to rule in the city only, I hereby decree that whenever he goes out, the city council and the people shall go out with him, and whenever he enters, they shall enter with him.'

Thus did the Holy One, blessed be He say: 'Since the moon humbled itself to rule by night, I hereby decree that when she comes forth, the stars shall come forth with her, and when she goes in, they shall go in with her' *(Midrash).*

dominate the night; and the stars. 17 *And God set*
them in the firmament of the heaven to give light
upon the earth, 18 *to dominate by day and by night,*
and to separate between the light and between the
darkness. And God saw that it was good. 19 *And*
there was evening and there was morning, a fourth
day.

powers of the constellations *(Ramban).*

וּלְהַבְדִּיל בֵּין הָאוֹר וּבֵין הַחֹשֶׁךְ — *And to separate between the light and between the darkness.*

I.e. to distinguish between the light of day and the dark of night *(Targum Yonasan).*

Thus, the functions of the luminaries are described in these verses as threefold:
(1) לְהָאִיר עַל הָאָרֶץ, *to shine upon the earth;*
(2) וְלִמְשֹׁל בַּיּוֹם וּבַלַּיְלָה, *to rule during the day and night* [i.e. 'to exert some control over natural processes of earth by day and by night' *(Munk)*];
(3) וּלֲהַבְדִּיל בֵּין הָאוֹר וּבֵין הַחֹשֶׁךְ, *and to distinguish between the light and between the darkness.*

Ramban notes that the functions of the two luminaries are now defined. Their dominion is not equal, but consists of causing a distinction between the darkness and the light. The greater luminary will dominate by day and its light will be everywhere — even in places where [the *direct* rays of] the sun do not reach. The smaller luminary will dominate by night — although it will do no more than relieve the darkness.

וַיַּרְא אֱלֹהִים כִּי טוֹב — *And God saw that it was good* — i.e. that it could not be more perfect. Had the sun been larger than it is, or closer to the earth its heat would have burned the earth; or had its path been lower, parts of earth would have become frozen. Similarly — every one of the constellations is in its exact place *(Abarbanel).*

Meam Loez notes that the sun was created *after* the earth to dispel any notion that the creation of earth was a natural result of the sun's heat vaporizing the waters. Similarly, lest anyone contend that plant-life is a natural outgrowth of the earth [aided by the sun], God created the earth and all its properties on the third day, and only afterwards, on the fourth day, did He create the sun, to demonstrate unequivocally that everything materialized from God's direct will.

20-22. The fifth day. Marine life and birds.

Hirsch brilliantly prefaces the events of the fifth day with the observation that the creations of the first three days are paralleled by those of the subsequent three days: The light of the first day was provided with bearers [מְאֹרֹת] on the fourth day; *the water and atmosphere of the second day were filled with life on the fifth day;* and the dry land with its mantle of vegetation of the third day was provided with inhabitants on the sixth.

כ וַיֹּאמֶר אֱלֹהִים יִשְׁרְצוּ הַמַּיִם שֶׁרֶץ נֶפֶשׁ
חַיָּה וְעוֹף יְעוֹפֵף עַל־הָאָרֶץ עַל־פְּנֵי
כא רְקִיעַ הַשָּׁמָיִם: וַיִּבְרָא אֱלֹהִים אֶת־

20. יִשְׁרְצוּ הַמַּיִם שֶׁרֶץ נֶפֶשׁ חַיָּה — *Let the waters teem* [with] *creeping living creatures* [lit. *'souls'.*]

The translation of שֶׁרֶץ, *creeping things,* follows *Rashi* who states that the term is used to describe 'any living creature [which is the smallest of its species *(Gur Aryeh)*] that does not rise much above the ground.' [As *Rashi* explains in verse 24, s.v. רֶמֶשׂ, they creep low on the ground and their method of locomotion is not discernable.] Of the winged creatures: flies; of the creeping creatures: ants, beetles and worms; of the larger animals: the mole, rat, lizard, and all fish.'

[*Rashi* does not suggest that all his examples were created from water on the fifth day; for among the animals he cites, some are in the category of רֶמֶשׂ, *creeping things,* which were created on the *sixth* day from the earth. *Rashi* merely lists them to define the term שֶׁרֶץ: there is no implication, however, that the שֶׁרֶץ creation of the fifth day embraced anything other than aquatic life.]

Ramban, following *Targum,* explains that the noun implies ceaseless movement: *'moving things',* and suggests that it is a composite of the words שֶׁהוּא רָץ, that which runs.

The verb יִשְׁרְצוּ according to *Rashi,* connotes aimless wandering, teeming in great, confused numbers; according to *Ramban* it connotes 'walking about', and *Targum* renders it as having a reference to propagation, bringing forth abundant progeny as do insects. Accordingly, the phrase could be rendered: *'let the water bring forth.'*

HaRechasim leBik'ah comments that the words לֵידָה, *procreation,* שְׁרִיצָה, *teeming,* and הוֹצָאָה, *bringing forth,* all refer to reproduction. The first refers to terrestrial life, the second to marine life, and the third to plant life.[Occasionaly, however, the terms are interchanged, as for example, in verse 24 תוצא *'bring forth',* is used for animals, while in 9:7 it is used for man in the sense of 'propagate as abundantly' as insects.]

Thus, *Hirsch* concludes, that the phrase יִשְׁרְצוּ הַמַּיִם can be taken transitively — *the water shall germinate;* or intransitively — *'the water shall swarm with'* etc.

In the intransitive form, 'the existing floating material with the potential for marine life would, as it were, become living bodies; in the transitive form, the water would "produce" them' *(Munk,* p.82).

God's decree 'let the waters teem' did not give water this power eternally; it applied only to the period of Creation. Thereafter, like the animals which the earth brought forth, God endowed marine life with self-proliferating powers by specifically blessing them that they be fruitful and multiply *(Or Hachaim).*

נֶפֶשׁ חַיָּה means *'a living soul'* — i.e. a soul in which there is life. Only moving things have a 'soul', therefore no mention is made of soul on the third day in connection with plants *(R' Bachya).*

... *'Living soul'* is a term which is applied even to man as in 2:7 *'and man became a living soul' (R' Meyuchas).*

[The 'soul' of this verse, however, refers only to animal life, not

X

I
20-21

[20] *God said, 'Let the waters teem with creeping liv-*
ing creatures, and fowl that fly about over the earth
across the expanse of the heavens.' [21] *And God*

to the spirituality which is uniquely man's. Cf. *Comm.* of *N'tziv* to 2:7.]

וְעוֹף יְעוֹפֵף עַל הָאָרֶץ — *And fowl that fly about over the earth.* [This translation follows *Ramban,* who connects the creation of bird life to the sea, because the creation of the fifth day emanated from the waters; had bird life been created from earth, its creation would have been mentioned on the sixth day. *Ramban* cites *Pirkei d'Rabbi Eliezer* which maintains — from the context of the verse — that the birds were created from the waters. However the subject was disputed by the Sages, in the *Talmud, Chullin* 27b, some agreeing with this view, while others, citing *Gen.* 2:19, maintain that '[bird life] was created out of the alluvial mud', which, as *Ramban* concludes, is at the bottom of the ocean. Thus even though the mud is "land," their creation is mentioned on the fifth day. (See also *Hirsch*'s introductory comment to this verse cited above.)]

As *Targum Yonasan* renders: *'and the fowl which flies, whose nest is upon the earth.'*

— For though they were formed from the water, their growth will be on the earth *(Rashbam).*

The birds were indeed created from a compound of two elements, earth and water. For had they been created from only water they would be no more able than fish to exist out of it; and if from earth alone, which is a heavy element, they would not have been able to fly. But produced from a mixture of earth softened by water, they are capable of functioning in all elements *(Alshich).*

Chizkuni suggests that the waters produced only aquatic birds, such as geese, and swans, which live on the water. But those that live only on land such as turkeys and chickens, were formed from the earth.

[Compare also *Lev.* 11:20 where the word עוֹף, *fowl,* used in conjuction with שֶׁרֶץ, *swarming insects,* signifies certain winged insects.]

Following *Onkelos,* however, the phrase is taken as an additional clause: *'and fowl shall fly over the earth ...*

Munk similarly renders the verse: *And Elokim decreed: 'The water shall swarm with swarms of free-living breathing beings and of flying beings which will fly above the land facing the space of the sky.'*

עַל־פְּנֵי רְקִיעַ הַשָּׁמָיִם — *Across* [lit. *'in front of'*] *the expanse* [or *'firmament'*] *of the heavens.*

[Again 'the Torah speaks in the language of man' and this phrase lit. *'in front of the expanse of the heavens'* views the birds' flight from the vantage point of man gazing up from earth.]

'And let the way of the bird be upon the air of the expanse of the heavens' *(Targum Yonasan);* because the entire air space above the ground is referred to as *'across the expanse of the heavens'*

הַתַּנִּינִם הַגְּדֹלִים וְאֵת כָּל־נֶפֶשׁ הַחַיָּה ׀
הָרֹמֶשֶׂת אֲשֶׁר שָׁרְצוּ הַמַּיִם לְמִינֵהֶם
וְאֵת כָּל־עוֹף כָּנָף לְמִינֵהוּ וַיַּרְא אֱלֹהִים
כב כִּי־טוֹב׃ וַיְבָרֶךְ אֹתָם אֱלֹהִים לֵאמֹר פְּרוּ

(Ahavas Yonasan), 'heaven' being used often in Scripture to mean *'air' (Chizkuni).*

N'tziv observes that the verse speaks of two kinds of flying creatures: those that fly עַל הָאָרֶץ, *low, near the ground;* and those that fly עַל פְּנֵי רְקִיעַ הַשָּׁמָיִם, *high in the sky.* He notes that the double *piel* form 'יְעוֹפֵף' [instead of the *kal* 'יָעוּף'] suggests this broader application and two kinds of flight.

This phrase should not be construed as merely descriptive of birds' flying habits: it is the divine will that birds be able to fly in the heavens. Were it not for God's specific decree, they would not be able to soar to such heights *(Or HaChaim).*

21. וַיִּבְרָא אֱלֹהִים אֶת הַתַּנִּינִם הַגְּדֹלִים — *And God created the great sea-giants* — i.e. the gigantic fish in the sea *(Rashi).*[1]

Rashi goes on to quote *Bava Basra* 74b, according to which these *sea-giants* are Leviathan and its mate. He then slew the female and preserved her for the righteous in the Hereafter, for had they been permitted to be fruitful and multiply, their enormous bulk would not have allowed the world to continue its normal existence.

Perhaps, this is why it does not say וַיְהִי כֵן, *and it was so,* in reference to this creation. Such a phrase would have been inappropriate here, since, as the *Talmud* teaches, they did not continue to exist in the form in which they were initially created *(Ramban).*

Additionally, *'it was so'* [indicating a *fait accompli*] is not mentioned here because the creation of living beings was not completed until the sixth day — the works of the fifth day were a prelude to that which culminated on the sixth day *(Malbim).*

Abarbanel — as cited above to verse 1 s.v. בָּרָא — notes that this is the first time since the first day that *'created'* is used. It denotes that something fundamentally new came into being — in this case it stresses the unprecedented magnitude of the fishes' size ... *'Created'* also applies to *'the living souls'* — also unprecedented until that moment.

The inherent potential of each part of the universe was created on the first day, but each was established on the day when it was so commanded [see *Rashi* cited above verse 14, s.v. יְהִי מְאֹרֹת *'let there be luminaries'*]. Nevertheless, the word *'created'* is used here because the water which germinated the living beings was endowed on the first day

1. [*Specific* guidance on the etymology of the word תַּנִּינִם [sea giants] and its present-day identity are lacking.

According to *Hirsch*, the word תַּנִּינִם, is of doubtful derivation and meaning. He suggests that the word might be rendered etymologically as 'a fish, or a whole genus or family of fish.'

The word appears in various contexts throughout Scriptures implying different definitions — see, for example comm. to ArtScroll ed. of *Eichah*, 4:3 where we left the word untranslated as *'Tanim'.*]

I *created the great sea-giants and every living being*
22 *that creeps, with which the waters teemed after their*
kinds; and all winged fowl of every kind. And God
saw that it was good. [22] *God blessed them, saying, 'Be*

with the potential to produce only *bodies* of the living beings, but not the potential to produce their *'living soul'*. This creation *ex-nihilo* of the life-potential, came from HASHEM alone (who added the necessary 'forces'), and it is, therefore, ascribed to Him *(Sforno; Or HaChaim; Malbim).*

Because of their great size the Torah specifically ascribes the creation of the sea-giants to God to stress that they, too, were created from naught *(Ramban).*

וְאֵת כָּל נֶפֶשׁ הַחַיָּה — *And every living being* — i.e., which has life *(Rashi).*

Rav Saadiah Gaon perceives in the use of the article אֶת the amplification of *'with'* extending the meaning of אֶת *the sea-giants and* אֶת *every living being that creeps* to the entire range of marine life ...

'תַּנִּינִם, *sea giants,* being mentioned because they include amphibia which form an intermediate association between marine and terrestrial life' *(Munk).*

אֲשֶׁר שָׁרְצוּ הַמַּיִם — *With which the waters teemed* [in response to God's command.]

לְמִינֵהֶם — *after their kinds. Targum Yonasan* adds: the kinds which are clean and the kinds which are not clean [And, according to him, this is the meaning of the word לְמִינֵיהֶם wherever it appears.]

More commonly, however, *after their kinds* is interpreted as an injunction that living beings proliferate within their own species as the *Tanchuma* comments: God said to them: 'Every species shall cleave to its own king; other species are prohibited to it.' The laws prohibiting כִּלְאַיִם, *mixed species,* are enumerated in *Yoreh De'ah* 295-297.

עוֹף כָּנָף — *winged fowl.*

Targum Yonasan renders: *'every fowl that flies with wings.'*

According to *Radak* on 7:14, the category also includes small flying insects like locusts, hornets, and flies.

וַיַּרְא אֱלֹהִים כִּי טוֹב — *And God saw that it was good,* i.e. that they attained their level of perfection and function. They were perfect in essence and in the good [as food] which is derived from them *(Abarbanel).*

22. וַיְבָרֶךְ אֹתָם אֱלֹהִים — *(And) God blessed them. Rashi* notes that they needed a special blessing because so many are reduced, hunted down, and eaten. The other animals, too, needed such a blessing, but they did not receive it so as not to include the serpent which was destined to be cursed.

The blessing was necessary because their potential would not be realized unless they were numerous *(Sforno).*

לֵאמֹר — *Saying.*

אמר, *say,* has the intention of having an immediate result ...

א
כג־כד

וּרְבוּ וּמִלְאוּ אֶת־הַמַּיִם בַּיַּמִּים וְהָעוֹף
כג יִרֶב בָּאָרֶץ: וַיְהִי־עֶרֶב וַיְהִי־בֹקֶר יוֹם
חֲמִישִׁי:
כד וַיֹּאמֶר אֱלֹהִים תּוֹצֵא הָאָרֶץ נֶפֶשׁ חַיָּה
לְמִינָהּ בְּהֵמָה וָרֶמֶשׂ וְחַיְתוֹ־אֶרֶץ לְמִינָהּ

God's will, as expressed in His words of creation were followed by immediate action in order that His will be carried out. The intention of לאמר, *saying,* is that the purport of what is being said no matter how briefly, is to be completely understood and amplified upon by the Oral Law which is the companion to the Written Law. Here, as in the other Utterances of creation, לאמר implies immediate fulfillment. Because God blessed the creatures with fruitfulness, he endowed them with the potential to proliferate and at the same time the direction and urge for it *(Hirsch).*

... But, as the *Vilna Gaon* points out, words were not directed to them, literally, [cf. comm. to verse 3, s.v. וַיֹּאמֶר] for they are not endowed with reason enabling them to comprehend the word of God. Rather, God's will was within them as if He had told them: Be capable of carrying out the divine will.

פְּרוּ וּרְבוּ— *Be fruitful and multiply.*

Had the verse not added וּרְבוּ, *and multiply,* each creature would bring forth only one more — *'multiply'* implies multiple birth: One should bring forth many *(Rashi).*

'פְּרוּ is the production of progeny; רְבוּ is the care of the young on which this proliferacy depends' *(Hirsch).*

Ibn Ezra renders *'Be fruitful and multiply'* not as an imperative, because the power was not their own, but as a Divine blessing and endowment: *'You will be fruitful and multiply.'* (This is similar to *Deut.* 32:50 וּמוּת בָּהָר which according to him is not to be rendered, for the same reason, in the imperative: *and die on the mountain;* but as a statement of fact: *'and you will die on the mountain.')*

The meaning, then, of the blessing is: 'I have endowed you with the capability of proliferation and with the blessing that you multiply exceedingly.' Indeed, fish are far more abundant than animals' *(Radak).*

[If the blessing is understood as an *imperative,* it is clear why it was not addressed also to the plants in verse 11: Being inanimate, their proliferation is dependent on the pollination process, and is not controlled by their own conscious will, as is the case, to a very limited extent, with animate creatures. However, if interpreted as a divine *blessing,* then the omission regarding plant life is noteworthy.]

Ramban discusses this. He mentions that the term 'blessing' can apply to plants as well: *'And I will command My blessing upon you in the sixth year'* [*Lev.* 25:21]. However no such blessing was needed on the third day when plant-life was created, because initially each species of living beings was created in *single pairs* [such as man and women *(Tur);* and endowed with the reproductive ability to procreate] according to its kind. Since there was only one prototype male and female pair for each species, they required a blessing to multiply and be abundant. The plants, however, sprung up simultaneously in

fruitful and multiply, and fill the waters in the seas;
but the fowl shall increase on the earth.' 23 *And there*
was evening and there was morning, a fifth day.
24 *God said, 'Let the earth bring forth living*
creatures according to their kind: cattle, and creeping
things, and beasts of the land according to their

great abundance over the surface of the entire earth, just as they exist today [their abundance being a *fait accompli* at their very first moment of appearance.]

בַּיַּמִּים — *In the seas. 'Seas'* are mentioned because it is there that they are most abundant; in the streams they are few *(Ramban).*

וְהָעוֹף יִרֶב בָּאָרֶץ — *But the fowl shall increase on the earth.* The translation follows *Ramban* who notes that although fowl were originally created from the water, they would be fruitful and multiply *on the earth,* for all fowl — even those whose habitat is upon the water, lay their eggs on land, and there they are born.

24. The sixth day: Animals and man. [See prefatory comment to verse 20.]

תּוֹצֵא הָאָרֶץ — *Let the earth bring forth.*

תּוֹצֵא, *bring forth,* implies a concealed, dormant presence being transformed into existence *(Ahavas Yonasan);* for as explained earlier [verse 14] the potential for everything was created on the first day; it was subsequently only necessary to *bring them forth (Rashi).*

Once the substances of the earth had already been endowed on the fifth day with the faculty of producing life through existing forces, no further endowment of life was required for their reproduction ... as all the components for producing living bodies were already present. God's decree, therefore, takes the form of 'instructing' the earth to bring them forth on its own *(Munk).*

Hirsch notes that only when it comes to the living land-creatures does it say תּוֹצֵא הָאָרֶץ, that the earth is to *yield them up* and *set them outside* the earth — unlike the previous creations which still remain bound to the element which produced them.

נֶפֶשׁ חַיָּה לְמִינָהּ — *living creatures* [lit. 'a living soul'] *according to their* [lit. *'its'*] *kind.*

I.e. 'Free-living, breathing beings yielding their own species. ... The term could also include any living thing not specifically mentioned thereafter, as, for example, germs' *(Munk).*

This does not imply that the soul was formed from the earth. To the contrary! It is only the body that the earth yielded — the soul descended from the spiritual world. The phrase is to be understood as 'let the earth give up life which has a soul' *(Rav Avraham ben haRambam).*

According to the *Midrash,* the term *'living soul'* here has special reference to man: 'the soul of Adam.'

בְּהֵמָה — *cattle.*

Most commentators understand this to refer to domestic animals

כה וַיְהִי־כֵן: וַיַּעַשׂ אֱלֹהִים אֶת־חַיַּת הָאָרֶץ
לְמִינָהּ וְאֶת־הַבְּהֵמָה לְמִינָהּ וְאֵת כָּל־
רֶמֶשׂ הָאֲדָמָה לְמִינֵהוּ וַיַּרְא אֱלֹהִים כִּי־
כו טוֹב: וַיֹּאמֶר אֱלֹהִים נַעֲשֶׂה אָדָם בְּצַלְמֵנוּ

which serve man's needs *(Ibn Ezra),* such as the ox, donkey, mule, horse, camel, sheep, and cattle *(Lekach Tov; Radak).*

According to *Ramban,* בְּהֵמָה refers to grass-eating [herbivorous] animals.

[Comp. *comm.* to חַיְתוֹ־אֶרֶץ, *beasts of the land,* below.]

וָרֶמֶשׂ – *And creeping things* – i.e. that creep low on the ground. They appear as though dragged along, their method of locomotion not being discernable. In general רֶמֶשׂ and שֶׁרֶץ refer to locomotion *(Rashi).*

וְחַיְתוֹ־אֶרֶץ – *And beasts of the land* – i.e. wild-life: the gazelle, lion, wolf, panther, bear and other animals of prey *(Lekach Tov; Radak)* which dwell in the wilderness and uninhabited areas *(Ibn Ezra).*

According to *Ramban,* it refers to meat-eating [carnivorous] animals.

חַיַּת אֶרֶץ, *beasts of the land,* are differentiated from בְּהֵמָה [cattle] which is naturally domesticable.

Thus, *Munk* suggests that the sequence of beings listed in this verse might be interpreted as being arranged with the following significance: נֶפֶשׁ חַיָּה, 'the' free-living being, i.e. man; followed by בְּהֵמָה, *domestic beings,* – animals controlled by him; then רֶמֶשׂ, *roaming beings,* – those less controlled; and חַיַּת הָאָרֶץ, *free-living* (wild) beings of the land – those rarely controlled by him.

[The suffix ו, *vav,* in חַיְתוֹ (rather than the construct חַיַּת) is understood by most commentators – e.g. *Ibn Janach; Rashbam; Ibn Ezra,* etc. – to be a poetic form, akin to בְּנוֹ בְעוֹר = בֶּן בְּעוֹר, *son of Be'or, (Num.* 24:3) and לְמַעְיְנוֹ מָיִם = לְמַעְיַן מַיִם, *into a fountain of water (Psalms* 114:8).]

וַיְהִי כֵן – *And it was so.*

I.e. The earth complied with God's decree *(Radak),* and it became eternally established *(Rashbam).*

[This is a general statement which will be elaborated upon in the following verses.]

25. וַיַּעַשׂ אֱלֹהִים – [*And*] *God made:* i.e. he shaped them with their full volition and full-grown stature *(Chullin* 60b; *Rashi).* [cf. *comm.* to וַיַּעַשׂ in verses 7 and 16.]

And God made the beast of the earth after its own kind: i.e. He endowed each species with whatever senses and faculties it required *(Sforno)* – and endowed each with its own peculiar nature and instincts *(Minchah Belulah).*

Malbim observes that the term וַיִּבְרָא, *created* [which would imply an unprecedented act of creation] is not employed here because already on the fifth day, physical creatures were endowed with breath and soul, giving a higher form of life to the universe ... But because this act of 'completion' was beyond the innate powers of the earth to accomplish, the act is attributed specifically to *God* [וַיַּעַשׂ אֱלֹהִים] as above in verse 21.

רֶמֶשׂ הָאֲדָמָה – *Creeping beings of the ground.'*

The term אֲדָמָה, *ground,* is in-

kind.' And it was so. 25 *God made the beast of the*
earth after its own kind, and the cattle after its own
kind, and every creeping being of the ground after
their kind. And God saw that it was good.
26 *And God said, 'Let us make man in Our image,*

troduced here in distinction to אֶרֶץ, *earth.* The difference between them is that *'earth'* is a general designation that includes the waters in addition to dry land, while *'ground'* refers specifically to the dry land. Since the *'creeping beings* of the waters' were already created on the fifth day [*verse* 21], Scripture specifically qualifies the creeping things in this verse with *'of the ground'* because only they were created by this Utterance *(Ha'amek Davar).*

The *Vilna Gaon* [*Aderes Eliyahu* 2:5] comments that the distinction between the two terms lies in the intention of the speaker: אֲדָמָה, *ground,* implies either tillable soil or its fruit; אֶרֶץ, *earth,* is a geographical term, meaning either the entire world or the land of Israel.

[Note that for some unexplained reason, the sequence in this verse is different from that of God's decree in the previous verse. Additionally נֶפֶשׁ חַיָּה, *living soul* (which is understood by the *Midrash* to refer to man) is omitted here entirely. The creation of man, the crown and pinnacle of Creation, is separate from the animals, and is detailed beginning with the next verse.]

וַיַּרְא אֱלֹהִים כִּי טוֹב — *And God saw that it was good.* I.e. that even though there are creatures among them who would later prove to be injurious, the overall usefulness of animals was obvious *(Radak).*

Hence, before proceeding to the עֲשִׂיָּה, *making,* of man, God puts the seal of His approval on the developments that have taken place, thus far, on the Sixth Day. Only man has not yet attained 'completion' at this stage *(Munk).*

26. Having completed all forms of creation, God then said: *'Let us make man!'* Like a person who builds a palace and, after having furnished and decorated it, ushers in its owner so it is ready for his immediate dwelling *(Rav Saadiah Gaon).* [Cf. *Sanhedrin* 38a].

וַיֹּאמֶר אֱלֹהִים — *And God said.* There was a special אֲמִירָה, 'utterance' dedicated to the making of man in recognition of his superiority *(Ramban).*

נַעֲשֶׂה אָדָם — *Let us make man.*

This preamble indicates that man was created with great deliberation and wisdom. God did not associate man's creation with the earth by decreeing *'Let the earth bring forth'* as He did with other creatures, but instead attributed it to the deepest involvement of Divine Providence and wisdom *(Abarbanel).*

B'chor Shor notes that the verb נַעֲשֶׂה, *make,* here implies — as it does in verses 7, 16, and 25 — 'bringing to a state of final completion.' The intent is: 'Let us bring to perfection the as yet uncreated man, whose image and form awesomely equip him to rule and govern ...'

This announcement heralding

man's creation parallels the preamble preceding woman's creation: *'It is not good for man to be alone ... I will make him a helper'*. Such announcements were not made preceding the creation of other beings. This illustrates God's righteousness to all His creatures. When He was about to place man over them as ruler and governor, He did not do so suddenly. He first prepared them by saying *'Let us make man'*, like a king about to levy a tax on his people, who announces: 'Come, let us levy a tax on the land for your benefit.' *(HaRechasim leBik'ah).*

Man was created last, says the *Talmud* [*Sanhedrin* 38a], so he should find all things ready for him. If he is worthy, he is told: 'All things were created in your behalf.' At the same time his late appearance on earth conveys an admonition of humility: If man becomes too proud he is reminded: Even gnats preceded you in the order of creation.

The *Mishnah* offers ethical reasons why only one man [i.e. one 'pair'] was created: In order to prevent feuds ... so that one man should not be able to say to his fellow, 'my ancestor was greater than yours!' Finally, the creation of only one man exhibits the power of God, Who, by means of only one 'mold' produces so many various types. Adam is the single progenitor of all mankind, and how different men are from one another! [*Sanhedrin* 4:5].

נַעֲשֶׂה — *Let us make.*

[The use of the plural is noted by the commentators.]:

Targum Yonasan paraphrases:

'And God said to the Ministering Angels who had been created on the second day of the creation of the world, "Let us make man!" '[1]

— These are the angels who minister before Him continually, such as Michael, Gabriel, etc. They are the ones referred to by the Sages as פַּמַלְיָא שֶׁל מַעְלָה, *'the heavenly household'*, and it was with them, the Sages tell us, that He consulted before creating man *(Ahavas Yonasan).*

Rambam discusses this verse:

'Our discourse deals only with angels, which are identical with the intellect, for our Torah does not deny that He governs that which exists, through [the intermediary vehicle of] angels. In some passages there is the plural form of God, e.g. *'Let us make man in our image'; 'Come let us go down'* [*Gen.* 11:7] ... The Sages have interpreted this verse to mean: God does nothing without first consulting the Heavenly *famalia* ... The intention of these verses is not, as thought by the ignorant, to assert that God spoke, deliberated, or that he actually consulted with and sought the help of other beings. How could the Creator seek help from those He created? They show only that all parts of the Universe are produced through angels, for natural forces and 'angels' are identical *(Moreh,* 2:6).

God spoke to the angels: 'Let us make man! We ourselves will engage in his creation, not the water or earth!' *(Ibn Ezra)*

Ramban is of the opinion that the plural denotes God and the earth:

"Concerning the 'living soul' God commanded: *'Let the earth bring forth.'* But in the case of man He said *'Let us make'* — i.e. I and the earth: The earth to produce the animal body from its elements as it did the cattle and beasts [cf. 2:4], and the higher spirit would come

1. [When Moses wrote the Torah and came to this verse (which says, *let 'us' make*) he said: 'Sovereign of the Universe! Why do You thus furnish an excuse to the heretics for maintaining that there is a plurality of divinities ח״ו?

'Write!' God replied. 'Whoever wishes to err will err ... Let them rather learn from their Creator who created all, yet when He came to create man He took counsel with the Ministering Angels' *(Midrash).*

As Rav Yochanan said: In all the passages that the heretics have misinterpreted as grounds for their heresy, their refutation is found near at hand. Thus it says (in the plural) 'Let *us* make man in *our* image', while the next verse continues (in the singular) *'and God* בָּרָא, *created man in 'His' image' (Sanhedrin* 38b).]

from the 'mouth' of God" [2:9]

According to the *Vilna Gaon,* God was addressing *all of creation* bidding each to contribute a portion of its characteristics to man. For man's strength is traced to the lion; his swiftness to the eagle; his cunning to the fox; his capacity for growth to the flora; and his living soul to the living beings — all of which are harmonized within man.

Many see the plural form as *pluralis majestatis* [the royal 'we']:

Those who say that this verse points to a plurality of creators are ignorant ... because they do not know that the Hebrew language gives *a distinguished person* license to say: 'Let *us* do,' 'Let *us* make,' though he is but a solitary individual. Thus Balak said [*Numbers* 22:6] *'Perhaps I shall prevail that we may smite them';* similarly, Daniel said: *(Dan.* 2:36) *'This is the dream, and we will tell its interpretation to the king'* ... There are many other examples in Scripture *(Rav Saadiah Gaon).*

The use of the *pluralis majestatis,* with which human kings proclaim their will to their subjects, suggests that the ruler does not issue orders to satisfy his personal whim, but only for the general interest and well-being. It is only as representative of the people that the king rules. Similarly, the Creator announces to the world the appearance of its master — man — as an act of consideration for the world's interest *(Hirsch).*

Others — e.g. *Ibn Janach; Rabbeinu Meyuchas; Ibn Caspi* — hold that the plural form here is non-restrictive, and they cite many passages where Scripture changes gender, tense, and number as a matter of course.

אָדָם — *Man.* A general term for mankind as a whole. As evidenced in 5:2, the term applies to both the male and female: 'He called *their* name Adam' *(B'chor Shor; Chizkuni).*

As *Sforno* interprets: 'It refers to one of the species of living creatures which I formed known as אָדָם, *man.'*

The etymology of the term אָדָם, *adam,* [man], is the subject of divergent views:

Radak holds that it is related to אֲדָמָה, *adamah,* [ground], wherefrom man was created: When God created man from the upper and lower elements He called him Adam, as if to say, Although his spirit is from the heavens, he is nevertheless *adam,* for his body was formed from the *adamah.*

N'tziv suggests that it is derived from the root דמה, *resemble,* as in *Isaiah* 14:14: אֲדַמֶּה לְעֶלְיוֹן, 'I shall *resemble* the Most high' — because man is in the likeness of God.

— Or perhaps, from אֵד, mist — 'the being made of earth wetted by mist, as *Rashi* [2:6] explains: 'He ... moistened the dust and man was created *(Munk).*

בְּצַלְמֵנוּ — *In our image.* In our mold *(Rashi)* — i.e. in the mold which We have prepared for man — it being impossible to say that God has a 'mold' *(Sifsei Chachamim).*

Hirsch renders: *'In a form worthy of us.'*

Perhaps צֶלֶם, *image,* is related to

Rashi explains that God did not allow the spurious interpretation of future heretics to deter Him from implying, by use of the plural form, the ethical lesson that one should always consult with others.

Nevertheless, the *Talmud* (*Megillah* 9a) records that when King Ptolemy [Philadelphus] assembled seventy-two elders and placed them each in separate rooms ordering them to translate the Torah, God prompted each one of them and (instead of writing נַעֲשֶׂה אָדָם בְּצַלְמֵנוּ *'let 'us' make man in 'our' image')* they all wrote ... אֶעֱשֶׂה אָדָם בְּצֶלֶם, *'I will make man in image and likeness ...'* [This was done so that Ptolemy would not have a pretext to claim that the Torah implicitly recognizes the existence of a duality of Creators.]

א
כז

כִּדְמוּתֵנוּ וְיִרְדּוּ בִדְגַת הַיָּם וּבְעוֹף
הַשָּׁמַיִם וּבַבְּהֵמָה וּבְכָל־הָאָרֶץ וּבְכָל־
כז הָרֶמֶשׂ הָרֹמֵשׂ עַל־הָאָרֶץ: וַיִּבְרָא
אֱלֹהִים | אֶת־הָאָדָם בְּצַלְמוֹ בְּצֶלֶם

צֵל, shadow, indicating that one must cleave to the Creator, and follow in His every way, as a shadow which faithfully follows the movements of its illuminated form *(Abarbanel).*

[Cf. *Psalms* 124:5: ה׳ צִלְּךָ עַל יַד יְמִינֶךָ, *HASHEM is your shade upon your right hand.*']

The *Vilna Gaon* explains that צֶלֶם, form, refers to an object's spiritual 'image' and content. A living creature is superior to a plant becaue of its unique *image.* A living soul, just as a plant, by virtue of its ability to reproduce, is superior to an inanimate object. Man, as the sovereign of creation unites within himself the 'images' of all lower forms of being. Thus בְּצַלְמֵנוּ, *in our image,* is addressed to all of creation [see *Vilna Gaon* above] commanding all of its facets to give of their content to man. Man was also granted a degree of divine holiness so that he might properly serve God.

כִּדְמוּתֵנוּ — *After our likeness.* With the power of understanding and intellect *(Rashi).*[1]

— Man thus has similarity to both his origins: physically he is similar to the earth from which he was taken, while spiritually he is similar to the higher beings because the soul is immortal *(Ramban).*

Ramban goes on to explain that צֶלֶם means appearance; and דְמוּת refers to likeness. Thus man's body resembles the earth while his soul resembles the higher beings.

But, as *Munk* perceives, the prefix 'כּ', [*'like'*] denotes that man's similarity to his two sources is only an approximation, for his freedom is limited by unavoidable physical requirements, and thus his similarity to God is not absolute. [See *Munk*, p.89-90.]

'Man alone among the living creatures is endowed — like his Creator — with moral freedom and will. He is capable of knowing and loving God and of holding spiritual communion with Him; and man alone can guide his actions in accordance with reason. He is therefore said to have been made in the form and likeness of the Almighty' *(Rambam).*

'Hirsch renders: *'as is commensurate with our likeness.'* He explains that צֶלֶם refers to an outer covering, a sheath. If all the compassion and love, and truth and equity and holiness of the divine rule were to be represented in an exterior form, it would be embodied in the form which the Creator gave man— thus: בְּצַלְמֵנוּ, *our sheath.* This form proclaims him as God's representative — the divine on earth. It is כִּדְמוּתֵנוּ from דמה, *like,* for it complies with, is adequate to, the calling of being 'god-like'. But similarity also implies that there is no contradiction, hence דמה also means silent — i.e. non-contradictory to its mission ...'

[For a fuller analysis, see *Overview*]

Man is a miniature world and his soul is likened to his Creator in five ways, as the *Talmud* [*Berachos* 10a] comments: 'Just as God fills the whole world, so the

1. *Rabbi Simcha Zisel Ziev* elaborates that man's God-like uniqueness lies in his willingness always to utilize his intellect as the basis of his decisions. Once he succumbs to temptation he forfeits his superiority.

I
27 *after Our likeness. They shall rule over the fish of the sea, the birds of the sky, and over the cattle, the whole earth, and every creeping thing that creeps upon the earth.'* [27] *So God created man in His image,*

soul fills the body; God sees but is not seen,so is the soul; God sustains the world, so does the soul sustain the body; God is pure, so is the soul; God abides in the innermost precincts, so does the soul: Let that which has these five qualities come and praise Him who has the five qualities.' This is the meaning of 'in our *likeness' (Vilna Gaon).*

[Taken in sum total, then, the two parallel terms צֶלֶם and דְמוּת describe man in his spiritual resemblance to his Creator: his endowment with the intellectual perception that gives him preeminence over the animals, that guides him consciously in the exercise of his free-choice, his moral sense of right and wrong, and finally that gives man his fundamental distinction of approximating some spiritual resemblance to his Creator. For, according to *Akeidas Yitzchak* צֶלֶם and דְמוּת are in reality synonymous, indicating that man must strive to imitate and resemble his Creator in His existential virtues of Unity and Reason.

Thus, man is bidden to subdue his impulses in the service of God, and is endowed with dominion over nature. As the Psalmist said of man:

'HASHEM, ... You have made him a little lower than the angles, and have crowned him with glory and honor. You have given him dominion over the works of Your hands ...' [*Psalms* 8:6*f*).]

וְיִרְדּוּ בִדְגַת הַיָּם וכו׳ – *And they* [i.e. mankind] *shall rule over the fish of the sea,* etc.

The plural form וְיִרְדּוּ, and *they* shall rule' implies that this does not refer to the original man as an individual – but to mankind as a whole *(Radak).*

Radak notes that יִרְדּוּ implies both *'dominion'* [from רדה] and *'descent'* [from ירד]: when man is worthy he *dominates* the animal kingdom; when he is not worthy he *descends* lower than them [i.e. becomes subservient to them], and the beast rules over him.

The order of the species: *fish, birds, cattle,* follows their order of Creation *(Reb Avrohom ben HaRambam).* Additionally the fish – being in an element alien to man – pose the greatest problem for dominion. Man conquered them by his ingenuity and aids such as nets, etc. They are therefore mentioned first because they posed the prime difficulty; the rest were easy *(Radak).*

וּבְעוֹף הַשָּׁמַיִם – *The birds of the sky* [lit. *'and over the fowl of the heaven'.*]

וּבְכָל הָאָרֶץ – [*And over*] *the whole earth.* i.e. literally the power to rule over earth itself: to uproot, dig, and extract metals *(Ramban).*

27. וַיִּבְרָא אֱלֹהִים אֶת הָאָדָם בְּצַלְמוֹ – *So God created man in his image* – i.e. in the mold made for him. For everthing else was created by a creative utterance, while man was

☙ This is a verse that must constantly be uppermost in the minds of man for it is a basic principle in Judaism. Man was created in God's image, and it is his responsibility always to act in such a way that he reflects favorably upon God whose image he bears. This is not the task of great men only, every human being is made in God's image and,therefore, was created with the ability to live up to it *(Harav Nosson Zvi Finkel).*

א אֱלֹהִים בָּרָא אֹתוֹ זָכָר וּנְקֵבָה בָּרָא אֹתָם:
כח וַיְבָרֶךְ אֹתָם אֱלֹהִים וַיֹּאמֶר לָהֶם אֱלֹהִים כח
פְּרוּ וּרְבוּ וּמִלְאוּ אֶת־הָאָרֶץ וְכִבְשֻׁהָ וּרְדוּ

created by [His] hands' as it is written [*Psalms* 139:5]: *'and You have laid Your hand upon me.'* He was made with a stamp like a coin which is made by a die *(Rashi)*. [Yet all men are different! (see *Mishnah Sanhedrin* 37a cited in previous verse s.v. נַעֲשֶׂה אָדָם).]

Thus, the subject of *his image* is man: i.e. the mold which God prepared for him; the next phrase specifying that the mold was in *'God's image' (Maharal).*

The *Vilna Gaon* renders *'in his image'*; in an image commensurate with his [lofty] soul.

The verb וַיִּבְרָא, *created*, is used because it refers to the creation — ex nihilo — of man's living soul, something unprecedented in creation. נַעֲשֶׂה, *make*, is used in verse 26 because that refers to the *formation* from existing material of man's body *(Malbim).*

בְּצֶלֶם אֱלֹהִים בָּרָא אוֹתוֹ — *In the image of God He created him.*

i.e. that image was in the form of the image of his creator *(Rashi).*

Munk renders: 'In a form (derived) of supreme power He caused him.' — His form would allow him close association with *Elokim'* [cf. 5:1 and 9:6.]

Some render this 'in the image of the angels' — for men and angels have similar images *(Rashbam; Radak; Chizkuni)*, while *HaRechasim leBik'ah* renders: 'in a beautiful and glorious image.'

זָכָר וּנְקֵבָה בָּרָא אֹתָם — *Male and female He created them.*

Rashi notes an apparent contradiction between this verse and verse 2:21 which details the creation of woman from man's side:

Rashi interprets that the Torah informs us here that both were created on the sixth day, while the *details* of their creation are expanded upon later on. According to the *Midrash*, man was created originally with two פָּנִים faces — i.e. male and female halves — and afterwards He divided them [See *Eruvin* 18a and *comm.* to 5:2.] [1]

[The change from singular to plural in this verse is noted]:

'Man is endowed with both individual [i.e. spiritual] permanence, and permanence of the species. Because of his rational power, he has individual permanence, like the celestials; and because of his material being, the human species has permanence ...

This will explain why the singular is used in the expression בְּצֶלֶם אֱלֹהִים בָּרָא אוֹתוֹ, *'in the image of God He created him'*, while in the expression זָכָר וּנְקֵבָה בָּרָא אֹתָם, *'male and female He created them'* the pronoun is in plural. The former refers to man's [spiritual] permanence as an individual which he enjoys over and above the other animals. The latter refers to the permanence of the species which is due to the union of male and female' *(Ikkarim* 1:11; *Malbim).*

1. The word פָּנִים, faces, also means outlook, approach, perspective. There are two facets to a concept. The original man contained a duality which was later separated into male and female, each with its own personality and outlook *(Harav Gifter).*

I *in the image of God He created him; male and female*
28 *He created them.*
[28] *God blessed them and God said to them, 'Be fruitful and multiply, fill the earth and subdue it; and*

Although all living creatures were created in both sexes, this is noted specifically only in the case of human beings to stress that both sexes were created directly by God in equal likeness to Him *(Hirsch).*

The *Midrash* notes that the expression וַיְהִי כֵן, *'and it was so'* — i.e. became firmly established: is not used at the creation of the heavens; of the sea-giants; and of man. The reason is that in each of these cases the term בָּרָא, *created,* is used; therefore וַיְהִי כֵן *and it was so,* does not apply. [*Munk:* i.e. 'because the term *and it was so* applies solely to a development from an existing source without, as it were, an intervention from 'outside'.

Similarly, the absence of כִּי טוֹב, *'that it was good',* [i.e. that it reached the intended state] in the narrative of man is noted. *Rav Yosef Albo* suggests it is absent because the standard intended for man is higher than for other beings: He is bidden not to stagnate, but to constantly strive for a higher standard ... to reach that potential intended for him. Man must thus exercise his free will in this quest, or he has not achieved his level of perfection. [Thus, man was not given a final state.]

[Cf. also *Ramban* to 2:18. *'Good'* is not used in the creation of man because he did not remain eternally in this state as a being alone.]

28. וַיְבָרֶךְ . . . וַיֹּאמֶר . . . פְּרוּ וּרְבוּ — *God blessed them ... and said ... be fruitful ...*

[Although the commentators agree that פְּרוּ וּרְבוּ, *'be fruitful and multiply'* is one of the 613 commandments obligatory upon a Jew,[1] they differ on whether it is inferred from *this* verse, which many interpret (as they do verse 22) as a divine *blessing*] ...

Rashi on 8:7 comments that the phrase in our verse is a divine *blessing,* but there it is a *command* [v. *Kesubos* 5a.]

This is formulated by *Tosafos Yevamos* 65b s.v. וְלֹא: "Although *'be fruitful and multiply'* was said to Adam, it was a general blessing and not a command." [cf. *Maharsha Sanh.* 59b s.v. גְּמָרָא] [Thus the *Vilna Gaon* notes that this utterance is not counted among the 'ten sayings by which the world was created' (see *comm.* 1:1) because it is not a creative utterance, but a blessing.] *Harav Gifter* suggests that the verse is a command that applies only to man, but it also contains a blessing that includes woman as well.

This verse is meant as a blessing, but to propagate is also a command-

1. It is so codified by *Rambam, Ishus:* 15:1; and in his *Sefer Hamitzvos,* pos. comm. 212:

'We are thus commanded to be fruitful and multiply for the perpetuation of the species. This is the law of propagation, being implicit in His words: *Be fruitful and multiply.*

In the *Sefer HaChinuch* it is counted as the first *Mitzvah:*

'In Chapter *Bereishis* there is one positive commandment: propagation, as it is written *'And God blessed them ... be fruitful and multiply.'*

The root of this *Mitzvah* is that in accordance with the Divine wish, the world is to be inhabited, as it is written [*Isaiah* 45:18]: *He did not create it a waste land; He formed it to be inhabited.* This is a great *mitzvah* upon which all the *mitzvos* of the world exist, because it was given to man and not angels ... One who neglects this has reglected a Positive Commandment, incurring great punishment, because he thereby demonstrates that he does not wish to comply with the divine will to populate the world.' [See *Even HaEzer* 1:1]

א בִּדְגַת הַיָּם וּבְעוֹף הַשָּׁמַיִם וּבְכָל־חַיָּה
כט הָרֹמֶשֶׂת עַל־הָאָרֶץ: כט וַיֹּאמֶר אֱלֹהִים הִנֵּה
נָתַתִּי לָכֶם אֶת־כָּל־עֵשֶׂב | זֹרֵעַ זֶרַע אֲשֶׁר

ment which the Sages symbolically attached to this verse *(Ibn Ezra; Radak).*

Rabbeinu Bachya explains that the interjected phrase וַיֹּאמֶר לָהֶם אֱלֹהִים, *and God said to them,* implies that there are two blessings in the verse: The first is a blessing for their general welfare implied in the phrase וַיְבָרֶךְ אֹתָם אֱלֹהִים, *and God blessed them* — i.e. He endowed them with a blessing of divine [spiritual] eternity; the second blessing is introduced by וַיֹּאמֶר לָהֶם אֱלֹהִים, *and God said to them,* werewith He blessed them with profligacy and earthly dominion.

Abarbanel views the interjected phrase similarly, but comes to a different conclusion: *'and He blessed them'* implies that He endowed them with a general all-encompassing blessing, After blessing them *God said to them* imperatively: *'Be fruitful, etc.'* as if to say: though I created you in My image, do not be so engrossed in the spirit and intellect that you neglect the physical and thus destroy the world; my desire is that you populate the world, not destroy it.

[See *Hirsch* who distinguishes between the procreative instinct of animals which is a purely physical act, and that of humans which is a free-willed moral carried out *as duty.*]

The verse is a blessing, but also a command that it be implemented by conscious propagation. The previous reference to propagation (v.22) implied a blessing only because it was said regarding fish which are incapable of being commanded *(Ha'amek Davar).*

There are thus two parts to the blessing: that they be fruitful and prolifigate, and that they govern the world *(Avrohom ben HaRambam).*

וּמִלְאוּ אֶת הָאָרֶץ — *[And] fill the earth.*

I.e. do not congregate in one location but disperse yourselves throughout the globe. It was the sin of the דּוֹר הַפְּלָגָה, Generation of the Dispersion [Chapter 11] that they defiantly wished to assemble in one place *(Aderes Eliyahu).*

... Man's mission on earth is thus not attached to any particular zone or climate ... the whole world being meant to be אֲדָמָה, the human kingdom, 'Adam's earth' *(Hirsch).*

Man is thus the one of the few creatures who can acclimate himself to thrive in any part of the world *(Malbim).*

HaKsav V'Hakaballah perceives in the word מִלְאוּ an implication of *'seek fulfillment of what you lack.'* Man was last in Creation, and though he found a 'ready' world filled with vegetation he found it difficult to enjoy it due to lack of proper utensils ... The blessing here was that man harness his ingenuity to benefit from the storehouse of nature to his fulfillment. Render, therefore: וּמִלְאוּ אֶת הָאָרֶץ — find fulfillment in the land and satisfy your needs.

וְכִבְשֻׁהָ — *And subdue it.*

I
29 *rule over the fish of the sea, the bird of the sky, and*
every living thing that moves on earth.'
[29] *God said, 'Behold, I have given to you all herb-*
age yielding seed that is upon the entire earth, and

[The word is usually used in the context of *subjugating* conquered land, hence many translate: *'and conquer it'*; or *'and master it.'* Cf. for example, *Numbers* 32:22.]

Rashi observes that the word כִּבְשׁוּהָ is spelled without a ו after the ש [so that its consonants could be read first-person singular masculine: וְכִבְשָׁהּ, and subdue *her*] to teach that it is the male who subdues the female that she should not be a gadabout, [since it could also be rendered 'and you (masculine) subdue *it*'] it also teaches that the obligation to be fruitful and multiply was directed specifically to the male whose function it is to *subdue* [the land in battle; *Rashi, Kiddushin* 35a] and not to the woman [Cf. *Yevamos* 65b].[1]

[This is the accepted view and is so codified as Halachah. Cf. *Rambam, Ishus* 15:2 and *Even Haezer* 1:1. The *Maharsha, Yev.* 65b notes that the above comment, based upon *Rashi* in *Kiddushin, that man's function to subdue applies to his function to subdue the land,* might also be interpreted as a reference to man's nature to *rule over woman,* as in 3:16 וְהוּא יִמְשָׁל בָּךְ, *and he shall rule over you.* See his comm.]

The simple sense of the verse, however, is that man should rule the creatures of the earth and bring them under his control *(Radak).*

— Utilize your ingenuity by ruling the animals and preventing them from entering your domain *(Sforno).*

[And if you are found worthy] ... וּרְדוּ בִּדְגַת הַיָּם — *And rule over the fish of the sea.*

I.e. Ensnare them with nets and compel them to serve you *(Sforno).*

This does not mean that man was created for this purpose, but only that this was the nature which God gave him *(Rambam* Moreh 3:13).

The verse lists them in the order of their creation: first the fish and fowl, and then the animals *(Ramban).*

וּבְכָל חַיָּה הָרֹמֶשֶׂת — *And every living being that moves.*

— Cattle, beast and insect: They all 'move' upon the earth *(Radak).*

[*Some translate: 'And every beast that creeps.'* Our translation follows *Targum* and the *Vilna Gaon* who interpret חַיָּה, which has the dual meaning of 'living being' and 'beast', as meaning, in our verse, the former thus including every living being created from the earth. (Cf. comm. to שרץ and רמש in verses 20,21 where our interpretation agrees with those who explain the verb as indicating *'movement',* rather than *'creeping'.*)]

29-30. *Rashi, Ibn Ezra,* and most commentators group these two verses together ... לָכֶם יִהְיֶה לְאָכְלָה, וּלְכָל חַיַּת הָאָרֶץ, *'it shall be your for food and to every beast of the earth ...'* indicating that man and beast

1. The mission of פרו ורבו, propagation, is given to both sexes, for united cooperation of both sexes is equally essential. Nevertheless, its implementation is essentially dependent upon the possession of means as implied in the word וְכִבְשֻׁהָ — the transforming of the earth and its products for human purposes. It is primarily the male's function to force the earth to yield them, and as the Talmud notes from the spelling of וְכִבְשֻׁהָ, the duty of marrying and establishing a home is given directly and unconditionally to the man *(Hirsch).*

א
ל

עַל־פְּנֵי כָל־הָאָרֶץ וְאֶת־כָּל־הָעֵץ אֲשֶׁר־
בּוֹ פְרִי־עֵץ זֹרֵעַ זָרַע לָכֶם יִהְיֶה לְאָכְלָה׃
ל וּלְכָל־חַיַּת הָאָרֶץ וּלְכָל־עוֹף הַשָּׁמַיִם
וּלְכֹל | רוֹמֵשׂ עַל־הָאָרֶץ אֲשֶׁר־בּוֹ נֶפֶשׁ
חַיָּה אֶת־כָּל־יֶרֶק עֵשֶׂב לְאָכְלָה וַיְהִי־כֵן׃

shared the same diet — all were to eat herbs. Man was thus forbidden to kill animals for food, this becoming permitted only after the flood [cf. 9:3 and *Sanhedrin* 59b].

Ramban, however, perceives a distinction in the verses. According to him verse 29 is addressed to man and his wife. In it God gave them every form of herb-yielding seed and all fruit of the trees. Verse 30, however, is directed to the beasts of the earth and the fowl of the heaven who were confined to כָּל יֶרֶק עֵשֶׂב, all green herbage, specifically excluding the fruit of the tree or the seeds. Thus, according to *Ramban*, man and animal did not share the same diet.

He continues that meat was prohibited because בַּעֲלֵי נֶפֶשׁ הַתְּנוּעָה moving creatures have a certain spiritual superiority — somewhat akin to בַּעֲלֵי נֶפֶשׁ הַמַּשְׂכֶּלֶת rational creatures.[1] It was only after they sinned [6:12] and God decreed that they perish in the Flood, that He saved some of them to preserve the species, and He permitted the sons of Noah to slaughter and eat them. However, there were restrictions: they could not eat a living animal, nor could they eat a limb cut off from a living animal or the blood because it is the basis of the soul [*Lev.* 17:14] Similarly, they were commanded to ritually slaughter the animals before partaking of their flesh.

הִנֵּה נָתַתִּי לָכֶם — *Behold! I have given* [i.e. *'hereby permit'*; or *'have provided'*] *to you.'* — I.e. for human consumption *(Sforno*, who agrees with *Ramban;* [according to *Rashi*, *'you'* in this verse would include the *beasts*, etc., mentioned in the next verse.])

[Man was thus given dominion over God's creatures only in the sense that he could harness them in his service (cf. *Sanhedrin* 59b), but he could not slay them for his consumption. He was to subsist entirely upon vegetables, a prohibition which was modified after the Flood (9:2-5).]

[Cf. *Isaiah* 11:7; 65:25 where in

1. That Adam was not permitted to eat meat is derived in *Sanhedrin* 59b from our verses: *'to you shall it be for food and to all the beasts of the earth'* [i.e. the herbs, etc., have been given as food to you and the beasts of the earth] — but the beasts of the earth themselves have not been given to you.

Whether this prohibition, before the Flood, extended also to animals that died by themselves, or to fish and fowl is uncertain [cf. *Tosaf. ibid.; Pesikta Zutresa; Maharshak (Imre Shefer)* and *Ran*. See also *Munk* p.100*f* and *Hirsch*.]

Interesting is the comment in *Midrash Agaddah:* 'From this verse you learn that Adam was prohibited from eating meat, for God had not created His creatures in order to have them die [and provide food for other species.] Had Adam not sinned, creatures would never have died

*every tree that has seed-yielding fruit; it shall be
yours for food. [30] And to every beast of the earth, to
every bird of the sky, and to everything that moves
on earth, within which there is a living soul, every
green herb is for food.' And it was so. [31] And God*

the Messianic Age even the carnivorous beasts will return to feeding only on vegetation.' *'The lion will eat straw like the ox.'*]

Noting that *'Behold I give to you'* in the beginning of the verse does not include the words *'for food'*, *Hirsch* explains that the verse is to be understood: 'See, I have given all vegetation, etc., לָכֶם, to you. Their further preservation and continuation for food depends upon your attention and care ... *'They are to be your food'*: it is therefore in your own interest that you give them wise and heedful care.

Targum Yonasan paraphrases: 'Behold I have given you every herb ... and every unfruitful tree for building and for burning ...'

[Thus man's dominion included his right to use for lumber and fuel those trees which did not yield fruit.]

פְּרִי עֵץ זֹרֵעַ זָרַע — *Seed-yielding fruit* [lit. *The fruit of a tree*] *yielding seed.*

—I.e. which yields fruit *(Ibn Janach).*

30. וּלְכָל חַיַּת הָאָרֶץ — *And to all the beasts of the earth.*

This translation follows *Rashi,* above, who renders verses 29-30 as a unit.

According to *Ramban, Sforno* and *Targum Yonasan* this verse is a separate clause addressed not to man in conjunction with verse 29, but to the animals limiting their diet. Hence the ו should be rendered as a preposition: *'But* to all the beasts, etc. .. [I have given] all green herbs.'

רוֹמֵשׂ ... אֲשֶׁר בּוֹ נֶפֶשׁ חַיָּה — *Thing that moves ... that has a living soul. Munk* [who apparently interprets the verse like *Ramban* in that animals are restricted to *'green herbs'*] brilliantly comments, therefore, that a רוֹמֵשׂ (moving thing) *without* a living soul — perhaps including low living organisms which do not move around freely — are thus excluded from the restriction limiting them for their growth to 'green herbs'. They can thrive on anything to which they can assimilate themselves.

וַיְהִי־כֵן — *And it was so.*

I.e. that every creature became endowed with the desire for that food which was meant for them *(Radak).*

Hirsch explains: Thus did the present condition of the earth: its habitation by animals and men and their relationship toward one another — come into existence.

The earth's creatures were thus to be satisfied with the restrictions upon them, while God, for His part, will 'open His hands and nourish the desire of every living thing' [cf. *Psalms* 14:16] (*R' Avraham ben HaRamban*).

The *Tur* quotes his father, the *Rosh,* that וַיְהִי כֵן in this verse

א לא וַיַּ֣רְא אֱלֹהִים֙ אֶת־כָּל־אֲשֶׁ֣ר עָשָׂ֔ה וְהִנֵּה־
לא טֹ֖וב מְאֹ֑ד וַֽיְהִי־עֶ֥רֶב וַֽיְהִי־בֹ֖קֶר י֥וֹם
הַשִּׁשִּֽׁי׃
ב א וַיְכֻלּ֛וּ הַשָּׁמַ֥יִם וְהָאָ֖רֶץ וְכָל־צְבָאָֽם׃
א

denotes that '[the command] was firmly established,' for God instilled in their hearts a distaste for eating meat and a recognition not to take the life of any creature — just as we today recognize the prohibition of taking a human life. Were it not for this, they could not have endured God's command.

[The commentators note that this statement is not concluded with כִּי טוֹב, *that it was good,* i.e., it became eternally established' because these dietary rules — prohibiting meat — would be changed after the Flood.]

31. וַיַּרְא אֱלֹהִים אֶת־כָּל־אֲשֶׁר עָשָׂה — *And God saw all that He had made.* — Even the evil inclination — *'and it was very good'* — because, as the Sages teach, were it not for the evil inclination, man would neither marry nor have children, with the result that the world would remain barren *(Chizkuni).*

וְהִנֵּה טוֹב מְאֹד — *And behold it was very good,* i.e. everything in creation was fit for its purpose and continually able to act accordingly *(Rambam, Moreh* 3:13).

Munk renders the verse: *'And Elokim willed all He had completed to be one entity, and this became now apparent,'* explaining that all the stages of development now formed one entity. Not only had each individual part of creation attained its intended state,they interacted cooperatively, and, as one whole, exceed the sum total of its parts.

As the *Vilna Gaon* explains: Something can be 'good' by itself, but no longer 'good' when fitted to another thing. The divine works of creation, however, are good in themselves and also together with others ...

From the combination of these elements arises a lofty and new character, which is not present in the parts but only in the whole *(Meshech Chachmah).*

This verse includes the creation of those destructive forces which, when viewed in context with the rest of creation, are necessary and integral *(Ha'amek Davar).*

[The verse thus expresses that viewing His work of creation in its completed state He perceived that not only were the specific details *'good'* — as mentioned in the previous verses — but that in totality each act harmonized with the rest and in unison were טוֹב מְאֹד, *very good.*]

הִנֵּה, *behold,* always introduces us to something new ... that whereas each unit of creation was considered *'good'* in isolation, now when creation was complete and all of its units were perceived as part of a whole, it was recognized as *'very good'.* ... Everything relatively evil appears so only when viewed separately, but even יְסוּרִים, suffering; מָוֶת, death; יֵצֶר הָרַע, temptation; becomes good — even 'very good' — as soon as we view it in the context of the whole. Thus Rabbi Meir and the Sages comment: *'Very*

I
31
II
1

saw all that He had made, and behold it was very
good. And there was evening and there was morning,
the sixth day.
[1] Thus the heaven and the earth were finished, and

good' refers to death ... to suffering ... to temptation. If we could but perceive at one glance the entire picture of God's management of intertwining events as He sees it, we would indeed agree with His verdict: וְהִנֵּה טוֹב מְאֹד, *'behold it is very good'! (Hirsch).*

In this connection *Harav Gifter* notes the statement of the Sages that in Time to Come, people will make the same blessing for evil as for good, because in those times they will realize that every manifestation of God's will is genuinely good.

וַיְהִי עֶרֶב וַיְהִי בֹקֶר יוֹם הַשִּׁשִּׁי — *And there was evening and there was morning the sixth day.*

The commentators note the unusual use of the definite article ה, *the,* before the word שִׁשִּׁי, sixth]:

— It designates 'the day that is distinguished among the other days of creation as the day on which His work was completed' *(Chizkuni).*

We are clearly meant to regard this day as the culmination of the first five, the day in which the list of creations found a goal and were fulfilled *(Hirsch)*

— The letter ה [which numerically equals 5] is added to the word שִׁשִּׁי, six, to imply that God stipulated with the works of the six days of creation that they endure only on condition that Israel would accept the Five Books of the Torah *(Shab.* 88a; *Rashi).*

— *Rashi* alternately suggests that *'the sixth day'* refers to the sixth day of Sivan, the day on which the Torah would be given to Israel. [The phrase is thus made to read: *There was evening and there was morning* — only because of — *the sixth day* — of Sivan, the date the Torah was given at *Sinai.*]

[It is also kabbalistically pointed out in this context that this group of words יוֹם הַשִּׁשִּׁי וַיְכוּלוּ הַשָּׁמַיִם with which the *kiddush* is begun, form an acrostic of the Divine Name.]

[And so, with the expression of *'very good',* the Six Days of Creation — preparatory to the Seventh Day, Sabbath — come to a close.]

II

1. The Seventh day: Sabbath.

וַיְכֻלּוּ הַשָּׁמַיִם וְהָאָרֶץ — *Thus* [lit. *'and'*] *the heaven and the earth were finished* [i.e., now, with the end of the sixth day, the heavens and

[The division of the Bible into chapters is of non-Jewish origin, introduced in the Middle Ages by Christian Bible printers. Most Jewish Bibles follow these divisions for identification purposes. In Masoretic manuscripts the text is divided according to several traditional systems — some of which unfortunately have never found their way into printed editions. Most notable among them is the traditional system of פְּתוּחוֹת *[open line divisions], and* סְתוּמוֹת *[closed spaces] as found in ancient Hebrew manuscripts and* סִפְרֵי תוֹרָה, *Torah Scrolls.*

According to the Masorah, therefore, *this verse does not begin a new chapter and a new trend of thought. Rather it is a continuation of the previous verses. Hence, the commentators view this verse in the context of the verses that preceded it and so interpret it.*

ב וַיְכַל אֱלֹהִים בַּיּוֹם הַשְּׁבִיעִי מְלַאכְתּוֹ אֲשֶׁר

earth stand before us in their final intended state in complete, harmonious perfection.]

Hirsch etymologically explains that וַיְכֻלּוּ, from the root כלה, combines two apparently opposite meanings: to be completely destroyed to the point of non-existence; and to reach the highest degree of perfection. Both meanings are true because perfection presupposes complete cessation of any positive or negative hindrances to its attainment. Partial perfection is a contradiction in terms: If one wishes to be perfect in various things at the same time, he will only be half perfect in each of them ... Thus כלה implies striving for a certain goal — hence תַּכְלִית, the goal, the purpose. In addition it implies כְּלִי, anything which serves a definite purpose, tool, vessel, clothes, etc. Hence וַיְכֻלּוּ *'they were brought to their destined end.'*

The transitive nature of the verb is stressed by *Hirsch:* וַיְכֻלּוּ, 'they had been *brought* to this end; they had not always been there, they *became.'* They are not the result of some blind force, but the work of One thinking being, creating them with intention and purpose.

Deriving וַיְכֻלּוּ from כְּלִי, utensil, the *Midrash* renders: 'The heaven and the earth became finished utensils . . .'

Rav Eliezer said: This may be compared to a bath full of water in which were two beautiful bas-reliefs; as long as it was full of water the work of the bas-relief could not be seen, but when the water was emptied, the bas-reliefs became visible. Similarly, as long as formlessness and void were in the world, the work of heaven and earth could not be seen; but as soon as formlessness and void were eradicated from the world the work of heaven and earth could be seen; hence *'the heaven and the earth were made into completed utensils' (Midrash).*

The oceans are included in the term *'earth'* for they are like one unit *(Ibn Ezra).*

צְבָאָם — *And all their array* [lit. *'host'*.][1]

Ramban explains that the *'host' of the earth* refers to the beasts, creeping things, fish, all growing things, and man; *the 'host' of the heavens* refers to the luminaries and the stars, as in *Deut.* 4:19: *'and lest you lift up your eyes to heaven and when you see the sun and the moon and the stars: all the host of heaven.'* The phrase also alludes to the formation of the angels as part of the work of creation, and the souls of man [of all generations, which, according to *Ramban* were created in the work of creation *(Chavel).*]

[The word צָבָא, literally means *'host'* in the sense of a regimented and disciplined (not necessarily military) body standing ready to do the will of its leader. Cf. *Exod.* 38:8, and *Numb.* 4:23 where it has the meaning of one engaged in group service. The use of the term in reference to the earth is unusual. The phrase צְבָא הַשָּׁמַיִם, *host of the heavens,* occurs frequently in Scriptures where, as in *Deut.* 4:19 cited by *Ramban* above, it refers to the celestial bodies, and occasionally, as in *I Kings* 22:19, it refers to the angels and what *Ramban* refers to as הַשְּׂכָלִים הַנִּבְדָּלִים the 'Separate Intelligences' — i.e. intelligences without matter; the incorporeal Celestial Beings. In our verse the term refers to the array of organized matter on earth which stands in testimony to God's sovereignty in creation.]

. . . These, in our verse, are called *'His*

1. The *Talmud, Rosh Hashanah* 11a formulates a basic concept:
All creatures of creation were brought into being with their full stature, their full capacities and their full beauty, as it is written: *Thus the heaven and the earth were completed and all their array.* Read not צְבָאָם, *their array,* but צִבְיוֹנָם, *their full beauty.*

all their array. ²*By the seventh day God completed*

host' in the sense that they totally subordinate themselves to the will of their Creator — as do royal troops who are totally obligated to fulfill the monarch's will *(Avraham ben HaRambam).*

For, as *Hirsch* elaborates: 'Everything created in heaven and on earth forms one great צָבָא, *host,* whose central point is its creator and master . . . Great and small we all stand on our post with powers given us to accomplish our task, all members of God's one great host. His is the power and the greatness . . . ours the obedience, the punctuality, the loyalty . . .'

Noting in this context that everything in creation serves a purpose, the *Midrash* comments: 'God caused drugs to spring forth from the earth; with them the physician heals the wound and the apothecary compounds his preparations.'

[This paragraph attests to the divine nature of creation and its completion on the Sabbath. Therefore it was appended to the Friday evening service and also recited to introduce the Sabbath Kiddush, santification because Sabbath, too, bears testimony to the fact that the Creator rested after completing the universe in six days (see *Sabbath* 119b and *Orach Chaim* 268).]

2. וַיְכַל אֱלֹהִים בַּיּוֹם הַשְּׁבִיעִי — [And] *by the seventh day God completed.*

[This phrase presents a difficulty noted by the commentators, for God completed His work not on the *seventh* day, but on the *sixth!* Our rendering of *'by'* solves the difficulty by incorporating the comments of the *Midrash* and major commentators]:

As *Sforno* comments: God completed His work at the moment which marked the inception of the seventh day, but yet was not part of it, as the Sages commented: נִכְנַס בּוֹ כְּחוּט הַשַּׂעֲרָה, He entered into it by a hair's breadth.[1]

Rashi incorporates the *Midrash* cited in the footnote below and offers both explanations: (a) that unlike a human being who cannot accurately determine points in time, God, 'who knows his times and moments' began the seventh day very precisely 'to a hair's breadth' and it therefore appeared [to human beings, as the Torah speaks in the language of man], as if He completed His work *on* that [seventh] day*; and (b) the world lacked rest, and בָּאת שַׁבָּת בָּאָה מְנוּחָה with the Sabbath came rest — and thus the work was completed [i.e. the work ended with the onset of the rest *on* the seventh day *(Maharal).*][2]

* It only appeared so, but it was not actually so because the very onset of the seventh day cannot rightfully be called part of the seventh day [as *Sforno* above], 'just as the beginning of a line cannot be considered as a line', for if it is actually considered part of the seventh day then there was activity on the seventh day! The Sages could could not expect Ptolemy to understand this concept in a literal translation and they therefore rendered it 'on the *sixth* day' (*Megillah* 9a). [See footnote]

1. *Rav Simcha Zisel Ziev* notes that constant striving is the source of all woes, because when man rushes from goal to goal, — never satisfied, never contemplating — he cannot evaluate his actions and change his directions. With the Sabbath came blessed, holy rest — the opportunity to take stock and assess the spiritual content of life.

2. The *Midrash* comments:

Rabbi asked Rav Yishmael ben Rav Yose: Have you heard from your father the actual meaning of *and on the seventh day God finished,* etc.? [For surely God finished His work on the *sixth,* not on the seventh day.]

He answered: It is like a man striking the hammer on the anvil, raising it by day and bringing it down by nightfall [i.e. in the second between raising it and bringing it down, day has

ב עָשָׂה וַיִּשְׁבֹּת בַּיּוֹם הַשְּׁבִיעִי מִכָּל־
ג ג מְלַאכְתּוֹ אֲשֶׁר עָשָׂה: וַיְבָרֶךְ אֱלֹהִים אֶת־

Why, then, does the verse not read 'on the *sixth* day', and avoid misinterpretation? This is not a difficulty for, had the verse used that version, one might have inferred that the work ended midway through the sixth day and that the inactivity of the Sabbath was purely coincidental because there was nothing left to do. The way that the verse *is* structured: *and He finished on the seventh day . . . and He ceased on the seventh day* forces us to interpret that He performed work *until* the very moment of the seventh day and ceased from all work thereon — *as part of His master plan,* the Sabbath having been conceived of initially as a day of rest *(Gur Aryeh).*

[*Ibn Ezra* notes that the preposition בְּ [lit. *'in'*] often means *'prior to', 'by',* as e.g. *Ex.* 12:16: אַךְ בַּיּוֹם הָרִאשׁוֹן, and similarly, *Ex.* 16:30 וַיִּשְׁבְּתוּ הָעָם בַּיּוֹם הַשְּׁבִעִי.]

Therefore, in accordance with *Ibn Ezra's* interpretation our verse could be rendered: *And by* — i.e. the very onset of — *the seventh day God completed,* etc.

B'chor Shor explains that with God's inactivity on the seventh day it became apparent that He had completed His work . . .

For on the eve of the seventh day Adam presumed that on the morrow God would continue to create as He had done until then. When he observed that God had ceased, he recognized that the work had ended *(Yosafos; Hadar Zekeinim; Chizkuni).*

A most fundamental interpretation is offered in *Akeidas Yitzchak:*

Although God gave existence to everything in the six days, it was not until the onset of the seventh day, which He blessed, that they commenced to function naturally, thus attaining the goal for which they were created. In this manner וַיְכַל is said to be derived from תַּכְלִית, *goal* [see *Hirsch* in verse 1], implying that on the seventh day God reached the goal of His work and therefore, ceased from making any new creation.

The definite article ה, *the* seventh day, indicates that this is *the* seventh day which the Jews were later commanded to observe as a day of rest *(Avraham ben HaRamban).*

מְלַאכְתּוֹ אֲשֶׁר עָשָׂה — *His work which He had done* — throughout the six days; everything was now in a state of completion *(R'Myuchas).*

Thus, God concluded His purposeful work (מְלַאכְתּוֹ) so that no further creative or developing action of His would follow other than

ended and night has commenced. Similarly, in the most precise terms, God finished his work at the exact instant when the sixth day ended so that the Sabbath commenced at that moment.]

Rav Shimon bar Yochai said: Mortal man who cannot calculate exact minutes or hours must add from the ordinary to the sacred [by beginning the Sabbath early to avoid possible miscalculation]; but God, who knows precisely the minutes or hours, can enter it by a hair's breadth.

Genibah and the Rabbis discussed this. Genibah said: This is comparable to a king who made a fully adorned bridal chamber. What did the bridal chamber lack? A bride to enter it. Similarly, what did the world lack? The Sabbath [for it was by means of the Sabbath itself that God completed (i.e. brought to perfection) His work, for without the higher longings inspired by the sanctity of a day consecrated by God, mankind is incomplete. Thus, as the verse states, *God* actually *'completed' his work on the seventh day.*

the maintenance of the existing universe in its existing working condition *(Munk).*

[*When applied to man, the term* מְלָאכָה commonly translated as 'work' is misleading. For in its *halachic* sense מְלָאכָה is by no means identical with physical strain or exertion. (Regarding prohibited 'work' on the Sabbath, מְלָאכָה is defined in its simplest form as those specific activities — and their derivatives — which were necessary for the construction of the Tabernacle).]

As *Hirsch* explains, 'work' is a term which refers to the effort involved in an activity without consideration of the result; while מְלָאכָה considers only the result, the product of activity.

Dayan Grunfeld thus defines מְלָאכָה as: 'an act that shows man's mastery over the world by the constructive exercise of his intelligence and skill.

[Therefore, when applied to God, מְלָאכָה must be understood in this context: *not* as 'toil', a concept inapplicable to God, but as a reference to the *result* of His creative activity.]

וַיִּשְׁבֹּת בַּיּוֹם הַשְּׁבִיעִי ... — *And He abstained on the seventh day from all His work which He had done.*

Munk renders: *'And He discontinued, on the seventh day, all His purposeful work which He had brought to its final state'* — For He created nothing after the sixth day *(Radak).*

It was by this abstention from creative activity that this day was distinguished from the six days preceding it *(Sforno).*

[Our translation of וַיִּשְׁבֹּת, *'He abstained'*, rather than the traditional *'He rested'* follows *Rav Saadiah Gaon* who explains that the Torah characterizes the positive and negative acts of creation by saying וַיַּעַשׂ אֱלֹהִים, *and God made,* וַיִּשְׁבֹּת, *and He rested.* However, just as the וַיַּעַשׂ, *and He made,* implies production, but not Godly motion or exertion, so undoubtedly, וַיִּשְׁבֹּת, *and He rested,* implies nothing more than the discontinuance of Creation. Although the Torah says of God וַיָּנַח, *'and He rested' (Exodus* 20:11), it means only that He discontinued His work of creation and production.]

Rambam explains that the concept of שָׁבַת, *rested,* is used here anthropomorphically. Since אמר, *to say,* has been figuratively used to express the will of the Creator throughout the account of the 'six days of creation,' the expression וַיִּשְׁבֹּת, *He rested,* has likewise been applied to God in reference to the Sabbath day on which there was no creation, for cessation from speech is likewise expressed by the verb שבת as, for example: וַיִּשְׁבְּתוּ שְׁלֹשֶׁת הָאֲנָשִׁים הָאֵלֶּה מֵעֲנוֹת אֶת אִיּוֹב, *so these three men 'ceased' to answer Job* [*Job* 32:1]. Similarly, in the verse *'They spoke to Naval according to all these words in the name of David,* וַיָּנוּחוּ, *and ceased* [*Sam. I* 25:9], וַיָּנוּחוּ [lit. *'and they rested'*] means 'they ceased to speak' and waited for the answer. No allusion to exertion was associated with their gentle speech. It is in this sense that the verb is used in the phrase וַיָּנַח בַּיּוֹם הַשְּׁבִיעִי 'and He *ceased* on the seventh day.'

[The *Midrash* interprets וַיִּשְׁבֹּת in the transitive sense: 'He created a resting' *(Yefe To'ar)*]:

'As long as the hands of the Master were busy with them they continued developing, but when the hands of their Master abstained from them rest was given to them *'and He gave rest, to His world, on the seventh day'* [Cf. *Ex.* 20:11] *(Midrash).*[1]

מִכָּל מְלַאכְתּוֹ אֲשֶׁר עָשָׂה — *From all*

1. The matter and forces which had been called into development were in a state of continuously progressive development; then — וַיְכֻלּוּ, *God set a goal to their development;* then

ב ג

יוֹם הַשְּׁבִיעִי וַיְקַדֵּשׁ אֹתוֹ כִּי בוֹ שָׁבַת מִכָּל־מְלַאכְתּוֹ אֲשֶׁר־בָּרָא אֱלֹהִים לַעֲשׂוֹת׃

His work which He had done. 'All' signified *all* the creatures which He had created *(Ibn Ezra).*

The abstention was absolute: even the *thought* of creative activity did not exist *(R' Meyuchas).*

3. וַיְבָרֶךְ אֱלֹהִים אֶת־יוֹם הַשְּׁבִיעִי וַיְקַדֵּשׁ אֹתוֹ—*[And] God blessed the seventh day and hallowed it.*

'Blessing' refers to abundant [spiritual] goodness, for on Sabbath there is a renewal of physical procreative strength, and there is a greater functioning capacity in the power of reasoning and intellect. *He hallowed it* by having no work done on it as on the other days *(Ibn Ezra).*

According to *Rav Saadiah Gaon* the blessing and sanctification prophetically refer to those who observe the sanctity of the Sabbath, for they will be blessed and sanctified.

Or HaChaim comments that the *Midrash* quoted by *Rashi* is an allusion to future events, but the plain meaning of the verse is that God gave the Sabbath a blessing that raised it above the vicissitudes of this world. Creation demands labor to provide food, drink, and all the other human necessities. Such labor is forbidden on the Sabbath while simultaneously the Sabbath is honored through three prescribed meals and more physical indulgence than weekdays. God blessed the Sabbath with abundance despite the abstinence from 'necessary' labor. What is more the sanctity of the Sabbath provides the blessing of success for the activity of the weekdays.

Rashi, too, perceives this verse as having been written in anticipation of the future:

He *blessed* it through the Manna, a double portion of which fell on the sixth day in preparation of the Sabbath; and *hallowed* it through the Manna, none of which fell on the Sabbath [see *Exodus* 16:22.] (Cf. *Mechilta, Yisro).*

Ramban, however, explains that the blessing on the Sabbath is the fountain of all blessing, and is the foundation of the world; *He hallowed it* by having it draw from the Sanctity above.

According to *Radak, 'blessing'* is the abundant well-being brought about by the Sabbath. It is the day when, free from mundane worry, man can immerse himself in wisdom and spirituality. God thus *blessed this day* by commanding the Jews themselves to rest on it and hallow it. *He hallowed it* by sanctifying and distinguishing it from ordinary days. It is the day during which the Jews abstain from work as a sign between them and God that they are holy by virtue of their observance of the Sabbath which testifies to the divine creation of the world.

He was שַׁדַּי, שֶׁאָמַר לְעוֹלָמוֹ דַּי, He who said to His world, 'it is enough!' As the *Midrash* comments: Had He not called His 'enough' to heaven and earth, they would still be today in a state of continuous progressive development *(Hirsch).*

II *done.* 3 *God blessed the seventh day and hallowed it,*
3 *because on it He abstained from all His work which*
God created to make.

[The blessing of the Sabbath, it must be noted, was that it was endowed with a spiritual exaltation, a sanctity which distinguished it from all other days.

In contrast to the festivals which were dependent upon the observance by witnesses of the new moon and the calendaric calculations of the rabbinic courts, the Sabbath was imbued with its *own* sanctity — independent of human activity. This holiness was endowed by the Creator — ['וַיְקַדֵּשׁ אֹתוֹ'] — Who ordained that it continually and faithfully manifest itself *every seventh day without interruption* in testimony to God's sovereignty over the universe.]

The *'blessing'* was that people would not experience need because of not working on Shabbos, *'it is the blessing of HASHEM that makes rich'* [*Proverbs* 10:22] . . .

And He hallowed it: By blessing it He thereby hallowed it. Cf. *Numbers* 7:1: *'He anointed them and sanctified them'* i.e. the anointing *was* the sanctification; here, too,the blessing *was* its sanctification *(Minchah Belulah).*

כִּי בוֹ שָׁבַת מִכָּל מְלַאכְתּוֹ — *Because on it He abstained from all His work.* I.e. He abstained from further creative activity [see *comm.* to previous verse] *(Chizkuni).*

אֲשֶׁר בָּרָא אֱלֹהִים לַעֲשׂוֹת — *Which God created to make* — i.e. to be self-reproductive according to their species *(Radak).*

I.e. from now on there will be no new creation; the species will reproduce [לַעֲשׂוֹת, to continue acting] throughout time by the unceasing operation of Divine laws *(Rav Yaakov of Vienna).*

[Our literal translation of the phrase preserves the ambiguity of **the subordinate clause לַעֲשׂוֹת, *to make,* in the Hebrew.]**

Ibn Ezra interprets that God created roots in all the species endowing them with the power to reproduce [lit. *'make*] their likeness. [The phrase would thus translate: *'which God had created in order to make'* (i.e. reproduce).]

Ramban offers two explanations: (a) that He *created* [בָּרָא, *ex-nihilo*] on the first day the elements from which to subsequently *make* all the works that are mentioned on the other days, translating: *He abstained from all His work which He had created* — out of nothing — לַעֲשׂוֹת, *to make* from it *all the works mentioned on the six days* [see *comm.* 1:1-2]; (b) reading לַעֲשׂוֹת, *to make,* as if it were מִלַּעֲשׂוֹת, *from making,* with the מ, *from,* implied: translating *that on it He abstained from all His work which He created, from making.* Cf. similar grammatical construction in *Gen.* 41:49: כִּי חָדַל [מִ]לִּסְפֹּר, *ibid.* 11:8: וַיַּחְדְּלוּ [מִ]לִּבְנֹת.

In a different vein, *Malbim* perceives לַעֲשׂוֹת *to make,* as an object of שָׁבַת, abstained:

'God's abstention from creative activity was not due to idleness, but לַעֲשׂוֹת, to begin an even loftier 'doing', the working of Divine Providence which is higher than nature . . . He abstained from ruling the world by the rigid laws of nature to rule by Divine **Providence which regulates the universe ac**cording to reward and punishment for man's deeds.

Noting that throughout the epic of Creation עָשָׂה has had the meaning of 'bringing to a state of completion', here too, the very abstention was לַעֲשׂוֹת, because His wisdom decreed that the cessation from work would

ב ° שני ד °אֵלֶּה תוֹלְדוֹת הַשָּׁמַיִם וְהָאָרֶץ בְּהִבָּרְאָם
ד בְּיוֹם עֲשׂוֹת יהוה אֱלֹהִים אֶרֶץ וְשָׁמָיִם׃

bring the world into a state of completion (*Chizkuni*).

Rashi, however, following the *Midrash,* explains that the verse does not say *'which God created and made'* but 'which God created *to make'* [implying a future action — indicating that some parts of Creation should logically have been created on the seventh day (*Mizrachi*)]. Instead God created them on the sixth day [because as the *Midrash* states, three things were created every day except for Friday when six things were created: its own quota plus that of the Sabbath.]

[The commentators note the absence of the formula which marks the close of each of the first six days: וַיְהִי עֶרֶב וַיְהִי בֹקֶר, *and it was evening and it was morning*]:

The phrase *'and it was evening,* etc.' serves to distinguish between the creations of one day and the next. However, since no creative activity took place on the Sabbath, the concluding phrase is unnecessary (*B'chor Shor*).

Additionally, since the *Midrash* tells us that the primal light functioned incessantly during that first Shabbos — for the entire 36 hour period commencing with Friday morning — there was, on the seventh day, neither 'evening' nor 'morning' (*Chizkuni*).

Thus, with the concluding phrase אֲשֶׁר בָּרָא, reminiscent of the introductory phrase בְּרֵאשִׁית בָּרָא, the narrative of the seven days closes (*Minchah Belulah*).

4. Certain events of Creation were described only briefly above because the primary purpose of that narrative was to stress the sovereignty of God who created the Universe in six days, and abstained from creative activity on the seventh day and hallowed it. Now the Torah returns to elaborate and supplement the narrative by focusing primarily on the details leading to the emergence of man, the 'offspring' of heaven and earth (*B'chor Shor; Ralbag; Akeidas Yitzchak*).

אֵלֶּה — *These are.* — i.e. the things mentioned above (*Rashi*).

[*Rashi* thus maintains that the formula אֵלֶּה תּוֹלְדוֹת refers, in summation, to what was stated in the preceding verses, while others treat this phrase rather as introductory to that which follows. See *Hoffman* below.]

תּוֹלְדוֹת הַשָּׁמַיִם וְהָאָרֶץ בְּהִבָּרְאָם — *The products* [i.e., the inherent potential developments (*Rashi*); or: *'generations'; 'offspring'; 'particulars'*] *of the heaven and the earth when they were created,* i.e., which were already inherent in them since their creation (*Sforno*).

As *Hirsch* interprets: 'The following series of the developments from the heavens and the earth have their origin in Creation.'

[Cf. *Rashi* to next stich, below.]

In a lengthy dissertation *Hoffman* views the phrase אֵלֶּה תּוֹלְדוֹת [lit. *'these are the generations'*] not as relating to the preceding verses [as *Rashi,* above] but as introductory to that which follows. He notes that although *'heaven and earth'* are both mentioned, only that of the *earth* is elaborated upon. He compares this to such verses as *Numbers* 3:1: *'these are the generations of Moses and Aaron',* where in succeeding verses only *Aaron* is treated. Moses is mentioned because he was spoken of in the preceding chapter — here, too, the heavens are mentioned because they were spoken of in relation to earth in the previous chapter. Additionally, *'heaven and*

II
4

⁴ *These are the products of the heaven and the earth when they were created in the day that HASHEM God made earth and heaven —*

earth' should here be understood as referring to the cosmos as a whole in its relationship to man.

He sums up that תּוֹלְדוֹת should be best translated as *'the history of'* and the phrase viewed as an introductory clause treating the *development* of the world, now that its creation had already been described.

[Incorporating, then, the above with the commentary of Abarbanel who understands the prefix בְּ (lit. *'when'* or *'in'*) in בְּהִבָּרְאָם as a preposition meaning *'from'* in this context (cf. *Lev.* 8:32 בַּבָּשָׂר, *'from* the flesh'; Prov. 9:5 בְּלַחְמִי, *'from* my bread'). Therefore: בְּהִבָּרְאָם *from* (i.e. *since*) their *creation.* The verse may be rendered: *'These — that which follows — are the developments of the World since their Creation.'*]

The *Talmud* [*Menachos* 29b] comments homiletically that בְּהִבָּרְאָם, *when they were created,* may be read as two words: בְּהֵ בְּרָאָם He created them with a ה, *he* [one of the letters of the Four Lettered Name.] The ה was chosen because this world resembles that letter: i.e. closed on three sides and open on the fourth: Whoever wishes to stray from the right path may do so and descend into the depths through the opening on the bottom; but whoever wishes to repent may re-enter through the small opening left for him on the side (v. *Rashi; Ramban).*

The *Midrash* comments that He created them [heaven and earth] with the letter *he,* for, it is noted, all letters demand an effort to pronounce them whereas, the *he,* being a mere aspirate, demands no effort. Similarly, God's creative activity was effortless: not with labor or wearing toil did God create His world, but with a mere word was His work accomplished, as in the verse: בִּדְבַר ה׳ שָׁמַיִם נַעֲשׂוּ, *by the Word of God were the heavens made* וּבְרוּחַ פִּיו כָּל צְבָאָם, *and by the breath of His mouth all their host* [*Psalms* 33:6.]

It is also noted in the *Midrash* that בְּהִבָּרְאָם is identical in lettering [although in different order] to בְּאַבְרָהָם, *for Abraham:* i.e. He created the world for the sake of Abraham *(Midrash),* who was the epitome of loving-kindness, one of the foundations upon which the world rests *(Zohar).*

[The traditional small ה in בְּהִבָּרְאָם has profound mystical kabbalistic connotations, as explained by the commentators. According to *Me'am Loez* however the reason for its small size is to draw attention to the *Midrashic* interpretations of that letter, noted above.]

בְּיוֹם עֲשׂוֹת ה׳ אֱלֹהִים — *In the day that HASHEM God made.*

Rashi interprets the word בְּיוֹם, in the *day,* literally. Consistent with his comm. to 1:14 [see there], he explains that this verse teaches us that all *the productions* — i.e. inherent potential developments — *of heaven and earth* were created on the first day *when God made earth and heaven.*

Abarbanel, as above on בְּהִבָּרְאָם, explains the preposition בְּ as meaning *from* [*since*] *the day ...*

Many commentators — e.g. *Rav Saadiah Gaon; Avraham ben HaRambam; R' Meyuchas* — explain 'day' as idiomatically having the broader meaning of *'at the time when'* — in this case the Six Days of Creation. [Cf. e.g. the use of 'day', in *Num.* 3:1; *Deut.* 8:1 where *'time'* is clearly meant.]

ה׳ אֱלֹהִים — *HASHEM God.*

[As explained in the comm. to 1:1 (s.v. אֱלֹהִים), the Holy Four lettered Name, יהוה (pronounced reverently as *Adonoy* and referred to as *HASHEM,* 'The Name') refers to God under His Attribute of Mercy, and also refers to the eternal self-existence of He Who is in the source of all existence and continuity, while אֱלֹהִים, *Elohim,* (translated as *'God'*) describes Him as a God of Judgment.][1]

[The *Shulchan Aruch Yoreh De'ah* 276:9 lists these Names of

1. The use of *'HASHEM'* in this verse is commented upon in the *Midrash.*

'This may be compared to a king who had some empty glasses. The king said: 'If I pour hot

ב
ה

ה וְכֹל ׀ שִׂיחַ הַשָּׂדֶה טֶרֶם יִהְיֶה בָאָרֶץ וְכָל־
עֵשֶׂב הַשָּׂדֶה טֶרֶם יִצְמָח כִּי לֹא הִמְטִיר
יְהוָה אֱלֹהִים עַל־הָאָרֶץ וְאָדָם אַיִן לַעֲבֹד

God among His seven Names which may not be erased.

The deeply rooted custom of not writing or pronouncing God's name unnecessarily (using instead '*HASHEM*' or '*Elokim*') is traced to the Third Commandment (Ex. 20:7; *Deut.* 5:11) which, *Rambam* in *Hil. Shevuos* 12:11 explains, prohibits not only *swearing* in God's Name in vain, but even *mentioning* one of the Divine Names unnecessarily.]

Throughout the saga of Creation אֱלֹהִים alone is used. Only afterwards is He referred to by His Holy and Awesome Name HASHEM. As the Sages [*Midrash* to verse 5] beautifully put it: 'The full name of God is employed in connection with a full world.' There was no vehicle adequate to receive this Name, the mysterious meaning of which I will explain, with God's help in my comm. to *Exodus* 6:3. *(Ibn Ezra).*

אֶרֶץ וְשָׁמָיִם — *Earth and heaven.*

The *Talmud* notes that sometimes *'heaven'* is mentioned first, while here *'earth'* is mentioned first. This teaches us that both are equally important *(Yerushalmi Chagigah* 2:1).

[See *Kli Yakar* cited in footnote below.]

5. וְכֹל שִׂיחַ הַשָּׂדֶה טֶרֶם יִהְיֶה בָאָרֶץ וכו' — *Now* [lit. *'and'*] — *no tree of the field was yet on the earth,* etc.

This verse describes the state of the earth on the sixth day before man was created. Although vegetation was *'brought forth'* from the earth on the third day [cf. *comm.* to 1:12] it did not emerge beyond the surface of the earth until the sixth day [see below] *(Rashi; Chullin* 60b).

According to *Ramban*, the simple meaning of the verse is that the verdure were indeed created on the third day in their full stature, but that Scripture now tells us that there was no one to further plant and sow them, nor could the earth be productive until the mist ascended and watered it and man was formed to cultivate and guard it.[1]

Since these verses lead up to the incident of the Tree of Life and Tree of Knowledge, the narrative begins

water into them, they will burst; if cold they will contract and snap. So he mixed hot and cold water and poured it into them and they therefore remained unbroken ...

Similarly, God said: If I create the world on the basis of mercy alone [represented by '*HASHEM*'], its sins will abound; on the basis of judgment alone ['*Elohim*'], it cannot endure. Therefore, I will create it on the basis of both judgment and mercy and may it then stand! Hence the combined expression: '*HASHEM God!*

Thus, in telling of the Creation of the Universe as a whole, אֱלֹהִים is used, and *'heaven'* is mentioned first, for, indeed, the celestial beings can endure being governed by Justice alone. But when man is to enter the scene, *'earth'* is mentioned first and the added use of '*HASHEM*' signifies that His justice must be tempered with mercy (Kli Yakar).

1. *Hoffmann* thus perceives the continuity of verses 5-7 as follows: Before anything sprang forth from the earth ... mist ascended from the earth and watered the soil ... from which God created man.

II
5 [5] *Now no tree of the field was yet on the earth and
no herb of the field had yet sprouted, for HASHEM
God had not sent rain upon the earth and there was
no man to work the soil.*

by describing how plant life came about *(Radak)*.

[*The translation of* שִׂיחַ as *'tree'* follows *Targum* ['אִילָנֵי']; *Menachem; Rashi* (below, and to *Job* 30:4) and *Ibn Ezra* (who adds that in his opinion it refers to fruit-bearing trees).

Avraham ben HaRambam suggests that שִׂיחַ is in the singular because it is a collective term designating tree-life; while according to *Radak* the term refers to shrubbery in general. Cf. 21:15 תַּחַת אַחַד הַשִּׂיחִם.

Hirsch, however, renders שִׂיחַ as *'growth'* and explains that in our verse it must mean the activity of growth, for plants were in existence on the third day but they made no progress and did not grow.]

[Many commentators perceive in שִׂיחַ a relationship to שִׂיחָה, *prayer, meditation,* as the commentators explain *Gen.* 24:63 לָשׂוּחַ בַּשָּׂדֶה *to pray in the field (Avodah Zarah 8)* cf. also *Psalms* 102:1 *'and pours out his petition* (שִׂיחוֹ) *before* HASHEM.*'*]

N'tziv elaborates upon this and interprets this verse on a deeper level as describing the state of the world 'before there was prayer which is described as שִׂיחַ הַשָּׂדֶה ... and before there was man who would pray ...' For as the Sages tell us, God desires the prayers of the righteous.

[Cf. *Song of Songs'* 2:14: הַשְׁמִיעִנִי אֶת־קוֹלֵךְ, *'let Me hear your (supplicating) voice'* upon which the *Midrash,* ad. loc. queries: Why were the matriarchs so long barren? — Because God loved to hear their prayers. In our verse, too, the Sages explain that God withholds sustenance — and rain — from the world because God loves the prayers of the righteous.]

כִּי לֹא הִמְטִיר ה׳ אֱלֹהִים עַל הָאָרֶץ — *For HASHEM God had not sent rain upon the earth.* And the reason He had not sent rain was because *'there was no man to work the soil'* and no one to recognize the utility of rain.* But when man was created he recognized its importance for the world. He prayed, and rain fell causing the trees and vegetation to spring forth *(Rashi)*.

* Interestingly, *Maharal* comments in this context that 'it is prohibited to perform a kindness on behalf of someone who will not recognize the favor.'

The name ה׳ אֱלֹהִים is explained by *Rashi: 'HASHEM* is His [personal] 'Name' whereas אֱלֹהִים designates Him as Ruler and Judge over all. The plain meaning of the combination where it occurs is: *HASHEM who is God* [*'Elohim'* — Ruler and Judge.] (See also *comm.* to preceding verse and 1:1; *Mizrachi; Gur Aryeh).*

Malbim explains that מָטָר, *rain,* is a symbol of divine providence, and it descends in response to man's prayers. He notes that there is a 'natural' rain which descends as a result of the vapor ascending to the clouds from earth. This rain is called גֶּשֶׁם and is not propitious. There is also a rain which is a gift of Divine Providence. It descends from the Upper Waters only in response to man's merits and prayers. This rain is called מָטָר and carries with it divine propitiousness.

Thus, the verse tells us that *the trees of the fields* — symbolic of the verdure which grow in cultivated fields and which depend on man's labor — *were not yet on the earth ...* because there was no man to plant the trees and till the land; while the herbs of the field — symbolic of the

ו אֶת־הָֽאֲדָמָה: וְאֵד יַֽעֲלֶה מִן־הָאָרֶץ
ז וְהִשְׁקָה אֶת־כָּל־פְּנֵי הָֽאֲדָמָה: וַיִּיצֶר
יהוה אֱלֹהִים אֶת־הָֽאָדָם עָפָר מִן־

wild-growing species not requiring man's labor, still did not grow, because they depend upon the מָטָר, *rain*, of blessing. And as the verse explains, *'HASHEM had not yet sent* מָטָר, this symbol of divine providence, *upon the earth'*, for there was no man to cause it to descend by virtue of his merits and prayers.

As *Hirsch* comments: Rain was lacking, for God would not grant it to the physical world, but only to mankind.

וְאָדָם אַיִן לַעֲבֹד אֶת הָאֲדָמָה — *And there was no man to 'work' the soil.* — Man, whose moral government on earth was demanded by God, its master, for the earth's further development ... Man's activity in mastering the earth is called עֲבוֹדָה, *service* [lit. *'work'*], for by his work on it man raises its purely physical nature ... Man's mastery over the earth is thus truly עֲבוֹדַת הָאֲדָמָה, service of the earth, by furthering its true purpose. In response to this 'service' of man to earth, God — as *HASHEM Elokim* — gives rain *(Hirsch).*

[*The translation of* אֲדָמָה as *'soil'* is an attempt to incorporate the distinction noted by the *Vilna Gaon* between אֶרֶץ and אֲדָמָה (as cited in 1:25 s.v. רֶמֶשׂ הָאֲדָמָה). According to him, אֲדָמָה *('ground')* has an agricultural connotation implying *'soil'*, while אֶרֶץ *('earth')* is a geographical term meaning the world in general or specifically the land of Israel ... Thus, in our verse: *'had not sent rain upon the* אֶרֶץ, *earth,'* — the world in general; *'and there was no man to work the* אֲדָמָה, *soil'* — the cultivatable land.]

6. וְאֵד יַעֲלֶה מִן הָאָרֶץ — [*And*] *a mist* [or *'cloud'*] *ascended from the earth.*

[This verse is understood by *Rashi* and many commentators to mean that this watering was preliminary to the formation of man. According to them, this mist did not take the place of the hitherto absent rain]:

This verse describes the preliminary steps of man's creation: God caused the deep to rise filling the clouds with water to moisten the dust, and man was created. It is similar to a kneader who first pours in water and then kneads the dough. Here, too: First, *'He watered the soil'*, and then *'He formed man' (Rashi).*

Additionally, the verse tells us that through the mist, the world was kept in a state of preparation for Man's arrival and for his work on it *(Hirsch).*

According to *Ramban*, it was the immutable course of the world that due to the earth's mist the heaven will bring down rains upon the earth and cause the seeds to grow.

For, as *Sforno* explains, when God established the eternal existence [of plant life], a vapor ascended from which there emanated rains and dew, the prequisites necessary for their continuity.

[Although יַעֲלֶה is in future tense and would normally be translated *will ascend*, our translation *ascended* (or, past-perfect, *had ascended) follows Targum* and many commentators. *Hirsch* renders: *'and vapor rose continuously'*, the future tense designating a continuous state of events *(Aderes Eliyahu).*

II
6-7

[6] *A mist ascended from the earth and watered the whole surface of the soil,* [7] *and HASHEM God formed man of dust from the ground, and He blew into his*

[*Rav Saadiah Gaon* interprets this verse that since it follows ... וְאָדָם אַיִן, *and there was no man ...*, the negative refers also to this verse. Thus: *'neither was there even any mist ascending from the earth to water the surface of the soil'.*]

וְהִשְׁקָה אֶת כָּל פְּנֵי הָאֲדָמָה — *And watered the whole surface of the soil.*

The moistening was only on the surface, unlike rain whose moisture penetrates deep into the soil. The impending creation of man required only surface moisture *(Ha'amek Davar).*

7. וַיִּיצֶר ה׳ אֱלֹהִים אֶת הָאָדָם — *And HASHEM God formed* [the] *man.*

Rashi notes that וַיִּיצֶר, *formed,* is spelled here [in reference to the creation of man] with two *yuds* unlike verse 19, where in describing the creation of animals, the verb is spelled with one *yud.* This denotes that man was endowed with a double *'formation'*: once for this world and once for resurrection after death.

The word אָדָם, *man,* is derived from אֲדָמָה, *earth,* from which he was taken, or it is derived from דָם, *blood,* for man is flesh and blood *(Midrash HaGadol).*

[For additional etymological definitions of this word see comm. to 1:26 s.v. אָדָם.]

עָפָר מִן הָאֲדָמָה — [*of*] *dust from the ground.* Although there were other elements combining in man, *'dust'* is specifically mentioned because it formed the largest single ingredient *(R' Meyuchas).*

The earth from which man was created was gathered from the four corners of the earth so that the earth should receive him for burial wherever he might die *(Rashi).*

This combination of earth from all corners of the globe further distinguished man from animal. It enabled him to live in any climate — from areas of extreme heat to extreme cold — and to adjust accordingly *(Ha'amek Davar).*

Another interpretation is that it was collected from the future site of the מִזְבַּח אֲדָמָה *'altar of earth' (Exodus* 20:21); i.e. the Sanctuary] to symbolize that it would be an atonement for him that he might be able to endure *(Rashi).*

The *Midrash* homiletically reads this as עֹפֶר, *young man: 'God created man as a young man in his fulness',* as Rav Yochanan said: Adam and Eve were created as at the age of twenty. Rav Eleazar ben Rav Shimon said: Eve, too, was created fully developed.

[Unlike the animals who were brought forth *entirely* from the earth (cf. 1:24), man is distinctive in that *God formed him* and breathed into his nostrils the soul of life] ...

1. Additionally, the *Midrash* notes that the two yuds in וַיִּיצֶר connotes double formations:
— Adam and Eve;
— With the nature of both celestial beings and earthly creatures;
— The Good and Evil Inclinations ...

Hirsch observes that the one *Yud* is audible, the other quiesent: One יְצִירָה [formation, impulse] is predominant and the other silent, but it is always there ... The loftiest man is still an earthly being, and even the loftiest deed of the Good Inclination requires a struggle to conquer the Evil Inclination and vice versa.

ב
הָאֲדָמָה וַיִּפַּח בְּאַפָּיו נִשְׁמַת חַיִּים וַיְהִי
ח ח הָאָדָם לְנֶפֶשׁ חַיָּה: וַיִּטַּע יהוה אֱלֹהִים גַּן
בְּעֵדֶן מִקֶּדֶם וַיָּשֶׂם שָׁם אֶת־הָאָדָם אֲשֶׁר

Hirsch thus notes that it does not say that God formed man מִן הֶעָפָר, *from* the dust of the ground, but He formed him עָפָר, *dust of the earth.* God formed from the עָפָר, *dust,* only that which is earthly in man, and which will eventually return to earth. Man's human life, however, was not taken by God from the earth: God breathed that part into his countenance and only *thereby* did man become a living creature ... For man is unlike animals, in that only the dead material came from the earth to form him, but it was the Breath of God that transformed that lifeless dust into a living being which raises man above the animal forces of physical necessity and makes him free, endowed with the ability to master and rule over the earthly within him *(Hirsch).*

וַיִּפַּח בְּאַפָּיו נִשְׁמַת חַיִּים — *And He blew into his nostrils the soul* [or *'breath'*] *of life.*

God thus made man out of both lower [i.e. earthly] and upper [heavenly] matter: his body from the dust and his soul from the spirit *(Rashi).*

נְשָׁמָה, *soul,* is a term that applies to man only *(Ibn Ezra; Radak).* It refers to the uppermost soul that comes from God, and which provides man with his superiority of knowledge, speech, and intellect beyond all animals ... and which will one day submit to judgment *(B'chor Shor).*

Soul of life, therefore, refers to the soul which lives on forever and does not die with the body *(Chizkuni).*

According to *Sforno:* 'He breathed into him a vivifying soul ready to receive the image of God'.

Ramban comments that since this soul was breathed into his nostrils by God, it follows that man's soul was of Divine essence and that Scripture specifically mentioned the Source of man's soul in order to make it clear that the soul did not come to man from the elements.

וַיְהִי הָאָדָם לְנֶפֶשׁ חַיָּה — *And man became a living being* [or: *'soul'.*]

According to *Onkelos* and *Rav Saadiah Gaon:* 'It became in man a Speaking Spirit.'

Rashi explains that even animals are referred to in 1:30 as possessing 'living souls'.[1] That of man, is more 'living' [i.e. developed] than theirs, however, for it was additionally endowed with reason and speech.

According to various opinions man has three souls: נֶפֶשׁ הַגְּדוֹל, the soul of growth — like that in plants; נֶפֶשׁ הַתְּנוּעָה, the soul of movement — like that of animals, fish and creeping things; and נֶפֶשׁ הַמַּשְׂכֶּלֶת, the rational soul. Others hold that man's God-given soul comprises these three forces combined into one soul. The former seems to be the opinion of the Sages, as rendered by *Onkelos* according to which this rational soul which God breathed into man's nostrils became a speaking soul. The verse is therefore to be interpreted that at first God formed man into a moving creature with life

1. *Ibn Ezra* explains that from the use of the phrase *'living soul'* in describing both the soul of man and that of animals, it is evident that, unlike human babies, Adam was able to get up and walk about as do animals.

II
8

nostrils the soul of life; and man became a living being.

[8] *HASHEM God planted a garden in Eden, to the east, and placed there the man whom He had formed.*

and perception, then He breathed into his nostrils, in addition, a living soul from the Most High, and consequently the unified whole man became a living soul which reasons, speaks, and performs tasks *(Ramban).*

N'tziv cites several of the interpretations quoted above regarding man's superiority over animals, but he states that it is not clear how the term נֶפֶשׁ חַיָּה lends itself to a different interpretation when used in reference to man than it does when used in reference to animals.

He explains that the above interpretations are based on the fact that חַי, *living,* in Hebrew suggests that a being has attained the highest degree of perfection possible for that particular creature. Animals achieve that state of being entitled נֶפֶשׁ חַיָּה, *a living soul,* just by existing according to their intended state. Man, however, attains this status only when his rational soul functions perfectly, whereas a Jew reaches this state of נֶפֶשׁ חַיָּה when he perceives his role as a servant of God, for this is the motive of his creation. This fundamental concept is alluded to in *Habakkuk* 2:4: וְצַדִּיק בֶּאֱמוּנָתוֹ יִחְיֶה [which, according to this interpretation should be rendered: *And the righteous shall, by virtue of his faith, be called 'living'.*]

HaK'sav V'Hakaballah comments that with the phrase נֶפֶשׁ חַיָּה, *living soul,* the Torah describes man in his most distinctive character: a rational being capable of free-choice. The word נֶפֶשׁ alludes to this concept of choice, as the word is used in 23:8: אִם יֵשׁ אֶת נַפְשְׁכֶם, *'if it is your wish';* while חַיָּה, *'living', being',* denotes man's *raison d'etre* of living a life expressive of that free will.

8. The Garden in Eden.

These verses elaborate upon the very brief general statement in 1:27: *'And God created man* ... Now, Scripture gives further information concerning man's whereabouts and activities *(Rashi; Rav Saadiah Gaon).*

וַיִּטַּע ה׳ אֱלֹהִים גַּן־בְּעֵדֶן מִקֶּדֶם — [And] *HASHEM God planted a garden in Eden to the east.* The translation of מִקֶּדֶם, *'to the east',* i.e. to the east part of Eden follows *Rashi.*

Onkelos, following the *Midrash* which comments that the Garden in Eden preceded man; *Ibn Ezra* [וַיִּטַּע = 'He *had* planted']; *R' Meyuchas* and others interpret מִקֶּדֶם as *'previously'; from the beginning,* and render the verse: 'And HASHEM God had planted a garden in Eden *from aforetime.'*[1]

'In reality the Garden had preceded man's creation but אֵין מוּקְדָּם וּמְאוּחָר בַּתּוֹרָה, the Torah does not concern itself with chronological sequence ...' *(Avraham ben HaRambam).*

1. Rav Shmuel bar Nachman said: You may think that מִקֶּדֶם means before [קֶדֶם] the creation of the world, but that is not so; rather it means before Adam, for Adam was created on the sixth day whereas the garden in Eden was created on the third *(Midrash).*

ב יָצָר: ט וַיַּצְמַח יהוה אֱלֹהִים מִן־הָאֲדָמָה
ט כָּל־עֵץ נֶחְמָד לְמַרְאֶה וְטוֹב לְמַאֲכָל וְעֵץ
הַחַיִּים בְּתוֹךְ הַגָּן וְעֵץ הַדַּעַת טוֹב וָרָע:

וַיִּטַּע ה׳ אֱלֹהִים —*[And] HASHEM God planted.* God's full Name is mentioned in connection with this planting to demonstrate that these were His plantings, the prearranged work of His hands about which he decreed precisely where the garden and each tree would be, unlike the other places on earth where the trees grow without specific order *(Midrash; Ramban).*

גַּן בְּעֵדֶן — *A garden in Eden. A place on earth whose exact location is unknown to any human being (Midrash HaGadol).*

Some interpret עֵדֶן as an adjective, and render גַּן בְּעֵדֶן, *a garden in a place of delight (Radak; R' Meyuchas)* or: *'a garden of delight, (HaRechasim leBik'ah).*

[For the hashkafa — philosophic — implications of the concept of the garden in Eden (which also signifies the heavenly Paradise where the souls of the righteous repose), see *Overview.*]

וַיָּשֶׂם שָׁם אֶת הָאָדָם אֲשֶׁר יָצָר — *And placed there the man whom He had formed.*

God *'placed'* him there but he was not created there. *'Placed'* in this context means that He placed him in charge *(Radak).*

As *Hirsch* comments: וַיָּשֶׂם שָׁם does not mean merely *placing* there, but it indicates the position he was to occupy.

Had man originated in the Garden in Eden he would have thought that the whole world was like that garden. Instead, God formed him outside the garden so he saw a world of thorns and thistles. Only then did God lead man into the choicest part of the garden. *(Chizkuni).* [See *Overview*]

[The commentators note that the definite article ה, *the,* before אָדָם, *man,* signifies that it is not the personal name *Adam* that is referred to in these verses, but mankind as a whole, personified in the First Man.]

9-14. The following parenthetic verses describe in detail the garden that was created especially for man. The narrative of his inhabiting the garden is continued in verse 15 *(Or HaChaim).*

9. וַיַּצְמַח ה׳ אֱלֹהִים מִן הָאֲדָמָה — *And HASHEM God, caused to grow from the ground* — i.e., from the ground of the garden of Eden *(Rashi; Radak).*

Sforno interprets the phrase to mean that God caused man's food to grow without man's toil.

נֶחְמָד לְמַרְאֶה וְטוֹב לְמַאֲכָל — *That was pleasing to the sight and good for food.*

There were no barren trees among them: The trees were esthetically magnificent and their fruit made excellent food *(Radak).*

'Pleasing to the sight' — i.e. gladdening and broadening the heart to make it receptive of intelligence, as in the verse: *'And it came to pass when the minstrel played that the hand of HASHEM came upon him'* [*I Kings* 3:15] *(Sforno).*

II
9 *⁹ And HASHEM God caused to grow from the ground every tree that was pleasing to the sight and good for food; also a tree of life in the midst of the garden, and a tree of the knowledge of good and bad.*

וְעֵץ הַחַיִּים בְּתוֹךְ הַגָּן — *also [He planted (Radak)] a tree of life in the midst* [i.e. *'the center' (Rashi)*] *of the garden* [see comm. below].

One who would eat its fruit would benefit from greatly increased longevity ... not that one would live *forever*! *(Ibn Ezra* to 3:6) [But cf. *Ramban* to 2:17; *comm.* to 3:22 and *Overview.*]

וְעֵץ הַדַּעַת טוֹב וָרָע — *And a tree of the knowledge of good and bad.*[1] [i.e. which was also, 'there in the midst of the garden' (see below).]

— 'And the tree of whose fruit they who ate would know between good and bad' *(Onkelos).*

The translation follows *Onkelos* who, following the traditional punctuation interprets עֵץ הַדַּעַת not as a unit meaning *Tree of Knowledge,* but as the עֵץ, *tree,* הַדַּעַת טוֹב וָרָע, *which causes knowledge of good and bad.*

Targum Yerushalmi [also *Ibn Ezra*] perceives this as a unit with an implied adjective: *knowledge,* and renders:

'And the tree of knowledge, of which anyone who ate would distinguish between good and bad.

[Many early commentators (eg. *Ibn Ezra; Radak)* perceive in the word *'knowledge'* a euphemism for sexual desire which was the result of eating the fruit of the tree. This is evidenced by the fact that as soon as Adam and Eve partook of its fruit they bcame aware of their nakedness (3:7), and Adam *'knew'* his wife (4:1).]

According to *Sforno,* the knowledge of good and bad refers to man's ability to choose the sweet even when it is harmful and reject the bitter even when it is beneficial [i.e. to perceive beyond the seemingly obvious.]

Hirsch says that, as is plain from the chapter, the tree's fruit was succulent and tempting, yet man was forbidden to eat from it. Because it was against God's will that man partake of it, its eating was intrinsically 'bad' no matter what the senses might dictate. Thus the tree was there to demonstrate that 'good

1. The *Midrash* discusses what kind of tree it was whereof Adam and Eve ate. Several opinions are offered:

— It was wheat ... which [at that time] grew lofty as the cedars of Lebanon;

— It was grapes ...'

— It was the esrog (citron), as it is written [3:6] *'and when the woman saw that the 'tree'* [הָעֵץ] *was good for food.'* For what tree is it whose wood [עֵץ] can be eaten like its fruit? — None but the esrog (see *Overview);*

— It was a fig ...

Rav Azariah and Rav Yehudah ben Rav Shimon in the name of Rav Yehoshua ben Levi said:

Heaven forfend that we should conjecture what the tree was! The Holy One, blessed be He did not, and will not reveal to man what the tree was ... for He was anxious to safeguard mankind's honor and His own ... [He did not reveal the nature of the tree so that it might not be said, 'through this tree Adam brought death into the world.']

י וְנָהָר֙ יֹצֵ֣א מֵעֵ֔דֶן לְהַשְׁק֖וֹת אֶת־הַגָּ֑ן
יא וּמִשָּׁם֙ יִפָּרֵ֔ד וְהָיָ֖ה לְאַרְבָּעָ֥ה רָאשִֽׁים׃ שֵׁ֥ם
הָֽאֶחָ֖ד פִּישׁ֑וֹן ה֣וּא הַסֹּבֵ֗ב אֵ֚ת כָּל־אֶ֣רֶץ
יב הַֽחֲוִילָ֔ה אֲשֶׁר־שָׁ֖ם הַזָּהָֽב׃ וּזֲהַ֛ב הָאָ֥רֶץ
הַהִ֖וא ט֑וֹב שָׁ֥ם הַבְּדֹ֖לַח וְאֶ֥בֶן הַשֹּֽׁהַם׃

and bad' are concepts that are dependent on the will of God, not the senses of man.

The commentators query: How could each of two trees be *exactly* in *'the center* of the garden'?

Ramban explains that in the middle of the garden there was something like an enclosed garden bed which contained these two trees. Additionally, since no one knows the true central point of anything except God alone, this 'middle' means 'the approximate middle'.

There are also opinions cited in the commentary of the *Tur* that the *branches* of the Tree of Knowledge encircled the Tree of life with the effect that they visually merged and appeared to be both in the center, with the effect that only *after* partaking of the fruits of the former could one 'make way' and partake of the latter.

The *Tur* cites an opinion of *Rav Yosef Kimchi* according to whom there was only one tree: the tree of life which was also a tree of knowledge [The repetitive phrase is similar to the double description of the same person as being both 'a wise man' and 'righteous man' when in reality both qualities are facets of the same person. For later (3:3) there is only *one* tree, (the *tree of knowledge)* that is described as *the* tree in the center of the garden.] *Tur* is doubtful that this interpretation is correct for, he queries, if it was truly the same tree what will they do with the verse [3:33] *'and now, lest he put forth his hand and take also of the tree of life and eat* ...? If it was one tree, he had already eaten from it!

R' Bachya seems to answer this difficulty with his interpretation that they were both in the center because they were attached and shared a common trunk, so that they were truly 'both' in the center.

10. וְנָהָר יוֹצֵא מֵעֵדֶן לְהַשְׁקוֹת אֶת־הַגָּן — *[And] a river issues forth from Eden to water the garden* — i.e. the river in Eden overflows and waters the garden *(B'chor Shor)* without need of man or his toil *(Sforno)*. For man was placed there to 'tend and guard it' [verse 15] but he did not have to water it; that was taken care of by the river *(Radak)*.

וּמִשָּׁם יִפָּרֵד וְהָיָה לְאַרְבָּעָה רָאשִׁים — *And from there it is divided and becomes four [river]-headwaters;* i.e., the excess water flowing out of the garden in Eden forms four parts: each of them becoming the head of a new river *(Targum; Radak)*.

Hirsch comments that some criticize the geographical description in this verse because it has been taken to refer to a river which divides into four streams, and no such river has been found ... But רָאשִׁים does not mean branches but four separate heads. The river starts as a single stream, and outside Eden, after it has watered the garden, it evidently disappears into the ground and springs up again in four different locations as four separate rivers.

11. שֵׁם הָאֶחָד פִּישׁוֹן — *The name of the first is Pishon.*

Rashi and most commentators [*Midrash; Zohar; R'Avraham ben HaRambam; Ramban*] identify *Pishon* with the Nile.

Abarbanel comments that the

II
10-13

[10] *A river issues forth from Eden to water the garden, and from there it is divided and becomes four
headwaters.* [11] *The name of the first is Pishon, the
one that encircles the whole land of Chavilah, where
the gold is.* [12] *The gold of that land is good; b'dolach
is there, and the shoham stone.* [13] *The name of the*

Greeks identify Pishon with the River Ganges, and that Chavila is a section of India which the Ganges surrounds, and in which there is gold. [Cf. *Targum Yonasan* which also identifies Chavila with הִינְדְקִי *(India?)* see below.]

הוּא הַסֹּבֵב אֵת כָּל־אֶרֶץ הַחֲוִילָה אֲשֶׁר שָׁם הַזָּהָב — *The one that encircles the whole land of Chavilah where the gold is.*

It must be borne in mind that the description refers to rivers and places which were well known when the Torah was written *(Hirsch).*

There are two different Chavilahs mentioned in the Torah: Seba and Chavilah [10:7]; and Ophir and Chavilah [*ibid.* 29]. This being the case, in order to identify this Chavilah, the Torah describes it as the place 'where there is gold', which is clearly the Chavilah near Ophir which *II Chron.* 9:10 describes as having gold. Since Cush and Ashur do not share their names with any other countries, no further description of them is needed *(B'chor Shor; R' Meyuchas).*

Apparently, the land of Chavilah was the closest in proximity to the Garden of Eden, and is therefore superior to other lands in its characteristics. The verse, therefore, mentions that it possesses gold. Furthermore, the word זָהָב, *gold,* is preceded with the definite article ה, *the,* to indicate that although many countries have gold, its gold was better and in great abundance *(Radak)*[1]

12. וּזֲהַב הָאָרֶץ הַהִוא טוֹב — [*And*] *the gold of that land is good* — i.e. better than of all other lands *(R' Meyuchas);* and free of all impurities *(Minchah Belulah).*

שָׁם הַבְּדֹלַח — [*The*] *b'dolach is there.* [We have left the word בְּדֹלַח (usually translated *'bdellium')* transliterated only. It is mentioned in *Numbers* 11:7 where the Manna is compared to it. The definite article הַ, *the,* indicates that it was a well-known substance.]

Rashi to *Num.* 1:7 translates *'crystal'.*

According to *Rav Saadiah Gaon, Ibn Ezra, Radak,* and *R' Avraham ben HaRambam,* however, it means *'pearl'.*

וְאֶבֶן הַשֹּׁהַם — *And the shoham stone.* [Translations vary from *beryl (Targum),* to *onyx,* and *lapis lazuli.* Although it is mentioned in *Exodus* 28:17-20; 39:10-13 as one of the *stones for setting* affixed to the breastpiece, its exact identity, can-

1. The *Midrash* notes that at this chronological point in time *Chavilah, Cush and Asshur* did not yet exist as countries, but the Torah refers to them by the name which those districts would bear in the future (cf. *Rashi; Kesubos* 10b).

יג וְשֵׁם־הַנָּהָר הַשֵּׁנִי גִּיחוֹן הוּא הַסּוֹבֵב אֵת
יד כָּל־אֶרֶץ כּוּשׁ: וְשֵׁם הַנָּהָר הַשְּׁלִישִׁי
חִדֶּקֶל הוּא הַהֹלֵךְ קִדְמַת אַשּׁוּר וְהַנָּהָר
טו הָרְבִיעִי הוּא פְרָת: וַיִּקַּח יהוה אֱלֹהִים
אֶת־הָאָדָם וַיַּנִּחֵהוּ בְגַן־עֵדֶן לְעָבְדָהּ

not be ascertained *(Ibn Ezra)* except that it is a precious stone. We have therefore left the word untranslated.

13. גִּיחוֹן – *Gichon.* [The identity of this river, too, is a matter of uncertainty, for as *Rashi* notes in *Berachos* 10b, the *Gichon* mentioned in *II Chron.* 32 is *'not the large river'*, which does not lie in *Eretz Yisrael,* but it is the Siloam pool near Jerusalem referred to in *I Kings* 1:33.]

כּוּשׁ – *Cush.* [Also left untranslated, for although it is usually identified with Ethiopia or Abyssinia, that, too, is a matter of conjecture upon which the Sages do not give conclusive guidance.]

14. חִדֶּקֶל – *Chidekel.* Most traditional sources identify this with the Tigris *(Aruch; Abarbanel).*

Although *Onkelos* has not translated any of the other rivers, he translated *Chidekel:* דִּיגְלַת [= טִיגְרִס, *Tigris (Nesinah laGer)*] *(Lechem V'Simlah).*

קִדְמַת אַשּׁוּר – *Toward the east of Ashur.* Associated with Armenia and Assyria *(Abarbanel).*

פְּרָת – *The Euphrates. Rashi* comments that this is the most important of the four rivers on account of its connection to *Eretz Yisrael* of which it was to be the ideal boundary, as in 15:18 *'To your seed I have given this land, from the river of Egypt, unto the great river, the river Euphrates.'* [*See Rashi* there, where he comments that because it is associated with *Eretz Yisrael* it is called 'great' although it was the last river to issue from Eden.]

Since, as Israel's boundary, this would be the most familiar of the rivers, no further geographical elaboration was necessary. The verse therefore identifies it as only הוּא פְּרָת, *this is the Euphrates* – i.e. the Euphrates you are familiar with *(Radak; Chizkuni).*

... This is the Euphrates that flows through Babylon into the Sea ... forming the northern border with Eretz Yisrael *(Abarbanel).*[1]

15. Man in the Garden.

After the paranthetical description of the Garden and its rivers which began in *v.* 9, the narrative resumes where it left off at the end of verse 8: the theme of man's entry into the Garden in Eden. Details are added here in elaborating upon the event *(Radak; R' Meyuchas).*

1. [It is codified in *Shulchan Aruch, Orach Chaim* 228:2 that one who sees any one of these four rivers (in a place where we are certain it is *running its natural course* unchanged by man) is obligated to pronounce the benediction עוֹשֶׂה מַעֲשֵׂה בְרֵאשִׁית *'Who made the works of the beginning,'* because we should praise God when we see things that we know He established in the six days of Creation that are still in existence *(Eliyahu Rabbah; Mishneh Berurah).*]

II
14-16 *second river is Gichon, the one that encircles the*
whole land of Cush. 14 *The name of the third river is*
Chidekel, the one that flows toward the east of
Ashur; and the fourth river is the Euphrates.
15 *HASHEM God took the man and placed him in*
the Garden of Eden, to work it and to guard it. 16 *And*

וַיִּקַּח . . . אֶת הָאָדָם — *[And] HASHEM God took the man* — i.e. He took man from the place where he was created *(Radak)*, inducing him to enter the Garden with kind words *(Midrash; Rashi)*.

וַיַּנִּחֵהוּ בְגַן עֵדֶן — *And placed him in the Garden of Eden* — As one who gently places down a precious treasure giving it fullest care and attention *(Rechasim leBik'ah)*.

'He showed him the garden from end to end and made him its king and ruler' *(Midrash)*.

The *Midrash* connects וַיַּנִּיחֵהוּ with מְנוּחָה, *repose*, and renders: וַיַּנִּיחֵהוּ בְּגַן עֵדֶן, *and He gave him repose in the Garden of Eden* (following *R' Yudan*; see *Mat. Kehunah*).

Homiletically, the *Midrash* comments that וַיַּנִּיחֵהוּ means: He gave him the precept of Sabbath [rendering: *'He commanded him concerning repose.*]

לְעָבְדָהּ וּלְשָׁמְרָהּ — *To work it and to guard it* — i.e. to water it and guard it against wild animals *(Chizkuni)*. [But cf. *Radak* cited in *comm.* to verse 10][1]

Great is work because even Adam tasted nothing before he worked, as it is said, *'and He put him into the Garden of Eden to work it and guard it'*, and only then *'from every tree of the garden you may eat'* . . . *(Avos d'Rabbi Nosson)*.

[I.e., only after God told him to cultivate and keep the garden did He give him permission to eat of its fruits] for it is improper for man to benefit from this world without contributing something beneficial towards the settlement and upkeep of the world *(Torah Temimah)*.

[Many commentators note that the feminine pronominal suffix *mappik* ה in לְעָבְדָהּ וּלְשָׁמְרָהּ — to work *it* and to guard *it*, refers to the אֲדָמָה, *ground* [fem.] because גַּן, *garden*, is in the masculine.

This is also the view expressed by *Ramban* in verse 8, above, that although the trees in the garden required no one to tend or prune them, he put man there *to work* [i.e. cultivate] *it and guard it* — i.e. to sow wheat for himself ... and rows of spices, reaping, plucking, and eating at will. It therefore refers to his cultivating the *ground*.

Ramban goes on to point out that *garden* is also found in fem. gender as in the verse [*Isaiah* 61:11] 'and as the garden causes the things that are in *her* to spring forth.' Hence the object of the verb may be the Garden.

1. The *Midrash*, however, gives an allegorical interpretation of this 'work' in Eden:

'What labor was there in the midst of the garden that the verse should say *to work it and guard it?*

Perhaps you will say: To prune the vines, plough the fields, and pile up the sheaves.

— But, did not the trees grow up of their own accord?

Perhaps you will say: There was other work to be done, such as watering the garden.

— But did not a river flow through and water the garden [verse 10]?

What, then, does *to work it and guard it* mean? — To indulge in the words of Torah and to 'guard' all its commandments, as it says further [3:24]: to guard the way of the tree of life — and the 'tree of life' signifies the Torah, as it is written [*Proverbs* 3:18]: *it is a tree of life to those that grasp it (Pirkei d'Rabbi Eliezer 12; Rabbeinu Bachya).*

טז וּלְשָׁמְרָהּ: וַיְצַו יְהוָה אֱלֹהִים עַל־הָאָדָם
יז לֵאמֹר מִכֹּל עֵץ־הַגָּן אָכֹל תֹּאכֵל: וּמֵעֵץ
הַדַּעַת טוֹב וָרָע לֹא תֹאכַל מִמֶּנּוּ כִּי בְּיוֹם

This agrees with the commentary of *Ibn Ezra* who, on *Ecclesiastes* 2:5 comments that: 'גַּן, *garden*, occurs sometimes in masc. as in *Song of Songs* 4:12 גַּן נָעוּל, *a garden locked-up*, and in *Gen.* 2:15 it occurs in the fem. לְעָבְדָהּ וּלְשָׁמְרָהּ. Similarly in the plural גַּנִּים (masc.) and גַּנּוֹת (fem.).]

16–17. וַיְצַו ... עַל הָאָדָם — *And HASHEM God commanded* [עַל, lit. *'upon'*] *the man.*

'Upon man': i.e. for man's benefit *(Aderes Eliyahu).*

The word *'commanded'* must here be understood as *'warned'* *(Sifri, Naso* 1).

Additionally, the phrase *'commanded upon'* carries with it an emphasis on the prohibitory aspect of the command: 'although I have permitted to you all the *other* trees of the garden, do not eat the fruit of the tree of knowledge.'

לֵאמֹר — *saying.* [lit. *'to say'* implying that he should relay the commandment to another], i.e. that he should in turn tell his wife *(Aderes Eliyahu).*

מִכֹּל עֵץ־הַגָּן אָכֹל תֹּאכֵל — *Of every tree of the garden you may freely eat.*

[The translation follows the majority of commentators who perceive this verse as *permission* to eat of any of the trees. Others, however, interpret this as part of the command that man *must* partake of the trees].

— The meaning is that these are *permitted* to you, similar to *'six days may you work'* [*Exodus* 20:9 — divine permission — which is then followed by the *prohibition* of 'work' on the Sabbath.] This verse is not a *command.* The command is only the prohibition against eating of the tree of knowledge (*Rav Saadiah Gaon; Ibn Ezra* 13; v. *Midrash HaGadol).*[1]

[According to the following, the verse should be rendered *'Of all the trees in the garden you shall surely eat'*]:

— The command may be understood to refer to the prohibition, or to both aspects, for it is a *mitzvah* for one to sustain himself with what is permitted him *(Radak).*

— It was a *mitzvah* for him to nurture his soul from the fruits of the garden as the *Talmud Yerushalmi* (end of *Kiddushin; Korban ha'Eidah)* exhorts: 'man will have to give an account and reckoning for everything from which he unnecessarily restrained himself in this world and did not partake of'. Adam sinned in not

1. *Hoffman* explains that the *'knowledge of good and evil'* means the *recognition* of good and evil, or more properly, discerning righteousness and its converse and distinguishing between them: 'to discern between good and evil [*I Kings* 3:9] — to choose the good out of deep conviction and to dispel everything evil. This is a capacity not possessed by young children [*Deut.* 1:39]; it is acquired but later lost again in extreme old age during the second childhood *(II Sam.* 14:17, 20]. Only during young manhood does man acquire this capacity [*Isaiah* 7:15*ff*], and it is a pre-eminent trait of divine beings [3:5, 22.]

[Why then, should man be prohibited from partaking of a tree the fruits of which can so greatly ennoble him? And why was man created without this capacity?]

II *HASHEM God commanded the man, saying, 'Of*
17 *every tree of the garden you may freely eat;* [17] *but of*
the tree of the knowledge of good and bad, you must

conveying this positive aspect of the command to his wife. Had she known that the eating of permitted food was the divine will, her enjoyment of food, even without doing so for the sake of a commandment, would have constituted performance of God's will. This merit would have 'protected' her from transgressing ... *(Meshech Chochmah).*

The *Talmud* connects this verse to the seven 'Noachide Laws' [i.e. 'universal laws obligatory upon all nations of the world. (The nations of the world are referred to as בְּנֵי נֹחַ, *'Noah's children'* because *'from him were the nations branched out after the flood'* [*Gen.* 10:32] — *Torah Temimah)*]:
וַיְצַו = institute law and order [i.e. establish courts of law and observe social justice];
ה =a prohibition again blasphemy;
אֱלֹהִים = an induction against idolatry;
הָאָדָם =bloodshed;
לֵאמֹר = adultery;
מִכֹּל עֵץ הַגָּן, *of every tree of the garden* =but not of robbery;
אָכֹל תֹּאכֵל, *you may freely eat* = but not flesh cut from a living animal.

[Proof verses are cited for each. For etymological connection between the verse and the Noachide Laws cited, see *Hirsch* to our verse. (Cf. also verse 24 below).]

וּמֵעֵץ הַדַּעַת טוֹב וָרָע — *But of the tree of the knowledge of good and bad.*

[Cf. *comm.* to verse 9]

לֹא תֹאכַל מִמֶּנּוּ — *You must not eat thereof.*

It is noted that God did not specifically prohibit eating from the tree of life because the tree of knowledge formed a hedge around it; only after one had partaken of the latter and cleared a path for himself could one come close to the tree of life [cf. *comm.* cited by *Tur* in verse 9] ... *(Chizkuni).*

The tree of life is not mentioned because had man not sinned he would have lived forever regardless, and the question of his partaking of the tree of life was academic. It was only *after* he sinned and was punished with mortality that God said [3:22]: *'and now* — i.e. after having already sinned and been sentenced to eventual death — *lest he put forth his hand,* etc.' *(Minchah Belulah).*

[The word מִמֶּנּוּ, *thereof,* is seemingly redundant since it already says וּמֵעֵץ, 'and *from* the tree.' But since nothing in the Torah is superfluous, the commentators explain its connotation]:

— It means: eat nothing of the tree; not even a morsel of it *(Ibn Ezra; Vilna Gaon).*

כִּי בְּיוֹם אֲכָלְךָ מִמֶּנּוּ מוֹת תָּמוּת — *For on the day you eat of it you shall surely die* — i.e. you will be deserving of death *(Targum Yonasan; Rav Saadiah Gaon; Lekach Tov).*

Hirsch renders: *you are 'liable' to death.* God did not threaten immediately death [for Adam reached the age of 930!], but that death

[The answer is that man's capacities for moral attainment must be drawn out and developed through discipline and testing. Man cannot be born with this full knowledge; it must be the result of living a life subordinated to the Will of God as revealed in His Torah even when the reasons underlying God's commands are beyond man's understanding. For man's instinctive perception of the best may be contrary to the lofty calling of man and judged by God as a capital crime (see *Overview).*]

יח אֲכָלְךָ מִמֶּנּוּ מוֹת תָּמוּת: וַיֹּאמֶר יְהוָה אֱלֹהִים לֹא־טוֹב הֱיוֹת הָאָדָם לְבַדּוֹ

would be the ultimate result of the sin. The exact nature of death is recognized, even today, as a still unsolved physiological problem. The prophet proclaims that death will disappear from the world *(Isaiah* 25:8) when mankind once again achieves the closeness to God that was intended at Creation.

According to the *Midrash*, therefore, יוֹם, *day*, is interpreted as יוֹמוֹ שֶׁל הקב״ה 'day of God' — i.e. a thousand years, as in *Psalms* 90:4 כִּי אֶלֶף שָׁנִים בְּעֵינֶיךָ כְּיוֹם אֶתְמוֹל, *for a thousand years are like a day gone by in Your eyes.*

[Difference of opinion abounds on whether or not man was initially created as an immortal being and that as a result of his sin he became mortal[1] or whether he was always destined to be mortal but that the sin hastened his death. (See *Overview*).]

You will surely die: I.e. you will be condemned to die an earlier death than was originally contemplated for you *(Radak).*

'... You will become mortal and eventually die. Some explain that the intent of the verse is that had he sinned before eating it he would not be subject to punishment because he would have had no knowledge [of good and evil], but henceforth were he to eat it and thereby gain this knowledge he would be held accountable and be punished *(Tur).*

Ramban, in a lengthy dissertation, notes that men versed in the sciences of nature are of the opinion that man would have died a natural death even had he *not* eaten because man is a composite of the four elements and hence (as *Ramban* explains later) according to the opinion of those wanting in faith, a composite, by its very nature, cannot exist indefinitely. If he sins, however, he will die prematurely as a result of his sin like those who are liable to death at the hands of heaven for their sins.

But according to the opinion of our Sages [cf. *Shabbos* 55b] if Adam had not sinned he would *never* have died, since his Higher Soul and the Will of God would always cleave to him and sustain him forever...

It has also been suggested that the intent of the verse is: if you partake of the fruit of the tree of knowledge you will be denied access to the tree of life thus making it impossible to gain eternal life by eating of its fruit. Thus you will literally *'die'*, because, by virtue of your act at that moment, you will be compelled to succumb to eventual death.

— *For on the day you eat of it*: On that day the evil impulses of jealousy, lust, and honor will be aroused making it impossible for you to attain the goal of spirituality on earth. Thus, eternal life would be an intolerable burden for you *(Malbim).*

[The double form of the verb indicates continuous action: מוֹת תָּמוּת, *you will die many times.* The arousal of lust, jealousy and all the other base instincts cause man to die in ceaseless stages.]

According to *Midrash* the double form of the verb מוֹת תָּמוּת [lit. *die, you shall die'*] is, as usual, understood as an extension:

1. They asked Adam: 'Who brought death upon you?' 'I brought it upon myself,' he replied. — 'I am like the sick man whom the physician warned: "You may eat such and such a thing, but not such and such a thing which will be deathly dangerous to you." But the sick man ate and when he was about to die, people asked him, "Was it perhaps the physician who is causing you to die?" He replied: "I have caused my own death. Had I heeded the physician's instructions I would not be dying."

not eat thereof; for on the day you eat of it, you shall surely die.'

[18] *HASHEM God said, 'It is not good that man be*

This intimates death for Adam, death for Eve, and death for their descendants *(Midrash).*

Ibn Ezra [to 3:8] cites Rav Yonah who suggests the following in explaining the use of *'the day'*:

— *'The day'* means *'a day of God'* i.e. one thousand years as in *Psalms* (90:4) during which time (930 years) he died *(Midrash);*

— He was born on a Friday and died on a Friday;

— On that day you will become guilty of death;

— *'Death'* is sometimes synonymous with 'punishment' as in (*II Sam.* 12:5);

Ibn Ezra concludes that the interpretation most plausible to him is that Adam was really guilty of death on that very day but that he repented and God tempered the severity of His judgment.

R' Meyuchas comments that in any event בְּיוֹם, does not necessarily mean in that *day*, but has the idiomatic meaning of *'when'; 'in the time.'* [Cf. *comm.* to 2:4 s.v. בְּיוֹם.]

18. The Creation of Woman.

לֹא טוֹב הֱיוֹת הָאָדָם לְבַדּוֹ — *It is not good that* [*the*] *man be alone.*

So that it should not be said that there are two Deities [governing the universe]: The Holy One blessed be He is alone in the upper worlds without a mate, and man is alone in the nether world without a mate *(Pirkei d'Rabbi Eliezer; Rashi).*

[Thus to maintain the equilibrium of creation man could not remain alone; he would have begun considering himself a god].

Rashi bases his comm. on the implication of the wording. It does not say *'It is not good for man to be alone'* but *'It is not good that man should be alone.'* The stress is on his 'aloneness', suggesting that uniqueness is in itself deleterious *(Ibn Crecas).*

Ramban explains לֹא טוֹב, *it is not good:* i.e. it cannot be said of man *'it is good'* in his present state when it is impossible for him to maintain his existence in this manner, for God has ordained that man have a mate and companion. [For as *Ramban* explains on 1:10, כִּי טוֹב, *that it was 'good'*, means that 'existence was thus permanently established in the form desired by Him.'] Hence, *good* was not said of man until woman was created.

The *Midrash* perceives the human factor in this need:

One who has no wife dwells without good, help, joy, blessing, and atonement. 'Without good' as it is written: *'it is not good that man should dwell alone'* ... He is also incomplete ... and He even impairs the Divine likeness ... *(Midrash;* cf. *Yevamos* 62b)

So when Adam was asked: 'Was it not the Holy One, blessed be He, who caused you to die?' He replied: 'No I myself am the cause of my death, for it was said to me, *Of every tree of the garden you may eat* — i.e. from every tree which is good for you; *but of the tree of the knowledge of good and evil* — which is deathly dangerous to you — *you shall not eat thereof.* And because I trespassed against His injunction and ate, I caused my own death' *(Midrash Tehillim* 92:14).

ב יט אֶעֱשֶׂה־לּוֹ עֵזֶר כְּנֶגְדּוֹ׃ וַיִּצֶר יהוה אֱלֹהִים
יט מִן־הָאֲדָמָה כָּל־חַיַּת הַשָּׂדֶה וְאֵת כָּל־
עוֹף הַשָּׁמַיִם וַיָּבֵא אֶל־הָאָדָם לִרְאוֹת
מַה־יִּקְרָא־לוֹ וְכֹל אֲשֶׁר יִקְרָא־לוֹ הָאָדָם

Harav Gifter (in his Foreword to the ArtScroll edition of *Shir HaShirim)* notes that love and devotion to another human being is an essential forerunner to love and devotion to God. In this sense the Torah says, *It is not good for man to be alone.*

Sforno interprets the spiritual need of a partner for man:

The goal implicit in his likeness and image would not be realized if man would have to devote himself, all on his own, to supplying his daily needs.

'Alone' does not imply that man would have been unable to propagate, for, as noted in 1:27, man was created with two 'faces' — i.e. endowed with both the male and female characteristic, so that as a single being he could have conceived and given birth. Rather God then declared that it would be good that the עֵזֶר, *'help'*, separate from him and be כְּנֶגְדּוֹ, *facing him,* and hence be more functional *(Ramban; Vilna Gaon).*

'It is not good' — neither for man or for the world *(Sefer Haparshios).*

אֶעֱשֶׂה־לּוֹ עֵזֶר כְּנֶגְדּוֹ — *I will make him a helper corresponding to him* [lit. *'a helper as in front of him'*; or *'a helper against him' (Ibn Janach).*]

[Lit.] *'A helper against him':* If man is worthy, the woman will be *'a helper'*; if he proves to be unworthy she shall be *against him' (Yevamos* 63a; *Rashi).*

Maharal elaborates: Man and woman represent two opposites, who if they are worthy merge into a unified whole ... but when they are not worthy the very fact that they are opposites causes her to be 'against him'.

[A wife is neither man's shadow nor his servant, but his other self, a 'helper' in a dimension beyond the capability of any other creature.]

19. וַיִּצֶר ה׳ אֱלֹקִים מִן הָאֲדָמָה — *Now, HASHEM God had formed out of the ground.* This verse does not describe a new creation. *Rashi* notes that the formation spoken of here elaborates upon the making of the animals already referred to in 1:25. Our verse repeats it, however, in order to indicate that the fowl were created from the alluvial mud since this verse says they were created from the *earth* while verse 1:20 associates them with the *water.* [See comm. there, s.v. וְעוֹף יְעוֹפֵף] The verse also implies that the animals were taken to man for naming on the same day they were created [when Adam was but one hour old] *(Midrash).*

Following the *Midrash* [cited also by *Rashi*] which relates וַיִּצֶר to צרר, subjugation, *Hirsch* renders the phrase *'God "drove" all the animals ... to man.'* He notes that this rendering seems confirmed by the fact that only the wild animals and birds — which require driving and forcing — are mentioned here. בְּהֵמָה, *cattle,* which naturally are domesticated and submissive to

II alone; I will make him a helper corresponding to
19 him.' [19] Now, HASHEM God had formed out of the
ground every beast of the field and every bird of the
sky, and brought them to the man to see what he
would call each one; and whatever man called each

man, would not have to be *driven* to man, and are, therefore, not mentioned until verse 20.

מִן הָאֲדָמָה . . . וְאֵת כָּל עוֹף בַּשָּׁמַיִם — *out of the ground...and every bird of the sky* [see *Rashi*, above, and cf. *comm.* 1:20.]

The fowl are described as having been formed from the earth, but when their formation was detailed originally [in 1:20], they were described as having been formed from the water. In reality both are true as they were formed from the water near the shore, as the Sages commented [*Chullin* 27b]: they were formed from the alluvial mud. Or, 'ground' is mentioned here, for after their creation from the sea they were placed on earth which was to be their domicile *(Radak).*

וַיָּבֵא אֶל הָאָדָם לִרְאוֹת מַה יִּקְרָא לוֹ—*And brought [them] to [the] man to see what he would call each of them.*

[God brought the animals to man for a double purpose: to have man name the animals and thus establish his lordship over them; and to satisfy man that he could not hope to find from among them a suitable companion — to serve the dual function of helping him physically and spiritually, and at the same time be his intellectual equal (cf. *Sforno).* It is probably for this reason that fish (aside from the fact that they dwell in the water — *Chizkuni)* are not mentioned here: they could not possibly be expected to fulfill the role of man's companion.][1]

Additionally, the folly of man's response to God after eating the fruit of the tree of knowledge wherein he put the blame for his sin on *'the woman whom You gave to be with me'* [3:12] is even more profound in the light of man's anxiety in seeking a mate. [See *Midrash* cited end of next verse.]

לִרְאוֹת, *to see,* does not imply that God was curious to see whether man would identify them correctly. Read together with that which follows, the phrase rather means: to observe, and establish that whatever names man would use would be their designations *(HaRechasim leBik'ah).*

[The word לוֹ, (lit. *'to him'* or *'it'*) is in singular but implies the entire spectrum of creatures: *'each one of them'* as in our translation.

1. The question arises: Why did God put Adam through this series of tasks? Why was man not originally created with a separate female counterpart as were the other creatures?

Harav David Feinstein cites the *Talmud (Kesubos* 8a): 'At first the intention was to create two, but ultimately only one was created.' He explains that the *Talmud* does not imply that God 'changed His mind' but that the preamble *'it is not good that man should be alone'* and man's quest for a companion and helper from among the animals — although this quest was obviously known by God in advance to be abortive — was designed to stress the sacred and precious nature of this partnership.

God willed that man should experience life without a woman for a brief time before her creation so that her arrival would be precious to him.

ב °שלישי כ נֶפֶשׁ חַיָּה הוּא שְׁמוֹ: °וַיִּקְרָא הָאָדָם שֵׁמוֹת
כ לְכָל־הַבְּהֵמָה וּלְעוֹף הַשָּׁמַיִם וּלְכֹל חַיַּת
הַשָּׂדֶה וּלְאָדָם לֹא־מָצָא עֵזֶר כְּנֶגְדּוֹ:

[God as Master of the universe proclaimed His sovereignty: He named the light, the darkness, the heavens and earth. But it is man, in his God-given role as governor of the earth [1:28], who is called upon to name his subjects — the animal world.]

וְכֹל אֲשֶׁר יִקְרָא לוֹ הָאָדָם נֶפֶשׁ חַיָּה הוּא שְׁמוֹ — *And whatever man called each living creature, that remained its name [forever.]*

The translation of the verse [which literally reads: *'and all that man will call to it* נֶפֶשׁ חַיָּה, *a living creature that is its name'*] is based upon *Rashi* who thus rearranges the verse in his interpretation, for the sake of clarity, and upon *Ibn Ezra's* suggestion that a ל, *to*, is implied preceding the words נֶפֶשׁ חַיָּה, rendering: *Whatever man shall call [to] every living creature . . .*

Ramban suggests that נֶפֶשׁ חַיָּה here refers to man [cf. verse 7], and that God brought before him all species of creatures so that 'every species among them that man would name, indicating that he regarded it as a נֶפֶשׁ חַיָּה, *living creature*, like himself, would retain the name permanently and become his helper.'

The *Vilna Gaon* explains that *'everything that man designated with a name by perceiving it as* נֶפֶשׁ חַיָּה, *living soul* [i.e., via its innermost characteristics rather than external appearance] — that *remained it's designation . . .*

According to *HaRechasim leBik'ah* the verse should be rendered: 'every name that man, the *living soul par excellence,* shall call it, that shall be its name forever.

It is this latter interpretation that is expounded upon by *Hirsch:*

Man assigns names subjectively as a נֶפֶשׁ, an individual, חַיָּה who, because he is himself alive, forms impression of the things about him, and according to whether and to what extent he accepts or rejects them, ranks and labels them in appropriate categories. אֲשֶׁר יִקְרָא לוֹ הָאָדָם stresses the subjectivity: *how man calls things for* לוֹ, *himself* [i.e. he regards them in relation to himself] for it is only God who sees things as they really are. Nevertheless the very fact that God led His creatures to man for naming and for consideration as a suitable companion, assures us that man's impressions — however subjective — are not deceptive.

20. וַיִּקְרָא הָאָדָם שֵׁמוֹת — *And the man assigned* [lit. *'called'*] *names* — i.e. *'the* man' — endowed by God with a superior intellect — perceived the nature of each creature and named it accordingly *(Radak).*

And as *Ramban* comments: God brought the creatures before him in pairs so that he should name also the females, the males of certain species are called by one name, such as שׁוֹר, *bull;* תַּיִשׁ, *he-goat;* כֶּבֶשׂ *ram;* while their female counterparts are called by another name such as פָּרָה, *cow;* תְּיָשָׁה, *she-goat;* כִּבְשָׂה, *ewe,* etc.

Furthermore, according to *Ramban,* this *'naming'* implied recog-

II
20

living creature, that remained its name. 20 *And the*
man assigned names to all the cattle and to the birds
of the sky and to every beast of the field; but as for
man, he did not find a helper corresponding to him.

nizing their nature and separating them by species, clarifying which are fit to mate with one another. As the verse continues, among them all he did not find a natural companion for himself.

'... God said to man: 'And what is your name?' — 'It is fitting that I be called Adam because I was created from the ground [''Adamah''.] ...' *(Midrash).*

לְכָל הַבְּהֵמָה — *To all the cattle.*

The cattle are not mentioned in the previous verse among the animals 'brought' to man. The domestic animals were either already with him or came of their own volition *(Chizkuni; R'Meyuchas).*

וּלְאָדָם לֹא מָצָא עֵזֶר כְּנֶגְדּוֹ — *But, as for man,* [lit. *'and for man'*] *he did not find a helper corresponding to him.*

Most commentators [e.g. *Ibn Ezra; Radak*] hold that אָדָם, *man,* takes the place of the reflexive pronoun לוֹ *'himself'*, and render *'but for himself he did not find a helper corresponding to him'*

[*Compare similar usage in I Sam.* 12:11: *And Jephtah and Samuel* (where Samuel is the speaker and *'Samuel'* takes the place of the reflexive pronoun *'myself'*).]

According to *Ramban,* however, the verse is to be explained: *But for the name* אָדָם, *man, he found no helpmate suited to correspond to himself.** ... It was thus God's will that man not be given a wife until he came to the realization that he had had no suitable mate among the living creatures and he would therefore crave for fitting companionship as befitting as she.

* As *Hirsch* expresses it: 'But for an *'Adam'*, a vice-regent of God on earth, he found none that would be parallel to himself, none that could share his obligation with him.

Man, indeed, found animals which would be helpful and serviceable to him. They could qualify as עֵזֶר, *help.* What he could not find among all the creatures that passed before him was כְּנֶגְדּוֹ, one that would *correspond to him* on an equal social and intellectual level *(Chizkuni; Ibn Latif).*

God then paraded all the creatures before Adam in pairs of every kind, male and female. Adam said: Every one of these has a mate except for me! (And why did God not create her for him at the beginning? — Because God foresaw that he will complain against her and she was therefore not given him until he expressly asked God for her) [see also *Mishnah Sanhedrin* 4:5 cited in end of *comm.* to 1:26 for other reason that Adam was created alone.]

... But as soon as man demanded her, then immediately: *HASHEM God caused a deep sleep to descend on man (Midrash; Rashi)*[1]

1. When the earth heard what God resolved to do it began to tremble and quake. 'I do not have the strength', it said, 'to provide food for the herd of Adam's descendants.'

But God pacified it by saying, 'I and you together, will find food for the herd'. Accordingly time was divided between God and earth. God took the night and earth took the day.

Refreshing sleep nourishes and strengthens man, it gives him life and rest, while the earth

כא וַיַּפֵּל יהוה אֱלֹהִים | תַּרְדֵּמָה עַל־הָאָדָם
וַיִּישָׁן וַיִּקַּח אַחַת מִצַּלְעֹתָיו וַיִּסְגֹּר בָּשָׂר
כב תַּחְתֶּנָּה: וַיִּבֶן יהוה אֱלֹהִים | אֶת־הַצֵּלָע
אֲשֶׁר־לָקַח מִן־הָאָדָם לְאִשָּׁה וַיְבִאֶהָ אֶל־
כג הָאָדָם: וַיֹּאמֶר הָאָדָם זֹאת הַפַּעַם עֶצֶם

21. תַּרְדֵּמָה — *A deep sleep.*

תַּרְדֵּמָה signifies a deeper sleep than שֵׁינָה, [sleep,] which, in turn, is deeper than תְּנוּמָה, [*slumber*]. God cast this deep sleep upon him to spare him the pain of the removal of his side. For although God could have spared him this pain while conscious, know that God never performs a miracle unnecessarily ... *(Radak).*

וַיִּישָׁן — *And he slept.* To spare him the sight of seeing the piece of flesh from which she was formed so she would not become repulsive to him *(Sanhedrin* 39a; *Rashi).*

Additionally, He spared him the discomforting sight of witnessing the creation of woman wallowing in blood ... and at the same time man would benefit from the sudden joy of awakening to discover this treasure God had granted him ... *(Abarbanel).*

וַיִּקַּח אַחַת מִצַּלְעֹתָיו — *And He took one of his sides.* Although the word is commonly rendered as *one of his 'ribs'*, the commentators are nearly unanimous in translating צַלְעֹתָיו as *one of his sides.* Cf. *Exodus* 26:20 וּלְצֶלַע הַמִּשְׁכָּן הַשֵּׁנִית, 'and for the second *side* of the Tabernacle.' As *Hirsch* observes the word צֶלַע never appears elsewhere in Scriptures as a 'rib' but always as a 'side'.

Targum Yonason, however, paraphrases: '... *and He took one of his ribs, it was the thirteenth rib on the right side and closed it up with flesh.*'

This interpretation is based on a controversy in the *Midrash,* according to which Rav Shmuel bar Nachman is of the opinion that the woman was taken from his side, while Shmuel maintains that it was a rib.

'It seems obvious to me that when man was created he had an additional "side" not vital for the functioning of his own body *(Abarbanel).*

וַיִּסְגֹּר בָּשָׂר תַּחְתֶּנָּה — *And He filled in* [lit. *closed*] *flesh in its place* [following *Onkelos.*]

I.e. He filled up the amputated area with flesh so it would not be deficient *(R' Meyuchas).*

22. וַיִּבֶן ... אֶת־הַצֵּלָע ... לְאִשָּׁה — *Then HASHEM God fashioned* [lit. built up] *the side which He had taken from the man into a woman.*

Built up — i.e. He took the flesh and bone from man and built it up forming a new creature, אִשָּׁה, a creature having the same general appearance and qualities as אִישׁ, *man,* differing from him only in sex *(Radak; Abarbanel; Sforno).*

Unlike man, the material for woman's body was not taken from the earth. God built one side of man into woman — so that the single human being now became two.

brings forth produce with the help of God who waters it. Yet man must work the earth to earn his food *(Pirkei d'Rabbi Eliezer* 12; *Midrash HaGadol).*

21 So HASHEM God cast a deep sleep upon the man
and he slept; and He took one of his sides and He
filled in flesh in its place. 22 Then HASHEM God
fashioned the side that He had taken from the man
into a woman, and He brought her to the man. 23 And
the man said, 'This time it is bone of my bones and

Thereby, the complete equality of man and woman was irrefutably demonstrated *(Hirsch).*

לְאִשָּׁה — *Into a woman.* i.e. into the female species called 'woman' which would be a companion to the male *(R' Meyuchas).*

[*The Talmud* perceives in the word וַיִּבֶן *and he built,* a similarity to בִּינָה, *understanding,* and renders: *And God endowed with more understanding the side which He took from the man for woman*]:

'The vows of a girl are binding at the age of twelve [while a boy's vows are not binding until the age of thirteen] ... because it is written וַיִּבֶן, which means that God endowed woman with more בִּינָה, understanding [which also develops at an earlier age] than man *(Niddah* 45b).

[Additionally, וַיִּבֶן is homiletically related to הִתְבּוֹנֵן, *consider well*]:

וַיִּבֶן is written, signifying that He considered well from what part to create her. God said: 'I will not create her from man's head, lest she be swell-headed [or: lightheaded; frivolous]; nor from the eye, lest she be a coquette; nor from the ear lest she be an eavesdropper; nor from the mouth lest she be a gossip; nor from the heart, lest she be prone to jealousy; nor from the hand, lest she be light-fingered [i.e. thievish]; nor from the foot lest she be a gadabout; but from the modest part of man [taking צֵלָע as *rib*], for even when he stands unclothed, that part is covered.'

And when God created each limb He ordered her: Be a modest woman!' *(Midrash).*

The Sages in the *Midrash* ascribe all the special characteristics of woman — her delicate voice, character and temperament, as being derived from this formation of woman from the already feeling, sensitive body of man; in contrast to man himself who was created from the dead, unfeeling earth.

וַיְבִאֶהָ אֶל הָאָדָם — *And He brought her to the man.* i.e. God Himself brought her *(R' Meyuchas)* ...

... Suddenly, so that man would experience the profound joy of receiving an unexpected gift *(Minchah Belulah).*

The use of the phrase 'and He *brought* her' [which would imply from a distance, while in reality she was formed from his side] is explained by *Ibn Ezra* as being Adam's reaction upon awakening and seeing this woman. He surmised that, like the other creatures, she was brought to him from elsewhere. It was only when he gazed upon her and realized that part of his body was missing, that he was moved to declare *'bone of my bones and flesh of my flesh!' (Cf. Chizkuni).*

[Perhaps, then, וַיְבִאֶהָ should be understood as *'and He presented her.'*]

The *Midrash* relates that God brought her to Adam amidst great fanfare. 'God made a canopy for her of the most precious stones and he Himself led her to Adam ... Happy is the man who is privileged to see his mate taken by the King and led to his home *(Tanchuma Yashan Vayera).*

23. זֹאת הַפַּעַם — *This time,* [lit. *'this, the time'*]

I.e. finally, after having unsuccessfully sought a mate from among every creature ... *(Rashi;* as explained by *Lekach Tov; Toledos Yitzchak* and *Vilna Gaon).*

ב מֵעֲצָמַ֔י וּבָשָׂ֖ר מִבְּשָׂרִ֑י לְזֹאת֙ יִקָּרֵ֣א אִשָּׁ֔ה
כד כִּ֥י מֵאִ֖ישׁ לֻֽקֳחָה־זֹּֽאת: כד עַל־כֵּן֙ יַֽעֲזָב־אִ֔ישׁ
אֶת־אָבִ֖יו וְאֶת־אִמּ֑וֹ וְדָבַ֣ק בְּאִשְׁתּ֔וֹ וְהָי֖וּ

— This time I have found the help for me which I did not find till now, for she is *'bone of my bones and flesh of my flesh' (Ramban).*

Or, according to *Targum Yonasan:* 'This time and not again, is woman 'created from man'.

I.e. *'this time'* only will woman come forth from man. From now on the contrary will be true: Man will come forth from woman! *(Rashbam).*

[The above translation *'this time'* which renders זֹאת, *this,* as an adjective modifying הַפַּעַם, *the time,* follows *Targum, Rav Saadiah Gaon, Ramban,* the implication of *Rashi*'s comm., and *Ibn Caspi.*]

[Others, however, perceiving that הַפַּעַם in itself means: *'this time', 'now', 'finally', 'at last',* explain that זֹאת refers to the woman. Therefore, according to them renders: *'This* [i.e. the woman], *at last',* or: *'this, is now'*]:

'None of these creatures which were previously brought to me were suitable. *This one* [i.e. the woman] *which was brought to me now* is truly *bone of my bones.* Now I have found what I sought *(R' Meyuchas).*

It means *'At last this is the goal!* Or: *'this at last is bone of my bones* etc.' The word הַפַּעַם expresses attainment of what has hitherto been striven after in vain *(Hirsch).*

עֶצֶם מֵעֲצָמַי וּבָשָׂר מִבְּשָׂרִי — [It is] *bone of my bones and flesh of my flesh.* I.e. '... She is as dear to me as my own body.' (The phrase is to be understood like the phrase [29:14]: אַךְ עַצְמִי וּבְשָׂרִי אַתָּה, *'you are truly my bone and flesh') (Rechasim leBik'ah)* [cf. also *Judges* 9:2; *I Chron.* 11:1.]

לְזֹאת יִקָּרֵא אִשָּׁה — [*To*] *this shall be called Woman* — i.e. 'this one is fit to be called Woman *(Targum Yonasan).*[1]

He was not referring to her specifically: every female would be designated by the term 'Woman'; her proper name was Chavah *(Radak).*

Ramban explains: *'she is bone of my bones and flesh of my flesh* and therefore, all the creatures to whom I have given names she is worthy of being called by the same name as mine.'

כִּי מֵאִישׁ לֻקֳחָה־זֹּאת — *For from man she was taken.*

[The stress is on the assonance of the Hebrew words *Ish,* man, and *Ishah,* woman.]

The *Midrash* derives from the fact that since only in Hebrew 'man' and 'woman' are phonetically similar, this proves that the language used at the time of creation was the Holy Tongue [Hebrew] *(Rashi).*

24. *Rashi* explains that the following is not a continuation of Adam's words, but a kind of bracketed statement interjected by God, carrying with it a prohibition of incest to the 'children of Noah' [i.e. the nations of the world. Cf. verse 16]:

1. The word אִישׁ, man, contains the letter *yud,* and the word אִשָּׁה contains the letter *he.* These two letters יָהּ, a name of God, indicate that as long as man and woman form a partnership in the service of God, He will protect them. If God is removed from their lives, however, the remaining letters of each name are אֵשׁ, *fire, destruction,* indicating that they would be consumed *(Pirkei d'Rabbi Eliezer).*

II
24

flesh of my flesh. This shall be called Woman, for
from man was she taken.' — 24 *Therefore a man shall*
leave his father and his mother and cling to his wife,
and they shall become one flesh. —

עַל כֵּן יַעֲזָב אִישׁ אֶת אָבִיו וְאֶת אִמּוֹ — *Therefore a man shall leave his father and his mother.*

'Therefore' — i.e., because woman is part of man's own bones and flesh, *therefore* he should leave his father and mother ... *(Mizrachi).*

'Therefore' — As long as man was alone his condition was not 'good' [v. 18], and once the division between man and woman had been made, it was no longer possible for man to find fulfillment alone. Without his wife, his עֵזֶר כְּנֶגְדּוֹ *helper corresponding to him,* he was only half a man. He can achieve wholeness only with her ... *(Hirsch).*

The verse is not to be construed to imply that man should not serve or honor his parents to his fullest capacity. It implies only a *physical* separation; that man's attachment to his wife should be so strong that he should move out of his parents' house and establish a new home with his wife *(Radak; R' Meyuchas).*

... As the *Midrash* observes:

'Until a man marries, his love centers on his parents; when he marries, his love is bestowed upon his wife, as it said: *therefore shall a man leave his mother and father and cling to his wife' (Pirkei d'Rabbi Eliezer* 34).

וְדָבַק בְּאִשְׁתּוֹ — *And cling to his wife.*

And cling — but not to a male [i.e., a prohibition against pederasty; for it is natural only for the opposite sexes to cling to each other];

To his wife — but not to his neighbor's wife [a prohibition against adultery] *(Sanhedrin* 58a; cf. *Rambam Hil. Melachim* 9:5).

According to the *Vilna Gaon,* however, the phrase *'and cling to his wife'* refers to a husband's responsibility to support his wife. His economic responsibilities to his parents must be deferred in favor of the needs of his wife.

Man is not unique among living beings in having a sexual life. But other creatures require mating only for the purpose of breeding; because male and female were created simultaneously, they can function independent of one another. Man is different: woman was created from man to show that only in partnership do the two form a complete human being *(Hirsch).*

וְהָיוּ לְבָשָׂר אֶחָד — *And they* [or: *'so that they'*] *shall become one flesh.*

Ibn Ezra renders: 'and let them comport themselves with one another as if they were one entity'; or, perceiving וְהָיוּ in the past tense, *and they were,* render: 'and let them once again be as Adam and Eve originally were: of one body.'

As the *Tur* comments: Let him be worthy of clinging to his wife and to none other because man and his wife are in reality one flesh as they were at the beginning of Creation.

... But that can only take place if at the same time they become one

ב כה
לְבָשָׂר אֶחָד׃ וַיִּהְיוּ שְׁנֵיהֶם עֲרוּמִּים כה
הָאָדָם וְאִשְׁתּוֹ וְלֹא יִתְבֹּשָׁשׁוּ׃ וְהַנָּחָשׁ א
הָיָה עָרוּם מִכֹּל חַיַּת הַשָּׂדֶה אֲשֶׁר עָשָׂה
ג א

mind, one heart, one soul ... and if they subordinate all their strength and efforts to the service of a Higher Will *(Hirsch)*.

For a man should seek to marry a woman harmoniously suited to him, so that together they form *one flesh* — a perfect whole *(Sforno)*. Because both parents are united in the child, their flesh is thus united into one *(Rashi)*.

... This excludes cattle, beasts of chase, and fowl, because man and any of these cannot become *one flesh (Rambam, Hil. Melachim* 9:5; *Sanhedrin* 58a; *Mizrachi)*.

Following the *Vilna Gaon* [see above] becoming *'one flesh'* refers to the familial ties, as in the verse [37:27] *'he is our brother, our own flesh.'* For the consanguineous restrictions apply to the relatives of one's wife as to his own.

וַיִּהיוּ שְׁנֵיהֶם עֲרוּמִּים — [*And*] *they were both naked.* Standing before one another as innocently as animals *(Lekach Tov)*.

וְלֹא יִתְבֹּשָׁשׁוּ — *And* [*they*] *were not ashamed.* For they did not yet have a concept of modesty [i.e. they had no need for 'modesty' since the Evil Inclination was not yet active *(Tzeidah LaDerech)*] to distinguish between good and bad. Although Adam had been endowed with the knowledge to name the creatures [verse 19], the יֵצֶר הָרַע, Evil Inclination, was not activated within him until he had eaten from the tree *(Rashi)*.

Sforno comments: 'All their acts and organs were exclusively in the service of their Maker [for the propagation of the species *(Malbim)*] and not at all for the satisfaction of desire. Consequently, the act of cohabitation was to them as innocent as eating or drinking, and they regarded the reproductive organs as we regard the mouth, face and hands' [Also *Ramban* to verse 9.][1]

[יִתְבֹּשָׁשׁוּ is lit. in the future tense *would be ashamed.* Rendered in the past tense, it designates a continuous state indicating that *there was not even a spark of shame within them,* nor would there have been had they not sinned. (Cf. translation of יַעֲלֶה, *ascended,* in *v.*6, p. 90). It was only *after* they ate of the Tree of Knowledge (see later, chapter 3), that they became aware that these acts could be directed toward evil ends and lust, that shame *was aroused in them.*]

III

1. The Serpent.

Rashi notes that the continuity of the verses — the nakedness of the man and his wife followed by the story of the serpent — indicates that the serpent's seductive counsel was due to its lustful desire for Eve which was aroused when he saw them engaged, unashamed and un-

1. *Harav Gifter* in *Pirkei Torah II* cites the above *Sforno* and comments: Man's awareness that his reproductive organs could become the tools of lust and sin aroused within him a sense of shame. It was only then that he felt the need to wear clothing. Thus, modesty is the product of an awareness of sin and an attempt to contain and control it. To the extent that he loses his recognition of the gravity of sin, he becomes immodest. This accounts for the decline in modesty that accompanies the relaxation of moral codes.

II
25

III
1

[25] *They were both naked, the man and his wife,*
and they were not ashamed.

[1] *Now the serpent was cunning beyond any beast*

concealed, in their native function *(Midrash).* [V. *Mizrachi; Gur Aryeh;* and *Sifsei Chachamim.*] [1]

וְהַנָּחָשׁ הָיָה עָרוּם מִכֹּל חַיַּת הַשָּׂדֶה — *Now the serpent was cunning beyond any beast of the field* — except for Man *(Ibn Ezra).*

No mention is made in the Torah of how much time elapsed between the creation of woman and their placement into the Garden of Eden and their sin and expulsion. The Sages, however, tell us explicitly *(Yalkut, Tehillim* 49; *Midrash; Pirkei d'Rabbi Eliezer* 11) that *all the events related here* — including the birth of Cain and Abel [*Tosaf. Sanhedrin* 38b excludes Abel; see *Maharsha ad. loc.*] *occurred on the very first day of Adam's creation.* [2]

Hoffman states that it was not planned that man should live his entire life under the restriction of only one prohibition. Man had to be tested to determine whether he had the moral strength to withstand the temptation of transgressing God's single command. This temptation came to him in the guise of the serpent — *'the most cunning of all the beasts of the field.'* The Torah does not specifically guide us as to the exact nature of the serpent. The narrative relates the incident simply as it appeared to man, without detailing the underlying factors. [See *Ha'amek Davar,* below.]

According to *Zohar Chadash:*

Rav Yitzchak said: The serpent is the יֵצֶר הָרָע, Evil Tempter; *Rav Yehudah* said it means literally a serpent. They consulted *Rav Shimon* who told them: Both these views are identical. It was Samael [the accuser; Angel of Death] who appeared as a serpent, for in this form the serpent is indeed the Satan ... For it is because the serpent was in reality the Angel of Death that it brought death into the world.

[As *Ha'amek Davar* notes citing *Ramban* (who is conspicuously silent in these verses): in matters that are beyond human understanding, the Torah alludes rather

1. *N'tziv* cites this interpretation and expresses wonder at how one species could be lustful for another [cf. *Bava Metzia* 91a]. Also, the serpent was not lacking a mate of its own! As to the fact that man and woman indulged in the open, the serpent, too, knew no shame! *Nitziv* explains that in viewing the man and woman together he perceived that their relationship was unique. The serpent realized that, unlike other beings whose mating is instinctive and only in times of arousal, human couples have a relationship that transcends the physical, a closeness that is born of their creation one from another and that surpasses even that of brother and sister. It was this that the serpent envied.

2. The day [on which Man was created] consisted of twelve hours: In the first hour Adam's dust was gathered; in the second it was kneaded into a shapeless Man; in the third his limbs were shaped; in the fourth, a soul was infused into him; in the fifth, he arose and stood on his feet; in the sixth he named the animals; in the seventh Eve became his mate; in the eighth they procreated — 'ascending as two and descending as four' — [i.e. Cain and his twin sister were born, for Abel and his twin sisters were born *after* they sinned. *v. Tosafos; Maharsha;* also *v. Yevamos* 62a]; in the ninth, he was commanded not to eat of the tree; in the tenth he sinned; in the eleventh he was judged; and in the twelfth he was expelled [from Eden] and departed *(Sanhedrin* 38b).

ג יְהוָה אֱלֹהִים וַיֹּאמֶר אֶל־הָאִשָּׁה אַף כִּי־
א אָמַר אֱלֹהִים לֹא תֹאכְלוּ מִכֹּל עֵץ הַגָּן׃

than specifies. Therefore the narrative of the serpent was left vague.]

Sforno, too, is of the opinion that the serpent represents the Satan, the Evil Inclination. The Satan is called a serpent figuratively just as a king is called 'lion' or enemies are called 'snakes' and 'demons'. The term serpent is used because it is an animal with limited utility but enormous potential to do harm.

[The consensus of the Commentators, however, is that the serpent is to be interpreted literally. Their differences seem to lie in what the snake *embodied* and by what force he was harnessed: the Evil Inclination; the Satan; or some other counterforce represented by the most cunning of the beasts of the field, who according to the *Midrash*, stood erect and was endowed with some facility of communication before he was cursed.]

[For the broader *Hashkafa* (philosophical perspective) interpretations of the serpent, see *Overview*.]

מִכֹּל חַיַּת הַשָּׂדֶה — *Beyond any beast of the field.*

Rashi notes that commensurate with the serpent's cunning and greatness was his ultimate downfall. *'More cunning than all the beasts'* = *'more cursed than all the beasts'* [v. 14.] *(Midrash).*

וַיֹּאמֶר אֶל הָאִשָּׁה — *And he said to the woman.*

[The commentators differ on whether there was literally a communication — either by the serpent or an angel acting through him — through spoken words or some other manner intelligible to Adam and Eve, the 'products of God's hands'; or whether this is to be understood allegorically]:

***Ibn Ezra* interprets the verse literally: The serpent actually spoke. Before he was cursed he also stood erect, and God Who gives wisdom to man, gave it to the serpent, too. For, if it was not the serpent itself that spoke but an angel, why was the serpent punished?**

Radak is of the opinion that the serpent was miraculously given the power of speech in order to test the woman ...

As *Chizkuni* explains, God opened the mouth of the serpent just as He opened the mouth of Balaam's ass.

According to *Abarbanel*, the serpent did not actually *speak* 'for the serpent is not a creature of speech.' He notes that the Torah does not say *'God opened the mouth of the snake'* as it does of Balaam's ass. The explanation, rather, is that the snake *spoke* by his actions. By continually crawling up the tree and eating its fruit — he demonstrated that no harm came to him — and Eve deduced from this, as if he were actually speaking to her, and saying: **'See, *you will not die.'*** It is in the manner of the verse in *Job* 35:11: *'Who teaches us by the beasts of the earth.'*

However, as *Hoffmann* suggests, it is not farfetched to assume that the original serpent communicated in a manner that was understood by Adam and Eve who were close to life in its natural state, but that the

III
1

of the field that HASHEM God had made. He said to the woman, 'Did, perhaps God say: You shall not eat of any tree of the garden?'' '

Torah garbs these communicated expressions in precise words intelligible to the reader. [It should be noted, too, that Solomon, wisest of men, was also able to understand the 'speech' of all creatures.]

The serpent approached the woman, rather than the man, because he reasoned that women are easier to beguile than man *(Midrash).*

אַף כִּי אָמַר אֱלֹהִים לֹא תֹאכְלוּ מִכֹּל עֵץ הַגָּן — *Did, perhaps, God say, 'You shall not eat of any tree of the garden'?*

— Although he saw them eating of the other fruits he struck up a general conversation with her so she should answer him and he would have the opportunity to focus on the subject of that particular tree *(Rashi).*

The serpent said: 'Is it possible that God forbade you to eat of any of the trees? Why has He created them if they are not to be enjoyed? *(Midrash HaGadol).*

[The translation of אַף כִּי follows *Rashi* who interprets the phrase as שֶׁמָּא, *perhaps,* although it is not clear whether *Rashi* interprets it as a question or a statement. Our translation of the phrase as a question follows the majority of early commentators — *Targum, Rav Saadiah Gaon; Ibn Janach; R' Meyuchas* — who so interpret it.] *Targum Yonasan* also renders it as a question: *'Is it true that HASHEM God said ...?'* — And even if God *did* say it, what of it?

Other commentators perceive this not as a question, but as the conclusion of a longer speech, the preceding part of which the Torah did not consider necessary to record. They surmise that the conversation went something like the following: 'God must hate you', said the serpent to the woman, for though He made you greater than the other creatures He really did not do you a favor ... אַף כִּי, *moreover because HASHEM God, prohibited to you all the trees of the garden.' (Radak)* [Cf. *Ibn Ezra* who also interprets this as the conclusion of a longer speech, but does not conjecture what that speech consisted of.]

Akeidas Yitzchak and *Sforno* explain אַף כִּי as meaning *'although'*, and explain that the serpent had intended to say: *"Even though God had said, 'You shall not eat of any of the trees in the garden lest you die'* — you will not die ..." But the woman interrupted him after he said the word 'garden' and corrected him [next verse]: *'We may eat of the fruit of the garden! It was only about the fruit of the tree in the middle of the garden that God had said ...'*

אֱלֹהִים — *God.* — The serpent did not utter God's Personal Name, *HASHEM,* [nor did the woman] because that Name was unknown to it *(Ibn Ezra).*

לֹא תֹאכְלוּ מִכֹּל עֵץ הַגָּן — *You shall not eat of any tree of the garden.*

The serpent, in his cunning, knew this was not the case. He purposely expanded the prohibition in order to incite her and engage her in open debate *(Akeidas Yitzchak;* cf. *Rashi* cited in beginning of verse).[1]

1. *Kli Yakar* (on 1:11) refers to the *Midrashic* interpretation that the earth 'disobeyed' God's command: it was ordered to produce trees with bark that tasted like their fruit. Instead, the earth produced inedible trees with tasty fruit. The serpent cunningly used that phenomenon to influence Eve. "Why were you commanded not to eat from an inedible *'tree'*, rather than from its fruit? Obviously because the original divine prohibition would have referred to the

ב וַתֹּאמֶר הָאִשָּׁה אֶל־הַנָּחָשׁ מִפְּרִי עֵץ־הַגָּן
ג נֹאכֵל: וּמִפְּרִי הָעֵץ אֲשֶׁר בְּתוֹךְ־הַגָּן אָמַר
אֱלֹהִים לֹא תֹאכְלוּ מִמֶּנּוּ וְלֹא תִגְּעוּ בּוֹ
ד פֶּן תְּמֻתוּן: וַיֹּאמֶר הַנָּחָשׁ אֶל־הָאִשָּׁה
ה לֹא־מוֹת תְּמֻתוּן: כִּי יֹדֵעַ אֱלֹהִים כִּי בְּיוֹם

2. מִפְּרִי עֵץ־הַגָּן נֹאכֵל — *Of the fruit of any tree of the garden we may eat.* [This translation follows *Rav Saadiah Gaon.* Lit. the Hebrew reads: *'of the fruit of the trees of the garden we (shall) eat'*]

3. וּמִפְּרִי הָעֵץ אֲשֶׁר בְּתוֹךְ־הַגָּן — *But* [lit. *'and'*] *of the fruit of the tree which is in the center of the garden.*

[I.e. *'It was only of the fruit of the tree which is in the center of the garden that God had said ...'*]

The woman did not describe it as a 'tree of knowledge of good and bad' because Adam probably never told her of the tree's special characteristic for he was apprehensive that if he told her she would crave to eat of it *(Ha'amek Davar).*

[According to *Midrash Tadshe* 7 and *Midrash Aggadah,* however, God never told Adam that it was a Tree of Knowledge — He simply called it 'the Tree in the midst of the Garden.' When Moses was told to write the Torah, he was given its name עַל שֵׁם סוֹפוֹ, according to the final result (cf. *Hirsch* to 2:9). And why did God prohibit this tree? So that whenever Adam would look upon it he would think of his Creator, recognize his responsibilities to Him, and not be haughty.]

אָמַר אֱלֹהִים . . . וְלֹא תִגְּעוּ בּוֹ — *God had said . . . nor touch it.* She added to the prohibition [which did not include touching] and as a result diminished from it *(Rashi).*

As the verse says [*Proverbs* 30:6]: *'Add not to His words lest He reprove you, and you be found a liar!' (Midrash).*

[*Rashi*'s interpretation here is based upon the *Talmud Sanhedrin* 29a which infers from this verse that כָּל הַמּוֹסִיף גּוֹרֵעַ, 'he who adds (to the word of God) subtracts (from it)', for as *Rashi* ad. loc. explains: 'God did not warn her against touching it, and as a result of her exaggeration it was diminished because the serpent pushed her into contact with the tree and told her, 'See, just as death did not ensue from the touch, so it will not follow from the eating of it!'

Rashi's interpretation that Eve was faulted for her exaggeration is followed by most commentators.

But if there was truly no prohibition against touching the tree, why was she deceived by the serpent's argument that the touch did not result in death?'

Torah Temimah discusses this and cites *Avos d'Rabbi Nosson I* according to which it was *Adam* who, when he related the injuction to Eve, added the prohibition of touching as an additional 'fence' around the prohibition.

However, the Rabbis also added 'fences' to safeguard the Torah and these are considered praiseworthy. Why does the *Talmud* cited above criticize this 'fence' as tantamount to a *subtraction* of God's word? — The commentators explain that this prohibition was not justifiable halachically, and moreover, as *Chizkuni* notes, the added prohibition against touching cannot be termed a סְיָג לַתּוֹרָה, *preventive fence guarding the Torah,* because she attributed it to God by saying אָמַר אֱלֹהִים . . . לֹא תִגְּעוּ בּוֹ, *'God' said . . . you shall not touch it.* (I.e. A Rabbinic ordinance must be clearly designated as such and never be endowed with the

trees themselves, had the earth followed God's command. Yet the earth was not punished for its disobedience! You, too, may ignore His command without fear of punishment.'' (See *Overview*).

III
2-5

[2] *The woman said to the serpent, 'Of the fruit of*
any tree of the garden we may eat. [3] *But of the fruit*
of the tree which is in the center of the garden God
had said: You shall neither eat of it nor touch it, lest
you die.'
[4] *The serpent said to the woman, 'You will not*
surely die; [5] *for God knows that on the day you eat*

character of a command embodied in the Written or Oral Law. Cf. *Rambam Hil. Mamrim* 2:9).]

As *Hirsch* comments: 'The Sages admonish us not to exaggerate and set the 'fence' too high lest it fall and destroy the plants it was erected to protect ... They warn us never to forget the origin and significance of these laws that are, in the final analysis, man-made expressions of Jewish conscientiousness, and not God-given laws ... If we forget this, and equate them with divine law, then transgressing them will make it easier to transgress God's law too.'

פֶּן תְּמֻתוּן — *Lest you die.*

Lest by virtue of touching this poisonous tree we will come to eat of it and die *(B'chor Shor; Radak).*

[That Adam and Eve thought that the tree was naturally poisonous rather than spiritually lethal, and that the prohibition was designed to safeguard them from the natural death which would follow partaking of it is shared also by *Malbim* and *N'tziv.*]

N'tziv notes that פֶּן תְּמֻתוּן, *lest you die,* implies that there is a possibility, but not a certitude of death. Adam told her this because he included a precaution against touching in his prohibition to her, an offense that could only lead to death through eating, but was not of itself punishable by death.

4. לֹא־מוֹת תְּמֻתוּן — *You will not surely die.*

— The serpent pushed her against the tree and said: 'Just as you did not die from touching it, so will you not die from eating it!' *(Midrash; Rashi)* [see *comm.* to previous verse.]

According to *Chizkuni:* 'You have already incurred the death penalty by merely touching the tree, so you may as well eat.'

'Fool! God did not prohibit this tree out of any great love for you! It is not poisonous or harmful to you and you won't die from it! He threatened you with death so you should exercise greater restraint regarding it, because He does not want you to attain more than He already alloted to you' *(B'chor Shor; Radak).*

— *You will not surely die!* The words פֶּן תְּמֻתוּן, *'lest* you die' imply that the Creator was *doubtful* as to what would ensue' (see *N'tziv* above). With this statement, the serpent introduced doubt into her mind. He convinced her that God threatened them with death merely to intimidate them so they would not eat thereof. This is typical of a tempter — he insinuates that the punishment threatened will never really come to pass *(Ha'amek Davar).*

5. כִּי יֹדֵעַ אֱלֹהִים — *For God knows.*

The reason He forbade it to you is not because it would cause your death but because He knows ... *(Sforno).*

ג אֲכָלְכֶם מִמֶּנּוּ וְנִפְקְחוּ עֵינֵיכֶם וִהְיִיתֶם
ו ו כֵּאלֹהִים יֹדְעֵי טוֹב וָרָע: וַתֵּרֶא הָאִשָּׁה כִּי
טוֹב הָעֵץ לְמַאֲכָל וְכִי תַאֲוָה־הוּא לָעֵינַיִם
וְנֶחְמָד הָעֵץ לְהַשְׂכִּיל וַתִּקַּח מִפִּרְיוֹ

וְנִפְקְחוּ עֵינֵיכֶם — [*And*] *your eyes will be opened,* i.e., you will become rationally aware and see whatever is around you in the proper perspective *(Midrash Aggadah).*

[See *comm.* to וַתִּפָּקַחְנָה on verse 7.]

As *Hirsch* comments: 'He has forbidden you to eat only to keep you in childish dependence of Himself. Eat, and your eyes will be opened! You will gain understanding, be able to know for yourselves what is good and what is bad. With this understanding you will become independent of God and thus, yourselves godlike. Even the smallest animal around you possesses the understanding of what is good and what is bad for itself.'

וִהְיִיתֶם כֵּאלֹהִים — *And you will be like God* — able to create worlds; and every artisan hates his fellow artisans *(Rashi).*

This follows the *Midrash:*

Rav Yehoshua of Siknin said in Rav Levi's name: The serpent began speaking slander of his Creator saying: He ate of this tree and created the world, He therefore ordered you not to eat thereof so you will not create other worlds, for every person hates his fellow craftsman.

[The translation of *Elohim* here as *'God'* follows the inference of *Rashi* and the *Midrash* cited above (see *Sforno* below).]

According to *Onkelos,*[1] *Yonasan, Rav Saadiah Gaon, Lekach Tov, Ibn Ezra, Radak,* and most others, however אֱלֹהִים, here is to be interpreted *'angels' — 'divine beings.'*

— God spared you nothing, but He does not want you to reach the level of the angels with the capability of distinguishing between good and bad' *(B'chor Shor).*

Those opinions follow Tractate *Soferim* 4:4 which had earlier formulated that the first *Elohim* in our verse is sacred [and refers to God] and that the second is secular [referring to angels or to rulers] and so subject to erasure if miswritten. [Also *Minchas Shay.*]

[See *Bamidbar Rabba* 10 which also states that *Elohim* appearing in this phrase is not holy.]

Therefore, perhaps a better translation which would convey the ambiguity of the phrase would be *'and you shall be godly . . .'*]

1. It is in the sense of 'ruler' that *Rambam* in *Moreh Nevuchim I*:2 interprets אֱלֹהִים:

'Every Hebrew knew that the term *Elohim* has many meanings. It denotes: God, angels, judges, and rulers of countries. *Onkelos* in his *Targum* rendered it in its true and correct manner by taking the words וִהְיִיתֶם כֵּאלֹהִים in the last-mentioned meaning by rendering them וּתְהוֹן כְּרַבְרְבַיָּא, 'and you shall be like rulers.'

[It is noteworthy that in 6:2 *Onkelos* also translates בְּנֵי־הָאֱלֹהִים as בְּנֵי רַבְרְבַיָּא which *Rashi* renders *'the sons of princes and rulers.'* See *comm.* there.]

HaKesav V'Hakabballah renders *Elohim:* 'Judge and ruler, as *Rambam* explained. The meaning here is that you yourselves will have the capability of judging what is good and choosing

III
6
of it your eyes will be opened and you will be like God, knowing good and bad.'
[6] *And the woman perceived that the tree was good for eating and that it was a delight to the eyes, and that the tree was desirable as a means to wisdom, and she took of its fruit and ate; and she gave also to her*

יֹדְעֵי טוֹב וָרָע — *knowing* [or: *'who know'*] *good and bad.*

[The verse is then to be understood either: *'And you shall know good and bad like God'*; or: *'and you shall be like the angels who know good and bad.'*]

God did not prohibit this tree out of any concern for your death, but because He is aware that by eating from it you will attain extra awareness and thereby you will become omniscient like Him.

6. וַתֵּרֶא הָאִשָּׁה — *And the woman perceived* [lit. *'saw'*]

— She was convinced by the words of the serpent: they pleased her and she believed him *(Rashi).*

The verse does not say *'she hearkened to the voice of the serpent'*, but rather *'she saw'* i.e. she perecived in it qualities of her own volition and understanding thanks to the encouragement of the serpent *(Abarbanel; Akeidas Yitzchak; Ibn Caspi).*

[The tempter did not tell the woman to eat the fruit, but he had enveloped her in his spell. She looked on the tree with a new longing — it was good to eat, a delight to the eyes, and it would give her wisdom.]

כִּי טוֹב הָעֵץ לְמַאֲכָל — *That the tree was good for eating* [or: *'for food'*]

She had thought that He admonished them against eating the fruit of the tree because it was bitter and poisonous; but now she saw that it was good and sweet food *(Ramban).*

Rashi explains *'was good':* [as referring to the words of the serpent]: to become godly.

וְכִי תַאֲוָה הוּא לָעֵינַיִם — *And that it was a delight to the eyes* — i.e. that it was beautiful to the sight *(Midrash).*

Ramban explains תַּאֲוָה as *desire:* 'that its fruit would awaken desire and cause one to stray after the sight of his eyes.'

— As the serpent had told her: *'and your eyes shall be opened' (Rashi).*

וְנֶחְמָד הָעֵץ לְהַשְׂכִּיל — *And that the tree was desirable as a means to wisdom* [lit. *'for becoming wise'*]

As God Himself said that it was *'a tree of knowledge of good and evil' (Sforno).*

— And as the serpent had said: *'knowing good and bad' (Rashi).*

... It was a source of intellectual benefit *(R' Meyuchas);* for it was

it, and what is bad and avoiding it, and thus not resemble other living creatures that are compelled to act as they do, and are not endowed with the ability to conduct themselves of their own volition and choice ... Additionally, *'Elohim'* has the significance of strength and competence (cf. *comm.* to 1:1) and implies: Be competent to distinguish with your own reason between good and bad and have no need of commands upon you; i.e. זֶעלְבְּסטְמאֶכטיג, independently strong.

ג וַתֹּאכַל וַתִּתֵּן גַּם־לְאִישָׁהּ עִמָּהּ וַיֹּאכַל׃
ז ז וַתִּפָּקַחְנָה עֵינֵי שְׁנֵיהֶם וַיֵּדְעוּ כִּי עֵירֻמִּם
הֵם וַיִּתְפְּרוּ עֲלֵה תְאֵנָה וַיַּעֲשׂוּ לָהֶם

'appealing to the understanding' (Hirsch).

וַתִּתֵּן גַּם־לְאִישָׁהּ עִמָּהּ — *And she gave also to her husband with her.*

She persuaded him with kind words *(Midrash)* so that she should not die and leave him alive to take another wife *(Rashi).*[1]

She then brought it to her husband who was elsewhere in the garden and repeated everything the serpent had told her. He was עִמָּהּ, *at one with her,* and not blameless (i.e. he was not hopelessly tempted or unreasonably deceived) and therefore liable to punishment *(Radak; Ibn Ezra).*

He was receptive both because he was אִישָׁהּ, *her husband,* and because he was עִמָּהּ, *with her (Sforno).* [I.e. for him it sufficed that *she* gave him the fruit.]

If, however, we want to judge her favorably, we can conjecture that she offered Adam the fruit not out of malice but out of love — that he, too, should become wise *(Minchah B'lulah).*

The *Midrash* notes that גַּם, *also,* is an extension which includes the cattle and beasts [see footnote.]

7. [And as a result of eating the forbidden fruit] ...

וַתִּפָּקַחְנָה עֵינֵי שְׁנֵיהֶם — *Then* [lit. *'and'*] *the eyes of both of them were opened.* This is not to be taken literally. The verse refers to their eyes being 'opened' with newfound intelligence and awareness *(Rashi).*

— As in the verse [*Psalms* 119:18]: גַּל עֵינַי וְאַבִּיטָה נִפְלָאוֹת מִתּוֹרָתֶךָ *'Open my eyes* [i.e. grant me intelligence] *that I may behold wondrous things out of Your Torah' (Ramban).*

According to the *Zohar:*

Rav Chiyah said: Their eyes were opened to the evil of the world which they had not known before. They knew that they were naked, since they had lost the celestial luster which had formerly enveloped them, and of which they were now divested.

Rambam [*Moreh I:*2] similarly explains that פקח [open] is used exclusively in the sense of receiving new sources of knowledge, not in that of regaining the sense of sight.

Targum Yonasan renders: 'And the eyes of both were enlightened.'

They now displayed a desire for every base pleasure despite its harmfulness *(Sforno).*

1. Eve could not bring herself to utterly disobey God's command, so she compromised with her conscience. First she ate only of the outside skin of the fruit, and then, seeing that death did not befall her, she believed the serpent, and ate the fruit itself *(Ibn Sabba; Midrash Tadshe).*

When she touched the tree she saw the angel of death before her and exclaimed: Woe is me! I shall now die and God will make another woman and give her to Adam. I will therefore make him eat with me. If we die, we will die together; and if we live, we shall both live *(Pirkei d'Rabbi Eliezer).*

The *Midrash* continues that it took tears and lamentations on her part to prevail upon Adam to take the step. Not yet satisfied, she gave of the fruit to all living beings, that they, too, might be subject to death.

III
7

husband with her and he ate. 7 Then the eyes of both
of them were opened and they realized that they were
naked; and they sewed together a fig leaf and made
themselves aprons.

וַיֵּדְעוּ כִּי עֵירֻמִּם הֵם — *And they realized* [lit. *'knew'*] *that they were naked.*

Even a blind person knows when he is naked! It signifies that they realized that they had stripped themselves of even the one precept with which they were entrusted [i.e. they were naked of obedience] *(Midrash; Rashi).*

It is not said 'And the eyes of both were opened and they *saw*', for what man saw previously and what he saw now were precisely the same; there had been no blindness which was now removed, but he received a new faculty whereby he found things wrong which previously he had not regarded as wrong *(Moreh I*:2).

They perceived that it is proper to conceal their private organs inasmuch as their primary function had now become satisfaction of sensual desire *(Sforno).*

The serpent was right: they had become enlightened people. But their first realization was — that they were naked! ... Man need not be ashamed of his body as long as it stands in the service of God. ... But when this condition is not entirely there he feels shame in his nakedness. This shame awakens the voice within us, the voice of conscience that reminds us we are not meant to be animals *(Hirsch).*

וַיִּתְפְּרוּ עֲלֵה תְאֵנָה — *And they sewed together a fig-leaf.*

And those who cynically note that they had no needle are foolish because any thin stick can be used for sewing! *(Ibn Ezra)*

According to the *Talmud* [*Berachos* 40a] the forbidden tree was a fig-tree, and by the very thing by which they were disgraced were they restored *(Rashi).*[1]

For as the *Midrash* states, Adam tried to gather leaves from the trees to cover parts of their bodies but he heard one tree after the other say: 'this is the thief that deceived his Creator ... Take no leaves from me!' Only the fig-tree allowed him to take its leaves, because it was the forbidden fruit. Adam had the same experience as that prince who seduced one of the maid-servants in the palace. When the king, his father, banished him, he vainly sought refuge with the other maid-servants, but only she who had caused his disgrace would help him.

And, as *Rashi* comments, why was the tree not explicitly identified in the Torah? — Because God never wishes to shame His creatures. He did not identify it so that people should not point to it and say 'this is the tree because of which the world suffers!'*(Tanchuma).*

According to *Ibn Ezra,* however, the two trees — the tree of life and the tree of knowledge — were unique and not to be found outside the Garden of Eden.

R' Meyuchas notes that עֲלֵה תְאֵנָה *fig-leaf,* is in the singular to stress the great size of the produce of the Garden. From only one leaf they were able to make many garments.

1. *For alternate interpretations of the species of the tree, see comm.* to verse 2:9.

ג ח חֲגֹרֹת: וַיִּשְׁמְעוּ אֶת־קוֹל יהוָה אֱלֹהִים
ח־י מִתְהַלֵּךְ בַּגָּן לְרוּחַ הַיּוֹם וַיִּתְחַבֵּא הָאָדָם
וְאִשְׁתּוֹ מִפְּנֵי יהוָה אֱלֹהִים בְּתוֹךְ עֵץ
ט הַגָּן: וַיִּקְרָא יהוָה אֱלֹהִים אֶל־הָאָדָם
י וַיֹּאמֶר לוֹ אַיֶּכָּה: וַיֹּאמֶר אֶת־קֹלְךָ

The *Midrash* regards this action as an immediate consequence of their sin:

Rav Yitzchak said: You have acted sinfully — take thread and sew! [i.e. because of your sin you must henceforth toil.]

וַיַּעֲשׂוּ לָהֶם חֲגֹרֹת — *And they made themselves aprons* [lit. *'girdles'*] — the *Midrash* understands it: various kinds of garments.

8. וַיִּשְׁמְעוּ אֶת קוֹל ה׳ אֱלֹהִים — [*And*] *they heard the sound* [or: *'voice'*] *of* HASHEM *God.*

— It was unlike any sound they had ever heard before *(Ibn Ezra).*

God caused His sound to be heard to afford them the opportunity of hiding *(Radak);* and also to teach etiquette: Do not look upon a man in his disgrace. God did not appear to them immediately after they sinned and were disgraced; he waited until they had sewn fig-leaves together and only then *'they heard the sound of* HASHEM *God.'* It also teaches that one should never enter another's home suddenly and unannounced *(Derech Eretz Rabbah* 5).

מִתְהַלֵּךְ בַּגָּן — *Manifesting itself* [lit. *'walking about'; 'moving about'*] *in the garden.*

The translation *'manifesting itself'* follows *Ramban* who interprets the verb as suggesting the revelation of the Divine Presence, while *Lekach Tov* perceives it as referring to the withdrawal of the Divine Presence on account of Adam's sin.

It is the *sound,* not *God,* that is being modified by the verb 'walking' (*Rashi* [according to *Levush*]; *Ibn Ezra; Rambam* [*Moreh I:*24]; *Radak* and others).

This is based on the *Midrash:* 'Rav Chilfi said, from here we may learn that a sound 'walks' for it is said [lit.] *'and they heard the sound of* HASHEM *God walking.*

לְרוּחַ הַיּוֹם — *Toward evening* [lit. *'in the wind, breeze, spirit, direction, of the day'*]

— In the רוּחַ, direction, in which the sun [synonymous with יוֹם, *day (Haamek Davar)*] sinks, viz. the west, for towards evening the sun is in the west and they sinned in the tenth hour [*Sanhedrin* 38b — cf. footnote to 3:1] *(Rashi).*

Ibn Janach explains: when the breeze of the day is strongest — toward evening.

This fact is mentioned because sounds carry further in the wind *(Radak).*

The *Vilna Gaon* notes that before they sinned, Adam and Eve communicated with God personally. When they sinned, however, they heard his voice only as a *Bas Kol* — His voice as it was transmitted by the wind.

Ramban states that wind is mentioned because the manifestation of the Divine Presence is portended by a strong wind [cf. *I Kings* 19:11.] ... However, in our verse *'the wind of the day'* implies a wind of ordinary days — not a gusty wind as in the vision of

[8] *They heard the sound of HASHEM God manifesting itself in the garden toward evening; and the
man and his wife hid from HASHEM God among the
trees of the garden.* [9] *HASHEM God called out to the
man and said to him, 'Where are you?'*

other prophecies — so that they should not be frightened. Yet the Torah tells us that despite the mildness of wind, they hid on account of their nakedness.

Hirsch renders the phrase: *They heard the voice of God withdrawing in the garden in the direction of the day — the West. This is profoundly significant because, in the Holy Temple, the Holy of Holies was in the west and the eternal light of the Menorah was turned toward the west, implying that God withdrew His Presence westward. According to the Midrash,* this was the first tragic withdrawal of the Divine Presence in the history of the world ...'

וַיִּתְחַבֵּא הָאָדָם וְאִשְׁתּוֹ מִפְּנֵי ה׳ אֱלֹהִים — *And the man and his wife hid from HASHEM God.*

They perceived that the voice they had heard was God who was coming to admonish them for their sin. They were ashamed of their nakedness and they hid, for the newly made aprons covered them insufficiently. Although they knew that they could not hide from Him, they displayed the kind of shame one has for his fellow man, and surely for HASHEM.

The man and woman crept away, מִפְּנֵי ה׳, *from before God.* Not only could they no longer stand upright לִפְנֵי ה׳, they feared even His proximity. They had lost the worthy status of human beings, and slunk away in hiding among the lower creatures *(Hirsch).*

בְּתוֹךְ עֵץ הַגָּן — *Among the trees of the garden.*

The Hebrew is singular, *'tree'*, but it has a collective sense *(Radak; R' Meyuchas).*

Abarbanel however, derives from the singular, that it is *'the tree'* that is here referred to: the tree from which they sinned, the Tree of Knowledge. It is that same tree from which they ate, from which they made themselves aprons, and in which they were forced to hide themselves.

9. אֶל הָאָדָם — *To the man.*

God addressed His call to the man, and not to the woman because it was Adam who had originally been commanded *(Abarbanel).*

וַיֹּאמֶר לוֹ אַיֶּכָּה — *And [He] said to him: 'Where are you?'* I.e. 'Is not all the world which I created manifest before Me; the darkness as well as the light? How have you presumed to hide from Me? Do I not know your hiding place? Where is the commandment I commanded you? *(Targum Yonasan).*

God knew where he was, but the question was merely a means of initiating a dialogue with him so he would not be terrified to repent [or: to reply] as he would be if God were suddenly to punish him. God acted similarly with Cain [4:9]; with Balaam [*Numb.* 22:9]; and with Hezekiah [*Isaiah* 39] *(Rashi; Ibn Ezra).*

For God, in His mercy, desires the repentance of the wicked so He can avoid punishing them *(Mizrachi).*

God said: 'Consider well how you have fallen from your heights;

ג
יא־יב

שָׁמַ֫עְתִּי בַּגָּ֑ן וָאִירָ֛א כִּֽי־עֵירֹ֥ם אָנֹ֖כִי
וָאֵחָבֵֽא׃ וַיֹּ֕אמֶר מִ֚י הִגִּ֣יד לְךָ֔ כִּ֥י עֵירֹ֖ם יא
אָ֑תָּה הֲמִן־הָעֵ֗ץ אֲשֶׁ֧ר צִוִּיתִ֛יךָ לְבִלְתִּ֥י
אֲכָל־מִמֶּ֖נּוּ אָכָֽלְתָּ׃ וַיֹּ֖אמֶר הָֽאָדָ֑ם הָֽאִשָּׁה֙ יב
אֲשֶׁ֣ר נָתַ֣תָּה עִמָּדִ֔י הִ֛וא נָֽתְנָה־לִּ֥י מִן־הָעֵ֖ץ

where is your exalted status? *(Aderes Eliyahu).*[1]

HaRechasim LeBik'ah notes that in Hebrew, אֵיפֹה expresses a simple question as to one's whereabouts; אַיֵּה expresses surprise at finding Adam where he should not have been found.

Moralistically, God's conversation with Adam and Eve teaches that before a human judge condemns someone he should first confront him personally to ascertain whether he has an explanation. For though God was fully familiar with all the facts, He did not punish them until He conversed with them and afforded them the opportunity to reveal any excuse they might have had *(Ralbag).*

10. וַיֹּאמֶר אֶת קוֹלְךָ שָׁמַעְתִּי בַּגָּן — *And he said, 'I heard the sound of You in the garden.'*

[It was apparently obvious, even to Adam, that God's question, *'Where are you?'* was but rhetorical and introductory. He does not answer by identifying *where* he is hiding; he explains only *why* he is hiding.]

וָאִירָא כִּי עֵירֹם אָנֹכִי — *And I was afraid because I am naked.*

Adam's answer makes it clear that he considered himself still to be naked, obviously, the fig-leaf aprons covered only a small portion of their bodies *(Chizkuni).*

Adam did not confess to his actual sin. According to him, he hid only out of modesty. But God presses harder ... *(Abarbanel).*

Hirsch notes that this feeling of fear rather than shame, proves that the consciousness of being naked is related to a sense of moral purpose as explained above on verse 7.

וָאֵחָבֵא — *So* [lit. *'and*] *I hid.* Out of shame *(Targum Yonasan).*

11. מִי הִגִּיד לְךָ — *Who told you.* I.e. How did this consciousness come to you? *(Hirsch).*

כִּי עֵירֹם אָתָּה — *That you are naked.* I.e. that nakedness is shameful? *(Rashi; Sforno).*

You were always naked until

1. God admonished him and said: 'Where has your heart gone?' *(Sanhedrin* 38b).

'How lowly you have become! Yesterday you were ruled by My will, and now by the will of the serpent ...'

[And by homiletically revocalizing the word אַיֶּכָּה to אֵיכָה the *Midrash* additionally comments that God lamented over Adam and said: אֵיכָה, *Alas!* [How have you fallen!] *(Midrash;* cf. *comm.* to *Lamentations, ArtScroll* ed. 1:1).

Having eaten from the forbidden tree, Adam and Eve lost the consistent inner purity that enabled them to treat all bodily organs and functions as tools in the service of God. To this extent they had 'dishonestly' appropriated their bodies for the use of evil impulses, and found it necessary to clothe themselves to help control their new-found lust. The words for traitorous, disloyal abuse of property or position are בְּגִידָה and מְעִילָה. They are derived from words for garments, בֶּגֶד and מְעִיל. Thus, a perfidious person uses another's 'garment' for his own purposes. Adam and Eve used bodily impulses that should have been solely in the service of God for their satisfaction of their own desires. For this they felt shame which had to be clothed *(Harav David Cohen).*

10 *He said, 'I heard the sound of You in the garden,*
and I was afraid because I am naked, so I hid.'
11 *And He said, 'Who told you that you are naked?*
Have you eaten of the tree from which I commanded
you not to eat?'
12 *The man said, 'The woman whom You gave to*
be with me — she gave me of the tree, and I ate.'

now, and yet you never hid. Who revealed something to you that you were never aware of before? *(Abarbanel).*

הִגִּיד, *tell,* implies revealing something new which the listener never before knew, while סַפֵּר, *relating,* denotes repeating something the listener might have already heard *(Ibn Ezra).*

הֲמִן־הָעֵץ . . . — *Have you eaten of the tree ...?*

It is obvious that you ate of the tree. Had you not eaten of it, your nakedness would not be a source of shame to you *(Malbim).*

God knew the answer, but He wanted to elicit Adam's response ... [and repentance] *(Radak).*

God opened the dialogue to give Adam the opportunity to acknowledge his sin and be pardoned. But Adam did not confess. Instead, as the next verse shows, he hurled against God the very kindness which God had shown him, the gift of Eve, by implying that God had caused him to sin by giving him that woman *(Midrash Aggadah).*

12. הָאִשָּׁה אֲשֶׁר נָתַתָּה עִמָּדִי — *The woman whom You gave to be with me.*

I.e. You are the cause of my sin because it was You who gave me the woman who enticed me *(Radak).*[1]

You gave her to me as a helpmate and I was justified in assuming that her counsel was good *(Ramban).*

Adam thus displayed his ingratitude [for God's gift to him] *(Rashi).*

[Additionally, it must be stressed that Adam was unjustified in implying that God thrust Eve upon him. Recall, from *comm.* to 2:20 that God did not create woman until Adam *demanded* her.]

הִוא נָתְנָה־לִּי מִן הָעֵץ — *She gave me of the tree.*[2]

— And I didn't even know from which tree she had taken the fruit! I trusted her and accepted it *(Chizkuni).*

— What do You want of me? She had already eaten of the tree and knew good and bad; I did not yet possess this knowledge, and she thus deceived me *(Tur* citing *Rosh).*

1. Adam pleaded before God:

'Master of the Universe! When I was alone did I sin in any way against You? But it was the woman whom You had brought to me, that enticed me away from Your bidding' *(Pirkei d'Rabbi Eliezer* 14).

2. According to *Baal HaTurim,* since *'the tree'* was the subject of conversation [*Have you eaten from the tree ...?*], Adam should have said in his reply merely מִמֶּנּוּ, from *'it'.*

He therefore interprets הָעֵץ as *'the stick'* and suggests that in its literal sense the verse means:

'She beat me with a stick until I ate.'

יג וָאֹכֵל: וַיֹּאמֶר יהוה אֱלֹהִים לָאִשָּׁה מַה־
זֹּאת עָשִׂית וַתֹּאמֶר הָאִשָּׁה הַנָּחָשׁ
יד הִשִּׁיאַנִי וָאֹכֵל: וַיֹּאמֶר יהוה אֱלֹהִים ׀
אֶל־הַנָּחָשׁ כִּי עָשִׂיתָ זֹּאת אָרוּר אַתָּה
מִכָּל־הַבְּהֵמָה וּמִכֹּל חַיַּת הַשָּׂדֶה עַל־

The *Vilna Gaon* observes that God asked him two questions. To the first question [*'Who told you that you are naked?'*] Adam remained silent thus acknowledging that the realization came from his own intuition. As to why he transgressed God's command, Adam offered two replies: firstly, *'the woman whom you gave to be with me'* the implication being that since God brought him the woman after having given him the command, he assumed that she knew that God annulled His prohibition; secondly, he replied: *'she gave me of the tree'* — i.e. he assumed that he was prohibited from personally approaching the tree, plucking its fruit, and eating [ממנו, directly from it] but that he was allowed to eat fruit already plucked by someone else, in this case, Eve (Cf. *Malbim).*

וָאֹכֵל — *And I ate.*

According to *N'tziv,* the words *'and I ate'* here and in the following verse, must be understood as a confession of sorts on the part of Adam and Eve that they did, in fact, sin by eating.

God does not reply to Adam's puny rationale; silence conveys His rejection *(Ibn Latif).*

13. מַה־זֹּאת עָשִׂית — *What is this that you have done?* I.e. How could you have done so dastardly an act! *(R' Meyuchas).*

Another rhetorical question, the answer of which He already knew from Adam's statement, but which He posed anyway to urge Eve toward repentance *(Sforno; Aderes Eliyahu).*

Ramban explains that Eve had been included in the prohibition given to Adam since at that time she was part of him — 'bone of his bones.' She was therefore included in the punishment.

Additionally, *Ramban* comments that her punishment for misleading Adam and causing him to sin was greater than for her eating.

Seeing that Adam and Eve had not expressed regret, God turned to Eve saying *'what is this that you have done?* in the hope that she would confess so He could forgive them both. But she did not do this; instead she attempted to exonerate herself by thrusting responsibility on the serpent *(Midrash Aggadah).*

הַנָּחָשׁ הִשִּׁיאַנִי וָאֹכֵל — *The serpent deceived me* [so *Rashi;* other's render: *'beguiled', 'seduced'*] *and I ate.*

... And if I am accused of having deceived Adam, the serpent, in turn deceived me, and You created that tempter! *(Radak).*

By saying *'and I ate'* she implied: How can I be accused of impropriety in giving it to my husband? I also ate of it, and it is obvious that I did not want to die ... and, furthermore, he also ate of it freely! *(Abarbanel).*

... This, then, was at once her defense and her complaint; that all this happened at the instigation of the serpent *(Or HaChaim).*

14. וַיֹּאמֶר ... — *And HASHEM God said.* Not that God actually *spoke* to the serpent, but that He so *decreed*

III
13-14

[13] *And HASHEM God said to the woman, 'What is
this that you have done!'*
*The woman said, 'The serpent deceived me, and I
ate.'*
[14] *And HASHEM God said to the serpent, 'Because
you have done this, accursed are you beyond all the
cattle and beyond all beasts of the field; upon your*

concerning him, as in Psalms 33:9 כִּי הוּא אָמַר וַיֶּהִי, *'For He spoke and it came to pass'* and ibid. 105:31 אָמַר וַיָּבוֹא עָרֹב, *'He spoke, and there came swarms of gnats'*, and all such similar instances where אָמַר implies 'decreed' *(Abarbanel).*

— *'And HASHEM God said'* — to His heavenly *famalia (Aderes Eliyahu).*

אֶל הַנָּחָשׁ — *To the serpent.* [i.e. regarding the serpent.] He was the instigator of it all so he was cursed first; then Eve, and finally Adam *(Chizkuni).*

As the *Midrash* comments: 'In bestowing honors we begin with the greatest, while in meting out punishment we begin with the smallest.'

כִּי עָשִׂיתָ זֹאת — *Because you have done this.*

The *Midrash* notes that with Adam, God first discussed the matter; with Eve He first discussed the matter; but with the serpent He entered into no discussion [but immediately cursed him.] The reason being that God said: 'The serpent is ready with answers: If I discuss it with him, he will answer me: "You commanded them and I commanded them: why did they ignore Your command and follow mine?" God therefore pronounced His sentence immediately.

This is formulated in the *Talmud Sanhedrin* 29a:

We learn from this incident that we do not plead on behalf of a מֵסִית ['seducer'; one who entices another to idolatry]. For as Rav Simlai said: The serpent had many pleas to put forward but did not do so. Then why did God not plead on its behalf? — Because it offered none itself. What could it have said [to try to justify itself]? דִּבְרֵי הָרַב וְדִבְרֵי הַתַּלְמִיד דִּבְרֵי מִי שׁוֹמְעִין 'When the words of the teacher and those of the pupil [are contradictory], whose words should be hearkened to; surely the teachers'!' [So Eve, although seduced by me, should have obeyed the command of God!]

[Cf. *Tosafos, Sanhedrin,* ibid.; *Mizrachi; Gur Aryeh; Torah Temimah*]

אָרוּר אַתָּה מִכָּל־הַבְּהֵמָה וּמִכֹּל חַיַּת הַשָּׂדֶה — *Cursed are you beyond* [lit. *'from*] *all' the cattle and beyond* [lit. *'from*] *all' beasts of the field.*

— The whole world, including its animal life, had been doomed by man's sin to suffer as a means of his betterment, but the serpent most of all *(Hirsch; Malbim).*

According to the greatness of the serpent so was his downfall; because he was *'cunning beyond all the beasts of the field* [v. 1], he is *'cursed beyond all' (Rashi).*

The curse was that which follows: henceforth he would crawl on his belly *(Ibn Ezra; Radak).*

According to *Sforno,* the curse was that the serpent would attain its desires and needs with difficulty and less pleasure than all other living creatures.

גְּחֹנְךָ תֵלֵךְ וְעָפָר תֹּאכַל כָּל־יְמֵי חַיֶּיךָ׃
טו וְאֵיבָה | אָשִׁית בֵּינְךָ וּבֵין הָאִשָּׁה וּבֵין
זַרְעֲךָ וּבֵין זַרְעָהּ הוּא יְשׁוּפְךָ רֹאשׁ וְאַתָּה
תְּשׁוּפֶנּוּ עָקֵב׃ טז אֶל־הָאִשָּׁה אָמַר

[*Rashi* comments regarding the apparently superfluous words וּמִכֹּל חַיַּת הַשָּׂדֶה, *and beyond all the beasts of the field,* ('if it was cursed more than הַבְּהֵמָה, *the cattle,* does it not necessarily follow that it was cursed more than חַיַּת הַשָּׂדֶה, *the beasts of the field?'*) by citing the *Talmud, Bechoros* 8a which relates the curse to the serpent's seven year period of gestation which is seven times longer than that of cattle (twelve months) which is in turn seven times longer than that of beasts (52 days); and which was been borne out by experimentation. (We must surmise, therefore, from the different gestation periods noted today, that natural cycles have changed, for as *Ramban* notes: 'The *Midrash* interpretations of Scripture and their allusions are all handed down [by God (see *Overview)*] and they perceived in them profound secrets on procreation and all matters, as I mentioned in my introduction').]

עַל־גְּחוֹנְךָ תֵלֵךְ — *Upon your belly shall you go.* Upon your intestines shall you scrape along *(Targum Yerushalmi).*

For the serpent originally had feet which were now removed *(Rashi).*

— [This is fundamental to the abomination in which *'whatever goes on its belly'* (*Leviticus* 11:42) would be later held.]

— 'If you are allowed to remain on an equal footing with the other animals you will corrupt the whole world!' *(Aderes Eliyahu).*

וְעָפָר תֹּאכַל כָּל־יְמֵי חַיֶּיךָ — *And dust shall you eat all the days of your life.* A fitting punishment; measure for measure. The serpent tried to entice man to sin by eating; he was punished in the same way *(Radak).*[1]

Actually, snakes do not eat earth, but feed on living creatures. The *'eating of dust'* may be a figurative picture of creeping about on its belly similar to Psalms 72:9 *'and his enemies shall lick the dust'.* Or, possibly, snakes, whose tongues seem ill-adapted for tasting, lack the sense of taste altogether. They eat only to satisfy their hunger but derive no enjoyment from it. Hence the explanation of our Sages in *Yoma* 75a that 'the most tasty food tastes to it only like dust' may be an actual physiological fact *(Hirsch).*

Since all food tastes the same to the serpent, its sources of sustenance are virtually unlimited; why, then, is this considered a curse?

The *Mechilta* cites the beautiful parable of a king who decreed that his son be given an annual stipend so that he would have no cause to see his father all year long. The prince was heartbroken because he was denied access to the love and concern of his father. So, too, the snake. The serpent was denied the

1. What the serpent set its eyes on was not proper for it; what it sought was not granted to it, and what it possessed was taken from it. God said: I designed you to be king over every animal and beast; but now *'cursed are you beyond all cattle and beyond every beast of the field'*; I intended you to walk with an erect posture; but now *'you shall go upon your belly'*; I intended that you eat of the same dainties as man; but now *'dust shall you eat'*. You schemed to kill Adam and take Eve; but now: *'I will put enmity between you and the woman and between your seed and her seed.' (Tosefta Sotah 4; Tal. Sotah 9b).*

III *belly shall you go, and dust shall you eat all the days*
15 *of your life.* [15] *I will put enmity between you and the*
woman, and between your offspring and her off-
spring. He will pound your head, and you will bite
his heel.'

need to pray to his Creator for sustenance as do the other animals. This was its curse *(Harav Shmuel Greineman* in *Chofetz Chaim al Hatorah).*

And, as *Minchah Belulah* notes from *Yoma* 75a, cited above, the serpent's curse is that whatever dainties it eats tastes like dust to it.

All the days of your life — i.e. as long as the species of serpents will remain on earth *(Radak).*

— Including the days of the Messiah. This curse will never be removed. Even in Messianic times [when *'the wolf and the lamb shall eat together, and the lion shall eat straw like the ox'*] *'the serpent's food shall be dust'* [*Isaiah* 65:25] *(Malbim).*

15. וְאֵיבָה אָשִׁית בֵּינְךָ וּבֵין הָאִשָּׁה — [*And*] *I will put enmity between you and* [*between*] *the woman.* You intended that Adam would eat first and die [because it is the practice of women to honor their husbands by feeding them before themselves; and consequently Eve, seeing that her husband died, would not eat *(Gur Aryeh)*] and you would then be free to marry Eve. Additionally, you spoke to Eve first only because women are more easily seduced and they know how to pursuade their husbands; the fitting punishment is that the reverse will occur: [you will neither marry her nor have any further rapport with womankind]. *'I will put enmity between you and between the woman' (Rashi; Midrash).*

— In inciting her you pretended that your motive was love; I will turn that love into hatred *(Radak).*

וּבֵין זַרְעֲךָ וּבֵין זַרְעָהּ — *And between your offspring and* [*between*] *her offspring.*

— The enmity will not be limited to you and Eve only *(Sforno).* It will extend to your descendants and hers because you are the cause of the pain entailed by the bearing and rearing of children *(Midrash Tadshe).*

Hirsch notes that among the four higher classes it is only the amphibians, of which snakes are representative, which are completely strange and hostile, and by the innate aversion and repugnance to mankind are completely apart from them.

הוּא יְשׁוּפְךָ רֹאשׁ וְאַתָּה תְּשׁוּפֶנּוּ עָקֵב — *He* [i.e. the descendants of the woman] *will pound your head, and you will bite* [lit. *hiss at*] *his heel.*[1]

1. Rav Yose asked: On the view that the serpent is man's Evil Inclination, how can one explain this verse?

He answered: It teaches that the only way to destroy the serpent is to crush him with the head; and who is the head? — The head of the Yeshivah; [that is, only with Torah can the Evil Inclination, personified by the serpent, be crushed.] Conversely, the 'serpent' can slay a man only through the heel — when one transgresses and tramples God's commandments under his heel. That is the meaning of the verse: *'and you will bite his heel'* — the Evil Inclination slays man by inducing him to trample the commandments *(Midrash Ha'Ne'elam).*

ג הַרְבָּה אַרְבֶּה עִצְּבוֹנֵךְ וְהֵרֹנֵךְ בְּעֶצֶב
יז תֵּלְדִי בָנִים וְאֶל־אִישֵׁךְ תְּשׁוּקָתֵךְ וְהוּא
יִמְשָׁל־בָּךְ׃ יז וּלְאָדָם אָמַר כִּי שָׁמַעְתָּ

— Man will wield the advantage in the conflict between himself and the serpent, for man will pound the serpent's head, but the serpent will bruise him only in the very heel with which man crushes its brain *(Ramban).*

And since the serpent is low it will be able to bruise man only in his heel *(Rashi).*

It may be said that the snake has become the symbol of man's struggle against his lusts. Thus the verse says significantly: *Man is given greater strength over his lusts, than they have over him.* Man can stamp his lusts on the head, they can at most catch him on the heel. Furthermore, lusts, like a snake, are of greatest danger to man when he is careless. By vigilance, he can avoid them. And just as snakes are most dangerous when incited, lusts should not be awakened and excited *(Hirsch).*[*see footnote*].

Rashi notes that יְשׁוּפְךָ and תְּשׁוּפֶנּוּ [have different meanings but] constitute a 'play on words' because of their assonance, and therefore both are used here.

16. Sentence on the woman.

הַרְבָּה אַרְבֶּה עִצְּבוֹנֵךְ — *I will greatly increase your suffering;*

— of rearing children *(Eruvin* 100b; *Rashi);*

— of menstruation *(R' Meyuchas; Sforno).* Since this natural discomfort comes upon her monthly, the verb is duplicated: הַרְבָּה אַרְבֶּה, *I will greatly increase (R' Bachya).*

Abarbanel renders: — *'I will greatly increase your vulnerability to pain',* women being less able to endure pain than men.

וְהֵרֹנֵךְ — *And your childbearing* — i.e. the travails of pregnancy *(Eruvin* 100b; *Rashi).*

— The duration of pregnancy *(Radak).*

This was the reverse of their condition prior to the sin, of which time the Sages said: On the very same day that they were created they lived together and she gave birth *(Sforno).*

Menachem, HaRechasim leBik'ah and others explain עִצְּבוֹנֵךְ וְהֵרֹנֵךְ as a hendiadys [= וְעִצְּבוֹן הֵרֹנֵךְ] 'the suffering of your childbearing'.

בְּעֶצֶב תֵּלְדִי בָנִים — *In pain shall you bear children.* This refers to the pangs of childbirth *(Rashi).*

עֶצֶב, like עִצָּבוֹן refers to forms of discomfort: *physically,* it denotes ailment, toil, fatigue; *mentally* it refers to anxiety and grief *(Ibn Janach).*

[Cf. use of verb in וַיִּתְעַצֵּב אֶל לִבּוֹ in 6:6 and comm. there.]

Rav Yochanan said: The struggle for food is twice as fierce as labor in childbirth. For childbirth is described with the word בְּעֶצֶב, *in pain,* whereas of the struggle for sustenance, [the more emphatic form denoting greater suffering] בְּעִצָּבוֹן, *in toil shall you eat* is used [next verse] *(Pesachim* 118a).

וְאֶל אִישֵׁךְ תְּשׁוּקָתֵךְ — *Yet* [lit. *'and'*] *your craving shall be for your husband.*

תְּשׁוּקָה [*craving*] refers to any spi-

III
16-17

[16] *To the woman He said, 'I will greatly increase
your suffering and your childbearing; in pain shall
you bear children. Yet your craving shall be for
your husband, and he shall rule over you.'*
[17] *To Adam He said, 'Because you listened to the*

ritual craving *(Malbim).*

When a woman is in the throes of labor she declares: 'I will henceforth never fulfill my marital duties,' whereupon God says to her: 'You will return to your craving; you will return to the craving for your husband' *(Midrash;* v. *Niddah* 31b).

— The conjugal initiative will always be man's *(Rashi);* the curse being that woman will never be able to satiate her longing fully *(Or HaChaim).*

According to *N'tziv:* In the most literal sense, the woman always strives to find favor in her husband's eyes.

[Cf. comm. to *Shir HaShirim* 7:11 ArtScroll ed. p.187: *'I am my beloved's and his longing is upon me.'*]

וְהוּא יִמְשָׁל בָּךְ — *And he shall rule over you.*

Woman's punishment is measure for measure. She influenced her husband and he ate at her command, her punishment was that she would now become subservient to him *(Ramban).*[1]

Hirsch notes that the new condition of life, that sustenance will be drawn only through hard labor, makes woman more dependent on man, the breadwinner. Obedience to Torah makes man and woman equally God-serving priests and restores the wife to her role as *'crown of her husband'* and *'invaluable pearl of his life' (Proverbs* 12:4, 31:10).

17. וּלְאָדָם אָמַר — *And to Adam He said.*

Now God turns to pronouce sentence on man who had been the prime recipient of the command, and hence the prime sinner *(Abarbanel).*

כִּי שָׁמַעְתָּ לְקוֹל אִשְׁתֶּךָ — *Because you listened to the voice of your wife* — and not to Mine. She made you privy to the serpent's plot and you are as guilty as she *(Chizkuni).*

Man was not blamed for willful arrogant transgression. His sin was that he meekly succumbed to his wife's ploy *(Sefer Haparshiyos).*

According to the view that Adam

1. 'The Sages have ordained that a man should honor his wife more than himself, and love her as himself; if he has money, he should increase his generosity to her according to his means; he should not cast fear upon her unduly and his conversation with her should be gentle — he should be prone neither to melancholy nor anger.

'They have similarly ordained that a wife should honor her husband exceedingly and revere him; she should arrange her affairs according to his wishes, and he should be in her eyes as if he were prince or a king while she behaves according to his heart's desire, and refrains from anything that is repugnant to him.'

'This is the way of the daughters and sons of Israel who are holy and pure in their union, and in these ways will their life together be seemly and praiseworthy' *(Rambam, Hil. Ishus* 15:19-20).

ג
יח

לְקוֹל אִשְׁתֶּךָ וַתֹּאכַל מִן־הָעֵץ אֲשֶׁר
צִוִּיתִיךָ לֵאמֹר לֹא תֹאכַל מִמֶּנּוּ אֲרוּרָה
הָאֲדָמָה בַּעֲבוּרֶךָ בְּעִצָּבוֹן תֹּאכֲלֶנָּה כֹּל
יח יְמֵי חַיֶּיךָ: וְקוֹץ וְדַרְדַּר תַּצְמִיחַ לָךְ

was unaware at the time that the fruit he was eating was of the forbidden tree, the verse is quite correct: Adam was not primarily blamed for *eating of the tree*, because he was unaware; he was accused of *'listening to the voice of his wife'* — for accepting his wife's counsel blindly without investigation. He succumbed to her *'voice'* without examining the content of her words *(Or HaChaim)*.

אֲשֶׁר צִוִּיתִיךָ — *About which I commanded you* [singular]. 'My command was directed to you and you should have been more conscientious in obeying it ...' *(Midrash HaGadol)*.

אֲרוּרָה הָאֲדָמָה בַּעֲבוּרֶךָ — *Accursed is the ground because of you* [or: *'for your sake'*].

It will produce for you accursed things such as flies, fleas, and ants. This is comparable to one who perpetrates evil with the result that people curse the bosom from which he was suckled *(Rashi)*.*

— It will yield its harvest, but only in scant measure; many of the seeds sown will never sprout forth *(Ibn Ezra; Radak)*.

— It will no longer yield up its crop effortlessly and without toil *(Sforno)*, for had man not sinned the trees would have borne fruit on the day they were planted *(Tanchuma)*.

[Note that man himself was not cursed as was the serpent because mankind (in 1:28) had already been blessed by God.] [1]

[See also *comm.* to 8:21.]

* The key word in this verse is בַּעֲבוּרֶךָ which can be variously explained as *'because of you'*, *'for your sake'* (with a positive or negative connotation) or, as *R' Meyuchas* renders: *'because of your sin'*.

Mizrachi perceives alternate interpretations in *Rashi's* comm. above: (a) The earth *per se* is not accursed, but it will bring forth evil beings in order to punish man — בַּעֲבוּרֶךָ meaning 'for your sake' i.e. toward you, to your detriment; and (b) the earth *itself* is cursed for having yielded up such sinful products as Adam and Eve, בַּעֲבוּרֶךָ here meaning 'because of you'.

The commentators perceive a difficulty and query: Why does the earth deserve punishment because of man's sin?

Several reasons are given:

☙ The earth was punished because it was created only for mankind ... The result being that when the earth does not yield its produce, man must turn to his Father in Heaven *(Midrash HaGadol)*;

☙ The earth is, in a sense, the 'mother' of man, for he was taken from it, and a mother is 'cursed' when her children sin, as in 27:13: *'upon me is your curse, my son' (Midrash)*;

☙ The earth 'sinned' on the third day of Creation when it yielded up trees whose barks were inedible [see *comm.* 1:11,12] *(Midrash)*;

☙ According to *Pirkei d'Rabbi Eliezer:*

1. *Hirsch* notes that only the earth and the serpent were cursed, but not mankind. Man was punished but not placed under a ban for his disobedience. His mission is still to be Godly. That he is expected to and capable of attaining this goal is proven by Jewish history and the emergence of such figures as Abraham, Moses, Isaiah, and the great men of all generations.

voice of your wife and ate of the tree about which I
commanded you saying, "You should not eat of it,"
accursed is the ground because of you; through
suffering shall you eat of it all the days of your life.
18 *Thorns and thistles shall it sprout for you, and you*
shall eat the herb of the field. 19 *By the sweat of your*

Because the earth did not 'speak out' against the evil deed, it was cursed ... For when men transgress less vital sins God smites the fruit of the earth [with the result that man's toil tilling the earth is in vain];

☙ *'Cursed is the ground'* — because it did not show you your guilt *(Targum Yonasan).*

[Another apparent difficulty is why the entire human race continues to suffer because of Adam's sin. See *Overview.*]

בְּעִצָּבוֹן תֹּאכֲלֶנָּה — *Through suffering shall you eat of it.* No longer shall you be able to sit idly by and eat of the land's produce. Henceforth you will obtain and eat the fruit of the earth only through your own hard labor and suffering *(Midrash Aggadah; Radak).*

It is no contradiction that in 2:15 man is described as having been put into the garden לְעָבְדָהּ וּלְשָׁמְרָהּ, *to till and guard it,* implying only light work [see *comm.* ad. loc.] From now on heavy labor would be the rule *(Radak).*

[Other commentators interpret עִצָּבוֹן as *'grief'* (see *comm.* of *Ibn Janach* cited to verse 16 s.v. בְּעֶצֶב] and render: *'In grief* shall you partake of it']:

When man was in the garden he knew no grief and anguish. It was when he was driven out and had children, one of whom murdered the other and in turn was condemned to become a wanderer, that Adam experienced the grief of this world. This is the sentence imposed upon him: May all his days be grief-filled *(Abarbanel).*

כֹּל יְמֵי חַיֶּיךָ — *All the days of your life.*

— As long as mankind is upon the face of the earth *(Radak).*

Some commentators see in this verse an allusion that the brunt of the curse would be in effect throughout Adam's life. Following his death it would be somewhat abated as indeed it was with the birth of Noah.

18. וְקוֹץ וְדַרְדַּר תַּצְמִיחַ לָךְ — [And] *thorns and thistles shall it sprout for you.* When you plant various types of seeds, the earth shall bring forth thorns and thistles [which are identified in the *Midrash* with] artichokes and cardoons (thistle-like plants) which are edible only if prepared *(Rashi).*

The translation *'thorns and thistles'* follows *Ibn Ezra* who comments that this is the additional evil that thorns will sprout amidst the wheat.

— Not only will you have a scanty harvest, but additionally, thorns and thistles will grow to aggravate you *(R' Meyuchas).*

Chizkuni interprets תַּצְמִיחַ not in the third-person fem. *'it will sprout'*, but in the second-person imperative: *'you will cause to grow'*:

'You will henceforth have to encircle your gardens with barriers of thorns and thistles to protect them from wild beasts, a protection which was unneeded before you sinned.'

יט וְאָכַלְתָּ אֶת־עֵשֶׂב הַשָּׂדֶה: בְּזֵעַת אַפֶּיךָ
תֹּאכַל לֶחֶם עַד שׁוּבְךָ אֶל־הָאֲדָמָה כִּי
מִמֶּנָּה לֻקָּחְתָּ כִּי־עָפָר אַתָּה וְאֶל־עָפָר
כ תָּשׁוּב: וַיִּקְרָא הָאָדָם שֵׁם אִשְׁתּוֹ חַוָּה כִּי
כא הִוא הָיְתָה אֵם כָּל־חָי: וַיַּעַשׂ יהוה

וְאָכַלְתָּ אֶת עֵשֶׂב הַשָּׂדֶה — *And you shall eat the herbs of the field.*

[*'Herbs of the field'* is apparently understood by the commentators to refer in this context to *wild* herbs and weeds]:

— Since the earth will yield thorns, thistles, and other weeds, you will have no choice but to eat them *(Rashi);*

You will now be forced to eat herbs rather than the fruits of the garden to which you were heretofore accustomed *(Radak).*

19. בְּזֵעַת אַפֶּךָ תֹּאכַל לֶחֶם — *By* [lit. *'in'* or *'with'*] *the sweat of your brow* [i.e. after excessive labor *(Rashi)*] *shall you eat bread* [i.e. food, in general *(Onkelos)*]

Rashi stresses that man can partake of bread only after shedding the 'sweat of the brow'. The verse is not to be understood as suggesting that his bread must be literally intermingled with sweat *(Mizrachi).*

Man, in this respect, is worse off than the animals. Originally, he simply ate wheat with no preparation. But now, before man can partake of food he must first sow, thresh, knead and bake ... *(Ibn Ezra).*

Hirsch observes that אַפַּים, which he translates *'countenance'*, has a meaning much higher and more characteristic of humanity than פָּנִים, *'face'*. It implies man's striving. It is thus Godlike countenance — the mind, insight, and divine light, which man must direct toward the struggle to earn a livelihood.

The *Midrash* records that when Adam heard the words *'thorns and thistles shall it bring forth and you shall eat the herb of the field,* he broke out in a sweat and said: 'What! Shall I and my cattle eat from the same manger?' God had mercy upon him and said: 'In consideration of the sweat of your face, you shall eat bread' (But cf. *Pesachim* 118a for a slightly different version).

עַד שׁוּבְךָ אֶל־הָאֲדָמָה — *Until you return to the ground* — i.e. this state will prevail all through your life *(R' Meyuchas).*

— Only with death will you be relieved from your labor *(Abarbanel).*

כִּי מִמֶּנָּה לֻקָּחְתָּ — *From which you were taken.*

[Following *Targum* and *Rav Saadiah Gaon* who understand the introductory כִּי as a modifier of 'ground'. Others, e.g. *R' Meyuchas,* take this phrase as a causative to the preceding: Why will you return to the ground? — *'For from it you were taken'.*]

כִּי־עָפָר אַתָּה וְאֶל עָפָר תָּשׁוּב — *For you are dust and to dust you shall return.*

As I have forewarned you: when you eat of the fruit of that tree, you will become mortal *(Sforno).*

III
20

brow shall you eat bread until you return to the
ground, from which you were taken: For dust are
you, and to dust shall you return.'
20 *The man called his wife's name Eve, because she*
had become the mother of all the living.

According to others, however, this is not part of the curse but an explanation of why death is inevitable:

Aderes Eliyahu explains that this is not a curse but a natural consequence of man's earthly origin. Had he not sinned, he could have purified his physical being and risen above his origin. Having sinned, he could no longer do so.

Since everything eventually disintegrates into the four elements [fire, air, earth, and water], why was Adam especially told 'unto *dust* you shall return'?

The reason is because the human structure consists *for the greater part,* of dust. [c.f. Comm. 2:7 s.v. עָפָר] And everything capable of decay does not revert immediately to its four elements during this process. It first disintegrates into something else [dust is the first thing *(Ibn Caspi)*] which in turn changes into still another thing. Ultimately it resolves into the elements, and so continues the cycle *(Rambam, Yesodei HaTorah* 4:4).

[Cf. *Ecclesiastes* 3:20: *'all originate from dust and all return to dust';* and *ibid.* 12:7: *'the dust returns to the ground as it was'* (i.e., death is the great equalizer) and the spirit returns to God Who gave it' (see *comm.* to *ArtScroll* ed.). This theme appears also in other verses throughout the Bible and is apparently based upon our verse and 2:7.] [1]

20. The Torah resumes the narrative of man naming all creatures [2:20] which had been interrupted to teach that through the giving of names Adam perceived that he was lacking a mate which God then supplied him. [See *comm.* to 2:20-23.] Having mentioned that the man and woman were both naked and unashamed, the Torah went into the sequence of the serpent to indicate that it was due to her lack of shame that the serpent desired her and enticed her with his seductive counsel in the matter of the tree of knowledge with its ensuing results [see *comm.* to 3:1] *(Rashi).*

וַיִּקְרָא הָאָדָם שֵׁם אִשְׁתּוֹ חַוָּה — [*And*] *the man called his wife's name Eve.* He named her, just as he named all the creatures. By use of the general term אִשָּׁה, *woman* [2:23], Adam identified her as the female of the human species. Now he gives her a *personal* name, Chava [Eve] *(Radak).*

The *Midrash* perceives in the name Chavah a play on the Aramaic word חִוְיָא, *Chivya,* serpent: 'She was given to him for an adviser but she counseled him like the serpent.'

כִּי הִוא הָיְתָה אֵם כָּל־חָי — *Because she had become the mother of all* [*the*] *living* — i.e. of all mankind *(Targum)*

Rashi explains that חַוָּה, *Chavah,* is similar to חַיָּה, *living,* meaning that she gives life to her children,

1. Man is thus bidden, even in his youth, to contemplate the day of his death. Adam, at the dawn of his creation had nearly a thousand more years to live after he sinned, yet God reminded him of his ultimate destiny: *'You are dust and unto dust you shall return.'*

ג אֱלֹהִים לְאָדָם וּלְאִשְׁתּוֹ כָּתְנוֹת עוֹר
כב וַיַּלְבִּשֵׁם: °רביעי כב °וַיֹּאמֶר | יהוה אֱלֹהִים הֵן
הָאָדָם הָיָה כְּאַחַד מִמֶּנּוּ לָדַעַת טוֹב וָרָע

the ו, *vav*, and י, *yod*, being interchangeable.

Although other women also become mothers, Adam gave her the name because she was the first *(Sforno)*.

The *Vilna Gaon* suggests that this name denotes woman's primary role as matriarch after the sin.

[*Harav David Cohen* elaborates that her original name was אִשָּׁה, *woman*, because her role prior to the sin was to interact with man to perfect creation. Following the sin, the mission of mankind shifted to future generations and countless people (see *Overview*). Thus her new name *'mother of all living'*.]

— Individuals die, mankind lives; and it is through woman that man lives on in children. Adam could well have castigated his wife for causing the loss of Paradise, yet he names her by the loveliest calling of woman! ... She became the savior from death, the dispenser of life, the guarantor of mankind's immortality. She is not only the physical, but the spiritual and intellectual perpetuator of mankind's higher calling *(Hirsch)*.

21. וַיַּעַשׂ ה׳ אֱלֹהִים — *And* HASHEM *God made* — i.e. inspired them with the industry to make garments for themselves (*Malbim;* but see *Radak* below).

כָּתְנוֹת עוֹר — *Garments of skin.*

They were uncomfortable in their scanty aprons of fig leaf, and, though they were sinners, God had compassion upon them and clothed them (*Mishrash Aggadah; R' Bachya*).

Rashi cites the various *Midrashim:* Some say the garments were smooth as fingernails, attached to their skin [כָּתְנוֹת עוֹר = *'garments attached to their skin'*, while others say they were *'garments made out of products of skin'*]; i.e. he made them garments of wool, which is soft and warm.

Additionally, according to *Pirkei d'Rabbi Eliezer,* these garments were made from the skin which the serpent sloughed off.

Do not wonder how God fashioned skin garments for them. It is no greater mystery than any other one of His wondrous acts of creation! *(Radak).*[1]

וַיַּלְבִּשֵׁם — *And He clothed them.*

The verse should have read *'and God made them garments of skin to wear.'* However, God Himself clothed them to demonstrate that

1. The *Midrash* comments that these garments were embroidered with pictures of all the animals and birds. When Adam and Eve wore them they had dominion over the animals, and were invincible. They were handed down from generation to generation to Methuselah and to Noah who took them into the Ark. Ham stole the garments passing them on to Cush who in turn hid them for many years until he passed them on to his son Nimrod. Nimrod's prowess as *'a mighty hunter'* [10:9] is directly attributable to these garments. When Esau slew Nimrod, Esau appropriated them. These were the *'coveted garments of Esau'* [27:15]. These were the garments worn by Jacob when he received Isaac's blessing, after which they were concealed. (See *Torah Sh'lemah* 3:184; *Sefer HaYashar* 7:24; Sefer HaParshiyos).

21 *And HASHEM God made for Adam and his wife
garments of skin, and He clothed them.*
22 *And HASHEM God said, 'Behold Man has
become like the Unique One among Us, knowing*

although they had sinned, His great love for them did not wane *(R' Bachya).*

He also did not exile them naked lest they dress themselves as a result of their own efforts and interpret the feat as proof of an added attainment *(Sforno).*

The Talmud cites this verse as an example of one of the ways that man should figuratively 'walk after God' [*Deut.* 13:5] by emulating His virtues. Just as He clothes the naked, so must man clothe the naked *(Sotah* 14a).

22. וַיֹּאמֶר ה' אֱלֹהִים — *And HASHEM God said* — to the angels that minister before Him *(Targum Yonasan).*

הֵן הָאָדָם הָיָה כְּאַחַד מִמֶּנּוּ — *Behold, Man has become like the Unique One among Us.*

[This translation, (as opposed to the more familiar translation: *'behold man has become like one of us')* follows the comm. of *Rashi* (as explained by *Gur Aryeh), Targum* and *Midrash.* (See further).]

[The more familiar translation has God addressing Himself to His heavenly *famalia* and in the manner of 1:26 modestly including Himself as one of them in a gesture of *pluralis majestatis* and saying: *Behold man has become like one of Us to know* (i.e. in his knowledge of) *good and bad.* This translation takes מִמֶּנּוּ as the heavenly *famalia* with God included among them, and renders *like one of Us.* This rendering is preferred by *B'chor Shor, Ibn Ezra ('behold man thinks he has become like one of Us' — Tzafnas Pane'ach), R'Bachya, R'Meyuchas* and many other commentators.

(In fact, *Abarbanel* and *HaRechasim leBik'ah* interpret the statement as God ironically jeering at the evil intent of man who believed the serpent's blasphemy when he said, *'and God knows ... that you shall become as God knowing good and bad* [v. 5]. They render this verse as God saying to the angels: *'Behold man has — according to the Tempter — become like one of Us to know good and bad.* Now, he might further heed the serpent's wicked counsel and put forth his hand. Let us show him how false these words are:)

This familiar translation has its basis in the *Midrash* where Rav Pappyas explained כְּאַחַד מִמֶּנּוּ as meaning 'like one of the ministering angels.' But R'Akiva with the words דַּיֶּיךָ פַּפְּיָס, 'let that suffice you Pappyas' (i.e. you go too far; it is incorrect) reproved him for the impropriety of placing God Himself on par with the angels regarding the knowledge of good and evil.

Instead, R' Akiva suggested that God placed two paths before Adam, the path of life and the path of death, and (by eating of the forbidden tree) he chose the latter. [Accordingly כְּאַחַד מִמֶּנּוּ is to be rendered *'like one of them* (i.e. of the paths) by his action, he has become like one of the alternatives from which he was to choose.' (See *Hirsch).* Or, according to *Yefe To'ar:* 'Behold, man has become as one who knows good and evil of himself, of his own free will' (see *Overview).*]

The *Midrash* continues that according to Rav Yehudah ben Rav Shimon the interpretation of כְּאַחַד מִמֶּנּוּ is: 'Like the Unique One (of the Universe)' [translating: *'the man has become like the Unique One among his kind.'*]

It is the latter interpretation that is adopted by *Rashi* when he comments: Behold he is unique among the terrestrial ones, just as I am unique among the celestial ones; and in having his own ability to discriminate between good and bad, a quality not possessed by cattle and beasts.

This also follows *Onkelos:* 'Behold man has become unique in

ג
כג־כד

וְעַתָּה ׀ פֶּן־יִשְׁלַח יָדוֹ וְלָקַח גַּם מֵעֵץ
כג הַחַיִּים וְאָכַל וָחַי לְעֹלָם: וַיְשַׁלְּחֵהוּ יהוה
אֱלֹהִים מִגַּן־עֵדֶן לַעֲבֹד אֶת־הָאֲדָמָה
כד אֲשֶׁר לֻקַּח מִשָּׁם: וַיְגָרֶשׁ אֶת־הָאָדָם

the world by himself, knowing good and bad.'[1]

Targum Yonasan renders similarly, but attaches מִמֶּנּוּ to the following phrase and translates it *'from him': 'Behold man is unique on earth as I am unique in the heavens above; and there will descend* מִמֶּנּוּ, *from him,* those who will know to discern between good and bad.'

Similarly, *Lekach Tov:* מִמֶּנּוּ, *from him* [i.e. from his sinful act] will future generations learn *to know good and bad.*

לָדַעַת טוֹב וָרָע — *Knowing* [lit. *'to know'*] *good and bad.*

This limits the comparison כְּאַחַד מִמֶּנּוּ [according to the various interpretations explained above] to only this one aspect: *'by his knowledge of good and bad' (Ibn Latif).*

וְעַתָּה ... גַּם מֵעֵץ הַחַיִּים — *And now, lest he put forth his hand and take also of the tree of life.*

God desired the fulfillment of His decree ordaining the mortality of man. Were Adam to eat of the tree of life which was created to give everlasting life to those who partook of its fruit, the decree would have been nullified. At first there was no need to guard the tree because Adam had no need for it [for, as the commentators explain, the tree of life would have had no effect before the sin because man was immortal regardless 'and it is like giving medicine to a healthy person' *(Hadar Zekeinim).*] But now that Adam had sinned and became endowed with free choice [and subject to ultimate death] the apprehension that he might reach out for that tree, too, was very real *(Ramban; Chizkuni; Tur).*

Minchah Belulah sums up that 'regarding this chapter we are all like blind men bumping into walls, and only those few who are endowed with special divine wisdom can properly comprehend the events. This narrative in its most literal sense demonstrates the paradox that 'All is in the hands of heaven except the fear of heaven'.

וָחַי לְעֹלָם — *And live forever.*[2]

— And this would enable him to deceive people into saying 'he, too, is a god' *(Rashi).*

Sforno explains: Man, by having been created in Our image already

1. It is *Onkelos'* interpretation that *Rambam* adopts in *Hilchos Teshuvah* 5:1:

"Free Will is bestowed on every human being. If one desires to turn towards the good way and be righteous, he has the capacity, and if one wishes to turn towards the evil way and be wicked he has the capacity. And thus it is written in the Torah *'Man has become unique of himself'* — which means that the human species had become unique in all the world, there being no other species like it in that man, of himself, and by the exercise of his own intelligence and reason, knows what is good and what is evil, and there is none who can prevent him from doing that which is good or bad. This being the case, there was apprehension *'lest he put forth his hand,* etc.' "

III good and bad; and now, lest he put forth his hand
23-24 and take also of the tree of life, and eat and live
forever!'
23 So HASHEM God banished him from the Garden
of Eden, to work the soil from which he was taken.
24 And having driven out the man, He stationed at the

knows good and bad. If he will also attain immortality he will spend all his days pursuing gratification and he will cast away intellectual entertainment and good deeds. He will thus fail to achieve the spiritual bliss which God intended in creating him in His image and likeness.

[Regarding the question whether man had been originally intended to be immortal see comm. to 2:17.]

23-24. Man's expulsion from Eden.

23. וַיְשַׁלְּחֵהוּ ... מִגַּן עֵדֶן — *So HASHEM God banished him* [lit. *sent him forth*] *from the Garden of Eden* —

As indirect punishment for his sin *(HaRechasim leBik'ah).*

... And to prevent him from eating of the tree of life *(B'chor Shor).*

'See what misfortune his sin caused! Because of Adam's one sin, his stature diminished, his glory dwindled, his food deteriorated and he became a fugitive and vagabond over all the earth. And he and his descendants, to the end of time were all doomed to die!' *(Midrash HaGadol).*

לַעֲבֹד אֶת הָאֲדָמָה אֲשֶׁר לֻקַּח מִשָּׁם — *To work the soil from which he was taken.* [cf. 2:7 and 3:19.]

This banishment is in fulfillment of God's decree [in 3:17] *(Hoffman).*

God had originally created man outside of the Garden of Eden (see comm. to 2:9, 16), and placed him there where all his needs were supplied with a minimum of effort. He had only to till the land and guard it against wild animals. But Adam proved unequal to even this light task; by his negligence he allowed the serpent to enter the garden with calamitous results. Therefore, God removed him and returned him to his source where he would have to toil excessively just to provide his own sustenance *(Radak; B'chor Shor; R'Meyuchas; Aderes Eliyahu).*

24. וַיְגָרֶשׁ אֶת הָאָדָם — *And having driven out the man ...*

— That neither he nor his descendants should ever return there *(Sforno)* ...

[Literally the Hebrew reads: *And He drove out the man.* Our translation follows *Ibn Ezra* and *Radak* who render this as a parenthetical

2. Why did God object to the possibility that man would live forever? — Because God in His mercy wanted man to achieve atonement for his sins through death *(Nefesh HaChaim* quoting *Vilna Gaon).*

Rabbi Y. L. Chasman comments homiletically that this teaches us the gravity of sin: Even eternal life is worthless if it is purchased at the cost of remaining stained with sin.

ג וַיְשַׁכֵּן מִקֶּדֶם לְגַן־עֵדֶן אֶת־הַכְּרֻבִים וְאֵת
כד לַהַט הַחֶרֶב הַמִּתְהַפֶּכֶת לִשְׁמֹר אֶת־דֶּרֶךְ
עֵץ הַחַיִּים׃
ד א וְהָאָדָם יָדַע אֶת־חַוָּה אִשְׁתּוֹ וַתַּהַר וַתֵּלֶד
א אֶת־קַיִן וַתֹּאמֶר קָנִיתִי אִישׁ אֶת־יהוה׃

phrase and thus resolve the seeming redundancy of this and the preceding verse (*'and HASHEM God sent him forth'*). In this verse, the phrase introduces the placement of the Cherubim.]

However, *Tur* quotes *Rav Yosef Kimchi* who suggests that the repetition of the verses implies that after man was *sent forth* from the garden, he returned. God therefore *'drove him out'* [וַיְגָרֶשׁ — a harsher term of expulsion implying finality] and placed the Cherubim there to make future return impossible.

Hirsch explains that וַיְגָרֶשׁ*, drove out,* implies man's greater separation from God. Having disobeyed God, man was forced to fend for himself in exile from His presence to learn the necessity for the guidance of God and to feel the yearning for His nearness.

וַיַּשְׁכֵּן — [*And*] *He stationed* [lit. *'caused to dwell'*] — i.e. before they had departed *(Sforno).*

מִקֶּדֶם לְגַן עֵדֶן — *At the east of the Garden of Eden.* Outside of the garden *(Rashi).*

Apparently, the entrance to the Garden was to its east *(Radak).*

אֶת הַכְּרֻבִים — *The Cherubim.*

— Destroying angels *(Rashi);*

— Terrifying apparitions *(Radak; Chizkuni).*

וְאֵת לַהַט הַחֶרֶב הַמִּתְהַפֶּכֶת — *And the flame of the ever-turning sword.*

The revolving sword had a לַהַט, a flashing flame, to frighten him from re-entering the garden. The *Targum,* however, translates לַהַט as *'blade' (Rashi).*

According to the *Midrash* this refers to the angels, 'which sometimes turn into men, sometimes into women, sometimes into spirits and sometimes appear as angels', while *R' Meyuchas* explains that it refers specifically to the Angel of Death

Rambam [*Moreh* 1:49] derives from the above *Midrash* that the angels have no fixed corporeal shape [since as the Midrash states they assume various forms] but that whatever form they assume depends on the prophetic vision of the prophet.

לִשְׁמֹר אֶת דֶּרֶךְ עֵץ הַחַיִּים — *To guard the way to the tree of life.*

So he would not partake of it on his way out *(Sforno).*

Although they also guarded the *entire* garden, the verse specifies that they guarded the way to the tree of life because that was their *primary* function *(Aderes Eliyahu).*

This 'guarding' was not in the sense of protecting it, but in honor of its exalted status [see *Rambam, Hilchos Bais HaBechirah* 8:1] *(Harav David Cohen).*

Hirsch, in a lengthy dissertation, explains that on a lofty plane, *guarding the way to the tree of life,* can mean to protect and preserve the way so that *it shall not be lost* for mankind, so that he will be able to find it again and ultimately go back on it ... He finds support for this in the fact that this task was

III
24

east of the Garden of Eden the Cherubim and the
flame of the ever-turning sword, to guard the way to
the tree of life.

IV
1

[1] Now the man had known his wife Eve, and she
conceived and bore Cain, saying, 'I have acquired a

entrusted to Cherubim, the same word used to describe the golden protectors of the Holy Ark in the Tabernacle and Temple.

For, as *Malbim* concludes: *They guard the way to the tree of life,* preparing it so that man can attain it after his soul separates from his body and returns to its Father. ...

IV

1. Cain and Abel.

וְהָאָדָם יָדַע אֶת חַוָּה אִשְׁתּוֹ — *Now the man had known his wife Eve.*

The translation in the past-perfect follows *Rashi:* he *'had known'*, i.e. the events of this verse: the conception and birth of Cain had occurred *before* the sin and expulsion of Adam and Eve from Eden.

[Cf. *footnote* to 3:1. It should be noted that acording to the *Midrash,* Adam and Eve's creation, sin, and expulsion took place in the first day of their creation. Accordingly, the commentators explain that prior to the sin, conception and birth were painless and immediate, thus explaining how it was possible for Cain's birth to occur before the expulsion.]

Rav Saadiah Gaon, Ibn Ezra, and others, hold that the events of this verse *follow* the expulsion. According to them the translation should be: *'And the man knew'*, because Cain was conceived and born only after the expulsion from the garden:

'Seeing that he was expelled from the garden, and as a result of his sin would not live forever, Adam decided to perpetuate the race' *(R' Bachya).*

[יָדַע, *'know'*, is used throughout Scriptures as a delicate term for marital intimacy.]

The verb implies 'recognition' of one's partner as his married mate. It raises marriage to sanctity rather than promiscuity in contrast to animals who mate with any partner out of instinct and desire *(Haamek Davar).*

Homiletically, however the *Midrash* in this case takes *'knew'* in its literal sense when it states:

Adam knew [i.e. became aware] that he had been robbed of his tranquility; he knew what his serpent [i.e. Eve, his temptress] had done to him.

Harav Gifter explains that the relationship of husband and wife in its highest state involves a *'knowledge'* of the spiritual resources of the partner. After the sin and the resultant decline of man, Adam and Eve had to *know* one another in their newly diminished state.

וַתַּהַר וַתֵּלֶד אֶת קַיִן — *And she conceived and bore Cain.*

The verse is to be understood as if it read: *'and she conceived and bore a son whom she named Cain, saying ...' (Radak; Ramban).*

וַתֹּאמֶר קָנִיתִי אִישׁ אֶת ה׳ — *Saying* [lit. *'and she said'*], *'I have acquired* [Heb. *'kanisi'*, a word resembling

ד ב וַתֹּסֶף לָלֶדֶת אֶת־אָחִיו אֶת־הָבֶל וַיְהִי־
ב הֶבֶל רֹעֵה צֹאן וְקַיִן הָיָה עֹבֵד אֲדָמָה:

'Cain'] a man with HASHEM.'

I have acquired a man: i.e. I have brought another man into the world *(Abarbanel).*

The *Midrash* suggests: 'I have acquired the lasting love of my man [through the birth of Cain] with the help of HASHEM.'

אֶת ה׳ – *With HASHEM:* – As partners with HASHEM. 'My husband and I were created by God alone, but in the birth of Cain we are partners along with Him' *(Rashi).*

Cf. *Niddah* 31a:

Our Rabbis taught: there are three partners in man: the Holy One, blessed be He, the father, and the mother.

The father and mother supply the bodily characteristics while God gives life and intelligence.

When one's time comes to depart from the world, God takes away His share and leaves the share of the father and mother.

Radak explains that קָנִיתִי here means 'maker', 'possessor', and is analogous to 14:19 קֹנֵה שָׁמַיִם וָאָרֶץ, *'maker of heaven and earth'.* Therefore render: *'I have made* [i.e. brought into the world] a man whose creation was not like our own, but one whom I, as a woman, made in partnership with God.'

Abarbanel explains similarly and suggests that the woman was boasting by attributing this birth only to herself and not Adam. It was as if she was saying: 'Although woman originally came from man, now, with the help of God, man has come from woman.'

'... With my own body and travail, I – with God's help – brought a man into His world to inhabit it. If I am guilty of having brought about the death of one man, I have, at least, brought about the completion of another' *(B'chor Shor;* apparently following interpretation of *Rav Saadiah Gaon* above).

The translation אֶת = *'with'* thus follows *Rashi.*

Onkelos renders: *'from before* [i.e. in the presence of] *HASHEM',* while *Ramban* seems to imply *'unto HASHEM'* – i.e. 'this child shall be an acquisition unto HASHEM: when we die, he will serve God in our place.'

The commentators note the use of *HASHEM* in this verse:

From the beginning of *Bereishis* until 2:4, God is referred to exclusively as אֱלֹהִים, *God,* indicating His attribute of strict justice with which He initially created the world [see *comm.* to 1:1]. From 2:4 until this verse He is designated as ה׳ אֱלֹהִים, *HASHEM* God (except for verses 3:1-5 where the conversation is with and by the serpent) indicating that He tempered His justice with mercy as implied in His name *'HASHEM'* [see *comm.* to 2:4] so that the world could exist. From the birth of Cain, when the Evil Inclination increased, He is referred to only as *'HASHEM'* indicating that God discarded His attribute of strict justice and rules the world with mercy alone, for the world could not endure otherwise *(Chizkuni; Tur).*

2. וַתֹּסֶף לָלֶדֶת אֶת אָחִיו אֶת הָבֶל – *And additionally she bore* [lit. *'and she increased to bear'*] *his brother Abel.*

Rashi explains that the three instances of אֶת [lit. *'with'*] in these two verses: אֶת קַיִן ... אֶת אָחִיו אֶת הָבֶל [lit. *'with'*] *Cain* . . . [*with*] *his brother* [*with*] *Abel,* imply an extension to the text teaching that a

IV
2
man with HASHEM.' 2 And additionally she bore his
brother Abel. Abel became a shepherd, and Cain
became a tiller of the ground.

twin sister was born with Cain, and that with Abel two were born. Therefore it says וַתֹּסֶף lit. *and she increased* [i.e. more than previously. (Cf. *comm.* to 1:1 s.v. אֵת הַשָּׁמַיִם).]

הֶבֶל — *Abel.* —[The name means 'futility', 'vanity', 'breath'. Cf. *comm.* to *Ecclesiastes* 1:2.]

He was therefore called *'Hevel'* because:

⋄ Man's hold on earth is but 'vanity'; however, she did not wish to state explicitly this grim view, therefore she did not explain Abel's name as she did Cain's *(Ramban; Radak).*

⋄ His life ended in futility *(Midrash HaGadol);*

⋄ Eve said: 'In vanity we came into this world and in vanity we shall be taken from it' *(Sefer HaYashar).*

⋄ In contrast to his more robust brother, Abel was insignificant; vanity *(Hoffman).*

Hirsch cites the view that Cain was born before the dismissal from Paradise, but that Abel was born after the expulsion. Thus Abel was born into a post-Eden world where a child can be considered a burden instead of a blessing. Eve's heart was heavy when she called her second son הֶבֶל, *Hevel,* 'transitoriness'.

[*Hirsch* also cites the alternate opinion according to which Cain and Abel were both born while still in Paradise.]

וַיְהִי הֶבֶל רֹעֵה צֹאן — [*And*] *Abel became* [or: *'was'*] *a shepherd.*

Because he feared the curse which God had pronounced against the ground, he turned to caring for sheep and herds *(Midrash; Rashi).*

Meat was still prohibited to them [being permitted only in the days of Noah, see 9:3]. Nevertheless, milk, butter, wool, and the skins of dead animals were permitted to them. Abel's work, thus, consisted of shearing the sheep for their wool, and milking the cows *(Mizrachi).*

HaK'sav V'haKaballah wonders how Abel could have been so involved with shepherding that Scripture lists it as his seemingly all-encompassing vocation? He explains that shepherding is a term used to describe those who wish to devote their lives — away from mundane toil — to solitude and carefree contemplation of things spiritual. It was therefore the profession chosen by our Patriarchs, Moses and David, for it enabled them to devote their lives and dedicate their every thought to God and His wondrous ways. It was to this lofty ideal that Abel dedicated himself, while Cain chose agriculture.

Hirsch notes that agriculture was the natural profession for a son of Adam (see 3:23). In plying it, man becomes attached to the soil, fertilizing it with his own sweat. Although agriculture has stimulated great progress in the human condition, man comes to worship the forces of nature and to enslave other men to labor for him in the effort to attain and develop property. The agricultural peoples were the first to beget slavery and polytheism. Although Abel was younger, his occupation is mentioned first because he chose a more

ד ג וַיְהִי מִקֵּץ יָמִים וַיָּבֵא קַיִן מִפְּרִי הָאֲדָמָה
ג־ה ד מִנְחָה לַיהוָה: וְהֶבֶל הֵבִיא גַם־הוּא
מִבְּכֹרוֹת צֹאנוֹ וּמֵחֶלְבֵהֶן וַיִּשַׁע יהוה
ה אֶל־הֶבֶל וְאֶל־מִנְחָתוֹ: וְאֶל־קַיִן וְאֶל־

spiritual pursuit. (See *HaK'sav V'haKaballah* above.)[1]

וְקַיִן הָיָה עֹבֵד אֲדָמָה— *And Cain became a tiller* [or: *'worker'*] *of the ground.*

Thus, as the oldest, he took on his father's trade [cf. 3:23] *(Hoffmann).*

Pirkei d'Rabbi Eliezer notes that they would exchange with each other the products of their respective pursuits. (Thus the system of bartering goods and services was instituted by God from the very beginning of creation — *Radak).*

3. וַיְהִי מִקֵּץ יָמִים — [*And*] *after a period of time* [lit. *'and it came to pass after the end of days'.*]

— From the time he began to cultivate the soil *(Radak).*

Various interpretations of *'days'* are offered by the *Midrash* and commentators ranging from 'an indefinite period' to 'forty years'. *Ibn Ezra* and *Radak* cite various verses *(Lev.* 25:29; *Exod.* 13:10) where 'days' means a full year.

After the passage of a significant period of time during which Cain's fields and Abel's flocks flourished under God's blessing, the brothers came to acknowledge God's goodness to them *(Hirsch).*

Midrash Aggadah interestingly comments that it was the season of Passover and Adam said to his sons: 'At some time in the future all the people of Israel will bring their Paschal sacrifices during this season, and they will be favorably received by God. This is therefore a propitious time for you, too, to bring a sacrifice to God, and He will be pleased with you.'

Harav Gifter points out that this *Midrash* illustrates the theme of *Bais Halevi* that the history of Israel follows the pattern of the Torah. Thus, Adam's injunction to his sons foreshadowed the future history of the Jews. (See *Overview).*

מִפְּרִי הָאֲדָמָה — *Of the fruit of the ground.*

From the subtle contrast between the simple description of Cain's offering and the more specific description of Abel's offering in the next verse *('from the choicest firstlings of his flock')* the Sages derive that Cain's offering was from the inferior portions of the crop, while Abel chose only the finest of his flock. Some say Cain's was from the leavings, while there is *Midrash* which says it was flax-seed.[2] His sacrifice was therefore not accepted *(Ibn Ezra; Radak).*

Cain brings to God מִפְּרִי הָאֲדָמָה,

1. [It has also been suggested that this chiastic arrangement of elaborating on the last-named person (Cain-Abel, Abel-Cain etc.) in these verses is reminiscent of the symmetry mentioned in *Berachos* 2a where 'the Tanna begins with the evening *Shema* and then proceeds to the morning *Shema.* While on the subject of the morning *Shema,* he expounds on the matters related to it and then he returns to the matters relating to the evening *Shema.*

Hence, having recorded Cain and Abel's birth chronologically, it proceeds to relate first Abel's profession and then Cain's. Continuing now with Cain and his offering, it proceeds to Abel's and goes on to mention that it was acceptable while Cain's was not, going on to describe Cain's violent reaction.]

[3] *After a period of time, Cain brought an offering to HASHEM of the fruit of the ground;* [4] *and as for Abel, he also brought of the firstlings of his flock and from their choicest. HASHEM turned to Abel and to his offering,* [5] *but to Cain and to his offering He did*

some of the produce of the earth, but without troubling to choose the finest. He is content with a minimum. Such a person devotes only spare time to God; donates only *'the lame and the sick'*, and whatever is expendable *(Hirsch).*

4. וְהֶבֶל הֵבִיא גַם הוּא — *And as for Abel, he also brought* [lit. *'and Abel brought, also he'*] — either before Cain or after *(Radak).*

He was inspired by his brother's act, but he surpassed him *(Harav Gifter).*

Others suggest that, in deference to his older brother, Abel sacrificed last *(Tz'ror HaMor).Alshich* notes the words גַם הוּא, lit. *also himself* suggest that Abel was not content to bring from his material substance. He was totally devoted to God; he was ready to offer all of *himself* in addition to his animals. Therefore, his sacrifice was so much more acceptable.

מִבְּכֹרוֹת צֹאנוֹ וּמֵחֶלְבֵהֶן — *Of the firstlings of his flock and from their choicest* — Before he derived any personal benefit from their milk or shearings *(Radak).*

Midrash Aggadah renders the phrase as a hendiadys: *'from the choicest firstlings of his flock.'*

— For Abel took of the very best firstlings of his flock. He who brings the first and the best, places his relationship to God in the foreground; for him this relationship is the first and most important. Everything else in life is secondary *(Hirsch).*

They did not build an altar, because they were prohibited from slaughtering animals *(R' Yosef Kimchi; Tur). Radak* suggests that he tied the live sacrifice to a certain spot where he left it to be consumed by a heavenly fire.

וַיִּשַׁע ה׳ אֶל־הֶבֶל וְאֶל־מִנְחָתוֹ — [*And*] *HASHEM turned to Abel and to his offering.*

— A fire descended and licked up his offering *(Rashi),* which was the way that God showed His regard for pleasing sacrifices, as He did in the Tabernacle [*Lev.* 9:24], and with Elijah [*I Kings* 18:38] *(B'chor Shor).*

Another indication of God's acceptance was that Abel's affairs prospered, while Cain's languished *(Lekach Tov; Ha'amek Davar).*

The verse does not read אֶל מִנְחַת הֶבֶל, *'to Abel's offering'*, but rather *'to Abel and to his offering':*

Abel *himself* was pleasing and so was his offering *(Sforno);* for as *HaK'sav V'haKabballah* explains, it was not merely the better quality of Abel's offering that made his sac-

2. *Midrash Tanchuma* relates that, according to the Sages, Cain's offering consisted of [lowly] flax-seed, while Abel's consisted of wool. For this reason, the blending of flax and wool was later forbidden [*Deut.* 22:11] because God said: It is not proper to mingle the offering of a sinner with the offering of the righteous.

ד
ו־ז

מִנְחָתוֹ לֹא שָׁעָה וַיִּחַר לְקַיִן מְאֹד וַיִּפְּלוּ
ו פָּנָיו: וַיֹּאמֶר יהוה אֶל־קָיִן לָמָּה חָרָה לָךְ
ז וְלָמָּה נָפְלוּ פָנֶיךָ: הֲלוֹא אִם־תֵּיטִיב שְׂאֵת
וְאִם לֹא תֵיטִיב לַפֶּתַח חַטָּאת רֹבֵץ

rifice more acceptable, and Cain's less; it was their conduct that was decisive. Abel was accepted because of his lofty deeds, while his brother was rejected because of his despicable ways ...

Abel's offering was in a spirit of humility while Cain's was in a spirit of arrogance *(Zohar).*

The translation of וַיִּשַׁע, *turned* (i.e. regarded) follows *Rashi* and *Ibn Janach. Targum* renders: It was acceptable; while the *Midrash* translates: He was satisfied with it.

— He found it acceptable *(R' Saadiah Gaon; Ibn Ezra).*

5. לֹא שָׁעָה — *He did not turn.* I.e. He did not find it acceptable *(Midrash).*

A fire did not descend to consume his sacrifice *(Lekach Tov),* neither did he prosper in his affairs *(Ibn Janach).*

— God detested both Cain and his offering, because Cain did not offer his sacrifice until he filled his own belly, and then gave of the leavings; whereas Abel gave of the *firstlings,* before enjoying any personal benefit *(B'chor Shor; Tur).*

וַיִּחַר לְקַיִן מְאֹד — *This annoyed Cain exceedingly.*

... Through jealousy of his brother's acceptability *(Sforno).*

... Because he did not understand how he had sinned *(Aderes Eliyahu).*

He thought to himself: 'I sacrificed first, and my offering should have been received first.' He was annoyed when he saw that it was not accepted at all *(Tzror haMor).*

[The translation of וַיִּחַר, *annoyed* follows *Rashi* to *Numbers* 16:15: נִצְטַעֵר מאד].

Others render: *'And Cain was very vexed'* cf. *Rashi to Exod.* 15:8.

Cf. *Hirsch:* 'This *burnt* Cain very much'. חָרָה is the feeling of irritation, anger provoked by an occurrence which we consider unfair.

וַיִּפְּלוּ פָּנָיו — *And his countenance fell* — in shame *(Ibn Janach,* et al.)

6-7. וַיֹּאמֶר ה׳ אֶל־קָיִן — *And HASHEM said to Cain.*

God addressed him in order to teach him and succeeding generations the way of repentance. A sinner can atone for his sins if he will but repent sincerely *(Radak).*

לָמָּה חָרָה לָךְ וְלָמָּה נָפְלוּ פָנֶיךָ — *Why are you annoyed, and why has your countenance fallen?*

'Why are you annoyed' as though My acceptance of your brother's sacrifice was arbitrary? It was *not* arbitrary or unjust! *And why has your countenance fallen?* When a fault can be remedied, one should not grieve over what has passed, but rather concentrate on improving matters for the future *(Sforno).*

Why do you indulge in self-pity? The option is yours to rise above your brother, and perfection lies in higher goals *(Abarbanel).*

The *Vilna Gaon* explains that לָמָּה, *why,* suggests 'in vain'; i.e. לָמָּה, why are you vainly annoyed —

IV
6-7

not turn. This annoyed Cain exceedingly, and his countenance fell.

[6] *And HASHEM said to Cain, 'Why are you annoyed, and why has your countenance fallen?* [7] *Surely, if you improve yourself, you will be forgiven. But if you do not improve yourself, sin*

you have only yourself to blame: you should have sacrificed from your firstlings; וְלָמָּה, *and why* has your countenance vainly fallen? — Just because I did not accept your one sacrifice you display an attitude that 'there is no justice and no judge' [cf. *Targum Yonasan* next verse.]

In this verse God tells Cain [in a theme later echoed by the Prophets] that He does not desire sacrifice but obedience ... *(Malbim).*

7. הֲלוֹא אִם־תֵּיטִיב שְׂאֵת — *Surely, if you improve yourself* [lit. *'do well'*], *you will be forgiven.*

[The commentators note that this is one of the most obscure Biblical passages. In fact, the *Talmud (Yoma* 52b) lists this among the five most indeterminate phrases because of the obscurity of the syntatic relationship of the word שְׂאֵת.

[The translation we have adopted follows *Rashi* and *Targum* which like *Menachem, Ibn Janach,* and others, interpret שְׂאֵת as 'forgiveness' as in *Exod.* 34:7:נֹשֵׂא עָוֹן, *forgiving iniquity.*]

Ibn Ezra, however interprets שְׂאֵת as in *Job* 11:15 תִּשָּׂא פָנֶיךָ, *lift up your countenance,* [rendering: *'if you will improve yourself,* שְׂאֵת, *your countenance will be lifted'* (i.e. you will be elated; your disposition will improve).] This is God's advice in response to Cain's depression which caused his countenance to fall.

According to *Ramban,* שְׂאֵת implies dignity, eminence of rank (as in יֶתֶר שְׂאֵת, *pre-eminence of dignity'* [49:3]). Accordingly, the phrase is interpreted: Why are you annoyed at your brother? *Surely if you improve yourself you will gain pre-eminence over him* for you are the firstborn.

לַפֶּתַח חַטָּאת רֹבֵץ — *Sin rests at the door* —

At the entrance to your grave, your sin will be kept *(Rashi)* [i.e. punishment will await you in the future world unless you repent.]

... But if you do not make your deeds good in this world, your sin will be retained until the day of the great judgment, and at the door of your heart it lies *(Targum Yerushalmi).*

— If you succumb to your Evil Inclination, punishment and evil will be as everpresent as if they lived in the very doorway of your house *(Sforno).*[1]

According to *Ramban:* 'If you do not improve your ways evil will come upon you not only because of your brother, for at the door *of your house* your sin lurks causing you to

1. The Evil Inclination is like a guest ... At first he is shy and undemanding, then he will begin making requests and — unless he is controlled by his host — will continue to take liberties and impose until he becomes virtual master of the house. So, too, the Evil Inclination. He

ד וְאֵלֶיךָ תְּשׁוּקָתוֹ וְאַתָּה תִּמְשָׁל-בּוֹ:
ח ח וַיֹּאמֶר קַיִן אֶל-הֶבֶל אָחִיו וַיְהִי בִּהְיוֹתָם

stumble in all your endeavors.'

Midrash HaGadol explains:

... If you mend your ways you will be able to bear, i.e. you will find forgiveness for past iniquities; but if you do not improve, *sin rests at the door* — you will succumb to the Evil Inclination which lurks at the door.

God explained to him that the Evil Inclination is ever ready and man should study his motives and not allow his baser instincts to overpower him since they always lay ready to poison his behavior *(Malbim).*

The *Talmud* derives from this verse that the Evil Inclination holds sway over man from birth rather than from the formation of the embryo, as it is written *'sin rests at the door'* [of man's entrance into the world] *(Sanhedrin* 91b).

[Similarly, sin rests at the entrance to life because the Torah is forgotten]:

A child is taught the entire Torah in its mother's womb. But when it is about to enter the world, an angel comes and strikes it on the mouth which makes it forget the whole Torah. Therefore, *sin rests at the door (Niddah* 30b).

The translation רֹבֵץ = *rests,* rather than *'couches'* (with the implication of lurking viciously) follows *Hirsch* who protests strongly that this verse has been twisted into a theory that there is an element of evil lurking in the world, like a wild beast, lying in wait for men, eager to spring upon them, overpower them, and 'bring about their fall'!

He continues that mature reflection shows that the sentence implies the opposite.

Wherever רֹבֵץ is found, it always refers to peaceful undisturbed *resting,* with no premeditation to attack or molest; never does it imply a lying-in-wait attitude ...

But the power of חַטָּאת, *sin,* the appeal of the senses, should not be underestimated. While it is powerless to overpower you, it remains quietly behind your door. It does not enter uninvited. If it is comfortable with you, finally to become master of your home, you must have *invited* it in ... By itself it remains quietly before your door hoping that you will master it; only by your own weakness can you succumb to it.

וְאֵלֶיךָ תְּשׁוּקָתוֹ — *[And] its desire is toward you.*

'Its desire' — i.e. of sin, referring to the Evil Inclination which continually seeks to entice you *(Rashi).*

For man's baser instincts long to lead him into sin and demoralize him *(Malbim).*

Ibn Ezra, however, explains this in the reverse: sin is willing to submit to you if you only desire it [cf. *Hirsch,* above.]

HaRechasim LeBik'ah [as well as several other commentators] explain the subject of this phrase as being Abel, it reverts back to the beginning of the verse, which when rearranged would translate thus: Why are you downcast that I accepted the offering of Abel, your younger brother, while yours I did not accept? If you will better your ways, שְׂאֵת, you will have preeminence above him as the eldest [cf. *Ramban* above], וְאֵלֶיךָ תְּשׁוּקָתוֹ, and you will be the object of his love and desire, וְאַתָּה תִּמְשָׁל בּוֹ, and you will rule over him as a master over a servant. However, וְאִם לֹא

will never seek to drive man to major sins at first, for people will not obey. He begins with small sins and, unless held in check, develops in man a pattern of sin until he is powerless to stop *(Me'am Loez).*

Thus again with the *Midrash:* 'Sin is at first like a passing visitor, then like a guest who lingers on, then like the master of the house.'

IV
8
rests at the door. Its desire is toward you, yet you can
conquer it.'
8 *Cain spoke with his brother Abel. And it hap-*

תֵיטִיב, if you do not better yourself לַפֶּתַח חַטָּאת רֹבֵץ, your punishment (חַטָּאת = punishment, as in חַטַּאת מִצְרָיִם, *'the punishment of Egypt'* — [*Zech.* 14:19] awaits you at the door of your tent and you will not be absolved.

וְאַתָּה תִּמְשָׁל־בּוֹ — *Yet you can conquer it* — i.e. you can prevail over it if you wish *(Rashi),* for you can mend your ways and cast off your sin. Thus God taught Cain about repentance, and that it lies within man's power to repent whenever he wishes and God will forgive him *(Ramban).*

... It lies within man's province to conquer his baser instincts by exercising the freedom of will given to him. Man is only free when he conquers the bestial portion of his instincts, and not when he permits it to conquer him *(Malbim).*

Cf. *Ibn Ezra* to *Numbers* 6:2.

As *Targum Yerushalmi* paraphrases: 'Yet into your hand have I delivered power over the Evil Inclination. You have dominion over it to become righteous or to sin.'

Others render the phrase not as God's comforting advice: 'Fear not, you have the ability to prevail over your baser instincts', but as a command: *'Sin seeks to entice you, but you must conquer it, and not let it overpower you!' (R' Meyuchas)*

8. וַיֹּאמֶר קַיִן אֶל הֶבֶל אָחִיו — [*And*] *Cain spoke with* [lit. *'said to'*] *his brother Abel.*

[The Torah does not specify *what* he said].

Rashi, based on *Midrash,* explains that he quarreled with him, engaging him in conversation to seek a pretext to kill him.[1]

1. [Cain sought a pretext to slay Abel]:

Cain said to Abel: 'Let us divide the world. I am the oldest and I get a double share' ... strife ensued and he killed him *(Tanchuma).*

The *Midrash* also adds that when they divided the world, one took the land and the other took the movables. The former said, 'you are standing on my land', while the other said 'what you are wearing is mine!' One said 'strip', while the other retorted 'Fly [off my land]'...

According to another view they fought about the additional twin that was born with Abel [see *v.* 2] with each one desiring her. Cain claimed her: 'I will have her because I am the firstborn', while Abel maintained 'I will have her because she was born with me!'

There are also divergent views about Abel's burial. Having never before seen death, Cain did not know what to do with the corpse. According to *Sefer HaYashar,* he dug a hole and buried him, while *Me'am Loez* cites a *Midrash* that he observed how some clean beasts and fowl were fighting, and when one was killed, they dug a hole and buried it. Cain followed their example and buried Abel.

According to *Pirkei d'Rabbi Eliezer* Cain left him in the field unburied.

The most common version of this *Midrash* is that of the *Yalkut (Tanchuma)* according to which Adam and Eve later came upon the still unburied corpse of Abel in the field. They did not know what to do with it. The mourning parents observed how a raven scratched the earth and buried a dead bird of its own kind in the ground. Adam followed the example and buried Abel. The raven was rewarded in that, though its young are deserted by their parents because they are born with white feathers and therefore unrecognized, God pities them and feeds them until their plumage turns black. Additionally, God grants their petition when they pray for rain. (Cf. *Psalms* 147:9)

ד בַּשָּׂדֶה וַיָּקָם קַיִן אֶל־הֶבֶל אָחִיו וַיַּהַרְגֵהוּ:
ט־י ט וַיֹּאמֶר יהוה אֶל־קַיִן אֵי הֶבֶל אָחִיךָ
וַיֹּאמֶר לֹא יָדַעְתִּי הֲשֹׁמֵר אָחִי אָנֹכִי:
י וַיֹּאמֶר מֶה עָשִׂיתָ קוֹל דְּמֵי אָחִיךָ צֹעֲקִים

The *Targumim* [also *Ramban*] quote Cain as saying something to the effect of *'Let us go into the field'*. [The divergences in wording between the *Targumim* prove that they did not intend to 'correct' the text of the Torah ח״ו by supplying some common original reading, but that they based their exposition on some ancient *Aggadah (Ahavas Yonasan).*]

According to *Rabbeinu Nissim:* Cain related to Abel what God had said to him. Perceiving that Abel was apprehensive, Cain engaged him in conversation to draw him away from their parents. Repeating everything that God had said, Cain lulled Abel into thinking that he was no longer angry. But when he got him in the field alone, Cain killed him.

Others interpret similarly but explain that he related what God said to him and blamed Abel for his misfortune. A quarrel broke out and he killed him *(Ibn Ezra; Radak).*

[Cf. *Targum Yerushalmi* below.]

וַיְהִי בִּהְיוֹתָם בַּשָּׂדֶה — *And it happened when they were in the field.* — Each engaged in his own profession, away from their parents' presence *(Ibn Ezra; Radak; Sforno).*

... While Abel was off his guard *(Tz'ror HaMor).*

When they were in the field Cain said to Abel: 'The fact that your offering was accepted and mine not proves that there is neither judgment nor judge, nor another world; the righteous are not rewarded nor will the wicked be punished. The world was not created in goodness, nor is it conducted in goodness...'

Abel answered: 'What you said is false. The world is conducted according to the fruit of good deeds. Because my deeds were better than yours my offering was accepted, and yours was not ...'

As they disputed, Cain attacked Abel his brother and killed him with a stone *(Targum Yerushalmi)*

וַיָּקָם ... וַיַּהַרְגֵהוּ — *That* [lit. *'and'*] *Cain rose up against* [lit. *'to*] *his brother Abel and killed him.*

Without cause, out of pure jealousy *(Tz'ror HaMor).*

His intention in killing Abel was in order that he would be built up through his own descendants, for he thought that his parents would not have any more children. Cain also feared that the development of the world might be primarily through his brother [which seemed likely since it was he] whose offering had been accepted *(Ramban).*

The *Midrash* relates that Abel was the stronger of the two, and the expression *'rose up'* can only imply that Cain had already been thrown down and lay beneath Abel. But Cain begged for mercy, saying: We are the only two in the world. What will you tell our father if you kill me?' Abel was filled with compassion, and released his hold. Cain then *'rose up and killed him.'*

As the *Talmud* [*Sanhedrin* 37b] relates: not knowing which blow

IV pened when they were in the field, that Cain rose up
9-10 against his brother Abel and killed him.
9 *HASHEM said to Cain, 'Where is Abel your brother?' And he said, 'I do not know. Am I my brother's keeper?'*
10 *Then He said, 'What have you done? Hark, the blood of your brother cries out to*

would be fatal, Cain pelted all parts of Abel's body, inflicting many blows and wounds, until he killed him by striking him on the neck (Cf. *comm.* to *v.* 10). According to the *Zohar*, he bit him to death with his teeth; and the *Midrash* suggests that he beat him with a cane (homiletically קַיִן = קָנֶה; Cain = cane).]

9. אֵי הֶבֶל אָחִיךָ — *Where is Abel your brother?*

A rhetorical question. God knew full well where he was — He entered with him into gentle conversation to give him the opportunity to confess and repent *(Rashi; Radak; Sforno).*

The question can also be taken in the form of rebuke *(HaRechasim LeBik'ah).*

Tanchuma homiletically renders אֵי, as *woe!: 'Woe to Abel your brother* for pitying you and not killing you when you were beneath him! Now you have, alas, murdered him!'

וַיֹּאמֶר לֹא יָדַעְתִּי — *And he said, 'I do not know.'*

He acted as if he could deceive God *(Rashi).*

Since God asked where Abel was, and did not ask: *'Why did you murder Abel?'*, Cain thought that God was unaware *(Radak);* and he thought he could deny it *(Ralbag).* [See *Kli Yakar* cited below.]

הֲשֹׁמֵר אָחִי אָנֹכִי — *Am I my brother's keeper?*

You are the Guardian of the world and yet You ask *me* where my brother is? *(Tanchuma).*

Did You then appoint me his guardian to keep constant watch over him, that You now demand him of me *(R' Meyuchas)* as one demands a treasure from its watchman? *(Aderes Eliyahu).*

'Do I watch him every moment that he is with his sheep?' *(Radak).* You imply that he is the important one and I am merely his guardian! *(Akeidas Yitzchak).*

Kli Yakar notes that since Cain had offered a sacrifice to God, he must have recognized that God is aware of human deeds and could not therefore have thought that God was oblivious to his act. This response to God is therefore not to be understood as an incredulous question. He attaches it instead to the previous statement [לֹא יָדַעְתִּי] and renders: *'I was not aware that I was to guard my brother* and protect him from murder. I had no idea that murder is sinful!'

Since the prohibition against murder was one of the Naochide laws transmitted to Adam, how could we say that Cain was unaware of it?

Me'am Loez suggests that in those early days in the history of the world, people were as yet unaware of which blow could be painful and which could be lethal. Cain, in his jealous rage, attacked Abel and sought to hurt him, but he did not know that death would result from his blows [although he probably *was* aware that murder was sinful.]

10. מֶה עָשִׂיתָ — *What have you done!*

A rhetorical question, implying rebuke *(Ibn Janach),* as if to say: See how much evil you have done! *(R' Meyuchas).*

יא אֵלַי מִן־הָאֲדָמָה: וְעַתָּה אָרוּר אָתָּה מִן־
הָאֲדָמָה אֲשֶׁר פָּצְתָה אֶת־פִּיהָ לָקַחַת
יב אֶת־דְּמֵי אָחִיךָ מִיָּדֶךָ: כִּי תַעֲבֹד אֶת־
הָאֲדָמָה לֹא־תֹסֵף תֵּת־כֹּחָהּ לָךְ נָע וָנָד

קוֹל דְּמֵי אָחִיךָ צֹעֲקִים אֵלַי — *Hark!* [lit. *'a sound!'* or: *'the sound* (or: *voice) of'*] the *blood* (plural in the Hebrew: *'bloods') of your brother cries* (plural in the Hebrew: *'cry') out to Me.*

— [I.e. for vengeance.]

The plural form, דְּמֵי, *bloods,* means: his blood and the blood of his potential descendants. Alternatively, the plural form teaches that his blood [from the many wounds inflicted upon him *(Gemara;* see above)] was splashed over the trees and stones *(Mishnah, Sanhedrin* 37a; *Rashi).*

Seeing that Cain was being insolent, God challenged him forthright by revealing that He was aware of Cain's crime *(Midrash Aggadah).*

This is like the case of a man who entered another's garden, gathered mulberries and ate them. The owner of the garden chased him, demanding 'What are you holding?' 'Nothing', he replied.

'But look! Your hands are stained with juice.'

Similarly, when Cain defiantly answered 'Am I my brother's keeper?' God said: 'Wretch! Hark! *Your brother's blood cries to Me from the ground!' (Midrash).*

[The translation of קוֹל = *Hark!* follows *Hirsch,* who cites *HaRechasim LeBik'ah.* This translation, which takes קוֹל independently is supported by the cantillation on קוֹל which is a separating one. *Ibn Ezra* also comments that the phrase צֹעֲקִים, *cry,* modifies the plural דְּמֵי, *blood* (on *Hirsch:* 'drops of blood') and not the singular קוֹל, sound, (which therefore leaves קוֹל to be interpreted independently).

Targum Yerushalmi, however, paraphrases: 'the voice of the bloods of the multitude of the righteous who were to arise from Abel, your brother, cry before Me from the earth.'

Cf. *Song of Songs* 2:8: קוֹל דוֹדִי, *'Hark! my Beloved!').*]

Following *Kli Yakar:* God answered that Cain's own common sense should have dictated that murder is sinful. Even the earth resounds with the murdered man's blood ...

מִן הָאֲדָמָה — *From the ground.* The earth is the terrain entrusted to mankind on which to live a life dedicated to God. But it does not belong to a murderer. The earth itself demands from God that He should execute justice on one who destroys a man *(Hirsch).*

11. וְעַתָּה אָרוּר אָתָּה מִן הָאֲדָמָה — [*And*] *therefore* [lit. *'now'*] *you are cursed more than the ground* [lit. *'from the ground'*]

Following *Rashi: 'more than the ground';* even more than the ground had been cursed previously because of its own sin [cf. 1:11, 3:17] *(Rashi).*

Others take the phrase literally: *'From the ground will come your curse'* as specified later on [v. 12] *(Radak).*

For Cain was a farmer and his punishment was that the land would not yield its full produce and he would be forced to wander far away seeking more fertile farmland. Thus his curse came *'through the ground' (Ibn Ezra; Ramban; Sforno).*

IV Me, from the ground! 11 Therefore, you are cursed
11-12 more than the ground, which opened wide its mouth
to receive your brother's blood from your hand.
12 When you work the ground, it shall no longer yield
its strength to you. You shall become a vagrant and a
wanderer on earth.'

Hirsch renders: 'You are already cursed by the very ground which you forced to accept your brother's blood.'

אֲשֶׁר פָּצְתָה אֶת פִּיהָ ... — *Which opened wide its mouth to receive your brother's blood from your hand.*[1]

[And, as a result, you and the earth are partners in a heinous act . . .]

You have killed your brother and covered his blood with the earth, and I will decree that it uncover the blood, *'and she shall no more cover her slain'* [*Isaiah* 26:21], for the earth, together with all that is covered up in it, such as seed and plant will be punished. Blood-letting which *'pollutes the land'* [*Numbers* 35:33] brings a curse upon its produce [cf. *Haggai* 2:16] *(Ramban).*

As you have used earth to cover the traces of your murder, so will you be punished by being denied the full use of the earth to produce your needs *(Sforno).*

[On the earth *'opening its mouth'* see such similar expressions as *Numbers* 16:30 (in the episode of Korach; also cf. *Psalms* 106:17).

12. כִּי תַעֲבֹד אֶת־הָאֲדָמָה — *When you work the ground.*

This is the curse. It is directed to Cain as a worker of the ground *(Radak).*

לֹא־תֹסֵף תֵּת־כֹּחָהּ לָךְ — *It shall no longer yield its strength* [i.e. its potential] to you.

There is a double curse here: That the earth would no longer yield its natural fertility for his benefit by making fruit trees productive; and that it would not even respond to his plowing and sowing as before *(Ramban).*

— When the man tears asunder the bond between himself and God, then God tears asunder the bond between man and the earth *(Hirsch).*

The Sages stress לָךְ, *to you,* explaining that this curse applied only to Cain:

Rav Eleazar said: *'To you* it shall not yield its strength, but to another it shall yield it *(Midrash).* Therefore the curse was specifically directed to him [previous verse], while in the case of Adam's curse [3:17], which was meant to apply eternally to all mankind, the curse was directed to the earth *(Radak).*

1. The *Mechilta* relates that when the Egyptians drowned, the Sea refused them and cast them upon the dry land, but the land, too, refused to harbor them and cast them back into the Sea saying:

'For receiving the blood of Abel, who was but an individual, I was cursed. How then shall I receive the blood of this vast multitude?'

The land persisted in her refusal until God reassured her that He would not bring her to judgment. (See *Overview*).

ד יג תִּהְיֶה בָאָרֶץ: וַיֹּאמֶר קַיִן אֶל־יְהוָה גָּדוֹל
טו יד עֲוֹנִי מִנְּשֹׂא: הֵן גֵּרַשְׁתָּ אֹתִי הַיּוֹם מֵעַל
פְּנֵי הָאֲדָמָה וּמִפָּנֶיךָ אֶסָּתֵר וְהָיִיתִי נָע
וָנָד בָּאָרֶץ וְהָיָה כָל־מֹצְאִי יַהַרְגֵנִי:
טו וַיֹּאמֶר לוֹ יהוה לָכֵן כָּל־הֹרֵג קַיִן
שִׁבְעָתַיִם יֻקָּם וַיָּשֶׂם יהוה לְקַיִן אוֹת

נָע וָנָד תִּהְיֶה בָאָרֶץ — *You shall become a vagrant and a wanderer on* [*the*] *earth.*

— You shall not have the right to dwell in one place *(Rashi).*

This is the third curse: that he will be a vagrant and a wanderer in the world, i.e. he will always wander, without the tranquility to remain in one place, for the punishment of murderers is banishment *(Ramban).* [See *Exodus* 21:13]

The commentators discuss why Cain was not sentenced to death like any other murderer:

'Cain's judgment shall not be as the judgment of other murderers for Cain had no one from whom to learn *(Midrash).* [see v. 15.]

And since the death sentence was not imposed, he was punished with exile, as prescribed by the Torah for unwitting killers *(Akeidas Yitzchak).*

Since *'the earth will not yield its strength',* he would always strive to find new areas to cultivate. Never finding blessing, he will wander aimlessly in search of more fertile land *(B'chor Shor; Ralbag);* but the quest is futile; the land is accursed to him. He must wander about restlessly, knowing no peace, like the blood of his brother *(Tz'ror HaMor).*

13. גָּדוֹל עֲוֹנִי מִנְּשֹׂא — *Is my iniquity too great to be borne?* i.e. to be forgiven, as in Ex. 34:7 נֹשֵׂא עָוֹן, *forgiving iniquity (Ibn Janach)* for one who forgives, *'lifts up'* the transgression from the sinner and lightens his burden, figuratively bearing it for him *(Ibn Caspi).*

Is my guilt greater than can be forgiven? *(Onkelos)*

— You, (God), bear the worlds above and below, yet You cannot bear my iniquity? *(Midrash; Rashi)* ... *But You are known as the All-merciful! (Lekach Tov).*

This proves how great, indeed, my iniquity is *(Me'am Loez).*

Others read this not as a question but as a statement and confession:

'More heavy is my rebellion than that can be borne away; nevertheless Yours is the power to forgive it' *(Targum Yonasan);*

My sin is greater than my father's. He transgressed but a slight command and was banished from the Garden of Eden, how much greater is my terrible crime of murder' . . . *(Midrash).*

My punishment is too great to be borne, עָוֹן meaning both *'sin'* and *'punishment'* [cf. 15:16; *I Sam.* 28:10] *(Ibn Ezra),* i.e. 'too overpowering is my punishment for me to bear; I shall not be able to endure it' *(B'chor Shor; Ralbag).*

14. [For, in consequence of my sin] ...

הֵן גֵּרַשְׁתָּ אֹתִי . . . — *Behold, You have banished me this day from the face of the earth.* I.e. away from my

13 *Cain said to HASHEM, 'Is my iniquity too great
to be borne?'* 14 *Behold You have banished me this
day from the face of the earth — can I be hidden from
Your presence? I must become a vagrant and a
wanderer on earth; whoever meets me will kill me!'*
15 *HASHEM said to him, 'Therefore, whoever slays
Cain, before seven generations have passed will be
punished.' And HASHEM placed a mark upon Cain,*

father and mother *(Radak).*

Or, according to *Ramban:* as a fugitive I am constantly *'driven from the land'* and I am unable to stay and find rest in any one place.'

וּמִפָּנֶיךָ אֶסָּתֵר — [*And*] *can I be hidden from Your Presence* [lit. *'face'*]? — Should I wish to dwell where You will not know what I do, *can I possibly be hidden from Your Presence?* Surely not! For everything is known to You *(Midrash Aggadah; Midrash)*

[This reading of the phrase as a question also follows *Targum Yonasan; Rav Saadiah Gaon.*]

Others render in reverse:

'And from Your countenance I will be hidden' — i.e. You will detest me and no longer watch over me *(B'chor Shor);* with the result that I will be exposed to all and unprotected *(Radak).*

Ramban: 'I will not be able, out of shame, to stand before You in prayer or bring a sacrifice ...'

וְהָיִיתִי . . . כָל־מֹצְאִי יַהַרְגֵנִי — [*'And*] *I must become a vagrant and a wanderer on earth; whoever meets me will kill me.'* — 'Yet You in Your boundless mercy have not decreed death upon me ... Behold, my sin is great and You have punished me exceedingly. Protect me that I should not be punished with more than You have decreed, for if I must be a fugitive and wanderer, unable to build myself a house and fence at any one place, and without Your protection, the beasts will kill me.' Thus Cain confessed that man is powerless to save himself by his own strength, but only by the watchfulness of the Supreme One *(Ramban).*

If Your protection were still upon me I would not worry. He Who commanded the earth to give its fruit will command the Heavens to sustain me. My fear is that bereft of Your presence and watchfulness I will be easy prey for anyone who wishes to molest me. Having no secure place, any creature could kill me and no one will avenge me *(Aderes Eliyahu).*

[Thus, my punishment is truly more than I can endure] ...

15. וַיֹּאמֶר לוֹ ה׳ — *And HASHEM said to him.*

Not אֵלָיו, *to him* but לוֹ, i.e. *concerning him (Hirsch).*

לָכֵן כָּל־הֹרֵג קַיִן שִׁבְעָתַיִם יֻקָּם — *Therefore, whoever slays Cain before seven generations have passed will be punished.*

The verse which reads literally *'therefore, anyone who slays Cain sevenfold shall he be avenged'* is obscure and open to several translations. Our rendering follows *Rashi* [and *Ibn Ezra*] who interprets this

ד טז לְבִלְתִּי הַכּוֹת־אֹתוֹ כׇּל־מֹצְאוֹ: וַיֵּצֵא קַיִן
טז מִלִּפְנֵי יהוה וַיֵּשֶׁב בְּאֶרֶץ־נוֹד קִדְמַת־

as 'an abbreviated verse with an implied clause: *Whoever slays Cain* will be punished (this phrase unstated, but understood); as for Cain, only *after seven generations will I execute My vengeance upon him,* when Lamech, one of his descendants will arise and slay him.'

Harav David Feinstein explains that the postponement of the ultimate punishment of Cain is a manifestation of God as אֶרֶךְ אַפַּיִם, long suffering and patient. Nevertheless, Cain was punished in a limited manner by being forced to wander the earth. It is similar to a man who lends someone a large sum of money and accepts payment at the rate of a penny a day. He is patient and merciful, but he does not forfeit the right to payment. So, too, God is patient and merciful in deciding upon the mode of punishment, but he exacts it nonetheless. As a result of his infinitesimal daily suffering as a wanderer Cain's punishment was deferred for hundreds of years.

Radak explains the verse: *'Whoever slays Cain, I will avenge him sevenfold'*, be it man or beast. *'Seven'* means several times over.

God said: 'Whoever slays Cain will have sevenfold vengeance taken on him. I will punish his slayer seven times for his sin, because I have promised Cain that, in the merit of his awe of Me and his confession, he will not be slain. *(Ramban to v.22).*

'Fear not, Cain, because you will be a wanderer and hence unable to defend yourself properly, I therefore decree that whoever slays you shall suffer a sevenfold vengeance — more than for any other murderer' *(Rabbeinu Nissim).*

וַיָּשֶׂם ה׳ לְקַיִן אוֹת ... — *And HASHEM placed a mark upon Cain* (or: *'set a sign for Cain'*]. — [A protective sign.]

The animals, led by the serpent, came to God demanding that Abel's death be avenged. God answered that Cain had no precedent from which to learn the severity of his crime (see above v. 13), and He warned the animals not to kill Cain *(Me'am Loez).*

He set a letter of His Name on Cain's forehead. According to another interpretation: Since Cain sinned he feared the wild beasts. God therefore set a sign for Cain: He made the animals fear him again *(Rashi).*

Ibn Ezra records that various opinions exist as to the nature of this 'sign' [depending on whether one takes Cain to be a remorseful penitent or the reverse *(Hirsch)*]: A horn *(Midrash);* He gave him courage or some sign to allay his fears; but more probably God gave him some sign until Cain was reassured, but the Torah did not reveal what the sign was.

He gave him some sort of permanent sign. Wherever Cain wandered he had a sign from God indicating the safe way to go, and by that he knew that no misfortune would overtake him on his perilous road *(Rambam).*

He made *Cain himself* into a sign or warning for murderers or penitents *(Midrash).*

He assigned a dog to accompany Cain on his travels.[1]

He made the sun shine upon Cain as a sign of divine benevolence.

1. *Chofetz Chaim* explained why a dog was chosen as the sign. A dog is outstanding in its loyalty to a master who has done it a good turn. Abel had overpowered Cain and then released him (see *Midrash,* above *v.* 8). Nevertheless, instead of feeling gratitude, Cain killed him. The dog was a constant reminder to Cain of the gravity of his sin of ingratitude.

IV 16 *so that none that meet him might kill him.* [16] *Cain left the presence of* HASHEM *and settled in the land of Nod, east of Eden.*

[God then reassured Cain of His protection because he was a repentant sinner, but only until the seventh generation.]

16. וַיֵּצֵא קַיִן מִלִּפְנֵי ה׳ — *[And] Cain left the presence of* HASHEM.

He left the hallowed environs of the garden abode of the Divine Presence where the Shechinah had communicated with Adam and Eve and their children *(Radak).*

— He departed joyous that God had promised him protection from physical harm *(Aderes Eliyahu).*

As our Sages understand it, Cain did not simply leave the place; he turned his back on God's wishes. Spurned by earth and man alike, Cain sought to found a new life for himself *(Hirsch).*

— He departed in [pretended] humility as though he could deceive the Most High *(Rashi)* [i.e. since actual *departure* from God's presence is impossible, *'departure'* is interpreted figuratively: he departed spiritually, as if it were possible to shrug off the Shechinah from himself *(Gur Aryeh).*][2]

According to *Ramban,* Cain never stood before Him anymore, as he implied when he said [v.14] *'and from Your countenance I will be hidden.'*

Cain's repentance

[As explained by most commentators, even at this point Cain did not repent *fully* — and he was therefore vulnerable to vengeance after the seventh generation as he was warned in the previous verse. (See *footnote* below). In this context, the *Midrash* cites several views that in departing from God, Cain 'threw God's words behind him' in rejection; another view pictures him departing hypocritically 'like one who shows the cloven hoof' (— a swine shows his cloven hoof pretending to be clean); while a third view has him departing in a 'joyful mood'.

This 'joyful mood' is also variously explained. Some commentators suggest that he was happy that he could now continue in his evil ways (citing in the parallel *Midrash, Shocher Tov* 100, *Esther* 5:9: *'then Haman went forth joyful ...'*), while others maintain that Cain *had* repented fully and rejoiced in his judgment (citing in *Bereishis Rabbah, Exod.* 4:14).

In *Devarim Rabbah* 8, however, Cain's repentance is viewed as more sincere. I quote it fully:

Great is prayer in God's eyes. Rav Eliezer said: If you wish to know the power of prayer, realize that if it does not achieve its entire objective, it achieves at least half of it. Cain rose up against his brother Abel and slew him and the decree went forth: *You shall become* נָע *a vagrant* and נָד *a wanderer on earth* (*v.*12) but immediately he confessed before God and said: Master of the Universe: 'You bear with the whole world and yet with my sin You will not bear? (*v.*13) ... Pardon my iniquity for it is great.' Immediately he found favor before God and He withheld from him the curse of נָע, *vagrant* — which is half

2. It is obvious that Cain did not actually deceive God. God 'sees the heart' and was fully aware that once Cain received clemency, he would resume his evil ways. Nevertheless, Cain claimed sincerity and God allowed him a degree of clemency assured that in the course of time Cain's wickedness would become apparent to all. At that time God would exact full punishment *(Harav David Feinstein).*

ד
יז עֵדֶן: וַיֵּדַע קַיִן אֶת־אִשְׁתּוֹ וַתַּהַר וַתֵּלֶד
יז־יח אֶת־חֲנוֹךְ וַיְהִי בֹּנֶה עִיר וַיִּקְרָא שֵׁם הָעִיר
יח כְּשֵׁם בְּנוֹ חֲנוֹךְ: וַיִּוָּלֵד לַחֲנוֹךְ אֶת־עִירָד
וְעִירָד יָלַד אֶת־מְחוּיָאֵל וּמְחִיָּיאֵל יָלַד
אֶת־מְתוּשָׁאֵל וּמְתוּשָׁאֵל יָלַד אֶת־לָמֶךְ:

the decree — for so it is written: *he dwelt in the land of Nod* [i.e. now after his repentance his wandering was not as compulsive. He apparently spent at least some of his time dwelling in one place. (He was now only a נָע, *wanderer,* not a נָד, *vagrant).*] For, according to *Malbim* נָע refers to one who *wanders* from country to country throughout the world, while נָד refers to being a vagrant within the confines of a certain region.

[Returning to *Bereishis Rabbah*]: Adam met Cain and asked him 'How did your case go?' 'I repented and was granted clemency,' he answered.

Thereupon Adam beat himself and cried: 'so great is the power of repentance and I did not know!' Whereupon he arose and said [*Psalms* 9:21]: מִזְמוֹר שִׁיר לְיוֹם הַשַּׁבָּת, *A psalm for the Sabbath day* [either because this happened on the eve of Sabbath and with the approach of Sabbath he was forgiven *(Ibn Caspi);* or because he took שַׁבָּת Sabbath, homiletically as related to תְּשׁוּבָה, repentance = the day that God accepted repentance *(Yefe To'ar)*] טוֹב לְהֹדוֹת לַה׳, *'it is good to confess to HASHEM'* [cf. *Midrash Tehillim* 100.]

וַיֵּשֶׁב בְּאֶרֶץ־נוֹד קִדְמַת־עֵדֶן — *And settled in the land of Nod; east of Eden.*

The land of Nod [נוֹד =wandering] — i.e. the land where exiles wander about ...

To the *east of Eden,* where his father had been exiled when he was driven out of the garden [cf. 3:24.]. Notably, the eastern region always forms a place of refuge for murderers, for the cities of refuge that Moses later set aside were also to the east, *'the place of sun-rise'* [cf. *Deut.* 4:41] *(Rashi).*

Taking נוֹד, *Nod,* in the sense of 'trembling', *Rashi* offers an alternate interpretation: Wherever Cain went the earth trembled beneath him, and people said: 'Turn away from him: this is the one who killed his brother!'

Radak interprets the word נוֹד as an adjective modifying Cain; thus: *'And he settled in the land as a wanderer'* [cf. *Sanhedrin* 37a; *Torah Temimah.*] He dwelt in the land as a wanderer far from his parents, until he finally settled in the east of Eden. But he found no rest there, either, for it was his fate to be a ceaseless wanderer. He is identified with this region, however, because it was there that he spent most of his time; his family resided there; and it was there that he would return periodically during his wanderings (also *Abarbanel).*

[Or, as suggested by the *Midrashim* cited above, Cain's repentance resulted in clemency from the original decree of vagrancy and wandering. Now he spent at least some of his time dwelling in one place.]

According to *Ramban,* the sense of the verse is that instead of wandering the entire world, Cain remained permanently in one land, perpetually wandering through it without rest. It was named *'the land of Nod'* [wandering] for that reason.

IV 17-18

17 *And Cain knew his wife, and she conceived and*
bore Chanoch. He became a city-builder, and he
named the city after his son Chanoch. 18 *To Chanoch*
was born Irad, and Irad begot Mehujael, and Mehu-
jael begot Methusael, and Methusael begot Lamech.

17. The descendants of Cain

וַיֵּדַע קַיִן אֶת אִשְׁתּוֹ — *And Cain knew his wife.*

Alone, and banished from his parents, he strove to father children with whom to associate, and he begot Chanoch *(Abarbanel).*

According to *Ramban,* it is in order to demonstrate that God is long-suffering [cf. *Exod.* 34:6, this being one of God's Attributes] and that He delayed the time of his punishment that the Torah enumerates Cain's children and works. For Cain did not perish until he lived to see many descendants, the last of whom ultimately perished in the flood. [*Ramban* also cites a *Midrash* that Cain himself perished in the flood. But see *comm. to v.*23.]

Ramban also notes that Cain's descendants consisted of only six generations [Chanoch, Irad, Mehujael, Methushael, Lamech, and his three children: Jabal, Jubal, and Tuval-Cain] while among the descendants of Seth [Adam's third son — see Chapt. 5] there were an additional two generations before the Flood [totalling eight: Enosh, Kenan, Mahalalel, Jared, Chanoch, Methuselah, Lamech and Noah]. *Ramban* suggests that there might have been more descendants, but the Torah had no need to record them, limiting its narrative to the names of those who began the building of cities, the grazing of sheep, the art of music, and metal-working.

וַיְהִי בֹּנֶה עִיר — [*And*] *he became a city-builder.* This refers to Cain *(Rashi).*

At first he thought that he would be childless. When he saw this was not so he built a city *(Ramban).*

— It does not say וַיִּבֶן עִיר, *he built a city.* The term *'builder of a city'* implies that his personality is being described. Cut off from the earth, from God, and from his fellow men, Cain was left only with his own intelligence and talent which he utilized to build cities. Urban life, unlike rural life, 'cultivates' its inhabitants. Hence, the following verses list the sophisticated skills that were developed in his inhabitants *(Hirsch).*

... He still wandered. The wording of the verse indicates that, because his efforts were cursed, he indulged in building the city all his days. He would build a little with great effort, and then wander away only to return and build more *(Ramban).*

Radak comments that the phrase means 'and it happened that he was building a city' — i.e. when his wife gave birth to Chanoch he was in the midst of constructing a city, which he named in honor of his newborn son.

וַיִּקְרָא שֵׁם הָעִיר כְּשֵׁם בְּנוֹ חֲנוֹךְ — *And he named the city after his son Chanoch* [lit. *'and he called the name of the city like the name of his son Chanoch'*]

— He thus proclaimed that he did not build it for himself, because he was cursed and a wanderer. Rather it would be as if Chanoch had built it for himself *(Ramban).*

ד
יט־כג

°חמישי יט °וַיִּקַּח־לוֹ לֶמֶךְ שְׁתֵּי נָשִׁים שֵׁם הָאַחַת
כ עָדָה וְשֵׁם הַשֵּׁנִית צִלָּה: וַתֵּלֶד עָדָה אֶת־
יָבָל הוּא הָיָה אֲבִי יֹשֵׁב אֹהֶל וּמִקְנֶה:
כא וְשֵׁם אָחִיו יוּבָל הוּא הָיָה אֲבִי כָּל־תֹּפֵשׂ
כב כִּנּוֹר וְעוּגָב: וְצִלָּה גַם־הִוא יָלְדָה אֶת־
תּוּבַל קַיִן לֹטֵשׁ כָּל־חֹרֵשׁ נְחֹשֶׁת וּבַרְזֶל
כג וַאֲחוֹת תּוּבַל־קַיִן נַעֲמָה: וַיֹּאמֶר לֶמֶךְ

19. וַיִּקַּח לוֹ לֶמֶךְ — *And Lamech took to himself* ...

The verse could have said simply *'and Lamech begot Jabal* ... etc.' listing the births of generations as it does in succeeding chapters *(Mizrachi)* but the Torah goes into the narrative [*vss.* 23-24] to inform us that God kept the promise that *'vengeance shall be taken on Cain after seven generations.'* For after Lamech had children — the seventh generation — he arose and slew Cain. [See *comm.* to *v.*23] *(Rashi).*

שְׁתֵּי נָשִׁים — *Two wives.*

Such was the practice of the generation of the flood. They would take two wives: One for childbearing and the other for pleasure. The latter would be given a sterility drug and be pampered like a bride, while the former would be bereft of companionship, and left mourning like a widow throughout her life [cf. *comm.* to *Job* 24:21.] *(Midrash; Rashi).*

שֵׁם הָאַחַת עָדָה . . . צִלָּה — *The name of one was Adah, and the name of the other* [lit. *'second'*] *was Tzilah.*

Adah was the childbearing wife, while Tzilah was reserved for pleasure [cf. *comm.* to v. 22] *(Rashi).*

According to the *Midrash,* Adah's name homiletically indicated 'turning away', for she became repulsive to her husband and he turned away from her, while Tzilah's name indicated that she constantly dwelt in his צֵל, *shadow.*

Or, as *Yerushalmi Yevamos* 6:5 holds that the roles were reversed: Adah was so named because Lamech luxuriated [מִתְעַדֵּן] in her; Tzilah was so named because she dwelt in the shadow of her children.

20. הוּא הָיָה אֲבִי יֹשֵׁב אֹהֶל וּמִקְנֶה — *He was the first* [lit. *'father'; 'ancestor'*] *of those who dwell in tents and breed cattle.*

[*'Breed'* is not in the Hebrew but implied. *Targum* renders: 'Masters of cattle'; *Radak* suggests 'with' [i.e. amidst cattle.]

Rashi explains that he was the first to pasture cattle. He dwelt in tents, leading a nomadic existence, moving on to new pastures whenever the grass in one place was finished.

— He was the first to study husbandry. By introducing this, the void left by the death of Abel — with whom the art died — was filled *(Ralbag).*

These occupations are listed to show how the world's various crafts originated *(Aderes Eliyahu).*

According to a *Midrash* cited by *Rashi* he was the first to provoke

IV
19-22

19 Lamech took to himself two wives: the name of
one was Adah, and the name of the other was Tzilah.
20 And Adah bore Jabal; he was the first of those who
dwell in tents and breed cattle. 21 The name of his
brother was Jubal; he was the first of all who handle
the harp and flute. 22 And Tzilah, too — she bore
Tuval-cain, who sharpened all cutting implements of
brass and iron. And the sister of Tuval-cain was
Naamah.

God's jealousy [מְקַנֵּא = being jealous] by erecting temples for idol worship.

21. כָּל־תֹּפֵשׂ כִּנּוֹר וְעוּגָב — *Who handle the harp and flute.*

I.e. he was the originator of the art of music *(Radak).*

According to *Rashi,* he used these musical instruments to make music for idol-worship.

22. וְצִלָּה גַם־הִוא יָלְדָה — *And Tzilah, too — she bore.*

Although she was the wife intended for frivolity rather than childbearing [see. *comm.* v.19] she nevertheless bore; the contraceptive potion was ineffective and she conceived *(Da'as Zekeinim).*

— She was perpetually downcast and God showed her compassion. She bore first *(Aderes Eliyahu).*

God had wanted her to bear seed and whatever Lemech did to prevent it was ineffective *(R' Bachya).*

תּוּבַל קַיִן — *Tuval-Cain.*

— Indicating that he 'improved upon' [תבל] Cain's work by preparing the weapons for bloodshed [i.e. making it easier to continue Cain's murderous precedent] *(Rashi).*

לֹטֵשׁ כָּל־חֹרֵשׁ נְחֹשֶׁת וּבַרְזֶל — *Who sharpened all cutting implements of brass and iron* [following *Rashi.*]

אֲבִי, 'the first', as found in *v.* 21, is extended by implication to this verse *(Ibn Janach).* Or: the 'master' of all those who understand the working of brass and iron *(Targum);* the first to forge brass and iron into utensils *(Midrash HaGodol).*

וַאֲחוֹת תּוּבַל־קַיִן נַעֲמָה — *And the sister of Tuval-Cain was Naamah.*

Her name (meaning 'lovely') is mentioned because she was the wife of Noah, and her deeds were lovely and pleasant *(Rashi).* She was famous and, being a righteous woman, she gave birth to righteous children. Thus, a token remembrance of Cain was left in the world *(Ramban).*

Noting that according to certain *Midrashim* she was not the same Naamah who was Noah's wife, *Ramban* counters that if she were not the woman from whom Noah begot his three sons, there would have been no reason for the Torah to mention her.

According to *Zohar Chadash,* she was righteous and lovely in her deeds as her name suggests. Rav Abahu said that the 'and' refers to the beginning of the verse: *'he sharpened'* ... and so did she. He created the art and she collaborated with him ... Rav Yitzchak said, quoting Rav Yochanan: she was called Naamah because of her beauty. She was the progenitor of those because of whom the בְּנֵי הָאֱלֹהִים erred. (See 6:2)

ד
כד־כה

לְנָשָׁיו עָדָה וְצִלָּה שְׁמַעַן קוֹלִי נְשֵׁי לֶמֶךְ
הַאְזֵנָּה אִמְרָתִי כִּי אִישׁ הָרַגְתִּי לְפִצְעִי
כד וְיֶלֶד לְחַבֻּרָתִי: כִּי שִׁבְעָתַיִם יֻקַּם־קָיִן
כה וְלֶמֶךְ שִׁבְעִים וְשִׁבְעָה: וַיֵּדַע אָדָם עוֹד
אֶת־אִשְׁתּוֹ וַתֵּלֶד בֵּן וַתִּקְרָא אֶת־שְׁמוֹ

23-24. Lamech's Plea

עָדָה צִלָּה שְׁמַעַן קוֹלִי — *Adah and Tzila, hear my voice.*

Even if you were not my wives you should, as intelligent women, hear my anguished voice *(Ha'amek Davar).*

נְשֵׁי לֶמֶךְ הַאְזֵנָּה אִמְרָתִי — *Wives of Lamech give ear to my speech.*

... But since you *are* my wives you should definitely give close attention to what I am about to say *(ibid.)*

Rashi explains that Lamech was blind and his son, Tubal-Cain used to lead him. One day, Tubal-Cain saw Cain and mistook him for an animal. He bade his father shoot an arrow which killed Cain. When he approached and realized it was his forefather Cain, Lamech beat his hands together [in grief] and [accidentally] struck his son, killing him. This angered his wives who denied themselves to him, and he now tried to appease them: *'Hear my voice'* — Obey me and return to me. [The bracketed words are added on the basis of *Tanchuma.*]

כִּי אִישׁ הָרַגְתִּי לְפִצְעִי — *Have I slain man by my wound?* i.e. Did I slay him [i.e. Cain] with premeditation so that the wound should be considered my deliberate act? *(Rashi).*

פֶּצַע indicates a wound inflicted by the sword *(Aderes Eliyahu).*

וְיֶלֶד לְחַבֻּרָתִי — *and a child by my bruise?*

I.e. and the child that I slew [my son], was he slain by a blow directed *intentionally* by me? *(Rashi).*

... חַבּוּרָה is a wound inflicted by a stone [i.e. by concussion] *(Aderes Eliyahu).*

24. כִּי שִׁבְעָתַיִם ... שִׁבְעִים וְשִׁבְעָה — *If ... at seven generations ... seventy-seven.*

— I.e. If the punishment of Cain, an intentional murderer, was delayed until the seventh generation, surely my punishment will be deferred many times seven because I killed accidentally! He thus used *'seventy-seven'* to denote many times seven [i.e. a long period, not meaning exactly seventy-seven] *(Rashi).*

Rashi adds that according to *Midrash Rabbah,* however, Lamech killed no one, but his wives separated from him because of God's decree that Cain's descendants would be destroyed after seven generations, and they refused to bear children who [according to them] were doomed to perish in a flood. Accordingly, Lamech asks, "Did *I* slay Abel — who was a *'man'* in deeds but a *'child'* in years — לְפִצְעִי, so that *I* should be wounded; so that *my* descendants should be exterminated in punishment for it? If Cain who *had* killed had his punishment delayed seven generations, it is certain that punishment against me — as I am blameless — will be delayed for many generations."

But this argument is absurd, for if God would endlessly postpone His decrees, He could never exact His debt or fulfill His word!

IV 23-25

[23] *And Lamech said to his wives, 'Adah and Tzilah,
hear my voice; wives of Lamech, give ear to my
speech: Have I slain a man by my wound and a child
by my bruise?* [24] *If Cain suffered vengeance at seven
generations; then Lamech at seventy-seven!'*
[25] *Adam knew his wife again, and she bore a son*

Targum unlike *Rashi*, renders the verses as a statement of assurance rather than a rhetorical question:

"I have not slain a man that I should bear guilt on his account; or destroyed a young man that my posterity [חַבָּרָתִי = my חַבּוּרָה, *company, posterity*] should be consumed. If seven generations are suspended for Cain, will there not be to Lamech, his son, seventy-seven?"

The *Midrash* continues that they went to put their case before Adam who told them to do their duty and procreate and not be concerned with what God might do in the future; 'You do your duty and God will do His!'

They responded to Adam: 'Perfect yourself first! Have *you* kept apart from Eve a hundred and thirty years for any reason but to avoid having children? [They did not realize that he separated from Eve these 130 years as an act of repentance, not because he feared the future. But such abstention was nevertheless improper *(Me'am Loez).*]

Upon hearing them, however, Adam resumed having children [next verse.]

Ramban cites several interpretations: In response to his wives, who feared having children because they would be the seventh generation from Cain, Lamech comforted them by saying that he would pray on their behalf and God would be long-suffering with them yet another generation ...

Ramban concludes that in his opinion Lamech's wives feared that he would be held accountable by God for having taught his son Tuval-Cain to forge implements of war and murder. He therefore assured them that they had nothing to fear: *'I have not slayed a man by wounds nor a child by bruises',* meaning, I did not murder someone as Cain did. The mere manufacture of a sword is not equivalent to murder. God will surely protect me for I have shed no blood.'

Rav Yosef Kara [cited by *B'chor Shor*] comments that Lamech's wives always wrangled with each other, and he complained to them: "What is my sin that there is no peace in my house? Have I slain man or child that such misfortune has befallen me, and no other man? I can no longer endure it and I will die because of your constant altercations. God, who will avenge Cain though he sinned, will certainly avenge my death ..."

25. Seth and his descendants.

וַיֵּדַע אָדָם עוֹד *And Adam knew ... again.*

This occurrence happened previously but first the Torah completed the entire narrative of Cain and Abel and now returned to detail the generation of Seth and his descendants. This is an example of אֵין מוּקְדָם וּמְאוּחָר בַּתּוֹרָה, 'the Torah does not concern itself with chronological sequence', the Torah arranges each general topic (such as the story of Cain and Abel) separately *(Aderes Eliyahu).*

— Adam saw that Abel was dead, Cain was cursed, and Cain's descendants had gone in evil ways. He 'knew' his wife again — after a

ד שֵׁת כִּי שָׁת־לִי אֱלֹהִים זֶרַע אַחֵר תַּחַת
כו כו הֶבֶל כִּי הֲרָגוֹ קָיִן׃ וּלְשֵׁת גַּם־הוּא יֻלַּד־בֵּן
ה וַיִּקְרָא אֶת־שְׁמוֹ אֱנוֹשׁ אָז הוּחַל לִקְרֹא
א °ששי א בְּשֵׁם יהוה׃ °זֶה סֵפֶר תּוֹלְדֹת אָדָם

separation of 130 years *(Midrash)* — to ensure that worthwhile forebears of mankind would be produced *(Malbim)*.

כִּי שָׁת לִי אֱלֹהִים זֶרַע אַחֵר — *Because* [she said *(Radak)*]: *'God has provided me'* [or: *'appointed for me'*] *another child* [lit. *'seed'*] — lasting seed *(Malbim)*; unlike the former *(Lekach Tov)*.

Eve does not accentuate her part in the birth of the child as she did when she first gave birth [*v.*1]. Then she said קָנִיתִי, *'I' have acquired*, stressing *her* role; Now she says *'God* has provided me; not as אִישׁ, *man*, but as זֶרַע, *seed*, the means for a new future' *(Hirsch)*.

כִּי הֲרָגוֹ קָיִן — *For Cain had killed him.*

— And he left no descendants *(Radak)*.

26. אֱנוֹשׁ — *Enosh.*

Seth was indeed a great man. He called his son *Enosh*, meaning 'man' (as in *Psalms* 8:5 *what is* אֱנוֹשׁ, *man, that You are mindful of him?)* although everyone else in his generation was *'calling upon God's name'*, by associating their own names with God's, e.g. Mechu*yael*, Mesusha*el* [i.e. the suffix *el* is a name of God] *(B'chor Shor)*.

But development does not progress only positively, sometimes it regresses, negatively. Seth also begot a son. He called him Enosh, a name (related to אנס, force, and ענש, punishment) which designates a troubled stage of mankind in contrast to the pure state of Adam *(Hirsch)*.

אָז הוּחַל לִקְרֹא בְּשֵׁם ה׳ — *Then to call in the Name of* HASHEM *became profaned.*

Following *Rashi* and *Midrash*: who interpret הוּחַל as לְשׁוֹן חוּלִין, meaning *'profane'*: Man and lifeless objects were called by the Name of God, and idolatry began.

Some commentaries on *Rashi* suggest, based upon early manuscripts of *Rashi*, that the words לְשׁוֹן חוּלִין 'meaning profane' should be omitted, for *Rashi* also holds that הוּחַל means הִתְחִיל, *began.* This will bring *Rashi* into close harmony with his own commentary to *Shabbos* 118b where, commenting upon the generation of Enosh, he states: — 'during which they *started* to serve idols as it is written אָז הוּחַל [then it was begun.]'

The translation of הוּחַל = הִתְחִיל, *began* also results in diametrically opposite interpretations:

'That was the generation in whose days they began to err, and to make themselves idols, and surnamed their idols by the name of the Word of HASHEM' *(Targum Yonasan; Tur)*.[1]

1. This is how *Rambam* treats the subject. It is so very fundamental that we cite it at length:

In the days of Enosh, the people fell into gross error, and the wise men of the generation began to give foolish counsel. Enosh himself was among those who erred. Their error was as follows: 'Since God created these stars and spheres to guide the world, set them on high and allotted them honor, and since they are ministers who serve before Him, they deserve to be praised and glorified, and honor should be rendered them. It is the will of God, blessed be He, that men should aggrandize and honor those whom He aggrandized and honored — just as a king wants respect to be shown to the officers who stand before Him, thereby honoring the

IV *and named him Seth, because: 'God has provided me*
26 *another child in place of Abel, for Cain had killed*
him.' 26 And as for Seth, to him also a son was born,
and he named him Enosh. Then to call in the Name of
V *HASHEM became profaned.*
1 *1 This is the account of the descendants of Adam—*

Others, conversely, perceive the verse as a statement of renewed worship of HASHEM:

Then did the righteous begin to pray in the Name of HASHEM *(Rashbam; Ibn Ezra; Ibn Caspi).*

The righteous then began to publicly expound the Name of HASHEM to counter the idolaters whose teachings began during that period as the Sages note *(Sforno).*

Hirsch interprets similarly and explains that the Name HASHEM represents man's realization that he must sanctify his earthly existence in submission to the dictates of God. Man never forgot Elokim, that there is a God who created heaven and earth, but that is not enough. It is the fulfillment of the HASHEM calling that is man's vital mission, and which became neglected in the time of Enosh.

V

1. The Genealogy of Mankind

זֶה סֵפֶר תּוֹלְדֹת אָדָם — *This is the account* [or lit. *'book'*] *of the descendants of Adam* [or: *'man'*].

A new narrative begins, enumerating the generations from Adam to Noah. The genealogy traces the line through Seth for it was through him that the human race survived; Abel died without issue, and Cain's descendants perished *(Radak; Chizkuni).*

Malbim, too, comments that in a real sense the entire history of the 'generations of Adam' begins with this verse. For this reason there is an

king.' When they conceived this idea, they began to erect temples to the stars, offered up sacrifices to them, praised and glorified them in speech, and prostrated themselves before them — to obtain the Creator's favor, according to their corrupt notions. This was the root of idolatry, and this was what the idolaters, who knew its fundamentals, said. They did not however maintain that, except for the particular star which was the object of their worship, there was no God. All knew that He alone is God; their error and folly consisted in imagining that this vain worship was His desire.

In course of time, false prophets arose who asserted that God had commanded and explicitly told them, 'Worship that particular star, ... offer such and such sacrifices to it. Erect a temple to it. Make a statue of it, to which all the people — the women, children, and the rest of the community — shall bow down' ... They began to make figures in temples, where they would assemble, bow down to the figures, and tell all the people that this particular figure conferred benefits and inflicted injuries, and that it was proper to worship and fear it.

So gradually the custom spread throughout the world to worship figures with various types of worship, such as offering them sacrifices and bowing to them. As time went on, the honored and revered Name of God was forgotten by mankind, vanished from their lips and hearts, and was no longer known to them. All the common people and the women and children knew only the figure of wood and stone, and the temple edifice in which they had been trained from their childhood to prostrate themselves to the figure, worship it, and swear by its name. Even their wise men, such as priests and the like, also fancied that there is no God save for the stars and heavenly spheres for which the figures were made.

But The Creator of the Universe was known to none, and recognized by none, save a few solitary individuals, such as Enosh, Methuselah, Noah, Shem, and Eber. The world moved on in this fashion, until the Pillar of the World, the Patriarch Abraham, was born *(Hilchos Avodas Kochavim* 1:1,2).

בְּיוֹם בְּרֹא אֱלֹהִים אָדָם בִּדְמוּת אֱלֹהִים
ב עָשָׂה אֹתוֹ: זָכָר וּנְקֵבָה בְּרָאָם וַיְבָרֶךְ
אֹתָם וַיִּקְרָא אֶת־שְׁמָם אָדָם בְּיוֹם
ג הִבָּרְאָם: וַיְחִי אָדָם שְׁלֹשִׁים וּמְאַת שָׁנָה

opinion in the *Midrash* that this verse forms the true beginning of the Torah, in the sense that everything preceding it rightfully belongs to the 'history of heaven and earth' [2:4] rather than of man. The descendants of Cain are considered insignificant because they did not survive.[1]

According to *Sforno*, the phrase is to be rendered: *'this is the history of the events which befell the human race.'*

[This translation of סֵפֶר [lit. *'book'*] as *'account'* follows *Rashi* who apparently relates it to the cognate verb meaning enumerate, count, tell, narrate.]

This has its basis in the *Talmud Avodah Zarah* 5a:

What is the meaning of the verse [lit.] *this is the book of the generations of Adam?* Did Adam have a book? — What it implies is that God showed to Adam every generation with its expositors, every generation with its Sages, every generation with its leaders ...'

When God showed these generations to Adam, he saw among them David who was destined to live for only three hours. Adam then turned to God, asking: 'Can his fate not be changed?'

'Thus have I decreed', was His reply.

'What is the span of my life? Adam asked.

On being told that he would live one thousand years, he asked whether he would be permitted to make a gift. When God agreed, Adam exclaimed: 'I hereby give to David seventy years of my own life!'

Adam then said: 'O Master of the world, how beautiful is his reign and the gift of song given him, to sing of Your glory, for seventy years!

בְּיוֹם בְּרֹא אֱלֹהִים אָדָם ... — *On the day that God created man He made him in the likeness of God.*

I.e. he was created in the perfection of God's likeness *(Ralbag)* from the very day of his creation ...[2]

The verse mentions that man was created in God's likeness to emphasize that he was created with free will. This justifies God's punishment of man when he sins *(Sforno).*

2. זָכָר וּנְקֵבָה בְּרָאָם — *He created them male and female.* [cf. *comm.* to 1:27.]

— Adam had neither father nor mother. Just as God created him out of nothing, so He created his wife *(Ramban).*

— Right from the very beginning God created 'mankind' male and female, with equal Godliness and of equal worth. Neither was more in the likeness of God than the other, both were given the same blessing by God, both together were given

1. There is an interesting comment in *Yerushalmi Nedarim* 9:4:

R' Akiva said: the dictum וְאָהַבְתָּ לְרֵעֲךָ כָּמוֹךָ *You shall love your fellow as yourself* [*Lev.* 19:18] is the great principle in the Torah. *Ben Azzai* said *'This is the account of the descendants of Adam'* is an even greater principle [because by stating clearly that all mankind descends from Adam it emphasizes even more profoundly the Brotherhood of Man; [cf. *Torah Temimah* who further explains that this verse stresses that man was made in the likeness of God, so that no person should ever fail to honor his fellows properly. Man must never slight the honor due to his fellows.]

On the day that God created man, He made him in
the likeness of God. [2] *He created them male and*
female. He blessed them and called them Man on the
day they were created.—
[3] *When Adam had lived one hundred and thirty*

the name 'Adam' ... *(Hirsch).*

וַיְבָרֶךְ אֹתָם — [*And*] *He blessed them.*

By endowing them with the power of procreation [cf. 1:28]. This indicates that begetting children is not simply a natural function, but comes as a specific *'blessing'* of God. Adam and Eve were not 'born'; they were created from nothing and were blessed with the ability to procreate *(Ramban).*

The *Talmud* comments that a man without a wife is not a man, for it is said, *'male and female He created them* ... and called their name Man' [i.e. only together, as man and wife, is he called *'Man'*] *(Yevamos* 63a).

וַיִּקְרָא אֶת־שְׁמָם אָדָם בְּיוֹם הִבָּרְאָם — *And He called them Man* [lit. *'and He called their name Man'*] *on the day they were created* — i.e. He called both of them Man — including Eve — because her formation was from the man. Individually, however, she was called Eve *(R' Meyuchas).*

Harav David Cohen points out that male and female components were originally created in the single body of Adam *(Eruvin* 18a). Thus, when God named him Adam, it was implicit that his female part — which was later to become a separate human being — was also called Adam, because male and female were two halves of one whole.

And as *Abarbanel* comments:

They were called Adam, *man,* rather than נְעָרִים, *youths, or* יְלָדִים, *children,* to indicate, as the Sages say, that they were created as adults — twenty years old, mature in body, physical development, and knowledge. [Cf. *comm.* to 2:1 צְבָאָם = צִבְיוֹנָם.]

For in sum total the verse is to be understood that He created them male and female and called them Adam when they were created. I.e. they were fully endowed with their essential nature from the day they were created; no new essential characteristics were added afterwards *(Ralbag).*

This recalls Solomon's conclusion: [*Eccles.* 7:29] *'God has made man* [or: *'Adam'*] *simple, but they sought many intrigues' (Malbim).*

Torah Shelemah 5:32 cites the *Midrash Sh'loshah V'Arbaah:*

Adam has seven different meanings: (1) It is the name of the first man; (2) of his wife; (3) all his children; (4) people, too, in general, are called Adam; (5) it signifies man as distinct from woman; (6) and woman as distinct from man. (7) It is also the name of a city [*Joshua* 3:16.]

3. וַיְחִי אָדָם שְׁלֹשִׁים וּמְאַת שָׁנָה — *When* [lit. *'and'*] *Adam had lived one hundred and thirty years.*

2. Man's true state of nature is not that of a mentally and morally restricted savage, as most people think. On the contrary, his true natural state is his likeness to God. Then, as the world blossoms around him as a paradise, he is mentally awake and morally pure, listening to the Voice of God wandering in the garden; for 'on the day that God created man,' he was Godlike and pure, striving upwards to God *(Hirsch).*

ה
ד־ו

וַיּוֹלֶד בִּדְמוּתוֹ כְּצַלְמוֹ וַיִּקְרָא אֶת־שְׁמוֹ
ד שֵׁת: וַיִּהְיוּ יְמֵי־אָדָם אַחֲרֵי הוֹלִידוֹ אֶת־
שֵׁת שְׁמֹנֶה מֵאֹת שָׁנָה וַיּוֹלֶד בָּנִים וּבָנוֹת:
ה וַיִּהְיוּ כָּל־יְמֵי אָדָם אֲשֶׁר־חַי תְּשַׁע מֵאוֹת
ו שָׁנָה וּשְׁלֹשִׁים שָׁנָה וַיָּמֹת: וַיְחִי־

[The specifics of the genealogies are now recorded, enumerating the ten generations from Adam to Noah. Tracing the genealogy of mankind through Seth, the Torah notes that one hundred and thirty years elapsed from Adam's creation and since his sin and expulsion from the Garden of Eden, which, as explained by the *Midrashim,* all happened on the first day of his existence — see *footnote* to 3:1).]

Rashi comments that during this 130 year period he kept from his wife [see *comm.* to 4:24-25.]

וַיּוֹלֶד בִּדְמוּתוֹ כְּצַלְמוֹ—*[And] he begot in his likeness and his image.* I.e. he begot Seth who was in Adam's own likeness. Eve had previously given birth to Cain who was not similar to Adam, and who slew Abel. Cain was then cast out and his descendants are not even listed in this genealogy of Adam. But afterwards there was born one like Adam and he was named Seth *(Targum Yonasan).*

Everything born of the living is in the likeness of that which bore it! The verse particularly points out that he begot in his likeness and his image to indicate that God gave Adam, who himself was created in God's likeness, the capacity to reproduce offspring who were also in this ennobled likeness. This is not mentioned concerning Cain or Abel because, since their seed perished anyway, the Torah did not wish to prolong the descriptions of them *(Ibn Ezra; Ramban).*

Sforno notes that Seth emulated Adam, and he was even more righteous than his older brothers, for even Abel did not sacrifice until Cain did so first! [But cf. *comm.* to 4:4.]

וַיִּקְרָא אֶת־שְׁמוֹ שֵׁת — *And he named him Seth* — meaning 'permanence', 'endurance', for Adam perceived in his wisdom that this child and his descendants would endure in this world *(Abarbanel).* [cf. 4:24.]

4. **שְׁמֹנֶה מֵאֹת שָׁנָה** — *Eight hundred years.*

The exceptional longevity of these personages is noted by the commentators.

Rambam [in *Moreh Nevuchim* 1:7] holds that only those distinguished individuals mentioned in this chapter lived so long. Other people lived an ordinary life-span. These people were exceptions either because of their diet or mode of living, or because a special miracle was wrought for them.

Radak adds that these longer life-spans were necessary to allow them to learn and preserve for their posterity the wisdom and art that would serve as the foundation for future generations. A normal seventy or eighty year life-span would not have sufficed.

V
4-5

years, he begot in his likeness and his image, and he
named him Seth. [4] *And the days of Adam after beget-*
ting Seth were eight hundred years, and he begot
sons and daughters. [5] *All the days that Adam lived*
were nine hundred and thirty years; and he died.

Ramban is of the opinion that Adam, as God's handiwork, was physically perfect, and the same applied to his children. As such it was his nature to live a long time. After the flood, however, a deterioration of the atmosphere caused a gradual shortening of life until it would appear that in the times of the Patriarchs people lived a normal lifespan of seventy and eighty years, while only the most righteous ones lived longer ...

[Cf. *comm.* to *Peleg* and *Joktan* in 8:25.]

וַיּוֹלֶד בָּנִים וּבָנוֹת — *And he begot sons and daughters* — i.e. during those eight hundred years *(Targum Yerushalmi).*

Ibn Ezra thus renders, *'having begotten sons and daughters.'*

5. וַיִּהְיוּ כָּל־יְמֵי אָדָם אֲשֶׁר־חַי — [*And*] *all the days that Adam lived were* [i.e. in the aggregate. It follows from what has already been stated that all the days that Adam lived came to so-and-so many years.]

The total number of years is given even though the parts are listed [i.e. age when begetting and years lived thereafter] so that a chronologist will not err. Thus each number proves the other *(Radak).*

תְּשַׁע מֵאוֹת שָׁנָה וּשְׁלֹשִׁים שָׁנָה — *Nine hundred and thirty years.*

N'tziv notes that sometimes the Torah lists the larger number of years first and then the smaller number [as in the case of Adam: *nine hundred years and thirty years*] while sometimes the procedure is reversed as in 5:8. He explains that when the closing years of a person's life are relatively as productive and righteous as the bulk of his lifetime, the larger figure is given first, the implication being that all of his years were as productive as the major period of his life.

Following the *Midrashim* cited earlier in the commentary, Adam originally had one thousand years to live [because he was to die on *'the day'* he ate of the tree, 'day' being understood as יוֹמוֹ שֶׁל הקב״ה 'a day of God' to whom a thousand years are but a day that has passed *(Ps.* 90:4).] However, Adam bequeathed 70 years of his life to David; hence he died at 930 *(Zohar;* cf. *Avodah Zarah* 5a cited in *v.*1).

וַיָּמֹת — *And he died.*

And was buried by Chanoch *(Seder Olam).*

The Torah specifically says *'and he died'* in all these verses to emphasize that even the wicked among them died a natural death and were not destroyed in the Flood *(R' Bachya; Kli Yakar).*

When Adam died Eve did not know what became of his remains. She petitioned God that since she had come from Adam's side, and they were together in Paradise, that God not separate them in death, and that she be buried together with

שֵׁת חָמֵשׁ שָׁנִים וּמְאַת שָׁנָה וַיּוֹלֶד אֶת־ ה
אֱנוֹשׁ: וַיְחִי־שֵׁת אַחֲרֵי הוֹלִידוֹ אֶת־אֱנוֹשׁ ז ז־כ
שֶׁבַע שָׁנִים וּשְׁמֹנֶה מֵאוֹת שָׁנָה וַיּוֹלֶד
בָּנִים וּבָנוֹת: וַיִּהְיוּ כָּל־יְמֵי־שֵׁת שְׁתֵּים ח
עֶשְׂרֵה שָׁנָה וּתְשַׁע מֵאוֹת שָׁנָה וַיָּמֹת:
וַיְחִי אֱנוֹשׁ תִּשְׁעִים שָׁנָה וַיּוֹלֶד ט
אֶת־קֵינָן: וַיְחִי אֱנוֹשׁ אַחֲרֵי הוֹלִידוֹ אֶת־ י
קֵינָן חֲמֵשׁ עֶשְׂרֵה שָׁנָה וּשְׁמֹנֶה מֵאוֹת
שָׁנָה וַיּוֹלֶד בָּנִים וּבָנוֹת: וַיִּהְיוּ כָּל־יְמֵי יא
אֱנוֹשׁ חָמֵשׁ שָׁנִים וּתְשַׁע מֵאוֹת שָׁנָה
וַיָּמֹת: וַיְחִי קֵינָן שִׁבְעִים שָׁנָה יב
וַיּוֹלֶד אֶת־מַהֲלַלְאֵל: וַיְחִי קֵינָן אַחֲרֵי יג
הוֹלִידוֹ אֶת־מַהֲלַלְאֵל אַרְבָּעִים שָׁנָה
וּשְׁמֹנֶה מֵאוֹת שָׁנָה וַיּוֹלֶד בָּנִים וּבָנוֹת:
וַיִּהְיוּ כָּל־יְמֵי קֵינָן עֶשֶׂר שָׁנִים וּתְשַׁע יד
מֵאוֹת שָׁנָה וַיָּמֹת: וַיְחִי מַהֲלַלְאֵל טו
חָמֵשׁ שָׁנִים וְשִׁשִּׁים שָׁנָה וַיּוֹלֶד אֶת־יָרֶד:
וַיְחִי מַהֲלַלְאֵל אַחֲרֵי הוֹלִידוֹ אֶת־יֶרֶד טז
שְׁלֹשִׁים שָׁנָה וּשְׁמֹנֶה מֵאוֹת שָׁנָה וַיּוֹלֶד
בָּנִים וּבָנוֹת: וַיִּהְיוּ כָּל־יְמֵי מַהֲלַלְאֵל יז
חָמֵשׁ וְתִשְׁעִים שָׁנָה וּשְׁמֹנֶה מֵאוֹת שָׁנָה
וַיָּמֹת: וַיְחִי־יֶרֶד שְׁתַּיִם וְשִׁשִּׁים יח
שָׁנָה וּמְאַת שָׁנָה וַיּוֹלֶד אֶת־חֲנוֹךְ: וַיְחִי־ יט
יֶרֶד אַחֲרֵי הוֹלִידוֹ אֶת־חֲנוֹךְ שְׁמֹנֶה
מֵאוֹת שָׁנָה וַיּוֹלֶד בָּנִים וּבָנוֹת: וַיִּהְיוּ כָּל־ כ

Adam. She raised up her eyes to God and said: 'Dear God, receive my soul!' and she died *(Zohar Chadash)*.

Eve was then buried in the Cave of Machpelah near Adam (cf. *Eruvin* 53a).

Adam had prepared the sepulcher for himself very deep within the earth lest his descendants venerate

V
6-20

6 When Seth had lived one hundred and five years
he begot Enosh. 7 Seth lived eight hundred and seven
years after begetting Enosh, and he begot sons and
daughters. 8 All the days of Seth were nine hundred
and twelve years; and he died.

9 When Enosh had lived ninety years, he begot
Kenan. 10 And Enosh lived eight hundred and fifteen
years after begetting Kenan, and he begot sons and
daughters. 11 All the days of Enosh were nine
hundred and five years; and he died.

12 When Kenan had lived seventy years, he begot
Mahalalel. 13 And Kenan lived eight hundred and
forty years after begetting Mahalalel, and he begot
sons and daughters. 14 All the days of Kenan were
nine hundred and ten years; and he died.

15 When Mahalalel had lived sixty five years, he
begot Jared. 16 And Mahalalel lived eight hundred
and thirty years after begetting Jared, and he begot
sons and daughters. 17 All the days of Mahalalel were
eight hundred and ninety five years; and he died.

18 When Jared had lived one hundred and sixty-
two years, he begot Chanoch. 19 And Jared lived eight
hundred years after begetting Chanoch and he begot
sons and daughters. 20 All the days of Jared came to

his remains as a god after his death.

He found the spot when he noticed a small light shining forth from it and he became attracted to it *(Zohar).*

When a man dies he is presented to Adam whom he accuses of being the cause of all humankind's death. But Adam repudiates this, saying: 'True, I committed one sin. But is there even one among you — even the most pious, who has not been guilty of more than one?' *(Zohar).*

The Ten Generations from Adam to Noah

There were ten generations from Adam to Noah. This demonstrates how long-suffering God was, for all the generations kept provoking Him until he brought upon them the waters of the flood *(Avos* 5:2).

Observe: all the generations between Adam and Noah provoked God by their evil ways, yet He restrained His wrath during all these generations. Ultimately,

יְמֵי־יֶרֶד שְׁתַּיִם וְשִׁשִּׁים שָׁנָה וּתְשַׁע
כא מֵאוֹת שָׁנָה וַיָּמֹת: וַיְחִי חֲנוֹךְ
חָמֵשׁ וְשִׁשִּׁים שָׁנָה וַיּוֹלֶד אֶת־מְתוּשָׁלַח:
כב וַיִּתְהַלֵּךְ חֲנוֹךְ אֶת־הָאֱלֹהִים אַחֲרֵי
הוֹלִידוֹ אֶת־מְתוּשֶׁלַח שְׁלֹשׁ מֵאוֹת שָׁנָה
כג וַיּוֹלֶד בָּנִים וּבָנוֹת: וַיְהִי כָּל־יְמֵי חֲנוֹךְ
חָמֵשׁ וְשִׁשִּׁים שָׁנָה וּשְׁלֹשׁ מֵאוֹת שָׁנָה:
כד וַיִּתְהַלֵּךְ חֲנוֹךְ אֶת־הָאֱלֹהִים וְאֵינֶנּוּ כִּי־

however, he brought the waters of the flood upon them because He will not be patient forever!

This is how we must think of our present state of Exile. Do not think that He will restrain Himself indefinitely against our oppressors because He is a long-suffering God! Be assured that He will certainly requite them according to their evil ways, and He will yet redeem and save us *(Rabbeinu Yonah).*

The Chronology of the generations

(Based upon *Seder Olam.* See Chronology/Time Line p. xii).

- ☙ אָדָם — *Adam*: died in 930;
- ☙ שֵׁת — *Seth:* born in the year 130 from creation. After him the generations began doing evil [see *Rambam* cited in *footnote* to 4:26]; died in 1042;
- ☙ אֱנוֹשׁ — *Enosh:* 235-1140.
- ☙ קֵינָן — *Kenan:* 325-1235.
- ☙ מַהֲלַלְאֵל — *Mehalalel:* 395-1290;
- ☙ יֶרֶד — *Jared:* 460-1422;
- ☙ חֲנוֹךְ — *Chanoch:* 622-987;
- ☙ מְתוּשֶׁלַח — *Methuselah;* 687-1656;
- ☙ לֶמֶךְ — *Lamech:* 874-1651;
- ☙ נֹחַ — *Noah:* 1056-2006.

Thus, Noah was born 126 years after Adam died; Lamech was the farthest descendant Adam lived to see.[1]

22. Chanoch

וַיִּתְהַלֵּךְ חֲנוֹךְ אֶת הָאֱלֹהִים — *And Chanoch* [usually transliterated *'Enoch'*] *walked with God.*

— I.e. he was wholly righteous, dedicating his life solely to the service of God, to the exclusion of all other interests *(Ibn Caspi).*

This is in contrast to the others who merely existed and preserved the race physically *(Hoffmann).*

As it says [*Deut.* 13:5]: *'You shall walk after HASHEM your God';* [6:9]: *'Noah walked with God' (Ibn Ezra).*

1. The *Talmud* notes that there were seven men whose lives spanned the entire history of man:

For Methusaleh saw Adam; Shem [son of Noah] saw Methusaleh; Jacob saw Shem; Amram [father of Moses] saw Jacob; Ahijah the Shilonite saw Amram; Elijah saw Ahijah [who did not die in the wilderness and enjoyed exceptional longevity]; and Elijah is still alive *(Bava Basra* 121b).

nine hundred and sixty two years; and he died.
[21] *When Chanoch had lived sixty-five years, he*
begot Methuselah. [22] *Chanoch walked with God for*
three hundred years after begetting Methuselah; and
he begot sons and daughters. [23] *All the days of*
Chanoch were three hundred and sixty-five years.
[24] *And Chanoch walked with God; then he was no*

[The *Talmud* comments *(Sotah* 14a): "Is it possible, then to 'walk' before God? — It means to serve Him and emulate His ways."]

As *Targum Yonasan* renders: *'He served God in truth.'*

The sense of the verse is: From the age of sixty-five he channeled all his desire in the love of God; he pursued wisdom and recognized his creator *(Radak).*

But, apparently, before that age he did not serve God, but followed the evil ways of the rest of his generation *(Ralbag).*

Sefer HaYashar devotes the entire Chapter 3 to the righteous life of Chanoch. It begins 'And Chanoch lived sixty-five years and he begot Methuselah; and Chanoch walked with God after having begot Methuselah, and he served HASHEM and despised the evil ways of man. And the soul of Chanoch was wrapped up in the instruction of HASHEM, in knowledge and in understanding, and he wisely retired from the sons of men and he separated himself from them for many years ...' [See *footnote* to *v.* 24.]

24. **וַיִּתְהַלֵּךְ חֲנוֹךְ אֶת הָאֱלֹהִים** — *And Chanoch walked with God.*

— [The repetition of the phrase from v. 22 here is noteworthy. The commentators are silent on the seeming redundancy but the repetition might be interpreted to connote his *'going with God'* as a euphemism for death, or it might be rendered (although not literally): *'And having walked with God ...'* i.e. since he devoted his life in the service of God, *therefore ... he was taken by God,* and did not die naturally (see *B'chor Shor,* below).]

Rashi [which the printed versions append to the identical phrase in *v.* 22 but which, on the basis of the *Midrash,* seems better suited to the context of *this* verse] comments that although Chanoch was a righteous man, he was liable to go astray. To avert this, God cut his life short, hence the use of the expression *'he was no more', rather than 'he died'* — *i.e. 'he was not':* he was not in the world to complete his allotted years.

Accordingly, the verse might be rendered, according to *Rashi: 'While Chanoch yet walked with God'* — i.e. while he was still righteous — *'he was not':* he died.

Or according to others: he disappeared at such a comparatively young age that it seemed as though he never existed *(Chizkuni).*

[The commentators point out that וְאֵינֶנּוּ, *and he was no more* as a delicate expression for death or for sudden disappearance is not uncommon in Scriptures. See, for example, such phrases as *Job* 7:21: *You shall seek me* וְאֵינֶנִּי*, and I shall not be'; Psalms* 39:14: *'Before I depart* וְאֵינֶנִּי*, and will be no more'; Prov.* 12:7: *'the wicked are overthrown* וְאֵינָם*, and are no more.'*]

°שביעי כה לָקַח אֹתוֹ אֱלֹהִים: וַיְחִי
מְתוּשֶׁלַח שֶׁבַע וּשְׁמֹנִים שָׁנָה וּמְאַת שָׁנָה
כו וַיּוֹלֶד אֶת־לָמֶךְ: וַיְחִי מְתוּשֶׁלַח אַחֲרֵי
הוֹלִידוֹ אֶת־לֶמֶךְ שְׁתַּיִם וּשְׁמוֹנִים שָׁנָה
וּשְׁבַע מֵאוֹת שָׁנָה וַיּוֹלֶד בָּנִים וּבָנוֹת:
כז וַיִּהְיוּ כָּל־יְמֵי מְתוּשֶׁלַח תֵּשַׁע וְשִׁשִּׁים
שָׁנָה וּתְשַׁע מֵאוֹת שָׁנָה וַיָּמֹת:
כח וַיְחִי־לֶמֶךְ שְׁתַּיִם וּשְׁמֹנִים שָׁנָה וּמְאַת
כט שָׁנָה וַיּוֹלֶד בֵּן: וַיִּקְרָא אֶת־שְׁמוֹ נֹחַ

כִּי לָקַח אֹתוֹ אֱלֹהִים — *For God had taken him* — i.e. he died *(Rashi)*, his death being so described as a mark of honor *(Ibn Ezra)*.

He mysteriously disappeared and only God knew his whereabouts *(Aderes Eliyahu)*.

B'chor Shor suggests that since Chanoch had a comparatively short life span — others living approximately 900 years while he lived approximately 300 — some might suspect that he died prematurely in punishment for being wicked. The Torah, therefore, specifically says: *And Chanoch walked with God*, i.e. he was wholly righteous, *and he was not* allowed to remain any longer in this world despite his young years *for God took him*, and plucked him away from the wicked ones.[1]

The entire verse is paraphrased in *Targum Yonasan:* 'And Chanoch served in truth before God, and behold, he was not with the sojourners of the earth, for he was withdrawn and he ascended to heaven by the word of God, and he was called Metatron, the great Scribe.'

25. מְתוּשֶׁלַח — *Methuselah.*

He was a wholly righteous man *(Yalkut)*.

According to *Seder Olam Rabbah*, he studied under Adam for 243 years, and according to *Bava Basra*

1. [Chanoch is much discussed in the *Aggadah* and he is the subject of various *Midrashim.*

The *Midrash* states that all sevenths are favorites and greater sanctity rests upon them: thus Chanoch was the seventh generation ... Moses was the seventh generation from the beloved Abraham ... David was the seventh son of Jesse.

Although his generation was sinful and served idols (see *footnote* end of Chapter 4), Chanoch recognized his Creator and, having been endowed with the knowledge of the 'secret of intercalation', *(Pirkei d'Rabbi Eliezer)*, and instructed in sublime and mystic wisdom regarding the nature of heaven and earth *(Zohar)*, he taught men to walk in the ways of God. He turned many people — including kings and princes — to righteous conduct and during this time peace and prosperity reigned in the world.

At the age of 300, the *Midrashim* continue, God took him up to heaven in a fiery chariot, to serve Him there, and appointed him ruler over the angels *(Sefer HaYashar; Targum Yonasan; Midrash HaNeelam)*.

Chanoch is counted among the nine righteous men who entered Paradise without suffering the pangs of death *(Derech Eretz Zota 1)*.

V
25-29

more, for God had taken him.
25 *When Methuselah had lived one hundred and*
eighty-seven years, he begot Lamech. 26 *And Methu-*
selah lived seven hundred and eighty-two years after
begetting Lamech, and he begot sons and daughters.
27 *All the days of Methuselah were nine hundred and*
sixty-nine years; and he died.
28 *When Lamech had lived one hundred and*
eighty-two years, he begot a son. 29 *And he named*

121b as cited in the *footnote v.* 6 he is one of the seven 'links' in the eternal chain which bridged the life-span of mankind.

His righteousness was such that the angels eulogized him, and the Flood was withheld from the world until his seven day mourning period ended [see 7:10] *(Sanhedrin* 108b; *Avos d'Rabbi Nosson).*

28. וַיּוֹלֶד בֵּן — *And he begot a son.* One by whom the world would be rebuilt *(Rashi).*

Rashi's comment is based on the fact that Noah's birth is not described *'and he begot Noah'* as are the others: *'and he begot Kenan', 'and he begot Mehalalel'.* Following *Tanchuma,* he interprets בֵּן, son, as an allusion to בנה, build *(Mizrachi).*

... In Noah was fulfilled the Jewish conception of a son, בֵּן, as one through whom the 'upbuilding' of the world continued *(Hirsch),* for the son is the constructive continuation of the father's work and hence the root of בן is בנה. בַּת, *daughter,* is similarly related to בנת but, as is common in Hebrew, the letter נ *nun* is dropped. In its plural form, however, בָּנוֹת, *daughters,* retains the 'nun' thus proving its derivation from בנה, *building (Gur Aryeh).*

Da'as Zekeinim comments that the verse alludes to the fact that Lamech did not name the child immediately at birth. This was at the advice of the righteous Methuselah who cautioned him to delay naming the child because the people of that generation were sorcerers who would have placed a spell upon him had they known his name.

Yalkut Shimoni cites the above

However, as *Tosafos Yevamos* 16b notes there are contradictory versions concerning his end, some maintaining he was transported alive to the heavens. *Midrash Rabbah* upon which *Rashi* bases himself, interprets that Chanoch died a natural — although premature death. The *Midrash* refutes those who attempt to prove that Chanoch did not die because the same phrase *'taken away'* is used in connection with Elijah *(II Kings* 2:3) who was taken up to heaven in a whirlwind but did not die in the usual sense *(ibid.,* v.11). The Sages refuted this by pointing to other verses where 'taking away' definitely refers to natural death. In fact, the *Midrash* records a view that Chanoch was righteous only intermittently vacillating between righteousness and sinfulness, and God removed him from the world before he lapsed into continuous sin.

And, the *Zohar Chadash* concludes: This is what is meant by the text *'and he was no more for God took him'* — i.e. he was no longer in this world to complete his allotted time, because God removed him prematurely in order to deal graciously with him by bestowing upon him the life of the Hereafter.

ה
ל-לא

לֵאמֹר זֶה יְנַחֲמֵנוּ מִמַּעֲשֵׂנוּ וּמֵעִצְּבוֹן
יָדֵינוּ מִן־הָאֲדָמָה אֲשֶׁר אֵרְרָהּ יהוה:
ל וַיְחִי־לֶמֶךְ אַחֲרֵי הוֹלִידוֹ אֶת־נֹחַ חָמֵשׁ
וְתִשְׁעִים שָׁנָה וַחֲמֵשׁ מֵאֹת שָׁנָה וַיּוֹלֶד
לא בָּנִים וּבָנוֹת: וַיְהִי כָּל־יְמֵי־לֶמֶךְ שֶׁבַע
וְשִׁבְעִים שָׁנָה וּשְׁבַע מֵאוֹת שָׁנָה וַיָּמֹת:

Midrash and explains that sorcery is ineffective unless one knows the correct name. Accordingly, Methuselah named him Noah, but advised Lamech to publicly call him *Menachem,* meaning 'comforter'. [See *Sefer HaYashar* in *comm.* to next verse.]

29. זֶה יְנַחֲמֵנוּ – *This one will bring us rest* [or: *'comfort'*]

[The literal translation (*'will comfort us')* raises etymological difficulties because the root נוּחַ Noah, is not related to נחם, comfort. For, as the *Midrash* observes: 'the name does *not* correspond to its interpretation nor does the interpretation correspond to the name']

Our rendering, as usual, follows *Rashi* who relates נֹחַ, Noah, to the root נוּחַ, *rest:* i.e. *'He will bring us rest* [יְנַחֲמֵנוּ] (in the sense of 'relief') *from the toil of our hands.'* This was said [prophetically] in reference to the invention of farming tools which were attributed to Noah. Until his time, in consequence of the curse decreed upon Adam [3:18]; the earth produced thorns and thistles when one planted wheat. In Noah's days this ceased.[1] *Rashi* contends that had *'Noah'* been related to נֶחָמָה, 'comfort' [*'he will bring us comfort'*] he should have been named מְנַחֵם, *Menachem* [comforter.]

Ibn Ezra comments that Noah's name may have been given him in prophetic anticipation of the comfort and rest he would bring them; or it was a name he earned later for ending the grief of man by successfully working the ground and inventing the plow. He explains that *'Noah'* denotes both 'comfort' and 'rest', for names do not always follow strict etymological or grammatical rules.

Radak reviews the above, and

1. There was a tradition from Adam to his descendants that the curse on the earth: 'in sorrow shall you eat of it ... *thorns and thistles shall it produce for you ... with the sweat of your brow shall you eat bread'* [3:17-19] would be in effect only during Adam's lifetime as the verse [*ibid.*] indicates: *'all the days of* your *life ... until* you *return to the earth.'* Chronologically, Noah was the first one — in our genealogical list of the leaders of the various generations — born after Adam's death. Beginning with him the *severity of the curse would abate.* Lamech was aware of this tradition,and therefore gave him that name *(Pirkei d'Rabbi Eliezer; Abarbanel).*

The *Midrash* also notes that Adam was told that the curse would last until one of his descendants was born circumcised. When Lamech saw Noah born that way, he knew that with this child the curse 'rested' *(Tanchuma).*

... Also, Noah was the first to fashion agricultural tools, giving them respite from the laborious toil of farming manually *(Tanchuma).* Also, with his birth they 'rested' from the famine that began in the days of Lamech *(Rabbah).*

*him Noah, saying, 'This one will bring us rest from
our work and from the toil of our hands, from the
ground which HASHEM had cursed.'* [30] *Lamech lived
five hundred and ninety-five years after begetting
Noah, and he begot sons and daughters.* [31] *All the
days of Lamech were seven hundred and seventy-
seven years; and he died.*

also concludes that in Hebrew, grammatical rules do not apply to names. He adds that both interpretations are correct because 'respite from grief is comfort', and that the Sages said that naming the child Noah in anticipation of the future proves that Lamech was a prophet ... *Radak,* however [also *Sforno; R' Meyuchos*], maintains that this naming was not prophetic but a fervent prayer made by a jubilant parent upon the birth of his child: *May this child bring us relief from our grief-filled work, the toil of agriculture from which we have been enjoying no benefit ...'*

Sefer HaYashar incorporates both interpretations, 'comfort' and 'rest':

"And Methuselah called his name Noah saying, 'the earth rested and was free of corruption in his days', but his father Lamech called him Menachem saying: *'this one will comfort us ...'* "

מִמַּעֲשֵׂנוּ וּמֵעִצְּבוֹן יָדֵינוּ — *From our work and from the toil of our hands.*

I.e. from our works that are not prosperous, and from the labor of our hands *(Targum Yonasan).*

מַעֲשֵׂנוּ, *our work,* refers specifically to husbandry (cf. *Judges* 19:16); עִצָּבוֹן, *toil,* refers to the manual labor in which fruitlessly we indulged *(Radak).*

[On עִצָּבוֹן, *toil,* see *comm.* of *Ibn Janach* to 3:16 s.v. בְּעֶצֶב: 'עֶצֶב, like עִצָּבוֹן, refers to forms of discomfort: *physically,* it denotes ailment, toil, fatigue; *mentally,* it refers to anxiety and grief'.]

מִן הָאֲדָמָה אֲשֶׁר אֵרְרָהּ ה׳ — *From the ground which HASHEM had cursed.*

[I.e. ... from the toil of our hands *arising from the very ground which God had cursed by decreeing to Adam* (3:17): *'accursed is the ground because of you, in toil you shall eat of it all the days of your life ...'* (But, presumably, now that Adam was dead, relief would be at hand).]

Man would still have to toil, but the intent is that Noah considerably lightened the burden by ingeniously introducing agricultural tools *(Radak).*

Ralbag relates the *'curse'* to that which God pronounced upon *Cain* [4:11-12]: *'Cursed are you* from the ground ... *it shall no longer yield to you its strength ...'* but that since Cain's seed was to perish in the Flood, that curse would be abated.

30. וַיּוֹלֶד בָּנִים וּבָנוֹת —*And he begot sons and daughters.*

[The phrase, *'and he begot sons and daughters'* occurring after every name in the genealogy is not redundant. It is the Torah's way of telling us that there were many more children, both male and female, born to each of those men-

ה
לב

לב וַיְהִי־נֹחַ בֶּן־חֲמֵשׁ מֵאוֹת שָׁנָה
וַיּוֹלֶד נֹחַ אֶת־שֵׁם אֶת־חָם וְאֶת־יָפֶת׃

ו
א

א וַיְהִי כִּי־הֵחֵל הָאָדָם לָרֹב עַל־פְּנֵי

tioned. They remain unidentified because the Torah is concerned only with the genealogy leading directly to Noah.]

Ibn Ezra adds that the fact that the Torah specifically mentions that girls were born to each of them is the best response to those cynics who question from where they found wives, and how the population grew so quickly.

32. בֶּן חֲמֵשׁ מֵאוֹת שָׁנָה – *Five hundred years old.*

The *Midrash*, [cited by *Rashi*,] notes why all his contemporaries begot at the age of one hundred to two hundred years, while Noah did not beget until he was five hundred years old. The Holy One, blessed be He reasoned: 'A flood is soon to come. If I give him children now and they are wicked, they will have to drown in the flood, and I do not wish to grieve this righteous man. If, on the other hand, they are righteous [and over the next few hundred years they will multiply greatly and will each have large families], I will have to trouble him to build many arks ... ' [i.e. Although a potentially large family would have been available to assist Noah in the construction, the burden of responsibility of building several arks and protecting them from the wicked people who taunted and attempted to hamper him would have been overwhelming *(Maharzu)*.] . . .

God therefore withheld children from him until he was 500 years old so that even Japheth, the eldest [see on 10:21 and below] would be less than a hundred at the time of the Flood. Before the giving of the Torah, as in Messianic times, someone younger than 100 was considered a minor in matters of responsibility for sin and liability to divine punishment.

Cf. *Isaiah* 65:20: *for the lad of a hundred years old shall die* i.e. shall be liable for punishment *(Rashi)*.

Me'am Loez adds that after the Torah was given, the age of responsibility for punishment was twenty. When people lived to such advanced ages, a 100-year old was comparable to a present-day teen-ager. However, Adam was punished although he was but a day old when he sinned because, as God's handiwork. he was endowed with more intelligence. Additionally his responsibility was greater because he heard the prohibition directly from God.[1]

Midrash Tanchuma suggests that Noah did not have children until such an advanced age because he perceived that it would be futile to bring into the world children who would anger God ... but when he was 500 years old, he reflected that he would die childless whereas God

1. *Harav David Cohen* notes that following the Flood, as the human lifespan was shortened drastically, so, too, there were other changes, all of which followed an apparent ratio of 1:5. Shem, the last person born before the Flood, lived 600 years; Moses lived 120 years, a typical life-span for the righteous of the period. Similarly, the age of divine punishment went from 100 to 20; and the age at which men could beget children went from 65 [5:16] to 13. Thus, as man's lifespan shortened, so did his physiology in the same proportion.

V
32 ³² *When Noah was five hundred years old, Noah begot Shem, Ham, and Japheth.*
VI
1 ¹ *And it came to pass when man began to increase upon the ground and daughters were born to them,*

had commanded Adam to propagate the species. Then, Shem, Ham, and Japheth were born to him.

Sefer HaYashar elaborates on this:

'Noah the son of Lamech, refrained from taking a wife, for he said, surely God will destroy the earth; why should I beget children? Now, Noah was a just man, perfect in his generation, and God chose him to raise up seed from his seed on the face of the earth. And God said to him,take a wife and beget children ...'

... And Noah went and chose Naamah, daughter of Chanoch ...

אֶת שֵׁם וְאֶת חָם וְאֶת יָפֶת – *Shem, Ham, and Japheth.*

Japheth was the eldest, but Shem is mentioned first because he was a righteous man, he was born circumcised [a sign of righteousness], and Abraham descended from him *(Rashi)*. ... He was also a High Priest, and the Temple would one day he built in his territory *(Midrash)*.

According to the *Talmud* [*Sanhedrin* 69b] Shem is mentioned first because Scripture enumerates them according to their wisdom, not age. The proof is that had they been listed according to age Shem would have to be at least two years older than Japheth [i.e. one year older than Ham who in turn would have to be one year older than Japeth.] Noah begot children when he was 500 years old and the flood began when he was 600 years old (7:6). Now, in 11:10 Shem is described as being 100 years old when he begot Arphaxad *'two years after the flood.'* If Shem were the oldest, he would have been slightly less than 100 when the flood commenced and 102 years old by the time he begot Arphaxad! Therefore, we must conclude that Shem was the youngest.

And beginning with the youngest the Torah enumerates them in ascending order to Japheth *(B'chor Shor)*.

However, there are views, based on 10:21, that *Shem* is the elder and Japheth the younger. See *comm.* there, 9:24, and 11:10.

Compare, also *Sefer HaYashar* 5:16 'And Naamah [Noah's wife] conceived and bore a son, and named him Japheth ... and conceived again and bore a son and he called him Shem ...'

VI

1. Prelude to the Flood

וַיְהִי – *And it came to pass.*

The *Talmud* notes that it is a tradition that wherever the term וַיְהִי, *and it came to pass,* occurs in Scripture it presages trouble. Thus, וַיְהִי here introduces *'and HASHEM saw that the wickedness of man was great'* [*v.* 5] *(Megillah* 10b).

כִּי הֵחֵל הָאָדָם לָרֹב עַל פְּנֵי הָאֲדָמָה– *When man began to increase upon the* [*surface of*] *the ground* ... [i.e. throughout the inhabited world.]

Having mentioned the birth of Noah and his sons, the Torah introduces the account of the flood by telling us that *as soon as man began*

ו ב ב הָֽאֲדָמָה וּבָנוֹת יֻלְּדוּ לָהֶם: וַיִּרְאוּ בְנֵי־
הָֽאֱלֹהִים אֶת־בְּנוֹת הָֽאָדָם כִּי טֹבֹת הֵנָּה

to multiply they began to sin. God, however, waited until they were steeped in their full measure of sin before he punished them *(Ramban).*

The word לָרֹב, *to increase,* is also interpreted homiletically in the *Talmud* as related to the word ריב, strife, rendering: *'When man began to introduce strife into the world' (Bava Basra* 16a).

וּבָנוֹת יֻלְּדוּ לָהֶם — *And daughters were born to them.*

... [As repeated throughout the previous chapter: *'and he begot sons and daughters'.*]

Radak comments that the daughters are specifically mentioned here because they are crucial to the narrative; it was through them that the wickedness was perpetrated.

2. בְּנֵי הָאֱלֹהִים — *The sons of the rulers,* i.e. the sons of the princes and the judges, for *Elohim* always implies rulership [cf. *comm.* to 1:1], as in *Exodus* 4:16 *'and you shall be his* אֱלֹהִים*, Master' (Rashi).*

[There are several interpretations of the expression בְּנֵי אֱלֹהִים. Our translation, as usual, adheres to *Rashi* and the majority of commentators who follow *Targum* and understand it as referring to the judges, potentates, and the sons of nobility, basing themselves on the interpretation of אֱלֹהִים in *Exodus* 22:7 *'and the owner of the house shall come near to* אֱלֹהִים*, the judges',* while *'daughter of man'* is interpreted as maidens of lower rank.]

Ramban cites this interpretation and comments that 'if so, the Torah relates that the very judges who should have administered justice committed open violence while no one interfered.'

This follows, also, the view cited in the *Midrash:*

The verse indicates that aristocratic youths took as wives the daughters of people who were powerless to resist. These marriages were the outgrowth of unrestrained passion and demonstrate man's moral descent to oppression and license, as Rav Shimon bar Yochai interpreted: *'the sons of the nobles'.*

Why, then, were they called בְּנֵי אֱלֹהִים, lit *'godly beings'?* Because [like divine beings] they lived a long time without trouble or suffering ... [They lived such long lives] to enable them to understand the astronomical cycles and calculations [a long life being required to make the necessary observations]; the Rabbis said: it was in order that they become liable for punishment [for their own sins accumulated through their long lives].

⁂ According to many commentators [eg. *Ibn Ezra, Radak, Rav Yehudah Halevy,* and more recently *Rav Samson Raphael Hirsch*] בְּנֵי אֱלֹהִים (lit. *'sons of God')* are the God-fearing descendants of Seth, while *'the daughters of men'* (implying less spiritual people) are the iniquitous descendants of Cain.]

This interpretation is also expounded by *Ramban* who explains 'it seems to me that Adam and his wife are called בְּנֵי אֱלֹהִים because they were God's handiwork. *'Adam begot Seth in his likeness and in his image'* [5:3] and as such he, and quite probably his descendants were also endowed with this Godly likeness ...

Hirsch thus explains that the Sethite line in whom the divine stamp devolved were the בְּנֵי אֱלֹהִים, for they continued to devote themselves to man's spiritual calling while the בְּנוֹת הָאָדָם represented the Cainite development of mankind who devoted themselves to agriculture and industry, and in whom 'the Godly was entirely eradicated — מְחוּיָאֵל (a contraction of מָחָה אל, he erased God).

— They are referred to as *Elohim,* meaning 'mighty', because they were awesome in appearance *(Rosh).*

HaK'sav V'HaKabballah suggests that just as an individual may be referred to as אִישׁ הָאֱלֹהִים, *'man of God'* in recognition

VI
2

[2] *the sons of the rulers saw that the daughters of man were good and they took themselves wives from*

of his dedication to Godliness, the term בְּנֵי אֱלֹהִים, 'people of God' may refer collectively to a group of people who are so dedicated ...

[The verse portrays the disastrous results of a merger between the righteous line of Seth with the proponents of a Godless culture whose 'progress' ended in depravity. Because of this marriage, the descendants of Seth sunk as well and suffered the doom that overtook all mankind with the exception of Noah and his family.]

[In support of the above interpretations it may be noted that according to the *Masorah* the word אֱלֹהִים in this verse is non-sacred (*Minchas Shay;* see also on 3:5).]

☙ There is a third view that explains *B'nai Elohim* as 'godly beings', or 'angels'.

This is the sense of the term in *Job* 1:6, and, as evidenced in *Gen.* 3:22 the existence of angels in a heavenly *famalia* is taken for granted.

The *Talmud* [*Yoma* 67b] states that the rite of Azazel on Yom Kippur [*Levit.* 16] is so called 'because it obtains atonement for the affair of Uzza and Azael.'[1]

Rashi ad. loc. explains Uzza and Azael as 'angels of destruction who descended to earth in the days of Naamah, sister of Tuval-Cain [see above regarding her beauty.] Referring to them the verse says *"and the godly beings saw the children of man."*

Accordingly, the Azazel obtains atonement for immorality.'

It is to this interpretation that *Rashi* to our verse refers when he says: 'Another explanation is that these were שָׂרִים, princely agents [i.e. angels; or according to another reading in *Rashi* cited by *Hoffmann:* שֵׁדִים, *demons*] who executed a divine commission; they, too, intermingled with them.'

For as explained in *Pirkei d'Rabbi Eliezer,* upon descending to earth these angels took on human form.

It is to such as these that the *Talmud, Chagigah* 16a refers when it says that 'they propagate like human beings.'

Ramban, after offering several of the above interpretations of these verses, concludes, in his commentary to 5, that the interpretation that best fits the text is that of 'the Midrash of Rabbi Eliezer HaGadol [i.e. *Pirkei d'Rabbi Eliezer*] which refers this to the angels 'fallen' from heaven, as discussed in *Yoma* 67b, but it requires lengthy delving into the mysteries of this subject.

[According to *Pirkei d'Rabbi Eliezer,* although the angels were the chief offenders, they were enticed by the women whose manner tempted them, leading them astray. As mentioned in the above *footnote,* the angels, having

1. A most esoteric *Midrash* quoted by *Torah Shelemah* 6:16 from the introduction to *Midrash Aggadas Bereishis* elaborates upon the *Talmudic* allusion cited above:

בְּנֵי אֱלֹהִים are the angels Uzza and Azael whose abode was in the heavens but descended to earth to prove themselves. While still in heaven they heard God say: *'I will blot out man whom I have created from the face of the earth.'* They replied, *'what is man that You are mindful of him, the son of man that You think of him?'* [*Psalms* 8:5; i.e. 'You are right; man did not deserve to be created!']

God said to them: 'If you lived on earth like these people and beheld the beauty of their women, the Evil Inclination would enter you, too, and cause you to sin!'

They replied: 'We will descend and yet not sin.' They then descended, and, as the verse says, *'the godly beings saw the daughters of man'.* When they saw them they asked to return to heaven, and they pleaded to God: 'This trial is enough for us!'

But God answered: 'You have already become defiled, and you shall never again become pure!' [cf. similar *Midrash* in *Yalkut Shimoni.*]

ו ג וַיִּקְחוּ לָהֶם נָשִׁים מִכֹּל אֲשֶׁר בָּחָרוּ:
ג וַיֹּאמֶר יהוה לֹא־יָדוֹן רוּחִי בָאָדָם לְעֹלָם

descended below, could no longer return to heaven and were doomed together with mankind.[1]

אֶת בְּנוֹת הָאָדָם — *The daughters of man* — i.e. the daughters of the general populace *(Rav Saadiah Gaon);* the multitude, the lower classes *(Rambam, Moreh* 1:14) who did not have the power to resist their superiors *(Radak).*

According to the second interpretation: The descendants of Cain *(Ibn Ezra);* [and according to the third interpretation the phrase is interpreted literally: the daughters of mortal man in contrast to the angels who desired them.]

כִּי טֹבֹת הֵנָּה — *That they were good* — i.e. beautiful; of good appearance *(Radak).*

וַיִּקְחוּ לָהֶם נָשִׁים מִכֹּל אֲשֶׁר בָּחָרוּ — *And they took* [to] *themselves wives from whomever* [lit. *'from all'*] *they chose'* — even a married woman, or a man, or an animal *(Rashi)* [thus interpreting נָשִׁים here in the sense of 'spouses.']

And they took — even by force, and there was none to protest for they were the children of the judges *(Ibn Ezra).* They thereby destroyed the entire social order *(B'chor Shor).*

Ramban comments that they would take them as wives by force. Thus Scripture stresses the חָמָס, *violent crime,* and mentions further מִכֹּל אֲשֶׁר בָּחָרוּ *'from whomever they chose'* to imply that they took even married women. The prohibition against their crime is not mentioned clearly by the Torah but it is self-understood and requires no specific injunction *(Ramban).*

Hirsch notes conversely, however, that לקח אשה, *taking a woman* is, in fact, the term for marriage, thus indicating that there was nothing dishonorable involved. The sin may lie in the phrase *'from whomever they chose'.* They married girls as they pleased, without considering the suitability of the match.

[The interpretations above of *'they took'* are not necessarily mutually exclusive. *'They took',* as *Rav Hirsch* points out, does indeed carry with it the connotation of marriage. It is the phrase *'from whomever they chose'* however, that carries with it an implication that they acted wantonly and did as they pleased. Not only did they act wantonly among themselves but they spread their violence and immorality throughout society destroying the social fabric. This was their sin.]

However, *Maharzu* suggests that לקח לאשה, take *as* a woman (wife), is the expression for legal marriage; here the verse only says וַיִּקְחוּ . . . נָשִׁים *and they took women* [without the ל, as] implying that true marriage was not intended.[2]

3. The Warning of the Flood

וַיֹּאמֶר ה׳ — *And God said.* Probably to be understood in the sense of

1. These giants with superhuman strength had to derive their power from some higher force, just as Samson's awesome strength was a divine gift. To indicate the source of this strength, the verse calls the giants *b'nai Elohim,* indicating that their strength and size was conferred by evil angels. Although it is difficult for us to conceive that spiritual beings like angels have the Freedom of Choice to rebel against the will of God, the Torah and the words of the Sages make it clear that such is indeed the case *(Hoffmann).*

VI
3

whomever they chose. 3 *And HASHEM said, 'My spirit shall not contend evermore concerning man*

'and God resolved'; or possibly He was addressing Noah *(Radak)*.

Ralbag, however, insists that 'God must have communicated the decree to His prophet, Noah, who in turn transmitted it to the people of the generation so that they should repent and avert the decree.

לֹא יָדוֹן רוּחִי בָאָדָם לְעֹלָם — *My Spirit shall not contend evermore concerning Man.*

I.e. My Spirit shall not be discontent and contentious within Me concerning man much longer; not for long will My Spirit continue to contend within Me whether to destroy or to show mercy *(Rashi)*.

[This verse lends itself to legions of interpretations touching upon fundamental principles of Torah-perspective. Our basic translation follows *Rashi* who thus explains יָדוֹן to mean strife, contention (as in *II Sam.* 19:10 כָּל־הָעָם נָדוֹן, *all the people were at strife).* He interprets the preposition ב (lit. *'in'*) in בָּאָדָם as *concerning* man, and לְעוֹלָם (lit. *'forever'*) as 'for a long time' *(Mizrachi)*.]

Radak similarly explains יָדוֹן as 'strife' but renders: 'No longer shall the exalted Spirit which I have lowered to reside in man be in constant strife with the body which draws him to animal lust.

Targum Yonasan paraphrases: The generations which are yet to arise will not be judged [יִתְדָּנוּן = יָדוֹן] like the Generation of the Flood which is to be destroyed and exterminated from the midst of the world. Have I not imparted My Holy Spirit to them that they may do good deeds? — and see, their deeds are wicked ...'

The *Mishnah* [*Sanhedrin* 107a] always interprets the verse as a reference to judgment: 'The generation of the flood has no share in the World to Come nor will it stand in judgment, as it says *'My spirit will not enter into judgment with man* לְעוֹלָם [i.e. *in the World to Come*]; [it shall have] neither *judgment*, nor *spirit* [of resurrection.]

Among the several interpretations recorded in the *Midrash*, one interprets יָדוֹן as related to נָדָן, *a sheath*; i.e. the casing of the spirit — [i.e. the body]:

'God said: When [in the resurrection] I restore the spirit to the sheath [i.e. return the souls to their bodies], I will not restore their spirit [i.e. of this wicked generation] to their sheath.' [לְעֹלָם is rendered: *'in the world* to come' as in the *Mishnah* above] (also *Yerushalmi Sanhedrin* 10:3).

The familiar translation is expressed in *Onkelos, Ibn Ezra*, and with some variation in *Ramban*: *'My Spirit* — in the sense of God's life-giving spirit [above 2:7; cf. *Eccles.* 12:7] — *shall not abide* [lit. *'be sheathed'* or from the root דנן — *'remain'*] *in man forever* — but since

2. *Harav David Feinstein*, explains that לָקַח אִשָּׁה connotes the 'taking of a spouse as a permanent relationship whether or not it becomes a legal marriage.' Indeed, the expression קיחה is used even for illicit relationships that cannot attain the status of marriage. The Generation of the Flood was not content to satisfy its lust and then continue its normal life. It took forbidden women — and even, as the *Midrash* says, man and beast — as mates in order to make perverted lust a permanent condition.

ו בְּשַׁגָּם הוּא בָשָׂר וְהָיוּ יָמָיו מֵאָה וְעֶשְׂרִים
ד שָׁנָה: ד הַנְּפִלִים הָיוּ בָאָרֶץ בַּיָּמִים הָהֵם

he is but flesh his soul shall return to Me, while his body shall return to the dust.

Or HaChaim perceives this verse as God's determination to no longer enter into dialogue with His creatures to reprove and debate with them as was His practice earlier when He addressed the serpent, the woman, Adam, and Cain. Now that their abominations increased, God said: My Spirit will no longer enter into direct, personal judgment with man.

N'tziv renders יָדוֹן from דַּיָּן, שׁוֹפֵט, a judge; one who determines a course of action. Man is composed of two parts: רוּחַ, the spirit; and בָּשָׂר, the flesh. Life is a struggle for domination between these two forces. In this verse, God foretells that man will continue to fall victim to his physical lust. Thus the verse is rendered: My Spirituality will not dominate man for he is a creature of flesh.

בְּשַׁגָּם הוּא בָשָׂר — *Since he is [but] flesh* — He does not submit to My rule even though he is but flesh [interpreting בַּאֲשֶׁר=בְּשֶׁגַם=בְּשַׁגָּם גַּם, *even though* (cf. *Judges* 5:7) שֶׁקַּמְתִּי = שַׁקַּמְתִּי)]. How much more rebellious would man be if he were made of a more durable substance! *(Rashi).*

Akeidas Yitzchak renders: 'My Spirit shall not always seek to judge man favorably by pleading that he is but human ...'

I.e. I will not always defend man's trespasses (as I did for Adam and Cain by giving them the benefit of the doubt and not destroying them immediately when they sinned) by justifying their trespass as being but the result of the שְׂאוֹר שֶׁבְּעִיסָּה, 'the yeast in the dough' [i.e. the Evil Impulse which causes a ferment in the heart [*Berachos* 17a; (see *ArtScroll Shir HaShirim* p.163)], and therefore absolve them. This generation does not deserve such sympathy ... *(Abarbanel).*

Sforno interprets similarly when he comments '... No longer will I deliberate whether man deserves punishment because he was created in My image and likeness [and must maintain a high standard of conduct] or whether he merits compassion because he is but flesh [cf. *Rashi.*]

R' Bachya interprets: Man is not worthy that My Spirit, that is, the Rational Intellect should dwell in him permanently in that he is also [= בְּשֶׁגַם] but flesh like every other creature, and his soul is drawn after his flesh, rather than after his Rational Intellect.

— And therefore the Spirit of God will no longer be sheathed in him forever for he is corporeal and not godly. The verse then, is reminiscent of *Psalms* 49:13: *'He remembered that they were but flesh, a wind that passes away ...' (Ramban).*

Minchah Belulah offers the following comment [possibly interpreting בְּשַׁגָּם = בְּשׁוֹגְגָם, *their erring ways*]:

'I implanted My Spirit in man so he should be guided by it. But by his evil ways man has turned even his spirit into flesh. This is unlike the righteous who transform their

VI since he is but flesh; his days shall be a hundred and
4 twenty years.'
4 The Nephilim were on the earth in those days —

physical selves into spiritual beings.

וְהָיוּ יָמָיו מֵאָה וְעֶשְׂרִים שָׁנָה — [*And*] *his days shall be a hundred and twenty years.*

— I will not inflict punishment on mankind immediately; I will grant them a probationary period of 120 years in which to repent. If they refuse I will *then* bring a Flood upon them (*Targumim; Rashi; Ramban* and most commentators).

יָמָיו, *his days,* therefore means: the extended [probationary] period I have allotted them (*Radak*).

Although the Torah records this decree *after* the birth of Noah's children we must remember that אֵין מוּקְדָם וּמְאֻחָר בַּתּוֹרָה events in the Torah are not always related in chronological order [*Pesachim* 6b] and we must assume that since Japheth, Noah's oldest son was born a hundred years before the Flood, the decree must have been issued twenty years before Noah had any children (*Seder Olam; Rashi; Ibn Ezra*).

Several commentators however, [cited by *Ibn Ezra* and *Abarbanel*] interpret this verse as meaning: Henceforth, the *average human life-span* constantly decreasing, will stabilize, not to exceed a hundred and twenty years.[1]

— As human beings with long life-spans they live corrupt and sinful lives since the fear of imminent death is not upon them; therefore I shall shorten their average life-spans (*Chizkuni*).

This interpretation gains credence from the *Midrash:*

Longevity was one of the beneficent powers lost through the sins of the Generation of the Flood, for though Adam sinned he lived to the age of 930 [5:5] but, when the Generation of the Flood sinned, God reduced the normal life span to a hundred and twenty years. In the Messianic future, however, God will restore Man's longevity as in *Isaiah's* prophecy [65:22]: *They shall not build and another inhabit, they shall not plant and another eat; for as the days of a tree shall be the days of My people, and My chosen shall long enjoy their handiwork* (*Midrash HaGadol*).

[If the entire verse is viewed in the context of the interpretation that *'b'nai Elohim'* are 'fallen angels' and hence their offspring were an intermixture of celestial and terrestrial elements, then God's

1. In response to the observation, however, that many individuals subsequently recorded in Scriptures lived greater life-spans than 120 years, *R' Eliezer Ashkenazi ('Rokeach')* explains that going from one extreme to another is not done without passing through intermediates, therefore the divine decree was not put immediately into force. But from that period human life-span greatly diminished until it was ultimately reduced to 120 years when the decrease stabilized, many not attaining even that age from frailty of constitutions. Moses, however, lived exactly that long.

Harav David Cohen suggests that '120 years' is also a reference to man's potential for eternity because, in the six thousand years which the universe in its present state is destined to endure, there will be 120 יובל, Jubilee years (i.e. a Jubilee is the fiftieth year of a cycle). The Torah calls the Jubilee year עולם, an *eternity.*

ו וְגַם אַחֲרֵי־כֵן אֲשֶׁר יָבֹאוּ בְּנֵי הָאֱלֹהִים
אֶל־בְּנוֹת הָאָדָם וְיָלְדוּ לָהֶם הֵמָּה
הַגִּבֹּרִים אֲשֶׁר מֵעוֹלָם אַנְשֵׁי הַשֵּׁם׃

resolve as expressed in this verse has the interpretation of: *'My spirit* of eternal life *shall not endure in man* — i.e. in the offsprings of this angelic-human union — *forever, since these children are also human,* they shall not be endowed with the immortality of their fathers, *but shall live a hundred and twenty years.*]

The *Talmud* [*Chullin* 139b] apparently also accepts the interpretation that man's general life span is referred to in this verse when it notes that Moses is alluded to in our verse because the numerical value of בְּשַׁגַּם = מֹשֶׁה, Moses. And the verse continues: *'therefore shall his days be a hundred and twenty years'* which corresponds with the life-span of Moses.

Interesting in this context is the *Midrash* recorded in *Yalkut Shimoni* 815 to *Deut.* 3:23: Moses requested that he be granted a longer life-span because he had been permitted to communicate with God 'face to face', an access even greater than that of the angels who live forever. In reply, God cited this verse saying: 'I cannot do otherwise, I have already decreed your life-span (of 120 years) from the beginning of days.

4. The Nephilim

הַנְּפִלִים — *The Nephilim* — i.e. Giants. They were so called because they fell [נָפְלוּ] and caused the world to fall *(Rashi)*, and because the heart of whoever saw them fell in amazement at their collosal size *(Ibn Ezra)*.

Rashi's comm. is based on the *Midrash* which explains *Nephilim* as derived from הִפִּילוּ, they hurled [the world down]; נָפְלוּ, they themselves fell; and נְפָלִים, abortions: [they filled the world with abortions through their immorality].

Onkelos renders for both נְפִלִים and גִּבֹּרִים: גִּבָּרַיָּא, mighty men, while *Ralbag* identifies them with the *'b'nai Elohim'* of *v.* 2 [see *Ramban* below.]

According to *Pirkei d'Rabbi Eliezer,* Anakim [giants] were the offspring of the illicit union of the descended angels and the daughters of Cain. They haughtily walked about committing robbery, violence and bloodshed. They are the Nephilim to whom the spies referred when they said [*Numbers* 13:33]: *And there we saw the Nephilim, the sons of Anak.*

[The verse in *Numbers* continues: '... *'and we looked like grasshoppers to ourselves and so we must have appeared to them.' Rashi,* there, comments: *'Nephilim* — Giants who descended from Shemchazai and Azael who fell from heaven in the days of Enosh' [cf. *Targum Yonason; Rashi, Niddah* 61a. Comp. also *Rashi* to *Yoma* 67b cited in *comm.* to v.2 where he identifies Uzza and Azael as the *'b'nei Elohim'*, godly beings who descended to earth.]

Targum Yonasan cites Shemchazai and Azael *themselves* 'as the Nephilim who fell from heaven.'

Many commentators etymologically attach נְפִלִים to נִפְלָא, *wondrous,* and render: 'Men of wondrous stature' *(Chizkuni);* men, who were of such height that it appeared as if they would fall over themselves *(B'chor Shor).*

Hirsch notes that the term נפל, falling, is often used by Scripture to connote the overpowering of a weaker force by a far more powerful one, as if to say that the strong one 'befell' the weak. Thus, *Nephilim* would indicate the overwhelming strength and superiority of this race of giants. As our verse indicates, *Nephilim* were common in those antediluvian days. They were

VI *and also afterward when the sons of the rulers would consort with the daughters of man, who would bear to them. They were the mighty who, from old, were men of devastation.*

products of the Cainite line which submerged the spiritual thus causing gigantic physical growth. Had the mixture of the spiritual line of Seth with the physical line of Cain [see *comm.* above 6:2] achieved the ideal result, a race of spiritually inclined giants would have resulted. Unfortunately, the physical overpowered the spiritual.

הָיוּ בָאָרֶץ בַּיָּמִים הָהֵם — *Were on the earth in those days* — i.e. in the days of Enosh and the children of Cain *(Rashi).*

Before the generations sinned *(B'chor Shor).*

וְגַם אַחֲרֵי־כֵן — *And also afterward.*

Although they witnessed the destruction of the generation of Enosh when the ocean rose and flooded a third of the world, they still did not humble themselves and repent *(Rashi).*

Sforno explains it as the period of probation that God had given for repentance.

According to *Ibn Ezra 'also after'* means: after the Flood.

[This would imply either that Noah's son married a daughter of the Nephilim and hence there were born to them after the Flood children who were descendants of Nephilim; or *Ibn Ezra* might be in agreement with the Talmudic opinion [*Niddah* 61a] that Og survived the Flood and he might add that others survived with him *(Ramban; Karnei Ohr).*

אֲשֶׁר יָבֹאוּ . . . וְיָלְדוּ לָהֶם — *When the sons of the rulers would consort ... who would bear* [lit. and they bore] *to them* — i.e. and begot giants like them *(Rashi).*

הֵמָּה הַגִּבֹּרִים — *They* [i.e. the Nephilim *(B'chor Shor)*] *are the mighty* — i.e. mighty in rebellion against God *(Rashi).*

They are the mighty who, from old — They are the ones who are mentioned by later generations as having existed from ancient times *(Radak).*

אֲשֶׁר מֵעוֹלָם אַנְשֵׁי הַשֵּׁם — *Who from old, were men of devastation* [lit. *'men of name'; 'men of renown'; 'men of distinction' (Aderes Eliyahu).*]

The translation 'men of devastation' follows *Rashi:* אַנְשֵׁי שִׁמָּמוֹן, men who brought devastation upon the world.

Although *Ramban* comments that the interpretation of these verses as referring to 'fallen' angels fits into the language of the verse more than all other interpretations, he avoids delving into this because of the mysteries it involves [see *comm.* v.2], and prefers to interpret that the *b'nei Elohim,* who were the Sethite line and were endowed with Adam's distinguished godly likeness, took women by force and their offspring stood out from their fellow men by virtue of their great stature. They were termed *'Nephilim'* which means 'inferior ones' (as in *Job* 12:3: *I am not 'nophel' — inferior — to you)* because they were inferior to their parents although they were גִּבּוֹרִים, mighty men in comparison with the rest of the generation.

[Following *Ramban,* then, the verse is to be rendered:
The Nephilim — who had been descendants of Adam through Seth — *were on the earth in those days* —

ו °מפטיר ה °וַיַּרְא יהוה כִּי רַבָּה רָעַת הָאָדָם בָּאָרֶץ
ה־ו וְכָל־יֵצֶר מַחְשְׁבֹת לִבּוֹ רַק רַע כָּל־הַיּוֹם:
ו וַיִּנָּחֶם יהוה כִּי־עָשָׂה אֶת־הָאָדָם בָּאָרֶץ

and also after that when the Nephilim themselves begot children.
when the b'nei Elohim had come in unto the daughters of man and begot children — i.e. when the first generation who were called *b'nai Elohim* because they were of absolute perfection, caused the daughters of men to beget Nephilim (who were inferior to them);
these were the mighty men — in comparison with the rest of the generation;
that were evermore [rendering מֵעוֹלָם *(of old)* = forever] — i.e. after the flood those who beheld the mighty ones would recall these Nephilim and exclaim: 'Mightier men than these preceded them in the ages preceding us';
the men of renown — they were the men of renown in later generations.]

5. וַיַּרְא ה׳ — *[And] HASHEM saw.*

I.e. 'It was manifest to HASHEM — which is how the phrase 'seeing' should be understood when connected with wrong, injury, or violence *(Moreh Nevuchim* 1:48).

Rav Saadiah Gaon renders: *'When* HASHEM saw ...'

In the literal sense *Aggadas Breishis* understands *'HASHEM saw'* in this verse as belying the wicked cynics who say: God does not see us when we sin, because He is far away, and seven heavens separate between us. But God retorts, as the verse in *Psalms* (94:9) states: *He that forms the eye shall He not see?* ... *'And HASHEM saw that the wickedness of man was great.'*

כִּי רַבָּה רָעַת הָאָדָם — *That the wickedness of man was great.*

— I.e., was increasingly greater *(Midrash).* [Cf. *Rashi* to 18:20 s.v. כִּי רַבָּה.].

When God looked down, He saw that man had brought great evil — harm and injustice — into the world. The present was immeasurably bad; the future would be worse *(Hirsch).*

בָּאָרֶץ — *Upon the earth.*

The verse stresses *upon the earth* because it was the violence that man was perpetrating upon his fellow man that *most* angered God ... *(Lekach Tov).*

[See *comm.* to *ArtScroll Koheles* 8:6 *'For everything has its time and justice, for man's evil overwhelms him':* — i.e. when man's evil goes beyond God's forbearance then punishment is heaped upon him *(Rashi, ibid.).* Our verse is cited there with the comment: "This description of sin and punishment is similar to the sequence found concerning the Generation of the Flood: *And HASHEM saw that the wickedness of man was great in the earth'* ... (and then) ... *'HASHEM said, I will destroy man.'* "[1]

וְכָל־יֵצֶר מַחְשְׁבֹת לִבּוֹ רַק רַע כָּל־הַיּוֹם —

1. [The description of man's sin as *'great'* does not necessarily describe their number, but their magnitude.

Rambam in *Hilchos Teshuvah* 2:2 discusses the evaluation of merit and iniquity:

'... So it is with the whole world. If the merits of its human population exceed its sins, it is a virtuous country, if its iniquities preponderate, it is an evil country ... and they are destroyed immediately as it is said, *And HASHEM saw that the wickedness of man was great* ...

This evaluation takes into account not the quantity but the quality of merits and sins. There may be a single merit that outweighs many iniquities, ... and there may be one iniquity that offsets many merits ... God alone makes this determination; He alone knows how to set off merit against sin.

VI
5-6

5 *HASHEM saw that the wickedness of man was
great upon the earth, and that every product of the
thoughts of his heart was but evil always.* 6 *And
HASHEM reconsidered having made man on earth,*

And [*that*] *every product of the thoughts of his heart was but evil always* [lit. *'all the day'*.]

I.e. every thought conceived by man [*'heart'* being considered throughout the Bible on the seat of the intellect] was continually motivated only toward evil, not good *(R' Meyuchas);* they would not listen to rebuke and there was no prospect of repentance [their corruption was total and complete] *(Sforno).*

HaRechasim leBik'ah renders *'thoughts of the heart'* as man's determined intentions.

According to *Radak,* of the two inclinations, good and evil, that are normally found in man's heart, that generation of man turned both to absolute evil. This lust is called יֵצֶר because the heart יוֹצֵר, 'fashions' man's desire for good or for evil. [See also *comm.* to 8:21.]

— The phrase implies that they were governed by their Evil Inclination and strayed after their own ideas *(Midrash HaGadol).*

God said: Look at the ways of the wicked! When I created man I gave him two servants, one good and one evil ... Not only have they failed to turn the Evil Inclination towards good; they have made the good one evil!' *(Midrash Aggadas Bereishis).*

Hirsch stresses that יֵצֶר does not imply a driving force, a strong cord dragging mankind along. He explains that the root of יֵצֶר contains no suggestion of compulsion, but rather of forming. It does not mean the 'molder' [יוֹצֵר], but that which is formed and subordinate to its master, as in חוֹמֶר בְּיַד הַיּוֹצֵר, clay in the hand of the artisan.

יֵצֶר מַחְשְׁבוֹת [*products of the thoughts*] are the 'formations of our weaving soul.' The notion of what we are capable of achieving impels us to attempt it, but it is we who have formed it.

Hirsch concludes that the expression כָּל יֵצֶר, *'every product'* refers to their ideas and notions: every goal was without merit. All man's thought formations in that generation pointed toward evil.

כָּל־הַיּוֹם — *Always* [lit. *'all the day'*] — this evil tendency to evil was continuous, and uninterrupted in their every pursuit *(Hirsch).*

'All the day' is interpreted literally in the *Talmud:*

Rav Yitzchak said: The [Evil] Inclination of a man grows stronger within him from day to day as it says *'only evil all the day'* [i.e. as the days go on the evil increases] ... and were it not that God comes to man's assistance, he would not be able to withstand it *(Sukkah* 52a).

'All the day' — from the rising until the setting of the sun there was no hope of good in them *(Midrash).*

6. וַיִּנָּחֶם ה׳ כִּי עָשָׂה אֶת הָאָדָם בָּאָרֶץ — *And HASHEM reconsidered having* [lit. *'that He'*] *made* [*the*] *man on* [*the*] *earth.*

I.e. He reconsidered and His thoughts were turned from His attribute of Mercy to the attribute of Justice [i.e. from that of upholding the world to that of destroying it] *(Rashi).*

[Literally the verb נחם, depending on its conjugation, can have the meaning of consolation, comfort, consideration,

ו ז ז וַיִּתְעַצֵּב אֶל־לִבּוֹ: וַיֹּאמֶר יהוה אֶמְחֶה

regret. The translation *'reconsidered'* reflects *Rashi's* alternate interpretation of the verse cited above.]

In *Rashi's* primary translation, (based upon the *Midrash),* he renders: *'God was consoled* [translating וַיִּנָּחֶם = נֶחָמָה, consolation] *that He made man on earth'* [stressing the seemingly superfluous mention of *'on earth' (Gur Aryeh)*] and comments:

'It was a consolation to God that He created man among the *earthly beings,* for had He made him a celestial being, man would have instigated revolt among the angels.'

For as we see in the *Midrash* (see *footnote* to *v.* 2) the angels Uzza and Azael came to earth and were, indeed, corrupted — how much more would man have been a danger to the angels had he lived in heaven and would have been their equal! *(Harav David Cohen)*

The *Zohar* also interprets נחם according to both renderings:

Rav Yesa said that the word נחם used of God means *'regret'* implying that God meditates to Himself that sinners are His handiwork and He therefore pities them and is grieved because they sin before him. Rav Chizkiah says that it means *'consoled'* implying that when God resolves to destroy the wicked He comforts Himself for their loss like one who resigns himself to the loss of an article.

The *Talmud* accounts for the presence of the seemingly superfluous word בָּאָרֶץ, *'in the earth',* in this verse and incorporates the dual interpretation of וַיִּנָּחֶם as *'consolation', 'comfort'* and *'regret'.*

Rav Dimi taught: 'God exclaimed: I did well in preparing graves for man' [rendering: *'God was comforted that he made man in the earth'*; i.e. by decreeing death upon man and that He brought destruction upon so wicked a way of life *(Rashi)*]; while others maintain that God said 'I did *not* do well by preparing them graves' [rendering *'God regretted that He made man in the earth,* i.e. made them mortal', for perhaps they would have repented *(Rashi)*] *(Sanhedrin* 108a).

Ibn Ezra notes the difficulty of depicting God as 'regretting' and comments that such terms as 'regret' cannot be applied to the Creator, rather they are anthropopathic because 'the Torah speaks in the language of man.' Man perceives this Divine manifestation as if it were regret. Similarly, וַיִּתְעַצֵּב, *He was saddened,* is an anthropomorphic antonym of such concepts as יִשְׂמַח ה׳ בְּמַעֲשָׂיו, 'Let HASHEM *rejoice* in His handiwork' [*Psalms* 104:31] for God 'rejoices' when man earns His graciousness.[1]

Rav Joseph Albo [*Ikkarim* 3:14] explains the concept of 'The Torah speaks in the language of man ...'

Since in human phraseology, when a king punishes those who have rebelled against him, he is said to be jealous and revengeful and full of wrath, so it is said of God when He punishes those who violate His will that He is a jealous and avenging God and is full of wrath because the act which emanates from Him against those who transgress His

1. In his penetrating discourse on the anthropomorphic human concept of grief and regret, *Akeidas Yitzchak* explains that this 'grief' is not contradictory to the basic Jewish belief that God forsees the future.

He cites the example of one who plants a sapling for use as lumber. He tends and nurtures it, takes pride in its growth, and lovingly protects it from harm, although he knows that one day he will chop it down. When that day comes he looks back on his efforts and feels sorrow that the product of his long toil is cut down. This is in no way contradictory to his foreknowledge.

Expressed in human terms, this is the 'grief' God now experienced.

and He had heart-felt sadness. [7] *And HASHEM said, 'I*

will is similar to the act of a revengeful, grudging, and jealous person.

The attribution of sorrow to God must be explained in the same way. Just as human beings feel sorrow when necessity compels that their works be destroyed, so the Torah says *'it grieved Him at His heart'*, and in the immediate sequel we read: *'And HASHEM said, I will blot out man* whom I have made ... *for I regret having made them.'* 'Regret' is applied to God because He performs the act of a person who regrets what he has made and desires to destroy it ...'

וַיִּתְעַצֵּב אֶל־לִבּוֹ — *And He had heart-felt sadness* [lit. *'And He felt it saddened* (or: *'grieved')* to *His heart'*].

Continuing *Rashi*'s alternate interpretation: 'He mourned over the loss of His handiwork';[1]

Continuing *Rashi*'s primary interpretation however: Man brought grief to God; it entered God's mind to punish him measure for measure by causing him to grieve.

'It grieved Him to his heart' — i.e. concerning man's heart, for he was evil *(B'chor Shor).*

[This interpretation is in consonance with *Rambam*'s alternate explanation of עצב as transitively meaning 'vexation', 'provocation', 'rebellion' (as in *Isaiah* 63:10; *Psalms* 78:40; 56:6); and *'His heart'*, meaning *'His will'* as dependent on the heart. Thus, avoiding the implication of the common interpretation, the verse accordingly would be rendered: *'And HASHEM regretted that He had made man on the earth for he* — i.e. man — *had rebelled against His will.'*]

In response to heretics, *Rashi* cites the following *Midrash:*

A gentile asked Rav Yehoshua ben Karcha: 'Do you not admit that God sees the future?'

'Yes', he answered.

'But it is written "He grieved at His heart?"' the heretic asked. [And if God knows the future, why was He grieved?]

'Was there ever a son born to you?' Rav Yehoshua asked. 'Yes' came the reply.

'And what did you do?' Rav Yehoshua asked.

'I made everyone joyous.'

'And did you not know, Rav Yehoshua asked, that he would ultimately die?'

'At the time of joy let there be joy' said the heretic, 'and in the time of mourning, mourning.'

'So are the works of the Holy One blessed be He,' said Rav Yehoshua: 'Even though it is revealed before Him that they would ultimately sin and be destroyed, He did not refrain from creating them for the sake of the righteous who are destined to arise from them.'

[And the meaning is not that God did not foresee that they would sin and it was only now that He became aware, but 'in the time of joy, joy, and in the time of mourning, mourning!' (see *Akeidas Yitzchak* cited in footnote at end of previous verse).]

The phrase אֶל לִבּוֹ, *'to His heart'* is also explained as anthropomorphic 'since the heart is understood in Scripture as the seat of intellect [i.e. synonymous with 'mind'], the same term is applied also to God as being His seat of emotion if one can so express it *(Radak).*

According to *Ramban:* 'He kept His regret to Himself and did not send a prophet to rebuke them.'

This follows *Rambam* [*Moreh* 1:29]: "According to the interpretation that וַיִּתְעַצֵּב means 'angered' the sense of the verse is *'And God was angry with them on account of the wickedness of their*

1. *Sforno* renders: *'He was grieved'*, because God does not desire the death of the wicked [but that he should repent and live.]

... As Rav Yehudah said: God was grieved because the execution of judgment is always displeasing to Him. Similarly, at the time when Israel crossed the Red Sea, when the angels came as usual to chant their praises before God on that night, God said to them: 'The works of my hands are drowning in the sea and you will chant praises?' *(Zohar).*

ו אֶת־הָאָדָם אֲשֶׁר־בָּרָאתִי מֵעַל פְּנֵי הָאֲדָמָה מֵאָדָם עַד־בְּהֵמָה עַד־רֶמֶשׂ וְעַד־עוֹף הַשָּׁמָיִם כִּי נִחַמְתִּי כִּי עֲשִׂיתִם:

deeds; as for the phrase אֶל לִבּוֹ, *'to His heart'* this is an anthropomorphism which means *'to Himself'*, without conveying it to anyone, for in the Torah no *distinct mention* is made of any message sent to the wicked generation of the flood cautioning or threatening them with death ...''

[It would thus seem that *Rambam* and *Ramban* are in disagreement with the interpretation that verse 3 was said to Noah giving the people a 120 year period of probation to repent, and it also appears to conflict with the statement of the *Zohar* on the next verse. When a man wants to take vengeance on another he says nothing for fear that if he discloses his intention, the other will be on guard and escape him. Not so God ... for in vain one would try to be on guard against Him. So now *'God said: I will blot out man,* etc.' — He proclaimed His intention through Noah and warned them several times, but they would not listen. Only then did He execute judgment and exterminate them.''

Rambam's interpretation also apparently disagrees with the interpretation *(Rashi, v.*14) that during the long period that Noah built the ark he warned the people that a flood was imminent unless they repent.]

Chizkuni renders: God grieved over the heart of man [which had fallen prey to evil thoughts. Or alternatively: God's heart grieved over the imminent destruction of the world.

Hirsch cautions lest, in interpreting anthropomorphisms in order to remove speculation of God's corporality, we forget that God has free-will and personality, and that man, too has both qualities. When we are told that God saw the evil of man, it is to make us aware that man is not inherently evil. God had to see it before He 'knew' it, so to speak. Neither man's evil nor the resultant destruction of the world were predetermined by natural causes.

7. וַיֹּאמֶר ה׳ — *And HASHEM said*[1] — i.e. became determined *(Ibn Ezra).*

Or, according to *Radak* [and *Zohar,* see. *comm.* end of last verse]: proclaimed through Noah.

[God did not punish capriciously — it was only after mankind was irreversibly steeped in evil and God was grieved to the point of reconsideration from Mercy to judgment. Cf. *Lamentations* 3:33 *'For He does not torment capriciously nor afflict man ...'* — (everything is in just retribution for man's sins).]

Let no one delude himself: Although He is long-suffering, God does not overlook transgressions. Man must remember that he will ultimately be held accountable for his actions, because God collects His due and retribution

1 [Noting that *'HASHEM'* (which connotes God in His Attribute of Mercy — v. *comm.* to 1:1, 2:4) is used in these verses of judgment instead of the more appropriate *Elohim* ('God'), which connotes His Attribute of Justice, the *Midrash* (33:3) comments:

'Woe to the wicked who turn the Attribute of Mercy into the Attribute of Justice. For wherever *'HASHEM'* is used it connotes the attribute of mercy, as in the verse *'HASHEM, HASHEM, God merciful and gracious' (Exodus* 34:6); nevertheless, here it is written *'And HASHEM saw that the wickedness of man was great'*; *'and HASHEM reconsidered ...'*; *'and HASHEM said I will blot out man'*.

Torah Shelemah suggests that the point might be 'that man's wickedness was so great that even in His capacity *'HASHEM'*, the God of mercy, He had to decree destruction upon them; or: while it appeared that He was now acting as the God of judgment in truth that very judgment,

will blot out man whom I created from the face of the ground — from man to beast, to creeping things, and to birds of the sky; for I have reconsidered My having made them.'

finally comes ... He waits for the opportune moment when man's evil is great, as He acted toward the generation of the Flood, granting them an extended period of apparent immunity but: *'When HASHEM saw that man's wickedness was great in the earth'* ... *'HASHEM said: I will blot out man' (Bamidbar Rabbah).*

אֶמְחֶה אֶת הָאָדָם — *I will blot out* [*the*] *man.*

The term 'blot' instead of 'slay', 'destroy', 'annihilate' is used because God said: Man is dust and I will *blot him out* [in the sense of 'dissolve'] by bringing water upon him *(Tanchuma; Rashi).*

'I do not need armies to destroy them! Just as I created the world with a word, I will but utter a word and destroy them!' *(Midrash).*

According to the Sages in the *Midrash* מחה means a *total* dissolving. Not only death and the decay of soft tissue is decreed. Even that part of the skeleton which, our Sages say, never deteriorates, was completely dissolved *(Hirsch).*

מֵעַל פְּנֵי הָאֲדָמָה — *From the face of the ground* — The world itself was not destroyed, but *the surface, which is alloted to man for his mission (Hirsch).*

מֵאָדָם עַד בְּהֵמָה — *From man to beast* — because the latter, too, had corrupted their way *(Midrash);* or, since everything was created for the sake of man, and he is about to be destroyed, what need is there for beasts? *(Rashi).*

כִּי נִחַמְתִּי כִּי עֲשִׂיתִם — *For I have reconsidered My having made them* [lit. *'that I made them'*].

[Following *Rashi*'s alternate interpretation cited to verse 6.]

Rashi here comments: 'I considered what to do after having made them'.

Heaven forbid that this represents a literal change of the divine will. Rather it was foreordained that the order of creation be changed in the future. The original state of the world was required by the divine will so that it could be possible for people upon occasion to enjoy utter tranquility such as that which reigned in antediluvian times without it being considered an unprecedented condition *(Ha'amek Davar).*

stern though it was, would ultimately prove to be an act of mercy, for thereby a higher humanity was enabled to arise.'

As *Hirsch* elaborates:

'HASHEM, the same mercy, the same God of love that had placed man on earth, now proclaims his destruction. Man's corruption was so great, that the very extermination was an act of mercy.'

The more esoteric implications of these matters, according to *Ramban,* constitute 'a great mystery which may not be written. Whoever knows it will understand why the Four Letter Name, HASHEM, is written here while in the rest of the chapter and in account of the Flood the name *Elohim,* [God of Judgment] is used.'

ו
ח

ח וְנֹחַ מָצָא חֵן בְּעֵינֵי יהוה׃

The question is asked here, in *I Samuel* 15:11, and *Exodus* 32:14: How can we associate the concept of reconsideration and regret with God? We must understand that it is impossible for God to promise and then change His mind, or find Himself unable to carry out His promise. Such behavior is possible only for humans. But there is another form of regret: God created man to serve Him and to contribute to the divine Glory. If man sins and becomes unworthy of this calling, and, as a result, is wiped off the earth, it seems as if God recanted when it is actually man who falls short *(B'chor Shor).*

It is with this very interpretation that *Hirsch* here and in verse 6 renders: *For I have been caused to alter My decision* — i.e. by man's external provocations and a change of circumstances.

Or HaChaim notes that if the cause of man's destruction had been only his own sins, then people below the age of punishment would have been spared. Rather the reason is God's regret *for having made him.* If so, even the righteous would be included in the Decree. But Noah was spared by God's grace (next verse).

8. וְנֹחַ מָצָא חֵן בְּעֵינֵי ה׳ — *But* [lit. *'and'*] *Noah found grace* [or: *'favor'*] *in God's eyes* — i.e. all his deeds were beautiful and pleasant before Him *(Ramban).*

The translation *'but'* as antithetic follows the *Talmud, Sanhedrin* 108a according to which in the previous verse God's regret extended to all, Noah included, but that a special exception was made for his sake because he found grace in God's eyes (see *Or HaChaim above).*

... And were it not for this special grace Noah would have perished, too *(Midrash Aggadah).*

Since God's plan did not call for a *total reversal* of Creation, Noah was able to find favor and be found worthy of rebuilding the world as it was, but in an altered condition *(Ha'amek Davar).*

Interesting is the comment of the *Zohar:*

When Noah was born they gave him a name which connoted consolation in the hope that it would be fulfilled for them as well. His relation to God, however, is expressed by the same letters in reverse order — חֵן, *favor,* a condition that benefited only his family. Rav Yose said: 'the names of the righteous influence their destiny for good, and those of the wicked for evil. Thus the anagram of Er, the wicked son of Judah is רַע, evil, and of him it is written [*Gen.* 38:7] *and Er was evil in the sight of HASHEM.*

God's *grace* was to make possible the salvation of Noah's family, for otherwise only he would have been spared. Although Noah was a righteous man, he did not influence his generation to know God, therefore his merit was insufficient to save others. Only a righteous person who attempts to make others righteous can bring about their salvation, because he can then influence them to repent *(Sforno).*

Hirsch concludes the Sidrah with the thought that after 1656 years of history, God was ready to wipe away all creation and carry on His

VI
8 [8] *But Noah found grace with HASHEM.*

plan with one man and his family. As Psalm 29 proclaims, the Presence of God feels all that is awesome and sublime. Nevertheless, ה׳ לַמַּבּוּל יָשָׁב, *HASHEM sat at the Flood:* He remained firm and unshaken, refusing to compromise His plan for the education of mankind. Such firmness is the precondition of peace as the psalm concludes ה׳ עֹז לְעַמּוֹ יִתֵּן ה׳ יְבָרֵךְ אֶת עַמּוֹ בַשָּׁלוֹם *HASHEM will give strength to His people, HASHEM will bless His people with peace.*

According to the Masoretic note appearing at the end of the Sidrah there are 146 verses in the *Sidra* numerically corresponding to the mnemonic אֲמַצְיָ״ה and יְחִזְקִיָּה״וּ. The *Haftorah* begins with *Isaiah* 42:5 כֹּה אָמַר.

סדר נח

Sidra Noach

— An Overview

An Overview
Noah and Abraham

עשרה דורות מאדם ועד נח להודיע כמה ארך אפים לפניו שכל הדורות היו מכעיסין לפניו עד שהביא עליהם את מי המבול
עשרה דורות מנח ועד אברהם להודיע כמה ארך אפים לפניו שכל הדורות היו מכעיסין לפניו עד שבא אברהם אבינו ונטל שכר כלם

There were ten generations from Adam to Noah to show how long-suffering [God] is, since all these generations antagonized Him until He brought the waters of the Flood upon them.
There were ten generations from Noah to Abraham to show how long-suffering He is, since all these generations antagonized Him until our Father Abraham came and took the merit of them all (Avos 5:2-3).

I. Tzaddik — Righteous

Three Words

Three words formed from the same root, expressing the same concept צדק, צדיק, and צדקה.

There are three words formed from the same root, expressing the same concept צדיק, צדק, and צדקה. *Tzaddik* is a righteous person; *tzedek* is justice in a court of law; *tzedakah* is 'charity.' Three words. In common parlance and understanding they are commonly taken as three widely varying ideals: People think of a *tzaddik* as a 'righteous person' who engages in religious ritual, other-worldly pursuits, or even asceticism. *Tzedakah,* charity and benevolence based on the circumstances of one in need, is far removed from *tzedek* the strict and scrupulous application of principles of law without regard to the need or circumstances of the litigants.

But the Hebrew language teaches us otherwise. All three words are derived from צדק, justice. All three concepts are different expressions of the same theme: that God has created the world with a plan and that every human being must see himself as an executor of that plan. Whether in his personal life, his legal dealings, or his disbursements to the needy, a Jew must see himself as an administrator of justice, apportioning his emotions, time, wisdom, and resources according to the wishes of their ultimate Owner.

Whether in his personal life, his legal dealings, or his disbursements to the needy, a Jew must see himself as an administrator of justice.

Three Forms of Justice

לֹא תַעֲשׂוּ עָוֶל בַּמִּשְׁפָּט לֹא תִשָּׂא פְנֵי דָל וְלֹא תֶהְדַּר פְּנֵי גָדוֹל בְּצֶדֶק תִּשְׁפֹּט עֲמִיתֶךָ

Do no wrong in judgment. Do not favor the poor, and show no honor to the great; with justice shall you judge your neighbor (Lev. 19:15).

The verse concludes with the positive command that complements and summarizes the three negative commands with which it begins. In order to do צֶדֶק, *justice,* properly, the judge must see every person standing before him, rich or poor, as עֲמִיתוֹ, his neighbor, entitled to the same rights and privileges, subject to the same obligations and duties as he is himself. His judgments are not handed down from on high; they are simply expressions of fairness and right as defined by the Torah *(Hirsch).*

Judgments are not handed down from on high; they are simply expressions of fairness and right as defined by the Torah.

הָשֵׁב תָּשִׁיב לוֹ אֶת הָעֲבוֹט . . . וּבֵרֲכֶךָּ וּלְךָ תִּהְיֶה צְדָקָה לִפְנֵי ה׳ אֱלֹקֶיךָ

You must return the security to him ... that he may bless you, and it shall be for you as a righteous duty (tzedakah) before HASHEM, your God (Deut. 24:13).

The holder of a security pledge from a poor man must return it if it is needed: bedding by night and clothing by day. This is absolutely required, yet the Talmud *(Shavuos* 44a) infers from the use of the word *tzedakah* that the return is an act of *generosity.* From this is derived the legal principle that בעל חוב קונה משכון, a creditor acquires certain rights of ownership in a pledge *(ibid).* A strange paradox: the creditor *owns* the pledge yet he is dutifully required to pursue the needy debtor to return it as is needed; the law requires him to return, yet it is regarded as an act of charity! There is no paradox at all. Even 'charity' is no more the doing of what is right.

The law requires him to return, yet it is regarded as an act of charity!

> As soon as you perceive that what you are doing is only your duty, your vocation, your task as a human being and as a Jew ... [you will] act with no other purpose than to fulfill the will of your Father in Heaven, and to give light and warmth and nourishment just as a ray of sunlight gives light in the service of God. Why should God give you more than you need unless He intended to make you the administrator of this blessing for the benefit of others, the treasurer of his treasures? Every penny you can spare is not yours, but should become a tool for bringing blessing to others. ... That is why our Sages prefer to give the beautiful name of *tzedakah* to this act of charity by means of material goods. For *tzedakah* is the justice which gives to every creature that which God allots to it *(Horeb).*

Why should God give you more than you need unless He intended to make you the treasurer of his treasures?

Tzaddik as Judge

A tzaddik, too, is one who exercises justice.

A *tzaddik,* too, is one who exercises justice. He knows that he is but the treasurer, not the owner, of the entire store of human and material resources. The marching orders of his life are contained in the Torah. For him to do otherwise than to carry them out meticulously would be a lack of justice that is comparable to robbery? For, indeed, if he were to make use of the breath of life, the spark of intelligence, the potential of wealth in ways opposed to the will of God, is he not misappropriating them from the Owner who has entrusted him with their management?

Therefore, the prophet says of the wealthy who do not assist the needy גְּזֵלַת הֶעָנִי בְּבָתֵּיכֶם, *the robbery of*

If the rich were entrusted with abundance, are they not thieves if they hoard it all for themselves?

the poor is in your homes (Isaiah 3:14). If the rich were entrusted with abundance, are they not thieves if they hoard it all for themselves?

Therefore, the *Zohar* says that the person who performs a sin or neglects a commandment has stolen from the Divine Presence. If life and strength were given him to serve God and he appropriates them for the satisfaction of his own desires, has he not stolen them from their Giver?

Whether man will deal justly or be a 'thief' is left to him.

Whether man will deal justly or be a 'thief' is left to him. Before an embryo is conceived, an angel says before God, 'What shall this drop become — a strong man or a weakling, a wise man or a fool, a rich man or a pauper? But whether he will be wicked or righteous is not foreordained *(Niddah* 16b).

Man is created with his treasury of potential and, as life goes on, it is filled or depleted. What he is to have has been decided before his birth; what he does with it is left to him. Each individual human being is born with a mission all his own. The magnate's is not that of the scholar, and vice versa. Obviously, the child born with the mission of being the teacher of the generation is endowed with the brilliance of intellect, memory, and analytical powers to do so. The one who is expected to become a supporter of Torah and the poor will be given great wealth. The mental and material treasures of a human being are the tools he is given to accomplish the goal God set for him, and the tools can be used well or they can be wasted. Money can find its way to worthy causes or it can be invested in a quest for more wealth; or it can be squandered at roulette wheels. Man will be called to account for how wisely and 'righteously' he has utilized the gifts placed in his trust. But one thing must be clear: whatever he needs for his mission will be provided him *(Michtav MeEliyahu).*

But one thing must be clear: whatever he needs for his mission will be provided him.

II. Noah

נֹחַ אִישׁ צַדִּיק תָּמִים הָיָה בְּדֹרֹתָיו
Noah was a righteous man; he was perfect in his generation (Gen. 6:9).

Perfect Tzaddik

The Torah testifies that Noah was totally righteous, a *tzaddik*. By definition he was a man whose life was an unending pattern of justice. Like the righteous judge who apportions fairly between the claims of those who appear before him, Noah dealt with the myriad conflicting claims that make up every human life, and apportioned his time and patience, his wisdom and knowledge, his wealth and property between himself, his family, and his neighbors. God's testimony to Noah's righteousness is the most eloquent of statements; an unimpeachable guarantee that his every act was measured and considered — and just.

The Midrash says that Noah was saved not because he was deserving!

Yet we find declarations about Noah that seem to contradict the lofty characterization of him as a *tzaddik*. The *Midrash* says that Noah was saved from the Flood only because he found grace in the eyes of God — *but not because he was deserving!* Noah himself is quoted in the Midrash as saying to God, ואני כאשר עשו כן עשיתי ומה ביני לבינם, 'And as for me, what they [the sinful generation] have done, I have done equally; what is the difference between me and them?'

Noah declared himself guilty of their sin.

What was the sin of the generation that caused the verdict against them to be sealed? Robbery (see 6:13 and Comm.). Yet Noah declared himself guilty of their sin, and the *Midrash* states that his salvation was nothing but an act of mercy because he found grace in God's eyes. How are we to understand that 'righteous' Noah, the *tzaddik* who apportioned every aspect of his existence to the proper service of God could be considered on a par with the corrupt and degenerate rabble that caused 1656 years of the history of creation to be washed away in the

How can we associate the sin of robbery with Noah?

cataclysmic Flood? And how can we associate the sin of robbery with Noah?

Zohar says that Noah sinned in not having chastised his fellow men. Therefore, the destructive, murderous waters of the Flood are called מֵי נֹחַ, *the waters of Noah (Isaiah* 54:9) — the waters were his responsibility because, had he fulfilled his responsibility fully, the waters might never have come. Had he chastized and taught, done more than set a towering personal example of righteousness, then mankind might have listened and heeded and survived. And the mission of Adam might not have ended in torrential failure.

Had he chastized and taught, mankind might have listened and heeded and survived.

Yet he did chastise:

כרוז אחד עמד לי בדור המבול — זה נח . . .
שהיו מבזין עליו וקרו ליה ביזיא סבא

[*God said*] *I had one spokesman in that generation, Noah! They humiliated him, called him reviled old man! (Midrash).*

Withholding Speech

Yes, righteous Noah indeed fulfilled his minimum obligations without flaw. His 'justice' could not be faulted. But he could have done more, and great people can be dealt with as severely for not doing right as for doing wrong. To speak sinfully incurs God's wrath. In the time of the Temple, malicious gossip was punished by צרעת, divinely visited leprosy, but there was another way to earn this punishment that forced its victim into isolation from his fellows and embarrassing spiritual impurity — *withholding* speech at a time when it could be beneficial to others. To live amid sin and to have the opportunity to help eradicate it by speaking up, by reasoning, by chastising, by teaching, by pleading — and not to do so, is equally guilty *(Zohar).*

What is more, to withhold speech where it is needed is itself considered robbery.

What is more, to withhold speech where it is needed is itself considered robbery. When Sarah accused Abraham of not supporting her against arrogant, rebellious Hagar, she said, חֲמָסִי עָלֶיךָ, *my wrong* [*that I endure*] *is upon you (Gen.* 16:5). *Rashi* explains that Abraham was to blame for Sarah's humiliation because he refrained from reproving Hagar. Sarah used the same word in berating Abraham that God used in sealing the decree against the generation of the Flood — חָמָס, *robbery* — for not to offer support can be equivalent to educating for evil.

Sarah used the same word in berating Abraham that God used in sealing the decree against the generation of the Flood.

In this sense, Noah who chastised, but not enough, condemned himself for sharing the sin and the guilt of his generation. He, too, was guilty of חָמָס, *robbery,* because he refrained from doing more than the strict dictates of righteousness required him to *(Shem MiShmuel).*

Noah who chastised, but not enough, condemned himself

III. Noah and Abraham

The Difficulty

בְּדוֹרוֹתָיו יש מרבותינו דורשין אותו לשבח ויש שדורשין אותו לגנאי

The verse says that Noah was a righteous man in *his generation.* Some of our Sages explain this in praise of Noah: if he was righteous in an evil generation, imagine how much greater he would have been in a time of righteous people. Other Sages interpret it as an indirect criticism: he was considered righteous in *his* generation compared to the corruption surrounding him. Had he lived in Abraham's time, he would have been insignificant (see *Rashi; Gen.* 6:9).

The righteousness of Noah is beyond dispute — the Torah proclaims it unequivocally. *Tanchuma Yashan* (quoted in *Torah Sheleima)* says that Noah's righteousness was equivalent to Abraham's. How are we to understand and resolve these differing views of Noah?

In the brilliant insights of the Sages, contradictions and disputes are really nothing more than different views of the seventy facets of Torah.

The explanation lies in a heightened perception of human capability. The key question is not whether Noah's greatness was equal to Abraham's. As we often find in the brilliant insights of the Sages, contradictions and disputes are really nothing more than different views of the seventy facets of Torah. The heavenly scales weigh differently than do ours. Righteousness in God's eyes is measured by how well one judges in the universe of his own being. The genius must serve God in his way by utilizing his abilities to their maximum. So must the baker, the laborer, the teacher, the homemaker. Each one must attain perfection on *his own* terms. In the heavenly scale, the great scholar who uses half of his mind's potential is honored but slightly for the great knowledge gained by using half his capacity; he is dealt with harshly for not having done twice as much. On the other hand, the laborer whose free moments are spent struggling over a chapter of Mishnah to the limits of his mental capacity, may rightly earn immense reward. אין הקב״ה מונה דפים אלא שעות, The Holy One, blessed be He, does not count the pages, but the hours.

The genius must serve God by utilizing his abilities. So must the baker, the laborer, the teacher, the homemaker.

When the Torah testifies that Noah was a *perfect tzaddik,* no room is left for quibble about his greatness. Wherein, then, lay the superiority of Abraham? It is a superiority that we find expressed not only in the Talmudical statement quoted by *Rashi;* but in the *Mishnah (Avos* 5:2-3) cited above: Noah *survived* the destruction caused by the failure of the first ten generations, but Abraham did much more: he was so great that he earned for himself all the reward that should have been the lot of the ten generations that preceded him. Abraham succeeded where all others failed, but how did he become more righteous than Noah? If we properly understood the term *tzaddik* as referring to a person who attains the standard set for him by God, then the same pedestal should have borne both Noah and Abraham.

If we properly understood the term tzaddik, then the same pedestal should have borne both Noah and Abraham.

Abram Outgrows His Mission

A human has the capacity to rise above his mission.

Abraham was born Abram (11:26). His destiny was to be אַב אֲרָם, the moral leader of the nation of Aram. Had he fulfilled that mission and nothing more, he would have been 'righteous.' But he did more. A human has the capacity to rise above his mission. Through dedication, prayer, love of God — all the attributes of the greatest figures — it is possible for a person to fulfill the mission set forth for him and be granted a new, higher one — just as it is possible for someone to fail so utterly that it becomes impossible for him ever to attain the good for which he was created. When that tragedy occurs, he becomes one of the most miserable of people: those for whom the possibility of repentance is foreclosed.

Abram's name was changed to Abraham.

Abram's name was changed to Abraham because, as the Torah says, אַב הֲמוֹן גּוֹיִם נְתַתִּיךָ, *I have made you the [moral] father of a multitude of nations (Gen. 17:5).* As *Rashi* explains, he had outgrown his mission. No longer was he the 'father' merely of Aram, henceforth he was to become the 'father' of all mankind setting a moral standard that would become the goal of the next four millenia of human history and that would bring the Glory of God to earth on Mount Sinai, in the parchment and letters of the Torah, and, finally, in the very being of his descendants. This aspect of Abraham's greatness overshadowed Noah's. Noah fulfilled his mission — he even attempted to reprove his generation. But Abraham rose above his mission and thereby gained a new one. Because he sanctified God's Name far above the extent for which he was created, he earned the merit which would have belonged to all the others had they done what they were created to.

Noah fulfilled his mission, but Abraham rose above his mission and thereby gained a new one.

Noah faulted himself for not having done more. He could have. Abraham did. That a 'perfect *tzaddik*' is taken to account for not having done much more than he should have been expected to is in itself an eloquent tribute to his greatness. Awesome achievement is expected only from people of awesome greatness *(Michtav MeEliyahu).*

Awesome achievement is expected only from people of awesome greatness

Ten Generations

The number 'ten' is a reference to the Ten Heavenly Emanations

The number 'ten' in Scripture or the Oral Torah, is a reference to the Ten Heavenly Emanations by means of which God's Presence descends from heaven and makes itself manifest. Thus we have the עשרה מאמרות, the ten statements with which God created heaven and earth; עשרת הדברות, Ten Commandments; עשרה נסיונות, ten tests of Abraham; and עשר

מכות, the ten plagues upon Egypt. All of these phenomena were aspects of revelation. Through each, man and the universe were elevated to new perceptions of God's holiness and presence.

Of the same order were the ten generations from Adam to Noah and the ten from Noah to Abraham.

Of the same order were the ten generations from Adam to Noah and the ten from Noah to Abraham. The number ten was not coincidental; God had a plan of development which was to proceed and develop until it reached its spiritual culmination in ten generations. The master plan of creation was Torah and it was to enable man to perfect himself through the study of Torah and the performance of its commands that heaven and earth were created (see *Overview:* Torah). The divine intention was that God's Presence be revealed behind the obscurity of earth's hiddenness (see *Overview:* Creation) through Adam, and that man's perception of it grow and intensify stage by stage, emanation by emanation, until the tenth generation when it was to reach its climax. Then, the Torah would be given and all mankind would achieve God's final purpose and become מַמְלֶכֶת כֹּהֲנִים וְגוֹי קָדוֹשׁ, *a kingdom of priests and a holy nation (Exodus* 19:6).

Zohar writes that this goal is alluded to in the word בְּשַׁגָּם — בְּשַׁגָּם הוּא בָשָׂר *'since he is but flesh' (Gen.* 6:3) — which has the numerical value of מֹשֶׁה, Moses.

Had man been worthy, the equivalent of Moses would have appeared to receive the Torah. But mankind was not worthy.

Had man been worthy, the equivalent of Moses would have appeared to receive the Torah. But mankind was not worthy; instead of attaining perfection,man moved in a downward spiral of idolatry, degeneration, and corruption until the Flood blotted him out.

Once again God set in motion the chain of development that was to culminate in man's perfection and the giving of the Torah.

The process was to begin again from righteous Noah who signaled a new and better beginning by bringing offerings of thanksgiving and dedication to God after the deluge. Once again God set in motion the chain of development that was to culminate in man's perfection and the giving of the Torah. Again, man did not rise to the challenge. The ten generations sinned increasingly, angering God more and more, even attempting to challenge His mastery of the earth and do battle with Him by erecting their Tower of Babel *(Gen.* 11:1-9; see *comm.).* But this chain of ten had a different ending than the earlier one. Had it ended in total failure, then no one can know what sort of misfortune might have been visited upon man. Instead it ended with Abraham. By his own greatness, a greatness he proved by elevating himself through a succession of ten tests, he achieved in his person what all ten generations had failed to do.

Until Abraham

The first series of generations was wiped out without a memory; the second series attained in Abraham what it was destined to accomplish.

The first series of generations was wiped out without a memory; the second series attained in Abraham what it was destined to accomplish. By not being equal to its mission, the rest of mankind lost its birthright of holiness: before then, all of mankind was meant to share the gift of Torah and be the chariot bearing God's Presence. All of mankind bore within itself the sparks of holiness that should have grown into a fire of spirituality. But they weren't nurtured and would have become extinguished — had not Abraham risen to such heights that he could become the abode of all the world's holiness. The unwelcome holy sparks left their unwilling hosts and lodged in Abraham. They all antagonized God, עד שבא אברהם וקבל שכר כולם, until Abraham came and earned the merit of them all.

'His two kidneys became like two teachers teaching him Torah and wisdom'.

'Abraham performed the commandments of the Torah before they were given,' even the Rabbinic injunctions of the future *(Yoma* 28b). 'His two kidneys became like two teachers teaching him Torah and wisdom' *(Midrash),* because he reached so high a level that his own words and thoughts became Torah; he united himelf with the mind of God until his own thoughts and wisdom became identical with God's (see *Overview:* Torah). Thus, in more than a symbolic sense, the Divine Plan was fulfilled and Torah was 'given' — not to the flawed generation of Babel — it was dispersed; not by giving the Tablets and the Torah in its present form — that was left for Moses and the children of Israel. But the Torah *was* given and nurtured in Abraham who, in a real sense, began a new history of the world. Now, there are בני נח, the children of Noah: the non-Jewish world which has the Noachic Laws and its own capacity to fulfill the Divine Will; and בני אברהם יצחק ויעקב, the Children of the Patriarchs whose history begins with Abraham. Fittingly does the *Zohar* say that the word הִבָּרְאָם, *when they were created (Gen.* 5:2), which introduces the Book of the Generations of Man, is spelled with the letters אַבְרָהָם, Abraham; the creation of man is an allusion to Abraham because he became its culmination and purpose.

The word הִבָּרְאָם, which introduces the Book of the Generations of Man is spelled with the letters אַבְרָהָם, Abraham.

IV. Crucial Moments

The Sixth Century

The Divine Plan has decreed that there be times when particular manifestations of holiness are visited upon earth. It is so in the annual calendar: the first ten days of Tishrei are days of judgment, Passover is a time of freedom, Tisha B'Av is a time of potential greatness that, unrealized, became the day of suffering and woe (see *Overview*, ArtScroll edition of *Eichah).* It is also so in the broad sweep of history: there are years and generations that were destined for revelation. One of them was the year of the Flood; another was the year of the dispersion.

There are years and generations that were destined for revelation.

בִּשְׁנַת שֵׁשׁ מֵאוֹת שָׁנָה לְחַיֵּי נֹחַ . . .
נִבְקְעוּ כָּל מַעְיְנוֹת תְּהוֹם רַבָּה וַאֲרֻבֹּת הַשָּׁמַיִם נִפְתָּחוּ

In the six hundredth year of the life of Noah . . . all the fountains of the great deep burst forth and the windows of the heavens were opened (Gen. 7:11).

Zohar comments that the *'wellsprings of the deep'* refers to the wisdom from below, man's capability through the Oral Torah to broaden and develop the wisdom of Torah. The *'windows of heavens'* refers to the Written Torah, God's gift from heaven. From the moment of creation, that year was foreordained to be a time of awesome Godly manifestation. Had man been worthy, he would have received the Writ-

From the moment of creation, that year was foreordained to be a time of awesome Godly manifestation.

ten and Orah Torahs and been worthy of broadening and deepening it through the Oral Torah.

The six hundredth year of Noah's life was chosen as a year when a flood of wisdom would descend upon earth.

The six hundredth year of Noah's life was chosen as a year when a flood of wisdom would descend upon earth. But like all heavenly gifts, man is free to decide how he will use it or whether he will be worthy to receive it. *Rambam* points out that material blessings can be extended to a pious person to enable him more easily to fulfill commandments. Secure in his livelihood, he can study Torah without anxiety, purchase what he needs to follow the Torah's precepts, and contribute generously to charities. The recipient of such blessings can easily find himself tempted by his new-found ability to gratify his senses and savor the earth's pleasures. By abusing God's blessing, he may cause it to be removed from him or it may remain with him to become the instrument of his punishment as he falls prey to the anxiety, rivalry, jealousy, and greed that so often follow in the train of misused wealth.

So unworthy were they that 'water' — which in God's spiritual world refers to wisdom — became the water of the Flood that blotted out man.

The generation of Noah should have been beneficiary of אין מים אלא תורה, Water as an allegorical reference to Torah. But they were unworthy. So unworthy were they that 'water' — which in God's spiritual world refers to wisdom — became the water of the Flood that blotted out man.

A New Potential

The generation of the Dispersion, too, was destined for a blossoming of knowledge. They settled in the land of Shin'ar which, the Sages teach, was Babylonia, the land where the Oral law flourished most in Talmudic times. They united to build a city, וּמִגְדָּל וְרֹאשׁוֹ בַשָּׁמַיִם וְנַעֲשֶׂה לָּנוּ שֵׁם, *and a tower whose top may reach to heaven, and let us make a name* (*Gen.* 11:4). In the land of Torah they resolved to ascend to heaven and make their mark. What a mark they could have made! How heavenly they could have become! How apt their setting was! The gift of Torah was ready for them, but instead of purifying themselves to receive it from God, they became the

In the land of Torah they resolved to ascend to heaven and make their mark. What a mark they could have made!

They became the vassals of Nimrod, hunter of animals and captor of humans.

vassals of Nimrod, hunter of animals and captor of humans.

They had unity — a blessed virtue that was a prerequisite to Israel's acceptance of the Torah at Sinai *(Exodus* 19:2 see *Rashi).*

The generations during the closing period of the First Temple committed the three cardinal sins of idolatry, adultery, and murder, causing the Destruction and Exile. The generations of the Second Temple were pious and studied Torah but they were conquered and exiled because of שנאת חנם, hatred without cause (see *Overview,* ArtScroll edition of *Eichah).* Which generation was greater? Look at the result: the Exile after the First Temple was relatively brief and a new Temple was built. The last Exile still endures *(Yoma* 9a).

Unity and brotherhood are so precious before God that He even overlooks grievous sins when they are present.

Unity and brotherhood are so precious before God that He even overlooks grievous sins when they are present *(Meshech Chochmah).*

The generation of the Dispersion had all the prerequisites for greatness, but they abused them and, so, lost the opportunity to become the fulfillment of God's plan.

But there was one man. He was forty-eight years old and he knew that his master was HASHEM, not Nimrod.

But there was one man among them who was not swept along by the tide. He was forty-eight years old and he knew that his master was HASHEM, not Nimrod. Because he persevered, the blessing of Torah that was destined for his countrymen concentrated upon him. He recognized at the age of three that there had to be a single God Who created and ruled the universe. Now, at forty-eight, he experienced a new revelation of Godly wisdom — of Torah — in the year and the place destined for revelation — and recognized his Creator as he never had before. His name was Abram and the Sages say בן מ״ח שנה הכיר אברם את בוראו, at the age of forty-eight, Abram recognized his Creator *(Midrash).*

Another Opportunity

Zohar wrote that there would be another deluge of wisdom upon the earth — in the sixth century of the sixth millenium: the years 5500-5600 (1739-40 — 1839-40 CE). It would seem that the world again stood at a crossroads during that century. Had Israel been completely worthy, it would have been bathed in the primeval light that was stored in Torah (see *Overview:* Torah); it would have been elevated beyond description, and — who knows? — perhaps the final redemption would have come. Had Israel been entirely unworthy, the wisdom might have gone through other channels and found its way to secular elements, or worse.

The sixth century of the sixth millenium was indeed a fateful one.

A cursory study of history reveals that the sixth century of the sixth millenium was indeed a fateful one. For Israel, it produced the parallel schools of the Baal Shem Tov and Vilna Gaon; in Poland Rabbi Akiva Eiger set standards of profundity; in Hungary the Chasam Sofer emerged, in Germany Rav Samson Raphael Hirsch began saving a lost nation with the *Nineteen Letters* and *Horeb*, the seeds of the Lithuanian Yeshiva movement were planted in Volozhin, and throughout Europe so brilliant a galaxy of gaonim was active in writing and teaching that the century has been described as דּוֹר דֵּעָה, the Generation of Knowledge, the same title used for the generation that spent forty years in the desert, living through daily miracles and learning from Moses, Aaron, and Miriam.

In the secular world, the Industrial Revolution began, ushering in the Age of Technology; in political life the American and French Revolutions changed man's thinking about government; and Marx and Engel were writing the books that would change his thinking about himself. In art, science, communication, medicine and other fields, what we call modern society was beginning to take shape. And the United States was becoming the future refuge for Jewish dispersions of the next century and a half.

Unlearned Lessons

Let us think only at our peril that man learns easily from the mistakes of his past. Rational man has a confounding capacity to rationalize and explain away the hand of God.

Rational man has a confounding capacity to rationalize and explain away the hand of God.

In Babel, Abram recognized his Maker and Nimrod recognized his own sword and bow. Noah was still alive as were his three sons — four people who were eye witnesses to the Flood, including the noble, righteous patriarch of the human race. Surely Noah cried out against the lunacy of building the futile tower in an insane effort to ascend to heaven and compete with God. Surely he told his great grandchildren that a merciful God could turn wrathful in the face of such iniquity. And Abram who would spend a lifetime of kindness in drawing people close to God's service was unafraid of Nimrod and his threats of death; Abram, too, surely protested. But the people didn't listen.

Abram recognized his Maker and Nimrod recognized his own sword and bow.

Surely he told his great grandchildren that a merciful God could turn wrathful in the face of such iniquity.

אמרו אחת לאלף ותרנ״ו שנים הרקיע מתמוטט כשם שעשה בימי המבול. בואו ונעשו לו סמיכות

They said: Once every 1656 years, the heavens tremble [causing a deluge] as it did in the days of the Flood. Let us build a support for it! (Midrash).

Had there been a Flood? Of course! But it was due to material causes and we can prevent it from ever happening again. How often man sees but refuses to observe! We read our history books and understand how wars and famines could have been prevented, but we do not prevent the next one. Instead we concoct schemes that justify past failures or create worse ones. Most tragic of all, we refuse to see the gloved Hand of God regulating the universe — and we lose priceless opportunities to climb out of the morass of a life where God is hidden. He knocks at the door, but we install pick-proof locks to keep out intruders.

Most tragic of all, we refuse to see the gloved Hand of God. He knocks at the door, but we install pick-proof locks to keep out intruders.

Noah was perfect and righteous. He could save his family, but not the world. Abram, too, was perfect and righteous and he salvaged the sparks of holiness from the madness of Babel. But then he added a new dimension to his mission by becoming Abraham, leader of all the world. He was so great that he acquired all the merit that had been trodden underfoot by his own generation and all those before. In so doing, he realized and fulfilled the purpose of creation and earned for his children the most treasured gift that God could bestow on any of his creatures — Torah.

V. The Ark

The Robber

The Flood was precipitated by חמס, *robbery*. God can endure patiently all varieties of sin, waiting for repentance, exacting punishment, building for better times in the future. But robbery represents an unpardonable low in human behavior because it shows man as a selfish being concerned with himself alone even at the expense of others. By definition, one who engages in robbery is not merely one whose primary interest is the satisfaction of his own appetite. The robber gratifies his own lust by taking from another. His life is a series of taking, stealing, looting. That another human being must suffer in the interest of his self gratification does not faze him.

That another human being must suffer in the interest of his self gratification does not faze him.

As *Meshech Chochmah* demonstrates, God tolerated Israel's most grievous sins as long as they were loyal to and considerate of one another. The present exile, *Golus Edom,* the Exile of Edom, was brought about by Rome which, the Sages teach, was descended from Esau. His dominant characteristic was violence and murder. That, too, is akin to robbery. The murderer wants the object of his lust. So much does he want it that he will allow nothing to stand in his way. And if the life of another human being bars the achievement of his goal — he will shed blood to gain it. Because Israel in the declining years of the Second Commonwealth sinned in its social life through jealousy, hatred, and failure to extend themselves for the benfit of one another, they were placed under the domination of the nation that ex-

The murderer wants the object of his lust. And if the life of another human being bars the achievement of his goal — he will shed blood to gain it.

emplified cruel selfishness.

The form of an exile is always determined by the sin that caused it.

The form of an exile is always determined by the sin that caused it because the purpose of an exile is to expiate the sin and bring about repentance. The destruction of the *First Temple* was caused because Israel sunk into lust (see *Overview*, ArtScroll edition of *Eichah*). It was exiled in the hands of Babylonia, a nation that was the leading oriental example of pleasure-seeking hedonism. The exile fit the sin. The next exile, too, brought about by selfishness was imposed by the most cruelly selfish of nations (*Michtav MeEliyahu*).

The Ark's Lesson

To save earthly life by means of an ark and miraculous salvation from the ravages of the Flood would hardly have sufficed if the sin that finally caused the Flood had remained totally unredeemed. Therefore, the ark had to be more than a protection against the raging elements without; it had to enclose within it a disparate collection of thousands of creatures led and cared for by Noah and his family, forcing them together, imposing upon them an awesome regimen of selflessness that allowed not a free moment for self-indulgence. Thereby, a human tradition was re-imposed. Cain asked 'Am I my brother's keeper?' Noah answered, 'Yes. I am the keeper of everyone, from human being to gnat, from docile lamb to voracious lion.'

For Noah personally, this was a vital lesson. He was taken to task for not having shown sufficient concern for his generation, for not reproving them, praying for them — saving them. He had been content to protect his own righteousness. His labors in the ark demonstrated to him that he must feel a responsibility for all others (*Harav David Cohen*).

The total care and maintenance of the ark and its inhabitants became the responsibility of Noah. The *Midrash* relates that he was crippled by a blow from a lion angry that its repast was once delayed. There were miracles enough in the ark and it would have been a simple matter for God to provide each animal with fresh sustenance day by day in its own chamber. At the very least, there could surely have been a way to spare Noah the excruciating task of trudging from chamber to chamber throughout the day to bring food for each living creature.

Of course, his task could have been eased, but that would have destroyed a vital function of the ark. For the ark was an incubator of goodness. A necessary ingredient of the salvation was God's command that the conditions for future survival be developed in the ark. So Noah and his family became caretakers for all surviving animal life, laboring, trudging, serving, so that when the progenitors of humanity emerged from the ark to rebuild the deluged remains of the earth, they would do it with a reborn awareness of the role of man as a caring, unselfish being *(Harav Gifter).*

VI. Shem and Japheth

Greece and Israel

The characteristics of Shem and Japheth were different, but they were intended to be complementary.

The characteristics of Shem and Japheth were different, but they were intended to be complementary. Every nation has its particular role in the development of the world. One has strength, another agricultural, another maritime, another business skills. Japheth was blessed with beauty and sensitivity; Shem with holiness and the Divine Presence. Of the many nations descending from both, the blessing of Japheth took root in *Yavan,* Greece, while the blessing of Shem rested on Israel.

But these blessings were never meant to exist in equal independence of one another. Noah said,

יַפְתְּ אֱלֹהִים לְיֶפֶת וְיִשְׁכֹּן בְּאָהֳלֵי שֵׁם

> *May God extend [the boundaries of] Japheth, but He will dwell in the tents of Shem* (9:27 see *Commentary).*

The Sages see another teaching in the name יֶפֶת, Japheth, and in the word Noah used to bless him: יַפְתְּ, *may He extend.* They find both words derived from יָפֶה, beautiful. Thus Japheth, as exemplified by

Grecian culture, became the primary expression on earth of the arts, the spiritual ancestor of drama, poetry, music, sculpture, sport, philosophy, and so on. But these gifts are no different from other tools which God has provided man to attain his primary calling in creation. They are meant to be used with צדק, justice, to do the will of He Who created and implanted them within the human mind (see above *Overview:* Noah and Abraham). Therefore, the Talmud teaches:

These gifts are meant to be used with צדק, justice, to do the will of He Who created and implanted them within the human mind.

> אמר ר׳ חייא בר אבא יפיופיתו של יפת (היינו שפת יונית עי׳ רש״י שם) יהא באהלי שם
>
> *The beauty of Japheth [the Greek language, the most beautiful of tongues (Rashi)] should be in the tents of Shem (Megillah* 9b).

This interpretation of Noah's blessing was used by the Sages to permit the translation of the Five Books of Moses into Greek *(ibid.).* Greek language and culture is an empty flourish if it is used for its own sake; its existence is justified only if it is utilized to beautify the *tents of Shem* — the study of Torah and the pursuit of holiness. It is true that sages from Solomon to the Vilna Gaon knew the sciences, but this knowledge was pure and holy only as an outgrowth and handmaiden of Torah, its ultimate source and purpose. If beauty and culture are deified for their own sake, then they become a curse instead of a blessing.

Greek language and culture is an empty flourish if it is used for its own sake.

If beauty and culture are deified for their own sake, then they become a curse instead of a blessing.

Japheth's Role

As *Hirsch* explains Noah's blessing:

> Japheth represents the meeting-place of the hot, unbridled sensuality of Ham and the spiritual, intellectual striving of Shem. The seeker of beauty, the artist, is open to external stimuli. He is sensitive and easily moved. He sees beauty in form and structure, and in words, sounds, and shapes, expresses the elegance, grace, and warmth he finds in the mundane and sensual. But the tragedies of history — past and ongoing —

The tragedies of history — past and ongoing — bear eloquent testimony to the eternal truth that perceptions of beauty are not enough.

bear eloquent testimony to the eternal truth that perceptions of beauty are not enough. Without an external ideal which controls and directs both the perceptions and expressions of beauty, man descends to immoral, unethical hedonism. He becomes a sensitive animal. Because he is intelligent and expressive, he can gild the chariots of his descent in impassioned rhetoric; lofty ideals, and sensuous beauty. He can build temples of passion and call them tents of a new godliness, golden calves and deify them as the purpose of existence. He can distort the human figure to fit the gorgeous clothing of his *haute couture,* and mold the human mind to fit the passions of his sensual heart.

Because he is intelligent and expressive, he can gild the chariots of his descent in impassioned rhetoric; lofty ideals, and sensuous beauty.

Noah used the name Elokim in giving his blessing to Japheth. It is the name of God that represents His dominance over nature for, as the commentators note, אלהים has the same numerical value, 86, as הטבע, the law of nature. Noah bestowed upon Japheth the blessings of nature, the ability to perceive and create beauty in this world, but he told his gifted, open, expressive, perceptive, gifted son that his achievements must *'dwell in the tents of Shem.'* Otherwise, his gifts would be worse than wasted; they would become a destructive, corrupting force. Beauty can elevate man and it can corrode him. It can inspire man and it can degrade him. For man is more susceptible to his heart and his senses than to his mind and his soul.

Noah bestowed upon Japheth the blessings of nature, but he told his son that his achievements must 'dwell in the tents of Shem.'

The Conflict

The beauty of Japheth and the tents of Shem reached their confluence during the period of the Second Temple. It was begun upon the command of Cyrus, a descendant of Japheth. His motives were pure at first, but later his respect for God and love for the Jews changed to wickedness (*Rosh Hashanah* 4a-b). Had his motives remained pure, the Second Temple might have achieved the holiness and Divine

Had his motives remained pure, the Second Temple might have achieved the holiness and Divine Presence of the First

Presence of the First *(Sfas Emes)*, but because he fell from his grandeur, the Temple that originated with his benevolence could not become worthy of so lofty a stature *(Yoma* 9b-10a). Alexander the Great conquered the world, but fell to his knees in awe and reverence before Shimon HaTzaddik, the High Priest and leader of Israel. He commanded that the Grecian culture of which he was spokesman should not be permitted to interfere with Israel's Torah and service of God.

Then came the reign of Antiochus and the Syrian-Greeks — and a Kulturkampf in Eretz Yisrael. The Syrians, bearers of the blessing of Japheth, imposed their culture upon Israel and attempted to destroy its allegiance to the God Who dwelt in the tents of Shem. They defiled the Temple and chose three commandments as their prime targets:

Greek culture would have to stand aside and bow humbly before the tents of Shem.

The Sabbath — eternal witness to the existence of God as the Creator of יש מאין, existence from absolute nothingness. If God was the eternal Creator and continuous resuscitator of the universe and if His Torah formed the blueprint and formula for the existence and purpose of Creation, then Greek culture would have to stand aside and bow humbly before the tents of Shem. This, Antiochus could not countenance.

The festivals enter the calendar and raise it from a record of material pursuit and struggle to a vehicle of holiness.

The New Moon — symbol of man's obligation to instill holiness into time. Time as the symbol of nature's tyranny over man could be subjugated. Time is meaningless until the Sanhedrin hallows it by proclaiming מקודש החדש מקודש, 'The new moon is sanctified, it is sanctified!,' and when this is done, מועדים, the festivals — the appointed meeting places in time between God and man — enter the calendar and raise it from a record of material pursuit and struggle to a vehicle of holiness. Antiochus and his culture were not absolute: they were either servants of holiness or crude intrusions upon the human purpose.

Milah — Circumcision — the declaration that the physical and the spiritual must be intertwined. The physical world is not separate from and independent of the spiritual. The body must bear the mark of allegiance to God's covenant, the restraining mark which tells it, 'You are a servant not a master; you are host to a soul and you must elevate yourself to its exalted level.' Beauty and pleasure were not the independent virtues Antiochus said they were. They were confined by Torah or they were nothing.

'You are a servant not a master; you are host to a soul and you must elevate yourself to its exalted level.'

A world without a Creator, a calendar without holiness, a body without restraint — these were the goals of a culture that had accepted the gifts but not the goals of Noah's blessing to Japheth. External grace and splendor covering a corrosive emptiness. To this had the beauty of Japheth been brought (*Sefer HaToda'ah*).

A culture that had accepted the gifts but not the goals of Noah's blessing — to this had the beauty of Japheth been brought

Small wonder that the *Midrash* comments that the primeval חֹשֶׁךְ, *darkness* (1:2) signifies יון, Greece. A tragic miscarriage of purpose! Greece should have placed its culture at the service of Shem, used it to help provide a glorious dwelling place for the Divine Presence. Instead, it's splendor became darkness.

It's splendor became darkness.

The darkness was lit not by the resolve of a righteous Japheth, but by the courage, sacrifice, and devotion of the priestly family of Chashmonaim. They prevailed in battle, but made the memory of their triumph eternal with the flame of a menorah. The flame symbolizes Torah, תּוֹרָה אוֹר, the antithesis of darkness, the blessing of Shem, the testament that Israel is the nation of Torah and that unless humanity is guided by its light, then the more brilliant its culture, the more intense and petrifying its darkness.

How apt that *Chizkuni* and others render that the צֹהַר, *illumination* which Noah was commanded to make for the ark (6:16) was an oil lamp (צהר = יצהר = oil), the same oil that symbolized Israel's bond to Torah in the Temple, provided the illumination for those who survived corruption to build anew — and charged that all culture can be darkness, unless it is illuminated by emanations from the tents of Shem.

All culture can be darkness, unless it is illuminated by emanations from the tents of Shem.

סדר נח

Sidra Noach

ו ט אֵלֶּה תּוֹלְדֹת נֹחַ נֹחַ אִישׁ צַדִּיק תָּמִים
ט הָיָה בְּדֹרֹתָיו אֶת־הָאֱלֹהִים הִתְהַלֶּךְ־נֹחַ׃

9. Noah

Noah — who re-established the human race after the Flood, was like Adam in that he too was the father of mankind. Therefore, although it has already listed Noah as the last link in the genealogy of his predecessors, the Torah begins the narrative anew, mentioning him and his children again, as the ancestors of mankind after the Flood *(Akeidas Yitzchak; Abarbanel).*

As *Hirsch* expresses it: Just as verse 2:4: *'these are the developments of heaven and earth'* introduces the development of mankind, here a new series in its development is introduced. The rest of mankind perishes. Noah, like a second Adam, heads a new generation of mankind.

אֵלֶּה תּוֹלְדֹת נֹחַ — *These are the offspring* [or: generations, descendants, products, history] *of Noah.* [Cf. comm. to 2:4 and 5:1]

The literal translation *'offspring' 'generations,'* follows *Onkelos,* and *Ramban; Yonason* renders: 'These are the genealogies of the race of Noah.'

According to *Ibn Ezra* and *B'chor Shor* the phrase is to be rendered: *'This is the history of Noah,'* as in 37:2: *'This is the history of Jacob': The word* תולדת [lit. 'generations'] in this case means 'that which time [יָלַד], brings forth' cf. *Proverbs* 27:1.

Rashi comments that since Noah was mentioned [to introduce his offspring or history, depending on the differing interpretations] Scripture praises him, saying *'Noah was a righteous man ...'*

נֹחַ אִישׁ צַדִּיק — *Noah was a righteous man. Rashi* alternately comments that he is described as a righteous man [before his offspring are named] to teach that good deeds are the real progeny of the righteous.[1]

Ramban explains that it is necessary to interrupt the genealogy with this praise of Noah to explain why he alone was chosen to build the ark. According to *Ibn Ezra* who interprets the word תּוֹלְדֹת as *'history',* i.e. the events of his life, this description is no digression for it is an integral part of his life story.

According to *Chizkuni,* this phrase describing Noah as *'a righteous man'* serves to explain why *'Noah found favor in God's eyes'* [verse 8.]

... And therefore deserved to be saved from annihilation *(B'chor Shor).*

נֹחַ — *Noah. Alshich* notes that the רְבִיעִי accent on the second *'Noah'* implies an exclamation: *'This Noah* whom I so greatly praised, *behold he was a righteous man* ... etc.'

אִישׁ צַדִּיק תָּמִים — *A righteous man, whole-[hearted;* or *'perfect,' blameless'.*]

1. *Kli Yakar* notes that after the phrase *'these are the descendants of Noah'* one would expect to see the names of his children. Instead it says *'Noah was a righteous man.* He cites a *Midrash* which quotes the verse [*Proverbs* 11:30] *'The fruit of the righteous is a tree of life'* which the Sages apply to Noah, for he did not die until he saw the world repopulated and seventy nations descended from his loins. Yet his righteousness is recorded as his offspring. For the sequence of the verse is: *These are the descendants of Noah: Noah was a righteous man:* his righteousness is his primary offspring.

VI 9 [9]These are the offspring of Noah — Noah was a righteous man, perfect in his generations; Noah

The *Talmud* explains: *'righteous'* in his deeds; *'perfect'* in his attributes *(Avodah Zarah* 6a).

Ibn Ezra renders: righteous in deed and *'perfect'* [i.e. sincere; whole] in his heart, while *Ramban* perceives *'perfect'* as modifying *'righteous'* and renders *'perfect in his righteousness'*; [or as a hendiadys: *perfectly righteous.*]

צַדִּיק — *Righteous.* i.e. he conducted himself righteously in contrast with his contemporaries who committed violence; *'perfect'* implies 'whole'; without fault *(Radak).*

Malbim notes that throughout Scriptures the term צַדִּיק, *righteous,* encompasses exemplary social conduct, while the term תָּמִים *perfect,* means that someone acts without thought of personal gain or aggrandizement. For a person may deal justly to gain honor or a good reputation, but if this incentive is removed he may change his behavior. A *'perfect'* person however, acts purely out of love for righteousness.

According to *Avos d'Rabbi Nosson* the term *'perfect'* in this case connotes, as noted earlier, that Noah was born circumcised. [This connection between circumcision and perfection is strengthened by the fact that Abraham was not called upon to attain *'perfection'* [17:1] until he was enjoined to undergo circumcision *(Torah Temimah).*]

אִישׁ, *man,* in conjunction with *'righteous'* is used to emphasize his virtue *(Lekach Tov);* while the plural term תָּמִים, perfect, instead of the singular תָּם, has the same emphatic connotation *(Ibn Caspi).*

The term אִישׁ, man, in Scripture is a designation of high honor. It is God's testimony [cf. Moses, Boaz, David, Mordechai] of a person's exemplary character. Noah stood the supreme test of manliness by living as an almost solitary righteous person for six hundred years in contrast to the violence around him, and as תָּמִים, *perfect,* in contrast to the moral corruption of his era *(Hirsch).*

תָּמִים הָיָה בְּדֹרֹתָיו — *He was perfect* [*or: 'wholehearted'; 'faultless'*] *in his generations.*

Rashi explains that there are different interpretations of *'in his generations':* some Sages maintain that it is in his praise: Noah was righteous even in his corrupt generation, how much more righteous would he have been had he lived in a truly righteous generation! According to other Sages, however, it is critical of him: Only *'in his generations',* i.e. by comparison with his exceptionally wicked contemporaries did Noah stand out as a righteous man; but had he lived in the time of Abraham he would have been insignificant.

Rashi's comment is based on *Sanhedrin* 108a where the *Talmud* cites two examples: In the former view Noah is like a phial of fragrant perfume lying amid refuse; if it is fragrant where it is, how much more so amid spices! In the latter view Noah is like a barrel of wine lying in a vault of vinegar. Only by comparison with the vinegar is the wine fragrant; elsewhere its scent would not be particularly fragrant.

All agree that he was not as great as Abraham. The Sages seek to point out, however, that the righteous of each generation must be judged and respected in terms of their *own* time and are placed by God in their particular generation according to its needs *(Sefer Haparshios).*

The plural form בְּדֹרֹתָיו, *in his generations, is noted:*

He spanned many generations and maintained his level of righteousness throughout them all *(Lekach Tov; Abarbanel; Ralbag);*

ו
י־יב

י וַיּ֥וֹלֶד נֹ֖חַ שְׁלֹשָׁ֣ה בָנִ֑ים אֶת־שֵׁ֖ם אֶת־חָ֥ם
יא וְאֶת־יָֽפֶת׃ וַתִּשָּׁחֵ֥ת הָאָ֖רֶץ לִפְנֵ֣י הָֽאֱלֹהִ֑ים
יב וַתִּמָּלֵ֥א הָאָ֖רֶץ חָמָֽס׃ וַיַּ֧רְא אֱלֹהִ֛ים אֶת־

and he was distinguished throughout all the generations for being the only one worthy of salvation *(B'chor Shor; R' Bachya).*

Ibn Ezra [apparently of the opinion that Noah's righteousness would have been exemplary even in Abraham's time] comments that the plural *'in his generations'* indicates that he was righteous in the generations both before and after the Flood; he lived till Abraham was fifty-eight years old.

Hirsch notes that בְּדֹרֹתָיו, *in his generations,* is mentioned only in connection with תָּמִים, *morally perfect* and not with צַדִּיק, *socially righteous.* This is because it is far harder to remain moral in the face of immorality than to remain honest in the face of dishonesty.

הָיָה — *Was.* Whenever this expression is used concerning a person, it indicates that he was consistent without deviation from beginning to end *(Midrash).*

אֶת הָאֱלֹהִים הִתְהַלֶּךְ נֹחַ — *Noah walked with God.* I.e. he walked in the fear of God *(Targum).*

אֶת has the meaning of *'with'*, while *'walking'* has the connotation of walking in the paths of God's service *(Ibn Janach).*

[Cf. comm. to similar phrase describing Chanoch in 5:22, 24.]

Rashi notes that it is written of Abraham [24:40]: ה׳ אֲשֶׁר הִתְהַלַּכְתִּי לְפָנָיו, HASHEM, *before* Whom I walked' Noah walked *with* God, in the sense that he needed His support [to maintain his righteousness], while Abraham was morally strong enough in his righteousness to walk alone, *before* God.

— It furthermore implies that he did not go out and try to influence his generation to repent, but his righteousness consisted of living *'with God'* in pious seclusion, content only with the thought of protecting his own family *(Alshich).*

Sforno, however, is of the reverse opinion. He explains: *He walked in God's ways.* He did good to others and he reproved his contemporaries (See *Overview).*

Radak explains that the sense of the phrase is: He clung to God and his every action was for His sake; he was not affected by the violence of his contemporaries.

He feared God alone, and was not enticed by astrology, etc., and certainly not by idolatry. He walked in the way God taught him for he was a prophet *(Ramban).*

10. וַיּוֹלֶד נֹחַ שְׁלֹשָׁה בָנִים — *[And] Noah had begotten three sons.*

[Translating past perfect, *'had'*, follows *Ibn Ezra.*]

These were his only children. Unlike his ancestors, he had no daughters *(Ramban).*

Radak notes that although his children had been named previously (5:32), they are mentioned here again following the statement that *'Noah walked with God'* to indicate that just as he served God he inculcated this training in his sons as well.

Sforno comments that Noah was given children as a reward for reproving his generation (see *comm.* above *v.* 9).

אֶת שֵׁם אֶת חָם וְאֶת יָפֶת — *Shem, Ham, and Japheth.* Japheth was the eldest, but Shem is mentioned first

walked with God. — [10] *Noah had begotten three sons:*
Shem, Ham, and Japheth.
[11] *Now the earth had become corrupt before God;*
and the earth had become filled with robbery. [12] *And*

because Scripture enumerates them according the their wisdom, not age [*Sanhedrin* 69b].

[For discussion of the chronology of Noah's children, see comm. to 5:32 and 10:21.]

Hirsch comments that the names of Noah's children indicate their sharply differing personalities. Shem (from שֵׁם, name) is the thinking person because man's wisdom lies in his ability to understand the nature of a concept or thing and define it, 'name it', so to speak. Ham (from חום, heat) is the sensuous, passionate person. Japheth (from פתה, openness) is the seeker after beauty who is open to external impressions. All three characteristics were saved from the Flood and all can be turned to the service of God when guided by the spiritual greatness of a Noah.

11. וַתִּשָּׁחֵת הָאָרֶץ — *Now* [lit. *And*] *the* [*inhabitants of (Ibn Ezra)*] *earth had become corrupt.*

Corrupt — with immorality and idolatry.

Cf. *Sanhedrin* 57a: 'A Tanna of the School of Rabbi Yishmael taught: Wherever the word הַשְׁחָתָה, *corruption,* is mentioned it must refer to immorality and idolatry.

לִפְנֵי הָאֱלֹהִים — *Before God.*

The significance of this phrase is discussed by the commentators:

Ibn Ezra cites conflicting opinions: the phrase signifies that they sinned 'in public'; or that their corruption was covert and known only to God. The interpretation that *Ibn Ezra* considers most plausible is that the phrase is anthropomorphic connoting that they transgressed brazenly like a servant who defiantly sins in the presence of his master and is not afraid.

According to the *Zohar* the verse implies that they sinned covertly at first so they were corrupt only *'before God'*, but, persisting in their evil ways, they later sinned openly. Therefore the later verse reads *'and the earth had become filled with violence'* — their violence had become obvious to all.

Others hold that אֱלֹהִים here is non-sacred and refers to the leaders of the generation: The people sinned defiantly and shamelessly in the presence of their leaders who did not rebuke them *(Ralbag).*

[However, as regards erasure when writing a Torah Scroll אֱלֹהִים in this verse is considered Halachically sacred.]

וַתִּמָּלֵא הָאָרֶץ חָמָס — *And the earth had become filled with robbery.*

The translation of חָמָס as *robbery* follows *Rashi* and nearly all commentators.[1]

1. *Mizrachi* notes that the *Talmud* differentiates between גָּזֵל and חָמָס as two forms of robbery: גָּזֵל is ordinary robbery and חָמָס is taking by force, but giving money in return. He concludes that this difference in semantics is a Talmudic usage, but that in the Torah the two words are treated as synonyms — hence *Rashi*'s definition of חָמָס as גָּזֵל.

Gur Aryeh disagrees for, if that were so, the Torah should use the word גָּזֵל which is com-

ו הָאָרֶץ וְהִנֵּה נִשְׁחָתָה כִּי־הִשְׁחִית כָּל־
יג בָּשָׂר אֶת־דַּרְכּוֹ עַל־הָאָרֶץ׃
יג וַיֹּאמֶר אֱלֹהִים לְנֹחַ קֵץ כָּל־בָּשָׂר בָּא

The phrase indicates that there was not a place on the whole earth which did not witness their sins *(Zohar).*

According to *Ibn Ezra* חָמָס refers additionally to the taking of wives by force.

Or HaChaim goes even further. He explains that חָמָס is the ultimate of wickedness: The term encompasses robbery, immorality, murder, and idolatry.

12. וַיַּרְא אֱלֹהִים אֶת הָאָרֶץ — *And God saw the earth.* — i.e. He took note of their actions *(R' Meyuchas).*

This refers to their idolatry which is essentially a matter of the heart and which only God can 'see' *(Kli Yakar).*

וְהִנֵּה נִשְׁחָתָה — *And behold it was corrupted.*

— [I.e. totally immersed in lewdness and idolatry.]

The entire social fabric had disintegrated. Force and lawlessness prevailed *(B'chor Shor).*

Sforno [interpreting שחת (corrupt) in its other meaning of *destruction*] explains that the phrase means: *'behold it was on the path to destruction'* — even without divine punishment — for immorality corrupts progeny and violent robbery corrupts the social order.

The *earth* is here described as being corrupt, explains the *Zohar,* because man constitutes the essence of the earth so that his corruption infects the earth ... The earth which failed to please God by raising up for Him righteous children, was ashamed, like a faithless wife who hides her face from her husband, as it is written elsewhere [*Isaiah* 24:5]: *and the earth was defiled under its inhabitants* ... Here, too, 'the earth was corrupt'. Why? *'Because* all flesh had corrupted their way.'

According to the *Midrash* [28:8] however, even the earth *itself* acted lewdly: wheat was sown and it yielded weeds. Indeed the weeds we now find among wheat stem from that time.

כִּי הִשְׁחִית כָּל בָּשָׂר אֶת דַּרְכּוֹ עַל הָאָרֶץ — *For all flesh had corrupted its way upon the earth* — i.e. they deviated from their natural character and habit *(Ibn Janach).*

Even animals mated with species other than their own *(Rashi).*

Most commentators, however, — e.g. *Onkelos, Lekach Tov, Radak,*

monly used throughout Scripture. He explains that since the generation was so utterly corrupt that virtually all people stole from one another, even the victims of crime would invariably have stolen property from their victimizers. Thus, the robbery fell into the general category of חָמָס, because money was taken in return.

Hirsch refers to the *Midrash* which defines חָמָס, robbery, as crime too petty to be adjudicable by courts [i.e. stealing less than a *perutah,* a definition that *Mizrachi* above holds to be applicable only in Talmudic terms.] Nevertheless, this sort of crime is more damaging morally. Society will not deteriorate as a result of גָּזֵל, open robbery, because it recognizes the evil and can defend itself from it. Subtle, conniving crime (חָמָס), however, because it stays within the letter of the law and is not subjected to human justice weakens the conscience, saps morality, and kills the instinct to be concerned with others. By corrupting the social fabric, it leads to the destruction of society.

VI 13 *God saw the earth and behold it was corrupted, for all flesh had corrupted its way upon the earth.*
13 *God said to Noah, 'The end of all flesh has come*

R' Meyuchas — understand בָּשָׂר, *flesh,* as referring to human beings only:

The simple meaning of the verse is that *'all flesh'* means 'all men,' for in verse 17 the Torah explicitly qualifies *'all flesh wherein is the breath of life'* meaning all living bodies, while here *all flesh* must mean 'all people' ... *(Ramban).*

13. The Decree is revealed

וַיֹּאמֶר אֱלֹהִים לְנֹחַ — *And God said to Noah.*

[The parenthetical digression in praise of Noah begun with verse 9 (see *Rashi* cited there) is ended. This verse continues the narrative of verses 3, 6, and 7 as God explicitly informs Noah that the decree which had until now been (if one may so express it) 'fermenting within Him' — אֶל לִבּוֹ, *in His heart* (see *comm.* to v.6) — to blot out man from the face of the earth was now an imperative and that Noah should make the necessary preparation.

[In the chronological sequence of events, then, this announcement must have come to Noah 120 years prior to the flood which began in the year 1656. Thenceforth, as explained by the commentators, Noah diligently constructed the Ark. God made His intentions known to Noah in advance, to demonstrate that He is patient and will allow them this grace period for repentance (see *comm.* to verse 3, 6 and 7).]

[This verse is not redundant because here it tells of the *announcement* to Noah, whereas verses 3 and 7 above, *'And God said'* can be interpreted as meaning that God said to Himself i.e. He became *determined,* but did not tell Noah of His decision.

[According to *Radak* and *Ralbag* וַיֹּאמֶר אֱלֹהִים in those verses means that God revealed His plans ('spoke') *then* to Noah, and advised him of the 120 year repentance period (see *comm.* there). Accordingly, the phrase *'the end of all flesh has come before Me'* would mean 'the 120 year probationary period has ended without repentance; instead, man has become ever more corrupt'.]

קֵץ כָּל בָּשָׂר בָּא לְפָנַי — *The end of all flesh has come before Me* [i.e. has come before Me for judicial decision.]

The meaning of the verse is: The Decree concerning man's impending doom has reached this world from before Me in the uppermost heavens *(Ahavas Yonasan).*

Hirsch derives קֵץ from קצץ, to 'cut off', hence the 'end', or conclusion. He suggests two interpretations of the stich: 'Humanity has descended to such a state that I must bring it to an end;' or, more likely: 'unless I intervene, humanity will continue on a course that will inevitably result in its own ruination.' The קֵץ, *end* was implicit in man's behavior; had God not intervened, even the spark of purity still alive in Noah would eventually have been extinguished [see *Overview*].

But Noah was unmoved. Instead of begging for mercy on behalf of the world, Noah asked God what would become of him. Scripture, therefore, rightfully calls the Flood 'the waters *of Noah'* [*Isaiah* 54:9]; they are attributed to him because once he was assured of his own survival in the ark he did not seek

ו לְפָנַי כִּי־מָלְאָה הָאָרֶץ חָמָס מִפְּנֵיהֶם
יד וְהִנְנִי מַשְׁחִיתָם אֶת־הָאָרֶץ: עֲשֵׂה לְךָ

mercy for the world *(Zohar).*[1]

[Cf. *comm.* to 7:1 s.v. בַּדּוֹר הַזֶּה.]

In view of the fact that the impending punishment was to engulf *all, Rashi* comments that immorality and idolatry are punished by 'אַנְדְּרוֹלוֹמוּסְיָא', indiscriminate punishment, which does not differentiate between the relatively righteous and the wicked. [2]

If the decree was all-encompassing why was Noah saved?

Noah was saved as a special dispensation in order to repopulate this world and because he found favor in God's eyes *(Yefe To'ar* to *Midrash,* and commentators).

Turei Zahav answers that the command to Noah to build the ark was meant to symbolize that henceforth Noah would be under a separate 'roof' and, therefore, no longer a part of the corrupt society that was doomed to total destruction. An ark,was chosen as the method of saving Noah because, as a 'house', the ark had the same property of protection against the angel of death that was expressed in the directive given by Moses to the children of Israel on the night that God slew the Egyptian firstborn [*Exodus* 12:22]: *'and none of you shall go out of the door of his house until the morning.'*

כִּי מָלְאָה הָאָרֶץ חָמָס מִפְּנֵיהֶם — *For the earth is filled with robbery through them* — i.e. because of their evil deeds *(Targum).*

Although they transgressed all laws, the decree of punishment was finally pronounced [lit. *'sealed'*] only on account of robbery, the *'violence',* mentioned in this verse *(Sanhedrin* 108a; *Rashi).*

Ramban explains that the reason חָמָס, robbery and oppression, is given as the prime cause of their destruction is because of the prohibition against חָמָס [robbery and oppression] is a rational commandment not requiring the admonition of a prophet, and it is, simultaneously, a transgression against both heaven and man.

מִפְּנֵיהֶם, *through them,* refers to

1. The *Baal Shem Tov* notes that the Hebrew word for Noah's ark, תֵּיבָה, also means 'a word'. Noah, clothed in his righteousness, withdrew into his 'תֵּיבָה' — into the words of Torah-study and prayer. — *He walked with God,* and cut himself off from the sinfulness of his society.

Moreover, when men came to him and inquired about the huge ship he was building, he told them of the impending Divine punishment — the Flood. But only *then,* when he was approached, did he scold and rebuke them and tell them to mend their ways; he did not take the initiative. He was content to save himself.

This type of conduct is called in Yiddish: *'A tzaddik in peltz'* — 'a righteous man in a warm fur coat.' There are two ways to warm oneself in a cold room: One is to build a fire — in which case everyone in the room benefits from the warmth; a second way is to put on a fur coat — in which case the wearer of the coat is warm but everyone else in the room remains cold. Wrapped up in the cozy warmth of his own righteousness, he is not really concerned with the bitter cold of those 'outside' *(Adapted from Likkutei Sichos — Lubavitch).*

2. *Harav David Feinstein* suggests a reason for the apparently indiscriminate punishment against righteous and wicked alike. God perceives that even the righteous who are exposed to the constant, pervasive influence of evil will fall prey to its corrosive effects. Because the evil is imperceptibly and unalterably germinating within them, God plucks them away before they become corruptive. It is similar to a farmer who disposes of nearly rotten fruit before it spoils completely.

VI before Me, for the earth is filled with robbery
14 through them: and behold, I am about to destroy
them from the earth. [14] Make yourself an ark of

their *willful* acts of violence.

The word is derived from פָּנִים, face, to indicate that they behaved with full awareness of the moral implications of their misdeeds. They were not oblivious of their evil nor did they steal out of hunger or need. They did so because they believed in evil as a way of life. Therefore, they were punished so severely *(HaKsav V'HaKaballah).*

וְהִנְנִי מַשְׁחִיתָם אֶת הָאָרֶץ — *And behold, I am about to destroy them from the earth.*

הִנֵּה, behold, is the term used for granting whatever is called for by particular circumstances or requests. Hence: 'In response to man's current situation, I present the proper alternative — destruction' *(Hirsch).*

Rashi explains that אֶת הָאָרֶץ in this verse can be rendered either *'from* the earth' as in *Exodus* 9:29 where אֶת הָעִיר means *'from the city'*; or אֶת הָאָרֶץ can be rendered *'together with* the earth' [as in *Exodus* 1:1 אֶת יַעֲקֹב, *'with* Jacob'] because the topsoil of the earth itself was washed away up to a depth of three handbreadths.

If man sinned, how did the earth deserve destruction?

— *Midrash HaGadol* cites a parable:

This is comparable to a king who allowed people to dwell in his country. Once, when he was abroad, they proclaimed the courtyard as their own. When the king heard of the rebellion he became enraged and exclaimed: 'Not only have they paid no rent; they even rebel against me! I will destroy the courtyard. Now let he who claims to be its owner stand up against me!'

14. The Ark

עֲשֵׂה לְךָ — *Make yourself* [lit. *'to you'*].

Radak renders: *'Make if you wish.'*

According to *Abarbanel,* the intent of *'yourself'* is that Noah himself should construct the ark and not delegate the task to another.

Alshich perceives this verse in a different light: 'Make an ark corresponding to your own behavior. You remained aloof from your compatriots instead of mingling with them and chastising them. Now, isolate yourself in an ark with the beasts and animals.

[Cf. *comm.* to 12:1 where the word לְךָ is used in God's command to Abraham לֶךְ־לְךָ (lit. *'Go for yourself')* is interpreted to mean: for your own benefit, for your own good.]

Rashi [following *Tanchuma*] queries:

There are numerous ways by which God could have saved Noah. Why then did God burden him with the task of constructing an ark? — So that when the curious would see him cutting down lumber and involved in building the ark for 120 years they would ask him why it was being made. He would answer, 'God is about to bring a Flood on the world because of your sins', and

ו תֵּבַת עֲצֵי־גֹפֶר קִנִּים תַּעֲשֶׂה אֶת־הַתֵּבָה
טו טו וְכָפַרְתָּ אֹתָהּ מִבַּיִת וּמִחוּץ בַּכֹּפֶר׃ וְזֶה
אֲשֶׁר תַּעֲשֶׂה אֹתָהּ שְׁלֹשׁ מֵאוֹת אַמָּה
אֹרֶךְ הַתֵּבָה חֲמִשִּׁים אַמָּה רָחְבָּהּ

they will thus be given an opportunity to repent.

... 'But', concludes the *Tanchuma,* 'Noah's contemporaries paid no attention to him.'

[See also *Turei Zahav* cited to *v.* 13 s.v. קֵץ.][1]

תֵּבַת עֲצֵי גֹפֶר — *An ark of gopher wood.*

The name תֵּבָה, *ark,* [indicating in its most literal meaning a chest or box-like object] is used instead of 'boat', because it was not shaped like a ship and it had no oars *(Ibn Ezra).*

For it was not designed to glide through the waters but to be afloat on them *(Hirsch).*

[This accentuates the fact that Noah's deliverance was not dependent on navigating skills. The ark was a free-floating vessel and, as such, he was saved entirely by God's will.]

עֲצֵי־גֹפֶר, *gopher wood,* is mentioned nowhere else in Scriptures.

The *Targum* identifies it as 'cedar' while *Menachem* and *Ibn Ezra* identify it only as a light-floating wood, which *Abarbanel* suggests is pine.

Rashi does not specifically identify gopher. He comments, however, that gopher was used because [its name is suggestive] of the גָּפְרִית, brimstone, by which the world was decreed to be destroyed. [For, as noted in *Sanhedrin* 108a, the waters of the Flood were scalding hot. *Cf.* 7:11,22; 8:2,11.]

קִנִּים תַּעֲשֶׂה אֶת הַתֵּבָה — *Make the ark* [*with*] *compartments;* for each species *(Rashi; Ibn Ezra).*

Hirsch observes that it does not say לַתֵּבָה, *for the ark,* but אֶת הַתֵּבָה, the ark. The structure was planned for its compartments. It was not meant as a home for Noah and his family with the incidental purpose of accommodating animals, rather it was intended for the salvation of all life.

וְכָפַרְתָּ אֹתָהּ מִבַּיִת וּמִחוּץ בַּכֹּפֶר — *And cover it* [*from*] *inside and* [*from*] *out with pitch.*

[To render it watertight] ... so that if the outer pitch is peeled off by the pressure of the water, the pitch from within will remain *(Radak).*

1. We have a dictum that when death rages in a town or the world at large, no man should show himself in the street because the destroying angel is then authorized to kill indiscriminately. Hence the Holy One, blessed be He said to Noah, 'Take heed and do not expose yourself to the destroyer so he will be powerless over you.'

You may think that there was not any destroying angel here but only the onrush of overwhelming waters. This is not so; no doom is ever executed on the world, whether of annihilation or any other chastisement, without the destroying angel in the midst of the visitation.

So here: there was indeed a flood, but this was only an embodiment of the destroyer who assumed its name *(Zohar).*

VI
15

gopher wood; make the ark with compartments, and
cover it inside and out with pitch. [15] *This is how you*
should make it — the length of the ark: three hundred
cubits; its width: fifty cubits, and its height: thirty

כֹּפֶר [pitch] is synonymous with זֶפֶת [used in waterproofing the box in which Moses was placed *(Exodus* 2:3).]

Rashi explains that the waters where Moses was placed were calm so that pitch was not needed inside the box. Another reason for its omission was to spare the righteous child [Moses] from the unpleasant odor of pitch.

Ibn Ezra notes that וְכָפַרְתָּ, [and you should] *cover,* is the verb form of the noun כֹּפֶר, *pitch.* [Accordingly the phrase could be rendered: *'and pitch it with pitch.'*]

Ibn Caspi, however, suggests that כֹּפֶר is a noun of the verb וְכָפַרְתָּ. According to him, the phrase is to be rendered: *And cover it with a covering* ... the nature of which is not specificed.

15. וְזֶה אֲשֶׁר תַּעֲשֶׂה אֹתָהּ — *[And] this is how you should make it.*

I.e. These are the details concerning its dimension and construction *(Ibn Ezra; Radak).*

The word *'this'* indicates that God [anthropomorphically] pointed out to Noah exactly how to proceed and build the ark *(Pirkei d'Rabbi Eliezer* 13.]

שְׁלֹשׁ מֵאוֹת אַמָּה ... — *Three hundred cubits* ...[1]

The commentators note that the proportions of the structure — the height a tenth of its length and its width a sixth of its length — ensured that it would not overturn even in the most violent storm *(Midrash; Ibn Ezra).*

These verses are paraphrased as follows by *Targum Yonasan:*

'Make yourself an ark of cedar wood; a hundred and fifty compartments shall you make for the ark in its left side, and thirty-six in its breadth, with ten cabins in the midst in which to store provisions, and five repositories on the right and five on the left, and you shall protect it within and without with pitch ...'

The cubit denotes a measurement similar to the human forearm measured from the elbow to the tip of the middle finger. In *Halachic* terms, according to *Menachos* 98a, the standard cubit equals six טְפָחִים, handbreadths, or twenty-four אֲגוּדָל, thumbwidths. The measure does not vary, but is standard and the same for all people.

The size of a cubit in contemporary measurements is the subject of a Halachic dispute. Estimates range from 18-24 inches [48-62.4 cm.] (See *Encylopedia Talmudica* s.v. אַמָּה).

[Thus, even according to the *smallest* estimate of 18 inches per cubit, the dimensions of the ark were 450x75x45 feet = 1,518,750 cubic feet. Each of its three storys had 33,750 sq. feet of floor space for a total of 101,250 sq.ft. This is in *addition* to the pitched roof which, the commentators explain, began after the thirty-cubit walls ended. *Kli Yakar* comments that the Torah went into such detail regarding the dimensions to emphasize the magnitude of the miracle, for without the miracle the structure would have been incapable of containing all its inhabitants. (See *comm.* to *v.* 18.]

1. *Midrash Abba Gorion* to *Esther* 5:14 comments that the fifty-cubit beam which Haman used to build the gallows for Mordecai was a plank from Noah's Ark:

'Haman searched for a 50-cubit beam but could not find one. So his son Parshandasa, who was governor of the Mt. Ararat area supplied him with a remnant of Noah's Ark which was 50 cubits long.'

טז וּשְׁלֹשִׁים אַמָּה קוֹמָתָהּ: צֹהַר | תַּעֲשֶׂה
לַתֵּבָה וְאֶל־אַמָּה תְּכַלֶּנָּה מִלְמַעְלָה
וּפֶתַח הַתֵּבָה בְּצִדָּהּ תָּשִׂים תַּחְתִּיִּם שְׁנִיִּם
יז וּשְׁלִשִׁים תַּעֲשֶׂהָ: וַאֲנִי הִנְנִי מֵבִיא אֶת־
הַמַּבּוּל מַיִם עַל־הָאָרֶץ לְשַׁחֵת כָּל־בָּשָׂר

16. צֹהַר תַּעֲשֶׂה לַתֵּבָה — *A light shall you make for the ark.*

[The translation *'light'* (in the sense of 'a source for illumination') for צֹהַר follows *Onkelos*, and preserves the ambiguity allowing for the differences in interpretation as follows.]:

According to the *Talmud, Sanhedrin* 108b: The Holy One blessed be He instructed Noah: 'set therein precious stones and jewels so that they may give off light, bright as צָהֳרָיִם, the noon' [when the light of the day reaches its zenith.]

Rashi, however, records a controversy: Some say it was a skylight [חַלּוֹן, *window*] while others say it was a precious stone.

The *Midrash* comments:

'Rav Pinchas said in Rav Levi's name: During the entire twelve months that Noah was in the ark he did not require the light of the sun by day or the light of the moon by night, but he had a polished gem which he hung up: when it was dim he knew that it was day, and when it shone he knew it was night.'

In fact, the *Ba'al HaTurim* notes that the numerical equivalent of צהר = לאור האבן, *'to the light of the stone'*, (295).

Most commentators — *Ibn Janach; Ibn Ezra; Radak;* [*Ramban* to 39:20] — relate צֹהַר to צָהֳרָיִם, *noon* (as above) and explain it as referring to the window which Noah opened as mentioned in 8:6.

Chizkuni adds that while the rains descended and the window was closed he set a transparent stone [glass?] therein to refract the light. This interpretation blends the divergent views of the Sages, concerning whether it was a window or a precious stone. There was, in fact, a window as explicitly mentioned later in the text. [However, except for the implication of this verse we are not expressly told that Noah built it.]

Furthermore, *Chizkuni* suggests that צֹהַר might be related to יִצְהָר, *oil,* rendering: *prepare oil for the ark to use for lighting.*

וְאֶל־אַמָּה תְּכַלֶּנָּה מִלְמַעְלָה — *And to a cubit finish it from above.*

[The translation conveys the ambiguity of the phrase.]

Rashi, based on the *Midrash* — and in agreement with most commentators — explains the phrase as referring to the roof which sloped inward [like a vaulted carriage *(Midrash)*] until it narrowed to only a cubit on top, so that the water should smoothly run off on each side.

According to *Ibn Ezra* the four sided roof sloped proportionately until it was one cubit in length and a sixth of a cubit in width [relative to the overall structure which was 300:50=6:1.]

Other commentators suggest that the phrase refers to the *window* 'which should be placed to within a

VI 16-17

cubits. [16] *A light shall you make for the ark, and to a cubit finish it from above. Put the entrance of the ark in its side; make it with bottom, second, and third decks.*

[17] *'And as for Me — Behold I am about to bring the Flood-waters upon the earth to destroy all flesh in*

cubit of the roof so it will be protected by the overhang *(Chizkuni; Da'as Zekeinim; Haamek Davar).*

וּפֶתַח הַתֵּבָה בְּצִדָּהּ תָּשִׂים — [*And*] *put the entrance of the ark in its side.*

The door was placed on the side of the ark [rather than a hatch on top as is usual for ships *(Mizrachi)*] to keep the rain from penetrating *(Rashi).*

Of course, the entrance was positioned on the upper third of the ark [above the projected water level] *(Chizkuni)* and they entered by means of ladders *(Ibn Ezra).*

Sforno makes an interesting etymological note that צַד indicates that the door was along the *breadth* of the ark; the *long* side is known in Hebrew as צֶלַע.

תַּחְתִּיִּם שְׁנִיִּם וּשְׁלִשִׁים תַּעֲשֶׂהָ *Make it with bottom, second and third decks.* I.e., three stories: the upper story for humans; the middle one for animals; and the bottom one for the refuse.

[The commentators add that obviously Noah and his family did not need a whole story for themselves. They explain that the clean birds and provisions for the period shared the upper story with them.]

17. וַאֲנִי — *And as for me* [lit. *'And I'*]

— You, for your part, complete the ark, and I, for mine, will immediately bring on the Flood *(Sforno).*

God now reveals to Noah the purpose of the ark: 'I will bring about a flood and the ark will serve as a refuge for you and your family' *(Abarbanel).*

The use of *'I'* in this verse specifically emphasizes that the Flood was not a natural phenomenon, but an act of special divine providence *(Malbim).*

Rashi cites the *Midrash* in accounting for the term *'and* I': 'I, too, must now concur with those who cautioned Me long ago at man's creation [*Ps.* 8:5]: *'What is man that You are mindful of him?'*

Ramban observes that the above *Midrash* is plainly difficult because God *did* indeed insure that life would go on by sparing Noah, his family, and pairs of all living things to renew life on earth! Perhaps the intent is that God concurred with the angels that barring a display of divine Mercy, there is no point in continuing life on earth.

הַמַּבּוּל מַיִם — *The Flood-waters* [or with the implied construct form: *'the flood of waters'* — 'waters' being explanatory *(Ibn Ezra).*]

The translation of *'Flood'* for מַבּוּל follows the generally accepted use of the term although, as noted by the commentators, the root of the word is related to נבל, *destruction* — implying the wholesale destruction of life on earth which then took place rather than a mere flood of water.

Sforno thus renders: 'I will bring about by means of water the destruction (מַבּוּל) to which I alluded earlier.'

Ibn Ezra and *Radak* explain that

ו אֲשֶׁר־בּוֹ רוּחַ חַיִּים מִתַּחַת הַשָּׁמָיִם כֹּל
יח יח אֲשֶׁר־בָּאָרֶץ יִגְוָע: וַהֲקִמֹתִי אֶת־בְּרִיתִי

the word means נובל 'falling' and is also related to בלולה, intermingling. Since the word can apply to anything that falls from heaven such as snow, fire or hail, the verse further identifies it by saying *'flood of water'.*[1]

[The *Talmud* apparently also takes it for granted that מַבּוּל does not necessarily mean a flood of *water.*

Cf. *Sanhedrin* 108b: When Noah rebuked his contemporaries and warned them of an impending flood they jeered: 'A flood of what? If a flood of fire [we can combat it]...if a flood of water [we can cope with that, too.]' Cf. also *Zevachim* 116a: 'They conjectured: He will not bring a מַבּוּל שֶׁל מַיִם, flood of water, but perhaps He will bring a מַבּוּל שֶׁל אֵשׁ, a flood of fire!']

Rashi explains that *'mabul'* is so named because it בִּלָּה, *destroyed* everything; because it בִּלְבֵּל, *confounded* everything; and הוֹבִיל, *brought down* everything from an upper to a lower level. The last underlies the interpretation of *Onkelos* who translates it as related to 'float' because the Flood 'floated' everything about and brought them to Babylonia which lies on a low level. Therefore Babylonia is also called Shinar because all those who died in the Flood were shaken out there [שֶׁנִּנְעֲרוּ שָׁם] (cf. *Shab.* 113b).

לְשַׁחֵת כָּל בָּשָׂר — *To destroy all flesh.*

[The Hebrew word for *'destroy'* שחת is the same as for *'corrupt'*]:

The punishment was thus measure for measure: כִּי הִשְׁחִית כָּל בָּשָׂר — *for all flesh had become corrupt* [verse 12]: now I have decreed לְשַׁחֵת כָּל בָּשָׂר — *to destroy all flesh (Lekach Tov).*

[As noted in the *comm.* to verse 7, the animals were created to serve man; if man was to perish what need was there for animals? *(Rashi; Midrash HaGadol).*]

כֹּל אֲשֶׁר בָּאָרֶץ יִגְוָע — *Everything that is in the earth shall expire.*

According to *Pesikta Zutresa* this means that the decree did not extend to the fish of the sea.

[Cf. *comm.* to 7:22 s.v. *'whatever was on the dry land'* where *Zevachim* 113b is cited with a similar comment.]

The term יִגְוָע, here translated with the delicate expression 'expire', carries with it, according to the commentators — *Ibn Ezra, Radak,* etc. — a connotation of quick death without prolonged sickness.

The *Midrash* [perceiving that in our verse the term includes the plant life to which 'death' in the sense of giving up the soul does not apply *(Yefe To'ar)*] renders the word: 'will shrivel'.

[The *Talmud, Bava Basra* 16b explains that wherever the term וַיִּגְוַע is mentioned together with וַיֵּאָסֶף, *'gathering'* it refers to the death of righteous people.]

Ramban to 25:17 holds that the word וַיִּגְוַע does not connote death, because after stating in 7:21 that all flesh וַיִּגְוַע [expired], Scripture nevertheless says in the next verse that they *'died'*. Obviously the term וַיִּגְוַע alone cannot include a connotation of death. He concurs with *Targum* that it should be translated יִתְנַגֵּד, 'faint', 'emaciate'. [See *Chavel*'s note ad. loc.]

Hirsch establishes etymologically that the word refers to a mass of non-responsive, non-feeling material. It would thus connote that death was a painless process because it was preceded by a state of numb torpor. God

1. [Interesting in this context, is the comment of *Radak* to *I Kings* 6:38 that the month of Cheshvan is referred to in the Bible as *Bul,* because of the abundant rains that usually fall in that month.]

VI *which there is a breath of life under the heavens;*
18 *everything that is in the earth shall expire.* [18] *But I*
will establish My covenant with you, and you shall

thus assured Noah that the generation would die without suffering. [Cf. 7:21-23 for the sequence of וַיִּגְוַע, מֵתוּ, וַיִּמַּח — unconsciousness, death and dissolution.]

18. וַהֲקִמֹתִי אֶת בְּרִיתִי אִתָּךְ — *But I will establish My covenant with you.*

[The verse can apparently be interpreted as in our translation above, that God refers to a covenant which He was *about to establish now, or at some later date;* or that God refers to *a previously existing covenant,* the establishment of which had not been recorded in the Torah. Our translation, reflecting the former view, follows *Targum.*]

As *Sforno* comments: *My Covenant* (which I will make) after the Flood.

Rashi, following the *Midrash* comments that this covenant was needed to guarantee that the food in the ark would not spoil, and that the wicked of the generation would not kill him.[1]

According to *Ibn Ezra* this was the sign that God had previously sworn to Noah that neither he nor his children would die in the flood. Although we find no mention of such a covenant, this is similar to *Deut.* 1:22 where Moses alludes to an incident which had not been recorded in the Torah. The word וַהֲקִמֹתִי should accordingly be rendered: and *'I will fulfill* My oath.' *Ibn Ezra* concludes, however, that the interpretation most acceptable to him is that 'convenant' refers to the rainbow (9:13) [which God was to establish after the Flood as a covenant rewarding Noah for complying with His command (*Tzafnas Pane'ach).*]

— It refers to the covenant immediately at hand; that Noah and his family would be spared while all others would perish *(R' Bachya; Ralbag* and *Chizkuni).*

Ramban interprets that בְּרִית signifies an unconditional covenant, and the verse is to be understood as God saying: 'When the Flood comes, My covenant will have been established with you guaranteeing that you, your family, and a pair from each species will be saved in the ark.

Ramban goes on to explain that kabbalistically, the intent of the verse is *'Through you* — as the sole survivor of the Deluge — *shall My covenant of the continuity of the universe and the preservation of the species* [interpreting בְּרִיתִי *My covenant* = בְּרִיאָתִי, My creation] *be fulfilled.'*

— Which covenant does this refer to? The covenant that heaven and earth will never entirely cease, as in the verse [*Jeremiah* 33:25]: *'If not for My covenant by day and by night, I had not appointed the ordinances of heaven and earth'* [i.e., the apparent meaning is: 'were it not for My covenant at the night and day of creation, heaven and earth would not enjoy permanence'; cf. *Pesachim* 68b] *(Midrash HaGadol).*

Abarbanel similarly cites the verse from *Jeremiah* which identifies the act

1. The *Midrash* comments ... 'You were indeed the builder, but were it not for My covenant which stood you in good stead could you have entered the ark?

Therefore it is written: *'But I will establish My covenant with you'* — [which will be proven] when you are brought into the ark.

ו אִתָּ֑ךְ וּבָאתָ֙ אֶל־הַתֵּבָ֔ה אַתָּ֕ה וּבָנֶ֛יךָ
יט־כ יט וְאִשְׁתְּךָ֥ וּנְשֵֽׁי־בָנֶ֖יךָ אִתָּֽךְ׃ וּמִכָּל־הָ֠חַי
מִֽכָּל־בָּשָׂ֞ר שְׁנַ֧יִם מִכֹּ֛ל תָּבִ֥יא אֶל־הַתֵּבָ֖ה
כ לְהַחֲיֹ֣ת אִתָּ֑ךְ זָכָ֥ר וּנְקֵבָ֖ה יִהְיֽוּ׃ מֵהָע֣וֹף
לְמִינֵ֗הוּ וּמִן־הַבְּהֵמָה֙ לְמִינָ֔הּ מִכֹּ֛ל רֶ֥מֶשׂ

of creation as God's 'covenant'. He explains that our verse refers specifically to the covenant which God had made during the Six Days of Creation confining the waters to one place [1:9]. In the face of this generation's corruption, He was suspending that covenant; however, He promised Noah that for the purpose of saving him and his family, He would nevertheless fulfill His covenant regarding the established order of creation.

וּבָאתָ אֶל הַתֵּבָה — *And you shall enter the ark.*

This is not necessarily a *command* but a divine promise: although the ark appeared to be far too small to contain Noah's family as well as the multitude of creatures, God assured him that they would be able to *enter the ark* and remain for the duration of the Flood *(Ma'aseh Hashem; HaKsav V'Hakaballah).*

אַתָּה וּבָנֶיךָ — *You and your sons,* etc.

From the sequence in which the people are listed: first the men and then separately the women, in contrast to 8:16 where the wives are listed together with their husbands, the *Talmud* [*Yerushalmi Taanis* 1:6 and *Bavli Sanhedrin* 108b] derives that marital intimacy was forbidden when Noah entered the ark, but that it was permitted again when he departed *(also Rashi).*[cf. *comm.* to 7:7 and *Gur Aryeh* cited there.]

19. וּמִכָּל הָחַי — [*And*] *from all that lives.*

I.e. of all those that have retained the vitality of life, and have not been corrupted by the degeneracy that was prevalent on earth. *(Hirsch;* see *Rashi* next verse).

שְׁנַיִם מִכֹּל — *Two of each* [lit. *'two from all'*]

This was the minimal requirement, for, as we see later, there were seven pairs taken from each of the 'clean' animals and birds *(Mizrachi):*

— Even from the least numerous species there was to be not less than two: one male and one female *(Rashi).*

Ramban observes that there are many huge beasts, such as elephants, and so many species of all sizes that ten such arks could not contain them along with the provisions they would need for one year! It was a miracle that the small ark could contain so much.

If there was such a miracle anyway, then why did God not relieve Noah of the burden of construction and have him make a smaller ark? There were two reasons: (a) an imposing structure would be noticed and possibly influence people to repent; and (b) the larger the structure the less obvious the miracle; people should try to reduce their reliance on miracles as much as possible.

תָּבִיא אֶל־הַתֵּבָה — *Shall you bring into the ark.*

VI 19-20

enter the ark — you, your sons, your wife, and your
sons' wives with you. 19 *And from all that lives, of all flesh, two of each shall you bring into the ark to keep alive with you; they shall be male and female.* 20 *From the birds according to each kind, and from the animals according to each kind, and from each thing*

I.e. you shall not abandon them, but shall permit them to accompany you *(Ibn Ezra)*.[1]

The command here cannot mean that God intended for Noah to actually *bring in* these animals; the next verse specifically says that the animals will come of their own accord [see *comm.* there.] The meaning of the verse is rather that he should help them enter and provide for their welfare *(R' Bachya)*.

לְהַחֲיֹת אִתָּךְ — *To keep alive with you* — i.e. to provide for their welfare daily *(Radak)*.

... And to strive on their behalf as you would for your own life *(Ramban)*.

The verse reads לְהַחֲיֹת *'to keep alive'* not לִחְיוֹת, *to live,* because Noah *kept them alive* by providing their sustenance. Had he not been righteous the world would have ceased to exist; the world could not have been saved for the sake of animals alone *(Alshich)*.

זָכָר וּנְקֵבָה יִהְיוּ — *They shall be male and female* — to ensure the survival of each species *(Abarbanel)*.

The meaning of *'two of each'* is thus defined *(Radak)*.

20. The general directive of the preceding verse is now specified *(Ibn Caspi)*:

מֵהָעוֹף לְמִינֵהוּ — *From the birds according to each kind.*

The phrase *'according to each kind'* [i.e. 'with whom no sin had been committed' *(Sanhedrin* 108b)] throughout the verse implies that he was to take only those that had kept to their own species, and who had not committed the perversion of mating with other species *(Rashi; Mizrachi)*.

According to *N'tziv:* Within each species of animal there are many different breeds. They did not all exist at the time of creation, however. The various breeds developed over the years from the original species.

הַבְּהֵמָה — *The animals.*

בְּהֵמָה usually refers to cattle [i.e. domesticated animals], here, however, the term includes חַיָּה, beasts *(Radak)*.

מִכֹּל רֶמֶשׂ הָאֲדָמָה לְמִינֵהוּ — *From each* [lit. *'all'*] *thing that creeps on the ground, after its kind.*

The reason that כֹּל, *all,* is used in this connection is to impress upon Noah that although insect life seemed unnecessary and dispen-

1. This verse reads *'you shall bring'* while the next verse reads *'shall come to you.'* What is the reconciliation of the contradiction?

— When God told Noah to bring the animals to the ark he asked, 'How can I possibly gather them?'

'It is not as you think', God responded. *'They will come to you to remain alive.'* Open the ark for them and they will come of their own accord *(Midrash HaGadol)*.

ו הָאֲדָמָה לְמִינֵהוּ שְׁנַיִם מִכֹּל יָבֹאוּ אֵלֶיךָ
כא־כב כא לְהַחֲיוֹת: וְאַתָּה קַח־לְךָ מִכָּל־מַאֲכָל
אֲשֶׁר יֵאָכֵל וְאָסַפְתָּ אֵלֶיךָ וְהָיָה לְךָ וְלָהֶם
ז כב לְאָכְלָה: וַיַּעַשׂ נֹחַ כְּכֹל אֲשֶׁר צִוָּה אֹתוֹ
א °שני א אֱלֹהִים כֵּן עָשָׂה: °וַיֹּאמֶר יהוה לְנֹחַ בֹּא־

sable to him, nevertheless, its utility was known to God, and he was therefore to be even more punctilious in assuring that *each one* of their species was accounted for *(Toldos Yitzchak).*

יָבֹאוּ אֵלֶיךָ לְהַחֲיוֹת – *Shall come to you to keep alive.*

'They shall come' of their own accord. He led the past the ark: the ark accepted those which had not been the object of sin, and them Noah permitted to enter; the ark rejected the others who had been the object of sin, and then Noah turned away Sanhedrin 108b; *Zevachim* 116a; *Rashi; Gur Aryeh).*

Ramban explains that only once they came, male and female, of their own accord, would Noah bring them into the ark [see 7:16]. God's decree was that only those animals whose purpose it was to be preserved [7:3] would come of their own accord. But God did not decree that animals should come to be slaughtered. Therefore, Noah *'took'* only those *'clean'* beasts which God commanded him to *'take seven and seven of each'* [7:2], to be later sacrificed as offerings.

21. וְאַתָּה קַח־לְךָ ... אֲשֶׁר יֵאָכֵל – *And* [*as for*] *you, take yourself . . . that is eaten.* i.e. take the appropriate food for the various species *(Sforno).*[1]

Noah was not to expect them to bring along their own food the way animals usually prepare their winter food during the summer. This was to be Noah's responsibility; he would gather the food and the animals would be sustained through him *(Malbim).*

He was to bring in all kinds of fruits, seeds, and herbs, because for the duration of the Flood even the carnivorous creatures abstained from meat, just as when they were created *(Radak).*

The *Midrash* comments that the greater part of his provisions consisted of pressed figs along with various greens for the different animals. He also stored away vine-shoots, fig-shoots, olive-shoots, and various seeds for future planting after the Flood. This is implied by the term וְאָסַפְתָּ אֵלֶיךָ, *and gather it in to yourself* — because 'a man does not gather [in the sense of 'store away'] anything unless he needs it for later.'

Ralbag suggests that for Noah to have known how much food to

1. According to *Kli Yakar* the phrase קַח־לְךָ is to be interpreted: *take from your own possessions and not from another's.*

Noah might have rationalized that since the generation was about to perish anyway, he could expropriate their belongings. Therefore God told him: Take only from your own possessions, however limited and seemingly insufficient they are for the intended purpose, in order to accentuate the miracle.

VI 21-22 that creeps on the ground according to its kind, two
of each shall come to you to keep alive.

21 'And as for you, take yourself of every food that
is eaten and gather it in to yourself, that it shall be as
food for you and for them.' 22 Noah did so; just as
God commanded him, so he did.

VII 1

1 Then HASHEM said to Noah, 'Come to the ark,

gather he must have been told approximately how long God was planning for them to stay in the ark (see *footnote)*. Others maintain that Noah did not know how much to prepare; that the food sufficed was itself part of the miracle (see next).

וְהָיָה לְךָ וְלָהֶם לְאָכְלָה — *That* [lit. *'and'*] *it shall be as food for you and for them.*

I.e. it will be sufficient and satisfactory for all the creatures. This was God's promise *(Ha'amek Davar).*

22. וַיַּעַשׂ נֹחַ ... כֵּן עָשָׂה —*[And] Noah did* [*so*]*; just as* [lit. *'according to all that'*] *God commanded him, so he did* — This refers to the construction of the ark *(Rashi)*; and to the gathering of the food. The repetition of כֵּן עָשָׂה, *so he did,* emphasizes that he followed God's command scrupulously; he omitted nothing from all that God commanded him *(Radak; Ramban).*

Thus, Noah complied with the first part of God's command regarding the ark, which he began immediately, and the gathering of the food preparatory to the Flood. The command to bring the species did not apply until the start of the Deluge *(Malbim).*

Radak derives from the reference to two 'doings' in this verse, that the first וַיַּעַשׂ נֹחַ, *Noah did so,* refers to the initial construction which he undertook as soon as God gave the command. The reiteration of כֵּן עָשָׂה refers to the completion of the ark indicating that he worked diligently during all the extended time [opinions range from 52 to 120 years] needed to complete the task in full compliance with God's will. Therefore in 7:5 concerning his entry into the ark, there is no need to repeat the phrase, because there was no extended intervening time lapse.

VII

1. The final call

The time for the Flood drew near. Noah had spent many decades building the ark and his work was complete. In this verse, the ark is referred to as הַתֵּבָה, *'the' ark,* with the definite article, for it is no longer a goal, but a reality. With the Flood to begin *'in seven days'*, God bids him to enter the ark with his family *(Ibn Ezra; Abarbanel).*

וַיֹּאמֶר ה׳ לְנֹחַ — *Then* [lit. *And*] *HASHEM said to Noah.* Since *v.* 4 tells us that the Flood was to begin in seven days, the seventeenth day of the second month (*v.* 11), it follows that this command to enter the ark came on the tenth day of that month *(Ramban).*

[The commentators note this paragraph refers to the Deity as

ז אַתָּה וְכָל־בֵּיתְךָ אֶל־הַתֵּבָה כִּי־אֹתְךָ
ב ב רָאִיתִי צַדִּיק לְפָנַי בַּדּוֹר הַזֶּה: מִכֹּל |
הַבְּהֵמָה הַטְּהוֹרָה תִּקַּח־לְךָ שִׁבְעָה

HASHEM, in contrast to the previous chapter where He is called אֱלֹהִים, *God,* the Name indicating the Attribute of Justice]:

Noah was informed that he and his family would be saved by *'HASHEM',* the Name which indicates God in His Attribute of Mercy [see *comm.* to 1:1 and 2:4]. In addition, by using the Name HASHEM, which is used exclusively concerning sacrifices (see *Ramban Lev.* 1:9), God suggested to Noah that He would mercifully accept his sacrifice and assure that the world would never again be destroyed by flood waters *(Ramban).*

N'tziv and *Malbim* perceive a different meaning in the use of HASHEM, indicating mercy, in this verse. The entire chapter speaks of Elohim, *God,* for that name indicates not only the God of Judgment, but also the God of Nature Who controls the functioning of the universe. In that Elohim-role, God provided for the continued existence of the world after the Flood. In this verse, God showed special mercy to Noah, His chosen righteous one, by permitting him to take along all of his personal effects — even non-essential ones — and household animals [according to *N'tziv,* even slaves]. This kindness was intended solely as a personal show of mercy to Noah.

וְכָל בֵּיתְךָ — *And all your household.*

Following *Targum.* [Lit.: *'and all your house'.*]

— It refers to his sons, wife, and sons' wives mentioned previously *(Ramban).*

It also includes personal household effects *(Malbim).*

כִּי אֹתְךָ רָאִיתִי צַדִּיק לְפָנַי — *For it is you that I have seen* [*to be*] *righteous before Me.* [1]

For you are righteous — and not the members of your household. Therefore the verse says, *come, you and all your household into the ark* — it is only for your sake that they are being saved *(Sforno).*

This interpretation is strengthened by the fact that 8:1 says: *And God remembered Noah,* and makes no mention of his children *(Minchah Belulah).*

According to *Radak: 'That you are righteous'* — and you therefore deserve to be saved along with your entire household, so that the world can be repopulated.

לְפָנַי, *before Me,* is essential. Noah was צַדִּיק לְפָנַי, *righteous before Me* — for it is God's assessment, not popular opinion, which

1. The *Talmud* derives a moral lesson from this verse.

Rabbi Yirmiyah ben Eleazar said: Only a part of man's virtues may be recited in his presence, but all of it in his absence.

[*Rashi* gives as the reason that excess praise would give the appearance of insincere flattery. *Maharsha* explains that it may lead the person being praised to conceit and overconfidence.]

In Noah's presence, i.e. when addressing him directly, God mentioned only a part of his virtues: *'For I have seen that you are righteous';* but when referring to Noah in his absence, God describes his full virtues: [6:9] 'Noah was righteous *and wholehearted' (Eruvin* 18b).

VII 2 *you and all your household, for it is you that I have seen to be righteous before Me in this generation.*
2 *Of every clean animal take unto you seven pairs, a*

determines man's true worth *(Hirsch).*

[As pointed out above, this communication took place seven days before the Flood, immediately following the death of the righteous Methuselah, Noah's grandfather (see *comm.* to *v.* 4).]

Kli Yakar notes, therefore, that God had never before singled out Noah as *the* righteous man of that generation as long as Methuselah was still alive and there was also the possibility that the generation might repent. When Methuselah died and they persisted in their wickedness, however, God singled out Noah and finalized the decree.

בַּדּוֹר הַזֶּה — *In this generation.*

[See *comm.* to 6:9 s.v. בְּדֹרֹתָיו, *in his generations.*]

The *Zohar* comments: Rav Yehudah said, when the sinners were to be destroyed in Noah's time, God was anxious to save the world, but there was none who could protect it, for Noah's whole efforts were required to save himself and to repopulate the world. It is written *'For I have seen that you are righteous only by comparison with this generation ...*

Rav Yose said: To the contrary! This description enhances his praise, and implies that even in that wicked generation he remained as righteous as if he had lived in the days of Moses. Yet, he could not save the world because there were not ten righteous men in it (as a minimum for saving others; cf. Abraham's pleading for Sodom, *Gen.* 18:32: *What if ten should be found there?).*[1]

It is in this praiseworthy manner that *Hirsch* interprets it:

Every person is affected by the terror and mores of his time. Nevertheless, God stressed to Noah that, because he remained righteous and faithful despite the degeneracy surrounding him, he was the fitting nucleus for the future God intended to build.

2. [The directive is now clarified. Of all 'unclean' animals, two of each species would come to Noah, but of the 'clean' animals he was to *take* seven pairs]:

מִכֹּל הַבְּהֵמָה הַטְּהוֹרָה — *Of every clean animal.*

— I.e. from every animal which will one day be declared 'clean' [i.e. as food for Israel]. This shows that Noah studied Torah *(Rashi).*

Ramban explains that God had fully explained to Noah the signs of ritual cleanliness for beast and fowl, as found in *Lev.* 11. For the sake of brevity, the Torah described them here as *'clean'.* The reference to *'clean'* does not refer to physical cleanliness, but to ritual acceptability.]

1. In a further dissertation, however the *Zohar* (67b) draws a parallel between Noah and Moses: When God was angry at the Jews in the time of Moses, he interceded on their behalf and sought mercy *(Exod.* 32:11) going so far as to offer his own life, as *ibid.* in *v.* 32: *'and if not, erase me, please, from Your book which You have written',* with the result that God forgave them (*v.* 34).

But Noah did not act this way. He was content to build an ark and save himself only, and did not intercede on behalf of his generation, but let them perish.

It is for this reason that the waters of the Flood are named after him, as it is written: [*Isaiah* 54:9] *'for this is as the waters of Noah unto Me'* ... But Moses is called *'he that brought them up out of the sea'* [*ibid.* 63:11] because their deliverance at that time was due to his prayer, and the achievement is ascribed to Moses because he risked his life for Israel [see *Overview*].

ז
ג

שִׁבְעָה אִישׁ וְאִשְׁתּוֹ וּמִן־הַבְּהֵמָה אֲשֶׁר
ג לֹא טְהֹרָה הִוא שְׁנַיִם אִישׁ וְאִשְׁתּוֹ: גַּם
מֵעוֹף הַשָּׁמַיִם שִׁבְעָה שִׁבְעָה זָכָר וּנְקֵבָה

The commentators vary on the definition of טָהֹר, *'clean'*, in this context.

From *Ibn Ezra, Ramban, Radak, Ra'avad Halevi, Sforno,* it is evident that 'fit for later sacrifice' is meant;

According to *Lekach Tov*, and to *N'tziv*'s citation of *Rashi*, the intent is 'clean [i.e., kosher] for food.'

According to *Zevachim* 116a: 'It means those with which no sin had been committed' [see *comm.* to 6:20.]

The concept of בְּהֵמָה טְהוֹרָה, 'clean' animal is mentioned here for the first time. It can have no other connotation than acceptability for sacrifice, because heretofore, animal flesh for food was forbidden. When bringing offerings to God, Noachides were never allowed to use other than 'clean' animals *(Zevachim* 115b). It is clear, therefore, that the Jewish table is required to maintain the same standard of purity as a Noachic altar. The word טָהֹר, *clean,* is related to צֹהַר, *window.* Both, therefore, indicate something which is receptive to rays of light. A 'clean' animal is one which, when consumed by man, does not decrease his susceptibility to spiritual rays. Were it to do so, it could not be permitted as food for Jews whose mission is to be receptacles of spirituality. The clean animals are those whose docile nature renders them submissive to human influences. The name HASHEM is used here to emphasize that the abundance of clean animals was not in order to preserve the species — for that, a pair would have sufficed — but to carry on the spiritual role of man represented by the name HASHEM *(Hirsch).*

תִּקַּח לְךָ שִׁבְעָה שִׁבְעָה — *Take unto you seven pairs* [lit. *'seven, seven'*]

In order that he might be able to sacrifice some of them when he left the ark *(Rashi).*

Radak suggests that the seven pairs could not have been just for sacrificial needs, for nowhere do we see that Noah offered more than one sacrifice; and he could have taken a single pair and used their offspring after waiting a year or two. The additional purpose was to provide an abundant supply of 'clean' livestock for food in anticipation of the removal of the prohibition against eating meat [9:3]. One should not ask 'why seven and not six or eight.' Know that God in His wisdom ordained that seven would serve the higher purpose He intended *(Radak).*[1]

The animals that came to preserve their species came of their own accord, prompted by the Divine Will. God gave Noah the merit of catching those that were destined to be slaughtered, for, in his great benevolence, God would not have these animals offer themselves for death. At the same time this teaches man that clemency must be exercised even toward animals *(Ramban; R' Nissim; R' Bachya).*

Chizkuni adds that Noah had to have larger quantities of clean

1. According to *Pirkei d'Rabbi Eliezer* this decree was necessary because 'Before the Flood, the unclean animals were more numerous than the clean animals. But when the waters of the Flood came, God wished to increase the clean animals and diminish the unclean animals. He therefore told him to take seven pairs of clean animals, but only one pair of unclean animals.

VII
3

male with its mate, and of the unclean animals, two, a
male with its mate; 3 *of the birds of the heavens also,*
seven pairs, male and female, to keep seed alive upon

animals, otherwise he would not have been able to offer sacrifices without completely exterminating the species involved.

The translation of *'seven pairs'* for lit. *'seven seven'* follows the *Midrash* which explains: 'seven males and seven females'. For if you explain it seven individual animals, one of them would lack a partner!

[The commentators explain additionally, that these seven pairs were not *in addition* to the original pair mentioned for all creatures; rather, the *total* for the 'clean' species was to be seven pairs.]

R' Bachya emphasizes that there are great secrets connected with the number 'seven' in relation to sacrifices. See, for example, *Numbers* 23:1,4.

אִישׁ וְאִשְׁתּוֹ — *Each with its mate* [lit. *'man and his wife'*] — i.e. male and female *(Targum).*

The two nouns אִישׁ, *man,* and אִשָּׁה, *woman* [wife], originally designated male and female of human beings, but were later applied to the male and female of animals as well *(Rambam, Moreh* 1:6).

The expression thus refers to pairs. When the pairs are equal in gender and/or quality, then Scripture says of them אִשָּׁה אֶל אֲחוֹתָהּ, *'woman to her sister'* [*Ex.* 26:3,5,6; *Lev.* 18:18, *Ezek.* 1:9]; but when they are not equal, but can mate with one another, then this expression *'man and his wife'* is applicable *(Karnei Or).*

וּמִן הַבְּהֵמָה אֲשֶׁר לֹא טְהֹרָה — *And of the unclean animals* [lit. *'and of the animal that is not clean'*].

The use of the longer expression אֲשֶׁר לֹא טְהֹרָה, *that is not clean,* instead of the forthright expression טָמֵא, *unclean,* teaches a moral lesson as noted by the *Talmud* [*Pesachim* 3a]:

'Rabbi Yehoshua ben Levi said: One should never utter a gross expression with his mouth, for the Torah added eight letters [in the Hebrew text of our verse which would be saved by use of the single word טָמֵא *'unclean'*], rather than utter a gross expression.

Rashi ad. loc. notes that the Torah *does* usually use the term טָמֵא, unclean. It is the unusual *change* from the normal expression to this more roundabout phrase that accentuates and draws attention to the moral lesson to be derived.

3. **גַּם מֵעוֹף הַשָּׁמַיִם** — *Of the birds of the heavens also.*

Rashi explains that this verse, too, refers to *clean* fowl [analogous to the distinction in the previous verse which refers to clean animals *(Ramban).*] Thus — לָמֵד סָתוּם מִן הַמְפֹרָשׁ, 'the non-explicit [of this verse] may be inferred from the explicit [previous verse].'

Bertinoro cites 8:20: *'every clean beast and every clean fowl'* which Noah sacrificed, as the explicit proof that *clean* fowl are here referred to.

Of the unclean fowl, however, two were sufficient *(R' Bachya).*

זָכָר וּנְקֵבָה — *Male and female.*

Animals who bear their young alive and whole like humans, are referred to in the previous verse as *'man and woman'*; but birds which

ז
ד

ד לְחַיּ֥וֹת זֶ֖רַע עַל־פְּנֵ֥י כָל־הָאָֽרֶץ׃ כִּי֩ לְיָמִ֨ים
ע֜וֹד שִׁבְעָ֗ה אָֽנֹכִי֙ מַמְטִ֣יר עַל־הָאָ֔רֶץ
אַרְבָּעִ֣ים י֔וֹם וְאַרְבָּעִ֖ים לָ֑יְלָה וּמָחִ֗יתִי
אֶֽת־כָּל־הַיְקוּם֙ אֲשֶׁ֣ר עָשִׂ֔יתִי מֵעַ֖ל פְּנֵ֥י

lay eggs, are referred to only as *'male and female' (R' Bachya).*

לְחַיּוֹת זֶרַע עַל פְּנֵי כָל הָאָרֶץ — *To keep seed alive upon the face of all the earth.* I.e. to assure the preservation of the species *(Ralbag).*

'To keep alive' indicates the preservation, flourishing, and development of the species rather than mere propagation *(Heidenheim).*

'Not that I need them,' said God [because sacrifices are to provide merit for those who offer them *(Yefe Toar)*], 'but *to keep seed alive upon the face of all the earth' (Midrash).*

If the reason, according to *Rashi* in *v.* 2, that Noah was to take these seven pairs of clean animals was for future sacrifice, then how does the reason given in this verse: לְחַיּוֹת זֶרַע, *to preserve the species,* apply?

The answer lies in the comment of *Ramban* to *v.* 1, where he explains that this phrase refers not to the animals, but to *Noah*'s descendants: God hinted to Noah that by the merit of his offering, *Noah's offspring will be preserved,* and will not perish in the Flood *(HaK'sav V'Hakaballah).*

According to the *Talmud (Avodah Zarah* 6a) this phrase suggests to Noah that he was to take into the ark with him only such animals as were healthy and physically capable of *'keeping seed alive'* — i.e. of bearing young and preserving the species.

'Upon the face of all the earth' — This is mentioned because their habitats are spread throughout the world *(Radak).*

4. כִּי לְיָמִים עוֹד שִׁבְעָה — *For in seven days' time* — These are the seven days of mourning for Methuselah in whose honor God delayed the Flood.

... Additionally, עוֹד, *another,* indicates an *additional* grace period of several days beyond the original period which God allotted in the hope that they would repent *(Avos d'Rabbi Nosson; Rashi).* [1]

אָנֹכִי מַמְטִיר עַל הָאָרֶץ — *I will send rain upon the earth.*

Hirsch notes that throughout Scripture the personal pronoun אָנֹכִי *'I'*, used of God designates a manifestation revealing of God's love and grace, whereas the personal pronoun אֲנִי designates the One who is מאנה, causes things to

1. What purpose was served by these seven days?

— Rav said: These were the days of mourning for Methuselah, thus teaching that lamenting for the righteous postpones retribution;

— Another meaning is: After the seven days during which the Holy One blessed be He, reversed the order of nature [lit. *'the beginning'*], the sun rising in the west and setting in the east [that the wicked might be arrested by the phenomenon and led to repentance] ...

— Another interpretation: God showed them the bounty of the righteous in the World to Come so that they might closely examine their own ways and say 'Woe unto us over this good which we are forfeiting!' — for they had corrupted their way on the earth *(Avos d'Rabbi Nosson).*

VII 4-5

the face of all the earth. [4] *For in seven days' time I will send rain upon the earth, forty days and forty nights, and I will blot out all existence that I have made from the face of the ground.'* [5] *And Noah did exactly*

happen, but Himself remains aloof from the affected creatures.

Thus אָנֹכִי in our verse is significant: 'Although I bring death and destruction to the entire world, I am still the same 'אָנֹכִי' whose main purpose is the happiness and well-being of the universe. The destruction itself is a manifestation of My ultimate love and benevolence.

[Perhaps the use in this verse of מָטָר, signifying rains of benevolence (see *comm.* of *Malbim* cited to 2:5) has the same significance: true, these rains will cause the obliteration of mankind, but even this harsh treatment has only God's love and fatherly chastisement as its higher purpose.]

אַרְבָּעִים יוֹם וְאַרְבָּעִים לָיְלָה — *Forty days and forty nights.* Although, as stated in 8:3, the rains lasted 150 days, nevertheless the obliteration of all subsistence would be accomplished in forty days *(Ha'amek Davar).*

Rashi, states that 'the forty days correspond to the period of a child's formation,' for by sinning they had troubled the Creator to form illegitimate children.

According to the *Midrash:* 'They have transgressed the Torah which was later given after forty days' ... 'they corrupted the features [of the human embryo] which take shape after forty days ...'

[Cf. *Vayikra Rabba* 23:12: During the whole of the forty days following conception the Holy One, blessed be He, is engaged in the fashioning the embryo's image ...']

This, then, is the corruption of the features referred to. It might correspond to their having corrupted *their own features* by following their evil designs *(Maharzu);* or it might correspond to their having corrupted their own features by causing their own obliteration from the earth; or the features of their children, or by having committed murder, destroying humankind as a whole.

It was all measure for measure: Forty days corresponding to the forty-day period of the formation of the embryo which they destroyed *(Yefe Toar).*

Forty is also the numerical equivalent of גֵּזֶל robbery, in which they were steeped *(Kli Yakar).*

וּמָחִיתִי אֶת כָּל הַיְקוּם — *And I will blot out all existence.*

The translation of יְקוּם, *existence,* follows *Ibn Janach* who derives it from the root קוּם, stand: 'everything that stands in the universe — i.e. all existence.'

According to *Ibn Caspi,* it refers to those living beings which can stand by their own strength; while *Abarbanel* explains it as referring to whatever 'stands' whether living or not, such as houses, etc.

The *Midrash,* also relating יְקוּם to 'stand', explains the verse as referring to Cain who 'stood up' against his brother [4:8], and renders: 'I will blot out the one who arose against him [his brother]. For as Rav Levi said in the name of Resh Lakesh: God held Cain's punishment in abeyance until the Flood came and swept him away. Hence, it is written (7:23): *'And He blotted out every one that had arisen.'*

מֵעַל פְּנֵי הָאֲדָמָה — *From the face of the ground* — i.e. anything on dry land, excluding the fish of the sea and whatever was in the ark *(Radak).*

ז
ה־ט

ה הָאֲדָמָה: וַיַּעַשׂ נֹחַ כְּכֹל אֲשֶׁר־צִוָּהוּ
ו יהוָה: וְנֹחַ בֶּן־שֵׁשׁ מֵאוֹת שָׁנָה וְהַמַּבּוּל
ז הָיָה מַיִם עַל־הָאָרֶץ: וַיָּבֹא נֹחַ וּבָנָיו
וְאִשְׁתּוֹ וּנְשֵׁי־בָנָיו אִתּוֹ אֶל־הַתֵּבָה מִפְּנֵי
ח מֵי הַמַּבּוּל: מִן־הַבְּהֵמָה הַטְּהוֹרָה וּמִן־
הַבְּהֵמָה אֲשֶׁר אֵינֶנָּה טְהֹרָה וּמִן־הָעוֹף
ט וְכֹל אֲשֶׁר־רֹמֵשׂ עַל־הָאֲדָמָה: שְׁנַיִם
שְׁנַיִם בָּאוּ אֶל־נֹחַ אֶל־הַתֵּבָה זָכָר

5. Noah complies

וַיַּעַשׂ נֹחַ כְּכֹל אֲשֶׁר צִוָּהוּ ה׳ — *And Noah did exactly as HASHEM had commanded him.*

This refers to his coming to the ark *(Rashi).*

Or, according to the *Midrash,* it refers to the taking in of the animals, beasts, and birds.

Ibn Ezra explains that he approached the ark with his family but did not enter until, as *v.* 7 implies, the rains forced him in.

[The commentators to *Rashi* ask how Noah complied with God's command by *approaching,* but not *entering* the ark. On the contrary, the implication of *v.* 7 indicates that he failed to comply until the raging water forced him in. The same difficulty apparently applies to *Ibn Ezra.*]

Or Hachaim explains that the compliance referred to in this verse is Noah's efforts to assemble seven pairs of clean animals and birds. The verse makes clear that Noah obeyed *all* God's commands, even though the entry of the seven pairs is not specifically mentioned later (see *v.* 9, 15).

— It refers to his entering and leaving the ark all during that seven day period — bringing in the animals as God had commanded, and making last-minute preparations in anticipation of the Flood *(Akeidas Yitzchak).*

6. וְנֹחַ בֶּן שֵׁשׁ מֵאוֹת שָׁנָה — *[And] Noah was six hundred years old.*

Rav Yehudah said: The year of the Flood is not counted in the number (of Noah's years). [For he was 600 years old when the Flood commenced, the Flood lasted a year in all, and he lived 350 years after the Flood (9:28) yet his lifetime is given as 950 years *(ibid.* 29), not 951. The reason for this was that it was a year of such suffering and tribulation that it was as if he had been dead during that year *(Mattanos Kehunah)*] But, said Rav Nechemiah to him, it is counted in the chronological reckoning [of the total number of years from the world's creation when we determine the seasons and intercalations *(Mattanos Kehunah).*]

וְהַמַּבּוּל הָיָה מַיִם עַל הָאָרֶץ — *When* [lit. *'and'*] *the Flood was water upon the earth.*

The translation follows *Ibn Janach* and *Radak* — i.e. 'when the Flood, which was a flood of water [see *comm.* to 7:17] was upon the earth.'

Rav Saadiah Gaon renders simply: *'When the Flood of water was upon the earth.'*

7. נֹחַ וּבָנָיו וְאִשְׁתּוֹ וּנְשֵׁי בָנָיו אִתּוֹ — *Noah, with his sons, his wife and his sons' wives with him.*

The men separately and the women separately because they

as HASHEM had commanded him.
6 Noah was six hundred years old when the Flood
was water upon the earth. 7 Noah, with his sons, his
wife, and his sons' wives with him, went into the ark
because of the waters of the Flood. 8 Of the clean
animals, of the unclean animals, of the birds, and of
each thing that creeps upon the ground, 9 in pairs,
they came to Noah into the ark, male and female, as

were forbidden marital intimacy while the whole world was in distress [cf. *comm.* to 6:18 and 8:16] *(Rashi).*

Gur Aryeh notes, however, that although permission to resume marital relations was implied in God's command to leave the ark in 8:16, nevertheless the males and females left the ark separately (8:18) because Noah feared a new Flood until God swore to him that He would never again inundate the world in such a deluge.

מִפְּנֵי מֵי הַמַּבּוּל – *Because of the waters of the Flood.*

Rashi interprets this phrase to mean that Noah entered only at the last moment:

'Noah was of little faith, believing and yet not believing that the Flood would come, and he did not enter until the rising water forced him to do so.' As the *Midrash* comments: 'He lacked faith; had the waters not reached his ankles, he would not have entered the ark.'

How can we say that the righteous Noah was lacking in faith? — Noah could not bring himself to believe that the Merciful God would truly destroy all life. Or, Noah thought that the onslaught of the water would cause the generation to repent and win God's mercy; he did not reckon on their continued stubbornness. Nevertheless, Scripture implies a criticism of Noah because he should have obeyed despite his calculations *(Me'am Loez).*

Ibn Ezra translates: Because of fear of the waters of the Flood.

Others interpret that they entered the ark immediately, in *anticipation* of the impending Flood. The fact that their entry is related again in *v.* 13 implies that the first entry was not their final one; they still would go in and out, making preparations *(Radak; Ralbag, Akeidas Yitzchak).*

According to *Ramban,* these verses are not in chronological order: Noah and his family with all the beasts entered the ark because of the waters of the Flood *in fulfillment of God's command.* Beginning with *v.* 11, however, the Torah repeats its general narrative of these events but in more detailed description, specifying the month and day he entered the ark, and stating that on that very day — and not prior to it — Noah entered the ark together with all living things.

8. מִן הַבְּהֵמָה הַטְּהוֹרָה – *Of the clean animals,* etc.

— All during that seven day period these animals assembled from all the corners of the world, it being beyond the capabilities of Noah to have sought them all out *(Ibn Ezra).*

9. שְׁנַיִם שְׁנַיִם בָּאוּ אֶל נֹחַ – *In pairs* [lit. *'two, two'*] *they came to Noah*

ז
י-יא

י וּנְקֵבָה כַּאֲשֶׁר צִוָּה אֱלֹהִים אֶת־נֹחַ: וַיְהִי
לְשִׁבְעַת הַיָּמִים וּמֵי הַמַּבּוּל הָיוּ עַל־
יא הָאָרֶץ: בִּשְׁנַת שֵׁשׁ־מֵאוֹת שָׁנָה לְחַיֵּי־נֹחַ
בַּחֹדֶשׁ הַשֵּׁנִי בְּשִׁבְעָה־עָשָׂר יוֹם לַחֹדֶשׁ
בַּיּוֹם הַזֶּה נִבְקְעוּ כָּל־מַעְיְנוֹת תְּהוֹם רַבָּה

— of their own volition [see *comm.* to 6:19, 20; 7:2] *(Tanchuma; Radak).*

Rashi comments that the *'two'* mentioned here was the *minimum* number common to all of them. [However, there were seven pairs of the 'clean' animals *(Mizrachi).*]

... These were the twos — male and female — that came *of their own accord.* While Noah busied himself with God's command to go out and assemble the seven pairs of 'clean' ones who were destined for a sacrifice *(Ramban).*

The verse thus stresses that two of every species came of their own accord. That Noah took the six additional pairs in accordance with God's command is already implicit in *v.* 5: *'And Noah did all that God had commanded him' (Or HaChaim).*

כַּאֲשֶׁר צִוָּה אֱלֹהִים אֶת נֹחַ — *As God had commanded Noah.*

Ha'amek Davar notes that it is said only of the animals that they came because of God's command, but not of the people *(v.* 7):

He explains that the people who approached the ark knew that they were doing so מִפְּנֵי מֵי הַמַּבּוּל *because of the Flood-water* which God had decreed; but the beasts had no idea why they were coming to Noah; it was the Spirit which was drawing them; they came because ... צִוָּה אֱלֹהִים אֶת נֹחַ, *God had so commanded Noah ...*

10. וַיְהִי לְשִׁבְעַת הַיָּמִים — *And it came to pass on the seventh day.*

— When the mourning period for Methuselah had ended *(Targum Yonasan).* [See *comm.* to *v.* 4.]

— After the seven days that the Holy One, blessed be He, mourned for His world before bringing the Flood *(Midrash).*

... The *Talmud* [*Yer. Mo'ed Katan* 3:5] adduces from our verse that the dead are mourned for a period of seven days. The *Talmud* asks: Does then one mourn *before* another's death? — Human beings who do not know what the future brings mourn after a relative dies; God, who knows the future, mourns in advance.

Far from the non-Jewish view that searches for natural causes to explain such calamities as the Flood, we see here that nature functions in obedience to the will of God: birds, insects, animals — all found their way in pairs to Noah *'at God's command.'* In the same way, the Flood burst upon the world precisely at the moment decreed by God *(Hirsch).*

וּמֵי הַמַּבּוּל הָיוּ עַל הָאָרֶץ — *That* [lit. *'And'*] *the waters of the Flood were upon the earth.*

— [Just as God, in *v.* 4, had said they would be.]

11. The final entry into the ark

בִּשְׁנַת שֵׁשׁ מֵאוֹת שָׁנָה לְחַיֵּי נֹחַ — *In the*

VII
10-11

God had commanded Noah. 10 *And it came to pass on the seventh day that the waters of the Flood were upon the earth.*

11 *In the six hundredth year of Noah's life, in the second month, on the seventeenth day of the month, on that day all the fountains of the great deep burst*

six hundredth year of Noah's life — in the year 1056 from Creation *(Seder Olam).*

The narrative up to now consisted mainly of generalities about the preparations for the Flood and about Noah's scrupulous compliance with God's commands. Now, Scripture returns to give us the exact date of the Flood and to detail the events as they happened *(Ramban).*

בַּחֹדֶשׁ הַשֵּׁנִי — *In the second month.*

Rashi noting the controversy in the *Talmud Rosh Hashanah* 11b, comments:

According to Rabbi Eliezer it was Marcheshvan, while according to Rabbi Yehoshua it was Iyar.

The difference of opinion is consistent with the differing views of when the world was created: Rabbi Eliezer holds that it was created in Tishrei, and hence Marcheshvan is the *'second month'*; while according to Rabbi Yehoshua the world was created in Nissan, and *'the second month'* refers to Iyar.

Targum Yonasan paraphrases: 'In the six hundredth year of the life of Noah, in the second month, which was the month of Marcheshvan, for prior to this, the months had been numbered from Tishrei, which was the beginning of the year, at the completion of the world ...'

Radak explains it as follows:

'It was already mentioned above [*v.* 6] that the Flood began after Noah's six-hundredth year. There it came to tell us Noah's age at the time of the Flood; here the intention is to give the specific month and date when it began. This date is disputed by the Sages in the *Talmud* ... and *Targum Yonasan* in *I Kings* 8:2 decides like Rabbi Eliezer. It appears that the ancients referred to Tishrei as the first month, for in it creation was completed. When the Jews left Egypt, God said *(Exodus* 12:2): *'This month shall be for you the beginning of months,'* thus ordaining that, for Jews, Nissan is to be counted as the first month. Since *'for you'* is emphasized, it follows that for gentiles Nissan is not *'the beginning of months.'*

The *Talmud* concludes that we follow Rabbi Eliezer in dating the Flood [i.e., in using Tishrei to calculate the years of Noah and the calendar; Tishrei being the New Year for years *(Rosh Hashanah* 2a)], and Rabbi Yehoshua in dating the תְּקוּפוֹת, seasons [i.e. annual cycles, for the year is divided into four cycles called *Tekufos:* The *tekufah* of Nissan (Vernal Equinox); Tammuz (Summer Solstice); Tishrei (Autumnal Equinox); Teves (Winter Solstice). Accordingly, Nissan is the first *tekufah: 'the first of months'*.]

[We will, therefore, in the calculations that appear in later verses follow *Rashi* and date the events of the Flood according to its beginning on the seventeenth of Marcheshvan.]

בַּיּוֹם הַזֶּה נִבְקְעוּ כָּל מַעְיְנוֹת תְּהוֹם רַבָּה — *On that day all the fountains of the great deep burst forth; and the windows of the heavens were opened.*

יב וַאֲרֻבֹּת הַשָּׁמַיִם נִפְתָּחוּ: וַיְהִי הַגֶּשֶׁם עַל־
הָאָרֶץ אַרְבָּעִים יוֹם וְאַרְבָּעִים לָיְלָה:
יג בְּעֶצֶם הַיּוֹם הַזֶּה בָּא נֹחַ וְשֵׁם־וְחָם וָיֶפֶת
בְּנֵי־נֹחַ וְאֵשֶׁת נֹחַ וּשְׁלֹשֶׁת נְשֵׁי־בָנָיו
יד אִתָּם אֶל־הַתֵּבָה: הֵמָּה וְכָל־הַחַיָּה
לְמִינָהּ וְכָל־הַבְּהֵמָה לְמִינָהּ וְכָל־הָרֶמֶשׂ
הָרֹמֵשׂ עַל־הָאָרֶץ לְמִינֵהוּ וְכָל־הָעוֹף
טו לְמִינֵהוּ כֹּל צִפּוֹר כָּל־כָּנָף: וַיָּבֹאוּ אֶל־נֹחַ

I.e. the subterranean fountains burst forth and the waters inundated the earth in a great seismic upheaval filling up the valleys, while simultaneously the torrential rains fell from heaven in such force that, figuratively speaking, the very 'windows of the heavens' opened up, causing complete havoc and obscuring day and night *(Lekach Tov; Ibn Ezra; Radak; Ralbag).*

The waters were scalding hot, notes the *Talmud* [*Sanhedrin* 108b].

The *Talmud* notes that the word *'great'* in this verse emphasizes that their punishment was 'great', measure for measure: Their wickedness was characterized as רַבָּה *'great'* [6:5], and they were punished by תְּהוֹם רַבָּה 'great' deep [*Sanhedrin* 108a.]

וַאֲרֻבֹּת הַשָּׁמַיִם נִפְתָּחוּ — *And the windows of the heavens were opened.*

אֲרוּבָּה is an aperture in a roof through which one raises and lowers objects *(Rashi, Menachos* 34). In Scriptures it is used metaphorically to refer to the heavenly influence which came down to earth as in *Malachi* 3:10: *'If I will not open the windows of the heavens for you and pour down for you an overflowing blessing.'* In our verse the term is employed to describe the abundance of heavenly waters waiting to stream down as if through opened windows *(HaK'sav V'Hakaballah).*

12. וַיְהִי הַגֶּשֶׁם — *And the rain was.*

Noting that later [*v.* 17], the narrative mentions *'Flood'* while here it refers to *'rain'*, *Rashi* explains that when the water descended, it began gently because it still could have become a rain of blessing had the people belatedly repented. Only when they refused did it become a Flood [*Zohar* 1:25.]

אַרְבָּעִים יוֹם וְאַרְבָּעִים לָיְלָה — *Forty days and forty nights.* As God had foretold *(Radak).*

Rashi calculates that according to Rabbi Eliezer [according to whom the reckoning begins with Tishrei (see *comm.* to *v.* 11)], this forty day period ended with the twenty-eighth day of Kislev.

This calculation omits the day the rain began, the seventeenth of Marcheshvan, because it rained for only part of that day *(v.* 13). In a typical year, Marcheshvan is a 'defective' month of 29 days. We therefore have twelve days of Marcheshvan (18th through 29th = 12], plus 28 days in Kislev totaling 40.

[On the significance of the Flood lasting forty days, see *comm.* to *v.* 4.]

VII forth; and the windows of the heavens were opened.
12-15 12 *And the rain was upon the earth forty days and*
forty nights.
13 *On that very day Noah came, with Shem, Ham,*
and Japeth, Noah's sons with Noah's wife and the
three wives of his sons with them into the ark —
14 *they and every beast after its kind, every cattle*
after its kind, every creeping thing that creeps on the
earth after its kind, and all birds after its kind, and
every bird of any kind of wing. 15 *They came to Noah*

13. בְּעֶצֶם הַיּוֹם הַזֶּה — *On that very day* — i.e. the seventeenth of the month *(Ibn Ezra).*

It was thus one of the miracles of the Flood that God had caused every one of the world's creatures to finally assemble and enter the ark *on that one very day* as Scripture here attests *(Rokeach: Ma'aseh Hashem).*

As *Ramban* explains in *Lev.* 23:28: We find that Scripture mentions the phrase בְּעֶצֶם הַיּוֹם in the case of events which have been decreed to come at certain set times. Since one may think that Noah had been bringing many animals beforehand and coincidentally happened to finish his task on that day, after which he entered, therefore Scripture emphasizes that *all* the particular events took place on the day decreed by God.

[Interpreting בְּעֶצֶם, 'during the strength' — i.e. at mid-day, in broad daylight *(Ibn Janach)*], *Rashi* comments: Scripture teaches you that his neighbors threatened to kill him and smash the ark if they saw him entering it, whereupon God said: 'I will have him enter the ark before the eyes of everyone and we shall see whose word prevails!' [*Midrash.*]

בָּא נֹחַ וְשֵׁם וְחָם וָיֶפֶת בְּנֵי נֹחַ וְאֵשֶׁת נֹחַ — *Noah came, with Shem [and] Ham and Japheth, the sons of Noah, with Noah's wife.*

— [As mentioned in the less detailed account in *v.* 7.]

It would have been briefer to simply state *'the sons of Noah'* without naming them. However, they are specifically listed, and Noah's name is repeated three times in this verse, to emphasize that each entered and was saved by his merit *(Ibn Caspi).*

14. לְמִינָהּ — *After its kind.*

[See *comm.* to 6:20 s.v. לְמִינֵהוּ.]

כֹּל צִפּוֹר כָּל כָּנָף — *Every bird of any kind of wing* — i.e. every kind of winged creature, even locusts *(Rashi).*

[The translation of the phrase (lit. *'every bird' 'every wing'*) follows *Rashi* who interprets 'all birds' as an adjective in the construct form with an implied preposition *'of'.*]

[According to the *Talmud, Chullin* 139b, צִפּוֹר, *bird,* refers only to clean birds, and כָּנָף, *winged,* includes both unclean birds and locusts.

Accordingly both words are nouns and

ז
טז־יז

אֶל־הַתֵּבָה שְׁנַיִם שְׁנַיִם מִכָּל־הַבָּשָׂר
טז אֲשֶׁר־בּוֹ רוּחַ חַיִּים: וְהַבָּאִים זָכָר וּנְקֵבָה
מִכָּל־בָּשָׂר בָּאוּ כַּאֲשֶׁר צִוָּה אֹתוֹ אֱלֹהִים
°שלישי יז וַיִּסְגֹּר יהוה בַּעֲדוֹ:°וַיְהִי הַמַּבּוּל אַרְבָּעִים

rendered: *'All (clean) birds, and all (unclean) winged creatures.'*]

The *Midrash*, explaining כל צִפּוֹר כָּל כָּנָף as: *'all birds [possessing] all their feathers'* explains that the verse thus excludes all those who were moulting or maimed [i.e. lacking 'all their feathers'] as unfit for sacrifices of the Noachides.

Ramban to *Lev.* 14:4 also interprets our phrase as two distinct nouns, and comments:

The correct interpretation appears to me to be that the term צִפּוֹר *tzipor*, is a generic term for all small birds that rise early in the morning to chirp and to sing, the term being associated with the Aramaic word צַפְרָא *tzafra* (morning). Similarly, the expression כֹּל צִפּוֹר כָּל כָּנָף *'every tzipor (bird) of every sort'* refers to two kinds: 'all the little ones and the big ones'.

15. Here we find man in his loftiest state. The entire animal world comes to him to save and preserve it *(Hirsch).*

וַיָּבֹאוּ אֶל נֹחַ . . . שְׁנַיִם שְׁנַיִם — [*And*] *they came to Noah . . . in pairs* [lit. *'two, two'*].

Two of every species — male and female — came of their own volition on that very day when the rains began and not before, because it was God *that commanded, and His spirit which gathered them* [*Isaiah* 34:16] *(Ramban).*

... All this could not have happened with such precision except by a miracle *(R' Bachya).*

They came in matched pairs — not one species missing — that was the wonder! *(Ibn Ezra; Radak).*

The translation *'in pairs'* follows *N'tziv* who explains: They came in pairs: one pair [for the unclean animals], and seven pairs [for the clean.]

Malbim says that every phrase in this verse is laden with the wondrous spectacle of the event:
And they came to Noah — although most animals run away from man;
to the ark — although animals despise confinement and cling to their freedom to roam;
'two and two' — and not more;
of all flesh — not even one species was missing.

אֲשֶׁר בּוֹ רוּחַ חַיִּים — *In which there was a breath* [lit. *'spirit'*] *of life.*

I.e. implying that sickly animals which were liable to die from a disease during the duration of the Flood were excluded *(Lekach Tov).*

16. . . . וְהַבָּאִים — *Thus* [lit. *'and'*] *they that came* — i.e. to the ark *(Ibn Ezra).*

— I.e. those pairs referred to in the previous verse *(Ha'amek Davar).*

זָכָר וּנְקֵבָה . . . כַּאֲשֶׁר צִוָּה — *Male and female as God had commanded him.*

They did not come simply in twos but in exact pairs — *male and female* precisely as God had commanded Noah; that is how he brought them into the ark *(Ramban).*

וַיִּסְגֹּר ה' בַּעֲדוֹ — *And HASHEM shut it on his behalf.*[1]

VII 16 *into the ark; in pairs of all flesh in which there was a breath of life.* [16] *Thus they that came, came male and female of all flesh, as God had commanded him. And* HASHEM *shut it on his behalf.*

I.e., by surrounding the ark with wild beasts which killed whoever approached it. God protected him against would-be destroyers who would smash the ark [see *comm.* to *v.* 13]. But according to the literal meaning of the verse, 'He shut him in against the waters' [by protecting the vessel against the violence of the storm *(Mizrachi)*] *(Rashi).*

Rashi continues that wherever בְּעַד occurs in Scripture it means כְּנֶגֶד in front of; on behalf of — as *Psalms* 3:4: מָגֵן בַּעֲדִי, *'a shield in front of me'* — i.e. *in my behalf; I Sam.* 12:19: *pray* בְּעַד, *on behalf of,* your servant.

Midrash HaGadol explains that God protected Noah from the wild beasts of the ark, *'shutting',* as it were, their mouths, as in *Daniel* 6:23.

According to *Ibn Ezra* and *Radak* the object is the Ark. God, in His compassion [indicated by the use here of *'HASHEM'*] sealed the ark so there was not a single split, and ensured that every crevice was waterlight so that not a single leak developed during forty days of the most violent storms; otherwise they would all have perished.

Though Noah had obeyed every command, the rescue was not guaranteed. It was God in His merciful manifestation of HASHEM, who protected him in order to preserve life *(Hirsch).*

B'chor Shor explains the stich more literally: Noah had left the door of the ark open allowing all the creatures to enter. He was afraid to close the door for fear that perhaps some species had not yet come. But once they had all entered, God closed the door for him.

Abarbanel views it figuratively: The rains came down in such force that they could no longer leave the ark; it was as if HASHEM Himself had closed them in ...

1. On that day God caused the whole earth to shake; the sun darkened, the fountains raged, lightning flashed, and thunder roared as never before. But the sons of man remained obstinate.

When the Flood began to rage, seven hundred thousand men surrounded the ark and begged Noah to let them in.

'Have you not all rebelled against God and said He does not exist?' Noah said to them. 'That is why God is now destroying you just as I have been warning you for the past 120 years, and you would not heed the call. Yet now you desire to be spared?'

'We will repent now!' they cried. 'Only open the door of your ark for us.'

'Now that you are in trouble, you finally agree to repent? Why did you not repent these last 120 years which were extended to you just for that very purpose? Now that you are beset with problems you finally come. But it is too late; God will not now hearken to you. You are doomed, and your pleas are to no avail.'

The people tried to forcibly enter the ark to escape the rains but the wild animals surrounding the ark drove them away, to meet their death in the Flood ... *(Sefer HaYashar).*

יוֹם עַל־הָאָרֶץ וַיִּרְבּוּ הַמַּיִם וַיִּשְׂאוּ אֶת־
יח הַתֵּבָה וַתָּרָם מֵעַל הָאָרֶץ: וַיִּגְבְּרוּ הַמַּיִם
וַיִּרְבּוּ מְאֹד עַל־הָאָרֶץ וַתֵּלֶךְ הַתֵּבָה עַל־
יט פְּנֵי הַמָּיִם: וְהַמַּיִם גָּבְרוּ מְאֹד מְאֹד עַל־
הָאָרֶץ וַיְכֻסּוּ כָּל־הֶהָרִים הַגְּבֹהִים אֲשֶׁר־
כ תַּחַת כָּל־הַשָּׁמָיִם: חֲמֵשׁ עֶשְׂרֵה אַמָּה
מִלְמַעְלָה גָּבְרוּ הַמָּיִם וַיְכֻסּוּ הֶהָרִים:

17. The Ravages of the Flood[1]

וַיְהִי הַמַּבּוּל אַרְבָּעִים יוֹם עַל הָאָרֶץ — *When the Flood was on the earth forty days.*

The translation *'when'* for lit. *'and'* follows *Ibn Ezra.* He notes that this fact was already stated in *v.* 12, and therefore this verse is not repetitious nor superfluous; it is to be understood as circumstantial: *'when'* — i.e, only after forty days of rainfall lay on the ground was the ark lifted up, but until then it remained stationary.

'Nights' are here implied in the word *'days'*: the incessant, heavy rains obscured all differences between night and day *(Lekach Tov).*

וַיִּרְבּוּ הַמַּיִם וַיִּשְׂאוּ אֶת הַתֵּבָה — [*And*] *the waters increased and raised the ark so that* [lit. *'and'*] *it was lifted above* [lit. *'from upon'*] *the earth.*

Rashi explains why the ark did not lift off the ground until the fortieth day, by which time, according to his calculation [in *v.* 7] the water must have reached 11 cubits. He makes the following comment *(Mizrachi):* 'The ark was sunk in eleven cubits of water like a heavily laden ship, partially sunk in the water. The verses that follow prove this' *(Rashi)* [cf. 8:4].

18. וַיִּגְבְּרוּ הַמַּיִם וַיִּרְבּוּ מְאֹד — [*And*] *the waters prevailed and increased greatly.*

— By themselves *(Rashi)* i.e. from the deep; because the rainfall had already ceased after forty days *(Gur Aryeh).*

The waters prevailed — i.e. beyond the eleven cubits of water which lifted the ark, as will be explained later *(Lekach Tov).*

According to *Ramban* the terms וַיִּגְבְּרוּ in this verse and גָּבְרוּ in the next are related to גבר, *strength,* which is the Hebrew expression for

1. In his prefatory remarks to these verses, *Hoffmann* notes that: There is an abundance of repetition in this narrative in order to give vivid expression to the great deluge. Therefore, entire verses are devoted to illustrate each aspect of the miracle.

Accordingly, *v.* 17 tells of the abundance of water and the lifting of the ark; *v.* 18: the floating of the ark; *v.* 19: the total submergence of the mountains; *v.* 20: the 15 cubit height of the water over the mountains.

Similarly, when describing the destruction of the earth, an entire verse is devoted to each point; *v.* 21 declares that all earthlings died; *v.* 22: that this death was the fate only of those creatures who live on land; *v.* 23: in the almost total calamity only Noah and those who were with him were saved.

[17] *When the Flood was on the earth forty days, the*
waters increased and raised the ark so that it was
lifted above the earth. [18] *The waters prevailed and in-*
creased greatly upon the earth, and the ark drifted
upon surface of the waters. [19] *The waters prevailed*
very much upon the earth, all the high mountains
which are under the heavens were covered. [20] *Fifteen*
cubits upward did the waters prevail, and the moun-

great abundance. He suggests that the meaning here is that the rains came in a gushing, powerful downpour, uprooting trees and toppling buildings.

Rav Saadiah Gaon renders: *'And as the waters prevailed ...'*

וַתֵּלֶךְ הַתֵּבָה עַל פְּנֵי הַמָּיִם — *And the ark drifted* [lit. *'went'*] *upon the surface of the waters.*

Verse 17 tells us that the waters lifted it above the water; here we are told that when the waters became more violent they tossed it to and fro [i.e. aimlessly about] *(Radak).*

19. וְהַמַּיִם גָּבְרוּ מְאֹד מְאֹד — [*And*] *the waters prevailed very much* [lit. *'much, much'*]

— The word 'much' is repeated to emphasize that they prevailed to the greatest extent possible, until nothing could exceed it *(Ibn Ezra).*

The verses describe the pathos and increasing intensity of the Deluge, from *'the waters increased'* [*v.* 17] to *'increased greatly'* [*v.* 18], to *'prevailed greatly'* in this verse, — *'prevail'* being a stronger term than *'increased'*. The second מְאֹד, *much*, is added to stress even further that the water had risen so high that it covered even the high mountains *(Radak).*

20. חֲמֵשׁ עֶשְׂרֵה אַמָּה מִלְמַעְלָה — *Fifteen cubits upward* [lit. *'from above'*].

Above the summits of all the mountains after the waters reached the tops of the mountains *(Rashi).*

I.e., the fifteen cubits are not above the ground but above the level reached previously [*v.* 19] when *'all the high mountains were covered'*, this itself being a level of several thousand cubits above the ground level *(Mizrachi).*

Rav Yehudah said: The waters were fifteen cubits over the mountains and fifteen cubits over the plains [thus becoming a fifteen cubit covering miraculously following the contours of the earth]. Rav Nechemiah said: Fifteen cubits over the mountains, but over the plains any height [i.e. the waters had only one level and therefore one cannot gauge how high it was above the individual plains] *(Midrash).*

[Cf. *Yoma* 76a: '... All the fountains of the great deep came up first until the water was even with the mountains, then the water rose fifteen more cubits!]

[Thus, the ark, which was submerged in the water to a depth of 11 cubits *(Rashi v.* 17), easily cleared even the highest mountain peaks with a margin of four cubits.]

N'tziv holds that Mount Ararat was the world's highest mountain at the time of the Flood, and the

ז
כא־כג

כא וַיִּגְוַע כָּל־בָּשָׂר | הָרֹמֵשׂ עַל־הָאָרֶץ בָּעוֹף
וּבַבְּהֵמָה וּבַחַיָּה וּבְכָל־הַשֶּׁרֶץ הַשֹּׁרֵץ
כב עַל־הָאָרֶץ וְכֹל הָאָדָם׃ כֹּל אֲשֶׁר נִשְׁמַת־
רוּחַ חַיִּים בְּאַפָּיו מִכֹּל אֲשֶׁר בֶּחָרָבָה
כג מֵתוּ׃ וַיִּמַח אֶת־כָּל־הַיְקוּם אֲשֶׁר | עַל־פְּנֵי
הָאֲדָמָה מֵאָדָם עַד־בְּהֵמָה עַד־רֶמֶשׂ

waters rose to 15 cubits above Ararat. The numerous mountains that are now far higher than Ararat came into being as a result of the upheavals of the Flood.

21. וַיִּגְוַע כָּל בָּשָׂר — *And all flesh expired* — i.e. *had* perished during the first forty days of the Flood. They obviously did not survive until the waters reached a level of fifteen cubits above the highest mountain peaks! *(Ibn Ezra/Or Yohel).*

Even those who climbed to the highest mountain peaks now found nowhere else to flee and they perished *(B'chor Shor; Rosh).*

[Thus, God's intention expressed to Noah in 6:17 was fulfilled.]

[For explanation of וַיִּגְוַע in this context meaning *'expired' — 'fainted'*, rather than 'died', see *comm.* of *Ramban* and *Hirsch* cited at end of 6:17.

According to *Radak*, however, וַיִּגְוַע connotes quick death, such as by drowning.

But as the consensus of commentators indicates, וַיִּגְוַע here is to be understood as signifying the transitional moment between life and death, while מֵתוּ, died, in the next verse represents death itself.]

הָרֹמֵשׂ עַל הָאָרֶץ — *That moves upon the earth* — A general statement, followed by a detailed enumeration of the species. רֹמֵשׂ, *that moved,* is an all-encompassing term embracing *all moving creatures (Ibn Ezra);* but in many contexts it is specifically applied to insect-life [see *comm.* to 1:24 s.v. רֶמֶשׂ] *(Karnei Or).*

וְכֹל הָאָדָם — *And all mankind* [lit. *'and every man'*] — [except for those in the ark, and Og; see *v.* 23.]

The verse lists the creatures in the order in which they were overcome by the Flood: First the birds and finally man *(Ha'amek Davar).*

The birds were overcome first, because they were too frail to withstand the downpour — then the domesticated animals; then the wild beasts many of whom dwelled in caves high in the mountains which protected them somewhat longer from both the lower and upper waters: they perished when the waters covered the mountain peaks; man probably tried every method known to him to survive: he climbed the highest trees atop the highest mountains; tried building rafts, etc. There were individuals who survived longer than others. But by the time the waters reached a level of fifteen cubits above the mountain peaks, combined with the strength and ravages described in these verses even man perished *(Malbim).*

Me'am Loez suggests that man perished last to give him that one last opportunity to repent.

22. נִשְׁמַת רוּחַ חַיִּים — *The breath of the spirit of life* — A term embracing

VII 21-23 tains were covered. 21 *And all flesh that moves upon*
the earth expired — among the birds, the cattle, the
beasts, and all the things that creeps upon the earth,
and all mankind. 22 *All in whose nostrils was the*
breath of the spirit of life, whatever was on dry land,
died. 23 *And He blotted out all existence on earth —*
from man to animal to creeping things and to the bird

every living creature that breathes *(Mizrachi; Gur Aryeh).*

[The above follows *Mizrachi*'s and *Gur Aryeh*'s interpretation of *Rashi.* They explain that נְשָׁמָה is a term that applies only to man as in 2:7 (see *Ibn Ezra* below). How, then, can Scripture use this term in a context clearly referring to animals? They therefore suggest that the proper reading in *Rashi* is not נְשָׁמָה שֶׁל רוּחַ חַיִּים, 'soul' of the spirit of life, but נְשִׁימָה rendering: נְשִׁימָה שֶׁל רוּחַ חַיִּים, the *breath* of the spirit of life — any living creature that breathes.]

Ibn Ezra, however, comments that the phrase in this verse probably refers only to man because we never find נְשָׁמָה referring to anything but נִשְׁמַת אָדָם, *the soul of man.*

Radak synthesizes both opinions and comments: Both nouns are in the construct form as if it said: 'the breath of life' and 'the spirit of life', the former referring to man, the latter to the other living creatures; or as if it read: *'whatever had* נְשִׁימַת רוּחַ*, the breath of spirit'* — i.e. locomotion *(Sefer Shorashim).*

מִכֹּל אֲשֶׁר בֶּחָרָבָה מֵתוּ — *Whatever* [lit. *'of all'*] *was on dry land died.* — This excludes the fish in the sea *(Sanhedrin* 108a; *Rashi).*

Maharsha, citing *Zevachim* 113b states that the scalding heat of the flood-waters did not affect the fish because the ravages of the Flood were directed to dry land. The fish did not participate in man's sins, and they were spared.

This is also implied by *v.* 17: *'The Flood was on the earth'* — not on the sea *(R' Bachya).*

Ramban suggests that it is conceivable that the flood-waters mingled with the seas and heated only the upper waters while the fish descended to the depths and thereby survived ... For none of the fish were brought into the ark to keep their seed alive, and no mention is made of fish in the covenant in 9:9-10.

Hirsch comments that this may explain why the geological diluvial strata contain mainly the remains of land, rather than marine animals. If it is true that these strata are products of the Flood, then, as this verse indicates, only land animals were affected.

According to *Malbim,* חָרָבָה specifically denotes moist places. Our phrase embraces those amphibians who dwell in moist areas — they, too, perished.

23. וַיִּמַח אֶת כָּל הַיְקוּם — *And He blotted out all existence.* [As He decreed in *v.* 4.]

After having stated in the previous verse that וַיִּגְוַע, they *expired,* it now adds that the Flood *blotted out,* i.e. dissolved, their bodies, and this is the meaning of the verb in *Numbers* 5:23: 'and he shall *blot them out* in the waters of bitterness' (Ramban).

ז וְעַד־עוֹף הַשָּׁמַיִם וַיִּמָּחוּ מִן־הָאָרֶץ
כד וַיִּשָּׁאֶר אַךְ־נֹחַ וַאֲשֶׁר אִתּוֹ בַּתֵּבָה: כד וַיִּגְבְּרוּ
הַמַּיִם עַל־הָאָרֶץ חֲמִשִּׁים וּמְאַת יוֹם:

Malbim points out that the upheaval of those months of enormous heat and turmoil caused a great shifting and turning of geological strata and a deep burial of animal remains. Thus, the attempt to date the earth and fossils is futile.

[The translation of וַיִּמַח as a verb transitive, *'and He blotted out'*, rather than the passive, *'and they were blotted out'*, follows *Rashi.*]

וַיִּמָּחוּ מִן הָאָרֶץ — *And they were blotted out from the earth.*

— The repetition of the verb emphasizes their total obliteration. Their very names were blotted out from the world; they left no seed *(Ibn Ezra).*

Ramban adds that the repetition might be to indicate that not even an egg of fowl or insect was left on a tree or under the earth: *everything* was blotted out.

— Not a trace of them was left, not even a building *(Radak),* nor towers, nor tools — anything that ever existed was wiped off the face of the earth leaving no trace whatsoever *(Abarbanel).*

The *Talmud* [*Sanhedrin* 108a] derives from the repetition that their destruction was from both worlds: 'The generation of the Flood has no portion in the World to Come,' as it is written: *'And He blotted out all existence . . . which was upon the ground . . . and they were blotted out from the earth.' And He blotted out all existence* — from this world: *'and they were blotted out from the* (אָרֶץ) — from the World to Come.

[*Torah Temimah* suggests that the reason the latter part of the verse is interpreted as referring to the World to Come is because אָרֶץ, *earth,* is elsewhere also interpreted as referring to the World to Come, as in *Sanhedrin* 90a: All Israel has a share in the World to Come, as it is written *(Isaiah* 60:21): *'Your people are all righteous; they shall inherit the land'* (אָרֶץ) ...']

וַיִּשָּׁאֶר אַךְ נֹחַ — *Only Noah survived.*

This follows *Rashi*'s literal interpretation. Aggadically, *Rashi* cites the *Midrash* that אַךְ implies an exclusion [implying that even Noah was not unaffected *(Mizrachi)* — rendering *'and Noah was left* אַךְ, *diminished'*: Noah was groaning and spitting blood because of his exertions in caring for the cattle and beasts. Others say that he delayed in bringing food to a lion and it bit him. Regarding him it is said [*Prov.* 11:31]: הֵן צַדִּיק בָּאָרֶץ יְשֻׁלָּם *'Behold even the righteous is paid* [*for his sins*] *in this world.'*

[There is a similar *Midrash Tanchuma:* because Noah was tardy in feeding him, the lion struck him with a blow which left him with a limp. He was therefore rendered unfit to sacrifice (because one with a physical defect may not perform the sacrificial service. See *Lev.* 21:17) and his son Shem sacrificed instead of him.]

Me'am Loez cites the above and comments that Noah was punished this way because feeding the animals was to him a divine command [6:21] and he should have been more scrupulous in carrying out his duty to provide for them punctually.

The verse thus tells us that God's promise was now fulfilled. One man, Noah was spared from God's Decree to *'blot out . . . from upon the ground from man to beast* [6:7]

VII *of the heavens; and they were blotted out from the*
24 *earth. Only Noah survived, and those with him in*
the ark. [24] *And the waters prevailed on the earth a*
hundred and fifty days,

— and, for his sake וַאֲשֶׁר אִתּוֹ, his family and representatives of all species. But even these were spared only בַּתֵּבָה, *in the ark* which alone was exempt from the Decree *(Malbim).*

Og, however, did survive the Flood *(Niddah* 61a; cf. *comm.* to *v.* 21).

Pirkei d'Rabbi Eliezer relates that Og King of Bashan, saved himself by sitting on the ark. He begged Noah to let him stay, vowing to become his servant forever. Noah bored an aperture in the ark through which he put out food daily, and Og thereby survived, as it is written [*Deut.* 3:11]: *'For only Og, king of Bashan, remained of the remnants of the giants.'*

It is quoted in the name of Rav Yehudah HaChasid that the Scriptural allusion to Og's survival is found in the words אַךְ נֹחַ, *only Noah,* the numerical value of which (79) equals עוֹג, *Og.*

24. וַיִּגְבְּרוּ ... חֲמִשִּׁים וּמְאַת יוֹם — *And the waters prevailed . . . a hundred and fifty days.*[1]

It continued to rain intermittently during this period, the proof for this being that 8:2 distinctly states וַיִּכָּלֵא הַגֶּשֶׁם, *and the rain was restrained (Ibn Ezra)* [implying that it *had* rained, at least intermittently, until that time, when it finally stopped *(Tzafnas Pane'ach).*]

[The commentators differ as to the exact chronology implied by this verse. The reckoning depends upon these factors:

(a) Whether or not the 150 days included the original 40 days;

(b) whether, as *Rashi* explains in verse 12, the months alternated: one 'full' consisting of 30 days, and the next 'defective' consisting of 29 days; or

(c) as *Radak,* all months in those times were counted 'full', each consisting of 30 days.

[The various chronological views will be cited in the commentary to 8:3-5 while for simplicity we cite the view of *Seder Olam* that this 150 day period ended on the first of Sivan.]

Additionally, the commentators differ on whether וַיִּגְבְּרוּ, *prevailed,* implies that:

(a) The water increased in intensity throughout this period *(Ibn Ezra; Chizkuni; Sforno).*

(b) That they maintained their force throughout this period but gradually subsided. By the one hundred and fiftieth day they still had not subsided the fifteen cubits to mountain top-level and hence they are described as *'prevailing' (Akeidas Yitzchak).*

(c) That the waters reached their highest point on the fortieth day, maintaining that level for the balance of the 150 days

1. The storm prevailed and all the living creatures in the ark were terrified. The lions roared, the oxen lowed, and the wolves howled ... and Noah and his children cried and wept, thinking that death was at hand.

Noah prayed to God and said: 'HASHEM, help us, for we have no strength to bear this evil that has encompassed us, for the waves of the waters have surrounded us, mischievous torrents have terrified us, the snares of death have come before us; answer us, HASHEM, answer us, light up Your countenance toward us and be gracious to us. Redeem and deliver us.'

God listened to his voice, *'and God remembered Noah . . .' (Pirkei d'Rabbi Eliezer; Zohar).*

ח
א

א וַיִּזְכֹּר אֱלֹהִים אֶת־נֹחַ וְאֵת כָּל־הַחַיָּה
וְאֶת־כָּל־הַבְּהֵמָה אֲשֶׁר אִתּוֹ בַּתֵּבָה
וַיַּעֲבֵר אֱלֹהִים רוּחַ עַל־הָאָרֶץ וַיָּשֹׁכּוּ

after which they began to decline *(Rav Saadiah Gaon; B'chor Shor).*

(d) The waters were gradually receding during these 150 days but the verse is written from the perspective of Noah, who saw only a mass of water and had no way of gauging its relative level because all the mountain tops were submerged *(Malbim).*

[According to others however, Noah did not even see the waters; he was totally enclosed within the ark, and did not open its window until later [8:6] *(Radak; Karnei Or).*]

Rav Saadiah Gaon interprets this verse as circumstantial to the following verse [which, it must be remembered does *not* begin a new chapter according to the Massorah], and renders: *'when the waters prevailed upon the earth for a hundred and fifty days, then God remembered Noah . . .'*

1. The waters recede

וַיִּזְכֹּר אֱלֹהִים — [*And*] *God remembered* — the covenant he had made to save Noah. His family need not be mentioned because Noah was its head *(Ibn Ezra).*

[Whether the events described in the following verses happened after the initial forty days or the 150 days depends upon the various chronological views set forth in *v.* 4.]

Noting the use here of *'Elohim', Rashi* comments: 'This Name denotes Him in His Attribute of Justice, which is transformed into the Attribute of Mercy through the prayers of the righteous; conversely, the evil deeds of the wicked transform the Attribute of Mercy into the Attribute of Justice, as in 6:5: *And* HASHEM [usually indicative of God's mercy] *saw that the wickedness of man was great;* and 6:7: *And* HASHEM *said, I will blot out,* etc.[1]

According to *Hirsch* the name of Judgment is used because God found Noah to be deserving of rescue entirely apart from His concern for the future of mankind.

[Perceiving that there is no forgetfulness before God, the *Midrash* assumes that *'remembered'* implies that He took cognizance of some virtuous act]:

"What did He *'remember'* in his [Noah's] favor? — That he provided for the animals in his care for the

1. [*Rashi* apparently notes that it is unusual for a verse speaking of God's compassionate 'remembering' of Noah to employ the name of God which designates Him in His strict Attribute of Justice. 'HASHEM', which designates Him as a *Merciful* God would seem more appropriate in this context. Obviously, there is a lesson to be learned.

Rashi explains it by basing himself upon a *Midrash,* part of which is cited in a *footnote* to 6:7: 'Woe to the wicked who turn the Attribute of Mercy into the Attribute of Justice ...'

The *Midrash* continues: 'Happy are the righteous who turn the Attribute of Justice into the Attribute of Mercy. Wherever *Elohim* is used, it connotes the Attribute of Justice ... yet it is written: *And Elohim ['God'] remembered Noah; And Elohim remembered Rachel* (30:22); *And Elohim heard their groaning (Exodus* 2:24).

Thus, *Rashi* concludes, it is the prayer of the righteous that transforms Justice into Mercy, and while the wrath of His fury was obliterating Creation, He nevertheless displayed Mercy to Noah and to those with him in the ark.]

VIII 1 ¹ *God remembered Noah and all the beasts and all the cattle that were with him in the ark, and God caused a spirit to pass over the earth, and the waters*

entire twelve months in the ark."

Rashi asks: 'What [virtuous act] did He remember *regarding the cattle?* — That they had not previously perverted their way [see *comm.* to 6:12,20] and that they had refrained from mating in the ark.' [Cf. *v.* 17.]

According to *Ramban,* God took cognizance of Noah's virtues as a perfectly righteous man, and of His covenant to save him. Scripture mentions only Noah, not his family, because they were all saved in his merit. *Ramban* maintains, however, that *'remembering',* meaning taking cognizance of a virtue, cannot apply to animals 'for among living creatures there is no merit or guilt, save in man alone.' He accordingly explains that 'remembering', concerning the animals refers to His plan that the world should continue with the same species as before. Thus He now saw fit to bring them forth so they do not perish in the ark.

Radak emphasizes that there is no forgetfulness with God, so the term *'remembering'* in its literal sense cannot apply to Him. Rather, the Torah employs human speech. Compare such expressions as *'I will remember for them the covenant of their ancestors'* [*Lev.* 26:45]; *'I will remember My covenant with Jacob'* [*ibid.* 42]. The meaning here is that He perceived that they had already suffered sufficiently in the ark, and that from then on the waters should decline.

In this vein, *Ibn Ezra* comments: Heaven forbid that there be even a semblance of forgetfulness before even the least of the Ministering Angels! How much less before the Creator Himself! Rather, when one observes the manifestation of God's benevolence upon earth, Scripture describes it as if He 'remembered' ...

וְאֵת כָּל־הַחַיָּה וְאֶת־כָּל־הַבְּהֵמָה — *And all the beasts and all the cattle* — general terms including all wild and domesticated animals respectively *(Ibn Ezra);* they are specifically included with man to show that they all stand equally under the general Divine Providence *(R' Bachya).*

וַיַּעֲבֵר אֱלֹהִים רוּחַ — *And God caused a spirit to pass.*

[Just as in *v.* 1:2, here, too, the commentators perceive different meanings in רוּחַ which is variously translated as *'spirit', 'wind',* or *'breath'.*]

Our translation follows *Rashi,* who is consistent with his interpretation of 1:2, and comments: 'It was a spirit of comfort and appeasement that passed before Him.'

I.e. *Rashi* does not translate *'wind'* because wind has the effect of stirring up the water, not assuaging it [cf. *Psalms* 147:18: *'He causes* His wind *to blow and the waters flow'!*] It was rather His *compassion* that calmed the turbulent water *(Mizrachi).*

Sifsei Chachamim notes that had 'wind' been meant, the verse should have stated *'upon the waters';* for how could wind pass over the *'earth'* which was completely submerged in water! Therefore *Rashi* translates *'spirit of comfort'* which He caused to pass before Him for the sake of the earth-bound creatures.

Thus *Rashi* comments: עַל הָאָרֶץ, *upon the earth* — i.e. concerning matters of the earth.

[Many other commentators seem to imply that it was a wind, but it is difficult from the context of their interpretations to be absolutely certain because the word רוּחַ is ambiguous, and can be translated as either *'wind'* or *'spirit'.*]

Only *Ramban* makes it absolute-

ח ב הַמָּיִם: וַיִּסָּכְרוּ מַעְיְנֹת תְּהוֹם וַאֲרֻבֹּת
ב־ד ג הַשָּׁמָיִם וַיִּכָּלֵא הַגֶּשֶׁם מִן־הַשָּׁמָיִם: וַיָּשֻׁבוּ
הַמַּיִם מֵעַל הָאָרֶץ הָלוֹךְ וָשׁוֹב וַיַּחְסְרוּ
ד הַמַּיִם מִקְצֵה חֲמִשִּׁים וּמְאַת יוֹם: וַתָּנַח
הַתֵּבָה בַּחֹדֶשׁ הַשְּׁבִיעִי בְּשִׁבְעָה־עָשָׂר

ly clear that he interprets 'wind':

'A great and powerful wind came forth from the innards of the earth upon the surface of the deep ad hovered over the waters' *(Ramban)*.

Onkelos, too, seemingly renders רוּחַ as wind:

'And God sent forth רוּחָא, a wind, upon the earth, and the waters rested.'

עַל הָאָרֶץ — *Over the earth*, i.e. over the waters which covered the earth *(Radak)*.

וַיָּשֹׁכּוּ הַמָּיִם — *And the waters subsided*, i.e. they calmed from their fury, as the verb is used in *Esther* 2:1: כְּשֹׁךְ חֲמַת הַמֶּלֶךְ, *when the wrath of the king subsided (Rashi)*.

The word suggests the opposite of boiling, for, as the Sages said, the Flood-waters seethed and bubbled *(Hirsch)*.

That very same רוּחַ [wind or spirit] which hovered [during Creation, 1:2], went forth upon the waters during the Flood and returned the waters to their original [chaotic] state. Then He sent forth this same רוּחַ to calm the waters *(Da'as Zekeinim)*.

2. וַיִּסָּכְרוּ מַעְיְנֹת תְּהוֹם — [*And*] *the fountains of the deep were closed.*

I.e. after one hundred and fifty days God caused a very strong wind to pass through the heavens and across the earth, sealing the fountains of the deep. The water that flowed from the deep returned to its place before the Flood, and the openings of its fountain were closed as were the windows of heaven ... *(Ramban* to *v.* 4).

Thus, there was the positive action of the wind which caused the water to evaporate, and the closing of fountains of the deep and the windows of heaven. This caused the accumulation of waters to cease from both below and above *(Radak)*.

Rashi notes however, that unlike 7:11 which says that *all* the fountains burst forth, our verse does not say that *all* of them closed because some fountains, such as the hot springs of Tiberias were left open to benefit the world *(Rashi)*. [It must be remembered that the waters of the Flood — even those which flowed into Eretz Yisrael (see 8:11) — were hot. Cf. 6:14; 7:11; *Sanhedrin* 108a.]

וַיִּכָּלֵא הַגֶּשֶׁם מִן־הַשָּׁמָיִם — *And the rain from heaven was restrained.* — They were restrained in the storehouse ofcain *(Ibn Ezra)*; even a little rain did not fall *(Radak)*.

Neither dew nor rain fell until they left the ark, and the air lost its moisture *(Ramban)*.

God did this so that Noah should not grow frightened at seeing new rain and think that a new Flood was coming. God, therefore, withheld all precipitation until He made the

VIII 2-4

subsided. 2 *The fountains of the deep and the win-*
dows of the heavens were closed, and the rain from
heaven was restrained. 3 *The waters then receded*
continuously from upon the earth, and the waters
diminished at the end of a hundred and fifty days.
4 *And the ark came to rest in the seventh month, on*

covenant with Noah promising him never again to bring a flood upon the world [9:11] *(Karnei Or).*

3. וַיָּשֻׁבוּ הַמַּיִם מֵעַל הָאָרֶץ הָלוֹךְ וָשׁוֹב — *The waters then* [lit. *'and the waters'*] *receded* [lit. *'returned'*] *continuously from upon the earth* [lit. *'going and returning'.*]

— I.e. *'they returned'* — to their reservoirs beneath the earth *(Ibn Ezra).*

וַיַּחְסְרוּ הַמַּיִם מִקְצֵה חֲמִשִּׁים וּמְאַת יוֹם — *And the waters diminished at the end of a hundred and fifty days.*

I.e. at the end of the 150 days [mentioned in 7:24], which coincided with the first of Sivan, the waters *began to diminish.* The calculation is as follows: On the 27th of Kislev the 40 days of rain [7:17] ended. Since Kislev had 30 days, there were 3 days remaining in Kislev, 29 in Teves, and 118 in Shevat, Adar, Nissan and Iyar together [29+30+29+30] for a total of 150 days.

Rashi here comments that the rain ended on 27 Kislev, an apparent contradiction to his commentary on 7:12 where he says that the rain ended on 28 Kislev. *Daas Zekenim* there notes the discrepancy and offers an alternate interpretation of the verses. (See *Daas Zekenim* on 7:12). *Sifsei Chachomim* resolves *Rashi:* The rain began on the morning of 17 Marcheshvan. Since it rained for 40 consecutive 24 hour periods, the rain stopped on the morning of 28 Kislev. However, the last *full* day of rain was 27 Kislev. Therefore in listing the beginning of the 150 day period after which the water subsided, *Rashi* here begins the count from 28 Kislev because the water remained at its full height until that morning from which point the 150 days began.

Rashi explains that וַיַּחְסְרוּ means that the waters *began to diminish* after the 150 days. Otherwise, *they diminished* would seem to imply a *fait accompli* indicating that the waters were all gone by then, which is not so, because they *continued* to recede until the following 27th of Marcheshvan when the earth was finally completely dry.

According to *Ramban* [see *v.* 4] these 150 days *include* the original 40 days, and end on the 17th of Nissan.

4. וַתָּנַח הַתֵּבָה בַּחֹדֶשׁ הַשְּׁבִיעִי — *And the ark came to rest in the seventh month.* I.e. Sivan, which is the seventh month from Kislev when the rains ceased *(Rashi).*

According to *Ramban* [see below] this verse is to be read in continuity with the previous verse. That is, at the end of the 150 days — on the 17th day of Nissan, the seventh month from Tishrei, the waters decreased so much that the ark came to rest on the mountains of Ararat.

בְּשִׁבְעָה עָשָׂר יוֹם לַחֹדֶשׁ — *On the seventeenth day of the month.*

According to *Rashi,* this proves that the ark was submerged eleven cubits in the water [cf. 7:17]: The next verse tells us that the tops of the mountains appeared on *the first day of the tenth month,* which is Av, the tenth month from Marcheshvan when the rains began. Hence from the first day of Sivan [previous verse] until the first of Av which is a period of sixty days, the fifteen cubits of water covering the

ח ה יוֹם לַחֹדֶשׁ עַל הָרֵי אֲרָרָט: וְהַמַּיִם הָיוּ
ה הָלוֹךְ וְחָסוֹר עַד הַחֹדֶשׁ הָעֲשִׂירִי

mountains [7:20] receded at a rate of 1 cubit every four days [¼ cubit per day; (15÷60=.25).] Therefore, by the sixteenth of the month, the water had receded only four cubits [16x.25=4] and the ark rested in eleven cubits of water [15-4=11.]

Thus, although the waters were continually receding since the end of the 150 days, according to *Rashi* and *Seder Olam,* this could not have been known to Noah. The decrease became apparent to him only through the resting of the ark which made him aware that the waters must have diminished to a considerable extent *(Y'mos Olam).*

[Thus verses 3 and 4 are to be read together: it became apparent that *the waters were diminishing after a hundred and fifty days* — because, seventeen days later, *the ark came to rest* ...]

⚭§ The chronology according to Ramban

Ramban disagrees with this chronology. He excuses himself for departing from the interpretation of *Rashi* which is based upon the *Midrash.* 'However, because elsewhere *Rashi* carefully analyzes Midrashic interpretations and also labors to explain the plain meaning of the verses, he permitted us to do the same for there are seventy facets to the Torah.'

In a lengthy dissertation *Ramban* first suggests that it is improbable that Scripture should employ different starting points in calculating the *second month,* the *seventh month* and the *tenth month,* as *Rashi* suggests. Secondly, he disagrees with *Rashi*'s proof concerning the depth of the submergence of the ark [*v.* 3] because *Rashi* calculates an equal decrease of water to each day — a quarter of a cubit per day — while *Ramban* holds that it is a known fact that a great river tends to recede at an increasing rate. *Ramban* also holds that, structured as it was, the ark would have sunk had it been submerged 11 cubits which is more than a third of its [30 cubit] height.

He suggests that the most plausible interpretation assumes that all months originate from Tishrei, the first month of the calendar, as follows:

The 150 days [7:24 and 8:3] are from the 17th of the second month, Marcheshvan. They *include* the 40 days of rain [7:17] and end on the seventeenth of the seventh month, Nissan [assuming, as he apparently does, that all the months are counted 'full', that is, 5 months of 30 days each = 150 days.]

On Nissan 17 the ark rested on the mountains of Ararat because on that day a powerful wind caused a sudden fall in the waters, this being the meaning of verses 1-3 which lead up to the immediate landing of the ark in *v.* 4. [This is radically unlike *Rashi* who holds that it took 17 days of gradual recession before the ark rested.]

Seventy-three days later, on the first day of Tammuz, the tenth month [*v.* 5], [according to *Rashi,* counting from Marcheshvan the tenth month was Av — 43 days later] the peaks of the mountains were seen.

At the end of 40 additonal days, the tenth of Av [according to *Rashi,* the same additional forty days (counting from Av) comes to the tenth of *Elul;* while according to *Seder Olam* (in its only divergence from *Rashi)* it is the tenth of Tammuz!], Noah opened the window of the ark [and sent forth the raven.]

Three weeks later [Elul 1; and according to *Rashi,* Tishrei 1] the dove left him permanently.

Thirty days after dispatching the dove [*v.* 13], on the first of Tishrei, he removed the covering of the ark. [According to *Rashi,* he removed the cover on the same day he sent out the dove, 1 Tishrei. Thus, *Rashi* and *Ramban* both agree that the cover was removed on 1 *Tishrei.*]

[*Ramban*'s chronology is virtually identical with *Targum Yonasan,* and is followed by *R' Bachya, Tur* and later *Malbim.*]

עַל הָרֵי אֲרָרָט — *Upon the mountains of Ararat.*

According to the *Midrash, Onkelos* and *Rav Saadiah Gaon* this

VIII *the seventeenth day of the month upon the moun-*
5 *tains of Ararat.* [5] *The waters were continuously*
diminishing until the tenth month. In the tenth

refers to the mountain range of Cordeyne.

Targum Yonasan paraphrases:

'Upon the mountains of Cordeyne. The name of one mountain is Cordania, and the name of the other mountain is Irmenia. The city of Armenia was built there in the land of the east.'[1]

[Ararat was the name of a country to the north of Assyria. When the Armenians invaded that area they named the area Armenia. Ararat is mentioned in *II Kings* 19:37 and *Isaiah* as the haven to which the sons of Sennacherib escaped after murdering their father. It is also mentioned in *Jeremiah* 51:27 in the prophecy against Babylon.]

Radak comments that these were probably the *'high mountains'* referred to in 7:19, or that the ark happened to be in that vicinity. In any event, they were among the highest mountains. Possibly, there were higher mountains than these, but there were definitely lower ones, because they did not all become visible until the tenth month.

As *Ramban* explains: The mountains of Ararat, which are among the highest mountains under the heavens had fifteen cubits of water above their summit. But this is difficult because it is known that there are mountains which are much higher than they [therefore there were fifteen cubits of water above these high mountains and hence much more above Ararat! Accordingly, the waters over Ararat must have receded more than fifteen cubits when the ark rested there.] — Perhaps the solution is that the decrease of the waters by the seventeenth of the seventh month was, indeed, more than fifteen cubits, and before the mount of Ararat became visible, the higher mountains were first exposed, but it just happened that the ark was over Ararat at that time and it rested over the tops of those mountains.

N'tziv, concerned with the same question, offers a different explanation. As noted in 7:19, he explains that Ararat was the highest mountain range prior to the Flood. Whatever mountains are now higher resulted from changes in the earth's contours during the Flood, and although their peaks protruded through the water's surface earlier, Scripture is concerned only with Ararat, over which the Ark was floating at the time.

5. עַד חֹדֶשׁ הָעֲשִׂירִי — *Until the tenth month.*

The verse does not mean that the waters diminished *entirely* by the tenth month, for in fact they did not recede until the earth was visible. The intent of the verse is that after the ark landed, the waters continued to abate until, on the tenth

1. It is interesting to note that Josephus [*Antiquities I*:3:5] mentions that Noah's Ark still existed in his time: 'Its remains are shown there by the inhabitants to this day.'

The 12th century Jewish traveler, Benjamin of Tudela [*The Itinerary of Benjamin of Tudela* p.52] notes that:

... 'It is two days to Geziret Ibn Omar which is surrounded by the Tigris at the foot of the mountains of Ararat.

'It is a distance of four miles to the place where Noah's ark rested, but Omar ben al Khataab took the ark from the two mountains and made it into a mosque for the Mohammedans. Near the ark is the Synagogue of Ezra to this day, and on the Ninth of Av, Jews assemble there from the city to pray ...'

Sefer Yuchasin also records that for many generations people would come to the spot where the ark rested to view its remains, and the sick would come there to be healed.

ח
ו־ז

בָּעֲשִׂירִי בְּאֶחָד לַחֹדֶשׁ נִרְאוּ רָאשֵׁי
ו הֶהָרִים: וַיְהִי מִקֵּץ אַרְבָּעִים יוֹם וַיִּפְתַּח
ז נֹחַ אֶת־חַלּוֹן הַתֵּבָה אֲשֶׁר עָשָׂה: וַיְשַׁלַּח
אֶת־הָעֹרֵב וַיֵּצֵא יָצוֹא וָשׁוֹב עַד־יְבֹשֶׁת

month, the tops of the mountains were visible. The waters continued receding until the earth became visible *(Radak)*.

This *tenth month* was Av, counting from Marcheshvan, when the rain began *(Rashi)*.

... For a fraction of a month [the 12 or 13 days left in Marcheshvan] count as a whole month *(Seder Olam)*.

Rashi explains that the counting of the tenth month must commence from Marcheshvan, when the rains began. It is impossible to reckon it from Kislev when the rains ended, for if so, it would be Elul — an impossibility, for two months elapsed before the earth dried [40 days until 8:6, and another 21 days for the dispatching of the birds]. If the tenth month is Elul, then the earth would have dried Marcheshvan, yet the Torah calls it the *first month!* [8:13] If, however, the *tenth month* is Av, then the drying occurred in Tishrei, as clearly indicated in 8:13.

Consistent with his chronology, however, *Ramban* reckons this as Tammuz, the *tenth month* from Tishrei, 73 days after the landing of the ark.

נִרְאוּ רָאשֵׁי הֶהָרִים — *The tops of the mountains became visible* [lit. *'were seen'*]

This refers to the mountains of Ararat *(Malbim)*.

[When the ark first touched down upon them 43 days earlier (according to *Rashi)* Ararat was submerged eleven cubits. The waters gradually continued to sink these eleven cubits at the rate of 1 cubit every 4 days, until now the tops of these mountains were finally visible.]

6. וַיְהִי מִקֵּץ אַרְבָּעִים יוֹם — *And it came to pass at the end of forty days.*

The forty days began when the tops of the mountains became visible [i.e. since the first of Av *(v.* 5), making this the tenth of Elul] *(Rashi)*.

According to *Seder Olam* [with whom *Rashi* now differs]: From the time when the waters began to diminish [i.e. from the first of Sivan *v.* 3] making this the tenth of Tammuz [23 days after the ark landed. Accordingly, no dry land was yet visible, as the mountains themselves, according to this view, were not exposed until the first of Av, three weeks later!]

[*Ibn Ezra* agrees with *Rashi* that the *forty days* is to be reckoned from the last-mentioned date: when the mountain tops became visible. But since he calculates from Nissan (see 7:11), this date falls out on the tenth of Shevat.]

Radak [who, until this point closely follows *Rashi*'s chronology] cites *Seder Olam*, but concludes that it appears to him that the forty days are to be reckoned from [the 17th of Sivan] when the ark landed on the mountains of Ararat [= 27th of Tammuz], because until then Noah had no way of knowing that the waters were receding. But when he perceived that the ark had landed on *terra firma* he waited another forty days to allow the waters to recede further and then he sent one of the birds on its exploratory mission.

According to *Ramban* [see *v.* 4] this forty day period ended on the tenth of Av.

אֶת חַלּוֹן הַתֵּבָה אֲשֶׁר עָשָׂה — *The window of the ark which he had made* — for light [צֹהַר, see 6:16]. This was not the door of the ark which

VIII 6-7 *month, on the first of the month, the tops of the*
mountains became visible.
6 *And it came to pass at the end of forty days, that*
Noah opened the window of the ark which he had
made. 7 *He sent out a raven, and it kept going and*

was used for entry and exit *(Rashi).*

Although *Rashi* leaves the interpretation of צֹהַר in 6:16 undecided by citing both views in the *Midrash,* here he does interpret it as being the חַלּוֹן, because, as the *Midrash* here comments: 'this verse supports the view that it [i.e. צֹהַר] was a window' *(Mizrachi).*

Noah knew that the rains had stopped earlier. He waited until sufficient time had elapsed since the ark had landed [see his *comm.* above] before he opened the window because until then he was afraid that waves might suddenly rise up and rush in through the opening *(Radak).*

Malbim suggests, however, that he had opened it regularly for a brief time to watch the progress of the waters; this time he left it open permanently.

This is also the view of *Ramban* who comments that after the cessation of the rains, Noah would open and close the window at will. Seventy-three days [twenty-three, according to *Rashi*] after the ark landed he peered out the window. He saw the peaks of the mountains of Ararat, and again closed the window. Scripture then relates that forty days later he sent forth the raven, because he thought that by that time the towers and trees [which, according to *Ramban,* were not destroyed by the Flood] would be visible and the birds would find in them a place to nest, so he opened the window and sent forth the raven.

Ha'amek Davar comments that אֲשֶׁר עָשָׂה *which he had made,* refers to the window [not the ark], which he had intentionally made — on his own initiative — to open and close.

7. Sending forth the raven

וַיְשַׁלַּח אֶת־הָעֹרֵב — *[And] he sent out a* [lit. *'the'*] *raven.*

Since Noah's purpose for sending forth the raven is not explicitly stated as it is in the case of the dove in *v.* 8, the commentators offer differing views:

According to *Pirkei d'Rabbi Eliezer,* 'Noah sent forth the raven to ascertain what was the state of the world.'

Malbim explains that had Noah's intention been *'to see if the waters subsided'* as in the case of the dove, the verse would have said so. Rather, the ancients considered the raven to be a bird which could indicate the future. They would build special cages where the priests would study the motions and flying formations of the ravens which they would interpret as divinations for the future. [See *comm.* to *Eccles.* 10:20 *'For a bird of the skies may carry the sound', ArtScroll ed.* p.82]. Noah therefore set the raven free to learn from its flying habits the state of the world.

According to *Sforno,* however, although not explicitly stated, the reason Noah sent the raven was to

ח הַמַּיִם מֵעַל הָאָרֶץ: וַיְשַׁלַּח אֶת־הַיּוֹנָה
מֵאִתּוֹ לִרְאוֹת הֲקַלּוּ הַמַּיִם מֵעַל פְּנֵי
ט הָאֲדָמָה: וְלֹא־מָצְאָה הַיּוֹנָה מָנוֹחַ לְכַף־

see if the air was dry enough for the raven to endure it.

— Noah reasoned: Ravens feed on carrion of man and beast. If the raven will bring some back he would know that the water had descended enough for the raven to have found some carrion on the ground *(Radak)*.

Why did Noah send a raven which was an unclean bird [see *Lev.* 11:15] and of which there were only two in the ark, thus risking a mishap that would have made an entire species extinct?

In answer, the *Talmud* [*Sanhedrin* 108b] notes that the raven was one of the three creatures who transgressed the prohibition of mating in the ark [see 7:7]: Noah's son Ham, the dog, and the raven.

The raven's mate had thus already been impregnated and was incubating her eggs. Therefore Noah reasoned that it was permitted to dispatch the raven because the survival of the species was assured.

Indeed, *Shaar Bas Rabim* suggests that the raven's incontinence is the very reason Noah banished it [וַיְשַׁלַּח having the connotation of absolute sending forth; see *comm.* next verse]. It also explains why, in the case of the raven, Noah did not stretch forth his hand to bring it back into the ark, as he did for the dove. Noah was angered that the raven, dog, and his son Ham transgressed the prohibition, but he was helpless. He could not banish the other creatures from the ark because they would have drowned; the raven was the only one of the three that could fly and survive outside of the ark for the duration the Flood.

וַיֵּצֵא יָצוֹא וָשׁוֹב — *And it kept going and returning.*

The raven kept returning and circling around the ark and did not carry out its mission because the raven was suspicious that Noah had designs on its mate as we learn in the *Talmud (Rashi)*.[1]

Maharsha explains that the dove had no such suspicions because doves are loyal to their mates. Ravens, however, are not and they would therefore tend to suspect their mates of similar infidelity.

According to *Malbim:* The mission was successful; Noah was indeed able to derive information from the bird's flight formations;

Sforno: The raven's mission was a failure. It returned with nothing in its mouth. It repeatedly returned to its nest in the ark and flew out again to see if it could find a place to rest.

עַד־יְבֹשֶׁת הַמַּיִם מֵעַל הָאָרֶץ — *Until the waters dried from upon the earth.*

I.e. it continually flew to and fro

1. Cf. *Sanhedrin* 108b:

Resh Lakish said: The raven gave Noah a devastating retort: 'Your Master hates me and you hate me. Your Master hates me since He commanded you to save seven pairs of the clean creatures but only one pair of unclean creatures. You hate me because you leave the species of seven and send me when I am one of only two. Should the angel of heat or cold attack me, will not the world be short of one species? Or perhaps you desire my mate!'

'Evil one!' Noah replied. 'Even my wife who is usually permitted to me, has been forbidden me in the ark; how much the more [your mate] which is always forbidden me! [See *comm.* to 6:18.]

According to the parallel *Midrash*, Noah is answering the raven's complaints [homiletically interpreting יָצוֹא וָשׁוֹב, *going out and refuting,* lit. answering] that it was singled out from all the birds to be sent away, by saying:

'What need has the world for you? You are fit for neither food nor sacrifice!'

The *Midrash* goes on to show how the raven was indeed a necessary species. It was the raven that would one day feed Elijah and keep him alive [*I Kings* 17:16].

VIII returning until the waters dried from upon the earth.
8-9 8 *Then he sent out a dove from him to see whether*
the waters had subsided from the face of the ground.
9 *But the dove could not find a resting place for the*

until they all left the ark when the earth dried *(Ibn Ezra).*

Rashi concurs with the literal interpretation but adds that according to the *Midrash* [cited in the latter part of the *footnote* below] the verse suggests that ravens had been designated for yet another mission *'when the waters were dried from the earth'* [i.e. when rain would be denied the earth]: in the days of Elijah as in *I Kings* 17:6: *'and the ravens brought him bread and meat.'*

8. The dove

וַיְשַׁלַּח אֶת הַיּוֹנָה מֵאִתּוֹ — *The he sent out a* [lit. *'the*] *dove from him.*

After seven days. Since it says in *v.* 10: *'and he waited again another seven days',* it implies that on this first occasion, too, he waited seven days *(Rashi).*

[According to the various chronologies (see *v.* 4), this happened on:
— The seventeenth of Elul *(Midrash; Rashi);*
— The seventeenth of Av *(Ramban* et al.);
— The seventeenth of Tammuz *(Seder Olam; Da'as Zekeinim).*]

When Noah saw that the raven's mission had been fruitless, he dispatched the dove, for doves have the ability to bring a response to their sender *(Radak).*

Rashi notes that the verb וַיְשַׁלַּח, *sent forth,* does not denote 'sending forth' on an errand, but setting it free. He sent it forth on its own, and he would thus see if the waters had subsided: If it would find a resting place it would not return to him.

Gur Aryeh explains that in connection with the Raven, *Rashi* need not explain that it was set free because it is understood; in connection with the dove, however, the verse *'to see whether the waters had subsided'* could be interpreted to mean that an errand was indeed involved

From the word מֵאִתּוֹ, *from* [*with*] *him,* [which is not mentioned in connection with the raven] the *Talmud* [*Sanhedrin* 108b] deduces that the clean birds lived together with the righteous [i.e. in the same living quarters as Noah and his family in the ark.]

Malbim suggests that Noah had brought along pairs of trained courier birds as part of his own personal belongings [see *comm.* to 7:1]. It was of מֵאִתּוֹ, *from his own,* that Noah sent forth this dove, not of the seven pairs he was required to bring into the ark and from which he would not diminish.

לִרְאוֹת הֲקַלּוּ הַמַּיִם — *To see whether the waters had subsided.*

If the waters subsided it would [not return but] nest instinctively on the mountains or towers *(Sforno).*

9. וְלֹא־מָצְאָה הַיּוֹנָה מָנוֹחַ לְכַף רַגְלָהּ — *But the dove could not* [lit. *'did not'*] *find a resting place for the sole of its foot.*

This is to be understood metaphorically: It could not sustain itself in the world [as in *Deut.* 28:65: *And among these nations you shall find no ease, nor shall the*

רַגְלָהּ וַתָּשָׁב אֵלָיו אֶל־הַתֵּבָה כִּי־מַיִם ח
עַל־פְּנֵי כָל־הָאָרֶץ וַיִּשְׁלַח יָדוֹ וַיִּקָּחֶהָ י־יא
י וַיָּבֵא אֹתָהּ אֵלָיו אֶל־הַתֵּבָה׃ וַיָּחֶל עוֹד
שִׁבְעַת יָמִים אֲחֵרִים וַיֹּסֶף שַׁלַּח אֶת־
יא הַיּוֹנָה מִן־הַתֵּבָה׃ וַתָּבֹא אֵלָיו הַיּוֹנָה
לְעֵת עֶרֶב וְהִנֵּה עֲלֵה־זַיִת טָרָף בְּפִיהָ

sole of your foot have rest (R' Meyuchas).[1]

[According to the chronology of *Rashi* and *Ramban,* the dove's errand took place 47 days *after* the mountain tops became visible. Why did the dove not find *a resting place for its foot?*]:

Ramban answers that birds do not rest on mountain tops which are bare of trees, particularly since water covered the surface of the earth. In *v.* 12, however, when she saw trees in whose branches she could build a nest, she went her way.

Sforno suggests that the mountain tops, although uncovered, were still too saturated to afford her a resting place.

— The tops were muddy and she could not rest on them *(Moshav Zekeinim).*

[It should be stressed, as pointed out in the *comm.* to *v.* 6, that according to *Seder Olam* the question is moot, because this occurred two weeks before the mountain tops were visible, hence there was obviously no resting place at that time for the dove.]

וַתָּשָׁב אֵלָיו אֶל־הַתֵּבָה — *And it returned to him to the ark.*

The verse emphasizes *'to the ark'* because she had not brought anything as a sign *(Radak),* and she tarried outside for fear that her master would not let her return without accomplishing her mission *(Ha'amek Davar).*

And when Noah saw her *(Radak)*...

וַיִּשְׁלַח יָדוֹ וַיִּקָּחֶהָ — *So* [lit. *'and'*] *he put forth his hand and took it.*

— To examine her wings and the bottoms of her feet for signs of mud or earth which might help him determine the state of the water on the ground *(B'chor Shor).*

— Out of pity. Noah's compassion teaches that one should treat a disappointing messenger just as well as a successful one if the failure of the mission was beyond the control of the messenger *(Ha'amek Davar).*

1. Rav Yehudah bar Nachman said:

Had it found a place of rest, it would not have returned. The *Midrash* also perceives the dove as an allegorical symbol of Israel [see *comm.* to *Shir HaShirim* 1:5, *ArtScroll ed.* p.92-93]: Similarly *'she dwelt among the nations, but found no rest'* [*Lam.* 1:3], but had she [i.e. Israel] found rest, she would not have longed to return [to God and her land.]

Midrash Aggadah adds:

Just as the dove found no resting place, so would Israel not find a haven of rest in Exile; but just as the dove returned to the ark, so will Israel return from Exile to their land, in the face of the burden of the nations who are likened to water.

Zohar Chadash refers this to the Shechinah:

As long as the Shechinah is in Exile [*Megillah* 29a; see *footnote* to *Shir HaShirim* p.134.] It may be said of her *'The dove found no rest'* because no righteous one was found who would give her rest.

VIII
10-11

sole of its foot, and it returned to him to the ark, for
water was upon the surface of all the earth. So he put
forth his hand, and took it, and brought it to him to
the ark.
[10] He waited again another seven days, and
again sent out the dove from the ark.
[11] The dove
came back to him in the evening, and behold, an
olive-leaf it had plucked with its bill! And Noah

According to *Malbim*, the dove was trained to perch on his outstretched arm. He therefore needed only to extend his arm and she alighted on it.

10. וַיָּחֶל עוֹד שִׁבְעַת יָמִים אֲחֵרִים — *[And] he waited again another seven days.*

In addition to the seven days he had waited between sending the raven and the dove *(Radak).*

— The reason he waited a week was to give the water ample time to noticably recede *(B'chor Shor).*

[The translation of וַיָּחֶל, *waited*, follows *Midrash, Rashi,* and most commentators who derive it from חול, waiting, and cite such verses as *Job* 29:21: לִי־שָׁמְעוּ וְיִחֵלּוּ, *to me they listened and waited. Targum Yerushalmi,* interpreting it as related to הַתְחָלָה, *beginning,* renders: 'and he began to count another seven days.]

11. וַתָּבֹא אֵלָיו הַיּוֹנָה — *[And] the dove came* [back] *to him* — i.e. she returned directly to Noah with an olive leaf that constituted the fulfillment of her mission *(Ha'amek Davar).*

[The emphasis is apparently on אֵלָיו, *to him.* The dove did not return to her nest, or return because she was tired; she returned *to Noah* in fulfillment of her Providential mission to bring back a sign of God's response.]

לְעֵת עֶרֶב — *In the evening* — of the same day he sent it *(Radak).*

וְהִנֵּה עֲלֵה זַיִת טָרָף בְּפִיהָ — *And behold, an olive leaf it had plucked* [lit. *'torn'*] *with its bill.*

[The translation of טָרָף = טָרַף as a masculine verb meaning 'plucked' follows *Rashi* as well as *Ibn Ezra;* compare such similar double *Kametz* forms as *Hosea* 6:1: כִּי הוּא טָרָף, *for He has torn; Amos* 3:8 אַרְיֵה שָׁאָג, *the lion has raged,* etc.]

Rashi comments that *'dove'* usually take a feminine form in Scriptures. The use of the masculine form in our verse [טָרָף] indicates that the dove was a male.

Rashi continues that Aggadically טָרָף is interpreted as a noun meaning food [as in *Prov.* 30:8: הַטְרִיפֵנִי, *feed me; Psalms* 111:5: טֶרֶף נָתַן לִירֵאָיו *He has given food to those who fear Him*]. The word בְּפִיהָ, *with its mouth,* is interpreted as a reference to symbolic speech; thus: 'and behold, she had an olive leaf as food, as if to say.'] For, the Sages explain her gift of a bitter olive branch as a message that: 'Rather that my food be bitter but from God's hand, than sweet as honey

ח
יב־יג

וַיֵּדַע נֹחַ כִּי־קַלּוּ הַמַּיִם מֵעַל הָאָרֶץ:
יב וַיִּיָּחֶל עוֹד שִׁבְעַת יָמִים אֲחֵרִים וַיְשַׁלַּח
אֶת־הַיּוֹנָה וְלֹא־יָסְפָה שׁוּב־אֵלָיו עוֹד:
יג וַיְהִי בְּאַחַת וְשֵׁשׁ־מֵאוֹת שָׁנָה בָּרִאשׁוֹן
בְּאֶחָד לַחֹדֶשׁ חָרְבוּ הַמַּיִם מֵעַל הָאָרֶץ

but dependent on mortal man.'[1]

Hirsch elaborates on this. He explains that טָרָף, like טֶרֶף, is a noun meaning food independently seized by one's own efforts. For a full year, the dove had not had the opportunity to earn its own food. It found a resting place to spend the entire day, but hunger could have forced it back to Noah's kindness. Then it found something it would ordinarily not eat — a bitter olive leaf! It carried the leaf back to Noah preaching the lesson of our Sages: even the bitterest food eaten in freedom is preferable to the sweetest food in servitude.

The familiar translation, *'in her mouth was an olive leaf torn off'* takes טָרָף as an adjective modifying leaf, and follows *Ibn Ezra, B'chor Shor, Radak,* and many other commentators, who explain that טָרָף, *torn off,* was used to emphasize that it was obvious to Noah that the leaf was freshly plucked, not found floating on the waters.

[It should be noted, however, that the familiar translation, structured as it is, does not appear to fit in as well with the Masoretic cantillation *('trop')* of the verse which recognizes a *tip'cha* pause between עֲלֵה זַיִת, and טָרָף בְּפִיהָ. A better translation, recognizing both the adjectival interpretation and the *trop* would be: *'And behold, there was an olive leaf, plucked by its mouth.'*]

Ramban notes that the verse seems to imply that trees were not uprooted. This is contradicted, however, by the declaration of the Sages that 'even lower millstones [exceedingly heavy objects] were obliterated' Accordingly, the *Midrash* says that the leaf was brought from the Mount of Olives since Eretz Yisrael was not inundated. This should not be taken to mean that the land remained unaffected, for as stated by *Pirkei d'Rabbi Eliezer,* there was no wall around the country. Rather, the rains did not *fall* upon Eretz Yisrael nor did the deep *overflow* it. The waters did *stream in* from other lands, however, although not with sufficient force to uproot its trees.

[The people in Eretz Yisrael, however, *were* overcome, because, as pointed out, the waters of the Flood were scalding hot. The fact

1. *Rashi*'s comm. is derived from *Sanhedrin* 108b, *Erubin* 18b and the *Midrash.*

The *Midrash* asks: From where did the dove bring it?

Rav Abba said: She brought it from the young shoots of Eretz Yisrael. Rav Levi said, she brought it from the Mount of Olives, for Eretz Yisrael was not submerged by the Flood.

Rav Birai said: The gates of the Garden of Eden were opened for her and from there she brought it.

Rav Abbahu said: Had she brought it from the Garden of Eden, should she not have brought something better, such as cinnamon or balsam leaf? — But in fact she hinted to him,saying in effect: Noah, better is bitterness from God, than sweetness from you!

knew that the waters had subsided from upon the
earth. 12 *Then he waited again another seven days*
and sent the dove forth; and it did not return to him
any more.
13 *And it came to pass in the six hundred and first*
year, in the first month, on the first of the month, the
waters dried from upon the earth; Noah removed the

that the hot springs of Tiberias still exist, indicates there were hot Flood-waters in Eretz Yisrael (see *comm.* 8:2). Those in the ark, however, were spared the devastating heat because the water was miraculously cooled at the side of the ark (cf. *Zevachim* 113b).]

וַיֵּדַע נֹחַ כִּי־קַלּוּ הַמַּיִם מֵעַל הָאָרֶץ — *And Noah knew that the waters subsided from upon the earth.*

I.e., he inferred from the fact that the dove had not *'found' it, but, as implied by the verb,* טָרָף, *plucked it* afresh, that the waters had almost entirely subsided from the earth because olive trees are not high *(Radak; Hadar Zekeinim).*

He also inferred it from the fact that the dove waited until nightfall to return, implying that she was able to rest.

12. וַיִּיָּחֶל עוֹד שִׁבְעַת יָמִים אֲחֵרִים — *Then* [lit. *'and'*] *he waited again another seven days* [to give the waters still more time to recede.]

[According to the various chronologies (*v.* 4) this took place on:
The first of Tishrei *(Rashi).*
The first of Av *(Seder Olam).*
The first of Elul *(Ramban).*

Rashi explains that וַיִּיָּחֶל, is synonymous with וַיָּחֶל, *waited,* in *v.* 10 but is of a different conjugation which does not affect its meaning.

וְלֹא־יָסְפָה שׁוּב אֵלָיו עוֹד — *And it did not return to him any more.*

Noah was now positive that the earth had dried and that the dove must have found rest among the trees *(Radak).*

13. The earth dries

וַיְהִי בְּאַחַת וְשֵׁשׁ מֵאוֹת שָׁנָה — *And it came to pass on the six hundred and first year.* I.e. calendar year of Noah's life — which commenced with the onset of the very first day of Tishrei *(Seder Olam; Radak).*

בָּרִאשׁוֹן בְּאֶחָד לַחֹדֶשׁ — *In the first* [month] *on the first* [day] *of the month.*

— According to Rav Eliezer, Tishrei; according to Rav Yehoshua, Nissan *(Rashi;* see *comm.* to 7:11).

Ramban, whose chronology commences consistently from Tishrei, explains that the Sages agreed that it was in Tishrei that the world was created as indicated by the text of the Rosh Hashanah prayer, זֶה הַיּוֹם תְּחִלַּת מַעֲשֶׂיךָ זִכָּרוֹן לְיוֹם רִאשׁוֹן, on this day, of the beginning of Your work, a remembrance of the very first day. Therefore, all references to the numerical order of months referred to Tishrei until the Exodus when the Torah ordained that months be counted from Nissan.

[It should be noted, as pointed out above, that according to *Rashi*'s chronology, the first of Tishrei coincides with the day that

ח
יד־טז

וַיָּסַר נֹחַ אֶת־מִכְסֵה הַתֵּבָה וַיַּרְא וְהִנֵּה
יד חָרְבוּ פְּנֵי הָאֲדָמָה׃ וּבַחֹדֶשׁ הַשֵּׁנִי
בְּשִׁבְעָה וְעֶשְׂרִים יוֹם לַחֹדֶשׁ יָבְשָׁה
°רביעי טו הָאָרֶץ׃ °וַיְדַבֵּר אֱלֹהִים אֶל־נֹחַ
טז לֵאמֹר׃ צֵא מִן־הַתֵּבָה אַתָּה וְאִשְׁתְּךָ

the dove finally departed, while according to *Ramban* and *Seder Olam* it is after a lapse of one month and two months respectively.]

חָרְבוּ הַמַּיִם מֵעַל הָאָרֶץ — *The waters dried from upon the earth.*

— Only the surface had dried: the earth had become swampy like clay and not firm enough to walk upon *(Rashi; Ibn Ezra).*

[It must be assumed here that the Torah is telling us a fact of which Noah himself was not aware until he uncovered the ark and saw it himself.]

[This translation of חָרְבוּ as not meaning entirely dry land is also consistent with *Malbim*'s translation in 7:22 of חָרָבָה, which he interprets as muddy, moist land.]

וַיָּסַר נֹחַ אֶת־מִכְסֵה הַתֵּבָה — [*And*] *Noah removed the covering of the ark.*

Although we are not specifically told that Noah built a 'covering' for the ark; it stands to reason that an ark designed to keep out the rain would have a covering *(R' Shlomo Kluger).*

[See *comm.* to 6:16.]

וַיַּרְא וְהִנֵּה חָרְבוּ פְּנֵי הָאֲדָמָה — *And* [*he*] *looked* [lit. *'saw'*] — *and behold the surface of the ground had dried* — but not so dry as to enable him to leave the ark and walk upon it *(Sforno).*

Therefore, God did not order him to leave the ark. Noah waited because he knew that at the appropriate time God would command him to leave just as He had commanded him to enter *(Radak).*

[It would seem then, that the window of the ark which opened on one side only was too small to allow Noah an ample view of the ground. Only after Noah removed the cover was he able to observe, first hand, what *we* already know from the earlier part of the verse.]

Additonally, אֶרֶץ connotes a larger area than אֲדָמָה, *earth* [see 47:20]. The Torah tells us that the entire *earth* was dry; when Noah peered through the roof of his ark he was able to view only the אֲדָמָה, the *ground* in the immediate periphery of the ark *(Ha'amek Davar).*

According to *Abarbanel,* however, the intent of the verse is that Noah perceived from the aridity of the air that the water had evaporated and exposed the earth. He removed the covering of the ark and he saw with his own eyes a devastating sight: וְהִנֵּה חָרְבוּ פְּנֵי הָאֲדָמָה, *and behold! the surface of the earth lay desolate* [interpreting חָרְבוּ not *dry,* but *devastated, desolate*] — the entire earth lay waste and devoid of life. There was neither growth nor buildings nor walls.

14. וּבַחֹדֶשׁ הַשֵּׁנִי בְּשִׁבְעָה וְעֶשְׂרִים יוֹם לַחֹדֶשׁ יָבְשָׁה הָאָרֶץ — *And in the second month, on the twenty-seventh day of the month, the earth was dried out,* i.e. it became hard,

VIII 14-16

covering of the ark, and looked — and behold! the
surface of the ground had dried. [14] *And in the second*
month, on the twenty-seventh day of the month, the
earth was dried out.
[15] *God spoke to Noah, saying,* [16] *'Go forth from*
the ark: you and your wife, your sons, and your

and returned to its natural condition *(Rashi);* יָבֵשׁ being a stronger term than חָרֵב *(Ibn Caspi).*

The second month — Marcheshvan *(Targum Yonasan; Seder Olam).*

Thus the cycle was complete. The Flood had commenced on the 17th of the second month of the previous year, and a complete *solar* year which was the period of punishment of the Generation of the Flood had elapsed before the earth returned to its original state. Since a solar year is eleven days longer than a lunar year, the additional eleven days from the sixteenth of the month [the end of the lunar year] to the twenty-seventh of the month complete the solar year, making 365 days in all *(Rashi* and *comm.).*

Rabban Shimon ben Gamliel said: If you wish to prove for yourself that the solar year exceeds the lunar year by eleven days, make a mark on a wall on the day of the summer solstice; the following year at that season, the sun will not reach it until eleven days later *(Seder Olam).*

But Noah still did not venture to leave the ark of his own will; he obediently waited for God's command *(R' Bachya).*

15. The command to leave the ark

וַיְדַבֵּר . . . לֵאמֹר — *[And] God spoke . . . saying* [lit. *'to say'*]

This expression is explained by the commentators:

— *To say:* i.e. that he should, in turn, tell his children, wife, and daughters-in-law *(Lekach Tov).*

The *Talmud, Yoma* 4a, derives an ethical lesson from the use of לֵאמֹר, *to say* [in *Lev.* 1:1]:

'Whence do we know that if a man was told something by his neighbor that he may not spread the news without being told לֵךְ אֱמוֹר *Go and say it? — From the verse [Lev.* 1:1]: וַיְדַבֵּר ה׳ . . . לֵאמֹר, *HASHEM spoke to him . . . to say* [i.e., to say to others]

אֱלֹהִים — *God.*

The name *Elohim* is used throughout the narrative because it represents Him as the God of nature who created and preserves it *(Ha'amek Davar).*

16. צֵא מִן הַתֵּבָה — *Go forth from the ark.*

Noah had said: Just as I entered the ark only with permission, so will I not leave without permission ... Thus, *'Go into the ark . . . and Noah went in'; 'Go forth from the ark . . . and Noah went forth' (Midrash).*

אַתָּה וְאִשְׁתְּךָ . . . — *You and your wife,* [and] *your sons and your sons' wives with you.*

The husbands and wives are now grouped together because they were now permitted to resume family life

יז וּבָנֶיךָ וּנְשֵׁי־בָנֶיךָ אִתָּךְ׃ כָּל־הַחַיָּה אֲשֶׁר־
אִתְּךָ מִכָּל־בָּשָׂר בָּעוֹף וּבַבְּהֵמָה וּבְכָל־
הָרֶמֶשׂ הָרֹמֵשׂ עַל־הָאָרֶץ הוצא° אִתָּךְ °הַיְצֵא קרי
וְשָׁרְצוּ בָאָרֶץ וּפָרוּ וְרָבוּ עַל־הָאָרֶץ׃
יח וַיֵּצֵא־נֹחַ וּבָנָיו וְאִשְׁתּוֹ וּנְשֵׁי־בָנָיו אִתּוֹ׃
יט כָּל־הַחַיָּה כָּל־הָרֶמֶשׂ וְכָל־הָעוֹף כֹּל
רוֹמֵשׂ עַל־הָאָרֶץ לְמִשְׁפְּחֹתֵיהֶם יָצְאוּ
כ מִן־הַתֵּבָה׃ וַיִּבֶן נֹחַ מִזְבֵּחַ לַיהוָה וַיִּקַּח

[which had been prohibited throughout their stay in the ark]. [Cf. grouping of names in 6:18 and 7:17 and *comm.* there] *(Rashi).*

17. כָּל־הַחַיָּה אֲשֶׁר אִתְּךָ מִכָּל־בָּשָׂר — *Every living being that is with you of all flesh.*

חַיָּה [which also means: *'beast', 'animal'*] is here translated *'living being'* because in this verse it is used as a general term for all life, followed by various individual species, מִכָּל־בָּשָׂר, *of all flesh: fowl, cattle, creeping things,* etc. *(Radak).*

הַיְצֵא אִתָּךְ – *Order them out with you.*

Rashi notes that the כְּתִיב [the Masoretic *spelling* of the word] is הוצא, while the קְרֵי [the Masoretic *pronunciation*] is הַיְצֵא. He explains that הַיְצֵא means *'order them out',* i.e. tell them to leave on their own, while הוֹצֵא carries with it the connotation that 'if they refuse to leave, *force them out.'*

... For the verb הוֹצֵא denotes passive acquiescence to the prodding of another while הַיְצֵא indicates the independent act of one who exits by choice: merely give them permission and they will go *(Hirsch).*

N'tziv explains the verb to mean that he was not simply to open the door and let them stampede out, but was to lead them out himself, supervising that they do not injure one another, as explained in *v.* 18 [s.v. לְמִשְׁפְּחֹתֵיהֶם.]

וְשָׁרְצוּ בָאָרֶץ וּפָרוּ וְרָבוּ ... *And let them teem on the earth and be fruitful and multiply* ... i.e. let them out that they may breed prolifically just as the fish were bidden to do at the beginning of Creation [cf. 1:20,22.] This command was directed to all creatures leaving the ark because they were few, and it was God's desire that they re-populate His world *(Radak; Ralbag).*

בָאָרֶץ, *on the earth;* i.e. but not in the ark. This teaches that animals and birds too were separated, male and female [i.e. not permitted to mate] in the ark *(Rashi).*

18. וַיֵּצֵא־נֹחַ וּבָנָיו וְאִשְׁתּוֹ ... — *So* [lit. *'and'*] *Noah went forth, and his sons,* [and] *his wife and his sons' wives with him.*

Here again, the sequence is changed: the men and women listed separately. Possibly, the men are mentioned first because the women

VIII
17-20

sons' wives with you. [17] *Every living being that is*
with you of all flesh, of birds, of animals, and creep-
ing things that creep on earth — order them out with
you, and let them teem on the earth and be fruitful and
multiply on the earth.' [18] *So Noah went forth, and his*
sons, his wife, and his sons' wives with him. [19] *Every*
living being, every creeping thing, and every bird,
everything that moves on earth came out of the ark
by their families.

[20] *Then Noah built an altar to HASHEM and took of*

were afraid to leave the ark until the men had gone out, the dread of the Flood still being upon them *(Radak).*

Gur Aryeh to 7:17 holds that this separation of men and women after the sanction to resume marital life (*v.* 16) indicates that Noah refrained from his marital duties, fearing another Flood [as the *Midrash* puts it: Noah said, 'Am I to go out and beget children for a curse?' Cf. *comm.* to 4:24,25] until God swore to him that He would never again bring a Flood upon mankind.

19. כָּל־הַחַיָּה — *Every living being.*

As in *v.* 17, חַיָּה here has the general signification of *all living beings*: all creeping things and all fowl. *Everything that* רוֹמֵשׂ, *moves, on the earth* in this case, embraces cattle and beasts *(Radak).*

According to the *Targumim*, however, the translation is: *every animal, every fowl, everything that creeps on earth . . .* [apparently leaving a redundancy between רֶמֶשׂ and רוֹמֵשׂ which *Radak* overcomes by rendering חַיָּה as a general term and interpreting רוֹמֵשׂ not as a synonym of רֶמֶשׂ, but as a general term encompassing all cattle and beasts. (Cf. use of רוֹמֵשׂ in 1:30).]

[See *N'tziv*, below.]

לְמִשְׁפְּחֹתֵיהֶם — *By their families,* i.e. they left the ark according to their species *(Rav Saadiah Gaon; Ibn Ezra; Radak).*

According to *Rashi,* leaving the ark as 'families', constituted an implied acceptance of the obligation to mate only with their own species.

As *Hirsch* explains: The supreme natural law of לְמִינֵיהֶם, *according to their own kinds,* was once again given them as they left the ark.

N'tziv takes חַיָּה, literally, as *beasts.* He notes that *'by their families'* indicates that Noah let them out in an orderly fashion so that they would not intermingle and injure one another. Because they are by nature docile, בְּהֵמָה, cattle, need not be mentioned in this context. [See above, s.v. הַיְצֵא.]

20. Noah brings an offering

וַיִּבֶן נֹחַ מִזְבֵּחַ לַה' — *And Noah built an altar to HASHEM.*

Noah sat and contemplated [rendering וַיִּבֶן, he *understood*]: 'God saved me from the waters of the Flood and brought me forth from that prison. Am I not obliged to bring before Him a sacrifice and

ח
כא

מִכֹּל | הַבְּהֵמָה הַטְּהֹרָה וּמִכֹּל הָעוֹף
כא הַטָּהוֹר וַיַּעַל עֹלֹת בַּמִּזְבֵּחַ: וַיָּרַח יהוה
אֶת־רֵיחַ הַנִּיחֹחַ וַיֹּאמֶר יהוה אֶל־לִבּוֹ

burnt offerings?' *(Pirkei d'Rabbi Eliezer).*[1]

Rambam comments in *Hil. Beis HaBechirah* 2:2:

There was a known tradition that the place where David and Solomon built the altar in the threshing floor of Aravnah [*II Chron.* 3:1], was the same place where Abraham built the altar upon which he bound Isaac. This is the same place where Noah had built an altar after leaving the ark, which was in the same place as the altar upon which Cain and Abel offered a sacrifice. It was there that Adam offered a sacrifice after he was created, for Adam was created from that very ground, as the Sages have taught: Adam was created from that place where he made atonement.

לַה' — *To* HASHEM.

The commentators note that in connection with sacrifices God is always referred to as HASHEM never *Elohim* [cf. 4:3,4.]

Hirsch explains: The perennial use of HASHEM, (the Name indicating the Attribute of Mercy), in connection with sacrifice proves conclusively that offerings are directed toward the merciful God who desires *life,* not death and suffering. The purpose of the sacrificial service is to bring about the closeness and dedication of a person to Godliness. The non-Jewish view of sacrifice as an appeasement of 'a vengeful God of nature' could never be connected with the Name, HASHEM. If such blasphemy were indeed the purposes of sacrifice, then the Name אֱלֹהִים would be used.

וַיִּקַּח מִכֹּל הַבְּהֵמָה הַטְּהֹרָה — *And took of every clean animal* — The term בְּהֵמָה includes חַיּוֹת, beasts *(Radak).*

Noah surmised that the reason God had ordered him to take seven pairs of clean creatures was to enable him to offer sacrifices after the Flood *(Rashi).*

— This sacrifice was in the manner of all those who go down to the sea in ships of whom it is said *'they offer sacrifices of thanksgiving'* *(Psalms* 107:22). So did Noah, who was greatly troubled because the world was destroyed while he escaped *(Chizkuni).*

Noah's gesture, in effect, demonstrated that HASHEM alone is to

1. When Noah left the ark and saw the world in a state of destruction, he wept and cried out to God: 'Master of the Universe! You are called All Merciful. You should have shown compassion upon the work of Your hand.

'Foolish shepherd!' God answered him. '*Now* you say this? Why did you not plead when I said *'I have seen that you are righteous before Me in this generation'*, and *'I will bring Floodwaters'*, and *'make unto yourself an ark of gopher-wood.'* I forewarned you to give you ample opportunity to seek mercy for My world. Instead, as soon as you heard that you would be spared you were complacent; it never occurred to you to pray on behalf of the others. You contently went into your ark and saved yourself. Now, that the world is in ruin, you open your mouth with meaningless petitions?

When Noah heard this, he built an altar and offered sacrifices *(Zohar).*

VIII
21

every clean animal and of every clean bird, and offered burnt offerings on the altar. 21 *HASHEM smelled the pleasing aroma, and HASHEM said in His*

be served, not the idols worshipped by the prior generations *(Ralbag);*

וַיַּעַל עֹלֹת בַּמִּזְבֵּחַ — *And* [*he*] *offered burnt offerings on* [lit. *'in'*] *the altar.*

The purpose of the offering was to thank God for all the wondrous goodness He had shown them. [For the offering Noah used some of the few domestic animals that were left him and his family for use in rebuilding their lives in a world laid waste. To show his gratitude, he diminished a supply that he might well have hoarded.] It was as if he declared: 'Everything is Yours, and I offer You merely what is Yours' *(Abarbanel).*

Noah said to himself, 'God has decreed the destruction of the world, and who knows if through my being saved I have used up all the merit I have accumulated?'

He therefore hastened to build an altar to HASHEM.

21. וַיָּרַח ה׳ אֶת־רֵיחַ הַנִּיחֹחַ — *And HASHEM smelled the pleasing aroma.*

— An obvious metaphor, which should be understood as: He accepted the offering and it was pleasing to him, as a man who is pleased by a sweet fragrance *(Ibn Ezra).* [As *Rashi* comments in *Lev.* 1:9, God is pleased. שֶׁאָמַרְתִּי וְנַעֲשָׂה רְצוֹנִי, 'for I have said, and My will has been done'.]

He accepted the sacrifice by consuming it with a heavenly fire, thus demonstrating that He was pleased with those who had survived the Flood *(Radak).*

[Cf. God's acceptance of Abel's sacrifice in *comm.* to 4:4.]

To avoid any anthropomorphic connotation of corporeality associated with smell or fragrances, the *Targum* renders: *'and HASHEM received with approval his oblation.'*

Hirsch notes that רֵיחַ, odor, and נִיחֹחַ, pleasing, are listed by the Talmud as two separate requirements *(Zevachim* 46b). He interprets רֵיחַ as the sort of knowledge converged by the sense of smell: a suggestion from afar. Thus רֵיחַ indicates a hint of a person's intentions. נִיחֹחַ indicates total compliance with the will of God. Thus רֵיחַ נִיחֹחַ means: a hint that the bringer of the offering is prepared to comply with God's will. This is the only time in Scripture where the positive article ה *the* is used in connection with an offering. רֵיחַ הַנִּיחֹחַ, *the* hint . . . This is to indicate that Noah's sacrifice was in a class of its own because he was the forerunner of reborn human life and was now dedicating the entire future of the race to God's service.

נִיחוֹחַ — *Pleasing.*

According to *Ibn Ezra* the term is related to מְנוּחָה, *rest* — i.e. a restful, soothing fragrance; while *Radak* suggests that it has the connotation of pacifying — i.e. a pacifying fragrance, which figuratively pacified God's anger at the world.

וַיֹּאמֶר ה׳ אֶל־לִבּוֹ — *And HASHEM said in* [lit. *'to'*] *His heart* [—i.e. to Himself.]

He resolved it, but He kept it in

ח
כב
לֹא אֹסִף לְקַלֵּל עוֹד אֶת־הָאֲדָמָה בַּעֲבוּר
הָאָדָם כִּי יֵצֶר לֵב הָאָדָם רַע מִנְּעֻרָיו
וְלֹא־אֹסִף עוֹד לְהַכּוֹת אֶת־כָּל־חַי כַּאֲשֶׁר
כב עָשִׂיתִי׃ עֹד כָּל־יְמֵי הָאָרֶץ זֶרַע וְקָצִיר

His heart and did not reveal it to Noah or his sons until they accepted His commandments and He made His covenant with them *(Ibn Ezra; Sforno).*

According to *Ramban, 'to His heart'* signifies that God did not reveal it to a prophet [or convey it to the people through a prophet *(Rambam)*] at that time. However, when He directed Moses to write the Torah he revealed to him that Noah's sacrifice was accepted and, that as a result, He had resolved never again to smite every living thing.

[Cf. similar interpretation of the parallel phrase *'to His heart'* in 6:6.]

Abarbanel emphasizes, to the contrary that God's resolution was entirely unrelated to Noah's sacrifice. It was an independent decision reached, as the verse continues, *because the imagery of man's heart is evil from his youth.*

לֹא אֹסִף לְקַלֵּל עוֹד . . . וְלֹא אֹסִף עֹד לְהַכּוֹת — *I will not continue to curse again the ground ... nor will I again continue* [lit. *'continue anymore'*] *to smite all that lives.*

God repeated the phrase לֹא אֹסִף, *'I will not again,'* so that it would constitute an oath [*Shevuos* 36a.] It is to this implied oath — no other more *explicit oath* being mentioned anywhere else in Scriptures — that *Isaiah* (54:9) refers: *For I have* sworn *that the waters of Noah will never again pass over the earth (Rashi).*

Ibn Ezra renders that the verse refers to two separate curses: 'I will not add any more to the curse which was pronounced against the ground because of Adam; *neither will I ever again smite* with a Flood. עוֹד can mean *'forever'* or *'a second time' (Ibn Ezra).*

According to the *literal* interpretation, however, the first phrase refers to *the earth;* the second to *living beings (Chizkuni).*

בַּעֲבוּר הָאָדָם — *Because of man,* i.e. because of man's sins *(Targum).*

[*Ramban* (like *Ibn Ezra,* above) apparently takes הָאָדָם here to refer not to mankind but to Adam.] He comments: They were punished because of Adam; had he been righteous they would have been spared although they, too, *had corrupted their way.*

כִּי יֵצֶר לֵב הָאָדָם רַע מִנְּעֻרָיו — *Since the imagery* [lit. *'formation'*] *of man's heart is evil from his youth.*

[See *comm.* to similar phrase in 6:5.]

God continues to find extenuating circumstances in man's sins, for he receives the Evil Inclination from birth, before he has the wisdom and maturity to combat it. Thus, man is undeserving of extermination for his sins *(Ramban).*

According to *Binah L'Ittim:* God decided to bring the Flood and blot out man's existence because his thought formations are purely evil (see 6:5). Here that very phrase is

VIII
22

heart: 'I will not continue to curse again the ground because of man, since the imagery of man's heart is evil from his youth; nor will I again continue to smite every living being, as I have done. [22] *Continuously,*

used in defense of man for, as the Sages said: 'Were it not for the Evil Inclination, man would never build a home, till fields, or marry . . .' In the time of the Nephilim, he used his material instincts only for evil. When Noah's first act upon leaving the ark was to bring an offering, God concluded [if one may so express it!] that, although man's animal instinct *was* completely evil, that condition existed only *'from his youth'* [i.e. in the early part of human history]. Now, however, he would harness his evil inclination for the service of God.

Rashi, noting that מִנְּעֻרָיו is spelled without a 'ו', *vav,* [after the *ayin* so that it can be read as being related to the root נָעַר *to stir*]. Therefore, the phrase can be rendered: *"man is given an evil inclination from the moment he is 'bestirred' to leave his mother's womb."*

According to *Radak,* it is called יֵצֶר, [lit. *'formation'*] because it is formed together with him, for, as the *Midrash* tells us, man acquires his evil inclination first; only later does he acquire his good inclination. He has no active inclination for good until he gradually acquires it, for he is born without wisdom but with an inclination toward evil. Only later does his heart begin developing virtues. Therefore I will not again destroy all life as I have done.[1]

[Cf. also *comm.* to 4:7, s.v. לַפֶּתַח חַטָּאת רֹבֵץ.]

Abarbanel explains that the intention here is not that because the imagery of man's heart is evil from his youth He will automatically forgive individual sinners; but rather He will not wipe out mankind totally. He will punish them in other ways.

Rav Chiyah the Elder said: How wretched must be the dough when the baker himself testifies it to be poor! Thus, man's Creator says: *Because the imagery of man's heart is evil from his youth.* Abba Yose said, How poor must be the leaven [a common simile for the Evil Inclination] when He who kneaded it testifies that it is bad!

כַּאֲשֶׁר עָשִׂיתִי — *As I have done.*

— For in the future God will never again punish the human family as a body; henceforth He will punish only the individual sinners as He later did in Sodom *(Radak).*

22. עֹד כָּל־יְמֵי הָאָרֶץ — *Continuously, all the days of the earth* — i.e. for the duration that God set for the world's existence *(Hoffmann).*

Hirsch holds that this clause is a self-contained promise: *'The days of the earth shall always endure.'*

This would seem to imply that the earth will exist only for a set period *(Ibn Ezra).*

— This refers to עוה״ז, This World — i.e. as long as we are in this world, structured as it is, the natural cycle will not cease; however, when

1. The exponents of the Mussar movement refer to the verse וְעַיִר פֶּרֶא אָדָם יִוָּלֵד, *man is born as a wild mule (Job 11:12).* Man is born as a totally selfish creature, virtually an animal. It is his task — and that of his parents and teachers to convert that animal into a human being.

ט וְקֹר וָחֹם וְקַיִץ וָחֹרֶף וְיוֹם וָלַיְלָה לֹא
א יִשְׁבֹּתוּ: א וַיְבָרֶךְ אֱלֹהִים אֶת־נֹחַ וְאֶת־בָּנָיו

God renews His world and brings on עוה"ב the World to Come, times and seasons *may* deviate *(Karnei Or)*.

This apparently has its basis in the *Midrash:*

Rav Yudan said in Rav Acha's name: What did the children of Noah [i.e. the idolators] think — that the covenant made with them would endure to all eternity? That is not so, but only as long as heaven and earth endure [i.e. as עוֹלָם הַזֶּה, This World] will their covenant endure. But when the day arrives [i.e. עוֹלָם הַבָּא the World to Come] of which it is written [*Isaiah* 51:6]: *For the heavens shall vanish away like smoke, and the earth shall be worn out like a garment,* then shall this verse be fulfilled [*Zech.* 11:11]: *And it* [i.e. the covenant] *will be broken that day.* [Brackets above are added from *Karnei Or*].

Rambam in *Moreh Nevuchim* Chapters 27-29 discusses the eternity of the universe and holds that the universe is to be eternal, but that many disagree. Since this is not an article of faith one may adopt either position, because 'since the world's beginning emanated from the Divine Will, its eternity or end depends also on that Will.'

Hirsch notes that the *Midrash* makes it very clear that the seasons as we now know them and described in this verse came into existence after the Flood. Prior to it, fields were cultivated only once in forty years, the climate was always spring-like and the entire land mass of earth was unbroken by seas and oceans. The *Midrash* also indicates that this ease of living was a major contributory factor in the corruption of the generation. The inference is plain that inactivity and excess leisure are deleterious to human moral development.

זֶרַע וְקָצִיר . . . לֹא יִשְׁבֹּתוּ — *Seedtime and harvest . . . shall not cease.*[1]

The *Talmud* [*Sanhedrin* 58b] derives from the phrase לֹא יִשְׁבֹּתוּ, *shall not cease,* that עוֹבֵד כּוֹכָבִים שֶׁשָּׁבַת חַיָּיב מִיתָה, a non-Jew who desists from work one day [declaring it a Sabbath] is guilty of the death penalty.

[The Sages apparently interpret the prohibition לֹא יִשְׁבֹּתוּ, *(v.* 22) as a reference to the human race which was discussed in *v.* 21 interpreting: '*they* (i.e. the Noachides) *shall not cease.*]

It should be understood that the *seventy facets of Torah* teach many equally valid derivations and interpretations in addition to the simple meaning. (See *Overview: Torah — Written and Oral).*]

The deduction is that during the Flood all the above *did cease. Seedtime and harvest* naturally ceased; there was no one to experience the seasons; similarly, those in the ark did not distinguish between night and day *(Radak).*

— But now they shall never again cease to take their natural course *(Rashi).*

The terms are explained:

According to *Rashi* — based on the emended reading by *Mizrachi* in consonance with *Bava Metzia* 106b,

1. The *Chofetz Chaim* saw every word of the Torah as a living fact that was even more valid than observable phenomena. 'How do we know the sun will rise tomorrow morning?' he asked. 'The scientist needs formulae and statistics to establish this fact. We *know* that the sun will rise because the Torah says: *'day and night shall not cease.'*

all the days of the earth, seedtime and harvest, cold and heat, summer and winter, day and night, shall not cease.'

1 *God blessed Noah and his sons, and he said to*

the year is thus divided into six periods of two months each, which, in that part of the world are:

זֶרַע, *seedtime,* the time of planting wheat: *Tishrei, Marcheshvan, and the first half of Kislev;*

חֹרֶף, *winter,* the time of planting barley and beans which are quick (חֲרִיפִין) to ripen: *The second half of Kislev, Teves, and the first half of Shevat;*

קוֹר, *cold,* which is more severe than winter: *The second half of Shevat, Adar and the first half of Nissan;*

קָצִיר, *harvest: The second half of Nissan, Iyar, and the first half of Sivan;*

קַיִץ, *summer,* a name which originally referred to summer fruit, as in *II Sam.* 16:2, but which is now applied to the season of such fruit; the time when the figs are gathered and laid out to dry in the fields: *The second half of Sivan, Tammuz and the first half of Av;*

חֹם, *heat,* the end of summer when the world is excessively hot, as expressed in *Yoma* 21a: the end of the summer is worse than summer: *The second half of Av, Elul and the first half of Tishrei.*

The fact that the verse specifies that יוֹם וָלַיְלָה, *day and night shall not cease, implies that during the Flood they did* cease, because as the *Midrash* says, the heavenly bodies did not function and the distinction between day and night was not apparent.

Mizrachi asks: According to the view that the heavenly bodies did not functin during the twelve months of the Flood, how should we interpret such verses as 8:13 where Noah removed the covering from the ark and *saw* that the earth was dry? He leaves his question unanswered.

[However, the *Midrash* says nowhere that there was no *illumination* during this period; only that the cycle of day/night was curtailed. The verses indicate that there was *some* light, although perhaps, heavily beclouded. As for the count of day and night throughout the Flood, the precious stone which hung in the ark telling Noah when it was night and day [see *comm.* to 6:16] easily provided him with that calculation.]

According to *Ibn Ezra,* the year is divided in this verse into two periods: *seedtime* and *harvest,* and then it is further divided into four antithetical periods: *cold* corresponding to *heat, summer* corresponding to *winter,* which in total correspond to the four seasons of the year. Finally it is divided into *day* and *night,* for the shortness of the day in one season (winter) is made up in its corresponding season (summer); similarly with night.

IX

1. Rebuilding a ruined world

וַיְבָרֶךְ אֱלֹהִים אֶת נֹחַ... — [And] *God blessed Noah and his sons.*

The world benefited from God's blessing to Adam [1:28] until the Generation of the Flood abrogated it with their corruption. When Noah left the ark, God renewed the blessing by repeating it to Noah and his sons *(Tanchuma Yashan; Torah Shelemah* 9:2).

Thus, standing with his family

ט
ב־ג

וַיֹּאמֶר לָהֶם פְּרוּ וּרְבוּ וּמִלְאוּ אֶת־
ב הָאָרֶץ: וּמוֹרַאֲכֶם וְחִתְּכֶם יִהְיֶה עַל כָּל־
חַיַּת הָאָרֶץ וְעַל כָּל־עוֹף הַשָּׁמָיִם בְּכֹל
אֲשֶׁר תִּרְמֹשׂ הָאֲדָמָה וּבְכָל־דְּגֵי הַיָּם
ג בְּיֶדְכֶם נִתָּנוּ: כָּל־רֶמֶשׂ אֲשֶׁר הוּא־חַי
לָכֶם יִהְיֶה לְאָכְלָה כְּיֶרֶק עֵשֶׂב נָתַתִּי לָכֶם

on the threshhold of the 'new' world, renewed and recreated from the overwhelming desolation and emptiness of the Deluge, Noah receives God's blessing, which follows *(Radak)*:

פְּרוּ וּרְבוּ וּמִלְאוּ אֶת הָאָרֶץ — *Be fruitful and multiply and fill the land.*

This verse is considered a divine *blessing*. The *command* to procreate is given in *v. 7*, as *Rashi* explains there *(Ha'amek Davar)*.

[Compare the identical blessing given to Adam in 1:28, and *comm.* there.]

And in the face of the total annihilation of mankind, this divine blessing that they would be enabled to procreate and repopulate the earth was indeed welcome *(Ibn Caspi)*.

When Noah departed from the ark and saw the world in ruins he was dismayed because only four men were left in the world. God, therefore, allayed his fear with the blessing that few though they were, they would, indeed, repopulate the world *(Abarbanel; Malbim)*.

2. וּמוֹרַאֲכֶם וְחִתְּכֶם ... — [And] *the fear of you and the dread of you.*

This additional blessing was given to allay any fear they might have had that being so few in number, they were subject to attack by animals. God assured them that their human countenance would exert a natural subjugation and mastery over all living creatures *(Abarbanel)*.

[The *Talmud, Shabbos* 151b, interprets חִתְּכֶם = חַיּתְכֶם, life, homiletically rendering: 'The fear of you *during your life* shall be upon every beast, etc.']:

Even a day old infant, alive, need not be guarded from weasels or mice, while [the giant] Og, king of Bashan, dead, needs to be guarded against attacks by such creatures, as in the verse *'the fear of you and the dread of you shall be upon every beast of the earth'*. — As long as man is alive, his fear lies upon dumb creatures; once he dies, this fear ceases *(Rashi)*.

Kli Yakar suggests that the reason for the blessing that animals would dread man is because God was about to permit the slaughter of animals for human consumption. Why should a beast allow itself to be taken for butchering without protest if it were not the hand of God that brought about its natural fear of man?

Malbim differentiates between מוֹרָא and חִתַּת. According to him, מוֹרָא is the *fear of harm* from another, while חִתַּת suggests the *submission* which the smaller naturally has for the greater.

וּבְכָל דְּגֵי הַיָּם — *And in all the fish of the sea.*

— Although they do not move upon the earth and are not with you on the dry land, nevertheless your

them, 'Be fruitful and multiply and fill the land. [2] *The*
fear of you and the dread of you shall be upon every
beast of the earth and upon every bird of the
heavens, in all that moves on earth and in all the fish
of the sea; in your hand they are given.
[3] *Every moving thing that lives shall be food for*
you; as the green herbage I give you everything.

mastery shall be over them *(Radak).*

According to *Tur,* this blessing establishing man's mastery over the animals was important because the animals had become overly familiar with man during their duration in the ark and had no fear of him.

And, as the *Zohar* comments, whereas the animals formerly feared man because they saw in him the supernal sacred impress of the *image of God,* now, after they had sinned it was man who dreaded the animal world, because the animals no longer saw in him the true Divine Image. But now the world was reinstated to its former position, God blessed them and bestowed upon them their former dominion over the creatures [see *footnote.*][1]

בְּיֶדְכֶם נִתָּנוּ — *In your hand they are given.*

To do with as you please *(Ralbag),* and to establish your mastery over them *(Caspi).*

[The translation follows *Malbim* and *N'tziv* who render that *'in your hand . . .* is a new clause, and that the categories listed previously are objects of the *fear of you . . . .*]

3. Permission to eat meat

כָּל רֶמֶשׂ אֲשֶׁר הוּא חַי — *Every moving thing that lives* — including cattle, beasts, birds, and even the fish of the sea — all of which are called רֶמֶשׂ, *moving things (Ramban).*

[Cf. 1:28 וּבְכָל חַיָּה הָרֹמֶשֶׂת, which according to this would be translated: *and every living being that moves* — cattle, beast, and insect: they all 'move' upon the earth *(Radak).*]

לָכֶם יִהְיֶה לְאָכְלָה — *Shall be* [*as*] *food for you.*

Meat, which was prohibited to Adam, was permitted to Noah because (a) it was because of him, and for his needs, that God had spared the animals; were it not for man they would not have been spared [cf. 6:7]; (b) he toiled over them and attended to their needs in the ark: of him it is said [*Psalms* 128:2]: *You shall eat the toil of your hands.* He had thus acquired rights over them *(Or HaChaim).*

— 'They were saved in an ark which you toiled to build, and through you came their salvation,

1. The *Talmud* continues that 'a beast has no power over man unless it takes him for an animal.'

This means that the man who was attacked by a beast must have been deserving of death for an unwitnessed transgression so that the death penalty could not be applied by the courts. God therefore sends one of His 'agents' — in any form it might take — to execute judgment. Having lost his human dignity, the sinner appears like an 'animal' and is prone to attack by brazen beasts. Had he maintained his human stamp, the animals would have fled in awe *(Zohar; Akeidas Yitzchak).*

ד אֶת־כֹּל׃ אַךְ־בָּשָׂר בְּנַפְשׁוֹ דָמוֹ לֹא
ה תֹאכֵלוּ׃ וְאַךְ אֶת־דִּמְכֶם לְנַפְשֹׁתֵיכֶם

therefore they are yours to do with them as you please — like the green herbs of the field' *(B'chor Schor; Chizkuni).*

[See *comm.* of *Ramban* cited to 1:29 and *footnote* there.]

Abarbanel suggests that meat was an accommodation to Noah who, upon emerging from the ark saw the earth barren of trees and plant-life — and was frightened of starvation. God therefore permitted him animal flesh as if to say: 'If you lack produce to eat, take from the animals for food.' Thus, meat will take the place of the vegetation given to earlier generations.

Hirsch comments that permission to eat meat might have been partly influenced by man's shortened life span requiring a more hectic pace of life and, hence, more nourishment, and climatic changes from the constant temperatures and ideal growing conditions that made vegetation so abundant before the Flood. He emphasizes that the Torah demands no vegetarianism nor does it have any aversion to eating meat, it even makes it a duty on festivals.

כְּיֶרֶק עֵשֶׂב נָתַתִּי לָכֶם אֶת כֹּל — *As the green herbage I give* [lit. *'gave'*] *you everything.*

Though I permitted only herbage, but not flesh, to Adam, I give you the same right to everything that he had for herbage *(Rashi).*

R' Bachya and *Chizkuni* comment that the comparison to *green herbage* is noteworthy: lest one think that *everything* was permitted, God qualified His permission by comparing it to herbage. Just as some herbs are beneficial to man while others are unfit for food and even poisonous, so among the animals and birds there are those that are permitted by the Torah and those that are prohibited. [See *comm.* of *Chavel* to his ed. of *R' Bachya*].

Malbim explains that it is logical and desirable for a lower form of life to be eaten by those absorbed into a higher form. Therefore, animals eat plant life, thus elevating it, and humans eat animals elevating them to become part of intelligent man.

4. [But, there are limitations] ...

אַךְ בָּשָׂר בְּנַפְשׁוֹ דָמוֹ לֹא תֹאכֵלוּ — *But flesh; with its soul its blood you shall not eat.*

[The translation, which follows the cantillation, is literal. Its ambiguity allows for the various interpretations that follow.]

Now that God permitted *all moving things* as food, He included a limitation [indicated by אַךְ, *but, however.*] God prohibited tearing a limb from a living animal and eating it, because it is one of the greatest barbarisms one can inflict upon animals, and if it were permitted, people would learn cruelty *(Radak; Abarbanel).*

Rashi explains that this verse prohibits אֵבֶר מִן הַחַי, a limb cut from a living animal — i.e., while its soul is still in it, you may not eat its flesh. [The preposition בְּ, in בְּנַפְשׁוֹ is accordingly rendered *with,* as if it read: *the flesh, while it is yet 'with' its soul, you shall not eat (Mizrachi).*][1]

4 *But flesh; with its soul its blood you shall not eat.*
5 *However, your blood which belongs to your souls I*

According to *Rashi* as explained by the commentators, the word בְּנַפְשׁוֹ, *with its soul,* relates to both the beginning and the end of the verse: בָּשָׂר בְּנַפְשׁוֹ = flesh while it is yet with its soul [i.e. life]; and דָמוֹ בְּנַפְשׁוֹ = while the blood is yet with its soul.

He accordingly interprets that there are *two* prohibitions implicit in the verse: both the flesh and the blood taken from a living animal are forbidden.

Rashi's interpretation follows the view of Rav Chaninah ben Gamliel in *Sanhedrin* 59, who holds that the verse prohibits both flesh cut from a living animal and blood drawn from a living animal. He interprets the verse thus: בָּשָׂר בְּנַפְשׁוֹ לֹא תֹאכֵלוּ, *flesh with its life you shall not eat,* and דָמוֹ בְּנַפְשׁוֹ לֹא תֹאכֵלוּ, *blood with its life you shall not eat.* The Sages, however, derived a different interpretation from the inclusion of the seemingly superfluous word דָמוֹ, maintaining that the phrase בְּנַפְשׁוֹ דָמוֹ teaches that flesh cut from live שְׁרָצִים, creeping things, is not included in the prohibition 'because the [prohibition of the] flesh of שְׁרָצִים is not distinct from their blood.' [i.e. in the case of animals, *flesh,* and *blood* are forbidden by separate Scriptural prohibitions whereas all parts of creeping things, blood as well as flesh, are included in the same proscription. The word דָמוֹ, *its blood,* indicates that our verse refers only to such creatures as have separate prohibitions for blood (see *Sanhedrin* 59 a-b).

Targum Yonasan renders:

But flesh which is torn from a living beast, while the life is in it, or that is torn from a slaughtered animal before all the breath has gone forth, you shall not eat.

[Thus, according to *Yonasan,* not only was a limb torn from a *living* beast prohibited, but even a *slaughtered* animal, while it still had a breath of life left in it (apparently implied by דָמוֹ, *his blood,* because *'the blood is the life'* — *Lev.* 17:14; see *Ramban)* was also not to be eaten by a Noachide (cf. *Chullin* 33b).]

Sforno, following *Rashi,* explains: אַךְ בָּשָׂר, however, *the flesh,* בְּנַפְשׁוֹ, *with its soul* — i.e. while it is still alive; דָמוֹ, and similarly, *its blood — while it is yet alive, you shall not eat. Sforno* adds that blood drawn from a *dead* animal is permitted to Noachides.

Accordingly, *Ramban* disagrees with *Rashi's* interpretation. He maintains that if the verse included a separate prohibition against blood, then the word *blood* would have been preceded by the connective ו, *and,* reading: בָּשָׂר בְּנַפְשׁוֹ וְדָמוֹ לֹא תֹאכֵלוּ, flesh with its soul *and* its blood you shall not eat. Additionally, as pointed out, the prevailing majority of Sages in the *Talmud* derive only the limb from the living to be forbidden by this verse; it is only Rav Chaninah ben Gamliel who holds that blood, too, is forbidden. He therefore suggests that the verse should be interpreted: But flesh with its soul, that is, its blood, you shall not eat — for the life of all flesh is its blood [*Lev.*

1. *Rambam* writes in his *Commentary to the Mishnah, Chulin,* end of Chapter 7:
Be aware of a fundamental concept, that whatever acts we do, or refrain from doing, are only the result of God having commanded concerning them to us through Moses, and not because God had previously related them to any prophets preceding him. For example, that we do not eat limbs torn from living animals is not due to God's having prohibited it to Noah, but because the Noachide prohibition was reaffirmed at Sinai. See what the Sages have proclaimed: '613 commandments were conveyed to Moses at Sinai' [*Makkos* 23b], this being among the commandments. [Cf. also *Sanh.* 59a,b.]

17:14 i.e. that is, 'blood', in the verse, is a synonym for 'life'].

[In an intricately grammatical dissertation, *Mizrachi* defends *Rashi* against *Ramban*'s primary criticism. Regarding *Ramban*'s latter criticism, however, it must be emphasized that it is well known that *Rashi*'s interpretation of Torah is not always in strict consonance with the established Halachah. Rather, as *Rashi* makes clear in his introduction and many times throughout his commentary, his intent is to interpret Torah according to פְּשׁוּטוֹ שֶׁל מִקְרָא, the most literal sense of the verse as he perceived it to be indicated by the text.

Additionally, it must be understood that the *seventy facets of Torah* touch many equally valid derivations in addition to the simple meaning. See *Overview* Torah — Written and Oral.]

Hirsch, rendering the verse in consonance with the Sages in *Sanhedrin* 59, stresses that blood from a living animal is not forbidden a Noachide... Following the cantillation on בָּשָׂר, which separates it from בְּנַפְשׁוֹ, *Hirsch* concludes that the verse cannot be rendered other than *nevertheless, flesh, while its blood is in its soul, you shall not eat* — clearly referring to the living state of the animal and prohibiting אֵבֶר מִן הַחַי, *flesh from a living animal.*

5. [There is another limitation]

וְאַךְ אֶת דִּמְכֶם לְנַפְשֹׁתֵיכֶם — [*And*] *however, your blood* [*which belongs*] *to your souls* ... [following *Hirsch*].

— I permitted you to take the lives of animals, but your own lives you may not take. I will require an accounting from one who spills his own blood — thus prohibiting suicide ...

The word לְנַפְשֹׁתֵיכֶם, *to your souls,* extends the prohibition of suicide to the situation where one takes his own life [soul] in a manner which does not involve the *spilling of blood* — for example, to one who hangs himself *(Rashi,* based on the *Midrash).*

The *Midrash* continues that lest one think that this prohibition of suicide includes even one like Saul's [who ordered that he be killed to avoid falling into the hands of the Philistines, see *I Sam.*31:4] and like that of Hananiah, Mishael, and Azariah [who were prepared to give up their lives עַל קִדּוּשׁ הַשֵּׁם, for the sanctification of God's Name, by choosing to be thrown into the fiery furnace rather than worship Nebuchadnezzar's idols, see *Dan. 3:17ff*. Now one could think that this verse expressly prohibits even such selfless forms of suicide ...] Therefore the Torah writes אַךְ, but [which in Talmudic exegesis is a limiting particle inferring that some forms of suicide are not prohibited.][1]

Ramban explains that לְנַפְשֹׁתֵיכֶם can be interpreted as if it were written without the ל, *lamed* [citing לְכֹל, *all* in *Exod.* 27:19, and לְאַבְשָׁלוֹם in *I*

1. This exegesis unfortunately is far more than theoretical. Countless Jews have committed suicide to sanctify God's Name rather than convert to another faith. These martyrs, respectfully called קְדוֹשִׁים, *holy ones,* made the ultimate sacrifice for the sake of Judaism, reaching a spiritual zenith of devotion to God.

Chron. 3:2 which are rendered as if they were written without the ל] meaning 'your blood which is your lives [lit. *'souls'*] ... Thus, the Torah says: *your blood which is your life I will require.* Thus, blood is synonymous with life, the intimation being that one incurs the death penalty for spilling the blood which is vital to life, but not for spilling the blood of limbs that are not vital to life. But, the Sages [*Bava Kamma* 91a] derived that this verse is an injunction against suicide and interpret: מִיַּד נַפְשֹׁתֵיכֶם אֶדְרֹשׁ אֶת דִּמְכֶם, from your own souls will I require tour blood.

— The intent, then is that the body, blood and life of *animals* are yours and at your disposal, but your own blood which belongs to your soul is Mine *(Hirsch).*

אֶדְרֹשׁ — *I will demand.*

I.e., I will avenge, as in *Psalms* 9:13: דֹרֵשׁ דָּמִים, *avenges blood (Ibn Ezra).*

אֶדְרֹשׁ thus means I demand as My property, and demand an account for every drop of it. דרש is a term used for demanding the return of property which is in someone else's possession. Cf. *Ezek.* 34:10 וְדָרַשְׁתִּי אֶת צֹאנִי מִיָּדָם, *and I will demand My flock from their hand.* God hereby claims the right to human blood consigned to human souls, as His possession and denies the right of disposal of one's own blood.

מִיַּד כָּל חַיָּה אֶדְרְשֶׁנּוּ — *Of [the hand of] every beast will I demand it.* The sinful generation of the Flood had been cast off as food to the animals. Now, [after *v.* 2 and 3] the animals were warned that they were not to exercise this dominion *(Rashi).*

According to the *Midrash:* This refers to one who turns another over to be killed by wild beasts *(Torah Shelemah* 31,21; *Radak).*

Although an animal has no reason and is not subject to punishment, nevertheless, in its relationship with man, animals are accountable for their deeds *(Radak):*

Every beast that kills a human being will itself be devoured, by Divine decree, [by another animal, or it will grow weak and become easy prey *(Abarbanel).*] Or, compare the case of an ox which is executed by the court for killing a human being [cf. *Exod.* 21:28].

Alternatively, this phrase means that the vengeance upon a murderer will be *at the hand of every beast,* for God will send wild beasts to avenge bloodshed, and He will send the *hand of man* against the murderer and he will not escape them *(Ramban).*

Rambam codifies in *Hil. Rotzeach* 3:2-5:

If one hires an assassin to kill another ... or ties him up and leaves him in front of a beast and the beast kills him ... the rule in each of these cases is that he is a shedder of blood, has committed the crime of murder, and the verb דרש, seek, in each of these cases is explicitly used to show that judgment is reserved for Heaven; but there is no capital punishment at the hands of the court ...[i.e. because direct act of murder has not been committed.]

Nevertheless, if a king of Israel wishes to put them to death by royal decree for the

Incidents are recorded where, during periods of צָרוֹת יִשְׂרָאֵל, *calamitous times for the Jews,* parents would even slaughter their own children rather than let them fall into the hands of apostasizers [see *Daas Zakeinim*].

ט הָאָדָם מִיַּד אִישׁ אָחִיו אֶדְרֹשׁ אֶת־נֶפֶשׁ
ו־ז ו הָאָדָם׃ שֹׁפֵךְ דַּם הָאָדָם בָּאָדָם דָּמוֹ
יִשָּׁפֵךְ כִּי בְּצֶלֶם אֱלֹהִים עָשָׂה אֶת־
ז הָאָדָם׃ וְאַתֶּם פְּרוּ וּרְבוּ שִׁרְצוּ בָאָרֶץ

benefit of society, he has the right to do so. Similarly, if the court deems it proper to put them to death as an emergency measure, it may do so provided that the circumstances warrant such action ...

In any event ... it is the duty of the court to flog them almost to the point of death and imprison them for many years in order to frighten and deter other wicked persons from feeling they can commit murder and be acquitted.

וּמִיַּד הָאָדָם — *But* [lit. *'and'*] *of* [*the hand of*] *man* — From the hand of one who deliberately murders without witnesses [and hence the human court is powerless to execute judgment]; in that even God will punish him *(Rashi).*

מִיַּד אִישׁ אָחִיו — *Of* [*the hand of every*] *man* [*for that of*] *his brother.*

At the hand of one who loves the victim as a *brother* having killed him בְּשׁוֹגֵג, through careless inadvertence, yet God will punish him if he does not expiate his crime by going into self banishment [cf. *Num.* 35:11*f.*], for even one who sins inadvertently requires atonement: Even if there are no witnesses to sentence him to exile and he does not voluntarily submit himself, then God will seek it of him...

Thus, our Sages [*Makkos* 10b] explained the text [*Exod.* 21:13]: וְהָאֱלֹהִים אִנָּה לְיָדוֹ, *and God caused it to come into his hand* — God causes the man who killed by accident and had not expiated the murder, and the man who killed with premeditation to meet at the same inn. The former in descending a ladder falls upon the latter and kills him and must therefore go into exile since the accident was seen by witnesses *(Rashi).*

The *Targum* renders —

From the hand of the man who sheds the blood of his brother will I require the life of man.

Man is punished for murder only when he is required to live in tranquility [connoted apparently by the word אָחִיו in this verse, suggesting brotherly co-existence.] However during a time of war these restrictions do not apply, for the world was so organized from its inception ... *(Ha'amek Davar).*

אֶדְרֹשׁ אֶת נֶפֶשׁ הָאָדָם — *I will demand the soul of man.*

If man does not deserve that I should save him, and he is slain by another, I will avenge the victim by punishing the slayer *(Sforno).*

From animals God demands a reckoning for דַּם הָאָדָם, *the blood of man,* (*v.* 5) but from men, a different expression is used: נֶפֶשׁ הָאָדָם, *the 'soul' of man.* Human beings must learn to respect not merely human *life,* but the human *soul,* for it is the spirit of God breathed into earthly man. Every moment of human life is sacred to God and He holds mortally responsible anyone who shortens a life by even a second *(Hirsch).*

6. שֹׁפֵךְ דַּם הָאָדָם — *Whoever sheds* [lit. *'spills' the*] *blood of man.*

— This refers to one who commits murder himself and not through an agent *(Rambam; Hil. Rotzeach* 2:2).

בָּאָדָם דָּמוֹ יִשָּׁפֵךְ — *By man* [i.e. by the court *(Radak)*] *shall his blood be shed* — I shall seek vengeance if there are no witnesses, but if there are witnesses the court must put him to death. Why? — *For in the*

man, of every man for that of his brother I will de-
mand the soul of man. 6 *Whoever sheds the blood of*
man, by man shall his blood be shed; for in the image
of God He made man. 7 *And you, be fruitful and*
multiply; teem on the earth and multiply on it.'

image of God ...' (Rashi; Radak).

כִּי בְּצֶלֶם אֱלֹהִים עָשָׂה אֶת הָאָדָם — *For in the image of God He* [i.e. the Maker *(Rashi)*] *made man* — [Cf. *comm.* to 1:26,27] And therefore whoever sheds blood is regarded as if he had impaired the divine likeness *(Midrash).*

One might think that since the murderer, too, was made in the image of God, it would be wrong to put him to death. Hence the verse comes to inform us that — no, the murderer expunged God's likeness from *himself* by his heinous act, and deserves himself to be killed *(Ralbag).*

Beloved is man for he was created in the image of God; but greater still was the love shown to him in that it was revealed to him that he was created in the image of God, as it is said: *For in the image of God He made man* [when God informed to man of this via Noah, the basis of the sanctity of human life in the re-created world was established] *(Avos* 3:14)].

This declaration assigns to human life a much higher value than to animal life; therefore, only man's murder is to be punished *(Sforno).*

7. וְאַתֶּם פְּרוּ וּרְבוּ — *And you, be fruitful and multiply.*

Having warned them concerning bloodshed, which destroys the world, he bade them to procreate abundantly and thereby build up the world *(Radak),* and increase mankind which was *'created in* the image of God' *(Malbim).*

According to the plain meaning, the similar statements made earlier to Adam [1:28] and to Noah [*v.* 1] which are preceded by the phrase *'and God blessed them'* constitute a *blessing* [see *comm.* there], like the one God gave the fish [1:22]. Here, the verse is understood as a *commandment.* In fact, the *Talmud, Sanhedrin* 59b cites *this* verse as the source of the commandment to procreate ...

Additionally, from the sequence of the verse, the *Talmud* [*Yevamos* 63b] derives that this command follows the prohibition of murder to liken one who refuses to procreate to one who sheds blood, and who diminishes the Divine Image *(Rashi; Ramban).*

שִׁרְצוּ בָאָרֶץ וּרְבוּ בָהּ — *Teem on the earth and multiply on it.*[1]

I.e. move about the world from one end to the other, each according

1. The *Midrash* derives from the phrase *'teem on the earth'* [i.e. the use of the apparently superfluous word *earth* in the phrase] that God implanted in everyone a love to dwell in his country of origin no matter how unattractive it may be *(Rashi; Matanos Kehunah):*

Resh Lakish said: A covenant has been made with climates [i.e. man prefers his native climate] ... Blessed is He who inspires citizens with love for their country because every race feels most comfortable in its own homeland, and becomes homesick even if its home is severe and unfriendly *(Hirsch).*

ט °חמישי ח וּרְבוּ־בָהּ: וַיֹּאמֶר אֱלֹהִים אֶל־נֹחַ
ח־יא ט וְאֶל־בָּנָיו אִתּוֹ לֵאמֹר: וַאֲנִי הִנְנִי מֵקִים
אֶת־בְּרִיתִי אִתְּכֶם וְאֶת־זַרְעֲכֶם אַחֲרֵיכֶם:
י וְאֵת כָּל־נֶפֶשׁ הַחַיָּה אֲשֶׁר אִתְּכֶם בָּעוֹף
בַּבְּהֵמָה וּבְכָל־חַיַּת הָאָרֶץ אִתְּכֶם מִכֹּל
יא יֹצְאֵי הַתֵּבָה לְכֹל חַיַּת הָאָרֶץ: וַהֲקִמֹתִי
אֶת־בְּרִיתִי אִתְּכֶם וְלֹא־יִכָּרֵת כָּל־בָּשָׂר

to his own way, and repopulate it *(Abarbanel).*

God added this phrase for emphasis, as if to say: carry it out with all your power *(Ramban);* since those who had departed from the ark were so few — only Noah and his children *(Radak).*

[The expression שִׁרְצוּ, *'teem',* indicates giving birth to many children, like the שְׁרָצִים, creeping insects which multiply very quickly and abundantly. Similarly, the abundant growth of Israel in Egypt is described as וַיִּשְׁרְצוּ, *and they teemed' (Exodus* 1:7).

8. The fulfillment of the covenant.

וַיֹּאמֶר אֱלֹהִים אֶל נֹחַ — *And God said to Noah.*

God's earlier resolve אֶל לִבּוֹ, *to His heart* [8:21], is now revealed to man as His unalterable decision *(Hirsch).*

וְאֶל בָּנָיו אִתּוֹ — *And to his sons with him.*

Opinions differ as to whether this means that God's words were transmitted to Noah's sons by their father, the sons being unworthy of divine revelation *(Ibn Ezra; Ramban);* or whether they all received God's word together so they should all be equally aware of God's promise to them and the other creatures of the world *(Ibn Ezra,* alt. opinion; *Radak).*

[See *comm.* of *R' David Feinstein* next verse.]

9. וַאֲנִי הִנְנִי מֵקִים אֶת בְּרִיתִי אִתְּכֶם — *And as for Me behold I establish My covenant with you.*

— *And I:* i.e., I agree with you that your fear is justified. [As pointed out in the *comm.* to 8:21], Noah was afraid to beget more offspring until God promised him not to destroy the world again. So He did [apparently referring to God's decision in 8:21], and now God added that He would ratify and strengthen His promise with a covenant, and give Noah a sign [*v.* 11, 12] *(Rashi;* see *Gur Aryeh; Levush).*

Cf. *Tanchuma:*

When God said *'Be fruitful and multiply',* Noah said: 'Master of the Universe! Perhaps You will bring another Flood? ...'

'I swear that I will never again bring another Flood,' God answered.

Harav David Feinstein suggests that this is why in the previous verse Noah's sons are described as still being אִתּוֹ, *with Noah:* they too, sharing Noah's concern, had not returned to their wives to resume their marital duties. [Cf. *comm.* to 8:16, 18.]

According to *Radak,* the phrase

[8] *And God said to Noah and to his sons with him:*
[9] *'And as for Me, behold I establish My covenant*
with you and with your offspring after you, [10] *and*
with every living being that is with you — with the
birds, with the cattle, and with every beast of the land
with you — of all that departed the ark, to every beast
of the earth. [11] *And I will ratify My covenant with*
you: never again shall all flesh be cut off by the

'and I' is to be understood in conjunction with verse 8: *and you, be fruitful and multiply* — i.e. you do your part and populate the world, and I, in turn, will do My part to sustain it so it will never again be destroyed.

Sforno explains that the covenant not to destroy the world was on the condition that they shed no innocent blood; if murder were to become rampant again, the world would be destroyed. [This is indicated by the fact that the covenant is preceded by the prohibition against murder.] Other sins, however, would be punished without total destruction.

[The word אִתְּכֶם can also be interpreted, as in 6:18: *'through you'* — i.e. God tells Noah that the covenant will be fulfilled *through* him, and his sons as the sole survivors of the Deluge. They will carry God's promise and act as the vehicle of His Word for posterity.]

10. [And this covenant will extend, not only to Noah and his descendants, but, to every living being] ...

וְאֵת כָּל נֶפֶשׁ הַחַיָּה אֲשֶׁר אִתְּכֶם — *And* [*with*] *every living being that is with you* — a general description referring to all those creatures which were with him in the ark and whom He now enumerates in somewhat more detail *(Radak).*

וּבְכָל חַיַּת הָאָרֶץ אִתְּכֶם — *And with every beast of the land with you.*

— *'With you'* refers to those animals that accompany man — the domestic animals *(Rashi).*

מִכֹּל יֹצְאֵי הַתֵּבָה —*Of all that departed the ark.*

— This includes creeping and crawling animals *(Rashi).*

They were with you in the ark and they therefore deserve the protection of My covenant with you *(Abarbanel).*

לְכֹל חַיַּת הָאָרֶץ — *To every beast of the earth.*

According to *Rashi,* this refers to מַזִּיקִים, wild, non-domesticated beasts, that are not included in the category of 'every domesticated beast of the earth' [*Gur Aryeh*]. *Mizrachi* and *Levush HaOrah* hold that *Rashi* refers to שֵׁדִים, semi-spiritual destructive beings that are invisible to man.

11. The Rainbow: Sign of the covenant.

וַהֲקִמֹתִי אֶת בְּרִיתִי אִתְּכֶם — [*And*] *I will ratify My covenant with you.*

Following *Rashi:* I will confirm [אֶעֱשֶׂה קִיּוּם = וַהֲקִמֹתִי] My covenant through the manifestation of My

ט עוֹד מִמֵּי הַמַּבּוּל וְלֹא־יִהְיֶה עוֹד מַבּוּל
יב־יג יב לְשַׁחֵת הָאָרֶץ: וַיֹּאמֶר אֱלֹהִים זֹאת אוֹת־
הַבְּרִית אֲשֶׁר־אֲנִי נֹתֵן בֵּינִי וּבֵינֵיכֶם וּבֵין
כָּל־נֶפֶשׁ חַיָּה אֲשֶׁר אִתְּכֶם לְדֹרֹת עוֹלָם:
יג אֶת־קַשְׁתִּי נָתַתִּי בֶּעָנָן וְהָיְתָה לְאוֹת

bow as described in the following verses.

According to *Radak* this refers to the covenant mentioned, but not specified in *v.* 9. Now the verse explains that the covenant is that *'never again shall all flesh be cut off by the waters of a flood.'*

This is the covenant that Isaiah referred to when he quoted God as saying [54:9]: *As I have sworn that the waters of Noah should go no more over the earth (Ibn Ezra).*

[See *Rosh* to *Shevuos* 36a; *Maharsha* regarding the repetition of וְלֹא in *this* verse constitutes the iteration of God's oath; and cf. *Rashi* cited 8:21.]

וְלֹא יִכָּרֵת כָּל בָּשָׂר עוֹד — *And never again shall all flesh be cut off.* Flesh is specified because it is the flesh, not the bones, that feels the pain *(Ibn Ezra).*

Or HaChaim explains that the flow of the verse is that God will never again cut off *'all'* flesh with flood waters. *Part* of the population, however, may be destroyed by flooding, but, as the verse continues, if God does bring a flood upon a segment of the population, it will not be the kind of flood that will destroy the world itself.

מִמֵּי הַמַּבּוּל — *By the waters of a flood.* This follows most commentators.

Or HaChaim [following *Rif*] interprets the phrase מִמֵּי הַמַּבּוּל *from the time of the waters of the Flood,* and that the verse means: *And never again shall all flesh be cut off* by any disaster, neither by fire or water — *from the period of the Flood* and henceforth.

וְלֹא יִהְיֶה עוֹד מַבּוּל לְשַׁחֵת הָאָרֶץ — *And never again shall there be a flood to destroy the earth,* i.e. there will never again be any sort of catastrophe to destroy the actual substance of the earth *(Sforno).*

— Even if the people sin *(Chizkuni).*

12. וַיֹּאמֶר אֱלֹהִים — *And God said* to Noah and his sons *(Radak).*

זֹאת אוֹת הַבְּרִית — *This* [the rainbow mentioned in the next verse] *is the sign of the covenant,* i.e. this is the token that I give you so you should not fear that every storm will become a flood *(Radak).*

Noah did not demand any token, but God, in His righteousness, wanted to give them a visible sign of the permanence of His unilateral assurance to them; this He accomplished by the manifestation of His bow in the skies *(Abarbanel).*

Hirsch comments that the rainbow is one of many **אוֹתוֹת**, *signs,* such as Sabbath, circumcision, and tefillin, all of which are designed to keep alive and fresh the great teachings which God gave man. The rainbow is the eternal sign that, no matter how bleak the future looks, God is not oblivious but He

waters of a flood, and never again shall there be a
flood to destroy the earth.'
12 *And God said, 'This is the sign of the covenant*
that I give between Me and you, and every living be-
ing that is with you, to generations forever: 13 *I have*
set My bow in the cloud, and it shall be a sign of the

will lead mankind to its ultimate goal.

וּבֵין כָּל נֶפֶשׁ חַיָּה אֲשֶׁר אִתְּכֶם — *And* [*between*] *every living being that is with you.*

Not that the animals will see the sign and be reassured; they do not have the intelligence to experience such emotion. Rather it is a sign that I will *fulfill* My covenant among Myself, you, and the animal world *(Imrei Shefer).*

לְדֹרֹת עוֹלָם — *To generations forever.*

The sign will be perpetual, for all generations *(Radak).*

Rashi notes that דֹרֹת is spelled defectively [without two *vavs* = דורות] indicating that the sign [which provides necessary reassurance for morally defective, underserving generations] is not required in perfectly righteous generations. For example, rainbows were not seen during the periods of Hezekiah, King of Judah, and of Rabbi Shimon bar Yochai *(Mizrachi).*

13. אֶת קַשְׁתִּי נָתַתִּי בֶּעָנָן — *I have set* [lit. *'given'*] *My bow in the cloud.*

Ibn Ezra interprets נָתַתִּי in the present tense: *I have now set.* He disagrees with Rav Saadiah who suggests that rainbows always existed. *Ibn Ezra* explains that the rainbow is caused by the rays of the sun against the clouds; after the Flood, God caused atmospheric changes so a bow would be produced. Prior thereto, the bow had never been seen.

However, nearly every commentator disagrees:

נָתַתִּי should be interpreted as Rav Saadiah Gaon, that the bow which I have set in the cloud shall be unto you a sign ... *(Radak).*

The use of the first person קַשְׁתִּי, *My bow,* and the past tense נָתַתִּי, *I have set,* indicate that the bow was previously in existence. The verse is therefore to be interpreted: The bow which I have set in the clouds since the beginning of creation — as a natural phenomenon resulting from the sun's rays refracting upon the moisture-laden air, similar to the rainbow visible in a container of water standing in the sun — shall henceforth serve as a sign of the covenant between Me and you *(Ramban).*

— *Hirsch* comments that there is no need to assume that the rainbow was a newly created phenomenon simply because God said נָתַתִּי, *I have placed* [in past tense]. Just as God showed Abraham the starry sky and told him that the already existing stars would symbolize the abundance of his children, God now designated the rainbow as an eternal symbol of the covenant never again to destroy humanity by a flood.

ט
יד־טז

יד בְּרִית בֵּינִי וּבֵין הָאָרֶץ: וְהָיָה בְּעַנְנִי עָנָן
טו עַל־הָאָרֶץ וְנִרְאֲתָה הַקֶּשֶׁת בֶּעָנָן: וְזָכַרְתִּי
אֶת־בְּרִיתִי אֲשֶׁר בֵּינִי וּבֵינֵיכֶם וּבֵין כָּל־
נֶפֶשׁ חַיָּה בְּכָל־בָּשָׂר וְלֹא־יִהְיֶה עוֹד
טז הַמַּיִם לְמַבּוּל לְשַׁחֵת כָּל־בָּשָׂר: וְהָיְתָה
הַקֶּשֶׁת בֶּעָנָן וּרְאִיתִיהָ לִזְכֹּר בְּרִית עוֹלָם

וְהָיְתָה לְאוֹת בְּרִית — *And it shall be a sign of the covenant.* — Henceforth and forever *(Ramban).*

The rainbow was chosen as a sign because it is symbolic of the Glory of God as described in *Ezekiel* 1:28. God thus implied: 'When it shall rain abundantly, I will present you with a symbol of My Glory,[1] so you shall receive the Shechinah [i.e. and repent], for were it My intentions to destroy you, I would not have manifested to you My Glory because a king does not deign to appear to his disgraced enemies *(B'chor Shor).*

Ramban explains that *any* visible object — e.g. *a heap of stones, a pillar* [31:52] *seven ewe lambs* [21:30] which serve to remind people of an agreement is called a 'sign', and every agreement is called a 'covenant.' ... Furthermore that the bow is inverted is symbolic that they are not shooting at the earth from the heavens, for it is the custom of warriors to invert the weapons they hold in their hands when calling for peace from their opponents.

According to *Bereishis Zuta,* the rainbow was chosen as the sign of the covenant because it is composed of fire and water in harmonious fusion. This is symbolic that God, who thus makes peace between opposites above, will similarly make peace on earth, and the earth will never again be overrun by a flood [also *Chizkuni*].

The rainbow symbolizes a bond between earth and heaven because it appears as an arc connecting earth with heaven .... In the midst of an overcast, foreboding sky, it comes as light; it is thus a reminder that even when God appears to be wrathful, His grace and mercy are still present *(Hirsch).*

14. וְהָיָה בְּעַנְנִי עָנָן עַל הָאָרֶץ — *And*

1. *Cf. the Midrash:*
אֶת קַשְׁתִּי = קִישׁוּתִי דָּבָר שֶׁהוּא מוּקָשׁ לִי, *My bow* = My likeness, something that resembles Me. Is that really possible? In truth the bow resembles God only as the chaff resembles the grain [i.e. it is but a faint reflection of God's glory.]

Cf. also what the Sages [*Chagigah* 16a] say concerning one who gazes at the rainbow [which, as derived from Ezekiel 1:28 is symbolic of God's Glory]: 'Whosoever takes not thought of the honor of his Maker would have been better off had he not come into this world.'

The *Halachah* is formulated in *Shulchan Aruch* O.Ch 258:1: One who sees a rainbow recites the following: בָּרוּךְ אַתָּה ה׳ אֱלֹהֵינוּ מֶלֶךְ הָעוֹלָם זוֹכֵר הַבְּרִית נֶאֱמָן בִּבְרִיתוֹ וְקַיָּם בְּמַאֲמָרוֹ, *Blessed are You,* H*ASHEM, our God, King of the universe, Who remembers His covenant, is faithful in His covenant, and upholds His word,* and one may not stare at it unduly long.

Avudraham comments on the phrases of the blessing: He *remembers* and *is faithful in His covenant* even when people are exceedingly wicked, *and He upholds His word* even if He is not bound to it by a covenant.

covenant between Me and the earth. 14 *And it shall*
happen, when I place a cloud over the earth, and the
bow will be seen in the cloud, 15 *I will remember My*
covenant between Me and you and every living being
among all flesh, and the water shall never again be-
come a flood to destroy all flesh. 16 *And the bow shall*
be in the cloud, and I will look upon it to remember

it shall happen, when I place a cloud over the earth.

וְהָיָה has two possible connotations in Scripture: *'and therefore'*; or: *'if it shall happen' (HaRechasim le'Bik'ah).*

This phrase is not to be taken in its literal sense, because a rainbow does not appear every time there are clouds *(Gur Aryeh);* or, according to *Mizrachi,* the typical rain storm is not capable of causing a flood. Rather, the phrase is to be understood: 'When it shall enter My thoughts to bring darkness and destruction upon the earth ...' *(Rashi).*

וְנִרְאֲתָה הַקֶּשֶׁת בֶּעָנָן — *And the bow will be seen* [*by mankind (Radak)*] *in the cloud ...*

[This verse introduces the next one which describes the significance of the rainbow. Thus, when the earth is beclouded and a rainbow is seen, God will remember. . . . *(Levush HaOrah* interpreting *Mizrachi). Levush,* however, renders: And *when I becloud the earth — then the bow will be seen in the cloud.*]

15. וְזָכַרְתִּי אֶת בְּרִיתִי — *I will remember My covenant.*[1]

'The Torah expresses [remembering] in human terms,' because there is no forgetfulness before His glorious throne *(Radak).*

[See *comm.* to the concept of 'remembering' in 8:1: *'and God remembered Noah'.*]

Midrash Aggadah queries: Is there any form of forgetfulness before God that He requires a bow to remember? — It is only because the Attribute of Justice indicts the wicked of the world.

וְלֹא יִהְיֶה עוֹד הַמַּיִם לְמַבּוּל — *And the water shall never again become a flood,* i.e., [rain] water shall never again accumulate in such abundance as to be termed a flood [inundating the entire world] *(Radak).*

16. וְהָיְתָה הַקֶּשֶׁת בֶּעָנָן — *And the bow shall be in the cloud* — i.e. it shall always be there in its potential. Even if it is concealed from mankind for natural reasons; to God it is always visible *(Ibn Ezra).*

Thus man is adjured not to despair if he does not see the rainbow. To God, it is always in evidence *(Abarbanel).*

1. *Hoffmann* notes that the implication of the verse is that without the reminder of the rainbow, God would not remember the covenant, an obviously impossible concept. The same difficulty exists in connection with the commandment to place the blood of the Paschal offering around the doorway in order to demonstrate that Jews lived in the house and thereby prevent the first-born from dying *(Exodus* 12:7,13); as if God had no other way of knowing where Jews lived. Hoffmann contends that the purpose of the signs was to make clear to man that a Merciful God was concerned with his fate and that the good deeds of man were valued by God and could influence the fate of mankind. Therefore, the signs of God's mercy had to be such as were plainly apparent to people.

ט
יז־יט

בֵּין אֱלֹהִים וּבֵין כָּל־נֶפֶשׁ חַיָּה בְּכָל־בָּשָׂר
יז אֲשֶׁר עַל־הָאָרֶץ: וַיֹּאמֶר אֱלֹהִים אֶל־נֹחַ
זֹאת אוֹת־הַבְּרִית אֲשֶׁר הֲקִמֹתִי בֵּינִי וּבֵין
כָּל־בָּשָׂר אֲשֶׁר עַל־הָאָרֶץ:
°ששי יח °וַיִּהְיוּ בְנֵי־נֹחַ הַיֹּצְאִים מִן־הַתֵּבָה שֵׁם
יט וְחָם וָיָפֶת וְחָם הוּא אֲבִי כְנָעַן: שְׁלֹשָׁה

וּרְאִיתִיהָ לִזְכֹּר בְּרִית עוֹלָם — *And I will look upon it* [lit. *'see it'*] *to remember the everlasting covenant.* This sign shall always be 'considered by Me' to recall the everlasting covenant *(Imrei Shefer).*

— *I can see it,* even when you cannot, and I thereby remember the everlasting covenant; *'remembering'* here again must be understood as an anthropomorphism *(Radak; Abarbanel).*

According to *Sforno,* [*v.*13 and here]: the rainbow is a sign to the righteous that their generation would have been punished were it not for the covenant. The righteous will pray as a result. Hence this phrase connotes: 'I will have regard to the prayers of the righteous, who stand in the breach [between Me and the wicked] to turn away My wrath.'

Abarbanel alternatively understands וּרְאִיתִיהָ as if it were causitive-transitive: 'I will *cause you to see it, to remember* ...'

As *HaK'sav V'Hakaballah* comments: 'I have instilled in the rainbow the quality to serve as a reminder to the people. לִזְכֹּר, *to remember,* refers to people who need help to remember that God rules the affairs of earth.

בֵּין אֱלֹהִים וּבֵין כָּל נֶפֶשׁ חַיָּה — *Between God and* [*between*] *every living being.* Noting that since God is the Speaker the verse should have said *between Me. Rashi* and *Radak* explain that *Elohim* represents His Attribute of Justice, and as the *Midrash* explains, the meaning of the verse is: when strict justice will demand that man be destroyed for his sins, I will see the sign and save you.

[Render, therefore, *and I will see it and remember the everlasting covenant between My strict Attribute of Justice* ...]

17. וַיֹּאמֶר אֱלֹהִים אֶל נֹחַ — *And God said to Noah.*

God, as *Elohim,* is used throughout the narrative of the rainbow, because this Name describes Him as the One Who possesses absolute power [see *comm.* to 1:1 s.v. אֱלֹהִים] and accordingly that is the name used throughout the original narrative of Creation. He is referred to by this designation in the case in the Flood as if to proclaim: He Who created the world from nothing is the same One Who destroyed the world in a Deluge, and Who now has promised to heal the world *(Abarbanel).*

זֹאת אוֹת הַבְּרִית — *This is the sign of the covenant.*

God actually showed Noah a rainbow and said to him: This is the sign of which I spoke *(Rashi).*

[This is why the verse is repeated

the everlasting covenant between God and every
living being, among all flesh that is on earth. 17 *And*
God said to Noah, 'This is the sign of the covenant
that I have established between Me and all flesh that
is upon the earth.'
18 *The sons of Noah who came out of the ark were*
Shem, Ham, and Japheth — Ham being the father of
Canaan. 19 *These three were the sons of Noah, and*

from *v.* 12. There, it is a general statement, here the verse tells us that God actually *showed* Noah the sign *(Mizrachi).*]

— This is a sign for you. When you and those like you see it, you must bestir yourselves to rouse people to repent and determine to do good *(Sforno).*

18. The intoxication and shame of Noah.

[For the moral lessons to be learned from the inclusion of this narrative in the Torah, see *Ramban* cited at end of *v.* 27. For the lessons of the blessings, see *Overview.*]

שֵׁם וְחָם וָיָפֶת — *Shem,* [*and*] *Ham, and Japheth.*

But, as the *Midrash* notes, Japheth was the eldest [see *comm.* to 5:32; 6:10; 10:2 and 11:11]. Shem is mentioned first because he was worthy and perfect with his Creator *(Tanchuma).*

Hirsch notes that although the three sons of Noah represented totally different types of character and striving, all were worthy of salvation. The three are named here to demonstrate that all families of man are equal as creatures of God and refugees from the flood. All are responsible to become pure human beings.

וְחָם הוּא אֲבִי כְנָעַן — [*And*] *Ham being the father of Canaan* — i.e. he was the source of the degradation *(Midrash).*

The Torah makes this preliminary announcement of Ham's genealogy in order that the reader will be able to understand how, in this episode which deals with Noah's intoxication, Canaan comes to be cursed through Ham's misdeed *(Rashi).*

Ibn Ezra comments that they are both mentioned because they were both evil — 'like father like son'. The episode was recorded to show that the descendants of the Canaanites, male and female, were already accursed since the days of Noah, and for this reason Abraham later cautioned against intermarriage with the Canaanites, as did Rebecca.

[See *Ramban* cited in *v.* 22.]

Malbim cites the *Midrash* that Ham was the only one of Noah's sons to cohabit in the ark. He comments, accordingly, that this verse alludes to Ham's transgression by saying that, upon leaving the ark, *Ham was* already *the father of Canaan,* because Canaan was born of this union in the ark.

[But cf. *comm.* to *v.* 25 and 10:6 where, according to many, Canaan was Ham's *youngest* child. *Malbim* cites *Ibn Ezra,* however, that Canaan was the oldest, but was mentioned last because he had been cursed by Noah.]

19. שְׁלֹשָׁה אֵלֶּה בְּנֵי נֹחַ —*These three were the sons of Noah.*

ט
כ־כב

אֵ֫לֶּה בְּנֵי־נֹ֑חַ וּמֵאֵ֖לֶּה נָֽפְצָ֥ה כָל־הָאָֽרֶץ׃
כ־כא וַיָּ֥חֶל נֹ֖חַ אִ֣ישׁ הָֽאֲדָמָ֑ה וַיִּטַּ֖ע כָּֽרֶם׃ וַיֵּ֥שְׁתְּ
מִן־הַיַּ֖יִן וַיִּשְׁכָּ֑ר וַיִּתְגַּ֖ל בְּת֥וֹךְ אָהֳלֹֽה׃
כב וַיַּ֗רְא חָ֚ם אֲבִ֣י כְנַ֔עַן אֵ֖ת עֶרְוַ֣ת אָבִ֑יו וַיַּגֵּ֥ד

Sforno explains that although a wicked one was among them, nevertheless, since *they were the sons of Noah* God blessed them that they 'be fruitful and multiply' with the result that ... *from these three was the entire earth ultimately peopled.*

The Torah again stresses in this phrase the phenomenon that one father so righteous and perfect produced three such radically different sons! *(Hirsch).*

וּמֵאֵלֶּה נָפְצָה כָל הָאָרֶץ – *And from these the whole world was spread out* [i.e. was populated]

– From them was everyone dispersed abroad to dwell on all the earth *(Targum Yonasan).*

Hirsch explains נפץ as related to מפץ, a hammer that shatters things into small fragments. All different human characteristics sprang from these three fundamentally different types.

This implies that they dispersed and divided the world among themselves. Now, it is well known that the ancients divided three continents: Asia was taken by Shem; Africa by Ham; and Europe by Japheth *(Abarbanel).*

20. וַיָּחֶל נֹחַ אִישׁ הָאֲדָמָה – [*And*] *Noah, the man of the earth, debased himself.*

The translation of וַיָּחֶל, *debased,* follows *Rashi* who relates the verb to חול, *profane:* 'he profaned himself because he should have started his planting with something other than a vineyard' *(Midrash).*

Ibn Ezra, Ramban, and most commentators interpret the verb from הַתְחָלָה beginning, i.e. the first, and render that *Noah, the man of the earth, was the first to plant a vineyard.* His predecessors planted single vines, but he was the first to plant many rows of vines in an orderly fashion, comprising a vineyard.

אִישׁ הָאֲדָמָה – *man of the earth.* I.e. master of the earth *(Rashi).*

Cf. *Zohar Chadash:*

Why was he called 'man of the earth' because the earth dried up on his behalf and, as the head of the lone surviving family, he became its master.

According to *Ibn Ezra,* it means 'skillful in the art of working the earth'; while *Ramban* explains it 'man of the earth', for Noah did not build cities, instead he devoted himself to the cultivation of the ground. Whoever dedicates himself to a purpose is referred to as אִישׁ, *man of,* that purpose. Similarly is one dedicated to the service of God called אִישׁ הָאֱלֹהִים, *a man of God* [*Deut.* 33:1].

וַיִּטַּע כָּרֶם – *And he planted a vineyard.*

He desired wine so greatly that he did not plant the vine singly, but instead planted an entire vineyard [see above] *(Ramban).*

Where did he get the vine to plant?

IX 20-22

from these the whole world was spread out.
20 *Noah, the man of the earth, debased himself and planted a vineyard.* 21 *He drank of the wine and became drunk, and he uncovered himself within his tent.* 22 *Ham, the father of Canaan, saw his father's*

— He had taken grapevines and young shoots for fig trees and olive trees into the ark with him *(Midrash; Rashi;* cf. *comm.* to 6:21).

Cf. *Targum Yonasan:* '... and he found a vine which the river had brought from the Garden of Eden and he planted it in a vineyard, and it flourished in a day; its grapes ripened and he pressed them out.'

21. וַיֵּשְׁתְּ מִן הַיַּיִן וַיִּשְׁכָּר — *[And] he drank of the wine* — To excess *(Midrash), and he became drunk.* Rav Chiyah said: He planted it, drank thereof, and was humiliated all in one and the same day *(Midrash).*

According to *Zohar Chadash,* the vine was already laden with grapes; he squeezed them out and drank the wine *(Torah Shelemah* 9:122).

וַיִּתְגַּל בְּתוֹךְ אָהֳלֹה — *And he uncovered himself within his tent* [i.e. in the innermost part of his tent, see *Hirsch* below.]

Rashi comments that וַיִּתְגַּל is in the *hithpael* conjugation [implying that he uncovered himself].

He was uncovered, not by himself, but by someone else whom the Torah does not identify. From the curse uttered later, it would seem that Canaan did it *(B'chor Shor; Ralbag).*

According to *Tur,* however, Noah was uncovered by Ham who told his brothers.

Rashi notes that the spelling of אָהֳלֹה is an allusion to the ten tribes of Israel, known collectively after the city of Samaria which was called אָהֳלָה *[Ezekiel* 23:4] and who were exiled [= גָּלוּ, homiletically related to וַיִּתְגַּל] on account of wine [cf. *Amos* 6:6]

[Therefore, the homiletical rendering of this verse, according to *Rashi* would be: those who dwelled in Oholah were exiled on account of wine.]

This follows the *Midrash* which also connects וַיִּתְגַּל to גָּלוּת, exile: He was the cause of exile for himself and subsequent generations.

Hirsch perceives from the cantillation of this verse that Noah had not *drunk the wine* בְּתוֹךְ אָהֳלֹה, in the innermost part of his tent, but וַיִּתְגַּל בְּתוֹךְ אָהֳלֹה, when he felt that the wine was going to his head he took refuge in the innermost part of the tent where he hoped nobody would see him.

22. וַיַּרְא חָם אֲבִי כְנַעַן ... — *[And] Ham, the father of Canaan, saw his father's nakedness.*

And he saw — i.e. he looked freely and unashamedly. He should have averted his gaze, but did not *(Lekach Tov).*

Some of our Sages maintain that Canaan saw and told his father; he is therefore associated with the matter and was cursed *(Rashi).*

According to *Sforno,* Ham saw the indignity which Canaan had perpetrated upon Noah [for according to *Pirkei d'Rabbi Eliezer* it was *Canaan* who emasculated him. See below.]

Shem and Japheth waited outside respectfully, but Ham who, as a father, should have best appreciated the dignity due a parent, went in to *see* the shame of his father and then went to his brothers gleefully telling what he had seen *(Hirsch).*

אֶת עֶרְוַת אָבִיו — *His father's nakedness.*

ט
כג-כד

כג לִשְׁנֵי־אֶחָיו בַּחוּץ: וַיִּקַּח שֵׁם וָיֶפֶת אֶת־
הַשִּׂמְלָה וַיָּשִׂימוּ עַל־שְׁכֶם שְׁנֵיהֶם וַיֵּלְכוּ
אֲחֹרַנִּית וַיְכַסּוּ אֵת עֶרְוַת אֲבִיהֶם
וּפְנֵיהֶם אֲחֹרַנִּית וְעֶרְוַת אֲבִיהֶם לֹא רָאוּ:
כד וַיִּיקֶץ נֹחַ מִיֵּינוֹ וַיֵּדַע אֵת אֲשֶׁר־עָשָׂה לוֹ

— Some say that he castrated him; others that he indulged his perverted lust upon him *(Rashi; Sanhedrin* 70a).

Hirsch suggests that the term עֶרְוָה sometimes means not literal nakedness, but the degraded condition of drunkenness as in *Habbakuk* 2:15. Thus it is possible that Noah was not naked but that Ham enjoyed his father's compromised condition.

Rav Shlomo Kluger suggests that the sin was a different one. Noah had become intoxicated and became uncovered in the privacy of his wife's tent as the *Midrash* interprets אָהֳלֹה = *her tent,* i.e., his wife's tent. No one of the sons dared enter and disturb their intimacy except for Ham, who then saw his mother in her immodesty. The phrase עֶרְוַת אָבִיו, *his father's nakedness,* alludes to his mother as in *Lev.* 18:8: *the nakedness of your father's wife you shall not uncover — it is your father's nakedness.*

וַיַּגֵּד לִשְׁנֵי אֶחָיו בַּחוּץ — *And* [*he*] *told his two brothers outside* — in the marketplace [i.e. publicly] *(Targum).*

— With mocking derision, thus making his father the object of ridicule *(Lekach Tov).*[1]

— He did not tell it to his brothers in order that they should cover him; if that were his intention, he could have covered him himself *(B'chor Shor).*

Ramban explains that Ham's sin was that he should have modestly covered his father's nakedness and concealed his shame by telling no one. Instead, he broadcast the matter to his two brothers in public in order to deride Noah. Our Sages have mentioned an additional sin that Ham committed [see *Rashi* and *Sanhedrin* 70a above.]

Following *Sforno:* He rejoiced at the indignity his son had inflicted, and joyfully told his brothers.

23. וַיִּקַּח שֵׁם וָיֶפֶת אֶת הַשִּׂמְלָה — *And Shem and Japheth took a* [lit. *'the'*] *garment.*

The verb *'took'* is in singular because Shem alone took the initiative in performing this meritorious deed, then Japheth came and joined him. Therefore, the descendants of Shem [i.e. the Jews] were rewarded with the precept of טַלִּית שֶׁל צִיצִית, fringed garments [*Numbers* 15:38]; those of Japheth were rewarded with burial in Eretz Yisrael as it is written [*Ezek.* 39:11]: *And it shall come to pass in that day that I will give unto Gog* [a descendant of Japheth] *a place fit for burial in Israel;* and those of Ham, who degraded his father, were eventually *'led away by the King of As-*

1. According to the *Midrash* [in apparent continuity of its interpretation that Noah had gone into *his wife's tent*] Ham said: 'Adam had but two sons yet one arose and slew his brother, and this man [Noah] had three sons and yet he wants four!' [*Rashi* cites this *Midrash* to *v.* 25 s.v. אָרוּר כְּנָעַן. See *footnote* there.]

IX
23-24 *nakedness and told his two brothers outside.* [23] *And*
Shem and Japheth took a garment, laid it upon both
their shoulders, and they walked backwards, and
covered their father's nakedness; their faces were
turned away, and they saw not their father's
nakedness.
[24] *Noah awoke from his wine and realized what his*

syria ... naked and barefoot' [*Isaiah* 20:4] *(Midrash; Rashi).*

Torah Shelemah cites *Midrash Zuta* to *Shir HaShirim* 1:15:

By what merit did Yavan [i.e., Greece a descendant of Japheth] govern Israel? — It was God's reward for Japheth who was concerned for his father's honor, for God overlooks nothing and He does not deprive any creature of its just reward.

וַיָּשִׂימוּ עַל שְׁכֶם שְׁנֵיהֶם — *And laid it upon both their shoulders* [lit. *'the shoulder of both of them.*] — i.e. each draped a part of the garment over his shoulder *(Ibn Ezra).*

They laid it on their shoulders to make it easy, when walking backward and approaching close to their father, to let the garment slip off their shoulders and cover their father without having to gaze upon him at all *(Imrei Shefer).*

וּפְנֵיהֶם אֲחֹרַנִּית — *And their faces were turned away* [lit. *'were backward'*]. — This is stated a second time to teach that when they approached him and had to turn around in order to cover him they turned their faces away *(Rashi).*

For not only did their eyes not glance at their father's shame, even their *faces* were turned away, *and they did not see their father's nakedness (Alshich).*

24. וַיִּיקֶץ נֹחַ מִיֵּינוֹ — [*And*] *Noah awoke from his wine.* i.e. the intoxicating and sleep-inducing effects of his wine wore off *(Midrash).*

Not only did he wake up from his sleep but even מִיֵּינוֹ, *from his wine,* i.e. his mind was completely lucid and therefore the prophetic spirit for which he was worthy returned to him and through it he knew what had transpired *(Ha'amek Davar).*

בְּנוֹ הַקָּטָן — *His small son.* This phrase raises several difficulties in the chronology of the children, and in the identity of its subject.

Rashi [following the *Midrash* which apparently agrees with *Sanhedrin* 69b that Japheth was the eldest, Ham the second, and Shem the youngest — (see *comm.* to 5:32)] explains that הַקָּטָן in this verse refers to Ham, who although not the youngest, is called *'small'* in the sense of *'the unfit and the despised'*, as the word is used in *Jeremiah* 49:15.

Ralbag interprets בְּנוֹ הַקָּטָן as *his youngest child,* and since Ham was not the youngest, this refers to Canaan, *Ham's* youngest son who, as pointed out, was implicated in the dastardly act. 'Grandchildren are like children.'

Following the translation *his youngest son, Ramban* perceives no difficulty. According to his chronology Ham was the youngest and it is he that is referred to: 'Noah knew that Ham had disclosed his disgrace to many, and he was ashamed of the matter.'

An entirely different interpreta-

כה בְּנוֹ הַקָּטָן: וַיֹּאמֶר אָרוּר כְּנָעַן עֶבֶד
כו עֲבָדִים יִהְיֶה לְאֶחָיו: וַיֹּאמֶר בָּרוּךְ יהוה
כז אֱלֹהֵי שֵׁם וִיהִי כְנַעַן עֶבֶד לָמוֹ: יַפְתְּ

tion is offered by *B'chor Shor* and *Chizkuni*. Understanding בְּנוֹ הַקָּטָן as *the youngest son,* they interpret the verse in a praiseworthy manner:

This verse refers to Shem, who took the initiative and acted righteously. Noah awoke from his wine and realized all the *goodness* his youngest son Shem had done on his behalf, and for this reason conferred upon him the choicest blessing [*v.* 26].

Hirsch introduces the next three verses by calling them the most far-reaching prophecy ever uttered. In it God allowed Noah to encapsule all of human history (see *Overview).*

25. אָרוּר כְּנָעַן — *Cursed is Canaan.*

Ham sinned and Canaan is cursed! — Rav Yehudah explains that God had already blessed Noah and his sons [*v.* 1] and there cannot be a curse where a blessing has already been given. Therefore, not being able to curse his son, he cursed his grandson. According to Rav Nechemiah, the curse is attached to Canaan because he originally saw Noah and informed the others *(Midrash)*[1]

Radak explains that Noah cursed Canaan because he prophetically foresaw that Canaan's descendants would be perpetually wicked. The curse was indeed fulfilled for we see that the patriarchs avoided intermarrying with the accursed Canaanites.

Noteworthy, also, is that it does not say אָרוּר יִהְיֶה כְּנַעַן, 'cursed *shall be* Canaan', but 'cursed *is* Canaan' which signifies he was already accursed from aforetime *(Tzror HaMor).*

עֶבֶד עֲבָדִים — *A slave of slaves.*

— I.e., a slave among slaves *(Ibn Ezra);* the implication was that his brothers, too, will become slaves, and he will be a slave unto them *(B'chor Shor; Radak).*

According to *Ralbag,* the phrase means 'the lowliest of slaves.'

Sforno comments that Canaan, as the most degraded of the family, would naturally have become a servant of his brothers. Noah's additional curse was that he would become a *slave of slaves.*

Indeed, many of the descendants of Shem and Japheth were, throughout history, sold into slavery, and conversely, not every Canaanite is a slave. The curse is that from birth they will be steeped in the spirit of slavery and will not even seriously desire their freedom. This is unlike the children of Shem and Japheth, whose inner spirit constantly aspires for freedom even when they are enslaved *(Haamek Davar).*

1. Noah grieved very much in the ark that he had no young son to wait on him and declared that after he left the ark he would beget another child. But when Ham acted thus to him [i.e. castrated him *(Sanh.* 70a)] he exclaimed: You have prevented me from begetting a young son to serve me, therefore I curse your fourth son [Canaan; see 10:6 (see also footnote to *v.* 23).] *(Midrash).*

IX small son had done to him. 25 And he said, 'Cursed is
25-26 Canaan; a slave of slaves shall he be to his brothers.'
26 And he said, 'Blessed is HASHEM, the God of
Shem; and let Canaan be a slave to them.'

The curse was that the raw, uncontrolled sensuality displayed by Canaan could never be permitted to rule. The person with self-control, on the other hand, will not allow himself to be enslaved *(Hirsch).*

יִהְיֶה לְאֶחָיו — *Shall he be to his brothers.* Cush, Mitzraim, and Phut [10:6] *(Ibn Ezra).*

According to *Ramban, 'his brothers'* might also refer to his father's brothers, Japheth and Shem, for one's father's brothers are called brothers' as in *Gen.* 14:14 where Lot, [a nephew] is referred to as Abraham's *brother.* It may also be that *to his brothers* means that he will be enslaved to the whole world; whoever will find him will enslave him.

26. בָּרוּךְ ה׳ אֱלֹהֵי שֵׁם — *Blessed is HASHEM the God of Shem* — who will keep His promise to Shem's descendants and give them the land of Canaan *(Rashi).* This interpretation is indicated by the following phrase: *'and let Canaan be a slave to them'* — but Canaan did not become a tributary of Shem's descendant until Israel conquered their land *(Mizrachi).*

Midrash Tanchuma [*Torah Shelemah* 9:160] notes that God's Name is not mentioned in connection with evil, but only in connection with good. Thus, only when Noah *blessed* his son does it say *Blessed is HASHEM, God of Shem;* but when he cursed Canaan, God's Name is not invoked, as it says: *Cursed is Canaan.*

Noah invoked HASHEM's unique Name in this blessing because he prophetically foresaw that Shem's descendants, the unique nation of Israel, would be dedicated to the service of HASHEM who is likewise Unique *(Radak; Ralbag).*

Shem's freedom was so absolute that he had no master over him but God *(B'chor Shor).*

Hirsch notes that HASHEM is not the exclusive God of Shem. He is referred to here as the God of Shem in the same sense that He is called the God of Abraham, Isaac, and Jacob: a) because He is especially revealed in their history and guidance; and b) because they are the ones who recognized and proclaimed His greatness.

וִיהִי כְנַעַן עֶבֶד לָמוֹ — *And let* [the descendants of *(Sforno)*] *Canaan be a slave* [or: *'servant'*] *to them* — to Shem's descendants, and may Canaan pay them tribute *(Mizrachi,* above).

Noah first blessed the God of Shem, thereby letting it be known that Shem will be a servant of HASHEM while Canaan will be subject to the descendants of Shem who were many. It is also possible that לָמוֹ, *to them,* reverts also to his aforementioned brothers *(Ramban).*

According to *Sforno,* this refers to the descendants of Canaan who will be compelled to serve *God and the descendants of Shem,* as it is

ט
כח־כט

אֱלֹהִים֙ לְיֶ֔פֶת וְיִשְׁכֹּ֖ן בְּאָֽהֳלֵי־שֵׁ֑ם וִיהִ֥י
כח כְנַ֖עַן עֶ֥בֶד לָֽמוֹ: וַֽיְחִי־נֹ֖חַ אַחַ֣ר הַמַּבּ֑וּל
כט שְׁלֹ֤שׁ מֵאוֹת֙ שָׁנָ֔ה וַחֲמִשִּׁ֖ים שָׁנָֽה: וַֽיְהִי֙
כָּל־יְמֵי־נֹ֔חַ תְּשַׁ֤ע מֵאוֹת֙ שָׁנָ֔ה וַחֲמִשִּׁ֖ים
שָׁנָ֑ה וַיָּמֹֽת:

written [*Josh.* 9:27]: *And Joshua made them that day hewers of wood and drawers of water for the congregation and for the altar of HASHEM.*

[*Ibn Ezra* explains that לָמוֹ is a poetic form for לָהֶם as in *Deut.* 33:2 וְזָרַח מִשֵּׂעִיר לָמוֹ, while *Heidenheim* points out that occasionally לָמוֹ may mean *to him,* which is how the *Targum* translates the word in *Isaiah* 44:15.]

27. יַפְתְּ אֱלֹהִים לְיֶפֶת — *May God extend Japheth* — i.e. May God extend Japheth's boundaries, and may he inherit many lands *(B'chor Shor).*

R' Bachya notes that 'until this very day the descendants of Japheth are countless and their lands are numerous.'

Hirsch concludes that יַפְתְּ is the *Hiphil* form of cognate verbs meaning: to open minds. He therefore renders: *'God will open the mind of Japheth ...'* i.e. will make him responsive to feelings. But educating people to a sense of beauty is not man's highest calling. His culture must be guided by a higher ideal, external to his own feelings and sense. This has been the role of Shem as bearer of the Torah. Thus, the two guiding lights of humanity have been Japheth as bearer of Greek culture, and Shem as bearer of God's spiritual calling (see *Overview).*

וְיִשְׁכֹּן בְּאָהֳלֵי שֵׁם — *But* [lit. *'and'*] *He will dwell in the tents of Shem.*

The subject of this is God. He will enlarge the boundaries of Japheth, but will cause His Shechinah to dwell [only] in Israel *(Rashi; Midrash).*

As the *Talmud (Yoma* 10a) explains: Although God extended Japheth, inasmuch as his descendant Cyrus built the Second Temple, yet the Shechinah did not dwell in it. — He rests only in the tents of Shem, for the Shechinah dwelt only in the First Temple which was built by Solomon, a descendant of Shem, [see *Shir HaShirim,* ArtScroll edition footnote p. 152 which interprets 5:5 in the light of this Talmudic reference] *(Rashi; Midrash).*

The Talmud also interprets this phrase with *Japheth* as the subject, relating יפת to יָפֶה, beauty:

The sacred books of the Scriptures may be written [in addition to Hebrew] only in Greek ... because it is written יַפְתְּ אֱלֹהִים לְיֶפֶת, implying, 'Let the chief beauty [יְפִיוּת] of Japheth, [i.e. Greek, the most beautiful of languages], be used in the tents of Shem' [i.e., the Jewish houses of study] *(Megillah* 9a).

This happened when King Ptolemy ordered seventy-two Sages to translate the Torah into Greek. Based on this verse and on a desire to make the Torah accessible to those who could not read it in Hebrew, the Sages permitted the translation to be made.

... Nowadays, however, since the beauty of the classical Greek has been corrupted, a Torah may be written only

IX 27-28

[27] *May God extend Japheth, but he will dwell in the tents of Shem; may Canaan be a slave to them.'*
[28] *Noah lived after the Flood 350 years.* [29] *And all the days of Noah were 950 years; and he died.*

in Hebrew *(Rambam, Hil. Tefilin* 1:19).

According to *Abarbanel,* there is also a prophetic suggestion here that Japheth's descendants will one day 'dwell in the tents of Shem' — i.e. will govern Eretz Yisrael when the Jews will be exiled [cf. *Midrash Zuta* cited to *v.* 23.]

Or, as *Targum Yonasan* paraphrases: God will grant a land of beauty to Japheth, and his sons will be proselytes dwelling in the academies of Shem.

Ibn Ezra points out that in this verse Noah blesses Japheth and Shem, because in the previous verse it is really *God* who is praised.

This is also how *Ramban* explains it: 'Noah then blessed Japheth with an extension of his territories. He blessed Shem that God cause His Shechinah to dwell in his tents, and finally said that Canaan be a servant *to them,* i.e. the two of them.'

וִיהִי כְנַעַן עֶבֶד לָמוֹ [*And*] *may Canaan be a slave to them.* i.e. to the descendants of Shem and Japheth, the repetition being for emphasis *(R' Bachya).*

Ramban explains that Noah made Canaan subservient to Shem twice [in this verse and the preceding] thus intimating that the descendants of Shem will inherit Canaan's land and all his possessions because [*Pesachim* 88b]: מַה שֶׁקָּנָה עֶבֶד קָנָה רַבּוֹ, 'whatever a slave acquires belongs to his master.'

According to *Rashi,* the repetition of the phrase indicates that even after Shem's descendants will go into exile, they will purchase Canaan's descendants as slaves.

Ramban concludes that the Torah recorded the incident to show that Abraham was granted Canaan's land because, the latter became an eternal servant as a result of his sin. Another reason is to show that intoxication can be so harmful that even the righteous Noah who saved the world was brought to curse his own grandchild due to wine-induced intoxication.

28. The death of Noah.

אַחַר הַמַּבּוּל — *After the Flood.*

Hoffmann points out that in distinction to Noah's predecessors [chapter 5] the dividing line between the two periods of Noah's life is not the birth of his children; it is the period of the Flood, the principle event in his life.

29. תְּשַׁע מֵאוֹת שָׁנָה וַחֲמִשִּׁים שָׁנָה — *Nine hundred and fifty years.*

[This chronological note yields us the following insight which will be important later]:

Noah was born in the year 1056 from Creation. The Flood commenced in 1656, his 600th year, and he died in 2006 ten years after the הַפְּלָגָה, Dispersion. Thus, Abraham, who was born in 1948 was 58 years old when Noah died *(Seder Olam; Midrash HaGadol). Ibn Ezra* points out as a mnemonic that the numerical value of נֹחַ is 58.

It is thus chronologically clear that Abraham, who *would command his children and his household after him that they may keep*

א וְאֵ֗לֶּה תּוֹלְדֹ֣ת בְּנֵי־נֹ֔חַ שֵׁ֖ם חָ֣ם וָיָ֑פֶת
ב וַיִּוָּלְד֥וּ לָהֶ֛ם בָּנִ֖ים אַחַ֥ר הַמַּבּֽוּל׃ בְּנֵ֣י יֶ֔פֶת

the way of HASHEM [18:19], saw Noah, who in turn saw Lamech, and who had seen Adam. Thus from Adam to Abraham there was a word-of-mouth tradition from creation spanning only four people. Similarly, Moses, who wrote the Torah saw Kehas [or Amram] who saw Jacob who saw Abraham. Thus, there were not more than seven people who carried the tradition first hand from Adam to Moses *(Abarbanel).*

[See *footnote to 5:22;* and Chronology/Time Line p. xii.]

וַיָּמֹת — *And he died.*

[There is no chronological sequence of events in the Torah. And, as pointed out, Noah lived much beyond this point in the narrative. His death is mentioned now because he was no longer pre-eminent and his later life had no bearing on the unfolding of history. Similarly, Abraham's death is stated before the histories of Ishmael and Isaac begin to become decisive.

[Cf. also *comm.* of *Ramban* cited regarding Terach's death in 11:32.]

Midrash Tanchuma comments that Noah did not die until he saw the entire world re-settled, and all seventy nations which descended from him.

X

1. The descendants of Noah. The Seventy Nations.

וְאֵלֶּה תּוֹלְדֹת בְּנֵי־נֹחַ שֵׁם חָם וָיָפֶת — *Now* [lit. *'and'*] *these are the descendants* [or: *'generations'*] *of the sons of Noah, Shem, Ham, and Japheth.*

The verse should be understood as if it read: 'The following are the descendants of Shem, Ham, and Japheth, who were Noah's sons' *(Radak; Ibn Caspi).*

Ramban suggests that the Torah's main purpose is to relate the history of Abraham and his family and for that reason, the genealogy of Shem, his ancestor, is also related in detail; Ham's genealogy is given to inform us of those nations whose lands Abraham was to inherit because of their ancestor's sin; and Japheth's line is given, and the story of the Dispersion, is related to account for the difference in languages and to show why mankind became dispersed although it had a common ancestor. Another reason for the genealogy is to demonstrate God's mercy in preserving man and maintaining the covenant with Noah [cf. *Moreh III:*50 cited in 11:1].

[See also *comm.* of *Abarbanel* to 9:29.]

אַחַר הַמַּבּוּל — *After the Flood.*

The verse thus tells us that although they were fit to beget children before the Flood — when people had children in their sixties — nevertheless God prevented Noah's sons from having children even at the age of a hundred, until *after* the Flood, lest the children be drowned in the deluge, and to avoid the necessity of accommodating too many in the ark *(Ramban).*

Me'am Loez stresses the poignancy of the phrase. It was *after* the Flood and the people should have realized that they could not defy God with impunity any more than

X
1 [1]*These are the descendants of Shem, Ham, and Japheth, the sons of Noah; sons were born to them after the Flood.*

had their ancestors of the generation that was blotted out (see *Overview*).

⋄§ The Seventy Nations.

The *Talmudic* tradition that there are seventy nations in the world is based upon the ensuing list of Noah's descendants *(R' Bachya).*

This tradition of seventy nations is deep-rooted. According to the *Midrash,* each of the seventy nations is placed under the protection of a special angel, except Israel, whose Protector is God Himself. [Cf *footnote* to 11:7.]

Just as there were seventy nations (cf. *Targum Yonasan* to 11:7), the words of the Torah engraved on the Tablets on Mount Ebal [*Deut.* 27:2 ff] were written in seventy languages (*Mishnah, Sotah* 7:5) so that all the nations might read it. For the same reason, God's voice at Sinai divided itself into seventy languages *(Shabbos* 88b).

The seventy bullocks sacrificed on Tabernacles were offered to atone for the seventy nations. 'Woe to the nations!' says Rav Yochanan; 'for they suffered a loss [by having destroyed the Temple] and do not realize the extent of the loss. While the Temple existed, the altar atoned for them, but now [that it is destroyed] who will atone for them?' *(Sukkah* 55b).

The seventy members of the Sanhedrin also corresponded to the seventy nations of the world *(Tar. Yerushalmi* to *Gen.* 28:3).

According to many commentators — e.g. *Radak, Ralbag, Chizkuni, Malbim* — this concept seems to underlie *Deut.* 32:8 which says that God *'established the boundaries of nations* [i.e. the seventy nations] ... *according to the number of the children of Israel'* — namely the seventy who descended to Egypt with Jacob *(Gen.* 46:27). [1]

There is some disagreement as to how the count of seventy nations is to be derived from the following verses. A counting of the names —

1. *Harav David Feinstein* explains the significance of the many parallels to the seventy nations: the seventy languages into which the Torah was translated, the seventy offerings of Tabernacles, the seventy members of the Sanhedrin.

Indeed, on the verse יַצֵּב גְּבֻלֹת עַמִּים לְמִסְפַּר בְּנֵי יִשְׂרָאֵל, *He established the boundaries of nations according to the number of the children of Israel (Deut.* 32:8), the Sages comment that God established seventy nations because Jacob's family numbered seventy when he descended to Egypt. Why was it necessary for the number of nations to correspond to the number of Jews? Moreover, at the conclusion of the forty years in the desert Moses explained the Torah to the Jews in all seventy languages (*Deut.* 1:5 see *Rashi*). Why was it necessary for him to use seventy languages when all his listeners were Hebrew-speaking Jews?

Each of the seventy nations represented a unique characteristic, as the Sages say, one excelled in warfare, another in licentiousness, another in beauty and so on. All of these national virtues and strains of character are present in Israel as well for each person has gifts to develop and temptations to overcome. God wants all nations to rise to their greatest spiritual potential.

These variations were present in the individuals of Jacob's family. And the seventy languages used by Moses parallel the seventy facets of Torah; each 'speaks' to one of the seventy characteristics with which God has populated the world. (It may also be suggested that each of the seventy offerings of Tabernacles atoned for the trespasses of each of these seventy national characteristics present within Israel, and consequently the nations of the world benefitted from this universal atonement).

Israel, as the spiritual model and leader of the world, was to demonstrate within itself that eminence is within reach of every nation; that every type of person can live a Torah life.

Therefore, a significant portion of Jewish life revolves around the number seventy to symbolize that every national trait can become harnessed for holy purposes.

י גֹּמֶר וּמָגוֹג וּמָדַי וְיָוָן וְתֻבָל וּמֶשֶׁךְ וְתִירָס׃
ג-ד ג ד וּבְנֵי גֹּמֶר אַשְׁכְּנַז וְרִיפַת וְתֹגַרְמָה׃ וּבְנֵי
יָוָן אֱלִישָׁה וְתַרְשִׁישׁ כִּתִּים וְדֹדָנִים׃

including Shem, Ham and Japheth, will reveal a total of seventy-four.

The *comm.* follows the most common system [following *Pesikta Zutresa; Torah Sheleimah* 9:110] of ascribing 14 nations to Japheth; 30 to Ham; and 26 to Shem, totalling seventy. Shem, Ham, and Japheth themselves are omitted as are the Philistines who, according to *v.* 14 are designated as a mixed race.

Others include the Philistines but omit Nimrod from whom a separate nation did not descend.

Yalkut Shimoni 61 attributes 15 nations to Japheth, 32 to Ham, and 27 to Shem, totalling 74. However, Shem, Arpachshad, Shelah and Eber were too righteous to be counted among the general rabble, leaving the total again at 70.

2. A. The line of Japheth (14 Nations).

[In the following genealogical history I have attempted to cull the classical sources for contemporary identification of the peoples. It must be emphasized however that where the guidance of our Sages is less than specific it is impossible to relate with certainty all of these names to contemporary geographic locations and ethnic ancestry].

בְּנֵי יֶפֶת — *The children of Japheth.*

Japheth is mentioned first because it is common Scriptural usage to continue a narrative with the last-named personage. Compare, for example, *Joshua* 24:4: *And I gave to Isaac, Jacob, and Esau; and I gave to Esau.* Here, too, Japheth was the last-named in the previous verse, and therefore this verse continues with him *(Ibn Ezra).*

[See similar explanation for the chiasmic arrangement of Cain-Abel, Abel-Cain in 4:2 s.v. וְקַיִן הָיָה.]

Ramban maintains, however, that Japheth is mentioned first because he was the oldest. It continues with Ham [although, according to *Ramban,* Ham was the youngest (see on 9:24)] so that the line of Shem [leading to Abraham] could be dealt with uninterruptedly.

[However, according to the genealogy of the *Talmud (Sanh.* 69b; see *comm.* to 5:32; 10:21 and 11:10) the names of Noah's sons are in the proper chronological order: Japheth, Ham, and Shem.]

(1)* גֹּמֶר — *Gomer,* i.e. Germania *(Yoma* 10a; *Yerushalmi* Megillah 1:11).

According to *Targum Yonasan* and *Midrash:* Africa.

[*Gomer* is mentioned in *Ezekiel* 38:6 as one of the Confederates of Gog of the land of Magog. (See below).]

[Some identify Germania with the Cimmerii, while more probably it refers to what in *Talmudic* times was the Roman province of Germania — גֶּרְמַנְיָא שֶׁל אֱדוֹם — *v. Meg.* 6a.]

See also *comm.* to *Ashkenaz,* next verse.]

(2) מָגוֹג — *Magog* — i.e. Kandia *(Yoma).*

* The names of each of the seventy nations will be preceded bv a number in parenthesis which will correspond to the charts of the Seventy Nations on page 313).

X
2-4

[2]*The children of Japheth: Gomer, Magog, Madai,*
Javan, Tubal, Meshech, and Tiras. [3]*The descendants*
of Gomer: Ashkenaz, Riphath, and Togarmah. [4]*The*
descendants of Javan: Elishah and Tarshish, the Kit-

According to *Targum Yonasan* and *Midrash*: Germania [see Gomer, above]; while according to *Yerushalmi Megillah* 1:11: Gothia, the land of the Goths.

[Magog is mentioned several times in Scripture, e.g. *Ezekiel* 38:2; 39:6 as the name of the land of Gog.]

Kesses HaSofer identifies them with the Mongols who lived near China, for in fact the very name Mongol is a corruption of Magog. He also cites Arab writers who refer to the Great Wall of China as 'the wall of Al Magog.'

(3) מָדַי — *Madia,* i.e. Macedonia *(Yoma),* while according to *Yonasan, Yerushalmi,* and the *Midrash,* the reference is to the Medes [who dwelt east of Assyria and are mentioned a number of times in Scripture. In fact, the mountain of Ararat lay in Median territory. In 550 B.C.E. Media was overthrown by Persia under Cyrus. Subsequently, they became a single kingdom and their names are often used interchangeably. See, for example, the references to Persia and Media in *Esther* 1:3, 14, 18, 19; 10:2; *Daniel* 5:28; 6:8; 8:20.]

(4) יָוָן — *Javan* — in its literal sense [i.e. Greece] *(Yoma).*

[They are thus identified with the Ionians, a tribe of the Hellenic race who settled on the mainland of Greece, the islands of the Aegean Sea, and the coast of Asia Minor. In *Talmudic* times יָוָן connoted the Greek peoples as a whole.]

(5) תֻבָל — *Tubal,* i.e., Beth-Unyaki *(Yoma).*

— Bithynia [a province in the Northwest of Asia Minor] *(Yer. Megillah).*

(6) מֶשֶׁךְ — *Meshech,* i.e. Mysia [a district in Asia Minor] *(Yoma).*

[Cf. *Ezekiel* 27:13, 38:2, where Tubal and Meshech are similarly mentioned together.]

(7) תִירָס — *Tiras,* i.e. Persia *(Rashi)* [i.e. the Euphrates region.]

Its identification is a matter of dispute in the *Talmud Yoma* 10a between Rav Shimon and the Rabbis. According to one, *Tiras* is to be identified with Beth Traiki [Thrace (?)], while the others held it was Persia.

Both opinions are recorded in the *Midrash,* while *Targum Yonasan* has Tarkei.

3. וּבְנֵי גֹּמֶר — *And the sons of Gomer.*

[Of the seven sons of Japheth mentioned in *v.* 2, only the further branches of Gomer and Javan are named. The Torah concerns itself only with those who developed into heads of new nations. The children who are not enumerated, apparently did not form separate nations. Cf. *Rashi* to *I Chron.* 1:7, and *Ramban* on 'Phut' in 2:6.]

According to *Radak* ad. loc. The descendants of the other sons were included under the families of Gomer and Javan, and hence they are not listed.

Similarly *Malbim* comments that Gomer had other children, too.

However, only those who themselves formed separate nations — Ashkenaz, Riphath and Togarmah —are enumerated. This is the system used throughout all the following genealogy.

(8) אַשְׁכְּנַז — *Ashkenaz.* i.e.; Asia *(Targum Yonasan; Midrash; Yerushalmi).*

[Ashkenaz is mentioned in *Jeremiah* 51:27 in association with the kingdoms of Ararat and Minni. Some have identified them with the Scythians and Asconians. *Yossippon* identified them with the Teutons, while according to Rav Saadiah Gaon, they are the Slavs.]

[It is interesting that in later Jewish literature Ashkenaz has come to denote Germany, although the origins of this identification are obscure. The first such mention of this appears in the *Siddur of Rav Amram Gaon* [about 850 C.E.] where he cites the 'customs of those Jews living in Ashkenaz'. In the first half of the 11th Century Rav Hai Gaon refers in his responsa to inquiries he received from Ashkenaz, by which term he undoubtedly means Germany. Cf. also *Rashi* to *Deut.* 3:9 and *Sukkah* 17a.

[The identification with Germany might be based upon the *Talmud's* identification of Ashkenaz's father Gomer with Germania, which evidently means German tribes or lands (although, as evidenced from parallel references in *Yerushalmi* and *Midrash,* in its original context Germanikia in northwestern Syria is probably meant. See *comm.* to *Gomer* in the preceding verse.) This is noteworthy, because, as *Kesses HaSofer* points out, in *Mishnaic* times the Germanic tribes were known only as strange peoples who, along with the Cushites, were enslaved to the Romans.]

(9) רִיפַת — *Riphath.* A tribe in Northern Asia *(Kesses HaSofer).*

Targum Yonasan repeats: Riphath, while *Targum Yerushalmi* renders: Parchavan; *Rav Saadiah Gaon* identifies them with the Franks — the whole of the Germanic tribes.

In the parallel Chronologies of *I Chronicles* 1:6 the name appears as דִיפַת, *Diphath. Metzudas Zion* ad. loc. comments: 'In the Torah the name appears as Riphath, and he was called by both names. This is a basic concept in explaining variant spellings of names wherever they appear.'

(10) תֹּגַרְמָה — *Togarmah.*

According to *Targum Yerushalmi:* Barbaria; *Midrash* and *Yer. Megillah:* Germania or Germanikia [see on Gomer and Ashkenaz, above.]

Kesses HaSofer identifies them with Armenia.

[*Ezekiel* (38:6) mentions: *Gomer and all his bands;* the house of Togarmah *on the uttermost parts of the North* ... In Ezekiel's lament on Tyre (*Chapter* 27), he mentions *Beth Torgamah* among those nations — e.g. Tarshish, Yavan, Tubal, Meshech — who had mercantile relations with Tyre.]

4. (11) אֱלִישָׁה — *Elishah,* i.e. Ellas [= Hellas (?)] *(Midrash).*

[*The coasts of Elishah* appears in *Ezekiel* 27:7 where the *Targum* renders: 'the coasts of Italia.']

(12) וְתַרְשִׁישׁ — *And Tarshish.* Taras; Tarsas (*Tar. Yonasan; Midrash).*

[Tarshish is mentioned frequently in Scripture as a flourishing, wealthy, distant seaport from which silver, iron, tin, and lead *(Ezek.* 27:12), (and according to *I Kings* 10:22: gold, silver, ivory, monkeys and peacocks) were imported to Israel.]

Although some identify it with Tartessus in ancient Spain beyond the Rock of Gibralter, *Kesses HaSofer* claims that this identification is without basis because the description of Tarshish in *Ezekiel* 27:12 placing it amid countries in Asia Minor, would appear, to mean Tarzia in the Balkans, although this is not certain.

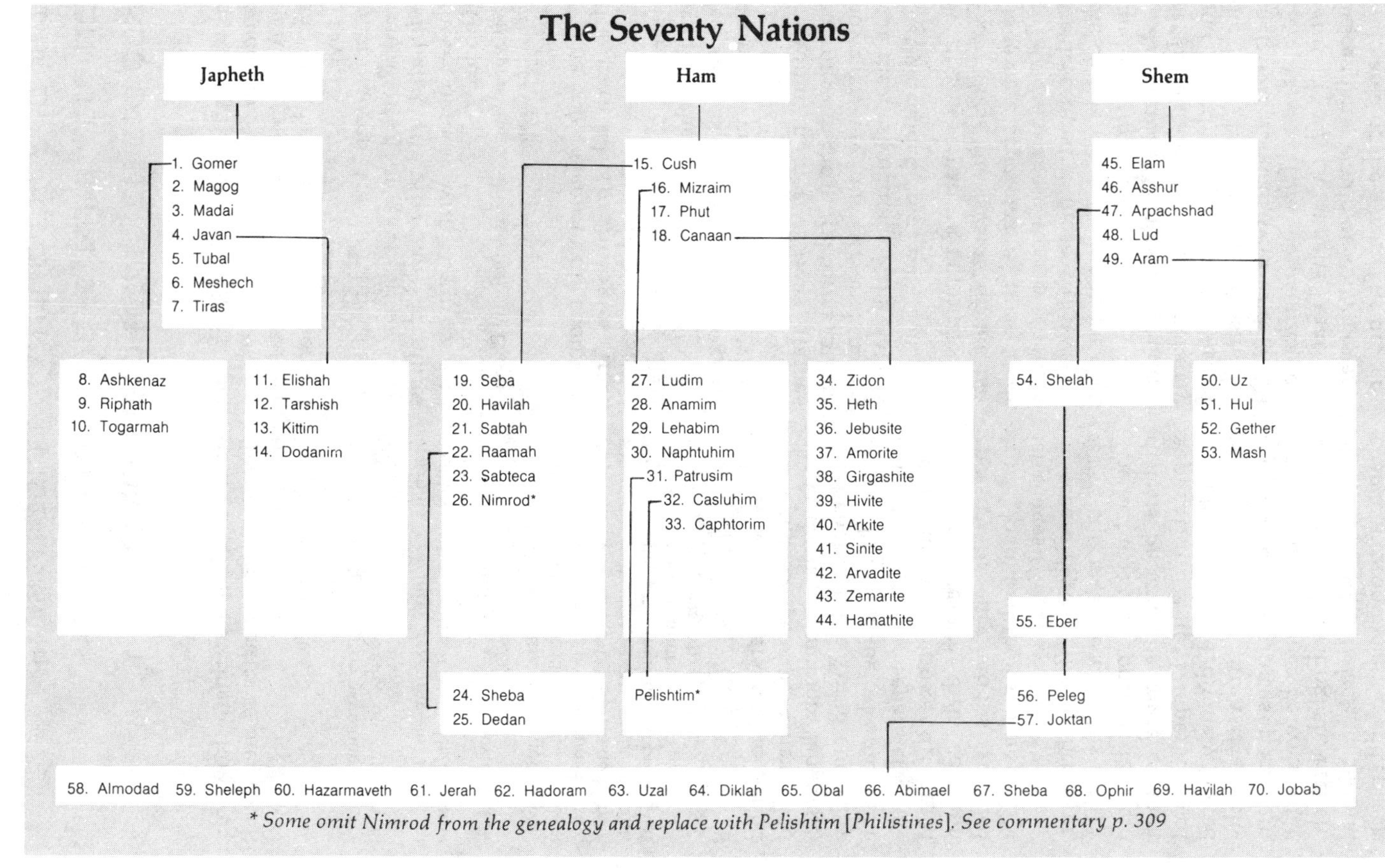
The Seventy Nations
Japheth
1. Gomer
2. Magog
3. Madai
4. Javan
5. Tubal
6. Meshech
7. Tiras
8. Ashkenaz
9. Riphath
10. Togarmah
11. Elishah
12. Tarshish
13. Kittim
14. Dodanim
Ham
15. Cush
16. Mizraim
17. Phut
18. Canaan
19. Seba
20. Havilah
21. Sabtah
22. Raamah
23. Sabteca
26. Nimrod*
24. Sheba
25. Dedan
27. Ludim
28. Anamim
29. Lehabim
30. Naphtuhim
31. Patrusim
32. Casluhim
33. Caphtorim
Pelishtim*
34. Zidon
35. Heth
36. Jebusite
37. Amorite
38. Girgashite
39. Hivite
40. Arkite
41. Sinite
42. Arvadite
43. Zemarite
44. Hamathite
Shem
45. Elam
46. Asshur
47. Arpachshad
48. Lud
49. Aram
54. Shelah
55. Eber
56. Peleg
57. Joktan
50. Uz
51. Hul
52. Gether
53. Mash
58. Almodad 59. Sheleph 60. Hazarmaveth 61. Jerah 62. Hadoram 63. Uzal 64. Diklah 65. Obal 66. Abimael 67. Sheba 68. Ophir 69. Havilah 70. Jobab
* Some omit Nimrod from the genealogy and replace with Pelishtim [Philistines]. See commentary p. 309

ה מֵאֵלֶּה נִפְרְדוּ אִיֵּי הַגּוֹיִם בְּאַרְצֹתָם אִישׁ
ו לִלְשֹׁנוֹ לְמִשְׁפְּחֹתָם בְּגוֹיֵהֶם: וּבְנֵי חָם
ז כּוּשׁ וּמִצְרַיִם וּפוּט וּכְנָעַן: וּבְנֵי כוּשׁ סְבָא

כִּתִּים וְדֹדָנִים (13,14) — *Kittim and Dodanim.*

According to the *Midrash:* Italia and Dardania [in the region of Troye *(Kessos HaSofer).*]

In *I Chron.* 1:3 the name is written *Rodanim* [see above on *Riphath*], and *Abarbanel* identifies these names with Cyprus and Rhodes.

[Cyprus was colonized largely by Phoenecians, but Greeks were also numerous on the island.]

The *Vilna Gaon* in his comm. to the parallel chronologies in *I Chronicles* 1:7 explains that all names occuring in these lists without the pronominal suffix ים, *im,* such as Gomer and Magog, are proper names of the children which their descendants assumed as national names. Those names ending with the plural forms, ים, *im,* however, are not personal names but the designation of the nations that descended from each son.

5. מֵאֵלֶּה נִפְרְדוּ אִיֵּי הַגּוֹיִם בְּאַרְצֹתָם — *From these the islands of the nations were separated in their lands.*

I.e., from these sons of Japheth are descended all those who dwell in the coastlands, each one in his own land *(Hoffmann).*

As *Ramban* explains, the children of Japheth each dwelt separately and spread far apart on the isles of the sea. This was the blessing of their father Noah who said [9:27] *God expand* [*the boundaries of*] *Japheth* which means that his descendants would be spread over a wide area of the earth. The descendants of Ham and Shem, however, lived near one another as they dwelt on the continents.

The term אִיֵּי can refer:
— to islands *(Radak);*
— to any foreign country adjoining the sea even if it is not surrounded by water on all four sides, as in the expression מְדִינַת הַיָּם, *maritime province,* referring to a distant country overseas *(Ibn Caspi; HaRechasim leBik'ah);*
— to any isolated place; hence an island or shut-in land.

Accordingly, the term refers not to particular geographical locations, but to the sort of relationships the nations assumed. From אֶרֶץ, *one land,* and גוי, *one nation,* they spread out to become אֲרָצוֹת, *lands,* and גוים, *nations.* Thus איים indicates a process of isolation from one another.

אִישׁ לִלְשֹׁנוֹ — *Each* [lit. *'man'*] *according to his language.*

This verse refers to the period *after* the Dispersion when God changed their common language, [next chapter], the Torah not being written in chronological order. The nations, dwelling separately one from another, spoke different languages, despite their common ancestry. Seventy nations decended from Noah, and they spoke seventy languages *(Radak).*

According to *Hirsch,* however, אִישׁ לִלְשֹׁנוֹ means *each to his dialect.* The fact that they spoke in different dialects became the *cause* of their separation. The Dispersion of Chapter 11 was a divinely forced scattering that intensified the already developing separation. There is a difference between שָׂפָה *language* (such as English, French, etc.) and לָשׁוֹן, *dialect,* a natural change in pronunciation and speech

X
5-6

tim and the Dodanim. [5]*From these the islands of the*
nations were separated in their lands — each ac-
cording to its language, by their families, in their na-
tions.
[6]*The children of Ham: Cush, Mitzraim, Phut, and*

pattern that results when people are separated from one another.

לְמִשְׁפְּחֹתָם בְּגוֹיֵהֶם — *By* [lit. *'to'*] *their families, in their nations* — i.e. divided according to the various families and political systems.

The distinct dialects became a means of uniting cohesive family units within the wider national groups *(Hirsch).*

6. B. The line of Ham (30 Nations)

(15) כּוּשׁ — *Cush* — i.e., Arabia *(Tar. Yonasan);* a sector in the southeast Sudan *(Rav Saadiah Gaon).*

Cush has come to be identified with Ethiopia, although the varying geographical descriptions in the Bible regarding Cush raise doubts about this interpretation. They might have originated in Ethiopia and migrated to other areas near Judah, Egypt and Midian. See, e.g. *I Chron.* 21:16; *ibid.* 14:8, 16:8; *Habbakuk* 3:7 *(Abarbanel; Shalsheles HaKaballah; Kesses HaSofer).*

[The darkness of the Cushites' skin has become a standing Scriptural and Talmudic analogy for anything unusual. It is also used for comparisons: just as 'black' persons are distinct from light skinned ones, so is Israel distinguished by their deeds from all men *(Moed Katan* 16b; cf. *Jeremiah 13:23).*

The term is also used as a euphemism meaning beauty. See *comm.* to *Numb.* 12:1 where Moses' wife is described as a Cushite. In the *Sifre* the question is raised: 'Was Moses' wife an Ethiopian?' — 'She was beautiful and thus distinguished by her beauty as is the Cushi by his color. In further development Cushi has simply become a synonym for 'black' *(Sukkah* 34b; *Bava Basra* 97b).

In *Isaiah* 11:11 the *Targum* renders Cush as הנראי (= India?) and the *Talmud Megillah* 11a in discussing *Esther* 1:1 records a difference of opinion whether Hodu and Cush are close to one another or are at the opposite extremes of the world.]

(16) מִצְרַיִם — *Mitzraim — i.e., Egypt.*

Hoffmann, suggesting that the plural form possibly designates 'the two *Matzors* [cf. *Isaiah* 19:6; 37:25; *and Micah* 7:12], referring to Egypt as a whole: both the upper and lower territorial regions.

(17) פּוּט — *Phut.*

Although difficult to identify, the name Phut occurs in conjunction with Lud and Cush in *Ezek.* 27:10; 35:5 and in *Nahum* 3:9.

Abarbanel identifies it with Libia [= Lybia?] in Africa, as the western part of lower Egypt is called Phiat in Coptic.

The *Midrash* notes that in the following verse the sons of Phut are not enumerated, as are the sons of Cush, Mizraim, and Canaan:

We should *not* think that the family of Phut did not exist as a separate entity and were absorbed by the others [neither becoming a nation or inheriting their own land], for *Ezekiel* [30:5] specifically mentions them as being a distinct entity in his days *(Midrash).*

— The reason they are not mentioned is because Phut became only one people formed under his own name, and did not branch off into

י
ח־ט

וַחֲוִילָה וְסַבְתָּה וְרַעְמָה וְסַבְתְּכָא וּבְנֵי
ח רַעְמָה שְׁבָא וּדְדָן: וְכוּשׁ יָלַד אֶת־נִמְרֹד
ט הוּא הֵחֵל לִהְיוֹת גִּבֹּר בָּאָרֶץ: הוּא־הָיָה
גִבֹּר־צַיִד לִפְנֵי יהוה עַל־כֵּן יֵאָמַר כְּנִמְרֹד

separate nations as did his brothers (*Ramban*).

(18) וּכְנָעַן — *And Canaan* — i.e., peoples of the low coastland of what was later known as Phoenecia, Philistia, and the Land of Canaan. Later the term Canaan had a wider connotation, embacing all the seven nations that were conquered by the Jews (*Abarbanel; Kesses HaSofer; Hoffmann*).

Describing the base characteristics of Canaan the *Talmud Pesachim* 113b comments that, 'Five things did Canaan charge his sons: Love one another, love robbery, love lewdness, hate your masters, and never speak the truth.

(19-23) סְבָא ... חֲוִילָה ... סַבְתָּה ... רַעְמָה ... סַבְתְּכָה — *Seba...Havila... Sabtah ... Raamah ... Sabteca.*

... And the name of their provinces, Sinirai, and Hindiki [=India?], and Semadai, and Lubai, and Zingai (*Targum Yonasan*).

[*Seba* is mentioned in *Psalms* 72:10 and *Isaiah* 63:3.] They are the Sabeans of Arabia in Asia Minor which divides Egypt from Canaan (*Abarbanel*).

[*Chavila* was the ancestor of certain tribes who lived on the African coast (*Abarbanel*) while a Chavilah near Ophir, apparently in northeast Arabia, appears as the descendants of Joktan in *v.* 29. See also 2:11 where the name Chavilah appears in connection with the rivers flowing from Eden. According to the *comm.* there, it is probably the Chavilah in *v.*29 that is referred to.]

The *Talmud* identifies Sabtah and Sabteca as 'Inner Sakistan and Outer Sakistan [Scythia?] (*Yoma* 10a).

(24) וּבְנֵי רַעְמָה שְׁבָא — *And the sons of Raamah: Sheba.*

The name occurs also among the children of Joktan [*v.* 28] and Keturah [25:3], the reference being to a nation of wealthy Arabian merchants which consisted of many tribes who apparently migrated from North Arabia to the south in the eight century B.C.E. (*Shalsheles Hakabbalah; Hoffmann; Kesses HaSofer*).

[It was the Queen of Sheba who visited King Solomon (*I Kings* 10).]

(25) דְּדָן — *Dedan.*

This name also occurs among the sons of Keturah [25:3]. They apparently resided on the shores of the Red Sea. They traded heavily with the Canaanites (*Kesses HaSofer*).

8. (26) וְכוּשׁ יָלַד אֶת נִמְרֹד — *And Cush begot Nimrod.*[1]

Nimrod is listed separately to draw attention to his might and kingdom (*Radak*).

1. *Me'am Loez* comments that, as a son of Cush, Nimrod should have been listed among Cush's other offspring in *v.* 7. This separate listing is to suggest that Nimrod proclaimed himself to be a god and people worshipped him thinking that he was not a mortal man born of woman. Therefore, Scripture makes a special point of saying that Cush begot him as if to ridicule those who believed he was an idol.

Canaan. [7]The children of Cush: Seba, Havilah, Sabtah, Raamah, and Sabteca. The children of Raamah:
Sheba and Dedan.
[8]And Cush begot Nimrod. He was the first to be a
mighty man on earth. [9]He was a mighty hunter
before HASHEM; therefore it is said: 'Like Nimrod a

According to *Ramban*, however, Nimrod is listed separately because he did not form a nation under his own name.

As *Hirsch* comments: Those mentioned up to now were founders of nations. That, Nimrod did not do, but introduced the new factor of might and domination into the development of nations.

הוּא הֵחֵל לִהְיוֹת גִּבֹּר בָּאָרֶץ — *He was the first* [lit. *'he began'*] *to be a mighty man on earth* — i.e. he was 'mighty' in causing the whole world to rebel against God by the plan that he devised for the generation of the Dispersion *(Rashi)*.

Mizrachi and *Gur Aryeh* disagree on *Rashi's* interpretation of הֵחֵל. *Mizrachi associates it with* הוּחַל (4:26) and וַיָּחֶל (9:20) both of which refer to defilement. Thus, Nimrod *became mighty in defiling* [God's Name] in the world by establishing idolatry.

Our translation follows *Gur Aryeh* who derives הֵחֵל from תְּחִלָּה, beginning. He agrees, however, that Nimrod was the first [i.e. *'began'*] to coerce people to idolatry, and adds that the word הֵחֵל is used by Scripture because of its similarity to חוּלִין, defilement, and because of its allusion to Nimrod's goal to indeed rebel against God by establishing idolatry among the nations under his mighty rule.

His very name described him. The Sages identify him with Amraphel, King of Shinar [see 14:1]. Why, then, was he called Nimrod? — Because he stirred up the whole world to rebel *(himrid)* against God's sovereignty *(Eruvin* 53a).

Radak explains that in the literal sense it certainly does not mean that there was never a *mighty man* before him, or that he was the only one in his generation. Behold, there were the Nephilim! Rather, the verse tells us that he was the first to subjugate others and proclaim himself a monarch over others, because until his time there was never a king; people were governed by judges and leaders. Furthermore, all of these events happened *after* the Dispersion.

For, as *Ralbag* explains, 'he was the first to seek dominion and conquest ...'

He was the first monarch. For preceding him there were neither wars nor reigning monarchs. He prevailed over the Babylonian people until they crowned him [*v.* 10], after which he went to Assyria and built great cities *(Ramban)*.

Before him every family lived under the authority of its own patriarch *(Malbim)*.

9. הוּא הָיָה גִבֹּר־צַיִד — *He was a mighty hunter.*

He ensnared [צַיִד = צָד] men with his words, and incited them to rebel against the Omnipresent *(Rashi)*.

As *Yonasan* paraphrases: He was

י י גִּבֹּור צַיִד לִפְנֵי יהוה: וַתְּהִי רֵאשִׁית
י מַמְלַכְתּוֹ בָּבֶל וְאֶרֶךְ וְאַכַּד וְכַלְנֵה בְּאֶרֶץ

a mighty rebel before HASHEM.

He became a mighty hunter of men, becoming the first to use his intellectual and physical superiority to bring lesser men under his domain. He kept people under his despotic rule until he was ready to exploit them *(Hirsch).*

According to the *Midrash* he instilled a false confidence in people and thereby entrapped them.

Midrash Aggadah takes the phrase literally: [Although meat became permitted after the Flood] no one ever partook of it until Nimrod. *He was the first who hunted and ate.*

This is followed by *Ibn Ezra:* He was the first, as a hunter, to exhibit man's might over the animals.[1]

לִפְנֵי ה׳ — *Before HASHEM,* i.e., his intention being to provoke God to His face *(Rashi).*

Ibn Ezra, however, interprets that in the most literal sense, this phrase would suggest that Nimrod built altars upon which he sacrificed unto God the animals he hunted.

[A basis for this interpretation is found in *Sefer Hayashar* 7:30 which states that in his youth, before he turned evil, Nimrod built altars upon which he offered the animals he trapped.]

Abarbanel qualifies this. He explains that he offered these sacrifices in a hypocritical pretext of piety in order to attract the masses.

Hirsch agrees that לִפְנֵי ה׳ indicates a hypocritical display of piety. He notes that לִפְנֵי ה׳ always refers to sincere devotion to God (see *Numbers* 32:20;32). Nimrod was the forerunner of those who hypocritically draped themselves in robes of piety as a means of deceiving the masses.

According to *Ramban,* the phrase suggests an exclamation that no one under the heavens rivalled his strength.

Sforno explains the phrase as denoting emphasis meaning 'an exceedingly strong hunter', just as God's name is used to emphasize the importance of Nineveh in *Jonah 3:3:* עִיר גְּדוֹלָה לֵאלֹהִים — [lit. *'a great city to God'*] where the meaning is an exceedingly great city. [Cf. *comm.* to 1:2 s.v. וְרוּחַ אֱלֹהִים.]

— In those times wild beasts were in abundance and people were in terror of them. Nimrod began his dominion by hunting down these animals, and, as a great hunter, people deified him, hence the phrase *before HASHEM (Malbim).*

Ha'amek Davar differs from all the above and interprets that Nimrod, unintentionally did indeed perform God's will. Without strong government, man cannot survive as a secure, civilized race. Nimrod was the first to establish such a strong political system. Thus, although his motives were base and selfish, he is considered as acting *'before*

1. As noted in the *comm.* to 3:21 the garments that God provided for Adam and Eve passed on to Cush who passed them onto his son, Nimrod. These garments were embroidered with animals and birds. When he put them on, God endowed him with strength, and all beasts, birds and animals crouched before him so that he had no difficulty in catching them. The people thought that these feats were due to his extraordinary strength, and they made him their king *(Sefer HaYashar* 7:30 al *Pirkei d'Rabbi Eliezer* 24).

X
10 *mighty hunter before HASHEM.' [10]The beginning of his kingdom was Babel, Erech, Akkad, and Calneh in*

HASHEM', because he was an instrument to carry out God's will.

עַל כֵּן יֵאָמַר — *Therefore it is said* — concerning any man who brazenly acts wickedly — knowing his Master yet acting rebelliously against Him *(Rashi).*

His prowess was proverbial: In the days of Moses if one wanted to describe a mighty hunter [or a vicious tyrant *(Ralbag)*] one would compare him to Nimrod *(Radak).*

According to *Ha'amek Davar* see above): it is said of any evil person who is an implement of fulfilling God's wish that he is like Nimrod.

10. וַתְּהִי רֵאשִׁית מַמְלַכְתּוֹ בָּבֶל ... — *And the beginning of his kingdom was Babylon,* etc. The verse can be interpreted in two ways. Either that the conquest which laid the foundation for his kingdom was Babylon, after which he conquered Erech, Akkad, and Calneh, the four of which are in the land of Shinar; or, he initially conquered these four and then conquered other countries which are not enumerated *(Radak).*

בָּבֶל — *Babel* [or: *'Babylon'*]

[Babel mentioned here refers to the *city* which later, under Nebuchadnezzar, became the center of the empire. It had the same Hebrew name, Babel, as the place of the Dispersion described in Chapter 11. In English Nebuchadnezzar's Babel is usually rendered Babylonia. It was one of the greatest cities of the ancient world. The reason it received this name (from בלל to *confound)* is given in the next chapter. *Jeremiah* (51:13) later describes the city which lies on the east bank of the Euphrates as being *upon many waters, abundant in treasures.* As Nebuchadnezzar himself describes the city [*Daniel* 4:27]: *Is this not the great Babylon that I built by the might of my power as a royal residence and for the honor of my majesty?*

According to *Imrei Shefer,* these verses are prefatory to the events of the Dispersion [Chapter 11; see *Malbim* next verse]. The word רֵאשִׁית in this verse does not necessarily mean *first* but *primary.* We are thus told that the seat of his empire was in the territory where the generation of the Dispersion later assembled to build their tower.

[It would seem then, that verses 8-12 are parenthetical to the genealogies. Since the Torah was listing the line of Ham to which Nimrod belonged, it went on to elaborate upon the events of his life and the places which would play a role in the events of the Dispersion that would be described in the next chapter.]

According to the *Midrash,* Shinar and Babylon are synonymous. The reference here to Babylon is prophetic because Shinar did not assume that name until after the Dispersion [11:9] *(Maharzu).*

אֶרֶךְ אַכַּד כַּלְנֵה — *Erech ... Akkad ... Calneh.* I.e., Urikath, Baskar, and Nuper-Ninpi [unidentified territories near Babylon] *(Yoma* 10a).

Rav Saadiah Gaon identifies them with areas in upper Mesopotamia and near Baghdad.

Kesses HaSofer identifies *Erech* with the Babylonian ruin on the left bank of the Euphrates now called

יא שִׁנְעָר: מִן־הָאָרֶץ הַהִוא יָצָא אַשּׁוּר וַיִּבֶן י
אֶת־נִינְוֵה וְאֶת־רְחֹבֹת עִיר וְאֶת־כָּלַח: יא

Warka in Arabic. In later writings it was called Uruch. It was a great city. Even today among its ruins there are walls over fifty feet in height.

He identifies *Akkad* as an ancient city which, already in the days of Amraphel lay in ruins. No further mention is made of it in Scriptures. Its name, however, remained in use as the standing title of Assyrian kings who identified themselves as 'King of Shumer [i.e. Shinar] and Akkad,' which designates Northern Babylonia.

In the *Midrash*, and *Targum Yerushalmi* Akkad is identified with Nisbis.

Kesses HaSofer adds that although the name *Calneh* appears in *Amos* 6:2 and *Isaiah* 10:9 we are at a loss to identify it further although some claim that on its ruins were built the great city of Ktesifon mentioned in *Eruvin* 57b.

בְּאֶרֶץ שִׁנְעָר — *In the land of Shinar.* I.e. *Babylonia (Midrash).*

As cited above, [see *comm.* to 6:17 s.v. מַבּוּל] *Rashi* explains that Shinar, denoting the low-lying country of Babylonia, was so called because the dead of the Flood were emptied out [שֶׁנִּנְעֲרוּ] there.

The *Midrash* adds: *Shinar* connotes that it is 'empty' [שְׁמְנוּעֶרֶת] of precepts lacking *terumah,* tithes, and the Sabbatical year [which, were observed in Eretz Yisrael only because they are conditional upon the soil of the Holy Land]; and that its princes die young [נְעָרִים]...

Kesses HaSofer and *Hoffmann* note that the name *Shinar* occurs also in 11:2; 14:1,9; *Josh.* 7:21; *Isaiah* 11:11; *Zech.* 5:11; *Daniel* 1:2. Shinar was the original name of Shumer, the different pronunciations being the result of dialectic variations. It was originally a region in southern Babylonia, and Sangir was the northern region. Later it had a wider signification referring to the entire territory of Babylonia.

11. מִן הָאָרֶץ הַהִוא יָצָא אַשּׁוּר — *Out of that land* [i.e. *Shinar*] *Asshur went forth.*

We are not told who Asshur was: Since he is listed with the descendants of Ham he was probably a Hamite, or perhaps he was the son of Shem mentioned in *v.* 22 *(Radak).*

[This verse is preliminary to the events of the Dispersion]:

He saw that his children were hearkening to Nimrod and rebelling against God by building a tower, so he left them *(Rashi).*

— He disassociated himself from that scheme and when he saw that they were defiant to God, he left the country. 'You departed from four places [Babel, Erech, Akkad and Calneh],' said God to him, 'by your life! I will give you four' — Nineveh, Rechovoth-Ir, Calah and Resen *(Midrash).*

According to *B'chor Shor, Ramban,* and *Chizkuni, Asshur* refers to the name of the country, i.e. Assyria, and the verse should be rendered as if it said אַשּׁוּרָה, *to* Asshur, the subject of the verse still being Nimrod:

the land of Shinar. [11]*From that land Asshur went forth and built Nineveh, Rechovoth-Ir, Calah,* [12]*and*

— After conquering the four cities mentioned above Nimrod expanded his domain and ruled also over Assyria. For this reason Assyria is called the Land of Nimrod as it is said: [*Micah* 5:5]: *And they shall waste the land of Assyria with the sword, the land of Nimrod with the keen-edge sword* — referring to Nineveh, the city of Rehoboth, and Calah.

According to *Malbim,* these verses relate that during the period when the generation of the future Dispersion assembled at Shinar [11:2] he was their king. After the building of the city and the tower had ceased [11:8] he built Babel, and Erech, etc. When the people had dispersed even further, to Asshur, he accompanied them and built cities there as well.

The usage of *Asshur,* meaning *to* Asshur is similar to *II Sam.* 10:14 where וַיָּבֹא יְרוּשָׁלָם means: 'and he came *to* Jerusalem'; *Numbers* 34:4: וְיָצָא חֲצַר־אַדָּר, 'and it shall go on *to* Hazar-addar'; and *Deut.* 3:1 אֶדְרֶעִי, '*to* Edrei.'

[On *Asshur,* cf. also on 2:14.]

וַיִּבֶן אֶת־נִינְוֵה — *And he built Nineveh.*

[According to *Rashi* and *Sforno,* the 'he' is *Asshur*]:

Because he disassociated himself from his wicked contempories, he was rewarded with the privilege of building the great cities which the Torah proceeds to enumerate *(Sforno).*

[According to *Ramban* and others, 'he' is Nimrod, whose further acts and conquests are now enumerated.]

This follows *Targum Yonasan:* 'From that land Nimrod went forth and reigned in Asshur ...'

The *Talmud, Yoma* 10a also understands Asshur as referring to a geographic location when it explains *Asshur* as Silok [or S'lika, *v. Kesubos* 10b] = Selucia, bordering Babylonia and Assyria.

Nineveh was the principal city of Assyriah and is mentioned often in Scriptures. It was the city of Senacherib *(II Kings* 19:36; *Isaiah* 37:37]. The city plays a predominant role in the prophecy of Jonah, where the city is described as having over120,000 inhabitants. Many associate Kfar Nunia mentioned in the *Talmud* with Nineveh, or at least with being located near Nineveh's ruins *(Abarbanel; Seder HaDoros; Kesses HaSofer).*

וְאֶת־רְחֹבֹת עִיר — *And Rechovoth Ir.*

An unidentified city. According to *Yoma* 10a: Perath of Meshan [= Messene(?).]

Malbim suggests that רְחֹבֹת עִיר is not the name of a city, but as its literal meaning implies, it means '*broad parts of the city.*' He explains that the verse indicates that when the population of Nineveh increased, he expanded the city; the newer parts being called רְחֹבֹת עִיר. When these, too, became congested, he proceeded to build Calah.

וְאֶת כָּלַח — *And Calah.*

— Perath d'Borsif [= Borsippa, near Babel] *(Yoma* 10a).

י
יב־טו

יב וְאֶת־רֶ֫סֶן בֵּין נִינְוֵה וּבֵין כָּלַח הוּא הָעִיר
יג הַגְּדֹלָה׃ וּמִצְרַיִם יָלַד אֶת־לוּדִים וְאֶת־
יד עֲנָמִים וְאֶת־לְהָבִים וְאֶת־נַפְתֻּחִים׃ וְאֶת־
פַּתְרֻסִים וְאֶת־כַּסְלֻחִים אֲשֶׁר יָצְאוּ מִשָּׁם
טו פְּלִשְׁתִּים וְאֶת־כַּפְתֹּרִים׃ וּכְנַעַן

12. וְאֶת־רֶסֶן — *And Resen.*

— Talsar [possibly Telasaar, on the upper Euphrates, mentioned in *Isaiah* 37:12] *(Targum Yonasan; Midrash).*

— Ctesiphon [a town on the eastern bank of the Tigris] *(Yoma* 10a).

הוּא הָעִיר הַגְּדֹלָה — *That is the great city.*

'One cannot be certain whether Nineveh or Resen was described as *the great city,* but since it is written [*Jonah* 3:3]: *Nineveh was an exceedingly great city* it follows that it is Nineveh that is here referred to as the great city' *(Yoma* 10a: *(Rashi).*

Chizkuni suggests that he merged Nineveh and Calah into one great metropolis, forming *'one great city.'*

13. [The Hamite genealogy, interrupted in *v.* 7 by the account of Nimrod, continues.]

וּמִצְרַיִם יָלַד אֶת־לוּדִים — *And Mizraim begot Ludim.*

Ibn Ezra maintains that the plural ים, *im,* ending indicates that these are the names not of families, but of countries, each of which was populated by a family. According to *Ramban,* if a family name does not coincide with the place name, then both are given separately (as in *v.* 10 and 11); otherwise we assume that the country was named after the family.

[See *comm.* of *Vilna Gaon* to *v.* 4, s.v. כִּתִּים.]

לודים . . . עֲנָמִים . . . לְהָבִים . . . (27-30) נַפְתֻּחִים — *Ludim ... Anamim ... Lehavim ... Naphtuhim.*

Ludim is mentioned in *Jer.* 46:9. *Targum Yonasan* renders 'Nyutai'; while *Rav Saadiah Gaon* identifies it with the city of Tunis.

Abarbanel comments that we cannot identify every name in these verses with certainty because Sannacherib came and forced migrations of all peoples from their home countries.

Anamim is identified by *Targum Yonasan* as Maryutai; *Rav Saadiah Gaon* identifies it with Alexandria of Egypt.

Lehavim: Pantpottai *(Targum Yonasan). Kesses HaSofer* identifies them with Lubim in *Nahum* 3:9 and *II Chron.* 12:3, while others identify it with Lybia.

Rashi, interpreting לַהַב = *flame,* suggests that the *Lehavim* were so called because their faces were fiery as flame. [For, *Gur Aryeh* explains, if a nation is given a name that has a definition of its own, such as לַהַב, *flame,* we must assume that the name was an outgrowth of their appearance or character.]

Naphtuhim: Secynai *(Targum Yonasan); residents of middle Egypt (Kesses HaSofer).*

14. (31) פַּתְרֻסִים — *Pathrusim.* Pilusai [= Pelusium in Egypt] *(Targum Yerushalmi).*

[The name פַּתְרוֹס, *Pathrus,* (apparently in upper Egypt) occurs again in *Isaiah* 11:11; *Jeremiah* 44:1,15; *Ezek.* 29:14; and 30:14.]

(32) כַּסְלֻחִים — *Casluhim.* Pontpolitai [Pentapolis, an Egyptian district] *(Targum Yonasan).*

Rav Saadiah Gaon identifies this

Resen between Nineveh and Calah, that is the great city.

13*And Mitzraim begot Ludim, Anamim, Lehavim, Naphtuhim,* 14*Pathrusim, and Casluhim, whence the Philistines came forth, and Caphtorim.*

area with Sa'id on the upper Nile.

אֲשֶׁר יָצְאוּ מִשָּׁם פְּלִשְׁתִּים — *Whence the Philistines came* [lit. *'went'*] *forth,* i.e. the Philistines descended from both Pathrusim and Casluhim. These two nations promiscuously mingled with each other and the Philistines were their illegitimate offspring *(Midrash; Rashi).*

Midrash Tanchuma derives this from the fact that the verse does not say *who begot the Philistines,* but *whence came forth* — intimating that they were the offspring of immorality.

[For this reason, as pointed out in the introductory comments to The Seventy Nations in *v.* 1, many omit the Philistines from the genealogy.

Ramban [in an apparent attempt to reconcile the view in *Jeremiah* 47:4 and *Amos* 9:7 according to which the Philistines originated from *Caphtor*], conjectures that the Casluhim were the inhabitants of a city by that name which was in the land of their brethren, the Caphtorim. The Casluhim left the country and conquered Philistia after which their descendants came to be called Philistines. This is the meaning of the verse in *Deut.* 2:22, the Caphtorim being of the sons of the Casluhim, who dwelt in the land of Caphtor.

According to *Ralbag,* this verse tells us that from the Casluhim two families descended: The Philistines *and* the Caphtorim.

The Philistines played an important — but antagonistic — role in the history of the Jews in Scriptural times. They founded five cities. Three of them on the southern coastland of Eretz Yisrael: Gaza, Ashkelon and Ashdod, and two inland: Gath and Ekron.

(38) כַּפְתֹּרִים — *Caphtorim,* i.e. Capudkai [Cappadocia in Asia Minor] *(Targum Yerushalmi).*

Rav Saadiah Gaon identifies this with Shafchu, to the west of Port Sa'id, while many identify this with the island of Crete on the Mediterranean.

15-18. [The descendants of Canaan]

Ramban explains that the enumerated sons all became heads of the Canaanite nations whose lands were promised to Abraham. *V.* 18 informs us that they dispersed, and it was then that some of their original names changed to the familiar ones listed in 15:19-21. The land of Canaan was originally destined for Israel [cf. *Deut.* 32:18], but at the time of the Dispersion God entrusted it to Canaan, a servant nation, until He was ready to present it to Israel, just as one may leave his legacy in trust with a servant until his son matures enough to acquire the treasure as well as the servant.

Phut's descendants are not mentioned because they are unnecessary for our narrative *(Rashi);* also, because his descendants jointly formed a nation under his name, they did not become separate nations *(Malbim).*

טז יָלַד אֶת־צִידֹן בְּכֹרוֹ וְאֶת־חֵת׃ וְאֶת־
יז הַיְבוּסִי וְאֶת־הָאֱמֹרִי וְאֵת הַגִּרְגָּשִׁי׃ וְאֶת־
יח הַחִוִּי וְאֶת־הָעַרְקִי וְאֶת־הַסִּינִי׃ וְאֶת־
הָאַרְוָדִי וְאֶת־הַצְּמָרִי וְאֶת־הַחֲמָתִי
יט וְאַחַר נָפֹצוּ מִשְׁפְּחוֹת הַכְּנַעֲנִי׃ וַיְהִי גְּבוּל
הַכְּנַעֲנִי מִצִּידֹן בֹּאֲכָה גְרָרָה עַד־עַזָּה
בֹּאֲכָה סְדֹמָה וַעֲמֹרָה וְאַדְמָה וּצְבֹיִם עַד־
כ לָשַׁע׃ אֵלֶּה בְנֵי־חָם לְמִשְׁפְּחֹתָם
לִלְשֹׁנֹתָם בְּאַרְצֹתָם בְּגוֹיֵהֶם׃

(34) צִידֹן — *Zidon.*

— Zidon was the capital of ancient Phoenecia *(Kesses HaSofer).*

[The name also stands for the whole country, and to differentiate the two, the *city* is referred to as *Great Zidon* in *Joshua* 11:8.]

בְּכֹרוֹ — *His first born,* i.e., he was actually the oldest and also superior in attainment to his brothers *(Radak).*

(35) חֵת — *Heth.*

They are mentioned several times in Scriptures. Abraham later met Hittites in Hebron [23:4]. Ephron was a Hittite [*ibid. v.* 10]; and Esau married Hittite women [26:34.]

(36) הַיְבוּסִי — *The Jebusites.*

These names refer collectively to the families which descended from them, not to individuals *(Radak).*

The Jebusites dwelt around Jerusalem which was formerly called *Jebus (Joshua* 11:3). David expelled them when he finally captured Jerusalem *(II Sam* 5:6,8).

(37-38) הָאֱמֹרִי וְהַגִּרְגָּשִׁי — *The Amorite and the Girgashite.*

They are mentioned often among the Canaanite nations. Parts of the Amorite, following references in *Num.* 21:13, *Deut.* 1:19, 27, 44 and *Joshua* 2:10, 10:5 lived in mountainous areas on both sides of the Jordan. These territories were ruled by the Amorite Kingdoms, Heshbon and Bashan.

17. (39-41) הַחִוִּי ... הָעַרְקִי ... הַסִּינִי ... — *The Hivvite ... Arkite ... Sinite.*

— I.e. Hildin [?], Arkasas of Lebanon and Ortosia [a Pheonecian seaport] *(Midrash).*

The Hivvites, too, are mentioned among the seven Canaanite nations displaced by the Israelites. Shechem, son of Hamor, is identified as a Hivvite (34:2).

Rav Saadiah Gaon identifies Sinite with Tripoli in Syria. [But cf. *Ezekiel* 30:15 where Sin is mentioned as *'the strength of Egypt'.*]

18. (42-44) — הָאַרְוָדִי ... הַצְּמָרִי ... הַחֲמָתִי — *The Arvadite ... Zemarite ... Hamathite.*

Arvadite: Aradus [on the Phoenician coast]; *Zemarite:* Chameatz [Emesa in Syria]. Why was it called *Zemarite?* — Because צֶמֶר, wool, was made there; *Hamathite:* Epiphania [in Syria] (cf. *Numb.* 34:8; *Amos* 6:14) *(Midrash).*

וְאַחַר נָפֹצוּ מִשְׁפְּחֹת הַכְּנַעֲנִי — *And afterward the families of the Canaanites were scattered.*

X
15-20

15 Canaan begot Zidon his first-born, and Heth;
16 and the Jebusite, the Amorite, the Girgashite,
17 the Hivite, the Arkite, the Sinite, 18 the Arvadite,
the Zemarite, and the Hamathite. Afterward, the
families of the Canaanites branched out. 19 And the
Canaanite boundary extended from Zidon going
toward Gerar, as far as Gaza; going toward Sodom,
Gomorrah, Admah, and Zeboiim, as far as Lasha.
20 These are the descendants of Ham, by their
families, by their languages, in their lands, in their
nations.

From these, in the course of time, there arose other families that were called by the generic name Canaanite *(Rashi,* as explained by *Mizrachi).*

— *Afterward,* meaning after the Dispersion, they were dispersed from their locality which was formerly in the east with the other families, to the land which was later called Canaan *(Radak).*

19. [The territory of Canaan]

וַיְהִי גְּבוּל הַכְּנַעֲנִי — *And the Canaanite boundary extended* [lit. *'was'.*]

'Boundary' means the extremities of a land, not a description of all the contours of its borders *(Rashi* according to *Mizrachi* and *Gur Aryeh).*

The Torah now proceeds to delineate the Canaanite's territory from Zidon to Sodom. All of the territory is not deliniated; this will be done later when the land is divided *(Joshuah* 13;21). The primary purpose of stating the borders is because Israel would later inherit the land. The verse teaches us that it was God's will that the Canaanite families dwell in the land until their time was up. God wanted Israel to occupy a developed, prosperous land, with houses, vineyards, and farms as He promised [*Deut.* 6:11] that they would enter the land and find *houses full of all good things which you did not fill, hewn cisterns which you did not hew, vineyards and olive groves which you did not plant (Radak).*

מִצִּידוֹן בֹּאֲכָה גְרָרָה עַד עַזָּה — *From Zidon going toward* [lit. *'your coming to*] *Gerar as a far as* [lit. *'until'*] *Gaza.*

[*I.e., from Zidonim* in the Northwest, down the coastline in the direction of Gerar as far as Gaza, Gerar being somewhat further south than Gaza. See *comm.* to 20:1.]

בֹּאֲכָה סְדֹמָה וַעֲמֹרָה ... עַד־לָשַׁע — *Going towards Sodom and Amorah ...as far as* [lit. *'until'*] *Lasha.*

[I.e., as one then goes in an easterly direction towards Sodom and Amorah ... as far as Lasha which the *Midrash* identifies with the later Callirhoe (a famous bathing resort on the east shore of the Salt Sea — *Hoffmann).*]

20. אֵלֶּה בְּנֵי חָם — *These are the descendants* [lit. *'sons'*] *of Ham (Rashi).*

— He thus ends the line of Ham with the same formula He used to end the line of Japheth [*v.* 5] and the line of Shem [*v.* 31] *(Ibn Ezra).*

כא וּלְשֵׁם יֻלַּד גַּם־הוּא אֲבִי כׇּל־בְּנֵי־עֵבֶר
כב אֲחִי יֶפֶת הַגָּדוֹל: בְּנֵי שֵׁם עֵילָם וְאַשּׁוּר
כג וְאַרְפַּכְשַׁד וְלוּד וַאֲרָם: וּבְנֵי אֲרָם עוּץ

21. The line of Shem. (26 Nations).

The genealogy of Shem which had been delayed until this point [for according to *Ramban*, Shem was older than Haran and his genealogy should have appeared first — see *comm.* to *v.* 2] is now given so the Torah can proceed to recount the history of Abraham and his descendants for they formed the primary nation of mankind.

וּלְשֵׁם יֻלַּד גַּם הוּא—*And to Shem, also to him were born.*

The phrase גַּם הוּא, *also he,* has this intent: Because the genealogy of Shem, an older brother who was mentioned previously, was delayed, we might have assumed that he had no children. Therefore, Scripture emphasizes that *also to him* were children born and that moreover he was the ancestor of the 'children of Eber' (see further) from whom the Patriarchs descended *(Radak).*

[Of course according to the view of *Rashi* in 5:32 and 9:24 based upon the *Talmud and Midrash* — see below — that Shem was the *youngest* of the sons, the first part of the above interpretation would not apply.]

אֲבִי כׇּל־בְּנֵי־עֵבֶר — [*He was*] *the ancestor of all those who lived on the other side* [of the river.]

This translation follows *Rashi* who understands עֵבֶר as a preposition referring to all those who lived עֵבֶר [הַנָּהָר] *across* [*the river*] rather than a proper noun referring to *Eber,* his grandson, for as *Ramban* comments in support of this interpretation: Why should the Torah associate him with Eber more than with any other of his offspring? [See further on the relationship of *Eber = Hebrews* on 11:14.]

[Cf. also *Rashi*'s comm to 14:13 אַבְרָם הָעִבְרִי, (familiarly translated *Abram the Hebrew,* but which *Rashi renders 'who had come from the other side of the river.'*]

— He was the father of all who dwelt across the river, whence came Abraham's family *(Ramban).*

According to others, however, the translation would be: *the father of all the sons of Eber* —

Shem was the primogenitor of all the descendants of Eber from whom came forth the Hebrews *(Radak; Ibn Ezra).*

[Cf. *Targum Yonasan* who interprets the phrase to mean: *the father of all the descendants of* עִיבְרָאֵי *the Hebrews.* [See further on 11:14, Eber = Hebrews.]

Although Shem had many descendants, Eber's children were the most favored of his offspring because they were righteous like him *(Abarbanel).*

Sforno comments that those who believed in God were called עִבְרִים, *Ivrim,* after Eber their teacher. Shem, because he was also their teacher, is called the 'father' of Eber's 'children', meaning his 'students', because students are called the children of their teacher.

אֲחִי יֶפֶת הַגָּדוֹל — *The brother of Japheth the elder.*

The subject of הַגָּדוֹל, *the elder,* in

X
21-23

[21]*And to Shem, also to him were born; he was the ancestor of all those who lived on the other side; the brother of Japheth the elder.* [22]*The sons of Shem: Elam, Asshur, Arpachshad, Lud, and Aram.* [23]*The*

this verse is grammatically ambiguous and could be either Japheth, [as suggested by our translation which is borne out by the cantillation of the verse], or to Shem [by rendering, *the older brother of Japheth.*]

The translation follows *Rashi* who admits that from this verse one cannot determine with certainty whether Shem or Japheth was the elder. He cites the chronology adduced from 11:10 [based upon the *Midrash* and *Sanhedrin* 69b cited in our *comm.* to 5:32] to prove that Japheth was the elder. Additionally, *Rashi* explains that the verse does not designate him as 'the brother of Ham', because Shem and Japheth honored their father, while Ham put him to shame [9:22].

According to *Ibn Ezra, Radak,* and *Ramban,* Shem was the eldest and the designation *'the elder'* reverts to Shem as in *Isaiah son of Amoz, the prophet* [*II Kings* 20:1] Isaiah, not Amoz being the prophet referred to.

[Cf. *comm.* to 5:32 and 9:24.]

Targum Yonasan [who apparently is also of the opinion that Shem is the oldest] renders יֶפֶת הַגָּדוֹל, *Japheth who was great in fear of* HASHEM.

22. בְּנֵי שֵׁם — *The sons of Shem.*

(45) עֵילָם — *Elam.*

They are mentioned often in Scriptures. According to *Rav Saadiah Gaon,* their territory lay between Shushan in Persia and Media with whom they are often associated [*Isaiah* 21:2; *Jeremiah* 25:25. Cf. *Daniel* 8:2 where the capital is designated as Shushan (on the Eulaeus).]

(46) אַשּׁוּר — *Asshur.*

Commonly translated as referring to the Assyrians who dwelt north of Babylon.

Cf. *comm.* to *v.* 11 where, according to *Rashi,* Asshur is described as having founded several cities.

In 2:14, Hidekel, on the rivers flowing from the Garden of Eden, is described as flowing to 'the east of Asshur.'

Much mention is made of Assyria in Scripture of their association with Israei.

(47) אַרְפַּכְשַׁד — *Arpachshad.*

He is considered by Josephus to be the ancestor from whom was derived the name כַּשְׂדִּים [etymologically related to the last three letters of his name כשד] = Chaldeans *(Hoffmann).*

The Chaldeans originally lived on the coastland of the lower Euphrates and afterwards moved inland. Abraham was later born in one of their principal cities, Ur.

[See also *comm.* to 11:10.]

(48) לוּד — *Lud.*

No positive ethnological identification of this name has been established. Apparently it is not the same as Ludim mentioned in *v.* 13 among the sons of Mizraim. The name Ludim, mentioned as archers in the Egyptian or Tyrian army appears in *Jeremiah* 46:9; *Ezek.*

כד וְחוּל וְגֶתֶר וָמַשׁ: וְאַרְפַּכְשַׁד יָלַד אֶת־
כה שָׁלַח וְשֶׁלַח יָלַד אֶת־עֵבֶר: וּלְעֵבֶר יֻלַּד
שְׁנֵי בָנִים שֵׁם הָאֶחָד פֶּלֶג כִּי בְיָמָיו

27:10; 30:5 (*Kesses HaSofer; Hoffmann*).

Josephus seems to identify them with the Lydians of Asia Minor.

(49) אֲרָם — *Aram.*

The Arameans, who lived on the fertile crescent, played an important role in the lives of the Jews during Scriptural times and later.

The main territory of Aramea was northeast of Eretz Yisrael, roughly in the area of Syria. The capital city of Aramea was Damascus [*Isaiah* 7:8], sometimes referred to as Aram-Damesek [*II Samuel* 8:6]. Aram-Zova [Aleppo] was to the northwest of Damascus [*ibid.* 10:6]. Further to the north, across the Euphrates, was Aram-Naharaim [Mesopotamia], also called *Paddan Aram* [28:2]; according to *Rashi, ibid.*, Paddan Aram *includes* Aram-Zova and Aram-Naharaim.

David, in his conquests annexed this territory to Eretz Yisrael. Later, the Greeks called the area Syria, the name by which the Talmud refers to it.

Laban is referred to as the Aramean, Aramea being the ancestral home of Nahor and his descendant Bethuel [22:20-24; 24:4,7,10.]

23. וּבְנֵי אֲרָם — *And the children of Aram.*

The genealogy commences with Aram because he was the last-named in the previous verse. [Cf. *comm.* to *v.* 2 s.v. יֶפֶת] The children of Elam, Asshur, and Uz are not given because they were insignificant. It may be that the children of Aram are given because Terach's family intermarried with them as indicated by the fact that Nachor named his first-born, Uz, and his grandson Aram, both being Aramean names (*Radak*).

(50) עוּץ — *Uz.*

[This name appears again only in *Jeremiah* 25:20; in *Job* 1:1. In *Lam.* 4:21 the name Uz appears in connection with Edom, but it is apparently not the same city, that being named after its early Edomite settler, Uz, Son of Seir (36:28).]

(51-53) חוּל ... גֶתֶר ... מַשׁ — ... *Hul ... Gether ... Mash.*

Malbim comments that Aram and Arpachshad had many more children, but the verse mentions only those that evolved into separate nations. Aram's other children became part of the Aramean nation and Arpachshad's other children formed a nation called Arpachshad.

These are unknown nations. Josephus identifies the land of *Hul* as Armenia. The parallel passage in *I Chron.* 1:17 reads *Meshech* instead of *Mash* (*Hoffmann*). This indicates that he was called by both names (*Radak loc. cit.*).

Kesses HaSofer suggests that Mash was the original name. He notes that there is a Mount Mash in Mesopotamia which may have been named after him.

Rav Saadiah Gaon interprets these as Hula, Gramka and Misha, but these locations are obscure.

24. The line of Arpachshad.

(54-55) שֶׁלַח ... עֵבֶר — *Shelah ... Eber.*

X
24-25 *sons of Aram: Uz, Hul, Gether, and Mash.* [24]*Ar-*
pachshad begot Shelah, and Shelah begot Eber.
[25]*And to Eber were born two sons: the name of the*
first was Peleg, for in his days the earth was divided;

[Eber was one of the righteous men of that time *(Midrash).* Along with his grandfather Shem, he established a yeshivah.]

Rambam [*Hil. Avodah Zarah* 1:1] counts Eber among 'the few solitary individuals — Enosh, Methuselah, Noah and Shem — who recognized God as the Creator even when all others were serving idols.

The name עֵבֶר [across] refers to their having come from *'across'* the river. Abraham the *'Ivri'* came from there [14:13], and subsequently Abraham's descendants came to be referred to as *Ivrim* [usually translated *'Hebrews'*] because, as the *Midrash Shemos Rabbah* 3 explains: they came from *ever hanahar,* the other side of the river [Euphrates], and because they descended from Eber [*Rashi* to 39:14.]

Mizrachi [to 39:14] asserts that the term *'Ivri'* was used only for someone who was both a descendant of Eber and also from the other side of the river, for Nachor was a descendant of Eber and Ishmael was from across the river, but neither was called an *'Ivri'* [i.e. only Isaac, not Ishmael, is considered an offspring of Abraham].

[Cf. also *Joshua* 24:2,3: *'Your ancestors lived on the other side of the river in old times . . . and I took your father Abraham from the other side of the river . . .'*

According to *Meg.* 17a Jacob spent fourteen years in the house of Eber. [For chronology, see *Chronology / Time-Line — Adam to Jacob* on p. xii.]

25. וּלְעֵבֶר יֻלַּד שְׁנֵי בָנִים — *And to Eber were born two sons.*

He begot other children besides these as it specifically says [11:17] *he begot sons and daughters.* Only these two are mentioned here because their names indicate important historical events [see further] *(Radak).*

[Only Joktan's line is traced in the next verse. Eber's genealogy through Peleg, culminating in Abraham, is traced in 11:16*ff.*]

(56) פֶּלֶג — *Peleg.*

[*Abarbanel* cites the city of Palga at the junction of the Euphrates and Chaboras rivers.]

כִּי בְיָמָיו נִפְלְגָה הָאָרֶץ — *For in his days the earth was divided* — i.e. the languages were confused, and the nations were dispersed from the plain throughout the world [11:7,8] *(Rashi).*

Rashi cites *Seder Olam* that the Dispersion took place at the *end* of Peleg's life [see *Chronology / Time-Line p. xii*], therefore as the *Midrash* notes Eber must have been a prophet to give his son a name which signified division [Peleg = Niphlega = Division.]

[*Rashi* explains that one cannot conjecture that the Dispersion occurred at the *beginning* of Peleg's lifetime and that the name was therefore not prophetic but merely commemorative of an event that had already occurred *(Mizrachi),* because Joktan was

י כו-ל

כו נִפְלְגָה הָאָרֶץ וְשֵׁם אָחִיו יָקְטָן: וְיָקְטָן
יָלַד אֶת־אַלְמוֹדָד וְאֶת־שָׁלֶף וְאֶת־
כז חֲצַרְמָוֶת וְאֶת־יָרַח: וְאֶת־הֲדוֹרָם וְאֶת־
כח אוּזָל וְאֶת־דִּקְלָה: וְאֶת־עוֹבָל וְאֶת־
כט אֲבִימָאֵל וְאֶת־שְׁבָא: וְאֶת־אוֹפִר וְאֶת־
חֲוִילָה וְאֶת־יוֹבָב כָּל־אֵלֶּה בְּנֵי יָקְטָן:
ל וַיְהִי מוֹשָׁבָם מִמֵּשָׁא בֹּאֲכָה סְפָרָה הַר

younger than Peleg and he begot thirteen families [*vss.* 26-29] who were included in the Dispersion. Nor can one conjecture that it occurred in Peleg's middle age because Scripture comes not to conceal but to clarify [i.e., this would have been too vague to convey proper information about the time of the Dispersion, and Scripture would have been more specific]. Consequently, *in his days* can only mean that they were dispersed in the final year of his life.]

Rashi, on the parallel verse in *I Chron.* 1:19 explains that he was called Peleg: 'because in his days the life-span of man was cut in half. Originally man lived an average of 900 years; from the days of Arphachshad it was split to about 400 years, while from Peleg it was divided further to about 200 years.'

This explanation is also given in *Midrash Aggadah; Sefer Hayashar; Daas Zekeinim,* citing *Rav Yosef Kara;* and in *Chizkuni.*

It is this very explanation that is given by *Sforno* to our verse, who adds that this reduced longevity was a direct result of the punishment of the Dispersion: their vitality was lowered by the abrupt and sudden change of climates. [Cf. *comm.* to 5:4.]

[*B'chor Shor* cites both explanations [i.e. that the 'division' refers to the Dispersion and also to the life-span] and concludes that the name probably alluded to both.

[Peleg's sons are recorded below in 11:18.]

26. (57) יָקְטָן — *Joktan.*

— He was so called because he was humble and belittled himself [מַקְטִין]. He therefore merited to establish many families *(Midrash; Rashi).*

[The name is given this explanation because Eber was a prophet and the giving of a name meaning *'small'* must have had a significance *(Mizrachi; Gur Aryeh).* See also *Gur Aryeh* to 10:13 *Lehavim.*]

Ibn Caspi holds, however, that there was a reason for all the names but that the Torah did not find it necessary to record their meanings.

Radak attaches the explanation to Joktan which *Rashi* in *Chronicles* and *Sforno* explain regarding Peleg [cited above.] He comments that Joktan, from קָטָן, diminished, signifies that from his time man's longevity would be diminished. He explains that Eber knew that Joktan's years would be fewer from birth, because he was born physically smaller than those who preceded him. [This explanation is found in *Midrash Zuta.*]

(58-61) אַלְמוֹדָד ... שָׁלֶף ... חֲצַרְמָוֶת ... יָרַח — *Almodad, ... Shaleph, ... Hazarmaveth ... Jerah.*

Targum Yonasan esoterically paraphrases: 'And Joktan begot Elmodad who measured [דְמָשַׁח, i.e., דְמָדַד] the earth with lines; Shaleph who led forth [דְשָׁלַף] the waters of rivers ...'

Rashi explains that *Hazarmaveth*

and the name of his brother was Joktan. [26]*Joktan*
begot Almodad, Sheleph, Hazarmaveth, Jerah,
[27]*Hadoram, Uzal, Dikalah,* [28]*Obal, Abimael, Sheba,*
[29]*Ophir, Havilah, and Jobab; all these were the sons*
of Joktan. [30]*Their dwelling place extended from*
Mesha as far as Sephar, the mountain to the east.

was so called after his dwelling place.

The *Midrash* explains that it was an extremely impoverished town where the residents of a courtyard [חָצֵר] awaited death [מָוֶת] daily [to relieve them of their misery].

Kesses HaSofer identifies these with Arabian cities. Hazarmaveth is Hadarmaveth in Southern Arabia.

27. (62-64) הֲדוֹרָם ... אוּזָל ... דִּקְלָה — *Hadoram ... Uzal ... Diklah.*

Doram is the name of a fortress in the south; Uzal is the original name of what the Arabs call San'a, the capital of Yemen. [Uzal is mentioned in *Ezekiel* 28:19 as a place from which iron was brought.] Diklah refers to the palm-tree [*dekel*] region in Main [in Judea] *(Kesses HaSofer).*

28. (65-67) עוֹבָל ... אֲבִימָאֵל ... שְׁבָא — *Obal, ... Abimael ... Sheba.*

The Samaritans refer *Obal* to the Mt. Eibal region in Samaria, near Shechem [Nablus]; *Abimael* is unidentified but in Sabaean the name means 'One Father, He is God'; Sheba is mentioned as a distant and wealthy people, famed for their frankincense, gold, precious stones [cf. *I Kings* 10:2,10; *Isaiah* 60:6; Jeremiah 6:20] *(Kesses HaSofer).*

The name occurs also among the Hamites. See *comm.* to *v.* 7.]

Some identify them with the Sabaeans of Southwest Arabia.

29. (68-70) אוֹפִר ... חֲוִילָה ... יוֹבָב — *Ophir ... Havilah ... Jobab.*

'How many pens were broken and how much ink wasted' in trying to identify Ophir, from whence Solomon brought the gold for the Temple [see *I Kings* 9:28; 10:11; cf. also *Psalms* 45:9; *Isaiah* 13:12], but all the hypotheses would seem to be negated by this verse which lists Ophir among the tribes of Joktan in Arabia. However, the fact that its companion nation is Havilah would seem to indicate otherwise, for Havilah is not on the east coast of the Red Sea but to the southeast of Arabia toward the Persian Gulf and India where Havilah is as we find above in 2:11 and further in 25:18 *(Kesses HaSofer).*

[See also *comm.* to *Havilah* in *v.* 7. (There is a place Huvaila in Bahrein on the Persian Gulf).]

Jobab is identified as the Egyptian coastal city Jobabiti *(Kesses HaSofer).*

30. וַיְהִי מוֹשָׁבָם — *And their territory* [lit. *'dwelling'*] *was.*

I.e., this was where they dwelt before the Dispersion *(Rashi* to 11:2), this being the territory of the Shemites, while the others lived in the immediate vicinity. They did not settle in the respective countries enumerated in this chapter until after the Dispersion. Accordingly verses 5, 19, and 20 are to be interpreted as referring to where they

י
לא-לב

לא הַקֶּדֶם: אֵלֶּה בְנֵי־שֵׁם לְמִשְׁפְּחֹתָם
לב לִלְשֹׁנֹתָם בְּאַרְצֹתָם לְגוֹיֵהֶם: אֵלֶּה
מִשְׁפְּחֹת בְּנֵי־נֹחַ לְתוֹלְדֹתָם בְּגוֹיֵהֶם
וּמֵאֵלֶּה נִפְרְדוּ הַגּוֹיִם בָּאָרֶץ אַחַר
הַמַּבּוּל:

יא
א °שביעי א °וַיְהִי כָל־הָאָרֶץ שָׂפָה אֶחָת וּדְבָרִים

ultimately dwelt after the Dispersion *(Mizrachi; Gur Aryeh).*

According to *Ramban* ad. loc., this verse, too, refers to where the Shemites settled *after* the Dispersion; before the Dispersion, everyone dwelt in the Mountains of Ararat [see *comm.* to 11:2].

מִמֵּשָׁא בֹּאֲכָה סְפָרָה הַר הַקֶּדֶם — *From Mesha until you come to Sephar, the mountain of the earth.* east

The *Midrash* explains these as Arabian and Babylonian districts. Sephar refers to Taphar in Southern Arabia.

According to *Rav Saadiah Gaon,* Mesha is Mecca, and Sephar is Medina.

[Cf. 11:2 where this is interpreted by *Ramban* to refer to the Ararat region.]

31. לְמִשְׁפְּחֹתָם לִלְשֹׁנֹתָם — *According to their families to their tongues.* — Referring to the period after the Dispersion *(Radak).* Cf. *comm.* to similar wording in *v.* 5.

32. אֵלֶּה מִשְׁפְּחֹת בְּנֵי נֹחַ — *These are the families of Noah's descendants.*

The reckoning of the seventy nations [see *v.* 1] is complete. There are 70 descendants listed in this chapter: 14 Japhethites, 30 Hamites; and 26 Shemites. The territories they inherited carried their names *(Chizkuni).*

וּמֵאֵלֶּה נִפְרְדוּ הַגּוֹיִם בָּאָרֶץ אַחֲרֵי הַמַּבּוּל — *And from these, the nations spread forth over the earth after the Flood.*

But they did not spread forth until after the Dispersion! The phrase *after the Flood* reverts to the beginning of the verse. Explain the verse, therefore, this way: These are the families of Noah's descendants that were born after the Flood who later spread forth over the earth — after the Dispersion *(Radak).*

From these, the nations spread forth — i.e. even those who did not become separate nations nevertheless dispersed to many places until the entire world was settled *(Ha'amek Davar).*

XI

1. The Tower and Dispersion

כָּל־הָאָרֶץ — *The whole earth,* i.e., all the inhabitants of the earth *(Radak).*

This episode reverts to the period before the nations *'were separated in their lands'* [10:5; see *Radak* there]. The verse describes the time when man had a common language, and all mankind dwelled together *(HaRechasim l'Bik'ah).*[1]

1. *Rambam* in *Moreh* 3:5 introduces the narrative of the Dispersion:

It is one of the fundamental principles of the Torah that the Universe had been created *ex-nihilo,* and of the human race, one individual being, Adam, was created. As the time which

X [31]*These are the descendants of Shem according to*
31-32 *their families, by their languages, in their lands, by*
their nations.
[32]*These are the families of Noah's descendants, ac-*
cording to their generations, by their nations; and
from these the nations were separated on the earth
XI *after the Flood.*
1 [1] *The whole earth was of one language and of com-*

The year is 1996, 340 years after the Flood *(Seder Olam).* As the *Midrash* [Chapter 26] notes, God honored Shem by suspending the Dispersion until then: the numerical value of שֵׁם, *Shem,* is 340.

שָׂפָה אֶחָת — *One language* — Hebrew *(Rashi)* — the language with which the world was created *(Mizrachi);* the language of the Unique One of the world *(Yer. Meg.* 1:9).

Additionally, there is an opinion in *Yerushalmi Megillah* 1:9 that they all spoke the seventy languages — each person understanding the language of the other.

This common language, then, was the cause of their wanting to unify and dwell in one location, contrary to the will of God who created the world for habitation *(Ha'amek Davar).*

וּדְבָרִים אֲחָדִים — *And of common purpose.*

[The Hebrew is ambiguous and could allow several literal interpretations such as *'and a few words'; 'and a few things'.* Many interpretations are offered by the commentators.]

The translation adopted follows *Rashi,* and seems to best capture his primary interpretation when he comments:

They were of common counsel and said, 'He has no right to choose the celestial spheres for Himself and assign the earth to us; let us ascend to the heavens and make war against Him.'

Another interpretation offered by *Rashi* is: They spoke against יְחִידוֹ שֶׁל עוֹלָם, the *Unique One of the Universe,* (explaining אֲחָדִים as 'referring to the One'). [Cf. *comm.* to 3:22 s.v. כְּאַחַד מִמֶּנּוּ.]

Yet another interpretation: They spoke דְּבָרִים חַדִּים, shrewd words *(Maharshal):*

elapsed from Adam to Moses was not more than about two thousand five hundred years, people would have doubted the truth of that statement if no other information had been added, seeing that the human race was spread over all parts of the earth in different families and with different languages, one very unlike the other. In order to remove this doubt the Torah gives the genealogy of the nations *(Gen.* 5 and 10), and the manner in which they branched off from a common root. It names those among them who were well known, tells who their fathers were, and how long, and where they lived. It describes also the cause that led to the dispersion of men over all parts of the earth, and to the formation of their different languages, after they lived for a long time in one place, and spoke one language *(ibid.* 11) as would be natural for descendants of one person.

Malbim [*v.* 7] continues that this is why the sins of that generation are not described here at length, it not being necessary to the basic reason for including the narrative in the Torah, which was to establish that the divergence of nations and languages was a result of the Divine plan as explained above.

ב אֲחָדִים: וַיְהִי בְּנָסְעָם מִקֶּדֶם וַיִּמְצְאוּ
ג בִקְעָה בְּאֶרֶץ שִׁנְעָר וַיֵּשְׁבוּ שָׁם: וַיֹּאמְרוּ
אִישׁ אֶל־רֵעֵהוּ הָבָה נִלְבְּנָה לְבֵנִים
וְנִשְׂרְפָה לִשְׂרֵפָה וַתְּהִי לָהֶם הַלְּבֵנָה
ד לְאָבֶן וְהַחֵמָר הָיָה לָהֶם לַחֹמֶר: וַיֹּאמְרוּ

Once in every 1656 years [i.e. the year of the Flood] the heaven trembles just as it did in the days of the Flood [thereby implying that the Flood was a cyclic phenomenon, not a Divine visitation for evil]; therefore, come, let us make supports for it! *(Rashi; see Overview).*

The *Midrash* interprets אֲחָדִים in its Aramaic meaning of 'closed', and comments: That means דְּבָרִים אֲחָדִים, veiled deeds, for the deeds of the generation of the Flood are explicitly stated, while those of the Dispersion are veiled.

— Hence it was left to us, to perceive from the allusion of the narrative, what their sin was *(Malbim).*

Since they all spoke the same language, there was no communication barrier between them, and it was natural that they would share a common interest *(Radak).*

According to *Ibn Ezra,* both the learned and the ignorant had the same vocabulary [i.e. 'a unified vocabulary']; while *Ralbag* suggests that the syntax of their dialects were the same.

Malbim explains, in conclusion, that דְּבָרִים can be interpreted, *words* or *possessions.* Similarly אֲחָדִים allows a translation of *few* or *common.* The verse describes a period of tranquility, and the phrase can be interpreted either: *few words* or *few possessions.* Times were such that their needs were few and so were their possessions.

Abarbanel, in this vein, explains that no one had any private property and they all shared a common language. With the incident related here, strife set in and each one wanted to selfishly establish his ownership over his own property.

2. וַיְהִי בְּנָסְעָם מִקֶּדֶם — *And it came to pass when they migrated from the east.* — Where they had lived [cf 10:30]. They now journeyed in search of a place which would accommodate them all, finding only Shinar *(Rashi).*

The *Midrash* perceives in this phrase that 'they migrated away from the Ancient One, קַדְמוֹן, of the World saying: we refuse to accept Him or His Divinity!

They shirked off the past [קֶדֶם] *(Malbim).*

According to *Ibn Ezra, from the east* refers to Ararat which lay in the east, where they lived after the Flood. They were in search of a place to found a great state.

[Geographically, however, it would appear that Ararat was to the north of Shinar. In this case they would have been travelling in a southerly direction. וצ״ע.]

The east was where Adam was created, and where mankind was concentrated before the Flood. It would seem proper that Noah returned to his native land after he landed at Ararat which was also in the east. It was by popular consent that they journeyed westward in order to find a place large enough to accommodate them all, lest they would have to disperse when they became numerous.

It must be remembered that Noah and his children were alive at this time and Abraham was forty-eight years old, having already recog-

XI
2-4

mon purpose. 2 And it came to pass, when they
migrated from the east they found a plain in the land
of Shinar and settled there. 3 They said to one
another, 'Come, let us make bricks and burn them in
fire.' And the brick served them as stone, and the
bitumen served them as mortar. 4 And they said,

nized his Creator at that age according to certain Sages, and at the age of three according to others. It is certain that they did not participate in the sinister plot of that generation although they might have been helpless to prevent it *(Radak).*

[See also *Malbim,* further, on *v.* 7, and *footnote* to *v.* 26.]

וַיִּמְצְאוּ בִקְעָה בְּאֶרֶץ שִׁנְעָר וַיֵּשְׁבוּ שָׁם — *They found a plain in the land of Shinar and settled there.*

They found a spacious plain, free of mountain and rocks, and many miles across. Because they saw that the area was capable of sustaining them they settled there and decided to build a city large enough to accommodate them all *(Abarbanel).*

This is the same Shinar referred to above in 10:10, for, as we mentioned earlier, those events happened *after* the Dispersion, for the Torah does not concern itself with chronological sequence *(Radak).*

The word וַיִּמְצְאוּ, *they found,* implies that they came upon what they were seeking *(Ibn Caspi).*

Ibn Ezra explains that בִּקְעָה *plain,* [sometimes rendered *'valley'*] is related to the verb בקע, to split. Hence, it refers to flat terrain which appears to split apart the surrounding mountains.

3. וַיֹּאמְרוּ אִישׁ אֶל רֵעֵהוּ — *And they said one to another* [lit. *man to his neighbor'*] — i.e. one nation to another: Mitzraim to Cush, Cush to Phut, and Phut to Canaan ... *(Rashi).*

According to *Sforno* the words *man to his neighbor* indicate that this was the counsel of *individuals.*

הָבָה *Come,* i.e. prepare yourself. Wherever the word הָבָה, *come,* is used it denotes an invitation to unite for some common purpose *(Rashi).*

נִלְבְּנָה לְבֵנִים וְנִשְׂרְפָה לִשְׂרֵפָה — *Let us make bricks and burn* [*them*] *in fire* [lit. *'and burn to a burning';* the translation follows *Onkelos.*]

There are no stones in Babylon which is a plain; they therefore had to manufacture their own bricks by firing them in a furnace *(Rashi).*

[The intent, then, of the verse is that they would manufacture bricks — not sun-dried bricks, but substantial kiln-fired bricks of great durability.]

וַתְּהִי לָהֶם הַלְּבֵנָה לְאָבֶן — *And the brick served them* [lit. *'was to them'*] *as stone* [lit. *to stone*].

Thus, in a country where there was no stone, bricks had to take their place. *Kesses HaSofer* points out that archaelogical excavations in Babylon show that burnt bricks cemented together by bitumen were regularly used for the outer parts of the buildings.

Rav Huna said: Their work prospered. A man came to lay one stone and two were laid; he came to plaster one row and two were plastered *(Midrash).*

וְהַחֵמָר הָיָה לָהֶם לַחֹמֶר — *And*

יא הָבָה | נִבְנֶה־לָּנוּ עִיר וּמִגְדָּל וְרֹאשׁוֹ בַשָּׁמַיִם וְנַעֲשֶׂה־לָּנוּ שֵׁם פֶּן־נָפוּץ עַל־פְּנֵי

bitumen served them [lit. *'was to them'*] *as mortar* [lit. *'to mortar'*].

— To plaster the walls *(Rashi).*

[Although the exact identification of these terms are difficult, the translation follows *Chizkuni* and *R' Meyuchas.* According to *Radak* חֵמָר is mud, חוֹמֶר is lime].

חוֹמֶר means *building material* and חֵמָר means the *mortar* that holds them together. In Babel they were forced to use mortar for clay i.e., what is normally a binding material was put into the ovens to be baked into bricks *(Hirsch).*

4. וַיֹּאמְרוּ — *And they said. The pronoun 'they'* refers to the counsel of the princes who wished to make Nimrod king over the whole human race *(Sforno).* [Cf. *comm.* to 10:8,9].

According to *Chullin* 89a, it was Nimrod himself who primarily initiated the scheme, and as the *Talmud* notes in *Erubin* 53a: 'Why was he called Nimrod? — Because in his reign he led all the world in rebellion [הִמְרִיד = נִמְרֹד] against God.'[1]

נִבְנֶה לָּנוּ עִיר וּמִגְדָּל וְרֹאשׁוֹ בַשָּׁמַיִם — *let us build a city and a tower with its top in the heavens.*

A city for dwelling and a tower from which they could oversee their herds and flocks from a distance. It would also serve as a beacon so that shepherds could find their location from afar, and hence be able to graze their herds even further away without the fear of getting lost.

Its top in the heavens — i.e., an idiomatic expression for 'high in the air,' as in *Deut.* 1:28: Moses described the cities of Canaan as *cities great ... up to heaven (Radak).*

Ibn Ezra adds that a structure of this height would be visible from a considerable distance and become a rallying point to all people.

וְנַעֲשֶׂה לָּנוּ שֵׁם פֶּן נָפוּץ עַל פְּנֵי כָל־הָאָרֶץ — *And let us make a name for ourselves, lest we be dispersed across the whole earth.*

Make us a name, was their reason for building the tower; *lest we be dispersed,* was their reason for building the city *(HaRechasim l'Bik'ah).*

They wanted to acquire a name, because the popularity of the tower would spread from afar, giving them fame and renown — something they could not achieve if they

1. As culled from *Pirke d'Rabbi Eliezer,* the *Talmud,* and *Sefer HaYashar*:

After the Flood they multiplied greatly and they were all one people, one heart, and one language. They despised the pleasant land [i.e. Eretz Yisrael] and journeyed east, and settled in Shinar.

R' Akivah said: They cast off the kingdom of Heaven and appointed Nimrod over themselves: a slave son of a slave — are not all the sons of Ham slaves? Woe to the land where a slave rules!

By virtue of Adam's garments which passed on to him he established himself as a mighty hunter [see 10:9].

Nimrod said to his subjects: Come, let us build a great city for ourselves lest we be scattered over the earth. Let us build a great tower in its midst ascending to heaven and we will war against Him, for His power is only in the heavens and we will make us a great name on the earth.

XI *'Come, let us build us a city, and a tower with its top in the heavens, and let us make a name for ourselves, lest we be dispersed across the whole earth.'*

were dispersed *(B'chor Shor; Radak).*

They wanted to gain mastery over the entire human race; the fame of the tower would spread and all would come to see it *(Chizkuni).*

Hirsch explains that their intent was to establish *themselves.* They did not call on others בְּשֵׁם ה׳, to the service of God, but to their *own* service: נַעֲשֶׂה לָּנוּ שֵׁם. They saw their desires as an end instead of a means, an attitude that must end in moral decay. In their arrogant stress on original accomplishment, they said, 'the old people must have stone, but we can build even without stone.' Next they came to believe that they could dispense with God and His laws of morality.'

According to the *Talmud:*

And make us a name — this refers to idolatry *(Sanhedrin* 109a); as the *Zohar* interprets: 'let us make an object of worship.'

Rashi explains *lest we be scattered:* i.e. that He shall not be able to bring a plague upon us and cause us to be scattered from here.

Rav Shimon ben Chalafta quoted: *'a fool's mouth is his ruin'* [*Prov.* 18:7; for by saying *lest we be scattered;* they unconsciously prophesied their fate and were themselves responsible for it.]

R' Bachya summarizes the simple interpretation:

'... Their intention was only to find a place large enough for them to build a city and concentrate in a single location, lest they be dispersed. This is the very reason that God later dispersed them, because this scheme ran contrary to His Will for the nations to multiply and inhabit every part of the world according to His master plan of creation ...

The *Midrashim* perceive sinister and idolatrous motives in their plan, but, unfortunately, the verses themselves, close the doors upon mature reflection on the evil motives lurking within them. The Torah did not reveal them. The *Midrash* alludes to this with the comment: "the deeds of the generation of the Flood are explicitly stated, but those of the generation of the Dispersion are veiled."'

There were three sorts of rebels among the builders: One said, 'Let us ascend and dwell there'; the second said, 'Let us ascend and serve idols'; and the third said, 'Let us ascend and wage war with God.' The first group: God dispersed; the second group: He turned into apes and spirits; and the third group: He confused their languages *(Sanhedrin* 109a).

Many years were spent building the Tower. The ascending steps were on the east, and the descending steps were on the west. It reached so great a height that it took a year to mount to the top. A brick was, therefore, more precious in the sight of the builders than a human being. If a man fell and died they paid no attention to him; but if a brick fell down they wept because it would take a year to replace it. They were so intent in their project that they would not permit a pregnant woman to interrupt her work when her hour of travail came upon her.

They would constantly shoot arrows toward heaven, which, when returning, were seen to be covered with blood. They were thus fortified in their delusion, and they cried 'We have slain all who are in heaven!'

But God did this to cause them to err, and to have occasion to punish them for their rebellious ways ...

ה כָּל־הָאָֽרֶץ: וַיֵּ֣רֶד יהוה לִרְאֹ֣ת אֶת־הָעִ֔יר
וְאֶת־הַמִּגְדָּ֑ל אֲשֶׁ֥ר בָּנ֖וּ בְּנֵ֥י הָאָדָֽם:
ו וַיֹּ֣אמֶר יהוה הֵ֣ן עַ֤ם אֶחָד֙ וְשָׂפָ֤ה אַחַת֙
לְכֻלָּ֔ם וְזֶ֖ה הַחִלָּ֣ם לַעֲשׂ֑וֹת וְעַתָּה֙ לֹֽא־
ז יִבָּצֵ֣ר מֵהֶ֔ם כֹּ֛ל אֲשֶׁ֥ר יָזְמ֖וּ לַעֲשֽׂוֹת: הָ֚בָה

5. וַיֵּרֶד ה׳ — *And HASHEM descended.* This is an anthropomorphism *(Ibn Ezra).*

When God wishes to examine the deeds of lowly man, Scripture calls it *'descent' (Radak).*

Sforno comments that God is referred to as 'descending' when he inflicts punishment not because of iniquities already committed, but because of the inevitable outcome of a path of action chosen by man. Thus, the *Talmud* explains the punishment of בֵּן סוֹרֵר וּמוֹרֶה the rebellious, gluttonous son [*Deut.* 21:18-21] as יָרְדָה תוֹרָה לְסוֹף דַעְתּוֹ, the Torah descended to the depths of his intention, meaning that although his sins were not yet grievous, they would become far worse. The same expression is used in connection with Sodom, because their sins were becoming progressively worse.

Rashi explains that obviously HASHEM had no need to 'descend' in order to 'see' what was happening on earth. The Torah utilizes this language anthropomorphically depicting God as descending, to teach a moral lesson: A judge must not condemn the accused until he has personally investigated the case fully [*Tanchuma; Gur Aryeh*]

The *Zohar* explains:

He descended from the sacred to the profane in order to survey what man had built, and what steps had been taken to establish idolatry.

Ramban [*v.* 2] comments in a shrouded manner that kabbalistically the wise student will perceive that during the narrative of the Flood the Torah mentions *Elohim* while in the Dispersion, He is called HASHEM. The Flood came on account of the corruption of the land — a sin against nature that was punished by the Attribute of *Elohim,* as God of nature. The Dispersion came because they 'mutilated the shoots' [קִצְּצוּ בִּנְטִיעוֹת, a term in Kabbalah which describes the attempted disruption of the unity between HASHEM the Creator, and His Creation.] Therefore, the punishment of Dispersion [a disruption of *their* unity] was meted out 'measure for measure'. [And because their sin was directed against the Most Exalted Name, HASHEM is used in the narrative.]

Hirsch offers that HASHEM is used here because the sin of Babel was to negate the moral value and priceless worth of the individual. Such success would have destroyed God's plan for the happiness and the well-being of mankind, and consequently, of Creation. Therefore, God as 'HASHEM' intervened.

לִרְאֹת אֶת הָעִיר וְאֶת הַמִּגְדָּל — *To look at the city and the tower.*

'To look' here means 'to consider methods of punishment' *(Zohar).*

Hirsch [*v.* 3] observes that since, as the Sages explain, God desended to look into the matter before giving judgment, it is obvious that building the city or tower was not wrong in itself. The danger to the moral future must lie in the purpose for which it was built and the motives of the builders, as expressed in the previous verse: *let us make ourselves a name.*

אֲשֶׁר בָּנוּ בְּנֵי הָאָדָם — *Which the sons of man built* — i.e. which they had

5 *HASHEM descended to look at the city and tower*
which the sons of man built, 6 *and HASHEM said,*
'Behold they are one people with one language for all,
and this they begin to do! And now, should not all
they propose to do be withheld from them? 7 *Come,*

begun to build *(Radak).*

Was it then already built that the verse speaks of it in past tense? — Perhaps because God punishes the wicked for their intentions as if they were accomplished facts *(Tosafos HaRosh).*

The *Midrash* notes the use of the words בְּנֵי הָאָדָם, *sons of man:*

"Of course the *children of man* built it! Would we then have thought that asses or camels built it? — It means however *the children of Adam* [because they showed themselves his spiritual heirs, both being ungrateful]: Just as Adam, after all the good I bestowed upon him said *'The woman whom You gave to be with me she gave me of the tree,* etc.,' [thus making God's very goodness the excuse for his sin; see *comm.* to 3:12], so too, the generation of the Dispersion followed the generation of the Flood by only two years [the generation of the Dispersion having begun with the first post-deluvian descendant of Noah, Arpachshad, who was born two years after the Flood (11:10)] — And look how rebellious they are!"

— These people also were ungrateful, rebelling against the One who had showered kindness upon them and rescued them from the Flood *(Rashi).*

Mankind is called *'sons of Adam'* because it was Adam, the first man, who rebelled against his Master and brought death into the world *(Zohar).*

6. וַיֹּאמֶר ה׳ — *And HASHEM said* — to the angels *(Radak);* this was preliminary to His *'going down'* in the previous verse *(Ibn Ezra).*

[On God addressing the angels cf. *comm.* to 1:26.]

According to *R' Meyuchas* this phrase is also an anthropomorphism which suggests: And God deliberated; the plural is *pluralis majestatis.*

הֵן עַם אֶחָד וְשָׂפָה אַחַת לְכֻלָּם וְזֶה הַחִלָּם לַעֲשׂוֹת — *Behold, they are one people with one language for all and this they begin to do!*

As *Midrash Aggadah* interprets: 'See, it is only becaue they are one people and one language that their rebellion was possible! Each one understands precisely what the other wants, and only in this way were they able to unite in a common endeavor ...'

וְעַתָּה לֹא־יִבָּצֵר מֵהֶם כֹּל אֲשֶׁר יָזְמוּ לַעֲשׂוֹת — *And now, should not all they propose to do be withheld from them?*

— [The reading of this phrase as a rhetorical question follows *Rashi.*]

According to *Ibn Ezra* and *Radak,* it is to be read as a statement of fact: 'If I do not thwart them they will presume that they can successfully accomplish whatever they undertake to do! *Therefore, come let us go down,* etc.'

— People are thwarted in their plans by lack of a common language and a common philosophy. In Babel, however, all these differ-

יא נֵרְדָה וְנָבְלָה שָׁם שְׂפָתָם אֲשֶׁר לֹא
ח יִשְׁמְעוּ אִישׁ שְׂפַת רֵעֵהוּ: ח וַיָּפֶץ יְהוָה
אֹתָם מִשָּׁם עַל־פְּנֵי כָל־הָאָרֶץ וַיַּחְדְּלוּ

ences were non-existent. So unified were they in all areas that, were they not stopped, they would have set up idol-worship that would have endured for all time *(Sforno).*

7. הָבָה נֵרְדָה וְנָבְלָה שָׁם שְׂפָתָם — *Come, let us go down and there confuse their language.*

— In His great humility God thus took counsel with His [heavenly] court *(Rashi),* for 'the Holy One, blessed be He, does nothing without consulting His heavenly *famalia* *(Sanhedrin* 38b).[1]

[Cf. *comm.* to 1:26.]

The use here, as in *v.* 5, of the word הָבָה, *come,* is noted: The punishment corresponded to the deed, 'measure for measure.' They said, 'Come, let us build,' and God correspondingly said 'come let us go down.'

'Let us go down now!' God said. Let us not wait until they corrupt all of mankind *(Malbim).*

HaK'sav V'Hakaballah notes that according to many there was no sin implicit in the actual construction of the tower and city themselves. Rather, the construction was the vehicle from which much evil would ultimately spring, although its exact nature has not been revealed to us. That is why *v.* 6 reads אֲשֶׁר יָזְמוּ לַעֲשׂוֹת, *which they 'propose' to do;* it was for their unanimous evil *intent* that they were punished: the evil which would have materialized after the completion of the construction. This, then, is the meaning of נֵרְדָה — let us *crush* their evil intent; [similar to וַיִּרְדֶּנָּה, *and it crushed them,* in *Lam.* 1:13] so that their plans will never come to fruition.

וְנָבְלָה — *And confuse.*

This translation follows *Rashi* and *Ibn Ezra* who take the נ, *nun,* as the pronominal prefix indicating first-person plural future, synonymous with וּנְבַלְבֵּל. The suffix ה is superfluous in וְנֵרְדָה.

Several others *(R' Yosef Kimchi; B'chor Shor)* interpret נָבְלָה in the fem. niphal form, rendering: *let us go down and their language will be confounded* (by our very presence):

As *Hirsch* renders, relating the word to the root נבל, to cause to wither: 'we will go down, and their speech will at once become withered,' no further action being required — the withering of their speech being the direct result of God's descent.

אֲשֶׁר לֹא יִשְׁמְעוּ אִישׁ שְׂפַת רֵעֵהוּ — *That they should not understand* [lit. *'hear*] *one another's language.*

And so it happened. From then on, no one knew what the other spoke: One would ask for a brick and the other would bring lime. In a rage, the former would throw a brick at his fellow and shatter his brain *(Midrash; Rashi).*

... And as noted in *Pirkei d'Rabbi Eliezer,* the frustration became so great in the light of the lack of communication, that 'every one took his sword, and they fought one

1. The Holy One, blessed be He turned to the seventy angels who surrounded His Throne of Glory and said: Come, let us descend and confuse the seventy nations and the seventy languages. They then cast lots concerning the various nations. Each angel received a nation but Israel fell to the lot of God, as it is written [*Deut.* 32:9]: כִּי חֵלֶק ה׳ עַמּוֹ, *HASHEM's portion is His people (Pirkei d'Rabbi Eliezer; Targum Yonasan).*

XI let us descend and there confuse their language, that
8 they should not understand one another's language.
[8] *And HASHEM dispersed them from there over the face of the whole earth; and they stopped building*

another, and half the world fell there by the sword.'

— And in this way God destroyed their unity — the very prerequisite which underlay the success of their venture *(Akeidas Yitzchak).*

B'chor Shor, according to whom each one of the seventy nations previously knew all seventy languages, comments that they each suddenly forgot all but the one language asigned to them. The Holy Tongue with which God created the world, was reserved for Israel. The Holy Tongue thus passed on to Eber, the most illustrious of Shem's descendants, because of which it came to be called לָשׁוֹן עִבְרִי, Hebrew.

Ibn Ezra cites an opinion that God instilled such a hatred among them that each nation devised a new language. Another is of the opinion that He Who instills wisdom in man now made him forget his language.

Ibn Ezra concludes, that in his own opinion the birth of languages was the result of their dispersion and the subsequent rise of many kingdoms with the eventual result that common language was forgotten.

8. וַיָּפֶץ ה׳ אֹתָם מִשָּׁם — *And HASHEM dispersed them from there.* — What they had feared when they said *'lest we be scattered* [*v.* 4], now actually happened *(Rashi;* see *v.* 4).

This dispersion was a natural result of their language being confounded. Since they were no longer able to communicate, their scheme was automatically nullified and they dispersed in groups with each clan sharing a common language dwelling in another sector until over the years, the entire world was populated. The more temperate climates were naturally inhabited first *(Radak).*

According to *Ibn Ezra,* it was, in effect, for their good, and an act of blessing that God dispersed them from there in accordance with His words [1:28]: *And fill the earth ...*

Abarbanel cites the latter comment of *Ibn Ezra* but claims that as far as that generation was concerned, we must say that it was a punishment, for they were wicked and as the *Talmud* specifically notes 'The Generation of the Dispersion have no share in the World to Come. However, the meaning is that through them God's will was executed, and mankind actually found a blessing by inhabiting the entire world.

Cf. *Sanhedrin* 71b:

The scattering of the wicked benefits both them and the world [for being scattered they cannot take counsel together for evil]; the scattering of the righteous is injurious to both them and the world; the assembling of the wicked is injurious to them and the world; and the assembly of the righteous benefit both them and the world.

וַיַּחְדְּלוּ לִבְנֹת הָעִיר— *And they stopped building* [lit. *'to build'*] *the city,* i.e., they did not complete it, but, as *v.* 5 indicates, they had already built at least part of the tower *(Ibn Ezra).*

They gave up their grandiose plans to build a metropolis and a tower, but the group that remained behind did build a city on a much reduced scale. They named it Babel in commemoration of the event that had occurred there *(Radak).*

The *Midrash* comments that a

ט לִבְנֹת הָעִיר׃ עַל־כֵּן קָרָא שְׁמָהּ בָּבֶל כִּי־
שָׁם בָּלַל יהוה שְׂפַת כָּל־הָאָרֶץ וּמִשָּׁם
הֱפִיצָם יהוה עַל־פְּנֵי כָּל־הָאָרֶץ׃
י אֵלֶּה תּוֹלְדֹת שֵׁם שֵׁם בֶּן־מְאַת שָׁנָה
וַיּוֹלֶד אֶת־אַרְפַּכְשָׁד שְׁנָתַיִם אַחַר
יא הַמַּבּוּל׃ וַיְחִי־שֵׁם אַחֲרֵי הוֹלִידוֹ אֶת־
אַרְפַּכְשָׁד חֲמֵשׁ מֵאוֹת שָׁנָה וַיּוֹלֶד בָּנִים
יב וּבָנוֹת׃ וְאַרְפַּכְשַׁד חַי חָמֵשׁ
יג וּשְׁלֹשִׁים שָׁנָה וַיּוֹלֶד אֶת־שָׁלַח׃ וַיְחִי
אַרְפַּכְשַׁד אַחֲרֵי הוֹלִידוֹ אֶת־שֶׁלַח שָׁלֹשׁ
שָׁנִים וְאַרְבַּע מֵאוֹת שָׁנָה וַיּוֹלֶד בָּנִים

third of the tower sank into the earth, a third was burnt, and a third is still standing. The latter third is so tall that 'if one ascends to the top he sees the palm trees below like grasshoppers.'

[It is interesting to note that the *Talmud Shabbos* 36b identifies Babel with Borsippa. *Kesses HaSofer* notes that archaeologists have discovered the remains of what was apparently a gigantic tower in Borsippa, an area contiguous with Babylon. [Could this be the tower which the Sages in the above *Midrash* imply existed still in their day?]

9. עַל כֵּן ... בָּלַל שְׂפַת כָּל־הָאָרֶץ — *That is why it was called* [lit. 'he called] *Babel, because it was there that* HASHEM *confused the languages of the whole earth.*

It was so named by the group that remained behind, because it was there that God had introduced confusion into the language *(Radak).*

Ibn Ezra explains that Babel is thus composed of two words בָּא בֵּל, *confusion has come;* בֵּל being a form of בָּלַל just as חֵן is a form of חָנַן *(Radak).*

וּמִשָּׁם הֱפִיצָם ה׳ עַל פְּנֵי כָּל־הָאָרֶץ — *And from there* HASHEM *scattered them over the face of the whole earth.*

— But not all of them; one group remained there *(Radak).*

The *Mishnah, Sanhedrin* 107b interprets the redundancy of the two references to 'scattering' in verses 8 and 9 *(Mizrachi;* cf. *Torah Temimah)*:

'The generation of the Dispersion have no share in the World to Come as it is written ... *And* HASHEM *scattered them from there* — refers to This World; *and from there He scattered them* refers to the World to Come.'

[Apparently, therefore, as the verse is thus expounded, their *scattering* was total — they were scattered both in This World and the Next.]

Rashi queries:

Whose sin was greater, that of the generation of the Flood, or that of the generation of the Dispersion?

The former did not plan a rebellion against God and the latter did, yet the former were drowned while the latter were preserved in spite of their blasphemies!

The generation of the Flood,

the city. 9 *That is why it was called Babel, because*
it was there that HASHEM confused the languages of
the whole earth, and from there HASHEM scattered
them over the face of the whole earth.
10 *These are the descendants of Shem: Shem was*
100 years old when he begot Arpachshad, two years
after the Flood. 11 *And Shem lived five hundred years*
after begetting Arpachshad, and he begot sons and
daughters.
12 *Arpachshad had lived thirty five years when he*
begot Shelah. 13 *And Arpachshad lived four hundred*
three years after begetting Shelah; and he begot sons
and daughters.

however, who were violent robbers and bore hatred for one another, were utterly destroyed; while the generation of the Dispersion who dwelt amicably, in brotherly love toward one another, were spared despite their evil intentions. This demonstrates how hateful is strife and how great is peace! *(Midrash).*

10. Shem to Abraham

אֵלֶּה תּוֹלְדוֹת שֵׁם — *These are the descendants of Shem.* Shem's genealogy was given in the previous chapter with his brother's. It is repeated now with the emphasis on the descent of Abraham. The account of the years from creation to Noah to Abraham was given to enable us to calculate the age of the world, and thus clarify that the world came into existence as a creation of God at a definite point in time before which there was a total vacuum *(Radak).*

וַיּוֹלֶד אֶת אַרְפַּכְשָׁד — *When* [lit. *'and'*] *he begot Arpachshad.*

[The translation 'when' follows *Targum Yonasan* and *Rashi.*]

שְׁנָתַיִם אַחַר הַמַּבּוּל — *Two years after the Flood.*

[As already pointed out in the *comm.* to 5:32 s.v. *Shem, Ham, and Japheth,* this verse is cited by the *Talmud* to prove its thesis that Shem who, two years after the Flood, is described as 100 years old, could not have beeen the eldest, but was the youngest son of Noah.]

11. וַיּוֹלֶד בָּנִים וּבָנוֹת — *And he begot sons and daughters.*

Unlike the genealogy of the ten generations from Adam to Noah [Ch.5] where of each generation it says וַיָּמֹת, *and he died,* here their death is not recorded. This is because each of these generations populated the world permanently through it progeny and did not perish. Therefore, though they died, it is not mentioned *(Lekach Tov).*

According to *Sforno,* the deaths of these generations are not mentioned as are those of the generations preceding Noah because all of those died prior to the major historical event of the era — the

יד וּבָנוֹת׃ וְשֶׁלַח חַי שְׁלֹשִׁים שָׁנָה
טו וַיּוֹלֶד אֶת־עֵבֶר׃ וַיְחִי־שֶׁלַח אַחֲרֵי הוֹלִידוֹ
אֶת־עֵבֶר שָׁלֹשׁ שָׁנִים וְאַרְבַּע מֵאוֹת שָׁנָה
טז וַיּוֹלֶד בָּנִים וּבָנוֹת׃ וַיְחִי־עֵבֶר
אַרְבַּע וּשְׁלֹשִׁים שָׁנָה וַיּוֹלֶד אֶת־פָּלֶג׃
יז וַיְחִי־עֵבֶר אַחֲרֵי הוֹלִידוֹ אֶת־פֶּלֶג
שְׁלֹשִׁים שָׁנָה וְאַרְבַּע מֵאוֹת שָׁנָה וַיּוֹלֶד
יח בָּנִים וּבָנוֹת׃ וַיְחִי־פֶלֶג שְׁלֹשִׁים
יט שָׁנָה וַיּוֹלֶד אֶת־רְעוּ׃ וַיְחִי־פֶלֶג אַחֲרֵי
הוֹלִידוֹ אֶת־רְעוּ תֵּשַׁע שָׁנִים וּמָאתַיִם
כ שָׁנָה וַיּוֹלֶד בָּנִים וּבָנוֹת׃ וַיְחִי רְעוּ
שְׁתַּיִם וּשְׁלֹשִׁים שָׁנָה וַיּוֹלֶד אֶת־שְׂרוּג׃
כא וַיְחִי רְעוּ אַחֲרֵי הוֹלִידוֹ אֶת־שְׂרוּג שֶׁבַע
שָׁנִים וּמָאתַיִם שָׁנָה וַיּוֹלֶד בָּנִים וּבָנוֹת׃
כב וַיְחִי שְׂרוּג שְׁלֹשִׁים שָׁנָה וַיּוֹלֶד
כג אֶת־נָחוֹר׃ וַיְחִי שְׂרוּג אַחֲרֵי הוֹלִידוֹ אֶת־
נָחוֹר מָאתַיִם שָׁנָה וַיּוֹלֶד בָּנִים וּבָנוֹת׃
כד וַיְחִי נָחוֹר תֵּשַׁע וְעֶשְׂרִים שָׁנָה
כה וַיּוֹלֶד אֶת־תָּרַח׃ וַיְחִי נָחוֹר אַחֲרֵי הוֹלִידוֹ
אֶת־תֶּרַח תְּשַׁע־עֶשְׂרֵה שָׁנָה וּמְאַת שָׁנָה
כו וַיּוֹלֶד בָּנִים וּבָנוֹת׃ וַיְחִי־תֶרַח

Flood [see Chronology / *Time Line,* p. xii]. The forebears of these generations, however, were all still alive when the major event of their era occurred — the emergence of Abraham, who excelled all others in proclaiming the greatness of God and leading people to His service through his kindness. [Cf. *Tur.*]

[See *comm.* to 5:5 s.v. וַיָּמֹת.]

The Ten Generations from Noah to Abraham.

There were ten generations from Noah to Abraham. This demonstrates how long-suffering God was, for all the generations kept on provoking Him until the patriarch Abraham came and received the reward of them all *(Avos* 5:2).

— That is, Abraham did not

XI
14-25

[14] *Shelah had lived thirty years when he begot*
Eber. [15] *And Shelah lived four hundred three years*
after begetting Eber, and begot sons and daughters.

[16] *When Eber had lived thirty four years, he begot*
Peleg. [17] *And Eber lived four hundred thirty years*
after begetting Peleg, and he begot sons and
daughters.

[18] *When Peleg had lived thirty years, he begot Reu.*
[19] *And Peleg lived two hundred nine years after*
begetting Reu, and he begot sons and daughters.

[20] *When Reu had lived thirty two years, he begot*
Serug. [21] *And Reu lived two hundred and seven years*
after begetting Serug, and he begot sons and
daughters.

[22] *When Serug had lived thirty years, he begot*
Nachor. [23] *And Serug lived two hundred years after*
begetting Nachor, and he begot sons and daughters.
[24] *When Nachor had lived twenty-nine years, he*
begot Terach. [25] *And Nachor lived one hundred nine-*
teen years after begetting Terach, and he begot sons
and daughters.

adopt the evil ways of his predecessors, but to the contrary, he perceived the Truth and taught the way of God. Therefore, Abraham deserved to receive the reward which his predecessors would have earned had they been righteous (*Ibn Aknin;* see *Overview* p. 198).

Chronology of the generations
(Based upon *Seder Olam)*

◆§ שֵׁם — *Shem:* 1558-2158.

◆§ אַרְפַּכְשַׁד — *Arpachshad:* 1658-2096

◆§ שֶׁלַח — *Shelah:* 1693-2126

◆§ עֵבֶר — *Eber:* 1723-2187

◆§ פֶּלֶג — *Peleg:* 1757-1996 (The Dispersion occurred in the year of his death).

◆§ רְעוּ — *Reu:* 1787-2026

◆§ שְׂרוּג — *Serug:* 1819-2049

◆§ נָחוֹר — *Nachor:* 1849-1997

◆§ תֶּרַח — *Terach:* 1878-2083

◆§ אַבְרָהָם — *Abraham:* 1948-2123

19. וַיְחִי פֶלֶג — *And Peleg lived.* [With Peleg, we see a dramatic shortening of the average lifespan nearly cut in half from his immediate ancestors' lifespan of approximately 450 years to approximately 230 years. See *comm.* to 10:25.]

נָחוֹר — *Nachor.*

[The name Nachor, Abram's grandfather, also appears in *v.* 26 as Abram's brother.]

יא
כז־כח

שִׁבְעִים שָׁנָה וַיּוֹלֶד אֶת־אַבְרָם אֶת־נָחוֹר
כז וְאֶת־הָרָן: וְאֵלֶּה תּוֹלְדֹת תֶּרַח תֶּרַח
הוֹלִיד אֶת־אַבְרָם אֶת־נָחוֹר וְאֶת־הָרָן
כח וְהָרָן הוֹלִיד אֶת־לוֹט: וַיָּמָת הָרָן עַל־פְּנֵי
תֶּרַח אָבִיו בְּאֶרֶץ מוֹלַדְתּוֹ בְּאוּר כַּשְׂדִּים:

26. וַיּוֹלֶד אֶת אַבְרָם — *And he begot Abram* — In the year 1948, 48 years before the Dispersion, which, as described above, happened in 1996 *(Seder Olam).*

'Abram is the same as Abraham' [*I Chron.* 1:27] At first he became an אַב אֲרָם *father,* [in the sense of teacher] *to Aram* [i.e., Aram-Naharaim, his birthplace *(Rashi)*] but ultimately he became a father to the whole world [as it is written in 17:5: *Behold I have made you a father of a multitude of nations (Rashi)*] *(Berachos* 13a see *Overview).*[1]

[According to *Sefer HaYashar,* Terach apparently named the child 'Avram' in honor of Terach's *own* elevation in Nimrod's court]: '... And Terach named the son that was born to him *Avram* [i.e., 'exalted father'] because the king had exalted him in these days and dignified him above all the princes that were with him.'

'Abraham was worthy of being created before Adam, but God reasoned: He may sin and there will be none after him to set it right. Therefore I will create Adam, so that if he sins, Abraham will come and set it right' *(Midrash* 14:6).

— The name of Abram's mother was Amthela, daughter of Karnebo *(Bava Basra* 91a).

[See *comm.* to *v.* 28 for further *Midrashim* concerning Abraham. The wealth of Talmudic and Midrashic material on Abraham will be more fully dealt with in Vol. II.]

אֶת נָחוֹר וְאֶת הָרָן — *Nachor and Haran.*

The *Talmud Sanhedrin* 69b, assumes that Abraham, Nachor, and Haran are listed chronologically. But, in that case, the *Talmud* points out, Abram would have been at least one year older than Nachor, and two years older than Haran. Now, we know that Abraham was ten years old when Sarah was born. Haran her father, who was two years younger than Abraham, would have had to be only eight years old when he begot her!

[The *Midrash* goes even further; Sarah was the younger of his daughers, and allowing at least two years for the two pregnancies, Haran was only six years old when be begot Sarah!]

Therefore, the *Talmud* suggests; as it does concerning Shem, Ham,

1. Why did Shem and Eber not influence people to destroy their idols? It may be that they protested against idols, but the people merely hid them. Abram, however, destroyed the idols *(Ra'avad).* Alternatively, Shem and Eber lived in Canaan where they taught the way of God while Abram's activity against idols was in Babel. When Abram came to Canaan, he excelled Shem and Eber by actively traversing the land and preaching that the people repent *(Kesef Mishneh).*

[See also *comm.* to 11:2.]

XI
26-29

[26] *When Terach had lived seventy years, he begot*
Abram, Nachor, and Haran.
[27] *Now these are the chronicles of Terach: Terach begot*
Abram, Nachor, and Haran; and Haran begot Lot.
[28] *Haran died in the presence of Terach his father, in*
his native land, in Ur Kasdim. [29] *And Abram and*

and Japheth, that the order of the births of Terach's children are given in order of wisdom and importance, and although Abraham is therefore mentioned first he was not necessarily the oldest, Haran probably being older than he.

27. וְאֵלֶּה תּוֹלְדֹת תֶּרַח *Now these are the chronicles of Terach.*

The word תּוֹלְדוֹת can be rendered *'generations, descendants, products,* and *history.'* Cf. *comm.* to 2:4; 5:1;9] Our translation, *'chronicles'*, follows *Radak* who notes that the *generations* of Terach have already been listed in the previous verse, only Lot being added here. This verse introduces the narrative of the *events* that befell him and his family. First of all, mention is made of his children — the premature death of his son, then the marriage of his other children; his departure from Ur Kasdim; and his death in Charan.

The *Midrash* notes that whoever has his name repeated twice in close proximity — has a share in the World to Come. But it was objected that Terach's name is also repeated [in our verse, *Terach, Terach* and he had practiced idolatry!] But, it was answered, Terach ultimately repented and did have a share in the future world [cf.*comm.* to *v.* 32, and 15:15.]

וְהָרָן הוֹלִיד אֶת לוֹט — *And Haran begot Lot.*

[Only Haran is mentioned as having children. Nachor did not beget children until much later (see *Ramban* to 22:20), and Abram's wife was barren (*v.* 30). Lot is introduced here as Haran's son because subsequent to his father's death he accompanied Abram, and would later play an important role in the narrative. Haran's daughters are mentioned in *v.*29.]

28. וַיָּמָת הָרָן עַל פְּנֵי תֶּרַח אָבִיו — *And Haran died in the presence of Terach his father* — i.e. in his father's lifetime *(Rashi).* It says *'in his father's presence'* because his father saw him die. Similarly it is said [in the case of the death of Nadab and Abihu *Num.* 3:4]: *In the presence of Aaron their father* [i.e. in their father's lifetime *(Tanchuma).* See *Rashi* and *Ramban* there.]

According to the *Zohar,* this is specially mentioned 'because until that day no man had ever died in his father's lifetime, Haran being the first.'

The *Vilna Gaon* in *Kol Eliyahu* cites the above *Zohar,* and comments: This statement of the *Zohar* is on the surface, incomprehensible. Many *before* Haran died during the lifetime of their fathers: such as Abel, Chanoch, Lamech.

Some suggest that the explanation of the Holy *Zohar* is that Haran was the first *after* the Flood to precede his father in death. However, we see that even among the ten generations from Noah to Abraham there

°מפטיר כט °וַיִּקַּח אַבְרָם וְנָחוֹר לָהֶם נָשִׁים שֵׁם אֵשֶׁת־
אַבְרָם שָׂרָי וְשֵׁם אֵשֶׁת־נָחוֹר מִלְכָּה בַּת־
ל הָרָן אֲבִי־מִלְכָּה וַאֲבִי יִסְכָּה׃ וַתְּהִי שָׂרַי

were some who died in their father's lifetime, such as Arpachshad, Peleg and Nachor ...

However if one probes deeply into the chronology of the period, then the *Zohar's* statement becomes comprehensible. According to the chronology, when Haran died, his ancestors Arpachshad, Peleg, and Nachor were still alive! Thus, as the *Zohar* maintains Haran *was* indeed the first to die in his father's lifetime. [Note: The Gaon's intricate calculations have been omitted. Instead, the reader is directed to the *Chronology / Time Line* on p.xii. Cf. also *HaKsav V'Hakaballah.*]

Rashi adds that according to the *Midrashic* interpretation, עַל פְּנֵי signifies that Haran died *because of his father* [עַל פְּנֵי, lit. *in the presence of* = מִפְּנֵי, *because of (Mizrachi).*] The *Midrash* relates that Terach had complained to Nimrod because Abraham had crushed his idols, [see *Overview* to *Lech-Lecha* in Vol.II] and he had him thrown into a fiery furnace. Haran, who was present, could not decide with whom to side, and was prepared to join whoever emerged victorious. When Abraham was miraculously saved from the fiery furnace, Haran was asked to declare himself. He replied that he sided with Abraham, whereupon he was thrown into the furnace. His innards were seared and he emerged from the furnace and died in his father's presence. He was unworthy of a miracle since he was willing to defy Nimrod only because he fully expected to duplicate Abraham's miracle.

This, continues *Rashi,* is the significance of אוּר כַּשְׂדִּים [which, relating אוּר with *fire,* he renders: *And Haran died ... in the fire of Kasdim.*[1]

בְּאֶרֶץ מוֹלַדְתּוֹ בְּאוּר כַּשְׂדִּים — *In his native land, in Ur Kasdim,* commonly rendered *Ur of the Chaldees.* See *comm.* below.]

According to *Ramban, Ur Kasdim* was the native land of Haran only. He explains that Kasdim and Shinar were inhabited by Ham's descendants, while Abraham's family were Shemites. Abraham's ancestors were from Aram [Mesopotamia] which is beyond the Euphrates. He is therefore called in 14:13 *Abram the Ivri* [*'Hebrew'*] meaning from 'across' the River [see *comm.* to 10:20] never *Abram the Kasdi.*

In a lengthy discourse on this theme, *Ramban* bases himself on the implication of several verses, and cites *Rambam,* [*Moreh*

1. Abram's father, Terach, was a dealer in idols. One day he fell ill and asked Abram to tend the business. Abram, who recognized HASHEM when he was only three years old, asked his mother to prepare food. He took it to the room filled with idols as if waiting for them to reach out for it. Then he took a hammer and smashed all the idols except for the largest. When he finished, he put the hammer in the hand of the one remaining idol.

Terach, hearing the commotion, came running. Seeing the carnage, he demanded to know what happened.

Abram answered innocently, 'The small idols took food before the big one. He was angered by their lack of manners and shattered them all!'

Terach raged, 'You lie. The idols are dead. They cannot eat or move!'

'In that case,' Abram answered, 'why do you worship them?'.

The result of Abram's brave denunciations of idolatry was that Nimrod cast him into the furnace from which he was miraculously saved. *Ramban* asks why so great a miracle is not mentioned in the Torah. His reply (see here and *Gen.* 46:15) will be discussed in *Overview,* Vol. II.

Nachor took themselves wives; the name of Abram's wife was Sarai, and the name of Nachor's wife was Milcah, the daughter of Haran, the father of Milcah and the father of Iscah. 30 *And Sarai remained barren,*

3:29] that Abraham was born in *Cuthah*, a city 'across' the river, which lies near Charan and Assyria, between Mesopotamia and the Euphrates, adjacent to Eretz Yisrael.

Noting that we find Nachor, Abraham's brother, in the city of Charan [further, 29:4 which is in Mesopotamia, *not* Kasdim]. *Ramban* concludes that Terach begot his older sons, Abraham and Nachor in the area 'beyond the river', his ancestral land. He then went with his eldest son Abram to Kasdim, where his youngest son Haran was born. It was there that, as the Rabbis stated, Abram was miraculously saved from the fiery furnace. His son, Nachor, apparently remained in their ancestral home, Aram Naharaim [Mesopotamia], and settled in Charan [cf. 24:10]. Hence, according to *Ramban*, the phrase *in his native land, Ur Kasdim* refers only to Haran, as only he, among Terach's children, was born there.

According to *Rashi*, however [implied in 12:1 but more specifically stated in 24:7] Abraham's birthplace was Ur Kasdim [not Aram Naharaim.] *Mizrachi* [in a lenghty comm. on 12:1] explains that *Ivri* is a general, all-inclusive designation for that *entire* region which, from the perspective of Canaan, lay *'across the river.'*

See also *Maharal* in *Gevuros Hashem* chapt. 5 who emphasizes that *Ramban's* view is certainly not in harmony with the view of the Talmudic Sages who hold that Ur Kasdim was the birthplace of Abraham. He cites *Pesachim* 87b where this is specifically stated. [Cf. also *Bava Basra* 91a, and comm. to 12:1.]

אוּר כַּשְׂדִּים — *Ur Kasdim.*

As mentioned above, *Rashi* explains Ur Kasdim as meaning the *fires of Kasdim.* It was so called on account of the miracle by which Abraham was saved from the fiery furnace.

Rashi adds that according to *Menachem*, אור in its literal sense, means 'plain' as in *Isaiah* 24:15: בָּאֻרִים כַּבְּדוּ ה׳, *glorify HASHEM in the plains.*

R' Bachya comments that there are three possible literal interpretations of אור: plain, mountain, and fire. He cites verses illustrating each interpretation.

Radak notes that Kesed, son of Nachor, after whom this country is named was not born until much later [cf. 22:22]. Hence, the composite name Ur Kasdim postdates the period spoken of here, and the Torah recorded the name by which the city was ultimately known in the time of Moses.

[According to the view of those who perceive in the name Arpachshad a reference to Kessed (see *comm.* to 10:22) the designation *Ur Kasdim could* have already been its name in Abraham's time.]

29. **וַיִּקַּח אַבְרָם וְנָחוֹר** — *And Abram and Nachor took ...*

When their brother, Haran, died in relative youth, his brothers married his daughters to honor the memory of Haran and to assuage the grief of Terach (*Imrei Shefer*).

שָׂרָי — *Sarai.*

[Her name was later changed to Sarah (17:15).]

See further on *Iscah*, and *footnote* on page 350.

וְשֵׁם אֵשֶׁת־נָחוֹר מִלְכָּה — *And the name of Nachor's wife was Milkah.*

Nachor's wife is mentioned to establish the ancestry of, Rivkah, Rachel, and Leah [23:20; 24:15] (*Ibn Ezra*).

בַּת הָרָן אֲבִי־מִלְכָּה וַאֲבִי יִסְכָּה — *The daughter of Haran, the father of Milcah and the father of Iscah.*

יא לא עֲקָרָה אֵין לָהּ וָלָד: וַיִּקַּח תֶּרַח אֶת־
לא אַבְרָם בְּנוֹ וְאֶת־לוֹט בֶּן־הָרָן בֶּן־בְּנוֹ וְאֵת
שָׂרַי כַּלָּתוֹ אֵשֶׁת אַבְרָם בְּנוֹ וַיֵּצְאוּ אִתָּם

Iscah was Sarah. She was so called [from the word meaning to *see, gaze*] because she could 'see' the future by holy inspirations, and because everyone gazed at her beauty. Also *Iscah* denotes נְסִיכוּת, princeliness *(Rashi).*[1]

Heidenheim explains that the Torah now tells us that the father of Milkah was Haran. His fame rested on being the father of both the renowned Milkah and Iscah, whom the *Talmud, Sanhedrin* 69b, identifies with Sarai. Now, Milkah's importance lay in the fact that she was the matriarch of an important family; of the name Iscah we find no other mention. Why, then, should the Torah have attached Haran's identification to an unknown personage? It is clear therefore, that Milkah and Iscah are identical with the Milkah and Sarai mentioned in the verse, both of them so famous that they form the basis for Haran's role in posterity. Hence we understand that the name Iscah must be an indication of an aspect of Sarai's personality.

Haamek Davar observes that Abram was older and should have married the elder sister Milkah. But since Sarai was 'Iscah', a prophetess [who could 'gaze' at the future] it was more fitting for Abraham to marry her. Therefore only Milkah is identified as a daughter of Haran, but not Sarai: Abraham did not marry Sarai out of filial devotion, but because of her personal virtues.

The reason the Torah identified Haran as their father after having already mentioned that she was his daughter, is to inform us that Lot, the only offspring of Haran mentioned in *v.* 27, was not an only child. The *Talmud*'s identification of Iscah with Sarai is supported by the fact that Abraham later referred to Sarah as *'the daughter of my father'* [20:12; in the sense of the *granddaughter* of my father, i.e., my niece — see *Rashi* ad. loc.], therefore Sarah, too, was perforce Haran's daughter *(Radak).*

[It is not unusual for the Torah to

1. *Maharal elucidates a fundamental principle in understanding Torah. He raises the question that it would have been more appropriate to allude to Sarah's greatness in prophecy in Gen. 21:12 where God told Abraham to obey Sarah because, as Rashi comments there, her powers of prophecy were superior even to Abraham's.*

Maharal explains that the Torah can be understood on many different levels, and it makes no attempt to deliver all of its profundities to readers incapable of understanding them. The scholar will understand the allusion to Sarah's prophetic spirit in the name Iscah while others are free to assume that Iscah was a different person. No matter how much the Torah makes plain, there will still be profound mysteries hidden within its words (see Overview: Torah).

He comments further that a woman has two missions in life as if she were born twice: the first is hers from birth as an individual, while the second comes with marriage when, if she marries a righteous person, she is elevated to a higher mission.

Sarah's two names indicate her two missions; one is used in connection with her father and the other in connection with her husband. 'Iscah', the name indicating personal greatness, was Sarah's for her own mission and it is the one used in telling of her birth to Haran. 'Sarah', indicating that she joined Abraham in leading the world to its ultimate goal, was the name associated with the Abrahamitic mission and it is used from the time of her marriage.

XI *she had no child.*
31 [31] *Terach took his son Abram, and Lot the son of*
Haran, his grandson, and his daughter-in-law Sarai,
the wife of Abram his son, and they departed with

identify a father by his offspring. Above, 10:21 Shem is identified as *the father of all the children of Eber.* See also *Exod.* 18:1, where *Rashi* explains that originally Moses would ascribe greatness to his father-in-law, [cf. *Exod.* 4:38], but that after Moses became God's prophet and instrument, Jethro honored himself by saying 'I am the father-in-law of Moses.'

Here, too, Haran prided himself in his daughters and hence he is described as their father.]

[It is interesting to note that according to *Sefer HaYashar* 7:22 and 50, Haran was born to a different mother than Abraham, Terach apparently having had more than one wife. See also 20:12 where Abraham reveals to Abimelech that Sarah was *'indeed ... the daughter* [i.e. granddaughter] *of my father* [through Haran], *but not the daughter of my mother. Rashi,* ad. loc., following the *Midrash,* similarly explains that Haran was born of a different mother than Abraham.]

30. אֵין לָהּ וָלָד — *she had no child.*

[If the verse begins by saying *Sarai was barren,* it is obvious *she had no child.* Why the redundancy?]

— Some women are childless and later give birth. Scripture tells us that her barrenness was complete — she was entirely incapable of ever bearing a child *(R' Bachya).*

As the *Talmud* notes: her barrenness was total, she did not even have בֵּית וָלָד, a womb! *(Yevamos* 64b).

[Thus, the fact that God later promised Abraham that He would make him a great nation (12:2) was even more noteworthy.]

The verse emphasizes that Sarai had no children in order to underline Abram's merit in complying with God's command to forsake his native land [12:1]. Had he had a child whom he could have left behind to inherit his portion of the family estate, his compliance would not have been so extraordinary. The Torah therefore gives us this information now, in anticipation of God's command *(B'chor Shor).*

31. וַיִּקַּח תֶּרַח — *And Terach took.*

According to *Ibn Ezra* and *Radak* this journey was the result of God's call to Abraham [in 12:1] to leave his country. Abraham told his father, who agreed to accompany him. Since Terach was the head of the family, the Torah honored him by ascribing the initiative to him. [However, according to *Ramban* (see end of this verse) and *Rashi (12:1)* Terach's exodus from Ur Kasdim was unrelated to the Divine call which came to Abraham only later in Charan.]

וְאֶת לוֹט בֶּן־הָרָן בֶּן־בְּנוֹ — *And Lot, son of Haran, his grandson* — Terach took Lot along because Haran had died and Lot was now dependant upon his grandfather. He therefore wanted Lot to be under his care, come what may *(Radak).*

He took Lot with him to spare him a premature death like his father's. By changing his environment, Terach hoped to change his fortune *(Abarbanel).*

אֵשֶׁת אַבְרָם — *Wife of Abram.*

This is added, though she was already described as Terach's

יא
לב

מֵאוּר כַּשְׂדִּים לָלֶכֶת אַרְצָה כְּנַעַן וַיָּבֹאוּ
לב עַד־חָרָן וַיֵּשְׁבוּ שָׁם: וַיִּהְיוּ יְמֵי־תֶרַח
חָמֵשׁ שָׁנִים וּמָאתַיִם שָׁנָה וַיָּמָת תֶּרַח
בְּחָרָן:

daughter-in-law to indicate that it was primarily as Abraham's *wife*, in compliance with God's command that she willingly left her land. It was not because Abraham insisted, that she left for a strange land, but because, as the wife of a righteous man, she had faith in whatever he told her in the name of God and she willingly did His will *(Radak)*.

[The fact that Nachor is not mentioned here as accompanying his father (although we find him later in Charan) is discussed by the commentators]:

Nachor is not mentioned because, either he had gone earlier, or he arrived later *(Ibn Ezra*; see *Gevuros Hashem* chapter 5).

According to *Ramban*, cited in *v.* 28, Nachor was already in Charan because he was born there; while *R' Meyuchas* suggests that Nachor *did* accompany them but it was unimportant for the immediate flow of the narrative to mention him.

וַיֵּצְאוּ אִתָּם — *And they departed with them.*

The plural forms are used to accentuate the role of these who played the primary roles *(Gur Aryeh):*

Thus, the phrase means: *'They* [Terach and Abram] *departed with them* [Lot and Sarai] *(Rashi).*

Tur cites *Ramban* that the plural אִתָּם, *with them* [i.e., instead of *with Terach*] is used in deference to Abram, since it was for his sake that they all left, because Lot and Sarai continued to accompany him even after he separated from Terach. *Tur* concludes that although, for this reason, it should have said וַיֵּצְאוּ אִתּוֹ, 'they went with *him'*, i.e. with Abram, nevertheless in deference to his father the Torah ascribes it to both of them.

אַרְצָה כְּנַעַן — *To the land of Canaan.*

[Although God had not specified which land] Abraham chose Canaan as his destination because it was the most acceptable of the lands; its climate had not been adversely affected by the Flood as was that of other lands, and it had the greatest potential for spiritual development *(Sforno)*. [See 8:11, page 282.]

According to *N'tziv*, Canaan was chosen because he had perceived its holiness from afar.

וַיָּבֹאוּ עַד חָרָן וַיֵּשְׁבוּ שָׁם — *But when they came as far as Charan, they settled there.*

Although *Terach* had originally intended to go as far as Canaan, he could not bring himself to abandon his land entirely. He therefore settled in Charan [the plural'they' probably refers to his wife, and entourage who are not mentioned] which is near the border of Canaan so he could be in close proximity to Abraham. He settled there until his death, while Abraham went on to Canaan in accordance with God's command *(Radak)*.

[Apparently, however, Abraham did spend at least some time in Charan. See *comm.* to 12:4,5]

It must be remembered that according to *Ramban* [*v.* 28] Aram, in which Charan also lies, was the birthplace of Terach, Abraham,

XI them from Ur Kasdim to go to the land of Canaan;
32 but when they came as far as Charan, they settled
there.

32 All the days of Terach were two hundred and five years, and Terach died in Charan.

and Nachor. Ur Kasdim was the birthplace only of Haran.

Ramban [ibid.] explains that from the moment Abraham was miraculously saved from the furnace, Terach and Abraham intended to flee to Canaan, away from Nimrod. When they reached Charan, where their ancestors had always lived they settled there among their family. [*Abarbanel* explains that Nimrod's dominion did not extend over Charan.] It was there that Abraham was commanded to go to the land of Canaan, and so he left his father, who later died there in Charan, his native land.

32. וַיָּמָת תֶּרַח בְּחָרָן — *And Terach died in Charan.*

In the year 2083; Isaac was 35 years old at the time *(Seder Olam).*

Rashi comments that Terach's death occurred more than sixty years after Abraham's departure from Charan to Canaan (as related in the next chapter). For, *Abraham was seventy-five years old when he left Charan* [12:4]; Terach was seventy years old when Abraham was born [11:26] making Terach 145 when Abraham left Charan. Therefore, Terach lived sixty more years as he died at the age of 205 [*v.* 32.] Nevertheless, Terach's death is recorded here [this being noteworthy because his is the first death recorded in the Ten Generations from Shem to Abraham *(R' Bachya;* see *comm.* to *v.* 11)] to avoid the public implication that Abraham was disrespectful to his father by leaving him in his old age....

Now, one should not think that in shielding Abraham by recording Terach's death when he was still alive, that the Torah חָלִילָה contained an untruth *(Levush),* because, as *Rashi* goes on to explain, Terach was wicked and truly dead [in the spiritual sense], for indeed the wicked, even while alive, are called dead, and the righteous, even when dead, are called alive.

Rashi's comm. is based upon the *Midrash* [on 12:1]:

Terach's death is immediately followed by God's command to leave Charan, yet the chronology proves that Terach died at least sixty years later! First, you may learn from this that the wicked, even during their lifetime, are called dead. Abraham was afraid, saying: 'Shall I go out and bring dishonor upon the Divine Name, as people will accuse me of leaving my father in his old age?'

God therefore reassured him and said: Go! I exempt you, but none other, from the duty of honoring your parents. Moreover [since a wicked man is called dead] I will record his death before your departure.'

True, Terach *did* repent later, as *Rashi* himself comments in 15:15, for as the Sages said, Terach has a share in the World to Come. But *Rashi* apparently holds that at the time of Abraham's departure Terach had not yet repented, and that is why the implied announcement of Terach's repentance was made only much later, as expressed in 15:15 *(Mizrachi; Gur Aryeh).*

Ramban also shares the view that Terach did not repent until late in his life. Nevertheless, *Ramban* maintains that the simple explanation for Terach's death being prematurely recorded here is that it is common for the Torah to record the father's death before proceeding with the narrative of the son, even though the death occurred many years later. Thus, Noah's death was recorded in 9:29 although Noah was still alive in the days of Abraham and his son Shem lived throughout Abraham's lifetime [as the *Talmud, Bava Basra* 121b comments 'Jacob saw Shem'—see *Chronology/Time Line* p. xii. See also *Gevuros Hashem,* chapt. 5.]

בְּחָרָן — *In Charan.*

Rashi notes that the נ *nun* in בְּחָרָן is inverted [Although such an inverted *nun* does not appear in our Torah Scrolls, *Minchas Shay* writes that it may have in some ancient Scrolls or, more likely, that the 'crown' atop the letter may have been altered slightly.]...

An inverted *nun* is used to signify that a period has come to a close (see *Numbers* 10:35-36). On our verse *Rashi* comments that the world had been under God's wrath since Adam's sin [i.e. the word חָרָן is related to חֲרוֹן, wrath]. But the emergence of the righteous Abram ended the period of divine anger with man's shortcomings.

Rabbeinu Bachya interprets the inverted *nun* as the ending of שְׁנֵי אֲלָפִים תֹּהוּ, the 2,000 years of desolation with which the history of Creation began. With Abraham the next period begins — שְׁנֵי אֲלָפִים תּוֹרָה, two thousand years of Torah, the twenty centuries during which the Jewish people was formed, the Written Torah given at Sinai, the Temples built, and the Oral Torah developed.

With God's Call to Abram in the very next verse, the 2,000 years of Torah begin....

According to the Masoretic note appearing at the end of the *Sidrah* there are 153 verses in the *Sidrah* numerically corresponding to the mnemonic בצלא״ל [= 153, *Bezalel* = 'in God's protection' — an allusion to Noah's deliverance in the ark]; and אב״י יסכ״ה לו״ט [=153]. The Haftorah begins with *Isaiah* 54:1 רָנִּי עֲקָרָה.

Meir Zlotowitz
Rosh Chodesh Tammuz, 5737 / June, 1977
Brooklyn, New York

☙ סדר לך-לך

☙ Sidra Lech-Lecha

— *The Overviews*

Genealogical Table / The Patriarchal Family

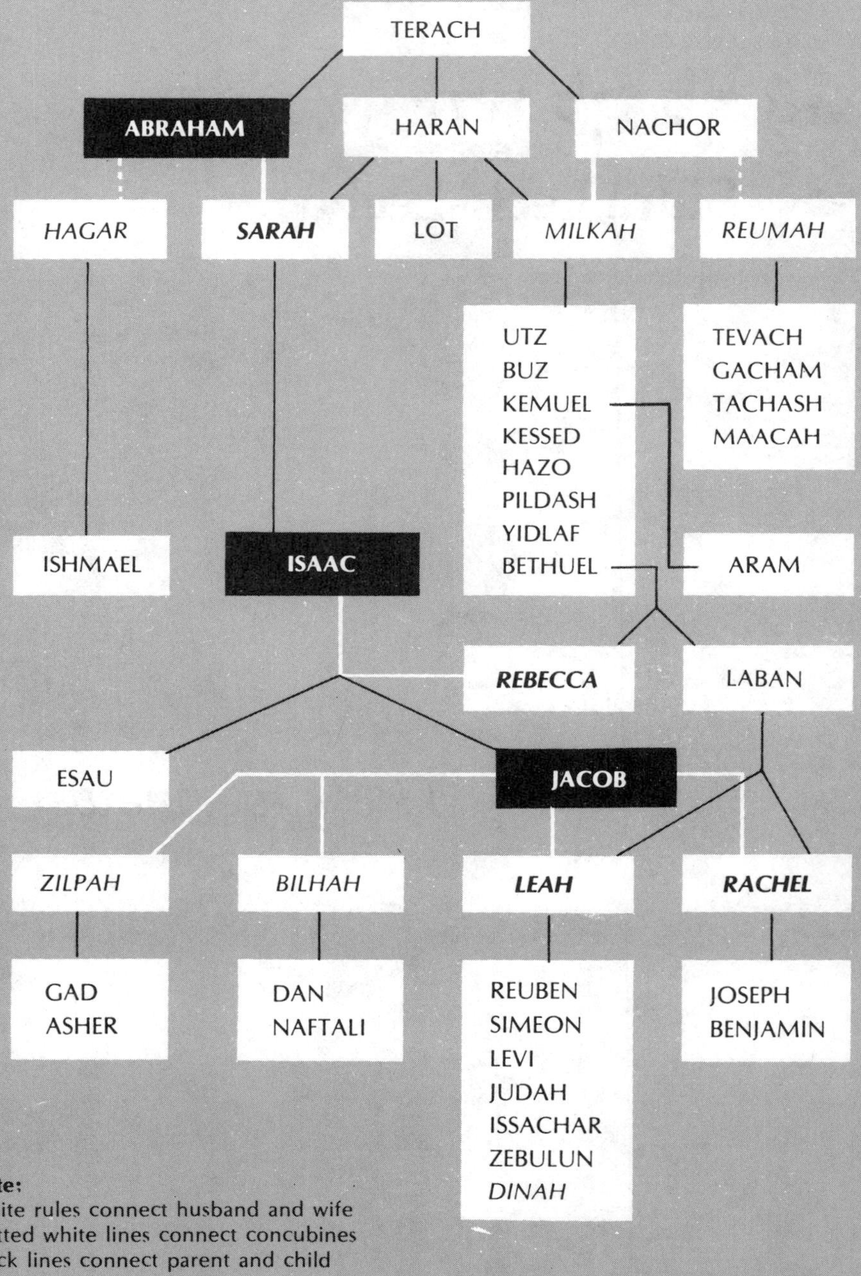

Note:
White rules connect husband and wife
Dotted white lines connect concubines
Black lines connect parent and child

An Overview —
The Patriarchs

תָּנָא דְבֵי אֵלִיָּהוּ שֵׁשֶׁת אֲלָפִים שָׁנָה הָוֵי הָעוֹלָם: שְׁנֵי אֲלָפִים תֹּהוּ, שְׁנֵי אֲלָפִים תּוֹרָה שְׁנֵי אֲלָפִים יְמוֹת הַמָּשִׁיחַ . . . שְׁנֵי אֲלָפִים תּוֹרָה מֵאֵימַת? . . . מִוְּאֶת הַנֶּפֶשׁ אֲשֶׁר עָשׂוּ בְחָרָן וּגְמִירֵי דְאַבְרָהָם בְּהַהִיא שַׁעְתָּא בַּר נ״ב הֲוָה

The Academy of Eliyahu taught: The world will endure for six thousand years: two thousand [years] of desolation, two thousand of Torah, and two thousand of the Days of Messiah ... When did the two thousand of Torah begin? ... From [the time of] 'and the souls whom they [Abraham and Sarah] made [which Targum translates "whom they brought under the yoke of Torah" (Rashi)] in Charan,' (12:5). *We have a tradition that at that time Abraham was fifty-two years old (Avodah Zarah 9a).*

I. The Emergence

The Chariot

God's Presence rests upon man to the extent that man permits. If he observes God's commands only so long as they do not conflict with a particular passion — be it a desire for food, lust, avarice, heretical intellectual stimulation — then to whatever extent that weakness conflicts with his dedication to the will of God, the *Shechinah* cannot rest upon him.

The bearer of God's Presence is referred to as a מֶרְכָּבָה*, chariot.*

The bearer of God's Presence is referred to as a מֶרְכָּבָה, *chariot.* A royal chariot can bear the king if it is free of external encumbrances. Fill it with extraneous burdens, and it will have no room for the king himself. And a royal chariot with no room for the king is a wagon, not a chariot.

הָאָבוֹת הֵן הֵן הַמֶּרְכָּבָה

The Patriarchs — they are the chariot (Bereishis Rabbah 47)

Abraham, Isaac, and Jacob are God's chariot on earth, because it was through them that His Presence descended to earth and found a place here.

Abraham, Isaac, and Jacob are God's chariot on earth, because it was through them that His Presence descended to earth and found a place here. So great were they that they were able to negate their selves entirely, dedicating every feeling and fiber of their being to His service. Never was there a selfish consideration. Their very existence — every moment of it — was an exercise in perfect service. Because they negated themselves as individuals with rights and desires, they could totally absorb Godliness and thus become bearers — the Chariot — of His *Shechinah.*

When Abraham received the honor of a visit from Abimelech and his field marshal, he greeted them as Abraham, servant of God, not as Abraham, the Ibri, who had attained status in a strange land, far from his family and servants. Personal considerations concerned the Patriarchs not at all; therefore God's Presence illuminated their every action and gave their every success an import that had implications millenia into the future.

They were the forerunners and the embodiment of the future nation of Israel, and therefore they alone are called אָבוֹת*, Fathers.*

They were the forerunners and the embodiment of the future nation of Israel, and therefore they alone are called אָבוֹת, *Fathers.* The twelve tribes, too are ancestors of the nation, but they are not called fathers. Moses was the shepherd, teacher, prophet, most faithful of God's household, but he is not a father. David represents the culmination of all God's plans of creation, the King Messiah who will fulfill the age-old potential that was dashed with Adam's failure, but David is not a father. Even Noah, literally the father of humanity, is not called the father of the Jewish people. Fatherhood, in the sense that the Patriarchs are fathers, is not measured in biological terms. All that a person is stems from his parents; whatever he becomes represents the development of the latent potential with which he was born. All that

Israel is and will yet become, represents the development of the national character that is the legacy of the Patriarchs.

The Torah Era Begins

Abraham, in a real sense, was as much the 'first man' as were Adam and Noah.

With Abraham, there began a new birth of the history of mankind. Abraham, in a real sense, was as much the 'first man' as were Adam and Noah. The Era of Desolation ended with the year 2000. It was indeed a bleak era in history. The fall of Adam, the murder of Abel, the introduction of idolatry, the failure of the first ten generations, the deluge, the failure of ten generations after Noah, the Dispersion. But in the year 1948 (from Creation) Abraham was born. When he was fifty-two years old — the year 2000 — he began gathering people together in Charan and teaching them to serving HASHEM. With that, an era began. Desolation was over and a new light began to shine upon humanity, the light of Abraham who embodied the light of Torah.

With that, an era began. Desolation was over and a new light began to shine upon humanity, the light of Abraham who embodied the light of Torah.

Abraham was a new phenomenon; there had never been anyone like him and he was completely apart from his birthplace and family, even from his parents.

The *Midrash (Bereishis Rabbah* 39) relates that when God commanded Abraham to leave Charan and begin a new life in Eretz Yisrael, he feared that by deserting his parents, he would cause a desecration of God's Name, for people would say, 'He abandoned his father to old age!'

> The Holy One, Blessed be He, said to Abraham, I absolve you from the obligation to honor your father and mother, but others will not be similarly absolved. What is more, I will relate the story of his death [in the Torah] prior to your leave-taking as it says first, *And Terach died in Charan* (11:32) and only afterward *And HASHEM said to Abram 'Go ... from your land'* (12:1).

Maharal explains that Abraham could be absolved from the commandment as was none other, because he was an entirely new and unique entity. In essence, he bore no relationship to Terach because he was the beginning of a new sort of existence on earth. Before him there was desolation and darkness; with him there was Torah and light. What relationship is there between light and darkness? None. When light appears, darkness flees. The prior existence of darkness does not give birth to light; it merely accentuates how different is the new from the old. Just as light causes darkness to disappear, so, too, the emergence of Abraham at the age of fifty-two as the bearer of Torah brought about the disappearence of any meaningful relationship between him and Terach. Therefore, *only* Abraham was absolved from the commandment to honor his father; no one else could claim to have his filial relationship so completely severed.

He bore no relationship to Terach because he was the beginning of a new sort of existence on earth.

What relationship is there between light and darkness? None.

And, therefore, when the Torah prefaced Abraham's departure from Charan with the declaration of Terach's death, it was no semantic pronouncement designed to deceive those who would fail to make the simple calculation that Terach lived for fully sixty years after Abraham left him. The announcement of Terach's death was a statement of *ultimate* truth, for Terach, though he still lived and breathed, was *truly* dead in all but the superficial sense, because רְשָׁעִים בְּחַיֵּיהֶם קְרוּיִים מֵתִים, *the wicked are considered to be dead even during their lifetimes (Midrash ibid.).* The Torah intended to make no secret of the fact that Terach was still physically alive; the chronology to prove it is right there in the verses of Scripture. Rather, God reassured Abraham that no desecration of the Name would be involved because his own contemporaries would acknowledge the truth that the Torah would indicate — Abraham had no relationship with Terach, for one was light and the other darkness, one was Torah and the other was desolation, one was life and the other was death *(Gevuras Hashem* 5).

The announcement of Terach's death was a statement of ultimate *truth, for Terach, though he still lived and breathed, was* truly *dead in all but the superficial sense.*

The new birth represented by Abraham was not completed until all three Patriarchs made their combined contribution. That Abraham's work was insufficient is demonstrated by the fact that he begot an Ishmael; that Isaac went further but did not complete the task his father began is demonstrated by Esau. But of Jacob the sages say מִטָּתוֹ שְׁלֵמָה, *his bed is perfect.* Every child of Jacob was a great person in his own right; together they formed the nation, the Tribes of God.

Every child of Jacob was a great person in his own right; together they formed the nation, the Tribes of God.

II. Three Attributes

The Traits

The three Patriarchs were different, and therein lay their greatness. Isaac and Jacob did not follow Abraham's well-trodden path to attain their own closeness to God. Each found his own way. In their three ways are the sum total of all possible variations of service to God. Therefore, they are the Fathers: whatever we do was foreshadowed by them; each succeeding generation of Israel with all its great individuals and differing paths to Torah, prayer, kindness and fulfillment of the commandments, is but further growth of their seeds. We are their children.

Abraham represents חֶסֶד, kindness; *Isaac represents* גְּבוּרָה, strength *or* פַּחַד, fear; *Jacob represents* תִּפְאֶרֶת, splendor *or* אֱמֶת, truth.

Each Patriarch had a prime characteristic: Abraham represents חֶסֶד, *kindness;* Isaac represents גְּבוּרָה, *strength* or פַּחַד, *fear;* Jacob represents תִּפְאֶרֶת, *splendor,* or אֱמֶת, *truth.* Let us examine these characteristics, attempt to define them, and see how they manifest themselves in the service of God. (The following discussion will be based primarily on *Michtav Me'Eliyahu* II, pp. 160-165, and III, pp. 33-37).

☙§ The attribute of חֶסֶד, *kindness,* is the feeling of a person that he must seek to define the needs of other people and fill them. This is an outer-directed trait. The *chesed*-person acts not out of selfishness nor pity, but out of a genuine desire to help others materially or spiritually, as the case may be. [This trait is different from רַחֲמָנוּת, *mercy.* The merciful person is moved by the suffering of his fellow. While mercy is one of the most exalted traits in the Jewish scale of values, it is tinged by a certain degree of selfishness: the merciful person has been moved by the plight of another. Had the need not been brought to his attention, or if the need of his fellow does not arouse his sympathy — for example, a frugal person might not feel pity if he were told that someone is suffering intense mortification for lack of a luxurious home — he will be loath to assist him. The *chesed*-person, however, will inquire after people who can be helped, and his desire to help will not be influenced by whether or not they move him to tears.]

The chesed-*person will inquire after people who can be helped, and his desire to help will not be influenced by whether or not they move him to tears.*

☙ The attribute of גְּבוּרָה, *strength* — or, as it is often called פַּחַד or יִרְאָה, *fear* [of God] — is inner-directed. The *gevurah*-person is driven by a fear of transgression and a powerful drive toward self-perfection. He examines his deeds and desires, and will tend to refrain from any act that may fall short of the high standards he seeks to attain.

The gevura-*person is driven by a fear of transgression and a powerful drive toward self-perfection.*

☙ The attribute of תִּפְאֶרֶת, *splendor* — or as it is often called אֱמֶת, *truth* — seeks to combine *chesed* and *gevurah,* kindness and strength. By exercising a passion for truth, the *tiferes*-person finds the middle course between indulgent *kindness* which can lead to undesirable excess (as we shall see later), and self-critical *strength* which can stifle achievement. By a passion for *truth,* the *tiferes*-person combines both extremes into the blend which results in the fulfillment of duty to oneself as well as to others.

By exercising a passion for truth, the tiferes-*person finds the middle course between indulgent* kindness *... and self-critical* strength.

The very word תִּפְאֶרֶת refers to such a properly balanced combination of traits and forces. A sunrise and a symphony are two examples of beauty, visual and aural. Can one ask which single color of the sunrise or which note in a symphony gives it its beauty? The question is ludicrous. If any *single* color were painted on the backdrop of the sky, it would hardly be worthy of a glance. If any single note were played by an orchestra for thirty minutes, the monotony would be maddening. Their beauty is provided by a perfect balance of different, even clashing, elements that are properly mixed and balanced. Therefore, *splendor* and *truth,* in the context of spiritual striving and development, are synonymous. When a course has been chosen because it is true, doing justice to the potential of the person, the demands of the environment, according to the wishes of God, there can be no greater truth, and therefore no greater splendor.

Each individual will have a character trait that is dominant, one that best expresses his own personality.

The three traits of kindness, fear, and truth are all desirable and, although every person will have them all in varying degrees, each individual will have a character trait that is dominant, one that best expresses his own personality. Within the broad boundaries of any one characteristic, however, there is room for variations.

Variations Within Attributes

The chesed-*person may be driven to indiscriminate acts of kindness. The* chesed-*person may be driven by a fear. Or the* chesed-*person may refine his kind instincts.*

The *chesed*-person is possessed of a kind, generous personality. His desire to benefit others may be so overpowering that he is driven to indiscriminate acts of kindness without analyzing whether a particular deed is truly beneficial to the recipient or to society — or if a kindness to one may result in cruelty to another. Conversely, this person may refrain from an act that others may consider necessary because he fears it will result in ill-feeling or embarrassment on the part of another. Such behavior is described in the language of the Kabbalists as חֶסֶד שֶׁבְּחֶסֶד, *the kindness within kindness* i.e., kindness for its own sake, as an overriding value.

The *chesed*-person may be driven by a fear; he may examine himself critically asking, 'Perhaps my kind instincts fall short so that I have not done enough. If I were as dedicated to kindness as I should be, I would not have rested when I did, or limited my largesse as I did, or set priorities as I did'. This is known as גְּבוּרָה שֶׁבְּחֶסֶד, *strength within kindness.*

Or the *chesed*-person may refine his kind instincts in the crucible of truth: 'Is my kindness real or imagined? In my desire to help a needy family, would they best be served if I give them money or if I give them food? Would the family benefit most if I channel my assistance through the husband, or through the wife, or should it be given through both? What would serve them best — charity to relieve their anxiety or a loan to salvage their pride and maintain their initiative. Such is known as תִּפְאֶרֶת שֶׁבְּחֶסֶד, *splendor* [i.e., truth] *within kindness.*

The gevurah-*person may seek to multiply his acts of kindness. Or the instinct may be so powerful that the* gevurah-*person refrains from the apparently desirable. Or he may subject his own introspectivve nature to the ultimate test of truth.*

The *gevurah*-person too, is not one-dimensional. In his fear of inadequately discharging his responsibilities, he may seek to multiply his acts of kindness because he knows that, as a Jew, he is obligated to help others. Thus, a person who by nature is entirely unsympathetic, even callous, to the needs of others may organize and direct major works of charity. He does so not because his emotions require it of him, but because his sense of reponsibility — the mainstay of his personality — demands it of him. This is חֶסֶד שֶׁבִּגְבוּרָה, *kindness within strength,* i.e., kindness resulting from strength.

Or the instinct for self-evaluation and self-criticism may be so powerful that the *gevurah*-person, demanding perfection of himself, refrains from the apparently desirable because he is unsure of his inner motives, because he feels that he will not do justice to the obligation incumbent upon him, because he fears that an intended good deed might have the opposite effect. This is an expression of גְבוּרָה שֶׁבִּגְבוּרָה, *strength within strength.*

Or he may subject his own introspective nature to the ultimate test of truth, striking a balance between his responsibilities to himself and his responsiveness to others, between the desirability of perfection and the necessity of accomplishment. This is תִּפְאֶרֶת שֶׁבִּגְבוּרָה, *splendor within strength.*

The tiferes-*person may seek his greatest fulfillment in the service of other people. Or he may be restrained by a fear. Or his dedication to truth may be such that he will refuse to be swerved.*

The *tiferes*-person seeks the path of truth, but this path, too, has more than one parallel lane. The honest, fair person recognizes the obligation to share with others, and his desire to find truth may motivate him to seek his greatest fulfillment in the service of other people. This is חֶסֶד שֶׁבְּתִפְאֶרֶת, *kindness within splendor.*

Or he may be restrained by a fear that, in his choice of a particular action or way of life, he has not chosen wisely, or that he may be involved with people or in situations that will have the effect of diluting his honesty. Thus, his zeal for truth may cause doubt and intensive self-examination. This is גְּבוּרָה שֶׁבְּתִפְאֶרֶת, *strength within splendor.*

Or his dedication to truth may be such that he will see the path of truth and refuse to be swerved by any extraneous considerations — he wants truth for the sake of truth. This is תִּפְאֶרֶת שֶׁבְּתִפְאֶרֶת, *splendor within splendor.*

The Human Challenge

One may wonder how these nine courses — and the infinite variations persisting within them — are significantly different. After all, isn't the behavior of the righteous Jew defined by the *Shulchan Aruch* and aren't his responsibilities already spelled out? Such a question betrays a failure to dig beneath the surface of human motivation, for there are indeed as many nuances to personality make-up as there are people on earth. The Torah speaks to all of them even when the course of action is as unambiguous as the eating of matzah on the evening of Passover, the recitation of a blessing, or the avoidance of labor on the Sabbath. The physical act may be the same for all, but it is not performed by unthinking automatons. How much more so is this true when one is engaged in the performance of commandments that by their very nature engage the intellecutal and emotional faculties.

The physical act may be the same for all, but it is not performed by unthinking automatons.

The recitation of Sh'ma whereby one accepts upon himself the yoke of God's heavenly reign cannot be divorced from the individuality of the person submitting himself to God's will. The scholar whose greatest love is to sit at his tractate and engage the thought of the great commentators of history and the person whose heart goes out to the sick and needy, both recite the same Sh'ma and accept the yoke of the same King. But if each remains with what he loves best in any case — the one with his studies oblivious to the obligation to help others, and the other with his charity caseload oblivious to the requirement to study Torah — then each, to a subtle but very real extent, has accepted upon himself the obligation to obey God's will in the areas to which he is already pre-disposed.

Obviously, the greatest commandment is the study of Torah; each individual is required also to serve God in accordance with his unique mission by utilizing all the skills, talent, and resources with which he had been endowed by the Creator, for all of them are the tools given him to make possible the performance of his assigned task. How is one to resolve the frequent conflict between one duty and the other? Or, better said, how is one to understand himself and his role sincerely and objectively enough to see through the conflict and find the proper course? And how is he to avoid the trap of the natural human instinct — frequently a synonym for the יֵצֶר הָרַע, *Evil Inclination,* — to clothe what he would *prefer* to do in the rational garb of what he is *obligated* to do? How simple for the indulgent person to relegate his books to the function of decorating his bookcase while he pursues business success 'because that way I'll have the financial security to study Torah myself and support worthy institutions — *eventually.'* Or how simple for the essentially selfish person to say that he cannot leave his studies despite the claims of fellows in distress 'because Torah comes before all.'

How is one to understand himself and his role sincerely and objectively enough to see through the conflict and find the proper course?

Of course there must be people who are able and willing to support the community, and, *of course* the very soul of the people is the Torah and blessed are those who are ready to give up all material opportunity to study it. But it is also true that God's service requires far deeper analysis and more intensive self-perfection than that provided by the easy way of first defining one's *own* desires and then decorating them with a philosophy.

God's service requires far deeper analysis and more intensive self-perfection than that provided by the easy way of first defining one's own desires and then decorating them with a philosophy.

III. Danger and Development

Fulfillment and Interaction

For someone to realize his potential, he must know his own strengths and weaknesses, and understand whether he is primarily motivated by *chesed, gevurah,* or *tiferes.* He must then recognize the possibilities and dangers of each course, then seek to maximize the former and minimize the latter. And he must create within himself a synthesis of all three.

Spiritual growth involves the tension of conflicting forces. The recipient earns the gratitude of the giver for having made possible the act of chesed.

Spiritual growth involves the tension of conflicting forces. The *chesed*-person, by definition, is giving and self-effacing. His goal is to satisfy the need of another. Rather than hoard for himself, he opens his heart and hand. But by giving he receives as well, both in terms of the personal satisfaction and sense of accomplishment, and in terms of the spiritual growth engendered by his generosity. Thus, the recipient earns the gratitude of the giver, for having made possible the act of *chesed.* As our Sages taught:

יוֹתֵר מִמַּה שֶּׁבַּעַל הַבַּיִת עוֹשֶׂה עִם הֶעָנִי, הֶעָנִי עוֹשֶׂה עִם בַּעַל הַבַּיִת

More than the householder does for the pauper, the pauper does for the householder (Vayikra Rabba 34:10).

כָּל אָדָם שֶׁאֵין לוֹ אִשָּׁה אֵינוֹ אָדָם

Any man who has no wife is not a man (Yevamos 63a).

The strongest basis of unified, harmonious living is the ability and wish to share with others — and to become enriched through sharing.

The giver and the receiver fulfill one another. Whether in the have and have-not, or in the husband-wife relationship, the strongest basis of unified, harmonious living is the ability and wish to share with others — and to become enriched through sharing. This brings in its train a growing and intensifying awareness that people are different and that they complement one another; that no individual is perfect, but that the community, by melding diverse outlooks and capabilities into a single unit, *can* approach a degree of perfection that is beyond the capacity of any of its individual components. Such a thriving, mutually fulfilling community of interests woven together into a fabric of *chesed*-induced harmony and development gives each of its members opportunities for spiritual growth that are denied the cloistered, introverted seeker of self-perfection.

Acquiring In Order to Give

The man with an abundance of Torah knowledge cannot fulfill his responsibility of chesed *by freely dispensing nickels while refusing to share his knowledge.*

But man can give only what he has. The man with an abundance of Torah knowledge and spiritual insight but a paucity of funds cannot fulfill his responsibility of *chesed* by freely dispensing nickels and pennies while refusing to share his knowledge. Conversely, the man rich in worldly goods but poor in Torah cannot carry out his obligations by freely dispensing advice and criticism but hoarding his wealth. To act in that manner, obviously, is not generous but mendacious; it displays a zeal not to give but to withhold, for it limits the giving to the inconsequential, to that which is of little use to the giver while clearly demonstrating to the recipient, 'What you need of me I shall not give you; what is useless to me, you are free to take.' That there are, unfortunately, so many people who flatter themselves by giving away fluff is merely an indication of the successful wiles of יֵצֶר הָרַע, the *Evil Inclination's* talent to dress sinners as saints, for it is far more pleasant and self-serving — and dangerous — for someone to dignify misdeeds as excursions into the heavenly spheres than to label them as what they are.

Only by giving what is of value to the giver does he enrich the receiver and, in turn, become enriched by having contributed to the common store of mutual development.

No — the *chesed*-person must give what he possesses. The magnate must give money, the mechanic must give skill, the sage must give insight, the scholar must give Torah. Only by giving what is of value to the giver does he enrich the receiver and, in turn, become enriched by having contributed to the common store of mutual development. Scavengers eagerly await spring-cleaning time when the well-to-do discard still useful items. Surely the poor family that finds serviceable furniture on a sidewalk has gained and the wealthy family that is redecorating has been the instrument of good. Furthermore, the desire for *chesed* surely finds expression in giving thought to how even so self-serving an end as purchasing new furniture can have the beneficial by-product of assisting the less fortunate. Nevertheless, those who help others only at minimum cost to themselves can hardly be considered *chesed*-people.

Those who help others only at minimum cost to themselves can hardly be considered chesed *people.*

This does not mean that the help must always be gratis. The person who earns his livelihood by exercising a laboriously cultivated skill cannot be expected to forgo his primary means of providing for himself and his family — nor should he. But there are ways to sell a product or charge for a service, and still be a giver. The grocer who earns a good living, but feels a responsibility to serve his customers honestly and faithfully, is giving even while he rings up his sale. The financial advisor who earns far more than his clients, but who conscientiously extends himself to ensure that their capital is invested where it will best serve *their* needs rather than his, is providing a service despite his own commission. The same holds true for the Torah scholar, the doctor, and the shoemaker. *Of course* there is often an obligation to help others without thought of personal gain, but the *chesed*-person does not cease to be a giver even while engaged in the pursuit of profit, as long as his first concern is that he give.

Rabbi Yisrael Salanter used to praise an innkeeper as a practitioner of chesed: *'He must charge in order to earn his livelihood, but that does not detract from the good he does!'*

Rabbi Yisrael Salanter used to praise an inn keeper as a practitioner of *chesed*. When his students protested that the man was charging for his services, Rabbi Yisrael replied,

'He must charge in order to earn his livelihood, but that does not detract from the good he does!'

Giving, however, is not enough. For his own perfection, the *chesed*-person must also develop *gevurah* instincts: he must look inward as well as outward, and to do so is by no means an exercise in selfishness. People are not stagnant; and even their obligation to others dictates that they facilitate personal growth so that they may be better able to help others. To become a bigger person requires a selfish focus upon oneself. What am I lacking? How can I improve? What school is best for me? What study companion can best stimulate me? Where should I pray? Whom should I seek out as a friend — and whom should I avoid? How can I go higher on the ladder of Divine Service? How can I best absorb a Torah outlook until it is part of my emotional as well as intellectual make-up?

To become a bigger person requires a selfish focus upon oneself. What am I lacking? How can I improve? As a result of this gevurah *preoccupation, one has new riches to bestow in his parallel role as a* chesed-*person.*

This concentration on self-development results in spiritual attainments just as, channeled in a different way, similar concentration can bring business or professional success with all its rewards. Having gained a new store of Torah knowledge, fear of God, and spiritual insight — or professional standing, expertise, and financial resources — as a result of this *gevurah* preoccupation, one has new riches to bestow in his parallel role as a *chesed*-person.

The human being who runs both lanes of this race — neglecting neither *chesed* nor *gevurah,* looking both outward and inward — is the most faithful servant of God, himself, and the community. But how is one to navigate his personal course in the human turmoil of constant obstacles, opportunities, temptations, triumphs, and failures? How is he to discern the call of true conscience from the mirage conjured up by self-interest masquerading as responsibility? Even more — what is to provide the initiative to embark and persevere on this endless course which allows no complacent respite?

The trait that provides the power and balance is tiferes, *the splendor of truth.*

The trait that provides the power and balance is *tiferes,* the splendor of truth. The possibility of achieving it was given to man in the form of Torah, God's own wisdom distilled from the world of the loftiest spheres to provide the formula for life on earth.

IV. Traits of the Patriarchs

Dangers of Chesed

As we have seen, Abraham represents *chesed,* for the decisive factor in Abraham's personality was the unceasing urge to help others. Isaac represents *gevurah,* for his prime trait was the introspective, self-critical fear of God that sought constantly to purify his motives and perfect his deeds. Jacob — the last of the Patriarchs — represents *tiferes,* for he was the weaver of the *triple thread* that eternally combined *chesed* and *gevurah* with *truth* as embodied in Torah. Not until Jacob's work was done was Israel's 'Fatherhood' stage complete, for until then, the national future was not secure. Abraham's *chesed* and Isaac's *gevurah* both contained the seeds of mortal danger, for although each of them had taken his own primary characteristic and nurtured, guided, chiseled, and polished it into a spiritual masterpiece, it was not yet enough. There is a danger in *chesed* and a danger in *gevurah.*

Not until Jacob's work was done was Israel's 'Fatherhood' stage complete. Abraham's chesed *and Isaac's* gevurah *both contained the seeds of mortal danger.*

The single-minded determination to help others requires one to ignore his personal needs. It requires total humility, for if one's own status, dignity, and comfort matter, then he will stand ahead of others. Even if his own desire for fulfillment can be achieved only by winning recognition as the unselfish protector of the weak, then his kindness is tarnished by an inherently selfish need to use the deficiencies of others as stepping stones to the attainment of his own ends. Or the zeal to obtain funds for charity can lead to excessive giving and borrowing.

Unbridled kindness can lead to results that are perversions of the generous spirit that inspired it.

Unbridled kindness can lead to results that are perversions of the generous spirit that inspired it. King Saul felt compassion for Agag, king of Amalek, and allowed him to live, in defiance of the heavenly command transmitted to him by the prophet Samuel. Another generation of Amalek was born and eventually Haman descended from Saul's 'kindness' (see *Overview*, the *Book of Esther*, Artscroll ed.). The Torah describes incest as *chesed*, for the indulgent wish to give pleasure can degenerate into the immorality that equates sin with love and filth with flowers.

The indulgent wish to give pleasure can degenerate into the immorality that equates sin with love and filth with flowers.

Control and Indulgence

Such are the dangers of uncontrolled *chesed*. Nevertheless *chesed* is good, it is sublime. God created the universe in order to provide the conditons that make His own kindness possible. The election of His chosen people waited twenty generations and two thousand years until the advent of the Patriarch who was, is, and shall always remain the epitome of kindness. Let us not fail to recognize, however, that Abraham's kindness was not unbounded by principle. When God's will demanded it, he could set aside his personal inclinations. When necessary, he could take up arms against the abductors of Lot and expel Hagar and Ishmael. *He* was in control of his *chesed* and not vice-versa, he said yes not because he was too weak to say no; he took his natural predilection toward kindness and utilized as a *God*-serving, not a *self*-serving vehicle. That was the greatness of Abraham.

A man with his nature could have become a crony of the licentious kings of Egypt and Canaan among whom he lived — for isn't immorality, too, a possible by-product of unchanneled kindness? His compassionate spirit could have found a place in his household for greedy Lot, murderous Ishmael, and idolatrous Hagar. Haven't many great and potentially great people been undone by an inability to be uncompromisingly strong in the face of entreaties by their loved ones?

The Two Thousand Years of Torah began with Abraham's initiation of Charanite converts. Abraham utilized every ounce of his chesed *for good, but he also harnessed its potential for excess.*

It is not incidental that the emergence of the Two Thousand Years of Torah began with Abraham's initiation of Charanite converts to the teachings of the Torah (see above). Abraham utilized every ounce of his *chesed* for good, but he also harnessed its potential for excess. He took Torah — the ultimate truth —

and allowed it to guide him to *gevurah* when called for, resulting in his product of תִּפְאֶרֶת שֶׁבְּחֶסֶד, the *chesed* personality that won fulfillment.

He had two sons, both of whom were heirs to his *chesed* teaching. During this embrionic era in Israel's development when the seeds of the entire national future were being sown, God wanted Isaac to forge a path all his own. Isaac was endowed with the archetypal *gevurah* personality. But Ishmael broke no new spiritual paths. He saw Abraham's kindness, but he failed to perceive the steel which underlay it, the principle which directed it. His challenge, like Abraham's was to face the test of *chesed* and arm himself with גְּבוּרָה שֶׁבְּחֶסֶד, *the strength within kindness,* that would result in תִּפְאֶרֶת שֶׁבְּחֶסֶד, *the splendor* of truth that could be developed *within kindness* to create the human masterpiece of an Abraham. But Ishmael failed. He perverted kindness into indulgence, a degeneracy that found apt expression when he descended with his mother to licentious Egypt, eventually to found a nation distinguished for lust, so dedicated to the satisfaction of its passion that it is quite ready to kill and plunder in its service.

God wanted Isaac to forge a path all his own. Isaac was endowed with the archetypal gevurah *personality. But Ishmael broke no new spiritual paths. He perverted kindness into indulgence.*

Strength and Selfishness

Isaac sublimated his trait just as Abraham had sublimated his. But in *gevurah,* too, there is a danger. The inward-looking person, dedicated to self-perfection can become obsessed with his own needs with the result that other people become inconsequential, even contemptible, in his eyes. If his own development is paramount, then he can come to regard others as his tools, meant to serve him, to be used by him. The *gevurah*-person must temper his nature with *chesed* in order to attain perfection. Otherwise, he can become an evil, rapacious monster.

The gevurah-*person must temper his nature with* chesed *in order to attain perfection. Otherwise, he can become an evil, rapacious monster.*

Isaac had two sons. Jacob was heir to Isaac's *gevurah* and Abraham's *chesed.* From his youth he was dweller in the tents of Torah. When he departed from Isaac and Rivkah to found his own home, he secluded himself for fourteen years in the Academy where he immersed himself uncompromisingly, indefatigably into the sea of Torah. With his passion for truth, he formed the perfect blend of attributes and became the final Patriarch, father of the family without blemish.

Esau inherited his father's strength without his grandfather's compassion and without his brother's quest for truthful splendor.

But Esau was different. He inherited his father's strength without his grandfather's compassion and without his brother's quest for truthful splendor. The result was the viciously selfish person who became the embodiment of callousness and disregard for others. Esau was a murderer because he deemed the lives of others to be too insignificant to stand in the way of his desires. Arrogance, cruelty, plunder, murder — all these are characteristics of Esau the strong, Esau the unbridled. Because Jacob was the ultimate in good, Esau was the ultimate in evil — resulting in his eternal war against all that Israel represents down through the ages. (This concept will be discussed at length in the *Overview* to *Toldos.)*

V. God is Master

Abraham's Contribution

מִיּוֹם שֶׁבָּרָא הקב״ה אֶת הָעוֹלָם לֹא הָיָה אָדָם שֶׁקְּרָאוֹ אָדוֹן עַד שֶׁבָּא אַבְרָהָם אָבִינוּ וּקְרָאוֹ אָדוֹן

From the day the Holy One Blessed be He created the universe there was no one who called Him, 'Lord' [*lit.* Master] *until our father, Abraham, came and called him, 'Lord' (Berachos* 7b).

The universe was created so that people would recognize that HASHEM is One *and that all emanates from Him and functions in accordance with His will.*

The various Names of God did not come into being with the creation of the universe, and certainly they were not coined by human beings. His Names are eternal just as He is eternal. The universe was created so that even in this mixture of good and evil, spiritual and material, people would come to recognize that *HASHEM is One* and that all emanates from Him and functions in accordance with His will. When Abraham came upon the scene, mankind recognized a multiplicity of gods, one for each aspect of the universe — one for light, one for darkness, one for fertility, one for vegetation and so on *ad infinitum.* There might be an אֱלָהָא דֶאֱלָהַיָא, a God of gods, an ultimate Creator, but He was far removed from the daily life of the planet. Abraham himself, at the age of only three, began his philosophical search for meaning with this same trend of thought, undoubtedly as a result of the conditioning he had received from his environment.

The next morning when the sun re-appeared, Abraham recognized the truth ה׳ הוּא הָאֱלֹהִים, HASHEM is the God.

'Who is God,' he wondered. He saw the sun rise and bathe the earth in its brilliant light. 'The sun must be god,' he proclaimed. But at night the sun gave away to the moon and young Abraham 'realized' that the moon must be god. The next morning when the sun re-appeared, Abraham recognized the truth — ה׳ הוּא הָאֱלֹהִים, *HASHEM is the God,* there had to be one Master of the universe and it is He alone Who rules it every moment of every day.

Abraham called HASHEM אָדוֹן, Master — *and no one had ever done so before. None had so enthroned* HASHEM *as had Abraham.*

Abraham called HASHEM, 'אָדוֹן, *Master'* — and no one had ever done so before. There had been righteous people on earth before him, people who had heard the word of God and served Him, but none had so enthroned HASHEM as Master of every aspect of existence as had Abraham. In a truly astounding gesture of reward, God reciprocated:

> לְדָוִד מִזְמוֹר נְאֻם ה׳ לַאדֹנִי שֵׁב לִימִינִי עַד־אָשִׁית אֹיְבֶיךָ הֲדֹם לְרַגְלֶיךָ.
>
> *To David, a psalm. The words of HASHEM: To My master, sit at My right; until I set your enemies as a stool for your feet (Psalms 110:1).*

Midrash Shocher Tov interprets the psalm as a praise of gratitude said by God *to Abraham.* God speaks to Abraham and calls him, *'My Master!'* The *Midrash* continues

> Rabbi Reuven said, 'The nations were in a slumber that prevented them from coming under the wing of God's Presence. Who aroused them to come ... Abraham! ... And not only the nations did Abraham

rouse, but [the concept of] kindness was asleep and he aroused it. How? He opened an inn and invited passersby.

God's Debt

God Himself was indebted to Abraham because, until he proclaimed Him as Master, the purpose of Creation had been frustrated. God created the universe so that man would perceive Him and serve Him despite the distractions of material existence. Until Abraham's time, the world had spun in a downward spiral of apathy and sin; creation had failed, lost meaning, served no purpose. Then Abraham revealed new vistas of recognition that HASHEM was everywhere and controlled everything. What is more, he would be father to a nation that would carry on his mission of standing up to skeptics and enemies until the day when all would acknowledge its message and accept its teaching. *Of course,* Abraham could be called master of mankind because, whether they realized or not, they owed their existence to him. But that was not all. *God* called him *My Master,* because he had presented God with a gift that even He in all His infinite power, could not fashion for Himself. For even God cannot guarantee that man's mind and heart would choose truth over evil, light over darkness, spirit over flesh, love of God over love of pleasure, recognition that the Master is God and not whatever inexorable force happens to find favor in the eyes of any current generation of non-believers.

God *called him* My Master, *because he had presented God with a gift that even He in all His infinite power, could not fashion for Himself.*

Abraham totally negated the chimera of material 'reality.' After leaving Charan and arriving in Eretz Yisrael Abraham *traveled southward,* הָלוֹךְ וְנָסוֹעַ הַנֶּגְבָּה (12:9). The word נֶגֶב, *south,* also means *dry, withered* — for that reason the desert was called Negev. Abraham's desire for the riches and pleasures of this world became ever more shriveled and withered as he advanced further into the holiness of God's Land and command (see *Overview, Eretz Yisrael and Sodom).* Stripping away the mask of physicality, he perceived more and more the

Abraham's desire for the riches and pleasures of this world became even more shriveled and withered as he advanced further into the holiness of God's Land and command.

Godliness that underlay all of existence. The more he perceived, the more he continued his travels הַנֶּגְבָּה, in the direction of further and deeper realization that physical reality was an empty facade with the result that the enemies of spirituality held no sway over him. They became his *footstool,* mere utensils for the mission of deriving light from darkness.

Abraham was the one who made God 'Master,' and because he accomplished what God had awaited vainly for two thousand years, God called him 'master.'

Thus Abraham was the one who made God 'Master,' and because he accomplished what God had awaited vainly for two thousand years, God called him *'master' (Bais Yaakov,* p. 87).

Adam and Circumcision

It was this new dimension of service to God based on all-embracing recognition that made Abraham the successor to Adam as the father of God's nation. Had Adam not sinned, all humanity would have borne the mantle; that privelege having been forfeited by Adam, it remained for someone to emerge who would be worthy (*Derech HASHEM:* see *Overview* to *Bereishis).* Before Abraham could become the father of Israel, he had to sanctify himself through circumcision. The sequence of chapter 17 makes it clear that the final gift of the Land and the gift of offspring — the nation and its home — were dependent upon circumcision. From the words of the Sages, we see that circumcision was a critical indication of a loyalty to God that transcended the limitations of the flesh — and even the strictness of natural law.

Before Abraham could become the father of Israel, he had to sanctify himself through circumcision.

Adam was born circumcised *(Avos d'Rabbi Nosson* 2:5), but after he disobeyed God by eating from the forbidden tree, his physiognomy changed: Rabbi Yitzchok said that he extended his foreskin and covered his circumcision *(Sanhedrin* 38b).

The term עָרְלָה, *surplusage* or *foreskin,* wherever it appears in Scripture, refers to a barrier standing in the way of a beneficial result. The fruits of trees in Eretz Yisrael are forbidden for the first three years; people are barred from deriving any benefits from them. They are called עָרְלָה. A person's resistance to repentance, the product of sinful behavior that insulates him against the call to a higher existence, is called עָרְלַת הַלֵּב, *the surplusage of the heart.* It is clear that the foreskin, too, is a barrier to holiness (see *comm.* to 17:11).

Circumcision teaches that man must rise above nature.

Circumcision teaches that man must rise above nature. The seven days of the week symbolize the rule of natural forces, for the physical world was created in seven days. *Milah,* circumcision, is performed on the eighth day of a child's life to symbolize that it represents the goal of rising above nature. Adam was born circumcised for he was a superior being (see *Overview* to *Bereishis),* but he failed to maintain his lofty standing. By succumbing to sin and imbibing evil, he fell prey to the natural forces that should have been his servants. He was instrumental in creating a barrier between himself and holiness. Having set his sights downward toward earth, he could no longer look to the heavens as he was created to do. The barrier of the spirit which he had erected was mirrored in his body as the symbol of his closeness to God, his circumcision, was covered by a barrier of flesh.

Adam was born circumcised but, by succumbing to sin and imbibing evil, he was instrumental in creating a barrier between himself and holiness.

Abraham tore down the barriers. He saw God everywhere, miracles were natural for him, natural abstractions withered away. He placed himself above the rule of the seven days. God recognized this change in his spiritual essence by giving him the commandment of circumcision *(Maharal Chiddushei Aggados).*

Perhaps it was in recognition of this overriding symbolism that Abraham refrained from circumcising himself before being specifically commanded to do so, unlike other commandments which he fulfilled voluntarily (see later *Overview, Eretz Yisrael — The Supremacy of the Land).* Because circumcision represented God's acknowledgment that the barrier caused by Adam's sin had been removed, Abraham could not perform it without a specific command. Circumcision without the inner portents of the deed would have no more value than removing some flesh from the elbow or shoulder. Only God could testify that Abraham had become worthy of the deed in all its meaning, that he had become father of the nation that would fulfill the failed hope of Adam.

VI. Fathers of History

Parents

The 'fatherhood' role of the Patriarchs was implicit in virtually every step they took, every deed they performed. *Ramban* (12:6) lays down the rule that is pivotal in understanding the narrative of the Patriarchs:

כָּל מַה שֶּׁאֵירַע לָאָבוֹת סִימָן לַבָּנִים
Everything that happened to the Patriarchs is a portent for the children.

The Patriarchs set down the moral principles and character traits by which Jews would live and be distinguished.

The Patriarchs embodied in their words and deeds the entire, still unfolding course of Jewish history. Even more significant, they set down the moral principles and character traits by which Jews would live and be distinguished.

There are prophecies which are dependent upon the merit of the recipient. But a prophecy accompanied by a symbolic act, cannot be abrogated.

There are prophecies which are dependent upon the merit of the recipient. So long as he, or his descendants, remain worthy of the divine promise, so long will it be carried out. The Jews who left Egypt should have entered Eretz Yisrael after receiving the Torah and remaining in the wilderness for a relatively brief period. They sinned and as result the nation remained in the desert for forty years and the adult generation which left Egypt was not granted the privilege of entering the Land. Similarly we find Abraham asking how he can be sure that his descendants will inherit the Land (15:8). As some commentators explain (see *comm.)* he was afraid that future generations would not be sufficiently righteous to merit fulfillment of the prophecy on their behalf. Jacob, too, feared that his own righteousness was inadequate to earn God's help in saving him from Esau's murderous army (32:11).

But a prophecy accompanied by a symbolic act, cannot be abrogated. This doctrine is enunciated by

Ramban who goes on to show how events of Abraham's life must be understood as prophetic symbols guaranteeing future blessings for his descendants (12:6). Other commentators follow *Ramban's* lead in searching the story of the Partriarchs for clues to the future of their children. Following, we will list a few of those interpretations and insights.

Heaven and Earth

The first city on Abraham's course through the Land was *Shechem. Rashi* notes that Shechem was to be a place of extreme danger for his grandchildren. There, Jacob's daughter Dinah was abducted and violated and there Simeon and Levi waged war against the entire city to free their sister and punish the wrong-doers. Abraham stopped at Shechem in order to pray for his children. Who knew better than Abraham how to pray and what prayer could accomplish? He knew that every place on earth is a physical fascimile of its spiritual equivalent in heaven. Thus, the Sages speak of a Holy Temple on high that will descend to earth when the deeds of Israel merit it: the Third Temple may be built by workmen with stone and beams, but even that will be only a physical representation of the ultimate world of the spirit. There is a Jerusalem on high.

Abraham stopped at Shechem in order to pray for his children. Who knew better than Abraham how to pray and what prayer could accomplish?

The city of Shechem, too, is a replica of a spiritual concept. Clearly, it is a place of danger for Jews — not only Jacob's family, but succeeding generations of Jews up to our day have found this to be true. Scripture says that Abraham passed through the Land עַד מְקוֹם שְׁכֶם, *until the site of Shechem* (12:6). The seemingly superfluous word מְקוֹם, *site,* indicates that Abraham directed his prayers to the *essential* Shechem, the spiritual area where the young Simeon and Levi must be strong to succeed in killing every man in a large city, even though the Shechemites had been weakened by circumcision.

Abraham directed his prayers to the essential Shechem, *the spiritual area where the young Simeon and Levi must be strong.*

Simeon and Levi had God's help and the family of Jacob was hardly lacking in the merit needed to earn such help, but anyone with an appreciation of the greatness of the Patriarchs must realize that Abraham's first prayer in the Land was as potent as the swords of his great-grandsons (*Noam Elimelech*).

Possession, Exile, War

Abraham stopped at Shechem to represent an acquisition of the city. And, indeed, Shechem was the first part of the land to come under the control of Israel.

Ramban adds that Abraham's stop-over at Shechem alluded to and influenced another phenomenon of the future. His brief encampment there symbolized the first act of possession: Abraham stopped at Shechem to represent an acquisition of the city. And, indeed, Shechem, as the conquest of Simeon and Levi, was the first part of the Land to come under the control of Israel. It was not a conquest that they maintained, for Jacob and his family left Shechem as soon as Dinah was rescued and the skirmish with the inhabitants was successfully concluded. This, too, is foreshadowed in our verse for it concludes וְהַכְּנַעֲנִי אָז בָּאָרֶץ, *the Canaanites were then in the Land:* although Abraham occupied Shechem, he could not keep it as yet for the time of Canaanite control was not over. Nevertheless, he was a prophet whose symbol of acquisition paved the way for future reality.

Soon after arriving in the Land, Abraham faced a famine which forced him to travel to Egypt for a brief sojourn. There he and his household were saved from famine, but Pharaoh abducted Sarah and attempted unsuccessfully to seduce her. Again, the deeds of the Patriarchs are a symbol for their children. In the time of Jacob, a hunger in Canaan would drive him and his family into Egypt where they would be exiled. The immoral Egyptians would have designs on Jewish women: only the *male* children were to be murdered. But Jewish women courageously rose to the challenge and remained as chaste as their mother Sarah. Abraham and Sarah had alluded to their fate and prepared the way for them. *(Ramban).*

Jewish women courageously rose to the challenge. Abraham and Sarah had alluded to their fate and prepared the way for them.

Abraham's first permanent settlement in the Land was at Hebron (13:18). He was still living there when God told him וּמְלָכִים מִמְּךָ יֵצֵאוּ, *and kings will descend from you* (17:6), and when He was promised that Sarah, too, would be blessed with a royal lineage: מַלְכֵי עַמִּים מִמֶּנָּה יִהְיוּ, *kings of nations will be from her* (17:16). Abraham and Sarah had been promised offspring on other occasions, but only in Hebron were they promised that kings would descend from them — this was a portent that in Hebron the greatest of all kings, David, would assume his throne. They were promised royalty at the site of royalty *(Niflaos MiToras Hashem).*

Only in Hebron were they promised that kings would descend from them. They were promised royalty in the site of royalty.

Irrevocable Covenant

After Abraham's conquest of the four kings (*ch.* 14. See *Overview, The Four Monarchies* for the significance of the kings and the war), God appeared to him again with a renewed promise that the Land would belong to his children. Then, however, the promise was accompanied by a covenant and thereby made irrevocable (see *comm.* to *Covenant Between the Parts,* 15:9-21), for a covenantal promise by God is not subject to change even if the recipient is undeserving. Abraham had just completed a war against the kings who symbolized the conquerors of the future. His pursuit of them had taken him throughout the length from Sodom in the south to Dan in the north. The places mentioned in the narrative of his victory are found again in *Numbers* and *Deuteronomy* in the listing of the territory of Israel. By his war and triumph, Abraham had physically demonstrated the possession that was to take legal effect in the future.

By appearing to him and making the unalterable covenant with him, God ratified this conquest.

By appearing to him and making the unalterable covenant with him, God ratified this conquest and demonstrated to Abraham that his triumph was much more than an isolated success unrelated to his destiny. God's concluding words were לְזַרְעֲךָ נָתַתִּי אֶת־הָאָרֶץ הַזֹּאת, *to your seed have I given this Land* (15:18). Note the use of the past tense, — the Land had *been given,* because Abraham had already acquired it.

[This interpretation would follow *Ramban* who holds that the Covenant chronologically followed the War of the Kings. According to *Rashi* based on *Seder Olam,* however, the Covenant took place when

Abraham was seventy, many years before the war. Even according to *Rashi,* however, the very fact that the Covenant is related out of chronological order and placed only following the narrative of the conquest of the kings (see *comm.*), lends support to the theory that the successful war constituted acquisition — a fact which the Torah 'ratifies' by relating that the Land had previously been covenantally promised to Abraham's offspring.

Three Lives Three Eras

The Oral Torah and the commentaries are replete with exegesis on the portentious deeds of the Patriarchs. Every event in their lives, every utterance of their lips, enwrapped the destiny of their posterity, for Jewish history as well as Jewish offspring is a product of their fatherhood. Just as commentators through the ages have found the nation's history foreshadowed in the narrative of the Patriarchs, there is no doubt that the tale is not yet complete: events yet to unfold will surely cast new light on the words of the pregnant chapters of Genesis as more of the future comes to be recognized in the allusions of the past. A recitation of even the classic writings on the matter would fill tomes; let us conclude, however, with the broad sweep taken from *Maharal's Derech HaChaim* (5:4).

The tale is not yet complete: events yet to unfold will surely cast new light on the words of the pregnant chapters of Genesis.

Abraham's life began in suffering and pursuit as Nimrod sought to silence his teachings, but from the time God plucked him from Ur Kasdim, his life was serene, secure, and productive. Israel, too, lived in distress during the early years of its national history; it was exiled and enslaved to Pharaohs who sought to bring about its destruction. But from the time God redeemed it from Egypt and pronounced to be His *first-born son,* it prospered and advanced to the zenith of David's and Solomon's reigns, to the Temple, and to the universal respect and acclaim that marked the golden years of the First Commonwealth.

Israel, too, lived in distress during the early years of its national history, but it prospered and advanced to the zenith of David's and Solomon's reigns.

Isaac began life basking in the glow of Abraham's eminence. But human illness and physical suffering began with Isaac *(Bereishis Rabbah* 65) as he became blind in his later years. The eminence of the Abrahamitic family, too, declined in Isaac's time (as four hundred years of exile began with the birth of Isaac who was not accorded the reverence shown Abraham (see *comm.* to 15:13). The middle period of Israel's history followed the pattern of Isaac's life: it began with the glory of previous greatness, but it declined in strife and subjugation as nations conquered Eretz Yisrael, extinguished the nation's 'light' — the Holy Temple (see *Bava Basra* 4a) — and exiled the people.

But the End of Days will bring fulfillment and vindication. The Temple — the eternal *Temple — will stand and Israel will be reunited in a spiritual summit.*

Jacob, the last Patriarch, embodied the final chapters of Israel's history. Nearly all of his life was a succession of tribulation and anguish until the last years of his life when he enjoyed peace and serenity in Egypt, his family restored and flourishing as it built toward the future redemption and the gift of Sinai. As the Talmud expounds in *Ta'anis* 5a, Jacob never died; only his physical shell was removed and interred, but the *essential* Jacob endures in the highest form of spirtual life. So, too, Israel. Beset by exile and pogrom, driven from continent to continent, reviled by foe and pseudo-friend, the nation suffers throughout its life. But the End of Days will bring fulfillment and vindication. The Temple — the *eternal* Temple — will stand and Israel will be reunited in a spiritual summit that will be vindication of all that has gone before, from which the rays of Torah will light the world, toward which mankind will stream to do His will with a complete and sincere heart.

An Overview — The Tests

עֲשָׂרָה נִסְיוֹנוֹת נִתְנַסָּה אַבְרָהָם אָבִינוּ עָלָיו הַשָּׁלוֹם וְעָמַד בְּכֻלָּם לְהוֹדִיעַ כַּמָּה חִבָּתוֹ שֶׁל אַבְרָהָם אָבִינוּ עָלָיו הַשָּׁלוֹם

Our father Abraham was tested with ten trials and he withstood them all, to demostrated how great was Abraham's love [for God] (Avos 5:3).

I. Purpose of Trials

The Difficult Question

What is the purpose of a trial?

God knows what a person will and will not do. He knows a person's capabilities. Further, the Sages teach that a person is never tested beyond his capabilities: the implication is that a divine test is inflicted only upon people of already proven greatness.

God inflicts trials for a purpose that goes far beyond one's normal life-experience.

Clearly, God inflicts trials for a purpose that goes far beyond one's normal life-experience. The businessman who takes a crushing loss or forgoes a huge profit because he, and no one else, knows that the profitable course of action will violate an obscure clause in the *Shulchan Aruch,* will surely be rewarded. He is to be admired, respected, and emulated; but his temptation and triumph do not fall within the category of *'trial'* which was the lot of the Patriarchs. Abraham, for example, was an immensely wealthy man who surely had business dealings of all varieties. He had as much opportunity as the next man for sharp dealing, even dishonesty; yet such matters are not included among his ten trials. The concept of 'trial' as used with relation to the Patriarchs goes infinitely deeper than the mere need

The concept of 'trial' as used with relation to the Patriarchs goes infinitely deeper than the mere need to cope with the normal vicissitudes and challenges of life.

to cope with the normal vicissitudes and challenges of life.

King David was told that he was inferior to the spiritual level of the Patriarchs because they had been tested while he had not been. Yet the agony of David's life is graphically and poignantly portrayed in the Book of Samuel, the verses of *Psalms*, the countless heart-rending Aggadic references to his history. We may well pray that we not face even a fraction of David's trials — yet his challenges were not considered נִסְיוֹנוֹת, *trials,* in the sense of Abraham's, Isaac's and Jacob's. (*Sanhedrin* 107a). If David's life was not a series of tests, than the Torah's definition of 'trial' surely involves more than the cliches of normal existence.

God's Intention

Ramban in introducing Abraham's climactic trial, the *Akeidah* of Isaac (see *comm.* to *ch.* 22), explains that the trial is not for God's benefit, in the sense that להבדיל a teacher may administer a test to evaluate the performances of a student. That sort of test is for the benefit of the teacher, but God's test is for the benefit of the person being tested. God already knows what he can and will do. A human being's primary reward is not for good potential and fine intentions. This world was created to serve as the medium for human free-willed *performance,* and God's reward and punishment are reserved primarily for deeds. Just as a person is not punished for a sin he was coerced to do since the lack of free will on his part renders the act null and void in terms of transgression, so too, a good but unfulfilled intention is hardly equivalent to a deed performed. Thus, when God puts a great man to the test, it is in order to permit him to translate potential into reality so that he becomes even greater for having overcome obstacles in the service of God and so that he can be rewarded for the performance itself.

God's test is for the benefit of the person being tested.

When God puts a great man to the test, it is in order to permit him to translate potential into reality so that he becomes even greater ... and so that he can be rewarded.

> *Know that HASHEM tests [only] the righteous; when he knows that the Tzaddik will do His will and He wishes to*

benefit him, He will command him [*to undergo*] *the trial. But He will not test the wicked who will not obey. Behold, therefore, that all trials in the Torah are for the benefit of the one being tested* (*Ramban* 22:1).

He will not test the wicked who will not obey.

Sforno adds that God wants the righteous to demonstrate in deed their love for and fear of God, for by translating their feelings into action they emulate God Himself Whose merciful deeds are continuing and endless. By realizing their great potential, the righteous fulfill the purpose of creation — which was that man should emulate God as much as possible.

By realizing their great potential, the righteous fulfill the purpose of creation — which was that man should emulate God as much as possible.

Banner and Miracle

The word נִסָּיוֹן, trial, *is related to* נֵס, *a* banner.

Trial is meant to 'raise up' the righteous by lifting them to new spiritual heights.

Great though Abraham already was, he became greater with each triumphant surmounting of a new trial.

As many commentators note, the word נִסָּיוֹן, *trial,* is related to נֵס, a *banner,* which is raised up high. The purpose of a trial is not to test in the usual sense of the word — and most assuredly it is not intended as a trap for the inadequate; if it were, the wicked would be tested — rather the trial is meant to 'raise up' the righteous by lifting them to new spiritual heights. Every person has observed countless times that someone who successfully survived the crucible of difficult experience emerges a better person. The lecturer, teacher, cook, mechanic, driver — no matter what the field, the one who turns theory into practice in difficult situations becomes a superior master of his craft. Great though Abraham already was, he became greater with each triumphant surmounting of a new trial. This, indeed, was the purpose of a trial — not to prove to God what *He* already knew, but to raise the subject to new heights just as a banner is lifted higher and higher on its pole.

As *Abarbanel* notes, a banner has other functions as well. It is meant to be an affirmation of identity, to hold the loyalties of its adherents, and to warn enemies to maintain their distance. Who would have known what the Patriarchs were capable of doing had they not been tested? And once they emerged as God's proven champions, they became 'banners'

Once they emerged as God's proven champions, they became 'banners' proclaiming that human beings are capable of attaining heights exalted beyond prior imagination.

proclaiming to all the world that human beings are capable of attaining heights exalted beyond prior imagination. And if mortals could accomplish so much, then why shouldn't everyone aspire to reach above his imagined limitations? As our Sages taught, a person should always say,

מָתַי יַגִּיעוּ מַעֲשַׂי לְמַעֲשֵׂי אַבְרָהָם יִצְחָק וְיַעֲקֹב
When will my deeds touch the deeds of Abraham, Isaac, and Jacob (Tanna d'Bei Eliyahu Rabbah 25).

That the Patriarchs could withstand the trials imposed upon them was entirely miraculous.

Maharal (Derech Chaim, Avos 5:3) derives נִסָּיוֹן from נֵס, *miracle.* The nature of a miracle is that it is supernatural. That the Patriarchs could withstand the trials imposed upon them was entirely miraculous. Human beings should not have succeeded. That is why David failed when at his insistence, he was tested with the temptation of Bathsheba *(Sanhedrin* 107a). Yet the trials of the Patriarchs, though surely difficult, do not seem to us to be unendurable. Even the climactic trial, the *Akeidah,* however awesome, has not gone unduplicated. How many Jewish parents have sacrificed everything to sanctify God's Name? But, as we shall now see, even that awesome degree of devotion is a direct result of Abraham's readiness to sacrifice even Isaac.

II. The Nation is Formed

Patriarchal Patterns

The character perfection and practical deeds of Abraham, Isaac, and Jacob set patterns that became part of the national grain.

As explained earlier *(Overview,* The *Patriarchs)* the character perfection and practical deeds of Abraham, Isaac, and Jacob were not limited to themselves as individuals. Rather, they set patterns that became part of the national grain. The Sages say that the children of Abraham are רַחֲמָנִים, בַּיְשָׁנִים, וְגוֹמְלֵי חֲסָדִים *compassionate, modest, and kind people* and that brazen, hard-hearted people are assuredly not descendants of Abraham. Clearly, the character traits of the Patriarchs were engraved in the national genes, so to speak — this, too, was part of the formative process of מַעֲשֵׂי אָבוֹת סִימָן לְבָנִים, *the deeds of the Patriarchs are a portent for the children* (see above *Overview, The Patriarchs).*

Rabbi Chaim of Volozhin infers this principle from the words of the *Mishnah.* In telling of the ten failed generations from Noah to Abraham, the *Mishna* does not refer to Abraham as *'our Father.'* In telling of the ten trials, however, he is described as אַבְרָהָם אָבִינוּ, *Abraham, our Father (Avos* 5:2-3). The inference to be drawn is that the trials endured by Abraham were part of the patrimony he bequeathed to his children. He endured them as the *Father* of the nation, not as a great and righteous individual.

The trials endured by Abraham were part of the patrimony he bequeathed to his children.

As King Solomon wrote, מִתְהַלֵּךְ בְּתֻמּוֹ צַדִּיק אַשְׁרֵי בָנָיו אַחֲרָיו, *When a tzaddik proceeds in his wholesomeness, praises go to his children after him (Prov.* 20:7). Many are the traits that a tzaddik acquires only through the hard, unremitting labor of character perfection — by conquering the most implacable of enemies: himself! But to his children after him, they are second nature. *(Ruach Chaim* to *Avos* 5:4).

Many are the traits that a tzaddik acquires only by conquering the most implacable of enemies: himself! But to his children they are second nature.

The awesome legacy of our forefathers may have faded from our consciousness, but because it is deeply rooted within the Jewish soul and psyche, every Jew willing to make the effort can retrieve past greatness from within himself. When the Sages insist that we take as models the deeds of Abraham, Isaac, and Jacob, they urge an attainable goal. Not, of course, that any of us can actually become even remotely as great as they were, but that our deeds can 'touch' theirs, because our deeds grow out of the seeds they planted just as we, ourselves, are their offspring. We need not fear the challenge of greatness because the ground has been broken by the Patriarchs and we are blossoms of their tree.

We need not fear the challenge of greatness because the ground has been broken by the Patriarchs and we are blossoms of their tree.

Sources of Traits

Ruach Chaim (ibid.) draws upon the Ten Trials of Abraham to find the source of Jewish traits that we have come to take for granted. How often we see ordinary folk, even people who have drifted far from Jewish observance, risk their lives and suffer all forms of privation and affliction for the Sanctification of His Name. Our century has seen Jewish suffering to rival any throughout the ages, and it has seen the heroism of both great and ordinary people who refused to deny their Jewishness even when to do so would save their lives, who stepped forward to identify with Jewish need, and who proudly donned Jewish identity during crises even though they may have worn it laxly in more serene times.

Where does this self-sacrifice come from when we find it in such unexpected places? From Abraham.

Where does this self-sacrifice come from when we find it in such unexpected places? From Abraham who entered Nimrod's furnace in Ur Kasdim rather than renounce his faith in God! That trial branded indelibly into Israel's character that faith comes above life, and that if death must come, it will be accepted with invigorated faith in God because it is but a trial that will raise us like a banner proclaiming that we are children of Abraham.

So it is with every trial of the Patriarchs. It remained with us and became part of us because God imposed it and the Patriarchs survived it in order to chisel a new trait into the eternity of Israel.

Why have Jews retained the longing to settle in, or at least visit, Eretz Yisrael? Because Abraham obeyed God's command to give up his entire past and travel to Eretz Yisrael.

Why have Jews endured pogrom, confiscation, discrimination, sickness, death, privation with the firm acceptance that כָּל דְעָבְדִין מִן שְׁמַיָא לְטַב עָבְדִין, *Whatever is done by Heaven is for the good?* Because immediately after sacrificing so much to go to Eretz Yisrael, Abraham was faced with famine and forced to descend to Egypt with its degenerate people and king, there to endure the bondage of his wife without knowing what her fate or his would be. The injustice of it! After having unquestioningly complied with God's command, Abraham should have been pelted with garlands, honored and revered! He and Sarah should have been the focus of adoration and imitation. Instead, his journey to Eretz Yisrael in obedience to God's wish was a fiasco.

Abraham did not question or complain. Whatever God willed was good, and if he did not understand why, the deficiency was his.

Abraham should have protested. But no! Abraham did not question or complain. Whatever God willed was good, and if he did not understand why, the deficiency was his. Only the wicked who have earned adversity complain when it comes. The righteous do not complain for they know that human affairs are guided by an Intelligence higher than theirs and by a Compassion unfathomable even to an Abraham *(Ruach Chaim, ibid).*

All Jewish fathers and mothers who have placed love of God above love of their cherished children, are echoes of Abraham and Isaac.

All Jewish fathers and mothers who have placed love of God above love of their cherished children, are echoes of Abraham and Isaac. We are heirs of the *Akeidah.* Every drop of blood, every crust of ash is a part of that sacrifice that almost was at the Binding of Isaac.

III. The Cycle of Ten

Ten Utterances

God created a universe with ten utterances.

Chapter Five of *Avos* lists a series of historical phenomena that are numbered in sets of ten. God created the universe with ten utterances, there were ten generations from Adam to Noah, another ten from Noah to Abraham, the ten trials of Abraham, and so on. The commentators note the significance of ten (see *Overview* to *Noah: Noah and Abraham)* and many explain the relationship of the various phenomena. Ten denotes perfection; the *Ten Sefiros, emanations,* represents a development from beginning to completion.

Ten denotes perfection — a development from beginning to completion.

As we have seen in the previous *Overview,* Abraham replaced Adam as the spiritual father of humanity, the one through whom God's purpose in the universe would be realized and through whom Israel would become the nation selected to receive the Torah. The ideal order of creation began with the realization engendered by the first utterance: בְּרֵאשִׁית, *In the Beginning.* That utterance was the clear indication that before God began His creative labor there was nothing save for God Himself. Thus,

In the Beginning *represents the realization that every facet of existence stemmed from his word and will.*

In the Beginning represents the realization that every facet of existence stemmed from His word and will. [This is especially the case according to those who agree with *Ramban* that the entire universe was created in a formless state at the beginning of the first day; the rest of the days of creation were spent by God molding and perfecting.]

From that initial realization, creation went from stage to stage until it reached its culmination with the creation of man whose task it was to bring God's word into even the minutest aspect of the world. When man was created, however, everything with all its potential of beclouding his senses and obscuring the source of it all was already in place. If mankind knew Who spoke the first utterance, then each succeeding stage represented a further glorification of the One Who could create so multi-faceted and interdependent a universe. If, however, man saw before him a universe without God, then each succeeding step in creation further obscured the Source. In order for him to comprehend the message of the Ten Utterances, he would have to start from the lowest stage of spiritual recognition and work his way upward. Only after having dismissed each succeeding level of obscurity could he stand at the summit of his spiritual potential and proclaim that God is Master of the universe.

If mankind knew Who spoke the first utterance, then each succeeding stage represented a further glorification of the One Who could create so multi-faceted and interdependent a universe.

Abraham Ascends

The Ten Trials were designed to raise Abraham to ever higher levels of greatness until he stood at the level of 'In the Beginning.'

When Abraham began his life of recognizing and proclaiming God, man had fallen from the cognition of creation through two successive ten-generation plunges into the spiritual abyss. The Ten Trials were designed to raise Abraham to ever higher levels of greatness until he stood at the level of *'In the beginning'*.

The first test was in Ur Kasdim where he defied the institutionalized idolatry of Nimrod's kingdom and thereby became an enemy of the people. According to *Pirkei d'Rabbi Eliezer,* his first trial came when he was but a child and all the kings of the area, already recognizing the danger this young renegade would pose to the established order, condemned him to death. Abraham spent thirteen years hidden in a cave until their wrath subsided. According to *Avos D'Rabbi Nosson*, the first trial was when Nimrod condemned him to death in a furnace for opposing idolatry. [The two sources disagree only on whether the first ordeal is included in the list of the ten, not whether it occurred.] In either case, Abraham's first trial involved a courageous stand — he refused to demean himself by worshiping man's own handiwork as his god.

Abraham's first trial involved a courageous stand — he refused to demean himself by worshiping man's own handiwork as his god. Thereby, he proclaimed his humanity.

Thereby, he proclaimed his humanity, for a man who denies the existence of God forfeits his right to God's protection and His gifts of life and breath. How can man ever hope to rise above the animal if he fails to acknowledge the sovereignty of his Maker, the source of all spiritual growth? Therefore, Abraham's first trial established his recognition of the last utterance of creation: נַעֲשֶׂה אָדָם, *Let us make man.* For, indeed, Abraham merited the mantle of Adam. Even in the days of Israel's degradation, just before the destruction of the First Temple, when the lowly remnant already lay in spiritual ruin and the Temple was but a glorious shell from which the *Shechinah* had departed, (see *Overview* to *Ezekiel,* ArtScroll ed.) the prophet Yechezkel told his unwilling listeners, אָדָם אַתֶּם, *you are man,* i.e., you are Adam, bearers of the mission of Adam; despite your fall you still carry the legacy that Abraham carried and bequeathed to you.

Yechezkel told his unwilling listeners, אָדָם אַתֶּם, you are man, *i.e., you are Adam, bearers of the mission of Adam; despite your fall you still carry the legacy that Abraham carried and bequeathed to you.*

Trial and Utterance

The commentators do not deal with the underlying relationship between each trial and its parallel utterance of creation. Nevertheless, we see some of the patterns just as we have seen the relationship of the first trial to the last utterance. The eighth trial according to *Pirkei d'Rabbi Eliezer* [and chronologically according to *Avos d'Rabbi Nosson* as well, although his listing of the trials is not chronological] was *circumcision.* Going back up the ladder from the last utterance to the first, the eighth step would be

יְהִי רָקִיעַ בְּתוֹךְ הַמָּיִם וִיהִי מַבְדִּיל בֵּין מַיִם לָמָיִם, *Let there be a firmament in the midst of the waters and let it separate between water and water* (1:6).

The separation between upper, spiritual waters and lower, material waters indicates the need to prevent the material from impinging upon the spiritual.

Rambam writes, 'Do not expect me to write anything about it since Scripture itself did not elaborate upon it.' Nevertheless, the separation between upper, spiritual waters and lower, material waters indicates the need to prevent the material from impinging upon the spiritual. The surplusage [i.e., foreskin] hiding the perfection of man is a barrier to his spiritual advancement (see *Overview: The Patriarchs).* Such barriers must be removed by man and his life must be dedicated to the continued prevention of mundane forces from diluting his spiritual potential.

By circumcising himself, Abraham removed from himself the material encumbrance which stood in the way of his spiritual advancement and his attainment of perfection (see *comm.* to 17:1). Indeed, Abraham feared that in doing so he would rise so far above the level of the heathen population that it would be impossible for him to maintain the relationship with them which had drawn so many to recognize the One God (see *comm.* 18:1).

The ninth trial was the expulsion of his first-born son Ishmael, together with Hagar. Sarah saw with her superior vision, Ishmael presented a danger to the emergence of Israel, and God instructed Abraham to heed her demand for his expulsion. The second utterance was יְהִי אוֹר, *Let there be light* (1:3).

Ishmael's presence would have extinguished the emerging light of Isaac. By preserving and nurturing that light, Abraham and Sarah attained the level of authentic spiritual light.

Ishmael's presence would have extinguished the emerging light of Isaac. By preserving and nurturing that light, Abraham and Sarah attained the level of authentic spiritual light, the light of Torah that illuminates more than do a thousand suns.

The final trial, *Akeidas Yitzchak* brought Abraham to the peak of his fulfillment. He could advance no higher. God said to him, *Now I know that you are God-fearing* (22:12), for he had been ready to comply with God's will even if it meant the slaughter of his most cherished possession — the son for whom he had waited so long and who was the guarantor of his future. This recognition that everything was God's and that nothing stood higher than His will was the living acknowledgment that *In the beginning* there was nothing except for Him and that therefore, even after the creation and elaborate development of the universe, there is *still* nothing except for His will.

In the Beginning *there was nothing except for Him and even after the creation and elaborate development of the universe, there is* still *nothing except for His will.*

[*Akeidas Yitzchok,* the Binding of Isaac upon the altar, will be discussed at length in the *Overview* to *Vayeira*].

IV. Individual Trials

God Above Self

Everyone's trial varies according to what he is. For someone to follow his instincts and preferences proves only whether or not his instincts are sound, but it does not prove that his love of God is great enough to lift him *above* his personal desires. Abraham could not be tested by asking him to search for guests, and Isaac could not be tested by asking him to dissect a deed to determine if it were acceptable to God. Those would not be tests, for they were nothing more than normal behavior of Abraham and Isaac (see *Overview: The Patriarchs).* But to ask Abraham to act callously or Isaac to forgo scrutiny of his deeds — that would be a trial.

To ask Abraham to act callously or Isaac to forgo scrutiny of his deeds — that would be a trial.

Therefore, many of Abraham's trials involved behavior which ran counter to his generous personality or which would have driven people away from his company. From this perspective we see a new dimension in many of the trials. The command of לֶךְ לְךָ מֵאַרְצְךָ, *Get yourself from your land* (12:1), can be seen as a break with family and past, never an easy thing to do for a man of seventy-five. However, it would have been far less difficult for a *gevurah*-person like Isaac. Abraham had already established a *chesed* way of life in Charan. He had become a center of spiritual activity; his students numbered in the hundreds and those upon whom he had at least some influence probably ran into the thousands. Now he was to leave the place where he was established and become a stranger in a new land with new customs where he would be forced to begin life anew and develop a network of relationships in order to spread God's message again. And he was acting cruelly toward his aged father, deserting him at a period in life where he would be needed more rather than less. [When Abraham had misgivings about his move, it was only this which bothered him; he was afraid that his unfeeling attitude toward Terach would cause a desecration of the Name. His personal sacrifice was never a consideration (see *Overview: The Patriarchs).*]

The War against the Kings involved him in strife, and raised the specter that his teaching would be rejected by people who would regard his as hypocritical.

The War Against the Kings involved him in strife, raised the possibility of bloodshed — and raised the specter that his teaching would be rejected by people who would regard him as hypocritical: 'Abraham preaches kindness so long as it suits him, but let a relative be endangered, and he becomes as bloodthirsty as a Nimrod!'

The command to despatch Hagar with Ishmael ran counter to his innermost instincts and the chesed *way of service which had become synonymous with his name.*

The command to despatch Hagar when she was pregnant, and again later to expel her with Ishmael ran counter to his innermost instincts and the *chesed* way of service which had become synonymous with his name. He who, three days after his circumcision, sat in the blazing sun scanning the sands for wayfarers whom he could serve and refresh — how could he drive out people who were part of him, who were dear to him, who were dependent on him and helpless without him?

It is inadequate to see this only in human terms. Abraham had based his service of God on the principle of kindness. How could he reconcile this with cruelty? Circumcision, too, was an act, he feared, that would drive people away from him. The populace would consider it bizarre and aberrant. They would sever their relationships with him. His inns and hostels would be emptied, and the chorus which proclaimed the Name of God would be stilled. The *Akeidah,* as we will see in the *Overview* to *Vayeira,* because it was climactic, the greatest of the trials, was also the most complex and difficult of all.

Not to Rationalize

Difficult tests can be made less difficult, for when one decides to accept the inevitable, his human nature compels him to clothe it attractively.

There is a further aspect of a trial. We know that there are two sides to every story and we have learned, especially in modern times, that an appealing argument can be made for almost any point of view or course of action. Difficult tests can be made less difficult — they can even be made appealing — for when one decides to accept the inevitable, his human nature compels him to clothe it attractively. 'Leave my land and desert my parents? — I am stifled here. My father is a idolator who opposes my way of life. I can benefit enormously from a change of scenery. What is more — *God* has commanded that I go and promised me great benefits if I obey. Why should I hesitate?'

How many of us would refuse to go to a new country if we had iron-clad assurances that we would gain immeasurably by the move in all aspects of our lives?

'Drive away Ishmael? True, he is my son and Hagar has been faithful to me for many years. But they are destructive influences in my household, and God has promised a great future for Ishmael even if he is not with me.'

The most 'irrational' behavior may be bizarre to the beholder, but the doer may easily consider it proper and even imperative. He may be able to marshal such an overwhelming array of justifications that it may seem useless to engage in discussion much less dispute. Unfortunately, people muster enormous powers of self-deception and rationalization in defense of a course that, once undertaken, must be made to seem logical.

Part of the trial was that Abraham not indulge in the luxury of justifying the required course of action.

The Patriarchs were not permitted this sophistry. Part of the trial was that Abraham not indulge in the luxury of justifying the required course of action. וַיֵּלֶךְ אַבְרָם כַּאֲשֶׁר דִּבֶּר אֵלָיו ה׳, *And Abram went as*

HASHEM told him (12:4): He did not think of the blessings and assurances which God had given him. Those guarantees of fame, prosperity, and posterity did not motivate him, they only made the test more difficult because they raised the new danger that he would comply primarily for his own benefit and only incidentally obey God's will. But if Abraham had done that, his obedience would have been selfish. All those thoughts he drove from his mind, He complied with God's word *only because it was God's will.* So it was with every trial, he obeyed because God willed it, not because he understood.

Those guarantees of fame, prosperity, and posterity did not motivate him, they only made the test more difficult.

Precedent Creators

We are part of a tradition. Israel is an old nation whose succeeding generations have laid brick upon brick, but all the bricks are laid atop the foundation that was poured by the Patriarchs. Our reactions to events and sense of national responsibility are predicated upon the lessons of the Torah and the experience of our history. But the Patriarchs had no previously-transmitted Torah and no national experience. They were originals. They created tradition. They shaped experience. The very title אָבוֹת, *Fathers,* tells what they were. They were our founders and we carry on their mission.

No one told them how to react to superhuman trials. But once their succession of trials was completed, the nation had a primer of conduct.

No one told them how to react to superhuman trials. But once their succession of trials was completed, the nation had a primer of conduct. Nothing else that was to happen in the future could be totally new because the Patriarchs had ingrained the response into the national character. It remained only for us to keep strong the national roots connecting us to the past.

The concept of מַעֲשֵׂי אָבוֹת סִימָן לַבָּנִים, *the deeds of the Patriarchs are a portent for the children,* refers to the distillation of the national *history* in the lives of the Patriarchs. But the nature of the trials, and the performance and motives of the Patriarchs in rising to meet them — thereby were formed the national *character.* All the noble strains of intense faith and spiritual exaltation that have ennobled Israel during its almost four thousand years, the determination which has maintained the nation throughout an exile that has far exceeded all its years of national tranquility and independence — these were molded in Ur Kasdim and on Mount Moriah, in Beer Sheba and Hebron, by unquestioning willingness to uproot families and bind children for a slaughter, by readiness to risk unpopularity and provoke hatred, by obeying God's will even when the obedience seemed to be the direct cause of greater suffering, without doubting for an instant that it was the God of Mercy Who commanded all and a Supreme Intelligence that decreed every event in its minutest detail.

The 'children', from David of old to an embattled entrepreneur of today, who follow in those exalted footsteps of old are walking a path that was trodden for them by Abraham, Isaac, and Jacob. Their manifestations of greatness had no precedent. And when they had finished molding Israel's character, the period of Fathers ended and the period of children began.

When they had finished molding Israel's character, the period of the Fathers ended and the period of children began.

An Overview —
Eretz Yisrael — The Supremacy of the Land

כָּל הַדָּר בְּאֶרֶץ יִשְׂרָאֵל דוֹמֶה כְּמִי שֶׁיֵּשׁ לוֹ אֱלוֹהַּ
וְכָל הַדָּר בְּחוּצָה לָאָרֶץ דוֹמֶה כְּמִי שֶׁאֵין לוֹ אֱלוֹהַּ
Whoever lives in Eretz Yisrael is like one who has a God, and whoever lives outside the Land is like one who has no God (Kesuvos 110b)

אַוירָא דְאֶרֶץ יִשְׂרָאֵל מַחְכִּים
The [very] air of Eretz Yisrael makes wise (Bava Basra 158b)

כָּל הַמְּהַלֵּךְ אַרְבַּע אַמּוֹת בְּאֶרֶץ יִשְׂרָאֵל מוּבְטָח לוֹ
שֶׁהוּא בֶּן עוֹלָם הַבָּא
Whoever walks four cubits in Eretz Yisrael is assured that he will merit the World to Come (Kesuvos 111a)

I. The Perception of Holiness

Fact and Illusion

The universe is full of God's glory. Everything proclaims it from the mightiest galaxy to the frailest blade of grass to the sub-microscopic organism. Can one even imagine that God is limited to the Temple Mount or the Holy Land? But human beings are trapped in a material world that obscures His existence and they must grope to find traces and rays of the holiness that is everywhere.

Any given set of facts can be variously interpreted to produce a kaleidoscope of conflicting results — all of them true according to the perceptions of this or that person.

Man sees on many levels. We like to speak of 'facts,' but facts and truth are hardly synonymous. Any given set of facts can be variously interpreted to produce a kaleidoscope of conflicting results — all of them true according to the perceptions of this or that person. Who can recall an economist or political leader who changed his entire philosophy because events proved him wrong? They are few and far between. By and large they persist in their views, explaining away deficiencies by pointing to an unexpected quirk, a failure of someone or something to cooperate, a lack of complete acceptance of their philosophy. The argument will seem eminently reasonable, even compelling to proponents of their point of view; to its opponents, it will seem like utter sophistry, a fantasy in search of an anchor.

To say that he should not let his philosophy interfere with his perception of reality is superficial, because perception so often is reality.

Man is a creature whose essence is intelligent imagination and articulate speech. To say that he should not let his philosophy interfere with his perception of reality is superficial, because perception so often *is* reality. A summer dry spell may be a vacationer's dream and a farmer's nightmare; a winter blizzard is a child's delight and a traveler's despair. One man sees peace in a balance of terror, and another in olive-garlanded borders. Sometimes only history can prove who was right, and sometimes even the history books are no more than dignified, annotated versions of current passions and perceptions.

Where God Is Seen

Where is God? He is everywhere, but some people see and others don't. And some places more readily provide the spiritual illumination for those who wish to see.

Of all the countries on earth, Eretz Yisrael is uniquely suited to the perception of holiness.

Of all the countries on earth, Eretz Yisrael is uniquely suited to the perception of holiness. *Whoever lives outside Eretz Yisrael is 'like' one who has no God.* Lacking the holy atmosphere of the Land, the conditions created by God to serve as the habitat for His Temple and His prophets, a person may fail to see the Godliness in every aspect of his existence. An uphill runner struggles, a blinkered lookout peers, and a hand-cuffed swimmer thrashes. They may achieve their goals, but only with exertion far greater than that of their unimpeded companions! And the same exertion without the external handicap could accomplish so much more!

This is what our Sages mean when they say that

one who lives in Eretz Yisrael is (דּוֹמֶה) *'like'* one who has a God, but one who lives outside the Land is (דּוֹמֶה) *'like'* one who is Godless. The key word is *'like'*. Both have a God. Every person has a God and He is everywhere. But there is a place where He is easily accessible to all who seek, a place where, because people find Him, He is present. That place is the Land whose very atmosphere conveys the wisdom of fear of God, whose hills and valleys echo with the footsteps of the Patriarchs, the words of the prophets — the handiwork of Him Who said, 'Let there be a universe.' One who lives in Eretz Yisrael and allows his spiritual eyes to remain open — sees; one who lives outside the Land denies himself that unique perception. Compared to the one who basks in its holiness and sees the hand of God caressing every blade of grass and infusing every thought, he is *'like'* one who has no God *(Sichas Malachei HaShares* 4).

One who lives in Eretz Yisrael and allows his spiritual eyes to remain open — sees; one who lives outside the Land denies himself that unique perception.

The Personal Eretz Yisrael

Since Eretz Yisrael is symbolic of the recognition of God, every Jew has a share in Eretz Yisrael. It is a Holy Land because it is a Land of Holiness.

Every human being was created with his own set of talents and handicaps, they are the tools given him to carry out his spiritual mission. His measure of potential is uniquely his, it is the measure of holiness which he was created to reveal and thus contribute to the fulfillment of the universe. Since Eretz Yisrael is symbolic of the recognition of God, every Jew has a share in Eretz Yisrael. For, in essence, Eretz Yisrael is not a geographical entity; its mountains and valleys, plains and seas, are but the physical manifestations of its spiritual being. It is a Holy Land because it is a Land of Holiness. Every Jew is charged with bringing to fruition his portion of holiness, *his own Eretz Yisrael,* wherever on earth he lives. Therefore, our Sages taught the legal principle that

אֵין לְךָ אָדָם שֶׁאֵין לוֹ אַרְבַּע אַמּוֹת בְּאֶרֶץ יִשְׂרָאֵל
There is no man who does not have four cubits in Eretz Yisrael (Tosafos, Bava Basra 44b)

Even the Jew who has never set foot in Eretz Yisrael, much less purchased a plot of its land, is considered the *owner* of four cubits [the minimum amount of space in which a person can function (*Bava Mezia* 10a)] there. The Sages understood that if the Jew can only attain his highest level of spiritual attainment in Eretz Yisrael, then it is inconceivable that part of the Land is not his. This being so, the principle that the Holy Land allows the Jew to develop his spiritual capacities to their maximum *dictates* that every Jew have his share in Eretz Yisrael. And because each person is an individual with a potential like no other, his own four cubits are his, and none other's. Exactly where in Eretz Yisrael those particular square inches are does not matter — they are his! (*Divrei Sofrim* 42-43).

If the Jew can only attain his highest level of spiritual attainment in Eretz Yisrael, then it is inconceivable that part of the Land is not his.

This does not guarantee that the Jew who lives in Eretz Yisrael will rise to the heights expected of him. Two people can be given identical financial resources. They may both erect palaces — one in heaven and one on earth. Two people may be given identical intellectual brilliance. They may both fight disease — one by removing symptoms that are measured by thermometers and electro-cardiograms and the other by fighting the spiritual sickness that is the source of physical malaise, the ultimate illness which can be cured only by returning to the realization that *'I am HASHEM, your Healer'* [*Exodus* 15:26].

Understood this way, much that the Sages have taught takes on deeper significance and meaning. Over the course of his lifetime, man is presented with many opportunities. Each is a test.

> חָכָם חָתָן נָשִׂיא — גְדוּלָּה מְכַפֶּרֶת
>
> *A wise man* [*appointed to a position*] *a bridegroom, and a leader* [*who have just attained their new stations*] *— their greatness atones (Yerushalmi Biccurim* 3:3)

The person raised to a new position enters a new realm of responsibility and judgment. The old standards no longer apply.

The person raised to a new position enters a new realm of responsibility and judgment. The old standards no longer apply. If he rises to the occasion with a new sense of dedication and the prayer that he not fall short of the challenge presented him, then he indeed merits that his earlier sins be forgiven. His new position was the cause of repentance. His old world disappeared when he was elevated to a new dimension of responsibility. The first accomplishment of the new mantle was to change the person upon whom it fell. He has changed, grown, repented — and so his sins are forgiven.

The first accomplishment of the new mantle was to change the person upon whom it fell. He has changed, grown, repented — and so his sins are forgiven.

But if he fails to discharge his new responsibilities properly, he is held responsible for the lack of accomplishment that resulted from his negligence. The emperor who fiddles while his city burns is not judged by the quality of his concerto. He is held responsible for the destruction of homes and the ruin of lives, and for the tragedy of human resources squandered on the clearing of rubble when they could have been building palaces.

Balance of Potential

He who was granted the privilege of living in Eretz Yisrael has the challenge of utilizing the capacity it provides him for spiritual growth.

He who was granted the privilege of living in Eretz Yisrael has the challenge of utilizing the capacity it provides him for spiritual growth. Being there is a challenge, and like all challenges, it carries with it the possiblity of success — or failure. As in all matters of the spirit, God provides an even balance. Opportunity is commensurate with pitfall. The enormous good that can be done by one who is elevated to greatness — good of such enormity that it can wipe away his sins and set him in a new world — is balanced by the evil that becomes his reponsibility if he fails to meet the challenge — or if he misuses his new power.

When *Ramban* migrated to Eretz Yisrael toward the end of his life, he was crushed by the spiritual desecration of the Land. It was virtually denuded of Jews, and those living there were subjected to a persecution even beyond that to which Jews had become accustomed. *Ramban* wrote to his family, 'כָּל הַמְקוּדָשׁ מֵחֲבֵרוֹ, מְחֻלָּל מֵחֲבֵרוֹ', *the holier a place is, the more desecrated it is.* Judah is more desecrated than the Galil, Jerusalem is more desecrated than Judah, and the site of the Holy Temple is the most desecrated of all.' His letter was more than a statement of historic fact. It was precisely the enhanced holiness of the place that created its potential for defilement, because זֶה לְעֻמַּת זֶה עָשָׂה הָאֱלֹהִים, *God has made the one as well as the other* [i.e., one to parallel the other] *(Koheles* 7:14). Just as the Galil could not equal the holiness of the Temple Mount, so was its potential for impurity not as great *(Michtav MeEliyahu* III p. 193).

Just as the Galil could not equal the holiness of the Temple Mount, so was its potential for impurity not as great.

Yehudah Halevi on the Land

To the question of why the signs of spiritual elevation are sometimes little apparent in those who dwell in Eretz Yisrael, *Rabbi Yehudah Halevi* responded:

> Your mountain is famous for the fruitfulness of its grapevines, but if vines are not planted and worked properly, surely no grapes would grow on it. [The same can be said of the Land.] Eretz Yisrael is the place which is ideally suited to the attainment of the principal spiritual quality [i.e., prophecy and closeness to God] by the treasured nation which is like the heart and essence of mankind. It is true that the Land assists in achieving this goal, but only on the condition that, combined with living in it, is the fulfillment of the commandments dependent on the Land. The commandments [to the Land] are like nurturing to a vineyard. By the same token, it is not conceivable that the treasured nation can merit Godly inspiration anywhere other than that place, just as it is inconceivable that the vineyard can be productive anywhere but on its fertile mountain *(Khuzari* II).

It is true that the Land assists in achieving this goal, but only on the condition that, combined with living in it, is the fulfillment of the commandments.

Rav Saadia Gaon says that Israel without Torah, is like a body without a soul; we may say the same of Eretz Yisrael: without the observance of the commandments, it, too, is like a body without a soul. But when it is host to a people that obeys the word of God, the potential of the Land is unlimited.

The *Khuzari* goes on to portray the greatness of

Cain and Abel contended over Eretz Yisrael; the brother chosen by God would gain the gift of prophecy and possession of the Land.

the Land. Every prophet prophesied either in it or concerning it — otherwise, no matter how great the person, he could not hear the word of God. Cain and Abel contended over Eretz Yisrael; the brother chosen by God would gain the gift of prophecy and possession of the Land, the other would be subservient to him like the shell to a fruit. And when Cain, murderer of his brother, was banished מִלִּפְנֵי ה׳, *from the Presence of HASHEM,* (4:16), it was from Eretz Yisrael that he was forced to go, for God's Presence is in His Chosen Land. Ishmael's strife with Isaac was over the same inheritance, and so was Esau's with Jacob. In Eretz Yisrael the Patriarchs erected their altars, and there God heard their prayers. Atop its Mount Moriah Abraham bound his son to the altar, the same mountain where David built an altar and where the Holy Temple stood and will stand again. And just as a farmer who finds a lovely tree in the wilderness will tenderly dig it up and transplant it in his finest soil, so too, when God found a treasure in Ur Kasdim and Charan, he brought him to Eretz Yisrael, tested him, found him worthy, sealed a covenant with him, made him father of His chosen nation, and gave him a new name, Abraham. Great though he was, even Abraham could not achieve fulfillment until he was brought to Eretz Yisrael.

Great though he was, even Abraham could not achieve fulfillment until he was brought to Eretz Yisrael.

II. The Unforgiving Land

A Double Standard

Because Eretz Yisrael is so saturated with holiness, demands higher standards of behavior than does any other corner of earth. Just as Israel's nature is unlike that of any other people, so the nature of its Land is unlike that of any other. *Ramban* deals at length with this phenomenon. The following exposition is taken almost in its entirety from his commentary to *Leviticus* 18:25.

After citing the full catalog of forbidden immorality *(Lev.* 18:1-24), the Torah exhorted Israel not to defile itself with these offenses, for the Canaanite inhabitants of the Land had done so with the result that

וַתִּטְמָא הָאָרֶץ וָאֶפְקֹד עֲוֺנָהּ עָלֶיהָ וַתָּקִא הָאָרֶץ אֶת־יֹשְׁבֶיהָ

The Land became impure, and I recalled its sin for it and the Land vomited out its inhabitants (ibid. v. 25).

Israel is warned against immorality because the Land *cannot abide immoral inhabitants and because* the Land *will expel immoral inhabitants.*

Israel was warned not to imitate the Canaanite abominations lest it too defile the land and be vomited out by it *(ibid. vs. 26-30)*. The verses are truly striking. Israel is warned against immorality not merely because God forbids it and is angered by it, not merely because it defiles Israel's own holy nature and derogates its mission as the Chosen People of God, it is warned not to sin *on the Land,* because *the Land* cannot abide immoral inhabitants and because *the Land* will expel immoral inhabitants just as the body vomits putrid food. The implication is clear — sin is forbidden everywhere, but in Eretz Yisrael it is worse. What can be abhorred but tolerated in Italy, America, or Australia, is expelled by Eretz Yisrael. And though the Land, like its Creator, may be patient and endure sin for generations and even centuries until a people exceeds its quota and reaches a point where forbearance becomes impossible (see *Genesis* 15:16 and *comm.*), nevertheless there is a threshold beyond which it will not endure further abomination.

The same is true of Israel, the nation. Israel is judged by a double standard. It is God's nation and He demands more of it.

The same is true of Israel, the nation. Israel is judged by a double standard. It is God's nation and He demands more of it. It cannot complain that it is judged more harshly than the nations for the same sins for its greatness demands that it adhere to higher standards than they. By the same token its rewards for fulfilling its obligations as the children of Abraham, Isaac, and Jacob, as the nation that stood at Sinai and accepted the Torah, are higher — no! they are of an entirely different order — than those of any other nation no matter how pious and noble it may be. For the Land and the Nation share one unique characteristic — they are the special province of God.

When God created the world, *Ramban* continues, he assigned constellations [מַזָּלוֹת], angels, and heavenly forces to guide its day-to-day functioning, much as a mortal ruler will assign officials to administer territories and departments. Each citizen is required to obey the king's decrees and is ultimately reponsible to him for infractions. Nevertheless the reward due a heroic firefighter or the task of irrigating a drought-ravaged territory need not cross his desk. His appointed official knows his master's will and carries it out as his deputy. In a similar fashion, God's heavenly hosts serve as his deputies in administering the affairs of men and nations. This is what the Sages mean by their frequent references to the שַׂר, the *master* or *angel* of individual nations.

God's heavenly hosts serve as His deputies. This is what the Sages mean by the master *or* angel *of individual nations.*

Israel and Land

Every country, stream, even blade of grass, has its heavenly minister. But one part of creation is different — *Eretz Yisrael.* It is not a land like any other land; it is uniquely *His* Land. Over it, no heavenly hand holds sway save for His alone.

Israel, too, is uniquely His people. Over it no heavenly hand holds sway save for His alone. These two unique entities — Land and People — come together: just as Israel is the People of HASHEM, so Eretz Yisrael is the Land of HASHEM. God further hallowed the nation dwelling in His land by forbidding to it immorality and licentious behavior, and instructing it in all the laws of the Torah.

וָאֹמַר לָכֶם אַתֶּם תִּירְשׁוּ אֶת־אַדְמָתָם וַאֲנִי אֶתְּנֶנָּה לָכֶם לָרֶשֶׁת אֹתָהּ . . . אֲנִי ה׳ אֱלֹהֵיכֶם אֲשֶׁר הִבְדַּלְתִּי אֶתְכֶם מִן־הָעַמִּים

And I said to you, 'You will inherit their soil and I will give it to you to inherit it ... I, HASHEM, your God, Who has separated you from the nations' (Vayikra 20:24).

It is clear that Israel's claim to the Land goes hand in hand with its separation from the nations.

It is clear that Israel's claim to the Land goes hand in hand with its separation from the nations. If it is unique, more holy, more dedicated to God Who does not surrender the destiny of His Land to His ministers, then it rightly belongs to Israel. But if Israel is no higher then the nations, then the Land will no more tolerate the presence of Israel than the presence of the Emorites.

> God says, 'Even though I exile you from the Land, to other places, remain distinguished through the performance of the commandments so that when I bring you back, the other commandments will not seem novel to you ... for the primary obligation to perform the commandments is only in Eretz Yisrael (*Sifri, Ekev* 43).

Of course, *Ramban* comments, the *Sifri* does not mean even to suggest that the Jew who leaves the Land is divorced from the commandments of the Torah. Nevertheless, he cannot achieve the same spiritual elevation in exile that he can in the abode of holiness. Eretz Yisrael's connection with commandments is not limited to those that are dependent on the Land itself — commandments such as tithes, the Sabbatical Year, and the Temple Service which can exist nowhere else. Even the great bulk of the commandments — those which the Torah emphasizes are obligatory בְּכֹל מוֹשְׁבֹתֵיכֶם לְדוֹרֹתֵיכֶם, *in all your habitations for your generations* — are of a different quality when they are performed in Eretz Yisrael.

Even the great bulk of the commandments are of a different quality when they are performed in Eretz Yisrael.

The Patriarchs' Perception

The Patriarchs recognized this connection. Who told them? Who taught them?

The Patriarchs recognized this connection. Their souls were so attuned to holiness that they could sense the affect of every deed. They knew that upon arising in the morning, one must accept upon himself the yoke of God's kingdom, that different species were not to be mixed, that work was not to be done on Sabbath, that certain marriages were incestuous. They complied with the entire Torah before it was given to Israel.

Who told them? Who taught them? The Sages say that Abraham's two kidneys were like two sages which taught him the commands of the Torah in all their detail. *Harav Mordechai Gifter* explains that the physical kidneys serve the function of separating and discarding foreign, harmful substances from the blood. Spiritual 'kidneys' so to speak would do the same: they will analyze ideas and deeds, accepting the beneficial and discarding the harmful, choosing the true from the merely attractive, permitting the healthy and refreshing 'blood' that sustains spiritual life to flow into the arteries and veins of someone's spiritual being. Abraham had such 'kidneys'. They filtered out the bad influences and provided him with a pure, exalted system of belief and deed, a system so all-embracing that it included even later-day Rabbinic enactments.

Despite their unfathomable spiritual greatness, even the Patriarchs needed the holiness of the Land to evoke this spiritual response.

Nevertheless, despite their unfathomable spiritual greatness, even the Patriarchs needed the holiness of the Land to evoke this spiritual response, the spiritual instinct that told them what must be done and what they dare not do. Therefore, it was when Jacob was in Eretz Yisrael that he instructed his household to remove from their midst any traces of idols or their appurtenances. (See also *Sforno* and *Or HaChaim.)*

Jacob would never have married two sisters in Eretz Yisrael, a liaison that the Torah would later forbid.

In a major pronouncement on the sanctity of the Land, *Ramban* continues that Jacob would never have married two sisters in Eretz Yisrael, a liaison that the Torah would later forbid. Because of Rachel's merit, she — the second sister, and, therefore, the forbidden one — did not die until she had entered the sacred environs of the Land; and because of Jacob's merit, he did not remain married to two sisters after having settled in the Land, for Rachel died soon after the family arrived. After coming to Eretz Yisrael, Jacob no longer lived with her and she must have conceived with Benjamin before they crossed the holy border. [Although Jacob and his family arrived at Succos two years before the birth of Benjamin, *Ramban* holds that the east bank of the Jordan, where Succos is located, lacks the holiness of the Land *(Techeles Mordechai).*]

Living in the Land and being permeated with its holiness, the Partiarchs and Matriarchs would not have — *could* not have — engaged in conduct which, while still permissible before the Torah was given, could not have passed the scrutiny of the spiritual 'kidneys' which filtered out any activity that could not attain the highest level of holiness. The Jacob of Charan was not the Jacob of Eretz Yisrael — such is the holiness of the Land, the holiness so sublime that the *Sifri* could say that *in comparison to righteousness inside the Land,* the Jew outside it is tantamount to one who has no God and who performs commandments for no other reason than to remember them for the day when he will once more be united with his Land.

The Jacob of Charan was not the Jacob of Eretz Yisrael — such is the holiness of the Land.

The Land Expels

Therefore Israel was commanded, exhorted, and warned to be moral in its Land. The expulsion of the Canaanites was not in punishment for their immorality. Egypt, too, was immoral, and Israel was instructed to avoid the licentious ways of Egypt no less than those of Canaan *(Lev.* 18:3). Indeed, Abraham's descent to Egypt and the later exile of his descendants to that vile land were to test their resistance to the lures of its fleshpots *(Bais Yaakov).* But no matter how much the immorality of Egypt may have been a factor in the plagues and punishment which decimated that haughty power, its land did not vomit out sinners. Only Eretz Yisrael did that. Had the Canaanites lived in Egypt, they would have retained it as their homeland; had the Egyptians lived in Eretz Yisrael, they would have been expelled by the Land whose bowels can abide no immorality.

Had the Canaanites lived in Egypt, they would have retained it as their homeland; had the Egyptians lived in Eretz Yisrael, they would have been expelled by the Land.

The fate of the seven nations of Caanan was sealed long before Joshua's armies carried out God's command to decimate them. They had long since been doomed: the Torah says וַתָּקִא הָאָרֶץ אֶת־יֹשְׁבֶיהָ, *the Land vomited* [past tense] *its inhabitants (ibid.* 18:25). Their immorality had condemned them; Israel was but the vehicle to carry out the decree. Had it not been Israel's time to enter its Promised Land, we may be certain that some other nation would have driven out the Canaanites. It was the *Land* that could not endure them, just as the Land would expel sinful Israel from its midst in the tragic days of Jeremiah and Ezekiel. For the Land of Israel on earth and Jerusalem on earth are reflections of Eretz Yisrael and Jerusalem on high *(Tanchuma, Vayakhel* 7). They are not geographical points on a map, but physical manifestations of spiritual levels (see *Overview* to *Breishis).* One does not commit immoral acts in heaven; one does not commit immoral acts on heaven on earth.

For the Land of Israel on earth and Jerusalem on earth are physical manifestations of spiritual levels.

Israel's Land

Rabbi Yitzchok said, It was unnecessary to begin the Torah except from 'This month is to you' *(Exodus* 12:2) *which is the first commandment with which Israel was instructed. Why did it [the Torah] start with 'In the beginning'? Because, 'The power of His deeds He related to His people to give them the lands of the nations' (Psalms* 111:6). *If the nations tell Israel 'You are bandits, for you have conquered the lands of seven nations', they [Israel] will reply, 'All the world belongs to the Holy One Blessed be He. He created it and gave it to whomever was fitting in His eyes. According to His will did He give it to them, and according to His will did He take it from them and give it to us' (Breishis Rabbah* and *Tanchuma).*

All the world belongs to the Holy One Blessed be He. He created it and gave it to whomever was fitting in his eyes.

Ramban to *Genesis* 1:1 explains the famous pronouncement of Rabbi Yitzchok. The entire story of creation is beyond human comprehension. After reading the story of the first week of human history, can we claim even a vague understanding of the process by which a vacuum was transformed into the universe? Nevertheless, God gave us the Torah including the narrative of creation and the succeeding story of mankind's sins, punishments, conquests, migrations, and most importantly — the story of Abraham and his offspring. The entire Book of *Genesis* and the first eleven chapters of *Exodus,* fully sixty-one chapters in a Book where every word, letter, and even the 'crowns of letters' are dissected for meaning and interpretation — all of this was transmitted to man only to make unmistakably clear that the Master of the Universe destined a corner of His creation for His nation. In early times it might be occupied by the Canaanites and Emorites. Later it would become the conquest of Babylonians, Romans, Moslems, Christians, Arabs, Turks, Britons. The catalogue of conquerors could be long and varied, but the Owner of the Land remains He Who created it. It was He alone Who could determine its destiny, and in His Torah He made clear that it would be the possession of Israel and none other.

The owner of the Land remains He Who created it and in His Torah He made clear that it would be the possession of Israel and none other.

Comfort in Exile

A not insignificant measure of Israel's tragic history is how much of its existence has been spent exiled from its Land. The nineteen centuries of the current exile alone are longer than the total number of years that Israel was true sovereign of all its Land. But even during the bitterest years of exile, there was no more eloquent testimony to Israel's eternal ownership of that slim strip of heaven on earth than the Land itself — the very Land that had banished, regurgitated, Israel as unworthy of its sanctity — that very Land testified that Israel is the single nation on earth that can claim title to its hills and valleys. Like a bereft mother shrouded in mourning pending the return of her children, Eretz Yisrael would not share its bounty with any other nation.

Like a bereft mother shrouded in mourning pending the return of her children, Eretz Yisrael would not share its bounty with any other nation.

וַהֲשִׁמֹּתִי אֲנִי אֶת־הָאָרֶץ וְשָׁמְמוּ עָלֶיהָ אֹיְבֵיכֶם הַיֹּשְׁבִים בָּהּ

And I will lay the Land waste, and upon it, your enemies who inhabit it will be desolate (Lev. 26:32).

Toras Kohanim finds comfort in this verse which, on its surface, is one more savage blow in the litany of God's Admonition to Israel. Israel would be flung down in disgrace, degradation, decimation. It would cannibalize its own children, roam an inhospitable planet, hungry, thirsty, naked to its enemies. Driven from its Land, it would see its cities, homes and fields occupied by oppressors.

But then — a verse of comfort. The Land that expelled Israel would welcome none other. Your enemies will inhabit your Land, *but they will be desolate upon it.* The Land that flowed with milk and honey for Israel would become dry and bitter. Valleys that were lush, plains that were green, would turn to wasteland and desert. No nation would find prosperity there. The grieving Land would wrap itself tight in its mourning shroud and refuse to nurse the children that came to replace her own. She would weep and wait.

Of course, the history books would supply answers for the anomaly of a once prosperous land turned barren. Centuries of neglect had allowed its topsoil to become eroded, they would say. It was inhabited by backward people who lacked the initiative and the knowledge to cultivate it properly. The tales of its earlier prosperity had been exaggerated in any case, they would say. Any modern, progressive nation could have made the desert bloom, they would say.

When 'logic' becomes the enemy of truth as set forth by the Written and Oral Torah, then it is simply a test of man's ability to find the truth through a smokescreen of deception.

All this can logically be argued, but that does not make it true. When 'logic' becomes the enemy of truth as set forth by the Written and Oral Torah, then it is simply a test of man's ability to find the truth through a smokescreen of deception. The more convincing the 'facts', the more difficult the test. Even so exacting a challenge as that of נָבִיא שֶׁקֶר, *a false prophet,* who buttresses his falsehood with a reputation for truth and with wonders and miracles is described by the Torah as *HASHEM, your God, is testing you to ascertain whether you love HASHEM, your God (Deut.* 13:4).

No nation has ever succeeded in Eretz Yisrael — except for the Jews. Let Israel fall short of its mandate and the Land will expel it.

No nation has ever succeeded in Eretz Yisrael — except for the Jews. The reason is clearly given by the Torah: the Land is Israel's. For Israel it will flow with milk and honey. Let Israel fall short of its mandate, and the Land will expel it, but even when that happens, it will withhold its blessings from any other claimant.

Abraham could not even receive God's blessings and covenant until he was in Eretz Yisrael. While he was still a resident of Charan at the age of seventy, he made a brief trip to Eretz Yisrael where God appeared to him and made the *Covenant Between the Pieces.* Abraham returned to his father's home and was not bidden to make the final break with his past until five years later when he was commanded to go to the land which God would show him (following the chronology according to *Seder Olam* and *Rashi*; see *comm.* to 15:7 and *Additional Note A).* Despite his already proven greatness, Abraham could not even *receive* God's promise anywhere but in the Holy Land, much less begin the long process of laying the foundation for the Chosen People.

Despite his already proven greatness, Abraham could not even receive *God's promise anywhere but in the Holy Land.*

Indeed, the first time Abraham journeyed to Eretz Yisrael, he was not bidden by God to do so. He himself perceived the holiness of the Land and wished to be in it *(Ramban, Sermon on Koheles).* Later, when God bid him to break with his homeland and family and travel *'to the land which I will show you'* (12:1), Abraham immediately set out for Eretz Yisrael; he knew that it was God's country and he believed implicitly that God could have meant no other place *(Ramban* to 12:1). Further, we do not find that God ever said to him, 'This is the Land which I mean.' When Abraham arrived in the Land it was as clear as if God had pointed a finger, so to speak, that he had arrived at the place where God wanted him to go — for who could feel its holiness better than Abraham *(Harav David Feinstein)?*

There is a way, albeit an imperfect one, to experience the exaltion of the Land even though one cannot be within it.

There is a way, albeit an imperfect one, to experience the exaltion of the Land even though one cannot be within it. With regard to the law of תְּחוּם שַׁבָּת, the maximum distance which one may walk on Sabbath, the halacha provides that one may make the decision that his dwelling place will be at a particular place. The decision alone gives him the right to walk the prescribed distance from that spot even though he had never actually engaged in any activity there. *Avnei Nezer* comments that this law makes clear that the carefully considered intention to be somewhere can be tantamount to the physical act. Similarly the firm resolve to live as holy a life as humanly possible and the strong desire to live it as if one were truly on the sacred soil can be considered in some measure equivalent to being there. May this inspiring thought help elevate our thoughts and deeds until the time when hope and reality merge.

The firm resolve to live as holy a life as humanly possible can be considered in some measure equivalent to being there.

An Overview —
The Four Monarchies*

וְהִנֵּה אֵימָה חֲשֵׁכָה גְדֹלָה נֹפֶלֶת עָלָיו

And behold — a dread! great darkness fell upon him (Genesis 15:12).

אֵימָה זוֹ בָּבֶל . . . חֲשֵׁכָה זוֹ מָדַי . . . גְּדֹלָה זוֹ מַלְכוּת אַנְטִיוֹכָס . . . נֹפֶלֶת עָלָיו זוֹ אֱדוֹם.

[This is an allusion to the four exiles.] אֵימָה*, dread, is Babylon [which destroyed the First Temple],* חֲשֵׁכָה*, darkness, is Media [which conquered Babylon and imposed the decree of Haman],* גְּדֹלָה*, great, is the kingdom of Antiochus [the Syrian-Greeks],* נוֹפֶלֶת עָלָיו*, fell upon him, this is Edom [the Roman Empire which destroyed the Second Temple] (Bereishis Rabbah 44:20).*

Vision and Conquest

God foretold to him that Israel would be subjugated by four Monarchies.

At the Covenant Between the Parts (15:7-21) when God made irrevocable the gift of Eretz Yisrael to Abraham, He foretold to him that even after receiving the Land, Israel would be subjugated by four powers, the Four Monarchies whose respective domination would end with the coming of Messiah and the building of the Third Temple. This prophecy was repeated in tangible form when Abraham mobilized his disciples and set out to wage war against the four kings who invaded Eretz Yisrael and took Lot captive (Ch. 14). Commenting on the *Midrash, Ramban* explains that the vision was intended to demonstrate to Abraham that four kingdoms would arise to dominate the world, but in

*This treatment is based primarily on *Pachad Yitzchak* to *Purim* Ch. 2 and *Pachad Yitzchok* to *Chanukah* Ch. 15

the end Israel would triumph over them. The last of the four invading kings whom Abraham defeated was Tidal, King of Goiim. The name of the kingdom, Goiim, literally *nations,* is an allusion to the Roman Empire for, as *Ramban* explains, the Roman Emperor ruled over a collection of nations and also because she extorted letters of domination [acknowledging its mastery, power, and usurpation *(Matanos Kehunah)*] from all the nations of the world.

Thus Abraham was shown, in a prophetic vision and in a symbolic microcosm, that four world powers would subjugate his children. Further, as the vision in 15:12 makes clear, the succession of exiles would become increasingly brutal as, indeed, Jewish history amply attests. For although the Divine plan allows periodic respites — after a period of oppression Israel will be permitted to revive and prosper before the next blow comes; or Jews may suffer in one part of the world while elsewhere they will have the influence and resources to assist their afflicted brethren — nevertheless, the general pattern would be one of increasingly oppressive difficulty leading up to the final redemption.

After a period of oppression Israel will be permitted to revive and prosper before the next blow comes; or Jews may suffer in one part of the world while elsewhere they will have the influence and resources to assist their afflicted brethren.

The Egyptian exile was not included in the vision of the Four Kingdoms; it was prophesied to him separately (15:13) because it was an exile of a different type: Egypt was the necessary prerequisite to nationhood, not an aggressive interruption of Israel's independent status. [The Egyptian Exile will be discussed in connection with Jacob's family and in Exodus.]

Ishmael and Esau

Ishmael is not included in the list of kingdoms?

But what of Ishmael? — Jews spent many centuries under Arab rule, much of it extremely oppressive, yet Ishmael is not included in the list of kingdoms? And why is Edom-Rome distinguished by the appelation 'Goiim', *nations,* implying that the persecution of many different nations fall under the heading of Roman subjugation? The Sages liken Israel's status during the current, seemingly endless exile to 'a solitary sheep among seventy wolves' — Israel's enemies are ubiquitous and numerous, yet the entire nineteen centuries of this final exile are all included in the fourth kingdom of Rome. The original Romans were conquered in ancient times; what is it about their particular form of oppression that puts their national stamp on all the Jewish suffering which has survived the demise of their empire?

Maharal (Ner Mitzvah) defines the Four Kingdoms as predicated upon one of two conditions: either they directly conquered Israel as did Babylon, or they succeeded to the sovereignty of Israel's conquerer as did the Persian-Median Emperor or the Greek Empire [which included Alexander the Great and his successors who divided his empire among themselves]. Ishmael, however, never directly conquered an independent Jewish nation nor was its greatness built on the ruins of one of Israel's conquerors. It arose independent of Israel and of Rome. That it held mastery over Israel was incidental, not central to its role in God's master plan, for there is a basic difference between the relationship of Isaac and Ishmael, and that of Jacob and Esau, the forefather of Edom-Rome.

Ishmael never directly conquered an independent Jewish nation nor was its greatness built on the ruins of one of Israel's conquerors.

Inimical Brothers

Until Jacob's time, impurity still existed in the seed of the Patriarchs, for Abraham and Isaac each begot an evil son. Because evil and good could exist side-by-side within them, there could be no such concept as כְּשֶׁזֶּה קָם זֶה נוֹפֵל, *when this one rises the other one falls* (see *Rashi* to 25:23). This rule could be said only of the relationship between Jacob and Esau. Jacob was the culmination of the Patriarchic era. He had attained perfection as was demonstrated with his totally righteous family (see above *The Patriarchs*). Therefore, good and evil as personified by Jacob and Esau could not exist concurrently, for they were diametrically opposed to one another. When one prospered, the other declined. This relationship would continue until the final redemption when Edom and all it reperesented would be erased from the earth (see *Overview* to *Ezekiel*). Until then, either

Good and evil as personified by Jacob and Esau could not exist concurrently. When one prospered, the other declined.

Israel or Edom would achieve greatness, one upon the ruins of the other, but both could never thrive simultaneously.

This condition of diametric opposition came into being with the birth of Jacob and Esau. Since evil had been purged from Jacob's strain and became embodied in Esau, the two could not co-exist in harmony. No such relationship prevailed between Isaac and Ishmael, however. True, there was conflict between them and it reached such proportions that Ishmael was expelled from Abraham's home (21:9 ff.), nevertheless that was not basic to the relationship of the two nations. Indeed, God blessed Ishmael with greatness, a blessing entirely independent of Israel's status. Esau's blessing, however, was predicated upon Jacob's failure to maintain the standards required of him (27:40). Ishmael, therefore, was never considered a direct conqueror of Israel: his dominion over Israel was incidental to Israel's status, not in conflict with it. Ishmael neither conquered a Jewish kingdom nor displaced one of Israel's conquerors.

No such relationship prevailed between Isaac and Ishmael.

God blessed Ishmael independent of Israel's status. Esau's blessing was predicated upon Jacob's failure.

Edom's uniqueness is thus two-fold: it cannot co-exist with Israel; and, because Edom is portended by Tidal, king of *nations,* there is in it an element of instigation. Edom is not merely an implacable opponent of Israel, it spreads its hatred to others and enlists them in its cause. This being so, other subjugators of Israel may seem to be independent players on the stage of history, but the roots of their enmity to Israel derive from Edom.

Edom's uniqueness is two-fold: it cannot co-exist with Israel; and, there is in it an element of instigation.

Esau's Instigation

When the fangs of a conqueror contain the poison of Edom, it is an agent of Edom. If that is its source then it, too, falls under the eternal rule of *'when this one rises, the other one falls.'* It may be any one of the seventy wolves surrounding the solitary sheep, it may not be the particular wolf named Edom-Rome, but it is Edom nonetheless, for its opposition to Israel derives from the venomous seed of Edom.

This condition began with the forerunner of the

fourth kingdom. As *Ramban* said, Tidal represented Rome which spreads its mastery, and hence its mission as Israel's foe, to other nations. The current exile is called גָלוּת רוֹמִי, *The Exile of Rome* [or, interchangeably גָלוּת אֱדוֹם, *the Exile of Edom*]. The reason is not merely because coincidentally it began with the Roman conquest of Judea, but because all the manifestations and ramifications of the unfolding exile are tentacles of Rome. The Torah implied this in the person of the symbolic Edom with whom Abraham did battle. Tidal was the king of *nations.* Some could be content to rule and gain domination over others, but Tidal enlisted other nations to his cause. Edom spread its message. The enmity of other nations could be traced back to Edom. Rome could have been removed from a central role in history more than a thousand years ago, but its venom pulses in other veins and continues to persecute the nation whose subjugation is the prerequisite of Esau's success.

All the manifestations and ramifications of the unfolding exile are tentacles of Rome.

Rome could have been removed from history more than a thousand years ago, but its venom pulses in other veins.

The first time we find this particular aspect of Edom is in the Persian Kingdom. Cyrus had authorized the construction of the second Temple. Then, Israel's foes in Eretz Yisrael sent hate-filled letters back to Ahauserus, the new king. He ordered the halt of construction. The Sages say that the writers of those epistles were the sons of Haman, a descendant of Amalek, the grandchild of Esau. Then came Haman's plot to destroy completely the entire Jewish people.

... וְנַהֲפוֹךְ הוּא אֲשֶׁר יִשְׁלְטוּ הַיְּהוּדִים הֵמָּה בְּשֹׂנְאֵיהֶם

... and it was turned about. The Jews gained the upper hand over their enemies (Esther 9:1).

Had the evil decree been the product of the Persians and the Medes alone — or of Ishmael — then the voiding of the plot would have been sufficient.

Had the evil decree been the product of the Persians and the Medes alone — or of Ishmael — then the voiding of the plot would have been sufficient salvation for Israel. But the decree stemmed from the offspring of Esau who indoctrinated others with their legacy of hatred for Israel. The Exile of Edom was still far off, but the seeds of the future were already being planted in the acts that enlisted Persia and Media into the cause of genocide. Other nations can co-exist with Israel — but the decree originated with Esau's offspring. *'When this one rises, this one falls.'* Israel's victory *had* to have the parallel result that Haman and his Amalekite brethren would be dashed to the ground; the same result that will come about in the End of Days when the evil of Esau is forever erased from the earth.

But the decree originated with Esau's offspring.

Israel's victory had to have the parallel result that Haman would be dashed to the ground.

סדר לך-לך

Sidra Lech-Lecha

לך לך
יב/א

א וַיֹּאמֶר יהוה אֶל־אַבְרָם לֶךְ־לְךָ מֵאַרְצְךָ
וּמִמּוֹלַדְתְּךָ וּמִבֵּית אָבִיךָ אֶל־הָאָרֶץ

XII

1. God's call to Abram.[1]

וַיֹּאמֶר ה׳ אֶל אַבְרָם — *[And]* HASHEM *said to Abram.*

When and *where* God said this to Abram is disputed among the commentators:

According to *Ibn Ezra* and *Radak* God had *already* said this to Abram in Ur Kasdim, and as a result, he and his family set out for Canaan [see 11:31]. According to them the words וַיֹּאמֶר ה׳ should be rendered in the past perfect: *Now HASHEM had [previously] said ...*

Cf. *Zohar:* Since Terach, an idolator, began the journey because he wanted to accompany Abraham, why did God, who delights in the repentance of sinners, not command them in the plural לְכוּ לָכֶם, *get yourselves,* thus including Terach and the others who were to comply? Rav Shimon replied. If you think that Terach left Ur Kasdim in order to repent of his past life, you are mistaken. The truth is that he was fleeing in order to save himself from his countrymen after the incident of Abraham in the fiery furnace [see. *comm.* of *Ramban* in 11:32.] But when he reached Charan [and no longer feared them], Terach went no further. Therefore the command was worded in the singular, only to Abraham, as if to say: go to give life to yourself and to all that follow you from now on. Terach, however, *'saw not the light'* and repented only late in life [see *comm.* to 11:32 and 15:15.]

According to *Rashi* and *Ramban* [but for different reasons], this command came to Abram when they were already in Charan. This is the view shared by most commentators.

לֶךְ לְךָ — *Get yourself* [lit. *'go to you'* or: *'go for yourself'.*]

[The addition of the seemingly superfluous word לְךָ, *to you,* is noted. Since nothing in the Torah is without specific significance, and since if the Torah merely wanted to say 'leave Charan and go to Canaan' the imperative לֵךְ, *go!,* should have sufficed. Therefore, the inclusion of לְךָ requires interpretation]:

1. This is one of the ten trials of faith with which God tested Abram, all of which Abram withstood. The commentators differ on the precise identity of the 'ten trials', for more than ten incidents in Abram's life could be so designated.

According to *Avos d'Rabbi Nosson* 33 he was tested:

□ *Twice* when he had to move [once here, and again in *v.* 10 when, after God's glowing promise of a good life in Canaan, Abram was forced to go to Egypt in the face of a famine];
□ *Twice* in connection with his two sons [the difficult decision to heed Sarah's insistence that he drive away Ishmael (21:10); and second, in the supreme test of binding his beloved son Isaac to the altar in preparation to sacrifice him (22:1-2)];
□ *Twice* with his two wives [when Sarah was taken from him to Pharaoh's palace (*v.* 15); and when he was required to drive Hagar from his home (21:10). (An alternate interpretation includes the banishment of Hagar with that of Ishmael as a single test. In its place among the list of the trials is the abduction of Sarah to the palace of Abimelech 20:2)];
□ *Once,* on the occasion of his war with the kings (14:14);
□ *Once,* at the Covenant between the Parts [(15:7*ff*) when he was told that his descendants would be enslaved and exiled for four hundred years];
□ *Once,* in Ur Kasdim [when he was thrown into a fiery furnace by Nimrod (see *comm.* to 11:28)]; and
□ *Once* at the covenant of Circumcision (17:9) [which was an unprecedented act and, at his advanced age, a dangerous operation].

XII
1-2

HASHEM said to Abram, 'Get yourself from your country, from your relatives, and from your father's house to the land that I will show you. 2 And

— *Rashi* interprets: Go לְהֲנָאָתְךָ וּלְטוֹבָתְךָ for your own benefit, for your own good. [And what is this 'benefit' and good? *(Mizrachi)*]: *That I will there make you a great nation,* but here you will not merit the privilege of having children. Moreover, I shall spread your fame throughout the world.[1]

— *Hirsch* notes that parallel usage in Scriptures of the verb הלך, *go,* followed by לְךָ, *for yourself* usually has the meaning of: *'go by yourself, to yourself, isolate yourself.'* (Thus, the similar usage by Jethro [*Exodus* 18:27]: וַיֵּלֶךְ לוֹ, *he went his way,* and renounced the advantages which his connections with Israel had brought him. See also *Joshua* 21:4). So here לֶךְ לְךָ means: go for yourself, detaching yourself from all your previous connections ... Thus the very isolation was the purpose of Abram's departure.

[See also *Rosh Hashanah* 16b where according to one view it was Abram's change of country that enabled him to have children — because immediately after leaving his former locale, childless, he was assured of becoming *a great nation;* according to another view it was the merit of Eretz Yisrael that benefited him.]

According to *Ramban,* however, *Rashi's* stress on the word לְךָ is unnecessary because the addition of לְךָ merely reflects common idiomatic usage in Hebrew. Cf. e.g. *Song of Songs* 2:11 הַגֶּשֶׁם חָלַף הָלַךְ לוֹ: [lit. *the rain is over and gone to itself*], *Deut.* 2:13: קֻמוּ וְעִבְרוּ לָכֶם אֶת נַחַל זָרֶד [lit. *'rise up and get you over the brook Zered'*].

Ramban adds that the Sages, however, assign *Midrashic* interpretations to such usage only when it is plainly not idiomatic. Examples are such commands to Moses as וְעָשִׂיתָ לְּךָ אֲרוֹן עֵץ [lit. 'make *to you* an ark of wood'] *(Deut.* 10:1), and עֲשֵׂה לְךָ שְׁתֵּי חֲצוֹצְרֹת כֶּסֶף [lit. 'make *to you* two trumpets of silver'] *(Numb.* 10:2), in contrast to the command concerning the Tabernacle, which states simply וְאֶת הַמִּשְׁכָּן תַּעֲשֶׂה, *and you shall make the* [*covering for*] *Tabernacle (Exod.* 26:1).

[*Ramban* apparently refers to *Yoma* 3b, where the *Talmud* discusses that the addition of לְךָ means מִשֶּׁלְּךָ, *from your own* (funds). The unusual use of לְךָ in the commands to Moses implies that God intimated to Moses: 'I prefer that which is made from yours to that which is from the community's.']

... In a dissertation fundamental to Torah exegesis, *Mizrachi* disagrees with *Ramban's* opinion that generally לְךָ is an insignificant idiomatic usage. He cites laws derived from such usage concerning *succah, lulav,* and *tzitzis* (see *Succah* 29b and 41b). There are also such Talmudic discussions in *Kiddushin* 4b, *Pesachim* 24a, and *Bava*

1. The numerical equivalent of לֶךְ לְךָ is one hundred. This intimates that the blessings mentioned in the following verses, that He would become a great nation, etc., would be realized when he would be one hundred years old [when Isaac was born] *(Yalkut);* it also intimates that Abraham would live an additional one hundred years after his departure at age seventy-five, from Charan. [He died at the age of 175 (25:7).]*(Baal HaTurim).*

Furthermore, God's command, *get yourself out,* had the implication of 'get out and experience first-hand the tribulations of travellers, and then you will practice hospitality with the greatest of sincerity and compassion' *(Zechusa d'Avraham).*

The *Midrash* compares Abraham to a tightly closed vial of myrrh, lying in a corner to protect its fragrance. As soon as its lid was taken off, however, its fragrance was disseminated. Similarly, God ordered Abraham to get out of his country and travel from place to place so his name would become great in the world. It was to this that Solomon referred when he wrote [*Song of Songs* 1:3 ArtScroll ed. p. 73]: *'Like the scent of goodly oils is the spreading fame of your great deeds.'*

Metzia 31a. *Mizrachi* concludes that הֵיכָא דְאִיכָּא לְמִידְרַשׁ דָּרְשִׁינָן, 'wherever it is possible to expound, we expound' [see also *Bechoros* 6b.] Here, too, although the use of לְךָ might be idiomatically correct, nevertheless its inclusion calls for an exposition. Thus, *Rashi*, basing himself on *Rosh Hashanah* 16b cited above, comments that the leaving was for Abram's benefit.

Levush HaOrah explains additionally that *Rashi*'s explanation *'for your benefit and for your good'* is not homiletical. Rather it is based on *Rashi*'s interpretation of the *simple meaning of the text*: there *I will make you a great nation,* which was to Abram's good and benefit for, as *Rashi* explains, 'here you will not merit the privilege of having children.' However, since the move's purpose was to benefit Abram, *Rashi* found it difficult to understand why God then caused him to wander about like a vagrant without being allowed to settle down peacefully. Therefore *Rashi* added his second interpretation: וְעוֹד שֶׁאוֹדִיעַ טִבְעֲךָ בָּעוֹלָם, 'moreover I shall spread your fame throughout the world.' The wandering, too, was beneficial and part of God's plan. It was designed to allow the inhabitants of Canaan and its environs to recognize and learn from Abram's pious deeds.

According to *B'chor Shor*, the emphasis of the command is: 'Abandon your land entirely; do not entertain the notion of ever returning to it!'

The Torah is written unvocalized and the Sages frequently uncover deeper meanings based on alternate vocalizations.

The *Midrash* thus notes that לֶךְ לְךָ may be homiletically vocalized לֵךְ לֵךְ, *go go:* Rav Yehudah said: *Go* is written twice: Once referring to his departure from Aram Naharaim and the other to his departure from Aram Nachor. According to Rav Nechemiah, the first לֵךְ refers to his departure from Aram Naharaim and Aram Nachor, and the second to intimate that God made him fly from the Covenant between the Parts (Ch. 15) and brought him to Charan. [This refers to the chronology of *Seder Olam* that Abram left Charan for Canaan at the age of 70, five years before he came to settle permanently in Canaan. During his first trip to Canaan, the Covenant between the Parts occurred, and then, at God's command, he returned to Charan. The departure referred to now was thus his *second* departure. See *comm.* to *v.* 4; 15:13; and Additional Note "A".]

Additionally, the words לֶךְ לְךָ occur both here and in the command of the binding of Isaac [22:2]: *'get yourself* [לֶךְ לְךָ] *to the land of Moriah,'* intimating that both trials — leaving his father's home and binding up his beloved son — were equally difficult.

The *Zohar* interprets God's command allegorically: Break away from the earthly matter that envelopes you: escape with all your might, from the imprisonment of your body, and from the lusts that are its jailers.

מֵאַרְצְךָ — *From your country.*

But had he not already left there [i.e., his country, Ur Kasdim] with his father and come to Charan? In effect, God was telling him: 'Go even further away from there [i.e., from Ur Kasdim] and leave your father's house as well!' *(Rashi).*

According to others, e.g. *Chizkuni, 'your country'* in this context refers to *Charan* — the land where you dwell presently.

וּמִמּוֹלַדְתְּךָ — *[And] from your relatives.*

[The translation of מוֹלֶדֶת as *relatives* (instead of *'native land')* follows the *Midrash* and many commentators (see below, and cf. use of the expression in *Esther* 8:6: *How can I bear to witness the destruction of* מוֹלַדְתִּי*, my relatives!)* It also makes it unnecessary to concern ourselves in this verse with the question of whether Abram's birthplace was Ur Kasdim or Charan, a problem with which the commentators grapple.

According to our translation, there is no difficulty in interpreting Charan as the place where Abram received this command — even if he was born in Ur Kasdim — because it was in Charan that his relatives lived following their earlier exodus from Ur Kasdim.

This will be further discussed in 24:4 where Abraham tells Eliezer to go to מוֹלַדְתִּי, *'my relatives.'* If he meant *'my birthplace'* Eliezer should have gone to Ur Kasdim, according to the view that that was Abraham's birthplace, and not to Aram Naharaim, city of Nachor (24:10).]

Following an alternate interpretation of the *Midrash:* מֵאַרְצְךָ means: *from your province;* וּמִמּוֹלַדְתְּךָ, *from the place where you are settled;* וּמִבֵּית אָבִיךָ means literally: *from your father's house.*

This interpretation agrees also with *Ramban* [who maintains that מוֹלֶדֶת can signify both birthplace and relatives]; *Lekach Tov:* מוֹלַדְתְּךָ means: your father's relatives; *Abarbanel:* the word signifies 'your loved ones among whom you were born and raised.' The expression signifies *'where you were brought up'* as in 50:23: יֻלְּדוּ עַל בִּרְכֵּי יוֹסֵף, 'were *brought up* on Joseph's knees' (see *comm.* there); *Bertinoro; Imrei Shefer;* and *HaRechasim l'Bik'ah*: the mother's relatives are also included in this expression. Cf. *Lev.* 18:9 מוֹלֶדֶת בַּיִת, *whether born at home* (see *comm.* there).'

[According to *Ibn Ezra* and *Radak,* however, who maintain that this command had already been addressed to Abraham in *Ur Kasdim* (see above), מוֹלֶדֶת is a clear reference to his *birthplace,* Ur Kasdim.]

וּמִבֵּית אָבִיךָ — *And from your father's house.*

[The commentators perceived that the order of the parallel terms *your country, your relatives,* and *your father's house* conveys a message. One would have expected them to be listed in reverse order because one leaves his father's house first, then his kindred, and finally his land. However, a different progression is indicated: First, the broadest concept — one's country; next the general ties of family, and finally the narrow, most cherished relationship — one's *father's house,* his intimate family circle] ...

As *Ramban* comments: It is difficult for a person to leave the country where he has all his associations; it is even more difficult if this is the land of one's kindred; and even more so his father's house. The Torah emphasizes that Abram was to leave all three [in ascending order of difficulty] to prove his great love for God.

The further implication of the verse is: Do not yearn for the riches of your country, kindred, and the inheritance of your father's estate. I will more than compensate you for them all [as detailed in the promises of the following verses] *(Chizkuni).*

B'chor Shor suggests that בֵּית אָבִיךָ should be understood, not literally as *your father's house,* but in the Biblical sense of בֵּית אָב, the family clan. [See *comm.* to *Exodus* 12:3.]

אֶל הָאָרֶץ אֲשֶׁר אַרְאֶךָּ — *To the land that I will show you.*

In order to keep him in suspense and thereby make the destination more beloved in his eyes, God did not specify it at the time of the command. God also wished to reward him for every step he took. This is similar to the case of the binding of Isaac where God said [22:2] *take your son, your only son, whom you love, Isaac;* God did not identify Isaac immediately in order to reward Abraham for every word spoken. For as Rav Huna said in Rav Eliezer's name: God first places the righteous in doubt and then reveals to them the meaning of the matter. [Cf. also *ibid.: upon one of the mountains which I will tell you*] *(Midrash; Rashi).*

ב אֲשֶׁר אַרְאֶךָּ: וְאֶעֶשְׂךָ לְגוֹי גָּדוֹל וַאֲבָרֶכְךָ
ג וַאֲגַדְּלָה שְׁמֶךָ וֶהְיֵה בְּרָכָה: וַאֲבָרְכָה

Midrash Tanchuma adds that having Abram embark on a journey and withholding the identity of the goal made the trial even more difficult. It called for unqualified devotion, and it carried with it much greater reward.

... Because, as *Malbim* explains, it is less of a hardship for one to relocate if he knows his destination. It was already Abram's intention to head toward Canaan, and had God revealed His will that Canaan was, indeed the final destination, his journey would not have proven selfless devotion to the will of God.

Hirsch [to *v.* 5] suggests that the implication of the command was, 'Go away, never mind where, and wander about until you come to a place where I shall let you see by some visible sign that there you are to remain.'

According to *Abarbanel,* God did not reveal the destination because He did not want the heathens to follow Abram to Canaan.

... Or, additionally, his father might have accompanied him as he did when they left Ur Kasdim, and it was God's will that Abram go alone *(Malbim).*

According to *Ibn Ezra* the intent of the phrase is *'to the land that I will show you* when you are ready to begin your journey.' He derives this from *v.* 5 which states that *they set out for Canaan* which, indicates that by that time God had already, revealed the destination to him [but see *comm.* to *v.* 5.]

Ramban comments that Abraham did not at this time know where God wanted him to go. It was his original intention, when he left Ur Kasdim [see 11:31], to travel toward Canaan but it was not yet his purpose to dwell there. He wandered about from country to country and, when he came to Canaan and God told him [*v.* 7]: *to your descendants I will give this land,* Abraham knew that this was the land God intended, and he settled there.

Ha'amek Davar suggests that Abraham was already aware of Canaan's holiness, and hence he set it as his goal. It was the specific site *within* Canaan that God would reveal to him only later, for the reasons set forth above.

Midrash HaGadol interprets: Do not read אַרְאֶךָּ, but אֶרְאֶךָּ *I will 'see' you,* i.e. to the land whereon My eyes gaze the whole year, as it says [*Deut.* 11:12] *the eyes of HASHEM are always upon it from the beginning of the year unto year's end.*

Additionally *Tanchuma* interprets: *unto the land in which* אֵרָאֶךָּ, *I will appear to you.* For, as the *Zohar* comments, it was only in Eretz Yisrael that Abraham would be worthy of Divine revelation. 'I will show you the power of that country, so profound that you would never be able to fathom it by yourself' *(Zohar).*

2. וְאֶעֶשְׂךָ לְגוֹי גָּדוֹל — *And I will make of you a great nation* [or: *'and I will make you into a great nation.'*]

Rashi notes that God gave Abraham the assurances in this verse to reassure him regarding three detrimental results usually caused by travel: מְמַעֶטֶת פְּרִיָּה וְרִבְיָה, it diminishes the possiblity of having children; וּמְמַעֶטֶת אֶת הַמָּמוֹן, it diminishes one's wealth; וּמְמַעֶטֶת אֶת הַשֵּׁם, and it lessens one's renown [because while travelling one cannot easily perform deeds deserving of fame *(Maharzu).*] Abraham therefore needed these three blessings [as counter-assurances]: God promised him children, wealth, and fame. [Cf. *Shabbos* 145b: People say, 'In one's own town his name is sufficient;

I will make of you a great nation; I will bless you, and
make your name great, and you shall be a blessing. 3 *I*

away from home — his dress' (i.e. where someone is unknown, people judge him by his external appearance).]

The *Midrash* continues: ... And though the proverb says, 'When you travel from house to house you lose a shirt, and from country to country you lose a life' [i.e., travel always carries with it the danger of loss of property or life], nevertheless, God assured Abraham, that he would lose neither life nor property.

One must view God's promise to Abraham in the context of Sarah's barrenness mentioned in 11:30. In effect, God said to Abraham: 'Here you do not beget children, but there, not only will you beget but I will make of you a great nation (*Akeidas Yitzchak*).

According to *N'tziv*, however, the promise that he would beget children was not given him until *v.* 7 after which he built an altar in gratitude. Here, it is possible to interpret *that* (or *the*) promise that he would become a great nation by becoming the spiritual father of a great multitude of people who would rally around him.

וַאֲבָרֶכְךָ — *(And) I will bless you.*

— With wealth (*Rashi*).

This interpretation is based on the *Midrash*. The basis for the relationship between 'blessing' and 'wealth' may be the verse in *Proverbs* 10:22: *It is the blessing of* HASHEM *that brings wealth,* which is interpreted to mean that a blessing, unless its nature is otherwise specified, is assumed to be wealth (*Tosefes Brachah*).

וַאֲגַדְּלָה שְׁמֶךָ — *And* [*I will*] *make your name great.*

The *Midrash* explains that this promise of greatness meant that Abraham's coinage would be accepted throughout the world like that of the greatest kings, a distinction held by only four personages: Abraham, Joshua, David, and Mordechai. What effigy did Abraham's coinage bear? An old man and an old woman [Abraham and Sarah] on one side, and a boy and girl [Isaac and Rebecca] on the reverse. According to others, the youthful couple represented Abraham and Sarah who were rejuvenated before bearing Isaac at the respective ages of one hundred, and ninety. See *comm.* to 18:11ff.

Tosafos Bava Kamma 97b explains that the coins did not bear images of an old man and lady, etc., the representation of human images being forbidden. Rather the coins were engraved on the one side with the *words* זָקֵן וּזְקֵנָה, 'old man and old woman', and on the other side בָּחוּר וּבְתוּלָה, 'boy and girl.'

'And I will make your name great' also alludes to the fact that God will add the letter ה, *he*, to his name, changing it from Abram to *Abraham* (*Midrash*; following *Radak*).

וֶהְיֵה בְּרָכָה — *And you shall be a blessing.*

[Several interpretations of this expression are suggested by the commentators]:

According to *Rashi*, following the *Midrash*, the meaning is: the power of blessing will be in your hand and you will bless whomever you wish, i.e., *'and you shall become the synonym of blessing'*.]

... People will flock around you to be blessed by you (*Ha'amek Davar*).

— You will succeed in whatever

מְבָרְכֶיךָ וּמְקַלֶּלְךָ אָאֹר וְנִבְרְכוּ בְךָ כֹּל
ד מִשְׁפְּחֹת הָאֲדָמָה: וַיֵּלֶךְ אַבְרָם כַּאֲשֶׁר

you undertake, as in *Isaiah* 19:24: *shall be ... a blessing in the midst of the land,* i.e. a repository of blessing *(B'chor Shor).*

Radak and *Ramban* suggest that the meaning is: You will be the standard of blessing by which people will bless themselves. They will take you as a classic example in formulating benedictions. When one wishes to bless his son he will say 'God make you like Abraham' [This is the interpretation *Rashi* gives to וְנִבְרְכוּ בְךָ in the following verse.] The word וֶהְיֵה is not to be understood in the imperative, i.e., *and become,* but as a promise: *and you will become (Radak).*

According to *Bereishis Zuta* the meaning is that Abraham would become the conduit of the blessings with which Noah blessed Shem. They will be carried onward and realized in the person of Abraham.

Da'as Zekeinim perceives this as a command: *Become a blessing!* Wherever you go, inspire your fellow man to recognize God and bless Him!

The blessing of God is that He should rejoice in His creation (see *Overview,* ArtScroll *Bircas Hamazon).* He thus told Abraham: Become a blessing to Me by acquiring perfection and transmitting it to the people *(Sforno).*

Rashi, following *Pesachim* 117b, alternately comments that *I will make of you a great nation* alludes to the fact that we mention [in the opening of the *Amidah* prayer] 'God of Abraham'; *and I will bless you* — that we say 'God of Isaac'; *and I will make your name great* — that we say 'God of Jacob.' One might think that we should conclude the blessing with a reference to all of them [i.e. by saying, 'Blessed are You, Shield of Abraham, Isaac, and Jacob'] therefore the verse says וֶהְיֵה בְּרָכָה, [only] *you* shall become a blessing — with you alone do we conclude the blessing [by saying 'Blessed are You, Shield of Abraham'], but not with them [*v. Maharsha.*]

In a similar vein the *Midrash* comments: *You will become a blessing* — God said, I will establish a special benediction in your name in the *Amidah,* yet you do not know which blessing will take precedence — yours or Mine ... Yours is *before* Mine — after having recited מָגֵן אַבְרָהָם, 'the Shield of Abraham', מְחַיֵּה הַמֵּתִים, 'He who resurrects the dead' is then said.

Is there then a greater blessing for a father than that his name and memory should remain upon the lips and hearts of his descendants for all time? *(KiTov).*

3. וַאֲבָרְכָה מְבָרְכֶיךָ וּמְקַלֶּלְךָ אָאֹר — *[And] I will bless those who bless you, and him who curses you, I will curse.*

Those who bless you are in the plural: they will be many; *him who curses you* is singular: they will be few *(Ibn Ezra).*

The meaning of the verse is: I will love your friends and detest your enemies. Lest you think that as a stranger in a new land you will lack friends to stand up for you, know that I will assume that role ... *(B'chor Shor; Chizkuni).*

I will bless those that bless you — i.e., those who are your companions and seek your welfare I will bless because of you and they will realize that their prosperity is the result of their friendship with you ... and conversely, *him who curses you I will curse* — if there arises a rare individual who seeks your harm — I will curse him *(Radak).*

'And I will bless the priests who

XII
3 *will bless those who bless you, and him who curses you I will curse; and all the families of the earth shall bless themselves by you.'*

will spread forth their hands in prayer and bless your descendants ...' *(Targum Yonasan).*

Cf. *Chullin* 49a: That the priests bless Israel is stated in *Numbers* 6:23; that the priests themselves will be blessed we learn from *Gen.* 12:3.

According to *Abarbanel, those who bless you* refers to those who will cleave to Abraham and subscribe to his teachings, while *him who curses you* refers to one who rejects him.

Ramban discusses the connotation of God's blessings to Abraham in these verses. Touching upon a theme from his *comm.* to 11:28 *Ramban* notes that before recording God's promise to Abraham that he would be totally provided for, the Torah should have explained that Abraham was deserving because of his righteousness and love of God [or by recounting his miraculous salvation from the furnace of Kasdim thanks to his total faith and self-sacrifice.] Obviously, the rewards are too great and unprecedented to be accounted for simply because Abraham left his native land. We must seek the guidance of the Oral Tradition to justify them.

Ramban continues that the intent of the verses may be that God would now compensate Abraham for the suffering and evil perpetrated upon him by wicked people of Kasdim. God would establish Abraham in Canaan where he could worship God and proclaim His greatness. Then those who formerly abused and cursed him would appreciate his greatness and bless themselves by him. The Torah, however, did not provide us explicitly with this background in order not to elaborate on the opinions of idolators in their controversies with Abraham regarding issues of faith, just as it dealt only briefly with the sinfulness of the generation of Enosh [4:26] and their innovations in instituting idolatry. [See *Moreh Nevuchim* 3:29.]

וְנִבְרְכוּ בְךָ כֹּל מִשְׁפְּחֹת הָאֲדָמָה — *And all the families of the earth shall bless themselves by you.*

[This translation which understands the *niphal* form of the word וְנִבְרְכוּ as reflexive follows *Rashi* who comments]: There are many Aggadic interpretations of this verse but the simple meaning is: A man will say to his son, 'Be like Abraham.' This is the meaning of the expression וְנִבְרְכוּ בְךָ whenever it occurs throughout Scriptures. The best proof that this is the correct interpretation is the indisputable usage of the similar phrase in 48:20 בְּךָ יְבָרֵךְ, *'by you shall Israel invoke blessings saying, "May God make you as Ephraim and Menasseh".'*

According to *Ramban* this is in addition to God's blessing in the previous verse וֶהְיֵה בְּרָכָה: Not only will the people *of his own country* cite Abraham's name in formulating benediction, but *all families of the earth* will do the same.

Ramban adds [in an interpretation shared by *Radak* and some others, that the word could also be understood in the passive, implying a certain universal doctrine later developed by the Prophets] that the phrase is to be rendered: בְךָ, *through you will all the nations of the earth be blessed* — i.e. you will become the source of all blessing to the

דִּבֶּר אֵלָיו יהוה וַיֵּלֶךְ אִתּוֹ לוֹט וְאַבְרָם
בֶּן־חָמֵשׁ שָׁנִים וְשִׁבְעִים שָׁנָה בְּצֵאתוֹ
ה מֵחָרָן׃ וַיִּקַּח אַבְרָם אֶת־שָׂרַי אִשְׁתּוֹ

world; by virtue of you they will be blessed. [Accordingly בְּךָ, following this interpretation, means, *for your sake*.]

And by your righteousness shall all the generations of the earth be blessed *(Targum Yerushalmi)*.

In order that the nations recognize and elevate you, I will begin to shower My blessings upon the lands of those in whose midst you will dwell, such as Philistia and Egypt, from the very day of your arrival *(Radak)*.

There is also an opinion — shared by *Rashbam* [to 28:14], *Chizkuni, Da'as Zekeinim*, and quoted by *Tur* — that the verb וְנִבְרְכוּ in this verse is related to the root ברך as in the *Mishnaic* term מַבְרִיךְ meaning *to intermingle, graft* [cf. *Kelaim* 7:1, *Sotah* 43a.] As *Heidenheim* explains it, this interpretation is inspired by the fact that nowhere else besides here do we find ברך (in the sense of 'blessing') in the *niphal* conjugation, while in the sense of 'grafting' it is common in that form.

... Accordingly the verse would mean: 'All the families of the earth will wish to intermingle with you, for you will not be considered a foreigner in their midst. That is the reason *families* is mentioned in this context' *(Chizkuni)*. This is exemplified by Abraham himself who married Sarah, a descendant of Shem; Hagar, a descendant of Ham; and Keturah, a descendant of Japhet *(Tur)*.[1]

4. וַיֵּלֶךְ אַבְרָם כַּאֲשֶׁר דִּבֶּר אֵלָיו ה׳ — *So Abram went as* HASHEM *had spoken to him.*

I.e., as HASHEM commanded him. He did not linger, but he left immediately. God said 'Go!', and he went *(Lekach Tov; Ibn Caspi)*.

As *Midrash Tehillim* 119:3 comments: When God said to Abraham, *'Get yourself out of your country, and away from your relatives*, etc.' Abraham did not argue the matter with Him by saying, 'What difference can it make to You whether a man remains here or moves on to another country? All such a move does is cause distress!' Abraham, however, did not hesitate. Immediately he did everything that God had commanded him.

וַיֵּלֶךְ אִתּוֹ לוֹט — *And Lot went with him.*

Since Lot's father, Haran, had died in Ur Kasdim for having sided with Abraham [see *comm.* to 11:28] the orphaned Lot remained in the care of his uncle, Abraham *(Chizkuni)*.

Lot was merely secondary to him *(Midrash)*. Abraham had no intention of taking him. But when Lot saw that Abraham was leaving, Lot insisted that he be allowed to follow. *And Lot went with him.* Abraham realized that Lot was determined, so he did not dissuade him *(Zohar Chadash)*.

Abraham's solicitude for Lot is viewed differently by the commentators. *Akeidas Yitzchak* observes that regarding *leaving*, Abraham scrupulously adhered to God's

1. All proselytes are considered 'children' of Abraham because it was his mission to draw all peoples toward the service of HASHEM (see *comm.* to 17:4). A member of any race or nation may become a member of Israel through the Halachic procedure of conversion, a concept that was initiated by the selection of Abraham and the designation of his mission. As *Rav Saadiah Gaon* puts it, Israel is not a race, but a community bound together by Torah which is our covenant with God *(Harav David Cohen)*.

[4] So Abram went as HASHEM had spoken to him,
and Lot went with him. Abram was seventy-five
years old when he left Charan. [5] Abram took his wife

Will, but regarding *abandoning his relatives* he did not comply entirely as evidenced by the fact that he permitted his [still idolatrous] nephew Lot to accompany him.

Cf. also *Midrash* [Ch. 41:11 to *v.* 13:14]: There was anger in heaven against our father Abraham when he asked his nephew Lot to leave his company. 'He makes everyone cleave to Me,' said God, 'yet he does not make his nephew cleave to Me!' Rav Nechemiah said: 'there was anger in heaven against the Patriarch Abraham, when Lot, his nephew, *went* with him ...

As the *Zohar* comments: Lot attached himself to Abraham to learn his ways, and in spite of it did not learn them too well.

Why, then did Abraham show compassion for Lot? — Because he foresaw that David and the Messiah were destined to descend from him, so he took him along. Also, because it was in defense of Abraham that Haran was killed, and Lot orphaned. Lot was his brother's son and his wife's brother, and Abraham showed compassion, but God was nevertheless displeased. The compassion was misplaced *(Zohar Chadash).*

According to *Bereishis Zuta,* however, Abraham's allowing Lot to accompany him was an act of זוכה ומְזַכֶּה, personal merit [i.e. in that he showed concern for his nephew] and bringing merit upon Lot [i.e. by placing him in an environment where he could learn to serve God.]

וְאַבְרָם בֶּן־חָמֵשׁ שָׁנִים וְשִׁבְעִים שָׁנָה בְּצֵאתוֹ מֵחָרָן — *[And] Abram was seventy-five years old when he left Charan.*

One reason for this chronological detail is to inform us indirectly that Terach was still alive at the time. Notwithstanding his natural reluctance to leave his aged father [for which he received special divine dispensation; see *comm.* to 11:32], Abraham did not hesitate but ran to do the will of his Creator *(B'chor Shor).*

[Another chronological fact, with perhaps even greater implications, is implicit in this verse: This departure from Charan at the age of 75, according to most commentators, was not Abraham's first departure to Canaan *but his second, and last.* He had to have gone from Charan to Canaan previously, because, as explained by most commentators, he was already in Canaan for the Covenant between the Parts five years previous at age seventy. Later he returned to Charan, and now departed again, at age 75.] [See Additional Note A p. 589.]

According to the view that Abraham was in Canaan previously, why did he return to Charan?

The *Midrash* (cited on *v.* 1 s.v. לֶךְ לְךָ) curiously states only that God 'made him fly from the Covenant between the Parts and brought him to Charan.' [i.e. God commanded him to return to Charan *(Rashi* on *Midrash),* and Abraham was speeded along miraculously, finding himself in Charan almost immediately; hence the expression 'made him fly'.]

Sefer HaYashar, cited above, suggests that he returned to Charan to visit his parents and family. *Chizkuni* suggests that upon hearing at the Covenant that his descendants would be *estranged in a foreign land for four hundred years* Abraham said to himself: 'Perhaps the time has already come for me to be blessed with children. It is better that the years of exile begin soon so that they will end sooner.'

לך לך
יב/ה

וְאֶת־לוֹט בֶּן־אָחִיו וְאֶת־כָּל־רְכוּשָׁם
אֲשֶׁר רָכָשׁוּ וְאֶת־הַנֶּפֶשׁ אֲשֶׁר־עָשׂוּ בְחָרָן
וַיֵּצְאוּ לָלֶכֶת אַרְצָה כְּנַעַן וַיָּבֹאוּ אַרְצָה

5. וַיִּקַּח אַבְרָם אֶת שָׂרַי אִשְׁתּוֹ — [*And*] *Abram took his wife Sarai.*

'Took' means that he persuaded her to accompany him, with soothing, gentle words, because a man is not permitted to take his wife with him to another country without her consent. [The word *take* is used in a similar sense in the texts *take Aaron (Numb.* 20:25) and *take the Levites (ibid.* 3:45).] He therefore persuaded her pointing out to her the evil deeds of their contemporaries *(Zohar).*

וְאֶת לוֹט בֶּן אָחִיו — *And his nephew* [lit. *'brother's son'*] *Lot.*

[This detail is repeated here as an amplification of the previous verse. There it states in general terms that Abram complied with the command and that Lot, being secondary to Abraham, showed his unwavering intention to accompany him. This verse, proceeds to relate in detail the preparations for the journey. It states among other things that Abram, as the head of the family and the prime mover, *took* Lot, perhaps in the sense of acquiescing to Lot's desire to accompany him.]

וְאֶת כָּל רְכוּשָׁם אֲשֶׁר רָכָשׁוּ — *And all their wealth which they had amassed.*

They trusted God implicitly. They did not say 'We will take only part of our wealth now: If things go well in Canaan, we will send for the balance, but if things do not work out we will return.' Rather, they took *all* their possessions with them and left Charan completely with no intention of ever returning, relying on God's promise entirely *(B'chor Shor).*

According to *Radak,* רְכוּשָׁם, *their wealth,* refers to all the money and property which Abram and Lot had amassed.

וְאֶת הַנֶּפֶשׁ אֲשֶׁר עָשׂוּ בְחָרָן — *And the people* [lit. *'soul'*] *they had acquired* [lit. *'made'*] *in Charan.*

This refers to those whom they had converted to the true faith and brought under the 'wings of the *Shechinah'*, for Abraham converted the men and Sarah converted the women. They [the converts] are therefore regarded as though they [Abraham and Sarah] had 'made' them. [This explains the plural form: עָשׂוּ, *they had made,* for both Abraham and Sarah had roles to play in the conversions *(Midrash).*] According to the simple meaning, however, it refers to the male and female slaves they had acquired for themselves, and עָשׂוּ is used here as it is in 31:1, as an expression for 'acquiring' and 'amassing' *(Rashi). Ibn Ezra,* too, refers to both interpretations.

Rashi's primary interpretation is also that of *Onkelos* and *Yonasan:* ... And all the souls they had made subject to the Torah in Charan.'[1]

This is based upon the *Midrash:*

1. The *Zohar* notes that it was a great entourage of proselytes that accompanied Abram [*Sefer HaYashar* puts the number at seventy-two] and he travelled fearlessly through the land. Furthermore the participle אֵת [which always exegetically implies an extension 'with' — see *comm.* to Vol. 1, p. 35] is explained by the *Zohar* as referring to the *merit* of these souls that

Sarai and his nephew Lot, and all their wealth that they had amassed, and the people they had acquired in Charan; and they embarked for the land of Ca-

Rav Leazar said: If all the nations united to create even a single insect, they could not endow it with life, yet the verse refers to 'all the souls they had *made* in Charan!' — It refers, rather to the proselytes they had made. Then why is the verb *'made'* used? Let the verse read 'that they had *converted*'! — The verse, as it is written is to teach you that he who brings a gentile near to God and converts him is as though he had created him.

Then why does the Torah not use the term אֲשֶׁר בָּרְאוּ, that they had *created*? — Possibly because the verb עשה, *made*, implies 'bringing an object into its ultimate state of perfection' as the commentators explain in *Deut.* 21:12 and *Gen.* 1:7. This word is thus more appropriate in this context, for it connotes improving something which already exists, rather than ברא, created, which connotes *creatio ex nihilo (Torah Temimah).*

[Cf. *Sanhedrin* 99b: Resh Lakish said, He who teaches Torah to his neighbor's son is regarded by Scripture as though he had *made* him.]

The *Talmud Avodah Zarah* 9a notes that there is a tradition that Abraham was fifty-two years old when he began proselytizing 'the souls he made at Charan.' and that period marked the end of שְׁנֵי אֲלָפִים תֹּהוּ, *the first two thousand years of void* [i.e., void of Torah, *v. Maharsha* and *Torah Temimah.* Abraham was born in the year 1948 after Creation, and he was 52 years old in the year 2000.] It was then the beginning of the next major historical epoch, שְׁנֵי אֲלָפִים תּוֹרָה, *the two thousand years of Torah* (see *Overview).*

[The interesting implication here is that Terach's migration to Charan with his family (11:31, see *comm.* there and on 12:4) occurred before Abraham was 52, because by that age, as the *Talmud* notes, Abraham was already converting souls in Charan.

See *Sefer HaYashar* cited in Chronology in *v.* 4.]

וַיֵּצְאוּ לָלֶכֶת אַרְצָה כְּנַעַן — *And they embarked for* [lit. *'went out to go'*] *the land of Canaan.*

I.e., they were unanimous in their intention to accompany Abraham on his noble mission *(Radak).* [On the choice of Canaan as their destination, although God had not specified to which land Abraham was to go, see *comm.* to 11:31 (p. 352).]

[It is also quite possible to assume that although not as yet given his final destination, Abraham assumed that Canaan would be the logical place for him to go first. This was because he had been promised that land as an inheritance [15:7] at the Covenant between the Parts only a few years earlier, a revelation that took place in Canaan [see Talmudic chronology in *comm.* to *v.* 4.] Consequently, he started out for Canaan as he awaited further revelation from God.

Even according to the opinion that this was his first departure from Charan, it would be only logical that Abram's first choice for a destination would be Canaan, to which his family had originally

augmented Abram's own merit and accompanied him.

What happened to the countless generations one would expect to have issued from these righteous proselytes whom Abram converted? No further mention is made of them thus suggesting that their new convictions did not survive the death of Abram and Sarai.

ו כְּנָֽעַן׃ וַיַּעֲבֹ֤ר אַבְרָם֙ בָּאָ֔רֶץ עַ֚ד מְק֣וֹם
שְׁכֶ֔ם עַ֖ד אֵל֣וֹן מוֹרֶ֑ה וְהַֽכְּנַעֲנִ֖י אָ֥ז בָּאָֽרֶץ׃

yearned to go when they intially set out from Ur Kasdim earlier.]

וַיָּבֹאוּ אַרְצָה כְּנָעַן — *And they came to the land of Canaan.*

The Torah tells us that Abraham and his entourage did not stop midway, but came directly to their intended destination. This is meant to point out the contrast to Terach who also set out for Canaan, but went only as far as Charan *(Radak).*

6. וַיַּעֲבֹר אַבְרָם בָּאָרֶץ — *[And] Abram passed into the land.*

Following *Rashi:* He entered *into* the land. [Not that he 'passed right through it' entering at one border and exiting at another *(Mizrachi).*]

It also apparently has the connotation that he *toured through the land,* going from place to place awaiting divine instruction which did not come to him until he arrived in Shechem. ... It was apparently God's will to have Abram see the whole land first hand, so he would fully appreciate the gift God was giving him when He promised to give the land to his descendants *(B'chor Shor).*

עַד מְקוֹם שְׁכֶם — *As far as the site of Shechem.*

[Later, in the time of Jacob, we find that Shechem was the name of the son of Chamor, lord of the city of Shechem (34:2).] *Ibn Ezra,* assuming that Chamor named the city in honor of his son, suggests that the Torah in our verse calls the city by its eventual name. *Ramban,* however, is of the opinion that Shechem was the name of the city in Abram's time, and that Chamor named his son after the city.

According to *Chizkuni,* the use of the word מָקוֹם, *place,* instead of עִיר, *city,* indicates that when this incident occurred, Shechem was not yet a *city.* The phrase, therefore, has the significance of: *the site of* [the future city of] *Shechem.*

Rashi comments that Abraham went to Shechem in anticipation of the future, in order to pray in behalf of Jacob's sons, who would one day fight against Shechem.[1]

[*Hoffmann* notes that after the destruction of the city of Shechem in the wars of Vespasian, the city was rebuilt under the name of Flavia Neapolis from which is derived its modern name *Nablus.*]

עַד אֵלוֹן מוֹרֶה — *Until the Plain of Moreh,* i.e., Shechem *(Rashi).*

The capitalization of Plain follows *Rashi* in 14:6 where he interprets Alon as a proper noun.

1. In a dissertation fundamental to the proper understanding of the Torah narratives concerning the Patriarchs, Abraham, Isaac and Jacob, *Ramban* cites the principle mentioned briefly in *Tanchuma:*

כָּל מַה שֶּׁאֵירַע לְאָבוֹת סִימָן לְבָנִים, 'Whatever happened to the Patriarchs is a sign to the children' [i.e., the lives of the Patriarchs is a sign of what will happen to their children.]

This is the reason that the Torah relates at length incidents in their lives such as various journeys, digging of wells, etc., which would otherwise seem to be unimportant. In reality, however, they serve as lessons for the future. Whenever a decree of God is clothed in a symbolic act that decree becomes permanent and unalterable. Examples are Jeremiah's command to Baruch that he cast a scroll of prophecy into the Euphrates River to symbolize the downfall of Babylon *(Jeremiah* 51:63-64), and the arrows shot by Elisha to symbolize the conquest of Aram *(II Kings* 13:17).

XII naan, and they came to the land of Canaan. [6] Abram
6 passed into the land as far as the site of Shechem, until the Plain of Moreh. The Canaanites were then in the land.

Ramban disagrees. See *comm.* there.

[Cf. *Sotah* 32a where the *Mishnah* comments that the plain of Moreh mentioned here is identical with the plains (plural) of Moreh mentioned in *Deut.* 11:30 in the vicinity of Mount Gerizim and Mount Ebal near the city of Shechem (see also *Joshua* 20:7, *Judges* 9:7).]

[*Rashi* apparently also derives from the fact that this stopover in Abram's itinerary is specifically mentioned, that] God showed him Mount Gerizim and Mount Ebal where his descendants would one day take upon themselves the oath of the Torah (cf. *Deut.* 27). [*Rashi* apparently relates אֵלוֹן homiletically with אָלָה, *oath,* and מוֹרֶה with *Torah (Maharshal).*]

The translation 'plain' for אֵלוֹן follows *Onkelos, Yonasan,* and *Radak.* According to *Ibn Ezra* it means אִילָן, 'tree', while *Ibn Janach* renders: 'grove'.

Moreh is explained by *Ibn Ezra, Radak,* and *Ramban* as the name of a person, Moreh, who owned the plain.

Bereishis Rabbasi interprets this name as the *'plain of instruction'* [הוֹרָאָה].

Two mountains, Ebal and Gerizim, rise from this plain. Although they share the same locale, they are in striking contrast to one another. Gerizim, upon which the blessings would later be recited by the Levites (*Deut.* 27) was green and smiling from its base to its peak — the embodiment of God's blessing. Ebal upon which the curse was recited (*ibid.*) was completely barren and desolate — the embodiment of God's wrath. It may be that the area around the mountains was called אֵלוֹן מוֹרֶה, the word *Moreh* signifying *teaching* — for by their very being, the two mountains 'taught' that blessing and curse are side-by-side, sharing the same conditions. The choice between them is man's.

וְהַכְּנַעֲנִי אָז בָּאָרֶץ — [*And*] *the Canaanites were then in the land.*

[The significance of the insertion of this historical detail is variously explained]:

Rashi explains that the Canaanites were then engaged in warfare, seizing the land from Shem's descendants to whom it had originally been allotted when Noah apportioned the earth among his sons, as in 14:18: *And Malchizedek* [identified in the *Talmud* (*Nedarim* 32b) as Shem] *king of Salem* [= Jerusalem, indicating that Shem had sovereignty over Canaan.] Hence, *unto your seed will I give this land* [*v.* 7] was a promise to ultimately restore it to Abraham's children who are the descendants of Shem.

Thus Abraham's first halt was in Shechem. In addition to the reason advanced by *Rashi,* that he prayed for his grandchildren, Abraham's encampment there [even before the promise of *v.* 7 that he would be given the land] was an indication that Shechem would be the first place to be conquered by his descendants [the sons of Jacob, 34:25] even before they would merit full possession of the land, an event that was not to take place for about another three hundred years later. For this reason it states that *the Canaanite was then in the land,* [to indicate that he symbolically took possession even though they were not yet ousted (*Tur*).] From there he journeyed and encamped between Beth-El and Ai, the latter being the first place conquered by Joshua [by use of the sword. The fall of Jericho was with the aid of a miracle.] The story of the Patriarchs will be replete with such symbolism [see *Overview*].

ז וַיֵּרָא יהוה אֶל־אַבְרָם וַיֹּאמֶר לְזַרְעֲךָ
אֶתֵּן אֶת־הָאָרֶץ הַזֹּאת וַיִּבֶן שָׁם מִזְבֵּחַ

Thus, *Rashi* interprets אָז as: *from that point on,* but not previously *(Gur Aryeh).*

[There is a second opinion (cited by *Rashi* in *Numb.* 13:22 from *Sotah* 34b — see also *Kesubos* 112a) that Canaan was originally the province of Ham, father of Canaan. Hence, *the Canaanites were then in the land,* but when Abraham came and received God's blessing, their title to the land was lost. (See also *Gur Aryeh, Da'as Zekenim,* and *Rashi*'s introductory comment to 1:1, p. 28).]

See also *Targum Yonasan* who interprets the phrase as meaning: *The Canaanites were already* [or: *still*] *in the land:*

'And the Canaanites were then in the land, for the time had not yet come for the children of Israel to possess it.'

Radak suggests that the significance of including this information in the narrative is to let us know God's miracles. Abraham, a stranger, sojourned in the land with his family, herds of cattle, and 'souls' he made in Charan — an imposing entourage. His cattle would graze in strange areas and his people would require sustenance. But, although *the Canaanites were then in the land,* they did not harm him — a miracle.

... Others say that although *the Canaanites were then in the land,* he did not learn their evil ways *(Pes. Zutresa).*

Chasam Sofer perceives this as a praise of Abraham's unswerving faith:

Abraham is told by God to leave his home and family with the promise that he will be blessed and a great nation will spring forth from him. The trial is great and he journeys to Canaan, as his inner spirit guides him. He tours the land, awaiting a divine word, a sign, but all the Torah tells is *'the Canaanites were then in the land.'* The land would not be Abraham's for the taking. What of God's promise? Others were living in the land! — But Abraham's faith was not shaken. When God's promise is communicated to him in the following verse, Abraham does not doubt for a moment that his children will, indeed, inherit the land [also *Midrash Rabbah.*]

Ramban, on the other hand, sees this reference as alluding to the fear felt by Abraham when he saw the Canaanites, *that bitter and impetuous nation* dwelling there. Abraham needed God's assurances in the following verse, after which he built an altar to God and worshipped him openly and fearlessly.

Additionally, this detail prefaces why Abraham found it necessary to move on again after God had appeared to him. The Canaanites were there, and engaged in battle, and Abraham felt it necessary to keep moving *(Bertinoro).*

There is something further implicit here: The Canaanites were *then* in the land, but in the future they will not be there. That is why in the very next verse he is promised *'to your seed will I give this land' (Minchah Belulah).*

Midrash HaGadol notes that the numerical value of אָז equals 8, the intimation being that the Canaanites would be in the land until Abraham's eighth generation when the land would be conquered by his descendants. Abraham, Isaac, Jacob, Levi, Kehath, Amram, and Moses equal seven generations. Joshua, the eighth generation, would conquer the land.

7. וַיֵּרָא ה׳ אֶל אַבְרָם — *[And]* *HASHEM appeared to Abram* — in a prophetic manner *(Ibn Ezra).*

XII
7 [7] *HASHEM appeared to Abram and said, 'To your offspring I will give this land.' So he built an altar*

And HASHEM made Himself visible to Abram: The stress is strongly on this *visibility*. The expression states that, not only was the Voice of God heard, but God Himself, so to speak, וַיֵּרָא, *appeared,* emerging from invisibility to visibility; revealing Himself. This is of far reaching importance because the Torah thereby specifically refutes the view of those who deny actual revelations and consider them products of human imagination and ecstasy. The means by which God spoke to human beings is an eternal mystery. It is enough to recognize that He did indeed speak and reveal Himself to them in some tangible way *(Hirsch).*

The commentators also point out previously, that outside the Land, Abraham had heard only the divine *voice.* When he arrived in the land that was destined to be dedicated to the service of God, he was given the additional privilege of a Divine vision, the nature of which is not described. This occurred in the year 2023 — after the first two millenia from the time of creation. Then began the period leading up to the giving and flowering of Torah (see *Ramban*'s Introduction to *Genesis).* Only then did God reveal Himself to the Patriarch of the nation to whom He would give His Torah.

לְזַרְעֲךָ אֶתֵּן אֶת הָאָרֶץ הַזֹּאת — *To your offspring* [lit. *'seed'*] *I will give this land.*

However, during the interim you will be free to *settle* in the choicest part of the Land and no one will deter you. But to your offspring who will be numerous, I will *give* the Land and will scatter its inhabitants before them *(Radak).*

[And although, as noted in the previous verse, the Land was then settled by the Canaanites and not ownerless, Abraham was undeterred.]

[See 9:27 and 10:15 where *Ramban* explains that Noah's curse to Canaan, proclaiming him a slave to Shem, intimated that the descendants of Shem will inherit Canaan's land and all his possessions because, as his servant, Canaan was merely the caretaker of Shem's property until God was ready for Shem to assume ownership.]

It must be emphasized that God never *commanded* Abraham to dwell in the land, for had that been so Abraham would have never left for Egypt in the face of the famine. Rather, God showed him the place and said: Here you *may* dwell *(B'chor Shor).*

וַיִּבֶן שָׁם מִזְבֵּחַ — *So* [lit. *'and'*] *he built an altar there.*

In gratitude for God's promise of children and the possession of the land *(Rashi).*

As explained at the end of *v.* 5, *Ramban* notes that after God appeared to him, Abraham was reassured that he could build an altar without fearing retaliation from the Canaanites.

Additionally, since God appeared to him there, Abraham knew that it was a site worthy of an altar *(Ha'amek Davar).*

ח לַיהוָה הַנִּרְאֶה אֵלָיו׃ וַיַּעְתֵּק מִשָּׁם הָהָרָה
מִקֶּדֶם לְבֵית־אֵל וַיֵּט אָהֳלֹה בֵּית־אֵל מִיָּם
וְהָעַי מִקֶּדֶם וַיִּבֶן־שָׁם מִזְבֵּחַ לַיהוָה
ט וַיִּקְרָא בְּשֵׁם יהוָה׃ וַיִּסַּע אַבְרָם הָלוֹךְ
וְנָסוֹעַ הַנֶּגְבָּה׃

לַה׳ הַנִּרְאֶה אֵלָיו — *To HASHEM Who appeared to him.*

The stress according to many commentators, is on *'that had appeared to him.'*

— He built an altar and offered upon it a sacrifice to give thanks that God had appeared to him. This was the first time that God had appeared to him in any form of prophetic vision. The command to leave his home came to him in a nocturnal dream or through רוּחַ הַקֹּדֶשׁ, the Holy Spirit [see *Moreh Nevuchim II*, 41-45 for a full discussion of prophetic experiences.]

... And he thus showed his gratitude for having been privileged to reach a level of prophetic vision (*Abarbanel*).

8. וַיַּעְתֵּק מִשָּׁם — *[And] from there he relocated.*

I.e. his tent (*Rashi; Ibn Ezra*).

Rashi notes that, because the verb *relocated* is in *hiph'il*, it must have an implied object: like *'his tent'*, rendering: and from there he removed his tent (*Mizrachi*).

Ibn Ezra alternately suggests that the implied object might be *himself*, rendering: *and from there he moved on.*

The use of וַיַּעְתֵּק [rather than וַיִּסַּע, *and he journeyed*] suggests that only a short distance was involved (*HaRechasim le'Bik'ah*).

הָהָרָה מִקֶּדֶם לְבֵית אֵל — *To the mountain, east of Bethel.*

He chose the hill country to escape the battles that were raging throughout the country at the time (*Abarbanel; Malbim*). *Sforno* suggests that he wished also to situate himself between two cities so that many people would come and hear him call upon the name of HASHEM.

Rashi to 28:17 differentiates this from Luz, a place near Jerusalem, which Jacob later renamed Bethel.

Others disagree [see *Hoffmann*] and maintain that both Bethel's are identical: According to their view, it was still known as Luz in Abraham's time, but the Torah uses its eventual name.

The *Midrash* comments that its name is now 'Bais Avan' [There is a city Beitin ten miles north of Jerusalem.]

וַיֵּט אָהֳלֹה — *And [he] pitched his tent.*

Radak notes that the word אָהֳלֹה is spelled in this case with the pronominal suffix ה, *he*, instead of a ו, *vav*. The meaning however does not change. It means אָהֳלוֹ, *his tent* [because it is a grammatical rule that the letters א,ה,ו,י are interchangeable.]

The Sages of the *Midrash*, however, perceive a deeper meaning the unusual spelling of the word. Noting that the word, as written, could be read אָהֳלָהּ *her tent*, they note that Abraham always honored his wife by pitching her tent before his own.

Additionally, it is noted that wherever Abraham sojourned he would pitch a tent which he would

there to HASHEM Who appeared to him. 8 *From*
there he relocated to the mountain east of Bethel and
pitched his tent, with Bethel on the west and Ai on
the east; and he built there an altar to HASHEM and
invoked HASHEM by Name. 9 *Then Abram journeyed*
on, journeying steadily toward the South.

use as a study-house [אָהֳלָהּ שֶׁל תּוֹרָה].

בֵּית־אֵל מִיָּם וְהָעַי מִקֶּדֶם — [With] *Bethel on the west and Ai on the east.*

[That is, he pitched his tent on a mountain range in an area to the west of which lay Bethel and east of which lay Ai.]

[Ai was the first place in the Promised Land that Joshua took in combat. Jericho, however, was conquered entirely through a miracle (see *Ramban* cited in *footnote* to *v.* 6).]

[*Hirsch* and other commentators note that עַי in Hebrew is always preceded by the definite article ה, *the Ai,* indicating that it is not simply a name. It may signify 'a heap of ruins', as already in Abraham's time the whole district seems to have been rich in ruins.]

מִיָּם, [lit. *'from the Sea'*] is synonymous with *from the west* because the Sea [i.e. the Mediterranean] lies to the west of Eretz Yisrael. [See *footnote* to 13:14.]

וַיִּבֶן שָׁם מִזְבֵּחַ לַה' וַיִּקְרָא בְּשֵׁם ה' — *And he built there an altar to HASHEM, and* [lit. *'in'*] *invoked HASHEM by Name.*

I.e. he prayed invoking HASHEM's Name *(Onkelos).*

He prophetically perceived that his descendants would stumble there through Achan's transgression [see *Joshua,* Ch. 7], he therefore prayed for them *(Rashi).*

And, indeed, his prayer proved indispensible. As the *Talmud, Sanhedrin* 44b comments:

Rav Eleazer said: One should always offer up prayer before misfortune comes; for had not Abraham anticipated trouble and prayed between Bethel and Ai, there would not have remained of Israel's sinners (a euphemism for Israel) [at the Battle of Ai in the days of Joshua] a single survivor.

According to *Ibn Ezra* and *Radak,* the phrase וַיִּקְרָא בְּשֵׁם ה' also means: he proclaimed God's Unity and summoned all men to worship Him.

The *Midrash* similarly comments: *And he called upon the name of HASHEM* — in prayer; another interpretation: he began to make converts [rendering: *he summoned people to the Name* (i.e. *Glory) of HASHEM*]; also: he caused the Name of HASHEM to be in the mouth of all people. [See *comm.* to 21:33].

Ramban elaborates further, interpreting that Abraham publicly proclaimed HASHEM's Name before the altar, teaching people to know God and recognize His Presence. In Ur Kasdim he did the same but they refused to listen. Now, however, after arriving in the land concerning which God promised him *I will bless them that bless you* [*v.* 3] he made it his practice to teach of HASHEM and proclaim His Majesty.

9. וַיִּסַּע אַבְרָם הָלוֹךְ וְנָסוֹעַ הַנֶּגְבָּה — *Then Abram journeyed on, journeying steadily* [lit. *'going and journeying'*] *toward the South.*

— He journeyed southward by stages, spending a month or more somewhere and then moving on and

י וַיְהִי רָעָב בָּאָרֶץ וַיֵּרֶד אַבְרָם מִצְרַיְמָה

encamping elsewhere, but always proceeding toward Jerusalem and Mount Moriah in what would become the territory of Judah *(Rashi)*.

— And he thus set his course toward the future site of the Temple *(Midrash)* ... And to where he would one day offer up his son *(Radak)*.

Ramban cites *Rashi* and adds that Abraham's action here, too, anticipated his offspring's future history, as it is written *Judges* 1:2]: *Judah shall go up first*, [i.e., just as Abraham settled first in the portion that would be Judah's, so too, Judah was the first tribe that would conquer its territory in Eretz Yisrael.]

The Torah does not specify the exact reason for Abraham's moving on. Perhaps the Canaanite civil war (see Ch. 14) reached the vicinity of Ai ... or perhaps having proclaimed God's Name publicly and thus drawing many adherents, Abraham's preaching was sought by others who thirsted for God's Word, influencing him to move on to other areas, spending a short time in each to further spread the true faith *(Imrei Shefer)*.

Ibn Ezra notes that the South was known as the Negev, meaning the dry country (related to the Aramaic נגב, to dry) because of its warmer, drier climate.

Hirsch notes that Abraham journeyed to the arid south and away from the cities of the flourishing north. He concludes that the spiritual fountainhead of the people was set in the desert, demonstrating that the success of the Torah requires no material riches. On the contrary, the prosperity of the future was to be based on spiritual wealth.

◈§ Abram in Egypt

[Immediately after Abram settled in Canaan, God forced him to undergo a new trial. Famine compelled him to leave the Land and move to Egypt. There Sarai was imperiled, but HASHEM saved her from Pharaoh, and she returned safely to Canaan with her family. There, at the very same altar that he had built in Bethel before going to Egypt, Abraham proclaimed the Name of HASHEM demonstrating that, though sorely tried, his faith in God was undiminished.] [1]

10. וַיְהִי רָעָב בָּאָרֶץ — *There was a famine in the land.*

— I.e. in that land [of Canaan] *only* [as indicated by the *kametz* vocalization, indicating the positive

1. The *Midrash* comments that God said to Abraham: 'Go forth and tread out a path for your children.' Thus you find that whatever is written in connection with Abraham foreshadowed the future.

Abraham went down to Egypt to sustain himself during a famine, the Egyptians oppressed him and attempted to rob him of his wife for which God punished them with great plagues; Abraham was then loaded with gifts and Pharoah even ordered his men to see that he left the country safely. [see *commentary* to *v.* 20.]

Similarly, his descendants went down to Egypt because of a famine; the Egyptians oppressed them with the intention of eventually taking their wives from them, this being the purpose of Pharaoh's edict to spare the daughters *(Exod.* 1:22) [i.e. they were to be spared for immoral purposes. However, it is clearly implied from Scripture and elucidated by the Sages that Israel maintained its morality. See *Rashi* to *Lev.* 23:11 and *Num.* 26:4, also *comm.* to *Shir haShirim* 4:12, *ArtScroll* ed.] But God avenged them by inflicting great plagues, and He brought them forth with great wealth, as the Egyptians finally pressed them to leave the country [*Exod.* 12:33] (*Ramban;* cf. also *Ramban* cited in *v.* 6; *Ha'amek Davar* to 26:1).

[10]There was a famine in the land, and Abram descended to Egypt to sojourn there, for the

article, under the ב, *beth,* i.e. *the Land* par excellence *(Levush).*] This was one of the ten trials (see *v.* 1); indeed, it was the first famine that had ever occurred since Creation, and its purpose was to test whether Abraham would protest God's justice. For Abraham had followed God's command scrupulously: he left his father, his relatives, and his native land and went to Canaan where he had received God's blessings. Yet, scarcely upon his arrival there, he was forced to leave it. One might have expected him to doubt God, but instead he *went down to Egypt to sojourn there (Pirkei d'Rabbi Eliezer; Tanchuma; Rashi).*

Canaan was almost entirely dependent on annual rainfall for its fertility. As will be seen many times throughout Scripture, famine was no infrequent occurrence there *(Hoffmann).*

וַיֵּרֶד אַבְרָם מִצְרַיְמָה — *And Abram descended to Egypt.*

A land not affected by famines because it is irrigated by the Nile and its fertility is not dependent upon rain water [Egypt was therefore the natural place to turn] *(B'chor Shor).* [Having migrated constantly southward and settling in the Negev, Abraham found Egypt, the nearest country, the most logical place to go.]

Ramban suggests that Abraham unintentionally sinned in endangering Sarai out of fear for his own life [*vs.* 12 and 13], and also for his very act of going to Egypt. In both cases he should have trusted that God would save him and his wife and all his possessions. It was because of this deed that the Egyptian exile was decreed for his children.

Most commentators, however, differ with *Ramban*'s comment:

Tur quotes *Ramban,* but disagrees saying: There appears to be no sin involved in Abraham's saying that Sarah was his sister. On the contrary, I see in it a merit because, although it was likely that the lustful, immoral Egyptians would kill him on account of Sarah, he refused to rely on a miracle.[1]

Abarbanel maintains that there was no sin attached either to Abraham's trip to Egypt or to his ruse concerning Sarah. The Canaanite hunger and the resultant sojourn in Egypt are listed among the ten challenges by which God tested Abraham. It is well-known that God challenges the righteous in order to prove their greatness. It is improper to say that one who survived the test [as the Sages testify concerning Abraham] can be labeled a sinner; nor dare one say that God tested Abraham in order to entrap him.

Concerning Sarah, *Abarbanel* contends that if it were indeed wrong for Abraham to endanger her by identifying her as his sister, then it is inconceivable that he would have repeated the error years later when he travelled to Philistia (20:2), or that Isaac, too, would have committed the same sin regarding Rebecca (26:7).

He goes on to say that Abraham had no idea that it was forbidden to leave Canaan temporarily until the end of the famine. Secondly, the purpose of God's commandments are that man should live by them, and not die by them [see *Lev.* 18:5.] Abraham reasoned that a famine is debilitating and one is not required to endure it, as the Sages proclaimed [*Bava Kamma* 60b]: 'When there is a famine in the land withdraw your feet' [i.e. migrate to another place.] For this reason, and from the implication of such phrases as *to sojourn there, for the famine was severe in the land* [see *comm.* further]

1. *Divrei Shaul* elaborates in a similar vein that Abraham, considering himself unworthy of a miracle feared that Sarah would be taken to Pharaoh by force and that God's Name would be desecrated as a result because people would ask, 'Why did God not protect His prophet? By passing her off as his sister, however, he hoped to avoid such treatment and, if a miracle were to occur, God's Name would be sanctified and His service made widely known.

יא לָגוּר שָׁם כִּי־כָבֵד הָרָעָב בָּאָרֶץ: וַיְהִי
כַּאֲשֶׁר הִקְרִיב לָבוֹא מִצְרָיְמָה וַיֹּאמֶר
אֶל־שָׂרַי אִשְׁתּוֹ הִנֵּה־נָא יָדַעְתִּי כִּי אִשָּׁה
יב יְפַת־מַרְאֶה אָתְּ: וְהָיָה כִּי־יִרְאוּ אֹתָךְ

the indication is clear that Abraham's motives were sincere.

Furthermore, as the *Midrash* [see *footnote*] makes clear, God inspired Abraham to go to Egypt 'to tread a path for his children.'

[Abraham's motive for having Sarah claim she was his sister, and the possible danger this may have caused will be discussed in *vs.* 12 and 13 (see also *footnote* to 20:2).]

Hirsch also discusses this question. In a dissertation fundamental to Torah perspective he cites the opinion of *Ramban* that Abraham sinned in these matters, and comments that *were we not in a position to explain all these superficial difficulties* we would have to agree with Ramban. But even were Abraham's act truly blameworthy, it need not trouble us because it is part of the Torah's greatness that it never attempts to gloss over the flaws of even the most righteous men. *The Torah does not present even our great men as being infallible.* The Torah does not conceal the faults and weaknesses of our great men (including Moses)! and thus *the Torah relates what occurred, not because it was exemplary but because it did occur. This attests to the unadorned truthfulness of what it relates.*

From the comment of *Ramban,* we learn that Truth is the seal of our Torah and we must not whitewash or appear as apologists for our spiritual heroes of the past.

But before we come to this decision and indeed consider Abraham blameworthy let us consider some facts more closely:

The danger must have been of such a threatening nature, so impossible of circumvention, that Abraham felt he could not possibly avoid it and so both he, in the later incident with Abimelech, and his son Isaac, in a similar plight, took refuge in exactly the same way. Now, when *Ramban* views this through the hindsight of history and says that Abraham should have stayed in Canaan he fails to take into account that Abraham had no precedents upon which to draw. We know that God protects his near ones because we can draw upon the experience of Abraham, Isaac, and Jacob, but Abraham in Egypt could only say to himself that he had no right to rely on miracles.

As for his behavior in Egypt, it was apparent to Abraham that Sarah's great beauty endangered her no less than it did him. As a married woman, she could not be wooed. The only way to win her was to murder her husband and take her — a fate worse than death. As a single woman accompanied by a 'brother', it would be more palatable for the Egyptians to curry favor with her and with him. In the interim, crisis would be postponed and God might help.

לָגוּר שָׁם — *To sojourn there.*

Not to *settle there permanently* but to *dwell there temporarily* until the end of the Canaanite famine *(Lekach Tov; Sforno).*

וַיֵּרֶד, *went down* is the usual term used in the Torah for the passage from the higher terrain of Canaan. The journey *to* Canaan is always referred to as עלה, *going up (Heidenheim).*

[Cf. the terms *aliyah and oleh* denoting 'going up' and one who emigrates to Eretz Yisrael.]

[Many commentators understand these terms in the spiritual sense. One *'goes up'* when he approaches the Holy Land, and *'goes down'* when he leaves it; see *footnote* to 13:1.]

כִּי כָבֵד הָרָעָב בָּאָרֶץ — *For the famine was severe in the land.*

This emphasizes the dire need. Had there been any alternative, Abraham would not have left the Land *(Lekach Tov; Abarbanel).*

As long as it was possible to sell

famine was severe in the land. 11 *And it occurred, as*
he was about to enter Egypt, he said to his wife Sarai,
'See now, I have known that you are a woman of
beautiful appearance. 12 *And it shall occur, when the*

his property and depend on his faith, he did so. Only when the severity of the famine reached proportions beyond endurance did he leave the land, as in the Rabbinic dictum *(Bava Kamma* 60b): 'When there is a famine in the land, withdraw your feet' *(Ha'amek Davar).*

11. וַיְהִי כַּאֲשֶׁר הִקְרִיב לָבוֹא מִצְרָיְמָה — *And it occurred as he was about* [lit. *'came near'*] *to enter* [*to*] *Egypt.*

[As they drew nearer to their destination, certain realizations and apprehensions surfaced in Abraham's mind. As *Sforno* notes, Egypt was known for its immorality. *Abarbanel* points out that Abraham was only a sojourner, and at the mercy of the Egyptians who might lust after his wife and do away with him. As he entered Egypt for the first time in his life, he saw their 'ugliness' (see *Rashi* below) and took special note of Sarah's beauty, and grew apprehensive.]

Now, as they neared their destination, he perceived her beauty. Some become uncomely because of the exertion of travel, but she had retained her beauty *(Midrash; Rashi).*

Ramban suggests that Abraham grew fearful because they were approaching a royal city where it was the custom to bring a very beautiful woman to the king and, if he was pleased with her, to slay her husband through some contrived charge.

הִנֵּה נָא יָדַעְתִּי כִּי אִשָּׁה יְפַת מַרְאֶה אָתְּ — *See now, I have known that you are a woman of beautiful appearance.*

[The emphasis is on the word נָא which usually denotes a request but which *Onkelos* always renders *'now'* and which, in several contexts such as here, below 19:2; 27:2; and *I Kings* 1:72, is rendered by *Rashi, Ibn Ezra* and *Radak* as *now*]:

The *Midrashic* interpretation is that until then he had not perceived her beauty because of their extreme modesty; now, however, through a coincidence, [in crossing the river Abraham saw in the water Sarah's reflection resplendent as the sun *(Tanchuma);* or in crossing the river she became exposed *(Targum Yonasan);* or according to *Mid. Aggadah* (see *Mizrachi; Gur Aryeh)* she fell while crossing a stream and Abraham saw her leg and became cognizant of her beauty. Additionally [as noted before] he perceived that she retained her beauty despite the exertion of the journey ...

Still, the simple sense of the verse [which the Translation reflects] is: 'Behold now the time has come when it is necessary to be anxious about your beauty. I have known for a long time that you are beautiful of appearance, but now I take special note of it particularly since we are coming among ugly people, brethren of Ethiopians, who are not accustomed to see a beautiful woman' *(Rashi).*

הַמִּצְרִים וְאָמְרוּ אִשְׁתּוֹ זֹאת וְהָרְגוּ אֹתִי
יג וְאֹתָךְ יְחַיּוּ: אִמְרִי־נָא אֲחֹתִי אָתְּ לְמַעַן
יִיטַב־לִי בַעֲבוּרֵךְ וְחָיְתָה נַפְשִׁי בִּגְלָלֵךְ:

In support of *Rashi's* interpretation *Abarbanel* comments that while in Ur and Charan Abraham was not especially concerned about Sarah's beauty in relationship to the other fine looking women of those countries. But as he neared Egypt, and saw the exceptional blackness and ugliness of the people he worried at how they might react to her beauty.

Abraham's choice of description יְפַת מַרְאֶה, *beautiful appearance,* referred to her light complexion.He was not concerned over her יְפַת תּוֹאַר *beautiful form* [i.e. features] because though the Egyptian women were black, they also had handsome features *(Rashi).*

Note also that in his *Midrashic* interpretation *Rashi* chose his words precisely. *Rashi* does not say 'עַד עַכְשָׁיו לֹא רָאָה אוֹתָהּ' 'until then he never *saw* her, [beauty]', but עַד עַכְשָׁיו לֹא הִכִּיר בָּהּ, 'until then he never *perceived* her [beauty]' — always having looked upon her with spiritual eyes, her physical appearance had never been of importance to him *(Arizal).*

Ramban comments that the *Midrash* concerning the modesty between Abraham and Sarah is traditional, but there is no need to adjoin it to an interpretation of נָא as *now.* He cites several verses indicating that נָא does not refer exclusively to something *new* but, can also refer to a long-existing condition. Thus the phrase here is to be interpreted: *'I have always known...'*

12. וְהָיָה כִּי יִרְאוּ אֹתָךְ הַמִּצְרִים — *And it shall occur, when the Egyptians will see you.*

... And perceive your beauty *(Targum Yonasan).*

וְאָמְרוּ אִשְׁתּוֹ זֹאת —[*And*] *they will say, 'This is his wife.'*

And they will be inconvenienced by this because adultery is prohibited to Noachides *(Midrash HaGadol).*

וְהָרְגוּ אֹתִי — *Then* [lit. *'and'*] *they will kill me* —

Knowing that I would not *willingly* consent to give you up *(Sforno).*

The commentators [*Radak; Chizkuni; Tur*] ask: Since both murder and adultery are prohibited to Noachides, is it not incongruous that the Egyptians would commit the crime of *murder* in order to avoid the crime of *adultery*? Why wouldn't they spare Abraham and simply take Sarah away from him?

The commentators explain that Abraham was convinced that the immoral Egyptians would rationalize and decide that it is better to murder once, thereby freeing a woman from her husband, than to let him live and commit countless acts of adultery with his still-married wife. Abraham further feared that if they murdered him she would remain without a protector. Therefore he must, at all costs, remain alive.

וְאֹתָךְ יְחַיּוּ — *But* [lit. *and*] *you they will let live.*

A euphemism! They will keep you alive for a fate worse than death *(Hirsch).*

XII *Egyptians will see you, they will say, "This is his*
13 *wife!" then they will kill me, but you they will let*
live. [13] *Please say that you are my sister, that it may*
go well with me for your sake, and that I may live on
account of you.'

13. אִמְרִי נָא אֲחֹתִי אָתְּ — *Please say that you are my sister.*

The translation *please* for נָא follows most commentators, *Targum Yonasan,* and also the following comment in *Midrash Hanagid:* Our patriarch Abraham, in his glory, pleads with Sarah and says אִמְרִי נָא, *'Say, I beg you',* וְאֵין נָא אֶלָּא לָשׁוֹן בַּקָּשָׁה, *na,* being nothing else but an expression of request *(Berachos* 9a).

Onkelos, as always, interprets נָא, *now,* [as in *v.* 11] and renders *'Say now* [i.e., this time] that you are my sister.'

[Although it is permissible to lie where a life is at stake, Abraham scrupulously adhered as closely as possible to the truth]:

Was she then his sister? She was his brother's daughter! [11:29]. — But a man often calls his kinswoman 'sister' *(Midrash haGadol)* [See also *comm.* to 20:12.]

Not only to Sarah did Abraham tell this, but he commanded all those who accompanied him and his nephew Lot to tell any Egyptian that might ask that Sarah is Abraham's sister *(Sefer haYashar).*

Ramban suggests that it was their usual procedure from the time they left Charan for Abraham to describe Sarah as his sister wherever they went [cf. 20:13]; the narrative mentions it only where something happened to them as a result ...

Ramban further suggests that it would seem from the literal meaning of the verses that Sarah did not consent to describe herself as Abraham's sister, but that it was Abraham who gave the information [*v.* 19]. She was taken to Pharaoh without being asked about her relationship to Abraham, and she offered no information. Therefore, when her identity was discovered, Pharaoh blamed only Abraham for the deception. But Pharaoh directed no accusations against Sarah, for it was proper that she not contradict her husband, but instead remain silent.

לְמַעַן יִיטַב לִי בַעֲבוּרֵךְ — *That it may go well with me for your sake* — i.e. they will give me gifts *(Rashi).*

— *Rashi* does not imply that Abraham was interested in profiting by the deception. Rather Abraham's plan was that the dignitaries who were vying for Sarah's hand would shower him with gifts in the hope of gaining his consent to marriage with her. Seeing how Abraham was honored, even the masses would be afraid to harm Abraham, and Sarah's safety would thus be assured *(Gur Aryeh).*

The above is also the interpretation of *Sforno* and *Malbim* who explain that it was customary in olden times to shower gifts upon the family of a prospective bride as inducement to gain permission for the marriage.

Malbim comments that בַעֲבוּרֵךְ

שני יד ° וַיְהִי כְּבוֹא אַבְרָם מִצְרָיְמָה וַיִּרְאוּ
הַמִּצְרִים אֶת־הָאִשָּׁה כִּי־יָפָה הִוא מְאֹד׃
טו וַיִּרְאוּ אֹתָהּ שָׂרֵי פַרְעֹה וַיְהַלְלוּ אֹתָהּ
אֶל־פַּרְעֹה וַתֻּקַּח הָאִשָּׁה בֵּית פַּרְעֹה׃

has the implication of: in order to win you. I will put off all offers, with the result that *I will live on account of you,* בִּגְלָלֵךְ connoting: *you will be the cause* of my being spared. In the interim we will arrange our escape.

וְחָיְתָה נַפְשִׁי בִּגְלָלֵךְ — *And that I* [lit. *'my soul'*] *may live* [i.e., remain alive] *on account of you* —

I.e. by your statement *(Onkelos).*

According to *Radak,* the second phrase explains the first: First Abraham said *that it may go well with me,* then he explained that by *'going well'* he meant *'that I may live on account of you.'* For God forbid that Abraham sought to gain anything but his life from Sarah's statement. Sarah's shame would be his as well!

[Abraham's choice of deception instead of fighting to protect Sarah was not an abdication of his responsibility for her safety. On the contrary, he knew full well that were he to be killed defending her — as would have been a virtual certainty — then her own plight would have been hopeless. She would have been at the mercy of the depraved Egyptians.]

See also *comm.* to *v.* 10.

Sifsei Chachamim [note 400] suggests that Abraham told Sarah to claim that he was her brother and that he was helping her search for her husband who had left her, in the hope of securing a divorce, or perhaps to establish that her husband had died and thus permit her to remarry. This would thus further Sarah's safety because they would not lust after a woman in such a circumstance [based upon *Chizkuni*].

14-15 But, as noted by *Ran,* events did not go according to Abraham's plan. Her *exceptional* beauty brought about a different turn of events ...

14. וַיְהִי כְּבוֹא אַבְרָם מִצְרָיְמָה — *But it occurred, with Abram's coming to Egypt* [lit. *'when Abram entered Egypt.'*]

Noting that only *Abram* is mentioned as entering Egypt, [in a verse where clearly Sarah is of prime concern and she certainly should have been mentioned along with Abraham, unlike many of the previous verses where it sufficed to mention Abraham alone as the head of the family and prime mover *(Gur Aryeh)*], *Rashi* cites the tradition that Abraham had hidden Sarah in a trunk. She was discovered when it was opened by the customs officials to assess the duty to be paid.[1]

וַיִּרְאוּ הַמִּצְרִים אֶת הָאִשָּׁה כִּי יָפָה הִוא מְאֹד — *And the Egyptians saw that the woman was very beautiful.*

Just as Abraham had foreseen:

1. *Rashi's* exegesis is based on the *Midrash:*

Where was Sarah? He had locked her in a chest. When he came to the customs house the officer demanded that Abraham pay the custom duties. Abraham agreed.

'You carry garments in that box', he said. 'Then I will pay the duty on garments', Abraham replied:

'You are carrying silks', he asserted. 'I will pay on silks', Abraham replied.

XII
14-16

[14] *But it occurred, with Abram's coming to
Egypt, the Egyptians saw that the woman was very
beautiful.* [15] *When the officials of Pharaoh's saw her,
they lauded her for Pharaoh, and the woman was
taken into Pharaoh's house.* [16] *And he treated Abram*

the Egyptian masses gazed at her beauty and were taken by it (*Sforno*).

However the effect of her beauty exceeded even Abraham's estimate. Whoever saw her said: This one is worthy of great princes. Their praise of her was so extravagant that she came to the attention of the King's officers who came to see her themselves (*B'chor Shor*).

[It must be realized that Sarah, being ten years younger than Abraham, was sixty-five years old, but she had retained her youthful beauty.]

15. וַיִּרְאוּ אֹתָהּ שָׂרֵי פַרְעֹה — [*When*] *the officials of Pharaoh saw her.*

They withheld her from the masses (*Sforno*), but the officials themselves feared touching her because they knew the king would desire her for himself (*Ramban*).

It would have been better for all wicked people to be blind, for their very eyes bring about evil upon the world as it says of the officers of Pharaoh who saw Sarah (*Bamidbar Rabbah* 20).

וַיְהַלְלוּ אֹתָהּ אֶל פַּרְעֹה — [*And*] *they lauded her for* [lit. '*to*'] *Pharaoh.*

The translation follows *Rashi* who comments: *And they lauded her* among themselves by saying: 'this one is suitable *for* the king' [i.e. she is suitable אֶל פַּרְעֹה *for Pharaoh.*]

Rashi chose this translation over the perhaps more literal rendering: 'and they lauded her *to* the king', which would indicate that the officers themselves praised Sarah's beauty to the king [which is how the verse is interpreted by *Ramban* and others] because if the latter were correct, the verse should have continued *and Pharaoh sent and took her* — as happened in the parallel incident with Abimelech [cf. 20:2] — Since the verse reads '*they saw ... they lauded ... and she was taken*', it implies that this all transpired among the officers. Additionally, if the latter interpretation were correct, the proper Hebrew expression would have been וַיְהַלְלוּ אֹתָהּ לִפְנֵי פַּרְעֹה [lit. '*and they lauded her before Pharaoh*'], or as *Mizrachi* suggests לְפַרְעֹה, *to Pharaoh.*

[Pharaoh was the royal title of all Egyptian kings, just as Abimelech was the official title of Philistine monarchs.]

According to *Sefer haYashar* the original Pharaoh was named Rikion. He was a man of great wisdom and cunning who usurped the throne of Egypt. His name Pharaoh was given him by the deposed king because of the פֵּרָעוֹן [payments, taxes] he exacted, bringing great wealth to the land.

וַתֻּקַּח הָאִשָּׁה בֵּית פַּרְעֹה — *And the woman was taken into Pharaoh's house,* i.e., palace (*Targum Yonasan*).

But the officer grew suspicious and insisted that Abraham open the chest so he could personally inspect the contents. As soon as he opened it the land of Egypt was irradiated with her beauty.

[*Sefer haYashar* notes that putting Sarah into the chest was Abraham's additional scheme in addition to his brother-sister plan, to minimize Sarah's exposure at all cost.]

טז וּלְאַבְרָם הֵיטִיב בַּעֲבוּרָהּ וַיְהִי־לוֹ צֹאן־
וּבָקָר וַחֲמֹרִים וַעֲבָדִים וּשְׁפָחֹת וַאֲתֹנֹת
יז וּגְמַלִּים: וַיְנַגַּע יהוה | אֶת־פַּרְעֹה נְגָעִים
גְּדֹלִים וְאֶת־בֵּיתוֹ עַל־דְּבַר שָׂרַי אֵשֶׁת

By force and against her will, as was Esther, who was likewise taken to the king's house [Esther 2:8] *(Aggadas Esther).*

As *Ramban* points out in *v.* 13, Sarah was taken with no questions asked, but Abraham apparently volunteered the information that she was his sister. [As implied by Pharaoh's accusation in *v.* 9 *'why did you say, she is my sister?'*]

How could a wife be taken without her husband weeping and rending his garments? — She was put into a room alone and Pharaoh did not approach her. The verse says: *'The woman was taken to Pharaoh's palace'*, not *unto Pharaoh (Midrash Or haAfelah,* ms. cited in *Torah Shelemah* 12:172).

Pirkei d'Rabbi Eliezer notes that Sarah's abduction to Pharaoh's house was one of Abraham's ten trials [see on *v.* 1. Abraham never lost his faith in God for a moment even in this most trying test.]

Midrash Tanchuma records that when Abraham saw his wife being taken he wept and prayed and so did Sarah. God answered that nothing would befall either of them, and further, He would make an example of Pharaoh and his household [*v.* 17].

16. וּלְאַבְרָם הֵיטִיב בַּעֲבוּרָהּ — *And he* [i.e. Pharaoh *(Rashi)*] *treated Abram well for her sake*[1]

וַיְהִי לוֹ — *And he* [i.e., Abram] *acquired* [lit. *'and there became his'*].

I.e., from Pharaoh who had given these to him. There follows a detailed explanation of *'and Abraham was well-treated' (Radak).*

[Apparently, this was in addition to *'all their possessions which they had amassed'* referred to in *v.* 5.]

Later Abraham vehemently refused to accept anything from the king of Sodom [see 14:23, even though he rightfully *deserved* a reward for having come to the Sodomite king's aid], while here he accepted many valuable gifts from Pharaoh. This apparent inconsistency must be viewed in the context of Abraham's claim that Sarah was his sister and the implicaion that he would allow her to marry a suitable person. Had he refused gifts, he would have aroused Pharaoh's suspicions *(Hoffmann;* see *Radak; Sifsei Chachamim* to *v.* 13; *Abarbanel, haK'sav v'haKabal-*

1. The *Talmud* derives a moral lesson from the word בַּעֲבוּרָהּ, *for her sake,* indicating that prosperity in the home as well as the blessings of home life are dependent upon the wife. It homiletically perceives *God* [not Pharaoh] as the implied subject and source of the goodness described in this and the next verse (see *Maharsha; Torah Temimah; Tosefes Brachah*):

'One must always observe the honor due to his wife,because blessings rest on a man's home only on account of his wife, as it is written: *and He dealt well with Abram for her sake.'*

Similarly did Rava say to the townspeople of Machuza: 'Honor your wives, that you may be enriched' *(Bava Metzia* 59a).

XII *well for her sake, and he acquired sheep, oxen,*
17 *donkeys, slaves and maidservants, female donkeys,*
and camels.
[17] *But HASHEM afflicted Pharaoh along with his*
household with severe plagues because of Sarai, the

lah, and *Imrei Shefer).*

[See *footnote,* below.]

צֹאן וּבָקָר . . . — *Sheep (and) oxen, ...*

Hirsch perceives that the seemingly haphazard order in which the gifts are enumerated here — interspersing gifts of servants among the animals and separating חֲמֹרִים, *donkeys* from אֲתוֹנוֹת, *female donkeys* — is significant and intentional. It indicates that Pharaoh was in a frenzy to win Abraham's favor. One day he sent him a nice ox, the next day an ass, then a slave, etc. Abraham dared not refuse lest he shatter Pharaoh's hopes of gaining Sarah legally and resort to force.

The word שְׁפָחֹת, *maidservants,* is written defectively [without the letter *vav*], implying that he was given only one maidservant, Hagar, Pharaoh's daughter by a concubine *(Pirkei d'Rabbi Eliezer: Midrash Hagadol).* [1]

Harav David Feinstein comments that, although as the Sages note, Sarah was given only one maidservant, the word appears in the plural form [שְׁפָחֹת] because it would not have been seemly for Pharaoh to give a miserly gift. Therefore, he gave one maidservant whose status *made her equivalent to many.*

[It may also be that, as a princess, Hagar had servants of her own. All of them would have accompanied her to Sarah, thus accounting for the plural form.]

17. וַיְנַגַּע ה׳ אֶת פַּרְעֹה נְגָעִים גְּדֹלִים וְאֶת־בֵּיתוֹ — *But* [lit. *'and'*] *HASHEM afflicted Pharaoh along with his house*[hold] *with severe* [lit. *'great'*] *plagues.*

Rashi explains that he was smitten with the plague of *raathan* [a debilitating skin disease] which makes cohabitation impossible.

This plague assured that Sarah's chastity would be safeguarded from Pharaoh. The wording of the verse [with the words *'with great plagues'* referring only to Pharaoh, and *with his household* mentioned only afterwards] indicates that only Pharaoh was afflicted with the *'great plagues'* which made cohabitation impossible. The

1. Rabbi Yehoshua ben Korchah said: Because of Pharaoh's love for Sarah he wrote her a document giving her his wealth — in silver, gold, manservants, and land. He also gave her the land of Goshen as a possession. Therefore, the children of Israel later dwelt in the land of Goshen [47:27], which belonged to our mother Sarah. He also gave her Hagar, his daughter from a concubine, as her handmaid *(Pirkei d'Rabbi Eliezer).*

As the *Midrash* [45:1] comments:

When Pharaoh saw what was done on Sarah's behalf to his own house [next verse], he took his daughter and gave her to Sarah, saying: Better let my daughter be a handmaid in this house than a mistress in another house.

What is Hagar? — הָא אַגְרֵךְ, 'here is your reward' [a homiletical play on the assonance of the name] *(Midrash HaGadol).*

יח אַבְרָם: וַיִּקְרָא פַרְעֹה לְאַבְרָם וַיֹּאמֶר
מַה־זֹּאת עָשִׂיתָ לִּי לָמָּה לֹא־הִגַּדְתָּ לִּי כִּי
יט אִשְׁתְּךָ הִוא: לָמָה אָמַרְתָּ אֲחֹתִי הִוא
וָאֶקַּח אֹתָהּ לִי לְאִשָּׁה וְעַתָּה הִנֵּה אִשְׁתְּךָ

others in his household were afflicted with other plagues [and according to a *Midrash,* Sarah herself was the only one in the palace complex not afflicted! *(Sforno)*] This led Pharaoh to question whether Sarah was, indeed unmarried *(Gur Aryeh).*

The night that Pharaoh was afflicted [with a plague that forced him to free Sarah] was [what would later be] the night of Passover. This paralleled how God would later greatly afflict the Egyptians [to force them to free the children of Israel] *(Pirkei d'Rabbi Eliezer* 26).

[This, then, is yet another example of 'whatever happened to the Patriarchs is an indication of what would happen to their children.' See *footnote* to *v.* 6.]

עַל דְּבַר שָׂרַי אֵשֶׁת אַבְרָם — *Because of Sarai, the wife of Abram.*

On account of the injustice they perpetrated against Sarai who was married to Abram, God sent a plague to protect the wife of His beloved. The plague was so severe that Pharaoh could not approach her *(Ibn Ezra).* Abram, too, is mentioned because it was in the merit of both that Pharaoh and his household were afflicted with these great plagues *(Ramban).*

Rashi interprets עַל דְּבַר literally — *'by the word of'* [i.e. *by order of*]: She said to the angel 'Smite!' and he smote.[1]

אֵשֶׁת אַבְרָם — *The wife of Abram.*

Do we not already know she was Abram's wife? — The verse comes to teach us that although Sarah gave the others the impression she was Abraham's sister, to Pharaoh [as noted in the *footnote* below] she revealed the truth thinking that the king would never stoop so low as to defile her if she told him she was a married woman. But she was wrong; he would not heed her, saying that she was telling him this merely to put him off. Therefore, God punished him with a debilitating skin disease which prevented any contact between the two ... Another explanation of *'on account of Sarai, Abram's wife'*: On account of his behavior towards Sarai, who was a married woman, wife of Abram *(Kli Yakar).*

This answers those who would ask why Pharaoh was punished

1. This follows the *Midrash* which interprets *by the word of Sarai* as: *by the prayer of Sarai* and *by order of Sarai:*

All of that night Sarah lay prostrate on her face crying, 'Sovereign of the Universe! Abraham went forth from his land on Your assurance while I went forth with blind faith; Abraham is without this prison while I am within!'

God answered her, 'Whatever I do, I do for your sake and all will declare "It is *because of Sarai, Abram's wife*".'

Rav Levi said: That entire night an angel stood, whip in hand. When she ordered, 'Strike!' [i.e. inflict him] he struck, and when she ordered, 'Desist!' he desisted. Why was Pharaoh so punished? — Because she had told him she was a married woman, yet he would not leave her.

Furthermore, the *Zohar* adds that with each blow the angel said, 'this is *because of Sarai who is Abram's wife!*' On learning that she was indeed Abram's wife, Pharaoh immediately called for Abram.

XII 18-19 wife of Abram. [18] Pharaoh summoned Abram and
said, 'What is this you have done to me? Why did
you not tell me that she is your wife? [19] Why did you
say, "She is my sister," so that I would take her as
my wife? Now, here is your wife; take her and go!'

without being warned as was Abimelech [see 20:3], for Pharaoh was indeed made aware of Sarah's true marital status *(Rav Yosef Kara;* see *Tur* and *footnote* below).

18. וַיִּקְרָא ... מַה זֹּאת עָשִׂיתָ לִּי — *Pharaoh summoned Abram and said, 'What is this you have done to me?'*

Pharaoh pondered upon this strange and sudden outbreak of disease, which coincided with the time Sarah was taken to his house. He suspected that Sarah was telling him the truth and the plague was indeed associated with her so he called Abraham and accused him. He was not certain she was his wife but he made the accusations in order to draw the truth from Abraham *(Ramban).*

לָמָּה לֹא הִגַּדְתָּ לִּי כִּי אִשְׁתְּךָ הִוא — *Why did you not tell me that she is your wife?*

The emphasis is on לִי, *me:* Even if you feared the people — perhaps, with justification — surely you could have told *me*! You certainly need not have suspected me, who as king rules the land righteously. You are surely aware that as king I would take nothing but a maiden! *(Ran; Sforno; Minchah Belulah).*

19. לָמָה אָמַרְתָּ אֲחֹתִי הִוא — *Why did you say, 'She is my sister'?*

Even if you would answer that I should have investigated the matter more fully, you should at least have remained silent. I relied on what you told me, for not only did you withhold that she is your wife but you even went out of your way to tell me she is your sister!

וָאֶקַּח אֹתָהּ לִי לְאִשָּׁה — *So that* [lit. *'and'* i.e. 'with the result that'] *I would take her to be my wife!* [lit. *'to me as a wife.'*]

[The commentators unanimously agree that Pharaoh was here expressing his *intention* to marry Sarah, not that had *already* taken her. The plagues prevented his defilement of her, and having seen the finger of God, Pharaoh desisted from his plan before it ever came to fruition.]

Pharaoh thus additionally implied that he chose her *because* he thought she was Abraham's sister, and he deemed it an honor to become related to such a wise and esteemed individual through marriage to his sister *(Ha'amek Davar).*

— I had not intended to defile her, but to make her my *legal wife* *(Radak).*

הִנֵּה אִשְׁתְּךָ קַח וָלֵךְ — *Now, here is your wife: take* [her] *and go!*

She is still אִשְׁתְּךָ, *your wife;* I hereby return her to you exactly as she was when I took her, I did not so much as touch her *(Radak).*

Why did Abraham not answer Pharaoh — as he later did to Abimelech under similar circumstances (see 20:11,12) — and justify his actions by expressing his fears and explaining that, as his niece, she

כ קַח וָלֵךְ׃ וַיְצַו עָלָיו פַּרְעֹה אֲנָשִׁים
וַיְשַׁלְּחוּ אֹתוֹ וְאֶת־אִשְׁתּוֹ וְאֶת־כָּל־אֲשֶׁר־

could truthfully be called his 'sister'?

The commentators answer that Pharaoh's reaction made it clear that he was in no mood for answers. True, he had 'asked' why Abraham said she was his sister, but he waited for no reply, immediately following his rhetorical inquiry with, *'Here is your wife, take her and go!'* — as if to say: You have brought us enough trouble, take your wife and be gone!

Abraham knew that he should not run the risk of further provoking the king's anger by engaging him in conversation. He did as the king told him: he took his wife and possesssions and departed. [Compare, however, the exchange in Ch. 20 where Abimelech conversed with Abraham and did not immediately permit him to leave. There, Abraham did respond to the king] *(Alshich; Minchah Belulah).*

Malbim suggests that Abraham could not possibly answer Pharaoh's question. Could he say that he placed no more trust in the morality of Pharaoh himself than in that of his people? Abraham decided it was better to remain silent.

According to *Ramban*'s interpretation of these verses, Pharaoh interpreted Abraham's silence — which was motivated by great fear — as his silent acquiescence that Pharaoh's suspicions were justified: Sarah was indeed his wife. He therefore ordered them to leave.

קַח וָלֵךְ — *Take* [her] *and go!*

Pharaoh did not say, as did Abimelech, [20:15] *Behold my land is before you, dwell wherever it pleases you;* Pharaoh was well aware that Egypt was steeped in immorality and judged it better, under the circumstances, that Abraham should depart *(Tanchuma; Rashi).*

[Furthermore, Pharaoh's order to *'take her and go'* presents a striking parallel: As pointed out several times, the entire episode of Abraham in Egypt presaged what would later occur to his descendants in Egypt — when a successor of Pharaoh would say to Moses and Aaron *(Ex.* 12:32): קְחוּ, *take* ... וָלֵכוּ, *and go!* (Cf. *Pes. Zutresa; Pirkei d'Rabbi Eliezer).*]

20. וַיְצַו עָלָיו פַּרְעֹה אֲנָשִׁים — *So Pharaoh gave men orders concerning him.*

— To escort and guard him *(Rashi).*

The use of the verb וַיְצַו [*gave orders*] indicates that; as a friendly gesture to Abraham, Pharaoh issued stern warning to his subjects to guarantee safe passage to this man and his wife and let them pass through unmolested lest others succumb and be punished as well *(Ibn Ezra; Minchah Belulah).*

Hirsch suggests, however, that the phrase צִוָּה עַל usually implies a restriction, suggesting that Pharaoh placed a restriction upon Abraham commanding him to leave the country unconditionally and appointed men to see that the command was executed — analogous to what would happen so often in later Jewish history.

XII 20 [20] *So Pharaoh gave men orders concerning him, and they escorted him and his wife and all that was his.*

וַיְשַׁלְּחוּ אֹתוֹ וְאֶת אִשְׁתּוֹ — *And they escorted him and his wife.*

The translation *escorted* for וַיְשַׁלְּחוּ [usually rendered: *'and they sent'*] follows *Rashi* who cites the translation of *Onkelos:* וְאַלְוִיאוּ, and they escorted.

Ibn Ezra also interprets the word *accompanied* intimating an honorable escort and quotes the parallel usage in 18:16: *'And Abraham went with them* לְשַׁלְּחָם, *to accompany them.'*

[Pharaoh thus hastens to rid himself of the source of his divine affliction, but, not wishing to incur God's further wrath by mistreating His beloved, he sends them away in honor, assuring that no evil will befall them.][1]

וְאֶת כָּל אֲשֶׁר לוֹ — *And all that was his.*

Pharaoh let them leave with all their property intact. He did not even suggest that Abraham had taken the gifts under false pretenses and should therefore return them *(Minchah Belulah).*

That he did not do so was one of the greatest miracles of the entire incident *(Ramban).*

It was thus God's providential Mercy that not only did Pharaoh not punish Abraham, or even take back his gifts, but that Pharaoh was so afraid of incurring further punishment from God, that he even had his men escort Abraham and Sarah lest anyone molest them *(Malbim).*

According to *Sefer HaYashar,* Pharaoh heaped additional gifts upon Abraham — cattle, servants, gold and silver — in order to appease him. Also it was now that Pharaoh gave Hagar to Sarah as a maidservant [see *comm.* to *v.* 16.]

According to *Seder Olam,* the entire incident in Egypt — from entering the country until being escorted out — took three months.

Abarbanel summarizes that among the moral lessons to be learned from the entire incident [see *Overview*] is that *there are many plans in a man's heart, but it is the purpose of HASHEM that shall prevail* [*Prov.* 19:21.] Witness the course of events: Abraham planned to escape a famine by fleeing to Egypt and save his wife with his scheme. But events did not work out quite as he had planned, and in

1. The *Talmud* [*Sotah* 46b] notes that in the merit of the four paces [*symbolic of the four cubits which represent the minimum fulfillment of the mitzvah of* לְוָיָה, *escorting (Torah Temimah)*] which Pharaoh accompanied Abraham, he enslaved the latter's descendants for four hundred years.

[Not that the four centuries were the *result* of these four paces; *that* was decreed at the Covenant between the Parts (15:13); the meaning of the *Talmud* is that by his action Pharaoh merited that the bulk of the four hundred years would be in his land *(Maharsha).*

Rav Avraham Gold notes that no subjugating nation is mentioned at the Covenant between the Parts; the choice of Egypt was Pharaoh's reward. Additionally, we learn from this that one who commands others to escort on his behalf, is considered as if he escorted personally; for Pharaoh, as the verse shows, did not escort them himself, but commanded others to do so.]

א לוֹ: וַיַּעַל אַבְרָם מִמִּצְרַיִם הוּא וְאִשְׁתּוֹ
ב וְכָל־אֲשֶׁר־לוֹ וְלוֹט עִמּוֹ הַנֶּגְבָּה: וְאַבְרָם
ג כָּבֵד מְאֹד בַּמִּקְנֶה בַּכֶּסֶף וּבַזָּהָב: וַיֵּלֶךְ

a short time he found himself back in Canaan, sustained for the balance of the famine by the generosity of God *'Whose eye is upon those who fear Him, upon those who hope in His lovingkindness'* [*Psalms* 33:18.]

XIII

1. וַיַּעַל אַבְרָם מִמִּצְרַיִם – *So Abram went up from Egypt.*

[The Torah always uses the verb וַיַּעַל, *went up,* when speaking of journeys *to* the higher terrain of Eretz Yisrael. Compare the use of וַיֵּרֶד, *went down* in 12:10.] [1]

הוּא וְאִשְׁתּוֹ וְכָל־אֲשֶׁר לוֹ – *He with his wife and all that was his.*

His entourage was already mentioned in the previous verse. It is repeated to emphasize the miracle that the Egyptians did not rob him of the gifts on the pretext that he had obtained them under false pretenses *(Ramban).*

וְלוֹט עִמּוֹ – *And Lot with him.*

[Lot is specifically mentioned here because of the role he is to play in the following narrative.]

Malbim notes that here, the verses say that Lot went עִמּוֹ whereas in 12:4, it says אִתּוֹ. Although both words are translated *'with him',* they have differing connotations. The word אִתּוֹ [12:4] implies a subservient, dependent relationship. At the time, Lot was an orphan who relied on his uncle, Abraham. The word עִמּוֹ, however, implies that one accompanied the other *as an equal.* During the interim, Lot had become independently wealthy *(v.* 5) and no longer displayed obedience to Abraham.

הַנֶּגְבָּה – *To the South,* i.e., to the South [the Negev region] of *Eretz Yisrael.*

Although Abraham was travelling northward from Egypt to Eretz Yisrael, his destination was the *Negev,* the southern part of the land. This is in contrast to 12:9 where, although heading for the same general destination, he was moving in a southerly direction for Charan *(Rashi).*

... As *HaRechasim leBik'ah* [to 12:9] explains: 'to the southern part of Eretz Yisrael which is called הַנֶּגֶב, *The Negev ...* ' [See on 12:9.]

2. וְאַבְרָם כָּבֵד מְאֹד – *Now* [lit. *'and'*] *Abram was very laden* [lit. *'heavy'*] – heavily burdened with bundles *(Rashi).*

The adjective *'heavy'* is used

1. The *Zohar* perceives in the word וַיַּעַל an indication that Abraham *ascended spiritually* from the 'lower degrees' of Egypt, reaching the highest degree of his former condition. He was not like Adam, who, when he descended [spiritually] was enticed by the serpent and brought death to the world; nor was he like Noah, who, when he descended, was enticed *and drank of the wine and became drunk and he uncovered himself within his tent* [9:21]. Unlike them, Abraham was not seduced, but *ascended* once again to his former condition.

XIII
1-3

[1] *So Abram went up from Egypt, he with his wife
and all that was his — and Lot with him — to the
South.* [2] *Now Abram was very laden with cattle,
silver and gold.* [3] *He proceeded on his journeys from*

because, with such an abundance of wealth, he was 'weighed down' and slow-moving *(Ibn Ezra)*.

For, anxious though he was to return home to his sacred calling he was forced to lead his flocks slowly *(Sforno)*. In addition, he travelled at a leisurely pace lest he appear to be fleeing from Pharaoh *(Minchah Belulah)*.

[Many also perceive the sense of the word to be synonymous with *'rich'* — i.e. 'heavy' with many possessions.]

בַּכֶּסֶף וּבַזָּהָב — *With [the] silver and [the] gold.*

The definite article *'the'* would seem to imply that he received these, too, in Egypt [although they are not mentioned among the gifts in 12:16]; or quite possibly he bartered the surplus of his other gifts for silver and gold *(Hirsch* to 12:16; *Hoffmann)*.

3. וַיֵּלֶךְ לְמַסָּעָיו ... — *And he proceeded* [lit. *'went'*] *on his journeys ...*

On his return trip he retraced his steps and lodged in the same places where he stayed on the outward journey [this is derived in *Arachin* 16b from the emphasis on his *journeys* — i.e. his [former] *journeys*: the journeys he had taken previously; and from the expression: *where his tent had been at the beginning* — retracing his former route.] This teaches good manners: One should not change his lodging.

The Talmud, *ibid.*, explains that one's lodging should not be changed unless one is the object of great harrassment and anguish. This is because a boarder who changes his lodging discredits both himself [because he will acquire the reputation of a man hard to please or of a man who acted improperly and was refused further lodging]; and he discredits the lodging place [which will be regarded as unsatisfactory] *(Rashi)*.[1]

Another interpretation: On his return he repaid the credit [which had been extended him for food and lodging on the way to Egypt] *(Midrash; Rashi)*.

How can it be that Abraham, the beloved of God, lacked funds to pay for such basic needs? — He had the funds, but because it was a time of famine, he was afraid to show that he had ready cash lest he be robbed. This counsel was later followed by Jacob [42:1] *(Devek Tov)*.

According to *Sforno*, the phrase *he went on his journeys* indicates that he went on a series of small journeys like the nomad shepherds who journey from place to place in search of new pastures.

Laden as he was with his burden of riches and abundant flocks his trip was really a series of short slow-moving journeys *(Radak)*.

1. *Mussar* masters derive from Abraham's behavior a lesson in frugality. When he went to Egypt in the midst of famine, he would have chosen inexpensive lodgings in order to conserve his dwindling resources. Upon his return he was exceedingly wealthy, yet he did not change his style of living.

לְמַסָּעָיו מִנֶּגֶב וְעַד־בֵּית־אֵל עַד־הַמָּקוֹם
אֲשֶׁר־הָיָה שָׁם אָהֳלֹה בַּתְּחִלָּה בֵּין בֵּית־
ד אֵל וּבֵין הָעָי׃ אֶל־מְקוֹם הַמִּזְבֵּחַ אֲשֶׁר־
עָשָׂה שָׁם בָּרִאשֹׁנָה וַיִּקְרָא שָׁם אַבְרָם
ה בְּשֵׁם יהוה׃ °וְגַם־לְלוֹט הַהֹלֵךְ אֶת־אַבְרָם
ו הָיָה צֹאן־וּבָקָר וְאֹהָלִים׃ וְלֹא־נָשָׂא אֹתָם
הָאָרֶץ לָשֶׁבֶת יַחְדָּו כִּי־הָיָה רְכוּשָׁם רָב

°שלישי

Malbim perceives in the use of the plural *journeys* that Abraham's intention was not to journey to one permanent destination, but to visit many places where he could lecture and disseminate the Word of the True God.

According to the *Targum,* the literal sense of the verse is: He returned via his original route which was from the south to Bethel, his destination being the altar, etc.

מִנֶּגֶב וְעַד־בֵּית־אֵל — *From the south* — [i.e. from Egypt which lies to the south of the land of Canaan *(Rashi)*] — *to Bethel.*

אֲשֶׁר הָיָה שָׁם אָהֳלֹה בַּתְּחִלָּה — *Where his tent had been formerly* [lit. *'at the beginning'*] — i.e., on the mountain, as it is written [12:8]: *And from there he removed towards the mountain, east of Bethel (Radak).*

[On the symbolism for future generations of Abram stopping at these particular places — Bethel, Ai, etc. — see *comm.* to 12:6.]

4. אֶל־מְקוֹם ... בָּרִאשֹׁנָה — *To the site* [lit. *'place'*] *of the altar which he had erected* [lit. *'made'*] *there at first.*

This informs us that he did not pitch his tent on a different part of the mountain but near the very spot where he had previously built an altar. This teaches that it is proper for a person to select a permanent place for his prayer and divine service. One's heart is better attuned in a familiar place *(Radak).*

וַיִּקְרָא שָׁם אַבְרָם בְּשֵׁם ה׳ — *And there Abram invoked HASHEM by Name.*

[See *comm.* to 12:8.]

I.e., upon returning to the land appointed for his mission, Abraham resumed his calling of teaching God's word summoning men to follow Him *(Hirsch).*

It is not clear from the verse whether the phrase *'and there Abram ...'* is an adjectivial modifier, i.e., Abraham returned to the place where he had *previously* erected an altar in order to invoke the Name of HASHEM, or whether, *after* having returned to the place, he proceeded to *invoke the Name of HASHEM. Rashi* cites both interpretations.

[Most commentators, agree with *Rashi*'s second interpretation, that Abraham 'invoked HASHEM by Name' to signify his resumption of his mission. For if the phrase were merely describing the location of the altar, than it would be superfluous to specifically mention *Abraham* as having called when he is already the subject of the dicates that a new thought is being introduced.]

XIII
4-6

the south to Bethel to the place where his tent had been formerly, between Bethel and Ai, [4] to the site of the altar which he had erected there at first. And there Abram invoked HASHEM *by Name.*

[5] Also Lot who went with Abram had flocks, herds, and tents. [6] And the land could not support them dwelling together for their possessions were abundant and they were unable to dwell together.

5. וְגַם־לְלוֹט הַהֹלֵךְ אֶת אַבְרָם — *[And] also* [to] *Lot who went with Abram.*

גַּם, *'also'* meaning: *'in addition to Abraham, a great fortune had accrued to Lot, as well.'*

Lot is further identified here as the one *who went with Abram* [although such identification is unnecessary since we have already been introduced to Lot several times previously] to indicate that it was in the merit of his accompanying Abraham that he accumulated this wealth *(Rashi; Radak).*[1]

6. וְלֹא־נָשָׂא אֹתָם הָאָרֶץ לָשֶׁבֶת יַחְדָּו — *And the land could not support* [lit. *'bear'*] *them dwelling* [lit. *'to dwell'*] *together.*

— I.e., could not provide sufficient pasture for their cattle *(Rashi).*

Rashi goes on to explain that the phrase is elliptical and a subject-word like *'pasture'* is implied but not stated. Such a subject should be understood as, for example: *'the pasture'* [מִרְעֶה (a masc. noun)] *of the land could not support them.* Therefore the masc. verb נָשָׂא, which agrees in gender with the implied subject מִרְעֶה, is used in this verse.

Rashi's comment would seem to imply that אָרֶץ, *the land,* (the ostensible subject of the verse) is a fem. word and thus incompatible with the masc. verb נָשָׂא. This, *Mizrachi* contends, is erroneous because there are verses — such as *Ps.* 105:30 *Isaiah* 9:18 — where אֶרֶץ clearly appears with masc. verbs. Rather, *Mizrachi* explains, *Rashi's* comment is based on the simple fact that the earth per se was obviously capable of bearing them. It could only be the available *pasture land* that was insufficient.

Gur Aryeh, on the other hand, is of the opinion that *Rashi*'s comment is, indeed, grammatically inspired by the fact that ארץ is fem. The few occasions where it appears with a masc. verb are clearly exceptions, and might be similarly explained as being elliptical.

According to the *Midrash* the inability of the land to support them went beyond natural considerations:

'Could it really be — a land that supported such a large population could not support them? It was the quarrels between their shepherds that was the true cause. Even the most abundant land cannot suffice for quarreling parties *(Pesikta Rabbasi, Midrash HaGadol).* [See *comm.* next verse.]

כִּי־הָיָה רְכוּשָׁם רָב וְלֹא יָכְלוּ לָשֶׁבֶת יַחְדָּו — *For their possessions were abundant and they were unable to dwell together.*

Why repetition of the phrase לָשֶׁבֶת יַחְדָּו, indicating that they could not dwell together?

— In truth Abraham and Lot were

1. The Talmud [*Bava Kamma* 93a] derives the popular saying 'drag chips behind a wealthy man' (i.e. in the company of a wealthy man — even by dragging chips behind him — you may become wealthy) — in the colloquial sense of 'money rubs off'] — from our verse. For *also Lot, who went with Abram, had flocks and herds and tents.*

ז וְלֹא יָכְלוּ לָשֶׁבֶת יַחְדָּו: וַיְהִי־רִיב בֵּין רֹעֵי
מִקְנֵה־אַבְרָם וּבֵין רֹעֵי מִקְנֵה־לוֹט
ח וְהַכְּנַעֲנִי וְהַפְּרִזִּי אָז יֹשֵׁב בָּאָרֶץ: וַיֹּאמֶר
אַבְרָם אֶל־לוֹט אַל־נָא תְהִי מְרִיבָה בֵּינִי
וּבֵינֶךָ וּבֵין רֹעַי וּבֵין רֹעֶיךָ כִּי־אֲנָשִׁים

separated by great ideological differences as alluded to by the Sages who interpreted the phrase [*v.* 11] וַיִּסַּע לוֹט מִקֶּדֶם as meaning that Lot removed himself [מִקַּדְמוֹן] from the Ancient One of the Universe saying 'I desire neither Abraham nor his God.' And on *v.* 14: 'As long as the wicked Lot was in Abraham's company God did not communicate with Abraham ...

Therefore our verse is to be interpreted: The land could not support them to dwell together because of their abundant possessions; וְלֹא יָכְלוּ לָשֶׁבֶת יַחְדָּו, neither could they themselves dwell together because of the ideological differences which separated them *(R' Eliezer of Germizah; Malbim).*

7. וַיְהִי רִיב . . . וְהַכְּנַעֲנִי וְהַפְּרִזִּי אָז יֹשֵׁב בָּאָרֶץ — *And there was quarreling between the herdsmen of Abram's flocks and* [*between*] *the herdsmen of Lot's flocks — And the Canaanite and the Perizites were then dwelling in the land.*

They quarreled because Lot's shepherds were wicked and they grazed their flocks on other people's pastures. When Abraham's shepherds rebuked them for this act of robbery, Lot's shepherds contended that they were within their rights because the land had been given to Abraham [12:7]. Since Abraham was childless, Lot was his heir; therefore, it was not robbery. The Torah specifically negates their contention by stating *'the Canaanites and Perizzites were then dwelling in the land'* to emphasize that Abraham was not yet the legitimate owner *(Rashi).*[1]

[Thus, according to the Sages, the quarrels were of a moral nature, concerning the definition of robbery]. According to the plain meaning, however, the quarrels were political and economic: The land could not bear them both and Lot's herdsmen would graze their cattle in Abraham's territory. Since Abraham and Lot were both strangers in the country, Abraham was afraid that their quarrels would draw the unfavorable attention of the Canaanites and Perizzites who inhabited the land, to the large number of foreign-owned cattle which were being pastured in the land. The result could be that both

1. This is elaborated upon more fully in the *Midrash:*

Abraham's cattle would go out to pasture muzzled [so as not to graze in other's fields] whereas those of Lot were not muzzled. Abraham's herdsmen would chide them: 'Has then robbery been permitted?' To which Lot's herdsmen would reply: 'Thus did God say to Abraham *'Unto your descendents will I give this land'*, and Abraham is as barren as a mule who cannot beget children. Therefore when Abraham dies, Lot will be his heir; even if they eat [of other's pastures] they are eating their own [because the land will ultimately be theirs.]'

XIII
7-8

7 *And there was quarreling between the herdsmen of*
Abram's flocks and the herdsmen of Lot's flocks —
and the Canaanites and the Perizzites were then
dwelling in the land.
8 *So Abram said to Lot: 'Please let there be no strife*
between me and you, and between my herdsmen and

Abraham and Lot would be driven out or slain *(Ramban).*

[In another interpretation, *Chizkuni* explains that the quarrels resulted because each had large herds but neither could enlarge his pastures because the Canaanites and Perizzites who were then in the land.]

Ramban continues that the life style of the Canaanites and Perizzites was typical of the nomads who dwelt in Canaan. The Canaanites and Perizzites אָז, *then,* lived there because their travels brought them there; but in later years the Jebusites and Emorites would wander there.

הַפְּרִזִּי — *The Perizzites.*

According to *Ibn Ezra,* Perizzi was one of the sons of Canaan [see 10:15-18] under a different name.

[They were called Perizzi because they lived in פְּרָזוֹת, 'open, unwalled villages,' indicating that peace prevailed and they had no fear of attack. The commentators explain that the phrase יֹשֵׁב בָּאָרֶץ, *were dwelling in the land,* indicates that although Canaanites and Perizzites had no great affinity for one another, they still dwelled together peacefully — in marked contrast to the feuds developing between Abraham and Lot. Abraham feared that the Canaanites and Perizzites might feel threatened by his and Lot's presence and, as a result, would unite against them *(Malbim; Kesses haSofer).*

8. וַיֹּאמֶר אַבְרָם אֶל־לוֹט — *So* [lit. *'and'*] *Abram said to Lot.*

Scripture speaks in praise of Abraham. Although it was arrogant and presumptuous of Lot to cause affront to Abraham, his protector and teacher, Abraham nevertheless pleaded with him *'let there be no strife.'* What is more, Abraham gave Lot the choice to settle wherever he wished *(Akeidas Yitzchak).*

אַל־נָא תְהִי מְרִיבָה בֵּינִי וּבֵינֶךָ — *Please let there be no strife between me and you.*

Malbim explains the difference between רִיב and מְרִיבָה, the two terms for *strife* found in *vs.* 7 and 8: רִיב is the actual dispute while מְרִיבָה is the *cause* of the strife. In this ause, Abraham explains that it was

God said to them: 'I have said that I give the land to his descendants. When? — When the seven nations are uprooted from it [see 15:18*ff*]. Meanwhile, however, *the Canaanites and Perizzites were then dwelling in the land.'*

[The version in *Pesikta Rabbasi* concludes: '... I promised the land to *Abraham's* descendants, and not to this wicked man (Lot), as you imagine ... and only when I drive the Canaanite and Perizzite from its midst. Abraham has still not been given children and the Canaanite and Perizzite are still the rightful owners, and you still say thus?]

ט אַחִים אֲנָחְנוּ׃ הֲלֹא כָל־הָאָרֶץ לְפָנֶיךָ
הִפָּרֶד נָא מֵעָלָי אִם־הַשְּׂמֹאל וְאֵימִנָה
י וְאִם־הַיָּמִין וְאַשְׂמְאִילָה׃ וַיִּשָּׂא־לוֹט אֶת־

because he and Lot were *kinsmen* — and therefore lived together — that disharmony developed. The land was large and rich enough to support them both had they lived separately. But because they were close relatives, they chose to live together resulting in competition over grazing land.

'In the future, when one of us selects a pasture let not the other claim it and cause strife' *(Sforno).*

The *Midrash* infers from this that just as there was strife between their herdsmen, so was there strife between Abraham and Lot themselves.

וּבֵין רֹעַי וּבֵין רֹעֶיךָ — *And between my herdsman and [between] your herdsmen.*

Now, while we still dwell here together *(Sforno).*

כִּי־אֲנָשִׁים אַחִים אֲנָחְנוּ — *For we are kinsmen* [lit. *'men who are brothers'*].

[And as such we should be expected to live in harmony.]

The fact that we are related makes our quarrels a source of embarrassment. Our neighbors will say: They cannot even dwell peacefully and tolerate one another as brother — how will they then act to strangers? They are a wicked people! *(B'chor Shor).*

According to *Malbim,* their quarrels were *because* they were kinsmen.

The translation *kinsmen* for the Hebrew אַחִים, lit. *brothers,* follows *Rashi.*

Pirkei d'Rabbi Eliezer comments: Was Lot his brother? Was he not his nephew? — It teaches that a brother's son is like one's own brother.

[Cf. also *Rashi's comm.* in 20:12 where Abraham referred to Sarah as his *sister.*]

See Abraham's magnanimity! Notwithstanding all the quarrels between them, Abraham calls him 'brother'! *(Tanchuma).*

Rashi additionally cites the Midrashic interpretation that Abraham called Lot his brother because they resembled one another.

[Their similarity of appearance will play an important part later in Lot's residence in Sodom and in the war of the kings. See *comm.* to 14:14 and *footnote* to 14:12; and 21:1.]

Referring to the interpretation that the quarrels between Abraham's and Lot's herdsmen were due to the accusation that Lot's herdsmen unlawfully grazed their cattle on private property, *Alshich* explains that Abraham's fear was that since he and Lot resembled one another so closely, people would blame Abraham for the trespasses. Therefore interpret: *'Let there not be strife between us ... because we resemble one another like brothers and others will not differentiate between the wickedness of your herdsmen and the righteousness of mine.'*

9. הֲלֹא כָל־הָאָרֶץ לְפָנֶיךָ הִפָּרֶד־נָא מֵעָלָי — *Is not all the land before you* — as it is before me? *(Radak)* — *Please separate from me.*

According to many commentators [*Rashi; Ibn Ezra; Radak; Ralbag; Akeidas Yitzchak; Abarbanel* etc.,] Abraham gave Lot unrestrained first choice of territories.

[In fact, according to *Rashi* (as explained by the commentators)

XIII your herdsmen, for we are kinsmen. [9] Is not all the
9-10 land before you? Please separate from me: if you go
left then I will go right, and if you go right then I will
go left.'

[10] So Lot raised his eyes and saw the entire plain of

Abraham did not want a total and unbreachable rift between himself and Lot; what he sought was a separation of ways with a promise that he would still come to Lot's aid should it be necessary]:

As *Rashi* comments: But wherever you go I will be near to render assistance in case of need; and so it happened: Lot was ultimately in need of him (see 14:14) and Abraham, indeed came to his aid.

Cf. also *Sefer haYashar;*

'... Please separate from me and choose a place where you may dwell with your cattle and all belonging to you ... But do not be afraid in leaving me, for if anyone will injure you, let me know and I will come to your aid. Only separate from me.'

אִם הַשְּׂמֹאל וְאֵימְנָה וְאִם הַיָּמִין וְאַשְׂמְאִילָה — *If you go left then I will go right, and if you go right then I will go left* [lit. *'if to the left and I go to the right; and if to the right and I go to the left'*] The translation follows *Rashi.*

— Thus: If you go toward the left, I will remain to your right, and if to the right I will remain to your left, always at your disposal in time of need. Abraham thus expressed himself figuratively: 'We are as one body with two arms: If you are the left (weaker) arm, I will be your right (stronger) arm, and *vice versa'* *(Malbim).*

[As paraphrased by *Targum, left* refers to the north, and *right* refers to the south — for, if one faces eastward, (קֵדְמָה=before him) the north will be to his left. Cf. *Psalms* 89:13: צָפוֹן וְיָמִין = *north and south*]. See *footnote* to *v.* 14.]

'If you [are] to the north, I [will be] to the south; but if you [are] to the south I [will be] to the north' *(Onkelos).* [Other editions conclude: וְאַצְפְּנָךְ *and I will cause you to go northerly.*]

Noting that it had been Abraham's intention to remain in the south [see 12:9], *R' Bachya* and the *comm.* to *Midrash* attributed to *Rashi,* explain that what Abraham meant was: 'If you take to the north then I will take to the south; but if you take to the south then אַשְׂמְאִילָה אוֹתְךָ I will cause you to go to the north even against your will', because my herds are many and I must at all cost remain in the south.' This is the interpretation of some editions of *Onkelos* [cited above.]

The above interpretation is also that of the *Midrash:* If you go to the left [north] I go to the south, while if I go to the south you go to the left — so that in either case I go to the south ... Rav Chaninah ben Yitzchak said: It is not written וְאַשְׂמְאֵלָה [intransitive, *I will go left*] but וְאַשְׂמְאִילָה, [transitive, *I will cause another to go left*] — in all events I will make that man [Lot] go to the left.

10. וַיִּשָּׂא לוֹט אֶת־עֵינָיו — *So* [lit. *'and'*] *Lot raised his eyes* — [a com-

עֵינָיו וַיַּרְא אֶת־כָּל־כִּכַּר הַיַּרְדֵּן כִּי כֻלָּהּ
מַשְׁקֶה לִפְנֵי | שַׁחֵת יהוה אֶת־סְדֹם וְאֶת־
עֲמֹרָה כְּגַן־יהוה כְּאֶרֶץ מִצְרַיִם בֹּאֲכָה
יא צֹעַר: וַיִּבְחַר־לוֹ לוֹט אֵת כָּל־כִּכַּר הַיַּרְדֵּן
וַיִּסַּע לוֹט מִקֶּדֶם וַיִּפָּרְדוּ אִישׁ מֵעַל אָחִיו:

mon Biblical expression meaning *looked about*]

Lot found Abraham's argument appealing. He sought an opportunity to leave Abraham and settle in a rich area of the land. *Lot lifted up his eyes* and let himself be guided by whatever appealed to his senses *(Hirsch).*

וַיַּרְא אֶת כָּל־כִּכַּר הַיַּרְדֵּן כִּי כֻלָּהּ מַשְׁקֶה – *And [he] saw the entire plain of the Jordan that it was well watered everywhere.*

From his vantage point atop the mountain where they had encamped [12:8; 13:3] Lot gazed across the whole area, and his gaze rested on the fertile Jordan plain *(Radak).*

[He based his decision only on the fertility of the area and paid no heed to the evil of his future neighbors.]

The term כִּכַּר הַיַּרְדֵּן, *plain* [or: *oval*] *of the Jordan* refers to the lower part of the Jordan valley from the sea of Kinneret to the Dead Sea, including apparently, the region is often referred to in Scriptures by the abbreviated term: הַכִּכָּר, *The Kikkar* [below, *v.* 12; 19:17; *Deut.* 34:3] *Hoffman; Kesses haSofer).*

Well watered — i.e., a land of streams of water *(Rashi).*

לִפְנֵי שַׁחֵת ה׳ אֶת־סְדֹם וְאֶת עֲמֹרָה – *Before HASHEM destroyed Sodom and Amorrah.*

This parenthetical note describes the exceptional fertility of the Jordan plains before the overthrow of the area as described in Ch. 19, as being comparable to *'the garden of HASHEM, like the land of Egypt.'*

כְּגַן ה׳ כְּאֶרֶץ מִצְרַיִם – *Like the garden of HASHEM, like the land of Egypt.*

Like the garden of HASHEM — with respect to trees; *like the land of Egypt* — with respect to seeds [i.e. vegetation] *(Midrash; Rashi).*

[I.e., just as the Garden of Eden was so favorable for trees, because it was watered by four rivers (see 2:10), so was the land of Egypt favorable for plant life in general because it was irrigated by the Nile. This describes the excellence and fertility of the region before God destroyed Sodom.]

Lot chose the area because a land which is so well irrigated is unlikely to be affected by drought and is good for pasture *(Ramban).*[1]

[The successive use of the prefix כ, *like,*

1. *Harav David Feinstein* comments that the basis of Lot's choice should be understood in the light of the *Midrashic* interpretation to the next verse that Lot departed from the Ancient One of the World, i.e., God (see *comm.* to *v.* 11). Lot saw a well watered plain, an area so rich and abundant that there was no need for God's assistance or intervention, nor would its inhabitants be required to pray for God's mercy.

XIII *the Jordan that it was well watered everywhere —*
11 *before* HASHEM *destroyed Sodom and Amorah — like*
the garden of HASHEM, *like the land of Egypt, going*
toward Zoar. [11] *So Lot chose for himself the whole*
plain of the Jordan, and Lot journeyed from the East;
thus they parted, one from another.

with each of two nouns is the Hebrew idiom to express complete similarity. (See *Ibn Ezra* to *Gen,* 18:25, and *Rashi* to *Numb.* 15:15. Cf. also *Sotah* 34b).]

Thus, it does not say *like the land of Babylon,* or *like the land of Assyria* because the Garden of Eden and Egypt are as one, neither of them require dew or rain, but both are irrigated by the overflow of the river. Yet, Eretz Yisrael is even richer, as it says [*Deut.* 11:10]: *For the land which you go in to possess, is not like the land of Egypt (Midrash Aggadah; Midrash haGadol).*

בֹּאֲכָה צֹעַר — *Going toward Zoar* — i.e. until Zoar *(Rashi).*

[The phrase is ambiguous. Many commentators seem to imply that it is part of the parenthetical description of the excellence of the area: *'as the land of Egypt as far as Zoar.'* Others suggest that the phrase reverts to the beginning of the verse and describes what Lot actually saw, the sense of the verse being: *'And Lot lifted up his eyes and saw the whole plain of the Jordan as far as Zoar that it was entirely well watered ...'*]

[*Zoar* is the name of a city to the south of the Dead Sea. (See 14:2 where it is identified with Bela). When God was about to destroy Sodom, Lot was allowed to escape to Zoar, 'a little city'. *Therefore the name of the city was called Zoar* — meaning 'little'.[See *comm.* to 19:22.]

Zoar is also mentioned in *Deut.* 34:3 as being the southernmost locality seen by Moses when he was shown Eretz Yisrael from Mt. Nebo.]

Rashi sums up, following *Horayos* 10b and *Midrash,* that, as pointed out above, the verse is interpreted to Lot's discredit. Lot followed his sensuous gaze, and chose this locale because its inhabitants were steeped in immorality.

11. וַיִּבְחַר־לוֹ לוֹט — *So* [lit. *'and'*] *Lot chose for himself.*

The inhabitants of the area pleased him although they were wicked. He *himself* chose the place, and did not consult with Abraham *(Da'as Soferim).*

... As *Tanchuma* notes: he perceived how debauched the Sodomites were and chose to be like them.

וַיִּסַּע לוֹט מִקֶּדֶם — *And Lot journeyed from the east.*

This translation follows *Rashi* and *Ibn Ezra,* i.e., he traveled in a westerly direction from Abraham. *Ibn Ezra* maintains that Sodom was thus to the west of Bethel.

But, as *Mizrachi* points out, it is geographically known that the Jordan Valley is the *eastern*most district of Eretz Yisrael while Bethel lay to its *west.* Consequently, Lot had to have traveled in an *easterly* direction. *Mizrachi* leaves the question unresolved.

[Perhaps, it is this very difficulty that leads *Rashi* to cite the *Midrashic* interpretation which interprets קֶדֶם here as a reference to

Conversely, during Israel's formative years in the Wilderness, God gave the manna day by day rather than once a year or once a month, in order to teach the people that they must look to Him constantly for their sustenance.

יב אַבְרָם יָשַׁב בְּאֶרֶץ־כְּנָעַן וְלוֹט יָשַׁב בְּעָרֵי
יג הַכִּכָּר וַיֶּאֱהַל עַד־סְדֹם: וְאַנְשֵׁי סְדֹם
יד רָעִים וְחַטָּאִים לַיהוָה מְאֹד: וַיהוָה אָמַר

God as the קַדְמוֹנוֹ שֶׁל עוֹלָם, the Ancient One of the Universe: Lot wandered away from the *Ancient One of the World*, saying: I want neither Abram nor his God! (Cf. similar interpretation of מִקֶּדֶם in 11:2).]

Several commentators attempt to harmonize *Rashi's* interpretation with the geographical difficulties. *Taz* suggests that Lot was ashamed to reveal to Abraham that he had chosen to dwell with the licentious people of Sodom. He therefore initially *journeyed from the east* — in a westerly direction so Abraham would not realize his destination; only later, after he was far away, did Lot turn around and head east to Sodom, avoiding Abraham. (See also *Malbim*).

Sifsei Chachamim suggests that the plains of the Jordan really encompassed a wide area, parts of which extended to the west of Bethel, so in a sense Lot did indeed travel west [but this apparently sidesteps the issue because in any event Lot's destination was Sodom, which was to the *east* of Bethel].

Radak suggests that in reality Lot journeyed *easterly* — the prefix מ in מִקֶּדֶם having the significance of a ב, *in* the east. Thus, the verse would be interpreted as if it read אֶל מִקֶּדֶם, *to the easterly regions.* For a similar construction, cf. *Josh.* 15:3: וְיָצָא אֶל־מִנֶּגֶב, *and it went out to the south side* (*Karnei Ohr*).

It has been also suggested that the rendering of the *Targum* וּנְטַל לוֹט מִלְקַדְמִין relates the word מִקֶּדֶם to קְדִימַת זְמַן, referring to an early time, the sense of the phrase therefore being: *And Lot departed first* (ibid.).

וַיִּפָּרְדוּ אִישׁ מֵעַל אָחִיו — *Thus* [lit. *'and'*] *they departed one from another* [lit. *'man from upon his brother'*].

There is great prophetic significance to this statement. Lot, in whom were hidden the sparks which would one day produce Ruth, the mother of Israel's royal family (see *Overview*, ArtScroll edition of *Ruth*), did not remain in the Camp of the Shechinah. *He departed from Abram,* and in time the rift would become absolute and irreversible, reaching the point where his male descendants would be prohibited from entering the congregation of Israel [*Deut.* 23:4: *An Ammonite or Moabite* (they were descended from Lot) *shall not enter the assembly of* HASHEM] (*Pesikta Zutresa*).

12. אַבְרָם יָשַׁב בְּאֶרֶץ־כְּנָעַן — *Abram remained* [lit. *dwelt*] *in the land of Canaan* — i.e. in the remainder of the land, in the areas not occupied by Lot. Abraham did not dwell in one place but roamed about (*Ralbag*).

[The verse seems to imply that only Abraham, not Lot, lived in Canaan — but Sodom was also part of the land of Canaan!] *Sforno* suggests that Canaan is differentiated from Sodom because the Sodomites were not of the family of Canaanites. In any event Abraham chose to dwell among the Canaanites who were at least not as wicked (see next verse) as were the Sodomites.

In a more positive vein, the *Zohar* perceives Abraham's remaining in Canaan as indicative of his desire to cling to the place which was to become the fountainhead of faith — Eretz Yisrael — and to learn wisdom so he could cleave to his Maker. Lot, on the other hand, *dwelt in the cities of the plain and pitched his tents as*

12 *Abram remained in the land of Canaan while Lot settled in the cities of the plain and pitched his tents as far as Sodom.* 13 *Now the people of Sodom were wicked and sinful toward HASHEM, exceedingly.*

far as Sodom, among the sinners who abandoned all faith. Thus, each chose a path befitting his own particular nature.

וְלוֹט יָשַׁב בְּעָרֵי הַכִּכָּר – *While* [lit. *'and'*] *Lot settled* [lit. *'dwelt'*] *in the cities of the Plain.* [i.e. while Lot limited himself to the cities of the plain which he had chosen].

The plural *cities* indicates that Lot, too, did not always dwell in one city. Due to the need to find adequate pasture for his many cattle, he roamed about within that region *(Ramban).*

וַיֶּאֱהַל עַד־סְדֹם – *And pitched his tents as far as* [lit. *until*] *Sodom.*

He pitched tents for his shepherds throughout the area, extending as far as Sodom *(Rashi).*

According to *Radak:* He roamed from place to place, constantly changing the site of his tents until he reached Sodom.

Until Sodom, but not actually in *Sodom,* ... as it is written [19:1]: *and Lot sat in the gate of Sodom.* His house was in the gate of the city from without *(Chizkuni).*

[See, however, the *comm.* to the same word in *v.* 17, below.]

13. וְאַנְשֵׁי סְדֹם רָעִים וְחַטָּאִים – *Now* [lit. *'and'*] *the people of Sodom were wicked and sinful.* And yet, Lot did not refrain from living with them ... They were *wicked* with their bodies [i.e., adulterous], and *sinful* with their money [by withholding financial assistance from the poor] *(Rashi* following Rav Yehudah in *Sanhedrin* 109a; *Targum,* following the first Tanna, reverses the interpretation).

An additional purpose of telling of the wickedness of the Sodomites, besides accusing Lot of not restraining himself from dwelling with them as *Rashi* explained, is the simultaneous implication of Abraham's merit in that *his* lot did not fall to be among the wicked *(Ramban).*

From the continuity of these verses [after the mention of Sodom, the wickedness of its inhabitants is stressed] the *Talmud (Yoma* 38b) derives the proper application of the text [*Prov.* 10:7] וְשֵׁם רְשָׁעִים יִרְקָב *'and the name of the wicked shall rot'* [viz., that whenever the name of the wicked is mentioned it should be followed by a term of opprobrium] *(Rashi).*

לַה' מְאֹד – *Toward HASHEM exceedingly.*

They knew their Master and yet deliberately rebelled against Him *(Rashi).*

Toward HASHEM — by practicing idolatry *(Tosefta Sanhedrin* 13).

[Cf. *comm.* to Artscroll ed. of *Ezekiel* 9:15.]

Since the Canaanites were themselves steeped in wickedness and sin, the Torah adds, when describing the Sodomites' sinfulness, the adjective מְאֹד, *exceedingly.* This emphasizes that their wickedness exceeded even that of the Canaanites. It will be described in more detail later *(Abarbanel).*

אֶל־אַבְרָם אַחֲרֵי הִפָּרֶד־לוֹט מֵעִמּוֹ שָׂא־
נָא עֵינֶיךָ וּרְאֵה מִן־הַמָּקוֹם אֲשֶׁר־אַתָּה
טו שָׁם צָפֹנָה וָנֶגְבָּה וָקֵדְמָה וָיָמָּה: כִּי אֶת־
כָּל־הָאָרֶץ אֲשֶׁר־אַתָּה רֹאֶה לְךָ אֶתְּנֶנָּה
טז וּלְזַרְעֲךָ עַד־עוֹלָם: וְשַׂמְתִּי אֶת־זַרְעֲךָ

14. The Repetition of the Promise

After Lot's departure from Abraham, God repeats His promise [12:7] to emphasize that it had been given exclusively to Abraham and his descendants *(Hoffman).*

אַחֲרֵי הִפָּרֶד לוֹט מֵעִמּוֹ — *After Lot had parted from him.*

— This is mentioned because as long as the wicked [Lot] was in his company, the word [of God] departed from him *(Rashi).*[1]

Rashi's interpretation is derived from *Tanchuma Yashan Vayetze* 8; and *Pesikta Rabbasi* 3:3.

The commentators note the obvious difficulty in this interpretation because, in 12:1 and 12:7, God plainly *did* communicate with Abraham although Lot was in his company.

Among the answers offered are:

— The earlier communications took place when Lot was still righteous. Only after he became wicked and *'wandered away from God'* [see on *v.* 11], did God refrain from speaking to Abraham. Now that Lot was no longer with Abraham, the communication resumed *(Moshav Zekeinim, Paaneach Raza).*

— The intent of *Rashi's* interpretation is that as long as Lot accompanied him Abraham did not receive *as lengthy and detailed a communication* as he did now *(Bertinoro; Akeidas Yitzchak).*

Sforno points out that this renewed promise of the Land could come only after Lot's departure. Had Lot still been with him, the Promise would have inflamed Lot's mercenary instinct still further and led to robbery on an even greater scale.

According to *Abarbanel,* God chose that moment to renew His assurance because Abraham may then have been depressed by the departure of his nephew whom he had loved dearly and regarded as the probable heir, through whom the Divine promise would to be fulfilled. God therefore communicated this prophecy to gladden him and reassure him of abundant progeny who would inherit the land.

שָׂא־נָא עֵינֶיךָ וּרְאֵה ... — *Raise now* [*v.* on נָא in 12:13] *your eyes and look out* [lit. *'see'*] *from* [*the place*] *where you are.*

— He did not even have to move from that spot! God caused him miraculously to view the entire land *from his present vantage point.* In this respect Abraham was greater even than Moses who, before he was shown the land, was told to *'get up to the top of Pisgah'* [*Deut.* 3:27] *(Midrash; Sifri).*

[See *Radak* next verse].

1. *Rav Yehudah* said: God was angry with Abraham when Lot parted from him. He said: 'He causes everyone else to cleave to Me except Lot, his brother.'

Rav Nechemiah maintained, that on the contrary, He was wroth with Abraham because he allowed Lot to *accompany* him! God said, 'Unto *your seed* have I given this land [15:18], yet he attaches Lot to himself as his heir! He might just as well bring two soldiers from the marketplace [and proclaim them his heirs, as he does his nephew!'] *(Midrash).*

[14] *HASHEM said to Abram after Lot had parted
from him, 'Raise now your eyes and look out from
where you are: northward, southward, eastward and
westward.* [15] *For all the land that you see, to you will
I give it, and to your descendants forever.* [16] *I will*

צָפֹנָה ... וָיָמָּה — *Northward ... and Westward.*[1].

Precise boundaries are not given, but the implication is broader than that of the first promise [12:7]. As Abraham's merits increased, he would be given yet another assurance in which the full extent of the Land would be revealed to him [15:18-21] *(Da'as Soferim).*

[The above follows those who interpret that the sequence of the promises in 12:7, here, and 15:18 are in chronological order. This is not the view followed by *Seder Olam* according to which the promise in 15:18 — as part of the Covenant Between the Parts — *preceded* the events of this chapter by five years (though it appears later in the Torah). See *comm.* to 15:7.]

15. כִּי אֶת־כָּל־הָאָרֶץ אֲשֶׁר אַתָּה רֹאֶה — *For all the land that you see* — including the Jordan plains which you gave to Lot *(Chizkuni).*

Bethel, where Abraham was standing, is in the central region of the Land. From that vantage point he was afforded a magnificent panoramic view of the whole country *(Hoffmann).*

לְךָ אֶתְּנֶנָּה וּלְזַרְעֲךָ — *To you will I give it, and to your descendants* [lit. *'seed'*], i.e., take possession of the gift now in order to bequeath it to your descendants, as our Sages have said [*Bava Basra* 119b]: 'Eretz Yisrael is an inheritance to the people of Israel from their Patriarchs'. According to the plain meaning of Scripture, the intent is: Even now you will be greatly honored by the inhabitants of the country as a ruler of the land *(Ramban; Sforno).*

To you will I give it — at the Covenant between the Parts [Ch. 15] *(Ha'amek Davar).*

[Or, according to the view (see 15:7) that the Covenant Between the Parts *preceded* this promise, the expression *to you will I give it* means: in fulfillment of the Covenant Between the Parts.]

עַד עוֹלָם — *Forever.*

Though they were exiled from it, they will eventually return to it. Thus it will be theirs forever even though they may not always occupy it *(Radak).*

As *Hirsch* comments, by this promise God does not proclaim that the Land will always be *in their possession,* but that they and the land will always be destined for one another, just as here it was given to Abraham without his ever taking possession of it.

1. [צָפוֹן means *'hidden'* and hence 'north' because the sun is 'hidden' and does not shine there as it does in the warmer, clearer south;
נֶגֶב means *'dry'* and hence refers to the 'south' because of the drier climate of *Eretz Yisrael*'s souther desert (see on 12:9);
קֶדֶם means *'before', 'first',* or *'early',* thus indicating the 'east' where the sun first rises;
יָמָּה means *'sea'.* It refers to the west because the 'Sea' is to the west of *Eretz Yisrael.*]

בַּעֲפַר הָאָרֶץ אֲשֶׁר | אִם־יוּכַל אִישׁ
לִמְנוֹת אֶת־עֲפַר הָאָרֶץ גַּם־זַרְעֲךָ יִמָּנֶה׃
יז קוּם הִתְהַלֵּךְ בָּאָרֶץ לְאָרְכָּהּ וּלְרָחְבָּהּ כִּי
יח לְךָ אֶתְּנֶנָּה׃ וַיֶּאֱהַל אַבְרָם וַיָּבֹא וַיֵּשֶׁב
בְּאֵלֹנֵי מַמְרֵא אֲשֶׁר בְּחֶבְרוֹן וַיִּבֶן־שָׁם

16. וְשַׂמְתִּי אֶת־זַרְעֲךָ כַּעֲפַר הָאָרֶץ — *[And] I will make* [lit. *'place'*] *your offspring* [lit. *'seed'*] *as the dust of the earth.*

Clearly, the verse does not refer to an enormous Jewish population during any particular generation. Jews were never *consistently* prominent numerically — cf. *Deut.* 7:7: *It is not because you are more numerous ... indeed, you are the fewest of all peoples.* Rather our verse refers to the countless total of all the generations of an immortal nation which will flourish throughout history *(Hirsch).*[1]

Hirsch contines that עָפָר, *dust,* is the basic material of earthly existence. From it, all is built and ultimately all return to it. Not an atom of it is ever lost. It is this property of dust which is used as an analogy for the seed of Abraham.

אֲשֶׁר אִם־יוּכַל אִישׁ לִמְנוֹת אֶת עֲפַר הָאָרֶץ — *So that if one can count the dust of the earth* — [an obvious impossiblity] ...

גַּם־זַרְעֲךָ יִמָּנֶה — *Then* [lit. *'and'*] *your offspring* [lit. *'seed'*], *too, can be counted.* And just as it is impossible for the dust to be counted, so will it be impossible to count your offspring *(Rashi).*

This divine promise, in its literal sense, refers to Messianic times when Jews will be numerous as foretold in *Hosea* 2:1: *Yet the number ot the children of Israel shall be like the sand of the sea which cannot be measured nor numbered (Lekach Tov).*

[Cf. also the description of the Jewish nation during King Solomon's reign *(I Kings* 4:20): *Judah and Israel were many, as the sand which is by the sea in abundance; they ate, they drank, and were happy.*]

17. קוּם הִתְהַלֵּךְ בָּאָרֶץ לְאָרְכָּהּ וּלְרָחְבָּהּ — *Arise, walk about the Land through its length and breadth.*

Ramban offers two interpretations:

1. The comparison to *dust of the earth* is explained in the *Midrash:*
— Just as the dust of the earth is found from one end of the world to the other, so shall your children be found from one end of the world to the other:
— As the dust of the earth can be blessed only through water, so will your children be blessed for the sake of Torah which is likened to water [cf. *Isaiah* 55:1];
— As the dust of the earth wears out even metal utensils yet itself endures forever, so will Israel exist forever while the nations of the world will cease to be;
— As the dust of the earth is trodden upon, so will your children be downtrodden under the heel of foreign powers ...
— But as the dust outlives those who tread upon it, so God said to Abraham, shall your sons outlive the nations of the world that persecute them.

make your offspring as the dust of the earth so that if one can count the dust of the earth, then your offspring, too, can be counted. [17] *Arise, walk about the Land through its length and breadth! For to you will I give it.'* [18] *And Abram moved his tent and came to dwell in the plains of Mamre which are in Hebron;*

(a) This was not a *command* to Abraham that he walk through the Land. Rather it was a *promise* of God's protection, telling Abraham that he could feel free to get up and walk fearlessly throughout the land כִּי לְךָ אֶתְּנֶנָּה, *for to you will I give it,* i.e., eventually it would be his;

(b) This *was* a command. The act of walking through the Land would denote taking possession of the gift [see on 12:6]. Abraham was now in the east; when he later went to the land of the Philistines in the west, he thereby fulfilled the command.

[*Ramban's* second interpretation is based upon a controversy recorded in *Bava Basra* 100a. According to Rav Eliezer, our verse proves that walking through the length and breadth of a newly purchased field constitutes a legal mode of acquiring possession. According to the Sages, walking is of no avail unless one has already taken possession of the land through חֲזָקָה (by performing some act of ownership such as leveling, fencing, breaking, etc. — see *Choshen Mishpat* 192). According to them, God commanded Abraham to walk through the Land in His love for him that his children might more easily conquer the country (i.e., the walk was merely a loving *symbol* of Abraham's acquisition, like a landowner surveying his fields, intimating that his descendants would enter as heirs and not as robbers, and also forestalling future complaints by Satan and the Attribute of Justice (*Rashbam*).]

18. וַיֶּאֱהַל אַבְרָם — *And Abram moved his tent.*

[The word וַיֶּאֱהַל conjugated from the noun אֹהֶל, *tent,* could be literally rendered, *'and he tented'.* It is often rendered, according to the context, as *'and he pitched his tent'* (*v.* 12 above). The sequence of verbs in our verse, as explained by the commentators, rules out such a translation]:

'The verse should have read: וַיָּבֹא... וַיֶּאֱהַל, *and he came... and pitched his tent,* not וַיֶּאֱהַל ... וַיָּבֹא, *and he pitched his tent ... and came.* Hence, the meaning of וַיֶּאֱהַל in our verse is not *and he pitched his tent,* rather it describes the action of *dismantling* his tent. It is not unusual in Hebrew for a word to have opposite meanings (*Lekach Tov; Chizkuni*).

[Following *Rashi's* commentary to וַיֶּאֱהַל in *v.* 12 rendering *'and he extended his tents',* we might offer an alternate interpretation: Abraham's wealth was of such magnitude that his shepherds and cattle required tents extending as far as Hebron, which he made his new home. Or, following *Radak,* we can render here: Abram roamed about, constantly changing the site of his tents until he finally settled in Hebron.]

בְּאֵלֹנֵי מַמְרֵא אֲשֶׁר בְּחֶבְרוֹן — *In the plains of Mamre which are in Hebron.*

—Mamre was the name of the owner (*Rashi*).

— He was an Emorite, as it says

מִזְבֵּחַ לַיהוָה:

°רביעי א °וַיְהִי בִּימֵי אַמְרָפֶל מֶלֶךְ־שִׁנְעָר אַרְיוֹךְ
מֶלֶךְ אֶלָּסָר כְּדָרְלָעֹמֶר מֶלֶךְ עֵילָם

[14:13]: *And he dwelt at the plains of Mamre, the Emorite, brother of Eshkol and brother of Aner.* However, whenever the Torah mentions Mamre alone rather than the *plains* of Mamre — as in 23:19 and 35:27 — it refers to the name of a city *(Ramban* to 12:6).

[The translation 'plains' for אֵלֹנֵי follows the *Targumim.* See *comm.* to אֵלוֹן in 12:6.]

Ramban in 14:6 discusses the etymology of this word. He cites *Isaiah 6:13* כָּאֵלָה וְכָאַלּוֹן [*'as a terebirth and as an oak'*] where the reference is to various trees, also *Ezek.* 27:6. He concludes that the correct translation of אֵלֹנֵי מַמְרֵא would be *'the oaks of Mamre'.* Nevertheless, Onkelos translates 'the *plain* of Mamre', meaning a plain containing Oak trees. This is in keeping with his method of conveying the *general intent and meaning of a verse* rather than translating the words literally.

[In *Wars of the Jews* IV 9:7, Josephus speaks of 'a very large turpentine tree six furlongs from Hebron. As the report goes, this tree has existed since the creation of the world.']

[Even today there is a tree which the Arabs revere as the 'Oak of Abraham.']

[Hebron, also called Kiryat Arba (23:2, 35:27), was an important city. According to *Numbers* 13:22 it was 'seven years older than Zoar in Egypt.' As shown in our verse Abraham resided there, and it was there that he buried Sarah in the Cave of Machpelah, and he himself was buried there. Later, Isaac and Rebeccah, and Jacob and Leah were also buried there. It ultimately became one of the עָרֵי מִקְלָט, *cities of refuge (Josh.* 20:7).

It was in Hebron that David was anointed and where he resided until the conquest of Jerusalem *(II Sam.* 2:11; 3:2*ff*; 5:1). Absalom's revolt began there *(ibid.* 15:7*ff).*

According to *Nehemiah* 11:25 Hebron was one of the towns which possessed a Jewish community after the return of the exiles from Babylon.]

וַיִּבֶן־שָׁם מִזְבֵּחַ לַה׳ — *And he built there an altar to HASHEM.*

To express his gratitude for the prophecy God had just given him [as in 12:7] *(Abarbanel).*

And to *'call upon the name of HASHEM'* and rally people to His *service [as explained in 12:8] (Radak).*

Or, wherever he built an altar, as he did here his mission became clearer to him *(Hirsch).*

XIV

◆§ The War of the Kings

Prefatory summary

[It is twenty-eight years after the Dispersion. Unsuccessful in unifying his kingdom by building the Tower, Nimrod (identified with Amraphel in *v.* 1) reigns over only Shinar (Babylon). Chedorlaomer (identified with Elam son of Shem), built an empire under his former name, Elam, and subjugated many other provinces — including Sodom and Amorrah, forcing them to pay tribute.

But peace did not last long. In the following narrative we learn how the kings of Sodom and Amorrah together with three other kings, rebelled for thirteen years.

In the fourteenth year, Chedorlaomer and three other kings allied with him took the initiative in crushing the revolt. They did not take the direct route to Sodom, but marched through the entire east of Eretz Yisrael southward toward Edom. In a display of might, probably designed to instill their dread in the inhabitants of the region and to bolster the morale of the soldiers, they conquered everything *en route,* taking spoils from the nations listed in *vs.* 5 and 6 who were probably allied with the five kings. Only then did they turn back northwards to their intended goal of Sodom.

The battle took place in the Valley of Siddim, and it was here that the first punish-

XIV and he built there an altar to HASHEM.

1 And it happened in the days of Amraphel, king of Shinar; Arioch, king of Ellasar; Chedorlaomer,

ment befell the wicked Sodomites who had always lived in luxurious tranquility in their blessed land. In history's oldest account of kings and wars, the five kings were quickly beaten and their treasures — which were always jealously guarded by the wicked Sodomites lest anyone derive pleasure from them — were carried away by strangers. Ironically, even Lot — who left Abraham to partake of the sensuous luxuries of Sodom — lost all his wealth and was himself carried away.

When Abraham became aware that his nephew Lot was a captive, he led his faithful followers and fearlessly pursued the four mighty kings who had by this time already vanquished twelve nations!

He pursued them as far as Chovah/Dan where his strength waned because he prophetically perceived that his descendants would one day erect an idol there. He pursued the aggressor kings no further, content that they had at least been driven from the Land.

Thus, the righteous Abraham, aided by heavenly forces, became the savior of Lot and the wicked Sodomites, and freed them and their possessions.

On returning from his defeat of the kings, Abraham was met by the king of Sodom who offered that Abraham keep the goods he recaptured.

But Abraham insisted that he will accept no personal benefit from bloodshed. War may sometimes be necessary to safeguard human life but it is not to be glorified. Abraham refused to take from the king of Sodom *even a thread or a shoe-strap, lest the king boast 'I have made Abraham rich.'*

Abraham thus disavowed all ungodly purposes, and thereby demonstrated that all his actions were selflessly motivated.]

1. וַיְהִי בִּימֵי — *And it happened in the days.*

Wherever we find in the Bible the term וַיְהִי בִּימֵי, *and it happened in the days,* it indicates the approach of trouble. Thus: *It happened in the days of Amraphel ... they made war.* [Cf also *Esther* 1:1, *Ruth* 1:1] (*Megillah* 10b).

The chronology according to *Seder Olam* (following *Ya'avetz)* is:

Abraham was forty-eight years old at the time of the Dispersion (1996). In the following year, the various cities were populated, and Chedorlaomer subjugated the five kings for a period of twelve years (2009). They revolted for thirteen years (until 2022) and in the fourteenth year (2023), coinciding with the year Abraham left Charan at the age of seventy-five (he was born in 1948), the war between the kings broke out. This occurred after Abraham had left Egypt (as related in Ch. 13). The Egyptian episode — from the time he left Eretz Yisrael until he returned — took three months.

[According to *Tosafos Berachos* 7b (as noted in *Additional Note "A")* the war occurred when Abraham was seventy-three years old. But according to this version, these events would have occurred during Abraham's *first* stay in Eretz Yisrael. Accordingly, it must be assumed that Lot accompanied Abraham back to Charan after his escapade in Sodom, ready for an amicable re-departure from Charan back to Canaan together with Abraham two years later (12:4). Because the text lends itself to this interpretation only with great difficulty, most commentators agree that the war occurred when Abraham was seventy-five. See *Hagahos* of Rav Elazar Hurwitz to Vilna ed. of *Berachos* 7b.]

אַמְרָפֶל — *Amraphel.*

He is identified with Nimrod [see 10:8ff; it was he who cast Abram into the furnace of Ur Kasdim, and

ב וְתִדְעָל מֶלֶךְ גּוֹיִם: עָשׂוּ מִלְחָמָה אֶת־
בֶּרַע מֶלֶךְ סְדֹם וְאֶת־בִּרְשַׁע מֶלֶךְ עֲמֹרָה
שִׁנְאָב | מֶלֶךְ אַדְמָה וְשֶׁמְאֵבֶר מֶלֶךְ
ג צבוים° וּמֶלֶךְ בֶּלַע הִיא־צֹעַר: כָּל־אֵלֶּה

°צְבוֹיִם ק׳

as related in the *comm.* to 11:4, it was he who initiated the scheme to build the Tower in rebellion against God.] As the *Talmud* notes, he was called Amraphel because he said [אָמַר] to Abram: 'Plunge [פּוּל] into the fiery furnace! [אָמַר = אַמְרָפֶל וְהִפִּיל] *(Rashi; Tanchuma; Eruvin* 53a; cf. the *Midrash).*

Chedorlaomer was the primary and most important of these kings as indicated in *v.* 5 'the kings who were *with him',* implying that the others were subservient to him. Nevertheless, in placing the incident in its historical perspective, Scripture speaks of Amraphel because he was the senior member of the alliance *(Paaneach Raza; Tur).*

שִׁנְעָר — *Shinar* — i.e. Babylon *(Targum).*

Babylon and Shinar are synonymous as is evident from 11:2 and 11:9 where it is explicitly stated that Shinar was called בָּבֶל, *Babel,* because the confusion of languages that happened there *(Nesinah laGer).*

[Cf. also *Rashi* to 6:17 (vol I p. 234) where he cites the *Talmud, Shabbos* 113b, that Babylonia is also called Shinar because all those who died in the Flood were shaken out there (שֶׁנִּנְעֲרוּ שָׁם).]

אַרְיוֹךְ מֶלֶךְ אֶלָּסָר — *Arioch, king of Ellasar.*

According to the *Midrash,* Ellasar refers to Greece. [The Greek name for Greece is Ellas.]

כְּדָרְלָעֹמֶר מֶלֶךְ עֵילָם — *Chedorlaomer king of Elam.*

He is identified in the *Midrash* with Elam, son of Shem, son of Noah.

וְתִדְעָל מֶלֶךְ גּוֹיִם — *And Tidal, king of Goiim.*

Goiim [lit. *'nations'*] was the name of a place which derived its name from its inhabitants who were of many nations and localities. They gathered there and proclaimed Tidal as their king *(Midrash; Rashi).*

Onkelos, however, interprets גּוֹיִם not as a proper noun, but, as a descriptive noun. He renders: *And Tidal king of nations.*

According to the *Midrash, Goiim* refers to Rome which levies troops from all nations [גּוֹיִם]. Rav Eleazar bar Abina said: When you see the powers fighting each other, look for the advent [lit. *'feet'*] of the King Messiah. The proof is that in the days of Abraham, because these powers fought against each other, redemption came to him [i.e. he was victorious over them.] [1]

It is not unusual that every city was under the sovereignty of a dif-

1. *Ramban* [drawing from the *Midrash,* and consistent with his interpretation that 'whatever has happened to the patriarchs is a sign to the children' (see *comm.* to 12:6)] perceives that the four kings in the narrative symbolize the four kingdoms who would, in turn, conquer the

XIV
2-3

king of Elam, and Tidal, king of Goiim, 2 *that these*
made war on Bera, king of Sodom; Birsha, king of
Amorah; Shinab, king of Admah; Shemeber, king of
Zeboiim; and the king of Bela, which is Zoar. 3 *All*

ferent king. This was the case even in the days of Joshua [see Ch. 14] *(Hoffman).*

2. עָשׂוּ מִלְחָמָה – *That these made war* [i.e. made a punitive war to squelch the rebellion of the following five kings, as we will learn from the continuing narrative. Or according to the latter majority interpretation cited in the next verse: they invaded territories with the intent of conquering them and making them tributaries.]

בֶּרַע ... בִּרְשַׁע ... שִׁנְאָב ... שֶׁמְאֵבֶר – *Bera ... Birsha ... Shinab ... Shemeber.*

The names are homiletically interpreted as reflecting their wickedness of the kings: *Bera* indicates that he was evil [*'ra'*] towards God and evil towards mankind [i.e., ב׳ רע = בֶּרַע, *two evils*: toward God and man]; *Birsha,* because he rose by means of wickedness [*'resha'*]; *Shinab,* because he hated [*'sana'*] his Father [*'ab*] in Heaven; *Shemeber,* because he made himself wings [*'sam ever'*] to fly, flapping them in rebellion against God *(Rashi; Tanchuma).*

וּמֶלֶךְ בֶּלַע הִיא־צֹעַר – *And the King of Bela, which is Zoar.*

Bela is the name of the city *(Rashi).*

[*Rashi* prevents a possible misinterpretation of the text. Without his comment one could render: *King Bela.* This interpretation is improbable, however, because it renders superfluous the phrase הִיא צֹעַר. (But see *Chomas Anach* below).]

Which is Zoar – [i.e. which later came to be called Zoar, as explained in 19:22.]

Ramban adds that his was a small kingdom consisting of only this one city, hence his name is not mentioned.

Additionally, the names of the other kings are mentioned because they allude to their wickedness; it is possible that the wickedness of the king of Bela = Zoar was not as extreme. No allusion of wickedness was to be derived from his name and hence it is not mentioned. This may also be the reason that Zoar was later spared as a refuge for Lot in the general destruction of Sodom and Amorah.

Chomas Anach suggests that the king may have assumed the name of his kingdom, hence King Bela. [Interestingly, according to *Sefer haYashar* 16:3, Bela was King of Zoar.]

3. כָּל־אֵלֶּה – ***All these.***

[Either: all nine kings mentioned

world and persecute Israel: Shinar, as noted, refers to Babylon; Ellasar refers to Media or Persia; Elam was the city in which the first Greek king, Alexander was crowned and from where his dominion spread over the entire world [see *Avodah Zarah* 10a]; *Goiim* [nations] refers to Rome which held sway over many nations.

Just as Abraham defeated the kings, so would his descendants ultimately defeat their conquerors and retrieve the captives and wealth which had been taken by the enemy.

חֻבְרוּ אֶל־עֵמֶק הַשִּׂדִּים הוּא יָם הַמֶּלַח:
ד שְׁתֵּים עֶשְׂרֵה שָׁנָה עָבְדוּ אֶת־כְּדָרְלָעֹמֶר
ה וּשְׁלֹשׁ־עֶשְׂרֵה שָׁנָה מָרָדוּ: וּבְאַרְבַּע
עֶשְׂרֵה שָׁנָה בָּא כְדָרְלָעֹמֶר וְהַמְּלָכִים
אֲשֶׁר אִתּוֹ וַיַּכּוּ אֶת־רְפָאִים בְּעַשְׁתְּרֹת

in *vss.* 1 and 2; or all the Jordanian allies just mentioned in *v.* 2.]

חֻבְרוּ אֶל־עֵמֶק הַשִּׂדִּים — *Had joined at the Valley of Siddim* — in battle *(Radak; Hirsch).* [The details of the war will be discussed in *v.* 8 after the parenthetical historical background in *vs.* 4-7.]

The above is the minority interpretation. It is shared also by *R' Meyuchas,* and *Hoffman.*

Most commentators, however — e.g. *Ran; Abarbanel; Sforno;* follow *Seder Olam* and perceive this verse as referring to a meeting in the Valley of Siddim to work out the peace accords which were to follow the end of the intial battle. The result was that the five kings agreed to serve and pay tribute to Chedorlaomer, the mightiest of the four victorious monarchs.[1]

עֵמֶק הַשִּׂדִּים, *the Valley of Siddim* was so called because it was full of fields [*sadeh*] *(Rashi).*

According to others *Siddim* refers to the abundance of lime [שִׂיד; cf. *Deut.* 27:2] contained in the area.

הוּא יָם הַמֶּלַח — *Now* [lit. *'that is'*] *the Salt Sea.*

[I.e. this *(Valley of Siddim)* is what later became the Salt Sea, so named because of its unusually high saline content; now known as the Dead Sea because it supports no life *(Me'or haAfelah, cited in Torah Shelemah).*]

4. שְׁתֵּים עֶשְׂרֵה שָׁנָה עָבְדוּ אֶת־כְּדָרְלָעֹמֶר — *Twelve years they* [i.e. the five kings enumerated in the previous verse *(Rashi)*] *served* [i.e. paid tribute to] *Chedorlaomer.*

וּשְׁלֹשׁ עֶשְׂרֵה שָׁנָה מָרָדוּ — *And they rebelled thirteen years* [by withholding their tribute].

This translation follows *Rashi* who goes on to explain that the phrase *'and on the fourteenth year'* in the next verse refers to the fourteenth year of the rebellion, [a total of twenty-six years being accounted for.]

This rendering also agrees with the interpretation of Rav Abin in *Shabbos* 11a, *Onkelos* [in most editions], *Seder Olam,* Rav Yose in the *Midrash, Tosafos Berachos* 7b,

1. *Sforno* interprets these verses as follows:

In the days of the famous Amraphel, King of Shinar, it happened that Arioch, Chedarlaomer and Tidal warred with Bera and his associates, and afterwards [*v.* 3] *all these,* i.e. Amraphel and the two warring sides gathered together in the Valley of Siddim, where the five vanquished kings agreed to serve the victorious Chedorlaomer. This agreement lasted twelve years and then they revolted.

The background is elaborated upon further in *Sefer haYashar, Ran,* and *Abarbanel.* As pieced together, the following emerges:

Nimrod [Amraphel] was the ruler of Babylon. Among his princes was Chedorlaomer. After the Dispersion, Chedorlaomer went to the land of Elam and reigned over it, and rebelled against Nimrod.

these had joined at the Valley of Siddim, now the Salt
Sea. 4 *Twelve years they served Chedorlaomer, and*
they rebelled thirteen years. 5 *In the fourteenth year,*
Chedorlaomer and the kings who were with him
came and struck the Rephaim at Ashtaroth-Karnaim,

and most commentators. Several chronological assertions are derived from this interpretation of the dates, among them *Seder Olam*'s view that the revolt of the five kings coincided with Abraham's first year in Canaan, when he was seventy-five years old [see chronological note in *v.* 1.]

Another possible translation (*Targum Yonasan,* Rav Shimon in the *Midrash, Ibn Ezra, Radak, R' Bachya, Hirsch)* is: *And in the thirteenth year they rebelled.* Accordingly, the phrase *'in the fourteenth year'* would date not from the beginning of the rebellion, but from the year they began serving Chedorlaomer.

Ibn Ezra explains that the above translation interprets the verse as if a prepositional prefix ב, *in,* were implied: [ו(ב)שְׁלֹשׁ עֶשְׂרֵה שָׁנָה, *and (in) the thirteenth year.*] This is similar to the implied preposition implied in *Exod.* 20:11: כִּי (בְ)שֵׁשֶׁת יָמִים עָשָׂה ה׳, *for (in) six days* H*ASHEM made.*

Other commentators — e.g. *Ralbag, Malbim* — suggest both interpretations as being equally possible — and 'we have no definitive determination in this matter.'

5. וּבְאַרְבַּע עֶשְׂרֵה שָׁנָה — [*And*] *in the fourteenth year.*

[Following *Rashi:* of the rebellion, being the *twenty-sixth year* since they first began serving Chedorlaomer; or according to the other interpretation (see above): the *fourteenth year* from when they began serving Chedorlaomer.]

בָּא כְדָרְלָעֹמֶר וְהַמְּלָכִים אֲשֶׁר אִתּוֹ — *Chedorlaomer and the kings who were with him came.*

Chedorlaomer is singled out. Because he was the leader, נִכְנַס בְּעָבְיֵי הַקּוֹרָה, 'he bore [lit. *'entered'*] the heavier side of the beam' [i.e. a *Talmudic* figure of speech meaning: 'he bore the brunt of it']: Since the five kings revolted against Chedorlaomer, he took the initiative, his allies playing a subordinate part *(Midrash; Rashi).*

וַיַּכּוּ — *And [they] struck.*

On the southward march to suppressing the rebellion, Chedorlaomer's forces conquered everything *en passant* and waged war against every nation they encountered whom they suspected of complicity in the rebellion, or who they feared would join the struggle of the five kings *(Hirsch; Malbim).*

רְפָאִים בְּעַשְׁתְּרֹת קַרְנַיִם — *The Rephaim at Ashtaroth-Karnaim.*

The Rephaim were the giants who lived in the northern part of Eretz Yisrael. When the four kings entered Canaan from Shinar /

Nimrod gathered a great army against Chedorlaomer, but Chedorlaomer emerged victorious and succeeded in making an alliance with Nimrod, Arioch, and Tidal who agreed to reign over the whole world with Chedorlaomer as the dominant figure.

At this point Ch. 14 begins. Together, these four kings attacked the five Jordan Valley kings and in a treaty made in the Valley of Siddim they agreed to serve Chedorlaomer in whose territory this area lay. [Cf. *Malbim* and *Me'am Loez* for minor variations.]

קַרְנַיִם וְאֶת־הַזּוּזִים בְּהָם וְאֵת הָאֵימִים
ו בְּשָׁוֵה קִרְיָתָיִם: וְאֶת הַחֹרִי בְּהַרְרָם
שֵׂעִיר עַד אֵיל פָּארָן אֲשֶׁר עַל־הַמִּדְבָּר:
ז וַיָּשֻׁבוּ וַיָּבֹאוּ אֶל־עֵין מִשְׁפָּט הִוא קָדֵשׁ

Babylon they encountered the Rephaim first. These giants were famous even much later. See, for example *Deut.* 3:11: *Only Og, King of Bashan, remained of the remnant of the Rephaim* [i.e. survived the foray against the Rephaim by Amraphel and his allies (see *Rashi* to *v.* 13)]; and *Joshua* 13:12. *Ashteroth-Karnaim* [lit. *'Ashtaroth of the twin-horns'*] was the capital city of Bashan, and is recorded in *Joshua* 12:4 as being the dwelling place of its king, Og *(Hoffman).*

Kesses haSofer comments that the name of the city was derived from the pagan goddess Astarte lying between the horns — i.e. between two mountains [see *Sukkah* 2a where *Rashi,* ad. loc. describes Ashtaroth-Karnaim as a glen between two peaked mountains where the sunlight does not penetrate.]

Onkelos renders Rephaim as גִּבָּרַיָּא, the giants.

They were so named [רְפָאִים is a term used in the Bible to describe the dead — see *Isaiah* 14:9] because their appearance made men's hearts die within them *(Ibn Ezra).*

וְאֶת הַזּוּזִים בְּהָם — *And the Zuzim in Ham.*

They are identical with the *Zamzumim* [mentioned in *Deut.* 2:20, 21: *'a people great and many and tall as the Anakim'*] *(Rashi).*

They later perished entirely and were succeeded in their territories by Ammon [*ibid.*] *(Da'as Soferim).*

Onkeles renders: The mighty who were in Hemta.

Ham was possibly the primitive name of the capital city of Ammon *(Hoffmann).*

וְאֵת הָאֵימִים בְּשָׁוֵה קִרְיָתָיִם — *And the Eimim at Shaveh-Kiriathaim.*

The Eimim are mentioned in *Deut.* 2:10 as the earliest settlers of the land of Moab. *Shaveh-Kiriathaim,* lit. 'the plains of Kiriathaim' [or 'of two towns'] almost certainly refers to the area north of Arnon. This was later in the territory of the tribe of Reuben [*Num.* 32:37; *Josh.* 13:19], and the later prophets describe it as being part of Moab [cf. *Jer.* 48:23; *Ezek.* 25:9] *(Hoffmann).*

Onkelos following his interpretation of these words as adjectives rather than proper nouns renders *Eimim* as 'the terrible ones' of Shaveh-Kiriathaim (אֵימָה = *fear* or *terror).*

6. וְאֶת הַחֹרִי — *And the Horites.*

They were the original inhabitants of Seir, [see 36:20]. The land was later occupied by Edom *(Hoffmann).*

בְּהַרְרָם שֵׂעִיר — *In their Mount Seir.*

[Following *Rashi*: בְּהַרְרָם=בְּהַר שֶׁלָּהֶם.]

The Land of Seir encompassed the mountainous regions from the Dead Sea southward toward the Gulf of Aqaba. Seir became the home of Esau and his descendants, the Edomites [cf. *Gen.* 32:3; 36:8, 20; *Josh.* 24:4; *Judges* 5:4] *(Hoffmann; Kesses haSofer).*

the Zuzim in Ham, the Eimim at Shaveh-Kiriataim;
6 and the Horites in their mount Seir, as far as Eil
Paran which is by the desert. 7 Then they turned back
and came to Ein Mishpat, which is Kadesh. They

עַד אֵיל פָּארָן — *As far as Eil Paran.*

As *Onkelos* renders: The plain of Paran. *Rashi* suggests, however, that *Eil* is not a generic word for plain; rather Eil in our verse is a proper noun, i.e. the plain of Paran was called *Eil.* Similarly, the plain of Mamre was called *Elonei;* and that of the Jordan, *Kikkar.* All these are translated by *Onkelos* as מִישׁוֹר, plain, but each had its own particular name.

Ramban disagrees holding that *Eil* is not a proper noun, but 'a forest of *terebinths*', as the word is used in *Isaiah* 1:29. *Elonei* is a forest of *oaks* as in *Isaiah* 6:13 and *Ezekiel* 27:6, for the word *Alon* in *Gen.* 35:8, specifically refers to an oak tree. *Onkelos* however translates them all *'plain'* in keeping with his method of conveying the *intent* of the verse rather than a rigid literal translation. Had *Onkelos* considered them to be proper names, he would have transliterated them by name — e.g. אֵילָא, אֵילוֹנֵי דְמַמְרֵא, דְפָארָן — as is his custom with names. Since he translates rather than transliterates them, it is clear that he considers them descriptive nouns, not names. In translating them all as *plain,* [instead of forest] *Onkelos* conveys the sense of the verse, since it was usual for forests to be planted in the plains around cities, and the verses refer to such areas.

Many commentators identify Eil Paran with the area of Eilat at the head of the Gulf of Aqaba to the south of Eretz Yisrael [cf. *Deut.* 2:8; *I Kings* 9:26. The Wilderness of Paran [cf. 21:21] is thus the desert bordering on Eilat.

אֲשֶׁר עַל הַמִּדְבָּר — *Which is by the desert.*

Probably what is now known as the Isthmus of Suez *(Kesses haSofer).*

7. וַיָּשֻׁבוּ — *Then* [lit. *'and'*] *they turned back.*

Now, from their southernmost penetration, the four kings turned back northwards to their real goal *(Hirsch).*

[But they stopped again and crushed whatever resistance — real or anticipated — they encountered on the way].

עֵין מִשְׁפָּט הִוא קָדֵשׁ — *Ein Mishpat, which is Kadesh.*

Rashi explains that it was called *Ein Mishpat* [lit. *'spring* or *fountain of judgment'*] in anticipation of a future event, for that place was identical with the 'waters of Meribah' [cf. *Num.* 20:1 and 13] where Moses and Aaron were to be *judged* for their sin at that *fountain.*

Ramban disagrees, and explains that the Kadesh mentioned here is the Kadesh-Barnea of the Desert of *Paran* [*Numbers* 13:26] whence the spies were sent by Moses in the second year after the Exodus from Egypt. However, the Kadesh where Moses and Aaron were judged was in the Desert of *Zin* where the Jews were encamped in the fortieth year after the Exodus [cf. *Num.* 20:1.] Therefore, the *Midrash* cited by *Rashi* probably means that in a place bearing this same name, *Kadesh* — but not this *particular* Kadesh — there will become a Well of Judgment.

Mizrachi answers that *Rashi's* interpretation is consistent with his thesis as set forth in his *comm.* to *Deut.* 1:46, where he explains that the Jews returned to Kadesh after nineteen years of aimless wandering. The Kadesh Barnea where they were encamped in the second year is thus identical to the Kadesh of Zin to which they returned later. The Wilderness of Paran and that of Zin bordered upon one another, and Kadesh was therefore referred to by both designations.

וַיַּכּוּ אֶת־כָּל־שְׂדֵה הָעֲמָלֵקִי וְגַם אֶת־
ח הָאֱמֹרִי הַיֹּשֵׁב בְּחַצְצֹן תָּמָר: וַיֵּצֵא מֶלֶךְ־
סְדֹם וּמֶלֶךְ עֲמֹרָה וּמֶלֶךְ אַדְמָה וּמֶלֶךְ
°צביים וּמֶלֶךְ בֶּלַע הִוא־צֹעַר וַיַּעַרְכוּ
ט אִתָּם מִלְחָמָה בְּעֵמֶק הַשִּׂדִּים: אֵת
כְּדָרְלָעֹמֶר מֶלֶךְ עֵילָם וְתִדְעָל מֶלֶךְ גּוֹיִם
וְאַמְרָפֶל מֶלֶךְ שִׁנְעָר וְאַרְיוֹךְ מֶלֶךְ אֶלָּסָר
י אַרְבָּעָה מְלָכִים אֶת־הַחֲמִשָּׁה: וְעֵמֶק
הַשִּׂדִּים בֶּאֱרֹת בֶּאֱרֹת חֵמָר וַיָּנֻסוּ מֶלֶךְ־
סְדֹם וַעֲמֹרָה וַיִּפְּלוּ־שָׁמָּה וְהַנִּשְׁאָרִים

°צבוים ק׳

Onkelos, renders it according to its literal meaning: 'the plain where the people of that district used to assemble for every lawsuit'.

וַיַּכּוּ אֶת־כָּל־שְׂדֵה הָעֲמָלֵקִי — *And [they] struck all the territory* [lit. *'fields'*] *of the Amalekites.*

The name is that which the area was called in the days of Moses — Amalek not having yet been born *(Rashi)*.

Ramban conjectures, however, that there lived in those days a distinguished Horite by the name of Amalek who ruled over that place. It was after this man that Eliphaz, Esav's first-born, named his son Amalek [see 36:12].

וְגַם אֶת־הָאֱמֹרִי — *And also the Emorites.*

[One of the Canaanite nations mentioned in 10:16.]

בְּחַצְצֹן תָּמָר — *In Hazazon-Tamar* — i.e. En-gedi as explicitly stated in *II Chronicles* 20:2 *(Rashi)*.

[The area is to the west of the Dead Sea. It was called *Hazazon Tamar*, (lit. *'the cutting place of dates')* because as the *Midrash* explains, En-gedi is abundant with palm-trees.]

8. The Battle of the Revolt

וַיֵּצֵא מֶלֶךְ סְדֹם — *And the king of Sodom went forth.*

They did not wait passively to be invaded, but took the initiative and attacked the enemy first *(Ha'amek Davar)*.

וַיַּעַרְכוּ אִתָּם מִלְחָמָה בְּעֵמֶק הַשִּׂדִּים — *And [they] engaged them in battle in the Valley of Siddim.*

It was no accidental encounter, but a carefully chosen battlefield because its nature was such that a small force thoroughly acquainted with the terrain could hold off a much larger and stronger force. Had the soft and wanton kings of Sodom and Amorrah been able and brave they would not have been routed. As it was they fled so ignominiously that they fell into the very pits they knew so well *(Hirsch)*.

The kings are mentioned in an order different from that of *v.* 2.

XIV 8-10

struck all the territory of the Amalakites; and also the
Amorites who dwell in Hazazon-Tamar.
[8] *And the king of Sodom went forth with the king*
of Amorrah, the king of Admah, the king of Zeboiim
and the king of Bela which is Zoar, and engaged them
in battle in the Valley of Siddim: [9] *With Chedorlao-*
mer, king of Elam; Tidal, king of Goiim; Amraphel,
king of Shinar; and Arioch, king of Ellasar — four
kings against the five.
[10] *The Valley of Siddim was full of bitumen wells.*
The kings of Sodom and Amorrah fled and fell into

Perhaps, now that war was about to begin, they are listed according to their military might *(Da'as Soferim).*

9. ... אֶת כְּדָרְלָעֹמֶר ... — *With Chedorlaomer.*

The translation here of אֶת = *with,* follows the implication of *Onkelos.*

אַרְבָּעָה מְלָכִים אֶת הַחֲמִשָּׁה — *Four kings against the five.*

And yet the four kings won, which proves their great might. Nevertheless, as we see later, Abraham did not hesitate to pursue them *(Rashi).*

10. The Defeat

בֶּאֱרֹת בֶּאֱרֹת חֵמָר — *Full of bitumen wells* [lit. *'wells, wells of bitumen'*]

בֶּאֱרֹת, *wells,* not בּוֹרוֹת, pits, as translated by some *(Hirsch).*

— The area was dotted with wells from which slime was taken for building *(Rashi).*

[For the def. of חֵמָר, see on 11:3.]

Again, as in *v.* 3 we have a description of the Valley of Siddim. It was submerged by the waters of the Dead Sea *(Malbim).*

וַיָּנֻסוּ מֶלֶךְ סְדֹם וַעֲמֹרָה וַיִּפְּלוּ שָׁמָּה — *And the king(s) of Sodom and Amorrah fled and fell into them* [lit. *'there'*].

[Well-prepared though they were, the five kings were unequal to the superior might of the four invading armies; they were routed. The kings of Sodom and Amorah panicked, and fleeing, fell into the wells. But, for the reason explained below, the king of Sodom was miraculously saved.]

Rashi cites the *Midrash* that the area was so swampy that only by a miracle was the king of Sodom able to escape it. [This miracle was wrought for him, unworthy as he was, for one reason]: Those who refused to believe in the miracle enabling Abraham to escape unharmed from the furnaces of Ur Kasdim now saw the miracle performed for the king of Sodom; and in hindsight, they believed in Abraham's miracle, too.

Ramban observes that faith in God would hardly be enhanced by a miracle performed on behalf of a heathen king. On the contrary, this miracle could only strengthen their idolatrous beliefs or cause them to attribute all miracles to witchcraft, and not to the God of Abraham! Thus, the effect would be the reverse!

Ramban goes on to suggest that the Sages of that *Midrashic* statement would interpret verse 17: *and the king of Sodom went out to meet him* as indicating that 'he went out'

יא הֶהָרָה נָּסוּ: וַיִּקְחוּ אֶת־כָּל־רְכֻשׁ סְדֹם
יב וַעֲמֹרָה וְאֶת־כָּל־אָכְלָם וַיֵּלֵכוּ: וַיִּקְחוּ
אֶת־לוֹט וְאֶת־רְכֻשׁוֹ בֶּן־אֲחִי אַבְרָם
יג וַיֵּלְכוּ וְהוּא יֹשֵׁב בִּסְדֹם: וַיָּבֹא הַפָּלִיט

from the well when Abraham passed by it looking for survivors. It was obvious to all that he emerged from the well miraculously, only in deference to Abraham, since he failed to get out previously. The king of Amorrah, however, had apparently died by the time Abraham arrived.

There is a basic difference between the verbs נוס and ברח [although both carry a connotation of flight]: לָנוּס, *to flee,* indicates flight from a pursuer or a *present* danger. לִברוֹחַ, *to escape,* indicates flight in *anticipation* of danger *(HaKsav V'HaKaballah).*

According to many, [e.g. *B'chor Shor; Hadar Zekeinim; Paaneach Raza; Tur; Malbim*] the word וַיִּפְּלוּ in our verse has the meaning of נפל in 25:18 where it means 'settle'. The connotation is that the kings did not accidentally *fall* into the well, but that they *jumped* into it to conceal themselves when they perceived that the armies of the four kings were imminently victorious. [But, as would appear from the *Midrash* they were unable to extricate themselves without a miracle].

וְהַנִּשְׁאָרִים הֶרָה נָּסוּ — *While the rest fled to a mountain.*

— Each person fled to the first mountain he came to; there is no definite article indicating that they all fled to a particular mountain *(Rashi).*

To whom does the phrase, *'the rest'*, refer? According to the *Midrash, and they fell there* refers to the kings; *the rest* refers to their armies. Another interpretation [in the *Midrash,* followed also by *Sforno*] explains *'the rest'* as referring to the kings of Admah, Zeboiim, and Bela who did not fall [or jump] into the pits.

11. Now the triumphant victors turn to claim the spoils of their defeated enemies *(Hoffmann):*

וַיִּקְחוּ אֶת כָּל רְכֻשׁ סְדֹם וַעֲמֹרָה — *They* [i.e., the invading conquerers] *seized* [lit. *'took'*] *all the wealth of Sodom and Amorrah.*

Scripture details the suffering from which the king and people of Sodom were rescued by Abraham in order to emphasize their wickedness. Despite their salvation they did not repent — and finally they were destroyed by God *(Da'as Soferim).*

[Spoils are not mentioned regarding the victories described in the previous verses. Perhaps the forces of Sodom and Amorrah were the most aggressive (they are given prominence by having been mentioned first in *v.* 8), and therefore, in revenge, the enemy seized their spoils more than that of the others. Or it may be that the Torah relates only those facts that are germane to the flow of the narrative.]

12. Lot taken captive

וַיִּקְחוּ אֶת לוֹט וְאֶת רְכֻשׁוֹ בֶּן אֲחִי אַבְרָם — *And they captured* [following *Onkelos;* lit. *'took'*] *Lot and his possession — Abram's nephew.*] *Abram.*]

It is strange that Lot's relationship to Abram is mentioned when it

them while the rest fled to a mountain.
11 *They seized all the wealth of Sodom and Amorrah and all their provisions and they departed.*
12 *And they captured Lot and his possesions — Abram's nephew — and they left; for he was residing in Sodom.*

is already well known. Equally puzzling is that the relationship is not mentioned after his name, but after *'and his possessions.'* It emphasizes that Lot's capture and the taking of his possessions was motivated [as pointed out below] first and foremost by his relationship to Abram *(Radal* to *Pirkei d'Rabbi Eliezer):*

The *Midrash* relates that they put Lot in a cage and made a spectacle of him. They marched around and boasted: 'We have captured Abram's nephew!' This proves that they had come only because of him *(Midrash haGadol).*[1]

According to *Sforno* they captured him especially *because* they knew he was Abram's nephew. They knew of Abram's wealth and they hoped to receive a large ransom for Lot.

וַיֵּלֵכוּ — *And they left* [lit. *'went'*]

[The object of their foray having been accomplished, they left.]

וְהוּא יֹשֵׁב בִּסְדֹם — *For* [lit. *'and'*] *he was residing in Sodom.*

This is mentioned to indicate that all of this befell Lot *because* he dwelt in Sodom *(Rashi).*

— He associated with wicked people and he deserved to be captured *(Yefe To'ar).*

Hirsch comments on the need for Scripture to repeat these two amply known facts — that he was Abraham's nephew and that he lived in Sodom. His relationship to Abram would have spared him from the vengeance of Chedarlaomer because Lot was known to be a stranger in Sodom. But he refused to remain a stranger there — he copied their ways and therefore fell victim to their fate. Throughout history, the Jew who remains separate is spared much. In the Middle Ages, the ghettoes and anti-Jewish persecution prevented Jews from becoming murderers and torturers like others. True, they were considered too inferior to become officials and knights, but, by the same token, their hands did not become blood-stained. And their ghettoes often protected them from the vengeance of conquerors because they were not contaminated

1. According to the *Midrash, Zohar,* and commentators, much of their campaign was directed as a spiritual war against Abram; Amraphel [Nimrod] remembering only too well his past experiences with this man in Ur Kasdim.

As the *Zohar* explains:

Note that when all those kings joined together their design was to root out Abram. But as our verse clearly states, as soon as they captured Lot, his nephew, they departed. The reason was that Lot closely resembled Abram [see *comm.* to 13:8]; thinking they had Abram they departed.

The reason for their enmity to Abram was that he weaned men from idolatry and taught them to worship Hashem. Also, God incited the kings to this invasion in order that Abram's name might be aggrandized through their defeat, and all would be attracted to His service.

by the corruption of their host countries. (See Overview to *Vayishlach.*)

13. וַיָּבֹא הַפָּלִיט — *Then* [lit. *'and'*] *there came the fugitive.*

Tradition identifies *the fugitive* with Og, King of Bashan.[1] The plain meaning (cited in *Tanchuma)* is that Og is called a fugitive because he escaped the *present* battle [i.e. the battle of the *Rephaim* in *v.* 5] and it is to this escape that *Deut.* 3:11 refers: *Only Og, King of Bashan was left of the remnant of Rephaim,* for he was not killed when they smote the Rephaim in Ashteroth-Karnaim.

According to the *Midrash,* however, Og is described as the fugitive because he was the only one who escaped from *the Flood.* According to this latter interpretation, the *Rephaim* mentioned in *Deut.* 3:11 are, identical with the Nephilim of *Gen.* 6:4. [Cf. *Niddah* 61a] *(Rashi).*

Cf. *Targum Yonasan:*

And Og came, who had been spared of the giants [6:4] that died in the deluge, and had ridden protected on the top of the Ark and sustained with food by Noah [see *comm.* to 7:23]: He was not spared by his righteousness, but that the inhabitants of the world would see the power of God and say: Were there not even *giants* who rebelled against the Lord of the world and they perished from the earth?

וַיַּגֵּד לְאַבְרָם הָעִבְרִי — *And told* [to] *Abram, the Ivri.*

Exactly *what* he told Abram is not recorded. Presumably he related to him the course of the battle: how the five kings were defeated; how Sodom was taken and its residents, including Lot, were taken prisoner *(Akeidas Yitzchak).*

Obviously, if the *only* thing the fugitive related to Abram was that Lot was captured, then our verse would have stated: וַיַּגֵּד לְאַבְרָם כִּי נִשְׁבָּה אָחִיו *and told Abram that his kinsman was taken captive.* [Hence it is apparent that he related the *entire episode* of events to him.]

His intention in telling him was not pure. He knew that the righteous Abram would not sit idly by once he became aware that his nephew was in peril. He, therefore, told him this news because he wished to incite Abram to engage the kings in battle with the expectation that Abram would be killed so that he himself might marry Sarai *(Midrash; Rashi).*

The *Midrash* continues:

'By your life!' said the Holy One, Blessed be He, '[Although your intentions were evil], you will be rewarded for your journey [to inform Abram in Hebron] by being granted long life. [He was still alive in the time of Moses]. But for your wicked scheme, intending Abram's death, you will see myriads of his descendants into whose hands you will ultimately fall [cf. *Num.* 32:33.]

One who performs a precept with

1. Why was he called Og?

— When he came he found Abram busy baking *ugos,* unleavened cakes [it was the eve of what would later be Passover and, as the Rabbis teach, Abram fulfilled all the precepts of the Torah even before they were promulgated.] He laughed to himself at what he thought was the absurdity of Abram's actions. In punishment he was nicknamed עוג — 'cookie' a name which would bring him ridicule in retaliation for his ridiculing Abram *(Midrash;* commentators).

13 *Then there came the fugitive and told Abram,*

sinister motives and in order to attain a sinful gain is severely punished. If so, why was Og rewarded for bringing the news to Abram since his intention was to gain Sarai? The answer is that every good deed deserves a reward. If, however, a person does it for selfish, sinful motives, God rewards him on this world so that he can be punished in the World to Come *(Meam Loez).*[1]

אַבְרָם הָעִבְרִי — *Abram, the Ivri* — the one who came from the 'other side' [עֵבֶר] of the River [Euphrates] *(Rashi).*

[This was the title used for Jews. After the exile of the Ten Tribes when the tribe of Yehudah remained the principal branch of the nation,the name *Yehudi (Jew)* came into general use.]

The *Midrash* offers several additonal interpretations of *Ivri:*

Rav Yehudah said: The name *Ivri* signifies that the whole world was on one side *(ever)* while Abram was on the other side [i.e., he alone of all mankind served the true God while all the others practiced idolatry];

Rav Nechemiah said: He was called *Ivri* as a desendant of Eber [10:25; 11:16-26.]

According to the Rabbis, it means that he came from across the river [see *Josh.* 24:3]; further that he spoke in the language of those who lived across the river.

This stresses the contrast between Abram and the implied criticism of Lot in the previous verse (see *comm.* of *Hirsch).* Abram is described as *Ivri* — one who stands on the other side — for he remained apart, unlike Lot who assimilated *(Hirsch).*

[We have already discussed the various meanings of *Ivri* in the comm. to 10:24 (p. 329); and to 11:28 (p. 348-9). See also *Mizrachi* to 39:14, who asserts that the term *Ivri* was used only for someone who was both a descendant of Eber and also from the other side of the river — therefore Isaac, not Ishmael, is considered an *Ivri* although Ishmael, too, descended from the Abrahamitic line.]

Radak explains *Ivri* as a descendant of Eber. He adds that although all Eber's descendants traced their lineage to him, Abram and his descendants are unique in being entitled *Ivrim,* for they alone remained loyal to the language of Eber [Hebrew; see *Maharzu* to the *Midrash* cited above], while Eber's other descendants spoke Aramaic. The latter are therefore referred to as *Arameans,* as, e.g. Laban, the Aramean, while Abram's line through Jacob was called *Ivrim.*

Is it possible that Og knew that Abraham was Lot's *relative?* He knew only that Lot was an *Ivri* — i.e. a believer in the religion of Eber — as was Abram, and as such he surmised he would come to his aid *(Sforno; Tur).*

וְהוּא שֹׁכֵן — *Who* [lit. *'and he'*] *dwelt.*

Hirsch points out that in this

1. When Moses warred on Og, God had to reassure him because he feared that Og would benefit from the merit of having warned Abram of Lot's danger. From this we learn a profound lesson: Og had only the selfish interest that he might marry Sarai. Moreover, Abram did not gain personally from the warning. Nevertheless, Og was rewarded for his deed which, contrary to his own motive, had a beneficial result. Surely if someone tried hard to do good and sincerely intended to do so, his reward will surely be very, very great *(Rabbi Israel Salanter).*

מַמְרֵא הָאֱמֹרִי אֲחִי אֶשְׁכֹּל וַאֲחִי עָנֵר
יד וְהֵם בַּעֲלֵי בְרִית־אַבְרָם: וַיִּשְׁמַע אַבְרָם
כִּי נִשְׁבָּה אָחִיו וַיָּרֶק אֶת־חֲנִיכָיו יְלִידֵי

phrase, too, the sharp distinction between Lot and Abram is drawn: of Lot it says וְהוּא יֹשֵׁב בִּסְדוֹם, *he settled in Sodom, (v.* 12) יֹשֵׁב [*settled*] having the connotation of belonging completely *to a place.* Just as in 13:7 *the Canaanites and Perizzites were then settled* [יֹשֵׁב] *in the land,* so, too, Lot *settled* in Sodom ...

Abram, on the other hand is described as שֹׁכֵן, [*dwelling*]. Although the Hebrew word has the connotation of resting quietly in a place, it does not connote the relation *to the ground,* but to the peaceful living *as neighbors,* without being entirely absorbed by each other. Thus, Abram was not ashamed to preserve his own special characteristics in the midst of the Emorites; he was Abram from 'the other side' — a tolerated stranger — and שׁוֹכֵן, 'living next to' the Emorites, living in friendly neighborly relations with them. [Cf. *Moreh Nevuchim* I:25; *Imrei Shefer.*]

[But cf. *comm.* to וַיָּגָר in 21:34, and to וַיֵּשֶׁב in 22:19.]

Chizkuni, in an alternate interpretation suggests that the subject *'he dwelt in the plains of Mamre'* could possibly refer to the פָּלִיט, *the fugitive — He* lived in the plains of Mamre, and therefore he told Abram.

בְּאֵלֹנֵי מַמְרֵא הָאֱמֹרִי — *In the plains of Mamre the Amorite.*

[See on 13:18. On Mamre's association with Abram as explained in the *Midrash,* see *comm.* to 18:1.]

וְהֵם בַּעֲלֵי בְרִית־אַבְרָם — *These being Abram's allies* [lit. *'these were confederates' ('masters of a covenant') of Abram.*]

They had entered into a treaty with Abraham *(Rashi).*

Hirsch observes that their relationship with Abraham was as בַּעֲלֵי בְּרִית, [lit. 'master of the covenant'] not אַנְשֵׁי בְּרִית ['(equal) members of the covenant'], suggesting that Abraham was subordinate to them. Aner, Eshkol, and Mamre were the בַּעֲלִים, masters, of the covenant because Abraham was the outsider in their land. They so admired Abraham that they accepted him into their fellowship. This is the eternal mission of the Jew — to remain loyal to his calling, but to set such a high example for integrity that others will respect him and invite him to participate in their covenant.

According to *Ha'amek Davar,* the phrase implies: *And these shared Abram's faith* — they, too, believing in God Who performs wonders.

14. Abraham saves Lot

וַיִּשְׁמַע אַבְרָם כִּי נִשְׁבָּה אָחִיו — *And* [*when*] *Abram heard that his kinsman* [following *Ibn Janach;* lit. *'brother'*] *was taken captive.* [The translation *'and when ...'* follows *Targum Yonasan* and *Ibn Janach.*]

[The term *'hear'* is often used in the sense of 'understand' as in שְׁמַע יִשְׂרָאֵל, *Hear O Israel ... Deut.* 6:4.]

According to *Akeidas Yitzchak,* the meaning of the phrase is *and Abraham reflected* on the significance of his *'brother'* having been taken captive. And immediately, the Spirit of God rested on him, and he bravely armed his trained ones.

The term *'his brother'* indicates that Abraham realized that the

the Ivri, who dwelt in the plains of Mamre, the Amorite, the brother of Eshkol and Aner, these being Abram's allies. 14 *And when Abram heard that his kinsman was taken captive, he armed his disciples*

primary reason Lot was taken captive was because he was Abraham's kinsman. At its source, their hatred was toward Abraham himself, and would intensify unless it was checked. Therefore he was even more determined to act against them *(Alshich; Tz'ror haMor).*

Initially Abraham had complacently trusted in God to save his nephew. However he heard that, due to Lot's strong resemblance to him, people were boasting that Abraham himself had been captured, and that Nimrod's easy victory proved the falsehood of the stories that Abraham had been miraculously saved from the furnaces of Ur! That such blasphemies could circulate was a חִילוּל ה׳, a desecration of God's Name; Abraham immediately armed his men and set out *(Me'am Loez).*

[See also *Ramban* to 19:29, that Abraham endangered himself to save Lot because Abraham felt personally responsible for him, for were it not for Abraham allowing Lot to follow him, Lot would still have been in Charan with his family. It was thus inconceivable that Abraham should allow harm to come to Lot because of him.]

וַיָּרֶק אֶת־חֲנִיכָיו — [*And*] *he armed his disciples* [lit. *'trained ones'*] — i.e. those youths whom he had educated in the true path towards service of God. The word is derived from חנך, *train, dedicate,* as in *Prov.* 22:6: *Train up* (חֲנוֹךְ) *a child.* The word thus signifies a person or thing which is dedicated [מְחֻנָּךְ] to some particular purpose *(Rashi; Radak*; see *Hirsch).*

According to *Ibn Ezra,* חֲנִיכָיו refers to those youths who were *trained for battle.*

The translation of וַיָּרֶק *'armed'* follows *Onkelos* [וְזָרֵיז = girded], and the word is so interpreted by *Ibn Janach, Rashi, Radak* and most commentators, who cite such parallel usages as *Lev.* 24:33 וַהֲרִיקֹתִי, *and I will gird myself; Exod.* 15:9 אָרִיק חַרְבִּי, *I will gird my sword; Ps.* 35:3 וְהָרֵק חֲנִית, *Gird yourself with the spear.* (Cf. *Rashi* to *Exod.* 15:9, and 13:18).

Ibn Ezra adds that the word also has the connotation of unsheathing a sword [leaving the sheath ריק=empty] as in 42:35: מְרִיקִים שַׂקֵּיהֶם *emptying their sacks.* [The connotation, therefore, is that Abraham quickly evacuated them from their homes — preparing them for battle.]

The *Talmud* interprets the phrase in the sense of 'empty', and the Sages find fault with Abraham for having pressed his disciples into battle:

Rav Elazar said: Why was Abraham punished and his descendants doomed to Egyptian servitude? — Because he used Torah scholars to wage war, as it is written, *he emptied his disciples (Nedarim* 32a; see *Maharsha).* [1]

1. *Harav David Feinstein* explains that the connotation of the above Talmudic explanation of וַיָּרֶק, Abraham *'emptied',* is that he *depleted the effect* of all his teaching. For Abraham had always devoted himself to training his disciples to order their priorities properly. He always taught them that nothing matters more than the study of Torah. Now he suddenly came and וַיָּרֶק אֶת־חֲנִיכָיו he *emptied out* his disciples of all their teaching, for, during a crisis when he felt

בֵּיתוֹ שְׁמֹנָה עָשָׂר וּשְׁלֹשׁ מֵאוֹת וַיִּרְדֹּף
טו עַד־דָּן: וַיֵּחָלֵק עֲלֵיהֶם | לַיְלָה הוּא וַעֲבָדָיו

יְלִידֵי בֵיתוֹ — *Who had been born in his house* — from the *'souls they had made in Charan'* [12:5] and in Canaan [i.e. for, as the Sages teach, 'One who teaches Torah to his fellow's son is considered as if he had given birth to him'] *(Radak).*

— This refers to those whom he trained in his house from the time of their birth *(Ralbag).* These, he could rely on most *(Hoffmann).*

Only because they were 'born in his household' could he make them חֲנִיכָיו, his proteges. Lot, however, had already formed his character when he fell under Abraham's influence: it was too late to change him. Education must begin with birth ... *(Hirsch).*

[*Rashi* to 17:12 explains יְלִיד בַּיִת as those born to the maidservants of the household.]

שְׁמֹנָה עָשָׂר וּשְׁלֹשׁ מֵאוֹת — *Three hundred and eighteen.*

Malbim observes that Abraham's courage reflected a concept elucidated in *Moreh Nevuchim:* A person clothed with the Spirit of God will don a spirit of wisdom and strength until he will even stand up against a large army without fear, just as Jonathan did when he singlehandedly defeated the Philistine army. So, too, Abraham did not seek the assistance of Aner, Eshkol, and Mamre relying instead on himself and the disciples whom he had raised in the service of God.

Harav David Cohen comments that the nature of the war dictated that Abraham take his *disciples,* but not his *allies.* Only those trained by Abraham to recognize God's omnipotence could fearlessly do battle against infinitely superior forces. Such faith could not be expected of Aner, Eshkol, and Mamre.

[Although it has become second nature for succeeding generations of righteous Jews to put reliance on God above superior might, Abraham did so *without relying on precedent.* It was his greatness to go into battle armed with this faith and without prior guarantee of victory. This may be considered another instance of מַעֲשֵׂה אָבוֹת סִימָן לְבָנִים, *Whatever happened to the Patriarchs is a sign to their children* (see *footnote* to 12:6).]

Midrashically, however, Rashi cites the *Talmud* [*Ned.* 32a] that it was his servant Eliezer alone whom he armed, 318 being the numerical equivalent of the name אֱלִיעֶזֶר, *Eliezer.*

Additionally, *Rashi* adds that the written form חנכו [spelled without a *yud* in the suffix] can be interpreted in the singular *'his trained one'* [although *Minchas Shay* reports never having come across this spelling in any Torah Scroll he has seen], referring to Eliezer whom Abraham trained in the Mitzvos.

R' Bachya seeks to explain the discrepancy between the simple meaning of the verse which makes it plain that Abraham drafted

he needed their help he removed them from the study hall in order to help him in his struggle.

It was for this that his descendants were punished by being drafted into the forced servitude of the enemies of HASHEM.

[According to the opinion that this was Abraham's sin which determined the Egyptian servitude, then the War of the Kings preceded the Covenant Between the Parts in Ch. 15. See *footnote* to *v.* 21.]

XIV who had been born in his house — three hundred and
15 eighteen — and he pursued them as far as Dan.
15 *And he with his servants deployed against them at*

his 318 disciples for the fray, and the *Midrashic* interpretation that only Eliezer fought. It is indeed true that only Eliezer fought. It is indeed true that Abraham called upon all 318 disciples to fight with him. They were afraid of the impossible odds, however. Knowing that the source of victory lies in merit rather than numbers, Abraham proclaimed that the faint-hearted need not come with him. In this he followed the future injunction of the Torah which freed the fearful from the battle *(Deut.* 20:8). [Cowardly people will tend to run away when the fighting grows fierce, thus throwing fear into the hearts of others *(Me'am Loez).*] In the end, only Eliezer was left and with him alone, Abraham went into battle. Thus, both interpretations of 318 are correct.

R' Bachya also perceives two interpretations in the word וַיָּרֶק in our verse. First: *and he armed,* for Abraham did indeed arm his disciples. Second: *and he emptied,* for he 'emptied' out — depleted — his force by encouraging the cowardly to leave.

וַיִּרְדֹּף עַד־דָּן — *And he pursued* [them] *as far as Dan.*

However, at Dan his strength waned because he prophetically foresaw that his descendant [Jeroboam] would one day set up an idolatrous calf there [*I Kings* 12:29] *(Sanhedrin* 96a; *Rashi).*

[He therefore gave up the chase in Chovah, as mentioned in the next verse.]

Dan, is used in anticipation of the area's future name in the days of the Judges. Formerly it was called Leshem [*Josh* 19:47] or Laish [*Judg.* 18:29]. It is located on the extreme northern border of Eretz Yisrael *(Heidenheim).*

Pirkei d'Rabbi Eliezer identifies Dan as Banias. *Targum Yonasan* renders: *Dan of Kisarion* [Caesarea Philippi, the Roman name for Banias which was named after the pagan god Pan.]

It is possible, however, that there existed in Abraham's time another place called Dan *(Radak).*

Torah Temimah suggests that this verse may be a case of a haplography [i.e. any omission of one of two adjacent and similar letters from neighboring words ending and beginning with the same consonants for example: עָזִּי וְזִמְרָתִי יָהּ=עָזִּי וְזִמְרָת יָהּ; לֹא יוּכַל לְשַׁלְּחָהּ= שַׁלְּחָהּ לֹא יוּכַל. There are many such instances, and it is possible that such is also the case in our verse, and that our phrase should accordingly read וַיִּרְדֹּף עַד־דְּדָן, *and he persued them as far as Dedan,* Dedan being a city already existing in Abraham's time, being named after Dedan son of Raameh [see 10:7]. The city of Dedan is also mentioned by *Jeremiah* [49:8], and by *Ezekiel* [27:15.]

15. וַיֵּחָלֵק עֲלֵיהֶם לַיְלָה הוּא וַעֲבָדָיו וַיַּכֵּם — *And he with his servants deployed against them at night* [lit. *'and was divided against them night, he and his servants, and* [he] *struck them.*]

Even at night he did not give up the pursuit. He split up his forces to follow the fugitives as they scattered in various directions *(Rashi).*

Thus, as *Ramban* explains the sequence of the verses, he pursued them with a united army as far as Dan; then, when night had fallen and he could not see by which road they fled, he divided his forces into several groups to pursue them in all directions smiting them as far as Chovah, which is to the north of Damascus.

Additionally, he split up his forces and attacked them from various fronts by night so they would be thrown into confusion. They would think his army was much greater than it really was, and would believe that they were completely surrounded by hostile forces *(Abarbanel).*

וַיַּכֵּם וַיִּרְדְּפֵם עַד־חוֹבָה אֲשֶׁר מִשְּׂמֹאל
טז לְדַמָּשֶׂק: וַיָּשֶׁב אֵת כָּל־הָרְכֻשׁ וְגַם אֶת־
לוֹט אָחִיו וּרְכֻשׁוֹ הֵשִׁיב וְגַם אֶת־הַנָּשִׁים

[On a similar strategem, see *Judges* 7:16*ff* and *I Sam.* 11:11]

The inverted order of the translation and the insertion of the implied preposition *at* (as if the verse read בַּלַּיְלָה), follows *Rashi* and most commentators. This translation clarifies the subject of the sentence as הוּא, *he*, for it was Abraham's *force* that *was divided* rather than the *night*. [*R' Meyuchas* cites such parallel examples of implied prepositions as *Exod.* 12:30: וַיָּקָם פַּרְעֹה לַיְלָה הוּא וְכָל עֲבָדָיו, *And Pharaoh rose up (at) night, he and all his servants; Num.* 16:5: בֹּקֶר וְיֹדַע ה׳, *(in the) morning, and* HASHEM *will make known; Hosea* 7:6: בֹּקֶר הוּא בֹעֵר, *(in the) morning it burns.*]

[For parallels of סָרֵס הַמִּקְרָא, inverting the order of words in a verse for better comprehension, cf. *Rashi* to 2:19; *Lev.* 1:15; 22:2; 23:16; *Num.* 19:7; 27:2; *Deut.* 4:38.]

Others interpret that the subject of *'divided'* was *the night*, rendering: *And the night was divided for them, him and his servants, and he defeated them,* i.e. when the night was divided for them [at midnight], their attack began. The implication is that the night was split for them: until midnight the four kings had the upper hand, but beginning with midnight they began fleeing from Abraham's attacking forces *(Radak;* cf. *R' Bachya).*

Sforno explains that Abraham chose the night in order to throw them into confusion and at the same time to hide the smallness of his own army.

According to the *Midrashic* interpretation cited by *Rashi,* the night was divided for him: during its *first half* a miracle was wrought for him [and he defeated the enemy], and the *second half* was reserved for the miracle which would occur at midnight in behalf of his children, in Egypt [cf. *Exod.* 12:29.]

וַיִּרְדְּפֵם עַד חוֹבָה אֲשֶׁר מִשְּׂמֹאל לְדַמָּשֶׂק — *[And] he pursued them as far as Chovah which is to the north* [lit. *'of the left'*] *of Damascus.*[1]

— I.e., he pursued the fugitive survivors of the force which he defeated, giving chase as far as Chovah *(Radak; R' Meyuchas).*

Ramban explains that he pursued them *for many days* as far as Chovah thus forcing them out of the land. He then turned homeward content that they were returning to Babylon, their country. According to the Rabbis, however, a great miracle occurred there, and Abraham traversed this great distance from his home in the plains of Mamre to Chovah in but a tenth of the normal time, taking such miraculously long steps that he hardly set foot on the ground.

1. Josephus [*Ant.* 10:1] relates the event as follows:

'When Abraham heard of their calamity, he was concerned about Lot his kinsman ... and marched hastily ... and fell upon the Assyrians near Dan, for that is the name of the other spring of the Jordan.

Before they could arm themselves, he slew some as they were in their beds, before they could suspect any harm. The others who had not yet gone to sleep but were so drunk they could not fight, ran away.

Abraham pursued them, till, on the second day he drove them *en masse* to Chovah, a place belonging to Damascus.

He demonstrated thereby that victory does not depend on multitude and number of hands ... '

XIV night and struck them; he pursued them as far as
16 Chovah which is to the north of Damascus. [16] He
brought back all the possessions; he also brought
back his kinsman, Lot, with his possessions, as well
as the women and the people.

Rashi explains that there is no place named Chovah. Rather, the city of Dan is called חוֹבָה, *Chovah* [= guilty city] because of the idolatrous service which would later be instituted there [by Jeraboam.]

In the previous verse we are told that he pursued them as far as the territory of Dan. Now we are told that he pursued them further until Chovah, i.e. that territory within Dan which lay to the north of Damascus, indicating that though his strength failed him there, Abraham did not rest until he drove them completely from Eretz Yisrael as noted by *Ramban* above *(Harav David Cohen).*

[The translation of שְׂמֹאל, (lit. *'left'*) as *'north'*, follows *Onkelos*. As explained above in 13:9 (Cf. footnote to 13:14) when one faces east, north is to his left.]

[He chased them only as far as Chovah. The Torah does not relate that he *massacred* them all. Apparently, as *Ramban* concludes, the rest of their scattered forces fled and returned home ingloriously.]

16. Abraham's Triumphant Return

וַיָּשֶׁב אֵת כָּל־הָרְכֻשׁ — [*And*] *he brought back all the possessions.*

— [Apparently, in their frantic flight the survivors left behind all the spoils they had amassed.]

The verse does not specify 'the possessions *of Sodom and Amorrah'* but states generally *'all* the possessions', to indicate that Abraham recaptured the spoils that had been taken from *all* the nations they had plundered *(Imrei Shefer).*

וְגַם אֶת לוֹט אָחִיו וּרְכֻשׁוֹ הֵשִׁיב — [*And*] *he also brought back his kinsman* [lit. *'brother'*], *Lot, with his possessions.*

Although Abraham's main purpose was the rescue of Lot, the minor triumph — the return of the possessions — is listed first. Then the verse goes on to a greater victory — the rescue of Lot, because we might have expected the defeated kings to avenge themselves by killing Lot *(Or HaChaim).*

וְגַם אֶת הַנָּשִׁים —*As well as* [lit. *'and also'*] *the women.*

— Lot's wives *(Sforno).*

וְאֶת הָעָם — *And the people,* i.e., the rest of the Sodomites who had been captured. It was these whom the king of Sodom wanted when he said [*v.* 21]: *'Give me the persons' (Sforno).*

He brought back the men and women as stated in this verse, but not the children. These he left there [rather than return them to their fathers' idolatrous ways *(Mattanos Kehunah).*] They thereupon arose and converted to the true faith *(Midrash).*

17. [Abraham returns triumphant and all gather to receive him in the Valley of Shaveh. The king of

יז וְאֶת־הָעָם׃ וַיֵּצֵא מֶלֶךְ־סְדֹם לִקְרָאתוֹ
אַחֲרֵי שׁוּבוֹ מֵהַכּוֹת אֶת־כְּדָרְלָעֹמֶר
וְאֶת־הַמְּלָכִים אֲשֶׁר אִתּוֹ אֶל־עֵמֶק שָׁוֵה
יח הוּא עֵמֶק הַמֶּלֶךְ׃ וּמַלְכִּי־צֶדֶק מֶלֶךְ שָׁלֵם

Sodom, who owes his life to Abraham's victory, shares in the reception]:

וַיֵּצֵא מֶלֶךְ סְדֹם לִקְרָאתוֹ — [*And*] *the king of Sodom went out to meet him.*

— He miraculously was enabled to leave the slime pit in which he had hidden [see *comm.* to *v.* 10] *(Chizkuni).*

That the *'going out'* referred to here is the escape *from the pit* is certainly פְּשַׁט, the simple meaning of the verse: Scripture informs us that the king extricated himself miraculously only thanks to Abraham. If, however, the king had somehow freed himself from the slime before Abraham's arrival, there would have been no purpose in narrating his fall without describing the escape *(Nimukei Shmuel).*

But the king of Sodom was hardly grateful. The *Midrash* relates that he put on airs, saying to him: Just as you descended into the fiery furnace and were saved, so did I descend into the slime and was saved!

The king of Amorah, however, is not mentioned here. He apparently died in the bitumen well *(Ramban* to *v.* 10).

אַחֲרֵי שׁוּבוֹ מֵהַכּוֹת ... אֲשֶׁר אִתּוֹ — *After his* [i.e., Abraham's] *return from defeating* [lit. *'striking'*] *Chedorlaomer and the kings* [*that were*] *with him.*

[This entire phrase, referring to Abraham, is paranthetic. The verse could perhaps be more easily understood if some of the words were rearranged in the translation, thus: *After his* (i.e. *Abram's) return from smiting Chedorlaomer and the kings with him, the king of Sodom went out to meet him in the Valley of Shaveh which is the Valley of the King.*]

אֶל־עֵמֶק שָׁוֵה — *To the Valley of Shaveh* [lit. *'level'* or *'smooth' valley.*] That was its name. *Targum* explains it *'to the empty plain'* because it was clear of trees and impediments *(Rashi).*

הוּא עֵמֶק הַמֶּלֶךְ — *Which is the king's valley.*

As *Onkelos* renders: בֵּית־רֵיסָא דְמַלְכָּא, the king's arena. A hippodrome thirty קָנִים [measuring rods] long [equal to 1 *rus*] was reserved as the king's private domain for sport *(Rashi).*

[A רוס is an area equal to 30 *kanim,* the word רו״ס itself being numerically equal to 266 cubits *(Aruch).* See *Rashi* to *Yoma* 87a.]

This area, as its names clearly indicate, consisted of smooth, [שָׁוֵה] level terrain, fit for use by the king of the area. From its mention in *II Sam.* 18:18 in connection with the location of Yad Absalom, we learn that it was near Jerusalem. Perhaps the 'king', for whom it served as a recreation area, was Malchizedek, who was king of Jerusalem [see *v.* 18] *(Imrei Shefer).*

According to the *Midrashic* interpretation the valley was so called

XIV
17-18

[17] *The king of Sodom went out to meet him after his return from defeating Chedorlaomer and the kings that were with him, to the Valley of Shaveh which is the king's valley.* [18] *But Malchizedek, king*

because it was there that all the nations unanimously agreed (הוּשְׁווּ) to accept Abraham as king and leader over them *(Rashi).*

As the *Midrash* relates:

Upon Abraham's triumphant return, all the peoples gathered. They felled cedars, erected a large dais, and set him on top while uttering praises before him [cf. 23:6]: *Hear us, my lord: You are a prince of God among us.* They said 'You are a king over us, you are a God over us!' But he replied: 'The world does not lack its King, and the world does not lack its God!'

18. Having met Abraham at the Valley of Shaveh, the king of Sodom paid him further homage by accompanying him to the city of Shalem where they were met by Malchizedek *(Ramban* to *v.* 20):

וּמַלְכִּי־צֶדֶק מֶלֶךְ שָׁלֵם — *But* [lit. *'and'*] *Malchizedek, King of Shalem.*

He is unanimously identified by the Sages [*Nedarim* 32b; *Midrash Tehillim* 76:3; *Targum Yonasan*] as Shem, son of Noah *(Rashi).*

He was so called because he was a king [*melech*] over a place known for its righteousness [*zedek*] *(Ibn Ezra);* a place which would not tolerate any form of injustice or abomination for an extended time *(Radak)*; or, according to *Ramban,* because he ruled over the future site of the Temple, the home of *zedek,* the righteous Shechinah, which was known even then to be sacred. Thus *Malchizedek* might designate him as 'king of the place of *zedek,* righteousness.'

That Shem was known by this title is not unusual. The kings of Jerusalem [see below] were called by the titles of 'Malchizedek' or 'Adonizedek' [see *Josh.* 10:1], just as the kings of Egypt were designated by the common title of *Pharaoh,* and those of the Philistines as *Abimelech (Ralbag).*

[On Shem, see also *comm.* to 6:10; 9:26; 10:21; and 12:6.]

Ramban explains that Shem was the most honored among the older generation of Canaanites, and he therefore became the priest of God the Most High in Jerusalem. The city was within the boundaries of the Canaanites who settled there [or according to *Rashi* on 12:6: who gradually conquered the land from the Shemites] until the time when God caused the seed of 'His friend' Abraham to inherit it. [See on 12:6.]

We have used the translation *but* for the prefix ו of וּמַלְכִּי־צֶדֶק at the beginning of our verse instead of the more commonly used *and.* The intent of the prefix thus emphasizes the stark difference between the king of Sodom and Malchizedek, for the verses intimate how the king of Sodom went to meet Abraham *empty-handed,* and with no display of gratitude for the salvation Abraham brought him. *'But* Malchizedek [who was not indebted to Abraham] ... was brought out bread and wine' *(Tosefes Brachah).* [1]

1. *Alshich* elaborates on this theme more fully: *V.* 17 which mentions the king of Sodom going out to meet Abraham, should have been followed by verse 21: *And the king of Sodom said to Abraham.* Why was the smooth flow of the narrative interrupted wth the episode of Malchizedek? It would have been more proper to first finish relating the exchange between the king of Sodom and Abraham, and then mention the episode with Malchizedek.

The interpretation of the episode with Malchizedek is inserted just at this point to

הוֹצִיא לֶחֶם וָיָיִן וְהוּא כֹהֵן לְאֵל עֶלְיוֹן:
יט וַיְבָרְכֵהוּ וַיֹּאמַר בָּרוּךְ אַבְרָם לְאֵל עֶלְיוֹן

[The phrasing of the text supports the above antithetic interpretation of Malchizedek's action. The common sentence structure of Scripture places the verb before the subject. An exception is when the subject is emphasized to contrast with a previous statement. Compare for example, 3:1 וְהַנָּחָשׁ הָיָה עָרוּם, *Now* (not *'and') the serpent* (the subject whose special characteristic the verse now wishes to emphasize) *was cunning ...;* also in a more contrasting manner, cf. 31:47: 'Laban called it Yegar Sahadusa, וְיַעֲקֹב קָרָא לוֹ גַּלְעֵד, *but* Jacob called it Gal-ed.' See also *comm.* of *Malbim* to 16:1 וְשָׂרַי ... לֹא יָלְדָה לוֹ, *'but* Sarai ... did not bear him a child.]

Thus, after the selfish, haughty behavior of the king of Sodom, our verse emphasizes *but* Malchizedek was different.]

As *Hirsch* explains: The king of Sodom must have felt very humiliated at his ignominious defeat and subsequent rescue by Abraham. Still, after the victory had been won he came out to meet Abraham as though they were on equal terms — as king. [Possibly rendering עֵמֶק הַשָּׁוֶה, *valley of equality* ed.] He 'demands,' for this is what a Sodomite king understands. It does not dawn on him that he has a responsibility to refresh the exhausted, hungry victors with a piece of bread and a drink of wine. Such decency is not included in the code of conduct of His Majesty of Sodom!

[As cited in *comm.* to *v.* 17, he even put on airs about his escape from the bitumen well, as if the credit were his!]

שָׁלֵם — *Shalem.*

An early name of Jerusalem. *Targum,* in fact, *translates* שָׁלֵם in our verse as 'Jerusalem'. This identification appears clearly in *Ps.* 76:3 where Shalem is mentioned in parallelism with Zion as the abode of God on earth.

The *Midrash* [56:16 to 22:14] explains that the name Jerusalem is a synthesis of the names *Yireh,* which Abraham later called it after the *Akeidah* [22:14], and *Shalem,* the name which Shem called it. In deference to both, God called it Yerushalem [יִרְאֶה שָׁלֵם = יְרוּשָׁלֵם]

Since time immemorial all knew by tradition that Jerusalem, which was the choicest of all places, was the exact complement on earth of the Heavenly Sanctuary where the Shechinah rested *(Ramban).*

הוֹצִיא לֶחֶם וָיָיִן — *Brought out bread and wine* — As customary on behalf of the returning battle-weary [cf. *II Sam.* 17:27 ff.], Malchizedek thereby demonstrated that he bore Abraham no malice for having slain his offspring *(Rashi).*

[The 'offspring' *Rashi* refers to must be Chedorlaomer, who is identified by the *Midrash* to *v.* 1 as Elam son of Shem! (See p. 313). Under the circumstances, then, Malchizedek's (=Shem's) gesture must be viewed as even more magnanimous.]

The *Midrash* comments: He instructed him in the laws of the

emphasize the contrast between the king of Sodom and Malchizedek. The king of Sodom did not go forth to meet Abraham in *personal* gratitude but, as the verse says, met him in the *Valley of Shaveh,* where, as the *Midrash* relates [see *v.* 17] all the peoples had unanimously gathered to praise and proclaim Abraham king. Everyone tumultuously received Abraham — and the king of Sodom merely joined them, though he was the only one who was *personally* indebted to Abraham. And moreover, as the verse implies, he came empty-handed.

This is in sharp contrast to Malchizedek. As a priest, he should have been the *recipient* rather than the *dispenser* of gifts; nevertheless he went forth bearing gifts, though not compelled to do so. [See also *Ramban* cited to *v.* 21.]

XIV *of Shalem, brought out bread and wine. He was a*
19 *priest of God, the Most High.* [19] *He blessed him say-*
ing: 'Blessed is Abram of God the Most High, Maker

priesthood: *bread* alluding to the showbread, and *wine* to libations.

וְהוּא כֹהֵן לְאֵל עֶלְיוֹן — *He was a priest ('kohen') of God, the Most High* — and not of the stars and idols *(Radak).*

This distinguishes him from those priests of the other nations who served *angels* called אֵלִים, *Eilim,* as it is written [*Exod.* 15:11] מִי כָמֹכָה בָּאֵלִם, *Who* is like You among the *Eilim* [*'mighty'* — which *Ramban* loc. cit. renders, 'who is like You among the angels who are called *Eilim?'*] He rather served HASHEM Who is called אֵל עֶלְיוֹן, *the Most High God,* which means, 'the Mighty One Who is Supreme over all.' Abraham [*v.* 22] went even further and identified Him as *HASHEM,* the Most High God *(Ramban).*

'Kohen' has the meaning of one designated to *serve* God and lead others in His service *(R' Meyuchas). HaRechasim le'Bik'ah* explains that it refers specifically to one who *offers sacrifices.*

[Cf. *Rashi* 47:22: The term *kohen* [priest] always means one who ministers to Deity except in those specific cases — such as 41:45: *The* כֹּהֵן [chief] *of On;* and *Exod.* 2:16 *Jethro the* כֹּהֵן [chief] *of Midian* — where the term denotes one of high rank.

[Cf. *Rashi* to *Exod.* 18:1 and *II Sam.* 8:18. Cf. also *Ramban* to 41:45 where he cites other Scriptural examples where *kohen* has a secular definition.]

Cf. *Bamidbar Rabbah* 4:6: Was Malchizedek really a priest? Surely the priesthood *per se* began only with Aaron? — But he was so designated because he performed the sacrificial rites just as do priests.

Hirsch emphasizes that the responsibility of a Jewish priest is to mold people and human affairs to satisfy the requirements and expectations of *God.* This is diametrically opposed to the modern concept of seeking to satisfy the religious needs of *man.* It is not man, but God Who must be "satisfied".

19. וַיְבָרְכֵהוּ וַיֹּאמַר — *[And] he blessed him, saying* [lit. *'and he blessed him and he said'*]

[The text does not read וַיְבָרְכֵהוּ לֵאמֹר, 'and he blessed him *saying'*, implying that the actual words of the blessing are quoted. Rather, Malchizedek made two statements]:

First he blessed him [the text of the blessing has not been recorded in the Torah] and then *he said: 'even without my blessing* בָּרוּךְ אַבְרָם לְאֵל עֶלְיוֹן, Abram is *already blessed* of God Most High', as it is written [12:2] וַאֲבָרֶכְךָ, *'and I will bless you' (Sforno;* see *Or HaChaim).*

בָּרוּךְ אַבְרָם לְאֵל עֶלְיוֹן — *Blessed is Abram of* [lit. *'to'*] *God the Most High.*

I.e may Abram's influence spread throughout the world, and as a result may the appreciation of God be magnified, Whose Name Abraham propogates *(Da'as Soferim).*

[The Sages take special note of the fact that Malchizedek first blessed Abram — as if the thanks for the victory went to *him* — and

כ קֹנֵה שָׁמַיִם וָאָרֶץ: וּבָרוּךְ אֵל עֶלְיוֹן אֲשֶׁר־מִגֵּן צָרֶיךָ בְּיָדֶךָ וַיִּתֶּן־לוֹ מַעֲשֵׂר

קֹנֵה שָׁמַיִם וָאָרֶץ — *Maker of heaven and earth* [lit. *'possessor of'*]

Having made them, He acquired them as His possession *(Rashi).*

Heaven and earth are God's possessions since there is no independent reason dictating their existence other than His will *(Sforno).*

The present tense קֹנֵה [*Maker*, or *Who makes*] is used rather than the past tense קָנָה [*Who made*] because God renews the act of Creation daily *(Ma'asei Hashem).*

According to the *Midrash,* however, קֹנֵה שָׁמַיִם וָאָרֶץ (lit. *'who has acquired heaven and earth')* refers to *Abraham* who, by diffusing the knowledge of God among men, was recognized as having acquired a partnership in the purpose of the Creation.[1]

20. וּבָרוּךְ אֵל עֶלְיוֹן — *And blessed be God the Most High.*

— I.e., by giving you this marvelous victory, the Highest God has shown Himself to be so near to those His who serve Him, that people are awakened and won over to His service. As a result, He and His kingdom become blessed *(Abarbanel).*

[There is great difficulty in comprehending the meaning of 'blessing' as applied to God — how can a frail, dependent human being bless the All-Power Creator?

Sefer haChinuch (430) observes that a blessing is nothing more than

only in the next verse did he bless God]:

Rav Zechariah said on behalf of Rav Yishmael:

The Holy One Blessed be He intended to bring forth the priesthood from Shem [identified with Malchizedek] but because he gave precedence in his blessing to Abraham over God, He brought it forth from Abraham, [for when Malchizedek had blessed Abraham and then God], Abraham had said to him: 'Is a servant's blessing to be given precedence over his Master's?'

Forthwith, God gave the priesthood to Abraham, as it is written: [*Psalms* 110:1,4]: *HASHEM said to my lord* (Abraham; cf. *Berachos* 7b] ... *'You are a priest forever after the manner* [דִּבְרָתִי] *of Malchizedek'* — which means, 'because of the words [דִּבְרַת] of Malchizedek whereby he gave Abraham prominence.'

Therefore our verse reads: *And he was a priest of God, the Most High — he* [only Malchizedek] was a priest, but not his descendants *(Nedarim* 32b).

Ran, ad. loc., explains that though Abraham was a descendant of Malchizedek, [Shem], and thus the priesthood *was,* in effect, inherited by the latter's seed, yet this was through the personal merit of *Abraham,* not as a legacy of Malchizedek. Furthermore, as *Torah Temimah* points out, Abraham was not descended through Shem's first-born, the natural heir. Therefore, the priesthood is regarded as Abraham's not Shem's.

1. Rav Yitzchak said: Abraham used to entertain wayfarers, and after they had eaten, he would say to them, 'Say a blessing.'

'What shall we say,' they asked.

'Blessed be the God of the Universe of Whose bounty we have eaten,' he replied.

Then God said to him: 'My Name was not known among My creatures, and you have made it known among them. I will therefore regard you as though you were associated with Me in the creation of the world *(Midrash;* see *comm.* to 21:33 s.v. וַיִּקְרָא).

XIV
20

of heaven and earth; [20] *and blessed be God the Most High Who has delivered your foes into your hand'; and he gave him a tenth of everything.*

our acknowledgement that God is the source from Whom we must seek all good.

Rashba and *Nefesh haChaim* derive the word בְּרָכָה from בְּרֵיכָה a *spring,* i.e. God is like a never-ending spring that His goodness flows out to His people (see *Bircas Hamazon,* ArtScroll ed. pp. 25-28).][1]

The identification of God as *'Most High'* in the exchanges between Malchizedek and Abraham served to disabuse listeners of the notion that any purpose could be served by worshiping idols. Hashem is the Most High and All-Powerful *(Akeidas Yitzchak).*

אֲשֶׁר מִגֵּן צָרֶיךָ בְּיָדֶךָ — *Who has delivered your foes into your hand.*

The word מִגֵּן, *delivered,* [in the sense of handed-over, surrendered, abandoned] has the same meaning here as in *Hosea* 11:8 אֵיךְ...אֲמַגֶּנְךָ יִשְׂרָאֵל *How can I abandon you, O Israel? (Rashi).*

וַיִּתֶּן לוֹ מַעֲשֵׂר מִכֹּל — *And he* [i.e. *Abram*] *gave him* [i.e. Malchizedek] *a tenth of everything.*[2]

That is, of everything that Abraham had, because Malchizedek was a priest [and, as such, entitled to the tithe] *(Rashi).*

He thereby indicated that his descendants would give מַעֲשֵׂר, *tithes,* to the priests *(Ramban).*

According to *Gur Aryeh,* the tithe was not taken from any of the proceeds of *this* conquest, because one does not tithe of that which is not his own, and in *v.* 22, Abraham specifically refrained from keeping any spoils of this victory. Rather, as *Rashi* explains, מִכֹּל was *from his general property.*

Many commentators *do* interpret the tithe as coming from the spoils of the war, and

1. [The meaning of בָּרוּךְ when applied to God might better be comprehended in its root meaning of 'kneel down to.' Perhaps a better translation would be *'worshiped'.*

He is *blessed* in the sense that he is blessed and extolled by all His creatures *(Midrashei Torah).*

As *Rav Shlomo Kluger* explains:

Just as every beneficial thing on earth is called a blessing, so, too, every personal virtue of a good person is called a blessing. This is the meaning of the 'blessings' which we recite to God: we acknowledge that all of his attributes are just and righteous.

2. In reward to Abraham for giving tithes מִכֹּל, *from all,* the three great pillars of the world, Abraham, Isaac, and Jacob, enjoyed prosperity. Of Abraham it is written [24:1]: *And HASHEM blessed Abraham* בַּכֹּל, *in all things;* of Isaac it is written [27:33]: *I have eaten* מִכֹּל *of all;* of Jacob it says [33:11]: *HASHEM has dealt graciously with me and I have* כֹּל, *all.* All the above in reward for *and he gave him a tenth* מִכֹּל, *of all (Midrash).*

This is the significance of the benediction in the Grace after Meals: כְּמוֹ שֶׁנִּתְבָּרְכוּ אֲבוֹתֵינוּ אַבְרָהָם יִצְחָק וְיַעֲקֹב בַּכֹּל מִכֹּל כֹּל, *just as our forefathers Abraham, Isaac, and Jacob were blessed in all, of all, all.* (See *comm.* to ArtScroll *Bircas Hamazon* p. 64.]

It is also noteworthy that all three Patriarchs gave tithes: Abraham in our verse; Isaac in 26:12 (see *Rashi);* and Jacob in 28:22.

Sefer HaChinuch gives reasons for the various tithes. The respective reasons correspond to the virtues of the respective Patriarchs:

— מַעֲשֵׂר עָנִי, *the tithe to the poor,* (commandment 66) 'so that God's creatures become accustomed to the attribute of mercy'. [This attribute corresponds to Abraham.]

— מַעֲשֵׂר רִאשׁוֹן, the *First Tithe* [to the Levites] (commandment 395) to assist the Levites 'for

כא מִכֹּל: °וַיֹּ֥אמֶר מֶֽלֶךְ־סְדֹ֖ם אֶל־אַבְרָ֑ם תֶּן־לִ֣י
כב הַנֶּ֔פֶשׁ וְהָרְכֻ֖שׁ קַֽח־לָֽךְ: וַיֹּ֥אמֶר אַבְרָ֖ם
אֶל־מֶ֣לֶךְ סְדֹ֑ם הֲרִמֹ֨תִי יָדִ֤י אֶל־יהוה֙ אֵ֣ל

they wonder how Abraham tithed that which was not his. They suggest that it was not Abraham who gave the tithe to Malchizedek, but *Malchizedek* who gave it to *Abraham* thereby demonstrating that, as the savior, the spoils rightfully were his *(Radak; Rav Yosef Kara; Midrash haNe'elam; Chizkuni.* Cf. also *Ra'avad* to *Hilchos Melachim* 9:1 and comm. there).

However, according to the primary view that it was Abraham who gave the tithe to Malchizedek, Abraham was probably following the concept as formulated in *Bava Kamma* 104a that 'if one rescued articles from heathens or from robbers [*if the owners have abandoned them*] they belong to him.' Now, since a *'chaver'*, a scrupulously observant person, does not let anything pass from under his hand, unless he first gave the required tithes, Abraham fulfilled the obligation to tithe the spoils that were legally his. This accomplished, he transferred the rest back to the king of Sodom *(Riva;* cf. *Tur).* [The opposing view would apparently emphasize the fact that the owners never entirely abandoned hope (נִתְיָאֵשׁ) for the return of the articles and hence Abraham had no claim on them.]

21. וַיֹּאמֶר מֶלֶךְ־סְדֹם אֶל־אַבְרָם — *And the king of Sodom said to Abram.*

Until this point, the king of Sodom had requested nothing of Abraham. But when he saw Abraham's generosity in giving the tithe to Malchizedek, he mustered up the courage to ask for the prisoners, as an act of charity *(Ramban).*

[This, according to *Ramban* is the reason the incident with Malchizedek was interpolated in the otherwise flowing narrative about the king of Sodom in *vss.* 17 and 21. The sequence of events demanded it. See also *Alshich* cited in *footnote* to *v.* 18.]

תֶּן לִי הַנֶּפֶשׁ — *Give me the people* [lit. *'the soul'*] — i.e., the freed captives ...

Return to me only the people *(Rashi),* so I can repopulate my city *(Lekach Tov).*

Rashi thus explains that in this context, נֶפֶשׁ, *soul,* refers in a general manner to *people,* the specific reference here being to those Sodomites whom Abraham had freed. Similarly תֶּן [*give*] has the meaning of *'return' (Mizrachi).*

[We must take note that even the king of Sodom must have recognized that as the victor, Abraham had the right to dispose of the rescued people however he desired. Hence, as *Ramban* points out above, the king of Sodom sought *an act of charity,* a request precipitated by Abraham's generosity in dispensing tithes to Malchizedek.]

[The Sages take Abraham to task for complying with the request *'give me the people'*, for had he kept the people with him, he would have taught them to know God]:

'Why was Abraham so punished that his descendants were enslaved to the Egyptians ... ? Rav Yochanan

God chose Levi from among his brothers for His service.' [Isaac represents the ideal of service.]

— מַעֲשַׂר בְּהֵמָה — *the Tithe from animals* [the same reason applies to מַעֲשֵׂר שֵׁנִי, the *Second Tithe*] which must be brought to Jerusalem (commandment 360) 'for God chose the Jewish people and desires for the sake of His righteousness that they all engage in Torah study' ... therefore He instructed them to go to Jerusalem, the center of Torah. [Jacob represents Torah study.] *(Rav Avie Gold).*

21 *The king of Sodom said to Abram: 'Give me the people and take the possessions for yourself.'*
22 *Abram said to the king of Sodom: 'I lift up my*

said: Because he hindered people from coming under the wings of the Shechinah (*Nedarim* 32a; cf. similar exegesis to *v.* 14). [1]

Abraham's rationale in returning the people was apparently that they were of wicked stock and no good would come of them in any event (*Ki Tov*).

[According to the *Midrash* cited end of *v.* 16, Abraham returned the adults only. It was to his credit that he kept the children behind and eventually converted them to the true faith.]

וְהָרְכֻשׁ קַח־לָךְ — *And take the possessions for yourself.*

It was not only the possessions of *Sodom* that were at issue here, but the spoils of Amraphel and his comrades too (*Ha'amek Davar*).

The Sages referred to this dialogue when they declared [*Avos* 5:10]: One who says, 'Mine is mine and yours is yours' ... that is the characteristic of Sodom (*Malbim*). [See *Overview*.]

22. [But Abraham declines the offer. In a magnanimous gesture of devotion to God, he takes a solemn oath rejecting any notion of personal gain from his recent victory]:

הֲרִמֹתִי יָדִי — *I lift* [lit. *'I lifted'*] *up my hand.*

An expression signifying an oath. Although lit. in past tense, the phrase is interpreted in the present tense as indicating such absolute determination to carry out the pledge, that the deed may be considered as good as done. Similarly in 23:13: נָתַתִּי כֶּסֶף הַשָּׂדֶה, *I give* [lit. *'I gave'*] *the money for the field* (*Rashi; Mizrachi; Devek Tov*).

The expression implying an oath, is similar to *Deut.* 32:40 *'I raise my hand to heaven ...'* (*Ibn Ezra*).

The implied meaning then is: 'I have lifted my hand to HASHEM to dedicate these things as sacred to Him, [and as such I may derive no personal benefit from them.] To declare things sacred is called תְּרוּמַת יַד, lifting the hand [see *Exod.* 35:24.] Thus Abraham vowed to derive no personal benefit from that which he sanctified as תְּרוּמָה לַה׳, *a heave offering to HASHEM*. The *Midrash* similarly relates הֲרִמֹתִי to

1. This insight of the Sages, that Abraham's sin in not seeking to bring God's teaching to the subjects of the Sodomite king resulted in the decree of the Egyptian exile, would seem to follow the view [of the *Midrash* cited by the Vilna Gaon in his *comm.* to *Seder Olam*, and of *Ramban*] that the narratives of this chapter and the next are in *correct* chronological sequence, and the War between the Kings accordingly preceded the Covenant Between the Parts in Ch. 15.

If, however, we follow according to this view, the usual Rabbinic chronology [*Seder Olam; Rashi; Tosafos*; see *comm.* to 15:7 and 'Additional Note A'], according to which the narrative is not in chronological order and the Covenant Between the Parts *preceded* this Sodomite war, then the exile had already been pre-ordained and could not have resulted from Abraham's sin (*Harav David Feinstein*).

[The usual Rabbinic chronology would apparently then follow that one view in *Nedarim* 32a (cited in 15:8) that Abraham sinned immediately before the covenant itself by asking בַּמָּה אֵדַע כִּי אִירָשֶׁנָּה — *'Whereby shall I know that I am to inherit it?'*]

כג עֶלְי֔וֹן קֹנֵ֖ה שָׁמַ֥יִם וָאָֽרֶץ׃ אִם־מִחוּט֙ וְעַ֣ד
שְׂרֽוֹךְ־נַ֔עַל וְאִם־אֶקַּ֖ח מִכָּל־אֲשֶׁר־לָ֑ךְ
וְלֹ֣א תֹאמַ֔ר אֲנִ֖י הֶעֱשַׁ֥רְתִּי אֶת־אַבְרָֽם׃

תְּרוּמָה, and interprets: Abraham made it a תְּרוּמָה, *heave offering (Ramban).*

Or, as *Ralbag* explains: הֲרִמֹתִי [past tense] *I have already dedicated my share to God* as the tithe in *v.* 20, and have therefore not benefited from the spoils one iota; וְאִם אֶקַּח [future tense] *neither will I take more,* nor benefit further (see *Or haChaim).*

Abarbanel, however, perceives the act of raising the hands toward heaven as an indication of one's affirmation that one's reliance is on our Father in Heaven. Thus, in response to the heathen king of Sodom, Abraham raises his hand away from all the gods, signifying that his faith is directed only to the Highest, to HASHEM Who, for him, is the only One. He thereby intimated: *'I lift up my hand to HASHEM'* ... as if to say, 'When I require gifts or favor, I will raise my hands in supplication *to God* for He is the Most High, Master of heaven and earth. Therefore, it is only from Him that I will accept gifts — from you, king of Sodom I will accept not even a thread or shoe strap.

[I will be provided for by the God Who promised me: *I will make you great.* My motives were only to make His wonders known throughout the world — I will accept no earthly rewards for my act.]

אֶל ה׳ אֵל עֶלְיוֹן — *To HASHEM, God Most High,* the same God in Whose Name this priest blessed me *(Ibn Ezra).*

To the אֵל עֶלְיוֹן, used by Malchizedek Abraham adds the name HASHEM, the most characteristic Name of God which places the God Most High, Possessor of heaven and earth in special relationship to mankind [see *comm.* to 1:1; 2:4; *footnote* on p. 192; 7:1; 8:21.] ... Abraham's designation of God thus expresses his conviction that God in His relationship to man does not differ from the author's conception of their gods merely in the degree of His power. In the Jewish conception, He is not only the God of nature, but the God of history and the Creator of the future Who determines the course of all events *(Hirsch).*

23. אִם מִחוּט וְעַד שְׂרוֹךְ נַעַל — *If so much as* [lit. *'from'*] *a thread* [*and*] *to a shoe strap* — shall I retain for myself from the spoils *(Rashi).*

— The general meaning is: Even the most insignificant spoils of my victories will I not retain — thus have I vowed to HASHEM *(Ibn Caspi).*

The translation *thread to a shoe strap,* follows *Ibn Ezra.*

חוּט, thread also refers to a head ornament [חוּטִין שֶׁבְּרָאשֵׁי הַבָּנוֹת] mentioned in *Shabbos* 57a, made of silken threads with which girls tie their hair; שְׂרוֹךְ נַעַל also refers to a foot ornament. The meaning, then, is 'even the slightest object, from the top of the head to the bottom of the foot' *(Chizkuni).*

According to *Rav Saadia Gaon,* Abraham thus disavowed the acceptance of anything, whatever its origin, whether it be *'thread',* [i.e. *vegetable:* wheat or fruit]; *a 'shoelace',* [i.e. *animal:* signifying animals or fowl]; *nor shall I take* ... [suggesting *mineral:* gifts of silver or gold] *(R' Bachya).*

*hand to HASHEM, God Most High, Maker of heaven
and earth,* [23] *if so much as a thread to a shoestrap;
nor shall I take from anything of yours! So you shall
not say, "It is I who made Abram rich."* [24] *Far from*

The *Talmud* [*Chullin* 88b] notes that as a reward for having refused to accept the thread and shoe-strap, Abraham's children received two precepts: the *thread* of blue [*Numb.* 15:38, referring to the precept of *tzitzis*], and the *strap* of *tefillin.*

Abraham is credited with instituting שַׁחֲרִית, morning services [*Berachos* 26b, based upon *Gen.* 19:27.] This is perhaps why it is during morning services specifically, that we don *tallis* and *tefillin* when in reality the *entire day* would be correct for the performance of these *mitzvos.* We envelop ourselves, therefore, in these *mitzvos* during *Shacharis* to demonstrate that it was by his merit that we received them *(Meshech Chochmah).*[1]

וְאִם־אֶקַּח מִכָּל אֲשֶׁר־לָךְ — *Nor* [lit. *'and if'*] *shall I take from anything of yours.*

Even if you offer me a reward — not from the spoils of my conquest which I have vowed not to retain — but even a gift *from your own treasures,* I will still accept nothing *(Rashi; Mizrachi).*

Throughout the Torah, the word אִם, [*if*], where it is not followed by a condition, has the implication of an oath, the meaning being: *'I will not' (Sforno; Heidenheim).*

This phraseology also signifies an implied consequence. The connotation implies that the full phrase is 'And may God do unto me such and such *if* I take ... ' See *I Kings* 2:23 *(Ramban; Tur).* [See also 21:23 and *Ruth* 1:17.]

וְלֹא תֹאמַר אֲנִי הֶעֱשַׁרְתִּי אֶת אַבְרָם — *So* [lit. *'and'*] *you shall not say,* '[it is] *I*

1. The *halachah* is that the left shoe should be tied before the right because the strap of tefillin is tied upon the *left* arm. The general rule, however, gives precedence to the right because Scripture preferred it in the Temple service. Therefore, for example, the right shoe is donned first. Why is the generally preferred order not followed with regard to *tying* as well? The answer is indicated by the *Talmudic* dictum that for refusing a shoe-strap, Abraham was rewarded with the strap of *tefillin.* Therefore, a shoe-strap has a special relationship to *tefillin*: since *tefillin* are tied on the left arm, the left in this case takes precedence and the shoe-lace is tied first *(Hagahas Rabbi Akiva Eiger, Orach Chaim* 2:4).

Additionally, according to other *Midrashim* the reward for Abraham denying himself *thread and shoe-strap* resulted in even more precepts:

- *For denying himself the thread* his children were rewarded with the Tabernacle which was adorned with blue and purple wool;

  Thread also alludes to the sacrifices: a thread-like scarlet line encircled the middle of the altar marking the division between the blood sprinkled on the upper part of the altar and the lower;

  In reward for *'thread'* his children were also rewarded with the scarlet thread which turned white on Yom Kippur [as a sign that Israel's sins were forgiven] See *Lev.* 16:10; *Isaiah* 1:18; *Yoma* 67a.

- *For denying himself the shoe-strap* his children were rewarded with the precept of *Chalitzah* of which it says [*Deut.* 25:9] *She shall loosen his shoe from his foot;*

  It refers to the feet of the festival pilgrims to Jerusalem of whom it says [*Song of Songs* 7:2 ArtScroll translation]: *But your footsteps were so lovely when shod in pilgrim sandals;*

  It also refers to the קָרְבַּן פֶּסַח, *Passover sacrifice,* which was eaten while wearing shoes [see *Exod.* 12:11.]

כד בִּלְעָדַי רַק אֲשֶׁר אָכְלוּ הַנְּעָרִים וְחֵלֶק
הָאֲנָשִׁים אֲשֶׁר הָלְכוּ אִתִּי עָנֵר אֶשְׁכֹּל
וּמַמְרֵא הֵם יִקְחוּ חֶלְקָם׃
א אַחַר
הַדְּבָרִים הָאֵלֶּה הָיָה דְבַר־יהוה אֶל־

[who] *made Abram rich,'* i.e., my reason for declining all personal gains here is so that you do not go about boasting that it was you who made me rich rather than God, on Whose promise of wealth I rely *(Rashi; Mizrachi).*

As *Chizkuni* comments:

'When I left my father's house, God promised me wealth [see *comm.* to 12:2]. Better that I take nothing of yours, and when I become wealthy I will attribute the wealth to its true Source — Him to Whom all wealth and honor belongs.'

Gur Aryeh raises the question that perhaps the Sodomite spoils were God's means of blessing Abraham, just as Pharaoh's gifts were in fulfillment of God's blessing. If so, why did Abraham refuse the king's offer? *Gur Aryeh* explains that a 'blessing' can never stem from human suffering. Since the king of Sodom offered gifts only in gratitude for having been rescued from certain death, Abraham realized that such gains could not be construed as God's blessing. Pharaoh, however, gave gifts in order to gain Abraham's favor. Thus his gifts were symbolic of the universal respect which God had promised Abraham. (See *comm.* to 13:16 for additional reason why Abraham accepted Pharaoh's gifts).

Some interpret that Abraham's intention was not to disparage the king's motive. What Abraham meant was: 'I am fully aware that your motive is sincere וְלֹא תֹאמַר *and you will not say* 'I made Abraham rich.' Nevertheless I will take nothing *(Kli Yakar).*

24. בִּלְעָדַי — *Far from me!* [lit. *'without me'*. Following *Ibn Janach; Nesinah laGer; Hirsch.*]

— This characteristic of desiring others' money is remote from me. Do not attempt to prevail upon me because I will not accept. Only what the young men have eaten ... *(haRechasim l'Bik'ah).*

According to *Sforno,* Abraham said: 'You can take what you desire בִּלְעָדַי *without me,* i.e. without my approval, as I make no claim. Only what the young men have eaten ...'

Malbim interprets בִּלְעָדַי, everything that transpired was done *without me,* in the sense of without any help from me. It is not *I* who fashioned victory in this war. Therefore, *I* claim nothing except for what the young men have eaten.

רַק אֲשֶׁר אָכְלוּ הַנְּעָרִים — *Only what the young men have eaten,* i.e. my disciples who accompanied me [*v.* 14.]

Only what the *young men* have eaten, not: 'what *we* have eaten.' Abraham did not partake of these possessions even for his own share of the food *(Ha'amek Davar).*

The *Talmud* [*Chullin* 89a] observes from our verse how grave, indeed, is theft which has been consumed, for even the perfectly righteous cannot restore it. [The *Talmud* is not suggesting that Abraham's servants ate stolen goods. Rather a general analogy is being drawn here. By refusing the spoils, he

me! Only what the young men have eaten, and the
XV share of the men who accompanied me: Aner,
1 Eshkol, and Mamre — they will take their portion.'
¹ After these events, the word of HASHEM came to

treated it as he would robbery and would have no part of it. Nevertheless even he could not restore what had *already* been wrongfully eaten by the young men. Such is the gravity of theft: Once it has been consumed, *complete* repentance is impossible.]

וְחֵלֶק הָאֲנָשִׁים אֲשֶׁר הָלְכוּ אִתִּי — *And the share of the men who accompanied me.* These were חֲנִיכָיו, *his disciples,* i.e., his students who were not his slaves, mentioned in *v.* 14 *(Levush; Malbim; Ha'amek Davar).*

עָנֵר אֶשְׁכֹּל וּמַמְרֵא הֵם יִקְחוּ חֶלְקָם — *Aner, Eshkol, and Mamre — they will* [or: 'may'] *take their portion.*

You are not to negotiate with them regarding their share; the prerogative is theirs to take any portion they consider fit *(Or haChaim).*

Abraham thus declared that Aner, Eshkol and Mamre, were entitled to share the spoils, even though they were not active combatants but remained behind to guard his property. David later emulated Abraham's example when he declared that the spoils of his wars were to be shared between combatants and non-combatants alike [See *I Sam.* 30:24, 25] *(Rashi).*

[Cf. also *Numb.* 31:26 ff.]

Sforno explains that Abraham would accept recompense only for that which his young men ate and on behalf of the men who accompanied him. As for Aner and his comrades, Abraham declared that it was not for him to allot them a share: they were chiefs and entitled to take it themselves.[1]

XV

1-6 God's Reassurance to Abraham

1. אַחַר הַדְּבָרִים הָאֵלֶּה — *After these events* [lit. *'things.'*]

— I.e. after his victory over the kings.

Whenever the term אַחַר occurs it signifies *immediately after* [and possibly as a result of] the preceding event. The term אַחֲרֵי signifies after the lapse of a considerable time *(Rashi).* [See *comm.* to 22:1 and 22:20.]

[*Rashi's* comment is based upon the *Midrash. Yafeh To'ar* notes that this distinction between the terms אַחַר and אַחֲרֵי, both of which mean *after,* is valid only when it occurs in the phrase *after these things.*]

1. The *Chofetz Chaim* notes that Abraham was especially stringent in his own conduct by refusing to benefit in any way from the king of Sodom — *'even so much as a thread to a shoestrap.'* For those who accompanied him, however, he was not as stringent. The lesson to be derived from this is that, regarding his own conduct, everyone has the prerogative to be more scrupulous than the law requires. But he may not impose this extra stringecy upon others.

אַבְרָם בְּמַּחֲזֶה לֵאמֹר אַל־תִּירָא אַבְרָם
ב אָנֹכִי מָגֵן לָךְ שְׂכָרְךָ הַרְבֵּה מְאֹד׃ וַיֹּאמֶר

בְּמַּחֲזֶה — *In a vision.*

I.e., in prophecy *(Onkelos);* a prophetic vision *(Ibn Ezra).*

The *Midrash* explains that prophecy is expressed by ten designations: נְבוּאָה [prophecy], חָזוֹן [vision], דִּבּוּר [speech], הַטָּפָה [influx, i.e. 'flow of words'], אֲמִירָה [saying], צִוּוּי [command], מַשָּׂא [burden], מָשָׁל [parable], מְלִיצָה [metaphor], and חִידָה [enigma; allegory]. The highest of these prophetic experiences is vision [מַחֲזֶה; חָזוֹן], and then speech [דִּבּוּר]. Great then, is the power of Abraham that his experience included both of these high levels of prophecy since the verse states that *the Word* [speech=דְּבַר] *of God came to Abraham in a vision* [מַחֲזֶה].

The word חָזוֹן [in our case, the cognate מַחֲזֶה] literally means viewing with the eye ... and also figuratively, to perceive mentally *(Moreh Nevuchim* 1:4).

... This communication is termed a *vision* because more than *speech* was involved. He was shown tangible things during this prophecy: He was taken outside and shown the stars, etc. *(Radak).*

Ramban explains that Abraham was now privileged to receive the divine communication in a daytime vision; hitherto it had come to him only at night. The esoteric implication of מַחֲזֶה, vision — known to the learned in Kabbalah [=לְיוֹדְעֵי חֵ״ן חָכְמוֹת נִסְתָּרוֹת, esoteric wisdom] is similar to the implications of the verse [in *Exod.* 20:15]: 'and all the people *saw* [rather than *heard*] the thundering' [see *comm.* there.]

לֵאמֹר — *Saying* [lit. *'to say'.*]

[As pointed out earlier (see *comm.* to 8:15, also 1:22; 2:16) the use of לֵאמֹר occurs frequently, but not always, in divine commands. It has different but not mutually exclusive connotations: In certain cases it signifies immediate fulfillment; in others that the intent of the command was perfectly comprehensible, and in others that the recipient of the command should, in turn, relay it to others. In this case the connotation might be a combination of the above: That God's promise of protection would comfort him and his descendants whenever they were faced with impending disaster, that the communication was crystal-clear and that he should pass on the promise to his descendants after him.]

אַל תִּירָא אַבְרָם — *Fear not, Abram.*

From God's assurance to Abraham, *'Fear not'*, it is clear that Abraham was strongly perturbed about something.

The *Midrashim* and commentators generally explain that when Abraham reflected on the miracle which enabled him to slay the kings although he was greatly outnumbered, he was anxious lest, the miracle had been possible only as שָׂכָר, *a reward,* for his previous righteousness and that he could not expect future divine assistance, and that he would be punished for the men he had slain in the foray *(Rashi),* some of whom — especially among the non-combatants — may have been righteous *(Midrash).* He was also apprehensive that the suc-

XV
1

Abram in a vision saying, 'Fear not, Abram, I am your shield; your reward is very great.'

cessors of the four kings would collect even greater armies than before and stage a reprisal attack on him. This time, since all his merit had been used to gain the previous victory, he would be defeated *(Midrash).* Additionally, he feared that he would die without children *(Ramban).*

God therefore appeared to Abraham in a prophetic vision and assuaged his fears.

Targum Yerushalmi paraphrases this verse as follows:

'After these words ... when Abram the Righteous ... had slain four kings, Abram the Righteous reasoned to himself: Woe is me that I have received my reward in This World, and have no portion in the World to Come; or perhaps the successors of the slain will combine and attack me; or perhaps I had until now the merit of a few mitzvos which made them fall before me, or that they were defeated by virtue of righteousness which was formerly found in me, but a second time it may not be found and the Heavenly Name will be profaned in me ...

'Then the word of prophecy from HASHEM was unto Abram the Righteous saying, Fear not Abram, though they should attack you in great numbers, My Word [i.e. I] shall be your reward and your shield in This World, and your protector throughout the World to Come. And though I cast down your enemies before you in this World, the reward for your good deeds is prepared by Me for you in the World to Come.'

Meshech Chochmah suggests that Abraham's fear was of a different nature. He reasoned that, had he prevented the Sodomites from reconstituting their wicked and selfish community, he might have succeeded in bringing them to repent. Instead he allowed them to return to Sodom where they became even more iniquitous than before. Thus, he was responsible for their sinfulness. God therefore assuaged his fear by saying, *Fear not, Abram ...*

[God's assurance, *Fear not!* was similarly given to Isaac (26:24), Jacob (46:3), and to nearly all the righteous ones in Scripture.]

אָנֹכִי מָגֵן לָךְ — *I am your shield* [lit. *'I am a shield unto you'*].

I am your shield against punishment; for you will not be punished on account of all these people you have slain *(Rashi)*; and I am your shield against your enemies. 'Just as a shield receives all spears and withstands them, so will I stand by you' *(Midrash).*

שְׂכָרְךָ הַרְבֵּה מְאֹד — *Your reward is very great* — Not only need you not fear punishment, but you need not be apprehensive concerning the future, *for your reward is very great (Rashi).* For, as the *Yalkut* notes [cf. *Targum Yerushalmi* above] Abraham was apprehensive lest his merits had been consumed in This World leaving nothing for the Hereafter, therefore God assured him concerning the great reward in store for him (see *Kli Yakar).*

God also assured him that there were no righteous people among those whom Abraham had slain; rather than deserving punishment for slaying them, he was worthy of reward for ridding the world of the wicked! *(Midrash).*

Ibn Ezra interprets:

I was your shield — when I saved you from the kings; similarly, *I shall reward you* for having risen to

אַבְרָם אֲדֹנָי יֱהוִה מַה־תִּתֶּן־לִי וְאָנֹכִי
הוֹלֵךְ עֲרִירִי וּבֶן־מֶשֶׁק בֵּיתִי הוּא דַּמֶּשֶׂק

the occasion of relying on Me in saving your nephew with only small forces.[1]

2. אֲדֹנָי ה׳ — *My Lord, HASHEM/ELOHIM.* [For explanation of this Name, see *comm.* to *v. 8.*]

מַה־תִּתֶּן לִי — *What can You give me?*

I.e. of what avail will Your gifts be to me ... *(B'chor Shor).*

וְאָנֹכִי הוֹלֵךְ עֲרִירִי — *Seeing that* [lit. *'and'*] *I go childless.*

Thus whatever You give me will be inherited by others *(B'chor Shor).*

Also, Abraham foresaw that the 'others' — those whom he had converted to the true faith, and even his own nephew Lot — had or would eventually abandon his teachings. Of all his disciples not one would remain upon whom Abraham could depend to carry forward the belief in the Creator. Given his own childlessness, with what could God reward him to assure the dissemination of belief in One God? *(Akeidas Yitzchak).* [2]

הוֹלֵךְ, *go, depart,* is explained by *Targum Yonasan, Radak,* and *Tur* as a euphemism connoting death: Abraham feared that he would 'pass from the world' [in the sense of *depart* from life] childless.

Ramban suggests however, that the verb is to be understood in its literal sense: Abraham incredulously said, 'Of what avail can a reward be seeing that I הוֹלֵךְ, *wander about* childless as a lone vagabond ... ?'

Although the commentators generally agree that the sense of עֲרִירִי is *'childless',* they differ on the etymology of the cognate verb.

Rashi quotes *Menachem* that עֲרִירִי derives from a word which, in different forms,has opposite meanings. Thus, when the word appears in the root form as עֵר it means *heir, child* [see *Targum* to עֵר וְעֹנֶה in *Malachi* 2:12], while as עֲרִירִי the same word means *childless.* Though he agrees that the implication of עֲרִירִי is *childless, Rashi* suggests that it is related to the cognate verb [ערה] meaning *destroy, lay* bare, as in *Ps.* 137:7 עָרוּ עָרוּ, *Destroy it! Destroy it!* [Thus, as *Rashi* notes to 16:2 a childless person is described as *destroyed* in terms of his memory in future generations.]

וּבֶן־מֶשֶׁק בֵּיתִי — *And the steward of my house.*

The translation follows *Onkelos,* and *Rashi* who explains it as *my administrator;* the man by whose authority my entire household is sustained. This is similar to the verb נשק, *sustenance* as in וְעַל פִּיךָ יִשַּׁק כָּל עַמִּי, *by your word shall all my people be sustained* [41:40].

1. The *Midrash* relates that Abraham entertained even further misgivings. He said to God: 'Sovereign of the Universe! You made a covenant with Noah not to exterminate his children. Yet, through my meritorious acts my covenant superceded his [and I was victorious and exterminated the forces of the four kings.] Perhaps another will arise who will accumulate even a greater store of precepts earning a new covenant that will supercede mine.'

God therefore reassured him that only to Abraham's children would He set up shields for the righteous [i.e., only to Abraham, but not to Noah, did God promise to be a shield; see *Radal*]; for there did not arise from Noah even one righteous person [aside from Abraham] whose righteousness could have served to spare his contemporaries. Moreover He assured him that there would always be a righteous one in each generation among Abraham's descendants who would shield his sinful contemporaries and atone on their behalf.

XV
2 [2] *And Abram said, 'My Lord, HASHEM/ELOHIM: What can You give me seeing that I go childless, and the steward of my house is the Damascene Eliezer?'*

הוּא דַּמֶּשֶׂק אֱלִיעֶזֶר — *Is the Damascene Eliezer* [lit. *'Damessek Eliezer*]

Our translation follows *Rashi* who, citing *Onkelos*, explains that he was a native of Damascus. According to the *Midrash*, however,he won this designation because it was with his assistance that Abraham pursued the kings as far as Damascus [see 14:14 regarding Eliezer's accompaniment of Abraham, and 14:15 that the pursuit was until the vicinity of Damascus.] The *Talmud, Yoma* 28b interprets the surname *Damessek* as if it were a composition of דּוֹלֶה וּמַשְׁקֶה, *one who draws and gives drink*, because Eliezer drew upon his master's teachings and transmitted them to others 'to drink'.

The translation also follows *Ibn Janach* who interprets the phrase as if it read הוּא אִישׁ דַּמֶּשֶׂק אֱלִיעֶזֶר, [*that is Eliezer, the man of Damascus*], or as if it read אֱלִיעֶזֶר מִדַּמֶּשֶׂק or אֱלִיעֶזֶר הַדַּמַּשְׂקִי.

Radak interprets similarly. He adds an alternative interpretation that his name was originally Damessek, but Abraham gave him the Hebrew name, Eliezer. At times, however, Abraham would call him by both names.

The general implication of Abraham's remark, then, is: If, I had a son, *he* [instead of this servant] would be in charge of my affairs *(Rashi).*

Had my heir been someone of my own kin it would not be so unpleasant. But it is distasteful, indeed, that a Damascene will inherit me *(Radak).*

... This stranger whom I brought to me from Damascus, neither from my family nor my country *(Ramban).*

Hirsch interprets: *And the heir who is longing* [מֶשֶׁק = תְּשׁוּקָה, *longing*] *for my house is Eliezer's Damascus i.e.,* not Eliezer, himself he is already old, but his relatives from Damascus. When Abraham pursued the defeated kings up to Damascus he learned that Eliezer's relatives were casting longing eyes at Abraham's inheritance. Therefore, Abraham said, Give me nothing; whatever You give me

2. In a dissertation fundamental to the understanding of the narrative, *Ramban* explains that the righteous grow apprehensive because they perceive that the righteous often suffer [see *Eccl.* 8:14]. Abraham feared that he would die childless; therefore God reiterated His assurance that his progeny would be as numerous as the stars of the heaven.

One may ask why Abraham felt such fear in view of God's earlier promise [above, 13:15-16] of the Land to his descendants who would be *as the dust of the earth?* Further, why would his belief in this second promise be more firm than his belief in the first?

The explanation is that the righteous never take their righteousness for granted. Abraham saw himself growing old and he was still childless. The first prophecy had not been fulfilled, and he feared that his own sin was the cause of its forfeiture; or as the *Midrash* notes, that he was being punished for having slain people in the war. Hence the principle that the righteous are never confident in this world; they need constant reassurance that they have not deprived themselves of God's blessing.

Jacob experienced a similar apprehension. See *Rashi* to 32:11: קָטֹנְתִּי מִכֹּל הַחֲסָדִים

ג אֱלִיעֶזֶר: וַיֹּאמֶר אַבְרָם הֵן לִי לֹא נָתַתָּה
ד זָרַע וְהִנֵּה בֶן־בֵּיתִי יוֹרֵשׁ אֹתִי: וְהִנֵּה
דְבַר־יְהוָה אֵלָיו לֵאמֹר לֹא יִירָשְׁךָ זֶה כִּי־
ה אִם אֲשֶׁר יֵצֵא מִמֵּעֶיךָ הוּא יִירָשֶׁךָ: וַיּוֹצֵא

would only pass on to Eliezer's Damascus relations.

3. וַיֹּאמֶר אַבְרָם — *Then* [lit. *'and'*] *Abram said.*

[In further verbalization of his apprehensions referred to earlier] —

The repetitive use of וַיֹּאמֶר, *and he said,* for the same speaker is not unusual in Scriptures. See, e.g. 30:27, 28; *Exod.* 1:15,16 *(Chizkuni).*

Hirsch suggests, however, that Abraham probably did not *express* this plaint to God. Rather he *thought* it; hence וַיֹּאמֶר in this case would mean *'he said [to himself'*], and it does not refer to a continuation of his earlier speech. That would explain why the next verse begins: וְהִנֵּה, *and behold!*; it was a sudden interruption of his thoughts. [See *Abarbanel,* next verse.]

הֵן לִי לֹא נָתַתָּה זָרַע — *See* [following *Hirsch* who relates הֵן to הִנֵּה], *to me You have not given offspring* [lit. *'seed'*]

— Of what value, then, is anything else You give me? *(Rashi).*

To me You have not given offspring although You promised me: *'I will make of you a great nation'* [12:2] and *'I will make your offspring as the dust of the earth'* [13:16.] Now, when Abraham said these things he did not, Heaven forfend, suggest that God would renege on His promise. Rather he was apprehensive that he had committed some offense which had forfeited his claim to the promise [see *Ramban, footnote* to *v.* 2]; or that he thought that the *'offspring'* was a relative whom God might be considering as equivalent as Abraham's own child *(Radak).*

Compare the words of Solomon in *Eccl.* 2:18, 19 who also expressed despair at the fate of one who leaves his estate to heirs whose prudence and wisdom are questionable *(Midrash haGadol).*

וְהִנֵּה בֶן־בֵּיתִי יוֹרֵשׁ אֹתִי — *And see, my steward* [lit. *'the son of my house;* transl. following *Targum Yonasan*] *is my heir* [lit. *'inherits me'*]

— And even were You to grant me a son now, in my old age, he will still be young after my demise and will be susceptible to Eliezer's maneuverings, and will be at the mercy of the elder servant who will, in effect, be his master *(Hadar Zekeinim; Sforno; Chizkuni; Bertinoro).*

The plural phrase בְּנֵי בַיִת [lit. *'children of the household'*] occurs in *Eccl.* 2:7 where, following *Targum, Midrash,* and *Metzudas David,* it is also translated *stewards.* According to *Ibn Ezra,* there the phrase refers to the slave-children born in the house [as distinct from slaves which were purchased.]

4. וְהִנֵּה דְבַר ה׳ אֵלָיו — [*And*] *suddenly* [lit. *'behold!'*] *the Word of* HASHEM [came] *to him.*

Following *Ramban:* suddenly; while Abraham was still speaking; or, according to *Hirsch* in *v.* 3: still thinking.

לֹא יִירָשְׁךָ זֶה — *That* [lit. *'this'*] *one will not inherit you.*

Regardless of *when* your son will be born to you, you need not be apprehensive. Your servant will not be your heir; your *own offspring will inherit you (Ramban; Tur; Sforno.* See previous verse).

*³ Then Abram said, 'See, to me You have given no
offspring; and see, my steward is my heir ... '
⁴ Suddenly, the word of HASHEM came to him,
saying: 'That one will not inherit you. None but him
that shall come forth from within you shall be your
heir.' ⁵ And He took him outside, and said, 'Gaze,*

כִּי־אִם אֲשֶׁר יֵצֵא מִמֵּעֶיךָ הוּא יִירָשֶׁךָ — *None but him that shall come forth from within you* [lit. *'your innards'*] *shall be your heir.*

The implication, then, of God's promise is that Abraham will father a son at some time in the future, and that the child will be an adult at Abraham's death so he will not require a guardian nor be susceptible to any servant. In this way *he,* and none other, would be assured of being the heir *(Abarbanel).*

The term מִמֵּעֶיךָ [lit. *'from your innards'*] is graphic. The general sense of the phrase is *from your issue,* the word meaning *from your body* a general reference to the male seed *(Radak).* The term may be used when referring to both male and female, so it should be interpreted *who shall come forth from you (R' Meyuchas).* In fact *Onkelos* avoids the symbolism entirely by rendering the phrase, אֱלָהֵין בַּר דְּתוֹלִיד הוּא יָרְתִינָךְ, *but a son whom you shall beget will be your heir.*

Hirsch finds it significant that מֵעֶיךָ [lit. *your innards*] not the usual terms חֲלָצֶיךָ [loins] or יְרֵכְךָ [thighs] is used here. The latter terms refer to the physical body and to intelligence, מֵעַיִם, however, refers uniquely to the source of such feelings as pity and sympathy. Such qualities are those most characteristic of the seed of Abraham. They are uniquely Jewish because they are the legacy of Abraham.

[A similar phrase addressed to a male occurs in *II Sam.* 7:12.]

5. וַיּוֹצֵא אֹתוֹ הַחוּצָה — *And He took him outside.*

The plain meaning is that He took him outside of his tent so he could gaze up at the stars. The *Midrashic* interpretation is צֵא מֵאִצְטַגְנִינוּת שֶׁלְּךָ, *abandon your astrological speculations* [the verse would thus be rendered: *He took him out of the realm of his constellation*]. Although you have seen by the מַזָּלוֹת, *constellations,* that you are not destined to have children, it is true only that *Abram* will have no son, but *Abraham* will have a son; *Sarai* will indeed be childless, but *Sarah* will bear. I will change your names [from Abram and Sarai to Abraham and Sarah] and your מַזָּל [constellation; luck] will change. An additional explanation is that God took him outside of the earthly sphere elevating him above the stars. Therefore, the verse uses the verb הַבֵּט, *gaze,* for this word especially signifies looking down from on high *(Rashi).* [1] [On *Constellations* see next page.]

The commentators elaborate upon these interpretations.

According to *Midrash HaGadol* and *Chizkuni,* this *'taking out'* and the subsequent prophetic promise were part of Abraham's vision begun in *v.* 1. *Abarbanel* suggests that after the promise of an heir in *v.* 5, Abraham awoke and he was

1. According to *Rashi*'s third interpretation, Abraham was raised 'higher than the stars', i.e., beyond the Laws of Nature, and God said to him כֹּה יִהְיֶה זַרְעֶךָ, *So shall your offspring be!* — The everlasting existence of your offspring shall also be beyond the laws of earthbound nature *(S'fas Emes).*

אֹתוֹ הַחוּצָה וַיֹּאמֶר הַבֶּט־נָא הַשָּׁמַיְמָה
וּסְפֹר הַכּוֹכָבִים אִם־תּוּכַל לִסְפֹּר אֹתָם
ו וַיֹּאמֶר לוֹ כֹּה יִהְיֶה זַרְעֶךָ׃ וְהֶאֱמִן בַּיהוָה

then brought outside to receive the subsequent prophecy introduced by the word וַיֹּאמֶר, *and He said.*

As for the *Midrashic* astrological interpretation cited by *Rashi, Ramban* notes that he begot Ishmael while his name was still *'Abram'* [How then could the *Midrash* say that *Abram* will have no son?] He answers that Abraham's fear, as expressed in *v.* 3 was that he would not have a son *as an heir;* God therefore assured him that as *'Abram'* he would not have a son who would be his heir [Ishmael was not his heir; see 21:12], only as *'Abraham'* would he father such a son. Additionally, it is possible that the astrological indication concerned Abram and Sarai only as a pair together [and Ishmael was born of Abram and Hagar!]

מַזָּלוֹת/Constellations

Although not in the scope of this commentary, a short note on the nature of מַזָּלוֹת, astrological calculations is in place.

At the outset, it should be perfectly clear that astrology, as spoken of in the Torah, was a science known to the wise men of ancient times. With it they could foretell events as Abraham did here and as we find concerning the sorcerors of Pharaoh. It bears no relationship, however, to horoscopes such as are used in modern times.

The commentators explain [as noted briefly in the comm. to *The Seventy Nations* in vol. I, p. 309 and in the *footnote* to 11:7] that each of the nations with the exception of Israel, is placed under the protection of a special angel. Israel's Protector is God Himself. Therefore the fate of each nation is under the influence of its guardian angel as determined by its מַזָּל, *planetary constellation.* Israel, however, because its Protector is God, is free from this planetary influence, as many Sages declared [*Shabbos* 156a]: אֵין מַזָּל לְיִשְׂרָאֵל, 'there is no *mazal* to Israel,' i.e., Israel is immune from planetary influence. *R' Bachya* [to our verse and more extensively in his *comm.* to *Deut.* 8:18] maintains that, although Israel as a *collective community* is above planetary influence, nevertheless 'there is *mazal* to each person *as an individual,* for the wisdom of planetary constellations is sublime and magnificent indeed, and the Sages do not deny this at all' (see also responsa in *Kisvei Ramban* 1:375).

Meshech Chochmah similarly explains that the concept of no *mazal* to Israel extends only to the nation, but that *individually* each Jew *is* subject to *mazal.* Abraham, however, as אַב הֲמוֹן גּוֹיִם, *father of a multitude of nations* [17:6], is considered the embodiment of the *community* rather than an individual. [Hence he can be freed from the personal affects of the astrological calculations he had seen regarding himself (see *Rav Yehudah Copperman's* commentary to *Meshech Chochmah).*]

The *Talmud (ibid.)* continues: Abraham pleaded with the Holy One, Blessed be He: 'I have looked at my constellations and find that I

XV now, toward the Heavens, and count the stars if you
6 are able to count them'! And He said to him, 'So shall
your offspring be!' [6] And he trusted in HASHEM, and

am not fated to beget a child.'

'Cease your planet-gazing,' said God ... for Israel [as a community; but cf. *Maharsha*] is free from planetary influence. [Nevertheless], what is [the basis of] your calculation? Because [your constellation] *Tzedek* stands in the West? [an inauspicious combination for begetting children]. Fear not! I will turn it back and place it in the East [so you will beget.] Thus it is written [*Isaiah* 41:2]: *Who has raised up Tzedek* [righteousness] *from the East; He has summoned it for his* [i.e., Abraham's] *sake.*

The implications of the above are that although the Sages agree that the destinies of private individuals *are* influenced by the celestial conjunctions, there are several factors capable of annulling these destinies. As *Rav Yosef Albo* states in *Sefer Ikkarim* 4:4 citing *Ibn Ezra's Sefer haMolados:* 'If a man trusts in God by Whom all actions are controlled, God will contrive means to deliver him from any evil which is indicated in his *mazal.*' This agrees with the opinion of the Sages in *Rosh Hashanah* 16b: Four things nullify the destiny indicated for man, namely: charity, prayer, change of name, and change of conduct ... some add change of place.

Furthermore, the Jew has always been cautioned against relying on horoscopes and various means of fortune-telling. He should rather place his trust in God. See *comm.* to *Deut.* 18:14.

Cf. *Pesachim* 113b: How do we know that one must not consult astrologers [lit. 'Chaldeans']? Because it is said [*Deut.* 18:14]: *You shall be wholehearted with HASHEM your God.*

הַבֶּט־נָא הַשָּׁמַיְמָה — *Gaze, now, toward the Heavens.* The Sages have explained that the verb הַבֵּט, *gaze,* always suggests gazing down from above, thus accounting for their explanation that Abraham was raised up *above* the stars, and as such he was told to gaze [down] upon them *(Malbim).*

[On the use of נא, *now,* see *comm.* to 12:13.]

כֹּה יִהְיֶה זַרְעֶךָ — *So shall your offspring be!*

As no nation can conquer the stars, so will no nation ever succeed in exterminating Israel *(Pesikta Zutresa).*[1]

Also esoterically suggested by the word כֹּה, which is the numerical equivalent of 25, is that in another 25 years, Abraham would have a child who would be his true heir. Abraham was 75 years old at the time, and Isaac was born when he was 100 years old *(Paneach Raza).*

The commentators generally agree that the comparison of Israel to the stars is not quantitative, i.e. telling him that his offspring would be 'as *countless* as

1. On the verse [*Lam.* 1:1] אֵיכָה יָשְׁבָה בָדָד, *Alas! she sits in solitude,* [which Jeremiah uttered in anguish over the fall of the Jews and Jerusalem], Rav Eliezer homiletically interpreted אֵיכָה [*Alas!* or *How!*] as two words: אֵי כֹּה, where is the כֹּה, the *so* which God promised to Abraham: כֹּה, *so, shall your offspring be!*

the stars'. God had already compared them to *the dust of the earth* [see *comm.* to 13:16] and the dust particles of the earth are even more numerous than the stars! Rather God was saying that his every descendant would be *qualitatively* as worthy and precious as the stars, each of which is individually counted by God for each star is a separate solar system or mighty force *(Malbim).* [Comp. *Isaiah* 40:26; *Rashi, Exod.* 1:1.]

Had God wished to direct Abraham's attention to the *quantity* of the stars, it would not have been necessary to show him the heavens, just as He did not show Abraham the dust when He promised: *'I will make your seed like the dust of the earth.'* Rather, God showed him the stars as if to say, 'Your national existence will be like that of the stars.' Here, on earth, everything we see is an evolving product of God's cause-and-effect natural law. The stars, however, are still pristine, unsullied products of God's hand, unchanged since the day He created them. Hence, God was, in effect, telling him, 'Abandon your earthly, natural speculations. Your offspring will be like the stars, drawing their sustenance from God, above all natural calculations' *(Hirsch).*

Noting that elsewhere [13:16; 28:14] God compared Abraham's offspring to the *dust of the earth,* while here they are likened to the *stars in heaven,* the Sages [*Megillah* 16a] derive an ethical lesson: When we do God's will, we are above all — like the stars. However, when we disobey God's will, we are trampled upon by all — like the dust of the earth.

6. וְהֶאֱמִן בַּה׳ — *And he* [*Abraham*] *trusted* [i.e., placed his confidence] *in* HASHEM.

Without, as *Rashi* explains, requesting a sign as he did with respect to the promise that he would possess the land [(*v.* 7); an event that although appearing later in the text actually happened several years earlier. See *Pref. Remarks* to next verse.]

Directing his trust completely to God's Providential care of every individual, Abraham discarded his astrological calculations *(Malbim).*

There was nothing new in this trust, it means that this unswerving faith which he now displayed had been innately a part of him for a long time. Had the meaning been that he trusted from that moment on, the Hebrew would have read וַיַּאֲמֵן בַּה׳ *(Ibn Caspi).*

He explains that the concept of believing someone, in the sense that his promise is accepted, would be expressed as הֶאֱמִין לְ־. The phrase הֶאֱמִין בְּ־, however, represents a much deeper concept than mere belief. It suggests total submission in the sense that one places his total confidence and seeks all his guidance and attitudes in God. In the same vein, when one responds *amen* to a blessing, he avows that he will be guided by the thought expressed in the blessing *(Hirsch).*

וַיַּחְשְׁבֶהָ לּוֹ צְדָקָה — *And He reckoned it to him (as) righteousness.*

I.e. God accounted this unswerving faith displayed by Abraham as an act of righteousness *(Rashi; Sforno).*

The subject of the phrase is ambiguous. As always, the translation follows *Rashi,* who interprets *God* as the subject.

Ramban, however, questions this interpretation because, as he points out, why should faith in God, especially by one as great as Abraham, be considered a virtue?

'God is not a man that He should lie' [*Num.* 23:19].

Moreover, we are speaking of a man who, on the basis of his faith was later prepared to sacrifice his beloved son, and had withstood all trials; how could he *not* show his faith in a good tiding? *Ramban* therefore suggests that the subject of the verse is *Abraham*: *He* [*Abraham*] *considered it an act of righteousness* on the part of God that He would promise him a child unconditionally [in God's righteousness] and without regard to Abraham's merit *(R' Bachya)*], *and* the possibility that he might sin. The verse says, therefore, that Abraham's trust in God's promise was total, for, since it was an act of Divine צְדָקָה *righteousness,* it was irreversible as in the verse [*Isaiah* 45:23]: *By Myself have I sworn, the word is issued from My mouth in righteousness, and shall not turn back.'*

[The latter concept is fundamental, and will be stressed in the following verses by many commentators. It is found in *Tanchuma Masei* 7, based on the verse, *God is not a man that He should lie (Num.* 23:19). When God promises to do good, he does not retract His promise even if the generation is guilty of infractions. *(*But cf. *Rambam* in the preface to his *Commentary to Mishnayos* that this applies only in cases where God had made this promise through a prophet. See *comm.* to 32:8). However, when He threatens to punish, He does retract if the guilty one repents. He promised Abraham the good tiding: *Gaze now at the heavens and count the stars ... so shall your offspring be,* and He has done so, for Moses said to the children of Israel *(Deut.* 1:10): *Behold you are this day as the stars of heaven.* (Hence, since Abraham was promised a good tiding, he was sure of its eventual fulfillment).]

In support of *Rashi*'s interpretation, however, *Mizrachi* emphasizes that the righteousness was not so much Abraham's *faith,* but the fact that he did not request a sign as he did when he was promised the Land. *Maharal* in *Gevuros Hashem* 7 elaborates on the primacy of אֱמוּנָה, faith, and explains how it is the Jew's faith that sustains him in his every endeavor. He expresses wonder at *Ramban*'s implication that Abraham's faith could be taken for granted.

We must also never forget that Abraham was the First Believer and thus had no one to look back upon. He established his own precedents; his faith was more difficult to come by than ours — for we are 'believers sons of believers', for our forebears already paved a road of unswerving Faith. It is no wonder then that the Torah emphasizes Abraham's faith as meritorious and noteworthy *(Akeidas Yitzchak).*

Rambam in *Moreh Nevuchim* 3:53 defines צְדָקָה, *righteousness,* as denoting 'giving everyone his due.' He explains, however, that the Torah uses the word in a different sense. In Scriptural terms, paying a laborer his wages or repaying a debt is *not* called צְדָקָה. In Scriptural usage, an act of *righteousness* is performed when we fulfill our duties to our fellow man prompted by our *moral conscience* — e.g. healing the wound of a sufferer; returning a pledge

יהוה אֲשֶׁר הוֹצֵאתִיךָ מֵאוּר כַּשְׂדִּים
לָתֶת לְךָ אֶת־הָאָרֶץ הַזֹּאת לְרִשְׁתָּהּ:
ח וַיֹּאמַר אֲדֹנָי יֱהוִֹה בַּמָּה אֵדַע כִּי

to a poor debtor [*Deut.* 24:13.] Similarly, acting virtuously and displaying faith in God is called *tzedakah* ['righteousness'] because we thereby act righteously toward our intellectual faculty. It is in this sense that God accounted Abraham's faith as righteousness.

Malbim comments that whenever the term מִשְׁפָּט, *justice*, is used in Scriptures *in reference to God*, it denotes those actions which He does in response to man's merits and good deeds; were his deeds to become corrupted, God's goodness would cease because it would no longer be earned. The term צְדָקָה, *righteousness*, denotes those righteous actions which He does as a benevolent God without regard to man's merits or deeds. Such goodness will continue despite man's actions. Abraham, convinced that he was undeserving, regarded God's promises to him as a manifestation of gracious *tzedakah*.

7-21. The Covenant Between the Parts:

⊷§ The Promise of the Land.

[The covenant described in the following verses was made when Abraham was seventy years old; chronologically it *preceded* the prophetic vision of the above verses which, as pointed out above, occurred when Abraham was seventy-five years old *(Seder Olam;* see *'Additional Note A'* regarding chronology of this period).

That the narrative of the Covenant between the Parts commences with this verse is derived from *Tosafos Berachos* 7b which cites it as an example of אֵין מוּקְדָּם וּמְאוּחָר בַּתּוֹרָה, that the Torah is not necessarily written in chronological order.

[While the commentators will generally assume events are chronologically given, there are frequent exceptions. For example, chapters are sometimes written out of sequence to indicate halachic or moral teachings derived from the association of seemingly unrelated concepts or events. Or, a particular topic may be narrated until its completion, before a new one is introduced. For example, the Torah tells of Terach's death before Abraham's departure to Canaan, while chronologically, Terach did not die until 60 years later (see *comm.* to 11:32); and Noah's death is recorded in 9:29 although Noah was still alive in the days of Abraham *(ibid.).* (See citation of above *Tosafos* in *comm* to *v.* 8.)

Rashbam offers a proof that God's reassurance to Abraham in *vs.* 1-6 took place at a different occasion from the Covenant Between the Parts in *vs.* 7-21. In *v.* 5, Abraham is bidden to gaze at the stars indicating that it was nightime, while *v.* 17 describes the sunset indicating that it was daytime. 'This proves that they are distinct chapters and did not occur consecutively, nor is there chronological order in the Torah' (see *Chizkuni).*]

7. אֲנִי ה׳ – *I am* HASHEM.

[God's identification of Himself as HASHEM does not conflict with *Exod.* 6:3 where God tells Moses

7 *He said to him, 'I am HASHEM Who brought you out of Ur Kasdim to give you this land as an inheritance.'*

8 *He said, 'My Lord, HASHEM/ELOHIM: Whereby shall I know that I am to inherit it?'*

Exod. 6:3 where God tells Moses that וּשְׁמִי ה׳ לֹא נוֹדַעְתִּי לָהֶם, *by My Name HASHEM I did not make Myself known to them* (i.e. the Patriarchs).

[That verse, as explained by the commentators, does not mean that we do not find the Name HASHEM already in the history and on the lips of the Patriarchs. Indeed Abraham here, and Jacob in 28:13 were spoken to by God Who identified Himself as HASHEM].

As *Rashi* points out in *Exodus,* it does not say וּשְׁמִי ה׳ לֹא הוֹדַעְתִּי לָהֶם, *I did not make known My Name HASHEM to them* [for, as we have seen, the Patriarchs *were* told the Name]. Rather it says לֹא נוֹדַעְתִּי, *did not become known,* i.e., the Name of HASHEM implies a certain level of awareness of God; that was not granted the Patriarchs. The sense of the Four-Letter Name is that God fulfills His promises. The Patriarchs did not 'know' God in that role, for the time of fulfillment had not yet arrived. *Rav Saadiah Gaon* interprets in this context that God did not make Himself known to the Patriarchs by His Name HASHEM *exclusively,* for He also addressed them with Names reflecting others of His Attributes. But to Moses He used only that Name, for His promises were about to be fulfilled. (see *Ibn Ezra; Ramban; Sforno;* and *Mizrachi* loc. cit.).

אֲשֶׁר הוֹצֵאתִיךָ מֵאוּר כַּשְׂדִּים — *Who brought you out of Ur Kasdim.*

I.e. Who miraculously saved you from the fiery furnace of Kasdim [see *comm.* to 11:28] *(Ramban).*

[*Ibn Ezra* suggests that the meaning is: *At Whose command you departed from (the city of) Ur Kasdim.* Since Ur Kasdim and not Charan is specified, this verse proves, according to *Ibn Ezra,* that God's command came to Abraham in Ur Kasdim. (See *comm.* to 11:31; 12:1.) This view is not shared by *Rashi* and *Ramban* who hold that the expression *'brought you'* refers only to the miraculous deliverance, but that the divine call first came to him in Charan.]

לָתֶת לְךָ אֶת־הָאָרֶץ הַזֹּאת לְרִשְׁתָּהּ — *To give you this land as an inheritance* [lit. *'to inherit it'*].

This decree giving you the Land is not new. I intended it from the time I saved you from Ur Kasdim *(Ramban)*; it was for this very purpose that I rescued you so that the Land would be an inheritance which you would pass on to your children as a father bequeathes his personal belongings to his heirs *(Radak;* cf. *Sforno).*

8. וַיֹּאמַר — *(And) he* [Abraham] *said.*

He was anxious, lest a condition of good deeds was attached to the inheritance of the Land *(Ramban).*

אֲדֹנָי ה׳ — *'My Lord HASHEM/ELOHIM'* [Read as *'Adonai Elohim'* meaning *'Merciful God'.*]

The *Talmud (Berachos* 7b) notes that Abraham was the first man ever to call Him *Adon,* [Master] and our verse is cited as proof of this (see *Overview: The Patriarchs).*

The obvious question arises why *our* verse is cited in this connection, rather than *v.* 2 where the same Name occurs first. It is in this connection that *Tosafos ibid.* explains that the Covenant Between the Parts [*vs.* 7-21] happened before the vision of *vs.* 1-6 (see above). Thus, Abraham's use of the Name *Adon* in our verse was the first in history.

[This, of course, coincides with the Chronology in *Seder Olam* that Abraham was 70 at the Covenant Between the Parts, as explained in *'Additional Note A'.* There are opinions, however, as noted there that the events *are* recorded here in correct chronological sequence and that the verses *do* follow sequentially. According to them, the question of why *v.* 2 is not cited by the *Talmud* as the earliest instance of man calling God *Adon* is not resolved. In fact, *Midrash haGadol* does cite *v.* 2 in that connection. Perhaps the answer lies in an interpretation attributed to R' Chananel that *v.* 2 was only *meditated* by Abraham (that is why *vs.* 2 and 3 are both preceded by וַיֹּאמֶר, *and he said*; cf. *comm.* there), while this verse was *spoken*. Therefore our verse is cited as the basis for the *Talmudic* interpretation (see *Torah Shelemah* 15:92, and *Maharsha* to *Berachos* 7b).

Netziv in *Herchev Davar* offers a different answer. The Name Adonai, from אָדוֹן, *master*, refers to two aspects of God: 1. As master, he can change or suspend natural law at will; 2. Even so-called natural law is but a hidden manifestation of the Master Who ordains that it function. In the first aspect of His mastery, there can be no doubt of God's power — who can deny that none but God splits the sea? But it is a greater measure of a man's greatness that he acknowledges God's Presence even where He appears to be absent. It was Abraham who first enunciated this concept.

◆§ The Name: My Lord HASHEM/ELOHIM

This combination of God's Names — אֲדֹנָי יֱהוִה — is most unusual, especially the second Name which has the spelling of the Four-Letter Name but the punctuation of *Elohim.*

According to *Mizrachi (Deut.* 3:24) whose interpretation we adopt in the translation, the name אֲדֹנָי in our context is the salutation by which Abraham and Moses addressed God, i.e., *my Lord*, for the word אָדוֹן means *master*; thus the Name is used to indicate complete obedience and acceptance.

The second Name has the spelling of the Four-Letter Name, but the punctuation of *Elohim.* It appears in the Five Books of Moses only four times: 15:2, our verse, *Deut.* 3:24, and 9:26. Although it is found in various books of Prophets and Hagiographa, it is used extensively only in *Ezekiel. 'HASHEM'* commonly refers to God's Attribute of Mercy while *Elohim* alludes to the Attribute of Judgment (see *comm.* to 1:1, 2:4). We have attempted to preserve this dual connotation in our translation *HASHEM/ELOHIM.* *Rashi* to *Deut.* 3:24 explains it as רַחוּם בְּדִין, *Merciful in Judgment.* According to *Mizrachi* whose interpretation we follow in the translation, this Name, combining mercy with judgment, implies the plea that even in judgment, God should temper his decree with mercy.

Gur Aryeh (ibid.) disagrees. He interprets אֲדֹנָי, with its connotation of mastery, as the Name implying judgment. The second Name, despite the pronounciation of ELOHIM, is indicative of mercy because of its spelling. [*Ramban ibid.* interprets the phrase as does *Gur Aryeh* according to *Rashi.* [1]

The question remains, according to *Ramban* and *Gur Aryeh,* why the second Name with its connotation of mercy, should be pronounced *ELOHIM*. *R' Bachya* explains that, because it is forbidden to vocalize the Four-Letter Name except in the Temple, we pronounce it *Adonai.* In our verse, however, since the Four-Letter Name is preceded by *Adonai,* the usual pronunciation would result in the pronuncia-

1. Rav Levi said: Abraham said before Him, Master of the Universe, if judgment decrees that offspring are due me, then give [them] to me. But if not, give me [offspring] with mercy *(Devarim Rabbah* and *Yelamdeinu* to *Deut.* 3:24).

tion of *Adonai* two times. Therefore, the pronunciation of ELOHIM is used instead. That pronunciation should, however, not be taken to indicate the new interpretation offered by *Mizrachi*.

Hirsch interprets the dual Name as the realization that even when God manifests Himself as the Executor of harsh judgment, His degree is in reality an expression of mercy. His severity, too, is ordained by His love, because it is necessary to lay the foundation of a brighter future.

Sefer Haparshiyos explains why the Four-Letter Name implies mercy. Its spelling suggests that God is היה, הוה, ויהיה, *He was, is, and will be* i.e., He is eternal. Because all of time is united within Him, He considers the merit of the past or the future in order to be merciful even when people in their *present* condition are undeserving. The Name used in our verse is another contribution of Abraham to mankind's perception of God. Abraham appealed to God with a juxtaposition of Names indicating that God's very justice requires that He be merciful to His creatures, and that even His severity is truly born of mercy.

בַּמָּה אֵדַע כִּי אִירָשֶׁנָּה — *Whereby shall I know that I am to inherit it?*

[In the most simple literal sense of the phrase one may be tempted to view Abraham as lacking complete faith and incredulously requesting a definite sign and reassurance that what God had just promised would indeed come to pass.

[But this is incongruous with Abraham's image as the Prime Believer, who was miraculously saved from the Furnace of Kasdim and who unquestioningly followed God's call to leave his father's house. Nor does it coincide with the interpretation of the great preponderance of commentators.

[True, one view in the *Talmud* (*Nedarim* 32a) cites as a reason that Abraham's descendants were doomed to Egyptian servitude, that by asking for a sign he went too far in testing God's attributes (i.e. promises; see also 14:4 and footnote to 14:21 for other reasons for the servitude). Nevertheless the prevalent view is that Abraham spoke not in complaint, but that he asked Him: 'Through what merit will I inherit the land?' (see below; cf. also *Meg.* 31b cited below).]

[The *Talmudic* interpretation in *Nedarim* which views Abraham's request as improper, is not irreconcilable with the view of the *Midrash* and commentators. His response could have been considered sinful because a person of Abraham's stature should not have felt the need to seek *any kind* of assurance from God for any part of the Promise. So great a person should have accepted God's promise gratefully and wholeheartedly with full confidence that the Merciful God would provide for all contingencies.

[This follows *Rashi* who explains that in addition to the plain meaning that Abraham sought a sign, another interpretation is: *By what merit will my descendants sustain themselves in the Land?* (i.e. Abraham was apprehensive about himself and his descendants: would they be sufficiently worthy?) His question is therefore to be interpreted as if the verse read בַּמָּה אֵדַע, *let me know how*, i.e. by what merit would he receive the Land *(Mizrachi)*, and how would his children merit to retain this gift in later generations: perhaps they will sin and forfeit all *(Maharzu)*.

God answered: 'By the merit of the sacrifices' which you are about to offer, and which I will institute as a means of atonement for your children. And because God would forgive Israel on account of their repentance and prayer for which sacrifices are a symbol *(Gur Aryeh)*.]

The *Talmud* (Megillah 31b) on which Rashi's latter comment is based continues:

... Abraham then said to Him: Sovereign of the Universe, this is very well for the time when the Temple will be standing, but when there will be no Temple what will befall them? ...

God replied: I have already established for them the סֵדֶר הַקָּרְבָּנוֹת [*the Order of the Sacrifice* said during the prayers.] Whenever they will read the section dealing with sacrifices I will consider it as if they were bringing Me an offering and forgive all their iniquities.

Ramban similarly explains that Abraham's request is not to be interpreted as asking for a sign as did Hezekiah in *II Kings* 20:8. Neither did God give him one. Rather, Abraham merely asked that he might know with a true inner knowledge that the gift of the Land would be an enduring one unaffected by his sin or that of his descendants. Additionally, he feared that the Canaanites [who were then in the Land and had to be driven away before Abraham's descendants could inhabit it (see *comm.* to 10:15; 10:19; 12:6; and *v.* 16 below)], might repent and thereby deserve to remain in the Land [see *Jeremiah* 18:7-8]. God therefore reassured him by making a covenant with him that he would inherit the Land despite all possible circumstances.[1]

... Abraham did not doubt that the promise would be fulfilled, what he was intimating was: *how* will I inherit it?; at what time?; during which generation?; how much of it will I inherit? *(B'chor Shor).*

The significance of Abraham's remark was, 'Indeed, You have assured me that I will inherit it, but the Land is occupied. Therefore, *whereby shall I make known that* I *am to inherit it?*, i.e. whereby shall I demonstrate to the nations of the world that it is my due inheritance and that I did not conquer it illegally?' [cf. *comm.* to יָדַעְתִּי in 22:12] *(Ma'asei Hashem).*

Abraham's primary concern was directed at his apprehension that *the other heirs of Shem* to whom the Land had been apportioned would protest his claims, he

1. Since the verb ידע is sometimes used in Scriptures with meanings other than its usual translation, *know,* some commentators perceive additional connotations to Abraham's question, בַּמָּה אֵדַע:

The *Talmud, Berachos* 5a, comments that 'God gave Israel three precious gifts, and all of them were given only through suffering. These are: The Torah, Eretz Yisrael and the World to Come.' Therefore, Abraham asked: בַּמָּה אֵדַע כִּי אִירָשֶׁנָּה, In what manner *shall I be made to suffer that I will be able to inherit the Land?* (This interpretation of אֵדַע as *suffer* follows the use of וַיֹּדַע, *chastised,* in *Judges* 8:16).

God, therefore, responded with יָדֹעַ תֵּדַע [*v.* 13, possibly meaning in this context *you shall surely be chastised*] and showed Abraham the subjugation to which his descendants would be subjected before they inherit the Land *(Ohev Yisrael).*

HaKsav v'Hakaballah relates אֵדַע to the word's use in 18:19 where יְדַעְתִּיו is interpreted by *Ramban* as 'raised and elevated', and its use in *Ps.* 144:3 מָה אָדָם וַתֵּדָעֵהוּ, *'What is man that You have exalted* [familiarly translated: *taken knowledge of*] *him?'*

He explains that Abraham, in his humility, was pensive about the profound implications of the favor God was bestowing upon him, and said: בַּמָּה אֵדַע, by virtue of what shall I become *so raised and elevated* in God's eyes that I will deserve to eternally inherit something so exalted.

9 *And He said to him, 'Bring Me three heifers,*

therefore asked for a sign that his inheritance would go unprotested *(Kli Yakar).*

Chizkuni cites this verse as further proof that this chapter is not in chronological sequence [see *prefatory comm.* to *v.* 1 and above.] For if the verses follow each other chronologically, how could Abraham, who was just lauded for his exemplary, unquestioning faith, now question God's promise? He therefore concludes that this second part is distinct from the first and preceded it.

Hirsch interprets the chapter in direct chronological order. Abraham had just conquered the four kings thanks to God's help and had just been praised for his perfect faith. He was fully prepared to undertake any action asked of him by God. The word לְרִשְׁתָּהּ, in *Hirsch's* view implies human initiative *to take into possession.* It suggests *capturing, conquering* as in עֲלֵה רֵשׁ, *go up and possess (Deut.* 1:21; also *ibid.* 1:8; 2:31; 9:23). Since he was commanded to conquer the Land, Abraham quite logically asked: *By what shall I know that the time has come for me to conquer the Land?*

9. קְחָה לִי – *Bring* [lit. *'take to'*] *Me.*

In order to sacrifice them to Me. I will thereby intimate to you the manner of your descendants' residence in the Land and their exile from it, and with the pieces I will enter into a Covenant with you so you will not falter *(Radak).*

For such was the method by which the ancients made a covenant – they would cut an animal in half and walk between the parts, as it is written [*Jeremiah* 34:18] *When they cut the calf in two and passed between its sections (Rashi; B'chor Shor).*[1]

God commanded him to take the following animals to seal the covenant and to give it the additional status of an irrevocable oath. It was to this that Moses later referred when he said to the Israelites *(Deut.* 9:5): *It is not for your righteousness ... that you go to possess their land, but because of the wickedness of these nations HASHEM is driving them out from before you, and in order to fulfill the oath that HASHEM swore to your fathers* [i.e., even if you do not merit possession of the Land, God must fulfill His oath] *(Sforno).*

[But, following *Rashi* to *v.* 8 the sacrifices were God's symbols of atonement. They represented the offerings that God would one day establish for them to atone for their sins, and in the merit of which they would remain in the Land]:

עֶגְלָה מְשֻׁלֶּשֶׁת – *Three heifers.*

Symbolic of the three sacrifices of bullocks which would later be brought by his descendants. פַּר יוֹם הַכִּפּוּרִים, the bullock which was brought (which was brought) on Yom Kippur [*Numb.* 29:8]; פַּר הֶעְלֵם דָּבָר שֶׁל צִבּוּר the bullock which was brought when the whole congregation sinned unintentional-

1. A covenant is a permanent bond between two parties, symbolizing a friendship so close that they are like a single body and that each is as responsible for the other as for himself.

Symbolic of this they cut an animal in two and pass between the parts, to signify that just as disease or injury afflicting one half of the animal affected the entire animal when it was a single, living organism, and only death separated the two parts – similarly, the two parties

מְשֻׁלֶּשֶׁת וְעֵז מְשֻׁלֶּשֶׁת וְאַיִל מְשֻׁלָּשׁ וְתֹר
י וְגוֹזָל: וַיִּקַּח־לוֹ אֶת־כָּל־אֵלֶּה וַיְבַתֵּר

ly by acting on certain types of erroneous decisions of the Sanhedrin [*Lev.* 4:13-21]; and עֶגְלָה עֲרוּפָה, the heifer whose neck was to be axed [*Deut.* 21:4] *(Rashi).*

[The translation of עֶגְלָה מְשֻׁלֶּשֶׁת as *three heifers* (lit. *'a heifer three-fold'*) follows *Onkelos, Midrash, Rashi,* and most commentators.]

Radak and *Ramban* concur with *Rashi's* translation, but disagree with *Ibn Ezra* [and *Targum Yonasan*] who translates מְשׁוּלֶּשֶׁת as *three years old. Ramban* cites the [*Mishnah Parah* 6:6] that עֶגְלָה, is a two-year old heifer; while a three-year old is called פָּרָה *'cow'*, [and since our verse mentions עֶגְלָה it cannot refer to a three-year old.] (Cf. *M'chok'kei Yehudah).*

Some commentators — *B'chor Shor, Chizkuni* — refer to the *Talmudic* expression עֶגְלָא תִּלְתָּא lit. *a third heifer,* which appears often in the *Talmud* and which *Rashi* variously explains as: 'a third-born heifer, for that is choicest because a young animal is yet frail, therefore first and second calves to which it gives birth are not as healthy' *(Shabbos* 11a); one-third grown because its meal is then tastiest (*Eruvin* 63a). [See also expression in *Pesachim* 68b; *Sanhedrin* 65b; *Tosafos Gittin* 56a.]

According to *Midrash HaGadol* the phrase means: Robust and strong like חוּט הַמְשֻׁלָּשׁ, a *three-ply cord.* [*Eccl.* 4:12.]

Hoffmann [who agrees with the interpretation of *'three years old'*] cites an interpretation by some who base themselves on the wording of a *Mishnah* in *Bava Metziah* 68a: 'and rear them until they become *meshulashin'* which *Rashi* ad. loc. explains as: 'until they reach a third of their growth.' The meaning here, too, according to them would be that Abraham was to take animals 'which reached a third of their growth.' [Cf. *Rashi Eruvin* 63a.]

וְעֵז מְשֻׁלֶּשֶׁת — *[And] three goats.*

Symbolic of the שָׂעִיר הַנַּעֲשֶׂה בִּפְנִים *goat which was offered within* the Temple on Yom Kippur [*Lev.* 16:15]; the goats brought as additional offerings [מוּסָף] on Festivals [*Num.* 28:15, 22, 30*ff*]; and of the goat brought as a חַטָּאת, *sin offering,* by an individual [*Lev.* 4:28] *(Rashi).*

וְאַיִל מְשֻׁלָּשׁ — *Three rams.*

Symbolic of: אָשָׁם וַדַּאי the guilt offering for definite commission of certain offenses [see *Lev.* 5:15; 14:24; 19:21 *Num.* 6:12]; אָשָׁם תָּלוּי, the guilt offering when there is doubt whether an offense was committed [*Lev.* 5:17-19]; and the lamb brought as a חַטָּאת, sin offering, by an individual [*Lev.* 4:32] *(Rashi).*

וְתֹר וְגוֹזָל — *A turtledove and a young dove.*

Radak explains that the word גּוֹזָל refers to any fledgling bird, just as young eagles are called גּוֹזָל in *Deut.* 32:11. The translation defining גּוֹזָל here specifically as *young dove* fol-

entering into the covenant are to be as one body, each ready to risk danger, if necessary, to help the other.

At the same time, each must reveal to the other his innermost thoughts, and not withhold knowledge about evil plots against the other ...

Therefore, as soon as God made a covenant with Abraham, He made known to him the evil that was destined to befall his descendants, symbolically showing him the subjugation of Israel to other nations, but simultaneously comforting him with the knowledge that *'afterward they shall out with great wealth* [*v.* 14] ...

Thus, the covenant symbolized that God would be with Israel in distress just as the whole body shares in the pain of one of its limbs. Our Sages say [*Ta'anis* 16a; See also *Megillah* 29a]: The Shechinah suffers with the suffering of Israel, as is said [*Ps.* 91:15], *'I will be with him in trouble' (Sefer halkkarim* 4:45).

XV *three goats, three rams, a turtledove and a young*
10 *dove.'* [10] *He brought all these to Him: he cut them in*

lows *Onkelos* [בַּר יוֹנָה] *Midrash,* and *Rashi.*

In choosing the animals listed in this verse, God alluded to future sacrifices of cattle and fowl all of which would be solely from these species. The גּוֹזָל mentioned here is identical with the bird fit for sacrifices in the *Book of Leviticus.* It is referred to here as גּוֹזָל, lit. *fledgling,* to indicate that only the young of this species would be fit for sacrifices [see *Lev.* 1:14 See also *Rashi* ibid *v.* 16 s.v. בְּנוֹצָתָהּ, that a גּוֹזָל is so called שֶׁנִּזּוֹן מִן הַגָּזֵל, because it sustains itself of other people's property (lit. *'from robbery').* Even *though the word* גּוֹזָל means any young bird, Abraham prophetically understood that young *doves* were being referred to as the specific species which would be selected by God as sacrificially fit. Or possibly Abraham chose the dove on his own initiative and set the precedent which the Torah later ratified *(Ramban).*

These birds are symbolic of Israel (see *Rashi,* next verse) because like doves, Israel is preyed upon [by the heathens] but does not prey, and as the female dove remains loyal to its mate [see *comm.* to *Shir haShirim* 1:15 ArtScroll ed. p. 93.] so has Israel, likened to a veritable widow in exile, remained loyal to HASHEM, and not strayed after other gods.

10. וַיְבַתֵּר אֹתָם בַּתָּוֶךְ – [*And*] *he* [i.e. *Abraham*] *cut them in the center.*

Dividing them into two parts *(Rashi).*

This is symbolic of the sacrifices which were likewise divided into parts [see e.g. *Lev.* 1:6, 1:12] *(Midrash Aggadah; Ramban).*

Rashi, however, departs from the symbolism of offerings, because offerings were not cut in half, and because the fact that a flaming torch passed between the pieces [*v.* 17] made it manifestly clear that a *Covenant* was being made here *(Mizrachi). HaRechasim leBik'ah* adds that the Hebrew term בתר for *cutting* is used in Scriptures only regarding covenants; cutting for other purposes [sacrifices, etc.] is described in the Torah by the term נתח.

With the above we are better prepared to understand *Rashi's* comment:

אֵין הַמִּקְרָא יוֹצֵא מִידֵי פְּשׁוּטוֹ *the text must primarily be understood in its plain sense.* God was making a covenant with Abraham that He would bequeath the Land to his children as expressly mentioned in *v.* 18. Therefore, in the plain sense, the cutting of the animals the passing between the parts and all that ensued must be interpreted as the ritual of those who enter covenant. The smoking furnace and flaming torch were emissaries of the *Shechinah* which is spoken of as fire [i.e. as if God were passing between the parts to symbolize His acceptance of the covenant.]

Allegorically, the cutting of the animals, symbolic of the heathen nations of the world, indicated that these heathen nations would become divided and cut into fragmented pieces by internal dissent ... *(Radak).*

אֹתָם בַּתָּוֶךְ וַיִּתֵּן אִישׁ־בִּתְרוֹ לִקְרַאת
יא רֵעֵהוּ וְאֶת־הַצִּפֹּר לֹא בָתָר: וַיֵּרֶד הָעַיִט
יב עַל־הַפְּגָרִים וַיַּשֵּׁב אֹתָם אַבְרָם: וַיְהִי

Radak adds that whatever Abraham did in this connection — the cutting and leaving whole — was at God's express command, though no reference to the command was recorded in the Torah.

According to *Akeidas Yitzchak*, the animals were divided in this case *lengthwise* with the result that the pieces were entirely alike, each having a foreleg and hindquarter.

וַיִּתֵּן אִישׁ־בִּתְרוֹ לִקְרַאת רֵעֵהוּ — *And* [*he*] *placed each piece opposite its counterpart.*

That is, he placed the divided parts each opposite its corresponding part: the classical position of the ancient covenant *(R. Meyuchas).*

וְאֶת הַצִּפֹּר לֹא בָתָר — *The birds, however* [lit. *'and the bird'*] *he did not cut up.*

The commentators almost unanimously explain that צִפּוֹר, *bird,* in this verse, although in singular, is a collective noun for *birds,* and refers to both the תֹּר וְגוֹזָל, *turtledove* and *young dove.* (See *Ramban* to *Lev.* 14:4 cited on p. 252, end of *Gen.* 7:14). It is not unusual for Scriptures to employ the singular form to denote an entire group or species. Cf. for ex. עֵץ פְּרִי, *fruit tree(s),* in 1:11, and throughout the Creation chapter]:

Abraham placed the turtledove and the young dove opposite one another for they were both included in the covenant, but he did not divide them in half, since regarding the fowl that is offered up the Torah states [*Lev.* 1:17]: *he shall not divide (Ramban).*

The symbolism of the animals chosen is that the nations of the world are compared to פָּרִים, *bullocks* (see *Ps.* 22:13), אֵילִים, *rams (Dan.* 8:3 Media and Persia), and שְׂעִירִים, *goats (ibid. v.* 21 = Greece). Israel is compared to young doves *(Song of Songs* 2:14). To indicate that the nations were destined to decline, Abraham divided the animals, but *the birds he did not cut up* suggesting thereby that Israel will live forever *(Rashi).*

Rav Eliezer said: At the Covenant Between the Parts, God showed our father Abraham the Four Kingdoms, [Babylon, Persia-Media, Greece, and Rome] their dominion, and their downfall.

... Rav Yehoshua said: Abraham took his sword and divided them, each into two parts. Had he not divided them [symbolically decimating Israel's enemies], the world would not have been able to exist, but because he divided them, he weakened their strength ... *But the birds he did not divide (Midrash).*

... Unlike the heathens who will become divided and cut up [see above], Israel, united by Torah and faith, will remain one people though they are scattered to the four directions of the heavens *(Radak).*

Additionally, the three animals he cut up represent the three generations which were oppressed in Egypt, as if they were cut up into pieces; the bird, uncut [= unoppressed], symbolizes the fourth

XV the center, and placed each piece opposite its counter-
11 part. The birds, however, he did not cut up.

[11] *Birds of prey came down upon the carcasses, and Abram drove them away.*

generation, the one which was liberated from Egyptian Bondage [*v.* 15] *(Alshich).*

11. וַיֵּרֶד הָעַיִט עַל הַפְּגָרִים — [And] *birds of prey came down upon the carcasses.*

— To eat them, as is the nature of birds *(Ramban).*

[The Heb. עַיִט, is in singular. But here, too, the commentators understand it as a collective noun referring to many.]

Levush haOrah comments that there was nothing unusual in birds of prey swooping down on carcasses. That this warranted special mention in the Torah, led the commentators to seek a symbolic interpretation.

The עַיִט, *bird of prey,* is so called because it flies about [עָט] and seeks carcasses upon which it darts quickly and feeds ... The פְּגָרִים *carcasses* refer to the בְּתָרִים, *pieces,* i.e. symbolically to the nations of the world whom David, son of Jesse, would come to destroy, only to be prevented by heaven from doing so, pending the arrival of King Messiah *(Rashi).*

The swooping down of the birds to consume the turtle-dove and young dove is symbolic of the nations of the world that try to exterminate us in every generation ... *(Radak).*

וַיַּשֵּׁב אֹתָם אַבְרָם — *And Abram drove them away,* by vigorously flapping his scarf until the *Shechinah* could conclude the Covenant *(Pirkei d'Rabbi Eliezer; Chizkuni), the verb* וַיַּשֵּׁב denotes *blowing* and *driving off* as in *Ps.* 147:18: יַשֵּׁב רוּחוֹ, lit. *He drives His wind (Rashi).*

This symbolizes how the Holy One, blessed be He, delivers us from the hands of our oppressors ['driving away the birds of prey'] in the merit of Abraham *(Radak).*[1]

According to *Ramban,* this symbolizes how the heathens would attempt to abrogate the sacrifices but would be driven away by the descendants of Abraham.

Cf. *Targum Yonasan:* 'And there swooped down idolatrous peoples who are likened to unclean birds, to snatch away the sacrifices of Israel; but the righteousness of Abram was a shield over them.'

[Thus, according to the above interpretations, the objective of the heathens in time to come would be to attack the spiritual strength of Israel by abrogating the divine service. By severing the spiritual link between God and Israel — the offerings and the study of Torah — the people would be spiritually asphyxiated. God's promise, therefore, was that the 'birds of prey' would be driven away without attaining their goal.]

1. Rav Assi said: Abraham took a flail and beat them but they were not killed. Nevertheless, וַיַּשֵּׁב אֹתָם אַבְרָם, *Abraham drove them away* — by תְּשׁוּבָה, repentance [i.e. Abraham, symbolic of Israel tried to beat the birds of prey, symbolic of the nations swooping down on Israel, by physical force, but without success. Only when Israel turns to God in repentance, are its enemies driven off. וַיַּשֵּׁב, *drove off,* is thus connected with תְּשׁוּבָה, *repentance.*] *(Midrash).*

הַשֶּׁ֙מֶשׁ֙ לָב֔וֹא וְתַרְדֵּמָ֖ה נָפְלָ֣ה עַל־אַבְרָ֑ם
וְהִנֵּ֥ה אֵימָ֛ה חֲשֵׁכָ֥ה גְדֹלָ֖ה נֹפֶ֥לֶת עָלָֽיו׃
יג וַיֹּ֣אמֶר לְאַבְרָ֗ם יָדֹ֨עַ תֵּדַ֜ע כִּי־גֵ֣ר ׀ יִהְיֶ֣ה

12. וַיְהִי הַשֶּׁמֶשׁ לָבוֹא — *And it happened, as the sun was about to set* [lit. *'to come'*]

It was still daytime, too early for someone to fall asleep *(Chizkuni)*.

This piece of information makes it clear that Abraham carried out all the tasks described in the above verses within that one day (*Ibn Ezra*).

וְתַרְדֵּמָה נָפְלָה עַל אַבְרָם — *A deep sleep fell upon Abraham.*

It was the deep sleep that accompanies prophetic manifestations (*Rambam Yesodei haTorah* 7:2; *Moreh* 2:41, 42).

Compare Daniel's prophetic slumber [*Dan.* 8:18]: *'As He was speaking with me, I fell into a deep sleep on my face toward the ground ...'* This was followed by a dark dread [*ibid. v.* 17]: *and when He approached me I was afraid (Radak)*.

It was during this deep sleep that the following prophecy came to him *(Da'as Zekeinim)*. God caused him to sleep during this prophecy so that he would not pray that his descendants be freed from subjugation by the Four Kingdoms *(Midrash haGadol)*.

וְהִנֵּה אֵימָה חֲשֵׁכָה גְדֹלָה נֹפֶלֶת עָלָיו — *And behold — a dread! great darkness fell upon him.*

Physical dread usually accompanied profound prophetic experiences: Their limbs trembled, their physical strength failed them, their thoughts became confused and thus the mind was let free to comprehend the vision it saw, as the Torah says with reference to Abraham ... and Daniel [*Dan.* 10:8] *(Rambam ibid.)*.

During the previous vision Abraham did not experience all of this, because the previous tidings were good. Now that God came to reveal the darkness and bitterness of the future exiles, He cast the deep sleep, fear, and darkness upon him to symbolize the difficult tribulations that lay ahead *(Rashi; Radak)*.

According to the *Midrash*, the fourfold expression, אֵימָה, *dread;* חֲשֵׁכָה, *darkness;* גְּדֹלָה, *great*; and נֹפְלָה, *fell* — all of which overtook his soul sequentially — referred to the Four Kingdoms. The *dread* is Babylon; *darkness* is Media-Persia; *great* is Greece; *fell* is Rome.

Thus, *Ramban* explains, God forewarned Abraham that if Israel sinned, they would be [kept in subjugation and] exiled from their land by these four powers. Following this general allusion, He explicitly told him that their possession of the Land would be preceded by the Egyptian exile.

13. God, Who has entered into a Covenant with Abraham, withholds nothing from His beloved, and reveals to him the future plight of his descendants *(Sefer HaIkkarim,* see footnote to *v.* 9):

יָדֹעַ תֵּדַע — *Know with certainty* [lit. *'know, you shall know'*].

XV
12-13

[12] *And it happened, as the sun was about to set, a
deep sleep fell upon Abram; and behold — a dread!
great darkness fell upon him.*
[13] *And He said to Abram, 'Know with certainty
that your offspring shall be aliens in a land not their*

Abraham is now told that although the land is assured him, actual *possession* of it will be delayed *'because the iniquity of the Emorite is not yet full'* [*v.* 16], and a nation cannot be expelled from its land until it has sinned to the point where God no longer forbears from depriving it of its homeland. During the interim his offspring shall be an alien nation. Not all will suffer *servitude,* however, for the bondage did not begin during the lives of the righteous; the servitude did not begin until after the death of Jacob's sons when it was deserved by their sinful children. He revealed all this to Abraham so that the last generation should know that whatever befell them was by the Word of HASHEM, and they should attribute it to no other cause, as the prophet declared [*Isaiah* 48:5]: *I have already from the beginning told it to you; announced things to you before they happened: that you might not say 'My idol has caused them; my carved and molten images commanded them' (Sforno).*

[The use of the compound יָדֹעַ תֵּדַע, *know, you shall know,* is noted. In the simple sense, the Torah uses the double verb form to add emphasis. Cf. for example, 2:16 אָכֹל תֹּאכֵל, 2:18 מוֹת תָּמוּת]

[*Midrashically,* however, the double verb signifies the double connotation of God's promise]:

— Know that I shall disperse your descendants, know that I will gather them together;

— know that I will take them in pledge [i.e., I will exile them to expiate their sins], know that I will redeem them;

— know that I will allow them to be enslaved, know that I will free them *(Midrash).*

כִּי גֵר יִהְיֶה זַרְעֲךָ בְּאֶרֶץ לֹא לָהֶם — *That your offspring* [lit. *'seed'*] *shall be aliens* [lit. *'a stranger'*] *in a land not their own.*

[Through the symbolism of the Covenant as explained above, God alluded in vague terms to the future exiles to be endured by Abraham's descendants. Now the vision is more clearly defined as it affects his immediate progeny. The commentators note that זַרְעֲךָ (lit. *'your seed')* although collectively referring to all his descendants, is in the singular to indicate that the גֵּרוּת, *sojourning,* of his future זֶרַע, *seed,* refers particularly to the time that a yet childless Abraham would have children, and to his זֶרַע, *seed par excellence,* Isaac (cf. 21:12). For, it was with the birth of Isaac thirty years after this Covenant (Abraham was seventy at the time of the Covenant and one hundred at Isaac's birth) that the 400 year calculation in this prophecy would begin (*Seder Olam; Midrash; Sechel Tov; R' Meyuchas;* see *Rashi* and *Ramban* below).]

Rashi notes that the verse does not specify Egypt because the exile in Egypt lasted for only 210 out of the 400 years. The 400 year period of exile began with the birth of Isaac, for it was from that time onward

זַרְעֲךָ בְּאֶרֶץ לֹא לָהֶם וַעֲבָדוּם וְעִנּוּ אֹתָם
יד אַרְבַּע מֵאוֹת שָׁנָה: וְגַם אֶת־הַגּוֹי אֲשֶׁר

that the family of Abraham was treated as גֵּרִים, *aliens,* even when they lived in Canaan as Isaac did all his life. Thus, the Torah states that soon after Isaac's birth *Abraham sojourned* [וַיָּגָר, from גֵּר, *stranger, alien*] *in the land of the Philistines* [21:34]; Isaac himself was commanded to *sojourn* [גּוּר] in the land [26:3]; *Jacob sojourned* [גָּר] in the land of Ham, [*Ps.* 105:23.] while his sons said that they came to Egypt לָגוּר, *to sojourn* [47:4.]

וַעֲבָדוּם — [*And*] *they* [i.e. your descendants] *will serve them.*

[I.e. the foreign Nation in whose midst your descendants shall be aliens].

After the exile-alien status, came this more severe phase, of the Bondage. It came to pass after the death of Joseph, when the Egyptians set taskmasters over the Jews [see *Exod.* 1:11] *(Malbim).*

[The translation of וַעֲבָדוּם with Israel as the subject: *they* (i.e. Israel) *will serve them* (the Egyptians), rather than the more familiar translation: *they* (i.e. the Egyptians) *will enslave them* (Israel) follows the parallel use of the same verb form in *Jeremiah* 8:2 אֲשֶׁר אֲהֵבוּם וַאֲשֶׁר עֲבָדוּם, *whom they have loved and whom they have served; Deut.* 31:20: וּפָנָה אֶל אֱלֹהִים אֲחֵרִים וַעֲבָדוּם, *and shall turn to other gods and serve them.* It is also related to the other conjugations, e.g. עֲבָדוּהוּ, עֲבָדוּךָ. This is also how the word is understood by *Malbim;* see below.]

Our translation also follows *Chizkuni,* and *HaRechasim leBik'ah* who comment that if *Egypt* was the subject of the word [the translation being *they will enslave them*], then the Hebrew should have read וְעָבְדוּ בָם. *Radak,* following *Targum* who translates וְיִפְלְחוּן בְּהוֹן [*they will enslave them*] agrees that Egypt is indeed the subject. In his alternate interpretation, however, he suggests that our translation is equally correct.]

וְעִנּוּ אֹתָם — *And* [*they*] *will oppress them.* —

[The subject is now the Egyptians.]

The *oppression* began with birth of Miriam *(Malbim).*

[This is based upon the *Midrashic* interpretation that Moses' sister was named מִרְיָם, lit. *bitterness,* because at the time of her birth the Egyptians increased the bitterness of the bondage upon the Jews, as it says *(Exod.* 1:14): וַיְמָרְרוּ אֶת חַיֵּיהֶם, *they embittered their lives.* Thus, the harshest part of the 210 years of the Egyptian bondage was the 86 years from the birth of Miriam. See below, and cf. *comm.* to *Shir HaShirim* 2:11, *ArtScroll* ed. p. 108.

Malbim explains why Israel is the subject of וַעֲבָדוּם [i.e., Israel served Egypt], while Egypt is the subject of וְעִנּוּ [i.e., Egypt oppressed Israel]. The Jews originally volunteered for national service so it is they who served Egypt, but oppression was perpetrated purely by Egypt.

The exile and especially the grinding servitude in Egypt must be seen from the perspective of כּוּר הַבַּרְזֶל, an *iron crucible,* as the Torah describes Egypt (*Deut.* 4:20). A crucible, by melting precious metal, removes the impurities from it. The purpose of exile in God's plan for Israel is to purify and elevate the nation. The extent of the suffering, however, will be increased if Israel is sinful *(Malbim, Da'as Sofrim;* see *Overview).*

XV *own, they will serve them, and they will oppress*
14 *them four hundred years.* [14] *But also upon the nation*

אַרְבַּע מֵאוֹת שָׁנָה — *Four hundred years.*

Abraham's prophecy did not clarify when these four hundred years would begin and end. He was told only that the total duration would extend for that period, but not how long or where each part of the bondage would be.

It is quite clear, that the phrase *four hundred years* stands by itself, preceded as it is by an אֶתְנַחְתָּא [Masoretic punctuation similar to the English semicolon] under the word אֹתָם, *them.* Accordingly, the 'four hundred years' refers to [the period which] גֵר יִהְיֶה זַרְעֲךָ, *Your offspring will be strangers,* and not to the *servitude and affliction* because, as explained above, only the sojourning extended four hundred years, from the birth of Isaac until the Exodus. The severity of the Bondage — slavery and oppression in Egypt — began only later and lasted a much shorter time *(Rashi* as explained by *R' Yosef Kara; Mizrachi;* and *Pa'aneach Raza).*

Therefore, as an aid in comprehension, *Ramban* suggests that the verse be transposed and interpreted as if it read: *Your offspring shall be a stranger for four hundred years in a land not theirs, and shall serve them, and they shall afflict them.* Thus, although the period they would be strangers has been defined, the length of the period of servitude and affliction remains unspecified.

Ramban cites many other verses which require transposition for proper understanding as, for example: 39:17; 41:57; *Exodus* 12:15; *Isaiah* 2:20; *Psalms* 66:16; *Hosea* 8:2; *Malachi* 3:17.

[For further examples of סָרֵס אֶת הַמִּקְרָא, transposing texts for clearer interpretation see *comm.* to 14:15.]

Rashi clarifies the chronology:

The period of 400 years extends from Isaac's birth until the Exodus. This total is arrived at because Isaac was 60 years old when Jacob was born [25:26]; Jacob, as he himself stated [*Gen.* 47:9], was 130 years old when he went down to Egypt, making a total of 190 years. They were actually in Egypt for 210 years, the numerical equivalent of רְדוּ [cf. *Rashi* to *Gen.* 42:2] making 400 years altogether.

Rashi goes on to explain that the verse cannot intend to suggest that they were actually *in Egypt* for 400 years, for Kehath, who accompanied Jacob to Egypt, lived 130 years [*Ex.* 6:18]; his son Amram lived 137 years[*ibid. v.* 20], and Moses was 80 years old when the children of Israel left Egypt [*ibid.,* 7:7] — totaling only 347. The actual figure, of course, is much less because their lifespans overlapped; the years that Kehath continued to live after Amram was born, and those that Amram lived after the birth of Moses must be deducted [which will then yield the total of 210 years as above.]...[1]

1. As noted in *Tanchuma Masei* 7, *God is not man, that He should lie* [*Numbers* 23:19]: When He promises good, though the generation is unworthy He does not retract; but when He threatens to bring evil he does retract, for, although He foretold Abraham that the affliction would endure *four hundred years,* yet the affliction lasted only two hundred and ten years! [Cf. also *comm.* to *Song of Songs* 2:8 where God is allegorically depicted as *'leaping and skipping'* to redeem the Jews before the pre-determined end.]

[*Rashi's* above comment is derived from *Seder Olam* which continues]: What, then, is meant by the references to servitude and affliction in our verse? — That the total period that *your offspring will be in a land not theirs* [probably including the Promised Land which did not yet belong to them] will be *400 years. They shall serve them* refers to the lesser period of servitude; *and they shall oppress them* to the period of actual oppression; together they amounted to four hundred years.

The *Mechilta, Bo* 14 notes that in *Exodus* 12:40 the length of Israel's stay in Egypt is given as *four hundred and thirty* years, while in our verse four hundred years were foretold. The texts are not contradictory, however. The additional thirty year period refer to the years between the Covenant [when Abraham was 70] and Isaac's birth [when Abraham was 100].

This, according to *Rav Saadiah Gaon* in *Emunos V'Deos* 8:4, encompasses the period that Abraham, himself, was a גֵּר, *stranger*, during his journeying.

But, as *Gur Aryeh* [next verse] notes, Abraham's sojourning was unlike that of his children. Even while wandering, he was never derogated; though he was a *stranger*, he was held in the highest esteem as [23:6] נְשִׂיא אֱלֹהִים, *a prince of God.*

[Therefore, perhaps, Abraham's *sojourns* are not included in the initial 400 years which began with Isaac, because the nature of Abraham's sojourns are different from those of his descendants. They are mentioned as part of the *additional* thirty years mentioned in *Exodus*, because they did, in fact, take place, but they are different in *kind*, rather than *degree*, from the sort of sojourning inflicted upon Isaac and his descendants.]

[There are, however, other interpretations of the additional thirty years, notably that of *Ramban* and *Ibn Ezra*, and these will be dealt with בעזהשי״ת in the *comm.* to *Exodus* 12:40. The English reader is referred to the excellent exposition of this matter in *The Conciliator* by Rav Menasheh ben Yisrael; N.Y., Hermon Press 1972; p. 60-64.]

14. וְגַם אֶת הַגּוֹי אֲשֶׁר יַעֲבֹדוּ דָּן אָנֹכִי — *But* [lit. *'and'*] *also* [*upon* (suggested by the otherwise untranslatable indefinite article אֶת)] *the nation which they shall serve, will I execute judgment.*

The nation that I have appointed for a fiery crucible, a melting pot for your descendants, is told here that when its mission is accomplished it will suffer the fate it will have richly earned *(Hirsch).*

[The word וְגַם (lit. *and also)* suggests a רִבּוּי, *amplification*, the subject of which is variously interpreted by the commentators]:

Rashi, following the *Midrash*, suggests that *also* is an allusion which the Four Kingdoms [who would subjugate Israel at a later date] They too, will perish because they subjugated Israel.

Ramban suggests that in the literal sense *also* implies: 'Just as I will execute judgment upon your children by subjecting them to servitude and affliction, so will I *also* punish the Egyptians for the violence they will do to them' [also *Sforno.*]

⊛§ Egypt as God's Agent

Free-Will and Foreknowledge

This verse evokes certain profound *hashkafah* (=philosophic) questions which touch on the very foundation of

XV 14 *which they shall serve, will I execute judgment, and*

man's Free-Will and God's Foreknowledge; reward and punishment.

Concisely formulated, the problem is: If God decreed that Abraham's descendants should be strangers in a land not their own, where they would be subjected to servitude and affliction, then why should the Egyptians be punished for having been the agents in carrying out God's Providential Will?

— *Rambam* in *Hilchos Teshuvah* 6:4 deals with this question. He answers that God was not addressing the *Egyptians* when He uttered this decree, nor did He decree that any *one person in particular* should enslave the Jews. God was merely instructing Abraham as to the course of future history. Just as no one similarly has the right to be wicked because the Almighty has informed Moses that there will be wicked men among Israel, so, too, with the Egyptians: every Egyptian who oppressed and ill-treated the Israelites could have refrained from doing so had he not wished to hurt them. [Since he *did* perpetrate these acts, however, he is subject to punishment] (see *comm.* ad. loc. *Ra'avad;* cf. also *Hirhurei Teshuvah* by *Harav Gifter).* [1]

— *Ramban* disagrees with the above, because the individual who takes the initiative to personally fulfill a king's general command, is deserving of the king's favor. [Therefore, the Egyptians who fulfilled God's decree should have been rewarded rather than punished.]

He explains that the Egyptians were punished not for *executing* God's decree but for their *overzealousness in carrying it out:* It was not included in His decree that they should throw Jewish children into the Nile, for this was not *'affliction'* — it was murder. The same applies to the general severity and vigor which they displayed toward the Israelites ...

This is the meaning of דָּן אָנֹכִי, :'I will bring them to *judgment* [a word which implies careful consideration of their deeds prior to determining whether and how they should be punished] to determine whether they complied with the decree, or if they increased the evil inflicted on them'. . . . [Cf. *Malbim.*]

Ramban continues: Understand well that a bandit who murders someone whose death has already been determined on Rosh Hashanah will nevertheless be punished [for he was unaware of the divine decree, and was acting from his own motives]; if, however, one heard the decree from a prophet and fulfills it *because he sincerely wishes to fulfill God's Will,* then he is guiltless and is even considered meritorious, as was the case with Jehu [see *II Kings* 10:30]. If, however, he murders out of *personal vindictiveness* or hopes of gain, then, though God's plan was accomplished through him, he is guilty. This is expressly stated with respect to Sancherev [see *Isaiah* 10:5, 6]. Pharaoh too, deserved punishment because he acted out of *personal* vindictiveness in enslaving the Israelites.]

This is also the case with Nebuchadnezzar, who, though the prophets unanimously called upon him and his people to destroy Jerusalem [see, e.g., *Jeremiah* 25:9; 32:28-29], and though the Chaldeans were aware that this was the command of God, nevertheless they were all punished because Nebuchadnezzar had his own personal glory in mind [see *Isaiah* 14:13, 14; 47:8], and because he added to the decree and overzealously perpetrated evil against Israel [see *Isaiah* 47:6.]

1. Even had no Pharaoh arisen, Israel was destined to servitude, as God specifically foretold. But מְגַלְגְּלִין זְכוּת עַל יְדֵי זַכַּאי, *good is brought through the worthy,* וְחוֹבָה עַל יְדֵי חַיָּיבִים, *while evil is brought through the guilty,* [Pharaoh was chosen for this mission because he was wicked, and therefore he deserved punishment] (*Semachos* 8).

טו גָּדוֹל: וְאַתָּה תָּבוֹא אֶל־אֲבֹתֶיךָ בְּשָׁלוֹם
טז תִּקָּבֵר בְּשֵׂיבָה טוֹבָה: וְדוֹר רְבִיעִי יָשׁוּבוּ

(The reader is directed to the *Overview; Meshech Chochmah; Or HaChaim*).

[The translation of יַעֲבֹדוּ *they shall serve,* agrees with the interpretation of the word וַעֲבָדוּם, *they shall serve them,* in the previous verse. This follows *Targum Yonassan* and *Ibn Ezra. Onkelos,* however, consistent with his interpretation in the previous verse, renders דִי יִפְלְחוּן בְּהוֹן, *who will enslave them,* as if the Hebrew implied the reading (בָּהֶם) אֲשֶׁר יַעֲבֹדוּ. (When עבד is followed by בָּהֶם or any word preceded by the prepositional prefix — בְּ changes the meaning of the verb עבד, *work,* from the intransitive to the causitive. Cf. for example, *Lev.* 25:39 לֹא תַעֲבוֹד בּוֹ עֲבוֹדַת עָבֶד, *do not cause him to serve as a bondservant;* and *Jeremiah* 34:9 *(Radak).*]

וְאַחֲרֵי־כֵן יֵצְאוּ בִּרְכֻשׁ גָּדוֹל — *And afterwards they shall leave with great possessions.*

I.e., with great wealth: the spoils of the Egyptians [*Ex.* 12:36] *(Rashi).*

Their wealth could not possibly be considered *payment* for the years of bitter enslavement and countless deaths, pain, and suffering, inflicted upon the Israelites by the Egyptians. Rather, what Abraham is being assured here is that when the time of redemption arrives, the awful past will not be recognizable in his descendants. They will leave Egypt not as pitiful slaves escaping from their master, but as a content nation which has amassed wealth and possessions (Da'as Sofrim).

15. וְאַתָּה תָּבוֹא אֶל אֲבֹתֶיךָ בְּשָׁלוֹם — *[And] as for you: you shall go* [lit. *'come'*] *to your ancestors* [lit. *'fathers'*] *in peace.*

A euphemism for death: You will go the way of all flesh in dignity *(Ibn Ezra),* and will not see all this [trial and tribulation] *(Rashi).*

Ramban disagrees because Abraham *himself* was included in the גֵּרוּת, *sojourning:* after Isaac's birth when the decree went into effect, Abraham, too, was a stranger in Philistia [21:34]. [And so he did ultimately see all this.] Rather, the intent of the verse is: Though I decree punishments of servitude and affliction upon your children, you will not be punished.

Mizrachi upholds *Rashi's* interpretation by explaining that *Rashi*'s comment, did not refer to the *sojourning;* the intent was merely that Abraham would not witness the *slavery* and *oppression.*

Gur Aryeh [as cited in *comm.* end of *v.* 13] explains that Abraham's sojourns are not in the same category as those of Isaac and his descendants. Even when Abraham was an alien in a strange land he was honored as a נְשִׂיא אֱלֹהִים, *a Prince of God* [23:6] and hence, according to *Rashi* our verse means: You will die peacefully, and not suffer alien status.

Abraham asked God! 'Will I too experience this servitude?' — He answered: '[No], you will go to your fathers in peace' *(Midrash).* For though the *sojourning* will commence during your lifetime, you will not be enslaved; instead you will experience nothing but peace from all sides *(Sechel Tov).*

It is possible that the word אֲבֹתֶיךָ in this verse is really derived from the word אבה, *desire* — i.e. אֲבֹתֶיךָ, *your yearnings.* The implication is: And you shall reach the zenith of your most lofty spiritual aspirations, amid spiritual tranquility *(HaK'sav v'Hakaballah).*

XV *afterwards they shall leave with great possessions. —*
15-16 *[15] As for you: you shall go to your ancestors in peace;*
you shall be buried in a good old age. — [16] And the
fourth generation shall return here, for the iniquity

In the literal sense, with אֲבֹתֶיךָ meaning *your fathers*, it is noted that the verse cannot be speaking of Abraham's *physical* interment alongside his ancestors: for he was entombed in Canaan, while his fathers were buried in Mesopotamia. [See 11:32: *'and Terach died in Charan'*.] Our verse thus eloquently refers to his immortal soul which will return to the eternal abode of his fathers, in peace.

Minchah Belulah suggests that our verse refers to the original ancestors of man, *Adam and Eve* who were entombed in the Cave of Machpelah.

Rashi notes that though Abraham's father, Terach, was an idolator, the verse still speaks of Abraham 'returning' to him! This proves that Terach repented his idolatry and returned to God [see *comm.* to 11:27; 11:32.]

[The translation, *as for you,* follows the cantillation which places a *t'vir* beneath וְאַתָּה, setting off the word and emphasizing it. I have followed this emphatic translation for similar pronouns throughout. Compare, for example 6:17: וַאֲנִי, *as for me;* 6:21: וְאַתָּה, *as for you.*]

תִּקָּבֵר בְּשֵׂיבָה טוֹבָה — *You shall be buried in a good old age.*

A Scriptural idiom meaning: spared from all suffering *(R' Meyuchas).*

By this promise, God announced to him that Ishmael would repent in Abraham's lifetime, and that [his grandchild] Esau would not go on the wicked path in his lifetime. To prevent Abraham from witnessing Esau's evil conduct, however, Abraham died five years earlier than he normally would have, because on the very day Abraham died Esau rebelled [and had Abraham lived, he would have witnessed it] *(Rashi).*

[This is based on the *Midrash* which notes that Abraham was destined to live 180 years like his son Isaac, but that God withheld five years of Abraham's life in anticipation of Esau's sins, as God said, I promised Abraham, *you shall be buried in a good old age.* Is it a *good old age* when he sees his grandson commit adultery and murder? Better let him die in peace!]

16. וְדוֹר רְבִיעִי יָשׁוּבוּ הֵנָּה — *And the fourth generation shall return here.*

I.e. the fourth generation after the beginning of the Egyptian exile will return הֵנָּה, *here — to Canaan* where this prophecy took place [as implied in *v.* 7 to give you *this land* as an inheritance]. So it happened: Jacob [who is not counted because he was of extremely advanced age and remained in Egypt but a short time *(Chizkuni; Mizrachi)*] descended to Egypt. Judah, Perez, and Chezron, three successive generations, were in Egypt, and Caleb [whose father Yefuneh is identified in *Sotah* 11b as Chezron] of the fourth generation was among those who entered the Promised Land *(Rashi).*

Others compute the four generations from Kehath [son of Levi]

הִנֵּה כִּי לֹא־שָׁלֵם עֲוֹן הָאֱמֹרִי עַד־הֵנָּה׃
יז וַיְהִי הַשֶּׁמֶשׁ בָּאָה וַעֲלָטָה הָיָה וְהִנֵּה

from whose time the actual Egyptian servitude began, because, as pointed out earlier, the servitude did not begin until after the death of the Tribes [i.e. Jacob's son's.] The three generations involved in the Egyptian Bondage are thus: Kehath, Amram, Moses. The *fourth* generation (i.e. the children of Moses) returned to the Promised Land, as foretold here.

Ramban disagrees with *Rashi's* interpretation [since as *Tur* points out, there seems to be no logical way to arrive at a total of exactly four generations. If alien status in other lands is to be included, than the Patriarchs would swell the total to seven. If it begins with the last of those who descended to Egypt, then only Chezron (who descended with Jacob) and Caleb would be counted. *Tur* answers, however, that the computation begins with Jacob's sons because Jacob was the prime exile and the count of four *begins from him onward.*]

Ramban suggests an entirely different interpretation. The fourth generations are not Israelite, but Emorite. By the time of the fourth generation, the allotted quota of Emorite sin will be full, for from the day their expulsion was decreed he allowed the Emorites an extension of time in the manner of His פֹּקֵד עֲוֹן אָבוֹת עַל בָּנִים עַל שִׁלֵּשִׁים וְעַל רִבֵּעִים לְשֹׂנְאָי, *visiting the iniquities of the fathers upon the sons, upon the third* [*generation*] *and upon the fourth* [*generation*] *of those that hate Me (Exodus* 20:5) ,[i.e., He permits three generations to continue in sin. If they persist after that, they are incorrigible, and He metes out their due punishment. (See *comm.* there).] Had the Emorites repented their iniquities God would *not* have brought about their utter destruction. Instead, they would have become bondservants, or they might have migrated elsewhere.

Tur cites an interpretation that דּוֹר encompasses three generations — grandfather, father, and son — with the computation beginning from Abraham. Thus the three 'generations' are: (1) Abraham, Isaac, and Jacob; (2) Judah, Peretz, and Chetzron; (3) Ram, Aminadav, and Nachshon. His son Shalmon was the beginning of the fourth generation, and he was among those who entered the Promised Land.

According to *R' Meyuchas* the implication is 'the fourth generation *after your death* will return here' — Levi was born after Abraham's death, and Moses' generation was the fourth from Levi. Moses' generation would have entered Eretz Israel had their sin in the wilderness not prevented them from doing so.

Or HaChaim gives a new interpretation. Two distinct terms are given in the verse — one for the end of the exile and the other for the entry to the Land. The exile would last no longer than 400 years. The time of entry into the Land, however, would be more flexible — the fourth generation — and it would be sooner or later within the lifetime of that generation, depending on the degree of its righteousness. The 'four generations' begin from the time the Egyptian servitude was imposed which was after the death of Jacob's twelve sons. Thus, the four are Perez, Chezron, Caleb, and Caleb's children. [Although Caleb entered the Land, he is not counted because the rest of his generation died in the wilderness.] The verse continues that the sins of the Emorites are also a determining factor. Had Israel been perfect in its righteousness, then the Emorites would have had to make way for them. However, since Israel sinned and could not be considered perfect, a different measuring rod was

XV *of the Emorites shall not yet be full until then.'*
17 17 *So it happened: the sun set, and it was very*

required. Israel was *better than* the Emorites, but not perfect. Therefore, the entry into the Land was delayed until the Emorite's alloted measure of sin will be competed.

כִּי לֹא שָׁלֵם עֲוֹן הָאֱמֹרִי עַד־הֵנָּה — *For the iniquity of the Emorite shall not* [lit. *'is not'*] *yet be full until then* [lit. *'until now,'* following *R' Meyuchos*; cf. *Deut.* 12:9].

That is, until that time they will not yet be sufficiently iniquitous to deserve expulsion, and God does not punish a nation until its measure is full [cf. *Isaiah* 27:8] *(Rashi).*

... And there is no suffering without iniquity [*Shabbos* 55a] *(Ibn Caspi).*

Radak explains: The time for punishment of the Emorite iniquity has not yet arrived because God is patient in meting out punishment to the wicked: everyone receives his due punishment at a time and in a manner predetermined by God and known only to Him. The *punishment* for עָוֹן, *iniquity,* is also termed עָוֹן as in 4:13: *My punishment* [עֲוֹנִי] *is too great to be borne* [see *Ibn Ezra* cited in *comm.* ad. loc. p. 154], just as the punishment for חַטָּאת, *sin,* is termed חַטָּאת as in *Zechariah* 14:19: חַטַּאת מִצְרָיִם, *the punishment of Egypt.*

[Thus, transfer of the Land to Abraham's descendants will not be a deprivation to its legitimate owners, as the former owners will have lost their claim through their sins. God is the Master of the Universe, and He allows a people to keep its land or He takes it from them according to moral principles established by Him. (See *comm.* of *Ramban* to 1:1).]

The *Emorite* represents *all* the Canaanite nations. It is singled out because it was the most powerful of them all, being described as *tall as cedars* [*Amos* 2:9] *(Ibn Ezra).*

The Israelites would not be able to overpower them until the time was ripe. Moreover, the Emorites were captured first, and their territory was the first one conquered *(Ramban).*

This is the crux of the entire prophecy: The Promised Land will not be given now, but to the fourth generation because only by then will the iniquity of the Amorites have reached sufficient dimension to warrant their expulsion from the Land. Another reason why God specified the Emorites is because Abraham then dwelled in the territory of Mamre, an Emorite *(Chizkuni; Hoffmann).*

Da'as Soferim makes an interesting point: Though their disposition made it clear that their measure would continue to fill up, with the result that they would lose their title to the Land, nevertheless this does *not* suggest that a war with them was inevitable. Before the Israelites entered *Eretz Yisrael,* they made peace overtures to the inhabitants [cf. *Rambam, Hil. Melachim* 6:1.] Had they accepted, the Canaanites would have remained in the Land together with Israel on the condition that they would accept the seven commandments enjoined upon the descendants of Noah.

17. The Ratification of the Covenant

וַיְהִי הַשֶּׁמֶשׁ בָּאָה — *So* [lit. *'and'*] *it happened: the sun set.*

תַּנּוּר עָשָׁן וְלַפִּיד אֵשׁ אֲשֶׁר עָבַר בֵּין
יח הַגְּזָרִים הָאֵלֶּה: בַּיּוֹם הַהוּא כָּרַת יהוה
אֶת־אַבְרָם בְּרִית לֵאמֹר לְזַרְעֲךָ נָתַתִּי
אֶת־הָאָרֶץ הַזֹּאת מִנְּהַר מִצְרַיִם עַד־

The word וַיְהִי is not the predicate of הַשֶּׁמֶשׁ, *the sun,* for this would require the fem. form וַתְּהִי since שֶׁמֶשׁ is a fem. noun *(Mizrachi).* Therefore, וַיְהִי is to be interpreted as a separate clause, with the missing predicate being implied: וַיְהִי דָבָר זֶה, *and this thing happened.* The same syntactical construction occurs in 42:35 and in *II Kings* 13:21 ...

The verb בָּאָה [set], is accented on the first syllable, בָּ, indicating that it is in past tense: *the sun already set.* Had the accent been on the second syllable, אָ, it would indicate the present tense: *the sun was in the process of setting,* a translation clearly not possible here because the process of the sun being *about* to set was already described in *v.* 12. Consequently, the events in this verse occurred *after* it was already dark. This rule that the tense of two-letter verbs is determined by the placement of the accent is a firm grammatical principle. Cf. שָׁבָה, *returned,* in *Ruth* 1:15; בָּאָה, *is coming,* further 29:6; and שָׁבָה, *would return,* in *Esther* 2:14 *(Rashi).*

וַעֲלָטָה הָיָה — [And] *it was very dark.*

The word signifies *thick darkness.* It is found nowhere else in Scriptures except for three times in *Ezekiel* [12:6, 7, 12]. The darkness was so all-enveloping that even the light of the stars was not visible *(Ibn Ezra; Yohel Or).*

וְהִנֵּה תַנּוּר עָשָׁן וְלַפִּיד אֵשׁ — *Behold there was a smoky furnace and a torch of fire.*

A vision symbolic of the Divine *Presence (Rashi* to *v.* 10).

The smoking furnace also symbolized Gehinnom into which the Four Kingdoms would descend *(Rashi,* here).

All of this occurred during Abraham's prophetic slumber *(Moreh Nevuchim* 1:21)...

He envisioned these things. The smoke [which rose up into the thick darkness *(Radak)*] was the *'Cloud and thick darkness'* which appeared at the revelation of the Torah; and the torch in its midst was 'the fire' which appeared at Sinai [see *Exod.* 19:18; *Deut.* 5:4].

אֲשֶׁר עָבַר בֵּין הַגְּזָרִים הָאֵלֶּה — *Which passed between these pieces.*

— In ratification of the Covenant *(Rashi v.* 10).

As pointed out above, Abraham did not pass through because he undertook no obligation under the terms of this Covenant. It was God Who was obligated under this Covenant regarding the gift of the Land, and, as such, He caused His Presence, symbolized by the fire, to pass through and conclude the Covenant *(Nimukei Rashi; Ralbag; Abarbanel).*

Thus, the Divine Glory passed through the parts of the offerings. This constituted ratification of the eternal covenant with Abraham. The following verse refers to this divinely executed ratification. One well-versed in the mysteries of the Torah will understand the implications of the foregoing *(Ramban).*

XV *dark. Behold there was a smoky furnace and a torch*
18 *of fire which passed between these pieces.* [18] *On that*
day HASHEM made a covenant with Abram, saying,
'To your descendants have I given this land, from the

[According to *Malbim,* the culmination of this vision was that the fire consumed the pieces, causing their smoke to ascend to heaven; or according to *Hirsch* that the pieces joined together, but these interpretations are apparently not shared by other commentators.]

Our verse uses the word גְּזָרִים, *pieces,* instead of פְּגָרִים, *carcasses,* as in *v.* 11. The use of the more respectful word in our verse is in deference to the *Shechinah* which passed between the pieces. *(Ralbag).*

18. [Thus, in culmination of all of the above]...

בַּיּוֹם הַהוּא כָּרַת ה׳ אֶת אַבְרָם בְּרִית לֵאמֹר — *On that day HASHEM made a covenant with Abram, saying.*

— I.e., the everlasting Covenant between God and Abraham was ratified by the events that occurred on that day: the visions, the division of the animals, the passing through of the Divine Presence and His promise *(Radak; Akeidas Yitzchak).*

[On the significance of the use of the word לֵאמֹר, *saying,* in this context, see *comm.* to that word in verses 1 and 4.]

לְזַרְעֲךָ נָתַתִּי אֶת הָאָרֶץ הַזֹּאת — *To your descendants* [lit. *'seed'*] *have I given this land.*

Scripture often uses the past tense in place of the future or present, as in 23:13: נָתַתִּי כֶּסֶף הַשָּׂדֶה, *I give* [lit. *'I gave'*] *you money for the field (R' Meyuchas).*

Rashi comments that the past tense is used here [besides its idiomatic correctness], because the promise of the Holy One, Blessed be He, is as reliable as if it were an accomplished fact.

Ramban [who, it must be remembered, views the narratives in *Lech Lecha* as being in *correct* chronological order, in contrast with the *Seder Olam* chronology which holds that the Covenant Between the Parts in this chapter occurred *before* the departure from Charan related in 12:1], comments that the promise of the Land was given to Abraham several times, each of them necessary. When he originally entered the country God told him [12:7]: *To your seed will I give this Land,* a pledge which included only the territory which he had traversed up to then, viz. Shechem. When his merits increased, God bestowed the additional promise [13:14-15]: *Lift up your eyes ... All the land which you see* — i.e., in every direction which you see — *to you will I give it, and your seed forever.* This promise was more comprehensive, and also added *and to your seed forever,* and that his seed would increase *as the dust of the earth.* In our chapter, God defines the boundaries of the Land [next verse], mentioning the ten nations [which presently occupied the Land and would be displaced, (verses 19-21)] and further made an irrevocable Covenant with him that he could not be abrogated through sin. When, He repeated the promise on the occasion of Abraham's circumcision for the final time, He added the words [17:8] 'for a *possession* forever', which meant that even if they were to be exiled, they would return and inherit it.

Thus, the first two instances are in the future tense. The promise during the Covenant, refers to a gift already given and is in past tense. At the circumcision, the promise involved a future return to the Land following exile; it is accordingly in future tense.

יט הַנָּהָר הַגָּדֹל נְהַר־פְּרָת: אֶת־הַקֵּינִי
כ וְאֶת־הַקְּנִזִּי וְאֵת הַקַּדְמֹנִי: וְאֶת־הַחִתִּי
כא וְאֶת־הַפְּרִזִּי וְאֶת־הָרְפָאִים: וְאֶת־הָאֱמֹרִי
וְאֶת־הַכְּנַעֲנִי וְאֶת־הַגִּרְגָּשִׁי וְאֶת־
א הַיְבוּסִי: וְשָׂרַי אֵשֶׁת אַבְרָם

מִנְּהַר מִצְרַיִם עַד־הַנָּהָר הַגָּדֹל נְהַר פְּרָת — *From the river of Egypt to the great river, the Euphrates River.*

The river of Egypt is variously explained as referring to either the Nile (so *Rashi* to *Josh.* 13:3), or, according to most commentators, (e.g., *Rav Saadiah Gaon, Ibn Ezra, Abarbanel* etc.), to נַחַל מִצְרַיִם, *the Brook of Egypt,* mentioned as Israel's ideal southern border in *Num.* 34:5, and *Josh.* 15:4. It is identified with Shichor, now known as *Wady el-Aris (Caftor Vaferach; Hoffmann).*

The *Euphrates,* because it is associated with *Eretz Yisrael,* is called 'great' although it was the last-mentioned of the rivers that issue forth from Eden [see on 2:14.]. Thus, goes the popular proverb [*Shevuos* 47b]: 'A king's servant is [also] a king; attach yourself to a captain and people will bow down to you' [i.e. proximity to the great makes one great; hence the Euphrates is called *'great'* only because it borders on Eretz Yisrael] *(Rashi).*

This frontier was, in fact, reached only during the days of David and Solomon [see *I Kings* 5:14; 8:65] but it was always considered the ideal border as in *Isaiah* 27:12; *Zech.* 9:10; *Psalms* 72:8.

19-21. [The ten nations of Canaan]:

The following are the inhabitants of Canaan who will one day yield their territory to the descendants of Abraham.

Rashi notes that although ten nations are mentioned here, God gave Israel the territory only of seven [*Deut.* 7:1]. The other three: Edom, Moab, and Ammon (identified respectively with the Kenites, Kenizzites, and Kadmonites in our verse), will become Israel's possession only in the future [see *Isaiah* 11:14].

[To the verse (*Deut.* 12:20): *When HASHEM your God shall enlarge your border as He has promised you,* the *Sifri* comments that this refers to the promise in our verse of the territory of the Kenites, Kenizzites, and Kadmonites...]

19. אֶת־הַקֵּינִי וְאֶת־הַקְּנִיזִּי וְאֵת הַקַּדְמֹנִי — *The Kennites, the Kenizzites, and the Kadmonites* — identified with Edom, Moab, and Ammon [see above] *(Rashi).*

This is based on the Sages in the *Midrash.* Other opinions in the *Midrash* identify these with: Arabia, the Shalamite, and the Nabatean; the Damascus region, Asia Minor, and Apamea; or Asia Minor, Thrace, and Carthage.

20. וְאֶת הַחִתִּי וְאֶת הַפְּרִיזִּי וְאֶת הָרְפָאִים — *The Hittites, the Perizzites, and the Rephaim.*

On *Heth,* son of Canaan, cf.

XIV river of Egypt to the great river, the Euphrates River:
21-22 [19] the Kennites, the Kenizzites, and the Kadmonites;
[20] the Hittites, the Perizzites and the Rephaim; [21] the
Emorites, the Canaanites, the Girgashites and the
XVI Jebusites.
1 [1] Now Sarai, Abram's wife, had borne him no

10:15. The *Perizzites* are mentioned in 13:7.

The *Rephaim* are mentioned in 14:5. *Rashi* identifies it with the land of Og [King of Bashan], which the verse clearly identifies with Rephaim [cf. *Deut.* 3:13].

According to the *Midrash*, the *Rephaim* are mentioned here instead of the Hivvites. The names are used interchangeably.

21. וְאֶת־הָאֱמֹרִי וְאֶת־הַכְּנַעֲנִי וְאֶת הַגִּרְגָּשִׁי וְאֶת הַיְבוּסִי — *The Emorites, the Canaanite, the Girgashites, and the Jebusites.*

For *Emorites, Girgashites* and *Jebusites,* see 10:16. For *Canaanite* see 10:7.

[The *Midrash* sums up with a note on the association of this verse with the next, which might also explain why the above verses of the Covenant Between the Parts, were placed here even though, according to the Sages, they are not in correct chronological sequence]:

The Holy One, Blessed be He, originally contemplated giving Israel possession of ten peoples, but He gave them only seven... Edom, Moab, and Ammon being the three nations that were not given them in this world... But in the days of the Messiah they shall once again belong to Israel [i.e. as though they had already belonged to Israel in accord with God's promise] in fulfillment of God's promise. Now, He has given them but seven...

Rav Yitzchak said: The swine grazes with ten of its young, whereas the sheep does not graze even with one. [This is proverbial: The unclean swine is always surrounded by a large litter of its offspring, whereas the clean sheep is alone.] Thus, all the above ten nations were promised to Israel, yet [next verse]: וְשָׂרַי אֵשֶׁת אַבְרָם לֹא יָלְדָה לוֹ, *Sarai, Abram's wife had borne him no children. . .*

XVI

☙ The Birth of Ishmael

1. וְשָׂרַי אֵשֶׁת אַבְרָם לֹא יָלְדָה לוֹ — *Now,* [lit. *'and'*] *Sarai, Abram's wife, had borne him no children.*

As it is written [11:30]: *And Sarai remained barren, she had no child (Radak).*

Rav Yehudah said: the Torah emphasizes 'she had borne *him* no child': she bore no children *to Abraham,* but would have borne had she been married to another. Rav Nechemiah said: Neither to him nor to anyone else ... How then is *to him* to be interpreted? — Read לֹא יָלְדָה לוֹ וָלָה *had*

לֹא יָלְדָה לוֹ וְלָהּ שִׁפְחָה מִצְרִית וּשְׁמָהּ
ב הָגָר: וַתֹּאמֶר שָׂרַי אֶל־אַבְרָם הִנֵּה־נָא
עֲצָרַנִי יהוה מִלֶּדֶת בֹּא־נָא אֶל־שִׁפְחָתִי
אוּלַי אִבָּנֶה מִמֶּנָּה וַיִּשְׁמַע אַבְרָם לְקוֹל

not borne to him and to her [i.e. this interpretation reads the verse as if there were no punctuation separating וְלָהּ, *and to her,* from the first clause]. The implication would thus be that her barrenness was not related exclusively to Abraham *(Midrash).*

In Abraham's plaintive cry [15:2]: מַה תִּתֶּן לִי, *'What can You give me seeing that I am childless?'* we see how deeply Abraham felt his childlessness ... Abraham's desire for children transcended that of the common childless person. His mission was to bring God's teaching to man for all time — how could he do this if he had no heir? Sarai's hurt, too, ran deep, Her role as Abram's true partner in every phase of their life's mission is stressed by our verse's emphasis on her as אֵשֶׁת אַבְרָם, *Abram's wife.* But, as the verse implies, though she was his wife she had not yet carried out the highest obligation of her mission — she *had borne him no children (Hirsch).*

According to *Malbim,* whenever the subject *precedes* the predicate, as in our verse [where *Sarai* precedes *had borne*], Scripture draws attention to a contrast with the foregoing. The verse means to emphasize that despite God's promise to Abraham of the above, *nevertheless,* Sarai had still not borne him a child. [See *Midrash,* end of previous verse. For this interpretation of the subject predicate sequence, see *comm.* to 14:18, s.v. וּמַלְכִּי צֶדֶק . . . הוֹצִיא. Accordingly the translation here should perhaps be *'But* Sarai, Abram's wife, etc.'] [1]

וְלָהּ שִׁפְחָה מִצְרִית וּשְׁמָהּ הָגָר — *She had* [lit. *'and to her there was'*] *an Egyptian maidservant, whose name was Hagar.*

She was a daughter of Pharaoh. When he saw the miracles that were wrought on behalf of Sarah [when she was in Egypt with Abraham; 12:17], he gave Hagar to Sarah, saying: 'Better that she be a servant in their house, than a lady in mine' *(Midrash; Rashi).*

[See *comm.* to 12:16 and *footnote* there.]

2. הִנֵּה־נָא עֲצָרַנִי ה׳ מִלֶּדֶת — *Look, now, HASHEM has restrained me from bearing.*

God has kept me from achieving that for which he gives women their unique capacity — giving birth *(Hirsch).*

Sarah thus realized from Whom her misfortune derived *(Midrash).* And she also realized that it was

1. *Malbim* continues that it was God's plan that Ishmael must be born before Isaac and that he be born to Hagar rather than to Sarai. Like silver from which all impurities are removed before it is put to its ultimate use, all but the holiest, most spiritual forces had to be removed from Abraham before he could beget Isaac. And Sarai, although she *could* have given birth with another husband (see *Midrash* above), was restrained from conceiving with Abraham until he had reached a state of complete spirituality. Therefore, Abraham married the Egyptian Hagar. Into Ishmael went any spiritual impurities that were in Abraham's makeup. Thus purified, and at an advanced age when earthly lust was gone and birth could be only a heavenly gift, Abraham and Sarah produced Isaac.

XVI
2

children. She had an Egyptian maidservant whose
name was Hagar. 2 *And Sarai said to Abram, 'See,*
now, HASHEM *has restrained me from bearing.*
Consort, now, with my maidservant, perhaps I will
be built up through her.' And Abram heeded the

from *her* — and not from Abraham — that a child had been withheld *(Midrash HaGadol).* For she was obviously aware of the promises of descendants that had been given her husband and was apprehensive that she was the obstacle to their fulfillment *(Abarbanel).*

[She said to Abraham]: 'Although He promised *you* offspring, He did not say it would issue from me' *(Sforno).*

The meaning of נָא, *now,* is: Still after all these years in Canaan *(Ibn Caspi).*

According to *Chida* [in *Chomas Anach*] the significance of נָא, *now,* is that *now* HASHEM has restrained me from bearing. But the condition will not last forever: eventually I *will* bear.

בֹּא־נָא אֶל שִׁפְחָתִי — *Consort* [lit. *'come'* [Scripture commonly uses this delicate expression for marital intimacy *(Ibn Janach)*] *now with* [lit. *'to'*] *my maidservant.*[1]

Sarai was apprehensive that in light of her barrenness, Abraham might take another wife. She therefore suggested that he consort with her personal maidservant Hagar *(Abarbanel)* ...

אוּלַי אִבָּנֶה מִמֶּנָּה — *Perhaps I will be built up through her.*

I.e. in reward for bringing a rival into my own house [God will have compassion upon me, *(Bereishis Zuta; Mizrachi)* and] I myself will have children. A childless person is considered as dead and demolished. As *dead,* for Rachel said to Jacob: [30:1]: *Give me children, or else I am dead.* As though *demolished,* for Sarah said, *perhaps I will be built up through her,* and one *builds up* only that which is already demolished *(Midrash; Rashi).*

Most commentators, however, interpret אִבָּנֶה, lit. *be built up,* as a play on the word בֵּן, *son,* and render: *perhaps I will obtain a son through her (Bereishis Zuta; Rambam* to *Mishnayos Nazir* 2; *Ibn Ezra).* The word *through her* thus has a more literal connotation:

Rachel expressed a similar desire (see 30:3) ... For in ancient times, the servant bore and the mistress reared the child which was then accounted to the latter *(Sechel Tov).*

Radak explains that a child is called בֵּן, *building block,* of the family edifice. By bringing children into the world, parents continue the task of building the eternal 'house' of the family and na-

1. King Solomon declared [*Prov.* 30:21]: *For three things the earth shudders, there are four it cannot tolerate: a slave who has become a king; a fool when he is filled with food; an unloved woman when she gets a husband; and a handmaid that is heir to her mistress.* And yet, here the mistress gives her domain to her handmaid!

This emphasizes the righteousness of Sarah who did not consider her own feelings at all but acted solely for the sake of Heaven *(Midrash HaGadol).*

ג שָׂרָי: וַתִּקַּח שָׂרַי | אֵשֶׁת אַבְרָם אֶת־הָגָר
הַמִּצְרִית שִׁפְחָתָהּ מִקֵּץ עֶשֶׂר שָׁנִים
לְשֶׁבֶת אַבְרָם בְּאֶרֶץ כְּנָעַן וַתִּתֵּן אֹתָהּ
ד לְאַבְרָם אִישָׁהּ לוֹ לְאִשָּׁה: וַיָּבֹא אֶל־הָגָר

tion. Childless parents, however, are unable to contribute to the building. Unable to conceive, Sarah still wished to have a share in building the House of Abraham. This she hoped to do by raising the son of her servant *(Hirsch).*

Sarah poured forth her soul in devising this desperate plan by which she would give her maidservant to her husband in marriage. She had hoped that God, Whose compassion is on all His handiworks, would feel compassion for her, and give her a son of her own. Similarly, He would later be merciful to Leah as it is written [29:31]: *And when HASHEM saw that Leah was hated, He opened her womb (Ibn Caspi).*

וַיִּשְׁמַע אַבְרָם לְקוֹל שָׂרָי — *And Abram heeded the voice of Sarai* — i.e., the voice of the Holy [prophetic] Spirit within her *(Midrash; Rashi).*

The Torah does not say simply וַיַּעַשׂ כֵּן, *and he did so.* Rather it emphasizes that *he heeded the voice of Sarah.* This indicates that despite his own deep longing for children, Abraham acted only with Sarah's permission. Even now his intention was not that *he* be 'built up' from Hagar, or that *his* offspring be from her. He acted only to carry out Sarah's wishes that *she* be 'built up' through Hagar, that she find satisfaction in her handmaid's children, or that she should merit her own children because of her unselfish act as explained above *(Ramban).*

Sforno further emphasizes that Abraham's compliance is so described because Abraham complied only out of a conviction that Sarah's suggestion was right; not because he wanted to consort with other women.

'It is clear to me that whenever the Torah uses the phrase שְׁמִיעַת קוֹל *heeding a voice,* attached to the preposition ל, *to,* the inference is that the advice was agreeable to the listener' [apparently, *without* the ל, as in וַיִּשְׁמַע קוֹל the phrase would imply a begrudging acquiescense to the other's wish] *(Malbim).*

3. וַתִּקַּח שָׂרַי אֵשֶׁת אַבְרָם אֶת הָגָר הַמִּצְרִית שִׁפְחָתָהּ – So [lit.*'and'*] *Sarai, Abram's wife, took Hagar the Egyptian, her maidservant.*

The *Midrash* perceives *took* to indicate not a *physical* taking, but that she pursuaded her with words: 'Fortunate are you to be united to so holy a man!' she urged *(Rashi; Gur Aryeh).* [Cf. *took* in 12:5.]

According to *Ramban, 'took'* here implies that Abraham did not rush into the matter but waited until Sarai herself took Hagar and *brought her* to him.

Sarah did not free Hagar by this marriage; she still remained שִׁפְחָתָהּ, her maidservant — her personal property *(Malbim; Or HaChaim).*

מִקֵּץ עֶשֶׂר שָׁנִים לְשֶׁבֶת אַבְרָם בְּאֶרֶץ כְּנָעַן — *After Abram lived in the land of Canaan ten years* [lit. *'at the end of ten years to the dwelling of Abram in the land of Canaan.'*]

XVI *voice of Sarai.*
3-4 [3] *So Sarai, Abram's wife, took Hagar the Egyptian*
her maidservant — after Abram lived in the Land of
Canaan ten years — and gave her to Abram her hus-
band, to him as a wife. [4] *He consorted with Hagar*

[As frequently pointed out earlier, the Torah is not a history book and tells us only what is necessary to convey the sense of the narrative. Hence every seemingly superfluous word must be measured to elicit the message embodied in its inclusion.] This seemingly gratuitous chronological detail is given to suggest the *halachah* that if a man spent ten childless years with his wife, he must remarry, for perhaps he is not destined to be built up [i.e., have children] by her *(Yevamos* 64a cited by *Rashi; Ibn Ezra).*

Rashi adds that *in the land of Canaan* is emphasized because their married years prior to coming to Canaan are not considered because God's promise of offspring, expressed in the phrase [12:2]: *and I will make of you a great nation,* was intended to be fulfilled only *after* he entered Eretz Yisrael.

Ramban disagrees, because *Rashi*'s reasoning would imply that only in the case of Abraham to whom a specific promise was made were the years outside the Land not reckoned. In fact, however, the *Talmud Yevamos* 64a clearly applies this principle universally and exempts the years that *every* husband and wife live outside of Eretz Yisrael from this total. Some, however, have misinterpreted this law to apply *only* to a couple living in *Eretz Yisrael.* This, however, is not the case, for the law *does* apply to those living outside of Eretz Yisrael; clearly a man who lives outside of Eretz Yisrael for ten years without children must divorce his wife and remarry, for if they have not merited children by then, he will never be 'built' through her [see Novellae of *Ramban* to *Yevamos* loc. cit.]

The intent of the exemption is, rather, that if a couple lived outside of the Land and then moved to Eretz Yisrael, then the years they lived outside the Land are disregarded and a new ten-year period is begun, for perhaps the merit of the Land will enable them to build a family *(Ramban).*

[See *Even HaEzer* 154:10 and commentators for the application and many exceptions to the halacha.]

Thus, from the time they entered the Land, they waited an additonal ten years, for they had hoped that there God would bless him with a son as He promised. When Sarah saw that she was already old, she despaired of being able to conceive, and she gave Abraham her maidservant as described above *(Radak).*

וַתִּתֵּן אֹתָהּ לְאַבְרָם אִישָׁהּ לוֹ לְאִשָּׁה— *And [she] gave her to Abram her husband to him as a wife.*

לוֹ, *to him* — and to no other [i.e., she remained Sarah's *personal* property and Abraham had no right either to free her or give her to another — he was permitted only to benefit from her productivity *(Malbim)*]; לְאִשָּׁה, *as a wife* — and not as a concubine *(Midrash).*

The earlier verse refers to Sarah as אֵשֶׁת אַבְרָם, *Abram's wife* [although we are already well aware of this fact]; similarly our verse refers to Abram as אִישָׁהּ, *her hus-*

וַתַּהַר וַתֵּרֶא כִּי הָרָתָה וַתֵּקַל גְּבִרְתָּהּ
ה בְּעֵינֶיהָ: וַתֹּאמֶר שָׂרַי אֶל־אַבְרָם חֲמָסִי

band. This implies that Sarah did not despair even now of having children with him, and they still remained as husband and wife. Nevertheless, she gave Hagar to him לְאִשָּׁה, i.e., with the full status of a wife, and not merely as a concubine. All this reflects Sarah's ethical conduct and the righteousness she showed her husband *(Ramban).*

[However see *Ramban* to *v.* 11 where he explains that Hagar lacked the courage to give the name Ishmael to her future son 'because she was a concubine'. It would seem that Hagar, by her later conduct, forfeited the privilege of being treated as if she were a wife of equal status with Sarah.]

4. וַיָּבֹא אֶל הָגָר וַתַּהַר — [*And*] *he consorted with* [lit. *'to'*] *Hagar and she conceived.*

From the first intimacy *(Midrash; Rashi).*

Otherwise why did the Torah mention *and he consorted with Hagar.* It should have said simply, *And she gave her to Abram her husband as his wife, and she conceived* as it says concerning Zilpah [30:9-10]: *And Leah ... took Zilpah her maid and gave her to Jacob as a wife, and Zilpah, Leah's maid bore (Mizrachi).*

The *Midrash* notes that this conception was unusual, because there is a Rabbinic dictum that 'a woman never conceives from the first intimacy,' the only other exceptions being Lot's daughters who (19:36): *came to be with child by their father* [*Tamar* in 38:18, and *Leah*] the circumstances there being unique (see *Overview* to *Ruth,* ArtScroll ed.).[1]

Heidenheim observes that the Rabbis' comment that Hagar conceived from the first intimacy is based neither on tradition nor prophecy, but from the simple meaning of the text. They derived this interpretation from the Masoretic punctuation [טְעָמִים, (*'trop'*; cantillation)] according to which most verses should be interpreted, and without which the commentator would be groping in the darkness.' Our Sages searched and found that in other appearances of the phrase וַיָּבֹא אֵלֶיהָ וַתַּהַר *and he consorted with her and she conceived,* the Torah divided the continuity of the phrase either with a pause in punctuation or by ending one verse with the phrase *and he consorted with her,* and beginning a new verse with the words *and she conceived.* Such is the case, for example, when the Torah relates Bilhah's pregnancy [see 30:4-5]. In our verse, however, there is no break in the continuity,

1. Rav Chaninah ben Pazzi remarked: Thorns are neither tended nor sown, yet they spring up on their own; whereas so much pain and toil are required before wheat can be made to grow! [Thus, Hagar conceived immediately, but Sarah underwent much anguish before she conceived.]

Why were the matriarchs barren for so long?

(a) — Because the Holy One, Blessed be He, yearned for their prayers, as it says [*Song of Songs* 2:14] הַשְׁמִיעִנִי אֶת קוֹלֵךְ, *let Me hear your voice* [in supplication; see *ArtScroll* ed. p. 111:12];

(b) — So that they might depend upon their husbands;

(c) — So that they might spend the greater part of their lives free from subjugation to their neighbors i.e., [The 400 years of alien status (15:13) which began with the birth of Isaac. Had the Matriarchs given birth earlier, they would have anguished at the sight of their children as *strangers* for a longer period of their lives *(Maharzu;* see *Radal).*]

(d) — So that they might preserve their youthful grace longer ... For the entire ninety years that Sarah did not bear children, she was like a bride in her canopy *(Midrash).*

XVI
5

and she conceived; and when she saw that she had conceived, her mistress was lowered in her esteem.
[5] *So Sarai said to Abram, 'The outrage against me is*

thus indicating that the consorting and conceiving followed immediately one upon the other. [Regarding Tamar, who also conceived after one intimacy with Judah (38:18), the verse is structured like ours.] *Rashi* in his wisdom, cited the entire phrase וַיָּבֹא אֶל הָגָר וַתַּהַר *he consorted with Hagar and she conceived* in introducing his commentary [rather than beginning only with וַתַּהַר, *and she conceived*] to intimate that he bases his exposition on the flow of the entire phrase as a unit.

וַתֵּקַל גְּבִרְתָּהּ בְּעֵינֶיהָ — *Her mistress was lowered in her esteem* [lit. *'her mistress became light in her eyes.'*]

She would boast to the ladies who would come to visit; Sarai is not the same inwardly as she appears to be outwardly. She cannot be as righteous as she seems, for so many years passed without her having children, whereas I conceived after one union!*(Rashi).*

She would also boast that all the promises made to Abraham would be realized only through *her* and *her* child, for it was only with *her* that Abraham would ever have children *(Midrash HaGodol).*

Hagar acted contemptuously toward Sarah [who is clearly defined as still being גְּבִרְתָּהּ, *her mistress*] because now it became manifestly obvious that it was Sarah and not Abraham who was barren. Now that Abraham's seed for posterity was through her, she felt that her status was no longer subservient to Sarah *(Radak).*

Thus, the commentators point out the contrast between the stinging mockery of the rival drunk with success and the righteous Sarah who in devotion to her husband made the enormous sacrifice of introducing this rival — as a wife of full status — into her home.

5. וַתֹּאמֶר שָׂרַי אֶל אַבְרָם — *So* [lit. *'and'*] *Sarai said to Abram.*

She could no longer contain herself in the face of Hagar's haughtiness, but she reasoned to herself: 'Shall I lower myself to this woman's level and argue with her? No; I will argue the matter with her master!' *(Midrash).*

חֲמָסִי עָלֶיךָ — *The outrage against me is due to you!* [lit. *'my violence; (my robbery) is upon you.'*]

[The translation, *the outrage against me,* in the sense of the wrong perpetrated upon me, rather than the equally possible translation *my outrage* — i.e., the wrong I commit — follows *Rashi*]:

Sarah said: I hold you responsible for my hurt, because when you prayed for a child and said [15:2] *'What can You give me seeing that I go childless?'* [and *ibid. v.* 3: 'You have not given *me* any offspring'], you prayed only for yourself; therefore God gives a child to you, but not to me. Had you prayed for *both* of us, then I, too, would have been 'remembered' by God [and the child being born to you would have been *mine* — not that of this ungrateful maidservant.][1] Moreover

1. The *Midrash* compares Sarah's former complaint to a parable of two prisoners. One day, as the king was passing by the prison, one of them cried: 'Have mercy on me!' The king had compassion and ordered his release.

When the other prisoner saw that his cellmate was to be released, he complained and said: 'I

עָלֶיךָ אָנֹכִי נָתַתִּי שִׁפְחָתִי בְּחֵיקֶךָ וַתֵּרֶא
כִּי הָרָתָה וָאֵקַל בְּעֵינֶיהָ יִשְׁפֹּט יהוה בֵּינִי
ו וּבֵינֶיךָ׃ וַיֹּאמֶר אַבְרָם אֶל־שָׂרַי הִנֵּה
שִׁפְחָתֵךְ בְּיָדֵךְ עֲשִׂי־לָהּ הַטּוֹב בְּעֵינָיִךְ

my additional complaint is that you חוֹמֵס, *rob,* me of your words of defense, in that you hear me insulted yet you remain silent *(Midrash; Rashi; Sforno).*

Why, indeed, did Abraham not pray for Sarah? *Harav David Cohen* notes that Abraham and Sarah were both infertile *(Yevamos* 64a), and Abraham considered it improper to pray for a double miracle. He was confident that if he prayed for himself, God would respond by helping them both. For this reason he was reluctant to take Hagar as a wife, agreeing to do so only upon the insistence of Sarah (see *Ramban* cited in *comm.* to *v.* 2) — He feared that Sarah might not be remembered with him if he had another mate.

[Note that although Abraham had a son with Hagar, that child was not the true response to his prayer: first, because only Isaac was to be considered his 'son' (21:12); and, second, because he considered Hagar no more than a concubine and the property of Sarah (16:6), and as such her son would not be regarded as an heir.]

אָנֹכִי נָתַתִּי שִׁפְחָתִי בְּחֵיקֶךָ — *It was I who gave my maidservant into your lap ...*

She recalls the series of events that led up to this outburst, and reminds him of the selfless manner in which she gave him her servant — not for her benefit, but so that her husband may realize a child through her, only to be flouted by this woman's mockery while Abraham held his peace. In deference to Abraham — because Hagar was his wife — Sarah did not wish to persecute her *(Radak).*

יִשְׁפֹּט ה׳ בֵּינִי וּבֵינֶיךָ — *Let HASHEM judge between me and between you!*

I am helpless against her because she is your wife, just as I am. I therefore implore you to intercede on my behalf. If you do not comply, let HASHEM judge us! I have acted righteously toward you, but you withhold the just response due me *(Abarbanel).* [1]

Rashi notes that wherever else in Scriptures the word בֵּינֶךָ, [second person masc.], *between you,* appears, it is spelled 'defectively' [i.e.,

have a grievance against you. Had you cried out, "Have mercy on *us*," he would have ordered my release too, just as he ordered yours. But since you petitioned only for yourself, he freed you but not me.'

Me'am Loez cites the following *Talmudic* incident in this context:

Rav Huna once appeared before his teacher, Rav, wearing a string as a belt. When asked why he was wearing a cheap string, Rav Huna replied that he had pledged his sash in exchange for wine for Kiddush.

Rav blessed him and said: May it be the will of heaven that you be smothered in silk robes. The blessing materialized, and he was soon wearing the finest garments.

When Rav heard this, he was chagrined. 'Why, when I blessed you,' he asked Rav Huna, 'did you not respond with "וְכֵן לְמַר, The same to you, Sir"?' [It was a propitious time and your blessing to me would have been fulfilled at the same time.] *(Megillah* 27b)

XVI *due to you! It was I who gave my maidservant into*
6 *your lap, and now that she sees that she has conceived, I became lowered in her esteem. Let HASHEM judge between me and you!'*

[6] *Abram said to Sarai, 'Your maidservant is in your hand; do to her as you see fit.' And Sarai dealt*

without the second *yod* = בֵּינֶךָ.] Here, however it is spelled 'full' so that it can be read בֵּינַיִךְ [second person feminine] indicating that Sarah addressed Hagar also and cast an עַיִן הָרַע, *evil eye,* upon her unborn child causing her to miscarry. [Her son Ishmael was born of a second pregnancy. See *comm.* to *v.* 11] *(Rashi).*

[Attention is drawn to this interpretation of וּבֵינֶיךָ by the dot appearing over the second *yod* in that word in all Torah Scrolls.]

6. שִׁפְחָתֵךְ בְּיָדֵךְ — *Your maidservant is in your hand.*

Although she is my wife she is still your maidservant as before *(Radak).*

...You have never set her free! *(Sforno)*

עֲשִׂי־לָהּ הַטּוֹב בְּעֵינָיִךְ — *Do to her as you see fit* [lit. *'do to her the good in your eyes'.*]

...As her mistress you exercise full control over her. If she mistreated you, punish her as you please *(Radak).*

To me she is a wife; I can do nothing. But you are her mistress: do as you please *(Haamek Davar).*

The *Midrash* explains that Abraham was frustrated and ambivalent. On the one hand, Sarah was suffering insult from her maidservant; on the other hand, this maidservant was now his wife, carrying his child. 'Having made her a wife shall we reduce her to a handmaid? I can therefore do her neither good nor evil.'

[Sarah, righteous though she was, could not bear the insolence of

1. The *Talmud* notes that he who is מוֹסֵר דִּין — i.e. invokes heavenly judgment, in a case where justice could be obtained in an earthly court of Law — against his fellow, is himself punished first ... For, as the Talmud continues, Sarah invoked heavenly judgment upon Abraham and as a result she predeceased him [see 23:2] ... For, it was taught: punishment is meted out first to the one who cries, and is more severe than for the one against whom justice is invoked *(Bava Kamma* 93a).

This is explained in *Rosh Hashanah* 16b: One of the things that call a man's iniquity to mind is calling for Divine Judgment on one's fellow man ... For he who invokes Divine Judgment on his neighbor is himself punished first [for, as *Rashi* explains: the Heavenly Court, on being invoked, declares: Let us consider whether this appellant is worthy that his neighbor be punished on his account.]

Thus, our *Midrash* concludes that whoever plunges eagerly into litigation will not escape from it unscathed. Sarah should have reached Abraham's years, but because she invoked God's judgment, her life was reduced by forty-eight years.

[For although Sarah's attitude was ultimately vindicated by God when He told Abaraham (21:12) *'all* that Sarah says to you, hearken to her voice,' which the sages *(Tosefta, Sota* 5:7) interpret to mean that God agreed with Sarah's attitude in our incident also, nevertheless since she invoked Heavenly Justice, she was punished.]

ז וַתְּעַנֶּהָ שָׂרַי וַתִּבְרַח מִפָּנֶיהָ: וַיִּמְצָאָהּ
מַלְאַךְ יהוָה עַל־עֵין הַמַּיִם בַּמִּדְבָּר עַל־
ח הָעַיִן בְּדֶרֶךְ שׁוּר: וַיֹּאמַר הָגָר שִׁפְחַת

her maidservant and responded harshly]:

וַתְּעַנֶּהָ שָׂרַי – *And Sarai dealt harshly* [lit. *'afflicted'*] *with her,* [The translation follows *Rashi.*]

According to *Hirsch,* the phrase is to be interpreted: *Then Sarai humbled her,* the cognate verb ענה meaning *to answer,* or *to be dependent.* It was basic to Sarai's plan that Hagar remain dependent on her so that the child could be raised by Sarah and treated as if it were hers. Therefore, she constantly brought this dependent condition home to Hagar's mind.

The *Midrash* comments:;

Rav Berachiah said: She slapped her face with a slipper;

Rav Berachiah said in Rav Abba's name: She bade her carry her water buckets and bath towels to the baths [servant's work.* Thus, Sarah's harshness consisted mainly of making her do work unsuited to her wifely status] *(Midrash).*

*[Cf. *Rashi* to *Lev.* 25:39 that such degrading chores are considered servants' work.]

Ramban comments that Sarah sinned in afflicting her, and so did Abraham for allowing it. God therefore heard Hagar's cry [*v.* 11], and gave her a son who would be a פֶּרֶא אָדָם, *wild – ass of a man, whose descendants persecute and afflict the seed of Abraham and Sarah.* [*See Chavel's* commentary to this citation and his reference to *Maasei* HASHEM.]

Most commentators disagree with *Ramban* and maintain that Sarah's intent was not malicious. Her intention was only to force Hagar to recognize her subordinate position and cease her insulting demeanor. Instead of accepting Sarah's admonition gracefully and constructively, Hagar fled *(Abarbanel; Sforno.* Cf. *Harchev Davar).*[1]

Cf. also *Tosefta Sotah* 5:7 (cited in footnote end of *v.* 5) where God's admonition to Abraham to heed Sarah's *every* directive (21:12) is interpreted to

1. *Harav Aryeh Levin* noted the apparent incongruity of Sarah's deeds – how could kind, benevolent Sarah stoop to petty retaliation because her servant grew arrogant? And if the situation at home was indeed so intolerable, why did the angel tell her to go back to her suffering?

He explains that the saintly Sarah never changed her behavior at all – it was Hagar who changed her attitude. It is similar to a rabbi whose disciples render him personal service. Whatever he may ask of them is not difficult or degrading to them for they feel privileged that they can serve him. Let an ordinary person request the same service of them, however, and they would be outraged.

So it was with Hagar. She had always regarded Sarah as an exalted person. Indeed, she had given up her father's palace in Egypt to become a servant in the home of Abraham and Sarah. But when she married Abraham and conceived, she grew arrogant and considered herself to be an equal of, if not greater than, Sarah. Then, Sarah's every routine request became an intolerable burden and Hagar fled the 'persecution.' The angel's advice to her was once more to accept Sarah as her mistress, her superior in spiritual qualities. Then the servitude would no longer be onerous. (Adapted from *A Tzaddik in Our Time,* Feldheim Pub., p. 440).

harshly with her, so she fled from her.

[7] An angel of HASHEM found her by the spring of water in the desert, at the spring on the road to Shur.

mean that this dismissal of Hagar, too, was consented to by God and in full consonance with His will, and that Sarah's action of oppression was thereby vindicated *(Minchas Biccurim).*

וַתִּבְרַח מִפָּנֶיהָ — *So* [lit. *and*] *she fled from her* [lit. *'from before her face'*]

A woman who had become a wife to Abraham could not act like a slave. His proximity would awaken her feelings of equality and break all bonds. So she fled *(Hirsch).*

7. Apparently Abraham, aggrieved though he surely was, did not send after her. Nevertheless, the call went out from Heaven for her to return *(Da'as Soferim).*

וַיִּמְצָאָהּ מַלְאַךְ ה׳ עַל עֵין הַמַּיִם בַּמִּדְבָּר — [*And*] *an angel of HASHEM found her by the spring of water in the desert.*

According to *Rambam,* all this happened in a prophetic vision for one should not imagine that an angel [meaning literally *messenger,* and applied to any agent of God] is seen or his word heard otherwise than in a prophetic vision ...

You can thus deduce that Hagar was not a prophetess ..., for the speech she heard was like a *Bas Kol* [lit. *a daughter* of a voice, i.e. a *faint echo* of the Divine Voice] frequently mentioned by our Sages, and is something that may be experienced even by men not fit for prophecy *(Moreh Nevuchim* 2:42).

According to most others, however, when executing their duty, angels *do* assume various tangible forms, and may actually communicate with man:

'... We should not be led to think that Hagar merely *imagined* these things. The *Bas Kol* referred to by our Sages is a physical sound which is actually heard in accordance with God's Will, and is no different from any of His other wonders. Thus, in a state inferior to prophecy, Hagar actually perceived, an angel in the form of a human being, and therefore did not become afraid. She did not experience this by virtue of her own merit, but by the merit of Abraham, so that she would return home and bear his child ...' *(Abarbanel).*

[That the angel *'found'* Hagar cannot be understood in the literal sense as if divine emmissary had to search for her. Obviously, the Torah, which speaks in human terms, informs us that God waited for the frightened, fleeing Hagar to rest at a spring before He communicated with her. When God considered the moment propitious, the angel *found,* in the sense of *revealed himself* to her at that moment, and not sooner (based on *Malbim*)] ... As *Sforno* comments: He found her ready for the Divine Vision, and therefore appeared to her.

עַל הָעַיִן בְּדֶרֶךְ שׁוּר — *At the spring on the road to Shur.*

The verse further identifies the spring of water as being specifically *the spring on the road to Shur,* to indicate that she was about to return to her birthplace Egypt, for Shur is near Egypt *(Radak).*

According to *Sforno,* עַיִן refers to a *crossroads.* Comp. 38:14.

Shur is identical with חַגְרָא,

שָׂרַי אֵי־מִזֶּה בָאת וְאָנָה תֵלֵכִי וַתֹּאמֶר
ט מִפְּנֵי שָׂרַי גְּבִרְתִּי אָנֹכִי בֹּרַחַת: וַיֹּאמֶר
לָהּ מַלְאַךְ יהוה שׁוּבִי אֶל־גְּבִרְתֵּךְ
י וְהִתְעַנִּי תַּחַת יָדֶיהָ: וַיֹּאמֶר לָהּ מַלְאַךְ

Hagra, as *Onkelos* renders; it is a town on the border of Canaan just outside of it. Her intention was to leave the Land [and it was there that the angel intercepted her] *(Sforno).*

Da'as Soferim points out that unlike her second flight she now found a spring without Divine intercession. [cf. 21:15 ff.] This time, when it was *Sarah* who expelled Hagar, Abraham's merit stood by her, but the second time it was *Abraham himself* who expelled her.

It was הָעַיִן, *the* well, because when the Torah was given, this site was already well-known by reason of the remembrance of this event. [As pointed out in *v.* 14, the descendants of Ishmael later revered it, and would hold commemorative festivities there each year] *(Hoffmann).*

The location of the well made it more conducive to fame, and therefore serve to maintain the memory of this event. The well was at the gateway to the driest, dreariest wilderness, so it became a natural resting place for caravans entering and leaving the desert *(Hirsch).*

8. וַיֹּאמַר — *And he* [i.e., the angel] *said.*

הָגָר שִׁפְחַת שָׂרַי — *Hagar, maidservant of Sarai.*

By addressing her as *maidservant,* he reminded her of her subservience to her mistress, and she acknowledged this subservience when, in her reply [next verse] she refers to Sarah as *'my mistress' (Chizkuni).*

For only to Abraham was Hagar now a 'wife'; to Sarah she remained but a 'maidservant' *(Midrash HaGadol).*

It is possible that by so addressing her he was intimating that only by virtue of the fact that she was *the maidservant of Sarai* did she merit this divine revelation. He also meant to ratify her subordination to Sarah as being in accordance with the Divine Plan *(R' Bachya).*

אֵי־מִזֶּה בָאת וְאָנָה תֵלֵכִי — *Where have you come from and where are you going?*

He knew the answer. He posed this leading question, not to elicit information, but to encourage her to speak *(Rashi).*

[Cf. similar rhetorical questions posed to Adam and Eve in 3:9, 11, and 13; to Cain in 4:9; and to Hagar again in 21:17.]

Rashi explains that the idiomatic expression אֵי מִזֶּה [lit. *'whence from this'*] is to be explained as: אֵי, *which,* is the place regarding which you would say מִזֶּה, *from this,* I came.

... Thus the proper interpretation of the phrase would include the implied word מָקוֹם, *place,* and is understood as: מֵאֵי זֶה (מָקוֹם) בָּאת *from which (place) have you come (R' Meyuchas).*

Sforno explains the angel's remark as cautionary: 'Consider well *from where you have come* — a holy place and house of the righteous; *and where you are going*

[8] *And he said, 'Hagar, maidservant of Sarai, where have you come from and where are you going?' And she said, 'I am running away from Sarai my mistress.'*
[9] *And an angel of HASHEM said to her, 'Return to your mistress, and submit yourself to her domination.'*

— to an unclean land and place of wicked people.'

He thus tried to inspire her to turn back for the spiritual nourishment of her soul *(Malbim).*

וַתֹּאמֶר — *And she said:*

[Hagar was accustomed to seeing angels in Abraham's house. She was unafraid, and answered directly (see *Rashi* to *v.* 13).]

מִפְּנֵי שָׂרַי גְּבִרְתִּי אָנֹכִי בֹּרַחַת — *I am running away from [before the face of] Sarai my mistress.*

I have no particular destination; I am merely fleeing from my mistress *(Sforno).*

... I am well aware of the futility of my actions; that I am leaving the good for the bad. But what can I do? The oppression is unbearable and it is the nature of one that flees to look only behind him and not to his destination *(Akeidas Yitzchak).*

The angel's argument that her flight was spiritually detrimental did not avail. The affliction was sufficient reason for her to flee; she was oblivious to her spirituality *(Malbim).*

On the same verse, the Talmud *(Bava Kamma* 92b) bases the proverb: 'If your neighbor calls you a donkey, put a saddle on your back.' Thus after the angel called her *Sarah's handmaid,* she responded by referring to Sarah as *'my mistress.'*[1]

9-11. Three separate speeches: *v.* 9: the condition; *v.* 10: the promise; and *v.* 11: the task and its result *(Hirsch):*

9. וַיֹּאמֶר לָהּ מַלְאַךְ ה׳ — *And an angel of HASHEM said to her.*

Angel is repeated in reference to each statement [*v.* 7; here, 10 and 11], because for each statement a different angel was sent to her. [This is in line with the dictum that an angel does not carry out two separate functions simultaneously (see *Rashi* to 18:2)] *(Rashi;* cf. *Meilah* 17b).

שׁוּבִי אֶל־גְּבִרְתֵּךְ — *Return to your mistress.*

He thereby hinted that she will always be subservient to Sarah, as Sarah's descendants will always dominate hers *(Ramban).*

[This is in apparent contradiction to *Ramban's* own comment in *v.* 6, where he comments conversely that Hagar's descendants would afflict Abraham's descendants וצ״ע. Perhaps this passage refers to what will happen in the future, or the implication is that although the Ishmaelites will *afflict* Abraham's descendants, the latter will always be *spiritually* dominant.]

וְהִתְעַנִּי תַּחַת יָדֶיהָ — *And submit yourself to her domination* [lit. *and be afflicted under her hands*].

1. The *Midrash* records the proverb: 'If one man tells you that you have donkey's ears, do not believe him; if two tell you, order a halter' [i.e., — do not argue the point]. Thus, after both Abraham [*v.* 6], and the angel [here] refer to Hagar as *Sarai's handmaid,* Hagar herself acquiesced by referring to Sarah as *'my mistress'.*

יהוה הַרְבָּה אַרְבֶּה אֶת־זַרְעֵךְ וְלֹא יִסָּפֵר
יא מֵרֹב: וַיֹּאמֶר לָהּ מַלְאַךְ יהוה הִנָּךְ הָרָה
וְיֹלַדְתְּ בֵּן וְקָרָאת שְׁמוֹ יִשְׁמָעֵאל כִּי־
יב שָׁמַע יהוה אֶל־עָנְיֵךְ: וְהוּא יִהְיֶה פֶּרֶא

It is worthwhile for you to endure her treatment, for it is to your advantage to dwell in proximity to Abraham: In his merit, your children will be abundant *(Radak)*.

As *Pesikta* remarks: Better affliction by Sarah, than the finest dainties from Pharaoh, King of Egypt.

10. Apparently, Hagar made no move to return, so the angel pressed further. Or, as the *Midrash* notes, there were several angels *(Radak)*. According to *Maasei Hashem*, however, Hagar *did* return, after which the following further promise was addressed to her:

הַרְבָּה אַרְבֶּה אֶת זַרְעֵךְ — *I will greatly increase* [lit. *increase, I will increase*] *your offspring.*

It was certainly not in the angel's province to increase her seed; he was merely using the first person, speaking in God's name as His emissary *(Radak;* cf. *Rashi* to 18:10).

[On this infinitive double use of the verb for emphasis cf. יָדֹעַ תֵּדַע in 15:13.]

וְלֹא יִסָּפֵר מֵרֹב — *And they will not be counted for abundance.*

[Unlike other promises, however, Hagar's progeny are compared neither to the stars nor to the dust, for those similes, as pointed out, were qualitative comparisons not quantitative (see *comm.* to 15:5).]

11. הִנָּךְ הָרָה — *Behold you will conceive,* i.e. when you return you will be with child. [The phrase is not to be interpreted in the present tense: *Behold you are pregnant,* for obviously Hagar was aware of her state as it plainly says in *v.* 4: *she saw she was pregnant.* Rather, *Rashi* is following his comment in *v.* 5, that as a result of Sarah's evil eye, Hagar miscarried. Accordingly, the angel now tells her that when she returns home she will conceive *again* and bear a son *(Mizrachi; Gur Aryeh).*] The expression הִנָּךְ הָרָה occurs also in the promise to Manoah's wife [*Judges* 13:5;7] where it also definitely refers to the future, i.e., *when you return home* you *will* conceive *(Rashi).*

וְיֹלַדְתְּ בֵּן — *And* [you] *shall have borne a son.*

The word וְיֹלַדְתְּ is similar to the present participle וְיֹלֶדֶת [and the perfect tense וְיָלַדְתְּ *(Devek Tov)* and should be rendered *'and you shall have borne a son'.*] Cf. *Jeremiah* 22:23 where יֹשַׁבְתְּ = יֹשֶׁבֶת, and מְקֻנַּנְתְּ = מְקֻנֶּנֶת *(Rashi; Ibn Janach).*

וְקָרָאת שְׁמוֹ יִשְׁמָעֵאל — [*And*] *you shall name him* [lit. *'call his name'*] *Ishmael* ['God will hear'].

This was a command *(Rashi).*

According to *Ramban*, however, this was not a command; God was merely telling her what the future would bring: A son would be born to her whose name would be Ishmael. [Thus, according to *Ramban*, the sense of the statement is not imperative, but factual: 'and

10 *And an angel of HASHEM said to her,'I will
greatly increase your offspring, and they will not be
counted for abundance.'*
11 *And an angel of HASHEM said to her, 'Behold
you will conceive, and shall have borne a son; you
shall name him Ishmael, for HASHEM has heard your
prayer.* 12 *And he shall be a wild-ass of a man: his*

you will call his name Ishmael.' See *comm.* to *v.* 17.]

כִּי שָׁמַע ה׳ אֶל עָנְיֵךְ — *For HASHEM has heard your prayer* [or *'cry'.*]

The translation of *prayer* for עָנְיֵךְ [otherwise translatable *'your affliction'*] follows *Onkelos* and *Rav Saadiah Gaon.*

Radak explains: The phrase means: *God has heard the cries* [*brought about by*] *your affliction.* This interpretation is necessitated by the fact that the verse employs the verb *heard* instead of *see* [which would have been the proper verb to use if עָנְיֵךְ meant *your affliction.*]

HaKsav V'haKaballah concurs with the above, and cites as an example, the parallel use of the verb in *Psalms* 22:25 where the expression עֱנוּת עָנִי means *the screams of the poor.*

Targum Yonasan, however, renders: 'because your *affliction* is revealed before God.'

12. וְהוּא יִהְיֶה פֶּרֶא אָדָם — *And he shall be a wild-ass of a man* [following *Ramban* (see below); or following *Targum Yonasan: Like a wild-ass among men*].

I.e. untameable *(Onkelos);* an image of unrestricted freedom among men: he would not submit to the rule of strangers, and would take what he wished by brutal force *(Ibn Ezra).*

Loving the wilderness [i.e. desert] and hunting wild animals, as is written of him (21:20): *And he dwelt in the wilderness and became an accomplished archer (Rashi).*

Pere Adam is in the construct form [as in our translation: *a wild-ass of a man*] meaning that he will be an אִישׁ פֶּרֶא, *wild-ass of a man,* accustomed to the wilderness, setting out early to plunder in search of food *(Ramban).*

This comparison of the Ishmaelites to wild-asses — wild and untameable — reflects their lives as 'free sons of the desert' who were wandering merchants. They are thus referred to as wild-asses, as it is written [*Jer.* 2:24]: *a wild-ass used to the wilderness,* and [*Job* 24:5]: *like wild-asses in the desert they go forth to their work ... (B'chor Shor).*[1]

His descendants will travel afar with their merchandise to places

1. The *Midrash* takes the name to connote savage: Rav Yochanan said: It means that while other people are bred in civilized surroundings, he would be reared in the wilderness. Resh Lakish said: It means a savage among men in its literal sense, for whereas all others plunder wealth, he plunders lives.

The *Zohar* [*Yisro* 86a] remarks that Ishmael was truly פֶּרֶא, *a wild-ass,* but he was only partly אָדָם, *man.* He possessed the beginnings of *'manhood'* because he was circumcised, but the *'manhood'* did not come to fruition in him because he rejected the Torah.

אָדָם יָדוֹ בַכֹּל וְיַד כֹּל בּוֹ וְעַל־פְּנֵי כָל־
יג אֶחָיו יִשְׁכֹּן: וַתִּקְרָא שֵׁם־יהוה הַדֹּבֵר
אֵלֶיהָ אַתָּה אֵל רֳאִי כִּי אָמְרָה הֲגַם הֲלֹם
יד רָאִיתִי אַחֲרֵי רֹאִי: עַל־כֵּן קָרָא לַבְּאֵר

where they are unknown, as we find אֹרְחַת יִשְׁמְעֵאלִים בָּאָה מִגִּלְעָד, *a caravan of Ishmaelites was coming from Gilead* (37:25). Any stranger is called *pere (Chizkuni).*

[For further interpretations, see *Sforno:* 'he will be a *wild-ass* from his mother and a *man* from his father ...'; *HaRechasim leBik'ah:* 'a wild-ass in the form of a man'; *HaKsav V'haKaballah:* He will be a *prolific* man (as in יַפְרִיא, *fertile* in *Hosea* 13:15) — and will have abundant progeny; *Ha'amek Davar:* He will be totally unruly (מַפְרִיא).]

יָדוֹ בַכֹּל וְיַד כֹּל בּוֹ וְעַל־פְּנֵי כָל־אֶחָיו יִשְׁכֹּן — *His hand against* [lit. *'in'*] *everyone, and everyone's hand against him; and over* [lit. *'upon the faces of'*] *all his brothers shall he dwell.*

I.e., he will be a brigand, and all will hate and fight him. Additionally his offspring will be numerous [so his boundaries will, of necessity, have to expand beyond their bounds into those of his brothers. See 25:18] *(Rashi).*

The phrase *his hand against everyone* indicates that at first his seed will be victorious against all people, but ultimately *everyone's hand,* etc., — they will conquer him *(Ibn Ezra).*

...The connotation, therefore, is that he will be a plunderer *(Radak).* The reference is to his descendants who will war with everyone *(Ramban).*

[According to *Onkelos,* the reference is to what may be currently termed an economic balance of power]: 'He will be dependent upon everyone and similarly everyone will be dependent upon him ...'

As *Chizkuni* interprets the verse: *His hand in everything* — i.e., in every type of business venture; *and everyone's hand in him* — i.e., associated with him commercially. *And over all his brothers he shall dwell* — his real estate holdings shall spread out among all his brothers throughout the world by virtue of his vast wealth.

[As interpreted by *Onkelos* and *Chizkuni,* the verse may be seen as a prophecy that has come to complete fulfillment in recent times. The Ishmaelites (the Arab states) are dependent upon other nations for technology, but other nations are dependent upon the Ishmaelites for their vast oil wealth. And as a result of their wealth, they have acquired vast holdings throughout the world. (See also *R' Bachya* cited in *comm.* to 21:18).]

Hirsch explains that עַל פְּנֵי often has the meaning of *standing in the way; hindering.* Cf. connotation of עַל פָּנָי in *Exod.* 20:3; *Isaiah* 65:3 *Jeremiah* 15:1. Thus Ishmael will take up his positions regardless of the feelings of his brothers. He will have no friends, but others will not dare oppose him.

13. וַתִּקְרָא ... אַתָּה אֵל רֳאִי — *And she named* [lit. *'called the name of'*] *HASHEM Who spoke to her* [via an

hand against everyone, and everyone's hand against
him; and over all his brothers shall he dwell.'
13 *And she named HASHEM Who spoke to her*
'You are the God of Vision,' for she said, 'Could I
have seen even here after having seen?' 14 *Therefore*

angel *(Ralbag)*]: *You are the God of Vision,* i.e., Who sees the humiliation and misery of the afflicted *(Rashi).*

For though it was only an angel that spoke with her, he was God's emissary, and Hagar therefore reacted as if God Himself had addressed her *(Hoffmann).*

Rashi goes on to explain that רֳאִי [which if punctuated differently might otherwise be interpreted to mean *Who sees me*] is punctuated with a *chataf-kametz* to denote that it is a noun, meaning [*God of*] *Vision.*

... [Cf. עֳנִי, *affliction (Ibn Ezra)*].

Calling the name of HASHEM signifies prayer in which she praised God Who spoke to her, by exclaiming: 'You are the God Who sees everywhere, not only in the house of Abraham' *(Sforno).*

הֲגַם הֲלֹם רָאִיתִי אַחֲרֵי רֹאִי – *Could I have seen even here after having seen?*

An exclamation of surprise: 'Could I ever have expected to see God's emissaries *even here* in the desert *after seeing* them in Abraham's house, where I saw many angels?' That Hagar was accustomed to seeing angels in Abraham's house may be deduced from the fact that Manoah [Samson's father] saw an angel only once and exclaimed [*Judges* 13:22]: *'We shall surely die!'* while Hagar saw *four* angels, one after the other, and she showed no fear *(Rashi).*

Although the angel appeared to her in human form, Hagar realized that he was an angel because he became invisible as soon as he had completed giving his message to her. Thus: 'Did I see him even here [i.e., in this very place] after having just seen him?' *(Radak).*

Ralbag, however, interprets מַלְאַךְ not as *angel,* but as *messenger* — i.e., a prophet who carries out God's mission. Hagar was surprised that there was a prophet of HASHEM other than Abraham, and if there was, surely, he would not be in the wilderness! She said: 'Have I seen even here [a prophet] who follows after He Who looks over me?'

14. עַל כֵּן קָרָא לַבְּאֵר – *Therefore the well was called* [lit. *therefore he called (to) the well*].

The identity of the one who named the well is ambiguous. [The verb קָרָא is masculine, singular: *'he called'*; therefore the subject could not be Hagar.] According to *Midrash Sechel Tov,* Abraham, in agreement with Hagar, gave it its name.

The descendants of Ishmael (the Arabs) gave the spring this name — when they later dug a well on that site — in commemoration of the miracle that occurred there for their matriarch, Hagar. *(Hoffmann;* see *Ibn Ezra* and *R'Bachya* below).

According to *Radak,* this *well* is identical with the *spring* referred to in *v.* 7.

בְּאֵר לַחַי רֹאִי הִנֵּה בֵין־קָדֵשׁ וּבֵין בָּרֶד׃
טו וַתֵּלֶד הָגָר לְאַבְרָם בֵּן וַיִּקְרָא אַבְרָם שֶׁם־
טז בְּנוֹ אֲשֶׁר־יָלְדָה הָגָר יִשְׁמָעֵאל׃ וְאַבְרָם
בֶּן־שְׁמֹנִים שָׁנָה וְשֵׁשׁ שָׁנִים בְּלֶדֶת־הָגָר
א אֶת־יִשְׁמָעֵאל לְאַבְרָם׃ וַיְהִי

בְּאֵר לַחַי רֹאִי — *Be'er Lachai Ro'i* [lit. *'the well of the Living One Who sees me'*].

As the *Targum* renders: 'The well at which the everlasting Angel appeared to me' *(Rashi).*

Lachai ['to the living one'] thus refers to the angel who exists eternally, and *Ro'i* means 'who appeared to me.' The entire phrase means: 'the well of the angel who appeared to me' *(Mizrachi).*

Or, the name means: the well of God Who is Eternal and is the First Cause for all that exists, but who nevertheless oversees every one of His creatures no matter how insignificant. Even a servant fleeing from her mistress is not ignored by God in her time of need. This serves as a lesson to all that no matter who someone is, he should bear in mind that חַי רֹאִי, the *Living God sees me (Hoffman).*

Another interpretation:

— *"The well of Him Who will yet be living in years to come."*

The word *'Chai'* has the significance here of a greeting as in *I Sam.* 25:6: כֹּה לֶחָי, *a hearty greeting!* For this was the greeting the Sons of Ishmael would use when they met annually at this site for their festivities, as if to say: next year when you are still alive [חַי] you will see me [רֹאִי] *(Ibn Ezra; R' Bachya).*

הִנֵּה בֵין־קָדֵשׁ וּבֵין בָּרֶד — [Behold] *it is between Kadesh and Bered.*

This site is further identified so that if a passerby should see it he should offer praise to the Almighty for having chosen the righteous. For it was out of His great love for Abraham that He sent His angel to Hagar though she was not acting as his emissary. *Bered* is identical with *Shur* mentioned in *v.* 7. It had two names and Scripture cites them both. *Onkelos* accordingly rendered them both identically *(Radak).*

For *Kadesh,* see 14:7. The site has tentatively been identified as Ain Muweileh, west of Ain Kadesh, and fifty miles south of Beersheba *(Hoffmann; Kesses HaSofer).*

Thus, Kadesh was to its east, and Bered to its west *(R' Meyuchas).*

15. [So, bolstered by the promise that her son would become the ancestor of a great people, Hagar returned to her mistress and after a short while, as the angel had foretold ...]

וַתֵּלֶד הָגָר לְאַבְרָם בֵּן — [*And*] *Hagar bore* [*to*] *Abram a son.*

She remained faithful. She bore *to Abram,* not to any other man *(Lekach Tov).*

וַיִּקְרָא אַבְרָם שֶׁם־בְּנוֹ ... יִשְׁמָעֵאל — *And Abram named* [lit. *'called the name of'*] *his son ... Ishmael.*

Abram was not present when the angel charged Hagar to name her child Ishmael [*v.* 11], nevertheless

the well was called 'Be'er Lachai Ro'i'. It is between Kadesh and Bered.

15 Hagar bore Abram a son and Abram named his son that Hagar bore him, Ishmael. 16 And Abram was eighty-six years old when Hagar bore Ishmael to Abram.

the [Prophetic] Holy Spirit rested upon him and he gave the child this name *(Rashi).*

Had Abraham heard from Hagar of the angel's command, he should have allowed her to name the child. Therefore *Rashi* explains that Abraham was prompted by the prophetic spirit and it therefore was as if *he* were the commanded one *(Gur Aryeh).*

Ramban, in *v.* 11, cites *Rashi*'s interpretation, but suggests that since Hagar was a concubine she hesitated giving a name to her master's son. She revealed the matter to him and Abram fulfilled God's will. The Torah had no need, however, to delve at length into the matter.

[*Ramban*'s interpretation of Hagar revealing her exchange with the angel to Abraham is valid even without his interpretation that Hagar was but a concubine. It is only natural that Abraham would have questioned Hagar as to the events that prompted her return; and she, in turn would have told him of the promises made by the angel and that the child's name would be Ishmael. According to *Ramban* there was no command per se that this name be given. See *comm.* to *v.* 11.]

[In support of *Rashi*'s interpretation, which is based on the *Midrash,* my father שליט״א emphasizes that Abraham's relationship with Hagar was purely an accommodation to Sarah. Hence it is quite probable that no subsequent exchange ever took place between him and Hagar. Therefore since Abraham is credited with naming the child, he must have known the name Ishmael through divine inspiration (Cf. *Malbim).*]

16. וְאַבְרָם בֶּן־שְׁמוֹנִים שָׁנָה וְשֵׁשׁ שָׁנִים — *And Abram was eighty-six years old ...*

[The year was 2034 from Creation.]

Abraham's age is recorded to give credit to Ishmael, for it is from here that we know that Ishmael was thirteen years old when Abraham circumcised him, yet he raised no objection *(Rashi).* Although Ishmael's age at the time of his circumcision is explicitly stated (17:24) in any case, we would not have known from the later verse that the statement of his age was intended to credit him rather than to cite the historical fact. Therefore, it is reiterated here *(Gur Aryeh).*

The fact that Abraham finally had his first child in itself is significant enough to merit mention of his age *(Da'as Sofrim).*

This chronological detail also serves to let us know that all the events in this chapter occurred within one year. For in *v.* 3 we are told that Sarah gave Hagar to Abraham *ten years after Abraham* dwelt in Canaan. Since Abraham was seventy-five when he left Charan (12:4), he was eighty-five when he married Hagar, and Ishmael was born that following year *(Ibn Sho'ib).*

אַבְרָם בֶּן־תִּשְׁעִים שָׁנָה וְתֵשַׁע שָׁנִים
וַיֵּרָא יהוה אֶל־אַבְרָם וַיֹּאמֶר אֵלָיו אֲנִי־

XVII

1. The Covenant of Circumcision

וַיְהִי אַבְרָם בֶּן־תִּשְׁעִים שָׁנָה וְתֵשַׁע שָׁנִים — [*And it happened*] *when Abram was ninety-nine years old.*

[The year is 2047 from Creation, Ishmael is thirteen years old, and Sarah, is eighty-nine.]

The momentous importance of this covenant required that it be precisely dated *(Hoffman).*

God waited thirteen years from the birth of Ishmael before instructing Abraham to circumcise himself [an act preparatory to Isaac's conception]. This was in order that Isaac be born when Abraham was a hundred years old, thus enhancing the miracle; and to display Abraham's love of God, for he circumcised himself when he was old and frail. The commandment was given prior to Isaac's birth in order that Isaac's conception take place in holiness and in order to emphasize the miracle that Abraham could have a child even though his organ had been weakened *(Radak).*

Because He wanted Isaac to be holy from his conception, God wanted Abraham's physical prowess to be diminished. This He accomplished by waiting until Abraham was advanced in age and by weakening him through circumcision. In addition, Isaac's conception and birth were miraculous. Thus he was ideally suited for holiness *(Malbim).*

וַיֵּרָא ה׳ אֶל אַבְרָם — [*And*] *HASHEM appeared to Abram.*

This 'appearance' was a lower form of prophecy *(Sforno).*

[See on 12:7]

אֲנִי־אֵל שַׁדַּי — *I am El Shaddai.*

[Cf. *Exod.* 6:3: *And I appeared unto Abraham, Isaac and Jacob as El Shaddai.* The commentators differ on the interpretation of this Name. Although familiarly translated *God Almighty,* we have merely transliterated this in consonance with *Targum* who treats it as a proper noun.

I am He in Whose Divinity [אֱלָהוּת] there is sufficiency [שֶׁיֵּשׁ דַּי] for every creature [i.e., I can provide every creature with (דֵּי מַחְסוֹרוֹ) its needs *(Rav Saadiah Gaon).*] Therefore, *walk before Me* and I shall be your God and Protector *(Rashi).*

Cf. the *Midrash:* I am God Who said to My world [during creation]: דַּי, enough! Had I not ordered *Enough!* heaven and earth would have continued expanding until this day. [See *Overview* to *Bereishis I,* p. 5.]

I, Who commanded My world, *Enough!,* now say to your suffering through childlessness, *Enough!* Not only Ishmael, but also Isaac, Zimran, Yokshan, Medan, etc. [see 25:2] will you father. But first circumcise yourself so you will beget children in purity *(Midrash HaChefetz: Torah Shelemah* 17:8);

... And now, regarding your uncircumcised state, I declare: *'Enough!' (Tanchuma Yashan).*

Rashi to 43:14 interprets: 'God, שֶׁ־דַּי, *Who is sufficient* in granting His mercies, and in Whose hand is

1 *When Abram was ninety-nine years old, HASHEM appeared to Abram and said to him, I am El*

sufficient [דַי] power to give. This is the real meaning.'

According to *Ibn Ezra,* שַׁדַּי is an adjective [for *El*], meaning *Mighty,* as in the expression [*Ezek.* 1:24]: קוֹל שַׁדַּי, *the noise of the mighty* [see *Radak* there], and [*Job* 22:25 according to *Ibn Ezra* ad. loc.]: וְהָיָה שַׁדַּי בְּצָרֶיךָ, *and strength shall be your silver. Ibn Ezra* continues that many relate it to the root שדד, implying that He *prevails and is mighty* over the legions of Heaven [see *Ramban.*] This particular Name was chosen for this communication to imbue Abraham with awe so that he should submit to the following command of circumcision.* He further notes that the Name Shaddai complements His Four Lettered Name הוי"ה, and is adjectival inasmuch as it sets boundaries to the attributes of that Name [for He creates with HASHEM, and He conquers, controls, and limits with *Shaddai (Tzafnas Paneach).*] The world exists on these two Names. The one who comprehends the mysteries of the Name will have faith [that the world, indeed, exists on the basis of the attributes described by these two Names *(Tzafnas Paneach).*] To this, *Ramban* adds that the Name *Shaddai* represents the attribute of might that guides and conducts the world ...

Ramban comments that *Shaddai* is not an adjective modifying *El,* [as *Ibn Ezra* maintains] but that it comprises a distinct Divine Name. He cites *Rashi*'s interpretation to which he appends *Rambam's* comment [in *Moreh Nevuchim* 1:63] that the Name means 'He who is self-sufficient,' i.e., entirely independent of any other being.

R'Bachya explains in 31:1, that in enabling Abraham to beget children by changing his מַזָּל, constellationary influence, (see *comm.* to 15:15), God performed a *hidden miracle* because it is a natural — though unusual — occurrence for such an old man to beget a child. Thus it was not incontrovertibly clear that natural law had been overturned by this.

Ma'or Vashemesh comments that the Name *Shaddai* implies such *hidden miracles.* Thus, God revealed Himself to Abraham as the Almighty, Who could bend the forces of nature to His service, in this case by enabling Abraham to transcend his natural fate of childlessness. He would now beget children with whom there would be an eternal covenant. This is the reason that God communicated the Name *Shaddai* to Abraham at this juncture.

This is unlike the miracles wrought by Moses i.e., the ten plagues, the splitting of the Sea, the Manna, etc., which clearly show Divine intervention. These 'open miracles' which clearly overpower nature are done with the Four Letter Name which was revealed to Moses [in *Exod.* 6:3.]

**R' Chananel* notes that this Name, implying Might was used in introducing the command of circumcision, because man is weakened when circumcised. Therefore lest Abraham be apprehensive that after he would undergo circumcision he would be incapacitated during his convalescence and easy prey for his enemies, God appeared to him with this Name as if to reassure him: I am God Who will grant you and your descendants sufficient strength to overcome your enemies. [See *footnote* to *v.* 22.]

אֵל שַׁדַּי הִתְהַלֵּךְ לְפָנַי וֶהְיֵה תָמִים׃
ב וְאֶתְּנָה בְרִיתִי בֵּינִי וּבֵינֶךָ וְאַרְבֶּה אוֹתְךָ

הִתְהַלֵּךְ לְפָנַי — *Walk before Me.*

As *Targum* renders [avoiding the anthropomorphic connotation of 'walking' in relation to God *(Levush)*]: worship before Me — cleave to My service *(Rashi).*

[Or, the phrase has the connotation of: *comport yourself in a manner pleasing to* Me.]

The *Midrash* contrasts the command in this verse that Abraham walk *before* God, with 6:9 where *Noah* is described as walking *with* God. The *Midrash* cites examples to illustrate that Noah walked *with* God in the sense that he needed His support [to maintain his righteousness] while Abraham was morally strong enough to walk alone, *before* God [cf. *Rashi* to 6:9 where 24:40 is cited as the contrasting verse.]

Tanchuma likens the description of the Patriarchs as walking before God [48:15] to a potentate whose elders walk before him and proclaim his glory. Similarly, the Patriarchs walked before God, proclaiming His glory *(Torah Shelemah* 17, 13-4).

וֶהְיֵה תָמִים — *And be perfect* [or: *wholehearted*]

This is a separate command: Be wholehearted in all the trials to which I will submit you. The *Midrash,* however, perceives this not as a separate command, but as a natural consequence of the former one: הִתְהַלֵּךְ לְפָנַי *Walk before Me* by observing the *mitzvah* of circumcision, וֶהְיֵה תָמִים, *and as a result of this you will become perfect*— for, so long as you remain uncircumcised, you lack perfection [lit. *'you are blemished'*] Another interpretation of *and be perfect:* [At present you are not *'whole'* in the moral sense because] you lack [mastery over] five organs [which lead man most to sin]: two eyes, two ears, and the membrum. I will therefore add a letter [ה=5] to your name [אַבְרָם which equals 243] so that your new name [אַבְרָהָם] will equal 248, corresponding to the [total number of] organs of your body. [That is, through circumcision, you will gain mastery over every organ of the body, including those which lead man to sin. As a result of this mastery you will be considered 'whole' *(Mizrachi; Gur Aryeh; Maharshal).*] *(Rashi).*

Midrash HaGadol notes that circumcision was one of the Ten Trials of Abraham [see 12:1 and *Overview.*] Although he was commanded to undergo this difficult ordeal in his advanced age, he did not disobey the words of his Creator.

According to *Ibn Ezra, 'be wholehearted'* implies: accept unquestioningly My commandment of circumcision.

... And by virtue of compliance with this commandment you will be 'perfect' because on your flesh will be a sign dedicated to Me. In addition to the above connotation of תָּמִים, *perfect,* Abraham would comprehend a second aspect. Precisely through removing some of his skin through circumcision — an apparent contradiction to physical perfection — you will become *perfect* because this slight diminuation of an organ will be the symbol of your

XVII *Shaddai; walk before me and be perfect.* [2] *I will set*
2 *My covenant between Me and you, and I will in-*

Covenant with God. This sign is possible only because circumcision is performed by man. Had he been born circumcised, the major significance would have been minimized. Therefore, some blood must be drawn even from one who is born already "circumcised" [(i.e.. without a prepuce) see *Yevamos* 71a] *(Radak).*[1]

Ramban connects this commandment with that in *Deut.* 18:13; תָּמִים תִּהְיֶה עִם ה׳ אֱלֹהֶיךָ *you shall be wholehearted with HASHEM your God.* Both verses signify that complete trust should be placed in the Omnipotent, Who alone has the power to do and undo, regardless of the natural fate portended by one's constellations. The Sages alluded to this concept when they elucidated God's exhortation to Abraham by saying, 'go forth from your astrological speculations' [See *comm.* to 15:5.]

[Cf. also *Rashi*'s comment to *Deut.* 18:13: Walk before Him wholeheartedly, put your hope in Him and do not inquire into the future; accept with wholehearted innocence whatever comes upon you. Then you will be one with Him and become His portion.]

According to *Sforno*, the command *'walk before Me and be wholehearted'* means: in all your ways *walk before Me,* i.e. seek to emulate My ways to the full extent of your capacity, in the manner of שִׁוִּיתִי ה׳ לְנֶגְדִּי תָמִיד, *I have set HASHEM before Me, always [Ps.* 16:8.] Additionally, *Be wholehearted:* seek the highest degree of שְׁלֵמוּת, perfection attainable by man, through knowing Me and emulating Me. Indeed this was the very purpose of [man's] Creation, at which time God said [1:26]: *Let Us make Man in Our image after Our form.*

2. And when you attain the wholehearted perfection ...

וְאֶתְּנָה בְרִיתִי בֵּינִי וּבֵינֶךָ — *[And] I will set My covenant between Me and [between] you.*

[The word *covenant,* in singular and not followed with a specification of *which* covenant, has a collective connotation *(Gur Aryeh)*]:

A covenant of Love, and the covenant to give this Land as a heritage to your children through [your observance of] the precept [of circumcision] *(Rashi).*

God now transferred irrevocably to Abraham all the covenants previously made with mankind. Because Abraham had made himself the suitable instrument for their fulfillment, he was appointed the germ from which the covenants would develop *(Hirsch).*

In the covenant of the Land, it was *God* Who had *made a covenant on that day* [15:18]; it was a *unilateral pledge by God,* requiring no reciprocal deed on the part of

1. Turnus Rufus [the Roman general] asked Rabbi Akiva: If your God desires circumcision why is a child not born circumcised?

Rabbi Akiva replied: Because God gave mitzvos to Israel only in order to purify them [by their practicing its tenets] i.e., God wished that man attain perfection by his own efforts through performance of the commandments *(Tanchuma).*

ג בִּמְאֹד מְאֹד׃ וַיִּפֹּל אַבְרָם עַל־פָּנָיו וַיְדַבֵּר
ד אִתּוֹ אֱלֹהִים לֵאמֹר׃ אֲנִי הִנֵּה בְרִיתִי

Abraham. In this covenant [of circumcision], however, Abraham undertook a reciprocal obligation — for this covenant would be בֵּינִי וּבֵינֶךָ, *between Me and you.* By his compliance, he and his descendants would be instrumental in 'perfecting' the Work of Creation, and this 'perfection' would begin within his own 'miniature world' — his body *(Malbim).*

[The two *'sides'* of the covenant are clearly defined. God's obligations are listed in verses 4-8. What God expected of Abraham and his descendants are enumerated in verses 9-14.]

וְאַרְבֶּה אוֹתְךָ בִּמְאֹד מְאֹד — *And I will increase you most exceedingly* [lit. *'and I will increase you with very much, very much.'*]

You need not be at all apprehensive that by undergoing circumcision your fertility will diminish; the reverse is true. By virtue of complying with the covenant, your progeny will be abundant *(B'chor Shor; Radak).*

According to *N'tziv* this promise of וְאַרְבֶּה does not refer to *numerical abundance of his progeny,* but to the qualitative esteem his descendants would enjoy in the eyes of others by virtue of their compliance with the covenant.

3. וַיִּפֹּל אַבְרָם עַל פָּנָיו — *[And] Abram fell upon his face.*

— In deference to the Presence of God. Until he was circumcised, Abraham was unable to stand while the Holy Spirit was above him, and so he literally *fell to the ground.* Cf. also *Num.* 24:4 *(Targum Yonasan; Rashi).*

Radak interprets וַיִּפֹּל as meaning that Abraham purposely *threw himself* upon his face in an expression of gratitude for the final ratification of the Covenant and the Divine Promise that was just revealed to him *(Radak; Maasei Hashem).*

[Cf. similar interpretation of וַיִּפְּלוּ, meaning *threw down* instead of *fell* in 14:10. See *Sefer Zikaron* cited to 30:13.]

In a similar vein *Ramban* comments that Abraham *threw himself upon his face,* with the intention of directing his attention toward the prophecy, in line with parallel instances in *Num.* 16:21-22.

For, as *Hirsch* elaborates, *throwing oneself down on one's face,* has a significance aside from the indication of total submission. It also involves a cessation of seeing, so that the individual can listen with uninterrupted concentration to the One before Whom he has prostrated himself. Such was the case when prophets were shown vi-

1. That the Torah does not mention in 12:7 that Abraham fell in the Divine Presence when God appeared to him is of no significance. [As pointed out many times earlier, the Torah relates *only* those things it deems necessary for conveying the deeper message inherent in the flow of the narrative.] Undoubtedly Abraham 'fell on his face' then as well, but the Torah mentions it only now — immediately before the commandment of circumcision — to emphasize that, in his uncircumcised state, he lacked the strength to stand up in the Divine Presence. After the circumcision, however, the verse says specifically [18:22]: *Abraham remained standing before HASHEM (Sifsei Chachomim).*

XVII *crease you most exceedingly.*
3-4 *3 Abram fell upon his face, and God spoke with*
him saying, 4 'As for Me, this is My covenant with

sions of angels around God's throne with their wings covering their faces (*Isaiah* 6 and *Ezekiel* 1). By this action Abraham indicated acceptance of the demands of the Covenant.

The *Midrash* notes that twice Abraham *fell upon his face* [here and in *v.* 17], portending the two times that his descendants would be deprived of circumcision: in Egypt and in the desert. [This might mean that he foresaw those two periods *and fell on his face* in intercession against the continuation of the deprivations. His prayers were answered (*Torah Shelemah*)]: In Egypt Moses came and circumcised them; in the desert Joshua arranged their circumcision before they captured the Promised Land.[1]

וַיְדַבֵּר אִתּוֹ אֱלֹהִים לֵאמֹר — *And God spoke with him saying,* i.e., clearly, and with the intention that he transmit the message to his descendants after him (*Radak; Hirsch*).

[Cf. *comm.* of לֵאמֹר, lit. *'to say'* in 15:1 and 4, and references there.]

The use of God's name *Elohim* from this point on in the narrative is noted:

Imrei Shefer explains that this Name, indicating the Attribute of Justice, signifies that whatever promises and rewards were given to Abraham were all fully deserved.

Malbim notes that *Elohim* ['God'] is the only Name that is associated with a creature, as in *God of Abraham,* or *God of the Universe.* For *Elohim* signifies God's manifestation in the world. When a person demonstrates Godly holiness, then he becomes, if one may say so, an extention of God. Similarly, the ordered nature of the universe is a manifestation of God's Providence. Further, the word אִתּוֹ, *'with' Him* implies a degree of joint action, or partnership. Thus, God recognized Abraham as acting with Him in manifesting His Presence on earth.

Hirsch comments that the use of *Elohim* signifies a decisive change in Abraham's nature. Prior to the covenant, Abraham had freedom of choice to refuse the obligations incumbent upon Israel; he could have chosen to remain a Noachide. Now, however, having entered into the Covenant, he was bound by the Attribute of Justice to fulfill it uncompromisingly (see *Overview*).

4. The details of the Covenant

אֲנִי — *As for Me,* [i.e., regarding My part of the covenant.]

1. Moses and Joshua, too, cast themselves down upon the ground symbolizing total submission: וַיִּשְׁמַע מֹשֶׁה וַיִּפֹּל עַל פָּנָיו, *and Moses heard and fell upon his face* (*Num.* 16:4); וַיִּפֹּל עַל פָּנָיו, *and Joshua fell upon his face* (*Joshua* 5:14). Because they submitted totally to the will of God, they were granted the privilege of being instrumental in the circumcision of the nation — Moses prior to the Exodus, and Joshua after the entry into the Land. At both of those times the majority of the nation was uncircumcised; in Egypt due to the rigors of the enslavement, and after the wilderness years because it had been medically dangerous to carry out circumcision in the desert. Because Moses and Joshua emulated Abraham, the task of supervising the masses of Israel was entrusted to them (*Reb Avi Gold*).

ה אִתָּךְ וְהָיִיתָ לְאַב הֲמוֹן גּוֹיִם: וְלֹא־יִקָּרֵא
עוֹד אֶת־שִׁמְךָ אַבְרָם וְהָיָה שִׁמְךָ אַבְרָהָם
ו כִּי אַב־הֲמוֹן גּוֹיִם נְתַתִּיךָ: וְהִפְרֵתִי אֹתְךָ

Verses 4-8 detail God's obligations in fulfilling *His* side of the covenant, while verses 9-14 detail those of *Abraham* and his descendants *(Hirsch).*

הִנֵּה בְרִיתִי אִתָּךְ — *This* [lit. *'behold; here'*] *is My covenant with you,* i.e., the covenant of circumcision which will be detailed below *(Ramban).*

With you — but with no other people *(Pesikta Zutresa).*

The meaning of the verse is: *As for Me, I already have a covenant with you* since the Covenant Between the Parts at which time I undertook certain obligations. As a result of that covenant *you will be the father of a multitude of nations,* as I promised you then. Now I have come to announce something greater: the change of name by which you will become a new person, greater in stature. This Covenant will be not only between you and Me, but will also include your *descendants for posterity,* without regard to time or place *(Akeidas Yitzchak; Abarbanel).*

וְהָיִיתָ לְאַב הֲמוֹן גּוֹיִם — [And] *You shall be* [as a direct result of complying with the covenant *(Ramban)*] *a father* [in the sense of Patron] *of a multitude of nations.*

Everyone who will undergo circumcision and conversion will consider you his Patriarch *par excellence (Midrash Aggadah).*

[*Rambam* in his *comm.* to *Mishnah Biccurim* 1:4 cites Abraham's universal patriarchy as the reason that, when converts bring their first fruits to the priest, they may recite the same formula as all Jews: 'I profess this day ... that I have come to the Land which HASHEM swore to *our* fathers to give us' *(Deut.* 26:3). Since the Land was not promised to the *fathers* of converts, how can they say the formula? However, because Abraham is *the 'father' of a multitude of nations,* all converts are considered as his descendants and a convert is therefore referred to as בֶּן אַבְרָהָם, *son of Abraham.*]

5. And in order to reflect your new mission:

וְלֹא יִקָּרֵא עוֹד ... וְהָיָה שִׁמְךָ אַבְרָהָם — *You shall no longer be called by your name Abram, but* [lit. *'and'*] *your name shall be Abraham.*

That is, your contemporaries and those after you will no longer refer to you by your former name. They will tell one another how God has changed Your name, and thereby the miracle which I am to perform for you will become manifest to all generations for eternity *(Radak).*

It is a deep-rooted custom to change someone's name when he rises in stature. The change signifies that the 'new' person has outgrown his old status. This was also the case with Sarah [=Sarai]; Joseph [=Tzafnas Paane'ach]; Joshua [=Hoshea]; Chananiah, Mishael and Azariah [=Shadrach, Mishach, Abed Nego] *(Chizkuni).*

כִּי אַב הֲמוֹן גּוֹיִם נְתַתִּיךָ — *For I have made* [lit. *'given'*] *you the father of a multitude of nations.*

The word נְתַתִּיךָ [*I have made*] is

XVII 5-6

you: you shall be a father of a multitude of nations;
⁵ you shall no longer be called by your name Abram,
but your name shall be Abraham, for I have made
you the father of a multitude of nations; ⁶ I will make

in past tense, but implies a future action. God's promise is like an accomplished fact *(R' Meyuchos).*

[Thus, his new name etymologically reflects his new role]:

The name אַבְרָהָם, *'Avraham'*, is a נוֹטְרִיקוֹן, contraction, of his new status as **אַב הֲמוֹן** *Av hamon, father of a multitude,* whereas אַבְרָם, *'Avram'*, denoted him in his former status as **אַב אֲרָם** *Av Aram,* father [i.e., lord and master] *of Aram,* his native country [see 11:28]. The letter ר, *resh,* in his former name remained after the change even though it was not needed to indicate the status denoted by the new name [and was now, for all purposes, rendered superfluous] *(Rashi).* [1]

Rashi homiletically explains that, although now unnecessary, the *Resh* remained because, as the *Midrash* comments, the י, *yod,* which was deleted from Sarai's name when it was changed to Sarah [שָׂרָה, שָׂרַי] complained to God until it was added to Joshua's name when Moses changed it from הוֹשֵׁעַ, to יְהוֹשֻׁעַ. [Therefore to avoid that situation here, the letter was retained. See *footnote* to *v.* 15.]

[See also *comm.* to *v.* 1 s.v. וֶהְיֵה תָמִים where the letter ה added to his name is symbolic of the additional five limbs he was able to control thanks to the 'wholeness' of circumcision.]

According to *Ibn Ezra,* however, the letter *resh,* is not superfluous, but an integral part of the new name, which is derived from אַבִּיר הֲמוֹן גּוֹיִם, *the strong one of a multitude (of nations).* He remarks that the new name was not given to delete a letter [or render it superfluous, as in *Rashi*'s interpretation *(Ba'er Yitzchak)*] but to add!

Hoffman approvingly cites the view of those who interpret the name as an expansion of אַב רָהָם, *raham* being an ancient Arabic word meaning 'horde, multitude'. The ancient Hebrew equivalent רָהָם might have already fallen into disuse by the time the Torah was given to Moses and it was therefore necessary for the verse to explain the etymology as being from הֲמוֹן, *multitude (of nations).*

The *Talmud* comments: Whoever refers to Abraham as Abram transgresses a positive command since it says, *Your name shall be Abraham.* Simultaneously he transgresses a negative command since it says: *You shall no longer be named Abram.* The Sages continue that this prohibition does not apply in the case of Sarai/Sarah because in that case God addressed His command to Abraham [hence it was *he,* not necessarily others, who was enjoined to call her only by the new name Sarah.]

It also does not apply to Jacob/Israel because the Torah itself later referred to him by the name *Jacob* [46:2], thus clearly showing that he retained that name. The reference to Abraham as *Abram* in *Nech.* 9:7 is no contradiction because it merely recounts Abraham's

1. *Notarikon* is a method of exegesis whereby words are broken up and letters or syllables are treated as abbreviations. In this treatment, only the *general* form of the word is treated, while a particular letter or so may be ignored. The *Talmud* [*Shabbos* 105a] deduces that *notarikon* is a permissible method of exegesis because our verse testifies that the name Abraham was derived from *Av Hamon* [*Goyim*], despite the presence of the superfluous *resh.*

בִּמְאֹד מְאֹד וּנְתַתִּיךָ לְגוֹיִם וּמְלָכִים מִמְּךָ
שביעי ז יֵצֵאוּ: וַהֲקִמֹתִי אֶת־בְּרִיתִי בֵּינִי וּבֵינֶךָ
וּבֵין זַרְעֲךָ אַחֲרֶיךָ לְדֹרֹתָם לִבְרִית עוֹלָם
לִהְיוֹת לְךָ לֵאלֹהִים וּלְזַרְעֲךָ אַחֲרֶיךָ:
ח וְנָתַתִּי לְךָ וּלְזַרְעֲךָ אַחֲרֶיךָ אֵת | אֶרֶץ

original name in the context of God's righteousness (*Berachos* 13a). [Cf. parallel in *Yerushalmi*]

Chizkuni suggests that the reason Abraham may not be referred to as Abram is because that name was given him before he became the forerunner of the Jewish nation. The name Jacob, however, may still be used because it was his while he had the mission and greatness of a Jewish patriarch.

Why were the names of Abraham and Jacob changed, but not that of Isaac?

Since both of the above were named by man, God changed their name [to reflect their new mission]. Isaac's name was not changed because the name, Isaac, was designated for him by God before birth [see *v.* 19.] (*Yerushalmi Berachos* 1:6).

Maharitz Chayes to *Berachos* ad. loc., explains that *Rambam* did not include this prohibition in his compilation of the mitzvos because, as *Rambam* explains in his *comm.* to *Mishnah Chullin* 100a, we do not list among the 613 those precepts from the pre-Sinaitic narratives of the patriarchs unless the prohibition was repeated at the giving of the Torah.

According to *Torah Temimah,* the *halachic* codifiers did not include this in the 613 commandments based on *Tosefta Berachos I* which explains that no *prohibition* is implied in this verse. Rather it is a narrative that emphasizes the exalted status implied in his new name.

[The *Shiyurei Knesses HaGedolah* (*Kelalim Nifradim* 25) explains that there is a *Rabbinic* prohibition inherent in calling him Abram, especially as evident from the commentators, if it is done in a derogatory manner. (See *M'lo HaRoim, Ber.* 13a). See also *Magen Avraham, Orach Chaim* 156:2 who mentions the prohibition.]

Me'am Loez emphasizes, therefore, that one should be scrupulous to carefully enunciate the name Abraham whenever it appears in our prayers, so that it not be slurred and sound like *Avram.*

6. וְהִפְרֵתִי אֹתְךָ בִּמְאֹד מְאֹד — *And I will make you most exceedingly fruitful* [lit. *'I will make you fruitful with very much, very much.'*]

The following elaborates on the promise above and explains *how* God intends to make Abraham into a *'father of a multitude of peoples'* (*R' Meyuchas*).

As mentioned in *v.* 2, the inner implication of the promise is an assurance to Abraham: do not think that circumcision will impair your potency. To the contrary, I will make you exceedingly prolific! (*Malbim*).

Abraham had *already* been promised abundant progeny. This blessing was to assure him that his descendants would be present on every corner of the world in sufficient numbers for them to instruct the nations in the true Faith (*Haamek Davar*).

[The translation *fruitful* relates הִפְרֵתִי to פְּרִי.]

XVII
7-8

you most exceedingly fruitful, and make nations of
you; and kings shall descend from you; [7] *and I will*
ratify My covenant between Me and you and be-
tween your offspring after you throughout their gen-
erations as an everlasting covenant, to be a God to
you and to your offspring after you; [8] *and I will give*
to you and to your offspring after you the land of

וּנְתַתִּיךָ לְגוֹיִם — *And [I will] make nations of you* [lit. *'and I will give of you unto nations.'*]

The reference is to Israel [his descendants through Jacob] and Edom [his descendants through Esau.] Because his son Ishmael was already living, the announcement of *future* descendants could not have referred to him *(Rashi).*

Ramban suggests, however, that Esau, the pregenitor of Edom who had not been commanded with circumcision [see *Sanhedrin* 59b and *comm.* to 21:12], is not referred to here. Rather the *nations* mentioned here, despite the plural, refers to Israel alone. In other verses as well — e.g. 35:11, 48:4; *Deut.* 33:3,19; *Judges* 5:14; (see commentaries there) — Israel is referred to by the collective term גּוֹיִם *nations* and עַמִּים, *peoples.*

Following *Haamek Davar,* the interpretation is *I will give you to the nations,* i.e. you will become the מְלַמֵּד דַּעַת לַגּוֹיִם, the teacher of wisdom to the nations. This is comparable to the similar charge to Jeremiah [1:5]: נָבִיא לַגּוֹיִם נְתַתִּיךָ, *I gave you* [i.e., I ordained you] *as a prophet to the nations.*

According to *Targum,* however, the translation of the phrase is: 'I will make tribes out of you,' while *Radak* suggests that the reference is to Abraham's descendants through his concubine, Keturah (enumerated in Ch. 25).

וּמְלָכִים מִמְּךָ יֵצֵאוּ — *And kings shall descend* [lit. *'come forth'*] *from you.*

Your descendants will not be dependent upon other kingdoms; they will have sovereigns of their own *(Daas Soferim).*

Continuing *Haamek Davar:* Not only will there descend from you *sages* who are qualified to instruct the nations, but there will come forth from you monarchs with the power to suppress idolatry from the nations. Such occurred during King Solomon's reign, and will again occur during the reign of King Messiah.

7. וַהֲקִמֹתִי אֶת בְּרִיתִי — *And I will ratify My covenant.*

Which covenant? — *To be your God ... (Rashi).*

לְדֹרֹתָם לִבְרִית עוֹלָם — *Throughout their generations* [i.e. throughout the ages; for all time] *as an everlasting covenant.*

לִהְיוֹת לְךָ לֵאלֹהִים — *To be a God to you* [lit. *'to be unto you a God'*].

The concept has a dual connotation: To be on the one hand the object of your worship and venerations, and on the other hand, to be your God, Protector and Benefactor *(Alshich).*

8. As a result of your compliance with the covenant, I will give the

מְגֻרֶיךָ אֵת כָּל־אֶרֶץ כְּנַעַן לַאֲחֻזַּת עוֹלָם
ט וְהָיִיתִי לָהֶם לֵאלֹהִים: וַיֹּאמֶר אֱלֹהִים
אֶל־אַבְרָהָם וְאַתָּה אֶת־בְּרִיתִי תִשְׁמֹר

land of your sojourn — i.e., the land in which you now dwell — the entire land of Canaan, to your descendants as an everlasting possession. There I will show myself to them as a protecting God provided they accept me as such *(Sechel Tov; Ibn Caspi)* [See *Malbim* below.]

We deduce from this verse that Israel inherited the land of Canaan only by virtue of circumcision, for the land was given to Abraham only on condition that he circumcise himself. Therefore, God ordered Joshua to circumcise the Israelites when they were to enter the Promised Land, [*Josh.* 5:2-9] for had they remained uncircumcised they could not have entered *(Midrash Aggadah,* see also *Bircas Hamazon,* ArtScroll ed. p. 43-44).

אֶרֶץ מְגֻרֶיךָ — *The land of your sojourns.* I.e., the land in which you tarried as a גֵּר, *alien,* a temporary resident — כָּל אֶרֶץ כְּנַעַן — *the whole of the land of Canaan.*

לַאֲחֻזַּת עוֹלָם — *For an everlasting possession.*

This expression does not imply that they would dwell eternally in the Land and never be exiled — that would depend on their deeds. Rather the expression means that the Land would remain their inalienable possession even though they may be in exile. The promise was that come what may the Land would always belong to them; they would eventually return to reclaim it and HASHEM would be their God *(Radak).*

This additional promise of *everlasting possession,* with the implication of ownership and eventual return after exile, is the primary difference between this promise and those given earlier (see *comm.* of *Ramban* cited in *comm.* to 15:18.]

[The concept of *and I will be their God* was already mentioned in the previous verse: nevertheless it is repeated here in connection with the land, indicating some special relationship *(Mizrachi).*] *Rashi* comments that 'only in *the land of their everlasting possession* will I *be their God;* one who dwells *outside* of Eretz Yisrael is as though he had no God' [*Kesubos* 110b.] (See *Overview).*

וְהָיִיתִי לָהֶם לֵאלֹהִים— *And I will be their God* [lit. *and I will be unto them a God.*]

[See *Sechel Tov* at beginning of verse.]

According to *Malbim:* When they will comply with the covenant and take possession of the land, then they will merit *in their own right* that I be their God, not only because I was the God of their fathers. At that time they themselves will be worthy of Godliness; HASHEM is called the God of Israel by virtue of their sanctity and righteousness.

9. The obligation on Abraham's part.

XVII *your sojourns — the whole of the land of Canaan —*
9 *as an everlasting possession; and I will be their God.'*
⁹ God said to Abraham, 'And as for you, you shall
keep My covenant — you and your descendents after

וְאַתָּה אֶת בְּרִיתִי תִשְׁמֹר — *And as for you,* [i.e., as far as you are concerned] *you shall keep My covenant.*

Rashi comments that the word וְאַתָּה begins with the conjunction *vav, and,* to imply that it is joined to the previous verses i.e., I have specified obligations to you *(v.* 4-8); as a result you must obligate yourself to comply with your obligations to Me as outlined in the following verses regarding circumcision.

Hirsch elaborates upon this concept. Since God pledged that His assurance was eternally valid, he charged Abraham and his descendants not to create conditions that would make them unworthy of God's gifts under the Covenant. Furthermore, they should remember that were it not for Abraham's pledge, Israel would not have existence for Isaac's birth was a direct result of the Covenant.

And this obligation does not rest upon you alone, but will extend as well to וְזַרְעֲךָ אַחֲרֶיךָ לְדֹרֹתָם — *your descendants after you throughout their generations* [i.e., *forever*] *(Malbim).*

Your descendants after you — but not any other people's *(Sanhedrin* 59b).

The *Talmud* [*Avodah Zarah* 27a] adduces from the wording וְאַתָּה, *as for you,* that the command was directed only to the Abrahamitic line [as it says וְזַרְעֲךָ אַחֲרֶיךָ, *and your descendants after you (Rashi)*] and that a circumcision performed by a heathen [on a Jew] is invalid. [See *Torah Temimah*]

Cf. *Sanhedrin* 59b: Every precept which was given to the sons of Noah and repeated at Sinai was meant for both Jew and non-Jew alike. But circumcision was given to the Noachides [i.e. Abraham who was considered a Noachide like all others; the separate status of Israel began with the Giving of the Law at Sinai] and repeated at Sinai [*Lev.* 12:3] yet was meant for Israel only? — The repetition [in *Lev.* reading *'on the eighth day the flesh of his surplusage shall be circumcised'*] was for a specific teaching, to permit circumcision on the Sabbath by specifying *on the day* [whenever it was] — even on the Sabbath. [Hence, since the repetition at Sinai was for a particular teaching, it is not considered a repetition and therefore was meant exclusively for Jews.]

... An alternative answer is that circumcision was originally commanded only to *Abraham* [and not to Noachides in general.]: *You shall keep My covenant* — you and your seed shall keep it but no others. Then let it be incumbent upon Ishmael [Abraham's son] also! — No, for Scripture states [21:12]: For in *Isaac* [i.e. and not Ishmael] shall be considered your seed. Then the children of Esau [Isaac's son] should be subject to the Law! — No, 21:12 is further interpreted; בְּיִצְחָק, *in* Isaac [the בְּ, *in,* being taken as a partitive preposition implying only part] but not *all* [the descendants] of Isaac.

Cf. also *Rambam* in his commentary to *Mishnah, Chullin* 100b: 'Reflect on a fundamental principle: Whatever we

י אַתָּ֫ה וְזַרְעֲךָ֫ אַחֲרֶ֫יךָ לְדֹרֹתָ֫ם: זֹ֫את בְּרִיתִ֫י
אֲשֶׁ֫ר תִּשְׁמְר֫וּ בֵּינִ֫י וּבֵינֵיכֶ֫ם וּבֵ֫ין זַרְעֲךָ֫
יא אַחֲרֶ֫יךָ הִמּ֫וֹל לָכֶ֫ם כָּל־זָכָ֫ר: וּנְמַלְתֶּ֫ם אֵ֫ת

perform today is only the result of God having so commanded us through Moses at Sinai, rather than what He commanded the prophets preceding him. We do not circumcise because Abraham did so to himself and his household, but because God expressly commanded us *through Moses* [*Exod.* 12:3] that we should circumcise ourselves as did Abraham [see also *comm.* to *Deut.* 33:4.]

10. The definition of the Covenant.

זֹאת בְּרִיתִי אֲשֶׁר תִּשְׁמְרוּ — *This is My covenant which you shall keep.*

It is possible that God actually *showed* Abraham — through a vision or otherwise — the manner in which the circumcision was to be accomplished. See, for example *Rashi*'s explanation of 9:17: זֹאת אוֹת הַבְּרִית, *This is the sign of the covenant* — i.e., God actually showed Noah a rainbow and said to him: *This* is the sign of which I spoke. Cf. also *Lev.* 11:2 *(Daas Soferim).*

[See *Aggadah Bereishis* 16 *(Torah Shelemah* 17:13) which describes God — if we may use such a bold anthropomorphism — as holding the knife for Abraham, while Abraham cut (See *comm.* to *v.* 24).]

[The anthropomorphic description of God as holding the knife can be understood as meaning that God gave Abraham the strength to go through with the act *(Harav David Cohen).*]

[The following rite of circumcision in addition to being the Covenant *itself,* is at the same time the אוֹת בְּרִית, the *external sign of the covenant* as the following verse clearly states. Although many reasons — for example, to counteract excessive lust, or as a hygienic measure — have been advanced to explain circumcision, those reasons, while they may be valid, cannot be taken as God's total purpose in assigning the commandment. It is symbolic of the mutual covenant between Israel and their Father in heaven, just as the rainbow — whatever its natural causes — assumed its primary significance because God proclaimed it the external sign of the covenant with Noah.]

(See *Overview).*

Hirsch notes an apparent discrepancy between our verse and *v.* 11. Here it is called *My Covenant,* implying that the physical act of circumcision is sufficient fulfillment of the covenant. Later it is described as the *sign* or *symbol* of the covenant, implying that the act is no more than a symbol, and not a complete fulfillment. He explains that there are two inseparable elements: the act without realization of the idea is insufficient; likewise the concept without the act is not enough. The act of circumcision must be performed, and it must be recognized as symbolic of the eternal bond between God and Israel.

בֵּינִי וּבֵינֵיכֶם — *Between Me and [between] you,* i.e., those of you who are now alive *(Rashi).*

וּבֵין זַרְעֲךָ אַחֲרֶיךָ — *And [between] your descendants after you,* i.e.,

you throughout their generations.
10 *This is My covenant which you shall keep between Me and you and your descendants after you: Every male among you shall shall be circumcised.*
11 *You shall circum-*

those to be born in the future *(Rashi).*

הִמּוֹל לָכֶם כָּל זָכָר – *Every male among you shall be circumcised.*

The translation follows *Rashi,* i.e., this is not the injunction to circumcise — that comes in *v.* 11 — rather it is the description of the covenant *(Sifsei Chachamim).*

[Since this command is in general terms, not particularly directed to the father, the *Talmud, Kiddushin* 29a adduces]: One whose father did not circumcise him, the Beth Din is bound to circumcise him. But if the Beth Din did not circumcise him, he is obligated to circumcise himself [see next verse and verse 14.] (Cf. *Yerushalmi Kidd.* 1:7).

◆§ Purposes of Circumcision

Although the rite of circumcision is a חוק, i.e., a law, whose reason is not given in the Torah, nevertheless the Jewish philosophers have, tried to elicit the *hashkafah* implications inherent in the mitzvah (see *Overview*). A *sampling* of the classical comments on the subject follow:

Rav Saadiah Gaon [*Emunos V'Deos* 3:10] states that 'perfection' implies a condition containing neither superfluity nor deficiency. The Creator created this part of man's body with a redundancy; when the redundancy is cut off a defect in man's formation is removed. What is left is a state of perfection.

Rambam [*Moreh* 3:49] holds that the commandment was not given 'as a complement to a deficient physical creature, but as a means for perfecting man's *moral* shortcomings ... for circumcision counteracts excessive lust...'

Sefer Hachinuch 2: Among the roots of the commandment are that HASHEM wished to establish a particular sign in the bodies of the people whom he had designated to be His own. This special sign differentiated their bodies, just as their souls are differentiated, to demonstrate that their source and mission are not like those of the other nations...

This symbol was placed in the reproductive organ because it represents the eternity of the race. God wanted to perfect His Chosen People, but he wanted this perfection to be accomplished through the deed of human beings. This symbolizes that just as the body must be perfected, so, too, people must strive to perfect their souls.'

Rav Yosef Albo [*Ikkarim* 4:45]: The commandment of circumcision was given as an external sign of the covenant binding God and Abraham's descendants who maintain His covenant. Since that sign exists continually in our nation, it shows that the divine bond is still with us ... The *Midrash* states that Abraham sits at the door fo Gehinnom and prevents the circumcised from going in. Therefore, as long as this sign of the Covenant is maintained in the nation we must not despair of redemption ... for it

בְּשַׂר עָרְלַתְכֶם וְהָיָה לְאוֹת בְּרִית בֵּינִי
יב וּבֵינֵיכֶם: וּבֶן־שְׁמֹנַת יָמִים יִמּוֹל לָכֶם כָּל־
זָכָר לְדֹרֹתֵיכֶם יְלִיד בָּיִת וּמִקְנַת־כֶּסֶף

points to the bond between God and us ... that through this bond the nation will return to its original strength and cleave to God as was prophesied.

[See also Hirsch's 'Symbolism in Jewish Law', *Collected Writings*, Vol. III (1906), pp. 254-396. Part of this important essay has been published in English translation in *Timeless Torah*, pp. 364 ff.]

11. וּנְמַלְתֶּם אֵת בְּשַׂר עָרְלַתְכֶם — *You shall circumcise the flesh of your surplusage*

This is a positive commandment requiring every father to circumcise his son, and obligating every child to have himself circumcised when he becomes a Bar Mitzvah if he had not been circumcised by his father or the Beth Din *(Radak).*

[See *Yerushalmi Kiddushin* 1:7. Cf. also *comm.* of *Rambam* cited at end of *v.* 9.]

Although עָרְלָה [*surplusage*] is commonly translated — in the context of our verse — *foreskin,* this familiar translation cannot by any means be considered literal. *Radak* [in *Sefer Shorashim*] notes that עָרְלָה refers, in its primary sense to anything superfluous and worthy of disposal.

[Accordingly the word עָרְלָה could designate any part of the body that would best be 'expendable' or removed.] According to *Hirsch* on *Lev.* 19:23, עָרְלָה could be translated 'hindrance', for the word refers to something which hinders spiritual development. [The Sages expound that Abraham deduced from the context of the passage which part of the body was to be removed. Since the promise that Abraham would have many descendants [*v.* 7] was repeated in connection with circumcision, Abraham reasoned that the commandment related to the part of the anatomy that produces descendants, and by virtue of circumcision he would also become תָּמִים, *wholehearted* and *perfect,* as God had commanded (see *comm.* to *v.* 1).]

[See *Rashi* to *v.* 14.]

Ibn Ezra to *Lev.* 12:3 explains that the word עָרְלָה always refers to the reproductive organ, unless it is used in a construct form such as the *'orlah* of the heart' [*Deut.* 10:16] in which case the context will clearly indicate its meaning.

Ramban [to *v.* 14] states that in his opinion the Torah itself is quite explicit in its intention inasmuch at it does not state ambiguously וּנְמַלְתֶּם אֵת עָרְלַתְכֶם, [You shall circumcise your *orlah* (i.e., that which obstructs; see further)], not does it say עָרְלַת בְּשַׂרְכֶם, 'the *orlah* of your flesh' implying, in the construct state, an obstruction *of* your flesh, as it says figuratively [*Deut.* 10:16] עָרְלַת לְבַבְכֶם, the *orlah* of your heart.' Instead our verse reads quite clearly: בְּשַׂר עָרְלַתְכֶם, the flesh of your *orlah,* which refers to the flesh which obstructs: there is no expendible flesh in the body which obstructs and covers a limb other than the 'flesh that covers the male organ.'

Additionally the very word בָּשָׂר, *flesh,* is a euphemism for the reproductive organ as in the expression *uncircumcised in flesh* [*Ezek.* 44:9]; *great of flesh* [*ibid.* 16:26]; and *an issue of his flesh* [*Lev.* 15:2].

The translation which takes וּנְמַלְתֶּם as a *kal* conjugation [you shall circumcise] in spite of the נ, *nun,* which would normally indicate a *niph'al* conjugation [*'you shall be circumcised'* (through removal of the flesh of your foreskin)] follows *Rashi* who explains that it is the same as the imperative וּמַלְתֶּם.

XVII
12

cise the flesh of your surplusage, and that shall be the sign of the covenant between Me and you. 12 *At the age of eight days every male among you shall be circumcised, throughout your generations — he that is born in the household or purchased with money from*

The נ, *nun,* is an addition to the [basic] root, [מל] and it is at times included [נמל] and at others omitted [מול]. This is similar to the נ, *nun,* of נוֹשֵׁךְ and נוֹשֵׂא [which is omitted in some forms, e.g. יִשָּׂא, יִשַּׁךְ; cf. *Rashi* to 49:10. *Onkelos* and *Ibn Ezra* render similarly.

According to *Ha'amek Davar* however, the verb is *niphal* i.e., you shall be circumcised. The command directs the uncircumcised to bear responsibility for his own circumcision.

וְהָיָה לְאוֹת בְּרִית — *And that shall be the sign of the covenant.*

— By which everyone may distinguish you as the seed which is blessed of God *(Sechel Tov).*

Circumcision will thus serve as a symbol and sign, just as *tzitzis* and *tefillin* function as reminders of Israel's bond and obligation to God. This, however is the supreme, unequaled sign inasmuch as it is indelibly sealed in the body of man *(Radak).*

... It is a perpetual reminder to walk in His ways, for it is, as it were, the Master's seal on His servant *(Sforno).*

Rav Nachman bar Yitzchak notes the expressions אוֹת, *sign,* בְּרִית, *covenant,* and לְדֹרֹתָם *throughout their generations* are used both in connection with circumcision and with the Sabbath [*for it* (the Sabbath) *is a sign* (אוֹת) *between Me and you* — *Exod.* 31:13; *the children of Isael shall keep the Sabbath ... for a perpetual covenant* (בְּרִית) — *ibid. v.* 16; *to observe the Sabbath throughout their generations* (לְדֹרֹתָם) — *ibid.*] From these common designations we learn that circumcision [in its proper time, the eighth day] supersedes the Sabbath *(Shabbos* 132a).

12. וּבֶן־שְׁמֹנַת יָמִים יִמּוֹל לָכֶם כָּל־זָכָר לְדֹרֹתֵיכֶם — [*And*] *at the age of eight days every male among* [lit. *'to'*] *you shall be circumcised, throughout your generations.*

The word יִמּוֹל is the *niphal* of the root מוּל meaning that the child should *be circumcised* by his father *(Radak; Rashi* to *v.* 11; *Ibn Ezra).*

[On the implication of לָכֶם, *among you,* see 'Note' in *comm.* to next verse.]

The *Talmud* derives from the use of the word יָמִים, *days,* that circumcision is performed by day and not by night *(Shabbos* 132a).

The *Mechilta* comments: Great is the Sabbath, for a child is not circumcised until he has lived through a Sabbath ...

Including ...

יְלִיד בָּיִת — *He that is born in household,* i.e., from a maidservant in the household *(Rashi).*

[Cf. *comm.* to same phrase in 14:14.]

וּמִקְנַת כֶּסֶף — *Or purchased with money.*

I.e., a slave purchased after he was born *(Rashi).*

Although the above are slaves, they must still be circumcised for they are, as the next verse continues, *homeborn in your house and purchased by your money* and hence subject to your obligations *(Abarbanel).*

מִכֹּל בֶּן־נֵכָר אֲשֶׁר לֹא מִזַּרְעֲךָ הוּא:
יג הִמּוֹל | יִמּוֹל יְלִיד בֵּיתְךָ וּמִקְנַת כַּסְפֶּךָ
וְהָיְתָה בְרִיתִי בִּבְשַׂרְכֶם לִבְרִית עוֹלָם:
יד וְעָרֵל | זָכָר אֲשֶׁר לֹא־יִמּוֹל אֶת־בְּשַׂר

13. ... הִמּוֹל יִמּוֹל יְלִיד בֵּיתְךָ — *He that is born in your house[hold] or purchased with your money shall surely be circumcised* [lit. *'circumcised shall he be circumcised'*] [1]

Essentially this repeats from the previous verse the command that one *born in the household* must be circumcised, but here the phrase *'at the age of eight days'* is not repeated. This indicates that in some cases those who are *born in the household* are circumcised לְאֶחָד, *on the first day* from birth or acquisition, [some editions of *Rashi* read לְאַחַר שְׁמֹנָה יָמִים, *after eight days*] as explained in *Shabbos* 135b *(Rashi).*

The Talmudic discussion referred to by *Rashi* is the controversy of Tannaim: 'For it was taught ... a slave born in his master's household is sometimes circumcised on the first day [from his birth] and sometimes on the eighth day; a slave purchased with money is sometimes circumcised on the first day [he was acquired, even if he was not yet eight days old], and sometimes on the eighth day.' [The general rule is that a child who was born a Jew is circumcised on the eighth day. A slave can be considered Jewish for this purpose because non-Jewish slaves owned by Jews are responsible for many commandments.]

The *Talmud* then proceeds to give various illustrations, as e.g. if one purchases a female slave together with her previously born infant child, that child is a 'slave bought with money' who is circumcised on the first day [of purchase.] However, if one purchases a female slave and she conceives in his house and gives birth, that is a 'slave born in his master's house' who is circumcised on the eighth day [from birth].

As regards the *converse* of the above, several views are cited. As formulated by *Rambam* in *Hilchos Milah,* if a pregnant slave is bought, and her still unborn child is purchased later, the child, is circumcised eight days after birth, for although he had been separately purchased, and therefore might be considered 'a slave bought with money,' nevertheless, since his mother had been acquired before the infants' birth he is circumcised on the eighth day.

However, when a female slave was acquired only for the right to her unborn child [with the purchaser having no share in the mother], or if she was acquired with the stipulation that she would not immerse in the ritual bath [without which she does not at-

1. The Sages perceive the compound expression הִמּוֹל יִמּוֹל as a support for many Rabbinic laws. To cite several:

One who is a *Mashuch* [surgically conceals his circumcison] must be recircumcised even a hundred times because it is written הִמּוֹל יִמּוֹל (apparently interpreting: though circumcised he must be recircumcised — see *v.* 14 s.v. אֶת בְּרִיתִי*) (Yevamos* 72a).

Circumcision performed by a heathen is invalid because it is written הִמּוֹל יִמּוֹל [which may be rendered homiletically הַמָּל יִמּוֹל, *He who is circumcised shall circumcise,* excluding a heathen] *(Avodah Zarah* 27a);

We learn from this that one who is born circumcised [i.e., without a foreskin] must let blood of the covenant drip from him [i.e. be pricked by a pin to cause some blood to flow] because it is written הִמּוֹל יִמּוֹל [which is interpreted to mean 'even he who is already (born) circumcised, must undergo a form of circumcision] *(Yer. Shabbos* 19:2);

Additionally, according to the *Yerushalmi* above, an uncircumcised Jew may not perform circumcision.

From this compound verb is also derived that circumcision consists of two parts: מִילָה, *circumcision,* and פְּרִיעָה, uncovering [the organ by splitting the prepuce and pulling it down.]

any stranger who is not of your offspring. 13 *He that is born in your household or purchased with your money shall surely be circumcised. Thus, My covenant shall be in your flesh for an everlasting covenant.* 14 *An uncircumcised male the flesh of whose surplusage shall not be circumcised — such a soul*

tain the Halachic status of a Jewish-owned slave], though her subsequently born child is born as the property of the Jew, he is circumcised on the day he is born because the infant was not born of a Jewess and is equivalent to a newly purchased slave. Should she, however, have immersed herself in the ritual bath after delivery, the infant is circumcised on the eighth day.

[Note: As explained by *Rashi* ad. loc., the law centers on the interpretation of our verse and the preceding verse. Whereas *v.* 12 specifies circumcision on the eighth day, *v.*13 does not — accordingly *the earliest possible moment* is implied. This is based on the several distinct circumstances indicated in *v.* 12 which refers to a slave who is most like a full Jew — one who was born in his master's house for his mother was the property of a Jewish master while pregnant; he is therefore circumcised on the eighth day like a full Jew. Otherwise — based upon the various illustrations — the child is not considered לָכֶם, *among you,* in the sense of being like a full Jew, and accordingly circumcised on the first day of birth or acquisition.]

Radak suggests that the covenant extended to all the members of Abraham's household, because it is inconceivable that Abraham's household should be divided between those who undertook the covenant of circumcision and those who did not.

וְהָיְתָה בְרִיתִי בִּבְשַׂרְכֶם לִבְרִית עוֹלָם — *Thus, My covenant shall be in your flesh for an everlasting covenant.*

Flesh is sometimes used in Scripture as a euphemism for the reproductive organ [see end of *Ramban* cited in *v.* 11] ... The verse thus indicates that since the Covenant is, in the physical sense, associated with the organ whereby the species is perpetuated, it symbolized the continuity of the Covenant upon his descendants for eternity *(Sforno; Hoffmann).*

... And just as the *symbol* of My Covenant will remain on your flesh throughout your lives, so will the covenant itself endure eternally *(Ralbag).*

14. As pointed out in the *comm.* to *vss.* 10 and 11, one who was circumcised neither by his father nor by Beth Din, is obligated from the time he reaches Bar Mitzvah to arrange for his own circumcision. The consequences for one who remains uncircumcised in violation of the commandment until the age of twenty, when he becomes liable to excision, are given in this verse.]

וְעָרֵל זָכָר — [*And*] *an uncircumcised male.*

The apparently unnecessary adjective *male* in this phrase is included to teach that circumcision must be performed on the member which distinguishes between male and female *(Shabbos Midrash; Rashi).*

[See *comm.* to עָרְלָה in *v.* 11.]

אֲשֶׁר לֹא יִמּוֹל אֶת בְּשַׂר עָרְלָתוֹ — *The flesh of whose surplusage shall not be circumcised.*

From when he reaches the age when he is liable to punishment [in

עָרְלָתוֹ וְנִכְרְתָה הַנֶּפֶשׁ הַהִוא מֵעַמֶּיהָ
טו אֶת־בְּרִיתִי הֵפַר: וַיֹּאמֶר אֱלֹהִים

this case twenty years old when a sinner becomes liable to heavenly punishment] — then וְנִכְרְתָה, *he shall be cut off* ... *(Rashi).* [1]

While he is still a minor, however, he is not liable *(Gur Aryeh).*

[The translation of יִמּוֹל as a reflexive verb *'shall* (not) *be circumcised'* follows *Rashi's* comm. in *v.* 11. *Targum* and *Ibn Ezra* translate it as an imperfect *kal: 'who will (not) circumcise.'*]

וְנִכְרְתָה הַנֶּפֶשׁ הַהִוא מֵעַמֶּיהָ — *Such a soul* [lit. *'that soul'*] *shall be cut off from its people.*

[Only *that soul,* i.e., the uncircumcised person shall be cut off] however, the *father,* by not having his son circumcised,does not incur the penalty of being 'cut off' although he has transgressed a positive commandment ... *(Rashi).*

The punishment of כָּרֵת, *excision* — being *cut off from his people* — involves dying a childless and untimely death *(Shabbos* 104a; *Rashi).*

Someone who has children is considered alive for his name is not cut off *(Ibn Ezra).* Thus, by this excision he will be completely cut off through 'the extinction of his descendants' *(Ralbag).* [See *comm.* to *Lev.* 20:4-5].

Gur Aryeh explains how the term *'shall be cut off'* implies that he will be childless. Young children are like branches growing from nourishment provided by the roots. If the roots are severed, the branches perforce die. Therefore, the excision of the parent makes impossible the survival of children dependent on the parent-root. [Grown children, however, are not included.]

However, the punishment is not only in This World. It extends into the Hereafter as well:

The severest retribution beyond which punishment cannot go, is that the soul should be cut off and not attain the life hereafter ... It is to this destruction that the prophets metaphorically apply such terms as בְּאֵר שַׁחַת, *Pit of Destruction,* [*Ps.* 55:24],etc. ... and all other expressions connoting cessation are applied to it because it is an irrevocable loss for which repentance is not possible *(Rambam, Hil. Teshuvah* 8:5).

In addition to the spiritual oblivion in the Hereafter, the *Talmud* [*Moed Katan* 28a] comments that one liable to כָּרֵת, *excision,* will die between the ages of the fifty and sixty [see version in *Semachos* 3:8 and *Tosafos* s.v. מֵת]. Rav Yosef, upon reaching the age of sixty, proclaimed a festive day for the Sages saying: 'I have just passed beyond [the limit of] excision.'

In the literal sense, the phrase indicates that the transgressor will no longer be associated with his nation and will be ostracized from the mainstream of his people inasmuch as he violated their beliefs by his

1. That twenty is the minimum age that one is liable for divine punishment is clearly stated by *Rambam* in his *comm.* to *Mishnah Sanhedrin* Ch. 7 s.v. הַבָּא:

All that we have elucidated [concerning the punishment of excision] applies even if the Rabbinical Court did not know of the sin and did not punish for it in a case where the testimony was not clarified — nevertheless, their sins are inscribed with the Creator, blessed be He. He shall punish the perpetrator of evil according to his evil as it seems fit according to His wisdom. But by Tradition we learned that the Holy One, blessed be He will not punish one

*shall be cut off from its people; he has invalidated
My covenant.'*
15 *And God said to Abraham, 'As for Sarai your*

transgression of this law, and does not bear their seal of servitude to God. This is the literal meaning of *'this soul shall be cut off'* whenever it appears in Scripture. Conversely, וַיֵּאָסֶף אֶל עַמָּיו, *and he was gathered unto his people* [49:33] is the expression used for the righteous *(B'chor Shor; Minchah Belulah).*

אֶת בְּרִיתִי הֵפַר — *He has invalidated My covenant.*

I.e., he has not *destroyed* the covenant, for it is not within the power of any person to do so. What he *has* done is to render the covenant 'ineffective' in the sense that it no longer assures him the eternal blessings of Abraham *(Hirsch).*

[Historically, the *Talmud (Yevamos* 72a) applies this to those who surgically stretched their membrum to pose as non-Jews by disguising their circumcision. There is a controversy among the Sages whether such a person — known as a מָשׁוּךְ [lit. *'one who is drawn'*] must be recircumcised. Those who rule that he must be recircumcised cite the compound phrase הִמּוֹל יִמּוֹל (see *footnote* to *v.* 11) as well as this verse. There are those who oppose recircumcision on the ground that it is a mortal danger to life. The Sages retorted that many such people did undergo recircumcison and were not endangered. Halachically, Rabbinic ordinance requires such a person to recircumcise himself.]

15. The Promise to Sarah

Previously the covenant was solely with Abraham ... Now Sarah is called upon as an equally essential factor in this convenant-promise. And just as Abraham's significance was to be perpetuated by a change of name, so was Sarai's importance to be perpetuated by changing her name *(Hirsch).*

וַיֹּאמֶר אֱלֹהִים אֶל־אַבְרָהָם — *And God said to Abraham* — [either in continuation of the prophetic vision begun in *v.* 1, or in a new communication.]

Abarbanel notes that throughout the prophecies up to this chapter, God manifested Himself in His Four Letter Name *HASHEM,* signifying the Attribute of Mercy by which He graciously promised the Land, safety, future progeny, and so forth. In this chapter, however, concerning circumcision and the childbearing of Sarah, He reveals Himself exclusively as *Elohim,* signifying the Attribute of Justice, He would fulfill His promises and obligations within the terms of His covenant. It also reflected true Justice that the righteous and deserving Sarah be 'remembered' by God and granted a child.

who is liable to excision except after twenty years of age, and there is no difference in this regard between male and female.

See also *Shabbos* 89b where it is accepted as axiomatic that ''twenty years of man's life is unpunishable''; and *Rashi* to [*Chaye Sarah*] 23:1; until the age of twenty one has not yet reached the age when one is subject to punishment. See also *Yoreh Deah* 376, *Pischei Teshuvah* sub. Ch. 3. [Cf. *Gur Aryeh* in footnote to 17:26 that in the Patriarchs' times, heavenly punishment was not inflicted until a sinner had become a hundred years old.]

אֶל־אַבְרָהָם שָׂרַי אִשְׁתְּךָ לֹא־תִקְרָא אֶת־
טז שְׁמָהּ שָׂרָי כִּי שָׂרָה שְׁמָהּ: וּבֵרַכְתִּי אֹתָהּ
וְגַם נָתַתִּי מִמֶּנָּה לְךָ בֵּן וּבֵרַכְתִּיהָ וְהָיְתָה
יז לְגוֹיִם מַלְכֵי עַמִּים מִמֶּנָּה יִהְיוּ: וַיִּפֹּל
אַבְרָהָם עַל־פָּנָיו וַיִּצְחָק וַיֹּאמֶר בְּלִבּוֹ

לֹא תִקְרָא אֶת שְׁמָהּ שָׂרָי כִּי שָׂרָה שְׁמָהּ — *Do not call her* [*by*] *the name Sarai, for Sarah is her name.*

[The new name signified her new universal status]: שָׂרָי, *Sarai* [with the pronominal suffix י, *yod*] designates *my princess* [= שָׂרָתִי]; שָׂרָה, *Sarah* without the limiting suffix, signifies 'princess to all the nations of the world'. Prior to the Covenant, Sarai's personal majesty made her the *princess* of Abraham and of his people Aram. Now, however, no limitations were placed on her. She was *princess* to all mankind *(Berachos* 13a; *Rashi).*

Malbim notes that *Iscah* [the name that alluded to her prophetic spirit] was her primary name [see end of *footnote* to 11:29; p. 350.] Sarai — [the name associated with her Abrahamitic mission and used from the time of her marriage] was given her by Abraham: שָׂרָתִי שֶׁלִּי, [*my princess.*] Abraham was now commanded that in his new status of אַב הֲמוֹן גּוֹיִם, *father of a multitude of nations,* his wife, too, was to take on a more universal status which would be reflected by the name שָׂרָה, *princess par excellence,* and not just *princess of Abraham.*[1]

16. וּבֵרַכְתִּי אֹתָהּ — *And I will bless her* —

With the blessing that will most appropriately precipitate her imminent childbearing *(Mizrachi):* I will restore her youthfulness. See *comm.* to 18:12 *(Midrash; Rashi).*

Resh Lakish said: She lacked ovaries [see *comm.* to 11:30], but God fashioned them for her and thus gave her the ability to conceive *(Midrash).*

The accent under the last syllable [the cantillation in the text appears under the ת] indicates future tense, the ו being *conversive*]; had the accent been under the ר, it would have indicated past tense, [and would have been *conjunctive*] ... *(Sechel Tov).*

[As reflected in the translation, this grammatical rule is evident in all the verbs throughout this verse: וּבֵרַכְתִּי, נָתַתִּי, וּבֵרַכְתִּיהָ, וְהָיְתָה, all of which are therefore rendered in the future tense.]

וְגַם נָתַתִּי מִמֶּנָּה לְךָ בֵּן — *Indeed,* [lit.

1. Rav Huna said, quoting Rav Acha:

The letter, *'yod',* which was removed from Sarai's name, has a numerical value of ten. It was divided into two letters [ה, *he,* has the numerical value of 5] one of which was added to Abram and the other to Sarai.

Rav Hoshiyah taught: The *yod* ascended to heaven and cast itself down before God crying out: "Master of the Universe! You have wrested me out of the [name of the] righteous woman!"

God comforted the *Yod.* 'Go forth. Up to now you were the last letter of a name; I will place you at the beginning of a name' ... So it is written [*Num.* 13:16]: *And Moses called* הוֹשֵׁעַ, *Hoshea the son of Nun* יְהוֹשֻׁעַ, *Joshua* [thus the change was effected by adding a י, *yod* to the beginning of Joshua's name *(Yerushalmi Sanhedrin* 2:6). [See *comm.* to יִצְחָק in *v.* 19].

wife — do not call her by the name Sarai, for Sarah is
her name. 16 *I will bless her; indeed, I will give you a*
son through her. I will bless her and she shall give
rise to nations; kings of peoples will rise from her."
17 *And Abraham threw himself upon his face and*
laughed; and he thought, Shall a child be born to a

and also] *I will give you* [lit. *have given you*] *a son through her.*

From this verse, the Sages [*Rosh Hashanah* 16b] inferred that a change of name brings about a change of man's fate. For after Sarai's name was changed she was blessed with a child *(Ralbag)*.

[Cf. *comm.* to 15:5: 'Give up your astrological speculations: Abram will not have a son but *Abraham* will have a son; Sarai will not bear a child but *Sarah* will.']

[It must also be noted that this is significantly the very first time God pronounces the word *'son'* directly to Abraham.]

Scripture's use of the past tense where the future is obviously meant, is known as the 'prophetic past.' This tense was used in most of God's promises to Abraham to indicate the absolute certainty of the fulfillment of the divine decree as if it had already come to pass. The specific connotation here is: 'I have already decreed that you be given a son through her, and My decrees are like accomplished facts' *(Ibn Ezra; Sechel Tov)*. [See *Sechel Tov* above.]

וּבֵרַכְתִּיהָ — [*And*] *I will bless her.*

By enabling her to nurse her own child [see *comm.* to 21:7.] *(Rashi)*.

— With abundant progeny who will stem from her *(Radak)*.

— She will bear and bring up the child without suffering *(Sforno)*.

וְהָיְתָה לְגוֹיִם — *And she shall give rise* [lit. *and she shall become*] *to nations.*

— To Jacob and Esau *(Midrash Aggadah)*.

מַלְכֵי עַמִּים מִמֶּנָּה יִהְיוּ — *Kings of peoples will rise* [lit. *'will be'*] *from her.*

— The descendants of Jacob and Esau *(Midrash Aggadah)*.

[Perhaps the inference here is that the parallel promises to Abraham in *v.* 6 — *'I will make nations of you', 'and kings shall descend from you'* — will be realized through Sarah.]

17. וַיִּפֹּל אַבְרָהָם עַל פָּנָיו — *And Abraham threw himself upon his face.*

In gratitude for the good tidings concerning Sarah *(Radak)*;

— To concentrate on the prophecy, and to pray concerning Ishmael *(Ramban* to *v.* 3).

Or, as *Rashi* interprets in *v.* 3: He *fell* in reverence of the *Shechinah*. [See *comm.* there.]

וַיִּצְחָק — *And laughed.*

Jubilantly; as *Onkelos* renders וַחֲדִי, *and he rejoiced*. In the case of Sarah, however, [see 18:12] *Onkelos* rendered the same verb וַתִּצְחַק as וְחַיְכַת, *she laughed* [with derision]. Abraham had faith and *rejoiced* while Sarah *sneered;* hence God was angry with Sarah but not with Abraham *(Rashi)*.

But even in his joy and faith Abraham was amazed *(Malbim)*:

וַיֹּאמֶר בְּלִבּוֹ — *And he thought* [lit. *'and he said in his heart'*].

הַלְּבֶן מֵאָה־שָׁנָה יִוָּלֵד וְאִם־שָׂרָה הֲבַת־
יח תִּשְׁעִים שָׁנָה תֵּלֵד: וַיֹּאמֶר אַבְרָהָם אֶל־
הָאֱלֹהִים לוּ יִשְׁמָעֵאל יִחְיֶה לְפָנֶיךָ:

הַלְּבֶן מֵאָה־שָׁנָה יִוָּלֵד — *Shall a child be born to a hundred year old man?*

[It is obvious that the question does not imply that Abraham *doubted* the power of Almighty God to give him a child of his own even at this advanced aged. Rather it is a naturally jubilant outburst at the prospect of fulfillment of his life's hope: 'Could it really be true that this is finally happening to me? I am overjoyed! (cf. such questions in *I Sam.* 2:2 and *Ezekiel* 8:6 for further example of questions which imply not doubt, but incredulous joy at the certainty embodied in God's word).]

Here, too, Abraham reacts by affirming to himself his joy of God's wonderful pronouncement by reflecting: could anyone [not expressly promised this by God] ever expect to beget a child at the age of a hundred? [Of course not! I am therefore gratefully overjoyed at this news] *(Rashi).*

וְאִם שָׂרָה הֲבַת תִּשְׁעִים שָׁנָה תֵּלֵד — *And Sarah — shall a ninety year old woman give birth?*

This, indeed is a wonder of God! *(Ralbag).*

Although previous generations commonly would beget at the age of five hundred, yet by Abraham's time lifespans were greatly reduced and physical strength waned. Cf., for example, that the generations between Noah and Abraham begot children at the average ages of sixty to seventy *(Rashi).*

Ramban explains that there was nothing extraordinary in a hundred-year-old person fathering children, for a man can beget as long as he remains virile, and Abraham begot children forty years later from Keturah. [Thus *Ramban* apparently disagrees with *Rashi*'s interpretation that Abraham's remark involved *his own* virility.] Rather the implication of this statement is: Since he did not beget a child from Sarah when they were younger, he was astonished that he would do so now when he was a hundred years old and she ninety, especially since he knew that she was incapable of bearing. Therefore Abraham did not express wonderment when he was told [in *v.* 6] that nations would descend from him, but only when he was told that these descendants would be begotten by Sarah.

Ramban concludes that it is certain that Abraham's remark was motivated by faith and joy. [It was, as *Rashi* explains above, a rhetorical affirmation expressed in wonderment.] The proof of this is that God commanded him to name his son *Yitzchak* [Isaac; see *v.* 19], a name commemorating his laughter, for had it been said in derision, God would not have told him to give his son a name denoting a lack of faith *(R' Bachya).*

According to *Malbim* there is a double statement here: אִם שָׂרָה, *will Sarah* — knowing that she is barren — *bear?*; and, even were she not barren, can *a ninety year old woman bear?*

XVII
18-19

hundred year old man? And Sarah — shall a ninety year old woman give birth?' [18] *And Abraham said to God, 'O that Ishmael might live before you!'* [19] *God*

18. [Abraham was overwhelmed at the abundant reward just promised him, and he replied]:

לוּ יִשְׁמָעֵאל יִחְיֶה לְפָנֶיךָ — *O* [lit. *if only* i.e. it would suffice *(Ramban)*] *that Ishmael might live before you!*

I am unworthy [not undesirous *(Sifsei Chachamim)*] of so great a reward as to have a son now; it will suffice me if only Ishmael lived righteously before You! [לְפָנֶיךָ, *before You,* being understood as בְּיִרְאָתֶךָ, *in Your reverence*] *(Rashi).*[1]

Cf. the *Midrash:* Imagine a king who wished to increase his friend's allowance. 'I intend to double your allowance', the king informed him. 'Do not fill me with hope,' he rejoined. 'I will be quite satisfied if you would only not withhold my present stipend.' Similarly, Abraham prayed, *'O, that Ishmael might live before you'* [and I shall not hope for another son.]

According to *Ramban,* since Ishmael was born first Abraham thought that *he* would be the heir promised him [see 15:4 where the promise of progeny occurs, to be followed by the birth of Ishmael]. Now that he was told that Sarah would bear him a son he understood that her son would be the heir, and he feared that it might imply Ishmael's death.

Rashi goes on to explain that the phrase יִחְיֶה לְפָנֶיךָ, *live before You* is to be interpreted: 'live in *reverence of You'* the emphasis being on לְפָנֶיךָ as *Onkelos* renders in *v.* 1: הִתְהַלֵּךְ לְפָנַי [lit. *walk before Me*] *serve before Me.* [*Rashi*'s interpretation of our verse is thus: I will be satisfied if Ishmael lives and grows up to be God-fearing.]

Ramban disagrees with this interpretation because God responded to Abraham's prayer by saying *And as for Ishmael, I have heard you* (*v.* 20). [And if the intent of Abraham's prayer was that Ishmael live in reverence of God, how could God assure him of that, since as the Sages have stated *(Berachos* 33b): 'Everything is in the hands of Heaven except the fear of Heaven'? *(Abohab).*] Rather the sense of Abraham's prayer was: *May he live and his seed exist eternally.*

Mizrachi defends *Rashi*'s interpretation by explaining that Abraham made two petitions here: that he live; and that he be God-fearing If, however, his prayer was for life alone,

1. When the time arrives for Israel's consolation, God will dispatch the Patriarchs to offer comfort. Abraham will say, 'Arise and accept the cup of consolation from God, for the time of your consolation is at hand!' But Israel will refuse, saying: 'We cannot accept consolation from you, for you forsook us and instead prayed for Ishmael saying: *"O that Ishmael might live before You"* ' *(Midrash HaGadol Vayechi).*

It is written [*Isaiah* 63:16] *Abraham knew us not.* Although the world's very existence depended on him he did not implore You on our behalf as he did for Ishmael when he prayed *'O that Ishmael might live before You.'* (*Zohar* 1:205) [See *Torah Shelemah* 17:136 and note.]

Thus the *Zohar* [2:32a] records that Rav Chiyyah wept at the circumstances that led Abraham to marry Hagar and beget a son to whom he became so attached that, though God assured him that he would have a son through Sarah, Abraham prayed that Ishmael might live before Him. Subsequently Ishmael was circumcised even before Isaac was born. In reward for that circumcision — yet to insure that he would not encroach upon Isaac's peculiar rights — God endowed Ishmael with a portion below in the Holy Land, but thrust him out of the heavenly communion.

יט וַיֹּאמֶר אֱלֹהִים אֲבָל֙ שָׂרָה אִשְׁתְּךָ יֹלֶדֶת
לְךָ֙ בֵּן וְקָרָאתָ אֶת־שְׁמוֹ יִצְחָק וַהֲקִמֹתִי
אֶת־בְּרִיתִי אִתּוֹ לִבְרִית עוֹלָם לְזַרְעוֹ
כ אַחֲרָיו: וּלְיִשְׁמָעֵאל שְׁמַעְתִּיךָ הִנֵּה ׀
בֵּרַכְתִּי אֹתוֹ וְהִפְרֵיתִי אֹתוֹ וְהִרְבֵּיתִי
אֹתוֹ בִּמְאֹד מְאֹד שְׁנֵים־עָשָׂר נְשִׂיאִם

what need was there for the word לְפָנֶיךָ, *before You?* Because Sarah had just been promised a son, God assured Abraham that Ishmael would live. But Abraham's second petition was not relevant to the promise just made regarding the birth and future survival of Isaac; therefore God did not respond at all. Or, the failure to respond may have been because God knew that Ishmael would go in the evil path [and this God did not wish to disclose to Abraham to avoid causing him anguish.] [According to *Ramban's* interpretation, the word לְפָנֶיךָ, *before You,* remains unexplained.]

[But cf. *Ralbag* who explains that לְפָנֶיךָ, *before You* has the connotation of: *along with You* — the inference in our verse being: May Ishmael's descendants endure by Your support even though they are unworthy until they are at one with You in righteous existence. Or, as others explain: *Before You,* i.e., under your care and protection.]

Hirsch comments that Abraham was shocked and dismayed by the implied unworthiness of Ishmael. If it were necessary to profoundly upset natural law to provide a son worthy of the Abrahamitic mission, then how unsuitable Ishmael must be in God's eyes! Abaham exclaimed, therefore, 'Might not Ishmael be at least partially worthy of *walking before You!'*

19. God reaffirms the promise:

אֲבָל שָׂרָה אִשְׁתְּךָ יֹלֶדֶת לְךָ בֵּן — *Nonetheless, your wife Sarah will bear you a son.*

Allay your apprehension: You are under the impression that *Ishmael* is your primary progeny and that therefore you have no need of a son from Sarah. Not so! Only *Sarah* will bear you the son through whose seed I will ratify My covenant forever *(Ramban; Abarbanel).*

The translation of the word אֲבָל [usually rendered *'but'*] as *'nonetheless'* follows *Targum, Ibn Janach, Rashi,* and *Ibn Ezra* who interpret the word as implying a confirmation of a previously made statement: *Indeed, nevertheless, verily, in truth,* as in 42:21: *Indeed* [אֲבָל] *we are guilty.* — The context bears this out *(Menachem).*

Ramban interprets the word as connoting a limitation: *Only* Sarah will bear the son of whom I informed you [i.e., therefore do not place your hopes on Ishmael; our covenant will be carried forth not through him but through Isaac.]

Hirsch perceives the same overall connotation as the above, but he interprets the word as negating Abraham's trend of thought: *'Not so!'* The stress Abraham placed on Ishmael's future role would not be realized; it was Isaac with whom God would fulfill His covenant for posterity.

Or HaChaim translates *'but'* and interprets it as a response to Abraham's plea for Ishmael. God told Abraham that it was well and good for him to pray that Ishmael would be worthy, but what of Sarah's lifelong prayers that she give birth to Abraham's son? He had no right to frustrate her hopes by looking to Ishmael as his succesor.

וְקָרָאתָ אֶת שְׁמוֹ יִצְחָק — *And you shall name him* [lit. *'call his name'*] *Isaac.*

The name Isaac [יִצְחָק, lit. *'he will laugh'*] refers to [Abraham's] צחוק laughter [of *v.* 17] *(Rashi).*

[See 18:12,13; 21:3,6,9]

His name accordingly should have ben צְחוֹק. Since the name is יִצְחָק, the *Midrash* accounts for the י, *yod,* by ascribing a significance to

XVII *said, 'Nonetheless, your wife Sarah will bear you a*
20 *son and you shall name him Isaac; and I will fulfill*
My covenant with him as an everlasting covenant for
his offspring after him. 20 *But regarding Ishmael I*
have heard you: I have blessed him, made him fruit-
ful and will increase him most exceedingly; he will
beget twelve princes and I will make him into a great

the numerical value of each letter of the name: י, *yod,* [= 10] alludes to the ten Trials Abraham endured [see on 12:1]; צ, *tzadi* [= 90] to the age of Sarah at his birth; ח, *ches,* [= 8] to the eighth day, on which he was circumcised; and ק, *kof,* [= 100] to Abraham's age at his birth (*Rashi* as explained by *Gur Aryeh*).

[Perhaps, additionally, the י, *yod,* which 'complained' when it was removed from שָׂרַי, *Sarai* (see footnote end of *v.* 15) was here placated by being used to introduce her son's name (*Rabbi Avie Gold*).

וַהֲקִמֹתִי אֶת בְּרִיתִי אִתּוֹ — *And I will fulfill My covenant with him* — i.e., the covenant of circumcision. From the general promise made in *v.* 7, it might be interpreted to embrace the descendants of Ishmael and Keturah as well. God specifically declared, therefore, that the covenant will be perpetuated *only* through the descendants of Isaac, and no other [see also on *v.* 21] (*Rashi*).

According to *Sechel Tov* the Covenant refers to the Covenant Between the Parts [15:7 ff.] which will be fulfilled through him.

20. וּלְיִשְׁמָעֵאל שְׁמַעְתִּיךָ — But *regarding* [lit. *'and to'*] *Ishmael, I have heard you* [following *Ibn Ezra*].

I.e., although the covenant will be perpetuated by Isaac, nevertheless, since you prayed on behalf of Ishmael, I hereby accept your plea and he, too, will be successful (*Ramban; R' Meyuchas*).

בֵּרַכְתִּי אֹתוֹ — *I have blessed him.*

[This past tense might imply the 'prophetic past' (see *v.* 16) and hence be interpreted in the future, *I will bless him, make him fruitful* etc. indicating the absolute certainty of fulfillment. However, it is possible that the past tense refers to the similar blessings concerning Ishmael that God had already given, through His angel, to Hagar in the desert in 16:10-12.]

שְׁנֵים עָשָׂר נְשִׂיאִם יוֹלִיד — *He will beget twelve princes* [as enumerated in 25:13-16.]

Rashi [based on the *Midrash*] notes that the Torah used the word נְשִׂיאִים, *princes,* here rather than the terms it uses concerning Jacob's sons, שְׁבָטִים, or מַטּוֹת, *tribes* — both of which indicate enduring strength — or rather than other commonly used terms such as שָׂרִים, *officials* רָאשִׁים, *heads,* or אַלּוּפִים *rulers*.He explains that the term נְשִׂיאִים used here alludes to the fact that *their glory would be transient:* 'They will dissipate like clouds,' for the word נְשִׂיאִים has the secondary meaning of 'clouds' as in *Prov.* 25:14: נְשִׂיאִים וְרוּחַ, *clouds and wind* (*Gur Aryeh; Maharzu*).

כא יוֹלִיד וּנְתַתִּיו לְגוֹי גָּדוֹל: וְאֶת־בְּרִיתִי
אָקִים אֶת־יִצְחָק אֲשֶׁר תֵּלֵד לְךָ שָׂרָה
כב לַמּוֹעֵד הַזֶּה בַּשָּׁנָה הָאַחֶרֶת: וַיְכַל לְדַבֵּר
כג אִתּוֹ וַיַּעַל אֱלֹהִים מֵעַל אַבְרָהָם: וַיִּקַּח

[See also *Targum Yonason* to *Exodus* 35:27 where נְשִׂאִם is rendered עֲנָנֵי שְׁמַיָּא, *clouds of the heavens.*]

Additionally *Rashi's* interpretation is based on the fact that, if taken literally, Ishmael's blessing would be as great as Isaac's. Therefore *Rashi* interprets it as connoting *dissipating clouds* to indicate that though the groups descending from Ishmael may appear mighty, they will ultimately vanish like clouds *(Be'er Mayim Chayim).*

וּנְתַתִּיו לְגוֹי גָּדוֹל — *And I will make him into a great nation.*

R' Bachya cites R' Chananel's comment on this verse: We see that from this prophecy [in the year 2047 from Creation, when Abraham was ninety-nine], 2,337 years elapsed before the Arabs, Ishmael's descendants, became a great nation. [This would correspond to 624 C.E., two years after the Hegira. However, cf. *Chavel's comm.* to *R' Bachya.*] ... Throughout this period, Ishmael waited anxiously, hoping, until finally the promise was fulfilled and they dominated the world. Surely, we, the descendants of Isaac, for whom fulfillment of the promises made to us is delayed due to our sins ... should certainly anticipate the fulfillment of His promises and not despair.

21. וְאֶת בְּרִיתִי אָקִים אֶת יִצְחָק — *But* [lit. *'and'*] *I will maintain My covenant through* [lit. *'with'*] *Isaac.*

Rashi [on *v.* 19] explains that this seeming redundancy [for *v.* 19 gives essentially the same promise] includes the phrase, אֲשֶׁר תֵּלֵד לְךָ שָׂרָה, *whom Sarah will bear to you* in order to stress that Isaac was holy [and ordained for transmitting the Covenant] when still in the womb. [See *Rashi* to *Shabbos* 137b s.v. מִבֶּטֶן; cf. *Tosafos.* See also *Da'as Zekeinim* who notes that the word אָקִים is an abbreviation of the phrase which opens the benediction following the circumcision: אֲשֶׁר קִדֵּשׁ יְדִיד מִבֶּטֶן, *Who sanctified the beloved one from the womb.*]

Another explanation offered by *Rashi* for the repetition is based on the *Midrash:* Rav Abba said: The Torah draws a conclusion קַל וָחוֹמֶר, *a minori* which [Isaac] the son of the wife, could draw from [Ishmael] the son of the handmaid. If God blessed Ishmael so in *v.* 20, surely it follows logically that He will bless Isaac so much more by maintaining His covenant through him!

[The flow of *vss.* 19-21 according to *Rashi*'s latter interpretation is: Isaac's offspring will bear My covenant, but since you prayed on behalf of Ishmael I will make him great. Nevertheless the blessing I will heap on Isaac will surely be much greater for through him will My covenant be maintained through the ages.]

As *Hirsch* comments: Ishmael's very name [see on 16:10-12] bears the guarantee for the fulfillment of

XVII
21-22

nation. 21 *But I will maintain my covenant through*
Isaac whom Sarah will bear by this time next year."
22 *And when He had finished speaking with him,*
God ascended from upon Abraham.

My promises to him. But the covenant — the promise for the elevation of all mankind — will be fulfilled only through the descendants of Isaac who was born from Sarah.

Great is circumcision, says Rabbi Yishmael, for thirteen covenants were made over it; that is how many times the word בְּרִית, covenant, occurs in this chapter *(Mishnah, Nedarim* 31b; *Yerushalmi Ned.* 3:9).

לַמּוֹעֵד הַזֶּה בַּשָּׁנָה הָאַחֶרֶת — *By this time* [or *'season'*] *next* [lit. *'in the other'*] *year. (Rav Saadia Gaon).*]

Abraham was given a definite time-frame during which the birth would occur, thus assuring him that the fulfillment of God's promise was at hand *(Radak; Ibn Caspi).*

[Cf. similar use of אַחֵר meaning *next, subsequent,* in *Ps.* 109:13.]

22. וַיְכַל לְדַבֵּר אִתּוֹ — *And when He had finished speaking with him.*

The expression אִתּוֹ, *with him* indicates a *dialogue* in contrast to אֵלָיו, *to him,* which implies that one spoke and the other listened. Whenever God makes a statement or gives a command that does not require clarification, אֵלָיו, *to him,* is used, because it is the function of the prophet merely to listen and nothing more. Our verse, however, says אִתּוֹ, *with him,* as the Torah says whenever explanation, clarification, and questioning is required. This is in the nature of the Oral Law, where the prophet must ask questions thus engaging in a dialogue until the intricacies of the law are clear to him *(Ha'amek Davar).*

Ibn Ezra attaches this verse to the next one, as if to say: As soon as God departed from him, Abraham immediately set out to fulfill his obligation. Thus, the narative is concluded by *v.* 23.[1]

[The Traditional insertion of the *Maftir* pause after *v.* 23 tends to support *Ibn Ezra*'s view of reading *vss.* 22 and 23 as a continuation of the narrative with *v.* 24 beginning a summary. Had the ascension of the *Shechinah* been considered as a pause in the narrative and Abraham's compliance in *v.* 23 perceived as a new thought, then the *Maftir* pause would have been inserted after *v.* 22 instead.]

וַיַּעַל אֱלֹהִים מֵעַל אַבְרָהָם — [*And*] *God ascended from upon Abraham* — i.e., He returned on High.

The phrase depicts the *Shechinah* as ascending מֵעַל אַבְרָהָם, from *upon* Abraham, indicating that the *Shechinah* had been above him. [Since the *Shechinah* had been speaking to Abraham, we would have expected Its departure to be described as מֵאֵת אַבְרָהָם from *with* (or *besides*) Abraham.] *Midrashically,* this depiction of God as being

1. The *Midrash* notes when the Holy One Blessed be He commanded Abraham to circumcise himself he went and took counsel with his three friends, Aner, Eshkol, and Mamre [either to test their beliefs so he could ascertain whether to continue his friendship with them *(Chizkuni);* or because he was uncertain how to go about fulfilling God's command — whether to sanctify God's Name by doing it publicly during the day, or possibly to circumcise

אַבְרָהָם אֶת־יִשְׁמָעֵאל בְּנוֹ וְאֵת כָּל־יְלִידֵי
בֵיתוֹ וְאֵת כָּל־מִקְנַת כַּסְפּוֹ כָּל־זָכָר
בְּאַנְשֵׁי בֵּית אַבְרָהָם וַיָּמָל אֶת־בְּשַׂר
עָרְלָתָם בְּעֶצֶם הַיּוֹם הַזֶּה כַּאֲשֶׁר דִּבֶּר
כד אִתּוֹ אֱלֹהִים: וְאַבְרָהָם בֶּן־תִּשְׁעִים וָתֵשַׁע
כה שָׁנָה בְּהִמֹּלוֹ בְּשַׂר עָרְלָתוֹ: וְיִשְׁמָעֵאל

upon Abraham [implying, as it were, that God *rode* upon him] indicates that the righteous [or as *Ramban* cites from the same *Midrash*: the Patriarchs] are the מֶרְכָּבָה, *chariot,* of the omnipresent, i.e., His vehicle, the direct bearers of His Glory on earth *(Rashi,* as explained by *Mizrachi; Gur Aryeh* and *Isserlein.* See *Overview: The Patriarchs).*

23. Abraham complies with the covenant. [See *Ibn Ezra* to *v.* 22.]

וַיִּקַּח אַבְרָהָם — *Then* [lit. *'and'*] *Abraham took* — [in the sense of 'drew along with persuasive words' — explaining to them the great significance of the mitzvah they were about to perform (see *Bamidbar Rabbah* 18:2; *Rashi* to 2:15 וַיִּקַּח אֶת הָאָדָם: and *comm.* to 12:5 וַיִּקַּח אַבְרָם אֶת שָׂרַי אִשְׁתּוֹ).]

אֶת־יִשְׁמָעֵאל בְּנוֹ — *His son Ishmael.*

Ishmael is here identified as Abraham's *son* [though the fact is quite familiar] for although thirteen years old at that time and in a position to refuse, Ishmael acted like a true son of Abraham and eagerly consented to being the first to submit to circumcision *(Alshich).*

Abraham did not circumcise himself first for fear that, at his advanced age, he would have then been to weakened to circumcise the others. Therefore he first concerned himself with the circumcision of his son and every last member of his household; then he circumcised himself *(Ramban).*

[But cf. *Or HaChaim,* further and footnote to *v.* 13.]

He circumcised Ishmael, his only child, first, so he would serve as a model for the others to emulate. Then he circumcised all יְלִידֵי בֵיתוֹ, *those servants born in his household* [i.e., the minors *(Midrash)*] who were most dependent upon him, and would lovingly comply first with their master's wish; then he circumcised those *servants whom he had purchased for*

himself secretly, at night to avoid becoming a spectacle to scoffers, and to avoid possible assault by his enemies *(Midrash; Mizrachi).*]

Aner tried to dissuade Abraham entirely: 'You are a man of a hundred years and you would inflict such pain upon yourself?'

Eshkol also was discouraging: 'Why should you go and thereby make yourself distinguishable [מְסֻמָּן = מְסַיְּים] to your enemies?'

Only Mamre — whose name indicates that he *himrah* [rebuked; showed a stern countenance] to Abraham — was vigorously encouraging and showed the firmest faith:

'Was there ever a circumstance when God did not firmly stand by you — in the fiery furnace, in famine, in the war with the kings? Will you not obey him then in this matter!

It was in reward for his good advice that God said He would appear *to Abraham only in the fields of Mamre* as written in 18:1.

23 *Then Abraham took his son Ishmael and all
those servants born in his household and all those he
had purchased for money — all the male members of
Abraham's house — and he circumcised the flesh of
their surplusage on that very day as God had spoken
with him.* 24 *Abraham was ninety-nine when he was
circumcised on the flesh of his surplusage;* 25 *And his*

money, [i.e., the adults *(Midrash)*] and finally *all* the members of his household, leaving not a single one uncircumcised *(Abarbanel).*

וַיָּמָל ... בְּעֶצֶם הַיּוֹם הַזֶּה — *And he circumcised...on that very day* [i.e.' in the *strength* of that day — at midday, in broad daylight, noontime *(Ibn Janach;* see 7:13).]

On the very day that he received the command; by day and not by night being afraid neither of the heathens nor the cynics. For, as the *Midrash* explains, he performed this in broad daylight so that his enemies should not be able to boast: Had we seen him we would have prevented him from circumcising and fulfilling God's command *(Rashi)* *

Therefore, he circumcised himself *that very day,* in broad daylight with the challenge: 'Let him who objects, speak!' *(Midrash).*

[Cf. similar *comm.* to Noah's entering the Ark in broad daylight, in 7:13, and see footnote to *v.* 26.]

*[However, according to the *Midrash* cited in footnote to *v.* 22, which *Rashi* himself cites in 18:1, Abraham first consulted with Aner, Eshkol, and Mamre before actually undergoing the ritual. Apparently, however, this all transpired *immediately* after the command.]

כַּאֲשֶׁר דִּבֶּר אִתּוֹ אֱלֹהִים — *As God had spoken with him.*

[I.e., adhering scrupulously to God's word in every detail.]

Or HaChaim comments that implied in this statement that he complied with God's command are his persuasive manner with his household in order that they submit willingly, and his immediate compliance without delay. In addition, *Or HaChaim* comments, that although not specifically mentioned in the Torah, Abraham circumcised himself *first* in accordance with the *halachah* that only a circumcised Jew may act as a *mohel,* and in order to set an example for others. [See summary in *v.* 26 where Abraham is mentioned first.]

[Cf. *Ramban* above, however, who maintains that Abraham first circumcised the others and then himself.]

24-27. The Torah now proceeds, in its usual custom, to recapitulate the substance of the previous verses, but in more detail and with additional emphasis:

24. בְּהִמֹּלוֹ בְּשַׂר עָרְלָתוֹ — *When he was circumcised on the flesh of his surplusage.*

The translation follows *Rashi* who explains that בְּהִמֹּלוֹ is a *niphal* [passive] form as 2:4 בְּהִבָּרְאָם, *when they were created.*

Some old mss. of *Rashi* cite here the *Midrash* [already quoted in the *comm.* to *v.* 10] that God Himself, as it were, held the knife with Abraham. "Therefore," the *Mid-*

בְּנוֹ בֶּן־שְׁלֹשׁ עֶשְׂרֵה שָׁנָה בְּהִמֹּלוֹ אֵת
כו בְּשַׂר עָרְלָתוֹ: בְּעֶצֶם הַיּוֹם הַזֶּה נִמּוֹל
כז אַבְרָהָם וְיִשְׁמָעֵאל בְּנוֹ: וְכָל־אַנְשֵׁי בֵיתוֹ
יְלִיד בָּיִת וּמִקְנַת־כֶּסֶף מֵאֵת בֶּן־נֵכָר
נִמֹּלוּ אִתּוֹ:

rah concludes, "the verse in *Nechemiah* 9:8 reads: וְכָרוֹת עִמּוֹ הַבְּרִית 'God cut the covenant [together] *with* him'."

[Cf. *Da'as Zekeinim; Pirkei d' Rabbi Eliezer* which records a view that Abraham summoned Shem, son of Noah, himself born circumcised, who circumcised him and his son, Ishmael.]

The *Midrash* notes that only in connection with Abraham is the indefinite particle אֶת [which in *Talmudic* exegesis denotes an extension (see *comm.* to אֶת in 1:1)] absent before the words בְּשַׂר עָרְלָתוֹ, *the flesh of his surplusage,* while in reference to the others the phrase reads אֵת בְּשַׂר עָרְלָתוֹ. The absence of this extending particle in connection with Abraham indicates that because of Abraham's advanced age his flesh was flattened and the operation was somewhat easier than in the case of the younger men whose flesh was firmer and who needed both 'cutting' and פְּרִיעָה 'uncovering.'

Mizrachi notes that although Abraham is credited with having fulfilled all the Laws of the Torah before they were given [see e.g. *comm.* to 14:13 where Abraham is described as baking matzos for Passover] he did not perform the mitzvah of circumcision until he was commanded to do so. Because he foresaw that this commandment would be promulgated later in his lifetime, he therefore waited until he was specifically commanded to do so, in recognition of the dictum: 'greater is he who is *commanded* and fulfills the command, than he who fulfills it without having been previously commanded.' And by performing this after he was commanded, it became obvious to all that he was undertaking this at great risk in fulfillment of God's wishes, and not for a therapeutic or cosmetic reason; as mocking skeptics would have claimed had he undertaken it on his own initiative.

Other mitzvos, such as Eruv, were not to be given him, therefore he performed them of his own volition. Accordingly, he performed פְּרִיעָה, *uncovering,* (on Ishmael) in anticipation, [though it would be commanded only later to Joshua. See *Tosafos Yev.* 71b s.v. לא] *(Tur).* [1]

25. וְיִשְׁמָעֵאל בְּנוֹ בֶּן שְׁלֹשׁ עֶשְׂרֵה שָׁנָה — *And his son Ishmael was thirteen years old.*

The ages of Abraham and Ishmael are specified to show that Abraham, despite his age, and Ishmael, despite his youth, went with vigor to perform the will of God. One might have expected them to fear the pain, or Ishmael's mother to object, or that they would wait to see the affects of the circumcision on the other members of the

1. Why was Abraham not commanded to circumcise himself at an *early* age?

In order not to discourage older proselytes who might otherwise be reluctant about undertaking this operation at an advanced age; or who might feel it was futile to undertake the yoke of heaven in their old age. Abraham therefore was commanded at the age of one hundred so he could serve as an example to all future proselytes ...

And why, then, now [before Isaac's birth!] So that Isaac should be conceived from pure and holy seed *(Midrash).*

*son Ishmael was thirteen years old when he was cir-
cumcised on the flesh of his surplusage.* [26] *On that
very day was Abraham circumcised with Ishmael his
son,* [27] *and all the people of his household: born in
his household and purchased for money from a
stranger, were circumcised with him.*

household. In their righteousness, however, they performed the commandment on that very day *(Abarbanel).*

26. Thus:

בְּעֶצֶם הַיּוֹם הַזֶּה — *On that very day.*[1]

When Abraham and Ishmael attained the ages of nintety-nine and thirteen respectively [i.e., their birthday] *(Rashi).*

Ramban disagrees with *Rashi*'s interpretation on chronological grounds relating to the birthdays of the Partriarchs (see *Rosh Hashanah* 11b) maintaining that Abraham was not circumcised on his birthday. *Ramban* suggests instead that the verse emphasizes the eagerness with which they complied with God's command *on the very day* it was promulgated.

Mizrachi defends *Rashi*'s chronology and adds that if the Torah merely wanted to recount Abraham's eagerness in fulfilling the decree, this verse would be redundant, for that was already stated in *v.* 23.

נִמּוֹל אַבְרָהָם וְיִשְׁמָעֵאל בְּנוֹ — *Was Abraham circumcised with Ishmael, his son.*

This does not indicate the order in which they were circumcised, for as *v.* 23 clearly indicates *Ishmael* was the first. [See *comm.* and cf. *Or HaChaim* there] *(Ramban).*

27. ... וְכָל אַנְשֵׁי בֵיתוֹ — *And all his household* [lit. *'and all the men of his house.'*]

1. The same expression בְּעֶצֶם הַיּוֹם הַזֶּה, *on that very day* is used in connection with Yom Kippur [*Lev.* 23:28]. The Sages derive by analogy that Abraham performed these circumcisions on that day [the tenth of Tishrei], and every year the Holy One, Blessed be He, sees the blood of our father, Abraham's, circumcision, and forgives all the sins of Israel as it says [*Lev.* 16:30] *for on this day* בַּיּוֹם הַזֶּה [i.e., the event that marked this day] *atonement shall be made for you, to cleanse you.*

In that place [Mount Moriah] where Abraham was circumcised and where his blood remained, the altar was subsequently built. Therefore the sacrificial blood was required to be poured out at the base of the altar [*Lev.* 4:30]

Tosafos (Rosh Hashanah 11a s.v. אֶלָּא) mentions this *Midrash* that the circumcision took place on Yom Kippur. There are, however, divergent views according to which it took place on Passover. The phrase *'on that very day'* being also used in connection with the Exodus (12:41). Cf. *Midrash Sechel Tov.*

Gur Aryeh adds that the Torah stressed the ages of Abraham and Ishmael. In those times, heavenly punishment was not inflicted until a sinner had become a hundred years old. God did not want Abraham to reach that state uncircumcized. Ishmael, having become thirteen, would attain his majority and — no longer subject to Abraham's domination — would have refused to circumcize himself. Therefore, the Torah stresses that he was barely thirteen and still amenable to his father's guidance.

The reason the Torah stresses that it took place on that day was to point out Abraham's dedication to God. Having already circumcised all members of his household, Abraham would have had no one to assist him during his recuperation for all his servants would have been ailing. Nevertheless he did not delay *(Abarbanel).*

According to *Chizkuni* this verse speaks of the members of *Ishmael's* household, who were circumcised as well; the members of Abraham's household had already been mentioned in *v.* 23.

[But the above interpretation evokes the obvious question of what 'household' would Ishmael have had at the age of thirteen? Perhaps the reference is to those servants who lived with Ishmael in Hagar's home. However, most commentators infer that this verse, too, speaks of the members of Abraham's household.]

Pirkei d' Rabbi Eliezer 29 notes that we cannot trust the sincerity of a proselyte until seven generations have passed. This insincerity is evidenced by the fact that none of the slaves Abraham had circumcised, neither they nor their descendants, remained true converts to Israel.

... Furthermore, why did Abraham circumcise every member of his household [on that day? — He could have facilitated the functioning of his household by waiting until some members were fully healed before circumcising the others.] — He wanted to immediately rid his house of impurity for 'whoever eats with an uncircumcised person is as though he were eating with a dog' [var. reading: as though he were eating the flesh of abomination.] (See *Torah Shelemah* 170-171).

נִמֹּלוּ אִתּוֹ — *Were circumcised with him.*

The phrase *with him* indicates they were under this obligation only as a result of being subject to Abraham's will; had they left his service they would not have had to be circumcised. Thus, the obligation did not pass on to their children *(Malbim).*

The passive form is used because he did not coerce them; they submitted willingly [therefore, the verse does not read *he circumcised them*]*(Chizkuni).*

Abraham entered the covenant of circumcision openly, in broad daylight. Circumcision is not an occult blood ritual of obeisance to the powers of darkness. With it, a Jew rises above those forces. It is like a new birth — a spiritual one. With it, a Jew proudly, publicly places himself in sharp contrast to those whose dedication is to physical forces *(Hirsch).*

According to the Masoretic note appearing at the end of the *Sidrah,* there are 126 verses in the *Sidrah* numerically corresponding to the mnemonic נמל״ו [=126='they were circumcised'] and also to מכנדי״ב [=126. The allusion is obscure. נְדִיב is interpreted in the *Talmud* [*Chagigah* 3a] and *Midrash* to *Song of Songs* 7:2 as a reference to Abraham. (See *comm.* there). The meaning of מָךְ may be derived from *Sotah* 10b where the same word is given two meanings with reference to David: 1) He was humble and self-effacing [מָךְ=*a poor person*], and 2) He was born circumcised [מָךְ=מַכָּה, *a wound*]. Either interpretation can be applied to Abraham, who was humble and who circumcised himself. The *Haftorah* begins with *Isaiah* 40:27 לָמָּה תֹאמַר יַעֲקֹב.

נשלם סדרה לך לך בעזרת האל

Additional Note A —

◆§ The Chronology of Abraham's Departures

Seder Olam 1 is the source of the chronology suggesting that Abraham's departure from Charan described in 12:1*ff* was not his first but his second and final one. According to *Seder Olam*, Abraham was seventy years old when God spoke with him at the Covenant between the Parts [Ch. 15; (the fact that that incident is recorded later is immaterial since אֵין מוּקְדָּם וּמְאוּחָר בַּתּוֹרָה, 'the Torah is not written to reflect chronological sequence') — see *Tosafos, Berachos* 7b.]

This age of seventy is established because Abraham was informed at the Covenant that his descendants would be enslaved for four hundred years [15:13.] As explained by the commentators, these four hundred years would be calculated from the birth of Isaac (which occurred thirty years later when Abraham was a hundred years old; see *comm.* to 15:13). It is further stated in *Exodus* 12:41 that the actual Exodus took place *'at the end of four hundred and thirty years'*, an apparent *lengthening* of the four hundred years prophecied to Abraham. The contradiction is resolved by counting the four hundred and thirty years from the time of the Covenant, thus assuming that Abraham was seventy years old at the time of the Covenant. Since 12:4 states that Abraham was seventy-five when he was commanded to leave Charan for good, it is plain that he came to Canaan for the first time five years previous.

[From his involvements in the events that occurred during these five years, it would seem that Lot accompanied Abraham the first time he went to Canaan as well. On the Chronology of the Egyptian bondage which lasted 210 years, see ArtScroll *Shir HaShirim, footnote* to p. 105.]

Seder Olam concludes that after the Covenant between the Parts, Abraham returned to Charan and spent five years there. [Lot apparently returned during this period with him because he was present at the second departure, too.]

It was after these five years that the command of God came to him *'Get yourself out of your country . . .'*

[There are several variations within the broad framework of this chronology. For example, when did the war of the kings (Ch. 14) occur? According to *Seder Olam* it occurred after the second departure when Abraham was seventy-five; while according to *Tosafos Berachos* 7b it occurred after the first departure when Abraham was seventy-three. These variations will be dealt with in their appropriate places, but the opinion that Abraham left Charan twice follows the chronology of the Sages in the *Talmud* and *Midrash*.

[See also *Avodah Zarah* 9a (cited in *comm.* to 12:5) that there is a tradition that the *'souls that Abraham and Sarah converted in Charan'* dated from the time Abraham was fifty-two years old. This does not affect our chronology, but it sheds light on the *Talmudic* opinion that places Abraham in Charan already from this age, eighteen years before we find him in Canaan for the covenant, and twenty-three years before he left Charan permanently.

This is also in consonance with *Sefer HaYashar* 13:3 which puts Abraham's age at fifty-two when he reached Charan. He was fifty-five when he left Charan for Canaan *(ibid.* 13:9). At the age of seventy Abraham, his wife with their belongings returned to Charan to visit his family. He remained there for five years *(ibid.* 13:20).]

Following *Ibn Ezra,* however, according to whom God's call to Abraham already had occurred in *Ur Kasdim* [see *comm.* to *v.* 1] there were not two departures to Eretz Yisrael. According to him, as he explains in *Exod.* 12:40, Abraham left Ur Kasdim with his family at the age of seventy and they all settled in Charan, as stated above in 11:31. Terach wished to go no further, and in deference to him Abraham tarried there for five years, at which time, he continued on to Canaan as described in 12:4, and 5, never again to return. He was then seventy-five. It was then that the War of the Kings and Covenant Between the Parts occurred as detailed in the Torah. The four hundred year period of bondage was reckoned from Isaac's birth when Abraham was 100, but the additional thirty years of exile began from the time Abraham left his home in Ur Kasdim at th age of seventy. [*Radak* concurs with this view but suggests that Abraham's departure from Charan after five years might have been the result of a second call from God not mentioned in the Torah.] See similarly *comm.* of *Vilna Gaon* to *Seder Olam.*

For further research into this matter, see *Tosafos Berachos* 7b s.v. לא; *Shabbos* 10b s.v. וְשֶׁל; *Tosafos Avodah Zarah* 9a s.v. וּגְמִירִי; *Rashi* and *Ramban* to *Exod.* 12:40; *Ramban's HaEmunah V'HaBitachon,* Ch. 12; *Tzemach David;* and the *comm.* of *Harav M. Weinstock* to *Seder Olam.* See also *Rav Saadiah Gaon, Emunos V'De'os* 8:4, *Da'as Zekeinim, Tur, Abarbanel* and *Chizkuni. (Cf. also alternative opinion of Ramban* on *Exod.* 12:40, where he suggests that in the plain sense the thirty years might indeed have been in addition to the four hundred, but that God had given Abraham an approximate round number rather then an exact figure.

An Overview — Sodom

אַנְשֵׁי סְדוֹם לֹא נִתְגָּאוּ אֶלָּא בִּשְׁבִיל טוֹבָה שֶׁהִשְׁפִּיעַ לָהֶם הקב״ה . . .
אָמְרוּ וְכִי מֵאַחַר שֶׁאֶרֶץ מִמֶּנָּה יָצָא לֶחֶם וְעַפְרוֹת זָהָב לוֹ לָמָּה לָנוּ עוֹבְרֵי דְרָכִים שֶׁאֵין בָּאִים אֶלָּא לְחַסְּרֵנוּ מִמָּמוֹנֵנוּ?

The people of Sodom became arrogant only because of the abumdance which the Hol One, Blessed be He, showered upon them . . .
They said, 'Since the land produces bread and it has gold dust, why should we allow wayfarers who come only to deprive us of our wealth?

Canaan and Sodom

When the Jewish nation was crossing the Wilderness on its way to Eretz Yisrael, it was instructed that it must not allow the Seven Nations of Canaan to remain in the Land. Israel was warned that the Land would spew forth its sinful inhabitants (see *Overview: The Land* to *Lech Lecha).*

But there was another element in Eretz Yisrael, one even more wicked than the Seven Nations; a culture even more corrupt than Canaan — Sodom. Despite the abominations that were so intolerable to the very essence of the Land, the Canaanite Nations were permitted to remain there for four hundred and seventy years after Abraham first received title to it at the Covenant Between the Parts. At that time he was told that a four hundred year exile would intervene —

one that began with the birth of Isaac thirty years later. Even thereafter his descendants spent another forty years in the wilderness, before the Canaanite and Emorite quota of sin was reached *(Genesis* 15:16 see *comm.),* but Sodom and its tributary cities were wiped from the earth in an unprecedented manner after only fifty-two years of settlement (see *comm.* to 19:20). The generation of the Flood was wiped out, but the world was rebuilt on its remains. The generation of the Dispersion was banished and scattered, but it lived to populate and develop the earth. Sodom, on the other hand, was overturned; its people were killed, its possessions totally destroyed, and its very locale — the rich, verdant plain which had enticed Lot to leave his mentor and protector (13:10-11) — was transformed into the salty, sulphuric wilderness that to this day is called the Dead Sea. What was it about Sodom?

What was it about Sodom?

The Sodom Motivation

Not unless we find the pattern behind their excesses can we understand the extent of their evil and the revulsion God felt for them.

The cruelties of Sodom have entered the language as the epitome of selfishness, callousness and depravity (see *comm.* to Ch. 19). But there was a method, a rationale, behind their perverse behavior. Not unless we find the pattern behind their excesses can we understand the extent of their evil and the revulsion God felt for them.

The region of Sodom was rich and fertile. Of all the Land lying before him, Lot chose only Sodom in which to settle and make his fortune. We can well imagine that if it held such a powerful attraction for someone like Lot who, for all his deficiencies, had still been raised by Abraham and Sarah and who was a relatively righteous person as well as a wealthy one, then it must have been even more attractive for thousands of others. In our own century, we see in nation after nation, how millions upon millions of people go from region to region and from country to country in search of a secure roof and a better livelihood. In those days, Sodom should surely have been no less a magnet than the large urban and industrialized areas of today.

The Sodomites knew this, too. And they were the first to devise policies to close their gates to the unwelcome rabble who threatened to dilute the economic base and mar the prosperity of the limited, but comfortable, population of the region. In effect, Sodom was the originator of anti-immigration laws.

In effect, Sodom was the originator of anti-immigration laws.

They did more than take down the welcome signs. They made it a terrifying experience for a stranger even to visit Sodom. A traveler would find no door open to him. Not a crust of bread nor a drop of water would be offered him. If he dared to seek lodging, he would be violently tormented, even maimed. The wayfarer in Sodom would be subject to perverse sexual abuse. The Sodomite who dared violate the social and legal strictures against hospitality would be treated as an enemy of the people and would be subject to abuse even worse than that meted out to the unsuspecting visitor — for, after all, the unwelcome migrant was but an unwitting and relatively harmless annoyance, but the citizen who broke with Sodomite tradition was a corrupting influence and a danger to the social and economic order.

Seeds of Sodom

The *Mishnah*, in describing attitudes toward fellow humans, says

הָאוֹמֵר שֶׁלִּי שֶׁלִּי שֶׁלְּךָ שֶׁלָּךְ, זוֹ מִדָּה בֵּינוֹנִי, וְיֵשׁ אוֹמְרִים זוֹ מִדַּת סְדוֹם

The one who says 'What is mine is mine and what is your is yours [i.e., he wishes neither to give to nor to receive from others] — this is the manner of ordinary people. Some say it is the manner of Sodom (Avos 5:10)

The Sages have given us an insight into the source of Sodomite iniquity and at the same time a sobering lesson in the evaluation of our own behavior. We are not surprised to read that 'the manner of ordinary people' calls for one neither to give nor to receive. 'Neither lender nor borrower be' has come into the language as a well-accepted maxim of conduct. This runs counter to the Torah's teaching that a Jew is required to lend and to give — nevertheless, it is hardly a code of conduct that can be described as wicked. Therefore, the first opinion cited by the *Mishnah* describes it as the code of ordinary people: it shows little sensitivity to the needs of others, but one would prefer it to the grasping, selfish attitude that has been the cause of suffering and misery throughout history.

The second opinion sees it differently. In itself, the code is not evil, but what seeds of wickedness it contains! Sodom, too, began as a society that said 'what is mine is mine and what is yours is yours.' Sodom was not an aggressive, warrior nation that plundered its neighbors. To the contrary, the one time in Scripture where we find Sodom engaged in battle, it was ignominiously defeated (14:10-11). But Sodom was concerned in protecting what it had and in not sharing it with others. To do so, it erected a new social code, one that did not stop with 'charity begins at home,' but which erected barriers against the hapless, terror against the helpless, that pronounced a sentence of a slow and painful death upon a girl whose only crime was that she secretly gave a crust of bread to a hungry stranger. People can go to frightening lengths to protect 'legitimate interests.' The person or nation whose eyes turn inward in selfish concern for the protection of only his own concerns, should search long and hard lest he become a Sodomite *(Harav David Feinstein).*

Sodom was concerned in protecting what it had and in not sharing it with others.

Unforgivable Sin

In the eyes of God, the greatest abomination of all is a social contract founded on selfishness, descending to cruelty, resulting in perversion of decency. The founding Patriarch was Abraham whose overriding characteristic was חֶסֶד, *kindness* (see *Overview, the Patriarchs),* a clear indication that God wished to found His chosen People upon the basis of kindness. Indeed עוֹלָם חֶסֶד יִבָּנֶה, *the very universe was built upon kindness (Psalms* 89:3). Without it mankind cannot endure; to bestow it, God created heaven and earth (see *Overview* to *Berei-*

shis). Licentiousness is a grievous sin; because of it the nations of Canaan were vomited out of the Land, and Israel was warned against it in the harshest terms. But it is understandable that human beings, possessed of animal passions, may fail to control them. Even a selfish unwillingness to help others is understandable. But to erect a society with a social and legal code in defense of selfishness and in opposition to kindness — that is an abomination which, both in God's eyes and in Jewish tradition is described with the contemptuous epithet מִדַּת סְדוֹם, *the manner of Sodom.* That behavior, God will not countenance. It resulted in the total upheaval that left no trace of the period's wealthiest city-state.

But to erect a society with a social and legal code in defense of selfishness and in opposition to kindness — that is an abomination.

The Sages liken the crime of Sodom to that of עִיר הַנִּדַּחַת, *a city led astray* after idolatry *(Tosefta Sanhedrin* 14:1). The fate of the *city led astray,* as *Rambam* makes clear in *Moreh Nevuchim* (3:41), is not entirely in punishment for the transgression of idolatry. If that were the case, it would not be required that all the property of the sinners be burned. In all other cases, the property of ordinary sinners condemned to death goes to their heirs. That the *city* must be destroyed in its entirety is to demonstrate that an entire community has reviled and rebelled against the Law — highhandedly, brazenly, publicly. *Rambam* holds that the same treatment would be meted out to any community that acts as a unit to oppose *any* commandment, even one not as serious as idolatry.

That the city must be destroyed in its entirety is to demonstrate that an entire community has reviled and rebelled against the Law — highhandedly, brazenly, publicly.

Indeed, the people of Sodom, unanimously and brazenly, acted to oppose the elementary dictates of decency; for that reason they could not be endured nor permitted to survive. The property of Canaan was neither destroyed nor forbidden; the property of Sodom was removed from the face of the earth, so grievous was the sin of its selfish owners.

Would the same thing have happened if Sodom had been in Africa, Europe, or America?

Most assuredly not. The sin would have been grievous, and it would have been punished somehow

But the Sodomites committed their blight in Eretz Yisrael, *the Land of holiness, the land which cannot abide sin.*

and at some time. *But the Sodomites committed their blight in Eretz Yisrael,* the Land of holiness, the land which cannot abide sin. A sin there is worse. In the words of *Ramban:*

> *Know that the judgment of Sodom was due to the spiritual elevation of Eretz Yisrael, for it is the inheritance of God and it does not tolerate abominable people. Just as it would later vomit out the entire nation [of Canaan] because of their abomination, it preceded and vomited out this nation [Sodom] which was the worst of all, to heaven and to humans, and rained desolation upon it from heaven and earth, and ravaged the land beyond cure forever. For they were haughty because of their prosperity, and God saw that it [the total destruction of the selfish society] would be an omen for rebellious people, for Israel which was destined to inherit it [the Land] ... For there are among the nations very wicked and sinful people, but He did not [utterly destroy] them. But [he did so to Sodom] because of the spiritual elevation of Eretz Yisrael for it is the Temple of* HASHEM *(Gen.* 19:5).

An Overview — The Akeidah

אָמַר לֵיה לְיִצְחָק רוֹאֶה אַתָּה מַה שֶׁאֲנִי רוֹאֶה? אָמַר לוֹ אֲנִי רוֹאֶה הַר נָאֶה וּמְשֻׁבָּח וְעָנָן קָשׁוּר עָלָיו. אָמַר לִנְעָרָיו רוֹאִין אַתֶּם כְּלוּם? אָמְרוּ לוֹ אֵין אָנוּ רוֹאִין אֶלָּא מִדְבָּרוֹת

[Abraham] said to Isaac, 'Do you see what I see?' He answered him, 'I see a beautiful, praiseworthy mountain and a cloud attached to it.' [Abraham] said to his attendants, 'Do you see anything?' They said, 'We see nothing but deserts!' (Midrash Tanchuma, Vayeira 23).

אָמַר לְפָנָיו, רִבּוֹן הָעוֹלָם הֲוֵי רוֹאֶה דָמָיו שֶׁל אַיִל זֶה כְּאִילוּ דָמוֹ שֶׁל יִצְחָק בְּנִי, אֵימוּרָיו כְּאִילוּ אֵימוּרָיו שֶׁל יִצְחָק בְּנִי

[Abraham] said before Him, 'Master of the Universe, consider the blood of this ram as if it were the blood of my son, Isaac; its parts as if they were the parts of my son, Isaac (Bereishis Rabbah 56:14)

I. Extent of the Trial

The Human Level

The *Akeidah* was the final and the supreme trial of Abraham. As we have seen *(Overviews* to *Lech Lecha)* it was necessary to submit Abraham to ten trials in order to elevate him to his spiritual zenith. After the *Akeidah,* he had thirty-eight years to live, but he was not tested again because he had already gained his ultimate height; nothing could be gained by testing him further. The *Akeidah* has assumed a central role in Jewish liturgy. It is a repeated refrain in the prayers of the Days of Awe. The Sages and the commentators discuss it extensively. Let us attempt to mine a few of those rich veins of insight and inspiration.

[A reading of the narrative and commentary in Chapter 22 is recommended as a necessary preliminary to this discussion.]

Like every trial, the Akeidah *forced its subject to make a painful choice that ran counter to his nature and inclination.*

Like every trial, the *Akeidah* forced its subject to make a painful choice that ran counter to his nature and inclination. The test can be understood on many levels and in many dimensions — all of them valid. That it was the climactic test of Abraham's greatness is reason enough for it to have been of such complexity, for it stands to reason that the extent of the reward called for an ordeal of parallel proportions.

Abraham had waited a hundred years for the gift of a son. He had been told by God that his heir must be borne from Sarah, but it was a physical impossibility for them to have a child together. God raised him above the stars which are His emissaries to preside over the natural functioning of the universe and told him that the rules of nature do not apply to him and Sarah. As Abram and Sarai they would not have children, but as Abraham and Sarah they would (15:5, *Rashi).* The couple waited many years after that vision until Isaac was finally born to them. Now they were both old, Abraham was 137 and Sarah was 127. Their rejuvenation had not continued; they had had no other children together. Isaac was thirty-seven, a mature man who had proven himself to be a deserving successor to Abraham's mantle. Now Abraham was asked to slaughter him. In human terms, the task of him was incomprehensible. An only son! There was no chance short of a miracle that another son would be born — could another miracle be expected? To bring him to the altar and to inflict the cut with *his own hands!*

In human terms, the task asked of him was incomprehensible. An only son!

The Spiritual Level

Abraham had built an empire of accomplishment in the service of God. In the sense that the offspring of the righteous are their good deeds, *(Genesis* 6:9, *Rashi).* Abraham had armies and armies of children.

From the time he was fifty-two he had been teaching the multitudes and leading people under the wings of the *Shechinah.* Though he lived in an immoral, idolatrous society, even they considered him a *Prince of God* (23:6) and he gained respect wherever he went. Everywhere his teaching was that people must emulate God who abhors cruelty and loves kindness, that human sacrifice is murder, and that idolatry is a denial of the true God.

What would happen to his followers and those who admired him if he slaughtered Isaac and the world learned that Abraham's teachings had been violated in the grossest manner by the preacher himself?

What would happen to his followers and those who admired him if he slaughtered Isaac and the world learned that Abraham's teachings had been violated in the grossest manner by the preacher himself? His entire lifetime of achievement would have been nullified. He would have been despised, vilified, ridiculed. Human nature being what it is, not only his detractors, but even his erstwhile followers, would probably have embarked on orgies of excess, because the one supreme moral force acting as the conscience of the world would have been irreparably discredited. Human beings can endure many forms of suffering, but none is more difficult than disgrace — the fate awaiting Abraham when he returned from Mount Moriah without Isaac at his side. Could he endure all that in order to satisfy the wish of God?

Let us dig deeper. Human beings commonly function on two levels. As members of an organization, they have the goal of furthering the larger community of which they are part, be it society, company, school or whatever. Simultaneously they have their personal role in that larger organization. A mature, established person inevitably comes to consider his own niche as vital and his energies become directed toward assuring its maximum success. An outside consultant may decide that a corporation might be well served if it eliminated a division and laid off its entire staff. The director of the division would surely feel otherwise. Even if he accepted his dismissal gracefully, he could hardly be expected to applaud his good fortune at having contributed, through his professional demise, to the greater glory of the company to which he had unselfishly given his best efforts for all of his professional life.

The Ultimate Level

Abraham had been as loyal a servant of God as had ever lived. He had been assured by God that his destiny would be continued through Isaac and none other. Now there would be no Isaac and as a result the work of Abraham himself would not endure. On the other hand, he understood that the greater goal of sanctifying God's Name would be enhanced by his deed. For the sacrifice asked of him would demonstrate conclusively that Abraham held back nothing from God — not his son, not his reputation, not even his lifetime of spiritual fulfillment. In God's scale of values, that degree of dedication outweighed all the jeers of scoffers and skeptics. It mattered not that Abraham would lose his following or that not a soul would understand the magnitude of his deed. He was alone when he began his work, but that did not detract from his greatness; he would be alone when he finished his work and be even greater because he would give up so much. God does not measure value in numbers. What is more, his supreme obedience would prove that accomplishment on earth, accomplishment measurable in human terms, had no ultimate value at all if God's will were otherwise. Because it was the Divine will, the destruction of his life's spiritual edifice would be his greatest and most genuinely tangible achievement because, in the Heavenly balance, it would outweigh everything else he had ever done.

Because it was the Divine will, the destruction of his life's spiritual edifice would be his greatest and most genuinely tangible achievement because, in the Heavenly balance, it would outweigh everything else he had ever done.

Intellectually, Abraham could surely have understood that infinitely better than we. Could he also feel it in the depths of his soul and with all his emotions? It was *his* son, *his* loss, *his* sacrifice. Could he feel the same joy in serving God by slaughtering Isaac that he had in raising him?

As explained earlier *(Overview: Trials)* the character traits of Israel became engraved into the national spiritual 'genes' through the acts and particularly the trials of the Patriarchs. We are

Abraham's offspring and the heirs of his submission to God's will. We are descendants of Abraham, but he was a son of Terach. Therefore, it is impossible for us to fully comprehend the awesome nature of his response to God's call to slaughter Isaac. To say that we benefit from his legacy is not to imply that we would do equally well — far from it. But we cannot divorce ourselves from our heritage; therefore we cannot imagine how severe the trial was for Abraham who had no patriarchal ancestor named Abraham. Suffice it to say that Abraham proved himself so well that he attained perfection in the eyes of the Supreme Judge. That there are those who question his uniqueness on the ground that countless Jewish parents throughout the ages have made similar sacrifices is testimony to how well he succeeeded. So totally did Abraham sublimate his personal ambitions and needs to the will of his Master, that the heritage remains strong almost thirty-seven centuries later.

We cannot imagine how severe the trial was for Abraham who had no patriarchal ancestor named Abraham.

The heritage remains strong almost thirty-seven centuries later.

II. Uniquely Abraham's

To Live Like a Jew

What of Isaac? The *Akeidah* is counted as one of Abraham's tests, but surely Isaac was being tested as well. As we shall see, Isaac's achievement was awesome and his performance during those fateful three days leading up to his ascent to the altar has remained part of the national heritage as has Abraham's. They were partners in approaching the *Akeidah* and they are partners in affecting us today by their accomplishment. Why then is the trial aspect of the *Akeidah* not ascribed equally to Isaac — or, since he was the one who volunteered his own life, why is it understood *primarily* as *Abraham's* trial and only secondarily as Isaac's?

Since he was the one who volunteered his own life, why is it understood primarily *as* Abraham's *trial and only secondarily as* Isaac's?

In commenting on this question, Rabbi Yosaif Yoizel Horowitz of Novardok remarked, 'It is harder to live like a Jew than to die like a Jew.'

Isaac was ready to offer his life. That done, all would have been over. He was fully prepared to give

Isaac was fully prepared to give everything for the sake of God, but he would not have had to deal with the aftermath.

everything for the sake of God, but he would not have had to deal with the aftermath. He would *climb* Mount Moriah, but he would not have had to *descend* from it. He was ascending to one of the great spiritual experiences of all time, but he would not have had to go back down to face the world and answer the question, 'What have you done with your son?' He would not have had to face the bereaved Sarah.

The supreme sacrifice is not to be regarded lightly, but such acts of heroism are not uncommon in human experience. People risk their lives for far smaller causes and they are soon forgotten. Great moments evoke great responses even from ordinary people; surely one would not expect less from Isaac.

But Abraham would have to go on, facing Sarah ... once more opening his tent to wayfarers who would now be afraid to accept the hospitality of the 'barbarous old man' who had killed his own son.

But Abraham would have to go on, facing Sarah, facing the world, rebuilding his shattered life, once more opening his tent to wayfarers who would now be afraid to accept the hospitality of the 'barbarous old man' who had killed his own son, preaching the word of God to people who would call him a hypocrite, wondering if the lack of a Jewish posterity might not be his unforgivable sin for having allowed his fully-grown son to remain unmarried for so long. Isaac had to *die* like a Jew, but Abraham had to bear the infinitely harder burden of carrying on, of continuing to *live* like a Jew.

Challenge or Norm

Even without this consideration, however, Isaac's act did not parallel Abraham's. There is no such thing as a trial *per se;* one's man challenge is another man's norm. For Abraham it was a tremendous challenge to expel Ishmael and Hagar; for Sarah it was self-evident that the deed had to be done. Some people find it difficult to part with their money for charity, others are overly generous; the former would be severely tested by a situation that called for extreme generosity, the latter would take it in stride.

Abraham and Isaac had different primary traits in the service of God (See *Overview: Patriarchs).* Abraham was the person of *chesed,* [*kindness*],

Abraham was the person of chesed ... *whose primary drive was to help others and use his generous nature to draw them close to God.*

whose primary drive was to help others and use his generous nature to draw them close to God. For him, the *Akeidah* was a trial of awesome proportions both for what he was called upon to do to Isaac and for the effect it would have on his relationship to society. But Isaac was the person of *gevurah,* [*strength*]. He was inner-directed and self-critical. He sought to perfect himself and remove any hint of baseness or imperfection in himself. To Isaac, the call to give up his life was not difficult. If the way to purge his imperfections was to purge his very life, then his nature would dictate that he do so.

For Abraham to commit such an act, however, required that he rise above his own character as a *chesed*-person and act contrary to his way of serving God. To do so would be possible only if his faith were so great that his was so total that he was capable of acting counter to everything he had understood and believed.

Ripples in the Future

Abraham's conquest of his merciful instincts in obedience to God's will forced him to act 'cruelly' toward Isaac and Sarah — yet still remain the same merciful Abraham. This had a two-fold result in the future history of Israel. When Israel, led by Joshua, entered the Land and waged war with the nations of Canaan, it did so under the Divine injunction of לֹא תְחַיֶּה כָּל נְשָׁמָה, *do not allow a soul to live (Deut.* 20:16). Even women and children fell under the decree. One would expect the nation to be affected by such barbaric conduct with the inevitable result that its people would become indifferent to human suffering. Indeed, one of war's most unpleasant by-products throughout history has been what it does to those who wage it, especially when their role is not antiseptic and automated, but involves hand-to-hand conduct with sword and bayonet. That did not happen to Joshua and his people, because the Patriarch had prepared the way.

Whether Abraham was washing the feet of wayfarers or bringing the knife closer to the neck of

Kindness can be iniquitous and cruelty can be virtuous if they are exercised properly.

his son, his intention was unvarying: to serve God and sanctify His Name. Kindness can be iniquitous and cruelty can be virtuous if they are exercised properly. Indeed, our vocabulary has different words for cruelty that is exercised in a just cause. We call it strength, principle, single-mindedness even though the same act in an unpopular cause would be soundly attacked.

Abraham could act as he did and still remain the same kind and merciful person. That, too, became a part of the national character. Joshua and his people were able to do the same — they fought, killed, and exterminated yet remained the grandchildren of the Patriarch who rescued mankind from two thousand years of desolation through the exercise of kindness.

He acted contrary to his nature, but, because he did so only with the purpose of carrying out God's behest, his nature remained unsullied.

He acted contrary to his nature, but, because he did so only with the purpose of carrying out God's behest, his nature remained unsullied.

This eternal result of Abraham's devotion is alluded to in the Divine blessing which was bestowed upon him at the conclusion of the trial:

> ... יַעַן אֲשֶׁר עָשִׂיתָ אֶת הַדָּבָר הַזֶּה ... וְיִרַשׁ זַרְעֲךָ אֵת שַׁעַר אֹיְבָיו וְהִתְבָּרְכוּ בְזַרְעֲךָ כֹּל גּוֹיֵי הָאָרֶץ ...
>
> ... *Since you have done this thing* ... *And your offspring shall inherit the gate of its enemy and shall bless themselves by your offspring* ... (22:16-18).

The exercise of cruelty in a just cause is generally regarded as a necessary evil, but sensitive people will not bless their children with it. Certainly the victims and potential victims of the conqueror will find no cause for blessing in his conduct. But Abraham was promised that not only would his offspring wage war triumphantly — the wars of Joshua which required an enormous degree of bloodshed — but all the nations on earth would bless their own children that they might grow up to be like the virtuous warriors to whom the need to inflict death is a Divine duty when called for, but not a degrading at that turns them into murderers. On the contrary, civilian populations for whom violence and sadism is processed into daily entertainment become far more insensitive to suffering than even the most effective sword wielder in Joshua's army — another legacy of the Patriarchs's who refined every trait and drew from it, its potential for good *(Meshech Chochmah).*

Further, Abraham's success in controlling his merciful instincts was rewarded measure for measure. We pray:

> כְּמוֹ שֶׁכָּבַשׁ אַבְרָהָם אָבִינוּ אֶת רַחֲמָיו מֵעַל בֶּן יְחִידוֹ לַעֲשׂוֹת רְצוֹנְךָ בְּלֵבָב שָׁלֵם, כֵּן יִכְבְּשׁוּ רַחֲמֶיךָ אֶת כַּעַסְךָ מֵעָלֵינוּ
>
> *Just as Abraham, our Father, suppressed his mercy from his only son in order to do Your will with a complete heart, so let Your mercy suppress Your anger from upon us (Daily Shacharis)*

There remains the spark of Abraham's holiness within every son and daughter of Israel.

Abraham showed that his devotion came above all other considerations. He injected his unconditional faith into the national character so that no matter how encrusted Israel may become with sin, and no matter how enamored it may become with sin's fleeting pleasures, there remains the spark of Abraham's holiness within every son and daughter of Israel. Repentance, therefore, is an ever-present possiblity if, somehow, that spark can be reached and fanned. The *basic* urge of Abraham's children is to be righteous. *Rambam (Hilchos Gerushin* 2:20) bases upon this principle the law that under certain conditions a Bais Din may force a recalcitrant husband to give a bill of divorcement, although the Torah requires that a divorce must be voluntarily given in order to be valid. The application of force, *Rambam* explains, serves only to neutralize the extraneous forces — temptation, passion, hatred, and so on — that caused a Jew to stray from the path of Torah in the first place. If his misguided pursuit of this-worldly values is balanced by his fear of the court's punishment, we may assume that his compliance with the law of the Torah is an expression of his essential Jewishness. This being so, God responds in kind by not allowing the anger provoked by our deeds to overwhelm the mercy that is awakened by our essence (see *ibid.).*

III. Trial Intensified

The Love Must Grow

Let us contrast the command of the Akeidah *with the command to drive* Ishmael *from his home.*

So Abraham's very nature, as opposed to Isaac's, dictated that the *Akeidah* was more *his* test than his son's. But the trial was intensified further by the way it was presented. Let us contrast the command of the *Akeidah* with the command to drive Ishmael from his home. There, God commanded Abraham to follow the superior insight of Sarah. He told him to feel no regret at dispatching the boy, and what is more, He promised Abraham that Ishmael would become a nation for, although only Isaac would have the status of Abraham's true offspring, Ishmael would still be treated graciously as someone born of Abraham's seed. Combined with the command that Abraham go against his nature by cutting off his kindness to Ishmael and Hagar was the assurance that no harm would befall them and that Sarah's insistence, far from being vindicitive, was an expression of God's own wisdom.

What reassurance was he given with regard to the slaughter of Isaac? Was he told that Isaac did not deserve the mantle of Patriarch? ... that he had sinned? ... that another would take his place? ... that he should cease loving him?

No.

'Please' take your son (22:2) ... Isaac remains your son — his status is undiminished.

'Your only son' ... He remains unique. Ishmael cannot return to take his place. You were promised a son, and Isaac will always remain the fulfillment of that promise even after you slaughter him.

'Whom you love' ... *Continue* to love him. Do not take the easy way of convincing yourself that your

love was misplaced, that Isaac is unworthy either of your love or of carrying on your mission.

When God uttered those words to Abraham, the Patriarch was infused with a new and greater realization of what Isaac was. His son for whom he had waited a lifetime and for whom all the covenants and promises were made ... the bearer of Abraham's mission ... the fulfillment of creation. He was Abraham's *only* son. He was unique ... there was none like him ... he had forged a new way to serve God and no one could take his place.

When Abraham heard the words whom you love, *he was infused with a greater love for Isaac than he had ever felt before.*

Abraham loved Isaac. God now ratified that love and when Abraham heard the words *whom you love,* he was infused with a greater love for Isaac than he had ever felt before. Abraham was not to ascend Mount Moriah with the thought that, little though he understood why, he was excising an unworthy outgrowth of himself. No. He was to go with all the respect, love, expectation, and feeling that an Abraham could possibly feel for an Isaac. He was to go with the realization that Isaac was not expendable and replaceable, neither as a son nor as a Patriarch. And still he was to go. How awesome! Only by attempting feebly to imagine how difficult God made the trial can we hope to understand how great was the aged father who sought no way to delay or reinterpret, who arose early and with alacrity to make even the exhausting physical preparations himself *(Chidushei HaRim).*

The Legacy Applied

These lofty words of *Chidushei Harim* were given poignant application by his great-grandson Rabbi Abraham Mordechai Alter of Ger. He had a son named Yitzchok who died on the seventeenth of Cheshvan, 5695 (1934), just before the Sabbath of *Vayeirah* with its narrative of the *Akeidah.* Abraham had lost his Isaac. He sat with his disciples at the Sabbath table and delivered the weekly discourse on the Torah reading of the day:

> *'Take your son, your only son, whom you love — Isaac.* My great-grandfather said

But Abraham had to slaughter Isaac without *diminishing his love.*

that the trial was that he slaughter Isaac even though the love was not taken from him. That trial was much greater. The Talmud says that Torah knowledge can be maintained only if one is willing to be as cruel as a raven to his children in order not to allow his love to interfere with his studies *(Eruvin* 22a). But Abraham had to slaughter Isaac *without* diminishing his love. The *Midrash* relates that as Abraham reached out to pick up the knife for the slaughter, he wept and the tears poured into Isaac's eyes. The mercy of a father welled up in him, but his heart was joyous at the opportunity to do the will of his Creator. Both emotions must be there. Tears and a joyous heart.

The *Midrash* tells that, as they walked toward Mount Moriah, Isaac spoke to Abraham saying, 'My father, my father.' Why did he repeat himself? The *Midrash* explains that he wanted to arouse Abraham's mercy.

Why did Isaac do that? Was he trying to save himself? No, Isaac did *not* wish to *avert* the slaughter. His intention was that Abraham's love and mercy should grow — *so that he would do God's will while filled with mercy to his son!*

The reward was that the Creator, Blessed be His Name, maintains His love for us eternally even when we are unworthy. לְגוֹלֶה עֲמוּקוֹת בַּדִּין, *Who reveals depths in the judgment (liturgy of Days of Awe)* — the meaning is that even in the depths of the harshest judgment, there is also Divine mercy *(Likutei Yehudah* to *Rosh Hashanah).*

The Distant Place

We are not done. The dimensions of the Trial are even greater.

How exalted a person should feel when engaged in carrying out God's will at great personal sacrifice, especially if God commanded him directly. As Abraham approached Mount Moriah and saw the cloud of the *Shechinah* hovering over it, he should have experienced a feeling of intense and intensifying nearness to God. As he ascended its slope, he should have felt himself rising to the highest possible spiritual summit. Who had ever made such a sacrifice? Who had ever been so willing to give up everything that mattered to satisfy God's wish.

Rabbi Simcha Zisel Ziev of Kelm used to say that a person could tell that his prayers were accepted if he felt relieved and exalted at their conclusion. If an ordinary person can sense God's nearness to him, how much more should Abraham have felt it as he drew closer to the *Akeidah?*

If an ordinary person can sense God's nearness to him, how much more should Abraham have felt it as he drew closer to the Akeidah?

But the *Zohar* says that Abraham felt no such thing. The *Zohar* interprets בַּיּוֹם הַשְּׁלִישִׁי וַיִּשָּׂא אַבְרָהָם אֶת עֵינָיו וַיַּרְא אֶת הַמָּקוֹם מֵרָחוֹק *On the third day Abraham raised his eyes (22:4),* [i.e. as his ordeal reached its climax, Abraham raised his sights confident that he would perceive more of God's closeness than he had ever before experienced] and he saw *The Makom* [i.e. the Omnipresent God] at a distance! Instead of coming closer to God, Abraham saw God drawing away from him! Filled with an overwhelming love for Isaac and a reintensified sense of the tragedy his death would represent, Abraham saw slipping away from him the very Godliness for which he was sacrificing Isaac. Perhaps Satan's seductive arguments were correct — perhaps he should not go through with the *Akeidah* (see *comm.)!*

Despite all this, Abraham still continued. Not because it is easy and satisfying is the service of God the proper course. Faith in the Creator need not supply instant gratification. God need not spell out His reasons and campaign for our approval. It is for us to understand that we *need not* understand. What He wills is right even if our every instinct cries out against it; what He inflicts is merciful even if its immediate result is agony; what He desires is exalting even if its immediate result is despair.

For if Abraham followed God's command lovingly even when He was distant, then He would maintain His love for Abraham's children even when they were spiritually distant and downtrodden.

Abraham forged on and his steps etched an eternal path in the history of his children. For if Abraham followed God's command lovingly even when He was distant, then He would maintain His love for Abraham's children even when they were spiritually distant and downtrodden. Therefore, too, there remains an inextinguishable spark of love in every Jew. There is a piece of Abraham in every one of his children. It was this remnant that God promised to preserve when he told Abraham אָנֹכִי מָגֵן לָךְ, *I am your shield* (15:1), and it is for this eternal pledge that we bless God in our daily prayers saying, בָּרוּךְ אַתָּה ה׳ מָגֵן אַבְרָהָם, *Blessed are You, HASHEM, Shield of Abraham.* Not merely for the protection He afforded Abraham ages ago do we bless God. We thank Him for protecting the Abraham within us, the Abrahamitic spark of love and devotion that no tidal waves of materialism, oppression, and emancipation can ever extinguish *(Sefer HaZ'chus* to *Tazria).*

Abraham's ordeal is not done. Satan said to Abraham, 'Tomorrow God will call you a murderer!' Abraham replied, 'Even so, I will do His will' *(Midrash).*

How could Abraham even imagine that he could be accused of shedding blood for having done God's will? *Rashbam* maintains that the *Akeidah* was in punishment for Abraham's treaty with Abimelech (see *comm.* to 22:1). Because Abraham had promised away part of his children's inheritance to the Philistine king, he was to be punished by the near loss of his son. [The *Midrash,* too, comments that his treaty with Abimelech was improper. Because of the seven sheep he presented to Abimelech, the Holy Ark would be captured on the day Eli the Priest died, and kept by the Philistines for seven months.] According to *Etz HaDaas Tov*, God told Abraham that the purpose of the *Akeidah* was to atone for his lapse in the affair of Abimelech. That being the case, Abraham, himself, would bear the responsibility of Isaac's death! True, the wound would be inflicted at God's command, but it was Abraham's error that was the cause of the command *(Ne'os Ha'Desheh)*.

That being the case, could Abraham have avoided the need to slaughter Isaac? Obviously there cannot even be a suggestion that he would flout God's word. But if it were possible to comply and still not kill Isaac — to avoid being rightfully called a murderer and to avoid the irreparable loss of the unique, beloved bearer of Israel's future promise — couldn't Abraham be forgiven for seeking a way out?

A Way Out

There were ways. When the *Akeidah* was over, God revealed to Abraham that he had indeed complied with the original command: 'I did not tell you שְׁחָטֵהוּ, *slaughter him*, I told you הַעֲלֵהוּ לְעֹלָה, *bring him up* [to the altar] *as an offering* (see *comm.* to 22:12). Had Abraham been a subjective human being who considers his own needs as part of the Divine equation, he could have made that distinction himself, as well. It is a familiar truism in Talmudic scholarship that the party to a dispute is capable of devising the most arcane and complex arguments to prove himself right. Self interest is a powerful spur to intellectual achievement. If, as was indeed the case, it were possible for the command to be interpreted as the symbolic elevation of Isaac upon an altar, why didn't Abraham's self interest compel him to do so?

If, as was indeed the case, it were possible for the command to be interpreted as the symbolic elevation of Isaac upon an altar, why didn't Abraham's self interest compel him to do so?

Not only did Abraham seek no ways to mitigate the decree by interpretation of its language, he did not even pray for God's mercy upon Isaac. For the sake of the perversely wicked people of Sodom, Abraham had remonstrated with God, but for his own righteous son he said not a word! That he chose to pray for Sodom and not for Isaac was surely not because he considered the Sodomites — even the relatively righteous among them — more worthy than Isaac.

Abraham prayed for Sodom because his *chesed* character could not endure the destruction of the cities with their people. His prayer was not a personal one; he did not specifically ask for the salvation of Lot, his nephew. He begged for heavenly mercy upon the Sodomite sinners because his perception of God was derived from and based upon mercy. That being so, he could not conceive of the Judge of the entire world not doing justice (18:25), because his path to God was that of עוֹלָם חֶסֶד יִבָּנֶה, *the world is built upon kindness (Psalms* 89:4); in that view, even a lack of mercy is equivalent to injustice.

But for Isaac he could not pray just as he did not pray for Lot. To do so would have meant to pray for a selfish interest.

But for Isaac he could not pray just as he did not pray for Lot. To do so would have meant to pray for a selfish interest. No matter how much he might purify his motives and remove all sense of self from his prayer, no matter how much he would base his plea upon the righteousness of Isaac and the destiny of Israel, he was human and his prayer might well be colored ever so slightly with a selfish plea for Isaac, his own son. To whatever extent that were true, it would not be outer-directed *chesed* designed only to fulfill God's wish. It would be a plea for *himself.* Who more than Abraham had a *right* to make such a plea? That he did not make it demonstrates more than anything else the greatness of the Patriarch and the reason God never removes the memory of the *Akeidah* from the balance where the fate of Israel is measured *(Michtav MeEliyahu II).*

IV. Ashes and Life

The True Sacrifice

וְזָכַרְתִּי אֶת בְּרִיתִי יַעֲקוֹב וְאַף אֶת בְּרִיתִי יִצְחָק וְאַף אֶת בְּרִיתִי אַבְרָהָם אֶזְכֹּר וְהָאָרֶץ אֶזְכֹּר וְלָמָּה לֹא נֶאֱמַר זְכִירָה בְּיִצְחָק? אֶלָּא אֶפְרוֹ שֶׁל יִצְחָק נִרְאֶה לְפָנַי צָבוּר וּמוּנָח עַל הַמִּזְבֵּחַ

And I shall remember My covenant with Jacob, and also my covenant with Isaac, and also my covenant with Abraham shall I remember (Lev. 26:42)

Why does it not specify remembrance in connection with Isaac? Because [God says] the ashes of Isaac are visible before Me gathered together atop the altar (Toras Kohanim).

מִזְבֵּחַ מְנָא יָדְעִי?... ר׳ יִצְחָק נַפְּחָא אָמַר אַפְרוֹ שֶׁל יִצְחָק רָאוּ שֶׁמּוּנָּח בְּאוֹתוֹ מָקוֹם

How did they [the Men of the Great Assembly] know where to build the altar [of the Second Temple]? ... Rabbi Yitzchok Nafcha said, 'They saw the ashes of Isaac laying on that place' (Zevachim 62a).

How can the Sages speak of Isaac's ashes when Isaac was never sacrificed and burned?

Isaac's *ashes* lay before God. They identify the altar because the Sages knew that the altar of the Temple was built upon the site of Abraham's altar on Mount Moriah. But how can the Sages speak of Isaac's ashes when Isaac was never sacrificed and burned? There can be *no* ashes of Isaac who never became an actual sacrifice, yet the halachically specified placement of the altar was determined by the 'ashes of Isaac'. A strange paradox! Isaac lived, but his ashes mark the place of his sacrifice.

In every sense except the physical, Abraham did slaughter Isaac and burn his remains as an offering.

At the outset of this Overview, we cited Abraham's prayer that the sacrifice of the ram be considered as if Isaac had remained upon the altar. The plea was not rhetorical. Both Abraham and Isaac came with all their hearts to complete the offering. There was no hesitation, no attempt to seek a reprieve. In every sense except the physical, Abraham *did* slaughter Isaac and burn his remains as an offering. As the commentators note, the purpose of every offering was to demonstrate in a tangible manner that a Jew recognizes that all his faculties and resources belong to God and must be dedicated to His service, for, in His Presence, no part of this flesh-and-blood world has any significance. Animals were created to serve man. They serve him by providing labor, food, hides. They can also serve him by being the vehicle to show his total deference to God. A person has no right to demonstrate this awareness by sacrificing himself or another human, because every human being comes to earth with a mission and the potential to fulfill it. Were he to become or to offer a human sacrifice, he would *fail* to serve God because genuine service can be done only by utilizing every available means to carry out His will, not be enduring a life that can still make contributions; it is not for us to say when God's gift of life should be returned to him.

When an offering is brought with the called for intentions, it is truly a substitute for its owner.

When an offering is brought with the called for intentions, it is truly a substitute for its owner. Were it God's will that *he* mount the altar, he would do so. Unable to do so himself, he offers his living possession to represent his own dedication. No human being had ever done this as Isaac did. He truly became Abraham's offering. He mounted the altar and the knife was at his throat. It took a Divine command to gain his release. When he descended the altar, he was no less an offering than he was when he ascended it. The ram was his substitute in an even more tangible way than even the purest sacrifice that would ever be brought in fulfillment of God's commands, because it took Isaac's place on the altar. The ashes of the ram were on the altar in place of Isaac's. Thus the ashes of the ram *were* Isaac's in a very real sense *(Michtav MeEliyahu).*

Spiritual Sensors

We may see this on a deeper level. To the prisoner in a dungeon, 'light' is the bare bulb hanging over his head, to the draftsman it is the lamp illuminating his work, to the vacationer it is the brilliant sun, to the scholar it is the wisdom of Torah. Which is the *true* light? We may well say that the answer is relative, or that the true light is the sun, and the others are either approximations or allegories. But that isn't true. The spiritual person knows that the only true light is Torah — God's wisdom. All the others are material representations, just as a child's mathematics beads

The spiritual person knows that the only true light is Torah — God's wisdom.

and blocks are but symbols of real numbers and more mature concepts. We refer to this concept as the different worlds: the spiritual world and the physical world (see *Overview* to *Bereishis).* In a higher world, Isaac surely can be seen as ashes. His willingness to become a sacrifice never left God's cognizance. The spiritual effect of his deed remained imprinted on the top of Mount Moriah.

People attuned to spirituality see things that others don't see.

People attuned to spirituality see things that others don't see. When Abraham and Isaac approached the mountain, they knew without being told that they had found *the* place. They saw a beautiful mountain covered by a pillar of smoke — the *Shechinah.* Their two attendants looked at the same mountain and saw only deserts. Were all four in the same place? Geographically, yes. But in the truest sense they were worlds apart. Abraham and Isaac were at the mountain of God and Ishamael and Eliezer were in the Canaanite desert. From that perspective, the participation of Abraham and Isaac at the *Akeidah* created *his* ashes, for he was truly sacrificed in every world but the material one. And in the material world, the ram took his place.

The Men of the Great Assembly had spiritual sensors that could see Isaac's 'ashes' on Mount Moriah. It was as clear to them where the altar had to be as it was to Abraham and Isaac that they had arrived at the mountain. And if we don't see those ashes — well, neither did Ishmael and Eliezer see more than a desert.

Life's Purpose

Isaac's ashes were before Him always, *a living reminder of Isaac's covenant — because an ascent to such spiritual heights as the Akeidah* never dies.

One must 'remember' only what is past. One must remember what happened last week, last year; he need not remember what is before him at that very moment. God promised to *remember* the covenant of Abraham and Jacob, but there was no need to bring the covenant of Isaac back from the past. Isaac's ashes were before Him *always,* a living reminder of Isaac's covenant — because an ascent to such spiritual heights as the *Akeidah* never dies.

Therefore, too, Isaac's life after the *Akeidah* was

of a different order than any other. He was a living sacrifice, sanctified and spiritual. For that reason he was forbidden to leave the Land. Abraham had gone to Egypt and Jacob was to go to Charan and Egypt. But when famine struck in Isaac's time, God ordered him not to leave Eretz Yisrael; he was a holy offering — and offerings may not leave the holy soil.

When the *Akeidah* was over, Abraham sent Isaac to the Academy of Shem to study Torah, for he said, 'Whatever I have attained is only because of the Torah, therefore I want it to remain with my children forever' *(Midrash).*

The Akeidah *itself made Abraham more acutely aware than ever of the role that Torah must play in his life and that of his posterity.*

The *Akeidah* itself made Abraham more acutely aware than ever of the role that Torah must play in his life and that of his posterity. The voice he heard telling to spare Isaac, came from 'between the two cherubim,' the place where the Tablets of the Law would be placed in the Temple of the future. Abraham understood the significance of the place. It was the home of the *Shechinah,* for God's Presence rests where Torah is placed. In the *Second Temple* which lacked the Ark containing the Tablets, there was no *Shechinah (Yoma* 21b). Without Torah, Judaism is a ritual devoid of holiness. That the voice ordering the salvation of Isaac came from the place of Torah was a message to Abraham saying as it were,

'Isaac's life is precious and worth saving because of the Torah he has studied and that will become the eternal legacy of your offspring and his.'

Abraham responded by sending Isaac to the Academy of Shem.

Abraham responded by sending Isaac to the Academy of Shem. To the Patriarchs life is valueless unless it is molded by Torah and it serves Torah *(Mesech Chochmah).*

A New Life

Indeed, Isaac's life after the *Akeidah* was different in more than a symbolic way:

> *When the sword reached* [*Isaac's*] *neck, his soul left him. When God's voice came from between the two cherubim telling* [*Abraham*] *not to harm him, his soul returned to his body ... Isaac experienced*

the resuscitation of the dead and said 'Blessed are you HASHEM, Who makes the dead live (Pesikta d'Rabbi Eliezer 31).

As the *Zohar* says, the letters of יצחק, *Isaac,* form the words קֵץ חַי, *the end of life.* Isaac's earthly life had truly come to an end. Only the word of God brought his soul back to him. He blessed God for having given him the gift of life anew. As *Vilna Gaon* comments, the second blessing of the *Shmone Esrai,* מְחַיֵּה הַמֵּתִים, *Who makes the dead live,* represents Isaac's who had, indeed, come back to life. His new life was a gift of God; his *mortal* life had truly ended. Thus, the intention of Abraham and Isaac to offer everything to God became fulfilled. The Isaac who walked away from the *Akeidah* was not the same one who had come to it. He was even greater than he had been earlier for he had given his life as a gift to God. That earlier life, the earthly one before Isaac became a sacrifice, merged with the ashes of the ram, ashes that never leave the notice of God *(Harav Moshe Shapiro).*

The Isaac who walked away from the Akeidah *was not the same one who had come to it. He was even greater than he had been earlier for he had given his life as a gift to God.*

Depth in Triviality

Strangely, the name chosen for that climactic event hardly seems to symbolize its true essence: *Akeidas Yitzchock,* the binding of Isaac. True, upon placing himself upon the altar, Isaac asked his father to bind him tight lest he interfere with the knife-stroke by inadvertantly moving, thereby rendering the sacrifice unfit *(Midrash),* but that is so minor an aspect of the incident that it hardly seems appropriate to base the title of the event upon it. *Sacrifice* of Isaac! *Slaughter* of Isaac! *Gift* of Isaac! *Selflessness* of Isaac! Why *'Binding* of Isaac?'

However, the name was well chosen indeed, for the very triviality it expressed reveals the greatness of Isaac.

Abraham and Isaac walked together for three days. We can imagine the turbulence in the heart of Abraham who *knew* why they were going, and the serenity of Isaac who thought that he would join with his father in offering an animal on the holy mountain of the future Temple. How different their feelings must have been! But the Torah testifies that וַיֵּלְכוּ שְׁנֵיהֶם יַחְדָּיו, *the two of them went together* (22:6). In unison they went, equal in resolve equal in serenity — one to bind and the other to be bound; one to slaughter and the other to be slaughtered *(Midrash). Neither* thought of tragedy, only of the Creator Whose will they were going to perform.

Then Isaac learned of his destiny. '*You* are the "sheep" my son!' And again: *the two of them went together* (22:8). Now it was Isaac who should have been broken and depressed, but he wasn't. The mood remained the same. The only thing that mattered was God's will — whatever form its fulfillment would take.

The true test is not how one reacts when the trial comes, for a person is not himself when he is struck by tragedy. The test is how well has he lived his life in order to be prepared for the crisis.

It was asking enough of Isaac that he volunteer himself as the sacrifice. Surely he could not have had the presence of mind to worry about details. Few are the people who can maintain their calm in trying circumstances. No one can be faulted for failing to make a check-list in the midst of a crisis. As the *Chidushei HaRim* commented, the true test is not how one reacts when the trial comes, for a person is not himself when he is struck by tragedy. The test is how well has he lived his life in order to be prepared for the crisis. It is too late when the awful moment comes to make the preparations or develop the personality to cope with it. There is no time to study the Shulchan Aruch when a house is aflame on Sabbath or a patient is dangerously ill. If the answers to burning questions are to be found, they will have to flow from years of prior preparation. Abraham's response, Isaac's response, were not born on Mount Moriah. Their reaction had been nurtured within them for years — the trial was no more than the means to reveal what had been present within them.

Precious for Purpose

The measure of Isaac's greatness was that he was conscious even of the danger that a reflex movement might ruin the slaughter. Of all things to think of! It was a vital detail, but surely not a noticeably major aspect of the panorama of the trial. How could he be so calm? But he *did* think of that, and he *was* so calm.

Did his life mean so little to him? No, his life was exceedingly *precious* to him because it was the tool with which to serve God, and without his life his service would be over. Life is priceless! To the Patriarchs even insignificant earthenware jars were important (32:25 see *Rashi)* because they could be used to serve God in some small way — and if something can be put to proper use then it is precious. To the judge, a case involving a *perutah* is as vital as a case involving a fortune, because ultimately every judgment involves the disposition of resources which God put on the world for a purpose. The purpose, not the market value, is the measure of importance.

The greatest indication of his greatness is that, in the last moments of his worldly life, he thought of a reflex action, a sudden movement, a misplaced stroke of the knife, a life that might be squandered if it were not returned to its Maker through a proper slaughter.

Isaac's life was precious beyond value, but only because it was a tool with which to serve God. The greatest indication of his greatness is that, in the last moments of his worldly life, he thought not not of his last will and testament, of the future generations he would never produce, or of the aged parents whom his loss would bereave. He thought of a reflex action, a sudden movement, a misplaced stroke of the knife, a life that might be squandered if it were not returned to its Maker through a proper slaughter *(Harav David Feinstein).*

> *'Bind me tight lest I move due to fear of the knife and I cause you anguish. And perhaps the slaughter will be unfit and the offering will not be credited to you. Bind me well, very well.'*

Only the greatest people rise to the smallest needs.

At such a time, Isaac thought of 'small' things. People can rise up to great occasions and often do — even little people. But only the greatest people rise to the smallest needs.

Rabbi Nosson Scherman

סדר וירא
Sidra Vayeira

א וַיֵּרָא אֵלָיו יהוה בְּאֵלֹנֵי מַמְרֵא וְהוּא
ב יֹשֵׁב פֶּתַח־הָאֹהֶל כְּחֹם הַיּוֹם: וַיִּשָּׂא עֵינָיו

XVIII

1. Visiting the Sick

וַיֵּרָא אֵלָיו ה׳ — *[And]* HASHEM *appeared to him.*

To visit the sick. Rav Chama [in *Bava Metzia* 86b] taught that it was the third day after Abraham's circumcision [the third day after an operation being the most painful for adults (see 34:25); for *children* it would appear from the *Talmud Shabbos* 134b that the first and second days are the most severe and that by the third the danger has lessened *(Mizrachi)*] and God came and inquired after his welfare *(Rashi).*

The above reason for God's visit is suggested by the fact that nowhere else in Scripture do we find God *appearing* without a direct communication immediately following *(Chizkuni).* Since no other reason is given for God's appearance to Abraham, and since it is our verse that is traditionally cited in the *Talmud* [*Sotah* 14a] as the reason for visiting the sick — as the *Talmud* expounds: 'imitate HASHEM: *He* visits the sick (as in our verse), *you* visit the sick' — therefore, *Rashi* cites this tradition as the *simple meaning* of the text that this was God's primary purpose *(Mizrachi).*

Noting that the purpose of God's visit might be construed as being for the purpose of revealing to Abraham the impending destruction of Sodom, the revelation of which properly begins with the address of *v.* 17, *Levush* suggests that *Rashi*'s interpretation that God's purpose was rather to visit the sick may be inspired by the unusual order of this Hebrew passage. The usual order of similar phrases is וַיֵּרָא ה׳ אֵלָיו [i.e., with *HASHEM,* the subject, coming immediately after the verb וַיֵּרָא. Cf., e.g. 12:7.] The Hebrew in our verse — וַיֵּרָא אֵלָיו ה׳ — emphasizes that God's *primary* purpose was to appear אֵלָיו, *to him,* which, in the light of Abraham's recent circumcision, refers to His visiting the sick. This is notwithstanding the possible *secondary* purpose of revealing the impending destruction of Sodom in *v.* 17, for if that were the *primary* purpose, God had no need to personally appear — *that* could have been accomplished through an emissary.

Additionally, had God's only reason for appearing been to advise Abraham of Sodom's destruction, then this verse would not have been written here; it would have been inserted immediately preceding *v.* 14.

[*Tur* notes that there are some, however, who *do* interpret that God's *primary* reason for appearing to Abraham at that time was to advise him of the impending destruction of Sodom, but that the Torah interrupted the narrative with the visit of the angels and their mission.]

Rashi states in general terms 'to visit the sick' rather than more specifically 'to visit *him*', because as pointed out above, God meant to establish a general precedent for man to emulate. Had *Rashi* stated that it was specifically to visit *Abraham* in his sickness, then people might be misled to construe that only the *righteous* ill are to be visited *(Sifsei Chachomim).*

According to *Ramban,* this revelation came to Abraham purely as a mark of distinction, and not to impart some communication to him. Rather, God visited the convalescing Abraham to signify Divine approval of his compliance with God's command; the revelation itself constituting the reward for his obedience. Parallel revelations constituting purely a mark of grace

XVIII 1-2

[1] HASHEM *appeared to him in the plains of Mamre while he was sitting at the entrance of the tent in the heat of the day.* [2] *He lifted his eyes and saw:*

may be found in the case of Jacob when *'the angels of God met him'* [32:1], and the vision shown the Jewish people as a whole at the splitting of the sea where, our Sages [*Mechilta Beshalach*] say, 'the handmaid at the Red Sea witnessed what the Prophet Ezekiel was not granted to see.'

Ramban continues that [although this begins a new chapter], this verse is closely connected with the narrative of circumcision which immediately precedes it. A new chapter was begun only to give prominence to the honor accorded Abraham following his circumcision. It was therefore sufficient to write אֵלָיו, *to him,* and not identify Abraham as the subject[1] ... Possibly the intent of the Sages in saying that God revealed Himself to Abraham to visit the sick was that the vision of the *Shechinah* was itself a cure.

Rambam in *Moreh Nevuchim* 3:43 interprets this section of the Torah as beginning with a *general statement* that HASHEM appeared to Abraham — in a prophetic vision. It then continues with a detailed description of the vision: namely that [*v.* 2] *Abraham lifted up his eyes* in the course of that vision and saw three angels ... He continues that the entire exchange depicted in this chapter took place *in the course of that vision. Rambam* similarly interprets Jacob's wrestling with the angel [32:24] as a prophetic vision.

Ramban challenges this vigorously, posing many questions [for example: Why does the narrative begin with *God* appearing, when he saw only *angels*? If it was only a vision, then Sarah did not bake cakes, nor did she laugh! Similarly if Jacob's wrestling was but a vision, why did he limp when he awoke?]

Ramban agrees with *Rambam* to the extent that whenever seeing or hearing an angel is described in the Torah, it refers to a vision since the human senses cannot perceive an angel. (The perception of angels, however, is still below the level of prophecy.) However, wherever the Torah specifically depicts angels garbed in human appearance as *men,* as in our case, then these angels are endowed with, what is known among students versed in *Kabbalah,* as a 'garment', and are thus sensually perceptible to the pure human vision of the pious and disciples of the prophets even when they are awake. *Ramban* concludes, 'I can explain no further.'

The *Midrash* emphasizes that God appeared to Abraham as *HASHEM,* as the God of Mercy and healing, אֵלָיו, *to him* but not to the other circumcised members of his household *(Pesikta Zutresa).*

Hirsch explains: God's Presence is everywhere but is not apparent to everyone. Only after an act of devotion such as Abraham had just performed, and as he constantly performed, does it become apparent. [See *Hirsch*'s comment on וַיֵּרָא cited in 12:7.]

1. The later philosophic commentators also note the use of אֵלָיו, *to him,* rather than the specifications of Abraham by name, as well as the failure to follow the more common construction וַיֵּרָא ה׳, *and* HASHEM *appeared.*

Pri Zaddik and *Shem MiShmuel* explain that a person's name indicates his spiritual qualities while אֵלָיו, *to him* indicates all aspects of his being, including the physical. In addition, the use of *'*HASHEM *appeared'* would indicate that God took the initiative even though the person was unworthy, whereas וַיֵּרָא אֵלָיו, lit. *and* [He] appeared to *him* indicates that no aspect of the person's being interfered with the revelation. Thus, after having circumcised himself and bringing even his basest instincts under his control, Abraham was totally ready for and worthy of God's revelation.

בְּאֵלֹנֵי מַמְרֵא — *In the plains of Mamre.*

The Torah does not usually mention the sites of revelations, and we already know from 14:6 that Abraham's home was in the plains of Mamre *(Mizrachi). Rashi* explains that the location is given because it was Mamre who had given Abraham [encouraging] advice regarding the circumcision. Therefore God honored Mamre by appearing to Abraham on his land. [See *footnote* to 17:26.]

This is where Abraham and his household were circumcised. God appeared to Abraham and not to the others because he was the worthiest for that vision which had as its purpose the acknowledgement of the circumcision as the fulfillment of the Covenant. Perhaps it is for this reason that it is customary to set a chair [of Elijah] at a circumcision [at which Elijah, as God's emissary, acknowledges the fulfillment of the Covenant] *(Sforno).*

[The translation of אֵלֹנֵי as *plains* — instead of groves, oaks, terebinths, etc. — follows *Onkelos.* See *comm.* to 12:6 and 14:6.]

וְהוּא יֹשֵׁב פֶּתַח הָאֹהֶל — *While* [lit. *'and'*] *he was sitting* [*at the*] *entrance of the tent.*

In order to see whether any travelers were passing by [עֹבֵר וָשָׁב] to whom he might offer hospitality *(Rashi).*[1]

Rashi [following the *Midrash*] additionally notes that יֹשֵׁב, *was sitting,* is spelled defectively without the usual ו [instead of יוֹשֵׁב], a spelling that could be vocalized יָשַׁב, *he sat.* This duality implies that when God appeared, Abraham wished to rise [so that his sitting would be יָשַׁב, a thing of the past]. God, however, told him to remain seated [so that he remained יוֹשֵׁב, *still sitting,* even after God appeared to him.] By this God implied: You will be an example to your descendants, for I will stand in the assembly of the judges while they sit,' as it says [*Ps.* 82:1]: *God stands in the assembly of the judges.* [Cf. *comm.* to יֹשֵׁב in 19:1.]

Or, according to the version in *Tanchuma:* Abraham replied, 'Is it proper that I should remain seated while You stand?' ... 'Do not be grieved,' God answered ... 'You are aged, a hundred years old. Just as now you sit and I stand, your children shall sit in their schools and synagogues when they are but three or four years old, and I will stand over them.'

In the literal sense, the Torah mentions that *Abraham was sitting by the door of his tent* to inform us that Abraham had not expected a prophetic vision. He had neither 'fallen on his face' [to make himself fit to receive prophecy; see on 17:3, 17] nor was he engaged in prayer; it came upon him unexpectedly as a sign of favor, as explained above *(Ramban).*

The *Midrash* derives that in the Hereafter, Abraham will sit at the entrance of Gehinnom and permit no circumcised Jew to descend therein.

כְּחֹם הַיּוֹם — *In* [lit. *'about'*] *the heat of the day* [i.e., at noon *(Berachos* 27a), as it is written *(II Sam.* 4:5): *and they came about the heat of the day ... as he was lying down for his midday rest.*]

The *Talmud* [*Bava Metzia* 86b] explains that God 'withdrew the sun from its sheath' causing great heat, to spare Abraham the imposition of being burdened by travelers. But seeing that Abraham was grieved that no travelers came, God

1. *Rashi*'s expression עֹבֵר וָשָׁב [passersby] instead of אוֹרְחִים, *guests,* might homiletically signify that Abraham sat at the entrance of his tent to see if there was anyone who was sinful [עֹבֵר עֲבֵירָה] and desirous of repenting [וָשָׁב], for Abraham's foremost activity, was to bring the sinful back to God *(Minchah Belulah).*

sent him three angels in the form of men *(Rashi).*

[God obviously knew that Abraham would be grieved by the lack of travelers to whom he could display hospitality. The Midrashic exposition (that God first spared Abraham from the impositions of travelers, and then sent angels to allay Abraham's grief at the lack of visitors) must be understood in this context. God wanted Abraham to earn reward for sitting in the intense heat grieving over the absence of passersby instead of seeking shade and comfort on this, the third, and most painful day of his convalescence. Thus when visitors finally arrived, he could earn the maximum reward for being hospitable to them in his weak physical state. Abraham thereby attained the spiritual heights prerequisite to perceiving the Shechinah.]

There is a view in the *Midrash* that God 'withdrew the sun from its sheath' excessively because the heat would speed Abraham's healing process.

The interpretation that the day was *intensely* hot is inspired by the conjunctive prefix *Kaf* in the expression כְּחֹם הַיּוֹם, lit. *like* the heat of the day, which indicates a comparison to the intense heat of some other well-known day. As the *Midrash* comments: this indicates that the heat was *like the day* [of Judgment] of which it is written [*Malachi* 3:19]: *for behold the day comes which burns like a furnace (Divrei David)* ...

[The *Talmud* comments on that verse, 'On the day of Judgment God will bring forth the sun from its sheath (creating intense heat); the wicked will be consumed by it; and the righteous will be healed by it *(Avodah Zarah* 3b).] [1]

[In the literal sense, however, the כ, *Kaf,* in the expression כְּחֹם הַיּוֹם is idiomatic and appears several times in Scripture, among them *II Sam.* 4:5. It has the significance of *'at about the* hottest time of the day', and is similar to the expression *(Exod.* 11:4): כַּחֲצֹת הַלַּיְלָה, *at about midnight.* In fact, in *I Sam.* 11:9 the *ksiv, written text* of a similar expression reads בְּחֹם הַשָּׁמֶשׁ, [lit. *in the heat of the sun*] while the *kri, traditional reading* is כְּחֹם הַשָּׁמֶשׁ [lit. *about the heat of the sun*]. *Radak* there explains that both expressions are idiomatic and synonymous.

In the literal sense the verse mentions that it was day-time to explain why Abraham did not offer his guests lodgings as did Lot [19:3.]. The angels came to Lot *in the evening* [19:1] when guests are in need of sleeping accommodations, but to Abraham they came *in the heat of the day* when passersby customarily do not sleep but take refreshment and continue on their way *(Rashbam).*

2. Visit of the Angels.
Hospitality to Strangers.

וַיִּשָּׂא עֵינָיו וַיַּרְא — *And he lifted his eyes and saw.*

[Though God had appeared to him and, from the context, was still present, Abraham continued to be engaged in his work of seeking travellers to whom he could display hospitality. Therefore the verse says, *'he lifted up his eyes'* implying that he was actively *seeking out* transients (see *comm.* to *v.* 3).]

1. *Kli Yakar* accounts for the use of the conjunctive prefix כ, *like,* in a novel manner: Abraham was כְּחוֹם, *'like'* the hot, warming sun. His only concern was to find guests for whom he could perform acts of kindness, just as the pleasant sun warms and heals. Because he ignored his own physical discomfort and sought to emulate the sun, he was rewarded with a visit from God.

וַיַּ֫רְא וְהִנֵּה֙ שְׁלֹשָׁ֣ה אֲנָשִׁ֔ים נִצָּבִ֖ים עָלָ֑יו
וַיַּ֗רְא וַיָּ֤רָץ לִקְרָאתָם֙ מִפֶּ֣תַח הָאֹ֔הֶל
ג וַיִּשְׁתַּ֖חוּ אָֽרְצָה׃ וַיֹּאמַ֑ר אֲדֹנָ֗י אִם־נָ֨א
מָצָ֤אתִי חֵן֙ בְּעֵינֶ֔יךָ אַל־נָ֥א תַעֲבֹ֖ר מֵעַ֥ל

וְהִנֵּה שְׁלֹשָׁה אֲנָשִׁים — *And behold! Three men.*

The word הִנֵּה, *behold,* suggests the unexpected [*Baal HaTurim Lev.* 13:6]. the 'men' had not approached from afar, but were suddenly standing there as though materializing from thin air! *(Ibn Sho'ib).*

The three *'men'* were really angels [as obvious from the specific reference to them as angels in 19:1] in the guise of men *(Bava Metzia* 86b; *Rashi* to *v.* 1 s.v. כְּחוֹם הַיּוֹם; *Ramban).*

Three different angels were sent because each had a different function: One [Michael] to inform him of Sarah's conception [*v.* 14]; one [Gabriel] to overthrow Sodom [19:24]; and one [Raphael] to heal Abraham, [no Scriptural verse is cited for the latter; it is a Rabbinic tradition] for one angel does not perform two missions [and likewise two angels do not perform one *(Midrash)*] *(Rashi).*

Rashi goes on to explain that the interpretation [that each mission was performed by a single angel rather than all the angels sharing the performance of each mission *(Mizrachi)*] is evident from the text itself, for the Torah speaks of their eating [*v.* 8] and talking [*v.*9] in the *plural;* while the performance of each of their commissions is related in the singular. For example regarding the announcement of Sarah's child [*v.* 10]; and the destruction of Sodom [19:21, 22] the angels are referred to in singular, [especially 19:25: *'he* overthrew those cities' *(Bava Metzia* 86b).] Raphael, who healed Abraham, went on from there to save Lot. [That Raphael was charged with both missions did not violate the principle of 'one angel does not perform two missions' for the missions were not simultaneous as the second mission was in another place and the angel was commanded about it only after he had completed his first mission; therefore a fourth angel was not required. Additionally, since healing and rescue are related missions, and both were done for the benefit of Abraham, one angel could be charged with both tasks *(Ramban);* see *Gur Aryeh.*]

Malbim, in a lengthy dissertation to *v.* 3, disagrees with those who maintain that Abraham saw these angels in a vision or that they assumed human corporeality visible only to him. He emphasizes that a proper understanding of the text dictates that the angels were visible to everyone as men, for even the people of Sodom — who were surely not prophets! — saw and spoke to them [see *Ramban* cited to *v.* 1].

נִצָּבִים עָלָיו — *Were* [i.e., *remained* (see *Rashi* below)] *standing over him* — i.e., *near him,* the phrase *'over him'* being a more delicate expression to use when referring to angels in order to avoid the suggestion that man and angel are on equal footing *(Rashi).* [Cf. *comm.* to 17:22].

וַיַּרְא — [*And*] *he perceived* [lit. *'saw'*].

Rashi notes that this is the second time in this verse that the verb וַיַּרְא, [lit. *and he saw*] appears. He explains that the first time it has its ordinary meaning *and he saw;* the second time it means *he under-*

And behold! three men were standing over him. He perceived, so he ran toward them from the entrance of the tent, and bowed toward the ground. 3 *And he said, 'My Lord, if I find favor in Your eyes, please*

stood; perceived. First, וַיַּרְא*, he saw* that they remained נִצָּבִים עָלָיו *standing near him* — but made no move *toward* him. Then וַיַּרְא*, he perceived* that they did not wish to trouble him [and he feared they were about to depart] — [For their part they knew he would take the initiative, but stood still in a display of respect, to show that they wished to spare him trouble *(Divrei David).*] — *Therefore, the verse continues, he* took the initiative and ...

וַיָּרָץ לִקְרָאתָם — *So* [lit. *'and'*] *he ran toward them.*

[If they were *standing near him* why did he have to *run toward them?*] — At first they came and stood near him, but when they saw him adjusting his bandages they perceived he was in great pain and they said, 'It is not proper to stay here.' When they were departing from him *he ran toward them (Bava Metzia* 86b).

At that moment he forgot his pain. Though previously he was in such pain that he could only *sit,* he was now so intent on the performance of the mitzvah of hospitality that he was able to *run (Akeidas Yitzchak).*

וַיִּשְׁתַּחוּ אָרְצָה — *And* [*he*] *bowed toward the ground.*

— In reverence, and as an expression of salutation *(Ramban).*

3. אֲדֹנָי — *My Lord.*

According to *Rashi*'s second interpretation — which closely follows the majority interpretation of this verse — the word אֲדֹנָי is sacred, referring to God. Abraham was *taking leave from God,* imploring *Him* to *pass not away from Your servant,* but wait while he attended to his guests.

[The translation of *'Lord'* with a capital *'L'*, therefore reflects the *halachah* that this Name refers to God and is sacred, in the sense that the special requirements related to the writing of God's Names must be exercised by the scribe who writes this Name in the Torah, and regarding the prohibition to erase it if it is miswritten (see *Soferim* 4:4; *Rambam Hilchos Yesodei HaTorah* 6:9; *Minchas Shay* and *comm.* further.]

Rashi's primary interpretation, as explained by the commentators, reflects his understanding of פְּשׁוּטוֹ שֶׁל מִקְרָא*,* the *literal* flow of the narrative that Abraham noticed that the angels intended to leave and asked *them* to stay. Accordingly, *he addressed himself to them* saying: אֲדֹנָי*, my lords.* Abraham essentially directed his request to the chief of the angels [obviously the one in the center *(Yoma* 37) in this case Michael *(Divrei David)*] imploring him to remain. The title אֲדֹנָי [lit. *'my lords'*] he directed to *all* of them, while to their chief he said [in singular]: *'please pass not away from your servant'*, confident that if the chief would remain the others would certainly remain [cf. *Or HaChaim*]. Consequently according to this interpretation, the word אֲדֹנָי does not signify God and has a

ד עַבְדֶּךָ: יֻקַּח־נָא מְעַט־מַיִם וְרַחֲצוּ רַגְלֵיכֶם
ה וְהִשָּׁעֲנוּ תַּחַת הָעֵץ: וְאֶקְחָה פַת־לֶחֶם

secular sense [being merely a term of address: 'Sirs'] (one opinion in *Shevuos* 35b).

A lesson in ethics is derived from the former interpretation of this incident:

'Greater is hospitality to wayfarers than receiving the Divine Presence' [for although the Divine Presence had appeared to Abraham, he took leave of Him in order to be hospitable to his guests] *(Shevuos* 35b; *Shabbos* 127a).

The *Talmud, Shabbos* 127a continues:

Rav Elazar said: Come and observe how the conduct of the Holy One, Blessed be He, is not like that of mortals. The conduct of mortals is such that an inferior person cannot say to a greater man: 'Wait for me until I come to you'; whereas in the case of the Holy One, Blessed be He, Abraham asked Him to wait.[1]

Ramban observes that the *kametz* vocalization in the word אֲדֹנָי indicates that it refers to God. [Had Abraham meant the secular *'my masters'*, it would be vocalized אֲדֹנַי]. Since *Ramban* agrees that according to the plain meaning of these verses Abraham was addressing the *angels,* and at the same time that the Name is sacred, he suggests that Abraham realized that they were angels, and addressed them by their Master's Name, *Adonai,* for we find that even angels are referred to by the divine name *Elohim* and *Eilim* [see *comm.* to אֵל in 14:18; *Ramban* to *Exod.* 15:11; 20:3; *Lev.* 18:27.] It was for this reason that he reverently prostrated himself before them.

4. יֻקַּח־נָא מְעַט־מַיִם — *Let some* [lit. *'a little'*] *water be brought* [lit. *'taken'*].

[According to all interpretations — even those who interpret *v.* 3 as having been addressed to God — this verse records what Abraham said *to the angels.*]

Abraham recognized that it was early in the day and that they would wish to continue their journey; he therefore showed them the most ap-

1. True, we, know from Abraham's behavior that hospitality takes priority over the Divine Presence, but how did Abraham know?

— If a king is someone's house guest and, during the royal visit, the king's child comes with an urgent request, the host will hasten to care for the child. The king will not feel slighted, for a service to his child is a service to him. So, too, with Abraham. After his circumcision, his every instinct and organ was devoted to God's service (see *footnote* to 18:1). By hurrying to extend hospitality to God's creatures, he was still engaged in the service of God *(Tanchuma Yashan).*

— Abraham knew that God had caused the heat to be unbearable so that no guests would come to trouble him. But, if one is forbidden to depart from the *Shechinah* in order to give hospitality to wayfarers, then the heat was unnecessary! From this Abraham understood that hospitality took precedence even over the *Shechinah (Rav Yaakov Shimshon of Shpetivka).*

As a young man, Rav Leib Chasman spent a Sabbath as a guest of the Chofetz Chaim. To his surprise, the Chofetz Chaim recited Kiddush and began the Friday night meal as soon as they arrived home from the synagogue. Only after the fish was eaten did the venerable sage recite the customary *Shalom Aleichem* which should be said before the meal. When Rav Chasman inquired over the strange reversal of order, the Chofetz Chaim answered,

'I knew you were hungry. It is more important to feed a hungry person as soon as possible. The angels can wait a few minutes before they are greeted.'

pass not away from Your servant.'
[4] *Let some water be brought and wash your feet,*
and recline beneath the tree. [5] *I will fetch a morsel of*

propriate hospitality for that hour of the day and offered that they refresh themselves and recline under the tree *(Ramban).*

The phrase *let some water be brought* indicates bringing by a servant [not by himself]. Therefore when Abraham's descendants required water in the desert, God recompensed Abraham by providing them with water through His servant Moses [and not directly Himself] as it says [*Numb.* 20:11]: *And Moses lifted his hand and struck the rock (Rashi).*

That they were provided water through a messenger was 'measure for measure'. Regarding *food,* however, they were provided with Manna directly by God, as He said [*Exod.* 16:4]: 'Behold *I* will rain bread from heaven,' because Abraham said [*v.* 5]: *'I' will take bread,* and [*v.* 8]: *'he' [himself] took butter and milk (Maharshal).*

Cf. also *Bava Metzia* 86b:

Rav Yehudah said in Rav's name, whatever Abraham personally did for the Ministering Angels, God did Personally for his descendants; and whatever Abraham did through an emissary, God did for his descendants though an emissary ... Rav Chama said, ... As a reward for *let a little water be brought,* they were rewarded with Miriam's well.

וְרַחֲצוּ רַגְלֵיכֶם — *And wash your feet.*

[According to *Rashi*'s exegesis, Abraham was not yet aware they were angels]:

He thought that they were [like] Arabs who worship the dust of their feet, and he scrupulously avoided bringing anything connected with idolatry into his house [*Midrash*]. Lot, however, was not particular about this. First he offered them lodging in his house, and only after did he mention washing the feet [see 19:2] *(Rashi).*[1]

[We do not find, however, that they did, in fact wash their feet. Possibly this is the intent of the angels' response recorded in *Bava Metzia* 86b: Do you suspect us of being (like) Arabs who worship the dust on their feet? Ishmael has already issued from you (i.e. your own son does so! — you were punished with such a son because you wrongfully suspected us and — *Shabbos* 97a; — whoever suspects the innocent is bodily afflicted' — *Maharsha;* cf. *Torah Temimah).* It should be noted, however, that Ishmael had not yet sinned. The first reference to his idolatry is in 21:8-9, see *comm.,* when he was approximately seventeen. Thus the implication of the angels' retort as interpreted by the Talmud is that Abraham had a son who would one day abandon his father's faith, and worship the sand *(Rabbi Avie Gold).*]

וְהִשָּׁעֲנוּ תַּחַת הָעֵץ — *And recline beneath the tree.*

In the shade, until I prepare your refreshment *(Radak).*

The translation *'tree'* follows *Rashi,* who briefly comments: תַּחַת הָאִילָן, *beneath the tree.*

The commentators to *Rashi* ex-

1. *Kli Yakar* wonders why Abraham should have been disturbed by the foolishness of those who worship earth. Would he have kept the sunlight out of his home because there are sun-worshipers? Just as idolators cannot render the sun forbidden, so they cannot render the dust forbidden. *Kli Yakar* interprets Abraham's request homiletically. Water is symbolic of purity, hence Abraham was attempting to influence them to repent by giving them 'water of purity.'

וְסַעֲדוּ לִבְּכֶם אַחַר תַּעֲבֹרוּ כִּי־עַל־כֵּן
עֲבַרְתֶּם עַל־עַבְדְּכֶם וַיֹּאמְרוּ כֵּן תַּעֲשֶׂה
ו כַּאֲשֶׁר דִּבַּרְתָּ׃ וַיְמַהֵר אַבְרָהָם הָאֹהֱלָה

plain that *Rashi*'s interpretation is inspired by *Onkelos* who renders the word עֵץ here as אִילָנָא, *tree,* to differentiate it from those instances where *Onkelos* renders עֵץ as אָעָא, *wood.* The meaning of the phrase, as implied by the translation of *Onkelos,* is that Abraham beckoned them to recline beneath a *live tree* rather than beneath a wooden shanty.

Midrash Or Ha'afelah [Torah Shelemah 18:62] perceives *tree* as an allusion to Torah which is described in *Prov.* 3:18 as a *tree of life.* Thus, it is proper that a host should ask his guests figuratively to 'repose under the tree,' i.e., he should entertain his guests with a Torah discourse.

By serving his guests out of doors, Abraham wanted to publicize the need to invite strangers in the hope that others would learn from his example; and to be able to notice other passersby whom he could invite in *(Rabbi Avie Gold).*

5. וְאֶקְחָה פַת־לֶחֶם – *[And] I will fetch a morsel of bread.*

An understated, modest description of the sumptuous meal about to be served. The *Talmud* derives from this that 'the righteous say little and do much' *(Bava Metzia* 87a).

וְסַעֲדוּ לִבְּכֶם – *That you may* [lit. *'and'*] *sustain yourselves* [lit. *'and support your heart'*]

Hunger weakens the heart causing it to 'fall'; food *supports* it to stand firm. Whoever translates this phrase 'refresh your heart' has failed to convey the Hebrew word סַעֲדוּ *(HaRechasim l'Bik'ah).*

The *Midrash* notes that in the Torah, Prophets, and Writings, we find that bread is the sustenance of the heart. In the Torah, in our verse: *I will fetch a morsel of bread and sustain your heart;* in the Prophets [*Jud.* 19:5]: *Sustain your heart with a morsel of bread;* and in the Writings [*Ps.* 104:15]: *Bread sustains man's heart...*

Rav Chama said: The term used here for 'heart' is not the usual form *l'vavchem'* [the longer form for 'hearts' which, in Rabbinic homiletics denotes the heart as the seat of *two* Inclinations – Good and Evil (see *Mishnah Ber.* 9:1], but *'libchem'* [the shorter form, which is regarded as a limitation indicating only one heart, or inclination]. This teaches that angels are free of the Evil Inclination. [The use of the shorter term indicates that there were no conflicting desires in their hearts. Their only desire was to do good] *(Rashi).*

Gur Aryeh asks: But Abraham did not know that they were angels; why then did he use the term *libchem*? He replies that Abraham treated guests with great respect. He addressed them as if it were a foregone conclusion that, angel-like, they had no desire for evil. Or, this may have been an instance of נִבָּא וְלֹא יָדַע מַה נִבָּא, *he prophesied* [i.e., uttered words of great significance] *without realizing that he was prophesying.*

אַחַר תַּעֲבֹרוּ – *Then go on* [lit. *'pass'*]

I.e., after that you may continue on your way *(Rashi).*

Rashi points out that this is an independent clause: *first* refresh yourselves, and *then go on (Mizrachi; Gur Aryeh).* His interpretation thus precludes joining this phrase [which could otherwise be rendered literally: *after you will go*] with the preceding phrase, resulting in the rendering: *I will fetch a morsel of bread that you may refresh yourselves after you go* [see *Nedarim*

bread that you may sustain yourselves, then go on — inasmuch as you have passed your servant's way.' They said, 'Do so, just as you have said.'
6 *So Abraham hastened to the tent to Sarah and*

37b; *Ran; Torah Temimah*].

[If it *were* to be thus rendered then the sense of the verse would be that Abraham was offering to prepare צֵידָה לַדֶּרֶךְ, food which they would take along to eat during their travels *after* having refreshed themselves *(Rabbi Avie Gold).*]

כִּי־עַל־כֵּן עֲבַרְתֶּם עַל עַבְדְּכֶם — *Inasmuch as* [lit. *'for therefore'*] *you have passed your servant's way* [lit. *'passed upon your servant'*].

— Seeing that you have passed my way it would not be fitting that you should not partake of my hospitality *(Ramban).*

[The connotation then would be: For this is the very reason that Providence caused you to come my way.]

As *Rashi* comments: כִּי, *for,* I ask this of you only עַל כֵּן, *inasmuch as,* you have honored me by calling upon me. This is the meaning of this phrase whenever it occurs in Scriptures [cf. 19:8; 33:10; 38:26; *Num.* 10:31.]

Hirsch takes the phrase as elliptical: *for therefore* [do I do or wish this, etc.] *because* ... etc. He explains that wherever this form of conjunction is found in Scripture, it appears to mean: contrary to what *you* may have supposed, there is a different reason for a particular course of action. Thus: 'I invite you to join me — not because you are in need, but because my tent's hospitality is available to every passerby.'

כֵּן תַּעֲשֶׂה כַּאֲשֶׁר דִּבַּרְתָּ — *Do so, just as you have said.*

— A courteous response: 'A morsel of bread will be sufficient, do not trouble yourself more than that' *(Ibn Ezra; Radak).* [1]

According to *Ramban* the response meant: Let us recline under the tree and then pass on immediately, as we are messengers. Do not detain us by inviting us into the tent or to lodge with you.

... Therefore, to comply with their wishes and not detain them, Abraham *ran* into Sarah's tent and asked her to hurry *(Sforno).*

Note that they did not say נַעֲשֶׂה, *'we* will comply with your wishes', because human activities such as eating, drinking, and washing do not apply to angels (*Ha'amek Davar).*

Also, from the future tense תַּעֲשֶׂה, lit. *you will do,* rather than the imperative עֲשֵׂה, *do,* the Sages perceived that the angels thereby intimated a blessing to Abraham: So may you always merit — in the future — to be hospitable to strangers *(Akeidas Yitzchak).*

6. וַיְמַהֵר אַבְרָהָם הָאֹהֱלָה אֶל־שָׂרָה — *So Abraham hastened to the tent to Sarah.*

1. The *Talmud* [*Bava Metzia* 87a] notes that the angels accepted Abraham's invitation immediately, whereas in the case of Lot he had to *'urge them greatly'* [19:3].

The ethical lesson derived from this is: מְסָרְבִין לְקָטָן וְאֵין מְסָרְבִין לְגָדוֹל, 'one may show unwillingness — [i.e. reluctance to accept an invitation] to an inferior person, but not to a great man.'

אֶל־שָׂרָה וַיֹּאמֶר מַהֲרִי שְׁלֹשׁ סְאִים קֶמַח
ז סֹלֶת לוּשִׁי וַעֲשִׂי עֻגוֹת: וְאֶל־הַבָּקָר רָץ

'Hastened' both to fulfill the *mitzvah,* and not further tax the patience of his obviously hurried guests *(Rashbam; Ramban).*

That Sarah remained within the tent illustrates the verse: כָּל כְּבוּדָּה בַת־מֶלֶךְ פְּנִימָה, *all-glorious is the king's daughter within* [*Ps.* 45:14; see *comm.* there.] *(Pesikta Zutresa)*

מַהֲרִי — *Hurry!*

Himself eager to perform a *mitzvah* he fired her with the same eagerness *(Lekach Tov).*[1]

שְׁלֹשׁ סְאִים קֶמַח סֹלֶת — *Three se'ahs of meal, fine flour.*

The סֹלֶת, *fine flour,* was for the cakes. The קֶמַח, inferior *meal,* was for the dough which cooks placed over the pot to absorb the froth *(Rashi).*

Rashi thus accounts for the combination of the two mutually exclusive nouns *meal* and *fine flour.* The phrase cannot be interpreted in the construct form: *fine flour* as some translate, because if so the Hebrew would have been סֹלֶת קֶמַח *(Mizrachi; Gur Aryeh).*

Ramban notes that this was a very large quantity for three men. Perhaps, aware that they were angels and would 'consume' the food, he considered the cakes to be made from the flour as burnt-offerings on the altar. Or possibly the principal men of Abraham's house dined with them.

[*Harav David Cohen* points out, however, that the Talmud in *Beitzah* 17a notes that an oven bakes better if it is full. This would explain why Abraham specified an amount of flour far larger than could be consumed; he wanted his guests to have the best-tasting bread.]

1. *Messilas Yesharim* in Ch. 7 treats זְרִיזוּת, *zealousness,* in serving God:

As soon as a man has taken hold of a *Mitzvah,* he must rush to bring it to a conclusion, not as though he were anxious to get rid of a burden, but in the spirit of apprehension lest he fail to consummate it ...

Whatever the righteous undertake, they carry out with haste. Of Abraham it is written, *"Abraham hastened into the tent to Sarah and said, 'Hurry, three se'ahs of meal, fine-flour, knead it and make cakes.' And Abraham ran unto the herd, and fetched a calf ... "* We are similarly told of Rebecca, *And she hastened and emptied her pitcher into the trough"* [24:20]. Commenting upon the verse, *"And the woman made haste, and ran, and told her husband"* *(Judges* 13:10), the *Midrash* adds, "We may learn that the deeds of the righteous are always performed expeditiously; no time is lost in undertaking a *Mitzvah* or in the execution thereof" *(Bamidbar Rabbah* 10:5).

See then that a man who is righteous does not act sluggishly in the performance of His *Mitzvos.* He moves with the swiftness of fire, and gives himself no rest until his object is attained. Note, further, that as enthusiasm calls forth zeal, so zeal calls forth enthusiasm, for when a man is engaged in the performance of a *Mitzvah,* he feels that as he hastens his outward movements, his emotions are aroused and his enthusiasm grows stronger. But if his bodily movements are sluggish, the movements of his spirit also become dull and lifeless ...

In the worship of the Creator, blessed be His name, it is most important that the heart truly yearn after Him and the soul feel a longing for Him.

Therefore it were best for a man in whom this desire does not burn as it should, deliberately to bestir himself, so that this zeal might become part of his nature, for the outer action awakens the inner attitude. And the outer action being certainly more subject to man's control than the inner attitude, if he avails himself of that which is within his control, he will in time acquire that which is beyond his control. As a result of deliberate effort, there will arise within him an inner joy and an ardent desire to do the will of God.

said, 'Hurry! Three se'ahs of meal, fine flour! Knead and make cakes! [7] Then Abraham ran to the herd,

Ramban continues that in his opinion the simple meaning of the verse is: Prepare quickly three se'ahs of קֶמַח, *meal,* to make of them סֹלֶת, *fine flour.* The entire three se'ahs of meal yielded only a bit of fine flour.

He specified *'three'* because he wanted an equal portion for each to demonstrate that they were all equally important to him in order to avoid jealousy at the meal [cf. *Meg.* 12a] *(R' Bachya).*

Hirsch, in effect, elucidates *Ramban's* interpretation. He explains סֹלֶת as the flour derived from the innermost and best kernel which, if repeatedly sifted, can be separated from the inferior קֶמַח which mingles with it in the form of fine dust *(Menachos* 76b). In describing the לֶחֶם הַפָּנִים, *showbread* of the Temple, the Talmud *(ibid.)* relates that of one *se'ah* of meal, one עִשָּׂרוֹן, *tenth* of an *ephah* of fine flour could be obtained. That amount, a tenth of an *ephah,* is one *omer,* the amount of food an average person consumes in a day. Thus, our verse would mean: *Out of three se'ahs of flour, sift out the finest.* The yield would be one *tenth* for each guest, an amount quite proper for an ample meal. [1]

Even according to *Rashi* only the סֹלֶת, *fine flour,* was used for baking, but *Rashi* avoided the above rendering because if the ordinary meal was not used at all; it would have sufficed to say 'Take סֹלֶת, *fine flour,* and make cakes'! Since the verse mentions both terms, *Rashi* accounts for them both the kneading of the *fine flour* being for the cakes, and the kneading of the *meal* for the 'bakers' dough' *(Divrei David).*

לוּשִׁי וַעֲשִׂי עֻגוֹת — *Knead and make cakes* [i.e., *matzos;* (see below).]

According to the *Midrash,* this occurred during what would later be Passover, and these cakes were unleavened bread [*matzos*] which are also referred to in *Exod.* 12:39 as עֻגֹת מַצּוֹת, *cakes of unleavened bread.* This intimated that his descendants would one day hastily bake *matzos,* and since he scrupulously adhered to all the precepts of the Torah, even before they were given [*Yoma* 28b], he prohibited leavening during the Passover period *(Pesikta Rabbasi* 6).[1]

Here, the word used is עֻגוֹת, *cakes,* while in the case of Lot, the Torah specifically states that he served *matzos* [19:3] in order that one chapter shed light on the other. The entire Torah is filled with allusions and lessons; what one part omits is supplied by another. So we find in many parts of the Torah. *(R' Bachya;* see *Overview* to *Bereishis* Vol. I).

Although it is obvious that flour must be kneaded to make dough, Abraham nevertheless specified to Sarah לוּשִׁי, *knead it.* He thereby intimated to Sarah that she should not share with a servant the *mitzvah* of providing hospitality, rather she

1. Homiletically, however, the *Talmud, Bava Metzia* 87a notes that our verse uses both terms: קֶמַח, *meal* — a general term encompassing all grades of flour, and סֹלֶת, *fine flour.* Said Rav Yitzchak: This teaches that אִשָּׁה עֵינֶיהָ צָרָה בְּאוֹרְחִים, a woman looks with a [more] grudging eye upon guests [than a man].

[Thus Abraham first said *meal* as a general term, but fearing that, because 'a woman looks with a grudging eye upon guests', she might choose an inferior grade, he felt compelled to further clarify that she use סֹלֶת, *fine flour.* (This follows interpretations of *HaKsav VhaKabalah.* Cf. comment of *Rashi* ad loc.: Sarah said: 'Shall I use קֶמַח, *plain* flour?' Abraham answered, סֹלֶת, *'Fine flour').*]

אַבְרָהָם וַיִּקַּח בֶּן־בָּקָר רַךְ וָטוֹב וַיִּתֵּן אֶל־
ח הַנַּעַר וַיְמַהֵר לַעֲשׂוֹת אֹתוֹ: וַיִּקַּח חֶמְאָה

should do even the *kneading* herself. According to the *Midrashic* interpretation that it was Passover and these were *matzos*, the significance was that she should *knead* and *make the cakes* without any intervening delay, lest they become *chametz (Alshich).*

7. וְאֶל הַבָּקָר רָץ אַבְרָהָם – *Then Abraham ran to the herd.*

This is mentioned in his praise. Since he 'said little and planned to do much' [see *comm.* to *v.* 5], he ran in order to expedite the preparations, which were more elaborate than the 'morsel of bread' he had promised them *(Rashbam).*

Ramban emphasizes how this portrays Abraham's great desire to show hospitality. Though he had many servants who were eager to serve him and he was old and still weak from his circumcision, he nevertheless *personally* ran to choose the animals for the meal.

From this verse we learn that the righteous *run* to perform a mitzvah (*Midrash Aggadah*; see *footnote v.* 6).

We see similarly in the *Talmud Shabbos* 119a that although many of the sages of the *Talmud* had servants, they would be scrupulous to participate personally in the Sabbath preparations, considering it a great honor: ... Rav Huna would light the lamp; Rav Papa would plait the wicks; Rav Chisdah would cut vegetables; Rabbah and Rav Yosef would chop wood; Rav Zeira would kindle the fire, and Rav Nachman would carry home the marketing (see *Orach Chaim* 250).[1]

Comp. the Talmudic dictum: מִצְוָה בּוֹ יוֹתֵר מִבִּשְׁלוּחוֹ, 'it is more meritorious through oneself than through one's agent' *(Kiddushin* 41a).

וַיִּקַּח בֶּן־בָּקָר רַךְ וָטוֹב – [*And he*] *took a calf, tender and good.* [2]

The *Talmud (Bava Metzia* 86b) interprets that the triple phraseology – *calf, tender, good* – indicates that there were three calves ... because he wished to offer them three tongues with different relishes [a delicacy.] His intention was that by offering the same to each, no favoritism would be shown and they would each have the broadest choice *(Akeidas Yitzchak).*

וַיִּתֵּן אֶל הַנַּעַר – *And* [*he*] *gave it to the youth.*

– His son, Ishmael; it being Abraham's purpose to train him in good deeds [hospitality to guests] *(Rashi).*

Others, in the *Midrash,* hold that it refers to his servant, Eliezer.

וַיְמַהֵר לַעֲשׂוֹת אֹתוֹ – *Who* [lit. *'and he'*] *hurried to prepare* [lit. *'make'*] *it.*

The *Talmud,* noting the singular

1. *Rabbi Levi Yitzchak of Berditchev* was famous for his hospitality, to the point where he would perform even demeaning, menial chores to assure the comfort of his guests. Once his father-in-law was annoyed with his excessive troubles:

'For a few pennies you can hire a servant to do those chores!' he shouted.

Rabbi Levi Yitzchak replied, 'Shall I give away the *mitzvah* of hospitality and even pay someone to taking away my privilege?

took a calf, tender and good, and gave it to the youth who hurried to prepare it. [8] *He took cream and milk*

'it' although there were *three* calves, answers that he gave *each* calf to a different young man to prepare [either in order to hasten the preparation process, or to train his men in hospitality] *(Bava Metzia* 86b).

8. וַיִּקַּח חֶמְאָה וְחָלָב — *He [Abraham] took cream and milk.*

Yet he brought no bread before them [although the preparation of bread-cakes are mentioned in *verses* 5 and 6!] — For Sarah became *a Niddah*: although she was aged, her menstrual cycle resumed on that day. As a result the dough became טָמֵא, ritually unclean *(Rashi).*

The phenomenon of the return of her menses was indicative of the rejuvenation which was to make the birth of Isaac possible, although, as it would appear from her incredulous response in *v.* 12, (see *Sifsei Chachomim* there) she was not aware that the menstruation was more than a passing phenomenon, perhaps brought about by the hectic rush of the day.]

Since Abraham was scrupulous in matters of ritual purity, he ate even *chullin,* ordinary unhallowed food, only when it was ritually pure *(Bava Metzia* 87a); and since he would not eat the [defiled] bread himself, he would not serve it to others *(Terumas HaDeshen).*

There are opinions — [eg. *Rashbam; Radak*], that according to the simple meaning of Scripture, Abraham *did* serve bread, but since bread is the staple of the meal, it was unnecessary to mention it. [This is also the opinion of the Rabbis in the *Midrash*].

[It would appear, even according to *Rashi's* alternate interpretation in *v.* 9, that bread was served, because the angels inquired after Sarah in order to pass her the cup of wine over which the Grace After Meals had been recited, a ritual dependent upon the eating of bread. *Me'am Loez* citing *Ahavas Zion* suggests that Abraham's *disciples* ate bread and recited the Grace over a cup which Michael then sent to Sarah. This interpretation is difficult, for it assumes that the servants would have eaten something which was not served to the angels, a breach of etiquette. It ignores the commentaries who explain that Abraham would not serve that which he himself would not partake of.]

[It is, however, possible to suggest that *after the first batch of dough became defiled,* a new batch was prepared by the servants, for it is difficult to suggest that the guests should be deprived of such a staple as bread because of Sarah's ritual uncleanness. The Torah which records only that which it deems essential for the narrative, did not include this detail. By not mentioning bread here, the Torah draws our attention to the tradition that with the return of Sarah's menses that original batch became defiled and was not served. But this does not exclude the probability that a new batch was prepared, although the Torah found no need to mention

2. An interesting *Midrash* is preserved in *Pirkei d'Rabbi Eliezer* 36:

A young calf that Abraham was about to fetch ran into the cave of Machpelah. He followed it and found Adam and Eve reclining on their couches, candles burning above them, enveloped in incense-like fragrance. He, therefore, desired the possession of the Cave of Machpelah as his future burial site.

וְחָלָב וּבֶן־הַבָּקָר אֲשֶׁר עָשָׂה וַיִּתֵּן
לִפְנֵיהֶם וְהוּא עֹמֵד עֲלֵיהֶם תַּחַת הָעֵץ
ט וַיֹּאכֵלוּ׃ וַיֹּאמְרוּ אֵלָיו אַיֵּה שָׂרָה אִשְׁתֶּךָ

it. For, as the *Midrash* comments, "if he served them what he had not offered [milk, cream, meat] he certainly served them what he *had* offered!"]

The traditional translation of חֶמְאָה, is *butter*. Our translation of *cream*, however, seems to best reflect *Targum* [שְׁמַן], and *Rashi* who interprets: 'the fatty part of the milk which is skimmed off its surface.' [Some render *curdled milk*, or *leben*.] That the word also means *butter* is evident from such verses as [*Prov.* 30:33]: 'the *churning* of milk brings forth butter' [*churning* being the process by which butter, not cream, is processed.]

וּבֶן הַבָּקָר אֲשֶׁר עָשָׂה — *And the calf which he* [i.e., through his young men] *had prepared* [lit. *'made'* — following *Rashi*.]

[According to *Rashi* in *v.* 7, there were *three* calves, while here only *one* is mentioned.] *Rashi* therefore answers: He served them as they became ready, i.e., one at a time. *(Mizrachi; Gur Aryeh).*

Others see in *Rashi's comm.* a solution to the difficulty of why Abraham served meat and milk in seeming contravention of the *Kashrus* laws. *Rashi's* explanation would thus imply that, following the order of the verse, Abraham first served the dairy items for they naturally required less preparation and were ready first. Only afterwards, after they slaked their thirst, and hunger, did he bring out the full meal which consisted of calves' meat *(Da'as Zekeinim; Malbim*; see *Midrash Hachefetz* [*Torah Sheleimah* 110]: 'from this we learn that butter and milk may precede meat').

Da'as Zekeinim also cites a conflicting *Midrash* [similarly found in *Pesikta Rabbasi* 25] that when God wished to give the Torah to Israel, the angels begged Him to leave His Torah in Heaven [for man would not adhere to its laws.] He refuted them, saying: 'The Torah prohibits milk with meat together, and yet when you descended below you ate meat and milk!' [Therefore why are you better than man?] They immediately acquiesced.

וַיִּתֵּן לִפְנֵיהֶם — *And he* [i.e., Abraham himself] *placed* [*these*] *before them (Radak).*

וְהוּא עֹמֵד עֲלֵיהֶם — [*And*] *he stood over them*, i.e., he waited upon them just as a king's servants stand and attend his needs while he eats *(Abarbanel).*

According to *Midrash HaGadol* [on 26:5] *he stood over them*, lest they mix the meat with the milk [and thereby render his utensils ritually unfit]. (See *Yoreh De'ah* 88).

וַיֹּאכֵלוּ — *And they ate* — i.e., they *appeared* to be eating; this teaches that one must not deviate from the custom *(Rashi).*

As the *Talmud* [*Bava Metzia* 86b] expresses it: One should never depart from custom, for behold Moses ascended on High and ate nothing, whereas the Ministering Angels descended below and ate.

XVIII and the calf which he had prepared, and placed these
9 before them; he stood over them beneath the tree and they ate.
⁹ They said to him, 'Where is Sarah your wife?'

'They ate' — can you really think so? Say rather 'appeared to eat'.

[For an esoteric interpretation of the 'eating' of the angels, see *Overview* to *Bircas HaMazon*, ArtScroll edition.]

Cf. *Zohar*. They 'ate' [i.e., *'consumed'*] whatever Abraham offered them in the sense of אֵשׁ אֹכֶלֶת, fire invisibly consuming fire [and in the sense that *the* bush shown to Moses *(Ex.* 3:2) was not אֻכָּל, *consumed (Da'as Zekeinim)*], as well as in the sense of being sustained on High from Abraham's offering, [sacrifices being also called the 'bread of God' *(Malbim)*.] Furthermore, the expression *'they ate'* is also to be figuratively understood in the sense that they were spiritually sustained from the words of his Torah lessons *(Yefas Toar)*.

Cf. also *Tosafos Bava Metzia ibid.* who cites *Tanna Debe Eliyahu*, that in deference to the righteous Abraham and the trouble he had taken, God 'opened their mouths' and they actually ate.

According to *Midrash HaGadol*, the phrase refers to the *others* from Abraham's household, Ishmael, etc., who were present at the meal and who ate (see *Ramban* to *v.* 6).

9. וַיֹּאמְרוּ אֵלָיו אַיֵּה שָׂרָה אִשְׁתֶּךָ — *(And) they said to him, 'Where is Sarah your wife?'*

The angels certainly knew where Sarah was. They asked this question in order to draw attention to her modesty — to bring out the fact that she was in the tent — and so endear her all the more to her husband. According to Rav Yose bar Chaninah [in *Bava Metzia* 87a] they inquired where she was in order to pass her the כּוֹס שֶׁל בְּרָכָה, the cup of wine over which the Grace after meals has been said *(Rashi)*. [See bracketed *comm.* to *v.* 8.]

According to *Rashbam* the question was merely rhetorical, serving as an opening for their conversation, much in the manner that God asked Adam [3:9]: אַיֶּכָּה, *'Where are you?'*

[Interestingly, according to the *Zohar*, the angel's question as to Sarah's whereabouts was sincere for angels do not know what is happening in this world except what is necessary for their mission. (See *Tosafos Shabbos* 12b s.v. שֶׁאֵין).

(Apparently those who maintain that the angels *did* know would hold that knowledge of Sarah's whereabouts *was* a necessary part of their mission).]

Sforno explains that they inquired after Sarah, because the purpose of their mission was to give Sarah the joy of hearing *personally* that she would have a child; Abraham had already been promised this by God Himself [17:16]. [See *footnote* to *v.* 12.]

Thus Abraham's answer הִנֵּה בָאֹהֶל, *she is in the tent* [in addition to *Rashi*'s Talmudic interpretation that this served to emphasize her modesty], indicated that she is near at hand to hear whatever you tell her *(Or HaChaim)*.

Midrash Sechel Tov notes that וַיֹּאמְרוּ, *they* [*all three*] *asked*, for had only one asked he would have cast suspicion upon himself. Subsequently, however, only the angel Michael conveyed the good tidings about the birth of a son.

י וַיֹּאמֶר הִנֵּה בָאֹהֶל: וַיֹּאמֶר שׁוֹב אָשׁוּב
אֵלֶיךָ כָּעֵת חַיָּה וְהִנֵּה־בֵן לְשָׂרָה אִשְׁתֶּךָ
וְשָׂרָה שֹׁמַעַת פֶּתַח הָאֹהֶל וְהוּא אַחֲרָיו:

Rashi — citing the *Midrash* and *Talmud* — notes that the letters א י ו of the word אֵלָיו, *to him*, have dots over them in the Torah [the dotted letters form the word אַיּוֹ, *where is he?*] Rav Shimon ben Elazar said: wherever you find [a word] in which the undotted letters exceed the dotted ones, one must give a special interpretation to the undotted letters. [The *Midrash* continues, if the dotted letters exceed the others, one must give special interpretation to the dotted ones.] Since the dotted letters here [איו] exceed the other one [ל], you must interpret the dotted ones: They also asked Sarah אַיּוֹ, where is he [Abraham]? — [just as they asked him about her *(Tosafos)*. Since they had seen Abraham before, they probably inquired after him when he went to the herd and was involved in preparing the meal *(Gur Aryeh)*.] ...

... The Torah thereby teaches etiquette: A man should inquire of the host about the hostess, and of the hostess about the host *(Rashi)*.

Hirsch cites the same Talmudic explanation and elaborates that it is indeed proper to inquire after the hostess, for, in all probability, it is she who is respsible for the hospitality being enjoyed. Nevertheless, the inquiry should not be made directly of her, but through her husband.

10. The Promise of a Son is revealed to Sarah.

וַיֹּאמֶר — *And he* [i.e., one of the three angels, the angel Michael *(Midrash)*] *said.*

שׁוֹב אָשׁוּב אֵלֶיךָ — *I will surely return to you* [lit. *'return, I will return to you.'*]

Surely the angel was not announcing that *he* would return, he was speaking only as God's agent [indicating that God would return]; this is similar to the angel who addressed Hagar [16:10] in first person, but was speaking only as God's messenger ... *(Rashi)*.

Rashi compares this with Elisha who, when promising the Shunamite [in *II Kings* 4:16] a child, could not promise that *he* would return. An angel, who lives forever, could make such a promise [for he spoke as an angel of God]; but Elisha as a human could not determine for himself that he would still be alive. He therefore said that *at this season, when the time comes around* [whether or not I am personally able to return] *you will embrace a child.*

Ibn Ezra adds as proof that the angel spoke in God's Name, that in *v.* 14 God Himself reiterates that it is He Who will return. Though it is not recorded that He did indeed return at the promised time, a reference to this return may lie in 21:1: *And* HASHEM *remembered Sarah as He had said, and* HASHEM *did to Sarah as He had spoken (Ramban;* see his other interpretation below s.v. כָּעֵת חַיָּה).

כָּעֵת חַיָּה — *At this time next year* [following *Rashi;* lit. *'as the time that lives'.*]

— It was Passover, and on the next Passover Isaac was born. That [it was *exactly* a year later from the date of God's promise in 17:21 *(Mizrachi* to 18:14)] is deduced from the definite article כָּ [כָּעֵת] 'at *this* [time]', rather than the indefinite כְּ [כְּעֵת] 'at *a* [time]' *(Rashi)*.

[See *comm.* to 21:2 s.v. לַמּוֹעֵד, where *Rashi* intimates that the *appointed time* was that which God intended when He announced to Abraham further, *v.* 14: *'at the appointed time I will return to you;* which in turn, as *Rashi* explains there, refers to the time *originally intended* by the announcement *God* had made to Abraham (three days earlier) at the circumcision when He promised to return [17:21] *at this season next year.*]

XVIII
10

And he said, 'In the tent!'
[10] *And he said, 'I will surely return to you at this time next year, and behold Sarah your wife will have a son.' Now Sarah was listening at the entrance of the tent which was behind him.*

According to *Midrash Tanchuma,* the angel had made a mark on the wall and said to him: 'When the sun reaches this point next year she will give birth.' [According to *Rashi* in 21:2, it was *God* Who had made this mark. See *comm.* there.]

[There are differences of opinion as to when this visit took place: after Yom Kippur, or Passover (15th of Nissan). There is, however, no dispute regarding Isaac's birth; all agree that he was born on the first day of Passover *(Rosh Hashanah* 11a; [see *Maharsha* and *Mizrachi*]; *Seder Olam; Ramban* to 17:26; cf. *Da'as Zekeinim).* See *footnote* to 21:2.]

[In any case, the promise of the angel in this verse וְהִנֵּה־בֵן לְשָׂרָה אִשְׁתֶּךָ, *and behold Sarah your wife will have a son* is not to be understood to imply that on this day next year *Sarah will give birth,* but that by this time next year Sarah will *already have given birth on the originally appointed day* promised in 17:21, and will by then *already have a son.*]

Rashi goes on to explain that כָּעֵת חַיָּה is a colloquial expression [which like all idioms defies literal interpretation]. It signifies: *at this time next year: at this time when there will be life* [חַיָּה] *to you,* i.e., when you will all be healthy and alive — [the intent idiomatically being similar to the expression כֹּה לֶחָי, lit. *so to life (I Sam.* 25:6) which signifies a form of blessing: so shall it be next year and many years — לֶחָי, colloquially connoting *next year* when you are חַי וְקַיָּם alive and well *(Menachem; Ibn Janach)*].

According to *Radak,* חַיָּה is a term used for a woman who has given birth (see *Mishnah Yoma* 73b). The verse therefore has the meaning of: *I will surely return to you at this time when she will give birth and Sarah will have a son.*

— The implication is: When the חַיָּה, *childbearing woman,* shall enter into labor, then אָשׁוּב אֵלֶיךָ, *I [Myself] shall return to you, and behold Sarah shall have a son* without the aid of a midwife! *(Karnei Or).*

Ramban suggests that the phrase שׁוֹב אָשׁוּב *[I will surely return]* might be interpreted in the causitive, [= אָשׁוּב אָשִׁיב]*: I will bring back to you.* The entire phrase would then mean: 'I will surely bring back for you a time exactly like this [in the cycle of the year] in which you will all be alive, and at which time Sarah will have a son.' This is similar to the promise Abraham already received in 17:21.

Ralbag maintains that in Hebrew עֵת חַיָּה refers to the present: *'the living moment',* as opposed to the past which is dead and gone, and the future which is not yet born. Thus, the angel promises a return at *this precise living moment,* in the annual cycle, i.e., next year.

As *Hirsch* explains: עֵת designates a particular point in time. Every moment represents the momentary terrestial and cosmic relation of the world. Thus עֵת חַיָּה indicates the identical moment in the 'recurring' cycle of time. [See *Overviews* to *Eichah* and *Haggadah,* ArtScroll ed.] Thus our phrase means: *Just as the present moment will recur in the living cycle of time so will I return.'*

וְשָׂרָה שֹׁמַעַת פֶּתַח הָאֹהֶל — *Now* [lit. *'and'*] *Sarah was listening at the entrance of the tent.*

She was in the tent, but when she heard them speaking about her she drew near the opening of the tent to

יא וְאַבְרָהָם וְשָׂרָה זְקֵנִים בָּאִים בַּיָּמִים חָדַל
יב לִהְיוֹת לְשָׂרָה אֹרַח כַּנָּשִׁים: וַתִּצְחַק
שָׂרָה בְּקִרְבָּהּ לֵאמֹר אַחֲרֵי בְלֹתִי הָיְתָה־

hear what they were saying *(Radak).*

She did not merely happen to overhear; *she was listening.* Although modesty kept her from the table, she did not want to miss the conversation, for Abraham's every word with guests was surely well worth the trouble of listening *(Hirsch).*

[Cf. the *Talmudic* dictum: 'Even the ordinary talk of scholars needs studying' *(Avodah Zarah* 19b).]

וְהוּא אַחֲרָיו — *Which was behind him* [lit. *'and he was behind him'.*]

I.e., the entrance was behind the angel *(Rashi);* she therefore was able to hear what he was saying *(Rashbam);* but, at the same time, the angels were unable to see her *(Radak).*

It was for this reason that the angel did not address her directly as Elisha did the Shunnamite [*II Kings* 4:15] *(Sforno).*

11. וְאַבְרָהָם וְשָׂרָה זְקֵנִים — *Now* [lit. *'and'*] *Abraham and Sarah were old.*

This verse is meant to explain Sarah's incredulous laughter in *v.* 12 *(Radak).*

בָּאִים בַּיָּמִים — *Well on in years* [lit. *'coming into the days.'*]

This expression is used to describe one upon whom old age weighs heavily; one who has 'entered into those days' when he knows he must go the way of all flesh *(Radak);* one upon whom life has taken its toll *(Heidenheim).*

According to *Malbim,* the phrase indicates that they were not *prematurely* aged, but were 'old' as a result of having lived a long life.

חָדַל לִהְיוֹת לְשָׂרָה אֹרַח כַּנָּשִׁים — *The manner of women had ceased to be with Sarah* [lit. *'it had ceased to be with Sarah the manner like the women'.*]

I.e., her regular menstrual cycle had ceased *(Rashi).*

This does not preclude that flow which came upon her while she was preparing the cakes, as *Rashi* explains in *v.* 8, [and which she perceived merely as an unusual phenomenon attributing no special significance to it.] It is the *regular* monthly cycle — prerequisite for childbearing — that had ceased *(Divrei David; Gur Aryeh).*

12. Sarah Laughs

וַתִּצְחַק שָׂרָה בְּקִרְבָּהּ לֵאמֹר — *And Sarah laughed at herself* [lit. *'within herself'*], *saying.*

I.e., derisively, unlike Abraham who laughed joyfully *(Onkelos; Rashi* to 17:17).

Following *Rashi:* She reflected on her withered physical condition [i.e., the phrase is to be translated: she laughed בְּקִרְבָּהּ, at her insides (rather than בְּקִרְבָּהּ *within herself)* — *(Mizrachi)*] and incredulously wondered whether in her withered state she could produce a child *(Tanchuma; Rashi).*

This reaction indicated her utter disbelief in the possibility of the prediction, as if such a thing were beyond God's powers. Therefore, God was angry with her and not with Abraham *(Midrash Aggadah);* [see *footnote* to *v.* 13.]

[It is apparently insignificant that

[11] *Now Abraham and Sarah were old, well on in
years; the manner of women had ceased to be with
Sarah —*
[12] *And Sarah laughed at herself, saying, 'After I
have withered shall I again have delicate skin? And*

Sarah was not aware they were angels; someone of Sarah's righteousness should never have sneered at the possibility of God's bringing about miraculous events. There is possibly also an element here from Sarah's perspective of the dictum *(Meg.* 15a): אַל תְּהִי בִּרְכַּת הֶדְיוֹט קַלָּה בְעֵינֶיךָ *'let not the blessing of an ordinary man be lightly esteemed in your eyes.'* As *Ramban* explains (see *v.* 13) she should have demonstrated faith and at least said: 'Amen, so be it.']

The word לֵאמֹר, *saying,* does not suggest that she laughed *audibly.* According to *Radak,* the verse rather has the meaning of *'she thought in her heart as follows.'* [As explained several times previously, לֵאמֹר has the connotation of *'clearly.'* That is, her purpose for laughing was quite clear; it was not impulsive and ambiguous.]

She laughed in disbelief because she thought that the guest's statement was simply the courteous blessing of a human prophet [like that of Elisha (see *II Kings* 4:16)] and not a prophecy from God. She thought, therefore, that his blessing was unattainable in view of her advanced age. Such a miraculous rejuvenation would be as great a miracle as the resurrection of the dead, which only the command of God Himself could accomplish *(Radak; Sforno).*[1]

[For the *Hashkafah* philosophical implications of Sarah's laughter, see *Overview.*]

Sifsei Kohen notes that as a prophetess — in many ways even greater than Abraham [*Megillah* 14a; see *Rashi* to 21:12] — Sarah should have perceived the truth of the guests' prediction. Why, then was she blinded to it? However, with the onset of ritual uncleanness which her rejuvenation brought about, she was temporarily not privy to prophetic perception.

אַחֲרֵי בְלֹתִי הָיְתָה לִי עֶדְנָה — *After I have withered shall I* [*again*] *have* [lit. *'was there to me'*] *delicate skin?*

1. A fundamental question arises: Abraham was already assured in 17:19 that Sarah would bear a son. Why, then, does Sarah now react with incredulous disbelief after God Himself — only three days earlier — made the promise?

Ramban [to *v.* 15, below] discusses this and concludes that Abraham had not revealed to Sarah what God had told him before his circumcision. Perhaps Abraham thought that God would undertake nothing until He revealed His plans to Sarah, His prophetess (see *Amos* 3:7). Or it is possible that in the hectic days in which Abraham in righteous diligence undertook to circumcise himself and his household, and the painful days of convalescence that followed, Abraham neglected to mention it to Sarah.

Additionally, as noted later, Sarah did not know they were angels, and therefore lent no credence to their words.

As *Hirsch* [to *v.* 1] explains, it appears that Abraham felt he had no right to tell Sarah because he had not been specifically told to do so. Apparently, Sarah was meant to hear the news suddenly so that the very idea should appear ridiculous to her. She would laugh just as Abraham did (17:17 [but for different reasons; see *comm.* there]); and in the future they would always bear in mind that the birth of a child seemed to them to be an impossibility.

יג לִי עֶדְנָה וַאדֹנִי זָקֵן: וַיֹּאמֶר יהוה אֶל־
אַבְרָהָם לָמָּה זֶּה צָחֲקָה שָׂרָה לֵאמֹר

[This verse does not exclude the accepted interpretation that Sarah had menstruated that day. She had not realized that her flow was more than an unrelated occurrence, certainly not the resumption of childbearing capability.]

The translation *delicate, smooth, glistening,* follows *Rashi* who explains that this is the Mishnaic use of the term [see *Menachos* 86a]. Alternatively the word is related to עִידָן, *time*: the menstrual period.

[*HaKsav V'HaKabbalah* explains that עֶדְנָה means period. It is used for menstruation because it usually occurs at fixed periods.]

According to *Ibn Ezra,* the word is related to עֵדֶן, *pleasure, satisfaction,* the intent of the statement being: After I have withered and aged shall there be renewed in me the pleasures of a rejuvenated youth?

Abarbanel perceives the *pleasure* as suggestive of the joy of marital intimacy which Sarah had despaired of resuming in light of her deteriorated physical state.

The past tense הָיְתָה *there was,* in the verse creates difficulties. Our rendering follows *Ibn Ezra* and most commentators who interpret it in the future tense as an incredulous, rhetorical question *shall there be?*

Hirsch suggests that it means: 'It seemed laughable to her to think that in the future people would say that in her old, worn-out age she obtained [past tense] the satisfaction of her deepest, innermost earthly desires.'

[According to the *Talmud, Bava Metzia* 87a, this was not a rhetorical question, but a statement of fact]: *After I have withered, I have had smooth skin!* I.e., after my skin has worn and the wrinkles have multiplied, lo! my skin is rejuvenated, my wrinkles smoothed out, and my former beauty returned.

It is apparently on the above interpretation that *Malbim* bases his entire exposition of this verse:

Having just witnessed her rejuvenation, in the form of the return of her menses, *Sarah laughed joyfully* with the knowledge that God's promise would be fulfilled inasmuch as her youthfulness had returned to her and she would now be able to conceive in a normal fashion without reliance on a further miracle which would have resulted in a reduction of her merit. Thus the interpretation of the verse is: I am overjoyed! *After having withered, I have now regained my youth* — and my merits will not be affected. [See continuation in *v.* 13 לָמָּה זֶּה]

וַאדֹנִי זָקֵן — *And my husband* [lit. *'my master'*] *is old!*

[In line with *Rashi* and *Ramban's* interpretation: Not only am I withered, but my husband, too, is old. Between the both of us, conception is impossible!]

According to *Da'as Zekeinim, Abarbanel, Malbim:* even though a miracle was performed for *me* with the return of my menses, nevertheless no perceptible change has come upon my husband; *he* remains old. Only a new miracle could alter this!

Ha'amek Davar sums up this interpretation when he comments: 'When she was first told, she did not doubt it for a minute. Nothing

XVIII my husband is old!'

13 [13] Then HASHEM said to Abraham, 'Why is it that Sarah laughed, saying: "Shall I in truth bear a child,

is beyond God; if He wished it, even a stone could conceive. When she, however, saw that her youthfulness returned, it became obvious that it was God's plan that her childbearing should be accomplished in a natural manner. She wondered, however, at the fact that her husband had not been rejuvenated. Therefore, she exclaimed: אַחֲרֵי בְלֹתִי הָיְתָה לִּי עֶדְנָה, *after I had been withered, my youthfulness has returned,* but alas! וַאדֹנִי זָקֵן, *my husband remains old!'*

Sarah reasoned: The change that has come about in me might be the result of my merits; perhaps my husband's merits were depleted by his victory over the kings and therefore it is futile to expect a further miracle. Additionally, we are both old and even if we were to have a son now, who knows if we will live to raise him and see him married? The rejuvenation I feel in myself may also mean that I will live long enough to raise him, but since it does not appear that my husband is any more youthful, the promised blessing is not 'whole' *(Kli YaKar).*

13. וַיֹּאמֶר ה׳ אֶל אַבְרָהָם — *Then* [lit. *'and'*] *HASHEM said to Abraham.*

According to *Levush* on *v.* 1, and *Ibn Ezra* to *v.* 10 [as well as *Rashi* and *Sforno* who in the following verses, paraphrase in first-person with God as the speaker] God Himself had been, if one may so express it, waiting patiently while Abraham entertained the angels. Now He interjects in response to Sarah's incredulous laughter.

According to *Rashbam, Radak,* and *R' Bachya, 'HASHEM'* here refers to the chief angel, who, as God's emissary is called by the name of his master. Cf. also *Judges* 6:16.

לָמָּה זֶּה צָחֲקָה שָׂרָה — *Why is it that Sarah laughed?*

HASHEM accused her in Abraham's presence of considering His promise to be impossible of fulfillment.

Instead of laughing derisively — although she did not know they were angels — she should have believed; at least she should have said 'Amen, May God do so!' [Especially since the resumption of her menses was a sign from heaven] *(Ramban* to *v.* 15).[1]

Malbim, following his comment to *v.* 12, interprets God's accusation: Why does Sarah rejoice that she can give birth despite her age because her rejuvenation makes a

1. Why did God rebuke Sarah for her laughter and not Abraham for his [17:17]? — This is comparable to a wise woman who wished to rebuke her daughter-in-law. Instead she directed the rebuke to her daughter, and the daughter-in-law understood the indirect message. Here, too, God rebuked Abraham indirectly in order to spare his feelings*(Chizkuni).*

[Perhaps the meaning is that when the offense was duplicated God no longer wished to overlook it; He had not rebuked Abraham earlier but now that Sarah

יד הַאַף אֻמְנָם אֵלֵד וַאֲנִי זָקַנְתִּי: הֲיִפָּלֵא
מֵיהוָה דָּבָר לַמּוֹעֵד אָשׁוּב אֵלֶיךָ כָּעֵת
°שני טו חַיָּה וּלְשָׂרָה בֵן: °וַתְּכַחֵשׁ שָׂרָה | לֵאמֹר
לֹא צָחַקְתִּי כִּי | יָרֵאָה וַיֹּאמֶר | לֹא כִּי
טז צָחָקְתְּ: וַיָּקֻמוּ מִשָּׁם הָאֲנָשִׁים וַיַּשְׁקִפוּ

further miracle unnecessary? As *v.* 14 continues, *Is anything beyond* HASHEM? Since only HASHEM holds the key to conception, it is He Who will cause her to give birth. That being the case, age was never a factor because the laws of nature are neglected in the face of God's will.

הַאַף אֻמְנָם — *Shall I in truth?* [Following *Rashi.*]

An incredulous question: Shall such a wondrous thing come true? *(Radak).*

וַאֲנִי זָקַנְתִּי — *Though* [lit. *'and'*] *I have aged.*

Her actual words in *v.* 12 were וַאדֹנִי זָקֵן, *my husband is old,* but for the sake of peace between husband and wife, Scripture [i.e., God] now changed the uncomplimentary reference from her husband to herself *(Rashi).*

Cf. *Bava Metzia* 87a: Peace is precious, for even the Holy One, Blessed be He, made a variation for its sake.

Ramban notes that God did, in effect, quote her truthfully, because the phrase וַאֲנִי זָקַנְתִּי, *I am old,* was really her intent when she had said אַחֲרֵי בְלֹתִי, *after I have withered.* Rather, for the sake of peace, He merely omitted her remark about Abraham וַאדֹנִי זָקֵן, *my husband is old.* [Had He not been concerned about peace He would have reported that she laughed about both of them.]

14. הֲיִפָּלֵא מֵה׳ דָּבָר — *Is anything beyond* [lit. *'hidden from'*] HASHEM? [i.e., from *Me,* according to *Rashi* and *Ibn Ezra* in *v.* 10; or: *from* HASHEM, Who sent us [the angels] *(Rashbam)*].

Following *Targum:* הֲיִתְכַּסֵּא, *is anything hidden:* Is anything so far distant and concealed from Me that I cannot accomplish whatever I wish? *(Rashi).*

According to *Chizkuni* the phrase implies: Is it hidden from Me that Sarah did, indeed, laugh?

— Is anything too difficult and improbable for God to cause it to happen? *(Ramban).*

— Do I not know that Sarah is old? Nevertheless it is *I* Who promised, and there is no room for doubt! *(Abarbanel).*

The inclusion here of HASHEM indicates that the angel was not merely giving you his own blessing;

laughed too, He rebuked her for the offense, with the result that Abraham, too, was indirectly rebuked for *his* earlier laughter.]

According to *Midrash HaGadol,* this teaches that when the lesser is rebuked, then the greater will understand also [but, in the reverse case, if the greater were rebuked the lesser might consider himself exempt because being greater obviously imposes greater obligations.]

[See also *Midrash Aggadah* cited at beginning of *v.* 12.]

though I have aged?'' 14 *— Is anything beyond*
HASHEM?! At the appointed time I will return to you
at this time next year, and Sarah will have a son.'
15 *Sarah denied it, saying, 'I did not laugh,' for she*
was frightened. But he said, 'No, you laughed in-
deed.'
16 *So the men got up from there, and gazed down*

he was speaking in My name! *(Sforno).*

[The word הֲיִפָּלֵא may also be derived from פֶּלֶא, *wonder,* yielding in a similar sense: *Is anything too wondrous for HASHEM?* (comp. *Ibn Ezra).*]

[*HASHEM's Name in this context might also imply: Is anything beyond HASHEM — in His Attribute of Mercy — to accomplish on behalf of His beloved?*]

לַמּוֹעֵד אָשׁוּב אֵלֶיךָ כָּעֵת חַיָּה — *At the appointed time I will return to you at this time next year.*

At the appointed time — i.e., the time I originally intended when I promised you to return [17:21] *at this time next year (Rashi).*[See *v.* 10 and 21:2.]

This intended time was Passover, when everyone agrees that Isaac was born. In fact, the numerical value of לַמּוֹעֵד [*at the appointed time* = 150] equals בַּפֶּסַח [*on Passover*]. *(Chizkuni).*

God Himself reiterated the promise now to reassure Abraham that in His displeasure with Sarah He did not withdraw the promise, but that He would surely fulfill it at the destined time *(Alshich; Or HaChaim).*

[The Traditional pause for שֵׁנִי, the second *aliyah* in the Torah reading, is inserted at this point rather than after the next verse which would at first glance seem to be a more natural break. The next verse ends with a rebuke, an inappropriate place for a pause. It is customary to insert the pause after an auspicious phrase, such as the ending of this verse: וּלְשָׂרָה בֵן, *and Sarah will have a son.* (See *Rama; Orach Chaim* 138).]

15. וַתְּכַחֵשׁ שָׂרָה — *Sarah denied it.*

[Apparently *to Abraham* when he confronted her *(based on Ramban and Sforno).*]

כִּי יָרֵאָה — *For she was frightened.*

To admit that she sinned. However, inwardly she repented *(Sforno).*

Or according to *Hirsch*: She was afraid that her laughter had offended the guests.

וַיֹּאמֶר לֹא כִּי צָחָקְתְּ — *But* [lit. *'and'*] *he* [Abraham (following *Ramban* and *Sforno*)] *said 'No, you laughed indeed.'* [1]

You need not deny it; rather you are not to forget that you did laugh *(Hirsch).*

16. Abraham escorts his guests

וַיָּקֻמוּ מִשָּׁם הָאֲנָשִׁים — *So the men got up from there.*

1. *Rashi* explains that the first כִּי in this verse is used in the sense of *because*: 'Sarah denied it *because* she was afraid'; the second כִּי is used in the sense of *but*: And he said, 'It is not as you said *but* you did, indeed, laugh!' For the Sages [*Rosh Hashanah* 3a] said that the word כִּי has four meanings: if; perhaps; but; because.

עַל־פְּנֵי סְדֹם וְאַבְרָהָם הֹלֵךְ עִמָּם
יז לְשַׁלְּחָם: וַיהוָה אָמָר הַֽמְכַסֶּה אֲנִי
יח מֵֽאַבְרָהָם אֲשֶׁר אֲנִי עֹשֶׂה: וְאַבְרָהָם הָיוֹ

From the house where they had received hospitality *(Sforno).*

According to *Rashbam,* two of them went on to Sodom, as it is written [19:1] *and the two angels arrived in Sodom,* and their chief remained behind to converse with Abraham. Beginning with *v.* 20 it is the angel of God [and not God Himself] who is the speaker.

According to most opinions, however, God Himself is the speaker in the dialogue with Abraham. He had come to visit with Abraham in *v.* 1, and if one may so express it, had been 'waiting' all this time while Abraham had taken leave of Him to show hospitality to his guests.

וַיַּשְׁקִפוּ עַל־פְּנֵי סְדֹם — *And* [*they*] *gazed down toward* [lit. *'upon the face of'*] *Sodom.*

— Which offered the most complete contrast to the simple pure atmosphere from which these men were just emerging *(Sforno;* cf. *Hirsch).*

The term *'gazed down'* is used because they were in Hebron, probably standing on one of the peaks of the Judean mountains from which they *gazed down* upon the panorama of the valley of Sodom *(Hoffman).*

Rashi notes that wherever the verb form of הַשְׁקָפָה, *gazing down* [i.e., in the *Hiph'il* form]; occurs in Scripture [specifically in the Five Books of the Torah *(Taz)*] it is always used in connection with calamity [i.e., it always denotes gazing for the purpose of bringing evil], except *Deut.* 26:15: הַשְׁקִיפָה מִמְּעוֹן קָדְשְׁךָ ... וּבָרֵךְ אֶת עַמְּךָ, *gaze down from Your holy habitation ... and bless Your people.* [The above verse deals with declarations that the required tithes, including that given to the poor, have been given] for so great is the virtue of charity that it changes [what would ordinarily be an expression portending] evil, into mercy.

וְאַבְרָהָם הֹלֵךְ עִמָּם לְשַׁלְּחָם — *While* [lit. *'and'*] *Abraham walked* [lit. *'was walking'*] *with them to see them off* [lit. *'to send them'*]

I.e., to escort them. He [still] thought that they were [ordinary] travelers *(Rashi).*

Alshich notes that after they had 'eaten', the angels could have transformed themselves into their spiritual non-corporeal states, and been in Sodom in an instant. Therefore, the verse specifically states that *the men rose up from there* on foot just as do human beings. They *gazed down upon Sodom* rather than instantaneously transmitting themselves there in order to enable Abraham to escort them. Therefore they accommodated their pace to his, so that he might complete his hospitality by escorting them.

The *Zohar* emphasizes the importance of escorting a departing guest:

Rav Yesa said: 'That Abraham escorted them shows that he was not aware that they were angels; for if he was aware, what need had he to send them off? ... '

toward Sodom, while Abraham walked with them to see them off.

[17] *And HASHEM said, 'Shall I conceal from Abraham what I do,* [18] *now that Abraham is surely to*

'No', answered Rav Elazar. 'Although he knew, he kept to his usual custom with them and escorted them. It is highly incumbent to escort a departing guest, for this crowns a good act.

That is why the present tense הֹלֵךְ, *was walking* is used, because this escorting is linked with the next verse. For while Abraham was accompanying them, God appeared to him to reveal His intentions ... Thus when one escorts his departing guest, he draws the Shechinah to accompany him on the way as a protection.

17. Sodom's destruction revealed.

וַה' אָמָר — *And HASHEM said.*

To the legion of Heaven, or to His angels. Or perhaps *said* means 'reflected' *(Ramban).*

The phraseology denotes the past perfect: HASHEM *had* said — he had long before determined that He would reveal His intentions to His prophets [see *footnote*] *(Hoffman).*

Sforno explains that while Abraham was still engaged in the precept of escorting his guests, God revealed Himself to him *so that he will command his children and his household after him,* for 'the reward of one *mitzvah* is another *mitzvah'.* [I.e., his reward for performing the *mitzvah* of escorting would be the fulfillment of the further *mitzvah* of commanding his children after him to keep God's way.]

[It must be noted that in any event God's reasoning reflected in *vs.* 17-19 was not *verbalized* to Abraham. They were not revealed to mankind until Moses committed the Torah to writing, as *Ramban* explains in 8:21. God's actual *revelation* to Abraham begins with *v.* 20.]

הַמְכַסֶּה אֲנִי מֵאַבְרָהָם אֲשֶׁר אֲנִי עֹשֶׂה — *Shall I conceal from Abraham what I do?* [I.e., what I am about to do] in Sodom. Since I have given him this land — including these Sodomite cities [see 10:19] — is it proper that I carry out My plan without his knowledge? Furthermore I called him Abraham, meaning *the father of a horde of nations* [17:5]: should I then destroy the children [the Sodomites] without first informing the father who loves Me? *(Rashi)* [1]

The question is rhetorical, i.e., *'of course I cannot conceal from Abraham!' (Hoffman).*

Alshich asks why it would be unusual for God to do something without first revealing it to Abraham. He explains that had Abraham not been given the opportunity to plead for Sodom, he would have thought that the destroying

1. The prophet Amos similarly expressed it [3:7]: *Surely My Lord HASHEM/ELOHIM will do nothing without revealing His secret to His servants the prophets.*

From our verse we see why God reveals His ways to the prophets. The reason is so that they can interpret historical events to their contemporaries, making history a teacher of the people. Abraham was not primarily a prophet to his own time — although he did proclaim the greatness of God. His primary function was to teach the דֶּרֶךְ ה', *the way of HASHEM,* to the future descendants of Israel. In order that he might derive the appropriate lessons from the destruction of Sodom, God revealed what he intended to do *(Hoffman).*

יט יִהְיֶה לְגוֹי גָּדוֹל וְעָצוּם וְנִבְרְכוּ־בוֹ כֹּל
גּוֹיֵי הָאָרֶץ׃ כִּי יְדַעְתִּיו לְמַעַן אֲשֶׁר יְצַוֶּה

angels had done their work without sparing any righteous people, or that God had acted through the strict Attribute of Justice without tempering it with mercy. Thinking it inconceivable that there were no significant numbers of righteous people even in Sodom, Abraham would have been deeply grieved.

Or, according to *Sforno:* Should I not at least reveal My Goodness to Abraham, that if there is a hope of repentance due to the presence of righteous people among the wicked Sodomites, then I would spare the wicked, for I do not desire their death but their repentance.

18. וְאַבְרָהָם הָיוֹ יִהְיֶה לְגוֹי גָּדוֹל וְעָצוּם — *Now that Abraham is surely to become a great and mighty nation.*

The translation and punctuation which emphasizes the continuity between this verse and the preceding, follows *Rashi* who comments: Shall I conceal it from him? He is so beloved of Me as to become a great nation and a source of blessing to the families of the earth!

Rashi also notes that the *Midrash* [also *Talmud, Yoma* 38b] applies this to the verse in *Prov.* 10:7 זֵכֶר צַדִּיק לִבְרָכָה, *The mention of the righteous shall be for a blessing,* therefore since He *mentioned* him, He *blessed* him. [See similar *comm.* concerning Noah in 6:9.]

This is why, notes *Torah Temimah,* that even today when we mention someone in writing we add after his name שליט״א, נ״י, שיחי׳, *may he live,* etc., or other some appropriate blessing. We should also do this in speech, as is the custom in certain Yemenite communities.

Ramban interprets that God felt constrained to inform Abraham because, seeing that Abraham is destined to become a great and mighty nation, future nations will ask 'How could God have hidden this from him?' or 'How could Abraham have been so callous about his close neighbors that he refrained from praying on their behalf?' He recognizes that I love righteousness, and he will charge his children to cultivate these virtues. Now, if there is a righteous cause to pardon the Sodomites, he will beseech Me to do so. If, on the other hand they are completely guilty, he, too, will desire that their judgment be carried out.

וְנִבְרְכוּ בוֹ כֹּל גּוֹיֵי הָאָרֶץ — *And all the nations of the earth shall bless themselves by him.*

The translation follows *Rashi* who in his *comm.* to the parallel expression in 12:3 explains: A man will say to his son, 'Be like Abraham,' and comments that 'this is the meaning wherever the expression appears.'

Ibn Ezra, however, differentiates between the *niphal* form וְנִבְרְכוּ in our verse which he renders: *they shall be blessed because of him,* [as *Onkelos* renders: *For his sake*] and the *hispael* form וְהִתְבָּרְכוּ בְזַרְעֲךָ [below 22:18] which he renders *they shall bless themselves by your offspring.*

[See also *comm.* to 12:3.]

Hirsch sees not Abraham but 'the great and mighty nations' that will descend from him as the subject of וְנִבְרְכוּ בוֹ. He renders: *For Abraham is indeed to become a great and mighty nation, and through it* [i.e.,

XVIII *become a great and mighty nation and all the nations*
19 *of the earth shall bless themselves by him?* [19] *For I*
have loved him, because he commands his children

the nation of Israel] *all the nations of the earth are to be blessed.*

19. כִּי יְדַעְתִּיו — *For I have loved him,* [lit. *'known'*] *him.*

The rendering of יְדַעְתִּיו, *known,* as *loved,* follows *Rashi* who explains that *affection* is the secondary meaning of *know,* for one who loves another brings him close to himself and thus knows him well. [Cf. the colloquial expression 'to know him is to love him.']

And why have I known [loved] him? — לְמַעַן אֲשֶׁר יְצַוֶּה אֶת־בָּנָיו וְאֶת־בֵּיתוֹ אַחֲרָיו, *because he commands* [the future imperfect form יְצַוֶּה, lit. *'will command'* expressing constant action, i.e., *regularly commands*] *his children and his household after him,* ... If, however, you render the verse as does *Onkelos*: 'I know of him *that* he will command, ... 'then the word לְמַעַן does not fit into the context *(Rashi)*

Ramban disagrees. He explains that *know* has the connotation of raise and elevate, as in *Exod.* 33:12: יְדַעְתִּיךָ בְשֵׁם [lit. *'I have known you by name',* which would accordingly mean: *I have made you great in name*] and as in *Ps.* 144:3 *What is man that You have known him* [וַתֵּדָעֵהוּ, i.e., *that You have elevated him?*] The sense of our verse would then be: I have elevated him so that he shall command his children after him to do that which is right before Me, and therefore I will make him a great and mighty nation so that he should serve Me.

Ramban also suggests, like *Onkelos,* that the verse might state: *I know that he will command, ...,* and [differing with *Rashi* who states that according to this interpretation לְמַעַן does not fit into the context] *Ramban* proceeds to show from *Exod.* 23:12 that in the verse לְמַעַן יָנוּחַ שׁוֹרְךָ וַחֲמוֹרְךָ, the words לְמַעַן יָנוּחַ mean שֶׁיָּנוּחַ, *that* [your ox and donkey] *will rest.* Here, too, as *Chavel* explains לְמַעַן אֲשֶׁר יְצַוֶּה can mean שֶׁיְצַוֶּה, *that he will command,* and accordingly לְמַעַן does fit into the context.

Ramban goes on to comment that *knowing* in its literal sense alludes to God's intimate Providence. He extends His Providence to all, but He does so more intimately and more constantly to His pious as it is written [*Job* 36:7] *He withdraws not His eyes from the pious.* There are many additional verses — such as *Ps.* 33:18 — which support this theme. [See also *Moreh Nevuchim* 3:51; and *Ramban* to אֵדְעָה in *v.* 21.] [1]

1. *Hirsch's* interpretation sheds much light on the above. He explains that ידע means *to perceive, to know.* When the word refers to the relationship of man to woman it designates the most intimate act of married life [see *comm.* to 4:1]; concerning the relationship of God to man it designates His *special* care, the *special* consideration of His Providence.

There are those whose attitudes to God are merely casual, who allow other considerations to come before their obligations to God — such people, are under His general protection, but God leaves them to the haphazard vicissitudes of life.

But there are people who place themselves completely under God's guidance and wish only to be His messengers on earth, leaving everything else to Him — God takes such people under His *special* guidance and care. This is what is called ידע. [*Hirsch* accordingly renders our verse: *For I have given him My special care so that he will command his children,* etc.]

אֶת־בָּנָיו וְאֶת־בֵּיתוֹ אַחֲרָיו וְשָׁמְרוּ דֶּרֶךְ
יהוה לַעֲשׂוֹת צְדָקָה וּמִשְׁפָּט לְמַעַן הָבִיא
יהוה עַל־אַבְרָהָם אֵת אֲשֶׁר־דִּבֶּר עָלָיו׃
כ וַיֹּאמֶר יהוה זַעֲקַת סְדֹם וַעֲמֹרָה כִּי־רָבָּה

לְמַעַן אֲשֶׁר יְצַוֶּה אֶת־בָּנָיו וְאֶת־בֵּיתוֹ אַחֲרָיו — *Because he commands* [lit. future perfect: *'will always command'*] *his children and his house*[*hold*] *after him.*

[It is noteworthy that Abraham's greatness is ascribed to his role as spiritual mentor of his posterity. Despite the many converts whom he and Sarah had brought under the wings of the *Shechina,* it is not *they* who are mentioned in this testament to Abraham's greatness — indeed, their belief in God did not survive the passing of Abraham. It is clear that Jewish posterity is built primarily upon the constant dedication of parents in raising *their own children* to walk the way of God in charity and justice.]

Happy are the righteous! Not only do they themselves perform God's will, but they also charge others to do the same, as stated by our verse. And woe to the wicked! Not only do they themselves not perform His will, but they even hinder others from doing so *(Midrash HaGadol).*

וְשָׁמְרוּ דֶּרֶךְ ה׳ — *That they keep the way of HASHEM.*

According to *Rashi* these words, until the end of the verse, form a part of Abraham's charge to his children: *'Keep the way of HASHEM ... in order that HASHEM may bring upon Abraham,'* etc.

Hirsch explains that the *way of HASHEM* has a dual connotation: the way of God that He takes; and that which He wishes us to tread. The two are really identical, since the way of good runs parallel with the way in which God leads and guides the world. That is why the way of the wicked clashes against it. As the prophet Hosea says [14:10]: *The ways of HASHEM are right: the righteous walk in them, but transgressors shall stumble in them.*

לַעֲשׂוֹת צְדָקָה וּמִשְׁפָּט — *Doing* [lit. *'to do'*] *charity and justice.*

[The word צְדָקָה can be translated as both righteousness and charity, the latter being regarded as but a particular application of the former. Since the Talmud and commentators derive the supremacy of charity in Jewish life from this verse, it is translated as *charity,* although in some cases the context of the verse will require the rendering of *'righteousness.'*]

The Talmud [*Yevamos* 79a] notes that the Israelite nation is distinguished in three ways: they are compassionate, bashful, and benevolent. The last is derived from our text: *to do charity.*

Rambam, therefore, codifies in his *Hilchos Matanos Aniyim* 10:1: 'We must therefore practice the mitzvah of *charity* more than any other because it is the characteristic of the true descendant of Abraham.' In support, he cites our verse.

The concepts of צְדָקָה, *charity, righteousness,* as compared with מִשְׁפָּט, *justice,* have already been noted in the *comm.* to 15:6. מִשְׁפָּט is

XVIII and his household after him that they keep the way
20 of HASHEM, doing charity and justice,' in order that
HASHEM might then bring upon Abraham that
which He had spoken of him.
[20] So HASHEM said, 'Because the outcry of Sodom

simply *justice;* צְדָקָה, is *the duty of benevolence,* the Jewish conception of *tzedakah* with which Abraham is to imbue children. Charity of this sort does not make the giver proud and humble the recipient. Rather it is an act of *duty'* which makes the rich administrators of a treasury which belongs to the poor and upon which they have a legitimate claim *(Hirsch).*

Hirsch continues that here the concept of צְדָקָה, *righteousness,* precedes the מִשְׁפָּט, *justice.* Sodom, too, had a kind of 'justice' but it was far from God's justice. Sodomite justice becomes a double-edged sword which lives by the maxim שֶׁלִּי שֶׁלִּי שֶׁלְּךָ שֶׁלָּךְ, 'I keep what is mine, you keep what is yours' [*Avos* 5:10] Its philosophy branded the needy as criminals endangering the public welfare. Rich men like Lot may be admitted, because they brought profit to the community, but 'begging is prohibited', and hungry unfortunates are jailed or told to move on. Thus justice without *tzedakah* becomes perverted into cruelty and harshness. For this reason, in contrast, the testament of Abraham to his children stresses *tzedakah* before righteousness.

לְמַעַן הָבִיא ה׳ עַל אַבְרָהָם אֵת אֲשֶׁר־דִּבֶּר עָלָיו — *In order that HASHEM might then bring upon Abraham that which He had spoken of him* — i.e., to ensure his descendants their continued presence in the Promised Land. And this being so, how can I destroy part of his inheritance without first telling him? *(Rashbam).*

[According to *Rashi,* this passage, too, is part of Abraham's charge to his descendants.]

Rashi notes that since it says עַל אַבְרָהָם, *upon Abraham* [himself] rather than *upon Abraham's children,* we may learn that he who leaves a son as righteous as himself is as though he had not died. [Therefore *Abraham himself* — not spiritually dead because he left righteous children — will personally be the recipient of God's blessings.]

20. וַיֹּאמֶר ה׳ — *So* [lit. *'and'*] *HASHEM said* — to Abraham, thus doing what He had determined: Not to conceal [Sodom's impending destruction] from Abraham *(Rashi).*

According to *Rashbam* it was the chief angel who had remained behind [see *v.* 16] who was now addressing Abraham in God's Name. [However, most commentators agree with *Rashi*'s interpretation that God *Himself* was speaking.]

Abraham was now accorded a higher degree of prophecy than the vision in *v.* 1:, וַיֹּאמֶר, *And He* [*God*] *said,* implies a closer revelation than וַיֵּרָא, *appeared (Sforno).*

According to *Ibn Ezra,* God said this to Abraham after the angels had already appeared in Sodom; *v.* 22, which tells of

כא וְחַטָּאתָם כִּי כָבְדָה מְאֹד׃ אֵרְדָה־נָּא
וְאֶרְאֶה הַכְּצַעֲקָתָהּ הַבָּאָה אֵלַי עָשׂוּ |

the angels traveling toward Sodom, preceded our verse chronologically.

זַעֲקַת סְדֹם וַעֲמֹרָה כִּי־רָבָּה — *Because the outcry of Sodom and Amorrah has become great* [lit. *'the outcry of Sodom and Amorrah because it is great.*]

— The outcry of its rebellion against God or the cry caused by its violence *(Ibn Ezra).* Or, according to *Ramban:* The cry of the oppressed begging for liberation.[1]

Sometimes the outcry resulting from oppression is greater than is actually warranted; in this case, however, the sin was even greater than the outcry *(Alshich).*

[It must be remembered that the description of the outcry as *'great'* does not necessarily describe its number but its magnitude]. As *Rambam* notes in *Hilchos Teshuvah* 3:2: ' ... If the iniquities of the inhabitants of a country are abundant, it perishes forthwith, as it says, *Because the outcry of Sodom and Amorrah is great* ... This evaluation takes into account not the quantity, but the quality of merits and sins. There may be a single merit that outweighs many iniquities ... and there may be one iniquity that offsets many merits ... God alone makes this determination; He alone knows how to set off merit against sin.'

Thus in the opinion of the Sages (see *footnote)* it was specifically the cry of that רִיבָה, young girl, cruelly put to death which finally sealed the fate of Sodom.]

The terms צְעָקָה and זַעֲקָה indicate the anguished cries of the oppressed; the agonized pleas of the victim for help in some great injustice. The terms are used between man and his fellow. The term שַׁוְעָה, however, is used to describe only outcries to God *(HaRechasim leBik'ah).*

The translation of רָבָּה in the past tense, *has become great,* follows *Rashi* who notes that wherever else the word occurs the accent is on the second syllable and accordingly the meaning is in the present tense: *great* or *becoming increasingly greater.* In this case however, the accent appears on the first syllable which indicates past tense, as explained in the *comm.* to the word בָּאָה, *had gone down* in 15:17.

Our translation of כִּי in its usual sense of *because* follows *Onkelos* [אֲרֵי]. We have moved the word to the beginning of the sentence in the translation for stylistic reasons. *Hoffman* points out that very often when כִּי appears in the midst of a sentence it is an adjective meaning *indeed, exceeding* [see *Isaiah* 7:9.] Hence, the verse would be

1. The *Talmud* [*Sanhedrin* 109b] specifically relates this to the incident of a רִיבָה, young girl, [some say she was Lot's daughter, Pelotis *(Pirkei d'Rabbi Eliezer)*] who, in defiance of the laws of Sodom which forbade the giving of charity, once carried out bread concealed in a pitcher, to a poor man. When the matter was discovered they daubed her with honey and placed her atop a wall; bees came and consumed her. [See *comm. v.* 21; and 19:14].

The *Talmud ibid.* records many similar instances of the horrendous deeds of the Sodomites. To cite a few: They had beds upon which travelers slept. If the guest arrived who wished to rest, he was led to one of the beds. If the guest was too tall his feet would be cut off to make him fit; if, on the other hand he was too short they would stretch him out. They would kill and steal the money of wealthy men who entered their cities. If one laid out his fruits, they would each take a 'sample' until nothing was left, claiming 'I have taken only one.'

Also their laws were so perverse that the *victim* of a crime would often be fined! Also, adultery, incest, and other sexual aberrations were the norm.

It was these cries that ascended to God, and which caused the Rabbis to exclaim: The people of Sodom have no share in the World to Come. [See *Overview.*]

XVIII *and Amorrah has become great, and because their sin*
21 *has been very grave,* [21] *I will descend and see: If they*
act in accordance with its outcry — then destruction!

rendered: *the outcry of Sodom and Amorah is indeed great.*

וְחַטָּאתָם כִּי כָבְדָה מְאֹד — *And because their sin has been very grave* [lit. *'heavy'*]

— And the earth cannot endure it *(Ibn Ezra).*

21. Therefore ...

אֵרֲדָה־נָּא וְאֶרְאֶה — *I will descend and* [*I will*] *see.*

An obvious anthropomorphism *(Ibn Ezra).* [See *comm.* to 11:5.]

This is one of the ten instances that the Shechinah is recorded as having *'descended'* into this world *(Avos d'Rabbi Nosson* 34).

[God obviously had no need to 'descend' in order to 'see' what was happening on earth *(Mizrachi)*], *Rashi* therefore explains, as he does in 11:5, that the Torah uses this expression to teach a moral lesson: A judge must not render a verdict in capital cases without personally investigating the matter. Another interpretation: I will descend to the very end of their doings [i.e., I will fathom the depths of their wickedness.]

Hence our Sages taught [*Avos* 2:4]: Do not judge your neighbor until you come to his place *(Midrash HaGadol).*

The intent then, was to investigate and determine whether there was an area for clemency, in order to avoid punishing them *(Radak).*

Ramban esoterically interpreting this 'in the opinion of those who received the truth' explains that, in formulating what courses to follow, God descended from Attribute to Attribute. He was saying: *I will descend* from My Attribute of Mercy to My Attribute of Justice, *and see* in mercy, *have they done in accordance with its outcry that has come to Me* through My Attribute of Justice ... [See *Ramban*, below s.v. וְאִם לֹא אֵדָעָה.]

Ralbag explains the *'going down'* in the sense of testing them once more by sending two angels to them in the guise of men [Ch. 19] and seeing how the Sodomites will treat them — thus indicating that their doom was not yet finally sealed and they were given a final opportunity to repent.

הַכְּצַעֲקָתָהּ — [Whether] *in accordance with its* [lit. *her*] *outcry.*

I.e., the outcry of the country [*'country'*, being a feminine, singular noun in Hebrew, for if the 'outcry' was that of the people, the verse should have said הַכְּצַעֲקָתָם, *whether in accordance with* 'their' *outcry*] *(Rashi).*

Rashi continues that the Sages explained the word as referring specifically to *her* cry, i.e., the cry of a certain girl whom the Sodomites killed in an unnatural manner because she had given to the poor [see *footnote* to *v.* 20. (The sense, then, is that that girl's cry ascended to God, and was indicative of the city's wickedness which had reached intolerable proportions. God therefore — anthropomorphically — resolved to make a personal investigation of the facts).]

As the parallel *Midrash* in *Pirkei d' Rabbi Eliezer* concludes:

She cried out: 'Sovereign of the Universe! Maintain my right and my cause at the hands of the men of Sodom!' Her cry ascended to the throne

כב כָּלָה וְאִם־לֹא אֵדָעָה: וַיִּפְנוּ מִשָּׁם הָאֲנָשִׁים וַיֵּלְכוּ סְדֹמָה וְאַבְרָהָם עוֹדֶנּוּ

of Glory and God said: *'I will descend and see whether they have done in accordance with her cry which has come to me,* and if they have indeed done everything implied by the cry of that young woman, I will turn its foundation upwards and the surface downward ...'

'For even should I desire to be silent,' said God, 'the maiden's cry for justice would not permit Me' *(Midrash).*[1]

The social iniquity of the Sodomites is echoed by Ezekiel [16:49]:

See! This was the sin of Sodom, your sister: pride, surfeit of bread and undisturbed peace were hers and her daughters' but the hand of the poor and the needy did she not support.

כָּלָה — [Then] *destruction!* i.e., then I will make an end of them *(Rashi).*

The translation of this ambiguous phrase follows *Onkelos, Rashi, Rashbam,* the primary interpretation of *Ibn Ezra, Radak,* and *Ramban.*

The above rendering takes into account the Massoretic vertical line [*'psik'* — a strong disjunctive] separating the word כָּלָה from that which precedes it. Hence the noun כָּלָה is interpreted as an elliptic separate clause related to כְּלָיָה, *destruction, extermination.*

The sense, then, of the phrase as explained by *Rashi* is: If they have indeed been as evil as the cry suggests, and they persist in their rebellious ways, כָּלָה, *an end will I make of them!*

To which *Onkelos* adds: 'If they do not repent.'

Hirsch, also deriving the word from כְּלָיָה, *destruction,* notes that, the cantillation indicates that כָּלָה is the object of עָשׂוּ, i.e., the sinners themselves have brought about the destruction of the city and its inhabitants. Thus the verse is rendered: *I will go down and see whether, in accordance with the cry which has come to Me they have achieved complete destruction.'* [This is apparently based on *Abarbanel: To see whether ... they have destroyed their souls;* i.e., whether their degeneracy had already reached its depth, so that they had doomed themselves to complete destruction.]

Rav Saadiah Gaon; Ibn Ezra in his alternate *comm.; Sforno,* and others interpret כָּלָה as synonymous with כֻּלָּה, כֻּלָּם *all of it; all of them.* [See *Exod.* 11:1.] Accordingly they render: הַכְּצַעֲקָתָהּ הַבָּאָה אֵלַי עָשׂוּ כָּלָה, 'Have they *all* done in accordance with its outcry that has come to me?'

[Although in *Exod.* 11:1 *Rashi does* render כָּלָה as *everyone,* he does not use that translation here. It seems to me that there are two reasons: first because such a translation would not account for the Masoretic division between עָשׂוּ | כָּלָה; and second, because such an interpretation implies that God was descending to determine if *all* the Sodomites were guilty, and presumably, (as *Tur* explains) if the wickedness was not unanimous, God would spare them.]

1. The *Midrash* notes that the real prosperity of Sodom lasted only fifty-two years [since its founding after the Dispersion in 1996 until its destruction in its fifty-second year in 2047 *(Seder Olam;* cf. *Tosafos Berachos* 7b; *Tosafos Shabbos* 10b).] For twenty-five of those years [since the war of the kings when Abraham was 73 according to *Tosafos Berachos, ibid.;* see *Additional Note A* : Chronology of Abraham's departures'] God made the mountains tremble and terrified them so they might reform. But they did not.

Therefore it is written [*Job* 9:5] *Who removes the mountains and they knew it not when He overturned them in anger.*

XVIII And if not, I will know.'
22 [22] — The men had turned from there and went to
Sodom, while Abraham was still standing before

[If this were indded God's intention, then Abraham had no need to approach Him in *v.* 23 to ask if He would slay the righteous with the wicked; he was already told that God would not! *Rashi*'s interpretation avoids this difficulty, and makes it quite understandable why, in light of God's threat to destroy the city, Abraham felt compelled to intercede.

Rav Saadiah Gaon, Ibn Ezra, and *Sforno* would probably defend their interpretation by explaining that the Masoretic vertical line is only secondary to the accents which *do* blend the words into a single phrase, and that Abraham asked God his question because he was unsure of just *how many* blameless people God would consider a substantial enough number to revoke His decree.]

Abarbanel suggests an interesting translation which also seems to take the *psik* into account interpreting כָּלָה as modifying צַעֲקָתָהּ: He renders: *Have they done everything implied by the outcry that comes to Me?*

וְאִם לֹא אֵדָעָה — *And if not, I will know.*

If, however, they do not persist in their rebellious ways [and they repent *(Onkelos)*], *I will know* what I shall do — punish them only with suffering, but I will not destroy them entirely. Cf. a similar thought in *Exod.* 33:5 *(Rashi).*

[The verb אֵדָעָה thus, carries with itself the connotation of chastisement as translated by *Onkelos:* אֶתְפְּרַע, *I will exact punishment.* This is the meaning of וַיֹּדַע, *he chastised,* has in *Judges* 8:16, *(R' Bachya)*]

[See also *footnote* to 15:8 — בַּמָּה אֵדַע]

According to *Ramban,* the word אֵדָעָה, *I will know,* implies 'I will show divine Mercy', as it does in *Exod.* 2:25 [where *Ramban* explains that וַיֵּדַע אֱלֹהִים, *and God knew,* means that He directed His mercies upon the children of Israel because he was cognizant of their suffering.

— If they are not worthy of utter destruction, then *I will know,* and I would expect Abraham to seize the opportunity and intercede on their behalf *(Radak).*

22. וַיִּפְנוּ מִשָּׁם הָאֲנָשִׁים וַיֵּלְכוּ סְדֹמָה — *The men turned* [their faces] *from there* — [from the place to which Abraham had escorted them *(Rashi)*] — *and* [they] *went to Sodom.*

[Only two of them entered Sodom, (see 19:1). The third one, his mission of advising Sarah of her son's birth completed, apparently returned to his abode. According to *Rashbam,* he remained behind to converse with Abraham as God's emissary.]

As explained earlier, this verse is parenthetical and chronologically preceded the events in *v.* 20 *(Ibn Ezra).*

According to *Mizrachi,* the *chronological* sequence of events is:

1. Abraham saw the angels in the guise of men. Thinking they were guests, he begged God to *not pass away from Your servant,* but to wait while he showered his guests with hospitality. God acceded to Abraham's request and waited until they deparated;

2. The angels turned from there to go to Sodom, while *Abraham remained standing before* HASHEM [*v.* 22];

3. *HASHEM reflected* [*v.* 17]: *Shall I conceal from Abraham what I am doing?;*

4. *HASHEM said (to Abraham)* [*v.* 20]: *The outcry of Sodom and Amorah has become great ...* [*v.* 21] *and if not, I will know;*

5. [*V.* 23] *And Abraham came forward.*

[Cf. *Sforno* below.]

As explained by *Ramban,* this verse is placed here because after having told of God's intention, the narrative reverts to relate how the men [= angels] who glanced down at Sodom [*v.* 16] went there, and how, from the time Abraham

כג עֹמֵד לִפְנֵי יהוה: וַיִּגַּשׁ אַבְרָהָם וַיֹּאמַר
כד הַאַף תִּסְפֶּה צַדִּיק עִם־רָשָׁע: אוּלַי יֵשׁ

was advised of the true nature of their mission until their arrival at Sodom, Abraham prolonged his supplication.

Abarbanel comments that this verse is placed here to indicate that the angels departed without taking leave while *Abraham still stood before God.* They saw him in supplication before God, and they left stealthily because they were 'Angels of Mercy' and did not wish to disturb his devotions.

According to *Midrash Aggadah,* however, *they turned from there* — completely drained of all mercy.

וְאַבְרָהָם עוֹדֶנּוּ עֹמֵד לִפְנֵי ה׳ — *While* [lit. *'and'*] *Abraham was still standing before* HASHEM.

[This is *Midrashically* interpreted to mean that God, Who had appeared to Abraham in *v.* 1 and from Whom Abraham had taken leave to offer hospitality to the three angels, had still waited for him throughout all this time]:

But surely it was not Abraham who had gone to stand before Him, but God Who appeared to Abraham and said *'The outcry of Sodom and Amorrah is great',* [and He was still there.] The verse should therefore have read *And* HASHEM *was still standing before Abraham.* This however, is a תִּקּוּן סוֹפְרִים, *literary refinement* [made to avoid an apparently irreverent expression] *(Rashi)* [1]

According to some commentators who interpret that the verses are in proper chronological order and hence Abraham already knew from *v.* 17 of the angels' mission, this verse, is not a 'literary refinement, but is to be interpreted literally as *'Abraham standing before God.'* For, upon realizing the destination and purpose of the angels, Abraham understood that the destruction was imminent and seized the opportunity to stand in prayer. As *Onkelos* renders: *And Abraham still ministered in prayer before* HASHEM.

Although the angels who were to destroy Sodom had already reached their destination, Abraham still stood in prayer on the Sodomites' behalf. This follows our Sages' teaching [*Berachos* 10a]: One must not desist from prayer even when a sharp sword is upon his neck *(Sforno).* [Cf. *Rashi* to 19:1.]

1. God forbid that one heretically misinterpret the term תִּקּוּן סוֹפְרִים to suggest that later Scribes dared tamper with the Holy text of the Torah and alter it in any way by replacing it with an "improved" expression, regardless of the sensitivities involved! ...

Rather, as the commentators explain, the Torah was originally composed by God to convey a sense of reverence and propriety. In minutely investigating every letter of the Torah, the Sages found verses which clearly indicate this underlying principle for, otherwise, they would have been differently rendered. Our verse is a case in point *(Ikkarim; Mizrachi; Taz; Minchas Shay).*

... And just as 'the Torah expresses itself in the language of man', the Torah likewise chooses reverent expressions just as would be expected from human scribes. Therefore such transparently reverent expressions which appear, on first hand, not to reflect the simple sense of the verse, are called תִּקּוּנֵי סוֹפְרִים, delicate expressions reflecting the kind of adjustments Scribes and Sages normally make when composing their own literary works *(Gur Aryeh;* cf. *Mizrachi* to *Num.* 11:15)

[See *comm.* to *Job* 7:20, and *Rashi* to *Job* 32:3.]

XVIII
23

HASHEM. —

[23] *Abraham came forward and said, 'Will You also stamp out the righteous along with the wicked?*

23. Abraham intercedes on behalf of Sodom.

In the following verses Abraham exemplifies his new role as *'father of a multitude of nations'* in its most sublime, noble form. Even the wicked inhabitants of Sodom will embrace his sympathy, and he overflows with sorrow over their impending doom *(Akeidas Yitzchak).*

His intercession on their behalf demonstrates his cognizance of the need for both justice and mercy. He recognized that only through merit could the wicked be saved; nevertheless he felt anguish at the thought that human beings were about to perish *(Abarbanel).*

It is this characteristic of Abraham — in contrast to Noah who held his peace when told of the impending flood — that has ennobled him as the compassionate patriarch of the Jewish nation *(Zohar;* see *Overview* to *Noach; comm.* to 6:13-14).

Hoffman notes however, that to Noah the decree was presented as a *fait accompli: The end of all flesh has come before Me ... behold I am about to destroy them from the earth* (6:13). No room was left for intercession, and indeed Noah maintained his silence because he thought the decree was irreversible. However, to Abraham God merely said that *because the outcries of Sodom were great* He would *descend and investigate further,* thus affording Abraham the opportunity — as father of a horde of nations — to intercede on their behalf. He grasped the moment as the text eloquently testifies.

וַיִּגַּשׁ אַבְרָהָם — [*And*] *Abraham came forward* [lit. *'drew near'.*]

— In prayer *(Onkelos).*

Rashi [citing *Midrash*] notes that we find the term וַיִּגַּשׁ, *came forward* in connection with *battle* [*II Sam.* 10:13]; *appeasement* [*Gen.* 44:18]; and *prayer* [*I Kings* 18:36]. Abraham *came forward* for all three purposes: to 'battle' i.e., argue even with God [*v.* 25]; appease [*v.* 27], and pray [*v.* 24.]

[This is the first time we find one man praying on behalf of another. Thus Abraham mustered all his inner resources — having no precedent to look back upon, both his gentle and hard qualities — to intercede on behalf of the inhabitants of Sodom.]

הַאַף תִּסְפֶּה צַדִּיק עִם רָשָׁע — *Will you also stamp out* [following *Ibn Ezra* = תְּכַלֶּה] *the righteous along with the wicked?*

The translation follows *Rashi* who explains אַף as a form of אֲפִילוּ, *even, also.* He cites *Onkelos* who perceives אַף as *anger.* Accordingly the rendering would be: *Will* אַף, *anger, persuade You to stamp out?* ... etc.

I.e., would the anger You harbor against the wicked cause You to slay undiscriminatingly the righteous among them as well? *(Radak).*

Rav Yochanan commented: Abraham said, 'A mortal is dominated by his anger but

חֲמִשִּׁים צַדִּיקִם בְּתוֹךְ הָעִיר הַאַף תִּסְפֶּה
וְלֹא־תִשָּׂא לַמָּקוֹם לְמַעַן חֲמִשִּׁים

You are always in control of Your wrath, as it says [*Nach.* 1:2] *'HASHEM avenges and masters wrath.'* Rav Huna interpreted this as a petition: הַאַף תִּסְפֶּה, *this wrath You should stamp out:* You dominate anger, but anger cannot dominate You!

Ramban explains that God's *anger* is manifested by His Attribute of Justice. Abraham was unaware that God had determined to temper His justice with mercy [as explained in the *comm.* to *v.* 20], He was apprehensive therefore that God would stamp out the righteous along with the wicked.

[Or as *Sforno* explains: Abraham had assumed that such was God's intention because He had spoken of the sin of the *cities* of Sodom and Amorah *collectively,* rather than of the individuals. Also, as *Malbim* notes, once the Destroyer has been given permission to destroy he does so indiscriminately *(Bava Kamma* 60a) unless an intended victim is *thoroughly* righteous in which case he is spared *(Avodah Zarah* 4a). That is why, in Egypt, God *Himself* and not an emissary killed the Egyptian first-born; had an angel done so, he would have killed Jews as well. Since Abraham saw that the angels proceeded alone and God remained in dialogue with him, he feared that the angels would punish indiscriminately (see *Ezekiel* 9)].

Ramban continues that Abraham therefore pleaded that it would be proper — according to the Divine Attribute of Mercy — that God should spare the entire group of five cities if they contained fifty righteous men. Furthermore, it would be inconceivable *in any event* — even according to His Attribute of Justice — that He slay the righteous along with the wicked [*v.* 25], for if so *the righteous will be as the wicked* and people will say it is vain to serve God. This is the significance of the double use of חָלִלָה לְךָ, *it is sacrilege to You* — [once for the Attribute of Mercy and once for the Attribute of Justice; for actually there are two pleas in the following verses: a request that the entire city, *including the wicked,* be forgiven for the sake of the righteous; and that, at the very minimum the righteous be spared and not be stamped out along with the wicked.]

Ramban concludes that God conceded that He would deal mercifully. He notes that God's Name is significantly written here as HASHEM [signifying Divine Mercy, denoting that He would act according to His Attribute of Mercy], while Abraham addressed Him throughout the dialogue as *Adonai* (My Lord) [signifying Divine Justice.] From this we infer that Abraham was under the impression that they would be judged only by Divine Justice.

24. חֲמִשִּׁים צַדִּיקִם — *Fifty righteous [people].*

Five cities were involved [see *v.* 29 and 14:2]. Abraham therefore mentioned fifty — ten righteous people [a quorum; see *v.* 26], for each city *(Rashi).*

[בְּתוֹךְ הָעִיר *in the city* would consequently have, according to *Rashi,* a collective sense meaning *in the combined group of cities;* according to others it refers to Sodom, the chief place of the threatened area (see *v.* 26; *Radak*).]

XVIII
24

[24] *What if there should be fifty righteous people in the city: Would You still stamp it out rather than spare the place for the sake of the fifty righteous peo-*

בְּתוֹךְ הָעִיר — *In the [midst of the] city.*

— I.e., righteous people who are *openly* God-fearing. (*Ibn Ezra* to *v.* 26.)

[In other words the righteous must be ones who fear God not only in the safety and privacy of their home, but *in the midst of the city* — playing a prominent part in public life and exerting their influence in its many fields of activity. Only in such a manner, and not by remaining anonymous, could these righteous hope to possess the spiritual merit of saving the city. If the moral climate of a city is such that it forced its righteous into seclusion, then that city is not worthy of being saved by virtue of a handful of men, who lead a secluded life within it.]

Hirsch stresses the parallel between the deficiencies of Sodom and those of Jerusalem prior to the destruction of the First Temple. There, too, righteous people were not בְּתוֹךְ הָעִיר; they failed to fulfill their responsibility to influence their brethren. Thus, in Sodom as well, a person more righteous than his fellows could not earn salvation by withdrawing into his own private existence. Cf. *Radak* to *Jeremiah* 5:1 who comments that no one could be found *'who acted justly and seeks the truth in the streets of Jerusalem'*, for the righteous were forced to remain inside by the animosity of the wicked. Therefore, there was no hope for the Holy City. See also *comm.* to *Ezekiel* 9:4, ArtScroll ed.

According to *Ramban* [*v.* 26]: Even if these righteous people are *strangers* in the city they should be worthy of saving it. Abraham had Lot in mind, and perhaps he thought that there were others as well.

Following *Malbim* the question was: If there are fifty people whose righteousness is only relative — בְּתוֹךְ הָעִיר, *in midst of the city* i.e., in comparison with the rest of the population — would they be prone to indiscriminate punishment by the Destroyer? [1]

Thus, the phrase בְּתוֹךְ הָעִיר, *in the city,* is not intended to describe their *whereabouts* because the same phrase occurs also in *v.* 26 where *Sodom* is specified as the place. Rather, it describes the צַדִּיקִים, *righteous people,* qualifying their righteouness as being only relative to the general wickedness of Sodom. Had they lived in other cities with a civilized citizenry, they would be considered worthless. This is similar to the description of Noah as צַדִּיק תָּמִים הָיָה בְּדֹרֹתָיו, *a righteous man, perfect in his generations* [as the commentators

1. Abraham knew very well that there were no truly righteous people in Sodom. If Lot was the greatest among them — and Abraham was painfully aware of Lot's shortcomings — how righteous could the others be? However, Abraham was also convinced that no matter how immersed Lot had become in the evil ways of Sodom, he could not have become deserving of destruction.

Abraham thought that there must be others who were similar, people who submitted to wrongdoers as long as they were ascendant, but who could be saved. If Sodom were punished rather than destroyed, perhaps there were people who could take the lead in achieving repentance *(Sefer HaParshios).*

הַצַּדִּקִם אֲשֶׁר בְּקִרְבָּהּ: חָלִלָה לְּךָ
מֵעֲשֹׂת | כַּדָּבָר הַזֶּה לְהָמִית צַדִּיק עִם־

explain: only as *compared to* his own generations.] *(HaKsav V'HaKabbalah)*

The *Midrash* thus notes that wherever the word צַדִּיקִים, *righteous people,* is used in connection with Sodom it is spelled defectively [= צַדִּקִם, i.e., without the second *yod*] to indicate that their righteousness, too, was doubtful and defective. Abraham's request was that if even such inferior righteousness could be found in fifty people, all the towns should be saved in their merit *(Kitov).*

הַאַף תִּסְפֶּה וְלֹא־תִשָּׂא לַמָּקוֹם ... — *Would You still stamp it out rather than* [lit. *and not*] *spare* [lit. *bear,* i.e., *forgive*] *the place for the sake of the fifty righteous people within it?*

— And thereby spare the wicked for the sake of the righteous *(Taz).*

On the meaning of תִשָּׂא see *Ibn Caspi* cited to 4:13: 'for one who forgives, *'lifts up'* the transgression from the sinner and lightens his burden, figuratively *"bearing it"* for him.'

According to *Ibn Ezra* [based apparently on *Pirkei d'Rabbi Eliezer*] Abraham's use of the word מָקוֹם, *place,* did not refer to the entire five-city area [as the other commentators explain] but specifically to *Sodom* where his nephew Lot resided. Hence, he interprets God's response in *v.* 26 that He would spare *Sodom,* as a reference only to Sodom, proper, rather as a collective name for the entire area. [But see *Hirsch* end of *v.* 26]

Ramban [in the view shared by the majority of commentators except *Rashi*] comments that it is inconceivable that Abraham could have been concerned about anything less than *all* of the cities as one entity . [See *comm.* to *v.* 29 s.v. אוּלַי.]

On the meaning of תִשָּׂא see *Ibn Caspi* cited to 4:13: 'for one who forgives, *'lifts up'* the transgression from the sinner and lightens his burden, figuratively *"bearing it"* for him'.

25. And should You maintain that the righteous cannot *save* the wicked, why, then, should You kill the righteous? [I.e., even if my prayer prevails upon you to spare the wicked for the sake of the righteous, surely you will at least spare the righteous. That they be spared is not a matter of special favor, for it is only justice that the presence of a significant number of righteous should be a reason for clemency *(Divrei David)*] *(Rashi).*

חָלִלָה לְּךָ — *It would be sacrilege to You!,* i.e., it is a profanation [חוּלִין; from חוּל a secondary root of חָלַל, *desecration,* in the sense of *foreign* to Your nature *(Midrash; Avodah Zarah* 4a); or: *far be it from You*] *to do so.*

For if You did, people would say: This is what He busies himself with — He indiscriminately destroys the righteous along with the wicked; He did so to the generation of the Flood and to the generation of the Dispersion, and still He does not abandon His craft *(Tanchuma; Rashi).*

Of course this was not the case, for Noah survived the Flood and the victims of the Dispersion were *scattered,* not massacred. Abraham's intention, however, was that God's Name would be desecrated if He were to kill the righteous and wicked alike. People would then say that many more people deserved to be saved from the Flood, but that God killed unjustly; Noah and his children were saved only in order to preserve the species. At the time of the Dispersion, people would say, all of the people in that particular

XVIII *ple within it?* 25 *It would be sacrilege to You to do*
25 *such a thing, to bring death upon the righteous along*

region were killed just as all the people of Sodom would be killed. The historic fact that no one was killed during the Dispersion would be denied by the skeptics *(Sifsei Chachomim).*

The *Tanchuma* concludes: God replied, 'How do you say this? Come and I will let you review all the generations which I destroyed and show you that I did not exact full retribution from them!

[The word חָלִילָה has become a common expression of repudiation, which in current idiom has the connotation of: *God forbid!*]

Onkelos renders: קוּשְׁטָא אִנּוּן דִּינָךְ, *'Your judgments are too true for You to do such a thing, to destroy the just with the guilty.'* [The etymology of his rendering is obscure but it is understood to be a reverential idiom in addressing the Deity.]

Ibn Ezra explains the term as essentially meaning 'it is inconceivable'; some connect it with חָלוּל, 'empty, hollow' indicating that 'it would be empty; unworthy of You; beneath Your dignity' ... *(Radak).*

HaKsav V'HaKabbalah suggests that, as the commentators explain it, the word seems less than respectful for Abraham to use in addressing God. Also if the word means *it is a profanation for You,* then the following verb should have been לַעֲשׂוֹת, *to do,* not מֵעֲשׂוֹת *from* doing. He therefore suggests that the term is to be interpreted as an expression of *tarry, delay.* This is the sense of the verb in *I Sam.* 10:8: *Seven days shall you tarry* [תּוֹחֵל]; *ibid* 13:8: *and he tarried* [וַיּוֹחֶל] *seven days; Num.* 30:3 as interpreted by *Rashbam: he shall not delay* [יַחֵל] *his word* ... [See also 8:10 וַיָּחֶל — *he waited;* i.e., restrained himself]. Therefore in our verse the word would have a more respectful connotation if defined as a petition: חָלִלָה לְּךָ, *may there be a suppression by You* [i.e., suppress Yourself] מֵעֲשׂת *from doing such a thing.*

מֵעֲשׂת כַּדָּבָר הַזֶּה — *To do* [lit. *'from doing'*] *such a thing.*

The Torah does not say דָּבָר הַזֶּה, *this* thing, but כַּדָּבָר הַזֶּה, *such* a thing, the implication being: do neither this *nor anything like it* — even of a lesser nature *(Midrash; Rashi).*

[For example, were God to determine that the Sodomites deserved not total annihilation but punishment (see *comm.* end of *v.* 21), these words would imply that God should not even afflict the righteous along with the wicked. Each person has his own measure of guilt and should be punished only commensurate with his own wickedness *(Divrei David).*]

Abraham pleaded with God: You made an oath to Noah not to bring a מַבּוּל, *deluge,* upon the earth: Would You then evade the oath by bringing a deluge *of fire* instead of a deluge *of water* [see *comm.* to מַבּוּל in 6:17.] Then you will not have kept your oath! [This is the implication of 'it would be sacrilege to You to do *such* a thing' — even something not technically covered by Your oath *(Maharzu).*]

[The answer to this argument may be derived from *Tosefta Taanis* 2: We may be assured that God will never again bring a deluge of *water* (see 9:11), but His oath does not prevent Him from bringing a deluge of *fire.* Also His oath prevented him from bringing a deluge to destroy כָּל בָּשָׂר, *all living things,* but it does not prevent Him from bringing a deluge to destroy *individuals* who are sinful.]

'How could I make such an all-encompassing oath?' says God. 'It

רָשָׁע וְהָיָה כַצַּדִּיק כָּרָשָׁע חָלִלָה לָּךְ
הֲשֹׁפֵט כָּל־הָאָרֶץ לֹא יַעֲשֶׂה מִשְׁפָּט:
כו וַיֹּאמֶר יהוה אִם־אֶמְצָא בִסְדֹם חֲמִשִּׁים

would free people from fear of punishment and they would sin with impunity!' *(Alshich).*

וְהָיָה כַצַּדִּיק כָּרָשָׁע — *Letting the righteous and wicked fare alike* [lit. *'and it would be like the righteous as the wicked'*].

And if the two are treated alike, people will say, *It is vain to serve God (Ramban v.* 23).

And if this comes about, Free Will and service of God will cease, and heresy will flourish in the world *(R' Bachya).*

For although the righteous will undoubtedly receive their due reward in the Spiritual World, nevertheless their punishment will have an adverse effect in This World *(Da'as Sofrim).*

Radak explains that the successive use of the prefix כ is an abbreviated idiomatic form of mutual comparison, such as כָמוֹךָ כְּפַרְעֹה *You are as Pharaoh* [44:18]; וְהָיָה כָעָם כַּכֹּהֵן, *as it shall be with the people, so shall it be with the priest* [*Isaiah* 24:2]. As *Ibn Ezra* explains, it expresses *complete* similarity. See *comm.* to 13:10 כְּגַן ה' כְּאֶרֶץ מִצְרַיִם.

חָלִלָה לָּךְ — *It would be sacrilege to You!*

In the World to Come *(Rashi).*

[The commentators struggle with the meaning of *Rashi's* comment here, and many strained solutions are suggested]:

Mizrachi admits that the meaning of *Rashi's* comment eludes him but he suggests that this comment is possibly based upon the *Midrash: 'Chalilah* is written twice in the verse, implying: It would profane the Divine Name, it would desecrate the Divine Name' [i.e. the repetition emphasizing the degree of desecration.] Since profanation of Heaven's Name is such a serious transgresssion, one achieves atonement only after death in the World to Come. It is to this that *Rashi* alludes here.

Justice in an indivisible concept. If injustice is done in This world, its effects extend even to the World to Come *(Gur Aryeh).*

[An explanation which seems to reconcile the difficulties is that the source for *Rashi's* comment is *Tanchuma Yashan* (which unlike the regular *Tanchuma* was not available until it was rediscovered in the last century by S. Buber): 'The phrase חָלִלָה לָּךְ is repeated twice in this verse, because Abraham indicated thereby: *It would be sacrilege to You* — not to forgive any creature neither in This World *nor in the next.'* It is apparently upon this *Midrash* that *Rashi* based his comment, the second חָלִלָה referring to the World to Come.]

[On the dual use of the expression חָלִלָה לָּךְ in this verse — one for the Attribute of Justice, and one for Mercy — see also *Ramban's* interpretation of this verse cited above to *v.* 23, s.v. הַאַף תִּסְפֶּה.]

Or, as *Gur Aryeh* suggests: one חָלִילָה refers to the deliterious effect of God's action on the current generation [עוֹלָם הַזֶּה] and the other on future generations [עוֹלָם הַבָּא] who would find it incomprehensible that God should treat the righteous and the wicked equally.

הֲשֹׁפֵט כָּל־הָאָרֶץ לֹא יַעֲשֶׂה מִשְׁפָּט — *Shall the Judge of all the earth not do justice?*

[Following *Rashi* who explains that the *chataf-patach* under the הֲ identifies it as an interrogative participle]:

As *Ibn Ezra* renders: How is it feasible that the Judge of all the earth would not act justly?

If it is the duty of a human judge

XVIII *with the wicked; letting the righteous and wicked*
26 *fare alike. It would be sacrilege to You! Shall the*
Judge of all the earth not do justice?
[26] *And HASHEM said, If I find in Sodom fifty*

to acquit the righteous, how much more is to be expected of God, the Judge of all the earth? *(Imrei Shefer).*

Abraham pleaded: In the case of an earthly judge a decision may be appealed, from the commander to the prefect and then to the governor. Will You not act justly simply because no one can appeal Your decision? *(Midrash).*

How can You merely deliver a verdict against people and not scrutinize each one individually? If you allow unmitigated justice to prevail, Your Name will be profaned by the unbelievers who will accuse You of murdering the innocent. They will claim that There is neither judge nor justice in this world! *Shall the Judge of the World not act justly? (Akeidas Yitzchak).*

If you desire the world to endure You cannot let unmitigated justice prevail, and if You do demand unmitigated justice, then there can be no world. Yet You hold the cord by both ends and desire both the continued existence of the world and unmitigated justice! Unless You forego a little, the world cannot endure! God answered him: *You have loved righteousness* [*Ps.* 45:8]: you have loved to justify My creatures, *and hated wickedness:* by refusing to condemn them. *Therefore HASHEM Your God has anointed you with the oil of gladness above your fellows.* What does *'above your fellows'* mean? — From Noah to you there were ten generations, and out of them I spoke to none but you *(Midrash).*

Sforno interprets this as an appeal that God not exercise judgement strictly. For if He is to act as a judge who follows the majority, then there will never be hope for an outnumbered *tzaddik.* Since most people are not righteous, the result will be that all righteous people will go down together with the wicked.

Following *Malbim*: You are the Judge over the entire earth and You must therefore scrutinize the righteous men of Sodom in comparison with their wicked contemporaries. It is not proper for them to be swept away by the general destruction seeing that within their own milieu they are considered righteous.

26. אִם־אֶמְצָא בִסְדֹם — *If I find in Sodom,* — through My angelic emissaries whom I have sent there [to test them] *(Sforno).*

Sodom was the capital and most important city of the district. [Compare the expression *Sodom and her suburbs* (lit. *daughters) Ezekiel* 16:46 *(Sforno)*] Therefore, although there were four more cities, they were subordinate to it *(Rashi).*

Ten people are the minimum which comprise an עֵדָה, *community.* Hence *Rashi* understands the number fifty to represent five groups of ten in whose merit the corresponding cities would be saved. [From God's answer it is apparent that only if all the fifty resided in

צַדִּיקִם בְּתוֹךְ הָעִיר וְנָשָׂאתִי לְכָל־
כז הַמָּקוֹם בַּעֲבוּרָם: וַיַּעַן אַבְרָהָם וַיֹּאמַר
הִנֵּה־נָא הוֹאַלְתִּי לְדַבֵּר אֶל־אֲדֹנָי וְאָנֹכִי
כח עָפָר וָאֵפֶר: אוּלַי יַחְסְרוּן חֲמִשִּׁים

Sodom — most important and debased of all the cities, and presumably the city from whence originated all the evil practices of the satellite cites — would each group of ten save not only a corresponding city but the entire area as well. It would not have sufficed, judging from the wording of this verse, for these fifty to be divided in groups of ten among the various cities.]

According to *Ibn Ezra* [see *v.* 24] Sodom itself is meant, that being the area of Abraham's prime concern because Lot lived there.

חֲמִשִּׁים צַדִּיקִם — *Fifty righteous people,* who protest against the wicked of the city *(Sforno).*

[See on *v.* 24].

בְּתוֹךְ הָעִיר — *In the midst of the city.*

[It has already been noted that this phrase is not intended to describe the location of the righteous people, for the verse has already specified Sodom. Rather, it modifies the *righteous men,* i.e., they are righteous only *in the midst of the city,* in comparison with the depraved populace. See *comm.* to *v.* 24.]

וְנָשָׂאתִי לְכָל הַמָּקוֹם בַּעֲבוּרָם — *Then I would* [lit. *'and I will'*] *spare* [lit. *'bear; forgive'*] *the entire place* [i.e., all of the cities *(Rashi)* and not only the righteous people *(Sforno)*] *on their account.*

God thus answered that He would go even beyond what Abraham requested: 'If fifty righteous people were found *in Sodom,* I will not only forgive the sins of the other four cities ... I will even spare the *entire place* — even the surrounding villages — for their sake' *(Radak;* comp. *Me'am Loez).*

Since there is a *full quota* of righteous people, the forgiveness would be absolute; I would not even subject them to punishment. *(Da'as Zekeinim* see footnote).

Not only in the merit of these righteous ones, but בַּעֲבוּרָם, *through them* — because of the very existence of these righteous ones and the fact that they are tolerated, the whole city deserves forgiveness. The tolerance of these righteous people by the rest of the populace would itself be a proof that the degeneration had not yet reached the lowest possible depth *(Hirsch).*

Hirsch notes also that the word מָקוֹם, *place,* is used for an entire district [*Numb.* 32:1] and even for an entire country [*ibid.* 10:29; 14:40]. [But cf. *Ibn Ezra* to *v.* 24.]

27. [God acquiesces to Abraham's petition. Abraham realizes, however that his first request would be unavailing because fifty righteous men would not be found in Sodom. But, encouraged by his success, he petitions further and begs God's indulgence]:

הִנֵּה־נָא הוֹאַלְתִּי לְדַבֵּר אֶל־אֲדֹנָי — *Behold, now, I desired* [or: *have begun; undertaken* or *been granted indulgence*] *to speak to My Lord.*

Although I am unworthy, my intention is not to dispute You, but

righteous people in the midst of the city, then I would spare the entire place on their account.

27 Abraham answered and said, 'Behold, now, I desired to speak to my Lord although I am but dust and ashes. 28 What if the fifty righteous people

merely to resolve my personal questions regarding Divine Justice and to fathom Your methods *(Sforno; Radak).*

[The root of הוֹאַלְתִּי is יאל. The translation *desired* [i.e., been granted the indulgence to desire *(Midrashei HaTorah)*] follows *Rashi, Ibn Ezra Radak* [*'desire to speak further'*] and *Ralbag*. *Rashi* cites *Exod.* 2:21 וַיּוֹאֶל מֹשֶׁה which he renders [along with *Onkelos* וּצְבִי]: *And Moses desired.* See also *Joshua* 7:7; *Judges* 19:6.

Ibn Ezra, in supporting this translation, differentiates it from the word הֲחִילוֹתִי, *I have begun.*

In our verse, however, *Onkelos* renders הוֹאַלְתִּי = שָׁרֵיתִי, *I have begun, undertaken,* which is the way *Rashi* translates הוֹאִיל מֹשֶׁה in *Deut.* 1:5: *Moses began.* There, strangely, *Rashi* cites *our verse* in support of that translation — an apparent conflict with his own interpretation here! The same is true of *Ibn Ezra* who also renders הוֹאִיל מֹשֶׁה *Moses began,* in discrepancy with his interpretation here.

Mizrachi and *Terumas Hadeshen* point out that in most early editions of *Rashi,* his explanation is attached *not to* הוֹאַלְתִּי of our verse, but *v.* 31, where the word appears a second time. Thus, it is possible that since *Rashi* is silent on this verse and offers his comment only later, that even *Rashi* agrees that the translation here is *I have begun.* The second time the word appears, however, in *v.* 31, when that translation would not fit the context, *Rashi* offers the translation *I have desired;* I have become determined, or I desire to speak further [see below.]

According to *Rav Saadiah Gaon,* the translation is: *I have prolonged my discourse,* while *Ibn Janach* explains it as *I have diligently persevered in presuming to address You.*

HaRechasim leBik'ah suggests that the word means *I am determined,* which, as *HaKsav V'HaKaballah* explains, is what *Rashi* means by his interpretation of 'desired': He refers to the highest motivation which inspires someone to an undertaking. As *Hirsch* comments [in *Exod.* 2:21] the verb יאל refers to the first decision to undertake a course of action; the resolution. Hence הוֹאִיל means to cause a decision to mature; to set about doing something; to take upon oneself.

Another connotation of the word, when it appears in *niphal* passive form [clearly *not* the case in our verse!] is *foolishness, thoughtlessness,* as e.g. *Num.* 12:11: אֲשֶׁר נוֹאַלְנוּ, *we have acted foolishly;* the passive form indicating frustrated hindrance: sins which we have committed without previous consideration or real intention.

[Synthesizing, then, the various versions, the intent of Abraham's expression of humility is:

'Although unworthy ...

— I desired to address You;

— I desire to address You further;

— I have been granted the indulgence to address You;

— I have taken it upon myself to address You;

— I have begun to address You;

— I have prolonged my discourse with you;

— I was diligent in presuming to address You;

— I was inspired to address You.']

וְאָנֹכִי עָפָר וָאֵפֶר — *Although* [lit. *'and'*] *I am* [*but*] *dust and ashes.*

— That is, I would long ago have been reduced to dust by the kings [Ch. 14] and to ashes by [the furnaces of] Nimrod [see 11:28] had it not been for Your mercy *(Rashi).*

הַצַּדִּיקִם חֲמִשָּׁה הֲתַשְׁחִית בַּחֲמִשָּׁה אֶת־
כָּל־הָעִיר וַיֹּאמֶר לֹא אַשְׁחִית אִם־אֶמְצָא
כט שָׁם אַרְבָּעִים וַחֲמִשָּׁה: וַיֹּסֶף עוֹד לְדַבֵּר

[The sense of the verse, then, following *Rashi* is: 'Behold, now, I desired to speak with You *because* (the prepositional prefix ו, lit. *'and')* I have known from personal experience how, were it not for Your mercies, I would have been by now but dust and ashes; or: I have desired, [i.e., been motivated] to address You, although I am but human and I would have been reduced to dust and ashes, but for Your compassion; or possibly: ... and what have I to lose? I am but human and my life is precarious in any event; any mishap in life could reduce me to dust and ashes!]

Following *Sforno*: 'And as such [i.e., being but human] I have still not been able to fathom the implications of Your response.'

Alshich interprets the sentence as an expression of the deepest humility, prefatory to the forthcoming petition: Here, I wish — i.e., presume — to speak further with HASHEM, Creator of the Universe — yet I am but *dust and ashes* — a self deprecating metaphoric expression for the unworthiest of creatures.

Dust is the lowliest of matter, trampled by everyone; *ashes* are its most useless remnant *(Akeidas Yitzchak).*

Abraham stressed his unworthiness in this way to dispel any possible notion that he considered himself worthy and righteous enough in God's eyes to pray on another's behalf. He therefore stressed that he felt compelled to present his pleas to God *in spite of his unworthiness (Minchah Belulah)*[1]

God said to Israel: I delight in you, because even as I confer greatness upon you, you humble yourselves before Me. I conferred greatness upon Abraham, and he said *I am but dust and ashes.* Upon Moses and Aaron and they declared [*Exod.* 16:8]: *Yet what are we?* Upon David and he declared [*Ps.* 22:7] *But I am but a worm, and no man (Chullin* 89a).

Cf. also *Sotah* 17a: In reward for Abraham's saying *'I am dust and ashes'* his children were rewarded with two commandments: The ashes of the פָּרָה אֲדוּמָּה, *Red Heifer* [which purify the unclean] and the dust [of the ordeal of] the סוֹטָה, *suspected woman* [which helps to restore the confidence of a husband in his wife, or punishes immorality.]

28. אוּלַי יַחְסְרוּן חֲמִשִּׁים הַצַּדִּיקִם חֲמִשָּׁה — *What if the fifty righteous people should lack five?*

[Leaving, according to *Rashi,* a representative group of nine for each of the five cities (see below)].

According to the *Midrash* [as explained by *Maharzu*] Abraham's question literally means: *What if there would be lacking the* [entire] *fifty righteous* [and there would be no more than] *five?* Abraham's expressed intention being: *Would You destroy* בַּחֲמִשָּׁה *despite the five* the entire city? God therefore told him following the *Midrash*: 'Revert to the beginning', i.e., to a number closer to your first and count down more gradually — it is too great a jump [as five are too few a number to save the cities *(Rashi* to Midrash)]! God made this clear to him by His specifically worded response which completely clarified the ambiguity: *I will not destroy if I find there forty-five* — [not the five you suggest *(Radak)*]. *Abraham*

1. 'Every Jew must possess two standards' — said the *Kotzker.* 'On one hand he must think of himself as being *but dust and ashes;* on the other he must declare, "For me was the world created!"'

XVIII should lack five? Would You destroy the entire city
29 because of the five?' And He said, 'I will not destroy
if I find there forty-five.'
[29] He further continued to speak to Him and he

therefore worded his following petitions more carefully, gradually lowering the figure to forty, thirty, twenty and then, finally, ten.

[See *Ibn Ezra's* interpretation on reduction cited in *footnote* to *v.* 29.]

הֲתַשְׁחִית בַּחֲמִשָּׁה אֶת־כָּל־הָעִיר — *Would You destroy the entire city because of the five?*

That is, because of the five that would be lacking from the total of fifty? *(Ibn Ezra)*

— There would still be nine for each city, and You, O righteous One of the Universe, could be added to the, total making the required ten for each! *(Midrash; Rashi)*

Kli Yakar offers a different explanation for the salvation despite the missing five. He comments that if forty-five were *still* present, they would suffice provided there had at one time been another five righteous people who had since departed from the city. This explanation would account for the fact that, wherever complete sets of ten are found, the word בַּעֲבוּר, *on account of,* is used i.e. each set of ten, on its own, is sufficient to save a city. In the case of *forty-five* — constituting sets of nine — however, salvation could not come about on their account alone.

[Abarbanel and some others suggest that Abraham pleaded that *his own merit* be counted along with that of the lesser number in order to effect a redemption. (See *Sechel Tov* and *Targum Yonasan* cited below beginning next verse).]

וַיֹּאמֶר לֹא אַשְׁחִית אִם־אֶמְצָא שָׁם אַרְבָּעִים וַחֲמִשָּׁה — *And He said, 'I will not destroy if I find there forty-five.'*

I.e., I will not *destroy* it, but I will exact punishment *(Da'as Zekeinim;* see *footnote* to next verse.)

Note that throughout this dialogue, God assured him that He would not destroy the city if that number were found there. He did not tell him, however, that the number of righteous would not be found there, for their trial had not yet been completed [see on *v.* 21 *I will descend and see.*] *(Ramban).*

Note also, that here God did not specify that the righteous had to be בְּתוֹךְ הָעִיר, *within the city,* i.e., influential and prominent in public life [see *comm.* to בְּתוֹךְ הָעִיר in *v.* 26.] God thus indicated that He would not measure righteousness by this criteria, and moreover, as Abraham requested, He would not destroy even if there were five lacking *(Kli Chemdah).*

29. וַיֹּסֶף עוֹד לְדַבֵּר אֵלָיו — *He* [Abraham] *further continued to speak to Him.*

Since Abraham was encouraged by God to continue his supplication [see beginning of previous verse] Abraham seized the opportunity and pleaded further.

The *Midrash* further compares this to a water-clock [used in courts of justice for measuring the time given for argument]: As long as it contains water, the defending

אֵלָיו וַיֹּאמַר אוּלַי יִמָּצְאוּן שָׁם אַרְבָּעִים וַיֹּאמֶר לֹא אֶעֱשֶׂה בַּעֲבוּר הָאַרְבָּעִים׃

counsel may plead; when the water runs out the defense must halt. Yet sometimes the judge wishes him to plead further, in which case he would order more water to be added to it.

Here, too, God indicated to him in each instance that he might plead further, but at a gradual rate. God figuratively 'added water to the water clock', and Abraham pleaded further while reverently begging His indulgence before each new request *(Mattanos Kehunah; Radal; Yafeh Toar).*

אוּלַי יִמָּצְאוּן שָׁם אַרְבָּעִים — *What if forty would be found there?*

Then only four of the cities would be saved. He similarly pleaded in the following verses that thirty should save three of them; or twenty save two of them; or ten save one of them *(Rashi).*

Why then, once the principle of fifty saving five cities, was conceded by God, was it necessary for Abraham to continue beseeching God? Once God agreed to the principle of saving a city for the sake of ten righteous people, it would be understood that if there were forty or thirty He would save the corresponding four or three cities without further supplication! — Perhaps Abraham thought that a larger group would effect a proportionately greater salvation than a smaller group. The smaller the group the less merits it had. Therefore Abraham felt compelled to plead separately for each, and God graciously demonstrated that the principle would prevail regardless of the size of the group [with differences, however; see *footnote.*] Regarding the matter of God's willingness to include Himself in the number of righteous, however, once God consented to associate with five groups of nine and spare the cities if there were forty-five, there was no further need for Abraham to allude to this concept again and ask for thirty-six, twenty-seven, etc., for surely if He consented to associate with a larger group God would certainly associate, in His righteousness, with a smaller group and save as many of the cities as possible *(Ramban; Tur; R'Bachya).*

Ramban, in interpreting *the simple meaning* of the verses however, disagrees with *Rashi* and suggests that when Abraham decreased the number throughout his beseeching, he was still pleading for all *five* cities, "And I do not know what prompted the Rabbi [i.e., *Rashi*] to say what he did."

[What, indeed, inspired *Rashi's* interpretation?] —

Kessef Mezukak defends *Rashi* by noting that his is the most plausible explanation of why Abraham reduced the number first by five, to forty-five, [i.e., nine in association with God for each city], and then by tens [thirty for three cities, twenty for two, etc.][1]

Cf. *Midrash Sechel Tov* [based on *Targum Yonasan*]:

The forty will atone for four of the cities. Since Zoar has been only recently populated [see *Shabbos*

XVIII *said, 'What if forty would be found there?' And He*
29 *said, 'I will not act on account of the forty.'*

10b; cf. *comm.* to 19:20] and has less iniquities, forgive her for the sake of Your compassion. And God agreed.

Ibn Ezra holds, however, that when Abraham's first two requests were granted, he became encouraged and realized that the reduction of fifty to forty in both steps came to a fifth; he thenceforth pleaded for a greater reduction: forty to thirty = a quarter; then even greater: thirty to twenty = a third; then a full half: twenty to ten. Further he did not plead.]

לֹא אֶעֱשֶׂה בַּעֲבוּר הָאַרְבָּעִים — *I will not act* [lit. *'do'*] *on account of the forty.*

I.e., since the number 'forty' represents four 'complete' groups of ten, I will do *nothing* to the respective cities — not even subject them to punishment *(Da'as Zekeinim;* see *footnote).*

1. *Rashi*'s interpretation that Abraham's requests involved the corresponding number of cities is further enhanced by the wording of the verses themselves:

In connection with the *fifty righteous,* God answers וְנָשָׂאתִי לְכָל הַמָּקוֹם בַּעֲבוּרָם *I would spare* [lit. *forgive*] *the entire place on their account.* In response to Abraham's pleas for the *forty-five, twenty,* and *ten* God answers לֹא אַשְׁחִית, *I will not destroy;* while in connection with the *forty* and *thirty,* He says לֹא אֶעֱשֶׂה, *I will not do.*

Da'as Zekeinim discusses this at length, and explains that God responded that if there were fifty he would totally forgive the entire area because fifty represented a 'complete number' of ten for each of the five cities. Furthermore, God's response indicates that the *forgiveness* would be absolute — they would not even be subject to punishment.

The number *forty-five,* as *Rashi* explains, represented five groups of nine — one for each city. God Himself would then join with each group thereby making the required ten. God consented and said לֹא אַשְׁחִית, *I will not destroy* — i.e., I will not *utterly destroy* them. However I will *punish* them [to effect betterment *(Hirsch)*] since there is not a 'complete number' for each city without My joining them.

The *forty* and *thirty* represented 'complete numbers' corresponding to four and three cities respectively, and as such they represented the majority of the five cities. Accordingly God used the expression לֹא אֶעֱשֶׂה, I will not act — i.e., I will do nothing — neither to destroy nor to punish — since the number is 'complete' and the affected cities represent the majority [and also, perhaps because they constitute sufficient moral elements amongst the masses so that a betterment from within is not impossible *(Hirsch).* As *Rashi* says, these numbers of righteous would affect salvation for only three or four of the cities.]

Regarding twenty and ten, however, although these righteous people represented 'complete' numbers for their respective cities, nevertheless they represented only a minority of the total five. Therefore, God again used the term לֹא אַשְׁחִית, *I will not utterly destroy,* but I *will* exact punishment. [The implication is that despite the fact that there are righteous people in sufficient numbers to save one or two of the cities, they cannot be spared retribution because the spared cities are but a minority of the total Sodomite complex.]

[The conclusion is that *Rashi* pursued his interpretation of corresponding groups of ten righteous people for individual cities because it most closely follows the literal sense of the dialogue between Abraham and God.]

ל וַיֹּאמֶר אַל־נָא יִחַר לַאדֹנָי וַאֲדַבֵּרָה אוּלַי
יִמָּצְאוּן שָׁם שְׁלֹשִׁים וַיֹּאמֶר לֹא אֶעֱשֶׂה
לא אִם־אֶמְצָא שָׁם שְׁלֹשִׁים: וַיֹּאמֶר הִנֵּה־נָא
הוֹאַלְתִּי לְדַבֵּר אֶל־אֲדֹנָי אוּלַי יִמָּצְאוּן
שָׁם עֶשְׂרִים וַיֹּאמֶר לֹא אַשְׁחִית בַּעֲבוּר
לב הָעֶשְׂרִים: וַיֹּאמֶר אַל־נָא יִחַר לַאדֹנָי
וַאֲדַבְּרָה אַךְ־הַפַּעַם אוּלַי יִמָּצְאוּן שָׁם
עֲשָׂרָה וַיֹּאמֶר לֹא אַשְׁחִית בַּעֲבוּר

30. Undeterred, Abraham begs God's indulgence for yet a further request:

אַל־נָא יִחַר לַאדֹנָי וַאֲדַבֵּרָה — *Let not my Lord be annoyed and I* [*will*] *speak.*

[The translation *annoyed* for יִחַר, follows *Rashi* to *Num.* 16:15. See *comm.* above to 4:5 וַיִּחַר לְקַיִן, *this annoyed Cain.*]

אוּלַי יִמָּצְאוּן שָׁם שְׁלֹשִׁים — *What if thirty would be found there?*

— Then let three cities be saved (*Rashi* to previous verse).

Following *Sechel Tov* [*Targum Yonasan*]:

Ten each for Sodom, Amorrah, and Admah. Forgive Zeboiim out of mercy, and grant Zoar to me, whose merit is small, because of my intercession. And God agreed.

לֹא אֶעֱשֶׂה — *I will not act* [lit. *do.*]

[See previous verse and *footnote* there.]

31. הוֹאַלְתִּי — *I desired* [see *comm.* to *v.* 27.]

עֶשְׂרִים — *Twenty.*

Enough to save two of the cities (*Rashi* to *v.* 29).

Following *Sechel Tov* [*Targum Yonasan*]:

One 'congregation' each for Sodom and Amorrah. You have agreed to spare Zeboiim in Your mercy, and Zoar because of my intercession. This leaves only Admah. Grant it Your clemency since it is but a minority against the others. And God agreed.

לֹא אַשְׁחִית בַּעֲבוּר הָעֶשְׂרִים — *I will not destroy on account of the twenty.*

— But I will subject them to *punishment* because they represent only a minority of the five cities (*Da'as Zekeinim*; see *footnote* to *v.* 29).

32. ['God loves to hear the prayers of the righteous'] ...

וַאֲדַבְּרָה אַךְ הַפַּעַם — *And I will speak but this once.*

[Abraham apparently knew that the following would have to be his final request; below ten he could not ask (see next verse).]

עֲשָׂרָה — *Ten.*

One עֵדָה, assembly. Sufficient to save one of the cities (*Rashi* to *v.* 29).

XVIII
30-32

30 *And he said, 'Let not my Lord be annoyed and I will speak: What if thirty would be found there?' And He said, 'I will not act if I find there thirty.'*

31 *So he said, 'Behold, now, I desired to speak to my Lord: What if twenty would be found there?' And He said, 'I will not destroy on account of the twenty.'*

32 *So he said, 'Let not my Lord be annoyed and I will speak but this once: What if ten would be found there?' And He said, 'I will not destroy on account of the ten.'*

Following *Targum Yonasan:*

'Perhaps ten may be found there. They and I will pray for mercy upon all the land, and You will forgive them. And God agreed.'

As the *Midrash* notes: Why ten? — So that there might be sufficient for an assembly [= quorum] of righteous men to pray on behalf of all of them.

Rashi explains that Abraham did not ask about less than ten because he reasoned: There were *eight* righteous people — Noah, his three sons and their wives — yet *they* could not save *their* generation *(Midrash)*; and regarding *nine* in association with God, he had already inquired [i.e., God already conceded to Abraham when He agreed to spare the forty-five (*v.* 28) that He would spare the cities by associating Himself with the various groups of nine, thus bringing the total of each to ten. Therefore there was no need for Abraham to repeat the request now *(Mizrachi; Gur Aryeh)*.] But, *Rashi* observes, He did not find find [i.e., *Rashi* concludes with this observation, for, in retrospect, since God did *not* spare them, obviously there were not even nine righteous *(Sifsei Chachomim)*.]

Others suggest that Abraham did not consider it *necessary* to ask for less than ten: He thought that Lot and his wife along with his four daughters and four sons-in-law, totaling ten, would be sufficiently worthy to save the town *(Da'as Zekeinim)*. But he was mistaken in thinking them righteous *(Mattanos Kehunah)*.

According to *Radak's* lone interpretation however, Abraham did not specify Lot in his ptayers [although Lot was primary in his mind] because he thought that if the area were to be destroyed, the Lot *would* be consumed along with the rest of the populace, since he had chosen to dwell in Sodom and remain with them. Additionally, Abraham was unsure whether Lot was innocent or whether he had learned from their ways. [But cf. *footnote* to *v.* 24.]

לֹא אַשְׁחִית בַּעֲבוּר הָעֲשָׂרָה — *I will not destroy on account of the ten.*

Hence our Sages said: If a place contains ten righteous people, then the place is saved on their account *(Pirkei d' Rabbi Eliezer)*.

I will not destroy — but I will subject them to *punishment* because they are such a small minority

לג הָעֲשָׂרָה: וַיֵּלֶךְ יהוה כַּאֲשֶׁר כִּלָּה לְדַבֵּר
אֶל־אַבְרָהָם וְאַבְרָהָם שָׁב לִמְקֹמוֹ:
°שלישי א °וַיָּבֹאוּ שְׁנֵי הַמַּלְאָכִים סְדֹמָה בָּעֶרֶב

(Da'as Zekeinim; see *footnote* to *v.* 29).

I will not destroy because of the ten but it is revealed and known to Me that there are not more than a third of a 'congregation' [of righteous] there: Lot and his two betrothed daughters. These are so few as to be inconsequential *(Sechel Tov).*

33. וַיֵּלֶךְ ה׳ כַּאֲשֶׁר כִּלָּה לְדַבֵּר אֶל אַבְרָהָם – [*And*] HASHEM *departed* [lit. *'went'*] *when He had finished speaking to Abraham.*

— As soon as the advocate [Abraham] became silent [i.e., had nothing more to say], the Judge departed *(Rashi).*

And conversely: As long as the Judge indicates that he is willing to listen the advocate pleads, but when the Judge rises, he becomes silent. So it was when HASHEM departed *(Midrash).*

Because HASHEM did not wish Abraham to intercede further, the Holy Presence and Spirit of Prophecy departed from him as soon as Abraham finished his last plea. Abraham understood that it was God's will that he pray no further *(Ha'amek Davar).*

וְאַבְרָהָם שָׁב לִמְקֹמוֹ – *And Abraham returned to his place.*

That is, Hebron *(Ibn Ezra).*

The Judge departed and the advocate did likewise. The accuser, however, continued his accusation, as a result of which *'the two angels came to Sodom'* [next verse] to destroy it *(Rashi).*

His place may also mean 'his characteristic', i.e., his usual hospitality, for Abraham's 'place' was the constant preoccupation with helping others. As an alternate interpretation, 'his place' may be rendered as *'his realm.'* A person's realm or place is the sum of his talents, feelings, strengths, and limitations. During God's revelation to him, Abraham ceased to be a physical being, rising to a level of prophetic spirituality. With the departure of the *Shechinah,* Abraham returned to his physical *realm (R' Bachya).*

Abraham could have been expected to be distraught. He had prayed and won God's pledge to spare a wicked population for the sake of only ten people, only to discover that all of his prayers had been in vain because there was no semblance of righteousness in any of the five cities. Nevertheless, *Abraham returned to his place.* He did not grieve over his failure for he had full faith that whatever God did was merciful and just *(Mei HaShiloach).*

XIX

1. וַיָּבֹאוּ שְׁנֵי הַמַּלְאָכִים – *The two angels came.*[1]

One to destroy Sodom and the other — Raphael, who had healed Abraham (see *comm.* 18:2) — to save Lot. The third angel who had

XVIII 33 *And HASHEM departed when He had finished*
33 *speaking to Abraham, and Abraham returned to his*
XIX *place.*
1 *The two angels came to Sodom in the evening*

made the announcement to Sarah had departed after concluding his mission *(Rashi).*

Rashi notes additionally that here they are referred to as *angels* while previously [18:2] they are referred to as *men*! — When the Divine Presence was with them [as It was during their visit to Abraham] they were described as *men* [i.e., in relation to God's Presence their superior status as angels faded to insignificance and, relatively, they were like mere mortals. But now that the Divine Presence had ascended, they resumed their full status as angels.] Alternatively, in connection with Abraham to whom visiting angels were no novelty, they were referred to simply as *men*; but Lot was overawed by their presence in his house, and the Torah therefore calls them *angels* *(Rashi; Gur Aryeh).*

Despite the above-noted reference to them as 'angels', it is clear that they appeared to Lot also as men, as evidenced by the fact that he, too, made a feast for them [*v.* 3]. The Torah's differentiation between the cases of Abraham and Lot applies only to *the third-person narrative.* Both to Abraham and Lot, however, they *appeared as men* as further evidenced by the fact that the Sodomites referred to them as such [*v.* 5]. Regarding the view of Rav Levi in the *Midrash* who [apparently interprets the verses literally when he] comments: 'To Abraham whose religious strength was great, they actually *appeared* as men [because he was as familiar with angels as with men]; but to Lot they *appeared* as angels because his strength was feeble [hence he was overawed by them]' — I fail to understand how Rav Levi will justify Lot's feeding them and the Sodomite's reaction *(Mizrachi).*

Yafeh To'ar answers the latter by reiterating that the Torah refers to them here as angels in its narrative to record the actual facts of the matter, [lit. 'the truth of the thing']. Rav Levi in the

1. There is a surface similarity between the behavior of the Sodomites in regard to Lot's visitors, and that of the Benjaminites in the notorious episode of the פִּלֶגֶשׁ בְּגִבְעָה, Concubine of Gibeah *(Judges* 19).

Ramban in *v.* 8 gives a lengthy dissertation to point out the basic differences:

In Sodom, cruelty to visitors was an *established policy with the Sanction of law and custom.* Its purpose was to avoid sharing the largesse of Sodom's lush prosperity with the needy [see *Overview*].

Gibeah had no such law, its populace tended to be ungenerous and inhospitable, but there was no sanctioned institutionalized policy to achieve exclusion of outsiders. The perpetrators of the atrocity in Gibeah were a powerful hoodlum element; whereas in Sodom the entire population came to torment the visitors. The Gibeanites did not commit a capital crime and there was no intention to kill the concubine who had previously committed adultery. The entire nation of Israel by rising up in war against the sinful city, demonstrated conclusively that the atrocity was an unprecedented aberration, while in Sodom there had never been a protest against the prevailing behavior.

וְלוֹט יֹשֵׁב בְּשַׁעַר־סְדֹם וַיַּרְא־לוֹט וַיָּקָם
ב לִקְרָאתָם וַיִּשְׁתַּחוּ אַפַּיִם אָרְצָה: וַיֹּאמֶר

Midrash does not suggest that Lot *actually perceived them as angels,* rather they are described as מַלְאָכִים in the sense of *Godly, distinguished emissaries* who deserved his utmost hospitality. [Therefore Rav Levi's comment should be understood as implying that because such distinguished visitors were not unusual to Abraham, the Torah describes them simply as *'men'*; because they were unique to Lot, their true status is recorded.]

Yafeh To'ar continues that Abraham was so righteous that he was superior to these angels — especially because he was human and subject to temptations which he controlled — unlike the angels who have no Evil Inclination. The Torah thus alluded that compared to him, they were like men.

סְדֹמָה — *To Sodom.*

The *Midrash* notes a grammatical rule: When a word requires the prepositional prefix *lamed* [ל=to ...], the prepositional suffix ה, *heh* may be substituted. For example סְדֹמָה, *to Sodom* [instead of לִסְדֹם]; שֵׂעִירָה, *to Seir* [instead of לְשֵׂעִיר] (33:16); מִצְרַיְמָה, *to Egypt* [instead of לְמִצְרַיִם] (12:10); חָרָנָה, *to Charan* [instead of לְחָרָן] (28:10).

בָּעֶרֶב — *In the evening.*

It certainly did not take the angels so long to travel from Hebron to Sodom! [According to the *Midrash* they left Abraham in the *mid-afternoon,* and since angels move with 'the swiftness of lightning' what took so long from the time they left Abraham until they entered the city?] But they were angels of Mercy and so they waited [until Abraham finished his pleading] on the chance that Abraham would succeed in his intercession for the place. When they saw that he did not succeed, they entered the city to perform their mission *(Midrash; Rashi).*

[Note in this context, that according to *Ralbag* in 18:21 these angels were sent to the Sodomites in the guise of men to test how the Sodomites will treat them — thus indicating that their doom was not yet finally sealed and they were given this final opportunity to repent. (See also *Midrash* cited to *v.* 5 and *Rashi* to *v.* 12.]

[It must be re-emphasized that the Torah is not merely a 'history book' and would not tell us that they arrived *in the evening* unless a message was to be derived from the fact.]

According to *Or HaChaim* they entered *in the evening* to provide Lot the opportunity of offering them hospitality and thereby justify his being saved. For though it was said that he was saved in Abraham's merit, nevertheless, some *personal* merit had to be found. Furthermore, had they arrived *by day,* the citizens might have prevented them from entering the city altogether.

When Lot came to Sodom he emulated Abraham and practiced hospitality. When the decree was promulgated in Sodom: 'Whoever supports the poor with food shall be burned by fire' he was afraid and did not venture to be hospitable *by day,* but did it *at night.* That is why Lot was sitting at the gate of Sodom *in the evening.* He was looking for night-travelers to whom he could secretly show hospitality *(Pirkei d'Rabbi Eliezer).* [Cf. *Midrash HaGadol*].

וְלוֹט יֹשֵׁב בְּשַׁעַר־סְדֹם — *And Lot was sitting at the gate of Sodom.*

[The gates of a city, like the gates around the Old City of Jerusalem

XIX and Lot was sitting at the gate of Sodom; now Lot
2 saw and stood up to meet them and he bowed, face to
the ground. [2] And he said, 'Behold now, my lords;

today, were fairly large edifices. They were not gathering places for idlers, but for the assembly of the dignitaries of the land. So we find throughout Scriptures that the elders, and judges, stationed themselves at the gate of a city. *Boaz* who was a judge sat at the gate *(Ruth* 4:1); as did *Mordechai* (who stationed himself at the gate of the King; see *comm.* to *Esther* 2:19). Solomon praises the woman of valor whose *husband is known at the gates, where he sits among the elders of the land (Prov.* 31:23). Commercial transactions took place and disputes were settled at the gate of a city.]

[With this background, since Lot is described as *sitting at the gate of Sodom* and the gate was where justice was administered] the *Midrash* cites the tradition that he sat there *as a judge.*

The *Midrash* additionally notes that יוֹשֵׁב, *was sitting* is written defectively [=יֹשֵׁב, without the *vav* which — since the Torah is written unvocalized — can be read יָשַׁב, *sat.*] This intimates that they appointed him as their judge that very day *(Rashi).*

[*I.e., the full spelling would have indicated that Lot was sitting constantly, past as well as present. The defective spelling, however, indicates that his sitting was 'incomplete', i.e., a recent development (Harav David Feinstein;* comp. 23:10).]

In a radical departure from the usual interpretation *B'chor Shor* [followed by *Chizkuni*] suggests that Lot resided in a secluded place near the city gate *outside* of Sodom [see his *comm.* to 13:12.] That is why he was bold enough to defy Sodom's ordinances against hospitality and offer the angels lodging. According to this interpretation, יֹשֵׁב should be rendered *dwelled.*

[Perhaps, according to the above, the fact that Lot resided outside the city's walls was a *contributing factor* in his being spared the fate of the others.]

וַיַּרְא־לוֹט וַיָּקָם לִקְרָאתָם — *Now* [lit. *'and'*] *Lot saw* [them] [*and*] *stood up to meet them* [lit. *'toward them'*].

From having lived in Abraham's house he learned to seek out travelers *(Rashi).*

When they had come *to Abraham* it was mid-day and he was able to see them approaching from afar. Therefore Abraham *ran toward them* [18:2]. Since it was evening when they arrived *in Sodom,* Lot did not see them until they were very close. Hence *he* simply *rose to meet them (R' Bachya).* [This differs from the general *comm.* to 18:2; see there.]

According to *Malbim,* the angels did not approach Lot to avoid endangering him by giving the appearance that they sought lodging in defiance of the city's ordinances. Rather *he saw them,* and *he* took the initiative.

וַיִּשְׁתַּחוּ אַפַּיִם אָרְצָה — *And he bowed, face to the ground.*

In a display of deference to their

הִנֶּה נָּא־אֲדֹנַי סוּרוּ נָא אֶל־בֵּית עַבְדְּכֶם וְלִינוּ וְרַחֲצוּ רַגְלֵיכֶם וְהִשְׁכַּמְתֶּם וַהֲלַכְתֶּם לְדַרְכְּכֶם וַיֹּאמְרוּ לֹּא כִּי בָרְחוֹב

obviously awe-inspiring appearance *(Sforno).*

And since it was nighttime he did not fear that he was being watched at the moment *(Yafeh To'ar).*

The word אַפַּיִם familiarly rendered *face,* essentially refers to the *nostrils,* the most protruding portion of the face *(Ibn Ezra).*

This expression denotes *completely outstretched prostration,* [פִּשּׁוּט יָדַיִם וְרַגְלַיִם], of the kind usually reserved for prayer. *Abraham* did not bow in this manner to human beings, therefore, when *he* bowed to his guests, the Torah describes it as [18:2] וַיִּשְׁתַּחוּ אָרְצָה, *and he bowed to the ground.* The word אַפָּיִם, *face,* i.e., total prostration, is omitted (See *Rashi* to *Harayos* 4a bot., s.v. בְּפִשּׁוּט).]

2. הִנֶּה נָּא־אֲדֹנַי — *Behold now, my lords.*

אֲדֹנַי, *my lords,* in our verse is not sacred. It is a humble reference to the two gentlemen *(Ibn Ezra).*

[The first נָּא in our verse is interpreted by *Rashi* to mean *now;* the second means *please* (see *comm.* to 12:11; *Mizrachi)*]:

Behold, *now that you have passed by my house,* you are my lords [i.e., consider me at your disposal]. Another interpretation: You should *now* exercise caution with regard to these wicked people that you not be noticed. And the following is good advice: *Turn aside, please, to your servant's house ... (Rashi).*

The *nun* of the first נָּא, *now,* has a *dagesh* [dot] in it according to the Masorah, although this is uncalled for according to the rules of grammar. It emphasizes that only נָּא, *now,* did Lot feel compelled to flout the restrictive ordinances of the city and invite guests into his home. Otherwise the unusually distinguished visitors would have been forced to sleep in the street for night had fallen and Sodom, obviously, had no guest-house *(Ha'amek Davar).*

[Were it still day-time, however, he might not have risked the consequences of so bold an offer; instead he might have simply brought them refreshments without inviting them into his home. It should be noted, however, that according to the Midrashim, guests were not unusual in Lot's house; perhaps the idea of harboring *two* at one time, however, involved more than the usual risk. These events should also be viewed in the light of the Midrashim which explain that the young girl who was smeared with honey and left to her painful death for feeding strangers was none other than Lot's daughter (see on 18:20-21). One can only imagine the deadly fear under which Lot must have made his offer. Nevertheless his upbringing in Abraham's house, in which he was exposed to incessant hospitality, had its effects on Lot throughout his life — even while a resident of debauched Sodom.]

[He dared invite them only under cover of dark and even then he had to use every manner of precaution,

XIX
2 *turn about, please, to your servant's house; spend the night and wash your feet, then wake up early and go your way! And they said, 'No, rather we will spend*

bidding the angels to follow him in devious ways]:

סוּרוּ נָא אֶל־בֵּית עַבְדְּכֶם — *Turn about, please, to your servant's house,* i.e., take a roundabout route to my house so you can enter unnoticed *(Rashi).*

And, rather than entering my home from the street, please use a back door so you will not be seen *(Me'am Loez).*

וְלִינוּ וְרַחֲצוּ רַגְלֵיכֶם — *Spend the night and wash your feet.*

Surely he should have *first* washed their feet as did Abraham [18:4], and *then* invited them to spend the night. — However, Lot feared that if the visitors washed their feet first and were then discovered in his house, the Sodomites would accuse him of having harbored them for several days without reporting it. He therefore reasoned that it would be better that their feet remain unwashed, so it would appear that they had just arrived *(Rashi);* therefore, he asked them not to wash their feet until after they left his house in the morning *(Me'am Loez).*[1]

There is an alternate opinion in the *Midrash* that Lot did not ask them to immediately wash their feet, as did Abraham, because Abraham objected to the pollution of idolatry [see *comm.* to 18:4] while Lot was unconcerned.

וְהִשְׁכַּמְתֶּם וַהֲלַכְתֶּם לְדַרְכְּכֶם — *Then [you shall] wake up early and [you shall] go [to] your way.*

— Before your presence in town is discovered *(Ramban).*

Or the intention is: Do not fear; I presume you are in a rush and I will not detain you. You may leave as early as you like *(Tur).*

[But the angel's reply is abrupt]:

וַיֹּאמְרוּ לֹּא — *And they said, 'No'.*

They declined Lot's invitation, but they accepted Abraham's invitation immediately, saying [18:5]; *Do as you have said.* We therefore infer that one may decline the invitation of an inferior, but not that of a superior *(Midrash; Rashi).*

Their refusal was merely an act of ethical conduct *(Ramban).*

1. How, indeed, were the guests discovered after such elaborate precautions?

According to *Pirkei d'Rabbi Eliezer* a young boy saw the guests and summoned the others.

The more familiar version [which does not necessarily exclude the above], is the *Midrash* records that Lot's wife was not anxious to entertain her husband's guests, and accordingly did not permit them in *her* portion of the house. [That is what Lot implied in describing them as guests who have come under the shadow of *my* rafters (*v.* 8).]

As a result an argument ensued [which is alluded to Midrashically by the word *matzos (v.* 3) which can also be translated *quarrel* (see *Ex.* 2:13, 21:22, *Lev.* 24:10)].

When Lot requested that a little salt be given his guests, his wife retorted: 'Is it not bad enough that you invite these people into the house? Do you wish to introduce the evil practice of giving salt also?'

So she betrayed him. She went to a neighbor to borrow some salt. When asked why she could not have prepared salt during the day, she replied: 'We had enough salt. But we need more for some guests.'

In this way, news of the visitors spread through the city.

ג נָלִין: וַיִּפְצַר־בָּם מְאֹד וַיָּסֻרוּ אֵלָיו וַיָּבֹאוּ
אֶל־בֵּיתוֹ וַיַּעַשׂ לָהֶם מִשְׁתֶּה וּמַצּוֹת אָפָה
ד וַיֹּאכֵלוּ: טֶרֶם יִשְׁכָּבוּ וְאַנְשֵׁי הָעִיר אַנְשֵׁי
סְדֹם נָסַבּוּ עַל־הַבַּיִת מִנַּעַר וְעַד־זָקֵן כָּל־
ה הָעָם מִקָּצֶה: וַיִּקְרְאוּ אֶל־לוֹט וַיֹּאמְרוּ לוֹ

כִּי בָרְחוֹב נָלִין — *Rather we will spend the night in the square* [lit. *'broad place'*].

— According to *Me'am Loez*: 'You need not endanger yourself; we can lodge in the town square.'

— We will thereby make our presence and mission publicly felt; perhaps the Sodomites will be moved to repent *(Chizkuni)*.

3. וַיִּפְצַר־בָּם מְאֹד — [*And*] *he* [i.e., Lot] *urged them very much.*

His urging was sincere and to his merit. The angels declined at first in order to increase his merit [by having him insist further]. Finally they consented *(Ramban)*.

וַיָּסֻרוּ אֵלָיו — *So* [lit. *'and'*] *they turned toward him.*

I.e., taking a roundabout route toward his house *(Rashi)*.

וַיַּעַשׂ לָהֶם מִשְׁתֶּה — [*And*] *he made a feast for them.*

The word מִשְׁתֶּה [from שתה, to *drink*] indicates a feast where wine is served. Lot was a lover of wine as we see later (*vs.* 32-35), and therefore offered it as a part of his hospitality. In the case of Abraham, however, we find mention of (21:8) this sort of feast only when the weaning of Isaac was celebrated, for among the guests were the important people of the land, the sort who indulge in drink.

וּמַצּוֹת אָפָה — *and* [*he*] *baked matzos.*

It was [the date that would later become] Passover *(Rashi)*.

[See *comm.* to 18:6]

Lot is described as baking the matzos himself, to assure that they would not become *chametz (Or HaChaim)*.

In the literal sense, however, the verse portrays Lot as preparing the meal, and even baking the matzos himself — what a sad contrast with the cheerful spirit of hospitality that prevailed in Abraham's entire household: Here, neither wife nor child shared the *mitzvah* of the father and husband. Even in his own home Lot stands alone *(Hirsch)*.

Nevertheless, Lot did not hesitate to maintain the teachings of Abraham even though he faced the opposition not only of his adopted city but of his own family, and rendered *personal* service to his guests *(Harav David Cohen)*.

וַיֹּאכֵלוּ — *And they ate.*

[I.e., they appeared to eat. See on 18:8.]

4. טֶרֶם יִשְׁכָּבוּ וְאַנְשֵׁי הָעִיר אַנְשֵׁי סְדֹם נָסַבּוּ עַל־הַבַּיִת — *They had not yet lain down* [lit. *'before they would lie down'*] *when* [lit. *'and'*] *the townspeople, Sodomites, converged upon* [lit. *'surrounded'*] *the house.*[1]

The simple meaning of the verse is: ... The men of the city, wicked men [i.e., true Sodomites] surrounded the house. The term

the night in the square.'
[3] *And he urged them very much so they turned*
toward him and came to his house. He made a feast
for them and baked matzos, and they ate.
[4] *They had not yet lain down when the towns-*
people, Sodomites, converged upon the house, both
young and old, all the people from every quarter.
[5] *And they called to Lot and said to him, 'Where are*

Sodomite became a generic word for wicked people, for the Torah specifically describes *the men of Sodom* as *wicked and sinners* [13:13] ... *(Rashi).*

Thus, the Torah identifies them as *Sodomites* although we already know where *the townspeople* were from, to emphasize that by their deeds they showed themselves to be true citizens of the debauched city of Sodom *(Radak).*

By use of this phrase, the Torah indicates that those who gathered around Lot's house were not a disreputable, lawless rabble. On the contrary, they were אַנְשֵׁי הָעִיר representative *townspeople.* Moreover, they were אַנְשֵׁי סְדֹם, *citizens of Sodom,* who came in defense of their social code that was under attack by this interloper who dared flout the long-established laws and customs of the city *(Hirsch).*

The verse stresses טֶרֶם יִשְׁכָּבוּ, *they had not yet lain down,* to indicate how morally debased the Sodomites were. They did not even wait until morning. As soon as the news of the strangers' presence spread among them, they all poured out from their remotest corners to vent their fury *(Abarbanel).*

Rashi cites the *Midrashic* interpretation of this verse:

Before they had laid down, the angels questioned Lot about the character of *the townspeople,* and Lot replied that they were wicked. While the discussion ensued, *the Sodomites surrounded the house.*

מִנַּעַר וְעַד־זָקֵן — *Both young and old* [lit. *'from youth until aged.'*]

— The *old* were as wicked as the *youth*: everyone converged on Lot's house *(Radak).*

כָּל־הָעָם מִקָּצֶה — *All the people from every quarter,* i.e., from one end [קָצֶה] of the city to the other. There was not even one righteous person among them to protest *(Midrash; Rashi).*[1]

This refers even to those who lived far away from Lot's house — so unusual was the spectacle of visitors in Sodom that they all wanted to participate in castigating them *(Akeidas Yitzchak).*

This graphically emphasizes how even the ten righteous ones on

1. The most striking and most illustrative feature of this public degeneracy was that it united every shade of the population. Young people are given to sexual excess, but they tend to sympathize with the persecuted. Older people tend to be callous of suffering, but intolerant of public licentiousness. The powerful and wealthy are accustomed to treading upon the unfortunate, but they quell public scandal. But not in Sodom! In that debauched city, all joined in their perverse inhumanity *(Hirsch).*

אַיֵּה הָאֲנָשִׁים אֲשֶׁר־בָּאוּ אֵלֶיךָ הַלָּיְלָה
ו הוֹצִיאֵם אֵלֵינוּ וְנֵדְעָה אֹתָם: וַיֵּצֵא אֲלֵהֶם
ז לוֹט הַפֶּתְחָה וְהַדֶּלֶת סָגַר אַחֲרָיו: וַיֹּאמַר
ח אַל־נָא אַחַי תָּרֵעוּ: הִנֵּה־נָא לִי שְׁתֵּי בָנוֹת
אֲשֶׁר לֹא־יָדְעוּ אִישׁ אוֹצִיאָה־נָּא אֶתְהֶן
אֲלֵיכֶם וַעֲשׂוּ לָהֶן כַּטּוֹב בְּעֵינֵיכֶם רַק

whose behalf Abraham had interceded could not be found in the city *(Rashbam)*; and hence justifies God's decree against them *(Radak)*.

[The vice of Sodom was proverbial among the prophets; see *Isaiah* 1:10; 3:9, 13:19; *Jeremiah* 49:18; *Ezekiel* 16:46-57; *Amos* 4:11; *Lam.* 4:6.].

5. אַיֵּה הָאֲנָשִׁים אֲשֶׁר־בָּאוּ אֵלֶיךָ הַלָּיְלָה — *Where are the men who came to you tonight?*

They stressed *tonight* to indicate that they were fully aware of the guests' presence and even knew that they had just arrived earlier that night; there would be no point in Lot's trying to deny their presence *(Ibn Sho'ib)*.

Rav Yehoshua ben Levi said in the name of Rav Padiah: Lot had been praying for mercy on behalf of Sodom that entire night, and the angels were inclined to hearken to his petition. [Note that according to several views the angels were sent to Sodom as God's emissaries to make a final determination of the Sodomites' guilt as explained in 18:21, the Sodomites' fate had not yet been firmly sealed.] When all the people of the city converged upon the house with *degenerate* intent however, the angels warded off his prayers saying: Until now you could intercede on their behalf, but after such iniquitous demands, have you still a mouth to plead for them? Plead no further! *(Midrash)*.

וְנֵדְעָה אֹתָם — *That* [lit. *'and'*] *we may know them.*

— i.e., know them carnally; cf. *v.* 8 *(Rashi; Ibn Ezra)*. The same expression is used in connection with the men of Gibeah [*Judges* 19:22] *(Rashbam)*.

[This interpretation is based on the fact that ידע, *know*, is used in Scripture as a delicate term for carnal knowledge and marital intimacy. See *comm.* to 4:1. In this case the Sodomites wished to vent their lust upon the visitors, as was their usual practice as noted in *Pirkei d'Rabbi Eliezer*. The term 'sodomy' for such acts is derived from here.]

Ramban's opinion is that their purpose [in so mistreating stangers] was to prevent the entry of strangers into their land. Because their fertile land was as excellent as *the garden of HASHEM* [13:10], they imagined that their territory would attract many impoverished fortune-seekers, and they refused to share their bounty with the less fortunate. Although they were notorious for every kind of wickedness their fate was sealed because of their persistent selfishness in not supporting the poor and the needy [see *Ezek.* 16:49], and because no other nation could be compared to the cruelty of Sodom. (When Lot came to settle in Sodom, an exception was made, either because of his vast wealth or because he was the nephew of Ab-

XIX
6-8

the men who came to you tonight? Bring them out to
us that we may know them.' [6] *Lot went out to them to*
the entrance having shut the door behind him, [7] *and*
he said, 'I beg you, my brothers, do not act wickedly.
[8] *See, now, I have two daughters who have never*
known a man. I shall bring them out to you and do to
them as you please; but to these men do nothing in-

raham [whose fame had apparently been widespread.]

... *Ramban* continues that Sodom was so severely judged because it was part of the *inheritance of* HASHEM — Eretz Yisrael, and would not allow men of abomination in its midst. Just as the land later vomited out the entire Canaanite nation because of its wickedness, He utterly laid waste the Sodomites who were the most evil of all and who grew haughty because of the material wealth bestowed upon them. This later became an object lesson on Israel who were warned that their inheritance of the land would not endure if they engaged in abominable conduct [See *Lev.* 18:25 and *Ramban* there; *Num.* 35:33-34; *Deut.* 29:22.] (See *Overview).*

6. וַיֵּצֵא אֲלֵהֶם לוֹט הַפֶּתְחָה — *Lot went out to them to the entrance.*

— In order to appease them *(Hoffman).*

וְהַדֶּלֶת סָגַר אַחֲרָיו — *Having shut the door behind him* [lit. *'and the door he closed behind him'*].

7. אַל־נָא אַחַי תָּרֵעוּ — *I beg you, my brothers, do not act wickedly!*

Da'as Sofrim notes that even in these circumstances, Lot refers to them as *'my brothers'*. Perhaps he hoped to placate them thereby, or it may well be that even this gross injustice did not inspire him to re-evaluate his relationship to the wicked Sodomites.

8. הִנֵּה־נָא לִי שְׁתֵּי בָנוֹת אֲשֶׁר לֹא־יָדְעוּ אִישׁ — *See, now, I have two daughters who have never* [lit. *'not'*] *known a man.*

[But they were betrothed. See *Rashi* to *v.* 14.]

[On *know* as a euphemism for *consort,* see 4:1; and cf. *v.* 5 above.]

וַעֲשׂוּ לָהֶן כַּטּוֹב בְּעֵינֵיכֶם — *And do to them as you please* [lit. *as the good in your eyes*].

The narrative up to this point related Lot's hospitality; now it relates his wickedness: He made every effort to protect the guests because they had come into his home, but he shows himself ready to appease the Sodomites by offering his daughters for immorality, which was apparently not repugnant to him, nor did he feel he was doing a great injustice to his daughters ... It is for this reason that the Sages have said [*Tanchuma*]: Usually a man will fight to the death for the honor of his wife and daughters, to slay or be slain, yet this man offers his daughters to be dishonored! Said the Holy One, Blessed be He to him: 'By your life! It is for *yourself* that you keep them [for eventually school children will read *(v.* 36) that

לָאֲנָשִׁים הָאֵל אַל־תַּעֲשׂוּ דָבָר כִּי־עַל־כֵּן
ט בָּאוּ בְּצֵל קֹרָתִי: וַיֹּאמְרוּ | גֶּשׁ־הָלְאָה
וַיֹּאמְרוּ הָאֶחָד בָּא־לָגוּר וַיִּשְׁפֹּט שָׁפוֹט

Lot's daughters came to be with child by their father] (*Ramban*; brackets are from the portion of the *Midrash* not cited by *Ramban*).

[However, cf. *Mishnah Horayos* (13a) that the prevention of *perversion* can take priority over the prevention of natural forms of immorality (*Harav David Cohen*).]

Hoffman notes that even today ... an Easterner regards the duty of protecting his guest as sacred and above all other considerations. However, Lot's impulsive gesture of offering his daughters without first seeking any other avenues reveals that the wickedness of Sodom had not passed over him without having left its mark.

[There are opinions however, that Lot's gesture was noble]:

'Just as Moses offered his life for Israel, so did Lot by offering his daughters to the people instead of his guests; but the Sodomites would not accept them' (*Pirkei d'Rabbi Eliezer*).

Heaven forbid that he abandoned his daughters. It is rather like one who tells another: 'My house is open; take whatever you please!' Or like one who thrusts himself upon his attacker and offers, 'Slay me!' knowing that he wouldn't. They therefore ordered him to stand back knowing his offer was insincere (*R' Chananel*).

According to *Abarbanel*, Lot made the insincere gesture of offering his daughters in order to gain time; he hoped against hope that in the interim his guests would be able to flee.

רַק לָאֲנָשִׁים הָאֵל אַל־תַּעֲשׂוּ דָבָר — *But to these men do nothing.*

הָאֵל, *these*, is an abbreviated form of הָאֵלֶּה or הָאֵלּוּ common in the Bible (*Rashi*).

The *Midrash*, however, interprets אֵל in the sense of strength: *they are powerful men*; or alternately in the sense of godly: *they are men of God.*

כִּי־עַל־כֵּן בָּאוּ בְּצֵל קֹרָתִי — *Inasmuch as they have come under the shelter of my roof* [lit. *'Because therefore they have come under the shade of my rafter'*].

— To avoid trouble such as this! (*Chizkuni*).

I am asking this — not as an act of benevolence to the visitors — but for my sake. I have asked them in and they are under my protection (*Rashi; Hirsch*).

— And it was not due to my own merit that they came, but for Abraham's. [צֵל, *shadow*, is accordingly interpreted as a metaphor for protector rendering: Inasmuch as they have come because of צֵל קֹרָתִי, the protector of my roof — Abraham [*Matanos Kehunah*).] (*Midrash*)

The *Midrash* notes that Lot's expression *'my* roof' implies that his wife had protested their presence and Lot sheltered them in *his* portion of the house. [See *footnote* to *v.* 3.]

You must understand that these

XIX
9

asmuch as they have come under the shelter of my roof.'
[9] *And they said, 'Stand back!' Then they said, 'This fellow came to sojourn and would act as a*

are not ordinary visitors, — Abraham said — 'they are great men (as indicated by the adjective הָאֵל *mighty* [see above]). This is obvious from the fact that כִּי עַל כֵּן *it was for this reason only* that I allowed them to stay in my home, something which I do not ordinarily do' *(Ha'amek Davar).*

9. וַיֹּאמְרוּ גֶּשׁ־הָלְאָה — *And they said, 'Stand back!'* [an idiomatic expression which literally means: *'approach yonder'.*]

— I.e., step aside and keep away from us; withdraw further away. (גֶּשׁ always means *approach; withdraw aside* [cf. *Isaiah* 65:5; 49:20], and הָלְאָה always means *yonder; further away* [cf. *Num.* 17:2; *I Sam.* 20:22].) The intent is one of contempt as if to say: 'We do not take any notice of you! How dare you presume to intercede for these strangers!' *(Rashi).*

According to *Hirsch* the rendering is *they said* [to one another] *'Push up closer!'*

וַיֹּאמְרוּ — *Then they said.*

Both expressions are introduced by וַיֹּאמְרוּ, *they said,* to indicate that there were two distinct replies to Lot's statement in *v.* 8 *(Divrei David):*

— To Lot's offer of his daughters the Sodomites calmly answered *'Stand back!';* but to his attempt to be protective of the strangers [in defiance of every Sodomite law against hospitality] they retorted הָאֶחָד בָּא לָגוּר, *'This fellow came to sojourn ...' (Rashi).*

הָאֶחָד בָּא־לָגוּר וַיִּשְׁפֹּט שָׁפוֹט — *This fellow* [lit. *'this one'*] *came to sojourn* [i.e., as an alien] *and would act as judge?* [lit. *'and he judged to judge?'*]

— You are the only stranger among us, having come here to immigrant [i.e., as a גֵּר, *stranger; alien*], and you make yourself a reprover of us?

[*Rashi* presumably interprets this as an incredulous statement, interpreting the ה, of הָאֶחָד as the definite article: *'the* one' — the only one (יְחִידִי) whom we ever allowed in our midst as an immigrant. *He* would now dare to act as judge!']

Rav Saadiah Gaon interprets that the ה, of הָאֶחָד is a ה הַשְּׁאֵלָה, the interrogative article: *Shall one who has come to sojourn presume to judge us?*

— We have already proclaimed this stranger as a judge over us [see *comm.* to *v.* 1]; *shall he now presume to* [*re-*]*judge* [יִשְׁפּוֹט] the validity of that which *has already been judged* [שָׁפוֹט] and, is established law in our community — that no travelers may be admitted to our city? Even a judge may not transgress this law! And you are no more than a stranger in our midst! *(Divrei David; Kli Yakar)*[1]

1. *Rav Yisrael Isserlein* [*'Terumas HaDeshen'*] explains the double form וַיִּשְׁפֹּט שָׁפוֹט as: ... and now he presumes to *judge the judges?*

Cf. *comm.* to *Ruth* 1:1: *And it happened in the days when* שְׁפֹט הַשֹּׁפְטִים, *the Judges judged,* which the *Talmud* explains as: when *the judges were judged*: it was a generation which judged its judges.

עַתָּה נָרַע לְךָ מֵהֶם וַיִּפְצְרוּ בָאִישׁ בְּלוֹט
י מְאֹד וַיִּגְּשׁוּ לִשְׁבֹּר הַדָּלֶת: וַיִּשְׁלְחוּ
הָאֲנָשִׁים אֶת־יָדָם וַיָּבִיאוּ אֶת־לוֹט
יא אֲלֵיהֶם הַבָּיְתָה וְאֶת־הַדֶּלֶת סָגָרוּ: וְאֶת־
הָאֲנָשִׁים אֲשֶׁר־פֶּתַח הַבַּיִת הִכּוּ בַּסַּנְוֵרִים
מִקָּטֹן וְעַד־גָּדוֹל וַיִּלְאוּ לִמְצֹא הַפָּתַח:

The above interpretation is apparently based on the *Midrash:*

'You wish to destroy the judgments of your predecessors [who forbade hospitality?' Rendering: וַיִּשְׁפֹּט שָׁפוֹט *and he would* [*re-*]*judge the judgments;* condemning them and introducing new ones?] For the Sodomites made an agreement among themselves that whenever a stranger visited them they should force him to submit to sodomy and rob him of his money.

עַתָּה נָרַע לְךָ מֵהֶם — *Now, we will treat you worse than* [we will treat] *them!*

Now that you even defend your action you are more punishable than they are; a greater danger to us than they are! *(Hirsch).*

They do not, however, *specify* what evil they plan to do *(Hoffman).*

'The same perversity we plan to inflict on them we will inflict on you [נָרַע being an allusion to sodomy]' *(Tanchuma).*

וַיִּפְצְרוּ בָאִישׁ בְּלוֹט מְאֹד — *They pressed exceedingly upon the man, upon Lot.*

They vigorously tried to *persuade* Lot to stand aside and allow them in; only when he persistently refused did they approach to break the door *(Ramban).*

Cf. *Midrash Sechel Tov:* He is described here as an אִישׁ, *man* — a term denoting prominence — because with every word he uttered he became greater in their eyes [he became more of a *man* in their eyes] and they grew frightened of him; they therefore sought to ensnare and cajole him when they saw that he refused to listen to them.

Onkelos, however, renders the verb וַיִּפְצְרוּ as connoting *physical* force: וּתְקִיפוּ בְגַבְרָא בְּלוֹט לַחֲדָא, *and they prevailed against the man, against Lot, greatly.*

According to *HaKsav V'HaKabballah* the connotation of אִישׁ, *man,* in this verse is that although he was an אִישׁ, *prominent person,* one whom they themselves had proclaimed a magistrate over them, nevertheless they *pressed exceedingly upon him, and approached to break the door.*

וַיִּגְּשׁוּ לִשְׁבֹּר הַדָּלֶת — *And* [*they*] *approached to break the door,* [i.e., to gain entrance and perpetrate their lustful acts upon the visitors.]

10. הָאֲנָשִׁים — *The men,* [*i.e., the angels*].

אֶת־יָדָם — *Their hand.*

This was 'measure for measure.' When Lot had invited them into his home he extended his hand to them and provided for their safety. Now they reciprocated by extending a

judge? Now we will treat you worse than them!' They pressed exceedingly upon the man, upon Lot, and they approached to break the door.

*10 The men stretched out their hand and brought Lot into the house with them, and closed the door.
11 And the men who were at the entrance of the house they struck with blindness, both small and great; and they tried vainly to find the entrance.*

hand to protect him. *(Midrash Or HaAfeilah— Torah Shleimah* 19:59)

וְאֶת־הַדֶּלֶת סָגָרוּ — *And* [*they*] *closed the door.*

So that in trying continuously to find the entrance until they exhausted themselves [*v.* 11], the Sodomites would demonstrate how utterly dedicated they were to wickedness *(Sforno).*

Torah Sheleimah 19:61 explains that the angel's power was such that they had no need to close the door. Even had the door been left open the Sodomites could not have entered, for in any event the angels smote them with blindness. Rather, as *Midrash Sechel Tov* explains it, they closed the door lest they come to test God [by relying on a miracle.]

11. [The wickedness could not be allowed to proceed in this way. Stern measures were called for to subdue the frenzied mob]:

וְאֶת־הָאֲנָשִׁים אֲשֶׁר־פֶּתַח הַבַּיִת — *And the men who were at the entrance of the house.* [i.e., the Sodomites.]

הִכּוּ בַּסַּנְוֵרִים — *They* [i.e., the angels] *struck with blindness.*

The translation *'blindness'* follows *Rashi.* However, in his comm. to the same term in *II Kings* 6:18 *Rashi* further defines סַנְוֵרִים as חוֹלִי שֶׁל שִׁמָּמוֹן, *hysteria,* a delusion where one sees and knows not what he sees.

Onkelos renders: שַׁבְרִירַיָּא, and *Yonasan renders* חֲוַודְרוּרַיָּא both of which terms express bedazzlement; bewilderment; temporary disorientation; and *Talmudically:* temporary blindness. cf. *Yoma* 28b; *Gittin* 69a.

Radak suggests that the term is a composite of the two words סַנֵי רְאִיָּה, *despising sight.*

מִקָּטֹן וְעַד־גָּדוֹל — *Both small and great* [lit. from *small to great*]

The *small* [*young*] had initiated the wrongdoing, as it is said [*v.*4]: מִנַּעַר וְעַד זָקֵן, *from young to old;* therefore they are mentioned here first — they are the first to be punished. *(Midrash; Rashi)*

וַיִּלְאוּ לִמְצֹא הַפָּתַח — *And they tried vainly to find the entrance.*

I.e., *they could not* find the door; cf. *Exod.* 7:18 נִלְאוּ, and ibid *v.*21 where the meaning is=וְלֹא יָכְלוּ *they could not (Rashbam; Ibn Ezra* ad. loc.)

The *Midrash* explains the word as אִישְׁתַּטוּן, they were maddened, as in *Jeremiah* 4:22 *for my people* is foolish [אֱוִיל].

How degenerate! Though stricken with blindness, they still did not redirect their efforts and

יב וַיֹּאמְרוּ הָאֲנָשִׁים אֶל־לוֹט עֹד מִי־לְךָ פֹה
חָתָן וּבָנֶיךָ וּבְנֹתֶיךָ וְכֹל אֲשֶׁר־לְךָ בָּעִיר
יג הוֹצֵא מִן־הַמָּקוֹם: כִּי־מַשְׁחִתִים אֲנַחְנוּ

cease their evil plan. Though blind, they still sought the door, vainly trying to gain entrance. (*Alshich; Sforno*)

Onkelos, Ibn Janach and *Radak* [*Shorashim*] expain וַיִּלְאוּ [from the root לָאָה], *and they became weary* searching for the entrance. See *Deut.* 25:18 עָיֵף וְיָגֵעַ, *faint and weary* — *Onkelos* renders: מְשַׁלְהֵי וּלְאֵי.

12. The wickedness of the Sodomites had become irreversible and their doom is announced to Lot (*Hoffman*).

עֹד מִי־לְךָ פֹה — *Whom else do you have here?*

I.e., what other relatives do you have in this city besides your wife and the daughters who are home with you? The above is the literal sense of the verse. The *Midrashic* interpretation homiletically reads עוֹד מִי לְךָ פֶּה: *on behalf of whom do you still have a mouth,* i.e., since the Sodomites perpetrated so disgraceful an act, can you still be so bold as to "open a mouth" in their defense? For, as the *Midrash* notes [See *comm.* to *v.*5], Lot had pleaded for them that entire night. (*Rashi*)

חָתָן וּבָנֶיךָ וּבְנֹתֶיךָ — *A son-in-law,* [lit. *'and'*] *your sons, or* [lit. *'and'*] *your daughters.*

If you have any of these in the city *get them out from the place.* [Lot had no sons] בָּנֶיךָ, *your sons,* therefore refers to your *grandsons* — the sons of your married daughters (Rashi). ['Grandchildren are like children'; cf. *comm.* to 20:12.]

[*Rashi* explains in *v.* 14 that Lot had four daughters: two who were betrothed and still lived in his home, and two who were married and no longer lived with him. It is apparently necessary to so interpret because in *v.* 8 Lot describes his daughters who *have never known a man,* while here *sons-in-law* are mentioned. Apparently then there were *sons-in-law* who were married to *other* daughters, and *betrothed suitors* to the two who were with Lot at home.]

Ramban takes *sons* in the literal sense and explains that the angels were speaking as if they were ordinary people who were unaware that he had no sons. Or it is possible that Lot had grown-up married sons.

וְכֹל אֲשֶׁר־לְךָ בָּעִיר — [And] *all that you have in the city* —

Such as cattle, silver, gold, and clothing (*Radak*).

[However, Lot ultimately escaped with no possessions, only with his wife and two of his daughters (see *v.* 16). He may have forfeited the opportunity by delaying until it was too late. Alternately, the phrase *all that you have in the city* could be interpreted as: *whomever you have in the city,* referring not to *possessions,* but to *people,* such as grandchildren or relatives.]

הוֹצֵא מִן־הַמָּקוֹם — *Remove from the place.*

XIX
12-13

[12] *Then the men said to Lot, 'Whom else do you have here — a son-in-law, your sons, or your daughters? All that you have in the city remove from the place,* [13] *because we are about to destroy this*

Take them out not only from *the city* but from the entire region [*the place*] *(Radak).*

Cf. *Tosefta Sanhedrin* 13 that in the case of עִיר הַנִּדַּחַת, *a city led astray* [see *Deut.* 13:13], even the possessions of righteous people *within* the city are destroyed. The *Tosefta* derives this from Lot whose possessions were ultimately destroyed because he did not remove them *before the destruction began* as indicated in *v.* 17. See *comm.* there.

13. כִּי־מַשְׁחִתִים אֲנַחְנוּ אֶת־הַמָּקוֹם הַזֶּה — *Because we are about to destroy* [lit. *'for we are destroying'*] *this place.*

[The present tense *are destroying* expresses absolute determination, although the act had not yet begun.]

See *Ramban's* explanation in *v.* 5 that although there were other very wicked nations on earth, they were not as severely punished as Sodom. This is because Sodom was part of Eretz Yisrael which, as God's heritage, could not tolerate such abominations in its midst ... and it was also God's purpose to make it an example to the children of Israel who were to inherit it as it says [*Deut.* 29:17-24]: *Lest there be among you ... whose heart turns from HASHEM our God ... HASHEM will not spare him ... and shall blot his name from under the heaven ... The land shall be brimstone and salt and burning ... like the overthrown Sodom and Amorrah, Admah and Zaboiim which HASHEM overthrew in His anger (Tur).* [See *Overview.*]

They used the plural form *'we'* although only *one* of them was the emissary of Destruction [for 'two angels do not perform one task'; see *Rashi* to 18:2] because they were standing before him together and they did not wish it to appear that one of them was merely an attendant. Or perhaps the implication of the plural was *Gabriel* [the angel charged with the destruction] *and his legions*; or the implication of *'we'* was that since Gabriel could not perform his task of destruction until Raphael [Lot's savior] effectively removed Lot, it could be said that Raphael, too, participated in the destruction of Sodom. This [indirect cause] is not considered 'two tasks' *(Or HaChaim;* see *Rashi* to *v.* 16 s.v. וַיַּחֲזִיקוּ).

[*Tosafos Bava Metzia* 86b s.v. הַהוּא mentions *Gabriel* as the angel of the destruction, and *Michael* as Lot's savior.]

The *Midrash* comments that for revealing God's secret and intimating that *they* were going to destroy the place, the ministering angels were banished from their abode in the Divine presence for a period of 138 years [until they re-ascended at Beer Sheba in Jacob's dream. These were the angels who Jacob saw ascending the ladder to return to their sacred precincts *(Matnas Kehuna;* cf. *R'Bachya* here and to 28:12).

The calculation is as follows: The overthrow of Sodom took place when Abraham was 99. He lived until 175, leaving 76 years until his death. Jacob

אֶת־הַמָּקוֹם הַזֶּה כִּי־גָֽדְלָה צַעֲקָתָם֙ אֶת־
יד פְּנֵי יהוה וַיְשַׁלְּחֵנוּ יהוה לְשַׁחֲתָהּ: וַיֵּצֵא
לוֹט וַיְדַבֵּר | אֶל־חֲתָנָיו | לֹקְחֵי בְנֹתָיו
וַיֹּאמֶר קוּמוּ צְּאוּ מִן־הַמָּקוֹם הַזֶּה כִּי־

was 77 when he saw the dream, making a total of 153. Deduct the 15 years that Jacob lived during Abraham's lifetime [Jacob was born when Abraham was 160] and that leaves a total of 138 years from the overthrow of Sodom until Jacob's dream *(Maharzu).*

כִּי־גָדְלָה צַעֲקָתָם אֶת־פְּנֵי ה׳ — *For their outcry* [— i.e., the anguished cry of the oppressed *(Radak)*] *has become great before* [lit. *'the Face of'*] *HASHEM.*

[The adjective *great* refers to the magnitude of the cries rather than to their number. See *comm.* to 18:20.]

וַיְשַׁלְּחֵנוּ ה׳ לְשַׁחֲתָהּ — *HASHEM has therefore sent us* [lit. *'and HASHEM has sent us'*] *to destroy it.*

Having initially intimated that *they* were going to destroy the city — thus ascribing the act to themselves — they were now required to admit that the matter was not in their control but in HASHEM's, and that they were but His emissaries. Therefore they restated the fact and said *'HASHEM has sent us to destroy it' (R' Bachya*; cf. *Rashi* to *v.* 22 s.v. כִּי לֹא אוּכַל).

It is significant that in the whole story God is called *HASHEM* — the Name signifying His Attribute of Mercy and His care for the future of mankind. It was in His Attribute of Mercy that He decreed the destruction of Sodom. To such depravity, complete annihilation itself is an act of merciful love [for Mankind] *(Hirsch).*

[See *footnote* to 6:7, and further, *v.* 24.]

14. וַיֵּצֵא לוֹט — *So Lot went out.*

Apparently after the Sodomites grew weary and went their way *(Sforno).*

וַיְדַבֵּר אֶל חֲתָנָיו — *And* [*he*] *spoke to his sons-in-law.*

Who were married to his two daughters who lived in the city *(Rashi).*

He did not speak to his daughters because women tend to defer to their husbands *(Radak).*

Lot's initiative to his sons-in-law rather than to his daughters does not indicate an indifference to them. In the Middle East more than anywhere else, a woman becomes totally subservient to her husband from the time of her marriage. By the nature of the relationship, Lot could speak only to the husbands *(Hoffman).*

Ibn Ezra, however, interprets that the two married daughters had died, for *v.* 15 refers to the two betrothed daughters as הַנִּמְצָאֹת, *present,* the implication being that no other children were 'present' i.e., alive.

Ramban in *v.* 12 mentions that the reference to *sons* there suggests that it is possible that Lot had grown-up married sons. [No reference in our verse, however, is made of an attempt by Lot to speak

XIX
14

place; for their outcry has become great before
HASHEM and HASHEM has therefore sent us to
destroy it.'
14 *So Lot went out and spoke to his sons-in-law,*
[and] the betrothed suitors of his daughters, and he
said, 'Get up and leave this place, for HASHEM is

to his *sons.*] *Ramban* therefore suggests that Lot spoke with his sons-in-law first because he was certain that his sons would obey him [without persuasion], but his sons-in-law laughed at him and their dialogue apparently continued until dawn when the angels rushed him and permitted him to take only those who were at hand. However, Lot's merit would have been sufficient [had they not laughed and time run out] to save his entire family, not as Abraham had thought, that God would destroy the righteous along with the wicked.

לֹקְחֵי בְּנֹתָיו — [And] *the betrothed suitors* [lit. *'the takers'*] *of his daughters* —

Those to whom his daughters at home were betrothed *(Rashi).* [I.e., those who were in the *process of taking* but who had not yet completed their taking *(Midrash)*].

[The conjunctive *and* is not in the Hebrew, but is contextually suggested. See *Mizrachi* below.]

Rashi — following the *Midrash* — holds that Lot had four daughters: two married who lived in the city, and two betrothed who lived in his home. Accordingly, חֲתָנָיו, *sons-in-law* refers to those who were *married* to two of his daughters. לֹקְחֵי בְּנֹתָיו, lit. *takers of his daughters,* could be interpreted as an adjectivial phrase further identifying the sons-in-law: חֲתָנָיו לֹקְחֵי בְּנֹתָיו, *his sons-in-law who took* [i.e., *married*] *his daughters. Rashi* rejects this interpretation and instead considers the phrase לֹקְחֵי בְּנֹתָיו a participle referring to a *second pair of persons. Rashi's* interpretation is based on several premises:

(a) If only one pair were being referred to, what need would there be to further describe his *sons-in-law* as *the takers of his daughters* when this is obvious? Hence it must refer to different persons *(Mizrachi);*

(b) The term חֲתָנָיו suggests sons-in-law after חֲתוּנָה *marriage;* had the second phrase been further identifying them it would have read: בַּעֲלֵי בְּנֹתָיו, *husbands of his daughters.* Since the term used is לֹקְחֵי, *takers* it is indicative that betrothed suitors are meant and that these are distinct from the married *sons-in-law (Gur Aryeh).*

(c) [As pointed out in a bracketed comment to *v.* 12 s.v. חָתָן, since Lot described the daughters in his house as *'never having known a man,'* [*v.* 8], it follows that these daughters could not be married. Therefore, the terms here חֲתָנָיו, *sons-in-law,* and לֹקְחֵי בְּנֹתָיו, *takers of his daughters* could not both refer to *married husbands* of those daughters. Rather חֲתָנָיו must refer to *sons-in-law* already married to *other daughters* while לֹקְחֵי בְּנֹתָיו must refer to as yet unmarried suitors of those daughters living with Lot.]

Furthermore, the fact that the words חֲתָנָיו and לֹקְחֵי בְּנֹתָיו are not separated by the conjuctive ו, *and,* [חֲתָנָיו וְלֹקְחֵי בְּנֹתָיו] is not entirely unusual. Comp., for example [*Habakuk* 3:11] שֶׁמֶשׁ יָרֵחַ עָמַד זְבֻלָה [lit. *sun moon stood still in their habitation;* the prepositional prefix ו, *and,* preceding יָרֵחַ, *moon,* is implied] *(Mizrachi).*

Therefore, in consonance with *Rashi's* interpretation we have supplied the bracketed *and* in the translation as required by the English syntax.

Divrei David suggests that exegetically the absence of *and* is intended to liken the two phrases one to the other. Thus we infer that just as his betrothed daughters were two in number *(v.* 16) so too were the married daughters two in number.

מַשְׁחִית יהוה אֶת־הָעִיר וַיְהִי כִמְצַחֵק
טו בְּעֵינֵי חֲתָנָיו: וּכְמוֹ הַשַּׁחַר עָלָה וַיָּאִיצוּ
הַמַּלְאָכִים בְּלוֹט לֵאמֹר קוּם קַח אֶת־
אִשְׁתְּךָ וְאֶת־שְׁתֵּי בְנֹתֶיךָ הַנִּמְצָאֹת פֶּן־
טז תִּסָּפֶה בַּעֲוֺן הָעִיר: וַיִּתְמַהְמָהּ | וַיַּחֲזִיקוּ

כִּי מַשְׁחִית ה׳ אֶת־הָעִיר — *For HASHEM is about to destroy* [lit. *'is destroying'*] *the city.*

[Note that Lot did not attribute the impending destruction to the angels but to HASHEM.][1]

וַיְהִי כִמְצַחֵק בְּעֵינֵי חֲתָנָיו — *But he seemed like a jester in the eyes of his sons-in-law.*

They said to him [with the typical self-assurance of a native Sodomite]: 'Absurd! Organs and cymbals are in the land — [i.e., everything in the land is in order, and its inhabitants carefree] — and you say that the land is to be overthrown!' Grievous is mockery for punishment did not overtake the Sodomites until they mocked Lot *(Midrash; Matnos Kehunah).*

Lot referred to God destroying the city by His name *'HASHEM'* which indicates His Attribute of Mercy. They therefore did not take Lot seriously because, they reasoned, shall HASHEM in His Mercy destroy a city? But indeed it is so, for 'the wicked turn the Attibute of Mercy into the Attribute of strict Justice' *(Kli Yakar).* [See *footnote* to 6:7 p. 192; *footnote* to 8:1 p. 260; and *Hirsch* end of *v.* 13.]

15. וּכְמוֹ הַשַּׁחַר עָלָה — *And just as* [or: *at about the time that (Targum Yonasan)*] *the dawn was breaking* [lit. *'rose up'*].

[As *Ramban* explains (see *v.* 14), Lot's conversation with his sons-in-law extended throughout the night, until the angels could wait no longer.]

The angels waited until dawn when the Sodomites began to awake so Lot could depart in full view of them all *(Midrash Or HaAfeilah-Torah Sheleimah* 19:80).

The idiomatic expression הַשַּׁחַר עָלָה refers to the time of day when the שַׁחֲרוּת, *darkness* of night עָלָה, *rises,* i.e., departs *(Heidenheim).*

וַיָּאִיצוּ הַמַּלְאָכִים בְּלוֹט — [*And*] *the angels urged Lot on,* i.e., as *Targum* takes it וּדְחִיקוּ [*they pressed him*] — they hurried him *(Rashi).*

1. *Bris Shalom* [cited in *Likutei Anshei Shem, Chumash Rav Pninim*] explains that Lot did not attribute the impending destruction to *angels* but to *God Himself.* His sons-in-law laughed because unlike an angelic Destroyer who does not distinguish between the good and the wicked [*Bava Kamma* 60a], God *does* distinguish [see *comm.* to 18:23.] Therefore, they reasoned that if God *Himself* was the Destroyer, any attempt to escape would be futile for He would find them wherever they might flee, while if He wished to spare them they could remain in the midst of the city and no harm would befall them. Therefore they looked at him as foolish to suggest that they flee.

[They did not realize however, that the target of destruction was the *city* as an organized society that has selfishness and cruelty at the base of its social order. Therefore, those who escaped before the destruction would not be overtaken in the Destruction about to take place, but would of course be judged on their own merit. Furthermore, while the Attribute of Mercy *decreed* the destruction, the *execution of the decree* was through an angel.]

XIX
15-16

about to destroy the city!' But he seemed like a jester
in the eyes of his sons-in-law.
15 *And just as dawn was breaking, the angels urged Lot on saying: 'Get up — take your wife and your two daughters who are present, lest you be swept away in the punishment of the city!'*

Cf. *Exod.* 5:13 וְהַנֹּגְשִׂים **אָצִים** לֵאמֹר *and the taskmasters pressed them,* i.e., urged them *(Ibn Ezra).*

Now that their true mission has been revealed they are referred to as *'angels'* for the first time since their arrival *(Ralbag)..*

Rashi to *v.* 23 [see *footnote* there] explains that the angels hurried him because the 'rains' of sulphur and fire began descending at the break of dawn, [and the danger was real making it imperative that Lot hurry his departure.]

According to *Sforno* they hurried him so that Sodom's destruction could take place at sunrise, the sun being their chief deity [thus the sun's impotence to save its worshippers would be demonstrated.]

[See *Rashi* to *v.* 24.]

אֶת־אִשְׁתְּךָ וְאֶת־שְׁתֵּי בְנֹתֶיךָ הַנִּמְצָאֹת — *Your wife and your two daughters who are present* [lit. *'found'*] — in the house, ready to be saved *(Rashi).*[1]

[Lot could save only his immediate family who lived with him in his home; the others forfeited whatever merit they had by sneering at his warning.]

The salvation of Lot's immediate family was perhaps in reward for his hospitality, as it is befitting for messengers to save their host and all his belongings, just as the messengers of Joshua similarly saved all the families of their hostess, Rachab [*Joshua* 6:23]. As the *Midrash* notes: 'Because Lot honored the angel by offering him hospitality, he accordingly befriended Lot' *(Ramban* to *v.* 12).

פֶּן־תִּסָּפֶה בַּעֲוֹן הָעִיר — *Lest you be swept away in the punishment of the city.*

[Or: *'lest you be swept away for the sin of the city,'* the word עָוֹן meaning both *punishment* and *sin.* Cf. 4:13; 15:16; *I Sam.* 28:10.]

Rashi explains תִּסָּפֶה, *swept away* as derived from סוֹף, *end*: i.e., *an end will be made of you;* see *Onkelos* to *Deut.* 2:14 תֹּם, *completely ended* = דְּסַף.

1. The *Midrash* comments on הַנִּמְצָאֹת, *that are found:*

Rav Toviah ben Rav Yitzchak said: Two מְצִיאוֹת, 'finds' [i.e., precious things would descend from Lot's daughters]: Ruth the Moabitess [ancestress of King David] and Na'amah the Ammonitess [wife of King Solomon]. Rav Yitzchak commented [*Ps.* 89:21]: *I have found* (מָצָאתִי) *David my servant.* Where did I find him [i.e., from where did he originate]? — In Sodom [see *vs.* 37 ff.]

Cf. *Midrash Aggadah*: They were saved in the merit of David and the Messiah, David as descendant of Ruth the Moabitess, and Rehaboam [son of Solomon] from Na'amah the Amonitess. The Messiah will be descended from both.

[This topic is dealt with fully in the *Overview* to the ArtScroll edition of *Ruth* — 'Ruth and the Seeds of Mashiach.']

הָאֲנָשִׁ֜ים בְּיָדוֹ֙ וּבְיַד־אִשְׁתּ֗וֹ וּבְיַד֙ שְׁתֵּ֣י
בְנֹתָ֔יו בְּחֶמְלַ֥ת יהוה עָלָ֑יו וַיֹּצִאֻ֥הוּ
יז וַיַּנִּחֻ֖הוּ מִח֥וּץ לָעִֽיר׃ וַיְהִי֩ כְהוֹצִיאָ֨ם אֹתָ֜ם
הַח֗וּצָה וַיֹּ֙אמֶר֙ הִמָּלֵ֣ט עַל־נַפְשֶׁ֔ךָ אַל־

16. וַיִּתְמַהְמָהּ — *Still* [lit. *'and'*] *he lingered*, in order to save his wealth *(Rashi)*.

The *Midrash* relates וַיִּתְמַהְמָהּ to תְּמָהוֹן, *astonishment*: He exclaimed in amazement: 'What a loss of gold, silver and gems!' [The commentators explain that this is the reason for the שַׁלְשֶׁלֶת cantillation of this word. Its long, reverberating tones emphasize the pathos and utter bewilderment which Lot experienced.]

Hirsch interprets וַיִּתְמַהְמָהּ from the root מהה, from which the word מַה, *what*, is derived. Thus the compounded וַיִּתְמַהְמָהּ connotes: *indecision*, i.e., Lot *tarried indecisively*. Lot could not easily bring himself to abandon his children and grandchildren to destruction.

[But the angels could wait no longer; God had contained His wrath for the fifty-two years of Sodom's existence. Now its measure of iniquity was full and its doom was sealed. Although the angels had told him to gather his possessions (*v.* 12), he had squandered the precious moments allowed him. They could not wait merely to allow Lot to gather his material wealth (see *Radak*).]

וַיַּחֲזִיקוּ הָאֲנָשִׁים בְּיָדוֹ וּבְיַד־אִשְׁתּוֹ וּבְיַד שְׁתֵּי בְנֹתָיו — *So* [lit. *and*] *the men grasped him by his hand,* [and] *his wife's hand and the hand of* [each of] *his two daughters.*

Ibn Ezra explains that וַיַּחֲזִיקוּ, *grasped,* [apparently relating it to חָזָק, strength] implies that *they strengthened Lot,* for in his terror he grew too weak to flee. *Ramban* cites the use of the same verb in *Exod.* 12:33 and holds that it means that they forcibly pulled them and sped them on.

Here the angels are once again called *'men'* because they acted like mortals by grasping the hands of and tugging along those who were being saved *(Radak)*.

Rashi explains that the angels are referred to in plural because one was there to save Lot and the other to destroy the city. [Since the latter could not commence the destruction until Lot and his immediate family were safely out of the city, the acts of *removal* are described in plural because *both angels* participated in expediting Lot from the center of destruction for this reason *(Be'er Mayim Chaim)*. See *Or HaChaim* cited in *v.* 13 who explains that this joint participation in the removal of Lot does not constitute a 'second' mission for the destroyer; otherwise this would run counter to the rule that one angel does not perform two missions. Cf. *Tosafos Bava Metzia* 86b s.v. הַהוּא.]

[When the actual *saving* begins, however, the speaker changes to singular. See *comm.* to וַיֹּאמֶר in *v.* 17.]

בְּחֶמְלַת ה׳ עָלָיו — *In HASHEM's Mercy on him.*

I.e., they pulled him out forcibly not because of his great merit but

XIX
16-17

[16] *Still he lingered — so the men grasped him by his
hand, his wife's hand, and the hand of his two
daughters in HASHEM's Mercy on him; and they
took him out and left him outside the city.* [17] *And it
was as they took them out that one said: 'Flee for*

because of HASHEM's mercy on him. [Therefore, had he continued to linger in Sodom, he would have forfeited the opportunity to be saved *(Sforno).*] Or, perhaps, the verse is stating that *they grasped his hand* ... to save him while *God's mercy was still upon him,* lest God's wrath go forth and he perish *(Ramban).*

The *Midrash* suggests that God spared Lot *for Abraham's sake,* in reward for Lot's loyalty: when Abraham was in Egypt and claimed that Sarah was his sister, Lot did not reveal the secret.

Hirsch explains that the verb חמל connotes undeserved mercy, or, at least, the mercy that arises only out of compassion. Lot did not truly deserve to be saved for he had allowed greed to draw him to Sodom, keep him there, and even to allow his children to become so degraded that they laughed at his entreaties that they escape the impending destruction. His life was saved, but he was not unpunished. His entire ill-gotten fortune was left behind in the upheaval.

17. וַיְהִי כְהוֹצִיאָם אֹתָם הַחוּצָה — *And it was as they took them out.*

Since the verse should have read וַיְהִי כְהוֹצִיאָם הַחוּצָה [i.e., without אֹתָם, in which case the suffix ם would refer to Lot and his family, unlike the present reading in which the subject *they* refers to the angels — see *Ibn Ezra* below], the inclusion of אֹתָם, *them,* is interpreted as a limitation: *them* only, i.e., Lot's wife and his immediate family — but not his property *(Chizkuni).*

The translation reflects *Ibn Ezra* who explains that the subject of כְּהוֹצִיאָם is the angels — i.e., *when they* [the angels] *took out* אֹתָם, *them* [Lot and his family]. This is unlike the word [*Jer.* 31:31] לְהוֹצִיאָם where the possessive suffix ם refers to the object: *to their being taken out* [rather than *to their* (the subject) *taking out.*]

וַיֹּאמֶר הִמָּלֵט עַל־נַפְשֶׁךָ — *That one* [lit. *'and he',* i.e., one of the angels] *said: 'Flee for your life!'* [lit. *'escape upon your soul.'*]

The previous acts, having been performed by both angels in order to expedite Lot's departure, are described in plural. The verb וַיֹּאמֶר, and *he* said, however, is in singular. This is because no longer are *both* angels assisting Lot. Now that Lot had been removed from the impending holocaust, Gabriel, the angel of destruction, was free to begin his mission, and he returned to perform his task. Therefore, *the angel whose mission it was to save Lot* (Raphael or Michael) now performed his mission and directed Lot to flee for his life *(Rashi* to *v.* 16 as explained by *Levush;* see *comm.* to וַיַּחֲזִיקוּ in *v.* 16; cf. *Rashi* to 18:2).

Rashi perceives the inclusion of the words עַל נַפְשֶׁךָ, *for your life* (lit. *'upon your soul')* as implying: הִמָּלֵט עַל נַפְשֶׁךָ, Be satisfied with הַצָּלַת נְפָשׁוֹת, saving *your lives;* do not think about saving your wealth also!

תַּבִּיט אַחֲרֶיךָ וְאַל־תַּעֲמֹד בְּכָל־הַכִּכָּר
יח הָהָרָה הִמָּלֵט פֶּן־תִּסָּפֶה: וַיֹּאמֶר לוֹט
יט אֲלֵהֶם אַל־נָא אֲדֹנָי: הִנֵּה־נָא מָצָא

You have wasted valuable moments reflecting upon material possessions — run for the safety of your lives! *(Abarbanel).*

Rashi comments that the root meaning of הִמָּלֵט wherever it occurs in Scriptures is *detach, slip away.*

Examples of the derivative meanings are: [*Isaiah* 66:7] וְהִמְלִיטָה זָכָר, *and she bore a male,* i.e., an embryo *slipped out* of the womb; [*Ps.* 124:7]: *Our soul* נִמְלְטָה *escaped like a bird.* [Cf. also *Rashi's comm.* to מַלֵּט in *Isaiah* 46:2 where he explains it as to *extract* from the absorbed.]

אַל־תַּבִּיט אַחֲרֶיךָ — *Do not look behind you.*

You are as wicked as they are and you are being saved only because of Abraham. It is not proper for you to look upon their punishment while you yourself are being spared *(Rashi).*

According to *Rashbam* . . . turning around causes delays. Furthermore one is not to gaze unnecessarily upon angels performing their task, as [Manoach said after he realized he had seen an angel — *(Judges* 13:22)]: *We shall surely die because we have seen God;* and Jacob's exclamation [32:30]: *For I have seen God face to face and yet my life was preserved.*[1]

The angel gave this instruction to Lot in the singular אַחֲרֶיךָ, *behind you,* but his family was included in the charge: *'you* and all who are with you.' This is similar to God's command to Adam regarding the Tree of Knowledge [2:17]: *'you shall not eat of it'* which, although directed to Adam in the singular, embraced Eve as well *(Ibn Ezra; Chizkuni).*

Ramban comments that *no punishment would be inflicted for violation of the angel's command not to look backward.* Rather the angel was warning them of dire consequences that would be a *natural result of such a glance,* for the mere sight of the atmosphere of destruction and all contagious diseases has a very harmful effect. Even thinking about them would be psychologically dangerous. Furthermore, the destroying angel *stood between the earth and heaven* enveloped in fire as did the angel seen by David [*I Chronicles* 21:16]. It is for this reason that he was prohibited from gazing.

The *Zohar* explains that the *Shechinah* was about to descend and one such as Lot may not gaze in the Presence of the *Shechinah 'for man may not see HASHEM and live'* [*Ex.* 33:20.]

1. *Kli Yakar* interprets this as an injunction not to look back in regret for the wealth they left behind. Lot's wife, however, could not make peace with this loss of possessions. Had she been concerned with having money with which to help others she would have been spared. But her punishment revealed her true intention. She was converted to salt, a corrosive substance that eats away the substance of coins. So, too, Lot's wife. In her hands, money was corrosive, a tool of greed rather than goodness, for it was only Lot who provided hospitality for guests (see *comm.* above). When his wife turned around it was in selfish grief and fear that when her husband died penniless, none would provide for her. Therefore, the Torah says that she looked מֵאַחֲרָיו, *behind 'him'* [*v.* 26] — her concern was for the time when he would be gone.

XIX
18-19

your life! Do not look behind you nor stop anywhere in all the plain; flee to the mountain lest you be swept away.'
[18] *Lot said to them; 'Please, no! My Lord —* [19] *See,*

וְאַל־תַּעֲמֹד בְּכָל־הַכִּכָּר — *Nor stop anywhere* [lit. *'and do not stand'*] *in all the Plain,* i.e., the plain of Jordan *(Rashi).* [See 13:10-11.]

Do not dally, for the destruction could not begin until you reach your destination, and the angel could not delay the time to any considerable further degree *(Ramban).*

הָהָרָה הִמָּלֵט פֶּן־תִּסָּפֶה — *Flee to the mountain lest you be swept away.*

I.e., he indicated thereby that Lot should flee to Abraham who was dwelling in the mountain, for as evidenced by 12:8 and 13:3, he still resided in his tent on the mountain where he originally lived when he came to Canaan. Although Abraham had many tents which extended as far as Hebron [13:18] his primary home did not change *(Rashi).*

18. וַיֹּאמֶר לוֹט אֲלֵהֶם אַל־נָא אֲדֹנָי — [*And*] *Lot said to them: 'Please, no! My Lord.'*

I.e., *Please do not tell me to escape to the mountain,* נָא meaning *please. Targum* renders *I beg of You now ... (Rashi).*

The Sages interpret that the word אֲדֹנָי [Adonai], *My Lord* in this case is sacred and refers to God. The reason for not rendering it as an address to the angel is because Lot continues in the next verse to say that he was speaking to the One Who showed mercy לְהַחֲיוֹת אֶת נַפְשִׁי *in keeping me alive.* Therefore this entire phrase — beginning with the introductory *My Lord* — must refer to Him in Whose power it is to put to death and to keep alive: the Holy One, Blessed be He *(Shev.* 35b; *Rashi).*

According to the above interpretation, the flow of the verse *(as reflected by the punctuation of the translation)* would be: *And Lot said to them* [i.e., the angels] אַל־נָא *O please do not!,* i.e., do not tell me to flee to the mountain. Then, directing his prayer to God, — indicated further by his change to the singular — he said: *O my Lord — see now, Your servant,* etc. *(Maharsha Shevuos* 35b).

Mizrachi interprets that the word נָא, *please,* introduces the petition addressed to God: *Lot said to them* [the angels]: אַל, *'do not',* i.e., do not ask me to flee to the mountain. Then he turned to God: נָא, *'Please, my Lord ... '*

[See *Gur Aryeh* who explains that *Onkelos* renders בְּבָעוּ, *I beg you,* as reflecting the inner implication of אַל, *do not,* and כְּעַן, *now,* is his rendering, as usual, of נָא. Comp. *Onkelos'* same rendering to אַל נָא in *v.* 7. This is in answer to *Mizrachi* who questioned how *Onkelos* rendered the same word נָא as *both* a request בְּבָעוּ, *I beg you,* and כְּעַן, *now,* while apparently not rendering the word אַל, *do not,* at all.]

[That *'my Lord'* in this case is sacred is the accepted *halachah,* and is so formulated in the *Talmud Shevuos* 35b; *Soferim* 4:7; *Rambam: Yesodei HaTorah* 6:9. This *halachah* primarily affects the writing of a Torah Scroll, and whether or not this word is subject to erasure if miswritten. See also *comm.* to 18:3.]

There are however several opinions — e.g. *Ibn Ezra; Radak; R' Chananel; R' Bachya* [to 18:3] that the *literal sense* of the word אֲדֹנָי here is *non*-sacred. It is the plural of אֲדֹנִי, *my master,* and the end-of-verse form of אֲדֹנָי [cf. *comm.* to 18:3]. They explain that *v.* 8 was addressed to the two angels whom he ad-

עַבְדְּךָ חֵן בְּעֵינֶיךָ וַתַּגְדֵּל חַסְדְּךָ אֲשֶׁר
עָשִׂיתָ עִמָּדִי לְהַחֲיוֹת אֶת־נַפְשִׁי וְאָנֹכִי
לֹא אוּכַל לְהִמָּלֵט הָהָרָה פֶּן־תִּדְבָּקַנִי
כ הָרָעָה וָמַתִּי׃ הִנֵּה־נָא הָעִיר הַזֹּאת
קְרֹבָה לָנוּס שָׁמָּה וְהִוא מִצְעָר אִמָּלְטָה

[was addressed to the two angels whom he addressed with the courteous term *'my lords'*, while Lot's request in *v.* 9 which is in the singular was addressed to that angel who, in *v.* 17, urged Lot to *'escape for your life.'* *Radak* adds that such a request imputing power over life and death to an angel is proper, for, in the performance of their mission, angels, and even prophets such as Elijah and Elisha could be addressed in terms that would seem to impute such power to them. The sense of the verse is that, since they act as agents of God, He is addressed through them.

Ramban to *v.* 12 explains, however, that angels only *seem* to have this power — in reality they are acquainted with the knowledge of God and merely fulfill His Will.

[Perhaps it is possible to synthesize both views by drawing an analogy from a similar controversy in 18:3 regarding whether the word אֲדֹנָי in that passage is sacred, and refers to God, or whether it is 'non-sacred' and is a courteous form of address to the angels. *Ramban* there agrees that according to the plain meaning of the verse Abraham was addressing the angels, while at the same time he agrees that the Name is sacred, as formulated in *halachah.* He therefore suggests that Abraham addressed the angels referring to them by their Master's name *Adonai* (see *comm.* there). Although *Ramban* offers no comment to our verse, possibly the interpretation applies here as well, that Lot addressed the Angels referring to them by the Name and Attributes of the Holy One, Blessed be He. This is further evidenced in *v.* 24 where *HASHEM* is interpreted by *Radak* and *Ramban* to refer to the angel Gabriel, the destroyer, who is designated by the Name of his Master.]

Furthermore, see *Ritva* to *Shevuos* 35b according to whom וַיֹּאמֶר לוֹט אֲלֵהֶם, *Lot said to them,* is interpreted as וַיֹּאמֶר לוֹט לִפְנֵיהֶם, *Lot said in their presence:* perceiving they were angels, he directed his prayer to God.

Ibn Ezra preserves an interesting etymological opinion from *Rav Shmuel HaSefaradi* that the word אַל might be related to הוֹאֵל, *desire* [i.e., and the phrase אַל־נָא would accordingly mean: *'please grant indulgence'* (lit. *'be desirous, please'),* interpreting אַל as the imperative form of the root יאל, just as דַּע, *know,* is the imperative form of the root ידע *(Karnei Or);* see *comm.* to הוֹאַלְתִּי in 18:27, and *Gur Aryeh* above.] *Ibn Ezra* continues, however, that he prefers to render אַל in its usual sense *do not.*

19. [As explained above, according to The Sages this verse was addressed in prayer to God in Whose power it is to keep alive and put to death, while there are opinions that it was addressed to the chief angel *(Ibn Ezra)* or to the one who had urged him to escape to the mountain *(Radak).*]

הִנֵּה־נָא מָצָא עַבְדְּךָ — *See now, Your servant has found ...*

Lot introduces his petition by gratefully acknowledging all that already has been done for him *(Alshich).*

לֹא אוּכַל לְהִמָּלֵט הָהָרָה — *I cannot* [lit. *'I will not be able to*] *escape to the mountain.*

[I.e., I am unable to maintain the pace required to flee as far as the mountain (based on *Ramban*'s interpretation of the literal meaning of the text; see further).]

As *Hirsch* elaborates: 'Your act of saving me is magnanimous, but if

XIX *now, Your servant has found grace in Your eyes and*
20 *Your kindness was great which you did with me to*
save my life; but I cannot escape to the mountain lest
the evil attach itself to me and I die. 20 *Behold, please,*
this city is near enough to escape there and it is small;

it can be completed only by unbroken flight directly to the mountain, the journey itself will kill me.'

פֶּן־תִּדְבָּקַנִי הָרָעָה וָמַתִּי — *Lest the evil attach itself* [lit. *'cling'*] *to me and I die.*

If I am too long in my effort to reach the mountain, the evil [i.e., the fire and brimstone *(Chizkuni)*] of the destruction will overtake me while I am still in the plain, for You will not defer the time much longer *(Ramban).*

The *'evil'* refers to the 'fallout' of the Destruction — the brimstone, salt and fire — which will spread over a large area *(B'chor Shor; Chizkuni)* [But see *Alshich* to *v.* 25.]

[*Rashi,* based upon the *Midrash,* continues his interpretation of *v.* 17 that Lot was ordered to flee to *the mountain* where Abraham resided.]:

Lot pleaded, 'Please do not ask me to go to the mountain to my uncle Abraham. When I dwelt among the Sodomites, God compared my righteousness to theirs and in comparison to them, I deserved to be saved. But if I go to the righteous one [i.e., Abraham] I will be considered wicked by comparison' *(Rashi).*

Rashi adds that this is similar to the response of the woman of Zarefath to Elijah [see *I Kings* 17:18] that although she had been considered righteous compared with others, now that Elijah had entered the scene, in comparison with him she was wicked.

[Thus it would appear that *Rashi* interprets our verse: *I cannot flee to the mountain* — i.e., to Abraham — for by doing so I would risk that תִּדְבָּקַנִי הָרָעָה, *the evil of my ways will cling to me* (i.e., my sinfulness will become obvious in comparison with the righteous Abraham) וָמַתִּי, *and I will die* (i.e., I will no longer merit being saved, so I will perish).]

According to *Pesikta Rabbasi* Lot replied that he could not rejoin Abraham because the latter had already told him [13:9]: הִפָּרֶד נָא מֵעָלָי, *please separate from me.*

Ibn Ezra discusses the grammatical form of וָמַתִּי which should be וָמַתְתִּי but the ת of the root drops because of the double consonant. Comp. the form וְכָרַתָּ [*Deut.* 20:20] which should similarly be, were it not for the double consonant, וְכָרַתְתָּ.

20. הִנֵּה־נָא הָעִיר הַזֹּאת קְרֹבָה — *Behold, please, this city is near.*

Rashi explains *near* as referring to *nearness* in time: קְרוֹבָה יְשִׁיבָתָהּ, it was populated [relatively] recently and so its measure [of sin] is not yet full.[1]

1. This interpretation is based on *Shabbos* 10b: 'A man should always seek to dwell in a city שֶׁיְּשִׁיבָתָהּ קְרוֹבָה, which was but recently populated, for since it was but recently populated, its sins are few, as it is said, *Behold, please, this city is* קְרֹבָה, *near and* מִצְעָר, *small.* What does קְרֹבָה, *near,* mean? Shall we say that it means [geographically] *near* and מִצְעָר means [physically] *small?* But surely they [the angels] could see that for themselves [and as *Be'er Mayim Chaim* points out why should Lot choose it on the basis of its *physical proximity to Sodom*; he would have been better off seeking a haven *further away* and hence safer from the impending disaster!] — Rather he meant: Because it has been recently populated [lit. 'inhabited a *near* time'] its sins are few.

נָא שָׁמָּה הֲלֹא מִצְעָר הִוא וּתְחִי נַפְשִׁי׃
כא °וַיֹּאמֶר אֵלָיו הִנֵּה נָשָׂאתִי פָנֶיךָ גַּם

°רביעי

Rashi continues to explain the chronology: How recently had it been settled? It dated from the generation of the Dispersion when mankind was scattered and men began to settle, each in his own place [for prior to that time all people lived together in Shinar as is evident from 11:1-2 *(Rashi; Shabbos* 10b)].

This Dispersion took place in the year of Peleg's death [see *Rashi* to 10:25] during Abraham's forty-eighth year [see *Chronology/Time-Line* p. xii]. When Sodom was destroyed, Abraham was ninety-nine years old. [Of the angels who visited Abraham, one was to destroy Sodom, and one announced that Isaac would be born one year later. Since Isaac was born when Abraham was 100, obviously he was 99 at the destruction]. Therefore, fifty-two years elapsed between the time that Sodom was populated, and its destruction. Traditionally, Zoar was populated one year after Sodom. This fact is alluded to homiletically in the *Talmud ibid.* by the phrase אִמָּלְטָה נָא, *let me escape* to the city which is נ״א, 51, in numerical value. (See *Tosafos* and *Maharsha ibid*; and *footnote* to 18:21 אֵרְדָה־נָּא.] [See also *Sechel Tov* cited to 18:29.]

In the literal sense, the distance between Sodom and Zoar was approximately five *mil* [*Pesachim* 93b], while according to the *Midrash* it was four *mil.* [See *comm.* to *v.* 23.]

וְהִיא מִצְעָר — *And it is small.*

I.e., its sins are few [מוּצְעָרִין 'עֲוֹנוֹתֶיהָ] *(Shabbos* 10b; see above).

[See *Ibn Ezra* and *Heidenheim* further.]

Hirsch comments upon Lot's emphasis on Zoar as being מִצְעָר which he explains as a noun meaning *it is a petty thing; insignificant*; offering no wealth or comfort. Because he had been forbidden even to look back, Lot understood that he was meant to be left with no possessions — nothing but his life. Now he argued that the poverty of living in insignificant Zoar would be equivalent to being left with only his life.

הֲלֹא מִצְעָר הִוא וּתְחִי נַפְשִׁי — *Is it not small? — and I will live* [i.e., *survive*; lit. *'and my soul will live.'*]

— Are not its sins yet few so that it may be spared and I may be allowed to survive in it? The above is the *Midrashic* interpretation. The simple meaning [of this latter phrase, (see *Sifsei Chachomim* below)] is: Is it not a small city with but a small population? It can be spared [since there cannot be many sinners in it *(Rashbam)*] so I can survive there *(Rashi).*

To *Rashi's* 'simple' interpretation *Mizrachi* raises the *Talmud's* objection cited in the footnote to the beginning of this verse that if מִצְעָר meant 'small' then it would have been superfluous for Lot to mention the obvious to angels. *Sifsei Chachomim* responds that *Rashi does* follow the *Talmudic* interpretation of מוּצְעָרִין עֲוֹנוֹתֶיהָ, its sins are few', the *first* time the word מִצְעָר appears in the verse. However, that word is repeated, and *Rashi* holds that it would be redundant to ascribe the same connotation to both ap-

I shall flee there. Is it not small? — and I will live.'
[21] *And he replied to him: 'Behold, I have granted you consideration even regarding this, that I not*

pearances of the same word. Therefore, *Rashi* cites the simple meaning with reference only to the *second* use of מִצְעָר.

Levush, however, comments that *Rashi's* simple interpretation applies to *both* parts of the verse. In mentioning the obvious — that the city was *'small'* — Lot was laying the foundation for his request: *'The city is* מִצְעָר, *small,* and therefore it cannot be heavily populated; hence its measure of wickedness must be proportionately מִצְעָר, *small,* and it should be possible to spare it so that I may survive there.

Ibn Ezra [as explained by *Yohel Or*] supports the interpretation that מִצְעָר, *small* (which he derives from צָעִיר, *young; little),* is an adjective modifying *city* rather than a noun meaning *'something insignificant'.* The fact that עִיר, *city,* is feminine in gender and hence its adjective should be in the feminine form (מִצְעֶרֶת) does not matter, since such is the Scriptural idiom.

Heidenheim notes however, that depending upon the context, מִצְעָר, *small,* may denote both: *few in number* as in *II Chron.* 24:24 בְּמִצְעַר אֲנָשִׁים *with a small group of men;* or *small in time* as in *Isaiah* 63:18: לַמִּצְעָר, *in a little while.* In our verse the word can have both connotations, מִצְעָר meaning both *smaller* and *younger* than Sodom.

Ha'amek Davar observes that Lot gave two reasons for his request that Zoar be spared: (1). — it was but a *small city* and it is natural for a village to be less steeped in immorality than a big city, in line with the *Talmudic* interpretation to *Song of Songs* 7:12 in *Eruvin* 21b [see *comm.* to *ArtScroll* ed. *ad loc.*]. Therefore Zoar had not descended to Sodom's level of wickedness; (2). — *So I may live,* i.e., spare it so I can survive. The difference between the two reasons is that according to the former the city should be spared entirely, while according to the latter its destruction should be postponed until such time as Lot departs from it.

It is small — it is sparsely populated and it is not very old. As a result, its measure of sin is not yet full, and although its destruction has been decreed along with the rest of the Plain, any merit I have will be sufficient to protect the city until I can depart from it when the plague is over *(Malbim).*

21. וַיֹּאמֶר אֵלָיו — *And he replied* [lit. *'said'*] *to him.*

I.e., the *angel* replied in God's Name, for Lot was not worthy of direct communication from God *(Radak).*

הִנֵּה נָשָׂאתִי פָנֶיךָ גַּם לַדָּבָר הַזֶּה — *Behold, I have granted you consideration even regarding this* [lit. *'Behold I have lifted up your face also to this thing.'*]

Even regarding this — i.e. not only will *you* be saved, but I will also save the *entire city of Zoar* for your sake *(Rashi).*

Radak derives from this that angels, as intelligent beings, are granted the authorization from God to modify their instructions according to their own judgment and assessment of particular circumstances. *Ramban* [*v.* 12], however, perceives no suggestion of independence in the angel's sudden concession; rather the angel was ac-

לַדָּבָר הַזֶּה לְבִלְתִּי הָפְכִּי אֶת־הָעִיר אֲשֶׁר
כב דִּבַּרְתָּ: מַהֵר הִמָּלֵט שָׁמָּה כִּי לֹא אוּכַל
לַעֲשׂוֹת דָּבָר עַד־בֹּאֲךָ שָׁמָּה עַל־כֵּן קָרָא
כג שֵׁם־הָעִיר צוֹעַר: הַשֶּׁמֶשׁ יָצָא עַל־הָאָרֶץ
כד וְלוֹט בָּא צֹעֲרָה: וַיהוה הִמְטִיר עַל־סְדֹם

quainted with the intentions of God Who had granted Lot's request.

The expression נָשָׂאתִי פָנֶיךָ, [lit. *'I have lifted up your face'*] translated as: *I have granted you consideration*, follows *Hoffman* who explains that this is the intent of the phrase [See *footnote* to 22:12.]

The expression occurs again in the בִּרְכַּת כֹּהֲנִים, *Priestly Blessing*, in *Num.* 6:26 יִשָּׂא ה׳ פָּנָיו אֵלֶיךָ [lit. *'may HASHEM lift up His face unto you,'*] which *Rashi* there explains as: *May HASHEM suppress His anger toward you. Ibn Ezra* there elaborates that the phrase has the opposite connotation of *Isaiah* 1:15: אַעְלִים עֵינַי מִכֶּם, *I will avert My eyes from you*, its connotation being: wherever you turn, His face will be lifted up toward you in benevolence [i.e., for one who is angry at another averts his face from him — cf. *Deut.* 31:18. When one *lifts his face* toward a person, it is evidence that he bears no ill-will.]

Cf. *Sifrei*, to *Naso* 6:26: *May HASHEM lift up His face unto you* [i.e. grant your prayer] when you stand and pray, as it says [in our verse] הִנֵּה נָשָׂאתִי פָנֶיךָ, *behold I have granted you consideration*, for it stands as simple logic: If I granted Lot's petition for the sake of Abraham, My friend, shall I not grant your's [i.e. that of the Children of Israel who receive the Priestly Blessing], both for your sake and for the sake of your ancestors?

לְבִלְתִּי הָפְכִּי אֶת־הָעִיר אֲשֶׁר דִּבַּרְתָּ — *That I not overthrow the city about which you have spoken.*

[According to the *Midrash, the city itself* was not overthrown but its *residents* were ultimately destroyed. Perhaps this is why Lot *was afraid to remain in Zoar (v.* 30), filled as it was with corpses. In the literal sense, however, the commentators maintain that Zoar was spared intact with its citizens.]

In a grammatical note *Rashi* comments that the י in הָפְכִּי is a subjective [*I overthrow*] suffix. Examples cited for such parallel grammatical forms are: [48:5] עַד בֹּאִי, *until I come;* [16:13] אַחֲרֵי רֹאִי, *after I saw;* [*Jeremiah* 31:19] מִדֵּי דַבְּרִי בּוֹ, *whenever I speak of him.* This is to distinguish it from such forms as הַמַּשְׁפִּילִי [*Ps.* 113:6], הַהֹפְכִי [*ibid.* 114:8], where the *yod* is reflexive and the word would be rendered *'my being overthrown' (Gur Aryeh; Devek Tov).*

22. כִּי לֹא אוּכַל לַעֲשׂוֹת דָּבָר עַד־בֹּאֲךָ שָׁמָּה — *For I cannot do a thing until you arrive there.*

This refers to the *upheavel* which had to wait for Lot's safe arrival in Zoar; the sulphur and fire from God, however, had begun descending with dawn (*Gur Aryeh v.* 24; see *footnote* there).

This forced admission by the

overthrow the city about which you have spoken.
[22] Hurry, See there, for I cannot do a thing until you
arrive there.' He therefore named the city Zoar.
[23] The sun rose upon the earth and Lot arrived at
Zoar. [24] Now HASHEM had caused to rain upon

angel of his powerlessness was his punishment for having boasted [*v.* 13] *we are about to destroy this place,* implying an independent initiative. Now the matter could not be concluded until they were compelled to make this admission that they were powerless *(Rashi;* [see *R' Bachya* end of *v.* 13 — accordingly this would be the angel's *second* such admission]).

Rashi also notes that the singular pronoun, *'I* cannot' etc., [as noted in 18:12] proves that only *one of them* was sent to destroy the city, and the other to save Lot, for two angels are not sent to perform the same mission. *(Rashi)* [See *comm.* to *v.* 16 s.v. וַיַּחֲזִיקוּ; *v.* 17 s.v. וַיֹּאמֶר.]

עַל־כֵּן קָרָא שֵׁם־הָעִיר צוֹעַר — *He therefore named* [lit. *'called the name of'*] *the city Zoar* [meaning *'small'.*]

Therefore, i.e., because Lot referred to it as a *'small'* city [מִצְעָר, *v.* 20], and because its salvation was due to its being smaller and of lesser iniquity, it came to be called *'Zoar'* — i.e., hamlet. It was originally called *Bela* [see comm. to 14 ff.] *(Rashi;* cf. *Radak; Hoffman).*

23. הַשֶּׁמֶשׁ יָצָא עַל־הָאָרֶץ וְלוֹט בָּא צֹעֲרָה — *The sun rose* [lit.*'went out'*] *upon the earth and Lot arrived at Zoar.*

This refers to *sunrise,* at which time the sun becomes visible on the horizon. It is later than the *dawn* mentioned in *v.* 15 when Lot departed from Sodom on his hurried escape. Thus, the entire journey is estimated in the *Midrash* as having taken as long as the lapse of time between dawn and sunrise. Therefore, the distance between Sodom and Zoar is reckoned as four or five *mils.* [See *comm. v.* 20 above.]

24. וַה׳ הִמְטִיר עַל־סְדֹם וְעַל־עֲמֹרָה — *Now* [lit. *'and'*] *HASHEM had caused to rain upon Sodom and Amorrah.*

The phrase וַה׳, *'and* HASHEM' always means He and His Celestial Court *(Midrash; Rashi).* [1]

This interpretation of וַה׳ is used only in cases where a conjunctive ו, *and,* is uncalled for by the context of a verse. Since the letter ו indicates an amplifica-

1. *Rashi* further interprets הִמְטִיר in the pluperfect, *had rained down* — i.e. the sulphur and fire had already begun raining down from the moment the morning broke, referring to *v.* 15: *just as dawn broke,* the time when the moon is in the sky together with the sun.

Because some of the Sodomites worshiped the sun and others the moon, God said: 'If I punish them by day the moon-worshipers may say, "Had it taken place at night when the moon holds sway, we would not have been destroyed." However, if I punish them by night the sun-worshipers might say, "Had it taken place by day when the sun holds sway, we would not have been destroyed." '

Therefore, it is written *just as dawn broke,* for He punished them at a time when

וְעַל־עֲמֹרָה גָּפְרִית וָאֵשׁ מֵאֵת יהוה מִן־
הַשָּׁמָיִם: כה וַיַּהֲפֹךְ אֶת־הֶעָרִים הָאֵל וְאֵת

tion, it is interpreted as HASHEM taking counsel together with His Celestial court *(Rakanati Vayera* 25:1; see there).

Mizrachi explains that *Rashi* does not *always* cite this interpretation of the word 'וה, *and* HASHEM, as embracing His celestial court [e.g. 13:14; 18:17; 21:1] although he *does* interpret so, for example, in *Exod.* 12:29. Wherever there is another literal reason for the form: for example, when a narrative resumes after an interruption, the *and* is obviously connective to the preceeding trend in the narrative; or in such cases where it is interpreted in the past-perfect, *and* HASHEM had previously [21:1]; or in cases where the form suggests a *contrast* to the preceding: *But* HASHEM. Thus *Rashi* interprets the various occurrences of 'וה, *and* HASHEM, according to their respective contexts.

Ramban points out that *Rashi* cites only one view, when in reality there are conflicting views of the Sages regarding this phrase: (a) That this first *HASHEM* in the verse refers to the Angel Gabriel, the messenger to destroy the city, who is referred to by the name of the Master [see 18:3]; (b) it refers to Him together with His Celestial Court; (c) it refers to God Himself.

Cf. *Sifri Zuta Naso* 6:26 [*Torah Sheleimah* 19:12], Such is the way of God, King of Kings: When He goes forth in peace He is accompanied by legions and armies but when He goes forth in battle He goes alone, as when He punished the five cities of Sodom. He punished them alone, as it says: Then *HASHEM* [i.e. Himself] rained down upon Sodom and Amorah sulphur and fire from *HASHEM* [i.e. Himself] out of the heaven.

[The use of *HASHEM* — the Name indicating His Attribute of *Mercy* — in conjunction with this description of Him wreaking destruction, (an act for which one would expect the name *Elohim,* indicating the Attribute of *Justice)* indicates that the Sodomites reached the lowest level of depravity. In such a case, complete annihilation itself is an act of love (for mankind). 'Woe to the wicked', comments the *Midrash,* 'who turn the Attribute of Mercy into the Attribute of Justice. (See *comm.* end of *v.* 13, and to *v.* 14).]

הִמְטִיר ... גָּפְרִית וָאֵשׁ — *Caused to rain ... sulphur and fire.*

[The term *rain* is used] because it both the moon and sun [-light] are in the sky [which coincides with the 15th of Nissan *(Midrash).*]

[Thus, according to *Rashi,* the descent of the sulphur and fire does not sequentially *follow* Lot's entrance into Zoar when the sun had already risen upon the earth (*v.* 23) but *preceded it* and began at dawn. This is why the angels urged him on 'lest he be swept away', and it is thus that Abraham upon waking up early in the morning (*v.* 27-28) was already able to see the smoke rising *(Mizrachi).* The angel's remark: *I cannot do anything until you arrive there (v.* 22), referred only to the *overthrowing* of the cities; the sulphur and fire from God, however, had already begun descending since dawn (*Gur Aryeh).*]

Be'er Yitzchak adds that the best proof that the Destruction described in these verses began *before* Lot entered Zoar lies in the narrative itself for in *v.* 25, Lot's wife is described at having peered behind her [during their flight to Zoar] and having been turned into a pillar of salt from witnessing the Destruction which had obviously *already begun.*

Sodom and Amorrah sulphur and fire; from HASHEM, out of heaven. [25] *He overturned these cities*

descended first as rain to see whether they would repent (see *Rashi* to 7:12 וַיְהִי הַגֶּשֶׁם) and was then changed to *sulphur* and *fire* (*Mechilta; Rashi*).

Cf. *Tanchuma:* Nothing evil descends directly from heaven: first it descended as beneficent rain; only when it approached earth did it become sulphur and fire.[Some render גָּפְרִית וָאֵשׁ as a hendiadys: *sulphurous fire.*]

מֵאֵת ה׳ מִן הַשָּׁמָיִם — *From HASHEM, out of the heaven.*

I.e., from the upper atmosphere (*Radak*).

This is emphasized to make it clear that the *sulphur and fire* were not natural phenomena from the earth, but were Divinely originated visitations *from HASHEM, out of heaven,* without any natural cause (*Sforno*)[1]

Additionally, *Rashi* notes that the connotation of the phrase *out of the heaven* is referred to in *Job* 36:31: *For by these* [i.e. the heavens; see the preceding verses there] *He judges the peoples.* For when God wishes to *punish* mankind He causes fire to descend upon them *from heaven* as he did to the Sodomites [see ibid *v.*32], but when He caused the Manna to fall it was also *from heaven* as it says [*Exod.* 16:4] 'Behold, I will rain down bread *from heaven* for you' [see *Job* ibid. second half of *v.* 31; cf. *Sanhedrin* 104b and note of *Torah Sheleimah* 19:126.]

One's understanding of *Rashi's* comment above can be enhanced by comparison with the following:

Woe to the wicked who transform a source of compassion [i.e. heaven] into a source of retribution. David extols God: *Praise HASHEM from the heavens* [*Psalms* 148:1] where there is neither fire, hail, nor sulphur [see *Midrash Tehillim ad. loc.*] How then does it say *HASHEM rained down sulphur and fire out of the heavens?* Only to teach you that the very beginning of their creation, God decreed to them: Be a source of whatever you perceive mankind to deserve. To the Sodomites and the children of Esau provide *sulphur and fire;* for Israel [provide] dew (*Tanchuma Yashan*).

[Cf. *Tanchuma* above s.v. הִמְטִיר.]

The repetition of *HASHEM* in the second half of this verse instead of the pronoun *Him* is noted by the commentators.

According to *Rashi* [following *Sanhedrin* 38b] it is the Scriptural style in many cases to repeat the subject, as for example in 4:23: *and Lemech said to his wives ... wives of*

1. *From HASHEM, out of the heaven,* is apparently redundant, for what *other* source could there be for rain?

The phrase is added to refute the eminently 'logical' explanation that the salty, sulphuric nature of the Sodomite terrain derives from its volcanic nature. Because the *effect* of the upheaval was to make the region volcanic, non-believers pontificate that the volcano was not effect, but cause. To emphasize the truth, the Torah makes clear that the nature of Sodom is a phenomenon that was caused by God. So it is, as well, regarding theories of evolution and the origin of the universe. The data on which the theories are based are true, but the postulators of the hypotheses are again confusing cause and effect. The observable phenomena are *products* of God's creation, not its *causes* (*Hirsch*).

כָל־הַכִּכָּר וְאֵת כָּל־יֹשְׁבֵי הֶעָרִים וְצֶמַח
כו הָאֲדָמָה׃ וַתַּבֵּט אִשְׁתּוֹ מֵאַחֲרָיו וַתְּהִי

Lemech rather than *my wives;* Ahasuerus said [*Esth.* 8:8]: *in the king's name* rather than *in my name.* Here, too, it says *from* HASHEM rather than *from Him.*

As indicated by the *Midrash* quoted by *Ramban,* above, *Rashi* cites only one view. According to view (a), the first HASHEM refers to the angel Gabriel; while according to view (b), the first refers to HASHEM together with His celestial court. Presumably both interpretations agree that the second mention of HASHEM refers to God Himself. *Rashi* follows Rav Yitzchak who retorted: In all of the Scriptures we find that the names of mere mortals are mentioned twice in one verse, yet you are surprised that God mentions His name twice in one verse! [I.e. it is not necessary to assume that different meanings are implied by the double use of HASHEM in the same verse.] (See *Mizrachi; Gur Aryeh*).

25. וַיַּהֲפֹךְ אֶת־הֶעָרִים הָאֵל — (And) *He overturned these cities. Overturned* literally: These four cities* were all built on the same rock which He overturned *(Midrash; Rashi).*

*[The *Midrash* mentions *'five'* — including Zoar. *Rashi* apparently does not consider Zoar because it was spared, while the *Midrash* includes it, presumably because according to the *Midrash,* Zoar was saved only through a miracle, but it had been included in the *original* decree of the upheaval.]

Others take it figuratively in the sense of 'reversed' — what had previously been a fertile region, *'Well watered ... like the garden of HASHEM'* [13:10] He now turned it into barren desolation; *its stones had been the place of sapphires; it had dust of gold; earth out of which comes bread, was overturned as if it were fire* [*Job* 28:6-5.] He rained down sulphur and fire upon it and utterly devastated it, from man to beast to vegetation *(Radak; Abarbanel).*

The verse emphasizes *these cities* [though it might have sufficed, after the specific reference in the previous verse to Sodom and Amorrah to simply say וַיַּהֲפֹכֵם *and He overturned them*] to stress that though it is the nature of such catastrophes to spread and do damage beyond the primary area of destruction [as Lot originally feared; see *comm.* to 19:20 s.v. פֶּן] God nevertheless contained the path of destruction limiting the catastrophe to הֶעָרִים הָאֵל, *these* cities, and not beyond *(Alshich).*

וְצֶמַח הָאֲדָמָה — *And the vegetation of the soil.*

The obliteration was total and extended to everything that the wicked Sodomites valued as being for their exclusive use *(Akeidas Yitzchak)*

Even plants were smitten. Rav Yehoshua ben Levi said: To this very day if one collects rain from the atmosphere of Sodom and pours it into a furrow, it will not promote growth! *(Midrash).*

26. וַתַּבֵּט אִשְׁתּוֹ מֵאַחֲרָיו — [*And*] *his* [i.e., Lot's] *wife peered behind him.* i.e. behind Lot *(Rashi),* who was acting as a rear guard for his entire household *(Ramban)*

According to *Ramban* [in *v.* 17] quoting *Pirkei d'Rabbi Eliezer,* the compassion of Edis, Lot's wife

XIX and the entire plain; with all the inhabitants of the
26 cities and the vegetation of the soil. 26 His wife peered

[other versions read 'Iris'] welled up for her two married daughters who had been left behind in Sodom [see *vs.* 14-15], and she turned around to see if they were following her. She saw the *Shechinah* [אֲחוֹרֵי הַשְּׁכִינָה: (the version in *R'Bachya* reads הַשְּׁכִינָה אַחֲרֶיהָ), *the Shechinah after her,* and she became a pillar of salt.

Ralbag explains that by her very act of showing compassion upon 'the hated of God' who did not believe enough to join in saving themselves, she thereby also sinned. Thus, when her compassion caused her thoughts to cleave to them and she turned around, the punishment overtook her as well.

According to *Abarbanel* the phrase וַתַּבֵּט אִשְׁתּוֹ מֵאַחֲרָיו is to be rendered 'and his wife, *who was behind him,* glanced back' — she was in the rear engrossed in attempting to save their wealth when the evil, i.e. the *sulphur* and *fire,* overtook and consumed her [turning her into a pillar of salt (see *Ibn Ezra* below).]

This follows *Radak* who explains that Lot's wife was of little faith and she turned around to see whether, indeed, the city had been overturned, although the angel had warned her against doing so.

Tur points out, however, that the death of Lot's wife was a necessary precondition to the matter of his daughters' conceiving through him; had their mother been alive, the event could not have occurred.

וַתְּהִי נְצִיב מֶלַח — *And she became a pillar of salt.*

She sinned through salt and was therefore punished through salt. When Lot asked her to bring salt for guests and she replied, 'Do you wish to institute this evil custom of hospitality, also, into our city?' [see footnote to *v.* 3] *(Rashi).*

According to *Ibn Ezra* her bones were burned and encrusted with salt which descended with the sulphur, as it is written [*Deut.* 29:22]: *the whole land is sulphur and salt ... like the overthrow of Sodom and Amorah, Admah and Zeboiim.* That verse, by omitting Zoar proves that it was spared the fate of the others.

Ramban explains in *v.* 17 that the mere sight of destruction could have a harmful effect. Perhaps Lot's wife turned into a pillar of salt for the plague entered her mind when she saw the sulphur and salt [see *Ibn Ezra* above] which descended from heaven ...

And just as the earth became encrusted with salt, so, too, did Lot's wife as a result of gazing upon the destructive forces; nevertheless, the *Midrash* notes, had Lot's wife been righteous she would not have come to harm — certainly not in this manner.

According to *Rav Saadiah Gaon, R' Chananel, Abarbanel,* and *Chizkuni,* the subjects of וַתְּהִי is *the earth*: 'Lot's wife glanced behind him and lo! It [i.e., the earth] had become a column of salt, since it had become destroyed through *sulphur and salt* [cf. *Deut.* 29:22.]

[It is noted that ancient writers

כז נְצִיב מֶלַח: וַיַּשְׁכֵּם אַבְרָהָם בַּבֹּקֶר אֶל־
הַמָּקוֹם אֲשֶׁר־עָמַד שָׁם אֶת־פְּנֵי יהוה:
כח וַיַּשְׁקֵף עַל־פְּנֵי סְדֹם וַעֲמֹרָה וְעַל כָּל־פְּנֵי
אֶרֶץ הַכִּכָּר וַיַּרְא וְהִנֵּה עָלָה קִיטֹר
כט הָאָרֶץ כְּקִיטֹר הַכִּבְשָׁן: וַיְהִי בְּשַׁחֵת

refer to this pillar as still being in existence. Josephus claims to have seen it][1].

Cf. *Pirkei d'Rabbi Eliezer*: She beheld the *Shechinah* and became a pillar of salt, which still stands [at the time that *Midrash* was redacted.] Oxen lick it every day until it dwindles down to the toes of her feet; by the morning it has risen up again.

27. Abraham views the disaster.

When Abraham had concluded his pleading for Sodom, God did not tell him what the outcome would be. Therefore, he arose in the morning to see what the final judgment had been *(Da'as Sofrim).*

וַיַּשְׁכֵּם אַבְרָהָם בַּבֹּקֶר — [*And*] *Abraham arose early next* [lit. *'in the'*] *morning.*

The rule that a scholar should not go out alone at night is derived in *Chullin* 91b from our verse [for he certainly would have gone out *before* morning to pray in their behalf had it been permitted].

See *Tosafos Pesachim* 4a which indicates that Abraham could easily have resolved this objection by taking others with him. However, he did not want others to witness the scene of destruction. Further, he did not pray at home during the night because this, as the place where HASHEM had appeared to him, was a propitious place to pray [see further] *(Harav David Feinstein).*

[Cf. *comm.* to 22:3.]

In *Berachos* 6b this verse is cited to support the view that Abraham instituted morning prayers. [See *Radak* further, and see *comm.* to 14:23.]

אֶל־הַמָּקוֹם אֲשֶׁר־עָמַד שָׁם אֶת־פְּנֵי ה׳ — [Hurrying back] *to the place where he had stood before* [lit. *'in the face of'*] *HASHEM.*

I.e., to the place to which he had accompanied the angels [18:16, 22-23.] for it was there that the 'hand of HASHEM' had come upon him [i.e. it was a propitious spot.] Having failed to find justly earned merit in their behalf, he now came to

1. Our sages taught in the *Mishnah*: If one sees [the pillar of salt of] Lot's wife ... he should utter thanksgiving and thank the Almighty.

But, the *Gemara* asks: The transformation of Lot's wife was a case of *punishment* over which one should say בָּרוּךְ דַּיַּן הָאֱמֶת, 'Blessed be the True Judge' [the formula recited on hearing bad news], yet [the *Mishnah*] says, 'Thanksgiving and praise'?

Therefore, the *Gemara* answers, that the *Mishnah* should read: "For Lot and his wife two blessings are said: For his wife we say, 'Blessed be the True Judge', and for Lot we say בָּרוּךְ זוֹכֵר אֶת הַצַּדִּיקִים, 'Blessed be He Who remembers the righteous" [i.e., for having remembered Abraham (*Rashi* ad. loc.).]

Rav Yochanan said, Even in the hour of His anger, the Holy One Blessed be He remembers the righteous *(Berachos* 54b).

behind him and she became a pillar of salt.
[27] *Abraham arose early next morning to the place*
where he had stood before HASHEM. [28] *And he gazed*
down upon Sodom and Amorrah and the entire sur-
face of the plain; and saw — and behold! The smoke
of the earth rose like the smoke of a kiln. [29] *And so it*

plead for mercy *(Sforno).*

[But it was too late: destruction had alrady begun, as Abraham was soon to witness.]

Radak comments: *To the spot where he had stood,* as it is written [18:22] *And Abraham was still standing before* HASHEM. Based upon this, the Sages expounded that Abraham originated *Shacharis,* the morning prayer, for *standing* [before God] refers only to prayer as it is written *and Phineas 'stood' and prayed (Ps.* 106:30). Thus, Abraham taught mankind that it is proper to pray in the morning and thank God for giving the light of the new day and pray before embarking on the day's activities. The Sages [*Berachos* 6b] further based on this verse that it is proper for a person to have a set place for prayer as it says, *to the spot where he had stood.*

[The phrase *hurrying back* is not in the Hebrew but such a phrase implying *rushing* is certainly implied by the expression וַיַּשְׁכֵּם ... אֶל, *and he arose early ... (hurrying) ... to.*]

28. וַיַּשְׁקֵף עַל־פְּנֵי סְדֹם וַעֲמֹרָה — *And he gazed down upon Sodom and Amorrah ...*

... To see whether or not there were ten righteous people found there so that the city could be spared *(Rashbam).*

As explained earlier, the expression הַשְׁקָפָה denotes gazing in anguish. Abraham knew what would happen. Now, in anguish, he gazed to see what the evil of Sodom had wrought *(Da'as Sofrim).*

וַיַּרְא וְהִנֵּה עָלָה קִיטֹר הָאָרֶץ כְּקִיטֹר הַכִּבְשָׁן — *And [he] saw — and behold! The smoke of the earth rose like the smoke of a* [lit. *'the'*] *kiln.*

[I.e., the fusion of the heavenly sulphur and fire which had scorchingly rained down since the crack of dawn (*footnote* to *v.* 24) had by now created a column of smoke so thick that it resembled the smoke rising from a kiln.]

Rashi explains that קִיטֹר signifies a column of smoke; and כִּבְשָׁן refers to an excavation [=kiln] in which stone is burned to lime [or in which ceramics are fired *(Radak).*]

Ibn Ezra adds that קִיטֹר refers to *smoke* and is related to קְטֹרֶת, smoke of the incense.

29. The summary:

The Torah, in its usual style now proceeds to summarize that to which it had earlier alluded: That Lot had been spared was due entirely to his uncle, Abraham *(Ran).*

וַיְהִי בְּשַׁחֵת אֱלֹהִים אֶת־עָרֵי הַכִּכָּר — *And so it was, when God destroyed the cities of the plain.*

[The translation of וַיְהִי, *and so it was,* follows the intent of the cantillation, and reflects the paranthet-

אֱלֹהִים֙ אֶת־עָרֵ֣י הַכִּכָּ֔ר וַיִּזְכֹּ֥ר אֱלֹהִ֖ים
אֶת־אַבְרָהָ֑ם וַיְשַׁלַּ֤ח אֶת־לוֹט֙ מִתּ֣וֹךְ
הַהֲפֵכָ֔ה בַּהֲפֹךְ֙ אֶת־הֶ֣עָרִ֔ים אֲשֶׁר־יָשַׁ֥ב
ל בָּהֵ֖ן לֽוֹט׃ וַיַּעַל֩ ל֨וֹט מִצּ֜וֹעַר וַיֵּ֣שֶׁב בָּהָ֗ר

ical, summing-up nature of the passage.]

וַיִּזְכֹּר אֱלֹהִים אֶת־אַבְרָהָם — *That* [lit. *'and'*] *God remembered Abraham.*

What bearing does God's remembering of Abraham have to do with the rescue of Lot?

— He remembered that Lot, compassionately kept silent and did not betray Abraham when he told Pharaoh that Sarah was his sister [see 12:13 ff]; therefore God now had compassion upon Lot *(Rashi)*[1]

Mizrachi finds the *Midrashic* question quoted by *Rashi* to be most difficult: why is it hard to understand the implication that Lot was saved for Abraham's sake; is it not clear from the entire narrative of the preceding chapters that Abraham loved Lot and that Lot left Charan to accompany Abraham?

— The verse should have said, *and God remembered 'Lot'*, not that He remembered *Abraham.* To this the *Midrash* answers that He remembered Lot only for the sake of Abraham *(Mizrachi).*

— Any mention of a remembrance of Abraham can be understood only in the historic context of the Abrahamitic mission. Therefore, such a remembrance can refer only to Abraham himself or his direct descendants, not to Lot. The reply is that Lot was instrumental in assuring Abraham's survival *(Gur Aryeh).*

— Lot accompanied Abraham for purely selfish reasons: he expected to be Abraham's heir. Therefore, his greatest merit was that he kept Abraham's secret in Egypt, for had he divulged Sarah's identity he would have been rewarded by Pharoah and inherited Abraham's fortune *(Sifsei Chachamim).*

According to *Ramban,* since Lot had accompanied Abraham he deserved to be saved on account of Abraham's merit. God 'remembered' [in the sense of 'took cognizance of his virtue'] that Lot was in Sodom only because he had followed Abraham; otherwise he would have still been in Charan with his family. Therefore it was inconceivable that Lot should die on account of his association with Abraham who had left his country at his Creator's command. For this same reason, Abraham had endangered himself by pursuing the kings on Lot's behalf [14:14].

Be'er Mayim Chaim comments that *Rashi* rejects *Ramban's* interpretation on the grounds that Lot's decision to follow Abraham out of Charan was insufficient to evoke God's mercy because thereafter Lot's greed led him to associate with the Sodomites whom he knew to be grossly sinful. *Rashi,* therefore, chose the *Midrashic* interpretation that God had compassion upon Lot because Lot had earned Divine mercy by virtue of his loyalty to Abraham in Egypt. Since Abraham owed his survival to Lot's silence, God rewarded Lot despite his subsequent greed.

1. The primary factor determining reward and punishment is a person's own deeds. When someone is saved for the sake of a *tzaddik*, it is not in the nature of a prize for the sake of the righteous. Rather it is because someone who considers bound up with the life of a righteous person deserves to survive on his account. Lot still felt an attachment to Abraham. He had endured hardship for Abraham's sake, had accompanied him, learned from him and — as history testifies — was to become part of Abraham's destiny because Ruth and Naamah descended from him. Ishmael's descendants, however, who severed their tie with Abraham, received no Divine favor on his account *(Da'as Sofrim).*

XIX *was when God destroyed the cities of the plain that*
30 *God remembered Abraham; so he sent Lot from amidst the upheaval when He overturned the cities in which Lot had lived.*

30 *Now Lot went up from Zoar and settled on the*

[The use of *Elohim* in this context indicates tht His Attribute of Justice came into play. However, it would seem more apropos to have used the Name HASHEM, indicating the Attribute of *Mercy*. Therefore, whenever the concept of *Elohim's* remembrance is mentioned in a merciful context — as in our verse and in 8:1 — *Rashi* takes pains to explain the apparent anomaly of the Attribute of Justice exercising mercy.

Rashi, accordingly, to 8:1 comments that through the prayers of the righteous, the Attribute of Justice is transformed into the Attribute of Mercy. In our verse, *Rashi* explains God's *remembrance* of Abraham as referring to His taking cognizance of Lot's virtuous acts אֶת אַבְרָהָם *with Abraham.* On the concept that God's *remembering* connotes the manifestation of His benevolence on earth, see *comm.* to 8:1: *'and God remembered Noah',* much of which is applicable here.]

Hirsch also explains in this context that from Lot's viewpoint, his salvation was an act of *mercy.* From Abraham's viewpoint, however, it was an act of *justice* because it was an instance of a wicked person being shown mercy only to prevent the righteous from feeling undeserved anguish.

וַיְשַׁלַּח אֶת־לוֹט מִתּוֹךְ הַהֲפֵכָה — *So He sent Lot out from the midst of the upheaval.*

The Torah emphasizes that he was not taken away *before* the upheaval began for this would not have been such an obvious miracle; rather Lot was plucked away *from the midst* of the upheavel which *had already begun.* Had he left Sodom earlier, when the angel wanted him to, his own merit would have sufficed to save him. But because he waited until the destruction began, the verse makes clear that he was saved only because God remembered Abraham *(Ha'amek Davar).*

בַּהֲפֹךְ אֶת־הֶעָרִים אֲשֶׁר־יָשַׁב בָּהֵן לוֹט — *When He overturned the cities in which Lot had lived.*

He certainly did not live in *all* of the cities. The verse idiomatically means *'in one of which* Lot had lived', as in *Judges* 12:7: *and he was buried in the cities* [i.e., in *one of* the cities] *of Gilead (Tur).*

Cf. 13:12 where Lot is similarly described as living in *'the cities of the plain';* yet it is evident from 14:12 that his specific place of residence was Sodom *(Hoffman).*

[See *Ramban* and *R' Bachya* cited to end of *v.* 5 as to the reason for the uncompromising severity of Sodom's punishment.]

30. Lot's daughters.

Moab and Ammon — The Roots of Jewish Monarchy [see *comm.* to *v.* 15; and *Overview* to *Ruth.*]

Lot's daughters were modest, righteous women whose actions were motivated for the sake of heaven. Therefore, they did not *ask* their father to consort with them and the Torah does not label their actions as adulterous. They sincerely thought there was no other way to

וּשְׁתֵּי בְנֹתָיו עִמּוֹ כִּי יָרֵא לָשֶׁבֶת בְּצוֹעַר
וַיֵּשֶׁב בַּמְּעָרָה הוּא וּשְׁתֵּי בְנֹתָיו׃ וַתֹּאמֶר לא
הַבְּכִירָה אֶל־הַצְּעִירָה אָבִינוּ זָקֵן וְאִישׁ
אֵין בָּאָרֶץ לָבוֹא עָלֵינוּ כְּדֶרֶךְ כָּל־הָאָרֶץ׃

insure the propagation of the species. Because their intentions were pure, they merited that Ruth, ancestress of David, and Naamah, queen of Solomon and mother of Rechavam, should descend from them *(R' Bachya).*

וַיַּעַל לוֹט מִצּוֹעַר — *Now Lot went up from Zoar,* at the first opportunity, once the agencies of destruction had subsided *(Radak).*

וַיֵּשֶׁב בָּהָר — *And settled on the mountain.*

The mountain to which the angel had originally directed him when he said [*v.* 17] *escape to the mountain lest you be swept away (Radak).*

כִּי יָרֵא לָשֶׁבֶת בְּצוֹעַר — *For he was afraid to remain* [lit. *'to dwell'*] *in Zoar.*

Because it was near to Sodom *(Rashi),* and he feared that the destruction would engulf him similar to those who live in the environs of an earthquake who are destroyed by the effect of its tremors *(Mizrachi).*

Ramban disagrees because once the angel assured him *(v.* 21) that he would not overthrow Zoar, it was in no danger although it was near Sodom ...

Mizrachi holds, however, that the angel's assurance could guarantee only that Zoar would not be destroyed directly, but not that it would suffer no natural side effects.

Gur Aryeh adds that he feared fires resulting from the destructive rain; or that Zoar's inhabitants would soon sin enough to cause their own destruction.

Ramban goes on to suggest that Lot was afraid to live there because Zoar had been one of the original targets of destruction, and was exempted only because he could not reach the mountain in time. Now that he had had sufficient time to go on, Lot thought that the angel would no longer accede to his request, and that Zoar, too, would be destroyed.

And now that he lived among them and witnessed their wickedness, he feared that as soon as their measure of iniquity was full, they, too, would be doomed *(Radak).*

... And according to *Rashi's* chronology in *v.* 20 that Zoar was as wicked as Sodom, but it was saved because it was a year younger, Lot may have left the city because he assumed its destruction was only one year away *(Ohel David).*

[According to the Midrash cited in *v.* 21 s.v. לְבִלְתִּי הָפְכִּי, the *residents* of Zoar were annihilated, and this is why Lot was afraid to remain there.]

וַיֵּשֶׁב בַּמְּעָרָה הוּא וּשְׁתֵּי בְנֹתָיו — *[And] he dwelt in a cave* [lit. *'the cave'* — it might have been a well-known cave *(Hoffman);* in *Sefer Hayashar* 19:55 it is identified as the cave of Adullam] *he with his two daughters.*

— But he did not seek out Abraham, presumably out of shame *(Alshich).*

XIX
31-32

mountain, his two daughters with him, for he was
afraid to remain in Zoar. He dwelt in the cave, he
with his two daughters. 31 *The older one said to to the*
younger, 'Our father is growing old and there is no
man to marry us in the usual manner. 32 *Come,let us*

As *Hoffman* remarks: Having seen Abraham's concern for Lot and that Lot's life had been saved for the second time thanks to Abraham, we would have expected Lot to return gratefully to his loving uncle. But it was not to be. Instead, an act occurred that caused the final break between them. From Lot were born two nations conceived in impurity. Abraham no longer cared to associate with Lot, who is never again mentioned in the Torah.

Midrash HaGadol, Vayeshev, notes that wherever it says וַיֵּשֶׁב, *he dwelt,* it indicates imminent trouble. Our verse says: *and he dwelt,* and then in *v.* 36: *thus, both of Lot's daughters became pregnant from their father.*

31. וַתֹּאמֶר הַבְּכִירָה אֶל־הַצְּעִירָה — [*And*] *The older one said to the younger.*

The word בְּכִירָה is understood by *Ibn Ezra* to be the fem. form of בְּכוֹר, *first-born.* Since Lot had married daughters who remained behind, the betrothed daughters were surely the younger ones as it was customary for the older ones to marry before the younger [see 29:26.] How then could the Torah refer to these daughters as the *first-born? (Yohel Or)* — *Ibn Ezra* therefore concludes that it is possible that these daughters, of which the בְּכִירָה was the *first-born,* were from another wife who had died earlier.

Our translation *older* [of the two daughters] follows *Ramban* who explains that *Ibn Ezra*'s interpretation is unnecessary for the term is *relative.* The older one is referred to as בְּכוֹרָה, *older,* in contrast to the צְעִירָה, *younger one,* just as the *first fruits* of the year are called בִּכּוּרִים, relative to that year's crop, and just as the expression [*Isaiah* 14:30] בְּכוֹרֵי דַלִּים refers to the *most desolate* relative to the other poor.

Similarly, *Onkelos* did not translate our passage with the usual Aramaic rendering for first born: בּוּכְרָא, but רַבְּתָא, *older one.*

אָבִינוּ זָקֵן — *Our father is* [*growing*] *old.*

— And if not now, when? He may die or become impotent *(Rashi).*

וְאִישׁ אֵין בָּאָרֶץ לָבוֹא עָלֵינוּ כְּדֶרֶךְ כָּל־הָאָרֶץ — *And there is no man to marry us* [idiom. *consort with us*] *in the usual manner* [lit. *'in the manner of all the earth'*].

According to *Rashi* they thought that the whole world had been destroyed as it was during the Flood.

— For she thought that with her father's departure from Zoar, that that city, too, was destroyed *(Ramban).*

[According to the *Midrash* cited above that the inhabitants of Zoar were killed as part of the upheaval, the fear of Lot's daughters is easily understandable.]

Rav Yosef Kara suggests that the motivation behind Lot's daughters'

לב לְכָ֨ה נַשְׁקֶ֧ה אֶת־אָבִ֛ינוּ יַ֖יִן וְנִשְׁכְּבָ֣ה עִמּ֑וֹ
לג וּנְחַיֶּ֥ה מֵאָבִ֖ינוּ זָֽרַע׃ וַתַּשְׁקֶ֧יןָ אֶת־אֲבִיהֶ֛ן
יַ֖יִן בַּלַּ֣יְלָה ה֑וּא וַתָּבֹ֤א הַבְּכִירָה֙ וַתִּשְׁכַּ֣ב
אֶת־אָבִ֔יהָ וְלֹֽא־יָדַ֥ע בְּשִׁכְבָ֖הּ וּבְקוּמָֽהּ׃
לד וַֽיְהִי֙ מִֽמָּחֳרָ֔ת וַתֹּ֤אמֶר הַבְּכִירָה֙ אֶל־

scheme was prompted rather by their observation that *their father was old* and it was futile to expect him to take a new wife, while at the same time they would not find a husband, for *they would not find a man willing to marry them* since they had lived among people who had deserved such a disaster. They therefore devised their scheme to assure continuity of their father's line.

32. וּנְחַיֶּה מֵאָבִינוּ זָרַע — *That* [lit. *'and'*] *we may give life to offspring through our father.*

For one who leaves no offspring to carry on his name is considered as if he were dead *(Radak).*

[Comp. *Rashi* to 16:2 s.v. אוּלַי אִבָּנֶה 'a childless person is considered as dead and demolished.']

Perhaps Lot's daughters were motivated by a sense of sincere duty [being under the impression that the destruction was universal] to take whatever steps they could to give birth to a son and daughter through whom the earth could be rebuilt, and thereby demonstrate that it was not in vain that God had saved them. They could have asked Lot to marry them, since a Noachide [a universal designation for a non-Jew] is permitted to marry his daughter, but their modesty prevented them; or perhaps such a thing was generally regarded with abhorrence and was never done *(Ramban).*

33. וַתַּשְׁקֶיןָ אֶת־אֲבִיהֶן יַיִן — *So* [lit. *'and'*] *they plied their father* [with] *wine.*

Where did they procure wine in the cave? Obviously they did not bring it along with them in their hurried exodus! — This wine had been [providentially] prepared for them in the cave for the specific purpose that they might bring forth two nations *(Rashi).*

This wine was in the nature of a foretaste of the Messianic days when *'it shall come to pass that the mountains shall drop down sweet wines'* [*Joel* 4:18] *(Midrash).*

According to the first view in the *Midrash,* however, wine was available there because, owing to the abundance of wine in the area, the Sodomites used to store wine in caves.

Mizrachi queries why *Rashi* chose the opinion that the wine was providentially prepared for them which would imply that they acted for the sake of heaven, instead of adopting the other view in the *Midrash* which states simply that wine was routinely stored in caves. Moreover, *Rashi* [below] comments that the older daughter originated this *unchaste* conduct indicating that their *intent was immoral,* as opposed to alternate opinions that their motives were pure, and for the sake of heaven?

He answers that the wine was providentially prepared for them, even though their intentions were unchaste. This indicates not

ply our father with wine and lay with him that we
may give life to offspring through our father.'
33 *So they plied their father with wine on that*
night; and the older came and lay with her father,
and he was unaware of her lying down or of her get-
ting up.
34 *And it was on the next day that the older one*

that they acted 'for the sake of heaven', but that God had willed it so, in order that the two nations might descend from them.

בַּלַּיְלָה הוּא — *On that night.*

Radak notes that הוּא lacks the definite article ה: הַהוּא. This is grammatically not unusual, as for example, in the following passages (II *Sam.* 6:3): אֶת הָעֲגָלָה חֲדָשָׁה: [=הַחֲדָשָׁה] (*Num.* 28:4): אֶת הַכֶּבֶשׂ אֶחָד [=הָאֶחָד]; (*I Sam.* 13:18): וְהָרֹאשׁ אֶחָד [=הָאֶחָד], etc.

Talmudically, however, the anomalous form הוּא [lit. *'he'*] in place of the regular הַהוּא refers to God, *'He'* being a designation of God [the *He* par excellence] for thus have the Sages remarked: 'The Holy One, Blessed be He assisted in that matter; and providentially provided the wine; *(R' Bachya)*, [see similar interpretation of הוּא, *He*, in 30:16; and see *Niddah* 31a.]

וַתִּשְׁכַּב אֶת־אָבִיהָ — *And [she] lay with her father.*

Of the younger daughters it is merely stated [*v.* 35] *'she lay with him'* [without explicitly stating *her father.*] Since the younger sister merely followed the example of the older, the Torah [relatively] obscured her sin and did not explicitly specify her shame, but in the case of the elder who *initiated* this incestuous act the Torah exposed her shameful act explicitly *(Rashi)* [cf. *comm.* to *v.* 37: *Moab.*]

Of course, both forms are grammatically correct. However, this interpretation favoring the younger sister is derived from the variance in expression; it therefore *appears* as though the Torah purposely refrains from emphasizing her shame *(Mizrachi).*

Ha'amek Davar notes that the act of the older one is described with the indefinite article אֶת, [וַתִּשְׁכַּב **אֶת** אָבִיהָ]. This indicates that she took the *initiative* in forcing the act upon her father. The act of the younger in *v.* 35 is decribed as being עִמּוֹ, *'with him'*, indicating that the deed was a *joint one*; her sense of shame would not allow her to take the lead, instead she *enticed* her father [and *he* took the lead]. (See on עִמּוֹ in 12:3.)

וְלֹא־יָדַע בְּשִׁכְבָהּ וּבְקוּמָהּ — *And he was unaware of her lying down or* [lit. *'and'*] *of her getting up.*[1]

The word וּבְקוּמָהּ [and of her getting up] occurring in reference to the older sister has a dot over it [a traditional method of drawing attention to a special interpretation (cf. for example אֵלָיו in 18:9)] to indicate that though he was not aware בְּשָׁכְבָהּ, *of her lying down,* he was well aware of וּבְקוּמָהּ, *her getting*

1. Rav Shimon says, וְלֹא יָדַע, *and he was not aware* means that he was not aware that it was God's purpose to raise from her King David, King Solomon, all the other kings, and ultimately King Messiah *(Zohar).*

הַצְּעִירָה הֵן־שָׁכַבְתִּי אֶמֶשׁ אֶת־אָבִי
נַשְׁקֶנּוּ יַיִן גַּם־הַלַּיְלָה וּבֹאִי שִׁכְבִי עִמּוֹ
לה וּנְחַיֶּה מֵאָבִינוּ זָרַע: וַתַּשְׁקֶיןָ גַּם בַּלַּיְלָה
הַהוּא אֶת־אֲבִיהֶן יָיִן וַתָּקָם הַצְּעִירָה
וַתִּשְׁכַּב עִמּוֹ וְלֹא־יָדַע בְּשִׁכְבָהּ וּבְקֻמָהּ:
לו־לז וַתַּהֲרֶיןָ שְׁתֵּי בְנוֹת־לוֹט מֵאֲבִיהֶן: וַתֵּלֶד
הַבְּכִירָה בֵּן וַתִּקְרָא שְׁמוֹ מוֹאָב הוּא

up, yet he was not more vigilant on the second night than he was on the first [for, as the *Talmud* concludes: Matters might have been different; he should not have drunk again on the second evening *(Horayos* 10b).] *Rav Levi* said, 'Whoever is inflamed by sexual desire will ultimately be made to eat his own flesh' [a euphemism meaning 'will commit incest'] *(Rashi; Midrash).*

34. וַתֹּאמֶר הַבְּכִירָה אֶל־הַצְּעִירָה הֵן שָׁכַבְתִּי אֶמֶשׁ אֶת־אָבִי — *And the older one said to the younger, 'Behold, I lay with my father last night.'*

The older one planned and orchestrated the entire episode. In naming the sons, she was the more brazen of the two. Indeed, we find that of the descendants, the Moabites, were more licentious than her sister's Ammonite nation as in *Numbers* 25:1 *(Hoffman).*

35. וַתַּשְׁקֶיןָ גַּם בַּלַּיְלָה הַהוּא אֶת־אֲבִיהֶן יָיִן — *So* [lit. *'and'*] *they plied their father with wine that night also.*

The גַּם, *also,* is exegetically regarded as a particle of extension: They gave him *more* that night than they had the night before, because, when his older daughter arose, he perceived what had happened (see *v.* 33) *(Sechel Tov).*

[On גַּם as an exegetical amplification, see also *comm.* to 20:5.]

וַתָּקָם הַצְּעִירָה וַתִּשְׁכַּב עִמּוֹ — *And the younger got up and lay with him.*

The expression וַתָּקָם, *she arose,* [in the sense of *'prevailed upon herself'*] is used because the matter was difficult for her. It was only at the prodding of the stronger willed older sister that she mustered up daring and courage. Cf. a similar use of the verb in 46:5 וַיָּקָם יַעֲקֹב, *and Jacob rose up* [i.e. prevailed upon himself and continued on] *(Haamek Davar).*

וְלֹא־יָדַע בְּשִׁכְבָהּ וּבְקֻמָהּ — *And he was not aware of her lying down or* [lit. *'and'*] *of her getting up.*

[In this case he was apparently so drunk that the verse is to be taken literally, unlike the night before when he was aware of her getting up (see *v.* 33 וּבְקוּמָהּ).]

36. וַתַּהֲרֶיןָ שְׁתֵּי בְנוֹת־לוֹט מֵאֲבִיהֶן — *Thus,* [lit. *'and'*] *Lot's two daughters conceived from their father.*

— I.e. from the first intimacy. Although a woman does not generally conceive from the first intimacy, they took special measures *(Midrash; Rashi).*

Rav Chaninah ben Pazzi observed:

said to the younger, 'Behold, I lay with my father last
night; let us ply him with wine tonight as well, and
you come lay with him that we may give life to off-
spring through our father.'
35 *So they plied their father with wine that night*
also. And the younger got up and lay with him and
he was not aware of her lying down or of her getting
up.
36 *Thus, Lot's two daughters conceived from their*
father.
37 *The older bore a son and named him Moab; he is*

Thorns are neither weeded nor sown, yet of their own accord they grow and spring up, whereas how much pain and toil is required before wheat is made to grow *(Bereshis Rabbah* 45:4) [i.e., thus Lot's incestuous daughters (=*'thorns')* conceived immediately while how much pain and anguish did the Matriarchs endure before they conceived!]

[See *comm.* to 16:4 regarding Hagar's conception also being the result of the first intimacy.]

That this was their first intimacy is vouched for by Lot's description of them in *v.* 8 as having *never known a man (Maharzu).*

We are thus informed that they conceived from the intimacy of that night, for there was never any further contact between them, their only purpose being to *'give life to offspring' (Radak).*

Additionally the phrase *their father* is included, although apparently superfluous, to accentuate Lot's shame. He was lecherous and allowed himself to be caught in such a situation. Therefore he deserved to have his shame inscribed in the Torah for all posterity, and for all to hear when this portion is read in the Synagogues *(Midrash; Yafeh Toar)* [1].

37. וַתֵּלֶד הַבְּכִירָה בֵּן וַתִּקְרָא שְׁמוֹ מוֹאָב — *[And] the older bore a son and named him Moab* [i.e., 'from father.']

This daughter who was immodest openly proclaimed his origin as being *from her father,* [thus publicizing her indecent act], but the younger delicately veiled the name in euphemistic anonymity [by naming him *Ben-Ami* meaning 'a son of my people']. She was rewarded for this in the time of Moses, who was commanded regarding the Ammonites [*Deut.* 2:19]: *Do not contend with them* — in any manner; it was even forbidden to *annoy* them.

1. When the Holy One, blessed is He, came to give the Torah to Israel, He revealed Himself not to Israel alone, but to all the peoples ...

He went to the peoples of Ammon and Moab and asked them, 'Will you accept the Torah?'

'What is written in it?' they queried.

He replied, *'You shall not commit adultery' (Exod.* 20:13).

They answered: 'Sovereign of the Universe! How can we accept the Torah? We epitomize immorality for our very existence originated through incest!' *(Sifri* to *Zos HaBrachah,* 33:2).

לח אֲבִי־מוֹאָב עַד־הַיּוֹם: וְהַצְּעִירָה גַם־הִוא
יָלְדָה בֵּן וַתִּקְרָא שְׁמוֹ בֶּן־עַמִּי הוּא אֲבִי
א בְנֵי־עַמּוֹן עַד־הַיּוֹם: וַיִּסַּע מִשָּׁם
אַבְרָהָם אַרְצָה הַנֶּגֶב וַיֵּשֶׁב בֵּין־קָדֵשׁ וּבֵין

Regarding the Moabites, however, it was forbidden only to wage war against them [*ibid.* 2:9]; annoying them, however, was permitted *(Horayos* 10b; *Rashi).*

[As the *Talmud, ibid.* remarks in this connection: אֵין הקב״ה מְקַפֵּחַ אֲפִילוּ שְׂכַר שִׂיחָה נָאָה, The Holy One, Blessed be He, does not deprive one even of the reward for a delicate expression.]

... And although the Sages proclaimed [*Bava Kamma* 38b]: 'Let a man do a good deed at the earliest opportunity, for on account of the one night whereby the elder preceded the younger, she merited to precede the younger by four generations in Israel: Obed, Jesse, David, and Solomon [who were descended from Ruth the Moabitess], whereas the younger had to wait until Rehaboam [son of Na'amah the Ammonitess through Solomon]'. Nevertheless she is criticized for having disgraced her father's honor for all eternity by giving the child that indecent name *(Tur).*

הוּא אֲבִי־מוֹאָב עַד־הַיּוֹם — *He is the ancestor of the Moabites until this day.*

I.e., the days of Moses [when the Torah was given]. This is the meaning of the expression *unto this day* throughout Scriptures: unto the time of the Scribe who recorded the matter *(Rashbam).*

This follows *Ibn Ezra* who explains that the expression *'he is the ancestor ... until this day'* indicates that they remained Moabites to the present; or it means: this fact is known to this day.

38. וְהַצְּעִירָה גַם־הִוא ... וַתִּקְרָא שְׁמוֹ בֶּן־עַמִּי — *And the younger also* [lit. *'also she'*] ... *and she named him Ben-Ami* [i.e., *'son of my kin'*]

[A more delicate name than *Moab* — *'from father'*. See *Rashi v.* 37.]

גַּם הִיא, *Also* [*she*] — *she also* gave birth to royalty as did her sister *(Chizkuni).*

הוּא אֲבִי בְנֵי־עַמּוֹן עַד־הַיּוֹם — *He is the ancestor of the people of Ammon* [lit. *'of the children of Ammon'*] *until this day.*

XX

1. Abraham moves to Gerar.

וַיִּסַּע מִשָּׁם אַבְרָהָם — [*And*] *Abraham journeyed from there,* i.e., from his former dwelling, the Plains of Mamre near Hebron [13:18; 18:1] *(Radak;* see below).

When he perceived that the region was destroyed and there were no more wayfarers to whom he might extend hospitality, he moved away. Another interpretation: He wished to be far from Lot who had gained a notorious reputa-

XIX
38

the ancestor of the Moabites until this day. 38 *And*
the younger one also bore a son and she named him
Ben-Ami. He is the ancestor of the people of Ammon
until this day.

XX
1

1 *Abraham journeyed from there to the region of the*
South and settled between Kadesh and Shur, so-

tion through his intimacy with his daughters *(Rashi).*

Rashi offers the second interpretation because the primary one does not fully account for why he moved so *far* away; surely there were closer places where Abraham could have resettled to find wayfarers *(Maharshal).*

Also, *Rashi's* secondary interpretation is supported by the fact that, as noted in the *comm.*: to 13:8 and *footnote* to 14:12, Lot physically resembled Abraham. Abraham therefore left the area to avoid being mistaken for Lot who committed the sin *(Me'am Loez* citing *Sefer HaYashar; Kessef Mezukak).* [1]

Radak observes that the *Torah* does not specify why Abraham made this journey in his hundredth year, after having lived in Canaan for twenty-five years *(Seder Olam).* He discounts the possibility that he was forced to leave Canaan by famine, like his earlier journey to Egypt, because 26:1 clearly implies that there was only one famine in Abraham's lifetime. He suggests, therefore, that Abraham journeyed to the land of the Philistines to establish his presence throughout Eretz Yisrael, for Philistia, too, was part of the Promised Land.

[On walking through the land to establish presence, see *comm.* to 13:17 קוּם הִתְהַלֵּךְ בָּאָרֶץ.]

[That Gerar was considered part of the Land to be inherited by the Children of Israel is evident from the fact that God instructed Isaac to live in Gerar after having commanded him not to leave the Land which would become his inheritance (26:2-3).]

אַרְצָה הַנֶּגֶב — *To the region* [lit. 'land'] *of the South.*

For the land of the Philistines, which was later to become part of the territory of Judah, lay in the Southern region of Eretz Yisrael *(Radak).*

[On נֶגֶב, *South,* see *comm.* to 12:9, 13:1; and footnote to 13:14.]

וַיֵּשֶׁב בֵּין־קָדֵשׁ וּבֵין שׁוּר — *And* [*he*] *settled between Kadesh and* [*between*] *Shur.*

These were two large cities. He chose this area for it was heavily populated and would thereby provide him the opportunity to spread belief in God *(Sforno).*

The region of *Kadesh* and *Shur*

1. In its *comm.* to 12:4, the *Zohar* discusses why Abraham took Lot with him when he left Charan? Among the reasons given was that Abraham prophetically perceived that the Messianic House of David was destined to descend from Lot and his daughters. Abraham therefore wished to keep him close by so he could watch over him. That is why Abraham sped to Lot's aid when he was captured in the War of the Kings [14:14], and desperately interceded on his behalf when Sodom was to be overturned.

Now that Lot's daughters had given birth there was no further need for Abraham to remain in Lot's proximity *(Zeis Ra'anan).*

ב שׁ֖וּר וַיָּ֥גָר בִּגְרָֽר׃ וַיֹּ֧אמֶר אַבְרָהָ֛ם אֶל־
שָׂרָ֥ה אִשְׁתּ֖וֹ אֲחֹ֣תִי הִ֑וא וַיִּשְׁלַ֗ח אֲבִימֶ֙לֶךְ֙
ג מֶ֣לֶךְ גְּרָ֔ר וַיִּקַּ֖ח אֶת־שָׂרָֽה׃ וַיָּבֹ֧א אֱלֹהִ֛ים

[the fortifications on the Egyptian frontier] was where the angels had appeared to Hagar. Perhaps Abraham chose the site of *Be'er Lachai Ro'i* which lay between Kadesh and Bered, Bered being identified with Shur *(Radak; Sechel Tov)* [see *comm.* to 16:14 and 16:7. On *Kadesh* see also on 14:7.]

וַיָּגָר בִּגְרָר – *Sojourning* [lit. *'and he sojourned'*] *in Gerar.*

The capital city of the Philistines *(Rashi* to 21:32).

Gerar did not lay *'between Kadesh and Bered'* but to the northwest of that area, and southeast of Gaza [see *comm.* to 10:19.] The intent of the verse is that Abraham's *primary residence* was between Kadesh and Shur, and his travels *occasionally* brought him to Gerar, where he resided temporarily [וַיָּגָר]; or that *first* he dwelt in the area between Kadesh and Shur and *then* in Gerar *(Radak; Hoffman; Hirsch).* [Gerar is mentioned in 10:19.]

According to *Radak's* primary interpretation, however, Gerar *was* located between Kadesh and Shur [perhaps Gerar is then to be identified, as some suggest, with the *Wady Jerur,* about thirteen miles west of *Kadesh.*] Accordingly the verse tells us first that Abraham dwelt in the general area of Kadesh-Shur, and then goes on to further identify the site as Gerar, the terms וַיֵּשֶׁב and וַיָּגָר being synonymous.

2. Sarah and Abimelech –
[One of the Ten Trials (see 12:1, footnote).]

וַיֹּאמֶר אַבְרָהָם אֶל־שָׂרָה אִשְׁתּוֹ אֲחוֹתִי הִוא – [*And*] *Abraham said of* [lit. *'to'*] *Sarah his wife, 'She is my sister.'*

'Sister' here means 'relative', but the Philistines took it literally *(Rav Saadiah Gaon* cited by *Torah Sheleimah).*

אֶל, *to,* has in this context the meaning of עַל [*upon*], i.e., *regarding; of;* as it does in *I Sam.* 1:27 and 4:21 *(Rashi, Ibn Ezra).*

Rashi notes that [unlike 12:13 where Abraham specifically asked her permission] this time he did not consult with her, but announced that she was his sister against her inclination, for she had previously been taken to Pharoh's palace through such a deception, and he knew that she would not consent *(Gur Aryeh).*

Perhaps he did not request Sarah to *offer* this information as he did in Egypt, because there the people were ugly [see *Rashi* to 12:11] and since her beauty was so striking he found it necessary for her to join in the ruse, for unless the Egyptians were convinced of his story, his life would have been in serious jeopardy. In Gerar, however, her beauty was not so outstanding. For this reason, Abimelech asked Abraham why he felt compelled to resort to this ploy and, unlike Pharaoh, even invited Abraham to remain in his land for they were basically safe there. Abraham, therefore, found it sufficient that he alone say that she was his sister *(Or HaChaim).*

[*Ramban* in 12:13 suggests however, that the literal sense of the narrative would indicate that in Egypt, too, Sarah had not consented to describe herself as Abraham's sister; she did not contradict him, however, but respectfullly remained silent, *offering* no information. Therefore when her true identity was discovered Pharaoh blamed only Abraham for the deception.]

According to *Yafeh To'ar* the point is

journing in Gerar. 2 *Abraham said of Sarah his wife,*
'She is my sister;' So Abimelech, King of Gerar sent,
and took Sarah. 3 *And God came to Abimelech in a*

not that Sarah would not consent, but that after their unfortunate experience with Pharaoh, there was no need to seek her permission. She realized that miracles do not happen every day and that every possible precaution had to be taken to minimize the danger [see *footnote.*]

[*Ramban* in 12:13 explains that Abraham and Sarah had no fear until they came to a royal city for it was customary to bring very beautiful woman to the king and to slay her husband through some contrived charge. He suggests, that, as evidenced from 20:13, it may have been their common custom from the time they left Charan to say that Sarah was his sister. The Torah, however, mentions it only when something happened to them on account of it.][1]

[Cf. *Radak* to *v.* 13 s.v. אֶל כָּל־הַמָּקוֹם and bracketed *comm.* following.]

וַיִּשְׁלַח אֲבִימֶלֶךְ מֶלֶךְ גְּרָר וַיִּקַּח אֶת־שָׂרָה — *'So* [lit. *'and'*] *Abimelech King of Gerar sent* [*for*] *and took Sarah,* i.e., with the intention of making her his wife, after having heard of her beauty. As to the wonder that at the age of ninety she

1. [The rationale behind Abraham's resort to the device of claiming Sarah as his sister despite their experience in Egypt requires explanation.

That even his son Isaac later resorted to the same tactic in light of his mother's experience would seem to indicate that the manners of the time made such an approach imperative.

As noted in the *comm.* to the parallel episode in Chapter 12, Abraham clearly feared for his life, for had they known she was his wife they would have murdered him knowing that he would never willingly consent to giving up his wife. The immoral ones would deem it preferable to transgress but once and *murder* the husband of a woman after whom they lusted, and thus be rid of him, rather than transgress constantly by being adulterous with a still-married woman. That Abraham was afraid of being murdered in godless Philistia as well was clearly stated by him in *v.* 11. (See bracketed comment there).

Claiming he was her brother minimized the danger. Among *the masses,* unmarried maidens were apparently much safer than married women, for the people would befriend the brother of a maiden hoping to win her through his consent. Meanwhile, Abraham could contrive delays until, with God's help, he was able to escape. (See also *Divrei Shaul* in *footnote* to 12:10).

As *Ramban* explains, Abraham claimed her as his sister whenever he traveled to a new location, and usually there were no repercussions. (As pointed out in 12:13 it was a half-truth for a man often calls his kinswoman 'sister', and Sarah was indeed the [grand-]daughter of his father as he explains here in *v.* 12.)

The contingency that Abraham did not anticipate was that Sarah's beauty would come to the attention of the king, the one person whom such a stranger would have to fear. For it was only the king who would dare take a maiden without wooing her brother, and who later would have no scruples in admitting it. Indeed, only in Egypt, notorious for its licentiousness — had such a thing happened.

Perhaps *Rashi's* comment implies that Sarah had more sensitivity in the matter than did Abraham and in this case she may have had prophetic intuition not to use this ploy. But her husband did not consult her; for her part since he insisted she acquiesced.]

אֶל־אֲבִימֶלֶךְ בַּחֲלוֹם הַלָּיְלָה וַיֹּאמֶר לוֹ
הִנְּךָ מֵת עַל־הָאִשָּׁה אֲשֶׁר־לָקַחְתָּ וְהִוא
ד בְּעֻלַת בָּעַל: וַאֲבִימֶלֶךְ לֹא קָרַב אֵלֶיהָ

was still so attractive that the king desired her, it may be that, as the Rabbis assert, when the angels brought her the tidings of her imminent child-bearings her youthfulness returned in preparation for conception *(Radak; Ramban;* cf. *comm.* to 18:11, 12).

Cf. *Bava Metzia* 87a: [When the angels brought their tidings] her skin became smooth, her wrinkles disappeared, and her former beauty was regained.

According to *Ran,* Abimelech took Sarah, not because of her beauty, but because she was Abraham's 'sister' and he wished to marry into so distinguished a family.

[This points to the lack of fear of God in that place. Their attitude was that 'the king may do as he pleases'. A stranger comes to their city, and no one asks him if he wants refreshment. The first thing they do is take note of the beautiful woman with him and ask 'Is she your wife? Is she your sister'? Perceiving great danger to himself if he were to identify himself as her husband, he answers: 'She is my sister', and she is immediately abducted to the King's palace. (see *comm.* to *v.* 7 and *Rashi* to *v.* 11).]

The commentators explain that Abimelech was the official title of all Philistine kings, just as Pharaoh was the title of the Egyptian monarchs. Literally, the name means *'father of king'* in the sense of *'patron of kings',* or *'king is father'.*

3. 'That night a deep sleep came upon Abimelech. He fell asleep on his throne and slept until morning' *(Sefer HaYashar)*:

וַיָּבֹא אֱלֹהִים אֶל־אֲבִימֶלֶךְ בַּחֲלוֹם הַלָּיְלָה — [*And*] *God came to Abimelech in a dream by night* [following *Hirsch;* lit.: *'in the dream of the night'.*]

For, to protect the honor of the righteous, God comes to gentiles in prophetic dreams as occurs often in Scriptures. To Pharoah He did not appear in a dream, for he was unworthy even though the honor of the righteous was involved. Instead he received punishment from God. It is as Elihu said: *'God speaks once, even twice, yet man does not perceive it. In a dream, a vision of the night, when deep sleep falls upon men, in slumberings upon the bed, then He opens the ears of men, and with discipline seals their instruction, that he may withdraw man from his purpose ...* ' [*Job* 33:14-16.] The *twice* refers to the dream and subsequent punishment *(Radak).*

The *Midrash* notes that God appears to heathens only at night. This was the case also with Balaam [*Num.* 22:20] and Laban [*Gen.* 31:24.]

הִנְּךָ מֵת עַל־הָאִשָּׁה אֲשֶׁר־לָקַחְתָּ וְהִוא בְּעֻלַת בָּעַל — *Behold you are to die because of the woman you have taken, moreover* [lit. *'and'*] *she is a married woman* [*Hirsch: 'the wife of a husband'*; (lit. *'she is possessed*

dream by night and said to him, 'Behold you are to die because of the woman you have taken; moreover she is a married woman.'

4 *Now Abimelech had not approached her. So he*

of,' i.e., has been intimate with, *a husband).*]

And as such she is prohibited to you since Adam was commanded concerning adultery as it says [above, 2:24] וְדָבַק בְּאִשְׁתּוֹ, *and cling to his wife,* and the Sages [*Sanhedrin* 58a] interpreted: 'but (was) not to his neighbor's wife'. This was a prohibition against adultery, a prohibition which they apparently observed zealously since they would sooner murder a man than take his wife [see footnote *v.* 2]. The Sages further derived from the use of the term בְּעֻלַת בָּעַל ['having been intimate with a husband'] instead of אֵשֶׁת אִישׁ ['married woman'] that to a Noachide 'marriage' does not take affect until it is consummated. [Therefore by telling Abimelech that Sarah was a בְּעֻלַת בָּעַל, i.e., a woman whose marriage had been consummated, God clarified why he would incur the death penalty] *(Radak).*

Malbim perceives in this verse that Abimelech committed two wrongs for which he deserved the death penalty: (1) *For the woman you have taken* — i.e. for *kidnapping her against her will* for which *Rambam* in *Hilchos Melachim* prescribes the death penalty whether or not the victim was married, as was the case with Shechem and Dinah [34:1 ff.] ; (2) *Moreover, she is a married woman,* and thus you have commited a further transgression. [Accordingly, the conjunction ו in וְהוא introduces an additional reason; we have, therefore, rendered it *moreover.*]

— *You will die;* no one has the right to take anything that is not his, least of all a woman. It remains immoral even, though you are a king, and even though it is the accepted custom. He added further: she is בְּעֻלַת בָּעַל, *the wife of a husband* — another has already the right to her *(Hirsch).*

4. וַאֲבִימֶלֶךְ לֹא קָרַב אֵלֶיהָ — *Now* [lit. *'and'*] *Abimelech had not approached her.*

He had been *prevented from doing so* by an angel [by denying him the strength to touch her *(Rashi* to *v.* 6) or, according to *Radak,* because God deadened his desire], as it says [*v.* 6]: *I therefore kept you from sinning against Me (Rashi).*

Ramban to *v.* 17 notes that 'approach' is a euphemism for intimacy, and Abimelech was punished for having taken Sarah by being rendered impotent.

[Others explain that his desire left him when she revealed to him that she was a married woman. See *comm.* to *v.* 5 וְהִיא־גַם־הִוא.]

It was necessary for the Torah to *explicitly testify* that Abimelech had not been intimate with her, moreso in this case than in the case of Pharaoh, because Isaac was conceived shortly after the incident with Abimelech *(Chizkuni).*

ה וַיֹּאמַר אֲדֹנָי הֲגוֹי גַּם־צַדִּיק תַּהֲרֹג: הֲלֹא
הוּא אָמַר־לִי אֲחֹתִי הִוא וְהִיא־גַם־הִוא
אָמְרָה אָחִי הוּא בְּתָם־לְבָבִי וּבְנִקְיֹן כַּפַּי
ו עָשִׂיתִי זֹאת: וַיֹּאמֶר אֵלָיו הָאֱלֹהִים

הֲגוֹי גַּם־צַדִּיק תַּהֲרֹג — *Will You slay a people* [lit. *'a nation'*] (the ה of הֲגוֹי being the interrogative rather than the definitive article) *though it is righteous.*

[The above translation follows *Rashi* and the majority of commentators who explain צַדִּיק, *righteous,* as modifying גוֹי, *nation.* They render the passage as if it read הֲגַם גוֹי צַדִּיק תַּהֲרֹג.]

Will You slay a nation even though it is righteous — is it Your practice to destroy nations without cause? If so, I must assume that You destroyed the generations of the Flood and of the Dispersion without just cause, just as You now wish to do to me! *(Rashi;* cf. *Rashi* to 18:25 חָלִלָה לְּךָ).

In comparison with the bestiality of Sodom, Abraham and Sarah were treated hospitably, and even the abduction of Sarah could be seen in a positive light, for Abimelech was doing her the honor of making her his queen *(Hirsch).*

By *nation* he meant himself [for the king is the personification of his people], his household, and his people *(Ibn Ezra).*

Sforno understands צַדִּיק to be a *noun* referring to himself: Is it, indeed, just for You to destroy an entire *nation* by slaying its king, who is a צַדִּיק, *righteous one,* for he has not sinned? [Read: הֲגוֹי גַּם־צַדִּיק תַּהֲרֹג, *will You slay a nation along with its righteous one?* (For by putting its leader to death, You destroy the entire nation).]

Or, according to *Ba'al HaTurim: If You slay me* [the personification of my גוֹי, *nation*] then you should also slay Abraham the צַדִּיק, *righteous one,* because he is the cause of this incident [*Read:* הֲגוֹי *if a nation* i.e., me, גַּם צַדִּיק *then also the righteous one,* Abraham, תַּהֲרֹג *You must slay.*]

5. הֲלֹא הוּא אָמַר־לִי אֲחֹתִי הִוא — *Did not he himself* [the הוּא inserted for emphasis: *he himself* (so *Hirsch*)] *tell me: 'She is my sister'?*

I.e., When I made personal inquiry and asked him directly about her — not relying on the reports of my servants — did *he himself not tell me* that she was his sister? *(Radak)*

וְהִיא־גַם־הִוא אָמְרָה אָחִי הוּא — *And she, too, herself* [lit. *'and she, also she'*] *said: 'He is my brother.'*

[The word גַּם, *also,* in the expression גַּם הִוא, lit. *'also she'* is seen as a רִבּוּי, *exegetical amplification,* presupposing that others also were involved — i.e., not *she alone* but *'also she'*: others as well. For had only Sarah been meant, it would have sufficed to say וְהִיא אָמְרָה, *and she said,* the word גַּם being superfluous since Abraham had already been mentioned previously]:

גַּם, *also,* includes her servants, camel drivers, and donkey drivers. I inquired of all of them and they told me, *'He is her brother' (Rashi).*[1]

[See *comm.* to 21:20 on the similar use of אֶת as an exegetical amplification.]

'I was misled! I asked him, "Is she your wife?" To which he replied: "She is my sister." Yet in spite of that I inquired further of the members of his household, and they all told me, "She is his sister".' *(Pesikta Rabbasi* 42)

— I even made personal inquiry of

XX said, 'O my Lord, will You slay a people though it is
5 *righteous?* [5] *Did not he himself tell me: "She is my*
sister"? And she, too, herself said: "He is my
brother"! In the innocence of my heart and integrity
of my hands have I done this.'

her, after I took her, in order not to rely on her husband's statement, and she corroborated his story. Why should I have doubted her? Therefore what sin have I transgressed? *(Radak; Ralbag).*

Some interpret that Sarah did reveal her true status to Abimelech. They note that in reference to Abraham Abimelech said הֲלֹא הוּא אָמַר **לִי** 'did he himself not tell *me*?' while in reference to Sarah he does not use the expression לִי, *to me.* Sarah had said *to others* that Abraham was her brother but to Abimelech she revealed her true status as Abraham's wife. Nevertheless, Abimelech's rationalization was that since she had told everyone else that she was Abraham's sister, he could discount whatever she told him privately. For perhaps she had found some fault with him and falsified her status in order to discourage him *(Me'am Lo'ez; Kessef Mezukak; Ha'amek Davar).*

בְּתָם־לְבָבִי וּבְנִקְיֹן כַּפַּי עָשִׂיתִי זֹאת — *In the innocence of my heart* [so *Hirsch;* lit. *'in the perfection of my heart',* i.e., *in a blameless manner*] and [*in the*] *integrity* [so *Hirsch*; lit. *'cleanness'*] *of my hands have I done this.*

In the innocence of my heart — i.e., I had no intention of sinning; *and the cleanness of my hands* — i.e., I am innocent of actual sin for I have not touched her *(Rashi).*

As *Radak* explains, the general intent of the statement is: My intention ['heart'] was pure for had I seriously suspected that she was a married woman I would never have even considered her, *and in the cleanness of my hands,* for when I took her it was honorably, with the intention of marrying her.

[Cf. the expression in *Ps.* 24:4 נְקִי כַפַּיִם, *clean hands,* i.e., impeccable integrity, with hands clean of all unlawful gain *(Metzudas David).*]

Abimelech expressed a not unusual sentiment: if his intentions were good, then he is automatically blameless. Judaism rejects this view. Good intentions do not purify a wrong deed. It must be measured by the standard of whether it complies with God's will. If it is wrong in His eyes, then good intentions do not sanction it. Moreover, lack of knowledge concerning its impermissibility is itself sinful, for a person has the obligation to seek instruction. A person in Abimelech's position has the further obligaton to set an example of appropriate behavior, for, is it right that even an unmarried woman must fear the whim of every prince? *(Hirsch)*

1. The loyalty of Sarah's servants indicates what a considerate mistress she must have been. Servants ordinarily feel resentment against and jealously of their employer. They would rejoice at the opportunity to win the favor and reward of a king by informing against their master or mistress. But in this case the servants maintained their loyalty and corroborated their master's story. The servants were surely rewarded for the merit of their loyalty as was Lot for not informing against Abraham and Sarah in Egypt [see *Rashi* to 19:29] *(Rabbi Yosef Weinbaum).*

בַּחֲלֹם גַּם אָנֹכִי יָדַעְתִּי כִּי בְתָם־לְבָבְךָ
עָשִׂיתָ זֹּאת וָאֶחְשֹׂךְ גַּם־אָנֹכִי אוֹתְךָ
מֵחֲטוֹ־לִי עַל־כֵּן לֹא־נְתַתִּיךָ לִנְגֹּעַ אֵלֶיהָ:
ז וְעַתָּה הָשֵׁב אֵשֶׁת־הָאִישׁ כִּי־נָבִיא הוּא

6. God is very much aware of Abimelech's good intentions; it was *He* who had kept him from the sin of adultery.

וַיֹּאמֶר אֵלָיו הָאֱלֹהִים בַּחֲלֹם — [*And*] *God said to him in the dream.*

[Since 'dream' is mentioned a second time] it is apparent that Abimelech's response in the previous verse was given to God after he awoke from the first dream. Then God came to him in this second dream *(Ha'amek Davar).*

[In the literal sense however, the *pasach* under the *beth* in בַּחֲלֹם indicates the definite article: *'the* dream' i.e., in the *aforementioned* dream.]

גַּם אָנֹכִי יָדַעְתִּי ... וָאֶחְשֹׂךְ גַּם־אָנֹכִי אוֹתְךָ מֵחֲטוֹ־לִי — *I, too, knew ... and I, too, prevented you from sinning against Me.*

'I knew that you acted in *the innocence of your heart* without intention to sin. According to the principle of [*Avodah Zarah* 55a]: הַבָּא לְטַהֵר מְסַעְיין אותו, 'One who comes to be cleansed is helped,' *I prevented you from sinning against Me (Rashi / Mizrachi)* ...

[However, God did not mention *'cleanness of hands'* in his reply (see *Rashi,* further).]

עַל־כֵּן לֹא־נְתַתִּיךָ לִנְגֹּעַ אֵלֶיהָ — *That is why* [i.e., because I knew your intention was innocent *(Rashi)*] *I did not permit* [lit. *'give'*] *you to touch her.*

Continuing *Rashi*: ... 'You therefore cannot claim *cleanness of hands,* however, because it was not of your own will that you did not touch her; rather it was *I* [i.e. though My angel *(Rashi* to *v.* 4)] who *prevented you from sinning* by denying you the strength to touch her.' (For similar instances of נתן, *give,* in the sense of *permit,* cf. 31:7 and *Judges* 15:1).[1]

I prevented you from committing adultery which is a sin *against Me;* but regarding the transgression against Abraham, you are guilty for even a king may not kidnap another's wife. Therefore, while you may not have *thought* you were guilty as reflected by בְּתָם־לְבָבְךָ, *the innocence of your heart* — but in *deed,* there is no נִקְיוֹן כַּפַּיִם, *cleanness of hands* here *(Malbim).*

To touch her — I deprived you even of the lust to embrace or kiss her *(Radak*; see *Ramban v.* 4 and *v.* 17).

7. וְעַתָּה הָשֵׁב אֵשֶׁת־הָאִישׁ — *But* [lit. *'and'*] *now, return the man's wife.*

And do not think that she will be repulsive to her husband and he will

1. Rav Aibu said: It is like the case of a warrior who was riding his horse at full speed, when seeing a child lying in the path he reined in the horse so the child was not hurt. Whom do we praise: the horse or the rider? — Surely the rider! Similarly, God said: '*I* did not permit you to touch her' [and the credit is accordingly Mine, not yours] *(Midrash).*

[6] *And God said to him in the dream, 'I, too, knew
that it was in the innocence of your heart that you did
this, and I, too, prevented you from sinning against
Me; That is why I did not permit you to touch her.*
[7] *But now, return the man's wife for he is a prophet,*

refuse to accept her, or that he will hate you and refuse to pray for you.

כִּי־נָבִיא הוּא ... — *For he is a prophet* and he knows that you did not touch her; therefore וְיִתְפַּלֵּל בַּעַדְךָ וֶחְיֵה, *he will pray for you and you will live (Rashi).*

The *Talmud* asks: And were she not a prophet's wife, would she not have to be returned?

— The verse must be interpreted: *Return the man's wife* no matter who he is. Regarding your defense that it is wrong of Me to *kill a righteous nation* [*v.* 4] because they themselves told you she was his sister [*v.* 7], be aware that Abraham *is a prophet* and as such he perceived from your actions and the questions put to him that his life would have been in danger had he not responded as he did. A stranger coming to a city should be asked whether he needs food and drink. Should he be asked: 'Is this your wife? Is this your sister?' *(Makkos* 9a) [see bracketed *comm.* end of *v.* 2.]

[Therefore it was your own improper conduct that caused him, as a prophet, to be cautious of revealing his true marital status. You are therefore worthy of the death penalty for having taken his wife.] [See *Rashi* to *v.* 11.]

Cf. the *Midrash*: 'Who will assure him that I did not touch her?' Abimelech asked.

'He is a prophet,' God answered, 'and as such he knows it without need for your assurance.'

'But who will make it known to *all* that I did not touch her?' Abimelech asked.

God answered, *'He will pray for you, and you will live,'* [and all will realize from the fact that he prayed for you that you were guiltless.]

As *Radak* explains: because he is a prophet, he is close to me, and I heed his prayer. I will not forgive you unless you appease him and he prays for you, for even if she were unmarried you sinned by taking her against her will.

Cf. *Bava Kamma* 92a:

A man who injures his neighbor, even if he pays [the five-fold compensation — for sustained injury; pain; medical care; loss of working 'time'; and humiliation], he is not forgiven until he asks him for pardon, as it says *but now return the man's wife for he is a prophet and he will pray for you and you will live.*

The word וֶחְיֵה [lit. imperative: *and live!*] is a form of prophetic future implying *and you shall surely live*; cf. וֶהְיֵה = וְתִהְיֶה *and you shall surely be (Ibn Janach).*

Here the implication is: *You shall recover from your sickness* [see *vs.* 17-18] *(Malbim).*

The word נָבִיא [prophet] is related to נִיב שְׂפָתַיִם *expressions of the lips,* [*Isa.* 57:19] i.e., one who is

וְיִתְפַּלֵּל בַּעַדְךָ וֶחְיֵה וְאִם־אֵינְךָ מֵשִׁיב דַּע
כִּי־מוֹת תָּמוּת אַתָּה וְכָל־אֲשֶׁר־לָךְ׃
ח וַיַּשְׁכֵּם אֲבִימֶלֶךְ בַּבֹּקֶר וַיִּקְרָא לְכָל־
עֲבָדָיו וַיְדַבֵּר אֶת־כָּל־הַדְּבָרִים הָאֵלֶּה
ט בְּאָזְנֵיהֶם וַיִּירְאוּ הָאֲנָשִׁים מְאֹד׃ וַיִּקְרָא
אֲבִימֶלֶךְ לְאַבְרָהָם וַיֹּאמֶר לוֹ מֶה־עָשִׂיתָ
לָּנוּ וּמֶה־חָטָאתִי לָךְ כִּי־הֵבֵאתָ עָלַי וְעַל־
מַמְלַכְתִּי חֲטָאָה גְדֹלָה מַעֲשִׂים אֲשֶׁר

frequently near Me and speaks My teaching; I love his words and listen to his prayers *(Rashbam)*[1]

As *Hirsch* points out, it is not the function of a prophet to foretell the future. To whatever extent he does that, it is incidental to his primary role which is to be the vessel and organ through which God's will reaches mankind.

וְאִם־אֵינְךָ מֵשִׁיב — *But* [lit *'and'*] *if You do not restore her.*

The threat is repeated, (now in the negative form), to emphasize the severity and import of the matter. Cf. 41:32 where in the case of Pharaoh having the same dream twice, means that the matter has been determined by God, and that God will soon carry it out: *(Da'as Soferim;* see *Ṭanchuma Yashan).*

מוֹת תָּמוּת — *You shall surely die* [lit. *'die, you shall die,'* the verb being idiomatically intensified by the addition of the infinite absolute].

— You are guilty of two death penalties: For kidnapping and because she is a married woman *(Malbim).*

The *Midrash* derives from this that a heathen need not be *warned* of consequence *before* he commits a transgression. [For Abimelech received no warning in advance, yet now he is threatened with the death penalty.]

אַתָּה וְכָל־אֲשֶׁר־לָךְ — *You and all that is yours.*

Your entire household *(Alshich);* including even the unborn children of your wife and maids *(Sforno).*

According to *Malbim,* this extended to the *entire nation,* because Noachide law makes everyone responsible for the institution of courts to administer justice. It was for their failure to do so that the people of Shechem were guilty when they allowed Shechem to go unpunished for abducting Dinah. See *Rambam, Hilchos Melachim* 9:14.

1. *Hirsch* defines *Tefillah* as man's obligation to penetrate all phases of his life and existence with God's truth, thereby to make his entire being harmonious with God's will. [Prayer as an expression of man's overflowing heart is described by words other than *Tefillah.*] This explains why there are set times and texts for the regular prayers. Whether or not man is emotionally ready or spiritually moved to pray does not matter — he is required to absorb the message of prayer, and his lack of inner desire to do so makes it even more imperative that he submit himself to God's will.

XX
8-9

and he will pray for you and you will live. But if you
do not return her be aware that you shall surely die:
you and all that is yours.'
8 *Abimelech arose early next morning. He sum-*
moned all his servants and told them all of these
things in their ears, and the people were very
frightened. 9 *Then Abimelech summoned Abraham*
and said to him, 'What have you done to us? How I
sinned against you that you brought upon me and
my kingdom such great sin? Deeds that are not to be

8. וַיַּשְׁכֵּם אֲבִימֶלֶךְ בַּבֹּקֶר — [*And*] *Abimelech arose early next morning.* He was filled with dread because of the message that he would require the forgiveness and prayers of the prophet even though he would return his wife *(Radak).*

— As *Tanchuma Yashan* notes, he twisted and turned waiting for morning so he could get up and summon his courtiers and repeat his dream.

בְּאָזְנֵיהֶם — *In their ears,* [i.e., discretely.]

וַיִּירְאוּ הָאֲנָשִׁים מְאֹד — *And the men were very frightened.* This refers to his servants who had agreed to his taking of Sarah and who had initially brought her to his attention *(Radak).*

[*They were frightened* because they perceived the obvious divine favor which Abraham enjoyed, and they were worried about the consequences to them.]

... Or because they were afraid that Abraham would refuse to pray for them, and thus the death penalty would not be remitted *(Ha'amek Davar).*

According to the *Midrash,* they had [miraculously, from afar *(Yafeh To'ar)*] seen the smoke of Sodom ascending like that of the fiery furnace and they said: Perhaps Abraham will summon the angels that destroyed Sodom! Therefore, fearing a similar fate they were terrified *(Midrash).*

9. וַיִּקְרָא אֲבִימֶלֶךְ לְאַבְרָהָם — *Then* [lit *'and'*] *Abimelech summoned* [lit. *'called to'*] *Abraham.*

In order to hear his explanation, and to beg his forgiveness so he would pray for him *(Radak).*

מֶה־עָשִׂיתָ לָּנוּ — *What have you done to us?* By telling us she was your sister, thereby exposing me and my servants to such a retribution *(Radak).*

וּמֶה־חָטָאתִי לָךְ — *And how have I sinned against you* [lit. *to you*].

I.e., how have I ever wronged you that you now retaliate against me in this way and expose me to mortal punishment? *(Radak).*

כִּי־הֵבֵאתָ עָלַי וְעַל־מַמְלַכְתִּי חֲטָאָה גְדֹלָה — *That you brought upon me and my kingdom such great sin?*

For the sin of the king, as representative of the nation, affects all; cf. *v.* 4 *(Radak).*

As *Midrash HaGadol* notes: The

י לֹא־יֵעָשׂוּ עָשִׂיתָ עִמָּדִי: וַיֹּאמֶר אֲבִימֶלֶךְ
אֶל־אַבְרָהָם מָה רָאִיתָ כִּי עָשִׂיתָ אֶת־
יא הַדָּבָר הַזֶּה: וַיֹּאמֶר אַבְרָהָם כִּי אָמַרְתִּי
רַק אֵין־יִרְאַת אֱלֹהִים בַּמָּקוֹם הַזֶּה
יב וַהֲרָגוּנִי עַל־דְּבַר אִשְׁתִּי: וְגַם־אָמְנָה

king to his country is like the heart to the body. If the heart ails, the entire body is ill. So, too, if the king sins, the country is sinful and may suffer destruction thereby.

[Since, as pointed out in *Radak*'s comm. to 15:16 s.v. כִּי לֹא שָׁלֵם, that the word חֲטָאת also refers to *punishment*, the verse might be rendered: '... *That you brought upon me and my kingdom such great punishment?*']

מַעֲשִׂים אֲשֶׁר לֹא־יֵעָשׂוּ עָשִׂיתָ עִמָּדִי — *Deeds that ought not be done have you done to me.*

It is beneath the dignity of a man like yourself to cause harm to people you have not known and with whom you have no quarrel; one does not go about claiming his wife is unmarried *(Radak; Sforno; Akeidas Yitzchak).*

Accroding to *Rashi*, *deeds* refers to the punishments visited upon the royal household. I.e., 'We have suffered the effects of an unheard of plague because of you — the closing up of all our bodily orfices: the reproductive organs, bowels, ears and even the nose [see *v.* 17-18; *Bava Kamma* 92a.]

Rashi thus rejects the possibility that the plural term מַעֲשִׂים, *deeds*, can refer to the claim that he was Sarah's brother *Gur Aryeh).*

10. The early questions were merely rhetorical, and Abimelech required no answer. Now, seeking an answer Abimelech asks Abraham to clarify what his true motives were *(Radak):*

מָה רָאִיתָ כִּי עָשִׂיתָ אֶת־הַדָּבָר הַזֶּה — *What did you see that you did such a thing?*

— What wickedness have you noticed in my conduct that made you fear that I would abduct your wife? I have never taken women away from their husbands! *(Ramban* to *v.* 12).

— It is impossible for one like yourself to have acted in this manner without a reason *(Radak).*

Have you seen any instance of murder, robbery, or adultery among us which aroused your suspicions about us? *(Malbim).*

Wherever else you traveled, you were the bearer of blessings, while to us you brought this catastrophe. Why? *(Midrash).*

11. רַק אֵין־יִרְאַת אֱלֹהִים בַּמָּקוֹם הַזֶּה — *There is but no fear of God in this place.*

'You are partially right' Abraham answered. 'The country is good, and the people well-mannered, but nevertheless the basic flaw here is that your subjects *do not fear God*, וַהֲרָגוּנִי עַל־דְּבַר־אִשְׁתִּי, and therefore it would not be beyond them to *slay me because of my wife*, for only the fear of God acts as a deterrent to

done have you done to me!'
10 *And Abimelech said to Abraham, 'What did you see that you did such a thing?'*

11 *And Abraham said, 'Because I said, There is but no fear of God in this place and they will slay me because of my wife.*
12 *Moreover, she is indeed, my*

unrestrained lust' *(Radak; Malbim).* [1]

My fear was not based upon any prior personal knowledge about you, but out of my general knowledge that in most places in the world [where I have traveled *(Tur)*] there is no fear of God *(Ramban).*

I especially noted their lack of God-fearing qualities when I entered the city. For when a man enters a town should he be asked about what he would like to eat or drink, or about the identity of the woman with him: whether she is his wife or sister? [Surely, they should inquire about one's need for food and drink.] Since the people of Gerar were concerned only with the identity of Sarah, Abraham immediately perceived that they lacked fear of God, and as such were void of moral restraint [*(Mizrachi; Tzeidah LaDerech)*] *(Rashi;* cf. *Makkos* 9b cited in *v.* 7; and *Bava Kamma* 92a).

[The extent to which Abraham feared that godless people would stoop, apparently motivated even Isaac to repeat the scenario when he traveled to Gerar many years later and identified Rebecca as his sister (26:7). Although Abraham doubtless told him of all that occurred, Issac, too, could expect no safety in a place *'where there is no fear of God'.* In such a place, an innocent traveller could be casually disposed of for the sake of his wife.]

[*Sforno* takes אֱלֹהִים in our verse in the sense of *judges* (cf. 6:2 and *Exod.* 22:7)]: There was no יִרְאַת אֱלֹהִים, *fear of the ruling authority* in that place and so lawlessness prevailed.

12. [Having defended his action, Abraham goes on to explain that his claim of being Sarah's brother even *in the literal sense* was not untrue; he never claimed that Sarah was *not* his wife, but emphasized that she was his sister *(Malbim).* This demonstrates that even where one is compelled to dissemble, he should remain as close to the truth as circumstances allow.]

1. Abraham informed Abimelech that there can be no assurance of safety even among a nation of well-bred, sophisticated people. Their code of conduct may be based on an appreciation of decent and honorable behavior, but that will avail them only so long as lust and temptation are not aroused. Let them be tested by a powerful desire for wealth or lust for physical gratification, and they will disregard all the behavioral norms. Only one thing can stand in the way of such desire — a powerful fear of God based on the knowledge that He is aware of even the minutest deed *(Malbim).*

אֲחֹתִי בַת־אָבִי הִוא אַךְ לֹא בַת־אִמִּי
וַתְּהִי־לִי לְאִשָּׁה: יג וַיְהִי כַּאֲשֶׁר הִתְעוּ אֹתִי

וְגַם־אָמְנָם אֲחֹתִי בַת־אָבִי הִוא — *And moreover, she is indeed, my sister, the daughter of my father,* and as such he was permitted to marry her, for a Noachide [a universal term for non-Jews] is permitted to marry his half-sister from his father, since the paternal relationship is not taken into consideration in the case of idolators. Abraham told him this in order to justify his earlier statements that she was his sister. In fact, however, you may retort that she was his *brother's* daughter [and not his *father's* daughter as he had claimed; therefore what justification did he have to tell this untruth?] — Since "grandchildren are considered as children" she may truly be regarded his sister. . .

Furthermore, we similarily find that Abraham used the term *'brother'* in reference to Lot (13:8) [although he was Lot's *uncle,* not brother. Here, too, as Sarah's uncle, it was just as legitimite for him to refer to her as *'sister'*] *(Rashi).*

Note also that Sarah is identified with Lot's sister, Iscah, the daughter of Haran who died early, and whose children, according to 11:31, seemed to have been raised by their grandfather Terach. Thus Abraham said: 'She was my foster-sister before she became my wife. She is the daughter of a brother who died early and she grew up with me under the same paternal roof. In spirit we are like brother and sister, and it is because we became so compatible that it was natural for us to marry *(Hirsch).*

Ramban finds it difficult to see how this response met Abimelech's complaint; the critical factor in Abimelech's predicament was that she was also Abraham's wife. Abraham withheld *that* fact and therefore Abimelech accused him of bringing about much sin [*v.* 9].

Ramban therefore maintains that Abraham's explanation of his motive was given in the previous and the next verse that this manner of identifying Sarah had been *routinely adopted* as a life-saving measure. The statement in this verse is merely an *additional justification* that he spoke the truth by declaring her his sister. Abraham asserted, 'I spoke the truth. Had the people been God-fearing, they would have asked whether Sarah was also my wife since one may marry his paternal half-sister. Since your servants took her without making any such inquiry, I perceived that there was no fear of God in this place and I remained silent' [apparently hopeful — as outlined in the footnote to *v.* 2 — of gaining a delay and eventually escaping with God's help.]

According to *Ibn Ezra,* Abraham's statement was merely intended to put off Abimelech for the moment, and thereby appease his anger [for, as the Sages ruled (*Yevamos* 65b) 'One may modify a statement in the interests of peace' (*Karnei Or*)]. *Cf. Comm.* to 27:19: *'I am Esau your firstborn'.*

אַךְ לֹא בַת־אִמִּי — *Though* [lit. *'but'*] *not my mother's daughter.*

Sarah's father Haran, was born of a different mother than Abraham [apparently Terach had remarried] *(Rashi; Sefer HaYashar;* see *comm.* end of 11:29).

וַתְּהִי־לִי לְאִשָּׁה — *And she became my wife.*

— Because a Noachide is permit-

XX sister, my father's daughter, though not my mother's
13 daughter; and she became my wife. [13] And so it was,
when God caused me to wander from my father's

ted to marry his paternal sister *(Malbim).*

[See *Rashi* and *Hirsch* above.]

13. This was Abraham's third justification: Since he had, at God's command, become a wanderer, he has resorted to this plan whenever entering a new place; it does not imply low esteem for this particular region *(Malbim).*

כַּאֲשֶׁר הִתְעוּ אֹתִי אֱלֹהִים — *When God caused me to wander,* i.e., when the Holy One, Blessed be He, brought me forth from my father's house to be a nomad, wandering from place to place, I knew that I would often be in the habitation of wicked men. *Onkelos* renders it in another manner [see below] *(Rashi).*

Rashi goes on to explain that the term הִתְעוּ [*'caused to wander'*] is applicable, for anyone exiled from his home without a permanent abode is called a תּוֹעֶה, *wanderer* [lit. one who 'strays' about aimlessly], as for example, 21:14: *Hagar ... strayed about* [וַתֵּתַע] *in the desert; Ps.* 119:176:*I have gone astray* [תָּעִיתִי] *like a lost sheep;* and *Job* 38:41: *they wander* [יִתְעוּ (in the sense of wandering about to seek food)] *for lack of food.*

Rashbam, Ibn Ezra, and *Radak* similarly render הִתְעוּ as *exiled,* for one who is exiled *wanders about* unfamiliar roads. The implication here is: *God exiled me* from my native place when He summoned me with לֶךְ־לְךָ, *Get yourself out, . . .* [12:1.]

Ibn Janach perceives the relationship of the root to the cognate verb טעה, *to err,* as also indicative of this wandering state.

The verb [הִתְעוּ, *caused to wander*] attached to אֱלֹהִים occurs here in a plural construction.

Rashi observes that it is not unusual for the Deity [אֱלָהוּת] or other terms of authority [מָרוּת] to be grammatically treated as plural, as for example, *II Sam.* 7:23: הָלְכוּ אֱלֹהִים, *God went* [plural]; *Deut.* 5:23: אֱלֹהִים חַיִּים *the living* [plural] *God; Josh.* 24:19 אֱלֹהִים קְדֹשִׁים, *a Holy* [plural] *God.* [Cf. also the use of the *pluralis majestatis* (the royal *'we')* in the creation of Adam in 1:26, see *comm.* there.]

The above translation interpreting the Name to be sacred, follows *Rashi.* However, the *Talmud* records a difference of opinion as to whether or not the word אֱלֹהִים, in our verse refers to God and is sacred, or whether it has non-sacred connotations [cf. *comm.* to בְּנֵי אֱלֹהִים in 6:2]. 'All the Names of God written in connection with Abraham are holy except the one in our verse which is non-holy. Some maintain that this too is sacred, the meaning being: But for God, they [i.e., the nations] would have caused me to wander astray' [from the true belief] *(Yerushalmi Megillah* 1:9).

The *Midrash,* too, perceives the difficulty of the plural verb in relationship with God, and separates the verb הִתְעוּ from God:

Rav Chanan said: If we could only adequately interpret this verse in three ways and so discharge our responsibility of achieving the true interpretation! — (a) *when the nations sought to assail me* [i.e., כַּאֲשֶׁר הִתְעוּ אוֹתִי, when they (the nations) swerved (to an improper path and wished to slay me because I rejected it)] אֱלֹהִים מִבֵּית אָבִי, *God* [saved me] *from* [i.e., while I was still in] *my father's house;* (b) *when they* (the nations) *tried to mislead me, God* [ordered me out] *of my father's house;* (c) *when they* (the nations) *erred from the Holy One's ways,* God raised two great men out of my father's house, Shem and Eber, to warn them [i.e., either אֱלֹהִים God (raised men) out of my fathers house; or He raised אֱלֹהִים מִבֵּית אָבִי, *judges, teachers, out of my father's house.*] As *Radak* notes according to the latter interpretation, אֱלֹהִים, does not refer to God but to *judges* [cf. *Exod.* 22:7] and hence is non-sacred. [See *Soferim* 4:6; *Minchas Shay*]

אֱלֹהִים֮ מִבֵּ֣ית אָבִי֒ וָאֹמַ֣ר לָ֔הּ זֶ֣ה חַסְדֵּ֔ךְ
אֲשֶׁ֥ר תַּעֲשִׂ֖י עִמָּדִ֑י אֶ֤ל כָּל־הַמָּקוֹם֙ אֲשֶׁ֣ר
יד נָב֣וֹא שָׁ֔מָּה אִמְרִי־לִ֖י אָחִ֥י הֽוּא׃ וַיִּקַּ֨ח
אֲבִימֶ֜לֶךְ צֹ֣אן וּבָקָ֗ר וַעֲבָדִים֙ וּשְׁפָחֹ֔ת וַיִּתֵּ֖ן
לְאַבְרָהָ֑ם וַיָּ֣שֶׁב ל֔וֹ אֵ֖ת שָׂרָ֥ה אִשְׁתּֽוֹ׃
טו וַיֹּ֣אמֶר אֲבִימֶ֔לֶךְ הִנֵּ֥ה אַרְצִ֖י לְפָנֶ֑יךָ בַּטּ֥וֹב

Torah Temimah explains that each of the above interpretations presupposes that our passage is לָשׁוֹן קָצָר, elliptical, and a word must be inferred to better gain the meaning, as for example the bracketed additions: וַיְהִי כַּאֲשֶׁר הִתְעוּ אֹתִי [הַתּוֹעִים, הִצִּילַנִי] אֱלֹהִים מִבֵּית אָבִי, *when they* [the nations] *wished to cause me to swerve, God* [saved me] *from the house of my father.* There are countless such elliptical passages throughout Scriptures. He goes on to list over twenty — for example: *Rashi* to 4:15: *whoever slays Cain* [will be punished]...; *Numbers* 21:8: *make yourself a* [נָחָשׁ] שָׂרָף *fiery* [*serpent*]; *Ramban* to 25:28: כִּי [נָתַן] צַיִד בְּפִיו, *'he* [placed] *prey in his mouth.* He concludes that there is no need to elaborate further. Whoever is familiar with Scriptures will find many additional such elliptical passages.'

Onkelos renders similar to the *Midrash* above: *'When the people erred after their own handiwork, God brought me close to Himself from the house of my father'* [Cf. *Targum Yonasan*].

Sforno, and *R' Bachya,* render the word as non-sacred, referring to the *gods* Abraham's parents served, the detestable service which forced him to leave his home: *And it came to pass when the idolatry* [i.e., *the idolatrous service of my parents and kinsmen*] *caused me to leave my home for an unknown destination, I said to my wife...'* [Cf. *HaKsav V'Hakabbalah*].

וָאֹמַר לָהּ — [*And*] *I said to her.* Knowing that we would find ourselves in strange, and perhaps dangerous, surroundings *(Akeidas Yitzchak).*

I.e., I said this to her many years ago and we have followed this practice ever since, whenever we traveled; this is not something we devised only when we entered your country *(Ramban v.* 12).

[See *Radak* further.]

זֶה חַסְדֵּךְ אֲשֶׁר תַּעֲשִׂי עִמָּדִי — *Let this be your kindness which you shall do for* [lit. *'with'*] *me.*

[Abraham emphasizes that Sarah did not *initiate* this scheme, but agreed to cooperate as a *kindness to him,* prompted by his urgings. See 12:31.]

אֶל כָּל־הַמָּקוֹם אֲשֶׁר נָבוֹא שָׁמָּה — *To whatever place we come* [*there*].

The Torah explicitly mentions this plan only twice. The true intent of his statement is: 'Whenever we are *aliens in a new place,* and there is reason to believe that the wickedness of the population makes our position precarious, *say, you are my sister.'* Apparently, wherever Abraham maintained a *permanent residence,* he was held in great esteem [see for example 23:6] and there was no reason to hide Sarah's true status *(Radak).*

Ramban (see 12:13, and *v.* 2 above) consistently disagrees with the first part of the above exposition. He is of the opinion that Abraham *always* resorted to this strategy whenever he entered a new locale whether or not there were particular grounds for fear.

house, I said to her, 'Let this be your kindness which you shall do for me — to whatever place we come, say of me: "He is my brother".'

14 *Then Abimelech took sheep, cattle, male and female slaves and gave them to Abraham. And he returned his wife Sarah to him.*

15 *And Abimelech said, 'Behold my land is before*

[However, it would seem reasonable to assume that after residing in a certain place for a time and coming to feel secure there, he would reveal the truth. The Torah mentions only those two occasions where something happened to them on account of the ruse.]

אִמְרִי-לִי — *Say of* [lit. *'to'*] *me.*

The translation reflects *Rashi* who comments that in this context, לִי, *to me,* has the meaning of עָלַי, *concerning* [lit. *'upon'*] *me.* Cf. 26:7: לְאִשְׁתּוֹ, *regarding his wife; Exod.* 14:3 לִבְנֵי יִשְׂרָאֵל *regarding the children of Israel; Judges* 9:54: לִי, *regarding me.*

14. וַיִּקַּח אֲבִימֶלֶךְ צֹאן וּבָקָר וַעֲבָדִים וּשְׁפָחֹת — Then [lit. *'and'*] *Abimelech took sheep,* [and] *cattle, and male and female slaves.*

The *Midrash (Bereishis Rabbah* 15:1) records that Abimelech followed the earlier example of Pharaoh. When he saw the miracles performed in his house on Sarah's behalf, he gave his daughter to her, saying: 'Better that my daughter Hagar, be a handmaid in your house than a mistress in another!' (cf. *comm.* to 12:16 where *Pirkei d'Rabbi Eliezer* bases this on the defective spelling שְׁפָחֹת female slaves implying that Pharaoh gave Abraham only one female slave).

וַיִּתֵּן לְאַבְרָהָם — *And* [*he*] *gave* [them] *to Abraham.*

So that he might be appeased and pray for him *(Rashi).*

[For it must be remembered that God warned him that he would avoid the death penalty only if Abraham interceded on his behalf.]

Also, he gave them *to Abraham,* because it is improper for a man to give a gift to a woman *(Alshich).*

Cf. *Midrash HaGadol:* Pharaoh had given his gifts directly to *Sarah* (see *footnote* to 12:16) [intimating that he still desired her], while Abimelech gave only to *Abraham,* because Abimelech was decent. He wanted to appease him so he might pray on his behalf.

15. הִנֵּה אַרְצִי לְפָנֶיךָ — *Behold, my land is before you.*

[The commentators note the contrast between Abimelech and Pharaoh; Abimelech displayed courteous hospitality by inviting Abraham to settle in whatever part of the land he chose; in similar circumstances *Pharaoh* had said to him: *'Behold your wife; take her and go'* (12:19)]: *Rashi* therefore explains [in Pharaoh's defense] that Pharaoh, knowing that his people were steeped in immorality, bade him to leave the country [for Abraham's own safety, to avoid further incidents (see *comm.* to 12:19).]

Toldos Yitzchak notes that the Philistines had become terrified

טז בְּעֵינֶיךָ שֵׁב: וּלְשָׂרָה אָמַר הִנֵּה נָתַתִּי
אֶלֶף כֶּסֶף לְאָחִיךְ הִנֵּה הוּא־לָךְ כְּסוּת
עֵינַיִם לְכֹל אֲשֶׁר אִתָּךְ וְאֵת־כֹּל וְנֹכָחַת:

because of what had happened in Sodom, and they were afraid that they, too, might be subject to destruction because of what had been done to Sarah. Therefore they invited Abraham to remain in their midst so his merit would protect them *(Me'am Loez).*

Additionally, by inviting Abraham to remain, Abimelech was demonstrating to all that he had not violated her, for a woman with whom the king had been intimate would never be permitted to return to a commoner husband in the king's own land *(Abarbanel).*

בַּטּוֹב בְּעֵינֶיךָ שֵׁב — *Settle wherever you see fit* [lit. *'in the best in your eyes settle'.*]

It has been noted that in conferring full rights of citizenship upon Abraham by allowing him to dwell where he chose, Abimelech showed his recognition of Abraham's qualities. It was a prelude to the covenant Abimelech later made [21:22ff] with Abraham *(Akeidas Yitzchak).*

Abimelech was a righteous heathen and desired to live near a righteous man *(Pesikta Zutresa).*[1]

16. וּלְשָׂרָה אָמַר — *And to Sarah he said.* — In deference to her in order to appease her *(Rashi).*

הִנֵּה נָתַתִּי אֶלֶף כֶּסֶף לְאָחִיךְ, — *Behold I have given your brother a thousand* [pieces of] *silver,* i.e., it was as a token of honor *to you* that I gave this money to your brother *(Rashi).*

The commentators explain *Rashi's* basis: since Abimelech had given gifts to Abraham in order to prevail upon him to pray (see *comm.* to *v.* 19) this declaration to Sarah could have been only to appease her, for, in fact, he had not given the money for her sake. How did *Rashi* know, however, that the gifts were, indeed, for the purpose of the prayer?

— For they were given after God told Abimelech that it was necessary that Abraham pray for him *(Mizrachi).*

1. According to *Bereishis Rabbah* 54:2 Abraham *declined* Abimelech's offer to dwell in his land, and [in *ibid.* 61:1] Abraham is praised for this refusal as one who [*Ps.* 1:1] *'sat not in the session of scorners'* [as the Philistines are described in *Avodah Zarah* 19a *(Radal).*]

This seemingly contradicts 21:34 and *Rashi's Seder Olam* chronology there according to which Abraham sojourned *in the land of the Philistines during that period.*

Mattanos Kehunah and *Maharzu* explain that the intent of the *Midrashim* is that Abraham declined Abimelech's offer by refusing to live *in the capital city of Gerar in Abimelech's close proximity.* However, Abraham did decide to dwell in what would later be called Beer Sheba, which, as *Ramban* in 21:32 explains, was then part of the land of Philistines. Thus, he accepted Abimelech's offer to the extent that he settled in Philistia, although not in the capital city. [When Eretz Yisrael was apportioned, it was in the territory of Judah.]

Accordingly, following the above, which most closely accords with the Rabbinic interpretation of the narrative, Abraham resided in Beer Sheba. It was there, apparently, that Isaac was born, the great feast was held to celebrate his weaning, Hagar was expelled, and the treaty was made with Abimelech. Abraham 'planted an *eshel*' there, and in fact, after the *Akeidah* it was to Beer Sheba that Abraham went first, even though he and Sarah lived in Hebron at that time.

In the opinion of *Ibn Ezra* and *Radak* however, Abraham did dwell in the environs of Gerar, and their varied opinions regarding his places of residence during the events of the narrative of Chapter 21 will be noted in the commentary there. [See *comm.* to 21:22, 22:19, and cf. *Ramban* to 23:3.]

XX
16 *you: settle wherever you see fit.'* [16] *And to Sarah he said, 'Behold I have given your brother a thousand pieces of silver. Behold! Let it be for you an eye-covering for all who are with you; and to all you will be vindicated.*

— If his original intention was only to appease Sarah, then he should have given the gifts directly to her *(Gur Aryeh).*

According to *Rashbam,* this money is different from the *gifts* enumerated in *v.* 14 which Abimelech gave to appease Abraham after he returned Sarah. This *money,* of our verse, is the *dowry* which Abimelech had given Abraham previously as the 'brother' of Sarah. Thus, Abimelech attempts to appease Sarah by reminding her how noble were his intentions; how he had not *abducted* her but had instead taken her honorably and paid an exhorbitant dowry to the man she identified as her brother ... For if Pharaoh gave gifts to Abraham for taking her [see 12:16], Abimelech certainly must have done the same.

Ramban, however, interprets that Abimelech *was* referring to the sheep, cattle, etc. which he had given him [*v.* 14] and which were worth that sum of a thousand pieces of silver.

לְאָחִיךָ — *To your brother,* i.e. to Abraham whom you have described as your brother *(Rashi).*

I gave the money to *your brother* for had I given the money to *you,* people might say it was a harlot's hire. That I gave it to your brother makes it obvious that I was forced against my will to redeem myself; thus it will serve to vindicate you to all *(R' Bachya).*

הִנֵּה הוּא־לָךְ — [*Behold!*] *Let it* [i.e., the aforementioned money and token of respect *(Rashi)*] *be for you* [lit. *'Behold! It is unto you.'*]

כְּסוּת עֵינַיִם לְכֹל אֲשֶׁר אִתָּךְ — *An eye-covering for all who are with you.*

The meaning of the idiomatic phrase *'eye-covering'* is obscure, but as perceived by the commentators it probably implies: *a diversion of attention from you; a prevention against looking contemptuously; a vindication. Hirsch* renders: *blinkers for the eyes.* [See below.] [1]

Rashi interprets: The gifts I showered upon you will serve to put a *'covering over the eyes'* so that none will regard you contemp-

1. The *Talmud* perceives this as a curse of blindness which was fulfilled in Isaac:

Rav Yitzchak said: אַל תְּהִי קִלְלַת הֶדְיוֹט קַלָּה בְעֵינֶיךָ, Let not the curse of an ordinary man be considered a trifling matter in your eyes for when Abimelech [who, although he was a king, was an *ordinary man* in the spiritual sense] cursed Sarah, it was fulfilled in her descendants, as it says, *Behold! Let it be an eye-covering for you,* which means: 'Since you *covered* the truth from me by not disclosing that he is your husband and causing me all of this trouble, may you have children of *covered eyes* [i.e., blind].'

This was actually fulfilled in her offspring, as it is written [27:1]: *When Isaac grew old, his eyesight faded (Bava Kamma* 93a)

... As the *Midrash* renders: *Let there be to you an eye-covering* — i.e. you covered my eyes [by deceiving me], therefore may the child that you will beget be of covered eyes.

יז וַיִּתְפַּלֵּל אַבְרָהָם אֶל־הָאֱלֹהִים וַיִּרְפָּא

tuosly. Had I sent you back empty-handed, however, they might have said: 'After he abused her he sent her back'; but now that I have been forced to expend money and appease you in this fashion they will know that it was against my will, and because of a miracle.

Rashi [further, s.v. וְנֹכָחַת] goes on to explain that according to *Onkelos'* rendering, the verse is interpreted: *It shall be to you a veil of honor for my eyes which had gazed* [lit. *'had power'*] *upon you and all who are with you.* As indicated, however, *Rashi* prefers his interpretation because it better reflects the contextual flow of the verse.

Malbim explains that a damaging rumor must be combatted in two ways: The indiscriminating masses must be shown a dramatic refutation; the more discriminating intelligensia must be given rational proof that the rumor was false. Abimelech told Sarah that the large gifts he had presented to Abraham would serve both functions, for everyone would realize that a king would not be forced to appease commoners so generously unless God had forced him to.

Continuing *Rashbam's* explanation [see above] '... and this dowry-money which I gave you serves to *'cover the eyes'* of those who look contemptously upon you as if you were taken wantonly; instead that dowry money makes it plainly evident that I took you honorably and released you against my will'.

According to *Ramban:* The gift will serve to 'close the eyes' of those who would gaze upon you and all that belongs to you. It will make them fear you; they will *'cover their eyes'* and avert their gazes for they will realize that even the king had to redeem himself for having stretched forth his hand to the prophet's wife.

As *R'Bachya* comments: The *Midrash* interprets כְּסוּת, *covering,* by its other meaning: *'garment'* —

Rav Yehudah bar Ilia explained: [Abimelech said to him]: Make yourself a garment that people may gaze at *it* and not your beauty [i.e., a garment that will divert people's attention from your physical beauty]; Rav Berachiah explains that the text means *a garment for the eyes* [i.e., a veil] which would hide her from the public gaze.

וְאֵת־כֹּל — *And to* [lit. *'with'*] *all,* i.e., and before all the people of the world *(Rashi).* ...

וְנֹכָחַת — [*And*] *you will be vindicated* [lit. *'proven'* i.e., your honor will be clearly proven.]

[*Ibn Ezra* notes that in this case the ו, *and,* is idiomatic and is omitted in the translation, as if it read וְאֵת כֹּל נֹכָחַת].

The word וְנֹכָחַת is obscure and variously interpreted by the commentators. As usual our translation follows *Rashi* who notes that, although there are many Aggadic interpretations, the one best reflecting the context relates the word to the root יכח, *to prove* ...

The flow of the passage, then, according to *Rashi,* is:

The gifts I have given to you will serve to close the eyes of all those who would otherwise have regarded you contempously, וְנֹכָחַת, *and you* will now have the opportunity לְהִתְוַכֵּחַ, *to be proven* [in the sense of *justified, vindicated*] *before all the people of the world* with these already evident facts.

17 *Abraham prayed to God, and God healed*

[Perhaps a better comprehension of the word could be gained by mentally revocalizing the word in second-person fem. imperative: וְנֹכַחַתְּ.]

Onkelos renders this particular phrase וְעַל כָּל מַה=וְאֶת־כֹּל וְנֹכָחַת דַאֲמָרַת אִתּוֹכָחַת, and for everything you have said, *be reproved* [i.e., *rebuked, admonished* (from the Hebrew תּוֹכָחָה).]

Rashbam, however, emphasizes the positive connotation — following *Rashi*'s interpretation — 'for Abimelech said all of these things to *appease* Sarah, not to chide or admonish her'.

Ramban also emphasizes that Abimelech appeased Abraham with money and Sarah with words so he would not be punished on either of their accounts [see *Mizrachi* cited beginning of this verse.] However, according to *Ramban* and *R'Bachya* the phrase וְאֶת־כֹּל וְנֹכָחַת is to be interpreted *and despite all this* [i.e., Abimelech's attempts at appeasement] *she remonstrated* [i.e., she continued arguing with him מִתְוַכַּחַת עִמּוֹ] honorably insisting that she would never forgive him for the flagrant abuse of her modesty. (On the use of the verb יכח, in the sense of *argue,* cf. *Micah* 6:2; *Job* 23:7). Abraham however was appeased and he prayed for the king.

R' Bachya goes on to add a novel interpretation: After having referred to Abraham as אָחִיךְ, *your brother,* Abimelech says that this expression may be regarded by you as a כְּסוּת עֵינַיִם — i.e., a delicate and modest way of referring to him — but henceforth you should be careful to so describe him only *to all who are with you,* your servants and retainers, for they know you are married so no misunderstanding can result. As for אֵת כֹּל, *all* others, וְנוֹכָחַת, *be convinced,* that such a description can lead to disaster and must never again be used (cf. also *Akeidas Yitzchak* and *Abarbanel).*

Hirsch, however, renders: *'And with everyone you can now stand openly'.* I, the king, atoned so publicly and ignominiously, and was forced to be so generous in gaining a reconciliation. This will 'place blinders over the eyes' of anyone who might have been tempted even to glance at you improperly. Henceforth, there will be no need for you to deny your relationship to Abraham.

According to *Ibn Ezra* and *Radak* in *Sefer HaShorashim* s.v. יכח, the three words וְאֵת כֹּל וְנֹכָחַת are not part of Abimelech's statement but are stated by the Torah in third-person as a comment about Sarah. The meaning is: וְאֵת כֹּל, with all that had happened to her because she said to Pharaoh and Abimelech that Abraham was her brother, Sarah was chastened [נוֹכְחָה] and admonished, resolving never again to refer to Abraham as her brother.

17. Abraham magnanimously forgives Abimelech and intercedes on his behalf.

וַיִּתְפַּלֵּל אַבְרָהָם אֶל־הָאֱלֹהִים — *[And] Abraham prayed to God.*

[Although he had returned Sarah and placated Abraham, Abimelech could not be spared from the death penalty, as God warned him in *v.* 7, unless the prophet, Abraham, would pray on his behalf. This was to make it manifest to all that it was

אֱלֹהִים אֶת־אֲבִימֶלֶךְ וְאֶת־אִשְׁתּוֹ
יח וְאַמְהֹתָיו וַיֵּלֵדוּ: כִּי־עָצֹר עָצַר יהוה בְּעַד
כָּל־רֶחֶם לְבֵית אֲבִימֶלֶךְ עַל־דְּבַר שָׂרָה

on Abraham's account that he had been punished.]

This is the first time of Torah that this expression is used [i.e., that we find anyone praying to God on behalf of another *(Rashi)*]. But as soon as Abraham prayed this 'knot' was untied *(Midrash)*.

Midrash HaGadol derives from this to what extent Abraham's magnanimity extended: Let every man be pliable as a reed; easy to pacify and hard to anger. Every man should learn forgiveness from our father Abraham. Although Abimelech committed what is perhaps the gravest of all sins against him by forcibly taking his wife, yet, when Abimelech asked his forgiveness Abraham bore no malice, but did so with a good heart; and moreover he even prayed for mercy on his behalf.[1]

וַיִּרְפָּא אֱלֹהִים אֶת־אֲבִימֶלֶךְ — *And God healed Abimelech, his wife, and his maids.*

[From the plague which had stopped the function of all their bodily orifices as *Rashi* comments in *v.* 9.]

וַיֵּלֵדוּ — *And they were relieved.*

[The verb literally means *'and they bore* (children).' The translation *'brought forth'*; *'relieved'*, is based upon *Rashi* following *Onkelos* (וְאִתְרְוָחוּ), who finds the literal translation *'bore'* difficult since Abimelech, too, is included in this term. Additionally how could it have happened that coincidentally all of them were ready to bear just at that time? (See *Ramban; Mizrachi*; and *Gur Aryeh* further).]

Rashi therefore explains that it means that their orifices [including Abimelech's] were opened [see above] and they were *relieved* [from their intense pain which was akin to that of labor pains] — and they 'brought forth'. This was their *'birth'* [i.e., this is the reason for the figurative expression *'birth'* in the text.]

According to *Ibn Ezra*, the word וַיֵּלֵדוּ is to be interpreted in its literal sense *and they bore*; it applies, however, only to Abimelech's wife and maids.

Ramban explains that a literal interpretation of וַיֵּלֵדוּ, *and they bore* [*children*] would be difficult as it would take into account only

1. Thus, the *Mishnah, Bava Kamma* 92a derives from Abraham's magnanimity in praying for Abimelech, that an injured person who refrains from forgiving an offender who has asked forgiveness, is called cruel.

Maharsha ad. loc. explains that Abraham's forgiving Abimelech was considered an act of compassion and therefore it is noted in *Beitzah* 32b that כָּל הַמְרַחֵם עַל הַבְּרִיּוֹת בְּיָדוּעַ שֶׁהוּא מִזַּרְעוֹ שֶׁל אַבְרָהָם אָבִינוּ, Whoever is merciful to his fellow-men is certainly of the children of our father Abraham.

Additionally, *Tanchuma Yashan* notes that Yom Kippur makes atonement for man's sins against God but not for man's sins against his fellow man until he becomes reconciled with him [see *Mishnah, Yoma* 85b]. The offended party must be compassionately forgiving, for when you have compassion on your neighbor, God has compassion on you. Thus Abraham was compassionate and immediately received his reward, for when Abraham prayed on Abimelech's behalf, his wife was *remembered by HASHEM* [21:1] and bore him a son.

XX 18

Abimelech, his wife, and his maids and they were
relieved; [18] *for HASHEM had completely restrained*
every orfice of the household of Abimelech, because

Abimelech's wives and maids *'whose wombs were restrained'* [next verse]. This interpretation is difficult because there was no time for the women to experience a 'restraining of the womb' since the verses imply that it was in one day that all these events occurred: the dream, the early rising to summon his servants and Abraham, . . .

— He suggests that perhaps the women happened to be in labor just at that time; or perhaps Abraham delayed his prayer and, in the interim, they were unable to give birth. However, none of the above takes *Abimelech's* recovery or illness into account [and it is also unlikely that they all happened to be in a childbirth stage simultaneoulsy on that very day *(Mizrachi*; see next verse).]

Ramban therefore proceeds to cite *Rashi*'s figurative interpretation of וַיֵּלֵדוּ as *bringing forth* in the sense of *relieved,* for indeed the term is so used in such contexts as *Ps.* 7:15: ... *and bring forth* [וְיָלַד] *falsehood; Prov.* 27:1: ... *what a day may bring forth* [יֵלֶד]. This, then, is why *Onkelos,* followed by *Rashi,* rendered it in the figurative sense because he wished to include Abimelech in the word וַיּוֹלֶד. *Ramban,* however, disagrees with the figurative interpration of רֶחֶם, *womb,* as *orifice.* [See next verse.]

Michlol Yofi suggests that the term וַיֵּלֵדוּ, even in its literal sense, *bore,* includes Abimelech in the sense that there was a return of his virility which had been taken from him during Sarah's detainment, and he regained his procreative abilities.

18. כִּי־עָצֹר עָצַר ה׳ בְּעַד כָּל־רֶחֶם לְבֵית אֲבִימֶלֶךְ — *For HASHEM had completely restrained* [lit. *'restrain, He restrained'* the idiomatic form for intensifying the verb by the addition of the infinite absolute] *every orifice* [lit. *'womb'*] *of the household of Abimelech.*

In continuation of *Rashi*'s interpretation of *v.* 17: the term רֶחֶם, *womb,* in this verse refers to the bodily *orifices* of the Philistines which God had closed — including *all* the male and female secretory orifices: the mouth, the nose, the eyes (i.e., tear ducts), the urinary, and semen orifices, etc. — as *Midrashically* noted from the use of the compound form עָצֹר עָצַר *(Bava Kamma* 92a; *Rashi* end of *v.* 9); (see further).

In the preceding verse *Ramban* agrees with *Rashi* that וַיֵּלֵדוּ, [and they bore], is to be rendered figuratively as *brought forth; relieved.* Here, however, he holds that רֶחֶם [figuratively rendered by *Rashi* as *orifices*] must be rendered only in its literal meaning of *womb,* for the word רֶחֶם in Scriptures never refers to any orifice other than the *womb.* Even *Onkelos* upon whom *Rashi* bases his interpretation of וַיֵּלֵדוּ rendered רֶחֶם literally as *womb.* It was only to include Abimelech that he rendered וַיֵּלֵדוּ as וְאִתְרְוָחוּ, *brought forth.* The Sages in *Bava Kamma* 92a who interpret that *all* the orifices were restrained derive this from the compounded use of עָצֹר עָצַר, but nowhere suggest that כָּל רֶחֶם should be interpreted except as *all the wombs.*

The commentators explain *Rashi's* interpretation. They agree that רֶחֶם means *womb,* but explain that our verse uses it generically to include *all* the orifices because:

אֵשֶׁת אַבְרָהָם׃ א וַיהוָה פָּקַד אֶת־
שָׂרָה כַּאֲשֶׁר אָמָר וַיַּעַשׂ יהוָה לְשָׂרָה

— The womb is the most important orifice of the body; although *all* were affected, it is therefore the only one specified *(Mizrachi).*

— Those who suffered the most were the pregnant women, therefore the *womb,* as the primary object of the punishment, is mentioned *(Gur Aryeh).*

Both agree that *Ramban's* literal interpretation of רֶחֶם as *womb* is difficult because it would assume the unlikely fact that all the women in the royal household were pregnant; and because ham's prayer, a patent impossibility if only the *womb* were meant. [Cf. *Maharsha, Bava Kamma* 92a.]

Ramban goes on to explain that [as pointed out the *comm.* to *vs.* 4 and 6] from the day Sarah was brought to Abimelech's house, Abimelech's punishment — which was delicately not mentioned in the Torah — was to be unable to relieve himself. He was, in effect, rendered impotent and unable to *approach her* [*v.* 4], a euphemism for intimacy; and at the same time *the wombs of his wife and maids* who were pregnant *were restrained* and they could not give birth. (The expression עָצַר רֶחֶם or סָגַר רֶחֶם as in *I Sam.* 1:5 denotes inability to *conceive;* while the wording in our verse עָצַר בְּעַד רֶחֶם denotes inability to *deliver a child)* ...

The situation then, as *Ramban* concludes, is that all of this did not occur in one day. Sarah stayed in Abimelech's house for a while and he persisted in detaining her without repenting [although impotent throughout this time] until God spoke to him in the dream. After Abraham prayed for him, Abimelech was cured and his wife and maid-servants gave birth.

According to the *Talmud* the restraining of *all the wombs* [as derived from the word *all*] was so total that even the fowl in his household did not lay their eggs *(Bava Kamma* 92a).

Ha'amek Davar suggests that the Philistines did not realize that this 'closing of the wombs' had anything to do with Sarah. Only after Abraham prayed and they had instant relief did everyone realize that this had come upon them *'because of Sarah, Abraham's wife.'*

עַל־דְּבַר שָׂרָה — *Because of Sarah,* i.e., at Sarah's bidding *(Midrash; Rashi).*

Cf. *Rashi*'s comment to the parallel phrase in 12:17, where עַל דְּבַר שָׂרַי [because of *Sarai*] is interpreted literally: *by the word of* [i.e., *by order of*] *Sarai,* for, as the *Midrash* notes: She said to the angel 'Smite!' and he smote [see *footnote* there]. *Mizrachi* notes that *Rashi*'s interpretaion is based on the wording עַל דְּבַר, lit. *by the word of* instead of עַל אודות, *because of.*

Ibn Ezra [to 12:17] explains the phrase: עַל דְּבַר, 'Because of the injustice they perpetrated against Sarah who was the wife of Abraham.'

Or according to *Akeidas Yitzchak:* Because of the *word* of Sarah, who announced she was Abraham's sister.

אֵשֶׁת אַבְרָהָם — *The wife of Abraham.*

[She is described here as *Abraham's wife* though this is superfluous, to emphasize that the plague had come to Abimelech *because she was Abraham's wife,* and, as the *Midrash* notes to *v.* 5, Sarah had indeed revealed privately *to him* that she was Abraham's wife, but he did not believe her. But cf. *Ha'amek Davar* above.]

XXI of *Sarah, the wife of Abraham.*

1 HASHEM *had remembered Sarah as He had said; and HASHEM did for Sarah as He had spoken.*

XXI

1. The Birth of Isaac.

וַה׳ פָּקַד אֶת־שָׂרָה — [*And*] *HASHEM had remembered* [following *Onkelos;* lit. *appointed; visited; considered; took note*] *Sarah*[1].

— *Had* remembered — before He healed Abimelech *(Rashi).*

[I.e., the *kal* form פָּקַד after the subject suggests the pluperfect tense, as it does in 4:1, וְהָאָדָם יָדַע, *Now the man had known,* and 19:24, וַה׳ הִמְטִיר, *and HASHEM had rained down.* This, in contrast to the usual imperfect form with the conversive ו׳, *vav,* וַיִּפְקֹד שָׂרָה *(Mizrachi).* It thus refers to the statement in the last verse, and accordingly means that God had *already remembered Sarah* when Abimelech and his household were still unrelieved of the plague that had befallen them.]

That this section is in proximity to the preceding one teaches that כָּל הַמְבַקֵּשׁ רַחֲמִים [or: הַמִּתְפַּלֵּל] בְּעַד חֲבֵרוֹ וְהוּא צָרִיךְ לְאוֹתוֹ דָּבָר, הוּא נֶעֱנֶה תְּחִילָּה, 'Whoever prays for mercy on behalf of another when he himself needs that very same thing, he is answered first.' For in the previous section it is said: *And Abraham prayed for Abimelech ... and they brought forth,* and here it says *and God had* [*already*] *remembered Sarah* — even before He healed Abimelech. [I.e., Abraham and Sarah were childless; when Abraham prayed that Abimelech's household be cured of the inability to give birth, he was answered first, for Sarah conceived before anyone in the royal household was enabled to give birth] *(Rashi).*

1. *Midrash Tanchuma* notes that wherever you find the phrase וַה׳, *'And* HASHEM*',* the prepositional prefix ו, *and,* implies a רִבּוּי, *exegetical amplification,* which adds something to the predicate noun, in this case meaning: *HASHEM together with His celestial court.* [See *comm.* to 19:24 וַה׳ הִמְטִיר, *And HASHEM* — He with His celestial court *(Rashi) — caused to rain.*] This teaches that HASHEM sat in judgment and said to the Ministering Angels: 'Is Sarah worthy of bearing a son?' They unanimously agreed that she was, and HASHEM immediately sealed her decree. [That *Rashi* does not cite this interpretation of וַה׳ as implying *'HASHEM together with His celestial court* to our verse although he does cite it in 19:24 (ה׳ הִמְטִיר) is discussed *ad. loc.*]

Another רִבּוּי, *exegetical amplification,* is derived in our verse from the untranslated indefinite article אֶת which has the implied meaning *with*: Had the verse read וַה׳ פָּקַד שָׂרָה, *And HASHEM remembered* [lacking אֶת] *Sarah,* it would imply that only Sarah was remembered; the phrase אֶת־שָׂרָה implies an exegetical amplification: *'With* Sarah — every barren woman in the world was remembered together with Sarah *(Midrash).*

As noted in the *comm.* to 22:20 it was at this time that Milcah, Sarah's sister who had been barren, also conceived. In fact, the *Midrash* notes that on the day Isaac was born many deaf and blind people regained their hearing and sight.

[On the concept of אֶת indicating an exegetical amplification, see bracketed *comm.* to 1:1 on p. 35 beginning 'The Sages ... '. On גַּם, *also,* indicating exegetical amplification, see 20:5.]

ב כַּאֲשֶׁר דִּבֵּר: וַתַּהַר וַתֵּלֶד שָׂרָה לְאַבְרָהָם

The above is drawn from *Bava Kamma* 92a according to which the subject of כַּאֲשֶׁר אָמָר, *as he had said* is not God, but *Abraham,* rendering: *And* HASHEM *had remembered Sarah as he* [i.e., Abraham] *had* [prayed and] *said* on behalf of Abimelech.

According to *R' Bachya* this section is placed near the previous verse [20:18] *for HASHEM had completely restrained the wombs,* in order to emphasize that it is *HASHEM Himself* Who *restrains,* and He Himself Who *remembers,* and none other. It is in this connection that the *Tanchuma* cites *Ezekiel* 17:24 and expounds: *All the trees of the field* — i.e., people in general — *shall know that I, HASHEM, have brought down the high tree* — an allusion to Sennacherib; *have exalted the low tree* — Israel, who make themselves lowly, (cf. *Malachi* 2:9); *have dried up the green tree* — Abimelech; *and have made the dry tree flourish* — an allusion to Sarah.

[Cf. in this connection, *Pirkei d'Rabbi Eliezer*: God has entrusted three 'keys' to no creature, but has retained them in His own hand: the key of rain, the key of resurrection, and the key of childbirth (lit. 'womb'). The latter is derived from our verse: *HASHEM* (i.e., Himself, and no other) *had remembered Sarah.* Similarly, is it written (30:22): *And HASHEM remembered Rachel ... and opened her womb.* (Cf. *Ta'anis* 2b; *Midrash Tehillim* 78:5).]

וַה׳ פָּקַד אֶת שָׂרָה כַּאֲשֶׁר אָמָר ... כַּאֲשֶׁר דִּבֵּר — *And HASHEM had remembered Sarah as He had said; and HASHEM did* [i.e., *now,* following *Hirsch* (as evidenced by the imperfect with *vav* conversive וַיַּעַשׂ rather than וַה׳ עָשָׂה)] *for Sarah as He had spoken.*

— *Remembered Sarah as He had said* by causing her to conceive; *as He had spoken* i.e., to Abraham, by causing her [and no other of Abraham's wives *(Maharshal)*] to give birth [to his heir] *(Pesikta; Rashi; Gur Aryeh).*

Thus, chronologically, *He remembered* refers to the initial conception; while *He did* [וַיַּעַשׂ] refers to childbirth, as the next verse states: *and she conceived and bore (Be'er Mayim Chaim;* cf. *Mizrachi).*

Where do the expressions אֲמִירָה, *saying,* and דִּבּוּר, *speech,* occur in these connections?

— *Saying: And God said, Nonetheless, your wife Sarah will give birth to a son* (17:19); — *Speech: The word* [דְּבַר=*speech*] *of* HASHEM *came to Abram* (15:1), which introduced the Covenant Between the Parts at which time Abraham was promised an heir (15:4). It was that heir which was now brought forth from Sarah *(Rashi).*

[*Ramban,* as interpreted by *Mizrachi* understood *Rashi* to imply that the *meaning* of פָּקַד is *caused to conceive.*] *Ramban* therefore explains that פקד is rather an expression of *remembrance* and הַשְׁגָּחָה, *Providential attention,* to the one being remembered. Cf. its use in 50:25; *Exod.* 3:16; *Judges* 15:1. *'Remembering'* [זְכִירָה] is similarly used in reference to all barren women who later gave birth, as in the case of Rachel [30:22] and Hannah [*I Sam.* 1:19].[1] Also, as evidenced by the statement of the

1. *Rav Yosef Kara* explains why three different descriptions of remembrance are used for Sarah, Rachel, and Hannah. In Sarah's case only the word פְּקִידָה is used because the word also alludes to the menstrual period *(Niddah* 2a), a condition that had been absent from Sarah and which had to be returned. Because Rachel was young and the above condition represented by

2 *Sarah conceived and bore a son unto Abraham in*

Sages [in *Rosh Hashanah* 32b, regarding the Biblical verses cited in the זִכְרוֹנוֹת, 'Remembrances' section of the Rosh Hashanah *Musaf* service: פִּקְדוֹנוֹת הֲרֵי הֵן כְּזִכְרוֹנוֹת, 'Biblical verses containing the term *pikdonos* are equivalent to verses containing the term *zichronos'* — [both referring to Divine Remembrances.

[In fact, it has been advanced that the very reason this chapter was chosen for the Torah reading of the first day of Rosh Hashanah, is because it contains this theme of *remembrance* (זִכְרוֹנוֹת), and because Sarah's *remembrance* took place on Rosh Hashanah. (See *Rosh Hashanah* 11a; *Megillah* 31a).]

Mizrachi, however, explains that *Rashi* had no intention of implying, as *Ramban* inferred, that conception is *the definition* of פקד. *Rashi* agrees that it means *remembrance;* he says merely that God *remembered her* by *enabling her to conceive.*

Abarbanel suggests that the meaning of the verse is: *And* HASHEM *remembered Sarah as He had said* — by giving her offspring; *and* HASHEM *did for Sarah as He had spoken* — in that the child born to her was a son rather than a daughter, and was named Isaac; as He had spoken.

Another interpretation: *And* HASHEM *remembered Sarah* — by giving her a son; *and* HASHEM *did for Sarah as He had spoken* — by restoring her youth and blessing her with milk [i.e., with the capability of nursing in her old age.] According to Rav Yudan, she lacked ovaries which God now fashioned for her [see *comm.* to 11:30 and 17:16] *(Midrash).*

[Of course the term *'remembered'* when said of God is anthropopathic because there is no forgetfulness before Him. See *comm.* to 8:1 *God remembered Noah*; and 19:29: *God remembered Abraham.*] The intent of the expression is that God manifests His Providence as if he remembered to carry out an earlier plan or promise. Since a long span of time has elapsed from the promise until the event, God is spoken of — *in human terms* — as *'remembering',* although such an expression, in absolute terms, is inappropriate to Him.]

2. וַתַּהַר וַתֵּלֶד שָׂרָה — [*And*] *Sarah conceived and bore.*

Since her *conception* has never been mentioned, it is now noted together with the mention of her having given birth. Comp. 4:1 *'and she conceived and bore Cain' (Radak).*

לְאַבְרָהָם — *Unto Abraham.*

The use of *unto* is noted. *Radak* explains that a wife is figuratively like the soil which nurtures a seed until it is ready for harvest. So, too, the husband's seed grows until she 'presents' him with a child.

According to the *Midrash,* however, the *Torah* specifies that Sarah bore this son *to Abraham* in emphatic testimony that this child was Abraham's and no one else's.

פְּקִידָה was still present, only the word זְכִירָה is used (30:22). In Hannah's case, both words [זְכִירָה *(I Sam.* 1:11,19); פְּקִידָה *(ibid.* 2:21)] are used because she gave birth to her first son when she was young and continued to have children even in her old age.

בֵּן לִזְקֻנָיו לַמּוֹעֵד אֲשֶׁר־דִּבֶּר אֹתוֹ
ג אֱלֹהִים: וַיִּקְרָא אַבְרָהָם אֶת־שֶׁם־בְּנוֹ
הַנּוֹלַד־לוֹ אֲשֶׁר־יָלְדָה־לּוֹ שָׂרָה יִצְחָק:

[It may be that the Torah specifies the names of Abraham and Sarah in order to emphasize that a child was born to *Abraham,* not Abram; and to *Sarah,* not Sarai. See *comm.* to 15:5 *(Rabbi Avie Gold).*]

לִזְקֻנָיו — *In* [lit. *'to'*] *his old age.*

This is mentioned not as a chronological note, for we already know that Abraham was old at Isaac's birth, but to emphasize that the event was a special divine favor even to Abraham *(Abarbanel).* For although Sarah had regained her youthfulness [see *comm.* to 18:11,12 and 20:2 s.v. וַיִּשְׁלַח] Abraham had remained unchanged — an old man — yet he fathered a child *(Radak).*

The *Midrash,* homiletically reading זְקוּנָיו, *his old age,* as זיו אִיקוּנָיו, the *luster of his visage* — i.e., physiognomy — notes that the phrase implies that the child's features resembled Abraham's (comp. also *Targum Yonasan).*

Cf. *Bava Metzia* 87a: ... The heathens still scoffed: 'Granted that Sarah could give birth at the age of ninety, but could Abraham beget a child at the age of a hundred?' Immediately Isaac's physiognomy changed and became unmistakingly like Abraham's, whereupon they all cried out: 'Abraham begot Isaac'. [See *comm.* to 25:19.]

The son who is the worthiest heir of his father is, so to speak, the *spiritual image* of his father. Thus the interpretation of the *Midrash* means to indicate the spiritual significance of the physical resemblance *(Harav David Feinstein).*

Hirsch explains זְקֻנִים, *old age,* as the time when a person reflects upon the accomplishments and experiences of his life, and looks forward to passing them on to a child who can take his place and carry his work forward. The son who is best suited to succeed his father is called his בֶּן זְקֻנִים, *the child of his old age,* i.e., the heir to his fund of experience (cf. 44:20).

לַמּוֹעֵד־אֲשֶׁר דִּבֶּר אֹתוֹ אֱלֹהִים — *At the appointed time of which God had spoken.*

I.e., at the appointed time He intended when He said [18:14]: *'At the appointed time I will return to you.'* He (according to *Midrash Tanchuma,* the angel speaking in God's Name) had made a mark on the wall and said to him, 'When the sun's rays come round to this mark next year she will give birth' *(Rashi)* [1]

The translation follows *Rashi,* who, citing *Onkelos,* interprets אֹתוֹ as an accusative after the verb דִּבֶּר, *spoke,* rendering אֲשֶׁר דִּבֶּר אֹתוֹ,

1. According to the most generally accepted chronology, the angels visited Abraham on what would later be Passover and announced that Sarah would bear a son *'at this time next year'* [18:10].

The פְּקִידָה, *remembering,* [according to *Rashi,* her *conceiving*] took place on the following *Rosh Hashanah* [1 Tishrei; 5½ months later]; according to *Tosefta Megillah* Ch. 4 (cf. *Megillah* 31a), this chapter is read in the Synagogue on *Rosh Hashanah* for that reason.

Isaac was born on the following Passover, 7½ months later [that year, according to *Rosh*

XXI his old age, at the appointed time of which God had
3 spoken. ³ Abraham named his son who was born to
him — whom Sarah had borne him — Isaac.

of which He spoke [lit. *'as he had spoken it'*, i.e., as He had intended the מוֹעֵד, *appointed time,* to be. According to *Radak,* אֹתוֹ is equivalent to אִתּוֹ, meaning עִמּוֹ, *with him.* Accordingly he renders: 'at the appointed time that God had spoken *with him.*'

3. וַיִּקְרָא אַבְרָהָם — *[And] Abraham named.*

In compliance with God's command to him [17:19]: *Sarah your wife shall bear you a son and you shall call him Isaac (Radak).*

בְּנוֹ הַנּוֹלַד־לוֹ אֲשֶׁר יָלְדָה־לּוֹ שָׂרָה — *His son who was born to him — whom Sarah had borne him.*

This emphasizes both facts: That a son was born to Abraham, though he was a hundred years old, and that Sarah first became a mother when she was ninety *(Hirsch).*

[The repeated emphasis on *born to 'him'* testifies against the scoffers that the child was born of *Abraham's* seed and of none other (see *comm.* to לִזְקֻנָיו in the previous verse, and *Rashi* to 25:19), and that it was the child of Sarah — that aged woman! She was not merely raising another's child.]

Haamek Davar notes the superfluity in this verse of the phrases הַנּוֹלַד לוֹ, *which was born to him,* and לוֹ, *to him,* which do not appear in 16:15 which tells of the naming of Ishmael. The verse implies at the moment when he named his son, Abraham announced to all that this was *his* child.

יִצְחָק — *Isaac.*

He neither changed the name, nor added to it; for so had he been specifically commanded to name the child *(Ibn Ezra).*

The birth of this child was צְחֹק, *laughter,* for by all the laws of nature, the very possibility that he could be born was laughable. When Abraham called his son יִצְחָק, *Isaac,* these facts were vividly in his mind *(Hirsch;* see his *comm.* to 17:17).

[See *Overview.*]

[*Ramban,* end of 17:17, explains that this name reflected the *rejoicing* of Abraham, for as *R' Bachya* ad loc. explains, this name would not have been given had it commemorated derisive laughter.]

[On *when* Abraham gave him this name, see next verse.]

The *Midrash* homiletically notes that the numerical value of the Hebrew letters of Isaac's name are significant: י, *yod* [= 10] stands for the Ten Commandments [which would be given to his descendants; צ, *tzadi* [= 90] corresponds to Sarah's age of ninety when he was born; ח, *ches,* [= 8] corresponds to the eighth day in which he was circumcised [he was thus the first Jewish child to be circumcised on the prescribed day]; and ק, *kof* [= 100] corresponds to

Hashanah 11a, was a leap year, a second Adar being interpolated], one year after the angels made the announcement (see *comm.* to 18:10; *Rosh Hashanah* 11a. Cf. *Tanchuma Vayera* 14:5: The four 'barren ones' were 'remembered' on *Rosh Hashanah*: Sarah, Rebecca, Rachel and Leah.)

[There are, however, differing versions of the chronology. For further research see *Tosafos Rosh Hashanah* 11a s.v. אֶלָּא; *Maharsha* ad loc.; *Mizrachi; Maharsha* to *Bava Kamma* 92a s.v. כַּאֲשֶׁר אָמַר. (There is also the difficulty that the mark on the wall would await the *sun's* rays the following year, thus indicating that it was a *solar* year that was being reckoned, while the chronologies — reckoning the Hebrew festivals, seem to be following the *lunar* calendar. וצ״ע.]

ד וַיָּמָל אַבְרָהָם אֶת־יִצְחָק בְּנוֹ בֶּן־שְׁמֹנַת
יָמִים כַּאֲשֶׁר צִוָּה אֹתוֹ אֱלֹהִים:
חמישי° ה °וְאַבְרָהָם בֶּן־מְאַת שָׁנָה בְּהִוָּלֶד לוֹ אֵת
ו יִצְחָק בְּנוֹ: וַתֹּאמֶר שָׂרָה צְחֹק עָשָׂה לִי
ז אֱלֹהִים כָּל־הַשֹּׁמֵעַ יִצְחַק־לִי: וַתֹּאמֶר מִי

Abraham's age of one hundred when he was born. [See *comm.* to 17:19.] The name also homiletically signifies: יָצָא חֹק, *Law has gone forth* to the world, a gift was made to the world.

Radal and *Maharzu* explain that חֹק, *Law,* refers to the law of *circumcision on the eighth day,* since Isaac was the first Jewish child to be circumcised on the eighth day; cf. *Tosafos Shabbos* 137b where the *Midrashic* reference to *law* and *gift* are discussed: The liturgical phrase חֹק בִּשְׁאֵרוֹ שָׂם, *He placed a law in his flesh,* is referred to Isaac (cf. *Taz Yoreh De'ah* 265:5); the reference to *gift* is that, with Isaac's birth, all barren women gave birth as well and all sick were healed as noted in the *footnote* to *v.* 1 *(Yafeh Toar).*

4. בֶּן־שְׁמֹנַת יָמִים — *At the age of eight days.*

Abarbanel suggests that the phrase *at the age of eight days* refers not only to the time of circumcision, but also to the time when Abraham named the child. *Ramban* however, [cited by *Abarbanel,* but not in the extant editions of *Ramban*] suggests that Abraham named Isaac *on the very day he was born,* because that name had been commanded by God [17:19], and with the very moment of the child's birth, Abraham was obliged to comply with the command. The circumcision, however, was in its proper time, on the eighth day. [See *Tosefes Brachah.*]

כַּאֲשֶׁר צִוָּה אֹתוֹ אֱלֹהִים — *As God had commanded him.*

In 17:12: *'At the age of eight days every male among you shall be circumcised' (Midrash).*

[And according to *Abarbanel* above, this phrase would refer also to the *naming* of the child Isaac, as *God had commanded him* in 17:19.]

The Sages [in *Kiddushin* 29a] derive from the word אֹתוֹ, *him,* that only the *father* is obliged to circumcise the son, but not the mother, for it is written, *'As God had commanded him'* — him, but not her.

5. וְאַבְרָהָם בֶּן־מְאַת שָׁנָה ... — *And Abraham was a hundred years old when his son Isaac was born to him.*

And yet Abraham circumcised his son, undaunted by tender concern for the infant of his old age *(Sforno).*[1]

1. The *Talmud,* [*Gittin* 57b] notes that the verse [*Ps.* 44:23] כִּי־עָלֶיךָ הֹרַגְנוּ כָל־הַיּוֹם, *for your sake we are killed all the day,* can be applied to circumcision, a commandment that involves danger, and is painful to the infant and father. That is why, according to our custom, the *'Shehechiyanu'* benediction is not made for it, (as in *Responsa Rashba* 245), for that blessing thanks God for having sustained one until he could perform a particular commandment — a blessing that is improper when its performance requires the suffering of another creature. Nevertheless, God's holy people are ready to risk themselves and their children to comply with His will that they circumcise their newborn infants. The commentators liken the father who circumcises his own child to one who brings an offering and sprinkles its blood upon the

XXI
4-7

[4] *Abraham circumcised his son Isaac at the age of*
eight days as God had commanded him. [5] *And*
Abraham was a hundred years old when his son Isaac
was born to him. [6] *Sarah said, 'God has made*
laughter for me; whoever hears will laugh for me.'
[7] *And she said, 'Who is the One Who said to*

6. [Sarah joyfully reflects on the poetical aspect of the moment] ...

צְחֹק עָשָׂה לִי אֱלֹהִים — *God has made laughter for me.*

I.e., joy at an astonishing event *(Rashbam).*[2]

כָּל־הַשֹּׁמֵעַ יִצְחַק־לִי — *Whoever hears will laugh for* [lit. *'to'*] *me.*

I.e., will rejoice for my sake. [The *Midrash* asks: If Sarah was remembered and had cause to rejoice, why should others rejoice with her? What did it matter to them?] The reason for the universal joy was that when Sarah was 'remembered' many barren women were remembered along with her, many sick were healed on that day, many prayers were answered along with hers, and there was much joy [שְׂחוֹק, *laughter*] in the world *(Rashi).*

Will laugh ... filling his mouth with song and [good natured] laughter for the wonder that has been wrought for me *(Ramban).*

— It is also possible that Sarah's intent was that: *'Whoever hears of my childbirth will laugh at me'* in derision at my earlier skeptical laughter when the angel first brought the tidings of his birth [18:12.] *(Abarbanel).*

7. וַתֹּאמֶר מִי מִלֵּל לְאַבְרָהָם — *And she said, 'Who is the One Who said to Abraham ...'.*

This rhetorical question is an exclamatory expression of praise i.e., *who but God could have done this?*

altar, for it is extremely difficult for a father to bring himself to perform a circumcision on his own child.

How much more does this apply to Abraham who finally was given a son in his old age after all hope had been abandoned. Nevertheless he did not perform his son's circumcision through another, but he repressed his compassion and circumcised him himself. All this because a deed is more meritorious if it is performed by oneself instead of through an agent, and so its performance should not appear to be burdensome [See *Rashi; Kiddushin* 41a.]

This, then, is the significance of our verse: *And Abraham circumcised ... as HASHEM had commanded him,* i.e., he *himself* circumcised the child — not through an emissary or agent *(Ksav Sofer).*

2. *Hirsch* to our verse and to 17:17 defines the *Kal,* simple verb, צָחַק as *involuntary laughter* at an obvious absurdity, and the *Piel,* intensive verb, צִחֵק as *derisive mocking* at something patently ridiculous.

At the news that Isaac was to be born, Abraham and Sarah both laughed. When he was born the world laughed. God commanded that the idea of laughter be embodied in his name. Just as the belief and ideals of Abraham and Sarah were considered absurdities by their contemporaries, so too, God did not give them an offspring until an age when there was no rational reason for them even to hope that they could still bear a child.

Isaac, a patriarch of the nation, was given a name that expressed this universal derision, for Judaism will endure the mockery of humanity throughout its history — until the End of Days when all will recognize its grandeur (see *Overview).*

מִלֵּל לְאַבְרָהָם הֵינִיקָה בָנִים שָׂרָה כִּי־
יָלַדְתִּי בֵן לִזְקֻנָיו: וַיִּגְדַּל הַיֶּלֶד וַיִּגָּמַל ח
וַיַּעַשׂ אַבְרָהָם מִשְׁתֶּה גָדוֹל בְּיוֹם הִגָּמֵל

(Sefer Zikkaron) [as in *Isaiah* 41:4: *Who has wrought and done it? ... I, HASHEM; ibid.* 40:26: *And behold who has created these things? (Kessef Mezukak)*]. Sarah exclaimed: *'See Who He is* [*Who said to Abraham that Sarah would suckle children*], and how He keeps His promise! God promises and indeed fulfills *(Rashi; Da'as Zekeinim; Rashbam).*

Ramban notes that the expression ... מִי, *Who* ... , usually appears in Scriptures in a *derogatory* sense as for example [*Judges* 9:28]: *Who* [מִי] *is Abimelech, and who* [מִי] *is Shechem?*; [*I Sam.* 25:10]: *Who* [מִי] *is David, and who* [מִי] *is the son of Jesse?* He therefore suggests that the interpretation is that the possibility that she could become a mother was so remote that *who would ever have said to Abraham* — even to console him — *that Sarah would nurse children?* Even the suggestion would never have occurred to anyone!

The verb מלל suggests *speaking with absolute certainty*, as in *Job* 33:3: *My lips shall utter* [מִלֵּלוּ] *knowledge in clarity;* [*Ps.* 106:2]: *Who can tell* [יְמַלֵּל] *the mighty acts of HASHEM, i.e., Who is* capable of verbalizing with absolute certainty and comprehension God's mighty deeds? In our verse, too, the connotation is: who is it that could have ever said to Abraham *with absolute certainty* that Sarah would nurse children? *(HaRechasim l'Bik'ah; HaKsav V'Hakaballah).*

Rashi homiletically notes that the Torah employs the unusual verb מִלֵּל, *said*, instead of the more common דִּבֵּר. This is an oblique reference to Abraham's begetting a child *at the age of one hundred*, the numerical value of מלל [מ=40; ל=30; ל=30.]

הֵינִיקָה בָנִים שָׂרָה — *Sarah would nurse children?*

According to *Abarbanel*: Although Sarah's *childbearing* had been foretold by God on many occasions, no mention was ever made of a capability to *nurse*. Therefore Sarah exclaimed: 'Who would ever have gone so far as to suggest to Abraham that Sarah would be capable of *nursing* this child born in old age?' — There is no doubt that this act of divine graciousness was wrought in Isaac's honor, so he should not have to nurse from Canaanite women.

Why the plural form *'children'?* — Many had scoffed and alleged that the old couple, Abraham and Sarah, had brought a foundling from the market-place and passed it off as their own child. Therefore, Abraham invited the skeptics to a great banquet and Sarah asked the women to come with their suckling infants. A miracle happened and Sarah nursed *their* children as well as her own! *(Bava Metzia* 87a; *Rashi).*[1]

In the literal sense *children* is in

1. The *Midrash* notes that many matrons brought their children to be nursed from that righteous woman. The Sages said: Whoever came לְשֵׁם שָׁמַיִם, *for the sake of Heaven* [i.e., that

XXI
8

Abraham "Sarah would nurse children?" For I have borne a son in his old age!'
[8] *The child grew and was weaned. Abraham made*

plural because once Sarah was rejuvenated and given the capability to nurse this *one* child, she presumably was given the capability of bearing *others* and nursing them as well *(Radak).*

According to *Midrash HaGadol,* the plural expression *children* teaches that the son given her was equivalent to many sons, in the manner of *I Sam.* 1:8: *'Am I not better to you than ten sons?';* and similarly we derive the same inference from *Joshua* 24:3: *'I multiplied his* (Abraham's) *offspring and gave him Isaac'* — all of which indicates that Isaac was equal to many sons.

For, as *Hirsch* elaborates, Sarah perceived the whole future of a nation in Isaac; through him she felt herself to be the mother of all Abraham's descendants. Thus, it was not only one child whom she nursed — but in nurturing him she was bringing up *sons,* the destiny of the entire nation!

כִּי יָלַדְתִּי בֵן לִזְקֻנָיו — *For I have borne a son in his old age!*

[Following *Rashi*: God promises and indeed fulfills! I have borne a son in Abraham's old age!]

According to *Radak*: No one would have dared suggest it, but God willed it so, and *indeed,* to everyone's surprise, *I have borne him a son in his old age.*

[Or perhaps this is a second part of the incredulous outburst begun in the beginning of the verse, and the כִּי, accordingly, is to be interpreted *'that'*:

'Who would ever have told Abraham that Sarah would nurse children; (and) *that I would have borne him a son in his old age?'*]

8. וַיִּגְדַּל הַיֶּלֶד וַיִּגָּמַל — [*And*] *the child grew and* [*he*] *was weaned,* from his mother's milk — at the age of twenty-four months *(Rashi;* cf. *Gittin* 75b).

There is a minority view in the *Midrash* that *'weaned'* is to be understood figuratively: he attained the age of thirteen, i.e., he was weaned from the *Evil Inclination* for *he grew* to religious majority and responsibility for the performance of the commandments. At that point *he was weaned* from the Evil Inclination as his Good Inclination became dominant. Cf.*Rashi* to 25:27: וַיִּגְדְּלוּ הַנְּעָרִים, *and lads grew,* i.e. they reached adulthood at age thirteen *(Matnas Kehunah; Maharzu).*

וַיַּעַשׂ אַבְרָהָם מִשְׁתֶּה גָדוֹל — [*And*] *Abraham made a great feast.*

It was called *'great'* because the great men of the generation attended: Shem, Eber, and Abimelech *(Tanchuma; Rashi)*

For after Abraham prayed on his behalf, Abimelech became

their child might be imbued with a spirit of righteousness by drinking Sarah's milk] became God-fearing. Rav Acha said: Even one who did not come for the sake of Heaven [but merely to see whether the miracle was really true] was granted dominion in this world. [The verse is homiletically rendered *Sarah nursed* בֹּנִים, *builders* — i.e., ones who were granted dominion to build up the world, as it were]. Yet they did not retain it, for when they remained aloof at Sinai and refused to accept the Torah, that dominion was taken from them.

ט אֶת־יִצְחָק: וַתֵּרֶא שָׂרָה אֶת־בֶּן־הָגָר
הַמִּצְרִית אֲשֶׁר־יָלְדָה לְאַבְרָהָם מְצַחֵק:

righteous and came to participate in Abraham's feast *(Mizrachi).*

[It was presumably at this occasion that Abimelech initiated his request for a treaty with Abraham. See *v.* 22.]

According to the *Midrash,* the feast was called 'great' because the Great One of the Universe attended. [i.e. he approved of the feast and took part in it, as it were.]

According to *Sefer HaYashar* 2:16, Terach and Nachor, Abraham's father and brother, came from Charan with a great entourage to join the festivities, so overjoyed were they that Sarah had borne Abraham a child. They remained with him a while in the land of the Philistines.

מִשְׁתֶּה, *feast,* from שָׁתֹה, *drink,* refers primarily to a *wine*-feast. See on 19:3 *(Sforno).*

בְּיוֹם הִגָּמֵל אֶת־יִצְחָק — *On the day Isaac was weaned.*

The weaning of a child was regarded as a joyous occasion. Similarly, we find that when Samuel was weaned, his mother took him to the Tabernacle at Shilch and offered sacrifices [*I Sam.* 1:23-24] *(Rashbam).*

R' Bachya notes that instead of making a banquet when Isaac was born or circumcised, Abraham delayed the 'great feast' until the weaning, i.e., the day he began his Torah studies. It is not strange that Torah studies should be begun at so early an age, for, as the *Midrash* notes, Abraham was three years old when he recognized God. It is also well-known that paternal love reaches its peak not when a child is born or circumcised, but when he is weaned.

Abarbanel suggests that this banquet was given to publicize the miracle that for all of these two years Sarah's milk had not ceased to flow and that she was provided with sufficiently nutritious milk to continue nursing her child until he was weaned. Therefore it says, *and the child grew,* to emphasize that Sarah was not forced to wean him at an early age because she did not have enough milk. On the contrary! She did not wean him *until he was grown!* This was the miracle that Abraham now publicized. [1]

According to *Tosafos Shabbos* 130a this feast took place at the child's *circumcision,* the passage being homiletically rendered בְּיוֹם ה״ג מָל אֶת בְּנוֹ, *on the eighth day* [ה״ג, 5+3=8] *when he circumcised his son.*

9. אֶת־בֶּן־הָגָר הַמִּצְרִית — *The son of Hagar, the Egyptian.*

From the time of Isaac's birth, Ishmael is never mentioned by name as long as he was in Abraham's house, because dross is never mentioned in the presence of gold. Further, Sarah contemptuously considered Ishmael to be *Hagar's son,* but not Abraham's *(Zohar* 118b).

Sforno explains that Ishmael is entitled the *son of Hagar* because Sarah assumed that his scoffing echoed the attitude of his mother.

1. [Many years later when Isaac was an adult, the Satan used this banquet as an excuse to criticize Abraham as being ungrateful to God. To demonstrate Abraham's total sincerity and devotion to Him, God put Abraham to the test by ordering him to bring his beloved, only son to the slaughter on the *Akeidah.* (See *comm.* to 22:1); cf. *Zohar* 1a.]

XXI a great feast on the day Isaac was weaned.
9 [9] Sarah saw the son of Hagar, the Egyptian, who
had borne to Abraham, mocking. [10] So she said to

[Cf. *Sukkah* 56b: 'The talk of a child in the market-place is either that of his father or his mother.']

מְצַחֵק — *Mocking* [or: *playing; making sport.*]

The verb as it occurs in Scriptures has several connotations. *Rashi,* citing various views in the *Midrash,* comments that the verb denotes the three cardinal sins of idolatry, adultery, and murder; in the root form צחק it denotes *idolatry* with reference to the Golden Calf [*Exod.* 32:6]; and *adultery* with reference to Potiphar's wife [39:17]; in the related root form שחק it refers to *murder* [*II Sam.* 2:14] (*Rashi*).

Further, [citing a differing view in the *Midrash*], *Rashi* infers from Sarah's insistence that Ishmael *not be a co-heir with her son* (*v.* 10) that Ishmael had insisted that he, as the first-born, was entitled to a double portion. Pursuing this quarrel, Ishmael went into the field with Isaac, and while pretending to engage in target practice, aimed his arrows at him. Cf. *Prov.* 26:18-19: *As a madman who casts firebrands and says I am only* מְשַׂחֵק, *jesting.*

Ramban cites the differing sources [*Midrash; Tosefta Sotah* 6:6; (cf. *Rosh Hashanah* 18b)] upon which *Rashi* based his attempt to synthesize ostensibly *opposing* views. The latter interpretation that mocking refers to the quarrel over the inheritance is based upon Rabbi Shimon ben Elazar who said, 'Heaven forbid to suggest that Abraham of whom it was written' [18:19]: *'For I have known him that he will instruct his children and his posterity to keep the way of HASHEM'* would permit idolatry, sexual immorality and murder in his house.

[To *Ramban*'s objection, *Gur Aryeh* replies that Abraham did not condone Ishmael's sins. He surely reprimanded him and assumed that the child would repent. Sarah, however, was more sensitive to Ishmael's *'mocking'* and ordered his expulsion because she prophetically foresaw that Ishmael would continue his evil way.]

Ramban continues: Furthermore, *Rashi's* comment that Ishmael quarreled directly *with Isaac* [and not, as the *Midrash* notes, that he boasted *to others*] would presuppose that the controversy occurred when Isaac was already grown up. But if this were so, Ishmael, who was fourteen years older than Isaac, would have been too big for his mother to carry on her shoulder [see *v.* 14]. Another objection to *Rashi*'s interpretation is the statement of the Sages [*Yalkut Shimoni* 95] that Ishmael was seventeen years old when he left his father's house. Accordingly Isaac was only three at the time — too young to have quarreled about an inheritance with Ishmael.

[*Gur Aryeh* answers that we cannot attempt to understand the ancients by contemporary standards. If she could carry him as a young man of seventeen, she could have carried him just as well were he older. Furthermore, *v.* 14 might simply mean that she carried the *pitcher of water* on her shoulder, not necessarily the boy, or that she 'carried' her son only figuratively, in the sense that she *supported* him.]

[It must also be remembered that it was at the age of three that Abraham recognized God; hence at that age, by ancient standards, Isaac could very well have carried on a dialogue regarding his inheritance.]

Ramban goes on to suggest that

י וַתֹּאמֶר לְאַבְרָהָם גָּרֵשׁ הָאָמָה הַזֹּאת
וְאֶת־בְּנָהּ כִּי לֹא יִירַשׁ בֶּן־הָאָמָה הַזֹּאת
יא עִם־בְּנִי עִם־יִצְחָק: וַיֵּרַע הַדָּבָר מְאֹד
יב בְּעֵינֵי אַבְרָהָם עַל אוֹדֹת בְּנוֹ: וַיֹּאמֶר

this incident occurred on the day of the weaning and Sarah noticed Ishmael *deriding Isaac,* or *jeering at the feast itself.* Sarah resented that the son of a bondwoman should presume to do this, which explains her allusion to him as the *son of Hagar, the Egyptian.*

Cf. *Ralbag:* He mocked at the great feast because he, too, was Abraham's son, yet no feast was made when *he* was weaned!

According to *Ibn Ezra* מְצַחֵק simply means *'playing',* as children usually do, and Sarah was jealous because Ishmael was bigger than her son. [*Be'er Mayim Chaim* explains that *Rashi* did not pursue such an interpretation because it is inconsistent with Sarah's character to ascribe such pettiness to her.]

Kessef Mezukak conjectures, however, that Sarah perceived that this *playing* was too intensive, was unwholesome, and consumed too much time. She feared the effect this would have on Isaac's spiritual development, and she was determined to curtail Ishmael's bad influence.

10. The Expulsion of Ishmael.
The ninth of the Ten Trials, *See footnote* to 12:1. *(Pirkei d'Rabbi Eliezer* 30).

גָּרֵשׁ הָאָמָה הַזֹּאת וְאֶת־בְּנָהּ — *Drive out that* [lit. *'this'*] *slavewoman with her son.*

The slave who mocks his master deserves a much harsher punishment, but I demand only that he not share your inheritance with my son. Moreover, the mother must be driven out as well, for the son would die if he were forced to leave his mother *(Ramban).*

Radak observes that, in any event, Hagar would not stay behind if her child were expelled.

[Note the contemptuous expression בְּנָהּ, *her* son, not בִּנְךָ, *your* son. In the next verse, however, Abraham refers to Ishmael as *his* son. See *comm.* there.]

The term גָּרֵשׁ, *drive out,* implies dismissing, discarding, by which all connection with the home ceases. Thus a divorced woman is called אִשָּׁה גְרוּשָׁה מֵאִישָׁהּ, a woman *driven out* from her husband [*Lev.* 21:7] *(Hirsch)* [1]

כִּי לֹא יִירַשׁ בֶּן־הָאָמָה הַזֹּאת — *For the son of that* [lit. *'this'*] *slavewoman shall not inherit.*

Inasmuch as הַוָּלָד הוֹלֵךְ אַחַר הַפָּגוּם 'a child follows the status of the tainted parent' [in this case his slavewoman mother; for the dictum see *Kiddushin* 66b], he is not entitled to inherit *(Sforno).*

[His quarreling with my son about the inheritance is pointless.

1. Despite the apparent harshness of Sarah's request, it must be understood that it was dictated by the conditions. In order to avoid the influence of Hagar and Ishmael upon the future house of Israel, it was necessary to banish them in such a manner that it was unmistakably clear that they were slaves, not integral parts of the family.

Sarah's repeated reference to הָאָמָה הַזֹּאת, *'this' slavewoman,* indicates the crux of her objection. In principle, the son of a slave could indeed have carried on the Abrahamitic tradition — that had been Sarah's intention in giving Hagar to Abraham. But the unsuitable character of this particular slavewoman made such a course impossible *(Hirsch).*

Abraham, 'Drive out that slavewoman with her son, for the son of that slavewoman shall not inherit with my son, with Isaac!'

11 *The matter greatly distressed Abraham regarding his son,* 12 *so God said to Abraham, 'Be not dis-*

Let him not even *consider* sharing the inheritance! (See *Rashi v.* 9).]

HaKsav V'haKaballah discerns Sarah's intent by noting her use of word יִירַשׁ, *shall inherit,* rather than its synonym יִנְחַל. The subtle difference between the roots ירש and נחל will explain what concerned Sarah. The verb נחל is used when an inheritance is divided among more than one heir as in בְּיוֹם הַנְחִילוֹ אֶת־בָּנָיו, *the day when he will cause his sons to inherit (Deut.* 21:16); and עַל־פִּי הַגּוֹרָל תֵּחָלֵק נַחֲלָתוֹ, *According to the lot will its inheritance be divided (Num.* 26:56). The word ירש, however, indicates an inheritance taken by a single heir as in וְהִנֵּה בֶן־בֵּיתִי יוֹרֵשׁ אֹתִי, *behold, a member of my household inherits me* (15:3). [This expression is also used when a group of people inherits jointly.] Thus, Sarah's use of the words יִירַשׁ indicates what she feared. A division of the inheritance would not have concerned her, but she feared that Ishmael's superior physical prowess and his seniority would enable him to seize the *entire* inheritance for himself.

עִם־בְּנִי עִם־יִצְחָק — *With my son, with Isaac.*

[Why the redundant expression *with my son, with Isaac?* Either one would have sufficed to adequately describe her child. Rather, Sarah alluded to *two reasons* why Isaac, not Ishmael, must be the heir]:

'Since Isaac is *my son* even were he not so worthy, he should be your sole heir. Or, even if someone other than my son had the superlative qualities *of Isaac,* he would deserve to be your heir and Ishmael would not deserve to share the inheritance with him. How unworthy is Ishmael compared with someone who is not only *my son,* but who also posesses the righteousness of *Isaac*! *(Rashi).*

According to *Radak,* she added *with Isaac* to remind Abraham that it was regarding this child that God declared [17:21]: I will establish My covenant *with Isaac* whom Sarah will bear to you.

11. But Abraham finds the matter painful ...

וַיֵּרַע הַדָּבָר מְאֹד בְּעֵינֵי אַבְרָהָם עַל אוֹדֹת בְּנוֹ — *The matter greatly distressed* [lit. *'was very evil in the eyes of'*] *Abraham regarding his son.*

Regarding his son, i.e., because he learned [from this matter] that his son had falled into evil ways [*Sh'mos Rabbah* 1]. The *plain meaning* is that he was distressed because she demanded that he drive him away *(Rashi).*

The commentators explain that *Rashi's plain meaning* does not suffice because if Abraham's distress was caused purely by Sarah's demand, then the phrase *regarding his son* is superfluous since the previous verse makes reference to Sarah's demand *(Mizrachi);* or because he was not yet *bound* to comply with her demand for expulsion.

To the question of why Abraham should

אֱלֹהִים אֶל־אַבְרָהָם אַל־יֵרַע בְּעֵינֶיךָ עַל־
הַנַּעַר וְעַל־אֲמָתֶךָ כֹּל אֲשֶׁר תֹּאמַר אֵלֶיךָ
שָׂרָה שְׁמַע בְּקֹלָהּ כִּי בְיִצְחָק יִקָּרֵא לְךָ

have felt compassion for Ishmael in view of his indulgence in the three cardinal sins, *Gur Aryeh* and *Levush HaOrah* reply that Abraham feared that all opportunities for reproof and repentance would be lost if Ishmael were forced from his father's household.

As *Hirsch* explains: What Sarah noticed had certainly not escaped Abraham. But Abraham must have felt that he dared not allow Ishmael to leave the wholesome influence of his home, for if Hagar had succeeded in corrupting the boy at home, how much worse would he become if he were subjected *only* to her!

According to *Ramban,* the Torah emphasizes in this verse that Abraham's displeasure was not caused by the prospect of casting out his maidservant, but specifically: *on account of his son.* God therefore told him in the following verse that he should not be displeased at all — neither for the son nor for the maidservant. He should rather listen to Sarah's bidding for only through Isaac — and not Ishmael — would his name be carried on.

Cf. *Rambam, Commentary to Mishnah Avos* 5:3 who explains: *On account of his son* — and not on account of Hagar. This emphasizes the extent to which Abraham kept aloof from Hagar, having originally married her only at Sarah's bidding.

... But all things being said and done, Abraham considered Ishmael *his son.* It is for this reason that God directed Abraham to *heed Sarah* in regarding Ishmael as the *'son of the maidservant',* and no longer to regard him as a son, for only in Isaac would his name be carried on. That is why, in *v.* 12, God justified Sarah by referring to him as הַנַּעַר, *'the youth,'* rather than בִּנְךָ, *'your son';* and in *v.* 14 which relates the expulsion of Hagar and Ishmael, Abraham's concession to this concept is alluded to by the fact that Ishmael is referred to as *'the boy'* rather than *'his son' (Or HaChaim).*

Radak, pursuing a trend different from most of the above [except *Ibn Ezra*], suggests that Abraham was displeased because Ishmael, though the son of a maidservant, was nevertheless בְּנוֹ, *his son,* whom he loved as his firstborn, and for whom he had compassion as a father for his children. Moreover, as a son of the righteous Abraham it is only reasonable to assume that Abraham — who brought everyone else close to God — would also raise his own son in the proper manner. For the sake of domestic peace, however, he maintained his silence, but he grieved over the matter until the specific divine directive to comply was given him.

12. [But God comforts Abraham by telling him that Sarah's directive is prophetic and in accordance with His will] ...

On that night God appeared to Abraham and said: 'Abraham, do you not know that Sarah your wife was destined to you from birth? She is your companion and wife of your covenant [i.e., wife of your youth (see *Rashi* to *Malachi* 2:14)]. Sarah is called your *wife* [17:19], but Hagar is only *your handmaid.* Everything that Sarah has spoken is

XXI
12
tressed over the youth or your slavewoman: Whatever Sarah tells you, heed her voice, since through Isaac will offspring be considered yours.

true. Do not be distressed' *(Pirkei d'Rabbi Eliezer* 30).

אַל־יֵרַע בְּעֵינֶיךָ עַל־הַנַּעַר וְעַל־אֲמָתֶךָ — *Be not distressed* [lit. *'let it not be evil in your eyes'*] *over the youth or* [lit. *'and over'*] *your slavewoman.*

From this reply, *Radak* deduces that in his *innermost heart* Abraham also had pangs on account of *this woman* who had served him for so many years and from whom he had begotten a son. In the earlier verse she is not mentioned because it was Ishmael and not Hagar who was the source of the conflict [or Abraham did not mention his pangs on account of *Hagar*'s expulsion out of sensitivity to the feelings of Sarah *(Tosefes Berachah).*] But God, Who knows the innermost thoughts of man, included her as well in His statement.

[See *Ramban, Mizrachi, Gur Aryeh,* and *Levush* to *v.* 11 that Abraham's *primary concern* was for Ishmael.]

כֹּל אֲשֶׁר תֹּאמַר אֵלֶיךָ שָׂרָה שְׁמַע בְּקֹלָהּ — *Whatever* [lit. *'all that'*] *Sarah tells you, heed her voice* — To the voice of the prophetic Spirit within her [comp. 16:2.] From this admonition we may deduce that Abraham's prophetic powers were subordinate to Sarah's *(Sh'mos Rabbah* 1; *Rashi).*

Whatever Sarah tells you — both about demoting Hagar to the status of a handmaid though she bore you a child, and now about expelling her with the boy — hearken to her voice' for so has HASHEM decided (see *Tosefta Sotah* 5; *Torah Sheleimah* 21:69; cf. *footnote* end of 16:5).

... *Heed her voice,* because she is justified in her demand *(Sforno).*

According to *Radak*: 'She is quite right in this matter when she says that *the son of the slavewoman will not inherit together with Isaac ...* '

Ha'amek Davar notes the preposition ב, *beth* — שְׁמַע בְּקֹלָהּ, literally, *listen 'in' her voice,* in contrast to Abraham's earlier obedience to Sarah's request that Hagar be banished where the verse says that Abraham listened לְקוֹל שָׂרָי, *'to' the voice of Sarai* (16:2). He comments that the preposition *'in* her voice' implies that God instructed Abraham to analyze Sarah's *intention* and thereby understand the justice of her demand.

Abraham was told to heed בְּקוֹל, *the voice,* rather than בִּדְבַר, *the word.* True obedience is to the person, regardless of whether or not the listener understands the reason for the command or agrees with it. Abraham was told to rely on Sarah's judgment because, as women do, she had a deeper insight into character than he did *(Hirsch).*

כִּי בְיִצְחָק יִקָּרֵא לְךָ זָרַע — *Since through Isaac will offspring be considered yours* [lit. *'because in Isaac will be called to you seed'*].

[I.e., for it is only through Isaac — and not Ishmael — that you will have achieved continued posterity, for only the righteous Isaac will follow in your footsteps and be considered your genuine offspring and consequently inherit the divine covenant sealed with you.]

... Ishmael, however, will not be

יג זָרַע: וְגַם אֶת־בֶּן־הָאָמָה לְגוֹי אֲשִׂימֶנּוּ כִּי
יד זַרְעֲךָ הוּא: וַיַּשְׁכֵּם אַבְרָהָם | בַּבֹּקֶר וַיִּקַּח־
לֶחֶם וְחֵמַת מַיִם וַיִּתֵּן אֶל־הָגָר שָׂם עַל־
שִׁכְמָהּ וְאֶת־הַיֶּלֶד וַיְשַׁלְּחֶהָ וַתֵּלֶךְ וַתֵּתַע

referred to as *your* child (see *Ramban* to *v.* 11).

For though Ishmael is referred to in *v.* 13 as זַרְעֲךָ הוּא, *your offspring*, that is because he was born of you; he has much of his *material* and *some of his spiritual being* from you. But he cannot be your spiritual heir; he cannot be called 'son of Abraham' *(Hirsch)*.

Whenever I mentioned *your offspring* [for example 12:7; 13:15; 15:18; 17:7-9] I referred only to Isaac, since only he is to be considered your *offspring (Radak)*.

... And it is only through *him* that the promises of this Land will be fulfilled *(Rashbam)*.

For although God called Abraham [17:5]: *'a father of a multitude of nations'*, He was referring only to the nations who followed in Abraham's footsteps. Idol-worshipers are not considered Abraham's children *(Me'am Loez)*. [1]

... For even from Isaac, not all will remain your spiritual heirs: On the best of trees not every fruit ripens, and to assure the purity of the People of God, some of Isaac's seed will be separated as unfit *(Hirsch)*.

13. [Greatness is in store for Ishmael as well] ...

וְגַם אֶת־בֶּן־הָאָמָה לְגוֹי אֲשִׂימֶנּוּ — *But the son of the slavewoman as well will I make into a nation.*

[As I promised Hagar in 16:10, and specifically told you in 17:20.]

Therefore do not fret over him *(Radak)*.

This was repeated to Abraham now to reassure him, for he was afraid that harm might befall Ishmael in the desert *(Ramban)*.

כִּי זַרְעֲךָ הוּא — *For he is your offspring* [lit. *'your seed.'*]

I.e., he indeed issued from you *(Ramban)*, [and because he is your physical descendant, he shall be rewarded with greatness].

Sarah was justified in matters concerning the inheritance *which affected Isaac*. But in other matters where Ishmael alone is concerned and which do not affect Isaac, then he is indeed, your seed *(Ha'amek Davar)*.

14. [Learning that the expulsion of Hagar and Ishmael is God's will, Abraham complies at once] ...

וַיַּשְׁכֵּם אַבְרָהָם בַּבֹּקֶר — *So* [lit. *'and'*]

1. As noted in the *Talmud* [*Nedarim* 31a], although Esau, too, was of Isaac's seed, he was not included among 'Abraham's descendants' as the preposition בְּ, *in*, of the word בְּיִצְחָק, *'in* Isaac' is explained as a partitive preposition indicating only part. Hence the verse is interpreted, *For* בְּיִצְחָק, *in Isaac* [i.e., only a *portion* of Isaac's descendants] *shall be considered your offspring* but not *all* the descendants of Isaac.

[Cf. *comm.* to 17:9 where the above is cited to exclude Ishmael and Esau from the Abrahamitic commandment of circumcision.]

XXI
13-14

13 *But the son of the slavewoman as well will I make into a nation for he is your offspring.'*
14 *So Abraham awoke early in the morning, took bread and a skin of water, and gave them to Hagar. He placed them on her shoulder along with the boy, and sent her off. She departed, and strayed in the*

Abraham awoke early in the morning.

— Eager to obey God's command in spite of his natural reluctance *(Abarbanel).*

It would also thus appear that God's directive came to him in a nocturnal vision *(Ralbag).*

[Cf. *comm.* to similar passages in 19:27 and 22:3.]

וַיִּקַּח־לֶחֶם וְחֵמַת מַיִם וַיִּתֵּן אֶל־הָגָר — *[And he] took bread and a skin of water, and gave* [them] *to Hagar.*

But he did not give him silver or gold because Abraham hated him for having fallen into evil ways *(Rashi* following his primary interpretation in *v.* 11 citing *Sh'mos Rabbah*]).

According to *Rashi's plain* interpretation of *v.* 11 that despite Ishmael's shortcomings Abraham was distressed *at having to banish him,* Abraham did not give them silver or gold because he hoped that the departure would not be permanent; when Sarah's anger would subside he would call them back *(Maharshal;* see *Sifsei Chachomim).*

Ibn Ezra comments that many wonder how the merciful Abraham could have banished them penniless? However, this question is groundless for it was God's command that Abraham obey Sarah and expell them; he therefore, had no right to give them gifts against Sarah's wishes. [*Ramban* interprets similarly]. After Sarah's death, however, he did give gifts to the children of his concubines. It may also be that he did give Hagar money, but the verse has no need to mention it.

Radak and *Ralbag* agree with the *latter* interpretation.

As *Radak* comments: He gave them sufficient provisions for a journey of several days because she could not carry more. He also gave her water because her route, returning to her family in Egypt, would take her through the desert. Undoubtedly, he gave them gold and silver too, even though these are not mentioned, because he would not have sent her and the boy away empty-handed.

According to *Rashbam* the provisions he gave them would have sufficed had they gone straight to the nearest settlement and not strayed along the way.

The translation of חֵמַת מַיִם as *skin of water* follows *Ibn Ezra* who explains that the word חֵמַת refers to a water vessel probably made of leather or wood, as a ceramic bottle would certainly be too fragile for such a journey.

שָׂם עַל־שִׁכְמָהּ וְאֶת־הַיֶּלֶד — *Placed them on her shoulder along with the boy.*

The Hebrew text and the dangling phrase *'along with the boy'* is unclear.

טו בְּמִדְבַּר בְּאֵר שָׁבַע: וַיִּכְלוּ הַמַּיִם מִן־

This translation which attaches שָׂם עַל שִׁכְמָהּ, *'placed on her shoulder,'* to the phrase וְאֶת הַיֶּלֶד, *'along with the boy,'* reflects *Rashi*'s understanding of the verse:

He placed the child, too, on her shoulder, for [though Ishmael was seventeen years old at the time *(Yalkut, Bereishis* 95)] he was unable to walk because Sarah had cast an evil eye upon him, and a fever seized him *(Midrash; Rashi).*[1]

[*Gur Aryeh* in *v.* 9 suggests that this phrase does not necessarily mean that she actually *carried* her seventeen year old sick son upon her shoulder, but that she *supported him* by having him lean on her shoulder (see *Hirsch* below).]

According to *Ramban*, however, only the *bread and skin of water* were placed on her shoulder, but not Ishmael. The phrase וְאֶת הַיֶּלֶד, *and the boy,* reverts to וַיִּתֵּן, *and he gave.* The verse is therefore to be explained: *he gave the bread and water to Hagar and* [he also gave her] *the child.*

Thus, as *Hirsch* explains [in consonance with *Ramban*'s interpretation], the phrase שָׂם עַל שִׁכְמָהּ, *placed on her shoulder,* is parenthetical. That is why the Hebrew does not read וַיָּשֶׂם, that *'he'* placed the provisions on her shoulder. The identity of the one who placed the provisions is insignificant; what matters is the *manner* in which she was sent away: as a slave — and not as the wife of Abraham and the mother of his son. The conditions and purpose of this whole dismissal inexorably demanded this.

[Cf. *Targum Yonasan*: 'Abraham rose up in the morning and took bread and a cruse of water, and gave to Hagar to bear upon her shoulder, and bound it to her loins to signify that she was a servant, and the child, and dismissed her with a letter of divorce (or: manumission).]'

Hirsch goes on to explain that the designation of the seventeen year old Ishmael, as יֶלֶד, *boy,* is not unusual, because Joseph, too, was called יֶלֶד, *boy* [37:30] when he was seventeen. According to the ratio of the average life-span in those days to the present time, a proportion of 120 to 70, a seventeen year old person of that era would be equivalent to a ten year old of today.

Abarbanel suggests that the phrase וְאֶת הַיֶּלֶד, is to be understood: *and upon the boy* [the *'upon'* being implied from the previous phrase], rendering: 'he placed provisions upon her shoulder *and upon the boy's* [shoulder as well].'

וַיְשַׁלְּחֶהָ — *And* [*he*] *sent her off.*

The word is either to be taken literally: *He sent her from his home,* or that he graciously *escorted* her until the outskirts of the city *(Radak; Sforno).*

[On the latter meaning, *escort,* see *Rashi* to 12:20 and 18:16.]

According to *Midrash Sechel Tov,* it has the significance of *and he divorced* [or *freed*] *her* [cf. *Targum Yonasan* above.]

1. According to the Talmud *Bava Metzia* 87a, until the time of Jacob there was no sickness in the world. How then could Ishmael have been ill?

The *Talmud* refers to illness from *natural* causes; Ishmael's illness, however, was the result of Sarah's evil eye; such illness was not included in that dictum *(Da'as Zekeinim* to *v.* 15).

XXI desert of Beer Sheba.
15 [15] When the water of the skin was consumed, she

In any event the term וַיְשַׁלְּחֶהָ *sent her* is milder than Sarah's גָּרֵשׁ *drive out* in *v.* 10 *(Ibn Latif).*

וַתֵּלֶךְ וַתֵּתַע בְּמִדְבַּר בְּאֵר שָׁבַע — [*And*] *she departed and strayed in the desert of Beer Sheba.*

According to *Rashi* [once in the desert and away from Abraham's control *(Zohar Chadash Ruth* 82a), she reverted to the idolatry of her father's house *(Midrash).*

[On the verb וַתֵּתַע indicating *straying* in idolatrous ways, see *comm.* to 20:13 וַיְהִי כַּאֲשֶׁר הִתְעוּ וכו׳.]

Gur Aryeh explains why *Rashi* chose this interpretation rather than the more obvious one that she *strayed* and became lost: Had she not reverted to her evil ways, Abraham's merit surely would have been sufficient for God to guide her through the desert., Because she was not wandering aimlessly, according to this interpretation, why did the water run out? This, *Rashi* explains in the next verse.

Rashbam apparently takes the phrase literally: *she got lost.* That is why she ran short of water [next verse], for had she gone directly to the closest settlement without straying she would have had sufficient water. [But see *Rashi* next verse.]

Ibn Ezra, too, points out that she had been given enough water for the journey from Gerar to Beer Sheba. (See *Karnei Or).*

[But cf. *footnote* to 20:15, according to which Abraham's permanent *residence* during this period was in Beer Sheba. Accordingly, Hagar's straying caused her to roam in the desert of Beer Sheba, apparently not very far from home.]

The first time she was expelled, she found a spring immediately (16:7). Now, although the succeeding verses indicate that water was close by, she was near death before it was shown her. Apparently, she did not deserve to find it easily *(Da'as Soferim;* see *Overview).*

[The place was not named Beer Sheba until the later incident narrated in *v.* 31. As the Torah often does regarding geographical locations, it uses the later name even when describing prior events.]

Beer Sheba is 28 miles southwest of Hebron. It is 25 miles southeast of *Umm et Jarar,* and 58 miles northeast of *Wady Jerur,* the two possible sites for the location of the ancient city of Gerar. In later times Beer Sheba became the southernmost city of Judah [comp. the expression *(I Sam.* 3:20): *'from Dan unto Beer Sheba'.*]

15. וַיִּכְלוּ הַמַּיִם מִן־הַחֵמֶת — *When* [lit. *'and'*] *the water of the skin was consumed.*

[The commentators all agree that Abraham had given them adequate water. They offer different explanations for the subsequent *lack* of water]:

— *Rashi* [who interprets *v.* 14 not that she *got lost,* but that *she reverted to idolatry,* and hence should have had sufficient water to reach the nearest settlement] explains that the water was used up because sick persons [in this case, Ishmael; see *v.* 14] drink much water.

[*Rashi* does not consider the possibility that Abraham gave them insufficient water for the trip. Therefore he comments that the water ran out *due to Ishmael's unusual thirst.* However, the question arises, if Ishmael was obviously so sick that Abraham had to *'place him on her shoulder',* why didn't he provide

הַחֵמֶת וַתַּשְׁלֵךְ אֶת־הַיֶּלֶד תַּחַת אַחַד
טז הַשִּׂיחִם׃ וַתֵּלֶךְ וַתֵּשֶׁב לָהּ מִנֶּגֶד הַרְחֵק
כִּמְטַחֲוֵי קֶשֶׁת כִּי אָמְרָה אַל־אֶרְאֶה
בְּמוֹת הַיָּלֶד וַתֵּשֶׁב מִנֶּגֶד וַתִּשָּׂא אֶת־קֹלָהּ
יז וַתֵּבְךְּ׃ וַיִּשְׁמַע אֱלֹהִים אֶת־קוֹל הַנַּעַר

additional water? — The answer is either that Ishmael's illness became worse and more thirst-provoking during the journey, [*Mizrachi*], or that Abraham mistakenly thought that his illness was not physical but a result of his temporary depression at being forced to leave home *(Gur Aryeh).*]

Rashbam and others explain that the water supply was depleted *because they got lost* [and in the hot desert, water would certainly be consumed faster than food.]

וַתַּשְׁלֵךְ אֶת־הַיֶּלֶד — [*And*] *she cast off the boy.*

[The word *'cast off'* clearly implies that at least at some point she must have been physically *carrying* him.]

According to the *Midrash* [see *Rashi, v.* 14] she had been carrying [or suporting *(Gur Aryeh, ibid.)*] the ill Ishmael *from the time they had left.* Now that the water had run out and the child was dying, she gave up hope and *cast him off.*

[The other commentators, e.g. *Ibn Ezra, Ramban,* etc. who do *not* interpret the phrase וְאֶת הַיֶּלֶד, in *v.* 14 to mean that the boy was originally placed on her shoulder, variously explain the connotation of our passage]:

Ibn Ezra interprets וַתַּשְׁלֵךְ literally as does the *Midrash: she cast off.* He explains that she held him in her lap when he became sick through dehydration. When she perceived that he was dying she *cast him off.*

Ramban does not hold that she had been carrying him at all. He interprets וַתַּשְׁלֵךְ in the figurative sense: *she abandoned* the child, as the word is used in *Ps.* 51:13: אַל־תַּשְׁלִיכֵנִי מִלְּפָנֶיךָ, *'cast me not* [i.e., do not forsake me] *from Your presence.'*

תַּחַת אַחַד הַשִּׂיחִם — *Beneath one of the trees.*

To afford him some shade from the sun *(Akeidas Yitzchak).*

[The translation of שִׂיחִים as *trees* follows *Onkelos* and *Ibn Ezra.* Cf. 2:5: וְכֹל שִׂיחַ הַשָּׂדֶה.]

16. וַתֵּלֶךְ וַתֵּשֶׁב לָהּ מִנֶּגֶד — [*And*] *she went and sat herself down at a distance* [lit. *'opposite'*].

The translation of מִנֶּגֶד, *at a distance,* follows *Rashi* who feels that it fits the context of the verse. The literal *'opposite'*, however, implies *nearness* and accordingly contradicts Hagar's stated reason for casting him off, which was: *'not to see the death of the child'. Rashi,* therefore, apparently takes the prefix מ to be antithetical: she sat מִן נֶגֶד, *from opposite,* i.e., at a distance *(Be'er Mayim Chaim; Sifsei Chachomim).*

הַרְחֵק כִּמְטַחֲוֵי קֶשֶׁת — *Some bowshots away* [lit. *'the distance of bowshots'*.]

I.e., the distance of about two bowshots [the word מְטַחֲוֵי being plural and two being the minimum plural number *(Mizrachi).*] *(Rashi).*

cast off the boy beneath one of the trees. 16 *She went*
and sat herself down at a distance, some bowshots
away, for she said, 'Let me not see the death of the
child.' And she sat at a distance, lifted her voice, and
wept.
17 *God heard the cry of the youth, and an angel of*

The *Midrash* estimates this distance as a *mil* [= 2,000 cubits (see on 6:15).]

Rashi goes on to explain that the root is טחה, a verb implying *shooting arrows,* and which is used in *Sanhedrin* 46a in a related sense. Moreover the introduction of a ו in the *conjugation of the root* טחה [מְטַחֲוֵי *instead of* מְטַחֵי] is quite regular. Comp. חַגְוֵי, *clefts,* in *Song of Songs* 2:14 which is from the root חגא, *breach,* in Isaiah 19:7, and קַצְוֵי, *ends* [*Ps.* from the root קָצֶה.

Hirsch, however, [following *Radak*] differs with this interpretation, explaining that מְטַחֲוֵי [in the form and conjugation of our verse] is a *hapax legomenon* [i.e., a word that does not occur elsewhere]; accordingly its meaning must be drawn from the context of our verse. He explains [as does *Radak*] that grammatically, מְטַחֲוֵי is the active participle of the *pi'el* [intensive] and would therefore seem to mean the *shooter* rather than the *bowshot.* Thus, the passage means that she retreated some distance *after the manner of archers,* i.,e., like archers who walk backwards from a target to the extreme point from which they can still see it, Hagar walked backward from Ishmael to avoid seeing his distress, but remained close enough to observe him ...

כִּי אָמְרָה אַל־אֶרְאֶה בְּמוֹת הַיָּלֶד — *For she said, 'Let me not see the death of the child.'*

Hagar's behavior was disgraceful; it clearly revealed her flawed Hamitic character. A Jewish mother would not have abandoned her child even though her presence would have done no more than provide momentary comfort. For Hagar to leave because *she* could not bear to see his suffering is not compassion but selfishness. She considered not Ishmael, but herself. Therefore, although both Hagar and Ishmael wept, it was only *the cry of the youth* which God heard (*v.* 17). Her self-pitying tears were worthless in God's eyes *(Hirsch).*

וַתֵּשֶׁב מִנֶּגֶד — *And she sat at a distance.*

The repetition indicates that she moved still further away when she realized that he was nearing death *(Rashi).*

וַתִּשָּׂא אֶת־קֹלָהּ וַתֵּבְךְּ — [*And she*] *lifted her voice and wept* [i.e., and wept in a loud voice.]

The Torah emphasizes that she 'threw' away the child in utter despair rather than gently place him down, but like all compassionate women she reviews her plight and is driven to tears *(Minchah Belula).*

17. וַיִּשְׁמַע אֱלֹהִים אֶת־קוֹל הַנַּעַר — [*And*] *God heard the cry* [lit. *'voice'*] *of the youth.* [See *Overview.*]

For though not specifically mentioned, he, too, wept *(Radak).*

Cf. *Pirkei d'Rabbi Eliezer* 30: Ishmael, weakened from thirst,

וַיִּקְרָא מַלְאַךְ אֱלֹהִים | אֶל־הָגָר מִן־
הַשָּׁמַיִם וַיֹּאמֶר לָהּ מַה־לָּךְ הָגָר אַל־
תִּירְאִי כִּי־שָׁמַע אֱלֹהִים אֶל־קוֹל הַנַּעַר
יח בַּאֲשֶׁר הוּא־שָׁם: קוּמִי שְׂאִי אֶת־הַנַּעַר

cried out, 'Master of the Universe, if You plan to grant me water please do so and let me drink now rather than suffer from thirst, for death of thirst is the cruelest of all deaths.' Then God hearkened to his prayer.

[Interestingly, God is here named in His Attribute of strict Justice: *Elohim.* Even in this attribute He was aroused to answer the boy's prayers. God judges a person according to his present state, regardless of past or future wickedness. At that moment, Ishmael deserved compassion even under the Attribute of Justice; (see end of verse בַּאֲשֶׁר הוּא־שָׁם).

[Hagar, too, wept, but the verse specifically states that God answered the voice *of the youth (Sifsei Chachomim)*], the inference is that a sick person's prayer for himself is more readily accepted than the prayer offered by others *(Rashi).*

מִן־הַשָּׁמַיִם — *From heaven* — Indicating that she heard the angel's voice but did not see him as she did at the *Be'er Lachai Ro'i* during her first expulsion from Abraham's house [see 16:13-14] *(Radak).*

[Compare also *comm.* to *from heaven* in 22:11.]

וַיֹּאמֶר לָהּ מַה־לָּךְ הָגָר — *And* [*he*] *said to her, what troubles you, Hagar?* [lit. *'what is unto you, Hagar?'*]

[An obviously rhetorical question, serving as a means of initiating the communication. See *comm.* to 3:9: אַיֶּכָּה, *where are you?*]

בַּאֲשֶׁר הוּא־שָׁם — *In his present state* [lit. *'in which he is there'*].

The translation follows *Rashi* who explains that God told her not to fear because he will be judged *according to his present deeds* and not according to what he would become in the future.

[Cf. *Rosh Hashanah* 16b: A man is judged only for his deeds at the time (of judgment)].

This differs from the case of בֵּן סוֹרֵר וּמוֹרֶה, *stubborn and rebellious son (Deut.* 21:18ff) who according to *Sanhedrin* 72a 'is tried on account of his *ultimate destiny'*, because, although he had not yet committed a capital offense, *in that case* he has already taken up the evil ways that would inexorably lead to the death penalty *(Mizrachi).*

Furthermore, even in the case of a *stubborn and rebellious son,* the human court judges only on the basis of deeds that have actually been done. The value judgment of the severity of the deed, however, is ordained by the Torah. If the Torah decrees that the *son* be put to death even though the transgressions he has actually committed appear to us to be relatively minor, then that judgment should be considered no more incomprehensible than is the death penalty of the desecrator of Sabbath — both are enacted by the Torah. That the Sages tell us what his *ultimate destiny* would be should not be construed to mean that he is executed for events that never happened. Further, the punishments of a human court are ordained by the Torah in order that the sinner leave this life with atonement for his sins so that he be absolved of heavenly punishment *(Gur Aryeh).*

XXI God called to Hagar from heaven and said to her,
18 *'What troubles you, Hagar? Fear not, for God has heeded the cry of the youth in his present state.*
18 Arise, lift up the youth and grasp your hand upon

As *Rashi* continues, the angels remonstrated with God: 'Will You create a well for him whose descendants will one day kill Your children by thirst?'[1]

God said to them: 'But *at the present,* is he righteous or wicked?'

'He is righteous',* they replied.

'Then I will judge him according to his present deeds.' This then, is the meaning of בַּאֲשֶׁר הוּא־שָׁם, *according to his present deeds.*

According to *Ramban,* the *simple meaning* of the verse is: 'God has heard the prayer of the lad *in the place where he was,* and that she need not search elsewhere for water, but that he will be enabled to quench his thirst *in that very place.* שָׁם, therefore has the meaning in our verse as it does in *Judges* 5:27 and *Job* 39:30: where it means *there,* i.e., *in that place.*

Tosefes Brachah elaborates on the *simple meaning* of the verse as given by *Ramban* and cites parallel passages where the word בַּאֲשֶׁר similarly appears as a contraction of בְּמָקוֹם אֲשֶׁר [*'in the place that'*] such as *Ruth* 1:16 בַּאֲשֶׁר תָּלִינִי, אָלִין, *'where* [i.e., בְּמָקוֹם אֲשֶׁר, *'in the place that'*] *you lodge, I will lodge*; similarly in *Judges* 5:27; *I Sam.* 23:13.]

18. קוּמִי שְׂאִי אֶת־הַנַּעַר — *Arise, lift up the youth,* i.e., do not abandon him *(Ibn Caspi).*

**Mizrachi* explains that when the angels referred to Ishmael as *'righteous',* they meant that he was innocent *in terms of their particular accusation,* for he had not yet slain anyone by thirst [see *footnote*], but he was guilty of the several transgressions implied by מְצַחֵק, *mocking,* as *Rashi* explains in *v.* 9. The angels did not cite those transgressions, however, either because the question at hand was whether or not he should be allowed to die of thirst and they therefore cited a transgression concerning thirst, although not yet perpetrated; or possibly this *Midrash* reflects the other view cited by the *Midrash* [see *Rashi* and *Ramban v.* 9] according to which *mocking* does not connote transgression, [but a dispute over the inheritance] and he was indeed righteous at the present time.

According to *Zohar Chadash* [see *Sifsei Chachomim*] they did not cite his current transgression because he was seventeen years old at the time and the Heavenly Court does not punish before the age of twenty [see *footnote* to 17:14]; also, concerning his own transgressions, the angels knew he would ultimately repent [see *comm.* to 25:9.]

Divrei David further suggests that they cited the transgression of his children because they thought that God wanted to save him because of good descendants who would spring forth from him. They therefore said: 'To the contrary! The offspring which will descend from him will kill the Israelites.' Why do You then save him from death by thirst?' (See *Gur Aryeh).*

1. When did Ishmael's descendants kill Israel with thrist?

At the destruction of the First Temple when Nebuchadnezzar carried the Israelites into exile, they were brought near the Arabs [Ishmael's descendants]. The thirsty Israelites begged their captors to lead them to their cousins, descendants of Ishmael who, they thought, would certainly pity them ... They begged for water, and instead the Ishmaelites brought them salted meat and fish, and water-skins inflated with air. Believing that these skins were filled with water, they put them to their mouths, and the air pressure distended their stomachs and killed many of them. *(Rashi; Midrash; Tanchuma Pesikta Rabbasi; Eichah Rabbah* 2:2; cf. *comm.* to *Lam.* 1:19: *I called for my 'lovers' and they deceived me).*

וְהַחֲזִיקִי אֶת־יָדֵךְ בּוֹ כִּי־לְגוֹי גָּדוֹל
יט אֲשִׂימֶנּוּ: וַיִּפְקַח אֱלֹהִים אֶת־עֵינֶיהָ
וַתֵּרֶא בְּאֵר מָיִם וַתֵּלֶךְ וַתְּמַלֵּא אֶת־
כ הַחֵמֶת מַיִם וַתַּשְׁקְ אֶת־הַנָּעַר: וַיְהִי
אֱלֹהִים אֶת־הַנַּעַר וַיִּגְדָּל וַיֵּשֶׁב בַּמִּדְבָּר
כא וַיְהִי רֹבֶה קַשָּׁת: וַיֵּשֶׁב בְּמִדְבַּר פָּארָן

וְהַחֲזִיקִי אֶת־יָדֵךְ בּוֹ — *And grasp your hand upon him.* I.e., soon you will not have to carry him, because his strength will return and he will be able to walk alone; you will merely have to hold his hand. Also inherent in this statement is that *your hand will be strengthened* — i.e., you will receive support — *through him,* for, as the angel explains, *I will make a great nation of him (Ha'amek Davar).*

Along similar lines, *Hirsch* notes that the verse does not read הַחֲזִיקִי בְּיָדוֹ, which would mean 'hold tight to his *hand',* but הַחֲזִיקִי אֶת־יָדֵךְ בּוֹ, i.e., *let your hand keep a firm hold on him.* Support and guide him strongly and firmly, for I have destined him for a great future.

19. וַיִּפְקַח אֱלֹהִים אֶת־עֵינֶיהָ וַתֵּרֶא בְּאֵר מָיִם — *Then God opened her eyes and she perceived* [lit. *'saw'*] *a well of water.*

This does not imply that she was physically blind before then; it means that He now gave her the intelligence and spiritual resources to notice the well which was there [but which her state of anguish did not permit her to see.]

[Cf. *Rashi* to 3:7 where in reference to Adam and Eve he explains that the passage וַתִּפָּקַחְנָה עֵינֵי שְׁנֵיהֶם, *the eyes of both of them were opened,* 'is not to be taken literally, but refers to their eyes being opened with newfound intelligence and awareness.' Cf. also *Targum Yonasan* there: *'And the eyes of both were enlightened* ...']

For as *Ramban* explains in *Moreh Nevuchim* 1:2, 'the verb פקח is used exclusively in the figurative sense of receiving new sources of knowledge, not in that of regaining the sense of sight ... for what was seen previously and what was seen *after* this circumstance were precisely the same.'

According to *Radak,* however, the well might have been obscured by bushes, or been distant from her. God now sharpened her eyesight temporarily so that she saw it. Or possibly there had been no well previously, but God cleft the ground and caused water to spring forth, as in the narrative of Samson. [Cf. *Judges* 15:19: *God split the hollow place ... and water came forth.*]

20. וַיְהִי אֱלֹהִים אֶת־הַנַּעַר — *God was with the youth,* i.e. He caused him to prosper through great deeds *(Radak).*

Although the indefinite article אֶת is grammatically required in this verse, Rabbi Akivah, a student of Nachum of Gamzo who interpreted every אֶת in Scriptures as an exegetical amplification [see footnote to *v.* 1], interpreted the אֶת in our verse similarily: Not only was *God with the lad,* but also with

him, for I will make a great nation of him.'
19 *Then God opened her eyes and she perceived a*
well of water. She went and filled the skin with water
and gave the youth to drink.
20 *God was with the youth and he grew up. He*
dwelt in the desert and became an accomplished
archer. 21 *He lived in the desert of Paran, and his*

all that eventually were his: his donkey drivers, camel drivers, and household; they *all* prospered *(Midrash).*

וַיִּגְדָּל — *And he grew up.*

The translation follows the usual understanding of the word. According to *Radak* the interpretation is: *and he became great,* i.e., with wealth and prosperity.

וַיְהִי רֹבֶה קַשָּׁת — *And [he] became an accomplished archer* [lit. *'an archer, a bowman'.*]

He lived in the wilderness and robbed travelers, as it is written [16:12] *his hand against everyone (Rashi).*

The Torah relates this narrative because Ishmael's children learned their martial skills from him. Through their strength and their skill as bowsmen they extended their sway everywhere *(Radak).*

Rashi explains that the word רֹבֶה is a common noun meaning 'one who shoots arrows with a bow', while קַשָּׁת vocalized as it is with a *pasach* beneath the ק and a *dagesh* in the שׁ [rather than קֶשֶׁת (bow)] indicates that it, too is a common noun, meaning *bowsman,* designating his occupation, just as חַמָּר [from חֲמוֹר, *donkey*] means *donkey-driver;* גַּמָּל [from גָּמָל, *camel*] means *camel-driver;* צַיָּד [from צוּד, *hunt*] means *hunter.*

Thus, our translation follows *Levush's* interpretation of *Rashi,* wherein he explains that both nouns together are to be construed as a hendiadys implying that his skill as a רֹבֶה *archer,* was so accomplished that he was truly worthy of being termed a קַשָּׁת, *skilled bowsman.* Thus the word וַיְהִי, *and he became,* tacitly applies to both words: *he became an archer and became a bowsman.*

According to *Ibn Ezra* and *Radak,* the double nouns are explained as: רֹבֶה (וְ)קַשָּׁת, *an archer* and *bow-maker* [מוֹרֶה הַחִצִּים וְעוֹשֶׂה הַקְּשָׁתוֹת] (see *Radak, Sefer Shorashim).*

According to *Ramban,* however, the term רֹבֶה can refer either to 'an archer' or a 'hurler of stones'. Therefore the term קַשָּׁת qualifies the ambiguous term רֹבֶה by explaining that his expertise as a רֹבֶה was as a *bowman* and not as a hurler of stones, i.e., rendering: *he was a shooter [of arrows] as a bowman.*

The *Targum* renders: 'He became a skillful master of the bow.'

As the *Midrash* notes in alternative interpretation: *while a lad* [רֹבֶה, related to רַבְיָה, *youth*] *he became a* קַשָּׁת, *archer;* or: *he became the master* [רַבָּה] *of archers.*

21. וַיֵּשֶׁב בְּמִדְבַּר פָּארָן — *He lived* [lit. *'settled'*] *in the desert of Paran.*

And while there, according to *Targum Yonasan,* he married a woman by the name of Adisha, and ultimately he divorced her. [Apparently on the advice of his father whom she mistreated many years later when he came to visit. See the footnote to 22:1.]

[On *Paran,* see comm. to 14:6.]

וַתִּקַּח־לוֹ אִמּוֹ אִשָּׁה מֵאֶרֶץ מִצְרָיִם׃
כב °וַיְהִי בָּעֵת הַהִוא וַיֹּאמֶר אֲבִימֶלֶךְ וּפִיכֹל
שַׂר־צְבָאוֹ אֶל־אַבְרָהָם לֵאמֹר אֱלֹהִים
כג עִמְּךָ בְּכֹל אֲשֶׁר־אַתָּה עֹשֶׂה׃ וְעַתָּה
הִשָּׁבְעָה לִּי בֵאלֹהִים הֵנָּה אִם־תִּשְׁקֹר לִי

וַתִּקַּח־לוֹ אִמּוֹ אִשָּׁה — *And his mother took a wife for him.*

[It was usual for parents to seek a wife for their children. Cf. 24:3; 34:4.]

[Ishmael's first, ill-fated marriage had been with a woman taken, apparently, without his mother's consent. Hagar now chose for him a new wife by the name of Fatima from the land of Egypt (see *Targum Yonasan; Pirkei d'Rabbi Eliezer* 30).]

מֵאֶרֶץ מִצְרָיִם — *From the land of Egypt.*

The land of her upbringing, Hagar being identified in 16:1 as an *Egyptian*. [She was Pharaoh's daughter; see comm. there.] This is the intent of the popular proverb: 'Throw a stick into the air and it will come back to its source' [i.e., the earth, from which it was originally cut. This refers to Hagar who, as soon as she was free from the influence of Abraham's home, returned to idolatrous Egypt] *(Rashi).*

22. The Alliance with Abimelech.

וַיְהִי בָּעֵת הַהִוא — *At that time* [lit. *'and it was at that time'*.]

[Perhaps at the feast for Isaac's weaning.]

The time when Isaac was born. Knowing all the miracles which God did for Abraham, Abimelech came to seal a covenant with him *(Rashbam).*

אֲבִימֶלֶךְ — *Abimelech* [king of Gerar, Abimelech being the royal title of all the Philistine kings (see on 20:2.]

פִיכֹל — *Pichol.*

Some maintain that Pichol was actually his name, while others maintain that Pichol was a title descriptive of his military position: the פֶּה, *mouth,* to whom כֹּל, *all,* his troops rendered obedience. Cf. 41:40 *According to your word* [פִּיךָ] *shall all* [כָּל] *my people be ruled (Midrash).*

Radak notes that when Isaac was born Abraham still resided in Gerar, near Abimelech. Therefore it does not say that Abimelech *went* to Abraham, but simply that he *spoke* to Abraham.

[This does not agree with the accepted Rabbinic interpretation (elaborated upon in the footnote to 20:15) according to which Abraham *declined* Abimelech's offer to dwell in Gerar and instead took up residence in Beer Sheva. Although the commentators do not discuss the matter in these verses, it is probable that the feast on the occasion of Isaac's weaning took place in Abraham's home in Beer Sheba; Abimelech attended (*v.* 8) and approached Abraham regarding an alliance. They made the pact there, and Abraham remained and planted an *eshel* after Abimelech departed.]

אֱלֹהִים עִמְּךָ בְּכֹל אֲשֶׁר־אַתָּה עֹשֶׂה — *God is with you in all that you do.*

mother took a wife for him from the land of Egypt.

[22] *At that time, Abimelech and Pichol his general said to Abraham, 'God is with you in all that you do.* [23] *Now swear to me here by God that you*

— As evidened by your departure from the locality of Sodom in safety; your defeat of the kings [chapter 14]; the birth of your child in your old age *(Rashi);* and also by the fact that your wife was saved from two powerful kings [Pharaoh and myself] *(Abarbanel).*

... It is only because God is with you that I fear you and desire a treaty; not because of your wealth or might *(Sforno).*

Abimelech is surely not addressing Abraham as an individual, for nations do not seek treaties of peace with elderly people who may soon die. Abimelech plainly knew that God had promised that an entire nation would descend from Abraham and therefore sought the friendship of the nation's ancestor. Thus understood, בָּעֵת הַהִוא, *at that time,* assumes special significance. It is after the expulsion of Ishmael, Abraham is an old man who may not live long, the future lies with his barely weaned child, and the king of the land comes seeking a treaty with the nation represented by the little boy. — Soon afterward, God commanded Abraham to sacrifice that very child! *(Hirsch).*

23. וְעַתָּה הִשָּׁבְעָה לִּי בֵאלֹהִים — *Now, swear to me here by God.*

I.e., by the most solemn and binding oath *(Malbim).*

For even Abimelech realized that an oath taken by Abraham in the name of God would be the most binding oath possible *(Ha'amek Davar).*

The Hebrew word for *oath,* שְׁבֻעָה, is related to שִׁבְעָה, *seven.* Sabbath, the seventh day of creation, is the eternal symbol of God's continuing connection with the universe as its Creator and Master. Thus, the person who violates an oath, שְׁבֻעָה, calls down upon himself the wrath of God, Who is symbolized by the number seven. Therefore, if someone says, as did Abimelech, 'swear אִם, *if* you do such and such,' he says, in effect, if you carry out this forbidden act, you bring God's wrath upon yourself. Conversely, if someone swears to *do* something, he says 'swear אִם לֹא, *if you do not',* i.e. if you *fail* to carry out your oath, you will suffer God's anger *(Hirsch).*

[*See Ramban* next page.]

הֵנָּה — *Here.*

I.e., in your own home, where there can be no charge of coercion, unlike a treaty made elsewhere *(Malbim).*

[Apparently, this meeting took place in Beer Sheba, Abraham's residence.]

אִם־תִּשְׁקֹר — *That you will not* [lit. *'whether* (or: *if) you will'*] *deal falsely.*

If you will not be ungrateful for the kindness I have shown you by letting you dwell peacefully in my land, and you will not betray my

וְלְנִינִ֖י וּלְנֶכְדִּ֑י כַּחֶ֜סֶד אֲשֶׁר־עָשִׂ֤יתִי עִמְּךָ֙
תַּעֲשֶׂ֣ה עִמָּדִ֔י וְעִם־הָאָ֖רֶץ אֲשֶׁר־גַּ֥רְתָּה
כד־כה
בָּֽהּ׃ וַיֹּ֙אמֶר֙ אַבְרָהָ֔ם אָנֹכִ֖י אִשָּׁבֵֽעַ׃ וְהוֹכִ֥חַ

love and esteem for you which were faultless except for [*v.* 25]: *the well of water which Abimelech's servants took away (Ramban).*

[Although אִם־תִּשְׁקֹר, lit. is *whether you 'will' deal falsely,* we have rendered is in the negative following *Onkelos: that you will not deal falsely.*]

This also follows the rule of *Sforno* and *Heidenheim* to 14:23 s.v. וְאִם אֶקַּח [see *comm.* there] that 'throughout the Torah the word אִם, *if, where it is not followed by a condition,* has the implication of an oath, the meaning being: *will not.* See also *Hirsch* above.

Ramban, however, emphasizes that אם [which he would render literally: *if*] always expresses *doubt* and should not be thought of in any other way [see *Rashi* and *Ramban* to אם in *Lev.* 2:14]. It usually appears in connection with oaths, as in *Deut.* 1:34-35, *I Sam.* 3:14; *Ps.* 89:36; 95:11. Since oaths are given with imprecation, the phrase signifies an *implied consequential phrase,* as if Abimelech were saying: *'Swear to me* [saying: May *God do unto me such and such (II Sam.* 3:35)] *if you will deal falsely with me.'* In this case, and all the parallel verses, the Torah shortens and modifies the expression, not wishing to expressly state the condition implied.

Ibn Ezra observes that this is the only place in Scripture where the verb שקר appears in the *kal* conjugation [תִּשְׁקֹר instead of תְּשַׁקֵּר.]

HaRechasim L'Bikah notes that in the *Kal* conjugation, תִּשְׁקֹר means to *act falsely in deed,* to betray; while in the *Pi'el* conjugation, תְּשַׁקֵּר means to *utter falsehood.* The oath asked of Abraham was not that he never *lie* to Abimelech's offspring, but that he not *deal unfaithfully* with them.

לִי וּלְנִינִי וּלְנֶכְדִּי — *With* [lit. *'to'*] *me, nor with my son nor with my grandson.*

I.e., neither you, your son, nor your grandson, with me, my son and my grandson, I ask you to swear because I know that once you take such an oath you will not deal treacherously with me and your son and grandchildren will respect your oath *(Radak).*

Why did Abimelech request that the oath extend only as far as his grandchildren?

— For so far does a father's compassion for his descendants extend [i.e., one is not apprehensive about what will happen to one's descendants after the third generation] *(Midrash; Rashi).*

According to *Chizkuni,* when Sarah gave birth, the kings of the earth were convinced that God would keep His oath to give Abraham and his descendants the Land, as He had promised [15:18]: *'To your offspring have I given this land from the river of Egypt unto the great river, ...'* Abimelech, therefore, proposed that as a reward for the kindness he had shown Abraham, they undertake a pact that the land would not be wrested from him, his son, or grandson. More than this he could not ask, however, because God had specifically said that in the fourth genera-

XXI *will not deal falsely with me nor with my son nor*
24 *with my grandson. According to the kindness that I*
have done with you, do with me, and with the land in
which you have sojourned.' 24 *And Abraham said, 'I*
will swear.'

tion Abraham's descendants would return to conquer the land [see *comm.* to 15:16.]

It is characteristic that while Abimelech demanded an oath of Abraham, he did not offer nor did Abraham request a reciprocal oath from him. Historically, the word of Abraham's descendants has been good, while the assurances made to them have been broken at will. Abraham and Abimelech both knew the worthlessness of such oaths *(Hirsch).*

כַּחֶסֶד אֲשֶׁר־עָשִׂיתִי עִמְּךָ — *According to the kindness that I have done with you,* i.e., by permitting you to dwell in whatever part of my land you wished [20:15] *(Rashi),* and heaping great honor upon you *(Radak).*

As pointed out above, *Ramban* notes that Abimelech did, indeed, deal kindly with Abraham as evidenced by the fact that Abraham's only complaint concerned the theft of some wells by Abimelech's servants.

תַּעֲשֶׂה עִמָּדִי — *Do with me,* i.e., reciprocate by taking the oath on behalf of your children *(Sforno).*

And when you eventually conquer the land as God promised, do not drive out my descendants but deal with them kindly as I have dealt with you *(Ha'amek Davar).*

וְעִם־הָאָרֶץ — *And with the land,* i.e., with the inhabitants *(Radak).*

As in the passage [45:2]: *and Egypt* [i.e., the inhabitants thereof] *heard (Michlol Yofi).*

24. אָנֹכִי אִשָּׁבֵעַ — *I will swear,* but you must reciprocate *(Radak).* [*Hirsch,* above, differs from this interpretation.]

I will do the kindness of acceding to your request, but your claim of having done kindness to me is not as justified as you imply, for your servants stole my well *(Sforno).*

According to one interpretation in *Or HaChaim,* the emphasis is on *I: 'I* can swear not to harm you, but I cannot bind my offspring.'[1]

According to *Rashbam* in 22:1,

1. The Sages considered it improper for Abraham to enter into a treaty whereby he limited his descendant's rights to the Promised Land. In fact the oath is credited with having prevented the Israelites in the days of Joshua from conquering Jerusalem where the Philistines had settled as *Rashi* and *Radak* note in their *comm.* to *Joshua* 15:63. *Midrash Or Ha'Afeilah* cited in *Torah Sheleimah* 21:126 notes that when these seven sheep died, idolatrous images of them were placed at the entrance of Jerusalem, and when the Jews came to conquer the city, the Philistine inhabitants displayed this representation of Abraham's covenant and prevented the Jews from possessing the city. These were the הַעִוְרִים וְהַפִּסְחִים, *the blind and the lame,* which David ordered removed so the city could be taken *(II Sam.* 5:6-8). [See *footnote to v.* 28.]

See *Radak ibid.* The עִוְרִים, *blind,* represented Isaac [cf. 27:1] — while the פִּסְחִים, *lame,* represented Jacob [cf. 32:32]. These were the נִין וְנֶכֶד, *son and grandson,* to whom Abimelech would apply the oath.

אַבְרָהָם אֶת־אֲבִימֶלֶךְ עַל־אֹדוֹת בְּאֵר
כו הַמַּיִם אֲשֶׁר גָּזְלוּ עַבְדֵי אֲבִימֶלֶךְ: וַיֹּאמֶר
אֲבִימֶלֶךְ לֹא יָדַעְתִּי מִי עָשָׂה אֶת־הַדָּבָר
הַזֶּה וְגַם־אַתָּה לֹא־הִגַּדְתָּ לִּי וְגַם אָנֹכִי
כז לֹא שָׁמַעְתִּי בִּלְתִּי הַיּוֹם: וַיִּקַּח אַבְרָהָם

this alliance by which Abraham covenanted to forego part of the land which had been promised to his descendants was a cause for the *Akeidah* (see *comm.* to 22:1).

It has been suggested that Abraham undertook this oath because he knew that it would be several generations before the Promised Land would come into his descendants' possession *(Da'as Soferim).*

The *Talmud* [*Sotah* 10a] comments that this oath between Abraham and Abimelech remained valid until it was abrogated by Philistine violations in the days of Samson. [Not until Samson's time do we find that the Philistines persecuted Israel although they later became bitter enemies of the Jews. In his time, the Jews were evil, and God gave them into the hands of the Philistines for a period of forty years (see *Judges* 13:1, and *footnote* to *v.* 28.)]

25. וְהוֹכִחַ אַבְרָהָם אֶת־אֲבִימֶלֶךְ — *Then Abraham disputed with Abimelech.*

[Although the peace-loving Abraham agreed to enter into the alliance, he seized the opportunity to state a grievance regarding a disputed well, for, as the *Midrash* notes: 'Reproof leads to peace, for such was the case with Abraham: First, *Abraham reprimanded Abimelech,* then: *the two of them made a treaty.*]

However, the translation *disputed,* follows *Rashi* who explains הוֹכִחַ as meaning וְהִתְוַכַּח, *disputed,* [indicating that they got into a misunderstanding over the matter. Also, *Rashi,* cites this rendering because the more familiar rendering *reprimanded* is difficult in regard to one reprimanding a reigning monarch (see *Gur Aryeh).*]

However, the *Midrash* and most commentators do understand the phrase in its more familiar sense: *And Abraham reprimanded Abimelech.*

עַל־אֹדוֹת בְּאֵר הַמַּיִם אֲשֶׁר גָּזְלוּ עַבְדֵי אֲבִימֶלֶךְ — *Regarding the well of water that Abimelech's servants had seized* [lit. *'robbed'.*]

Although the incident was not mentioned previously, *Sefer HaYashar* and *Pirkei d'Rabbi Eliezer* explain that Abraham's servants had dug a well in the area of Beer Sheba which was on the extreme border of Philistia; but Abimelech's servants came and took the well by force claiming they were the owners [see *Rashi v.* 30.]

As *Radak* elaborates, once the two of them entered into an oath and a treaty, Abraham voiced his claim to the well which Abimelech's servants had stolen from him claiming that it was in Philistine Territory. Although Scripture does not

[25] *Then Abraham disputed with Abimelech*
regarding the well of water that Abimelech's servants
had seized. [26] *But Abimelech said, 'I do not know*
who did this thing; furthermore, you have never told
me, and moreover I myself have heard nothing of it
except for today.'

say so explicitly, it appears that they went to Beer Sheba to inspect the well.

Abraham accordingly rebuked Abimelech for tolerating flagrant violence in his country, and also for harboring such wicked people in his household *(Sforno).*

Abraham did not say 'that Abimelech's servants had seized *from me'*. Instead he made a general statement, for his concern was not a personal one. He uttered his displeasure at the lack of fear of God — that very God by whom Abimelech wished Abraham to take an oath — which allowed such violence to prevail in the land *(Ha'amek Davar).*

26. [Abimelech claims complete ignorance of the entire incident.]

לֹא יָדַעְתִּי מִי עָשָׂה אֶת־הַדָּבָר הַזֶּה — *I do not know who did this thing.*

Even now that you tell me that this act was perpetrated by servants of mine, I have no idea who could have done it, for I would not harbor in my court one who would be suspect of such violence *(Sforno).*

וְגַם־אַתָּה לֹא־הִגַּדְתָּ לִּי — *Furthermore, you* [lit. *'and also, you'*] *have never told me,* so that I could have properly investigated the matter and punished the guilty party *(Ralbag).*

Consequently, you cannot blame me *(Radak).*

וְגַם אָנֹכִי לֹא שָׁמַעְתִּי בִּלְתִּי הַיּוֹם — *And moreover,* [lit. *'and also'*] *I myself have heard nothing of it except for today.*

I.e., I — even in my position as ruler — have heard nothing of the clamor and repercussions of the violence which you claim was perpetrated in my kingdom *(Sforno).*

Ibn Sho'ib suggests that Abimelech responded to Abraham's accusation by saying, *'I do not know who did this thing.'* Further responding to Abraham's insinuation that as king Abimelech should have been aware of everything happening in his kingdom, Abimelech accused Abraham, too, of impropriety in not asking the king to intercede on his behalf. Therefore it is Abraham's fault that Abimelech remained ignorant of it until this very moment.[1]

1. A similar interpretation accounting for seemingly repetitious statements is attributed to *Ma'aseh Hashem* (see *Tzeidah La'Derech*):

Abimelech first said, *'I do not know who did such a thing,'* and then turned to Pichol the general of his troops and accused him, *'You also have never told me,'* [and it is your responsibility to keep me abreast of whatever goes on in the kingdom]. Pichol defended himself saying, *'I, too, have heard nothing until today.'*

צֹאן וּבָקָר וַיִּתֵּן לַאֲבִימֶלֶךְ וַיִּכְרְתוּ
כח שְׁנֵיהֶם בְּרִית׃ וַיַּצֵּב אַבְרָהָם אֶת־שֶׁבַע
כט כִּבְשֹׂת הַצֹּאן לְבַדְּהֶן׃ וַיֹּאמֶר אֲבִימֶלֶךְ
אֶל־אַבְרָהָם מָה הֵנָּה שֶׁבַע כְּבָשֹׂת
ל הָאֵלֶּה אֲשֶׁר הִצַּבְתָּ לְבַדָּנָה׃ וַיֹּאמֶר כִּי
אֶת־שֶׁבַע כְּבָשֹׂת תִּקַּח מִיָּדִי בַּעֲבוּר
תִּהְיֶה־לִּי לְעֵדָה כִּי חָפַרְתִּי אֶת־הַבְּאֵר

27. Having expressed his complaints, Abraham prepares the covenant:

וַיִּקַּח אַבְרָהָם ... וַיִּכְרְתוּ שְׁנֵיהֶם בְּרִית — *So Abraham took ... and the two of them entered into* [lit. *'cut'*] *a covenant.*

This was distinct from the oath they took later [*v.* 31.] This covenant was a mutual covenant of affection *(Ha'amek Davar).*

[On the ancient, classical manner of *'cutting'* a covenant, see *comm.* and *footnote* to 15:9.]

In this case, however, the commentators explain, the ratification of the covenant took the form of an exchange of gifts *(Ralbag).* Abraham wished to be under no obligation for the gifts Abimelech had given him [20:14], so now that he was entering this alliance in equality with him, Abraham made it a point to present gifts to the king *(Akeidas Yitzchak).*

Midrash HaBiur [cited in *Torah Sheleimah* 21:122] notes that slaves and maidservants were not included among the reciprocal gifts which Abraham gave Abimelech, although they had been among Abimelech's earlier gifts to him. This teaches that slaves who have undergone circumcision and maidservants who have undergone ritual immersion, thereby converting to Judaism, may not be given by their Jewish master to a non-Jew.

For, as *Rosh* comments, they had already come under the 'Wings of the Shechinah' and Abraham could not part with them.

28. וַיַּצֵּב אַבְרָהָם אֶת־שֶׁבַע כִּבְשֹׂת הַצֹּאן לְבַדְּהֶן — [*And*] *Abraham set seven ewes of the flock* [lit. *'sheep'*] *by themselves* [i.e., separately.]

The definite article הַצֹּאן, *the* sheep indicates that the reference is to *the flock of sheep* mentioned above *(Sechel Tov).*

I.e., from the gift of sheep and cattle mentioned in the previous verse, Abraham took seven female sheep — שֶׁבַע, *seven,* corresponding to the שְׁבוּעָה, *oath* [see *comm.* to *v.* 23 and *v.* 31] — and set them aside to symbolize the seven/oath significance of the word שֶׁבַע in their alliance *(Radak).*[1]

And according to *Hirsch* he set them aside as special ratification for his legal right of possession of the well [as Abraham explains to Abimelech in *v.* 30.] כְּבָשׂוֹת, *ewes,* the female of the species, were selected for they are the animals upon which the whole future of a flock depends.

XXI
27-30

[27] *So Abraham took sheep and cattle and gave*
them to Abimelech; and the two of them entered in-
toa covenant. [28] *Abraham set seven ewes of the flock*
by themselves, [29] *and Abimelech said to Abraham,*
'What are these seven ewes which you have set by
themselves?'
[30] *And he replied, 'Because you are to take these*
seven ewes from me, that it may serve me as

Midrash HaGadol states that the number seven symbolized the seven Noachide laws which were then in effect. Abraham set them up in permanent testimony [of his sovereignty over the well] just as Jacob and Laban later set up a heap and pillar to act as 'a witness' [see 31:44-52.] These seven sheep served the same function and, whenever one of the sheep would die, Abimelech would replace it with another one so the 'testimony' would remain permanent [see *footnote* to *v.* 24.]

29. אֲשֶׁר הִצַּבְתָּ לְבַדָּנָה — *Which you have set by themselves?*

— You have already given them to me with the cattle, what is the significance of your now setting them apart?

The word לְבַדָּנָה [= לְבַדְּהֶנָּה *(Hoffman)*] is synonymous with לְבַדֶּן, it being usual of Scriptures to end words with the pronominal third-person fem. suffix ןָ, as וַתֹּאמַרְןָ, וַתֵּלַדְןָ, וַתָּבֹאןָ, sometimes written ןָ, other times, נָה, as in וַתֹּאמַרְנָה, וַתָּבֹאנָה, וַתֵּלַדְנָה. *(Sechel Tov).*

30. כִּי אֶת־שֶׁבַע כְּבָשֹׂת תִּקַּח מִיָּדִי — *Because you are to take these seven ewes from me* [lit. *'from my hand'*].

As a token of your acknowledgment of my rights [to the well.] This is similar to the ancient mode of acquisition of property by a symbolic barter effected by removing one's shoe and giving it to the other party [see *comm.* to *Ruth* 4:7] *(Sforno).*

בַּעֲבוּר תִּהְיֶה־לִּי לְעֵדָה — *That it* [lit. *'she'*, i.e., this group of seven sheep] *may serve me as testimony* [lit. *'as*

1. The *Midrash* consistently stresses that God was displeased with this treaty.

God said to Abraham: You gave him seven ewes: As you live, I will delay the joy of your children for seven generations [for the Jews were not able to conquer Eretz Yisrael until seven generations had passed — Abraham, Isaac, Jacob, Levi, Kohath, Amram and Moses]:

You gave him seven ewes: As you live, Abimelech's descendants will slay seven righteous men of your descendants: Hofni, Phineas, Samson, and Saul with his three sons [see *Judges* 16:30; *I Sam.* 4:11; and *ibid.* 31:2,4];

You gave him seven ewes: accordingly your descendants' seven sanctuaries will be destroyed [or: cease to be used]: the Tent of Appointment, the sanctuaries at Gilgal, Nob, Gibeon and Shiloach, as well as the two Temples;

You gave him seven ewes: My ark will therefore be exiled for seven months in Philistine territory [see *I Sam.* 6:1.]

Furthermore, the *Midrash* notes that when the Israelites left Egypt, the Torah mentions that *God did not lead them by the way of the Land of the Philistines* כִּי קָרוֹב הוּא, *for it was near,* [*Exod.* 13:7] [i.e., the alliance with Abimelech was still chronologically 'near'] — his grandson, the third generation covered by the alliance — was still alive then. [For another example of קָרוֹב, *near,* interpreted as chronological 'nearing in time' rather than geographic nearness. See קְרֹבָה in 19:20.]

לא הַזֹּאת: עַל־כֵּן קָרָא לַמָּקוֹם הַהוּא בְּאֵר
לב שָׁבַע כִּי שָׁם נִשְׁבְּעוּ שְׁנֵיהֶם: וַיִּכְרְתוּ
בְרִית בִּבְאֵר שָׁבַע וַיָּקָם אֲבִימֶלֶךְ וּפִיכֹל
שַׂר־צְבָאוֹ וַיָּשֻׁבוּ אֶל־אֶרֶץ פְּלִשְׁתִּים:
לג וַיִּטַּע אֶשֶׁל בִּבְאֵר שָׁבַע וַיִּקְרָא־שָׁם בְּשֵׁם

witness' עֵדָה being the fem. form of עֵד *(Rashi).*]

I.e., that you admit that I dug this well *(Sforno).*

כִּי חָפַרְתִּי אֶת־הַבְּאֵר הַזֹּאת — *That I dug this well.*

Rashi, drawing on the *Midrash* explains that to settle the disputed ownership of the well, it was agreed that the well would belong to whomever the water would rise up for when he approached the well [with his flocks *(Midrash)*]. At the approach of Abraham [with his flocks *(ibid.)*] the water immediately rose up *(Rashi).*

[Thus, in *Rashi*'s interpretation of the events, these seven sheep were those at whose appearance Abraham's rights in the well were clearly settled. He therefore set them aside to present to Abimelech, as testimony to his undisputed ownership.]

[The gift of the sheep was perhaps also meant to demonstrate to Abimelech that the rising of the water was not due to any magical powers possessed by the animals. When they became the king's property, the water no longer rose to meet them *(Harav David Cohen).*]

31. עַל־כֵּן — *Therefore,* i.e., in commemoration of all the foregoing events *(Malbim).*

קָרָא לַמָּקוֹם הַהוּא בְּאֵר שָׁבַע — *That place was called* [lit. *'he called that place'*] *Beer Sheba.*

[Lit. *'well of seven',* or *'well of swearing.'*]

That place alone [i.e., the well *(Akeidas Yitzchak)* or the region in general] was called Beer Sheba at that time; the *city* itself did not receive that name until the days of Isaac [see 26:33] *(Chizkuni).*

The phrase means either that that place came to be called *by others* 'Beer Sheba' in commemoration of what happened there [cf. 11:9; and 16:14], or that Abraham himself gave it that name in order to publicize the oath and establish thereby his undisputed title to the well so it would not again be subject to theft *(Alshich).*

32. וַיִּכְרְתוּ בְרִית בִּבְאֵר שָׁבַע — *Thus,* [lit. *'and'*] *they entered a covenant at Beer Sheba.*

[Since the making of the covenant had already been noted in *v.* 27, this verse would seem to be merely repetitious of that fact. Therefore, following *Ibn Sho'ib* and *Hoffman* the rendering *'thus'* reflects the interpretation of this verse as a summary of the foregoing, as is common in Scriptures. Cf. 15:18.]

According to *Ha'amek Davar,* however, this verse is not a sum-

testimony that I dug this well' [31] *Therefore that place*
was called Beer Sheba because there the two of them
took an oath. [32] *Thus, they entered into a covenant at*
Beer Sheba. Abimelech then arose, with Pichol, his
general, and they returned to the land of the
Philistines.
[33] *He planted an* 'eshel' *in Beer Sheba, and there he*

mary but refers to a *second covenant* into which they entered in order to reinforce their solemn oath.

וַיָּשֻׁבוּ אֶל־אֶרֶץ פְּלִשְׁתִּים — *And they returned to the land of the Philistines.*

I.e., they returned to Gerar, the royal city of the land of the Philistines. Abraham, however, resided in Beer Sheba which was considered part of the valley of Gerar *(Ramban).*

According to *Sforno,* however, Beer Sheba [merely bordered upon but] was not part of Gerar. Hence the term *'returned'* for Abimelech and his entourage had come to Beer Sheba to meet with Abraham who was there to oversee his herds. It was there that the covenant was made.

Radak suggests that Abraham spent a few days there, tending his sheep, planting the *eshel,* etc. [*v.* 33] and then also returned to his permanent residence in Gerar or Philistia.

[The accepted Rabbinic view, however, is that of *Ramban.* See *footnote* to 20:15.]

According to *Ha'amek Davar,* they did not return *directly* to Gerar, but first traversed the land making its citizens aware of the new alliance [which, as noted in the *comm.* to *v.* 24, was honored for many centuries.]

33. וַיִּטַּע אֶשֶׁל בִּבְאֵר שָׁבַע — *He planted an* eshel *in Beer Sheba.*

[The translation *'eshel'* (instead of the familiar rendering *'tamarisk')* preserves the ambiguity allowing for the various differing Rabbinic interpretations]:

[The Talmudic Sages] Rav and Shmuel differ as to the meaning of *eshel.* Rav understands אֶשֶׁל to mean that he planted an *orchard* from which he took fruits to serve to wayfarers, while the other interprets [*figuratively*] that it was an *inn for lodging* in which he maintained a supply of fruit for wayfarers. [According to the latter opinion that it means *'inn'*, how can the verb *planted* be used in that connection?] — We find the term *planted* used in the case of structures, as in *Daniel* 11:45: *He will plant* [in the sense of *'establish'*] *the tents of his palace (Sotah* 10a; *Rashi).*

In *Rashi's* comm. to the *Talmud* ibid., he explains that according to the figurative interpretation the word אֶשֶׁל is perceived as an acrostic of the words אֲכִילָה, eating, שְׁתִיָּה, *drinking,* and לְוָיָה, *escorting* — the three services a host should provide his guests. (See also *Rashi* to *Kesubos* 8b; *Lekach Tov; Midrash Tehillim* 110:1, and *Midrash HaGadol.)*

[There are some who explain the acrostic as being composed of: אֲכִילָה *eating,* שְׁתִיָּה *drinking, and* לִינָה, *lodg-*

לד יְהוָה אֵל עוֹלָם׃ וַיָּגָר אַבְרָהָם בְּאֶרֶץ פְּלִשְׁתִּים יָמִים רַבִּים׃

ing, while *Rabbeinu Chananel* preserves a *Midrashic* reading — not in our edition — of אֲכִילָה *eating,* שְׁכִיבָה, *reclining* (i.e. lodging), and לְוָיָה, *escorting.* The most common reading, however, is the primary אֲכִילָה שְׁתִיָּה לְוָיָה.] [1]

The above three items are the chief 'ingredients' of hospitality, and the last one of them, לְוָיָה, *escorting,* in the most meritorious act of all. For in reward for *escorting* the departing angels [18:16] Abraham was graced with divine revelation regarding Sodom. *(R'Bachya)* .

[Pharaoh, too, was rewarded for providing Abraham with לְוָיָה, *escort.* See *comm.* to 12:20.]

[*R' Bachya* also notes that Masoretically there are only two verses which begin with the word וַיִּטַּע, *and he planted*: our verse, and 2:8: *'And He* (God) *planted a garden in Eden.'* This teaches that whoever seizes onto (the good deed of) bringing guests into one's home (according to the version in *Kad HaKemach*: 'whoever grasps onto *implanting* this trait'), inherits the Garden of Eden.]

According to the *Midrash,* too, the word *eshel* means *orchard* [in the figurative sense], the word אֶשֶׁל homiletically being rearranged to read שְׁאַל, *ask.* That is, Abraham established an inn, [i.e. an 'asking place'] where he would tell wayfarers: 'ask for whatever you desire: fish, grapes, wines, meat, eggs,' etc., and he would readily fulfil their request.

Radak, in *I Sam.* 31:13 explains *eshel* in a *literal* sense as a name of a type of tree, probably an oak tree. In our verse, he explains that Abraham's action of improving the site was a public demonstration of his now undisputed ownership of the well. And in the *Rabbinic* sense it tells how he inculcated in the residents of Beer Sheba that they, too, should greet visitors with every amenity: food, drink, and escort.

[The familiar rendering *tamarisk* is cited by *Michlol Yofi.*]

Akeidas Yitzchak cites the interpretation of *eshel* which all agree means in the literal sense *tree* or *orchard* [*Rashi*'s primary interpretation from *Sotah* 10a; see *Maharsha* there]. He explains however, that the mere planting of an orchard would certainly not have been recorded in the Torah were it not that Abraham's purpose was spiritual, i.e. to feed wayfarers and bring them close to him for spiritual nourishment as well, as the verse proceeds to inform us: *And there he proclaimed* the name of *HASHEM, God of the Universe.* Therefore the word *eshel* is interpreted in its figurative sense as well.

וַיִּקְרָא־שָׁם בְּשֵׁם ה׳ אֵל עוֹלָם — *And there he proclaimed* [lit. *'called in'*] *the Name of HASHEM, God of the Universe.*

Onkelos renders: *And he prayed there* [i.e. called upon in prayer.]

As in *Ps.* 30:9 *to You, HASHEM I call,* i.e. pray *(R' Bachya).*

1. The story is told of a man who offered generous hospitality to guests. His home was destroyed by fire and people wondered why so kind a person should have been punished so. *Vilna Gaon* explained that the host's hospitality was incomplete for he omitted the לְוָיָה, *escorting,* aspect of *eshel.* He was left with only אֲכִילָה, *food,* and שְׁתִיָּה, *drink,* the initials of which form the word אֵשׁ, *fire*!

XXI
34

proclaimed the Name of HASHEM, God of the Universe. [34] *And Abraham sojourned in the land of the Philistines many years.*

According to the *Talmud* [*Sotah* 10a] followed by *Rashi* to our verse, [the word is taken in the literal sense: *call, proclaim*]: Read not וַיִּקְרָא, *he called*, but in the causitive וַיַּקְרִיא, *he caused others to call*, for through that *eshel* the Name of the Holy One, Blessed be He came to be called *'God of the entire Universe'* [or *Rashi* may be *rendered:* through that *eshel* the Name of the Holy One Blessed be He, God of the Universe came to be uttered] by every passerby. 'For after guests ate and drank at that *eshel*, they would get up to bless Abraham for his generosity. But he would say to them, 'Bless God of Whose possessions you have eaten! Do you then think that you have eaten of what is *mine?* — you have eaten from His Who spoke and the world came into being!'

[Cf. 12:8 where a similar passage is rendered: *'and he invoked HASHEM by Name'*; see also on 13:4.]

The rendering of אֵל עוֹלָם as *God of the Universe* follows the implication of the *Talmud* above and *Onkelos*.

It also agrees with one of the interpretations of *Ramban* who elaborates that it signifies that Abraham proclaimed the secret of God's leadership of the entire universe which is by His Name HASHEM as the Mighty One in strength [הַחֲסִין בְּכֹח] Who is Supreme [אֱילוּת] over all others.

[The Name אֵל עוֹלָם is unusual and does not appear again. A similar form, however, appears in *Isaiah* 40:28 where He is called אֱלֹהֵי עוֹלָם.]

In his primary interpretation, however, *Ramban* prefers to render this phrase as *HASHEM*, the *God of Eternity* [or *Eternal God*]: portraying Him as the *God Who directs time*, for as *Rambam* explains in *Moreh Nevuchim* [2:13; see also 3:29] this alludes to God as the First Cause, Who is Eternal and existed before the creation of time; the world He created, however, is not eternal but was created within the limitations of time [see *comm.* to *Bereishis*, 1:1.] (Cf. *Sforno)*.

34. וַיָּגָר אַבְרָהָם בְּאֶרֶץ פְּלִשְׁתִּים — *And Abraham sojourned in the land of the Philistines.*

[Apparently in Beer Sheba which was considered part of the Philistine kingdom because as it was on their border *(comm.* to *v.* 32; *comm.* to *v.* 25; and *footnote* to *v.* 14.]

Now that Abraham had concluded his treaty with Abimelech, he remained there for he feared no man. We see, too, that the land of the Philistines is one of plenty as evidenced by the fact that the Shunnamite dwelt there for a period of seven years because of a famine in Eretz Yisrael [*II Kings* 8:1] *(Radak)*.

[However, even notwithstanding this alliance, the verse does not read וַיֵּשֶׁב אַבְרָהָם *and Abraham settled*, usually implying *permanent residence*. Rather the term used is וַיָּגָר, *sojourned*, i.e., as a גֵּר, *alien*. For as *Rashi* points out in his *comm.* to 15:13, the years Abraham

°וַיְהִי אַחַר הַדְּבָרִים הָאֵלֶּה וְהָאֱלֹהִים נִסָּה אֶת־אַבְרָהָם וַיֹּאמֶר אֵלָיו אַבְרָהָם

sojourned in the land of the Philistines since the birth of Isaac were reckoned as part of the 400 years his descendants were to be *'strangers in a land not theirs' (ibid.).*]

[There are, incidentally, exceptional instances where even וַיֵּשֶׁב, *settled,* is interpreted as connoting only a *temporary stay.* See, for example, *Rashi* to 22:19: וַיֵּשֶׁב אַבְרָהָם בִּבְאֵר שָׁבַע.]

יָמִים רַבִּים — *Many years* [lit. *'many days'*].

I.e., longer than the preceding days in Hebron. For in Hebron he spent twenty-five years* and here he stayed twenty-six years. That this excess in Philistia is only one year is evident from the verse itself, for the rule is that לֹא בָא הַכָּתוּב לִסְתּוֹם אֶלָּא לְפָרֵשׁ, 'Scripture does not come to conceal but to explain', [i.e., the Torah does not intend a passage to be obscure, but to instruct' (see *Rashi* to 10:25)]. Thus, if the phrase יָמִים רַבִּים, *many days,* were meant to indicate a period of at least *two* years longer than the preceding period in Hebron, then the Torah would have explicitly given the length of its duration [for the term *'many days'* is too vague to convey this information]. Therefore we must assume that only one year longer — the minimum meaningful period — is meant. After this period, Abraham returned to Hebron [with the 25 year old Isaac], where he spent the next twelve years *(Rashi)* [since Isaac was 37 at the time of the *Akeidah* according to *Seder Olam.* During these twelve years he commuted between his *eshel* in Beer Sheba and his wife in Hebron].

*The calculation of twenty-five years in Hebron is supplied by *Rashi*: Abraham was 75 years old when he left Charan [12:4], and the first place we find him settling was the Plains of Mamre [13:18]. Previously on his way to Hebron, he was merely a transient wherever he went as clearly noted by the phrases וַיַּעֲבֹר אַבְרָהָם, *and Abraham passed* [12:6], וַיַּעְתֵּק, *and he removed* [*ibid.* 8], etc. Even in Egypt he spent but three months before *he continued his journeys* [13:3] and finally *settled* [וַיֵּשֶׁב] *in the plains of Mamre* [*ibid.* 18] where he made his permanent home until Sodom was overthrown when he was ninety-nine. [The angels came to him on the third day after his circumcision.] Thereafter he left the area out of shame for Lot's doings [20:1] and sojourned in the land of the Philistines. Thus [including part of Abraham's seventy-fifth year] 25 years elapsed from the year Abraham settled in Hebron until he came to the land of the Philistines.

XXII

1. The Tenth Trial: The Akeidah (See *footnote* to 12:1).

'This section constitutes the very reason for Israel's existence in God's eyes. It has therefore become part of our daily prayers and accordingly warrants a more penetrating study than other sections' *(Abarbanel).* It is dealt with extensively in the *Overview.*]

וַיְהִי אַחַר הַדְּבָרִים הָאֵלֶּה — *And it happened after these things.*

[The phrase always denotes a close connection with the preceding. (See

XXII
1

And it happened after these things that God tested Abraham and said to him, 'Abraham,' and he

comm. to 15:1). In the case of our chapter, however, the opening phrase cannot refer to the preceding incidents because, according to *Rashi*'s chronology (which follows *Seder Olam)* a period of twelve years elapsed between Abraham's treaty with Abimelech and the *Akeidah. Rashi,* therefore draws on two Aggados which relate events that occurred immediately prior to the *Akeidah,* and which are viewed by the Sages as precipitating the test that follows *(Mizrachi)*]:

Some of our Sages explain that this event occurred *after the words* of Satan [דְּבָרִים, *things,* also means *'words'*] who accused Abraham [to God] saying: 'Of all Abraham's banquets he did not offer a single sacrifice to You! ... '

God answered, ' ... He prepared it all for his son's sake yet if I were to bid him: "Sacrifice your son to Me," he would not refuse.' [Therefore, *immediately after these words God tested Abraham.*] ...

[Apparently Satan delayed the test until Isaac was mature, accomplished, and fully grown. Then, unless Abraham's dedication were absolutely total, he would have found it impossible to sacrifice Isaac.]

Others say that it means: *After the words* of Ishmael who boasted to Isaac that he — Ishmael — had *willingly* allowed himself to be circumcised at the age of thirteen [when he was old enough to have resisted; see *comm.* to 16:17 and 17:25; whereas Isaac was circumcised as an infant (21:4) and could not protest. By this taunt, as the *Midrash* further notes, Ishmael was indicating that he was dearer to God than Isaac.] Isaac retorted: 'You intimidate me by boasting about [your sacrifice of] one part of your body? If God were to tell me to sacrifice myself [i.e., offer my *whole* being for slaughter although I am now thirty-seven years old*] I would not refuse!' [Therefore, as our verse relates, *immediately after these words,* i.e. the sort of words which would precipitate such a test, God put Abraham to the test.] *(Rashi* — bracketed additions are from *Sanhedrin* 89b and *Yalkut).*[1]

*[That Isaac's age was thirty-seven at the *Akeidah* is derived as follows: Sarah was ninety years old at his birth, and 127 years at her death. Since Sarah died when she heard that her son had been taken to be slaughtered (see *comm.* to 23:2), it follows that Isaac was thirty-seven years old at the time.]

[The above is the accepted chronology, based on *Seder Olam.* There are, however, other opinions according to which Isaac was 26 years old at the *Akeidah.* (See *Tosafos Yevamos* 61b; glosses of *Vilna Gaon* to *Seder Olam; Tzemach David; Seder HaDoros).* According to this view, Rebeccah was fourteen years old when Isaac married her at the age of forty (see *comm.* to 25:20) rather than the accepted Rabbinic view that she was three years old.]

1. [According to *Rashi*'s alternate *Midrashic* interpretation, how could Ishmael have been present to taunt Isaac immediately preceding the *Akeidah*? He had been sent away with his mother, many years previous! Where are we told that he returned to his father?]

— *Pirkei d'Rabbi Eliezer* chapter 29 and *Sefer HaYashar* relate that Abraham missed Ishmael greatly and, after several years, went to visit him.

He arrived at Ishmael's tent and found Ishmael's wife sitting with her children. Abraham asked about his son and she told him that he had gone with his mother to fetch fruit. Abraham asked for some water and bread. She refused and took no further notice of him, not even ask-

According to *Rashbam,* the phrase *after these things,* refers to the events of the preceding chapter: Abraham's unauthorized treaty with Abimelech angered God because the Land had been promised to Abraham's descendants [See on 21:23] whom God would later command, through Moses and Joshua, to show no mercy to the residents of the Land, contrary to Abraham's treaty. In fact, the descendants of Abimelech used the treaty to thwart Israel's conquest of the Land. [See *II Sam.* 5:8 and *Rashi* there. See also *comm.* to 21:17.] Therefore God *aggrieved* him [rendering נִסָּה as *aggrieved*] with so distressing a trial as if to say: 'You became haughty because I gave you a son, and you went so far as to make a treaty between your descendants and theirs. Now sacrifice that son and see what value your treaty will have!'

Or HaChaim interprets *after these things* — i.e., *after all that Abraham endured* until he was finally blessed with a child in his old age. He had raised Isaac who, as God assured him would be considered his only 'seed' — and now God tells him to sacrifice that son! Without hesitancy, Abraham complied. Additionally, in the literal sense, the verse implies: *After the preceding events* [which included Ishmael's expulsion]. Before that, God could not have referred to Isaac as *your only son.*

Ha'amek Davar, interpreting הַדְּבָרִים with both its meanings — *things* and *words* — explains the phrase: *After all the preceding events and dialogues between God and Abraham enumerated above,* in the course of which God had raised him to great heights. Now, He subjected him to the *Akeidah* by which Abraham and his descendants attained the pinnacle of greatness. The *Midrash* renders נִסָּה in the sense of *elevated,* like a נֵס, *banner,* which flies high above a ship [See also *Numb.* 21:8.] Hence the phrase is rendered: And God *exalted* Abraham [through the *Akeidah*] ... trial upon trial, greatness after greatness, in order to try the righteous and exalt them in the world like a ship's ensign [נֵס] flying aloft (based on the *Midrasic* exposition of *Ps.* 40:6). Nothing higher could be achieved and after these events God never addressed him again for there was no higher purpose for which he could possibly be elevated.

וְהָאֱלֹהִים — *That God* [lit. *and The God*], the *same* God Who had revealed Himself to Abraham and had given him Isaac as the culmination of his life's aim *(Hirsch).*

God, the just; through His Name *Elohim* — the Attribute of His divine Justice *(Or HaChaim).*

נִסָּה אֶת אַבְרָהָם — *Tested Abraham*
This was the tenth trial [see on 12:1] but it is the only one of the ten that is specifically described in the Torah as a test. That is because God actually required Abraham to carry the other nine to completion, while this was not meant to be more than a נִסָּיוֹן, *test;* God never intended that Isaac actually be slaughtered *(Abarbanel).*

☙ The Concept of Trial

[The concept of נִסָּיוֹן, *Trial,* has broad *hashkafah* implications and the reader is directed to the *Overview* for a fuller discussion. In the following, only several major points will be mentioned]:

ing who he was. She then went into her tent and Abraham heard her beating her children and cursing her husband.

'When your husband returns home,' Abraham told her, 'tell him: "An old man from Canaan came to see you. He said to tell you to change the threshold of your house for it is not good".

When Ishmael returned home and heard what happened, he understood his father's allusion and divorced his wife.

Three years later, Abraham repeated the journey and again did not find Ishmael at home, His new wife, however, asked Abraham to dismount and refresh himself in the tent. Abraham declined, asking only for water. She brought him water and bread and urged him to partake of

There are philosophical difficulties in the concept of God's submitting persons to trial. God certainly does not require this in order to convince *Himself* of a man's sincerity, for He foresees everything. Nothing is unknown to Him, yet this foreknowledge does not *compel* man to act in any manner; man acts of his own free will *(Ran).*

The greatest commentators since medieval times have grappled with the question of how the principle of free choice can be reconciled with God's prior knowledge of all events. If God knows beforehand what a person will do, how can he be free to choose an opposite course?

Malbim points out that the difficulty is more apparent than real. Just as we do not and cannot have any conception of God's essence, so too, we can have no conception of His intelligence. Therefore, what is an obvious contradiction in terms of human intelligence would not be so if we could understand His intelligence.

He adds that according to the Kabbalists, while God knows all, He judges, rewards, and punishes human beings only in terms of human existence. Thus, while in a higher realm of knowledge He is aware of what people will do, this does not affect His dealings with men. Only in terms of their exercise of free will and the quality of their deeds are they rewarded or punished.

Rambam [*Moreh Nevuchim* 3:24] discusses the concept of *Trial* and explains that the act was intended to demonstrate *to the world* how properly to obey God's Will. Hence the sole object of the trials mentioned in the Torah is to teach man what is expected of him, hence the performance of the trial is not the desired end, but an example for our instruction. Hence the word: לָדַעַת *'to know whether you love,'* in *Deut.* 13:4 does not imply that God was forced to submit Israel to a trial in order to know whether the nation truly loved Him. Rather the word has the same connotation as in *Exod.* 31:13: *to know (*לָדַעַת*) that I am HASHEM Who sanctifies you,* i.e., that what God already knows should become so obvious that even all the nations shall know ... [cf. *Rashi* to *Exod.* 20:17].

Rambam continues that the *Akeidah* narrative includes two great principles of our faith. First, it portrays the extent of fear of God: ... At the age of one hundred, Abraham finally is rewarded with a child who, he is promised, will become father of a great nation. How intensely he must have had his hopes on Isaac! Yet as soon as he is commanded to slaughter him, he sets aside all considerations and undertakes to comply with God's command not out of *fear* that God would punish him but because it is man's *duty* to love and fear God ... That is why the angel told him [*v.* 12]: *For now I know,* i.e., your action proves that you truly deserve to be called a God-fearing man, and all people shall learn from you the extent of the fear of God. This was accomplished because Abraham was commanded to perform an act that surpasses any other sacrifice of property or life and belongs to the class of actions which are believed to be contrary to human feelings.

The second purpose was to demonstrate by Abraham's example how a prophet must unquestioningly confirm the principles of the truth of prophecy — regardless of how difficult the commandment is to perform. His compliance with the command to slaughter his beloved Isaac would have been impossible were he not to believe in the truths of the vision he perceived.

Abarbanel adds that a third purpose was to display unequivocally that there

it, showering him with hospitality. He blessed his son for having chosen so considerate a mate. Again Abraham left a cryptic message for Ishmael, but this time it was warm and laudatory. When Ishmael returned home, his heart rejoiced that his father still had compassion for him, and that his new wife had found favor in Abraham's eyes.

It is further related that from that time on, knowing that his father would favorably receive him, Ishmael repeatedly visited Abraham; apparently he was there when God commanded Abraham regarding the *Akeidah*.

ב וַיֹּאמֶר הִנֵּנִי: וַיֹּאמֶר קַח־נָא אֶת־בִּנְךָ

is a firm belief in הַשְׁאָרַת הַנֶּפֶשׁ, the eternity of the soul, and its spiritual reward. Without such a belief, Abraham could not have undertaken to slaughter his heir leaving himself bereft on This World. Believing in the Hereafter, however, he would recognize that whatever the implications of his deed in this existence, they would be only transitory.

[Note that according to the *literal flow of the narrative* of Scripture, Abraham had never seen Ishmael again after having expelled him many years previous. This made the test of sacrificing Isaac all the more challenging for, as a practical matter, Isaac was the only 'son' he had left. This, of course, does not take account of *Pirkei d'Rabbi Eliezer* cited in the footnote below nor does it take into account the *Midrash* cited by *Rashi* in *v.* 2 according to which Ishmael was very much in Abraham's mind, for in the dialogue following God's command to take his *'only'* son, Abraham expressed doubt as to which of his sons God was referring to.]

Akeidas Yitzchak elaborates on *Rambam*'s primary interpretation that God wished to demonstrate Abraham's righteousness *to the world* [although, as *Ibn Ezra* notes, not even Abraham's servants were to be present at the actual slaughter!], by explaining that since the events were recorded in the Torah it is as if every Jew, past, present, and future, witnessed the trial. Anyone who has ever read Scripture's account of the *Akeidah* could not fail to recognize the awesome nature of the trial and the extraordinary extent of Abraham's faith. His belief in God has become indelibly inscribed in all who learned of his deed.

Ramban explains the concept of *trial* as follows:

Since man has full charge over his own actions, the concept of נִסָּיוֹן, *trial,* refers to the perspective of the person who is being tested. To God who knows all, the outcome is not in doubt. Nevertheless, He imposes the trial in order to translate into actuality the latent potential of the person being tested [מֵהַכֹּחַ אֶל הַפּוֹעַל] so that he can be rewarded for the actual *deed,* not only for the good intention ... Know further that God tries only the righteous who He knows will comply with his will. Desiring to demonstrate his righteousness, God confronts him with a trial. He does not, however, try the wicked who would not do his will. Thus, all trials described in the Torah are for the benefit of the one being tested.

Cf. the *Midrash:*

HASHEM examines [or *tests*] *the righteous ones* [*Ps.* 11:5] ... A potter does not examine defective vessels [i.e. demonstrate their strength to a potential buyer] because he cannot give them a single blow without breaking them. What then does he examine? Only the sound vessels, for even many blows will not break them ... Rav Elazar said: When a man has two cows, one strong and the other feeble, upon which does he put the yoke? — Surely upon the strong one! Similarly God tests none but the righteous. [See also *comm.* to ArtScroll edition of *Ps.* 11:5, and *Overview* there.][1]

וַיֹּאמֶר אֵלָיו אַבְרָהָם — *And [He] said to him, 'Abraham!'*

Malbim notes that in other verses, a name is repeated, as for example in the subsequent call [*v.* 11]: *Abraham, Abraham; Jacob, Jacob* [46:2] The *Midrash* explains that repetition of a name indicates affection and haste, i.e., that God's addressing someone *by name* is a sign

1. [The question of why this is referred to as *Abraham's* trial, when in reality it was *Isaac* who submitted to this martyrdom, and also the question of why the *akeidah* ('binding') was chosen as the most significant aspect of this trial, are treated in the Overview.]

replied, 'Here I am.'
2 *2 And He said, 'Please take your son, your only*

love; His *repeating* the name indicates urgency. Here, the name was not repeated because God did not wish to throw Abraham into a frenzy, for fear, as the *Midrash* explains elsewhere [see *Rashi* to next verse and *comm.* to *v.* 4], that skeptics might assert that Abraham was so overcome by God's repetitive call of urgency that his decision to slaughter Isaac was not a lucid one.

הִנֵּנִי — *Here I am.*

Such is the answer of the pious, the expression denoting both humility and readiness *(Rashi).*

2. קַח־נָא — *Please take.*

נָא being primarily an expression of entreaty *(Rashi).*

[Although in other cases *Rashi* interprets נָא as *now* (cf. 12:11; 19:2) here he interprets it in its primary meaning denoting *'please'* because he wishes to avoid the implication that God *caused* him to panic. Rather, everything about God's command was expressed mildly and with the utmost delicacy. At the same time, the very fact that it was given to Abraham in the form of a Divine supplication denotes the importance that God attached to this, the most decisive of the Ten Trials.]

Rashi continues: God said, 'I beseech you: Stand firm for Me in this [your most difficult] trial, so that people will not say that your vindication in the earlier trials was without substance.

The *Talmud* [*Sanhedrin* 89b] compares this to a king who was confronted with many wars which he won by the aid of a great warrior. Subsequently he was faced with the severest of battles. The king said to that warrior: 'Please assist me in this decisive battle, so that people will not say that your previous victories were in vain'.

Additionally, the mildness of the request was itself part of the test. Sensing that this was not a harshly worded absolute command, Abraham might have been encouraged to beseech God to rescind it, especially since God had repeatedly promised him that his seed would descend from Isaac who was to be the link with the future destiny upon which God's promises to Abraham were based. Thus, Abraham's undertaking to sacrifice that son is perhaps among the profoundest personal experiences recorded. In addition to offering his son, it involved giving up the objectives toward which his life had been focused, for they had revolved around Isaac and the mission to preach that God loves goodness and abhors human sacrifice. Yet, true to his faithfulness, Abraham unquestioningly complied although the command was worded in a mild, supplicating manner *(Rav Saadiah Gaon; Akeidas Yitzchak).*

Abarbanel likewise notes that קַח נָא may be interpreted either as a plea: *please take,* as above, or as *take now,* the connotation being: *Now* is the appropriate time to perform the mission of taking your son and offering him as a sacrifice.

Or HaChaim similarly explains: *take now,* i.e., immediately, part of the test being that he not request additional time, unlike the daughter of יִפְתָּח, *Jephtah* who when her father wished to sacrifice her as an offering requested a two-month delay [*Judges* 11:37].

The *Zohar* adds that *'take'* does not mean 'take forcibly' since

אֶת־יְחִידְךָ אֲשֶׁר־אָהַבְתָּ אֶת־יִצְחָק וְלֶךְ־
לְךָ אֶל־אֶרֶץ הַמֹּרִיָּה וְהַעֲלֵהוּ שָׁם לְעֹלָה

Abraham was too old to do so [and Isaac was thirty-seven at the time!] Rather, it has the same sense as *take Aaron and Elazar his son* [*Num.* 20:25], which means: Persuade them by your words and lead them to do the will of God.[1]

[Cf. similar explanation of *take* in 2:15; 12:5; 17:23.]

קַח נָא אֶת בִּנְךָ — *Please take your son.*

— 'But I have *two* sons,' Abraham said. [Which should I take?]

אֶת יְחִידְךָ, *'Your only one,'* God answered.

'But each of them is the *only one* of his mother,' said Abraham.

אֲשֶׁר אָהַבְתָּ, *'Whom you love,'* God answered.

'But I love them both,' Abraham said.

אֶת יִצְחָק, 'I am referring to *Isaac*,' God replied ... *(Sanhedrin* 89b; *Rashi).*

Why did God not simply reveal this to him originally, [i.e., why not simply say 'Take Isaac'?] rather than engage in this dialogue?

First, to avoid shocking Abraham with the sudden command that he sacrifice his beloved Isaac lest he be accused of complying only in a state of disoriented confusion. Also the slow unfolding of the offering's identity was intended to make *the command** more precious to him by arousing his curiosity and to reward him for complying with each and every word of the command. *(Rashi*; see also similar explanations in 12:2 s.v. אֶל הָאָרֶץ, and further at end of this verse).

*[The wording in the *Midrash* is כְּדֵי לְחַבְּבוֹ בְּעֵינָיו, to make him (Isaac) more precious in his (Abraham's) eyes (apparently by stressing that he was the *'only'* and *'beloved'* son)] [1]

Ramban adds that God referred to Isaac as the *'only'* son because he was the son of Sarah, and because Abraham's name would be carried forth only through him.

וְלֶךְ־לְךָ — *And get yourself* [lit. *go to you*, or *go for yourself*.]

[Cf. *Rashi's comm.* on 12:1 to the same expression. Possibly here, too, the expression לְךָ indicates that God's intent is *go for your benefit and for your good*, since, as *Ramban* explains above, all trials are for the benefit of the one being tested.]

1. The Sages likewise commented that Abraham spent that entire night persuading Sarah. He could not bring himself to let her know of the plan, for he was afraid she would thwart it. On the other hand, he was afraid she would die of grief if he were to take Isaac without telling her. He therefore asked her to prepare a banquet during which he engaged her in conversation and told her that he recognized God when he was but three years old, yet Isaac was already an adult and not yet fully trained in God's commandments.

'There is a place not far from here,' Abraham told Sarah, 'where youths are educated. I will take him there and have him educated' [see *v.* 19]. Sarah cautiously consented and prepared provisions for the way, giving Abraham extensive instructions regarding the care of their son. She then gave Isaac one of the beautiful garments Abimelech had given her.

Sarah kissed her son and bade him farewell, praying that she live to see him again. The entire household wept at the touching scene, which lasted until sleep overtook them.

This is one of the reasons that Abraham *awoke early in the morning,* — planning to leave before Sarah awoke, lest she change her mind and not consent to let them go. *(Tanchuma Yashan; Midrash HaGadol; Sefer HaYashar; Yalkut Shimoni;* cf. *Or HaChaim).*

one, whom you love — Isaac — and get yourself to the Land of Moriah; bring him up there as an offering

It is noteworthy that the rare expression לֶךְ־לְךָ, *get yourself* is used here and in 12:1. These two separations have much in common: They indicate his two most important departures — there from his parents, denoting his break from his past; and here from his future, his son *(Abarbanel).*

אֶל־אֶרֶץ הַמֹּרִיָּה — *To the land of* [the] *Moriah,* i.e., Jerusalem; cf. *II Chron.* 3:1: *To build the House of* HASHEM *at Jerusalem, on Mount Moriah.*

The Sages explained that it was so named because הוֹרָאָה, *teaching,* went forth from it to the world. *Onkelos* renders it לְאַרְעָא פּוּלְחָנָא, *to the land of Divine Service.* Apparently he takes the word *Moriah* as derived from מוֹר, *myrrh,* nard, which along with other spices was offered in the Temple as incense *(Rashi).*

Ramban notes that the above interpretation [that the word *Moriah* alludes to the Temple Mount in Jerusalem although there was no Temple in Abraham's time] would suggest that the name Moriah, already in use in those days, was prophetically given. Or that God implied: *Get yourself to the Land which will be called Moriah in the future.* Furthermore, *Ramban* states that *Onkelos'* rendering, *land of worship,* is not derived from the *myrrh of the incense* as *Rashi* conjectures. Rather the intent of *Onkelos* is: to the land *in which they will worship God,* deriving the word, *Moriah,* as the Sages did, from the word מוֹרָא, *fear,* for in that land the people feared God and served Him.

[It should be remembered that Moriah was in the area of Jerusalem *(Shalem)* where Malchizedek (Shem son of Noah) maintained a Torah Academy.]

Ramban continues that in the literal sense the verse means: *Get yourself to the land where myrrh grows abundantly.* See *Song of Songs* 4:6 [ArtScroll *Shir HaShirim* p. 133.] From the verse in *Chronicles* cited above it would seem that originally the Temple Mount alone was called Moriah, and the adjacent territory received its name from the mountain. Hence in the literal sense our verse would mean: *Get yourself to the land of,* i.e., the land which contains, [mount of] *the Moriah.*

According to *Rashbam,* the name מוֹרִיָּה, *Moriah,* refers to the Land of the אֱמוֹרִי, *Amorite,* with the elision of the *alef,* this not being unusual.

[The Amorites were the foremost Canaanite tribe living in the area later populated by the tribe of Judah, of which Jerusalem was part. Hence, *Rashbam* does not disagree with the above interpretation that the destination was Jerusalem; he disagrees only regarding the word's etymology.]

וְהַעֲלֵהוּ שָׁם לְעֹלָה — [*And*] *bring him up there as an offering.*

Rashi notes that God did not say וְשַׁחֲטֵהוּ, *slaughter him,* because it was never His intention that Isaac should, in fact, be slaughtered, but

1. *Chidushei HaRim* comments that God's words to Abraham intensified the trial in a different way. Had Abraham been told simply to sacrifice Isaac, he could have rationalized that Isaac was not as righteous as he seemed, he was even unworthy of life. Therefore, God said

עַל אַחַד הֶהָרִים אֲשֶׁר אֹמַר אֵלֶיךָ׃
ג וַיַּשְׁכֵּם אַבְרָהָם בַּבֹּקֶר וַיַּחֲבֹשׁ אֶת־חֲמֹרוֹ

only that he be *brought up* to the mountain and be *prepared* as a burnt-offering. Therefore, once Abraham had [complied with the literal terms of the trial and] brought him up, God told him to bring him back down [*v.* 12. By means of this comment *Rashi* resolves the difficulty of how God could later contradict His earlier order to slaughter Isaac; Abraham was commanded to *bring him up* as an offering, but not to carry out the process of slaughter. See *Overview.*]

[We find in *Rashi* a very basic doctrine regarding the philosophy of God's relationship to man.

Rashi does not suggest that הַעֲלֵהוּ, *bring him up,* is a term that by definition, has no meaning other than 'bring him up to the mountain but do not actually sacrifice him'. On the contrary, as evidenced by the many times the verb *bring up* is used in connection with sacrificial offerings (for example *Lev.* 14:20; 17:8; *Josh* 22:23; *Judg.* 6:26; 11:31; *I Sam.* 13:9; *Jer.* 14:12; *Ezek.* 43:24) that term clearly implies carrying out the sacrifice *completely* in every aspect. Furthermore, it was clearly so understood by Abraham. And it was God's intention that he understand it as implying actual slaughter; otherwise there would have been no test!

Rather, what *Rashi* suggests is that instead of the explicit וְשַׁחֲטֵהוּ, *slaughter him,* God deliberately chose the expression הַעֲלֵהוּ, *bring him up* which generally indicates complete sacrifice, but which also allows for the alternate interpretation. For had the expression not allowed for both connotations, *God would never have uttered it, later to annul His clear command* because as the Torah states *(Num.* 23:19) לֹא אִישׁ אֵל וִיכַזֵּב, *God is not a man that He should lie.* Therefore, He did not command Abraham, specifically *'slaughter him',* because it was never His intention that Isaac should die. As *Rashi* explains in *v.* 12: God said, *'I will not alter that which went out from my lips (Ps.* 89:35); I did not tell you to *slay him,* but *to bring him up* (to the mountain). You complied by bringing him up; now bring him back down again.']

עַל אַחַד הֶהָרִים — *Upon one of the mountains.*

God first keeps the righteous in suspense in order to increase their reward. [Therefore, He did not tell Abraham in advance exactly what his destination would be.] *(Rashi).* For [as pointed out in the *comm.* to 12:1, s.v. אֲשֶׁר אַרְאֶךָּ, *that I will show you*] embarking on a journey without knowing the final destination makes the trial even more difficult and calls for unqualified devotion, therefore carrying with it much greater reward *(Tanchuma).*

Following *Ramban's* interpretation of the literal sense of the verse, the name *Moriah* referred to both the country and the *mountain* of that name. Abraham was familiar with the *land of Moriah,* but not with the *mountain.* Therefore God told him to go to that *country* where he would be directed to the particular mountain. God chose that mountain because it was to be the

אֲשֶׁר אָהַבְתָּ, *whom you love.* With these words, Abraham's love for Isaac increased to an unprecedented extent. Thus the trial was made infinitely more difficult.

In a similar view, *Malbim* comments that by increasing Abraham's regard for Isaac, (see *Midrash* cited in *comm.)* Abraham came to feel as never before how precious Isaac was to him. Then he was tested to see whether he could subvert his love for Isaac to his love for God. Thus his willingness to comply with God's will was even more extraordinary. It was like a loyal subject who offers his king the most precious possession he has.

XXII *upon one of the mountains which I shall indicate to*
3 *you.'*
[3] *So Abraham awoke early in the morning and he*
saddled his donkey; he took his two young men with

site of His future abode; He therefore wanted the merit of the *Akeidah* to be perpetuated in the sacrifices which would be offered there.

Malbim suggests that the phrase אֲשֶׁר אֹמַר אֵלֶיךָ, *that I shall indicate* [lit. *'tell'*] *to you,* does not describe the *mountain* which God would later point out to him, but that it modifies וְהַעֲלֵהוּ, *and bring him up.* The verse would accordingly mean: *Take your son ... and get yourelf to the land of Moriah,* and *bring up there ... him which I shall tell you,* i.e., the ram. Therefore God told him, in a separate communication: *Do not stretch out your hand against the lad!* There is the ram, take that, for it was never My intention that Isaac be the sacrifice.

3. וַיַּשְׁכֵּם אַבְרָהָם בַּבֹּקֶר — *So* [lit. *and*] *Abraham awoke early in the morning.*

In eagerness to fulfill the command *(Rashi).*[1]

Cf. the *Talmudic* dictum, זְרִיזִים מַקְדִּימִים לְמִצְוָה, the zealous hasten to perform their religious duty *(Pesachim* 4a).

From the fact that Abraham waited until morning instead of beginning his preparations immediately, the *Talmud* derives that there is no religious merit in hastening to begin preparations before dawn. The objection may be raised, however, that Abraham may have refrained from going out at night only because a scholar should not go out alone at night, which is the reason Abraham went to view the fate of Sodom only with daybreak (see *comm.* to 19:27). *Tosafos* replies that the above objection would not apply in our case for two reasons: 1 — He was accompanied by Isaac and the two attendants; and 2 — Night-time presents no danger to one who is carrying out a specific command of God, for שְׁלוּחֵי מִצְוָה אֵינָם נִיזָּקִין, no harm befalls those who are engaged in the performance of a mitzvah.

Radak comments he did not relate the matter to Sarah lest she harm herself in her grief upon learning the intended fate of her beloved son. [See *footnote* to previous verse].

וַיַּחֲבֹשׁ אֶת־חֲמֹרוֹ — *And he saddled his donkey.*

He did it *personally* instead of ordering one of his servants to do so, because, [as the *Talmud Sanhedrin* 105b explains]: הָאַהֲבָה מְקַלְקֶלֶת אֶת הַשּׁוּרָה, 'love [in this case love of God] disregards the rule of normal conduct' [The saddling of a donkey is beneath the dignity of a great man such as Abraham, but in

1. The implication of וַיַּשְׁכֵּם, *awoke,* is clear that Abraham actually slept that night. One can only marvel at his complete trust in God which allowed him to remain calm and serene despite the knowledge that he would set out the next morning to slaughter his beloved son (*Harav Michael Munk).*

וַיִּקַּח אֶת־שְׁנֵי נְעָרָיו אִתּוֹ וְאֵת יִצְחָק בְּנוֹ
וַיְבַקַּע עֲצֵי עֹלָה וַיָּקָם וַיֵּלֶךְ אֶל־הַמָּקוֹם
ד אֲשֶׁר־אָמַר־לוֹ הָאֱלֹהִים׃ בַּיּוֹם הַשְּׁלִישִׁי

his eagerness to perform God's will, Abraham ignored his own honor and did it] *(Rashi)*.[1]

The *Talmud ibid.* adds conversely that 'hate, likewise disregards the rule of dignified conduct' as is deduced from Balaam who, in his hatred for Israel, also ignored his own dignity and *rose up early and saddled his she-ass* [*Num.* 22:21].

וַיִּקַּח אֶת־שְׁנֵי נְעָרָיו אִתּוֹ — [*And*] *he took his two young men with him.*

Without first summoning them and explaining the journey, so as to avoid unnecessary questions *(Abarbanel)*.

They were Ishmael [who had returned to visit Abraham; see *footnote* to *v.* 1] and [Abraham's servant] Eliezer *(Midrash)*.

[The reason he took them both along was because a man of importance should not travel without two attendants, so that he will not remain unattended should one servant take leave to ease himself *(Midrash; Pirkei d'Rabbi Eliezer; Rashi)*.

[The term נַעַר, *youth, young man,* is here applied to Ishmael and Eliezer although they were not young. Ishmael, being fourteen years older than Isaac, was fifty-one at the time, and Eliezer was probably close to Abraham's age if not even older. *Ibn Ezra* to *Exod.* 33:11 explains that the term נַעַר, *youth, young man,* can be applied to anyone who renders such service as is usually provided by a young attendant. *Rambam ibid.* likewise observes that in Hebrew the word נַעַר is a general term for 'attendant' (regardless of age), just as אִישׁ, *man,* is used for a person of high office.]

Ha'amek Davar notes that our verse uses the word אִתּוֹ in saying that the young men went *with him.* In the incident of Balaam [*Num.* 22:22 וּשְׁנֵי נְעָרָיו עִמּוֹ], however, the word used for *with him* is עִמּוֹ; and similarly in the case of Saul [*I Sam.* 28:8: וּשְׁנֵי אֲנָשִׁים עִמּוֹ]. There is a basic difference between the two words: עִמּוֹ has the connotation of equality, suggesting that those who went with Balaam and Saul were regarded as of equal status. Abraham, however, did not become excessively convivial by lowering

1. *And he* [Pharaoh] *hitched his chariot* [to pursue the Israelites] *(Exod.* 14:6). With his own hand, he hitched it. It is the manner of kings to stand aside while others prepare the chariot and hitch it, but the wicked Pharaoh did it all himself ...

Four people hitched their mounts joyfully:

Abraham did so (our verse). Didn't he have many servants? — Yes, but he did it in honor of God.

Joseph hitched his wagon [to go and greet Jacob] (46:29). Didn't he have many serants? — Yes, but he did it in honor of his father.

Balaam saddled his she-ass joyfully to curse Israel *(Num.* 22:21).

Pharaoh hitched joyfully *(Exod.* 14:6).

Abraham's saddling in God's service withstood Balaam's saddling to curse Israel, and Joseph's hitching in honor of his father withstood the hitching of wicked Pharaoh in pursuit of Israel *(Mechilta Beshalach)*.

XXII *him and Isaac, his son. He split the wood for the*
3 *offering, and rose up and went to the place which God had indicated to him.*

himself to the status of his servants.

Kol Eliyahu to *Balak* comments that עִמּוֹ indicates that both parties were of the same mind while אִתּוֹ means that their intentions were dissimilar. [Cf. אִתּוֹ־עִמּוֹ in 19:32.]

וְאֵת יִצְחָק בְּנוֹ — *And Isaac his son.* — Making it appear as if he were taking him along only as an afterthought, so as not to arouse questions *(Alshich).*

וַיְבַקַּע עֲצֵי עֹלָה — *And he split the wood for the offering.*

In his zeal to fulfill the commandment, he feared that he might not find wood there, so he brought his own. It may be that he wanted to be certain that the wood he used for the offering would be free of worms, as is the law of sacrifices [*Middos* 2:5] so he selected perfect wood from his own area rather than rely on the unforeseen *(Rambam).*

... This follows *Midrash HaGadol: Wood for the offering,* i.e., wood worthy of being used for an offering.

Note, also that he first waited until he was away from his home before he split the wood, so as not to arouse Sarah's suspicions *(Akeidas Yitzchak).*

The attendants probably assumed that the wood would be used as cooking-fuel during the journey *(Radak).*

As a reward for *splitting* [וַיְבַקַּע] the wood himself, Abraham merited that God Himself should split the Sea for his descendants, as it is written [*Exod.* 14:21] וַיִּבָּקְעוּ הַמָּיִם, *and the waters were split (Midrash).*

[Now that the preparations for the mission are complete, the actual journey can begin]:

וַיָּקָם וַיֵּלֶךְ — *And he rose up and* [*he*] *went.*

He was not faint-hearted nor did he feel weak as a result of the emotional ordeal he was about to undertake. Instead, he stood up and firmly set out on foot for a journey of several days. Only the heavy wood did he load onto the donkey *(R. Meyuchas).*

The *Midrash* derives that Abraham was rewarded separately for both acts: for *rising up* and for *going.* [Otherwise it would be redundant to specify that he *rose up* — how else could he go? *(Matnas Kehunah).*

[Although it is apparent that they *all* went, the singular form is used because Abraham was the principal — the others were under his jurisdiction. See comm. to *v.* 19.]

אֶל־הַמָּקוֹם אֲשֶׁר־אָמַר־לוֹ הָאֱלֹהִים — *To the place which God had indicated* [lit. *'told'*] *to him,* i.e., the *land of Moriah,* for he did not yet know which *mountain (Radak).*

According to *Ha'amek Davar,* had it meant to the *land,* the verse would have read אֶל הָאָרֶץ, *to the land.* Since it reads *to the place;* it means *to the mountain,* the *particular site* He had chosen. Though Abraham still did not know his exact destination, Divine Providence guided his steps in that direction.

וַיִּשָּׂא אַבְרָהָם אֶת־עֵינָיו וַיַּרְא אֶת־
ה הַמָּקוֹם מֵרָחֹק׃ וַיֹּאמֶר אַבְרָהָם אֶל־
נְעָרָיו שְׁבוּ־לָכֶם פֹּה עִם־הַחֲמוֹר וַאֲנִי

4. בַּיּוֹם הַשְּׁלִישִׁי — *On the third day.* Of the journey *(Ibn Ezra).*[1]

Why did God choose a place so distant that three days were consumed by travel? — So that people should not say that Abraham had acted impetuously, but would not have complied with God's request had he had time to reflect upon the matter *(Tanchuma; Rashi).*

וַיִּשָּׂא אַבְרָהָם אֶת עֵינָיו — [And] *Abraham looked up* [lit. *'lifted up his eyes'*].

נָשָׂא עַיִן always denotes an intentional looking up and around. Abraham had been looking constantly, but failed to see an indication that he had come to the place intended by God, until, on the third day of looking, he finally saw it *(Hirsch).*

וַיַּרְא אֶת־הַמָּקוֹם מֵרָחֹק — *And [he] perceived* [lit. *'saw'*] *the place from afar.*

— He saw a cloud hovering over the mountain *(Rashi).* [See *Midrash* further].

According to the literal meaning: He saw the *land of Moriah,* which was well known to him, from afar *(Ramban)* [cf. *comm.* end of *v.* 2].

Sforno explains: He sighted the place for the sacrifice on Mount Moriah; Divine Providence directed his gaze to that spot and he perceived that that would be the chosen place.

The *Midrash* ascribes to מָקוֹם, *place,* its other meaning. The word מָקוֹם is also used as a Name of God for it is symbolic of His Omnipresence. Thus:

Abraham saw a cloud he recognized as the manifestation of God's Presence *(Pirkei d'Rabbi Eliezer)* enveloping one of the mountains, he turned to his son and said: 'Isaac, my son, do you see the same thing I see?' 'Yes', he replied. Upon hearing this from Isaac, Abraham understood that he had been granted such spiritual might because he was to be the offering. Abraham then turned to the two attendants and asked 'Do you see the same thing I see?' They answered in the negative.

5. שְׁבוּ־לָכֶם פֹּה עִם־הַחֲמוֹר — *Stay here by yourselves* [lit. *'unto you'*] *with the donkey.*

Continuing the above *Midrash:* when the attendants told Abraham that they saw nothing unusual, he put them in the same category as the donkey and said: 'The donkey sees nothing and you see nothing, therefore *stay here by yourselves with the donkey'* [See *Overview.*]

1. There is a difference of opinion on which day the *Akeidah* occurred.

According to *Pesikta Rabbasi* 40:6, it was the first of Tishrei — *Rosh Hashanah* [see *footnote* to *v.* 13 and to *v.* 16.] This is the opinion cited by *Abudraham* [Jerusalem ed. 1963, page 269] in the name of 'a *Midrash.'*

According to *Recanati* [familiarly spelled *'Rakanti'*] the *Akeidah* occurred on *Yom Kippur;* and by virtue of it, Abraham's descendants were granted atonement on that day. According to *Midrash Shmos Rabbah* 15:11, the *Akeidah* occurred in Nissan, on Passover — [on Isaac's birthday, since the righteous are destined to die on the date of their birth *(Maharzu).*]

[4] *On the third day, Abraham looked up and perceived the place from afar.* [5] *And Abraham said to his young men, 'Stay here by yourselves with the donkey, while I and the lad will go yonder; we will*

The *Midrash* homiletically reads the phrase עַם הַחֲמוֹר, *'O nation of the donkey'*, i.e., עַם הַדּוֹמֶה לַחֲמוֹר, *the nation similar to the donkey* [in its lack of spiritual perception].

[The fact that the 'donkey-like' people were Eliezer and Ishmael indicates how exalted Abraham and Isaac were. Compared to them, even Eliezer and Ishmael were totally lacking in vision.]

He also intimated thereby that the donkey should not enter that holy place *(Radak).*

As *Sechel Tov* comments: So scrupulous was he that he began to exercise such respectful behavior when he was fully twelve *mils* away [the distance of מֵרָחוֹק, *'from afar'* as noted by the commentators to that word in *Exod.* 20:18] from the holy site. It was then that he bade them remain behind, for one may not enter the precinct of a sacred spot with an unclean beast.

Sforno suggests that Abraham told them to remain behind so that they would not attempt to prevent him from bringing the sacrifice.

Stay here by yourselves. Abraham was telling them that the spectacle about to unfold was beyond their capacity to comprehend. They could never have understood Abraham's motivation to slaughter his son; they might even have tried to prevent it. For the *Akeidah* marked the difference between זֶרַע אַבְרָהָם, *the seed of Abraham,* and בְּנֵי נֹחַ, *the children of Noah* [i.e. universal man]. Abraham and his descendants ignore the objections of the senses, the protestations of the rational and obvious. To them the only reality is the will of God. Until Moriah, all could go together; but now Abraham and Isaac had to walk alone *(Hirsch).*

Malbim comments that Abraham had never hesitated to fulfill a commandment, even those which had not been ordained for him, because his inner spiritual self sensed what was required by the will of God. In the case of the *Akeidah,* however, even his spiritual being rebelled against the act of slaughter, for unknown to Abraham, it was truly not God's desire that he go through with the slaughter. Because he felt this lack of inner desire, he was ashamed to perform the deed in the presence of his servants. His trial consisted in whether he could bring himself to go through with it nevertheless.

וַאֲנִי וְהַנַּעַר — *While* [lit. *'and'*] *I and the lad* [i.e. Isaac].

He was thirty-seven years old and yet Abraham calls him נַעַר, *lad!* — It is, however, common for the Torah to use this expression for mature people: Joshua, Moses' servant, is referred to as נַעַר, *lad; young man* [*Exod.* 33:11] although he was 42 years old *(R' Bachya).* [See *comm.* to נְעָרָיו in *v.* 3. and to יֶלֶד in 21:14.]

נֵלְכָה עַד־כֹּה — [*We*] *will go yonder* [lit. *'until thus'*], i.e. a short distance: to the place in front of us. The *Midrash* notes the use of the

וְהַנַּעַר נֵלְכָה עַד־כֹּה וְנִשְׁתַּחֲוֶה וְנָשׁוּבָה
ו אֲלֵיכֶם: וַיִּקַּח אַבְרָהָם אֶת־עֲצֵי הָעֹלָה
וַיָּשֶׂם עַל־יִצְחָק בְּנוֹ וַיִּקַּח בְּיָדוֹ אֶת־הָאֵשׁ
וְאֶת־הַמַּאֲכֶלֶת וַיֵּלְכוּ שְׁנֵיהֶם יַחְדָּו:

rare word כֹּה, *thus,*and interprets it as an allusion to God's earlier promise to Abraham [which began with the same word]: כֹּה, *thus shall be your descendants as the stars of the heavens* (15:5) [i.e., I go to comply with God's will, confident that I will see how God's promise of many descendants will be fulfilled even though He bids me to slay the very son through whom He promised the realization of His promise.]

וְנִשְׁתַּחֲוֶה וְנָשׁוּבָה אֲלֵיכֶם — *[And] we will worship* [lit. *'prostrate ourselves'*], *and we will return to you.*

The attendants understood that in addition to worshipping, he would offer sacrifices, because they brought wood and fire. Cf. *I Sam.* 1:3: *Elkanah went up* לְהִשְׁתַּחֲוֹת וְלִזְבֹּחַ, *to worship and to sacrifice (Radak).*

With complete simplicity and with total lack of grandiloquence does Abraham announce the great deed he is about to do! 'We shall just go there, prostrate ourselves, and return to you' (*Hirsch).*

[Since he planned to sacrifice Isaac, he should have used the singular and said 'and *I* will return to you']:

— He [unwittingly] prophesied that *both* of them would return *(Rashi).*

This *Midrashic* interpretation is based upon *Mo'ed Katan* 18a which derives from our verse the dictum בְּרִית כְּרוּתָה לִשְׂפָתַיִם, 'a covenant has been made with the lips' [i.e. the spoken word, even if unintentional, often becomes fulfilled].

The commentators *R' Yosef Albo; [Maharsha; Yefeh Toar]* explain that Abraham's statement was divinely inspired and hence a form of prophecy, as *Rashi* notes. God often causes the spirit of prophecy to enter the righteous as He did here in allowing Abraham to unwittingly prophesy that Isaac would return unscathed.

Ibn Ezra cites 'some who explain' that Abraham used the plural form *'we'*, because it was his initial — although concealed — intention that Isaac's *bones* would return with him.

6. וַיִּקַּח אַבְרָהָם אֶת־עֲצֵי הָעֹלָה — *And Abraham took the wood for the offering.* From the donkey which had been carrying it *(Sechel Tov).*

וַיָּשֶׂם עַל־יִצְחָק בְּנוֹ — *And* [*he*] *placed it on Isaac, his son.*

Like one who carries on his own shoulder the stake upon which he is to be executed *(Midrash).*

— In order to arouse his interest in the preparations so that he might question his father and the truth would dawn on him *(Alshich).*

וַיִּקַּח בְּיָדוֹ אֶת־הָאֵשׁ וְאֶת־הַמַּאֲכֶלֶת — *[And] he took* [i.e. carried] *in his hand the fire and the knife.*

From his attendants who had been carrying it until them *(Sechel Tov).*

To further arouse his interest in what was about to happen *(Alshich).*

XXII *worship and we will return to you.'*

6 [6] *And Abraham took the wood for the offering, and placed it on Isaac, his son. He took in his hand the fire and the knife, and the two of them went*

[The אֵשׁ, *fire* may be taken literally, i.e. torches which they carried with them throughout the journey; or the tools which they used to kindle a fire.]

Rashi explains that a knife is called מַאֲכֶלֶת [from אכל: eat, consume, devour] either because:

(a) it *devours* meat as in *Deut.* 32:42: *My sword devours* [תֹּאכַל] *flesh*; or,

(b) because it makes meat ritually fit for eating [אֲכִילָה; i.e. the knife מַאֲכֶלֶת, 'feeds' others, for through the slaughter process an otherwise non-ritually-fit food becomes permissible *(Mizrachi).*]

(c) Another explanation: That particular knife is called מַאֲכֶלֶת [i.e. *feeder*] because whatever Israel still *'eats'* [i.e. enjoys] in this world is only through the merit of that knife [by which Abraham was about to subject his son to the supreme sacrifice *(Mizrachi)*] *(Tanchuma).*

As an etymological observation, *Sechel Tov* remarks that knife is known as סַכִּין because it endangers [מְסַכֵּן] mankind.

וַיֵּלְכוּ שְׁנֵיהֶם יַחְדָּו — *And the two of them went* [or: *walked off*] *together,* i.e. in complete harmony. Abraham who knew that he was going to slay his son went with the same willingness and joy as Isaac who knew nothing of it *(Rashi).*[1]

As the *Midrash* comments, *the two of them walked off together* — one to bind and the other to be bound; one to slaughter and the other to be slaughtered.

... One to bind, and the other to prostrate himself *(Sechel Tov).*

As *Hirsch* explains: This inspiring phrase, repeated in *v.* 8 represents father and son facing a difficult challenge *together,* in total unity and harmony.

7. Until now Isaac was still not aware of the true purpose of the journey. [But the elaborate preparations; their secrecy-shrouded early-morning departure; the specially

1. The *Midrashim* [*Pirkei d'Rabbi Eliezer; Tanchuma; Yalkut* 1:98] record that the Satan appeared to Abraham as an old man and tried unsuccessfully to thwart his plans.

He asked Abraham: 'Should an old man like you kill his son who was given to him in old age?'

'God Himself has commanded it,' Abraham retorted.

To Isaac he appeared as a young man and accosted him: '... Your father plans to sacrifice you!'

'It does not matter; I shall follow him,' Isaac answered.

The Satan seeing that his scheme was spurned disguised himself as a deep river. Abraham and Isaac entered the water which reached their necks.

Abraham then cried out to God: 'I did not refuse even Your command to sacrifice my beloved son, although You had promised me that through him Your Name shall be known throughout the world. But *the waters have reached the soul* [*Ps.* 69:2]: If I or my son Isaac drown, who will assert the Unity of Your Name?'

God then rebuked the Satan and the water disappeared.

The Satan then appeared to Sarah and asked her where Abraham and Isaac were. 'He took Isaac to an academy to study,' she answered.

'You will never see your son again' the Satan said coldly.

'May God do as He wills,' Sarah replied.

[Nevertheless, she died from the shock of later hearing the account of the *Akeidah.* See *comm.* to 23:2]

ז וַיֹּאמֶר יִצְחָק אֶל־אַבְרָהָם אָבִיו וַיֹּאמֶר
אָבִי וַיֹּאמֶר הִנֶּנִּי בְנִי וַיֹּאמֶר הִנֵּה הָאֵשׁ
ח וְהָעֵצִים וְאַיֵּה הַשֶּׂה לְעֹלָה: וַיֹּאמֶר
אַבְרָהָם אֱלֹהִים יִרְאֶה־לּוֹ הַשֶּׂה לְעֹלָה
ט בְּנִי וַיֵּלְכוּ שְׁנֵיהֶם יַחְדָּו: וַיָּבֹאוּ אֶל־
הַמָּקוֹם אֲשֶׁר אָמַר־לוֹ הָאֱלֹהִים וַיִּבֶן שָׁם
אַבְרָהָם אֶת־הַמִּזְבֵּחַ וַיַּעֲרֹךְ אֶת־הָעֵצִים

selected firewood; the fire, and the knife all began to take on a new significance to him. Everything else was so carefully planned, but where was the lamb for the sacrifice? The truth was now becoming apparent to Isaac.]

וַיֹּאמֶר יִצְחָק אֶל־אַבְרָהָם אָבִיו וַיֹּאמֶר אָבִי — *Then* [lit. *'and'*] *Isaac spoke to Abraham his father and said:* [*My*] *'Father!'*

Isaac did not as yet ask Abraham the question with which the verse concludes; he merely addressed him as, *'My father'*, and paused. For Isaac sensed that he intended him to be the offering. But if this were so, did it not indicate that the loving father-son relationship had ceased? How else could Abraham fail to have compassion on his beloved son? *(Kli Yakar)*[*See continuation below.*]

... As the *Midrash* comments: Why the stress on the paternal relationship: *his father, ... my father?* — So that Abraham should have compassion upon Isaac. For as the *Midrash* points out, though the Satan could not dissuade Isaac (see *footnote* end of last verse), his attempt nevertheless had some minor effect upon him and induced him to plead indirectly to his father.

וַיֹּאמֶר הִנֶּנִּי בְנִי — *And he said, 'Here I am, my son.'*

Kli Yakar, continues his interpretation of Isaac's expression *'My father'*: Abraham responded to Isaac's implied doubt. *'Here I am, my son,'* i.e. you are still my son, my love for you is undiminished. Now that Isaac was reassured about his father's love, he was convinced that Abraham could not wish to slaughter him. That being the case, Isaac asked, *'Where is the lamb for the offering?'* Abraham replied *(v.* 8), that the choice of the offering was the will of God: 'You are to become a sacrifice because He desires it — and we both place His command above all else.' Hearing this, Isaac's resolved to fulfill God's will and, as the next verse declares, *'the two of them went together'* — of a single mind and with a single purpose.

הִנֵּה הָאֵשׁ וְהָעֵצִים וְאַיֵּה הַשֶּׂה לְעֹלָה — *Here are the fire and the wood, but where is the lamb for the offering?*

[I.e., you made elaborate preparations regarding everything but the lamb for the offering; what will you do about *that?*]

Note that Isaac's question specified only the fire and the wood. It was not unusual to bring along a

together. 7 *Then Isaac spoke to Abraham his father*
and said, 'Father — '
And he said 'Here I am, my son.'
And he said, 'Here are the fire and the wood, but
where is the lamb for the offering?'
8 *And Abraham said, 'God will seek out for*
Himself the lamb for the offering, my son.' And the
two of them went together.
9 *They arrived at the place which God designated*
to him. Abraham built the altar there, and arranged

knife, for it could be needed on any journey as protection against beasts and bandits. But Abraham's unusual decision to carry fire and wood such a long way — especially in the absence of the animal — suggested something unusual (*Abarbanel*).

8. אֱלֹהִים יִרְאֶה־לּוֹ הַשֶּׂה לְעֹלָה בְּנִי — *God will seek out for Himself* [lit. '*look for Himself*'] *the lamb for* [lit. 'to'] *the offering, my son.*

I.e. God will seek out and select for Himself the lamb, but if there is no lamb then לְעֹלָה בְּנִי, *you,* my son, will be the offering. Isaac then understood (*Rashi*).

It is for us but to be prepared for the offering — with wood, fire, and knife. God will choose the lamb and whatever His will decrees, we will do, knowing it is right (*Hirsch*).

Kli Yakar, concluding his interpretation of the dialogue, has Abraham replying, 'It is not I who have chosen you for an offering, but God. Both of us are equally obligated to honor Him.' Hearing this , Isaac felt no more misgivings, and the two of them went together, in renewed harmony.

וַיֵּלְכוּ שְׁנֵיהֶם יַחְדָּו — *And the two of them went* [or: *walked off*] *together.*

[This is repeated to emphasize that] although Isaac now became aware that he was going to be slain, they still walked forward with a common purpose, [and with no change in attitude] (*Rashi*).[1]

9. אֲשֶׁר אָמַר־לוֹ הָאֱלֹהִים — *Which God designated to him* — i.e., which God *now* designated to him, saying: 'This is the mountain of which I spoke to you' (*Ramban*).

וַיִּבֶן שָׁם אַבְרָהָם אֶת־הַמִּזְבֵּחַ — [*And*] *Abraham built the altar there.*

Not *an* altar, but *the* altar, which the *Midrashim* explain as referring to a previously existing altar. It was

1. *Hirsch* [to *v.* 3] comments that Isaac's greatness in this trial ranks equal to Abraham's. Isaac had not been commanded directly by God; he heard from his father as Oral Law. Nevertheless, the first Jewish son is ready to sacrifice himself for a tradition he knew only from his father This created the precedent for the devotion of future generations to the traditions of their fathers. The Sages ask [*Sanhedrin* 89b] how Isaac could believe in such a הוֹרָאַת שָׁעָה, an extraordinary ruling, and allow himself to be a human sacrifice? How dared he do so? The answer is הֵיכָא דְמוּחְזָק שָׁאנֵי, where a prophet's veracity is proven, one may obey his prophecy. (See *Overview*).

וַֽיַּעֲקֹד֙ אֶת־יִצְחָ֣ק בְּנ֔וֹ וַיָּ֤שֶׂם אֹתוֹ֙ עַל־
י הַמִּזְבֵּ֔חַ מִמַּ֖עַל לָעֵצִֽים׃ וַיִּשְׁלַ֤ח אַבְרָהָם֙
אֶת־יָד֔וֹ וַיִּקַּ֖ח אֶת־הַֽמַּאֲכֶ֑לֶת לִשְׁחֹ֖ט אֶת־

the altar on which the ancients had sacrificed, and which Abraham now rebuilt after centuries of disuse.

God pointed out the altar to Abraham and said: This is the altar where Adam sacrificed; where Cain and Abel sacrificed; and where Noah and his sons sacrificed *(Pirkei d'Rabbi Eliezer).*

Cf. *Rambam, Hilchos Beis HaBechirah* 2:2:

'There was a known tradition [*Midrash Tanchuma*] that the place where David and Solomon built the altar in the threshing floor of Aravnah [*II Sam.* 24:18. (See also in *II Chron.* 3:1 where he is called Arnon)] was the same place where Abraham built the altar upon which he bound Isaac ... it was the soil from which Adam was created.'

[The previous verses speak of Abraham and Isaac going *together*; now only Abraham is mentioned as building and arranging the altar.]

— The *Midrash* asks: Where was Isaac? Abraham had hidden him in a cave out of fear that the Satan would throw a stone at Isaac and maim him, thus disqualifying him from serving as a sacrifice [cf. *Lev.* 22:21.]

Yafeh Toar explains that Abraham's attitude was based on the dictum that 'when the plague rages in a town no man should show himself *in the street'* [cf. *footnote* to 6:14 p. 230.] Therefore Abraham took every precaution and concealed Isaac in a cave, not leaving him in the open where he would be exposed to Satan's designs.

וַיַּעֲרֹךְ אֶת־הָעֵצִים — *And* [*he*] *arranged the wood.*

The Torah again emphasizes the orderliness with which Abraham proceeded: First he built the altar, then arranged the wood, then tied his son, etc. Abraham maintained his full presence of mind throughout and no act was impulsive *(Abarbanel).*

In the normal procedure, an offering is not killed on the altar. It seems that Abraham wanted to perform the great act in such a way that there would be nothing further to do after the slaughter. Therefore he planned to sacrifice Isaac directly on the stack of wood so that the flames would immediately engulf his body *(Hirsch).*

וַיַּעֲקֹד אֶת יִצְחָק בְּנוֹ — [*And*] *he bound Isaac his son,* by tying him hand to foot behind him. The term עֲקִידָה, *binding,* refers to the tying of hand-to-foot, hand-to-foot. Cf. the word הָעֲקֻדִּים in 30:35 *(Rashi).* [See *Shabbos* 54a].

Why did he tie him?

— According to the *Midrash,* Isaac said: 'Father, I am a vigorous young man and you are old. I fear that when I see the slaughtering knife in your hand I will instinctively jerk and possibly injure you, I might also injure myself and render myself unfit for sacrifice. Or my in-

XXII the wood; he bound Isaac, his son, and he placed him
10 on the altar atop the wood. [10] Abraham stretched out
his hand, and took the knife to slaughter his son.

voluntary movement might make you unable to perform the ritual slaughter properly. Therefore bind me well so that at the final moment, I will not be deficient in filial honor and respect, and thereby not fulfill the commandment properly. Thereupon, Abraham immediately *bound Isaac his son*. Could he bind a thirty-seven year old man without his consent? *(Midrash; Pirkei d'Rabbi Eliezer; Targum Yonasan; Tanchuma; Yalkut HaMachiri).*[1]

[Although the *Akeidah* is reckoned as a trial of Abraham rather than of Isaac (see *Overview*), it may be that the episode is entitled עֲקֵידַת יִצְחָק, the *Binding of Isaac,* to give recognition to Isaac's concern, even at this final moment, to take care that he do nothing — even inadvertently — to render the sacrifice less than perfect.]

וַיָּשֶׂם אֹתוֹ עַל־הַמִּזְבֵּחַ מִמַּעַל לָעֵצִים — *And he placed him on the altar atop the wood.*

The *Midrash* notes that when completed, the altar was as beautiful as a wedding canopy.

10. וַיִּקַּח אֶת־הַמַּאֲכֶלֶת לִשְׁחֹט אֶת־בְּנוֹ — *And took the knife to slaughter his son.*

To slaughter his son is mentioned [although that was obviously his intention] so that we may infer the principle that כַּוָּנָה, *specific intention,* is required for the slaughter of sacrifices *(Midrash HaChefetz — Torah Shelemah* 117; cf. *Chullin* 13a where another Scriptural verse is cited in this connection.]

The Sages movingly depict the intensity of emotion that enveloped Abraham and the heavenly angels. Abraham felt a mixture of joy, that he was fulfilling God's will, and sadness, that his beloved son was about to die: He stretched forth his hands to take the knife, while in fatherly compassion, the tears streamed from his eyes and dripped into Isaac's eyes. Yet in spite of that he rejoiced to do his Creator's will *(Midrash).* Abraham looked at Isaac, and Isaac looked up at the angels on high. Isaac saw them, but Abraham did not *(Targum Yonasan).* The angels were also weeping as it were, and their tears fell into

1. Isaac then said: 'Father, make haste and execute the will of your Creator. Do not delay. After you have slaughtered and thoroughly burned me as an offering, gather my ashes, bring them to my mother, and place them in a casket in her chamber. Whenever she enters the chamber and sees the casket, she will remember her son and weep for him.'

'O beloved father,' Isaac continued, 'what will you tell Mother when she asks what became of me? What will you both do in your old age?'

The tears welled up in Abraham's eyes and he answered: 'My son, we know we will not long survive you, and our death is near. But meanwhile, He Who comforted us before you were born will comfort us until the day of our death' *(Midrash Vayosha; Yalkut Shimoni;* cf. *Sefer HaYashar).*

יא בְּנוֹ: וַיִּקְרָא אֵלָיו מַלְאַךְ יהוה מִן־הַשָּׁמַיִם
וַיֹּאמֶר אַבְרָהָם | אַבְרָהָם וַיֹּאמֶר הִנֵּנִי:
יב וַיֹּאמֶר אַל־תִּשְׁלַח יָדְךָ אֶל־הַנַּעַר וְאַל־

Isaac's eyes (*Rashi* to 27:1). ... The angels appealed, 'Sovereign of the Universe ... was Abraham not hospitable to strangers and did he not lead them into Your service by proclaiming You as the source of all the blessings of the world? Did not Sarah's menses return in Abraham's merit that she could bear Isaac? Will now the promises made to Abraham regarding this offspring be broken? Lo! The knife is at his throat; how long will You wait?' *(Pirkei d'Rabbi Eliezer).*

11. וַיִּקְרָא אֵלָיו מַלְאַךְ ה' מִן־הַשָּׁמַיִם — *And an angel of HASHEM called to him from heaven.*[1]

[Note that God's Name appears here as *HASHEM*, indicating His Attribute of Mercy.]

Why *'from heaven'*?

— Because this indicates that he heard a sound, but saw no vision *(Radak).*

How could Abraham obey an angel contradicting what he had heard expressly from God Himself? Furthermore, how could the angel have spoken in the first person? [See however *comm.* to 16:10 that, as God's emissary, the angel speaks in His Name in first person. See also *Malbim,* further and footnote to *v.* 12 s.v. מִמֶּנִּי] — The answer may be, as the Rabbis explained in *Vayikra Rabbah* 1:9, that the meaning is הַמַּלְאָךְ קוֹרֵא וְהַדִּבּוּר מְדַבֵּר, the angel 'called' and the divine Word 'spoke' — i.e., the actual communication came from God; the angel merely called Abraham's name to draw his attention to the communication about to be heard from God *(HaK'sav V'HaKaballah).*

This is supported by *Tanchuma Yashan:* When the angel called him, Abraham asked: 'Who are you?'

— 'An angel,' he replied.

'When God told me to sacrifice him,' Abraham answered, 'He told me so Himself. I therefore now request that He Himself [not an angel] tell me.'

Immediately God opened the heavens and said [*v.* 16]: *'By Myself I have sworn ...'*

Thus a prophecy coming directly from God cannot be annulled by another prophet until the first prophet hears directly from God that the original prophecy was countermanded. Therefore, in I *Kings* 13:11, the man of God was punished because based on the words of the old prophet of Bethel who said [*ibid. v.* 18] *'I am a prophet like you are,'* the man acted contrary to the order he had received directly from God. Similarly, Abraham was reluctant to heed the angel until God Himself appeared to him *(Malbim* to *v.* 14; see *Ikkarim* 3:18).

1. When the Ministering Angels saw how the father wholeheartedly bound, and the son wholeheartedly allowed himself to be bound, the angels pleaded to God.

'Lord of the Universe, do not let Abraham's progeny be erased from the world.'

God replied: 'Was it not you who approached Me with charges [about Abraham's ingratitude, which instigated this trial? (see *comm.* to *v.* 1)]. Now you come to Me to plead for compassion!'

He [nevertheless] beckoned an angel of mercy to call Abraham, as it is written *'an angel of HASHEM called to him from heaven' (Tanchuma; Midrash HaGadol).*

[11] *And an angel of HASHEM called to him from
heaven, and said, 'Abraham! Abraham!'
And he said, 'Here I am.'*
[12] *And he said, 'Do not stretch out your hand*

אַבְרָהָם אַבְרָהָם — *Abraham, Abraham.*

The repetition expresses love *(Rashi).*

According to the *Midrash,* it also expresses urgency [see *Malbim* cited to *v.* 1]:

Abraham was hastening and was about to slaughter his son so the angel called out in great urgency like a man crying out in distress: 'What are you doing? — *Do not lay your hand on the lad!' (Pesikta Rabbasi* 40).

Alshich comments, See with what great desire Abraham performed God's will! When he was commanded to slaughter his son, it was sufficient that his name be mentioned but once. But when he was engaged in carrying out the commandment, he became so suffused with love of God and determination to fulfill His word, that he did not heed the call to desist until he was called twice.

Others, too, were so addressed: *'Jacob, Jacob'* [46:2]; *'Moses, Moses'* [*Exod.* 3:4]; *'Samuel, Samuel'* [*I Sam.* 3:10]; — The repetition indicates that He spoke both to him and to future generations: There is no generation which does not contain men like Abraham, and there is no generation which does not contain men like Jacob, Moses and Samuel [each of whose name was likewise repeated. *Yafeh Toar* explains that the four respectively represent philanthropy, service of God, Torah study, and civil justice, which may be regarded as the fundamentals of civilization — and accordingly each age must have some who represent them] *(Midrash).*

The *Midrash* [*Sh'mos Rabbah* 2:6] notes that the punctuation of the various verses reveals a difference in the quality of prophecy experienced by the four prophets. The two Abrahams are separated by a disjunctive mark [פְּסִיק, *pause:* אַבְרָהָם | אַבְרָהָם] as are the repeated names 'Jacob' and 'Samuel'. But in the case of 'Moses Moses', no disjunctive mark ['pause'] separates them. This is because God interrupted [פָּסַק, *paused*] his discourse with all other prophets [i.e. He spoke only at intervals, and accordingly there are marks of interruption between the two mentions of their names], but with Moses, He never broke off [פָּסַק, *paused*] His communication all his life.

Kabbalistically, the angel repeated Abraham's name in order to animate him with a new spirit, and spur him to a new activity with a new heart *(Zohar).*

וַיֹּאמֶר הִנֵּנִי — *And he said 'Here I am.'*

About to complete God's command *(Abarbanel).*

12. וַיֹּאמֶר — *And he said.*

[The speaker may have been either the angel speaking in God's name, or God Himself. See *comm.* to *v.* 11.]

אַל־תִּשְׁלַח יָדְךָ אֶל־הַנַּעַר — *Do not stretch out your hand against* [lit. *'to'*] *the lad,* i.e. to slaughter him.

תַּעַשׂ לוֹ מְאוּמָה כִּי | עַתָּה יָדַעְתִּי כִּי־יְרֵא
אֱלֹהִים אַתָּה וְלֹא חָשַׂכְתָּ אֶת־בִּנְךָ אֶת־

Abraham protested, 'Then I will have come here for no purpose,I will wound him and cause some blood to flow!'

God thereupon answered, וְאַל תַּעַשׂ לוֹ מְאוּמָה *'Nor do anything* [מְאוּמָה] *to him,'* i.e. create no blemish [מום] in him, *for now I know, ...'(Midrash; Rashi).*

[This must be understood in the light of how intensely Abraham wished to perform God's command. The dialogue is not meant to imply that he was eager to *harm* his son. Rather, Abraham's reaction should be understood in the light of the *Zohar* which explains that when the angel said to him: *Do not stretch out your hand against the lad,* Abraham was distressed because he *erroneously understood it to indicate* (not that God changed His mind, so to speak, or that it was only a test, but) that *his offspring was unacceptable* and that his labor and preparation had been for naught.' He therefore attempted to demonstrate his desire to comply with the original command even in some lesser form than originally intended.]

Rashi continues to quote the *Midrash:* Abraham said: 'I will explain my words, [i.e., express my grievance *(Divrei David)*]: Previously You promised me כִּי בְיִצְחָק יִקָּרֵא לְךָ זָרַע, *that through Isaac will offspring be considered yours* (21:12); then You said קַח־נָא אֶת־בִּנְךָ, *please take your son* to the *Akeidah;* yet now You tell me: אַל תִּשְׁלַח יָדְךָ אֶל הַנַּעַר, *Do not stretch out your hand against the lad.* [I.e. I cannot comprehend the mysteries of Your ways. Do You then change Your mind or speak idle words?']

God then answered him [in the words of *Ps.* 89:35]: *'I will not profanely covenant, nor alter that which went out of My mouth.* When I told you *'take your son'* I did not alter what had gone out of My lips [by abrogating My earlier covenant that through Isaac will you have descendants.] I never said שַׁחֲטֵהוּ, *slaughter him,* but הַעֲלֵהוּ, *bring him up* [upon the altar]. You *have* brought him up [and by so doing you have completely complied with my command.] Now bring him down again.'

[It was only now at the *conclusion* of the *Akeidah,* that Abraham raised the apparent contradiction between God's two statements. For Abraham to have posed the question earlier would have implied that he wished to avoid educated compliance with God's command. Now, however, that Isaac was spared, Abraham asked the question in an effort to understand the precise meaning of God's pledge and subsequent commands *(Divrei David).* See also bracketed comm. to וְהַעֲלֵהוּ in *v.* 2.] [1]

1. Abraham then said: 'Master of the Universe. I swear that I will not descend from this altar until I tell You my petition. You promised me seed through Isaac, yet when You commanded me to sacrifice him I restrained my most natural emotional instincts, and did not hesitate. So, too, when my descendants sin and thereby become oppressed, may you remember this *Akeidah.* May it be considered before You as if Isaac's ashes were gathered upon the altar and

XXII
12 *against the lad nor do anything to him for now I know that you are a God-fearing man, since you have not withheld your son, your only one, from Me.'*

The *Midrash* notes the phrase: 'Stretch not your *hand* against the lad.'

Where was *the knife?* — Tears had fallen from the angels and dissolved it. Upon seeing that he was prevented from carrying out the slaughter, Abraham attempted to sacrifice Isaac by means of מְלִיקָה, the sacrificial slaughter of birds in which the thumbnail is used (see *Lev.* 1:15 and *Rashi* there). The angel then cautioned Abraham to inflict *not even a bruise* upon Isaac (*Midrash* as interpreted by *Etz Joseph*).

Radak comments that in the literal sense of the verse God added the phrase וְאַל תַּעַשׂ לוֹ מְאוּמָה, *nor do anything to him,* for extra emphasis.

כִּי עַתָּה יָדַעְתִּי — *For now I know* [lit. *I knew* or *have known*].

[*Rashi* resolves the difficulties: How could it say that He knew only '*now*' that Abraham feared Him? Further, there is an apparent contradiction between עַתָּה, *now,* and יָדַעְתִּי, *knew* which is in past tense. Therefore *Rashi* interprets]: Now I can prove to Satan and all skeptics what I have long since known, for you have conclusively demonstrated that you are God-fearing. (As explained by *L'shon Chaim*).

According to *Rambam* [see comm. to *v.* 1 s.v. נִסָּה] it means *Now it has become known* [i.e. I have *made known* to the world הוֹדַעְתִּי=יָדַעְתִּי; (*Rav Saadiah Gaon*).]

As *Kli Yakar* elaborates: when God sees that an individual has within himself great love for and devotion to Him, He tests him so that his spiritual greatness can be demonstrated and thus revealed to all.

Ramban [following his *comm.* to *v.* 1] explains: Now Abraham's *potential* fear of God has become known in actuality.

There are some who interpret יָדַעְתִּי as: I have *loved* him. Cf. *comm.* to 18:19 כִּי יְדַעְתִּיו (*HaK'sav v'HaKaballah*).

Kli Yakar explains that the expression עַתָּה, *now,* does not imply an exclusion of the preceding period, i.e. *now* I *know,* but before I didn't know. We find, for example, the verse [*Deut.* 10:12]: *And now,* [וְעַתָּה], *Israel, what does HASHEM your God require of you but to fear* ... Did God not require *before* that moment that Israel fear Him? Rather the word '*now*' there has the connotation of *'Behold,' Israel.* Here, too, the expression means: *'Behold, I have known ...'*

his blood was sprinkled upon the altar, and may You forgive their sin' (*Tanchuma; Rabbeinu Bachya*).

[Cf. the prayer said during שַׁחֲרִית, Morning Services, after the reading of this chapter: 'Master of the World! Just as Abraham restrained his compassion to do Your will with a loyal heart, so may Your mercy restrain Your anger from us; let Your compassion prevail over Your attributes (of justice and punishment) ...' (see *Overview*).]

יג יְחִידְךָ מִמֶּנִּי: וַיִּשָּׂא אַבְרָהָם אֶת־עֵינָיו
וַיַּרְא וְהִנֵּה־אַיִל אַחַר נֶאֱחַז בַּסְּבַךְ

Alshich, on the other hand, suggests that this be read in the interrogative as God's incredulous question: *For do you then think that I became aware that you are a God-fearing man only now, because you did not withhold your only son from Me?*

כִּי־יְרֵא אֱלֹהִים אַתָּה — *That you are a God-fearing man.*

God is identified here as *Elohim* because the command to *take your son* was given in His attribute of אֱלֹהִים, Justice, as it is written *And God* [אֱלֹהִים] *tested Abraham (Alshich).*

The mention in our verse of *'fear'* rather than *'love'* is noted by the commentators:

The *Sages (Sotah* 31a) state that *'Fear of God'* as practiced by Abraham was an outgrowth of love, as it is written זֶרַע אַבְרָהָם אֹהֲבִי, *the seed of Abraham who loved Me,* [*Isaiah* 41:8], i.e. the essence of Abraham's character was love of God.

מִמֶּנִּי — *From Me.*

[Those who interpret that this is spoken by the angel explain that he speaks in the name of God in first person.] [1]

According to *Sforno* the verse means: *Now I* [the angel] *know* from *My* own observation of your actions which are *now* actual, rather than only potential *that you are* יְרֵא אֱלֹהִים, *God-fearing,* מִמֶּנִּי, *more than I, because you have not withheld your only son.* This is as the Sages proclaimed: [*San.,* 93a]: גְּדוֹלִים צַדִּיקִים יוֹתֵר מִמַּלְאֲכֵי הַשָּׁרֵת the righteous are greater than the Ministering Angels.

Radak explains that Abraham's 'fear' as expressed in this trial was an expression of love, for he did not fear in the physical sense that one seeks to avoid pain or punishment. Rather he 'feared' lest his soul be deemed unworthy. He loved his son more than himself, yet he was prepared to sacrifice Isaac in order to safeguard his own place in the World to Come — so great was his love for God and his reluctance to forfeit the opportunity to cleave to Him.

HaKsav V'HaKaballah comments that love and fear are not separate and distinct forms of divine service, rather they are one. Love leads to fear; fear complements love but is even a higher level than love. The more a parent loves his child, the more he will fear that the child may be endangered. Similarly, the more one loves God, the more he will fear committing a deed that will cast dis-

1. This is explained in *Ikkarim* 2:28:

Angels are spiritual beings that are not subject to the flaws to which material beings are liable, such as envy, hatred, strife. They are free from all evil, and always choose what is good and right in the eyes of God. Therefore, when they are sent to man, they are given permission to speak in the name of God, as we clearly see in many instances where an angel speaks in the name of the One Who sent him. [Our verse is among the several cited.] The reason for this is because the angel cannot disobey the command of God and alter the message or speak of his own volition. For this very reason an angel is called [מַלְאָךְ, (lit.) 'messenger'] because he is not a distinct intellect, but the bearer of a mission from God. If he changed the message he would no longer be an angel ...

[13] *And Abraham looked up and saw — behold a ram! — afterwards, caught in the thicket by its horns.*

honor upon His Holy Name. Thus it was only from Abraham's fear of God that the extent of his love was determined.

Ha'amek Davar notes that, in contrast to his lengthy prayers for the salvation of Sodom, Abraham made no attempt to intercede for his beloved son. It was as though the command had come not from God whom Abraham loved, but from a cruel human king before whom he stood in mortal fear of even appealing for mercy. Thus, although Abraham's love of God was well-known, the extent of his fear of God was demonstrated now as never before.

13. וַיִּשָּׂא אַבְרָהָם אֶת־עֵינָיו — *And Abraham looked up* [lit. *'lifted up his eyes'*][1]

[See *comm.* to *v.* 4].

He looked about to see if there were another ritually clean animal which he could offer instead of his son *(Radak).*

... Abraham felt the urge to dedicate the future life of his descendants just as he had been ready to offer the life of his son. The 'binding' represented total submission to God's will; Abraham sought to make this concept eternal by bringing an offering now in Isaac's place, the daily Temple offerings are a national continuation of Isaac's *Akeidah (Hirsch).*

וְהִנֵּה־אַיִל — *[And] behold, a ram!*

It had been predestined for this occasion from the six days of creation *(Rashi).*

Cf. *Avos* 5:6: 'Ten things were created on the eve of the Sabbath at twilight of the sixth day of creation ... Some maintain, that Abraham's ram was also among them.'

אַחַר נֶאֱחַז בַּסְּבַךְ בְּקַרְנָיו — *Afterwards, caught in the thicket by its horns.*

The translation follows *Rashi* and *Onkelos:* אַחַר, *afterwards,* i.e. after the preceding events when the angel had told him not to harm the lad, *he looked up and saw a ram caught in the thicket.*

The ram had been running toward Abraham [to offer itself up as a sacrifice instead of Isaac *(Pirkei d'Rabbi Eliezer)*], but Satan [in order to thwart Abraham's offering *(ibid.)*] caused it to get caught by its horns in the thicket *(Rashi).*

Hirsch and *HaKsav V'Hakabalah* render that Abraham looked up and saw the ram; אַחַר, *after which it* [the ram] *was caught.*

According to *Ibn Ezra* the verse is to be interpreted ... *Abraham saw a*

1. The *Tanchuma* relates that after Abraham stated his grievance and swore not to leave the altar until he received assurance that his descendants would always benefit from the merit of the *Akeidah* [see *comm.* to *v.* 12], God answered him that on that day [*Rosh Hashanah* or *Yom Kippur,* the anniversary of the *Akeidah* (see *footnote* to *v.* 4)] God would judge all, and that if future generations wish Him to recall for them the merit of the binding of Isaac and forgive them, they should sound the *Shofar,* [*ram's horn.*] 'What is the shofar?' asked Abraham. 'Turn around and see it,' God answered. Thereupon *Abraham looked up, and behold a ram!*

Cf. *Rosh Hashanah* 16a: Why do we sound the *Shofar* of a ram on *Rosh Hashanah?* — Because God said: 'I will thereby recall in your favor the Binding of Isaac and regard it as though you yourselves were bound before Me.'

בְּקַרְנָיו וַיֵּלֶךְ אַבְרָהָם וַיִּקַּח אֶת־הָאַיִל
יד וַיַּעֲלֵהוּ לְעֹלָה תַּחַת בְּנוֹ: וַיִּקְרָא אַבְרָהָם
שֵׁם־הַמָּקוֹם הַהוּא יהוה | יִרְאֶה אֲשֶׁר
טו יֵאָמֵר הַיּוֹם בְּהַר יהוה יֵרָאֶה: וַיִּקְרָא

ram אַחַר נֶאֱחַז, *after it had become caught*, etc.

Others render: *After* he had first sighted a ram roaming wild, he *now saw it caught* by its horns in the thicket. God caused the ram to be caught in order to facilitate his catching it unharmed *(Tur)*.

Sforno explains that it was only *immediately after* the preceding events that he saw the ram caught in the thicket, *whereas there had been no ram there before*, Abraham, therefore, realized that the ram had been sent to him through the will of God and that it was not private property.

Malbim explains: Abraham was pondering what to sacrifice when וְהִנֵּה אַיִל, *and behold a ram!* He suddenly caught sight of a ram which had not been there earlier; אַחַר, *and then* he saw that the ram נֶאֱחַז בַּסְּבַךְ בְּקַרְנָיו, *had become caught in the thicket by his horns*. He recognized the Divine Providence in this event, Abraham went and untangled the ram, and sacrificed it.

תַּחַת בְּנוֹ – *Instead of his son.*

The Torah specifies this to indicate that with each part of the sacrificial service which he performed on the ram Abraham prayed to God that He accept that particular act as if it were being done to his son: '... As though *his* blood were sprinkled; as though *he* were flayed; as though *he* were consumed and became ashes' *(Rashi)*.

The very phraseology תַּחַת בְּנוֹ, *instead of his son*, is a refutation of that narrow minded misconception which refuses to acknowledge the deep symbolic significance of offerings. Were it not for this profound symbolism it would have been absurd, even obscene, to suggest that a stray animal could be *'instead'* of a beloved son who was to bear the destiny of the nation. It would be like substituting a worthless pin for a precious fortune *(Hirsch)*.

According to others, the phrase implies that Abraham prayed: 'Sovereign of the Universe! Regard it as though I had sacrificed my son Isaac first and then this ram [תַּחַת] following him', the word תַּחַת being understood as *after him*, as in the verse *II Kings* 15:7 *Jotham his son reigned in his stead* [תַּחְתָּיו, in the sense of: *as his successor*] *(Midrash)*.

14. ה׳ יִרְאֶה – *HASHEM Yireh* [i.e., '*HASHEM will see*'].

The plain meaning is as *Onkelos* renders: *God will* [choose and] *seek out* for Himself this place for the dwelling of His Shechinah and the offering of sacrifices *(Rashi)*.

Radak perceives this name as an allusion of Abraham's prophetic assurance to Isaac in *v.* 8: *God* [יִרְאֶה] *will seek out for Himself the lamb for the burnt offering*. This name was meant to memorialize forever that God indeed provided for the sacrifice.

HASHEM will see to it for all generations, that the merit of the

XXII 14 *So Abraham went and took the ram and offered it up as an offering instead of his son.* [14] *And Abraham named that site 'HASHEM Yireh,' as it is said this day, on the mountain HASHEM is seen.*

Akeidah shall remain with Isaac's descendants for all time *(R'Bachya).*

But the name ה׳ יִרְאֶה, *God sees,* is related to Moriah [see *comm.* to *Moriah* in *v.* 2]. It is also reminiscent of אֱלֹהִים יִרְאֶה לוֹ, *God will seek out,* of *v.* 8. The names indicate הוֹרָאָה, *instruction.* Here at Moriah, Abraham bequeathed to his descendants the concept that God always sees. Whenever and wherever we fail to see, the deficiency is ours, and we must subordinate our judgment to His *(Hirsch;* see continuation below).

As noted in the *comm.* to 14:18 the name of that place was originally *Shalem,* the name given it by Shem, son of Noah [whom the Sages identify with Malchizedek, king of Jerusalem.] After the *Akeidah,* Abraham called it *Yireh.* In deference to Shem and Abraham, God synthesized both names and called it Yerushalayim [יְרוּשָׁלֵם = יִרְאֶה שָׁלֵם] *(Midrash).*

אֲשֶׁר יֵאָמֵר הַיּוֹם בְּהַר ה׳ יֵרָאֶה — *As it is said this day, on the* [i.e., *this*] *mountain HASHEM is seen.*

The translation follows *Rashi: It shall be said by future generations* — (the word הַיּוֹם, *this day* being explained by *Rashi* as synonymous with *'until this day';* all future generations who read this phrase will apply the phrase to the time in which they live) — *'On this mountain the Holy One, Blessed be He, manifests Himself to His people.'*

[Thus *Rashi* in this interpretation connects ה׳ with יֵרָאֶה (ה׳ יֵרָאֶה=*HASHEM is seen)* rather than with הַר, *mountain* (הַר ה׳= *mountain of HASHEM).*

The phrase אֲשֶׁר יֵאָמֵר הַיּוֹם (lit. *that it shall be said this day)* is accordingly understood to mean: *hence the common proverb.*]

Rashi continues that according to the *Midrashic* interpretation the entire verse is to be explained: ה׳ יִרְאֶה *May HASHEM see* this Akeidah every year [on the anniversary of this day; see below] to forgive and save Israel from punishment, *so that it may be said on this day* — in every generation — בְּהַר ה׳, *on the Mountain of HASHEM,* יֵרָאֶה metaphorically *shall be seen,* the ashes of Isaac heaped up and serving as means of atonement.

Cf. *Pesikta Rabbasi* 40:6:

Abraham prayed:

ה׳ יִרְאֶה, *May HASHEM take note*

1. So said Abraham: May it be the will of Him Who saw the ram which I offered in place of my son, that it be considered as if I had indeed offered my son, him and all his future descendants. May the name of this place be יִרְאֶה, *He shall see,* and may the prayer of everyone who will ever recite His Name be included in my prayer today.

The Spirit of Holiness replied: אֲשֶׁר יֵאָמֵר הַיּוֹם, *that which is said today* [by Abraham], בְּהַר ה׳ יֵרָאֶה, *will be seen on the Mountain of HASHEM.*

When? — When God will choose this mountain as the resting place for His Name [i.e., the Holy Temple where the *Shechinah* will rest] and it is known as the Mountain of HASHEM, then — three times a year — will all Jewish men be seen [יֵרָאֶה] before God[*Deut.* 16:16]. At that time all Israel which comes here will be perceived as the descendants of Isaac who sanctify themselves before Me and sacrifice burnt-offerings before Me *(Midrash Tehillim).*

מַלְאַךְ יהוָה אֶל־אַבְרָהָם שֵׁנִית מִן־
טז הַשָּׁמָיִם: וַיֹּאמֶר בִּי נִשְׁבַּעְתִּי נְאֻם־יהוָה
כִּי יַעַן אֲשֶׁר עָשִׂיתָ אֶת־הַדָּבָר הַזֶּה וְלֹא

[lit. *'see'*] [of what happened here] אֲשֶׁר יֵאָמֵר, *so that it will be said*: [What took place] הַיּוֹם בְּהַר, *today on the mountain* — where truly the ashes of Isaac are heaped up and kept for expiation of Israel's sins — ה׳ יֵרָאֶה, *is still seen by* HASHEM.

As *Radak* explains: *This day* is a prophetic reference to the day when God's glory will be visible on that mountain; i.e. when the Temple will be built it will be said that HASHEM is seen on the mountain.

According to *R'Bachya*: God will see and remember this place forever, for Abraham's prayer at that most propitious moment was both for the present and for all his future descendants.

[Compare the impassioned prayer of King Solomon uttered before the newly finished altar of the Temple *at that very spot. I Kings* 8:22 ff.]

Hirsch continues his exposition of this verse: ... 'But now that the Torah, embodying the concept of God's Omnipotence, has been given us to spell out our obligations to Him, it is our *mission* to present ourselves to God to demonstrate how well we have succeeded in carrying out His mission. This was done, primarily when all Jews ascended to the Temple on Mount Moriah. Thus: בְּהַר ה׳, *on the mountain of God*, יֵרָאֶה, *one is seen*.

Hoffman suggests that in its most literal meaning, the phrase *as it is said 'this' day* refers to the time of Moses when the Torah was given. In Moses' time, the facts of the *Akeidah* were well known among the nation, and the site was spoken of as that place where HASHEM's Presence revealed itself to Abraham in order to save the life of Isaac. Abraham then chose a ram as a substitute sacrifice for his beloved son. Thus, idiomatically, the phrase has come to mean: *The mount where God sees/selects*, i.e., wherever God's salvation is most needed, there He appears and chooses those who merit His salvation.

15. וַיִּקְרָא ... שֵׁנִית מִן־הַשָּׁמָיִם — *The angel of* HASHEM *called to Abraham a second time from heaven.*

— Because the angel's first address had been interrupted by the sacrifice of the ram *(Tz'ror HaMor).*

[Again, the angel speaks in God's name, in first person. But cf. *Tanchuma* cited to *v.* 11, that it was God Himself who opened the heavens and addressed Abraham.]

Hirsch explains that the angel appeared a *second time*, because after having sacrificed the ram and named the mountain, Abraham had turned this epochal event into the external standard of behavior for his descendants. Only then did the angel announce the great blessing that lay in store.

16. בִּי נִשְׁבַּעְתִּי — *By Myself I swear.*

An irrevocable oath: Just as I am eternal, so is My oath eternal *(Radak).*

[This oath which emphatically summarizes all the previous promises, is the only formal one taken by God in the story of the

XXII
15-16

15 *The angel of HASHEM called to Abraham a*
second time from heaven, 16 *and said, 'By Myself I*
swear, declared HASHEM, that since you have done

Patriarchs. It is the oath referred to in many subsequent passages e.g. *Exod.* 32:13 and *Deut.* 26:15.]

What need was there of an oath? — This oath was given in direct response to Abraham's begging of God to assure him that never again would he or his son be subjected to additional trials *(Midrash).*

Before the *Akeidah,* God's commitment to Abraham had been merely a בְּרִית, *covenant* — something that was dependent upon the mutual fulfillment of both parties, although it was not dependent on external conditions. Now, however, it became a שְׁבוּעָה, *oath* — completely unconditional. Abraham had fulfilled the highest possible demand and thereby had indelibly inscribed in his descendants the ultimate allegiance to God no matter how far they might stray along the way *(Hirsch).* [1]

God had already promised that He would increase Abraham's children as the stars of the heaven [15:5] and the dust of the earth [13:16]. Now God assured Abraham by an oath in His name that his descendants would possess the gates of their enemies. Thus, even should they sin grievoulsy they would never be *completely* destroyed nor *permanently* fall into the hands of the enemy. Accordingly this was a solemn assurance of the ultimate redemption *(Ramban).*

[*The translation of* נִשְׁבַּעְתִּי in the present tense *I swear* rather than in the past tense *I have sworn* follows *Rashi* to 14:22 s.v. הֲרִמֹתִי where he cites this word as an example of the past which indicates the present as though the act is ready accomplished.]

נְאֻם ה׳ — *Declared HASHEM.*

The translation follows the commentators who explain the phrase as a solemn asseverative interjection used constantly by the prophets meaning, as *Onkelos* renders: *'HASHEM said'* [or: *'declared God'.*]

HaKsav V'HaKaballah explains that the word נְאֻם is related to the root אם = cognate of אֱמוּנָה, אָמֵן, *truth, faith, stability.* The phrase therefore suggests permanence: the oath will remain eternally true and permanent.

כִּי יַעַן אֲשֶׁר עָשִׂיתָ אֶת־הַדָּבָר הַזֶּה — *That since you have done this thing.*

The *Midrash* asks: There were *ten* trials, yet God attaches everything to *this one thing?* — This, however, was the final trial which counterbalanced all the others, for had he not submitted to it the merit of the others would have been lost [see *Rashi*'s alt. *comm.* to *v.* 2 s.v. קַח־נָא.]

The merit of the *Akeidah* is twofold: through it, the highest moral perfection became part of Isaac and his descendants, and its example

1. It is because God took this oath to Abraham that on Rosh Hashanah He would recall the *Akeidah* in Israel's merit, that Rev Berachiah took the words [introducing the law of Rosh Hashanah, in *Lev.* 23:24]: בַּחֹדֶשׁ הַשְּׁבִיעִי *in the seventh* [*'shevii'*] *month* to intimate 'In the month of God's שְׁבוּעָה, *oath* to Abraham. *(Pesikta Rabbasi* 46:6).

יז חָשַׂכְתָּ אֶת־בִּנְךָ אֶת־יְחִידֶךָ׃ כִּי־בָרֵךְ
אֲבָרֶכְךָ וְהַרְבָּה אַרְבֶּה אֶת־זַרְעֲךָ כְּכוֹכְבֵי
הַשָּׁמַיִם וְכַחוֹל אֲשֶׁר עַל־שְׂפַת הַיָּם וְיִרַשׁ
יח זַרְעֲךָ אֵת שַׁעַר אֹיְבָיו׃ וְהִתְבָּרְכוּ בְזַרְעֲךָ
כֹּל גּוֹיֵי הָאָרֶץ עֵקֶב אֲשֶׁר שָׁמַעְתָּ בְּקֹלִי׃

remained before them at all times. This assured that Israel would always survive as the nation of God *(Hirsch).*

Ibn Ezra explains יַעַן [since] as derived from the root עָנָה, *answer.* The literal rendering accordingly would be *'in response'* to your having done this thing.

וְלֹא חָשַׂכְתָּ — *And* [*you*] *have not withheld.*

HaKsav V'HaKabbalah notes that in *v.* 12 where the identical clause appears, it concludes with the word מִמֶּנִּי, *from Me,* whereas in our verse the concluding word is omitted. He further notes the apparent redundancy in our verse, for the prior phrase: יַעַן אֲשֶׁר עָשִׂיתָ, *since you have done ...* , already refers to the act of bringing Isaac to the *Akeidah*; why the repetitive reference to conclude the verse. He explains that there were two aspects of Abraham's devotion: 1 — The act of placing Isaac upon the altar and the readiness to slaughter him. 2 — Abraham's reluctance to free Isaac from the altar thereby forfeiting the opportunity to serve God by giving up what was more precious to him than anything on earth (see *comm. v.* 12). In *v.* 12 the reference is *solely* to the first aspect of the trial. Our verse enumerates both: אֲשֶׁר עָשִׂיתָ, *what you have done,* refers to the positive act of sacrifice; וְלֹא חָשַׂכְתָּ, *and you have not withheld,* refers to Abraham's unwillingness to withhold Isaac without at least symbolically drawing blood from him.

17. כִּי בָרֵךְ אֲבָרֶכְךָ — *That I shall surely bless you* [lit. *'for bless I shall bless you'.*]

The compound of the verb ברך signifies a double blessing: One for the father [Abraham] and one for the son [Isaac; or all of his future descendants.] Similarly in the next phrase וְהַרְבָּה אַרְבֶּה [lit. *and increase I shall increase*] *(Midrash; Rashi).*[1]

כְּכוֹכְבֵי הַשָּׁמַיִם וְכַחוֹל אֲשֶׁר עַל־שְׂפַת הַיָּם — *Like the stars of the heavens and like the sand on the seashore.*

[Cf. *comm.* to 13:16 and 15:5.]

When Israel complies with the will of God they resemble the stars of the heavens; then no kingdom or nation can dominate them. But when they flout His will, they resemble the sand on the seashore — trampled by every tyrannical foot *(Midrash Or HaAfelah; Torah Shelemah* 22:195).

Midrash Aggadah comments:

1. The blessings given to Abraham were unconditional; God did not say that they would be granted only if his descendants scrupulously obeyed the commands of the Torah. It is this promise to which we refer when we beseech God זְכוֹר אֲשֶׁר נִשְׁבַּעְתָּ לַאֲבוֹתֵינוּ כְּכוֹכְבֵי הַשָּׁמַיִם אַרְבֶּה אֶת זַרְעֲכֶם, *Remember what you swore to our forefathers, 'Like the stars of heaven will I increase your seed* (the *Tachnun* prayer). We pray that God will fulfill his oath even though we are undeserving *(Chafetz Chaim al HaTorah).*

XXII
17-18

this thing, and have not withheld your son, your only
one, [17] *that I shall surely bless you and greatly in-*
crease your offering like the stars of the heavens and
like the und on the seashore; and your offspring shall
inherit the gate of its enemy; [18] *and all the nations of*
the earth shall bless themselves by your offspring,
because you have listened to My voice.'

Just as the sand is a wall against the sea whose raging waves break on it, so the nations of the world throw themselves against Israel, but their fury is in vain for they cannot prevail [see *Jer.* 5:22] and they break before Israel. Such was the case with Pharaoh, Sisera, Babylon, Haman, and the Greeks. Similarly will the Edomites [= Rome; also a generic term for Israel's oppressors] fall before them as it is written [*Ezek.* 25:14]: *I will exact My vengeance upon Edom, through My people Israel.*

[See also *comm.* to 1:9 s.v. יִקָּווּ הַמַּיִם.]

וְיִרַשׁ זַרְעֲךָ אֵת שַׁעַר אֹיְבָיו — *And your offspring shall inherit* [or: *seize; possess; capture* (see *Hirsch* on 15:8: אִירָשֶׁנָּה)] *the gate of its enemy.*

[The capture of the gate, the stronghold of a city, is symbolic of its downfall. Therefore *'gate'* is used in this connotation, for they will possess the city by inheriting or siezing its gate.]

Abarbanel explains that the three blessings of this verse and the next, were given Abraham measure for measure. 1 — Because he was prepared to render himself childless, he was blessed with abundant progeny. 2 — Because he would have forfeited his inheritance [by slaughtering his only son], he was promised that his offspring would inherit the Land. 3 — Because he was ready to incur the curses of the populace for having slaughtered his son, he was promised that all would bless themselves by his offspring.

18. וְהִתְבָּרֲכוּ בְזַרְעֲךָ — *Shall bless themselves by your offspring.*

— I.e., the nations will pray to God: 'Bless us as You have blessed the offspring of Abraham' *(Radak).*

When nations will [in the Time to Come] *call upon HASHEM's Name to serve Him unanimously* [*Zeph.* 3:9] they will seek blessings through your seed and endeavor to emulate them *(Sforno).*

The translation follows *Rashi* and *Ibn Ezra* to 18:18. [See below]. *Onkelos* renders: *Shall be blessed for the sake of your children.*

[As explained in the *comm.* to 18:18 *Onkelos* and *Rashi* do not distinguish between the *hispa'el* [the reflexive] form of this verb and the *niph'al* [passive: וְנִבְרְכוּ], while *Ibn Ezra* and *Radak* do perceive differences in meaning between the forms. They render נִבְרְכוּ *be blessed* and הִתְבָּרְכוּ, *bless themselves.* See also *comm.* to 12:3.]

עֵקֶב אֲשֶׁר שָׁמַעְתָּ בְּקֹלִי — *Because* [lit. *'as a result of that'*] *you have listened to* [lit. *'in'*] *My voice* [i.e., *My command.*]

Verse 17 listed the blessings which I will bestow upon your descendants in reward for your not

יט וַיָּשָׁב אַבְרָהָם אֶל־נְעָרָיו וַיָּקֻמוּ וַיֵּלְכוּ
יַחְדָּו אֶל־בְּאֵר שָׁבַע וַיֵּשֶׁב אַבְרָהָם בִּבְאֵר
שָׁבַע׃

having *withheld your only son.* Now I bestow a further blessing: *all the nations of the earth shall bless themselves by your offspring because you have listened to My voice* — i.e., because you responded to My command of וְהַעֲלֵהוּ, *bring him up.*

Ramban in *Deut.* 7:12, discusses the word עֵקֶב, *because.* He cites commentators [*Ibn Ezra* and *Radak*] who comment that it signifies *ultimate consequence. Ramban* explains the derivation on this definition: The Hebrew language employs organs of the human body as the source of figurative expressions. Thus, the *beginning* or *best* of something is called רֹאשׁ, *head;* while the *conclusion, consequence,* or *end* is called עֵקֶב, *heel.* Similarly, when referring to relative value, the most important is called רֹאשׁ, *head,* while the least important is called זָנָב, *tail.*

In a similar vein, *Ramban* ad loc. cites *Onkelos* who renders the word חֲלַף, *in exchange.* The connotation is a *circular course* of events, i.e. it is as if a person's deed returns to him, for his reward or punishment is commensurate with his act. The primary meaning of the root עקב, in this view, is *round;* therefore, the heel, which is rounded, is called עָקֵב.

[It would seem that the English idiom which best conveys the meaning of עֵקֶב, is: *on the heels of,* i.e., closely following; *'as a result of'*; hence 'because'.][1]

Heidenheim adds that the word עֵקֶב also refers to *footsteps* [cf. *Song of Songs* 1:8: בְּעִקְבֵי הַצֹּאן, *the footsteps of the sheep.* It has the same connotation as בִּשְׁבִיל, *because,* which is derived from שְׁבִיל, *footpath.* Therefore, either word may be used to indicate a consequence which comes as a direct result of a prior cause i.e., the cause is the 'path' leading to their consequence which comes 'on the heels' of the cause.

19. וַיָּשָׁב אַבְרָהָם אֶל־נְעָרָיו — [*And*] *Abraham returned to his young men.*

Although only Abraham is mentioned as having returned, Isaac's presence may be assumed. Only Abraham is mentioned because he was the principal figure and his son Isaac was secondary to him. Cf. *v.* 3 וַיָּקָם וַיֵּלֶךְ, 'And *he* [Abraham] rose up and went' where only Abraham is mentioned although it is obvious that Isaac and the two attendants accompanied him; and *Exod.* 10:1 where God's command was addres-

1. *Harav David Feinstein* further suggests that there are two connotations inherent in the expression עֵקֶב, *heel:*

(a). Abraham was rewarded because he complied with God's will *'on the heels'* of the command — i.e., immediately. He did not procrastinate in the hope that in the interim the decree might be changed. This is expressed in *v.* 3 *Abraham awoke early in the morning* — 'for the zealous are early to perform their religious duty.'

(b). By עֵקֶב, *footpath* [cf. *Song of Songs* 1:8] God was indicating that Abraham had thereby *trod the path* in the sense that he set an external pattern for his children to emulate throughout history. He was therefore deserving of all these blessings for setting the standard.

XXII
19 [19] *Abraham returned to his young men, and they rose up and went together to Beer Sheba, and Abraham stayed at Beer Sheba.*

sed only to Moses although Aaron was to accompany him *(Ibn Ezra; Radak; Yohel Or).*

According to the *Midrash,* however, the absence of Isaac's name *is* significant:

— 'And where was Isaac? — Rav Berachiah said in the name of the Rabbis: Abraham sent him to Shem* [son of Noah] to study Torah *(Midrash).*

... And he remained there three years *(Targum Yonasan).* [1]

According to another view in the *Midrash,* Abraham sent him at night for fear of עַיִן הָרַע, *the evil eye* [i.e., he feared that the jealousy aroused by his narrow escape from death might result in an evil eye which would adversely affect him]. The efficacy of an evil eye was demonstrated at the time of Chananiah, Mishael, and Azariah who were never again mentioned in Scripture from the time they emerged from the fiery furnace [*Daniel* Ch. 3] ... They died as a result of an evil eye being cast upon them.

[Abraham therefore sent him on alone — safe from the gaze of Ishmael and Eliezer, who, as the *Midrash* relates, disputed which of them would inherit Abraham should Isaac die — each of them claiming priority. Abraham was not apprehensive that an evil eye would be cast upon Isaac in the academy where it is possible that the matter of the *Akeidah* was not yet known at the time.]

וַיָּקֻמוּ וַיֵּלְכוּ יַחְדָּו — *And they rose up and went together.*

Hirsch notes that this clause appears here for the third time in the chapter. The first two indicated the joint ascent of Abraham and Isaac to new dimensions of greatness. Here it shows how, even after having attained awesome spiritual heights, they returned to their two attendants and went together with them. They were unaffected by pride. Instead of being consumed with 'I' and 'myself', they considered themselves no better than anyone else.

וַיֵּשֶׁב אַבְרָהָם בִּבְאֵר שָׁבַע — *And Abraham stayed at Beer Sheba.*

The translation of וַיֵּשֶׁב [lit. *dwelt*] as *stayed* follows *Rashi* who explains that Abraham stayed there, only *temporari-*

*[On Shem see *Overview* to *Noach (vol. I)* p. 216 ff; *comm.* to 6:10; 9:27; and 10:21,24. As indicated in the "Chronology/Time Line: Adam to Jacob" on p. xii, Shem was born in 1558 and died in 2158. Isaac was born in 2048 and was 37 years old at the *Akeidah* in 2085. Shem (who is identified with Malchizedek, king of Shalem = Jerusalem; see *comm.* to 14:18; and who, according to tradition founded a Torah academy in association with his great-grandson Eber) was therefore 527 years old at the time.]

1. *Me'am Loez* explains why it was necessary for Abraham, who was unequalled in his knowledge of Torah, to send Isaac to the academy of Shem. Pedagogy is a unique talent which Shem possessed to a superior degree. In addition, in Shem's academy Isaac would find the vital stimulation of discourse with fellow students. Furthermore, a child, because he is so familiar with his parent, can often not learn from him successfully. Previously, Sarah would not allow Isaac to leave home. Having succeeded in taking Isaac away from home on the pretext that he would go to study Torah, [see *footnote* to *v.* 2] Abraham sent him to Shem.

°וַיְהִי אַחֲרֵי הַדְּבָרִים הָאֵלֶּה וַיֻּגַּד
לְאַבְרָהָם לֵאמֹר הִנֵּה יָלְדָה מִלְכָּה גַם־
כא הִוא בָּנִים לְנָחוֹר אָחִיךָ׃ אֶת־עוּץ בְּכֹרוֹ

ly, for his *permanent residence* for the past 12 years was once again in Hebron to where he had returned after having lived in Beer Sheba for the 26 years following the destruction of Sodom as explained in 20:1 and in the chronology (which is based upon *Seder Olam), Rashi* interprets וַיֵּשֶׁב in this case as indicating only *temporary dwelling.*]

According to *Midrash HaGadol* Abraham felt compelled to return to Beer Sheva, site of his *eshel* [21:33], because it was there that he had experienced spiritual tranquility and had carried on his mission of proclaiming God's Name. [And as *Ramban* suggests in 23:3, he went first to the site of his *eshel,* there to give thanks for the miracle that befell him.]

[It was also the birthplace of Isaac who had just been saved.]

Malbim comments that the literal flow of the verses suggests that Abraham sent Isaac ahead to Hebron where Sarah dwelt to tell her the outcome of the recent events. Abraham, however, returned to spend some time at Beer Sheba which, although later part of the territory of Simeon, was then under Philistine control. When Sarah died in Hebron, Abraham hastened there (23:2) to eulogize her and arrange for her burial. Since Isaac was already in Hebron with his mother, Scripture has no need to specify that he, too, came to eulogize her.

◆§ The Birth of Rebecca

20. וַיְהִי אַחֲרֵי הַדְּבָרִים הָאֵלֶּה — *[And] it came to pass after these things* [or lit. *'words'*]

I.e., after the deep reflections [הרהורי דְבָרִים] which were inspired by the *Akeidah.* The *Midrash* comments that when Abraham returned from Mount Moriah he mused: 'Had my son actually been sacrificed he would have died childless. Perhaps I should have married him to one of the daughters of Aner, Eshkol or Mamre.'* God therefore caused him to be informed that Rebecca, Isaac's future mate, had been born. This, then, is the meaning of אַחֲרֵי הַדְּבָרִים, *after these words* — i.e., after the *words* [meditations] which were inspired by the *Akeidah (Rashi).*[1]

*[The version in the *Midrash* reads: Abraham said: 'What shall I do now? — I will marry him to one of the daughters of (my covenant-brothers 14:13) Aner, Eshkol, and Mamre who are virtuous women, for of what concern to me is their (accursed Canaanite) birth?'

God then said to him: 'Do not entertain such a notion — for Isaac's mate has already been born.']

[The commentators point out that the *Midrash* to 15:1 (which follows the War of the Kings) also interprets אַחַר הַדְּבָרִים הָאֵלֶּה to refer to deep reflections on the part of Abraham. See *comm.* there.]

[*Rashi* explains in 15:1 that when the term אַחֲרֵי, *after* is used it signifies a long lapse of time from the preceding, unlike אַחַר, *after,* which signifies *immediately following.* Since our verse is usually interpreted to mean that Abraham was informed of Rebecca's birth *immediately* after the *Akeidah* it would seem that the term אַחַר should have been used. *Mizrachi* comments that אַחַר would indicate

1. *After these things* — After Abraham had bound Isaac, the Satan came and told Sarah that Abraham had killed Isaac. Sarah cried out in grief and died *(Targum Yonasan).*

XXII
19

20 *It came to pass after these things, that Abraham*
was told, saying: Behold, Milcah too has borne
children to Nachor, your brother: 21 *Utz, his first-*

something which occurred immediately — without any delay. Since there was at least a slight time lapse between the *Akeidah* and the news of Rebecca's birth, the use of אַחֲרֵי is indeed proper.

Gur Aryeh comments that the passage of time *per se* is not the determining factor in whether to use אַחַר or אַחֲרֵי. If the second narrative is dependent upon and inseparable from the first, then אַחַר is used. If, however, the two narratives are not inherently unified, then אַחֲרֵי may be used, even though, coincidentally, there was little lapse of time. Abraham's concern at not having arranged Isaac's wedding was not the reason for Rebecca's birth.

Levush HaOrah explains that *Rashi* interprets our verse as a reference to 'deep reflection' rather than elapsed time because the context of the verses makes it plain that little time elapsed. Therefore, it should have said simply that Abraham was informed of the birth. Hence the phrase can refer only to something other than time, i.e. after reflecting.]

Midrash Sechel Tov explains that the term אַחֲרֵי, *after*, in this verse, refers to the long lapse of 37 years from when Milcah began to bear children. For as the *Midrash* notes, when Sarah conceived so did Milcah. The matter is mentioned here rather than above because this narrative centers around the birth of Rebecca who was born in the same year as the *Akeidah*.

Tur suggests, that אַחַר *always* signifies *immediately following* while אַחֲרֵי can signify either *after a long lapse*, or *immediately after*, depending upon the context.

הִנֵּה יָלְדָה מִלְכָּה גַם־הִוא בָּנִים לְנָחוֹר אָחִיךָ — *Behold, Milcah* [lit. *she*] *too has borne* [*children*] *to Nachor your brother.*

[For their relationship to Abraham see 11:29, and Genealogical Table on p. xii].

Hoffman points out that the birth of Rebecca at this time is another instance of the Divine Providence with which the story of the Patriarchs is replete. Because she was born, Isaac, who had submitted himself to becoming a 'perfect offering', did not have to be defiled by marriage to one of the debauched Canaanite women. It is to accentuate this fact that the Torah does not mention the genealogy of Terach's family previously.

Ramban observes that God must have performed a miracle in giving children to Nachor and his wife in their old age, for it appears from the verse that Abraham was unaware previously that they had children. Had children been born to them when they were young, Abraham would certainly have heard of it previoulsy since the distance between Mesopotamia [Nachor's home] and Canaan was not great. This is the intent of גַּם הִוא, *she too* — as the Sages explained, Milcah, like her sister Sarah [miraculously] gave birth to children in her old age.

— The primary *news* however was not the birth of Milcah's *children*, which apparently took place in the years after Abraham departed from Charan, but the birth of Rebecca which coincided with the *Akeidah (Hoffman).*

For, obedient to the command [12:1] *Get yourself ... from your father's house*, Abraham had kept himself so isolated from his relations that he came to know of their offspring only when the time came to seek a wife for Isaac *(Hirsch).*

Cf. also *Yalkut Shimoni, Balak* 1:766: When God promised Abraham

וְאֶת־בּוּז אָחִיו וְאֶת־קְמוּאֵל אֲבִי אֲרָם׃
כב וְאֶת־כֶּשֶׂד וְאֶת־חֲזוֹ וְאֶת־פִּלְדָּשׁ וְאֶת־
כג יִדְלָף וְאֵת בְּתוּאֵל׃ וּבְתוּאֵל יָלַד אֶת־
רִבְקָה שְׁמֹנָה אֵלֶּה יָלְדָה מִלְכָּה לְנָחוֹר
כד אֲחִי אַבְרָהָם׃ וּפִילַגְשׁוֹ וּשְׁמָהּ רְאוּמָה
וַתֵּלֶד גַּם־הִוא אֶת־טֶבַח וְאֶת־גַּחַם וְאֶת־
תַּחַשׁ וְאֶת־מַעֲכָה׃

[*v.* 18]: *all the nations of the earth shall bless themselves by your offspring,* Abraham reflected: others shall bless themselves by my merit, should not my relative Milcah, sister of my wife, also be remembered? Immediately he was notified that — *'Behold! Milcah, she too, had borne children.'*

For, as the *Midrash* notes, when God had 'remembered' Sarah, He 'remembered' all the other barren women in the world and they too, including Milcah, conceived. [See *comm.* to *v.* 1.]

Rashi cites the *Midrash* that גַּם הִוא, *she too,* implies that Milcah had families equal in number to Abaham's — namely twelve: Of the twelve tribes descended from Abraham, eight were children of Jacob's wives and four of his maid-servants, so in Milcah's case, eight were sons of the wife and four were sons by the concubine.

It is noteworthy that the same number of tribes — twelve — descended from Ishmael as well [25:16] *(Hoffman).*

21. אֶת־עוּץ בְּכוֹרוֹ — *Utz, his first-born.*

According to one view in *Yerushalmi Sotah* 5:6, Utz is identified with Job ...

For the Holy One, Blessed be He told Abraham after the *Akeidah* that many, more severe trials, should have befallen him, but now that Utz, (who was in fact Job) was born, they would not. For God told Abraham [*Eccles.* 9:7]: *'Go, eat your bread with joy ... God has already approved your deed.'* [i.e., He will not subject you to further sacrifice.] *(Tanchuma Yashan Sh'lach).*

[See *comm.* to Job 1:1, and *ArtScroll* ed. *Eccles. ibid.* Cf. also *comm.* to *Gen.* 10:23. On *Midrashic* derivation of the identification of Utz as Job, see *Torah Temimah* to our verse.]

בּוּז — *Buz*

The name Buz occurs also in *Jeremiah* 25:23. Elihu ben Barachel, the fourth friend of Job, was a Buzite [*Job* 32:2] *(Hoffman).*

קְמוּאֵל — *Kemuel.*

The *Midrash* identifies Kemuel with Balaam [according to *Radal*'s emendation], because he arose [קָם] against the people of God [אֵל].

קְמוּאֵל אֲבִי אֲרָם — *Kemuel, the father of Aram.*

Kemuel may be associated with Aram because the son was a more famous personage than the father [cf. *the father of Milcah* in 11:29 and *comm.* p. 351]. Or it may be

XXII born; Buz, his brother; Kemuel, the father of Aram;
20-21 *22 and Kessed, Hazo, Pildash, Yidlaf, and Bethuel;*
23 And Bethuel begot Rebecca. These eight Milcah
bore to Nachor, Abraham's brother. *24 And his con-*
cubine whose name was Reumah, also bore children:
Tevach, Gaham, Tahash, and Maacah.

that there was more than one Kemuel in that generation, so the Torah identified the one under discussion by specifying that the Kemuel son of Milcah was the father of Aram *(Ramban).*

The name *Aram* also appears in 10:22 as one of the sons of Shem. See *comm.* there. This would indicate that there were two Aramean peoples — a Semite one which was more ancient, and a younger, Nachorite one *(Hoffman).*

22. כֶּשֶׂד — *Kessed.*

— The ancestor of the Chaldeans. [=Kasdim.] *(Radak).*

Hoffman suggests that Kessed may have been the ancestor of the Kasdim [Chaldeans] who stole the camels of Job (1:17). However, the Chaldeans who later became a world power were apparently descendants of Arpachshad.

[Cf. *comm.* to 11:28 s.v. *Ur Kasdim.*]

23. וּבְתוּאֵל יָלַד אֶת־רִבְקָה — *And Bethuel begot Rebecca.*

The entire genealogy was recorded only to lead up to this key verse *(Rashi).*[1]

Laban is not mentioned here although he was older than Rebecca, because the Torah was concerned only with mentioning the eight children of Milcah [of whom Bethuel was the eighth, and not the *grand*children.] Rebecca was mentioned only because her genealogy was necessary for the narrative *(Ramban).*

The *kal* form יָלַד, [*(begot)* lit. *'gave birth'* instead of the *hiphil* causative הוֹלִיד (lit. *'begot')*] is not unusual even when the subject is a male. See for example, 4:18; and 10:8 *(Hoffman).*

24. וּפִילַגְשׁוֹ ... וַתֵּלֶד גַּם־הִוא — *And his concubine ... [she] also bore.*

'She also' — For, as noted above, when Sarah was 'remembered' and granted a child, all barren women — *even slaves* — gave birth at the same time *(Torah Sheleimah* 225).

מַעֲכָה — *Maacah.*

In *I Chron.* 19:6 Aram is referred to in association with Maacah. The name occurs often in Scriptures [*Deut.* 3:14; *Josh.* 12:5; 13:11; *II Sam.* 10:6. Cf. *Beth Maacah* in *II Sam.* 20:14.] This people apparently dwelt in the Hermon region *(Hoffman).*

The Torah includes the genealogy of the concubine as well to establish that *all* of these children

1. Before the Holy One, Blessed be He made Sarah's sun set, He made Rebecca's sun rise. First: בְּתוּאֵל יָלַד אֶת רִבְקָה — *Bethuel begot Rebecca;* then: וַיִּהְיוּ חַיֵּי שָׂרָה, *the life of Sarah was ... (Midrash).*

of Nachor were worthy to marry the children of Abraham, and they were *all* included in Abraham's injunction to Eliezer in 24:38 *(Ramban).*

According to the Masoretic note appearing at the end of the *Sidrah* there are 147 verses in the *Sidrah* numerically corresponding to the mnemonic אמנו״ן [= 147; apparently a reference to the profound אֱמוּנָה, *faithfulness,* of Abraham which is the primary theme of this *Sidrah.* This faithfulness reached its zenith when Abraham was confronted by the command to sacrifice the very son in whom his every future promise was to have been fulfilled. Yet his utter אֱמוּנָה, *trust,* in God: was such that Abraham complied unhesitatingly.] The Haftorah begins with *II Kings* 4:1: וְאִשָּׁה אַחַת.

נשלם כרך ב מספר בראשית בעזרת האל

Meir Zlotowitz
Rosh Chodesh Shevat 5738/January 1978
Brooklyn, New York

An Overview —
The Days of the Perfect

יוֹדֵעַ ה׳ יְמֵי תְמִימִם וְנַחֲלָתָם לְעוֹלָם תִּהְיֶה. כְּשֵׁם שֶׁהֵן תְּמִימִים כַּךְ שְׁנוֹתֵיהֶם תְּמִימִים. בַּת כ׳ כְּבַת ז׳ וכו׳ ד״א זוֹ שָׂרָה שֶׁהָיְתָה תְמִימָה בְּמַעֲשֶׂיהָ.

HASHEM is aware of the days of the perfect; their inheritance will endure forever (Psalms 37:18). Just as they [the righteous] are perfect, so their years are perfect. When she [Sarah] was twenty, she was just as she was at seven ... Another interpretation: this refers to Sarah who was perfect in her deeds (Bereishis Rabbah 58:1).

I. Two Forms of Perfection

Sarah was perfect. In wisdom, in beauty, in innocence, in accomplishment, in consistency, her life was a tapestry of perfection. She was the first of the Patriarchs and Matriarchs to die, and the Torah chose her to display the standard of כּוּלָן שָׁוִין לְטוֹבָה, *all [her years] were equally good (Rashi* to 23:1. See *comm.).*

The word תָּמִים, *perfect, has two connotations, both applicable to Sarah: without blemish, and of complete faith.*

Sfas Emes expounds that the word תָּמִים, *perfect,* has two connotations, both applicable to Sarah: without blemish, and of complete faith.

Unblemished Time

Just as people, animals, and things can be without blemish, so can time. For time, too, is a creation. Before the existence of heaven and earth, there was no such concept as time. Existence was limited to God alone, and He is beyond time, without either beginning or end. That He included time in the universe means that it is the tool, and therefore also the challenge, of man. Just as man is charged with wisely using his ability, his possessions, and his surroundings, so he is charged with making proper use of the moments allotted him on earth. We may liken a lifetime to a huge needlepoint canvas with millions upon millions of holes to be filled with the threads of achievement. The holes are the countless instants, the fleeting 'nows' of life.

We may liken a lifetime to a huge needlepoint canvas with millions upon millions of holes to be filled with the threads of achievement.

As the saying goes, הֶעָבַר אַיִן הֶעָתִיד עֲדַיִן וְהַהֹוֶה כְּהֶרֶף עַיִן, *the past is gone, the future is not yet, and the present is like the blink of an eye.* True, but the past, however glorious or inglorious, is the accumulation of those blinks and the future, whatever it may bring, is built upon them. What does 'everyman's' needlepoint of life resemble? For most, it is a series of random patches and blanks. Perhaps not even a recognizable pattern emerges after all the years of effort. For others, there may be only a few scattered, ill-fitting stitches. For still others there may be imperfect but still distinguishable pictures that testify to purposeful weeks and months.

And then there are the Sarahs. Their canvas has no bald spots. It is full, perfect, lush with color, meaning, and accomplishment.

And then there are the Sarahs. Their canvas has no bald spots. It is full, perfect, lush with color, meaning, and accomplishment. Every thread is related to the one before and the one after. It reflects what God knows — that just as they are perfect, so their years are perfect; and had they not been perfect they could never have achieved the perfection of a lifetime without blemish.

In this vein, *Chiddushei HaRim* explains the meaning of Hillel's famous exhortation וְאִם לֹא עַכְשָׁיו אֵימָתַי, *If not now— when? (Avos* 1:14). Simply understood, the *Mishnah* warns that time is not forever. No man knows how long he will live nor can he be sure that he will have the ability or opportunity tomorrow or next week to perform the good deed he seeks to postpone today. There is a deeper meaning as well, the *Rim* maintains.

Can the obligation of any instant be postponed to a later moment? No — for that later moment has an obligation of its own.

Every עַכְשָׁיו, every point in time, has a particular purpose for each human being. Its purpose was ordained by the Creator for every person who shares that particular point in time: For some it is Torah study, for others the performance of a commandment. It may be earning a livelihood, eating, sleeping, relaxing, traveling. Can the obligation of any instant be postponed to a later moment? No — for that later moment has an obligation of its own. Today's 2:34 p.m. was never here before and it will never return. Tomorrow's 2:34 — or today's 2:35 — has a mission of its own. To do tomorrow what should have been done today is to deprive tomorrow of its due. 'If not now — when?' — Hillel asks: What will become of *this* 'now' if it is not utilized? It will be lost forever!

The Light of Day

A day that has the glow of spiritual accomplishment is a day; a twenty-four hour period without such meaning is but the unrealized potential of a day that never was.

Sfas Emes often quotes *Chiddushei HaRim*'s homiletical interpretation of וַיִּקְרָא הָאֱלֹהִים לָאוֹר יוֹם, *and God called to the light — Day! (Genesis* 1:5): It was not the emergence of the morning sun that God entitled *Day*, nor was it the passage of twenty-four hours on a clock. The essence of *Day* is its אוֹר, its *spiritual light.* A day that has the glow of spiritual accomplishment is a day, a twenty-four hour period without such meaning may be called a day for the sake of convenience or convention, or for crossing off another number on a calendar — but in the truest sense, it is but the unrealized potential of a day that never was.

God renews his creation constantly, daily [הַמְחַדֵּשׁ בְּטוּבוֹ בְּכָל יוֹם תָּמִיד מַעֲשֵׂה בְרֵאשִׁית]. Because there are always new opportunities, they must be received with freshness and vigor. Time and duty never become stale to truly perceptive — to the righteous Sarahs — because they accept every challenge as novel and never-to-be-repeated. As *Sifri (Devarim* 6:6) teaches, God urges us always to bear in mind the commandments אֲשֶׁר אָנֹכִי מְצַוְּךָ הַיּוֹם, *which I command you 'today'* — never are we to think of them as ancient vestiges of miraculous days in Egypt and the Wilderness. They are *new.* Given *daily.* And our response must be one of anxious anticipation of each day's store of light-filled moments.

Just as each limb and organ of the body has its role and function within the whole, so each day has its role in the perfection of an individual lifetime.

Just as each limb and organ of the body has its role and function within the whole, so each day has its role in the perfection of an individual lifetime. The righteous person pursues the spiritual roots beneath the external trappings of each moment. By so doing he gives it completion and fashions it into a sound part of the whole. This analogy of the moments of life to the organs of the body is borne out by the context of the very verse upon which the Sages expound that the days of the righteous are perfect. The preceding verse *(Psalms* 37:17) laments כִּי זְרוֹעוֹת רְשָׁעִים תִּשָּׁבַרְנָה, *For the arms of the wicked will be broken* ... then the Psalmist speaks of the perfection with which the righteous invest not only their deeds but their moments on earth. Is it not plain that every עַכְשָׁיו, every *now,* is as vital as a cell, a capillary, a nerve?

Perfect in Faith

There is a second connotation of the word תמים — perfection and wholeheartedness in faith (see *Genesis* 17:1 and *Deuternomy* 18:13). This, too, relates as much to the *days* of the righteous as to their deeds and attitudes, for man passes through many periods — good times and bad — during his sojourn on earth. It is relatively easy to have perfect faith in God while He smiles at Israel. Only the wicked and spiritually corrupt could fail to 'see' God's smiling countenance and 'feel' His gentle hand during the golden years of King Solomon. Israel basked in a universal recognition of its glory such as it had never before known. Such was its magnificence that hordes of gentiles streamed to embrace the religion of God's successful people — and the Sages of the period refused to accept proselytes because conversion came too easily. Why should one not wish to join a proven success?

The Sages of the period refused to accept proselytes because conversion came too easily. Why should one not wish to join a proven success?

Why not join a nation which knew only cloudless days?

The perfect faith of the righteous remains impaired and unblemished even in times of darkness and suffering. Truly — 'just as they are perfect, so their years are perfect!'

But the perfect faith of the righteous remains unimpaired and unblemished even in times of darkness and suffering. It is strong enough to endure the buffeting of eras when God's countenance is clouded by anger, and the hand Israel feels is not the gentle one of His beneficence, but the mailed fist of its persecutors. Through *all* periods, the righteous remain perfect in their faith. Such was Sarah's life. Growing up in the moral filth of Ur Kasdim and Aram or living in the sanctuary of Abraham's tent; dragged off to the harems of Pharaoh and Abimelech, or playing hostess to angels and proselytes; giving her maidservant Hagar to Abraham that he might have an heir despite her own barrenness or nursing her own Isaac amid joy and rejuvenation — all were the same to Sarah. Whatever external winds might blow, her faith was unimpaired. Truly — 'just as they are perfect, so their years are perfect!' *(Sfas Emes).*

II. Sarah's Eternal Teaching

Unlike Abraham

Such was the unique lesson of Sarah — that in all varieties of time and experience one must maintain faith.

Such was the unique lesson of Sarah — that in all varieties of time and experience one must maintain faith based on the conviction that all conditions are dictated by God for the fulfillment of His ultimate will. Originally her name had been שָׂרַי, *Sarai,* [literally, *my mistress*] for she had been the dominant figure only to Abraham, but then a new dimension was added, both to her name and to her mission. She became שָׂרָה, *Sarah,* a name with the connotation that she was the spiritual mistress of all the world *(Rashi* to *Genesis* 17:15. See ArtScroll Ed.). But if Abraham had been elevated to the status of אַב הֲמוֹן גּוֹיִם, *Father of the Multitude of Nations* (17:5), and he was subservient to *Sarai* — for such was the import of her original name — then why was it necessary to rename her as well? The answer lies in the different characteristics of Abraham and Sarah. Abraham represented מִדַּת הַחֶסֶד, *the Attribute of Kindness* [see *Overview* to *Lech Lecho.*] In his life all flowed from God's manifestation of kindness. Abraham was honored wherever he was. He was respectfully addressed as נְשִׂיא אֱלֹהִים, *prince of God* (23:6), even by the idolatrous accursed Canaanites of Heth, and Divine intervention spared him from living long enough to see Esau's descent into wickedness (see *comm.* to 29:25). Neither his descendants nor the world at large could learn from Abraham how to face dark moments, for he had none. But Sarah knew. She taught how to perfect time and how to recognize that every moment emanated from God in order that we might fill it with faith and service. If only Abraham's way of life and faith was to serve as the model for all people, then the weak of spirit would not find the strength to cope with adversity. But from Sarah they could learn strength and constancy no matter what the odds. That was Sarah's great role in the development of man *(Siach Sarfei Kodesh).*

Neither his descendants nor the world at large could learn from Abraham how to face dark moments, for he had none.

Hagar Learns It

This lesson was taught Hagar when she fled from Sarah's chastisement of her. She sat by a well pondering when an angel came to her and asked:

> הָגָר שִׁפְחַת שָׂרַי אֵי מִזֶּה בָאת וְאָנָה תֵלֵכִי
> *Hagar, maidservant of Sarai, where have you come from and where are you going?* (16:8).

The question was not meant to gather information. The angel knew — she had fled from the house of Abram and Sarai and she was going back to Egypt; she was traveling the road from sanctity to profanity. The facts were plain. But were the implications? Hagar! Do you realize what you have left behind? Have you evaluated the fool's gold for which you trade the precious moments in the service of the righteous? Why are you crestfallen, Hagar, because you have been forced to submit to the

Hagar! Do you realize what you have left behind? Have you evaluated the fool's gold for which you trade the precious moments in the service of the righteous?

domination of Sarai? Is that reason enough to turn your back on the Abrahamitic universe? Remember, Hagar, you are שִׁפְחַת שָׂרַי, *the maidservant of Sarai* — from whom can you learn better than from her to have faith even in the blackest moments? Where will you find as holy a place as Sarai's tent? And how can you forsake such lofty teaching merely to seek comfort?

Where will you find as holy a place as Sarai's tent? And how can you forsake such lofty teaching merely to seek comfort?

שׁוּבִי אֶל גְּבִרְתֵּךְ וְהִתְעַנִּי תַּחַת יָדֶיהָ

Return to your mistress and submit to her domination (16:9).

Hagar relented for she had indeed been taught the lesson of Sarai there by the well. *'You are the God of Vision'* (16:13), she said, 'Who sees the humiliation and misery of the afflicted' *(Midrash).* So she called the well *Be'er Lachai Ro'i, the well of the Living One Who sees me.*

It was that well that Isaac went regularly to pray and where he settled after marrying Rebecca. The well had a special meaning for him.

It was to that well that Isaac went regularly to pray and where he settled after marrying Rebecca (25:11). The well had a special meaning for him — Isaac, whose life began Israel's descent into exile, had to live according to his mother's lesson — the lesson that had been exemplified by Hagar's experience. Indeed, that was God's intention in dispatching the angel to bring the lesson home to Hagar. Ishmael did not benefit by his mother's experience; Isaac — and after him, scores of Jewish generations that lived through every manner of privation — did. To accentuate that lesson for Isaac, God sent an angel to show Hagar the lesson of Sarah *(Sefer HaZechus).*

Sarah's Heiress

רַבִּי עֲקִיבָא הָיָה יוֹשֵׁב וְדוֹרֵשׁ וְהַצִּבּוּר מִתְנַמְנֵם. בִּקֵּשׁ לְעוֹרְרָן אָמַר מַה רָאֲתָה אֶסְתֵּר שֶׁתִּמְלֹךְ עַל קכ״ז מְדִינוֹת אֶלָּא תָּבֹא אֶסְתֵּר שֶׁהִיא בַּת בִּתָּהּ שֶׁל שָׂרָה שֶׁחָיְתָה ק׳ וכ׳ וז׳ וְתִמְלוֹךְ עַל ק׳ וכ׳ וז׳ מְדִינוֹת.

Rabbi Akiva sat and expounded, but the congregation drowsed. He sought to arouse them. He said, 'Why was Esther worthy to reign over 127 provinces? — Let Esther, a granddaughter of Sarah who lived 127 years, come and reign over 127 provinces (Bereishis Rabbah 58:3).

What is the connection between Sarah's years and Esther's kingdom? And why should Rabbi Akiva's comparison between the two serve to stimulate a drowsing audience?

Rabbi Akiva lived in a time of perhaps the most intense persecution Israel had known. The Roman Empire in all its infamous barbarianism had destroyed the Temple, crushed the last embers of resistance, put down Bar Kochba's rebellion, and outlawed the teaching of Torah. This last edict would ח״ו have snuffed out the soul of the people; Rabbi Akiva defied it and eventually paid for his bravery with a martyr's death by torture.

The Jew who perceives the holiness of his Torah study feels no boredom. Excited people do not doze, but Rabbi Akiva's students did. Why?

His students had fallen into a stupor, a sure symptom that the Divine Countenance was masked from their perceptions. The Jew who perceives the holiness of his Torah study feels no boredom. The Jew who senses the cosmic effect of his good deeds feels no fatigue. Excited people do not doze, but Rabbi Akiva's students did. Why? He understood why. Deep down, they doubted that they and their studies made any difference. The glories of old might remain etched in memory, but never could they return to reality. To inspire them, Rabbi Akiva attacked the problem at its roots.

What was there in the heritage of the Patriarchs and Matriarchs that could enable Esther and her generation to surmount the darkness? There was Sarah.

Esther, too, lived in a time when God's Visage glowered at Israel. It was a generation of הַסְתָּרַת פָּנִים, *concealment of God's [Merciful] Face* (see *Overview* to ArtScroll *Megillas Esther).* What was there in the heritage of the Patriarchs and Matriarchs that could enable Esther and her generation to surmount the darkness? There was Sarah. She had lived all moments of her life with equal perfection. In Pharaoh's palace of lust or Abraham's temple of holiness, she never failed to perceive that all was from God.

Esther learned from her grandmother, Sarah. She learned not to fear the exile of her people or her personal exile as the wife of Ahasuerus. Her years were perfect. Her deeds were perfect. Sarah still lived in her granddaughter, Esther. So Sarah's years were translated into provinces; the Matriarch reigned over time and her granddaughter reigned over space.

And Rabbi Akiva's students? Grandsons of Sarah have no right to despair, because they know the lesson of her perfect life.

Not a Lost Moment

The *Midrash* states that Sarah died when she was told that Isaac had been slaughtered on the *Akeidah* (see *comm.* to 23:1). The implication is that her death was accidental, that she would have lived much longer had she only known the truth.

Harav Yaakov Kaminetzky proves that such an interpretation is untenable. The *Talmud* states that since heredity is a factor in determining a person's expected lifespan, a person should begin anticipating the end of his days when he comes to within five years of the age at which one of his parents died. Therefore, the Sages explain, when Isaac reached the age of 123, he prepared to bless his firstborn because his mother had died at 127 years of age. But if Sarah's death was purely accidental — the result of the shocking news — then why should Isaac draw any conclusions from it? Surely heredity is not a factor where external factors cause death?

But if Sarah's death was purely accidental — the result of the shocking news — then why should Isaac draw any conclusions from it?

No. Sarah lived out her full years. Indeed, it is axiomatic that a righteous person of Sarah's caliber fulfills her entire mission on earth — her days were יְמֵי תְמִימִים, *perfect days* of a perfect person. Her soul was taken from her because she had fulfilled her purpose on earth. In the natural world, God decrees that death have the appearance of a natural cause — a heart attack, a stroke, an accident, an earthquake, or a shocking lie — any one may be the 'natural' cause through which God carries out His will. But the days of Sarah are complete and perfect in quantity as well as quality.

Such was the storehouse of gems which Sarah presented to God. He had given her potential; she presented Him with fulfillment.

Such was the storehouse of gems — the moments of her life — which Sarah presented to God. He had given her potential; she presented Him with fulfillment.

An Overview —

The Matriarchs/Sarah and Rebecca

כָּל יָמִים שֶׁהָיְתָה שָׂרָה קַיֶּמֶת הָיָה עָנָן קָשׁוּר עַל פֶּתַח אָהֳלָהּ כֵּיוָן שֶׁמֵּתָה פָּסַק אוֹתוֹ עָנָן. וְכֵיוָן שֶׁבָּאת רִבְקָה חָזַר אוֹתוֹ עָנָן. כָּל יָמִים שֶׁהָיְתָה שָׂרָה קַיֶּמֶת הָיוּ דְלָתוֹת פְּתוּחוֹת לִרְוָחָה ... הָיְתָה בְּרָכָה מְשׁוּלַּחַת בְּעִיסָּה ... הָיָה נֵר דוֹלֵק מִלֵּילֵי שַׁבָּת וְעַד לֵילֵי שַׁבָּת ... כֵּיוָן שֶׁבָּאת רִבְקָה חָזַר. וְכֵיוָן שֶׁרָאָה אוֹתָהּ שֶׁהִיא עוֹשָׂה כְּמַעֲשֵׂה אִמּוֹ ... מִיָּד וַיְבִאֶהָ יִצְחָק הָאֹהֱלָה.

All the years that Sarah lived, a cloud hung by the entrance of her tent; as soon as she died, the cloud left. But as soon as Rebecca came, that cloud returned. All the years that Sarah lived, the doors were wide open [to welcome all wayfarers] ... a blessing was dispatched to her dough ... the lamp would burn from Sabbath eve to the next Sabbath eve ... as soon as Rebecca came it [all of the above] returned. As soon as [Isaac] saw that she did as his mother did ... immediately [the Torah relates]: Isaac brought her to the tent (Bereishis Rabbah 60:16).

I. Complimentary Functions

A Name

When God fashioned Eve and presented her to Adam as his mate and helpmeet, he named this new breed of human as he had named all other living things.

לְזֹאת יִקָּרֵא אִשָּׁה כִּי מֵאִישׁ לֻקֳחָה זֹּאת

This shall be called woman for from man was she taken (2:23).

Woman is called אִשָּׁה, *Ishah*, because she was fashioned from אִישׁ, *Ish* [*man*]. The Torah gives this as the reason for *her* name, but it does not tell us why man was called *Ish*. We know the derivation of man's other name, *Adam* — he was fashioned from the *adamah*, earth (2:7) — but why is he called *Ish*? What is the significance of each of the two names? And why is there a feminine form of *Ish*, but not of *Adam*?

Not only man, but all animal life was fashioned from earth. But human beings have within them a characteristic of another prime element — fire.

Not only man, but all animal life was fashioned from earth. All breathe, eat, sleep, propagate. God's plan was to give life to clods formed from earth, whether the life was human or animal. But human beings have within them a characteristic of another prime element — fire. Fire represents verve and enthusiasm, lust and initiative. It represents the uniquely human traits that *give* man dominance and enable him to attain wisdom, develop culture and pass them on to his children. The name אִישׁ, *Ish*, derives from the element of אֵשׁ, *eish* [*fire*].

In man's 'fire' aspect, however, God must be present, otherwise he can become a source of danger and destruction.

There is a major difference between these two facets of life. Simply to live and vegetate — although impossible without God's gift of life — can be managed without Godliness. Animals do it; so do Godless humans. If man lives that way, he imitates an animal, becomes a caricature of what he should be, but he is not destructive. In man's 'fire' aspect, however, God must be present, otherwise he can become a source of danger and destruction. No elaboration is needed. A glance at the morning paper, a slight acquaintance with the history of any century, will show all too well what happens when man fans his instincts into a flaming conflagration, and does it without God's guidance.

Only Together

Nowhere is the spirit of God more essential than in the union between man and woman that produces future generations. When His spirit is present from the moment of conception, the future has holiness as an ingredient of its growth from a cell to a finished being whose lustful drives have been tempered by God's Presence. Man alone cannot bring it; woman alone cannot bring it — only the two of them together can invite holiness to join.

Man alone cannot bring it; woman alone cannot bring it — only two of them together can invite holiness to join.

This is implied by the names *Ish* and *Ishah.* The Sages teach that man's name, אִישׁ, contains a י, *yud.* Woman's name, אִשָּׁה, contains a ה, *he.* When man and woman unite with sincerity and holiness, he contributes his *yud* and she contributes her *heh* forming יָהּ, *Yah,* a Name of God. But if man and woman deny God entry into their lives, he surrenders his *yud* and she surrenders her *he.* Remaining is אֵשׁ, *eish* — the *fire* of destruction *(Sotah* 17a, see *Rashi; Pirkei d'Rabbi Eliezer).*

Adam, God's own handiwork, perceived when the first woman was brought to him that they were to be partners in ennobling the fiery instincts within them both. Woman as a creature ultimately formed from the earth needed no particular name — both man and woman are *adam.* But the function of taming fire and turning it into a Godly force must be carried out jointly with each of the partners taking separate but complementary roles. Adam knew that he needed her as she needed him in order that — together — they could stamp God's Name on the future of humanity. And so he named her *Ishah,* assigning to her the second letter of God's Name *(Sifsei Zaddik).*

Adam knew that he needed her as she needed him in order that — together — they could stamp God's Name on the future of humanity.

II. Sarah's Temple

Matriarch's Tent

Sarah was the classic Jewish mother, the first and the only Matriarch who is named as one of the seven prophetesses quoted in Scripture. Her home was no ordinary tent. It had extraordinary qualities: a cloud of holiness, doors which proclaimed their openness to all passers-by, a blessing in her dough, a Sabbath lamp that remained lit all week long. These miracles were not Abraham's doing; they ceased with Sarah's death.

There was a special significance in these blessings. They paralleled the miracles of the Mishkan *in the wilderness and the Temple in Jerusalem.*

There was a special significance in these blessings. They paralleled the miracles of the *Mishkan* in the wilderness and the Temple in Jerusalem. The cloud represented God's Own Presence, the same Presence which rested on the *Mishkan*. Only one other human being had a comparable sign of holiness hovering over his private residence: Moses *(Ex.* 33:9). Sarah's open doors symbolized the Temple which was a repository of holiness beckoning every Jew to come and draw closer to God through its agency.

There was a blessing in her dough; her guests ate and then went away with lingering feelings of satisfaction that kept hunger away for a long time. In the Sanctuary of the Temple, loaves of show-bread, לֶחֶם הַפָּנִים, were emplaced every Sabbath. All week long they remained as warm and fresh as they were when they were set on the sacred Table. The Sages teach that the bread of the Temple was the source of prosperity for the entire nation. Because it was blessed it never became stale, unlike material things which begin to deteriorate from the moment they come into existence. The blessing in Sarah's dough was a spiritual one, a blessing that protected it from the elements and helped all who ate it absorb its holiness within themselves.

The נֵר מַעֲרָבִי, *western lamp*, of the Temple Menorah burned longer than all the others. It was the first lit and the last to go out, its flame burning bright until the moment of the next day's lighting.

This symbolized a principle of spiritual growth — yesterday's greatness need not fade away; it should become the starting point for today's further development.

This symbolized a principle of spiritual growth — yesterday's greatness need not fade away; it should become the starting point for today's further development. Of course, when one deserts the world of the spirit and plunges into the material here and now, his earlier attainments become diminished, for holiness is not static; it cannot be stored away for future use. Sarah's Sabbath candles ushered in a יוֹם מְנוּחָה וּקְדֻשָּׁה, *day of contentment and holiness*, God's precious gift to Israel. But so do our Sabbath flames. What happens when Sabbath is over? Do the Sabbath flames of holiness survive the six days of banality and material striving? Sarah's did. Her Sabbath lamp, like the western lamp of the Menorah, endured and shed a glow that lit the darkness of the week. When the next Sabbath came, she brought new holiness into her home — not replacing its predecessor, but *enhancing* it.

Because God's Presence was in Sarah's tent, on her table, her menorah, He set His cloud atop her dwelling.

Thus the heavenly cloud that hovered over her tent — like that which adorned the Temple — was God's testimony to what went on within. Because God's Presence was in Sarah's tent, on her table, her Menorah, He set His cloud atop her dwelling *(Shem MiShmuel).*

The True Mishkan

The Sages often refer homiletically to the Jewish home as a sanctuary. Simply understood, this serves as an inspiring exhortation to every Jew: Your home is not a structure of brick and mortar, wood and plaster. It can be imbued with God's Own holiness. Jews built a *Mishkan* and a Temple which became resting places for the *Shechinah* — and you can make the same of your home.

Inspiring though this is, it barely touches on the magnitude of a Jewish home. In his introduction to the Book of *Exodus, Ramban* writes:

When they arrived at Mount Sinai and made the Tabernacle, they returned to the eminence of their forefathers who had God's mystery upon their tents.

> ... The exile [in Egypt] was not completed until the day they [Israel] returned to their place and returned to the eminence of their forefathers. When they left Egypt, even though they left the house of slavery, they were still considered exiles because they were in a land not their own, confounded in the wilderness. When they arrived at Mount Sinai and made the Tabernacle, and the Holy One, Blessed be He, returned and rested His *Shechinah* among them — then they returned to the eminence of their forefathers who had God's mystery upon their tents, and who were themselves the 'chariot' [i.e., the bearers] of His

> *Shechinah.* Then, they were considered finally redeemed...

The Mishkan *itself was meant to be a replica of the Jewish home — not vice versa.*

As *Ramban's* words make clear, the *Mishkan* itself was meant to be a replica of the Jewish home — not vice versa. Sarah's tent was the Temple upon which God placed His Presence. The *Mishkan* was built to recapture that eminence — and so can every Jewish tent, hovel, home.

III. Sarah's Successor

Prerequisites

When Eliezer was dispatched to find a suitable mate for Isaac, he set his priority on her character. Brilliance and beauty might be attractive and impressive, but they were not sufficient to make a Jewish Matriarch, to make a woman worthy to wear the mantle of Sarah. Beseeching God to make his mission successful, Eliezer set up a test of character and kindness. The story is familiar enough (see Chapter 24 and *comm.).* As many commentators have noted, Abraham's kindred in Charan were no less idol worshippers than his Canaanite neighbors, but despite all their many deficiencies, his family still retained a level of decency that allowed one of its daughters to emerge untainted from the abomination of idolatry. A daughter of such a family could shed the layers of religious impurity that may have adhered to her from being raised by a Bethuel and living with a Laban, but someone who lacked the moral and ethical virtues of Abrahamitic greatness could never be 'educated' to them.

A daughter of such a family could shed the layers of religious impurity that may have adhered to her, but someone who lacked the moral and ethical virtues of Abrahamitic greatness could never be 'educated' to them.

The *Brisker Rav, Harav Yitzchak Zev Soloveitchick,* was asked why the Torah does not make specific comments concerning character traits. The Sages and ethical works liken bad character traits to such sins as idol worship, and teach that the unvirtuous person is unwelcome — even despised — by

God. If so, why does not the *Torah* state: Do not be quick to anger. Do not be depressed. Do not be arrogant ...?

The perfection of character — a never-ending obligation — is a prerequisite to proper acceptance of the Torah and fulfillment of the commandments.

The *Rav* answered that the Torah was given to *people*, not animals. The perfection of character — a never-ending obligation — is a prerequisite to proper acceptance of the Torah and fulfillment of the commandments; its necessity is implicit.

As *Rabbi Chaim Vital* writes:

> Bad character traits are much worse than transgressions themselves. Thus you can understand why the Sages say, for example, that one who becomes angry is as if he had served idols, or one who is coarse of spirit is as if he had denied the primary principle [of God's existence] and he should be uprooted like an *asheirah* [a tree worshiped as an idol] ... Understand this well, for it is because they are principles and fundamentals that they are not reckoned among the 613 Commandments, which depend on man's intellectual capacity. Therefore, one must beware of bad character traits even more than he is zealous in the positive and negative commandments, for by being a virtuous person, he will readily perform the commandments. Thus, you can also understand the astounding words of the Sages concerning virtues, that modesty and humility lead one to Divine Inspiration, [רוּחַ הַקֹּדֶשׁ] and the *Shechinah* rests upon him ... and many such statements. They speak not of the performance of commandments but of character virtues! ... Understand this well — how the foundation of performance of the commandments is moral excellence — and vice-versa *(Sha'arei Kedushah* 2:2).

They speak not of the performance of commandments but of character virtues! Understand this well — how the foundation of performance of the commandments is through good virtues.

The *Brisker Rav* points out the revealing process of Isaac's decision to take Rebecca as his wife. Eliezer came back to Canaan with her and told Isaac all that had happened on his trip (24:66): God's intervention enabled him to make in a matter of hours a round trip that should have taken five weeks; the water rose up toward Rebecca; Eliezer had prayed that God indicate the proper maiden and the choice had fallen upon Rebecca; Bethuel tried to poison him, but was himself killed through an angel's intervention. Miracle after miracle Eliezer related, but still Scripture does *not* say that Isaac married Rebecca. Miracles are surely impressive, but they are not enough to determine an Isaac's choice of his Matriarch.

Only when Isaac saw Rebecca's deeds and virtues did he take her for his wife. Then *came love and comfort for the loss of his mother.*

He took Rebecca into the tent, *Sarah*'s tent, and behold! — *she was Sarah*! The tent became a Temple again. There was kindness and blessing in the tent. Visitors felt welcome and satisfied. Holiness came and remained, and the *Shechinah* was a welcome guest. Only when Isaac saw Rebecca's deeds and virtues did he take her for his wife (24:67). *Then* came love and comfort for the loss of his mother.

A Revealing Comparison

The emergence of Rebeca as Sarah's successor reveals much about Sarah herself. The two Matriarchs seem to be totally different personalities.

The emergence of Rebecca as Sarah's successor reveals much about Sarah herself. The two Matriarchs seem to be totally different personalities:

Rebecca comes to us as a model of self-effacing kindness. Even when she initiated the tactics which resulted in Esau's loss of the blessings to Jacob (see Chapter 27), she did it quietly, gently, without confronting Isaac with a demand that a son as unworthy as Esau should be banished, not blessed.

Our picture of Sarah, at least as it takes shape from a superficial reading of the Torah's narrative of her life, is quite different. Scripture tells us of her courage and strength. She followed Abraham from Charan to an unknown future, let herself be abducted by Pharoah and Abimelech because to do otherwise could have caused Abraham's death. Seeing herself barren, she surrendered her privileged position by giving her maidservant to Abraham as a wife so that he might have an heir. But when Hagar became arrogant she punished her harshly — at least in Hagar's eyes (see *comm.* to 16:6). When Ishmael presented a danger to her Isaac, Sarah banished him to the heat and thirst of the desert though he was too sick to travel. It was a move that Abraham refused to permit until God instructed him to obey Sarah because she was superior to him in prophecy (21:12). So grievous an act was it in Abraham's judgment, that it is reckoned by the Sages as one of his ten tests, but for Sarah it was not a test, her conscience was not troubled. Indeed, she insisted that Hagar and the feverish Ishmael be expelled to an uncertain fate without animals or generous provisions.

So Sarah was strong and decisive — but was she kind and generous? Rebecca was kind and generous — but was she strong and decisive?

So Sarah was strong and decisive — but was she kind and generous? Rebecca was kind and generous — but was she strong and decisive? The lesson of the Sages would appear to be that they were very much alike. Isaac took Rebecca not because she was *unlike* Sarah, but because she was *like* her. And God bore witness to the fact by showing that Sarah's temple and Rebecca's temple were one and the same. To the casual observer, nothing could be more different than a down featherbed and a mosquito netting. In reality, though, they are identical in the sense that each is the correct protection against a particular condition. One mother covers her child gently with the featherbed, the other drapes his cradle with netting; both are doing what must be done *then* and both are equally concerned and caring.

The underlying substance of Sarah and Rebecca was identical: virtue, kindness, humility, and all the traits that, as *R' Chaim Vital* wrote, are the prerequisites of obedience to the commandments.

The Midrash *comments that just as wool and linen are forbidden in the combination, so, too, Sarah understood that Isaac and Ishmael could not remain together in the same family.*

Midrash Tanchuma (Chayei Sarah) states that part of Abraham's eulogy for Sarah was the verse

דָּרְשָׁה צֶמֶר וּפִשְׁתִּים

She sought out wool and linen (Proverbs 31:13).

The *Midrash* comments that just as wool and linen are forbidden in combination, so, too, Sarah understood that Isaac and Ishmael could not remain together in the same family. Each had his mission, and Isaac's mission could not be contaminated by the presence of Ishmael. Would it have been merciful to allow Ishmael to present a mortal threat to the Jewish nation — God's purpose in creation — for even another moment? Or would it have been false mercy akin to Saul's disastrous pity that permitted the survival of King Agog of Amalek and led to the eventual birth of Haman, and who knows how many other shedders of Israel's blood. (See *Overview* to ArtScroll *Megillas Esther.)*

Was Sarah indeed lacking in mercy? God Himself testified twice that she was not.

Was Sarah indeed lacking in mercy? God Himself testified twice that she was not: He ratified her decision by telling Abraham to obey her, and He showed that gracious, selfless Rebecca was Sarah reborn!

Corresponding and Against

Indeed, Sarah embodied the concept of *Ish* and *Ishah* which Adam recognized when the first wife in history was brought to him. Together, the two could harness the fiercest human drives by placing them at the service of יָ־הּ, *God.* It was a mission neither could perform alone. Man and woman, husband and wife are separate beings, yet they are one. In unison, by complementing one another, they bring holiness to one another, to their posterity, to the universe.

Man and woman, husband and wife are separate beings, yet they are one. In unison, by complementing one another, they bring holiness to one another.

When He saw Adam living alone without a companion, God said לֹא טוֹב הֱיוֹת הָאָדָם לְבַדּוֹ אֶעֱשֶׂה לּוֹ עֵזֶר כְּנֶגְדּוֹ, *It is not good that man be alone; I will make him a helper corresponding to him* (2:18). The word כְּנֶגְדּוֹ can be understood either as *corresponding to him,* in the sense that she complements him, compensating for his flaws as he does for hers and accentuating his strengths as he does hers; or it can be translated *against him* in the sense that she opposes and hinders him. Thus our Sages teach that if a man is worthy, his wife will help him, but if he is unworthy she will hinder him *(Yevamos* 63a). Experience teaches that the way to help someone is not always by agreeing. Sometimes a person insists upon following the wrong course; then it is the highest duty of a dear friend — and surely of a loving mate — to cajole, coax, insist, deceive, bully, persuade so that, willingly or not, the enticing course of disaster will be forsaken. Sometimes the mate is truly כְּנֶגְדּוֹ, *corresponding* [i.e., helpful] *to him,* only if she is כְּנֶגְדּוֹ, willing to be *against him.*

Abraham was blind to the shatnez *in his home, but Sarah was wiser.*

Abraham was blind to the *shatnez* [i.e., forbidden combination of 'wool and linen'] in his home. In his impassioned kindness, he hoped yet to raise up Ishmael from the filth of Hagar's heritage and his own uncouth and undisciplined ways. But Sarah was wiser. She acted *not* as Isaac's anxious, protective mother — for the verses Abraham chose for her eulogy were from אֵשֶׁת חַיִל, *a woman* [i.e., *wife*] *of valor.* She acted as Abraham's *wife* in excising the forbidden combination from their home. Of course she was strong — for strength was the necessary complement to Abraham's חֶסֶד, *kindness.*

Rebecca, too, lived in a house with two sons. She, too, saw what her husband could not see. That she acted differently from Sarah does not change their essential sameness.

Rebecca, too, lived in a house with two sons. She, too, saw what her husband could not see. She, too, acted in the called-for manner. That she acted differently from Sarah does not change their essential sameness, for each did what had to be done in her particular circumstances.Isaac judged correctly when he saw in Rebecca the image of Sarah. Justifiedly was he comforted after his mother when he took the Charanite treasure into his home which she transformed into Sarah's temple *(MiSod Chachamim).*

III. God Alone Chooses

Bogus Acquiescence

The choice of a Matriarch of Israel is not a random task. She must have human qualities of the highest order, accept the principles which God ordains as the foundation stones of His people, and be chosen by His standards of holiness and dedication. For no less than the Patriarch is she the forebear of the nation, the bearer of the measure of Godliness that, combined with her husband's, results in the

Name of God that is stamped upon their offspring from the instant of conception.

In the choice of Rebecca, we find that her family at first acquiesced to the match,piously declaring מֵה׳ יָצָא הַדָּבָר, *the matter stems from HASHEM* (24:50). Later, however, they tried to delay the marriage 24:55 — according to the Sages, they tried to prevent it entirely — unsuccessfully. Why the change of heart?

Let not the idolators of Charan ever say that they were instrumental in the birth of Israel!

Shem MiShmuel explains that God wanted them to have no share whatsoever in the match of Isaac and Rebecca. Let not the idolators of Charan ever say that they were instrumental in the birth of Israel! He likens it to the *Talmudic* passage which relates that when the Messiah comes, the nations will demand a share in the beneficence being showered upon those who trusted God's promise and obey His commandments through all the horrors of exile.

> 'Master of the Universe, many markets did we set up, many bathhouses did we make, much silver and gold did we amass ... Many bridges did we build, many cities did we conquer, many wars did we wage. — We did it all only for Israel's sake so that it might study Torah.'
>
> The Holy One, Blessed be He, will reply, 'Whatever you did, you did for yourselves...' (*Avodah Zarah* 2b).

The bogus obsequiety of Rebecca's parents and brother could indeed have enabled them to claim that without them there would have been no Jewish people. 'We gave up our sister for the sake of Israel's future! We, too, have a share in God's Temple!'

When they realized that Eliezer had no precious gifts for them, that he had no intention of 'buying' a bride for his master, their refrain changed.

But then, when they realized that Eliezer had no precious gifts for them, that he had no intention of 'buying' a bride for his master, their refrain changed. They tried to prevent the marriage, delay it, even murder Eliezer. That later behavior proved beyond a doubt that there had never been sincerity in their earlier cooperation. Indeed, without realizing what they were saying, they had told the truth: מֵה׳

יָצָא הַדָּבָר, *the matter stems from HASHEM*, for the match between Isaac and Rebecca had never been in their hands. It was ordained by God.

Rebecca's Acceptance

So God chose the Matriarch for His people. He ratified Abraham's vision of Charan and Canaan: underlying decency can overcome an overlay of idolatry, but underlying corruption cannot be easily rooted out.

Before Rebecca could be returned to Eretz Yisrael *to bring holiness back to Sarah's tent, she had to be ready to accept the fundamentals of a Jewish nation.*

Before Rebecca could be returned to *Eretz Yisrael* to bring holiness back to Sarah's tent, she had to be ready to accept the fundamentals of a Jewish nation. Shimon HaZaddik, last survivor of the Men of the Great Assembly, taught:

עַל שְׁלֹשָׁה דְבָרִים הָעוֹלָם עוֹמֵד עַל הַתּוֹרָה וְעַל הָעֲבוֹדָה וְעַל גְּמִילוּת חֲסָדִים

On three things does the world stand: on the Torah, on Service, and on the performance of kindness (Avos 1:2).

Rebecca had demonstrated her kindness — demonstrated it so nobly that Eliezer was dumfounded — but that is not enough upon which to establish God's nation.

Greedy Laban was enticed by the glitter of the gold and jewels which Eliezer gave her, but their true value was beyond his comprehension.

Eliezer presented her with gifts. Greedy Laban was enticed by the glitter of the gold and jewels which Eliezer gave her, but their true value was beyond his comprehension. *Rashi* cites and *Gur Aryeh* explains the *Midrashic* interpretation of the underlying meaning of Eliezer's gifts. He gave her a gold nose ring weighing a בֶּקַע, *a half-shekel.* That was a message to her that her descendants would each give a half shekel a year to share in purchasing the offerings of the *Mishkan* and Temple. There would be no exceptions, no pity on the poor, no lavish gifts by the rich. For their individual offerings, donors could give what they would, what they could — but the nation in its entirety shared equally in the dedication to עֲבוֹדָה, the pillar of service, the second leg of the tripod that supports the universe.

Eliezer gave her two bracelets weighing ten *shekalim.* They symbolized the acceptance of the

Torah, the day when Israel would stand at Sinai and receive *two* tablets inscribed with *ten* commandments. That was Torah, the third leg of the tripod. No matter how great the kindness of Rebecca, she could not become a Jewish Matriarch unless she was prepared to subordinate herself to all three parts of Israel's mission.

No matter how great the kindness of Rebecca, she could not become a Jewish Matriarch unless she was prepared to subordinate herself to all three parts of Israel's mission.

She was willing — and so she became Sarah. She and Isaac combined to create a new manifestation of God's Name that gave form, meaning and eternity to the flames burning within them.

An Overview —
Eliezer — Blessed Servant

כְּנַעַן בְּיָדוֹ מֹאזְנֵי מִרְמָה, זֶה אֱלִיעֶזֶר שֶׁהָיָה יוֹשֵׁב וּמַשְׁקִיל אִם בִּתּוֹ רְאוּיָה הִיא אוֹ אֵינָהּ רְאוּיָה לְיִצְחָק.

The Canaanite [merchant] — in his hands are scales of deception (Hoshea 12:8): this is Eliezer who sat and considered whether or not his daughter was worthy of Isaac (Bereishis Rabbah 59:9)

דַּמֶּשֶׂק אֱלִיעֶזֶר שֶׁדּוֹלֶה וּמַשְׁקֶה מִתּוֹרַת רַבּוֹ לַאֲחֵרִים

Eliezer of Damesek (15:2) who drew and gave others to drink of his master's Torah (Yoma 28b).

זְקַן בֵּיתוֹ שֶׁהָיָה זִיו אִיקוּנִין שֶׁלּוֹ דּוֹמֶה לוֹ

The eldest of his household (24:2) for his [Eliezer's] features resembled his [Abraham's] (Bereishis Rabbah 59:8).

עַל יְדֵי שֶׁשָּׁרֵת אוֹתוֹ צַדִּיק בֶּאֱמוּנָה יָצָא מִכְּלַל אָרוּר לִכְלַל בָּרוּךְ

Because [Eliezer] served that Tzaddik [Abraham] faithfully, he went from the category of 'accursed' to the category of 'blessed' (ibid. 60:7).

I. Saintly Servant

Personal Greatness

It is no small matter that Eliezer is described in such lofty spiritual terms. Following the rule that the physical details given by the Torah have spiritual significance as well, the Sages derive that Eliezer was as much in control of his Evil Inclination as was Abraham, that he was as great as 318 of Abraham's students combined, that he knew all of Abraham's teachings and transmitted them to others — even that he came to resemble Abraham.

This resemblance can be understood only in spiritual terms. It is surely impossible that Eliezer the Canaanite could have physically resembled Abraham the Semite. But on a scale of values where spiritual attainment is paramount, people are envisioned in terms of wisdom, righteousness, and kindness. In our own experience, we often see how a person's developing character stamps itself on his features. A keen observer can usually tell the difference between a saint and a sadist even though their external measurements are the same. When Moses came down from Mount Sinai, rays of spiritual brilliance shone from him, constant witnesses to the heights he had attained.

When Laban first glimpsed Eliezer he thought the stranger before him was Abraham. But Laban had never seen Abraham.

According to the *Midrash*, when Laban first glimpsed Eliezer he thought the stranger before him was Abraham — because Eliezer *resembled* Abraham. But Laban had never seen Abraham; how can the *Midrash* speak of a resemblance? Undoubtedly, Eliezer's saintliness shone from his face and Laban imagined that so pure-looking a person could only be Abraham.

Eliezer's great spiritual stature can be deduced from his very success in gaining Rebecca's firm insistence that she wished to accompany him to Canaan.

Eliezer's great spiritual stature can be deduced from his very success in gaining Rebecca's firm insistence that she wished to accompany him to Canaan. As a child of only three [according to most commentators, see *comm.*] she surely knew little or nothing of her faraway uncle, Abraham, and she may never even have heard of Isaac. Her parents may have had memories of Abraham and Sarah, but she did not. Her only conception of the household where she was asked to spend the rest of her days came from Eliezer. She saw his righteousness, delicacy, tact, consideration, gentility, humility. She saw the servant and concluded that if such was the product of Isaac's home, then she wanted to be part of it.

Eliezer was indeed the teacher of Abraham's Torah — not only from lectures, but more importantly, from living example (*Oznaim LaTorah).*

Total Selflessness

It is instructive that in all sixty-seven verses of the narrative of Eliezer's mission (chap.24), he is not once mentioned by name. Even when he introduces himself to Bethuel's family, he says simply עֶבֶד אַבְרָהָם אָנֹכִי, *I am a servant of Abraham* (24:34). A more accurate translation than the bland and antiseptic *servant* would be *slave.* So he introduced himself and so he is described throughout the chapter: a *slave.* A slave is the property of his master. He has no possessions, rights, or priviliges. Moses, too, is described as a *slave,* he is עֶבֶד ה׳, *a slave of HASHEM (Joshua* 1:1). The connotation is simple: Moses dedicated himself totally to the service of God, no personal considerations ever entered into his thinking. Like a loyal slave, he was nothing and deserved nothing except as his master wished. In this sense, too, Eliezer was a slave — the total and perfect reflection of Abraham's personality and will. In this manner he proceeded upon his mission.

In this sense, too, Eliezer was a slave — the total and perfect reflection of Abraham's personality and will.

Abraham had given him *carte blanche,* but he did not rely upon his own merits or wisdom. Although he formulated his plan to test the moral qualifications of Isaac's future bride, he relied only on prayer for success. He directed his prayer to the God of *Abraham* and asked that *kindness* be shown Abraham. Merit did not enter into his thoughts. The prayer was not for his personal success; it was for the fulfillment of *Abraham's* need. And he did not call upon Abraham's merit — for no one knows better than the greatest people how insignificant is their merit — but upon God's mercy.*

He did not call upon Abraham's merit — for no one knows better than the greatest people how insignificant is their merit — but upon God's mercy.

Eliezer's choice of total reliance upon God's guidance instead of upon his own considerable wisdom and good judgment, and his prayers for God's kindness in a matter where people of lesser stature

*But see *Ta'anis* 4a that Eliezer erred in not inquiring into such matters as Rebecca's health.

generally rely on common sense and keen insight — these demonstrate how great was the concentration of the powers of evil to thwart his effort to continue the development of the nation of Israel. The sapling of Israel was indeed fragile at that point: Abraham and Sarah had not had their son until infertility and old age made miraculous intervention necessary; the *Akeidah* nearly ended Isaac's life before he had married; it appeared that in all the world, only Rebecca was a suitable match for him; as events later unfolded, even this marriage was infertile until prayer and miracle combined to produce Jacob and Esau. It was not the only time in the history of the world when the forces of evil girded in battle against an event of overriding significance for the achievement of God's ultimate purpose (*Shem MiShmuel*).

It was not the only time in the history of the world when the forces of evil girded in battle against an event of overriding significance.

II. Homes of the Patriarchs

אָמַר רַבִּי אַחָא, יָפָה שִׂיחָתָן שֶׁל עַבְדֵי בָּתֵּי אָבוֹת לִפְנֵי מְתּוֹרָתָן שֶׁל בְּנֵיהֶם שֶׁהֲרֵי פָּרָשָׁה שֶׁל אֱלִיעֶזֶר כְּפוּלָה בַּתּוֹרָה וְהַרְבֵּה גּוּפֵי תוֹרָה לֹא נִתְּנוּ אֶלָּא בִּרְמִיזָה

Rabbi Acha said, the conversation of the servants of the Patriarchs' homes [this word בָּתֵּי, *homes,* is not found in the text quoted by *Rashi* in 24:42; it is, however, in the *Midrash*] *is more beautiful before the Omnipresent than the teaching of* [their] *descendants: for the chapter of Eliezer is repeated in the Torah while many essentials of the Torah were given only by allusion (Bereishis Rabbah* 60:8).

Service of Scholars

Not only is Eliezer's mission narrated by the Torah in unusually great detail, it is given a second time in Eliezer's own words as he described his experience to Rebecca's family. Not surprisingly, the Sages, as well as the later commentators, find this lengthy repetition to be remarkable. The Sages exclaim that even the casual conversation of the Patriarchs is given a more honored place in the Torah than complex and far-reaching laws. The commentators scour chapter 24 for subtle changes of expression between the first account and the second, changes which they explain exhaustively and from which many laws are derived [see *comm.* to entire chapter and appendix at the end of *Sidra*]. Why then, did the Sages seem to question the necessity of this chapter? The Sages did not mean to imply that the chapter is redundant, for many teachings are derived from the subtle differences between the two accounts. Their point is that the very *conversation* of Abraham's servant is laden with meaning and teaching.

Their point is that the very conversation *of Abraham's servant is laden with meaning and teaching.*

Eliezer's behavior, his way of dealing with a complex situtation, his response to God's sign, his treatment of Rebecca, his tactful, carefully shaded dialogue with her family — all of these are reflective of the home where he grew and developed. They *are* Torah, because Abraham's every movement, speech, and inflection is as much Torah as the tort Laws of *Mishpatim* or the ritual laws of *Leviticus.* As the *Brisker Rav* expressed it, 'The Torah was given to human beings, not animals'(see previous Overview) — what greater book of laws and principles in the attainment of the status of 'Human Being' than a glimpse at a typical day in the lives of human beings *par excellence* like Abraham and Sarah — and Eliezer who was the conduit to humanity of *all* facets of Abraham's Torah — his personal conduct as well as his learning.

Abraham's every movement, speech, and inflection is as much Torah as the tort Laws of Mishpatim *or the ritual Laws of* Leviticus.

גְּדוֹלָה שִׁמּוּשָׁהּ שֶׁל תּוֹרָה יוֹתֵר מִלִּמּוּדָהּ

[Personal] service of Torah [scholars] is superior to its study (Berachos 7b).

Through devotion to the service of great people, one can observe the personal traits that they brought to Torah and that were an outgrowth of Torah. Eliezer, as Abraham's devoted servant for many decades, had become a reflection of Abraham. From

We learn not only about his own character and wisdom, but about the Abrahamitic home.

closely studying chapter 24, we learn not only about his own character and wisdom, but about the Abrahamitic home where he became the the trusted expositor of his master's Torah, and great enough an exemplar of goodness to convince Rebecca to commit her life to the building of a home whose nature she could guess only by observing the majestic behavior of its servant.

God Loves the Temple

Harav David Cohen points out a parallel that illustrates tellingly the importance which the Torah attaches to the teachings of the Patriarchal home. *Ramban (Exodus* 36:8), in discussing the extensive repetition concerning the plans and construction of the *Mishkan,* concludes:

> All this is indicative of affection and eminence, as if to say that God desires the work and mentions it in His Torah many times to increase the reward of those who occupy themselves with it. It is similar to what they said in the *Midrash*: 'the conversation of the servants of the homes of the Patriarchs is more beautiful before the Omnipresent than the teaching of their descendants,' for the chapter of Eliezer takes up two or three columns.

Simply understood, *Ramban* seems to do nothing more than cite Eliezer's chapter as a second example of repetitive narration. *Harav Cohen* notes, however, that *Ramban's* meaning goes much deeper. As we have pointed out (see above Overview) *Ramban* himself, in his introduction to *Exodus,* maintains that the *Mishkan* was meant to replicate the homes of the Patriarchs and Matriarchs. Thus, Ramban's example of the two or three columns devoted to Eliezer is of a piece with the extensive treatment given to the construction of the *Mishkan.* The two are one and the same: Eliezer's behavior represented the human embodiment of God's Temple; it was that sort of behavior which the *Mishkan* was intended to

The two or three columns devoted to Eliezer is of a piece with the extensive treatment given to construction of the Mishkan. *The two are one and the same.*

symbolize. So much does God love the *Mishkan* that He did not hesitate to devote to it several complete columns in His Torah where He cherishes each letter and crown of a letter, where He teaches the most complex laws through nuance and allusion. Rabbi Acha, the Sage who taught the significance of Eliezer's conversation, was careful to refer to him as the servant of בָּתֵּי אָבוֹת, *the 'homes' of the Patriarchs. Home* is the key word, for the 'home'of God is equally where Abraham and Sarah dwell and where the Tablets of the Law are set.

Home is the key word, for the 'home' of God is equally where Abraham and Sarah dwell and where the Tablets of the Law are set.

III. Lessons of Self Interest

Seeing is Not Believing

Many of the subtle changes which Eliezer inserted in his narrative of the events are explained by the commentary as dictated by his desire to gain approval for the match. Had he related the facts to Bethuel and his family exactly as they occurred, he might have been misunderstood or they might have been insulted. An extra word here, a deleted phrase there, and occasional change in the sequence of events would be needed to avoid a refusal and the failure of his mission. But was Eliezer not thereby practicing deception? Far from showing us the superiority of this representative of the Patriarchal home, does it not show us a side more in keeping with his Canaanite ancestry than his Abrahamitic upbringing?

Michtav MeEliyahu detects in these very changes one of the vital lessons of the episode. The most objective people have their own blind spots. Where their own interests are involved they 'see' things a certain way. Two sincerely honest and truthful people will see the same accident differently if they are parties to it. They may seek to avoid blame and place upon the other the maximum responsibility to pay

The most objective people have thier own blind spots. Where their own interests are involved they 'see' things a certain way.

or, with excessive zeal to be fair, they may absolve a guilty party and unfairly blame themselves. No matter what, they are not reliable witnesses. The *halachah* recognizes this fact by disqualifying a נוֹגֵעַ, *interested party,* as a judge or witness.

Similarly, there are other bounds beyond which a person does not see. Upon hearing about the personal honesty of the *Chofetz Chaim* and the zeal with which he avoided benefiting from another's mistake, one person may hear the stories, marvel and take such stories as the standard by which to measure his own behavior. Another person may regard them as foolish legends about an impractical saint. It is a truism that a person may be judged according to whom and what he admires. The person who reveres the legacy of the *Chofetz Chaim* will be revolted at tales of shrewd 'heroes' of the business world. He fails to see the difference between such 'shrewdness' and legalized thievery. And vice-versa — the person who admires the conquests of sharp operators, may find little to emulate in the *Chofetz Chaim*

Telling the Truth

Even before he inquired about her identity, he was confident that she had to be the girl designated by God! But could he tell that to her avaricious and idolatrous family?

Eliezer, with his implicit faith in God, could rush to bestow valuable gifts upon Rebecca as soon as she demonstrated the selfless generosity he sought in the future wife of Isaac. Even before he inquired about her identity, he was confident that she had to be the girl designated by God! But could he tell that to her avaricious and idolatrous family? Would he not stamp himself as a fool by revealing to them how quickly he and his gold were parted? And if he had permitted them to doubt his wisdom — even his *sanity* — according to *their* code of behavior — he would have been telling the ultimate lie, for they would have refused to accept the absolute truth that God had given them a Rebecca only in order that she would become Isaac's wife and a Matriarch of Israel. Eliezer, the teacher of Abraham's Torah, acted like an accomplished pedagogue. When a classful of youngsters has a wasted year, the teacher can hardly plead innocence if the only motivation he gave them was that Torah is the source of infinite spiritual qualities. 'I told them the truth' he will shout in his own defense. But he did *not* tell them the truth. To the young child, 'infinite spiritual values' have no meaning. He understands carrots and sticks, praise and criticisms, honor rolls and failure. To tell him something beyond his comprehension is to distort the truth.

To the young child, infinite spiritual values have no meaning. He understands carrots and sticks. To tell him something beyond his comprehension is to distort the truth.

So Eliezer carefully considered what he could tell them in order not to mislead them. If they could not understand the saintliness of Abraham and Isaac, there would be no point in extolling virtues which they would regard as patronizing or foolish. With this background, we can better understand much of Eliezer's narrative — and gain a deeper appreciation of the stature of one who learned Godliness in the Temple of Abraham and Sarah.

No one is immune from the blinding influence of self-interest, not even an Eliezer. In repeating the story to the family, he included an allusion that he had hoped his *own* daughter could be selected for Isaac's wife. But the allusion does not appear when Eliezer was speaking directly to Abraham. [See *comm.* to 24:39 for the allusion and various explanations of why it does not appear earlier.]

Michtav MeEliyahu comments that when Eliezer spoke to Abraham, he was convinced of his own sincerity. Never did it enter his mind that his seemingly logical question to Abraham was actually an opening wedge for the eventual introduction of his own daughter for Abraham's consideration. Only after God had shown him that Rebecca was Isaac's intended could Eliezer dispassionately analyze his own earlier behavior. As long as an unknown bride was being sought for Isaac, Eliezer had his own candidate though he remained silent about her. He was affected by self-interest and he had been blind — but now he knew! All along he had been subconsciously thinking of himself as the father-in-law of Isaac, and of his daughter as the wife of Isaac. This, too, is a les-

Only after God had shown him that Rebecca was Isaac's intended could Eliezer dispassionately analyze his own earlier behavior.

son from the seemingly casual conversation of Abraham's servant!

Unlike the slave whose honor depends on the rod held over his head, Eliezer went on his mission with uncompromising zeal.

Though Eliezer had a compelling personal reason to wish for the failure of his mission, he rose above all selfish considerations. With loyalty, faith, dedication, and wisdom, he proceeded to prove that Abraham's trust in him was well placed. Unlike the slave whose honor depends on the rod held over his head, Eliezer went on his mission with uncompromising zeal. In so doing, he completed the transformation of himself from accursed Canaanite to בְּרוּךְ ה׳, *blessed of God.* Such is the effect of life in the tent of the Patriarchs. Small wonder the Sages taught that every Jew should set as his constant goal in life the question

מָתַי יַגִּיעוּ מַעֲשַׂי לְמַעֲשֵׂי אַבְרָהָם יִצְחָק וְיַעֲקֹב
When will my deeds approach the deeds of Abraham, Isaac, and Jacob? (Tanna d'Bei Eliyahu 25).

— *Rabbi Nosson Scherman*

◆ סדר חיי שרה

◆ Sidra Chayei Sarah

XXIII

Prefatory Synopsis

Abraham and Sarah had moved back to Hebron twelve years before the Akeidah, *when Sarah was 115 years old. They had lived in Hebron once before — it was their first permanent home in* Eretz Yisrael, *and they lived there for twenty-five years, leaving it after the destruction of Sodom and the incest of Lot and his daughters (20:1). At that time, they settled in Beer Sheba (21:13) where Abraham established his famous* eishel, *the place where he extended hospitality to wayfarers and proclaimed God's teaching (see* commentary *to 21:33). Even after moving to Hebron, he maintained the* eishel *in Beer Sheba and went there frequently, as he did on his way home from the* Akeidah *(see* commentary *to 22:19).*

The question arises, why did Abraham and Sarah choose to leave Beer Sheba after twenty-six years to return to Hebron?

For many years, Abraham and Sarah had longed to be buried in the final resting place of Adam and Eve, but no one knew where it was. Then, on the day when God transmitted to them the news for which they had hoped all their lives, the imminent birth of a son, He allowed them to learn this secret as well. When the angels came to inform Abraham that Sarah would give birth to Isaac, the Patriarch went to his herd to select animals for the feast with which he honored his guests (18:7). One of the calves ran away, and Abraham gave chase. The calf ran into a cave. Abraham followed and, as soon as he entered, he found Adam and Eve reclining on their couches, a spiritual light of unparalleled brilliance burning above them, and the entire scene was enveloped in incense-like fragrance. He immediately desired the possession of that cave as his future burial site. The place was the Cave of Machpelah in the field of Ephron, just outside Hebron. Abraham kept the secret, and told no one except his wife of the cave's significance.

When Sarah was 115 years old, she felt that the end of her life was drawing near. As residents of Beer Sheba, then under Philistine control, she and Abraham could have no legitimate claim to burial in the Hittite city of Hebron, in the land of Canaan. Therefore, they moved back to their original home, there to re-establish residency and eventually to claim the right, as permanent residents, *to purchase a burial plot. Accordingly, when Sarah died, it was natural for Abraham to come to the leaders of the city as an 'alien and resident' and ask them to intercede with Ephron to negotiate the sale of the plot he had chosen for his wife's burial* (Seder Olam; Pirkei d'Rabbi Eliezer *36;* Zohar; Abarbanel; *see chronology in* commentary *to 21:34 [page 780] and 22:19 [page 814]).*

א וַיִּהְיוּ֙ חַיֵּ֣י שָׂרָ֔ה מֵאָ֥ה שָׁנָ֛ה וְעֶשְׂרִ֥ים שָׁנָ֖ה
ב וְשֶׁ֣בַע שָׁנִ֑ים שְׁנֵ֖י חַיֵּ֥י שָׂרָֽה׃ וַתָּ֣מָת שָׂרָ֗ה

1. Sarah's lifespan, and the purchase of a burial site.

וַיִּהְיוּ חַיֵּי שָׂרָה — *Sarah's lifetime was* [lit. *and they were the lives* (or *life*) *of Sarah*].

Rashbam observes that although the lifespans of other women are not recorded in the Torah, it was necessary to mention Sarah's death in order to connect it to the purchase of the Cave of Machpelah. Having mentioned her death, the Torah also informs us of the age at which she died after having given birth at the age of ninety.

[Generally, the Torah gives genealogies and lifespans in order that the chronological order of historical events can be fixed. In the case of women, this purpose would not be served, hence *Rashbam*'s need to find a reason for the mention of Sarah's lifespan. His explanation follows פְּשׁוּטוֹ שֶׁל מִקְרָא, *the literal meaning of Scriptures.* Exegetically, however, the Sages derive much from *how* Sarah's age is expressed. See *Rashi* further.]

The *Midrash* observes that all the righteous women died before their husbands, so they should be spared the degradation [of being widows] *(Pesikta Zutresa).*

Minchah Belulah adds that Sarah is given this special distinction of being the only woman whose age is mentioned in the Torah, because she is the Matriarch and prime ancestress of the Jewish nation. As the Prophet declares [*Isaiah* 51:2]: *Look to Abraham your father, and to Sarah that bore you.*

The *Da'as Zekeinim* notes that the גִּמַטְרִיָּא, *numerical value,* of וַיִּהְיוּ [*and they were*] equals 37. Since Sarah had a child only at the age of ninety, she is regarded as having truly *'lived'* only for the subsequent thirty-seven years of her life [127-90 =37] since 'a childless person is considered as dead' [*Nedarim* 64b]. [Thus, the verse would be rendered homiletically: וַיִּהְיוּ חַיֵּי שָׂרָה, *thirty-seven* [*years*] *comprised the (primary) 'life' of Sarah; one hundred and twenty-seven years being* שְׁנֵי חַיֵּי שָׂרָה, the *(entire)* life-span of Sarah. (Cf. *Baal HaTurim).*]

[In the light of the above, שְׁנֵי, may be translated as *two* i.e., Sarah had *two* lives, her total life span, and her years of fulfillment following the birth of Isaac.]

[According to *Rashi*, however, (s.v. שְׁנֵי חַיֵּי שָׂרָה) all her years were equally good.]

The Hebrew word חַיִּים, *life* (lit. *lives*; in the construct-state: חַיֵּי), always takes the plural form [in this case וַיִּהְיוּ, *were,* instead of וַיְהִי, *was*], although by definition 'life' is singular *(Ibn Ezra).* [This is akin to words like שָׁמַיִם, *heaven,* מַיִם, *water,* פָּנִים, *face,* etc. (see *comm.* of *Harav Gifter* to 1:1, page 34).]

מֵאָה שָׁנָה וְעֶשְׂרִים שָׁנָה וְשֶׁבַע שָׁנִים — *One hundred years,* [*and*] *twenty years, and seven years.*[1]

Rashi explains that the reason the

1. Rabbi Akiva was once giving a lecture when he noticed that his students were drowsing. In order to rouse them he asked, "Why was it seen fit that Esther should rule over one hundred and twenty-seven provinces? Because thus said God: 'Let the daughter of Sarah who lived one hundred and twenty-seven years come and reign over one hundred and twenty-seven provinces' "*(Midrash).*

Chidushei HaRim asks: Why would these words alert the drowsing students more than the topic of the day? Rabbi Akiva wanted to impress upon his students the importance of time

23 Sarah's lifetime was one hundred years, twenty
1 years, and seven years; the years of Sarah's life.

word שָׁנָה, *years*, is repeated after *every* stage [i.e., *one hundred years, and twenty years, and seven years,* instead of: *one hundred and twenty-seven years*, or as is customary in Scriptures: *one hundred years and twenty-seven years*] is to teach that each term must be interpreted independently [and, because each term is a fragment of the whole, that term shares a particular characteristic of its neighboring term]: At a hundred she was like a woman of twenty with relation to sin. — Just as she was still without sin at the age of twenty, having just reached the age when one becomes subject to heavenly punishment,* so was she still sinless at the age of a hundred. And at twenty she was like seven with relation to beauty [i.e., at twenty she was as *naturally* beautiful, without cosmetics, as a child of seven who does not use cosmetics *(Chizkuni)*.] [2]

Rashi follows the same pattern of interpretation in 25:7 where, in describing Abraham's lifespan, Scripture repeats the word *years* inordinately.

* [See *footnote* to 17:14 (p. 574); *Gur Aryeh* in *footnote* to 17:26 (p. 587); cf. also *Rashi* to 5:32 (p. 178).]

and the duty to use every second to best advantage. It was because Sarah's one hundred and twenty-seven years were perfect and completely sin-free that her granddaughter could hold sway over one hundred and twenty-seven provinces. Each second meant a family; each minute, a farm; each day, a village. Had Sarah idled away her time, Esther's kingdom would have been diminished. Time is too precious to waste. Sarah's well-spent time was rewarded during Esther's reign. Each of us, too, is presented with the fleeting gift of time — and the mission of utilizing it fully and well. Who can say what the rewards will be for each fully utilized minute; or the penalty for each wasted minute?

This implied admonition brought Rabbi Akiva's students to attention.

Another explanation has been offered. Rabbi Akiva lived during a period of intense persecution by the Romans. It was forbidden to teach Torah, and Rabbi Akiva was later executed for doing so. During such times, it was inevitable that the morale of Torah scholars would suffer because they would see no benefit in their efforts. Therefore, Rabbi Akiva consoled them by showing that Sarah's good deeds did not go unrewarded even though many centuries went by before the time of Esther. Nevertheless, when the reward was bestowed, it was enormous *(Yalkut Yehudah)*.

2. *Hagaon Rav Moshe Feinstein* שליט"א notes the apparent incongruity of the last comparison. To us it seems plain that the physical beauty of a twenty-year old far surpasses that of a seven-year old, yet the *Midrash* quoted by *Rashi* indicates that the greatest beauty is that of the child. *Harav Feinstein* comments that the beauty of a seven-year old is natural and devoid of any incitement to lust. A twenty-year old, on the other hand, has a destructive beauty that can tempt others to go astray. That sort of beauty is impure and not praiseworthy. The greatness of Sarah was that even in the prime of her life, those who saw her recognized a purity and innocence that, despite her unique physical beauty, was no more conducive to sin than that of a beautiful child. [Only in Egypt and Philistia, whose populations were particularly lustful, did her beauty cause danger.]

As *Hirsch* explains, we are told of Sarah's years in such a manner as to indicate that there are three distinct periods in a person's development: childhood, mature youth, and advanced age. It is the mark of a spiritually perfected life that one acts in accordance with his age: when

Ramban disagrees sharply with *Rashi*'s comment on three grounds. First, the same construction is used in giving the life-span of Ishmael: *one hundred years, and thirty years, and seven years* (25:17). According to the rule enunciated by *Rashi*, the division into three separate terms would indicate that all of Ishmael's years were equally good. However, as the Sages teach, Ishmael repented only toward the end of his life, thus his earlier years cannot be considered equal to his later ones; second, this sort of construction is common in Scriptures and cannot be understood as an indication of the need for a homiletical exegesis. Third, the use of *years* to separate the various periods of life should more logically be taken to *differentiate* between the stages, rather than to liken them one to another.

Da'as Zekenim, too, cites the verse regarding Ishmael. He comments that it may be inferred that Ishmael's repentance was so sincere that none of his earlier sins was considered; thus his life was equivalent to an unbroken chain of righteousness, a fact implied by the repeated use of *years*.

Therefore, *Ramban* concludes, the exegesis cited by *Rashi* is to be derived only from the concluding phrase of the verse: שְׁנֵי חַיֵּי שָׂרָה, *the years of Sarah's life*, an expression which is all-encompassing and equates them all. It is the conclusion of the verse, therefore, that indicates the equal status in all respects of all the years of her life.

Rashi's comment, which is derived primarily from the *Midrash*, inspires much comment from the supercommentaries who seek to defend it against the objections of *Ramban*.

Mizrachi (as interpreted by *Gur Aryeh*) notes that in common usage, Scripture cites the word *year* in connection with hundreds and again in connection with the other numbers. Thus, had our verse followed the accepted procedure, it would have read: מֵאָה שָׁנָה וְשֶׁבַע וְעֶשְׂרִים שָׁנָה – *one hundred years and twenty-seven years*. The third use of the word *years*, therefore, would be superfluous were it not meant to indicate an exegetical interpretation. The use of the words *years* could indeed be understood to imply a distinction between the periods as *Ramban* contends, but since the verse ends with שְׁנֵי חַיֵּי שָׂרָה, *the years of Sarah's life* — which, *Ramban* agrees, implies a likening of the different stages — we infer that the three stages are to be *likened* rather than *distinguished*. As for Ishmael — regarding whom Scripture does not make implicit that all periods of his life are to be similarly interpreted — the triple use of *years* is meant to imply *only* a dissimilarity between the periods, i.e., Ishmael fluctuated between righteousness and wickedness. That *Rashi* indicates a likening of the periods in the case of Abraham (see *comm.* to 25:7) is based on the introductory phrase וְאֵלֶּה יְמֵי שְׁנֵי חַיֵּי אַבְרָהָם, *these are the days of the years of the life of Abraham*, i.e., the phrase implies that all of his life formed a single unit rather than a series of inconsistent stages of development.

Gur Aryeh offers a different interpretation. He agrees with *Ramban* that it is common for Scriptures to separate terms with the word *years*. Here, however — and in the case of Abraham — no such separation should have been made because the verse begins וַיִּהְיוּ חַיֵּי שָׂרָה, *And Sarah's life was*, implying that the totality of her years would be given, hence there should not have been a division between the mention of the various periods. *Gur Aryeh* says further that each distinct period is mentioned to imply that she remained consistent throughout — i.e., each succeeding number of years is to be regarded as a unit of her life during which she remained the same Sarah from beginning to end. There is hardly a human being who does not change during a period of twenty years; Sarah, however, remained true and consis-

one is a child, he should act like a child; when an adult, like an adult, and so on. Further, our Sages teach that one should take along into each succeeding stage of life, the major attainments of the prior period. If an accomplishment was truly his, he should not allow advancing years to rob him of it. Thus, Sarah took her childhood beauty into her womanhood, and her womanly innocence into her most advanced years.

That the Sages find 'innocence' in the twenty-year old is in itself a remarkable lesson. The seven-year old who has never tasted sin cannot be called innocent — she knows no other way. True 'innocence' implies that temptation was met and conquered. The twenty-year old Sarah, having matured to beautiful womanhood, struggled against her senses and won. She could truly be called innocent.

tent from beginning to end. Her righteousness, like her beauty, was an undeviating characteristic of her life. The Sages cite beauty and righteousness for the respective periods because those happen to be the characteristics that best relate to the age under discussion; however, beauty and righteousness were traits that prevailed throughout her life.

As to *Rashi*'s comment that when she was one hundred years old, she was as sinless as a twenty year old because heavenly punishment is not inflicted until one is *twenty* years old, *Mizrachi* cites *Rashi* to 5:32 quoting the *Midrash* that prior to the giving of the Torah, heavenly punishments were not inflicted prior to the age of *one hundred;* it was only thereafter that the age was reduced to twenty. *Mizrachi* ventures that *Rashi* may have meant that even by latter-day standards, Sarah would have been considered sinless.

Both *Mizrachi* and *Gur Aryeh* ask how we can know that she was free of sin by the standards of human courts before which one is liable from the age of thirteen. *Gur Aryeh* replies that the heavenly standard is far more exacting than the earthly one. Thus an act which would not be considered sinful by earthly legal standards might be deemed punishable in God's judgment. Therefore, we find, for example, that the righteous are culpable for relatively minor infractions. [This would also explain why the age of responsibility is deferred until one is more mature]. If, then, we are told that she was sinless even by heavenly standards, then surely she was free of sin so blatant that even human courts would take action.

[*Maharzu* in his commentary to the *Midrash* cites a parallel in *Midrash Tehillim* 37 where the reading is: 'At a hundred she was like twenty in beauty, and at twenty like seven in sin.' *Maharzu* defends the version in *Midrash Tehillim* as the correct reading since a person reaches maximum beauty at age twenty, as evidenced by the fact that the *Midrash* itself (14:7 cited in *comm.* to עָפָר in 2:7, p. 91) describes Adam and Eve as being created in their fullness, *as at the age of twenty.* And in the case of Sarah her youthfulness returned to her late in life as evidenced by the fact that even at the age of ninety she was considered a beautiful woman and taken to the palace of Abimelech (20:2). At the age of twenty she was as sinless as a child of seven. The preponderance of commentators, however, defend *Rashi*'s reading of the *Midrash* on various grounds.]

[Sometimes the Torah lists the larger number of years first and then the smaller numbers (as in our verse) while at other times the procedure is reversed. See *Haamek Davar* cited in 5:5 (p. 169), for an explanation, although, as he notes, there are exceptions to his generality.]

שְׁנֵי חַיֵּי שָׂרָה — *The years of Sarah's life.*

They were all equal in goodness *(Rashi),* i.e., they were all equally devoted to the service of God.[1]

2. וַתָּמָת שָׂרָה — *[And] Sarah died.*

From the shock of being told by Satan that Abraham had killed Isaac [at the *Akeidah*]; she cried out in grief and died *(Targum Yonasan* to 22:20). [See *Rashi* and *footnote* below *s.v.* וְלִבְכֹּתָהּ.]

The Torah records the birth of Rebecca [22:23] before mentioning the death of Sarah to draw attention to the tradition that Sarah lived until the birth of Rebecca who was worthy to succeed her, for there is a tradition that a righteous person is not taken until his successor has been born, as the verse implies [*Eccles.* 1:5]: *The sun rises and the sun sets.* Thus, Sarah did not die until Abraham was informed of the birth of Rebecca, the next Matriarch *(Sforno, Baal HaTurim).*

Cf. *Midrash Koheles* ad. loc.: Do we not know that the sun rises and sets? Rather the verse (using the rising and setting sun to symbolize the life-death cycle) tells us that before the 'sun' of one righteous man sets, God causes the

1. Although Sarah certainly experienced difficult years during her lifetime, she paid them no attention, but accepted everything graciously and with good cheer — the bad along with the good. This is what *Rashi* means by *'all equal in goodness'* — even the bad she accepted lovingly *(HaDrash V'halyun).*

בְּקִרְיַת אַרְבַּע הִוא חֶבְרוֹן בְּאֶרֶץ כְּנָעַן
וַיָּבֹא אַבְרָהָם לִסְפֹּד לְשָׂרָה וְלִבְכֹּתָהּ:

'sun' of another righteous man to rise ... and so on, generation after generation. [See examples cited in ArtScroll *Koheles* p. 55.]

בְּקִרְיַת אַרְבַּע — *In Kiriath Arba* [lit. *the city of four.*]

— So called because of the *four* giants who lived there: Ahiman, Sheshai, Talmai, and their father [see *Numbers* 13:22.]; others explain the name as [prophetically] alluding to the *four* couples buried there: Adam and Eve, Abraham and Sarah, Isaac and Rebecca, and Jacob and Leah *(Midrash; Rashi).*[1]

Ibn Ezra suggests that אַרְבַּע in our verse is not the number *four,* but a proper noun. *Arba* was one of the *Anakim* [giants] who lived in that city, and the city was named after him. Thus, קִרְיַת אַרְבַּע would be rendered: *city of Arba.*

[See *Joshua* 14:15: *And the name of Hebron was formerly Kiriath Arba, (Arba being) the greatest man among the Anakim; ibid.* 15:13: *And to Caleb son of Yephuneh, [Joshua] gave ... Kiriath Arba the father of the giant, that is Hebron.*]

The question is raised why does *Rashi* interpret אַרְבַּע as *four* instead of translating קִרְיַת אַרְבַּע as *City of Arba* in line with the Scriptural statement that *Arba* was the name of the head of the *Anakim.*

Mizrachi suggests that *Arba* the giant was named after the city rather than vice-versa because it is most unlikely that a number [arba=four] should be used as the name of a person.

Gur Aryeh comments that, if *city of Arba* is a descriptive term — i.e., Hebron was the city led by a man named Arba — then proper Hebrew sentence structure would call for the name Hebron to be given first: חֶבְרוֹן הִיא קִרְיַת אַרְבַּע, *Hebron which is the city of Arba.*

Others hold that Arba cannot be construed as a proper noun since the word appears with a definite article [קִרְיַת הָאַרְבַּע, lit. *city of the Arba*] in both 35:27 and *Nechemiah* 11:25 which demands that אַרְבַּע be rendered *four (Minchah Belulah).*

הִוא חֶבְרוֹן — *Which is Hebron* [i.e., which later came to be called Hebron *(Joshua* 14:15 and *Judges* 1:10).]

[On *Hebron,* see also *comm.* to *v.* 19 below and 13:18.]

The commentators explain that Ham, son of Noah, built the city for Canaan his son and called it Hebron. Later the family of the Anakim — Achimon, Sheshai, Talmai, and their father, Arba, settled there, and the city was referred

1. The *Midrash* notes that the city had four names: *Eshkol; Mamre; Kiriath Arba;* and *Hebron.* The *Midrash* goes on to enumerate several reasons why it was named Kiriath Arba ['the city of four']. Among the reasons offered:

a. Because four righteous men resided and were circumcised there: Abraham, Aner, Eshkol and Mamre;

b. Because the four righteous patriarchs of the world were buried there: Adam, Abraham, Isaac and Jacob;

c. Because the four matriarchs of the world were buried there: Eve, Sarah, Rebecca and Leah;

d. Because of its four owners [or founders] Anak and his three sons [see *Numbers* 13:22 and *Josh.* 15:13.];

e. Because from there Abraham went forth and pursued the four mighty kings.

23
2 Sarah died in Kiriath Arba which is Hebron in the
land of Canaan. And Abraham came to eulogize
Sarah and to bewail her.

to as Kiriath Arba in deference to them. There was a period when it was called 'Mamre'. In the days of Joshua it resumed its former identity and was again called Hebron.

[As pointed out in the *comm.* to 22:19 (p. 814) Hebron had been the permanent residence of Abraham and Sarah for the past twelve years, as it had been for their first twenty-five years in Canaan See *Prefatory Synopsis* above, and *comm.* further.]

בְּאֶרֶץ כְּנָעַן — *In the land of Canaan.*

This is mentioned to emphasize that it was in the precincts of the Holy Land that she merited to die *(Abarbanel;* see *Malbim).*

וַיָּבֹא אַבְרָהָם — *And Abraham came.*

From Beer Sheba *(Rashi),* [where Abraham had gone temporarily after the *Akeidah,* as explained in [22:19 (p. 813).]

Where was Isaac? The commentators answer that either his presence is implicit: he returned to Hebron earlier, or now, together with his father *(Abarbanel);* or he was in the Academy of Shem and Eber unaware, as yet, of his mother's demise *(Midrashim).*

Ramban discusses Abraham's residences and, commenting on the Midrashic interpretation, concurs with the view of the Sages cited by *Rashi* in 21:34; 22:19; *comm.* to 21:22; and *footnote* on p. 736, that the primary residence during this period was Hebron. It was there that Abraham received the command regarding the *Akeidah.* Accordingly, upon his return from the *Akeidah* atop Mount Moriah, he stopped briefly at Beer Sheba, site of his *Eishel.* There he heard of Sarah's death and he came to Hebron, as this verse tells us. [However, according to *Ramban,* Abraham later returned to Beer Sheba. This differs from the implication of *Rashi* in 22:19 that he *remained in Hebron,* his permanent residence.]

Regarding the *literal sense* of the expression *and Abraham came,* however, *Ramban* goes on to suggest that in his opinion the phrase does not necessarily imply an arrival in Hebron from another city, for if that were the case the Torah would have mentioned the place from which he embarked, saying, *and Abraham heard, and he came from such and such a place.*

Rather, *Ramban* concludes, the verse implies either that Sarah had her own tent (as Leah and the two maid-servants [31:33]), and Abraham now went [וַיָּבֹא=came] into Sarah's tent where she had died; or the phrase וַיָּבֹא אַבְרָהָם is idiomatic and means *Abraham proceeded* [or *prepared; undertook*] *to eulogize Sarah.* The latter usage of the verb בא, *come,* is quite common in the *Talmud,* where it refers to one who bestirs himself to undertake something. Cf. such expressions as בָּא לוֹ לְדוֹפֶן הַשְּׂמָאלִית, *he came to the left flank* [*Tamid* 4:3]; *I have not attained* [בָּאתִי, *come*] *to this principle* [*Berachos* 20a]; בָּא לְטַהֵר, *one who undertakes to be purified* [*Shabbos* 104a]; and in the Torah itself [*Exodus* 22:14]: בָּא בִּשְׂכָרוֹ, *he came for his hire,* i.e., he *undertook it* for the purpose of his hire. [*Ramban*'s latter interpretation concurs with *Rashbam.*].

לְסְפֹּד לְשָׂרָה — *To eulogize [to] Sarah.*

I.e., to eulogize for her sake and in her honor. [Thus the verse specifically mentions *Sarah* to emphasize that the eulogy was in *her* honor] for as the *Talmud* [*Sanhedrin* 46b] notes, the funeral lament [eulogy] is in honor of the *dead* [in contrast to the other opinion there that the funeral lament is in honor of the *living* (survivors). A halachic distinction between the two opinions will arise when one leaves instructions that he is not to be eulogized, or when the heirs are asked to pay for the eulogy from the estate] *(Sforno).*

Additionally, Scriptures specifies Sarah's *name* rather than stating simply; 'to eulogize *her,'* because it was not Sarah's *physical* departure from the world that Abraham bewailed; he knew that this righteous woman would enjoy the fruits of her righteousness in the Spiritual World of eternity; rather, the verse informs us, Abraham eulogized *Sarah,* i.e., the loss of that which her very name Sarah connoted — princess *par excellence;* princess of all mankind [see *comm.* to 17:15 (p. 576)] *(Kli Yakar).*

[We have adopted the more limited rendering of לִסְפֹּד as *to eulogize,* but the Scriptural connotation of the word, as pointed out by the commentators, is broader: *to mourn* (so *Hirsch); wail (Radak); lament (Heidenheim)* in a *loud manifestation of grief.* As *Hirsch* explains, the word may be related to the root זבד, *a portion,* i.e., to apportion publicly that which the deceased had accomplished during his lifetime; to express his value.

[It also refers to the mournful lamentations for which professional mourning women were hired in later times *(Jer.* 9:16; see also *II Chron.* 35:25).

[*Talmudically,* the technical meaning of *hesped* is 'lamenting with striking upon the breast', as it is written *(Isaiah* 32:11-12): *Tremble ... strip ... put cloth about your loins* עַל־שָׁדַיִם סֹפְדִים, *striking upon the breast (Moed Katan* 27b). However, in *Sanhedrin* 46b, as well as in *Halachic* literature, the word *hesped* generally connotes a *eulogy* delivered in a lamenting, bewailing manner rather than a speech given in praise of the deceased. Also, it is not necessarily given as part of the funeral oratory.]

The commentators note that the Torah — in which every word is measured and laden with profound implication — found it necessary to detail so obvious a fact as Abraham eulogizing and weeping for his wife. This was done not for narrative purposes, but to teach how important it is to mourn a good person and eulogize him *(Rav Yaakov Culi).*[1]

וְלִבְכֹּתָהּ — *And to bewail her.*

The Torah [thus tells us that Abraham *came* (directly from Beer Sheba following the *Akeidah) to eulogize Sarah and to bewail her (Beer Mayim Chaim),* and] recounts the narrative of her death closely after that of the *Akeidah,* because her death was caused by Isaac's near sacrifice. The shock of hearing that her son had almost been slaughtered caused her soul to flee from her and she died *(Rashi; Pirkei d'Rabbi Eliezer* 32. See also *Gur Aryeh).*[2]

In relating the circumstances leading up to Sarah's death, the *Midrash* uses the expression that she was told כִּמְעַט שֶׁלֹּא נִשְׁחַט, *he*

1. *Yoreh De'ah* 344:2 cites the halachah that women are eulogized. Proof for the law is derived from *Megillah* 28b where it is related that *Rafram* eulogized his daughter-in-law. It seems strange, however, that the commentators do not base the law on Abraham's eulogy of Sarah.

It may be that Abraham's mourning would be insufficient proof to establish a general principle because the personal grief of a husband for his dead wife is so great that he would feel compelled to give it expression even if the halachah did not require him to do so. As the Talmud *(Sanhedrin* 22b) puts it: אֵין אִשָּׁה מֵתָה אֶלָּא לְבַעְלָהּ, *a woman dies only for her husband (Torah Temimah).*

was almost slaughtered. Terumas HaDeshen gives a different interpretation: כִּמְעַט, *she had almost been told* שֶׁלֹּא נִשְׁחַט, *that he had not been slaughtered* — when she died. I.e., before the messenger was able to conclude his story, telling her that the intended slaughter had not been carried out, she died.

[This traditional Rabbinic chronology which relates Sarah's death to the *Akeidah* forms the basis for much Biblical dating. Foremost, it dates the *Akeidah* as having taken place in the same year as Sarah's death, 2085, when Isaac was thirty-seven years old.]

The word וְלִבְכֹּתָהּ, *and to weep for her,* is written in the Torah with a small כ, *kaf,* to indicate that Abraham did not weep *excessively,* for she was old [and one restrains his mourning for one who dies — as all mankind must — after having led a full life.]

Additionally, [as noted in the *footnote* to 16:5 (p. 545)], Sarah had, in a sense, brought about her own [premature] death by invoking Heavenly judgment against Abraham, and was therefore punished by predeceasing him. Accordingly, since Sarah was responsible for her premature death, Abraham curtailed his lament as one does for a person who takes his own life *(Baal HaTurim).*

Furthermore, the Talmud has provided us with a norm for mourning a close relative: the first three days for weeping, the first week for lamenting, the first thirty days for refraining from cutting the hair and donning pressed clothes. Thereafter, the Holy One, Blessed be He, says: 'You are not more compassionate [toward the departed one] than I'. [For one must accept the loss with forbearance] *(Moed Katan* 27b).

Hirsch suggests, accordingly, that the small כ might indicate that Abraham did not parade his grief

2. There are several basic *Midrashic* recensions dealing with Sarah's death; they vary in minor details:

A. Satan was frustrated at his inability to dissuade Abraham and Isaac from heeding God's command. He thereupon went to Sarah and said, 'Alas, Sarah, have you not heard what has happened?'

'No', she replied.

'Your husband took Isaac, slaughtered him, and offered him up as a sacrifice on the altar,' Satan said. 'The boy wept, but there was none to save him.'

Hearing this, Sarah burst into a fit of wailing, crying aloud three times like the three sustained notes of the *Shofar.* She then sobbed three *Teru'ah* (i.e., broken) sounds of the Shofar; her soul departed and she died *(Pirkei d'Rabbi Eliezer). Midrash HaGadol* concludes that we therefore make similar blasts with the Shofar on Rosh Hashanah, signifying Sarah's lament, so that her cries should be atonement for us.

B. In *Vayikra Rabbah* 20:2 it was Isaac *himself* who went to Sarah and told her all that had occurred, saying: 'Had the angel not called down from heaven, I would have been slaughtered.' The very thought of that killed Sarah. In *Midrash Tanchuma* it is Satan disguised as Isaac who tells the tale.

C. According to *Sefer HaYashar* when Satan informed Sarah [who had been waiting, according to this version, in Beer Sheba], what had happened, Sarah threw herself on the ground, cast ashes on her head, and sobbed: 'O, my son Isaac, I wish I would have died today in your stead ... I who first bore you at ninety, now mourn over you! But I console myself in that you have performed God's will, for who can transgress the word of our God in Whose hands is the soul of every living creature?'

'O God!' she continued, 'You are just! While my eye weeps bitterly, my heart rejoices.' She then laid her head down and wept.

She wandered about inquiring of everyone she encountered as to the whereabouts of her husband and son. She sent some servants to the academy of Shem and Eber, and she herself went to Hebron. But no one could verify what had happened to her son.

Sarah was delirious. Suddenly, the Satan reappeared to her in the guise of an old man and said: 'I lied to you before, Abraham did not kill his son and he is not dead!'

When Sarah heard this, she was so elated that her soul departed through joy.

ג וַיָּקָם אַבְרָהָם מֵעַל פְּנֵי מֵתוֹ וַיְדַבֵּר אֶל־
ד בְּנֵי־חֵת לֵאמֹר: גֵּר־וְתוֹשָׁב אָנֹכִי עִמָּכֶם

publicly. We know what Sarah had been to Abraham, and how infinitely deep his grief must have been. He mourned and wept, but the full measure of his pain he concealed in his heart and in the privacy of his home.

This follows the comment in the *Zohar*, that it is improper for a sage to weep excessively in public.

Minchah Belulah cites a *Midrash* that the small כ indicates that it is to be omitted for the purpose of exegesis. The phrase should be interpreted as if it read לִסְפֹּד לְשָׂרָה **וּלְבִתָּהּ**, 'to eulogize Sarah *and her daughter'*; who also died on that day, for as the Sages derive from 24:1 s.v. בַּכֹּל, Abraham had a daughter [from Sarah], and the Torah, which does not necessarily concern itself with chronological order, alluded to it out of sequence.

Kli Yakar notes that *weeping* usually precedes *hesped*, as in *Moed Katan* 27b cited above: ג׳ לִבְכִי וז׳ לְהֶסְפֵּד, *three days for weeping and seven for 'hesped'* [*lamenting*], while in our verse the order is reversed. That is because the overpowering grief which induces weeping, tends to dissipate with the passage of time; hence, emotional weeping comes first, to be followed by הֶסְפֵּד, a more intellectual appreciation of the person who died. In Sarah's case, however, the degree of loss — the absence of her wisdom and righteousness — was recognized more and more as the days went by. Therefore, the weeping continued after the eulogies ended.

According to *Riva*, the usual order is reversed in our verse because Abraham arrived only after the three-day period of weeping was already over and his household was then engaged in eulogizing her. Abraham joined them and began his own weeping at the conclusion of the eulogies.

[See *Sanhedrin* 46b, however, that Sarah's funeral was delayed until Abraham's arrival; see also *Ha'amek Davar*].

3. וַיָּקָם אַבְרָהָם מֵעַל פְּנֵי מֵתוֹ — *And Abraham rose up from the presence of* [lit. *from upon the face of*] *his dead.*

I.e., weeping in mournful lament, he had been literally bending over the body of his departed wife. Now he stood up *(Abarbanel).*

According to *HaKsav V'haKaballah,* Abraham purposely stood *near* her body in order to evoke the sympathy of those present.

The Torah specifies that Abraham *rose up,* to teach that it is proper to stand while addressing a gathering. Apparently, it was the custom for an individual to sit after he had concluded addressing a gathering. Accordingly, when Abraham wished to speak further, he again stood up [*v.* 7] *(R' Bachya).*

We derive from the wording of the phrase *'from upon the face of his dead'* that a corpse should be laid down on its back *(Or HaChaim).*

Homiletically, the *Talmud* derives from this verse that as long as one has not fulfilled his obligation of burial to the dead, it is con-

³ *Abraham rose up from the presence of his dead,*
and spoke to the children of Heth, saying: ⁴ *'I am an*
alien and a resident among you. Grant me an estate

sidered as if he is in the *presence* of the deceased *(Berachos* 18a).

The *Midrash* homiletically renders the phrase: *And Abraham rose up from the face of his death* — he saw the Angel of Death challenging him [i.e., now with the death of his wife he saw his own death staring him in the face.]

וַיְדַבֵּר אֶל בְּנֵי־חֵת — *And he spoke to the children of Heth.*

I.e., Heth being the son of Canaan [10:15], the Hittites were the leaders of the region. Abraham gathered them together so that his request could be negotiated and approved by the proper authorities. As a result, the property would legally remain the uncontested possession of his family forever *(Radak; Akeidas Yitzchak).* [1]

[Even later in the days of Moses and Joshua we find the children of Heth dwelling in the mountains of Judah *(Numbers* 13:29; *Joshua* 11:3).]

4. גֵּר־וְתוֹשָׁב אָנֹכִי עִמָּכֶם — *I am an alien* [or: *foreigner*] *and a resident among* [lit. *with*] *you.*

I.e., I am a *foreigner* from another land and have *settled* in your midst [i.e., although I came here as a *foreigner* from another land, I am not merely a *transient* here; I have *settled* among you, and as such I deserve special consideration *(Mizrachi)*]. The *Midrashic* interpretation is: If you are agreeable [and accede to my request to sell me the land] then I can be regarded as a גֵּר, *foreigner* [who lacks the privileges of a citizen] and therefore, I am entirely dependent on your good will and will pay for the land. If you do *not* accomodate me, I shall claim it as a תּוֹשָׁב, *resident,* [and citizen] and *take* it as my *legal right,* since God promised this Land to my seed [12:7] *(Rashi).*

How could Abraham threaten to claim the land as his *legal right* since, as *Rashi* notes in his *comm.* to 13:7 s.v. וְהַכְּנַעֲנִי וְהַפְּרִזִּי אָז יֹשֵׁב בָּאָרֶץ, that Abraham was *not yet the legitimate owner of the land* [apparently, because the Canaanites and Perizzites still resided there]?

Mizrachi answers that the birth of Isaac constituted fulfillment of God's condition of *to your offspring will I give this land* [12:7]. Now Abraham had the offspring to whom the land would legally belong. Hence he could lay claim to it on behalf of his descendants although the Canaanites still dwelt there.

1. The *Midrash* notes that *speaking* sometimes connotes *comfort* as in *Isaiah* 40:2: *Speak* [i.e., *comfortingly*] *to the heart of Jerusalem.* Thus, by telling us that Abraham *spoke* consolingly to the Hittites, the Torah implies that the death of Sarah was a loss not only for Abraham and his family, but for the whole country.

So long as Sarah was alive, all went well in the land. With her death confusion ensued. The weeping, lamenting, and wailing over her death was universal, and Abraham — instead of receiving consolation — had to console others.

Abraham arose and comforted them: 'My children: Be not grieved. There is one event [death] unto all, the pious and impious alike. Favor me, I pray you, by granting me a burying place — not as a gift but for money.' *(Midrash HaGadol).*

תְּנוּ לִי אֲחֻזַּת־קֶבֶר עִמָּכֶם וְאֶקְבְּרָה מֵתִי
ה מִלְּפָנָי׃ וַיַּעֲנוּ בְנֵי־חֵת אֶת־אַבְרָהָם
ו לֵאמֹר לוֹ׃ שְׁמָעֵנוּ | אֲדֹנִי נְשִׂיא אֱלֹהִים

According to *Yafeh Toar*, Abraham could not yet lay claim to the *entire* land since the measure of the Canaanite residents' sins were not full; but he *did* — even at this time — *have the right to expropriate what he needed*, such as a burial site. [1]

Ramban explains that the natives had separate sepulchres reserved for each family, while there was a common burial ground set aside for the interment of all strangers. Therefore, Abraham told the children of Heth: 'Having come here as a *stranger*, I inherited no family sepulchre; now that I wish to become a *resident* among you, give me a permanent family burial-place.'

Akeidas Yitzchak notes that Abraham clearly defined his request; it was a *burial site* he was seeking, not fields or vineyards.

Hirsch explains the connotation: 'I have no *right* to your land, but I have lived among you for a long time.'

According to *Ibn Ezra*, the word גֵּר refers to a *transient foreigner*; the combined phrase גֵּר וְתוֹשָׁב is a *hendiadys* (essentially a single thought expressed by means of two words connected by 'and'). It should be understood as if the conjunctive ו, *and*, were absent, the meaning being: *a resident alien* [see *Avi Ezer; Karnei Or*].

[*Rashi* in *Lev.* 25:47 similarly renders the phrase גֵּר וְתוֹשָׁב, as a hendiadys: *strange resident* (resident alien), as does *Onkelos* there: עֲרַל תּוֹתָב *an uncircumcised resident*. See *comm.* ad. loc.]

Some explain the inclusion of the word עִמָּכֶם, *with you*, in this phrase as intimating: 'In truth I am a resident *alien* here *along with you* — i.e., just as you are. Do not delude yourselves that, in the spiritual realm, your foothold is any more permanent here than mine. Whatever our transient material possessions, we are both *foreigners* in this world. The end of all mankind is death — and I must make the necessary preparations.' *(Alshich;* [cf. *Dubner Maggid*]*)*.

T'cheles Mordechai similarly observes that Abraham meant to imply that the Hittites, like himself, were aliens. The bulk of the Hittite nation resided in Transjordan. Only the Hittite clans to which Ephron belonged had settled in Canaan. Abraham therefore said — 'I am a

1. The Sages regard this episode as constituting one of the many trials to which Abraham had been subjected [*Sanhedrin* 111a; see *Ramban* to *v.* 19 and *Rashi* to *Exodus* 6:3]. They draw the contrast between God's many promises to Abraham to 'give you the land', and Abraham's need to prostrate himself before the children of Heth, begging for a sepulchre in which to bury his wife:

Observe Abraham's humility! God had promised the entire land to him and his descendants forever, yet now he was landless and had to *purchase* a burial plot. Nevertheless, he never doubted God's ways, nor did he express resentment. He furthermore addressed himself to the citizens of the country in terms of utmost humility, describing himself as *a foreigner and a resident*.

Said the Holy One, Blessed be He to him: 'You humiliated yourself; by your life I shall make you a lord and prince over them!' *(Midrash HaGadol)*.

for a burial site with you, that I may bury my dead from before me.'

5 *And the children of Heth answered Abraham saying to him:* 6 *'Hear us, my lord: You are a prince*

resident alien, *with you,* for you, too, are but foreigners who took up residence here.'

תְּנוּ לִי אֲחֻזַּת קֶבֶר עִמָּכֶם — *Grant* [lit. *give*] *me an estate for a burial site* [lit. *possession of a grave* (see *Rashi* below)] *with you.*

With you — i.e., just as one of you *(Ramban).*

Or: give it to me *with you* — i.e., in your presence, publicly, so the transfer will be uncontestable *(Ralbag).*

אֲחֻזַּת קֶבֶר refers to the permanent possession of a known family sepulchre *(Hoffman).*

It has been noted that terms like *buying* and *selling* do not appear in this exchange. Gentlemen in those times and in that culture did not transact business, but made each other 'presents', although they made certain that the counter-present was at least as valuable *(Akeidas Yitzchak; Ibn Caspi).*

The term *give* is then to be understood to imply: *permit me to acquire (Sforno).* [Hence our rendering: *Grant*].

[There are, however, other connotations in the use of the word *give.* See *Ramban* and *Malbim* further. *Targum Yonasan* throughout this dialogue renders *give* as וְיִזְבּוּן, *sell.*]

The phrase אֲחֻזַּת קֶבֶר, [lit. *possession of a grave*] is elliptical and should be rendered, אֲחֻזָּה, *possession of land,* to serve as a קֶבֶר, *burying place.* A grave, being in a technical sense a hole in the earth, is an intangible, which one cannot be said to *possess.* Rather, one possesses the *land,* which serves as a burial place *(Rashi* as explained by commentators).[1]

וְאֶקְבְּרָה מֵתִי מִלְּפָנָי — *That I may* [lit. *and I will*] *bury my dead from before me* [or as *Hirsch* renders: *out of my sight*].

Wishing to stress the urgency of his request, Abraham emphasized that his dead was still *in his presence,* since it is known that the sooner the dead are buried, the greater their peace *(Ralbag).*

5-6. The Hittites consider the matter and give Abraham their reply:

5. לֵאמֹר לוֹ — *Saying to him.* I.e., through their representative [see

1. *Hirsch* explains that the word אֲחֻזָּה, *estate,* derives from אחז, *to grasp.* However, it cannot refer to the owner 'grasping' his possessions, so to speak, because the word אֲחֻזָּה is never used with reference to movable objects which an owner can literally grasp, but only to land. Furthermore, the root אחז referring to property ownership is used exclusively in the נִפְעַל, *passive* form suggesting that the owner is held *by* his property. Thus the concept of אֲחוּזָּה is that of a *landed estate* which outlives its owner and remains permanently in place. The owner is *grasped* by his immovable property. Since Abraham's Godly calling had been to be a wanderer, he never purchased land in Canaan. Now, however, that he was to accord Sarah her final honor, he would not consider leaving her to rest in another's property. Her burial site was to be his first possession in the land, the first instance where the land would hold him in its *grasp.* Thus, Sarah's grave would become the first permanent bond attaching Israel to its land.

אַתָּה֙ בְּתוֹכֵ֔נוּ בְּמִבְחַ֣ר קְבָרֵ֔ינוּ קְבֹ֖ר אֶת־
מֵתֶ֑ךָ אִ֣ישׁ מִמֶּ֔נּוּ אֶת־קִבְר֖וֹ לֹֽא־יִכְלֶ֥ה
ז מִמְּךָ֖ מִקְּבֹ֥ר מֵתֶֽךָ׃ וַיָּ֧קָם אַבְרָהָ֛ם וַיִּשְׁתַּ֥חוּ

further] *(Ha'amek Davar).* [Comp. *Comm.* to *v.* 14.]

6. שְׁמָעֵנוּ אֲדֹנִי — *Hear us, my lord.*[1]

One speaker was appointed to respond on behalf of them all, therefore, he used the plural form שְׁמָעֵנוּ, *hear 'us'*. However, the spokesman did not address Abraham as אֲדֹנֵנוּ, *our lord*, because it is impolite to ascribe to a stranger lordship over one's colleagues *(Ibn Ezra; Radak).*

נְשִׂיא אֱלֹהִים אַתָּה בְּתוֹכֵנוּ — *You are a prince of God in our midst.*

I.e., we do not regard you as a *foreigner* or *sojourner* — as you so humbly describe yourself; rather you are a king. God has made you king over us, and we and our land are your subjects. You need not *ask* for the land — it is yours! Take any burial ground you desire in which to inter your dead *(Ramban).*

The term 'prince of God' is used here as an honorific title. *Targum Yonasan* renders: רַב קֳדָם ה׳, *great before God*; a term of magnificence — for you are a prophet *(Ibn Ezra)*; you are one *elevated* [נָשִׂיא=*raised*] *by God*, and are so considered by us *(Radak).*

The word אֱלֹהִים in this verse is sacred *(Soferim* 4:6). [This precludes treating אֱלֹהִים as an adjective, and rendering נְשִׂיא אֱלֹהִים as *mighty* prince.]

'You are a king over us, you are a prince over us ...' the Hittites told Abraham, to which Abraham replied: 'The world does not lack its King, nor does it lack its God' *(Midrash*; comp. *Midrash* to 14:17 [p. 493]).

[It must be remembered that Abraham had lived among the Hittites in Hebron for a total of thirty-seven years: beginning twenty-five years before he moved to Beersheva, as noted in the Prefatory Synopsis to *v.* 1. It was from there that he went forth to conquer the invading Kings (ch. 14); that he undertook to circumcise his household, and where the call came for the *Akeidah.* His fame — from the days of his miraculous delivery from the furnaces of Nimrod at Ur Kasdim — was widespread and preceded him. The Hittites' references to him as *Prince of God* or *lord*, were certainly not empty praises; they knew Abraham intimately, and he was probably on friendly terms with many of them.]

בְּמִבְחַר קְבָרֵינוּ קְבֹר אֶת־מֵתֶךָ — *In the choicest of our burial places bury your dead.*

And it shall become your eternal possession *(Ramban).*

[They had been under the impression that Abraham was interested only in *a single grave*, and

1. Observe that the Hittites referred to Abraham several times throughout this episode by the reverential term אֲדֹנִי, *my lord*, while Abraham, in turn, never once reciprocated by using this term in addressing them.

... Abraham gave them his money; he even humbled himself to them, but the term אֲדֹנִי, *my lord*, he would not use, for there is no *lord* for Abraham except the Almighty *(Rav Yosef Hurwitz of Novardok).*

23
7

of God in our midst. In the choicest of our burial
places bury your dead. Any of us will not withhold
his burial place from burying your dead.'
7 *Then Abraham rose up and bowed down to the*

therefore accorded him the honor of offering him the grave of his choice.]

אֶת קִבְרוֹ — *His burial place.*

— I.e., even the grave reserved for his very own use *(Avraham ben HaRambam).*

לֹא יִכְלֶה — *Will not withhold.*

This translation follows *Rashi* and *Ibn Ezra.* Although the root of יִכְלֶה is כלה which, as used for example in 18:21, means *destruction* [כִּלָּיוֹן], this definition would clearly be out of context here. Thus, *Rashi* and *Ibn Ezra* relate יִכְלֶה to the cognate root כלא, *withhold, restrain,* as the verb is used in *Psalms* 40:12: לֹא תִכְלָא רַחֲמֶיךָ, *withhold not Your mercies;* and *Gen.* 8:2: וַיִּכָּלֵא הַגֶּשֶׁם, *and the rain was restrained (Divrei David).* For although the verbs differ in that they end with a ה and א respectively, they are synonymous and appear interchangeably *(Mizrachi).*

מִקְּבֹר מֵתֶךָ — *From burying your dead.*

But the fact that none of them would withhold *his burial place* did not satisfy Abraham's request. The bereaved Abraham was not satisfied merely to acquire *a grave* in which to inter his wife on another's land, a grave next to which strangers could later be buried; he wanted to acquire *permanent possession* of a *family sepulchre* for the eventual burial of his *entire family (Radak; Rokeach).*[1]

[And, as pointed out in the *Prefatory Synopsis,*] Abraham desired *specifically* the cave of Machpelah, but in order not to prejudice his negotiating position, he did not reveal that this was his desire lest the price become outrageously inflated [which it eventually did in any event] *(Alshich; Zohar).*

7. Abraham acknowledges their response and entreats further.

וַיָּקָם אַבְרָהָם — *Then* [lit. *and*] *Abraham rose up.*

Wishing to address them further, he respectfully stood up *(R' Bachya* to *v.* 3).

וַיִּשְׁתַּחוּ — *And bowed down.*

In gratitude, not servitude *(Avraham ben HaRambam).*

Implying thereby that he did not regard himself as a prince over them, but, to the contrary, that he considered *them* as superior *(Or HaChaim).*

1. According to *Malbim,* the intent of the Hittite response in this verse was as follows:
Hear us, my lord — and discern our words well: Do not think that we refuse your request for a family sepulchre because we do not hold you in esteem. To the contrary! — we regard you as *a prince of God among us.* But our common law limits the *possession of a burial site* [i.e., a family sepulchre] exclusively to natives. However, you have one option: *bury your dead in one of the graves from the choicest of our burial places* from our common burial sites; or if you wish to select a private grave then *none of us will withhold his* own private *burial place from you from burying your dead.*

לְעַם־הָאָרֶץ לִבְנֵי־חֵת: וַיְדַבֵּר אִתָּם לֵאמֹר אִם־יֵשׁ אֶת־נַפְשְׁכֶם לִקְבֹּר אֶת־מֵתִי מִלְּפָנַי שְׁמָעוּנִי וּפִגְעוּ־לִי בְּעֶפְרוֹן

According to *Radak,* the verse signifies that Abraham stood up and *bowed his head down* to them in gratitude and deference to their accommodating reply [although he proceeded to indicate that he would not take advantage of it.]

Ibn Ezra also explains הִשְׁתַּחֲוָיָה as referring to *bowing the head* [see also his *comm.* to 43:28.] Similarly, *Targum Yonasan* renders it as גחן indicating *bowing* rather than prostration.

Rashi, however [42:6; 43:26; *Lev.* 26:1] explains the word as denoting פְּשׁוּט יָדַיִם וְרַגְלַיִם, *stretching out of hands and feet* [i.e., complete prostration], and the term is so interpreted — with *Halachic* implications — by the Sages in the *Talmud: Berachos* 34b; *Megillah* 22b (see *Maharsha* there); *Shevuos* 16b. [Cf. *comm.* to 19:1, and see *HaKsav V'haKabbalah.*]

לְעַם הָאָרֶץ לִבְנֵי חֵת — *To the members of the council* [lit. *the people of the land*] *of the sons of Heth.*

This rendering follows *Hirsch,* who explains that the phrase עַם הָאָרֶץ [lit. *people of the land*] in this context does not refer to the citizenry or peasantry [as the phrase *Am HaAretz* came to mean in later *Talmudic* Hebrew: a boor, ignorant person.] Rather it is a *political term* that refers to the *representatives of the country* — who are empowered to grant aliens the right to acquire possession of land. (Comp. the use of עַם הָאָרֶץ in *Lev.* 20:4 where it also refers to the representatives of the people). It is to them that Abraham directs his remarks. Accordingly, לִבְנֵי חֵת [lit. *to the children of Heth*], is not a distinct phrase paralleling לְעַם הָאָרֶץ, [i.e., to the people ... to the sons ...]. Instead, both expressions form a single unit: To the members of the council of the sons of Heth — i.e., *to the Hittite council.*

Sforno interprets: To the assembled chiefs who represented the local population.

8. וַיְדַבֵּר אִתָּם לֵאמֹר — *And* [*he*] *spoke to them, saying*

[לֵאמֹר, *saying,* i.e., *as follows,* in a clear unambiguous manner (see *comm.* to 15:2).]

אִם־יֵשׁ אֶת נַפְשְׁכֶם — *If it is truly your will* [lit. *if you have with your soul.*]

I.e., if your *inner motivation* is as sincere as your *expressed offer* to accommodate me in burying my dead *(Avraham ben HaRambam).*

The rendering follows *Hirsch* based upon *Rashi* who comments that נַפְשְׁכֶם, *your soul,* in our verse figuratively means רְצוֹנְכֶם, *your will.* [This is similar to the figurative expression: *If you have it in your heart.*]

Radak cites a similar use of the word in *Psalms* 27:12: *Deliver me not over to the will* [נֶפֶשׁ] *of my enemies.*

The intent of Abraham's comment is: I will not inter my dead in another's grave. However, if it is indeed your intention that I bury my dead ... *(Ramban).*

If it is your sincere intention that my wife's burial be in one of your choicest burial sites *(Sforno).*

לִקְבֹּר אֶת־מֵתִי מִלְּפָנַי — *To bury* [i.e., *that I bury (Ramban)*] *my dead from before me.*

The implication of the word מִלְּפָנַי, *from before me,* is that I will otherwise be forced to keep her always *before me* by entombing her

23
8 *members of the council of the sons of Heth, [8] and*
spoke to them, saying: 'If it is truly your will to bury
my dead from before me, heed me, and intercede for

in a casket [a clearly unacceptable course of action, especially in view of the respect in which Sarah was held by the Hittites] unless you provide me with a proper burial ground. Alternatively, it is possible that the phrase is to be rendered: 'to bury my dead *who still remains before me'* — and I must hurry her burial *(Ramban).*[1]

וּפִגְעוּ־לִי בְּעֶפְרוֹן בֶּן־צֹחַר — *And intercede for me with Ephron son of Tzochar.*

Ephron was a rich and distinguished person, and Abraham knew that it would not befit his status and wealth to sell his ancestral inheritance as in the case of Naboth, who told King Ahab [*I Kings* 21:3]: *HASHEM forbid it to me that I should give the inheritance of my fathers to you.* Abraham, therefore, did not approach Ephron directly and offer an inflated price for the field. Instead he asked the people of the city to entreat Ephron dignifiedly on his behalf to magnanimously *'give'* the property to Abraham, though Abraham would be prepared to pay handsomely for it and still consider it a gift *(Ramban).*

The rendering of פִּגְעוּ [lit. *encounter*] as *intercede* [in the sense of 'use your influence'] follows *Rashi* who explains that the word signifies entreaty [לְשׁוֹן בַּקָּשָׁה], as it does in *Ruth* 1:16: אַל תִּפְגְּעִי בִי, *do not urge me.* The word signifies an important request which would not be granted but for the petitioner's influence *(Heidenheim).*[2]

The *Midrash* offers the dual connotation of פִּגְעוּ *to meet* and *to entreat*: 'Let me *meet* him, but if he is not willing, *beseech* him on my behalf.'

1. *Kli Chemdah* notes that *Ramban* himself writes in *Toras Ha'Adam (Sha'ar HaKevurah)* that Torah law requires burial *in the ground.* If so, how can *Ramban* say that Abraham was prepared to leave Sarah entombed *in a casket above ground?*

In reply, *Kli Chemdah* cites two reasons for underground burial: 1. Since Adam was fashioned from the earth, man's body must be returned to its source; and 2. To avoid desecration of the body through leaving it exposed. The second reason would not apply to entombment in a casket for that, too, preserves the dignity of the deceased. As to the first reason, a person *who is free of sin, as was Sarah,* has elevated his or her body to the point where it is no longer like the material earth. There would be no obligation to return such a body to its 'source' for it is no longer of the same nature as its source. Therefore, Abraham could be justified in refusing to bury Sarah if a suitable site were unattainable.

2. Abraham decided not to approach Ephron directly. Instead, he asked the Hittites to intercede on his behalf. Similarly, Joseph asked the 'house of Pharaoh' to seek the monarch's permission to take Jacob to *Eretz Yisrael* for burial [50:4]. The use of an intermediary places greater pressure for compliance on the object of the plea because the prestige of two people, the intermediary as well as the supplicant, is involved. Both are accommodated by agreement and both are insulted by refusal. This may also be the factor in the efficacy of public prayer which, as the Sages note in *Berachos* 8a, is not rejected by God. Also, a prayer for the benefit of another person is more readily accepted than a personal plea because the merits of more than one person are involved *(Tosefes Berachah).*

ט בֶּן־צֹחַר: וְיִתֶּן־לִי אֶת־מְעָרַת הַמַּכְפֵּלָה אֲשֶׁר־לוֹ אֲשֶׁר בִּקְצֵה שָׂדֵהוּ בְּכֶסֶף מָלֵא

According to *Me'am Loez,* Abraham consulted the entire Hittite community in order to avoid violation of the law of בַּר מְצְרָא. This Talmudic law gives the first right of refusal to neighboring property owners. Had Abraham gone directly to Ephron, the owner of an adjoining property could have challenged his right to purchase the land.

9. Abraham specifically reveals that the cave is the object of his intention.

וְיִתֶּן־לִי — *That* [lit. *and*] *he may grant* [lit. *give*] *me.*

[On the use of *give me* see *Comm.* to *v.* 4 s.v. תְּנוּ לִי, and *Ramban* below s.v. בְּכֶסֶף מָלֵא.]

מְעָרַת הַמַּכְפֵּלָה — *The cave of Machpelah* [lit. *the cave of the double*].

It was so called because it contained an upper and a lower story; or it was called 'doubled' on account of the זוגות, *couples,* who were [to be] buried there [i.e., the root כפל which signifies *multiplication* as well as *doubling*, denotes that it was so called because it had *multiple couples* interred within it] *(Rashi;* see on *v.* 2: קִרְיַת אַרְבַּע).

Although only Adam and Eve were as yet buried there, the name signified that the cave was spacious enough for the eventual interment of four couples *(Gur Aryeh).*

Cf. *Eruvin* 53a: Rav and Shmuel differ as to the cave of Machpelah. One holds that it consisted of two chambers — one within the other; and the other holds that the cave consisted of a lower and an upper chamber. According to the one who holds that the chambers were one above the other, the term *machpelah* is well justified [since *machpelah* depicts double stories], but according to him who holds that it consisted of two chambers one within the other, what could be the meaning of *machpelah* [since such a term is inappropriate to two adjacent chambers *(Rashi* ad loc.) — According to the latter the name *Machpelah* signified that it had *multiples of couples* [but his opinion that there were in fact two chambers within the cave is not implied by the name *Machpelah* (see *Maharsha).*]

Ibn Ezra maintains that it was so called because it was a *double cave,* one within the other. *Abarbanel* understands *Ibn Ezra* to agree with *Rashi* that the cave consisted of double *stories* though his language can be interpreted otherwise. *Radak* in *Sefer HaShorashim* explicitly suggests that *machpelah* [doubled] signifies that there were inner and outer caves separated by a wall, and that such an arrangement *could* properly be termed 'double'.

Rashbam and *Ramban* suggest that the entire *plain* was called *Machpelah* as evidenced from *v.* 17: 'the field of Ephron *which was in Machpelah'* [and hence the cave which was within that plain quite naturally came to be known as the Cave of Machpelah]. And, as *Ramban* comments: It is unnecessary to seek reasons for the names of places [in seeking the simple meaning of Scriptures.] [See *Chidushei Rashash* to *Bereishis Rabbah* 59:8].

Midrashically, however, *Ramban* notes that the Holy One, Blessed be He, bent double [i.e., folded in half] the stature of Adam [in order that the very tall Adam could fit into the cave] and He buried him there [in the cave] *(Bereishis Rabbah* 55:10). Accordingly, the area was always referred to by that name [which signified the 'doubling' of Adam] though the people [of Heth] were unaware of the name's significance, and that there was a grave in the cave.

[That Abraham *was* aware of the name's

23
9 me with Ephron son of Tzochar. 9 That he may grant
me the cave of Machpelah which is his, on the edge
of his field — let him grant it to me for its full price! —

true significance is evidenced by the fact that he referred to the *cave* as Machpelah. The Hittites, however, being unaware of the cave's significance, had no particular name for the cave. They referred to the entire *area* as Machpelah [*v.* 17] *(Abohab).*]

[As the *Zohar* mentions (see *Prefatory Synopsis)* since the time that Abraham learned that Adam and Eve were buried in the cave, he longed to establish it as the sepulchre for him and his children.]

[For the Kabbalistic implication of *Machpelah,* see *Zohar* 1:128b.]

אֲשֶׁר לוֹ — *Which is his.*

By stressing that the cave was Ephron's property, Abraham specifically negated a facile rationalization that could have been utilized in his behalf: i.e., since the cave was *on the edge of Ephron's field,* its use would not interfere with Ephron's exploitation of the field. Since Ephron had no use for that section, the council of the Hittites might have been tempted to allow Abraham to use the cave without Ephron's permission and without paying him [in the vein of *Bava Kamma* 20b]. This reasoning, Abraham categorically rejected *(Harav David Feinstein).*

[The commentators note that there is profound mystical significance in the fact that many places of great holiness were originally the possessions of simple or profane people. Thus, the cave belonged to Ephron, the site of the Temple was originally the threshing-floor of Ornan the Jebusite from whom David purchased it [*II Samuel* 24:18-25]; Bathsheba, ancestress of the Davidic dynasty, was married to Uriah [ibid. 11:3], and *Eretz Yisrael* was inhabited by the Canaanites for many centuries. Similarly, many proselytes achieved holiness although they were born as non-Jews. Such mysteries of the Torah resulted from Adam's sin, and are beyond our comprehension *(Sifsei Cohen).*]

[A similar mystical concept underlies the descent of the Davidic dynasty from Ruth the Moabitess whose roots grew from the incestuous union of Lot and his daughters. David's family descended from the 'tainted' union of Judah and Tamar. For a discussion of these phenomena as examples of שֹׁחַד לְשָׂטָן, *a bribe to Satan,* see Chapter V of *Overview* to ArtScroll ed. of *Ruth.*]

אֲשֶׁר בִּקְצֵה שָׂדֵהוּ — *Which is on the edge of his field.*

Abraham stressed that the cave was at *the extreme edge of his field,* so that separating it would not interfere with Ephron's use of the field *(Hirsch),* nor would it impair his estate *(Sforno).*

— And the field itself could be retained by Ephron, since Abraham was anxious only to acquire the cave *(Ramban).*

It would also seem that, because it was at the very edge of his field, the cave could be entered from the public thoroughfare. Therefore Abraham had no need to purchase the adjacent field for easement purposes *(Harav David Feinstein).*

בְּכֶסֶף מָלֵא יִתְּנֶנָּה לִי — *Let him give it to me, for its full price* [lit. *'in full silver'* i.e., *for its full value (Rashi).*]

— With coins that contain their full weight in silver and not of a short measure *(Radak).*

— So did King David say to

י יִתְּנֶנָּה לִּי בְּתוֹכְכֶם לַאֲחֻזַּת־קָבֶר: וְעֶפְרוֹן
יֹשֵׁב בְּתוֹךְ בְּנֵי־חֵת וַיַּעַן עֶפְרוֹן הַחִתִּי
אֶת־אַבְרָהָם בְּאָזְנֵי בְנֵי־חֵת לְכֹל בָּאֵי
יא שַׁעַר־עִירוֹ לֵאמֹר: לֹא־אֲדֹנִי שְׁמָעֵנִי
הַשָּׂדֶה נָתַתִּי לָךְ וְהַמְּעָרָה אֲשֶׁר־בּוֹ לְךָ

Ornan [whose threshing floor he purchased as a site for the altar, which later became the site of the Temple]: בְּכֶסֶף מָלֵא, *for its full price* [*I Chron.* 21:22] *(Rashi).*

Abraham implied: 'Although I stand ready to pay any price Ephron may designate, I will still consider it a generous courtesy that so important a person will agree to cede his ancestral estate to me.' Abraham therefore made no mention of the word 'sale.' A similar idea is to be found in the phrases [*Deut.* 2:28] *You shall sell me food for money ... and* give *me water for money* — i.e., for the gift of water I shall give you money. Perhaps, *give* is merely idiomatic when describing sales transactions *(Ramban).*

Following *Malbim* [see end of *v.* 6]: Let Ephron make me a *gift* of the insignificant piece of property on the edge of his field; in that way he will not violate your common law which prohibits only the *sale* of property to aliens. At the same time I will make him a gift of a substantial amount of money to offset any possible loss he may suffer by this transaction.

בְּתוֹכְכֶם — *In your midst.*

I.e., *in the presence of all of you,* that none may subsequently dispute it *(Midrash HaGadol).*

'And I will pay him immediately while you are all still present; I do not ask for any extended time to settle the finances.' And so it happened: as soon as Ephron named his price, Abraham paid him immediately [*v.* 16] *(Sforno).*

לַאֲחֻזַּת־קָבֶר — *As an estate for a burial site* [lit. *'as (permanent) possession of a grave'*].

I.e., that it meet with your *unanimous approval* (בְּתוֹכְכֶם) for it to become my אֲחֻזַּת קָבֶר, permanent estate as a burial site *(Rashbam).*

Lest Ephron later contest his right to bury someone near his boundary, Abraham emphasized that he was buying the property for use as a *burial site (Sforno).*

10. וְעֶפְרוֹן יֹשֵׁב בְּתוֹךְ בְּנֵי חֵת — *Now,* [lit. *and*] *Ephron was sitting in the midst of the children of Heth.*

I.e., *sitting* as a magistrate *(Midrash;* cf. 19:1). This is derived from the fact that the verb ישב, *sitting,* in conjunction with תוך, *midst,* implies authority as in *II Kings* 4:13: בְּתוֹךְ עַמִּי אָנֹכִי יֹשָׁבֶת, *I sit among my people* [i.e., I am in a position of authority among my own people *(Mizrachi)*].

The verb יושב, *was sitting,* is written defectively [יֹשֵׁב, without the *vav*] which — since the Torah is written unvocalized — can be read יָשַׁב, *sat,* in the past tense, [a form indicating that the event happened for the first time *(L'shon Chaim),*

23
10-11

in your midst as an estate for a burial site.'
10 *Now, Ephron was sitting in the midst of the children of Heth. And Ephron the Hittite responded to Abraham in the hearing of the children of Heth for all who come to the gate of his town, saying:* 11 *'No, my lord; heed me! I have given you the field, and as for the cave that is in it, I have given it to you. In the*

or, because the spelling was defective, implies that his sitting was 'incomplete', i.e., a recent development (*Harav David Feinstein*; see *comm.* to 19:1).] This intimates that *on that very day* they had appointed Ephron to be their magistrate.

— It was because of the high standing of Abraham that Ephron was elevated to this dignified position [so that Abraham would negotiate with a dignitary and not a common person] (*Tzeidah LaDerech; Rashi*).

וַיַּעַן עֶפְרוֹן הַחִתִּי אֶת אַבְרָהָם — *And Ephron the Hittite responded* [*to*] *Abraham.*

[It is not clear whether, in fact, the Hittites had transmitted Abraham's request to Ephron who now offered his response, or whether Ephron *who had been sitting,* either as a magistrate (see above) or as an observer, took the initiative and addressed Abraham directly when he heard his name specifically mentioned and perceived that the council was generally inclined to favor Abraham's wish].

בְּאָזְנֵי בְנֵי־חֵת — *In the hearing* [lit. *ears*] *of the children of Heth.*

— I.e., publicly, for all to hear (*Radak*).

לְכֹל בָּאֵי שַׁעַר עִירוֹ — *For all who came to the gate of his town.*

— I.e., all those who were assembled at the city gate — great and small alike. The term בָּאֵי שַׁעַר, in the sense of all those who pass through the gate, is idiomatic, and denotes the entire population of the city. Scriptures interchangeably uses the expressions בָּאֵי שַׁעַר, *arrivals through the gate,* and, יוֹצְאֵי שַׁעַר, *departers through the gate.* See *Jer.* 17:19 where both expressions occur synonymously (*Radak*).

The phraseology implies that they had all left their work and come to pay their last respects to Sarah (*Rashi*).

[As noted in the *comm.* to 19:1, the gates of a city, like the gates around the Old City of Jerusalem today, were fairly large edifices. They were not gathering places for idlers, but for the assembly of the dignitaries of the Land ... it was the place where commercial transactions took place and justice was administered. (See also *Ruth* 4:1-11).]

11. לֹא־אֲדֹנִי — *No, my lord.*

— You need not *purchase* it (*Rashi*).

הַשָּׂדֶה ... וְהַמְּעָרָה ... לְךָ נְתַתִּיהָ — *I have given you the field, and* [*as for*] *the cave that is in it have I given to you.*

I.e., I have decided to give it to you (*Abarbanel*), and it is as if I have already given it to you (*Rashi*).

But his promises were empty! For the

נְתַתִּיהָ לְעֵינֵי בְנֵי־עַמִּי נְתַתִּיהָ לָּךְ קְבֹר
יב מֵתֶךָ: וַיִּשְׁתַּחוּ אַבְרָהָם לִפְנֵי עַם־הָאָרֶץ:
יג וַיְדַבֵּר אֶל־עֶפְרוֹן בְּאָזְנֵי עַם־הָאָרֶץ
לֵאמֹר אַךְ אִם־אַתָּה לוּ שְׁמָעֵנִי נָתַתִּי

wicked promise much but perform not even little; they would anoint with oil from an empty flask!

Three times in this verse does Ephron speak of *giving* the property to Abraham as a *gift*, yet he concludes by taking only *negotiable* currency [*v.* 16]. The wicked are empty as are their words and deeds; but as for the righteous, their words and their deeds are truth *(Midrash HaGadol*; see Rashi to *v.* 16).

— Not as you proposed, that I sell it to you בְּכֶסֶף מָלֵא, *for its full price.* To the contrary! I will make you a *gift* of it; and not merely the cave as you requested, but the entire field! *(Radak).*

For if you were to acquire only the cave without the field, you would lack the easement for legal access to the cave *(Chizkuni*; [but cf. *Harav Feinstein* comment on *v.* 9 אֲשֶׁר בִּקְצֵה שָׂדֵהוּ]).

Ephron was unaware that there was a grave [of Adam and Eve] on his property. Abraham was interested only in acquiring the cave itself; he was content that the adjacent field remain Ephron's. Ephron, on the other hand, by way of good conduct or trickery [possibly in the hope that if he combined the field with the cave, he would receive a higher price for the larger transaction *(Chavel)*] said he would give him the field as well as the cave on it, for it would be unbecoming for one as honorable as Abraham to own a *cave* as a sepulchre while the ownership of the *field* belonged to another. Abraham rejoiced at Ephron's offer [next verse] and he purchased it in its entirety for the full price Ephron suggested *(Ramban).*[1]

לְעֵינֵי בְנֵי־עַמִּי נְתַתִּיהָ לָּךְ קְבֹר מֵתֶךָ — *In the view* [lit. *'to the eyes'*] *of the children of my people have I given it to you. Bury your dead.*

— Behold all my people are

1. [The question can be raised that Abraham would seem to have been guilty of questionable conduct since he knew of the cave's immense value as the sepulchre of Adam and Eve, a fact of which he did not make Ephron aware. The explanation of Abraham's action lies in the *Zohar*. The *Zohar* explains that 'Ephron never perceived anything (of spiritual value) inside the cave, *since such things are never revealed except to their rightful owner, in this case Abraham,* but not to Ephron who had no portion in it, and who therefore saw only darkness in it.'

Accordingly, even in the hypothetical case that if the cave's true value could become known, the transaction could not be termed retroactively questionable since *without Abraham's prophetic revelation, the value of the cave would have forever remained a mystery.*

Indeed, while the spirituality of the cave was a priceless treasure to Abraham, it was essentially meaningless to an Ephron.

Furthermore, the sum Ephron demanded for the property was astronomical and Abraham immediately paid it. He *did not haggle nor deprecate the property by suggesting a lower price.* Therefore, *Ephron* was the one who dealt unfairly by taking advantage of Abraham's bereavement to gouge a hapless customer.]

23
12-13

view of the children of my people have I given it to
you; bury your dead.'
12 *So Abraham bowed down before the members of*
the council, 13 *and spoke to Ephron in the hearing of*
the members of the council, saying: 'Rather, if only
you would heed me! I give you the price of the field,

witnesses to this transaction, you need not fear denial or retraction; you may confidently *bury your dead (Ramban).*

Ha'amek Davar adds that a second connotation is discernable between the lines of Ephron's statement: 'You understand, of course, Abraham, that I make you this magnanimous offer of a gift *only in the presence of my people*; between us, however, you certainly realize that I cannot make a *gift* of so valuable a property.'

Following *Malbim*: No, Abraham, you misunderstood our common law. There is no difference whether we make a *gift* of the property or *sell* it. It is a *burial site* that we are prohibited from transferring to strangers. Therefore, I will give you the entire field to use for planting, and the cave will be included as part of the entire property. I make this transaction incontestible, in the presence of all of my countrymen — *after which you may bury your dead,* i.e., once it is yours you may do with your property as you see fit, though I make it clear that I am not selling it to you as a sepulchre, but as farmland.

12. וַיִּשְׁתַּחוּ אַבְרָהָם לִפְנֵי עַם הָאָרֶץ — *So,* [lit. *and*] *Abraham bowed down before the members of the council* [*Am Ha'aretz*; see on *v.* 7].

I.e., he bowed down to Ephron *in the presence of* the members of the council *(Targum Yonasan; Ibn Ezra; Rashbam).*

According to *Sforno,* the verse implies that Abraham bowed down *to the members of the council* in gratitude, implying that he recognized that it was out of respect to *them* that Ephron had consented to comply with his wishes.

According to the *Midrash,* [the phrase לִפְנֵי עַם הָאָרֶץ, *in the presence* of the council, instead of לְעַם הָאָרֶץ, *to* the council, as in *v.* 7, indicates that] it was *God* to whom Abraham bowed *in the presence of* the council, to give thanks to the Divine Name. 'From this we learn that one must give thanks for good tidings' *(Yafeh Toar).*

13. וַיְדַבֵּר אֶל־עֶפְרוֹן — *And* [*he*] *spoke to Ephron.*

— Directly, there being no further need for intermediaries *(Ibn Caspi).*

בְּאָזְנֵי עַם הָאָרֶץ — *In the hearing* [lit. *ears*] *of the members of the council.*

[Concerned throughout that they should witness the negotiations, and thereby prevent possible denials or retractions later.]

אַךְ אִם אַתָּה לוּ שְׁמָעֵנִי — *Rather, if only you would heed me.*

The word אַךְ: *however, but, nevertheless, rather,* always implies a limitation, negating or further defining that which had been expressed earlier. In this case the intent is: You told me to listen to you [*v.* 11] and accept it without pay-

כֶּ֤סֶף הַשָּׂדֶה֙ קַ֣ח מִמֶּ֔נִּי וְאֶקְבְּרָ֥ה אֶת־מֵתִ֖י
יד שָֽׁמָּה׃ וַיַּ֧עַן עֶפְר֛וֹן אֶת־אַבְרָהָ֖ם לֵאמֹ֥ר
טו לֽוֹ׃ אֲדֹנִ֣י שְׁמָעֵ֔נִי אֶ֗רֶץ אַרְבַּ֨ע מֵאֹ֧ת שֶֽׁקֶל־
כֶּ֛סֶף בֵּינִ֥י וּבֵינְךָ֖ מַה־הִ֑וא וְאֶת־מֵתְךָ֖

ment. I do not accept the field on such a basis. אַךְ, *rather,* אִם אַתָּה לוּ שְׁמָעֵנִי, *if you would only heed me...* (*Rashi* as explained by *Mizrachi*).

נָתַתִּי כֶּסֶף הַשָּׂדֶה קַח מִמֶּנִּי – *I give* [lit. *have given*] *you the price* [lit. *money* or *silver*] *of the field, accept* [lit. *take*] *it from me.*[1]

Abraham indicated that he was ready to pay the value of the *entire field* for the cave alone. The money was ready – there it was! He no longer considered it his own. Let Ephron pick it up and the matter would be concluded (*Hirsch*).

Cf. *Pesikta Zutresa*: The [Torah testifies that the] word of the righteous is their deed; not 'I *will* give', but 'I *have* given.'

Apparently Abraham was concerned that if he considered it a *gift,* Ephron might later retract, and wish to inter Hittite dead alongside the righteous Sarah. Abraham therefore insisted on a formal *sale* (*Abarbanel*).

According to *Sforno,* Abraham's response was: You ask me to bury my dead [*v.* 11]. I accept your offer, אַךְ, *only* on this condition – אִם אַתָּה לוּ שְׁמָעֵנִי, *if you would but listen to me,* נָתַתִּי כֶּסֶף הַשָּׂדֶה, *if I have first given you the money* [and the cave is no longer considered a gift] only then וְאֶקְבְּרָה אֶת מֵתִי שָׁמָּה, *will I bury my dead there.*

An interesting interpretation of Abraham's response is offered by *Chizkuni,* who notes that the word

1. Our verse contains one of the best known examples of גְּזֵרָה שָׁוָה, the method of exegesis whereby the use of similar words or phrases in two different Scriptural passages indicates that the law or connotation of one passage applies to the other as well. Our verse refers to the act of קִיחָה, *taking,* i.e., קַח מִמֶּנִּי, *take it from me.* From this is derived that the act of legal acquisition of property can be accomplished by the transfer of funds, since Abraham specified that he turned over payment for the field to Ephron.

Deut. 22:13 refers to the consecration of a bride: כִּי יִקַּח אִישׁ אִשָּׁה, *if a man takes* [i.e., *acquires*] *a wife.* However, the legal method of *acquisition* is not specified. The Sages expound קִיחָה קִיחָה מִשְּׂדֵה עֶפְרוֹן, [lit. *taking, taking* is derived from Ephron's field] i.e., the concept of קִיחָה, *taking,* is mentioned regarding Ephron's property; the concept of קִיחָה is also mentioned regarding the taking of a bride. The use of similar phrases teaches that a bride is consecrated to her groom [i.e., *acquired* or *taken*] in the same manner that a field is acquired, namely through the transfer of money or something of value. The traditional קדושין, *consecration,* ceremony involving the giving of a ring from man to woman is valid because the ring has monetary value. (See *Kiddushin* 2a).

I.e., the money is ready for you; I wish I had given it to you already (*Rashi*).

[Although the verb נָתַתִּי, lit., is in past tense, *have given, Rashi* in 14:22 interprets this verse in the present tense: *I give.* This is based on the following phrase קַח מִמֶּנִּי, *take it from me,* which implies that the money was immediately made available. The past tense is used to indicate such determination to carry out the act that the deed may be considered as good as done. Additionally, the word לוּ [=הַלְוַאי], *if only,* above, is applied to this phrase as well; hence *Rashi*'s interpretation: לוּ ... נָתַתִּי, *I wish* [הַלְוַאי] *I had given it to you already* (*Sechel Tov; Maharshal; Sefer HaZikaron; Mizrachi* to 14:22). [Comp. also 15:18.]

23
14-15

accept it from me, that I may bury my dead there.'
[14] And Ephron replied to Abraham, saying to him:
[15] 'My lord heed me! Land worth four hundred silver
shekels — between me and you — what is it? Bury
your dead.'

נָתַתִּי, *I have given,* is separated from the rest of the phrase כֶּסֶף הַשָּׂדֶה, *the money for the field,* by a disjunctive cantillation [*Azlah Geresh*]. Thus, the three words are not to be understood as a single thought. Instead, נָתַתִּי refers to *v.* 11 where Ephron used the same word, saying, נָתַתִּי, *I have given you the field* ... Accordingly, Abraham said: *Listen to me.* [You said,] *I have given you the field.* No, rather, כֶּסֶף הַשָּׂדֶה קַח מִמֶּנִּי, *the money for the field, take from me.*

14-15. Ephron names the price ...

14. לֵאמֹר לוֹ — *Saying to him.*

This phrase, like the similar one in *v.* 5, implies something relayed through an intermediary. However, unlike the pompous public gestures of generosity which he had earlier made, Ephron intended this statement only for Abraham: לוֹ, [*directly*] *to him.* The inflated price was such that Ephron was ashamed to request it personally, nor would he make it known to the public. He preferred to make it known to Abraham privately, through an intermediary *(Hirsch;* cf. *Ha'amek Davar; Tzror HaMor).*

Me'am Loez suggests that the constant repetition of לֵאמֹר, *saying,* indicates that all of these negotiations took place through an interpreter, since Abraham did not speak the Hittite language well.

[This interpretation is difficult, however, since Abraham was a resident in Hebron for over thirty-seven years, and, being so intent on hospitality to strangers and on drawing others close to God, it is inconceivable that he would not have learned to communicate effectively with the local residents.]

15. אֶרֶץ אַרְבַּע מֵאֹת שֶׁקֶל כֶּסֶף — *Land worth* [lit. *of*] *four hundred silver shekels.*

The word *worth* follows the translation of *Onkelos* who renders שַׁוְיָא.

Ramban, citing *Onkelos,* explains that according to that interpretation, the sum of four hundred silver shekels was indeed the *value* of the property in accordance with the current market price. The *simple* interpretation would be that Ephron or his forebears had bought the land for that sum. According to the Sages, however, Ephron set an astronomically exorbitant price, and Abraham graciously paid it.

בֵּינִי וּבֵינְךָ מַה־הִוא — *Between me and you — what is it?*

I.e., between such friends as we, of what significance is it? *(Rashi).*

[The commentators observe that in this apparently unconcerned tone the seller nonchalantly names his excessive price. As Rabbi Aryeh Kaplan points out in his notes to *Torah Anthology* II, we find that King Omri paid only six thousand shekels for the entire territory of Samaria *(I Kings* 16:25), and that Jeremiah paid only seventeen shekels for a property that was at least

טז קְבֹר: וַיִּשְׁמַע אַבְרָהָם אֶל־עֶפְרוֹן וַיִּשְׁקֹל
אַבְרָהָם לְעֶפְרֹן אֶת־הַכֶּסֶף אֲשֶׁר דִּבֶּר
בְּאָזְנֵי בְנֵי־חֵת אַרְבַּע מֵאוֹת שֶׁקֶל כֶּסֶף
°שני יז עֹבֵר לַסֹּחֵר: °וַיָּקָם | שְׂדֵה עֶפְרוֹן אֲשֶׁר

as large as the field of Machpelah! (*Jeremiah* 32:9).]

וְאֶת מֵתְךָ קְבֹר — [*And*] *bury your dead.*

I.e., put aside the question of 'purchase' and bury your dead! (*Rashi*).

The indefinite article אֶת indicates a רִבּוּי, exegetical amplification, with the implied meaning being *with* or *in addition to* [see *footnote* to 21:1, p. 743]. Therefore, the *Vilna Gaon* comments that exegetically the phrase וְאֶת מֵתְךָ קְבֹר [and bury something *in addition to* your dead] alludes to Esau's head which was also buried in the cave of Machpelah. [See *comm.* to 49:21].

16. Abraham consummates the purchase.

וַיִּשְׁמַע אַבְרָהָם אֶל עֶפְרוֹן — [*And*] *Abraham heeded* [to] *Ephron.*

— 'A hint to the wise is sufficient' (*Rashbam*).

According to *Sforno*: He accepted Ephron's evaluation [i.e., without protestation or counter-offer.]

וַיִּשְׁקֹל אַבְרָהָם לְעֶפְרֹן — [*And*] *Abraham weighed out* [in order to ascertain their exact value] *to Ephron.*

[The rendering *weighed* follows most commentators. According to *Sforno*, however, in this context the word merely means *paid out*, as in *I Kings* 20:39: or else you shall *pay* (תִּשְׁקוֹל) a talent of silver.]

The *Midrash* notes that the name Ephron is usually spelled with a ו, *vav*, i.e., עֶפְרוֹן. In this case it is spelled עֶפְרֹן defectively without the *vav*. This indicates that there was something missing in Ephron — his stature was reduced — because he promised much but performed not even a little (*Bava Metzia* 87a and *footnote* to *v.* 11). [It was as if he were an עֶפְרֹן, one who speaks with עָפָר, *dust*, in his mouth (*Bertinoro*; see *Bava Basra* 16a)]; for in the end he demanded from Abraham large shekels: *centenaria* [valued at a full one hundred smaller units] as it is said עֹבֵר לַסֹּחֵר, *negotiable currency* [see below] (*Rashi*).[1]

אֶת הַכֶּסֶף אֲשֶׁר דִּבֶּר בְּאָזְנֵי בְּנֵי חֵת — *The amount* [lit. *money* or *silver*]

1. The *Midrash* [*Bereishis Rabbah* 79:7] comments that this is one of the three places where the gentiles cannot besmirch Israel by saying: 'You hold stolen property'.

They are the following: The cave of Machpelah; the site of the Temple, and Joseph's sepulchre.

— *The cave of Machpelah*, for it is written *And Abraham listened to Ephron, and weighed out ... four hundred shekels;*

— *The site of the Temple*, as it is written [*I Chron.* 21:25]: *So David gave to Ornan for the place six hundred shekels of gold.* [The term *full price* is used there (*v.* 22) as well];

— *Joseph's sepulchre*, as is written [33:19]: *He bought the parcel of ground* [i.e., Shechem, where Joseph's bones were finally interred. (See *Joshua* 24:32).]

[In all three cases, payment was made in uncontested currency, and without negotiation; the first asking price was given without haggling.]

23
16-17

[16] *Abraham heeded Ephron, and Abraham weighed out to Ephron the amount which he had mentioned in the hearing of the children of Heth — four hundred silver shekels in negotiable currency.*
[17] *And Ephron's field which was in Machpelah, fac-*

that he had mentioned in the hearing [lit. *ears*] *of the children of Heth.*

I.e., the payment that he previously promised he would make for a burial site [vs. 9-13]. In giving the payment to Ephron, he simultaneously fulfilled his promise of *v.* 9 to pay כֶּסֶף מָלֵא, *its full price (Hoffman).*

עֹבֵר לַסֹּחֵר — *Negotiable currency* [lit. *passing over to the merchant.*]

As *Targum Yonasan* explains it: אַרְבַּע מְאָה סִלְעִין דִּכְסַף טַב עָבְרִין בְּכָל פְּתוֹר וּמִתְקַבְּלִין בְּכָל פְּרַקְמַטְיָא, *four hundred selaim of good silver passing at every* [*banker's*] *table, and receivable in all transactions.*

The phrase refers to coins which were everywhere accepted in value as a full shekel — for there are places where their shekels are large, called קַנְטָרִין, *centenaria* [worth a hundred smaller units] *(Rashi).*

[As the Talmud *Bava Metzia* 87a explains, Ephron refused to accept anything but *centenaria,* hence Abraham gave him four hundred *centenaria* instead of ordinary shekels as Ephron had originally demanded. This is deduced from the phrase עֹבֵר לַסֹּחֵר implying that it was recognized everywhere as a shekel — even in those places where *centenaria* were used as ordinary shekels.]

For whenever else the Torah refers to a *shekel* it means a coin weighing a *sela.* Abraham's shekels, however, weighed a *centenaria (Bava Metzia* 87a). As *Rashi* explains there, each *centenaria* weighed one hundred *mannah.* A *mannah* is twenty-five *shekels.* [Thus, according to *Rashi,* each *centenaria* is worth 2,500 ordinary *shekels* and Abraham paid a total of one million ordinary *shekels* for the cave.]

According to *Ibn Ezra,* the phrase עֹבֵר לַסֹּחֵר indicates currency readily acceptable by merchants who recognize and accept only coins of *the finest silver.*

17. וַיָּקָם שְׂדֵה עֶפְרוֹן — *And Ephron's field ... passed* [lit. *rose up; became elevated*].

I.e., the ownership of the field, cave, etc. *became established* as Abraham's property. This is the literal meaning of *vs.* 17-18 [which although they are separate verses are to be *rendered* as one unit.] The *Midrashic* interpretation of וַיָּקָם is that the property became *elevated* in importance ['תְּקוּמָה הָיְתָה לוֹ'] because it passed from the possession of a commoner [Ephron] to that of a king [i.e., Abraham; see *comm.* to נְשִׂיא אֱלֹהִים in *v.* 6] *(Rashi).*

The version in the *Midrash* reads: It had been lowly, and now it *rose up;* it had belonged to a humble man and it now became the property of a great man.

According to *Sforno,* this phrase intimates that the *deed of purchase was validated* [וַיָּקָם] by its signatories.

Rambam in *Moreh Nevuchim* 1:12 discusses the various definitions of the verb קום.

בַּמַּכְפֵּלָה אֲשֶׁר לִפְנֵי מַמְרֵא הַשָּׂדֶה
וְהַמְּעָרָה אֲשֶׁר־בּוֹ וְכָל־הָעֵץ אֲשֶׁר
יח בַּשָּׂדֶה אֲשֶׁר בְּכָל־גְּבֻלוֹ סָבִיב: לְאַבְרָהָם
לְמִקְנָה לְעֵינֵי בְנֵי־חֵת בְּכֹל בָּאֵי
יט שַׁעַר־עִירוֹ: וְאַחֲרֵי־כֵן קָבַר אַבְרָהָם

Among the verses he cites to illustrate the different meanings, is our verse which he interprets to denote confirmation and verification: *The field of Ephron was verified* (as the property of Abraham). Cf. similar connotations in *I Sam.* 1:23; *ibid.* 24:20; *Lev.* 25:30.

[The Torah now proceeds to delineate the exact location of the purchase]:

אֲשֶׁר בַּמַּכְפֵּלָה — [*Which was*] *in Machpelah.*

[I.e., the territory which was known — after the cave — as Machpelah. See *comm.* to *v.* 19, further].

From the wording of this phrase, the *Midrash* homiletically renders: Which was *doubled* — i.e., for its value doubled in the eyes of everyone [now that it was in Abraham's ownership], for whoever was buried there was assured that his reward was doubled and even trebled. Rav Abbahu said: the name signifies that the Holy One, Blessed be He, bent Adam double and buried him in it [see *Ramban* cited to *v.* 9.]

אֲשֶׁר לִפְנֵי מַמְרֵא — *Facing Mamre* [lit. *which was before Mamre*].

One of the four names of Hebron, as the *Midrash* explains [see *comm.* to *v.* 2 s.v. הִוא חֶבְרוֹן.]

As noted in the *comm.* to 13:18, whenever the Torah mentions Mamre alone — as in this verse and 35:27 — it refers not to the name of its *owner* (Mamre, Abraham's comrade; 14:13) — but to the city (*Ramban* to 12:6).

Rashi to 35:27 explains that Mamre refers more specifically to the *plain* which lay before the city.

Chizkuni comments that Ephron's field ran parallel to and along the length of the city. In this episode it is referred to as *Mamre which is Hebron* [*v.* 19], in *v.* 2 it is called *Kiriath Arba which is Hebron*, in 35:27 it is identified as *Mamre — Kiriath Arba* whereas in 13:18 Abraham is described as dwelling *in the plains of Mamre which are in Hebron.* This teaches that Mamre built a town facing Hebron — Hebron itself being a Hittite city — and he named it Mamre after himself, the 'plains of Mamre' being before it, and Machpelah adjacent to it. After Mamre's death it fell under the sway of the giant [*Anak*] named Arba who renamed the entire territory *Kiriath* [i.e., *city of*] *Arba.* Later, when the Israelites prevailed over the Hittites, they renamed it Hebron.

הַשָּׂדֶה וְהַמְּעָרָה אֲשֶׁר־בּוֹ — *The field and the cave within it.*

— Both of which lay *before Mamre (Radak).*

וְכָל הָעֵץ אֲשֶׁר בַּשָּׂדֶה אֲשֶׁר בְּכָל־גְּבֻלוֹ סָבִיב — *And all the trees* [which were] *in the field* [which were] *within all its surrounding boundaries* [lit. *within all of its boundary around.*]

The *Midrash* derives from the fact that even the *trees* are men-

ing Mamre — the field and the cave within it and all the trees in the field, within all its surrounding boundaries — passed 18 *to Abraham as a purchase in the view of the children of Heth, among all who came to the gate of his town.* 19 *And afterwards Abraham*

tioned in this verse [especially since nothing in the Torah — not even a letter — is superfluous] that one who sells his field must enumerate the distinctive features of its boundaries. [Cf. *Mishnah Bava Basra* 68b-69a,b].

Furthermore, this fact indicates that the purchase was *absolute* — he even purchased every shrub in the field to assure that no stranger would retain a foothold in what was now Abraham's absolute possession *(Da'as Soferim).*

18. לְאַבְרָהָם לְמִקְנָה — *To Abraham as a purchase.*

מִקְנָה [from the root קנה, *to purchase*] referring to the *object* purchased *(Ibn Ezra),* while *Sforno* explains it as referring to the *legal document* recording a purchase.

לְעֵינֵי בְנֵי־חֵת — *In the presence* [lit. *eyes*] *of the children of Heth.*

I.e., the citizens of the city *(Ibn Ezra).*

In front of whom Abraham weighed out the silver *(Radak).*

The *Midrash* notes that [although the Torah scrupulously avoids unnecessary repetition], *the children of Heth* is repeated no fewer than ten times [eight times in the present chapter and again in 25:10; 49:32], corresponding to the number of the Ten Commandments. 'How much ink has been spilled and how many quills have been broken' to write this phrase over and over again. This teaches that he who is instrumental in executing a purchase by the righteous [such a purchase being put to lofty uses] is considered as though he has fulfilled the Ten Commandments.

בְּכֹל בָּאֵי שַׁעַר־עִירוֹ — *Among* [lit. *in*] *all who came to the gate of his town.*

This refers to the transient passersby and observers to the sale *(Ibn Ezra).*

For it was *in the midst of all of them* [this being the interpretation of the prepositional prefix *beth* of בְּכֹל, *'in all' (Divrei David)*], and with *all of them* standing by, that he gave him legal possession of it *(Rashi).*

Thus, since all were expected to be present, no one could come later and lay claim to the property either with בַּר מֶצְרָא challenges [see *Me'am Loez* cited, end of *v.* 8], or by producing earlier liens *(Or HaChaim).*

[On the expression *all who came to the gate of his town* see *v.* 10.]

19. וְאַחֲרֵי־כֵן קָבַר אַבְרָהָם — *And afterwards Abraham buried.*

— *Afterwards,* i.e., only *after* all aspects of the negotiations had been completed did Abraham proceed to bury his wife; before this he did not do so since, as the Talmud [*Bava Basra* 112a] notes, it is degrading for the righteous to be buried in alien soil *(Ha'amek Davar).*[1]

1. The burial of Sarah took place amid great magnificence of the kind usually reserved for royalty. Shem and his great-grandson Eber, Abimelech king of the Philistines, Aner, Eshkol,

אֶת־שָׂרָ֣ה אִשְׁתּ֗וֹ אֶל־מְעָרַ֞ת שְׂדֵ֧ה
הַמַּכְפֵּלָ֛ה עַל־פְּנֵ֥י מַמְרֵ֖א הִ֣וא חֶבְר֑וֹן
כ בְּאֶ֥רֶץ כְּנָֽעַן׃ וַיָּ֨קָם הַשָּׂדֶ֜ה וְהַמְּעָרָ֛ה

אֶת שָׂרָה אִשְׁתּוֹ — *Sarah his wife.*

His wife is mentioned here to emphasize that it was because Sarah was *Abraham's wife* that she came to be buried in this holy sepulchre. Therefore, in 49:31: *there they buried Abraham and Sarah,* Abraham is mentioned first although Sarah's burial preceded his, because Abraham was primarily meritorious; Sarah benefited because she was his wife *(Midrash Ariel).*

אֶל מְעָרַת שְׂדֵה הַמַּכְפֵּלָה — *In* [lit. *to*] *the cave of the field of Machpelah.*

[See *Ramban* to *v.* 9 according to whom this verse supports the view that it was the *area* that was called Machpelah by the residents; Abraham, who knew the true meaning of the name, had referred to the *cave* as Machpelah.]

According to *Malbim,* the verse indicates that after the interment of Sarah, the field remained unsown and became merely secondary to the cave of Machpelah, becoming known merely as the field surrounding the cave.

The term אֶל lit. *to* the Cave of Machpelah, is idiomatic and means *in* the Cave of Machpelah. Cf. for example, אֶל הַמְּעָרָה, *in the cave* (49:29), וְאֶל הָאָרוֹן, *in the ark* [*Exod.* 25:21] *(Radak).*

עַל פְּנֵי־מַמְרֵא הִוא חֶבְרוֹן — *Facing* [lit. *upon the face of*] *Mamre, which is Hebron.*

[See on *v.* 17].

Da'as Sofrim notes the varying nuances of the essentially similar phrases used here and in *v.* 17. Our verse describes the place as עַל פְּנֵי מַמְרֵא, lit. *'upon the face of Mamre,* meaning that the cave ran along the full length of the area called Mamre. Verse 17 uses the term לִפְנֵי מַמְרֵא, lit. *before Mamre,* indicating that Mamre was closer to Hebron than was the cave. He comments further that the extensive descriptions of the cave's location were necessary in order that it not be forgotten with the passage of time, and so that the future generations which would enter the Land could locate the site and properly safeguard the sanctity of the cave. [Especially in view of the fact that 250 years would elapse from Jacob's journey to Egypt until his descendants came back to *Eretz Yisrael* after the Exodus, it was essential to give the extensive listing of the boundaries.]

The word Machpelah derives from כפל, *double,* signifying that the cave bore a special relationship to pairs. The name Hebron has a similar connotation — חבר, *unite,*

and Mamre, as well as the great of the land followed her bier. A seven-day mourning period was observed for her, and all the inhabitants of the land came to comfort [לְנַחֵם] the bereaved Abraham and Isaac *(Sefer HaYashar).*

[Incidentally, it is chronologically noted that Abraham suffered the loss of several of his close relatives during this relatively short period. His father Terach had died two years previously; Lot died two years later at the age of one hundred and forty, and Abraham's brother, Nachor, died shortly afterward at the age of one hundred and seventy-two *(ibid.).*]

buried Sarah his wife in the cave of the field of Machpelah facing Mamre, which is Hebron, in the land of Canaan.

20 *Thus, the field with its cave passed to Abraham*

attach. Thus, the first Jewish possession in Eretz Yisrael was a place that stood for the attachment of husband and wife, and the loyalty of succeeding generations to one another in closeness and intimacy. Centuries later, the Temple service was not begun until the priestly lookout saw the sun's rays shining on the graves of the Patriarchs — the symbol that honor of parents is a prerequisite to honor of God *(Hirsch).*

Esoterically, the name *Hebron* from חבר, *unite,* indicates that it was there that the souls of the interred reunite to their roots beneath the Throne of Glory *(R' Bachya).*

It is there, the place of חִבּוּר, *joining,* that heaven meets earth in an ultimate acknowledgement of the single origin of both. The patriarchs and their wives, the יְשֵׁנֵי חֶבְרוֹן, *those who sleep in Hebron,* in the burial ground of Machpelah, achieved in their lifetimes this perfect dedication of their earthly activities to the will of God; therefore they were buried in Machpelah, at the entrance to the Garden of Eden *(Zohar);* to signify their achievement in uniting the two worlds (Miller; *Sabbath Shiurim).*

בְּאֶרֶץ כְּנָעַן — *In the land of Canaan.* — This is repeated [although already stated in *v.* 2] to emphasize that burial anywhere in *Eretz Yisrael* is meritorious, although not on as great a scale as the cave itself *(Ha'amek Davar).*

This is further mentioned to re-emphasize that the righteous Sarah died and was interred in the Land of Canaan, for the Hittites were of the families of Canaan *(Ramban).*[1]

20. וַיָּקָם הַשָּׂדֶה ... לְאַבְרָהָם לַאֲחֻזַּת־קָבֶר — *Thus* [lit. *and*], *the field passed to Abraham as an estate for a burial site* [lit. *as a (permanent) possession of a grave*].

Verses 16-18 inform us that the

1. *Ibn Ezra* comments that the reason this incident — with its lengthy portrayal of the dealing and bargaining over a burial plot — was recorded in the Torah was "to make known Eretz Yisrael's superiority over all other lands, both for the living and the dead, and also to fulfill God's promise that the land would be Abraham's inheritance."

According to *Ramban* [who is also apparently bothered by the fact that the Torah preoccupied itself at such length with this narrative], the episode is recorded to emphasize God's kindness to Abraham inasmuch as Abraham — who had come to the land as a stranger, was regarded as נְשִׂיא אֱלֹהִים, *a prince of God (v.* 6), in addition to being reverently addressed as אֲדֹנִי, *my lord,* though he never made pretentious claims. Thus, God's promise to make his name great (12:2) was fulfilled in his own lifetime. The Torah also wished to tell us that his wife was buried in the "inheritance of the Land" [*Eretz Yisrael*]. Thus it informs us of the sepulchre of our patriarchs since we are obligated to honor the graves of our sainted forefathers.

Additionally [as noted in the *footnote* to *v.* 4], the Sages regard this episode as one of Abraham's trials inasmuch as he had to negotiate for a plot of land in which to bury his wife. [Although the entire land had been *promised* him, he did not question God's ways, and responded humbly.]

אֲשֶׁר־בּ֖וֹ לְאַבְרָהָ֑ם לַאֲחֻזַּת־קָ֑בֶר מֵאֵ֖ת
א בְּנֵי־חֵֽת׃ וְאַבְרָהָ֣ם
זָקֵ֔ן בָּ֖א בַּיָּמִ֑ים וַֽיהוָ֛ה בֵּרַ֥ךְ אֶת־אַבְרָהָ֖ם

property became Abraham's upon payment of the purchase money. But it did not become an אֲחֻזַּת קָבֶר, *a permanent possession as a sepulchre*, until Abraham completed the act of burying his wife there *(Rashbam; Chizkuni)*. For, as the *Midrash* notes, the קִנְיָן, *legal acquisition*, of the property was *finalized* through Abraham's formal act of חֲזָקָה, *possession*, in this case the digging of the grave *(Mizrachi)*.

[According to others, this verse, as is customary in Scriptures, summarizes in one sentence the essence of the preceding episode: the intent of the verse being: *'and thus it happened that Ephron's field ... passed to Abraham.'* Cf. for example 11:9; 17:26; 19:36.]

מֵאֵת בְּנֵי־חֵת — *From the children of Heth.*

— All of whom agreed in writing that it should be his undisputed burial site forever *(R' Bachya, Sforno)*. And that no one should later contest Ephron's right to sell Hittite property as a grave site *(Chizkuni)*.

XXIV

1. Seeking a wife for Isaac.

וְאַבְרָהָם זָקֵן — *Now* [lit. *and*] *Abraham was old.*

Abraham's old age was already noted above in 18:11. It is repeated here since God had earlier restored Abraham's youth [i.e., by restoring his procreative abilities prior to Isaac's conception]. Now that Abraham again became old, the Torah restates the fact. According to Rav Ammi, 18:11 refers to the first case of old age without the loss of לַחְלוּחִית, *vitality* [i.e., virility], while our verse refers to old age without vitality *(Bereishis Rabbah 48:16)*.

Ramban notes that Rav Ammi's interpretation (see above) of the distinction between 18:11 and our verse is implied by the very wording of both texts. The expression in 18:11 is in *present* tense: בָּאִים בַּיָּמִים, lit. entering *into the days*, indicating the *onset* of old age. Here the expression is in *past* tense: בָּא בַּיָּמִים, lit., 'had entered *into the days*,' indicating a *fait accompli*: he was *already* old [and his vitality was no more].[1]

In the *literal* sense, the Torah

1. The *Talmud* observes: Until Abraham, there was no [visible indication of *(Maharsha)*] old age. Whoever saw Abraham thought him to be Isaac, and *vice* versa. Abraham then prayed for [visible] old age, and his prayer was answered, as it is written: *Now Abraham was old* [i.e., *visibly* old; for though old age is mentioned prior to this, as for example regarding Abraham and Sarah in 18:11; the *elders* of Sodom (19:4); Lot (19:31), in those cases only *chronological age* is meant. Our verse, however, traditionally alludes to the *appearance* of old age — grey hair — which originated with Abraham]. *(Sanhedrin* 103b; *Bava Metzia* 87a; [bracketed additions are from *Maharsha*]. [*Pirkei d'Rabbi Eliezer* interprets our verse as referring to gray hair — 'a hoary head']).

24 *as an estate for a burial site, from the children of*
1 *Heth.*

Now Abraham was old, well on in years, and HASHEM had blessed Abraham with everything.

restates Abraham's old age to explain why he did not undertake the mission himself *(Ramban).*

Midrash Tanchuma suggests that Abraham's age is *now* mentioned to emphasize that it was *immediately after Sarah's death* that the strains of old age set upon Abraham and became obvious to all.

בָּא בַּיָּמִים — *Well on* [or: *advanced*] *in years* [lit. *he had entered into the days*].

I.e., one who has 'entered into those days' when he knows he must go the way of all flesh *(Radak)*; [see *comm.* to same phrase in 18:11].

— The days of which it is written *(Eccles.* 12:1): *Remember your Creator in the days of your youth before the evil days come (Midrash).*

Abraham therefore decided that the time had come to see his son married in his lifetime *(Rashbam).*

Due to his age, Abraham could no longer undertake the strains of a journey; he therefore sent his servant *(Chizkuni).*

His life's work was finished; he had nothing more to strive for and his concern was for his son and the household who would survive him *(Hirsch).*

The *Midrash* observes: One may have the dignity of old age without its years, or longevity without dignity. In this case, however, it was זָקֵן בָּא בַּיָּמִים — the dignity of *old age* was matched by *length of days,* and *longevity* was matched by the *dignity of age.*[1]

וַה׳ בֵּרַךְ אֶת אַבְרָהָם — *And HASHEM had blessed Abraham.*

— [Not that HASHEM *now* blessed Abraham in his old age. Had the blessing been a new one, the phrase would have read: וַיְבָרֶךְ ה׳ אֶת אַבְרָהָם, in the *vav*-conversive. As noted in the *comm.* several times previously (e.g. 4:1 וְהָאָדָם יָדַע; 21:1 וַה׳ פָּקַד) whenever the subject precedes the verb without the *vav*-conversive as in our passage, וַה׳ בֵּרַךְ, it denotes past-perfect: 'HASHEM *had* blessed.']

Midrash Tanchuma notes, however, the blessing is mentioned only after Sarah's death, because God did not want people to say that Abraham was blessed only on account of Sarah. Therefore God said: 'I will *declare* his blessing *after* her death.'

Kabbalistically, the phraseology וַה׳, *and HASHEM* is interpreted [as it is in 21:1; see *footnote* p. 743] as an exegetical amplification meaning: *HASHEM together with His Celestial Court,* i.e., the Attribute with which

1. The *Mussar* masters perceive in this expression that Abraham's life was full and meaningful in every aspect. Every day of life represented a new challenge and a new mission. Thus, while a great person looks back upon a life full of fruitful days, a wicked one has a full catalog of wasted and abused days. In this sense, our verse describes Abraham's accumulated years as בָּא בַּיָּמִים, *he came with the days* — i.e., he brought along into his old age *all* of his days. Not one moment of his life was wasted or spent in anything but service to his Creator.

Abraham was blessed in all spheres, was that of *Kol (Ramban; R' Bachya;* see *comm.* further s.v. בַּכֹּל).

בַּכֹּל — *With everything*[1]

He lacked nothing, and the only concern he had in this world was to provide his son with a suitable spouse *(Radak).*

Rashi notes that the numerical value (גִימַטְרִיָּא) of בַּכֹּל, *with everything* (=52) equals that of בֵּן, *a son*: having been blessed with a son, Abraham now proceeded with the task of finding a wife for him.

Sifsei Chachomim explains that *Rashi*'s reasoning is based on the context which uses this statement to introduce Eliezer's mission to Aram Naharaim. Rather than explicitly stating that Abraham had been blessed with a son, the verse alludes to the birth of Isaac with the word *everything,* suggesting the concept expressed by *Akeidas Yitzchak* below.

Akeidas Yitzchak also explains that the blessing referred to his having begotten a son. This was the true blessing, for before then he had regarded all blessings as valueless, and he had exclaimed [15:2] *My Lord, HASHEM/ELOHIM: What can You give me seeing that I go childless?*

Ramban explains the verse essentially like *Radak* [see above] and elaborates that Abraham was blessed בַּכֹּל, with all the essential treasures to which man aspires: riches, possessions, honor, longevity, and children. The one thing he lacked was to see his son have children to inherit his status and honor; this was Abraham's strongest desire now.

Rashbam explains the mention of Abraham's abundant blessing as a necessary preface to the following narrative. He sent his servant to Aram Naharaim *not* because the people in Canaan did not wish to give their daughters in marriage to Isaac. On the contrary! He was a wealthy man — having been blessed with everything — and a match with his son was much sought after by the community. But he insisted that his son take a bride only from his family. His servant, too, made this clear when he said [*v.* 35]: *HASHEM has greatly blessed my master, and he has prospered.* Thus, it was necessary for the Torah to first state this preamble, just as in 9:18 the Torah parenthetically notes *Ham being the father of Canaan* [to inform us of Canaan's evil roots].

The *Talmud* [*Bava Basra* 16b] records several interpretations of *HASHEM had blessed Abraham* בַּכֹּל, *with everything*: What is meant by *with everything*? R'

1. The *Talmud (Bava Basra* 16b-17a) teaches that the Patriarchs, Abraham, Isaac, and Jacob, were given an inkling of the World to Come, and that the Evil Inclination had no dominion over them. This is derived from the fact that expressions with the word כֹּל, *everything* — which implies perfection, a totally unflawed blessing — are used in the Torah referring to each of the Patriarchs.

Regarding Abraham, our verse [בַּכֹּל] is cited; regarding Isaac, it is written [27:33]: וָאֹכַל מִכֹּל, *and I* [Isaac] *have partaken from everything*; regarding Jacob [33:11]: כִּי חַנַּנִי אֱלֹהִים וְכִי יֶשׁ לִי כֹל, *for God has been gracious to me* [*Jacob*] *and I have everything.*

[This is the intent of the blessing in Grace After Meals: 'The compassionate One! May He bless ... ours and all that is ours — just as our forefathers Abraham, Isaac, and Jacob were blessed בַּכֹּל, *in everything,* מִכֹּל, *from everything,* כֹּל, *everything. Cf. comm.* to ArtScroll *Bircas HaMazon.*]

²And Abraham said to the senior servant of his

Meir said: [he was blessed] in the fact that he had no daughter; R' Yehudah said: in the fact that he *had* a daughter; others say that Abraham indeed had a daughter whose name was *Ba-Kol.*[1] [See *comm.* of *Minchah Belulah* cited in 23:2 s.v. וְלִבְכֹּתָהּ, that she died on the same day as Sarah.]

[The commentators dwell heavily on explaining the various views in the above controversy of Tannaim.] In the most simple sense, however, *Maharsha* ad. loc. explains that the controversy surrounds the differing views of whether a daughter is a blessing or not. R' Meir maintains that Abraham's primary blessing lay in the birth of his son since man, Adam, was created first while the female was secondary, having been created from his side. R' Yehudah holds that the blessing lay in the fact that Abraham *did* have a daughter, since the male cannot propagate alone; it is only in partnership with his female counterpart that he is truly called Man. For as the Sages [in *Yevamos* 63a] comment on 5:3: 'a man without a wife is not a man, for it is said: *Male and female He created them ... and called their name Man.*' The 'others' who hold that her name was *Ba-Kol* [i.e., that *HASHEM had blessed Abraham with* (a daughter named) *Ba-Kol*] would maintain that her very name [which means 'with everything'] reflects her role, since the *Talmud* itself introduces this controversy with the statement that with the birth of a daughter 'increase has come to the world.' Thus, daughters represent an all-encompassing blessing since it is they who give birth; a multitude of males with only one female can produce but a single child.

Ramban discusses this Talmudic interpretation which he describes as 'a wonderful insight of the Sages'. He explains that R' Meir felt that Abraham's blessing of being complete — with *everything* — would indicate that Abraham had no daughter because a daughter would have been a constant source of anxiety since he could not have married her to anyone but accursed Canaanites; and even among his own family [in Aram Naharaim] the men were still idolators [see *Joshua* 24:2: *Your fathers dwelt of old beyond the River — even Terach the father of Abraham and the father of Nachor, and they served other gods*] and a woman would be subject to the authority of her husband. Abraham furthermore did not want his worthy children from Sarah to leave the land [which may be a reason why he sent Eliezer to fetch a wife for Isaac].

Had Abraham had a daughter, however, the prevailing etiquette would have demanded that she dwell in her new husband's home. [As *Hirsch* points out, a son of Abraham who brought a bride to his ancestral home, would have won her over to Abraham's righteous ways whatever her background, but Abraham's daughter uprooted to an idolatrous environment could have become like her new family. Surely, her children could have been idol-worshippers. What could have caused Abraham greater heartbreak than to have a daughter who would suffer such a fate?]

Ramban continues that in R' Yehudah's opinion, however, implicit in being blessed *with everything* is that God did not withhold even a daughter from Abraham. The 'others', however, in stating that this one daughter was named *Ba-Kol,* have interpreted this verse as alluding to a profound mystery of the Torah. The word *bakol,* esoterically refers to one of God's Attributes called *Kol,* so named because it is the Foundation of Everything. Another Attribute emanating from this is esoterically called בַּת [*Bas;* literally, 'daughter'] by which He controls everything ... This is the sublime meaning of the metaphoric use of 'daughter' ... which alludes to כֹּל, *Kol* ... [*Ramban* proceeds to cite several verses in support of his mystical interpretation, which we omit because of its profoundly Mystical nature.]

Ramban therefore sums up that Hashem blessed Abraham with the Attribute called *Bas,* which is also called *Kol* because it is an element of the Attribute *Kol.* Thus Abraham was given all blessings of heaven and earth, for they are included within this all-embracing Attribute.

2. עַבְדּוֹ זְקַן בֵּיתוֹ — ***The senior servant of his household*** [lit. ***his servant, the elder of his house***].

1. The *Talmud, ibid.* cites several additional interpretations of how Abraham was blessed *with everything:*

R' Eliezer the Modiite said: Abraham possessed a power of reading the stars for which he

המשֵׁל בְּכָל־אֲשֶׁר־לוֹ שִׂים־נָא יָדְךָ תַּחַת
ג יְרֵכִי: וְאַשְׁבִּיעֲךָ בַּיהוה אֱלֹהֵי הַשָּׁמַיִם

This is obviously Eliezer, who was mentioned previously in 15:2. Sixty years have passed since then, and he is not only the senior servant titularly, but actually *the elder of his household (Hoffman).*

Radak explains that the term זְקַן בֵּיתוֹ may either mean that he grew old in his service, or that he was the oldest one in the household. In either case, it emphasizes his loyalty and worthiness for the mission on which he was about to be sent.

The commentators emphasize that Eliezer's loyalty was such that his name is never mentioned throughout this entire narrative, and appears only once in 15:2. This is eloquent testimony to the extent that Eliezer's entire self was devoted to his master; the righteous servant sublimated his own identity in order to be known as *Abraham's servant.* In fact, the *Midrash* notes, Eliezer's features even came to resemble Abraham's, and as the *Talmud* [*Yoma* 28b] comments, Eliezer was entitled זְקַן בֵּיתוֹ, indicating that he sat on Abraham's council and had acquired his master's learning [see *comm.* to 15:2]. Yet, as a descendant of the accursed Canaan, he could not intermarry with Abraham *(Shem MiShmuel).*

On Eliezer, see *comm.* to 15:2. According to *Pirkei d'Rabbi Eliezer,* when Abraham left Ur Kasdim, he was presented with many gifts. Nimrod assigned Eliezer [who is identified as Nimrod's son by some *Midrashic* views] to Abraham. After Eliezer successfuly executed this mission on Isaac's behalf, Abraham gave him his freedom [see *Torah Sheleimah* 24:2, note 34 and *Overview.*]

In a grammatical note, *Rashi* observes that since the word זְקַן is in the construct state it is punctuated זְקַן. *Radak* adds that this is similar to כְּבַד פֶּה = כְּבֵד פֶּה.

הַמֹּשֵׁל בְּכָל־אֲשֶׁר־לוֹ — *Who controlled* [lit. *the ruler of*] *all that was his.*

I.e., he was the executor of Abraham's will; one whom even Isaac would have to obey in the event of his father's death *(Ramban).*

According to the *Midrash* this passage indicates that *he controlled all that was his* [own]— i.e., Eliezer was in complete control of *his own emotions and passions,* and as such could be completely relied upon to do justice to the delicate and sensitive task at hand.

שִׂים־נָא יָדְךָ תַּחַת יְרֵכִי — *Place now your hand under my thigh.*

[Traditionally, *thigh* is explained

was much sought after by the potentates of the East and West.

R' Shimon bar Yochai said: Abraham had a precious stone suspended from his neck which brought immediate healing to any sick [or: wounded *(Tosafos* s.v. שֶׁכָּל)] person who gazed upon it. When Abraham our father departed from the world, God suspended it from the orb of the sun [i.e., allowed the sick to heal 'naturally' *(Maharsha)*]. Abaye said: This bears out the popular saying: As the day advances the illness lightens.

Another explanation of how Abraham was blessed *in everything*: In that [his grandson] Esau did not rebel so long as he was alive [see *comm.* to 25:29]. Another explanation is that Ishmael repented while Abraham was still alive [see *Rashi* to 15:5 and 25:9.].

Kabbalistically, the phrase implies that the *Shechinah* dwelt with him *(Zohar Chadash).*

24
3
household who controlled all that was his: 'Place now
you hand under my thigh. 3 *And I will have you*
swear by HASHEM, God of heaven and God of earth,

as a euphemism for the *membrum virile,* for even offspring are euphemistically described as יוֹצְאֵי יֶרֶךְ, lit., *coming out of their father's 'thigh'* (46:26; *Exod.* 1:5).]

Thus, *Rashi* explains that one who takes an oath must place his hand on some sacred object such as a Torah scroll or *tefillin* [see *Shevuos* 38b]. Because circumcision was the first precept given to Abraham and came to him only through much pain, it was therefore particularly precious to him, and Abraham selected the organ as the object upon which to take this oath. [*Targum Yonasan* renders similarly; cf. *Tanchuma.*]

And since, as *Rashi* notes, this mitzvah had come to Abraham through so much travail it was *particularly* precious to him. He therefore did not tell Eliezer: 'place your hand under *your* thigh' although Eliezer, too, had been circumcised *(Devek Tov).*

Furthermore, the sign of circumcision had been esteemed so greatly by the Patriarchs, and used as a sacred object of an oath — like *tefillin* today — because it was the covenant of circumcision that set apart the Patriarchal families from the surrounding heathens *(Tzeidah laDerech).*

Rashbam notes that this same form of oath was used by Jacob in adjuring Joseph [47:29], because such an oath is used when a superior adjures an inferior, such as a master his servant, or a father his son. When *equals* are parties to a covenant, however, then כַּף אֶל כַּף, *clasping of hand to hand,* is used [see *Ezek.* 17:18]. Sometimes the treaty is made binding by dividing an animal and passing between its parts [see *comm.* to 15:10].

According to *Abarbanel,* this does not *necessarily* suggest that Abraham would actually allow his servant to grasp his *organ,* as such an act would be an indignity. Rather the form of oath was such that the servant symbolically placed his hand under his *thigh* as if to signify: Remember the covenant of circumcision by which we have both bound ourselves.

Ibn Ezra explains that it was the custom in those days for a servant to place his hand under his master's thigh as a symbol of fidelity and homage, the latter sitting on his servant's hand to signify his mastery. Such is still the practice in India.

According to this interpretation, the act of 'placing the hand beneath the thigh' was an act of fidelity only; the fact that he was also to swear was a separate, unrelated act *(R' Bachya).*

3. וְאַשְׁבִּיעֲךָ — *And I will have you swear* [or: *and I will adjure you.*]

Realizing the infirmities of his old age, Abraham feared that he might die before Eliezer's return. Accordingly, by having the servant undertake a *sacred oath* Abraham assured himself of unwavering loyalty to his plan because he knew that Isaac would follow the counsel of Eliezer, who *controlled all that was his* [*v.* 2] *(Ramban* to *v.* 1).

According to *Sforno,* Abraham deemed it necessary not simply to *command* Eliezer but to have him undertake *a solemn oath* because

וְאלֹהֵי הָאָרֶץ אֲשֶׁר לֹא־תִקַּח אִשָּׁה לִבְנִי מִבְּנוֹת הַכְּנַעֲנִי אֲשֶׁר אָנֹכִי יוֹשֵׁב בְּקִרְבּוֹ׃

Abraham was apprehensive that — in the event of his death — Eliezer might be bribed to arrange an improper match for Isaac. Once bound by an oath, however, Eliezer would not do something disloyal.

Or HaChaim suggests that Abraham framed the oath in general terms against marriage with a Canaanite, but his intention was to direct it at Eliezer himself. Abraham wished to allay his apprehension that Eliezer, who had reached such a pinnacle of power, might — after Abraham's death — entertain a notion of marrying *his own daughter* to Isaac. Abraham, therefore, adjured him generally so the servant would take no offense at the clear implication that he — as an accursed Canaanite [9:25] — could harbor no thoughts of intermarrying with the blessed Isaac. [See *comm.* to *v.* 39.][1]

The obvious question arises: Why did Abraham direct this oath *to his servant*? He should have commanded *Isaac* directly.

Since Abraham could not undertake the journey himself, and under no circumstances would he allow his son to leave the land [*v.* 6], he decided to dispatch his servant during his lifetime to his country and family to seek a wife for Isaac. He therefore directed the command to the one who was about to be charged with the mission. Once he adjured his servant regarding this, it was pointless to reiterate the command to Isaac as well, for he would surely not flout his father's wish, nor break his servant's oath. It is also possible that Eliezer was the executor of Abraham's will — as implied by the expression *v.* 2, *who controlled all that was his* — and Abraham accordingly imposed his will upon him, with the sanctity of an oath, making it a *condition of Isaac's inheritance* that he marry only in accordance with his father's wishes *(Ramban).*[2]

בַּה׳ אֱלֹהֵי הַשָּׁמַיִם וֵאלֹהֵי הָאָרֶץ — *By HASHEM, God of* [*the*] *heaven and God of* [*the*] *earth.*

God is also designated in this context as *God of the earth* to emphasize that He closely oversees that which happens on earth, for

1. Since Abraham knew that Eliezer's loyalty was complete, why did he find it necessary to administer an oath? *Shem MiShmuel* comments that every person has within him strength and fortitude of which he himself is not aware. In time of crisis, he can draw upon them — if he is determined enough to do so — to conquer seemingly insurmountable obstacles. Abraham knew that Eliezer's mission could be beset by unpredictable pitfalls and difficulties, so much so that Eliezer could decide in all sincerity that he had no chance of success. By swearing, however, Eliezer dedicated himself to such an extent that he would persevere in the face of the 'impossible.' Precisely because he took the oath, the obstacles failed to materialize — because they could not have deterred him in any case.

2. From the fact that Abraham did not adjure Isaac directly concerning his choice of a mate, *Meshech Chochmah* derives support for the *halachah* cited by *RaMA* in *Yoreh Deah* 240:25 that a son is not required to obey a parental order forbidding him to marry the woman of his choice. Isaac's instruction to Jacob [28:1] not to take a Canaanite wife should not be understood as a direct command. Rather, as indicated by 28:4, Isaac was informing Jacob that, as a condition of his retaining the Abrahamitic blessings and the right to inherit the Land, he could not allow his posterity to be descended from Canaanite women.

that you not take a wife for my son from the daughters of the Canaanites, among whom I dwell.

marriages on earth are preordained in heaven *(Ibn Ezra).*

— He is the God Who is as directly the God of the earth as He is the God of heaven *(Hirsch).*

Accordingly, do not think that if you violate my oath you will go unpunished: He will certainly exact punishment from you as *God of the earth!* When Abraham was referring to himself in *v.* 7, however, he had no need to reiterate that HASHEM was God over the earth as well; to Abraham it was obvious *(Radak).*

According to *Ramban,* אֱלֹהֵי הָאָרֶץ does not refer generally to Him as *God of the earth,* but God of the *Land — par excellence*: the Land of Israel. Therefore in *v.* 7, where God is referred to as having 'taken me from my father's house' He is not referred to [by His unique Attribute of] *God of the Land,* because that event took place in Charan or Ur Kasdim, outside of *Eretz Yisrael.* This is what the Sages meant when they said [*Kesubos* 110b]: He who lives outside *Eretz Yisrael* is as if he had no God [because such a person lacks the manifestation of His Attribute as *God of the Land*].

[Thus, *Ramban* seems to emphasize that the *God of the Land* will assure that Isaac would not have to forsake the Land in order to obtain a bride. For although one is permitted to leave *Eretz Yisrael* in order to marry, Isaac was different: he was an עוֹלָה תְּמִימָה, *perfect offering,* completely devoted to God. (See *comm.* to *v.* 6 s.v. הִשָּׁמֶר לְךָ, and see *Overview).*]

Sforno perceives that *God of heaven* refers to the World to Come, and *God of earth* refers to This World. The implication, then, is: 'If you prove false to the oath He will exact punishment from you both in This World, and the World to Come.'

מִבְּנוֹת הַכְּנַעֲנִי — *From the daughters of the Canaanites.*

A generic name for the eleven descendants of Canaan who populated the land *(Ibn Ezra* [see *Ibn Ezra* to 15:19. *Yohel Or* enumerates: Zidonite; Hittite; Jebusite; Emorite; Girgashite; Hivvite; Arkite; Sinite; Erodite; Zimrite; Hamite].)

[It was not a question of racial 'purity'.] — The seed of Canaan was specifically *cursed* [9:25] while Abraham's seed was *blessed* [22:18]. The two, could therefore not mingle *(Rashi* and *Radak)*[1]

1. *Hirsch* comments that Abraham's rejection of the daughters of Canaan was not based on their worship of idols, for, if so, the idolatrous Arameans would have been just as unacceptable. Rather it was the *moral degeneracy of Canaan* which motivated him. Idolatry is an intellectual perversion which can be remedied, but a lack of morality, ethics, and modesty affects a person's entire nature. Thus, a woman from his family could be found whose character was worthy of Abraham's household, but not from morally corrupt Canaan (based on *Drashos HaRan).*

Cf. also in this context *Rashi* to *Lev.* 18:3 who states that the deeds of the Egyptians and Canaanites were more corrupt than those of any other nation, and that those peoples which the Israelites conquered were even more corrupt than other Canaanites.

ד כִּי אֶל־אַרְצִי וְאֶל־מוֹלַדְתִּי תֵּלֵךְ וְלָקַחְתָּ

[See *comm.* to *v.* 39.]

As *Midrash HaGadol* comments: Why did Abraham object to them? — Because they were all under the ban, as it says [*Deut.* 20:17] *You shall utterly destroy them.*

Abraham also wanted to avoid any implication that his offspring later acquired the land by virtue of having intermarried with the original inhabitants; he wanted it unmistakably clear that he had acquired it solely through God's promise *(Chizkuni; Ralbag).*

אֲשֶׁר אָנֹכִי יוֹשֵׁב בְּקִרְבּוֹ — *Among whom* [lit. *in whose midst; proximity*] *I dwell.*

— And with whose base ways I am accordingly fully familiar *(Da'as Soferim).*

According to the *Midrash,* implicit in בְּקִרְבּוֹ, *among whom,* [rather than the broader phrase: בְּאַרְצוֹ, *in whose land*] was that Eliezer should not consider even the daughters of Abraham's *closest* allies — in whose *closest proximity he dwelt*: Aner, Eshkol and Mamre, although they were righteous [see *Rashi* to 22:20, and to *v.* 8, cf. below.]

Abraham thus cautioned Eliezer not to reason that Abraham would not have dwelt *among them* unless they were righteous, and accordingly, those in whose closest proximity he dwelt *would* be suitable for marriage with Isaac. Abraham cautioned Eliezer not to take a wife even from among the most righteous Canaanites *(Tzror HaMor).*

Hirsch explains that the influence of a Canaanite wife on his son would be all the greater since 'I dwell *among* them. Not only the girl, but her family, relatives, and friends will cumulatively influence my son.'

4. כִּי אֶל־אַרְצִי — *Rather, to my land.*

[I.e., to the land whence I originated — the area beyond the River Euphrates *(Mizrachi* to *v.* 7). This should not be interpreted as the specific land of Abraham's birth because, according to *Rashi,* Abraham was born in Ur Kasdim, not Charan. — See further.]

וְאֶל מוֹלַדְתִּי — *And to my kindred.*

I.e., to my family, in Charan *(Ramban* [and *Rashi* according to *Sifsei Chachamim*]*).*

— To my relatives who are in my land *(Rashbam).*

Abraham thereby indicated that Eliezer would find his family there. In reality, he was alluding to Rebecca of whose birth he had been informed earlier *(Radak).*[1]

This was the second part of the command; the first part being that he not take a Canaanite wife for his son ... *(Malbim*; see *Ramban* to *v.* 8).

Abraham's kindred, too, were idolators [see *comm.* above, and *Josh.* 24:2]

1. As *Rashi* comments in 22:20 citing the *Midrash,* after the *Akeidah* Abraham was concerned that Isaac was still unmarried and he considered marrying him to one of the daughters of Aner, Eshkol and Mamre 'for they are virtuous women and of what concern to me is their (accursed Canaanite) birth?' God therefore caused Abraham to be informed that Isaac's mate had already been born in his family. For until that time, there had been no births in Abraham's family, and the righteous daughters of his comrades would have been the logical choice for

4 *Rather, to my land and to my kindred shall you go*

and he had departed from them. Nevertheless, he said that since he engaged in proselytizing in any case, he should do so among his own relatives, especially since they were more prone to penitence. In so doing, he acted in accordance with the Sages who stress that one should always strive to act first for the benefit and welfare of his own kindred, as in the verse [*Isaiah* 58:7]: *From your own flesh do not hide (Midrash HaGadol).*

The definition of כִּי as *rather* [in the sense of *but*] is one of the four definitions of כִּי offered by the Sages in *Rosh Hashanah* 3a. The other definitions are: if; perhaps; because.

[The translation of מוֹלֶדֶת as *kindred* (i.e., relatives) follows the implication of *Rashi* cited by *Ramban* in *v.* 7, and more specifically in 12:1. There *Ramban* notes that although the term can signify both *birthplace* and *relatives* (cf. use of the expression in *Esther* 8:6: *How can I bear to witness the destruction of* מוֹלַדְתִּי*, my relatives!)* the context implies clearly that it means *my relatives*. For if Abraham meant *my birthplace*, Eliezer should have gone to Ur Kasdim, according to the view that that was Abraham's birthplace, and not to Charan in Aram Naharaim, city of Nachor [*v.* 10].

[It is noteworthy that in Eliezer's account (*v.* 38), he reports that Abraham adjured him: אֶל בֵּית אָבִי וְאֶל מִשְׁפַּחְתִּי תֵּלֵךְ, *Go to my father's house and to my family*, specifically mentioning *family* rather than *birthplace*. Cf. also 43:7 where *Rashi* himself renders מוֹלַדְתֵּנוּ as *families*, and similarly 48:6 where he explains מוֹלַדְתְּךָ as *your offspring*.

[*Rashi* is silent on our verse. This divergency of interpretation derives from the varying views of where Abraham was born. As noted in the *comm.* to 11:28 (p. 349) *Ramban*, quoting *Rambam*, is of the opinion that Abraham was born in Cuthah, a city adjacent to *Eretz Yisrael*. It was 'across' the river, near Charan and Assyria. According to *Rashi*, however, (implied in 12:1 but more specifically stated in 24:7) Abraham was born in Ur Kasdim (not Aram Naharaim). See *Maharal* in *Gevuros Hashem* ch. 5 who emphasizes that *Ramban*'s view is not in harmony with the view of the Talmudic Sages who hold that Ur Kasdim was Abraham's birthplace, as specifically stated in *Pesachim* 87b (cf. also *Bava Basra* 91a and *comm.* to 12:1).]

Ramban in *v.* 7 goes on to suggest, however, that מוֹלַדְתִּי in *our* verse can indeed signify *my birthplace*, the reference being, according to him, to Charan in Mesopotamia where [according to *Ramban* in 11:28 and 12:1] Abraham was born and from where his family had originated. Or it means *family;* consequently the intent of Abraham's command was as Eliezer paraphrased in *v.*38: that he select Isaac's wife from the family.

The commentators conjecture that *Rashi* is silent on our verse because there are sufficient parallel uses of the term מוֹלֶדֶת as *relatives* to justify that rendering here as well. In *verse* 7, however, the term אֶרֶץ מוֹלַדְתִּי*, land of my* מוֹלֶדֶת stands in contrast to בֵּית אָבִי*, my father's house*, leaving *Rashi* no alternative but to interpret it there as *birthplace* which, following the Sages, was Ur Kasdim. However, even if *Rashi* were to interpret the term here as *birthplace*, Ur Kasdim, [As does *Ibn Ezra* in our verse!] then the fact that Eliezer traveled to Charan presents no difficulty since Abraham may have used *birthplace* in general terms, referring not to his native *city*, but to the region of his native land beyond the River. If so, Charan was Eliezer's obvious destination since Abraham's relatives now dwelt there.

תֵּלֵךְ — *Shall you go.*

I.e., do not send another in your stead; but *go yourself* and choose whoever seems suitable to you *(Ha'amek Davar).*

him. Now that the revelation of the birth was given him, he dispatched his trusted servant to his family.

It is noteworthy that Abraham did not clearly command Eliezer to bring back Rebecca. Perhaps he relied on Divine Providence to guide Eliezer to the preordained spouse. Or he may have felt that if Eliezer were told that there was only a single acceptable girl, he might have felt that the mission was too difficult — what if she preferred not to go?

ה אִשָּׁה לִבְנִי לְיִצְחָק: וַיֹּאמֶר אֵלָיו הָעֶבֶד
אוּלַי לֹא־תֹאבֶה הָאִשָּׁה לָלֶכֶת אַחֲרַי
אֶל־הָאָרֶץ הַזֹּאת הֶהָשֵׁב אָשִׁיב אֶת־בִּנְךָ
ו אֶל־הָאָרֶץ אֲשֶׁר־יָצָאתָ מִשָּׁם: וַיֹּאמֶר
אֵלָיו אַבְרָהָם הִשָּׁמֶר לְךָ פֶּן־תָּשִׁיב אֶת־

וְלָקַחְתָּ אִשָּׁה לִבְנִי לְיִצְחָק — *And take a wife for my son — for Isaac.*

[The redundant expression לִבְנִי לְיִצְחָק, *for my son — for Isaac,* is noted]:

Two considerations are to guide Eliezer in choosing the woman: her character must be such that she can become Abraham's daughter, even as Isaac is his son; thus she must be worthy לִבְנִי, *for my son.* but that is not enough: she must be suitable לְיִצְחָק, for Isaac's personality, because two individuals may be of excellent character yet not be suitable for one another *(Hirsch).*

[*For a discussion of the character and personality differences between Abraham and Isaac, see Overview: Three Attributes,* Vol. II, pp. 361*ff.*]

[Comp. *Rashi's comm.* to Sarah's outburst in 21:10: *with my son with Isaac;* where it indicates the superlative qualities of an Isaac even if he were not her son].

Me'am Loez [citing *Ahavas Olam*] suggests that Abraham mentioned Isaac by name because he was appointing Eliezer as his agent to betroth a woman [וְלָקַחְתָּ, *take,* being interpreted in the Biblical sense of 'take' in betrothal or marriage]. Therefore, in effect, Abraham was cautioning Eliezer that when he performed the act of betrothal he should mention Isaac by name.

In the same vein, *Ha'amek Davar* notes that if one betroths a woman to 'one of his sons' without specifying which, she is forbidden to all of them because the definite identity of her husband is unknown. This is so even though there are reasonable grounds to assume which of the brothers was intended (see *Kiddushin* 64b). Therefore, were Isaac not to be specified as the betrother, the vague term 'my son' could have been interpreted as a reference to Ishmael.

5. אוּלַי לֹא־תֹאבֶה הָאִשָּׁה לָלֶכֶת אַחֲרַי — *Perhaps the woman* [i.e., the woman to whom I will speak, or: the woman who is suitable for Isaac *(Ramban)*] *will not wish to follow me.*

I.e., she may deem it beneath her dignity to go to a foreign country with a slave, and might require Isaac to come and fetch her *(Abarbanel).* [Cf. *Rashi, Numbers* 22:13.]

Eliezer does not doubt that he will find the suitable mate who will consent to marry Isaac; he is apprehensive, however, that she might not want to go with him and forsake her family *(Hoffman).*

Hirsch notes etymologically that the verb אבה, *wish,* means to conform to the *wishes of someone else,* as distinct from חפץ which refers to a *self-inspired wish.*

[However, see *Rashi* to *Exodus* 23:6 that אבה means to desire for oneself.]

אֶל הָאָרֶץ הַזֹּאת — *To this land.*

The land of Canaan; a land foreign to her *(Abarbanel).*

הֶהָשֵׁב אָשִׁיב אֶת־בִּנְךָ — *Shall I take*

and take a wife for my son — for Isaac.'
5 *The servant said to him: 'Perhaps the woman will
not wish to follow me to this land; shall I take your
son back to the land from which you departed?'*
6 *Abraham answered him, 'Beware not to return*

your son back [lit. *return shall I return your son*]?

Eliezer was asking: What if I no longer find you alive upon my return from my mission. Tell me now whether I should bring your son back there in the event she refuses to accompany me? *(Radak).*

I.e., 'shall I take him back there *to marry her* in the event the woman I select does not wish to come here?' *(Abarbanel)*; or the question means: 'Shall I take him back there to search for a wife in the event *I* am unsuccessful in finding someone suitable?' *(Ralbag).*

Eliezer speaks of 'bringing Isaac *back*' [implying that Isaac would be returning to his former home] even though Isaac had never been there before, because this is said from the standpoint of Abraham, whose ancestral land was being referred to *(Sforno; Heidenheim).*

[This is similar to 15:16: *And the fourth generation shall return here.* The Jews after the Exodus are thus spoken of as 'returning' to the Promised Land though they had never been there because it was their ancestral home and the prophecy was given from the standpoint of Abraham.]

According to *Minchah Belulah, bring back* is the appropriate expression since Eliezer — who was going there — was the speaker.

In the Hebrew, the verb *return* is repeated for emphasis. *Malbim,* however, perceives that the connotation of the repetition is a double return: ... הֶהָשֵׁב אָשִׁיב, 'shall I take your son back there to fetch her *on condition that after the marriage he return here with her?'* Eliezer suggested this as a compromise that might satisfy the terms of Abraham's oath yet gain the agreement of his reluctant family.

אֶל־הָאָרֶץ אֲשֶׁר יָצָאתָ מִשָּׁם — *To the land from which you departed?*

I.e., your ancestral home *(Radak).*

— And which, by leaving, you rejected *(Sforno).*

6. ... הִשָּׁמֶר לְךָ פֶּן — *Beware not to return* [lit. *guard yourself, lest you return*] *my son to there.*

— For Abraham would not let Isaac lose the special sanctity with which he had been invested when he was brought as an עוֹלָה תְמִימָה, *an offering completely devoted,* to God *(Pesikta Zutresa)*; Abraham thus emphasized that Isaac was on no account to leave the precincts of the Land which God had promised to his descendants *(Radak).*

And as a perfect offering, Isaac was *figuratively* invested with the sanctity of offerings, including the prohibition not to remove sacrifices from the sacred environs of the Temple *(Deut.* 12:13) [in this case the environs of *Eretz Yisrael*] *(Minchah Belulah).* [It is significant that both our verse and *Deut.* 12:13 begin with the same phrase: הִשָּׁמֶר לְךָ פֶּן.]

[Isaac, alone of the Patriarchs, never left Canaan. God later forbade him to do so, even in days of famine (see 26:28).]

The idiomatic expression פֶּן תָּשִׁיב, *lest you*

ז בְּנֵי שֵׁמָה: יהוה | אֱלֹהֵי הַשָּׁמַיִם אֲשֶׁר
לְקָחַנִי מִבֵּית אָבִי וּמֵאֶרֶץ מוֹלַדְתִּי וַאֲשֶׁר
דִּבֶּר־לִי וַאֲשֶׁר נִשְׁבַּע־לִי לֵאמֹר לְזַרְעֲךָ
אֶתֵּן אֶת־הָאָרֶץ הַזֹּאת הוּא יִשְׁלַח

return, means *do not return*, just as in 3:3, פֶּן תְּמֻתוּן, *lest you die* really means: *so that you do not die (Radak)*.

7. ה׳ אֱלֹהֵי הַשָּׁמַיִם — *HASHEM, God of [the] heaven.*

[Abraham's response as reflected in this verse implies: God cannot be inconsistent. The God of Heaven whose Providence manifests itself on earth has demonstrated countless times by a series of promises and covenants that He has special plans for my descendants. He will certainly make your mission successful in finding a suitable bride for Isaac, regarding whom I have been expressly promised [17:21] that through *him* God's covenant would be maintained, and whose offspring will be considered mine (21:12).]

In this verse Abraham did not identify Him as 'the God of the earth' as he did in *v.* 3, for in effect, Abraham said, 'Now he is acknowledged as the *God of the heavens* as well as *God of the earth* because I made His name known as such. But when I speak of the time when He took me out of my father's house, I can designate Him only as *God of heaven* and not *God of the earth,'* for men did not then acknowledge Him on earth, nor was His name commonly known on earth *(Rashi)*. [*See also Radak* to *v.* 3, s.v. 'בַּה'].

Here, Abraham only refers to HASHEM, *God of the heaven,* in contrast to *v.*3 where he adds *God of the earth.* There, where he administers the oath to Eliezer, he stresses God's omnipotence on earth to punish one who fails to obey His word. In our verse, however, Abraham refers to the heavenly plan in accordance with which God's Providence had guided Abraham's destiny in the past and which will continue to do so in bringing success to Eliezer's mission *(Hirsch).*

אֲשֶׁר לְקָחַנִי — *Who took me ...*

— And having taken me from there in order to give my descendants this land, He certainly would not want my son to return there! *(Radak).*

Not הוֹצֵאתַנִי, *brought me out,* but לְקָחַנִי, *took me,* implying that He selected me for His special purposes ... *(Hirsch).*

מִבֵּית אָבִי — *From the house of my father.*

— I.e, Charan *(Rashi).*

וּמֵאֶרֶץ מוֹלַדְתִּי — *And from the land of my birth.*

Ur Kasdim *(Rashi).*

[See *comm.* of *Ramban* cited in *v.* 4 regarding the proper rendering of מוֹלֶדֶת, and the controversy regarding Abraham's birthplace. Cf. also *comm.* to 11:28 and 12:1].

וַאֲשֶׁר דִּבֶּר־לִי — [*And*] *Who spoke concerning me.*

— Not אָמַר לִי, *said to me,* which would have indicated a promise, but דִּבֶּר לִי, *made statements about me,* such as וֶהְיֵה בְּרָכָה, *you shall* be a blessing [12:2], וְשָׁמְרוּ דֶּרֶךְ ה׳, *that*

24 *my son to there.* [7] *HASHEM, God of heaven, Who*
7 *took me from the house of my father and from the*
land of my birth; Who spoke concerning me, and
Who swore to me saying, "To your offspring will I
give this land," He will send His angel before you,

they [his children and his household] will keep the way of HASHEM [18:19] *(Hirsch).*

This follows *Rashi* who explains that it is a grammatical rule that whenever the pronouns לִי, לוֹ, and לָהֶם [lit. *to me; to him; to them*] follow the verb דבר, *speak,* they are to be rendered in the sense of עָלַי, עָלָיו, עֲלֵיהֶם, *concerning me, him* or *them.* Were it to mean *to me...* then the proper pronouns would be אֵלַי, אֵלָיו and אֲלֵיהֶם. However, in the case of the verb אמר, *say,* pronouns לִי, לוֹ, and לָהֶם are appropriate to mean *to me....*

Ramban disagrees with this distinction and cites verses [e.g. *Exod.* 32:34] where the verb דבר is found in connection with לך and yet means *to you* and not *concerning you* as *Rashi* suggests.

Mizrachi defends *Rashi* by stressing the distinction in connotation between דַּבֵּר, *speak,* and אֱמֹר, *say,* and noting that at times the verbs are substituted for one another as the context demands, as *Ramban* himself comments in *Lev.* 21:1. Therefore, in such cases where דַּבֵּר has the connotation of אֱמֹר, forms of the pronoun לִי may be used in the sense of *to* me rather than *concerning* me.

According to *Radak,* לִי has the literal meaning of *to me,* the phrase denoting, *Who spoke to me* — before I departed from there.

According to *Sforno* this refers to God's promise [21:12] כִּי בְיִצְחָק יִקָּרֵא לְךָ זָרַע, *since through Isaac will offspring be considered yours* [and accordingly, it is part of God's Master Plan that a *suitable* wife will be found for Isaac to assure the continuity of the Abrahamitic mission].

וַאֲשֶׁר נִשְׁבַּע לִי — *And Who swore to me.*

— At the Covenant Between the Parts [15:7 ff.] *(Rashi).*

לְזַרְעֲךָ אֶתֵּן אֶת הָאָרֶץ הַזֹּאת — *To your offspring will I give this land.*

Accordingly I am certain that He does not wish my son to leave this land; He will therefore guide your way and make your mission successful *(Rashbam).* You will find a suitable spouse for my son to marry and bear seed to fulfill His oath *(Sforno).*

הוּא יִשְׁלַח מַלְאָכוֹ לְפָנֶיךָ — *He will send His angel before You.*

I.e., in the light of His many promises to me, I am confident that He will grant you His Special Providence and aid in finding a suitable mate *(Rashbam; Akeidas Yitzchak).*

He will send His angel not *with* you but *before* you; the angel will smooth the way, leaving nothing for you to do but travel *(Hirsch).*

See the *Midrash* where it is specifically stated that a *particular angel* was meant *(Ha'amek Davar).*

This is derived from the possessive *His* angel, rather than *an* angel. It refers either to Michael, or to the angel in charge of marriage *(Minchah Belulah).* [*But cf. implication of Rashi* in *Exodus* 23:20

According to *Ibn Ezra* this was not a statement of *prophecy,* but a prayer: *May He send His angel before you,* etc. for if it was *prophetic,* why would Abraham allow himself the contingency, *But if the woman would not want to follow you?*

מַלְאָכוֹ לְפָנֶיךָ וְלָקַחְתָּ אִשָּׁה לִבְנִי מִשָּׁם׃
ח וְאִם־לֹא תֹאבֶה הָאִשָּׁה לָלֶכֶת אַחֲרֶיךָ
וְנִקִּיתָ מִשְּׁבֻעָתִי זֹאת רַק אֶת־בְּנִי לֹא
ט תָשֵׁב שָׁמָּה׃ וַיָּשֶׂם הָעֶבֶד אֶת־יָדוֹ תַּחַת
יֶרֶךְ אַבְרָהָם אֲדֹנָיו וַיִּשָּׁבַע לוֹ עַל־הַדָּבָר

וְלָקַחְתָּ אִשָּׁה לִבְנִי מִשָּׁם — *And you will take* [i.e., be successful in obtaining] *a wife for my son from there.*

— Without my son having to go there *(Sforno).*

For He Who knew that I was to be withdrawn from my father's house will also ensure that you find the right girl for my son out of my relative's house. This thought is implied by the parallel usage: לְקָחַנִי, *He took me;* וְלָקַחְתָּ, *you will take (Hirsch).*

8. וְאִם לֹא תֹאבֶה ... — *But* [lit. *and*] *if the woman will not wish to follow you.*

Back here, to a country foreign to her *(Ha'amek Davar).* Since — although we depend fully on His Providence — God forces nobody to act against his free will *(Hirsch).*

Abraham was completely confident of God's Providential assistance in fulfilling his request, but he was, at the same time, prepared for a *possible* Divine denial of success. This absolute trust exemplified by the righteous is a fundamental principle of faith *(Da'as Soferim).* [See *Chovos Halevavos, Sha'ar Bitachon* ch. 5].

וְנִקִּיתָ מִשְּׁבֻעָתִי זֹאת — *You shall then be absolved* [lit. *and you will be cleansed* (i.e., *cleared*)] *of this oath of mine.*

— And you may, in such a case, take a wife for him from the daughters of Aner, Eshkol, and Mamre *(Rashi).*

Abraham's oath that Eliezer not take a wife for Isaac from among the Canaanites applied only prior to the trip to Charan. If, however, a suitable bride could not be found among Abraham's relatives, the oath would be null and void. This is clearly indicated in Eliezer's account of the oath (*vs.* 37-41). The question is raised, however, how *Rashi* inferred that the bride would then be sought from among the daughters of Abraham's three comrades in preference to other Canaanites.

The answer may be found in the phrase אֲשֶׁר אָנֹכִי יוֹשֵׁב בְּקִרְבּוֹ, *among whom I dwell* (*v.* 3): The word, בְּקִרְבּוֹ, lit. *in his midst,* implies that the oath not to take a Canaanite woman applied particularly to those among whom Abraham lived, i.e., Aner, Eshkol, and Mamre. Conversely, if the trip to Charan ended in failure, it was to *them* that Abraham would turn in search of a bride *(Mizrachi).* [See difficulty raised by *Mizrachi* cited in *comm.* to *v.* 49 s.v. וְאֶפְנֶה.]

Ramban maintains that it is inconceivable that Abraham would ever have allowed his son to marry a Canaanite. Rather, Abraham was telling him that *he,* Eliezer, would be free of the oath in that eventuality, and that God would then do whatever He saw fit. Abraham was confident that his righteous son would not violate his wishes, and would [if Eliezer's mission proved unsuccessful] avoid [the accursed] Canaan and turn instead to Ishmael, Lot, or the other nations.

Ramban goes on to explain that, as noted previously, there were two parts to the oath. By specifying שְׁבֻעָתִי זֹאת, *this* my oath, Abraham thereby implied

and you will take a wife for my son from there. [8] But if the woman will not wish to follow you, you shall then be absolved of this oath of mine. However, do not return my son to there.'

[9] So the servant placed his hand under the thigh of Abraham his master and swore to him regarding this

that Eliezer would be free from only *that part* of the oath — which he had just expressed in the last verse: that he go to his family *and take a wife for his son from there;* Eliezer would, however, still be bound by the other part of the vow — that he not take a daughter of the Canaanites.

It is possible, as *Hoffman* points out, that Abraham was not more specific in commanding Eliezer *exactly* what to do should the mission fail, because of his powerful faith that it would succeed. Only to reassure Eliezer, whose faith may not have been so strong, did Abraham tell him that he would be absolved if she refused to come.

רַק אֶת בְּנִי לֹא תָשֵׁב שָׁמָּה — *However* [lit. *only*], *do not return my son to there.*

— Even for a short stay; even just for one day to fetch her and return here *(Malbim;* see *v.* 5 s.v. הֶהָשֵׁב אָשִׁיב).

— *And HASHEM will do that which is good in His sight* [*II Sam.* 10:12] *(Ramban)* [i.e., in His own way God will see to it that Isaac marries his worthy, predestined wife].

Rashi explains that the word רַק [*however; only*] exegetically denotes a limitation, thus narrowing the sense of the exclusion: it is *only* my son who may not go back there; but my grandson Jacob will, eventually, go there [in a similar quest].

9. Eliezer undertakes the oath.

וַיָּשֶׂם הָעֶבֶד ... — *So* [lit. *and*] *the servant placed ...*

Midrash Yelamdenu and *Midrash HaGadol* note a distinction between the responses of Eliezer and Joseph to the requests that they 'place their hand under the thigh' [see 47:29]:

Rav Yehudah said: The slave acted as befit his servile station; the free man as befit his freedom. Regarding the slave it is written: *so the servant placed his hand under the thigh* etc. Regarding the free man, however, it is written [47:30-31]: *He* [Joseph] *said: I will do as you said ... and he swore to him.*

[Joseph did not accompany his oath with a placing of his hand beneath his father's thigh because it was not seemly for a son to do so (as the Sages teach — *Pesachim* 51a: A man may bathe with all except with his father, his father-in-law, his mother's husband and his sister's husband) *(Chizkuni;* see note to *Torah Sheleimah* 24:68).]

וַיִּשָּׁבַע לוֹ עַל הַדָּבָר הַזֶּה — *And* [*he*] *swore to him regarding this matter* [lit. *upon this thing*].

According to *Hoffman,* the phrase עַל הַדָּבָר הַזֶּה signifies that Eliezer undertook the oath only because of the concession that Abraham agreed to at the end of his

י הַזֶּה: °וַיִּקַּח הָעֶבֶד עֲשָׂרָה גְמַלִּים מִגְּמַלֵּי
°שלישי אֲדֹנָיו וַיֵּלֶךְ וְכָל־טוּב אֲדֹנָיו בְּיָדוֹ וַיָּקָם
וַיֵּלֶךְ אֶל־אֲרַם נַהֲרַיִם אֶל־עִיר נָחוֹר:

command [i.e., that in the event the woman would not consent to return with him, he would be free from the bonds of the oath].

Eliezer accepted upon himself the judgment of Abraham although it may have seemed bizarre. For there was no *apparent* difference between the idolators of Aram where Abraham was sending him, and those of Canaan. Surely, the future of the nation would be determined by upbringing and education rather than geographic origin ... and Eliezer had a righteous daughter of his own! Nevertheless, the loyal Eliezer took an oath to carry out his master's will in every regard *(Da'as Soferim).*

10. וַיִּקַּח הָעֶבֶד — *Then* [lit. *and*] *the servant took.*

— I.e., immediately after swearing, *the servant himself took* — on his own initiative. Since he was הַמֹּשֵׁל בְּכָל אֲשֶׁר לוֹ, *in charge of all that was his* [*v.* 2], and accordingly was authorized to take whatever he desired *(Chizkuni).*

עֲשָׂרָה גְמַלִּים מִגְּמַלֵּי אֲדֹנָיו — *Ten of his master's camels* [lit. *ten camels of his master's camels*].

— [The Torah mentions that they were *his master's camels* although it is obvious that they belonged to his master and no one else. This draws attention to the fact that] they were distinguishable from the camels of others because they were muzzled to prevent robbery, i.e., so that they could not feed on other persons' fields *(Rashi).*

And although God does not bring about mishaps through the animals of the righteous [see *Chullin* 7a], in this case *extra precautions* were scrupulously exercised to avoid their grazing even at the edge of public thoroughfares, areas where owners surrender their rights to the public *(Sifsei Chachamim).* According to *Mizrachi,* Abraham kept them muzzled although he was confident that no sin would come about through them, because one may not rely on miracles. [See elaboration of the topic in *comm.* to *v.* 32 s.v. וַיְפַתַּח.]

The number *ten* need not necessarily be taken literally. It may simply mean *many,* as in *I Sam.* 1:8: *Am I not more to you than ten sons?* For ten is a round number meaning many *(Or HaChaim).*

וַיֵּלֶךְ — *And* [*he*] *set out* [lit. *he went*].

[The verb וַיֵּלֶךְ, *he went,* or *departed,* is repeated in this verse. The first is interpreted by *Sforno* to mean that Eliezer *took leave* from his master after having prepared the camels. The second, as reflected in the Translation, refers to his actual *departure.*]

Hirsch, however, suggests that the first וַיֵּלֶךְ in our verse is to be taken in the literal sense: Although the servant took ten of his master's camels, nevertheless *he walked* — Eliezer himself set out on foot to preserve his image as a *servant* [see *Eccles.* 10:7].

וְכָל־טוּב אֲדֹנָיו בְּיָדוֹ — *With* [lit. *and*] *all the bounty* [lit. *good*] *of his master in his hand.*

[I.e., *in his hand* literally *(Be'er*

24
10

matter. [10] *Then the servant took ten of his master's camels and set out with all the bounty of his master in his hand and made his way to Aram Naharaim to the city of Nachor.*

Mayim Chaim)], he held *a deed of gift* by which Abraham had written over all his possessions to Isaac, so that everyone would be eager to have his daughter marry him *(Rashi)*.

Cf. the *Midrash*: He carried with him a דְיַתִּיקִי, *disposition of property*.

According to *Ramban* the phrase is elliptic and implies that the camels were loaded מִכָּל טוּב אֲדֹנָיו, with *all manner of his master's goods* [i.e., a *great part* of his master's wealth, not a deed of gift] of which Eliezer took בְּיָדוֹ, *along with him* [not literally *in his hand*]. *Rashi*, however, follows the literal translation *in his hand*, and therefore interprets that Eliezer held a deed.

Cf. 41:57: *and the whole earth came to Egypt* where whole is used in the sense of *a great part*; here, too, it means *a great part of his master's wealth (Radak)*.

Following *Chizkuni* [see above] this clause is parenthetical and explains why Eliezer was able to take whatever he desired: because כָּל־טוּב אֲדֹנָיו בְּיָדוֹ, *all his master's goods were in his hand*, i.e., in his control, he being the controller of all Abraham owned.

Rashbam suggests that כָּל טוּב is to be understood in the sense of *the important personages of Abraham's household* who joined Eliezer's entourage. That others accompanied Eliezer is expressly stated in *v.* 32, and *v.* 54. *Or HaChaim* explains the phrase as referring to the *choicest of his master's possessions*: gold, precious gems, ... to bedazzle and encourage them into making a match with Isaac.

Hirsch, however, suggests that the camels were not laden because they were saddled for riding, not equipped for carrying baggage — Eliezer was leading the camels to Charan for use on the return trip by the bride and her attendants. As for the valuables, he literally carried *all the best of his master in his hand*, since the most precious jewelry can quite easily be carried in a small box.

אֲרַם נַהֲרַיִם — *Aram Naharaim* [lit. *Aram of the two rivers*].

The country was so called because it was situated between two rivers [Euphrates and Tigris] *(Rashi)*.

[The area is generally identified with today's Iraq; formerly Mesopotamia. On its identity with *Paddan Aram* see *Rashi* to 28:2, and cf. *comm.* to 10:22 regarding Aramea and its identity with Syria.]

אֶל עִיר נָחוֹר — *To the city of Nachor*.

— Which is Charan, in Mesopotamia the ancestral home of Abraham's family *(Ramban* to 11:28; see *comm.* there, p. 349).

[According to *Rashi* as well (see *comm.* to 12:1, p. 427), it is Charan, that is referred to here as the *city of Nachor*. This is also the prevailing *Talmudic* view as noted in the

יא וַיַּבְרֵךְ הַגְּמַלִּים מִחוּץ לָעִיר אֶל־בְּאֵר
הַמָּיִם לְעֵת עֶרֶב לְעֵת צֵאת הַשֹּׁאֲבֹת:
יב וַיֹּאמַר | יהוה אֱלֹהֵי אֲדֹנִי אַבְרָהָם
הַקְרֵה־נָא לְפָנַי הַיּוֹם וַעֲשֵׂה־חֶסֶד עִם

comm. to *v.* 3 s.v. מוֹלַדְתִּי. However, Nachor was not born there, (since according to the *Talmudic* view followed by *Rashi*, Ur Kasdim was Abraham's birthplace), but because Abraham's relatives (of whom Nachor was *the* oldest surviving kin) *lived* in Charan following their earlier exodus from their ancestral home, Ur Kasdim (11:31), Charan came to be called the *city of Nachor*. Accordingly Abraham directed Eliezer to go there when he commanded him in *v.* 3 to go to מוֹלַדְתִּי, *my relatives.*]

According to the *Midrash,* Eliezer miraculously arrived there on the *same day* that he set out, although the journey should normally have taken seventeen days [See *comm.* to *v.* 42.]

11. וַיַּבְרֵךְ הַגְּמַלִּים — *He made the camels kneel down.*

In order to water them, and afford them rest. Meanwhile, he prayed to God to fulfill his needs *(Radak).*

מִחוּץ לָעִיר — *Outside the city.*

He reasoned that someone who would let his daughter draw water from a well *outside the city* would not object to letting her go to a foreign country to marry a wealthy husband *(Malbim).*

אֶל בְּאֵר הַמָּיִם — *Towards a well of water.* [Following *Hirsch: Towards* a well, not besides it.]

He chose a well since it is the sort of central place where a stranger seeking information would usually station himself *(Midrash HaGadol;* see note to *Torah Sheleimah* 24:76).

Lekach Tov observes that all the righteous who departed from their homes went to wells. Moses: *He sat down by a well* [*Exod.* 2:15]; as did Jacob [29:2].

[On *well* as distinct from *spring,* see *Malbim* cited to *v.* 20].

לְעֵת עֶרֶב לְעֵת צֵאת הַשֹּׁאֲבֹת — *At evening time, the time when women come out to draw* [lit. *at the time when the water-drawers go out*]. [1]

— I.e., for the evening meal *(Abarbanel).*

[And this would be a most suitable location to observe the habits of young girls and select a suitable wife for Isaac].

Furthermore, Eliezer was expressly not interested in a *wealthy* girl for Isaac. He was searching for someone of modest means; the kind who would go to draw water

1. The *Zohar* notes that this timing, too, was part of the Divine Plan. For when Eliezer reached Charan and met Rebecca *at evening time* it was the time of מִנְחָה, *the afternoon prayer.* Thus, the moment when Isaac began the afternoon prayer coincided with the moment when the servant encountered Rebecca.

So, too, it was at the very moment of his afternoon prayer [see *comm.* to *v.* 63] that Rebecca came to Isaac himself. Thus, all was fittingly disposed through the working of the Divine Wisdom.

11 He made the camels kneel down outside the city
towards a well of water at evening time, the time
when women come out to draw. 12 And he said,
'HASHEM, God of my master Abraham, may You so
arrange it for me this day that You do kindness with

herself, not have servants do it for her *(Malbim).*

12. Eliezer prays for a sign.

Eliezer was apprehensive that the family of the girl might object to her leaving home for a distant marriage. He therefore proposed the test in the following verses in order that Abraham's relations would recognize God's hand in the ensuing events. Since he implored God in His Providence to perform certain signs, and God fulfilled them in every detail — they would recognize that everything led to exclaim: *The matter stems from HASHEM!* [which they in fact did; see *v.* 50], and would consent to allow their daughter to leave home and accompany the man.

And as the servant surmised, so it came to pass *(HaKsav V'HaKabal-lah).*

וַיֹּאמַר — *And he said.*

[I.e., he meditated; see *v.* 45].

[The cantillation over the word וַיֹּאמַר, *and he said,* is a *shalsheles* which indicates a pause and which occurs only four times in the Torah. It has been suggested that its placement here possibly indicates the servant's hesitation to address God directly.]

ה׳ אֱלֹהֵי אֲדֹנִי אַבְרָהָם — *HASHEM, God of my master Abraham.*

Eliezer was not so brazen as to pronounce the Divine Name as *God of the heaven and God of the earth* as did Abraham [*v.* 3], because he felt himself unworthy. Instead he contented himself to refer to Him as the God of his master who knows the Attributes by which God is called *(Abarbanel).*

According to the *Midrash,* Eliezer knew he was of accursed stock, and therefore he calls upon Hashem as the *God of Abraham,* meaning thereby to invoke the merit of the Patriarch.

הַקְרֵה־נָא לְפָנַי הַיּוֹם — *May You so arrange it for me this day* [lit. *please cause to happen before me today*].

I.e., arrange that it should so happen. Cf. 27:20: *HASHEM your God has caused it to chance* [*happen*] *before me (Ibn Ezra).*

This plea, which may be literally rendered as *cause to chance before me today,* is paradoxical. As *Abarbanel* formulates the difficulty, how could one who relied on Divine Providence, pray for a *chance happening* when these categories are mutually exclusive; what transpires Providentially cannot be termed *chance.*

In lengthy discourse on this matter, however, the expositors conclude that Eliezer's faith in God as the Prime Mover caused him to acknowledge even those events which appear to mortal man as *chance occurrences* of the universe, are not to be attributed merely to nature. Rather they have been so caused by Divine Providence, the prime cause of all things, to appear as if they were random events [see *Ramban, Exodus* 13:16.]

יג אֲדֹנִי אַבְרָהָם: הִנֵּה אָנֹכִי נִצָּב עַל־עֵין
הַמָּיִם וּבְנוֹת אַנְשֵׁי הָעִיר יֹצְאֹת לִשְׁאֹב
יד מָיִם: וְהָיָה הַנַּעֲרָ אֲשֶׁר אֹמַר אֵלֶיהָ הַטִּי־

Accordingly, Eliezer entreated God, to *arrange* that matters should work out in accordance with his desires, although the course the events would take would appear in the eyes of blind mortals as pure *chance.*

As *Hirsch* observes: Nothing is further from the Jewish concept than the idea of *chance* with which events generally are associated. Rather, the term מִקְרֶה refers to the moments of life that one does not direct, but which direct him. Such unanticipated or unintended events could be the most intentional messages sent by the One Who directs and brings about all things ...Thus, instead of *chance,* the term מִקְרֶה refers to the situations where one was lead by a higher force...

Hirsch concludes, therefore, that Eliezer prayed that God take in hand what Eliezer could not bring to its desired end. That is, he prayed that God consummate his mission.

The word לְפָנַי implies: make it happen *in my presence,* so I can witness it, and הַיּוֹם, *today,* so I am assured that it is by Your guiding Providence and not mere coincidence *(Malbim);* furthermore let it be הַיּוֹם, *today,* so I need not *tarry* here in search of a bride *(Abarbanel).*

You have already indicated Your favor to me today [by miraculously speeding me on the way (see *Rashi* to *v.* 42)], please complete it [i.e., see to the successful fulfillment of my mission] today as well *(Midrash).*

וַעֲשֵׂה חֶסֶד עִם אֲדֹנִי אַבְרָהָם — *That* [lit. *And*] *do kindness with my master Abraham.*

[He thus invoked the merit of the Patriarch in assuring the success of his mission.]

For, if You act as I am about to propose, it will be a sure sign to me that You have done so as an act of graciousness *for my master Abraham (Radak).*

— חֶסֶד, *graciousness, kindness,* refers to magnanimity beyond what is naturally expected. It was this *extra* grace for which Eliezer was now beseeching *(Malbim).*

All need [God's] kindness, notes the *Midrash.* Even Abraham, for whose sake kindness is shown to the world, needed kindness himself, as our text indicates.

13. The criteria are established:

הִנֵּה אָנֹכִי נִצָּב־עַל עֵין הַמָּיִם — *See, I stand here by the spring of water.*

— I.e., away from a home atmosphere, and hence in a better perspective to judge the character of a prospective bride. For here the girl will act freely in accordance with her own innate character, while what a girl does at home may not necessarily reflect her own nature because there she might be under constraint of her relatives' orders or expectations *(Chizkuni).*

Furthermore, standing here by the spring of water will be a further test of her character. When I ask her for a drink it would be quite easy for someone of less than generous character to say: 'You are right by the spring, why don't you simply take the water *yourself?' (Malbim).*

[On differences between *spring* and *well,* see *v.* 20.]

24
13-14

my master Abraham. [13] *See, I stand here by the spring of water and the daughters of the townsmen come out to draw.* [14] *Let it be that the maiden to*

14. וְהָיָה הַנַּעֲרָ אֲשֶׁר אֹמַר אֵלֶיהָ — *Let it be that the maiden* [ie., the maiden who will find favor in my eyes *(Malbim)*] *to whom I shall say* ...

Eliezer *beseeched* God that this chain of events should come to pass so that he might thereby recognize Isaac's destined wife. Because Eliezer acted prayerfully and with total reliance on God, this did not fall under the category of forbidden נִיחוּשׁ, *divination* [in the sense of discovering omens, or drawing auguries from certain events, which is prohibited in *Lev.* 19:26]. This is similar to the case of Jonathan who predicated a military decision on the choice of words of the Philistine sentries [(*I Samuel* 14:9-10). [There, too, Jonathan acted with trust in God as is indicated by his statement *ibid.* 14:6] *(Sforno).*

Sforno continues, noting the statement of the Sages in *Chullin* 95b: An omen which is not after the form pronounced by Eliezer, Abraham's servant, or by Jonathan, the son of Saul, is not considered a divination [indicating that the course followed by Eliezer and Jonathan was forbidden]. *Sforno* explains, however, that the Sages refer only to a situation whereby the diviner uses the same *form* as they, [and *without* invoking God's Name as did Eliezer in *v.* 12 *(Torah Temimah)*], as a divination, saying that if such and such would occur, he would take such and such course of action. [However, *Tosefos, Chullin* 95b s.v. כאליעזר and s.v. וכיונתן responds differently. See also gloss of *Raavad* to *Rambam, Hilchos Avodah Zarah* 11:4 and *Kessef Mishneh* there.][1]

Ran to *Chullin* 95b, expounded upon by *Hirsch* explains why Eliezer's behavior was not forbidden even though his *formula*, taken out of context, is cited as an example of forbidden divination. The Torah prohibits only decisions that are based on unrelated events e.g., if it rains tomorrow I will marry this woman. However, if the event is material to the decision, such a means of determination is permitted. In Eliezer's case, he sought a wife for Isaac who had Jewish compassion and displayed selfless generosity toward others. Thus, far from a magical incantation,

1. The Sages, however, frowned on Eliezer's haphazard request:

R' Shmuel bar Nachman quoting R' Yonasan said: Three men made improper requests. Two of them were fortunate in the reply they received, and one was not: [One of the fortunate ones was] Eliezer the servant of Abraham, as it is written: *Let it be that the maiden to whom I shall say* ... She might have been lame or blind! But he was fortunate in that it was *Rebecca* who came out *(Ta'anis* 4a).

Radak points out, however, that Eliezer did not leave *everything* to the test, for he would not have addressed his request to one who was lame or blind. However, the girl could have turned out to be a servant or not of Abraham's family. It is for this reason that he invoked God and prayed [*v.* 12]: הַקְרֵה־נָא לְפָנַי, *grant me good fortune this day.*

And, in any event, as *Chizkuni* notes, Eliezer did not rely on this test completely, for he did not give her the presents before ascertaining her family. [See *Tosafos, Chullin* 95b s.v. כְּאֱלִיעֶזֶר; *Torah Temimah*; but cf. *comm.* to *v.* 22-23].

Furthermore, Gur Aryeh to *v.* 13 notes that even total dependence on the sign does not constitute divination, since the test is a reasonable one. [See *Ran* above.]

Abarbanel, too, maintains that Eliezer resorted neither to divination, or arbitrary sign, but simply applied a *character* test in order to find out about her inner qualities, and this he did by the 'drink and I shall water your camels too' formula.

נָא כַדֵּךְ וְאֶשְׁתֶּה וְאָמְרָה שְׁתֵה וְגַם־
גְּמַלֶּיךָ אַשְׁקֶה אֹתָהּ הֹכַחְתָּ לְעַבְדְּךָ
לְיִצְחָק וּבָהּ אֵדַע כִּי־עָשִׂיתָ חֶסֶד עִם־

the test he chose for Rebecca would provide him with information upon which he could logically base his decision.

Throughout our chapter, the word נַעֲרָה *maiden*, is spelled defectively (נַעֲרָ), as if it were the masculine *lad*. The *Talmud (Kesubos* 40b) notes that throughout the Torah it is spelled fully only once (*Deut.* 22:19) and there the full spelling indicates that the maiden is at least twelve years old i.e., a fully developed maiden. Otherwise, Scripture refers to a girl similar to a lad i.e., one who is not yet, or not necessarily, twelve years old, the age of feminine maturity. In the case of Rebecca, as our Sages say, she was only three years old. The use of the word נַעֲרָה, as noted by *Mizrachi* in 25:20, implies in Rebecca's case *intellectual maturity* [see footnote to *v.*16].

הַטִּי־נָא כַדֵּךְ וְאֶשְׁתֶּה — *Please tip over your jug so I may* [lit. *and I will*] *drink.*

— A moderate request *(Sforno).*

But at the same time the character test would be most revealing. Since I am standing empty-handed right by the spring, it would be reasonable for her to become indignant at my request that she lower her laden jug from her shoulder to give me a drink when I could easily take some water *myself* directly from the spring, or I could pick on another girl who is still holding the water jug in her hand *(Malbim).*

וְאָמְרָה שְׁתֵה וְגַם גְּמַלֶּיךָ אַשְׁקֶה — *And who replies* [lit. *and she shall say*'], *'Drink, and I will even water your camels.'*

— I.e., her response will go *beyond* my request, and she will offer all that is needed *(Sforno).*

And she would not demur by resorting to any of the indignant replies conjectured above, instead she would graciously accede to my request *(Malbim).*

[Note that even in offering water for his camels, she would not simply say 'and take water for your camels as well', but she would offer to *water* his camels herself! Compare her actual response, however, in *v.* 19, and comment of *Hadar Zekeinim* there.]

This response would be a barometer of her wisdom and tenderness, showing that she had said to herself: This man is obviously handicapped if he cannot lower a jug to draw himself water from the well. If he cannot give *himself* a drink then most certainly he is unable to water the camels. Her concern over the thirst of the camels would indicate her kindness to animals *(Malbim).*

Harav Moshe Feinstein notes that in fact, however, when Rebecca responded to Eliezer's entreaty, she did not *offer* to water the camels, but watered them anyway. This was in contradiction both to his prayer, which mentioned an explicit response on her part, and to Eliezer's repetition of the incident (*v.*44). *Harav Feinstein* explains that Rebecca's kindness was so great that she took it for granted that another's needs should be provided for whatever they were. That his camels had to be watered

24 *whom I shall say, "Please tip over your jug so I may*
14 *drink," and who replies "Drink and I will even water*
your camels," — her will You have designated for
Your servant for Isaac, and may I know through her
that You have done kindness with my master.'

was so obvious to her that it was unnecessary for her to announce her intention to do so (*Igros Moshe, Orach Chaim II* responsa 52).

[As we see from *v.*32, servants traveled with Eliezer, yet he made no request for water on their behalf.] *Akeidas Yitzchak* and *Abarbanel* comment that Eliezer ordered his escorts to remain distant from him so that Rebecca would not see him surrounded by strong, healthy men fully capable of drawing their own water. Then, appearing to be a lone, weary traveler, he put her to the test.

Rashi to *v.*44, however, cites the *Midrash* that Rebecca gave them water as well. On the surface, at least, it would seem that *Rashi* does not agree with *Akeidas Yitzchak* that the men had removed themselves from the scene. Noting *Rashi, Da'as Soferim* comments that Eliezer requested water *only* for himself because it would have been extremely improper for him to make the request for his men, as well. At most, he could have borrowed her jug for their benefit. But her kindness was so extraordinary that she served them all in addition to Eliezer and the camels.

אֹתָהּ הֹכַחְתָּ לְעַבְדְּךָ לְיִצְחָק — *Her will You have designated* [or: *appointed*] *for Your servant for Isaac.*

— I.e., she is the one whom God has designated as a fitting mate for Isaac, since she will possess a charitable nature and therefore be worthy of admission into Abraham's household. The word הֹכַחְתָּ means *selected; designated (Rashi; Radak; Ibn Janach).*

[Cf. *Rashi* to 20:16 where the root יכח is explained as making something *evident.* Here, too, accordingly, the sense is: it is she *whom You have made evident* as being the suitable wife for Isaac.]

Ha'amek Davar renders this as a prayer: *May it be Your will that she be the one whom You have designated.* It would follow then that if the one You have designated were not here, then no maiden would respond to my test.

Sforno, in a departure from most interpretations of הֹכַחְתָּ, renders it *have taught* (or: *reproved) her,* and accordingly interprets the phrase: 'she will be the one *whom You have taught the right way',* and she will make a good wife for Isaac.

וּבָהּ אֵדַע — *And may I know through her.*

This rendering follows *Rashi* who perceives the phrase as a petition [not as others render: *and through it,* the test, *shall I* (automatically) *know,* or: *and thereby*

1. An interesting *halachah* is derived from our verse:

Although one is forbidden to eat before he has fed his animals [see *comm.* to *Deut.* 11:15 where it *first* says: *I will give grass in your fields for your cattle* (and only *then* does it say) *and you shall eat and be satisfied*], this applies only to food. Concerning drink, however, man takes precedence, as we derive from this verse where the order is *drink, and I will also water your camels. (Magen Avraham* to *Orach Chaim* 167:18 citing *Sefer Chassidim)* [See *Igros Moshe, Orach Chaim II,* responsa 52, for an extensive discussion of this *halachic* derivation.]

Or HaChaim to *v.* 19 suggests that the reason Rebecca gave water to him first was that —

אֲדֹנִי: וַיְהִי־הוּא טֶרֶם כִּלָּה לְדַבֵּר וְהִנֵּה
רִבְקָה יֹצֵאת אֲשֶׁר יֻלְּדָה לִבְתוּאֵל בֶּן־
מִלְכָּה אֵשֶׁת נָחוֹר אֲחִי אַבְרָהָם וְכַדָּהּ

shall I know, which would intimate that as *a direct result of the foregoing omen* I would know that she is the right woman, for that would savor of divination. Rather, this was Eliezer's *prayer* to God that He direct his path and make His intentions evident to him *(Tzeidah LaDerech; Maharshal).*

Ha'amek Davar adds that if Eliezer meant 'through this test I will know' he would have said וּבְזֶה אֵדַע, by virtue of *this* I will know. וּבָהּ means *to her* — and refers to *the girl* who meets his criteria.

Ramban, however, transposes the word order to gain the sense of Eliezer's plea in accordance with his recounting the incident in *v.* 43-44 as follows: 'Make it happen to me today that the maiden to whom I will speak will be the one whom You have designated for Your servant Isaac. By this [i.e., by directing me toward the right person] show kindness to my master Abraham *for by her* [or: *by this*] *shall I know* that You have shown kindness to him if she be of his kin, intelligent, and beautiful'.

כִּי עָשִׂיתָ חֶסֶד עִם אֲדֹנִי — *That you have done kindness with my master.*

— For if she turns out to be both of his family *and* a fitting companion for him, I shall know that You have shown kindness to my master *(Rashi).*

— *With my master* — since I am acting on his behalf, and it is in *his merit* that I am requesting all of this *(Ha'amek Davar).*

15. וַיְהִי־הוּא — *And it* [=הוּא] *was.*

The translation follows *HaKsav V'HaKaballah* who reads וַיְהִי הוּא together as indicated by the cantillation, as implying: *And so the thing happened.* See *Rashi* to 15:17.

טֶרֶם כִּלָּה לְדַבֵּר — *Before he had finished speaking*

— I.e., while he was still in the midst of the foregoing meditation. Cf. similar syntax in *Isaiah* 65:24: טֶרֶם יִקְרָאוּ וַאֲנִי אֶעֱנֶה, *before they call I will answer, and while they are yet speaking I will hear (Radak).*

[For so swift was the Divine response to his petition, that while he was still in the midst of his supplication, Providence had already caused Rebecca to leave her house and go to the well. This may be compared to God's interjected response to Abraham's prayer for children in 15:4].

וְהִנֵּה רִבְקָה יֹצֵאת — *That suddenly there came out Rebecca*[lit. *And behold, Rebecca was going out*].

[The word הִנֵּה, *behold,* suggests something unusual (see *comm.* to *Ruth* 2:4). *Midrashically,* it is interpreted to indicate that Rebecca's coming to the well that day was un-

even in matters of food — when there is possible danger to human life involved, man takes precedence over animals. Since, in fact, the weary old man approached her and requested 'a sip of water,' she filled his needs first — as his need was the most urgent — and then that of his camels.]

24
15 ¹⁵ *And it was before he had finished speaking that
suddenly there come out Rebecca — who had been
born to Bethuel the son of Milcah the wife of Nachor,
brother of Abraham — with her jug upon her*

usual; it was the guiding hand of Divine Providence that led her there on that particular day to meet Eliezer.]

Cf. *Pirkei d'Rabbi Eliezer* 16: Everything is revealed before the Holy One, Blessed be He. A daughter of kings [i.e., Rebecca (for Bethuel was the king of Aram; see *Yalkut Shimoni* 109)], who in all her life had never gone forth to draw water went out to draw water at that hour. And the girl, who did not know who the man [Eliezer] was, accepted the proposal to marry Isaac. Why? Because she had been destined for Isaac from her mother's womb. [Cf. also *Midrash HaBiur* cited in *Torah Sheleimah* 24:89.]

The phrase should have read וְהִנֵּה רִבְקָה בָּאָה, behold Rebecca *came out,* rather than יֹצֵאת, *was going out.* Accordingly, the *Zohar* kabbalistically perceives that the Torah is testifying that Rebecca was יוֹצֵאת מִן הַכְּלָל, *an exception to the rule,* for everyone else in the city was wicked, and she alone was righteous.

אֲשֶׁר יֻלְּדָה לִבְתוּאֵל בֶּן־מִלְכָּה אֵשֶׁת נָחוֹר אֲחִי אַבְרָהָם — *Who had been born to Bethuel the son of Milcah the wife of Nachor, brother of Abraham.*

Milcah is mentioned here to draw attention to the fact that Bethuel was the son of Milcah, Nachor's *wife,* not of the *concubine* Reumah [see 22:24] *(Ramban; Sforno).*

[The Publisher apologetically notes that due to a graphic arts error on the Patriarchal family geneological table on p. xii of the first edition of *Bereishis* vol. II, the names of *Milcah* and *Reumah* have been inadvertently transposed. On the *corrected* version, *Milcah* is shown as the mother of Utz, Buz, etc., while *Reumah* is the mother of Tevach, Gacham etc.]

Hirsch observes how wonderfully Abraham's wish was being granted. Bethuel — as this verse emphasizes — was doubly related to Abraham: Bethuel's father was Abraham's brother, and his mother was both Abraham's niece and a sister of Sarah. Rebecca's mother is not named at all. She was probably not of Abraham's family. Further, it may well be that Rebecca took after her father and grandmother, absorbing the character traits of the Abrahamitic spirit. Her brother, Laban, however, as the narrative reveals, was far different. Apparently, Rebecca's mother and brother ran the household, and 'old-fashioned,'' Abrahamitic Bethuel was shunted to the side and ignored.

וְכַדָּהּ עַל שִׁכְמָהּ — *With her jug upon her shoulder.*

— This was the *Syrian* [*Aramean*] fashion of carrying a pitcher. In many *other* Eastern countries, as among the Arabs today, pitchers are carried on the *head (Otzar Yisrael).*

Although this was the *first time* she had gone to draw water, and as the daughter of wealthy parents, she could have had her servants carry the jug, it is remarkable — and part of the Divine Plan — that she was carrying *her own* jug in unknown anticipation of the test to which Eliezer was about to subject her to *(Alshich; Malbim).*

טז עַל־שִׁכְמָהּ: וְהַנַּעֲרָ טֹבַת מַרְאֶה מְאֹד
בְּתוּלָה וְאִישׁ לֹא יְדָעָהּ וַתֵּרֶד הָעַיְנָה
יז וַתְּמַלֵּא כַדָּהּ וַתָּעַל: וַיָּרָץ הָעֶבֶד

16. וְהַנַּעֲרָה טֹבַת מַרְאֶה מְאֹד — *Now, the maiden was very fair to look upon* [lit. *exceedingly good of appearance*].[1]

Hirsch attempts to distinguish between טֹבַת מַרְאֶה which, as our Translation reflects, denotes a *pleasing appearance,* more a spiritual beauty of the face, an impression of grace, and יְפַת מַרְאֶה, *beautiful of appearance* which he explains as actual beauty. In objection to his thesis, he notes that Vashti, too, is described as טֹבַת מַרְאֶה הִיא, [*Esther* 1:12]. It may be, however, that Vashti's appearance, too, was pleasing rather than beautiful. Her refusal to appear before Ahasuerus may well speak for spirit, and feelings of decency.

[Sarah, in 12:12, is described as יְפַת מַרְאֶה which, according to *Hirsch,* denotes only *skin-deep* beauty. However, see *comm.* there that the planned descent to Egypt to escape Canaanite famine posed a new danger that Sarah's beauty would attract the attention of the Egyptians. Thus, the verse specifies her *skin-deep* beauty to emphasize the danger, rather than to imply that she was deficient in spiritual beauty. On the other hand, Abraham had been fully cognizant of Sarah's spiritual greatness for many decades before the Egyptian episode. He would certainly not have meant that he had only then become aware of her *spiritual beauty;* as *Rashi* explains there, it was her *physical beauty* which he just perceived for the first time. Indeed the spiritual aspect of Sarah's character is implicit in the entire Scriptural narrative of her life.]

בְּתוּלָה וְאִישׁ לֹא יְדָעָהּ — *A virgin whom no man had known* [lit. *a virgin, and a man had not known her*].

[On *know* as a delicate term for marital intimacy see on 4:1, וְהָאָדָם יָדַע].

According to *Rashi* the phrase *and a man had not known her* is not merely a redundancy parallel to the word בְּתוּלָה, *virgin.* Rather, following the *Midrash,* he explains that heathen maidens preserved their virginity, yet freely practiced unnatural intimacy. He accordingly distinguishes between the two terms and renders בְּתוּלָה as a *virgin* — in the literal sense; *and man had not known her* — unnaturally.

— It further denotes that no man had *known* her even before the age

1. According to the traditional chronologies Rebecca was three years old at the time. The calculation given by *Seder Olam* is as follows:

Sarah died at the age of 127 upon hearing of Isaac's Binding. Thus, since she was ninety at his birth, Isaac would have been thirty-seven. Rebecca was born immediately after the *Akeidah* [22:20-23], while Isaac was 40 when he married her [25:20.] Hence, she was three years old at the time (see *comm.* 25:29).

This follows the view of *Seder Olam* which interprets that Rebecca's birth coincided with the *Akeidah,* making her three years old at this time [see *comm.* beginning of 25:20].

Tosafos (Yevamos 61a s.v. וְכֵן), cites a different opinion. *Tosafos* observes that the term נַעֲרָה, *maiden,* indicates a girl much older than three. Accordingly, *Tosafos* records another opinion that Rebecca was fourteen years old at her marriage to Isaac [either Rebecca's birth preceeded the *Akeidah* by eleven years and Abraham was told it only at the *Akeidah,* or Isaac was twenty-six at the *Akeidah* (see *Mizrachi* to 25:20 and glosses of *Vilna Gaon* to *Seder Olam*). This chronology is based on the *Sifri* which states that Rebecca's life-span equaled that

24 *shoulder.* 16 *Now the maiden was very fair to look*
16 *upon; a virgin whom no man had known. She*
descended to the spring, filled her jug and ascended.

of three. Such an intimacy would not have altered her status as a virgin because בְּתוּלוֹתֶיהָ חוֹזְרִין, *her mark of virginity grows back,* in such ayoung child *(Tur).*

Hirsch [following the *Midrash*] also explains that *man had not known her* could not refer merely to her *virginity* for that was already stated by בְּתוּלָה. Rather it means that she was so extraordinarily modest and retiring, and possessed such innate morality and dignity, *that no* man *had dared become intimately friendly with her.* This was certainly remarkable, especially in Aram.

Cf. *Rashbam* who explains that the reference to *any undue familiarity.*

Another interpretation: No one had יְדָעָה *perceived her* true exalted nature: that she was wholly righteous — amid the evil of Aram — and that she was destined to become one of the Matriarchs of Israel *(Chupas Eliyahu).*

In the simple sense, some interpret that since Rebecca was a daughter of wealthy parents, and did not regularly come down to the well, the Torah is merely telling us that *no one* [at the well] *knew her;* she had always kept to herself and no one recognized her *(Be'er Mayim Chaim II).*

וַתֵּרֶד הָעַיְנָה — [*And*] *she descended to the spring.*

— [I.e., *toward* the spring. She did not have to descend all the way *down to the water level,* for when she got close enough, a miracle occurred; see further.]

וַתְּמַלֵּא כַדָּהּ וַתָּעַל — [*And*] *filled her jug and ascended.*

— Unlike the other girls who, when they go to draw water, waste their time in idle chatter, Rebecca did her task quickly and without delay; *she filled her jug and* immediately *came up (Minchah Belulah).*

Since the verse does not read וַתִּשְׁאָב, *and she drew water,* and filled her jug, the *Midrash* interprets the verb וַתָּעַל, *and ascended,* as referring to the water: All other women went down and *drew* from the well; in her case, however, as soon as the water saw her, a miracle occurred: וַתָּעַל, *it* [the

of Kehath = 133. [Although Kehath's life-span is recorded in the Torah (*Exodus* 6:18), that of Rebecca is unrecorded in the Torah except by a *Midrashic* comment to 35:8 that Rebecca died at the same time as Deborah, when Jacob entered Canaan (at the age of 99)]. In calculating the various known chronologies [see *comm.* to 35:8], it is clear that Rebecca could not have been 133 years old at her death unless she was 14 years old when she was married (add twenty years of barrenness before she bore Jacob [=34] to Jacob's age at her death and we have 133). For if she were there three years old at her marriage, she would accordingly have been 122 years old at her death.

Tosafos concludes that these *Midrashim* are indeed conflicting. *Mizrachi* in his dissertation to 25:20 concludes similarly, but adds that the *primary* Rabbinic chronology agrees that Rebecca was *three* at her marriage. Rebecca, accordingly, is referred to as נַעֲרָה, *maiden* not to be taken in the *technical* sense, but as referring to her maturity and intelligence. [See the exhaustive *comm.* of *Reb Moshe Weinstock* ז״ל to *Seder Olam;* Jerusalem 1957. See also *Kesubos* 40b cited in *comm.* to *v.* 14.]

לִקְרָאתָהּ וַיֹּאמֶר הַגְמִיאִינִי נָא מְעַט־מַיִם
יח מִכַּדֵּךְ: וַתֹּאמֶר שְׁתֵה אֲדֹנִי וַתְּמַהֵר וַתֹּרֶד
יט כַּדָּהּ עַל־יָדָהּ וַתַּשְׁקֵהוּ: וַתְּכַל לְהַשְׁקֹתוֹ
וַתֹּאמֶר גַּם לִגְמַלֶּיךָ אֶשְׁאָב עַד אִם־כִּלּוּ

water] *immediately rose (Ramban v. 17).*

[But this miracle occurred only the first time. See *v.* 20 s.v., וַתִּשְׁאַב.]

17. וַיָּרָץ הָעֶבֶד לִקְרָאתָהּ – *The servant ran toward her.*

– [Toward *her* and no other] because he saw that the water rose in the well when she approached it *(Rashi;* see *Ramban* above).[1]

It is in the demeanor of הָעֶבֶד, *the slave,* that Eliezer hurried to meet her *(Hirsch)* ...

הַגְמִיאִינִי נָא מְעַט מַיִם מִכַּדֵּךְ – *Let me sip, if you please, a little water from your jug.*

He begs for just 'a little water' to gulp down *(Hirsch).*

– I.e., just a single mouthful *(Midrash);* for the word הַגְמִיאִינִי is similar to גְּמִיעָה, *sip (Rashi).*

Hoffman relates it to the verb גמא, *drink,* in *Job* 39:24.

18. Rebecca proves equal to the test.

שְׁתֵה אֲדֹנִי – *Drink, my lord.*

– I.e., do not content yourself with only a *sip.* Here! – *drink* as much as you wish! *(Or HaChaim).*

– This illustrates her fine character. She did not know him yet she courteously addresses him as אֲדֹנִי, *my lord,* and hurries to serve him graciously *(Radak).*

She answers: 'Drink,' and adds 'my lord' although he stands as a slave before her ... Thus, step by step, she shows her Abrahamitic feelings, and proves herself worthy to succeed Sarah as the family matriarch *(Hirsch).*

וַתְּמַהֵר וַתֹּרֶד כַּדָּהּ עַל יָדָהּ וַתַּשְׁקֵהוּ – *And quickly she lowered her jug* [from her shoulder *(Rashi)*] *to her hand* [lit. *and she hurried, and she lowered her jug upon her hand*] *and gave him drink.*

[The translation *gave him drink* does not quite have the force of the Hebrew וַתַּשְׁקֵהוּ, which connotes more forcefulness and abundant beneficence. A better rendering might be *'and she plied him with drink'* in the sense of she *watered him,* if such a term could be used for humans. (See *comm.* in *v.*43, and compare this use in 19:33).]

She acted in a most supreme manner: She immediately lowered her jug herself to spare him the effort, and וַתַּשְׁקֵהוּ, which implies that she actually brought the jug near his mouth, so he would not even have to hold the jug *(Or HaChaim).* [This interpretation is probably based on the fact that the verse does not read *she handed it to him.*']

Her energetic personal service atoned for Abraham's failure to do the same for the angels. Then, Abraham ordered that water be fetched, but he did not bring it himself (Machazeh Avraham).

1. Though Eliezer saw so astounding a miracle, he did not forgo the test he had set for the prospective bride. The caliber of a person is proven by character, not miracles *(Rabbi Yisroel of Modzhitz).*

24 17-19 [17] *The servant ran toward her and said, 'Let me sip,*
if you please, a little water from your jug.' [18] *She said,*
'Drink my lord,' and quickly she lowered her jug to
her hand and gave him drink.
[19] *When she finished giving him drink, she said, 'I*
will draw water even for your camels until they have

19. וַתְּכַל לְהַשְׁקֹתוֹ – *When* [lit. *and*] *she finished giving him* [or: *plying him with*] *drink.*

— She did not speak until he was finished, because as the Sages cautioned [*Ta'anis* 5b]: אֵין מְשִׂיחִין בִּסְעוּדָה one should not speak while eating 'lest the windpipe acts before the gullet' [i.e., lest the food get caught in the windpipe] *(Sforno).*[1]

Scripture should have said וַיְכַל לִשְׁתּוֹת, *when 'he' had finished drinking.* The text indicates that she held the jug and poured water into his mouth. Possibly she feared that in the great weariness and thirst occasioned by the journey, he might drink more than was good for him; therefore, she regulated the amount. Yet lest he think that she was limiting the water merely to lessen her own efforts, she added that she would draw even for his camels *(Or HaChaim;* see *footnote* to *v.* 14).

Furthermore, *Or HaChaim* [*v.* 18] suggests that the reason she did not *initially* tell him that she would water his camels as well was that he should not drink too quickly or too little, out of consideration for the extra trouble she would be undertaking. By not speaking of her intention, she was assured that he would drink his fill slowly without feeling guilty that he was unduly taxing her.

According to *HaK'sav V'haKaballah,* Rebecca weighed her every word carefully so as not to give offense to anyone. She did not repeat the same words Eliezer had contemplated, *'Drink* and *I will water your camels also',* since by this she would be equating him with the camels. She, therefore, stopped short and said, *'Drink, my lord.'* Later on, she made her offer to water the camels.

For what would be the point in mentioning the second part of an act she could not perform at this moment anyway? It would appear that she was boasting and wanted him to be beholden to her *(Kedushas Levi).*

The Jewish woman does not boast of grandiose plans. She speaks only when she is ready to act, and when she does, her generosity is as complete as was Rebecca's in giving the camels their fill *(Hirsch).*

Igros Moshe cited above explains that the care of the camels was so obvious a duty in her eyes that she felt no need to mention it.

[For *Halachic* implications, see *footnote* to *v.* 14 s.v. וְאָמְרָה].

גַּם לִגְמַלֶּיךָ אֶשְׁאָב עַד אִם כִּלּוּ לִשְׁתֹּת – *I will draw* [water] *even for your camels until they have finished drinking.*

— He now understood that God had responded to his prayer *(Rashbam).*

1. *Harav David Feinstein* notes that the *Talmud* uses the expression מְשִׂיחִין, the *causative* form. Thus it should be interpreted to forbid someone who is *not* eating to enter into conversation with someone who *is* eating. To do so will *cause* the eater *to speak,* and thereby endanger him. This explains why Rebecca did not speak while Eliezer was eating: she was afraid she might say something that would provoke Eliezer to a response.

כ לִשְׁתֹּת: וַתְּמַהֵר וַתְּעַר כַּדָּהּ אֶל־הַשֹּׁקֶת
וַתָּרָץ עוֹד אֶל־הַבְּאֵר לִשְׁאֹב וַתִּשְׁאַב
כא לְכָל־גְּמַלָּיו: וְהָאִישׁ מִשְׁתָּאֵה לָהּ מַחֲרִישׁ

Rebecca did not respond by saying אַשְׁקֶה, I will *water* your camels as Eliezer had anticipated in formulating his criteria in *v.* 14. Rather she offered only to *draw* the water (אֶשְׁאָב) for them. This was further proof of her modesty, since the Sages in *Kesubos* 61b perceive it to be immodest for a woman to *feed* male beasts [i.e., from her hand]. Therefore, she modestly proposed to *draw* the water for them and fill the troughs after which they would drink their fill themselves. It is also possible that since there was a trough from which the animals could drink themselves, when Eliezer said *water* them, he anticipated only that she would *draw* the water and fill the troughs *(Hadar Zekeinim).*

Kedushas Levi suggests that she offered to *draw* the water rather than *water* them, was an indication of compassion. If she were to give water directly to the camels, how could she choose which to water first? Therefore, she kept pouring water into *the trough* so they could *all drink at once*, and she continued drawing water until they all finished drinking.

Rashi explains that the word אם in this verse idiomatically means אֲשֶׁר, *that*, and the phrase is literally to be rendered: *until that they have finished drinking.* He notes that *Onkelos* renders our phrase: עַד דִּי־סַפְקוּן לְמִשְׁתֵּי, *until they have had sufficient to drink.* [This is distinct from 43:2 where *Rashi* explains כַּאֲשֶׁר כִּלּוּ לֶאֱכֹל אֶת הַשֶּׁבֶר as implying that *they finished eating* not because they were satiated after having eaten enough, but because the food had run out (see *comm.* there).]

20. וַתְּמַהֵר וַתְּעַר כַּדָּהּ אֶל הַשֹּׁקֶת — *So* [lit. *And*] *she hurried and* [she] *emptied* [lit. *poured*] *her jug into the trough.*

I.e., a hollowed out stone from which animals drink *(Rashi).*

This, too, displayed her manners, in that she did not pour Eliezer's left-over water back into the *well* from which *people* also drink, but into the *trough (Chizkuni).*

Rashi explains that the word וַתְּעַר means 'pour out' and so occurs Talmudically (e.g., *Avodah Zarah* 72a). In Scripture it is used figuratively as *'to pour out' the soul* [*Psalms* 141:8; *Isaiah* 53:12.]

וַתָּרָץ עוֹד אֶל הַבְּאֵר לִשְׁאֹב — *And kept running* [lit. *ran again*] *to the well to draw* [water].

[Rebecca *runs* eagerly when she performs an act of kindness, as did Abraham when he was providing for *his* guests (see 18:7); a further sign of her suitability to join Abraham's household.]

Malbim distinguished between עַיִן, *spring*, in *v.* 13, and בְּאֵר, *well*, here. A *spring* is the source from which water flows from the depths of the earth; a *well* is usually dug nearby into which the spring water collects. Water for *humans* is usually drawn directly from the *spring* where it is cooler and fresher; water for the *animals* is drawn from the *well.* Therefore, *well* is mentioned when the animals are referred to, as in *v.* 11 and the present verse; whereas when the water was for humans as in *v.* 13, and *v.* 16., the *spring* is mentioned.

וַתִּשְׁאַב לְכָל גְּמַלָּיו — *And she drew for all his camels.*

[This time it specifically states that *she drew*; for the miracle of the rising water happened only the first time *(Ramban* to *v.* 17).]

finished drinking.' 20 *So she hurried and emptied her*
jug into the trough and kept running to the well to
draw water; and she drew for all his camels.
21 *The man was astonished at her, reflecting silent-*

The first time she was drawing for her own needs — and so a miracle could be performed to assist the righteous in their own task. Now that she was performing a *mitzvah,* she would be rewarded in proportion to the effort expended. Therefore, now *she drew* the water herself and no divine aid was given her *(Kedushas Levi).*

I. Levy, in a bracketed comment to *Hirsch,* notes that in their first drink, ten camels would consume at least 140 gallons of water! The task so eagerly undertaken by Rebecca of drawing such large quantities of water for a stranger's camels was indeed not a token gesture.

21. וְהָאִישׁ מִשְׁתָּאֵה לָהּ — *[And] the man was astonished at her.*

I.e., he was מִשְׁתּוֹמֵם, *astonished,* and perplexed [over the immediate fulfillment of his prayer which surpassed all his expectations *(Hirsch)*] ... and was *wondering* about her [i.e., whether she was of his family (see *Rashi* further).]

According to *Onkelos* the phrase has the connotation of 'the man lingered ... '

He was waiting and wondering whether she had made an empty promise, or she would indeed water his camels 'until they will have finished drinking.' When [in the next verse] he perceived that *all* the conditions to determine her character had been met, he gave her the gifts and spoke further to her *(Or HaChaim).*

Sforno explains he was admiringly bewildered by her industriousness to do a kindness.

[Perhaps the rendering which best captures the sense of the above would be: *And the man was fascinated by her.*]

The Commentators — e.g. *Rashi, Ibn Janach, Ibn Ezra, Radak* — agree that the word מִשְׁתָּאֵה is from the root שאה, *waste, desolate,* a term which is figuratively applied to one who is perplexed and speechless, sunk in contemplative thought regarding what is happening around him.

That the ת in מִשְׁתָּאֵה is not part of the root is not unusual, since there is a grammatical rule that when a root-verb beginning with שׁ, (like שאה) is used in the *hispa'el*—reflexive state, the added ת, *tav,* of *hispa'el* comes after the *shin* of the rest: מִשְׁתָּאֵה [instead of the more common *hispa'el* conjugation of מִתְשָׁאֵה. Similarly, שלל becomes מִשְׁתּוֹלֵל as in *Isaiah* 59:15. However, those who would render the word as derived from the root שתה, מִשְׁתָּאֵה=*drink* [i.e., *the man was drinking*] render erroneously since an א would never replace the ה of the root שתה [i.e., if מִשְׁתָּאֵה were from the root שתה, *drink,* the word, in *hispa'el,* would be מִשְׁתָּתֵה] *(Rashi).* [*Midrashically,* however, there *is* an interpretation that the word refers to drinking. See *footnote* below. *Karnei Or,* furthermore notes that *Rav Saadiah Gaon* renders: *was drinking.*] [1]

Rashi goes on to explain that לָהּ (lit. *to* her) has the meaning in this context of *about, regarding,* as לִי in 20:13 means *'about* me', and as does the

1. The *Midrash* ascribes to R' Yochanan of Sephoris that the verse means: מְמַצְמֵץ וּמַבִּיט בָּהּ. There are several conjectural translations of the word מְמַצְמֵץ. According to *Matnos Kehunah*

לָדַעַת הַהִצְלִיחַ יהוה דַּרְכּוֹ אִם־לֹא׃ וַיְהִי
כַּאֲשֶׁר כִּלּוּ הַגְּמַלִּים לִשְׁתּוֹת וַיִּקַּח הָאִישׁ
נֶזֶם זָהָב בֶּקַע מִשְׁקָלוֹ וּשְׁנֵי צְמִידִים עַל־

pronominal prefix ־לִ in 26:7. [See also *comm.* to *v.* 7, וַאֲשֶׁר דִּבֶּר לִי.]

מַחֲרִישׁ — *Reflecting silently* [or more literally: *maintaining silence*].

Although he was overawed by her compulsion to do such kindness, *he maintained his silence* instead of saying, as courtesy would have dictated, 'Do not go to so much trouble,' *(Sforno).*

According to *Radak,* although fascinated by her, *he remained silent* and did not yet ask her identity — the knowledge of which was decisive in determining whether God had made his search successful — until the camels had completely finished drinking.

לָדַעַת הַהִצְלִיחַ ה׳ דַּרְכּוֹ אִם לֹא — *To learn* [*Hirsch: to get to know* (i.e., with certainty)] *whether* HASHEM *had made his journey* [or: *errand*] *successful or not.*

— For he saw that his plan was *nearly* successful but he was as yet unsure *whether she was of Abraham's family or not (Rashi).*

And thus he restrained himself until he could ascertain whether the girl who so marvelously conformed to all his requirements concerning her character would also conform to Abraham's familial conditions *(Hirsch).*

— Continuing *Sforno*: [He maintained his silence ...] because he wanted to ascertain from observing her further actions, *whether God had made his journey successful* — i.e., whether her kindness was sincerely motivated [and hence she was the predestined wife for Isaac, thus rendering his mission successful], *or not* — but all her actions were performed only in the hope of receiving a reward [and if so the test was a failure].

22. וַיְהִי כַּאֲשֶׁר כִּלּוּ הַגְּמַלִּים לִשְׁתּוֹת — *And it was, when the camels had finished drinking.*

— This must naturally have taken a considerable amount of time [see *comm.* end of *v.* 20]. Since she did not ask for any payment he now knew that she possessed graciousness befitting the wife of his master's son, and her motives were entirely altruistic *(Sforno).*

וַיִּקַּח הָאִישׁ נֶזֶם זָהָב ... וּשְׁנֵי צְמִידִים עַל יָדֶיהָ — *The man took a golden nose ring, ... and two bracelets, on her arms* [lit. *hands*].

The word נֶזֶם can refer to either a nose-, or earring *(Ibn Ezra; Chizkuni).* That *nose* ring is meant here may be inferred from *v.* 47.

Since our verse does state explicitly that he gave her these gifts now, there is a difference of opinion

and *Yafeh Toar* the meaning is: He scrutinized her, and focused his entire concentration on her.

According to an interpretation in *Karnei Or,* however, the word מִשְׁתָּאֵה is homiletically related to שתה, *drink,* and the *Midrash* accordingly means: he sipped his drink (מְמַצְמֵץ) [i.e., he toyed with his drink] and all the while he was really scrutinizing her, wondering whether HASHEM had blessed his mission with success.

24 *ly to learn whether HASHEM had made his journey*
22 *successful or not.*
22 *And it was, when the camels had finished drink-*
ing, the man took a golden nose ring, its weight was a
beka, and two bracelets on her arms, ten gold shekels

among the expositors as to whether Eliezer actually presented her with these gifts before inquiring as to her identity (next verse), or whether be *prepared* them in anticipation of the good news he would soon receive, but did not give them until he verified that she was a member of Abraham's family. The latter opinion is *apparently* substantiated by Eliezer's own account in *v.* 45.

According to *Rashi* (see next verse), as implied by this verse, Eliezer actually *gave* her the gifts before he asked her identity 'for he was confident that on account of Abraham's merit, God had made his journey successful.' [According to a version of *Rashi* cited by *Abarbanel* — a version not found in extant editions — Eliezer gave her these gifts before asking her identity, *as payment* (which she had earned) *for her efforts.*]

Cf. *Tosafos Chullin* 95b s.v. כֶּאֱלִיעֶזֶר; *Chizkuni* cited to *v.* 14 s.v. וְהָיָה הַנַּעֲרָה, and *Torah Temimah* ad loc.]

[*Rashi* notes in *v.* 47 that when Eliezer later recounted the story, he changed the sequence of the two events, because Rebecca's family would not have understood how he could squander precious gifts on blind faith; they would demand: 'How could you give her anything before you knew who she was?']

[Further, it seems that to achieve his interpretation here, *Rashi* perceives עַל יָדֶיהָ (lit. *upon* her hands) as an elliptical phrase which should be understood as if it read: וַיָּשֶׂם עַל יָדֶיהָ, that *he placed it upon her arms* (i.e., he actually *gave her* the gifts) and is so rendered by *Targum Yonasan.*]

Akeidas Yitzchak, too, explains that he gave her these gifts *before* establishing her identity her, for even if she were *not* to be of Abraham's family, he would nonetheless establish thereby a reputation for generosity which would aid him in his search. However, when recounting the story to her family, he mentioned that he inquired who she was — either because he did not want to give away his strategy, or to imply that he gave her the ornaments in honor of her family.

Malbim, notes that her identity did not matter. Abraham [according to *Malbim's* interpretation of מוֹלַדְתִּי in *v.*4] had insisted only that the woman be of his *country,* not necessarily of his *family.*

Ramban, however, interprets that Eliezer's account in *v.* 47 reflected the *true* sequence of events as they actually occurred: First Eliezer established her identity and *then* gave her the gifts as indicated by *v.*47. Our verse indicates only that he *prepared* the gifts for her — *a golden ring, and two bracelets which would be* עַל יָדֶיהָ, *upon her hands* [i.e., appropriate for her hands.] That the Torah omits mention of the giving in our verse in this case is not unusual.[1]

According to *Or HaChaim* the phrase עַל יָדֶיהָ indicates that *they fit her hands*

1. *Hirsch* agrees that the gifts were not presented until afterward, but he perceives a special purpose in Eliezer's preparation of the gifts at this point. Rebecca had already demonstrated that her character was sterling; but Eliezer's next request would be for hospitality for himself, and ten camels. To comply with such a request, not only Rebecca but her whole family would have to be of Abrahamitic character. To obtain such a show of generosity, Eliezer felt that it would be wise to display his wealth. Indeed, knowing the mercenary nature of Laban, the

כג יָדֶיהָ עֲשָׂרָה זָהָב מִשְׁקָלָם: וַיֹּאמֶר בַּת־מִי
אַתְּ הַגִּידִי נָא לִי הֲיֵשׁ בֵּית־אָבִיךְ מָקוֹם
כד לָנוּ לָלִין: וַתֹּאמֶר אֵלָיו בַּת־בְּתוּאֵל אָנֹכִי
כה בֶּן־מִלְכָּה אֲשֶׁר יָלְדָה לְנָחוֹר: וַתֹּאמֶר
אֵלָיו גַּם־תֶּבֶן גַּם־מִסְפּוֹא רַב עִמָּנוּ גַּם־

exactly as though they were made for her. Eliezer interpreted this as a further sign of the Providential success of his mission.

בֶּקַע מִשְׁקָלוֹ — *Its weight was a beka.*

The *beka* (from בקע, *split; fraction),* was equal to a *half* [i.e., a split] shekel *(Ibn Ezra).*

Rashi explains that this gift symbolized the half-shekel which each Israelite donated upon being counted, as it is written: [*Exod.* 38:26]: בֶּקַע לַגֻּלְגֹּלֶת מַחֲצִית הַשָּׁקֶל, *a beka for each head, half a shekel.*

For, as *R' Bachya* explains, the only reason the Torah recorded the weight of the respective gifts was to allude that from her would descend a nation that would accept the Torah, would donate *half-shekalim,* and would receive the twin tablets of the Ten Commandments containing 172 words [=the numerical value of בֶּקַע *(Toras Chaim)*]. [*See Rashi* below.]

וּשְׁנֵי צְמִידִים עַל יָדֶיהָ — *And two bracelets on her arms* [lit. *hands*].

— The *two* bracelets were symbolic of the *two* stone tablets of the Ten Commandments which were מְצוּמָדוֹת, *joined together (Rashi).*

עֲשָׂרָה זָהָב מִשְׁקָלָם — *Ten gold* [*shekels*] *was their weight.*

The word *shekels* is implied in the phrase *ten gold,* as it is above in 20:16 *(Hoffman).*

— This was symbolic of the Ten Commandments which were inscribed upon the tablets *(Rashi).*

23. וַיֹּאמֶר בַּת־מִי אַתְּ — *And he said, 'Whose daughter are you?'*

[See *comm.* to previous verse as to whether Eliezer's question *followed* his giving her the ornaments *(Rashi)*; or *preceded* it *(Ramban).*]

According to the latter opinion, this verse would be interpreted in the past-perfect: And he *had* said [i.e., *before* giving her the gifts] *(R' Bachya).*

הַגִּידִי נָא לִי — *Pray tell me.*

I.e., give me a *full detailed account.* This is implied by the verb הגד which denotes a more comprehensive, detailed, account [in contrast with אמר, *say,* which has a more superficial connotation.] Thereby, Eliezer was indicating that he wanted not only her name and her father's name, but *a full detailed genealogy.* [That is why she answered him accordingly (next verse)] *(Ha'amek Davar).*

Since he hardly expected the girl to tell this to a stranger, he repeats his question with more urgency *(Hirsch).*

dominant figure in the family, Rebecca may not have dared invite Eliezer had she not seen that he could make it worth Laban's while. In recounting these events in *v.*47, however, Eliezer tactfully omitted this point; another example of the subtle delicacy he displayed throughout his mission.

was their weight. [23] *And he said, 'Whose daughter*
are you? — pray tell me. Is there room in your father's
house for us to spend the night?' [24] *She said to him, 'I*
am the daughter of Bethuel the son of Milcah whom
she bore to Nachor.'
[25] *And she said to him, 'Even straw and feed is*
plentiful with us as well as place to lodge.'

הֲיֵשׁ בֵּית־אָבִיךָ מָקוֹם לָנוּ לָלִין — *Is there room* [in] *your father's house for us to spend the night* [or: *lodge*]*?*[1]

לִין, a noun [similar in form to רִיב (*Rashbam*)] meaning *one night's lodging.* In her generosity, however, she answered [next verse] using the verb לָלוּן, *to lodge,* which signifies *many nights' lodging (Rashi;* see *comm.* there).

[*Hadar Zekeinim* interprets in reverse, however: Eliezer asked for a place לָלִין, to spend *several* nights to recuperate from the long journey, while she offered a place לָלוּן to spend *one night only* as if to say: you can not stay long because of the idolatry in the house.]

According to *Sforno,* לָלִין is a transitive verb implying: 'Where we may *stable* [our camels].'

Da'as Soferim notes that Eliezer asks about a place to lodge even before receiving an answer about her family. Apparently he wished to benefit from the hospitality of this generous family even it were not related to Abraham.

24. בַּת בְּתוּאֵל אָנֹכִי ... — *I am the daughter of Bethuel the son of Milcah whom she bore to Nachor.*

She answered his first question first and last one last *(Rashi).* [Cf. *Pirkei Avos* 5:9].

[Again, she referred to her ancestress Milcah as if to emphasize that she was descended from Nachor's *wife,* not his concubine. See *comm.* to *v.* 15].

25. וַתֹּאמֶר אֵלָיו — *And she said to him.*

[I.e., in response to his second question].

גַּם־תֶּבֶן גַּם־מִסְפּוֹא רַב עִמָּנוּ — *Even straw and* [*even*] *feed is plentiful with us.*

These were offered as an expression of her own hospitality; Eliezer had not asked for these *(Rashbam).*

[... As if to assure him: You ask for lodging only. There is even food for your camels as well!]

... All of this was further evidence of her sterling character and noble soul *(Radak).*

Or following *Sforno*: Not only do we have room to *stable* (לָלִין) your camels, we even have *feed* for them.

Rashi explains that מִסְפּוֹא refers to all kinds of food for camels — e.g., straw and barley. [Cf. the Aramaic verb ספא, *to feed (Hoffman).*]

1. The לָנוּ, *us,* is emphasized: 'Do you have a place suitable for *us* — i.e., a place free of idolatry, since we are members of Abraham's household — to spend the night?' Therefore, having been so informed, when she replied she simply answered that there was ample space in her home for lodging but she did not say *'for you'*, since, in effect, the house had to be first cleansed of its idolatry, as *Rashi* notes in *v.* 31 *(Pardes Yosef* citing *Imrei Zvi).*

כו מָקוֹם לָלוּן: וַיִּקֹּד הָאִישׁ וַיִּשְׁתַּחוּ לַיהוָה:
כז °וַיֹּאמֶר בָּרוּךְ יהוה אֱלֹהֵי אֲדֹנִי אַבְרָהָם
°רביעי אֲשֶׁר לֹא־עָזַב חַסְדּוֹ וַאֲמִתּוֹ מֵעִם אֲדֹנִי
אָנֹכִי בַּדֶּרֶךְ נָחַנִי יהוה בֵּית אֲחֵי אֲדֹנִי:

Radak explains similarly, that מִסְפּוֹא refers to all animal feed — such as barley and oats, etc. except for straw.

[It would seem that since this verse already mentions *straw* separately, *Radak*'s interpretation is more appropriate. However in support of *Rashi*'s interpretation it might be possible to suggest that the תֶּבֶן, *straw*, mentioned in the verse was not meant for *feed*, but for use as mattresses to accommodate the guests. The all-inclusive term מִסְפּוֹא, would include the straw which was the *feed* for the camels (*Karnei Or*).]

[It is common for Scriptures to repeat the adverb גַּם to denote *'this as well as that,'* as in 46:34: גַּם אֲנַחְנוּ גַּם אֲבֹתֵינוּ; 47:19 גַּם אֲנַחְנוּ גַּם אַדְמָתֵנוּ; *I Kings* 3:26: גַּם לִי גַּם לָךְ].

גַּם מָקוֹם לָלוּן — *As well as place to lodge.*

I.e., לָלוּן, to spend *several nights*, not only room for *one night* as implied by your request לָלִין (*Rashi*, previous verse).

Following *Sforno*: '... Not only do we have room for you to stable [לָלִין] your camels and provide for them, but we have room even for you and your retinue to lodge [לָלוּן]!

[But she did not say לָךְ, *for you*. See *Pardes Yosef* in *footnote*, end of *v.*24.]

26. וַיִּקֹּד הָאִישׁ וַיִּשְׁתַּחוּ לַה׳ — *So* [lit. *and*] *the man bowed low and prostrated himself to* HASHEM.

Prostration (הִשְׁתַּחֲוָיָה) is more than bowing (קִידָה). The Sages have explained [*Berachos* 34b] that *bowing low* refers to the bowing of the head; *prostration* is spreading out hands and feet (פִּשּׁוּט יָדַיִם וְרַגְלַיִם). [See *comm.* to 23:7]. Thus, in this prostrate position, he thanked God for having made his mission successful (*Radak*).

Hirsch explains that קִידָה, *bowing* without bending the knees, signifies submission of one's *head*, one's *mind* completely to whomever one bows. הִשְׁתַּחֲוָיָה, *prostrating* the entire body, signifies placing oneself entirely at the disposal of the one before whom one prostrates himself ... Here, too, Eliezer first bows his *intellect* before the management and guidance of the Divine Providence which had so clearly been demonstrated to him, and then gives himself up entirely to it.

Hence, we learn that one must render thanks on hearing good tidings (*Midrash*; comp. 23:12).

27. בָּרוּךְ ה׳ אֱלֹהֵי אֲדֹנִי אַבְרָהָם — *Blessed be* HASHEM, *God of my master Abraham.*

Abraham was the first to proclaim Him; therefore He is described as *Abraham's* God (*Ha'amek Davar* to *v.* 48).

[On the meaning of 'blessing' when applied to God — for how can a frail, dependent human being bless the All-Powerful Creator? — see *comm.* to 14:20 and *footnote* 1 on page 497. See also *Overview* to ArtScroll *Bircas HaMazon*.]

אֲשֶׁר לֹא עָזַב חַסְדּוֹ וַאֲמִתּוֹ — *Who has not withheld His kindness and* [*His*] *truth.*

[Cf. the expression חֶסֶד וֶאֱמֶת in *v.* 49].

[The commentators seek to define

24
26-27

26 *So the man bowed low and prostrated himself to*
HASHEM 27 *and said, 'Blessed be HASHEM, God of my master Abraham, Who has not withheld His kindness and truth from my master. As for me, HASHEM has guided me on the way to the house of my master's brothers.'*

the difference between *kindness* and *truth.*] When one seeks good, it is fitting that God do good for him; that is *truth* i.e., rewarding a person measure for measure. *Kindness* refers to an abundance of good; in the case of Eliezer, it is the fact that he found a bride who was from Abraham's family *(Radak).*

According to *HaRechasim l'Bikah,* extraordinary favors are referred to by the dual expressions חֶסֶד וֶאֱמֶת, lit. *kindness and truth,* or חֶסֶד וֶאֱמוּנָה, *kindness and faith.* It may well be that because kindness is the finest of deeds and truth is the finest of character traits, these two characteristics are combined to describe an extraordinary favor. Accordingly, the dual phrase would be a hendiadys meaning 'steadfast kindness.'

Hirsch interprets אֱמֶת, *truth* as a limitation on חֶסֶד, *kindness. Kindness* is an outgrowth of love; it puts the emotion into action. But blind love can accede to the wish of the beloved even if it is harmful. Truth is a limiting factor which prevents love from going astray. In the case of Eliezer, the desire for truth would prevent the false kindness of a marriage with an unsuitable mate. [See *Overview,* Vol II, pp. 361-5.]

מֵעִם אֲדֹנִי — *From my master.*

— [On whose behalf I undertook this mission. Accordingly, I acknowledge that whatever success I experienced is due to *his* merit not mine (see similar expression in *v.* 14).]

אָנֹכִי בַּדֶּרֶךְ נָחַנִי ה׳ — *As for me, HASHEM has guided me on the way.*

The syntax is difficult. The cantillation separates אָנֹכִי from the rest of the phrase. This indicates a change in subject from 'Abraham,' the subject of the first part of the verse, to 'Eliezer,' the subject of the next part. Our Translation emphasizes this transition to a new subject, and at the same time preserves the sense of *Rashi* [see below.] Thus, the flow of the verse is gratitude for the kindness God showed — to Abraham, and specifically to Eliezer — in having eased his mission by guiding him to his destination [see *HaKsav V'HaKaballah.*]

Rashi [following *Onkelos*] perceives the definite article *patach* [equivalent to הַ, *the*] under the ב of בַּדֶּרֶךְ as indicating *the* way — i.e., the designated way, *the right way,* the way which Eliezer really required [cf. *v.* 48.] *Onkelos* accordingly renders: *And me has HASHEM led in a right way to the house of my master's brother.*

As *Da'as Soferim* explains:

אָנֹכִי, *'I* — although I am but Abraham's *servant,* far away from him and his land — *nevertheless,* God has

כח וַתָּ֙רָץ֙ הַֽנַּעֲרָ֔ וַתַּגֵּ֖ד לְבֵ֣ית אִמָּ֑הּ כַּדְּבָרִ֖ים
כט הָאֵֽלֶּה׃ וּלְרִבְקָ֥ה אָ֖ח וּשְׁמ֣וֹ לָבָ֑ן וַיָּ֨רָץ לָבָ֧ן
ל אֶל־הָאִ֛ישׁ הַח֖וּצָה אֶל־הָעָֽיִן׃ וַיְהִ֣י ׀

guided me and brought me directly to my destination.' These words of Eliezer, Abraham's servant, are reminiscent of the exclamation of Sarah's maidservant Hagar [16:13]: *'Could I have seen even here after having seen?'*

According to *Radak*, [not taking the cantillation into account] the sense of the verse is: אָנֹכִי בַּדֶּרֶךְ, *while I was still on the way* — and had no idea of even where I would find lodging, נָחַנִי ה׳, *God led me,* in His Providence, בֵּית אֲחֵי אֲדֹנִי, *to the house of my master's brothers,* on the beginning of my journey. The connotation in the *Midrash* is that since a miracle had occurred — the way having contracted for him, allowing him to make the long journey in but one day [see *comm.* to *v.*42] — Eliezer was now intimating that: אָנֹכִי בַּדֶּרֶךְ, *I was at the beginning of my journey, and I miraculously found myself speedily led by God to the house of my master's brothers! (R' Bachya).*

בֵּית אֲחֵי אֲדֹנִי — [*To*] *the house of my master's brothers* [i.e., *kinsmen*].

In the literal sense, the plural *brothers* is used since Nachor was Abraham's brother, and Milcah was his niece [the daughter of his other brother, Haran (see 11:27:29)] *(Radak).*

[Cf. use of singular in *v.* 48].

28. וַתַּגֵּד לְבֵית אִמָּהּ — *And told* [to] *her mother's household.*

The women had separate houses where they did their work, and a daughter, of course, confides only in her mother *(Rashi).* [In the case of Rachel, however, she told her *father* (29:12) because her mother had died and there was no one else to tell but her father *(Midrash).*]

Ha'amek Davar observes that it would follow from *Rashi*'s interpretation that the verse should have read: *the maiden ran to her mother's house and told her mother.* Reading as it does, the verse indicates that she told it to her *mother's* entire *household,* and news of it reached Laban also. It would also seem from this narrative, that her mother was the real head of the house, and her father was subordinate even to Laban, as the narrative makes it clear. [See *comm.* of *Hirsch* to *v.* 15.]

כַּדְּבָרִים הָאֵלֶּה — *According to these events.*]

The rendering of the prefix כ in כַּדְּבָרִים [lit. *like* these things] as: *approximately what had occurred* follows *Radak* who explains that her narrative was a *general* account of what had occurred, since it is inevitable that some miscellaneous details would be omitted.

This also indicates Rebecca's tact in not divulging details — such as the stranger's offer of gifts before he even ascertained her identity — [details which would otherwise have conflicted later with Eliezer's account of the event] *(Kli Chemdah).*

[28] *The maiden ran and told her mother's house-*
hold according to these events.
[29] *Rebecca had a brother whose name was Laban.*
Laban ran to the man, outside to the spring. [30] *For*

29. Laban

וּלְרִבְקָה אָח וּשְׁמוֹ לָבָן — [*And*] *Rebecca had a brother whose* [lit. *and his*] *name was Laban.*[1]

Laban — a central character in this narrative — is now introduced for the first time. It would appear — from the profound influence he exercised in his household — that he was either the *only* son or the oldest *(Hoffman).*

There is a difference of opinion in the *Midrash* regarding the significance of the name *Laban,* which means 'white'. According to one opinion it simply refers to his skin which was exceptionally white. Others give it derogatory meanings: he was 'whitened in wickedness ...' and 'whitened the faces of Israel' [by shaming them; Laban often being described as an archetype of Israel's enemies.]

This man was the brother of Rebecca and father of the matriarchs Rachel and Leah. Although usually portrayed as a schemer — specifically in his later dealings with Jacob — he seems to have had certain admirable characteristics which occasionally emerged among his otherwise sinister traits (see *footnote*) and which reflected the shining character of his righteous sister and daughters. *Rashi,* following the *Midrashic* perspective, views Laban's every action in the most sinister light as motivated by greed — thus anticipating the character of Laban as it reveals itself later in his relations with Jacob. *Ramban,* however, in interpreting Laban's character strictly on the basis of how he emerges from the simple sense of the Biblical text in the narrative, views him here in more sympathetic terms as being *basically* straightforward and honorable.

וַיָּרָץ לָבָן אֶל הָאִישׁ — [*And*] *Laban ran to the man.*

Why did he *run* and what was his purpose? [It is known that Laban was not righteous and, unlike *Rashi*'s comment about Lot in 19:1, Laban certainly was not simply being *hospitable (Maskil L'David).*] The next verse clarifies it — He was prompted to do so because *he saw*

1. *Or HaChaim* cites the *Midrash* that in the case of righteous people, the word שֵׁם, *name,* is mentioned before their name as in וּשְׁמוֹ שָׁאוּל, *and his name was Saul* [*I Samuel* 9:2]. In the case of the wicked, however, the names are given first as in גָּלְיָת שְׁמוֹ, *Goliath was his name* [*ibid.* 17:4]. If so, why is the wicked Laban introduced as are the righteous, with his name given first? The reason is suggested by the seemingly difficult sequence of the verses, for, in *v.*29, which contains the allusion to Laban's righteousness, he is described as running toward Eliezer even before he heard the full account of the episode from Rebecca (*v.*30). When he heard that a stranger had accosted his sister, he hurried to defend her honor (*v,* 29).—Only later, when he heard the full story did he learn that Eliezer had acted properly and honorably. Because Laban is introduced to us as a brother acting virtuously in what he thought was defense of his sister, he is described in accord with his deed — righteously.

כִּרְאֹת אֶת־הַנֶּזֶם וְאֶת־הַצְּמִדִים עַל־יְדֵי
אֲחֹתוֹ וּכְשָׁמְעוֹ אֶת־דִּבְרֵי רִבְקָה אֲחֹתוֹ
לֵאמֹר כֹּה־דִבֶּר אֵלַי הָאִישׁ וַיָּבֹא אֶל־
הָאִישׁ וְהִנֵּה עֹמֵד עַל־הַגְּמַלִּים עַל־הָעָיִן:
לא וַיֹּאמֶר בּוֹא בְּרוּךְ יְהוָה לָמָּה תַעֲמֹד
בַּחוּץ וְאָנֹכִי פִּנִּיתִי הַבַּיִת וּמָקוֹם

the ring, and the bracelets; judging Eliezer to be a wealthy man, Laban had an eye on his money *(Rashi).*

Thus *Rashi* accounts for the unusual order of these two verses and notes that the next verse explains the reason for his running: he *saw the jewelry* and judged Eliezer to be wealthy; as well as the fact that he *overheard Rebecca's account;* for were it Laban's intention to be hospitable rather than avaricious, there would be no need for the Torah to mention his *seeing the jewelry;* the fact that he *heard the account* would have sufficed *(Mizrachi; Divrei David).*

Sforno, too, agrees that hospitality was not Laban's motivation in running. He explains that he ran simply out of curiosity to see the wealthy visitor who had come to town. [According to him the next verse does not clarify this one, but is to be interpreted independently.]

הַחוּצָה אֶל הָעָיִן — *Outside to the spring.*

[Where Eliezer had apparently remained, waiting while Rebecca had gone home to advise her parents of the man's presence].

30. וַיְהִי כִּרְאֹת אֶת הַנֶּזֶם ... — *For* [lit. *and it was*] *upon seeing the nose ring and bracelets ...*

[This verse, according to *Rashi* above, elaborates on the previous verse and explains *why* Laban had run out to the man: he had seen the ornaments Rebecca was wearing] ...

This teaches how begrudging Laban was in regard to his sister: it was when he saw the jewelry on her that he ran out to greet the man *(Radak).*

[But see *Sforno* below, who portrays Laban in a more compassionate light].

וּכְשָׁמְעוֹ אֶת דִּבְרֵי רִבְקָה אֲחֹתוֹ — *And upon his hearing* [i.e., *overhearing* from her conversation in her mother's house *(Radak)*] *his sister Rebecca's words ...*

[I.e., that the stranger who had given her these ornaments was still waiting by the well].

Or according to *Malbim*: That there was a stranger who presented himself as a servant of Abraham [*v.* 27], and whom Laban assumed to be an emissary to bring gifts to Abraham's family. If Rebecca, his sister, had been given such extravagant gifts, Laban could only imagine what lay in store for him!

[See *Or HaChaim, footnote* to וּשְׁמוֹ לָבָן above].

לֵאמֹר כֹּה־דִבֶּר אֵלַי הָאִישׁ — *Saying: 'Thus has the man spoken to me.'*

According to *Radak,* Eliezer had apparently informed her of the purpose of his mission.

Or, more simply, he asked her if there were room for lodging in her home [see *Sforno* below.]

upon seeing the nose ring and bracelets on his sister's arm, and upon his hearing his sister Rebecca's words, saying, 'Thus has the man spoken to me,' he approached the man, who was still standing by the camels by the spring,
31 and said, 'Come, O blessed of HASHEM! Why should you stand outside when I have cleared the house, and place for the camels?'

וַיָּבֹא אֶל הָאִישׁ — [*And*] *He approached* [lit. *came to*] *the man.*

— Since he judged the stranger to be wealthy, and he was covetous of his money (*Rashi v.* 29).

Sforno views Laban in a more sympathetic light. He suggests that Laban had *initially* run out to see the man merely out of curiosity and with no intention of inviting him in. But, as this verse tells us, as Laban became aware of all the gifts, etc., and *when he heard his sister Rebecca's words* that the man had requested lodging in their house, Laban wished to show gratitude — so, as the verse continues, *he approached the man* to invite him in.

וְהִנֵּה עֹמֵד עַל הַגְּמַלִּים — *Who was still* [lit. *and behold he was*] *standing by* [lit. *upon*] *the camels.*

I.e., attending to his camels. The idiomatic expression עֹמֵד עַל, lit. *standing upon* occurs also in 18:8 where Abraham is described as עוֹמֵד עֲלֵיהֶם, *standing over them* [the angels] — i.e., to wait upon them (*Rashi*).

עַל־הָעָיִן — *By* [lit. *upon*] *the spring.*

For Eliezer had not followed Rebecca home; he remained there — tending to his camels' needs — while patiently awaiting an invitation to lodge with Rebecca's family (*Radak*).

31. וַיֹּאמֶר — *And* [*he*, i.e., Laban] *said.*

בּוֹא בְּרוּךְ ה׳ — *Come, O blessed of HASHEM.*

— I.e., blessed with wealth, as I can see (*Radak*).

The Torah now records a prophetic expression placed — unbeknown to him — on Laban's lips. For his exemplary kindness to Abraham, Eliezer passed from the category of *accursed* Canaanite, into that of *blessed*. Laban, however, had thought he was addressing Abraham, because their features were similar (*Midrash*).

[See *Tur* cited end of *v.*39 for the significance of this unfamiliar appelation *blessed* in Eliezer's thinking.]

לָמָּה תַעֲמֹד בַּחוּץ — *Why should* [or *do*] *you stand outside?*

It does not befit a man of your dignity to stand outside (*Midrash*).

[Following *Sforno*]: You originally requested stabling only for your animals [see *comm.* to *v.* 23]. Why did you and your people wish to remain outside?

וְאָנֹכִי פִּנִּיתִי הַבַּיִת — *When* [lit. *and*] *I have cleared the house.*

—I.e., for you and your men (*Sforno*).

According to *Rashi* [citing the *Midrash*] the phrase implies: *I have cleared the house* — from the defilement of idols.

HaKsav V'haKaballah explains that this interpretation might be derived from the fact

לב לַגְּמַלִּים: וַיָּבֹא הָאִישׁ הַבַּיְתָה וַיְפַתַּח הַגְּמַלִּים וַיִּתֵּן תֶּבֶן וּמִסְפּוֹא לַגְּמַלִּים וּמַיִם לִרְחֹץ רַגְלָיו וְרַגְלֵי הָאֲנָשִׁים אֲשֶׁר אִתּוֹ:

that the verb used for *clear* is not the more common בִּעַרְתִּי, as e.g., in *Deut.* 26:13 בִּעַרְתִּי הַקֹּדֶשׁ מִן הַבַּיִת. The verb פִּנִּיתִי is generally used in reference to clearing away an obstruction or something which people find objectionable (as, for example, in *Isaiah* 54:14). Therefore, since Eliezer was the servant of Abraham who had been persecuted for his denunciation of idolatry, the commentators related this word to the idols, since nothing could be more objectionable to a member of Abraham's household than to lodge in the presence of idols.

[See *footnote* end of *v.* 23 where it is noted *how* Laban knew — before Eliezer introduced himself as a member of Abraham's household — that he should remove the idols from his house].

The commentators note that the use of אָנֹכִי is usually emphatic: *I* cleared the house personally for you — I, and not my servants.

וּמָקוֹם לַגְּמַלִּים — *And place for the camels.*

I.e., I have *cleared* an area for stabling the camels as well *(Sforno).*

For it was known that not even Abraham's camels would enter a place containing idolatry *(Avos d'Rabbi Nosson* 8).

Why did Laban go to all of this trouble on behalf of a stranger? Because he conjectured to himself: 'If that man was so generous to my sister only because she drew some water for him and his camels, imagine how generous he will be to me if I offer him and his camels lodging and even go to the trouble of cleaning the room for him!' *(Rav Yosef Caro).*

32. וַיָּבֹא הָאִישׁ הַבַּיְתָה — *So* [lit. *and*] *the man entered the house.*

The *man* refers to Eliezer *(Ramban).*

וַיְפַתַּח הַגְּמַלִּים — *And* [*he*] *unmuzzled* [lit. *loosened; ungirded*] *the camels.*

This refers to *Laban* who acted ethically toward his guests. That the subject changes within a single verse [in this case from Eliezer to Laban] is not unusual. Compare, for example 37:28 where the subject changes from the Midianites to Joseph's brothers, and in *II Samuel* 9:11 from Ziba to David. There are many such verses *(Ramban).*

The translation *unmuzzled* follows *Rashi* who explains [as noted in the *comm.* to *v.* 10] that the camels had been muzzled so that on the journey they would not graze in other people's fields.

Rashi's interpretation follows the *Midrash*, which then proceeds to ask: Were not the camels of our father Abraham equal to the donkey of R' Pinchas ben Yair? [the son-in-law of R' Shimon bar Yochai. He was celebrated for his great piety and the *Talmud (Chullin* 7a) records that even his donkey refused to eat untithed grain].

Ramban citing the above, notes that if the piety of R' Pinchas was great enough to protect even his unmuzzled animals from sin, surely there could have been no need for Abraham to muzzle his camels. He concludes, therefore, that there was no need to muzzle the them *for no injustice befalls the righteous* [*Prov.* 12:21].

Accordingly, *Ramban* interprets וַיְפַתַּח as: *he unyoked, unharnessed* them, since they used to travel tied together. *Rashbam* renders similarly.

[In defense of *Rashi*, however — as noted in the *comm.* to *v.* 10 s.v. מִגְּמַלֵּי אֲדֹנָיו —

24 [32] *So the man entered the house, and unmuzzled*
32 *the camels. He gave straw and feed for the camels,*
and water to bathe his feet and the feet of the men

several answers are suggested. Their essence is that Abraham as the *beacon of inspiration for his descendants* was *extra-scrupulous in such matters:* One does not rely on a miracle, especially in matters of possible damage to another's property (see *Kiddushin* 32). Furthermore, in the matter of R' Pinchas ben Yair's donkey, the food in question was forbidden only to Jews but not to animals, therefore, there was no reason to muzzle the donkey. In our case, however, where robbery was involved, the animal's theft was the responsiblity of the owner. Additionally, it should be remarked that Abraham was so scrupulous that although he could have rationalized that his camels would be eating the produce of land that had been promised to him, he still kept them muzzled to avoid even the *appearance* of robbery.]

Yafeh Toar observes in this context that the *Midrash* already noted [see *footnote* to 13:7 p. 460] that Abraham's cattle — in contrast with those of Lot — went out muzzled, but there *Ramban* offered no objection as he does here.

[Perhaps the reason *Ramban* appended his comment *here* and not *above* is because in our verse *Rashi* cites this as פְּשׁוּטוֹ שֶׁל מִקְרָא, *the simple meaning of Scripture;* and it is *Rashi's* view of this Midrashic interpretation as the *literal* meaning of וַיְפַתַּח with which *Ramban* disagrees.]

וַיִּתֵּן תֶּבֶן וּמִסְפּוֹא לַגְּמַלִּים וּמַיִם לִרְחֹץ רַגְלָיו — *[And] he gave straw and feed for the camels, and water to bathe his* [Eliezer's] *feet.*

The subject here, too, is Laban, who provided feed for the animals and water for Eliezer. It would be unlikely that Eliezer himself would fetch water for his own feet and that of his men *(Ramban;* see above).

First, he gave feed to the animals and only *afterwards* was food set before the guests [*v.* 33], for one must not partake of food until he has fed his animals, for it is written [*Deut.* 11:15]: 'I will give grass in your fields *for your cattle',* and after that: *'you shall eat* and be satisfied' *(Midrash HaGadol* [see *footnote* to end of *v.14*]*).*

Laban had heard that it was the practice in Abraham's home to wash the feet of visitors to remove idolatry [see 18:4]. In a gesture of presumed piety, he offered them water for this purpose. In reality, however, he showed such concern only for idols that were not his and which he did not worship *(Pesikta).*

The *Midrash* comments: Rav Acha said, The washing of the feet of the slaves of the Patriarch's household is more beautiful to God then the Torah [laws or discourses] of their children. For the Torah even finds it necessary to relate how they washed their feet, whereas the uncleanness of a reptile is an integral teaching of the Torah, yet we know that its blood causes defilement, as does its flesh, only from exegetical extensions and deductions. [Cf. prefatory *comm.* to *v.* 34-39 and *Overview*].

הָאֲנָשִׁים אֲשֶׁר אִתּוֹ — *Of the men who were with him.*

This is the first time that the Torah *explicitly mentions* that Eliezer was accompanied by others, although it is alluded to several times above. As noted in the *comm.* to *v.* 14, it has been suggested that while he tested Rebecca's character at the well, he had asked the men to remain out of sight *(Akeidas Yitzchak)* [but cf. *Rashi* to *v.*44]. *Midrash HaGadol* suggests that they accompanied him to attest to

לג °וַיִּישֶׂם לְפָנָיו לֶאֱכֹל וַיֹּאמֶר לֹא אֹכַל עַד
לד אִם־דִּבַּרְתִּי דְּבָרָי וַיֹּאמֶר דַּבֵּר: וַיֹּאמַר
לה עֶבֶד אַבְרָהָם אָנֹכִי: וַיהוָה בֵּרַךְ אֶת־אֲדֹנִי

°וַיּוּשַׂם ק׳

his power of attorney to negotiate on Abraham's behalf, and to keep watch over him on his return journey with Rebecca.

33. וַיּוּשַׂם לְפָנָיו לֶאֱכֹל — *Food was set before him* [lit. *and it was placed before him to eat*].

[Only *after* the animals had been provided for (see *Midrash HaGadol* above).]

The *ksiv,* traditional spelling, is וַיִּישֶׂם, the passive of the *kal,* as in 50:26: וַיִּישֶׂם בָּאָרוֹן, *and he was placed* [gently] in a coffin, the root being ישם. The *kri,* traditional *reading,* is וַיּוּשַׂם, in the *pu'al* [passive of the more intensive *pi'el*], the meaning being that the food *was placed* [with a sense of urgency] by the servants of the household *(Ibn Ezra; Radak).*

The *Midrashim* record a tradition that they placed a deadly poison before Eliezer [ויישם being homiletically suggestive of וַי סַם, *woe, poison! (Midrash HaGadol).* Or, according to *Baal HaTurim,* since the only other time וַיִּישֶׂם appears in Scripture (50:26), it refers to *placing in a coffin,* therefore, here too, where it appears as the *ksiv,* it also connotes an association with death and suggests that they wanted to kill Eliezer.] In Abraham's merit, however, the dish was changed: *Bethuel* ate of it and died later that evening. [Cf. *comm.* to *v.* 55.]

וַיֹּאמֶר לֹא אֹכַל עַד אִם־דִּבַּרְתִּי דְּבָרָי — *But* [lit. *and*] *he said, 'I will not eat until I have spoken my piece'* [lit. *until that I have spoken my words*].[1]

— The mission has thus far been successful: Divine Providence led Eliezer on the right path to the home of Abraham's relatives, and to the girl who, by the test of her character, proved to be worthy of marriage to Isaac. However, there was one obstacle still left — the doubt Eliezer had expressed earlier to Abraham: Perhaps the girl would not consent to follow him to Canaan. He therefore was resolved to complete his task; he would not eat until the matter was settled beyond a doubt *(Rashbam; Tz'ror HaMor; Malbim).*

[Other reasons for his refusal to eat are implicit in his statement in the next verse: *I am Abraham's servant.* See *comm.* there.]

Rashi explains that עַד אִם is idiomatically equivalent to עַד אֲשֶׁר *until that,* as well as being synonymous with עַד כִּי as in 49:10 עַד־כִּי יָבוֹא שִׁילֹה [*until Shiloh shall come*], אִם [Aramaic: אִי] being one of the four meanings ascribed to the word כִּי in *Rosh Hashanah* 3a (see *footnote* to 18:15). [That כִּי also means אֲשֶׁר, *that,* — a meaning which is not among the four listed in *Rosh Hashanah ibid.* — is only because both are equivalent to אִם, and is not to be construed as a *fifth* meaning of the word *(Mizrachi).*]

וַיֹּאמֶר דַּבֵּר — *And he said, 'Speak'.*

[It is not clear who the speaker is:] Laban or Bethuel [see *v.* 50] *(Radak).*

1. An interesting *halachah* is drawn from this verse:

If food is placed before a guest he may interpret it as an implicit invitation to eat without being specifically *invited* to do so, for, as we see, Eliezer declined to eat although he was not specifically invited to do so; since food was set before him, a *verbal invitation* was unnecessary *(Magen Avraham, Orach Chaim* 170:18).

24
33-34 *who were with him.* [33] *Food was set before him, but*
he said, 'I will not eat until I have spoken my piece.'
And he said, 'Speak.'
[34] *Then he said, 'A servant of Abraham am I.*

34-39. The Recapitulation.

Prefatory Comment

Radak emphasizes that Eliezer repeated the whole story in order to convince them that God willed this marriage, thus delicately hinting that their refusal would not hinder it.

[However, the Torah — which contains not even a *single letter* without a purpose — now proceeds to *record at length* Eliezer's recapitulation of the events which led him to Bethuel's house, when in reality, the Torah could merely have stated: *And Eliezer related to them these things,* etc.]

That the narrative was repeated in such detail led the Sages in the *Midrash* to exclaim: יָפָה שִׂיחָתָן שֶׁל עַבְדֵי אָבוֹת לִפְנֵי הַמָּקוֹם מִתּוֹרָתָן שֶׁל בְּנֵיהֶם, *The ordinary conversation of the Patriarchs' servants is more pleasing* [lit. beautiful] *before God than even the Torah* [i.e., religious discourses] *of their children,* for the chapter of Eliezer [the account of his journey] is repeated in the Torah, whereas many important principles of the Torah [גּוּפֵי תוֹרָה] are derived only from textual allusions [בִּרְמִיזָה]. [See *comm.* to *v.* 42]. From Eliezer's subtle changes in recounting the narrative, the expositors have perceived great ethical messages revealing his wisdom. These nuances will be treated in the *Overview* and commentary as they occur. [For a parallel representation of the two versions, see the Appendix at the end of this Sidra. See also the *Overview* and *comm.* to *v.* 42.]

Hoffman notes that it is common for the Torah to repeat a *halachic* or narrative passage בִּשְׁבִיל דָּבָר שֶׁנִּתְחַדֵּשׁ בָּהּ, because of a substantive detail which is added in the second version (*Sotah* 3a). As we shall note, Eliezer's repetition contains several such instructive additions and nuances.

34. עֶבֶד אַבְרָהָם אָנֹכִי — *A servant of Abraham am I.*

— This shows Eliezer's modesty. He does not seek grandeur by representing himself as Abraham's associate or agent, nor does he claim that the wealth was his. He immediately introduces himself as Abraham's servant and thereby indicates that that is why he must carry out his master's mission, even before breaking bread *(Radak; Ralbag; Alshich).*[1]

Also implied in this statement is: 'As a member of Abraham's household who observes the laws of the Torah, I may eat only permissible foods.' Possibly they placed forbidden food before him, and he therefore explained his refusal to eat *(Minchah Belulah).*

1. The *Talmud* [*Bava Kamma* 92b] derives from Eliezer's statement the popular saying 'Be the first to tell whatever is degrading in you' [i.e., one should take the initiative and admit to his defect rather than wait for others to discover it and mention it first].

The *Zohar* applies to Eliezer the verse *a slave honors his master* [*Malachi* 1:6], for in spite of all the precious valuables he brought along with him by virtue of which he could have pretended to be whatever he desired, he made no pretentious claims but informed them he was merely Abraham's slave — his purpose being to enhance Abraham's stature, so they could judge the greatness of his master.

מְאֹד וַיִּגְדָּל וַיִּתֶּן־לוֹ צֹאן וּבָקָר וְכֶסֶף
וְזָהָב וַעֲבָדִם וּשְׁפָחֹת וּגְמַלִּים וַחֲמֹרִים׃
לו וַתֵּלֶד שָׂרָה אֵשֶׁת אֲדֹנִי בֵן לַאדֹנִי אַחֲרֵי
זִקְנָתָהּ וַיִּתֶּן־לוֹ אֶת־כָּל־אֲשֶׁר־לוֹ׃
לז וַיַּשְׁבִּעֵנִי אֲדֹנִי לֵאמֹר לֹא־תִקַּח אִשָּׁה
לִבְנִי מִבְּנוֹת הַכְּנַעֲנִי אֲשֶׁר אָנֹכִי יֹשֵׁב

35. With feeling and enthusiasm, Eliezer tells his hosts about Abraham's miracle-filled life. His words are a glorious summary of Abraham's life and accomplishments *(Da'as Soferim).*

וַה׳ בֵּרַךְ אֶת־אֲדֹנִי מְאֹד — *HASHEM has greatly blessed my master.*

— With everything that man treasures [see *v.* 1] *(Ha'amek Davar).*

And being so blessed everyone in our country would want to marry into his family; it is *he* who refuses, however *(Rashbam).*

[Do not consider it strange that he sent me so far to seek a bride for his son; it is not because there is something wrong with him, or because no one wishes to marry into his family].

In commencing the conversation by ascribing his master's wealth to HASHEM, Eliezer wanted to establish his master's faith in God in the hope that his listeners, too, would accept it. As evidenced by their immediate response to his story [*v.* 50]; they believed: *The matter stems from HASHEM! (Minchah Belulah).*

He also intimated thereby that his master's wealth came *from HASHEM* [i.e., through His abundant blessing], not from robbery or violence *(Lekach Tov).*

וַיִּגְדָּל — *And he prospered* [lit. *became great*].

Having acquired great fame among men *(Ha'amek Davar).*

Such is the way of the world:

When a man wishes to marry a girl, he tells her of his lineage and the lineage of his family, in order to endear himself and his family to her. Eliezer acted accordingly: First he spoke in praise of Abraham and then in the praise of Isaac *(Midrash HaGadol).*

וַיִּתֶּן־לוֹ צֹאן וּבָקָר ... — *He has given him sheep,* [and] *cattle ...*

My master's wealth consists not merely of contentment with his lot — such wealth being intangible and not bequeathable to heirs — but his wealth consists of tangible substance: sheep, cattle, etc. *(Ha'amek Davar).*

36. וַתֵּלֶד שָׂרָה אֵשֶׁת אֲדֹנִי בֵן לַאדֹנִי אַחֲרֵי זִקְנָתָהּ — *Sarah, my master's wife, bore my master a son after she had grown old.*

— And therefore he was especially dear to them since birth *(Sforno).*

In mentioning that Sarah gave birth to Isaac *after she had grown old,* Eliezer was anticipating a possi-

[35] HASHEM has greatly blessed my master, and he
prospered. He has given him sheep, cattle, silver and
gold, servants and maid-servants, camels and
donkeys. [36] Sarah, my master's wife, bore my master
a son after she had grown old, and he gave him all
that he possesses. [37] And my master made me take an
oath saying, "Do not take a wife for my son from the
daughters of the Canaanites in whose land I dwell.

ble objection on their part: 'How can you expect to pair a *son* of Abraham with a *granddaughter* of Abraham's brother Nachor? This son must be an old man!' Therefore, Eliezer informed them that Isaac was born only after Sarah was old, and he was still relatively young. [He was forty years old at the time.] *(Ha'amek Davar).*

— And since God performed a miracle, allowing Sarah to give birth to him at the age of ninety, you can be certain that he is a perfect young man, for God would not perform such a miracle for the sake of an ordinary son *(Alshich).*

וַיִּתֶּן־לוֹ אֶת־כָּל־אֲשֶׁר־לוֹ — *And he* [i.e., *my master*] *gave him all that he possesses.*

— He will not have to share the inheritance with his brother *(Rashbam).*

Thus, if you wish to marry your daughter to a wealthy man, be assured that he has been given all his father's wealth *(Alshich).*

And to substantiate this, Eliezer showed them the deed of gift *(Rashi).* [See on *v.* 10].

37. וַיַּשְׁבִּעֵנִי אֲדֹנִי — [*And*] *my master made me take an oath ...*

I am here only because my master made me take such an oath since *he* rejects the girls in my country, and not because there is a shortage of women there *(Radak; Sforno).*

Thus, Eliezer proceeds to explain in further detail why he would not eat until he had spoken his piece. *He was under the heavy burden of a sacred oath* administered by his master and could therefore not waver from his mission until he had fulfilled the obligations imposed upon him *(Akeidas Yitzchak).*

לֹא תִקַּח אִשָּׁה לִבְנִי מִבְּנוֹת הַכְּנַעֲנִי — *Do not take a wife for my son from the daughters of the Canaanites.*

Unless [as *v.* 38 continues] you first go *to my father's house and to my family,* and the woman you choose there refuses to follow you *(Rashi).*

[This follows *Rashi's* comment on *v.* 8 where he explains that if the woman Eliezer selected would not wish to follow him, he may marry Isaac to a daughter of Aner, Eshkol, or Mamre. But cf. *Ramban* there, and *comm.* to *v.* 49].

אֲשֶׁר אָנֹכִי יֹשֵׁב בְּאַרְצוֹ — *In whose land I dwell.*

— 'Living in their land, I know their ways and morals.' Abraham in *v.* 3, had actually said **אֲשֶׁר אָנֹכִי יֹשֵׁב בְּקִרְבּוֹ** [lit. in whose *midst* I dwell]. But Eliezer, with great

לח בְּאַרְצוֹ: אִם־לֹא אֶל־בֵּית־אָבִי תֵּלֵךְ וְאֶל־
לט מִשְׁפַּחְתִּי וְלָקַחְתָּ אִשָּׁה לִבְנִי: וָאֹמַר אֶל־
מ אֲדֹנִי אֻלַי לֹא־תֵלֵךְ הָאִשָּׁה אַחֲרָי: וַיֹּאמֶר

delicacy, changed *in whose midst* to *in whose land.* They would have found Abraham's choice of words offensive, it would have suggested that he had a tendency to be critical of those around him; had he lived among his relatives, he might have been equally critical of their ways. [However, the *land* of Canaan was notorious for the prevalence of immorality.] *(Hirsch* to *v.* 3).

Or, as *HaKsav V'haKaballah* suggests: Abraham did not say *in whose land* and ascribe ownership of the land to the Canaanites since he was confident of God's promise that the land had been given him, and would one day be his, whereas Eliezer, in conversing with people of lesser faith, delicately alluded only to the present.

38. אִם לֹא אֶל בֵּית־אָבִי תֵּלֵךְ — *Unless you go to my father's house.*

[The Translation follows the implication of *Rashi* in *v.* 37 in viewing this verse as the condition of the previous verse — i.e., that he is not to take a Canaanite wife *unless he first attempts* to take a wife from Abraham's family.]

וְאֶל מִשְׁפַּחְתִּי — *And to my family.*

Abraham's instructions to Eliezer put less emphasis on his family than on his country: he did not say *to my father's house and to my family* but *to my land and kindred* (מוֹלַדְתִּי) [*v.* 4; see *comm.* there]. But since Abraham disapproved of his country, he might have indeed meant his actual family. Or perhaps the servant subtly changed Abraham's words [intimating that Abraham had specifically directed Eliezer to go to *his family*] in order to honor them so they would be more receptive *(Ramban* to *v.* 4).

The word מִשְׁפָּחָה, *family* — cognate to the root ספח, *attach* — denotes an intimate, close familial relationship. Since Abraham had departed from his family at God's command, and they remained idolatrous, Abraham did not maintain a close familial tie with them. Therefore, reflecting his true feelings, he referred them in his charge to Eliezer by the less intimate term: *my kindred.* Eliezer — trusted servant that he was — did not wish to convey Abraham's distant feelings to them, and therefore tactfully substituted the endearing term *family (HaKsav V'haKaballah).*

Akeidas Yitzchak explains that Eliezer, on his own initiative, added to Abraham's original testament the qualification of *father's house* in order to take advantage of the wonderful opportunity that had come his way in the girl's *happening* to belong to Abraham's immediate family. He took it for granted that Abraham's prohibition of Canaanite girls had been prompted by a wish to be reunited with his own family and father's house. For this reason he consistently substituted the words *family* and *father's house* for the wording of his master: *my land and kindred.*

24
38-39

[38] *Unless you go to my father's house and to my family and take a wife for my son."* [39] *And I said to my master, "Perhaps the woman will not follow*

39. אֻלַי לֹא־תֵלֵךְ הָאִשָּׁה אַחֲרָי — *Perhaps the woman will not follow me?*

[When Eliezer discussed with Abraham the possibility that the appropriate woman would not return to Canaan with him, he said אוּלַי לֹא **תֹאבֶה** הָאִשָּׁה, *perhaps the woman will not 'wish'* ... implying that her *willingness* would be the crucial factor. Here, however, he omitted any such reference, saying merely that she will—in fact—*not follow*. Originally, Eliezer envisioned only that the *woman* — of her own volition — might refuse to go to Canaan. Now, however, that he saw that Rebecca had not such objections, Eliezer realized that her *family* might hinder her. He therefore makes it clear to them that even if the woman will, *in fact,* not follow me *through no ill-will of her own, but because of family hindrance,* Abraham's oath would be nullified and Isaac would be forced to seek a wife from among the Canaanites. Eliezer alludes to this in *v.* 41 when he states: *and if they will not give her to you,* making the mission dependent on *their* consent, rather than, as Abraham had said (*v.* 8) on the *girl's* consent (as *Ha'amek Davar* explains there).]

Or, as *Harav David Feinstein* suggests, once Eliezer devised his elaborate test of character to determine Isaac's destined bride, it was inconceivable that a woman of such noble qualities should decline *of her own volition* to accompany him; only external factors could cause her not to follow him.

Rashi [following the *Midrash*] notes that אוּלַי, *perhaps,* is written here אֻלַי, which, since the Torah is not punctuated, could be read as אֵלַי, *to me.* Eliezer had a daughter whom he was anxious to marry off to Isaac, and for whom he was hopeful that Abraham would approach him. [*Rashi* would accordingly suggest that the verse be rendered: 'אֵלַי, *to me* (i.e., you may yet come *to me,* Abraham, for I hope that) לֹא תֵלֵךְ הָאִשָּׁה אַחֲרָי, *the woman* (I select in Charan) *will not want to follow me.'* But Abraham answered: 'My son is blessed [22:18] and you are accursed [9:25]; the accursed cannot unite with the blessed.' [Cf. *comm.* of *Or HaChaim* cited to *v.*3.] [1]

See *Hasav V'haKaballah* cited to 27:12 who explains the difference between אוּלַי, *perhaps,* and פֶּן, *lest.* The former implies a hope that the event *will* occur, while the latter

1. *Rashi* himself comments in *v.* 8 that if the woman whom Eliezer selected refused to accompany him then the oath would be void and Eliezer would *be free to take a wife for Isaac from the daughters of Aner, Eshkol, and Mamre.* The latter were also Canaanites. Why, then, were they preferable to Eliezer?

Possibly because the curse of Canaan [9:25: *a slave of slaves shall he be to his brothers*] found its *full expression* in Eliezer *since he was actually a slave* while the others were free men, thus the full onus of the curse was not apparent on them.

Furthermore, it would be even more degrading to marry his son to the daughter of his own Canaanite slave *(Da'as Zekeinim).*

אֱלֹהֵי יְהוָֹה אֲשֶׁר־הִתְהַלַּכְתִּי לְפָנָיו יִשְׁלַח
מַלְאָכוֹ אִתָּךְ וְהִצְלִיחַ דַּרְכֶּךָ וְלָקַחְתָּ
מא אִשָּׁה לִבְנִי מִמִּשְׁפַּחְתִּי וּמִבֵּית אָבִי: אָז
תִּנָּקֶה מֵאָלָתִי כִּי תָבוֹא אֶל־מִשְׁפַּחְתִּי
וְאִם־לֹא יִתְּנוּ לָךְ וְהָיִיתָ נָקִי מֵאָלָתִי:

implies a fear that an *undesired event* will take place.

Eliezer inserted this implication as if to say: Do not think that no one wants to marry Isaac. I myself would gladly marry *my own daughter* to him! But I am only a slave, a descendant of the accursed Canaan and hence blemished, since, as my master tells me, the accursed and blessed cannot intermarry. Were I not blemished, I would certainly not have come so far to seek a bride for his son *(Alshich; Yafeh Toar).*

Why, then, is the word אוּלַי not spelled אֻלַי in *v.* 5 to suggest the *Midrashic* allusion cited by *Rashi*? Perhaps it is because Eliezer — knowing that he was of the accursed Canaanites — could not *then* presume to think of marrying into Abraham's family. Now, however, that he was called *blessed one* [*v.* 31], he entertained such a notion as subtly alluded to here *(Tur).*

Several other answers are offered to the question of why the defective spelling with its implication is not used earlier. A few of them are as follows:

— Had the spelling אֻלַי, *to me,* been used earlier, it would have implied that Eliezer feared that her refusal to go might have been an objection to *him* personally: it might be beneath her to travel with a servant. In relating the event to Rebecca's family, however,he implied a warning that they should not make unfair demands as a condition of their consent; Eliezer's daughter was an eminently acceptable alternative choice *(K'li Yakar).*

— When Eliezer put the question to Abraham, he followed by asking whether he should bring Isaac to Charan if necessary. Thus, the context indicates that the question was meant seriously rather than as a subterfuge to inject his daughter into consideration. Here, however, his personal desire is implied *(Terumas HaDeshen).*

— In the holy presence of Abraham, Eliezer did not think of his personal interests. It was only after he left the Patriarch that he considered his ambitions for his daughter *(Sfas Emes).*

40. ה׳ אֲשֶׁר הִתְהַלַּכְתִּי לְפָנָיו — *HASHEM before Whom I have walked.*

[I.e., *before Whom* Abraham could walk alone unsupported — so strong was his righteousness. Noah, by contrast, is described as walking *with* God (6:9), in the sense that as *Rashi* explains there, Noah needed God's support to maintain his righteousness].

But Abraham added [*verse* 7]: 'HASHEM, God of heaven *Who took me from the house of my father and from the land of my birth....*

Eliezer omitted mention of God's command that Abraham withdraw from his family lest his relatives take offense that he purposely disassociated himself from them *(HaKsav V'haKaballah).*[1]

24
40-41

me?"[40] *He replied to me, "HASHEM, before Whom I*
have walked, will send His angel with you and make
your journey successful, and you will take a wife for
my son from my family and my father's house.
[41] *Then will you be absolved from my oath when you*
have come to my family; and if they will not give her
to you, then, you shall be absolved from my oath."

וְהִצְלִיחַ דַּרְכֶּךָ — *And make your journey successful.*

But Abraham said only that the angel's guidance would result in Eliezer's successful finding of a wife [*v.* 7]. Abraham was concerned with the end result of the mission and pronounced that the angel would help achieve this goal. In Eliezer's humble reverence for his master, however, he added that Abraham's blessing extended to all aspects of the journey. — Every step of the way succeeded thanks to Abraham's blessing *(HaKsav V'haKaballah).*

מִמִּשְׁפַּחְתִּי וּמִבֵּית אָבִי — *From my family and my father's house.*

[Emphasizing again Eliezer's delicate rewording of his master's more general command, as explained in *v.* 38].

— As if to suggest: It is not enough that she be simply *kindred* — she must be specifically *of my father's house (Ha'amek Davar).*

41. אָז תִּנָּקֶה מֵאָלָתִי כִּי תָבוֹא אֶל מִשְׁפַּחְתִּי — *Then will you be absolved* [lit. *cleansed* (i.e., *cleared*)] *from my oath when you have come to my family.*

[I.e., only then will you be absolved from my oath — when you have come to my family] ...

Eliezer did not use Abraham's term שְׁבוּעָה for *oath,* [see *v.* 8] but substituted the stronger term אָלָה which signifies an *oath reinforced by a curse.* He used this stronger term to impress them with the seriousness of Abraham's intention *(Ibn Ezra; Karnei Or; Baal HaTurim).*

Here he did not specify *my father's house* but, more generally, *my family* because, in effect, he would not be absolved from the oath unless he exhausted every possibility within the family. If Eliezer failed in Abraham's *father's house,* he still had to go to the *maternal* part of the family *(Baal HaTurim).*

וְאִם לֹא יִתְּנוּ לָךְ וְהָיִיתָ נָקִי מֵאָלָתִי — *And if they will not give* [*her*] *to you, then you shall be absolved from my oath.*

[... I.e., and if, after you come to my family, they refuse to give her to

1. Cf. *Midrash* quoted in *Torah Sheleimah* 24:157:

Why did Eliezer misquote Abraham who had actually said *HASHEM ... Who took me from my father's house*? He acted wisely, to refrain from reminding them of what had happened to Haran [Abraham's brother, who was cast into the furnaces in Kasdim after Abraham was miraculously delivered; see *Rashi* to 11:28], as it is written [*Prov.* 10:12]: *Hatred stirs up strifes.* Eliezer, however, had come to inspire them with *love* for Abraham, and one may misquote for the sake of peace.

מב וָאָבֹא הַיּוֹם אֶל־הָעָיִן וָאֹמַר יהוה אֱלֹהֵי
אֲדֹנִי אַבְרָהָם אִם־יֶשְׁךָ־נָּא מַצְלִיחַ דַּרְכִּי
מג אֲשֶׁר אָנֹכִי הֹלֵךְ עָלֶיהָ: הִנֵּה אָנֹכִי נִצָּב
עַל־עֵין הַמָּיִם וְהָיָה הָעַלְמָה הַיֹּצֵאת
לִשְׁאֹב וְאָמַרְתִּי אֵלֶיהָ הַשְׁקִינִי־נָא מְעַט־

you, only then will you be absolved from my oath.]

The clause: *you will be absolved from my oath* is repeated because of the dual nature of the oath that Eliezer go to the family, and that he not take a Canaanite woman [as explained by *Ramban* in *v.* 8]: *When you come to my family* you will have fulfilled the first part of my oath — my family; *and if they will not give her to you,* then you will be absolved from the second part of the oath; for in such a case you may indeed take a Canaanite wife [as *Rashi* explains in *v.* 8, but with which *Ramban* disagrees] *(Malbim).*

Eliezer immediately added that although Abraham had complete faith that God would make the mission successful, he was nevertheless prepared for the possibility that his wish would not materialize and the family would not cooperate. Eliezer emphasized this so that they would not miscalculate and believe that his promise to Abraham compelled him to bring back a bride *at any price,* with the result that he was completely dependent upon them *(Avraham ben HaRambam).*

Ha'amek Davar suggests that Eliezer judged it more tactful to make the mission dependent on *their* consent hence his remark: *if they will not* give her to you although Abraham [*v.*8] had specifically made it dependent on the *girl*'s consent.

Furthermore, he avoided an expression of Abraham's absolute distaste for his family's domicile by omitting the insinuation implied in Abraham's admonition in *v.* 6 not to return Isaac to that land *(Abarbanel).*

42. וָאָבֹא הַיּוֹם אֶל־הָעָיִן — *I came today to the spring.*

Today I left [i.e., commenced my journey] and *today* I arrived. The road contracted for him (קָפְצָה לוֹ הַדֶּרֶךְ) — [and in only three hours, he found that he had miraculously completed what would ordinarily be a seventeen-day journey *(Pirkei d'Rabbi Eliezer).*] *(Rashi).*

[See *footnote* to *v.* 45 s.v. וַתֵּרֶד הָעַיְנָה as to why Eliezer mentioned this miracle while intentionally omitting others.]

Rashi continues, citing the *Midrash*: Rav Acha said, The ordinary conversation of the Patriarchs' servants is more pleasing to God than even the Torah (discourse) of their children, for the chapter of Eliezer is repeated in detail in the Torah whereas many important laws are derived only from slight textual allusions. (See Prefatory Comment to *v.* 34, and *Overview).*

According to *Rashbam*, Eliezer's purpose in repeating all of this was to impress upon them that it was all

[42] 'I came today to the spring and said, "HASHEM
God of my master Abraham. If You would graciously
make successful the way on which I go — [43] Behold, I
am standing by the spring of water. Let it be that the
young woman who comes out to draw and to whom I
shall say, 'Please give me some water to drink from

divinely decreed, and, as *Radak* concludes, since Providence willed this marriage, even their refusal would not hinder it. [See their response in *v.* 50.]

Hirsch adds that all of Eliezer's variations can be based either on consideration of politeness, or to make the narrative more plausible to his hosts whom he seems to have understood perfectly ... Therefore, Eliezer sharply stressed the striking evidence which even a Laban would be loath to oppose.

וָאֹמַר ה׳ אֱלֹהֵי אֲדֹנִי אַבְרָהָם — *And* [*I*] *said: 'HASHEM God of my master Abraham.'*

[See *Ha'amek Davar* on *v.* 27].

אִם יֶשְׁךָ־נָּא מַצְלִיחַ דַּרְכִּי ... — *If You would graciously make successful the way on which I go* [*lit. if You have it* (i.e., intend to) *please, making successful my way on which I go*].

[The word יֶשְׁךָ, *you have,* meaning *you intend,* occurs again in *v.* 49 in the plural יֶשְׁכֶם. It appears to be idiomatic, implying: *if you have it* within you to do something. Cf. 23:8 אִם יֵשׁ אֶת נַפְשְׁכֶם, *if it is truly your will* [lit. *if there is had with your soul.*] The translation in our verse, following *Hirsch,* reflects the reverence of using this expression in addressing God.]

Hirsch notes that Eliezer omitted the הַקְרֵה נָא, *cause to happen,* of *v.* 12 and all his worry about the success of the enterprise. With some people it is dangerous to appear too emotional. They deride it as 'romantic', 'exaggerated', or they doubt its sincerity. They will be apt to doubt the feasibility of the project into which they are invited.

43. הָעַלְמָה הַיֹּצֵאת לִשְׁאֹב — *The young woman who comes* [lit. *goes*] *out to draw* [water].

In *v.* 16 Eliezer had used the word נַעֲרָה, *maiden.* Here he tactfully said עַלְמָה which denotes *a young woman in the vigor of her youth,* and carries a more discerning connotation than *maiden,* implying that he was being selective. Furthermore, that such a person would come to the well would be indicative of Divine Providence, since the more distinguished עֲלָמוֹת, *young women,* ordinarily left the menial task of drawing water to the poorer maidens *(Malbim).*

הַשְׁקִינִי־נָא מְעַט מַיִם מִכַּדֵּךְ — *Please give me some water to drink from your jug.*

[As pointed out in the *comm.* to *v.* 18, the Hebrew verb הַשְׁקָה has a more causitive, transitive sense than let me drink, just as הַאֲכִילִינִי would best be translated *feed me,* not *let me eat.* When referring to animals, this form would be translated as *watering.* The same sense is meant in our verse, but such a term is in-

מד מַיִם מִכַּדֵּךְ: וְאָמְרָה אֵלַי גַּם־אַתָּה שְׁתֵה
וְגַם לִגְמַלֶּיךָ אֶשְׁאָב הִוא הָאִשָּׁה אֲשֶׁר־
מה הֹכִיחַ יהוה לְבֶן־אֲדֹנִי: אֲנִי טֶרֶם אֲכַלֶּה
לְדַבֵּר אֶל־לִבִּי וְהִנֵּה רִבְקָה יֹצֵאת וְכַדָּהּ
עַל־שִׁכְמָהּ וַתֵּרֶד הָעַיְנָה וַתִּשְׁאָב וָאֹמַר
מו אֵלֶיהָ הַשְׁקִינִי נָא: וַתְּמַהֵר וַתּוֹרֶד כַּדָּהּ
מֵעָלֶיהָ וַתֹּאמֶר שְׁתֵה וְגַם־גְּמַלֶּיךָ אַשְׁקֶה

correct English usage when applied to humans.

In *v.* 14, Eliezer contemplated saying: *please tip over your jug so I may drink*; while he actually said: *please let me sip a little water from your jug (v.* 17). Here, in his recapitulation he changes it again.]

44. גַּם־אַתָּה שְׁתֵה — *You may also drink.*

The גַּם, *also,* suggests that Rebecca's offer included the men who accompanied him *(Rashi).*

[On גם denoting an exegetical amplification see *comm.* to 20:5 and *footnote* to 21:1.]

הִוא הָאִשָּׁה אֲשֶׁר הֹכִיחַ ה׳ לְבֶן אֲדֹנִי — *She shall be the woman* [or following *Ha'amek Davar* in *v.* 14: *Let her be the woman*] *whom HASHEM has designated for my master's son.*

— It must be so, for my master's household is generous; and if this woman is also generous then she must be the woman whom HASHEM has designated for my master's son, שֶׁאֵין מְזַוְוגִין לוֹ לְאָדָם אֶלָּא לְפִי מַעֲשָׂיו, *for a man is mated only according to his deeds (Lekach Tov).*

The translation of הֹכִיחַ again follows *Rashi,* who, as in *v.* 14, explains that it means *selected, designated. Rashi* adds here that this is the meaning the *hiph'il* form of the verb יכח throughout Scripture.

45. אֲנִי טֶרֶם אֲכַלֶּה לְדַבֵּר אֶל־לִבִּי — *I had not yet finished* [lit. *I, before I finished*] *meditating* [lit. *speaking to my heart.*]

He mentioned this to *further emphasize* that the Godly origin of the matter was demonstrated by the immediacy of the response to his prayers — coming as it did before he had even finished meditating *(Alshich; Sforno).*

Ramban to 27:41 explains that any decision which a person reaches after deliberation is referred to in Hebrew as *'speaking to the heart'* even if it is coupled with *actual speech.* He explains that in Eliezer's case speech was probably meant since *v.* 12 states: *And he 'said': HASHEM, God of my master Abraham* ... although it is possible that meditation is meant and the phrase אֲנִי טֶרֶם אֲכַלֶּה לְדַבֵּר אֶל לִבִּי means: *before I had concluded the thought in my mind.*

It is *Ramban*'s latter interpretation that is followed by the overwhelming majority of expositors, and which we incorporated into our Translation by rendering the phrase as *meditated.* [Cf. *HaKsav V'haKaballah*].

Or HaChaim notes that Eliezer stressed that he *meditated* so that no

24
44-46 *your jug,' [44] and who will answer, 'You may also*
drink and I will draw water for your camels, too,' —
she shall be the woman whom HASHEM has
designated for my master's son."
[45] 'I had not yet finished meditating when sudden-
ly Rebecca came out with a jug on her shoulder, and
descended to the spring and drew water. Then I said
to her, "Please give me a drink." [46] She hurried and
lowered her jug from her shoulder and said, "Drink,
and I will even water your camels." So I drank and

one might suspect that Rebecca accommodated him only because she overheard Eliezer's expressed wishes.

Rashi explains that the word אֲכַלֶּה is in future tense: *I will finish.* However, it is idiomatic in Hebrew to use future or even past tense to express an ongoing action. Thus the sense of the phrase is *before I was finishing* or, as we translate, *I had not yet finished.*

וְהִנֵּה רִבְקָה יֹצֵאת — *When suddenly* [lit. *and behold!*] *Rebecca came out* [lit. *was* (already) *going out*].

[The word וְהִנֵּה, *suddenly*, stresses the hand of God in her 'happening' to go out at that very moment. See *comm.* to *v.* 15].

That Eliezer knew Rebecca's name is not surprising. Either he overheard it in her house, or she mentioned it at the well, although the Torah did not record that part of the conversation *(Ramban).*

וַתֵּרֶד הָעַיְנָה וַתִּשְׁאָב — *And (she) descended to the spring and drew water.*

Eliezer portrayed her as *drawing* the water, and did not now mention the miracle of the water rising up to meet her [*v.* 16] because he thought that they would not believe in the miracle *(Ramban* to *v.* 17).[1]

46. **וַתֹּאמֶר שְׁתֵה** — *And (she) said, 'Drink'.*

She had actually said 'Drink, *my lord'*, [*v.* 18] but Eliezer modestly omits this appelation in his recapitulation *(R' Bachya).*

וְגַם גְּמַלֶּיךָ אַשְׁקֶה — *And I will even water your camels.*

Eliezer mentioned the response

1. If Eliezer hesitated to relate this miracle because they lacked belief, why did he not also refrain from relating that he arrived in Charan the same day he left Abraham, which was possible only because the road contracted for him [*v.*42].

Maharsha answers that Abraham had given him a deed of gift bequeathing all his possessions to Isaac as cited by *Rashi* on *v.*10. Further, in *v.* 36 s.v. וַיִּתֶּן לוֹ *Rashi* mentions that to substantiate this fact to Rebecca's family, Eliezer showed them the document.

The deed was certainly dated the day Eliezer departed. Had Eliezer not told them that the seventeen-day journey was miraculously accomplished on that one day, they would have suspected the veracity of the document with its apparently false date.

It may also be that Eliezer had no reason to avoid mentioning the first miracle since no one would hesitate to believe in miracles relating to Abraham or a servant carrying out his wish, but why would her idolatrous family believe that miracles could be associated with Rebecca?

מז וָאֵשְׁתְּ וְגַם הַגְּמַלִּים הִשְׁקָתָה: וָאֶשְׁאַל
אֹתָהּ וָאֹמַר בַּת־מִי אַתְּ וַתֹּאמֶר בַּת־
בְּתוּאֵל בֶּן־נָחוֹר אֲשֶׁר יָלְדָה־לּוֹ מִלְכָּה
וָאָשִׂם הַנֶּזֶם עַל־אַפָּהּ וְהַצְּמִידִים עַל־
מח יָדֶיהָ: וָאֶקֹּד וָאֶשְׁתַּחֲוֶה לַיהוָה וָאֲבָרֵךְ
אֶת־יהוה אֱלֹהֵי אֲדֹנִי אַבְרָהָם אֲשֶׁר
הִנְחַנִי בְּדֶרֶךְ אֱמֶת לָקַחַת אֶת־בַּת־אֲחִי
מט אֲדֹנִי לִבְנוֹ: וְעַתָּה אִם־יֶשְׁכֶם עֹשִׂים חֶסֶד

he *expected* [*v.* 14] rather than the response he actually got [*vs.* 18-19] since Rebecca in deed *waited until Eliezer had finished drinking* before she indicated she would water his camels as well. This is discussed in *Igros Moshe*; see *footnote* to *v.* 14.

47. וָאֶשְׁאַל אֹתָהּ ... וָאָשִׂם הַנֶּזֶם — *Then I questioned her ... and I placed the ring.*

Actually [according to *Rashi* in *v.* 22-23] Eliezer *first* gave her the gifts and *then* asked her identity. But here, he tactfully changed the order to *'I questioned her and I placed ...'* so that they should not catch him by his own words and say 'How did you give her [the gifts] before you knew who she was?' *(Rashi).*

Akeidas Yitzchak elaborates on *Rashi*'s explanation:

Eliezer had been emphasizing all along that he had come on a special mission to Abraham's family, for his master preferred them above all other people for his son. Had he said that he presented the ornaments to Rebecca before he even knew to which family she belonged, this would have contradicted his previous assertion, since a man will not give away valuables purposelessly; presumably, therefore, they were intended as marriage gifts to her, whoever she might have been. This is what *Rashi* meant when he stated that Eliezer was afraid they would catch him by his own words.

Eliezer was also anxious that in their trickery they not claim that the precious gifts were given her in payment for her services, and belonged to her father. Eliezer, therefore, insisted that he gave them after ascertaining that she was worthy to be Isaac's wife, and that he gave them as a bridal gift from her prospective groom. Accordingly her father had no legitimate claim to them *(Or HaChaim).*

[According to *Rashi*'s account of the true sequence of events in *v.* 23 Eliezer gave her the gifts — although he did not yet ask her identity — in full confidence that, in Abraham's merit, his quest had been successful. (See *Abarbanel*'s version of *Rashi* cited in *v.* 22). Following *Ramban*, however, Eliezer's account accurately reflected the sequence of events as they had actually occurred.]

The word וָאָשִׂם, *and I placed* [ordinarily spelled וָאָשִׂים], is spelled deficiently, to allude to the fact that it was a 'deficient' placing — he did not touch her skin; it is further the letter *yud* [=10] that is missing to suggest that he did not even touch one of her ten fingers *(Baal HaTurim).*

בַּת בְּתוּאֵל בֶּן נָחוֹר אֲשֶׁר יָלְדָה־לוֹ מִלְכָּה — *The daughter of Bethuel, son of Nachor, whom Milcah bore to him.*

She had actually described herself as [*v.* 25]: the daughter of

24 *she watered the camels also.* 47 *Then I questioned her*
47-49 *and said, "Whose daughter are you?" And she said,*
"The daughter of Bethuel, son of Nachor, whom
Milcah bore to him." And I placed the ring on her
nose and the bracelets on her arms. 48 *Then I bowed*
and prostrated myself to HASHEM *and blessed*
HASHEM, *God of my master Abraham, Who led me*
on a true path to take the daughter of my master's
brother for his son.
49 *'And now, if you intend to do kindness and*

Bethuel the son of *Milcah*, mentioning her father's *mother* first [see *comm.* there]. But the servant, observing proper etiquette, mentioned her father's *father*, Nachor. He added *whom Milcah bore to him* to acknowledge that Bethuel was the son of the wife [Milcah] and not of the concubine [Reumah] (*Ramban* to *v.* 15).

48. וָאֲבָרֵךְ אֶת ה׳ אֱלֹהֵי אֲדֹנִי אַבְרָהָם — *And [I] blessed* HASHEM *the God of my master Abraham.*

Eliezer related this to intimate his absolute conviction that she was indeed *the woman whom* HASHEM *had designated* and that he is merely seeking their consent to conclude the matter. He further wished to impress upon them that because of his conviction he *blessed* HASHEM, had there been any doubt, such a blessing would have been premature (*Ha'amek Davar*).

[On the appelation: *God of my master Abraham,* see on *v.* 27].

אֲשֶׁר הִנְחַנִי בְּדֶרֶךְ אֱמֶת — *Who led me on a true path.*

— I.e., *the way of truth,* upon which the words of HASHEM to do kindness to Abraham and his son were vindicated (*Rashbam*).

לָקַחַת אֶת־בַּת־אֲחִי אֲדֹנִי לִבְנוֹ — *To take the daughter of my master's brother for his son.*

[Rebecca was not a daughter, but a *grand*-daughter of Abraham's brother, Nachor. The word *brother* may refer to Bethuel, Abraham's nephew, for Lot, too, was called a *brother* (i.e., a close relative) in 14:16. Or the *brother* may indeed be Nachor because 'grandchildren are considered like children' (*Yevamos* 62b).]

In *v.* 27 Eliezer speaks of his master's *brothers* (plural), for there, not yet knowing who the bride would be, he was referring to the members of his master's family in general. Now that the choice was made, he refers to the girl more *specifically* in the singular: *my master's brother's daughter* (*Chizkuni*).

49. אִם יֶשְׁכֶם עֹשִׂים חֶסֶד וֶאֱמֶת אֶת־אֲדֹנִי — *If you intend* [lit. *if you have it (within you to;* see יֶשְׁךָ in *v.* 42)] *to do* [lit. *doing*] *kindness and truth* [lit. *to deal kindly and truly;* or: *deal with kindness and truth*] *with my master.*

חֶסֶד, *kindness*, denotes an action which one is not obligated to do,

וֶאֱמֶת אֶת־אֲדֹנִי הַגִּידוּ לִי וְאִם־לֹא הַגִּידוּ
נ לִי וְאֶפְנֶה עַל־יָמִין אוֹ עַל־שְׂמֹאל: וַיַּעַן
לָבָן וּבְתוּאֵל וַיֹּאמְרוּ מֵיְהוָה יָצָא הַדָּבָר
נא לֹא נוּכַל דַּבֵּר אֵלֶיךָ רַע אוֹ־טוֹב: הִנֵּה־

while אֱמֶת, *truth,* means to *fulfill* the promise of *kindness (Ibn Ezra).*

As *Ralbag* explains: *kindness* is goodness conferred voluntarily while *truth* is the fulfillment of an obligation. Thus, mercy conferred by God Himself after having promised to do so is called *truth* because it is in fulfillment of His promise. Therefore, Scripture says of God's gifts to Israel תִּתֵּן אֱמֶת לְיַעֲקֹב חֶסֶד לְאַבְרָהָם, *You give truth to Jacob, kindness to Abraham* [*Micah* 7:20]: the promise to Abraham was *kindness,* but its fulfillment to Jacob was *truth.*

Ibn Ezra explains that the word אֱמֶת, *truth,* is related to the root אמן, *trust, faith;* the root-letter נ grammatically dropping out in certain conjugations [thus, although the form should be אֲמֶנֶת, the נ drops out to form אֱמֶת, just as תֶּנֶת=תֵּת from the root נתן *(Yohel Or).*]

Radak explains similarly in *Sefer HaShorashim* [s.v. "אמן"]: 'truth' refers to the concept of trust and tradition which are outgrowths of אֱמוּנָה, *faith;* one with faith gives his trust and accepts the truth.

[Cf. חַסְדּוֹ וַאֲמִתּוֹ in *v.* 27].

The connotation here is: *Truth* refers to the honor you are obligated to show to members of your family — especially to one so notable as Abraham — by honoring his request for your daughter's hand in marriage to her son; the *kindness* will be shown by your permission to allow her to go to a distant country *(Radak).*

According to *Sforno*: If you will do my master the *kindness* of yielding to his wishes, in sending your daughter so far away, and simultaneously *do truth,* by having *her* true interest in mind ....

The *truth* is that it is obviously God's Will; the *kindness* is that you comply with His will by consenting to her accompanying me — a slave — and not insisting that Isaac himself come and fetch her *(Malbim).*

הַגִּידוּ לִי — *Tell me.*

[I.e., make your intentions clear].

וְאִם לֹא הַגִּידוּ לִי וְאֶפְנֶה ... — *And if not* [i.e., *if such is not your intention, then*] *tell me,* [i.e., advise me of that] *and I will turn* [lit. *face*] ...

I.e., you must tell me immediately, for the burden of the oath weighs heavily upon me to accomplish my mission speedily *(Abarbanel).*

וְאֶפְנֶה עַל יָמִין אוֹ עַל שְׂמֹאל — *And I will turn* [lit. *face*] *to the right or to the left* [lit. *upon right or upon left*].

— *To the right* refers to the daughters of Ishmael [who lived in the Wilderness of Paran in the south (=right; since the orientation of Biblical direction faces east)], *to the left* refers to the daughters of Lot who lived to the left (=north) of Abraham [see 13:9] *(Rashi).*

Rashi in *v.*8 interprets that if the woman would not accompany Eliezer, then he could marry Isaac to one of the daughters of the Canaanites, Aner, Eshkol, and Mamre. Why did *Rashi* not say there as he does here that the next best alternative would be the

24
50

truth with my master, tell me; and if not, tell me, and
I will turn to the right or to the left.'
50 *Then Laban and Bethuel answered, 'The matter*
stems from HASHEM.' We can say to you neither

daughters of Ishmael or Lot? *Mizrachi* raises this difficulty in *v.*8 and leaves the question unanswered.

According to *Rashbam*, this expression refers merely to the other members of the family.

Or: I will seek other avenues — either by a straight or circumspect route *(Ha'amek Davar).*

He did not, however, say that he would return *to Canaan*, since [according to *Ramban*] he was still not freed from the oath against taking a Canaanite wife for Isaac *(Ramban* to *v.* 8).

50. The matter stems from HASHEM!

There is no better evidence of Eliezer's success in having sensitively and discreetly carried out his mission, than the response his persuasive eloquence elicits: *'The matter stems from HASHEM!'*

וַיַּעַן לָבָן וּבְתוּאֵל — *Then* [lit. *and*] *Laban and Bethuel answered.*

Laban was a wicked person and, in his great impudence, he hastened to answer before his father *(Rashi).*

Radak suggests that Bethuel was infirm, and the household was, in effect, run by Laban. Therefore he spoke first.

מֵה׳ יָצָא הַדָּבָר — *The matter stems from HASHEM* [lit. *from HASHEM has the matter* (or: *word) gone forth*].

[Everything, as you say, has been preordained from Above ...][1]

The *Midrash* asks: From *when did it stem* [i.e., when did God decree this and how did these heathens come to acknowledge it]? Rabbi Yehoshua ben Nechemiah quoting Rav Chaninah ben Yitzchak said: It stemmed from Mount Moriah [i.e., it was preordained at Mt. Moriah when, as he was descending with Isaac after the *Akeidah*, Abraham was informed of Rebecca's birth (22:20-23)]. The Rabbis stated [that Rebecca's family became convinced as a result of *this incident* that the marriage was Divinely ordained, as in their statement *(v.* 51)]: *let her be a wife to your master's son as HASHEM has spoken* [i.e., the entire narrative of how Eliezer was led to Rebecca — which was a continuous story illustrating God's Providence — convinced them that it was divinely decreed].

לֹא נוּכַל דַּבֵּר אֵלֶיךָ רַע אוֹ־טוֹב — *We can say to you neither bad nor good.*

I.e., we cannot refuse this proposition flatly with *bad* (i.e., with a *bad* reason), or, with *good* (i.e., with a reasoned reply), for it is evident that the matter stems from

1. We learn from the Torah, the Prophets, and the Writings that a woman is destined for a man by God.

From the Torah — from our verse [for although it was spoken by Laban and Bethuel, the very fact that the Torah records it, gives it credence *(Rashba* to *v.* 31];

From the Prophets — *But his* [Samson's] *father and his mother knew not that it was of HASHEM* [*Judges* 14:4];

From the Writings — *House and riches are the inheritance of fathers; but a prudent wife is of HASHEM* [*Prov.* 19:14] (Moed Katan 18b).

Cf. *Sotah* 2a: 'Forty days before the formation of a child a Heavenly Voice issues forth and proclaims: The daughter of So-and-so shall marry So-and-so.'

רִבְקָה לְפָנֶיךָ קַח וָלֵךְ וּתְהִי אִשָּׁה לְבֶן־
נב אֲדֹנֶיךָ כַּאֲשֶׁר דִּבֶּר יהוה: וַיְהִי כַּאֲשֶׁר
שָׁמַע עֶבֶד אַבְרָהָם אֶת־דִּבְרֵיהֶם וַיִּשְׁתַּחוּ
°חמישי נג אַרְצָה לַיהוה: °וַיּוֹצֵא הָעֶבֶד כְּלֵי־כֶסֶף
וּכְלֵי זָהָב וּבְגָדִים וַיִּתֵּן לְרִבְקָה וּמִגְדָּנֹת
נד נָתַן לְאָחִיהָ וּלְאִמָּהּ: וַיֹּאכְלוּ וַיִּשְׁתּוּ הוּא
וְהָאֲנָשִׁים אֲשֶׁר־עִמּוֹ וַיָּלִינוּ וַיָּקוּמוּ בַבֹּקֶר

HASHEM since, according to your account He brought her to you *(Rashi).*

We cannot say anything to you, bad, i.e., to annul the decree; *or even good,* i.e., to confirm it, for it does not depend upon our confirmation *(Sforno).*

It might be possible to dispute your proof or even to doubt if you are telling the truth concerning your alleged request for an omen. Nevertheless, we cannot deny that we have never before sent Rebecca to do the menial task of drawing water. Today she went and met you; in itself this shows that God decreed the episode *(Maharit).*

R' Bachya observes that Laban's character and natural tendencies are reflected in the precedence he gave to the mention of 'bad.'

51. הִנֵּה רִבְקָה לְפָנֶיךָ קַח וָלֵךְ — *Here* [lit. *behold*], *Rebecca is before you; take* [her] *and go.*

— Even without our permission *(Sforno).*

[The expression קַח וָלֵךְ, *take her and go* has harsh overtones reminiscent of Pharoah's statement to Abraham in 12:19].

[According to *Rashi,* (but not *Rashbam* or *Radak*), it would appear that this reflected only familial consent *in principle* to the match; the *final* consent, however, would have to come from Rebecca herself. See bracketed comment *v.*58, s.v. הֲתֵלְכִי.]

כַּאֲשֶׁר דִּבֶּר ה׳ — *As HASHEM has spoken.*

I.e., as HASHEM has clearly *decreed* or *preordained.* Thus no specific text need be cited as a source for God having *spoken* these words; it is His Providential Will [as It manifests Itself in man's everyday activities] that is here referred to *(Ramban* to a similar phrase in *Lev.* 10:3).

— But surely they, as idolators, did not believe in HASHEM? — They meant: As you and your master Abraham believe HASHEM has spoken *(Midrash Mayan Ganim* cited in *Torah Sheleimah* 24:178).

52. כַּאֲשֶׁר שָׁמַע עֶבֶד אַבְרָהָם אֶת דִּבְרֵיהֶם — *When Abraham's servant heard their words.*

This is the only time in the entire chapter when he is given the title *Abraham's servant.* Having accomplished his mission in total obedience to Abraham's wishes, he feels entitled to such an honored designation *(Hirsch).*

וַיִּשְׁתַּחוּ אַרְצָה לַה׳ — [*And*] *he prostrated himself to the ground unto HASHEM.*

— In gratitude and joy *(Ha'amek Davar).*

24 *bad nor good.* 51 *Here, Rebecca is before you; take*
51-54 *her and go, and let her be a wife to your master's son*
as HASHEM has spoken.'
52 *And it was, when Abraham's servant heard their*
words, he prostrated himelf to the ground unto
HASHEM. 53 *The servant brought out objects of silver*
and gold, and garments, and gave them to Rebecca.
And delicious fruits he gave to her brother and
mother. 54 *They ate and drank, he and the men who*

[See *comm.* to 23:7, and 24:26]. From this we see that one must render thanks to God on receiving good tidings *(Rashi).*

53. וַיִּתֵּן לְרִבְקָה — *And gave* [them] *to Rebecca.*

— For the purpose of betrothal [לְשֵׁם קִדּוּשִׁין] to Isaac. The *first presents* at the well were only gifts since one does not betroth without arranging for consent; that having been done, Eliezer acted as Isaac's agent to betroth her. [cf. *Kiddushin* 12b: *Rav flogged those who betrothed without proper arrangements* רַב מַנְגִּיד עַל הַמְקַדֵּשׁ בְּלֹא מְשַׁדְּכִין] *(Lekach Tov).*

[Cf. *Or HaChaim* cited to *v.* 47].

וּמִגְדָּנֹת — *And delicious fruits.*

The rendering *delicious fruits* follows *Rashi* who relates the word to מְגָדִים [see *Song of Songs* 7:14], and comments that Eliezer had brought various fine fruits from *Eretz Yisrael* which he now gave them.

Ibn Ezra renders likewise but suggests as an alternative, that the root is גדן and the word מִגְדָנִים may refer to *precious garments.*

Ibn Janach suggests that the word refers to *precious gifts* in general and the exact meaning depends on the context. [See, for example, *Ezra* 1:6 where *Metzudas Zion* renders similarly].

נָתַן לְאָחִיהָ וּלְאִמָּהּ — *He gave to her brother and* [to her] *mother.*

Hoffman suggests that the father did not accept gifts because he considered it beneath his dignity to accept gifts from a slave.

[Of course, the above follows the opinion of those who hold that Bethuel was still alive at this time. Others, following the *Midrash,* hold that Bethuel had died in the interim as noted in the *comm.* to *v.* 55.]

54. וַיֹּאכְלוּ וַיִּשְׁתּוּ — [*And*] ... *ate and drank.*

Of Rebecca's סְעוּדַת אֵירוּסִין, *betrothal feast (Midrash HaGadol; Malbim).*

הוּא וְהָאֲנָשִׁים אֲשֶׁר־עִמּוֹ — *He and the men* [*who were*] *with him.*

Malbim notes that in *v.* 32 the Hebrew word for *with him* is אִתּוֹ. Consistent with his exegesis of these words [cf. for example *comm.* to וְלוֹט עִמּוֹ in 13:1], there are different connotations to these otherwise synonymous terms: עִם denotes *equality* while אִתּוֹ implies a *subservient, dependent relationship* The men, as *v.* 32 suggests, were clearly his *subordinates,* but now, while describing the betrothal feast,

נה וַיֹּאמֶר שַׁלְּחֻנִי לַאדֹנִי: וַיֹּאמֶר אָחִיהָ
וְאִמָּהּ תֵּשֵׁב הַנַּעֲרָ אִתָּנוּ יָמִים אוֹ עָשׂוֹר
נו אַחַר תֵּלֵךְ: וַיֹּאמֶר אֲלֵהֶם אַל־תְּאַחֲרוּ

the Torah alludes that they ate together in complete *equality;* at this happy occasion, Eliezer did not display superiority over his underlings.

Ha'amek Davar perceives a similar interpretation, commenting that *equality* is suggested here because true joy can come only from a common feeling of equality.[1]

וַיָּלִינוּ — *And they spent the night* [lit. *lodged*].

— Every expression of the verb לין in Scripture denotes only *one night's lodging (Rashi;* comp. *comm.* to לין־לון in *vs.* 23, 25).

וַיֹּאמֶר שַׁלְּחֻנִי לַאדֹנִי — *And he said: 'Send me to my master.'*

— I.e., permit me to leave with Rebecca. It was obvious that, having betrothed her [on Isaac's behalf] Eliezer would not leave her behind *(Ha'amek Davar).*

Since Eliezer specifically said *'to my master'*, the Sages inferred: One should never say: 'Do such and such for my sake'; but, 'Do it for my father's sake'. As in this case, 'for my master's sake' *(Midrash HaGadol).*

Tosefes Brachah comments that although Eliezer had already taken leave of them (*v.*51) he acted out of courtesy. This was in consonance with the *Talmudic* dictum that if one takes leave of his teacher but spends the night in the same city; he must take leave again prior to departing (*Moed Katan* 9a).

55. וַיֹּאמֶר אָחִיהָ וְאִמָּהּ — *Her brother and mother said.*

Where was her father Bethuel? — He wished to prevent the marriage, and therefore an angel killed him *(Midrash; Rashi).*

Although Laban and Bethuel had both agreed that *the matter stems from* HASHEM [*v.* 50], and bade Eliezer to take Rebecca [*v.* 51], apparently Bethuel reconsidered and now wished to prevent the marriage consequently he died.

Alshich maintains that they had expected extravagant gifts from this stranger and therefore consented to the match. When they got only *delicious fruits* they reconsidered and decided to do away with the disappointing stranger.

According to another account in *Midrash Aggadah,* Bethuel died because the angel who accompanied Eliezer took the poisoned dish which had been set before Eliezer and exchanged it with Bethuel's. He ate from it, and he died [see *comm.* to *v.* 33 s.v. וַיּוּשַׂם].

Da'as Zekeinim suggests that they wished to poison Eliezer so they could take his valuables for themselves.

Ibn Ezra [who in seeking the *simple* interpretation of Scriptures — where Bethuel's death is not specifically mentioned] suggests that her brother and

1. In his footnote *Herchev Davar, N'tziv* observes that this betrothal feast took place at night since Eliezer arrived at the well in the evening [*v.* 11] and by the time all of the above transpired it was certainly well into the night. This is the origin of the custom to make wedding feasts at night [he cites *Kiddushin* 65b], similar to the first Jewish betrothal.

24
55-56

were with him, and they spent the night. When they
arose next morning, he said, 'Send me to my master.'
55 *Her brother and mother said, 'Let the maiden re-*
main with us a year or ten [months]; then she will
go.'
56 *He said to them, 'Do not delay me now that*

mother spoke because it was they who received the gifts; or her brother may have spoken because he was wiser and held in greater esteem than Bethuel, as we find in *v.* 50 that he received precedence.

[Literally translated the verse begins: *And her brother said and mother,* since וַיֹּאמֶר is in the singular. The implication is that Laban took the initiative and his mother went along. This further emphasizes Laban's impudence in assuming the paternal role of speaking aggressively on behalf of the family, even in his mother's presence.]

תֵּשֵׁב הַנַּעֲרָה אִתָּנוּ יָמִים אוֹ עָשׂוֹר — *Let the maiden remain with us a year or ten* [*months;* lit. *days or ten*].

— So that she can adjust gradually for nature cannot tolerate sudden changes *(Sforno).*

The rendering of יָמִים אוֹ עָשׂוֹר [lit. *days or ten*] as: *a year or ten months* follows *Rashi* and most commentators and is drawn from *Kesubos* 57b where it is explained that they requested this year's delay because that was the period of time generally given a maiden to provide herself with a trousseau [lit. *ornaments*] before her marriage.

Rashi [following the *Talmud*'s reasoning] explains that יָמִים [*days*] means *year* in this context just as it does in *Lev.* 25:29 יָמִים תִּהְיֶה גְאֻלָּתוֹ, *for 'a full year' shall he have the right of redemption* [*since, as Rashi* notes *ad. loc., the days of a full year* are briefly referred to in certain contexts as *days*]. *If* יָמִים were taken to mean literally *days* in our case, it would have to mean the minimum plural of two days; *ten* accordingly would mean ten *days.* This, however, is illogical since a negotiator does not begin with a low figure and then go on to a higher one: 'Delay the matter *two days* [the minimum number of the plural form יָמִים], or, if this is not agreeable to you then delay it *ten days.'* Accordingly, יָמִים must denote *year* as in *Lev.* 25:29, and עָשׂוֹר, *ten,* is an elliptical reference to a shorter period — *months,* as if to say: *delay the matter a full year, or at least ten months.*

[Understood in this way the plural *days* signifies: *next year when this day comes around again.*]

A request for a year's delay is not excessive considering Rebecca's age and the fact that this would be a permanent departure from her mother *(Hoffman).*

אַחַר תֵּלֵךְ — *Then* [lit. *after*] *she will go.*

[If she is not accompanied by you at that time, then she will go with someone else. See *Radak* to *v.* 58 s.v. הֲתֵלְכִי].

The *Talmud* [*Nedarim* 37b] considers the word אַחַר, *after,* in this phrase as an example of עִטּוּר סוֹפְרִים, *stylistic embellishment.* As explained there by *Ran,* the word *after* is stylistically superfluous because the phrase would mean the same without it (presumably by the use of the copulative ו: וְתֵלֵךְ, *'and* she will go.').Every such embellishment is part of the God-given Torah, the *'halachah* from Moses at Sinai,' called for the insertion of the word to give the text a smoother flow.

56. אַל תְּאַחֲרוּ אֹתִי וַה׳ הִצְלִיחַ דַּרְכִּי — *Do not delay me now that* [or: *since;* lit. *and*] *HASHEM has made my journey successful.*

— [As Abraham had assured me He would *(v.* 40).]

אִתִּי וַיהוָה הִצְלִיחַ דַּרְכִּי שַׁלְּחוּנִי וְאֵלְכָה
נז לַאדֹנִי: וַיֹּאמְרוּ נִקְרָא לַנַּעֲרָ וְנִשְׁאֲלָה
נח אֶת־פִּיהָ: וַיִּקְרְאוּ לְרִבְקָה וַיֹּאמְרוּ אֵלֶיהָ
הֲתֵלְכִי עִם־הָאִישׁ הַזֶּה וַתֹּאמֶר אֵלֵךְ:
נט וַיְשַׁלְּחוּ אֶת־רִבְקָה אֲחֹתָם וְאֶת־מֵנִקְתָּהּ

— By miraculously shortening the road [see *comm.* to *v.*42], and by causing everything to happen as I requested *(Midrash Aggadah).*

It is thus apparent that He does not desire any delay since success is not total if there is a delay *(Rashbam).*

שַׁלְּחוּנִי וְאֵלְכָה לַאדֹנִי — *Send me,* [i.e., give me leave] *and I will go to my master.*

Since everything has gone so smoothly and God so speedily guided my mission, it is obvious that He wishes me to return to my master without delay *(Abarbanel).*

57. נִקְרָא לַנַּעֲרָ וְנִשְׁאֲלָה אֶת פִּיהָ — *Let us call the maiden (Radak)*] *and ask her personally* [lit. *ask her mouth*].

Let us ask her in your presence, otherwise you will accuse us of influencing her unfairly *(Radak).*

In any event, whether you agree to wait the year or ten months, or if you insist on going immediately, even if God wills this marriage, Rebecca is entitled to a twelve month period to gather her trousseau. Therefore, it is for her to make the final decision *(Rashbam).*

From this we learn that a woman may be given in marriage only by her consent [*Kiddushin* 11a] *(Rashi).* [*See next verse.*]

58. הֲתֵלְכִי עִם הָאִישׁ הַזֶּה — *Will you go with this man?*

— I.e., will you accompany *this man now,* or go to your destined husband accompanied by someone else after a year or ten months? *(Rashbam).*

[*The Midrash* emphasizes the negative form of their question. See further, s.v. וַתֹּאמֶר אֵלֵךְ.]

Radak, too, points out that probably they were asking her only about *when* she would accompany the man. Presumably, however, she had already consented to the marriage previously, even before they expressed their approval to Eliezer [*v.* 51]. Although this is not specifically mentioned in the text, one would certainly not give his daughter in marriage without first consulting her.

[The Rabbinic view cited by *Rashi,* however, would certainly not agree with the above.]

[The implication of the flow of the narrative would accordingly be that although they had perceived that *the matter stemmed from* HASHEM (although with some reservation, as *Mizrachi* detects from *Rashi*'s comment there) they consented to the match on that basis [*vs.* 50-51], *probably without yet consulting her.* Then, as *Da'as Zekeinim* to *v.* 55 comments, Bethuel, possibly angry that he had received no gifts (as *Alshich* and *Malbim* explain), changed his mind or was never sincere to begin with. He tried to prevent the marriage and steal Eliezer's wealth by poisoning him, and died. Laban, too, was probably in a quandary and hoped to delay the matter for a year or so [*v.* 55]. — Or as *Malbim* suggests, now that Bethuel died, Rebecca's mother wanted to delay the wedding to gain more time for preparations. But

*HASHEM has made my journey successful. Send me,
and I will got to my master.'*[57] *And they said, 'Let us
call the maiden and ask her personally.'*
[58] *They called Rebecca and said to her, 'Will you
go with this man?'*
And she said 'I will go.'
[59] *So they escorted Rebecca their sister, and her*

when Eliezer, again invoking God's hand in the success of the mission, insisted that he be allowed to leave *immediately* with Rebecca, they decided to leave the matter entirely to Rebecca's own discretion.

[Thus, the very fact that *Rashi* makes the comment *here* that a woman's consent is necessary prior to marriage, clearly indicates that he is of the opinion that they had not asked her permission when they had offered her earlier. (Cf. *Mizrachi* who distinguishes between *betrothal* and *marriage*. *Maharam Shiff* to *Kesubos* 57b and *Malbim* suggest gest that since it was Laban, a *brother*, who was finally consenting, they were trying to minimize the possibility that Rebecca would exercise the right of מִיאוּן, *retraction*, which a minor has if she is betrothed by anyone other than her father. Furthermore, the version in the *Midrash* reads: From this we learn that a יְתוֹמָה, *fatherless maiden*, may not be given in marriage without her consent וצ״ע.)]

[It might *simply* be that according to *Rashi*, they originally consented *in principle* to the *idea* of such a match, in the manner of parents agreeing to have their daughter meet a certain man, but marriage would still be dependent upon her consent. Here, too, although Rebecca's *family* had already consented *in principle*, they would not permit their daughter *to leave with this man* to consummate the marriage without her consent. It is *this* consent to which *Rashi* refers.]

וַתֹּאמֶר אֵלֵךְ — *And she said, 'I will go.'*

— I.e., by myself — even if you do not consent *(Rashi)*.

As the *Midrash* explains, she was prompted to this response by the strongly negative form of their question which the Hebrew implies but which the translation does not adequately reflect, and which, according to the *Midrash* was asked incredulously: *'Would you truly go with this man?'*

[According to *Rashbam* and *Radak* her response would imply: Yes, I will accompany this man *now*].

59. [Whether, as *Rashi* would interpret, they gave permission reluctantly to avoid her threatened defiance; or as *Radak* and *Ramban* would interpret, that they graciously acquiesced to her wishes, it must be noted that once Rebecca expressed her intention, they no longer hindered her. Immediately, they arranged a procession, and blessed her. As *Abarbanel* observes, however, no member of her immediate family accompanied her. Possibly they were angered by her firm response.]

וַיְשַׁלְּחוּ אֶת רִבְקָה אֲחֹתָם — *So they escorted* [lit. *sent*] *Rebecca their sister.*

From the wording *'their* sister' rather than *'his* sister' the *Midrash*

ס וְאֶת־עֶבֶד אַבְרָהָם וְאֶת־אֲנָשָׁיו: וַיְבָרְכוּ
אֶת־רִבְקָה וַיֹּאמְרוּ לָהּ אֲחֹתֵנוּ אַתְּ הֲיִי
לְאַלְפֵי רְבָבָה וְיִירַשׁ זַרְעֵךְ אֵת שַׁעַר

Sechel Tov derives that the plural refers to her being the 'sister' in a general sense in relationship to all her kinsfolk and townspeople who came to pay their respects and bid her farewell.

[The translation *'escorted'* for וַיְשַׁלְּחוּ (usually rendered *sent off)* follows *Rashi's* interpretation of the verb in 12:20 and 18:16 (see *comm.* there). It also follows *Targum Yonasan's* rendition here: וְאַלְוִיו. However, *Onkelos,* who rendered *escort* in both 12:20 and 18:16, renders here וְשַׁלְּחוּ, *sent off* (See *Ya'er).*]

Radak, too, renders *escorted* and explains that the blessing in the next verse came after they had escorted her some distance. [For if this verse were interpreted *sent off,* then the blessing in the next verse should have *preceded* the send-off. (*Ha'amek Davar* renders similarly; see below).]

[It would appear, however, from the implication of *Ramban's* comment in *v.* 61 that he interprets this verse *they gave permission to leave to* Rebecca and her nurse, as well as to Eliezer and his men. [They then blessed them (next verse)], and *v.* 62 tells us that they actually took off and departed.]

וְאֶת־מֵנִקְתָּהּ — *And her nurse.*

— For according to the most common Rabbinic chronology, Rebecca was but three years old at the time [see *footnote* to *v.* 16.]

Ibn Ezra [who is of the opinion that Rebecca was older, and hence had no need of the services of a nurse *(Karnei Or)*], explains that this was the nurse *of her infancy* [and it was usual for a nurse to remain with a girl even after she had grown up *(ibid.)*].

Apparently they sent *her maidens* with her as well, but they are not specified here as receiving the honor of a family escort [see previous verse] The *nurse* alone is mentioned as she was the most prominent among them. They are however, mentioned matter-of-factly in *v.* 61 *(Radak).*

The nurse's name was *Deborah,* as she is identified in 35:8 *(Lekach Tov).*

וְאֶת־עֶבֶד אַבְרָהָם וְאֶת אֲנָשָׁיו — *As well as* [or: *along with*] *Abraham's servant and his men.*

The way the verse is worded implies that they made an escort processional for Rebecca consisting of women, her nurse and maidens; while a separate one was made by the men and elders of the city for Abraham's servant and his men *(Ha'amek Davar).*

60. וַיְבָרְכוּ אֶת רִבְקָה — [*And*] *they blessed Rebecca.*

— As they were about to take their leave after having escorted her some distance *(Radak).*

In *Kallah Rabbosi* 1, this verse is cited as an *Asmachta* [a Biblical support (see *Overview* to *Bereishis I* p. lv)] for the custom of בִּרְכַּת חֲתָנִים, *marriage benedictions.* [See *Kesubos* 7b that the requirement for such blessings to be in the presence of *ten men* is derived from Boaz *(Ruth* 4:2). Cf. *Tosafos*

24 *nurse, as well as Abraham's servant and his men.*
60 [60] *They blessed Rebecca and said to her,*
'Our sister,
may you come to be thousands of myriads,
and may your offspring inherit
the gate of its foes.'

ad. loc. s.v. שֶׁנֶּאֱמַר that our verse is an *Asmachta* specifically for the benediction at the time of *Erusin* (betrothal) when a woman is married through an agent as was the case here.]

אֲחֹתֵנוּ — *Our sister.*

[The term refers to her not particularly as *Laban's* sister, but more generally as *kinswoman of the townsfolk* who had come to escort and bless her. See above.]

אַתְּ הֲיִי לְאַלְפֵי רְבָבָה — *May you come to be* [*unto*] *thousands of myriads.*

[The emphasis is on the pronoun אַתְּ, *you,* which is grammatically superfluous, and therefore denotes: may *you* (and no other woman) be the ancestress of the thousands of myriads promised to Abraham *(Mizrachi; Yafeh To'ar)*]:

May *you* and *your* offspring be the recipients of the blessing given to Abraham on Mt. Moriah [22:17]: *I will greatly increase your offspring* [*like the stars of the heavens and like the sand on the seashore* ...] May it be His will that these offspring descend from *you* [as Isaac's wife] and not from another woman *(Rashi).*[1]

Since the second part of the verse is almost a literal repetition of 22:17, Eliezer must have related to them the promise regarding Isaac that God had made to Abraham at the Akeidah. It was thus their blessing that the blessing be fulfilled through *her (Alshich).*

Hirsch suggests that this expected future of the house of Abraham was widely known as evidenced by Abimelech's visit after the birth of Isaac [21:22]. In this light, Laban's blessing is understandable, for we may assume that the people of Charan knew that Rebecca would now share in the destiny of the Abrahamitic nation.

וְיִירַשׁ זַרְעֵךְ אֵת שַׁעַר שֹׂנְאָיו — *And may your offspring inherit* [or: *seize; possess; capture* (see *Hirsch* on 15:8 אִירָשֶׁנָּה)] *the gate of its foes.*

[This blessing appears almost verbatim in God's blessing to Abraham after the *Akeidah* in 22:17. As explained there, the capture of the gate, the stronghold of a city, is symbolic of its downfall. Therefore, *gate* is used in this connotation, the blessing being that her offspring should possess cities by inheriting or seizing their gates.]

According to *Ha'amek Davar* the blessing refers to wise judges and counselors who sit at the gate of a city [see on 19:1]. Thus, the bless-

1. However, as the *Midrash* notes, their blessing was futile since God caused her to remain barren for twenty years, lest the heathens say, It was *our* prayer that bore fruit. For in fact Rebecca did not conceive until *Isaac* prayed for her as it says [25:21]: *Isaac entreated HASHEM opposite his wife because she was barren, and HASHEM allowed Himself to be entreated by him and his wife Rebecca conceived (Midrash Rabbah; Midrash HaGadol).*

סא שְׂנְאָיו: וַתָּקָם רִבְקָה וְנַעֲרֹתֶיהָ וַתִּרְכַּבְנָה
עַל־הַגְּמַלִּים וַתֵּלַכְנָה אַחֲרֵי הָאִישׁ וַיִּקַּח
סב הָעֶבֶד אֶת־רִבְקָה וַיֵּלַךְ: וְיִצְחָק בָּא מִבּוֹא
בְּאֵר לַחַי רֹאִי וְהוּא יוֹשֵׁב בְּאֶרֶץ הַנֶּגֶב:

ing was that Rebecca's descendants should achieve such a reputation for integrity and wisdom that even their enemies would seek their advice.

Ha'amek Davar further notes that our verse refers to the enemies as שֹׂנְאִים, whereas in 22:17 they are called אוֹיְבִים. A שׂונא is a foe who outwardly displays his hatred whereas an אויב conceals his feelings behind a veneer of friendship. God, to Whom all thoughts are known, blessed Abraham that even inner enemies would be subjugated to him. Laban's blessing was that even Israel's bitter enemies would be in need of its superior wisdom.

Avos d'Rabbi Nosson II notes that by uttering this blessing to Rebecca, Laban and his comrades unknowingly prophesied for they were actually cursing themselves.

61. וַתָּקָם רִבְקָה וְנַעֲרֹתֶיהָ — *Then* [lit. *and*] *Rebecca arose with her maidens.*

Following *Ramban:*

After having received permission to depart [*v.* 59], Rebecca *arose* [*arose* is in singular] and summoned her maids [who are not mentioned before]. Then they departed.

[According to *Radak* and others who explain that Rebecca had been escorted part of the way (*v.*59) and then blessed, (*v.*60), this verse would be interpreted as relating their *departure*, in a one-verse summary. Accordingly, the verse would be rendered: *Thus,* (i.e., and so it was) *Rebecca rose with her maidens,* etc. Cf. similar usage in 23:20.]

Spiritually, according to *Lekach Tov,* she indeed *rose up* in leaving a discredited house and entering a home of sanctity [comp. *Rashi* to 23:17 וַיָּקָם שְׂדֵה עֶפְרוֹן.]

וַתִּרְכַּבְנָה עַל הַגְּמַלִּים — [*And*] *they rode upon the camels.*[1]

— I.e., the camels that Eliezer brought with him *(Ibn Ezra)* [this is why the word *camels* is preceded by the definite article הַ, *the (Yohel Or).*]

וַתֵּלַכְנָה אַחֲרֵי הָאִישׁ — *And* [*they*]

1. The *Talmud (Pesachim* 3a) notes that although it is usually indecent form for a woman to be spoken of in the Torah as *riding* [in the usual, straddling fashion] since *sitting* [i.e., side-saddle] is more modest and decent. Nevertheless, there are instances where riding is unavoidable, among them this sort of case since a camel's great height would make a woman fear to ride it side-saddle lest she fall.

[The *Midrash* as explained by *Maharzu* defends by implication Rebecca's mode of riding on a camel]:

— Rav Levi said: That was because camels were bred in the east [i.e., in Rebecca's home land, hence they were the usual means of transit and had to be used by women, too *(Maharzu)*]. According to the Rabbis [the reference to Rebecca riding the camel was symbolic:] just as a camel possesses one mark of uncleanness and one of cleanness [it chews its cud, but does not have a cloven hoof (see *Lev.* 11:4)], so did Rebecca bear one righteous and one wicked son *(Midrash).*

24
61-62

61 *Then Rebecca arose with her maidens. They
rode upon the camels and proceeded after the man.
The servant took Rebecca and went.*
62 *Now Isaac came from having gone to the well of
Lachai Ro'i, for he dwelt in the south country.*

proceeded [lit. *walked; went*] *after the man.*

Because it is improper for a man to walk behind a woman [lest it lead to impure thoughts] *(Berachos* 61a).

According to *Ramban*, the *simple sense* of this verse is that they followed the man because he knew the way.

וַיִּקַּח הָעֶבֶד אֶת־רִבְקָה וַיֵּלַךְ — [*And*] *the servant took Rebecca and went* [his way].

I.e., he took her under his special care and stayed close by to guard her from any mishap *(Ramban).*

Ibn Ezra explains that he walked with Rebecca and was so engrossed in guarding her that he did not feel the weariness of the journey until Isaac met them. [That may be why Rebecca noticed Isaac before Eliezer did (*v.* 64).]

According to *Sforno*, the phrase: *the servant took Rebecca* means: in his capacity as Isaac's agent, he formally received her as the bride of his master. Thereby, he became her servant as well — [and from this point onward, Scripture once more refers to him as *the servant* rather than *the man*, as at the begining of this verse].

Pirkei d'Rabbi Eliezer 16 comments that they left at noon, and to prevent Eliezer from being alone with Rebecca at night, the road miraculously contracted for him on his return journey as well, and in three hours, at the time of *Minchah*, the Afternoon Prayer, they returned home.

62. Isaac meets his bride.

The Torah narrates that Isaac 'happened' to meet them on the road before they entered the city, just as Eliezer's encounter with Rebecca at the well, etc., occurred by what seemed to be 'chance'. In reality, it was a result of God's Providential Will, for 'God deals righteously with the righteous' *(Radak).*

וְיִצְחָק בָּא מִבּוֹא בְּאֵר לַחַי רֹאִי — *Now* [lit. *and*] *Isaac had come from having gone* [lit. *came from coming*] [to] *the well of Lachai Ro'i.*

He did not live there, but he returned from having *temporarily visited* the place. Or, the infinitive form מִבּוֹא, *from coming* might imply that he constantly went there [render, as does *Onkelos: he came from his* (usual) *coming*] possibly to oversee his cattle which grazed there, or to do business in that area *(Radak; Rashbam)*; or because it was a place of prayer for him since it was there that an angel revealed himself to Hagar [see 16:14]. According to *Onkelos*, who identifies Bered [16:14] with Shur [20:1], the area was near Beer Sheba and Abraham's *Eishel* — certainly a place Isaac would frequent in prayer *(Ramban).*

He went there to pray at the propitious site where Hagar's prayers had once been answered. Even *before* he prayed, his needs were answered in Charan and his wife was already approaching, in the manner of [*Isaiah* 65:24] טֶרֶם יִקְרָאוּ וַאֲנִי אֶעֱנֶה, *before they call I will answer (Sforno).*

Chizkuni [following *Ibn Ezra*] suggests that the word מִבּוֹא might be an adjectivial phrase meaning *from the frontier; entrance,* as in *I Kings* 8:65: מִלְּבוֹא חֲמָת, *from the entrance of Hamath,* the word בֹּא meaning *entrance.* Accordingly, our verse would be rendered: *And Isaac came from the frontier of Be'er Lachai Ro'i.*

According to *Rashi,* following the *Midrash,* Isaac had gone to *Be'er Lachai Ro'i* to bring [מִלְהָבִיא=מִבּוֹא *from bringing*] Hagar back as a wife for Abraham. [Apparently, she made her residence at the site where the angel had so auspiciously addressed her (see 16:8 ff). This follows the tradition which identifies Keturah of 25:1 with Hagar].

Cf. the *Midrash:* He had gone to bring Hagar, the one who sat by the בְּאֵר, *well,* and besought לַחַי, Him Who is *Life* of all worlds, saying רְאֵה, *'Look* upon my misery.'

[The Hebrew reader is directed to the novel interpretation of this phrase offered by *HaKsav V'haKaballah*].

וְהוּא יוֹשֵׁב בְּאֶרֶץ הַנֶּגֶב — *For* [lit. *and*] *he dwelt in the south country.*

The *exact* place of Isaac's residence is not mentioned. The interpretation of what is referred to by this generalization *south country* is open to conjecture.

According to *Rashi,* he dwelt near the well of Lachai Ro'i. *Rashi* cites 20:1 as proof that that area was referred to as the south country, and 21:14 that the well was located there.

[*Rashi* is apparently of the opinion, as he formulates in his *comm.* to 22:19, that during this period Abraham still maintained his *primary* residence not in the south, but in Hebron — presumably *together with Isaac* as suggested by 35:27, but that they often commuted to the site of Abraham's *eishel* in Beer Sheba. This *eishel,* as *Ramban* explains above was in the proximity of Be'er Lachai Ro'i. It is to this occasional *staying* in that southern region that this verse refers to. (Comp. *Rashi*'s interpretation of וַיֵּשֶׁב as *stayed* in 22:19).]

[Isaac's residence *after* Abraham's death, however, is specifically given in 25:11 as Be'er Lachi Ro'i.]

According to *Ramban* in 23:2, after Sarah's burial Abraham returned to the spiritual tranquility of his *eishel* in Beer Sheba, and resumed his permanent residence there along with Isaac.

According to *Midrash HaGadol* [and similarly *Radak*], the designation *south country* refers *in itself* to Hebron since Hebron is specifically described in 35:27 as the place where Abraham *and Isaac* had dwelt.

Midrash Sechel Tov concurs with the above and elaborates that when Isaac returned from the Academy of Shem and Eber where he studied for the three years since the *Akeidah,* he rejoined his father in Hebron which (as in 12:9) is referred to as the South — facing Jerusalem and Mount Moriah — in what would become the territory of Judah [see *Rashi* 12:9]. Accordingly, it was *toward Hebron,* to his father, that Isaac was now returning, after having gone to Be'er Lachai Ro'i.

63. וַיֵּצֵא יִצְחָק לָשׂוּחַ בַּשָּׂדֶה לִפְנוֹת עָרֶב — *Isaac went out to supplicate in the field toward evening.*

He turned off the road [on his return journey from the well of Lachai Ro'i] in order to pour forth his supplication before God in the field, undisturbed by passers-by. This, although he had already

[63] *Isaac went out to supplicate in the field toward*

prayed at the well, and had been answered. Compare *Daniel* 10:12: *From the first day that you ... humbled yourself before your God, your words were heard (R' Avraham ben HaRambam; Sforno).*

There is a tradition that *the field* where Isaac prayed was Mount Moriah [site of the *Akeidah,* and *future site of the Temple*] *(Tosafos Berachos* 34b s.v. חָצִיף; cf. *Pesachim* 88a); while according to the *Zohar Chadash* it was *the field* adjacent to the Cave of Machpelah which Abraham had purchased.

The translation *supplicate* follows *Rashi* who explains that לָשׂוּחַ means *to pray,* as in *Psalms* 102:1: *A prayer of the afflicted when he pours forth* שִׂיחוֹ, *his supplication, before* HASHEM.

This follows the *Talmud (Berachos* 26b) and *Midrash,* which derive from this verse the tradition that Isaac instituted the *Minchah* [afternoon] prayer. That Abraham instituted the *Shacharis* [morning] prayer is derived from 19:27; and that Jacob instituted the *Aravis* [evening] prayer is derived from 28:11.[1]

Rashbam relates לָשׂוּחַ to שִׂיחַ, *tree,* in 2:5, and explains that Isaac went to plant trees and oversee his laborers, and while he was in the field he saw camels approaching. He drew near them to see whether they were his father's camels which Eliezer had taken.

Ibn Ezra and *Radak* similarly relate it to *tree* and explain that the connotation of the verse is that Isaac went to stroll among the trees and meditate (see *Karnei Or).*

Ramban is ambiguous on his interpretation of the word but from the context of his comment, he seems to take it in the secular sense: He went out towards evening לָשׂוּחַ [possibly to *converse*] with his companions who were there.

Malbim, following *Abarbanel,* derives לָשׂוּחַ from שִׂיחַ, *speech.* It is used in the sense of words that flow in one's mind as he meditates and also for the flow of thoughts as he prays.

HaKsav V'haKaballah, however, comments that the term derives from שָׂח or, as it is often spelled סָח which refers to *movement.* The word designates an act of *removal* such as מֵשִׂיחַ דַּעַת, *to remove one's attention* from the task at hand. Thus, לָשׂוּחַ would refer to an act which is done to relieve oneself from preoccupation with something else. For example, לָשׂוּחַ בַּשָּׂדֶה in our verse could indicate that Isaac *strolled in the field to relieve himself from some anxiety.* It could also mean that Isaac relieved his

1. The Sages derive from this verse that Isaac was the one who instituted *Minchah,* the afternoon prayer, for we find that Isaac went out to the field to supplicate before God לִפְנוֹת עָרֶב, *toward evening.* From this verse, too, we find support for the *Talmudic* dictum that 'one should be especially scrupulous regarding the afternoon prayer' *(Berachos* 6b) for it was in the afternoon that Elijah's prayer was answered *(I Kings* 18:36-37). Presumably Isaac was praying for the success of Eliezer's mission and we find that his prayer was answered immediately with the appearance of Rebecca.

Although Abraham and Jacob, respectively, instituted the morning and evening prayers, we find nowhere that God responded to them *immediately.* That Isaac's request was granted without delay may, therefore, be taken as an indication that the afternoon prayer is especially efficacious *(Kli Yakar).*

וַיִּשָּׂא עֵינָיו וַיַּרְא וְהִנֵּה גְמַלִּים בָּאִים׃
סד וַתִּשָּׂא רִבְקָה אֶת־עֵינֶיהָ וַתֵּרֶא אֶת־יִצְחָק
סה וַתִּפֹּל מֵעַל הַגָּמָל׃ וַתֹּאמֶר אֶל־הָעֶבֶד
מִי־הָאִישׁ הַלָּזֶה הַהֹלֵךְ בַּשָּׂדֶה לִקְרָאתֵנוּ

soul from its troubles through prayer. It is in this sense that *Rashi* translates לָשׂוּחַ as *supplicate,* although a more literal translation would be *to relieve* or *to remove preoccupation.*

וַיִּשָּׂא עֵינָיו — *And he raised his eyes.* — After he completed his prayers. Before then his eyes had been shut in total concentration *(Tzror HaMor).*

וְהִנֵּה גְמַלִּים בָּאִים — [*And*] *behold! Camels were coming.*

[Such was the efficacy of his prayers — even before he completed his prayers he had been answered. See *Kli Yakar* above in *footnote*].

They were still too far away for him to distinguish *people;* at first all he saw was the form of camels *(Abarbanel).*

[According to those who interpret לָשׂוּחַ in the secular sense, the providential hand of God would also be evident in his unexpectedly meeting them now on his journey home. Isaac could not have expected to meet them because it was only yesterday that Eliezer had embarked on what should have been a seventeen-day journey in each direction, but which was miraculously shortened to but three hours each way as *Pirkei d'Rabbi Eliezer* notes in *comm.* to *v.* 42 and *v.* 61 s.v. וַיִּקַּח].

64. וַתִּשָּׂא רִבְקָה אֶת עֵינֶיהָ וַתֵּרֶא אֶת יִצְחָק — *And Rebecca raised her eyes and saw Isaac.*

Rebecca saw him before Eliezer since she was riding on the camel, while Eliezer was on foot *(Malbim).*

[Having never seen him, she could not *recognize* him *(Mizrachi)*] ... She perceived his dignified appearance and felt abashed in his presence causing her to *'fall' from the camel* [see further] *(Rashi).*

Hirsch suggests, however, that Eliezer had undoubtedly spoken to her about Isaac all through the journey, and from his descriptions, she surmised that it was him.

וַתִּפֹּל מֵעַל הַגָּמָל — [*And*] *she inclined herself while upon* [lit. *fell from upon*] *the camel.*

The commentators generally do not interpret *fall* in the literal sense for if she had actually *fallen off the camel* the verse would have read וַתִּפּוֹל מֵהַגָּמָל *(R' Bachya),* or the usual Scriptural form: וַתִּפֹּל אַרְצָה, *she fell to the ground (Maskil le-David).* Rather, upon being overawed by the dignity of the approaching man, Rebecca *inclined herself to one side — while still on the camel* — in order to modestly turn her face from him. *(Rashi* and *Onkelos* as explained by *Ramban* and *Mizrachi).*

Rashi cites *Psalms* 37:24: *Though he fall, he shall not be utterly cast down* where *fall* is not literal, but means: though he *inclines himself toward the earth,* yet he shall not touch the ground. [The *Midrash* similarly explains that she was *inclined to fall* but did not].

Ramban elaborates and cites the similar use of *fall* in his interpretation of *II Kings*

24
64-65

*evening and he raised his eyes and saw — Behold!
Camels were coming.* 64 *And Rebecca raised her eyes
and saw Isaac. She inclined while upon the camel,*
65 *and said to the servant, 'Who is that man walking
in the field toward us?'*

5:21: *And when Naaman saw one running after him* וַיִּפֹּל [lit. *he fell*] *from upon the chariot to meet him, and said, Is all well?* There, וַיִּפֹּל means that he *bent over* while in his chariot toward the runner, to inquire whether all was well [see *Malbim* below, and *Sforno*].

Ramban continues that accordingly the prepositional prefix מ, *mem*, of מֵעַל [lit. *from* upon] is superfluous, and the expression מֵעַל הַגָּמָל [*from* upon the camel] is like עַל הַגָּמָל, *on* the camel. Cf. such superfluous prefixes in *Psalms* 108:5 and 148:4 עַל הַשָּׁמַיִם=מֵעַל הַשָּׁמַיִם, and *Isaiah* 65:20 שָׁם=מִשָּׁם.

In the literal sense, however, it appears that *Ramban* agrees with *Ibn Ezra* that the phrase means: *she threw herself down* [in the sense of *alighted*] *willingly* from upon the camel.

Malbim, basing himself on *Rashi* [and perhaps more specifically on *Ramban*'s citation from *II Kings* 5:21], explains that upon seeing the man, she *inclined herself* while still upon the camel *toward* Eliezer, who was accompanying her on foot [in order to ask him the question in the next verse].

Rashbam similarly explains it as: *she dismounted* [*fell* probably having the connotation of 'quickly jumped'] because [as explained in the *comm.* to *v.* 61 s.v. וַתִּרְכַּבְנָה] she was riding the camel normally rather than side-saddle, and it would have been immodest for Isaac to see her in that position.

Hirsch also takes it in the sense of quickly dismounted', as a result of a spontaneous decision that it was unseemly to meet Isaac as if she were an aristocratic lady, riding toward him, especially since he was on foot.

Sforno explains it as 'she made obeisance from her seat upon the camel' [similarly, *Akeidas Yitzchak*]; while *Radak* explains that, overawed by the man's dignity, she dismounted the camel and then *fell to the ground.*

Yalkut Shimoni cites a *Midrash* [see also *Hadar Zekeinim* and *Midrash Aggadah*] that Rebecca perceived at that moment through a prophetic spirit that the wicked Esau was to issue from her; she trembled with horror and actually *fell* from the camel causing herself injury [see *Torah Sheleimah* note to 24:237].

65. מִי־הָאִישׁ הַלָּזֶה הַהֹלֵךְ בַּשָּׂדֶה לִקְרָאתֵנוּ — *Who is that man walking in the field toward us?*

[Following the implication of *Rashi*, she was so overawed by his lordly appearance that *first* she modestly *inclined herself*, and *then* she asked his identity. According to *Malbim*, she *leaned over* while seated on the camel in order to whisper this question to Eliezer.]

Did she then ask about every man she encountered? — Only here, but the verse is elliptic and implies: *Who is that man walking in the field* — who changed his direction and is now coming לִקְרָאתֵנוּ, *directly toward us? (Hadar Zekeinim*

וַיֹּאמֶר הָעֶבֶד הוּא אֲדֹנִי וַתִּקַּח הַצָּעִיף
סו וַתִּתְכָּס: וַיְסַפֵּר הָעֶבֶד לְיִצְחָק אֵת כָּל־
סז הַדְּבָרִים אֲשֶׁר עָשָׂה: וַיְבִאֶהָ יִצְחָק
הָאֹהֱלָה שָׂרָה אִמּוֹ וַיִּקַּח אֶת־רִבְקָה

citing a *Rashbam* which is not in our editions).

According to *Ibn Ezra*, the events of this verse *preceded* those of the previous verse and the phrase... וַתֹּאמֶר אֶל הָעֶבֶד מִי הָאִישׁ should be rendered 'and she had *already* said', i.e., she saw Isaac and alighted from the camel after having previously asked Eliezer who he was.

Ramban cites this opinion and acknowledges that there are, indeed, verses in the Torah whose order have to be exegetically transposed in order to achieve better continuity. In this case, however, in addition to transposing whole verses, one would also have to mix the interlocking phrases within the verses, as follows: She saw Isaac [*v.* 64], asked the servant who he was, and when he answered that it was his master [*v.*65], she alighted from the camel [*v.* 64], and veiled herself [*v.* 65.]

Ramban holds that such drastic transposition is uncalled for here. Rather, the *sequential* sense of the verses is: When Rebecca saw a man walking in the field and turning toward them, she realized that he was approaching them either to greet them or offer them lodging. As was proper for a woman, she reacted by alighting from the camel and stood modestly. [Then, as he was still approaching them, she inquired *exactly who* he was, and upon hearing that he was Isaac, she veiled herself.]

The expression הַלָּזֶה, [*that*], is used when speaking of someone *from a distance*, as [is the case with Joseph's brothers' who, seeing him *from afar* (37:18) said] בַּעַל הַחֲלֹמוֹת הַלָּזֶה בָּא, *that dreamer is coming* [ibid *v.* 19.] When one is *near*, however, הַזֶּה [*this*] is used, as in *Esther* 7:6 הָמָן הָרָע הַזֶּה, *this wicked Haman (Rashbam).*

[Those who homiletically interpret the *Notarikon* (abbreviation of words [see *footnote* to 17:5 p.563]) of the Torah, expound upon the word הַלָּזֶה: Who is that man who, at the age of thrity-seven (ל״ז=37) submitted to the *Akeidah*, and whose parents each had the letter *heh* added to their names (ה־ה with which the word הלזה begins and ends). This is a reference to Abraham and Sarah who were originally named Abram and Sarai (*Midrash* cited in *Torah Sheleimah* 24:241 and *Minchah Belulah*).]

הוּא אֲדֹנִי — *He is my master.*

[Although he did not specify that it was Isaac rather than Abraham, it was obvious from his age that it was Isaac who was standing before them.]

And since Abraham had bequeathed all his possessions to Isaac, as Eliezer himself mentioned in Bethuel's house [*v.* 36.] He therefore made reference to *Isaac* as his master *(Hoffmann).*

וַתִּקַּח הַצָּעִיף וַתִּתְכָּס — *Then* [lit. *and*] *she took the veil and covered herself.*

And the servant said, 'He is my master.' She then took the veil and covered herself.
66 *The servant told Isaac all the things he had done.*
67 *And Isaac brought her into the tent of Sarah his*

As an act of modesty *(Ralbag);* for she was afraid to gaze upon his awesome appearance*(Sforno).* [1]

The rendering of *covered herself* [instead of the causitive *covered someone else*] follows *Rashi* who explains that the verb וַתִּתְכַּס is in the הִתְפָּעֵל, *reflexive* form, indicating the *passive* form, as do the verbs וַתִּקָּבֵר, *and she was buried* and וַתִּשָּׁבֵר, *and she was broken.* [Although these illustrations are not הִתְפַּעֵל, *reflexive,* but נִפְעַל, *passive,* they illustrate the obvious *passive* nature of the verb, in contrast to the *causitive* form from which *Rashi* distinguishes them *(Mizrachi).*]

Targum Yerushalmi renders: *she took a veil and wrapped herself in it.*

66. וַיְסַפֵּר הָעֶבֶד לְיִצְחָק אֵת כָּל־הַדְּבָרִים אֲשֶׁר עָשָׂה — *[And] the servant told Isaac all the things he had done.*

He reported to him the miracles that had been wrought for him: how the earth had contracted for him, and how Rebecca had been ready for him in speedy response to his prayer *(Rashi).*

Cf. the *Midrash:* R' Elazar said: There are more general statements in the Torah than detailed accounts, for several columns could have been written regarding Eliezer's report [yet the narrative was kept to a minimal reference]. The Rabbis said: He related the more welcome incidents only, for example, that the earth had contracted before him.

The commmentators question *Rashi's* exegesis: If all he related were the miracles that had been wrought for him the verse should have read: 'the servant related all *that had been done for him'!* not: 'all that *he* [implying himself] *has done'!* But according to *Rashi's* interpretation the subject of the clause would be *God: The servant related to Isaac all the things* He [i.e., God] *had done (Divrei David).*

According to the simple sense of the verse, however, it was on the way back to Abraham's residence in Hebron that the servant related every detail of his mission. They reached Hebron, where Sarah's tent was located, on the morrow *(Radak).*

67. וַיְבִאֶהָ יִצְחָק הָאֹהֱלָה שָׂרָה אִמּוֹ — *And Isaac brought her into the tent of Sarah his mother.*[lit. *to the tent Sarah his mother*].

[The commentators note that since the word הָאֹהֱלָה *to the tent,* appears with the definite article, ה, *the,* it cannot be used in סְמִיכוּת, the construct state with שָׂרָה אִמּוֹ, *Sarah his mother.* Therefore the verse contains two distinct units: *To the tent,* and

1. Rebecca veiled her face out of awe of Isaac, and shame to be in his presence, as though to indicate that she considered herself unworthy of him. This set the pattern for their subsequent relationship which was unique among the Patriarchs and Matriarchs.

Sarah, Rachel, and Leah were often assertive in their relationships with their husbands. Rebecca, on the other hand, never confronted Isaac directly. Thus we find that she tolerated Isaac's favor toward Esau although she knew that Esau had been deceiving his father. When the time came for the blessings to be given, she employed *deception* to secure them for Jacob.

This sort of relationship was preordained by God in that the transmission of the blessings would take place in a seemingly underhanded manner. The purpose of His plan will be discussed in the succeeding chapters *(Ha'amek Davar).*

וַתְּהִי־ל֖וֹ לְאִשָּׁ֑ה וַיֶּאֱהָבֶ֑הָ וַיִּנָּחֵ֥ם יִצְחָ֖ק
אַחֲרֵ֥י אִמּֽוֹ׃

°ששי א °וַיֹּ֧סֶף אַבְרָהָ֛ם וַיִּקַּ֥ח אִשָּׁ֖ה וּשְׁמָ֥הּ קְטוּרָֽה׃

Sarah his mother, and is interpreted as elliptical.]

He brought her into the tent and behold! she was as *Sarah his mother!* That is, she became like Sarah his mother in every respect. For as long as Sarah was alive a lamp burned in her tent from one Sabbath eve to another, her dough was blessed, and a cloud [signifying the Divine Presence; see *Exodus* 40:34] hung over her tent. When Sarah died, these ceased, but when Rebecca entered the tent they returned *(Rashi).*

Onkelos renders: 'And Isaac brought her to the tent, and he saw, and behold! her deeds were righteous as the works of Sarah his mother, and he loved her.'

According to the *Zohar,* when Isaac brought Rebecca into the tent, the *image of Sarah* reappeared and permeated the tent, thus indicating to Isaac, unequivocably, Divine approval of his new wife.

Ibn Ezra explains the literal elliptical sense as: *to the tent,* the tent of *Sarah his mother,* rendering: *Into his mother Sarah's tent.*

Radak defends this rendering by citing such parallels which contain the definite article yet are interpreted in the construct sense as e.g., *Numbers* 34:2 הָאָרֶץ כְּנָעַן, *the land of Canaan; Joshua* 3:14 הָאָרוֹן הַבְּרִית, *the Ark of the Covenant.*

The verse thus stresses the devotion and respect which were posthumously given Sarah in that her tent remained dismantled from the time of her death. However, in honor of Rebecca he assigned that tent to her, and brought her into it. It was there that he took her as his wife *(Radak; Ramban).*

וַיִּקַּח אֶת רִבְקָה וַתְּהִי לוֹ לְאִשָּׁה וַיֶּאֱהָבֶהָ — [*And*] *he married* [lit. *took:* (in its Biblical sense of *take in marriage*)] *Rebecca;* [*and*] *she became his wife, and he loved her.* [1]

This was the exact order of events: It was only *after* he brought her into his mother's tent and observed that her actions were like Sarah's that *he married her (Malbim).*

Ha'amek Davar comments that Isaac betrothed her himself and then married her. He did not rely on Eliezer's betrothal on his behalf because a slave may not act as an agent, Eliezer's betrothal was valid

1. *Hirsch* notes that marriage preceded love; the more they were married, the more Isaac loved her. In this, the first Jewish marriage, the *Torah* illustrates the principle that has generally been followed by Jews: Jewish marriages are contracted not as a result of passion and romance, but as a result of good judgment and sound reason. If the couple is well-suited, the marriage will result in love and happiness. Marriages based on pre-marital infatuation, however, all too often fail the test of married life.

Hirsch continues that the chapter ends with words that exalt and ennoble the status of a Jewish wife. Isaac was a mature man when his mother died, but he could not be consoled as long as the sweetnesss and goodness of the Matriarch were gone from the home. In his wife he found consolation — she embodied worth, nobility, and greatness.

*mother. He married Rebecca, she became his wife,
and he loved her. And thus was Isaac consoled after
his mother.*

*Abraham proceeded and took a wife whose name
was Keturah.* 2 *She bore him Zimran, Yakshan,*

only to the extent that thereby Rebecca became engaged, but not halachically betrothed.

וַיֶּאֱהָבֶהָ וַיִּנָּחֵם יִצְחָק אַחֲרֵי אִמּוֹ — *And he loved her and thus was Isaac consoled after his mother*

I.e., *After* having grieved for his mother *(Radak).*

After having seen that Rebecca's deeds were like his mother's *(Chizkuni).*

He was deeply grieved for his mother and found no consolation until he was consoled by his wife through his love for her. This love was inspired by her righteousness and aptness of deeds, the only criteria upon which the Torah bases the love between a man and his wife *(Ramban).*

He was comforted to such an extent that it was as if his mother were still alive *(Midrash),* for as noted above, the *image of Sarah* reap- finds comfort in his wife *(Rashi).*

Thus is the way of the world: a man is attached to his mother during her lifetime; when she dies, he finds comfort in his wife *(Rashi).*

XXV

1. Abraham Remarries.

וַיֹּסֶף אַבְרָהָם וַיִּקַּח אִשָּׁה — *[And] Abraham proceeded* [lit. *continued; added*] *and took a wife.*

After Abraham arranged for Isaac's marriage, he *then* took a wife for himself as evidenced from the sequence of the verses. The *Midrash* observes that the Torah teaches propriety: a man [=widowed or divorced] with grown sons should first see them married and *then* take a wife himself.

The *Midrash,* interpreting *Eccles.* 11:6 in this context comments: If you have had children while young, take a wife in your old age and have more children. [As the parallel exegesis in *Tanchuma Yashan* concludes: for one does not know which of his children will be virtuous and Godfearing; (cf. *Yevamos* 62b; *Rambam, Yad, Hilchos Ishus* 15).]

That Abraham married again is not surprising when we remember that he survived Sarah by thirty-eight years. Apart from that, our Sages teach that man is not 'whole' without a wife, a human being's mission is too great to be fully accomplished by one person alone *(Hirsch).*

The word וַיֹּסֶף, *again,* in the phrase, which literally means: *and Abraham again took a wife,* is interpreted by the Sages to intimate that Abraham *remarried the wife* to

ב וַתֵּלֶד לוֹ אֶת־זִמְרָן וְאֶת־יָקְשָׁן וְאֶת־מְדָן
ג וְאֶת־מִדְיָן וְאֶת־יִשְׁבָּק וְאֶת־שׁוּחַ׃ וְיָקְשָׁן
יָלַד אֶת־שְׁבָא וְאֶת־דְּדָן וּבְנֵי דְדָן הָיוּ
ד אַשּׁוּרִם וּלְטוּשִׁם וּלְאֻמִּים׃ וּבְנֵי מִדְיָן

whom he had been married before: Hagar. [They cite the use of the same word וַיֹּסֶף in *Isaiah* 8:5 *And HASHEM spoke to me again* as proof that the verb *yet again* intimates a resumption of what had already existed previously (see *Sechel Tov* and note to *Torah Sheleimah* 25:9). Others interpret that the verse in *Isaiah* is cited to imply that just as that verse intimates prophecy, so too, does our verse suggest that everything was done in accordance with the Divine call (עַל פִּי הַדִּבּוּר)] (*Midrash; Pirkei d'Rabbi Eliezer* 30).

The *Zohar* specifically states that the term וַיֹּסֶף [lit. *and he again added*] here indicates not that Abraham took *another* wife, but that he took *again* his *former* spouse whom he had driven out with Ishmael.

Radak in his *commentary* to *I Chron.* 1:31 notes that Keturah was considered a concubine [and she is referred to as a *concubine* in *v.* 6 (see *Ramban* cited there).] The phrase וַיִּקַּח אִשָּׁה in our verse is accordingly not to be understood in its usual sense of *married* [i.e., took a wife], but in its more literal sense: *he took a woman* — to be his concubine.

וּשְׁמָהּ קְטוּרָה — *Whose* [lit. *and her*] *name was Keturah.*

— Keturah is Hagar, who received this name because her deeds were as beautiful as incense [*ketores*]; also because she remained chaste [קָשְׁרָה פִּתְחָהּ, (קָשְׁרָה) being a cognate verb of קטר, of which קְטוּרָה is the past participle)], from the time she had separated from Abraham (*Midrash; Rashi).*

In 21:14 s.v. וַתֵּלֶךְ וַתֵּתַע (p. 761) *Rashi* comments that Hagar reverted to the idolatry of her father's house. How then does he now call her action 'beautiful as incense'? — Rather, when she was expelled from Abraham's household she felt forsaken even by his God and she intended to revert to her idolatrous ways. But when the miracle occurred at the well, she repented *(Gur Aryeh).*

The *Zohar* similarly comments that although she *had* relapsed into her ancestral idolatry, she later repented and changed her name, after which Abraham sent for and married her. From this we see that a change of name makes atonement for guilt, for she made this change of name symbolic of her change of behavior.

[The phraseology וּשְׁמָהּ קְטוּרָה rather than וּקְטוּרָה שְׁמָהּ denotes that Keturah was righteous, and fit for Abraham. See *footnote* to 24:29.]

Although Hagar/Keturah was a first-generation Egyptian [16:1] and hence forbidden in marriage [see *Deut.* 23:9], nevertheless, since his first marriage to her was with God's sanction [see *Rashi* to 16:2 s.v. לְקוֹל], she remained permissible to him for *remarriage* as well. Furthermore, the *Midrash* [*Bereishis Rabbah* 60:4] specifically states that Abraham remarried Keturah/Hagar *by Divine command* (עַל פִּי הַדִּבּוּר) *(Tur).*

[It is conceivable that Abraham's action was in accordance with the minority view of Rabbi Shimon in the *Mishneh, Yevamos* 76b that Egyptian *women* were permitted (after Conversion) — *(Rabbi Avie Gold).*]

Targum Yonasan renders the verses: and Abraham added and took a wife, and her name was Keturah; she is Hagar who had been

25
2-4

Medan, Midian, Ishbak and Shuah. 3 *Yakshan begot*
Sheba and Dedan and the children of Dedan were
Ashurim, Letushim, and Leumim. 4 *And the children*

bound to him [קְטוּרָה is Aramaic for קְשׁוּרָה, *the bound one*] from the beginning.

According to the *simple* sense of the verse, however, Keturah is *not* Hagar *(Rashbam).*

Ramban in interpreting the literal sense also subscribes to the latter view, and distinguishes (in his *comm.* to *v.* 6) between Hagar and Keturah. He conjectures that since the Torah does give the genealogy of Keturah, we may assume that she was a neighboring Canaanite.

Whatever her nationality, *Ramban* continues, why did Abraham not seek a wife from among his kindred, in Charan, as he did for Isaac? The answer is that the Covenant (see 17:2, 19) was to be fulfilled only through *Isaac* [21:12], and hence *his* seed had to be guarded. [It would not matter with whom Abraham would beget other children, since *they* would not be bearers of the covenant in any event.]

2. **וַתֵּלֶד לוֹ** — *[And] she bore him*

Although Abraham was by now much older than he was at the birth of Isaac, nevertheless this is not considered a new miracle. His aged body had already been reinvigorated in order to make possible the birth of Isaac. God merely allowed him to retain that capacity *(Ha'amek Davar).*

אֶת־זִמְרָן וְאֶת־יָקְשָׁן וְאֶת־מְדָן — *Zimran [and] Yakshan [and] Medan.*

These tribes are largely unidentified. The 'Medanites' are referred to in 37:36 as traders with Egypt, but they seem to be identified with the Midianites in *v.*28 there. Perhaps, as *Hoffmann* suggests, being brother tribes they eventually merged.

The *Midrash,* in keeping with its method of seeking homeletical significance in names, comments that *Zimran* means that they sang [*mezamrin*] hymns to idols, and *Yakshan* — that they beat [*mekashin*] the timbrel in honor of the idols.

וְאֶת־מִדְיָן וְאֶת־יִשְׁבָּק וְאֶת־שׁוּחַ — *Midian* [and] *Ishbak and Shuah.*

Midian is a tribal name that frequently appears in the Bible. Further, [*Exodus* 3:1] we find Jethro [later, Moses' father-in-law], as the priest of Midian, while in *Numbers* 22 and 31 the Midianites appear as enemies of Israel. In *Judges* 6 we are told that they ruled Israel for a period of seven years until Gideon prevailed over them. [Ishbak is unknown], and Shuah, [the tribe of Job's friend, Bildad], is mentioned in *Job* 2:11 as a tribe of the land of Utz *(Hoffmann).*

3. **אֶת־שְׁבָא וְאֶת־דְּדָן** — *Sheba and Dedan.*

The names Sheba and Dedan appear also above 10:7, as the descendants of Raamah son of Cush; (see *commentary* there). Sheba occurs also as one of the children of Joktan in 10:28 *(Hoffmann).*

הָיוּ אַשּׁוּרִם וּלְטוּשִׁם וּלְאֻמִּים — *Were Ashurim,* [and] *Letushim* [and] *Leumim.*

Our translation, as always, follows *Rashi* who in this case views

עֵיפָה וָעֵפֶר וַחֲנֹךְ וַאֲבִידָע וְאֶלְדָּעָה כָּל־
ה אֵלֶּה בְּנֵי קְטוּרָה: וַיִּתֵּן אַבְרָהָם אֶת־כָּל־

these as proper nouns, the names of the chieftains of peoples.

Radak observes that it is not clear why these children were given names with an *im* ending which usually indicates the plural. Mitzraim also gave his sons names with an *im* suffix: [10:13]: Ludim, Ananim, Lehavim, etc. [see *The Seventy Nations,* on p. 313.] Perhaps they had a reason which eludes us.

The *Targumim,* however, perceive these words not as proper *names,* but as *adjectives* — describing the prime characteristics of Dedan's descendants: *Ashurim* — is rendered by *Onkelos* as *campers; Letushim* as *tent-owners* [who spread about in all directions *(Rashi)*]; *Leumim* as islands or *sea-districts.*

Rashi justifies *Onkelos'* rendering on grammatical grounds, explaining that אַשּׁוּרִם *Ashurim,* can be related to מַשִּׁירְיָן, *camps* [cf. שַׁיָּרָא, *a caravan*], since the א of אַשּׁוּרִם, is not part of the root. Compare the noun אֲנָךְ, *plumbline,* whose root is נכה, *stricken;* אָסוּךְ, *a cruse of oil,* which is related to the verb סכה, *anointing.* לְטוּשִׁם, *Letushim,* is rendered by *Onkelos* as *tent owners,* in the sense of נְטוּשִׁים, *spread about* [*I Sam.* 30:16], since they were spread out in all directions and traveled about. This, too, is valid, since ל and נ interchange, and hence לְטוּשִׁים, *Letushim* equals נְטוּשִׁים, *scattered ones.*

Nevertheless, *Rashi* concludes, 'I cannot make *Onkelos'* translation fit in with the syntax' [lit. language of the text.]

Ramban proceeds to further elaborate upon *Onkelos'* understanding of this verse by commenting that *Onkelos* rendered *Ashurim* as *camps* in the sense of camps of caravan drivers that travel from town to town as Ishmaelites regularly do [cf. 37:25.] This interpretation relates *Ashurim* to אֲשׁוּר, *footsteps* [see *Job* 23:11; *Psalms* 37:31]: *Letushim* [similar to *netushim, scattered ones,* as *Rashi* explains] refers to the nomadic *tent-dwellers* who are scattered over the face of the country. *Leumim* refers to the island-dwellers.

Ramban continues that *Onkelos* was drawn to view these names as descriptive, by the word הָיוּ, *were,* in the phrase: *'and the Children of Dedan* הָיוּ, *were* [which would imply that: their *characteristics were:* caravan drivers, tent dwellers, and island dwellers]. If these were proper names, however, this verse should have been expressed similarly to 10:13: *and Mitzraim begot Ludim, Ananim, Lehavim, Naphtuhim.*

Ramban cites the *Midrash* which interprets *Ashurim* as *merchants* [which *Ramban* explains as those who walk the roads, derived from אֲשׁוּר, *footstep*]; *Letushim* as *flaming ones* [i.e., men of wickedness] and *Leumim* to *heads of people* [רָאשֵׁי אומות]. The *Midrash* concludes with the view of Rav Shmuel, son of Rav Nachman, [with which *Ramban* concurs] that though the Translators are accustomed to render these names as descriptive, they are still the proper names of the heads of these nations bearing those names.

25
5-6

of Midian: Ephah [and] Epher, Chanoch, Abida, and
Eldah. All these were the descendants of Keturah.
5 *Abraham gave all that he had to Isaac.* 6 *But to*

[It is to this latter view that *Rashi*, in seeking the literal meaning of Scripture, follows. He apparently renders הָיוּ as *they became* the leaders of the peoples bearing those names.]

Ibn Ezra also follows this view [see *Avi Ezer* who remarks about the apparent inconsistency between the count of *sixteen* descendants of Keturah here, and the *thirteen* in *I Chronicles* 1:32 where these children of Dedan are omitted. He comments that according to *Onkelos' descriptive* interpretation, these are three characteristics of Keturah's other descendants, hence the Torah, too, lists thirteen children of Keturah. According to *Rashi*'s interpretation that these are *actual names*, there are sixteen, as *Rashi* specifically mentions in his commentary to *Song of Songs* 6:8 (see ArtScroll ed. p. 166). Thus there is a difficulty as to why the children of Dedan are omitted in *Chronicles*.]

Hirsch renders these as words descriptive of their national characteristics: *And the sons of Dedan were those living in the plains* [from אשר walking straight forward], *those living by themselves armed* [from לטש, sharpen], *and grouped nations.*

4. וּבְנֵי מִדְיָן עֵיפָה וָעֵפֶר ... — *And the children of Midian: Ephah, [and] Epher ...*

Midian had five sons; according to *Numbers* 31:8, Midian had five princes. In *Isaiah* 60:6, the Ephites are mentioned as a tribe of merchants bringing gold and frankincense from Sheba to the restored Jerusalem. The other tribes mentioned here appear no place else, although the names *Ephah* and *Epher* occur among the descendants of Judah, Manasseh and Reuben. According to Josephus (*Antiquities I*, 15:1) the descendants of Keturah captured territory southeast of Egypt, and the coastal regions east of the Red Sea *(Hoffmann)*.

כָּל־אֵלֶּה בְּנֵי קְטוּרָה — *All these were the descendants of Keturah.*

Of course, Keturah *eventually* had more descendants. Obviously, if one counts great grandchildren and great-great grandchildren one can go on *ad infinitum!* The expression *all these were the descendants of Keturah* means that *all* these were the sons of Keturah along with the grandchildren *who lived during her lifetime.* Possibly they lived during Abraham's lifetime as well, since if Abraham married Keturah immediately after Isaac's wedding, this would mean that Abraham lived for an additional thirty-five years from that time, certainly long enough for him to see grandchildren *(Radak)*.

They are referred to as the *descendants of Keturah,* since in fact, they are not reckoned in the Abrahamitic genealogy *(Malbim)*. [But cf. *v.* 6 אֲשֶׁר לְאַבְרָהָם.]

5. וַיִּתֵּן אַבְרָהָם אֶת־כָּל־אֲשֶׁר־לוֹ לְיִצְחָק — *and Abraham gave all that he had [or all that was his] to Isaac.*

Since Abraham's primary progeny was Isaac, Abraham distinguished him from his other children by giving him his physical and spiritual possessions *(Malbim)*.

In 24:10 the commentators note that Eliezer had taken with him a deed writing over all of Abraham's

ו אֲשֶׁר־לוֹ לְיִצְחָק: וְלִבְנֵי הַפִּילַגְשִׁים אֲשֶׁר לְאַבְרָהָם נָתַן אַבְרָהָם מַתָּנֹת וַיְשַׁלְּחֵם

possessions to Isaac. In 24:36 Eliezer specifically states that Abraham bequeathed all his possessions to Isaac, and as *Rashi* notes there, [Eliezer] *showed them the document*.

Accordingly, *Ramban* notes in his *commentary* to 24:10, that our verse [which is essentially the same as 24:36] means that Abraham had Isaac actually *taken possession* of his property [to take effect] at the time of his death so that the other children would not contest his ownership.

As the commentaries explain, *Rashi* does not accept the view that 24:36 speaks merely of a deed indicating *future* disposition of the estate. Rather, he holds that prior to Eliezer's departure to Aram Naharaim, Abraham already *had given Isaac possession* of all that was his, as Eliezer accurately reported. Accordingly, since the verse cannot be merely redundant, there must be, following *Rashi*, a deeper message in this verse.

Rashi therefore, selected — from among the several interpretations offered by the *Midrash* — the one which he deemed to be closest to the simple sense of the verse, that of R' Nechemiah [who interprets *all that he had* not in the material sense, but as a spiritual legacy]: Abraham transmitted to him 'the blessing' as a legacy [i.e., he conferred on Isaac the privilege of blessing others], for God had told Abraham [12:2] וֶהְיֵה בְּרָכָה, *and you shall be a blessing*, [which as *Rashi:* explains there means]: the privilege of blessing whomever you wish will be in your hand. It was this that Abraham now conferred upon Isaac [for the inclusive phrase *all that he had* denotes an *all-encompassing gift*, meaning even the privilege of blessing].

Among the other views in the *Midrash* are:

— He gave him the birthright;

— He gave him the right to burial in the cave of Machpelah and a deed of gift to his estate;

— He gave him gifts.

According to *Zohar Chadash* this legacy which Abraham now transmitted to Isaac refers to the *supernal knowledge* Abraham possessed inasmuch as he knew the Name of the Holy One, Blessed be He.

There is also an opinion that this gift refers to whatever wealth Abraham amassed in the ensuing period after he wrote the earlier deed to Isaac *(Ibn Caspi)*.

According to *Maharsha, Sanhedrin* 91a, the Talmudic understanding of the simple sense of the verse is that in 24:10 Eliezer took along with him not a *deed* of gift, but the *actual ornaments he later gave to Rebecca*. Accordingly, it is our verse which describes Abraham's transfer of all his possessions to Isaac.

[However, *Maharsha's* interpretation does not account for Eliezer's statement to Bethuel in 24:36 that Abraham had given all that was his to Isaac. Perhaps that verse that led *Rashi* to his interpretation that Eliezer had taken along a deed of gift to show Bethuel, and, following the *Midrash*, that our verse, accordingly, speaks of a spiritual legacy.]

6. וְלִבְנֵי הַפִּילַגְשִׁים אֲשֶׁר לְאַבְרָהָם — *But to the concubine-children whom Abraham had* [lit. *and to the children of the concubines that were unto Abraham*]. The translation follows *Hirsch* who explains that אֲשֶׁר, lit. *that were*, refers to *the children*

25
6 *the concubine-children whom Abraham had, Abraham gave gifts. Then he sent them away from*

and not to *the concubines.* Alternatively, אֲשֶׁר may be referred to the concubines: *but to Abraham's sons by the concubines that were to Abraham.*

[The prefix ו is translated *but* according to the context which emphasizes the contrast between *everything* that Abraham had given Isaac, and his token gifts to his children by his concubines. On such uses of the ו as *conversive,* especially in cases where the verb *follows* the subject, see comm. to 14:14, pp. 493-4.]

To whom does the plural פִּילַגְשִׁים, *concubines,* refer?

Rashi, citing the *Midrash,* notes that the word פִּילַגְשִׁים [according to an ancient Masoretic tradition recorded in the *Midrash**] is spelled deficiently: פִּלַגְשִׁים, without a י, [so it can homiletically be rendered as the singular פִּלֶגֶשׁ (with an appended ם)**]: There was only one concubine — Hagar, who is identical with Keturah.

Moreover, *Rashi* defines the difference between *wives* and *concubines:* Wives are married with a *kesubah* [a document providing, among other things, for a marriage settlement], while *concubines* have no *kesubah,* as explained in *Sanhedrin* 21a.

Rashbam [who does not identify Keturah with Hagar] maintains that the plural *concubines* refers to both Hagar and Keturah.

Ramban notes that although Hagar was a *concubine* [see bracketed *comm.* end of 16:3] and Keturah was his *wife,* she, too, is alluded to as his *concubine* here, as well as specificially as such in I *Chronicles* 1:32. Because only descendants of Isaac could be considered offspring of Abraham [21:12], he regarded all consorts except for Sarah as tantamount to *concubines,* since their children would not be his heirs. It is also possible that Keturah was referred to as a concubine since she was a handmaid who was descended from a family of slaves.

[See *Radak,* cited in *v.* 1 end of s.v. וַיֹּסֶף אַבְרָהָם].

Ramban disagrees with *Rashi* cited above that a concubine is a betrothed wife without a *kesubah,* because most *Tannaim* agree that a *kesubah* is only a Rabbinic ordinance. *Ramban* maintains that a concubine is taken for a consort without *kiddushin* [formal betrothal].

---

*[That in *our* Torah Scrolls the word is spelled *'full'* with two *yods,* פִּילַגְשִׁים, is not unusual since as *Tosafos Shabbos* 55b s.v. מעבירם, as well as *Beis Yosef, Yoreh Deah* 275, note, the *Talmud* is often at variance with the *Masorah* that is used in practice. Cf. *Minchas Shay*].

This is one of three places where *Rashi* cites spellings different from those current in our Torah Scrolls. The other two places are: *Exodus* 25:22: [(וְ)אֵת]; and *Deut.* 1:13 [וַאֲנָשִׁ(י)ם].

Sefer HaZikaron emphasizes that one must have wholehearted faith that despite the rare differences between our *Masorah* and the *Talmud*ic exegeses, our *Scrolls* are correct. An allusion to this is a paraphrase of *Avos* 1:17. 'The *Midrash* is not primary, but practice.'

**If, as *Rashi,* maintains, Abraham's only concubine was Hagar/Keturah, why was the final ם, *mem,* appended to the singular פִּלֶגֶשׁ, *concubine,* making it a modified plural?

Levush suggest that the modified plural is used because Abraham married Hagar on two different occasions: once in Sarah's lifetime and again after her death.

He also notes that the correct text in *Sanhedrin* 21a is: נָשִׁים בִּכְתוּבָּה וּבְקִידוּשִׁין פִּלַגְשִׁים בְּלֹא כְתוּבָּה וּ[בְלֹא] קִידוּשִׁין, 'wives have *kesubah* and *kiddushin;* concubines have no *kesubah* and [no] *kiddushin.*' [*Mizrachi* defends *Rashi* by stating that *Rashi* was citing from the version of the *Talmudic* text in his possession].

Ramban offers a possible defense of *Rashi*'s interpretation that the distinction lies in the *kesubah.* In the case of a Noachide [i.e. all men before the giving of the Torah] *kiddushin* does not apply in any event, but it is conceivable that when taking a *wife* by intercourse as is their law, Noachides were accustomed to write a *form* of *kesubah*, a contract providing for a dowry and gift. If a Noachide intended to take a woman as a concubine whom he could send away at will and whose children would not be among his heirs, then he would not give her this contract.

The inclusion of the phrase אֲשֶׁר לְאַבְרָהָם, *that were Abraham's,* attests to the fact that in however hidden a manner — they carried a spark of Abraham in their souls *(Zohar Chadash).*

נָתַן אַבְרָהָם מַתָּנֹת — *Abraham gave gifts.*

The gifts were given outright [so they would be uncontestable]; not merely bequeathed in the form a last will and testament *(Sforno).*

[What gifts did Abraham have left to give? He had previously given *everything* he owned to Isaac? (Mizrachi)]:

Rashi explains: according to the Sages [*Sanhedrin* 91a that *gifts* are not to be understood in the *material* sense, but rather]: He imparted to them the secrets of the impure or unclean arts.

This refers to the knowledge of demons and sorcery, etc. This does not suggest that Abraham intended them to *use* this knowledge [in idolatry and impure worship], since these unhallowed arts are clearly prohibited by the Torah. Rather, he imparted this knowledge to teach them to *counteract* sorcery, and exorcise demons which enter men *(Gur Aryeh).* [See *Maharsha*].

According to *HaKsav V'haKaballah,* Abraham imparted this knowledge to them so that they would know how to guard themselves from substituting impure names for hallowed names and inadvertently worshiping them.

Rashi adds: another interpretation: *Gifts* refers to those gifts which had been given him because of Sarah [20:14, 16], and the gifts he received from others. All of these he now gave to them since he wished to derive no benefit therefrom. [Previously, he had given Isaac all the *wealth* which he had *earned.*]

וַיְשַׁלְּחֵם מֵעַל יִצְחָק בְּנוֹ בְּעוֹדֶנּוּ חַי — *Then* [lit. *and*] *he sent them away from* [*upon*] *Isaac his son, while he was still alive.*

Lest they *quarrel over the estate (Radak),* and to avoid their laying claim to the Land *(Malbim).*

Abraham wanted to foreclose a possible claim by them that only Ishmael was excluded by God's promise in 21:12 'Since *through Isaac* will offspring be considered yours,' and that because the children of Keturah had not yet been born at that time, God had never intended them to be denied an opportunity to inherit equally with Isaac. To prevent this, Abraham sent them away during his lifetime *(Haamek Davar).*

While he was still alive — since he did not wish to rely on a will *(Sforno).*

[The phrase *while he was still alive* dangles, but the cantillation clearly makes it modify the phrase *he sent them away.* Otherwise, it could have been understood to

Isaac his son, while he was still alive — eastward to the east country.

modify the earlier phrase *Abraham gave gifts* in the sense that he *transferred* the gifts to them during his lifetime and then sent them away rather than making bequests for possession after his demise.]

This is apparently the message *Ralbag* derives from the verse when he comments: The Torah teaches that one should divide his possessions among his children during his lifetime to avoid disputes after his death.

Da'as Soferim notes the sharp contrast between Abraham's treatment of the concubine-children and his earlier treatment of Ishmael. He expelled Ishmael virtually empty-handed to teach him the error of his ways and perhaps influence him to repent. But he gave generous gifts to his children although they were still at an age when he could train them. Presumably he realized that they *could* improve no further under his guidance, or that they might cause harm to Isaac.

Hirsch notes that even Abraham could not succeed in educating *all* his children as he hoped, whereas now it is expected of all Jewish parents that they raise *all* of their children to be their spiritual successors. Then, there was not an inch of land outside his own home where Abraham's spirit was welcome. Now, Jewish children can find at least *some* companions who share their own values.

From the fact that Ishmael participated in Abraham's burial [*v.*9], it is apparent that he had not been driven away permanently as were the other concubine-children. But, as *Abarbanel* explains when Ishmael saw that the others were sent away and that he had no advantage over them, he submitted to Isaac's superiority *(Malbim).* [See also *footnote* to 22:1, pp. 781-783.]

Why did Abraham disinherit some of his sons when such action is forbidden? [see *Deut.* 21:16-17].

— Abraham was following the Divine command of 21:12 according to which only Isaac — of all his children — would be considered his heir *(Mizrachi);*

—When God had told Abraham in 21:12: *Whatever Sarah tells you heed her voice,* He was, in effect, agreeing with her statement [ibid *v.* 10]: *the son of that slavewoman* [*Hagar*] *shall not inherit with my son, with Isaac! (Kli Yakar).*[1]

קֵדְמָה אֶל אֶרֶץ קֶדֶם — *Eastward, to the east country.*

I.e., east of the land of Israel *(Ibn Ezra).* [see 29:1; *Judges* 6:3].

First the Torah states in general terms that Abraham sent them *in an easterly* direction, and then it specifies that it was to those regions that generally come under the heading of 'land of the east': Charan in Aram Naharaim and Ur

1. Cf. also Mishnah, *Bava Basra* 126b that if a man [on his death bed *(Rashi)*] disposes of his property by giving some children more than others, or if he assigned to his first-born a share only *equal* [rather than the double share due him] to that of the other children, his arrangements are valid, provided he declared it a *gift*. If, however, he declared it as an *inheritance* his wishes are disregarded [since Torah law requires that the first-born get a double portion, while the other sons receive equal shares.] This *Mishnah* [*without* the qualification that this disposition take place on a deathbed, as *Rashi* notes] is cited in *Midrash HaGadol* as support for Abraham's division of the inheritance in this case.

ז אֶרֶץ קֶדֶם: וְאֵלֶּה יְמֵי שְׁנֵי־חַיֵּי אַבְרָהָם
אֲשֶׁר־חָי מְאַת שָׁנָה וְשִׁבְעִים שָׁנָה וְחָמֵשׁ
ח שָׁנִים: וַיִּגְוַע וַיָּמָת אַבְרָהָם בְּשֵׂיבָה טוֹבָה

Kasdim. Since Abraham's kin lived in those lands, he sent his concubine-children there, confident that his kinsman would welcome them and offer them greater friendship there than they would find elsewhere *(Radak).*

Chizkuni also identifies 'east country' with Aram [=Syria / Iraq; see *comm.* to 10:22 and 24:10]. He cites *Isaiah* 9:11 that Aram was to the east of *Eretz Yisrael*, and further notes that the land of Utz, described in *Job* 1:3 as an *eastern country*, was named for Utz, one of the children of Abraham's brother Nachor [see 22:21.] Accordingly, *Chizkuni* explains that Abraham sent them there to claim the ancestral inheritance that was due him for his own family.

7. The death of Abraham.

וְאֵלֶּה יְמֵי שְׁנֵי חַיֵּי אַבְרָהָם אֲשֶׁר־חָי — *Now* [lit. *and*] *these are the days of the years of Abraham's life which he lived.*

— I.e., which he had lived *fully*; not one day of his life was wasted [cf. *Midrash HaGadol:* all his days were life, and none of them was death; and cf. *Berachos* 18a 'the righteous even in death are called living.']

[Chronologically, Abraham lived until his grandson Jacob was fifteen years old (since Abraham was a hundred at Isaac's birth, and Isaac was sixty when Jacob was born — *v.* 26) and accordingly his death took place *after* the events of the coming chapters. But in accordance with the Torah's usual method of narration, (as *Ramban* explains in 11:32) it bids farewell, so to speak, to Abraham when there is nothing further of his life that it must recount. Similarly, the Torah gives us whatever information it deems necessary about Ishmael's family. Then it can go on uninterrupted to the central figure of the succeeding narrative, Isaac.

In the same way, Noah's death is recorded in 9:29 before the history of his sons is mentioned although Noah was still alive well into the days of Abraham, and his son Shem lived to see Jacob, *(Bava Basra* 121b; see vol. I p. xii: *Chronology*/Time Line); the passing of Terach [11:32] is recorded before the story of Abraham, although he lived another sixty years(in that case the *Midrash* offers a special interpretation; see *Rashi* and *Ramban* there); and the death of Isaac [35:28-29) before the narratives of Esau and Jacob, although Isaac was still alive when Joseph was sold into slavery.]

מְאַת שָׁנָה וְשִׁבְעִים שָׁנָה וְחָמֵשׁ שָׁנִים — *A hundred* [*years*] *and seventy* [*years, and*] *five years.*

At a hundred he was like seventy and at seventy like five — without sin *(Rashi).*

Rashi compares him to a man of seventy regarding sin, because a man at seventy is at the twilight of his life, and since death stares him in the face he does not sin, just as a child of five is sinless *(Be'er Mayim Chaim).*

[*See comm.* to 23:1 in reference to Sarah's lifespan where *Rashi* offers a similar ex-

[7] *Now these are the days of the years of Abraham's*
life which he lived: a hundred and seventy-five
years. [8] *And Abraham expired and died at a good old*

egesis. That interpretation, however, unlike this one, is based on a *Midrash*, as *Ramban* ad. loc. point out. See there also the defense of *Mizrachi* and *Gur Aryeh* cited for *Rashi's* interpretation here.]

8. וַיִּגְוַע וַיָּמָת אַבְרָהָם — *And Abraham expired and died.*

The year was 2123 from Creation *(Seder Olam).*

The term וַיִּגְוַע here translated with the delicate expression *expired,* has been discussed in the *commentary* to 6:17 and 7:21.

Ibn Ezra and *Radak* explain it as quick death without prolonged sickness: 'The sudden departure of the spirit from the body without pain or delay.'

Ramban [to *v.* 17] cites the *Talmud (Bava Basra* 16b), [see *comm.* to *v.* 17] as proof that in conjunction with the terms מִיתָה, *death,* and וַיֵּאָסֶף, *being gathered in* וַיִּגְוַע refers to quick death without prolonged sickness. This is the death enjoyed by the righteous.

Ramban goes on to cite a different view [*Bereishis Rabbah* 62:1] that the early pious men used to suffer with intestinal disease for about ten or twenty days before death. That is the basis for the principle, that הַחוֹלִי מְמָרֵק, *illness cleanses* [*from sin;* or possibly that it physically *purifies* the internal organs so that the righteous may enter the life of the Hereafter in physical purity *(Yafeh Toar)*]. As the *Midrash* goes on to say, the very term וַיִּגְוַע implies death from intestinal disease [which, as noted in *Erubin* 41b, is a death that comes quickly while one is even alert enough to carry on a conversation *(Radal).*] According to this *Midrashic* interpretation, וַיִּגְוַע would mean *shriveled, emaciated,* etc. or *faint* which is how *Onkelos* renders it.

As noted in the *commentary* to 7:21, however, the consensus of commentators explain the term וַיִּגְוַע as signifying the *transitional moment between life and death* [Hirsch: *unconsciousness*] while וַיָּמָת represents *death* itself.

Karnei Or, on this basis, relates the word to the root יגע, *fatigue,* and explains the term וַיִּגְוַע to refer to the body's complete loss of vigor, prior to death [*HaKsav V'haKabbalah*].

בְּשֵׂיבָה טוֹבָה זָקֵן וְשָׂבֵעַ — *At a good old age, mature* [so *Hirsch;* lit. *old*] *and content.*

— For God promised him in 15:15, that the prophesied affliction of his descendants would not begin in his lifetime *(Rashbam).*[1]

Ramban explains the phrase *old and contented* as implying that he

1. [See *Rashi* in *commentary* to 15:15 that Abraham was destined to live 180 years like his son but God caused him to die five years earlier so that he would not witness Esau's evil conduct. For, as the *Midrash Aggadah* notes, the five years corresponded to the five sins Esau committed on the very day Abraham died [and had Abraham lived he would have witnessed them]: he stole, raped a betrothed maiden, murdered, denied the fundamental Principle [i.e. the existence of God], and despised the birthright. God therefore said, 'I promised Abraham, *you shall be buried in a good old age.* Is it *good old age* when he sees his grandson commit adultery and murder? — Better let him die in peace!']

[According to *Rashi* in *v.* 9, however, the specific reference here to *good old age* is that Ishmael had repented.]

ט זָקֵן וְשָׂבֵעַ וַיֵּאָסֶף אֶל־עַמָּיו: וַיִּקְבְּרוּ אֹתוֹ יִצְחָק וְיִשְׁמָעֵאל בָּנָיו אֶל־מְעָרַת הַמַּכְפֵּלָה אֶל־שְׂדֵה עֶפְרֹן בֶּן־צֹחַר הַחִתִּי

lived to see all the desires of his heart fulfilled, and was content with all good things. This is the mark of the righteous who are content with their lot and do not desire superfluous luxuries, in contrast with those of whom it is said *he that loves money shall not be satisfied with money* [*Ecclesiastes* 5:9]. As the Sages commented: No man leaves the world possessing half of his desires. If one has a hundred, he desires two hundred; if he acquires two hundred, he desires four hundred. Thus the wicked are dissatisfied when they die; only of the righteous, who seek no luxuries can it be said that they are *satisfied*.

According to the *Midrash* — *Ramban* continues — Abraham was content, because before he died he was shown, as are the righteous in this world, a vision of the reward stored up for them in the World to Come. Then immersed in joy, they die peacefully and satisfied.

Radak explains שֵׂיבָה טוֹבָה, *good old age*, as indicating that he lived to see children and grandchildren, and was steeped in goodness and honor.

וַיֵּאָסֶף אֶל־עַמָּיו — *And he was gathered to his people* [lit. *his peoples*] [i.e. to the members of his family who died before him (*Radak*).]

Some maintain that the phrase is idiomatic, i.e. that [in death] he went the way of his ancestors, and so, in a sense, joined them (*Ibn Ezra*). In this sense the phrase occurs whether the ancestors were righteous or wicked (*Radak*).

Most, however, connect this expression specifically to the soul, for while it is in the body it is, as it were, in isolation [from the Upper worlds]; when the soul leaves the body, it rejoins its Source and is gathered back to its glory (*Ralbag*).[1]

[That such phrases allude to the *soul's* ingathering to its honorable repose can be inferred also from God's promise to Abraham in 15:15: *You shall go to your fathers in peace.* Since Abraham was not *buried* near his fathers, that verse must refer to a *spiritual reunification* of the soul with his ancestors. As *Sechel Tov* points out, our verse teaches that he was *spiritually reunited* with his father Terach, who had repented and whose soul was in Gan Eden.]

Midrash HaGadol explains *his people* as implying that in the Hereafter, every person is gathered in accordance with his character: the righteous are gathered with the generation of their ancestors, and the wicked are hurled with theirs; one whose life exemplified silver eats out of silver utensils, while he whose life was earthen [i.e. base] eats out of earthenware utensils.

— He was gathered into the bond

1. In the matter of a soul returning to its source, we find many similar expressions in Scripture: *You will come to your forefathers* (15:15); *gathered in to his forefathers (Judges* 2:10). See also, for example, 47:30 and *I Kings* 2:10. Such expressions prove that belief in the Hereafter is an integral part of Jewish faith. Death, therefore, is viewed as a reunification with earlier generations. Conversely, the punishment of כָּרֵת, *excision*, cutting off of *the soul*, i.e., the denial to it of the opportunity to return to its forebears.

25 *age, mature and content, and he was gathered to his*
9 *people.* [9] *His sons Isaac and Ishmael buried him in*
the cave of Machpelah, in the field of Ephron the son

of eternal life with the righteous of all generations, who are *his people* because they are similar to him. The plural עַמָּיו, *his peoples,* implies that there are many 'nations' in the World to Come, an allusion to the fact that each righteous person has his own unique characteristics as if there is a multitude of worlds. This is because everyone's share in the World to Come is a product of his own unique accomplishments during life. Therefore, no two portions in the Hereafter are alike *(Sforno).*

Thus, the term *gathering* refers to restoration of anything to its proper place. In this case, since the body is only the soul's temporary home, when it leaves the body it is *gathered* to its true, permanent home *(Hoffmann).*

As *Hirsch* comments, the belief in immortality of the soul was so routinely accepted in ancient times that there was no need to 'teach' it as dogma. It was taken quite for granted that just as the dead body returned to earth, its source, so the soul would return to the spiritual world whence it orginated.

9. וַיִּקְבְּרוּ אֹתוֹ יִצְחָק וְיִשְׁמָעֵאל בָּנָיו — *And his sons Isaac and Ishmael buried him.*

We would expect to see Ishmael mentioned first as the older son *(R'Bachya)* ...

We infer from this that Ishmael repented and gave precedence to Isaac *(Rashi).*

As the Midrash comments: Ishmael, the son of the maidservant [Hagar] showed honor to the son of the lady [Sarah], for were this not the case they would have been listed according to their age with Ishmael first. In *Bava Basra* 16b it is deduced from this that Ishmael had repented. The *Talmud* asks: Perhaps the verse merely listed them in the order of their wisdom [and thus Isaac is properly mentioned first, with no suggestion of repentance on the part of Ishmael.] The *Talmud* answers that in this case, the Torah did not use relative wisdom as the criterion. The proof of this is in 35:29, which tells how Isaac was buried by his children: there Esau [the elder] is mentioned before Jacob [the wiser]. The prior mention of Isaac in our verse, therefore, must lead to the deduction that he repented in Abraham's lifetime *(Mizrachi).*

Gur Aryeh asks: Perhaps the Torah mentioned Isaac first simply because he was the son of the lady and as such clearly merited precedence over Ishmael the son of the maidservant? —But the traditional hatred of the wicked for the righteous is so intense, and so defies the norm of dignified conduct [מְקַלְקֶלֶת אֶת הַשּׁוּרָה], that if Ishmael were still wicked he would never — under any circumstances — have allowed the righteous Isaac, to precede him. Hence, the Sages derive from this verse that Ishmael repented.

Ha'amek Davar adds that implicit here is that Abraham had informed Ishmael of God's decree that he was a son in every respect, except in situations where Isaac was involved [in line with 21:12: *through Isaac will offspring be considered yours.*] Ishmael obediently refrained from contesting the inheritance, and accordingly now gave precedence to Isaac. Once Isaac is given this precedence, Ishmael is referred to as *son* which he was in every other sense.

אֶל מְעָרַת ... — *In the cave ...*

The Hebrew אֶל is literally *to* the cave, but here it means *in* the cave. Cf. *Exodus* 25:21 וְאֶל הָאָרֹן, and *in* the Ark. There are many such examples in Scripture *(Radak).*

י אֲשֶׁר עַל־פְּנֵי מַמְרֵא׃ הַשָּׂדֶה אֲשֶׁר־קָנָה
אַבְרָהָם מֵאֵת בְּנֵי־חֵת שָׁמָּה קֻבַּר
יא אַבְרָהָם וְשָׂרָה אִשְׁתּוֹ׃ וַיְהִי אַחֲרֵי מוֹת
אַבְרָהָם וַיְבָרֶךְ אֱלֹהִים אֶת־יִצְחָק בְּנוֹ
וַיֵּשֶׁב יִצְחָק עִם־בְּאֵר לַחַי רֹאִי׃
°שביעי יב °וְאֵלֶּה תֹּלְדֹת יִשְׁמָעֵאל בֶּן־אַבְרָהָם אֲשֶׁר

10. הַשָּׂדֶה אֲשֶׁר קָנָה אַבְרָהָם מֵאֵת בְּנֵי חֵת — *The field that Abraham had bought from the children of Heth.*

The Torah again emphasizes, when mentioning this field, that Abraham *purchased* it to stress Abraham's exemplary faith in God. For although God had promised him [13:15]: *All the Land that you see, to you will I give it* ... nevertheless he had to *buy* a small plot in order to bury his wife. Nevertheless, his faith remained unshaken throughout *(Radak).*

שָׁמָּה קֻבַּר אַבְרָהָם וְשָׂרָה אִשְׁתּוֹ — *There was Abraham buried, and Sarah his wife.*

The *Midrash* notes that thirty-eight years elapsed between Sarah's death and Abraham's — why, then, is Sarah's death mentioned here?

— To evoke memories, comparing both funerals. Whoever partook in Sarah's funeral also was privileged to participate in Abraham's.[1]

— Furthermore, Shem and Eber attended Sarah's funeral and they selected the site within the Cave of Machpelah which they felt would be suitable for Abraham whom they foresaw would also be buried there. Thus, Sarah was buried in the cave, and Abraham was now buried beside her.

11. וַיְהִי אַחֲרֵי מוֹת אַבְרָהָם וַיְבָרֶךְ אֱלֹהִים אֶת יִצְחָק בְּנוֹ — *And it was, after the death of Abraham, that* [lit. *and*] *God blessed Isaac, his son.*

By 'bless' is meant that He comforted him in his mourning [נִחֲמוֹ תַּנְחוּמֵי אֲבֵלִים, *He comforted him with the formula of consolation for mourners*] *(Rashi).*

[This is based on *Sotah* 14a where we are enjoined to imitate God's ways: 'The Holy One, Blessed be He comforted mourners (as it says in our verse); therefore you must comfort mourners.']

Rashi chose this as פְּשַׁט, the simple meaning of *bless* in our verse, for — since Abraham had already made *him* the source of blessing by conferring upon him the right to bless others (*v.*5) — what blessing could Isaac have needed aside from that of consolation *(Gur Aryeh).*

According to *Nachalas Yaakov* [cited by *Sifsei Chachomim*], *Rashi* cites the *Talmudic* explanation as the simple meaning because the verse emphasizes that this blessing was conferred *after* Abraham's death. Now, unless it was the blessing of comforting the mourner why would the Torah have to specify that it was conferred after Abraham's death?

Rashi continues with another explanation [possibly motivated by the fact that the verse specifies that *God* blessed Isaac rather than his father as was customary]:

Although God had empowered Abraham to bless whomever he wished, he feared to bless Isaac,

1. On the day of Abraham's death, the great of all the nations of the world lamented; 'Woe to the world that has lost its leader! Woe to the world that has lost its pilot!' *(Bava Basra* 91b).

of Zohar the Hittite, facing Mamre. 10 *The field that*
Abraham had bought from the children of Heth —
there was Abraham buried, and Sarah his wife.
11 *And it was after the death of Abraham that God*
blessed Isaac his son, and Isaac settled near Be'er
Lachai R'oi.
12 *These are the descendants of Ishmael, Abraham's*

because he foresaw that Esau would descend from him [and he was apprehensive that Isaac would in turn prefer to confer these blessings upon his favorite son Esau, rather than Jacob *(Terumas HaDeshen)*]. According to this interpretation we must assume that although Abraham was spared the ordeal of witnessing Esau's public sinfulness (see *Rashi* to *v.*30), he nevertheless foresaw that Esau would be wicked.] Abraham had therefore said, 'Let the Master of the blessings come Himself and bless whomever He sees fit.' — God now came and blessed him [since God knew that Jacob, and not Esau, would be the recipient of the blessings (ibid.)]

This latter interpretation of *Rashi* would then negate *Rashi's* own interpretation in *v.* 5 that Abraham *had* transferred to Isaac the divine power to bless whomever he wished. Verse 5 would accordingly have to be interpreted in one of the other senses cited by the Midrash *(Mizrachi; Gur Aryeh; Terumas HaDeshen).*

According to *Radak,* our passage means simply that *God prospered Isaac's endeavors.*

Hirsch suggests that the verse is telling us that now God blessed Isaac on his own account; for heretofore the blessing which Isaac enjoyed was derived only from the blessing granted to Abraham.

Kli Yakar suggests that God blessed Isaac only *after* Abraham's death. God withheld the blessing until then because, during his lifetime, Abraham had the privilege of blessing whomever he wished [12:2]; God did not wish to 'bypass' Abraham so to speak.

וַיֵּשֶׁב יִצְחָק עִם־בְּאֵר לַחַי רֹאִי — *And Isaac settled near* [lit. *with*] *Be'er Lachai Ro'i.*

— Near Hagar, Abraham's widow *(Midrash Aggadah).*

The Torah mentions the places of Isaac's residence because he spread the Name of God from each of them *(Da'as Soferim).*

Either the verse means that he lived near (עִם) the area of Be'er Lachai Ro'i, or since Be'er Lachai Ro'i was not a *city* but a *well* [see 16:14], the Torah mentions that he lived *near the well.* Presumably, if it were the name of a city the Torah would have written that he settled *in* Be'er Lachai Ro'i] *(Ramban).*

12. Ishmael's Genealogy

וְאֵלֶּה תֹּלְדֹת יִשְׁמָעֵאל בֶּן־אַבְרָהָם — [*And*] *these are the descendants* [lit. *generations; genealogies; chronicles*] *of Ishmael, Abraham's son.*

In the simple sense, Ishmael's descendants are enumerated, as well as his years, in deference to Abraham *(Radak),* [hence the appelation: *Abraham's son*], and to inform us that the seed of the righteous shall be blessed. However, in the

יָלְדָה הָגָר הַמִּצְרִית שִׁפְחַת שָׂרָה
יג לְאַבְרָהָם: וְאֵלֶּה שְׁמוֹת בְּנֵי יִשְׁמָעֵאל
בִּשְׁמֹתָם לְתוֹלְדֹתָם בְּכֹר יִשְׁמָעֵאל נְבָיֹת
יד וְקֵדָר וְאַדְבְּאֵל וּמִבְשָׂם: וּמִשְׁמָע וְדוּמָה
טו וּמַשָּׂא: חֲדַד וְתֵימָא יְטוּר נָפִישׁ וָקֵדְמָה:

case of Esau, his lifespan is not mentioned because he outlived Jacob [according to *Sotah* 13a, Esau was present at Jacob's burial; cf. *Rashi* and *footnote* to 27:45], and the narrative of that period would not be concluded until later, with the death of Jacob. When that took place, the Torah did not wish to revert to mentioning Esau since his genealogy had already been enumerated in its appropriate place [Chapt. 36] *(Ramban)*.

Ramban continues: although there are several *Midrashic* explanations for the Scriptural account of Ishmael's years, the correct one is that he deserved this recognition since he had repented, and died a religious man.

[*Rashi* cites one of the *Midrashic* explanations from *Megillah* 17a in his *commentary* to *v.* 17.]

According to *Yafeh Toar's* reading of the *Midrash*, Ishmael's genealogy deserved mention in the Torah because he came from the uttermost recesses of the wilderness to pay honor to his father [at his death].

אֲשֶׁר יָלְדָה הָגָר הַמִּצְרִית שִׁפְחַת שָׂרָה לְאַבְרָהָם — *Whom Hagar the Egyptian, Sarah's maidservant, bore to Abraham.*

This verse points out the dual spiritual characteristics stored up within Ishmael. On the one hand he is בֶּן אַבְרָהָם, *Abraham's son,* while on the other hand the blood of his Egyptian mother, Hagar, flows through his veins *(Alshich)*.

Although Ishmael was the son of the maidservant, Abraham loved him as his firstborn; and God accordingly blessed him for Abraham's sake, as it says [21:20]: *God was with the youth and he became great.* He begot twelve princes as God promised Abraham [17:20] *(Radak)*.

As had been noted previously, it is emphasized that Abraham regarded him as his son in every sense of the word; it was only relative to Sarah and her son that Ishmael was considered the son of the maidservant *(Haamek Davar)*.

... And as such the destiny of the Abrahamitic line was not to find expression in him *(Hoffmann)*.

Thus, as *Ramban* [to *v.* 19] explains, the phrase *whom Hagar the Egyptian bore* ... is included here in Isaac's honor, as if to signify that Ishmael's progeny is not traceable to *Abraham* they are considered to be exclusively the children of the maidservant, and they were blessed as promised to Hagar in 21:13. Therefore, when mentioning *Isaac's* genealogy in *v.* 19, the Torah specifically says *Abraham begot Isaac* — explicitly identifying Isaac as the primary son.

13. וְאֵלֶּה שְׁמוֹת בְּנֵי יִשְׁמָעֵאל — [*And*] *these are the names of the sons of Ishmael.*

בִּשְׁמֹתָם לְתוֹלְדֹתָם — *By* [lit. *in*] *their*

25 *son, whom Hagar the Egyptian, Sarah's maidservant,*
13-16 *bore to Abraham.* 13 *These are the names of the sons*
of Ishmael by their names, in order of their birth:
Ishmael's first born Nebayoth, Kedar, Adbeel, and
Mivsam, 14 *Mishma, Dumah, and Masa,* 15 *Hadad*
and Sema, Yetur, Nafish, and Kedmah. 16 *These are*

names, in order of their birth.

The rendering of לְתוֹלְדֹתָם as: *in order of their birth* follows *Rashi,* and most commentators. [It could also be rendered *to their generations; to their progeny; to their chronicles.*]

That this is so, is evidenced by the fact that, in the very next phrase, Nebayoth is specifically identified as Ishmael's first-born. It would seem, therefore, that the Torah is concerned with the order of their birth, in contrast to other genealogies in the Torah — such as Noah's, for example, where his children are listed in order of their *wisdom,* not their age [*Sanhedrin* 69b; see *comm.* to 6:10] (*Mizrachi;* cf. *Haamek Davar,* and *comm.* to *Exod.* 6:16).

Hirsch, noting from *v.* 16 that those who are named here were נְשִׂיאִים, *chieftains,* suggests that the expression בִּשְׁמֹתָם לְתוֹלְדֹתָם has the connotation of *whose names remained for their descendants* since these names remained the names of the Ishmaelite tribes. Thus, the verse informs us that the well-known names of the Bedouin tribes derived from the sons of Ishmael.

בְּכֹר יִשְׁמָעֵאל נְבָיֹת, וְקֵדָר — *Ishmael's first born Nebayoth,* [*and*] *Kedar.*

Nebayoth, the first-born, and *Kedar,* the second son, are the most important of the Ishmaelite tribes. They are mentioned together in *Isaiah* 60:7. One of Esau's wives was Mahalath, the sister of Nebayoth [28:9].

... Kedar, famous for its archers [*Isaiah* 21:16] appears as a wealthy merchant tribe in *Jeremiah* 49:28-29 *(Hoffmann).*

[As noted in the *commentary* to ArtScroll *Shir HaShirim* 1:5, David describes them as a barbarous people when he exclaims (*Psalms* 120:5): אוֹיָה לִי כִּי גַרְתִּי מֶשֶׁךְ שָׁכַנְתִּי עִם־אָהֳלֵי קֵדָר, *Woe is me that I sojourn in Meshech, that I dwell in the tents of Kedar!*]

וְאַדְבְּאֵל וּמִבְשָׂם — [*And*] *Adbeel, and Mivsam.*

— Unknown (*Hoffmann*).

14. וּמִשְׁמָע וְדוּמָה וּמַשָּׂא — [*And*] *Mishma,* [*and*] *Dumah, and Masa.*

Mishma is unknown. The *Dumah* mentioned in *Isaiah* 21:11 is apparently not the same tribe *(Hoffmann).* [Dumah is mentioned there together with Seir which would indicate that they were descended from Esau.]

15. חֲדַד וְתֵמָא יְטוּר נָפִישׁ וָקֵדְמָה — *Hadad and Tema, Yetur, Nafish and Kedmah.*

Hadad — unknown; the *Temites* were a trading tribe mentioned in *Job* 6:19; *Isaiah* 21:14; *Jeremiah* 25:23. In both Isaiah and Jeremiah Temais mentioned in relation to Dedan — one of the descendants of Keturah. The city of *Tema* was an important station bordering on the Syrian desert. ...

The tribes of Yetur and Nafish were expelled by Reuben, Gad, and

°מפטיר

טז °אֵלֶּה הֵם בְּנֵי יִשְׁמָעֵאל וְאֵלֶּה שְׁמֹתָם
בְּחַצְרֵיהֶם וּבְטִירֹתָם שְׁנֵים־עָשָׂר נְשִׂיאִם
יז לְאֻמֹּתָם: וְאֵלֶּה שְׁנֵי חַיֵּי יִשְׁמָעֵאל מְאַת
שָׁנָה וּשְׁלֹשִׁים שָׁנָה וְשֶׁבַע שָׁנִים וַיִּגְוַע
יח וַיָּמָת וַיֵּאָסֶף אֶל־עַמָּיו: וַיִּשְׁכְּנוּ מֵחֲוִילָה

Menasheh when they settled on the Transjordan; cf. *I Chron.* 5:18-19. The descendants of Yetur settled in the mountain ranges to the north and south of Damascus, in regions of difficult access. Aristobulus, a king during the latter period of the Second Temple period, forced the southern Yeturites to embrace Judaism [see *Josephus,* Antiquities 13:11:3]. *Kedmah* is not mentioned again in the Bible. The *children of Kedem* [east] mentioned in *Judges* 6:3 were not one tribe, but the appelation for several Arab tribes who dwelt in the east *(Hoffmann).*

16. אֵלֶּה הֵם בְּנֵי יִשְׁמָעֵאל – *These are the sons of Ishmael.*

As is customary in Scripture, the subject is closed with a general statement summing up the matter; the closing summary also being used as a means of further clarification *(Radak).*

וְאֵלֶּה שְׁמֹתָם בְּחַצְרֵיהֶם וּבְטִירֹתָם – *And these are their names by* [lit. in] *their open cities* [following *Rashi and Onkelos;* (lit. *courtyards*)] *and by* [lit. *in*] *their strongholds* [i.e., fortified cities *(Radak)*].

I.e. – whether they took up residence in *open cities* [denoting, according to *Hoffmann,* the circular *encampments* of nomadic tribes (cf. *Numb.* 31:10)] or in *encampments* – they lived in security and honor. All those bearing these tribal names [שְׁמֹתָם] – regardless of where they lived, were descendants of Ishmael (cf. *Radak).*

שְׁנֵים עָשָׂר נְשִׂיאִם לְאֻמֹּתָם – *Twelve chieftains* [or: *princes*] *for their nations.*

I.e. twelve chieftains of as many families. Each of the above was a prince, *and* the ancestor of a large family which carried his name, as we see from later appearances of these names in Scripture, representing distinct family clans *(Radak).*

This was in fulfillment of the promise made to Abraham in 17:20 *(Sechel Tov).*

[On the transient nature of their glory, like נְשִׂיאִים, *clouds,* see *Rashi* to 17:20. *Hirsch* to our verse, however, perceives a positive connotation in the use of the same word, נְשִׂיאִים, for *clouds* and for *princes.* All the moisture received by clouds comes from the earth and is eventually returned to the earth; so, the conscientious prince perceives himself as the servant of his people. What he has derives from them and is meant to be utilized for their benefit. This is in contrast to the princes of Esau's family. They are called אֲלוּפִים which *Hirsch* interprets as a term denoting selfish possession (see *comm.* to 36:15).]

Hoffmann notes that the word אֻמָּה is rare in Hebrew although common in Aramaic. Perhaps the word is used specifically to denote Ishmaelite tribal-clans; cf. *Numbers* 25:15 where it is used of a Midianite chieftain.

the sons of Ishmael, and these are their names by
their open cities and by their strongholds, twelve
chieftains for their nations.
17 These were the years of Ishmael's life: A
hundred and thirty-seven years. He expired and died,
and was gathered to his people. 18 They dwelt from

17. וְאֵלֶּה שְׁנֵי חַיֵּי יִשְׁמָעֵאל — [*And*] *these were the years of Ishmael's life.*

Ishmael's age is given because it assists in calculations with respect to [dating the various events which occurred in the life of] Jacob (*Rashi* [*Yevamos* 64a]).[1]).

According to *Ramban* [to this verse, but cited in *v.* 12] Ishmael's age is noted here because he repented and the age of the righteous is generally stated. *Rashbam* holds that it is recorded as a mark of honor for Abraham. Since the Torah had mentioned Abraham's age at Ishmael's birth, and Ishmael's age when he underwent circumcision, it now concludes by mentioning his lifespan.

מְאַת שָׁנָה וּשְׁלֹשִׁים שָׁנָה וְשֶׁבַע שָׁנִים — *A hundred* [years] *and thirty* [*years, and*] *seven years.*

[See *comm.* to 23:1 for a discussion of why each period of Ishmael's life is set off by the word *years.*]

וַיִּגְוַע וַיָּמָת וַיֵּאָסֶף אֶל־עַמָּיו — *And he expired and died and was gathered to his people.*

[On the meaning of the expressions *expired* and *gathered to his people,* see *commentary* to *v.* 8.]

Rashi comments that the word וַיִּגְוַע is mentioned only in the case of righteous people [such as Ishmael, since he repented as noted in the *commentary* to *v.* 9.]

The *Talmud Bava Basra* 16b, however, notes that the term וַיִּגְוַע, *expired* is used also with reference to the *wicked* Generation of the Flood [see above 6:17; 7:21]. The answer is that the term *expired* alludes to the death of the wicked only when it is used alone [as in the case of the victims of the Flood and the generation that died in the wilderness (*Numbers* 20:3).] However, when it is used in conjunction with the

1. *Rashi* goes on to explain that we calculate from Ishmael's age at his death that Jacob attended the Academy of Eber for fourteen years from the time he left his father's house [which coincides with Ishmael's death (see on 28:9)] to the time he arrived at Laban's house (as is explained in *Megillah* 17a).

[Briefly, according to the data cited in *Megillah* 17a, when Jacob stood before Pharaoh he should have been 116 years old, yet Jacob himself gave his age as 130 (47:9). The discrepancy is explained by the fact that he spent fourteen years in the Academy of Eber after leaving his father's house.]

According to the parallel exegesis in the *Midrash,* Ishmael's lifespan is given in order to assist in calculating Jacob's age when he was blessed. [Jacob received the blessings from Isaac at the time Ishmael died (see 28:9). Ishmael was 137 years old then he died and Isaac was Ishmael's junior by fourteen years, since Abraham was 86 years old when Ishmael was born (16:16) and 100 years old when Isaac was born (21:5)

Therefore, since Isaac was 123 years old at Ishmael's death, Jacob who was 60 years younger than Isaac (25:26) was 63 years old when he received the blessings.

עַד־שׁוּר אֲשֶׁר עַל־פְּנֵי מִצְרַיִם בֹּאֲכָה
אַשּׁוּרָה עַל־פְּנֵי כָל־אֶחָיו נָפָל׃

expression וַיֵּאָסֶף אֶל עַמָּיו, *and he was gathered to his people*, it alludes to righteous people. [Similarly when it comes in conjunction with וַיָּמָת, *and he died* as it does here and regarding Abraham, it refers to the righteous *(Ramban).*]

According to *R' Bachya* it is based on the use in our verse of both *expired* and *died* — which refer to the death only of the righteous — that the Sages said that Ishmael repented of his evil ways.

18. וַיִּשְׁכְּנוּ מֵחֲוִילָה עַד שׁוּר אֲשֶׁר עַל פְּנֵי מִצְרַיִם בֹּאֲכָה אַשּׁוּרָה — *They dwelt from Chavilah to Shur — which is near Egypt —* [lit. *upon the face of Egypt*] *toward Assyria.*

Chavilah is located to the southeast of Arabia toward the Persian Gulf of India, as in 2:11 *(Kesses HaSofer* to 10:29).

Shur is part of the Sinai Peninsula bordering on Egypt, as above 16:7 *(Hoffmann).* As *Sforno* notes there it is identical with *Hagra*, as *Onkelos* renders; a town on the Canaanite border or just beyond it.

On the phrase בֹּאֲכָה אַשּׁוּרָה, *toward Assyria,* compare the similar expression in 13:10 בֹּאֲכָה צֹעַר [*going toward Zoar*] which *Rashi* explains there as: *until Zoar.*

In our case the phrase means: *in the direction of Assyria* [i.e. they dwelt in the region from Chavilah *in a northeast direction* toward Shur which is near Egypt] *(Hoffmann).*

[There is also an opinion that the reference is to the land of *Ashurim* mentioned in *v.* 3, probably to the south, rather than the well-known Assyria, to the north,which does not fit in as well with the context.]

עַל פְּנֵי כָל־אֶחָיו נָפָל — *Over* [lit. *in the face of*] *all his brothers he dwelt* [lit. *fell.*]

[The essential meaning of this passage is the fulfillment of the promise to Hagar in 16:12: וְעַל־פְּנֵי כָל אֶחָיו יִשְׁכֹּן, *over all his brothers he shall dwell.* As *Rashi* explains there, the blessing meant that Ishmael's descendants would be so numerous that they would have to expand beyond their own bounds onto those of their brothers.]

The translation of נָפָל, [lit. *fell*], as *dwelt* follows *Rashi* to our verse

25 *Chavilah to Shur — which is near Egypt — toward*
18 *Assyria; over all his brothers he dwelt.*

who cites the parallel use of that verb in *Judges* 7:12. He notes that in our verse the verb *fell* is used, while the promise in 16:12 says יִשְׁכֹּן, *dwell,* is used. As the *Midrash* explains, while Abraham was alive it could be said that Ishmael would יִשְׁכֹּן, *dwell* [i.e. a term which connotes tranquility and security (*Maharzu*)]; after Abraham died, however, *he fell* [i.e. a term suggesting declining security.][1]

According to *Hirsch* and others the term *fell* is suggestive of 'alighting where one does not belong,' or more forcefully: *plunder, conquer, attack.* They would render accordingly: *He* [i.e. *his descendants*] *intruded against all his brothers.*

[This might account for the different verbs here and in 16:12: during Abraham's lifetime, Ishmael *dwelt peacefully;* after Abraham's death, however, נָפָל, he aggressively *intruded forcibly* on other's boundaries.]

According to the Masoretic note appearing at the end of the *Sidrah* there are 105 verses in *Chayai Sarah* numerically corresponding to the mnemonic יהויד״ע [= יה יודיע, = HASHEM *makes known*], an allusion to God's having made His will known through Eliezer (24:14). The *Haftarah* begins with *I Kings* 1: וְהַמֶּלֶךְ דָּוִד זָקֵן.

1. *Kli Yakar* raises the difficulty, however, that since Ishmael apparently repented after Abraham's death, it would be more appropriate to say that he *fell* only during Abraham's lifetime, when he was still sinful! — Therefore, *Kli Yakar* suggests a reverse interpretation: יִשְׁכֹּן, which is in future tense, should refer to Ishmael's continuing high status *after* his repentance, while נָפָל, in past tense, refers only to the relatively brief period until then.

Alternatively, he suggests that נָפָל, literally *he fell,* refers to the *repentant* Ishmael because an important feature of repentance is that the erstwhile sinner *fell* i.e., that he fell humble and submissive.

נשלם סדרה חיי שרה בעזרת האל

APPENDIX

Eliezer's Mission: Variations and Nuances

Chapter 24 describes Eliezer's mission to seek a wife for Isaac. Virtually every part of the chapter is given in two versions: The narrative of the event as given by Scripture, and the recapitulation given by Eliezer to Rebecca's family [see *Prefatory Comment* to 24:34-39]. The subtle differences between the two versions form the basis for much of the commentary of that chapter.

Similarly, there are differences between Eliezer's prayer calling for God's help in the test by means of which Rebecca was selected and its fulfilment.

Below we offer comparison charts prepared by Rabbi Avie Gold. The translation below sometimes departs from that of the Book in order to emphasize contrasts between the versions.

The Mission

The Narrative	Eliezer's Version
א. וְאַבְרָהָם זָקֵן בָּא בַּיָּמִים 1. *Now Abraham was old, well on in years,*	(see verse 36 below)
(see verse 2 below)	לד. וַיֹּאמַר עֶבֶד אַבְרָהָם אָנֹכִי׃ 34. *Then he said, 'A servant of Abraham am I.*
וַה׳ בֵּרַךְ אֶת אַבְרָהָם בַּכֹּל *and* HASHEM *had blessed Abraham with everything.*	לה. וַה׳ בֵּרַךְ אֶת אֲדֹנִי מְאֹד וַיִּגְדָּל וַיִּתֶּן לוֹ צֹאן וּבָקָר וְכֶסֶף וְזָהָב וַעֲבָדִם וּשְׁפָחֹת וּגְמַלִּים וַחֲמֹרִים׃ 35. HASHEM *has greatly blessed my master, and he prospered. He has given him sheep, cattle, silver and gold, servants and maidservants, camels and donkeys.*

The Narrative *(cont.)*	Eliezer's Version *(cont.)*
ד. כִּי אֶל אַרְצִי וְאֶל מוֹלַדְתִּי תֵּלֵךְ 4. *Rather, to my land and to my birthplace (or: kindred) shall you go*	לח. אִם לֹא אֶל בֵּית אָבִי תֵּלֵךְ וְאֶל מִשְׁפַּחְתִּי 38. *Unless you go to my father's house and to my family*
וְלָקַחְתָּ אִשָּׁה לִבְנִי לְיִצְחָק׃ *and take a wife for my son — for Isaac.'*	וְלָקַחְתָּ אִשָּׁה לִבְנִי׃ *and take a wife for my son."*
ה. וַיֹּאמֶר אֵלָיו הָעֶבֶד 5. *The servant said to him:*	לט. וָאֹמַר אֶל אֲדֹנִי 39. *And I said to my master,*
אוּלַי לֹא תֹאבֶה הָאִשָּׁה לָלֶכֶת אַחֲרַי אֶל הָאָרֶץ הַזֹּאת *'Perhaps the woman will not wish to follow me to this land;*	אֻלַי לֹא תֵלֵךְ הָאִשָּׁה אַחֲרָי׃ *"Perhaps the woman will not follow me?"*

(see verse 1 above)	לו. וַתֵּלֶד שָׂרָה אֵשֶׁת אֲדֹנִי בֵן לַאדֹנִי אַחֲרֵי זִקְנָתָהּ 36. *Sarah, my master's wife, bore my master a son after she had grown old,*
	וַיִּתֶּן לוֹ אֶת כָּל אֲשֶׁר לוֹ: *and he gave him all that he possesses.*
ב. וַיֹּאמֶר אַבְרָהָם אֶל עַבְדּוֹ זְקַן בֵּיתוֹ הַמֹּשֵׁל בְּכָל אֲשֶׁר לוֹ שִׂים נָא יָדְךָ תַּחַת יְרֵכִי: 2. *And Abraham said to the senior servant of his household who controlled all that was his: 'Place now your hand under my thigh.*	(see verse 34 above)
ג. וְאַשְׁבִּיעֲךָ בַּה׳ אֱלֹהֵי הַשָּׁמַיִם וֵאלֹהֵי הָאָרֶץ 3. *And I will have you swear by* HASHEM, *God of heaven and God of earth,*	לז. וַיַּשְׁבִּעֵנִי אֲדֹנִי לֵאמֹר 37. *And my master made me swear saying,*
אֲשֶׁר לֹא תִקַּח אִשָּׁה לִבְנִי מִבְּנוֹת הַכְּנַעֲנִי *that you not take a wife for my son from the daughters of the Canaanites,*	לֹא תִקַּח אִשָּׁה לִבְנִי מִבְּנוֹת הַכְּנַעֲנִי *"Do not take a wife for my son from the daughters of the Canaanites,*
אֲשֶׁר אָנֹכִי יוֹשֵׁב בְּקִרְבּוֹ: *in whose midst I dwell.*	אֲשֶׁר אָנֹכִי יֹשֵׁב בְּאַרְצוֹ: *in whose land I dwell.*

(continued above right)

הֶהָשֵׁב אָשִׁיב אֶת בִּנְךָ אֶל הָאָרֶץ אֲשֶׁר יָצָאתָ מִשָּׁם *shall I take your son back to the land from which you departed?'*	
ו. וַיֹּאמֶר אֵלָיו אַבְרָהָם 6. *Abraham said to him*	מ. וַיֹּאמֶר אֵלָי 40. *He said to me,*
הִשָּׁמֶר לְךָ פֶּן תָּשִׁיב אֶת בְּנִי שָׁמָּה: *'Beware not to return my son to there.*	
ז. ה׳ אֱלֹהֵי הַשָּׁמַיִם 7. HASHEM, *God of heaven,*	ה׳ *"*HASHEM,
אֲשֶׁר לְקָחַנִי מִבֵּית אָבִי וּמֵאֶרֶץ מוֹלַדְתִּי וַאֲשֶׁר דִּבֶּר לִי וַאֲשֶׁר נִשְׁבַּע לִי לֵאמֹר לְזַרְעֲךָ אֶתֵּן אֶת הָאָרֶץ הַזֹּאת *Who took me from the house of my father and from the land of my birth; Who spoke concerning me, and Who swore to me saying, "To your offspring will I give this land."*	אֲשֶׁר הִתְהַלַּכְתִּי לְפָנָיו *before Whom I have walked,*
הוּא יִשְׁלַח מַלְאָכוֹ לְפָנֶיךָ *He will send His angel before you,*	יִשְׁלַח מַלְאָכוֹ אִתָּךְ *will send His angel with you*
	וְהִצְלִיחַ דַּרְכֶּךָ *and make your journey successful,*
וְלָקַחְתָּ אִשָּׁה לִבְנִי *and you will take a wife for my son*	וְלָקַחְתָּ אִשָּׁה לִבְנִי *and you will take a wife for my son*
מִשָּׁם: *from there.*	מִמִּשְׁפַּחְתִּי וּמִבֵּית אָבִי: *from my family and my father's house.*

(continued next page)

The Narrative	Eliezer's Version
	מא. אָז תִּנָּקֶה מֵאָלָתִי כִּי תָבוֹא אֶל מִשְׁפַּחְתִּי 41. *Then you will be absolved from my imprecation when you have come to my family;*
ח. וְאִם לֹא תֹאבֶה הָאִשָּׁה לָלֶכֶת אַחֲרֶיךָ 8. *But if the woman will not wish to follow you,*	וְאִם לֹא יִתְּנוּ לָךְ *and if they will not give (her) to you*
וְנִקִּיתָ מִשְּׁבֻעָתִי זֹאת *you shall then be absolved of this oath of mine.*	וְהָיִיתָ נָקִי מֵאָלָתִי: *then, you shall be absolved from my imprecation."*
רַק אֶת בְּנִי לֹא תָשֵׁב שָׁמָּה: *However, do not return my son to there."*	
ט. וַיָּשֶׂם הָעֶבֶד אֶת יָדוֹ תַּחַת יֶרֶךְ אַבְרָהָם אֲדֹנָיו וַיִּשָּׁבַע לוֹ עַל הַדָּבָר הַזֶּה: 9. *So the servant placed his hand under the thigh of Abraham his master and swore to him regarding this matter.*	

(continued above right)

The Narrative *(cont.)*	Eliezer's Version *(cont.)*
י. וַיִּקַּח הָעֶבֶד עֲשָׂרָה גְמַלִּים מִגְּמַלֵּי אֲדֹנָיו וַיֵּלֶךְ וְכָל טוּב אֲדֹנָיו בְּיָדוֹ וַיָּקָם וַיֵּלֶךְ אֶל אֲרַם נַהֲרַיִם אֶל עִיר נָחוֹר: 10. *Then the servant took ten of his master's camels and set out with all the bounty of his master in his hand and made his way to Aram Naharaim to the city of Nachor.*	
יא. וַיַּבְרֵךְ הַגְּמַלִּים מִחוּץ לָעִיר אֶל בְּאֵר הַמָּיִם לְעֵת עֶרֶב לְעֵת צֵאת הַשֹּׁאֲבֹת: 11. *He made the camels kneel down outside the city towards a well of water at evening time, the time when women come out to draw.*	מב. וָאָבֹא הַיּוֹם אֶל הָעָיִן 42. *I came today to the spring*

The Character Test

The Narrative: The Prayer	The Narrative: The Fulfillment	Eliezer's Version: The Prayer	Eliezer's Version: The Fulfillment
	טו. וַיְהִי הוּא טֶרֶם כִּלָּה לְדַבֵּר 15. *And it was before he had finished speaking*		מה. אֲנִי טֶרֶם אֲכַלֶּה לְדַבֵּר אֶל לִבִּי 45. *Before I had finished meditating* [lit. *speaking to my heart*]
	וְהִנֵּה רִבְקָה יֹצֵאת *when suddenly Rebecca came out*		וְהִנֵּה רִבְקָה יֹצֵאת *when suddenly Rebecca came out*
	אֲשֶׁר יֻלְּדָה לִבְתוּאֵל בֶּן מִלְכָּה אֵשֶׁת נָחוֹר אֲחִי אַבְרָהָם *— who had been born to Bethuel, son of Milcah, wife of Nachor, brother of Abraham*		
	וְכַדָּהּ עַל שִׁכְמָהּ *— with her jug on her shoulder.*		וְכַדָּהּ עַל שִׁכְמָהּ *with her jug on her shoulder.*
	טז. וְהַנַּעֲרָ טֹבַת מַרְאֶה מְאֹד בְּתוּלָה וְאִישׁ לֹא יְדָעָהּ 16. *Now the maiden was very fair to look upon; a virgin whom no man had known.*		
יב. וַיֹּאמַר 12. *And he said,*		וָאֹמַר *and I said,*	
ה׳ אֱלֹהֵי אֲדֹנִי אַבְרָהָם *'HASHEM, God of my master Abraham,*		ה׳ אֱלֹהֵי אֲדֹנִי אַבְרָהָם *"HASHEM, God of my master Abraham,*	

(continued next page)

The Character Test *(cont.)*

The Narrative: The Prayer	The Narrative: The Fulfillment	Eliezer's Version: The Prayer	Eliezer's Version: The Fulfillment
הַקְרֵה נָא לְפָנַי הַיּוֹם וַעֲשֵׂה חֶסֶד עִם אֲדֹנִי אַבְרָהָם: *may You so arrange it for me this day that You do kindness with my master Abraham.*		אִם יֶשְׁךָ נָּא מַצְלִיחַ דַּרְכִּי אֲשֶׁר אָנֹכִי הֹלֵךְ עָלֶיהָ: *If You would graciously make successful my way on which I go*	
יג. הִנֵּה אָנֹכִי נִצָּב עַל עֵין הַמָּיִם 13. *Behold, I am standing by the spring of water*		מג. הִנֵּה אָנֹכִי נִצָּב עַל עֵין הַמָּיִם 43. *Behold, I am standing by the spring of water.*	
וּבְנוֹת אַנְשֵׁי הָעִיר יֹצְאֹת לִשְׁאֹב מָיִם: *and the daughters of the towns-men come out to draw.*			
	וַתֵּרֶד הָעַיְנָה *She descended to the spring,*		וַתֵּרֶד הָעַיְנָה *She descended to the spring*
	וַתְּמַלֵּא כַדָּהּ וַתָּעַל: *filled her jug and ascended.*		וַתִּשְׁאָב *and drew (water).*
יד. וְהָיָה הַנַּעֲרָ אֲשֶׁר אֹמַר אֵלֶיהָ 14. *Let it be that the maiden to whom I shall say,*	יז. וַיָּרָץ הָעֶבֶד לִקְרָאתָהּ וַיֹּאמֶר 17. *The servant ran toward her and said,*	וְהָיָה הָעַלְמָה הַיֹּצֵאת לִשְׁאֹב וְאָמַרְתִּי אֵלֶיהָ *Let it be that the young woman who comes out to draw and to whom I shall say,*	וָאֹמַר אֵלֶיהָ *Then I said to her,*
הַטִּי נָא כַדֵּךְ וְאֶשְׁתֶּה *"Tip over your jug, please, so I may drink,"*	הַגְמִיאִינִי נָא מְעַט מַיִם מִכַּדֵּךְ: *'Let me sip, please, a little water from your jug.'*	הַשְׁקִינִי נָא מְעַט מַיִם מִכַּדֵּךְ: *'Give me to drink, please, a little water from your jug,'*	הַשְׁקִינִי נָא *"Give me to drink, please."*
וְאָמְרָה שְׁתֵה *and who says, "Drink*	יח. וַתֹּאמֶר שְׁתֵה אֲדֹנִי וַתְּמַהֵר וַתֹּרֶד כַּדָּהּ עַל יָדָהּ וַתַּשְׁקֵהוּ 18. *She said, 'Drink my lord,' and she hurried and lowered her jug to her hand and gave him drink.*	מד. וְאָמְרָה אֵלַי גַּם אַתָּה שְׁתֵה 44. *and who says to me, 'You may also drink*	מו. וַתְּמַהֵר וַתּוֹרֶד כַּדָּהּ מֵעָלֶיהָ וַתֹּאמֶר שְׁתֵה 46. *She hurried and lowered her jug from upon her and said, "Drink,*

	יט. וַתְּכַל לְהַשְׁקֹתוֹ וַתֹּאמֶר 19. *When she finished giving him drink, she said,*		(see below וָאֵשְׁתְּ)
וְגַם גְּמַלֶּיךָ אַשְׁקֶה *and even your camels will I water,"*	גַּם לִגְמַלֶּיךָ אֶשְׁאָב עַד אִם כִּלּוּ לִשְׁתֹּת: *'Even for your camels will I draw, until they have finished drinking.'*	וְגַם לִגְמַלֶּיךָ אֶשְׁאָב *and even for your camels will I draw,' —*	וְגַם גְּמַלֶּיךָ אַשְׁקֶה *and even your camels will I water."*
	(see above וַתְּכַל)		וָאֵשְׁתְּ *So I drank*
	כ. וַתְּמַהֵר וַתְּעַר כַּדָּהּ אֶל הַשֹּׁקֶת וַתָּרָץ עוֹד אֶל הַבְּאֵר לִשְׁאֹב וַתִּשְׁאַב לְכָל גְּמַלָּיו: 20. *So she hurried and emptied her jug into the trough and kept running to the well to draw and she drew for all his camels.*		וְגַם הַגְּמַלִּים הִשְׁקָתָה: *and she even watered the camels.*
אֹתָהּ הֹכַחְתָּ לְעַבְדְּךָ לְיִצְחָק *— her will You have designated for Your servant for Isaac,*		הִוא הָאִשָּׁה אֲשֶׁר הֹכִיחַ ה׳ לְבֶן אֲדֹנִי: *she shall be the woman whom* HASHEM *has designated for my master's son."*	
וּבָהּ אֵדַע כִּי עָשִׂיתָ חֶסֶד עִם אֲדֹנִי: *and may I know through her that You have done kindness with my master.'*			

The Familial Test

The Narrative	Eliezer's Version
כא. וְהָאִישׁ מִשְׁתָּאֵה לָהּ מַחֲרִישׁ לָדַעַת הַהִצְלִיחַ ה׳ דַּרְכּוֹ אִם לֹא: 21. *The man was astonished at her, reflecting silently to learn whether* HASHEM *had made his journey successful or not.*	
כב. וַיְהִי כַּאֲשֶׁר כִּלּוּ הַגְּמַלִּים לִשְׁתּוֹת וַיִּקַּח הָאִישׁ נֶזֶם זָהָב בֶּקַע מִשְׁקָלוֹ וּשְׁנֵי צְמִידִים עַל יָדֶיהָ עֲשָׂרָה זָהָב מִשְׁקָלָם: 22. *And it was, when the camels had finished drinking, the man took a golden nose ring, its weight was a beka, and two bracelets on her arm, ten gold shekels was their weight.*	(see below verse 47, וָאָשִׂם)
כג. וַיֹּאמֶר 23. *And he said,*	מז. וָאֶשְׁאַל אֹתָהּ וָאֹמַר 47. *Then I questioned her and said,*
בַּת מִי אַתְּ הַגִּידִי נָא לִי *'Whose daughter are you? — pray tell me.*	בַּת מִי אַתְּ *"Whose daughter are you?"*
הֲיֵשׁ בֵּית אָבִיךְ מָקוֹם לָנוּ לָלִין: *Is there place in your father's house for us to spend the night?'*	

The Narrative *(cont.)*	Eliezer's Version *(cont.)*
כה. וַתֹּאמֶר אֵלָיו גַּם תֶּבֶן גַּם מִסְפּוֹא רַב עִמָּנוּ גַּם מָקוֹם לָלוּן: 25. *And she said to him, 'Even straw and feed is plentiful with us as well as place to lodge.*	
(see verse 22 above)	וָאָשִׂם הַנֶּזֶם עַל אַפָּהּ וְהַצְּמִידִים עַל יָדֶיהָ: *And I placed the nose ring on her nose and the bracelets on her arms.*
כו. וַיִּקֹּד הָאִישׁ וַיִּשְׁתַּחוּ לַה׳: 26. *So the man bowed and prostrated himself to* HASHEM	מח. וָאֶקֹּד וָאֶשְׁתַּחֲוֶה לַה׳ 48. *Then I bowed and prostrated myself to* HASHEM
כז. וַיֹּאמֶר בָּרוּךְ ה׳ אֱלֹהֵי אֲדֹנִי אַבְרָהָם 27. *and said, 'Blessed be* HASHEM, *God of my master Abraham,*	וָאֲבָרֵךְ אֶת ה׳ אֱלֹהֵי אֲדֹנִי אַבְרָהָם *and blessed* HASHEM, *God of my master Abraham,*
אֲשֶׁר לֹא עָזַב חַסְדּוֹ וַאֲמִתּוֹ מֵעִם אֲדֹנִי *Who has not withheld His kindness and truth from my master.*	
אָנֹכִי בַּדֶּרֶךְ נָחַנִי ה׳ HASHEM *has guided me on the path*	אֲשֶׁר הִנְחַנִי בְּדֶרֶךְ אֱמֶת *Who guided me on a true path*

לָקַחַת אֶת בַּת אֲחִי אֲדֹנִי לִבְנוֹ׃ *to take the daughter of my master's brother for his son.*	בֵּית אֲחֵי אֲדֹנִי׃ *to the house of my master's brothers.'*

כד. וַתֹּאמֶר אֵלָיו 24. *She said to him.*	וַתֹּאמֶר *She said,*
בַּת בְּתוּאֵל אָנֹכִי בֶּן מִלְכָּה אֲשֶׁר יָלְדָה לְנָחוֹר׃ *'I am the daughter of Bethuel, son of Milcah, whom she bore to Nachor.'*	בַּת בְּתוּאֵל בֶּן נָחוֹר אֲשֶׁר יָלְדָה לוֹ מִלְכָּה *"The daughter of Bethuel, son of Nachor, whom Milcah bore to him."*

(continued above right)

סדר תולדת

Sidra Toldos

— The Overviews

An Overview —
Isaac / Strength and Consolidation

מַיִם עֲמֻקִּים עֵצָה בְלֶב אִישׁ וְאִישׁ תְּבוּנָה יִדְלֶנָּה. רָצָה לוֹמַר כִּי הֶחָכְמָה ... בָּאָדָם ... כְּמַיִם הַטְמוּנִים בְּלֵב הָאָרֶץ ... וְהַנָּבוֹן ... יִשְׁאָבֶנָּה מִלִּבּוֹ כַּאֲשֶׁר יַחְקֹר עַל הַמַּיִם אֲשֶׁר בְּמַעֲמַקֵּי הָאָרֶץ

*Like deep waters is counsel within the heart of man, but a man of wisdom will draw it up (*Proverbs *20:5). This means to say that wisdom ... within ... man is like water that is hidden in the heart of the earth ... An understanding person ... will draw it from his heart just as one searches out water buried in the depths of the earth (Introduction to* Chovos Halevovos).

הָיָה דַעְתּוֹ לָרֶדֶת לְמִצְרַיִם ... אָמַר לוֹ אַל תֵּרֵד מִצְרַיְמָה שֶׁאַתָּה עוֹלָה תְמִימָה וְאֵין חוּצָה לָאָרֶץ כְּדַאי לְךָ

[*Isaac*] *planned to descend to Egypt* [*when famine struck Canaan*] *(26:2).* [*God*] *said to him, 'Do not descend to Egypt, for you are a perfect burnt-offering, and a country outside of* Eretz Yisrael *is not worthy of you' (*Bereishis Rabbah *64:3).*

I. Isaac's Uniqueness

No Less Exalted

Of the three Patriarchs, Isaac seems to be the least prominent.

Of the three Patriarchs, Isaac *seems to be* the least prominent. Several chapters of the Torah deal with Abraham, even more describe Jacob and the development of his family. Virtually throughout, Abraham and Jacob are the prime movers of their respective stories. But to Isaac, few chapters of the

Torah are devoted, and even there, he seems generally more passive than active. Eliezer was sent to choose his wife. Jacob and Rebecca matched wits with Esau to secure Isaac's blessings. In both of these major episodes, Isaac was less the actor than the acted upon.

Like many superficially 'obvious' assessments of the events and people chronicled in the Torah, this one is far wide of the mark.

The 'obvious' conclusion was that Isaac is less majestic than either his father or his son, that he was merely a bridge between the two major pillars of Israel's genesis. Like many superficially 'obvious' assessments of the events and people chronicled in the Torah, this one is far wide of the mark. The three Patriarchs are described by the Sages as equal to one another (*Bereishis Rabbah* 1:15), as the 'strong steeds' who galloped before God (*Sanhedrin* 96a), as the 'chariots' upon whom God rested His Presence on earth. Nowhere is there a suggestion that Isaac is not on the same pedestal as the others. What is more, the time will come when the salvation of his descendants will rest with Isaac:

> Rabbi Shmuel bar Nachmeni said in the name of Rabbi Yochanan, In time to come, the Holy One, Blessed be He, will say to Abraham, 'Your children have sinned.' [Abraham] will say before Him, 'Master of the Universe, let them be wiped out in sanctification of Your Name.'
>
> God will say, 'Let me tell this to Jacob who endured the suffering of raising children. Perhaps he will pray for mercy upon them ... '
>
> Jacob will say ... 'Let them be wiped out in sanctification of Your Name.'
>
> ... Isaac will say, 'Master of the Universe, are they *my* children and not *Your* children? When they said, *"We will do"* before they said, *"We will hear,"* You called them *"My firstborn"* — now you call them my children and not Yours? ... [Isaac proceeded to show that the extent of Israel's sinfulness was relatively small. He

Isaac will say, 'Master of the Universe, are they my *children and* not Your *children?*

'If You endure all [the sins], good. If You want them all to be upon me — I have already offered myself.

concluded:] 'If You endure all [the sins], good. If not, let half be upon You and half be upon me. If You want them all to be upon me — I have already offered myself before You [at the time of the *Akeidah*] (*Shabbos* 89b).

Isaac will prevail where neither his father nor his son will make the attempt. But when Israel will come to express its gratitude, he will point, as it were, to God and tell them to direct their praises to Him (ibid).

So august, yet so little mentioned in the Torah! Let us try to understand Isaac's way a little more — at least to the infinitesimal extent to which we can comprehend the way of a Patriarch.

A New Path

Abraham and Isaac represented two very different approaches to the service of God. Abraham's was that of *Chessed-Kindness.* Isaac's was that of *Gevurah-Strength.* [For a lengthy exposition of these traits and their ramifications, see *Overview/The Patriarchs* to ArtScroll *Lech Lecha* p. 357.] As *Michtav MeEliyahu* points out, it is axiomatic in our perception of the holy Patriarchs that their philosophies of life were not haphazardly based on personal whim or preference. Isaac could just as well have adopted Abraham's philosophy. In fact, it would have been eminently logical for him to follow in the footsteps of his illustrious father. Abraham had found the spark of Godliness in the spiritual debris of the ten failed generations from Noah's time to his own. He had recognized his Creator and had been rewarded with manifestations of the *Shechinah* that made even his idolatrous contemporaries regard him as נְשִׂיא אֱלֹהִים, *a prince of God.* Why should Isaac not have followed Abraham's pattern?

It is axiomatic in our perception of the holy Patriarchs that their philosophies of life were not haphazardly based on personal whim or preference.

Instead, Isaac chose to beat a new path. Rabbi Simcha Zissel of Kelm sees Isaac's greatness in this very refusal to choose the easy way of imitation. Had he been like Rebecca, coming from a land and a family of idolators, he would simply have broken with his

He had no inner compulsion to rebel against the teachings of Abraham and Sarah. To the contrary, what better teachers and models could there be?

past — as Abraham did before him. But he had no inner compulsion to rebel against the teachings of Abraham and Sarah. To the contrary, what better teachers and models could there be? Nevertheless he chose to learn from them *but not imitate them.* Isaac developed a new way to serve God, the path of *Gevurah-Strength.* Without doing violence to the heritage of Abraham, he formulated another essential way in the attainment of spiritual greatness. He played an essential role in creating the tripod upon which Judaism eternally rests, because his mode of service was fused with Abraham's to form the *Tiferes-Truth* way of Jacob. In succeeding Abraham but not becoming his carbon copy, Isaac demonstrated that he was not merely the heir of a Patriarch, but a Patriarch himself.

In succeeding Abraham but not becoming his carbon copy, Isaac demonstrated that he was not merely the heir of a Patriarch, but a Patriarch himself.

More Acceptable

This, Rabbi Simcha Zissel explains, is why his prayer for offspring was found more acceptable than Rebecca's (see 25:21 and *comm.*). Her status as צַדֶּקֶת בַּת רָשָׁע, a woman who became righteous despite her wicked forebears, is beyond reproach, but her difficult way was made a little easier by the knowledge that whatever she had seen in the house of Bethuel, Milcah, and Laban could be disregarded with contempt. She had the relative luxury of knowing that her past could serve as nothing more than a model for change. But Isaac? He had to become a צַדִּיק בֶּן צַדִּיק, an *original tzaddik* despite the fact that he was the son of a *tzaddik,* To become an Isaac rather than a second Abraham is truly an awesome feat. To seek independently to find the meaning and significance of thought and deed is a spiritual triumph of majestic proportions.

To become an Isaac rather than a second Abraham is truly an awesome feat.

This explains the lofty assessment given to Isaac's laboriously attained personal stature, but it still does not tell us why he was forced to choose a way which ignored many of Abraham's and Sarah precedents. They dedicated their lives to seeking out people to whom they could bring the message of God. Abraham had an 'army' of some 318 disciples of fighting age who were part of his own household (14:14); even before moving to Canaan from Charan, he and Sarah had proselytized untold numbers of people (12:5). Nowhere do we find Isaac engaged on a similar course of action. But if it was meritorious for the father to do so, surely it was no less meritorious for the son to do the same!

In summarizing the rise of Abraham and his descendants until Moses received the Torah, *Rambam* shows the sharp contrast between Abraham and Isaac:

> *On this path [of progressively more serious idolatry] the world went and developed until the birth of the pillar of the universe — our father Abraham ... He arose and called out in a great voice to the entire world to inform them that there is a single God ... from city to city and from kingdom to kingdom he went ... until he arrived in Canaan ... until he gathered to himself thousands and tens of thousands. They are the people of Abraham's household ... He set up Isaac to teach and to exhort. Isaac made this known to Jacob and appointed him to teach ... (Hilchos Avodah Zorah* 1:2-3).

Abraham was the inspirer ana teacher of tens of thousands. Isaac taught Jacob.

Abraham was the inspirer and teacher of tens of thousands. Isaac taught Jacob. Why did Isaac not create an army of adherents to God and His Torah?

Chessed and Gevurah

The answer lies in a clearer understanding of the ways of *Chessed* and *Gevurah.* Though they seem to be widely divergent, they are truly complementary. Neither can thrive — nor even continue to exist — without the other. Because we cannot climb the spiritual peaks of the Patriarchs, let us turn to analogies familiar to us from everyday life.

— A government seeks to benefit great masses of its citizens. It will institute programs and projects to deliver services to the needy. Money, health care, education, leisure time activities — the necessities and amenities of life will be made available, and sighs of relief and cries of gratitude will be heard throughout the land. But unless the implementation of policy is controlled and evaluated, it will gradually become the source of problems as acute as those it set out to remedy. Are all needy people dealt with fairly? Are lives made better, or just easier? Are people subtly being trained to forget that dipping into an open pocketbook is less important than inner-directed efforts at self-betterment? So, after a time, the benevolent governmen must pause and evaluate, improve efficiency, and consider how best to match the goodness of results with the goodness of the intentions.

But unless the implementation of policy is controlled and evaluated, it will gradually become the source of problems as acute as those it set out to remedy.

— A corporation seeks to expand. It opens new factories or new stores, or it acquires other companies. Can it continue to do so without periodically tightening its controls on the new activity and making sure that the expansion does not become a non-contributing drain?

— An individual seeks to help others by imparting to them his own Torah knowledge. Can he continuously give to others without pausing to further enrich himself, deepen his values, and rigorously force himself to grow?

The urge to give and grow is a function of Chessed. *It is sometimes generous and sometimes self-indulgent, sometimes altruistic and sometimes selfish.*

The urge to give and grow is a function of *Chessed.* It is sometimes generous and sometimes self-indulgent, sometimes altruistic and sometimes selfish. Clearly the expanding corporation is mainly interested in its own profits rather than in serving society. The government policy-maker may be dedicated to the common weal or he may be concerned only with increasing his own power and budget. The teacher of Torah may not always be motivated solely by the desire to serve God and Israel. This does not change the *essential nature* of their activity. Because the activities are directed toward others, they are manifestations of the *Chessed* impulse to give. Every such person faces a challenge: he can turn his motives, attitudes and deeds in the direction of Abraham, the 'pillar of the universe' whose kindness had the purpose of perfecting man and drawing him close to God — or he can turn his *Chessed* activities in the path of sloth, gratification of the senses, and a deadening of the will to strive for greatness. For *Chessed-Kindness can* have both effects. Indulgence without discipline, *Chessed* without *Gevurah* (or, as it is frequently called, *din*), will lead to degeneracy.

II. Complement

An Outgrowth

Isaac's philosophy was not a contradicition of Abraham's. *Sfas Emes* notes that the *sidra Toldos* begins with the conjunctive *vav:* וְאֵלֶּה תּוֹלְדֹת יִצְחָק בֶּן אַבְרָהָם, *'And' these are the offspring of Isaac, son of Abraham.* The verse follows the *Talmudic* dictum of וְאֵלֶּה מוֹסִיף עַל הָרִאשׁוֹנִים, the word וְאֵלֶּה [*and these*] indicates a continuation of what has been said earlier. So the story of Isaac's life is a continuation — but a continuation of what?

Sfas Emes *finds Isaac to be a continuation in cosmic terms.*

Sfas Emes finds Isaac to be a continuation in cosmic terms. We find אֵלֶּה תוֹלְדוֹת הַשָּׁמַיִם וְהָאָרֶץ בְּהִבָּרְאָם, *These are the generations* [i.e., *products*] *of the heaven and the earth when they were created (Genesis* 2:4). As the *Zohar* comments, הִבָּרְאָם has the letters of אַבְרָהָם, *Abraham:* the world was created for the sake of Abraham and his teachings, for his proclamation of Hashem as the only God and his infinite kindness were the purpose and foundation of creation. Abraham did his share to perfect creation. By employing love, goodness, and hospitality, he was indeed able to raise armies of converts in Charan and Canaan. But now there had to be a new epoch in achieving God's purpose. Abraham's work was not to be annulled — the world was created for his sake and it would continue to exist for his sake, but his very foundation would crumble unless it were tempered and consolidated. Isaac came on the

Abraham did his share to perfect creation. But now there had to be a new epoch in achieving God's purpose.

scene as the one who would be מוֹסִיף עַל הָרִאשׁוֹנִים, *continue the works* of his father. What Abraham had wrought with kindness, Isaac would refine with judgment; what Abraham had created with goodness, Isaac would consolidate with strength.

What Abraham had wrought with kindness, Isaac would refine with judgment; what Abraham had created with goodness, Isaac would consolidate with strength.

Now we see Isaac's life from a new perspective. אַבְרָהָם הוֹלִיד אֶת יִצְחָק, *Abraham begot Isaac* (25:9). In its many layers of meaning, the Torah is giving us more than the fact of genealogy or facial resemblance (see *comm.). The philosophy* of Abraham begot the *philosophy* of Isaac. Strength and kindness do not contradict one another; they complement and perfect one another. Not only must the expansiveness of *Chessed-Kindness* be followed by the consolidation of *Gevurah-Strength, but also* יִרְאַת ה׳, *fear and awe of God,* must flow from אַהֲבַת ה׳, *love of God.* 'Abraham' gave birth to 'Isaac'; love of God brought in its wake an awareness of God's power and majesty, and awakened an awe and a fear that made God's servants tremble, lest they overstep the bounds of His will in their zeal to serve him better and spread His Name more widely. From such a complementary tension between love and fear, between kindness and strength, is born — *Tiferes-Splendor,* — *Emes-Truth* — the final level of perfection represented by, Jacob (see *Overview* to *Lech Lecho.* Jacob's role will be discussed further in future *Overviews.*). Isaac, therefore, is the logical and necessary next step in the spiritual process begun by Abraham.

'Abraham' gave birth to 'Isaac'; love of God brought in its wake an awareness of God's power and majesty.

Ultimate Refinement

Indeed, Isaac's emergence and his contribution to the unfolding development of God's mission on earth brought an achievement that had not yet been possible in Abraham's day. The principal struggle between good and evil is represented by the implacable hostility between Jacob and Esau. For Isaac was left the task of slicing away the contamination of Esau from the emerging Abrahamitic nation. *Chessed* was inadequate to cope with an Esau; the task required the rigorous application of inner

For Isaac was left the task of slicing away the contamination of Esau from the emerging Abrahamitic nation.

strength and refinement that were Isaac's contribution to the Patriarchal strain. True, Abraham had his Ishmael who had to be removed from Israel, but there was an essential difference between Ishmael and Esau: Ishmael was not a son of Sarah and he was never considered to be an offsping of Abraham (21:12). Esau, However, was born to a Matriarch as well as to a Patriarch — and he *was* entitled to continue the lineage of Abraham and Isaac (see later *Overview, The Birthright*). That made the challenge so awesome: Jacob or Esau, which would it be? A choice of that magnitude had to await the coming of Isaac.

Clearly, therefore, the life of Isaac could not have the narrative prominence of the life of his father.

Clearly, therefore, the life of Isaac could not have the narrative prominence of the life of his father. Abraham was the doer, the propagator who strode from land to land proclaiming God's Name. Isaac's role was just as important and just as difficult, but far more modest. His stage was not the world, but his inner heart. His voice was not the one that carried to tens of thousands of proselytes, but the inner voice that demanded rigorous appraisal and merciless refinement. Abraham's academy was open to all who would listen; Isaac had one student — Jacob — but what a student! We do not know the ultimate results of Abraham's teaching — although it is axiomatic that despite the disappearance of his converts, the lifetime devotion of an Abraham surely had lasting results — but we *do* know that the single product of Isaac's academy become the father of the nation, the culmination of God's purpose in creating heaven and earth.

Abraham's academy was open to all who would listen; Isaac had one student — Jacob — but what a student!

III. The Wells

Portents for Children

The Torah gives much prominence to Isaac's efforts to reopen the wells which Abraham had once dug and which the Philistines had closed. The early and later commentators find much significance in these ostensibly mundane activities. More was at

More was at stake than water and more underlay the rivalry between Isaac and the Philistines than nascent anti-Semitism, jealously, or fear

stake than water and more underlay the rivalry between Isaac and the Philistines than nascent anti-Semitism, jealously, or fear of marauders (see *comm.* to chap. 27). *Ramban* follows his fundamental rule of מַעֲשֵׂה אָבוֹת סִימָן לַבָּנִים, *the deeds of the Patriarchs are portents for the future of the Jewish nation (see comm.* here and to chap. 12 and *Overview* to *Lech Lecho).* In our *Sidra, Ramban* interprets the Philistine success in closing Isaac's first two wells, *Esek* and *Sitnah,* as allusions to the destruction of the first two Temples. Isaac's third well, *Rechovos,* which marked the Philistine's failure to interfere with his freedom to live and thrive, is symbolic of the Third and eternal Temple. Such interpretation set a pattern, for wells and water are symbolic of much in the spiritual life of Israel and the opposition it must overcome before it can breathe freely and proclaim that God has finally removed obstacles from its path.

But the struggle is not only between Israel and Philistia and Jacob and Esau. The conflict between good and evil is not waged only — or even primarily — on the universal scale. It is a private struggle as well, and it goes on constantly within each human being. As Rabbi Yisrael Salanter used to say, 'During the *Shemona Esrei* of *Rosh Hashanah* and *Yom Kippur,* we should have in mind not only that God should be proclaimed as King of the entire universe. We must proclaim Him as King over *ourselves,* as well!

The Philistines in the land of Canaan could not endure Abraham's wells, nor can the Philistine within each individual endure the eternal flow of fresh life-giving spiritual waters within the sons and daughters of Abraham. Isaac reopened his father's wells, so must we. In his time, Isaac was called upon to perfect with inner strength the attainments of Abraham. In every generation, too, Isaac's offspring have the duty to return to the wells of their parents and grandparents, dig, open, protect, and perfect the always endangered legacy bequeathed them by the Abrahams of history.

In every generation, too, Isaac's offspring have the duty to return to the wells of their parents and grandparents, dig, open, protect, and perfect.

Buried Wealth

Wells symbolize the spiritual wealth that is buried beneath layers of 'earth', materialism, smugness, laziness. Abraham uncovered it and made it available to his neighbors, but they refused to accept his teachings. All the wells that Abraham had dug, the Philistines closed up (26:15-32). There is a resistance to the teachings of an Abraham, a refusal to sweep away the sand that obscures the flow of water, an instinctive reaction that makes people cover their eyes when the light breaks through. As *Chovos Halevovos* teaches, wise counsel is within a person just as life-giving water is beneath the earth. But to bring that 'water' to the surface requires effort, a willingness to break through barriers and dispose of the here-and-now reality upon which man plies his way through life. It takes a man of wisdom and understanding to do that, because only by first mustering up the resolve to be great can one find the strength and courage to do so, even against opposition and derision.

Wise counsel is within a person just as life-giving water is beneath the earth. But to bring that 'water' to the surface requires effort.

Sefer HaZ'chus writes that Isaac could easily have sent his servants immediately to dig *Rechovos*, the well that was his without opposition. Why did he first have them dig and fail and dig again? Because in this instance as in so many of the deeds of the Patriarchs, a way was prepared for the future. There would be dark times in Jewish history when Isaac's offspring would be beset by Philistines and worse — how would they *then* find the fortitude to continue as the children of Abraham, Isaac, and Jacob? To make such future Jewish accomplishment possible, Isaac uncovered 'water' in the face of hatred and opposition. The wells might be stopped up over and over again, as indeed they were, but the earth would have been softened and the spiritual legacy would be established: the water is there, the light is there — and people of wisdom can uncover it. Perhaps we are not capable of cutting hard rock, but we can remove the earth that has been softened for us by Isaac.

In so many of the deeds of the Patriarchs, a way was prepared for the future.

Perhaps we are not capable of cutting hard rock, but we can remove the earth that has been softened for us by Isaac.

The sequence of events surrounding the well-digging correspond to Isaac's mission is the *Gevurah* complement to Abraham's pioneering *Chessed.*

Return to Abraham

וַיָּשָׁב יִצְחָק וַיַּחְפֹּר אֶת בְּאֵרֹת הַמַּיִם אֲשֶׁר חָפְרוּ בִּימֵי אַבְרָהָם אָבִיו וַיְסַתְּמוּם פְּלִשְׁתִּים אַחֲרֵי מוֹת אַבְרָהָם וַיִּקְרָא לָהֶן שֵׁמוֹת כַּשֵּׁמֹת אֲשֶׁר קָרָא לָהֶן אָבִיו

And Isaac dug anew the wells of water which they had dug in the days of Abraham, his father, and the Philistines had stopped up after the death of Abraham; and he called them the same names that his father had called them (26:18).

We have already been told that the Philistines closed up Abraham's wells (*v.* 15), why the repetition only three verses later? Let us examine the verse again in our perspective of Isaac's mission and our understanding of the underlying significance of the wells. Abraham revealed emanations of spirituality — he dug wells. But his *Chessed* work could not endure unless it was tempered and consolidated by Isaac's *Gevurah.* Now let us look again at verse 18:

Abraham revealed sources of spiritual flow, but after he died the forces of evil stopped them up. Isaac returned to the same wells *and opened them anew.*

Abraham revealed sources of spiritual flow, but after he died the forces of evil stopped them up. Isaac succeeded him as God's emissary on earth, but Isaac did not seek to depart from his father's teachings. *He returned to the same wells* and opened them anew. And when his task was done, he gave them the same names they bore in Abraham's day. The book of *Genesis* is replete with the significance of names. A name given by God, or an Adam, Abraham, or Isaac carried within it volumes of meaning. Abraham named a 'well' according to its spiritual role and content. When Isaac reopened Abraham's wells, he gave them *Abraham's names,* because the content remained the same. Isaac was Abraham's son, the completion of his father's mission.

He gave them Abraham's names, *because the content remained the same.*

Sefer HaZ'chus sees in Isaac's *own* three wells an allusion to further spiritual phenomena in the lives of all his descendants. *Esek* and *Sitnah,* he maintains,

During the workweek, a Jew struggles against the unforgiving earth and unsympathetic Philistines. But God in His mercy gave 'a precious gift: the Sabbath'.

are allusions to the six days of labor; *Rechovos* symbolizes the Sabbath. During the workweek, a Jew struggles against the unforgiving earth and unsympathetic Philistines. The spiritual content of creation seems *so* clouded and obscured, that even when some of it is revealed, opposing forces always seem to rush in to check the flow. But God in His mercy gave 'a precious gift from His treasure house' (*Shabbos* 10b): the Sabbath. The Sages call it נַחֲלָה בְּלִי מְצָרִים, *a heritage without constrictions (Shabbos* 118a), because the Sabbath bears witness to God not only in His ancient role of Creator of heaven and earth, but to his constant role of Sustainer of the universe Who continuously breathes spiritual life into His creation. Fittingly, Isaac named it *Rechovos* — כִּי עַתָּה הִרְחִיב ה׳ לָנוּ וּפָרִינוּ בָאָרֶץ, *For now HASHEM has granted us ample space, and we can be fruitful in the land* (26:22).

This too, was a Patriarchal gesture with eternal implications for his children. Every moment of every day is further reflection of the teaching and legacy of Isaac, the Patriarch whose role was to provide the steel and cement which give eternity to the mission of his father and his son.

An Overview —
Isaac — Game and Sacrifice

וַיְהִי עֵשָׂו אִישׁ יֹדֵעַ צַיִד אִישׁ שָׂדֶה פרש״י לָצוּד וּלְרַמּוֹת אֶת אָבִיו בְּפִיו ... אָדָם בָּטֵל וְצוֹדֶה בְּקַשְׁתּוֹ חַיּוֹת וְעוֹפוֹת
*And Esau became one who knows hunting, a man of the field (25:27). [He knew how] to entrap and deceive his father with his mouth ... He was an unoccupied person who would entrap animals and birds with his bow (*Rashi, *ibid.).*

שְׁחוֹז מַאֲנֵי זַיְנָךְ שֶׁלֹּא תַאֲכִילַנִי נְבֵלוֹת וּטְרֵפוֹת
[*Isaac told Esau*] *sharpen your hunting gear [to make a proper ritual slaughter] so that you will not feed me improperly slaughtered meat (*Bereishis Rabbah 65:8).

הָאָבוֹת הֵן הֵן הַמֶּרְכָּבָה ... כִּי הַשְּׁכִינָה שׁוֹרָה עֲלֵיהֶם כְּמוֹ שֶׁהָיְתָה שׁוֹרָה עֲלֵיהֶם בְּמִקְדָּשׁ וּמֵעַתָּה הַמַּאֲכָל שֶׁהֵם אוֹכְלִים הוּא כְּקָרְבָּן שֶׁעוֹלֶה עַל גַּבֵּי הָאִשִּׁים
The Patriarchs were the 'chariot' ... for the Shechinah *rested upon them just as it rested upon [the vessels and implements] in the Sanctuary. Hence, the food that they eat is like an offering that is brought upon the flames [of the altar] (*Mesillas Yesharim *Ch. 26).*

I. Rigorous Evaluation

Beneath Deeds

How could Isaac be deceived by Esau? Let Esau ask all the pietistic questions possible — let him inquire how to tithe salt and straw (see *comm.*) — surely the Isaac who could uncover spiritual wellsprings beneath the land of the Philistines could perceive the emptiness beneath Esau's pious exterior. Concerning Isaac's sympathy toward Esau, the *Zohar* says כָּל זִינָא רַחִים לְזִינֵיה, *every type loves the same type.* These are truly astounding words, and they force us to delve into the parallels between Isaac and Esau.

Concerning Isaac's sympathy toward Esau, the Zohar *says* every type loves the same type.

As we have seen, above and in the *Overview* to *Lech Lecho*, Isaac's attribute was the inner strength to refine and perfect. Such a quality is particularly relevant when one is faced by the common sort of situation which is a mixture of good and evil, or with an act which can be either good or evil depending on how, why, and with what intentions it is done. A slap in the face can be violent or cruel — unless it is employed to revive a fainting person or prevent someone from an evil deed. Even when the slap is called for, it can be intermixed with evil if it is done partly as an outlet for hostile feelings or as a manifestation of personal rage.

A slap in the face can be violent or cruel — even when the slap is called for, it can be intermixed with evil.

In this sense, we can understand why Jacob was punished for denying Esau the opportunity to marry Dinah (see *Rashi* to 32:23). As the *Mussar* masters explain, Jacob was surely justified — even obligated — to protect his daughter from Esau, but when he hid her, it should have been with a feeling of compassion for a brother who *might* thereby be losing a final opportunity to repent under the influence of a righteous wife. Instead, Jacob may have felt too much the animosity toward Esau who had defiled the sanctity of the Abrahamitic household, deceived his father, sworn to kill his brother, and come after more than thirty-four years with an army of four hundred men to murder Jacob and his family. Where was Jacob's sin? At most it lay in the most delicate assessment of feelings. Such purging of emotions and motives is the function of *Gevurah-Strength*, the attribute of Isaac.

Where was Jacob's sin? At most it lay in the most delicate assessment of feelings.

Isaac and Shechitah

For this reason, *Neos HaDesheh* explains, Isaac in particular was commanded to be zealous in observing the commandment of שְׁחִיטָה, *ritual slaughter.* When he dispatched Esau to prepare game for him as a prerequisite to receiving the blessings, Isaac cautioned him to sharpen his implements carefully in order to prevent any possibility of improper slaughter (*Bereishis Rabbah* 65:8). Killing an animal and shedding its blood can easily an act of cruelty. There is a feeling of power in wielding the knife, pulling the trigger, outwitting the quarry. On its simplest level, *shechitah*, with its intricate laws designed to assure that the animal is killed quickly and painlesssly, injects mercy into the process. On a deeper level, *shechitah* is similar to all of the other commandments which bring holiness into otherwise mundane activities. The giving of tithes and charity elevates the pursuit of a livelihood. Proper observance of the major body of laws governing ethics and honesty in commerce turns the profane activity of engaging in business into a holy pursuit.

Shechitah *also gives meaning and holiness to the animal which becomes the vehicle for performance of the commandment.*

Shechitah also gives meaning and holiness to the animal which becomes the vehicle for performance of the commandment. Thus, *shechitah* is a prime manifestation of the inner strength represented by Isaac. It is the means by which holiness can be extracted from an activity that would otherwise be simply a form of the law of the jungle: The big animal kills the small animal, the bigger animal kills the big animal — and man, the most cunning, and therefore the most powerful animal of all, slaughters whatever it pleases him to serve on his table or make into clothes for his body. In the hands of an ordinary killer of animals, that is all slaughter would be, but *shechitah* is different — it is symbolic of Isaac.

Shedder of Blood

The *Talmud (Shabbos* 156a) teaches that one who is destined to shed blood has alternatives. He can become a *mohel* or a *shochet*, bringing infants into the covenant of Abraham or making the flesh of animals permissible as food for the servants of God. Otherwise, he would shed blood some other way — as a murderer.

Esau was this sort of person, and Isaac knew it.

Even at birth and before, he had all the symptoms of a violent, sinful person. As an embryo he fought to approach the temple of idols, he was born with the redness that is symbolic of bloodshed. As a youngster he was drawn to the excitement of the hunt. But this is not to say that he was destined to be evil and that there was no way for him to avoid becoming the epitome of violence. King David, too, had the redness of bloodshed, but he surmounted all obstacles to become the Sweet Singer of Israel [see *Overview* to ArtScroll *Tehillim*]. Esau *could* have become a righteous person. It would have demanded great strength on his part. It would have demanded the *Gevurah* personality of an Isaac. Indeed, Esau had such strength. The test was whether he would utilize it to direct his impulses toward the good or whether he would use his strength to satisfy his cruel, bloodthirsty nature.

Esau could *have become a righteous person. It would have demanded the* Gevurah *personality of an Isaac. Indeed, Esau had such strength.*

Eating is one of the acts that can be sublimated only by inner strength. Of all man's animal impulses, probably none must be indulged in so often, so publicly, and so lends itself to abuse. Huge industries have sprung up everywhere to cater, not to man's unavoidable need for nourishment, but to satisfy and encourage his lust for gastronomic excess. When the Sages likened the table to an altar, they presented a challenge by stating what a table's purpose should be. An ordinary meal can be a means of serving God no less than an offering brought to the Temple in Jerusalem. But the elevation of eating to the status of an offering, requires a person to assault his own nature no less than the hunt requires a huntsman to trap and attack his game.

The elevation of eating to the status of an offering, requires a person to assault his own nature no less than the hunt requires a huntsman to trap and attack his game.

Had Esau attempted to achieve such ends, even a partial success would have mattered greatly because he would have been fighting against his nature. He had physical strength and courage to unusual degrees. He fought mighty kings and fierce animals and conquered all. If that could have been directed inwardly — O what he could have become! And even if he were *not* perfect, if he were merely making the struggle — then, in his own way, he would have been like Isaac in the fields of Philistia, removing the earth from wells of spiritual water. This concept is symbolized by Esau's occupation of צָד צַיִד, *the hunter of game.* In spiritual terms, a 'hunter' is one who seeks to extract holiness from the 'jungle' of evil. Isaac perceived in Esau a man who was fighting against his imperfection and who chose to do it by turning his violent nature toward refining the bloody instinct of the huntsman through *shechitah* and self-control. [Isaac's view of Esau will be discussed further in the *Overview* on the Blessings.]

In spiritual terms, a 'hunter' is one who seeks to extract holiness from the 'jungle' of evil.

II. Isaac's Altar

Exalted Eating

Because Isaac dedicated himself to the enormously difficult task of analyzing and perfecting personal behavior, shechitah *and preparation of food loom so large in the relatively few chapters devoted to his life.*

Because Isaac dedicated himself to the enormously difficult task of analyzing and perfecting personal behavior, *shechitah* and the preparation of food loom so large in the relatively few chapters devoted to his life. *Neos HaDesheh* notes that the term זֶבַח, *zevach,* is most commonly used in Scripture to denote שְׁלָמִים, *peace offerings* (see *Rashi* to *Exodus* 18:12 and *Deut.* 22:17). Peace offerings, *shelamim,* are offerings, portions of which are eaten by the priest and by the owners of the offering. The term זֶבַח, *zevach,* however, refers to slaughter — why should the word for slaughter be used to refer particularly to offerings which are eaten? The answer lies in the similar nature of *shechitah* and the sort of eating which makes an altar of even the ordinary table. Both have the goal of taking dangerous behavior and making it sublime. Kosher slaughter removes killing from the level of bloodlust and transforms it into a holy act. Eating with the intention of preserving one's health in order to serve God better removes a feast from the level of epicurean indulgence and elevates it into a holy offering. Both the offering and the feast can be called *zevach* if they serve the same purpose as *shechitah.*

Isaac saw potential greatness in Esau because he turned his attention to the field — where he *could* have refined a coarse nature. And Isaac gave particular attention to the preparation of food in his own home in order to saturate even feasts with holiness instead of gluttony.

Esau's Offering

The feast requested of Esau was not meant to satisfy a gourmet's palate. Rather it was in the nature of an offering brought to the Temple of God.

Thus does Rabbi Yosaif Leib Block *(Sheiurei Daas II)* explain Isaac's need for delicacies preparatory to conferring the blessings upon his son. The feast requested of Esau was not meant to satisfy a gourmet's palate. Rather it was in the nature of an offering brought to the Temple of God. The bearer of an offering subordinated his person and his possessions to the will of God. He brought pleasure to God who savored the fragrance rising up from the altar and said, אָמַרְתִּי וְנַעֲשָׂה רְצוֹנִי, *I have spoken and My will has been done* (see *Rashi* to *Lev.* 1:9). As *Mesillas Yesharim* writes, the food and drink placed before a righteous person become elevated. The food is like an offering, like first fruits, the drink is like the נְסָכִים, *libations*, poured upon the altar. This explains, he continues, the *Talmudic* dictum that כֹּהֲנִים אוֹכְלִים וּבַעֲלִים מִתְכַּפְּרִים, *the priests eat and the owners receive atonement* — that an Israelite enables the righteous priests to eat from his offering and replenish their energies is in itself a source of untold merit for him; their eating too, is in the nature of an offering upon God's altar.

That an Israelite enables the righteous priests to eat from his offering and replenish their energies is in itself a source of untold merit for him;

As Isaac prepared to draw his son into the covenant of Abraham, how could he better bring him nearer to the service of God than by having him bring an offering to God with all the holy connotations contained in so sublime a deed? That is precisely what Isaac did. He asked Esau to bring an offering, prepare it well and slaughter it properly, to place it upon an altar and pour libations before God. For Isaac's food was an offering and his drink was a libation.

He asked Esau to bring an offering prepare it well and slaughter it properly, to place it upon an altar and pour libations before God. For Isaac's food was an offering.

Further, Isaac was signaling to him that his work of sanctifying his cruel instinct — the task Isaac thought was his — should be carried further by bringing nobility, control, purpose, and holiness into his life and upon his table.

Jacob Remembers

Sixty-seven years after the blessings were given, Jacob prepared to descend to Egypt with his family. He was afraid of what the future would bring, and before he departed from *Eretz Yisrael,* he went to Beer Sheba, the place that had been important in the lives of his father and grandfather. There, וַיִּזְבַּח זְבָחִים לֵאלֹהֵי אָבִיו יִצְחָק, *he slaughtered offerings to the God of his father, Isaac* (46:1). The commentators find it noteworthy that only Isaac, and not Abraham, is mentioned in connection with Jacob's offerings. *Neos HaDesheh* explains that Jacob was embarking on a task that was uniquely suited to his legacy from Isaac. The uniqueness of Isaac was his strength in taking the grain of good from its shell of evil. He had done it in Philistia and had symbolized it by his particular responsibility for the sanctity of *shechitah* and of eating. Jacob was about to descend to Egypt, the most corrupt, perverted country then on earth. His task and that of the succeeding generations of his children would be to remain pure even in Egypt and to draw out of that accursed place the scattered sparks of holiness that were there. Jacob was about to begin an Isaac-like mission — and he brought his offerings to God Who gave Isaac the strength to succeed. Jacob would need the qualities of his father more than of his grandfather to succeed in Egypt.

Only Isaac, and not Abraham, is mentioned in connection with Jacob's offerings.

Jacob would need the qualities of his father more than of his grandfather to succeed in Egypt.

Sforno there adds the thought that Jacob thought of Isaac at that juncture because Isaac had been forbidden by God from going to Egypt. Jacob sought mercy as he was about to do what his father was commanded not to do. Why, indeed, was Jacob able to go? Not because Isaac was inferior to him, but because Isaac had preceded him. Isaac had come upon the stage of history with the mission of perfecting Abraham's legacy. Abraham's expansive goodness required Isaac's introspective strength to

Why, indeed, was Jacob able to go? Because Isaac had preceded him.

perfect and purge it. Isaac had succeeded in uncovering holiness that was buried after Abraham's death, in bringing sanctity to potential bloodshed and holiness to potential gluttony. By responding to God's awesome challenge, he had even purged Esau from the seed of Abraham [see *Overviews* further]. His mission done, Jacob had within him the combined attributes of Abraham and Isaac. *He* was suited to descend to Egypt and conquer the evil and impurity of that shameful land — *because* Isaac had prepared the way for him.

An Overview —
The Birthright — Esau's or Jacob's

... כִּי בְיִצְחָק יִקָּרֵא לְךָ זָרַע. בְּיִצְחָק וְלֹא כָל יִצְחָק
... Since through Isaac will offspring be considered yours (21:12). Part of Isaac [i.e., a portion of this offspring] but not all of Isaac's [offspring will be considered descendants of Abraham] (Nedarim *31a).*

יַעֲקֹב נוֹצַר מִטִּפָּה רִאשׁוֹנָה וְעֵשָׂו מִן הַשְּׁנִיָּה צֵא וּלְמַד מִשְׁפוֹפֶרֶת שֶׁפִּיהָ קְצָרָה תֵּן בָּהּ שְׁתֵּי אֲבָנִים זוֹ תַּחַת זוֹ הַנִּכְנֶסֶת רִאשׁוֹנָה תֵּצֵא אַחֲרוֹנָה
Jacob was conceived from the first drop and Esau from the second. Go and learn from a tube with a narrow mouth. Put in two pebbles, one beneath the other. The first one in will go out last (Rashi *to 25:26).*

אָהַבְתִּי אֶתְכֶם אָמַר ה׳ וַאֲמַרְתֶּם בַּמָּה אֲהַבְתָּנוּ הֲלוֹא אָח עֵשָׂו לְיַעֲקֹב נְאֻם ה׳ וָאֹהַב אֶת יַעֲקֹב וְאֶת עֵשָׂו שָׂנֵאתִי ...
'I loved you,' said HASHEM.
And you said, 'By what have You loved us?'
'Was not Esau a brother of Jacob?,' the words of HASHEM, 'but I loved Jacob. And Esau I hated ...' (Malachi *1:2,3).*

I. The Intended Division

The Brothers

We fail to feel the drama of the conflict between Jacob and Esau because we heard the story when we were children and, by the time we were mature enough to appreciate the rivalry and the stakes it involved, the suspense was gone. But the stakes were indeed great. The struggle for primacy between the two carried as its prize the privilege of bearing for all time the covenant of Abraham and receiving the Torah.

The struggle for primacy carried as its prize the privilege of bearing for all time the covenant of Abraham and receiving the Torah.

Rambam writes in *Hilchos Melochim* 10:7:

> *The commandment of circumcision was directed to Abraham and his offspring exclusively ... Ishmael and his offspring are excluded because Scripture says* through Isaac will offspring be considered yours (Genesis *21:12). Esau is excluded because Isaac said to Jacob* and may He give the blessing of Abraham to you and your offspring *(ibid. 28:4), implying that he alone is the offspring of Abraham, who holds fast to his religion and to his righteous path.*

Why does *Rambam* cite 28:4 for the exclusion of Esau from the category of Abraham's offspring instead of following the *Talmud (Nedarim* 31a) which derives from *Genesis* 21:12 that only part of Isaac's offspring [i.e., Jacob] is so privileged and that both Ishmael and Esau are thereby excluded?

Rabbi Chaim Soloveitchick of Brisk explains that 21:12 tells us only that not all of Isaac's sons would be of equal status as the heirs of Abraham. But that verse leaves open the question of whether the heir would be Jacob or Esau. Had Esau been awarded the right to succeed Isaac, then Jacob would have been excluded despite his moral excellence. The final decision that Jacob would be the chosen part of Isaac was not proclaimed until Isaac summoned Jacob to instruct him to go to Paddan Aram to find his mate from among Abraham's kindred. At that time Isaac specifically told him that בִּרְכַּת אַבְרָהָם, *the blessing of Abraham,* was his — and therefore he was obligated in the corollary prohibition not to marry a Canaanite woman.

The final decision that Jacob would be the chosen part of Isaac was not proclaimed until Isaac summoned Jacob.

Therefore, too, Malachi began his prophecy with

Esau was a brother to Jacob. Indeed he was. Esau was Jacob's equal in every way — except that he was unworthy.

God's word that Esau was *a brother to Jacob.* Indeed he was. Esau was Jacob's equal in every way — except that he was unworthy, and, because he was, God hated him. Jacob earned Divine love and it was that — not his purchase of the birthright or the deception that brought him the first set of blessings — which *earned* him and his offspring the title זֶרַע אַבְרָהָם, *offspring of Abraham.*

Isaac's original decision to bless Esau now assumes awesome proportions. Although there are widely divergent opinions among the commentators concerning exactly what it was that Isaac wished to bestow upon Esau and what blessings, if any, he would have left for Jacob, the simplest understanding of the Torah's narrative makes unmistakably clear that Isaac's choice was crucial to the future development of the Abrahamitic nation. This section of the Overview will deal with the following questions:

How had Isaac intended to divide the blessings?

1. How had Isaac intended to divide the blessings between Esau and Jacob?

If the birthright was Esau's, how did Jacob justify his right to take it away?

2. If the birthright was Esau's, how did Jacob justify his right to take it away?

As the reader will see from a study of the *commentary,* many opinions have been expressed by the classic commentators. The following is not meant to be definitive; it is an attempt to offer insights that follow generally accepted basic trends.

Complementary Roles

The distinction of being the son who was to carry on the Abrahamitic tradition would in all likelihood have gone to Jacob in recognition of his infinitely superior righteousness. This is indicated by the very text of the Torah for the blessings (27:28,29) conferred by Isaac upon the disguised Jacob — the son whom Isaac took to be Esau — which makes no mention of בִּרְכַּת אַבְרָהָם, *the blessing of Abraham.* Only later when Isaac knew he was addressing Jacob (28:3,4) did he specifically confer the Abrahamitic blessings.

The implication is plain: Isaac had planned to con-

Isaac had planned to confer upon Esau blessings. But those blessings were entirely apart from the right to carry on the Patriarchal tradition.

fer upon Esau blessings which were essential to Jacob and which Providence decreed were indeed to go to Jacob, but those blessings were entirely apart from the right to carry on the Patriarchal tradition. Instead, Isaac planned to give Abraham's blessing to Jacob, but to give Esau a significant degree of superiority over Jacob, for as he said in 27:29 when he thought he was addressing Esau, *be a lord to your brother and the children of your mother will prostrate themselves to you.*

Esau was to have material wealth, power, and dominance. Jacob was to have spiritual ascendancy.

Isaac intended to divide the material and spiritual worlds. Esau was to have material wealth, power, and dominance. Jacob was to have spiritual ascendancy. This is implied by the Torah's description of the youthful Jacob and Esau: one was a man of the tent of Torah study and the other was a man of the field. While these are surely dissimilar characteristics, they need not conflict with one another. In future centuries, the tribe of Zebulun would engage in commerce and thereby support the Torah study of the tribe of Issachar (see *Rashi* to *Deut.* 33:18). Zebulun's mercantile pursuits, because they were dedicated to the end of spiritual greatness, were themselves elevated to the status of spirituality. An accountant might compare the merchants of Zebulun with the merchants of Tyre, but to the All-Seeing Eye they were no more similar than the real Mount Everest and stage set of a mountain. The unknowing eye might be deceived, but the essential reality was different beyond description.

Had Esau been worthy, he, too, would have been master of a material world and made it a sounding board for the voice of Jacob's Torah and prayer.

Had Esau been worthy, he, too, would have been master of a material world and made it a sounding board for the voice of Jacob's Torah and prayer. Though not sharing the title of Abraham's offspring, Esau would have been an essential and exalted complement to the fulfillment of Jacob's mission, for it is God's will that His commandments be carried out by earthlings through the agency of material factors. He did not create human life because He was short of angels, but because only man, not angels, could carry out His plan as it was conceived by His wisdom.

Voice and Hands

The concept of material ascendancy is described by the word יָדַיִם, *hands,* for sustenance must be wrung from the material world by the labor of hands. Spirituality is expressed by קוֹל, *voice,* for the voice is man's means of articulating the wisdom of the Torah and the words of prayer. Thus, Isaac described the attributes of his sons as הַקֹּל קוֹל יַעֲקֹב וְהַיָּדַיִם יְדֵי עֵשָׂו, *the voice is Jacob's voice but the hands are Esau's hands* (27:23).

The two — hands and voice, hard labor and sacred words — would seem to be gulfs apart, but they are not.

The two — hands and voice, hard labor and sacred words — would seem to be gulfs apart, but they are not. The world represented by the hands is the outer shell; its inner essence, is its spiritual content. Esau was intended to be lord of this world. Even after Jacob acquired the blessing originally meant for his brother, Esau was still granted ascendancy during periods when Jacob was undeserving (27:40). In effect, even the material mastery acquired by Jacob was not to be purely physical, for if he were not to be of sufficient spiritual worth, he would lose his superiority to Esau. Rather, Jacob would dominate his brother and attain dominion over the *material* world through *spiritual* means. But how does one gain material results with spiritual tools? Can an hour of Torah study plow a field or win a war?

Convince a man that his performance in a particular task will make a difference to whatever it is that he holds most dear — and wild horses will not stop him.

In the deepest sense it can. Let us use an analogy. One attempts to motivate a worker to surpass anything he has ever done. It may be done at gunpoint, or by offering large financial rewards. There is another way. If one knows his worker well enough, knows what is important to him as a human being, he may be able to touch the man's emotions more than he could with money or threats. Convince a man that his performance in a particular task will make a difference to his God, his family, his reputation, his country — whatever it is that he holds most dear — and wild horses will not stop him. His soul will have been touched and in the final analysis, that is the most powerful force there is. So, too, the uni verse. Tanks and bulldozers have an undeniable force, but strength cannot be measured only in horsepower.

> רוֹמְמוֹת אֵל בִּגְרוֹנָם וְחֶרֶב פִּיפִיּוֹת בְּיָדָם
> *Exaltation of God is in their throats and a double-edged sword is in their hands* (Psalms *149:6).*

When the voice is Jacob's voice, the hands of Esau become impotent. There is no other way for Jacob to control the course of material events.

When one has in his throat the exaltation of God — when his throat vibrates with the voice of Torah and prayer — then, his hands are armed with a double-edged sword that can overcome the powerful hands that hold the world in their sway. When *the voice is Jacob's voice,* the hands of Esau become impotent. There is no other way for Jacob to control the course of material events. The normal way is Esau's, but Jacob can overpower him by going to the source. Brawny Esau can push about a vehicle at will as long as its power source is inactive. Let Jacob turn on its engine and Esau's strength becomes immaterial. So long as Jacob neglects the exaltation of God which is the ultimate lever of power, he is subservient to his mightier brother, but if he recognizes that his strength is at the source of earth's existence, he truly becomes invincible.

Isaac's intention was to forge a harmony between his sons.

But it could not be because Esau would not allow it to be.

Isaac's intention was to forge a harmony between his sons that would place Esau's world at the service of Jacob's world. Had Esau been worthy of his calling, such would have happened without cause for alarm or deception. But it could not be because Esau would not allow it to be. Therefore, Rebecca had to find a way for Jacob to gain the blessing that would permit him to turn the material world to the service of his mission (*Sfas Emes).*

II. Unending Struggle

Opposites from Conception

Maharal explains that the natures of Jacob and Esau were so divergent that even before birth each displayed the powerful tendency that would govern his entire life — Jacob to good and Esau to evil. Even then, Jacob was unconcerned with physical wealth or pleasure. Esau had no care for spiritual perfection. Nevertheless, each wanted both worlds because each one, according to his own set of values and beliefs, could not tolerate the other. How can goodness tolerate the existence of evil and vice versa? Had there been no Esau, Jacob would have had both worlds; there would have been no possibility for the abuse of this world's riches for everything would have been Jacob's to use in the service of God. The present rivalry between good and evil and the centuries-long eclipse of Israel because it succumbed to the spirit — and, therefore to the power — of Esaù, would never have come to pass.

How can goodness tolerate the existence of evil and vice versa? Had there been no Esau, Jacob would have had both worlds;

The struggle between the two, began unrelentingly from the womb. For as Rebecca was told when she sought the reason for the abnormal agitation within her, the two nations she carried would never know equilibrium: when one rose the other would fall. They were unlike Israel and Ishmael or Israel and Canaan. Israel's destiny would not be linked of necessity to that of the other nations. The world could have fifty powerful empires without in the least affecting Israel. In the same prophecy which assured Abraham of the greatness awaiting Isaac's offspring, he was told that Ishmael would be a great and powerful nation. Israel and Ishmael can coexist as easily as can Israel and China. Geographical proximity need not necessarily be a hindrance to either. But Jacob and Esau cannot rise independently of one another. Indeed, *Drashos HaRan* maintains that all the conditions of their development, upbringing, blessings, and history were Divinely designed to foster conflict between the two brothers who were to become two nations. The history of the world would be played out in the rivalry between the philosophies of good and evil as represented by them. Obviously, then, there could be no compromise between two such diametrically opposed forces. Light and darkness cannot compromise.

Israel and Ishmael can coexist as easily as can Israel and China. But Jacob and Esau cannot rise independently of one another.

Nevertheless, if the two could not be equals in

either world and if there had to be a division of worlds between them, Jacob's choice was clear — he would surrender this world if he must in order to gain the world to come, the world of the spirit. True, as *Sfas Emes* explains above, where Jacob required the services of the material world to serve spiritual needs, his 'voice' gave him the means to attain it. But even that was a function of his choice of priority. The only world that mattered was the spiritual one, everything else flowed from that crucial choice.

Jacob's choice was clear — he would surrender this world if he must in order to gain the World to Come.

Each Chooses

בְּכֹר, first-born. *Each letter of that word is the second in its numerical set. Jacob wanted the world represented by that collection of second letters.*

This, *Maharal* explains, is indicated by the very combination of letters that expresses the status Jacob sought to retrieve from Esau: בְּכֹר, *first-born.* Each letter of that word is the second in its numerical set: ב, *bet* [=2], is the second in the set of ones; כ, *chaf* [=20], is the second in the set of tens; ר, *reish* [=200], is the second in the set of hundreds. A human being lives in two worlds. He lives first in the material world but his ultimate reward will come in the second one, the World to Come. Jacob begged of Esau that he sell him his status of בְּכֹר, *first-born,* his birthright (25:31). He wanted the second world represented by that collection of second letters. And Esau? He made clear by his request of Jacob which world mattered to him. Jacob spoke of spirituality and Esau spoke only of a pot of beans. Jacob reached toward exalted heights and Esau demanded only that his hunger be satisfied. Jacob spoke of going on to a meaningful life and Esau saw only death. If Esau gave up eternity for a stomachful of lentils, he received more than full value, because to him the birthright had no worth at all. The Torah testifies that Esau was not defrauded of his other world while his life hung in the balance, for when he turned and left with his innards filled there was not a murmur of protest: וַיִּבֶז עֵשָׂו אֶת הַבְּכֹרָה, *Esau despised the birthright* (25:34).

It would seem that Jacob held an independent claim to the birthright, entirely apart from his agreement with Esau. As *Rashi* comments based on the

Midrash, the newborn Jacob held on to Esau's heel (25:26) as if to insist that the right to be born first belonged to him. As *Rashi* explains, Jacob was conceived first even though Esau was born first and therefore he considered himself entitled to the status of the first-born. The difficulty of this claim is obvious, however. The Torah states clearly that the birthright belongs not to the one who is conceived first, but to the one who is *born* first (*Exodus* 13:2). Even if we were to know that the twin born second was conceived first, he would not have the *halachic* status of the first-born. Why, then, would the Torah stress a symbolic claim of Jacob that had no validity?

Jacob was conceived first even though Esau was born first and therefore he considered himself entitled to the status of the first-born.

Perhaps we may find the answer in an analysis of the general concept of the sanctity of the first-born, and the uniqueness of the Patriarchal mission.

Jacob's Claim

Not only human and animal first-born are accorded special status. The Torah describes many things as בְּכֹר, *first-born,* or by the related expression רֵאשִׁית, *first.* The *Midrash* expounds that the universe was created for the sake of Torah and Israel which are called רֵאשִׁית [see *comm.* to 1:1]. First fruits are described as בִּכּוּרִים, *biccurim;* tithes of grain, dough, and other varieties are called רֵאשִׁית. First shearings, [רֵאשִׁית הַגֵּז] are one of the priestly gifts. Interestingly enough, God describes the Jewish nation as בְּנִי בְכֹרִי יִשְׂרָאֵל, *My first-born son Israel (Ex.* 4:22) — but Israel is hardly the oldest, or 'first-born' among nations. What is the significance of first or first-born?

My first-born son Israel — *but Israel is hardly the oldest, or 'first-born' among nations. What is the significance of first or first-born?*

The first produce of a person's labor, is precious to him. One would expect a farmer to exult with the first finished fruits of his vine, tree, or field and bring them home to share with his family. How much travail and labor went into producing them! The first child. The first calf. The first portion of a finished crop. They all matter. They are all symbolic of a person's fulfillment. The goal to which he dedicates them tells much about what sort of person he is, for a person *is* the sum total of his aspirations and hopes. What does he do with what *really* matters

The goal to which he dedicates them tells much about what sort of person he is, for a person is the sum total of his aspirations and hopes.

to him? Where will he direct his *first* child, his *first* fruit, his *first* portion of the finished harvest? Israel is God's first-born because it is His most precious, His chosen nation. God calls the Torah 'first' because it matters most of all. When the Jew complies with God's will by sanctifying all these 'firsts' of his life and his productive capacities, he signifies that the thrust of his existence is dedication to the will of God. First, he satisfies his Creator; then, he turns to his private needs. Thereby he proclaims that God's wish *is* his own wish. The first child to be born is sanctified as an expression of this resolve.

In the existence of the Patriarchs, there was a further element. Each of them had his particular mission. As we have seen above and in the *Overview* of *Lech Lecha*, Abraham represented *Chessed-Kindness* Isaac's mission flowed from Abraham's; he was to refine and perfect Abraham's *Chessed* through his own *Gevurah-Strength*. But Isaac was not a contradiction to Abraham. His was a continuation of his father's mission as we have seen above. The successor to Isaac, whether it would be Jacob or Esau, would also continue his father's mission. He would complete the work of Abraham and Isaac by fusing their unique contributions into *Tiferes-Splendor*, *Emes-Truth*. Again, his had to be an outgrowth of their missions, not a contradiction or an unrelated one.

The successor to Isaac, whether it would be Jacob or Esau, would also continue his father's mission.

Embodiment of Potential

There is a further concept of first-born, one that is formulated by *Maharal* and elucidated by *Pachad Yitzchok (Pesach* ch. 20). Perhaps we may find in this concept the reason for Jacob's primacy in having been conceived first. *Maharal* comments that there is כֹּחַ הָאָב, the *capacity* or *potential of the father*. At the instant of conception, when the father's seed merges with the mother's egg, he has completed his role in the birth process. The further development of the embryo and its ultimate birth will take place within and from the mother's body, but conception represents the fulfillment of the father's role for it is then that he contributes his own potential to the future human being. If the father were to die immediately after conception, he would still be the father of the child when it is eventually born.

Clearly, without the development and childbearing of the mother, the father's role would be meaningless; conception without birth serves no more purpose than no conception at all. In the case of the Patriarchs, however, conception had a special meaning. Isaac's mission grew out of Abraham's and Jacob's grew out of Isaac's. They became Patriarchs of Israel precisely because they embodied the potential of their fathers, a potential which each in turn nurtured and brought to full realization according to his own particular mission.

How significant therefore, that Jacob could say that he was conceived first. He was the first of Isaac's potential.

The conflict between Jacob and Esau was over which would be the successor to Abraham and Isaac. Everything else was secondary. How significant therefore, that Jacob could say that he was conceived first. He was the first of Isaac's potential, the best representation of his father's seed, the embodiment of the concluding stage in the growth of the Patriarchal mission.

In this regard, it is instructive that we look at Esau's progression. As we have seen, Esau had the strength of Isaac, but he was the corruption of *Gevurah:* instead of using his inherited attribute to purge himself of baseness, he used it to subdue the world for the gratification of his lust, to acquire, and dominate for selfish ends. Ishmael, too, was heir to Abraham's attribute of *Chessed-Kindness*, but he corrupted the gift: instead of using it to benefit others, he became the epitome of *self*-indulgence. When Esau realized that he had forfeited his birthright and blessings to Jacob, he tried to impress his parents with a new resolve to live up to their standards of behavior. He had failed them by marrying Canaanite women, now he would please them by marrying someone from the family of Abraham. He took Ishmael's daughter in marriage (28:9).

How striking the contrast between the two

But Esau? He combined his own perversion of Isaac with Ishmael's perversion of Abraham.

brothers! Jacob combined the attributes of kindness and strength — of Abraham and Isaac at their best — into the splendor of truth. But Esau? He combined his own perversion of Isaac with Ishmael's perversion of Abraham to produce the lineage that continues to represent implacable opposition to good until the End of Days when God will judge the Mountain of Esau and take unto Himself the universally acknowledged reign over a world that will bow to the offspring of Jacob.

An Overview —
Esau Honors His Father

אָמַר רשב״ג כָּל יָמַי הָיִיתִי מְשַׁמֵּשׁ אֶת אָבִי וְלֹא שִׁמַּשְׁתִּי אוֹתוֹ אֶחָד מִמֵּאָה שֶׁשִּׁמֵּשׁ עֵשָׂו אֶת אָבִיו

*Rabban Shimon ben Gamliel said, 'All my life I served my father, but I did not serve him even a hundredth as well as Esau served his father (*Devarim Rabbah *1).*

שְׁלֹשָׁה שֻׁתָּפִים בָּאָדָם הקב״ה אָבִיו וְאִמּוֹ בִּזְמַן שֶׁהָאָדָם מְכַבֵּד אָבִיו וְאִמּוֹ אָמַר הקב״ה ... כְּאִלּוּ דַּרְתִּי בֵּינֵיהֶם וְכִבְּדוּנִי ... וּבִזְמַן שֶׁמְּצַעֵר אָבִיו וְאִמּוֹ אוֹמֵר ... אִילּוּ דַּרְתִּי בֵּינֵיהֶם צִעֲרוּנִי

*There are three partners in a person, the Holy One, Blessed be He, his father and his mother ... When the person honors his father and mother, [God] says, 'It is as if I dwelt among them and they honored me' ... When he causes his parents to suffer [God] says ... 'Had I dwelt among them they would have caused Me suffering' (*Kiddushin *31b).*

The Sages teach that the honor Esau rendered his parents was so awesome that in its merit alone he very nearly superceded Jacob. *Sefer HaZ'chus* and others comment that Jacob could earn the blessings for himself only by giving equivalent honor. Therefore, he was put to the test by Rebecca. She demanded unquestioning obedience from him in going to Isaac in the guise of Esau even though Jacob protested that if he were discovered, his father might well curse him. It was not only the curse that bothered him. Deception went against his very grain. Jacob remains the eternal epitome of truth yet he was

Only by completely subjugating himself to his mother's desire — in the face of danger and personal distaste — could he earn the right to displace Esau.

being asked to deceive. Only by completely subjugating himself to his mother's desire — in the face of danger and personal distaste — could he earn the right to displace Esau.

It is no accident that this particular commandment was the one that was so significant for Esau. *Mesech Chochmah* (to *Kedoshim*) comments that honor and obedience to parents is the key to the survival of tradition. Without it, the chain of the generations would be severed and Israel would cease to be the nation of Torah. The ultimate bond uniting us with the generation that stood at Sinai and with the Patriarchs is loyalty to parents. So vital is this need to honor parents that a child would be *required* to violate even the laws of the Torah itself at the behest of his parents. Only because the Torah clearly implies that children should not obey their parents in such instances are they absolved from the general requirement to obey [see *Rashi* to *Leviticus* 18:3]. Thus, as long as Esau retained his loyalty to his parents, he could be seen as part of the tradition of Isaac and Abraham; his allegiance to his parents might eventually be translated into broader loyalty to the ideals for which they lived. It may very well be that equal devotion to a different commandment instead might have availed him not at all in his effort to gain Isaac's favor.

The ultimate bond uniting us with the generation that stood at Sinai and with the Patriarchs is loyalty to parents.

So important is this honor to God's 'partners' in the creation of each individual human being, that He placed the commandment of *Honor your father and your mother (Exodus* 20:12) among the first five of the Ten Commandments; it is among those that deal with man's duties to God for by honoring the parents who shared with Him the task of giving him life, a person honors the Third Partner, but if he fails to show gratitude to his human parents, then by implication he fails to recognize his debt to God as well.

If he fails to show gratitude to his human parents, then by implication he fails to recognize his debt to God as well.

If Esau's honor of parents was great enough to make Rabban Shimon ben Gamliel's — and even Jacob's! — seem pale by comparison, then how could

Esau have been so wicked? And if honor of parents stands so high in God's estimation, then why is it so commonly found among people who otherwise place so little value in the Torah and its commandments?

He gave up his chance to make the fortune because he refused to awaken his father. The next year God rewarded him with a Parah Adumah.

In its discussion of the obligation to honor parents, the *Talmud* inquires as to how much one should sacrifice to fulfill this commandment (*Kiddushin* 31b). The *Talmud* tells of a non-Jew named Dama ben Nesina who possessed the precious stones needed for the *Kohain Gadol's* breastplate. The Sages offered him 600,000 shekels for the gems, but his key to the treasure was under the pillow of his sleeping father. He gave up his chance to make the fortune because he refused to awaken his father. The next year God rewarded him with a *Parah Adumah*, (red heifer), one of the rarest of all the animals required for the performance of a commandment (see *Numbers* 19:1-22). Again the Sages came to Dama. He told them that he knew he could command any price he chose, but he would ask only for the 600,000 shekels he had forgone a year earlier.

Dama ben Nesina set a standard that is surely hard to match; his achievement would seem to make Israel seem pale by comparison.

Two Perceptions

Perhaps no other commandment is as required by the dictates of simple logic as is the requirement to honor parents.

Maharal offers a deeper understanding of Dama's dedication to his father, of Esau's dedication to his — and of Israel's own brand of dedication to the will of God. Perhaps no other commandment is as required by the dictates of simple logic as is the requirement to honor parents. It is accepted by every culture and acknowledged even by hardened criminals. Esau, who was a product of Isaac's attribute of strength, approached this commandment with all the strength of his nature. Dama, too, recognized the obligation and carried it to an almost unbelievable extreme. Esau risked his life to honor Isaac; Dama risked his fortune to honor his father. Both acted valiantly for something they understood.

There are areas of obligation that are less well understood.

There are areas of obligation that are less well understood, even areas that are entirely beyond human comprehension. Classic among them is God's decree of the Red Heifer. Every aspect of its laws defies logic. But it was to satisfy *that* requirement that the Sages beat a path to Dama the following year. He remembered the events of the previous year and he remembered the price he had given up — to the *perutah*. Jews, too, understand the logic of such 'common sense' laws as: honor your parent; do not kill; and do not steal. Israel need not take a back seat to any civilization in its laws of decency and consideration, and its willingness to sacrifice profit for the sake of principle. But Israel is equally ready to sacrifice for laws it does *not* understand, in order to honor the wishes of its other Father, the Third Partner in the triumvirate of honor. Therein lies the greatness of Israel.

Israel is equally ready to sacrifice for laws it does not *understood, in order to honor the wishes of its other Father, the Third Partner in the triumvirate of honor.*

For all the greatness of Esau's service to his parents, it was flawed. *Neos HaDesheh* pinpoints the salient fault in Esau's character as a failure to recognize that he might be anything less than perfect. He was satisfied with himself; there was no room for improvement. For the *Midrash* relates that when he came home from his hunt one day to learn that Abraham had died, he exclaimed, 'If the Attribute of Justice could strike even at that righteous man, then there is surely no reward and no resuscitation of the dead!' With that, Esau threw away his birthright as a useless encumbrance. The gall of Esau! He saw such perfection in himself — and surely in Abraham — that there could be no justification for Abraham's death. And if someone whom 'perfect' Esau considered righteous could nevertheless be the victim of Divine judgment, then ח״ו God's judgment was without justification or purpose.

Neos HaDesheh *pinpoints the salient fault in Esau's character as a failure to recognize that he might be anything less than perfect. He was satisfied with himself:*

This strain of myopic selfishness colors his honor of parents as well. There is no contradiction between the regard shown parents by the self-centered person and his total preoccupation with himself. Because he is an extension of his parents, he honors *himself* by giving them their due. He honors them because they are *his* parents, not because he is indebted to them.

Because he is an extension of his parents, he honors himself *by giving them their due.*

Even in his concern for them he sees only himself. Had Esau truly meant the happiness and welfare of his parents, how could he have failed to foresee the heartbreak he would cause them by marrying Canaanite women?

Even in his concern for them he sees only himself. Had Esau truly meant the happiness and welfare of his parents, how could he have failed to foresee the heartbreak he would cause them by marrying Canaanite women? In his preoccupation with how to take tithes from salt and straw, did it not strike him that he was making a travesty of his parents principles by marrying daughters of an accursed nation? He married at the age of forty in imitation of his father, but he did not draw back from the matches which Abraham had specifically forbidden to Isaac. Not until twenty-three years later, when Isaac sent Jacob to Paddan Aram and also ratified the stripping from Esau of the Abrahamitic blessings did it dawn on him to please his parents by his choice of a wife!

In that callous attitude lay the measure of Esau's devotion to his parents.

In that callous attitude lay the measure of Esau's devotion to his parents. The lengths to which he went in order to serve them were truly awesome — and for that he would be fully rewarded, despite his own declaration that there was no reward. But at root, his dedication to them was of a piece with his entire character. Esau was selfish and exploited everything around him for his own ends. He honored Isaac and Rebecca because he owed them a debt for having raised him; by paying his debt to them, he would entitle himself to make demands upon his own children. It was not Isaac he honored, but himself *(Michtav MeEliyahu).*

An Overview — Isaac's Blessing

The following material is based on *Michtav MeEliyahu II.* As the *commentary* indicates there are different views as well.

I. Nature of Blessing

The Tzaddik's Role

The tzaddik *who blesses or who prays is aware of his own inability to influence events.*

Blessing and prayer are similar. The *tzaddik* who blesses or who prays is aware of his own inability to influence events. He wishes to save someone from tragedy or to bring unanticipated prosperity upon him, but he cannot. Only God can control events. So another's need has brought him to recognize anew, or more keenly, the omnipotence of God. If his prayer is answered or his blessing fulfilled, his recognition of God's majesty will grow even further, all because of the person who moved him to bless or pray. Perhaps the needy person was unworthy of the benefit sought for him, but the *tzaddik* is one whose deeds have earned him heavenly consideration. His goal is to serve God better and, since he now desires help for another, the success of that person will enhance the service of the *tzaddik.* To be the cause of such enhancement is in itself a source of great merit for the needful person, and it may well be enough to earn him the assistance he desires.

Prayer or blessing cannot *directly* change the state of a person's religious belief. One cannot expect a positive response to the prayer 'Give me greater faith in God.' All we can ask for is that the conditions of life be made more conducive to the achievement of such faith. For example, if one is able to study Torah and perform commandments amid relative prosperity, it is immeasurably easier for him to gain higher spiritual levels. If, however, he is beset by poverty, illness, and frequent failure, then his study and *mitzvah*-performance are hindered and he may well lose confidence in the efficacy of his way of life. In short, no prayer can make someone more pious, but it *can* bring about conditions that will help him along the road to greater piety.

No prayer can make someone more pious, but it can bring about conditions that will help him along the road to greater piety.

Two Causes

There are two general causes for God to provide a person with material benefits in return for his deeds.

There are two general causes for God to provide a person with material benefits in return for his deeds. The first is His desire to bestow blessing upon the great *tzaddik*. Its purpose is to enable him to better serve his Maker. Since his sole desire is to serve God, it is fitting that he be provided with the means to do so. The second general cause is because God desires to reward someone in This World, rather than in the World to Come, for superficial deeds. For example, one may wave his *esrog* and *lulav* habitually, mechanically, mindlessly. He deserves to be rewarded for his deed because, although lacking in meaning, it was still an act of compliance with God's will. But because the deed was shallow, the reward will be of a kind — it will come in the form of benefits in the fleeting material world. Nevertheless, the performer of the deficient *mitzvah* may well be a person with an active spark of goodness within him, a spark which may be helped to grow and add more meaning to future deeds as a result of the reward. In that case, the reward may be designed to help him improve the quality of his *mitzvah*-performance. On the other hand, a person may be devoid of any meaningful spiritual content; in that case, his reward is given in life only so he that he will gain nothing from the future life of the spirit in which he has no place.

The performer of the deficient mitzvah *may well be a person with an active sark of goodness within him.*

On the other hand, a person may be devoid of any meaningful spiritual content;

To one of Isaac's inner strength, outside assistance was detrimental to his service of God. To the extent that his task was eased, he was denied the opportunity to perfect himself in the face of adversity. True, wealth, good health, and friendly sur-

To one of Isaac's inner strength, outside assistance was detrimental to his service of God.

roundings make it easier to serve God, but the person who is strong enough to serve Him just as well amid poverty, illness and hostility reaches a far higher level of spiritual perfection. The Sages teach that Isaac requested suffering, so that he could exercise his inner strength to serve God despite the pain. Jacob, too, asked for strict judgment. To people of such caliber, material blessing is not a gift but a hindrance. In their world-view, blessing is a boon only to the spiritual weakling whose aspirations are good, but who lacks the strength to follow through on them.

To people of such caliber, material blessing is not a gift but a hindrance.

II. Isaac Chooses

His Love for Esau

Isaac knew that Jacob was a tzaddik *of such rare caliber that blessing held no benefits in terms of his* personal *striving.*

Isaac knew full well that there was a yawning chasm between Jacob and Esau. He was not at all mistaken in his assessment of Jacob's greatness. Isaac knew that Jacob was a *tzaddik* of such rare caliber that blessing held no benefits in terms of his *personal* striving. Jacob sought no blessing, needed no blessing for himself. And Isaac knew that Esau was far from a *tzaddik* in those lofty terms. In fact, according to the *Yalkut*, Isaac became reassured that the person in front of him was Esau and not Jacob when his prophetic insight foresaw that wicked people would descend from the man who had come for his blessings (see quotation below). To Isaac this seemed a clear indication that he was facing Esau. Obviously, then, he knew that Jacob's level of righteousness towered far above Esau's.

Did he realize that Esau was wicked? No. He thought that Esau was engaged in a constant, difficult struggle to perfect himself.

Did he realize that Esau was wicked? No. Therein lay Isaac's error. As mentioned above, he thought that Esau was engaged in a constant, difficult struggle to perfect himself, a struggle he could not win without assistance. Since, in Isaac's asssessment, Esau wished to utilize material success to help him reach his spiritual goal, Isaac constantly sought to help him. That was the reason Isaac loved Esau: it is human nature for a person to love someone whom he has helped. The more a parent does for a child, the more he loves him. The more a patron helps his ward, the greater his tenderness toward him. The reverse is not as true: The recipient may well resent his benefactor, but the giver's love will grow the more he gives. Isaac gave of himself to Esau because he saw him as one who fought mightily to better himself. And because he gave, he loved.

Obviously, we can assess the extent of the tzaddik's *elevation from the extent of the blessing.*

As explained above, a blessing is fulfilled because its realization becomes a vehicle for the elevation of the *tzaddik* who bestows it. Obviously, we can assess the extent of the *tzaddik's* elevation from the extent of the blessing. If one blessing results in a pauper being spared from going to bed hungry and a second blessing results in benefits that continue after thousands of years, there cannot be the slightest doubt that the second one elevated the *tzaddik* infinitely more than the first. Isaac's blessings upon Jacob were monumental. Their effects were never-ending. To achieve such results, Isaac must have overcome a truly enormous challenge. What was it?

Doubt and Decision

Isaac felt reassured when he sensed that wicked people descend from the person who stood before him. Those wicked people whom Isaac thought to be the progeny of Esau were in reality the descendants of Jacob. Isaac recognized that the ancestor of such people should be blessed in order that his sinful offspring could be kept from falling into the abyss. The *voice of Jacob* troubled him because it was the voice of Torah and prayer, a voice of one who resisted external help which would prevent him from realizing greatness on his own. The realization that this *tzaddik*, whoever he was, bore within him the seeds of wickedness was what swayed Isaac, for he had long since made peace with the idea that help *should* be given to an unworthy person in order to help make him worthy.

The realization that this tzaddik, *whoever he was, bore within him the seeds of wickedness was what swayed Isaac.*

וַיָּרַח אֶת רֵיחַ בְּגָדָיו — רֵיחַ בּוֹגְדָיו *He smelled his garments* [בְּגָדָיו]. *Read it as if it were* בּוֹגְדָיו, *his traitors, such as Yosaif Meshissa and Yokum of Tzeroros (*Yalkut Simoni Toldos *115).*

When the enemies wished to enter the Temple Mount, they said, let one of [the Jews] enter first. They said to Yosaif, 'Enter and whatever you remove is yours.' [He took a golden menorah which they did not let him keep. They sent him in again but he refused to go.] R' Pinchas said that they offered him three years' taxes, but he still refused saying, 'Is it not enough that I angered God once — shall I anger him again! ... They cut him to bits while he cried out, 'Alas, alas, that I angered my Creator!'

They cut him to bits while he cried out, 'Alas, alas, that I angered my Creator!'

Yakum of Tzeroros, a nephew of R'Yosi ben Yoezer, was riding a horse on the Sabbath [a forbidden act] and came upon the gallows where R'Yosi was to be hung. Yakum taunted R'Yosi ... [R'Yosi answered] 'If such is the fate of those who do His will, how much more so with those who anger Him!' This pierced Yakum's heart. [He repented and subjected himself to the four manners of execution]. R'Yosi said, 'Yakum has preceded me into the Garden of Eden' (*Bereishis Rabbah* 65:22).

'If such is the fate of those who do His will, how much more so with those who anger Him!'

As Isaac wondered who stood awaiting the blessing, he perceived that traitors would descend from this person, traitors like Yosaif Meshissa who went with impunity into the Temple and Yakum who desecrated the Sabbath while brazenly taunting R'Yosi who was about to be hung by the Romans. The forefather of such people needed his blessing, surely.

The Inner Self

Whom was he blessing, Jacob or Esau? Truthfully it did not matter. Spiritually exalted Isaac did not think in terms of personalities. He did not consider whether he was blessing the man called Esau or the man called Jacob — that was immaterial. A farmer does not consider the name of the land he plans to purchase. He weighs its suitability for farming. In his role as Patriarch, it was now his responsibility to bestow blessings upon the person who possessed the set of spiritual conditions that required those blessings. Isaac loved and respected both his sons, each in a different way. If he wanted Esau to come to him, it was because he was convinced that Esau was the one who needed, deserved, and could utilize the blessings. If, however, he perceived the proper set of conditions in a person whose name happened to be Jacob — so be it. Indeed, he now found those conditions — he would bless evildoers whose good was external, but who could become better if they were given help.

The Test

Then came his test. He felt the presence of the *Shechinah.* He savored the scent of the Garden of Eden, of righteous people who were worthy to be *bearers* of God's Presence, not merely its half-hearted or frantic pursuers. It was a signal to him that blessings of heavenly assistance should be given to the righteous, even the very great.

It was a signal to him that blessings of heavenly assistance should be given to the righteous, even the very great.

That was Isaac's great test. Like all tests, the message was not so clear that he could not rationalize it away if he preferred to do so. After all, all the experience of his lifetime of uncompromising, powerful effort at perfection cried out against this vague message. How could Isaac, the embodiment of *Gevurah-Strength* make peace with the idea that he should bless those who could fight on their own? Had the message been absolutely clear, it would not have been a test. Of course compliance would have been unpleasant, but the man who laid himself on the altar of the *Akeidah* could easily do God's bidding even if he found to be incomprehensible. But this test *did* leave room for doubt if Isaac chose to doubt. Which aspect of his son would he bless — only the sinful one or even the righteous one?

Which aspect of his son would he bless — only the sinful one or even the righteous one?

God had allowed Isaac to be deceived by Esau for over sixty years in order to set the stage for this test. Had he known the truth about Esau, the conditions for this painful test would never have existed.

Surely, the blessing of Isaac played no small role in enabling wicked, traitorous Yosaif and Yakum to repent and die heroes' deaths.

Now he was tested and he responded. He blessed Jacob, righteous Jacob, the Jacob who brought with him the scent of the Garden of Eden, of God's Presence, of people so righteous that they could become chariots bearing the *Shechinah*. But his original intention, too, was fulfilled. Surely, the blessing of Isaac played no small role in enabling wicked, traitorous Yosaif and Yakum to repent and die heroes' deaths.

The blessing of Isaac. Isaac, Patriarch of strength and refusal to compromise, bestows his blessing upon all who can benefit from God's help and because he surmounted his personal challenge, every Jew, whatever his ordeal, can more easily raise himself to heights he thought beyond him.

סדר תולדת

Sidra Toldos

יט וְאֵ֫לֶּה תּוֹלְדֹ֥ת יִצְחָ֖ק בֶּן־אַבְרָהָ֑ם אַבְרָהָ֖ם
כ הוֹלִ֥יד אֶת־יִצְחָֽק: וַֽיְהִ֣י יִצְחָ֗ק בֶּן־

19. Isaac's Genealogy.

וְאֵלֶּה תּוֹלְדֹת יִצְחָק בֶּן אַבְרָהָם — [*And*] *these are the offspring* [or: genealogies] *of Isaac, son of Abraham.* — The *offspring* are Jacob and Esau who are discussed in this section *(Rashi).*

For after listing the descendants of *Ishmael,* the Torah now reverts to the offspring of *Isaac* — Jacob and Esau — who are mentioned below *(Ibn Ezra);* but before actually mentioning them, the Torah parenthetically describes the circumstances surrounding their birth *(Gur Aryeh).*

Furthermore, the conjunctive *vav, and,* in וְאֵלֶּה, *these,* signifies a continuity with that which precedes it — in this case the offspring of Abraham. Just as Abraham begot both a righteous and a wicked son, so did Isaac *(Sifsei Chachomim).*

The translation of תּוֹלְדֹת as *offspring, progeny,* follows *Onkelos* and the implication of the commentators above who apply it directly to Jacob and Esau.

According to *Sforno,* however, תּוֹלְדוֹת in our verse means *chronicles* or *history*: the events that befell him. [This follows *Ibn Ezra* to 6:9 where he explains תּוֹלְדֹת to mean *history:* that which time (יָלַד), brings forth (Comp. *Proverbs* 27:1).]

Mizrachi notes that only *time* can produce *events;* mankind produces *offspring.* Therefore, since תּוֹלְדוֹת in our verse is in the construct state with Isaac, *Rashi* prefers to translate *offspring.* If the Torah meant to recount the *history* of Isaac the verse would have read וְאֵלֶּה תּוֹלְדֹת יְמֵי יִצְחָק, *these are the events* (or *history) of the days of Isaac.* Moreover, in context with the *offspring* of Ishmael listed above, it stands to reason that תּוֹלְדֹת here similarly refers to the *offspring* of Isaac although Jacob and Esau are not mentioned until later.

[Cf. however translation of תּוֹלְדוֹת הַשָּׁמַיִם in 2:4 as *products of the heaven;* and תּוֹלְדֹת תֶּרַח in 11:27 as *chronicles of Terach.*]

אַבְרָהָם הוֹלִיד אֶת יִצְחָק — *Abraham begot Isaac.*

The Torah felt compelled to add that *Abraham begot Isaac* (although it is obvious from the description of Isaac as *son of Abraham)* to allude to the fact that the cynics of Abraham's generation had been saying that Sarah, who had lived so long with Abraham without bearing a child, must have become pregnant by Abimelech [see *comm.* to 21:2 s.v. לִזְקֻנָיו, and 21:3 s.v. הַנּוֹלַד לוֹ]. In order to refute this slander, God made Isaac's features so undeniably similar to Abraham's that even the scoffers had to admit that אַבְרָהָם הוֹלִיד אֶת יִצְחָק, *'it was indeed Abraham who had begotten Isaac!' (Tanchuma; Rashi* as explained by *Mizrachi).*

[See also *Bava Metzia* 87a where the implication is that Isaac was not simply *born* resembling Abraham. At the feast Abraham made on the day Isaac was weaned, God miraculously changed Isaac's physiognomy — in the presence of all the skeptics assembled — to resemble Abraham's whereupon even the scoffers cried out 'Abraham begot Isaac!'][1]

1. The *Midrash* [*Tanchuma Yashan*] observes that some children are ashamed of their parents and some parents are ashamed of their children. Not so in the case of Abraham: [Isaac was proud to be Abraham's son] and Abraham was proud to have begotten Isaac, as it says

25 These are the offspring of Isaac, son of Abraham —
19-20 Abraham begot Isaac. 20 Isaac was forty years old

According to the *literal* sense of the narrative, however, since the Torah identifies Ishmael as the son *whom Hagar the Egyptian, servant of Sarah, had borne to Abraham* [*v.* 12 above], it now identifies Isaac as Abraham's primary son, whom *Abraham had begotten* from his true wife ... Similarly in *Chronicles* after listing Abraham's descendants as Isaac, Ishmael, and the children of Keturah, the text reverts and mentions *Abraham begot Isaac.*See *I Chron.* 1:34; see also ibid. *v.* 9 where Shem as the head of Abraham's ancestry is repeated after his descendants were already listed *(Rashbam).*

Ramban interprets similarly and notes that [as evidenced by the above-cited verses in *Chronicles*] when Scripture records the genealogy of distinguished people, it commonly reverts to the ancestral head of the family. He continues that the Torah uses this device regarding Isaac's progeny in order to give honor to Isaac as Abraham's primary son; otherwise the formula would be the same for Isaac as for Ishmael: *these are the offspring of Isaac son of Abraham* [see 25:12]. This also explains why 25:12 does not begin Ishmael's genealogy by saying: *these are the offspring of Abraham,* because Scripture does not wish to equate the other children with Isaac as descendants of *Abraham.* The significance, thus, of the phrase *Abraham begot Isaac,* is that Isaac alone is the son identified with Abraham. [See *comm.* of *Ramban* cited to Ishmael's genealogy in *v.* 12 s.v. אֲשֶׁר יָלְדָה הָגָר.]

Ibn Ezra suggests that הוֹלִיד should be interpreted in the sense of *reared (raised)* as in 50:23 יֻלְּדוּ עַל בִּרְכֵּי יוֹסֵף, *reared upon Joseph's knees.*

[The intent of the phrase in our passage would accordingly be that of all Abraham's sons, Isaac alone was reared by him, as evidenced by the fact that Abraham had sent all his other sons away from Isaac (*v.* 5).]

Abarbanel explains that the events and tribulations of Isaac's life so closely paralleled those of Abraham, that it was manifest to all that *Abraham begot Isaac.*

Abraham begot Isaac. For did Abraham beget no other children, such as Ishmael and children by concubines, that it says *Abraham begot Isaac* [as if Abraham had no other children]? But this verse comes to inform us that Isaac [like his father] was a righteous man and Abraham was proud to be his father.

When Abraham and Isaac would pass by, standersby would exclaim, 'You are fortunate, Abraham, to have Isaac for a son, and you, Isaac, are fortunate to have Abraham for a father' *(Midrash HaGadol).*

Midrash Rabbah conveys this idea by citing, *Proverbs* 17:6: *Children's children are the crown of old men, and the glory of children are their fathers.*

Cf. *Lekach Tov: Abraham begot Isaac* — whoever witnessed Isaac's righteous deeds would exclaim, 'Surely Abraham begot Isaac!', but this was not the case with Abraham's other progeny.

As *Ralbag* observes, it is common in many languages that when a son emulates his father, people say, 'He is his father's son.'

אַרְבָּעִים שָׁנָה בְּקַחְתּוֹ אֶת־רִבְקָה בַּת־
בְּתוּאֵל הָאֲרַמִּי מִפַּדַּן אֲרָם אֲחוֹת לָבָן

According to *Chizkuni* [in some *Chumashim* this appears as *Rashi's* primary interpretation] the phrase denotes: Only as *Abraham* [i.e. only after his name was changed to Abraham] did he bear Isaac; not as Abram.

[Cf. *comm.* to 15:5 and *Midrash* cited there: God said to Abram before He changed his name: 'Abandon your astrological speculations! Although you have seen by the מַזָּלוֹת, *constellations,* that you are not destined to have children, it is true only that *Abram* will have no son (as an heir), but *Abraham* will have a son; *Sarai* will indeed be childless, but *Sarah* will bear. I will change your names (from Abram and Sarai to Abraham and Sarah) and your מַזָּל, *constellation; luck* will change.']

20. בֶּן אַרְבָּעִים שָׁנָה — *Forty years old.*

According to the traditional Rabbinic chronology of *Seder Olam* followed by *Rashi,* Isaac was 37 years old at the *Akeidah* at which time Rebecca was born. He waited until she was physically capable of marriage [רְאוּיָה לְבִיאָה] — three years — and the married when he was forty. [This explains why Isaac did not marry earlier in compliance with the *mitzvah.* For when Isaac was younger, he would not intermarry with the accursed Cannanites. After the *Akeidah* Abraham was informed that Isaac's destined bride — Rebecca — had been born. Isaac then waited the necessary three years, and married her although she was not yet physically fit to bear children *(Mizrachi).*]

The other opinion — that of *Tosafos, Yevamos* 61b s.v. וְכֵן — that Rebecca was *fourteen* years old when she was married, is discussed in the *footnote* to 24:16. [That opinion, however, seems to leave unanswered the question of why Abraham waited three years from the time he was informed of her birth to arrange the marriage. Perhaps he wanted to wait until she was *physically fit to bear children* which, as *Rashi* notes in *v.* 26, is approximately at age thirteen.]

The Torah tells us that Isaac was forty years old when he married Rebecca, and sixty years old when his children were born [*v.* 26]. This informs us by implication that she was barren for twenty years *(Rashbam).* [See *comm.* to *v. 26.*]

בְּקַחְתּוֹ — *When he took.*

[I.e. *married,* 'take' being the Biblical idiom for 'taking in marriage.']

בַּת בְּתוּאֵל...מִפַּדַּן אֲרָם אֲחוֹת לָבָן— *Daughter of Bethuel ... from Paddan Aram, sister of Laban.*

Although we are already aware of her family background and native land, the Torah repeats these facts to proclaim her praise: She was the daughter of a wicked man, sister of a wicked man, and her native place was one of wicked people, yet Rebecca did not emulate their wicked ways *(Midrash; Rashi).*

... *Like a rose among the thorns (Song of Songs* 2:2) she developed instead into a righteous woman (see *Yevamos* 64a, *Midrash)* —

[This *Midrashic* interpretation is inspired by the superfluous repetition of אֲרַמִּי, *Aramean,* which is accordingly homiletically rendered as if it read רַמַּאי, *rogue* or *cheat.* See below.]

הָאֲרַמִּי — *The Aramean.*

The designation *Aramean* does not necessarily imply a *descendant*

25 *when he took Rebecca, daughter of Bethuel*
20 *the Aramean from Paddan Aram, sister of Laban the*

of Aram, which Bethuel was not [see 22:21 and *Genealogical Table* on p. xii of vol. 2], but one who *lived* in the land of Aram *(Midrash Or HaAfeilah,* cited in the note to *Torah Sheleimah* 25:67).

[See *Radak* cited in commentary to 14:13 p. 485 who explains that the term *Ivri* (= Hebrew) refers uniquely to the Abrahamitic line since they alone of the descendants of Eber remained loyal to Hebrew, the language of Eber, while Eber's other descendants spoke Aramaic. The latter are therefore referred to as *Arameans,* as for example, Laban the Aramean.][1]

פַּדַּן אֲרָם — *Paddan Aram.*

Since there were two localities named *Aram:* Aram Naharaim (see 24:10) and Aram Zova [=Aleppo] (see *II Samuel* 10:6), the Torah refers to it [i.e. the locality of both Arams] as *Paddan Aram,* [meaning the *pair of Arams*]. The word *paddan* means 'pair' as in the phrase צֶמֶד בָּקָר [*a yoke of oxen (I Samuel* 11:7)] which *Targum* there renders as פַּדַּן תּוֹרִין, *a pair of oxen.* There is an opinion that *Paddan Aram* is identical with שְׂדֵה אֲרָם, *the field-country of Aram* as it is called in *Hoshea* 12:13, since in Arabic a field is called *paddan (Rashi).*

According to *Tosafos HaRosh, Paddan Aram* refers only to Aram Naharaim for it was the 'Aram which lay between the pair of rivers.' Our verse therefore refers to *Aram Naharaim* [lit. *Aram of the pair of rivers;* see on 24:10] as *Paddan Aram* for it was named after the *pair of rivers.*

There were additional localities named Aram: *Aram Damessek* [=Damascus] *(II Sam.* 8:5), and *Aram Beth R'chov (II Sam.* 10:6). However, only Aram Naharaim and Aram Zova are spoken of as a 'pair' — *Paddan* — because they were near one another. Furthermore, the designation *Paddan Aram* incorporates Ur Kasdim, Charan, and other villages *(Radak).*

Hoffmann suggests that what is referred to in 24:10 by the broad designation *Aram Naharaim* embracing the *entire territory of Mesopotamia between the Tigris and Euphrates rivers,* is briefly referred to here as *Aram.* As noted above, the word *Paddan* in Aramaic means a *yoke* [or *pair*] (of oxen) and in Assyrian a *field.* Perhaps it designates an area which a pair of oxen can plow in a given time. Thus the name *Paddan Aram* (which occurs again in 28:2-7; 31:18; 33:18; 35:9; 46:15 [and as *Paddan* alone in 48:7]) refers to the *plains* or *fields* of the land of Aram as the term is indeed used in *Hoshea* 12:13. *Possibly* it refers to the area immediately surrounding Charan where there is a mound and settlement called *Tel Paddan.*

אֲחוֹת לָבָן הָאֲרַמִּי — *Sister of Laban the Aramean.*

[See *Rashi* above s.v. בַּת בְּתוּאֵל.]

Chizkuni observes that in the literal sense it is common for Scripture to identify a woman by her older brother. For example [further, 28:9]: *sister of Nebaioth;* [*Exod.*

1. The *Midrash* notes that although the family is placed in Paddan Aram, the Torah repeatedly refers to Bethuel and Laban in this verse as אֲרַמִּי, *Aramean.* Therefore, the word אֲרַמִּי, *Aramean,* is homiletically interpreted, by a play on words, as if it read רַמַּאי, *rogue* or *cheat,* and thus forms the basis for the *Midrash* cited above by *Rashi* which contrasts Bethuel and Laban who, were *rogues,* and the righteous Rebecca who came forth from among them *like a rose among thorns.*

כא הָאֲרַמִּי לוֹ לְאִשָּׁה: וַיֶּעְתַּר יִצְחָק לַיהוה
לְנֹכַח אִשְׁתּוֹ כִּי עֲקָרָה הִוא וַיֵּעָתֶר לוֹ

15:20]: *sister of Aaron;* [*Exod.* 6:23]: *sister of Nachshon.* [See *Rashi* there and *Rashbam* to 28:9.]

In this case, Laban was mentioned because he was more renowned and distinguished than his father *(Ibn Ezra)* [cf. on 24:51, 55.]

This genealogical note also alludes to the fact that she bore Esau *because she was the sister of* [*the wicked*] *Laban* [since as the *Talmud* *(Bava Basra* 110a) notes: sons tend to resemble the mother's brother] *(Sforno).*

Thus, we are prepared beforehand for the discord which arose later on. It is not surprising that an Esau was born; what is unusual is that a Jacob grew up alongside him! *(Hirsch).*

לוֹ לְאִשָּׁה — *As a wife* [lit. *woman*] *for* [lit. to] himself.

I.e., a woman suitable to be לוֹ לְאִשָּׁה, a wife to *him*: a righteous woman married to a righteous man *(Lekach Tov).*

21. Rebecca's Barrenness.

וַיֶּעְתַּר יִצְחָק לַה׳ — [And] *Isaac entreated* [to] HASHEM.

I.e. he prayed *abundantly* and *urgingly (Rashi).*

Rashi explains further s.v. וַיֵּעָתֶר לוֹ, that the root עתר throughout Scripture denotes *urging* or *abundance.*

As *Mizrachi* notes, however, *Rashi* does not suggest that 'praying' is the *definition* of וַיֶּעְתַּר in our verse, because, as *Rashi* himself notes later it denotes *urging* or *abundance.* Rather, in the *context of this verse, Rashi* comments that the *urging* took the form of persistent prayer.

[*Rashi* apparently follows the view of R' Yochanan in the *Midrash* who derives the word וַיֶּעְתַּר from עתר which in Aramaic means *wealth,* hence *abundance,* and accordingly explains that 'it means that he poured out petitions *in abundance.'*

[There is, however, another view recorded in the *Midrash:* Resh Lakish connects the verb to עָתֶר, *a pitchfork,* and comments that he 'overturned the Divine decree' (i.e. reversed her destiny), for as Rav Yitzchak in *Yevamos* 64a states: Why is the prayer of the righteous compared to a pitchfork (i.e. why is Isaac's prayer described by a term deriving from עָתֶר, *pitchfork,* rather than by a more familiar term such as וַיִּתְפַּלֵּל)? — Just as a pitchfork turns sheaves of grass from one place to another, so does the prayer of the righteous turn the dispensations of the Holy One, Blessed be He from the Attribute of Anger to the Attribute of Mercy.]

Another opinion [*Pesikta Zutresa; Lekach Tov;* see *Hirsch*] homiletically substitutes a ח for the ע and interprets וַיֶּעְתַּר as וַיֶּחְתַּר, *he bored into, tunneled,* the term used for the forcible propulsion of a ship against wind and billows [see *Jonah* 1:13]. Hence, the word denotes *a penetrating prayer and request.* [See *Midrash* cited below s.v. וַיֵּעָתֶר לוֹ. See also *Yerushalmi Sanhedrin* 10:2 to *II Chronicles* 33:11.]

The *Zohar* echoes this interpretation and explains that וַיֶּעְתַּר implies that Isaac's prayer 'dug a tunnel,' as it were, leading right up to the supernal department appointed over child-bearing, rising above the planetary influences [מַזָּלוֹת] ... In another explanation, the *Zohar* interprets וַיֶּעְתַּר as implying *prayer accompanied by offerings;* on an analogy with a kindred term in the passage, *So* HASHEM *was entreated* [וַיֵּעָתֵר] *for the land* [*II Sam.* 24:25]. There also the

25 *Aramean, as a wife for himself.* [21] *Isaac entreated*
21 *HASHEM opposite his wife, because she was barren.*

prayer was accompanied by offerings. Accordingly, the further phrase וַיֵּעָתֶר לוֹ ה׳, *and HASHEM allowed Himself to be entreated by him,* indicates that a celestial fire descended to meet the fire ascending from below.

Hoffmann cites a similar interpretation and quotes *Ezekiel* 8:11 where עָתָר occurs in the sense of incense.

According to *Pirkei d'Rabbi Eliezer* 32, seeing that she was barren Isaac took Rebecca and went to pray with her to Mount Moriah, the site of the *Akeidah.*

[As explained in the *comm.* to *v.* 26, it was in the twentieth year of their marriage that they began praying. When Isaac married Rebecca, she was, according to most opinions three years old. Until she was thirteen she could not be considerred sterile since, as *Rashi* to *v.* 26 points out, one does not usually bear children below the age of thirteen. Hence, they waited ten additional years as the *halachah* required (see *comm.* to 16:3 regarding Abraham's waiting ten years before taking Hagar), and only then did they begin to storm the gates of heaven with their prayers]

[See also *Rashi* to *v.*26 who explains why Isaac did not marry a maidservant to have children as did Abraham when he married Hagar.]

לְנֹכַח אִשְׁתּוֹ — *Opposite* [or *facing*] *his wife.*

The translation נֹכַח as *opposite* follows the *Talmud:*

— He stood in one corner and prayed, while she stood in the other corner and prayed *(Yevamos* 64a; *Rashi).*

And Isaac said, 'HASHEM, God of heaven and earth, whose goodness and mercies fill the earth, You took my father from his ancestral home and birthplace and brought him to this land. You said to him; *To your offspring will I give this land,* and You promised him, *I will multiply your seed as the stars of heaven and as the sand of the sea.* Now, may Your words which You spoke to my father be verified, for our eyes are directed to You only' *(Sefer HaYashar).*

[According to the *Midrash,* the word לְנֹכַח is also taken in the *figurative* sense as, 'Isaac prayed *compatibly* with his wife']: Isaac prayed: 'Sovereign of the universe, may all the children You promised to grant me be from that righteous woman!' Rebecca prayed likewise [for each desired that his destined children be through the other and no one else. See *comm.* to 24:60.]

As *Sforno* observes, although Isaac had already been assured of children. [see 17:19], he begged God that the promise be realized through *this worthy woman* who was standing *opposite* him.

He was certain that he would have children because God had promised him descendants. But he began to doubt that the Covenant of Abraham would be carried on by the offspring of someone from Laban's family. Therefore he prayed particularly לְנֹכַח אִשְׁתּוֹ, *referring to his wife,* Rebecca *(Hirsch).*

Rashbam renders לְנֹכַח אִשְׁתּוֹ as *on behalf of his wife.*

כִּי עֲקָרָה הִוא — *Because she was barren.*

כב יהוה וַתַּהַר רִבְקָה אִשְׁתּוֹ: וַיִּתְרֹצְצוּ הַבָּנִים בְּקִרְבָּהּ וַתֹּאמֶר אִם־כֵּן לָמָּה זֶּה

Why were our ancestors barren? — Because the Holy One, Blessed be He longs to hear the prayers of the righteous *(Yevamos* 64a). [Such prayers publicize the efficacy of prayer. God therefore gives them cause to pray, so He can miraculously fulfil their requests publicly *(Radak)*.[1]

In the specific case of *Rebecca,* however, as noted in the *footnote* to 24:60 Providence caused Rebecca to remain barren so long lest her heathen kin maintain that it was *their* prayer and blessings (given her before she departed with Eliezer in 24:60) that had been instrumental in her fruitfulness. Therefore as this verse makes clear, וַיֵּעָתֶר לוֹ ה׳, *HASHEM allowed himself to be prevailed upon by* him: Rebecca conceived as a direct result of God's response to *Isaac's* prayer.

According to a view in *Yevamos* 64a, the phrase *'opposite* his wife' rather than *'for* his wife' implies that they were *both* barren [the phrase meaning that he prayed complementary to his wife for her barrenness' — his prayer complemented hers, each praying on behalf of the other, for such prayers are more acceptable *(Maharsha).*]

Midrash HaGadol too, derives from the text that both were barren. This is alluded to by the word הוא which is, according to the Masoretic punctuation here, pronounced הִיא, *she,* but is spelled הוא, *he.* Thus, the duality of the word suggests the barrenness of both.

וַיֵּעָתֶר לוֹ ה׳ — *And* HASHEM *allowed Himself to be entreated* [lit. *was entreated*] *by him* [lit. *to him.*]

I.e., He accepted his entreaty [in the sense of *allowed Himself to be prevailed upon*] *(Onkelos).*

לוֹ, *by him,* and not לָהּ, *by her* [although, as explained above, they *both* prayed], because there is no comparison between the [efficacy of] the prayer of a righteous person [Isaac] who is the child of a righteous person [Abraham], and the prayer of a righteous person [Rebecca] who is the child of a wicked person [Bethuel] *(Yevamos* 64a; *Rashi).*

— For were this not the case, the phrase should have read, as the *Talmud* ibid. notes: וַיֵּעָתֶר לָהֶם ה׳, HASHEM allowed Himself to be entreated by *them (Mizrachi).*

Also, לוֹ, *by him,* because a prisoner cannot free himself from jail *(Berachos* 5b), [i.e. the prayers of Rebecca, for herself, cannot be as

1. Note that of the four Matriarchs, three were barren. Sarah [11:30]; Rebecca; and Rachel [29:31.] A simple explanation can be offered for their barrenness —

Sarah: to allow Ishmael to be born from Abraham [see 16:2] and to allow for her change of name, with its esoteric implications;

Rebecca: to delay the wicked Esau's birth until Abraham reached ripe old age, for it is known that Abraham was to die before Esau took to wicked ways [see 15:15, and comm. to *v.* 30, further];

And Rachel: to provide a reason for marrying Bilhah and Zilpah from whom were born Dan, Naftali, Gad, and Asher *(R'Bachya).*

[Additional reasons for our Matriarchs being so long barren are given in the *footnote* to 16:4, p. 542.]

25 *HASHEM allowed Himself to be entreated by him and*
22 *his wife Rebecca conceived.*
[22] *The children agitated within her, and she said,*

effective as Isaac's on her behalf. According to this interpretation, Isaac was capable of begetting a child.] (*Tur*).

The *Midrash* notes that 'in Arabic the word וַיֶּעְתַּר, *entreat*, is pronounced the same way as the word וַיַּחְתֵּר, *to bore; tunnel.*' [I.e., the Arabic equivalent of ע is pronounced there with a guttural sound like a ח making the two words homonyms; (see above *s.v.* וַיֶּעְתַּר)]. Rav Levi remarked: Our phrase [which the *Midrash* homiletically renders: *and HASHEM assisted him in digging*] is reminiscent of a prince who was tunneling into his father's treasury to take a pound of gold. The king [in an effort to assist his son] began to tunnel outwards [to meet his son 'halfway.' Similarly God assisted Isaac by receiving his pleas and granting his petition. See *Zohar* cited above s.v. וַיֶּעְתַּר יִצְחָק.]

וַתַּהַר רִבְקָה אִשְׁתּוֹ — *And his wife Rebecca conceived.*

The Torah mentions her name here to accentuate that it was as 'Rebecca' that she conceived; unlike Sarah her name did not have to be changed before she could bear a child (see *Kli Chemdah; Me'am Loez*).

22. A Portentious Pregnancy.

וַיִּתְרֹצְצוּ הַבָּנִים בְּקִרְבָּהּ — [*And*] *the children agitated within her.*

Since the Torah did not clarify the nature of this 'agitation' and mentioned it only briefly together with Rebecca's reaction, this phrase calls for a *Midrashic* interpretation [to enlighten us as to what the 'agitation' was all about since, as *Mizrachi* observes, if these were *normal pregnancy pains*, Rebecca would not have exclaimed, *If so, why am I thus?* Obviously something extraordinary was happening within her.] The Rabbis derive the word וַיִּתְרֹצְצוּ from the root רוץ *to run, move quickly:* When Rebecca passed the entrances of the Torah schools conducted by Shem and Eber, Jacob 'ran' [i.e. moved convulsively] and struggled to come forth [i.e. be born]; and when she passed the entrances of an idolatrous temple, Esau 'ran' and struggled to come forth [*Midrash*.][1] Another explanation [*Yalkut*]: they struggled with one another and quarreled as to how

1. The divergent tendencies of Jacob and Esau are manifestations of the cosmic nature of their conception, birth, and development, and no *generally applicable conclusions* can be drawn from the narrative. Nevertheless, the general question arises of whether an embryo can be influenced by the attraction of good or evil.

Gur Aryeh explains that the struggles of the embryoic Jacob and Esau were not influenced by their respective Good and Evil Inclinations [יֵצֶר טוֹב וְיֵצֶר הָרַע] because the Inclinations are not present before birth [see *comm.* to 4:7.] The Inclinations influence people to deeds and to a striving for fulfillment; since deeds are impossible before birth and it is the natural state of an embryo to be unfulfilled, the inclinations cannot function in an embryo (see also *Gur Aryeh* to 8:21, and *Sanhedrin* 91b cited in *comm.* to 4:7 s.v. לַפֶּתַח חַטָּאת רֹבֵץ).

The *essential nature* of Jacob was good even *before* birth, however, just as Esau's was evil. It was natural for each embryo to be drawn toward the expression of its underlying characteristic. Therefore, when Rebecca passed a study hall, the embodiment of good, Jacob struggled to draw closer to it. When she passed by an idol, the embodiment of evil, Esau struggled to cleave to it. [Cf. *Levush*.]

כג אָנֹכִי וַתֵּלֶךְ לִדְרֹשׁ אֶת־יהוה: וַיֹּאמֶר

they should divide the inheritance of the two worlds *(Rashi).*

— I.e., who would inherit this world, and who, the World to Come *(Midrash Aggadah).*

Rav Berachiah observed in Rav Levi's name: Do not imagine that only *after* they were born was Esau antagonistic to Jacob,for even while still in his mother's womb Esau's fist was stretched forth against him, as it is written [*Psalms* 58:4] *The wicked stretch out their fists in the womb (Midrash).*

They are called *children* [although before birth they should more properly be called *embryos*] since in due course they would become children. Cf. *Job* 22:6: *He stripped the naked of their clothes* [where the term *naked* is used while they are still clothed, in anticipation of the removal of their clothes] *(Ibn Ezra).*

וַתֹּאמֶר — *And she said.*

[Obviously unaware that the agitation was caused by twins enacting their drama inside her. She was concerned, rather over her painful feeling that something *extraordinary* was happening within her. As *Kli Yakar* comments, she had thought there was *one* embryo within her who became agitated each time she passed entrances of Torah schools and להבדיל, houses of idolatry. It was this conflicting duality of loyalty of one child being seemingly drawn to two deities ח"ו that concerned her and caused her to seek expression of God's word.]

אִם כֵּן — *If so.*

According to *Rashi:* if the pain of pregnancy is so extreme.[1]

Ibn Ezra [following the *Midrash*] suggests that [since one does not usually say 'if so' unless it is in continuation of an ongoing conversation *(Karnei Or)*] the expression implies that Rebecca had inquired of other women whether they had similar experiences [in the words of *Midrash:* whether they had endured similar suffering] and they answered her 'No'. She thereupon said, 'If the *usual* pregnancy is unlike mine ...'

לָמָּה זֶּה אָנֹכִי — *Why am I thus?*

[The translation of this phrase preserves the ambiguity of the Hebrew which literally means *why this I,* and allows for the various interpretations that follow.]

Following *Rashi:* '... why have I longed and prayed to become pregnant?' [apparently understanding the petition to mean: *why for this have I prayed? (Gur Aryeh).*]

— If this is the anguish of a mother, what good are children to me? *(Targum Yonasan).*

Following *Ibn Ezra:* '...why, then, am *I* beset with an unusual pregnancy?'

— Why am I different from all other women? *(Radak).*

1. The Sages expounded that righteous women were not included in the decree upon Eve that children be born in pain [*Sotah* 12a]. They further expounded that the Matriarchs were barren because God desired their prayers [*Yevamos* 64a]. In the light of these two teachings, Rebecca was counfounded:

If she was so righteous that God made her barren in order that she pray — then why did she suffer such pain?

And if she felt the pain because she was not righteous — then why did God render her barren to induce her to pray? *(Divrei Yosef).*

25 *'If so, why am I thus?' and she went to inquire of*
22 *HASHEM.*

Ramban disagrees with *Ibn Ezra's* interpretation that Rebecca inquired of other women, for such an inquiry is too central to the flow of the narrative to have been omitted in the text if indeed it took place. [Therefore, although it is based upon a *Midrash* it is too far from the 'simple meaning' of the text to be interpreted as such.] *Ramban* suggests that the meaning is: 'If it will so be with me, why am I in the world? — If only I did not exist; I should die or never have existed!' as in [*Job* 10:19] *I should have been as though I had not been.*

Compare, in this sense, Rebecca's outcry in 27:46: *I am disgusted with life ... what is life to me? (Hoffmann).*

She thought she was about to miscarry, so she exclaimed: 'If I am about to miscarry, why did God accept my prayer and allow me this futile pregnancy?' *(B'chor Shor; Tur).*

'If such is the case, why am I sitting idly by instead of seeking the reason?' *(Gur Aryeh; Tur).*

וַתֵּלֶךְ — *And she went.*

— To the academy of Shem *(Rashi)* [who, as a prophet, would seek God's Word on her behalf.]

This follows *Targum Yonasan* and *Tanchuma Yashan. Midrash Rabbah,* derives from this that visiting a Sage is like visiting the Divine Presence [since visiting Shem's school is here referred to as going to inquire (directly) of HASHEM *(Maharzu).*]

Otherwise, the verse would have read *she inquired of HASHEM! (Mizrachi);* what other need have we of *she went?* — a phrase which indicates a *specific destination* [intimating ח״ו that His presence is limited to one place] when in fact, the entire world is full of his glory! *(Sifsei Chachomim).*

[According to *Seder Olam* (see *Chronology/Time Line* in vol. 1 page xii), Shem lived until Jacob was 50 years old, and Eber until Jacob was 79.]

◆§ Why did Rebecca not go to Isaac or Abraham to inquire of HASHEM?

As the Sages expounded [*Sotah* 12a], righteous women were not included in the decree upon Eve [that she bear children in pain *(Gen.* 3:16)]. Therefore Rebecca was apprehensive that her unusual pregnancy pains were in punishment for some sin. She was reluctant, therefore, to reveal her travails to Isaac — lest he consider her distasteful as a sinner — or to Abraham — lest he urge Isaac to take another wife *(Gur Aryeh).* [See *footnote* on previous page.]

According to *Tur,* she wanted to spare the aged Abraham the grief of learning of her pain.

לִדְרֹשׁ אֶת ה׳ — *To inquire* [lit. *seek*] *of HASHEM.*

That He might tell her how it would end *(Rashi)* [and explain why she was having such a painful pregnancy.]

Onkelos renders: *To seek instruction before HASHEM. Targum Yonasan* renders: *To supplicate before HASHEM for mercy.*

According to *Ramban,* the phrase לִדְרֹשׁ אֶת ה׳ is to be interpreted in the context of prayer: *to seek HASHEM in prayer,* as in *Psalms* 34:5, *I sought* [דָּרַשְׁתִּי (i.e. *prayed to)*] *HASHEM and He answered me.*

יהוה לָהּ שְׁנֵי °גיים בְּבִטְנֵךְ וּשְׁנֵי לְאֻמִּים
מִמֵּעַיִךְ יִפָּרֵדוּ וּלְאֹם מִלְאֹם יֶאֱמָץ וְרַב

°גוים ק׳

Mizrachi defends *Rashi's* interpretation by pointing out that the answer given by HASHEM in the following verse bears out his interpretation that this verse speaks of *inquiry*, not of prayer. [*Ramban* would presumably defend his interpretation by claiming that God's answer was in response to her earnest *prayer*.]

23. The Prophecy.

The answer, as in the case of most prophecies, is cast in poetic form. The infants represent two nations: Israel and Edom, and the future irreconcilable rivalries between these two nations are prefigured in them. In the end the younger will prevail *(Hoffmann)*.

וַיֹּאמֶר ה׳ לָהּ — *And HASHEM said to her.*

— Through an intermediary. God spoke to Shem who, in turn, conveyed His word to her *(Rashi)*.

According to *Ibn Ezra*, the answer was given through a prophet, or through Abraham who did not die until her sons were fifteen years old [as calculated in *Seder Olam*.]

These interpretations that she was not addressed *directly* by HASHEM follow the *Midrash* and are supported by the fact that Rebecca is not counted with the seven prophetesses enumerated in *Megillah* 14a: Sarah, Miriam, Chuldah, Esther, Abigail, Chanah and Deborah. [But cf. 27:42 where *Rashi* interprets that Esau's intention to kill Jacob was revealed to Rebecca by Divine Inspiration. However, it is possible, as noted in the *comm.* there, that the communication did not come *directly* to her in that case either, but through a prophet. It may also have been a Divine Inspiration (רוּחַ הַקֹּדֶשׁ) that was not on the level of prophecy. Cf. also *comm.* to 27:8 and 27:45.]

The פְּשַׁט, *literal sense*, of the narrative, also demands an interpretation that the answer was given indirectly, since the previous verse 'she *went* [i.e. to an intermediary] to inquire', rather than וַתִּדְרֹשׁ, *she inquired*, implies that the response was now given to her by *the very same intermediary* from whom she initially made the inquiry.

Sifsei Chachomim derives this from the use of the phrase וַיֹּאמֶר ה׳ לָהּ which has a less direct connotation [=He said *concerning* her] instead of וַיֹּאמֶר אֵלֶיהָ [=*He said to her*]. Others derive it from the less common word order: וַיֹּאמֶר ה׳ לָהּ, which connotes indirect communication, rather than the more common order: וַיֹּאמֶר לָהּ ה׳.

HASHEM conveyed it to *her* and not to Isaac. Therefore, never having heard this prophecy that one of his children would be wicked Isaac never imagined Esau to be a sinner *(Chizkuni)*.

For though Isaac was a prophet, the mystery of the entire matter of Jacob and Esau remained unrevealed to him. ... It would seem that Rebecca was specifically bidden to withhold the matter from Isaac, in order that he not despair of educating Esau to serve God. Had Isaac not devoted himself equally to Jacob and to Esau, the latter would have had an excuse to ignore his obligations to God *(Daas Soferim)*. [See *Ramban* to 27:4, and *footnote* to *v.* 28.]

שְׁנֵי גוֹיִם בְּבִטְנֵךְ — *Two* [ancestors of] *nations* [i.e. peoples *(Targum)*] *are in your womb.*

He allayed her anxiety by informing her that the turmoil within her was natural because she was pregnant with *twins*. Possibly, His intimation was that since they, unlike most children born of the same parents, are destined to be enemies with one another, their pre-natal

25
23

23 *And HASHEM said to her:*
'Two nations are in your womb;
Two regimes from your insides
shall be separated;
the might shall pass from one regime
to the other,

struggling portends the struggle which will ultimately exist between them [and already from the womb they were demonstrating that the space was insufficient for them (*Malbim*).] But from now on, He assured her, they would rest and she would find tranquility [for the duration of her pregnancy] (*Radak; Ramban*).

According to *Kli Yakar,* the answer implied that she need not be apprehensive that there was one child within her who was drawn to two deities ח״ו, but rather that she was carrying twins — one of whom would serve HASHEM, and the other, idols, and that God's Unity is of course undiminished.

The Hebrew for *nations,* גוֹיִם, in this verse is traditionally spelled in Torah Scrolls גיים. This may homiletically be read as גֵיִים [=גֵאִים, *exalted ones, noble people.*] This is an allusion to [two great personages who would descend from the twin embryos in Rebecca's womb: from Esau, the Roman Emperor] Antonious, and [from Jacob] R' Yehudah the Prince [redactor of the *Mishnah*].

The *Talmud,* [*Avodah Zarah* 11a] records that they were both so wealthy that neither lettuce, nor radish, nor cucumber was ever absent from their table either in summer or winter. [This was an indication of great wealth since these vegetables — which the *Talmud* ad. loc. explains were healthful — could not be stored, and when not in season had to be imported from distant lands] (*Rashi*).

Tosafos ad. loc. s.v. צנון, notes that Rabbi Judah is described in *Kesubos* 104a as so righteously ascetic that 'he did not enjoy any worldly benefits even with his little finger.' The fact that he is described here as never lacking these condiments should not be construed as luxurious frivolity, but as his concern for the well-being of his extremely large household [especially since, as the *Talmud* notes, these vegetables were healthful as aids to digestion.]

The *Midrash* interprets similarly: There are two proud nations [גֵאִים] in your womb each taking pride in his world [Esau in This World and Jacob in the Hereafter (*Radak*)] and each in his kingdom. Another interpretation: In your womb are two rulers of the proudest nations — Hadrian of the gentiles and Solomon of Israel.

Rashi was led to offer the *Midrashic* interpretation of the unusual spelling of גיים to avoid a possible misconception. Taken literally, the verse would seem to indicate four peoples: two גוֹיִם, *nations,* **and** *two* לְאֻמִּים, *regimes.* To prevent such a misinterpretation, *Rashi* interprets גֵיִים [*exalted ones*] to personify certain notable descendants (*Devek Tov*).

וּשְׁנֵי לְאֻמִּים מִמֵּעַיִךְ יִפָּרֵדוּ — *[And] two regimes from your insides shall be separated.*

— While still in your very womb they already part from one another: one to wickedness, the other to integrity (*Rashi*).

Thus, the prophecy assured her that the turmoil within her was due specifically to the diametrically opposed characteristics of the agitating embryos (*Mizrachi*).

[As noted above, we have not translated the word וּשְׁנֵי as '**and** *two (regimes)*' to avoid the implication that there were two nations *and* two regimes. The prepositional prefix ו in Hebrew does not always take the conjunctive sense *and;* it also serves as an untranslatable conjunction to connect stiches in a verse *(Ibn Janach).*]

The rendering of לְאֻמִּים as *regimes* follows *Rashi* who explains that אֵין לְאוֹם אֶלָּא מַלְכוּת, the word לְאֹם always denotes a kingdom [i.e. a people living together under one form of government].[1]

According to *Radak:* From the moment they leave the womb they will already be *noticeably* different in physical appearance, and as they get older their *deeds* will set them even further apart; furthermore they will be ideologically at odds forever, for one will hate the other, as they already do now, before they are even born.

Sforno suggests that implicit in the statement *two regimes from your insides shall be separated,* is that both embryos will be born alive and none will die as a result of their הִתְרוֹצְצוּת, *agitation,* within her.

Midrash HaGadol identifies these *two regimes* as the kingdom of Edom [=Rome] which descended from Esau [see *v.* 30], and the kingdom of David who descended from Jacob.

וּלְאֹם מִלְאֹם יֶאֱמָץ — [*And*] *the might shall pass from one regime to the other* [lit. *and regime from regime shall be mighty.*]

— The two of them will never be mighty simultaneously: when one [i.e. one's regime] falls, the other will rise. The *Talmud* [*Megillah* 6a], citing our verse, derives this from *Ezekiel* 26:2 [in which Tyre — colonized by the descendants of Esau says of Jerusalem]: *I shall be filled, she is laid waste (Rashi).*

I.e., Tyre's rise depended upon the downfall of Jerusalem. Thus, the war between them is inevitable for the rise of one is contingent on the fall of the other. This condition began when each conquered its own land and will continue until the coming of Messiah *(Malbim).*

Thus according to *Mizrachi's* interpretation of *Rashi,* the prepositional prefix מ of מִלְאֹם means *from the regime:* one regime will derive might from the other i.e., the victorious power will draw wealth and strength from the vanquished. Thus, at no time in history were Israel and Edom [=Rome] both mighty.

Others render the מ as the comparative *than.* They render: One will always be mightier *than* the other. *Harechasim leBik'ah*: One will always be *braver* than the other (אמץ describing spiritual strength as opposed to חזק, physical strength); one will always compete with the other *(Haamek Davar).*

Hirsch renders: *One form of government will be mightier than the other.* He explains that Rebecca was prophetically informed that the two nations whose forebears she carried represented conflicting philosophies of government. One would base its greatness on the humane instincts of human beings — on their spiritual and moral greatness. The other would build on cunning and strength. One form of government would always be more powerful than

1. *Malbim* [here and more clearly in *Psalms* 54:4], explains that גוי refers to a nation of native people unified by purely physical factors such as geographic proximity and ethnic similarity. לְאֹם refers to a numerically large people unified by an idealogical, political, or spiritual bond.

The implication is that from their very birth they will become separate nations, and afterwards they will further separate idealogically into different spiritual beliefs — a separation which was already innately within them from their conception — Jacob's seed will accept the Torah, while Esau's descendants will serve idolatry.

25 *And the elder shall serve the younger.'*
24 24 *When her term to bear grew full, then behold!*

the other. History is the story of the struggle between the spirit and the sword. Or, in the metaphor of the Sages, between Jerusalem representing right and Caesaria representing might.

וְרַב יַעֲבֹד צָעִיר — *And* [*the*] *elder* [lit. *greater one*] *shall serve* [*the*] *younger.*

I.e. in the end the younger will prevail. The reference, as pointed out by the commentators is not really to the two *individuals* — but to the two nations they represent: Israel and Edom *(Hoffmann).*

According to *Midrash Or HaAfeilah* [cited in *Torah Sheleimah* 25:113] this prophecy will be fulfilled in the days of the Messiah.[1]

This is the view followed by *Malbim* [see above] who cites *Obadiah* 1:21 which describes Messianic times when *Deliverers shall go up to Mount Zion to rule the hill country of Esau and dominion shall be HASHEM's.* Another factor in the conflict is that submission by the greater to the younger is against the law of nature; it cannot take place without struggle and war.

According to *Rashbam* this prophecy explains why Rebecca loved Jacob [*v.* 28]: Jacob is portrayed by the prophets as the beloved of God, as in *Malachi* 1:2: *I* [God] *loved Jacob.*

Daas Zekeinim offers a unique interpretation: רַב [= הַרְבֵּה], *abundantly* יַעֲבֹד צָעִיר *will the younger serve* [the elder].

It is theoretically possible to translate our verse: אֶת הָרַב יַעֲבֹד צָעִיר, *the elders shall the younger serve* —i.e., as for the elder, the younger shall serve him. Our translation which treats *elder* as the subject who will serve the *younger,* follows *Onkelos,* most commentators, and specifically *Ibn Ezra* who draws from the parallel construction in *Malachi* 1:6: בֵּן יְכַבֵּד אָב, *a son honors a father* which corroborates this translation of our verse [since it is obviously not correct to render the latter verse *a son — shall a father honor* [*him*] *(Karnei Or).*]

It is this very ambiguity in the wording of the blessing that provides for sometimes the descendants of Jacob being superior, and the descendants of Esau at other times as *Rashi* explains above s.v. וּלְאֹם מִלְאֹם יֶאֱמָץ intimating that when one falls the other rises [see *footnote*] *(Ibn Caspi).*

Midrash HaGadol, however, cites 27:40 to corroborate that it is the intent that *Esau* would serve *Jacob.*

The translation of רַב as *elder* follows *Michlol Yofi.*

According to *Hirsch,* however, רַב means *great in number and power.* Although Esau's forces will be mightier and emerge triumphant in his quest for material strength, ultimately it will be seen that Esau's victories will have paved the way for Jacob's final triumph. The representative of strength will not be destroyed, but will submit to a new realization that spiritual principles are superior.

24. The Birth of Esau and Jacob.

וַיִּמְלְאוּ יָמֶיהָ לָלֶדֶת — *When her term* [lit. *days*] *to bear grew full.*

1. — When Jacob in later addressing Esau referred to himself as *your servant Jacob* [32:5], God said to him, not only have you profaned the holy [by referring to yourself as his *servant* and addressing him as *my lord Esau*], but additionally you thereby disregard My promise that the *elder shall serve the younger.* By your life! Your own words shall materialize: Esau will dominate you in this world, but you will dominate him in the World to Come *(Yalkut Shimoni* 1:133).

According to the *Midrash*: If Jacob is deserving, Esau shall *serve* [יַעֲבֹד] him; if not, Esau shall *enslave* [יְעַבֵּד, *subjugate*] him.

כה תוֹמִם בְּבִטְנָהּ: וַיֵּצֵא הָרִאשׁוֹן אַדְמוֹנִי
כֻּלּוֹ כְּאַדֶּרֶת שֵׂעָר וַיִּקְרְאוּ שְׁמוֹ עֵשָׂו:

I.e, *when two hundred and seventy days of pregnancy had passed ... (Targum Yonasan).*

Of Tamar's childbirth, however, Scripture does not record that her days of pregnancy 'grew full': וַיְהִי בְּעֵת לִדְתָּהּ, *and it came to pass in the time of her bearing,* [38:27] for Tamar gave birth in the seventh month *(Rashi).*

וְהִנֵּה תוֹמִם בְּבִטְנָהּ — *Then behold! There were twins in her womb.*

I.e., Behold, *the twins in her womb* came forth *(Radak).*

To the midwives, it was apparent *while she was still pregnant* [i.e., while still בְּבִטְנָהּ, *in her womb*] that she was carrying twins *(Sforno).*

In the Torah the word for twins is spelled *defectively,* (תוֹמִם), while in the case of Tamar it is spelled *full* [38:27]: וְהִנֵּה **תְאוֹמִים** בְּבִטְנָהּ, to imply that in Tamar's case both children proved righteous [i.e. they were completely similar] while here [the defective spelling implies that their similarity was incomplete] — one was righteous and the other was wicked *(Rashi* citing *Midrash).*

As the word is spelled it can be vocalized תּוּמָם, *perfect* or *wholesome,* and homiletically applied to *Jacob* only who is called in *v.* 27 אִישׁ תָּם, *a wholesome man (Lekach Tov).*

According to *Abarbanel,* this homiletical perfection refers to both of them: one was perfect in his righteousness; the other in his wickedness.

In a more esoteric manner, *Malbim,* who interprets this entire incident as portending Messianic times, explains that when her pregnancy reached full-term, the agitation of the twins ceased; this is indicated by the defective spelling of תוֹמִם. In Messianic times, which are symbolized by the term לֵידָה, *birth,* the conflict between Esau and Jacob will cease as Esau submits to Israel's spiritual superiority.

[The word הִנֵּה, *behold,* generally indicates a sudden or surprising development. In our case, however, the existence of twins had already been foretold to Rebecca — why, then, the implication of surprise?]

Ramban [27:4] comments that Rebecca was not permitted to reveal the above prophecy. In that case, the birth of twins would have been unexpected to all except her.

Hirsch comments that, in view of the sharp differences prophesied for the children, it was anticipated that they would be dissimilar from birth. *Unexpectedly, however, they were identical twins* except that Esau was more developed physicially. This external similarity combined with their divergent personalities and futures, and draws attention to the fact that the seeds of the future conflict lay deep beneath the surface and require intensive study.[1]

25. וַיֵּצֵא הָרִאשׁוֹן אַדְמוֹנִי — *And the first one emerged red.*

— According to *Midrash HaGa-*

1. If they were destined to be so dissimilar, why were they born as *twins?*
— There is no קַשׁ, *chaff,* without תְּבוּאָה, *wheat,* and no wheat without chaff.
Of Esau it is written [*Ovadiah* 1:18] וּבֵית עֵשָׂו לְקַשׁ, *the house of Esau shall be as chaff;* and

25 *there were twins in her womb.* [26] *The first one*
25 *emerged red, entirely like a hairy mantle; so they*

dol and most commentators, the 'redness' refers to *a ruddy complexion* [see below]; *Midrash HaChefetz* cited by *Torah Sheleimah* in note to 25:132 interprets it as *red hair.*

Chizkuni questions what redness has in common with *a hairy mantle* to which Esau is likened. Therefore he suggests that אַדְמוֹנִי in this context is cognate to אָדָם, *man,* and means *manly; like a hairy mantle.*

Rashi, in pursuing the *Midrashic* interpretation, comments that Esau's ruddiness was a portent that he would shed blood [since there is no other reason for the Torah to inform us of his ruddiness. The mention that he was *like a hairy mantle* was only to explain why he was named Esau; (see below; *Mizrachi).*]

King David is also described in *I Samuel* 16:12 as being אַדְמוֹנִי, *red.* The *Midrash* comments that Samuel feared that this might portend that David, too, was a murderer. But God reassured Samuel, saying that unlike Esau, David was [as the verse in *Samuel* ibid. continues] *of beautiful eyes,* for when Esau slew he consulted no one, but David slew only after consulting the Sanhedrin who are the 'eyes' of the community (see ArtScroll *Shir HaShirim* and *Overview* ArtScroll *Tehillim).* [I.e., David's redness is qualified by Scripture's testimony that his tendency toward bloodshed was exercised only when it was required as determined by the *eyes* of the community].

Midrash HaGadol, however, observes: If you see a ruddy man be aware that he will be either wholly wicked like Esau, or wholly righteous like David.

The *Midrash* goes on to cite *Ezekiel* 35:6 where Esau is described as *hating blood!* However, this is interpreted to refer to the *blood of sacrifices* whose preparation was the duty of the first born; or to the blood of circumcision.[1] The Rabbis said, He hated to let blood remain in another person's body.

כֻּלּוֹ כְּאַדֶּרֶת שֵׂעָר – *Entirely* [lit. *all of him*] *like a hairy mantle.*

— I.e. as hairy as a hairy woolen garment *(Rashi).*

This interpretation of *Rashi* follows *Nachalas Yaakov* who follows *Radak* in *Sefer Shorashim* s.v. אַדֶּרֶת. He explains that our phrase is elliptic with the word שֵׂעָר, *hair,* referring to כֻּלּוֹ as well as to אַדֶּרֶת. Thus: *he was as completely hairy as a hairy mantle.* This differs from *Mizrachi* and *Gur Aryeh* who interpret אַדֶּרֶת as not being in the construct state with שֵׂעָר. They maintain that a garment of *wool* could not be referred to as *hair,* since the term *hair* is used regarding *human hair* only. A mantle would be described only by the material of which it is made. They therefore interpret *Rashi* as expounding our verse as if it read כֻּלּוֹ שֵׂעָר כְּאַדֶּרֶת, *all of him hairy as a mantle.* [The latter agrees with *Ibn Ezra's* primary interpretation of our verse.] But, as *Nachalas Yaakov* points out, they apparently overlooked an identical phrase in *Zechariah* [13:4], where *hair* definitely modifies *mantle.*

of Jacob it is written [*Jeremiah* 2:3]: קֹדֶשׁ יִשְׂרָאֵל לַה' רֵאשִׁית תְּבוּאָתֹה, *Israel is holy to* H*ASHEM, the first fruits of His crops* [lit. *wheat*] *(Chizkuni).*

[From the language of this comment, *Torah Sheleimah* surmises that it is drawn from an unknown *Midrash*].

2. Since Scripture nowhere states that Esau was circumcised, as it does, by implication of Jacob and his sons (34:15), *Da'as Zekeinim* preserves a tradition that Isaac hesitated to circumcise Esau on the eighth day because his ruddiness might have been symptomatic of ill health in which case circumcision should be delayed. When it became apparent that ruddiness was his nature, Isaac decided he would wait to circumcise him until his thirteenth birthday, the age at which Ishmael was circumcised. But at the age of thirteen Esau hindered it. [See *Kli Chemdah* and note in *Torah Sheleimah* 25:133.]

כו וַאַחֲרֵי־כֵ֞ן יָצָ֣א אָחִ֗יו וְיָד֤וֹ אֹחֶ֙זֶת֙ בַּעֲקֵ֣ב
עֵשָׂ֔ו וַיִּקְרָ֥א שְׁמ֖וֹ יַעֲקֹ֑ב וְיִצְחָ֛ק בֶּן־שִׁשִּׁ֥ים

וַיִּקְרְאוּ שְׁמוֹ עֵשָׂו — *So* [lit. *and*] *they named him* [lit. *called his name*] *Esau.*

— Which means *completely formed* [= עָשׂוּי, *made (Rashbam).*]

[The plural form: *they named,* refers to the fact that] *everyone* called him Esau because he was *completely developed* with hair like a child several years old *(Rashi).*

According to *Tanchuma Sh'mos* 4, *'they'* refers to Esau's *parents* — Isaac and Rebecca — who gave him that name. [Compare the singular וַיִּקְרָא, *he called,* in the following verse.]

26. אַחֲרֵי־כֵן יָצָא אָחִיו — [And] *after that his brother emerged.*

[*Rashi* is troubled by why Jacob was born second *(Gur Aryeh);* or according to *Levush,* why this verse does not read *'the second* emerged' which stylistically would agree with the previous verse which reads 'the *first one* emerged.']

Rashi accordingly comments, 'I heard a *Midrash* [see *Midrash Rabbah* 63:8] which expounds this literally: Jacob was justified in trying to prevent Esau from issuing first, since Jacob had been conceived first and Esau second. Consider a narrow tube into which two stones are inserted in succession. The one inserted first will emerge last, and vice versa. Accordingly Esau, who was formed last emerged first, and Jacob who had really been formed first, emerged last. Accordingly וְיָדוֹ אֹחֶזֶת בַּעֲקֵב עֵשָׂו, *Jacob's hand was grasping onto Esau's heel,* since he wanted to emerge first, as the first one conceived, and legally be claimed *first born.* [Thus, as *Levush* concludes, the verse does not refer to Jacob as *second* but simply as *brother* since in terms of conception he was first.]

Another *Midrashic* interpretation: Why did Esau issue first? So that all the birth refuse might issue with him. Rav Abbahu said: Like the bath-attendant who first scours the bathhouse in preparation for the prince to bathe.

וְיָדוֹ אֹחֶזֶת בַּעֲקֵב עֵשָׂו — *With* [lit. *and*] *his hand grasping on to the heel of Esau.*

Portending that his [Esau's] period of dominion [which is interpreted to include all of Roman (=Western) civilization] will barely be complete before Jacob comes and wrests it from him [i.e. Jacob's dominion will come on the *'heels'* of Esau's] *(Rashi).*

Rashi interprets the grasping of Esau's *heel* to be no more than a sign, for if Jacob was really intent on *preventing* Esau from emerging first, he would have grasped Esau's *head (Maskil leDavid).*

And as he was given the name of Jacob, he will follow at the heels to commemorate the position he adopted rather than his outward appearance. He allowed Esau to precede him but he followed at Esau's heels. He is that צָעִיר, the weaker one [*v.* 23], who unexpectedly will be first *(Hirsch).*

Midrash HaGadol s.v. וַיִּתְרוֹצְצוּ comments: Jacob and Esau tossed up and down in Rebecca's womb like ocean waves, each one intending to be born first. Esau finally said to Jacob: 'If you do not let me be first, I will kill mother and

25 *named him Esau.* [26] *After that his brother emerged*
26 *with his hand grasping the heel of Esau; so he named*
him Jacob. Isaac was sixty years old when she bore
them.

emerge through the stomach wall.' Calling Esau a wicked murderer from his very inception, Jacob allowed him to emerge first.

וַיִּקְרָא שְׁמוֹ יַעֲקֹב — *So* [lit. *and*] *he named him* [lit. *called his name*] *Jacob.*

— I.e. *God* so named him [following *Tanchuma Sh'mos* 4; i.e. He commanded Isaac so to name him]. Another interpretation: His *father* [sc. Isaac] named him Jacob [=*Yaakov,* a play on the word *ekev,* heel] because he grasped Esau's heel *(Rashi).*

According to *Sforno,* the name means: At the end [עָקֵב] of time, he will endure [as the victor in the constant struggle with the evil forces represented by Esau]. This was symbolized by Jacob's grasping of his brother's heel, alluding to *end.* The symbolism was ratified by the fact that according to the Sages God named Jacob.

[*Rashi* offers the alternate interpretation that *Isaac* named him, because according to the primary opinion of the *Midrash* that *God* named him, it is difficult why his name was later changed from Jacob to Israel [for if *God* named him the name should have been permanently his and not subject to addition or change *(Maskil leDavid).* [See 35:10. Perhaps this is why the name Jacob remained even after Israel was added.]

Tur points out that in seeming contradiction to the former interpretation cited by *Rashi, Yerushalmi Berachos* 1:6 [cited in comm. to 17:5, p. 564] notes that since Abram and Jacob were originally named *by man* God changed their names, but Isaac's name was not changed because God designated his name before birth [see 17:19]. To resolve this contradiction, *Tur* answers that Isaac's name was not changed because God designated his name *before* birth, while Jacob was not given his name until *after* he was born. [See *R' Bachya* cited in *comm.* to 26:18 s.v. וַיִּקְרָא לָהֶן].

Or HaChaim supports the interpretation that *He called* in the beginning of our verse refers to God; if *Isaac* were the subject, then the verse would not continue *'Isaac' was sixty years old* etc. for it would be unnecessary to give his name; it would suffice to say, 'and *he* was sixty years old.'

[Those who maintain that *Isaac* was the implied subject in the beginning of the verse would explain that his name is specified in the second half of the verse to avoid any ambiguity of subject after Jacob's name was mentioned.]

וְיִצְחָק בֶּן־שִׁשִּׁים שָׁנָה בְּלֶדֶת אֹתָם — [And] *Isaac was sixty years old when she* [Rebecca] *bore them* [lit. *in bearing them.*]

[This seemingly gratuitous chronological detail serves to inform us that there was a total period of twenty years from her marriage at age three (see comm. to *v.* 20) until she bore children. *Rashi,* below, explains why he did not divorce her after being married for ten years without children (see *comm.* to 21:3), or take a second wife. (See also *Yevamos* 64a and *Even Haezer* 154:10 and commentators for the application of the *halachah* and the many exceptions to it)]:

Ten years passed from their marriage until she reached the age of thirteen and became capable of bearing children [so, in effect, the first ten years of their marriage were not considered childless in the *halachic* sense]. He waited these [latter] ten years as his father

כז שָׁנָה בְּלֶדֶת אֹתָם: וַיִּגְדְּלוּ הַנְּעָרִים וַיְהִי
עֵשָׂו אִישׁ יֹדֵעַ צַיִד אִישׁ שָׂדֶה וְיַעֲקֹב
כח אִישׁ תָּם יֹשֵׁב אֹהָלִים: וַיֶּאֱהַב יִצְחָק אֶת־

Abraham did [in regard to Sarah — see *comm.* to 16:3]. When she did still not conceive, he realized she was barren and prayed for her. But he did not want to marry one of his maids [as Abraham did in the case of Sarah] because he had been sanctified on Mount Moriah to be עוֹלָה תְּמִימָה, an *unblemished offering* [and could therefore not marry a slave] *(Rashi).*

[On Isaac as an *unblemished offering* in cosequence of his having been consecrated as an offering to God at the *Akeidah*, see *comm.* to 26:2.]

27. The Personalities Emerge.

וַיִּגְדְּלוּ הַנְּעָרִים — [*And*] *the lads grew up.*

[Although as *v.* 23 records, Jacob and Esau were distinct from the womb *(Mizrachi)*], there was no *conspicuous* difference between them when they were children. No one paid much attention to their characters [attributing Esau's pranks to childishness rather than wickedness *(Sifsei Chachomim)*]. But when they reached thirteen their varying dispositions became manifest: Jacob frequented houses of study, and Esau the idolatrous temples *(Rashi).*

How does *Rashi* specify *thirteen* as the age when their varying characteristics became manifest, when further, (in *v.* 30), *Rashi* makes it clear that Abraham died prematurely when Esau was *fifteen* years old so Abraham would not see Esau pursue a career of wickedness?

Mizrachi answers that during the two years until he was fifteen, Esau sinned privately; after that he sinned openly. According to *Nachalas Yaakov*, before Esau was fifteen he did not commit cardinal sins such as adultery with married women or murder.

וַיְהִי עֵשָׂו אִישׁ יֹדֵעַ צַיִד — [*And*] *Esau became* [lit. *was*] *one who knows hunting* [lit. *trapping*].

—I.e., *knowing* [that is, figuratively *attaining skill*] how to entrap and deceive his father with his mouth, asking him how tithes were to be taken from salt and straw [although he knew full well that these were not subject to the law of tithes]. Consequently, his father thought him to be punctillious in performing the *mitzvos (Tanchuma; Rashi).*

Rashbam interprets the phrase literally as *a cunning hunter.*

[The figurative *Midrashic* interpretation which *Rashi* follows is not opposed to the literal sense but reflects a profound perception into the nature of Esau. The term יֹדֵעַ צַיִד, one who *knows* hunting signifies, as *Hirsch* points out, that "the צַיָּד, *hunter*, must understand the art of stalking; he must be able to appear quite innocent and still have in his heart the thought of killing. It is the complete exercise of trickery, insidiousness ..." Hence, apparently, *Rashi* accepted as the underlying simple sense of the phrase, the *Midrashic* interpretation that the phrase implies Esau's devious character in deceiving his father.]

[Compare the description of Nimrod, whose spiritual heir Esau seems to have been, as גִּבּוֹר צַיִד לִפְנֵי ה׳, *a mighty*

[27] *The lads grew up and Esau became one who
knows hunting, a man of the field. But Jacob was a
wholesome man, abiding in tents.* [28] *Isaac loved Esau*

hunter before HASHEM, (above 10:9) which *Rashi* there explains as, 'he ensnared men with his words and incited them to rebel against the Omnipresent.'][1]

אִישׁ שָׂדֶה — *A man of the field.* — As it literally implies: A carefree person who hunted beasts and birds with his bow *(Rashi).*

[I.e., Esau was a man of the outdoors; unrestricted; in contrast with the description of Noah as אִישׁ הָאֲדָמָה, *man of the earth* (9:20), and Cain in 3:2 as עֹבֵד אֲדָמָה, *worker* (tiller) *of the earth,* both of which terms denote agricultural labor. That interpretation of agriculturalist, however, cannot be applied to Esau who was a hunter *(Mizrachi).*]

According to *Sforno,* however, the term *does,* even in this case, describe one *skilled in field work.*

The *Zohar* perceives the phrase *man of the field* to imply that he was a highwayman who robbed and murdered people while pretending to his father that he isolated himself to pray. Also, he was *a man of the field* in that his portion was not cast in inhabited land, but in wild and desolate places. [See *footnote* to *v.*28.]

Kli Yakar, based on *Bava Basra* 16b interprets that Esau went to the fields to commit adultery. There, far from towns, the cries of his victims would not be heard [cf. *Deut.* 22:25-7).

וְיַעֲקֹב אִישׁ תָּם — *But* [lit. *and*] *Jacob was a wholesome man* [lit. *a simple or perfect man,* in the moral sense].

I.e., not expert in all of the above: his heart and mouth were consistent with one another. One not ingenious in deceiving people is called תָּם [*plain; simple, wholesome*] *(Rashi).*

The description of Jacob as אִישׁ תָּם, *simple man,* contrasts with Esau as יֹדֵעַ צַיִד, *a man who knows trapping;* Jacob's יֹשֵׁב אֹהָלִים, *abiding in tents,* contrasts with Esau as אִישׁ שָׂדֶה, *a man of the field,* again emphasizing the starkness of their diametrically opposed characteristics *(Ibn Ezra; Abarbanel).*

The *Midrash* cites this verse to support the tradition that Jacob was born circumcised: תָּם, being interpreted in the sense of physically *perfect* and *whole.*

יֹשֵׁב אֹהָלִים — *Abiding* [lit. *dwelling; sitting*] *in tents.*

1. *Yalkut Shimoni* preserves a *Midrash* that Esau's skill as a hunter was directly attributable to a tunic which Esau took from Nimrod. As noted in the *footnote* to 3:21 and 10:10, this garment, originally made for Adam, passed on to Cush who in turn passed it on to his son, Nimrod. It was embroidered with animals and birds, and it was to this that Nimrod owed his prowess and renown.

As *Hadar Zekeinim* and *Da'as Zekeinim* record, Esau and Nimrod had been engaged in a bitter feud for a long time and finally resolved to leave the decision to a duel. Jacob, knowing that Nimrod was invulnerable as long as he was clad in Adam's garments, advised his brother not to enter into combat before his adversary had removed these garments. Whereupon Esau put those garments on steathily and killed Nimrod in the duel. This made Esau, too, a *cunning hunter.* These were the *coveted garments of Esau* [referred to in 27:15] which Jacob wore when he received Isaac's blessing.

עֵשָׂו כִּי־צַיִד בְּפִיו וְרִבְקָה אֹהֶבֶת אֶת־

In the tents [=schools] of Shem and Eber *(Rashi)*.[1]

According to *Radak*, the intent of the plural is that he studied with every sage he encountered, this being his sole desire; and he was *simple* — free of any deviousness.

— He dwelt among the tents of Abraham and Isaac and received instruction from both of them *(Racanati)*.

Sforno comments that there were two tents where Jacob divided his time: the shepherd's tent and the tent of meditation.

28. וַיֶּאֱהַב יִצְחָק אֶת עֵשָׂו — *[And] Isaac loved Esau.*

It goes without saying that he loved Jacob, for, indeed, he surely loved Jacob even more than Esau. This verse merely gives the specific reason Isaac entertained *any* liking for Esau *(Radak)*.

כִּי־צַיִד בְּפִיו — *For game* [lit. *trapping*] *was in his mouth.*

I.e., in *Isaac's* mouth [i.e., Esau supplied Isaac with venison, hence, *Rashi* interprets the phrase literally: 'because Esau's game was in Isaac's mouth.' — *he ate of Esau's game (Targum)*.] *Midrashically*, however, the phrase is interpreted as implying: in *Esau's* mouth; i.e., Isaac loved Esau because *there was entrapment in his mouth* — he used to deceive his father [by his speech; see on previous verse יֹדֵעַ צַיִד] *(Rashi)*.

— It was his *father* not mother towards whom he directed his deception since he wanted to be the recipient of Isaac's blessings *(Or HaChaim)*.

Ibn Ezra accordingly interprets that the phrase in the literal sense is elliptic and means, he *supplied* game in his [father's] mouth.

Ralbag, following the literal interpretation comments that this is indeed the reason Isaac loved him 'since it is only natural for one to love someone who caters to him.'

Ibn Ezra comments that Isaac lost the considerable fortune left him by Abraham. Therefore, he loved Esau who became the provider of food for the family.

Ramban, in *v.*34, disagrees sharply with *Ibn Ezra*. To the contrary, the Patriarchs were usually honored as kings, and it was the custom of royalty to prefer venison above all food. Esau flattered his father by supplying him with venison so that he could eat of it to his heart's content; furthermore, the love of a father for his firstborn is easily understood.

It was concerning a love like Isaac's to Esau that the Sages proclaimed [*Avos* 5:16]: All love that depends on a

1. He would sometimes study under Eber although Shem was the elder sage of the generation and more renowned.

Although in matters of *Torah law* one should strive to consult the *most* renowned sage, in matters of *Torah study* it is difficult: one must learn *Torah* from whomever he can — even from a younger sage since as the Sages proclaimed [*Avodah Zarah* 19a]: 'One should always study that part of the *Torah* which his heart desires' — even from a lesser scholar since 'not from every teacher can someone merit to learn' *(Gur Aryeh)*.

[The defective spelling ישב is usually perceived homilectically to imply 'sat for the first time that very day.' See, for example, *Rashi* to 19:1 וְהוּא ישֵׁב, and to 23:10 וְעֶפְרוֹן ישֵׁב. Here the commentators do not discuss the implication of this spelling.] *Harav David Feinstein* cites *Berachos* 63b that the Torah is as beloved every day to those who study it as the day it was given at Sinai. Thus, our verse alludes to Jacob's constantly renewed enthusiasm as he undertook each day's study of Torah.

specific factor [in this case כִּי צַיִד בְּפִיו, *for game was in his mouth*] will cease once that factor no longer exists. Conversely, as the verse continues, *Rebecca loved Jacob*: No motive is given for *that* love; none was necessary: her love for him was pure and unaffected by external factors. Such love never ceases *(Minchah Belulah)*.

Nevertheless the *Midrash* points to Esau's exemplary filial devotion, as a consequence of which he merited his father's love [see *Overview*.] In fact *Sefer Chassidim* Chapt. 341 cites that Esau's descendants were given dominion over the world in reward for Esau's filial devotion in constantly exposing himself to mortal danger to supply his father with game.

Meam Loez offers a novel interpretation: Isaac loved Esau כִּי, *when*, game was in his [Isaac's] mouth. Isaac felt love for Esau when the otherwise sinful son honored his father by supplying him with food. Although Isaac was aware of Esau's evil ways, he felt that as long as Esau scrupulously observed even this one commandment, there was still hope he would become righteous. [Citing *Kesef Nivchar*; cf. *Chizkuni*.]

וְרִבְקָה אֹהֶבֶת אֶת יַעֲקֹב — *But* [lit. *and*] *Rebecca loved* [lit. *loves*, signifying an increasingly unwavering love *(Chizkuni)*.]

Here, no reason need be given. It is only logical that Jacob should be loved *(Hoffmann)*.

Rebecca's love for Jacob was earned; she was not 'deceived' into loving him. Rather, he earned her love *(Hirsch)*. [*See Minchah Belulah* above.]

She loved *only* him. She recognized how Jacob clung to the paths of *Torah*, wisdom and life, and how Esau rejected these and chose instead a dangerous occupation, acted wantonly, and plundered. Isaac, who was aged and of poor sight, remained at home and to the extent that he was unaware of Esau's wickedness, he was charmed by Esau's obsequiety. The Torah mentions this detail to prepare us for the sale of the birthright as a display of Esau's recklessness *(Radak)*.[1]

Furthermore, it must be remembered that *Rebecca*, and not Isaac, was the recipient of the prophecy regarding *the elder serving the younger* and hence had a God-given truer perspective of the characteristics of her sons. [See *comm.* to *v.* 23 וַיֹּאמֶר ה׳ לָהּ] *(Rashbam; Chizkuni)*.

[The translation of the ו as *but*, follows the rule explained in the *comm.* to 14:19, 16:2, and 21:1 whereby it is expounded that the common sentence structure of Scripture places the verb before the subject: וַיֶּאֱהַב יִצְחָק. Whenever the subject *precedes* the predicate — even within the same verse — וְרִבְקָה אֹהֶבֶת, Scripture means to draw attention to a *contrast* with the foregoing. Hence the prepositional prefix ו is not interpreted *and*, but as the antithetical *but*. Cf. 31:47 'Laban called it Yager Sahadusa, וְיַעֲקֹב קָרָא לוֹ גַּלְעֵד, *but* Jacob called it Gal Ed.']

1. It may be asked, seeing that the *Shechinah* was with Isaac, how is it that he was unaware of Esau's evil deeds?

— The truth is that the *Shechinah*, although continually with Isaac, did not reveal to him Esau's evil career in order that Jacob should receive his blessing not by the will of Isaac, but by the will of the Holy One, Blessed be He. So it was destined to be, and when Jacob entered into the presence of his father the *Shechinah* accompanied him, and Isaac thus felt that there was before him one who was worthy of being blessed; and blessed he was by the will of the *Shechinah (Zohar)*. [See *comm.* to Chapt. 27, and *Overview*. See also *comm.* of *Chizkuni* and *Da'as Soferim* to *v.*23.]

כט יַעֲקֹ֑ב׃ וַיָּ֥זֶד יַעֲקֹ֖ב נָזִ֑יד וַיָּבֹ֥א עֵשָׂ֛ו מִן־
ל הַשָּׂדֶ֖ה וְה֥וּא עָיֵֽף׃ וַיֹּ֨אמֶר עֵשָׂ֜ו אֶֽל־יַעֲקֹ֗ב
הַלְעִיטֵ֤נִי נָא֙ מִן־הָֽאָדֹ֤ם הָֽאָדֹם֙ הַזֶּ֔ה כִּ֥י

29. The Sale of the Birthright.

וַיָּזֶד יַעֲקֹב נָזִיד — *Once,* [lit. *and*] *Jacob simmered a stew.*

The *stew* is unidentified. Not until *v.* 34 are we told it was a *lentil* stew.

Abraham died that day and Jacob cooked a stew of lentils to provide his father with the traditional mourner's meal *(Bava Basra* 16b; *Targum Yonasan;* see *Rashi* next verse).

The unusual verb וַיָּזֶד means *cook (Onkelos; Rashi).* The rendering *simmer* attempts to suggest the nuance perceived by *HaKsav V'haKaballah* that the verb וַיָּזֶד denotes the *early stage of cooking* when the contents of the pot just began to boil. The choice of this verb serves to emphasize Esau's character in wanting the stew — which was still unfinished — to be poured down his throat like an animal [see *comm.* to הַלְעִיטֵנִי and נָא in *v.* 30.]

Tzror HaMor citing *Midrash HaNeelam* perceives in the choice of the verb וַיָּזֶד as a suggestion of the verb זוד, meaning *premeditated scheme,* as in *Exodus* 18:11, and נָזִיד implying a *premeditated act* [cf. terms such as זָדוֹן, מֵזִיד.] The implication, according to the above is that וַיָּזֶד יַעֲקֹב נָזִיד, *Jacob devised* [colloquially: *cooked up*] *this scheme* after it had been suggested to him by Shem and Eber that if he could get Esau to relinquish his birthright this act would work against Esau's descendants on the Day of Judgment, and accordingly they would be powerless to halt the ascendancy of Jacob's descendants. [For, as *Ramban* states in 12:6: מַעֲשֵׂה אָבוֹת סִימָן לְבָנִים, 'whatever has happened to the Patriarchs is a sign to the children.' Every event that happened to any one of the three Patriarchs portends what is decreed to happen to his descendants.]

וַיָּבֹא עֵשָׂו מִן־הַשָּׂדֶה — [And] *Esau came in from the field.*

[The day of mourning for Abraham has arrived. Isaac and Rebecca weep; Jacob weeps; heaven and earth weep. The sick people Abraham had healed and all those upon whom he had showered hospitality — all mourn for him. The great of all the nations stood in the mourner's row and lamented, 'Woe to the world that has lost its leader; woe to the ship that has lost its pilot!' *(Bava Basra* 91b) — Even Ishmael who had repented mourns the great father he had just helped bury (see 25:7-9).

They return from the Cave of Machpelah — Isaac sits on the ground and mourns while Jacob prepares the customary mourner's meal from his own lentils since a mourner may not eat the first meal from his own food, but only from that of others.

Where was Esau? —

Esau, in contrast, is portrayed as going about his evil business as usual, uninvolved, as it were, in his family's bereavement: *Esau came in from the field.*

There is a *Midrash* that when Esau learned why Jacob was preparing lentils he exclaimed blasphemously, 'If Judgment has been able to overtake that righteous man (i.e. Abraham who did not reach the longevity of Adam or Noah —

[29] *Once, Jacob simmered a stew, and Esau came in*
from the field, exhausted. [30] *Esau said to Jacob, 'Pour*
into me, now, some of that very red stuff for I am ex-

[*Yafeh Toar*]) then there is neither reward nor resurrection!' To this the *Midrash* concludes, the *Shechinah* cried out, '*Weep not for the dead* — i.e. for Abraham — *nor bemoan him; but weep bitterly for him who went away* — that is, for Esau (who forsook the true faith).']

Further, the *Midrash* explains that *came in from the field* is a euphemistic reference to his having violated a betrothed maiden that very day. This is derived from the *Midrashic* interpretation that he stalked the fields to find women to violate. [Cf. the reference to *field* in this context in *Deut.* 22:25.]

וְהוּא עָיֵף [*And he was*] *exhausted.*

— After having committed murder, cf. *Jeremiah* 4:31 *for my soul is exhausted* [עָיְפָה] *before the murderers (Bava Basra* 16b; *Rashi).*

— For on that day he slew Nimrod *(Da'as Zekeinim;* see *footnote* to *v.* 27), and committed five heinous sins. See *comm.* next verse.

The translation *exhausted* follows *Onkelos. Ibn Ezra* renders it in the sense of *languishing; famished:* hungry and thirsty. Cf. *Isaiah* 32:12 בְּאֶרֶץ עֲיֵפָה, *in a languishing land.*

30. הַלְעִיטֵנִי נָא — *Pour into me now.*

[The Hebrew which is in the transitive has a very forceful connotation, much like the colloquial *stuff me!*] The sense of the expression, as *Rashi* explains it, is: *I will open my mouth; pour a lot into it!* The expression, as *Rashi* points out citing the *Mishnah* in *Shabbos* 155b, is normally used for feeding *animals* [and implies animal-like voracity.]

Onkelos, on the other hand, renders אַטְעֲמְנִי, *give me a taste.*

The word נָא in Scripture usually denotes a request [=*please*], but is always rendered by *Onkelos* as כְּעַן, *now,* and in certain contexts by *Rashi* and *Ibn Ezra* as well. See for example *comm.* to 12:11 הִנֵּה נָא יָדַעְתִּי.

Me'am Loez cites an interpretation by *Ahavas Zion* that נָא also means *raw* as in the verse regarding the paschal lamb [*Exodus* 12:9] *Do not eat of it* נָא, *raw.* Hence Esau [apparently seeing that the stew was still cooking, and unfinished (see *comm.* to וַיָּזֶד in *v.* 29)] asked that the stew be poured down his throat נָא, although still unfinished [*raw*].

מִן הָאָדֹם הָאָדֹם הַזֶּה — *Some of that very red stuff* [lit. *from this the red the red.*]

The repetition *red red* attests to his haste, for when one is urgent he repeats himself *(Rashbam)*; and indicates the intensity of one's desire for something *(Radak).*

Ramban observes that we are still not informed of the *kind* of stew it was. Esau saw a dish reddened by red lentils or it had been colored red by some red substance whose name Esau did not know, so he referred to it vaguely as *that very red stuff.*

The translation *very red* follows *Chizkuni* who explains that the repetition denotes an intensification; hence *very* red. Cf. אֲדַמְדָּם, *very red* in *Lev.* 13:49. [Cf. also שְׁחַרְחֹרֶת *in Song of Songs* 1:6.]

Rashi comments:

It was a stew of red *lentils* [as evidenced by the fact that in *v.* 29 Jacob is described as simmering a

עָיֵף אָנֹכִי עַל־כֵּן קָרָא־שְׁמוֹ אֱדוֹם:
לא וַיֹּאמֶר יַעֲקֹב מִכְרָה כַיּוֹם אֶת־בְּכֹרָתְךָ

stew, and in *v.* 34 the dish is referred to as a *lentil* stew *(Mizrachi).*] Abraham had died on that day in order to be spared seeing his grandson Esau enter upon a career of wickedness [for as the *Talmud, Bava Basra* 16b notes, on the day Abraham died, Esau began his sinful career (so in effect Abraham was spared witnessing it). Esau committed five crimes on that day: he violated a betrothed maiden; committed murder; denied God; denied resurrection of the dead; and spurned the birthright.] For had Abraham lived to see this he would not have enjoyed the *good old age* [see comm. to *v.* 8] promised him by God. Therefore, God cut his life short by five years — for he lived five years less than his son Isaac. Jacob was now preparing this lentil stew for the customary mourner's meal.[1]

כִּי עָיֵף אָנֹכִי — *For I am exhausted.*

I.e., and I haven't the strength to feed myself *(Ralbag).*

עַל־כֵּן קָרָא שְׁמוֹ אֱדוֹם — *He was therefore named* [lit. *he therefore called his name*] *Edom.*

— Meaning 'red.' He was ruddy and desired red food for the sake of which he sold his birthright. Thus Edom was a term of contempt (*Rashbam; Ramban* similarly).

The Hebrew is in the singular: *He* called his name Edom:

Esau gave *himself* this name *(Da'as Zekeinim); Jacob* gave him this name which should be rendered in the imperative אֱדוֹם, *be red* like the strew you wish to swallow! *(Sforno).*

According to *Abarbanel,* the phrase means· *Therefore* [i.e., because he was urgent and tired] *he called its name* [i.e., he referred to the stew as] *red* [*adom*].

Haamek Davar interprets: Esau, by his very act of referring to the stew as *adom,* caused himself to be so referred to after this episode. This was part of the Divine Plan so that everyone should become aware of what transpired and the matter would accordingly be ratified and not subject to change. Furthermore, the name *Edom* in itself was appropriate to him, as the *Midrash* comments: He was red, his food red, his land red [32:4: אֱדוֹם], his warriors were red [*Nachum* 2:4], their garments were red [*ibid.*].

31. מִכְרָה כַיּוֹם — ***Sell, as this day.***

— I.e. a binding sale. Just as this day is certain, so make a binding sale [i.e., make the sale as clear as the light of day to leave no room for dispute] *(Rashi).*

Rashbam renders: Sell your share

1. *Rashi* continues: Why lentils? Because as lentils are round like a wheel, so is mourning like a wheel, which revolves in the world [i.e. sooner or later it touches everyone just as every part of a wheel touches the ground in turn.]

Another reason is, as lentils have no opening [פֶּה, 'mouth'], so must a mourner not open his mouth [lit. 'have no mouth' (i.e. to greet others).] It is customary to give eggs to a mourner as his first meal since, just as eggs are round and have no mouth, so [as we learn in *Moed Katan* 21b] must a mourner during the first three days of his week of mourning neither greet nor respond to greeting; from the third to the seventh he may respond to a greeting but not extend greeting. [This paragraph is found in old texts of *Rashi*].

25
31
hausted.' (He was therefore named Edom.)
31 *Jacob said, 'Sell, as this day, your birthright to*
me.'

of our father's inheritance to me *as this day,* i.e., *immediately,* for a sum of money which I shall give you. Then I will give you the food as testimony and ratification of the deal. We find that food was used to signify conclusion of agreements as in [31:46] *they ate by the heap* — to ratify the covenant between Jacob and Laban. [*Radak* and *Ramban* also interpret that the food was not *payment* for the sale; but that *money* passed hands. See *v.* 34.]

Ramban notes that the literal translation of כַּיּוֹם is *at this time.* [It is apparently this interpretation that *Rashbam,* too, follows in rendering *'immediately.'* Sell it to me *now,* just as this day is now with us *(Chizkuni)*]. See this meaning in *I Samuel* 9:13, 27; ibid. 2:16; *Daniel* 9:7.

Hirsch [*v.* 34] suggests that מכר does not necessarily mean to *sell,* but has also the meaning of *relinquishing,* abandoning. (Cf. *Deut.* 32:30; *Judges* 4:9).

According to *Da'as Zekeinim* the phrase means: Sell it to me for the value it has *today,* i.e., a small sum, since, you must realize, if you die before our father you will not have inherited him and you will in effect have gained nothing from being firstborn; what have you then to lose? [Cf. *Sforno.*]

— Just as *this day* will pass never to return, make this sale binding never to be contested *(Kli Yakar).*

Ramban cites *Onkelos'* translation of כְּיוֹם דִּילְהֵן which he explains as *the day when it occurs'* — i.e., 'sell me your birthright with the sale to take effect as of whatever day our father's death occurs.' The *halachah* is that one can sell only what he actually possesses: 'One cannot sell something that has not yet come into existence' *(Bava Metzia* 33b). Thus, for example, one cannot 'sell' a property that he plans to purchase at some future date. Therefore, unless the birthright had some *tangible value during Isaac's lifetime,* it was not a commodity that could be bought or sold. As *Ramban* maintains in *v.* 31, the birthright carried no distinction until after the passing of the father. Therefore, had Esau tried to make the sale effective *immediately* the transaction could not be valid. But by stipulating, as *Onkelos* implies by his word דִּילְהֵן, effective on *whatever day it may occur* [rendering כַּיּוֹם = בַּיּוֹם, *on* the day the birthright shall come into your possession] — then the sale would be valid although Isaac was still alive and technically Esau did not yet possess it. [This is because, as codified in *Choshen Mishpat* 209:4 gloss: 'but if one stipulated to buy it when it shall come into existence it is a valid sale, although it is not yet in existence,' because the tangible possession will exist at the time of the transfer of ownership *(Techeles Mordechai).* The above interpretation of *Ramban* is condensed from Rabbi Chavel's annotations to his edition of *Ramban.*]

According to *Rivash* [cited in *Herchev Davar*], the sale of an intangible item was valid before the giving of the Torah, hence the sale was valid in this case.

[Note: It must be pointed out that *Ramban's* interpretation above differs substantially from *Rashi's* interpretation further that the firstborn had the privilege of carrying out the sacrificial service. What is remarkable is that *Ramban* makes no mention whatever in this case of *Rashi's* view, unlike most cases where *Ramban* cites *Rashi* in cases where he differs. Perhaps there is some area of agreement between them. וצ"ע (this requires further research).]

אֶת־בְּכֹרָתְךָ לִי — *Your birthright to me.*

The sacrificial service was then carried out by first born sons, and Jacob considered the wicked Esau

לב לִי: וַיֹּאמֶר עֵשָׂו הִנֵּה אָנֹכִי הוֹלֵךְ לָמוּת
לג וְלָמָּה־זֶּה לִי בְּכֹרָה: וַיֹּאמֶר יַעֲקֹב
הִשָּׁבְעָה לִּי כַּיּוֹם וַיִּשָּׁבַע לוֹ וַיִּמְכֹּר אֶת־

unworthy of sacrificing to the Holy One, Blessed be He *(Rashi)*.[1]

According to *Ibn Ezra's* primary interpretation, the birthright consisted of the firstborn's right of a double share in the father's estate [*Ramban* disagrees with this and maintains that this right was instituted later by Torah law]; alternatively since the Patriarchs fulfilled the whole Torah, Jacob felt obligated to show honor to his older brother. He considered the wicked Esau undeserving of this and therefore asked to purchase this privilege from him.

⊲§ But, the commentators query, could such a sale be valid? Could then a non-priest purchase the priesthood of a priest and expect to officiate?

[For *Ramban*'s opinion, see above.]

□ *Mizrachi* replies that the 'sale' was indeed *not* sufficient to give Jacob the right of priesthood. However, because Esau *swore to renounce his birthright*, he was bound to honor his own oath and refrain from performing the sacrificial service. Thereby, the wicked Esau was foreclosed from involvement in the holy service. It was this, rather than his own enhancement, which was Jacob's purpose.

□ *Gur Aryeh* contends that the objection has validity only with regard to a כֹּהֵן, *priest*, whose holiness is God-given and thus not transferrable. However, before the Torah was given, the priestly function was reserved for the firstborn purely in honorary recognition of his status. Therefore it was his personal right, and he had the power to sell it.

□ *Divrei David's* approach is similar. Before the Torah was given, anyone — even a non-priest or non-firstborn — was permitted to perform the sacrificial service. Once Esau was removed from consideration by his oath, the privilege remained Jacob's by default.

□ *Nachalas Yitzchak* comments that priesthood was God's gift to Abraham. It passed on to Isaac who would, in turn, transfer to his offspring. Since Esau had relinquished it, Jacob remained the only eligible son.

32. וַיֹּאמֶר עֵשָׂו — *And Esau said.*

To himself or to Jacob *(Radak)*.

הִנֵּה אָנֹכִי הוֹלֵךְ לָמוּת — *Look, I am going to die.*

Following *Rashi's* interpretation that the birthright's only immediate

1. Why did Jacob display such eagerness for the birthright? Because we learned [*Zevachim* 112b; see *Rambam Perush HaMishnayos* there]: Before the Tabernacle (מִשְׁכָּן) was erected the בָּמוֹת, *high places*, were permitted [i.e. sacrifice was not centralized but might be offered at privately erected altars], and the sacrificial service was performed by the firstborn; after the Tabernacle was erected the high places were forbidden and the sacrificial service was performed by priests. Jacob said: 'Shall this wicked man stand and offer the sacrifices!' Therefore he strove so ardently to obtain the birthright *(Midrash)*.

Furthermore, as *Chizkuni* notes, a priest who shed blood was not permitted to officiate; and in those times the priestly functions were performed by the firstborn, hence Jacob perceived that Esau was disqualified.

32 *And Esau said, 'Look, I am going to die so of*
what use to me is a birthright?'
33 *Jacob said, 'Swear to me as this day.' He swore to*

privilege was the right to perform the sacrificial service, Esau now reasoned: ...'My birthright is an unstable privilege.' ... For Esau learned that many breaches of the regulations governing the service — such as officiating after drinking much wine, or officiating bare-headed [see *Sanhedrin* 22b, are punishable by death at the hands of Heaven.] Esau then exclaimed: Look, *I am going to die* [as a result of this privilege since I am sure to transgress]; *why should I desire it?*

Following *Ramban's* interpretation that there were no tangible benefits in the birthright until after a father's death. Esau's reaction meant: *'Look, I am going to die,* i.e., I am constantly in mortal danger from hunting animals; it is likely that I will die while Father is still alive and the birthright carries no special distinction while he lives. *Of what benefit is a birthright to me?'* [The above is essentially followed by *Rashbam; Radak; Ibn Ezra; Da'as Zekeinim*].

According to the *Midrash* that Esau murdered Nimrod on that day [see *footnote* to *v.* 27, and *comm.* to *v.* 29 וְהוּא עָיֵף], Esau was fearful now that he was in mortal danger of being victimized by avengers of Nimrod.

וְלָמָּה־זֶּה לִּי בְּכֹרָה — *So of what use to me is a birthright?* [lit. *and why this to me a birthright?*]

— I do not desire it; it is sold to you! *(Ramban).*

When Esau uttered these words, the *Shechinah* exclaimed: וְלָמָּה זֶה לְךָ בְּרָכָה, then of what use is a blessing [a play on words between בְּכֹרָה, *birthright,* and בְּרָכָה, *blessing*] *to you? (Midrash HaGadol).*

— He rejected the birthright and concerned himself only with what was directly before him; he had no belief in the future *(Pesikta Zutresa).*[1]

33. הִשָּׁבְעָה לִּי כַּיּוֹם — *Swear to me as the day.* [i.e. make your oath as clear as day; see *comm.* to *v.* 31.]

— I. e. swear to me that you will never complain about the transaction *(Rambam);* perhaps once you have eaten you will regret it *(Radak).*

According to other opinions the oath was not merely a reinforcement and a precaution against later recrimination, but *an integral part of the sale.* For as *Mizrachi* comments above [*v.* 31], it was the *oath* itself that rendered the sale valid since, as *Tur* comments citing his father, the *Rosh,* although the intangible may not be sold, if one un-

1. The *Chofetz Chaim* comments that when a *tzaddik* thinks of impending death, his mind turns to repentance and fear of God. But when Esau said *I am going to die,* his only reaction was that the birthright was useless to him!

לד בְּכֹרָתוֹ לְיַעֲקֹב: וְיַעֲקֹב נָתַן לְעֵשָׂו לֶחֶם
וּנְזִיד עֲדָשִׁים וַיֹּאכַל וַיֵּשְׁתְּ וַיָּקָם וַיֵּלַךְ
וַיִּבֶז עֵשָׂו אֶת־הַבְּכֹרָה:

dertakes an oath the sale is valid.

וַיִּמְכֹּר אֶת בְּכֹרָתוֹ לְיַעֲקֹב — *And* [he] *sold his birthright to Jacob.*[1]

— For the price they agreed upon between themselves but which Scripture did not care to specify *(Sforno).*

This follows the interpretation of many exegetes [primarily *Rashbam, Radak's* father; *Tur* (the basis for which is a reference to the sale being for money in *Bamidbar Rabbah* 6:2 and *Pesikta Zutresa)*] who maintain that the *bread and lentil stew* mentioned in the next verse that Jacob gave Esau was *not* the purchase price for the sale but merely an amenity symbolic of the ratification of the transaction [just as gentlemen partake of a meal after concluding a deal *(Tur).*] The purchase price *was an unspecified amount of money which Jacob gave Esau. Ramban,* while citing this view rejects it, as does *Radak.* They favor the interpretation that the lentil stew, not money, .was the barter price of the birthright.

Sefer HaYashar [see also *Imrei Noam; Toldos Yitzchak*] records a tradition that this transaction included the sale to Jacob of Esau's right to be buried in the Cave of Machpelah.

34. וְיַעֲקֹב נָתַן לְעֵשָׂו — *Jacob gave* [to] *Esau.*

As noted above, this was either a ratification of the transaction, or it was the actual purchase price *(Radak).*

Although *Sforno* maintains that an unspecified amount of money eventually passed hands, and that the *bread and lentil stew* was *not* the purchase price, he suggests that the stew, or the pot containing it was the legal instrument of קִנְיַן חֲלִיפִין, 'acquisition by symbolic barter,' reminiscent of *Ruth* 4:7. [For according to *halachah,* whenever a transaction occurs, the transaction may be consummated — even before money changes hands — by a symbolic act signifying acquisition by the new owner. An example of this is חֲלִיפִין, *exchange.* In more recent times it came to be called, קִנְיַן סוּדָר, lit. *'acquisition of a cloth'* i.e. the symbolic grasping of a garment by both parties to the transaction.]

[Although not entirely analogous to our case the *halachah Sforno* cites is codified by *Rambam* in *Hilchos Mechirah* 5:5: 'Real Estate ... and movables may be acquired by symbolic barter. This act is called *Kinyan.* The fundamental principal of this mode of acquisition is that the transferee should give the transferor an article of some utility no matter how small its value and say to him, "Acquire this article in exchange for the yard ... you sold me for so much and so much." If this is done, then when the vendor lifts the article

1. The Torah, by mentioning that *he sold his birthright to Jacob* thereby testifies to the validity of the sale *(Or HaChaim).*

The *Midrash* notes that Esau brought in with him group of ruffians. They jeered at Jacob saying, 'Let's eat his food and mock at him!' As if the entire transaction had been in jest. But the Holy One, Blessed be He, consented to the sale, as it is written [*Exod.* 4:22]: *Thus says* HASHEM, *Israel* [i.e. Jacob] *is my first born.*

25 34 *him and sold his birthright to Jacob.* [34] *Jacob gave*
Esau bread and lentil stew, and he ate and drank, got
up and left. Thus, Esau spurned the birthright.

and takes possession of it, the purchaser acquires title to the article ... though he has not paid its price. Then neither party may renege.']

Hirsch notes the use of the pluperfect וְיַעֲקֹב נָתַן which he interprets *Jacob had given* instead of the usual form וַיִּתֵּן יַעֲקֹב, *and Jacob gave,* which is the usual sequential form [compare for example וַיֵּדַע הָאָדָם, Adam *had* known *Gen.* 4:1]. This implies, he explains, that Jacob *had already fed Esau earlier,* and did not force him to sell before giving him food.

HaKsav V'haKaballah interprets similarly and amplifies that immediately upon hearing Esau's request for food Jacob supplied him to his heart's content. After gluttonously stuffing himself, Esau made contemptuous remarks about the birthright, and Jacob seized the opportunity of asking him to sell it to him.

לֶחֶם וּנְזִיד עֲדָשִׁים — *Bread and lentil stew.*

Not until here does the Torah reveal what it was that Jacob was cooking; why was the *lentil* stew not mentioned earlier in *v.* 29? *R' Bachya* comments that mention of the type of food is left for after the sale to emphasize the grossness of Esau. For what did he give up his precious birthright — for a pot of beans!

וַיֹּאכַל וַיֵּשְׁתְּ וַיָּקָם וַיֵּלַךְ — [*And*] *he* [i.e. Esau] *ate and drank,* [and] *got up and left.*

I.e. he returned to the outdoors to pursue his hunting career *(Radak).*

— After eating and drinking he returned to his hunt which was the cause of despising the birthright. Thus acts the fool: he eats and drinks to fulfill his passing desire, not giving a care for the future *(Ramban).*

[The rapid succession of verbs accurately depicts Esau's gluttonous character. Decency would have called for him to sit and eat calmly, but Esau had no time or patience for the amenities. He wolfed down his food and drink, and left abruptly as soon as he had satisfied his ravenous appetite.]

וַיִּבֶז עֵשָׂו אֶת הַבְּכֹרָה — *Thus, Esau spurned the birthright.*

Thus the Torah itself testifies to Esau's wickedness in despising the Service of the Omnipresent! *(Rashi).*

[He forfeited the Spiritual in exchange for transitory physical gratification.][1]

For even after he had eaten he did not regret the sale *(Radak).*

According to *Rashbam,* since Esau *eventually* regretted his action, however, complaining that Jacob had taken his birthright [27:36] the Torah makes it a point to record his folly at *this stage* in spurning the

1. As *Rashi* comments to *v.*32 (see above). Esau discarded the birthright because he feared the death penalties associated with it. If so, he stood in awe of its responsiblities — why does the Torah accuse him of 'despising' it.

Harav Moshe Feinstein derives from this that one must accept the responsibility of serving God even though he may be subjected to danger and calumny. For one to refuse His service to avoid such burdens is equivalent to despising His Torah.

א וַיְהִי רָעָב בָּאָרֶץ מִלְּבַד הָרָעָב הָרִאשׁוֹן
אֲשֶׁר הָיָה בִּימֵי אַבְרָהָם וַיֵּלֶךְ יִצְחָק אֶל־
ב אֲבִימֶלֶךְ מֶלֶךְ־פְּלִשְׁתִּים גְּרָרָה׃ וַיֵּרָא

birthright which was of no value in his eyes.

Even after the sale, however, Esau considered the birthright unworthy of the price they agreed upon. Therefore the Torah emphasized that Esau eas not victimized since the birthright had little value in his eyes *(Sforno)*.

The intent is that Esau had *always* spurned the birthright and held it in little esteem; therefore Jacob took it from him! *Rav Yehudah HaChassid* [in *Sefer Chassidim*] notes that 'from this incident you may learn that if a Torah Scroll or some other *mitzvah* comes into the hands of a wicked person, it is permitted for a righteous person to scheme in order to acquire it *(Da'as Zekeinim)*.

HaKsav V'haKaballah observes that Jacob was interested only in the *spiritual* aspects of the birthright, not the physical benefit. We see,therefore, that Jacob always remained subservient to Esau, referring to him as *my lord*, and to himself as *your servant, Jacob*.

As *Hirsch* notes, we find Jacob deriving no material advantage whatever from the sale. To the contrary, in succeeding chapters, we find Esau growing powerful and mighty while Jacob became an exiled shepherd toiling for Laban. Jacob's desire was solely for the spiritual benefits of the birthright. That relationship between the brothers has been acted out in succeeding generations. Esau lusted for material wealth which Jacob gladly surrendered in return for spiritual growth.

XXVI

1. Isaac Becomes an Alien.

וַיְהִי רָעָב בָּאָרֶץ — [And] *there was a famine in the land.*

In *the* land *par excellence* — Canaan — *Eretz Yisrael* [*Rashi* to 12:10].

[As noted in the *commentary* to 12:10, Canaan was almost entirely dependent on an annual rainfall for its fertility. As seen many times throughout Scriptures, famine was no infrequent occurrence there.]

מִלְּבַד ... בִּימֵי אַבְרָהָם — *Aside from the first* [or *primary*] *famine that was in the days of Abraham* [as related in 12:10ff].

Ramban notes that the term הָרָעָב הָרִאשׁוֹן, *the first famine*, might suggest that the famine in Abraham's time was indeed the *first* since Creation and therefore the Torah uses it as a reference point.

Ramban goes on to suggest that the Torah uses the famine as a focal point because it left an indellible impression on men's minds due to Abraham's experience in Egypt and the greatness he achieved as a result. For this reason Isaac wished to emulate his father by going to Egypt.[1]

R' Bachya questions *Ramban*'s primary interpretation that Ab-

1. *Midrash Lekach Tov* and the commentators observe how this is yet another example of the great similarities between the lives of Abraham and Isaac ... There was a famine in the life of Abraham, and in that of Isaac.

This famine was far more severe than that in Abraham's time. But there was a far more

26
1 There was a famine in the land, aside from the first famine that was in the days of Abraham. And Isaac went to Abimelech king of the Philistines, to Gerar.

raham's famine was literally the *first* since Creation, since this view is contradicted by the *Midrash* that there were ten famines in the world, the *first* having occurred in the days of Adam [implied in 3:17]; another one in the days of Lamech [implied in 5:29]; in the days of Abraham [12:8]; Isaac [here]; Jacob [45:6]; in the days of the Judges [*Ruth* 1:1]; David [*II Samuel* 21:1]; Elijah [*I Kings* 17:1]; Elisha [II Kings 6:25]; and the spiritual famine which will occur in Messianic times [*Amos* 8:11].

R' Bachya proceeds to agree with *Ramban*'s implication that the word רִאשׁוֹן should be rendered in the *relative* sense: the *earlier* famine. Everyone remembered how Abraham descended to Egypt then, and the great honor God did him.

[*Harav Chavel* in his annotations to *R' Bachya* defends *Ramban*'s primary interpretation by citing *Pirkei d'Rabbi Eliezer* 26 that the famine in Abraham's time was indeed the *first* since Creation. *Radal ad. loc.* points out that while the *PdRE* follows in this case the more literal sense of our verse, it differs from the *Midrash Rabbah* (cited by *R' Bachya* that the famine in Abraham's time was actually the *third* since Creation). It is for this reason, *Harav Chavel* concludes, that *Ramban*, cognizant of the conflicting *Midrashim*, used the equivocal term "*might* suggest."]

Radak [apparently interpreting הָרָעָב הָרִאשׁוֹן in our context to mean *the preceding famine*] notes that the earlier famine in Abraham's days is referred to since there had been no famine since then.

וַיֵּלֶךְ יִצְחָק אֶל אֲבִימֶלֶךְ ... — *And Isaac went to Abimelech King of [the] Philistines.*

Following 24:62, Isaac had lived in *the south country* during Abraham's lifetime. This designation is variously interpreted by the commentators there to refer either to the area near the *Be'er LaChai Ro'i*, or Hebron. *After* Abraham's death, however, Isaac is clearly described in 25:11 as having settled near *Be'er LaChai Ro'i* which, in 16:14 is identified as being *between Kadesh and Bered*, about fifty miles south of Beersheba. Most consider this to be within the environs of Canaan, while others (most notably *Sforno*) hold that it was under Philistine sovereignty. As noted belowe, it becomes clear from the following episode that even Gerar, captial of Philistia, was considered part of the Land to be inherited by the Children of Israel since, as evidenced by God's command in *v.*3, living there was considered to

significant difference between them: the first famine was sent to test Abraham [see *comm.* to 12:8], and this famine was to demonstrate God's omniscient providence to Isaac.

Further, it manifested His compassionate kindness in that He does not forsake the righteous during a famine nor does He forsake their children, as it is written [*Psalms* 37:25] *I have not seen a righteous man forsaken, with his children begging for bread* [see *comm.* to ArtScroll *Tehillim* ad loc.] Instead, when a famine broke out in *Eretz Yisrael*, God made ample provision for Isaac and his family *(Tanchuma).*

Additionally, the *Midrash* notes that famines come only in the days of mighty men who can withstand them.

be still with the boundaries of *Eretz Yisrael*. [See also *footnote* on p. 736.]

אֲבִימֶלֶךְ – *Abimelech.*

Either this was the same king as in the time of Abraham [Chapter 20], or this was the dynastic name of the Philistine monarchy [as Pharaoh was of the Egyptian monarchs], for in David's time, the Philistine king was also called Abimelech [see *Psalms* 34:1] *(Ramban).*

As evidenced from *Onkelos'* interpretation of *v.* 28, this was the son of the Abimelech who reigned in the days of Abraham.

גְּרָרָה – *To Gerar.*

The capital city of the Philistines *(Rashi* to 21:32).

Though under separate sovereignty, Gerar was considered part of Canaan, as noted [for it is one of the lands God promised him in *v.* 3] *(Radak).*

[See also *comm.* to 20:2, and *footnote* on page 720.]

⊲§ Why did Isaac go to Abimelech in Gerar?

□ According to *Rashbam*, the verse implies that Isaac followed the earlier example of Abraham in going to Egypt to escape the famine. [As noted above to 12:10, Egypt was not affected by drought because it was irrigated by the Nile.] The shortest route to Egypt was through Philistia [see *Exodus* 13:17]. While Isaac was there en route to Egypt, God appeared to him, and commanded him not to leave *Eretz Yisrael* [*v.* 2].

[The above would assume that Gerar was located *south*west of *Be'er LaChai Ro'i*. Most commentators indeed subscribe to this view. (See *Chizkuni* further). If, however, as noted in the *comm.* to 20:2 (page 720) Gerar was to the *north*west of that area, then the circuitous route through Philistia would certainly not have been the shortest route to Egypt. Perhaps this prompted *Ramban* to suggest [see next comment] that Isaac had a specific reason for taking the detour to Abimelech. Or *Ramban* may also have reasoned that had Isaac merely been *passing through the land,* the verse need not have told us that he went specifically *to Abimelech.*]

□ Until commanded not to do so by God, it was Isaac's intention to follow in his father's footsteps and go to *Egypt*. However, he first went to Abimelech, his father's ally, to see [in the light of the mutual covenant he had with his father – extending to *son and grandson* (see 21:23) *(Radak)*] whether special arrangements could be made during the duration of the famine to avert the necessity of going down to Egypt *(Ramban).*

[Apparently *Ramban* and *Radak* are of the opinion that Abimelech's land was not affected by the famine in Canaan. Most commentators, however, hold that Philistia, too, *was* suffering famine.]

Ramban perceives great symbolic significance to Isaac's sojourn to Philistia, see *footnote.*[1]

□ In 15:13, it had been foretold to Abraham that his *offspring shall be aliens in a land not their own ... four hundred years.* As explained

1. **The seeds of the Babylonian Exile**
In a fundamental exposition, *Ramban* explained in his *commentary* to 12:10 [cited in *footnote*, page 436] that כָּל מַה שֶּׁאֵירַע לְאָבוֹת סִימָן לְבָנִים, every event in the lives of the Patriarchs symbolically presaged events in the future of their children.

26 2 *HASHEM appeared to him and said, "Do not*
2 *descend to Egypt. Dwell in the land that I shall in-*

by the commentators there, it was with the birth of Isaac that this period of גֵרוּת, *sojourning, alien-status,* would begin.

Apparently, this prophecy had been told to Isaac, and *Chizkuni, Alshich* and *Malbim* hold that his prophetic knowledge that he was to initiate an alien-status ending in Eyptian servitude convinced Isaac that the famine was a sign that the period of exile was now to begin.

He therefore set out for Egypt via the land of his father's compatriot, Abimelech.

There God appeared to him and told him that, contrary to what he thought, he should *not go down to Egypt.* Rather גוּר בָּאָרֶץ הַזֹּאת, *sojourn in this land;* the alien-status foretold to Abraham could be accounted from his residence as a foreigner in Philistia. He should not be concerned about the famine affecting that country as well, since God's Providence would be with him and grant him abundance amidst the famine.

☐ *Sforno* [who apparently holds that Isaac had already been living under Abimelech's sovereignty, and that Philistia, too, was affected by the famine] suggests that Isaac now appeared before Abimelech to request permission to leave for Egypt [which, as noted above, was irrigated by the Nile and not effected by droughts.]

2. וַיֵּרָא אֵלָיו ה׳ — [*And*] HASHEM *appeared to him* [i.e. *Isaac*].

— In a prophetic manner *(Ibn Ezra* to 12:7).

Hirsch in 12:7 renders וַיֵּרָא ה׳: *And* HASHEM *made Himself visible.* For implications of this emphasis on *visibility* see his comment cited there.

אַל תֵּרֵד מִצְרָיְמָה — *Do not descend to Egypt.*

For such had indeed been Isaac's intent following, as he was, the example set by his father, to go down to Egypt in time of the famine. [see *v.* 1 for various reasons he chose Egypt as his destination.] God ac-

Ramban accordingly explains here that just as Abraham's forced descent in the face of the famine portended his descendant's exile to Egypt [see *footnote* on page 442], so did Isaac's forced descent to the land of Abimelech — a land in which his father resided [see *footnote* on page 736] — portend the Babylonian exile which was also, in the ancestral land of Ur Kasdim. Abraham's descent to Gerar, by contrast, was not symbolic since it was not *forced* by famine; he went on his own volition.

Ramban observes that the other parallels between Isaac's experience with the Philistines, and the Babylonian Exile are striking:

Isaac descended there because of famine / they were exiled to Babylon *because of the fever of famine* [*Lamentations* 5:10];

Isaac's wife was not taken; he was mainly subject to fear / in Babylonia they were not oppressed and to the contrary their leaders rose to political eminence;

Abimelech vacillated: first issuing a protective decree [*v.*11], then regretting it and expelling them [*v.*16], followed by ultimately returning to make a covenant with Isaac [*vs.*25-31] / at first Israelite leaders were esteemed in Babylonia, whoever wished to, was permitted return — with the help of the governors — to build the Temple [*Ezra* 1:3], work on the Temple was halted for a period of time [see *Ezra* 4:24 and *Daniel* 7:12], and the ultimately, permission to build the House of God was restored.

ג שְׁכֹ֣ן בָּאָ֔רֶץ אֲשֶׁ֖ר אֹמַ֥ר אֵלֶֽיךָ׃ גּ֚וּר בָּאָ֣רֶץ
הַזֹּ֔את וְאֶהְיֶ֥ה עִמְּךָ֖ וַאֲבָרְכֶ֑ךָּ כִּֽי־לְךָ֣
וּֽלְזַרְעֲךָ֗ אֶתֵּן֙ אֶת־כָּל־הָֽאֲרָצֹ֣ת הָאֵ֔ל
וַהֲקִֽמֹתִי֙ אֶת־הַשְּׁבֻעָ֔ה אֲשֶׁ֥ר נִשְׁבַּ֖עְתִּי

cordingly said to him: *'Do not go down to Egypt* for you are an עוֹלָה תְּמִימָה, *an unblemished offering,* and [residence] outside the Land does not befit you' *(Rashi).*

I.e., [having been consecrated as an offering to God on the altar at the *Akeidah*], Isaac was compared to a perfect offering without a blemish. Just as an offering becomes unfit if it passes beyond the Temple enclosures [even if it is later returned *(Mizrachi)*] so would Isaac become 'unfit' if he left the environs of the Land *(Midrash).*

שְׁכֹן בָּאָרֶץ אֲשֶׁר אֹמַר אֵלֶיךָ — *Dwell in the land that I shall indicate* [lit. *say*] *to you.*

— That is, as a general rule establish residence throughout your life only in those places that *I shall indicate to you from time to time (Ramban).* [I.e. do not take into your own hands the right to decide where to go, to escape famine; rely on My Providence to direct you.]

In an alternate interpretation, *Ramban* suggests that this Divine charge came to Isaac earlier. Even before Isaac left his home God cautioned him against going to Egypt, and instead commanded him to *dwell in the land* — Canaan — which comprised many lands and peoples, and travel about until he reached *the land which God would indicate to him.* (This paralleled God's charge to Abraham, when he commanded him to take Isaac and *go to the land I shall indicate to you.* See *comm.* to 22:2). When he reached Gerar, God told him to *stay there a while.* [Thus, *v.* 2 is to be interpreted in the past perfect: HASHEM had *appeared to Isaac* — even before he left home because of the famine. There was, accordingly, a lapse in time between verses 2 and 3.]

[God does not immediately tell the righteous but holds them in suspense — even if but for a short while — to instill reliance upon Him and thereby increase their reward. See 12:1 and 22:2.]

Sforno interprets: Erect your shepherd's huts [שְׁכֹן from מִשְׁכָּנוֹת, *huts*] in the very place that I will tell you to sojourn, and do not fear lack of pasture.

The *Midrash* interprets the connotation of שְׁכֹן [*dwell*] to be: Cause the *Shechinah* to reside in the Land.

3. גּוּר בָּאָרֶץ הַזֹּאת — *Sojourn* [i.e., *be an alien*] *in this land.*

Following *Ramban's* primary interpretation, God said: 'I will indicate to you from time to time where to establish residence, *but for the time being* גּוּר בָּאָרֶץ הַזֹּאת, *stay awhile* [lit. *sojourn*] *in this land.'*

— And [regarding My command that you do not leave the Holy Land], this land is considered part of Canaan *(Sforno).*

וְאֶהְיֶה עִמְּךָ וַאֲבָרְכֶךָּ — *I will be with you and* [*I will*] *bless you.*

Although the land of Canaan is suffering famine *I will be with you* and assure that you do not lack pasture, *and I will bless you* with wealth and possessions *(Sforno).*

The expression *I will be with you,* is echoed often throughout Scripture and said also to Jacob (28:15); to Moses (*Exod.* 3:12); and Joshua (*Josh.* 1:5) and in different form to Abraham (15:1). All are explicit affirmations of Providence

26 *dicate to you.*[3] *Sojourn in this land and I will be with*
3 *you and bless you; for to you and your offspring will*
I give all these lands and establish the oath that I
swore to Abraham your father:

watching over the details of their various activities according to the measure of their perfection *(Rambam, Moreh Nevuchim* 3:18).

Ha'amek Davar renders: *I will be with you* — to save you from Abimelech's enmity; *and will bless you — with abundant crops.*

כִּי לְךָ — *For to you ...*

God proceeds to tell Isaac *why* He is ordering him to sojourn in Philistia rather than Egypt: כִּי לְךָ וּלְזַרְעֲךָ אֶתֵּן אֶת כָּל הָאֲרָצֹת הָאֵל, *because to you and to your offspring will I give all these lands.* You must establish your presence there and show your love for the land which is inherently yours and your offspring's *(Alshich; Haamek Davar).*

[Compare God's direcctive to Abraham in 13:17: קוּם הִתְהַלֵּךְ בָּאָרֶץ, *Arise, walk about the Land!* which, as explained by *Ramban* there, denotes taking possession of the gift. See *Sforno* end of this verse.]

וּלְזַרְעֲךָ — *And to your offspring.*

I.e. to your offspring through Jacob *(Radak).*

To *your* offspring, and not to Ishmael's because only you are counted as Abraham's son *(Chizkuni).*

אֶתֵּן־אֶת־כָּל־הָאֲרָצֹת הָאֵל — *I will give all these lands* [הָאֵל = הָאֵלֶּה, *these (Rashi).*] Philistia is included among these promised lands *(Ramban; Chizkuni; Or HaChaim).*[1]

And since this land is included in the Promised Land, your remaining here does not constitute a forbidden departure from the Holy Land *(Akeidas Yitzchak).*

I will give you the potential and abundance of *all of* these lands put together; so much will the produce of *Eretz Yisrael* be blessed *(Haamek Davar).*

וַהֲקִמֹתִי אֶת הַשְּׁבֻעָה אֲשֶׁר נִשְׁבַּעְתִּי לְאַבְרָהָם אָבִיךָ — *And [I will] establish the oath that I swore to Abraham your father.*

[As the following verse outlines, the oath referred to was made to Abraham on various occasions.]

The word וַהֲקִמֹתִי could mean either *I will fulfill* or *I will establish.* Our translation, *establish,* follows

1. The *Midrash* to 15:21 comments that, 'The Holy One, Blessed be He, originally contemplated giving Israel possession of ten peoples [see listing in 15:21] but He gave them only seven ... Edom, Moab and Ammon being the three nations that were not given them ... Those three will be inherited by Israel in the days of the Messiah.'

The *Midrash* to our verse similarly deduces this from the fact that the word הָאֵלֶּה in the phrase *these lands* is spelled in the abbreviated form הָאֵל. This abbreviation, the *Midrash* notes, implies a limitation: I will give you only *part* of the lands; the rest I will give you in the days of the Messiah.

HaKsav V'haKaballah suggests that the spelling הָאֵל alludes to the majesty of the Land. The word הָאֵל is Scripturally used to mean *strength* as in אֵילֵי הָאָרֶץ, *the mighty of the Land (Ezekiel* 17:13). Thus, on our verse, הָאֲרָצֹת הָאֵל would mean *these great and majestic lands.*

ד לְאַבְרָהָם אָבִיךָ: וְהִרְבֵּיתִי אֶת־זַרְעֲךָ
כְּכוֹכְבֵי הַשָּׁמַיִם וְנָתַתִּי לְזַרְעֲךָ אֵת כָּל־
הָאֲרָצֹת הָאֵל וְהִתְבָּרְכוּ בְזַרְעֲךָ כֹּל גּוֹיֵי

Ramban who maintains that it would be superfluous for God to assure Isaac that he would fulfill the *unambiguous* and *unconditional* oath he had already made to Abraham, for *God is not a man that He should regret* [*I Samuel* 15:29. See *Ramban* cited to 15:26.] Furthermore, in any event, Abraham had no offspring other then Isaac upon whom a covenant had been established with God. This is unlike the case of Jacob where (35:12) God did have to give an *assurance* that the Abrahamitic oath would be fulfilled in *Jacob* and not in Esau.

Since the Torah often refers to oaths made to Abraham, Isaac, and Jacob [*Exodus* 32:13 and *Deut.* 34:4] and we find no other oath made exclusively to Isaac, *Ramban* concludes that this phrase denotes a *fresh oath* with Isaac, since it was God's desire *to establish a separate oath with each of the Patriarchs individually* to demonstrate each one's worthiness to have the covenant made with him alone. For though the previous oath suffices, it is an additional benefit to their descendants that each Patriach's merit combines with that of the other two. Thus, it is to this distinction that God refers when He says [*Lev. 26:42*]: *I will remember My covenant wirth Jacob, and also My covenant with Isaac, and also My covenant with Abraham will I remember; and the Land will I also remember.*

Sforno comments: The reason I commanded you: *sojourn in this land and I will grant you goodness* is that I will thereby be fulfilling the covenant I made with Abraham to give him and his offspring this Land. By dwelling in it you will establish your right to it as a heritage for your descendants.

4. וְהִרְבֵּיתִי אֶת זַרְעֲךָ כְּכוֹכְבֵי הַשָּׁמַיִם — [*And*] *I will increase your offspring like the stars of the heavens.*

[The middle of this verse, if interpreted as an *additional blessing to Isaac,* appears to repeat verse 3. Therefore, it seems proper, as reflected in the Translation, to interpret verse 4, not as an additional blessing to *Isaac* but as clarifying *what* promise was made to *Abraham* on various occasions, as if verses 3 and 4 were connected by the word לֵאמֹר, *saying* or *namely.* The sense then is '... *that I swore to Abraham your father* by saying to him '*I will increase your offspring,* etc.]

[On this parallel Abrahamitic promise see 22:17 *I will increase your offspring like the stars of the heavens.* See also *comm.* to 13:16 and 15:5.]

Abarbanel suggests that this verse amplifies the previous one, the implication being: Lest you wonder how as a small number of people like your family will be able to take possession of *all these lands,* know that first, *I will increase your offspring like the stars of the*

26
4 [4] *'I will increase your offspring*
like the stars of the heavens;
and will give to your offspring all these lands;
and all the nations of the earth
shall bless themselves by your offspring.'

heavens and *then I will give to your offspring all these lands.*[1]

וְנָתַתִּי לְזַרְעֲךָ אֵת כָּל־הָאֲרָצֹת הָאֵל — *And I will give* [*to*] *your offspring all these lands.*

[Cf. promise to Abraham in 13:15: *For all the land that you see, to you will I give it, and to your descendants forever.* Compare also the additional promises of the land in 12:7; 13:6, 9; 15:7, 18; and 24:7.]

In using the term לְזַרְעֲךָ, *to your offspring,* God alluded to His promise to Abraham in 21:12 where He declared that only *part* of Isaac's offspring would be considered offspring of Abraham to qualify for the heritage of the land. Thus the descendants of both Ishmael and Esau were excluded. [See *footnote* to page 758] *(Or HaChaim).*

וְהִתְבָּרְכוּ בְזַרְעֲךָ כֹּל גּוֹיֵי הָאָרֶץ — *And all the nations of the earth shall bless themselves by your offspring.*

[This is repeated verbatim from 22:18; see *comm.* there.]

Throughout Scripture this phrase means that a man will bless his son by saying, 'May your offspring be like Isaac's! The source for this idea is 47:20 בְּךָ יְבָרֵךְ יִשְׂרָאֵל, *By you shall Israel bless their children saying, 'May God make you like Ephraim and Manasseh.* Conversely, in the case of a curse, the interpretation is similar. The verse [*Numbers* 5:27]: וְהָיְתָה הָאִשָּׁה לְאָלָה, *The woman shall become a curse* means: One who wishes to curse his enemy will say, 'Be like that woman!' *(Rashi).*

[Compare *commentary* to וֶהְיֵה בְּרָכָה in 12:2 and וְנִבְרְכוּ in 12:3 and 18:18.]

God was now also intimating that the blessing to Abraham that all the nations of the earth will bless themselves by his offspring [22:18] would now be realized in *Isaac himelf.* It was later reiterated to Jacob [28:14] *(Ramban).*

In applying this blessing to the context of the episode, *Ha'amek Davar* explains the intent as: All the nations of the earth will bless themselves by wishing to enjoy a comparable success with their crops as will be enjoyed by your descendants, Israel.

1. *Harav David Feinstein* notes in this context the promises made to the Patriarchs, discussed in *Shabbos* 118b, and *Exodus* 23:29, 30 where God tells the Israelites that, *I will not drive them* [i.e. the natives of all the Canaanite territories] *out before you in a single year lest the land become desolate* [because you are too few to occupy it] *and the wild beasts multiply upon you; I will drive them out before you little by little, until you have increased and* [are ready to] *possess the land.*

Thus, Israel will occupy increasingly larger portions of the land as its population grows and becomes better able to absorb the new territories. This is the sense of verse 4: As I increase your offspring, I will give you more and more of these lands.

ה הָאָֽרֶץ׃ עֵ֚קֶב אֲשֶׁר־שָׁמַ֥ע אַבְרָהָ֖ם בְּקֹלִ֑י
וַיִּשְׁמֹר֙ מִשְׁמַרְתִּ֔י מִצְוֺתַ֖י חֻקּוֹתַ֥י וְתוֹרֹתָֽי׃

5. עֵקֶב אֲשֶׁר שָׁמַע אַבְרָהָם — *Because* [*lit. as a result of that*] *Abraham obeyed* [lit. *listened to*].

Do not think that all of these blessings are granted only to induce you not to descend to Egypt. They were already *decreed in Abraham's days as the consequence of one thing:* עֵקֶב אֲשֶׁר שָׁמַע אַבְרָהָם, *As a result of Abraham's having listened,* etc. *(Abarbanel).*

The etymological connotation of עֵקֶב [derived from עָקֵב, *heel*] 'on the heels of' as denoting *circular course of events; a direct result of a prior cause,* hence *because,* in *consequence of,* has been discussed in the commentary to 22:18.

R' Chaninah and *R' Yochanan* both said: Abraham was forty-eight years old when he recognized his Creator. R'Levi said in the name of Resh Lakish: He was *three* years old, for Abraham listened to the voice of his Creator to keep His charge [for as many years as] the numerical value of *Ekev* [עֵקֶב=172] while altogether he lived 175 years *(Midrash).*[1]

בְּקֹלִי — *To* [lit. *in*] *My voice.*

— When I tested him *(Rashi);* he was even prepared to slaughter his only son *(Radak).*

As explained many times previously, the phrase שָׁמַע בְּקֹל does not mean merely that someone *heeded an injunction,* but that he *delved into the intent of the words (Haamek Davar).*

וַיִּשְׁמֹר מִשְׁמַרְתִּי — [*And*] *safeguarded My Ordinances* [*lit. my guard* — i.e. things I wished to you to *safeguard.*]

This refers to *Rabbinic enactments* which serve as barriers against infringement of Biblical prohibitions, for example the Rabbinic extensions to the forbidden degrees of consanguinity [e.g., the Torah forbids one to marry his mother; the ordinance forbids his mother's mother], and the enactments forbidding certain acts on Sabbath *(Rashi)* [see *Yevamos* 21a].

[*Rashi* thus sees מִשְׁמַרְתִּי, lit. my *ordinances* as referring to those 'protections' and 'restrictive measures' designed to *safeguard* God's original precepts. See *Lev.* 18:30 as interpreted in *Yevamos* 21a.]

Ibn Ezra in the literal sense perceives מִשְׁמַרְתִּי, as a general term defined further in the verse by: *commandments, decrees, and Torahs.*

Hirsch likewise explains it as a general term stating our obligation toward the Torah transmitted to us from God. It is a treasure which we are to *guard* and use according to the Will of its Owner. This involves two duties: (1) the positive one of study and care to fulfill its obligations and precepts; (2) to institute such protective ordinances as are necessary and desirable to prevent the violation of its laws.

1. [Comp. the slightly differing versions in *Nedarim* 32b; *Bamidbar Rabbah* 18:21; *Rambam, Hilchos Avodah Zarah* 1:2; and see *comm.* to 11:2 that Abraham was 48 years old at the Dispersion, and had already recognized his Creator. One version, cited in *Torah Sheleimah* does not interpret עֵקֶב by its numerical equivalent but by its meaning of *heel* interpreting that Abraham recognized his Creator from the moment he was able to lift his עָקֵב, *heel,* off the ground.

The differing opinions should be understood not as conflict, but as a reference to differing degrees of recognition. For example, Abraham recognized the *existence* of God at the age of three, but surely to a far lesser degree than he did at the age of forty-eight.]

26
5

⁵ Because Abraham obeyed My voice, and safeguarded My Ordinances, My Commandments, My Decrees, and My Torahs."

מִצְוֹתָי — *My Commandments.*

Such as those laws which the moral sense would have enacted even if they were not written in the Torah, for example the prohibitions against theft and murder *(Rashi)* [see *Yoma* 67b.]

חֻקּוֹתַי — *My Decrees.*

Laws which our Evil Inclinations and heathen nations would promptly disagree with, for example the prohibition against eating swine's flesh, and the wearing of *shaatnez* [garments made of a mixture of linen and wool] — laws for which reason can provide no explanation, and which are thus, as it were, *royal decrees* enacted on His subjects *(Rashi).*

— [See *comm.* to *Lev.* 18:4 and *Yoma* 67b.]

According to *Radak* חֻקּוֹתַי refers even to those *Noachide* laws for which their logical reason has not been made apparent except to the very wise: the prohibition against breeding mixed species of cattle, grafting together different species of trees, or eating a limb torn from a live animal.

וְתוֹרֹתָי — *And My Torahs* [or: *Teachings.*]

The plural number indicates [both the Written Torah and] the Oral Torah which includes those rules and interpretations transmitted to Moses at Sinai *(Rashi).*

[The word *Torah* is usually derived from ירה, *teaching.*]

In a novel interpretation, *Hirsch* derives Torah from הרה, *conceive.* Just as the embryo grows from a seed that is implanted at conception, so too, God's teachings plants a seed, so to speak, which develops within the recipient into even greater consciousness of good.

⇐§ To what extent the Patriarchs observed the Torah.

Ramban cites *Rashi's* interpretation which implies that Abraham fulfilled the Torah before it was revealed at Sinai. Indeed this is the opinion of the Sages [see *Yoma* 28b]: Our father Abraham kept the whole Torah before it was given ... even the law concerning עֵרוּב תַּבְשִׁילִין, [the Rabbinic provision through which it becomes permissible, under certain conditions, to prepare food on *Yom Tov* for use on a Sabbath which falls on the day after *Yom Tov*]. See also *Bereishis Rabbah* 95:2 which inteprets עֲגָלֹת, (lit. *wagons*) in 45:21 to refer to the Torah's chapter of *Eglah Arufah (Deut* 21:6) which Jacob expounded to Joseph; and *Bereishis Rabbah* 79:7 which says that Jacob was rewarded for observing the Sabbath. Thus it is clear that the Patriarchs knew and observed the Torah.

If so, *Ramban* continues, it is difficult to understand how Jacob erected a pillar upon which to bring sacrificial offerings [see 28:18] since such use of pillars is forbidden [*Deut.* 16:22], and how he married two sisters [prohibited in *Lev.* 18:18] ... and how [Moses' father] Amram married his aunt [*Exod.* 6:20], and how Moses erected twelve pillars for offerings [*ibid.* 24:4], when the Torah forbids all these things. How could such people violate explicit commandments if Abraham scrupulously transmitted his teachings to his children? [18:19].

Ramban explains that the consensus of Rabbinic opinion is that Abraham arrived at a knowledge of the *entire Torah*

ו־ז °וַיֵּשֶׁב יִצְחָק בִּגְרָר: וַיִּשְׁאֲלוּ אַנְשֵׁי
°שני הַמָּקוֹם לְאִשְׁתּוֹ וַיֹּאמֶר אֲחֹתִי הִוא כִּי

through Divine Inspiration and observed it voluntarily (כְּמִי שֶׁאֵינוֹ מְצוּוֶּה וְעוֹשֶׂה). Before the Torah was given, however, the Patriarchs observed the future commandments without exception only in *Eretz Yisrael* [see *Ramban* to *Lev.* 18:25]. This accounts for the marriages of Jacob and Amram which took place only outside of the Land.The erection of pillars was permitted in the time of the Patriarchs; they became prohibited only later when such forms of sacrificial service became particularly associated with idolatry [see *Sifre* to *Deut.* 16:22].That Joseph observed the the Sabbath in Egypt [(*Bereishis Rabbah* 92:4) although according to this premise he was not required to do so], was because of the Sabbath's great importance as the testimony to God's creation of the world *ex nihilo.* Joseph wished to instill this basic faith in his children and protect them from the idolatrous ways of the Egyptians. Jacob, too, observed even the Rabbinic minutiae of the Sabbath laws for the same reason.

Gur Aryeh, in a lengthy dissertation on 46:10, disagrees with *Ramban's* thesis that the Patriarchs observed the commandments *only* in *Eretz Yisrael. Gur Aryeh* offers several major points:

A. Just as God's Divine Inspiration informed the Patriarchs and their offspring of the future commandments, so, too, It informed them of instances when they were to marry close relations in order to give birth to children worthy to build the nation. Such marriages were not considered to be in violation of God's word because they were sanctioned by God Himself. Thus, even Jacob's marriage to two sisters was, in effect, in compliance with the Torah.

B. Prior to the giving of the Torah, different individuals were particularly suited to the observance of particular commandments. Thus, Abraham was unique in that he was suited to keep the entire Torah; the commandment of שְׁחִיטָה, *ritual slaughter,* was suited to Isaac (see *comm.* to 27:3); and the commandment of גִּיד הַנָּשֶׁה, *the thigh muscle on the hip-socket* [32:33] was given to Jacob. That Abraham kept all the commandments, therefore, is no indication that his descendants had to do the same before the Torah was given.

Furthermore, there is a fundamental difference between positive and negative commandments. The fulfillment of a positive commandment brings about a beneficial result in the universe. Therefore, even one who is not specifically instructed to do so is rewarded for its performance [such as women who listen to the *shofar* on *Rosh Hashanah*].

Observance of negative commandments, however, is commendable only because it signifies compliance with God's will. Prior to the giving of the Torah, God had not prohibited marriage to two sisters or to an aunt. Therefore, there was no reason for Jacob or Amram to refrain from such marriages especially since they knew that righteous children would ensue from them. Similarly, according to this thesis, the Patriarchs and their offspring were scrupulous in their observance of positive, but not of negative, commandments.

In accordance with its *plain* meaning, however, *Ramban* suggests that מִשְׁמַרְתִּי, *My charge,* refers to belief in the Unique Divine Name, i.e., Abraham believed in Him as the One God and safeguarded this belief. Thereby he differed from the idol worshipers and sought to teach this to others;

מִצְוֹתַי, *My commandments,* includes all that God had commanded him: to leave his home [12:1], sacrifice his son [22:1], and expel Hagar and her son [21:12];

חֻקּוֹתַי, *My ordinances,* to be gracious and merciful, to do justice and righteousness, and to command his chidren to do likewise;

תּוֹרֹתָי, *My teachings,* such as circumcision as well as all the מִצְוֹת בְּנֵי נֹחַ *Noachide Commandments.*

Rashbam — as do most commen-

[6] *So Isaac settled in Gerar.* [7] *When the men of the*
place asked about his wife, he said, "She is my

tators, with slight variations — interprets similarly, and notes that many of the interdictions against robbery, immorality, covetousness; the duty to establish legal courts of justice, to show hospitality to wayfarers, etc., were in force before the Torah was given, but were later separately and explicitly enjoined upon the Israelites who entered a covenant to observe them.

6. Isaac in Gerar.

וַיֵּשֶׁב יִצְחָק בִּגְרָר — *So* [lit. *and*] *Isaac settled in Gerar.*

— In fulfillment of God's command to him in *v.*3 *(Radak).*

For though Abimelech made no offers of assistance as Isaac had hoped he would, nevertheless Isaac trusted in God's promise and took up permanent residence there in Gerar *(Ha'amek Davar).*

7. וַיִּשְׁאֲלוּ אַנְשֵׁי הַמָּקוֹם לְאִשְׁתּוֹ — *When* [lit. *and*] *the men of the place asked about* [lit. *to*] *his wife.*

Abimelech, because of his covenant with Abraham, showed Isaac no malice. It was the *residents* who inquired out of curiosity about the identity of the woman he was with (*Ramban* to *v.*1).

That Rebecca was not taken to the king's palace as was Sarah is undoubtedly due to the many exhortations Abraham had given them about their mistreatment of strangers *(Radak;* see chapter 20).

The phrase אֶל אִשְׁתּוֹ, lit. *to his wife,* in this context means עַל אִשְׁתּוֹ, *concerning his wife.* Compare 20:2 אֶל שָׂרָה, *about Sarah;* 20:13 אִמְרִי לִי, *say of me (Rashi).*

Malbim interprets that the expression: וַיִּשְׁאֲלוּ...לְאִשְׁתּוֹ literally, asked *to* his wife, implies that they licentiously questioned Rebecca *directly* about her identity, and Isaac would interject out of fear, *'She is my sister.'*

וַיֹּאמֶר אֲחֹתִי הִוא — [*And*] *he said, 'She is my sister.'*

No mention is made in the Torah or *Midrashim* of Jacob and Esau during this episode.

Ramban observes that apparently the Philistines did not inquire about the children; they apparently assumed that the children were not Rebecca's.

Ramban, in expounding on the episode of Abraham in Egypt [12:11], suggests that from the time he had left Charan, Abraham *commonly* identified Sarah as his sister, because he knew they would often find themselves in strange and perhaps dangerous surroundings (20:13). The Torah mentioned this strategy only on the two occasions that something unusual happened. Isaac, on the other hand, felt secure in his own surroundings, and had no need for the ruse. Only when he came to the land of the Philistines did he adopt his father's plan.

According to *Midrash HaGadol,* however, Isaac resorted to this strategy only *after* the peeople of the place started asking about his wife and showing an interest in her. It was then that Isaac felt he should rely on his father's precaution.

[The rationale of resorting to such a strategy is fully discussed in the *footnote* on p. 721.]

Hirsch comments that Isaac's precaution was vindicated by the

יָרֵא לֵאמֹר אִשְׁתִּי פֶּן־יַהַרְגֻנִי אַנְשֵׁי
הַמָּקוֹם עַל־רִבְקָה כִּי־טוֹבַת מַרְאֶה הִוא׃
ח וַיְהִי כִּי־אָרְכוּ־לוֹ שָׁם הַיָּמִים וַיַּשְׁקֵף
אֲבִימֶלֶךְ מֶלֶךְ פְּלִשְׁתִּים בְּעַד הַחַלּוֹן
וַיַּרְא וְהִנֵּה יִצְחָק מְצַחֵק אֵת רִבְקָה
ט אִשְׁתּוֹ׃ וַיִּקְרָא אֲבִימֶלֶךְ לְיִצְחָק וַיֹּאמֶר
אַךְ הִנֵּה אִשְׁתְּךָ הִוא וְאֵיךְ אָמַרְתָּ אֲחֹתִי

fact that once the true relationship between himself and Rebecca became known, Abimelech found it necessary to protect them by a decree of the death penalty for any assault.

Unlike the case of Abraham and Sarah, [12:13] Isaac did not ask Rebecca to go along with his plan. As noted above, Rebecca was more subservient to her husband than any of the other Matriarchs and routinely went along with Isaac's decisions. [See *footnote* to 24:65] *(Ha'amek Davar).*

פֶּן־יַהַרְגֻנִי אַנְשֵׁי הַמָּקוֹם עַל רִבְקָה — [*For he thought*], *'Lest the men of the place kill me because of Rebecca.'*

It was their practice to spirit a wife away from her husband and murder him on some pretext (*Ramban* to 12:11).

[As Abraham explained to Abimelech nearly a century earlier (20:11): *There is but no fear of God in this place.* It would not be beyond them therefore to slay him because of his wife, for only the fear of God acts as a deterrent to unrestrained lust. Thus, although Abraham doubtless told Isaac of all that occurred, Isaac, too, could expect no safety in a place where there is no fear of God. This apparently motivated him to repeat the scenario, and resort to the same device.]

[On their rationale of murdering a husband to avoid the crime of adultery, see *comm.* to 12:12 s.v. וְהָרְגוּ. On the choice of deception *not* reflecting an abdication of responsiblity, see *comm.* to 12:13 s.v. לְמַעַן יִיטַב and וְחָיְתָה.]

The elliptic phrase *for he thought* is not in the Hebrew, but is implicit in the verse. This follows *Ibn Ezra* who cites a similar case in 41:52 which explains the reason for the name Joseph chose for his second son. There, a proper understanding of the expression: *he named Ephraim, for God has caused me* similarly demands that the phrase *he said* be implied, rendering: *he named Ephraim, for,* he said, *God has caused me.* [This interpretation is necessitated by the abrupt changes from first to third person.]

כִּי טוֹבַת מַרְאֶה הִוא — *For she was fair to look upon.*

In 24:16 she is described as *very* fair to look upon. Now she had already borne children and her beauty was not *as* pronounced *(Chizkuni).*

8. כִּי אָרְכוּ־לוֹ שָׁם הַיָּמִים — *As his days there lengthened* [i.e., when he had been there a long time].

And so, he ceased to be careful in concealing his true relationship to Rebecca thinking that since they did

26
8-9

sister," for he was afraid to say "my wife" — "Lest the men of the place kill me because of Rebecca for she is fair to look upon!"
8 *And it came to pass, as his days there lengthened that Abimelech king of the Philistines gazed down through the window and saw — behold! Isaac was jesting with his wife Rebecca.* 9 *Abimelech summoned Isaac and said, "But look! She is your wife! How could you say, 'She is my sister'?"*

not molest her all the while, he need no longer be apprehensive *(Rashi; Rashbam).*

וַיַּשְׁקֵף אֲבִימֶלֶךְ מֶלֶךְ פְּלִשְׁתִּים בְּעַד הַחַלּוֹן — *That* [lit. *and*] *Abimelech, king of the Philistines, gazed down through the window.*

I.e., he purposely gazed through the carelessly shuttered window of Isaac's dwelling *(Divrei David).*

Nachalas Yitzchak denies that the righteous Isaac could have carelessly left his window unshuttered while being intimate with his wife. Rather בְּעַד has the significance of *in front of* [see *Rashi* to 7:16] indicating that Abimelech gazed down *at* Isaac's window, and surmised from the fact that it was shuttered during the day, that the woman was not his sister.

[See *Rashi* to 18:16 who explains that the verb שקף, *gazing down,* throughout Scipture always denotes gazing for the purpose of bringing evil.]

Midrash HaGadol comments: Woe to the wicked who gaze only for immoral purposes. Scripture teaches us here that Abimelech would always take note of them in order to be able to gaze upon Rebecca.

וַיַּרְא וְהִנֵּה יִצְחָק מְצַחֵק אֵת רִבְקָה אִשְׁתּוֹ — *And saw* [*and*] *behold! Isaac was jesting with his wife Rebecca.*

All commentators agree that the term מְצַחֵק, *jesting* — which is the same term used of Ishmael in 21:9 — is, in this context (since Rebecca is specifically described as *his wife*), a euphemism for intimate relations *(Rashi)*; physical closeness *(Chizkuni)*; or at the very least undue familiarity which would be inappropriate between brother and sister *(Abarbanel).*

This does not suggest — even according to *Rashi*'s interpretation — that Abimelech actually *saw* them being intimate. Rather, Abimelech *perceived,* from observing them through the window that their relationship was the 'jesting' of a married couple *(HaKsav V'haKaballah).*

[This differs from *Nachalas Yitzchak* above.]

9. אַךְ הִנֵּה אִשְׁתְּךָ הִוא — *But, look!* [or: *behold!*] *She is your wife!*

She certainly is not your sister as you claimed! You 'jested' with her as one does not jest with a sister! *(Radak).*

הָוא וַיֹּאמֶר אֵלָיו יִצְחָק כִּי אָמַרְתִּי פֶּן־
י אָמוּת עָלֶיהָ: וַיֹּאמֶר אֲבִימֶלֶךְ מַה־זֹּאת
עָשִׂיתָ לָּנוּ כִּמְעַט שָׁכַב אַחַד הָעָם אֶת־
יא אִשְׁתֶּךָ וְהֵבֵאתָ עָלֵינוּ אָשָׁם: וַיְצַו
אֲבִימֶלֶךְ אֶת־כָּל־הָעָם לֵאמֹר הַנֹּגֵעַ
יב בָּאִישׁ הַזֶּה וּבְאִשְׁתּוֹ מוֹת יוּמָת: וַיִּזְרַע
יִצְחָק בָּאָרֶץ הַהִוא וַיִּמְצָא בַּשָּׁנָה הַהִוא

כִּי אָמַרְתִּי פֶּן אָמוּת עָלֶיהָ — *Because I was apprehensive* [lit. *said*] *that I would* [lit. *lest I*] *be killed* [following *Onkelos;* lit. *I would die*] *because of* [lit. *upon*] *her.*

— This was his tacit acknowledgment that she was, indeed, his wife *(Midrash HaGadol).*

Isaac could not offer the rationale given by Abraham: that she was indeed his 'sister' [see *comm.* to 20:12]; or that he always claimed her as her sister when he arrived at a new place and did not yet know the nature of the people. This, then was the only response he could honestly give to defend his action *(Malbim).*

10. מַה־זֹּאת עָשִׂיתָ לָּנוּ — *What is this that you have done to us?*

By telling us she was your sister!

And by lying because of a remote possibility of imagined danger *(Malbim).*

[Compare Abimelech's similar outburst to Abraham in 20:9.]

כִּמְעַט שָׁכַב אַחַד הָעָם אֶת אִשְׁתֶּךָ — *One of the people has nearly lain with your wife.*

Acording to *Rashi* and most commentators, this was an oblique reference to himself: *one of the people* — the most distinguished one, the king himself.

— And as king I would certainly not be expected first to seek your consent since it would be an honor for one to give his sister in marriage to the king *(Sforno).*

According to *Ramban* [in *v.*1], the implication was: 'I, Abimelech, did not touch her, and I exercised great restraint regarding her. However, *one of the men of the land* might easily have stumbled!'

— They would not have considered it sinful inasmuch as you identified her as your sister! *(Radak).*

וְהֵבֵאתָ עָלֵינוּ אָשָׁם — *And you would have brought guilt upon us!*

We would all have been punished on your account, for you are great and beloved of God *(Radak).*

— And a sin by the king would have repercussions on all his subjects *(Sforno).*

As happened when Sarah was taken and death was declared on my entire household [20:8] *(Malbim).*

For as *Midrash HaGadol* to 20:9 observes: A king to his country is like the heart to the body. If the heart ails, the entire body is ill. So, too, if the king sins, the country is sinful and may suffer destruction thereby.

[The Hebrew is in past tense: *you*

26
10-12

*Isaac said to him, "Because I was apprehensive
that I would be killed because of her."*
10 *Abimelech said, "What is this that you have
done to us? One of the people has nearly lain with
your wife, and you would have brought guilt upon
us!"* 11 *Abimelech then warned all the people saying,
"Whoever molests this man or his wife shall surely
die."*
12 *Isaac sowed in that land, and in that year he*

have brought, which, as reflected in the Translation, *Rashi* renders in the conditional past tense, rather than in the future]: had someone really lain with her, *you would have brought guilt upon us.*

Or, *Rashi* can be interpreted in the simple past tense: *If one has already lain with her, then you have brought guilt on us.*

Alshich interprets the phrase to mean: Had this sinfulness come about, וְהֵבֵאתָ, *then you would have had to bring* עָלֵינוּ, *on our behalf,* אָשָׁם, *a guilt offering,* [*because the sin would have been your responsiblity.*]

Chizkuni suggests that Isaac would have been obligated to sacrifice a guilt offering for having broken the covenant made with Abraham [21:24]: *That you will not deal falsely with me nor with my son nor with my grandson.*

11. וַיְצַו אֲבִימֶלֶךְ — *Abimelech then warned* [lit. *commanded*].

[Abimelech realized that no husband of a beautiful woman was safe in his land, and therefore found it necessary to assure Isaac's safety by issuing a *royal decree* on Isaac's behalf. What testimony this bears to vindicate Isaac's initial aprehensions when entering this Godless country!]

הַנֹּגֵעַ בָּאִישׁ הַזֶּה וּבְאִשְׁתּוֹ מוֹת יוּמָת — *Whoever molests* [lit. *touches*] *this man or* [lit. *and*] *his wife shall surely die.*

Whoever dares even throw a pebble at them will be put to death! *(Midrash).*

This exemplified God's beneficent Providence. Not only did Abimelech not become vindictive against Isaac for his deception, but he went so far as to issue this proclamation, to protect him and did not even expel him from his land *(Malbim).*

12. Isaac Prospers.

וַיִּזְרַע יִצְחָק בָּאָרֶץ הַהִוא — [*And*] *Isaac sowed in the land.*

In consonance with God's bidding that he remain *in that land* [he engaged in agriculture, a pursuit that requires residence for a significant length of time] *(Sforno).*

[The emphasis is on *that land*]: Isaac sowed in Gerar even though it was not as fertile as his former home, the part of Canaan which was occupied by the seven nations *(Rashi).*

וַיִּמְצָא בַּשָּׁנָה הַהִוא — *And in that year he reaped* [lit. *found*].

In *that* [relatively unfertile] *land* and *in that year* — a difficult year of

יג מֵאָה שְׁעָרִים וַיְבָרְכֵהוּ יהוה: °וַיִּגְדַּל
°שלישי הָאִישׁ וַיֵּלֶךְ הָלוֹךְ וְגָדֵל עַד כִּי־גָדַל מְאֹד:

drought. As the *Midrash* notes, the verses emphasizes the miraculous nature of Isaac's prosperity against two obstacles: the soil was hard, and the year was generally unfavorable *(Rashi).*[1]

— As the *Midrash* concludes: If Isaac's crop was so successful in that poor year, imagine how much more he would have prospered had the year been favorable!

מֵאָה שְׁעָרִים — *A hundredfold.*

I.e. a hundred times as much as the expected estimate. According to our Rabbis his estimation was made for the purpose of establishing the quantity due as מַעַשְׂרוֹת, *tithes (Rashi).*

This follows the *Midrash,* which gives two interpretations to the word שְׁעָרִים: *Measures* = a hundred *kor* [a *kor* being the largest measure]; and, from the verb שער: *Estimation* = a hundred times the initial estimate. [These comments are inspired by the use of the unusual term שער which implies a measure, instead of a more common term like פְּעָמִים.]

The *Midrash* asks, how could Isaac have estimated and counted his produce, is there not a dictum that: 'A blessing is not found in that which is weighed, measured, or counted, but only in that which is concealed from the eye'? [See *Bava Metzia* 42a.] — But, the *Midrash* answers, it was measured on account of the tithes [which of course is justified.]

According to the calculations in *Kesubos* 112a, in ordinary years one *se'ah* of seed sown in a *beth se'ah* [an area of fifty by fifty cubits] would yield five hundred *kor* [a measure equal to thirty *se'ahs.*] Therefore in the case of Isaac where the land yielded a *hundredfold,* the result was fifty thousand *kor* [100×500=50,000.]

That this verse refers to tithing is echoed by the *Midrash* and commentators. Isaac's subsequent blessing and prosperity is interpreted to be in merit of the tithes he gave. [See *Midrashim* cited below.] *Ramban* to *v.* 5 cites Isaac's tithing as another example that the Patriarchs observed the whole Torah before it was given.

In fact, *Rambam* in *Hilchos Melachim* 9:1 credits Isaac with *instituting* tithing. *Kessef Mishnah* there explains that although Abraham is already recorded in the Torah as having given a tenth to Malchizedek [14:20], he seems to have done so specifically on that occasion from the spoils, and not as a usual act of tithing which Isaac, indeed, instituted.

[But not all commentators agree with the *Kessef Mishnah's* interpretation of Abraham's tithing; see, for example, *Rashi* ad loc., who seems to imply that it was *common* in Abraham's time to tithe to a priest, and see gloss of *Raavad* who suggests that, accordingly, *Abraham* should be credited with the institution of tithing, וצ״ע.]

Although *Hirsch* agrees that in Rabbinic Hebrew שַׁעַר means *measure,* he maintains that

1. *Rabbi Yitzchak Vorkei* commented homiletically that God was pleased with Isaac for working the land in spite of the drought. Because he did so, God was able to provide for him in the natural way. Had Isaac not engaged in working his fields, however, God would have had to perform obvious miracles to provide for him. As his reward, God blessed him with hundred-fold prosperity.

reaped a hundredfold; thus had HASHEM blessed him.[13] *The man prospered and continually flourished until he was very prosperous.* [14] *He had acquired*

throughout Scripture it occurs only with the meaning of *gate* or *market place,* as for example in *II Kings* 7:1. Accordingly, he interprets the implication of our phrase in the Scriptural sense to be: *he reached a hundred markets.* His crop was not only sufficient for his own requirements, but he brought to market a hundred times the normal crop.

וַיְבָרְכֵהוּ ה׳ — *Thus* [lit. *and*] *had HASHEM blessed him.*

[I.e. by granting him the extraordinary crop despite the poor soil and famine.]

Cf. *Pirkei d'Rabbi Eliezer:* Isaac took a tenth of his wealth and distributed it as charity among the poor, that is why the Torah adds: *And HASHEM blessed him.*

— God granted him prosperity in his every undertaking *(Radak).*

Immediately following Isaac's tithes, *God's blessing* is mentioned. This is in consonance with God's declaration that although one is forbidden to 'test' Him by seeing if He will reward the performance of commandments in an obvious manner, it *is* permitted to put Him to the test regarding His promise of bountiful blessing in return for tithing. So it is stated in *Malachi* 3:10: *Bring all the tithes into the storehouse ... and put Me to the test thereby ...: If I will not open for you the windows of heaven and pour out for you blessing without measure! (Pesikta Zutresa).*

Following *Hirsch:* Because Isaac did not selfishly hoard the crop until the price went up in that famine-stricken year, but instead brought it generously to the markets and used his blessing for the general good, he became recognized as the man blessed by God.

13. וַיִּגְדַּל הָאִישׁ — [*And*] *the man prospered* [lit. *grew; became great*].

Became great — In wealth and property *(Radak).*

It is *the man* — Isaac — not the land or crops, with whom the blessing is associated *(Malbim).*

וַיֵּלֶךְ הָלוֹךְ וְגָדֵל — *And continually flourished* [lit. *and he went on increasingly and became greater*].[1]

— He increased in wealth by the day *(Radak).*

Since it never regressed at all, his success was manifestly Providential in nature *(Malbim).*

The translation of גָּדֵל in the present as an adjective meaning *increasingly greater* follows *Radak. Ibn Ezra* interprets it in past tense like זָקֵן, rendering: he went on increasingly *and he became great.*

עַד כִּי גָדַל מְאֹד — *Until he was very prosperous.*

— His greatness reached such a point that the Philistines were say-

1. The *Dubna Maggid* comments that this verse implies that Isaac's prosperity came upon him in a natural manner, gradually increasing by the day, rather than in one great thrust. The gradual nature of his growing prosperity was part of God's blessing because the sudden acquisition of great wealth presents a person with exceedingly difficult challenges. Many people cannot cope with the temptation that wealth brings within their grasp. As God saw that Isaac could handle increasing wealth, He kept giving him more *(Yalkut Yehudah).*

יד וַֽיְהִי־לוֹ֙ מִקְנֵה־צֹאן֙ וּמִקְנֵ֣ה בָקָ֔ר וַעֲבֻדָּ֖ה
טו רַבָּ֑ה וַיְקַנְא֥וּ אֹת֖וֹ פְּלִשְׁתִּֽים׃ וְכָל־
הַבְּאֵרֹ֗ת אֲשֶׁ֤ר חָֽפְרוּ֙ עַבְדֵ֣י אָבִ֔יו בִּימֵ֖י
אַבְרָהָ֣ם אָבִ֑יו סִתְּמ֣וּם פְּלִשְׁתִּ֔ים וַיְמַלְא֖וּם

ing: 'Rather the manure of Isaac's mules, than Abimelech's gold' *(Rashi* citing the *Midrash).* I.e., the populace deprecated Abimelech's wealth in comparison with Isaac's by insinuating that even the manure of Isaac's mules, so to speak, was worth more than Abimelech's gold.

14. וַעֲבֻדָּה רַבָּה — *And many enterprises.*

The translation reflects *Rashi* who interprets עֲבֻדָּה as a collective noun of עֲבוֹדָה [lit. *labor*] referring to *undertakings* or *enterprises. Ha'amek Davar* adds the nuance of *business enterprises.*

Ibn Ezra and *Ramban* relate the word to עֲבוֹדָה, *labor,* and render: *a retinue of male and female slaves.* According to *Rashbam* and *Sforno many lands and vineyards to be worked. Radak* suggests that the definition is *produce,* the fruits of one's agricultural *labor.*

Ramban observes that *monetary wealth* is not listed here as it is in the case of Abraham [13:2]. The wealth which Isaac accumulated in the land of the Philistines was in the form of *flocks and herds* etc., which are *visible* to all and accordingly, as the verse concludes, aroused the Philistine's jealousy of him.

וַיְקַנְאוּ אֹתוֹ פְּלִשְׁתִּים — *And the Philistines envied him.*

Because of the tangible wealth he had acquired, as enumerated above *(Ramban).*

He was especially hated by those who lived in Gerar, the capital city. Presumably many wealthy persons resided in the capital; one rich man is envious of another, particularly if the latter is a Jew *(Ha'amek Davar).*

Hirsch perceives from the expression that they envied אֹתוֹ, *him* [personally], rather the usual בּוֹ, *it* [i.e., *the wealth*] that their envy was directed more at Isaac, the man, than at his riches. They felt themselves threatened by the position and respect that his wealth brought him.

15. וְכָל הַבְּאֵרוֹת אֲשֶׁר חָפְרוּ עַבְדֵי אָבִיו בִּימֵי אַבְרָהָם אָבִיו — [*And*] *all the wells that his father's servants had dug in the days of Abraham, his father.*

[See 21:25 for a reference to one such well.]

סִתְּמוּם פְּלִשְׁתִּים וַיְמַלְאוּם עָפָר — *The Philistines stopped* [*them*] *up, and* [*they*] *filled them with earth.*

They claimed that these wells could become a menace because of marauding troops [i.e. wells might attract robbers; or an invading army could use them as its water supply] *(Rashi).*

☙ When were the wells stopped up?

There is a difference of opinion among the commentators:

☐ *Mizrachi* and *Gur Aryeh* hold that this verse is parenthetical, and the stopping up of the wells was *not a result of the jealousy* in the previous verse, but on account of an

26 *flocks and herds and many enterprises; and the*
15 *Philistines envied him.*
15 *All the wells that his father's servants had dug in*
the days of Abraham his father, the Philistines
stopped up, and filled them with earth.

event that occurred *long before* Isaac's entry into Gerar. They are of the opinion that *Rashi* interprets their action not as being malicious, but motivated only by fear of invading troops.

Hoffmann elaborates on this opinion and suggests that the Philistines considered these wells to be strategically menacing to them. While Abraham was alive they dared not interfere with them out of respect for the revered Patriarch, but when he died — and Isaac still had not come to their land — they viewed these wells to be as ownerless and stopped them up as a security measure. This interpretation seems supported by the fact that they did not interfere with Isaac's later reopening of these same wells [*v.*18].

Hirsch agrees that this happened immediately after Abraham's death even before Isaac lived amongst them. However, he differentiates between the Philistines respect for Abraham and their persecution of Isaac. As long as Abraham was alive, he was regarded as a 'prince of God' and no one dared tamper with his wells (except on one occasion only, when a similar tendency to enmity did manifest itself but was immediately disfavored by the king. See above 21:26). As soon as he died, however, the Philistines maliciously destroyed his wells notwithstanding the fact that water supply is of major benefit to everyone. This symbolizes the state of national exile that commenced with the advent of Isaac. [See *Hirsch's* full exposition of this verse.]

Although it is not entirely clear from *Rashbam's* comment when this occurred, he interprets that it was their motive to prevent Abraham's heirs from taking possession of them after his death. The verse is inserted here to introduce Isaac later redigging them.

[See significance of stopping up of the wells suggested by *HaKsav V'haKaballah* in footnote to *v.* 18.]

□ *Alshich* and *Nachalas Yitzchak*, based on the sequence of the verses, suggest that the Philistines stopped up the wells *as a direct result of their envy* of Isaac. They intended thereby to intimate to him that they wished him to leave the country. When Isaac did not respond, Abimelech personally ordered him to leave [*v.* 16]. According to this view, *Rashi's* comment about marauding troops should be understood merely as the *pretext* used by the Philistines.

This view basically follows *Ramban* [*v.* 17] who distinguishes between the wells mentioned here and the wells Isaac later redug in *v.* 18. He explains that the wells referred to in *this* verse were Isaac's by inheritance from his father and were located within the boundaries of the city of Gerar. They were stopped up when the Philistines lords of Gerar, the capital city, became envious of Isaac. [See his *comm.* to *v.* 17 regarding the other wells.]

Chizkuni interprets that it was their intention to prevent Isaac from laying claim to the wells and thereby gaining a foothold in their country.

— Further, in their envy, they stopped up the wells so he could not avail himself of their water for irrigation or watering his herds *(R' Bachya).*

... Thus, in effect, they acted out of

טו עָפָר: וַיֹּאמֶר אֲבִימֶלֶךְ אֶל־יִצְחָק לֵךְ
יז מֵעִמָּנוּ כִּי־עָצַמְתָּ מִמֶּנּוּ מְאֹד: וַיֵּלֶךְ מִשָּׁם
יח יִצְחָק וַיִּחַן בְּנַחַל־גְּרָר וַיֵּשֶׁב שָׁם: וַיָּשָׁב
יִצְחָק וַיַּחְפֹּר | אֶת־בְּאֵרֹת הַמַּיִם אֲשֶׁר
חָפְרוּ בִּימֵי אַבְרָהָם אָבִיו וַיְסַתְּמוּם
פְּלִשְׁתִּים אַחֲרֵי מוֹת אַבְרָהָם וַיִּקְרָא לָהֶן

sheer spite since they, too, could not now benefit from the wells *(Radak).*

[*R' Bachya* maintains, however, that when Isaac mustered up the strength, he definitely redug *those same wells* in *v.* 18.]

Sforno observes that the Philistines were afraid to harm Isaac himself because of Abimelech's decree [*v.* 11], so they stopped up the wells in a fierce display of their jealousy.

This act was done by the country dwellers. Because he lived in Gerar and had no way of knowing who was responsible, Isaac could not complain to the king. The government, too, turned a blind eye out of animosity *(Ha'amek Davar).*

□ Regardless of *when* this occurred, it must be emphasized that the Philistines thereby desecrated the covenant Abimelech made with Abraham [21:27] *(Midrash HaGadol).*

[See *Ha'amek Davar* next verse.]

16. כִּי עָצַמְתָּ מִמֶּנּוּ מְאֹד — *For you have become much mightier than we.*[1]

Though I am king I do not have in my home as many possessions as you. It is a disgrace to us that you should be wealthier than the king! *(Ramban).*

'Your wealth would enable you to attack us' *(Sforno).*

'Leave the town where the ministers of state have their homes, for your wealth is like thorns in their eyes. The king cannot tolerate the embarassment caused to his wealthy citizens. Therefore I am obliged to violate my treaty with Abraham in which I promised his descendants the right to live wherever they please in my country.' The episode foreshadows a similar fate that will befall the Jews in their Dispersions where they will be restricted in their right of domicile. Compare *Ramban* [in *footnote* to *v.* 1] who also explains the symbolic significance of this narrative as סִימָן לְבָנִים, presaging future events in

1. The *Midrash* perceives in this first expulsion order a prototype of what would unfortunately mark the history of the Jewish people who have known expulsions from place to place, homeland after homeland, throughout the centuries. The מ of מִמֶּנּוּ is interpreted as the comparative prefix: *You have become mightier* מִמֶּנּוּ, *than we.* The *Midrash,* however, prefers to translate the מ of מִמֶּנּוּ in the sense of *from us:* Accordingly, Abimelech said to Isaac, 'You have become mighty *from us.*' Did not all that you accumulated come *from us?* Previously, you had but a single flock, and now you have many!'

Thus, in spite of the fact that Isaac sowed the land with his own seed and received in that year of drought a hundredfold, and that he enriched himself by his own toil and the blessing of God and not by exploiting any other man, Abimelech accused him of deriving his wealth from him and his citizens *(Akeidas Yitzchak).*

[*Radak* records a similar interpretation in the name of his father.]

16 *And Abimelech said to Isaac, "Go away from us*
for you have become much mightier that we!"
17 *So Isaac departed from there and encamped in*
the valley of Gerar. 18 *And Isaac dug anew the wells*
of water which they had dug in the days of Abraham
his father and the Philistines had stopped up after

the history of Israel *(Ha'amek Davar).*

Ha'amek Davar adds that these symbolic connotations of later exiles are specifically derived from these episodes of *Isaac* because it is with *him* that the exile foretold to Abraham was to have begun.

17. וַיֵּלֶךְ מִשָּׁם יִצְחָק — *So* [lit. *and*] *Isaac departed* [lit. *went*] *from there.*

Although Isaac had a large retinue of servants he did not attempt to oppose the Philistines. God had told him to *be an alien in the land* [*v.* 3], so he did not want to remain there through militancy *(Malbim).*

וַיִּחַן בְּנַחַל גְּרָר — *And* [*he*] *encamped in the valley of Gerar.*

— Far from the city *(Rashi)* [*and hence residence there was in conformity with the expulsion order.*]

Radak and *Ramban* suggest the place was called *Gerar Valley* which was not part of Abimelech's domain although it was in Philistine land, or that possibly the valley by that name extended from Gerar to another land.

The rendering of נַחַל [literally *stream; wadi*] as *valley* follows *Radak* who explains that a valley is referred to by this name even when it is dry, as indicated by *Deut.* 2:36: *the town in the valley* [which, since there was a town there, implies that there was no water there.] Some find implicit in the name נַחַל a suggestion that there *had been* a wadi there that had since dried up, and that in such cases water may often be found by digging. *Meam Lo'ez* suggests that the area was in a valley next to a wadi in which water flows only during the rainy season.

18. וַיָּשָׁב יִצְחָק וַיַּחְפֹּר...אֲשֶׁר חָפְרוּ... וַיְסַתְּמוּם פְּלִשְׁתִּים — *And Isaac dug anew* [lit. *returned and dug*] *the wells of water which they had dug ... and the Philistines had stopped up ...*

The translation, follows *Rashi* who explains וַיְסַתְּמוּם פְּלִשְׁתִּים [is *not* to be misinterpreted to imply that *now* after he redug them *they again stopped them up,* but is to be interpreted] in the *past perfect,* i.e., which the Philistines *had* stopped up *after the death of Abraham.* Before Isaac was ordered out of Gerar, he had re-dug those wells.

According to *Maskil l'David*'s reading of *Rashi* קוֹדֶם שֶׁנָּסַע יִצְחָק מִגְּרָר חָזַר וַחֲפָרָן, the implication is that before Isaac left the boundary of the city of Gerar en route to the valley of Gerar he devoted himself to redigging his father's wells. While he had still been living there, he did not want to antagonize the Gerarites. Thus, the sequence of the narrative is: the Philistines became envious of him; we are parenthetically informed that there had been wells which had been stopped up; as a result of this envy Isaac was expelled and headed toward the valley of Gerar, but when he passed his father's wells he redug them. [See *Mizrachi; Nachalas Yitzchak* and *Levush* for different interpretations.]

Ramban notes *Rashi's* implication that these were the same wells mentioned in verse 15. He asks, however, how this could be so, for how would the

שֵׁמוֹת כַּשֵּׁמֹת אֲשֶׁר־קָרָא לָהֶן אָבִיו:
יט וַיַּחְפְּרוּ עַבְדֵי־יִצְחָק בַּנָּחַל וַיִּמְצְאוּ־שָׁם
כ בְּאֵר מַיִם חַיִּים: וַיָּרִיבוּ רֹעֵי גְרָר עִם־רֹעֵי
יִצְחָק לֵאמֹר לָנוּ הַמָּיִם וַיִּקְרָא שֵׁם־
כא הַבְּאֵר עֵשֶׂק כִּי הִתְעַשְּׂקוּ עִמּוֹ: וַיַּחְפְּרוּ

Philistines have permitted him to redig the wells which, as *Rashi* notes there, they claimed to be a possible menace to them because of marauding troops?

Ramban suggests therefore, that since Abraham must have dug many wells during his long residence in Philistia [see 21:34], it is logical to assume that these wells in Gerar Valley were *not the same* as those in Gerar itself. The wells *within* Gerar, as pointed out in *v.* 15, were stopped up as a result of the envy of the Philistine lords who resided with Isaac in the capital city of Gerar. The latter wells, in Gerar Valley, however, were not stopped up during Abraham's lifetime in deference to him, but were stopped up soon after he died since Isaac did not live there. But they did not do this out of enmity [see below].

Mizrachi notes that *Ramban* leaves unanswered *why* the Philistines stopped up these wells after Abraham's death if there was no hatred. He comments further that *Ramban* has no answer of his original question: Why did the Philistines allow Isaac to open the wells again? *Mizrachi* therefore concludes that *Rashi* could defend his interpretation — as could *Ramban* — by contending that the Philistines stopped up the wells with the excuse [contrived or real] that since there was imminent war, the stopping of the wells was a security measure against attackers, but now that times were peaceful, they had no legitimate reason to prevent him. Or, since Abimelech was afraid of Isaac's *might* [as noted above to *v.*16] perhaps they were powerless to *prevent* him from redigging them.

וַיִּקְרָא לָהֶן שֵׁמוֹת כַּשֵּׁמֹת אֲשֶׁר־קָרָא לָהֶן אָבִיו — *And he called them the same names that his father had called them,* [lit. *and he called them names like the names his father had called them*].

— So that no man could now dispute his possession of them *(Rashbam).*[1]

According to *R' Bachya,* Isaac's motivation was one of respect for his father. There is a great moral lesson in the fact that the Torah informs us of this meritorious act. It serves to teach us to what lengths one must go not to deviate from his father's ways since Isaac did not even wish to change the names that his father had given wells. This exemplifies the scrupulous manner in which the Patriarchs conducted their lives. Perhaps it was in the merit of this loyalty to his father's

1. *HaKsav V'haKaballah* suggests that Abraham had carefully given his wells names that would evoke recognition of the supremacy of the One God, and draw people near Him. Thus we find that the Patriarchs used names like HASHEM Yireh, Beth El, HASHEM Nisi, LaChai Ro'i — in order to evoke God's Name to passersby who would stop to drink at their wells. People would then be engaged in conversation, and persuaded to abandon their idolatry and believe in the Creator.

Therefore, the Philistines who reverted to their idolatrous ways after Abraham's death stopped up the wells in order to eradicate evidence of Abraham's religion.

That is why Isaac made it a point to reestablish the significance of the wells by returning to them their original names.

Abraham's death; and he called them the same names that his father had called them.

19 Isaac's servants dug in the valley and found there a well of fresh water. 20 The herdsmen of Gerar quarreled with Isaac's herdsmen saying, "The water is ours," so he named that well Esek because they involved themselves with him. 21 Then they dug

choice of names that Isaac was the only Patriarch whose own name was not changed.

[For, as *Midrash HaGadol* notes, Isaac merited by his modesty to be named before birth by the Holy One, Blessed be He (17:19), and his name therefore went unchanged throughout the generations. (See *comm.* to 17:5 p. 564 where *Yerushalmi Berachos* 1:6 is quoted in this context. See also *comm.* to 25:26 s.v. וַיִּקְרָא שְׁמוֹ).]

19. The dispute over the wells.

וַיַּחְפְּרוּ עַבְדֵי יִצְחָק בַּנָּחַל — [*And*] *Isaac's servants dug in the valley.*

— In search of even more water for his abundant herds *(Radak).*

וַיִּמְצְאוּ שָׁם בְּאֵר מַיִם חַיִּים — *And* [*they*] *found there a well of fresh* [lit., *living*] *water.*

I.e. flowing water [the opposite of stagnant water] *(Ibn Ezra).*

Malbim renders: *Spring water.*

After digging they uncovered an earlier well flowing with living water. That is why the verse speaks of finding a *well* rather than finding water *(Radak).*

The Torah testifies that it was a well gushing forth *fresh water,* from its *own source.* Contrary to the contention of those who disputed Isaac's right to the water [next verse], he did *not* draw water from their supply *(Ramban v. 17).*

20. לָנוּ הַמָּיִם — *The water is ours!*

'The well is located in the valley and draws its water from there at the expense of our own water supply, hence, it is ours.' But the Torah itself testified to the contrary [see *v.* 19] *(Ramban).*

Philistine law provided that everything — even the underground — belonged to the king, while Isaac's herdsmen claimed that the waters of the deep should be considered ownerless and become the property of anyone who discovers them *(Malbim).*

They quibbled in the exact style has been used against the Jews in Exile throughout the centuries: 'Yes, you dug the well; the *hole* belongs to you, but the *water* is ours!' *(Hirsch).*

וַיִּקְרָא שֵׁם הַבְּאֵר עֵשֶׂק — *So* [lit. *and*] *he named that well Esek.*

[*Involvement*], i.e. protest *(Rashi)* [see *Rashi* further].

According to *Radak, Shorashim,* the word עשק, synonymous with the Talmudic term עֵסֶק, means *contention, dispute.*

According to the Sages, as recorded by *Targum Yonasan,* it was the Will of Heaven that the water dry up while the Philistines held it; but when they returned it to Isaac, the water flowed again.

Accordingly, *HaKsav V'haKabal-*

בְּאֵר אַחֶרֶת וַיָּרִיבוּ גַּם־עָלֶיהָ וַיִּקְרָא
כב שִׁמָהּ שִׂטְנָה: וַיַּעְתֵּק מִשָּׁם וַיַּחְפֹּר בְּאֵר
אַחֶרֶת וְלֹא רָבוּ עָלֶיהָ וַיִּקְרָא שְׁמָהּ
רְחֹבוֹת וַיֹּאמֶר כִּי־עַתָּה הִרְחִיב יהוה לָנוּ

lah interprets עֵשֶׂק as derived from the term עֵסֶק meaning *to do one thing while intending something else,* or *to miss one's purpose.* Hence, following the Sages' interpretation that the Philistines quarreled over a well which became dry when they took it over, the name עשק commemorates this *non-attainment of their desired aims.* He wonders that according to those who interpret עשק as connoting *strife* or *dispute,* why Isaac did not name it *Merivah: strife,* or *quarrel.*

כִּי הִתְעַשְּׂקוּ עִמּוֹ — *Because they involved themselves with him.*

I.e. they involved themselves with him in strife and protest *(Rashi).*

The wording of *Rashi* proves that he does not *define Esek* as protest but intimates that the purpose of their *involvement* with him was to protest his success *(Sifsei Chachamim).*

— Each arguing the validity of his claim to ownership *(Malbim).*

Or according to *HaKsav V'ha-Kaballah* cited above: because they failed to attain the goal of their contention.

The purpose of their contention was to get Isaac to abandon the well *(Sforno).*

According to *Targum Yonasan,* the water dried up while the Philistines had the well and flowed again after they returned it. The implication, therefore, is that they failed in their contention and the well remained in Isaac's possession.

Subsequently his servants proceeded to dig *additional* wells as recorded in the following verses.

Abarbanel agrees with the above and observes that since one does not give names to something that does not belong to him, the fact that Isaac named the wells implies that they remained his.

According to *Malbim,* however, Isaac wanted no part of contention. He abandoned this well and had his servants dig another well.

This generally agrees with *Ramban* who makes an oblique reference to Isaac having derived no advantage from the wells.

21. וַיָּרִיבוּ גַּם עָלֶיהָ — *And they quarreled over that also.*

Once the Philistines saw that they had succeeded in stealing the well by a spurious claim, they continued to steal without any claim at all — just out of sheer enmity *(Ha'amek Davar).*

For this time the Philistines had no claim whatsoever — it was not *fresh water,* but rain water to which even the king had no claim *(Malbim).*

וַיִּקְרָא שְׁמָהּ שִׂטְנָה — *So* [lit. *and*] *he named it Sitnah.*

— I.e. *enmity (Rashi).*

— Related to the word *Satan*: adversary; hinderer *(Radak).*

Accordingly, the term commemorates how the Philistines quarreled with him without even a pretext. Thus, since it is self-

26
22

another well, and they quarreled over that also. So he
named it Sitnah. [22] *He relocated from there and dug*
another well. They did not quarrel over it, so he
named it Rechovos, saying, "For now HASHEM has

explanatory, there is no need for the Torah to give a reason for the name *(Chizkuni).*

As *Daas Zekeinim* comments, the first incident could have been interpreted as an exception, but now their habitual quarreling was obviously an expression of sheer enmity.[1]

22. וַיַּעְתֵּק מִשָּׁם — *[And] he relocated from there.*

In order to remove himself from conflict *(Midrash HaGadol),* to a place where the residents were not so wicked *(Haamek Davar).*

By moving he also made certain that he would no longer be in an area where they could contend that he was digging in their land *(Radak).*

[The implications of the term וַיַּעְתֵּק is discussed in the *comm.* to 12:8.]

וַיַּחְפֹּר בְּאֵר אַחֶרֶת — *And [he] dug another well.*

This time *he* himself presided over the digging, or perhaps he even dug the first clod to initiate the venture. It was in his merit that this venture met with no opposition *(Ha'amek Davar).*

וְלֹא רָבוּ עָלֶיהָ — *[And] they did not quarrel over it.*

... This being a manifestation of God's Providence *(Ha'amek Davar).*

— He was now far from their pastures *(Rashbam).*

וַיִּקְרָא שְׁמָהּ רְחֹבוֹת — *So* [lit. *and*] *he named it Rechovos* [i.e., wide open spaces].

— To make it obvious to all that this well was not the object of strife *(Radak).*

כִּי עַתָּה הִרְחִיב ה׳ לָנוּ — *For now HASHEM has granted us ample space.*

— In which to settle without contention *(Ha'amek Davar).*

HASHEM's Name is now mentioned because of the positive

1. *Ramban* further pursues his thematic interpretation that the Torah narrates at length these seemingly trivial incidents in the lives of the Patriarchs because of the significance they foreshadow in the future history of the children of Israel [see *footnote*, end of *v.* 1, and *footnote* to 12:10.]

He suggests, therefore, that the only point in narrating this incident is the esoteric implication that *well of living water* sublimely alludes to the בֵּית הַמִּקְדָּשׁ, *Holy Temple*, which Isaac's descendants would one day build.

He named the first well *Esek: contention*, to allude to the First Temple which signifies the strife and contention of the nations who finally destroyed it.

The second well, *Sitnah: hindrance, enmity*, a harsher name than the first, bespeaks the enmity of our enemies against us in the period of the Second Temple, until they finally destroyed it and exiled us.

The third well, *Rochovos: spaciousness*, auspiciously refers to the Third Temple, may it be built speedily in our days, which will be free of strife and feud.

The very reference to God enlarging our borders is prophetic (see *Deut.* 19:8).

The reference to being fruitful in the land [*v.* 22] alludes to the universal acknowledgment of God.

°רביעי

כג וּפָרִינוּ בָאָרֶץ: °וַיַּעַל מִשָּׁם בְּאֵר שָׁבַע:
כד וַיֵּרָא אֵלָיו יהוה בַּלַּיְלָה הַהוּא וַיֹּאמֶר
אָנֹכִי אֱלֹהֵי אַבְרָהָם אָבִיךָ אַל־תִּירָא כִּי־
אִתְּךָ אָנֹכִי וּבֵרַכְתִּיךָ וְהִרְבֵּיתִי אֶת־זַרְעֲךָ
כה בַּעֲבוּר אַבְרָהָם עַבְדִּי: וַיִּבֶן שָׁם מִזְבֵּחַ

aspects of this venture *(Akeidas Yitzchak).*

וּפָרִינוּ בָאָרֶץ — *And we can be fruitful in the land.*

— I.e. without hindrance or discord we can thrive *(Radak).*

For in the comfort and security of spaciousness, one is more prone to be fruitful *(Ha'amek Davar).*

23. Isaac Returns to Beer Sheba.

וַיַּעַל מִשָּׁם בְּאֵר שָׁבַע — [And] *he went up from there to Beer Sheba.*[1]

He did so out of fear, as is evident from the fact that God, in the following verse, tells him *'Fear not' (Rashbam).*

The significance of the following narrative impresses that in the more central area of *Eretz Yisrael* which was the heritage of Isaac's descendants, Isaac lived in security and was not harassed by the local populace as he was in Gerar which, though also technically part of the Promised Land, would not be conquered by his descendants until future times *(Radak).*

The Torah always speaks of going *up* when speaking of journeys *to* the higher terrain of *Eretz Yisrael.* Comp. *Judges* 15:9: *and the Philistines went up,* and *I Sam.* 14:36: *Saul said, 'Let us go down after the Philistines,'* and so very frequently *(Radak).*

[On the *spiritual* implication of *'ascending'* to the higher spiritual degree of *Eretz Yisrael,* see *Zohar* cited in *footnote* to 13:1.]

24. בַּלַּיְלָה הַהוּא — *That night.*

I.e. the very night after he left his former residence *(Daas Soferim).*

אָנֹכִי אֱלֹהֵי אַבְרָהָם אָבִיךָ — *I am the God of your father Abraham.*

— Hence I am particularly suitable to protect you, just as I was a *shield to Abraham* [15:1]. See *comm.* to 28:13 and *Exodus* 3:6 where this concept of *God of Abraham* is further explained as denoting *protection from enemies.* In contrast, the appelation *God of Isaac* refers to Him as Provider of sustenance *(Ha'amek Davar).* [In 24:26 *Ha'amek Davar* adds that God is called *God of Abraham* since Abraham was the first to proclaim Him.]

1. [As noted in the *footnote* on page 736 and *Ramban's comm.* to 21:32 which reflects the accepted Rabbinic view, Beer Sheba was then part of Philistia, in the Valley of Gerar. Thus, Isaac was still complying with God's command in *v.* 3 that he sojourn in Philistia. (When the land was later apportioned among the Tribes, Beer Sheba became part of the territory of Judah).

Beer Sheba was greatly significant to Isaac. It was there that Abraham had resided for many years and made his treaty with Abimelech. Isaac was born there; and there Abraham made the great feast to celebrate Isaac's weaning. Abraham established his *eshel* there, and went there after the *Akeidah,* where he heard the news of Sarah's demise.]

granted us ample space, and we can be fruitful in the
land,"
[23] *He went up from there to Beer Sheba.*
[24] *HASHEM appeared to him that night and said, "I*
am the God of your father Abraham. Fear not, for I
am with you; I will bless you and increase your of-
fspring because of Abraham my servant." [25] *He built*

אַל־תִּירָא — *Fear not.*

— 'That Abimelech, who drove you away, and the herdsmen or Gerar, who quarreled with you, will gather against you and slay you and your family' *(Ramban).*

According to *Sforno,* Isaac was apprehensive that he would experience loss through their enmity.

Haamek Davar suggests that Isaac was fearful that his neighbors in Beer Sheba might prove to be equally envious and troublesome to him.

[God's assurance, *Fear not!* was similarly given to Abraham (15:1), Jacob (43:3), and to nearly *all* the righteous ones in Scripture.]

כִּי אִתְּךָ אָנֹכִי — *For I am with you.*

[God's promise of being 'with' the Patriarchs is an affirmation of His Providence in watching over the details of their various activities according to the measure of their perfection, as noted in the *comm.* to God's promise *I will be with you* in *v.* 3.]

Or HaChaim adds that since Isaac was expelled by Abimelech and harassed by the herdsmen, he feared that God had forsaken him. God therefore appeared to reassure him that he need not fear for the God of his father remains at his side.

The fulfillment of this assurance can be recognized in the following episode. Providence influenced Abimelech to show Isaac even greater honor than he had shown Abraham, for, when he came to conclude a treaty with Isaac he was accompanied by Pichol and a retinue of friends [*v.* 26] *(Ramban).*

Following *Haamek Davar:* And your new neighbors will be powerless over you.

וּבֵרַכְתִּיךָ ... בַּעֲבוּר אַבְרָהָם עַבְדִּי — [*And*] *I will bless you ... because of Abraham my servant.*

The blessing will come to you by merit of זְכוּת אָבוֹת, *the merit of your father* Abraham which abides by you in This World. It is your own merit however, as a righteous son of a righteous father, which will secure you your place in the World to Come *(Midrash HaGadol).*

[See *v.* 5 for similar concept of Isaac's blessing materializing because of Abraham's righteousness.]

Abraham is referred to here as *servant* to signify how he obeyed all God's commands as a slave does *(Radak).* [*See Overview, Chayei-Sarah.*]

Meshech Chochmah notes the contrast to *verse* 5 where Abraham was not called a 'servant' of God. The implication of our verse is that Abraham engaged in God's *service* by offering sacrifices [see 12:8 and

וַיִּקְרָא֙ בְּשֵׁ֣ם יהוה וַיֶּט־שָׁ֖ם אָהֳל֑וֹ וַיִּכְרוּ־
כו שָׁ֥ם עַבְדֵֽי־יִצְחָ֖ק בְּאֵֽר׃ וַאֲבִימֶ֕לֶךְ הָלַ֥ךְ
אֵלָ֖יו מִגְּרָ֑ר וַאֲחֻזַּת֙ מֵֽרֵעֵ֔הוּ וּפִיכֹ֖ל שַׂר־

13:4]. This is what prompted Isaac to do likewise, as recorded in the next verse.

25. וַיִּבֶן שָׁם מִזְבֵּחַ — *[And] he built an altar there.*

To acknowledge God's beneficence and express gratitude for the prophecy God had just given him, as Abraham did in 12:7 and 13:18 *(Abarbanel).*

After God's earlier revelation in verse 3, however, Isaac made no such open display of gratitude because he was afraid to publicize that he had been promised the lands of his neighbors, lest he arouse their enmity, for Isaac had been a *wholesome man* [25:27] who had never engaged in warfare. Because *this* blessing was more general, however, he had no fears of publicizing it, so he built the altar. It was to this prophetic revelation that Abimelech later referred when he said [*v.* 28]: *We have indeed seen that HASHEM has been with you (Meshech Chochmah).*

וַיִּקְרָא בְּשֵׁם ה׳ — *[And] invoked HASHEM by Name.*

He prayed there [i.e. *called upon* in prayer] *(Onkelos).*

[See *comm.* to 12:8, 13:4 and 13:18. In 21:33 a similar passage is rendered: *He proclaimed the Name of HASHEM,* which would be closer to the sense of the *Meshech Chochmah* cited above.]

וַיֶּט שָׁם אָהֳלוֹ — *And there he pitched his tent.*

[I.e. established his residence.]

Midrash Or HaAfeilah cited in *Torah Sheleimah* perceives the implication to be that he set up a study house for Torah [אֹהֱלָהּ שֶׁל תּוֹרָה] as evidenced by the phrase *he proclaimed HASHEM's Name* [which *Radak* in 13:18 interprets as signifying that he rallied people to God's service.]

וַיִּכְרוּ שָׁם עַבְדֵי יִצְחָק בְּאֵר — *[And] there Isaac's servants began digging a well.*

This was the well he subsequently named Shibah when, after Abimelech departed, his servants apprised him that they had completed digging it [*v.* 32] *(Rashbam).*[1]

The translation *began digging* follows *Malbim* who draws a distinction between the verbs כרה and חפר, since they appear together with separate connotations in *Psalms* 7:16. The former denotes the *beginning* of digging, while the latter, the *culmination* of the digging [or as he explains in *Psalms,* the *deeper* digging]. Thus, in *v.* 32, his servants came to advise him of this well אֲשֶׁר חָפָרוּ, which they had *finished digging.*

Heidenheim observes in this context that the verb כרה expresses the *probing* for water preliminary to the actual חֲפִירָה, *digging* of a well.

26. Abimelech's Visit.
The Reaffirmation of the Treaty.

וַאֲבִימֶלֶךְ הָלַךְ אֵלָיו מִגְּרָר — *[And] Abimelech went to him from Gerar.*

1. It is to the credit of the righteous that whenever they go they dig wells and provide the populace with water that is a source of sustenance to all. Thus, too, is it written [*Prov.* 10:11]: *The mouth of the righteous is a fountain of life (Midrash HaGadol).*

26 *an altar there, invoked HASHEM by Name, and there*
26 *he pitched his tent; there Isaac's servants began digg-*
ing a well.
[26] Abimelech went to him from Gerar with a group
of his friends and Pichol his general.

God inspired him to take this initiative, in fulfillment of His promise to Isaac *(Ramban).*

According to the *Midrash,* Abimelech's trip was involuntary. The Sages note that the word מִגְּרָר, *from Gerar* is superfluous since it is obvious that he would have come from his capital. Hence, in seeking the deeper message inherent in its inclusion, the Sages homileticaly revocalized the word to read: *Abimelech went to him* מְגֹרָר, *wounded.*

Targum Yonasan similarly records that: 'When Isaac left Gerar the wells dried up and the trees bore no fruit. They felt that this befall them because they had driven him away, so Abimelech went to Isaac from Gerar ...

וַאֲחֻזַּת מֵרֵעֵהוּ — *With a group of his friends.*

The translation follows *Rashi* who, on the basis of *Onkelos* renders סִיעַת מֵרַחֲמוֹהִי, *a group,* from among his friends.

Rashi explains that the word אֲחֻזַּת — including the suffix ת — signifies a group who are נֶאֱחָזִין, held together, close-knit by some common consideration: in this case Abimelech's friendship. The prefix מ of מֵרֵעֵהוּ means that his entourage was chosen *from among* רֵעֵהוּ, *his* [many] *friends.*

Rashi defends his interpretation on grammatical grounds by pointing out that words ending with ת [like אֲחֻזַּת which is synonymous with אֲחֻזָּה] are often not used in the construct form. Examples are *Psalms* 60:13: עֶזְרַת מִצָּר [=עֶזְרָה מִצָּר] *help against the adversary; Isaiah* 51:21: וּשְׁכֻרַת וְלֹא מִיָּיִן [=וּשְׁכֻרָה] *drunken, but not from wine.* Accordingly, the suffix form ת of אֲחֻזַּת should *not* in this case be interpreted as indicating סְמִיכוּת, *construct state,* meaning אֲחֻזָּה *of.* Further, the prefix מ of מֵרֵעֵהוּ is the prepositional prefix: *from* or *of,* which modifies the noun רֵעֵהוּ, *his friends.* Another possible, but incorrect interpretation, would be that the מ is part of the noun מֵרֵעַ as in *Judges* 14:11 מֵרֵעִים, *friends.* If the latter were the correct interpretation, the implication would be that *all* of the king's friends went along, giving the insulting impression that the king had no friends other than this one group of people. Hence, the phrase should be translated as in the primary comment.

It is possible that this group included the Philistine herdsmen who had quarreled with Isaac over the wells [*vs.* 20-21]. Abimelech took them along as a gesture to strengthen the sincerity of his peace overture *(Meshech Chochmah).*

Rashi's primary translation based on *Onkelos,* follows one view in the *Midrash.*

According to another view in *Midrash Lekach Tov,* the phrase is interpreted *Ahuzzath, his intimate* friend, Ahuzzath being the name of מֵרֵעֵהוּ, *his intimate friend* [like the word מֵרֵעַ in *Judges* 14:11 and 15:16]. *Midrash Rabbah* records a view that *Ahuzzath Mere'eihu* was his actual name.

וּפִיכֹל שַׂר צְבָאוֹ — *And Pichol his general.*

כז צְבָאוֹ: וַיֹּאמֶר אֲלֵהֶם יִצְחָק מַדּוּעַ בָּאתֶם
אֵלָי וְאַתֶּם שְׂנֵאתֶם אֹתִי וַתְּשַׁלְּחוּנִי
כח מֵאִתְּכֶם: וַיֹּאמְרוּ רָאוֹ רָאִינוּ כִּי־הָיָה
יהוה ׀ עִמָּךְ וַנֹּאמֶר תְּהִי נָא אָלָה
בֵּינוֹתֵינוּ בֵּינֵינוּ וּבֵינֶךָ וְנִכְרְתָה בְרִית

Either [as noted in the *commentary* to 21:22] Pichol was his name, or it was a title descriptive of his military position which the *Midrash* here interprets to mean: the פֶּה, *mouth*, responsible for the weapons of כָּל, *all* Abimelech's troops.

In 21:22 the *Midrash* cites 41:40: *According to your word* [פִּיךָ] *may my people be ruled* [thus indicating that the title *Pichol* bespoke of the power to rule; everyone being dependent upon his good word.]

Radak who agrees with the view that Pichol was his name, suggests that he was the same one who had accompanied Abimelech to Abraham [at least seventy-five years earlier!]

[See *comm.* of *Ramban* s.v. אֲבִימֶלֶךְ in *v.* 1.]

27. מַדּוּעַ בָּאתֶם אֵלָי — *Why have you* [plural] *come to me?*

You surely could not have come for a social visit since you hate me and expelled me from your country! *(Haamek Davar).*

Isaac's cynical reception is certainly motivated by a common sense appraisal of Abimelech's credibility. This very same Philistine king — or his father; it does not really matter! — came in great urgency to Abraham and made a treaty with him that was to last for generations. But the king does not find it feasible to make proper arrangements for his covenant-brother's *son* even in time of famine, and the king's servants even stopped up his wells. This made it plain that a pact with Philistines was useless, and Isaac reacted to their overtures accordingly *(Abarbanel).*

Or Hachaim explains that they surely had no fear that Isaac would harm them because he was bound by Abraham's oath. In that case, they must have come for *Isaac's* benefit — but that was impossible because they had demonstrated their baseless hatred of him by drawing him away! This was the logic of Isaac's apparently harsh reception.

וְאַתֶּם שְׂנֵאתֶם אֹתִי וַתְּשַׁלְּחוּנִי מֵאִתְּכֶם — [And] *You* [plural] *hate me and drove me away from you.*

Isaac addressed Abimelech in the plural form for it was obviously in consonance with his councilors that Abimelech ordered Isaac to leave the land [*v.* 16] *(Radak).*

28. רָאוֹ רָאִינוּ כִּי הָיָה ה׳ עִמָּךְ — *We have indeed seen that* HASHEM *has been with you.*

[The verb *see,* רָאוֹ רָאִינוּ (lit. *see we have seen),* is repeated in the verse, to intimate]: We saw it with your father, and we have seen it with you also *(Rashi)*; and glorious is the son who fills the role of his father! *(Pesikta Zutresa).*

[27] *Isaac said to them, "Why have you come to me? You hate me and drove me away from you!"*

[28] *And they said, "We have indeed seen that HASHEM has been with you, so we said, Let the oath between ourselves now be between us and you, and let us make a covenant with you:*

— We perceived your success in every endeavor: *We saw it* in your crops and *we saw it* in your wells.

Originally we attributed your wealth to natural causes, accusing you of draining off our water supply and hence diminishing our blessing; now we truly perceive that it is *God* Who has constantly been with you and caused you to prosper *(Malbim).*

[See *Meshech Chochmah* cited in *v.* 25.]

And it is because we *perceive that God has been with you* — and not out of mortal fear of you — that we desire this treaty *(Sforno).*

[See *Ramban* further who in his primary interpretation suggests that they desired the treaty because they were afraid of retaliation by Isaac's *descendants.*]

וַנֹּאמֶר — *So* [lit. *and*] *we said.*

— I.e. we concluded among ourselves *(Haamek Davar).*

תְּהִי נָא אָלָה בֵּינוֹתֵינוּ בֵּינֵינוּ וּבֵינֶךָ — *Let the oath between ourselves now be between us and* [*between*] *you.*

The translation follows *Rashi* and *Rashbam* who interpret the gesture as suggesting that *the oath which had existed* בֵּינוֹתֵינוּ *between ourselves* since the days of your father, now by renewed בֵּינֵינוּ וּבֵינֶיךָ, *between us and you.*

[Apparently this interpretation can best be understood by rearranging the word order for comprehension: אָלָה בֵּינוֹתֵינוּ, *the oath between us,* i.e. your father and us תְּהִי נָא, *let it now be* בֵּינֵנוּ וּבֵינֶךָ, *between us and you.*]

[The above interprets אָלָה, *oath,* as if it were written with the difinite article הָאָלָה, *the oath.*]

Onkelos renders similarly: *Let now the oath which was between our fathers be confirmed between us and you.*

According to *Ibn Ezra,* the redundancy is for extra clarification. [I.e. the expression *between ourselves* could mean *between Abimelech and his subjects;* he therefore clarified any possible ambiguity by adding that the intent of *between ourselves* is: *between us and you.*]

Ramban, noting the severity of the term אָלָה, *dread oath* [which signifies an oath reinforced by an imprecation and hence is more severe than an ordinary שְׁבֻעָה, *oath* (see on 24:41 s.v. אָז)] interprets their gesture to mean: We now approach you with an oath to formulate a ban on whomever transgresses the covenant.

וְנִכְרְתָה בְרִית עִמָּךְ — *And let us make* [lit. *cut*] *a covenant with you.*

They were apprehensive — not that Isaac *himself* constituted a military threat to them — but that his descendants might not consider themselves bound by the pact. They had violated the covenant with Abraham and they were apprehensive that Isaac would retaliate by annulling his part of the covenant. His descendants would thus be free to drive

עִמָּךְ׃ כט אִם־תַּעֲשֵׂה עִמָּנוּ רָעָה כַּאֲשֶׁר לֹא
נְגַעֲנוּךָ וְכַאֲשֶׁר עָשִׂינוּ עִמְּךָ רַק־טוֹב
וַנְּשַׁלֵּחֲךָ בְּשָׁלוֹם אַתָּה עַתָּה בְּרוּךְ יהוה׃

Abimelech's descendants from the land. Therefore, they excused themselves and emphasized that not only did they not annul the previous covenant, but they have done him only good! It is conceivable, however, that they recalled *Abraham's* God-given military successes against the four kings [Chapter 14], and they were afraid that Isaac, too, would be able to defeat them since such an action would require a much smaller force. They might also have heard of the prophecy that God had promised the land to Abraham and feared that by expelling Isaac from the land, they might have aroused his ill will and he was harboring thoughts of retaliation *(Ramban v.* 29).

Thus, having violated their first oath in regard to the wells and the expulsion, they wished to reaffirm it *(Chizkuni).*

Similarly, when one party violates a treaty the *halachah* is that the other is no longer bound to it [*Sotah* 10a]. Hence the reaffirmation *(Yalkut Yehudah).*

On the 'cutting of a covenant' [the details of which are not given here], see *comm.* and *footnote* to 15:19.

29. אִם תַּעֲשֵׂה עִמָּנוּ רָעָה — *If you dare do evil to* [lit. *with*] *us ... !*

[The above translation allows for the various following nuances, all of which, as *Radak* points out, imply that Abimelech recognized Isaac's potential — spiritual or physical — to harm him.]

Their primary intent was not to create a friendly alliance, but to conclude a non-agression pact *(Ha'amek Davar).*

In 14:23 *Sforno* formulates the rule that throughout the Torah the word אִם, *if,* where it is *not followed by a condition,* has the implication of an oath, the meaning being: *that you will not* [do evil to us.]

This also follows *Onkelos,* who renders the oath which Abimelech administered to Abraham in 21:23 אִם תִּשְׁקֹר לִי: *That* [not *if*] *you will not* deal falsely with me.'

Ramban, however, in his commentary to 21:23, insists that אִם, appearing in connection with oaths means *if,* and explains that since oaths are given an imprecation, the phrase signifies an *implied consequential phrase,* as if Abimelech were saying [in 21:23]: *Swear to me* saying: May God do unto me such and such *if you will deal falsely with me.* He cites our verse as an example: אִם תַּעֲשֵׂה עִמָּנוּ רָעָה, *if you do evil to us* — then may God do such and such to you] for in all such cases the Torah shortens the expression, leaving the threatened consequences to the imagination rather than explicitly stating them.

In his *commentary* to our verse, *Ramban* tailors his interpretation of the implied imprecation to our specific passage: *If you will do evil to us,* then *just as we have not molested you*...because אַתָּה עַתָּה בָּרוּךְ ה׳, *you are* **now** *the blessed of* *HASHEM,* and accordingly we are powerless to harm you, be aware that if you harm us unjustly, God will remove his blessing from you. Some day you will have to return to our land — and then we will avenge ourselves. Therefore, to avoid all of

26
29 [29] *If you dare do evil to us ... !*
Just as we have not molested you,
and just as we have done with you only good,
and sent you away in peace —
Now, you, O blessed of HASHEM!"

this we propose that we enter into a treaty.]

Targum Yonasan interprets אִם in the negative: We will enter into a covenant with you *lest you do us evil.*

כַּאֲשֶׁר לֹא נְגַעֲנוּךָ — *Just as we have not molested you.*

When we told you to leave our land *(Rashi).*

Or according to *Ramban:* When we decreed that no one molest you or your wife [*v.* 11].

We submitted you only to social and economic pressures; not physical *(Ha'amek Davar).*

וְכַאֲשֶׁר עָשִׂינוּ עִמְּךָ רַק טוֹב — *And just as we have done with you only good.*

Guarding your possessions by warning the people against interfering with you *(Ramban).*

[How glaring is their omission of any reference to the herdsmen who quarreled over the wells, or stopped up Abraham's wells! The *Midrash* takes note of this when it comments that רַק is always interpreted as a limitation implying that their actions were not *entirely* good. Perhaps in their perverted way, they rationalized, as have anti-Semites through the ages, that their acts of harassment were justifiable (see *footnote*).]

וַנְשַׁלֵּחֲךָ בְּשָׁלוֹם — *And* [*we*] *sent you away in peace.*

— Although we were envious of you, we did not confiscate the wealth you amassed with us. We let you depart peacefully with all your possessions *(Ramban).*[1]

— To the contrary! We sent you away to protect you from the envy of our subjects *(Radak).*

[On the imprecative connotation of *in* peace instead of the auspicious *to* peace, see *v.* 31 s.v. וַיֵּלְכוּ.]

אַתָּה עַתָּה בְּרוּךְ ה' — *Now you, O blessed of* HASHEM.

Rashi [as explained by *Mizrachi*] and *Rashbam* render: *Now you, O blessed of* HASHEM — i.e., now you, who are blessed of HASHEM , act with us in a like manner and reciprocate our kindness to you by entering into a treaty with us. For as one who is manifestly the blessed of HASHEM it is indeed in your power to deal graciously with us.

1. The *Midrash* perceives the hypocracy of those gentile nations who insist that Israel was indebted to them nerely because of their 'benevolence' in allowing Israel to dwell among them unmolested.

The *Midrash* cites the parable of a wild lion that killed an animal and a bone stuck in his throat. He was unable to find any animal willing to extract it. He then promised to amply reward anyone who removes the bone.

A long-necked stork came. It placed its head in the lion's mouth and pulled out the offending bone. When he demanded his reward, the lion said, 'What? You want a reward too? Go! It is reward enough for you that you will be able to go about and boast that you put your head into a lion's mouth and came out in peace [unscathed]!'

ל °וַיַּעַשׂ לָהֶם מִשְׁתֶּה וַיֹּאכְלוּ וַיִּשְׁתּוּ׃
לא וַיַּשְׁכִּימוּ בַבֹּקֶר וַיִּשָּׁבְעוּ אִישׁ לְאָחִיו
וַיְשַׁלְּחֵם יִצְחָק וַיֵּלְכוּ מֵאִתּוֹ בְּשָׁלוֹם׃
לב וַיְהִי | בַּיּוֹם הַהוּא וַיָּבֹאוּ עַבְדֵי יִצְחָק

The exession *blessed of HASHEM,* then, is similar to the title Laban gave Eliezer in 24:31 [see *comm.* there] *(Rashbam).*

According to *Ramban's* interpretation of the oath as explained above, the connotation is *Now* you have the upper hand because you are the *blessed of HASHEM* and we are powerless against you, but beware that the balance of power will change and if you harm us now, we will one day be in a position to retaliate.

Cf. *Radak:* God has blessed you, and you can harm us if you wish, but this would be an unjust response to our kindnesses to you.

Following *Targum Yonasan's* interpretation: It is by virtue of the fact that we have not molested you, and that we have done only kindness with you and sent you away in peace *that you are now blessed of HASHEM.*

Continuing *Meshech Chochmah:* While you lived with us we accused you of having grown wealthy *through us* [see *footnote* to *v.* 16]. *Now,* however, we realize that *you are blessed of HASHEM* and your success and wealth have come to you as a direct result of the natural workings of His beneficent Providence.

According to *Daas Soferim* the connotation is simply: *You are now blessed of God* — and it is accordingly desirable to seek a treaty with you.

30. וַיַּעַשׂ לָהֶם מִשְׁתֶּה וַיֹּאכְלוּ וַיִּשְׁתּוּ — *[And] he* [Isaac] *made them a feast and they ate and drank.*

Since gentlemen partake of a meal after concluding a transaction, Isaac prepared the feast to consummate the mutual acceptance of the pact (*Radak* and *Tur* to 24:33-34).

— Such is the way of the truly righteous: they are easily appeased *(Ha'amek Davar).*

31. וַיַּשְׁכִּימוּ בַבֹּקֶר — *[And] they awoke early in the morning.*

— Specifically in the morning, after they had slept off the effects of the dinner wine so that no one could claim that the oath was undertaken in anything less than an alert, sober state *(Torah Sheleimah,* 126 note).

וַיִּשָּׁבְעוּ אִישׁ לְאָחִיו — *And [they] swore to one another.*[1]

1. According to *Pirkei d'Rabbi Eliezer 31,* [*see also Targum Yonasan*] the covenant stipulated that Isaac's descendants would not take possesson of the land of the Philistines.

To ratify the covenant, Isaac cut off a cubit of the bridle-rein of the donkey he was riding and gave it to them as a token of the covenant and oath between them.

Centuries later, when David became king and wished to enter the land of the Philistines, he was prevented from doing so because of this symbol of the covenant's ratification. He remained unable to enter until he first took from them this sign of Isaac's oath, as it is written: *David struck the Philistines and subdued them; and David took* מֶתֶג הָאַמָּה *the cubit of the*

30 *He made them a feast and they ate and drank.*
31 *They awoke early in the morning and swore to one another. Then Isaac saw them off and they departed from him in peace.*
32 *And it was on that very day that Isaac's servants*

— With the אָלָה, *dread oath,* mentioned above *(Ha'amek Davar).*

As noted in chapter 21 Abraham's alliance with Abimelech caused much woe for the Jews in later generations, but at the time, Abraham saw no way to avoid accomodating the king and entering into the alliance. His deeds became Isaac's guide. Indeed, Isaac tried to put them off [*v.* 27] but he was unsuccessful; he was as much as *forced* to make a treaty *(Daas Soferim).*

They swore not to harass each others' descendants, but the Philistines violated the oath when they warred against Israel in the days of the Judges and King Saul *(Midrash Or HaAfeilah).*

[The Torah does not record whether, as Abimelech suggested in *v.*28, they actually 'cut a covenant' in the classical sense by passing between cut up animals as explained in 15:19, and that the oaths they took were an *additional ratification*; or whether they relied on the classical covenant made with Abraham, and the *entire treaty* now consisted of the oaths they now exchanged (see footnote).]

וַיְשַׁלְּחֵם יִצְחָק — *Then* [lit. *and*] *Isaac saw them off* [lit. *sent them.*]

[I.e. *escorted them* in a hospitable manner befitting a departing royal entourage. This translation follows *Targum Yonasan* here, and *Rashi* and *Onkelos'* interpretation of the verb in 12:20. See *commentary* there to 18:16 and to 24:59.]

וַיֵּלְכוּ מֵאִתּוֹ בְּשָׁלוֹם — *And they departed from him in peace.*

The *Talmud* [*Berachos* 64a] advises that when a man takes leave of his fellow, he should not say to him לֵךְ בְּשָׁלוֹם, 'Go *in* peace', but לֵךְ לְשָׁלוֹם, 'Go *to* peace.' For Moses, to whom Jethro said [*Exodus* 4:18]: 'Go *to* peace,' went up and prospered, whereas Absalom to whom David said [*II Samuel* 15:9], 'Go *in* peace' went away and was hung.

Accordingly, concerning the Philistines who told Isaac hypocritically [*v.* 29]: 'We sent you away *in* peace,' Scripture now says, 'They departed from him *in* peace' *(Seichel Tov).*

32. וַיְהִי בַּיּוֹם הַהוּא — *And it was on that very day.*

While Abimelech was still with Isaac; this newly discovered prosperity was another sign of God's Providential beneficence toward Isaac so that the Philistine nobles should be impressed and stand in awe of him *(Radak).*

bridle-rein out of the hand of the Philistines [*II Samuel* 8:1; see *Radak* there, where this entire passage from *Pirkei d'Rabbi Eliezer* is cited.]

[For a similar *Midrash* regarding Abraham's oath, see *footnote* on page 771.]

וַיַּגִּדוּ לוֹ עַל־אֹדוֹת הַבְּאֵר אֲשֶׁר חָפָרוּ
לג וַיֹּאמְרוּ לוֹ מָצָאנוּ מָיִם: וַיִּקְרָא אֹתָהּ
שִׁבְעָה עַל־כֵּן שֵׁם־הָעִיר בְּאֵר שֶׁבַע עַד
לד הַיּוֹם הַזֶּה: וַיְהִי עֵשָׂו
בֶּן־אַרְבָּעִים שָׁנָה וַיִּקַּח אִשָּׁה אֶת־
יְהוּדִית בַּת־בְּאֵרִי הַחִתִּי וְאֶת־בָּשְׂמַת

וַיַּגִּדוּ לוֹ עַל־אדוֹת הַבְּאֵר אֲשֶׁר חָפָרוּ — *And they told him about the well they had dug.*

I.e., about the well they had *begun* digging before Abimelech came [*v.* 25] and which they now *finished* digging. On the day of his departure they came to Isaac with the news that they found water *(Ramban).*

וַיֹּאמְרוּ לוֹ מָצָאנוּ מָיִם — *And [they] said to him, 'We have found water!'*

I.e., spring water *(Malbim).*

Without strife or quarreling. Thus was Isaac's every effort successful in Eretz Yisrael *(Radak).*

33. וַיִּקְרָא אֹתָהּ שִׁבְעָה — *And he named* [lit. *called*] *it Shibah.*

On account of the covenant [connecting שִׁבְעָה to שְׁבוּעָה, *oath*] *(Rashi).*

According to *Ibn Ezra,* the name *Shibah* — which means *seven* as well as *oath* — commemorates both the *seven* ewes which Abraham had given to Abimelech (21:28-31) as well as the oath.

Ramban suggests that this is the *very same well* which Abraham had dug at the time he made his earlier covenant with Abimelech. As testimony to his ownership of the well and to the newly concluded treaty, Abraham had given Abimelech *seven* ewes. In commemoration, the well was named Beer Sheba. The Philistines had subsequently stopped it up along with the other wells; Isaac now redug it and *gave it the same name it had borne previously* [*v.* 18].

Rashbam maintains, however, that this was a different site than the Beer Sheba of chapter 21, there being two sites named Beer Sheba, as indicated by the reference to Beer Sheba *'which was in Judah'* in *I Kings* 19:3 [distinct from the Beer Sheba in Simeon (see *Joshua* 19:2).]

[But see *Radak* in *I Kings* 19:3 who notes that the Beer Sheba of Judah was the *same* Beer Sheba as that of Simeon, i.e., Simeon's territory was intermixed with that of Judah).]

According to *Sforno,* the name שִׁבְעָה, [*seven*], also signifies it was the *seventh* well they had dug. The earlier six included: *'all the wells'* in *v.* 15 implying a minimum of three which Isaac subsequently reopened [*v.* 18]; the three wells *Esek, Sitnah,* and *Rechovos;* and now this well for a total of seven.

On the 'seven' connotation of the word שִׁבְעָה, see *Hirsch* cited on page 769.

עַל כֵּן שֵׁם הָעִיר בְּאֵר שֶׁבַע — *Therefore, the name of the city is Beer* [i.e., the well of] *Sheba.*

On account of the בְּאֵר, *well,* which both the father and the son named to commemorate their שְׁבוּעָה, *oath (Ramban).*

The vocalization בְּאֵר שֶׁבַע alludes to the dual significance of both the *oath* and *seven.* In Abraham's case it was vocalized בְּאֵר שָׁבַע [21:31] since it symbolized the *oath* aspect

26 came and told him about the well they had dug, and
33-34 said to him, "We have found water!"[33] And he
named it Shibah. Therefore, the name of the city is
Beer Sheba until this very day.

When Esau was forty years old he took to wife
Judith daughter of Be'eri the Hittite, and

primarily as the verse there states (*Sforno*).

Ramban adds that this well alludes to the Tabernacle at Shiloh which the Philistines destroyed when they captured the Ark of God [*I Samuel* 4:11]. The *redigging* indicates the Ark's eventual return [*ibid.* 6:11] (see *footnote* to *v.* 20).

Abraham gave the name Beer Sheba only to the *well* or to the immediate *district* [21:31]; our verse informs us that Isaac gave the name to the עִיר, *city*, itself (*Radak*).

R' Menashe ben Yisrael [*The Conciliator*, Question 48] suggests that Abraham and Isaac both named the same site, but the name Abraham gave it did not remain firmly established until it was confirmed after Isaac's covenant. Then it remained permanent. This may be inferred from the texts themselves, for in Abraham's case it does not say *until this very day* — which is a Scriptural term to denote the permanence of a thing — as it does in Isaac's.

— Thus, in the case of Abraham this emphasis is on *why* the name was given; here, on its permanent aspect (*Ha'amek Davar*).

עַד הַיּוֹם הַזֶּה — *Until this very day.*

I.e., the days of Moses [when the Torah was given.] This is the meaning of *until this day* throughout Scripture: until the time of the Scribe who recorded the matter (*Rashbam* to 19:37).

[And, as noted above, it denotes permanence.]

34. Esau Marries.

בֶּן אַרְבָּעִים שָׁנָה — *Forty years old.*

Rashi comments: Esau is compared to a swine which, when it lies down stretches out its cloven hoof as if to say, 'See, I am a clean (i.e., kosher) animal.' [In reality animals are considered 'clean' only if they have a cloven hoof, and chew their cud. Swine do not have the second feature (see *Leviticus* 11:4, 5).]: In a similar manner, the princes of Esau rob and extort while they pretend to be honorable.

... So was it with Esau: For forty years he had been living an immoral life — enticing married women from their husbands — and when he reached the age of forty he hypocritically said that he would follow the example of his father who married at that age [see 25:20] (*Midrash*).

יְהוּדִית בַּת־בְּאֵרִי הַחִתִּי — *Judith daughter of Beeri the Hittite.*

Hittite is mentioned to emphasize that Isaac was not as careful as was his father in seeing that his son married a fitting wife, or that he not marry a Hittite [=Canaanite] (*Sforno*).

לה בַּת־אֵילֹן הַחִתִּי: וַתִּהְיֶיןָ מֹרַת רוּחַ
א לְיִצְחָק וּלְרִבְקָה: וַיְהִי כִּי־
זָקֵן יִצְחָק וַתִּכְהֶיןָ עֵינָיו מֵרְאֹת וַיִּקְרָא

— But the punishment for the failure to oversee their sons' activity came quick: Esau's wife immediately proved to be a source of spiritual rebellion, and introduced idolatrous practices into the house to the utter frustration of Isaac and Rebecca *(Hoffmann).*[1]

Ibn Ezra suggest that Esau had no children from Judith and she is therefore not mentioned with his other wives in the listing of his genealogy (36:2). *Rashi* suggests that she is the Oholibamah, daughter of Anah, mentioned there, both she and her father having two names.

בָּשְׂמַת בַּת אֵילֹן הַחִתִּי — *Basemath, daughter of Elon the Hittite.*

The *Midrash* notes that these women were indeed suited to be wives of the wicked Esau, and it is Providence that called out, 'Let Esau, may his name be blotted out, come and marry this woman, may her name be blotted out!'

In the genealogical history below [36:2], her name appears as *Adah,* daughter of Elon the Hittite. She apparently had two names which is common in Scripture [but see *Rashi* there] *(Ibn Ezra).*

With this marriage, accordingly, Esau set the seal on his complete unfitness to be the one who was to carry on the mission of Abraham. In a home ruled by two Hittite women, the Abrahamitic ideal lays buried *(Hirsch).*

35. מֹרַת רוּחַ — *A source of spiritual rebellion.*

The translation follows *Rashi* who derives the word from מרה, *to rebel* (as in the cognate word מַמְרִים, *rebellious,* in *Deut.* 9:24) rather than from מרה *bitter*: they were rebellious, intentionally seeking to provoke Isaac and Rebecca.

Compare *Onkelos*: 'They were rebels and irritants against the word of Isaac and Rebecca'; while *Targum Yonasan* renders: 'They set themselves to rebel in their evil conduct against Isaac and Rebecca.' *Targum Yerushalmi* paraphrases: 'They were refractory, swelling in spirit with idolatrous worship, and would not receive instruction either from Isaac or Rebecca.' [The implication of the latter is noteworthy since it dispels the image of Isaac and Rebecca sitting idly by while their daughters-in-law sinned; the parents were, apparently, helpless to control them.]

According to *Ibn Ezra,* the root is מרר, *bitterness,* hence: *a bitterness of spirit.*

Sforno derives the word from מוֹרָה, *razor* [*Judges* 13:5], signifying that they *cut short the spirit in* the lives of Isaac and Rebecca.

1. [The calculations of *Seder Olam* provide a possible defense for Isaac and Rebecca. Rachel and Leah were not born until the blessings were given, over twenty years later. There may therefore have been no righteous woman to whom Esau could be directed by his parents. Perhaps this is why Jacob did not marry earlier. It was only when Providence informed Isaac that Rachel and Leah had been born that Isaac sent Jacob to his kin.]

26 *Basemath daughter of Elon the Hittite.* [35] *And they*
35 *were a source of spiritual rebellion to Isaac and to*
Rebecca.

27 *And it came to pass, when Isaac had become old,*
1 *and his eyesight dimmed from seeing, that he*

— They were in complete opposition to the spirit that dominated Isaac and Rebecca *(Hirsch).*

And, as the *Midrash* notes, [the bitterness was that] they caused the *Shechinah* to depart from Isaac and Rebecca.

לְיִצְחָק וּלְרִבְקָה — *To Isaac and to Rebecca.*

— In that they worshipped idols *(Rashi).*

Isaac is mentioned first in this respect to signify that their idolatrous ways were a greater source of irritation to him, who had never been exposed to idolatry, than to Rebecca who had been accustomed to her family's idolatrous service since her youth. See *comm.* to 27:1 *(Midrash).*

Sforno notes that despite Esau's brazenness in marrying such women and in not controlling their idolatrous behavior, Isaac still refused to recognize the evil nature of his son. As a result, he wished to bless him and, even after having conferred the blessings on Jacob, Isaac blessed Esau to a certain extent. As a result, Jacob had to flee, and his descendants suffer from Esau's offspring to this day. Thus, these verses are a prelude to the next chapter.

Hirsch too, sees this episode as setting the stage for the blessings. Esau's wives were in total contradiction to the feelings and principles of Isaac and Rebecca. Significantly Isaac is mentioned first: even the loving father was repelled by the behavior of his daughters-in-law.

XXVII

1. Isaac's Blessing.

וַיְהִי כִּי־זָקֵן יִצְחָק — *And it came to pass, when Isaac had become old.*

[Isaac was 123 years old at this time. This is based on a simple calculation from *Seder Olam's* chronology that Jacob was 63 years old when he was blessed (see *Megillah* 17a; and *Rashi* to *v.* 2). Add to this Isaac's age of 60 when Jacob was born (25:26) and you arrive at 123. The year accordingly, was 2171 from Creation (see also chronology in 25:17).]

Kli Yakar notes that, unlike its description of Abraham's advanced age, Scripture does not say of Isaac בָּא בַּיָּמִים *well on in years* [24:1]. That expression, he comments, implies heightened perception, as if saying that one continuously emerges from the darkness of night into the light of spiritual day. In Isaac's case, however, regarding his

אֶת־עֵשָׂו | בְּנוֹ הַגָּדֹל וַיֹּאמֶר אֵלָיו בְּנִי

evaluation of Esau — the subject of this chapter — he remained in 'darkness', for he continued to regard Esau as righteous and more worthy of the blessings than Jacob.

Talmudically the term זָקֵן, *old*, refers to 'one who has acquired wisdom' and who sat on the elders' council. The Sages in *Yoma* 28b comment: Our ancestors were never left without the scholars' council ... Our father Isaac was an 'elder' and sat in the scholars' council as it says, *and it came to pass when Isaac was old* [see *Maharsha*.]

וַתִּכְהֶיןָ עֵינָיו מֵרְאֹת — *And his eyesight* [lit. *eyes*] *dimmed* [lit. *weakened*] *from seeing.*

Rashi offers three reasons for Isaac's failing eyesight.

1 — From seeing the smoke of the incense which his daughters-in-law [Esau's wives] offered to their idols. [Isaac's eyesight was more affected by the smoke than Rebecca's, because, as noted above, unlike Isaac Rebecca was born in a house where incense was constantly burned to idols and she was accustomed to the smoke *(sifsei Chachomim).* Further, God saw Isaac's distress at his daughters-in-law's wickedness and caused him this blindness to spare him from further seeing it *(Tanchuma).*

2 — Another reason: When Isaac lay bound on the altar at the *Akeidah* and his father was about to slay him, the heavens opened and the ministering angels wept over him. Their tears dropped into his eyes and dimmed them. [This second interpretation does not exclude the first; rather, it helps explain further why Isaac was more vulnerable to the smoke of his daughters-in-law's incense than was Rebecca: Isaac's eyes had already weakened, and the smoke aggravated them *(Maharshal)*]

3 — Another explanation: [*His eyes dimmed* מֵרְאֹת=*so he shall not see*]. Providence caused him to become blind for the specific reason that Jacob might receive the blessing [and Isaac would not realize whom he was blessing *(Tanchuma).*]

[Another reason for Isaac's blindness was the curse given by Abimelech to Sarah. This curse: 'May you have children of כְּסוּת עֵינַיִם, *covered eyes'* [20:16], was fulfilled in Sarah's offspring *(Bava Kamma;* see footnote to 20:16, page 737).]

The *Midrash* offers additional reasons: Providence caused Isaac to go blind so that he would not see Esau's wicked deeds. Further, so that Isaac's blindness would cause him to remain indoors and not suffer the shame of mingling with people and being constantly pointed out as the father of the wicked Esau. Similarly, God caused Ahijah the Shilonite to go blind in old age [*I Kings* 14:4] because he raised a wicked disciple.

— His eyesight failed because *he loved Esau for game was always in his mouth* [25:28 — i.e. because Isaac responded to Esau's flattery, a form of emotional bribery] and it is known that *a bribe blinds the eyes of the wise* [*Deut.* 16:19, so he no longer discerns things properly] *(Da'as Zekeinim).*

Ramban [end of Chapt. 25] comments that in line with the *simple meaning of Scripture,* Isaac's blindness was but a manifestation of his old age. Jacob, too, suffered from lack of vision in his old age [48:10]; as did Achiyah the Shilonite [*I Kings* 14:4]. Concerning Moses, however, the Torah mentions the *remarkable* fact that his eye was *not* dimmed in his old age [*Deut.* 34:7].

There is also a sentiment in the commentators that Isaac's blindness was in punishment for his failure to restrain Esau's wickedness. The same punishment befell Eli who also did not restrain his wicked children [*I Samuel* 3:12] *(Sforno).*

Akeidas Yitzchak emphasizes, however, that only Isaac's *vision* was impaired: Otherwise he was in control of all his faculties.

[It would appear from the narrative itself, that Isaac's vision had deteriorated to the point that he could no longer recognize people.]

וַיִּקְרָא אֶת־עֵשָׂו בְּנוֹ הַגָּדֹל — *[That] he summoned* [lit. *called*] *Esau, his older son.*

[*The word* גָּדוֹל means *greater* or *elder*. The translation *older* follows the literal sense of the context. According to the *Midrashim*, the implication is that Isaac *referred* to Esau as 'the greater']:

— From this description we learn that one may flatter the wicked while they are in ascendancy; additionally: the world was then in Esau's grasp and Isaac therefore called him *his great son (Da'as Zekeinim).*

The *Midrash* expounds that although Esau is described by his parents as *great* [see also *v.* 15], God said to them: Though in your eyes he is great, in Mine he is small, as it says concerning Edom, Esau's descendants [*Obadiah* 1:2]: *Behold I make you small among the nations.*

Or HaChaim notes that the Hebrew is not the usual וַיִּקְרָא אֶל עֵשָׂו, *he called 'to' Esau,* because Isaac's inability to see Esau made it impossible to direct a summons *to* him; rather the Hebrew וַיִּקְרָא אֶת עֵשָׂו, implies that *he called out the name 'Esau!'*

⁂ Why did Isaac summon Esau to receive the blessings, rather than Jacob who had purchased the birthright? Why was Esau not disqualified by having married Hittite women, thereby bringing misery upon Isaac and Rebecca (26:35)?

☐ *Or HaChaim* answers that perhaps Isaac was not aware of the sale [and hence still considered him the first born.]

☐ Isaac's intention in bestowing the paternal invocation of the Divine bounty upon *Esau* — though Isaac was aware of his wickedness — was that he hoped that as a result of the blessings Esau would be attracted to the right path and amend his ways. The righteous feel pain when their offspring are sinful and Isaac accordingly made every effort to improve Esau. Note that the Sages [*Bereishis Rabbah* 76:9; see *Rashi* to 32:22] say that Jacob was punished for withholding Dinah from Esau, because he failed to take into consideration the possibility that she might influence Esau to repent *(Or HaChaim).*

☐ *Ramban:* Isaac summoned *Esau* with the intent of blessing him since he was the first born. Presumably, Rebecca never told Isaac of the prophecy she had received during pregnancy that *the elder shall serve the younger,* nor did she reveal it to him now because she knew that in Isaac's great love for Esau he would leave everything to Providence instead of blessing Jacob. Therefore she maintained her silence

ב וַיֹּ֥אמֶר אֵלָ֖יו הִנֵּֽנִי׃ וַיֹּ֕אמֶר הִנֵּה־נָ֖א זָקַ֑נְתִּי
ג לֹ֥א יָדַ֖עְתִּי י֥וֹם מוֹתִֽי׃ וְעַתָּה֙ שָׂא־נָ֣א כֵלֶ֔יךָ

but arranged matters so that Isaac would in effect bless Jacob with an undivided heart *(Ramban).*

□ According to *Radak,* however, Isaac wished to bestow his blessings on *Esau* because he perceived that Esau was in need of his blessings since he was not righteous, whereas Jacob, who was righteous had no need of blessings. Isaac foresaw that it was in Jacob's descendants that Abraham's covenant to inherit the land would be fulfilled in any event.

[Thus, the blessing originally intended for Esau (verses 28-29) promised abundance, fertility, power, and dominion — material blessings. But the Abrahamitic mission, the blessing of seed and the promise of the Land were not bequeathed to Esau — They were reserved for Jacob and indeed, Isaac conferred them upon Jacob on the eve of his departure to Laban (28:3-4) — since such a spiritual blessing cannot be conferred by succession but only granted to the one who is deserving of it].

□ *Malbim* and *Hirsch* agree generally on Isaac's selection of Esau to receive the blessings. According to them, Isaac deemed it necessary for Israel to be composed both of people who would devote themselves to spiritual matters, and of others whose pursuits would be material, but who would be obligated to invest their everyday activities with higher motives. Thus, even the worker and businessman are expected to dedicate their activities to higher goals than the mere amassing of wealth and luxuries. Isaac recognized full well that Esau was not the righteous scholar of the family, but he wished to give him the blessing of material success which he would then use to assist Jacob in his higher calling. Therefore, he asked Esau to hunt down an animal and prepare it for Isaac as a prerequisite to gaining the blessings; this was symbolic of his intended role as one who would utilize material success to assist in the attainment of spiritual ends.

They differ, however, concerning Isaac's intentions *for Jacob.* According to *Malbim,* the role of God's spiritual surrogate on earth cannot be conferred by human blessing. It must be earned through accomplishment and ratified by God alone. Hence, Isaac did not intend a formal blessing for Jacob. *Hirsch,* however, maintains that Isaac had indeed meant to bless Jacob separately. Knowing this, Esau was confident that there was still left with Isaac a blessing to which he was entitled (*v.* 36 and 38). *That* blessing, however — the one intended for Jacob — could not be given to the materialistic Esau.

[See *Overview.*]

וַיֹּאמֶר אֵלָיו בְּנִי — *And he said to him, 'My son.'*

When the night of Passover arrived, Isaac summoned his elder son, Esau, and said, 'Tonight, my son, the whole world will be reciting special praises to God and the treasurehouses containing the dew of blessing will be open. Prepare delicacies for me and while I am still in this world, I will bless you' *(Pirkei d'Rabbi Eliezer).*

וַיֹּאמֶר אֵלָיו הִנֵּנִי — *And he* [Esau] *said to him, 'Here I am.'*

— An answer denoting readiness to comply. [Cf. *Rashi* to 22:1.]

2. הִנֵּה־נָא זָקַנְתִּי — *See, now* [following *Onkelos;* or: *Behold, if you please (Rashbam)*] *I have aged.*

I bring up this subject now because *I am old* and I wish to

son;" And he said to him, "Here I am."
[2] And he said "See, now, I have aged; I know not the day of my death. [3] Now sharpen, if you please,

bestow upon you the blessings while I am still alive *(Rashbam);* for a blessing is indeed more efficacious when given nearer to one's death — as we find that Jacob and Moses also pronounced their blessings soon before their deaths — because the soul is then freer from its physical bonds *(Sforno).*

לֹא יָדַעְתִּי יוֹם מוֹתִי — *I know not the day of my death.*[1]

The *Midrash* notes: When a man reaches within five years before and after the age at which his parents died he should be concerned about his own death. Now, Isaac was 123 years old [see *comm. v.* 1] — about five years younger than his mother at the time of her death at 127, and he was apprehensive that he might only reach her age. He therefore said, *I do not know the day of my death:* perhaps I may only reach my mother's age [and I will soon die]; or perhaps I may reach my father's age [of 175 (see 25:7) in which case there is much time *(Midrash).* Actually, Isaac lived to be 180 years old (38:28), five years more than Abraham whose life was shortened — as noted in *comm.* to 25:30] *(Rashi).*

3. וְעַתָּה שָׂא־נָא כֵלֶיךָ — *Now sharpen, if you please, your gear.*

The rendering *sharpen* follows *Rashi* who derives it from a *Mishnaic* term with that meaning in *Betzah* 28a. Accordingly, Isaac told Esau: Sharpen your knife and slaughter the animal according to the proper ritual so you do not feed me נְבֵלָה [carrion; flesh of animal not ritually slaughtered, since kosher slaughtering requires — among other things — a perfectly unflawed blade].

— Although [at least in the view of Isaac who always ate of Esau's game] Esau was reliable in such ritual matters, nevertheless Isaac verbalized these special precautions now because he feared that Esau in his haste to fulfill his father's specific request, might neglect to give proper attention to examining the knife. He, therefore, cautioned him to be scrupulous in the ritual requirements and not

1. The *Midrash,* as interpreted by *Yefei Toar,* records that there are seven things that are hidden from even the greatest prophets. They are:

1 — The day of death; because if people knew when their time would come, they would die from the terror of its imminence. Furthermore, they would not repent until the last possible moment. And they would fail to comply with God's will that the world be developed because they would lose interest in life.

2 — The time of Messiah's arrival; because if people had known throughout history that Messiah was not destined to come in their time, they would have gone mad with grief.

3 — When Edom (the dominant power of the current exile) will fall.

4 — The depth of the law; because if it were known, people would fail to study and clarify it through debate.

5 — The source of wealth; because if people knew how to become successful they would all engage in the same occupation.

6 — The thoughts of other people; because life would be impossible if thoughts were not private.

7 — The sex of a pregnant woman's child.

תולדת
כז/ד

תְּלְיְךָ וְקַשְׁתֶּךָ וְצֵא הַשָּׂדֶה וְצ֫וּדָה לִּי
°צידה: וַעֲשֵׂה־לִי מַטְעַמִּים כַּאֲשֶׁר
אָהַבְתִּי וְהָבִיאָה לִּי וְאֹכֵלָה בַּעֲבוּר

°צַיִד ק׳ ד

to place his emphasis on filial obedience *(Gur Aryeh* [Cf. *Mizrachi*].

Targum translates שָׂא in its more familiar sense of *take; carry.*

— This taking of weapons intimated that Esau's descendants would live by the sword *(R' Bachya).*

[Now the verse specifies *which* 'gear' *(Ibn Ezra)*]:

תְּלְיְךָ — *Your sword.*

The rendering *'sword'* follows *Onkelos,* and *Rashi* who derive it from תלה [*hang*] — that which is usually hung [at the side].

Rashbam, Targum Yonasan, Radak and *Ibn Ezra* in his primary interpretation agree with the derivation, but render the word as meaning 'quiver' — where arrows are kept hung.

וְקַשְׁתֶּךָ — *And your bow.*

[Possibly to defend himself against wild beasts.]

Or, possibly the bow was for hunting and Esau was to exercise such great care that if he shot at an animal, he would not maim it so as to render it ritually unfit for slaughter, but would merely slow it down so he could catch and properly slaughter it *(Sifsei Chachomim* citing *Nachalas Yaakov).*

וְצֵא הַשָּׂדֶה — [And] *go out to the field.*

— Perhaps Esau did not venture out every day *(Radak).*

Most commentators, however, perceive that Isaac sent Esau out to the field to hunt rather than ask him to select a domestic animal from their herd, so as to make the task more arduous and therefore the mitzvah more meritorious *(Alshich).*

וְצוּדָה לִּי צָיִד — *And hunt game for me.*

[The לִּי, *for me,* is emphasized: hunt game *suitable for me (Mizrachi)*]:

— Bring ownerless animals; not stolen ones *(Rashi).*

[For similar interpretations of the addition of the seemingly superfluous לְךָ, *for you,* as signifying *from your own,* in cases where it could have been omitted without changing the sense of the verse, see *Ramban* and *Mizrachi* to 12:1].

Although Isaac, as noted above, considered Esau trustworthy in such matters, he cautioned him to be *extra*-scrupulous in making certain that he hunt far away from private lands and hunt only ownerless game — since if he were to sin even *unintentionally,* the blessings would not be effective since God is not with sinners *(Gur Aryeh).*

The word צָיִד, *game,* is spelled in the Torah with a superfluous ה [=5] because Isaac was instructing him in the laws of ritual slaughter, and cautioned him to avoid the *five* acts which render ritual slaughter invalid: [שְׁהִיָּה, pausing while cutting; דְּרָסָה, pressing on the knife; חֲלָדָה, thrusting, i.e. burrowing into the throat; הַגְרָמָה, cutting outside of the prescribed region of the throat; and עִיקּוּר, tearing out the windpipe after cutting through the gullet *(Rashi, Chullin* 9a) or: slaughtering with a notched knife which tears rather than cuts the organs *(Tosafos* ibid.)] *(R'Bachya;* the *Midrash* is found in *Pesikta Zutresa).*

27 *your gear — your sword and your bow, and go out to*
4 *the field and hunt game for me.* [4] *Then make me*
delicacies such as I love and bring it to me to eat so

4. וַעֲשֵׂה לִי מַטְעַמִּים כַּאֲשֶׁר אָהַבְתִּי — *Then* [lit. *and*] *make me delicacies such as I love* [lit. past tense indicating a constant action: *I have loved (*and continue to love.)]

The *Midrash* explains that Isaac desired מַטְעַמִּים, *delicacies,* i.e. tasty food, since he was blind and could not derive satisfaction merely from the *sight* of food. 'Formerly', Isaac told Esau, 'I used to enjoy sight; now I can only enjoy flavor.' King Solomon said [*Eccles.* 5:10]: *What advantage, then, has the owner except what his eyes see* — which intimates that the blind are never satisfied [since they do not behold with their eyes]. You cannot compare him who sees an empty bread basket and remains hungry, to him who sees a full bread-basket and is satisfied [by the mere knowledge that he has something to eat].

⌘ What was Isaac's purpose in sending Esau to bring him delicacies prior to blessing him?

☐ *Radak* emphasizes that Isaac's request for food certainly was *not* — as *Ibn Ezra* seems to suggest — because Isaac was destitute and needed Esau's meal. [See *Ramban* to 25:34 who similarly attacks *Ibn Ezra* as having 'erred here exceedingly']. To the contrary, Isaac was exceedingly wealthy and owned much cattle. Rather, Isaac requested these delicacies, because old people are disgusted with life and desire something exotic and tasty to eat. Therefore, Isaac asked Esau to bring him vension that he might feel good of heart and bless him.

☐ *Ramban* [in 25:34] comments simply that the blessings are not to be construed as recompense for the food. Rather, Isaac's desire for food preliminary to blessing Esau was in order to derive a benefit from him so the blessing would be bestowed wholeheartedly. Perhaps Isaac discerned that he would be joyful and the Holy Inspiration would descend upon him, after he enjoyed the delicacies, as in the case of Elisha who said [*II Kings* 3:15], *But now, bring me a minstrel. And it came to pass, when the minstrel played, that the hand of HASHEM came upon him.* [For, as noted in *Shabbos* 30b: 'The *Shechinah* does not rest upon man through gloom ... but rather through joy' and the verse in *II Kings* is cited. *Maharsha* there explains that since the *Shechinah* does not rest on a man plunged into gloom, Elisha required the minstrel to dissipate the gloom occasioned by Jehoram's visit.][1]

☐ *Sforno:* Isaac's aim in making this request was that Esau involve himself in filial obedience so the blessing should be effective. Although Isaac was not aware of the extent of Esau's wickedness, he nevertheless did not consider him worthy of the blessing he had in store for him. In the case of Jacob whom he knew to be worthy, Isaac made no such request before blessing him prior to his departure to Paddan Aram [28:2] .

1. *Torah Temimah* cites the *Responsa* of *Maharam* 354 who explains Isaac's desire for delicacies as an effort to achieve joy, for one who confers blessings must be joyous. He further cites I *Kings* 8:66 that when the Jews returned to their homes *gladdened and good-hearted, they blessed the King* [Solomon]; again it is implied that blessing had to be preceded by happiness. Therefore, too, the halachah forbids a priest who is a mourner from delivering the Priestly Blessings.

ה תְּבָרֶכְךָ נַפְשִׁי בְּטֶרֶם אָמוּת: וְרִבְקָה
שֹׁמַעַת בְּדַבֵּר יִצְחָק אֶל־עֵשָׂו בְּנוֹ וַיֵּלֶךְ
ו עֵשָׂו הַשָּׂדֶה לָצוּד צַיִד לְהָבִיא: וְרִבְקָה
אָמְרָה אֶל־יַעֲקֹב בְּנָהּ לֵאמֹר הִנֵּה

5. Rebecca's scheme.

When Rebecca saw Esau leave to do his father's bidding, her jealousy was aroused. She did not realize that Jacob would be blessed irrespective of whether his father blessed him [see above], and that this was his father's intention as well. Her mind was thrown into a turmoil in her great love for Jacob, and this accounts for her subsequent action in advising him to circumvent the truth to receive the blessing from his father. She gave no concern to the sinfulness of the act *(Radak)*.

[It must also be remembered that Rebecca felt that the prophecy she had heard during pregnancy, וְרַב יַעֲבֹד צָעִיר, *the elder shall serve the younger* (25:23) would be subverted by the blessing about to be bestowed upon Esau. In her consternation, she devised the following ruse, convinced that since as *Ramban* notes, she never made Isaac aware of the prophecy all of these 63 years, it would be futile — recognizing his great love for Esau — to do so now that so few precious moments were left. See also *Zohar* in footnote to 25:28 that the Divine plan dictated that Jacob receive the blessings in such a manner.]

[See *Hirsch; Malbim*. The matter of the deception is dealt with in the *Overview*.]

וְרִבְקָה שֹׁמַעַת — *Now* [lit. *and*] *Rebecca was listening* or: *would listen; would overhear.*]

☐ As noted above [*v.* 1] *Malbim* and *Hirsch* explain Isaac's request as a device to symbolize the purpose of Esau's blessing: that he utilize his physical prowess and material success to enhance spiritual purposes.

וְאֹכֵלָה — *To eat* [lit. *and I will eat*].

Implying [perhaps unconsciously], it was because of food that you forfeited your birthright, and because of food it will revert to you *(Tur)*.

בַּעֲבוּר תְּבָרֶכְךָ נַפְשִׁי — *So that I may give you my innermost blessing* [lit. *so that my soul may bless you.*]

— From this we derive that one who bestows blessings must be of a joyful spirit (Responsa of *Maharam* 344; see *Torah Temimah* in *footnote)*.

— The expression that my *soul* may bless you is used because a blessing, as the Translation signifies, must emanate from man's *soul* and flow from the innermost recesses of one's being *(Hoffmann)*.

Isaac intended to bless Esau that he be the instrument of the fulfillment of God's covenant that Abraham's descendants inherit the land *(Ramban)*.

This differs from *Radak* who holds that Isaac intended to bless Esau only because he knew that Jacob would be the recipient of Abraham's blessings anyway.

בְּטֶרֶם אָמוּת — *Before I die.*

And, as *Sforno* explains in *v.* 2, a blessing is more effective when given nearer to one's death.

27
5-6

that I may give you my innermost blessings before I die."

5 *Now Rebecca was listening as Isaac spoke to Esau his son. And Esau went to the field to hunt game to bring.* 6 *But Rebecca had said to Jacob her*

This was her practice. When Isaac spoke to Esau she would eavesdrop to ascertain whether the conversation concerned Jacob *(Ha'amek Davar).*

The phrase is רִבְקָה שֹׁמַעַת, *Rebecca was listening* i.e. *always* listening, rather than וַתִּשְׁמַע רִבְקָה, *Rebecca listened,* or וְרִבְקָה הָיְתָה שֹׁמַעַת, *Rebecca had been listening,* both of which would imply that she was listening only on this occasion. The Torah thereby informs us *she always overheard Isaac's conversations* though they were not in her presence, for she had prophetic inspiration. Perhaps, Isaac spoke to Esau in a hushed voice to prevent being overheard [not realizing that Rebecca overheard him in any event]. Accordingly he unquestioningly assumed that the one who came to receive the blessings was Esau *(Or HaChaim).*

This follows the *Tanchuma* which specifically attributes Rebecca's 'hearing' in this case to her prophetic spirit.

וַיֵּלֶךְ עֵשָׂו הַשָּׂדֶה לָצוּד צַיִד — *And Esau went to the field to hunt game.*

This continues the narrative.

— He had departed immediately to do his father's bidding and this convinced Rebecca not to enter into a dialogue with Isaac to dissuade him; time was of the essence and she had to act immediately *(Abarbanel; Malbim).*

What she did not know, however, was that Providence caused Esau to be delayed. He repeatedly trapped animals, but angels released them to allow sufficient time for Jacob to carry out Rebecca's instructions and receive the blessings *(Pirkei d'Rabbi Eliezer; Tanchuma).*

לְהָבִיא — *To bring* [i.e., to bring home to Isaac].

What is implied by [the apparently superfluous] לְהָבִיא, *to bring?*

[Esau was determined — under any circumstances — *to bring* something back]: If he found game [ownerless venison of his own hunt as Isaac specified] well and good; if not he would bring a stolen animal *(Rashi).*

According to *Hirsch* who interprets that this mission was designed to compel Esau benevolently to utilize his love of hunting and trapping [see above *v.* 4], this verse accordingly implies that for once Esau went out on the hunt for the noble purpose of לְהָבִיא, *to bring* home.

[It would seem, however, that the *simple sense* of the narrative would also require use of the word *to bring,* as if to tell us that Esau had gone out not simply to *hunt* but *with the express intention* of fulfilling his father's command that he hunt and prepare a delicacy *and bring it to him (v.* 4).

6. וְרִבְקָה אָמְרָה אֶל יַעֲקֹב בְּנָהּ — *But* [lit. *and*] *Rebecca had said to Jacob her son.*

שָׁמַ֙עְתִּי֙ אֶת־אָבִ֔יךָ מְדַבֵּ֥ר אֶל־עֵשָׂ֖ו אָחִ֥יךָ
ז לֵאמֹֽר׃ הָבִ֨יאָה לִּ֥י צַ֛יִד וַעֲשֵׂה־לִ֥י
מַטְעַמִּ֖ים וְאֹכֵ֑לָה וַאֲבָרֶכְכָ֛ה לִפְנֵ֥י יהוה
ח לִפְנֵ֥י מוֹתִֽי׃ וְעַתָּ֥ה בְנִ֖י שְׁמַ֣ע בְּקֹלִ֑י לַאֲשֶׁ֥ר
ט אֲנִ֖י מְצַוָּ֥ה אֹתָֽךְ׃ לֶךְ־נָא֙ אֶל־הַצֹּ֔אן וְקַח־

[The subject-verb arrangement וְרִבְקָה אָמְרָה instead of וַתֹּאמֶר רִבְקָה suggests both the conversive and pluperfect: 'But Rebecca *had* said' — implying that even before, *Esau went out to the field to hunt,* Rebecca had already said to Jacob her son ... such was her urgency.]

הִנֵּה שָׁמַעְתִּי — *Behold, I heard.*

I.e. do not think it is too late to act. I *just* heard it, and there is plenty of time to carry out my plan *(Or HaChaim).*

לֵאמֹר — *Saying.*

I.e. not verbatim — since in effect Rebecca did not quote Isaac exactly — but the following was his *intent (Or HaChaim).*

7. הָבִיאָה לִי צַיִד — *Bring me* [some] *game.*

She omitted Isaac's command that he *sharpen his weapon and go out to the field* since Jacob, as a non-hunter would have demurred, Rebecca therefore implied that there was no *requirement* that the game be from the wild rather than from their domestic herds *(Malbim).*

[And, as *R' Chananel* notes in the *comm.* to *v.* 20 s.v. וְאָכְלָה מִצֵּידִי, the word צַיִד also refers to *food* in general.]

וַאֲבָרֶכְכָה לִפְנֵי ה' לִפְנֵי מוֹתִי — *And* [*I*] *will bless you in the presence of* HASHEM *before my death.*

In the presence of HASHEM — i.e., by His permission: with His approval *(Rashi).*

[See *Maskil leDavid* below].

Rebecca added the words לִפְנֵי ה', *in the Presence of* HASHEM, to impress upon Jacob the immensity of his father's blessing *inasmuch as it would be in the presence of* HASHEM, that is, with the prophetic

1. *Maskil leDavid* points out that the term פָּנִים is used to depict *desire, consent,* knowledge. Cf. 6:3: *The end of all flesh has come* לְפָנַי, *before Me* — i.e. to My attention.

In Rabbinic usage זָכִין לְאָדָם שֶׁלֹּא בְּפָנָיו means 'a benefit may be conferred upon someone without his knowledge or formal consent.' Thus, Rebecca's expression לִפְנֵי ה', *with* HASHEM*'s consent,* is equivalent to Isaac's statement *that my soul bless you. HaKsav V'haKabbalah* cites this and adds that blessing proceeding from the mouths of the righteous are not their own but are inspired from Above. When Isaac referred to the blessing as coming from נַפְשִׁי, *my soul,* his intention was that his soul, i.e. his *spiritual* self, would divorce itself from all physical and personal considerations and become God's tool in conferring the blessings as He willed them. Thus Rebecca paraphrased, but did not change the meaning of his words.

HaKsav V'haKabbalah goes on to explain that Rebbeca's deception may be accounted for by Isaac's intention to submit himself to God's will. Since she knew that God wanted Jacob to receive the blessings — for she had received the prophecy that the older son would be subservient to the younger — it became her duty not to permit Isaac to violate God's will by conferring the blessings upon Esau. [See *Overview*].

son, saying "Behold I heard your father speaking to
your brother Esau saying 7 *'Bring me some game and*
make me delicacies to eat, and I will bless you in the
presence of HASHEM before my death.' 8 *So now, my*
son, heed my voice to that which I command you.
9 *Go now to the flock and fetch me from there two*

spirit that would descend upon him while he would utter the benedictions *(Radak).**

... And as such the blessing would be irrevocable. Accordingly, if Esau was blessed with it, it would remain with his descendants forever and Jacob would never be able to lift his head before him *(Ramban).*

As *Malbim* explains, Rebecca meant to allay Jacob's concern that a blessing obtained through deception would not be efficacious in any case, because if Isaac intended to bless Esau, the blessing could not rest upon Jacob. Rebecca, therefore, added that the blessing is *before HASHEM* i.e. the prophet is merely God's tool. The blessing is God's, not Isaac's. If such is God's will, than the blessing will be Jacob's despite despite Isaac's intention, since Isaac is merely the conduit which God's Will would be manifested.[On the implication of לִפְנֵי ה׳, see ArtScroll edition of *Jonah* 1:3, p.83].

8. וְעַתָּה בְנִי שְׁמַע בְּקֹלִי — *So now, my son, heed* [in] *my voice.*

'Although the following appears deceitful I adjure you as בְּנִי, *my son,* to heed my voice.' Thus, Rebecca relates Jacob's compliance to filial *obedience,* thereby silencing any resistance *(Abarbanel; Malbim).*

— As you have always listened to me, listen to me now as well *(Midrash Aggadah).*

The seemingly superfluous בְּקֹלִי, lit. *in my voice,* implies *to my intent* [i.e., that which is implicit *within my voice*]: carefully scrutinize every word I say. She also implied thereby that she was addressing him with a prophetic spirit *(Haamek Davar).*

[Cf. *Rashi* to 21:12 *heed her voice,* i.e. to the voice of the prophetic spirit within her. Perhaps *Rashi* does not cite this exegesis here because, as noted in the *comm.* to *v.* 23, he apparently subscribes to the view that Rebecca was not a prophetess, for she was not counted among the seven prophetesses enumerated in *Megillah* 14a. But cf. *comm.* to verses 42 and 45, and 25:23.]

לַאֲשֶׁר אֲנִי מְצַוָּה אוֹתָךְ — *To that which I command you.*

[I. e. and for which I take full responsibility.]

Rebecca perceived Jacob's reluctance to participate in this devious scheme. She therefore emphasized that he was to 'listen to that which *I* — as your mother — command you *(Divrei Yirmiyah).*

9. לֶךְ־נָא אֶל הַצֹּאן — *Go now to the flock.*

* [Compare Jonah who is described as fleeing מִלִּפְנֵי ה׳, *from before HASHEM's Presence (Jonah* 1:3) where *Radak* similarly explains that it was not מִפְּנֵי ה׳, *from HASHEM's Presence Itself,* that Jonah presumed to escape, but מִלִּפְנֵי ה׳, *from* לִפְנֵי ה׳, *that which is before HASHEM* — from prophetic contact with Him.

לִי מִשָּׁם שְׁנֵי גְּדָיֵי עִזִּים טֹבִים וְאֶעֱשֶׂה
אֹתָם מַטְעַמִּים לְאָבִיךָ כַּאֲשֶׁר אָהֵב׃
י וְהֵבֵאתָ לְאָבִיךָ וְאָכָל בַּעֲבֻר אֲשֶׁר יְבָרֶכְךָ
יא לִפְנֵי מוֹתוֹ׃ וַיֹּאמֶר יַעֲקֹב אֶל־רִבְקָה אִמּוֹ
הֵן עֵשָׂו אָחִי אִישׁ שָׂעִר וְאָנֹכִי אִישׁ חָלָק׃
יב אוּלַי יְמֻשֵּׁנִי אָבִי וְהָיִיתִי בְעֵינָיו
כִּמְתַעְתֵּעַ וְהֵבֵאתִי עָלַי קְלָלָה וְלֹא

[See *comm.* to *v.* 7 that Rebecca did not ask Jacob to go out to the fields because he was not a hunter, Furthermore, Isaac's request for 'game' did not exclude domestic animals (see .*v.* 19 below).]

וְקַח־לִי מִשָּׁם שְׁנֵי גְּדָיֵי עִזִּים טֹבִים — *And fetch me from there two choice* [lit. *good*] *young kids of the goats.*

Did Isaac's meal consist of *two* kids of the goats? — Rather, it was Passover eve and one goat would serve as the Passover sacrifice, and the other as מַטְעַמִּים, *the delicacy* (*Rashi citing Pirkei d'Rabbi Eliezer*). [*See v.* 1 s.v. וַיֹּאמֶר אֵלָיו בְּנִי.]

In the literal sense, however, although Isaac could not consume so much, it was proper to prepare as sumptuous and generous a meal as possible in his honor due to the auspicious nature of the occasion. Compare Abraham's extravagant preparations for his guests in 18:6 (*Hoffmann*).

And fetch לִי, [*for*] *me* — i.e. from those which *belong* to me and are not taken from Isaac without his permission. [As the *Midrash* notes] her כְּתוּבָּה, marriage contract, provided that she receive, as part of her allowance, two goats every day (*Rashi*).

The adjective טֹבִים means *tasty* (*Chizkuni*).[1]

וְאֶעֱשֶׂה אֹתָם מַטְעַמִּים לְאָבִיךָ כַּאֲשֶׁר אָהֵב — *And I will make* [of] *them delicacies for your father, as he loves.*

Since [of all the domestic animals Rebecca could have instructed Jacob to bring] the goat tastes most like deer [=venison] which Isaac loved (*Rashi*).

Furthermore, as *Rashbam* notes, goats were chosen over sheep because goats' wiry hair more resemble a human's.

10. בַּעֲבֻר אֲשֶׁר יְבָרֶכְךָ לִפְנֵי מוֹתוֹ — *So that he may bless you before his death.*

1. Rebecca's choice of *goats* was not haphazard. As the *Midrash* relates, Rebecca intimated thereby:

They are *good* for you and *good* for your descendants. *Good for you personally* since you will receive blessings through them; and *good for your descendants* who will be pardoned through them on Yom Kippur, of which it is written [*Lev.* 16:5: *And he shall take of the congregation of Israel two he-goats* ...] *For on this day shall atonement be made for you* [ibid. *v.* 30] (*Midrash*).

[Just as you will prevail over Esau now by virtue of the goats, so in the future, will the two goats allow you to avoid the indictments of Esau's guardian angel — symbolized by the שָׂעִיר, goat, *Lev.* 16:22 (a play on שֵׂעִיר, a reference to Esau) — and will achieve atonement for your descendants (*R' Bachya*).]

27 *choice young kids of the goats, and I will make of*
10-12 *them delicacies for your father, as he loves.* [10] *Then*
bring it to your father and he shall eat, so that he may
bless you before his death."
[11] *Jacob replied to Rebecca, his mother, "But my*
brother Esau is a hairy man and I am a smooth-
skinned man. [12] *Perhaps Father will feel me and I*
shall appear as a mocker; I will thus bring upon

For he will then be in a joyful mood, joy being prerequisite for the Presence of the *Shechinah (Lekach Tov;* see *v.* 4; *Chizkuni).*[See *Overview.*]

In an esoteric sense the stimulus of food will bring about physical comfort and serve as a 'bribery' for the physical senses so they will not deter the soul from uniting with the Source of the Blessing *(Malbim).*

11. ['But', Jacob asks, 'have you considered the following difficulty?']:

וַיֹּאמֶר יַעֲקֹב אֶל רִבְקָה אִמּוֹ — [And] *Jacob replied* [lit. *said*] *to Rebecca, his mother.*

— The phrase *his mother* is repeated throughout these verses to emphasize that Jacob complied with a deception that he considered to be onerous for only one reason: his *mother* demanded obedience of him, and as a son he obeyed *(Hirsch).*

וְאָנֹכִי אִישׁ חָלָק — *Whereas* [lit. *and*] *I am a smooth-skinned man.*

12. אוּלַי יְמֻשֵּׁנִי אָבִי — *Perhaps* [*my*] *Father will feel me.*

— Not suspiciously, but to *affectionately caress me,* and he will discover that I am smooth-skinned. It is noteworthy that Jacob was not afraid of that Isaac would recognize his voice. Perhaps their voices were similar [see on *v.* 22], or Jacob could imitate Esau's voice *(Ramban).*

The word פֶּן, *lest,* has a negative undertone, used when the speaker does not wish something to occur [comp. 3:22; 4:4.] Thus, had Jacob wished to express the hope that his father would *not* feel him he should have said 'I am afraid [פֶּן]*lest* my father feel me.' The adverbial prefix אוּלַי, *perhaps,* has a positive undertone and is used when the speaker desires the matter to come to pass. [Comp. comm. to Eliezer's query in 24:39]. Jacob's inner reluctance to employ deception is thus revealed in his phraseology. He hoped that his mother would call off the attempt as a result of his plea, and so he used the word אוּלַי with its positive connotation as if to say that he hoped he would be discovered *(HaKsav V'haKaballah).*

Rashi explains יְמֻשֵּׁנִי as cognate to the expression [*Deut.* 28:29] מְמַשֵּׁשׁ בַּצָּהֳרַיִם, *groping at noon.* [This would thus reflect the groping of a blind man at an object.]

כִּמְתַעְתֵּעַ — *As a mocker.*

Following *Onkelos. Ibn Ezra* relates the word to the causative of תעה, *go astray,* hence one who leads another astray: a *deceiver, deluder.*

Malbim also interprets the word as *go astray* and renders: I will be in his eyes as one who strayed from the proper path, and will forfeit everything.

The *Midrash* interprets 'One who strayed [or טעה, *errs*] like an idolator.'

יג בְּרָכָה: וַתֹּאמֶר לוֹ אִמּוֹ עָלַי קִלְלָתְךָ בְּנִי
יד אַךְ שְׁמַע בְּקֹלִי וְלֵךְ קַח־לִי: וַיֵּלֶךְ וַיִּקַּח
וַיָּבֵא לְאִמּוֹ וַתַּעַשׂ אִמּוֹ מַטְעַמִּים כַּאֲשֶׁר
טו אָהֵב אָבִיו: וַתִּקַּח רִבְקָה אֶת־בִּגְדֵי עֵשָׂו
בְּנָהּ הַגָּדֹל הַחֲמֻדֹת אֲשֶׁר אִתָּהּ בַּבָּיִת

Midrash Tanchuma observes: He who deceives his father is as though he practiced idol worship. See also *Sanhedrin* 92a.

[Cf. כִּמְתַעְתֵּעַ in 20:13].

Hirsch observes that Jacob employed the prefix כְּ, *like.* He was not a cheat, but would appear *like* one. Isaac would be outraged and, without giving him time to explain, might curse him.

וְהֵבֵאתִי עָלַי קְלָלָה וְלֹא בְרָכָה — [*And*] *I will thus bring upon myself a curse rather than* [lit. *and not*] *a blessing.*

Even if he *had* planned to reserve a blessing for me, he will withhold it if he discovers a deception *(Sforno; Malbim).*

— My father will not give me even the single blessing that he would otherwise reserve for me *(Midrash).*[1]

13. עָלַי קִלְלָתְךָ בְּנִי — *Your curse be on me, my son!*

Upon me and upon my neck [i.e. I take full responsibility.] She had complete confidence in the prophecy that *the elder would serve the younger* [25:23] *(Rashbam).*

If he blesses you they shall be upon you and your descendants; if, however, he curses you, the curses shall remain upon me and my soul *(Targum Yonasan).*

— 'Have no fear that he will curse you. If he does curse you, may it alight on me, not you,' this being the way of women [to have compassion and want to suffer for their children *(Yohel Or)*] *(Ibn Ezra).*

Radak perceives the nuance as: If he *does* curse you, the malediction will affect not you, but me, since I incited you.

— He himself will perceive that *I* am responsible for the scheme and not you *(Chizkuni)*...

And in effect it is not *you* who will be cursed but עָלַי קִלְלָתְךָ, *the curse you speak about will be upon me,* since it is the way of the world that when a child acts improperly, one castigates the parents and says, 'Cursed are those who raised this one!' *(Daas Zekeinim; Tosafos HaRosh).*

Onkelos renders: עָלַי, *unto me,* has it been said in prophecy, that there shall be no curses upon you,

1. *Rabbi Elimelech* of *Lizhensk* [*Noam Elimelech*] homiletically interpreted this and the next verse as a dialogue between Jacob and the *Shechinah* speaking through the mouth of Rebecca.

Isaac intended to bless Esau with material wealth and give only spiritual riches to Jacob. The *Shechinah,* however, wanted Jacob to have wealth in This World as well. Jacob argued that the temptation of material wealth might cause flaws to develop in his erstwhile innocence. *'Perhaps my Father* [in heaven] *will feel me* [detect my unworthiness] and thus, by taking blessings for which I am unqualified, *I will bring a curse upon myself.'*

The *Shechinah* replied that it would take responsibility for the curse. As long as Jacob would obey its voice by devoting his material wealth to the performance of good deeds and the giving of charity, he need feel no ill effects.

myself a curse rather than a blessing."
13 *But his mother said to him, "Your curse be on me, my son. Only heed my voice and go fetch them for me."*
14 *So he went, fetched, and brought them to his mother, and his mother made delicacies as his father liked.*
15 *Rebecca then took her older son Esau's clean garments which were with her in the house, and clothed*

my son. *Ralbag* similarly comments that Rebecca might have been prophetically informed that Jacob would not be cursed.

Malbim explains that Rebecca instructed Jacob that if Isaac were to find out his deception and attempt to deliver a curse, Jacob was to tell him עָלַי, *upon me,* i.e. the responsibility was Rebecca's. Then Isaac would realize that Jacob had come not for personal gain, but in obedience to his mother. He would further realize that Rebecca would not have done so without a compelling reason. And even if he were to be angry, his anger would be directed only against her.

אַךְ שְׁמַע בְּקֹלִי — *Only heed* [in] *my voice.* [Cf. comm. *v.* 8].

— And take the risk on my word *(Radak).*

— Since I have informed you that such is God's Word, it is incumbent upon you to cooperate *(Malbim).*

Minchah Belulah suggests that the phrase *listen to my voice* implies that she coached him to listen to how she imitated Esau's voice, and follow suit. But in his wholesomeness, Jacob did not do so, and this caused Isaac to be suspicious.

14. וַיֵּלֶךְ וַיִּקַּח וַיָּבֵא לְאִמּוֹ — *So* [lit. *and*] *he went,* [*and*] *fetched, and brought* [them] *to his mother.*

Jacob undoubtedly valued the blessings, and under the circumstances he certainly had need to hurry and bring the delicacies to his father. There should, then, be some allusion to this haste as there was in the case of Abraham where the text notes he *ran* to meet his guests [18:2], and the many other references to his haste in the narrative there. Similarly in the case of Eliezer and Rebecca the text often notes their haste. Therefore, the text here, too, should have said וַיָּרָץ יַעֲקֹב, *Jacob ran,* and brought them to his mother. The verse, as it is written, indicates clearly that Jacob did not apply himself enthusiastically to this scheme but reluctantly carried out his mother's behest *(HaKsav V'haKaballah).*

Cf. the *Midrash* which also detects in the text a hint of Jacob's reluctance: *He went and got and brought to his mother* — under duress, bent, and weeping.

15. The disguise.

בִּגְדֵי עֵשָׂו ... הַחֲמֻדֹת — *Esau's clean garments.*

[The word חֲמֻדוֹת literally means *treasured, precious.*] The primary translation *clean* follows *Rashi* who

טז וַתַּלְבֵּשׁ אֶת־יַעֲקֹב בְּנָהּ הַקָּטָן: וְאֵת עֹרֹת
גְּדָיֵי הָעִזִּים הִלְבִּישָׁה עַל־יָדָיו וְעַל חֶלְקַת
יז צַוָּארָיו: וַתִּתֵּן אֶת־הַמַּטְעַמִּים וְאֶת־
הַלֶּחֶם אֲשֶׁר עָשָׂתָה בְּיַד יַעֲקֹב בְּנָהּ:
יח וַיָּבֹא אֶל־אָבִיו וַיֹּאמֶר אָבִי וַיֹּאמֶר הִנֶּנִּי
יט מִי אַתָּה בְּנִי: וַיֹּאמֶר יַעֲקֹב אֶל־אָבִיו

cites *Onkelos* [who apparently perceives the word as implying: those garments which Esau scrupulously kept *unsoiled* from hunting]. In an alternative translation, *Rashi* identifies these garments as the ones which Esau חָמַד, *coveted,* from the famous hunter Nimrod [see *footnote* to 25:27.]

These were the precious garments which Esau [renowned for his great filial devotion] would wear while he waited upon his father *(Rashbam).*

— He would wear these glorious garments while at leisure and while in the company of important personages. He kept them in fragrant grasses so they had a pleasant odor. This is why his fragrance was easily recognizable [see *v.* 27], and Rebecca chose them for that very reason *(Radak).*

אֲשֶׁר אִתָּהּ בַּבָּיִת — *Which were with her in the house.*

This provides an insight into Esau's married life. He left his best treasures in his mother's keeping because he knew his wives' ways and did not entirely trust them *(Rashi; see Hirsch).*

[According to *Rashbam's* interpretation (see above) they were presumably kept there *out of convenience* since those were the garments Esau wore when he served his father. Thus, they would be ready whenever Isaac summoned him. This follows the *Midrashic* understanding also.][1]

וַתַּלְבֵּשׁ אֶת יַעֲקֹב — *And* [she] *clothed Jacob.*

Jacob's reluctance is evident. With filial devotion he allowed his mother to dress him; he did not wait to put them on himself *(HaKsav V'haKaballah).*

בְּנָהּ הַקָּטָן — *Her younger son.*

As *Hirsch* notes in *v.* 11, it was as his *mother* that she demanded, and as *her son* that he obeyed.

That the narrative describes Esau as the *older* and Jacob as the *younger* is to the credit of Rebecca. Although a mother would normally recognize that the blessings belonged to the firstborn, she was

1. Esau's filial devotion was proverbial among the Rabbis.

Rabban Shimon ben Gamliel said, 'I attended to the needs of my father all my life but I did not do for him even a hundredth of what Esau did for his father. When I would care for my father, I would do so in soiled garments so as not to dirty my good clothing; but when I went outside, I would put on clean ones. But when Esau catered to his father he put on his most precious garments, for he would say, "Nothing but royal robes befits my father's honor" ' *(Midrash).* [See *Overview.*]

27
16-19

Jacob her younger son. [16] *With the skins of the goat-*
kids she covered his arms and the bareness of his
neck. [17] *She placed the delicacies and the bread which*
she had prepared into the hand of her son Jacob,
[18] *and he came to his father and said, "Father," and*
he said, "Here I am. Who are you my son?"
[19] *Jacob said to his father, "It is I, Esau your first-*

determined that they go to Jacob because she perceived Esau's unfitness for them *(Ramban).*[1]

According to *HaKsav V'haKabal-lah,* the sons are described as *younger* or *older* to imply that Rebecca did not act out of personal motives but only in fulfillment of the prophecy that *the elder would serve the younger* [25:23].

16. עַל יָדָיו וְעַל חֶלְקַת צַוָּארָיו -[*On*] *his arms and* [*on*] *the bareness of his neck.*

— To deceive Isaac into thinking that Jacob was the hairy Esau *(Tz'ror HaMor).*

17. וְאֶת הַלֶּחֶם — *And the bread.*

— Which she had baked to accompany his meal *(Radak).*

בְּיַד יַעֲקֹב בְּנָהּ — *Into the hand of her son Jacob.*

[Again symbolic of Jacob's lack of enthusiasm for the scheme. His mother had to place it into his very hand; it was only by virtue of the filial devotion due her as בְּנָהּ, *her son,* that he took it. He was passive and tearful throughout the preparations, as noted above by the *Midrash,* and she accompanied him as far as Isaac's door.]

18. וַיָּבֹא אֶל־אָבִיו — [*And*] *he* [Jacob] *came to his father.*

— With head bowed, and in tears *(Midrash).*

וַיֹּאמֶר אָבִי — *And* [*he*] *said,* '[*My*] *father.'*

A courteous form of announcing his presence since Isaac could not see him *(Radak; Ibn Caspi).*

Jacob called out this one word to test whether his father would recognize his voice. Were Isaac to recognize his voice, Jacob would have abandoned the scheme and pose as if he merely came to visit. *(Alshich).*

[See *Ramban* to *v.* 12 that either Jacob disguised his voice or his voice was similar to Esau's.]

מִי אַתָּה בְּנִי — *Who are you, my son?*

The scheme was working! Isaac was uncertain which son had just come in *(Alshich).*

1. The terms in Hebrew are גָּדוֹל and קָטָן, lit. *large* and *small,* instead of רַב and צָעִיר, *older* and *younger.* This implies that though Esau was of much *larger* build than Jacob the *smaller* brother, nevertheless the clothes fit Jacob perfectly. Rebecca perceived this as a sign that Heaven agreed with her plan that Jacob should receive the blessing. This is similar to the case of Saul, who was very tall [*I Sam.* 9:2] who clad the shorter David with his royal garments [ibid. 17:38], and they fit David perfectly. This was perceived as a divine sign that David's mission against Goliath would be successful, and that David would eventually reign as king in Saul's stead *(Yesod HaTorah).*

אָנֹכִי֙ עֵשָׂ֣ו בְּכֹרֶ֔ךָ עָשִׂ֕יתִי כַּאֲשֶׁ֥ר דִּבַּ֖רְתָּ
אֵלָ֑י קוּם־נָ֣א שְׁבָ֗ה וְאָכְלָה֙ מִצֵּידִ֔י בַּעֲב֖וּר
כ תְּבָרְכַ֥נִּי נַפְשֶֽׁךָ׃ וַיֹּ֤אמֶר יִצְחָק֙ אֶל־בְּנ֔וֹ
מַה־זֶּ֛ה מִהַ֥רְתָּ לִמְצֹ֖א בְּנִ֑י וַיֹּ֕אמֶר כִּ֥י
כא הִקְרָ֛ה יהוה אֱלֹהֶ֖יךָ לְפָנָֽי׃ וַיֹּ֤אמֶר יִצְחָק֙

19. אָנֹכִי עֵשָׂו בְּכֹרֶךָ — *It is I, Esau your first-born.*

[The commentators take pains to show that Jacob remained as close as possible to the truth during the course of his conversation with Isaac. Some of the interpretations seem very strained in the light of the translation. It should be borne in mind, however, that the construction of the Hebrew allows for such interpretation even where the English does not.][1]

The commentators agree that technically Jacob did not lie. He chose his words deliberately, the intent of his response being, as *Rashi* explains: אָנֹכִי, *It is I* who bring this to you; עֵשָׂו בְּכֹרֶךָ, *Esau,* (however) *is your first born.*

Thus, by adding בְּכֹרֶךָ, *your first born,* Jacob was presenting an ambiguity and intimating what was, in fact the truth; had he merely said אָנֹכִי עֵשָׂו, *It is I, Esau,* that would have been an outright lie *(Alshich; Or HaChaim).*

He meant, *'I am, who I am; Esau is your first born,'* while others suggest that he said under his breath אָנֹכִי, *'I'*, and loudly *'Esau is your first born,' (Ibn Ezra).*

Ibn Ezra continues that the latter interpretation is unwarranted since under certain circumstances one engaged in a divine mission may color the truth — within certain prescribed limits — without harm. Compare, for example where David *'man of God'* [*II Chron.* 8:14] misled Ahimelech out of dire need [*I Samuel* 21:6]; Elisha who ambiguously told Hazael to say to him *he will surely live* [*II Kings* 8:10] when in fact Elisha was shown that he would die [see *kri* of לו, *to him,* and *ksiv* of לא, *could not,* which preserved this dual connotation in that verse]; Micah similarly offered out of courtesy a futile prayer [*I Kings* 22:15] though he knew the other would die; Abraham also put off Abimelech out of fear by insisting that Sarah was truly his sister [see *Ibn Ezra* cited in *comm.* to 20:12], and when at the *Akeidah* Abraham told the youths that he would return with Isaac after praying [22:5].

Radak interprets similarly.

עָשִׂיתִי כַּאֲשֶׁר דִּבַּרְתָּ אֵלָי — *I have done as you told* [lit. *have spoken to*] *me.*

Continuing *Rashi,* the intimation is: *I have* — on many occasions — *done as you have told me.*

— I have done כַּאֲשֶׁר, *as if,* you would have told *me* to do it (attributed to *ARIzal).*

According to *Or HaChaim,* Jacob's rationale was that since he had purchased the birthright the blessings were legitimately his;

1. However, it must be understood that only the Divinely ordained nature of the mission justified Jacob's clever choice of words to avoid an outright lie. He *did* mislead his father, and in everyday affairs such behavior would be *halachically* forbidden as deceptive. Rather, Jacob's behavior must be understood as an attempt to remain as close as possible to the truth even in a situation where deception was not only *unavoidable,* but required *(Rabbi Yerucham Levovitz of Mir).*

born. I have done as you told me. Rise up, please, sit and eat of my game that you may give me your innermost blessing."

[20] *Isaac said to his son, "How is it that you found so quickly, my son?" And he said, "Because* HASHEM *your God so arranged it for me."*

therefore Isaac's instructions to Esau should rightfully have been addressed to Jacob. Accordingly, Jacob now said that he complied with the request since as the 'owner of the birthright,' the request is considered as if it had been addressed to him.

קוּם־נָא שְׁבָה — *Rise up, please, sit.* — I.e., sit at the table *(Rashi).*

According to *Radak,* Isaac had been reclining in his bed, so Jacob implied, *Rise up* from your reclining position, if you please, *and sit* up in bed to eat.

וְאָכְלָה מִצֵּידִי — *And eat of my game.* The imperative verb form with a suffix ה (in this case שְׁבָה instead of שֵׁב and וְאָכְלָה instead of the usual imperative וֶאֱכֹל) is used to reflect a courteous connotation of *request* rather than a *command (HaKsav V'haKaballah; Malbim).*

Although the word מִצֵּידִי literally means from my *trapping* [=game], the word צַיִד also means *food* in general, as for example in *Joshua* 9:5. Hence, Jacob who did not *hunt* but took animals from the herd was not lying when he spoke of צַיִד *(R' Chananel).*

20. וַיֹּאמֶר יִצְחָק אֶל בְּנוֹ — [And] *Isaac said to his son.*

The general term *his son* reflects Isaac's continued uncertainty. Apparently there was something in the voice that aroused Isaac's suspicions and inspired him to make further inquiry as described in this and succeeding verses *(Radak).*

מַה־זֶּה מִהַרְתָּ לִמְצֹא בְּנִי — *How is it that you found so quickly, my son?*

Isaac had specifically asked him to take his weapons and *go out to the field* in order to make the task more arduous and hence the *mitzvah* greater [*v.* 3]. When he saw the quick return, he was apprehensive that 'Esau' had not carried out the details as bidden.

HaKsav V'haKaballah suggests that from the cantillation it appears that מַה זֶּה is not a *question,* but an idiomatic exclamation of *surprise and gratitude* for his speedy return. Therefore, Jacob's response intimated, 'You owe me no gratitude; it was not due to my efforts, but to HASHEM Who so arranged it.'

כִּי הִקְרָה ה׳ אֱלֹהֶיךָ לְפָנָי — *Because* HASHEM *your God so arranged it for me* [lit. *so chanced it to happen before me*].

[The term מִקְרֶה, lit. *coincidence; chance* is used to refer to Providential destiny. See *comm. above to 24:12.*]

— It was apparently your merit that stood by me since it was for you that I was hunting *(Radak).*

Following *Malbim,* Isaac understood the reply to mean, 'I had actually planned to hunt far away, but *God arranged it* that game appeared

אֶל־יַעֲקֹב גְּשָׁה־נָּא וַאֲמֻשְׁךָ בְּנִי הַאַתָּה
כב זֶה בְּנִי עֵשָׂו אִם־לֹא: וַיִּגַּשׁ יַעֲקֹב אֶל־
יִצְחָק אָבִיו וַיְמֻשֵּׁהוּ וַיֹּאמֶר הַקֹּל קוֹל
כג יַעֲקֹב וְהַיָּדַיִם יְדֵי עֵשָׂו: וְלֹא הִכִּירוֹ כִּי־

before me near home where there is usually none to be found. This 'coincidence' was therefore taken as a sure sign that it was arranged by God — Who obviously did this in Isaac's merit.

21. וַיֹּאמֶר יִצְחָק אֶל יַעֲקֹב — [And] *Isaac said to Jacob.*

This time the narrative refers to him as *Jacob* rather than vaguely as *his son.* At this point Isaac was very suspicious that it might not be Esau who was standing before him, but Jacob *(Alshich).*

גְּשָׁה־נָּא וַאֲמֻשְׁךָ בְּנִי — *Come close, if you please, so I can feel you, my son.*

Isaac's suspicions were aroused since he knew that it was not characteristic of Esau to mention God's name so readily as did the person who now stood before him [verse 20] *(Rashi).*

... And Isaac, therefore, decided not to rely on voice recognition alone, but to decide the matter through the more conclusive test of actually touching him *(Malbim).*

But, *Ramban,* queries, since Esau was not wicked in Isaac's eyes how could the mention of God be a distinguishing mark for Jacob?

He answers that though Isaac thought Esau to be pious, he assumed that Esau had always made it a habit to avoid pronouncing God's Name since he often found himself in unclean places, or out of fear that he might pronounce it without proper *kavannah* [conentration and intention]. In fact, Isaac viewed this *favorably* to Esau's credit as symbolic of Esau's fear of heaven.

However, in the *literal* sense of the narrative, *Ramban* concludes that it was Jacob's *voice* that made Isaac suspicious. [For although, as *Ramban* notes in *v.* 12, Jacob and Esau had similar voices, or Jacob disguised his voice, it would seem that the unusual circumstances — such as the swiftness of his return; the mention of God's Name; and now the voice — combined to arouse Isaac's suspicions.]

22. וַיִּגַּשׁ יַעֲקֹב אֶל־יִצְחָק אָבִיו — *So* [lit. *and*] *Jacob drew close to Isaac his father.*

[The very test that Jacob dreaded (in verse 12) was at hand!]:

'Perspiration poured over his legs and his heart melted like wax. But the Holy One, Blessed be He, sent him two angels, one at his right side and one at his left who supported him by his elbows so that he should not fall' *(Midrash).*

הַקֹּל קוֹל יַעֲקֹב — *The voice is Jacob's voice.*

The Sages interpreted that Jacob and Esau had similar voices and that the *voice is Jacob's voice* refers not to his, Jacob's, *voice* but to his *manner of speaking,* inasmuch as he spoke gently and invoked the name of Heaven [when he said (v. 20):

[21] *And Isaac said to Jacob, "Come close if you*
please, so I can feel you, my son. Are you, indeed, my
son Esau or not?"
[22] *So Jacob drew close to Isaac his father who felt*
him and then said, "The voice is Jacob's voice, but
the hands are Esau's hands." [23] *But he did not*

'Because HASHEM, your God ...'] (*Ramban* to *v.* 7).

— The gentility of manner and address belongs to Jacob. Jacob spoke entreatingly קוּם נָא, *rise up, if you please,* while Esau spoke harshly [*v.* 31] יָקֻם אָבִי, *let my father rise (Rashi).*

וְהַיָּדַיִם יְדֵי עֵשָׂו — *But* [lit. *and*] *the hands are Esau's hands.*

Since there is really little resemblance between animal skin and hairy human arms, it would appear from Isaac's response that either much effort went into preparing the disguise, or Isaac's sense of touch had greatly deteriorated *(Sforno).*

The *Midrash* offers a wealth of insight into the implication of this verse. A short selection follows:

— *The voice is Jacob's voice:* Jacob wields power only by his voice [i.e. Jacob exemplifies spiritual strength]; *but the hands are Esau's hands*—Esau gains dominion only by his hands [i.e., Esau exemplifies material might.]

When Jacob's voice withdraws within itself [the word קֹל, *voice* is spelled defectively, without the ו so it can be read הֻקַל קוֹל יַעֲקֹב, 'the voice of Jacob is *lightened' (Yafeh Toar)*] — and Jews do not make proper use of their voices by praying and studying Torah, *then* הַיָּדַיִם יְדֵי עֵשָׂו, *Esau's hands have dominion,* ... but conversely when the voice of Jacob rings out in the synagogues, Jacob cannot be dominated — for Esau has no hands [i.e. In such a case *Esau's hands* have no power to encroach upon Jacob].

[On the latter *Midrash* see footnote to ArtScroll *Shir HaShirim* 8:13 page 203. Perhaps, as *Yafeh Toar* explains, the interpretation is that since these two opposites, *Jacob's voice* and *Esau's hands,* cannot coexist simultaneously, the Sages perceive the verse to intimate that either *the voice is the voice of Jacob* — or — *the hands are the hands of Esau:* while one is strong the other is powerless.]

— The *Midrash* continues:

The voice is the voice of Jacob — the voice of Jacob cries out at what *the hands* did to him [i.e. at the incredible slaughters perpetrated against Israel by the descendants of Esau/Edom (Rome). The *Midrash* specifically cites the cries of the accursed Hadrian who slew eighty thousand myriads at Bethar in approximately 135 C.E. where the Bar Kochba revolt was finally crushed with incredible slaughter.]

— The *Talmud* [*Gittin* 57b] interprets the reference of *Esau's hands* to refer to the Roman Empire which destroyed the Temple and exiled us from our land.

— Similarly, the *Talmud* [ibid.] observes that 'wherever a prayer is effective, a descendant of Jacob must be among those who uttered it; whenever a war is victorious, Esau's descendants must have had a hand in it.

23. וְלֹא הִכִּירוֹ ... — *But* [lit. *and*] *he did not recognize him because*

הָיוּ יָדָיו כִּידֵי עֵשָׂו אָחִיו שְׂעִרֹת
כד וַיְבָרְכֵהוּ: וַיֹּאמֶר אַתָּה זֶה בְּנִי עֵשָׂו
כה וַיֹּאמֶר אָנִי: וַיֹּאמֶר הַגִּשָׁה לִּי וְאֹכְלָה
מִצֵּיד בְּנִי לְמַעַן תְּבָרֶכְךָ נַפְשִׁי וַיַּגֶּשׁ־לוֹ
כו וַיֹּאכַל וַיָּבֵא לוֹ יַיִן וַיֵּשְׁתְּ: וַיֹּאמֶר אֵלָיו

his hands were hairy like those of Esau his brother.

Isaac placed more reliance on his sense of *touch* than he did on the *voice.* He apparently felt that the sound of the voice was inconclusive because a voice can be disguised.

[Similarly the intangible *mannerism* of the voice which was more respectful than usual (as *Rashi* explains above), was also not as conclusive as the feel of the hairy arms. Nor was the unusual invocation of the name of Heaven conclusive since Isaac — convinced by the hairy arms that it was Esau — probably surmised that Esau purposely spoke more gently and invoked God's Name on this ocasion in order to rise spiritually to the awesome challenge of becoming a worthy recipient of the benedictions (see *Haamek Davar).*]

וַיְבָרְכֵהוּ — *So* [lit. *and*] *he blessed him.*

I.e., so he *resolved* to bless him. The actual wording of the blessing is given in verse 28 *(HaKsav V'haKaballah).*

— He *prepared* to bless him by partaking of his food, the act of eating in this case, as noted above, being for the very purpose of preparing himself to be a conduit for the blessings *(Malbim).*

According to *Haamek Davar,* Isaac *praised* him for using his voice to invoke the Divine Inspiration.

Sforno cites the *Talmudic* dictum [*Berachos* 31b]: 'One who suspects his neighbor of a fault of which the other is innocent, must beg his pardon, and moreover must bless him.' Compare Eli who blessed Hannah after having suspected her of being drunk [*I Samuel* 1:13-18]. Therefore, since Isaac had suspected him of deceit, he blessed him [possibly indicating a short conciliatory blessing distinct from the blessing of the firstborn which commences in *v.* 28.]

24. וַיֹּאמֶר אַתָּה זֶה בְּנִי עֵשָׂו — *And he said, 'You are, indeed, my son Esau!'*

A statement of fact: Isaac was now convinced beyond a doubt that it was indeed so *(Rashbam; Or HaChaim).*

Haamek Davar, similarly, maintains that Isaac was sure that the one who stood before him was Esau. Had he been suspicious, he could not have been satisfied by Jacob's repeated affirmations, that he was indeed Esau. Rather, a prerequisite to blessing is that the one who confers it must feel love for the object of his blessing. Mentioning and hearing his name assists in arousing such warm feelings, as we find in

27
24-26 *recognize him because his hands were hairy like*
those of Esau his brother; so he blessed him. 24 *He*
said, "You are, indeed, my son Esau!" And he said,
"I am."
25 *He said, "Serve me and let me eat of my son's*
game that I may give you my innermost blessing." So
he served him and he ate, and he brought him wine
and he drank. 26 *Then his father Isaac said to him,*

48:8 where Jacob used this device to further arouse his love for Ephraim and Menashe prior to blessing them.

According to *Radak,* this is to be construed as a question, *Are you, indeed, my son Esau?* Although the interrogative particle ה is lacking, this not unusual in Scriptures (as for example *I Kings* 1:24: אַתָּה אָמַרְתָּ כו', *Did you say Adonijah shall reign after me ... ?)* Isaac asked this of him because convinced as he was, the strange voice caused him to doubt. Furthermore, he wanted to impress upon 'Esau' the seriousness which he attached to the blessings, to make it clear to him that he would not have approved if 'Jacob' had frivolously sought to come in place of 'Esau'.

Malbim perceives this as a rhetorical question. Now that Isaac was prepared to draw divine inspiration from the Source of Blessing, he wished to specify explicitly the identity of whom he was about to bless. Thus, the question and response.

... And if applicable, he wished to give him this final opportunity to confess *(Abarbanel).*

אֲנִי — *I* [*am*].

He did not utter an actual falsehood by saying אֲנִי עֵשָׂו, *I am Esau,* but simply אֲנִי, *I am* (Rashi). [His response can also be rendered: *'It is I.'*]

25. וַיָּבֵא לוֹ יַיִן וַיֵּשְׁתְּ — *And he brought him wine and he drank.*

In order to induce good humor [a requisite for the reception of the *Shechinah*] before the blessings. In general, most of their meals were without wine unless the meal is specifically described as a מִשְׁתֶּה [from שתה, *drink*] denoting a wine feast *(Radak).*

[See in this connection comm. to מִשְׁתֶּה, *feast,* in 19:3 and 21:8.]

Chizkuni adds that wine was brought to induce some lightheadedness in Isaac so he would be less prone to be suspicious about whether it was Esau or Jacob. [1]

Da'as Zekeinim compares this to the case of Malchizedek who gave wine to Abraham then blessed him [14:18-19].

1. *Midrash Tanchuma* credits this use of wine as one reason for the *halachah* that the wine blessing of *Kiddush* takes precedence over the blessing over bread. Wine is given this honor because Jacob used it to help secure Isaac's blessing, and also because wine was used as a libation on the Temple altar. [See also the commentaries *to Shulchan Aruch Orach Chaim* 211.]

כו יִצְחָק אָבִיו גְּשָׁה־נָּא וּשְׁקָה־לִּי בְּנִי: וַיִּגַּשׁ
וַיִּשַּׁק־לוֹ וַיָּרַח אֶת־רֵיחַ בְּגָדָיו וַיְבָרְכֵהוּ
וַיֹּאמֶר רְאֵה רֵיחַ בְּנִי כְּרֵיחַ שָׂדֶה אֲשֶׁר

26. גְּשָׁה נָּא וּשְׁקָה לִּי בְּנִי — *Come close, if you please, and kiss me, my son.*

Kabbalistically a kiss brings about the deep spiritual intimacy which Isaac wished to arouse in order to cause the *Shechinah* to alight upon him preparatory to invoking the blessings *(Alshich; Malbim).*

Midrash Lekach Tov notes that a kiss generally heralds greatness as in the case of Samuel who kissed Saul when he anointed him [*I Sam.* 10:1.]

Isaac did not say, *And I will kiss you* though it is usually the elder who kisses the younger, or when they are equals they are said to kiss one another. Rather, Isaac asked his son to *kiss him* since Isaac was blind and could not kiss another without seeing him *(Radak).*

27. וַיָּרַח אֶת־רֵיחַ בְּגָדָיו — [*And*] *he smelled the fragrance of his garments.*

I.e., while Isaac was kissing Jacob, he inhaled the fine fragrance of his garments, for as we noted earlier [*v.* 15] the garments were kept in fragrant grasses and so had a pleasant odor. Isaac did not perceive it from afar, but smelled it as soon as Jacob drew near to kiss him *(Radak).*

Rashi, citing the *Midrash,* asks: But the pungent smell of washed goatskin is most offensive! — This, however, implicitly teaches us that the fragrance of Garden of Eden entered the room with him [and it was to *this* fragrance that Isaac referred.]

[As noted in the footnote to 25:27 this garment had belonged to Adam, and passed onto Nimrod and then to Esau. Adam had worn it in Eden, and it still retained its fragrance *(Tanchuma Yashan Toldos* 16). *Maharsha* in *Taanis* 29b notes, however, that the *Midrash* cited by *Rashi* has an implication different from the *Tanchuma.* According to the *Midrash,* it was not Esau's *garments* that retained the fragrance of the Garden of Eden, but that the fragrance of the Garden of Eden permeated the room *in the merit of Jacob.* By contrast, when Esau later entered, Gehinnom entered with him (see *Rashi v.* 33).]

According to *Midrash Aggadas Bereishis,* Isaac smelled that same fragrance he had smelled when he was bound on the altar at the *Akeidah. Midrash Tanchuma* preserves a tradition that God had impregnated these garments with the aroma of the fragrant incense which would one day be offered in the Temple [see *Targum Yonasan* below].

Isaac wished to be elated by the fragrant scent, and so he deliberately inhaled the aroma. Cf. *Berachos* 43b: 'What is it which gives enjoyment to the soul and not to the body? — You must say that this refers to a fragrant aroma' *(Sforno).*

וַיְבָרְכֵהוּ — *And* [*he*] *blessed him.*

— After first acknowledging the fragrant aroma. Isaac thereby informed his son that the food, drink, and fragrant aroma had made him joyous. As a result, the Divine Inspiration descended upon him and he conferred the blessing *(Radak).*[1]

This is similar to the case of Elisha the prophet of whom Scripture says that *after the minstrel played* [*II*

27 *"Come close, if you please, and kiss me, my son,"*
27 *[27] So he drew close and kissed him. He smelled the*
fragrance of his garments and blessed him. He said,
"See, the fragrance of my son is like the fragrance of
a field which HASHEM had blessed —

Kings 3:15] *the hand of HASHEM came upon him* (Sforno).

וַיֹּאמֶר — *He said.*

— [I.e., he *remarked before* proceeding with the actual blessing.]

רְאֵה — *See.*

Isaac was not addressing anyone in particular, but thinking out loud — the imperative form רְאֵה, *see,* being merely idiomatic *(Radak).*

Sforno renders that Isaac was addressing his son, the verse meaning *See, my son, this fragrance which is like, etc.*

Rambam [*Moreh Nevuchim* 1:46] notes that in Hebrew, a description of the perception made by one sense is often substituted for that made by another. Thus Scripture says [*Jeremiah* 2:31] *See the word of HASHEM,* which is like *hear,* for the intended meaning is, *Perceive the meaning of His word.* Similarly, *see the fragrance my son,* has the meaning of *smell the fragrance of my son* since it relates to the perception of the fragrance.

רֵיחַ בְּנִי כְּרֵיחַ שָׂדֶה אֲשֶׁר בֵּרֲכוֹ ה׳ — *The fragrance of my son is like the fragrance of a field which HASHEM had blessed.*

[The phrase אֲשֶׁר בֵּרֲכוֹ ה׳ is ambiguous: בֵּרֲכוֹ can be translated

1. **The Nature of Isaac's Blessings: Prophecy or Prayer.**

The commentators deal with the very difficult question of the nature of Isaac's blessings. The primary approaches are: 1). Isaac was acting as *a prophet* in foretelling *the future* of the son who stood before him. If so, however, what objection could there be on the part of Rebecca, Jacob, or Esau to Isaac's blessing — a prophecy merely foretold an event that would occur in any case?; and 2). Isaac actually *conferred a blessing* in the sense that he prayerfully changed the destiny of his son by his words and 'laying of hands' upon him. If so, however, how could a blessing take effect upon Jacob if Isaac meant it for Esau? Some of the explanations are:

— *Ibn Ezra* comments that Isaac's blessings were in the nature of a prayer for the future good fortune of his son. It was meant to be fulfilled in *future* generations, for Esau was not subservient to Jacob during their lifetimes.

— *Ikkarim* holds that a righteous person becomes God's conduit by means of which a heavenly blessing comes upon the one he blesses. For example, if the recipient is a farmer, his blessing can cause a hundredfold abundance. Once the blessing has been delivered, it is a *fait accompli,* the objection or misapprehension of the blesser notwithstanding.

— *Ikkarim* and *Abarbanel* cite — but disagree with — a view that combines prophecy with blessing: the prophet foresees a condition and prays that it become even more blessed and beneficial.

— *Drashos HaRan* comments that the prophecy to Rebecca concerning Jacob's ascendancy could still have been reversed because it was made privately to Rebecca. Because it was not to be made public, it could have been revoked if Jacob proved to be unworthy or — and it was this which Rebecca wished to avoid — a righteous person of Isaac's stature blessed Esau to the contrary.

— *Drashos HaRan* offers a second view that Isaac remained in doubt as to the indentity of the person before him. He resigned himself to confer the blessings upon whomever God judged to be the proper recipient.

[See *Overview* for further discussion.]

כח בֵּרֲכוֹ יהוה: °וְיִתֶּן־לְךָ הָאֱלֹהִים מִטַּל

°ששי

either as *blessed it,* i.e., the field, or *blessed him,* i.e., the son. Our translation follows *Rashi* who explains that the phrase refers to the *field 'which* HASHEM *had blessed'*]

— By giving it a fragrant aroma. The Sages declared that it refers to the fragrance of a field of apple trees [*Ta'anis* 29b] *(Rashi).*[1]

[See *footnote* to ArtScroll *Shir HaShirim* 7:9, p. 185.]

According to *Rashbam,* it was like a field of sweet-smelling spices.

Sforno observes that the sustenance and prosperity afforded by a field are one blessing; the expansiveness of spirit afforded by its *pleasant, exhilirating scent* is a further blessing. By referring to *both* dimensions of God's blessed field, Isaac introduced his blessing to Jacob, implying that such was the nature of the bounty which God would bestow in the future.

— *Targum Yonasan* paraphrases: See, the fragrance of my son is as the scent of the fragrant incense to be offered on the Temple site which is called a *field,* [by Isaac; see *Pesachim* 88a] which HASHEM has blessed and chosen as a dwelling for His *Shechinah.*

According to *Ramban,* the phrase אֲשֶׁר בֵּרֲכוֹ ה׳, *which HASHEM has blessed,* refers back to the word בְּנִי, *my son,* the verse having the meaning of ... *the fragrance of my son is like the fragrance of a field by which God blessed him* — by making his hunt there successful and guarding him from any mishap.

Rashi, as explained by *Sifsei Chachomim* [next verse] also suggests that in the *literal* sense the phrase *which HASHEM has blessed* reverts to *my son,* the sense of the passage being, *See, the fragrance of my son whom HASHEM has blessed is like the fragrance of a field.* Following this literal sense, *Rashi* perceives that the next phrase continues the thought begun by this one [see further]

28. וְיִתֶּן לְךָ הָאֱלֹהִים — *And may God give you.*

I.e. may He give you repeatedly [lit. may He give you and again give you] *(Rashi).*

Ordinarily the conjunctive prefix ו, *vav* [*and*] would indicate a continuation of the thought begun in the previous verse. Here, however, the blessing clearly begins with *this* verse. Therefore, *Rashi* follows the *Midrash* in observing that the conjunction ו in וְיִתֶּן literally meaning *'and* (may God) give you', is, in effect, superfluous since it does not connect with the previous verse. He therefore, interprets it to denote a *constant and repetitive action:* 'May He give *and* give *and* give incessantly.' Compare the *Midrash:* 'May He give you again and again; may He give you blessings and the means for retaining them; may He give you yours and give you your father's; may He give you yours and give you your brother's' *(Mizrachi; Gur Aryeh).*

The literal interpretation of *Rashi's* comment, as noted above is 'may He give you and again give you.' *Devek Tov* perceives the implication in *Rashi's* language to be that the blessing was prophetic: Although there

1. In the *Biur HaGRA* to *Orach Chaim* 538:8 the *Vilna Gaon* suggests that the reason for eating an apple on Rosh Hashanah is to commemorate this incident which occurred on Rosh Hashanah [according to a view in *Zohar Chadash* 1:99. See *Maharil* cited in *Darkei Moshe* ad loc.]

[Following Rashi's chronology in *v.* 9, however, these events occurred on *Passover.* The latter is based on specific references to Passover in *Pirkei d'Rabbi Eliezer* 32; in *Sh'mos Rabbah* 16 to Nissan; *Targum Yonasan* to *v.* 1; and *Zohar.*]

[28] *And may God give you*

will be an interruption in the blessing following the destruction of the Temple, know that *He will resume giving it to you.* Or, the implication is that He will give you — in This World — and *again* give you in the World to Come.

Maharshal explains the implication as meaning, more generally, 'Even if your sins will cause an interruption, know that וְיִתֶּן, He will *again give you.*'

Rashi [as explained by *Mizrachi*] continues that in the *literal sense* the conjunction ו *and,* is quite justified as suggesting a continuity between the verses The phrase אֲשֶׁר בֵּרֲכוֹ ה׳, *whom HASHEM has blessed,* refers back to בְּנִי, *my son* [see *Sifsei Chachomim* cited at end of previous verse.], and serves to introduce the blessings. Thus, the flow of these verses is, 'See, my son, just as God blessed you by giving you a fragrance like the fragrance of the field, *in addition may He also give you of the dew of heaven, etc.*

[This is essentially the interpretation given to the sequence by *Ramban.*]

Rashbam interprets the conjunction as signifying: 'Just as He blessed the field, *so may He give you ...* all the blessings of productivity and abundance!

— As you reflect on God's bountiful blessings my son, so may He, inasmuch as He is God, grant you a blessed field ... *(Sforno).*

הָאֱלֹהִים — [the] *God.*

[The definite article *the* God *accentuates* that the reference is to God in His role as *Elohim* — i.e., as the Dispenser of Strict Justice, in contrast with the Name ה׳, *HASHEM* which depicts Him in His role as Dispenser of Mercy. (See *comm.* 1:1 and 2:5).]

Rashi, following *Midrash Tanchuma* comments: What is the significance here of the name *Elohim* which depicts Him as Dispenser of Justice? — Isaac meant: May He give it to you as *Elohim* — i.e., only if you are justifiably *worthy of it* may He give it to you, but not otherwise. But to Esau he stated unconditionally [*v.*39] *of the fat of the earth shall be your dwelling*— i.e., whether you deserve it or not, you will receive it.[1]

[The above *Midrash* may seem difficult because Isaac thought that *Esau* was receiving the blessing. We must say that since the blessings were divinely inspired, these words were placed into Isaac's mouth although it would be reasonable to assume that he himself was not aware of their *full* import until he discovered the ruse later.

[Further, it should be understood that at the moment Isaac was conferring this blessing, he still supposed Esau to be righteous and therefore, predicated the fulfillment of the blessing on the worthiness of the recipient. Later, however, when he was made aware of Esau's wickedness (see *comm.* to *v.* 33), he omitted the precondition of worthiness — otherwise, Esau's blessings would never have been fulfilled.

[In the *literal* sense, we will see many interpretations based on the fact that this blessing — which stresses the

1. *Rashi* continues that when Solomon dedicated the Temple, he emulated Isaac. Of the Israelites whom he knew were faithful and would unconditionally acknowledge the justice of God, he prayed [*I Kings* 8:39]: *Render to every man* [Israelite, cf. *v.* 38] *according to all his ways.* But with reference to the stranger who lacked faith, Solomon prayed [ibid. 43]: *Hear in Heaven ... and do according to all that the stranger calls upon You for* — i.e. whether the stranger deserves it or not grant him his request, lest he come to murmur against You.

הַשָּׁמַיִם וּמִשְׁמַנֵּי הָאָרֶץ וְרֹב דָּגָן וְתִירֹשׁ:

physical rather than the spiritual — was intended for Esau rather than Jacob. See *footnote.*]

According to *Ramban,* the addition of *God,* here, implies that as a *gift of God,* the blessing would contine uninterrupted. But in the case of Esau, [*v.* 39], Isaac did not similarly invoke God's Name implying that his lot would be good only as long as he lives, but ultimately, he [i.e., his seed] will perish and face oblivion [see *comm.* there].

מִטַּל הַשָּׁמַיִם — *Of the dew of the heavens.*[1]

The meaning is as the literal sense of the words imply. But there are many *Midrashic* explanations offering various interpretations *(Rashi).*

The blessing was not the *dew* per se, since God causes dew to descend universally in any event. Rather, this is a blessing of increase and abundance. 'Just as He has blessed you with success in the field [see above], so may He bless you uninterruptedly for the extent of your days on the land with the abundance generated by the dew of the heavens and the most fertile areas of the earth *(Ramban).*

He blessed him with *dew* rather than *rain* since dew carries within it *complete* blessing, unlike rain which has the disadvantage of being sometimes stormy, sporadic, and which hampers travel *(Radak; Sforno).* At the same time, dew is granted in sufficient quantities to ensure abundant crops *(Abarbanel).*

Chizkuni notes that since Isaac knew that the eternal heritage of his seed was *Eretz Yisrael* where the rainy season is meager, he, ap-

1. The Sages in the *Midrash* perceived many spiritual allusions implicit in the otherwise materialistic blessings:

The dew of the heavens — alludes to the *manna* which 'rained' down from heaven [together with the dew; see *Numbers* 11:9 *(Maharzu)*];

the fatness of the earth — alludes to the well [which followed the Israelites in the desert] and brought up for them various fat [i.e. rich] fish;

abundant grain — alludes to young men [see *Zechariah* 9:17];

wine — alludes to the maidens [see *Zechariah ad. loc.*].

Another interpretation:

The dew of the heavens — alludes to Zion [cf. *Psalms* 133:3];

the fatness of the earth — to the sacrifices [which consisted of the choicest ('fattest') of animals *(Maharzu)*];

abundant grain — to the first fruits [as it is written (*Deut.* 18:4): *The first fruit of your grain, wine,* etc. *Maharzu)*];

wine — to the libations [which consisted of wine *(Maharzu)*];

Another interpretation:

The dew of the heavens — alludes to Scripture [which came intact from heaven *(Maharzu)*];

the fatness of the earth — to *Mishnah* [which was transmitted by the Sages on earth *(Maharzu)*];

abundant grain — to *Talmud* [just as grain is the primary produce so is the *Talmud* the primary source for Torah Law *(Maharzu)*];

wine — to *Aggadah* [the homiletic expositions of the Sages] since wine, like the homiletic expositions, gladdens the hearts of men *(Maharzu).*

27
28

of the dew of the heavens
and of the fatness of the earth,
and abundant grain and wine.

propriately blessed him with an abundance of *dew* which the soil desperately needs throughout the rest of the year when it does not rain.

וּמִשְׁמַנֵּי הָאָרֶץ — *And of the fatness of the earth.*

That is, from the fattest [שָׁמֵן] (i.e., most fertile) portions of the earth *(Ramban).*

— A reference to *Eretz Yisrael* which *flows with milk and honey* [*Exodus* 17:5] *(Alshich).*

— May your produce be sweet as if grown in a place saturated with heavenly dew and fertility *(Haamek Davar).*

According to *Ibn Ezra,* the prepositional prefix מ [*from*] in מִטַּל *from the dew,* applies itself also to this word which should be interpreted as if it read וּמִמִּשְׁמַנֵּי הָאָרֶץ, *from the* מִשְׁמַנֵּי, *fine fruits,* of the land. [Such double applications of prepositions are common even in English where, for example, one would say 'from home and field,' where the implication is '*from* home and *from* field.']

וְרֹב דָּגָן וְתִירֹשׁ — *And abundant grain and wine.*[1]

— So you will be able to sustain others *(Sforno).*

Ramban suggests that the conjunctive ו, *and,* in this phrase must be superfluous; the connotation of the blessing actually means: *May* HASHEM *give you of the dew of heaven and the fat of the land* [namely]: *abundant grain and wine.*

That is, by virtue of the *dew of heaven* [i.e., effortlessly, by divine blessing, not as a result of excessive toil], may the earth yield up its fatness: abundant grain and wine *(Ibn Caspi).*

[The translation of תִּירֹשׁ as *wine* follows *Onkelos.* Although in the Torah the terms יַיִן and תִּירֹשׁ are synonymous, the *Talmud* notes that in common usage there is a distinction between תִּירֹשׁ, by which people used to refer to a sweeter, less fermented wine than יַיִן which referred to fully aged wine. (See *Rashi* to *Nedarim* 76b). Apparently, however, even תִּירֹשׁ would be intoxicating when consumed in quantity (see *Sanhedrin* 70b).]

1. In blessing Jacob, it was Isaac's intention to annul the curse placed upon Adam after his sin, and thereby to restore the world to its former beauty.

In contrast to Adam's curse [3:18]: *accursed is the ground because of you,* Isaac said: *May* HASHEM *give you of the dew of the heavens and of the fat of the earth.* This will bring joy in the world unlike the sadness caused by drought and famine which was inherent in Adam's curse [ibid.]: *in suffering shall you eat of it.*

Contrasting *thorns and thistles shall it sprout for you,* Isaac blessed him with *abundant grain and wine,* this further contrasting the curse given Adam of *you shall eat the wild herbs of the field.*

Contrasting *by the sweat of your brow shall you get bread to eat* since no one will help you do your farming, Jacob was told *peoples will serve you* — i.e. will till the ground for you, as in *Isaiah* 61:6 *sons of the alien shall be your plowmen and your vinedressers.*

Contrasting the curse, *for dust are you and to dust shall you return* humiliated and despised, Isaac now said, *be a lord to your brothers.*

Thus, Jacob is now divested of the curses of Adam and garbed in blessing. But moreover, he was now given the right to bring blessings and curses upon others as it says, *cursed be they who curse you, and blessed are they who bless you (Tzror HaMor* based on the *Zohar).*

כט יַעַבְדוּךָ עַמִּים וְיִשְׁתַּחֲוֻ לְךָ לְאֻמִּים הֱוֵה
גְבִיר לְאַחֶיךָ וְיִשְׁתַּחֲווּ לְךָ בְּנֵי אִמֶּךָ

29. יַעַבְדוּךָ עַמִּים — *Peoples will serve you* [or: *work for you.*]

— *Peoples*: the seventy nations *(Midrash).*

In the literal sense עַמִּים refers to peoples who are not independent nations unto themselves, but who dwell under the rule of others *(Haamek Davar).*

Your blessing of *abundant grain and wine* will not result from your own toil; othets will do your work for you, as the *Zohar* notes [see *footnote v.* 28 citing *Isaiah* 61:6] *(HaKsav V'haKaballah).*

וְיִשְׁתַּחֲוֻ לְךָ לְאֻמִּים — *And regimes* [see on 254:23] *will prostrate themselves to you.*

[Not from duress but as a result of their recognition of your superiority.]

— Entire kingdoms will come to pay obeisance to you. But וְיִשְׁתַּחֲוֻ is spelled defectively [without a double ו at the end, to imply that the prostration will be 'defective']: they will not prostrate themselves in a *servile* manner, but in a show of honor, as implied in *Isaiah* 25:3, *Therefore shall the strong people glorify you (Haamek Davar).* [Cf. full spelling of וְיִשְׁתַּחֲווּ further in the verse.]

The *Midrash* perceives *Leumim* to refer to the descendants of Ishmael and Keturah in connection with whom it is written [25:3]: The sons of Dedan were *Ashurim, Letushim,* and *Leumim.*

[Until this point, the blessing consisted of prayer to God in behalf of his son, or of prophetic portent of what the future will bring (see *footnote* to *v.26*: *'The Nature of Isaac's Blessings').* Now Isaac continues with further prophetic petition uttered as a *charge* directly to his son]:

הֱוֵה גְבִיר לְאַחֶיךָ — *Be a lord to your kinsmen* [lit. *brothers*].

Isaac thus referred to the Divine prophecy (25:23) *the elder shall serve the younger (Chizkuni).*

— This materialized during the period of the First Temple. Although Edom was an independent nation, it was subordinate to Judah [see *Rashi* to 36:31] *(Haamek Davar).*

... It will also be fulfilled in the days of the Messiah *(Radak).*

In a fundamental exposition, *Sforno* observes that since Isaac thought he was blessing Esau it is plain that he intended Esau to exercise mastery over Jacob. He intended this for Jacob's benefit because Isaac did not want him to be encumbered by material responsibilities which would hinder his spiritual development. Thus Jacob would have inherited *Eretz Yisrael* and been free to serve God within its holiness, while Esau, upon whom Jacob would be dependent, would rule the land and provide for its inhabitants.

Sforno continues that Isaac feared that Jacob's descendants would become corrupted by too much material wealth, success, and power — as indeed, we find the prophet Amos proclaiming, *'I* [*God*] *despise the pride of Jacob* [*Amos* 6:8]. That Isaac always intended Jacob to have *Eretz Yisrael* and the spiritual blessings of Abraham is

27
29

[29] *Peoples will serve you,*
and regimes will prostrate themselves to you.
Be a lord to your kinsmen,
and your mother's sons will prostrate themselves to you.

apparent from two facts: In these blessings which were intended for Esau, neither *Eretz Yisrael* nor Abraham are mentioned. In 28:4 where Isaac blessed Jacob directly, both blessings *are* specified.

Following *Hirsch:* Esau's blessings (for it was Esau whom Isaac thought he was addressing) were of a dual nature. In order to carry on Abraham's mission to be a source of blessing for the entire world, he had to gain the respect of the nations. This he could do only by having the material prosperity (*v.* 28) which they would value and admire. However, to win the respect of his brother, prosperity was not enough. He was commanded הֱוֵה גְבִיר לְאַחֶיךָ, *be a 'Man'* [i.e. a person of spiritual accomplishment] *to your brother* — be worthy of your brother's respect so that he will *bow to you,* in acknowledgment of your eminence. *Then,* those who bless you will be blessed and those who curse you will be cursed.

The rendering of אַחֶיךָ as *kinsmen* follows *Ibn Ezra* who explains that it refers to the children of the concubines, Hagar and Keturah. The word cannot be translated literally as *brothers* since he only had one brother. Therefore it has the sense of *kinsmen* as in 13:8 *(Yohel Or).*

According to the *Midrash, kinsmen* refers to *the chiefs of Esau* [see chapt. 36] (*Radak* interprets similarly).

וְיִשְׁתַּחֲווּ לְךָ בְּנֵי אִמֶּךָ — *And your mother's sons will prostrate themselves to you.*[1]

Mother's sons refers to Esau's descendants *(Ibn Ezra).*

Here וְיִשְׁתַּחֲווּ is spelled *'full'* in order to imply *complete servility.* This blessing was fulfilled during the time of the Second Temple when the Edomite nation was a vassal state of Israel. [Cf. spelling of וְיִשְׁתַּחֲוֻ above.]

According to the literal intent of the blessing whereby *Esau* is being addressed, *Malbim* explains that *Jacob's* descendants will honor *Esau* as the first born. See *Sforno*'s explanation above that Isaac considered it beneficial to Jacob's spiritual tranquility to be somewhat subservient to Esau.

Daas Soferim suggests that Isaac who thought that Esau stood before him emphasized *'children* of your mother' implying: 'Even if your mother does not value you, her *children* will come to recognize your worth.'

1. The *lordship* mentioned in the previous phrase implied that Jacob was to win his brothers over by means of his exemplary service to God — *then,* by virtue of such spiritual superiority, his mother's sons would prostrate themselves to him; otherwise brothers are not subservient one to another. Therefore, we see that no sooner does Israel falter in its service to God, then Edom rises to preeminence *(Or HaChaim).*

ל אֹרְרֶיךָ אָרוּר וּמְבָרְכֶיךָ בָּרוּךְ׃ וַיְהִי
כַּאֲשֶׁר כִּלָּה יִצְחָק לְבָרֵךְ אֶת־יַעֲקֹב וַיְהִי
אַךְ יָצֹא יָצָא יַעֲקֹב מֵאֵת פְּנֵי יִצְחָק אָבִיו

Rashi notes that when Jacob blessed Judah, however, he said [49:8]: 'your *father's sons* shall bow down to you.' Because Jacob had several wives the only way he could assure Judah dominion over the entire nation was by referring to his own sons. Isaac having had only one wife, alludes to her [since he did not want to associate himself with making his child subservient. Jacob, however, had no choice but to say *your father's sons (Gur Aryeh).*]

אֹרְרֶיךָ אָרוּר וּמְבָרְכֶיךָ בָּרוּךְ — *Cursed be they who curse you, and blessed be they who bless you.*

Whoever may wish to curse you is cursed from now, and accordingly will not be able to curse you; conversely, they who will bless you are retroactively blessed so their blessings will be effective *(Or HaChaim).*

— *Cursed be they who curse you* alludes to Balaam. *Blessed be they who bless you* alludes to *Moses and Aaron, David and Solomon (Midrash).*

Rashi [following the *Midrash*] notes that Balaam, in contrast, reversed the order by saying *Blessed be they who bless you, and cursed they who curse you* [*Numbers* 24:9]. The explanation is that the righteous first experience suffering [=curse] and then, happiness [=blessing] so that those who curse them (and cause them suffering) precede those who bless them. Therefore, the righteous Isaac spoke first of those who curse and only then of those who bless. But with the wicked it is the reverse: first they enjoy tranquility and then suffering. Therefore the wicked Balaam first mentioned those who bless and then those who curse.

Ramban cites the above comment and observes that in connection with Abraham God said [12:3], *I will bless those who bless you, and him who curses you I will curse* [first mentioning the blessing and then the curse!] He answers that by pointing out the contrast which is explained there: *the blessing* in 12:3 is expressed in the plural *'those' who bless you,* while the *curse* is expressed in the singular *'he' who curses you.* The verse gives priority to the *many* who will universally bless Abraham, and only *then* goes on to mention the rare *individual* who might curse him. Or, that sequence is used in Abraham's case since in that passage *curse* is not the concluding thought since God continues [ibid.]: *and all the families of the earth shall bless themselves by you.* Thus God's statement to Abraham begins and ends with blessing.

Why, indeed, is it written here *'they* who curse you' in the plural, while in the case of Abraham the singular *'he* who curses you' is used? — *Chizkuni* answers that in effect Isaac thought he was addressing Esau whom he knew to be engaged in mundane pursuits that

27
30
Cursed be they who curse you,
and blessed be they who bless you."
30 *And it was, when Isaac had finished blessing*
Jacob, and Jacob had scarcely left from the presence

were bound to make him *many enemies*, hence: *they* who curse you. Abraham, however, was known to be loved by all and hence his enemies would be few if any.

[Inasmuch as Jacob was the recipient of the blessings, the plural form was unfortunately prophetic. History testifies to the many enemies of Jacob's descendants, who seized every opportunity to curse us — in word and deed ל״ור].

The Hebrew is literally, *'they* who curse you *is* cursed, and *they* who bless you *is* blessed.' *Ibn Ezra* explains that the plural means *each and every one* who curses you will be cursed, and *each and every one* who blesses you will be blessed.'

30. Esau returns.

וַיְהִי כַּאֲשֶׁר כִּלָּה יִצְחָק לְבָרֵךְ אֶת־יַעֲקֹב — *And it was, when Isaac had finished blessing Jacob.*

As Isaac finished his blessing of Jacob, the Torah uses the word וַיְהִי which the Sages explain as portending *woe*. By implication, the Torah bemoans the fact that Isaac *finished* and did not bless Jacob with even more blessings. For had Isaac also given Jacob those additional blessings which he later conferred upon Esau (verses 39-40), then Edom [a reference to all anti-Semites through the ages] would have been without any semblance of hope *(Or HaChaim)*.

וַיְהִי אַךְ יָצֹא יָצָא יַעֲקֹב — *And Jacob had scarcely left* [lit. *and it was but that Jacob was leaving he left*].

The phrase emphasizes how as one was on the way out, the other entered *(Rashi)*.

The word אַךְ, *but*, is always interpreted as a מִיעוּט, *limitation.* It qualifies the compound verb יָצָא, *leave*, as being incomplete — one came *before* the other's leaving was complete *(Gur Aryeh)*.

The incident also emphasizes the miracle wrought for Jacob. Had Esau come but a minute sooner, Jacob would not have been blessed *(Rashbam)*.

... And had he come much later, an undue amount of time would have elapsed between the blessing and Isaac's confirmation גַּם בָּרוּךְ יִהְיֶה, *indeed, he shall remain blessed (Malbim)*.

The *Midrash* notes in this context that Providence arranged for Esau to be less successful than usual in his hunt 'so that Jacob who was the glory of the world might come and receive the blessings which had been determined as his from the very beginning of the world.'

The *Midrash* records an opinion that Isaac's tent had two entrances. Esau entered by one, and Jacob left by the other. According to the Rabbis, Jacob hid behind one of the hinged doors until Esau entered and then he departed. That is the significance of the expression אַךְ יָצֹא יָצָא, *had scarcely left* — his leaving was still incomplete: Jacob had *appeared* to have gone out, yet had not actually done so.

לא וְעֵשָׂו אָחִיו בָּא מִצֵּידוֹ: וַיַּעַשׂ גַּם־הוּא
מַטְעַמִּים וַיָּבֵא לְאָבִיו וַיֹּאמֶר לְאָבִיו יָקֻם
אָבִי וְיֹאכַל מִצֵּיד בְּנוֹ בַּעֲבֻר תְּבָרְכַנִּי
לב נַפְשֶׁךָ: וַיֹּאמֶר לוֹ יִצְחָק אָבִיו מִי־אָתָּה
לג וַיֹּאמֶר אֲנִי בִּנְךָ בְכֹרְךָ עֵשָׂו: וַיֶּחֱרַד יִצְחָק
חֲרָדָה גְּדֹלָה עַד־מְאֹד וַיֹּאמֶר מִי־אֵפוֹא
הוּא הַצָּד־צַיִד וַיָּבֵא לִי וָאֹכַל מִכֹּל בְּטֶרֶם

וְעֵשָׂו אָחִיו בָּא מִצֵּידוֹ — *That* [lit. *and*] *Esau his brother came back from his hunt.*

31. וַיַּעַשׂ גַּם־הוּא מַטְעַמִּים [And] *he, too, made delicacies.*

I.e. *after* he returned from the hunt; this being Isaac's implicit instruction [see *v.* 4] *(Haamek Davar).*

יָקֻם אָבִי וְיֹאכַל מִצֵּיד בְּנוֹ — *Let my father rise and eat of his son's game.*

[See *Rashi* to *v.* 22 where Esau's harsh tone in this verse (which is more striking in the Hebrew than in the translation) is compared with Jacob's entrating tone in *v.* 19, קוּם נָא שְׁבָה, *Rise up, please, sit,* etc.]

Also, Jacob added שְׁבָה, *sit,* as if to imply that by saying קוּם נָא it was not his intention that his father literally *stand up* and then *sit down,* but that it was to be taken as a polite request that he *move into a comfortable sitting position*; Esau omitted שְׁבָה — implying that he did not care whether his father was comfortable or not: his call יָקֻם אָבִי, let my father *rise* was to be taken literally — that his father *rise up* and prepare himself to partake of Esau's delicacies *(HaKsav V'haKaballah).*

Chizkuni suggests that יָקֻם, *rise,* in this context has the sense of *awaken,* since Isaac had been slumbering after having eaten Jacob's meal.

Furthermore, Esau said *from his son's game* as if he were Isaac's only son *(HaKsav V'haKaballah).*

32. מִי אָתָּה — *Who are you?*

Isaac thought that this might be Jacob who, having heard that Esau was to be blessed, also prepared and brought delicacies so that he, too, would be blessed *(Ramban).*

אֲנִי בִּנְךָ בְּכֹרְךָ עֵשָׂו — *I am your firstborn son, Esau.*

[Compare the self-assurance of this unambiguous response with Jacob's in verse 19.]

33. וַיֶּחֱרַד יִצְחָק חֲרָדָה גְּדֹלָה עַד מְאֹד — *Then* [lit. *and*] *Isaac trembled in very great perplexity.*

The verb חרד literally refers to *terror* or *trembling*. The translation *perplexity* follows *Rashi* who, in his primary interpretation, cites the rendering of *Onkelos:* וּתְוַה, *perplexed, overcome with anxiety.*

The commentators explain that *Rashi* chose not to use the stronger, literal connotation, *terror, trembling* because *terror* would not fit the context here. Certainly Isaac was not seized in the *literal* sense with terror *per se* over having discovered the scheme; it was rather a feeling of fear, anxiety and confusion associated specifically with a feeling of *utter perplexity* and *bewilderment* at the unfolding events.

27
31-33

of his father, that Esau his brother came back from
his hunt. 31 *He, too, made delicacies, and brought*
them to his father. He said to his father, "Let my
father rise and eat of his son's game, so that you may
give me your innermost blessing."
32 *His father Isaac said to him, "Who are you?"*
And he said, "I am your firstborn son Esau".
33 *Then Isaac trembled in very great perplexity,*
and said, 'Who — where — is the one who hunted
game, brought it to me, and I partook of all before

Rashi continues that following the *Midrash* [the term חֲרָדָה, which primarly means *terror, is* appropriately used to describe Isaac's reaction, because] when Esau entered the room Isaac perceived Gehinnom open open beneath him [i.e., *Esau. Hence Isaac was literally* seized with *terror (Gur Aryeh).*]

[Compare *v.* 27 where *Rashi* records that when Jacob entered the room the fragrance of the Garden of Eden entered with him.]

His terror at *perceiving Gehinnom* beneath him was due to the implication of punishment that Isaac felt awaited him.

As *Pirkei d'Rav Kahana* notes, when Isaac now realized that he had been constantly misled by Esau's flattery and feigned piety, *he was seized with exceedingly great terror* over the thought of the Day of Judgment.

According to *Midrash Tanchuma,* Isaac had intended to bless both his sons, but he had summoned Esau first because he was the firstborn. But when he realized that the younger had taken the blessing of the firstborn which was a serious matter [see *Deut.* 21:16-7], *he was seized with terror,* thinking: How have I sinned that I reversed the normal order by blessing the younger before the elder? [*Rashi* cites this *Midrash* in *v.* 36. See there.]

And although Isaac could not blame himself entirely for the error since he was terrified that God Who sees all, seemingly acquiesced in the supplanting of the firstborn *(Chizkuni).*

According to *Ramban,* Isaac's reaction was precipitated by his realization that Esau had lost the blessing irrevocably.

— Isaac visibly manifested great anxiety so that Esau should not suspect him of having mocked him by blessing Jacob intentionally *(Radak).*

The expression עַד מְאֹד, *very great,* denotes that his anxiety exceeded even that which he experienced when on the altar during the *Akeidah (Midrash).*

מִי־אֵפוֹא הוּא הַצָּד־צַיִד וַיָּבֵא לִי — *Who — where — is the one who hunted game,* [*and*] *brought* [it] *to me?*

— Another manifestation of the Divine Providence which was explicit throughout. *Who* came in so stealthily and unidentified; *where* could he have disappeared so quick-

לד תָּבוֹא וָאֲבָרְכֵהוּ גַּם־בָּרוּךְ יִהְיֶה׃ כִּשְׁמֹעַ
עֵשָׂו אֶת־דִּבְרֵי אָבִיו וַיִּצְעַק צְעָקָה גְּדֹלָה

ly; how could one have *hunted game* so quickly, even faster than you, who are such a skilled hunter; how could he have known to bring it to me — I did not instruct him to do so? *(Malbim).*

The translation follows *Rashi* who explains that אֵפוֹא is an independent particle whose definition depends on the context. In our case he defines it as a compound of the words אֵי פֹּה, *who, here,* the verse meaning: *Who and where here is he who hunted game?* [*Ibn Ezra* comments similarly.][1]

And as *Radak* [*Shorashim* s.v. איף] comments, although the conjunction *and* is missing between the words, it is implied, as if it were written מִי וְאֵיפוֹא, *who and where.* [Our translation *who — where* reflects the rhythm of the Hebrew which preserves Isaac's bewildered outburst.]

Sforno interprets the phrase as meaning, *Who,* **then**, *is it who hunted game?* He distinguishes between the spelling אֵיפֹה which [like *Rashi*] he explains as meaning *where,* as in 37:16 אֵיפֹה הֵם רֹעִים, *where they are pasturing,* and the spelling אֵיפוֹא, such as in our case, which he defines as *if so, then.*

וָאֹכַל מִכֹּל — *And I partook of* [lit. *from*] *all.*

— I.e. of all the delicacies he prepared for me *(Radak);* of all the goodness of the world *(Midrash; Maharzu);* of all the flavors of his delicacy — whatever taste I desired to find in it, I indeed found *(Rashi).*

[As noted in the *comm.* to 24:1, the word כֹּל, *Kol ('all')* has esoteric implications as one of the Attributes of God. In connection with each of the Patriarchs, the Torah uses the word כֹּל, *all, everything,* which implies *perfection,* totally unflawed blessing. This Kabbilistically teaches that each was given an inkling of the World to Come and that the Evil Inclination had no dominion over them. See *footnote* there and *comm.* to ArtScroll *Bircas HaMazon.*]

וַאֲבָרְכֵהוּ — *And I blessed him.*

— Since the Hand of God was implicit throughout *(Malbim).*

גַּם־בָּרוּךְ יִהְיֶה — *Indeed, he shall remain* [lit. *be*] *blessed.*

Isaac thus confirmed his blessing. Lest one think that Jacob would not have been blessed had he not engaged in deception, Isaac confirmed it, blessing him now of his own free will *(Midrash; Rashi).*

[See *Tanchuma* cited by *Rashi* in *v.* 36 s.v. אֶת בְּכֹרָתִי לָקָח.]

Having already blessed him, I confirm it since he, too, is my son *(Radak).*

Indeed, he shall remain blessed — for having rushed to serve me. Isaac now realized that Jacob had done everything in accordance with the instructions of Rebecca who perceived that Jacob was more worthy of the blessings *(Rashbam).*

Ramban notes that in the literal sense, it would be unlikely for one

1. *Da'as Zekeinim* interprets the verse Midrashically: Isaac asked מִי אֵפָה, "Who shall be 'baked' in Gehinnom?" And the Divine Spirit responded הַצָּד צַיִד, *"He who hunted the game"* — a reference to Esau. Therefore Isaac later said to Esau [*v.* 37]: וּלְכָה אֵפוֹא, *"And for you, where — what can I do, my son?,"* i.e. and for you — you are destined to be אָפוּי, *baked,* in Gehinnom; what can I possibly do for you?

27
34

you came and I blessed him? Indeed, he shall remain blessed!"

34 *When Esau heard his father's words he cried out an exceedingly great and bitter cry and said to his*

to *willingly* bless another who had deceived him and thus compound the deceit. Certainly this would arouse Esau's ire even more and cause him to distrust his father's sincerity.

Ramban accordingly offers two interpretations: 1. The verse should be rendered: Who — where is he that hunted and brought me game that I should bless him *for I know that indeed he is blessed*; 2. Even so, although he received the blessing dishonestly, *he must remain blessed,* even against my will, since I cannot revoke the blessing. Indeed Isaac knew by this time that it could be only Jacob since the blessings could not have rested on anyone but his offspring.[1]

— [Isaac saw God's Will in what he had done; though done involuntarily, it could not be revoked.]

Sforno suggests that Isaac was making a matter-of-fact statement that though Jacob's methods were questionable, Isaac had an inner assurance that his blessings had been effective and accordingly, Jacob *indeed,* would remain blessed. As it is said of R' Chaninah, he knew when prayers he had offered for the sick had been efficacious [see *Mishnah, Berachos* 34b.]

34. כִּשְׁמֹעַ עֵשָׂו אֶת דִּבְרֵי אָבִיו — *When Esau heard his father's words.*

I.e. Isaac's voluntary confirmation of Jacob's blessing *(Malbim).*

According to *Akeidas Yitzchak* the wording of this verse attests that it was not Esau's recognition of the importance of the blessing that made him cry out in bitter anguish. It was only Isaac's response and his anxiety and terror at the truth of events that impressed upon Esau the greatness of the blessings. However, he still did not comprehend their *true* mystery or he would have known that such a blessing could not be shared among two individuals.

וַיִּצְעַק צְעָקָה גְּדֹלָה וּמָרָה עַד־מְאֹד — [And] *he cried out an exceedingly great and bitter cry.*

The Torah gives eloquent testimony to Esau's intense desire to be a faithful son. Although he had not been deprived of anything tangible — only of the blessings — he reacted as though he had lost an immense fortune.

1. The *Midrash* notes that Isaac's first reaction was to *curse* Jacob, but he was told through Divine Inspiration that if he were to do so, he would be cursing himself since he had said [*v.* 29] *Cursed be they who curse you.* So, as we see, Isaac blessed him instead. Thus, it was due to Divine intervention that Jacob was spared, for Isaac's consternation might easily have resulted in his *cursing* Jacob upon finding out the scheme. But Jacob trusted in God Who inspired Isaac to bless him instead.

[The *Midrash* offers a similar comment in *Ruth* 3:8: although Boaz was startled [וַיֶּחֱרַד] and might easily have cursed Ruth, who secreted herself in his field, God put it into his heart to bless her (*v.* 10 there).]

וּמָרָה עַד־מְאֹד וַיֹּאמֶר לְאָבִיו בָּרְכֵנִי גַם־
לה אָנִי אָבִי: וַיֹּאמֶר בָּא אָחִיךָ בְּמִרְמָה וַיִּקַּח
לו בִּרְכָתֶךָ: וַיֹּאמֶר הֲכִי קָרָא שְׁמוֹ יַעֲקֹב
וַיַּעְקְבֵנִי זֶה פַעֲמַיִם אֶת־בְּכֹרָתִי לָקָח

The Sages compare Esau's bitter lament to Mordechai's outcry when he heard of Haman and Ahasuerus' edict to exterminate his people [see *footnote*].[1]

בָּרְכֵנִי גַם־אָנִי אָבִי — *Bless me too,* [*my*] *father.*

I, too, am your son, just as he is! *(Radak).*

Esau did not realize that his blessing was reserved for Jacob; therefore he protested that a father should be able to bless *all* his children with wealth, dominion and everything good *(Malbim).*

The word אֲנִי is vocalized אָנִי although it is not the end of a clause, becuase of the cantillation, a *tip'cha,* which is disjunctive *(Radak).*

35. בָּא אָחִיךָ בְּמִרְמָה — *Your brother came with cleverness.*

— By having disguised himself as a hairy person *(Radak).*

Although Isaac had asked incredulously *who* it was who took the blessings, he surmised that since Esau was now before him, his earlier visitor must have been Jacob since his blessing could rest only on his own offspring *(Tur;* see *Ramban* above).

The translation of the word מִרְמָה as *cleverness* [*wisdom*],instead of more common, *cunning* or *deceit,* follows *Onkelos* [בְּחָכְמְתָא] and *Rashi.*

The *Midrash* similarly renders 'by the wisdom of his Torah.'

Torah Sheleimah cites *Midrash Ha-Biur* that permissible cunning is called מִרְמָה; malicious *deceit* is called עָרְמָה.

[Perhaps the term מִרְמָה was used because it has a dual connotation; Esau was to understand it as meaning *deceit;* Isaac's intent was that Jacob acted with *wisdom.*]

Even those who preserve the literal connotation of *deceit* (for example, *Alshich, Malbim)* interpret that Isaac implied that only the manner of Jacob's *coming* [i.e. the disguise, etc.) was considered deceitful [בָּא בְּמִרְמָה], not the *taking* of the blessings; which was a valid 'taking' as Isaac himself intimated when he said וַיִּקַּח בִּרְכָתֶךָ, *and took your blessing,* implying a successful *fait accompli.* This validity is attested to by the fact that the fragrance of the Garden of Eden entered the room with him [*v.* 27], symbolic of God's consent to what was transpiring.

וַיִּקַּח בִּרְכָתֶךָ — *And* [he] *took your blessing.*

— I.e., it was *your* blessing because it would have been particularly appropriate for you inasmuch as it concerned material things *(Sforno).*

The blessing which is due a firstborn *(Akeidas Yitzchak).*

1. The *Midrash* notes that God is patient, but He eventually collects what is due. Thus, Jacob caused Esau to cry out once, and his descendants ultimately paid for this in the capital city of Shushan, as it says, in almost identical wording, that on hearing of the edict to exterminate his people [*Esther* 4:1]: וַיִּזְעַק זְעָקָה גְדוֹלָה וּמָרָה, *he* [Mordechai] *cried loudly and bitterly.*

The *Yalkut* there records that Mordechai cried out, 'My ancestor Isaac! What have you done to me? Esau *cried out* before you and you heeded his cries and blessed him. Now *we* are destined to be slaughtered [by Haman, a descendant of Esau]!

father, "Bless me too, Father!"
35 But he said, "Your brother came with cleverness
and took your blessing."
36 He said, "Is it because he was named Jacob that
he should outwit me these two times? — He took

36. הֲכִי קָרָא שְׁמוֹ יַעֲקֹב — *Is it because he was named Jacob ('Yaakov').*

This translation follows *Rashi* who views this as an incredulous question [the הֲ being the interrogative particle = *is it,* and כִּי = *because,* as in 29:15 הֲכִי אָחִי אַתָּה, *Is it because you are my brother?*]

See alternate view of *Ibn Ezra,* further, who renders: *His name is rightfully called Jacob,* and *Alshich* who explains that God is the subject of קָרָא שְׁמוֹ, *He named him.*]

וַיַּעְקְבֵנִי זֶה פַעֲמַיִם — *That* [lit. *and*] *he should outwit me these two times?*

There is a play on words here between the name *Yaakov* which connotes *heel* (see 25:26) and also the verb meaning *take a circuitous route* to achieve one's goal *(Haamek Davar); deceive (Radak); supplant.*

Following two interpretations of *Onkelos, Rashi* renders: *lie in wait, ambush* [see *Deut.* 19:11], or *outwitted me.* [It is the latter interpretation that we have followed in our translation.]

Continuing *Rashi:* Was he given the name Jacob in prophetic anticipation that he would one day outwit me? [For had the name commemorated a *current* event his name should have been עָקֵב [*heel*] or עָקַב, (past tense); the future verb form יַעֲקֹב signifies a future deception *(Divrei David-Taz).*]

Rashbam [interpreting פַעֲמַיִם in the sense of a *double portion,* renders]: Since he is younger than I, his share of the inheritance should have been only half of my first-born's double portion. Is it because he was given a name suggesting deception that he has the right to cheat me of my rightful inheritance and to take for himself the double portion of the first-born?

Sforno renders: *Did the fact that he was named Jacob influence him to deceive me?* For as the *Talmud* notes [*Berachos* 7b]: שְׁמָא גָרֵים, a man's name influences his character.

Alshich cites the view that at birth, *God* named him Jacob [see *comm.* to 25:26], and Esau accordingly did not say: *Is it because* קָרָאתָ *you* [father] *named him Jacob,* but said, *'Is it because of this that* קָרָא, *He named* i.e., God – Who forsees the future — *named him Jacob?* Now I understand why He gave him that name. It was not because Jacob had, at birth, grasped me by the עָקֵב, *heel,* as commonly thought, but as a portent that he would יַעֲקְבֵנִי, *outwit me.* But does that divine portent give him the right to do so פַעֲמָיִם, *twice?'*

His name Jacob was supposed to portend that his sovereignty will supplant mine in the *Time to Come!* [see *comm.* to 25:27 — he will rule 'on my heels,' i.e. after me]; how then does he presume to *outwit* me now by committing these two deceitful acts? Does he think that he was named Jacob to signify that he

וְהִנֵּה עַתָּה לָקַח בִּרְכָתִי וַיֹּאמַר הֲלֹא־
לז אָצַלְתָּ לִּי בְּרָכָה: וַיַּעַן יִצְחָק וַיֹּאמֶר
לְעֵשָׂו הֵן גְּבִיר שַׂמְתִּיו לָךְ וְאֶת־כָּל־אֶחָיו
נָתַתִּי לוֹ לַעֲבָדִים וְדָגָן וְתִירֹשׁ סְמַכְתִּיו

has the right to outwit me even now? *(Abarbanel; Malbim).*

According to *Ibn Ezra,* this is not a question but a *statement:* the word הֲכִי is an affirmation meaning *indeed, rightfully.* His name is rightfully called Jacob, because he supplanted me these two times [*Onkelos* renders similarly.]

Radak, too, follows this interpretation: He was properly called Jacob, since the name carries within it the connotation of deceit as well!

אֶת בְּכֹרָתִי לָקָח — *He took away my birthright.*

First he deceived me by taking advantage of me when I was famished; there is no greater deceit than that *(Radak).*

The wicked Esau had the audacity to lie to his father's face about Jacob 'taking' his birthright when in reality it was Esau himself who sold it under oath and thereby flagrantly despised it as the Torah attests [25:34] (cf. *HaKsav V'ha-Kaballah).*

But, his own mouth caused him to testify against himself by admitting that the birthright was now Jacob's *(Chizkuni).*

Rashi cites *Midrash Tanchuma* that Isaac was *seized with terror* [*v.* 33] because he thought he committed a serious transgression in blessing the younger before the elder [see *Deut.* 21:16-17]. When Esau cried out, *He outwitted me these two times,* Isaac asked, 'How?' When Esau replied, *He took away my birthright,* Isaac was relieved and said, 'It was on this account that I had feared I had overstepped the line of strict justice, but now that you tell me he has the birthright I realize that I actually blessed the firstborn, [I.e., Jacob was entitled to the blessing of the firstborn] — Indeed גַּם בָּרוּךְ יִהְיֶה, *indeed, he shall remain blessed!'*

According to this interpretation, of course, this exchange occurred *before* Isaac exclaimed [*v.* 33] *indeed he shall remain blessed;* accordingly, verse 34, *when Esau heard his father's words,* should be interpreted as a paranthetic elaboration in the past perfect: 'when Esau *had* heard' [his father's anxiety over having blessed someone else before Esau *v.* 33]. There is an allusion to such an interpretation even in the literal sense inasmuch as *v.* 34 does not begin with the usual sequential formula וַיְהִי כִּשְׁמֹעַ עֵשָׂו, *and it came to pass, when Esau heard.* The omission of וַיְהִי allows for such a past-perfect interpretation *(Divrei David).*

[Or it might be that the verses reflect the *actual sequence,* and the *Midrash* cited by *Rashi* is emphasizing how Isaac felt vindicated in retrospect for having confirmed the blessing now that he heard that the birthright was indeed Jacob's by Esau's own acknowledgment.]

וְהִנֵּה עַתָּה לָקַח בִּרְכָתִי — *And see, now he took away my blessing.*

[There is a further play on words here: בְּכֹרָתִי, *my birthright* — בִּרְכָתִי, *my blessing.*]

Since Rebecca had been told that the *elder son would serve the younger one* [25:23] Jacob's purchase of the birthright had the added effect of making him subser-

27 *away my birthright and see, now he took away my*
37 *blessing!" Then he said, "Have you not reserved a*
blessing for me?"
37 *Isaac answered, and said to Esau, "Behold, a lord*
have I made him over you, and all his kin have I
given him as servants. With grain and wine have I

vient to Esau who had been left with the status of the younger son. Now, however, Esau had the further complaint that Jacob had deceptively usurped the blessing of being a *lord to his kinsmen* [*v.* 29], with the result that he would dominate Esau *(Malbim).*

וַיֹּאמַר — *Then* [lit. *and*] *he said.*

Esau understood from his father's remark 'he took your blessing' that Isaac could not bless him equally. But certainly there was *something* his father had left to bestow upon him *(Haamek Davar).*

... Perhaps a loophole can be found.

הֲלֹא אָצַלְתָּ לִּי בְּרָכָה — *Have you not reserved a blessing for me?*

— Even an inferior one? *(Midrash).*

Even though you intended to bless me with the *superior* blessing you certainly did not intend to bestow *everything* on me and leave my brother entirely devoid of your blessing. You must have reserved *something.* Can you not give me that? *(Sforno).*

[Our translation of אָצַלְתָּ as *reserved* follows *Rashi* who interprets the word as meaning *separate, set aside* (cf. *Numbers* 11:25). *Targum* and *Ibn Ezra* render it as *hold back,* as does *Ramban* in *Numbers* 11:17.]

37. **הֵן גְּבִיר שַׂמְתִּיו לָךְ** — *Behold, a lord have I made* [lit. *placed*] *him over you.*

As implied in the expression (*v.* 29): *Be a lord to your kinsmen (Ramban).*

— This was the *seventh* in the series of blessings Isaac gave Jacob (see verses 28-29); why does Isaac single it out as if it were the *primary* blessing?

— Isaac's intention was to emphasize to Esau that the blessing of lordship had already been given Jacob, so whatever property Esau would acquire would automatically revert to Jacob in accordance with the rule מַה שֶּׁקָּנָה עֶבֶד קָנָה רַבּוֹ, *whatever a servant acquires belongs to his master* (cf. *Kiddushin* 23b). [Thus, in a sense, this blessing superceded the others.] *(Rashi).*

וְאֶת־כָּל־אֶחָיו נָתַתִּי לוֹ לַעֲבָדִים — *And all his kin* [lit. *brothers*] *have I given him as servants.*

— As implied in the expression [*v.* 29] *your mother's sons will prostrate themselves to you (Ramban).*

His kin, referring to the descendants of Ishmael and of Keturah *(Ibn Ezra; Sforno).*

[See *comm.* to *v.* 29].

וְדָגָן וְתִירֹשׁ סְמַכְתִּיו — *And* [*with*] *grain and wine have I supported him.*

'With' is not in the Hebrew, but is implied. This translation follows one opinion in *Radak.* Alternatively he suggests that the root סמך means

לח וּלְכָה אֵפוֹא מָה אֶעֱשֶׂה בְּנִי׃ וַיֹּאמֶר עֵשָׂו
אֶל־אָבִיו הַבְרָכָה אַחַת הִוא־לְךָ אָבִי
בָּרְכֵנִי גַם־אָנִי אָבִי וַיִּשָּׂא עֵשָׂו קֹלוֹ וַיֵּבְךְּ׃
לט וַיַּעַן יִצְחָק אָבִיו וַיֹּאמֶר אֵלָיו הִנֵּה
מִשְׁמַנֵּי הָאָרֶץ יִהְיֶה מוֹשָׁבֶךָ וּמִטַּל

near (סְמוּכִים לוֹ), rendering, *grain and wine have I kept near him.*

וּלְכָה אֵפוֹא מָה אֶעֱשֶׂה בְּנִי — *And for you, where ... what can I do, my son?*

After all the above, what is left? *(Radak).*

Where could I possibly seek out something to do for you? *(Rashi).*

— What blessing could I offer you that would be of any avail? *(Sforno).*

The question was rhetorical. It was a polite way of telling him that there was indeed nothing Isaac could do for him *(Abarbanel).*[1]

38. הַבְרָכָה אַחַת הִיא־לְךָ אָבִי — *Have you but one blessing, [my] father?*

The above is the usual rendering: *Radak* renders: Is there not even a *single blessing* that does not conflict with Jacob's blessing?

Torah Sheleimah cites *Tanchuma:*

Esau was one of three persons who argued indirectly with God. [The others are Cain (4:23) and Menashe (*II Chronicles* 33:12). See *Sanhedrin* 101b.] Esau said to Isaac: 'It appears that had Jacob and I *both* been righteous, your God would not have been able to provide blessings for both of us!' 'Silence!' God interjected. 'Jacob will eventually bless twelve tribes and not duplicate any of the blessings!' Nevertheless, Esau was shown compassion, and he was blessed.

The translation of this phrase follows *Rashi* who notes grammatically that the prefix ה in הַבְרָכָה is a ה הַשְּׁאֵלָה, *interrogative participle.* [This interpretation appears to violate the general rule, because it is not punctuated with a *chataf-patach* which usually identifies the interrogative prefix ה (see *comm.* to הֲשֹׁפֵט in 18:25), and it is followed by a letter with a *sheva* which usually indicates the definite article ה.] *Rashi,* therefore, cites other examples of interrogative prefixes which are similarly punctuated]: הַבְּמַחֲנִים, *are they in camps?* [*Numbers* 13:19]; הַשְּׁמֵנָה, *is it fat?* [ibid. *v.* 20]; הַכְּמוֹת, *Will it be like the death...?* [*I Samuel* 3:33.]

בָּרְכֵנִי גַם־אָנִי אָבִי — *Bless me, too,* [my]-*Father.*

— Enable me also to achieve wealth and dominion in this world, independently, and not in the shadow of Jacob. Bless me as a father blesses *each* of his children with abundance *(Malbim).*

1. Actually there *were* blessings Isaac *could* have given Esau, but Isaac perceived that, as Jacob's enemy, Esau would have been more deservant of being *cursed,* as Isaac had specifically said [*v.* 30]: *Cursed be they who curse you.* Isaac was therefore reluctant to bless Esau. The beginning of our verse intimates this with the words: וַיַּעַן יִצְחָק וַיֹּאמֶר, *And Isaac answered and said,* implying that he continued this 'answer' only for the purpose of 'saying' that nothing could be done for Esau rather than as a positive reply to Esau's plaint *(Or HaChaim).*

[The word אֵפוֹא, *where,* is discussed in *v.* 33. See also *Da'as Zekeinim* cited there.]

27 *supported him, and for you, where ... what can I do,*
38-39 *my son?"*
38 *And Esau said to his father, "Have you but one*
blessing, Father? Bless me too, Father!" And Esau
raised his voice and wept.
39 *So Isaac his father answered, and said to him:*
"Behold, of the fat of the earth shall be
your dwelling

וַיִּשָּׂא עֵשָׂו קֹלוֹ וַיֵּבְךְּ – *And Esau raised his voice and wept.*

Esau produced but a few tears ... But see how much peace and tranquility God bestowed in compensation upon Esau for those few tears! *(Tanchuma).*

For, as the *Zohar* notes, we will remain under Esau's power until we repent and shed tears that can outweigh his.

For these tears he was rewarded with Mount Seir where sufficient rain always falls. He enjoys the good of this world, and whatever punishment he deserves will be meted out to him in the World to Come *(Yalkut).*

It was these tears that influenced the *Shechinah* to consent to Isaac's blessing or Esau (*Alshich).*

39. Esau's Blessing.

וַיַּעַן יִצְחָק אָבִיו – *So* [lit. *and*] *Isaac his father answered.*

The Torah thus implicitly tells us *why* Isaac as אָבִיו, *his father, relented. His fatherly compassion* was aroused by Esau's tears – and so he blessed him *(Or HaChaim).*

I.e. it was as his compassionate *father* that Isaac answered him *(Malbim).*

הִנֵּה מִשְׁמַנֵּי הָאָרֶץ יִהְיֶה מוֹשָׁבֶךָ – *Behold, of the fat of the earth shall be your dwelling.*

I.e., may the land you inherit be the most fertile region on earth *(Radak).*

According to *Rashi,* this refers to אִיטַלְיָאָה שֶׁל יָוָן, the Grecian portions of Italy [i.e. southern Italy which includes Rome (cf. the term Magna Graecia).]

The *Talmud (Megillah* 6b) defines 'Greek Italy' as Rome. [Apparently Rome is so designated on account of the great influence of the Greek civilization on the Roman.]

Rashi ad loc. notes that the phrase אִיֵּי אֱלִישָׁה, *Isles of Elishah (Ezekiel* 27:7) is rendered by *Targum:* 'Isles of Italy.'

[This *Midrashic* interpretation follows the familiar identification of Esau/Edom (see 36:1) with Rome. *Rashi's* interpretation of our verse also serves to distinguish between the identical term מִשְׁמַנֵּי הָאָרֶץ, *of the fatness of the earth,* used in Jacob's and Esau's blessings. For Jacob it refers to abundant *crops,* and for Esau, according to the context, it refers to the fertile *region* where he would dwell – hence the association with Italy where Esau's descendants – the Romans – fourished (see *Mizrachi; Gur Aryeh).*][1]

1. There is a significance to Esau being given Rome as an ultimate heritage.

The *Talmud* [*Sanhedrin* 21b; *Yerushalmi Avodah Zarah* 1:1 [cf. version in *Rashi* to *Megillah* 6b] records that when King Solomon married the daughter of Pharaoh (*I Kings* 3:1), an

מ הַשָּׁמַיִם מֵעָל: °וְעַל־חַרְבְּךָ תִחְיֶה וְאֶת־
אָחִיךָ תַּעֲבֹד וְהָיָה כַּאֲשֶׁר תָּרִיד וּפָרַקְתָּ

°חצי הספר בפסוקים

The *Midrash* identifies the reference here as being to Beth Gubrin, the fertile Idumean town and fortress in southwestern Judea.

According to *Radak*, the reference is to Seir [the home of Esau and his descendants, the Edomites (see 32:3; 33:14,6)].

Noting that Seir was not the *most* fertile of lands, *Abarbanel* interprets the phrase as referring to *unspecified* fertile lands that his children would later occupy, as indeed came to pass.

וּמִטַּל הַשָּׁמַיִם מֵעָל — *And of the dew of the heavens from above.*

There was no conflict in the blessing since God's natural blessing is abundant enough for *both* of them. Furthermore, as noted in 28:4, as Abraham's heir, Jacob would realize his blessing *in the land of Canaan,* while Esau would realize his in another land. However, Isaac did not bless Esau with *abundant grain and wine* as he did Jacob since he wanted to honor the one who was blessed first *(Ramban).*

Rashi in *v.* 28 s.v. הָאֱלֹהִים notes that God's name is omitted here because unlike Jacob's, Esau's blessing was not dependent upon his righteousness. See *Ramban* cited there.

Tur adds that God's name is not invoked here since Esau himself made no reference to God as did Jacob [*v.* 20.]

As *Hirsch* notes: Isaac did not preface his blessing to Esau by saying וְיִתֶּן לְךָ הָאֱלֹהִים, May *God* give you, which implies that His blessings would be given under the *special management* and guidance of God as were Jacob's. Rather, Esau's blessings would come in the *normal* course of Nature's functioning on 'heaven and earth.'

[The suggestion by some 'moderns' that this was a left-handed blessing with the interpretation being, *'Away' from the fatness of the earth shall your dwelling be and away from the dew of heaven,* (the מ of מִשְׁמַנֵּי and מִטַּל being interpreted in the partitive sense *away from,* thus contrasting Esau's blessing with Jacob's), is devoid of Rabbinic exegitical basis and exhibits a merely fanciful departure from the simple context of the blessings.]

וּמִטַּל הַשָּׁמַיִם מֵעָל — *and of the dew of the heavens from above.*

I.e., may you benefit from abundant heavenly dew [which carries with it more blessing than *rain* — (see *v.* 28)] so you will be spared the toil of irrigating your fields *(Akeidas Yitzchak; Sforno).*

[Many Chumashim draw attention to a Masoretic note that this point marks half of the Book of *Bereishis* in number of verses.]

40. וְעַל חַרְבְּךָ תִחְיֶה — [*And*] *by* [lit. *upon*] *your sword you shall live.*

As a hunter *(Rashbam);* as a warrior *(Sforno).*

— All of this you earned by your merit because you *sharpened your*

angel planted a reed in the Mediterranean Sea. Mud and sand gradually accumulated around this reed, eventually building up the Italian peninsula on which subsequently Rome was built. [See *Overview* to ArtScroll *Eichah.*]

Tiferes HaGershuni suggests since all the world was created for the sake of Jacob, Esau was therefore given Rome as an *ultimate* heritage which as the Aggadah above notes, did not yet exist in the time of Jacob.

27 *and of the dew of the heavens from above.*
40 *[40] By your sword you shall live,*
but your brother you shall serve.
Yet it shall be that when you are aggrieved,

sword and bow as I bid you [*v.*3] *(Chizkuni).*

Esau's descendants would conquer other nations, and ultimately rule the entire world by the force of their sword; the fulfillment of this prophecy is well-known *(Abarbanel).*

The implication was not that Esau would be forced to become a brigand and plunderer with his sword, for he was blessed with sustenance from the *fatness of the earth and dew of heaven.* Rather, the blessing was that he be victorious in war and survive his battles *(Ramban).*

Rashi notes that the Hebrew עַל חַרְבְּךָ, *upon your sword,* has the meaning of בְּחַרְבְּךָ, *with,* or *by,* your sword. [Perhaps the connotation of עַל חַרְבְּךָ is accordingly: *with reliance upon* your sword.] *Ramban* cites *Deuteronomy* 8:3 *for man does not live* עַל הַלֶּחֶם [lit. *upon bread*] *alone,* which means בַּלֶּחֶם, *by bread.*

וְאֶת אָחִיךָ תַּעֲבֹד — *But* [lit. *and*] *your brother you shall serve.*

This, too, was a blessing: It would be better to serve his *brother* than to be in servitude to *others (Radak).*

The translation *but,* perceiving this as a qualification of the preceding blessing, follows *Ramban* who explains that although Esau was blessed with victory in battle, he was served notice that he would remain subservient to his brother. Esau would not prevail over his brother; instead Jacob would prevail over Esau [depending, as Isaac continued, upon Jacob's remaining righteous.]

Esau was not bidden to do menial chores for his brother; this 'serving' was with dignity. Esau was to act as Jacob's swordbearer in the sense of protecting him while leaving him free to attain the spiritual goals destined for him and his descendants *(Rav Saadiah Gaon).*

According to *Abarbanel,* the implication is: Your military pursuits should never take you against your brother: *him shall you serve.* ...This subjugation of Edom by Israel was fulfilled in the days of David and Solomon, Rechavam, Abijah, Asa, and Jehoshafat, kings of Judah, until the days of the sinful Jehoram when Edom revolted and appointed its own king. Even later, during the Second Temple period, Edom was subservient to Israel.

The *Midrash,* reflecting the implication that Esau's subservience depended upon Jacob's worthiness, *homiletically* renders: Isaac said, 'If Jacob is meritorious, you shall תַּעֲבֹד, *serve* him; if not, you may תְּאַבֵּד, *decree his destruction'* ... The *Midrash* concludes that for these words Isaac is not mentioned among the Patriarchs in *Isaiah* 63:16, for "shall he who says to Esau, 'Decree his destruction' be associated with the Patriarchs?"

However the fate of subjugation to Israel is limited and dependent upon Israel's righteousness.

וְהָיָה כַּאֲשֶׁר תָּרִיד — *Yet* [lit. *and*] *it shall be that when you are aggrieved.*

I.e., when Israel shall transgress the Torah so that you have a valid reason to be *aggrieved* over his hav-

מא עָלּוֹ מֵעַל צַוָּארֶךָ׃ וַיִּשְׂטֹם עֵשָׂו אֶת־יַעֲקֹב
עַל־הַבְּרָכָה אֲשֶׁר בֵּרֲכוֹ אָבִיו וַיֹּאמֶר

ing taken the blessings, *then you may cast off his yoke from your neck (Rashi).* [As noted in *v.*28, the implication was that Jacob would enjoy his blessing — including his subjugation of Esau — only so long as he is worthy of it *(Maharam):* When Israel *was* righteous, Esau had no right to be aggrieved over the loss of the blessings *(Mizrachi).*

Thus, the word תָּרִיד according to *Rashi*, signifies *grief, pain* as in *Psalms* 55:3 אָרִיד בְּשִׂיחִי, *I am aggrieved in my meditation.*

Ibn Ezra — citing this interpretation — understands *Rashi* to derive his interpretation from the root רוד which also denotes *complaint* (as he interprets the phrase in *Psalms*) [the implication being: when you have just cause to *complain to God* regarding Israel's unjustified oppression, then God will have compassion upon you (*Tur*).]

Rashbam also translates תָּרִיד as *suffer* but explains the implication as: *When the burden of his servitude shall be more than you can endure* — then you may *cast off, etc.*

Sforno similarly perceives the implication as the legitimate cry of protest resulting from the undue harshness of his overlordship.

Rashbam adds that this refers to suffering resulting from Israel's transgressions, since this was a hint to Israel not to deal harshly with Esau's descendants. Therefore, when they approached the Edomite border while marching through the wilderness after Exodus, the Israelites were forbidden to molest Edom [*Deut.* 2:4].

Similarly, the Sages [*Yerushalmi Rosh Hashanah* 1:1] note that in punishment for David's six-month campaign during which *he cut off every male of Edom* [*I Kings* 11:16], those six months did not accrue as part of his reign.

In his primary interpretation, *Ibn Ezra* explains the word as being related to the root רדה, *rule* [see use of this verb in *I Kings* 5:4], the connotation being — as explained by *Radak* and *Ralbag: When you are due to rule*, i.e., when your time to reign will come because Israel will have forfeited its lordship through sinfulness.

Hirsch follows a different approach. Esau's strength of sword and his world-conquest are for the *ultimate* purpose of his final submission to Jacob in acknowledgment that the sword is the servant of the spirit. Esau's greatest hope is כַּאֲשֶׁר תָּרִיד, *when you 'humble yourself' to Jacob,* by submitting yourself to his ideals — then you will no longer be subservient to him. Then you will be his equal partner in carrying out God's will.

וּפָרַקְתָּ עֻלּוֹ מֵעַל צַוָּארֶךָ —*[Then] you may cast off his yoke from upon your neck.*

I.e., God will then have compassion on your plight, and you will be successful in casting off Jacob's yoke from your neck *(Ibn Ezra; Ralbag).*[1]

— And as a result of his sinfulness, you will not be in servitude to him *(Radak).*

— As the *Midrash* notes: When the voice is not the voice of Jacob

27
41

you may cast off his yoke from upon your neck."
41 Now Esau harbored hatred toward Jacob because of the blessing wherewith his father had blessed him. And Esau thought, "May the days of

[i.e., when Israel's voice is not heard in the study of Torah and in prayer] then the hands are the hands of Esau [see *comm.* to *v.*22] *(Malbim).*

The fact that you will live as a warrior will qualify you for this *(Sforno).*

[Cf. Edom's revolt from Judah under Jehoram related in *II Kings* 8:20-22.]

41. Esau's Hatred.

וַיִּשְׂטֹם ... עַל הַבְּרָכָה אֲשֶׁר בֵּרְכוֹ אָבִיו — *Now Esau harbored hatred ... because of the blessing wherewith his father had blessed him.*

[The pronoun *him* is ambiguous: Does it refer to the blessing given *Jacob* or to the one given *Esau*? Esau's hatred may have resulted from the blessing *Jacob* gained deceptively, or he may have hated Jacob for having caused him, *Esau*, to receive only an 'inferior blessing.']

Alshich takes the former view, while *Malbim* suggests that Esau was angered at his father for confirming Jacob's blessing [*v.*33], and for telling him *You shall serve your brother*, in effect making Esau subordinate to Jacob.

The translation of וַיִּשְׂטֹם follows *Onkelos* and *Targum Yonasan* who render: *And Esau kept hatred in his heart ....*

The commentators define the verb שטם as synonymous with נטר, *bear a grudge* [see *Levit.* 19:18]. *Hirsch* explains that the root שטם is related to שתם [*Lamentations* 3:8] and סתם, *closed up, stopped up.* All designate a hate which is *repressed*, a similar conception to נטר which in general means *guarded: to retain hatred.*

וַיֹּאמֶר עֵשָׂו בְּלִבּוֹ — *And Esau thought* [lit. *and Esau said in his heart* — the 'heart' being considered in Scriptures as the *seat of the intellect.*]

This translation follows the implication of *Rashi* and *Midrash* which assume that Esau revealed his plan to no one. The fact that Rebecca was told of the scheme (next verse), implies that it was revealed to her by Divine Inspiration.

Ibn Ezra suggests that he may have revealed his secret to one of his friends [and Rebecca subsequently became aware of it.]

1. This does not suggest, in the literal sense, however, that when it came Esau's time to rule that Esau's yoke would henceforth necessarily be upon Jacob. Rather, one would not subjugate the other, but they would be equal. That in fact Esau did, later, achieve the dominion was due to the sins of Israel.

The implication was that once Esau would have cause to revolt, the dominion would never revert to Jacob. However Bilaam's pronouncement in *Numbers* 24:19 וְיֵרְדְּ מִיַּעֲקֹב, *one out of Jacob shall have dominion*, uses the same root, רדה, which expresses Esau's dispensation from servitude. The verse is interpreted to mean that dominion will indeed revert to Jacob. The end of that verse, ... *and shall destroy the remnant of the city* [*the city* being interpreted by *Rashi* there to refer to the most important city of Edom, Rome], implies that in the day of the Messiah, speedily in our days, Esau's memory will be obliterated and never rise again.

... And as the prophet predicts, in the end of days, Esau will indeed revert to servitude as it says [*Obadiah* 1:21]: *Deliverers shall go up to Mount Zion to rule the hill country of Esau and dominion shall be* HASHEM'*s (Abarbanel).*

עֵשָׂו בְּלִבּוֹ יִקְרְבוּ יְמֵי אֵבֶל אָבִי וְאַהַרְגָה
מב אֶת־יַעֲקֹב אָחִי: וַיֻּגַּד לְרִבְקָה אֶת־דִּבְרֵי
עֵשָׂו בְּנָהּ הַגָּדֹל וַתִּשְׁלַח וַתִּקְרָא לְיַעֲקֹב
בְּנָהּ הַקָּטָן וַתֹּאמֶר אֵלָיו הִנֵּה עֵשָׂו אָחִיךָ
מג מִתְנַחֵם לְךָ לְהָרְגֶךָ: וְעַתָּה בְנִי שְׁמַע

Ramban suggests, however, that in the literal sense the phrase *say in the heart* does not *necessarily* refer to pure *thought*; it refers to any decision reached after deliberation even when it is coupled with speech. [Thus, according to *Ramban*, the phrase should be rendered *and Esau resolved*, possibly even declaring his intention aloud. (This view is substantiated in *Avos d'Rabbi Nosson II* cited in *v.*42).] *Ramban* concludes that according to the *Midrash*, of course, the implication [as noted above] is that he kept these thoughts to himself.

יִקְרְבוּ יְמֵי אֵבֶל אָבִי — *May the days of* [lit. *the days of my father's mourning will approach.*]

My father is old and his death is near; I will wait until he dies *(Radak).*

I do not wish to cause my father grief while he is still alive *(Rashi; Ramban).* — Perhaps he feared that his father would curse him, and his blessing would then turn into a curse *(Ramban).*

The commentators emphasize that *Rashi*'s interpretation of Esau's intention in this statement being to spare Isaac aggravation was based on *Rashi*'s opinion that Esau retained — even now — his filial honor. This is supported by Esau's respectful and obedient reaction to his father's displeasure with the Canaanite women whom Esau married [28:8,9].

Following *Malbim* [who holds in 28:8 that Esau had sinister motives in contracting a new marriage that would please Isaac; see *comm.* there], Esau's intention was to avenge himself upon his father and brother *simultaneously*, by killing Jacob. He said, 'I will kill Jacob — as a result יִקְרְבוּ יְמֵי אֵבֶל אָבִי, *my father will soon be in mourning* — for his son Jacob.'

Ralbag interprets similarly: Even if it accelerates my father's death [lit. brings near the days of mourning for my father] I nevertheless will kill my brother Jacob (cited by *Tur).*

Some render Esau's intent as: My father is old; let the days of his mourning come already so I can kill my brother and inherit everything *(Rav Saadia Gaon).*

וְאַהַרְגָה אֶת־יַעֲקֹב אָחִי — *Then* [lit. *and*] *I will kill my brother Jacob.*

'Did not my father say עַל חַרְבְּךָ תִחְיֶה, *by your sword you shall live*? The first use to which I shall put my sword will be the killing of Jacob!' *(Hirsch).*

42. וַיֻּגַּד לְרִבְקָה אֶת דִּבְרֵי עֵשָׂו בְּנָהּ הַגָּדֹל — *When* [lit. *and*] *Rebecca was told of the words of her older son Esau.*

Esau's intention was revealed to her by רוּחַ הַקֹּדֶשׁ, *Divine Inspiration (Rashi).* [How else could she have become aware of his thoughts? (See *comm.* to previous verse for alternate views).]

There is a view in the *Midrash* that the Matriarchs, including Rebecca, were pro-

27
42

mourning for my father draw near, then I will kill my brother Jacob."

42 *When Rebecca was told of the words of her older son Esau, she sent for and summoned Jacob her younger son and said to him, "Behold, your brother Esau is consoling himself regarding you to kill you.*

phetesses. [See *v.*45. But it would seem — as noted in the *comm.* to 25:27 — that *Rashi* does not subscribe to this view since Rebecca is not listed among the prophetesses enumerated in *Megillah* 14a. Receiving a communication by Divine Inspiration, which *Rashi* mentions here, does not necessarily make her a prophetess.]

There is a possiblity — according to those who do not consider Rebecca a prophetess [see *comm.* to 25:23] — that she was informed by one of the prophets living at that time (Ms. *Or HaAfeilah, Torah Sheleimah* note 193).

Avos d'Rabbi Nosson II Chapt. 45 comments that Esau planned in his heart to slay his brother Jacob, but in effect he revealed this intention to everyone, as evidenced by Rebecca's having become aware of it. [This text supports *Ramban*'s interpretation in the previous verse, but is not cited by him.]

וַתִּשְׁלַח וַתִּקְרָא לְיַעֲקֹב — [*And*] *she sent for and summoned Jacob.*

— Jacob had gone into hiding, either out of fear or shame, from his brother Esau who was complaining about him *(Ramban).*

בְּנָהּ הַקָּטָן — *Her younger* [lit. *smaller*] *son.*

This was one of Rebecca's primary concerns that urged her to summon Jacob: Jacob was her *smaller* son, and hence defenseless against the brute strength of his 'big' brother Esau *(Malbim).*

הִנֵּה עֵשָׂו אָחִיךָ מִתְנַחֵם לְךָ לְהָרְגֶךָ — *Behold, your brother Esau is consoling himself regarding you to kill you* [i.e., is planning to kill you.]

[As noted in the lengthy exegesis to נחם in 6:6, the verb depending on its conjugation, can have the meaning of regret, comfort, consideration, consolation. *Rashi* offers several interpretations of this phrase; the translation follows the last one. As *Rashi* comments]:

He *regrets* the existing relationship and harbors thoughts of estranging himself from you to kill you. According to the *Midrash* [the word מִתְנַחֵם is interpreted *accepts consolation*]: As far as Esau is concerned, he regards you as being *already dead* and he has already drunk over you the 'cup of consolation' [which was drunk in a mourner's house after the burial of a near relative.]

Rashi continues that in the *literal sense* the word is interpreted as *consolation*, i.e., 'cup of consolation' *(Mizrachi)*]: *He consoles himself for the loss of the blessings with the thought that he plans to kill you.*

Onkelos renders: *Behold, Esau your brother lurks* [כָּמִין, i.e., waits for the opportunity] *against you to kill you.*

Ramban explains that the intent

בְּקֹלִי וְקוּם בְּרַח־לְךָ אֶל־לָבָן אָחִי חָרָנָה׃
מד וְיָשַׁבְתָּ עִמּוֹ יָמִים אֲחָדִים עַד אֲשֶׁר־
מה תָּשׁוּב חֲמַת אָחִיךָ׃ עַד־שׁוּב אַף־אָחִיךָ
מִמְּךָ וְשָׁכַח אֵת אֲשֶׁר־עָשִׂיתָ לּוֹ וְשָׁלַחְתִּי
וּלְקַחְתִּיךָ מִשָּׁם לָמָה אֶשְׁכַּל גַּם־שְׁנֵיכֶם

of *Onkelos'* explanation here which reflects the intent of the verse but not its language is that: he pretends to be consoled about the blessings so you will not be on guard, but in fact he intends to kill you.

Ramban goes on to suggest that the meaning of מִתְנַחֵם לְךָ is the same as either מִתְנַחֵם בְּךָ, *his comfort is in you* [i.e., in his intent to kill you], or מִתְנַחֵם עָלֶיךָ, *he is comforting himself regarding you.*

He comforts himself in the notion that by killing you the birthright and blessings will revert to him *(Or HaChaim).*

אָחִיךָ — *Your brother.*

He is, and remains, *your brother*. Whatever the extent of his evil, you may never forget that he is your brother *(Hirsch).*

— But since he is your *brother*, it will be much more difficult for you to elude him *(Malbim).*

43. Jacob is Advised to Flee to Laban.

וְעַתָּה בְנִי שְׁמַע בְּקֹלִי — *So now, my son, heed* [*in*] *my voice.*

I.e., carefully scrutinize every word I say; she also implied thereby that she was addressing him with a prophetic spirit *(Haamek Davar).*

[See *comm.* to same phrase in *v.*8.]

Although Esau implied that he would not carry out his intention until Isaac died, Rebecca could not be sure when that would happen. She therefore ordered Jacob not to procrastinate until it would be too late, but *now my son ... flee immediately*. Compare the Rabbinic dictum [*Avos* 2:10]: "Repent one day before your death," the idea being that since one is never certain on which day he will die, he should spend his entire life in penitence *(Or HaChaim).*

וְקוּם בְּרַח לְךָ — *And arise! Flee* [lit. *flee to yourself*].

I.e., flee, go as a fugitive *(Hirsch).*

The word לְךָ, *to yourself*, implies keep the matter to yourself; tell no one where you are going *(Haamek Davar).*

[*The word* לְךָ in such contexts often has the connotation of *for your own benefit, for your own good*; see *comm.* to 12:1 לֶךְ־לְךָ.]

אֶל לָבָן אָחִי חָרָנָה — *To my brother Laban, to Charan.*

— He will protect you if Esau attacks *(Or HaChaim).*

[It was also clearly her intention that he take a wife from her kin. See further.]

44. יָשַׁבְתָּ עִמּוֹ יָמִים אֲחָדִים — *And remain with him a short while* [following *Rashi*: lit. *a few days.*]

Her hope was that things would soon be smoothed over, but in fact, she never saw him again *(Akeidas Yitzchak).*

According to *Ibn Ezra*, יָמִים here

27
43-45

[43] *So now, my son, heed my voice and arise! Flee to my brother Laban, to Charan,* [44] *and remain with him a short while until your brother's wrath subsides.* [45] *— Until your brother's anger against you subsides, and he forgets what you have done to him. Then I will send and summon you from there. Why should I be bereaved of both of you on the same day?"*

means *years,* as in *Levit.* 25:29, the intent being: *a few years, few* meaning less than ten years, to allow Esau time to regain his composure. [See *comm.* to יָמִים as *year* in 24:55.]

[See 29:20: *Jacob served seven years for Rachel and they seemed to him but a few days.*]

עַד אֲשֶׁר־תָּשׁוּב חֲמַת אָחִיךָ — *Until your brother's wrath subsides* [lit. *turns away.*]

חֵמָה [*wrath,* lit. *heat*] refers to intensely glowing, burning anger *(Hirsch).* [See *Rashi* to *Exodus* 15:8 for explanation of אַף, חֵמָה, חָרוֹן, and חֲרוֹן אַף.]

45. עַד שׁוּב אַף אָחִיךָ מִמְּךָ — *Until your brother's anger against you subsides* [lit. *turns away.*]

The term אַף, *anger* [lit. *nose*], alludes to the flaring of the nostrils during one's anger *(Rashi, Exodus* 15:8). It is a lesser degree of anger than the חֵמָה, *wrath,* mentioned in the preceding verse.

The implication of Rebecca's remark was: 'We should not be satisfied merely with the cooling of Esau's חֵמָה, *burning wrath.* Let us wait until even his אַף, *anger,* subsides to the point where we need not fear even unfiendliness on his part *(Hirsch).*

According to *Malbim,* חֵמָה refers to inner, deep-seated anger which one represses, while אַף refers to the outer manifestations of anger. Thus, חֵמָה alludes to Esau's explicit fury, while אַף alludes to the implicit danger of his threat against Jacob's life.

According to *Sechel Tov, his fury* — in respect to the blessings; *his anger* — in respect to the birthright [*R' Bachya* interprets in the reverse.]

וְשָׁכַח אֵת אֲשֶׁר־עָשִׂיתָ לּוֹ — *And he forgets what you have done to him.*

Obviously, Rebecca had a high opinion of Esau. She thought that with the passage of time, he would forget the wrong which had been done him *(Hirsch).*

The *Midrash* notes that Rebecca had innocently hoped to wait until Esau's anger would subside. But she was mistaken. Instead, [*Amos* 1:11]: *Edom's ... anger tore perpetually and he kept his wrath forever.*

וְשָׁלַחְתִּי וּלְקַחְתִּיךָ מִשָּׁם — *Then* [lit. *and*] *I will send and summon* [lit. *fetch*] *you from there.*

But under no circumstances are you to return on your own *(Or HaChaim).*

— [For if you demur, and decide to stay here]:

לָמָה אֶשְׁכַּל גַּם שְׁנֵיכֶם יוֹם אֶחָד — *Why should I be bereaved of both of you on the same day* [lit. *one day.*]?

מו יָוֹם אֶחָֽד׃ וַתֹּאמֶר רִבְקָה֙ אֶל־יִצְחָק קַצְתִּי
בְחַיַּי מִפְּנֵי בְּנוֹת חֵת אִם־לֹקֵחַ יַעֲקֹב
אִשָּׁה מִבְּנוֹת־חֵת כָּאֵלֶּה֙ מִבְּנוֹת הָאָרֶץ
כח/א א לָמָּה לִּי חַיִּים׃ וַיִּקְרָא יִצְחָק אֶל־יַעֲקֹב

The word שכל refers to a parent who has buried his child *(Rashi).*

— If Esau attacks you, you are certain to die, for [even] if you succeed in killing him, his children [as his avengers *(Rashbam)*] will rise and kill you. A divine inspiration [רוּחַ הַקֹּדֶשׁ] was 'sprinkled into her' and she prophesied that they would die on one day. As stated in *Sotah* 13a, such was indeed the case *(Rashi).*[1]

— *Why should I be bereaved of both of you on the same day?* — You being slain, and he driven forth as Eve was bereaved of Abel whom Cain slew, both of them being removed from Adam and Eve all the days of their life? (*Targum Yonasan*).

The victim would be gone and she could no longer consider the murderer to be her son. Her fear of losing *both,* makes plain that she regards Esau as no less her son than she does Jacob. This casts all her action in a noble unselfish light (*Hirsch;* but cf. *Or HaChaim*).

Hirsch notes that שכל means to be bereft of children — and אֶשְׁכֹּל means grapes! He explains that perhaps אֶשְׁכֹּל does not designate so much the grapes as the cluster, the very short stalks on which the grapes hang. As long as the grapes are hanging there the stem in not seen. It is only visible when the grapes are plucked off. אֶשְׁתְּךָ כְּגֶפֶן פֹּרִיָּה, *the mother rich in children is like a vine full of grapes* (*Psalms* 128:3). Should her children die, she would be as bereft as a bare stem of grapes from which the grapes have been plucked.

Some suggest that by Rebecca's remark: *both of you,* she referred to *Isaac* and Jacob since Esau was plotting to kill Jacob on the day Isaac would die *(Tur).*

[The above interpretation does not agree with *Rashi* who holds that the term שכל refers only to being bereft of *children*].

46. וַתֹּאמֶר רִבְקָה אֶל־יִצְחָק — [*And*] *Rebecca said to Isaac.*

— In an effort to spare him the aggravation of knowing the truth *(Malbim).*

קַצְתִּי בְחַיַּי — *I am disgusted with my life* [following *Rashi*].

She expressed herself with gestures of utter abhorrance *(Midrash).*

Several homiletical reasons are offered for the small ק in קַצְתִּי.

— The numerical value of ק is 100. The ק is small to suggest that her disgust with life was because

1. The *Talmud* notes that when Jacob was brought by his family for burial in the Cave of Machpelah, Esau came and challenged their right to bury him there, claiming to have retained the right of the firstborn. Among those present was Chushim son of Dan who took a club and struck Esau on the head so that his eyes fell out and rolled to the feet of Jacob. At that time was the prophecy of Rebecca filled, as it is written, *why should I be bereaved of both of you on the same day?* For though the *death* of the two of them did not occur on the same day [obviously Jacob died first if Esau was attending his funeral], still their *burial* took place on the same day (*Sotah* 13a).

27 *[46] Rebecca said to Isaac, "I am disgusted with my*
46 *life on account of the daughters of Heth, If Jacob*
takes a wife of the daughters of Heth like these, of
the natives of the land, why need I live?"

she foresaw that the Temple which was 100 cubits high would one day be destroyed because of intermarriage, and thus Israel's glory would be diminished *(Zohar; R' Bachya).*

— The small letter implies that her *disgust* was not *real* but feigned to Isaac so he would send Jacob away *(Ms. Or Has'chalim* cited in *Torah Sheleimah).*

— According to the view that Rebecca was 14 years old at her marriage [*footnote* to 24:16] and hence 34 years old at Jacob's birth, since Jacob was 63 years old at the blessings, [*footnote* to 25:17] Rebecca was 97 years old by this time. The small ק [=100] thus alludes to her consternation at her nearly 100 years of life at this point which would in retrospect be considered as having been lived worthlessly if Jacob -whom she felt was the essence of her being — would marry a detestable Canaanite woman *(Harav David Feinstein).*

מִפְּנֵי בְּנוֹת חֵת — *On account of the daughters of Heth.*

Onkelos renders: *At the sight of the daughters of Heth.*

— [A reference to Esau's wives.]

אִם לֹקֵחַ יַעֲקֹב אִשָּׁה — *If Jacob takes* [i.e., marries] *a wife* [lit. *woman*].

Rather than tell Isaac that she wanted Jacob to leave home because his life was in danger, she used the unsuitability of the Hittite women as a pretext for her decision *(Rashbam).*

Righteous Rebecca did not utilize the opportunity to justify her deception by telling Isaac that Esau was a potential murderer and, therefore, clearly undeserving of the blessings. Instead, she preferred to give a natural and reasonable purpose for Jacob's journey to Paddan Aram *(Hirsch).*

מִבְּנוֹת־חֵת כָּאֵלֶּה מִבְּנוֹת הָאָרֶץ — *Of the daughters of Heth like these, of the natives* [lit. *daughters*] *of the Land.*

Like these — for unfortunately, we have come to know from our own daughters-in-law how inapproriate they are *(Hirsch).*

The *Midrash* records that as Rebecca said כָּאֵלֶּה, *like these* [i.e., in the direct form], she slapped each of them [Esau's wives] in turn.

לָמָּה לִּי חַיִּים — *Why need I live?* [lit. *why life to me?*]

She thus made it perfectly clear that she could not consider life worth living if her son married anyone other than her kin *(Abarbanel).*

Torah Temimah observes that although Rebecca cannot be said to have uttered this as a *prophecy* in the strict sense of the word, but rather was voicing her tragic apprehension, nevertheless the *Talmud*'s citation must be understood in the light of the dictum in *Moed Katan* 18a: בְּרִית כְּרוּתָה לַשְּׂפָתַיִם, *a covenant has been made with the lips,* i.e., the spoken word, even if unintentional, may contain a prognostication for the future, and often becomes fulfilled as if by prophecy [see *comm.* to 22:6 s.v. וְנִשְׁתַּחֲוֶה.] Furthermore, the dictum in *Makkos* 11a may be cited in this connection: 'A curse of a wise man, though uttered without cause, takes effect.'

וַיְבָרֶךְ אֹתוֹ וַיְצַוֵּהוּ וַיֹּאמֶר לוֹ לֹא־תִקַּח
ב אִשָּׁה מִבְּנוֹת כְּנָעַן: קוּם לֵךְ פַּדֶּנָה אֲרָם
בֵּיתָה בְתוּאֵל אֲבִי אִמֶּךָ וְקַח־לְךָ מִשָּׁם
ג אִשָּׁה מִבְּנוֹת לָבָן אֲחִי אִמֶּךָ: וְאֵל שַׁדַּי
יְבָרֵךְ אֹתְךָ וְיַפְרְךָ וְיַרְבֶּךָ וְהָיִיתָ לִקְהַל

XXVIII

1. The Admonition Against Marrying a Canaanite Woman; The Abrahamitic Blessing is Conveyed to Jacob.

וַיִּקְרָא יִצְחָק אֶל יַעֲקֹב וַיְבָרֶךְ אֹתוֹ — *So* [lit. *and*] *Isaac summoned* [lit. *called to*] *Jacob and blessed him.*

The *blessing* is the one given further in *v.* 3 *(Radak).*

According to *Malbim,* this verse merely informs us that Isaac blessed him; the *text* of the blessing, however, is not recorded. Rather, Isaac blessed him with an unrecorded blessing of spiritual bounty and cautioned him against taking a Canaanite wife (further in this verse). This was an *injunction.* Then he went on to give him a *positive command* to go to Paddan Aram and take a wife from his mother's kin (verse 2). Then Isaac blessed him again with the blessing in verse 3.

Now Isaac blessed him of his own free will and with full consciousness. Rebecca's ruse had succeeded in making him realize that *Jacob* was the deserving one of his sons *(Hirsch).*[1]

וַיְצַוֵּהוּ וַיֹּאמֶר לוֹ — *He instructed* [lit. *commanded*] *him and said to him.*

[Apparently, Rebecca's suggestion that Jacob go to her brother's home (27:43) was motherly *advice;* Isaac's summons now gave it the force of a *command.*]

[*And said to him,* i.e. clearly and unambiguously. *Immediate action* is implied by the association of the verbs *command* and *say.* See *Hirsch* on 1:22.]

לֹא־תִקַּח אִשָּׁה מִבְּנוֹת כְּנָעַן — *Do not take a wife* [lit. *woman*] *from the Canaanite women* [lit. *from the daughters of Canaan.*]

Included in the generic term *Canaanite* were the eleven descendants of Canaan who populated the land: the Zidonite, Hittite, Jebusite, Emonite, Girgashite, Hivvite, Arkite, Sinite, Erodite, Zimrite, Hamite *(Ibn Ezra* and *Yohel Or* to 15:19; 24:3).

He admonished Jacob even against marrying the daughters of Aner, Eshkol, and Mamre [with whom they were friendly; hence the need for this exhortation *(Yafeh Toar).*] *(Midrash).*

1. As the *Midrash* notes, until now, Jacob's right to the blessing had been open to question. Now his right became affirmed. Lest one say that Jacob would have had no blessing had he not deceived his father, the Torah tells us that *Isaac summoned Jacob and blessed him.* [See *Rashi* to 27:33].

Rav Berachiah said, It may be compared to a prince, who made a tunnel into his father's treasury to get himself a pound of gold. His father said to him, 'Why this secrecy? Come take it openly!' Thus *Isaac summoned Jacob and blessed him.*

28
1-3

[1] *So Isaac summoned Jacob and blessed him. He instructed him, saying to him, "Do not take a wife from the Canaanite women.* [2] *Arise, go to Paddan Aram to the house of Bethuel your mother's father, and take a wife from there from the daughters of Laban, your mother's brother.*

[3] *And may El Shaddai bless you,*
make you fruitful and make you numerous,

Cf. similar instructions Abraham gave to Eliezer regarding a wife for Isaac in 24:3, and *comm.* there.

However, as noted in the footnote to 24:3 *Meshech Chochmah* suggests that Isaac's instruction to Jacob here should not be understood as a direct command.

Rather, as *Meshech Chochmah* perceives from *v.* 4 Isaac informed Jacob that it was a *condition* of retaining the Abrahamitic blessings and the right to inherit the Land that he not allow his posterity to descend from Canaanite women.

2. קוּם לֵךְ פַּדֶּנָה אֲרָם — *Arise, go to Paddan Aram.*

Arise! is idiomatic for *set out quickly (Radak).*

This part, unlike the previous verse, was not a *command* but fatherly advice *(Ha'amek Davar; differing from Malbim* above).

בֵּיתָה בְתוּאֵל אֲבִי אִמֶּךָ — *To the house of Bethuel, your mother's father.*

[In charging Eliezer, Abraham was more vague, sending him generally to his native land and family (24:4, see *footnote* there) whereas Isaac specifies exactly to whom Jacob was to turn in search of a wife.]

מִבְּנוֹת לָבָן אֲחִי אִמֶּךָ — *From* [among] *the daughters of Laban, your mother's brother.*

In a home where a woman like your mother grew up in spite of the proximity of Laban, you can quite possibly find a worthy wife for yourself *(Hirsch).*

3. וְאֵל־שַׁדַּי יְבָרֵךְ אֹתְךָ — *And may El Shaddai bless you.*

Rashi explains the significance of this Name here as implying: He, Who suffices [שֶׁדַּי = שַׁדַּי] with His blessing to those who are blessed by him, *He will bless you.*

[This Name has been discussed in the commentary to 17:1. See also 43:14 and *Exodus* 6:3.]

— You need take nothing with you, but your trust in God. *He* will bless you, i.e., give you the means to found a household ... *(Hirsch).*

According to *Ha'amek Davar* this was not merely a blessing, it was a *prophetic premonition* that *God* as *El Shaddai* would indeed bless him after his return from Paddan Aram with those blessings of fruitful abundance, and that a community of people descend from him [see 35:11].

וְיַפְרְךָ וְיַרְבֶּךָ — *Make you fruitful and make you numerous* [or: *increase you*].

He will give you the strength to

ד עַמִּים: וְיִתֶּן־לְךָ֙ אֶת־בִּרְכַּ֣ת אַבְרָהָ֔ם לְךָ֖
וּלְזַרְעֲךָ֣ אִתָּ֑ךְ לְרִשְׁתְּךָ֙ אֶת־אֶ֣רֶץ מְגֻרֶ֔יךָ
°שביעי ה אֲשֶׁר־נָתַ֥ן אֱלֹהִ֖ים לְאַבְרָהָֽם: °וַיִּשְׁלַ֤ח
יִצְחָק֙ אֶת־יַעֲקֹ֔ב וַיֵּ֖לֶךְ פַּדֶּ֣נָֽה אֲרָ֑ם אֶל־
לָבָ֤ן בֶּן־בְּתוּאֵל֙ הָֽאֲרַמִּ֔י אֲחִ֣י רִבְקָ֔ה אֵ֥ם

have children and to bring them up in your own spirit. Through them you will become multiplied *(Hirsch).*

וְהָיִיתָ לִקְהַל עַמִּים — *And may you be a congregation of peoples.*

You will have what I did not succeed in having: קְהַל עַמִּים, a *congregation of peoples.* Your children will be עַמִּים, different kinds of people, who will be the forerunners of separate and distinct tribes, but none of them will be פָּסוּל [*disqualified*]: They will be a united קָהָל *(Hirsch).*

4. וְיִתֶּן־לְךָ אֶת־בִּרְכַּת אַבְרָהָם — [*And*] *may He grant you the blessing of Abraham.*

— I.e. [the blessing which God gave to Abraham] in which He told him [12:2]: *I will make of you a great nation;* and [the blessing He gave Abraham in 22:18 and repeated to Isaac in 26:4]: *And all the nations of the earth shall bless themselves by your offspring* — May all those blessings be said regarding you. May that *great nation* and *blessed seed* issue from *you (Rashi).*

— The blessing that he become the ancestor of a *horde of nations* [17:5] *(Ha'amek Davar);* the blessing that Abraham received when he was told [15:5] *Gaze, now, toward the Heavens, and count the stars if you are able to count them! ... So shall your offspring be! (Aggadas Bereishis).*

לְךָ וּלְזַרְעֲךָ אִתָּךְ — *To you and to your offspring with you.*

'With you' not *'after* you.' The kernel for a future generation will develop from you as well as from your offspring. You will not have to wait for some later era when your descendants will become worthy of the blessings. None of your children will be estranged from you; all of them will inherit *with* you the blessings that have been promised to you *(Hirsch).*

לְרִשְׁתְּךָ אֶת־אֶרֶץ מְגֻרֶיךָ — *That you may possess* [or: *inherit*] *the land of your sojourns.*

I.e. *Eretz Yisrael* the land where you now dwell *(Sforno).*

[The land in which you tarry as a גֵר, *alien.* See 17:8].

— In reward for not marrying one of the Canaanite women who are slaves, as Abraham commanded Isaac *(Rashbam).*

This blessing should be understood in conjunction with the earlier blessing [27:28] *May God give you of the dew of heaven,* etc. Isaac now specified that this blessing of material plenty should be fulfilled in the land of Canaan which God had given Abraham, while the material blessings given Esau [27:39] would be fulfilled in a different country (*Ramban* to 27:39).

and may you be a congregation of peoples.
4 *May He grant you the blessing of Abraham*
to you and to your offspring with you,
that you may possess the land of your sojourns
which God gave to Abraham."
5 *So Isaac sent away Jacob and he went toward*
Paddan Aram to Laban the son of Bethuel the Ara-
mean, brother of Rebecca, mother of Jacob and Esau.

אֲשֶׁר נָתַן אֱלֹהִים לְאַבְרָהָם — *Which God gave to Abraham.*

[See 17:8: *I will give to you and to your offspring after you the land of your sojourns — the whole of the land of Canaan — as an everlasting possession.*]

5. וַיִּשְׁלַח יִצְחָק אֶת יַעֲקֹב — *So* [lit. *and*] *Isaac sent away Jacob.*

No mention is made of Isaac sending wealth along with his son as would be expected. *Ramban* [to 25:34] suggests that Jacob was fleeing for his life and Isaac was afraid to give him wealth, servants, and camels, etc. lest he arouse the jealousy of his enemies. In fact, the *Midrash* comments that Jacob was robbed at the outset of his journey of whatever possessions he had. [See *Ibn Ezra* there].

וַיֵּלֶךְ פַּדֶּנָה אֲרָם — *And he went toward Paddan Aram.*

[The translation *toward* reflects the Rabbinic chronology cited by *Rashi* in verse 9 that Jacob set out for the *ultimate destination* of Paddan Aram, but *first* he went to the Academy of Eber (Shem was already dead by this time; see *Chronology / Time Line* vol. 1, page xii) and spent fourteen years there, studying day and night. Although, as *Rashi* calculates in *v.* 9, (see Chart B) Jacob was separated from his father a total of 36 years, the 14 years he detoured and spent studying were not accounted against him, and he was held liable only for the balance of 22 years. His punishment was that his beloved son Joseph was separated from him for a like amount of years (see Chart C). This will be further discussed in *Sidrah Vayeshev* אי״ה.]

The question arises: If Isaac *sent Jacob away* why was Jacob punished at all for the years he stayed away from his father's service?

— Perhaps their intention was that he go to Paddan Aram and take a wife — Leah — and be prepared to return as soon as they sent for him. But Jacob *voluntarily* offered to stay on and work an additional seven years for Rachel [29:18]; therefore *all* the years he was away [except for the fourteen years he studied in the Academy of Shem and Eber [see *Rashi* further, *v.* 9] were accounted against him *(R'Bachya).*

אֲחִי רִבְקָה אֵם יַעֲקֹב וְעֵשָׂו — *The brother of Rebecca, mother of Jacob and Esau.*

— I do not know what [the addition of this phrase] is intended to teach us *(Rashi).*

[*Rashi* was indeed aware of possible interpretations. He makes this comment rather than simply maintain silence because he wishes to emphasize that he does not find an interpretation which he considers to fit the

ו יַעֲקֹב וְעֵשָׂו: וַיַּרְא עֵשָׂו כִּי־בֵרַךְ יִצְחָק
אֶת־יַעֲקֹב וְשִׁלַּח אֹתוֹ פַּדֶּנָה אֲרָם לָקַחַת־
לוֹ מִשָּׁם אִשָּׁה בְּבָרְכוֹ אֹתוֹ וַיְצַו עָלָיו
לֵאמֹר לֹא־תִקַּח אִשָּׁה מִבְּנוֹת כְּנָעַן:
°מפטיר ז וַיִּשְׁמַע יַעֲקֹב אֶל־אָבִיו וְאֶל־אִמּוֹ וַיֵּלֶךְ
ח פַּדֶּנָה אֲרָם: וַיַּרְא עֵשָׂו כִּי רָעוֹת בְּנוֹת
ט כְּנָעַן בְּעֵינֵי יִצְחָק אָבִיו: וַיֵּלֶךְ עֵשָׂו אֶל־
יִשְׁמָעֵאל וַיִּקַּח אֶת־מָחֲלַת | בַּת־יִשְׁמָעֵאל
בֶּן־אַבְרָהָם אֲחוֹת נְבָיוֹת עַל־נָשָׁיו לוֹ
לְאִשָּׁה:

literal flow of the narrative *(Kitzur Mizrachi).*]

Ramban suggests that in the context of this command that Jacob marry a woman from among the daughters of Laban his mother's brother, the Torah added that Laban was also the brother of *Esau's* mother too, thereby implying that it would have been proper for Isaac to have instructed Esau, too, to go to Laban to seek a wife. The reason Isaac instructed only *Jacob*, however, was because he knew that the Abrahamitic blessing would be fulfilled only through *Jacob* and *his* offspring.

[See *comm.* to 25:1 for similar interpretation that Abraham married the Egyptian Keturah and was not particular in taking himself a wife from his kin, since his insistence that a suitable wife be chosen concerned him only in regard to his offspring who would bear the Abrahamitic covenant.]

Some interpret that Rebecca is again identified here as the sister of Laban and as both the mother of Jacob and Esau to remind us that she bore an Esau *because* she was the sister of Laban, since children resemble the mother's brother [see *Sforno* to 25:20]. Others suggest that by sending Jacob to her brother to avoid bloodshed between her children, Rebecca was compassionately acting as the mother of both of them *(Tur).*

6-9. Esau marries the daughter of Ishmael.

The following [parenthetical] verses form one unit: *When Esau saw that Isaac had blessed Jacob and sent him away to Paddan Aram ... and that Jacob had obeyed his father and had gone to Paddan Aram ... and that the Canaanite women were evil* — so *Esau went to Ishmael (Rashi).*

6. ... וַיַּרְא עֵשָׂו — *When Esau saw that Isaac blessed Jacob.*

In his second blessing to Jacob, Isaac conferred upon him the Abrahamitic gift of *Eretz Yisrael.* Esau calculated that this blessing had been stripped from him because he had wed Canaanite women. Therefore he now took a daughter of Ishmael in the hope that he might

28
6-9

[6] — *When Esau saw that Isaac had blessed Jacob and*
sent him off to Paddan Aram to take himself a wife
from there, charging him as he blessed him, "You
shall not take a wife from among the Canaanite
women;" [7] *and that Jacob obeyed his father and*
mother and went to Paddan Aram. [8] *Then Esau*
perceived that the Canaanite women were evil in the
eyes of Isaac, his father, [9] *so Esau went to Ishmael*
and took Mahalath, the daughter of Ishmael, sister of
Nebayoth, in addition to his wives, as a wife for
himself. —

yet regain the Abrahamitic blessing of the Land *(Rashbam).*

7. וַיִּשְׁמַע יַעֲקֹב — *And that Jacob listened ...*

[Unlike Esau himself who had been callous to the fact that he had married women who were a source of spiritual rebellion to his parents.]

8. וַיַּרְא עֵשָׂו כִּי רָעוֹת בְּנוֹת כְּנָעַן בְּעֵינֵי יִצְחָק אָבִיו — *Then Esau perceived* [lit. *saw*] *that the Canaanite women* [lit. *daughters of Canaan*] *were evil in the eyes of Isaac his father.*

Esau perceived — by Isaac's charge to Jacob. Although it had not been told directly to Esau previously, Esau had never reacted to Isaac's displeasure with the Canaanite wives. Only now, when he saw that the fulfillment of Isaac's blessing to Jacob seemed to be dependent upon the choice of wives, did he too, take the example, and react to his father's feelings. But his efforts were feeble; he neither divorced his Canaantite wives, nor took a new wife from Rebecca's family. Instead he simply went and married a daughter of Ishmael, to *partially* pacify his father *(Abarbanel; Malbim).*

9. וַיֵּלֶךְ עֵשָׂו אֶל יִשְׁמָעֵאל — *And Esau went to Ishmael.*

The fact that Esau responded to Isaac's verbalized displeasure and *went to Ishmael* proves that had Isaac exercised his authority over Esau earlier — as Rebecca inspired him to do now in the case of Jacob — he could have prevented Esau from marrying the Canaanite women [see on 26:34] *(Sforno).*

מַחֲלַת בַּת יִשְׁמָעֵאל — *Mahalath the daughter of Ishmael.*

The *Midrash* homiletically interprets the name Mahalath as derived from מַחֲלָה, *illness, disease,* hence adding grief to grief, adding evil to a house already full.[1]

אֲחוֹת נְבָיוֹת — *Sister of Nebayoth.*

Radak suggests that in the literal sense the identification here with Nebayoth — like that of *sister of*

1. Was then Mahalath her name? In 36:3 her name is given as Basemath! Rather the name Mahalath [is descriptive and] is derived from מחל, *forgiveness.* This teaches that his sins were pardoned. From this we derive that a man's sins are pardoned when he marries *(Yerushalmi Biccurim 3:3).*

See *Rashi* and *Ramban* to 36:3.

Laban [24:20] or *brother of Japheth* [10:21] — was because Nebayoth was a man of great renown.

Rashbam suggests that Nebayoth is mentioned because he was the first-born. This is the case with Miriam who is likewise identified as *sister of Aaron* [*Exod.* 15:2] since Aaron was the elder of the brothers [see *Ramban* there].

... Or it might be that Ishmael had daughters from several wives and Mahalath was the sister of Nebayoth from that same wife *(Ibn Ezra).*

Rashi [citing the Sages in *Megillah* 17] notes that the apparently superfluous description *sister of Nebayoth* is added to draw our attention to the tradition that **Ishmael died after he designated his daughter for Esau.** It was *Nebayoth* who actually gave her in marriage to Esau; hence he too, is mentioned in this connection [see *Chronological Deductions next page.*]

עַל נָשָׁיו — *In addition to* [lit. *upon*] *his wives.*

He did not divorce his first wives, but added wickedness upon wickedness *(Rashi).*

According to *Ha'amek Davar*, the phrase עַל נָשָׁיו, *'upon* his wives' suggests that she was placed in authority *over* them.

— Esau tried to impress Isaac by heeding the *negative* injunction in *v.* 1 against taking a Canaanite wife. However, he flagrantly ignored the *positive* command to marry one of the Abrahamitic family in Paddan Aram *(Abarbanel; Malbim).*

לוֹ לְאִשָּׁה — *As a wife* [lit.*woman*] *for himself.*

[Perhaps the connotation is here, too, as in 25:20: A woman suitable to be לוֹ לְאִשָּׁה, a wife to *him,* in this case, a wicked woman married to a wicked man.]

This section justifies the concept of Esau as a selfish person oblivious to all but his own desires. For twenty-three years he had caused anguish to his parents by the behavior of his Canaanite wives, yet it seems to have dawned on him only now. But instead of divorcing them, he merely took another unsuitable wife *in addition* to them. Thus he proved that he had no feeling for the House of Abraham, and Rebecca's assessment of his complete unfitness for the future guidance of that House fully and completely justified *(Hirsch).*

According to the Masoretic note appearing at the end of the *Sidrah* there are 106 verses in the *Sidrah* numerically corresponding to the mnemonic על״ו [*they* (i.e., Isaac and Jacob) *ascended* = 106; alluding to the primary themes of the Sidrah: the *ascendancy of Isaac* as a result of his experiences in Gerar (see *comm.* to 26:4,13, and 28); as well as the *ascendancy* of Jacob as a result of his having secured the birthright and the blessings.] The *Haftorah* begins with *Malachi* 1:1 מַשָּׂא דְּבַר ה׳.

Meir Zlotowitz
Aseres Y'mei Teshuvah 5739 / October, 1978
Brooklyn, New York

◆§ Chronological Deductions.

Rashi [following *Megillah* 14a and *Seder Olam*] deduces several important chronological calculations *from the above-mentioned fact that Ishmael's death coincided with the period when Jacob received the blessing and left home.* Among the most important, perhaps, is that when Jacob stood before Pharaoh he should have been, according to the relevant data, 116 years old, yet Jacob himself gave his age as 130 (47:29). This discrepancy is explained by the fact that he spent 14 years in the Academy of Eber *after leaving his father's house* before going to Laban. [Much of the relevant calculations, such as that Jacob was 63 years old at the time he received the blessings have been detailed in the *footnote* to 25:17, and will אי״ה be referred to in more detail in their appropriate places. See 33:17 and 47:9.]

Among *Rashi*'s calculations are:

[A]

Jacob's age when he left his father's house	63
***Years engaged in study at Academy of Eber**	**+ 14**
Years spent with Laban until Joseph was born	+ 14
Joseph's age when he became ruler in Egypt (see 41:46)	+ 30
Years of prosperity (7) and famine (2) until Jacob came to Egypt	+ 9
Jacob's age when he stood before Pharaoh (see 49:9)	= 130

*[*Without this assumption we lack 14 years from the total of 130 years*]

[B]

Years Jacob engaged in study at Academy of Eber	+ 14
Total years in Laban's service (7 for Leah, 7 for Rachel, and 6 additional service)	+ 20
Journey home	+ 2
Total years separated from father	= 36
[less the meritorious years engaged in Torah study]	− 14
Total accountable years Jacob was separated from his father	**= 22**

[*Equal to the years Joseph was separated from Jacob. See "C"*]

[C]

Joseph's age when he was separated from Jacob (see 37:2)	17
Age when reunited with father (30+9)	39
Total years Joseph was separated from his father (39-17)	**= 22**